2017 Harris New York Manufacturers Directory

Exclusive Provider of
Dun & Bradstreet Library Solutions

Published January 2017 next update January 2018

WARNING: Purchasers and users of this directory may not use this directory to compile mailing lists, other marketing aids and other types of data, which are sold or otherwise provided to third parties. Such use is wrongful, illegal and a violation of the federal copyright laws.

CAUTION: Because of the many thousands of establishment listings contained in this directory and the possibilities of both human and mechanical error in processing this information, Mergent Inc. cannot assume liability for the correctness of the listings or information on which they are based. Hence, no information contained in this work should be relied upon in any instance where there is a possibility of any loss or damage as a consequence of any error or omission in this volume.

Publisher

Mergent Inc.
444 Madison Ave
New York, NY 10022

©Mergent Inc All Rights Reserved
2017 Mergent Business Press
ISSN 1080-2614
ISBN 978-1-68200-388-6

TABLE OF CONTENTS

Summary of Contents & Explanatory Notes 4
User's Guide to Listings 6

Geographic Section
County/City Cross-Reference Index 9
Firms Listed by Location City 13

Standard Industrial Classification (SIC) Section
SIC Alphabetical Index 703
SIC Numerical Index 705
Firms Listed by SIC 707

Alphabetic Section
Firms Listed by Firm Name 883

Product Section
Product Index 1101
Firms Listed by Product Category 1125

SUMMARY OF CONTENTS

Number of Companies.. 17,531
Number of Decision Makers...................................... 44,202
Minimum Number of Employees.. 5

EXPLANATORY NOTES

How to Cross-Reference in This Directory
Sequential Entry Numbers. Each establishment in the Geographic Section is numbered sequentially (G-0000). The number assigned to each establishment is referred to as its "entry number." To make cross-referencing easier, each listing in the Geographic, SIC, Alphabetic and Product Sections includes the establishment's entry number. To facilitate locating an entry in the Geographic Section, the entry numbers for the first listing on the left page and the last listing on the right page are printed at the top of the page next to the city name.

Source Suggestions Welcome
Although all known sources were used to compile this directory, it is possible that companies were inadvertently omitted. Your assistance in calling attention to such omissions would be greatly appreciated. A special form on the facing page will help you in the reporting process.

Analysis
Every effort has been made to contact all firms to verify their information. The one exception to this rule is the annual sales figure, which is considered by many companies to be confidential information. Therefore, estimated sales have been calculated by multiplying the nationwide average sales per employee for the firm's major SIC/NAICS code by the firm's number of employees. Nationwide averages for sales per employee by SIC/NAICS codes are provided by the U.S. Department of Commerce and are updated annually. All sales—sales (est)—have been estimated by this method. The exceptions are parent companies (PA), division headquarters (DH) and headquarter locations (HQ) which may include an actual corporate sales figure—sales (corporate-wide) if available.

Types of Companies
Descriptive and statistical data are included for companies in the entire state. These comprise manufacturers, machine shops, fabricators, assemblers and printers. Also identified are corporate offices in the state.

Employment Data
This directory contains companies with 5 or more employees in the manufacturing industry. The employment figure shown in the Geographic Section includes male and female employees and embraces all levels of the company: administrative, clerical, sales and maintenance. This figure is for the facility listed and does not include other plants or offices. It should be recognized that these figures represent an approximate year-round average. These employment figures are broken into codes A through G and used in the Product and SIC Sections to further help you in qualifying a company. Be sure to check the footnotes on the bottom of pages for the code breakdowns.

Standard Industrial Classification (SIC)

The Standard Industrial Classification (SIC) system used in this directory was developed by the federal government for use in classifying establishments by the type of activity they are engaged in. The SIC classifications used in this directory are from the 1987 edition published by the U.S. Government's Office of Management and Budget. The SIC system separates all activities into broad industrial divisions (e.g., manufacturing, mining, retail trade). It further subdivides each division. The range of manufacturing industry classes extends from two-digit codes (major industry group) to four-digit codes (product).

For example:

Industry Breakdown	Code	Industry, Product, etc.
*Major industry group	20	Food and kindred products
Industry group	203	Canned and frozen foods
*Industry	2033	Fruits and vegetables, etc.

*Classifications used in this directory

Only two-digit and four-digit codes are used in this directory.

Arrangement

1. The **Geographic Section** contains complete in-depth corporate data. This section is sorted by cities listed in alphabetical order and companies listed alphabetically within each city. A County/City Index for referencing cities within counties precedes this section.

> IMPORTANT NOTICE: It is a violation of both federal and state law to transmit an unsolicited advertisement to a facsimile machine. Any user of this product that violates such laws may be subject to civil and criminal penalties, which may exceed $500 for each transmission of an unsolicited facsimile. Mergent Inc. provides fax numbers for lawful purposes only and expressly forbids the use of these numbers in any unlawful manner.

2. The **Standard Industrial Classification (SIC) Section** lists companies under approximately 500 four-digit SIC codes. An alphabetical and a numerical index precedes this section. A company can be listed under several codes. The codes are in numerical order with companies listed alphabetically under each code.

3. The **Alphabetic Section** lists all companies with their full physical or mailing addresses and telephone number.

4. The **Product Section** lists companies under unique Harris categories. An index preceding this section lists all product categories in alphabetical order. Companies can be listed under several categories.

USER'S GUIDE TO LISTINGS

GEOGRAPHIC SECTION

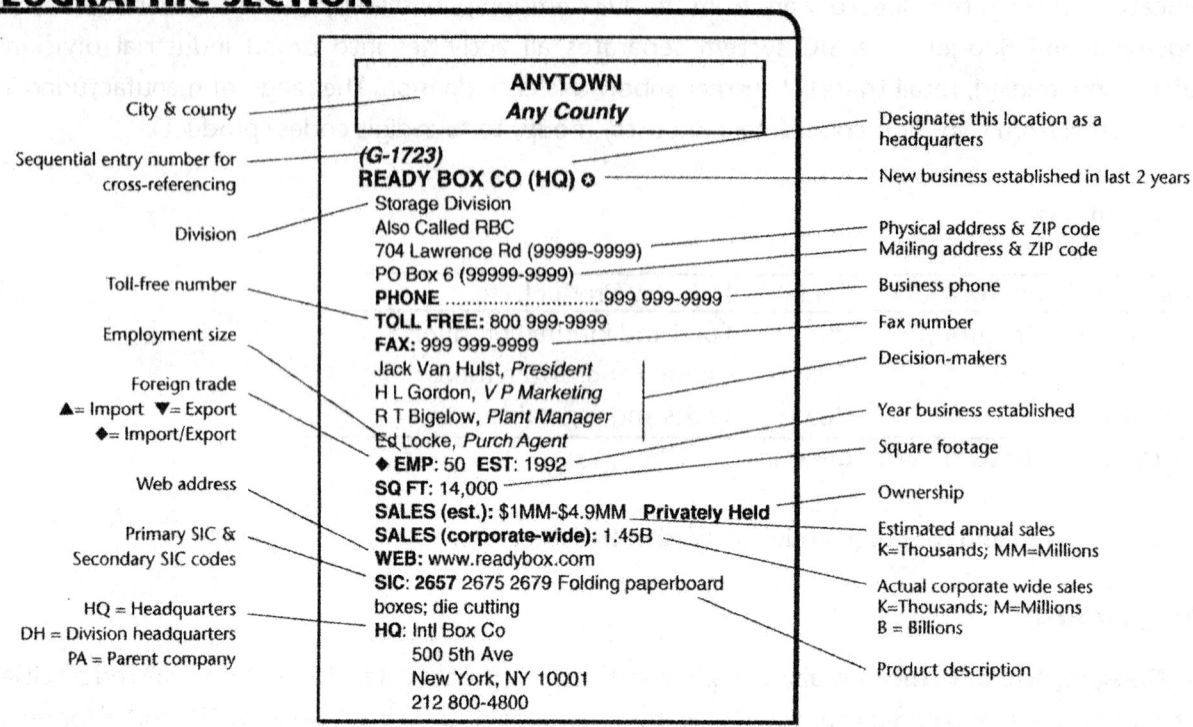

SIC SECTION

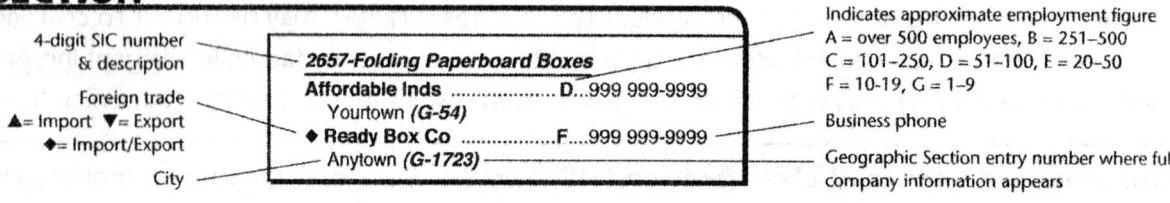

ALPHABETIC SECTION

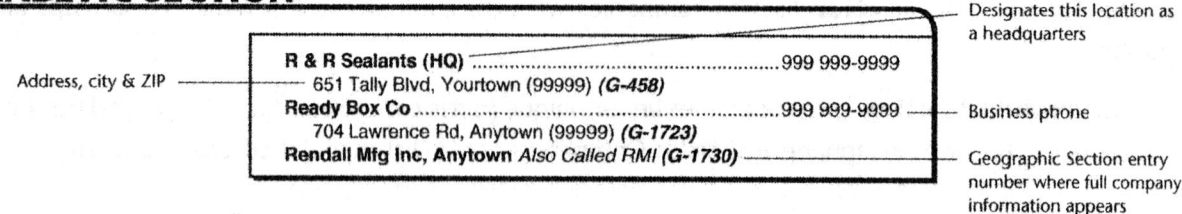

PRODUCT SECTION

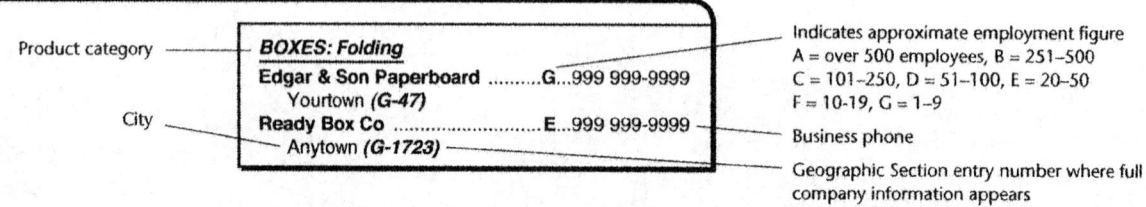

GEOGRAPHIC SECTION
Companies sorted by city in alphabetical order
In-depth company data listed

STANDARD INDUSTRIAL CLASSIFICATIONS
Alphabetical index of classifcation descriptions
Numerical index of classifcation descriptions
Companies sorted by SIC product groupings

ALPHABETIC SECTION
Company listings in alphabetical order

PRODUCT INDEX
Product categories listed in alphabetical order

PRODUCT SECTION
Companies sorted by product and manufacturing service classifications

New York
County Map

COUNTY/CITY CROSS-REFERENCE INDEX

Albany
City	Entry #
Albany	(G-33)
Alcove	(G-172)
Altamont	(G-206)
Coeymans	(G-3745)
Cohoes	(G-3747)
Colonie	(G-3819)
Delmar	(G-4244)
East Berne	(G-4381)
Feura Bush	(G-5172)
Glenmont	(G-5666)
Green Island	(G-5853)
Guilderland	(G-5902)
Latham	(G-7351)
Medusa	(G-8285)
Menands	(G-8363)
Ravena	(G-14020)
Selkirk	(G-15354)
Slingerlands	(G-15477)
South Bethlehem	(G-15514)
Troy	(G-16218)
Voorheesville	(G-16516)
Watervliet	(G-16679)
Westerlo	(G-17042)

Allegany
City	Entry #
Alfred	(G-193)
Alfred Station	(G-195)
Almond	(G-204)
Angelica	(G-376)
Belmont	(G-843)
Bolivar	(G-1159)
Canaseraga	(G-3362)
Cuba	(G-4068)
Fillmore	(G-5175)
Friendship	(G-5452)
Scio	(G-15321)
Wellsville	(G-16748)

Bronx
City	Entry #
Bronx	(G-1250)

Broome
City	Entry #
Binghamton	(G-884)
Castle Creek	(G-3417)
Chenango Bridge	(G-3596)
Conklin	(G-3864)
Deposit	(G-4276)
Endicott	(G-4795)
Endwell	(G-4835)
Johnson City	(G-7091)
Kirkwood	(G-7230)
Vestal	(G-16438)
Whitney Point	(G-17219)
Windsor	(G-17272)

Cattaraugus
City	Entry #
Allegany	(G-198)
Cattaraugus	(G-3436)
Delevan	(G-4234)
Ellicottville	(G-4640)
Franklinville	(G-5368)
Freedom	(G-5378)
Gowanda	(G-5748)
Hinsdale	(G-6424)
Kill Buck	(G-7166)
Limestone	(G-7450)
Little Valley	(G-7511)
Machias	(G-7993)
Olean	(G-13134)
Portville	(G-13874)
Randolph	(G-14016)
Salamanca	(G-15099)
South Dayton	(G-15517)

Cayuga
City	Entry #
Auburn	(G-476)
Aurora	(G-530)
Cato	(G-3425)
Genoa	(G-5590)
King Ferry	(G-7168)
Locke	(G-7568)
Moravia	(G-8616)
Port Byron	(G-13734)
Scipio Center	(G-15322)
Weedsport	(G-16746)

Chautauqua
City	Entry #
Ashville	(G-426)
Bemus Point	(G-844)
Brocton	(G-1248)
Cassadaga	(G-3414)
Clymer	(G-3733)
Dunkirk	(G-4331)
Ellington	(G-4644)
Falconer	(G-4889)
Findley Lake	(G-5177)
Forestville	(G-5333)
Fredonia	(G-5371)
Frewsburg	(G-5448)
Gerry	(G-5592)
Irving	(G-6765)
Jamestown	(G-6967)
Kennedy	(G-7153)
Lakewood	(G-7287)
Mayville	(G-8215)
Portland	(G-13873)
Ripley	(G-14135)
Sheridan	(G-15400)
Sherman	(G-15401)
Silver Creek	(G-15447)
Sinclairville	(G-15452)
Westfield	(G-17044)

Chemung
City	Entry #
Big Flats	(G-880)
Chemung	(G-3593)
Elmira	(G-4668)
Elmira Heights	(G-4708)
Horseheads	(G-6569)
Lowman	(G-7934)
Millport	(G-8480)
Pine City	(G-13550)
Pine Valley	(G-13556)
Wellsburg	(G-16747)

Chenango
City	Entry #
Afton	(G-8)
Bainbridge	(G-554)
Earlville	(G-4360)
Greene	(G-5862)
Mount Upton	(G-8658)
New Berlin	(G-8779)
Norwich	(G-13020)
Oxford	(G-13363)
Sherburne	(G-15389)
South Otselic	(G-15531)

Clinton
City	Entry #
Au Sable Forks	(G-475)
Champlain	(G-3537)
Chazy	(G-3562)
Keeseville	(G-7137)
Mooers	(G-8615)
Peru	(G-13527)
Plattsburgh	(G-13649)
Rouses Point	(G-15041)
Saranac	(G-15133)
West Chazy	(G-16842)

Columbia
City	Entry #
Ancram	(G-375)
Canaan	(G-3331)
Chatham	(G-3557)
Copake	(G-3887)
Copake Falls	(G-3888)
Germantown	(G-5591)
Ghent	(G-5607)
Hudson	(G-6602)
Kinderhook	(G-7167)
Livingston	(G-7560)
Philmont	(G-13540)
Stottville	(G-15781)
Stuyvesant	(G-15782)
Stuyvesant Falls	(G-15783)

Cortland
City	Entry #
Cincinnatus	(G-3653)
Cortland	(G-4011)
Homer	(G-6515)
Marathon	(G-8083)
Mc Graw	(G-8221)

Delaware
City	Entry #
Arkville	(G-411)
Bloomville	(G-994)
Davenport	(G-4080)
Delhi	(G-4236)
East Branch	(G-4384)
Halcottsville	(G-5904)
Hancock	(G-5962)
Hobart	(G-6425)
Margaretville	(G-8093)
Masonville	(G-8107)
Sidney	(G-15434)
Stamford	(G-15623)
Walton	(G-16547)

Dutchess
City	Entry #
Amenia	(G-215)
Barrytown	(G-619)
Beacon	(G-781)
Clinton Corners	(G-3724)
Dover Plains	(G-4314)
Fishkill	(G-5180)
Hopewell Junction	(G-6547)
Hyde Park	(G-6733)
Lagrangeville	(G-7253)
Millbrook	(G-8475)
Millerton	(G-8479)
Pawling	(G-13450)
Pine Plains	(G-13554)
Pleasant Valley	(G-13711)
Poughkeepsie	(G-13886)
Poughquag	(G-13941)
Red Hook	(G-14028)
Rhinebeck	(G-14056)
Staatsburg	(G-15617)
Stanfordville	(G-15627)
Stormville	(G-15779)
Wappingers Falls	(G-16566)
Wassaic	(G-16600)
Wingdale	(G-17274)

Erie
City	Entry #
Akron	(G-19)
Alden	(G-173)
Amherst	(G-218)
Angola	(G-378)
Blasdell	(G-960)
Bowmansville	(G-1170)
Buffalo	(G-2788)
Chaffee	(G-3532)
Cheektowaga	(G-3563)
Clarence	(G-3654)
Clarence Center	(G-3673)
Colden	(G-3772)
Collins	(G-3815)
Depew	(G-4247)
Derby	(G-4283)
East Amherst	(G-4361)
East Aurora	(G-4364)
East Concord	(G-4385)
Eden	(G-4585)
Elma	(G-4645)
Getzville	(G-5595)
Glenwood	(G-5703)
Grand Island	(G-5750)
Hamburg	(G-5918)
Holland	(G-6480)
Kenmore	(G-7145)
Lackawanna	(G-7242)
Lake View	(G-7279)
Lancaster	(G-7297)
North Collins	(G-12926)
Orchard Park	(G-13249)
Springville	(G-15609)
Tonawanda	(G-16132)
Wales Center	(G-16539)
West Falls	(G-16844)
West Seneca	(G-16938)
Williamsville	(G-17230)

Essex
City	Entry #
Crown Point	(G-4067)
Elizabethtown	(G-4626)
Jay	(G-7054)
Lake Placid	(G-7273)
Lewis	(G-7431)
Mineville	(G-8540)
Ray Brook	(G-14024)
Schroon Lake	(G-15318)
Ticonderoga	(G-16124)
Upper Jay	(G-16303)
Westport	(G-17067)
Willsboro	(G-17264)
Wilmington	(G-17267)

Franklin
City	Entry #
Akwesasne	(G-32)
Brainardsville	(G-1171)
Burke	(G-3266)
Chateaugay	(G-3556)
Hogansburg	(G-6427)
Malone	(G-8005)
Moira	(G-8546)
Paul Smiths	(G-13448)
Saranac Lake	(G-15134)
Tupper Lake	(G-16277)

Fulton
City	Entry #
Broadalbin	(G-1240)
Gloversville	(G-5704)
Johnstown	(G-7107)
Mayfield	(G-8213)
Northville	(G-13019)

Genesee
City	Entry #
Alexander	(G-187)
Batavia	(G-621)
Bergen	(G-845)
Byron	(G-3269)
Corfu	(G-3952)
East Bethany	(G-4382)
Le Roy	(G-7402)
Oakfield	(G-13064)
Pavilion	(G-13449)
Stafford	(G-15620)

Greene
City	Entry #
Athens	(G-464)
Cairo	(G-3270)
Catskill	(G-3426)
Coxsackie	(G-4056)
Durham	(G-4354)
East Durham	(G-4387)
Elka Park	(G-4629)
Greenville	(G-5884)
Palenville	(G-13397)
Prattsville	(G-13945)
Round Top	(G-15040)
Surprise	(G-15811)

Hamilton
City	Entry #
Lake Pleasant	(G-7277)
Speculator	(G-15563)

Herkimer
City	Entry #
Dolgeville	(G-4305)
Frankfort	(G-5349)
Herkimer	(G-6299)
Ilion	(G-6739)
Jordanville	(G-7132)
Little Falls	(G-7497)
Middleville	(G-8472)
Mohawk	(G-8542)
Newport	(G-12790)
Old Forge	(G-13132)
Poland	(G-13727)
Van Hornesville	(G-16432)
West Winfield	(G-16957)

Jefferson
City	Entry #
Adams	(G-2)
Adams Center	(G-4)
Alexandria Bay	(G-191)
Brownville	(G-2783)
Cape Vincent	(G-3384)
Carthage	(G-3407)
Clayton	(G-3684)
Dexter	(G-4285)
Felts Mills	(G-5167)

2017 Harris
New York Manufacturers Directory

COUNTY/CITY CROSS-REFERENCE

City	ENTRY #
Fort Drum	(G-5338)
Great Bend	(G-5783)
Henderson	(G-6290)
Henderson Harbor	(G-6291)
La Fargeville	(G-7235)
Three Mile Bay	(G-16123)
Watertown	(G-16633)
Woodville	(G-17367)

Kings
Brooklyn	(G-1511)

Lewis
Beaver Falls	(G-794)
Castorland	(G-3421)
Croghan	(G-4058)
Harrisville	(G-5995)
Lowville	(G-7935)
Lyons Falls	(G-7977)

Livingston
Avon	(G-538)
Caledonia	(G-3275)
Conesus	(G-3850)
Dansville	(G-4075)
Geneseo	(G-5564)
Hemlock	(G-6263)
Lakeville	(G-7282)
Leicester	(G-7420)
Lima	(G-7443)
Livonia	(G-7563)
Mount Morris	(G-8653)
Nunda	(G-13041)
Piffard	(G-13546)
Retsof	(G-14054)
York	(G-17505)

Madison
Canastota	(G-3363)
Cazenovia	(G-3442)
Chittenango	(G-3629)
De Ruyter	(G-4081)
Hamilton	(G-5947)
Madison	(G-7994)
Morrisville	(G-8619)
Munnsville	(G-8749)
Oneida	(G-13155)
West Edmeston	(G-16843)

Monroe
Brockport	(G-1243)
Churchville	(G-3633)
East Rochester	(G-4453)
Fairport	(G-4842)
Gates	(G-5561)
Hamlin	(G-5950)
Henrietta	(G-6292)
Hilton	(G-6417)
Honeoye Falls	(G-6525)
Mendon	(G-8380)
North Chili	(G-12924)
Penfield	(G-13497)
Pittsford	(G-13557)
Rochester	(G-14161)
Rush	(G-15046)
Scottsville	(G-15332)
Spencerport	(G-15565)
Webster	(G-16713)
West Henrietta	(G-16865)

Montgomery
Amsterdam	(G-332)
Canajoharie	(G-3332)
Esperance	(G-4839)
Fonda	(G-5315)
Fort Plain	(G-5347)
Fultonville	(G-5477)
Palatine Bridge	(G-13395)
Saint Johnsville	(G-15092)
Sprakers	(G-15577)

Nassau
Albertson	(G-152)
Atlantic Beach	(G-468)
Baldwin	(G-558)
Bellmore	(G-813)
Bethpage	(G-861)
Carle Place	(G-3385)
Cedarhurst	(G-3455)
East Meadow	(G-4418)
East Norwich	(G-4445)
East Rockaway	(G-4467)
Elmont	(G-4715)
Farmingdale	(G-4925)
Floral Park	(G-5189)
Franklin Square	(G-5359)
Freeport	(G-5379)
Garden City	(G-5492)
Garden City Park	(G-5539)
Glen Cove	(G-5608)
Glen Head	(G-5632)
Great Neck	(G-5784)
Greenvale	(G-5879)
Hempstead	(G-6264)
Hewlett	(G-6306)
Hicksville	(G-6318)
Inwood	(G-6750)
Island Park	(G-6777)
Jericho	(G-7060)
Lawrence	(G-7390)
Levittown	(G-7423)
Lido Beach	(G-7439)
Locust Valley	(G-7628)
Long Beach	(G-7637)
Lynbrook	(G-7943)
Manhasset	(G-8054)
Massapequa	(G-8176)
Massapequa Park	(G-8185)
Merrick	(G-8383)
Mineola	(G-8486)
New Hyde Park	(G-8814)
North Baldwin	(G-12904)
North Bellmore	(G-12914)
Oceanside	(G-13071)
Old Bethpage	(G-13124)
Old Westbury	(G-13133)
Oyster Bay	(G-13365)
Plainview	(G-13576)
Port Washington	(G-13795)
Rockville Centre	(G-14788)
Roosevelt	(G-15003)
Roslyn	(G-15016)
Roslyn Heights	(G-15025)
Sea Cliff	(G-15341)
Seaford	(G-15343)
South Hempstead	(G-15529)
Syosset	(G-15812)
Uniondale	(G-16288)
Valley Stream	(G-16397)
Wantagh	(G-16553)
West Hempstead	(G-16849)
Westbury	(G-16960)
Williston Park	(G-17260)
Woodbury	(G-17282)
Woodmere	(G-17310)

New York
New York	(G-8958)

Niagara
Barker	(G-612)
Burt	(G-3268)
Gasport	(G-5555)
Lewiston	(G-7432)
Lockport	(G-7569)
Middleport	(G-8420)
Newfane	(G-12787)
Niagara Falls	(G-12793)
North Tonawanda	(G-12953)
Ransomville	(G-14019)
Sanborn	(G-15113)
Wilson	(G-17268)
Youngstown	(G-17531)

Oneida
Ava	(G-531)
Barneveld	(G-614)
Blossvale	(G-997)
Boonville	(G-1161)
Camden	(G-3312)
Chadwicks	(G-3530)
Clayville	(G-3686)
Clinton	(G-3717)
Deansboro	(G-4084)
Forestport	(G-5331)
Holland Patent	(G-6487)
Marcy	(G-8090)
Mc Connellsville	(G-8220)
New Hartford	(G-8801)
New York Mills	(G-12720)
Oriskany	(G-13303)
Oriskany Falls	(G-13318)
Remsen	(G-14040)
Rome	(G-14803)
Sangerfield	(G-15132)
Sauquoit	(G-15199)
Sherrill	(G-15404)
Stittville	(G-15762)
Taberg	(G-16076)
Utica	(G-16304)
Vernon	(G-16433)
Vernon Center	(G-16437)
Waterville	(G-16677)
Westernville	(G-17043)
Westmoreland	(G-17062)
Whitesboro	(G-17192)
Yorkville	(G-17523)

Onondaga
Baldwinsville	(G-564)
Brewerton	(G-1202)
Bridgeport	(G-1235)
Camillus	(G-3321)
Cicero	(G-3641)
Clay	(G-3683)
De Witt	(G-4083)
East Syracuse	(G-4498)
Elbridge	(G-4623)
Fabius	(G-4841)
Fayetteville	(G-5163)
Jamesville	(G-7045)
Jordan	(G-7130)
Kirkville	(G-7227)
La Fayette	(G-7239)
Liverpool	(G-7512)
Manlius	(G-8067)
Marcellus	(G-8086)
Mattydale	(G-8212)
Nedrow	(G-8772)
North Syracuse	(G-12941)
Skaneateles	(G-15455)
Skaneateles Falls	(G-15467)
Solvay	(G-15506)
Syracuse	(G-15844)
Tully	(G-16273)

Ontario
Bloomfield	(G-981)
Canandaigua	(G-3335)
Clifton Springs	(G-3713)
Farmington	(G-5146)
Fishers	(G-5178)
Geneva	(G-5569)
Hall	(G-5917)
Honeoye	(G-6523)
Manchester	(G-8051)
Naples	(G-8764)
Oaks Corners	(G-13069)
Phelps	(G-13529)
Seneca Castle	(G-15359)
Shortsville	(G-15433)
Victor	(G-16458)

Orange
Bullville	(G-3263)
Central Valley	(G-3520)
Chester	(G-3598)
Cornwall	(G-3985)
Cornwall On Hudson	(G-3992)
Florida	(G-5210)
Goshen	(G-5731)
Greenwood Lake	(G-5896)
Harriman	(G-5970)
Highland Falls	(G-6410)
Highland Mills	(G-6411)
Huguenot	(G-6651)
Middletown	(G-8424)
Monroe	(G-8547)
Montgomery	(G-8592)
Mountainville	(G-8747)
New Hampton	(G-8797)
New Windsor	(G-8928)
Newburgh	(G-12748)
Otisville	(G-13344)
Pine Bush	(G-13548)
Pine Island	(G-13553)
Port Jervis	(G-13781)
Rock Tavern	(G-14780)
Salisbury Mills	(G-15112)
Slate Hill	(G-15474)
Southfields	(G-15556)
Sparrow Bush	(G-15562)
Sugar Loaf	(G-15804)
Tuxedo Park	(G-16283)
Unionville	(G-16302)
Walden	(G-16530)
Warwick	(G-16586)
Washingtonville	(G-16598)
West Point	(G-16930)
Westtown	(G-17068)

Orleans
Albion	(G-161)
Holley	(G-6489)
Kendall	(G-7143)
Lyndonville	(G-7968)
Medina	(G-8264)

Oswego
Bernhards Bay	(G-858)
Central Square	(G-3515)
Cleveland	(G-3692)
Constantia	(G-3880)
Fulton	(G-5453)
Hannibal	(G-5969)
Lacona	(G-7251)
Mexico	(G-8395)
Oswego	(G-13329)
Parish	(G-13414)
Phoenix	(G-13542)
Pulaski	(G-13946)
Sandy Creek	(G-15131)
West Monroe	(G-16909)
Williamstown	(G-17228)

Otsego
Cherry Valley	(G-3597)
Colliersville	(G-3814)
Cooperstown	(G-3883)
Edmeston	(G-4622)
Fly Creek	(G-5313)
Milford	(G-8473)
Morris	(G-8618)
Oneonta	(G-13171)
Richfield Springs	(G-14061)
Schenevus	(G-15314)
Unadilla	(G-16287)
West Burlington	(G-16841)
Worcester	(G-17368)

Putnam
Brewster	(G-1206)
Carmel	(G-3398)
Cold Spring	(G-3762)
Garrison	(G-5554)
Mahopac	(G-7996)
Patterson	(G-13437)
Putnam Valley	(G-13973)

Queens
Arverne	(G-424)
Astoria	(G-431)
Bayside	(G-762)
Bayside Hills	(G-779)
Bellerose	(G-809)
Cambria Heights	(G-3303)
College Point	(G-3773)
Corona	(G-3993)
Douglaston	(G-4310)
East Elmhurst	(G-4388)
Elmhurst	(G-4658)
Far Rockaway	(G-4919)
Floral Park	(G-5208)
Flushing	(G-5220)
Forest Hills	(G-5319)
Fresh Meadows	(G-5438)
Glen Oaks	(G-5640)
Glendale	(G-5642)
Hollis	(G-6494)
Howard Beach	(G-6597)
Jackson Heights	(G-6887)
Jamaica	(G-6890)
Kew Gardens	(G-7157)
Laurelton	(G-7386)
Little Neck	(G-7507)
Long Island City	(G-7643)
Maspeth	(G-8110)
Middle Village	(G-8409)
Oakland Gardens	(G-13067)

COUNTY/CITY CROSS-REFERENCE

	ENTRY #		ENTRY #		ENTRY #		ENTRY #		ENTRY #
Ozone Park	(G-13375)	Burnt Hills	(G-3267)	Massena	(G-8192)	Huntington	(G-6654)	Narrowsburg	(G-8768)
Queens Village	(G-13974)	Clifton Park	(G-3693)	Norfolk	(G-12897)	Huntington Station	(G-6693)	Roscoe	(G-15011)
Rego Park	(G-14031)	Corinth	(G-3957)	North Lawrence	(G-12935)	Islandia	(G-6785)	South Fallsburg	(G-15520)
Richmond Hill	(G-14064)	Galway	(G-5484)	Norwood	(G-13040)	Islip	(G-6806)	Thompsonville	(G-16115)
Ridgewood	(G-14096)	Gansevoort	(G-5485)	Ogdensburg	(G-13109)	Islip Terrace	(G-6814)	White Lake	(G-17071)
Rockaway Beach	(G-14781)	Greenfield Center	(G-5871)	Potsdam	(G-13876)	Jamesport	(G-6966)	Wht Sphr Spgs	(G-17221)
Rockaway Park	(G-14784)	Hadley	(G-5903)	South Colton	(G-15515)	Kings Park	(G-7169)	Woodridge	(G-17315)
Rosedale	(G-15013)	Halfmoon	(G-5907)	Star Lake	(G-15628)	Lake Grove	(G-7265)		
Saint Albans	(G-15083)	Malta	(G-8019)	Waddington	(G-16521)	Lake Ronkonkoma	(G-7278)	**Tioga**	
South Ozone Park	(G-15532)	Mechanicville	(G-8224)			Lindenhurst	(G-7452)	Berkshire	(G-853)
South Richmond Hill	(G-15534)	Middle Grove	(G-8404)	**Steuben**		Lloyd Harbor	(G-7566)	Candor	(G-3377)
Springfield Gardens	(G-15608)	Rexford	(G-14055)	Addison	(G-5)	Manorville	(G-8077)	Lockwood	(G-7627)
Sunnyside	(G-15805)	Rock City Falls	(G-14777)	Arkport	(G-410)	Mastic	(G-8202)	Nichols	(G-12892)
Whitestone	(G-17199)	Round Lake	(G-15036)	Avoca	(G-537)	Mastic Beach	(G-8204)	Owego	(G-13350)
Woodhaven	(G-17305)	Saratoga Springs	(G-15140)	Bath	(G-653)	Mattituck	(G-8206)	Richford	(G-14063)
Woodside	(G-17316)	Schuylerville	(G-15319)	Campbell	(G-3329)	Medford	(G-8233)	Spencer	(G-15564)
		South Glens Falls	(G-15522)	Canisteo	(G-3379)	Melville	(G-8286)	Waverly	(G-16699)
Rensselaer		Stillwater	(G-15759)	Coopers Plains	(G-3882)	Middle Island	(G-8405)		
Averill Park	(G-532)	Waterford	(G-16608)	Corning	(G-3960)	Montauk	(G-8588)	**Tompkins**	
Berlin	(G-855)	Wilton	(G-17271)	Hammondsport	(G-5953)	Mount Sinai	(G-8654)	Dryden	(G-4320)
Castleton On Hudson	(G-3418)			Hornell	(G-6560)	Nesconset	(G-8774)	Freeville	(G-5435)
		Schenectady		Lindley	(G-7496)	North Babylon	(G-12901)	Groton	(G-5897)
Cropseyville	(G-4060)	Alplaus	(G-205)	Painted Post	(G-13389)	Northport	(G-13008)	Ithaca	(G-6816)
Eagle Bridge	(G-4356)	Delanson	(G-4231)	Wayland	(G-16709)	Oakdale	(G-13057)	Lansing	(G-7348)
East Greenbush	(G-4401)	Duanesburg	(G-4324)	Woodhull	(G-17309)	Patchogue	(G-13415)	Trumansburg	(G-16265)
East Schodack	(G-4473)	Glenville	(G-5701)			Peconic	(G-13470)		
Hoosick Falls	(G-6539)	Niskayuna	(G-12893)	**Suffolk**		Port Jeff STA	(G-13763)	**Ulster**	
Nassau	(G-8770)	Pattersonville	(G-13447)	Amagansett	(G-213)	Port Jefferson	(G-13774)	Accord	(G-1)
Petersburg	(G-13528)	Rotterdam Junction	(G-15035)	Amityville	(G-273)	Quogue	(G-14015)	Bearsville	(G-792)
Poestenkill	(G-13722)	Schenectady	(G-15226)	Aquebogue	(G-383)	Ridge	(G-14091)	Bloomington	(G-993)
Rensselaer	(G-14042)	Scotia	(G-15323)	Babylon	(G-544)	Riverhead	(G-14137)	Boiceville	(G-1158)
Stephentown	(G-15756)			Bay Shore	(G-663)	Ronkonkoma	(G-14845)	Ellenville	(G-4632)
Troy	(G-16224)	**Schoharie**		Bayport	(G-755)	Sag Harbor	(G-15076)	Gardiner	(G-5547)
Valley Falls	(G-16396)	Central Bridge	(G-3482)	Bellport	(G-824)	Sagaponack	(G-15082)	High Falls	(G-6399)
West Sand Lake	(G-16931)	Charlotteville	(G-3555)	Blue Point	(G-998)	Saint James	(G-15086)	Highland	(G-6403)
Wynantskill	(G-17379)	Cobleskill	(G-3734)	Bohemia	(G-1001)	Sayville	(G-15203)	Kerhonkson	(G-7154)
		Howes Cave	(G-6601)	Brentwood	(G-1175)	Selden	(G-15348)	Kingston	(G-7175)
Richmond		Middleburgh	(G-8418)	Bridgehampton	(G-1232)	Setauket	(G-15374)	Lake Katrine	(G-7269)
Staten Island	(G-15629)	Richmondville	(G-14089)	Brightwaters	(G-1238)	Shelter Island	(G-15386)	Marlboro	(G-8105)
		Schoharie	(G-15316)	Brookhaven	(G-1505)	Shirley	(G-15411)	Milton	(G-8482)
Rockland		Sharon Springs	(G-15382)	Calverton	(G-3286)	Smithtown	(G-15481)	Mount Marion	(G-8650)
Airmont	(G-10)	Sloansville	(G-15479)	Center Moriches	(G-3464)	Sound Beach	(G-15513)	New Paltz	(G-8873)
Blauvelt	(G-969)	Warnerville	(G-16579)	Centereach	(G-3469)	Southampton	(G-15538)	Rifton	(G-14132)
Chestnut Ridge	(G-3623)			Centerport	(G-3475)	Southold	(G-15557)	Saugerties	(G-15178)
Congers	(G-3851)	**Schuyler**		Central Islip	(G-3483)	Speonk	(G-15575)	Shokan	(G-15432)
Garnerville	(G-5553)	Beaver Dams	(G-793)	Cold Spring Harbor	(G-3767)	Stony Brook	(G-15766)	Stone Ridge	(G-15763)
Haverstraw	(G-6237)	Burdett	(G-3264)	Commack	(G-3822)	Wading River	(G-16522)	Tillson	(G-16130)
Hillburn	(G-6415)	Cayuta	(G-3440)	Copiague	(G-3889)	Wainscott	(G-16529)	Ulster Park	(G-16285)
Monsey	(G-8566)	Hector	(G-6257)	Coram	(G-3941)	Water Mill	(G-16603)	Wallkill	(G-16541)
Nanuet	(G-8751)	Montour Falls	(G-8609)	Cutchogue	(G-4071)	West Babylon	(G-16760)	Wawarsing	(G-16708)
New City	(G-8781)	Odessa	(G-13108)	Deer Park	(G-4085)	West Islip	(G-16902)	West Hurley	(G-16901)
Nyack	(G-13043)	Rock Stream	(G-14779)	Dix Hills	(G-4288)	West Sayville	(G-16933)	Woodstock	(G-17362)
Orangeburg	(G-13217)	Watkins Glen	(G-16693)	East Hampton	(G-4405)	Westhampton	(G-17056)		
Palisades	(G-13400)	Wayne	(G-16712)	East Islip	(G-4417)	Westhampton Beach	(G-17058)	**Warren**	
Pearl River	(G-13454)			East Moriches	(G-4429)	Wyandanch	(G-17369)	Bakers Mills	(G-557)
Piermont	(G-13545)	**Seneca**		East Northport	(G-4432)	Yaphank	(G-17384)	Brant Lake	(G-1173)
Pomona	(G-13728)	Fayette	(G-5162)	East Patchogue	(G-4447)			Chestertown	(G-3621)
Sloatsburg	(G-15480)	Interlaken	(G-6746)	East Quogue	(G-4450)	**Sullivan**		Glens Falls	(G-5669)
Spring Valley	(G-15578)	Lodi	(G-7635)	East Setauket	(G-4474)	Barryville	(G-620)	Lake George	(G-7261)
Stony Point	(G-15773)	Ovid	(G-13345)	East Yaphank	(G-4581)	Bethel	(G-859)	Lake Luzerne	(G-7272)
Suffern	(G-15784)	Romulus	(G-14841)	Eastport	(G-4584)	Callicoon	(G-3284)	North Creek	(G-12933)
Tallman	(G-16077)	Seneca Falls	(G-15360)	Edgewood	(G-4589)	Cochecton	(G-3740)	Queensbury	(G-13986)
Tappan	(G-16078)	Waterloo	(G-16624)	Farmingville	(G-5159)	Ferndale	(G-5168)	Silver Bay	(G-15446)
Thiells	(G-16114)			Great River	(G-5850)	Harris	(G-5976)	Warrensburg	(G-16580)
Tomkins Cove	(G-16131)	**St. Lawrence**		Greenlawn	(G-5872)	Hurleyville	(G-6731)		
Valley Cottage	(G-16374)	Brasher Falls	(G-1174)	Greenport	(G-5876)	Jeffersonville	(G-7058)	**Washington**	
West Haverstraw	(G-16846)	Canton	(G-3380)	Halesite	(G-5905)	Kauneonga Lake	(G-7136)	Argyle	(G-408)
West Nyack	(G-16910)	Childwold	(G-3628)	Hampton Bays	(G-5960)	Liberty	(G-7436)	Cambridge	(G-3304)
		Cranberry Lake	(G-4057)	Hauppauge	(G-6006)	Livingston Manor	(G-7561)	Cossayuna	(G-4055)
Saratoga		Gouverneur	(G-5742)	Holbrook	(G-6429)	Long Eddy	(G-7642)	Fort Ann	(G-5337)
Ballston Lake	(G-579)	Hammond	(G-5952)	Holtsville	(G-6500)	Monticello	(G-8604)	Fort Edward	(G-5339)
Ballston Spa	(G-589)	Heuvelton	(G-6305)					Granville	(G-5773)
		Madrid	(G-7995)					Greenwich	(G-5886)

COUNTY/CITY CROSS-REFERENCE

	ENTRY #		ENTRY #		ENTRY #		ENTRY #		ENTRY #
Hampton	(G-5959)	Williamson	(G-17222)	Harrison	(G-5977)	Pound Ridge	(G-13942)	Attica	(G-471)
Hartford	(G-5996)	Wolcott	(G-17276)	Hartsdale	(G-5997)	Purchase	(G-13953)	Bliss	(G-980)
Hudson Falls	(G-6638)	**Westchester**		Hastings On Hudson	(G-6002)	Purdys	(G-13972)	Castile	(G-3416)
Middle Granville	(G-8398)	Amawalk	(G-214)	Hawthorne	(G-6242)	Rye	(G-15054)	Gainesville	(G-5483)
Salem	(G-15111)	Ardsley	(G-403)	Irvington	(G-6766)	Rye Brook	(G-15070)	Java Village	(G-7053)
Whitehall	(G-17189)	Armonk	(G-412)	Jefferson Valley	(G-7056)	Scarsdale	(G-15216)	North Java	(G-12934)
Wayne		Baldwin Place	(G-563)	Katonah	(G-7133)	Sleepy Hollow	(G-15475)	Perry	(G-13524)
Clyde	(G-3725)	Bedford	(G-796)	Larchmont	(G-7350)	Somers	(G-15509)	Portageville	(G-13872)
Lyons	(G-7970)	Bedford Hills	(G-799)	Mamaroneck	(G-8023)	South Salem	(G-15535)	Silver Springs	(G-15451)
Macedon	(G-7979)	Briarcliff Manor	(G-1231)	Mohegan Lake	(G-8543)	Tarrytown	(G-16084)	Warsaw	(G-16582)
Marion	(G-8094)	Bronxville	(G-1498)	Montrose	(G-8613)	Thornwood	(G-16116)	Wyoming	(G-17380)
Newark	(G-12728)	Buchanan	(G-2785)	Mount Kisco	(G-8621)	Tuckahoe	(G-16269)	**Yates**	
North Rose	(G-12936)	Chappaqua	(G-3550)	Mount Vernon	(G-8659)	Valhalla	(G-16365)	Branchport	(G-1172)
Ontario	(G-13195)	Cortlandt Manor	(G-4048)	New Rochelle	(G-8883)	Waccabuc	(G-16520)	Dresden	(G-4318)
Palmyra	(G-13405)	Croton Falls	(G-4061)	North Salem	(G-12939)	White Plains	(G-17072)	Dundee	(G-4326)
Red Creek	(G-14025)	Croton On Hudson	(G-4062)	Ossining	(G-13320)	Yonkers	(G-17410)	Himrod	(G-6422)
Savannah	(G-15202)	Dobbs Ferry	(G-4300)	Peekskill	(G-13473)	Yorktown Heights	(G-17506)	Penn Yan	(G-13506)
Sodus	(G-15503)	Eastchester	(G-4582)	Pelham	(G-13488)	**Wyoming**		Rushville	(G-15053)
Walworth	(G-16550)	Elmsford	(G-4731)	Pleasantville	(G-13712)	Arcade	(G-386)		
				Port Chester	(G-13737)				

GEOGRAPHIC SECTION

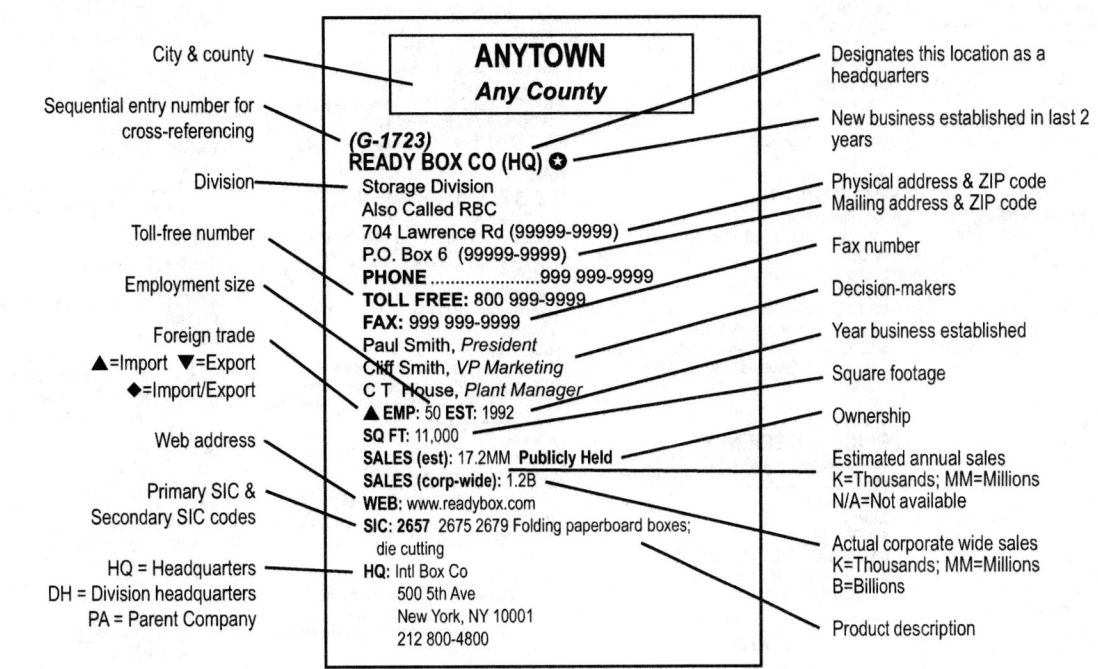

See footnotes for symbols and codes identification.
- This section is in alphabetical order by city.
- Companies are sorted alphabetically under their respective cities.
- To locate cities within a county refer to the County/City Cross Reference Index.

IMPORTANT NOTICE: It is a violation of both federal and state law to transmit an unsolicited advertisement to a facsimile machine. Any user of this product that violates such laws may be subject to civil and criminal penalties which may exceed $500 for each transmission of an unsolicited facsimile. Harris InfoSource provides fax numbers for lawful purposes only and expressly forbids the use of these numbers in any unlawful manner.

Accord
Ulster County

(G-1)
VIC DEMAYOS INC
4967 Us Highway 209 (12404-5723)
P.O. Box 253 (12404-0253)
PHONE.................................845 626-4343
Fax: 845 626-3335
Vic De Mayo, *President*
Eugene De Mayo, *President*
EMP: 6 EST: 1964
SQ FT: 4,000
SALES: 225K Privately Held
SIC: 3111 5941 Accessory products, leather; sporting goods & bicycle shops

Adams
Jefferson County

(G-2)
BENJAMIN PRINTING INC
Also Called: Minuteman Press
60 E Church St (13605-1103)
PHONE.................................315 788-7922
Fax: 315 788-8103
Charles Adams, *President*
Michael Biolsi, *General Mgr*
Vitusa Adams, *Vice Pres*
Ed Yancey, *Graphic Designe*
EMP: 14
SQ FT: 4,000
SALES (est): 1.1MM Privately Held
WEB: www.benjaminprinting.com
SIC: 2752 Commercial printing, lithographic

(G-3)
GREAT LAKES CHEESE NY INC
23 Phelps St (13605-1096)
PHONE.................................315 232-4511
Fax: 315 232-4055
Gary Vanic, *Ch of Bd*
Hans Epprecht, *President*
John Epprecht, *Vice Pres*
John Jennings, *Opers Mgr*
Tracy Stuckey, *Purch Dir*
EMP: 79
SQ FT: 88,000
SALES (est): 26.1MM
SALES (corp-wide): 1.3B Privately Held
WEB: www.greatlakescheese.com
SIC: 2022 Cheese, natural & processed
PA: Great Lakes Cheese Co., Inc.
   17825 Great Lakes Pkwy
   Hiram OH 44234
   440 834-2500

Adams Center
Jefferson County

(G-4)
R G KING GENERAL CONSTRUCTION
Also Called: Kings Quarry
13018 County Route 155 (13606-3104)
PHONE.................................315 583-3560
Fax: 315 583-3560
Ronald King, *President*
Bill King, *Vice Pres*
EMP: 5
SALES (est): 462K Privately Held
SIC: 1442 Construction sand & gravel

Addison
Steuben County

(G-5)
CRAWFORD PRINT SHOP INC
6120 Herrington Rd (14801-9235)
PHONE.................................607 359-4970
Adam Crawford, *President*
EMP: 5
SALES: 220K Privately Held
WEB: www.crawfordsprintshop.com
SIC: 2752 Color lithography

(G-6)
FICS INC
25 Community Dr (14801-1140)
P.O. Box 328, Painted Post (14870-0328)
PHONE.................................607 359-4474
Fax: 607 359-4478
Shawn E Smith, *President*
Michael Harold, *Corp Secy*
Steve E Boyer, *Vice Pres*
EMP: 20
SQ FT: 4,000
SALES (est): 5.6MM Privately Held
WEB: www.fics.cc
SIC: 3625 Electric controls & control accessories, industrial

(G-7)
HES INC
6303 Symonds Hill Rd (14801-9564)
PHONE.................................607 359-2974
John J Crane, *President*

Paula Spencer, *Office Mgr*
EMP: 8
SQ FT: 10,000
SALES: 450K Privately Held
SIC: 3621 3599 Electric motor & generator parts; machine shop, jobbing & repair

Afton
Chenango County

(G-8)
BABYSAFE USA LLC
251 County Road 17 (13730-3111)
PHONE.................................877 367-4141
Sagi Ben-Dov, *Mng Member*
Ron Berry, *Manager*
Mary Rosario, *Manager*
Jamie Baciuska,
Lynn Baciuska,
▲ EMP: 5
SQ FT: 8,000
SALES: 235K Privately Held
SIC: 3944 Baby carriages & restraint seats

(G-9)
COBRA OPERATING INDUSTRIES LLC
37 Main St (13730-3164)
PHONE.................................607 639-1700
Barbara A Wagner,
Richard W Wagner,
EMP: 6
SALES (est): 400K Privately Held
SIC: 3441 Fabricated structural metal

Airmont
Rockland County

(G-10)
1ROBOTICS LLC
360 Route 59 (10952-3415)
PHONE..................845 369-6770
Lonnie Ebner, *VP Finance*
Serge Seguin,
Aplonia Ebner,
EMP: 8
SALES (est): 690K **Privately Held**
SIC: 3812 Search & navigation equipment

(G-11)
901 D LLC
360 Route 59 Ste 3 (10952-3416)
P.O. Box 615, Tallman (10982-0615)
PHONE..................845 369-1111
Fax: 845 369-0531
Serge Seguin, *CEO*
Frank Duvergne, *General Mgr*
Aldric Seguin, *Exec VP*
Thomas Aspinwall, *CFO*
Andrew Eisenberg, *Program Mgr*
EMP: 48
SALES (est): 11MM
SALES (corp-wide): 52.9MM **Privately Held**
WEB: www.901d.com
SIC: 3499 8711 3812 3679 Aerosol valves, metal; engineering services; search & navigation equipment; antennas, receiving; computer terminals, monitors & components
PA: Graycliff Partners, Lp
   500 5th Ave Fl 47
   New York NY 10110
   212 300-2900

(G-12)
ART ESSENTIALS OF NEW YORK (PA)
25 Church Rd (10952-4108)
P.O. Box 38, Tallman (10982-0038)
PHONE..................845 368-1100
Bella Jacobs, *President*
Arnold A Jacobs, *Shareholder*
EMP: 2
SQ FT: 1,400
SALES: 1MM **Privately Held**
WEB: www.artessentialsofnewyork.com
SIC: 2499 Decorative wood & woodwork

(G-13)
CREATIVE KIDS FAR EAST INC
382 Route 59 (10952-3419)
PHONE..................845 368-0246
Samuel Lapa, *Chairman*
▲ **EMP:** 120
SALES (est): 12.8MM **Privately Held**
WEB: www.creativekidsltd.com
SIC: 3944 5092 Games, toys & children's vehicles; toys & hobby goods & supplies

(G-14)
DRT LABORATORIES LLC
331 Spook Rock Rd (10901-5319)
PHONE..................845 547-2034
Ronit Arginteanu,
EMP: 5
SALES (est): 556K **Privately Held**
SIC: 2844 2834 Cosmetic preparations; druggists' preparations (pharmaceuticals)

(G-15)
HANDY LAUNDRY PRODUCTS CORP (PA)
382 Route 59 Ste 318 (10952-3422)
PHONE..................800 263-5973
Edward Pinkesz, *President*
Aron Braun, *Principal*
Shlome Masri, *Office Mgr*
EMP: 6
SALES (est): 456.5K **Privately Held**
SIC: 2392 Laundry, garment & storage bags

(G-16)
JOMAR INDUSTRIES INC
382 Route 59 Ste 352 (10952-3484)
P.O. Box 379, Monsey (10952-0379)
PHONE..................845 357-5773
Fax: 845 357-5119
Alan Marks, *President*
Jonathan Marks, *Vice Pres*
▲ **EMP:** 20
SQ FT: 4,000
SALES (est): 1.6MM **Privately Held**
WEB: www.jomarindustries.com
SIC: 3993 2395 5961 2759 Advertising novelties; art needlework: made from purchased materials; gift items, mail order; commercial printing

(G-17)
NY CUTTING INC
Also Called: Uppercut
382 Route 59 Ste 286 (10952-3422)
PHONE..................845 368-1459
Solomon Katz, *CEO*
▲ **EMP:** 6
SQ FT: 2,500
SALES: 1MM **Privately Held**
SIC: 2392 2621 Placemats, plastic or textile; towels, tissues & napkins: paper & stock

(G-18)
PRINCETON SCIENCES
386 Route 59 Ste 402 (10952-3411)
PHONE..................845 368-1214
Todd Hoffman,
EMP: 7
SQ FT: 1,000
SALES (est): 360K **Privately Held**
SIC: 2833 Vitamins, natural or synthetic: bulk, uncompounded

Akron
Erie County

(G-19)
AAKRON RULE CORP (PA)
8 Indianola Ave (14001-1199)
P.O. Box 418 (14001-0418)
PHONE..................716 542-5483
Fax: 585 542-1537
Danielle Robillard, *Ch of Bd*
Devin Piscitelli, *Vice Pres*
Angel Alicea, *Plant Mgr*
George Vancleef, *Opers Mgr*
Jean Taylor, *Purch Mgr*
◆ **EMP:** 150 **EST:** 1967
SQ FT: 16,000
SALES (est): 36MM **Privately Held**
WEB: www.aakronline.com
SIC: 2499 3993 3952 3951 Rulers & rules, wood; paint sticks, wood; signs & advertising specialties; lead pencils & art goods; pens & mechanical pencils

(G-20)
AAKRON RULE CORP
2 Oak St (14001-1111)
PHONE..................716 542-5483
EMP: 76
SALES (corp-wide): 36MM **Privately Held**
SIC: 2499 Rulers & rules, wood
PA: Aakron Rule Corp.
   8 Indianola Ave
   Akron NY 14001
   716 542-5483

(G-21)
COUNTY LINE STONE CO INC
4515 Crittenden Rd (14001-9517)
P.O. Box 150 (14001-0150)
PHONE..................716 542-5435
Fax: 585 542-5442
John Buyers Jr, *Vice Pres*
Bruce M Buyers, *Vice Pres*
Wendy Seabo, *Admin Sec*
EMP: 30
SQ FT: 20,000
SALES (est): 4.2MM **Privately Held**
SIC: 1429 5032 Sandstone, crushed & broken-quarrying; asphalt mixture

(G-22)
FORD GUM & MACHINE COMPANY INC (PA)
18 Newton Ave (14001-1099)
P.O. Box 330 (14001-0330)
PHONE..................716 542-4561
Fax: 585 542-4610
George H Stege, *Ch of Bd*
Robert A R Clouston, *Ch of Bd*
George H Stege, *Ch of Bd*
George Stege, *President*
Luela Lo, *General Mgr*
▲ **EMP:** 100 **EST:** 1913
SQ FT: 125,000
SALES (est): 57.8MM **Privately Held**
WEB: www.fordgum.com
SIC: 2067 5441 Chewing gum; candy

(G-23)
G & S FARM & HOME INC
Also Called: Agway
13550 Bloomingdale Rd (14001-9801)
P.O. Box 214 (14001-0214)
PHONE..................716 542-9922
Gregg Brown, *President*
Sue Brown, *Admin Sec*
SQ FT: 6,000
SALES (est): 1.1MM **Privately Held**
SIC: 2879 5261 Agricultural chemicals; arsenates, arsenites (formulated); nurseries & garden centers

(G-24)
IGNITER SYSTEMS INC
12600 Clarence Center Rd (14001-9749)
PHONE..................716 542-5511
John Davis, *President*
EMP: 20
SQ FT: 90,000
SALES (est): 1.6MM **Privately Held**
WEB: www.ignitersystems.com
SIC: 3567 Heating units & devices, industrial: electric

(G-25)
NIAGARA LABEL COMPANY INC
12715 Lewis Rd (14001-9668)
P.O. Box 90 (14001-0090)
PHONE..................716 542-3000
Fax: 585 542-2608
Michael C Witmarsh, *CEO*
Marjorie Witmarsh, *Corp Secy*
Chris Whitmarsh, *Sales Mgr*
Tina Lemley, *Accounts Mgr*
Shannon Radlich, *Sales Associate*
EMP: 17
SQ FT: 5,000
SALES (est): 3MM **Privately Held**
WEB: www.niagaralabel.com
SIC: 2754 2759 Labels: gravure printing; labels & seals: printing

(G-26)
NIAGARA SPECIALTY METALS INC
12600 Clarence Center Rd (14001-9749)
P.O. Box 280 (14001-0280)
PHONE..................716 542-5552
Fax: 585 542-5555
Robert F Shabala Jr, *President*
Timothy Gelnett, *Vice Pres*
Ray Ferington, *Sales Staff*
Jeff Rich, *Sales Staff*
◆ **EMP:** 37
SQ FT: 110,000
SALES (est): 16.9MM **Privately Held**
WEB: www.nsm-ny.com
SIC: 3312 Hot-rolled iron & steel products

(G-27)
PERRYS ICE CREAM COMPANY INC
1 Ice Cream Plz (14001-1031)
PHONE..................716 542-5492
Fax: 585 542-2544
Robert Denning, *President*
Brian Perry, *Exec VP*
Diane Austin, *Vice Pres*
Nancy Lynch, *Human Res Mgr*
Jim Marshall, *Manager*
▲ **EMP:** 300 **EST:** 1918
SQ FT: 135,000
SALES (est): 79.1MM **Privately Held**
SIC: 2024 5145 Ice cream & frozen desserts; snack foods

(G-28)
RE-AL INDUSTRIAL CORP
Also Called: D & E Industrial
5391 Crittenden Rd (14001-9598)
P.O. Box 37, Newfane (14108-0037)
PHONE..................716 542-4556
Fax: 585 542-4558
Richard Bottom, *President*
EMP: 8
SQ FT: 8,000
SALES: 700K **Privately Held**
WEB: www.d-eind.com
SIC: 3535 1796 Conveyors & conveying equipment; machinery installation

(G-29)
STRIPPIT INC (DH)
Also Called: L V D
12975 Clarence Center Rd (14001-1371)
PHONE..................716 542-5500
Fax: 585 542-5957
John Lesebbre, *President*
James C Blackstone, *Vice Pres*
Pam Halchishak, *Vice Pres*
John J Quigley, *Vice Pres*
Bruce Turner, *Vice Pres*
▲ **EMP:** 200
SQ FT: 255,000
SALES (est): 49.3MM
SALES (corp-wide): 69.2K **Privately Held**
SIC: 3542 3544 3549 3545 Machine tools, metal forming type; special dies, tools, jigs & fixtures; metalworking machinery; machine tool accessories
HQ: L.V.D. Company Nv
   Nijverheidslaan 2
   Wevelgem 8560
   564 305-11

(G-30)
WHITING DOOR MFG CORP (PA)
113 Cedar St (14001-1038)
P.O. Box 388 (14001-0388)
PHONE..................716 542-5427
Fax: 716 542-5947
Donald J Whiting, *Ch of Bd*
Steve Shelby, *Vice Pres*
Bob Stoll, *Vice Pres*
Lauren Whiting, *Vice Pres*
Michael T Whiting, *Vice Pres*
▼ **EMP:** 330 **EST:** 1953
SQ FT: 371,000
SALES (est): 115.7MM **Privately Held**
SIC: 3714 Motor vehicle parts & accessories

(G-31)
WHITING DOOR MFG CORP
13550 Bloomingdale Rd (14001-9801)
PHONE..................716 542-3070
Fax: 716 542-1658
Craig Smith, *Plant Mgr*
Michael Whiting, *Manager*
Joe Lukasiewizd, *Info Tech Dir*
EMP: 60
SALES (corp-wide): 115.7MM **Privately Held**
SIC: 3493 Coiled flat springs
PA: Whiting Door Mfg Corp
   113 Cedar St
   Akron NY 14001
   716 542-5427

Akwesasne
Franklin County

(G-32)
OHSERASE MANUFACTURING LLC
26 Eagle Dr (13655)
P.O. Box 1221 (13655-1221)
PHONE..................518 358-9309
Justin Tarbell, *Vice Pres*
▲ **EMP:** 25
SALES (est): 3.4MM **Privately Held**
SIC: 3999 Barber & beauty shop equipment

▲ = Import ▼ = Export
◆ = Import/Export

Albany
Albany County

(G-33)
ACCESSIBLE BATH TECH LLC
6 Albright Ave (12203-4802)
PHONE.....................518 937-1518
Craig La Londe, *President*
EMP: 15
SALES: 950K **Privately Held**
SIC: 3999 Manufacturing industries

(G-34)
ACCUPRINT (PA)
2005 Western Ave Ste 1 (12203-5073)
PHONE.....................518 456-2431
Donald Blais, *Owner*
Geoff Ryan, *Prdtn Mgr*
EMP: 6
SALES (est): 538.8K **Privately Held**
SIC: 2752 Commercial printing, lithographic

(G-35)
ADIRONDACK SPCLTY ADHSIVES INC
4258 Albany St (12205-4614)
P.O. Box 13283 (12212-3283)
PHONE.....................518 869-5736
Fax: 518 869-3584
Jerald Casey, *President*
Debra Stoecker, *Controller*
Phil Desnoyers, *Systems Staff*
EMP: 15
SQ FT: 7,500
SALES (est): 3.6MM **Privately Held**
WEB: www.adktapes.com
SIC: 2891 Adhesives

(G-36)
AIRGAS INC
84 Karner Rd (12205-4730)
PHONE.....................518 690-0068
Lester Mackey, *Branch Mgr*
F Gay Dunn, *Co-Mgr*
EMP: 14
SALES (corp-wide): 189.3MM **Privately Held**
SIC: 2813 Oxygen, compressed or liquefied
HQ: Airgas, Inc.
  259 N Radnor Chester Rd
  Radnor PA 19087
  610 687-5253

(G-37)
ALBANY ASP & AGGREGATES CORP
101 Dunham Dr (12202-2106)
PHONE.....................518 436-8916
Frederick M Stutzman, *President*
Philip Carnevale, *Vice Pres*
Eugene D Hallock III, *Vice Pres*
John Stutzman, *Vice Pres*
Ray Lohrebsa, *Director*
EMP: 20 **EST:** 1948
SQ FT: 10,000
SALES (est): 4.3MM
SALES (corp-wide): 12.7MM **Privately Held**
SIC: 2951 Asphalt paving mixtures & blocks
PA: Hudson River Construction Co., Inc.
  101 Dunham Dr
  Albany NY 12202
  518 434-6677

(G-38)
ALBANY CATHOLIC PRESS ASSOC
Also Called: Evangelist, The
40 N Main Ave Ste 2 (12203-1481)
PHONE.....................518 453-6688
Fax: 518 453-6793
James Breig, *Principal*
Bishop Hubbard, *Principal*
Stephanie Zebrowski, *Manager*
Barbra Oliver, *Manager*
EMP: 9
SQ FT: 10,000
SALES: 1MM **Privately Held**
SIC: 2711 8661 Newspapers: publishing only, not printed on site; religious organizations

(G-39)
ALBANY LETTER SHOP INC
16 Van Zandt St Ste 20 (12207-1448)
P.O. Box 1003 (12201-1003)
PHONE.....................518 434-1172
Lawrence A Propp, *President*
EMP: 6
SQ FT: 2,900
SALES (est): 41.6K **Privately Held**
SIC: 2752 Commercial printing, offset

(G-40)
ALBANY MOLECULAR RESEARCH INC
21 Corporate Cir (12203-5154)
PHONE.....................518 512-2234
Kathryn Saybe, *Purch Agent*
EMP: 42
SALES (corp-wide): 402.3MM **Publicly Held**
SIC: 2836 8731 Biological products, except diagnostic; commercial physical research
PA: Albany Molecular Research, Inc.
  26 Corporate Cir
  Albany NY 12203
  518 512-2000

(G-41)
ALBANY MOLECULAR RESEARCH INC (PA)
26 Corporate Cir (12203-5121)
P.O. Box 15098 (12212-5098)
PHONE.....................518 512-2000
Fax: 518 464-0289
Thomas E D'Ambra, *Ch of Bd*
William S Marth, *President*
George Svokos, *COO*
Steven R Hagen, *Senior VP*
Lori M Henderson, *Senior VP*
◆ **EMP:** 249
SQ FT: 169,000
SALES: 402.3MM **Publicly Held**
SIC: 2836 8731 Biological products, except diagnostic; biotechnical research, commercial

(G-42)
ALBANY MTAL FBRCATION HOLDINGS
67 Henry Johnson Blvd (12210-1413)
PHONE.....................518 463-5161
Fax: 518 426-4232
Dave Warzek, *Principal*
EMP: 7
SALES (est): 1.1MM **Privately Held**
SIC: 3499 Fabricated metal products

(G-43)
ALBANY STUDENT PRESS INC
Also Called: A S P
1400 Washington Ave Cc329 (12222-0100)
PHONE.....................518 442-5665
Carey Qeen, *Manager*
EMP: 30
SALES: 12.4MM **Privately Held**
SIC: 2711 2741 Newspapers; miscellaneous publishing

(G-44)
ALL-LIFTS INCORPORATED
27-39 Thatcher St (12207-5016)
PHONE.....................518 465-3461
Fax: 518 465-0342
Steven R Dewey, *President*
Patrick Dewey, *Vice Pres*
Beth Wilson, *Accountant*
Jannes Scott, *Manager*
Glenn Simon, *Manager*
EMP: 25 **EST:** 1966
SQ FT: 12,400
SALES (est): 8.2MM **Privately Held**
WEB: www.all-lifts.com
SIC: 3496 2298 5063 Miscellaneous fabricated wire products; chain, welded; slings, rope; electrical construction materials

(G-45)
ALO ACQUISITION LLC (HQ)
26 Corporate Cir (12203-5121)
PHONE.....................518 464-0279
Thomas E D'Ambra, *Ch of Bd*
EMP: 4
SALES (est): 105.8MM
SALES (corp-wide): 402.3MM **Publicly Held**
SIC: 2833 5122 8733 Medicinals & botanicals; drugs & drug proprietaries; research institute
PA: Albany Molecular Research, Inc.
  26 Corporate Cir
  Albany NY 12203
  518 512-2000

(G-46)
AMERICAN BOILER TANK WLDG INC
53 Pleasant St (12207-1385)
PHONE.....................518 463-5012
Fax: 518 463-5087
William A Novak, *President*
Bill Engel, *Buyer*
Paul Engel, *Manager*
Brenda Longe, *Manager*
EMP: 20 **EST:** 1936
SQ FT: 30,000
SALES: 5MM **Privately Held**
WEB: www.americanboiler.com
SIC: 3443 Fabricated plate work (boiler shop)

(G-47)
AMRI RENSSELAER
26 Corporate Cir (12203-5121)
PHONE.....................518 512-2000
Thomas E D'Ambra, *President*
Kevin McGee, *General Mgr*
Christopher Conway, *Business Mgr*
Wendy Kriz, *Business Mgr*
Paul Brodfuehrer, *Project Mgr*
▲ **EMP:** 903 **EST:** 2010
SALES (est): 52.3MM
SALES (corp-wide): 402.3MM **Publicly Held**
SIC: 2833 Medicinals & botanicals
PA: Albany Molecular Research, Inc.
  26 Corporate Cir
  Albany NY 12203
  518 512-2000

(G-48)
ARCY PLASTIC LAMINATES INC (PA)
555 Patroon Creek Blvd (12206-5007)
PHONE.....................518 235-0753
Robert Cecucci, *Asst Sec*
EMP: 40 **EST:** 1952
SQ FT: 31,000
SALES (est): 4.3MM **Privately Held**
SIC: 2541 Counter & sink tops

(G-49)
ARDENT MILLS LLC
Cargill
101 Normanskill St (12202-2155)
PHONE.....................518 447-1700
Jim Hess, *Sales Staff*
Cody Meyers, *Manager*
Karen Horton, *Executive*
EMP: 100
SALES (corp-wide): 694.8MM **Privately Held**
WEB: www.cargill.com
SIC: 2041 0723 Flour & other grain mill products; flour milling custom services
PA: Ardent Mills Llc
  1875 Lawrence St Ste 200
  Denver CO 80202
  800 851-9618

(G-50)
ART & UNDERSTANDING INC
Also Called: A & U America's Aids Magazine
25 Monroe St Ste 205 (12210-2744)
PHONE.....................518 426-9010
David Waggoner, *Director*
EMP: 7
SALES (est): 690K **Privately Held**
SIC: 2721 Magazines: publishing only, not printed on site

(G-51)
BACKYARD FENCE INC
4204 Albany St (12205-4508)
PHONE.....................518 452-9496
Fax: 518 456-4568
Gerald Haley, *President*
EMP: 12
SALES: 1.2MM **Privately Held**
SIC: 3499 Barricades, metal

(G-52)
BARKER STEEL LLC
126 S Port Rd (12202-1087)
PHONE.....................518 465-6221
Fax: 518 465-6224
John Gradoni, *Sales Mgr*
Duane Miller, *Sales Staff*
Gary Wolfe, *Sales Staff*
David Legenbauer, *Branch Mgr*
Scott Henricks, *Branch Mgr*
EMP: 20
SALES (corp-wide): 122.1MM **Privately Held**
WEB: www.barker.com
SIC: 3449 8742 3441 Bars, concrete reinforcing: fabricated steel; management consulting services; fabricated structural metal
PA: Barker Steel Llc
  55 Sumner St Ste 1
  Milford MA 01757
  508 473-8484

(G-53)
BEN WEITSMAN OF ALBANY LLC
300 Smith Blvd (12202-1090)
P.O. Box 420, Owego (13827-0420)
PHONE.....................518 462-4444
Stephnen Green, *President*
Joel Root, *Vice Pres*
Daniel Innarella, *CFO*
Heather Davison, *Office Mgr*
Adam Weitsman,
EMP: 20 **EST:** 2013
SALES: 21MM
SALES (corp-wide): 54.3MM **Privately Held**
SIC: 3559 3341 Recycling machinery; copper smelting & refining (secondary)
HQ: Upstate Shredding, Llc
  1 Recycle Dr Tioga Indust K Industrial Par
  Owego NY 13827
  607 687-7777

(G-54)
BENWAY-HAWORTH-LWLR-LACOSTA HE
Also Called: Hearing Aid Office, The
21 Everett Rd (12205-1437)
PHONE.....................518 432-4070
Fax: 518 432-4070
Robert Lacosta, *President*
EMP: 12
SQ FT: 2,000
SALES (est): 1.4MM **Privately Held**
SIC: 3842 5999 Hearing aids; hearing aids

(G-55)
BEST PALLET & CRATE LLC
22 Railroad Ave (12205-5727)
PHONE.....................518 438-2945
Neil Manasse,
EMP: 6
SALES (est): 836.2K **Privately Held**
SIC: 2448 Wood pallets & skids

(G-56)
BIMBO BAKERIES
78 N Manning Blvd (12206-2294)
PHONE.....................518 463-2221
Joe Rebholtz, *Principal*
EMP: 16
SALES (est): 2.6MM **Privately Held**
SIC: 2051 Bread, cake & related products

(G-57)
BIMBO BAKERIES USA INC
40 Fuller Rd (12205-5122)
PHONE.....................518 489-4053
EMP: 18
SALES (corp-wide): 13B **Privately Held**
WEB: www.gwbakeries.com
SIC: 2051 Bread, cake & related products

Albany - Albany County (G-58) — GEOGRAPHIC SECTION

HQ: Bimbo Bakeries Usa, Inc
255 Business Center Dr # 300
Horsham PA 19044
215 347-5500

(G-58)
BULLEX INC (DH)
Also Called: Bullex Digital Safety
20 Corporate Cir Ste 3 (12203-5153)
PHONE.................518 689-2023
Ryan O Donnell, *CEO*
Simon Balint, *Sales Staff*
Damien Pinto-Martin, *Manager*
Jane Tezze, *Manager*
Tom Rossi,
▲ **EMP:** 10
SALES (est): 14.5MM
SALES (corp-wide): 79.8MM Privately Held
WEB: www.bullexsafety.com
SIC: 3569 8748 Firefighting apparatus; safety training service
HQ: Lion Training Resources Group, Inc.
7200 Poe Ave Ste 400
Dayton OH 45414
937 898-1949

(G-59)
BULLEX INC
Also Called: Bullex Digital Safety
20 Corporate Cir Ste 3 (12203-5153)
PHONE.................518 689-2023
Thomas Roffi, *Branch Mgr*
EMP: 50
SALES (corp-wide): 79.8MM Privately Held
WEB: www.bullexsafety.com
SIC: 3999 Fire extinguishers, portable
HQ: Bullex, Inc.
20 Corporate Cir Ste 3
Albany NY 12203
518 689-2023

(G-60)
CAPITAL REGION WKLY NEWSPAPERS
Also Called: Advertiser
645 Albany Shaker Rd (12211-1158)
P.O. Box 1450, Clifton Park (12065-0806)
PHONE.................518 877-7160
Fax: 518 877-7824
Patrick Smith, *President*
EMP: 29
SQ FT: 4,000
SALES (est): 1.3MM Privately Held
SIC: 2711 Newspapers, publishing & printing

(G-61)
CHAMPLAIN HUDSON POWER EX INC
600 Broadway Fl 3 (12207-2235)
PHONE.................518 465-0710
John Douglas, *CEO*
Donald Jensson, *President*
Scott Hargreaves, *CFO*
Sara Rong, *Coordinator*
EMP: 7
SQ FT: 500
SALES (est): 540K Privately Held
SIC: 3568 Power transmission equipment

(G-62)
CHAPMAN STAINED GLASS STUDIO
212 Quail St (12203-1223)
PHONE.................518 449-5552
Fax: 518 449-5594
Philip H Morgan, *President*
P Keith Morgan, *Vice Pres*
EMP: 7
SQ FT: 15,000
SALES (est): 430K Privately Held
SIC: 3231 1793 Stained glass: made from purchased glass; glass & glazing work

(G-63)
CHARLES FREIHOFER BAKING CO
1 Prospect Rd (12206-2229)
PHONE.................518 463-2221
Fax: 518 438-7721
Peter Rollins, *President*
Richard M Lee Jr, *Vice Pres*
EMP: 8

SALES (est): 720K Privately Held
SIC: 2499 Bakers' equipment, wood

(G-64)
CLEAR VIEW BAG COMPANY INC
5 Burdick Dr (12205-1405)
P.O. Box 11160 (12211-0160)
PHONE.................518 458-7153
Fax: 518 458-1401
William J Romer, *Ch of Bd*
Deborah S Romer, *Vice Pres*
Len Smith, *QC Mgr*
Todd Romer, *Human Res Mgr*
Angie Fullam, *Sales Executive*
EMP: 156 **EST:** 1957
SQ FT: 45,000
SALES (est): 29.7MM Privately Held
WEB: www.clearviewbag.com
SIC: 3081 2673 Polyethylene film; bags: plastic, laminated & coated

(G-65)
CMC-KUHNKE INC
1060 Brdwy (12204)
PHONE.................518 694-3310
Fax: 518 694-3311
Heinz Grossjohann, *President*
Alex Grossjohann, *Vice Pres*
Edward L Shively, *Technical Mgr*
Eric Mooberry, *Regl Sales Mgr*
Nicole Delavega, *Manager*
EMP: 12
SQ FT: 10,000
SALES (est): 2.2MM Privately Held
SIC: 3411 Food & beverage containers

(G-66)
CMP INDUSTRIES LLC (PA)
Also Called: Ticonium Division
413 N Pearl St (12207-1311)
PHONE.................518 434-3147
Fax: 518 434-1288
Walter Pietro, *Mfg Dir*
Stephen Pace, *Traffic Mgr*
Walter Piepro, *Mfg Staff*
Tim Brennan, *Purch Agent*
Ed Civiok, *CFO*
◆ **EMP:** 40 **EST:** 1889
SQ FT: 90,000
SALES (est): 9.3MM Privately Held
WEB: www.cmpindustry.com
SIC: 3843 Dental equipment & supplies

(G-67)
CMP INDUSTRIES LLC
Also Called: Nobilium
413 N Pearl St (12207-1311)
PHONE.................518 434-3147
William Regan, *Branch Mgr*
EMP: 5
SALES (corp-wide): 9.3MM Privately Held
WEB: www.cmpindustry.com
SIC: 3843 Dental laboratory equipment
PA: Cmp Industries Llc
413 N Pearl St
Albany NY 12207
518 434-3147

(G-68)
COCA-COLA BOTTLING CO OF NY
38 Warehouse Row (12205-5757)
PHONE.................518 459-2010
Fax: 518 435-8140
Dwayne Claire, *COO*
Dwayne St Claire, *COO*
Duane St Clair, *Plant Mgr*
Dwayne St Clair, *Opers Mgr*
Jeff Moore, *Safety Mgr*
EMP: 11
SALES (corp-wide): 44.2B Publicly Held
SIC: 2086 5149 Bottled & canned soft drinks; groceries & related products
HQ: The Coca-Cola Bottling Company Of New York Inc
2500 Windy Ridge Pkwy Se
Atlanta GA 30339
770 989-3000

(G-69)
COCCADOTTS INC
1179 Central Ave (12205-5436)
PHONE.................518 438-4937
Rachel Dott, *Owner*

EMP: 10
SALES (est): 1.1MM Privately Held
SIC: 2051 Cakes, bakery: except frozen

(G-70)
COMMERCEHUB INC (PA)
201 Fuller Rd Fl 6 (12203-3640)
PHONE.................518 810-0700
Richard N Baer, *Ch of Bd*
Francis Poore, *President*
Richard Jones, *Exec VP*
Bill Kong, *Exec VP*
Mark Greenquist, *CFO*
EMP: 3 **EST:** 1997
SQ FT: 49,500
SALES (est): 87.6MM Publicly Held
SIC: 7372 Prepackaged software

(G-71)
DAVIES OFFICE REFURBISHING INC (PA)
40 Loudonville Rd (12204-1513)
PHONE.................518 426-7188
Fax: 518 449-4036
William E Davies, *President*
Patty Cocca, *Regional Mgr*
Evelyn Davies, *Vice Pres*
Sue Risler, *Finance Mgr*
Joan Griffin, *Manager*
▲ **EMP:** 130
SQ FT: 96,000
SALES (est): 41.8MM Privately Held
WEB: www.daviesoffice.com
SIC: 2522 7641 Office furniture, except wood; office furniture repair & maintenance

(G-72)
DE LA RUE NORTH AMERICA INC
Swan Street Building (12210)
PHONE.................518 463-7621
Nick Iacobucci, *General Mgr*
EMP: 8 **EST:** 1986
SALES (est): 640.9K
SALES (corp-wide): 658.3MM Privately Held
SIC: 2759 Security certificates: engraved
HQ: De La Rue North America Inc.
6401 Commerce Dr
Irving TX 75063
972 582-1100

(G-73)
DIGITAL PAGE LLC
75 Benjamin St (12202-1137)
PHONE.................518 446-9129
Eugene R Spada II,
EMP: 11
SQ FT: 2,000
SALES (est): 131K Privately Held
SIC: 2791 Typesetting

(G-74)
DYNAMIC SCREENPRINTING
12 Vatrano Rd (12205-3404)
PHONE.................518 487-4256
Jeff Serge, *Mng Member*
EMP: 9
SALES (est): 753.9K Privately Held
SIC: 2261 Screen printing of cotton broadwoven fabrics

(G-75)
EASY BOOK PUBLISHING INC
260 Osborne Rd Ste 3 (12211-1856)
PHONE.................518 459-6281
Nydia Russum, *President*
John Russum, *Vice Pres*
EMP: 6
SQ FT: 1,500
SALES (est): 622.5K Privately Held
WEB: www.easy-book.net
SIC: 2741 Directories: publishing only, not printed on site

(G-76)
EDP RENEWABLES NORTH AMER LLC
1971 Western Ave 230 (12203-5066)
PHONE.................518 426-1650
Patrick Doyle, *Branch Mgr*
EMP: 8
SALES (corp-wide): 3.1B Privately Held
SIC: 3621 Windmills, electric generating

HQ: Edp Renewables North America Llc
808 Travis St Ste 700
Houston TX 77002
713 265-0350

(G-77)
EMPIRE AIR SPECIALTIES INC
40 Kraft Ave (12205-5428)
PHONE.................518 689-4440
Fax: 518 689-4442
Robert J Miner, *President*
Rebecca Miner, *Treasurer*
EMP: 35
SQ FT: 5,500
SALES (est): 5.4MM Privately Held
SIC: 3444 Sheet metalwork

(G-78)
ENGINEERED MOLDING TECH LLC
Also Called: Emt
59 Exchange St (12205-3326)
PHONE.................518 482-2004
Todd Eteffe, *CEO*
Carrie Eteffe, *Manager*
Michael Pandori,
EMP: 16
SQ FT: 5,000
SALES: 2MM Privately Held
SIC: 3089 Molding primary plastic

(G-79)
FASTSIGNS
1593 Central Ave (12205-2457)
PHONE.................518 456-7446
Fax: 518 869-1808
James Pritchard, *Principal*
EMP: 10
SALES (est): 1.1MM Privately Held
SIC: 3993 Signs & advertising specialties

(G-80)
FINGERPRINT AMERICA INC
1843 Central Ave (12205-4796)
P.O. Box 12542 (12212-2542)
PHONE.................518 435-1609
Fax: 518 435-1507
Chris Migliaro, *President*
EMP: 6
SQ FT: 3,000
SALES (est): 1MM Privately Held
WEB: www.fingerprintamerica.com
SIC: 3999 Fingerprint equipment

(G-81)
FORT ORANGE PRESS INC
11 Sand Creek Rd (12205-1442)
PHONE.................518 489-3233
Fax: 518 489-1638
Robert F Witko, *Ch of Bd*
Frank P Witko, *Ch of Bd*
Michael P Witko, *President*
Jamie Dickinson, *Vice Pres*
William Dorsman, *Vice Pres*
EMP: 37 **EST:** 1905
SQ FT: 33,000
SALES (est): 11.8MM Privately Held
WEB: www.fortorangepress.com
SIC: 2752 2791 Commercial printing, offset; typesetting

(G-82)
GENERAL ELECTRIC COMPANY
11 Anderson Dr (12205-1401)
PHONE.................518 459-4110
James Miner, *Safety Mgr*
Kyle Badeau, *Engineer*
Michael Davi, *Engineer*
David Ebbing, *Engineer*
Mark Seus, *Design Engr*
EMP: 50
SQ FT: 1,680
SALES (corp-wide): 117.3B Publicly Held
SIC: 3629 7694 Electronic generation equipment; electric motor repair
PA: General Electric Company
41 Farnsworth St
Boston MA 02210
617 443-3000

(G-83)
GREENBUSH TAPE & LABEL INC
40 Broadway Unit 31 (12202-1174)
P.O. Box 1488 (12201-1488)
PHONE.................518 465-2389

Fax: 518 465-5781
Alfred Chenot, *Corp Secy*
James Chenot, *Vice Pres*
EMP: 35 **EST:** 1966
SQ FT: 75,000
SALES (est): 4.4MM **Privately Held**
WEB: www.greenbushlabel.com
SIC: 2759 2672 Labels & seals: printing; coated & laminated paper

(G-84)
HANES SUPPLY INC
156 Railroad Ave Ste 3 (12205-5773)
PHONE..................518 438-0139
Fax: 518 438-5343
Bill Kenny, *Manager*
Kevin Sitterly, *Manager*
EMP: 26
SALES (corp-wide): 108.4MM **Privately Held**
SIC: 3315 Wire & fabricated wire products
PA: Hanes Supply, Inc.
  55 James E Casey Dr
  Buffalo NY 14206
  716 826-2636

(G-85)
HANGER PRSTHETCS & ORTHO INC
1315 Central Ave (12205-5282)
PHONE..................518 446-1774
Thomas Kirk, *CEO*
Sheryl Price, *Director*
EMP: 99
SALES (corp-wide): 500.5MM **Privately Held**
SIC: 3842 Surgical appliances & supplies
HQ: Hanger Prosthetics & Orthotics, Inc.
  10910 Main Dr
  Austin TX 78758
  512 777-3800

(G-86)
HEARST CORPORATION
Capital Newspaper Div
645 Albany Shaker Rd (12211-1158)
P.O. Box 15000 (12212-5000)
PHONE..................518 454-5694
Tony Pallone, *Editor*
Kurt M Vantosky, *Senior VP*
David P White, *Vice Pres*
George Hearst, *Vice Pres*
Geary Morgan, *Plant Mgr*
EMP: 550
SALES (corp-wide): 4.9B **Privately Held**
WEB: www.hearstcorp.com
SIC: 2721 2752 2711 Periodicals: publishing only; commercial printing, lithographic; newspapers
PA: The Hearst Corporation
  300 W 57th St Fl 42
  New York NY 10019
  212 649-2000

(G-87)
HOCKEY FACILITY
830 Albany Shaker Rd (12211-1054)
PHONE..................518 452-7396
Fax: 518 452-5408
Paul Hebert, *Manager*
EMP: 5
SALES (est): 494.1K **Privately Held**
SIC: 2329 Hockey uniforms: men's, youths' & boys'

(G-88)
HOEHN INC
Also Called: Hoehn.us
159 Chestnut St (12210-1905)
PHONE..................518 463-8900
James G Hoehn Jr, *President*
Melissa Nigro, *Vice Pres*
EMP: 15
SALES: 1.6MM **Privately Held**
WEB: www.hoehn.com
SIC: 2339 2389 Women's & misses' accessories; men's miscellaneous accessories

(G-89)
HP HOOD LLC
9 Norman Dr (12205-4721)
PHONE..................518 218-9097
EMP: 299
SALES (corp-wide): 1.9B **Privately Held**
SIC: 2026 Fluid milk

PA: Hp Hood Llc
  6 Kimball Ln Ste 400
  Lynnfield MA 01940
  617 887-8441

(G-90)
ION OPTICS INC
Also Called: Cosmo Optics
75 Benjamin St (12202-1137)
PHONE..................518 339-6853
Brian Sebastian, *Principal*
EMP: 13 **EST:** 2012
SALES (est): 967.4K **Privately Held**
SIC: 3229 Lens blanks, optical

(G-91)
ISIMULATE LLC
90 State St Ste 700 (12207-1707)
PHONE..................877 947-2831
Bobby Sied, *General Mgr*
Bobby Syed, *Info Tech Mgr*
EMP: 5
SQ FT: 1,000
SALES: 500K **Privately Held**
SIC: 7372 Educational computer software

(G-92)
JASON LADANYE GUITAR PIANO & H
605 Park Ave (12208-3217)
PHONE..................518 527-3973
Jason Ladanye, *Owner*
EMP: 50
SALES (est): 68.3K **Privately Held**
SIC: 3931 Harmonicas

(G-93)
KAL-HARBOUR INC
Also Called: Harbour Roads
11 Villa Rd (12204-2213)
P.O. Box 4087 (12204-0087)
PHONE..................518 266-0690
Laura Harbour, *President*
EMP: 10
SALES (corp-wide): 1.9MM **Privately Held**
WEB: www.harbourroads.com
SIC: 2951 Asphalt paving mixtures & blocks
PA: Kal-Harbour Inc
  21 Arch St
  Watervliet NY 12189
  518 266-0690

(G-94)
KEEBLER COMPANY
12 Selina Dr (12205-4724)
PHONE..................518 464-1051
Mike Raila, *Manager*
EMP: 25
SALES (corp-wide): 13.5B **Publicly Held**
WEB: www.keebler.com
SIC: 2052 Cookies
HQ: Keebler Company
  1 Kellogg Sq
  Battle Creek MI 49017
  269 961-2000

(G-95)
KING ROAD MATERIALS INC
Cordell Rd (12212)
P.O. Box 12699 (12212-2699)
PHONE..................518 382-5354
Mellisa Bennett, *Principal*
EMP: 15
SALES (corp-wide): 25.3B **Privately Held**
SIC: 3273 Ready-mixed concrete
HQ: King Road Materials, Inc
  1245 Kings Rd
  Schenectady NY 12303
  518 381-9995

(G-96)
KOEPPELS KUSTOM KITCHENS INC
16 Van Rensselaer Rd (12205-1413)
PHONE..................518 489-0092
Fax: 518 489-0363
Carl J Koeppel Jr, *President*
EMP: 5
SQ FT: 4,500
SALES (est): 520K **Privately Held**
SIC: 2541 1751 Counter & sink tops; cabinet building & installation

(G-97)
LIDS CORPORATION
131 Colonie Ctr Spc 429 (12205-2751)
PHONE..................518 459-7060
Dinelle Jackson, *Manager*
EMP: 5
SALES (corp-wide): 3B **Publicly Held**
WEB: www.hatworld.com
SIC: 2253 Hats & headwear, knit
HQ: Lids Corporation
  7555 Woodland Dr
  Indianapolis IN 46278

(G-98)
M&G DURAVENT INC
10 Jupiter Ln (12205-4947)
PHONE..................518 463-7284
EMP: 16
SALES (corp-wide): 123.5K **Privately Held**
SIC: 3444 Metal ventilating equipment
HQ: M&G Duravent, Inc.
  877 Cotting Ct
  Vacaville CA 95688
  707 446-1786

(G-99)
MAINE POWER EXPRESS LLC
600 Broadway Fl 3 (12207-2235)
PHONE..................518 465-0710
John Douglas,
Scott Hargreaves,
Donald Jensson,
Sara Rong, *Coordinator*
EMP: 7
SQ FT: 500
SALES (est): 440K **Privately Held**
SIC: 3568 Power transmission equipment

(G-100)
MCD METALS LLC
20 Corporate Cir Ste 2 (12203-5175)
PHONE..................518 456-9694
Jacek Wozniak, *Opers Mgr*
EMP: 11
SALES (est): 414.6K **Privately Held**
SIC: 3499 Shims, metal

(G-101)
MECHANICAL TECHNOLOGY INC (PA)
Also Called: MTI
325 Washington Avenue Ext (12205-5581)
PHONE..................518 218-2550
Fax: 518 533-2201
Kevin G Lynch, *Ch of Bd*
Frederick W Jones, *CFO*
Susan Landauer, *Consultant*
Jeuillie Keegan, *Executive*
EMP: 34 **EST:** 1961
SQ FT: 17,400
SALES: 6.3MM **Publicly Held**
SIC: 3829 Stress, strain & flaw detecting/measuring equipment; vibration meters, analyzers & calibrators

(G-102)
MOMENTIVE PRFMCE MTLS HOLDINGS
Also Called: Momentive Prfmce Mtls Holdings
22 Corporate Woods Blvd (12211-2374)
PHONE..................518 533-4600
Bradley J Bell, *Ch of Bd*
Mark Brammer, *Exec VP*
Douglas Johns, *Exec VP*
David Rusinko, *Vice Pres*
Nick Wilhelm, *Purch Mgr*
EMP: 9270
SALES (est): 461.8K **Privately Held**
SIC: 2869 3479 Silicones; coating of metals with silicon
PA: Momentive Performance Materials Inc.
  180 E Broad St
  Columbus OH 43215

(G-103)
MOTOROLA SOLUTIONS INC
251 New Karner Rd (12205-4627)
PHONE..................518 869-9517
EMP: 142
SALES (corp-wide): 5.7B **Publicly Held**
SIC: 3663 Mfg Communication Equipment

PA: Motorola Solutions, Inc.
  1303 E Algonquin Rd
  Schaumburg IL 60196
  847 576-5000

(G-104)
MTI INSTRUMENTS INC
325 Washington Ave 3 (12206-3012)
PHONE..................518 218-2550
Fax: 518 218-2506
Kevin G Lynch, *CEO*
Rick Jones, *Vice Pres*
Don Welch, *Engineer*
Patricia Phillips, *Human Res Mgr*
Tim Prentice, *Natl Sales Mgr*
EMP: 10
SALES (est): 1.8MM
SALES (corp-wide): 6.3MM **Publicly Held**
WEB: www.mtiinstruments.com
SIC: 3829 8731 Stress, strain & flaw detecting/measuring equipment; vibration meters, analyzers & calibrators; commercial research laboratory; engineering laboratory, except testing; energy research
PA: Mechanical Technology Incorporated
  325 Washington Avenue Ext
  Albany NY 12205
  518 218-2550

(G-105)
NBTY INC
120 Wash Ave Ext Ste 110 (12203-6448)
PHONE..................518 452-5813
Michael Austin, *Manager*
EMP: 19
SALES (corp-wide): 3B **Publicly Held**
SIC: 2833 Vitamins, natural or synthetic: bulk, uncompounded
HQ: Nbty, Inc.
  2100 Smithtown Ave
  Ronkonkoma NY 11779
  631 200-2000

(G-106)
NEW YORK PRESS & GRAPHICS INC
12 Interstate Ave (12205-5319)
PHONE..................518 489-7089
Fax: 518 489-8232
David J Goldstein, *CEO*
Adam Goldstein, *Vice Pres*
Gail Wilty, *Opers Mgr*
Daniel Goldstein, *CFO*
EMP: 16
SQ FT: 13,000
SALES: 2.4MM **Privately Held**
WEB: www.nypressandgraphics.com
SIC: 2752 Commercial printing, lithographic

(G-107)
NEWKIRK PRODUCTS INC (HQ)
15 Corporate Cir (12203-5177)
PHONE..................518 862-3200
Fax: 518 862-3399
Raymond Newkirk, *CEO*
Peter Newkirk, *President*
Kassie Scholz, *Assistant VP*
James B Salada, *Vice Pres*
John J Graham, *CFO*
EMP: 240
SQ FT: 135,000
SALES (est): 27.4MM
SALES (corp-wide): 2.8B **Publicly Held**
WEB: www.newkirk.com
SIC: 2731 Pamphlets: publishing & printing
PA: Dst Systems, Inc.
  333 W 11th St
  Kansas City MO 64105
  816 435-1000

(G-108)
NEWSPAPER TIMES UNION
Also Called: Capitol Newspaper
645 Albany Shaker Rd (12211-1158)
P.O. Box 15000 (12212-5000)
PHONE..................518 454-5676
David White, *President*
On April, *Publisher*
George R Hearst, *Vice Pres*
Janet Reynolds, *Opers Mgr*
Dan Couto, *Opers Staff*
EMP: 12

Albany - Albany County (G-109)   GEOGRAPHIC SECTION

SALES (est): 690K **Privately Held**
WEB: www.saratogasignature.com
SIC: 2711 Newspapers, publishing & printing

(G-109)
NORTHEAST COMMERCIAL PRTG INC (PA)
Also Called: Eastern Offset
1237 Central Ave Ste 3 (12205-5328)
PHONE..................518 459-5047
Fax: 518 459-5048
Anthony Mosca, *President*
EMP: 7
SQ FT: 4,000
SALES (est): 854K **Privately Held**
WEB: www.northeastcommercial.com
SIC: 2752 Commercial printing, offset

(G-110)
NORTHEASTERN AIR QUALITY INC
730 3rd St (12206-2007)
PHONE..................518 857-3641
Robert Kelley, *President*
Russell Hilton, *Opers Mgr*
EMP: 12
SALES (est): 5MM **Privately Held**
SIC: 1389 Testing, measuring, surveying & analysis services

(G-111)
ORACLE AMERICA INC
Also Called: Sun Microsystems
7 Southwoods Blvd Ste 1 (12211-2526)
PHONE..................518 427-9353
Frank Wickham, *Systs Engr*
Leslie Woodin, *Sales/Mktg Mgr*
Tom Karpowitz, *Technical Staff*
EMP: 52
SALES (corp-wide): 37B **Publicly Held**
SIC: 3571 Minicomputers
HQ: Oracle America, Inc.
500 Oracle Pkwy
Redwood City CA 94065
650 506-7000

(G-112)
OTIS ELEVATOR COMPANY
20 Loudonville Rd Ste 1 (12204-1509)
PHONE..................518 426-4006
Fax: 518 426-1101
Dorothy Mynahan, *Branch Mgr*
EMP: 33
SALES (corp-wide): 56.1B **Publicly Held**
WEB: www.otis.com
SIC: 3534 Elevators & equipment
HQ: Otis Elevator Company
10 Farm Springs Rd
Farmington CT 06032
860 676-6000

(G-113)
OUR DAILY EATS LLC
10 Burdick Dr Ste 1 (12205-1457)
PHONE..................518 810-8412
EMP: 12
SALES (est): 1.8MM **Privately Held**
SIC: 2068 Mfg Salted/Roasted Nuts/Seeds

(G-114)
PATRICK RYANS MODERN PRESS
1 Colonie St (12207-2434)
PHONE..................518 434-2921
Fax: 518 434-2954
Michael Ryan, *President*
Patrick Ryan, *Vice Pres*
Teresa Granger, *Graphic Designe*
EMP: 10 EST: 1946
SQ FT: 6,000
SALES (est): 1MM **Privately Held**
WEB: www.modernpress.com
SIC: 2752 2759 2791 Commercial printing, offset; letterpress printing; typesetting

(G-115)
PBR GRAPHICS INC
20 Railroad Ave Ste 1 (12205-5785)
PHONE..................518 458-2909
Fax: 518 458-7118
Robert Cullum Jr, *President*
Robert G Cullum Sr, *Vice Pres*
Barbara Cullum, *Treasurer*
Allen Kawa, *Manager*
EMP: 9
SQ FT: 11,000
SALES: 920K **Privately Held**
SIC: 2759 Laser printing

(G-116)
PEI LIQUIDATION COMPANY
1240 Central Ave (12205-5307)
PHONE..................518 489-5101
Fax: 518 489-5109
Dan Jesco, *Manager*
Aaron Laport, *Manager*
EMP: 14
SALES (corp-wide): 14.1MM **Privately Held**
WEB: www.patioenc.com
SIC: 3448 1521 Prefabricated metal buildings; sunrooms, prefabricated metal; patio & deck construction & repair
PA: Pei Liquidation Company
700 Highland Rd E
Macedonia OH 44056
330 467-4267

(G-117)
PENGUIN RANDOM HOUSE LLC
80 State St (12207-2541)
PHONE..................212 366-2377
David Shanks, *CEO*
EMP: 200
SALES (corp-wide): 18.4B **Privately Held**
SIC: 2731 5942 Book publishing; book stores
HQ: Penguin Random House Llc
1745 Broadway
New York NY 10019
212 782-9000

(G-118)
PETERSONS NELNET LLC
3 Columbia Cir Ste 205 (12203-5158)
PHONE..................609 896-1800
Randi Tobin, *Manager*
EMP: 220
SALES (corp-wide): 1.2B **Publicly Held**
WEB: www.culinaryschools.com
SIC: 2731 2741 Textbooks: publishing & printing; miscellaneous publishing
HQ: Peterson's Nelnet, Llc
3 Columbia Cir Ste 205
Albany NY 12203
609 896-1800

(G-119)
PHARMACEUTIC LABS LLC
15 Walker Way (12205-4945)
PHONE..................518 608-1060
Ernesto Samuel, *CEO*
Raleigh Hamilton, *CFO*
Amy Milani PHD, *Marketing Staff*
Samantha Mattison, *Pharmacist*
John Mather, *Director*
▲ EMP: 14
SALES (est): 2.2MM **Privately Held**
SIC: 2834 Pharmaceutical preparations

(G-120)
PHYLJOHN DISTRIBUTORS INC
Also Called: Gillette Creamery
6 Interstate Ave (12205-5309)
PHONE..................518 459-2775
Richard H Gillette, *Supervisor*
EMP: 10
SALES (corp-wide): 29.8MM **Privately Held**
WEB: www.gillettecreamery.com
SIC: 2024 Ice cream & frozen desserts
PA: Phyljohn Distributors, Inc.
47 Steves Ln
Gardiner NY 12525
845 419-0900

(G-121)
PIEDMONT PLASTICS INC
4 Access Rd (12205-4744)
PHONE..................518 724-0563
Dawn Carden, *Principal*
EMP: 8
SALES (corp-wide): 164.1MM **Privately Held**
SIC: 2295 Resin or plastic coated fabrics
PA: Piedmont Plastics, Inc.
5010 W Wt Harris Blvd
Charlotte NC 28269
704 597-8200

(G-122)
PINE BUSH PRINTING CO INC
2005 Western Ave (12203-7016)
PHONE..................518 456-2431
Don Blais, *President*
EMP: 7
SALES (est): 622.6K **Privately Held**
SIC: 2752 Commercial printing, lithographic

(G-123)
PRAXAIR INC
116 Railroad Ave (12205-5789)
PHONE..................518 482-4360
EMP: 20
SALES (corp-wide): 10.7B **Publicly Held**
SIC: 2813 Industrial gases
PA: Praxair, Inc.
39 Old Ridgebury Rd
Danbury CT 06810
203 837-2000

(G-124)
PRINTING RESOURCES INC
Also Called: The Printing Company
100 Fuller Rd Ste 1 (12205-5760)
PHONE..................518 482-2470
Fax: 518 482-2567
Darcy Harding, *President*
Denise Harris, *Cust Svc Dir*
EMP: 20
SQ FT: 15,000
SALES (est): 2MM **Privately Held**
SIC: 2759 2791 2789 2752 Commercial printing; typesetting; bookbinding & related work; commercial printing, lithographic

(G-125)
R & J SHEET METAL DISTRS INC
Also Called: R and J Sheet Metal
119 Sheridan Ave (12210-2426)
PHONE..................518 433-1525
Robert Gardner, *President*
EMP: 6
SALES (est): 892.1K **Privately Held**
SIC: 3441 Fabricated structural metal

(G-126)
RAFF ENTERPRISES
12 Petra Ln Ste 6 (12205-4973)
PHONE..................518 218-7883
Sean Raff, *Owner*
EMP: 9
SALES (est): 876K **Privately Held**
SIC: 2511 China closets

(G-127)
RATIONAL RETENTION LLC (PA)
Also Called: Rational Enterprises
2 Tower Pl Ste 13 (12203-3726)
PHONE..................518 489-3000
William W Duker, *Mng Member*
EMP: 33
SALES (est): 1.4MM **Privately Held**
SIC: 7372 7374 Prepackaged software; data processing & preparation

(G-128)
REM PRINTING INC
55 Railroad Ave (12205-5947)
PHONE..................518 438-7338
Paul Remmert, *President*
Matthew Remmert, *VP Sales*
EMP: 6
SQ FT: 5,000
SALES (est): 600K **Privately Held**
WEB: www.remprinting.com
SIC: 2752 Commercial printing, lithographic

(G-129)
RR DONNELLEY & SONS COMPANY
Moore Graphics Services
4 Executive Park Dr Ste 2 (12203-3717)
PHONE..................518 438-9722
Fax: 518 489-7080
Joe Benoit, *Manager*
EMP: 100
SALES (corp-wide): 11.2B **Publicly Held**
WEB: www.moore.com
SIC: 2759 Screen printing
PA: R.R. Donnelley & Sons Company
35 W Wacker Dr Ste 3650
Chicago IL 60601
312 326-8000

(G-130)
SARATOGA TRUNK AND FURNITURE
Also Called: Tomorrow Group, The
5 Macaffer Dr (12204-1207)
PHONE..................518 463-3252
Ronald Richardson, *President*
David Tamburelli, *Exec VP*
Sheila Richardson, *Admin Sec*
▲ EMP: 15 EST: 1924
SQ FT: 20,000
SALES: 1MM **Privately Held**
SIC: 3499 Novelties & giftware, including trophies

(G-131)
SCARANO BOAT BUILDING INC
194 S Port Rd (12202-1075)
PHONE..................518 463-3401
John S Scarano, *President*
William Hubert, *Controller*
EMP: 45
SALES: 950K **Privately Held**
WEB: www.scaranoboat.com
SIC: 3731 Shipbuilding & repairing

(G-132)
SCARANO BOATBUILDING INC
194 S Port Rd (12202-1075)
PHONE..................518 463-3401
John Scarano, *President*
Rick Scarano, *Vice Pres*
EMP: 27
SQ FT: 90,000
SALES (est): 4.8MM **Privately Held**
SIC: 3732 Boat building & repairing

(G-133)
SCHAAP BROTHERS
6 Brown Rd (12205-5702)
PHONE..................518 459-2220
Theodore Schaap, *President*
EMP: 1
SQ FT: 85,000
SALES (est): 5.7MM **Privately Held**
SIC: 1389 Oil & gas wells: building, repairing & dismantling

(G-134)
SMITHS GAS SERVICE INC
Also Called: J and M Schwarz
5 Walker Way Ste 1 (12205-4953)
PHONE..................518 438-0400
John Schwarz, *President*
EMP: 5
SALES (est): 522.4K **Privately Held**
SIC: 3494 Plumbing & heating valves

(G-135)
SOMML HEALTH LLC
43 New Scotland Ave Mc25 (12208-3412)
PHONE..................518 880-2170
Kurt Lozier, *Principal*
David Wood, *Mng Member*
EMP: 5
SQ FT: 200
SALES (est): 117.2K **Privately Held**
SIC: 7372 Prepackaged software

(G-136)
STANLEY PAPER CO INC
1 Terminal St (12206-2283)
PHONE..................518 489-1131
Fax: 518 453-2603
Matthew Jasinski II, *President*
Pearl Jasinski, *Corp Secy*
EMP: 11 EST: 1942
SQ FT: 6,000
SALES (est): 2.1MM **Privately Held**
SIC: 2679 5113 Conduits, fiber (pressed pulp): from purchased material; industrial & personal service paper

(G-137)
STEIN FIBERS LTD (PA)
4 Computer Dr W Ste 200 (12205-1630)
PHONE..................518 489-5700
Fax: 518 489-5713
Sidney J Stein III, *Ch of Bd*
Peter J Spitalny, *President*
David Knight, *Vice Pres*

Allen Greenburg, *CFO*
Tom Tesarano, *Controller*
◆ **EMP:** 18
SQ FT: 4,600
SALES: 291.8MM **Privately Held**
WEB: www.steinfibers.com
SIC: 2824 Polyester fibers

(G-138)
STOP N SHOP LLC
911 Central Ave Ste 149 (12206-1350)
PHONE.................................518 512-9657
Efasto Bowl, *Mng Member*
EMP: 6
SALES (est): 135.3K **Privately Held**
SIC: 7372 Business oriented computer software

(G-139)
SUPPLY TECHNOLOGIES (NY) (DH)
80 State St (12207-2541)
PHONE.................................212 966-3310
Jack Laufer, *CEO*
Samuel Laufer, *President*
Frank Negron, *Asst Controller*
▲ **EMP:** 18 **EST:** 1953
SQ FT: 10,000
SALES (est): 8.7MM
SALES (corp-wide): 1.4B **Publicly Held**
SIC: 3452 3599 5072 3451 Bolts, metal; rivets, metal; washers, metal; screws, metal; machine shop, jobbing & repair; bolts; rivets; washers (hardware); screws; screw machine products
HQ: Supply Technologies Llc
6065 Parkland Blvd Ste 1
Cleveland OH 44124
440 947-2100

(G-140)
TECHNICAL WLDG FABRICATORS LLC
27 Thatcher St (12207-5052)
PHONE.................................518 463-2229
Fax: 518 462-1360
Carol Boyer,
EMP: 10
SALES (est): 1.4MM **Privately Held**
SIC: 3315 Welded steel wire fabric

(G-141)
TEL TECHNOLOGY CENTER AMER LLC (DH)
255 Fuller Rd Ste 244 (12203-3663)
PHONE.................................512 424-4200
Fax: 518 292-4300
Hiroshi Takenaka, *President*
▲ **EMP:** 29
SALES (est): 5MM
SALES (corp-wide): 5.6B **Privately Held**
SIC: 3674 Semiconductors & related devices
HQ: Tokyo Electron U.S. Holdings, Inc.
2400 Grove Blvd
Austin TX 78741
512 424-1000

(G-142)
THERMOAURA INC
132 Railroad Ave Ste B (12205-5742)
PHONE.................................518 880-2125
Rutvik J Mehta, *Ch of Bd*
Benjamin Mitchell, *Manager*
Ganpath Ramanath, *Director*
EMP: 14
SALES (est): 2.1MM **Privately Held**
SIC: 3674 Wafers (semiconductor devices)

(G-143)
TOKYO ELECTRON AMERICA INC
255 Fuller Rd Ste 214 (12203-3604)
PHONE.................................518 292-4200
Fax: 518 320-1985
Adam Gildea, *Engineer*
Chris Krammer, *Branch Mgr*
Frank Ayala, *Manager*
EMP: 11
SALES (corp-wide): 5.6B **Privately Held**
WEB: www.telusa.com
SIC: 3826 Electrolytic conductivity instruments

HQ: Tokyo Electron America, Inc.
2400 Grove Blvd
Austin TX 78741
512 424-1000

(G-144)
U ALL INC
9 Interstate Ave (12205-5320)
PHONE.................................518 438-2558
Fax: 518 438-7282
James Holodak, *President*
Stephanie Marion, *Purchasing*
Peggy Holodak, *Controller*
Tom Clark, *Sales Dir*
Robert White, *Sales Mgr*
EMP: 25
SQ FT: 10,000
SALES (est): 3.2MM **Privately Held**
WEB: www.allu.com
SIC: 2759 2395 5199 2396 Screen printing; embroidery & art needlework; advertising specialties; automotive & apparel trimmings

(G-145)
UCC GUIDE INC (PA)
Also Called: Ernst Publishing Co
99 Washington Ave (12210-2822)
PHONE.................................518 434-0909
Gregory E Teal, *CEO*
Lisa Donahue, *Assistant VP*
Jan Clark, *Vice Pres*
Kathryn Teal, *Vice Pres*
Douglas Harff, *Opers Staff*
EMP: 10
SQ FT: 4,000
SALES (est): 2.6MM **Privately Held**
WEB: www.ernstinfo.com
SIC: 2741 Miscellaneous publishing

(G-146)
ULTREPET LLC
136c Fuller Rd (12205-5604)
PHONE.................................781 275-6400
M Scott Mellen, *President*
Carol C Forman, *Principal*
David B Spencer, *Chairman*
Leigh A Peritz, *Vice Pres*
Paul C Zordan, *Vice Pres*
▲ **EMP:** 65
SALES (est): 14.6MM
SALES (corp-wide): 47.2MM **Privately Held**
SIC: 3559 Plastics working machinery
PA: Wte Corporation
7 Alfred Cir
Bedford MA 01730
781 275-6400

(G-147)
UNIVERSITY AT ALBANY
Also Called: College Nnoscale Science Engrg
257 Fuller Rd (12203-3613)
PHONE.................................518 437-8686
Fax: 518 437-8687
Michael Liehr, *General Mgr*
Laura Babcock, *Assistant VP*
Sara Brenner, *Assistant VP*
Diana L Dumesnil, *Assistant VP*
Steven Novak, *Assistant VP*
EMP: 23 **Privately Held**
SIC: 3674 9411 Semiconductors & related devices;
HQ: University At Albany
1400 Washington Ave
Albany NY 12222
518 442-3300

(G-148)
VERTICAL LAX INC
20 Corporate Cir Ste 4 (12203-5157)
PHONE.................................518 669-3699
Curt Styres, *CEO*
Paul Gait, *President*
Lewis Staats, *Treasurer*
Kelly Anderson, *Accountant*
▲ **EMP:** 7 **EST:** 2010
SALES (est): 632.2K **Privately Held**
SIC: 3949 7389 Sporting & athletic goods;

(G-149)
WEST END IRON WORKS INC
4254 Albany St (12205-4684)
PHONE.................................518 456-1105
Fax: 518 456-1335
Eric R Frey, *President*

EMP: 5 **EST:** 1890
SQ FT: 9,000
SALES (est): 460K **Privately Held**
SIC: 3446 Architectural metalwork

(G-150)
WILD WORKS INCORPORATED
30 Railroad Ave (12205-5721)
PHONE.................................716 891-4197
William C Smith, *CEO*
EMP: 5
SALES (est): 536.4K **Privately Held**
SIC: 2891 Adhesives & sealants

(G-151)
ZELA INTERNATIONAL CO
13 Manor St (12207-3008)
PHONE.................................518 436-1833
Fax: 518 436-1533
Ike Sukljian, *President*
Cristina Samuels, *VP Sales*
▲ **EMP:** 25
SQ FT: 60,000
SALES (est): 2.2MM **Privately Held**
WEB: www.zela.com
SIC: 2844 5122 Toilet preparations; cosmetics

Albertson
Nassau County

(G-152)
BRAUN INDUSTRIES INC
Also Called: Braun Brush Company
43 Albertson Ave (11507-2102)
PHONE.................................516 741-6000
Fax: 516 741-6299
Max W Cheney, *Ch of Bd*
Lance W Cheney, *President*
Adam Czerniawski, *Vice Pres*
▲ **EMP:** 20 **EST:** 1875
SQ FT: 15,000
SALES (est): 3.5MM **Privately Held**
WEB: www.brush.com
SIC: 3991 Brooms & brushes

(G-153)
DAIGE PRODUCTS INC
1 Albertson Ave Ste 3 (11507-1444)
PHONE.................................516 621-2100
Fax: 516 621-1916
I M Harris, *President*
EMP: 15
SQ FT: 3,500
SALES (est): 2.8MM **Privately Held**
WEB: www.daige.com
SIC: 3555 Printing trades machinery

(G-154)
GEMSON GRAPHICS INC
820 Willis Ave Ste 2c (11507-1979)
PHONE.................................516 873-8400
Emanuel Manicone, *Chairman*
EMP: 5
SALES (est): 480K **Privately Held**
SIC: 2752 2759 Commercial printing, offset; flexographic printing

(G-155)
INTERNATIONAL BRONZE MANUFAC
810 Willis Ave (11507-1919)
PHONE.................................516 248-3080
Fax: 516 248-4047
Kenneth Klein, *President*
Rommi Klein, *Vice Pres*
▲ **EMP:** 15
SALES (est): 1.1MM **Privately Held**
WEB: www.internationalbronze.com
SIC: 3999 3993 5999 Plaques, picture, laminated; signs & advertising specialties; trophies & plaques

(G-156)
PATSY STROCCHIA & SONS IRON WO
Also Called: Strocchia Iron Works
175 I U Willets Rd Ste 4 (11507-1524)
PHONE.................................516 625-8800
Fax: 718 349-2852
Ralph J Strocchia, *Ch of Bd*
Leonard D Strocchia, *Vice Pres*
Michael Anne, *Manager*

Ralph Strocchia Jr, *Admin Sec*
EMP: 18 **EST:** 1922
SALES: 3.2MM **Privately Held**
SIC: 3441 Fabricated structural metal

(G-157)
PAYA PRINTING OF NY INC
87 Searingtown Rd (11507-1125)
PHONE.................................516 625-8346
Fax: 516 625-9658
Mohammad Samii, *President*
EMP: 5
SQ FT: 1,000
SALES (est): 482.9K **Privately Held**
SIC: 2754 2752 Commercial printing, gravure; commercial printing, lithographic

(G-158)
PELLA CORPORATION
Also Called: Pella Window Door
77 Albertson Ave Ste 2 (11507-2127)
PHONE.................................516 385-3622
Shanade Alton, *Branch Mgr*
EMP: 316
SALES (corp-wide): 1.9B **Privately Held**
SIC: 2431 Windows, wood
PA: Pella Corporation
102 Main St
Pella IA 50219
641 621-1000

(G-159)
PELLA CORPORATION
Also Called: Pella Window Door
77 Albertson Ave Ste 2 (11507-2127)
PHONE.................................516 385-3622
EMP: 316
SALES (corp-wide): 663.7MM **Privately Held**
SIC: 2431 Mfg Millwork
PA: Pella Corporation
102 Main St
Pella IA 50219
641 621-1000

(G-160)
SHRITEC CONSULTANTS INC
91 Searingtown Rd (11507-1125)
PHONE.................................516 621-7072
Rathi Raja, *President*
Venkat Raja, *Vice Pres*
EMP: 9
SALES: 1.7MM **Privately Held**
SIC: 7372 Prepackaged software

Albion
Orleans County

(G-161)
ALBION-HOLLEY PENNYSAVER INC
Also Called: Lake Country Pennysaver
170 N Main St (14411-1063)
P.O. Box 231 (14411-0231)
PHONE.................................585 589-5641
Fax: 585 589-1239
Karen Sawicz, *President*
Gary Hill, *Editor*
Brad London, *Sales Associate*
EMP: 64
SQ FT: 22,000
SALES (est): 7.9MM **Privately Held**
SIC: 2791 2711 2741 Typesetting; job printing & newspaper publishing combined; miscellaneous publishing

(G-162)
AUSTIN INDUSTRIES INC (PA)
3871 Oak Orchard Rd (14411-9536)
PHONE.................................585 589-1353
Alan Austin, *President*
Vernon Carl Austin, *Vice Pres*
Denise Austin, *Treasurer*
Simeon O Terry, *Program Mgr*
Tim Gregg, *Info Tech Dir*
EMP: 7
SQ FT: 7,200
SALES (est): 931.1K **Privately Held**
SIC: 3542 5085 Machine tools, metal forming type; welding supplies; industrial tools

Albion - Orleans County (G-163)

(G-163)
CDL MANUFACTURING INC
15661 Telegraph Rd (14411)
PHONE.............................585 589-2533
Kaz Laszewski, *President*
Steve Chiruck, *Vice Pres*
EMP: 5
SQ FT: 8,000
SALES (est): 662.1K Privately Held
WEB: www.cdlmfg.com
SIC: 3599 Machine shop, jobbing & repair

(G-164)
EAGLE HARBOR SAND & GRAVEL INC
4780 Eagle Harbour Rd (14411)
PHONE.............................585 798-4501
Paul D Pass, *President*
Tom Diamonte, *Vice Pres*
EMP: 5
SALES (est): 323K Privately Held
SIC: 1442 Construction sand mining; gravel mining

(G-165)
FREEZE-DRY FOODS INC
111 West Ave Ste 2 (14411-1500)
PHONE.............................585 589-6399
Fax: 585 589-6402
Alasdair Grant, *CEO*
Karen Richardson, *President*
Andy Rose, *Plt & Fclts Mgr*
Anna Marie Clift, *Controller*
Minh Pham, *Info Tech Mgr*
▲EMP: 40
SALES (est): 6.6MM
SALES (corp-wide): 623.7K Privately Held
WEB: www.freeze-dry.com
SIC: 2038 Frozen specialties
PA: Freeze-Dry Foods Limited
2916 South Sheridan Way Suite 300
Oakville ON L6J 7
905 844-1471

(G-166)
J PAHURA CONTRACTORS
415 East Ave (14411-1620)
PHONE.............................585 589-5793
James Pahura, *Owner*
EMP: 5
SALES (est): 210K Privately Held
SIC: 2951 Asphalt paving mixtures & blocks

(G-167)
ORLEANS PALLET COMPANY INC
227 West Ave (14411-1520)
PHONE.............................585 589-0781
Shawn R Malark, *President*
EMP: 11
SQ FT: 65,000
SALES: 954K Privately Held
SIC: 2448 Pallets, wood

(G-168)
PENASACK MACHINE COMPANY INC
49 Sanford St (14411-1117)
P.O. Box 396 (14411-0396)
PHONE.............................585 589-7044
Fax: 585 589-0046
Gerard Damore, *Ch of Bd*
Jeffrey Kinser, *Engineer*
Nancy Cole, *Accounts Mgr*
Jessica Tobin, *Manager*
EMP: 40 EST: 1967
SQ FT: 35,000
SALES (est): 7.2MM Privately Held
SIC: 3444 Sheet metal specialties, not stamped

(G-169)
RS AUTOMATION
Also Called: Richard Stacey Rs Automation
4015 Oak Orchard Rd (14411-9346)
PHONE.............................585 589-0199
Richard Stacey, *Owner*
Dawn Stacey, *Clerk*
EMP: 17
SQ FT: 12,000
SALES (est): 4.6MM Privately Held
SIC: 3441 5084 Fabricated structural metal; industrial machinery & equipment

(G-170)
SAINT-GOBAIN ADFORS AMER INC
14770 East Ave (14411-9709)
PHONE.............................585 589-4401
Ron Paeth, *Facilities Mgr*
Michele Guzman, *Human Res Mgr*
Joel Allen, *Branch Mgr*
Wendy Moriarty, *Personnel Assit*
EMP: 52
SALES (corp-wide): 207.6MM Privately Held
SIC: 2297 Nonwoven fabrics
HQ: Saint-Gobain Adfors America, Inc.
1795 Baseline Rd
Grand Island NY 14072
716 775-3900

(G-171)
WOODSIDE GRANITE INDUSTRIES (PA)
Also Called: Brigden Memorials
13890 Ridge Rd W (14411-9160)
PHONE.............................585 589-6500
Fax: 585 589-4221
Leo Lacroix, *President*
Mickey Babcock, *Office Mgr*
▲EMP: 3
SQ FT: 1,500
SALES (est): 1.2MM Privately Held
SIC: 3272 5999 Grave markers, concrete; gravestones, finished

Alcove
Albany County

(G-172)
NEW YORK QUARRIES INC
305 Rte 111 (12007)
PHONE.............................518 756-3138
Fax: 518 756-8000
Nancy O'Brien, *President*
▲EMP: 15
SQ FT: 1,200
SALES: 1.5MM Privately Held
WEB: www.newyorkquarries.com
SIC: 3281 1411 Cut stone & stone products; limestone, dimension-quarrying

Alden
Erie County

(G-173)
AGRI SERVICES CO
13899 North Rd (14004-9779)
PHONE.............................716 937-6618
James Guarino, *Owner*
EMP: 5
SALES (est): 125K Privately Held
SIC: 3714 5531 Automotive wiring harness sets; truck equipment & parts

(G-174)
ALDEN AURORA GAS COMPANY INC
Also Called: Reserve Gas Company
13441 Railroad St (14004-1389)
P.O. Box 207 (14004-0207)
PHONE.............................716 937-9484
Edward Harris, *Ch of Bd*
James C Gorom, *President*
Paul Tryanowski, *Treasurer*
Jacqueline Harris, *Shareholder*
Bernice Rosenbloom, *Shareholder*
EMP: 8
SQ FT: 1,200
SALES (est): 566.7K Privately Held
SIC: 1381 Drilling oil & gas wells

(G-175)
BENNETT MANUFACTURING CO INC
13315 Railroad St (14004-1390)
PHONE.............................716 937-9161
Fax: 585 937-3137
Steven L Yellen, *Ch of Bd*
Richard D Yellen, *Vice Pres*
Robert Cowing, *Purchasing*
Toby F Yellen, *Treasurer*
Mary Anaka, *Manager*
▲EMP: 150
SQ FT: 100,000
SALES (est): 32.1MM Privately Held
WEB: www.bennettmfg.com
SIC: 3441 2842 Fabricated structural metal; specialty cleaning, polishes & sanitation goods

(G-176)
D J CROWELL CO INC
2815 Town Line Rd (14004-9676)
PHONE.............................716 684-3343
Fax: 716 684-3345
David C Bressette, *President*
Jeffrey Minotti, *Vice Pres*
EMP: 6 EST: 1900
SQ FT: 6,000
SALES: 500K Privately Held
SIC: 3599 Machine shop, jobbing & repair

(G-177)
DUNDAS-JAFINE INC
11099 Broadway St (14004-9517)
PHONE.............................716 681-9690
Fax: 716 681-0011
James Feldmeyer, *Mfg Staff*
Debbie Patterson, *Production*
Bill Szajn, *CFO*
Colleen Ference, *Human Resources*
Dave Rockwell, *Natl Sales Mgr*
EMP: 50
SALES (corp-wide): 13.2MM Privately Held
WEB: www.dundasjafine.com
SIC: 3585 3564 3444 Heating equipment, complete; air conditioning equipment, complete; blowers & fans; sheet metal-work
PA: Dundas Jafine Inc
80 West Dr
Brampton ON L6T 3
905 450-7200

(G-178)
GAMMA NORTH CORPORATION
13595 Broadway St (14004-9736)
PHONE.............................716 902-5100
Matthew Baum, *President*
James Mitchell, *President*
Elliot Kracko, *Chairman*
Juan J Alpizar, *Senior VP*
Jose M Rodriguez, *Senior VP*
EMP: 50 EST: 2012
SALES (est): 9.3MM Privately Held
SIC: 3442 Store fronts, prefabricated, metal

(G-179)
HUBCO INC
2885 Commerce Dr (14004-8538)
PHONE.............................716 683-5940
Craig Huber, *President*
Paul Huber, *Vice Pres*
Mark Richardson, *Info Tech Mgr*
▲EMP: 5
SQ FT: 6,000
SALES (est): 856.6K Privately Held
WEB: www.hubcopads.com
SIC: 3569 Assembly machines, non-metalworking

(G-180)
INTEGER HOLDINGS CORPORATION
Also Called: Greatbatch Medical
11900 Walden Ave (14004-9706)
PHONE.............................716 937-5100
Fax: 716 937-5333
Ed Voboril, *Chairman*
Lorie Adamczak, *COO*
Scott Bowers, *Engineer*
Stan Bystrak, *Engineer*
Jeffrey Grisante, *Engineer*
EMP: 24
SALES (corp-wide): 800.4MM Publicly Held
SIC: 3675 Electronic capacitors
PA: Integer Holdings Corporation
2595 Dallas Pkwy Ste 310
Frisco TX 75034
716 759-5600

(G-181)
PHELINGER TOOL & DIE CORP
1254 Town Line Rd (14004-9672)
PHONE.............................716 685-1780
Fax: 716 685-9306
Gordon Phelinger, *President*
Scott Phelinger, *Vice Pres*
EMP: 7
SQ FT: 1,000
SALES (est): 1MM Privately Held
WEB: www.phelingertool.com
SIC: 3544 Special dies & tools; jigs & fixtures

(G-182)
RESERVE GAS COMPANY INC
13441 Railroad St (14004-1338)
P.O. Box 207 (14004-0207)
PHONE.............................716 937-9484
Sterlin Harris, *CEO*
James C Gorom, *President*
EMP: 8
SQ FT: 3,200
SALES (est): 1MM Privately Held
SIC: 1311 Natural gas production

(G-183)
SDR TECHNOLOGY INC
1613 Lindan Dr (14004-1113)
PHONE.............................716 583-1249
Charles Chauncey, *President*
EMP: 5
SALES (est): 381.2K Privately Held
SIC: 3663 Radio & TV communications equipment

(G-184)
TURBOPRO INC
1284 Town Line Rd (14004-9672)
PHONE.............................716 681-8651
Joseph Bantle, *President*
Brenda Bantle, *Vice Pres*
EMP: 4
SALES (est): 1MM Privately Held
SIC: 3563 Air & gas compressors

(G-185)
UNITED RBOTIC INTEGRATIONS LLC
2781 Town Line Rd (14004-9676)
PHONE.............................716 683-8334
John M Lass, *President*
William Penney, *Treasurer*
Michelle M Berger, *Admin Sec*
Paul Barker,
Melvin Bernhard,
EMP: 5
SALES (est): 530K Privately Held
WEB: www.unitedpmr.com
SIC: 3535 Robotic conveyors

(G-186)
WEISBECK PUBLISHING PRINTING
Also Called: Alden Advertiser
13200 Broadway St (14004-1313)
PHONE.............................716 937-9226
Leonard A Wiesbeck Jr, *President*
Leonard A Weisbeck Sr, *President*
EMP: 5 EST: 1948
SQ FT: 1,748
SALES (est): 467.9K Privately Held
WEB: www.aldenadvertiser.com
SIC: 2711 Newspapers, publishing & printing; job printing & newspaper publishing combined

Alexander
Genesee County

(G-187)
LENAPE ENERGY INC (PA)
Also Called: Leape Resources,
9489 Alexander Rd (14005-9795)
PHONE.............................585 344-1200
Fax: 585 344-3283
John Holko, *President*
Amy Holko, *Vice Pres*
Pat Sanders, *Office Mgr*
Jack Crooks, *Supervisor*
EMP: 2
SQ FT: 3,200

GEOGRAPHIC SECTION

Altamont - Albany County (G-210)

SALES (est): 1MM **Privately Held**
WEB: www.lenaperesources.com
SIC: **1381** 1389 1382 4923 Drilling oil & gas wells; haulage, oil field; gas compressing (natural gas) at the fields; oil & gas exploration services; gas transmission & distribution

(G-188)
LENAPE RESOURCES INC
9489 Alexander Rd (14005-9795)
PHONE.....................585 344-1200
John Holko, *President*
Amy Holko, *Vice Pres*
EMP: 10
SALES: 1MM **Privately Held**
WEB: www.lenaperesources.com
SIC: **1382** 4923 Oil & gas exploration services; gas transmission & distribution
PA: Lenape Energy Inc
    9489 Alexander Rd
    Alexander NY 14005
    585 344-1200

(G-189)
P & D EQUIPMENT SALES LLC
10171 Brookville Rd (14005-9783)
PHONE.....................585 343-2394
Josh Raines,
Brian Raines,
Dennis Raines,
Mark Raines,
Paul Raines,
EMP: 5
SALES (est): 538.5K **Privately Held**
SIC: **3523** Barn, silo, poultry, dairy & livestock machinery

(G-190)
RICHARD BAUER LOGGING
3936 Cookson Rd (14005-9718)
PHONE.....................585 343-4149
Richard Bauer, *Owner*
EMP: 5
SALES (est): 260K **Privately Held**
SIC: **2411** Logging camps & contractors

Alexandria Bay
Jefferson County

(G-191)
THOUSAND ISLANDS PRINTING CO
Also Called: Thousand Islands Sun
45501 St Rt 12 (13607)
PHONE.....................315 482-2581
Fax: 315 482-6315
Jeanne Roy Snow, *President*
William F Roy, *Vice Pres*
Helethea Roy, *Treasurer*
EMP: 9 EST: 1901
SQ FT: 3,250
SALES (est): 633.6K **Privately Held**
SIC: **2711** Job printing & newspaper publishing combined

(G-192)
THOUSAND ISLANDS WINERY LLC
43298 Seaway Ave Ste 1 (13607-2141)
PHONE.....................315 482-9306
Fax: 315 482-9302
Roxy Raymo, *General Mgr*
Steven J Conaway,
Erika Conaway,
EMP: 22
SQ FT: 4,771
SALES (est): 3.2MM **Privately Held**
WEB: www.thousandislandswinery.com
SIC: **2084** Wines

Alfred
Allegany County

(G-193)
CS MANUFACTURING LIMITED
56 S Main St (14802-1317)
PHONE.....................607 587-8154
Edward Fan, *Principal*
EMP: 50

SALES (est): 4.3MM **Privately Held**
SIC: **3312** 3089 3324 Pipes, iron & steel; stainless steel; forgings, iron & steel; injection molding of plastics; commercial investment castings, ferrous

(G-194)
SAXON GLASS TECHNOLOGIES INC
200 N Main St Ste 114 (14802-1000)
P.O. Box 575 (14802-0575)
PHONE.....................607 587-9630
Arun Varshneya, *President*
Darshana Varshneya, *Vice Pres*
EMP: 10
SQ FT: 4,500
SALES (est): 1.2MM **Privately Held**
WEB: www.saxonglass.com
SIC: **3211** Strengthened or reinforced glass

Alfred Station
Allegany County

(G-195)
ASK CHEMICALS HI-TECH LLC
6329 Rte 21 (14803)
P.O. Box 788, Alfred (14802-0788)
PHONE.....................607 587-9146
Dawn Gillish, *President*
Jamie Darcy, *Safety Mgr*
Jeannie Cartwright, *Purch Mgr*
Paul Bronson, *Plant Engr*
Rick Glenn, *Controller*
◆ EMP: 100
SALES (est): 16.2MM **Privately Held**
SIC: **3297** Nonclay refractories

(G-196)
BUFFALO CRUSHED STONE INC
638 State Route 244 (14803-9766)
P.O. Box 38 (14803-0038)
PHONE.....................607 587-8102
Fax: 607 587-8004
Douglas Drake, *Manager*
EMP: 9
SALES (corp-wide): 651.9MM **Privately Held**
SIC: **1442** Construction sand mining; gravel mining
HQ: Buffalo Crushed Stone, Inc.
    500 Como Park Blvd
    Buffalo NY 14227
    716 826-7310

(G-197)
NORTHERN TIMBER HARVESTING LLC
6042 State Route 21 (14803-9709)
P.O. Box 95 (14803-0095)
PHONE.....................585 233-7330
Adam Ricci,
EMP: 11
SQ FT: 10,000
SALES: 2.9MM **Privately Held**
SIC: **2411** Logging

Allegany
Cattaraugus County

(G-198)
ALLEGANY LAMINATING AND SUPPLY
158 W Main St (14706-1235)
PHONE.....................716 372-2424
Charles Cousins, *President*
Wanda Cousins, *Corp Secy*
Ron Lemon, *Treasurer*
David Koebelin, *Council Mbr*
Athena Silluzio, *Admin Sec*
EMP: 5
SQ FT: 8,300
SALES (est): 460K **Privately Held**
SIC: **2541** 3088 Table or counter tops, plastic laminated; partitions for floor attachment, prefabricated: wood; cabinets, except refrigerated: show, display, etc.; wood; tubs (bath, shower & laundry), plastic

(G-199)
E F LIPPERT CO INC
4451 S Nine Mile Rd (14706-9790)
PHONE.....................716 373-1100
Fax: 585 373-1100
Mary Stayer, *President*
Tom Stayer, *Vice Pres*
Bryan Howard, *Manager*
Cinda Warner, *Admin Sec*
EMP: 13 EST: 1945
SQ FT: 500
SALES (est): 725.7K **Privately Held**
SIC: **1442** 5261 Common sand mining; gravel mining; sod; top soil

(G-200)
EAST RESOURCES INC (DH)
51 W Main St (14706-1201)
PHONE.....................716 373-0944
Fax: 716 373-0946
Terrence M Pegula, *President*
Robert H Long Jr, *Vice Pres*
Marilyn Jacobi, *Treasurer*
EMP: 6
SQ FT: 6,400
SALES (est): 21.2MM
SALES (corp-wide): 264.9B **Publicly Held**
SIC: **1382** 1311 Oil & gas exploration services; natural gas production
HQ: Shell Oil Company
    910 Louisiana St Ste 1500
    Houston TX 77002
    713 241-6161

(G-201)
HANSON AGGREGATES EAST LLC
4419 S Nine Mile Rd (14706-9790)
PHONE.....................716 372-1574
EMP: 6
SALES (est): 326.8K **Privately Held**
SIC: **3272** Mfg Concrete Products

(G-202)
I & S OF NY INC
4174 Route 417 (14706-9787)
P.O. Box 380 (14706-0380)
PHONE.....................716 373-7001
Frank Steven, *President*
Mary Stephens, *Manager*
EMP: 10
SQ FT: 6,000
SALES (est): 1.5MM **Privately Held**
SIC: **1389** Servicing oil & gas wells

(G-203)
POTTER LUMBER CO INC
3786 Potter Rd (14706-9410)
P.O. Box 10 (14706-0010)
PHONE.....................716 373-1260
Fax: 716 373-1297
Robert G Potter, *President*
Theodore Potter, *Vice Pres*
Mary Frances Potter, *Treasurer*
Lucy Benson, *Admin Sec*
EMP: 40 EST: 1910
SQ FT: 700
SALES (est): 6.2MM **Privately Held**
SIC: **2421** 2426 Sawmills & planing mills, general; hardwood dimension & flooring mills

Almond
Allegany County

(G-204)
HANSON AGGREGATES NEW YORK LLC
Also Called: Hanson Ready Mix Concrete
546 Clark Rd (14804)
PHONE.....................607 276-5881
Jeffrey Feenaughty, *Manager*
EMP: 5
SALES (corp-wide): 14.4B **Privately Held**
SIC: **3271** Concrete block & brick
HQ: Hanson Aggregates New York Llc
    8505 Freport Pkwy Ste 500
    Irving TX 75063

Alplaus
Schenectady County

(G-205)
INDUSTRIAL HANDLING SVCS INC
209 Alplaus Ave (12008-1014)
P.O. Box 2922, Glenville (12325-0922)
PHONE.....................518 399-0488
Fax: 518 399-0491
Michael F Coffey, *President*
EMP: 9
SQ FT: 1,598
SALES: 1,000K **Privately Held**
SIC: **3531** Cranes

Altamont
Albany County

(G-206)
ALFRED B PARELLA
Also Called: Latham Seamless Gutters
20 Reservoir Rd (12009-3230)
P.O. Box 448 (12009-0448)
PHONE.....................518 872-1238
Fax: 518 872-9777
Alfred B Parella, *President*
EMP: 5
SALES: 400K **Privately Held**
SIC: **3444** Gutters, sheet metal

(G-207)
ALTAMONT SPRAY WELDING INC
133 Lewis Rd (12009-3220)
PHONE.....................518 861-8870
Fax: 518 861-7212
Mark C Schrowang, *President*
Sandra E Schrowang, *Vice Pres*
EMP: 9
SQ FT: 9,000
SALES (est): 730K **Privately Held**
WEB: www.altamontspraywelding.com
SIC: **3599** Machine shop, jobbing & repair

(G-208)
INDIAN LADDER FARMSTEAD BREWER
287 Altamont Rd (12009-2400)
PHONE.....................518 577-1484
Dietrich Gehring,
EMP: 5
SQ FT: 875
SALES (est): 185.3K **Privately Held**
SIC: **2082** Beer (alcoholic beverage)

(G-209)
INOVA LLC
6032 Depot Rd (12009-4313)
P.O. Box 644 (12009-0644)
PHONE.....................518 861-3400
Loren Sherman, *Owner*
Jerry Blackwell, *General Mgr*
EMP: 15
SALES (est): 2.5MM **Privately Held**
SIC: **2599** Furniture & fixtures

(G-210)
MET WELD INTERNATIONAL LLC
5727 Ostrander Rd (12009-4209)
PHONE.....................518 765-2318
Fax: 518 765-2310
William M Mc Grath, *Plant Mgr*
Kevin Shaw, *Engineer*
Betty Hill, *Bookkeeper*
Jim Kuba, *Financial Analy*
Laurel Collins, *Human Res Mgr*
EMP: 70
SQ FT: 55,000
SALES (est): 20.9MM
SALES (corp-wide): 31.2MM **Privately Held**
WEB: www.metweldintl.com
SIC: **3498** Fabricated pipe & fittings
PA: Gavial Holdings, Inc.
    1435 W Mccoy Ln
    Santa Maria CA 93455
    805 614-0060

Altamont - Albany County (G-211) — GEOGRAPHIC SECTION

(G-211)
ROBERT PIKCILINGIS
Also Called: Candy Kraft
2575 Western Ave (12009-9488)
PHONE................................518 355-1860
Robert Pikcilingis, *Owner*
EMP: 10
SQ FT: 4,000
SALES (est): 410K **Privately Held**
SIC: 2064 2066 Chocolate candy, except solid chocolate; chocolate & cocoa products

(G-212)
RSB ASSOCIATES INC
Also Called: Bruno Associates
488 Picard Rd (12009-3519)
P.O. Box 14825, Albany (12212-4825)
PHONE................................518 281-5067
Robert S Bruno Sr, *President*
Sean Bruno, *Vice Pres*
EMP: 11 EST: 2006
SQ FT: 4,000
SALES: 650K **Privately Held**
SIC: 3554 Die cutting & stamping machinery, paper converting

Amagansett
Suffolk County

(G-213)
COSMETICS PLUS LTD
Also Called: Pixy Dust
23 Deep Wood Ln (11930)
P.O. Box 2444 (11930-2444)
PHONE................................516 768-7250
Rose Evangelista, *President*
EMP: 8
SQ FT: 10,000
SALES (est): 626.4K **Privately Held**
SIC: 3942 Dolls & stuffed toys

Amawalk
Westchester County

(G-214)
JACKDAW PUBLICATIONS
2 Watergate Dr (10501-1105)
P.O. Box 503 (10501-0503)
PHONE................................914 962-6911
Roger Jacques, *Owner*
EMP: 10
SALES (est): 801.1K **Privately Held**
SIC: 2741 Miscellaneous publishing

Amenia
Dutchess County

(G-215)
CASCADE MOUNTAIN WINERY & REST
835 Cascade Rd (12501)
PHONE................................845 373-9021
William Wetmore, *President*
EMP: 10 EST: 1972
SALES (est): 680K **Privately Held**
SIC: 2084 5812 Wines; eating places

(G-216)
GREY HOUSE PUBLISHING INC (PA)
4919 Route 22 (12501-5585)
P.O. Box B, Millerton (12546-0640)
PHONE................................518 789-8700
Fax: 518 789-0556
Richard H Gottlieb, *Ch of Bd*
David Garoogian, *Editor*
Katie Keeran, *Editor*
Leslie McKenzie, *Vice Pres*
Vyonne Coburn, *Opers Mgr*
EMP: 26
SALES (est): 6.9MM **Privately Held**
WEB: www.greyhouse.com
SIC: 2741 2731 Miscellaneous publishing; book publishing

(G-217)
TIA LATTRELL
13 Powder House Rd (12501-5517)
PHONE................................845 373-9494
Tia Lattrell, *Owner*
Frederic Latrell, *Owner*
EMP: 5
SALES (est): 322.9K **Privately Held**
SIC: 2024 Ice cream & frozen desserts

Amherst
Erie County

(G-218)
3G GRAPHICS LLC
7138 Transit Rd (14221-7214)
PHONE................................716 634-2585
Robert Ganz,
EMP: 6
SQ FT: 5,000
SALES: 350K **Privately Held**
SIC: 2752 Commercial printing, lithographic

(G-219)
AIRSEP CORPORATION
Airsep Commercial Products Div
260 Creekside Dr Ste 100 (14228-2075)
PHONE................................716 691-0202
EMP: 100
SALES (corp-wide): 1.1B **Publicly Held**
SIC: 3569 Mfg Oxygen Generators
HQ: Airsep Corporation
    401 Creekside Dr
    Amherst NY 14228
    716 691-0202

(G-220)
ALLIED MOTION SYSTEMS CORP (DH)
Also Called: Hathaway Prcess Instrmentation
495 Commerce Dr Ste 3 (14228-2311)
PHONE................................716 691-5868
Ronald Meyer, *President*
Herbert Franson, *Controller*
Tracy Montford, *Human Res Dir*
Chester Clarridge, *Bd of Directors*
EMP: 15
SQ FT: 13,000
SALES (est): 2MM
SALES (corp-wide): 5B **Publicly Held**
SIC: 3825 Electrical power measuring equipment
HQ: Qualitrol Company Llc
    1385 Fairport Rd
    Fairport NY 14450
    586 643-3717

(G-221)
ALLIED MOTION TECHNOLOGIES INC (PA)
495 Commerce Dr Ste 3 (14228-2311)
PHONE................................716 242-8634
Fax: 716 242-8638
Richard S Warzala, *Ch of Bd*
Kenneth R Wyman, *Vice Pres*
Michael R Leach, *CFO*
Robert P Maida, *CFO*
Bjorn Karlstrom, *Senior Mgr*
▲ EMP: 191
SQ FT: 6,000
SALES: 232.4MM **Publicly Held**
WEB: www.alliedmotion.com
SIC: 3621 3825 Motors & generators; rotary converters (electrical equipment); function generators

(G-222)
ALLSAFE TECHNOLOGIES INC
290 Creekside Dr (14228-2031)
PHONE................................716 691-0400
Fax: 716 691-0404
James Pokornowski, *President*
Kristine Blackburn, *Opers Mgr*
Robert P Pokornowski, *Treasurer*
Christine Blackburn, *Marketing Staff*
Kyle Lysek, *Manager*
▲ EMP: 65
SQ FT: 35,000
SALES (est): 13.1MM **Privately Held**
WEB: www.allsafe.com
SIC: 3089 2759 Identification cards, plastic; commercial printing

(G-223)
AMERICAN BUSINESS FORMS INC
3840 E Robinson Rd # 249 (14228-2001)
PHONE................................716 836-5111
Larry Zavadil, *Branch Mgr*
EMP: 80
SALES (corp-wide): 17MM **Privately Held**
SIC: 2752 Commercial printing, lithographic
PA: American Business Forms, Inc.
    31 E Minnesota Ave
    Glenwood MN 56334
    320 634-5471

(G-224)
AMERICAN PRECISION INDS INC (HQ)
Also Called: Basco
45 Hazelwood Dr (14228-2224)
PHONE................................716 691-9100
Fax: 716 691-9181
James W Bingel, *CEO*
Brian Buzzard, *Engineer*
◆ EMP: 200 EST: 1946
SQ FT: 106,800
SALES (est): 211.2MM
SALES (corp-wide): 20.5B **Publicly Held**
WEB: www.apischmidtbretten.com
SIC: 3677 3621 3625 3443 Coil windings, electronic; inductors, electronic; motors & generators; electromagnetic clutches or brakes; heat exchangers: coolers (after, inter), condensers, etc.; condensers, steam; separators, industrial process: metal plate
PA: Danaher Corporation
    2200 Penn Ave Nw Ste 800w
    Washington DC 20037
    202 828-0850

(G-225)
AMHERST STNLESS FBRICATION LLC
60 John Glenn Dr (14228-2118)
PHONE................................716 691-7012
Fax: 716 691-8202
Gerald J Bogdan, *President*
Joseph B Huber, *Corp Secy*
Jim Mazur, *Engineer*
Christopher Bogdan, *Project Engr*
Mike Huber, *Manager*
▼ EMP: 40 EST: 1945
SQ FT: 35,000
SALES (est): 7.5MM
SALES (corp-wide): 9.4MM **Privately Held**
WEB: www.avinsfab.com
SIC: 3443 Tanks, lined: metal plate
PA: General Oil Equipment Co., Inc.
    60 John Glenn Dr
    Amherst NY 14228
    716 691-7012

(G-226)
API DELTRAN INC
45 Hazelwood Dr (14228-2224)
PHONE................................716 691-9100
Barry Bistis, *Chairman*
John Pieri, *Manager*
◆ EMP: 130
SALES (est): 42.6K
SALES (corp-wide): 20.5B **Publicly Held**
SIC: 3625 Electromagnetic clutches or brakes
PA: Danaher Corporation
    2200 Penn Ave Nw Ste 800w
    Washington DC 20037
    202 828-0850

(G-227)
BEKAERT CORPORATION
Also Called: Advanced Coating Technologies
6000 N Bailey Ave Ste 9 (14226-5102)
PHONE................................716 830-1321
Chandra Venkatraman, *Branch Mgr*
EMP: 20
SALES (corp-wide): 451MM **Privately Held**
WEB: www.bekaert.com
SIC: 3315 Wire & fabricated wire products
HQ: Bekaert Corporation
    3200 W Market St Ste 303
    Fairlawn OH 44333
    330 867-3325

(G-228)
BFC PRINT NETWORK INC (PA)
455 Commerce Dr Ste 6 (14228-2313)
PHONE................................716 838-4532
John Crainer, *President*
Nancy Zabka, *Treasurer*
Marlene Wirth, *Sales Executive*
EMP: 1
SQ FT: 5,800
SALES (est): 1.2MM **Privately Held**
WEB: www.bfcprintnetwork.com
SIC: 2759 Business forms: printing

(G-229)
BIRDAIR INC (HQ)
65 Lawrence Bell Dr Ste 1 (14221-7094)
PHONE................................716 633-9500
Fax: 716 633-9850
Mitsuo Sugimoto, *President*
Kimberly Boeheime, *General Mgr*
Jerry Lisowski, *Vice Pres*
Eiichi Okamoto, *Vice Pres*
David W Andrews, *Treasurer*
◆ EMP: 60 EST: 1956
SQ FT: 20,000
SALES (est): 14.5MM
SALES (corp-wide): 290.5MM **Privately Held**
SIC: 3448 Prefabricated metal buildings
PA: Taiyo Kogyo Corporation
    4-8-4, Kikawahigashi, Yodogawa-Ku
    Osaka OSK 532-0
    663 063-008

(G-230)
CCA HOLDING INC
300 Corporate Pkwy (14226-1207)
PHONE................................716 446-8800
Edward Bredniak, *President*
William F Sullivan, *Vice Pres*
◆ EMP: 245
SALES (est): 12.8MM **Privately Held**
SIC: 3313 Ferroalloys

(G-231)
CENTER FOR INQUIRY INC (PA)
Also Called: Councel For Sclar Hmnism Cscop
3965 Rensch Rd (14228-2743)
P.O. Box 664, Buffalo (14226-0664)
PHONE................................716 636-4869
Paul Kurtz, *President*
Chris Mooney, *Pub Rel Dir*
Lauren Foster, *Manager*
Nora Hurley, *Producer*
Nicole Scott, *Assoc Editor*
EMP: 15
SALES (est): 4.2MM **Privately Held**
WEB: www.centerforinquiry.net
SIC: 2721 Magazines: publishing only, not printed on site

(G-232)
CHART INDUSTRIES INC
Also Called: Airsep
260 Creekside Dr Ste 200 (14228-2047)
PHONE................................716 691-0202
Joe Priest, *COO*
Mark Mizerkiewicz, *Production*
Richard Boerdner, *Treasurer*
Dennis Fitzgerald, *Manager*
Peter Weisenborn, *Info Tech Mgr*
EMP: 20
SALES (corp-wide): 1B **Publicly Held**
SIC: 3569 Generators: steam, liquid oxygen or nitrogen
PA: Chart Industries, Inc.
    1 Infinity Corp Ctr Dr # 300
    Cleveland OH 44125
    440 753-1490

(G-233)
CHART INDUSTRIES INC
Also Called: Airsep
500 Commerce Dr (14228-2327)
PHONE................................716 691-0202
EMP: 25
SALES (corp-wide): 1B **Publicly Held**
SIC: 3569 Generators: steam, liquid oxygen or nitrogen

▲ = Import ▼=Export
◆ =Import/Export

GEOGRAPHIC SECTION   Amherst - Erie County (G-258)

PA: Chart Industries, Inc.
1 Infinity Corp Ctr Dr # 300
Cleveland OH 44125
440 753-1490

(G-234)
COLUMBUS MCKINNON CORPORATION
Also Called: C M
470 John Jmes Adubon Pkwy
(14228-1142)
PHONE..................716 689-5400
Linda Riggi, *General Mgr*
Kathleen Butler, *Commissioner*
EMP: 100
SALES (corp-wide): 597.1MM **Publicly Held**
WEB: www.cmworks.com
SIC: 3536 Hoists, cranes & monorails
PA: Columbus Mckinnon Corporation
205 Crosspoint Pkwy
Getzville NY 14068
716 689-5400

(G-235)
CRANE EQUIPMENT & SERVICE INC (HQ)
140 John Jmes Adubon Pkwy
(14228-1183)
PHONE..................716 689-5400
Jena Buer, *President*
Timothy T Tevens, *Chairman*
Karen L Howard, *CFO*
Rakesh A Jobanputra, *Treasurer*
Linda Wrobel, *Manager*
EMP: 3 **EST:** 1997
SQ FT: 3,000
SALES (est): 28.1MM
SALES (corp-wide): 597.1MM **Publicly Held**
WEB: www.broussardla.com
SIC: 3531 Crane carriers
PA: Columbus Mckinnon Corporation
205 Crosspoint Pkwy
Getzville NY 14068
716 689-5400

(G-236)
DANAHER CORPORATION
Also Called: Warner Electric
45 Hazelwood Dr (14228-2224)
PHONE..................716 691-9100
EMP: 6
SALES (corp-wide): 20.5B **Publicly Held**
SIC: 3566 Speed changers, drives & gears
PA: Danaher Corporation
2200 Penn Ave Nw Ste 800w
Washington DC 20037
202 828-0850

(G-237)
DELPHI AUTOMOTIVE LLP
Also Called: Delphi Amherst Test Operations
4326 Ridge Lea Rd (14226-1016)
PHONE..................716 438-4886
EMP: 5 **Privately Held**
SIC: 3714 Motor vehicle parts & accessories
PA: Delphi Automotive Llp
Courteney Road
Gillingham

(G-238)
EMC CORPORATION
500 Corporate Pkwy # 122 (14226-1263)
PHONE..................716 833-5348
Kent Lorence, *Accounts Mgr*
Diane Willmott, *Manager*
EMP: 25
SALES (corp-wide): 72.7B **Publicly Held**
WEB: www.emc.com
SIC: 3572 Computer storage devices
HQ: Emc Corporation
176 South St
Hopkinton MA 01748
508 435-1000

(G-239)
ENHANCED TOOL INC
90 Pineview Dr (14228-2120)
PHONE..................716 691-5200
Fax: 716 691-0109
Michael Emmert, *CEO*
David M Healey, *Vice Pres*
Pat Healey, *Manager*
EMP: 20

SQ FT: 6,000
SALES (est): 3.7MM **Privately Held**
WEB: www.enhancedtool.com
SIC: 3544 Special dies & tools

(G-240)
ESM GROUP INC (DH)
300 Corporate Pkwy 118n (14226-1207)
PHONE..................716 446-8985
Gregory P Marzec, *Ch of Bd*
William F Sullivan, *Exec VP*
Charles A Zak, *Exec VP*
◆ **EMP:** 15 **EST:** 1957
SQ FT: 15,000
SALES (est): 29.7MM
SALES (corp-wide): 306.6MM **Privately Held**
WEB: www.esmgroup.com
SIC: 2819 Industrial inorganic chemicals
HQ: Skw Stahl-Metallurgie Gmbh
Rathausplatz 11
Unterneukirchen 84579
863 462-7203

(G-241)
ESM II INC (DH)
300 Corporate Pkwy 118n (14226-1258)
PHONE..................716 446-8911
Fax: 716 446-8911
Charles F Wright, *President*
John Tobias, *VP Mktg*
Troy Kislak, *Manager*
Michael Mohan, *Manager*
▲ **EMP:** 50
SALES (est): 12MM
SALES (corp-wide): 306.6MM **Privately Held**
SIC: 3549 Metalworking machinery
HQ: Esm Group Inc.
300 Corporate Pkwy 118n
Amherst NY 14226
716 446-8985

(G-242)
ESM SPECIAL METALS & TECH INC
300 Corporate Pkwy 118n (14226-1207)
PHONE..................716 446-8914
Hartmut Meyer-Grnow, *CEO*
Sandyee Whipple, *Principal*
EMP: 20
SALES (est): 2.7MM **Privately Held**
SIC: 2819 Industrial inorganic chemicals

(G-243)
GENERAL OIL EQUIPMENT CO INC (PA)
60 John Glenn Dr (14228-2118)
PHONE..................716 691-7012
Fax: 716 691-7990
Gerald Bogdan, *Ch of Bd*
Joseph B Huber, *President*
Jim Mazur, *Engineer*
Karl B Huber Jr, *Treasurer*
Werner Wittmann, *Sales Mgr*
EMP: 49
SQ FT: 34,000
SALES (est): 9.4MM **Privately Held**
WEB: www.goe-avins.com
SIC: 3625 5084 7699 3443 Electric controls & control accessories, industrial; oil refining machinery, equipment & supplies; industrial machinery & equipment repair; tanks, lined: metal plate

(G-244)
GROVER CLEVELAND PRESS INC
2676 Sweet Home Rd (14228-2128)
PHONE..................716 564-2222
Fax: 716 691-6766
Michael Degen, *President*
Tom Degen, *Vice Pres*
EMP: 10
SQ FT: 12,800
SALES (est): 2MM **Privately Held**
WEB: www.grovercleavelandpress.com
SIC: 2752 2759 Commercial printing, lithographic; photo-offset printing; letterpress printing; embossing on paper

(G-245)
I-EVOLVE TECHONOLOGY SERVICES (PA)
501 John James Audubon Pk (14228-1143)
PHONE..................801 566-5268
Dan Larkin, *President*
Heidi Fischer, *VP Admin*
Nathan Brozyna, *Engineer*
Robert Dunmire, *Engineer*
Tracey Durst, *Engineer*
EMP: 12
SALES (est): 5.9MM **Privately Held**
SIC: 3433 Solar heaters & collectors

(G-246)
INTERNATIONAL IMAGING MTLS INC (PA)
Also Called: Iimak
310 Commerce Dr (14228-2396)
PHONE..................716 691-6333
Fax: 716 691-1133
Douglas Wagner, *CEO*
Richard Marshall, *Ch of Bd*
Susan R Stamp, *Senior VP*
Rick Johnson, *Engineer*
Joe Perna, *CFO*
◆ **EMP:** 327
SQ FT: 250,000
SALES (est): 133.8MM **Privately Held**
SIC: 3955 3555 Ribbons, inked: typewriter, adding machine, register, etc.; printing trades machinery

(G-247)
INTRI-CUT INC
90 Pineview Dr (14228-2120)
PHONE..................716 691-5200
Fax: 716 691-5344
Ronald Janson, *President*
EMP: 12
SQ FT: 6,000
SALES (est): 1.6MM **Privately Held**
WEB: www.intri-cut.com
SIC: 3544 Special dies & tools

(G-248)
JUICY VAPOR LLC (PA)
Also Called: Nixteria Crafted By Juicyvapor
188 Creekside Dr (14228-2031)
PHONE..................855 525-8429
Brad McNamara, *President*
Anthony Brancato, *Vice Pres*
EMP: 10
SALES (est): 1MM **Privately Held**
SIC: 2111 Cigarettes

(G-249)
LIBERTY DISPLAYS INC
4230b Ridge Lea Rd # 110 (14226-1063)
PHONE..................716 743-1757
Dean Rainer, *President*
EMP: 30
SQ FT: 57,000
SALES: 5MM **Privately Held**
SIC: 3999 Forms: display, dress & show

(G-250)
MAHLE INDSTRBETEILIGUNGEN GMBH
Also Called: Delphi-T Compressor Engrg Ctr
4236 Ridge Lea Rd (14226-1016)
PHONE..................716 319-6700
Tim Skinner, *Manager*
EMP: 75 **Privately Held**
SIC: 3563 Air & gas compressors
HQ: Mahle Industriebeteiligungen Gmbh
Pragstr. 26-46
Stuttgart
711 501-0

(G-251)
MAHLE INDUSTRIES INCORPORATED
4236 Ridge Lea Rd (14226-1016)
PHONE..................248 735-3623
Dennis Kimsey, *Director*
EMP: 12 **Privately Held**
SIC: 3714 Motor vehicle parts & accessories
HQ: Mahle Industries, Incorporated
23030 Mahle Dr
Farmington Hills MI 48335
248 305-8200

(G-252)
MOTIVAIR CORPORATION
85 Woodridge Dr (14228-2221)
PHONE..................716 691-9222
Fax: 716 689-0073
Graham Whitmore, *President*
Dan Arnold, *Opers Mgr*
Jeffrey Barnes, *Manager*
Randy Partin, *Manager*
▲ **EMP:** 20
SQ FT: 25,000
SALES (est): 6.7MM **Privately Held**
SIC: 3585 3443 Air conditioning condensers & condensing units; separators, industrial process: metal plate

(G-253)
NEXSTAR HOLDING CORP
Also Called: PHASE IL MARKETING DBA
275 Northpointe Pkwy (14228-1895)
PHONE..................716 929-9000
Fax: 716 929-9090
Gary Robinson, *President*
Richard S Elliott, *Vice Pres*
Danny Jayes, *Production*
Paula Bednarz, *Admin Asst*
EMP: 5
SALES (est): 911.2K **Privately Held**
SIC: 3564 Filters, air: furnaces, air conditioning equipment, etc.

(G-254)
NK MEDICAL PRODUCTS INC (PA)
80 Creekside Dr (14228-2027)
PHONE..................716 759-7200
Fax: 716 759-0700
Norman V Kurlander, *President*
Angela Hastings, *General Mgr*
Joseph Manzella, *Manager*
▲ **EMP:** 5
SQ FT: 1,600
SALES (est): 1.2MM **Privately Held**
WEB: www.nkmedicalproducts.com
SIC: 2514 2599 Cribs: metal; hospital beds

(G-255)
NOVUM MEDICAL PRODUCTS INC
80 Creekside Dr (14228-2027)
PHONE..................716 759-7200
Joe Mandella, *President*
Jennifer Cappello, *Manager*
◆ **EMP:** 10
SALES (est): 1MM **Privately Held**
SIC: 2514 2599 Cribs: metal; hospital beds

(G-256)
OERLIKON METCO (US) INC
6000 N Bailey Ave (14226-5102)
PHONE..................716 270-2228
Dan Wisniewski, *Branch Mgr*
EMP: 10
SALES (corp-wide): 2.6B **Privately Held**
SIC: 3399 Powder, metal
HQ: Oerlikon Metco (Us) Inc.
1101 Prospect Ave
Westbury NY 11590
516 334-1300

(G-257)
ONY INC
1576 Sweet Home Rd # 114 (14228-2710)
PHONE..................716 636-9096
Fax: 716 636-3942
Edmund Egan, *President*
Bill Ferguson, *CFO*
Judy Wetter, *Accounting Mgr*
Lynn Hlavaty, *Manager*
EMP: 26
SQ FT: 8,000
SALES (est): 6.2MM **Privately Held**
WEB: www.ony.com
SIC: 2834 Pharmaceutical preparations

(G-258)
PROMETHEUS BOOKS INC
59 John Glenn Dr (14228-2197)
PHONE..................716 691-2158
Paul Kurtz, *President*
Jonathan Kurtz, *Vice Pres*
Mary Read, *Human Resources*
Steven Mitchell, *Manager*

Amherst - Erie County (G-259) — GEOGRAPHIC SECTION

Gretchen Kurtz, *Director*
▲ **EMP:** 30
SQ FT: 28,000
SALES (est): 3.4MM **Privately Held**
WEB: www.prometheusbooks.com
SIC: 2731 Book publishing

(G-259)
SAINT-GBAIN ADVNCED CRMICS LLC
Boron Nitride Div
168 Creekside Dr (14228-2037)
PHONE 716 691-2000
Dawn Bell, *Prdtn Mgr*
William Hill, *Manager*
Mary Corbi, *Manager*
Linda A Broderick, *Administration*
Michael Rogers, *Maintence Staff*
EMP: 50
SALES (corp-wide): 189MM **Privately Held**
WEB: www.hexoloy.com
SIC: 3291 Abrasive products
HQ: Saint-Gobain Advanced Ceramics Llc
23 Acheson Dr
Niagara Falls NY 14303

(G-260)
SALLY BEAUTY SUPPLY LLC
310 Main St (14226)
PHONE 716 831-3286
Barbara Miller, *Manager*
EMP: 5
SALES (corp-wide): 3.8B **Publicly Held**
WEB: www.sallybeauty.com
SIC: 2844 Toilet preparations
HQ: Sally Beauty Supply Llc
3001 Colorado Blvd
Denton TX 76210
940 898-7500

(G-261)
SIEMENS INDUSTRY INC
85 Northpointe Pkwy (14228-1886)
PHONE 716 568-0983
EMP: 87
SALES (corp-wide): 83.5B **Privately Held**
SIC: 3822 Air conditioning & refrigeration controls
HQ: Siemens Industry, Inc.
1000 Deerfield Pkwy
Buffalo Grove IL 60089
847 215-1000

(G-262)
STERLING UNITED INC
Also Called: Sommer
6030 N Bailey Ave Ste 1 (14226-1000)
P.O. Box 374, Clarence Center (14032-0374)
PHONE 716 835-9290
Fax: 716 871-9085
John Giblin, *Ch of Bd*
Chuck Huynh, *Opers Staff*
EMP: 7
SALES (est): 994.7K **Privately Held**
SIC: 2752 Commercial printing, lithographic

(G-263)
SUITE SOLUTIONS INC
100 Corporate Pkwy # 338 (14226-1200)
PHONE 716 929-3050
Alan Perlmutter, *President*
Richard Wolney, *CFO*
Dennis Malinowski, *E-Business*
Kathleen Morabito, *MIS Staff*
Edward F O'Gara, *Bd of Directors*
EMP: 25
SALES (est): 1.2MM **Privately Held**
SIC: 7372 7371 Prepackaged software; custom computer programming services

(G-264)
SYNERGY TOOLING SYSTEMS INC (PA)
287 Commerce Dr (14228-2302)
PHONE 716 834-4457
Richard E Morrison Jr, *President*
Dan Witucki, *Facilities Mgr*
Patrick Quinlan, *Engineer*
William Reese, *CFO*
EMP: 35
SQ FT: 20,000
SALES (est): 4.8MM **Privately Held**
SIC: 3544 Special dies, tools, jigs & fixtures

(G-265)
TARGETPROCESS INC (PA)
1325 Millersport Hwy (14221-2932)
P.O. Box 1845 (14226-7845)
PHONE 607 346-0621
Michael Dubakov, *President*
Andrey Mihailenko, *Vice Pres*
David Hart, *Director*
EMP: 10
SALES (est): 1.8MM **Privately Held**
SIC: 7372 Prepackaged software

(G-266)
THOMSON INDUSTRIES INC
45 Hazelwood Dr (14228-2224)
PHONE 716 691-9100
Dan Daniel, *CEO*
EMP: 12
SALES (est): 1.7MM **Privately Held**
SIC: 3585 Heating equipment, complete

(G-267)
TRANSCONTINENTAL PRINTING GP
300 International Dr # 200 (14221-5781)
PHONE 716 626-3078
Louis J Continelli, *Branch Mgr*
EMP: 5
SALES (corp-wide): 693MM **Privately Held**
SIC: 2752 Commercial printing, lithographic
PA: Imprimeries Transcontinental 2005 S.E.N.C
1 Place Ville-Marie Bureau 3315
Montreal QC H3B 3
514 954-4000

(G-268)
TRI-METAL INDUSTRIES INC
100 Pineview Dr (14228-2120)
PHONE 716 691-3323
Fax: 716 691-3327
Donald Chatwin Jr, *President*
Jerry Stetter, *Foreman/Supr*
Brian McCracken, *Purchasing*
Douglas B Chatwin, *Treasurer*
EMP: 38 **EST:** 1960
SQ FT: 33,000
SALES: 2MM **Privately Held**
SIC: 3444 Sheet metalwork

(G-269)
UFC BIOTECHNOLOGY
1576 Sweet Home Rd # 225 (14228-2710)
PHONE 716 777-3776
EMP: 10
SALES (est): 2MM **Privately Held**
SIC: 2835 Microbiology & virology diagnostic products

(G-270)
ULTRA-SCAN CORPORATION
4240 Ridge Lea Rd Ste 10 (14226-1083)
PHONE 716 832-6269
John K Schneider, *President*
James Baker, *Vice Pres*
Leonard C Pratt, *Vice Pres*
Stephen Gojevic, *Design Engr*
David C Horan, *Admin Sec*
EMP: 11
SQ FT: 12,600
SALES (est): 2MM **Privately Held**
WEB: www.ultra-scan.com
SIC: 3575 Computer terminals, monitors & components

(G-271)
WATSON BOWMAN ACME CORP
95 Pineview Dr (14228-2121)
PHONE 716 691-8162
Fax: 716 691-9239
Markus Burri, *President*
Mike Turchiarelli, *Finance Dir*
Rick Patterson, *Director*
◆ **EMP:** 100
SALES (est): 37.6MM
SALES (corp-wide): 75.6B **Privately Held**
WEB: www.wbacorp.com
SIC: 3441 2899 3568 Expansion joints (structural shapes), iron or steel; concrete curing & hardening compounds; power transmission equipment
HQ: Basfin Corporation
100 Campus Dr Ste 301
Florham Park NJ 07932
973 245-6000

(G-272)
WELCOME MAGAZINE INC
4511 Harlem Rd (14226-3803)
PHONE 716 839-3121
Fax: 716 839-1187
Julie Kianof More, *President*
Margaret Ashley, *Manager*
Julie Kianof, *Manager*
EMP: 10
SQ FT: 500
SALES (est): 1MM **Privately Held**
WEB: www.welcome-magazine.com
SIC: 2721 Magazines: publishing only, not printed on site

Amityville
Suffolk County

(G-273)
A & G PRECISION CORP
680 Albany Ave (11701-1123)
PHONE 631 957-5613
Fax: 631 957-8722
Gus Georgopoulos, *President*
Nick Georgopoulos, *Vice Pres*
EMP: 15
SALES (est): 1.5MM **Privately Held**
SIC: 3599 Machine shop, jobbing & repair

(G-274)
ACRAN SPILL CONTAINMENT INC (PA)
599 Albany Ave (11701-1140)
PHONE 631 841-2300
John Deangelo, *President*
EMP: 8
SALES (est): 846.7K **Privately Held**
SIC: 2655 Containers, liquid tight fiber: from purchased material

(G-275)
AMITY WOODWORKING INC
Also Called: Amity Wood Industries
25 Greene Ave (11701-2943)
PHONE 631 598-7000
Daniel Demarco, *President*
EMP: 5
SALES (est): 490K **Privately Held**
SIC: 2431 Millwork

(G-276)
ANCON GEAR & INSTRUMENT CORP (PA)
29 Seabro Ave (11701-1201)
PHONE 631 694-5255
Fax: 516 694-5056
Joseph Markiewicz, *President*
Ed Markiewicz, *Vice Pres*
Micheal Chapman, *Manager*
EMP: 18
SQ FT: 6,000
SALES (est): 2.7MM **Privately Held**
WEB: www.ancongear.com
SIC: 3599 Machine shop, jobbing & repair

(G-277)
BAYWOOD PUBLISHING COMPANY
26 Austin Ave Ste 2 (11701-3052)
P.O. Box 337 (11701-0337)
PHONE 631 691-1270
Fax: 516 691-1770
Stuart Cohen, *President*
Edward Cohen, *Treasurer*
EMP: 9
SQ FT: 6,000
SALES (est): 1MM **Privately Held**
WEB: www.baywood.com
SIC: 2721 2731 Trade journals: publishing only, not printed on site; books: publishing only

(G-278)
CALICO COTTAGE INC
210 New Hwy (11701-1116)
PHONE 631 841-2100
Fax: 516 841-2401
Mark L Wurzel, *President*
David A Sank, *Exec VP*
Lawrence J Wurzel, *Vice Pres*
Steve Lohin, *VP Mfg*
Steven Nagle, *VP Mfg*
▼ **EMP:** 50
SQ FT: 45,000
SALES (est): 15.4MM **Privately Held**
WEB: www.calicocottage.com
SIC: 2064 Candy & other confectionery products

(G-279)
CALPAC INCORPORATED
44 Seabro Ave (11701-1202)
PHONE 631 789-0502
Fax: 631 789-0586
Pierre Lintault, *President*
EMP: 10
SQ FT: 11,000
SALES (est): 1MM **Privately Held**
SIC: 3086 2653 Packaging & shipping materials, foamed plastic; display items, corrugated: made from purchased materials

(G-280)
CASUAL HOME WORLDWIDE INC
Also Called: Prefered Directors Share
38 William St (11701-2916)
PHONE 631 789-2999
Fax: 631 789-2970
Ming Chiang, *CEO*
Su O Chiang, *Vice Pres*
Su Chiang, *Vice Pres*
Fang Chiang, *Treasurer*
▲ **EMP:** 6
SALES (est): 612.5K **Privately Held**
SIC: 2759 Imprinting

(G-281)
CONTINENTAL INSTRUMENTS LLC (HQ)
355 Bayview Ave (11701-2801)
PHONE 631 842-9400
Fax: 631 842-9135
Bob Weinstein, *Opers Staff*
Richard Soloway, *Mng Member*
Richard Tare, *Manager*
John Banks,
EMP: 34
SQ FT: 90,000
SALES (est): 2.9MM
SALES (corp-wide): 82.5MM **Publicly Held**
SIC: 3625 Control equipment, electric
PA: Napco Security Technologies, Inc.
333 Bayview Ave
Amityville NY 11701
631 842-9400

(G-282)
CONTROL RESEARCH INC
Also Called: Cri Graphic
385 Bayview Ave Unit C (11701-2801)
PHONE 631 225-1111
Robert Slomkowski, *President*
Sheryl Young, *Office Mgr*
EMP: 5 **EST:** 1963
SQ FT: 10,000
SALES (est): 597.5K **Privately Held**
WEB: www.stageresearch.com
SIC: 2759 2395 Screen printing; embroidery & art needlework

(G-283)
CRAFTMASTER FLAVOR TECHNOLOGY
23 Albany Ave (11701-2829)
PHONE 631 789-8607
Fax: 631 789-2721
Thomas Massetti, *President*
Ellen McDonald, *Vice Pres*
Joseph Massetti, *Treasurer*
EMP: 10
SQ FT: 4,000
SALES (est): 1.4MM **Privately Held**
SIC: 2869 2087 Flavors or flavoring materials, synthetic; extracts, flavoring

▲ = Import ▼ =Export
◆ =Import/Export

GEOGRAPHIC SECTION

Amityville - Suffolk County (G-305)

(G-284)
DANIEL DEMARCO AND ASSOC INC
25 Greene Ave (11701-2943)
PHONE.....................................631 598-7000
Fax: 631 598-1140
Daniel Demarco, *Ch of Bd*
Joe Corrente, *Manager*
Lyn Setffek, *Manager*
Mike Smith, *Director*
EMP: 35
SALES (est): 8.9MM **Privately Held**
WEB: www.danieldemarco.com
SIC: 3429 1751 2499 Cabinet hardware; cabinet building & installation; decorative wood & woodwork

(G-285)
EDO LLC (HQ)
Also Called: Edo Corporation
1500 New Horizons Blvd (11701-1130)
PHONE.....................................631 630-4000
Charles Greene, *CEO*
Joseph Cangelosi, *General Mgr*
Lawrence Schwartz, *Principal*
Jon A Anderson, *Senior VP*
Frank W Otto, *Senior VP*
◆ EMP: 9 EST: 1925
SQ FT: 6,000
SALES (est): 976.5MM
SALES (corp-wide): 7.4B **Publicly Held**
WEB: www.nycedo.com
SIC: 3812 3728 3663 3679 Search & navigation equipment; sonar systems & equipment; warfare counter-measure equipment; detection apparatus: electronic/magnetic field, light/heat; military aircraft equipment & armament; counter-measure dispensers, aircraft; research & dev by manuf., aircraft parts & auxiliary equip; antennas, transmitting & communications; satellites, communications; electronic crystals; piezoelectric crystals
PA: Harris Corporation
    1025 W Nasa Blvd
    Melbourne FL 32919
    321 727-9100

(G-286)
EDO LLC
Also Called: Antenna Products
1500 New Horizons Blvd (11701-1130)
PHONE.....................................631 630-4200
Peter Martin, *General Mgr*
Joseph Canova, *Business Mgr*
EMP: 1000
SALES (corp-wide): 7.4B **Publicly Held**
SIC: 3825 3812 3761 3699 Instruments to measure electricity; search & navigation equipment; guided missiles & space vehicles; electrical equipment & supplies; radio & TV communications equipment
HQ: Edo Llc
    1500 New Horizons Blvd
    Amityville NY 11701
    631 630-4000

(G-287)
EDO LLC
Also Called: Defense Systems
1500 New Horizons Blvd (11701-1130)
PHONE.....................................631 630-4000
Peter Martin, *General Mgr*
Joseph Canova, *Business Mgr*
Milo Hyde, *Vice Pres*
Ed Blasko, *Engineer*
Glenn Umstetter, *Engineer*
EMP: 123
SALES (corp-wide): 7.4B **Publicly Held**
WEB: www.nycedo.com
SIC: 3625 Control equipment, electric
HQ: Edo Llc
    1500 New Horizons Blvd
    Amityville NY 11701
    631 630-4000

(G-288)
G MARKS HDWR LIQUIDATING CORP
Also Called: G. Marks Hardware, Inc.
333 Bayview Ave (11701-2801)
PHONE.....................................631 225-5400
Fax: 631 225-6136
George Marks, *President*
Donna Gallagher, *Purch Mgr*
Florin Mirica, *Engineer*
Bert Weichselbaum, *Finance Mgr*
Dave Koogler, *Business Dir*
EMP: 90
SQ FT: 35,000
SALES (est): 14.3MM
SALES (corp-wide): 82.5MM **Publicly Held**
WEB: www.marksusa.com
SIC: 3429 Locks or lock sets
PA: Napco Security Technologies, Inc.
    333 Bayview Ave
    Amityville NY 11701
    631 842-9400

(G-289)
GKN AEROSPACE MONITOR INC
1000 New Horizons Blvd (11701-1138)
PHONE.....................................562 619-8558
Fax: 631 957-0179
Daniele Cagnatel, *CEO*
Kevin L Cummings, *Ch of Bd*
Fran Novak, *President*
David Maguire, *General Mgr*
Paul Kowack, *Vice Pres*
▲ EMP: 275 EST: 1947
SQ FT: 238,000
SALES (est): 94.7MM
SALES (corp-wide): 10.9B **Privately Held**
WEB: www.monair.com
SIC: 3728 3769 Aircraft assemblies, sub-assemblies & parts; guided missile & space vehicle parts & auxiliary equipment
PA: Gkn Plc
    Ipsley House
    Redditch WORCS B98 0
    152 751-7715

(G-290)
GRAND KNITTING MILLS INC (PA)
7050 New Horizons Blvd # 1 (11701-1179)
PHONE.....................................631 226-5000
Fax: 631 226-8336
▲ EMP: 40 EST: 1910
SQ FT: 35,000
SALES (est): 2.9MM **Privately Held**
SIC: 2361 5137 Mfg Girl/Youth Dresses/Blouses Whol Women's/Child's Clothing

(G-291)
HABCO CORP
Also Called: Habco Sales
41 Ranick Dr E (11701-2844)
PHONE.....................................631 789-1400
Herb Auleta, *CEO*
Steven Auleta, *President*
Philip Auleta, *Vice Pres*
▲ EMP: 50
SQ FT: 19,175
SALES: 9MM **Privately Held**
SIC: 2022 Processed cheese

(G-292)
HART SPECIALTIES INC
Also Called: New York Eye
5000 New Horizons Blvd (11701-1143)
P.O. Box 9003 (11701-9003)
PHONE.....................................631 226-5600
Fax: 631 226-5884
Arthur Jankolovits, *Ch of Bd*
Shannon Johnson, *Vice Pres*
Lucy Korn, *Vice Pres*
Jan Phillips, *Vice Pres*
Susan Conway, *Bookkeeper*
▲ EMP: 70
SQ FT: 25,000
SALES: 21.6MM **Privately Held**
WEB: www.newyorkeye.net
SIC: 3827 5995 Optical instruments & apparatus; optical goods stores

(G-293)
HELGEN INDUSTRIES INC
Also Called: De Santis Holster and Lea Gds
431 Bayview Ave (11701-2638)
PHONE.....................................631 841-6300
Fax: 631 841-6320
Gene De Santis, *Ch of Bd*
Helen De Santis, *Vice Pres*
Stacey Falek, *Manager*
▲ EMP: 125
SQ FT: 14,000
SALES (est): 18.6MM **Privately Held**
WEB: www.desantisholster.com
SIC: 3199 3172 Holsters, leather; personal leather goods

(G-294)
HI-TECH PHARMACAL CO INC (HQ)
Also Called: Hi-Tech Pharmacal - An Akorn
369 Bayview Ave (11701-2801)
PHONE.....................................631 789-8228
Fax: 516 789-8429
David S Seltzer, *President*
Gary M April, *President*
April Caccavale, *Counsel*
April Polikoff, *Counsel*
Kamel Egbaria, *Exec VP*
▲ EMP: 277
SALES (est): 96.1MM
SALES (corp-wide): 985MM **Publicly Held**
WEB: www.hitechpharm.com
SIC: 2834 Pharmaceutical preparations
PA: Akorn, Inc.
    1925 W Field Ct Ste 300
    Lake Forest IL 60045
    847 279-6100

(G-295)
IMC TEDDY FOOD SERVICE
Also Called: Sefi Fabricator
50 Ranick Dr E (11701-2822)
P.O. Box 338 (11701-0338)
PHONE.....................................631 789-8881
Rasik Patel, *Partner*
Madelin Fernandez, *Purch Agent*
Joan Brent, *Bookkeeper*
Joe Campbell, *Sales Mgr*
▲ EMP: 48 EST: 1956
SALES (est): 6.6MM **Privately Held**
WEB: www.imcteddy.com
SIC: 3589 Commercial cooking & food-warming equipment

(G-296)
INTERSTATE WOOD PRODUCTS INC
Also Called: Interstate Wood & Vinyl Pdts
1084 Sunrise Hwy (11701-2526)
PHONE.....................................631 842-4488
Fax: 516 842-4345
Jennifer Cerullo, *CEO*
John Hokanson, *Manager*
EMP: 25
SQ FT: 8,500
SALES (est): 3.6MM
SALES (corp-wide): 31.5MM **Privately Held**
SIC: 2499 5031 3496 1799 Fencing, wood; fencing, wood; miscellaneous fabricated wire products; fence construction
PA: Amendola Industries, Inc.
    1084 Sunrise Hwy
    Amityville NY 11701
    631 842-4427

(G-297)
ISLAND LITE LOUVERS INC
35 Albany Ave (11701-2828)
PHONE.....................................631 608-4250
Kristin Hill, *Ch of Bd*
Joe Serbo, *Manager*
EMP: 25
SALES (est): 3.6MM **Privately Held**
WEB: www.islandlitelouver.com
SIC: 3648 Reflectors for lighting equipment: metal

(G-298)
JAXSON ROLLFORMING INC
145 Dixon Ave Ste 1 (11701-2836)
PHONE.....................................631 842-7775
Fax: 631 842-7791
Alexander Trink, *President*
▲ EMP: 37
SALES (est): 8MM **Privately Held**
WEB: www.jaxsonrollforming.com
SIC: 3446 5031 Fences, gates, posts & flagpoles; partitions & supports/studs, including accoustical systems; molding, all materials

(G-299)
JEFFREY JOHN
Also Called: Creative Compositions
25 Elm Pl (11701-2815)
PHONE.....................................631 842-2850
John Jeffrey, *Owner*
EMP: 6
SALES (est): 370K **Privately Held**
SIC: 2499 Decorative wood & woodwork

(G-300)
KABCO PHARMACEUTICALS INC
2000 New Horizons Blvd (11701-1137)
PHONE.....................................631 842-3600
Fax: 516 842-6008
Abu Kabir, *Ch of Bd*
Saiful Kibria, *President*
Amir Hossain, *QC Mgr*
Belal Chowdhury, *Manager*
Alicia Johnston, *Manager*
▲ EMP: 4
SQ FT: 30,000
SALES (est): 1.4MM **Privately Held**
WEB: www.kabco.org
SIC: 2834 Vitamin preparations

(G-301)
KDO INDUSTRIES INC
32 Ranick Dr W (11701-2825)
PHONE.....................................631 608-4612
Lucelle Del Rosaio, *CEO*
George Koenig, *Vice Pres*
EMP: 7
SQ FT: 10,000
SALES (est): 1.3MM **Privately Held**
SIC: 3441 Fabricated structural metal

(G-302)
KEY CAST STONE COMPANY INC
113 Albany Ave (11701-2632)
PHONE.....................................631 789-2145
Fax: 631 920-5422
Filippo Pedalino, *President*
John Gonzalez, *Treasurer*
Carmelo Cicero, *Admin Sec*
▲ EMP: 20 EST: 1958
SQ FT: 20,000
SALES (est): 3.2MM **Privately Held**
WEB: www.keycaststone.com
SIC: 3272 Precast terrazo or concrete products; steps, prefabricated concrete; sills, concrete

(G-303)
KLEER-FAX INC
750 New Horizons Blvd (11701-1191)
PHONE.....................................631 225-1100
Elias Cruz, *CEO*
Louis Nigro, *President*
Larry Campbell, *Opers Mgr*
Dan Smith, *Safety Mgr*
Christopher Pascale, *Info Tech Mgr*
▼ EMP: 97
SQ FT: 50,000
SALES (est): 25.9MM **Privately Held**
WEB: www.kleer-fax.com
SIC: 2678 2677 3089 5943 Stationery products; envelopes; extruded finished plastic products; office forms & supplies; die-cut paper & board

(G-304)
LAMBRO INDUSTRIES INC (PA)
115 Albany Ave (11701-2632)
P.O. Box 367 (11701-0367)
PHONE.....................................631 842-8088
Fax: 516 842-8083
Shiv Anand CPA, *Ch of Bd*
Scott Racywolski, *Purchasing*
Mario Szczepanski, *Chief Engr*
Angela Candreva, *Bookkeeper*
Denise Botterio, *Human Res Mgr*
▲ EMP: 100
SQ FT: 56,000
SALES (est): 22.8MM **Privately Held**
WEB: www.lambro.net
SIC: 3444 Ventilators, sheet metal

(G-305)
LEMODE CONCEPTS INC
19 Elm Pl (11701-2815)
PHONE.....................................631 841-0796
Robert Tolda, *President*

Amityville - Suffolk County (G-306)

Bob Tolda, *President*
Susan Tolda, *Vice Pres*
EMP: 6
SALES (est): 430K **Privately Held**
WEB: www.lemodeconcepts.com
SIC: 2511 Kitchen & dining room furniture

(G-306)
LYNMAR PRINTING CORP
8600 New Horizons Blvd (11701-1154)
PHONE 631 957-8500
Lou Dilorenzo, *President*
Anthony Lisanti, *Vice Pres*
EMP: 8
SQ FT: 8,000
SALES: 1MM **Privately Held**
WEB: www.lynmarprinting.com
SIC: 2752 Commercial printing, offset

(G-307)
M & D MILLWORK LLC
178 New Hwy (11701-1117)
PHONE 631 789-1439
Darren Winter,
Marek Zaleski,
EMP: 10
SQ FT: 14,000
SALES (est): 1.6MM **Privately Held**
SIC: 2431 Millwork

(G-308)
MADJEK INC
185 Dixon Ave (11701-2840)
PHONE 631 842-4475
R Freeman, *Vice Pres*
Barbara Oneil, *Purchasing*
Philip Erickson, *Engineer*
Elaine Moore, *Human Resources*
Phil Erickson, *Legal Staff*
▲ **EMP:** 85
SALES (est): 14.4MM **Privately Held**
WEB: www.madjek.com
SIC: 2541 Store fixtures, wood

(G-309)
MAGNIFLOOD INC
7200 New Horizons Blvd (11701-1150)
PHONE 631 226-1000
Fax: 631 226-4444
Kenneth Greene, *President*
Anita Greene, *Admin Sec*
▲ **EMP:** 20 **EST:** 1977
SQ FT: 27,500
SALES (est): 5.2MM **Privately Held**
WEB: www.magniflood.com
SIC: 3646 Commercial indusl & institutional electric lighting fixtures

(G-310)
MASSAPQUA PRCSION MCHINING LTD
30 Seabro Ave (11701-1202)
PHONE 631 789-1485
Fax: 631 789-1798
Richard Beleski, *President*
EMP: 9
SQ FT: 7,000
SALES: 1.9MM **Privately Held**
SIC: 3599 Machine shop, jobbing & repair

(G-311)
MEGA CABINETS INC
51 Ranick Dr E (11701-2821)
PHONE 631 789-4112
Fax: 516 789-8394
Anthony Griffo, *President*
Arthur Griffo, *Vice Pres*
Alice Braun, *Bookkeeper*
EMP: 25
SQ FT: 20,000
SALES: 1.4MM **Privately Held**
WEB: www.megacabinets.com
SIC: 2434 5031 Wood kitchen cabinets; vanities, bathroom: wood; kitchen cabinets

(G-312)
MERLIN PRINTING INC
215 Dixon Ave (11701-2832)
PHONE 631 842-6366
Steven Vid, *CEO*
Mike Giardina, *President*
Jill Sisco, *Prdtn Mgr*
Julia Kezer, *Asst Controller*
Irene Post, *Finance Mgr*
EMP: 35 **EST:** 1963
SQ FT: 14,200
SALES (est): 7MM **Privately Held**
WEB: www.merlinprinting.com
SIC: 2759 7336 Commercial printing; newspapers: printing; graphic arts & related design

(G-313)
MG CONCEPTS (DE) LLC
185 Dixon Ave (11701-2840)
PHONE 631 608-8090
Jay Austrian, *Mng Member*
EMP: 9
SALES: 5MM **Privately Held**
SIC: 2541 Store & office display cases & fixtures

(G-314)
NAPCO SECURITY TECH INC (PA)
333 Bayview Ave (11701-2801)
PHONE 631 842-9400
Fax: 631 789-9292
Richard L Soloway, *Ch of Bd*
Michael Carrieri, *Senior VP*
Jorge Hevia, *Senior VP*
Byron Thurmond, *Vice Pres*
Kevin S Buchel, *Treasurer*
◆ **EMP:** 277
SQ FT: 90,000
SALES: 82.5MM **Publicly Held**
WEB: www.napcosecurity.com
SIC: 3669 3699 3429 1731 Emergency alarms; fire alarm apparatus, electric; security control equipment & systems; door locks, bolts & checks; safety & security specialization; systems software development services

(G-315)
NATURAL ORGANICS LABORATORIES
Also Called: Universal Proteins
9500 New Horizons Blvd (11701-1155)
PHONE 631 957-5600
Gerald Kessler, *President*
Heather Fairman, *QC Mgr*
Nancy Devera, *Research*
Liz Mendoza, *Manager*
Greg Madden, *Maintence Staff*
EMP: 500
SALES (est): 72.8MM **Privately Held**
SIC: 2834 2087 Vitamin preparations; flavoring extracts & syrups

(G-316)
NEW BUSINESS SOLUTIONS INC
Also Called: Nbs
31 Sprague Ave (11701-2618)
PHONE 631 789-1500
Michele Ruggeri, *CEO*
George J Ruggeri, *Ch of Bd*
Michael Filangeri, *Project Mgr*
Marleny Huggins, *Bookkeeper*
Maria R Avignone, *Manager*
▲ **EMP:** 28
SALES (est): 5.6MM **Privately Held**
WEB: www.newbusinesssolutions.com
SIC: 2542 2541 7389 Fixtures: display, office or store: except wood; store & office display cases & fixtures; window trimming service

(G-317)
OFFICIAL OFFSET CORPORATION
8600 New Horizons Blvd (11701-1183)
PHONE 631 957-8500
Fax: 631 957-4606
Benjamin Paulino, *Ch of Bd*
Frank Paulino, *Vice Pres*
Mary Paulino, *Admin Sec*
▼ **EMP:** 20 **EST:** 1957
SQ FT: 20,000
SALES: 4.5MM **Privately Held**
WEB: www.officialoffset.com
SIC: 2752 2791 Commercial printing, offset; typesetting

(G-318)
OIL AND LUBRICANT DEPOT LLC
Also Called: Oil Depot, The
61 Ranick Dr S (11701-2823)
PHONE 718 258-9220
Steven Krausman, *Mng Member*
Jeffrey Sanet, *Manager*
EMP: 10 **EST:** 2011
SALES (est): 1.4MM **Privately Held**
SIC: 2992 Lubricating oils & greases

(G-319)
P & M LLC
Also Called: Sefi Fabricators
50 Ranick Dr E (11701-2822)
P.O. Box 338 (11701-0338)
PHONE 631 842-2200
Fax: 516 842-2203
Tony Cabrera, *Sales Mgr*
Russ Middleton, *Sales Mgr*
Mark Shaw, *Sales Mgr*
Rasik Patel, *Mng Member*
Tom Zebrowski, *Associate*
EMP: 46 **EST:** 1997
SQ FT: 17,000
SALES (est): 10.5MM **Privately Held**
SIC: 3556 Food products machinery

(G-320)
PAULIN INVESTMENT COMPANY
8600 New Horizons Blvd (11701-1154)
PHONE 631 957-8500
Ben M Paulino, *Owner*
EMP: 27
SALES (est): 2.9MM **Privately Held**
SIC: 2759 Commercial printing

(G-321)
PEPSI BOTTLING VENTURES LLC
Also Called: Pepsico
550 New Horizons Blvd (11701-1139)
PHONE 631 226-9000
Fax: 631 226-4233
Carl Cariffunior, *General Mgr*
Stephen Ernst, *Executive*
EMP: 40
SALES (corp-wide): 64.4MM **Privately Held**
SIC: 2086 Carbonated soft drinks, bottled & canned
HQ: Pepsi Bottling Ventures Llc
4141 Parklake Ave Ste 600
Raleigh NC 27612
919 865-2300

(G-322)
PORTFAB LLC
Also Called: Wenig Company, The
45 Ranick Dr E (11701-2821)
PHONE 718 542-3600
Luz Ruiz, *Bookkeeper*
William Friedman, *Mng Member*
Rosemarie Friedman,
EMP: 32
SQ FT: 38,000
SALES (est): 5.2MM **Privately Held**
WEB: www.portfab.com
SIC: 3441 Fabricated structural metal

(G-323)
PRECISION SIGNSCOM INC
Also Called: Precision Engraving Company
243 Dixon Ave (11701-2830)
PHONE 631 842-5060
Fax: 516 842-0064
Michael Anzalone, *Ch of Bd*
Michelle Lorber, *General Mgr*
Gary Anzalone, *Vice Pres*
Kathy Winter, *Asst Controller*
Samantha Moore, *Accountant*
EMP: 51
SQ FT: 23,500
SALES (est): 8.2MM **Privately Held**
SIC: 3993 Signs & advertising specialties

(G-324)
SARAGA INDUSTRIES CORP
Also Called: Lenco
690 Albany Ave Unit D (11701-1199)
PHONE 631 842-4049
Fax: 516 842-3908
Robert Saraga, *President*
Pat Hermel, *Office Mgr*
EMP: 6
SQ FT: 4,000
SALES (est): 670K **Privately Held**
WEB: www.lencocoolers.com
SIC: 3443 Heat exchangers, condensers & components

(G-325)
STEIN INDUSTRIES INC
22 Sprague Ave (11701-2634)
PHONE 631 789-2222
Fax: 631 789-8888
Stuart Stein, *President*
Andrew Stein, *Vice Pres*
Andrew Jinks, *Manager*
Jane McCaffrey, *Manager*
EMP: 40 **EST:** 1937
SQ FT: 30,000
SALES (est): 5.8MM **Privately Held**
WEB: www.steinindustries.com
SIC: 2541 Wood partitions & fixtures

(G-326)
STRUCTURED 3D INC
188 Dixon Ave (11701-2812)
PHONE 346 704-2614
Mitchell Proux, *President*
EMP: 5
SALES (est): 157.3K **Privately Held**
SIC: 2759 Commercial printing

(G-327)
SUNDIAL BRANDS LLC
11 Ranick Dr S (11701-2823)
PHONE 631 842-8800
Richelieu Dennis, *CEO*
Nyema Tudman, *President*
Cyrus Dennis, *Senior VP*
Rick Smith, *VP Opers*
John M Perrone, *CFO*
▲ **EMP:** 215
SALES: 70MM **Privately Held**
SIC: 2844 Toilet preparations

(G-328)
SUNDIAL FRAGRANCES & FLAVORS
11 Ranick Dr S (11701-2823)
PHONE 631 842-8800
Fax: 631 842-4444
Richelieu Dennis, *CEO*
Nyema S Tubman, *Ch of Bd*
Mary Dennis, *Treasurer*
EMP: 24
SQ FT: 50,000
SALES (est): 8.1MM **Privately Held**
WEB: www.nhexec.com
SIC: 2869 5122 Perfumes, flavorings & food additives; perfumes

(G-329)
TOPIDERM INC (PA)
5200 New Horizons Blvd (11701-1189)
PHONE 631 226-7979
Burt Shaffer, *Ch of Bd*
Eric Stern, *VP Opers*
Bob Arnaiz, *Prdtn Mgr*
Carol Donaldson, *Mfg Staff*
Alice Dorschler, *Purch Mgr*
▲ **EMP:** 106
SALES (est): 37.6MM **Privately Held**
SIC: 2834 2844 Pharmaceutical preparations; cosmetic preparations

(G-330)
TOPIX PHARMACEUTICALS INC
5200 New Horizons Blvd (11701-1189)
PHONE 631 225-5757
Fax: 631 226-8588
Burt Shaffer, *President*
Marie Hughes, *Controller*
Jody Manganiello, *Human Resources*
Joe Ragosta, *VP Sales*
Eileen Hodge, *Manager*
▲ **EMP:** 30
SALES (est): 7.6MM **Privately Held**
WEB: www.topixpharm.com
SIC: 2834 Pharmaceutical preparations

(G-331)
TRITON BUILDERS INC
645 Broadway Ste T (11701-2118)
PHONE 631 841-2534
EMP: 20
SQ FT: 2,000

▲ = Import ▼ = Export
◆ = Import/Export

GEOGRAPHIC SECTION

Amsterdam
Montgomery County

(G-332)
AMSTERDAM PRINTING & LITHO INC
Go Promos
166 Wallins Corners Rd (12010-1899)
PHONE 518 842-6000
Melissa Santamaria, *Admin Mgr*
EMP: 15
SALES (corp-wide): 5.1B **Privately Held**
WEB: www.amsterdamprinting.com
SIC: 3993 2752 2761 Advertising novelties; commercial printing, lithographic; manifold business forms
HQ: Amsterdam Printing & Litho, Inc.
    166 Wallins Corners Rd
    Amsterdam NY 12010
    518 842-6000

(G-333)
AMSTERDAM PRINTING & LITHO INC
Baldwin Cooke
166 Wallins Corners Rd (12010-1899)
PHONE 518 842-6000
Melissa Santamaria,
EMP: 49
SALES (corp-wide): 5.1B **Privately Held**
WEB: www.amsterdamprinting.com
SIC: 3993 2752 2761 Advertising novelties; commercial printing, lithographic; manifold business forms
HQ: Amsterdam Printing & Litho, Inc.
    166 Wallins Corners Rd
    Amsterdam NY 12010
    518 842-6000

(G-334)
BECKMANN CONVERTING INC (PA)
14 Park Dr (12010-5340)
P.O. Box 390 (12010-0390)
PHONE 518 842-0073
Klaus Beckmann, *CEO*
Peter Piusz, *Vice Pres*
Ray Hart, *Opers Staff*
Chuck Gerardi, *Engineer*
Bill Wood, *Engineer*
▲ **EMP:** 40
SQ FT: 100,000
SALES (est): 5.4MM **Privately Held**
WEB: www.beckmannconverting.com
SIC: 2295 2262 Leather, artificial or imitation; fire resistance finishing: manmade & silk broadwoven

(G-335)
BEECH-NUT NUTRITION COMPANY (DH)
1 Nutritious Pl (12010-8105)
PHONE 518 839-0300
Jeffrey Boutelle, *President*
Tami Colby, *Editor*
Shen-Youn Chang, *Vice Pres*
Michael Maloney, *Opers Staff*
Linda Snell, *Purch Mgr*
◆ **EMP:** 295
SALES (est): 112.7MM
SALES (corp-wide): 1.3B **Privately Held**
SIC: 2032 Baby foods, including meats: packaged in cans, jars, etc.
HQ: Hero Ag
    Karl Roth-Strasse 8
    Lenzburg AG
    628 855-111

(G-336)
BRETON INDUSTRIES INC (PA)
1 Sam Stratton Rd (12010-5243)
PHONE 518 842-3030
Fax: 518 842-1031
Alfred Damofal, *CEO*
Peter A Lewis, *Senior VP*
G Eric Lewis, *Vice Pres*
G Richard Lewis, *Treasurer*
EMP: 96
SQ FT: 55,000
SALES (est): 19.4MM **Privately Held**
WEB: www.bretonindustries.com
SIC: 2394 2399 3443 2295 Canvas & related products; canvas awnings & canopies; canvas covers & drop cloths; shades, canvas: made from purchased materials; aprons, breast (harness); fabricated plate work (boiler shop); coated fabrics, not rubberized; narrow fabric mills

(G-337)
CAPITOL CUPS INC
1030 Riverfront Ctr (12010-4616)
PHONE 518 627-0051
Robert S Abrams, *President*
John Belfance Jr, *COO*
Robert N Sawyer, *CFO*
Robert L Thompson, *Controller*
EMP: 26
SQ FT: 10,000
SALES (est): 4.4MM **Privately Held**
WEB: www.capitolcups.com
SIC: 3089 Cups, plastic, except foam

(G-338)
CAPITOL PLASTIC PRODUCTS INC
1030 Riverfront Ctr (12010-4616)
P.O. Box 710 (12010-0710)
PHONE 518 627-0051
Robert Abrams, *Principal*
▼ **EMP:** 218
SALES (est): 8.4MM
SALES (corp-wide): 127.3MM **Privately Held**
SIC: 3085 Plastics bottles
PA: Cv Holdings, Llc
    1030 Riverfront Ctr
    Amsterdam NY 12010
    518 627-0051

(G-339)
CAPITOL PLASTIC PRODUCTS LLC
1030 Riverfront Ctr (12010-4616)
PHONE 518 627-0051
Robert S Abrams,
EMP: 5
SALES (est): 600.3K **Privately Held**
SIC: 3085 Plastics bottles

(G-340)
COBLESKILL RED E MIX & SUPPLY (PA)
Also Called: Cobleskill Concrete Ready Mix
774 State Highway 5s (12010-7668)
PHONE 518 234-2015
John Tesiero, *President*
Carol Whelly, *Admin Sec*
EMP: 10
SQ FT: 15,000
SALES (est): 13.9MM **Privately Held**
SIC: 3273 Ready-mixed concrete

(G-341)
CRANESVILLE BLOCK CO INC (PA)
Also Called: Cranesville Ready-Mix
1250 Riverfront Ctr (12010-4602)
PHONE 518 684-6000
John A Tesiero Jr, *Ch of Bd*
Elizabeth N Tesiero, *Corp Secy*
Steven Dow, *Opers Mgr*
Joe Nolan, *Opers Mgr*
Rj Kumpitsch, *Purchasing*
▲ **EMP:** 45 **EST:** 1947
SALES (est): 41.2MM **Privately Held**
SIC: 3271 3273 5211 Blocks, concrete or cinder: standard; ready-mixed concrete; concrete & cinder block; cement; masonry materials & supplies

(G-342)
CSP TECHNOLOGIES INC (HQ)
1031 Riverfront Ctr (12010-4616)
PHONE 518 627-0051
Robert Abrams, *CEO*
Bob Thompson, *Controller*
Laurie Gomula, *Accountant*
▲ **EMP:** 45
SALES (est): 9.5MM
SALES (corp-wide): 127.3MM **Privately Held**
SIC: 3089 Plastic processing

(G-343)
ELECTRIC CITY CONCRETE CO INC (HQ)
774 State Highway 5s (12010-7668)
PHONE 518 887-5560
John A Tesiero Jr, *President*
Carol Whelly, *Vice Pres*
Anthony Zarrelli, *Manager*
EMP: 25 **EST:** 1977
SALES (est): 1.3MM
SALES (corp-wide): 41.2MM **Privately Held**
SIC: 3273 Ready-mixed concrete
PA: Cranesville Block Co., Inc.
    1250 Riverfront Ctr
    Amsterdam NY 12010
    518 684-6000

(G-344)
EMBASSY MILLWORK INC
3 Sam Stratton Rd (12010-5243)
PHONE 518 839-0965
Michael Caruso, *President*
EMP: 12
SALES (est): 1.1MM **Privately Held**
SIC: 2421 Planing mill, independent: except millwork

(G-345)
FIBER GLASS INDUSTRIES INC (PA)
Also Called: Fgi
69 Edson St (12010-5247)
PHONE 518 842-4000
Fax: 518 842-4408
John Menzel, *CEO*
Mike Lanham, *President*
Ken Weiss, *Engineer*
James Farnan, *Controller*
Kathy Griffin, *Sales Mgr*
◆ **EMP:** 75 **EST:** 1957
SQ FT: 60,000
SALES (est): 31.1MM **Privately Held**
SIC: 2221 Fiberglass fabrics; glass broadwoven fabrics

(G-346)
FIBER GLASS INDUSTRIES INC
1 Homestead Pl (12010)
PHONE 518 843-3533
Bob Grant, *Branch Mgr*
EMP: 73
SALES (corp-wide): 31.1MM **Privately Held**
SIC: 2221 Fiberglass fabrics
PA: Fiber Glass Industries, Inc.
    69 Edson St
    Amsterdam NY 12010
    518 842-4000

(G-347)
FULMONT READY-MIX COMPANY INC (PA)
774 State Highway 5s (12010-7668)
PHONE 518 887-5560
Fax: 518 887-2561
Elizabeth Tesiero, *President*
John Tesiero III, *Vice Pres*
EMP: 16 **EST:** 1947
SALES (est): 1.1MM **Privately Held**
SIC: 3273 Ready-mixed concrete

(G-348)
GLENS FALLS READY MIX INC (HQ)
774 State Highway 5s (12010-7668)
PHONE 518 793-1695
Elizabeth Tesiero, *President*
John Tesiero III, *Vice Pres*
EMP: 1
SALES (est): 1MM
SALES (corp-wide): 1.1MM **Privately Held**
SIC: 3273 Ready-mixed concrete
PA: Fulmont Ready-Mix Company Inc
    774 State Highway 5s
    Amsterdam NY 12010
    518 887-5560

(G-349)
GREAT ADIRONDACK YARN COMPANY
950 County Highway 126 (12010-6287)
PHONE 518 843-3381
Patti Subik, *Owner*
Paul Subik, *Vice Pres*
EMP: 10
SALES: 400K **Privately Held**
SIC: 2281 2253 5949 5199 Natural & animal fiber yarns, spun; sweaters & sweater coats, knit; sewing & needlework; yarns

(G-350)
HYPERBARIC TECHNOLOGIES INC
1 Sam Stratton Rd (12010-5243)
P.O. Box 69 (12010-0069)
PHONE 518 842-3030
Peter Lewis, *President*
Richard Lewis, *CFO*
EMP: 2
SQ FT: 5,000
SALES (est): 4.5MM **Privately Held**
SIC: 3443 Chambers & caissons

(G-351)
J H BUHRMASTER COMPANY INC
Also Called: Amsterdam Oil Heat
164 W Main St (12010-3130)
PHONE 518 843-1700
Fax: 518 842-4678
Donald L Hosier, *Sales/Mktg Mgr*
EMP: 8
SALES (corp-wide): 15.9MM **Privately Held**
SIC: 3567 Industrial furnaces & ovens
PA: J. H. Buhrmaster Company, Inc.
    421 Sacandaga Rd
    Scotia NY 12302
    518 382-0260

(G-352)
KAPSTONE CONTAINER CORPORATION
28 Park Dr (12010-5340)
PHONE 518 842-2450
G Robertshaw, *Mfg Staff*
Linda Ruback, *Personnel*
Eugene C Mowry Jr, *Sales Mgr*
Paul Robbens, *Sales Staff*
Edward H Poulin, *Manager*
EMP: 60
SALES (corp-wide): 2.7B **Publicly Held**
SIC: 2411 2674 2621 2631 Wooden logs; shipping & shopping bags or sacks; kraft paper; container board; boxes, corrugated: made from purchased materials; boxes, solid fiber: made from purchased materials
HQ: Kapstone Container Corporation
    1601 Blairs Ferry Rd Ne
    Cedar Rapids IA 52402
    319 393-3610

(G-353)
KC TAG CO
108 Edson St (12010-7213)
PHONE 518 842-6666
Kevin Collins, *Ch of Bd*
EMP: 9
SALES (est): 1.2MM **Privately Held**
SIC: 3089 Plastics products

(G-354)
KEEP AMERICA BEAUTIFUL INC
Also Called: For A Safer America
1 Prospect St (12010-3637)
P.O. Box 229 (12010-0229)
PHONE 518 842-4388
Anna Podolec, *Branch Mgr*
EMP: 6
SALES (corp-wide): 9.1MM **Privately Held**
WEB: www.kab.org
SIC: 3993 Advertising novelties
PA: Keep America Beautiful, Inc.
    1010 Washington Blvd 22-1
    Stamford CT 06901
    203 323-8987

Amsterdam - Montgomery County (G-355)

(G-355)
LOSURDO FOODS INC
78 Sam Stratton Rd (12010-5244)
PHONE.................518 842-1500
Fax: 518 842-1594
Maria Hammill, *Branch Mgr*
EMP: 25
SALES (corp-wide): 100.9MM **Privately Held**
WEB: www.losurdofoods.com
SIC: 2041 Doughs & batters
PA: Losurdo Foods, Inc.
  20 Owens Rd
  Hackensack NJ 07601
  201 343-6680

(G-356)
MILLER PRINTING & LITHO INC
97 Guy Park Ave (12010-3225)
PHONE.................518 842-0001
Fax: 518 842-6397
Scott Miller, *President*
Eben Miller, *Vice Pres*
EMP: 6
SQ FT: 9,000
SALES (est): 914.7K **Privately Held**
SIC: 2752 Commercial printing, offset

(G-357)
MILNOT HOLDING CORPORATION
1 Nutritious Pl (12010-8105)
PHONE.................518 839-0300
Amy McGrath, *Human Res Dir*
Donna Dodson, *Info Tech Dir*
EMP: 7
SALES (est): 592K
SALES (corp-wide): 1.3B **Privately Held**
SIC: 2099 Food preparations
HQ: Hero Ag
  Karl Roth-Strasse 8
  Lenzburg AG
  628 855-111

(G-358)
MOHAWK FABRIC COMPANY INC
96 Guy Park Ave (12010-3241)
P.O. Box 587 (12010-0587)
PHONE.................518 842-3090
Fax: 518 842-3095
Gregory Needham, *President*
Dominic Wade, *Principal*
Blaine Harvey, *Plant Mgr*
EMP: 15 EST: 1922
SQ FT: 35,000
SALES (est): 4.4MM **Privately Held**
WEB: www.mohawkfabric.com
SIC: 2258 Lace & warp knit fabric mills

(G-359)
MOHAWK RESOURCES LTD
65 Vrooman Ave (12010-5321)
P.O. Box 110 (12010-0110)
PHONE.................518 842-1431
Fax: 518 842-1289
Steven Perlstein, *President*
Andrea Baldomar, *General Mgr*
Nancy Rogers, *Business Mgr*
Pamela Smith, *Hum Res Coord*
Sherri Abell, *Sales Mgr*
▲ EMP: 70
SQ FT: 55,000
SALES (est): 33.8MM **Privately Held**
WEB: www.mohawklifts.com
SIC: 3536 Hoists

(G-360)
MOHAWK SIGN SYSTEMS INC
5 Dandreano Dr (12010-5253)
P.O. Box 966, Schenectady (12301-0966)
PHONE.................518 842-5303
Fax: 518 842-5306
James Gryzbowski, *President*
Neale Dill, *Vice Pres*
Bettina Gryzbowski, *Vice Pres*
Loureen Hingle, *Manager*
EMP: 30
SQ FT: 10,000
SALES: 2.5MM **Privately Held**
WEB: www.mohawksign.com
SIC: 3993 Signs, not made in custom sign painting shops

(G-361)
NATIONWIDE TARPS INCORPORATED (PA)
Also Called: NTI Global
50 Willow St (12010-4219)
P.O. Box 189 (12010-0189)
PHONE.................518 843-1545
Stephen Raeburn, *Ch of Bd*
Anita Raeburn, *Vice Pres*
Barbara Salie, *Human Res Mgr*
▲ EMP: 75
SQ FT: 195,000
SALES (est): 16.7MM **Privately Held**
WEB: www.ntiglobal.com
SIC: 3081 2821 2394 2392 Polyethylene film; plastics materials & resins; canvas & related products; household furnishings; solar cells

(G-362)
NORTH E RGGERS ERECTORS NY INC
178 Clizbe Ave (12010-2935)
PHONE.................518 842-6377
Fax: 518 842-7248
Scott Egan, *President*
Michael Egan, *Vice Pres*
Charles Egan, *Treasurer*
Lynn Clough, *Admin Sec*
Thomas Egan, *Admin Sec*
EMP: 40
SQ FT: 6,000
SALES (est): 7.7MM **Privately Held**
SIC: 3441 Fabricated structural metal

(G-363)
NORTHEASTERN WATER JET INC
4 Willow St (12010-4219)
PHONE.................518 843-4988
Lenny Laporte, *President*
David Siiss, *General Mgr*
Andre Laporte, *Vice Pres*
Laport Lenny, *Administration*
EMP: 18
SQ FT: 176,000
SALES (est): 4.5MM **Privately Held**
WEB: www.newj.com
SIC: 3545 Cutting tools for machine tools

(G-364)
NOTEWORTHY INDUSTRIES INC
Also Called: Noteworthy Company, The
336 Forest Ave (12010-2723)
P.O. Box 490 (12010-0490)
PHONE.................518 842-2662
Fax: 518 842-8317
Anthony Constantino, *President*
Elsa Buseck, *President*
Tim Gralewski, *General Mgr*
John P Colangelo, *Vice Pres*
Nicholas Costantino, *Vice Pres*
▲ EMP: 148 EST: 1971
SQ FT: 400,000
SALES: 18MM **Privately Held**
WEB: www.noteworthy.com
SIC: 2673 2679 Bags: plastic, laminated & coated; paper products, converted

(G-365)
POWER AND COMPOSITE TECH LLC
Also Called: P C T
119 Genessee Ln (12010-1835)
PHONE.................518 843-6825
Robert Mylott, *CEO*
Phil Day, *Managing Dir*
Joseph Day, *Vice Pres*
Bill Pabis, *Vice Pres*
Fabio Tucci, *Vice Pres*
▲ EMP: 90
SQ FT: 55,000
SALES (est): 24MM
SALES (corp-wide): 228.7MM **Privately Held**
WEB: www.pactinc.com
SIC: 3621 Electric motor & generator parts
PA: Thayer Capital Partners, L.P.
  1455 Penn Ave Nw Ste 350
  Washington DC 20004
  202 371-0150

(G-366)
RAYCO OF SCHENECTADY INC
4 Sam Stratton Rd (12010-5244)
P.O. Box 408 (12010-0408)
PHONE.................518 212-5113
Fax: 518 843-8317
Ed Legere, *President*
Janis Legere, *Vice Pres*
EMP: 13
SQ FT: 6,000
SALES (est): 1.6MM **Privately Held**
SIC: 3471 Electroplating of metals or formed products; polishing, metals or formed products

(G-367)
REVOLUTION VAPOR LLC
4715 State Highway 30 (12010-7431)
PHONE.................518 627-4133
EMP: 8
SALES (est): 1.1MM **Privately Held**
SIC: 2111 Cigarettes

(G-368)
SARATOGA HORSEWORKS LTD
57 Edson St (12010-5238)
P.O. Box 549 (12010-0549)
PHONE.................518 843-6756
Fax: 518 843-5057
Michael Libertucci, *President*
Adrienne Libertucci, *Corp Secy*
Jordan Casey, *Manager*
EMP: 25
SQ FT: 15,000
SALES (est): 950K **Privately Held**
WEB: www.horseworks.com
SIC: 2399 Horse & pet accessories, textile

(G-369)
TAYLOR
166 Wallins Corners Rd (12010-1817)
PHONE.................518 954-2832
Shirley McAuliff, *Human Res Mgr*
Ron Baker, *Manager*
Ashleigh Simeone, *Technology*
William Rocas, *Prgrmr*
EMP: 5
SALES (est): 197.8K **Privately Held**
SIC: 2752 Commercial printing, lithographic

(G-370)
TONCHE TIMBER LLC
3959 State Highway 30 (12010-6509)
PHONE.................845 389-3489
Ronald Cohen, *Owner*
EMP: 6 EST: 2007
SALES (est): 391.6K **Privately Held**
SIC: 2411 Timber, cut at logging camp

(G-371)
TRI-VILLAGE PUBLISHERS INC
Also Called: Recorder, The
1 Venner Rd (12010-5617)
PHONE.................518 843-1100
Fax: 518 843-1338
Sidney Lafavour, *Publisher*
Elizabeth Mangle, *Sls & Mktg Exec*
John Deneuville, *Loan Officer*
Lisa Guadagno, *Manager*
Brian Krohn, *Manager*
EMP: 60
SALES (est): 3.8MM **Privately Held**
WEB: www.recordernews.com
SIC: 2711 Newspapers

(G-372)
UNIVERSAL CUSTOM MILLWORK INC
3 Sam Stratton Rd (12010-5243)
PHONE.................518 330-6622
Fax: 518 843-6622
Stephen R Chapman, *Ch of Bd*
Jeffrey W Pahl, *Vice Pres*
Robert Chapman, *Finance*
Lisa Gizara, *Manager*
Kelly Shaw, *Manager*
EMP: 60
SQ FT: 50,000
SALES (est): 7.3MM **Privately Held**
WEB: www.ucmillwork.com
SIC: 2431 Millwork

(G-373)
VIDA-BLEND LLC
1430 State Highway 5s (12010-8184)
PHONE.................518 627-4138
Freddy Luna, *Mng Member*
Edward Pragliabento, *Mng Member*
Michael Pragliabento, *Mng Member*
Levon Schilling, *Lab Dir*
EMP: 20 EST: 2013
SALES (est): 3.4MM **Privately Held**
SIC: 2834 Vitamin, nutrient & hematinic preparations for human use

(G-374)
WILLIAM J KLINE & SON INC (PA)
Also Called: Hamilton County News
1 Venner Rd (12010-5617)
PHONE.................518 843-1100
Sidney Lefavour, *President*
Kevin McClary, *Publisher*
Bill Brzezicki, *Business Mgr*
John Deneuville, *Finance*
Bruce Lafavour, *Manager*
EMP: 80 EST: 1878
SQ FT: 30,000
SALES (est): 4.3MM **Privately Held**
SIC: 2711 2752 Newspapers; commercial printing, lithographic

Ancram
Columbia County

(G-375)
SCHWEITZER-MAUDUIT INTL INC
2424 Route 82 (12502-5414)
P.O. Box 10 (12502-0010)
PHONE.................518 329-4222
R D Hotaling, *Opers Mgr*
Gary Kennedy, *Manager*
Dorothea Hotaling, *Executive*
EMP: 135 **Publicly Held**
SIC: 2141 2111 2621 Tobacco stemming & redrying; cigarettes; cigarette paper
PA: Schweitzer-Mauduit International, Inc.
  100 N Point Ctr E Ste 600
  Alpharetta GA 30022

Angelica
Allegany County

(G-376)
ANGELICA FOREST PRODUCTS INC
54 Closser Ave (14709-8746)
P.O. Box 685 (14709-0685)
PHONE.................585 466-3205
Fax: 585 466-3411
David Chamberlain, *Principal*
EMP: 9
SALES (est): 1.1MM **Privately Held**
SIC: 2421 Sawmills & planing mills, general

(G-377)
ANGELICA SPRING COMPANY INC
99 West Ave (14709-8713)
P.O. Box 681 (14709-0681)
PHONE.................585 466-7892
William Geoppner, *President*
EMP: 17
SQ FT: 4,400
SALES (est): 2.9MM **Privately Held**
WEB: www.angelicaspringcompany.com
SIC: 3493 3496 Coiled flat springs; flat springs, sheet or strip stock; miscellaneous fabricated wire products

▲ = Import ▼ = Export
◆ = Import/Export

GEOGRAPHIC SECTION

Angola
Erie County

(G-378)
ADVANCED ASSEMBLY SERVICES INC
35 S Main St (14006-1517)
PHONE.................................716 217-8144
Tim Kosmowski, *President*
Ra Kosmowski, *Vice Pres*
EMP: 6 **EST:** 2000
SQ FT: 5,000
SALES (est): 952.3K **Privately Held**
WEB: www.advancedassemblyservices.com
SIC: 3083 Plastic finished products, laminated

(G-379)
ANGOLA PENNYSAVER INC
19 Center St (14006-1305)
PHONE.................................716 549-1611
Fax: 716 549-1611
Daniel Guest, *President*
EMP: 12 **EST:** 1922
SQ FT: 5,950
SALES (est): 1MM **Privately Held**
SIC: 2711 Newspapers: publishing only, not printed on site

(G-380)
GOYA FOODS INC
Also Called: Goya Foods Great Lakes
200 S Main St (14006-1534)
P.O. Box 152 (14006-0152)
PHONE.................................716 549-0076
Robert J Drago Sr, *Principal*
Greg Drago, *Opers Staff*
Cynthia Badama, *Human Res Dir*
EMP: 75
SALES (corp-wide): 623.7MM **Privately Held**
SIC: 2033 2032 2035 2034 Canned fruits & specialties; canned specialties; pickles, sauces & salad dressings; dehydrated fruits, vegetables, soups; poultry slaughtering & processing
PA: Goya Foods, Inc.
    350 County Rd
    Jersey City NJ 07307
    201 348-4900

(G-381)
POLYTEX INC
1305 Eden Evans Center Rd (14006-8839)
PHONE.................................716 549-5100
Jacob H Ilioha, *President*
Jennifer Forgens, *Clerk*
▲ **EMP:** 100
SQ FT: 8,000
SALES (est): 5.9MM **Privately Held**
SIC: 2221 Fiberglass fabrics

(G-382)
TX RX SYSTEMS INC
8625 Industrial Pkwy (14006-9692)
PHONE.................................716 549-4700
Fax: 716 549-4772
David J Hessler, *Ch of Bd*
Wayne Newman, *General Mgr*
Anthony Delgobbo, *Plant Mgr*
Ken Pokigo, *Engineer*
Ken Charles, *Design Engr*
▲ **EMP:** 115 **EST:** 1976
SQ FT: 31,000
SALES (est): 22.5MM **Privately Held**
WEB: www.txrx.com
SIC: 3669 Intercommunication systems, electric
PA: Bird Technologies Group Inc.
    30303 Aurora Rd
    Solon OH 44139

Aquebogue
Suffolk County

(G-383)
ALTAIRE PHARMACEUTICALS INC
311 West Ln (11931)
P.O. Box 849 (11931-0849)
PHONE.................................631 722-5988
Fax: 631 722-9683
Teresa Sawaya, *President*
Al Sawaya, *President*
Joseph Sawaya, *Vice Pres*
Kelly Jeffries, *Admin Sec*
EMP: 130
SALES (est): 27.1MM **Privately Held**
SIC: 2834 Pharmaceutical preparations

(G-384)
CRESCENT DUCK FARM INC
10 Edgar Ave (11931)
P.O. Box 500 (11931-0500)
PHONE.................................631 722-8700
Fax: 631 722-5324
Douglas H Corwin, *President*
Douglas Corwin, *Vice Pres*
Jeffrey Corwin, *Treasurer*
Blake Corwin, *Manager*
Janet Wedel, *Admin Sec*
▼ **EMP:** 50 **EST:** 1959
SQ FT: 6,000
SALES (est): 8.2MM **Privately Held**
SIC: 2015 4222 2011 Ducks, processed: fresh; refrigerated warehousing & storage; meat packing plants

(G-385)
PAUMANOK VINEYARDS LTD
1074 Main Rd Rr 25 (11931)
P.O. Box 741 (11931-0741)
PHONE.................................631 722-8800
Fax: 631 722-5110
Charles Massoud, *President*
Ursula Massoud, *Vice Pres*
John Perry, *Manager*
Thomas Matthews, *Info Tech Dir*
▲ **EMP:** 20
SQ FT: 9,000
SALES (est): 2.8MM **Privately Held**
WEB: www.paumanok.com
SIC: 2084 Wines; wine cellars, bonded: engaged in blending wines

Arcade
Wyoming County

(G-386)
AMERICAN PRECISION INDS INC
Surface Mounted Devices Div
95 North St (14009-9196)
P.O. Box 38 (14009-0038)
PHONE.................................585 496-5755
Fax: 585 496-5072
Steve Chandler, *Plant Mgr*
Kevin Heffler, *Branch Mgr*
EMP: 100
SALES (corp-wide): 20.5B **Publicly Held**
WEB: www.apischmidtbretten.com
SIC: 3677 Coil windings, electronic; inductors, electronic
HQ: American Precision Industries Inc.
    45 Hazelwood Dr
    Amherst NY 14228
    716 691-9100

(G-387)
API HEAT TRANSFER INC
A P I Airtech Division
91 North St (14009-9196)
PHONE.................................585 496-5755
Jack Bellomo, *President*
Rudolph Kristich, *Div Sub Head*
Mike Williams, *Vice Pres*
Jason Williams, *Buyer*
Bob Mladenovic, *Engineer*
EMP: 200
SQ FT: 85,000
SALES (corp-wide): 411.7MM **Privately Held**
WEB: www.apiheattransfer.com
SIC: 3443 Heat exchangers: coolers (after, inter), condensers, etc.
HQ: Api Heat Transfer Inc.
    2777 Walden Ave Ste 1
    Buffalo NY 14225
    716 684-6700

(G-388)
BATAVIA ENCLOSURES INC
636 Main St (14009-1037)
PHONE.................................585 344-1797
Toll Free:..............................877 -
Fax: 585 344-1503
Leonard Roberto, *President*
EMP: 6
SQ FT: 10,000
SALES (est): 1MM **Privately Held**
WEB: www.bataviaenclosures.com
SIC: 3444 Sheet metalwork

(G-389)
BLISS MACHINE INC
260 North St (14009-1206)
P.O. Box 145 (14009-0145)
PHONE.................................585 492-5128
Fax: 585 492-5166
William Kanner, *President*
Randy Kanner, *Vice Pres*
Nichole Kanner, *Manager*
EMP: 18
SQ FT: 9,500
SALES (est): 3.5MM **Privately Held**
WEB: www.blissmachine.net
SIC: 3599 Machine shop, jobbing & repair

(G-390)
BRAUEN CONSTRUTION
1087 Chaffee Rd (14009-9779)
PHONE.................................585 492-0042
Fax: 585 492-0042
Floyd Brauen, *President*
EMP: 7 **EST:** 1983
SQ FT: 16,000
SALES (est): 1.1MM **Privately Held**
WEB: www.brauenmillwork.com
SIC: 2431 Woodwork, interior & ornamental

(G-391)
DEVIN MFG INC
40 Edward St (14009-1012)
P.O. Box 97 (14009-0097)
PHONE.................................585 496-5770
William A Devin, *President*
Anne Devin, *Vice Pres*
Erica Smith, *Purchasing*
Erica Bigos, *Admin Sec*
▼ **EMP:** 17 **EST:** 1959
SQ FT: 17,400
SALES (est): 3.1MM **Privately Held**
WEB: www.devinmfg.com
SIC: 3599 3537 3494 3949 Machine shop, jobbing & repair; engine stands & racks, metal; valves & pipe fittings; target shooting equipment; targets, archery & rifle shooting

(G-392)
EMKAY TRADING CORP
Also Called: Emkay Bordeaux
58 Church St (14009-1188)
PHONE.................................585 492-3800
Fax: 585 492-3700
Cathy Golman, *Branch Mgr*
EMP: 30
SQ FT: 51,500
SALES (corp-wide): 1.9MM **Privately Held**
WEB: www.emkaytrading.org
SIC: 2022 2026 Cheese, natural & processed; cream, sweet
PA: Emkay Trading Corp
    250 Clearbrook Rd Ste 127
    Elmsford NY 10523
    914 592-9000

(G-393)
GM PALMER INC
51 Edward St (14009-1012)
P.O. Box 343 (14009-0343)
PHONE.................................585 492-2990
Fax: 585 492-2991
Greg Palmer, *President*
Mary Palmer, *Corp Secy*
Mary Keenan, *Manager*
◆ **EMP:** 15
SQ FT: 47,500
SALES (est): 10MM **Privately Held**
SIC: 2421 Fuelwood, from mill waste

(G-394)
GOWANDA - BTI LLC
Also Called: Chiptek
7426a Tanner Pkwy (14009-9758)
PHONE.................................716 492-4081
Thomas Norsen, *Controller*
Don McElheny,
EMP: 66
SALES (est): 1.8MM **Privately Held**
SIC: 3677 Electronic coils, transformers & other inductors

(G-395)
J A YANSICK LUMBER CO INC
16 Rule Dr (14009-1019)
PHONE.................................585 492-4312
James Yansick, *President*
Ken Buckley, *Opers Staff*
Scott Holmes, *Controller*
EMP: 30 **EST:** 1966
SQ FT: 1,979
SALES (est): 3.1MM **Privately Held**
SIC: 2421 2426 Lumber: rough, sawed or planed; hardwood dimension & flooring mills

(G-396)
MAPLE GROVE CORP
Also Called: Maple Grove and Enterprises
7075 Route 98 (14009-9756)
P.O. Box 156 (14009-0156)
PHONE.................................585 492-5286
Phillip M Hobin, *Ch of Bd*
Rachel Bookmiller, *COO*
Ted Hobin Jr, *Vice Pres*
Jen Hobin, *CFO*
Michelle Hobin, *Admin Sec*
EMP: 25
SQ FT: 1,200
SALES (est): 4.9MM **Privately Held**
SIC: 7692 7213 Welding repair; coat supply

(G-397)
NEIGHBOR TO NEIGHBOR NEWS INC
Also Called: Arcade Herald
223 Main St (14009-1209)
PHONE.................................585 492-2525
Fax: 716 492-2667
Grant Hamilton, *President*
Judy Kessler, *Advt Staff*
EMP: 9
SQ FT: 1,200
SALES (est): 360K **Privately Held**
SIC: 2711 Newspapers: publishing only, not printed on site

(G-398)
NEW EAGLE SILO CORP
7648 Hurdville Rd (14009-1021)
PHONE.................................585 492-1300
Fax: 585 492-4029
Leonard Johnson, *President*
EMP: 8 **EST:** 1967
SQ FT: 6,000
SALES: 400K **Privately Held**
SIC: 3531 Cement silos (batch plant)

(G-399)
PRESTOLITE ELECTRIC INC
400 Main St (14009-1189)
PHONE.................................585 492-2278
Fax: 585 492-1660
Mick Cooper, *Opers Mgr*
Craig Schlau, *Opers Staff*
Michael Jefferlone, *Purch Mgr*
Ken Pritchard, *Buyer*
Ryan Slocum, *Engineer*
EMP: 150
SQ FT: 34,000
SALES (corp-wide): 273.2MM **Privately Held**
SIC: 3694 Alternators, automotive
HQ: Prestolite Electric Incorporated
    30120 Hudson Dr
    Novi MI 48377
    585 492-1700

Arcade - Wyoming County (G-400)

(G-400)
STEEL & OBRIEN MFG INC
274 Rte 98 S (14009)
PHONE 585 492-5800
Bryan Wells, *President*
Michael Lovelace, *Vice Pres*
Scott Wells, *Vice Pres*
Jim Maiorano, *Purch Agent*
Rick Smith, *Purch Agent*
▲ **EMP:** 72
SQ FT: 55,000
SALES (est): 15.6MM **Privately Held**
WEB: www.steelobrien.com
SIC: 3494 3492 Valves & pipe fittings; fluid power valves & hose fittings

(G-401)
TPI ARCADE INC
7888 Route 98 (14009-9601)
PHONE 585 492-0122
Fax: 585 492-0169
Jack Pohlman, *Ch of Bd*
Gerald Byrne, *Chairman*
Tom Wittmeyer, *Maint Spvr*
Traci Hemmerlin, *Controller*
EMP: 75
SALES (est): 16.1MM
SALES (corp-wide): 619.1MM **Privately Held**
WEB: www.tpicast.com
SIC: 3363 Aluminum die-castings
PA: Ligon Industries, Llc
   1927 1st Ave N Ste 500
   Birmingham AL 35203
   205 322-3302

(G-402)
WHATS NEXT MANUFACTURING INC
4 Rule Dr (14009-1019)
PHONE 585 492-1014
Fax: 585 492-1018
Brad Countryman, *President*
Deborah Fields, *Purch Mgr*
EMP: 20
SQ FT: 20,000
SALES (est): 2MM **Privately Held**
SIC: 3944 Games, toys & children's vehicles

Ardsley
Westchester County

(G-403)
ACORDA THERAPEUTICS INC (PA)
420 Saw Mill River Rd (10502-2605)
PHONE 914 347-4300
Fax: 914 347-4560
Ron Cohen, *President*
Jim Mack, *Adv Board Mem*
Melisa Palacio, *Project Mgr*
Charles Coggins, *Materials Mgr*
Nancy Lovallo, *Purchasing*
▲ **EMP:** 277
SQ FT: 138,000
SALES: 492.6MM **Publicly Held**
WEB: www.acorda.com
SIC: 2834 8731 2836 Drugs acting on the central nervous system & sense organs; biotechnical research, commercial; biological products, except diagnostic

(G-404)
ADVANCED COMM SOLUTIONS
38 Ridge Rd (10502-2226)
PHONE 914 693-5076
EMP: 5
SALES: 900K **Privately Held**
SIC: 3663 Mfg Radio/Tv Communication Equipment

(G-405)
IRTRONICS INSTRUMENTS INC
132 Forest Blvd (10502-1031)
PHONE 914 693-6291
Fax: 914 693-6290
John Jenkofsky, *President*
EMP: 15
SQ FT: 1,200
SALES: 870K **Privately Held**
SIC: 3822 3355 3672 Temperature sensors for motor windings; aluminum wire & cable; printed circuit boards

(G-406)
SUPRESTA US LLC (DH)
420 Saw Mill River Rd (10502-2605)
PHONE 914 674-9434
Peggy Viehweger, *CEO*
Thomas Emignanelli, *CFO*
Andrew Schemick, *Finance Dir*
Charlotte Jung, *Credit Mgr*
Pasqual Zottola, *Manager*
▼ **EMP:** 22
SALES (est): 34.6MM
SALES (corp-wide): 5.4B **Privately Held**
SIC: 2899 Fire retardant chemicals
HQ: Icl Performance Products Lp
   622 Emerson Rd Ste 500
   Saint Louis MO 63141
   314 983-7500

(G-407)
UPPER MANHATTAN ARTS PROJECT
73 Bramblebrook Rd (10502-2233)
PHONE 914 980-9805
Timothy Miller, *Chairman*
EMP: 8
SALES (est): 504.3K **Privately Held**
SIC: 3131 Uppers

Argyle
Washington County

(G-408)
ADIRONDACK PLAS & RECYCL INC (PA)
453 County Route 45 (12809-3514)
PHONE 518 746-9212
Fax: 518 638-8951
John Aspland, *CEO*
John S Clair, *Manager*
▲ **EMP:** 21
SQ FT: 125,000
SALES (est): 4.9MM **Privately Held**
SIC: 3089 3559 Plastic processing; recycling machinery

(G-409)
ADIRONDACK SCENIC INC
Also Called: Adirondack Studios
439 County Route 45 Ste 1 (12809-3514)
PHONE 518 638-8000
Fax: 518 761-3362
David Thomas Lloyd, *CEO*
Louis Allen, *Vice Pres*
Ken Crosby, *VP Prdtn*
Stephen Detmer, *Project Mgr*
Patrick Tynan, *Foreman/Supr*
▲ **EMP:** 100
SQ FT: 128,000
SALES: 180MM **Privately Held**
WEB: www.adirondackscenic.com
SIC: 2599 Factory furniture & fixtures

Arkport
Steuben County

(G-410)
HP HOOD LLC
25 Hurlbut St (14807-9706)
P.O. Box 474 (14807-0474)
PHONE 607 295-8134
Stephen Lally, *QC Dir*
Freeman Covert, *Manager*
EMP: 100
SQ FT: 5,184
SALES (corp-wide): 1.9B **Privately Held**
WEB: www.hphood.com
SIC: 2026 2099 2022 Cottage cheese; cream, sour; yogurt; food preparations; cheese, natural & processed
PA: Hp Hood Llc
   6 Kimball Ln Ste 400
   Lynnfield MA 01940
   617 887-8441

Arkville
Delaware County

(G-411)
CATSKILL MOUNTAIN PUBLISHING
Also Called: Catskill Mountain News
43414 State Hwy 28 (12406)
PHONE 845 586-2601
Fax: 845 586-3266
Richard D Sanford, *President*
Laurie Sanford, *Vice Pres*
Linda Schebesta, *Manager*
James Krueger, *Director*
Jenny Rosenzweig, *Director*
EMP: 11 **EST:** 1903
SALES (est): 881.7K **Privately Held**
WEB: www.catskillmountainnews.com
SIC: 2711 Newspapers: publishing only, not printed on site

Armonk
Westchester County

(G-412)
ARUMAI TECHNOLOGIES INC (PA)
175 King St (10504-1606)
PHONE 914 217-0038
P Stephen Lamont, *CEO*
David J Colter, *CTO*
Gregory B Thagard, *CTO*
EMP: 12
SALES (est): 592.8K **Privately Held**
SIC: 7372 Prepackaged software

(G-413)
IBM WORLD TRADE CORPORATION (HQ)
1 New Orchard Rd Ste 1 (10504-1722)
PHONE 914 765-1900
Fax: 914 765-6021
Virginia M Rometty, *CEO*
Asif Samad, *Partner*
Hoonmeng Ong, *General Mgr*
Val Rahmani, *General Mgr*
Robert Zapfel, *General Mgr*
EMP: 8
SQ FT: 417,000
SALES (est): 40.3B
SALES (corp-wide): 81.7B **Publicly Held**
WEB: www.lnn.com
SIC: 3571 3577 7377 7379 Electronic computers; computer peripheral equipment; computer rental & leasing; computer related maintenance services
PA: International Business Machines Corporation
   1 New Orchard Rd Ste 1
   Armonk NY 10504
   914 499-1900

(G-414)
INTERNATIONAL BUS MCHS CORP
Also Called: IBM
1 New Orchard Rd Ste 1 (10504-1722)
PHONE 914 345-5219
Stephen Ward, *Senior VP*
James J Kelly, *Engineer*
Prabjit Singh, *Engineer*
Sharon Stanley, *Engineer*
Jeffery K Thomas, *Engineer*
EMP: 10
SALES (corp-wide): 81.7B **Publicly Held**
SIC: 7372 Prepackaged software
PA: International Business Machines Corporation
   1 New Orchard Rd Ste 1
   Armonk NY 10504
   914 499-1900

(G-415)
INTERNATIONAL BUS MCHS CORP
Also Called: IBM
20 Old Post Rd (10504-1314)
PHONE 914 499-2000
Fax: 914 499-2188

David Leftwich, *General Mgr*
Andrew J Decustai, *Vice Pres*
Jim Gregory, *Vice Pres*
Ted Hoff, *Vice Pres*
Nancy Lewis, *Manager*
EMP: 50
SALES (corp-wide): 81.7B **Publicly Held**
WEB: www.ibm.com
SIC: 7372 Prepackaged software
PA: International Business Machines Corporation
   1 New Orchard Rd Ste 1
   Armonk NY 10504
   914 499-1900

(G-416)
JINGLEBELL INC
Also Called: JINGLENOG DBA
190 Byram Lake Rd (10504-1509)
PHONE 914 219-5395
Melissa Byrne, *President*
▲ **EMP:** 6 **EST:** 2008
SALES: 200K **Privately Held**
SIC: 3229 3231 7389 Christmas tree ornaments, from glass produced on-site; Christmas tree ornaments: made from purchased glass; design services

(G-417)
MAIN STREET CONNECT LLC
Also Called: Daily Voice
200 Business Park Dr # 209 (10504-1719)
PHONE 203 803-4110
Kathryn Desilva, *Sales Dir*
Carll Tucker,
EMP: 12 **EST:** 2012
SALES (est): 678K **Privately Held**
SIC: 2711 Newspapers, publishing & printing

(G-418)
NEFF HOLDING COMPANY
357 Main St (10504-1808)
PHONE 914 595-8200
EMP: 5
SALES (est): 1.2MM
SALES (corp-wide): 5.9B **Publicly Held**
SIC: 2741 Yearbooks: publishing & printing
HQ: Visant Corporation
   3601 Minnesota Dr Ste 400
   Minneapolis MN 55435
   914 595-8200

(G-419)
PRODUCTION RESOURCE GROUP LLC (PA)
Also Called: Prg Integrated Solutions
200 Business Park Dr # 109 (10504-1751)
PHONE 212 589-5400
Jeremiah Harris, *CEO*
Stephan Paridaen, *President*
John Hovis, *COO*
Steven Greenberg, *Exec VP*
Robert Manners, *Exec VP*
◆ **EMP:** 100
SQ FT: 140,000
SALES (est): 429.9MM **Privately Held**
WEB: www.prg.com
SIC: 3999 7922 Theatrical scenery; equipment rental, theatrical; lighting, theatrical

(G-420)
SUMMIT COMMUNICATIONS
28 Half Mile Rd (10504-1306)
PHONE 914 273-5504
Russell Dekker, *Owner*
EMP: 6
SALES (est): 283.9K **Privately Held**
SIC: 2741 Miscellaneous publishing

(G-421)
SURGICAL DESIGN CORP
Also Called: S D C
3 Macdonald Ave (10504-1935)
PHONE 914 273-2445
Fax: 914 786-2139
William Banko MD, *President*
Stanislava Banko, *Corp Secy*
EMP: 15
SQ FT: 10,000

GEOGRAPHIC SECTION

Astoria - Queens County (G-448)

SALES (est): 2.6MM **Privately Held**
WEB: www.surgical.com
SIC: 3841 3851 3827 Surgical instruments & apparatus; instruments, microsurgical: except electromedical; ophthalmic goods; optical instruments & lenses

(G-422)
TRINITY PACKAGING CORPORATION (PA)
84 Business Park Dr # 309 (10504-1717)
PHONE.................................914 273-4111
Fax: 914 273-4715
John H Freund, *CEO*
Peter Freund, *President*
Tim Shiley, *Plant Mgr*
Jacob Schreiber, *QA Dir*
William Motter, *Project Engr*
▲ EMP: 30
SQ FT: 9,000
SALES (est): 169MM **Privately Held**
SIC: 2673 2679 Plastic bags: made from purchased materials; paper products, converted

(G-423)
VISANT SECONDARY HOLDINGS CORP (DH)
357 Main St (10504-1808)
PHONE.................................914 595-8200
Kevin P Hayden, *President*
Paul B Carousso, *Vice Pres*
Marie Hlavaty, *Vice Pres*
Marc L Reisch, *Senior Mgr*
EMP: 4
SALES (est): 831.7MM
SALES (corp-wide): 5.9B **Publicly Held**
SIC: 2741 Yearbooks: publishing & printing
HQ: Visant Holding Corp.
  3601 Minnesota Dr Ste 400
  Minneapolis MN 55435
  914 595-8200

Arverne
Queens County

(G-424)
ARMOUR BEARER GROUP INC
Also Called: 2fish 5loaves Comminty Pantry
424 Beach 65th St (11692-1440)
PHONE.................................646 812-4487
Clinton Nixon, *President*
EMP: 5 EST: 2014
SALES (est): 234.8K **Privately Held**
SIC: 2099 Food preparations

(G-425)
DARRELL MITCHELL
Also Called: D.A.M. Construction, Company
704 Beach 67th St (11692-1314)
PHONE.................................646 659-7075
Darrell Mitchell, *Owner*
EMP: 5
SALES (est): 159.2K **Privately Held**
SIC: 1389 1799 8741 8742 Construction, repair & dismantling services; construction site cleanup; construction management; construction project management consultant

Ashville
Chautauqua County

(G-426)
CASTELLI AMERICA LLC
5151 Fairbanks Rd (14710-9796)
PHONE.................................716 782-2101
EMP: 80
SALES (corp-wide): 201.4MM **Privately Held**
SIC: 2022 Cheese, natural & processed
HQ: Castelli America, Llc
  277 Fairfield Rd Ste 208
  Fairfield NJ 07004
  716 782-2101

(G-427)
CHAUTAUQUA MACHINE SPC LLC
1880 Open Meadows Rd (14710-9793)
PHONE.................................716 782-3276
Fax: 716 782-4801
Dave Hishman, *Engineer*
Dennis Furlow,
EMP: 10
SQ FT: 8,000
SALES (est): 750K **Privately Held**
SIC: 3441 7692 Fabricated structural metal; automotive welding

(G-428)
CHAUTQUA PRCSION MACHINING INC
1287 Hunt Rd (14710-9612)
PHONE.................................716 763-3752
Jeff Christie, *President*
Mary Ann Attard, *Administration*
EMP: 12
SALES (est): 1.7MM **Privately Held**
SIC: 3599 Machine shop, jobbing & repair

(G-429)
FAIRBANK RECONSTRUCTION CORP
Also Called: Fairbank Farms
5151 Fairbanks Rd (14710-9796)
PHONE.................................800 628-3276
Fax: 716 782-2900
Ronald G Allen, *CEO*
Rick Fahle, *President*
A Joseph Fairbank, *Vice Pres*
Brenda L Fahe, *Treasurer*
Robert Anderson, *Director*
EMP: 90 EST: 1931
SQ FT: 100,000
SALES (est): 11.1MM
SALES (corp-wide): 43.5MM **Privately Held**
WEB: www.fairbankfarms.com
SIC: 2011 2013 Meat packing plants; sausages & other prepared meats
PA: Afa Group Inc.
  860 1st Ave Ste 9a
  King Of Prussia PA 19406

(G-430)
THAYER TOOL & DIE INC
1718 Blckville Watts Flts (14710-9538)
PHONE.................................716 782-4841
Fax: 716 782-3261
John Thayer, *President*
Jennifer Henry, *Office Mgr*
EMP: 15
SQ FT: 5,000
SALES (est): 577.6K **Privately Held**
SIC: 3544 Special dies & tools

Astoria
Queens County

(G-431)
4 OVER 4COM INC
1941 46th St (11105-1101)
PHONE.................................718 932-2700
Taso Panagiotopoulos, *President*
Elizabeth Salazar, *Prdtn Mgr*
EMP: 6
SALES (est): 660K **Privately Held**
SIC: 2759 Post cards, picture: printing

(G-432)
AKI CABINETS INC
2636 2nd St (11102-4130)
PHONE.................................718 721-2541
Mujo Todic, *Ch of Bd*
Gloria Henderson, *Principal*
▲ EMP: 18
SALES (est): 2.2MM **Privately Held**
SIC: 2434 Wood kitchen cabinets

(G-433)
ALPS PROVISION CO INC
2270 45th St (11105-1336)
PHONE.................................718 721-4477
Fax: 718 956-4050
Giulio Sottovia, *President*
Leonardo Castorina, *Vice Pres*
Remo Tozzi, *Treasurer*
EMP: 27 EST: 1928
SQ FT: 12,500
SALES (est): 4.1MM **Privately Held**
WEB: www.alpsinstyle.com
SIC: 2013 5143 5147 Sausages & other prepared meats; cheese; meats, fresh

(G-434)
COMFORT WAX INCORPORATED
3174 Steinway St Fl 5 (11103-3909)
PHONE.................................718 204-7028
Fei Qinhua, *Owner*
EMP: 11
SALES (est): 1.2MM **Privately Held**
SIC: 2842 Wax removers

(G-435)
D & S SUPPLIES INC
2067 21st St (11105-3507)
PHONE.................................718 721-5256
Paul Melky, *President*
EMP: 17
SALES (est): 1.2MM **Privately Held**
SIC: 3679 Electronic loads & power supplies

(G-436)
D-LITE DONUTS
4519 Broadway (11103-1625)
PHONE.................................718 626-5953
George Kaparakos, *Owner*
EMP: 5
SALES (est): 150K **Privately Held**
SIC: 2051 Doughnuts, except frozen

(G-437)
DF MAVENS INC
2420 49th St (11103-1017)
PHONE.................................347 813-4705
Malcolm Stogo, *Principal*
WEI Lo, *Assistant*
EMP: 20 EST: 2013
SALES (est): 970K **Privately Held**
SIC: 2024 Ice cream & frozen desserts

(G-438)
ECONOMY PUMP & MOTOR REPAIR
3652 36th St (11106-1304)
PHONE.................................718 433-2600
Fax: 718 433-2296
Elsie Domagala, *President*
EMP: 6
SALES (est): 540K **Privately Held**
SIC: 3433 3585 3586 5999 Heating equipment, except electric; heat pumps, electric; compressors for refrigeration & air conditioning equipment; measuring & dispensing pumps; motors, electric

(G-439)
ELECTROTECH SERVICE EQP CORP
2450 46th St (11103-1008)
PHONE.................................718 626-7700
Joseph Amendalara, *CEO*
Michael Gurello, *Manager*
EMP: 46
SQ FT: 15,000
SALES (est): 19.3MM **Privately Held**
SIC: 3613 5731 Switchgear & switchgear accessories; switchboard apparatus, except instruments; consumer electronic equipment

(G-440)
EMPIRE METAL FINISHING INC
2469 46th St (11103-1007)
PHONE.................................718 545-6700
Fax: 718 932-0300
Michael Vetrone, *President*
Lisa Vetrone, *Vice Pres*
EMP: 30 EST: 1922
SQ FT: 5,000
SALES (est): 3.2MM **Privately Held**
SIC: 3471 3499 3449 Gold plating; fire- or burglary-resistive products; miscellaneous metalwork

(G-441)
EXQUISITE GLASS & STONE INC
3117 12th St (11106-4801)
PHONE.................................718 937-9266
Fax: 718 473-4808
Buz Vaultz, *President*
EMP: 5
SQ FT: 900
SALES (est): 500K **Privately Held**
SIC: 3231 Decorated glassware: chipped, engraved, etched, etc.

(G-442)
FAME CONSTRUCTION INC
2388 Brklyn Queens Expy W (11103-1023)
PHONE.................................718 626-1000
Michael Andreou, *President*
Kosta Savelibis, *Manager*
EMP: 50
SQ FT: 1,700
SALES (est): 4.9MM **Privately Held**
SIC: 1389 Construction, repair & dismantling services

(G-443)
HEAT AND FROST INSLATRS & ASBS
Also Called: Insulators Local 12
3553 24th St (11106-4416)
PHONE.................................718 784-3456
Fax: 718 784-8357
Nino Grgas, *President*
Matt Aracich, *President*
Al Wassell, *President*
Sal Gargiulo, *Corp Secy*
EMP: 6
SQ FT: 500
SALES (est): 11.8MM **Privately Held**
WEB: www.asbestosworkers.com
SIC: 3644 8399 Insulators & insulation materials, electrical; community chest

(G-444)
HELLAS STONE INC
3344 9th St (11106-4902)
PHONE.................................718 545-4716
Esdavros Cayioulis, *CEO*
▲ EMP: 5
SALES (est): 505.2K **Privately Held**
SIC: 2514 Kitchen cabinets: metal

(G-445)
INTER CRAFT CUSTOM FURNITURE
1431 Astoria Blvd (11102-3691)
PHONE.................................718 278-2573
Chipiv Savva, *President*
EMP: 9
SALES (est): 840K **Privately Held**
SIC: 2511 Wood household furniture

(G-446)
KEYSTONE ELECTRONICS CORP (PA)
3107 20th Rd (11105-2017)
PHONE.................................718 956-8900
Fax: 718 956-9040
Richard David, *President*
Jim Magnuson, *General Mgr*
Joe Roosenblum, *General Mgr*
Joe Schmalzried, *Regional Mgr*
Bob Hubert, *Mfg Staff*
▲ EMP: 126
SQ FT: 40,000
SALES (est): 18.2MM **Privately Held**
WEB: www.keyelco.com
SIC: 3678 Electronic connectors

(G-447)
LEMODE PLUMBING & HEATING
3455 11th St (11106-5011)
PHONE.................................718 545-3336
Angelo Lemodetis, *Owner*
EMP: 30
SALES (est): 4.7MM **Privately Held**
SIC: 3494 Plumbing & heating valves

(G-448)
LENS LAB EXPRESS SOUTHERN BLVD
3073 Steinway St (11103-3801)
PHONE.................................718 626-5184
Fax: 718 626-5405
Jeffery Nesses, *President*
EMP: 7
SALES (est): 841.6K **Privately Held**
SIC: 3851 5048 Ophthalmic goods; ophthalmic goods

Astoria - Queens County (G-449)

(G-449)
MODERN ART FOUNDRY INC
Also Called: Jeffrey Spring Modern Art
1870 41st St (11105-1025)
PHONE.................................718 728-2030
Fax: 718 267-0819
Robert Spring, *President*
Jeffrey Spring, *Vice Pres*
Mary Jo Bursig, *Controller*
▲ EMP: 30
SQ FT: 14,000
SALES (est): 5MM Privately Held
WEB: www.modernartfoundry.com
SIC: 3366 3446 Castings (except die): bronze; architectural metalwork

(G-450)
NIEBYLSKI BAKERY INC
2364 Steinway St (11105-1913)
PHONE.................................718 721-5152
Anthony Niebylski, *President*
Rose Niebylski, *Vice Pres*
EMP: 7
SALES: 500K Privately Held
SIC: 2051 5461 Bakery: wholesale or wholesale/retail combined; bakeries

(G-451)
NY PHRMACY COMPOUNDING CTR INC
3715 23rd Ave (11105-1993)
PHONE.................................201 403-5151
Wesam Abdrabouh, *President*
EMP: 5 EST: 2014
SALES (est): 678.4K Privately Held
SIC: 2834 Pharmaceutical preparations

(G-452)
OMNICARE ANESTHESIA PC (PA)
3636 33rd St Ste 211 (11106-2329)
PHONE.................................718 433-0044
Evans Crevecoeur MD, *Ch of Bd*
Gina Duval, *Principal*
Michelle Vega, *Administration*
EMP: 25
SALES (est): 5.5MM Privately Held
SIC: 3841 Anesthesia apparatus

(G-453)
QCR EXPRESS CORP
2565 23rd St Apt 3d (11102-3393)
PHONE.................................888 924-5888
Oscar Bayona, *President*
Veronica Bayona, *Vice Pres*
EMP: 6
SALES: 1.2MM Privately Held
SIC: 3993 Signs & advertising specialties

(G-454)
RAGO FOUNDATIONS LLC
Also Called: Rago Shapewear
1815 27th Ave (11102-3744)
PHONE.................................718 728-8396
Fax: 718 728-8465
Steven H Chernoff, *General Mgr*
Iky Rahim, *Prdtn Mgr*
Chris Gayasingh, *Purch Agent*
Georgiana Petrobono, *Bookkeeper*
Kieran Hohammed, *Manager*
▼ EMP: 96 EST: 1944
SALES (est): 10.5MM Privately Held
WEB: www.ragoshapewear.com
SIC: 2342 Foundation garments, women's

(G-455)
ROSENWACH TANK CO INC (PA)
Also Called: Rosenwach Group, The
4302 Ditmars Blvd (11105-1337)
PHONE.................................212 972-4411
Fax: 718 482-0661
Andrew Rosenwach, *Ch of Bd*
Wallace Rosenwach, *Principal*
George Vassiliades, *Principal*
Alice Rosenwach, *Treasurer*
Robert Obus, *Admin Sec*
EMP: 35 EST: 1945
SQ FT: 23,000
SALES: 16.9MM Privately Held
SIC: 2449 3443 2531 Tanks, wood: coopered; fabricated plate work (boiler shop); public building & related furniture

(G-456)
SINGLECUT BEERSMITHS LLC
1933 37th St (11105-1118)
PHONE.................................718 606-0788
Rich Buececa, *Mng Member*
EMP: 14 EST: 2012
SALES (est): 1.2MM Privately Held
SIC: 3556 Brewers' & maltsters' machinery

(G-457)
SITECRAFT INC
Also Called: Rosenwach Tank Co
4302 Ditmars Blvd (11105-1337)
PHONE.................................718 729-4900
Andrew Rosenwach, *President*
Al Seabra, *Opers Staff*
Wallace Rosenwach, *Director*
EMP: 5
SQ FT: 10,000
SALES (est): 791.4K
SALES (corp-wide): 16.9MM Privately Held
SIC: 2511 Wood lawn & garden furniture
PA: Rosenwach Tank Co. Inc.
   4302 Ditmars Blvd
   Astoria NY 11105
   212 972-4411

(G-458)
SPONGEBATH LLC
2334 28th St Apt 2r (11105-2877)
PHONE.................................917 475-1347
Matthew Flannery, *Mng Member*
Tod Maitland, *Mng Member*
EMP: 6
SQ FT: 2,200
SALES: 2MM Privately Held
SIC: 2842 Disinfectants, household or industrial plant

(G-459)
STEINWAY AWNING II LLC (PA)
Also Called: Steinway Awnings
4230 24th St (11101-4608)
PHONE.................................718 729-2965
Fax: 718 729-2968
Cuzana Michalovicoug, *Executive*
EMP: 6
SQ FT: 4,000
SALES: 300K Privately Held
SIC: 2394 5999 Awnings, fabric: made from purchased materials; canopies, fabric: made from purchased materials; awnings

(G-460)
VSHIP CO
3636 33rd St Ste 207 (11106-2329)
PHONE.................................718 706-8566
Vindu Koil, *President*
Ali Siddiqui, *Manager*
◆ EMP: 12 EST: 2000
SALES (est): 1.1MM Privately Held
SIC: 3443 Containers, shipping (bombs, etc.): metal plate

(G-461)
WAINLAND INC
2460 47th St (11103-1010)
PHONE.................................718 626-2233
Fax: 718 626-9222
Donald Wainland, *President*
Mark Wainland, *Vice Pres*
Neil Wainland, *Vice Pres*
Karin Kovi, *Manager*
▲ EMP: 45
SALES (est): 8.2MM Privately Held
WEB: www.wainlands.com
SIC: 3645 3444 Residential lighting fixtures; sheet metalwork

(G-462)
WHITE COFFEE CORP
1835 38th St (11105-1076)
PHONE.................................718 204-7900
Fax: 718 956-6836
Carole White, *Ch of Bd*
Jonathan White, *Exec VP*
Gregory White, *Vice Pres*
John Bosco, *Opers Mgr*
Paul Harvey, *Safety Mgr*
▲ EMP: 85 EST: 1939
SALES (est): 33MM Privately Held
SIC: 2095 5149 Coffee roasting (except by wholesale grocers); tea

(G-463)
YOYO LIP GLOSS INC
2438 47th St (11103-1010)
PHONE.................................718 357-6304
Evangelia Parlionas, *President*
Margarita Parlionas, *CFO*
▲ EMP: 10
SQ FT: 25,000
SALES: 1.3MM Privately Held
SIC: 2844 Cosmetic preparations

Athens
Greene County

(G-464)
NORTHEAST TREATERS INC
796 Schoharie Tpke (12015-4306)
PHONE.................................518 945-2660
Frank Crowe, *Manager*
EMP: 25
SALES (corp-wide): 17.8MM Privately Held
WEB: www.netreaters.com
SIC: 2491 Wood preserving
PA: Northeast Treaters, Inc.
   201 Springfield Rd
   Belchertown MA 01007
   413 323-7811

(G-465)
NORTHEAST TREATERS NY LLC
796 Schoharie Tpke (12015-4306)
PHONE.................................518 945-2660
Fax: 518 945-2662
Joan Lamotte, *Office Mgr*
David A Reed, *Mng Member*
Douglas C Elder,
Charles Geiger,
Henry G Page Jr,
EMP: 20
SQ FT: 884
SALES (est): 1.7MM Privately Held
WEB: www.otda.state.ny.us
SIC: 2491 Wood preserving

(G-466)
PECKHAM INDUSTRIES INC
Uninn St (12015)
PHONE.................................518 945-1120
John R Peckham, *Branch Mgr*
EMP: 5
SALES (corp-wide): 192MM Privately Held
SIC: 2951 Asphalt paving mixtures & blocks
PA: Peckham Industries, Inc.
   20 Haarlem Ave Ste 200
   White Plains NY 10603
   914 949-2000

(G-467)
PECKHAM MATERIALS CORP
2 Union St Ext (12015-1298)
PHONE.................................518 945-1120
Mark Libruk, *Terminal Mgr*
Joe Widermuth, *Manager*
Art Coe, *Manager*
Joe Wildermith, *Manager*
Larry Fingar, *Maintence Staff*
EMP: 20
SQ FT: 242
SALES (corp-wide): 192MM Privately Held
SIC: 2951 Asphalt paving mixtures & blocks
HQ: Peckham Materials Corp
   20 Haarlem Ave Ste 200
   White Plains NY 10603
   914 686-2045

Atlantic Beach
Nassau County

(G-468)
ANCHOR COMMERCE TRADING CORP
53 Dutchess Blvd (11509-1223)
P.O. Box 238 (11509-0238)
PHONE.................................516 881-3485
Meryl P Benin, *President*
EMP: 6 EST: 1976
SALES (est): 200K Privately Held
SIC: 3714 3533 2819 3823 Motor vehicle parts & accessories; oil field machinery & equipment; industrial inorganic chemicals; computer interface equipment for industrial process control

(G-469)
HORIZON APPAREL MFG INC
115 Bayside Dr (11509-1608)
PHONE.................................516 361-4878
Mark Hassin, *President*
Bonnie Hassin, *Vice Pres*
▲ EMP: 5
SQ FT: 800
SALES: 25MM Privately Held
SIC: 2211 Apparel & outerwear fabrics, cotton

(G-470)
SMALL BUSINESS ADVISORS INC
2005 Park St (11509-1235)
PHONE.................................516 374-1387
Joseph Gelb, *President*
Dawson Vandam, *Manager*
Barbara Goetz Gelb, *Shareholder*
EMP: 10
SALES (est): 350K Privately Held
SIC: 2721 8721 Periodicals; accounting, auditing & bookkeeping

Attica
Wyoming County

(G-471)
ATTICA MILLWORK INC
71 Market St (14011-1023)
P.O. Box 118 (14011-0118)
PHONE.................................585 591-2333
Fax: 585 591-3240
Kevin Demars, *President*
Justin Papucci, *Vice Pres*
Doug Houghton, *Opers Staff*
Thomas Wackenheim, *Shareholder*
▲ EMP: 19 EST: 1945
SQ FT: 65,000
SALES (est): 3MM Privately Held
WEB: www.atticamillwork.com
SIC: 2431 Moldings, wood: unfinished & prefinished

(G-472)
ATTICA PACKAGE COMPANY INC
45 Windsor St (14011-1208)
P.O. Box 295 (14011-0295)
PHONE.................................585 591-0510
Fax: 585 591-3655
Douglas W Domes, *President*
Brittany Gadd, *Office Mgr*
Barbara Schmidt, *Administration*
EMP: 10
SQ FT: 16,000
SALES (est): 870K Privately Held
SIC: 2411 5199 5211 Logging; sawdust; millwork & lumber

(G-473)
HLW ACRES LLC
Also Called: Hlw Acres Poultry Processing
1727 Exchange Street Rd (14011-9627)
PHONE.................................585 591-0795
Hermann Weber, *Owner*
EMP: 9
SALES (est): 548.4K Privately Held
SIC: 2015 Poultry slaughtering & processing

(G-474)
PRECISION FABRICATION LLC
40 S Pearl St (14011-1207)
PHONE.................................585 591-3449
Donald McCulloch, *Owner*
EMP: 5
SALES: 530K Privately Held
SIC: 3444 3448 Sheet metalwork; prefabricated metal components

GEOGRAPHIC SECTION

Auburn - Cayuga County (G-498)

Au Sable Forks
Clinton County

(G-475)
COLD SPRING GRANITE COMPANY
Lake Placid Granite Co
Rr 9 Box S (12912)
P.O. Box 778 (12912-0778)
PHONE..................................518 647-8191
Fax: 518 647-8340
Rick Barber, *Manager*
EMP: 27
SALES (corp-wide): 298.9MM **Privately Held**
WEB: www.granitemountainstonedesign.com
SIC: **1411** Granite, dimension-quarrying
PA: Cold Spring Granite Company Inc
  17482 Granite West Rd
  Cold Spring MN 56320
  320 685-3621

Auburn
Cayuga County

(G-476)
4M PRECISION INDUSTRIES INC
4000 Technology Park Blvd (13021-9030)
PHONE..................................315 252-8415
Fax: 315 253-9611
Margaret Morin, *President*
Daniel Morin, *Vice Pres*
Allen Morin, *Purchasing*
Stephen C Morin, *Shareholder*
Edith Carroll Morin, *Admin Sec*
EMP: 51
SQ FT: 55,000
SALES (est): 11.3MM **Privately Held**
WEB: www.4mprecision.com
SIC: **3469** Metal stampings

(G-477)
AUBURN ARMATURE INC (PA)
Also Called: Aai
70 Wright Cir (13021-3163)
P.O. Box 870 (13021-0870)
PHONE..................................315 253-9721
Fax: 315 247-2271
Geoff Murphy, *CEO*
Edward Stefanak, *General Mgr*
Alice Wagner, *General Mgr*
Dan Ewing, *COO*
Art Burt, *Engineer*
EMP: 70 EST: 1946
SQ FT: 50,000
SALES (est): 38.3MM **Privately Held**
WEB: www.auburnarmature.com
SIC: **7694** 5063 5065 3621 Electric motor repair; motors, electric; electronic parts & equipment; motors & generators

(G-478)
AUBURN CUSTOM MILLWORK INC
4022 Technology Park Blvd (13021-9014)
PHONE..................................315 253-3843
Fax: 315 258-8613
Christopher Colella, *President*
Sherry Colella, *Manager*
EMP: 8
SALES (est): 1.3MM **Privately Held**
SIC: **2431** 2541 Millwork; cabinets, lockers & shelving

(G-479)
AUBURN FOUNDRY INC
15 Wadsworth St (13021-2257)
P.O. Box 715 (13021-0715)
PHONE..................................315 253-4441
Fax: 315 253-5918
David Boglione, *President*
Nicholas Boglione, *Vice Pres*
C Spagnola, *Manager*
Denise Boglione, *Admin Sec*
EMP: 17
SQ FT: 60,000
SALES (est): 1.7MM **Privately Held**
WEB: www.auburnfoundry.com
SIC: **3321** Gray & ductile iron foundries; gray iron castings

(G-480)
AUBURN PUBLISHING CO
Also Called: Citizen , The
25 Dill St (13021-3605)
PHONE..................................315 253-5311
Fax: 315 253-6031
Richard J Emanuel, *President*
Jean Bennett, *Editor*
Jeremy Boyer, *Editor*
David Wilcox, *Editor*
Carolyn Clark, *Accounts Exec*
EMP: 85
SALES (est): 5.6MM
SALES (corp-wide): 648.5MM **Publicly Held**
SIC: **2711** Newspapers: publishing only, not printed on site
HQ: Lee Publications, Inc.
  201 N Harrison St Ste 600
  Davenport IA 52801
  563 383-2100

(G-481)
AUBURN TANK & MANUFACTURING CO
Also Called: Atco EZ Dock
24 Mcmaster St (13021-2442)
P.O. Box 488 (13021-0488)
PHONE..................................315 255-2788
Fax: 315 253-9239
Carl Weber, *President*
April Amodei, *Safety Mgr*
Charles Masters, *Sales Mgr*
Kristy Weber, *Office Mgr*
EMP: 14
SQ FT: 12,000
SALES (est): 2.2MM **Privately Held**
WEB: www.auburntank.com
SIC: **3444** Sheet metalwork

(G-482)
AUBURN VACUUM FORMING CO INC
40 York St (13021-1251)
P.O. Box 489 (13021-0489)
PHONE..................................315 253-2440
Fax: 315 253-2203
Paul D Hickey, *President*
Kristine Hickey, *CFO*
EMP: 19
SQ FT: 71,000
SALES (est): 2.1MM **Privately Held**
SIC: **3563** Vacuum (air extraction) systems, industrial

(G-483)
AVSTAR FUEL SYSTEMS INC
15 Brookfield Pl (13021-2209)
PHONE..................................315 255-1955
EMP: 5
SALES (est): 609.7K **Privately Held**
SIC: **2869** Fuels

(G-484)
BIMBO BAKERIES USA INC
11 Corcoran Dr (13021-2213)
PHONE..................................315 253-9782
Bill Bos, *Plant Mgr*
EMP: 100
SQ FT: 28,668
SALES (corp-wide): 13B **Privately Held**
SIC: **2051** Breads, rolls & buns
HQ: Bimbo Bakeries Usa, Inc
  255 Business Center Dr # 200
  Horsham PA 19044
  215 347-5500

(G-485)
BLAIR CNSTR FABRICATION SP
13 Brae Ridge Rd (13021-9672)
PHONE..................................315 253-2321
Fax: 315 253-2302
Blair Longo, *President*
EMP: 6
SQ FT: 6,000
SALES (est): 360K **Privately Held**
SIC: **3599** Machine shop, jobbing & repair

(G-486)
BO-MER PLASTICS LLC
13 Pulaski St (13021-1105)
PHONE..................................315 252-7216
Thomas R Herbert, *President*
Robin Axton, *Office Mgr*
▼ EMP: 46 EST: 2001
SQ FT: 44,000
SALES (est): 10.5MM **Privately Held**
WEB: www.bo-mer.com
SIC: **3089** Thermoformed finished plastic products; plastic processing

(G-487)
BROOK NORTH FARMS INC
89 York St (13021-1135)
P.O. Box 1239, Weedsport (13166-1239)
PHONE..................................315 834-9390
Fax: 315 834-9675
Carolyn Kyle, *CEO*
Peter Kyle, *President*
◆ EMP: 12
SALES (est): 2.1MM **Privately Held**
WEB: www.northbrookfarms.com
SIC: **2515** 3496 5083 Mattresses & bed-springs; mats & matting; dairy machinery & equipment

(G-488)
CIERRA INDUSTRIES INC
491 Grant Avenue Rd (13021-8204)
PHONE..................................315 252-6630
F Paul Vanderpool, *President*
▲ EMP: 11
SQ FT: 4,000
SALES (est): 2.2MM **Privately Held**
SIC: **3568** Power transmission equipment

(G-489)
COPPER JOHN CORPORATION
173 State St (13021-1841)
PHONE..................................315 258-9269
Fax: 315 258-0529
Douglas A Springer, *President*
Eric Springer, *Vice Pres*
EMP: 19
SQ FT: 11,000
SALES (est): 1.9MM **Privately Held**
WEB: www.copperjohn.com
SIC: **3949** Archery equipment, general

(G-490)
CURRIER PLASTICS INC
101 Columbus St (13021-3101)
PHONE..................................315 255-1779
Fax: 315 252-6443
John Currier, *Ch of Bd*
Massimo A Leone, *President*
Tom Maloney, *Business Mgr*
James E Currier, *Vice Pres*
Dustin Dreese, *Project Mgr*
▲ EMP: 99
SQ FT: 60,000
SALES (est): 28MM **Privately Held**
WEB: www.currierplastics.com
SIC: **3089** Injection molding of plastics

(G-491)
DAIKIN APPLIED AMERICAS INC
Also Called: Applied Terminal Systems
4900 Technology Park Blvd (13021-8592)
PHONE..................................315 253-2771
Fax: 315 282-6417
Steve Henry, *Vice Pres*
Mary Currier, *Facilities Mgr*
Charlie Balko, *Engineer*
Jeff Cusyck, *Engineer*
Albert Eldik, *Engineer*
EMP: 55
SALES (corp-wide): 17.4B **Privately Held**
SIC: **3585** 3822 3564 3561 Heating & air conditioning combination units; auto controls regulating residntl & coml environmt & applncs; blowers & fans; pumps & pumping equipment; fabricated pipe & fittings
HQ: Daikin Applied Americas Inc.
  13600 Industrial Pk Blvd
  Minneapolis MN 55441
  763 553-5330

(G-492)
DE WITT PLASTICS INC
28 Aurelius Ave (13021-2231)
PHONE..................................315 255-1209
David M Hess, *President*
▲ EMP: 11 EST: 1972
SALES (est): 3MM **Privately Held**
WEB: www.dewittplastics.com
SIC: **2821** Plasticizer/additive based plastic materials

(G-493)
EMCOM INC
Also Called: Electomechanical Componets
62 Columbus St Ste 4 (13021-3161)
PHONE..................................315 255-5300
Fax: 315 255-5311
Endy China, *President*
Joseph Reding, *President*
Tony Pongipat, *Vice Pres*
Joseph D'Urso, *Production*
Sue Galbally, *Buyer*
▲ EMP: 100
SQ FT: 10,000
SALES (est): 36.3MM **Privately Held**
WEB: www.em-com.com
SIC: **3699** Electrical equipment & supplies

(G-494)
FINGER LAKES LEA CRAFTERS LLC
Also Called: Auburn Leathercrafters
42 Washington St (13021-2479)
PHONE..................................315 252-4107
Fax: 315 252-4734
Anita Dungey, *President*
Alan Dungey, *Vice Pres*
▼ EMP: 15
SQ FT: 13,000
SALES: 1.2MM **Privately Held**
WEB: www.auburndirect.com
SIC: **3199** Dog furnishings: collars, leashes, muzzles, etc.: leather

(G-495)
FIRST PRESBYTERIAN CHURCH
112 South St (13021-4891)
PHONE..................................315 252-3861
Gerald Rife Jr, *Pastor*
EMP: 6
SALES (est): 370K **Privately Held**
SIC: **3281** Cut stone & stone products

(G-496)
FLP GROUP LLC
301 Clark St (13021-2236)
PHONE..................................315 252-7583
Fax: 315 253-4370
Greg Kanane, *President*
Joseph Mirabito, *Production*
Gerard Mirabito Jr, *Executive*
Kathy Feocco, *Administration*
Rex Dean, *Recruiter*
EMP: 11 EST: 1928
SQ FT: 20,000
SALES (est): 1.7MM
SALES (corp-wide): 4MM **Privately Held**
WEB: www.fingerlakespress.com
SIC: **2752** 2791 2789 2759 Commercial printing, offset; typesetting; bookbinding & related work; commercial printing; automotive & apparel trimmings
PA: Kinaneco., Inc.
  2925 Milton Ave
  Syracuse NY 13209
  315 468-6201

(G-497)
GEN-WEST ASSOCIATES LLC
101 Columbus St (13021-3121)
PHONE..................................315 255-1779
Louri Hapkins, *Principal*
Pat Craine, *Accountant*
EMP: 5
SALES (est): 569.3K **Privately Held**
SIC: **3089** Injection molding of plastics

(G-498)
GOULDS PUMPS INCORPORATED
1 Goulds Dr (13021-3134)
PHONE..................................315 258-4949
Fax: 315 252-9713
Solly Durado, *Branch Mgr*
Kathy Dewaele, *Admin Asst*
EMP: 338
SALES (corp-wide): 2.4B **Publicly Held**
SIC: **3561** 5084 Pumps & pumping equipment; industrial pumps & parts; pumps, oil well & field; pumps, domestic: water or sump; industrial machinery & equipment

Auburn - Cayuga County (G-499)   GEOGRAPHIC SECTION

HQ: Goulds Pumps Incorporated
240 Fall St
Seneca Falls NY 13148
315 568-2811

(G-499)
HAINES PUBLISHING INC
Also Called: Haines and Company
144 Genesee St Ste 305 (13021-3526)
PHONE.................................315 252-2178
Fax: 315 252-8055
Bill Haines Jr, *CEO*
Steven Carey, *Director*
EMP: 30
SALES (est): 2MM **Privately Held**
SIC: 2741 Miscellaneous publishing

(G-500)
HAMMOND & IRVING INC (PA)
254 North St (13021-1129)
PHONE.................................315 253-6265
Fax: 315 253-3136
Edward Gallager, *President*
Edward C Gallagher, *Exec VP*
Barbara Zach, *Treasurer*
Crystal Reyes, *Sales Staff*
Jamie Moore, *Manager*
▲ EMP: 85
SQ FT: 20,000
SALES: 18MM **Privately Held**
WEB: www.hammond-irving.com
SIC: 3463 Nonferrous forgings

(G-501)
INTERNATIONAL FIRE-SHIELD INC
194 Genesee St (13021-3360)
P.O. Box 7305 (13022-7305)
PHONE.................................315 255-1006
Fax: 315 255-2765
Patrick D Bumpus, *CEO*
George Murray, *Ch of Bd*
Jean Graves, *Vice Pres*
EMP: 12
SALES (est): 1.4MM **Privately Held**
WEB: www.nyfs.com
SIC: 2899 Fire retardant chemicals

(G-502)
ITT CORPORATION
Also Called: ITT Water Technology
1 Goulds Dr (13021-3134)
PHONE.................................315 258-4904
Jim Jones, *Engineer*
Louis Juliano, *Branch Mgr*
Scott Liscum, *Manager*
EMP: 58
SALES (corp-wide): 2.4B **Publicly Held**
SIC: 3625 Control equipment, electric
HQ: Itt, Llc
1133 Westchester Ave N-100
White Plains NY 10604
914 641-2000

(G-503)
JACOBS PRESS INC
87 Columbus St (13021-3121)
P.O. Box 580 (13021-0580)
PHONE.................................315 252-4861
Fax: 315 253-3618
Michael K Trapani, *President*
Pat Nation, *Sales Staff*
Laura Poseczmick, *Business Dir*
Molly Trapani, *Admin Sec*
EMP: 10 EST: 1915
SQ FT: 7,228
SALES: 1.1MM **Privately Held**
WEB: www.jacobspress.com
SIC: 2752 Commercial printing, offset

(G-504)
JOHN G RUBINO INC
Also Called: Gleason-Avery
45 Aurelius Ave (13021-2249)
PHONE.................................315 253-7396
Fax: 315 253-8344
John G Rubino, *CEO*
John Rubino, *President*
▲ EMP: 30
SQ FT: 32,000
SALES: 4.8MM **Privately Held**
WEB: www.gleasonavery.com
SIC: 3621 3566 Motors, electric; speed changers, drives & gears

(G-505)
JOHNSTON PRECISION INC
7 Frank Smith St (13021-1145)
PHONE.................................315 253-4181
Fax: 315 253-4182
Theodore Johnston, *President*
EMP: 5
SQ FT: 2,400
SALES (est): 480K **Privately Held**
SIC: 3599 Machine & other job shop work

(G-506)
LOLLIPOP TREE INC
181 York St (13021-9009)
PHONE.................................845 471-8733
Laurie V Lynch, *Ch of Bd*
Robert Lynch, *President*
Denise Birch, *Accountant*
EMP: 20
SQ FT: 18,200
SALES (est): 2.6MM **Privately Held**
WEB: www.lollipoptree.com
SIC: 2045 2033 2099 2035 Prepared flour mixes & doughs; preserves, including imitation: in cans, jars, etc.; food preparations; pickles, sauces & salad dressings

(G-507)
MACK STUDIOS DISPLAYS INC
5500 Technology Park Blvd (13021-8555)
P.O. Box 917 (13021-0917)
PHONE.................................315 252-7542
Fax: 315 252-5786
Peter Maciulewicz, *President*
Walt Pinchak, *General Mgr*
Christine Lockrow, *Business Mgr*
Dan Fleischman, *Accountant*
EMP: 45
SQ FT: 125,000
SALES: 10.9MM **Privately Held**
WEB: www.mackstudios.com
SIC: 3999 Advertising display products

(G-508)
MATTEO & ANTONIO BARTOLOTTA
Also Called: Bartolotta Furniture
282 State St (13021-1144)
PHONE.................................315 252-2220
Fax: 315 252-9251
Matteo Bartolotta, *President*
EMP: 10 EST: 1976
SQ FT: 4,000
SALES (est): 1MM **Privately Held**
SIC: 2512 2521 2434 Upholstered household furniture; wood office furniture; wood kitchen cabinets

(G-509)
NEW HOPE MILLS INC
181 York St (13021-9009)
PHONE.................................315 252-2676
Fax: 315 497-0810
Dale E Weed, *President*
David J Weed, *Vice Pres*
Mamie Weed, *Marketing Staff*
EMP: 12
SQ FT: 11,500
SALES: 1.1MM **Privately Held**
WEB: www.newhopemills.com
SIC: 2045 0723 Pancake mixes, prepared: from purchased flour; flour milling custom services

(G-510)
NEW HOPE MILLS MFG INC (PA)
181 York St (13021-9009)
PHONE.................................315 252-2676
Douglas Weed, *CEO*
Dale Weed, *President*
Dana Weed, *Office Mgr*
EMP: 50
SQ FT: 30,000
SALES: 7.4MM **Privately Held**
SIC: 2051 5461 Bakery products, partially cooked (except frozen); bakeries

(G-511)
NUCOR STEEL AUBURN INC
25 Quarry Rd (13021-1146)
P.O. Box 2008 (13021-1077)
PHONE.................................315 253-4561
Fax: 315 253-5377
Mary E Slate, *General Mgr*
Dave Smith, *General Mgr*
Dan Dimicco, *Chairman*
Ed Wolf, *Plant Mgr*
Luke Scott, *Safety Mgr*
▲ EMP: 290 EST: 2001
SQ FT: 300,000
SALES (est): 117.8MM
SALES (corp-wide): 16.4B **Publicly Held**
WEB: www.nucorauburn.com
SIC: 3312 Blast furnaces & steel mills
PA: Nucor Corporation
1915 Rexford Rd Ste 400
Charlotte NC 28211
704 366-7000

(G-512)
OWASCO RECYCLING CENTER
38a E Lake Rd (13021)
PHONE.................................315 252-0332
Mike Wilson, *Manager*
EMP: 6
SALES (est): 593.7K **Privately Held**
SIC: 2611 Pulp manufactured from waste or recycled paper

(G-513)
OWENS-BROCKWAY GLASS CONT INC
7134 County House Rd (13021-5901)
PHONE.................................315 258-3211
Judy Johnson, *Purchasing*
Steven Gabel, *Manager*
EMP: 210
SALES (corp-wide): 6.1B **Publicly Held**
SIC: 3221 Glass containers
HQ: Owens-Brockway Glass Container Inc.
1 Michael Owens Way
Perrysburg OH 43551
567 336-8449

(G-514)
PRINTERY
55 Arterial W (13021-2730)
PHONE.................................315 253-7403
Fax: 315 253-0590
Pam Flaherty, *Owner*
EMP: 5
SALES (est): 190K **Privately Held**
SIC: 2261 Screen printing of cotton broadwoven fabrics

(G-515)
R P M INDUSTRIES INC
Also Called: RPM Displays
26 Aurelius Ave (13021-2212)
PHONE.................................315 255-1105
Roger P Mueller, *President*
David Hess, *Vice Pres*
Martin Lynch, *Asst Treas*
Roy P Mueller, *VP Sales*
Barb Loomis, *Manager*
▲ EMP: 50 EST: 1925
SQ FT: 60,000
SALES (est): 37K **Privately Held**
WEB: www.rpmdisplays.com
SIC: 3089 5046 2499 Boxes, plastic; plastic hardware & building products; mannequins; shoe trees

(G-516)
ROBINSON CONCRETE INC (PA)
Also Called: Vitale Ready Mix Concrete
3486 Franklin Street Rd (13021-9348)
PHONE.................................315 253-6666
Fax: 315 252-7595
Michael Vitale Jr, *President*
Norman Chirco, *Counsel*
Vincent Vitale, *Vice Pres*
Gale O'Neill, *Purch Mgr*
Art Dufore, *Sales Staff*
EMP: 50 EST: 1865
SQ FT: 2,500
SALES (est): 24MM **Privately Held**
SIC: 3273 3272 1442 Ready-mixed concrete; concrete products, precast; construction sand & gravel

(G-517)
SCHOTT CORPORATION
Also Called: Fiber Optics Schott America
62 Columbus St (13021-3167)
PHONE.................................315 255-2791
Hinz Keiser, *Plant Mgr*
EMP: 64 **Privately Held**
SIC: 3229 3827 3674 Pressed & blown glass; optical instruments & lenses; semiconductors & related devices
HQ: Schott Corporation
555 Taxter Rd Ste 470
Elmsford NY 10523
914 831-2200

(G-518)
SIGN GUYS LLC
67 Franklin St (13021-2154)
PHONE.................................315 253-4276
Thomas Shayler, *Mng Member*
EMP: 5
SALES: 220K **Privately Held**
SIC: 3993 Signs & advertising specialties

(G-519)
SIMPLEX MANUFACTURING CO INC
105 Dunning Ave (13021-4403)
P.O. Box 279 (13021-0279)
PHONE.................................315 252-7524
Fax: 315 252-0980
Robert C Merritt, *President*
Richard C Merritt, *Vice Pres*
Dan Bird, *Marketing Staff*
EMP: 19
SQ FT: 25,000
SALES (est): 3.1MM **Privately Held**
WEB: www.simplexco.com
SIC: 3469 Metal stampings

(G-520)
SPECTRUM MICROWAVE INC
Also Called: API Technologies Corp
23 N Division St (13021-2357)
PHONE.................................315 253-6241
Richard Southworth, *President*
Walt Gorden, *Manager*
EMP: 22
SALES (corp-wide): 232.2MM **Privately Held**
WEB: www.idt.com
SIC: 3679 Microwave components
HQ: Spectrum Microwave, Inc.
8061 Avonia Rd
Fairview PA 16415
814 474-4300

(G-521)
SUNNYCREST INC (PA)
58 Prospect St (13021-1699)
PHONE.................................315 252-7214
Fax: 315 252-7859
Robert Atkinson, *President*
William Atkinson, *Vice Pres*
Ron Shortsleeve, *Manager*
Eleanor Atkinson, *Admin Sec*
EMP: 30
SQ FT: 53,000
SALES (est): 4.4MM **Privately Held**
WEB: www.sunnycrest.com
SIC: 3272 7261 Concrete products, precast; funeral service & crematories

(G-522)
T SHORE PRODUCTS LTD
Also Called: Shore Products Co
5 Eagle Dr (13021-8695)
PHONE.................................315 252-9174
Fax: 315 252-9174
Thomas H Tutt II, *President*
Marlene Tutt, *Vice Pres*
EMP: 6
SQ FT: 8,500
SALES: 800K **Privately Held**
SIC: 3536 3448 5461 Hoists; boat lifts; docks: prefabricated metal; bakeries

(G-523)
TARO MANUFACTURING COMPANY INC
114 Clark St (13021-3325)
PHONE.................................315 252-9430
Fax: 315 252-9431
Mario Buttaro, *President*
Mark Buttaro, *Vice Pres*
Steve Buttaro, *Vice Pres*
Roxanne Foster, *Manager*
▲ EMP: 19
SQ FT: 17,000
SALES (est): 3MM **Privately Held**
WEB: www.taromfg.com
SIC: 3621 3694 3678 Rotors, for motors; ignition apparatus & distributors; electronic connectors

(G-524)
TOWPATH MACHINE CORP
31 Allen St (13021-9004)
PHONE.................................315 252-0112
Fax: 315 255-1580
Patricia Hanford, *President*
George Hanford, *Treasurer*
EMP: 7
SQ FT: 3,000
SALES: 500K **Privately Held**
WEB: www.towpathmachine.com
SIC: 3599 Machine shop, jobbing & repair

(G-525)
TRW AUTOMOTIVE INC
TRW Manufacturing
2150 Crane Brook Dr (13021-9516)
PHONE.................................315 255-3311
Fax: 315 253-8747
Larry Trent, *Branch Mgr*
Robert Nearpass, *Systems Analyst*
EMP: 300 **Privately Held**
SIC: 3469 3714 Metal stampings; motor vehicle parts & accessories
HQ: Trw Automotive Inc.
    12025 Tech Center Dr
    Livonia MI 48150
    734 266-2600

(G-526)
TRW AUTOMOTIVE US LLC
Also Called: T R W Automotive
2150 Crane Brook Dr (13021-9516)
PHONE.................................315 255-3311
David Cunningham, *Engineer*
Emmanuel Goodman, *Manager*
Jeffrey Hohman, *Manager*
EMP: 250 **Privately Held**
WEB: www.trw.mediaroom.com
SIC: 3469 Metal stampings
HQ: Trw Automotive U.S. Llc
    12001 Tech Center Dr
    Livonia MI 48150
    734 855-2600

(G-527)
VOLPI MANUFACTURING USA CO INC
5 Commerce Way (13021-8557)
PHONE.................................315 255-1737
Fax: 315 255-1202
Max Kunz, *CEO*
Scott Kittelberger, *COO*
Jennifer Ross, *Buyer*
James Casasanta, *Engineer*
Richard Cincotta, *Engineer*
◆ EMP: 38
SQ FT: 37,000
SALES (est): 6.6MM
SALES (corp-wide): 194.9K **Privately Held**
WEB: www.volpiusa.com
SIC: 3229 Glass fiber products
HQ: Volpi Ag
    Wiesenstrasse 33
    Schlieren ZH
    447 324-343

(G-528)
WEAVER MACHINE & TOOL CO INC
44 York St (13021-1136)
PHONE.................................315 253-4422
Fax: 315 253-0058
Victor Ianno, *President*
Susan Garrigan, *Prdtn Mgr*
Joe Artman, *Officer*
EMP: 15
SQ FT: 26,000
SALES (est): 3.2MM **Privately Held**
WEB: www.weavermachine.com
SIC: 3599 Machine shop, jobbing & repair

(G-529)
XYLEM INC
1 Goulds Dr (13021-3134)
PHONE.................................315 258-4949
Sally Dorado, *Branch Mgr*
EMP: 150 **Publicly Held**
SIC: 3561 Pumps & pumping equipment
PA: Xylem Inc.
    1 International Dr
    Rye Brook NY 10573

Aurora
Cayuga County

(G-530)
MACKENZIE-CHILDS LLC (PA)
3260 State Route 90 (13026-9769)
PHONE.................................315 364-7567
Fax: 315 364-5190
Lee Feldman, *CEO*
Kevin Grish, *Safety Dir*
Tony Ciccone, *Purch Mgr*
Julie Schneider, *Buyer*
Howard Cohen, *CFO*
◆ EMP: 150
SQ FT: 70,000
SALES (est): 43.8MM **Privately Held**
WEB: www.mackenzie-childs.com
SIC: 3263 2512 2511 Cookware, fine earthenware; upholstered household furniture; wood household furniture

Ava
Oneida County

(G-531)
ROBERT W STILL
Also Called: Ava Wood Products
11755 State Route 26 (13303-2251)
PHONE.................................315 942-5594
Robert Still, *Owner*
Nick Calogero, *Accountant*
EMP: 16
SALES: 1.2MM **Privately Held**
SIC: 2411 Logging

Averill Park
Rensselaer County

(G-532)
518 PRINTS LLC
1548 Burden Lake Rd Ste 4 (12018-2818)
P.O. Box 632 (12018-0632)
PHONE.................................518 674-5346
Jesse Brust, *Owner*
EMP: 6
SALES (est): 641K **Privately Held**
SIC: 2752 Commercial printing, lithographic

(G-533)
CAPITAL REG WKLY NEWSPPR GROUP
Also Called: Advertiser, The
29 Sheer Rd (12018-4722)
P.O. Box 70 (12018-0070)
PHONE.................................518 674-2841
Fax: 518 674-8680
Charles Hug, *Principal*
Alyson Regan, *Principal*
Karen Demis, *Manager*
EMP: 10
SALES (est): 850K **Privately Held**
SIC: 2721 Periodicals: publishing only

(G-534)
GARMENT CARE SYSTEMS LLC
Also Called: Laura Star Service Center
50 Blue Heron Dr (12018-4601)
PHONE.................................518 674-1826
James E Wells, *Mng Member*
▲ EMP: 6
SALES (est): 654.5K **Privately Held**
WEB: www.garmentcaresystems.com
SIC: 3499 Ironing boards, metal

(G-535)
L J VALENTE INC
8957 Ny Highway 66 (12018-5822)
PHONE.................................518 674-3750
Fax: 518 674-3228
Anthony Valente, *President*
Steve A Valente, *Vice Pres*
EMP: 8 EST: 1925
SALES (est): 1.4MM **Privately Held**
SIC: 2421 Building & structural materials, wood

(G-536)
NEXT ADVANCE INC (PA)
24 Prospect Ave (12018-9574)
PHONE.................................518 674-3510
Ian Glasgow, *President*
EMP: 15
SALES (est): 193K **Privately Held**
WEB: www.nextadvance.com
SIC: 3821 Clinical laboratory instruments, except medical & dental

Avoca
Steuben County

(G-537)
HAINES EQUIPMENT INC
20 Carrington St (14809-9766)
PHONE.................................607 566-8531
Fax: 607 566-2240
Patricia Haines, *President*
Jack Stewart, *Sales Executive*
EMP: 50
SQ FT: 50,000
SALES (est): 9.4MM **Privately Held**
WEB: www.hainesequipment.com
SIC: 3523 3565 3556 3535 Farm machinery & equipment; packaging machinery; food products machinery; conveyors & conveying equipment; tire cord & fabrics

Avon
Livingston County

(G-538)
B & B PRECISION MFG INC (PA)
310 W Main St (14414-1150)
P.O. Box 279 (14414-0279)
PHONE.................................585 226-6226
Gerald Macintyre, *President*
Lawrence Bailey, *Treasurer*
Shelly Guerin, *Accounts Mgr*
EMP: 26 EST: 1976
SQ FT: 15,900
SALES (est): 2.9MM **Privately Held**
WEB: www.bbprecision.com
SIC: 3545 Precision measuring tools

(G-539)
BARILLA AMERICA NY INC
100 Horseshoe Blvd (14414-1164)
PHONE.................................585 226-5600
Kirk Trofholz, *Principal*
Tj Dioguardi, *Controller*
Daniel Shirley, *Maintence Staff*
▲ EMP: 121
SALES (est): 20MM **Privately Held**
SIC: 2099 Packaged combination products: pasta, rice & potato
HQ: Barilla America Inc.
    885 Sunset Ridge Rd
    Northbrook IL 60062
    515 956-4400

(G-540)
KRAFT HEINZ FOODS COMPANY
140 Spring St (14414-1153)
PHONE.................................585 226-4400
Fax: 585 226-4306
Danny Agee, *Plant Mgr*
Jeff McMindes, *Purchasing*
Kenneth Rowe, *Engineer*
Greg Manning, *Manager*
Kathy Freeman, *Manager*
EMP: 450
SALES (corp-wide): 210.8B **Publicly Held**
WEB: www.kraftfoods.com
SIC: 2038 2099 Whipped topping, frozen; food preparations
HQ: Heinz Kraft Foods Company
    1 Ppg Pl Ste 3200
    Pittsburgh PA 15222
    412 456-5700

(G-541)
MONROE INDUSTRIES INC
5611 Tec Dr (14414-9562)
PHONE.................................585 226-8230
Fax: 585 226-8276
John C Webster, *President*

Cary Holdsworth, *Director*
EMP: 8
SALES (est): 720K **Privately Held**
SIC: 3281 Marble, building: cut & shaped

(G-542)
PENNY LANE PRINTING INC
Also Called: Penny Express
1471 Rte 15 (14414)
P.O. Box 340 (14414-0340)
PHONE.................................585 226-8111
Steven Harrison, *President*
Kimberly Dougherty, *Vice Pres*
Gina Doran, *Manager*
Jennifer Howe, *Manager*
EMP: 54
SQ FT: 25,000
SALES: 4.5MM **Privately Held**
SIC: 2759 7319 Commercial printing; distribution of advertising material or sample services

(G-543)
STAR HEADLIGHT LANTERN CO INC (PA)
455 Rochester St (14414-9503)
PHONE.................................585 226-9500
Fax: 585 226-2029
Christopher D Jacobs, *Ch of Bd*
Christopher D Jacob, *President*
David W Jacobs, *President*
Debra Blaszkow, *General Mgr*
Gary Starks, *Opers Spvr*
▲ EMP: 148 EST: 1889
SQ FT: 85,000
SALES (est): 36.7MM **Privately Held**
WEB: www.star1889.com
SIC: 3648 3669 Strobe lighting systems; railroad signaling devices, electric

Babylon
Suffolk County

(G-544)
A C J COMMUNICATIONS INC
Also Called: Beacon
65 Deer Park Ave Ste 2 (11702-2820)
PHONE.................................631 587-5612
Carolyn James, *Principal*
◆ EMP: 15
SALES (est): 54.3K **Privately Held**
SIC: 2711 Newspapers: publishing only, not printed on site

(G-545)
ADVANCED COATING TECHNIQUES
313 Wyandanch Ave (11704-1501)
PHONE.................................631 643-4555
Fax: 631 643-1412
Anthony Gaitan, *President*
Maria Gaitan, *Corp Secy*
EMP: 20
SQ FT: 50,000
SALES (est): 2.6MM **Privately Held**
WEB: www.advancedcoatingtech.com
SIC: 3479 Galvanizing of iron, steel or end-formed products

(G-546)
BEDROCK LANDSCAPING MTLS CORP (PA)
Also Called: Bedrock Plus
454 Sunrise Hwy (11704-5906)
PHONE.................................631 587-4950
David Cannetti, *President*
EMP: 9
SALES (est): 781.8K **Privately Held**
WEB: www.bedrockmaterial.com
SIC: 3291 Abrasive buffs, bricks, cloth, paper, stones, etc.

(G-547)
EAST PENN MANUFACTURING CO
790 Railroad Ave (11704-7820)
PHONE.................................631 321-7161
Fax: 631 321-6611
Timothy Dunn, *Principal*
EMP: 6

Babylon - Suffolk County (G-548)

SALES (corp-wide): 2.2B **Privately Held**
SIC: 3999 Barber & beauty shop equipment
PA: East Penn Manufacturing Co.
102 Deka Rd
Lyon Station PA 19536
610 682-6361

(G-548)
EDM MFG
141 John St Ste 600 (11702-2945)
PHONE...................631 669-1966
Dariusz Mejer, *Chairman*
EMP: 8
SALES (est): 801K **Privately Held**
SIC: 3999 Manufacturing industries

(G-549)
JEWELERS MACHINIST CO INC
400 Columbus Ave (11704-5599)
PHONE...................631 661-5020
Raymond Pawloski, *President*
John Pawloski, *Vice Pres*
Kathleen Pawloski, *Admin Sec*
EMP: 7 **EST:** 1946
SQ FT: 3,000
SALES (est): 1MM **Privately Held**
WEB: www.threadgrind.com
SIC: 3599 Machine shop, jobbing & repair

(G-550)
M C PACKAGING CORPORATION
Also Called: M C Packaging Corp Plant
300 Governor Ave (11704-1900)
PHONE...................631 643-3763
EMP: 40
SALES (corp-wide): 22.9MM **Privately Held**
SIC: 2679 5113 2759 2657 Mfg Converted Paper Prdt Whol Indstl/Svc Paper Commercial Printing Mfg Folding Paperbrd Box Mfg Corrugated/Fiber Box
PA: M C Packaging Corporation
200 Adams Blvd
Farmingdale NY 11735
631 414-7840

(G-551)
PHARMAVANTAGE LLC
15 Lakeland Ave (11702-1409)
PHONE...................631 321-8171
Susan Capie,
▲ **EMP:** 6 **EST:** 2000
SALES (est): 649.9K **Privately Held**
SIC: 2834 Druggists' preparations (pharmaceuticals)

(G-552)
PREMIER SYSTEMS LLC
41 John St Ste 6 (11702-2932)
PHONE...................631 587-9700
Joseph Pegno,
EMP: 6
SALES (est): 670K **Privately Held**
SIC: 3679 Electronic circuits

(G-553)
WOLTERS KLUWER US INC
400 W Main St Ste 244 (11702-3009)
PHONE...................631 517-8060
Thomas A Lesica, *President*
EMP: 30
SALES (corp-wide): 4.5B **Privately Held**
SIC: 2731 Books: publishing only
HQ: Wolters Kluwer United States Inc.
2700 Lake Cook Rd
Riverwoods IL 60015
847 580-5000

Bainbridge
Chenango County

(G-554)
SHEHAWKEN ARCHERY CO INC
40 S Main St (13733-1216)
P.O. Box 187 (13733-0187)
PHONE...................607 967-8333
Fax: 607 967-2828
EMP: 12
SQ FT: 17,000
SALES (est): 720K **Privately Held**
SIC: 3949 Mfg Archery Equipment

(G-555)
TRIMAC MOLDING SERVICES
13 Pruyn St (13733-1155)
P.O. Box 176 (13733-0176)
PHONE...................607 967-2900
Linda Pickwick, *Partner*
Harold Pickwick, *Partner*
EMP: 9
SQ FT: 60,000
SALES (est): 1MM **Privately Held**
WEB: www.trimacmolding.com
SIC: 3089 Injection molding of plastics

(G-556)
UPTURN INDUSTRIES INC
2-4 Whitney Way (13733-1007)
PHONE...................607 967-2923
Mike Horoszewski, *CEO*
Donna L Enck, *CEO*
Tomas Mahar, *Business Mgr*
Kelly Lanten, *Manager*
Nicole Vanpelt, *Administration*
▲ **EMP:** 31
SQ FT: 12,000
SALES (est): 5.3MM **Privately Held**
WEB: www.upturnindustries.com
SIC: 3599 Machine shop, jobbing & repair

Bakers Mills
Warren County

(G-557)
CHAD PIERSON
Also Called: Chad Pierson Logging & Trckg
Chad Pierson (12811)
P.O. Box 29 (12811-0029)
PHONE...................518 251-0186
Chad Pierson, *President*
Melissa Pierson, *Bookkeeper*
EMP: 7
SQ FT: 5,600
SALES (est): 701K **Privately Held**
SIC: 2411 Logging

Baldwin
Nassau County

(G-558)
ELLIQUENCE LLC
2455 Grand Ave (11510-3556)
PHONE...................516 277-9000
Fax: 516 277-9023
Paul Thau, *Controller*
Alan Ellman, *Mng Member*
Scott Goldsmith, *Manager*
▲ **EMP:** 19
SALES (est): 3.2MM **Privately Held**
SIC: 3841 Surgical & medical instruments

(G-559)
JAL SIGNS INC
Also Called: Sign-A-Rama
540 Merrick Rd (11510-3439)
PHONE...................516 536-7280
Fax: 516 536-1687
Agnes Lidner, *President*
James Lidner, *Admin Sec*
EMP: 10 **EST:** 1999
SALES (est): 1.3MM **Privately Held**
SIC: 3993 Signs & advertising specialties

(G-560)
NOTICIA HISPANOAMERICANA INC
53 E Merrick Rd Ste 353 (11510)
PHONE...................516 223-5678
Cinthia Diaz, *Owner*
Silvana Diaz, *Publisher*
Jeovanny Mata, *Director*
▲ **EMP:** 30
SALES (est): 1MM **Privately Held**
SIC: 2711 Newspapers

(G-561)
ROSE FENCE INC
345 Sunrise Hwy (11510-3054)
PHONE...................516 223-0777
Scott Rose, *Branch Mgr*
EMP: 10

SALES (corp-wide): 20.2MM **Privately Held**
WEB: www.rosefence.com
SIC: 2499 5211 3496 3315 Fencing, wood; fencing; miscellaneous fabricated wire products; steel wire & related products
PA: Rose Fence, Inc.
345 W Sunrise Hwy
Freeport NY 11520
516 223-0777

(G-562)
TECHNICAL PACKAGING INC
2365 Milburn Ave (11510-3349)
P.O. Box 504 (11510-0504)
PHONE...................516 223-2300
Fax: 516 223-0025
Don Romig, *President*
James Kane, *Vice Pres*
Maureen Romig, *Sales Mgr*
EMP: 15
SALES (est): 3MM **Privately Held**
WEB: www.technicalpackaging.com
SIC: 2653 2441 3053 3086 Corrugated & solid fiber boxes; packing cases, wood; nailed or lock corner; packing materials; packaging & shipping materials, foamed plastic; packaging materials; corrugated & solid fiber boxes

Baldwin Place
Westchester County

(G-563)
GOODWILL INDS OF GREATER NY
80 Route 6 Unit 605 (10505-1033)
PHONE...................914 621-0781
Herbert Wright, *Principal*
EMP: 153
SALES (corp-wide): 115.1MM **Privately Held**
SIC: 3999 Barber & beauty shop equipment
PA: Goodwill Industries Of Greater New York Inc
421 27th Ave
Astoria NY 11102
718 728-5400

Baldwinsville
Onondaga County

(G-564)
ACME SIGNS OF BALDWINSVILLE
3 Marble St (13027-2918)
PHONE...................315 638-4865
Dennis Sick, *Owner*
EMP: 6
SALES (est): 330K **Privately Held**
SIC: 3993 4226 Signs & advertising specialties; special warehousing & storage

(G-565)
ADVANCED RECOVERY & RECYCL LLC
3475 Linda Ln (13027-9217)
PHONE...................315 450-3301
Byron Tietjen, *President*
Peter Stockmann,
EMP: 10
SALES (est): 606.9K **Privately Held**
SIC: 2611 Pulp mills, mechanical & recycling processing

(G-566)
ANHEUSER-BUSCH LLC
2885 Belgium Rd (13027-2797)
P.O. Box 200 (13027-0200)
PHONE...................315 638-0365
Fax: 315 635-4404
Howard Triche, *General Mgr*
Chris Lukaczyk, *Area Mgr*
Stephen McMorick, *Plant Mgr*
James Macconaghy, *Opers Mgr*
Ryan Brown, *Warehouse Mgr*
EMP: 162

SALES (corp-wide): 1B **Privately Held**
WEB: www.hispanicbud.com
SIC: 2082 Beer (alcoholic beverage)
HQ: Anheuser-Busch, Llc
1 Busch Pl
Saint Louis MO 63118
314 632-6777

(G-567)
CAPCO MARKETING
Also Called: Gourmet Connection
8417 Oswego Rd 177 (13027-8813)
P.O. Box 1727, Cicero (13039-1727)
PHONE...................315 699-1687
Kirk Capece, *Owner*
EMP: 10
SALES (est): 453.3K **Privately Held**
WEB: www.capcomarketing.com
SIC: 2721 5812 Magazines: publishing & printing; eating places

(G-568)
COVERALL MANUFACTURING
Also Called: New Top Sales Company
3653 Hayes Rd (13027-8414)
PHONE...................315 652-2731
Joseph Peta, *President*
EMP: 8
SALES (est): 490K **Privately Held**
WEB: www.golfcarcovers.com
SIC: 2394 Canvas & related products

(G-569)
FRIEDEL PAPER BOX & CONVERTING
7596 Rania Rd (13027-9399)
PHONE...................315 437-3325
Nadim Jabaji, *President*
Douglas Andrews, *Manager*
EMP: 7
SALES (est): 1MM **Privately Held**
SIC: 2652 3554 Setup paperboard boxes; die cutting & stamping machinery, paper converting

(G-570)
INDIAN SPRINGS MFG CO INC
2095 W Genesee Rd (13027-8649)
P.O. Box 469 (13027-0469)
PHONE...................315 635-6101
Fax: 315 635-7473
Maurice J Ferguson, *CEO*
Shawn Ferguson, *President*
Robert Wolniak, *General Mgr*
Donna Miner, *Bookkeeper*
Beth White, *Info Tech Dir*
EMP: 18 **EST:** 1946
SQ FT: 9,000
SALES (est): 4.8MM **Privately Held**
WEB: www.indiansprings.com
SIC: 2812 3599 Chlorine, compressed or liquefied; machine & other job shop work

(G-571)
MATTESSICH IRON LLC
7841 River Rd (13027-9216)
PHONE...................315 409-8496
Michael Mattessich,
EMP: 5 **EST:** 2010
SQ FT: 4,000
SALES: 500K **Privately Held**
SIC: 3462 Iron & steel forgings

(G-572)
METROPOLITAN SIGNS INC (PA)
3760 Patchett Rd (13027-9454)
P.O. Box 3062, Liverpool (13089-3062)
PHONE...................315 638-1448
Fax: 315 638-1509
David R Razzante, *President*
EMP: 7
SQ FT: 4,000
SALES: 600K **Privately Held**
WEB: www.metropolitansigns.com
SIC: 3993 Signs & advertising specialties

(G-573)
PAPERWORKS INDUSTRIES INC
2900 Mclane Rd (13027-1319)
PHONE...................913 621-0922
Ronald Jenkins, *Principal*
EMP: 12
SALES (est): 2MM **Privately Held**
SIC: 3999 2671 Barber & beauty shop equipment; packaging paper & plastics film, coated & laminated

GEOGRAPHIC SECTION

Ballston Spa - Saratoga County (G-598)

(G-574)
PATIENT PORTAL TECH INC (PA)
8276 Willett Pkwy Ste 200 (13027-1328)
PHONE.....................315 638-2030
Brian Kelly, *CEO*
John O'Mara, *President*
Thomas Hagan, *CFO*
Kevin Kelly, *Director*
EMP: 19
SALES (est): 7.1MM **Publicly Held**
WEB: www.gambinoapparel.com
SIC: 7372 Prepackaged software

(G-575)
SPECIALIZED PACKG GROUP INC (DH)
Also Called: Paperworks
2900 Mclane Rd (13027-1319)
PHONE.....................315 638-4355
Carlton Highsmith, *Chairman*
Elizabeth Emig-Rosekrans, *Finance*
▲ **EMP:** 2
SALES (est): 50MM
SALES (corp-wide): 18.3B **Privately Held**
SIC: 2653 2657 Corrugated & solid fiber boxes; folding paperboard boxes
HQ: Paperworks Industries, Inc.
40 Monument Rd Ste 200
Bala Cynwyd PA 19004
215 984-7000

(G-576)
SPECIALIZED PACKG RADISSON LLC
8800 Sixty Rd (13027-1235)
PHONE.....................315 638-4355
Robert Gariepy, *COO*
Basciano Leo, *Plant Mgr*
Elizabeth Emig-Rosekrans, *Finance Dir*
Brenda Chapman, *Human Res Dir*
Tom Saylor, *Sales Executive*
EMP: 150 **EST:** 1998
SALES (est): 38.8MM
SALES (corp-wide): 18.3B **Privately Held**
SIC: 2653 2657 Boxes, solid fiber: made from purchased materials; folding paperboard boxes
HQ: The Specialized Packaging Group Inc
2900 Mclane Rd
Baldwinsville NY 13027
315 638-4355

(G-577)
SSAC INC
8242 Loop Rd (13027-1391)
PHONE.....................800 843-8848
Fax: 315 638-0333
EMP: 21
SALES (est): 3.3MM **Privately Held**
SIC: 3625 Mfg Relays/Industrial Controls

(G-578)
SYRASOFT LLC
6 Canton St (13027-2300)
PHONE.....................315 708-0341
Fax: 315 708-0819
Thomas Gardener, *Partner*
EMP: 10
SALES (est): 1MM **Privately Held**
WEB: www.syrasoft.com
SIC: 7372 7371 Prepackaged software; custom computer programming services

Ballston Lake
Saratoga County

(G-579)
ASTRO CHEMICAL COMPANY INC
3 Mill Rd (12019-2022)
P.O. Box 1250 (12019-0250)
PHONE.....................518 399-5338
Fax: 518 399-8859
Duane A Ball, *Ch of Bd*
Scott Fuller, *VP Opers*
Jay Arnold, *Manager*
▲ **EMP:** 20
SQ FT: 24,000
SALES (est): 5.7MM **Privately Held**
WEB: www.astrochemical.com
SIC: 2821 Epoxy resins

(G-580)
BENNETT STAIR COMPANY INC
1021 State Route 50 (12019-1915)
PHONE.....................518 384-1554
Fax: 518 384-1555
Dave Bennett, *President*
EMP: 8
SQ FT: 2,800
SALES (est): 650K **Privately Held**
SIC: 2431 Staircases, stairs & railings

(G-581)
CBM FABRICATIONS INC
15 Westside Dr (12019-2025)
PHONE.....................518 399-8023
Fax: 518 399-8064
Charles B McCormack II, *Ch of Bd*
Margaret Spoonogle, *Administration*
EMP: 30
SQ FT: 8,100
SALES (est): 8.6MM **Privately Held**
WEB: www.cbmfab.com
SIC: 3441 7692 3599 3444 Fabricated structural metal; welding repair; machine shop, jobbing & repair; sheet metalwork

(G-582)
LAKESIDE CIDER MILL FARM INC
336 Schauber Rd (12019-2104)
PHONE.....................518 399-8359
Fax: 518 399-6907
Richard Pearce, *President*
Jeffrey Pearce, *Vice Pres*
EMP: 8 **EST:** 1944
SQ FT: 5,000
SALES (est): 1MM **Privately Held**
SIC: 2099 5812 5431 Cider, nonalcoholic; eating places; vegetable stands or markets

(G-583)
MERCURY PEN COMPANY INC
245 Eastline Rd (12019-1810)
PHONE.....................518 899-9653
Fax: 518 899-9657
Jody Gentilesco, *President*
▲ **EMP:** 7 **EST:** 1946
SQ FT: 5,000
SALES (est): 216.6K **Privately Held**
WEB: www.mercurypen.com
SIC: 3951 Ball point pens & parts; penholders & parts; pencils & pencil parts, mechanical

(G-584)
MTS SYSTEMS CORPORATION
30 Gleneagles Blvd (12019-1014)
PHONE.....................518 899-2140
EMP: 116
SALES (corp-wide): 563.9MM **Publicly Held**
SIC: 3829 Measuring & controlling devices
PA: Mts Systems Corporation
14000 Technology Dr
Eden Prairie MN 55344
952 937-4000

(G-585)
NORTHEAST TONER INC
26 Walden Gln Fl 2 (12019-9234)
PHONE.....................518 899-5545
Gail Trietiak, *President*
Paul Trietiak, *Vice Pres*
EMP: 7
SALES (est): 800K **Privately Held**
SIC: 3955 Print cartridges for laser & other computer printers

(G-586)
SIXNET LLC
331 Ushers Rd Ste 14 (12019-1546)
P.O. Box 767, Clifton Park (12065-0767)
PHONE.....................518 877-5173
Fax: 518 877-8346
Steve Schoenberg, *CEO*
Stuart Eaton, *Vice Pres*
Rake W Jiang, *Vice Pres*
Mark Loperano, *Opers Staff*
Ryan Melchert, *Opers Staff*
EMP: 80
SQ FT: 20,000
SALES (est): 18.4MM
SALES (corp-wide): 1.8B **Privately Held**
WEB: www.sixnetio.com
SIC: 3823 Computer interface equipment for industrial process control
HQ: Red Lion Controls, Inc.
20 Willow Springs Cir
York PA 17406
717 767-6961

(G-587)
SIXNET HOLDINGS LLC
331 Ushers Rd Ste 10 (12019-1546)
PHONE.....................518 877-5173
Jason Koeferl, *Marketing Staff*
Hilton Nicholson,
Jason Koeserl, *Administration*
▲ **EMP:** 22
SALES (est): 12.1MM
SALES (corp-wide): 1.8B **Privately Held**
SIC: 3823 Industrial instrmnts msrmnt display/control process variable
HQ: Red Lion Controls, Inc.
20 Willow Springs Cir
York PA 17406
717 767-6961

(G-588)
TJB SUNSHINE ENTERPRISES
6 Redwood Dr (12019-2631)
PHONE.....................518 384-6483
Tom Brundige, *President*
EMP: 14
SALES (est): 1MM **Privately Held**
SIC: 2842 Window cleaning preparations

Ballston Spa
Saratoga County

(G-589)
ADVANCED COMFORT SYSTEMS INC
Also Called: ACS
12b Commerce Dr (12020-3631)
PHONE.....................518 884-8444
Fax: 518 884-8411
Roger M Kerr, *President*
Ray Hickey, *Sales Staff*
Kitty Stake, *Manager*
EMP: 10
SALES (est): 1.7MM **Privately Held**
WEB: www.advancedcomfortsys.com
SIC: 7372 1742 Application computer software; insulation, buildings

(G-590)
ALBATROS NORTH AMERICA INC
Also Called: Sepsa North America
6 Mccrea Hill Rd (12020-5515)
PHONE.....................518 381-7100
John Hanrahan, *CEO*
Nicholas Fuster, *President*
William D Kolberg, *Finance*
▲ **EMP:** 45
SQ FT: 36,000
SALES (est): 10.4MM
SALES (corp-wide): 533.5MM **Privately Held**
WEB: www.sepsa.es
SIC: 3679 3699 Static power supply converters for electronic applications; security control equipment & systems
HQ: Albatros SI
Calle De Albatros (Pol Ind La Estaci),
7 - 9
Pinto 28320
914 957-000

(G-591)
ALLYTEX LLC
540 Acland Blvd (12020-3074)
PHONE.....................518 376-7539
Alison Arakelian,
EMP: 5
SALES (est): 400.6K **Privately Held**
SIC: 2311 Men's & boys' suits & coats

(G-592)
BURNT HILLS FABRICATORS INC
318 Charlton Rd B (12020-3412)
P.O. Box 2, Burnt Hills (12027-0002)
PHONE.....................518 885-1115
Fax: 518 885-0526
James Fantauzzi, *President*
EMP: 15
SQ FT: 7,000
SALES (est): 1.8MM **Privately Held**
SIC: 3441 Fabricated structural metal

(G-593)
DIGITAL IMAGING TECH LLC
425 Eastline Rd D (12020-3617)
PHONE.....................518 885-4400
Fax: 518 885-4423
Michael Marino, *Mng Member*
Richard Siciliano,
EMP: 6
SQ FT: 5,000
SALES (est): 1MM **Privately Held**
WEB: www.digimtech.com
SIC: 2752 Commercial printing, lithographic

(G-594)
DIT PRINTS INCORPORATED
Also Called: Digital Imiging Technologies
425 Eastline Rd Ste D (12020-3617)
PHONE.....................518 885-4400
Deborah Libratore Le Blanc, *President*
Paul Le Blanc, *General Mgr*
EMP: 5
SQ FT: 2,400
SALES (est): 458.7K **Privately Held**
SIC: 2759 Commercial printing

(G-595)
DURA-MILL INC
Also Called: Newco Products Division
16 Stonebreak Rd (12020-4479)
PHONE.....................518 899-2255
Fax: 518 899-7869
Richard J Walrath, *President*
David Walrath, *Vice Pres*
Suzanne Walrath, *Accounting Mgr*
EMP: 33
SALES (est): 8.2MM **Privately Held**
WEB: www.duramill.com
SIC: 3545 5085 Cutting tools for machine tools; industrial supplies; abrasives; bearings, bushings, wheels & gears; industrial wheels

(G-596)
ELECTRIC BOAT CORPORATION
350 Atomic Project Rd (12020-2817)
PHONE.....................518 884-1270
EMP: 91
SALES (corp-wide): 31.4B **Publicly Held**
SIC: 3731 Submarines, building & repairing
HQ: Electric Boat Corporation
75 Eastern Point Rd
Groton CT 06340

(G-597)
GLOBALFOUNDRIES US INC
107 Hermes Rd (12020-4534)
PHONE.....................408 462-3900
James Depasquale, *Finance Mgr*
Norman Armour, *Branch Mgr*
Al Frank, *Manager*
Doug Rust, *Manager*
Raghawendra Balgi, *Database Admin*
EMP: 19 **Privately Held**
SIC: 3369 3674 Nonferrous foundries; integrated circuits, semiconductor networks, etc.
HQ: Globalfoundries U.S. Inc.
2600 Great America Way
Santa Clara CA 95054
408 462-3900

(G-598)
GREAT AMERICAN AWNING & PATIO
43 Round Lake Rd (12020)
PHONE.....................518 899-2300
Frank Rasalik, *President*
EMP: 15

Ballston Spa - Saratoga County (G-599)

SALES (est): 1.2MM **Privately Held**
SIC: 3271 Blocks, concrete: chimney or fireplace

(G-599)
HARVEST TECHNOLOGIES INC
36 Featherfoil Way (12020-4371)
PHONE.................................518 899-7124
Donna Morris, *Partner*
Turk Ellis, *Partner*
EMP: 2
SALES: 2MM **Privately Held**
SIC: 2611 Pulp manufactured from waste or recycled paper

(G-600)
JOHNSON CONTROLS INC
339 Brownell Rd (12020-3705)
PHONE.................................518 884-8313
David Bardsley, *Branch Mgr*
EMP: 95 **Privately Held**
SIC: 2531 Seats, automobile
HQ: Johnson Controls, Inc.
  5757 N Green Bay Ave
  Milwaukee WI 53209
  414 524-1200

(G-601)
LANE ENTERPRISES INC
825 State Route 67 (12020-3604)
PHONE.................................518 885-4385
M J Cathers, *Branch Mgr*
EMP: 20
SALES (corp-wide): 71.7MM **Privately Held**
WEB: www.lanepipe.com
SIC: 3444 3449 Pipe, sheet metal; miscellaneous metalwork
PA: Lane Enterprises, Inc.
  3905 Hartzdale Dr Ste 514
  Camp Hill PA 17011
  717 761-8175

(G-602)
MERIDIAN MANUFACTURING INC
27 Kent St Ste 103a (12020-1543)
PHONE.................................518 885-0450
Paul Michael, *President*
Robin Guarino, *Vice Pres*
EMP: 7
SQ FT: 8,100
SALES (est): 1MM **Privately Held**
SIC: 3599 Machine shop, jobbing & repair

(G-603)
MESSENGER PRESS
1826 Amsterdam Rd (12020-3323)
P.O. Box 376 (12020-0376)
PHONE.................................518 885-9231
Ed Bellamy, *Owner*
EMP: 8
SALES (est): 460K **Privately Held**
SIC: 2752 7336 Lithographic Commercial Printing/Commercial Art/Graphic Design

(G-604)
NORTH AMERICAN SVCS GROUP LLC (HQ)
Also Called: North American Service Group
1240 Saratoga Rd (12020-3500)
PHONE.................................518 885-1820
Fax: 518 885-7638
Frank Zilka, *President*
Rick Matteson, *General Mgr*
Will Hearn, *Regional Mgr*
Tim Zilka, *COO*
Michael Pickering, *Safety Dir*
EMP: 15
SQ FT: 40,000
SALES (est): 4.1MM
SALES (corp-wide): 94MM **Privately Held**
SIC: 3443 1799 Cryogenic tanks, for liquids & gases; service station equipment installation, maintenance & repair
PA: North American Industrial Services, Inc.
  1240 Saratoga Rd
  Ballston Spa NY 12020
  518 885-1820

(G-605)
NORTHWIND GRAPHICS
2453 State Route 9 (12020-4407)
PHONE.................................518 899-9651
Steve Richardson, *Owner*
EMP: 5
SQ FT: 3,500
SALES (est): 420.9K **Privately Held**
SIC: 2759 Screen printing

(G-606)
PARTS UNLIMITED INC
Also Called: Drag Specialties
10 Mccrea Hill Rd (12020-5515)
PHONE.................................518 885-7500
Mike Cornell, *Manager*
▲ **EMP:** 95
SALES (est): 12.2MM **Privately Held**
SIC: 3714 Acceleration equipment, motor vehicle

(G-607)
PREMIUM BLDG COMPONENTS INC
831 Rt 67 Bldg 46 (12020)
PHONE.................................518 885-0194
John Buyaskas, *Principal*
EMP: 20
SALES (corp-wide): 7.9MM **Privately Held**
SIC: 3713 Truck & bus bodies
PA: Premium Building Components, Inc.
  527 Queensbury Ave
  Queensbury NY 12804
  518 792-0189

(G-608)
SAND HILL INDUSTRIES INC
Also Called: T-Shirt Graphics
12 Grove St (12020-1814)
PHONE.................................518 885-7991
Fax: 518 885-8068
Dennis Albright, *President*
Eileen Albright, *Vice Pres*
EMP: 6
SQ FT: 10,000
SALES (est): 560K **Privately Held**
WEB: www.t-shirtgraphics.com
SIC: 2759 2395 2752 3081 Screen printing; embroidery & art needlework; commercial printing, offset; unsupported plastics film & sheet

(G-609)
SPECIALTY SILICONE PDTS INC
Also Called: SSP
3 Mccrea Hill Rd (12020-5511)
PHONE.................................518 885-8826
Fax: 518 885-4682
Daniel Natarelli, *CEO*
Randall Putnam, *President*
Paul Decaprio, *COO*
Randy Putnam, *COO*
Patricia S Babbie, *Senior VP*
▲ **EMP:** 45
SQ FT: 37,000
SALES (est): 14.6MM **Privately Held**
WEB: www.sspinc.com
SIC: 2869 2822 3714 2992 Silicones; silicone rubbers; motor vehicle parts & accessories; lubricating oils & greases

(G-610)
STEWARTS PROCESSING CORP (PA)
2907 State Route 9 (12020-4201)
P.O. Box 435, Saratoga Springs (12866-0435)
PHONE.................................518 581-1200
Gary C Dake, *Ch of Bd*
Shane Nolan, *Plant Supt*
Randy Mercier, *Buyer*
Michael Cocca, *Treasurer*
David Farr, *Asst Treas*
EMP: 85
SALES: 68.2MM **Privately Held**
SIC: 2026 2024 2086 Fluid milk; ice cream & ice milk; soft drinks: packaged in cans, bottles, etc.

(G-611)
WINDOW TECH SYSTEMS INC
15 Old Stonebreak Rd (12020-4900)
P.O. Box 2260 (12020-8260)
PHONE.................................518 899-9000
Fax: 518 899-4104
Philip H Frederick, *President*
Dave Bangert, *President*
Tracy Carpenter, *Manager*
Tracy Mason, *Admin Asst*
EMP: 22 **EST:** 1952
SQ FT: 30,000
SALES (est): 4.9MM **Privately Held**
WEB: www.windowtechsystems.net
SIC: 3442 3089 Screens, window, metal; windows, plastic

Barker
Niagara County

(G-612)
ATLANTIC TRANSFORMER INC
1674 Quaker Rd (14012-9616)
P.O. Box 276 (14012-0276)
PHONE.................................716 795-3258
Fax: 716 795-3101
John Khorrami, *President*
EMP: 10
SQ FT: 8,500
SALES (est): 400K **Privately Held**
WEB: www.mgs4u.com
SIC: 3677 Electronic transformers

(G-613)
JT PRECISION INC
8701 Haight Rd (14012-9630)
PHONE.................................716 795-3860
Jeff Thuman Sr, *President*
Brian Rakfeldt, *General Mgr*
Richard Meyers, *Principal*
Sarah Munn, *Principal*
Cristine O'Keefe, *Officer*
EMP: 34
SALES (est): 3MM **Privately Held**
SIC: 3714 Motor vehicle engines & parts

Barneveld
Oneida County

(G-614)
JET SEW CORPORATION
8119 State Route 12 (13304-2105)
PHONE.................................315 896-2683
Edward Wiehl, *President*
EMP: 15
SQ FT: 65,000
SALES (est): 550K **Privately Held**
WEB: www.jetsew.com
SIC: 3599 Custom machinery

(G-615)
MOHAWK ELECTRO TECHNIQUES INC
8063 State Route 12 (13304-2102)
PHONE.................................315 896-2661
Fax: 315 896-2954
Lee Broomfield, *President*
Fred Ingo, *Vice Pres*
Mike Locke, *Manager*
Kathy Hite, *Officer*
EMP: 90
SQ FT: 5,000
SALES (est): 10.8MM **Privately Held**
SIC: 3677 Coil windings, electronic; electronic transformers

(G-616)
ROLLING STAR MANUFACTURING INC
125 Liberty Ln (13304-2537)
P.O. Box 471 (13304-0471)
PHONE.................................315 896-4767
Fax: 315 896-5055
Jamie R Servello, *President*
Dean Beck, *Vice Pres*
Melissa Parzych, *Manager*
EMP: 20
SQ FT: 2,728
SALES (est): 3.8MM **Privately Held**
WEB: www.customizedtrailers.com
SIC: 3799 Trailers & trailer equipment

(G-617)
SAMPO INC
Also Called: Donmaar Enterprises
119 Remsen Rd (13304-2407)
P.O. Box 109, Rome (13442-0109)
PHONE.................................315 896-2606
Brian Butts, *President*
EMP: 23
SQ FT: 12,038
SALES (est): 2MM **Privately Held**
WEB: www.sampoinc.com
SIC: 3949 2298 Fishing equipment; cordage & twine

(G-618)
SQUARE STAMPING MFG CORP
108 Old Remsen Rd (13304)
PHONE.................................315 896-2641
Fax: 315 896-2734
David Allen, *President*
Dan Hart, *General Mgr*
Edward Allen III, *Treasurer*
Jeffrey Gouger, *Treasurer*
Beth McGovern, *Office Mgr*
EMP: 35 **EST:** 1926
SQ FT: 25,000
SALES (est): 7.1MM **Privately Held**
WEB: www.squarestamping.com
SIC: 3469 Stamping metal for the trade

Barrytown
Dutchess County

(G-619)
STATION HILL OF BARRYTOWN
120 Station Hill Rd (12507-5018)
PHONE.................................845 758-5293
Fax: 845 758-8163
George Quasha, *President*
Susan Quasha, *Vice Pres*
Siu Yuen, *Marketing Staff*
Sam Truitt, *Director*
EMP: 6
SALES (est): 430K **Privately Held**
SIC: 2731 5961 Book publishing; book club, mail order; record &/or tape (music or video) club, mail order

Barryville
Sullivan County

(G-620)
N A R ASSOCIATES INC
128 Rte 55 (12719)
P.O. Box 233 (12719-0233)
PHONE.................................845 557-8713
Fax: 845 557-6770
Nick A Roes, *President*
Nancy Bennett, *Vice Pres*
EMP: 6
SALES (est): 537.5K **Privately Held**
WEB: www.nickroes.com
SIC: 2731 Book publishing

Batavia
Genesee County

(G-621)
ALPINA FOODS INC
5011 Agpark Dr W (14020-3446)
PHONE.................................855 886-1914
Carlos Mejia, *Principal*
EMP: 13
SALES (est): 1.7MM
SALES (corp-wide): 642.8MM **Privately Held**
SIC: 2023 Dry, condensed, evaporated dairy products
PA: Alpina Productos Alimenticios S A
  Carrera 4 7 99
  Sopo
  160 516-16

(G-622)
AMADA TOOL AMERICA INC
4 Treadeasy Ave Ste A (14020-3010)
PHONE.................................585 344-3900
Hitoshi Iizuka, *President*
Michael Guerin, *Corp Secy*
Don Grower, *Manager*
▲ **EMP:** 55
SQ FT: 50,000
SALES (est): 10.6MM
SALES (corp-wide): 2.6B **Privately Held**
SIC: 3544 Special dies & tools

HQ: Amada North America, Inc
7025 Firestone Blvd
Buena Park CA 90621

(G-623)
AUTOMOTIVE LLC
4320 Federal Dr (14020-4104)
PHONE..................................248 728-8642
Douglas Delgrosso, *CEO*
EMP: 15
SALES (est): 2.1MM
SALES (corp-wide): 1.8B **Privately Held**
WEB: www.automotivecorporation.com
SIC: 3465 Body parts, automobile: stamped metal
HQ: Chassix, Inc.
300 Galleria Officentre
Southfield MI 48034
248 728-8642

(G-624)
BATAVIA PRESS LLC
3817 W Main Street Rd (14020-9402)
PHONE..................................585 343-4429
Becky Almeter, *Partner*
Robert Hodgins,
EMP: 32
SALES (est): 1.4MM **Privately Held**
SIC: 2752 7389 2759 Business form & card printing, lithographic; document embossing; engrossing: diplomas, resolutions, etc.; invitation & stationery printing & engraving; security certificates: engraved

(G-625)
BILL SHEA ENTERPRISES INC
Also Called: Deluxe Machine & Tool Co
8825 Alexander Rd (14020-9581)
PHONE..................................585 343-2284
Fax: 585 343-0480
William Shea, *President*
Ken Lowell, *General Mgr*
Steven Shea, *Vice Pres*
EMP: 11
SQ FT: 20,000
SALES (est): 880K **Privately Held**
WEB: www.trojanloaders.com
SIC: 3544 3599 Special dies, tools, jigs & fixtures; machine shop, jobbing & repair

(G-626)
BRACH MACHINE INC
4814 Ellicott Street Rd (14020-3420)
PHONE..................................585 343-9134
Fax: 585 343-1292
William H Brach, *President*
Nancy E Brach, *Vice Pres*
EMP: 12
SQ FT: 15,000
SALES (est): 1.7MM **Privately Held**
WEB: www.brachmachine.com
SIC: 3469 Machine parts, stamped or pressed metal

(G-627)
CHAPIN INTERNATIONAL INC
700 Ellicott St (14020-3744)
P.O. Box 549 (14021-0549)
PHONE..................................585 343-3140
Andris K Chapin, *Ch of Bd*
James W Campbell, *President*
James Grant, *Vice Pres*
William Kegler, *Materials Mgr*
Greg Klein, *Engineer*
◆ **EMP:** 225
SQ FT: 710,000
SALES (est): 27.5MM
SALES (corp-wide): 54.2MM **Privately Held**
SIC: 3499 3524 3085 3563 Aerosol valves, metal; lawn & garden equipment; plastics bottles; air & gas compressors
PA: Chapin Manufacturing, Inc
700 Ellicott St Ste 3
Batavia NY 14020
585 343-3140

(G-628)
CHAPIN MANUFACTURING INC (PA)
700 Ellicott St Ste 3 (14020-3794)
P.O. Box 549 (14021-0549)
PHONE..................................585 343-3140
Fax: 585 344-1775
James W Campbell, *Ch of Bd*
Andris K Chapin, *Ch of Bd*
James Grant, *Vice Pres*
Robert C Mathis, *Vice Pres*
Chuck Mattes, *Vice Pres*
◆ **EMP:** 220
SQ FT: 710,000
SALES (est): 54.2MM **Privately Held**
WEB: www.chapinmfg.com
SIC: 3499 3524 3085 3563 Aerosol valves, metal; lawn & garden equipment; plastics bottles; air & gas compressors; spraying outfits: metals, paints & chemicals (compressor); spreaders, fertilizer

(G-629)
CONSOLIDATED CONTAINER CO LLC
Also Called: Liquitane
14 Hall St (14020-3216)
PHONE..................................585 343-9351
Fax: 585 343-0086
Bob Henry, *Manager*
Michael Campbell, *Manager*
Robert Henri, *Manager*
Sharon Cummings, *Office Admin*
James Cervi, *Executive*
EMP: 15
SALES (corp-wide): 22B **Privately Held**
WEB: www.ccclic.com
SIC: 3089 Plastic containers, except foam
HQ: Consolidated Container Company, Llc
3101 Towercreek Pkwy Se
Atlanta GA 30339
678 742-4600

(G-630)
ENERGY PANEL STRUCTURES INC
Also Called: Fingerlakes Construction
5773 E Main Street Rd (14020-9621)
PHONE..................................585 343-1777
Fax: 585 344-3859
Kirt Burghdorf, *Vice Pres*
EMP: 8
SALES (corp-wide): 700K **Privately Held**
SIC: 3448 2452 Prefabricated metal buildings; prefabricated wood buildings
HQ: Energy Panel Structures, Inc.
603 N Van Gordon Ave
Graettinger IA 51342
712 859-3219

(G-631)
EXIDE TECHNOLOGIES
Also Called: Exide Batteries
4330 Commerce Dr (14020-4102)
PHONE..................................585 344-0656
George Hoffman, *Site Mgr*
Sam Manuele, *Sales/Mktg Mgr*
Deborah Cravatta, *Manager*
EMP: 9
SALES (corp-wide): 2.8B **Privately Held**
WEB: www.exideworld.com
SIC: 3691 Lead acid batteries (storage batteries)
PA: Exide Technologies
13000 Deerfield Pkwy # 200
Milton GA 30004
678 566-9000

(G-632)
FONTRICK DOOR INC
9 Apollo Dr (14020-3001)
PHONE..................................585 345-6032
Fax: 585 345-6033
Michael J Fontaine, *CEO*
Jacob Mingle, *Engineer*
Judy Brown, *Bookkeeper*
EMP: 30
SQ FT: 26,000
SALES (est): 5.2MM **Privately Held**
WEB: www.fontrickdoor.com
SIC: 2431 1751 Doors & door parts & trim, wood; cabinet building & installation

(G-633)
FRITO-LAY NORTH AMERICA INC
8063 Kelsey Rd (14020-9433)
PHONE..................................585 343-5456
Keith Matteson, *Branch Mgr*
EMP: 20
SALES (corp-wide): 63B **Publicly Held**
WEB: www.fritolay.com
SIC: 2096 Potato chips & similar snacks
HQ: Frito-Lay North America, Inc.
7701 Legacy Dr
Plano TX 75024

(G-634)
GENESEE PRECISION INC
4300 Commerce Dr (14020-4102)
PHONE..................................585 344-0385
Robert Shepard, *President*
Patricia Vincent, *Corp Secy*
Gregory Almeter, *Vice Pres*
Patty Drew, *Admin Asst*
▲ **EMP:** 43
SQ FT: 24,000
SALES (est): 4.1MM **Privately Held**
SIC: 3544 3089 Special dies, tools, jigs & fixtures; injection molding of plastics

(G-635)
GEORGIA-PACIFIC CORRUGARED LLC
Also Called: Majic Corrugated Inc
4 Etreadeasy Ave (14020)
PHONE..................................585 343-3800
Fax: 585 343-5236
Andrew Perkins, *Manager*
EMP: 65
SALES (est): 7.9MM
SALES (corp-wide): 26.7B **Privately Held**
WEB: www.gp.com
SIC: 2611 Pulp manufactured from waste or recycled paper
HQ: Georgia-Pacific Llc
133 Peachtree St Ne # 4810
Atlanta GA 30303
404 652-4000

(G-636)
GRAHAM CORPORATION (PA)
20 Florence Ave (14020-3318)
PHONE..................................585 343-2216
Fax: 585 343-1097
James J Malvaso, *Ch of Bd*
James R Lines, *President*
Alan E Smith, *Vice Pres*
Michele Engle, *Buyer*
Jeffrey F Glajch, *CFO*
◆ **EMP:** 277
SQ FT: 45,000
SALES: 90MM **Publicly Held**
WEB: www.graham-mfg.com
SIC: 3563 3585 3443 Vacuum pumps, except laboratory; compressors for refrigeration & air conditioning equipment; condensers, refrigeration; heat exchangers, condensers & components; heat exchangers, plate type; heat exchangers: coolers (after, inter), condensers, etc.

(G-637)
HANSON AGGREGATES EAST LLC
6895 Ellicott Street Rd (14020)
PHONE..................................585 344-1810
Scott Wheaton, *Manager*
EMP: 15
SQ FT: 6,406
SALES (corp-wide): 14.4B **Privately Held**
SIC: 3273 Ready-mixed concrete
HQ: Hanson Aggregates East Llc
3131 Rdu Center Dr
Morrisville NC 27560
919 380-2500

(G-638)
HEATH MANUFACTURING COMPANY
Also Called: Heath Outdoors Products
700 Ellicott St (14020-3744)
PHONE..................................800 444-3140
EMP: 6
SALES (corp-wide): 54.2MM **Privately Held**
SIC: 2048 Bird food, prepared
HQ: Heath Manufacturing Company
140 Mill St Ste A
Coopersville MI 49404
616 997-8181

(G-639)
HODGINS ENGRAVING CO INC
3817 W Main Street Rd (14020-9402)
PHONE..................................585 343-4444
Fax: 585 343-0412
Robert Hodgins, *President*
Elaine Skoczylas, *Purch Agent*
Becky Hodgins, *Cust Mgr*
Kathleen Dixson, *Comms Mgr*
Amy Fuchs, *Director*
◆ **EMP:** 70
SQ FT: 36,000
SALES (est): 13MM **Privately Held**
WEB: www.hodginsengraving.com
SIC: 3555 3953 Printing trades machinery; marking devices

(G-640)
INTERSTATE CHEMICAL CO INC
4 Treadeasy Ave (14020-3089)
PHONE..................................585 344-2822
Fax: 585 344-2608
Mark Shea, *Sales Staff*
Jeff Heverly, *Branch Mgr*
Jeff Heverley, *Executive*
EMP: 11
SQ FT: 72,000
SALES (corp-wide): 436.3MM **Privately Held**
WEB: www.interstatechemical.com
SIC: 2819 Industrial inorganic chemicals
PA: Interstate Chemical Company, Inc.
2797 Freedland Rd
Hermitage PA 16148
724 981-3771

(G-641)
LICKITY SPLITS
238 East Ave (14020-2704)
PHONE..................................585 345-6091
Fred Hamilton, *Partner*
Craig Hargrades, *Partner*
EMP: 8
SALES (est): 508K **Privately Held**
SIC: 2024 Ice cream & frozen desserts

(G-642)
MONDELEZ GLOBAL LLC
Also Called: Nabisco
4303 Federal Dr (14020-4105)
PHONE..................................585 345-3300
Phil Barter, *Branch Mgr*
Anthony Del Duca, *Maintence Staff*
EMP: 10
SALES (corp-wide): 29.6B **Publicly Held**
SIC: 2099 5141 Food preparations; groceries, general line
HQ: Mondelez Global Llc
3 Parkway N Ste 300
Deerfield IL 60015
847 943-4000

(G-643)
N Y WESTERN CONCRETE CORP
638 E Main St (14020-2812)
PHONE..................................585 343-6850
Fax: 585 343-8440
Joseph Penepent, *President*
Eugene Penepent, *Vice Pres*
Vincent Penepent, *Treasurer*
Jeanne Penepent, *Manager*
EMP: 5 **EST:** 1950
SQ FT: 2,000
SALES (est): 1.3MM **Privately Held**
SIC: 3273 Ready-mixed concrete

(G-644)
O-AT-KA MILK PRODUCTS COOP INC (PA)
700 Ellicott St (14020-3744)
P.O. Box 718 (14021-0718)
PHONE..................................585 343-0536
Fax: 585 343-4473
Robert Hall, *CEO*
Herbert Nobles, *Ch of Bd*
Joseph Valenti, *General Mgr*
Dan Wolf, *COO*
Clyde Rutherford, *Vice Pres*
◆ **EMP:** 277 **EST:** 1956
SQ FT: 205,000
SALES: 295.5MM **Privately Held**
WEB: www.oatkamilk.com
SIC: 2023 2021 2026 Concentrated skim milk; evaporated milk; dried nonfat milk; creamery butter; fluid milk

Batavia - Genesee County (G-645)

(G-645)
PINNACLE MANUFACTURING CO INC
56 Harvester Ave (14020-3357)
PHONE.....................585 343-5664
Fax: 585 344-3099
Kim Kisiel, *President*
Kevin Kisiel, *Vice Pres*
Luis Pulvino, *Plant Mgr*
Kevin Bishoff, *Foreman/Supr*
Lois Kisiel, *Controller*
▲ EMP: 25
SQ FT: 35,000
SALES (est): 5.2MM Privately Held
WEB: www.pinnaclemanufacturing.com
SIC: 3363 3364 Aluminum die-castings; zinc & zinc-base alloy die-castings

(G-646)
PROTECH AUTOMATION LLC
Also Called: Jiftt Tite
1 Mill St Ste 205 (14020-3141)
PHONE.....................585 344-3201
Scott Baubie,
EMP: 7
SALES (est): 714.6K
SALES (corp-wide): 17.3MM Privately Held
WEB: www.jiffytite.com
SIC: 3714 Motor vehicle body components & frame
PA: Jiffy-Tite Co. Inc.
    4437 Walden Ave
    Lancaster NY 14086
    716 681-7200

(G-647)
SEVEN SPRINGS GRAVEL PDTS LLC
8479 Seven Springs Rd (14020-9632)
PHONE.....................585 343-4336
Mike Doyle,
Carmen Pariso,
EMP: 6
SALES (est): 570K Privately Held
SIC: 1442 Gravel mining

(G-648)
STRONG FORGE & FABRICATION
20 Liberty St (14020-3208)
P.O. Box 803 (14021-0803)
PHONE.....................585 343-5251
Mitchell Strong, *President*
Debbie Buchinger, *Manager*
Brian Delillo, *Manager*
EMP: 37
SALES (est): 8MM Privately Held
WEB: www.strongforge.com
SIC: 3599 Machine shop, jobbing & repair

(G-649)
SUMMIT LUBRICANTS INC
4d Treadeasy Ave (14020-3010)
P.O. Box 966 (14021-0966)
PHONE.....................585 815-0798
Fax: 585 344-4302
Ronald Krol, *President*
Allan Ulrich, *Opers Mgr*
Brian Caputi, *Accountant*
Donna Kurek, *Manager*
Danielle Brinkman, *Administration*
▼ EMP: 47
SQ FT: 50,000
SALES (est): 19MM
SALES (corp-wide): 737.5MM Publicly Held
WEB: www.summitlubricants.com
SIC: 2911 Greases, lubricating
PA: Quaker Chemical Corporation
    901 E Hector St
    Conshohocken PA 19428
    610 832-4000

(G-650)
TOMPKINS METAL FINISHING INC
6 Apollo Dr (14020-3002)
PHONE.....................585 344-2600
Allen C Tompkins, *President*
John Tompkins, *Vice Pres*
Bill Schuler, *Safety Mgr*
Jim McCarrick, *QC Mgr*
EMP: 80
SALES (est): 20.1MM Privately Held
SIC: 3559 Metal finishing equipment for plating, etc.

(G-651)
TRACO MANUFACTURING INC
4300 Commerce Dr (14020-4102)
PHONE.....................585 343-2434
Fax: 585 343-2881
Tracy Jachimowicz, *President*
Daniel Jachimowicz, *Vice Pres*
Dave Morrill, *Mfg Staff*
Gary Buchholz, *Regl Sales Mgr*
Vince Pilletteri, *Sales Engr*
EMP: 5
SQ FT: 16,500
SALES (est): 582K Privately Held
WEB: www.tracomfg.com
SIC: 2542 Partitions & fixtures, except wood

(G-652)
VISUAL IMPACT GRAPHICS INC
653 Ellicott St Ste 6 (14020-3746)
P.O. Box 236, Byron (14422-0236)
PHONE.....................585 548-7118
Fax: 585 548-7139
Tom Chapell, *President*
EMP: 6
SALES (est): 544.2K Privately Held
WEB: www.visualimpactonline.com
SIC: 3993 Signs & advertising specialties

Bath
Steuben County

(G-653)
BABCOCK CO INC
36 Delaware Ave (14810-1607)
PHONE.....................607 776-3341
Mark McConnell, *President*
J Ward McConnell, *Chairman*
EMP: 25
SQ FT: 107,000
SALES (est): 4.9MM Privately Held
SIC: 2499 Ladders, wood

(G-654)
BOMBARDIER TRNSP HOLDINGS USA
7940 State Route 415 (14810-7571)
PHONE.....................607 776-4791
Carl Drum, *Branch Mgr*
EMP: 60
SALES (corp-wide): 18.1B Privately Held
SIC: 3441 8711 3799 3585 Fabricated structural metal; engineering services; cars, off-highway: electric; refrigeration & heating equipment; electrical apparatus & equipment; electrical equipment & supplies
HQ: Bombardier Transportation (Holdings) Usa Inc.
    1501 Lebanon Church Rd
    Pittsburgh PA 15236
    412 655-5700

(G-655)
CLARK SPECIALTY CO INC
323 W Morris St (14810-1030)
PHONE.....................607 776-3193
Fax: 607 569-3694
James L Presley, *Ch of Bd*
Thomas Presley, *Vice Pres*
Robert Schuck, *Plant Mgr*
Gene Patterson, *Opers Staff*
Robert Abbey, *Purch Mgr*
EMP: 37 EST: 1946
SQ FT: 90,000
SALES (est): 7MM Privately Held
WEB: www.clarkspecialty.com
SIC: 2542 3444 Telephone booths: except wood; sheet metalwork

(G-656)
GATEHOUSE MEDIA LLC
Also Called: Steuben Courier Advocate
10 W Steuben St (14810-1512)
PHONE.....................607 776-2121
Fax: 607 776-3967
Karen Causer, *Manager*
EMP: 7
SQ FT: 3,700
SALES (corp-wide): 1.2B Publicly Held
WEB: www.gatehousemedia.com
SIC: 2711 Newspapers: publishing only, not printed on site
HQ: Gatehouse Media, Llc
    175 Sullys Trl Ste 300
    Pittsford NY 14534
    585 598-0030

(G-657)
HANGER PRSTHETCS & ORTHO INC
47 W Steuben St (14810-1540)
PHONE.....................607 776-8013
Erico Webster, *General Mgr*
EMP: 7
SALES (corp-wide): 500.5MM Privately Held
SIC: 3842 Orthopedic appliances
HQ: Hanger Prosthetics & Orthotics, Inc.
    10910 Main Dr
    Austin TX 78758
    512 777-3800

(G-658)
KEELER SERVICES
47 W Steuben St Ste 4 (14810-1540)
PHONE.....................607 776-5757
Fax: 607 776-5777
Mathew Keeler, *Owner*
EMP: 6
SQ FT: 6,270
SALES (est): 457.9K Privately Held
SIC: 3585 Heating & air conditioning combination units

(G-659)
KNIGHT STTLEMENT SAND GRAV LLC
7291 County Route 15 (14810-8245)
P.O. Box 191 (14810-0191)
PHONE.....................607 776-2048
Tom Roye, *Controller*
Bryan Dickson,
Brett Dickson,
L Jay Dickson,
EMP: 38
SQ FT: 9,408
SALES (est): 5.7MM Privately Held
SIC: 1442 Gravel mining

(G-660)
LANE ENTERPRISES INC
Also Called: Lane Metal Products
16 May St (14810)
PHONE.....................607 776-3366
Fax: 607 776-3899
Richard A Walter, *Manager*
EMP: 10
SQ FT: 18,416
SALES (corp-wide): 70.1MM Privately Held
WEB: www.lanepipe.com
SIC: 3443 Culverts, metal plate
PA: Lane Enterprises, Inc.
    3905 Hartzdale Dr Ste 514
    Camp Hill PA 17011
    717 761-8175

(G-661)
PHILIPS ELEC N AMER CORP
Philips Lighting
7265 State Route 54 (14810-9586)
PHONE.....................607 776-3692
Fax: 607 776-3892
EMP: 110
SALES (corp-wide): 26B Privately Held
WEB: www.usa.philips.com
SIC: 3645 3641 Residential lighting fixtures; electric lamps
HQ: Philips Electronics North America Corporation
    3000 Minuteman Rd Ms1203
    Andover MA 01810
    978 687-1501

(G-662)
SMART SYSTEMS INC
320 E Washington St (14810-1323)
P.O. Box 158, Bohemia (11716-0158)
PHONE.....................607 776-5380
Fax: 607 776-5383
Marven Smith, *President*
EMP: 20
SALES (est): 2.2MM Privately Held
WEB: www.smartsystemsinc.com
SIC: 3711 5012 Snow plows (motor vehicles), assembly of; truck bodies

Bay Shore
Suffolk County

(G-663)
A AND K MACHINE AND WELDING
20 Drexel Dr (11706-2202)
P.O. Box 713, Deer Park (11729-0713)
PHONE.....................631 231-2552
Fax: 631 231-1616
Kenneth Melin, *President*
EMP: 5
SQ FT: 6,000
SALES: 300K Privately Held
SIC: 3599 1799 5046 Machine & other job shop work; custom machinery; welding on site; commercial cooking & food service equipment

(G-664)
ABS TALKX INC
34 Cleveland Ave (11706-1223)
PHONE.....................631 254-9100
Ron Bregman, *President*
Chuck Hedge, *Opers Staff*
EMP: 8
SQ FT: 7,300
SALES (est): 890K Privately Held
SIC: 3661 5999 4813 Telephones & telephone apparatus; telephone equipment & systems; voice telephone communications

(G-665)
ADEPTRONICS INCORPORATED
Also Called: Ziptswitch
281 Skip Ln Ste C (11706-1215)
PHONE.....................631 667-0659
EMP: 6
SALES: 850K Privately Held
SIC: 3625 Mfg Relays/Industrial Controls

(G-666)
ADVANCED ENGINEERED PRODUCTS
25 Drexel Dr (11706-2234)
PHONE.....................631 435-3535
Douglas Davis, *President*
Ken Donahue, *CFO*
Peter Canese, *Controller*
EMP: 10 EST: 1998
SQ FT: 10,000
SALES (est): 742.2K Privately Held
SIC: 3542 5051 Machine tools, metal forming type; tubing, metal

(G-667)
AIR INDUSTRIES MACHINING CORP
1479 N Clinton Ave (11706-4051)
PHONE.....................631 968-5000
Peter D Rettaliata, *President*
Dario A Peragallo, *President*
Anthony Schiappa, *Project Dir*
Keith Hispanski, *Prdtn Mgr*
Nancy Meehan, *Purch Mgr*
▲ EMP: 172
SALES (est): 37.8MM
SALES (corp-wide): 80.4MM Publicly Held
SIC: 3728 Aircraft parts & equipment
PA: Air Industries Group
    360 Motor Pkwy Ste 100
    Hauppauge NY 11788
    631 881-4920

(G-668)
ALL STAR CARTS & VEHICLES INC
1565 5th Industrial Ct B (11706-3434)
PHONE.....................631 666-5581
Fax: 631 666-1319
Steven Kronrad, *President*
Robert Conrad, *Vice Pres*
Gregory Kronrad, *Vice Pres*
Robert Kronrad, *Vice Pres*
Syed Zadi, *Accountant*

GEOGRAPHIC SECTION
Bay Shore - Suffolk County (G-695)

EMP: 51
SQ FT: 25,000
SALES (est): 8.6MM **Privately Held**
WEB: www.allstarcarts.com
SIC: 2599 3792 3444 2451 Carts, restaurant equipment; travel trailers & campers; sheet metalwork; mobile homes

(G-669)
ALTEC DATACOM LLC
70 Corbin Ave Ste I (11706-1039)
PHONE 631 242-2417
Fax: 631 242-2475
John Andreala, *Office Mgr*
Abraham Mendez,
Teresa Mendez,
EMP: 8
SQ FT: 1,500
SALES (est): 867.1K **Privately Held**
SIC: 3679 Harness assemblies for electronic use: wire or cable

(G-670)
AMERICAN PRIDE FASTENERS LLC
195 S Fehr Way (11706-1207)
PHONE 631 940-8292
Lynda Zacpal, *President*
George W Hughes III, *Vice Pres*
Nicholas Zacpal, *QC Mgr*
Kathy Sheirdan, *Controller*
Terrance Dillon, *Sales Mgr*
▲ EMP: 20
SQ FT: 10,000
SALES (est): 4.2MM **Privately Held**
SIC: 3965 3452 5085 Fasteners; bolts, nuts, rivets & washers; fasteners & fastening equipment

(G-671)
ANTENNA & RADOME RES ASSOC (PA)
15 Harold Ct (11706-2220)
P.O. Box 113, Old Bethpage (11804-0113)
PHONE 631 231-8400
Florence Isaacson, *President*
Robert Isaacson, *Controller*
EMP: 50 EST: 1957
SQ FT: 20,000
SALES (est): 21.7MM **Privately Held**
WEB: www.arra.com
SIC: 3679 Microwave components

(G-672)
ARTISTIC IRONWORKS INC
94 Saxon Ave (11706-7005)
PHONE 631 665-4285
Rick Portera, *President*
EMP: 8
SQ FT: 5,500
SALES (est): 973.6K **Privately Held**
SIC: 3446 3312 2431 Stairs, fire escapes, balconies, railings & ladders; rails, steel or iron; staircases, stairs & railings

(G-673)
ASTRO ELECTROPLATING INC
171 4th Ave (11706-7303)
PHONE 631 968-0656
Neil Weinstein, *CEO*
Jennifer Calderone, *Human Resources*
Chris Myers, *Manager*
EMP: 37
SALES (est): 5.2MM **Privately Held**
SIC: 3471 Electroplating of metals or formed products

(G-674)
BAIRD MOLD MAKING INC
195 N Fehr Way Ste C (11706-1234)
PHONE 631 667-0322
Fax: 631 667-0324
John Baird, *President*
Henry Quintin, *Vice Pres*
▲ EMP: 6
SQ FT: 3,000
SALES (est): 823.4K **Privately Held**
SIC: 3089 Molding primary plastic; injection molding of plastics

(G-675)
BFG MARINE INC
200 Candlewood Rd (11706-2217)
PHONE 631 586-5500
Glenn Burgos, *President*
Ellis W Konkel III, *Vice Pres*

EMP: 16 EST: 1959
SQ FT: 20,000
SALES (est): 2.6MM **Privately Held**
WEB: www.bfgmarine.com
SIC: 3429 5085 Marine hardware; industrial supplies

(G-676)
BIMBO BAKERIES USA INC
1724 5th Ave (11706-3444)
PHONE 631 274-4906
Mark Reynolds, *Manager*
EMP: 110
SQ FT: 161,172
SALES (corp-wide): 13B **Privately Held**
SIC: 2051 Bread, cake & related products
HQ: Bimbo Bakeries Usa, Inc
255 Business Center Dr # 200
Horsham PA 19044
215 347-5500

(G-677)
BIMBO BAKERIES USA INC
30 Inez Dr (11706-2204)
PHONE 203 531-2311
James Montgomery, *Branch Mgr*
EMP: 50
SALES (corp-wide): 13B **Privately Held**
WEB: www.englishmuffin.com
SIC: 2051 Doughnuts, except frozen; cakes, bakery: except frozen; pies, bakery: except frozen
HQ: Bimbo Bakeries Usa, Inc
255 Business Center Dr # 200
Horsham PA 19044
215 347-5500

(G-678)
BIMBO FOODS BAKERIES INC (DH)
Also Called: Bimbo Bakeries USA
40 Harold Ct (11706-2220)
PHONE 631 273-6000
▲ EMP: 150
SQ FT: 600,000
SALES (est): 2B
SALES (corp-wide): 13B **Privately Held**
WEB: www.gwbakeries.com
SIC: 2051 Mfg Bread/Related Products
HQ: Bimbo Bakeries Usa, Inc
255 Business Center Dr # 200
Horsham PA 19044
215 347-5500

(G-679)
BONDY PRINTING CORP
Also Called: Sir Speedy
267 W Main St (11706-8319)
PHONE 631 242-1510
Fax: 631 666-0979
William Bondy Jr, *President*
Donna Bondy, *Vice Pres*
EMP: 5
SALES (est): 864.3K **Privately Held**
SIC: 2752 2791 2789 2759 Commercial printing, lithographic; typesetting; bookbinding & related work; commercial printing; automotive & apparel trimmings

(G-680)
CABLE MANAGEMENT SOLUTIONS INC
Also Called: Jette Group
291 Skip Ln (11706-1206)
PHONE 631 674-0004
Fax: 631 674-0010
Roger Jette, *President*
Bob Renz, *Executive*
EMP: 30
SQ FT: 3,500
SALES (est): 6.9MM **Privately Held**
WEB: www.snaketray.com
SIC: 3496 Miscellaneous fabricated wire products

(G-681)
CCS MACHINERY INC
2175 Union Blvd (11706-8016)
PHONE 631 968-0900
Mark Wilenkin, *Ch of Bd*
EMP: 14 EST: 2001
SALES (est): 2.2MM **Privately Held**
SIC: 3531 Construction machinery

(G-682)
CENTURY METAL PARTS CORP
230 S Fehr Way (11706-1208)
PHONE 631 667-0800
Fax: 631 667-0802
Frank Swierzbin, *President*
Thomas Larkin, *IT/INT Sup*
EMP: 25 EST: 1967
SQ FT: 17,000
SALES (est): 4.3MM **Privately Held**
SIC: 3663 3451 Antennas, transmitting & communications; screw machine products

(G-683)
CHEM-TEK SYSTEMS INC
Also Called: Moldedtanks.com
208 S Fehr Way (11706-1208)
P.O. Box 473, Nesconset (11767-0473)
PHONE 631 253-3010
Shawn Sprague, *President*
EMP: 10
SQ FT: 4,000
SALES (est): 1.1MM **Privately Held**
SIC: 3089 Plastic & fiberglass tanks

(G-684)
CLAD METAL SPECIALTIES INC
1516 5th Industrial Ct (11706-3402)
PHONE 631 666-7750
Denise Marcoccia, *Exec VP*
Dominick Bodami, *Vice Pres*
Debra Worrell, *Production*
Phil Bunn, *Engineer*
Karen Gerkey, *Finance*
EMP: 19
SQ FT: 13,500
SALES (est): 3.6MM **Privately Held**
WEB: www.cladmetal.com
SIC: 3479 Bonderizing of metal or metal products; aluminum coating of metal products

(G-685)
COLONIAL LABEL SYSTEMS INC
Also Called: Colonial Rapid
50 Corbin Ave Ste L (11706-1047)
P.O. Box 812, Deer Park (11729-0976)
PHONE 631 254-0111
Ron Afzelius, *President*
EMP: 25
SALES (est): 4.1MM **Privately Held**
SIC: 2759 Commercial printing

(G-686)
COLONIE PLASTICS CORP
188 Candlewood Rd (11706-2219)
PHONE 631 434-6969
Fax: 631 434-6984
Paul Gurbatri, *President*
Laura Arzeno, *Controller*
Louie Passi, *Manager*
▲ EMP: 130
SQ FT: 11,500
SALES (est): 16.2MM **Privately Held**
WEB: www.colonieplastics.com
SIC: 3089 Injection molded finished plastic products

(G-687)
COLORFULLY YOURS INC
11 Grant Ave (11706-1007)
PHONE 631 242-8600
Fax: 631 242-8664
Joseph Lindner, *President*
Deborah Lindner, *Vice Pres*
EMP: 10
SQ FT: 5,000
SALES (est): 1.2MM **Privately Held**
WEB: www.colorfullyyours.com
SIC: 2752 Commercial printing, offset

(G-688)
COMMAND COMPONENTS CORPORATION
6 Cherry St (11706-7325)
PHONE 631 666-4411
Fax: 631 666-4422
Jerry Sukman, *President*
EMP: 8
SQ FT: 3,000
SALES (est): 1.2MM **Privately Held**
WEB: www.commandcomponents.com
SIC: 3643 Electric connectors

(G-689)
CYNCAL STEEL FABRICATORS INC
225 Pine Aire Dr (11706-1147)
PHONE 631 254-5600
Cynthia Callahan, *Owner*
Martha Gray, *Admin Asst*
EMP: 12
SALES (est): 760K **Privately Held**
SIC: 3441 Fabricated structural metal

(G-690)
D K P WOOD RAILINGS & STAIRS
1971 Union Blvd (11706-7956)
PHONE 631 665-8656
Dmitri Onishchuk, *President*
EMP: 11
SALES (est): 1.3MM **Privately Held**
SIC: 2431 Stair railings, wood

(G-691)
DAVID PEYSER SPORTSWEAR INC (PA)
Also Called: Weatherproof
88 Spence St (11706-2229)
P.O. Box 9171 (11706-9171)
PHONE 631 231-7788
Fax: 631 435-8018
Paul Peyser, *Ch of Bd*
Irwin Peyser, *Corp Secy*
Irwin Hosea, *Vice Pres*
Alan Peyser, *Vice Pres*
Bruce Lerit, *CFO*
▲ EMP: 245
SQ FT: 110,000
SALES (est): 94.2MM **Privately Held**
WEB: www.mvsport.com
SIC: 2329 Men's & boys' sportswear & athletic clothing

(G-692)
DECAL TECHNIQUES INC
40 Corbin Ave Ste I (11706-1048)
PHONE 631 491-1800
Fax: 631 491-1816
Eugene P Snyder, *President*
Terry Lomanto, *Vice Pres*
Helen Rider, *Admin Sec*
EMP: 8 EST: 1979
SQ FT: 4,000
SALES (est): 600K **Privately Held**
WEB: www.decaltech.com
SIC: 2752 Decals, lithographed; posters, lithographed

(G-693)
DEER PARK SAND & GRAVEL CORP
145 S 4th St (11706-1200)
PHONE 631 586-2323
David Ciardullo, *President*
Joe Ciardullo, *Vice Pres*
EMP: 20
SQ FT: 4,000
SALES (est): 3.6MM **Privately Held**
SIC: 3273 5032 Ready-mixed concrete; gravel; sand, construction

(G-694)
DEJAH ASSOCIATES INC
Also Called: Dejah Enterprises
1515 5th Industrial Ct (11706-3401)
PHONE 631 265-2185
Fax: 631 744-4560
Raymond Dejah, *President*
Loretta Temkin, *Office Mgr*
EMP: 20
SQ FT: 24,000
SALES: 4.5MM **Privately Held**
SIC: 2542 Office & store showcases & display fixtures

(G-695)
DELTA POLYMERS INC
130 S 2nd St (11706-1036)
PHONE 631 254-6240
Razia Rana, *President*
Riasat Rana, *Vice Pres*
EMP: 8
SQ FT: 10,000
SALES: 1.5MM **Privately Held**
WEB: www.deltapolymers.com
SIC: 2851 1752 Epoxy coatings; floor laying & floor work

Bay Shore - Suffolk County (G-696)

(G-696)
DURO DYNE MACHINERY CORP
81 Spence St (11706-2206)
P.O. Box 9117 (11706-9117)
PHONE..................................631 249-9000
Milton Hinden, *CEO*
Randall Hinden, *President*
Joe Auriemmo, *Vice Pres*
Carole D'Agosta, *Vice Pres*
Carole Dagosta, *Vice Pres*
◆ **EMP:** 40 **EST:** 1952
SQ FT: 25,000
SALES (est): 10.1MM
SALES (corp-wide): 120.9MM **Privately Held**
SIC: 3585 Air conditioning equipment, complete; heating equipment, complete
PA: Dyne Duro National Corp
 81 Spence St
 Bay Shore NY 11706
 631 249-9000

(G-697)
DURO DYNE NATIONAL CORP (PA)
81 Spence St (11706-2206)
P.O. Box 9117 (11706-9117)
PHONE..................................631 249-9000
Randall Hinden, *President*
Charlie Larocca, *Plant Supt*
Bob Ramotor, *Plant Mgr*
Tina Scheuer, *Mfg Spvr*
Steve Friedstein, *CFO*
▲ **EMP:** 125
SQ FT: 35,000
SALES (est): 120.9MM **Privately Held**
SIC: 3585 Air conditioning equipment, complete; heating equipment, complete

(G-698)
E F IRON WORKS & CONSTRUCTION
241 N Fehr Way Ste 3 (11706-1233)
PHONE..................................631 242-4766
Fax: 631 242-6873
Ed Frage, *President*
EMP: 6
SALES: 390K **Privately Held**
WEB: www.efiron.com
SIC: 3446 1799 Architectural metalwork; ornamental metal work

(G-699)
EMPIRE INDUSTRIAL SYSTEMS CORP (PA)
40 Corbin Ave (11706-1048)
PHONE..................................631 242-4619
Shali Roufberg, *President*
Rosemarie Price, *Office Mgr*
EMP: 10
SQ FT: 7,500
SALES (est): 1.1MM **Privately Held**
SIC: 3443 1711 7699 3441 Boilers: industrial, power, or marine; industrial vessels, tanks & containers; boiler & furnace contractors; boiler repair shop; fabricated structural metal

(G-700)
FENIX FURNITURE CO
Also Called: Mica America
35 Drexel Dr (11706-2235)
PHONE..................................631 273-3500
Fax: 631 273-3572
Jared Fenigstein, *President*
Sol Portnoy, *Vice Pres*
EMP: 30
SQ FT: 24,000
SALES (est): 3.4MM **Privately Held**
SIC: 2511 Wood household furniture

(G-701)
FRED M LAWRENCE CO INC (PA)
45 Drexel Dr (11706-2201)
PHONE..................................718 786-7227
Vincent Lanci, *President*
Angelo Lanci, *Shareholder*
▲ **EMP:** 25
SQ FT: 22,000
SALES (est): 2MM **Privately Held**
WEB: www.photoframes.net
SIC: 2499 Picture & mirror frames, wood

(G-702)
GBV PROMOTIONS INC
44 Drexel Dr (11706-2202)
PHONE..................................631 231-7300
Richard Goldstein, *President*
Allan Goldstein, *Manager*
Marilyn Goldstein, *Admin Sec*
EMP: 11 **EST:** 1960
SQ FT: 3,000
SALES: 1.4MM **Privately Held**
SIC: 2752 Commercial printing, offset

(G-703)
GNY EQUIPMENT LLC
20 Drexel Dr (11706-2202)
PHONE..................................631 667-1010
Bill Peil, *President*
Kathleen Archer, *Office Mgr*
Kathy James, *Office Mgr*
Louis Colon, *Manager*
Charlie Creamer, *Manager*
▲ **EMP:** 10
SQ FT: 20,000
SALES (est): 1.2MM **Privately Held**
WEB: www.gnyequipment.com
SIC: 3728 5084 5082 Refueling equipment for use in flight, airplane; pumps & pumping equipment; contractors' materials

(G-704)
HARBOR WLDG & FABRICATION CORP
208 S Fehr Way (11706-1208)
PHONE..................................631 667-1880
Fax: 631 242-2441
Joseph Awing, *President*
EMP: 11
SQ FT: 5,400
SALES: 1.8MM **Privately Held**
SIC: 3449 Bars, concrete reinforcing: fabricated steel

(G-705)
INNOVATIVE JEWELRY INC (PA)
Also Called: Fiora Italy
5 Inez Dr (11706-2203)
PHONE..................................718 408-8950
Abraham Rowe, *Vice Pres*
▲ **EMP:** 4
SQ FT: 3,000
SALES: 4MM **Privately Held**
SIC: 3911 Bracelets, precious metal

(G-706)
INTER MOLDS INC
26 Cleveland Ave (11706-1223)
PHONE..................................631 667-8580
Fax: 631 667-8581
Victor Goncalves, *President*
Francisco Silva, *Vice Pres*
Douglas Cooper, *Treasurer*
Mario Santiago, *Admin Sec*
EMP: 6
SQ FT: 5,000
SALES (est): 700K **Privately Held**
WEB: www.intermolds.com
SIC: 3544 Forms (molds), for foundry & plastics working machinery

(G-707)
INTERFACE PRODUCTS CO INC
215 N Fehr Way Ste C (11706-1209)
PHONE..................................631 242-4605
George Miller, *President*
Mary Ann Harrell, *Office Mgr*
EMP: 8
SQ FT: 2,125
SALES (est): 770K **Privately Held**
SIC: 3534 Elevators & equipment

(G-708)
ISLIP MINITURE GOLF
500 E Main St (11706-8502)
PHONE..................................631 940-8900
Mike Flemming,
EMP: 8
SALES (est): 392.9K **Privately Held**
SIC: 3999 Miniatures

(G-709)
JERRY CARDULLO IRON WORKS INC
Also Called: Cardullo, J Iron Works
101 Spence St (11706-2208)
PHONE..................................631 242-8881
Fax: 516 242-4326
Jerry Cardullo, *President*
EMP: 12
SQ FT: 3,000
SALES (est): 880K **Privately Held**
SIC: 3446 Architectural metalwork

(G-710)
LAMINATED WINDOW PRODUCTS INC
211 N Fehr Way (11706-1203)
PHONE..................................631 242-6883
Ismael Santiago, *President*
EMP: 10
SQ FT: 4,000
SALES: 800K **Privately Held**
SIC: 2391 2394 Draperies, plastic & textile: from purchased materials; shades, canvas: made from purchased materials

(G-711)
LANWOOD INDUSTRIES INC
Also Called: Fred Lawrence Co
45 Drexel Dr (11706-2201)
PHONE..................................718 786-3000
EMP: 30
SQ FT: 25,000
SALES (est): 193.4K **Privately Held**
SIC: 2499 2782 Mfg Wood Products Mfg Blankbooks/Binders

(G-712)
LASTICKS AEROSPACE INC
35 Washington Ave Ste E (11706-1027)
PHONE..................................631 242-8484
Fax: 631 242-8485
Guy T Russo, *President*
Keith Johns, *Vice Pres*
Steve Rizzi, *Purchasing*
Denise Walker, *Manager*
Gregory Nasta, *Software Dev*
EMP: 14
SQ FT: 5,000
SALES (est): 1.4MM **Privately Held**
WEB: www.lasticksaero.com
SIC: 3599 Machine shop, jobbing & repair

(G-713)
LEXAN INDUSTRIES INC
Also Called: Struthers Electronics
15 Harold Ct (11706-2220)
PHONE..................................631 434-7586
Fax: 631 434-7589
Florence Isaacson, *President*
Daniel Richardson, *General Mgr*
Daniel Gibbons, *Div Sub Head*
Roberta Simmons, *Purchasing*
Jayme Sohnis, *Manager*
EMP: 19
SQ FT: 11,000
SALES (est): 1.3MM **Privately Held**
SIC: 3679 3825 Microwave components; test equipment for electronic & electrical circuits

(G-714)
M F L B INC
Also Called: S D S of Long Island
7 Grant Ave (11706-1007)
PHONE..................................631 254-8300
Frank Baubille, *Vice Pres*
Michael Cafiero, *Admin Sec*
EMP: 13
SQ FT: 2,500
SALES: 450K **Privately Held**
WEB: www.mflb.com
SIC: 3677 Electronic coils, transformers & other inductors

(G-715)
MARKS CORPEX BANKNOTE CO (PA)
1440 5th Ave (11706-4149)
PHONE..................................631 968-0277
Fax: 631 968-0397
Henri Bertuch, *Principal*
Rhoda Bertuch, *Treasurer*
Linda Newton, *Administration*
EMP: 8
SQ FT: 12,000
SALES (est): 961.1K **Privately Held**
WEB: www.corpexnet.com
SIC: 2752 5085 Commercial printing, lithographic; industrial supplies

(G-716)
MBA ORTHOTICS INC
60 Corbin Ave Unit 60g (11706-1046)
PHONE..................................631 392-4755
Andrea Tamayo, *President*
EMP: 5 **EST:** 2015
SALES: 300K **Privately Held**
SIC: 3131 Sole parts for shoes

(G-717)
METAL IMPROVEMENT COMPANY LLC
210 Candlewood Rd (11706-2217)
PHONE..................................631 567-2610
William Halley, *Manager*
EMP: 14
SALES (corp-wide): 2.2B **Publicly Held**
WEB: www.mic-houston.com
SIC: 3398 Metal heat treating
HQ: Metal Improvement Company, Llc
 80 E State Rt 4 Ste 310
 Paramus NJ 07652
 201 843-7800

(G-718)
MILEX PRECISION INC
66 S 2nd St Ste G (11706-1000)
PHONE..................................631 595-2393
Fax: 631 595-1907
Aeric Misko, *President*
Dagmar Misko, *Vice Pres*
EMP: 14
SQ FT: 4,000
SALES: 1.5MM **Privately Held**
SIC: 3728 3599 Aircraft parts & equipment; machine shop, jobbing & repair

(G-719)
MINICO INDUSTRIES INC
66a S 2nd St Ste A (11706)
PHONE..................................631 595-1455
Fax: 631 595-1620
Nicholas Chonis, *President*
Constantine Chonis, *Vice Pres*
Michael Chonis, *Treasurer*
EMP: 9
SQ FT: 4,500
SALES (est): 1MM **Privately Held**
WEB: www.minicoindustries.com
SIC: 3089 Injection molding of plastics

(G-720)
MV CORP INC
Also Called: M V Sport
88 Spence St Ste 90 (11706-2229)
P.O. Box 9171 (11706-9171)
PHONE..................................631 273-8020
Joshua Peyser, *Ch of Bd*
Alan Peyser, *Principal*
Paul Peyser, *Principal*
Phil Potash, *Opers Mgr*
Joe Rodriguez, *Warehouse Mgr*
▲ **EMP:** 150
SQ FT: 40,000
SALES (est): 16.5MM
SALES (corp-wide): 94.2MM **Privately Held**
WEB: www.mvsport.com
SIC: 2311 2262 2759 2339 Men's & boys' suits & coats; screen printing: man-made fiber & silk broadwoven fabrics; screen printing; women's & misses' outerwear
PA: David Peyser Sportswear, Inc.
 88 Spence St
 Bay Shore NY 11706
 631 231-7788

(G-721)
NASSAU SUFFOLK BRD OF WOMENS
145 New York Ave (11706-3209)
PHONE..................................631 666-8835
Cris McNamara, *President*
EMP: 50
SALES (est): 1.7MM **Privately Held**
SIC: 2387 Apparel belts

GEOGRAPHIC SECTION

Bay Shore - Suffolk County (G-750)

(G-722)
NEW YORK GOURMET COFFEE INC
204 N Fehr Way Ste C (11706-1229)
PHONE..................................631 254-0076
Douglas Robinson, *President*
Deborah Robinson, *Vice Pres*
EMP: 5
SALES: 500K **Privately Held**
SIC: 2095 Roasted coffee

(G-723)
PHOTO MEDIC EQUIPMENT INC
Also Called: Precise Optics
239 S Fehr Way (11706-1207)
PHONE..................................631 242-6600
Fax: 631 242-4421
Len Corso, *Ch of Bd*
R Hannington, *Purchasing*
Ann Alonzo, *Controller*
R Corso, *Marketing Staff*
Gordon Kellogg, *Systems Mgr*
EMP: 90
SQ FT: 50,000
SALES (est): 7.4MM **Privately Held**
WEB: www.preciseoptics.com
SIC: 3844 X-ray apparatus & tubes

(G-724)
PLATINUM CARTING CORP
1806 Carleton Ave (11706-1632)
PHONE..................................631 649-4322
Carol Key, *President*
Zed Key, *Treasurer*
EMP: 15
SALES (est): 1.3MM **Privately Held**
SIC: 3639 Garbage disposal units, household

(G-725)
POLY SCIENTIFIC R&D CORP
70 Cleveland Ave (11706-1282)
PHONE..................................631 586-0400
John J Caggiano, *President*
John H Arnold, *Exec VP*
Joseph Caggiano, *Vice Pres*
Cory Gabe, *Executive*
EMP: 40 **EST:** 1969
SQ FT: 22,000
SALES (est): 9.3MM **Privately Held**
WEB: www.polyrnd.com
SIC: 2869 5169 2819 Industrial organic chemicals; chemicals & allied products; industrial inorganic chemicals

(G-726)
POLYCAST INDUSTRIES INC
130 S 2nd St (11706-1036)
PHONE..................................631 595-2530
Razia Rana, *President*
Riasat Rana, *Vice Pres*
EMP: 5
SQ FT: 100,000
SALES: 1MM **Privately Held**
SIC: 3679 2992 2891 2821 Electronic circuits; lubricating oils & greases; adhesives & sealants; plastics materials & resins

(G-727)
PRECISION METALS CORP
221 Skip Ln (11706-1206)
PHONE..................................631 586-5032
Thomas J Figlozzi, *Ch of Bd*
Anna Maria Figlozzi, *Corp Secy*
Tony Figlozzi, *Vice Pres*
Bill Bednarski, *Manager*
Carol Nudelman, *Admin Sec*
EMP: 45
SQ FT: 16,000
SALES (est): 13.8MM **Privately Held**
WEB: www.precisionmetalscorp.com
SIC: 3441 3599 3444 Fabricated structural metal; machine & other job shop work; sheet metalwork

(G-728)
PRESTIGELINE INC
5 Inez Dr (11706-2203)
P.O. Box 100 (11706-0703)
PHONE..................................631 273-3636
Scott Roth, *President*
Randy Gaumer, *Division Mgr*
Stuart Goldstein, *Senior VP*
Kenneth Golden, *Vice Pres*
▲ **EMP:** 82

SQ FT: 150,000
SALES (est): 11.1MM **Privately Held**
WEB: www.prestigelineinc.com
SIC: 3645 5063 Residential lighting fixtures; lighting fixtures, residential

(G-729)
PROTO MACHINE INC
60 Corbin Ave Ste D (11706-1046)
PHONE..................................631 392-1159
James Bailey, *President*
Eric Lindskog, *Vice Pres*
EMP: 11
SQ FT: 3,600
SALES: 1.2MM **Privately Held**
SIC: 3599 Machine shop, jobbing & repair

(G-730)
R G FLAIR CO INC
199 S Fehr Way (11706-1207)
PHONE..................................631 586-7311
Fax: 631 586-7316
Gerhard Raible, *President*
Dieter Thole, *Corp Secy*
Martin Sievers, *Vice Pres*
Chris Thole, *Manager*
EMP: 22
SQ FT: 13,000
SALES (est): 4.1MM **Privately Held**
WEB: www.rgflair.com
SIC: 3469 3915 Metal stampings; jewelers' materials & lapidary work

(G-731)
RAN MAR ENTERPRISES LTD
143 Anchor Ln (11706-8121)
PHONE..................................631 666-4754
Melvin Small, *President*
EMP: 12
SQ FT: 13,000
SALES (est): 1.4MM **Privately Held**
SIC: 2891 Adhesives

(G-732)
RASJADA ENTERPRISES LTD
1337 Richland Blvd (11706-5415)
PHONE..................................631 242-1055
Ronald C Cusano Jr, *President*
EMP: 12
SQ FT: 15,000
SALES: 2MM **Privately Held**
SIC: 2541 Cabinets, except refrigerated: show, display, etc.: wood

(G-733)
RFN INC
40 Drexel Dr (11706-2202)
PHONE..................................516 764-5100
Alex Treyger, *President*
EMP: 18
SQ FT: 28,000
SALES: 1.5MM **Privately Held**
SIC: 2759 8742 Commercial printing; marketing consulting services

(G-734)
RINALDI PRECISION MACHINE
Also Called: R P M
60 Corbin Ave Ste F (11706-1046)
PHONE..................................631 242-4141
Fax: 631 242-4422
Angelo Rinaldi, *President*
EMP: 10
SQ FT: 1,700
SALES: 1.5MM **Privately Held**
SIC: 3599 Machine shop, jobbing & repair

(G-735)
RIT PRINTING CORP
250 N Fairway (11706)
PHONE..................................631 586-6220
Fax: 631 586-6247
Anthony Buono, *President*
Maria Brown, *Manager*
EMP: 10
SQ FT: 8,000
SALES (est): 1.5MM **Privately Held**
WEB: www.ritprinting.com
SIC: 2752 2759 Commercial printing, lithographic; commercial printing

(G-736)
RIZE ENTERPRISES LLC
81 Spence St (11706-2206)
P.O. Box 1311, Brentwood (11717-0688)
PHONE..................................631 249-9000

Randy Hinden,
▲ **EMP:** 5
SALES (est): 551.6K **Privately Held**
SIC: 3429 Security cable locking system

(G-737)
ROCKET TECH FUEL CORP
20 Corbin Ave (11706-1004)
PHONE..................................516 810-8947
Richard Miller, *President*
Joseph Silhan, *Vice Pres*
EMP: 10 **EST:** 2004
SQ FT: 1,800
SALES: 90MM **Privately Held**
SIC: 1311 Crude petroleum & natural gas

(G-738)
ROMAN STONE CONSTRUCTION CO
85 S 4th St (11706-1210)
PHONE..................................631 667-0566
Fax: 631 667-0617
Thomas Montalbine, *President*
Layne Urbas, *Treasurer*
Richard Benz, *Sales Mgr*
Ryan Camberdella, *Sales Mgr*
Michelle Bou, *Sales Staff*
EMP: 45 **EST:** 1903
SQ FT: 25,000
SALES (est): 9.1MM **Privately Held**
WEB: www.romanstoneco.com
SIC: 3272 Pipe, concrete or lined with concrete

(G-739)
ROSSITER & SCHMITT CO INC
220 S Fehr Way (11706-1208)
PHONE..................................516 937-3610
Richard Shapiro, *Chairman*
David Shapiro, *Assistant VP*
EMP: 5
SALES: 1MM **Privately Held**
SIC: 3991 Brushes, household or industrial

(G-740)
ROYAL WINDOWS MFG CORP
Also Called: Royal Windows and Doors
1769 5th Ave Unit A (11706-1735)
PHONE..................................631 435-8888
Fax: 631 435-8899
Solomos Hajicharalambous, *Ch of Bd*
George Efthymiou, *Treasurer*
Tim Efthymio, *Controller*
Efthymios Efthymiou, *Controller*
Solon Efthymiou, *Manager*
EMP: 27
SQ FT: 60,000
SALES (est): 4.4MM **Privately Held**
WEB: www.royalwindow.com
SIC: 2431 5031 1751 Windows, wood; doors, wood; doors & windows; window & door (prefabricated) installation

(G-741)
RUBIES COSTUME COMPANY INC
Also Called: Collegeville Imagineering
158 Candlewood Rd (11706-2219)
PHONE..................................631 777-3300
EMP: 100
SALES (corp-wide): 464.8MM **Privately Held**
SIC: 2389 7299 Mfg Costumes
PA: Rubie's Costume Company, Inc.
 12008 Jamaica Ave
 Richmond Hill NY 11418
 718 846-1008

(G-742)
RUBIES COSTUME COMPANY INC
Also Called: Rubie's Distribution Center
1 Holloween Hwy (11706-1633)
PHONE..................................631 951-3688
Fax: 631 951-3723
Marc Beige, *Manager*
EMP: 120
SALES (corp-wide): 477.7MM **Privately Held**
SIC: 2389 7299 Costumes; costume rental
PA: Rubie's Costume Company, Inc.
 12008 Jamaica Ave
 Richmond Hill NY 11418
 718 846-1008

(G-743)
SIW INC
271 Skip Ln (11706-1206)
PHONE..................................631 888-0130
Lisa Gurcan, *President*
Dominic Amorosa, *Vice Pres*
▲ **EMP:** 12
SQ FT: 11,500
SALES (est): 1.2MM **Privately Held**
SIC: 3449 Bars, concrete reinforcing: fabricated steel

(G-744)
STANDARD INDUSTRIAL WORKS INC
271 Skip Ln (11706-1206)
PHONE..................................631 888-0130
Fax: 631 888-0133
Paul Spotts, *President*
Lisa Gurcan, *Software Dev*
EMP: 10
SQ FT: 11,800
SALES: 700K **Privately Held**
SIC: 3444 Sheet metalwork

(G-745)
SUFFOLK COPY CENTER INC
Also Called: Suffolk Printing
26 W Main St (11706-8383)
PHONE..................................631 665-0570
Fax: 631 665-0403
William Beitch, *President*
Florence Beitch, *Corp Secy*
Charles Beitch, *Vice Pres*
EMP: 6 **EST:** 1971
SQ FT: 4,000
SALES (est): 947.6K **Privately Held**
WEB: www.suffolkprinting.com
SIC: 2752 Commercial printing, offset

(G-746)
SUMMIT MANUFACTURING (PA)
Also Called: Summit Plastics
100 Spence St (11706-2231)
PHONE..................................631 952-1570
Lou Marineelo, *President*
Art Landi, *Partner*
Richard Rickman, *Partner*
Ping Hsia, *Vice Pres*
Mike Parisi, *Director*
EMP: 5 **EST:** 2015
SALES (est): 4.9MM **Privately Held**
SIC: 3089 Plastic containers, except foam

(G-747)
SUMMIT MANUFACTURING
59 Spence St (11706-2206)
PHONE..................................631 952-1570
EMP: 34
SALES (corp-wide): 4.9MM **Privately Held**
SIC: 3089 Plastic containers, except foam
PA: Summit Manufacturing
 100 Spence St
 Bay Shore NY 11706
 631 952-1570

(G-748)
SUMMIT PROMOTIONS LLC
59 Spence St (11706-2206)
PHONE..................................631 952-1570
Glenn Davis, *President*
EMP: 12
SALES (est): 2.6MM **Privately Held**
SIC: 2673 Food storage & frozen food bags, plastic

(G-749)
SUMNER INDUSTRIES INC
Also Called: Ateco Products
309 Orinoco Dr (11706-7111)
PHONE..................................631 666-7290
Fax: 631 666-1424
Jonathan Sumner, *President*
Danny Deprospo, *Manager*
Yewa Sawicka, *Manager*
▼ **EMP:** 15 **EST:** 1935
SQ FT: 10,000
SALES (est): 3.3MM **Privately Held**
SIC: 3728 Aircraft parts & equipment

(G-750)
TAPE-IT INC
233 N Fehr Way (11706-1203)
PHONE..................................631 243-4100

Bay Shore - Suffolk County (G-751)

Fax: 631 243-4326
Arnold Rabinowitz, *President*
Lorie Amuro, *Human Res Mgr*
Alex Aguirre, *Mktg Dir*
Arnold Robinwitz, *Director*
▲ **EMP:** 50
SQ FT: 55,000
SALES (est): 13MM **Privately Held**
WEB: www.tapeit.com
SIC: 2672 5113 5122 Tape, pressure sensitive: made from purchased materials; pressure sensitive tape; drugs, proprietaries & sundries

(G-751)
TENSATOR INC
Also Called: Tensator Group
260 Spur Dr S (11706-3917)
P.O. Box 400 (11706-0779)
PHONE..................................631 666-0300
Alan McPherson, *CEO*
Ben Gale, *CEO*
James Baker, *General Mgr*
David Cohen, *Business Mgr*
William Goebel, *Business Mgr*
◆ **EMP:** 94
SQ FT: 81,000
SALES (est): 26.5MM
SALES (corp-wide): 47.7MM **Privately Held**
WEB: www.lawrencemetal.com
SIC: 3446 Ornamental metalwork
HQ: Tensator Group Limited
  Unit 7 Danbury Court
  Milton Keynes BUCKS MK14
  190 868-4600

(G-752)
TROJAN METAL FABRICATION INC (PA)
Also Called: Trojan Powder Coating
2215 Union Blvd (11706-8015)
PHONE..................................631 968-5040
Fax: 631 968-5939
Carl Troiano, *CEO*
James Dunne, *Counsel*
Keith Rein, *Vice Pres*
Chris Banach, *Plant Mgr*
Dora Simpson, *Prdtn Mgr*
EMP: 50
SQ FT: 80,000
SALES (est): 7.7MM **Privately Held**
WEB: www.trojanpowder.com
SIC: 3479 Coating of metals & formed products

(G-753)
ULTIMATE STYLES OF AMERICA
27 Garfield Ave Unit A (11706-1052)
PHONE..................................631 254-0219
David Goldstein, *President*
EMP: 12
SQ FT: 4,000
SALES (est): 1.3MM **Privately Held**
SIC: 2499 5712 Kitchen, bathroom & household ware: wood; cabinet work, custom

(G-754)
VIATECH PUBG SOLUTIONS INC
1440 5th Ave (11706-4149)
PHONE..................................631 968-8500
Fax: 631 968-0830
Alyssa Graziano, *Prdtn Mgr*
Belinda Pearson, *Accounting Mgr*
Alison Seguna, *Accountant*
Tom Bergenholtz, *VP Sales*
Angie Benefield, *Accounts Mgr*
EMP: 48
SALES (corp-wide): 64.1MM **Privately Held**
SIC: 2752 7389 Commercial printing, offset; lithographing on metal; subscription fulfillment services: magazine, newspaper, etc.
PA: Viatech Publishing Solutions, Inc.
  11935 N Stemmons Fwy
  Dallas TX 75234
  214 827-8151

Bayport
Suffolk County

(G-755)
CARE ENTERPRISES INC
435 Renee Dr (11705-1237)
PHONE..................................631 472-8155
Lina Torre, *Vice Pres*
EMP: 6
SALES: 650K **Privately Held**
SIC: 3822 Air conditioning & refrigeration controls

(G-756)
CGW CORP (PA)
102 S Gillette Ave (11705-2239)
PHONE..................................631 472-6600
Fax: 631 472-3521
George Werner, *President*
EMP: 7
SALES: 800K **Privately Held**
WEB: www.cgwcorp.com
SIC: 3825 Network analyzers

(G-757)
CHIMNEY DOCTORS AMERICAS CORP
738a Montauk Hwy (11705-1621)
PHONE..................................631 868-3586
Nicole Newberg, *President*
EMP: 5
SQ FT: 500
SALES (est): 206.8K **Privately Held**
SIC: 3259 3271 3272 1799 Clay chimney products; blocks, concrete: chimney or fireplace; fireplace & chimney material: concrete; prefabricated fireplace installation

(G-758)
JOHNSON MANUFACTURING CO
326 3rd Ave (11705-1316)
PHONE..................................631 472-1184
David Johnson Sr, *Owner*
EMP: 7
SQ FT: 5,000
SALES: 350K **Privately Held**
SIC: 3089 Plastic processing

(G-759)
NBTY INC
Capsuleworks
10 Vitamin Dr (11705-1112)
PHONE..................................631 200-2000
Joe Moreno, *Supervisor*
EMP: 11
SALES (corp-wide): 3B **Publicly Held**
SIC: 2833 Medicinals & botanicals
HQ: Nbty, Inc.
  2100 Smithtown Ave
  Ronkonkoma NY 11779
  631 200-2000

(G-760)
PLASTIC SOLUTIONS INC
158 Schenck Ave (11705)
PHONE..................................631 234-9013
AVI Ben-Bassat, *Ch of Bd*
EMP: 32
SALES (est): 5MM **Privately Held**
SIC: 3089 3544 Plastic containers, except foam; special dies, tools, jigs & fixtures

(G-761)
WENNER BREAD PRODUCTS INC (PA)
33 Rajon Rd (11705-1101)
PHONE..................................800 869-6262
Fax: 631 563-6546
Richard R Wenner, *CEO*
Lawrence L Wenner, *Senior VP*
Daniel Wenner, *Vice Pres*
John J Wenner, *Vice Pres*
William W Wenner Jr, *Vice Pres*
▲ **EMP:** 388 **EST:** 1975
SQ FT: 140,000
SALES (est): 126.7MM **Privately Held**
WEB: www.wenner-bread.com
SIC: 2051 2053 5461 Bread, all types (white, wheat, rye, etc): fresh or frozen; frozen bakery products, except bread; bakeries

Bayside
Queens County

(G-762)
A & G FOOD DISTRIBUTORS LLC
21610 47th Ave Apt 3b (11361-3412)
PHONE..................................917 939-3457
Rocco Macri, *President*
▲ **EMP:** 3 **EST:** 2009
SALES: 1.5MM **Privately Held**
SIC: 2032 Italian foods: packaged in cans, jars, etc.

(G-763)
A AND K GLOBAL INC
3312 208th St (11361-1319)
PHONE..................................718 412-1876
Darrow Wu, *General Mgr*
EMP: 67 **EST:** 2008
SALES (est): 4.2MM **Privately Held**
SIC: 3651 Home entertainment equipment, electronic
PA: Dongguan Naifan Packing Engineering Co., Ltd.
  Dongguan
  769 827-8410

(G-764)
A T A BAGEL SHOPPE INC
Also Called: Bagel Club
20814 Cross Island Pkwy (11360-1187)
PHONE..................................718 352-4948
Anthony Lombardo, *President*
EMP: 5
SALES (est): 270K **Privately Held**
SIC: 2051 5812 5461 Bagels, fresh or frozen; eating places; bagels

(G-765)
ABSOLUTE FITNESS US CORP
21337 39th Ave Ste 322 (11361-2071)
PHONE..................................732 979-8582
Salvatore Naimo, *CEO*
Dina Destafano, *Director*
EMP: 100
SALES (est): 4.7MM **Privately Held**
SIC: 3949 Sporting & athletic goods

(G-766)
ALEXANDER POLAKOVICH
Also Called: Minuteman Press
4235 Bell Blvd (11361-2863)
PHONE..................................718 229-6200
Fax: 718 229-0485
Alexander Polakovich, *Owner*
EMP: 6
SQ FT: 2,000
SALES (est): 340K **Privately Held**
SIC: 2752 Commercial printing, lithographic

(G-767)
BAGEL CLUB INC
20521 35th Ave (11361-1245)
PHONE..................................718 423-6106
Rosa Lombardo, *President*
EMP: 13
SALES (est): 1.5MM **Privately Held**
SIC: 2051 Bagels, fresh or frozen

(G-768)
CANAAN PRINTING INC
20007 46th Ave (11361-3018)
PHONE..................................718 729-3100
Fax: 718 729-3159
Sang Miung Kim, *President*
EMP: 10 **EST:** 1980
SQ FT: 5,000
SALES (est): 840K **Privately Held**
WEB: www.canaanprinting.com
SIC: 2752 Commercial printing, offset

(G-769)
DADA GROUP US INC
22104 67th Ave Apt B (11364-2628)
PHONE..................................631 888-0818
Zhiqian Zhang, *President*
▲ **EMP:** 4
SALES: 3MM **Privately Held**
SIC: 2386 Garments, leather

(G-770)
FREEMAN TECHNOLOGY INC
2355 Bell Blvd Apt 2h (11360-2051)
PHONE..................................732 829-8345
Tim Freeman, *President*
John Yin, *Project Mgr*
EMP: 20 **EST:** 2012
SQ FT: 1,500
SALES: 2MM **Privately Held**
SIC: 3829 Measuring & controlling devices
PA: Freeman Technology Limited
  1 Miller Court
  Tewkesbury GLOS

(G-771)
G PESSO & SONS INC
20320 35th Ave (11361-1110)
PHONE..................................718 224-9130
Gidon Pesso, *Principal*
EMP: 7
SALES (est): 494.2K **Privately Held**
SIC: 2024 Ice cream & frozen desserts

(G-772)
HISPANIC COM PUB INC
Also Called: Schneps Publications
3815 Bell Blvd Fl 2 (11361-2058)
PHONE..................................718 224-5863
Victoria A Schneps, *President*
Josh Schneps, *Vice Pres*
Murial Vilectia, *Accounts Mgr*
EMP: 15
SALES (est): 770K **Privately Held**
SIC: 2711 Newspapers

(G-773)
KASTOR CONSULTING INC
3919 218th St (11361-2331)
PHONE..................................718 224-9109
Greg Manaris, *President*
EMP: 9
SALES (est): 780K **Privately Held**
WEB: www.kastor.com
SIC: 7372 Prepackaged software

(G-774)
NATIONAL PROSTHETIC ORTHOT
21441 42nd Ave Ste 3a (11361-2963)
PHONE..................................718 767-8400
Fax: 718 423-8708
Fernando Perez, *President*
Sibia Perez, *Manager*
EMP: 9
SQ FT: 1,500
SALES (est): 900K **Privately Held**
SIC: 3842 Limbs, artificial; braces, orthopedic

(G-775)
SCHNEPS PUBLICATIONS INC (PA)
Also Called: Forest Hills Courier
3815 Bell Blvd Ste 38 (11361-2058)
PHONE..................................718 224-5863
Fax: 718 224-5441
Victoria A Schneps, *President*
Katrina Medoff, *Editor*
Joshua Schneps, *Vice Pres*
Keith Fiocca, *Accounts Exec*
Michele Miller, *Accounts Exec*
EMP: 37
SALES (est): 5.6MM **Privately Held**
SIC: 2711 Newspapers

(G-776)
UL CORP
3812 Corporal Stone St # 2 (11361-2141)
PHONE..................................201 203-4453
Hyung Ho Kim, *President*
EMP: 8
SALES: 1.2MM **Privately Held**
SIC: 3953 Marking devices

(G-777)
URBAN RACERCOM
21333 39th Ave (11361-2091)
PHONE..................................718 279-2202
Jackie Yi, *Principal*
Bob Hernandez, *Editor*
Terren Lin, *Editor*
Eri Magara, *Opers Staff*
Erin Gross-luk, *Associate*
EMP: 5

SALES (est): 610.3K **Privately Held**
SIC: 2721 Periodicals: publishing only

(G-778)
VF IMAGEWEAR INC
333 Pratt Ave (11359-1119)
PHONE..................................718 352-2363
Martin Soto, *Manager*
Paul G Policarpio, *Administration*
EMP: 21
SALES (corp-wide): 12.3B **Publicly Held**
WEB: www.vfsolutions.com
SIC: 2311 2326 2339 Men's & boys' uniforms; work uniforms; women's & misses' outerwear
HQ: Vf Imagewear, Inc.
545 Marriott Dr Ste 200
Nashville TN 37214
615 565-5000

Bayside Hills
Queens County

(G-779)
CAPTURE GLOBA INTEG SOLUT INC
21214 48th Ave (11364-1204)
PHONE..................................718 352-0579
Harry Pateroulakis, *President*
EMP: 8 EST: 2003
SALES: 1MM **Privately Held**
SIC: 3577 Magnetic ink & optical scanning devices

(G-780)
CATHAY GLOBAL CO INC
Also Called: Vactronics
5815 215th St (11364-1839)
PHONE..................................718 229-0920
Fu Geng, *President*
Janet Jiang, *Vice Pres*
EMP: 6 EST: 1991
SQ FT: 2,000
SALES (est): 406.5K **Privately Held**
SIC: 3699 Electrical equipment & supplies

Beacon
Dutchess County

(G-781)
ARCHITECTURAL GLASS INC
71 Maple St Apt 2 (12508-2034)
PHONE..................................845 831-3116
Fax: 845 831-3321
Michael Benzer, *President*
Jennifer Smith, *Vice Pres*
EMP: 10
SQ FT: 8,000
SALES (est): 500K **Privately Held**
WEB: www.glasstiles.com
SIC: 3229 Glassware, art or decorative

(G-782)
CHEMPRENE INC
483 Fishkill Ave (12508-1251)
P.O. Box 471 (12508-0471)
PHONE..................................845 831-2800
Fax: 845 831-4639
John Nicoletti, *President*
Motria Iverson, *Accounts Mgr*
Debbie Tibido, *MIS Dir*
▲ EMP: 110
SQ FT: 200,000
SALES (est): 43.9MM **Privately Held**
WEB: www.chemprene.com
SIC: 3496 3069 3535 2295 Conveyor belts; rubberized fabrics; rubber hardware; conveyors & conveying equipment; coated fabrics, not rubberized; investment holding companies, except banks
HQ: Ammeraal Beltech International Beheer B.V.
Comeniusstraat 8
Alkmaar
725 751-212

(G-783)
CHEMPRENE HOLDING INC
483 Fishkill Ave (12508-1251)
PHONE..................................845 831-2800
Jami Goud, *Ch of Bd*

Paul Hamilton, *President*
▲ EMP: 180
SALES (est): 19.8MM **Privately Held**
SIC: 3496 3069 3535 2295 Conveyor belts; rubberized fabrics; rubber hardware; conveyors & conveying equipment; coated fabrics, not rubberized

(G-784)
DOREL HAT CO (PA)
1 Main St (12508)
PHONE..................................845 831-5231
Fax: 845 831-0481
Salvatore Cumella, *CEO*
Ramon Moreno, *Vice Pres*
EMP: 30
SQ FT: 28,000
SALES (est): 1.6MM **Privately Held**
WEB: www.aldohats.com
SIC: 2353 Hats, caps & millinery; hats, trimmed: women's, misses' & children's

(G-785)
HUDSON VALLEY CHOCOLATIER INC (PA)
Also Called: Alps Sweet Shop
269 Main St (12508-2735)
PHONE..................................845 831-8240
Sally Craft, *President*
Terry Craft, *Vice Pres*
EMP: 14
SALES (est): 1.8MM **Privately Held**
WEB: www.alpssweetshop.com
SIC: 2064 5441 Candy & other confectionery products; candy

(G-786)
MECHTRONICS CORPORATION (PA)
511 Fishkill Ave (12508-1253)
PHONE..................................845 231-1400
Fax: 914 989-2726
Richard J Fellinger, *Ch of Bd*
Anthony Squitieri, *President*
Keith Arndt, *Vice Pres*
John Cox, *Project Mgr*
Tony Siragusa, *Project Mgr*
▲ EMP: 40 EST: 1944
SQ FT: 20,000
SALES (est): 28.6MM **Privately Held**
WEB: www.mech-tronics.com
SIC: 3993 Displays, paint process

(G-787)
MECHTRONICS CORPORATION
511 Fishkill Ave (12508-1253)
PHONE..................................845 831-9300
Richard Fellinger, *Branch Mgr*
EMP: 40
SALES (corp-wide): 28.6MM **Privately Held**
WEB: www.mech-tronics.com
SIC: 3993 2542 2653 Displays, paint process; fixtures: display, office or store: except wood; corrugated boxes, partitions, display items, sheets & pad
PA: Mechtronics Corporation
511 Fishkill Ave
Beacon NY 12508
845 231-1400

(G-788)
METAL CONCEPTS
9 Hanna Ln 12 (12508-2868)
PHONE..................................845 592-1863
Herman Roggeman, *Owner*
Jan Roggeman, *Co-Owner*
EMP: 3
SALES: 1.5MM **Privately Held**
SIC: 3441 Fabricated structural metal

(G-789)
RECOMMUNITY RECYCLING
508 Fishkill Ave (12508-1255)
PHONE..................................845 926-1071
EMP: 381
SALES (corp-wide): 122.5MM **Privately Held**
SIC: 2611 Pulp manufactured from waste or recycled paper
PA: Recommunity Recycling
1007 Amble Dr
Charlotte NC 28206
704 598-8595

(G-790)
SIEGFRIEDS CALL INC
20 Kent St 109 (12508-2042)
PHONE..................................845 765-2275
Scott H Bacon, *Partner*
Andrea Bacon, *Officer*
EMP: 6
SALES (est): 100K **Privately Held**
SIC: 3931 Brass instruments & parts

(G-791)
TIGA HOLDINGS INC
74 Dennings Ave (12508-3624)
PHONE..................................845 838-3000
Gary Santagata, *President*
Timothy Hochberj, *Vice Pres*
Michael J Siciliano, *Director*
EMP: 24
SQ FT: 2,300
SALES (est): 1.9MM **Privately Held**
WEB: www.tigallc.com
SIC: 3911 Jewelry, precious metal

Bearsville
Ulster County

(G-792)
LIFELINK MONITORING CORP (PA)
3201 Route 212 (12409-5224)
PHONE..................................845 336-2098
Fax: 845 679-7938
Arthur G Avedisian, *President*
John K Holland, *Chairman*
EMP: 15 EST: 1994
SQ FT: 25,000
SALES (est): 1.1MM **Privately Held**
WEB: www.llmi.com
SIC: 2835 In vitro & in vivo diagnostic substances

Beaver Dams
Schuyler County

(G-793)
M & H RESEARCH AND DEV CORP
Also Called: M&H Soaring
471 Post Creek Rd (14812-9124)
P.O. Box 368, Big Flats (14814-0368)
PHONE..................................607 734-2346
Claude M Sullivan, *President*
Hinz Weissembuehler, *Principal*
Karen Schlosser, *Vice Pres*
EMP: 6
SALES: 450K **Privately Held**
WEB: www.mandhsoaring.com
SIC: 3721 Gliders (aircraft)

Beaver Falls
Lewis County

(G-794)
INTERFACE PERFORMANCE MTLS
9635 Main St (13305)
PHONE..................................315 346-3100
John Tabolt, *Principal*
Greg Peters, *Info Tech Mgr*
EMP: 15 EST: 2012
SALES (est): 253K **Privately Held**
SIC: 2679 Paper products, converted

(G-795)
OMNIAFILTRA LLC
9567 Main St (13305)
P.O. Box 410 (13305-0410)
PHONE..................................315 346-7300
Fax: 315 346-7301
Gino Fronzoni, *President*
Scott Sauer, *Mill Mgr*
Michele Moore, *Financial Exec*
Patty Flint, *Accounts Mgr*
▼ EMP: 35
SALES: 9.5MM **Privately Held**
SIC: 2621 Paper mills

Bedford
Westchester County

(G-796)
BEDFORD WDWRK INSTLLATIONS INC
200 Pound Ridge Rd (10506-1243)
PHONE..................................914 764-9434
EMP: 6
SALES (est): 440K **Privately Held**
SIC: 2493 Mfg Reconstituted Wood Products

(G-797)
LESANNE LIFE SCIENCES LLC
47 Brook Farm Rd (10506-1309)
PHONE..................................914 234-0860
Robert J Beckman,
Robert Beckman,
EMP: 5
SALES: 300K **Privately Held**
SIC: 2835 In vitro & in vivo diagnostic substances

(G-798)
TORY ELECTRIC
641 Old Post Rd (10506-1218)
PHONE..................................914 292-5036
EMP: 7
SALES (est): 131.2K **Privately Held**
SIC: 3699 Electrical equipment & supplies

Bedford Hills
Westchester County

(G-799)
BEDFORD PRECISION PARTS CORP
290 Adams St (10507-1910)
P.O. Box 357 (10507-0357)
PHONE..................................914 241-2211
Fax: 914 241-3063
Daniel L Kleinman, *President*
Paul Kleinman, *Chairman*
Evalyn S Kleinman, *Corp Secy*
David Kleinman, *Vice Pres*
Robert Kleinman, *Vice Pres*
EMP: 33
SQ FT: 14,000
SALES (est): 5MM **Privately Held**
WEB: www.bedfordprecision.com
SIC: 3993 3563 Signs & advertising specialties; spraying outfits: metals, paints & chemicals (compressor)

(G-800)
CUSTOM SPORTSWEAR CORP
Also Called: Sportswear Unlimited
375 Adams St (10507-2001)
PHONE..................................914 666-9200
Adam Giardina, *President*
Gene King, *Production*
Len Schlangel, *CFO*
Ryria Singer, *Administration*
EMP: 5 EST: 1988
SQ FT: 6,000
SALES (est): 500K **Privately Held**
WEB: www.sptunl.com
SIC: 2759 5136 Screen printing; uniforms, men's & boys'

(G-801)
DAVID HOWELL PRODUCT DESIGN
Also Called: David Howell & Company
405 Adams St (10507-2066)
PHONE..................................914 666-4080
David Howell, *President*
Gina L Nuccetelli, *District Mgr*
Jeanne M May, *Marketing Staff*
Susan Howell, *Admin Sec*
EMP: 20
SQ FT: 6,000
SALES: 2MM **Privately Held**
WEB: www.davidhowell.com
SIC: 3911 Jewelry, precious metal

Bedford Hills - Westchester County (G-802)

(G-802)
DISPERSION TECHNOLOGY INC
364 Adams St (10507-2048)
PHONE..............................914 241-4777
Andre Doukhin, *President*
Petty Rausa, *Office Mgr*
Betty Rausa, *Manager*
EMP: 4
SQ FT: 3,000
SALES: 2MM **Privately Held**
SIC: 3829 Measuring & controlling devices

(G-803)
EYEGLASS SERVICE INDUSTRIES
Also Called: Vision World
777 Bedford Rd (10507-1504)
PHONE..............................914 666-3150
EMP: 5
SALES (corp-wide): 7.1MM **Privately Held**
WEB: www.visionworld.com
SIC: 3841 5995 Surgical & medical instruments; opticians
PA: Eyeglass Service Industries Inc
420 Sunrise Hwy
Lynbrook NY 11563
516 561-3937

(G-804)
MALCON INC
405 Adams St (10507-2066)
P.O. Box 463 (10507-0463)
PHONE..............................914 666-7146
Peter Malavenda, *President*
Frances Malavenda, *Corp Secy*
EMP: 18
SQ FT: 15,000
SALES (est): 300.3K **Privately Held**
WEB: www.malcon.com
SIC: 3823 Panelboard indicators, recorders & controllers: receiver

(G-805)
PRODUCTION MILLING COMPANY
364 Adams St Ste 5 (10507-2047)
PHONE..............................914 666-0792
Frank G Servidio, *President*
EMP: 5
SQ FT: 1,900
SALES (est): 495K **Privately Held**
SIC: 3599 Machine shop, jobbing & repair

(G-806)
RAINBEAU RIDGE FARM
49 Davids Way (10507-2531)
PHONE..............................914 234-2197
Lisa Schwartz, *Owner*
Karen Sabath, *Partner*
Mark Schwartz, *Co-Owner*
Ron Brooks, *Manager*
Isaac Jahns, *Manager*
EMP: 9
SQ FT: 6,000
SALES (est): 310K **Privately Held**
SIC: 2022 8299 Cheese, natural & processed; educational services

(G-807)
RECORD REVIEW LLC
Also Called: Bedford Pund Rdge Rcord Review
264 Adams St Fl 2 (10507-1910)
P.O. Box 455 (10507-0455)
PHONE..............................914 244-0533
Fax: 914 244-0537
Felix Carroll, *Advt Staff*
Deborah White, *Mng Member*
EMP: 10
SALES (est): 415.3K **Privately Held**
SIC: 2711 Newspapers, publishing & printing

(G-808)
WATER TREATMENT SERVICES INC
Also Called: Water Treatment Svce
395 Adams St (10507-2001)
PHONE..............................914 241-2261
Fax: 914 241-2517
Carol Salis, *President*
EMP: 7
SALES: 425K **Privately Held**
SIC: 3589 Water treatment equipment, industrial

Bellerose
Queens County

(G-809)
ADVANTEX SOLUTIONS INC
24845 Jericho Tpke (11426-1912)
PHONE..............................718 278-2290
Giovanni Natale, *President*
Antonio Sferrazz, *Vice Pres*
Danielle Haselton, *Administration*
EMP: 6
SALES (est): 1MM **Privately Held**
SIC: 3822 Temperature controls, automatic

(G-810)
LEIGH SCOTT ENTERPRISES INC
Also Called: Minuteman Press
24802 Union Tpke (11426-1837)
PHONE..............................718 343-5440
Fax: 718 343-2329
Scott Levine, *President*
EMP: 6
SALES (est): 550K **Privately Held**
WEB: www.minutemanbellrose.com
SIC: 2752 2791 Commercial printing, lithographic; typesetting

(G-811)
RITNOA INC
24019 Jamaica Ave Fl 2 (11426-1054)
PHONE..............................212 660-2148
Shabbir Khan, *President*
EMP: 38 EST: 2006
SQ FT: 12,000
SALES (est): 3.1MM **Privately Held**
SIC: 7372 Business oriented computer software

(G-812)
ZINNIAS INC
24520 Grand Central Pkwy 4l (11426-2712)
PHONE..............................718 746-8551
▲ EMP: 12
SQ FT: 3,800
SALES: 1.4MM **Privately Held**
SIC: 2369 2361 Girls And Childrens Outerwear, Nec, Nsk

Bellmore
Nassau County

(G-813)
ARNOLD TAYLOR PRINTING INC
2218 Brody Ln (11710-5102)
PHONE..............................516 781-0564
Fax: 212 629-7345
Carey Platt, *President*
EMP: 5 EST: 1963
SALES (est): 350K **Privately Held**
SIC: 2752 Commercial printing, offset

(G-814)
BANNER TRANSMISSION & ENG CO
Also Called: Banner Transmissions
2765 Broadway (11710-5612)
PHONE..............................516 221-9459
Fax: 516 221-0813
Clifforddwin Hettinger, *President*
Christopher B Sweeny, *Admin Sec*
EMP: 10
SQ FT: 4,500
SALES (est): 860K **Privately Held**
WEB: www.bannertransmission.com
SIC: 3714 7539 Transmissions, motor vehicle; automotive repair shops

(G-815)
BELLMORE STEEL PRODUCTS CORP
2282 Bellmore Ave (11710-5627)
P.O. Box 825 (11710-0825)
PHONE..............................516 785-9667
Fax: 516 785-9631
Glenn S Suskind, *Ch of Bd*
EMP: 16
SQ FT: 3,000
SALES: 2.6MM **Privately Held**
SIC: 3443 Fabricated plate work (boiler shop)

(G-816)
CLPA EMBROIDERY
2635 Pettit Ave (11710-3630)
PHONE..............................516 409-0002
Fax: 516 409-2049
Joseph Clabby, *Owner*
EMP: 5 EST: 2001
SALES (est): 246.9K **Privately Held**
SIC: 2395 Art needlework: made from purchased materials

(G-817)
DECAL MAKERS INC
2477 Merrick Rd (11710-5751)
PHONE..............................516 221-7200
Fax: 516 221-7229
Audrey J Hastingscooper, *President*
Leslie A Hastings-Bensi, *Corp Secy*
Mark Harris, *Vice Pres*
Linda Hennessy, *Vice Pres*
Matthew Hennessy, *Plant Mgr*
EMP: 25 EST: 1923
SALES (est): 2.3MM **Privately Held**
SIC: 2752 3993 2396 Decals, lithographed; name plates: except engraved, etched, etc.: metal; automotive & apparel trimmings

(G-818)
METRO CITY GROUP INC
2283 Bellmore Ave (11710-5623)
PHONE..............................516 781-2500
Carlos Jaramillo, *President*
EMP: 4
SALES: 4.5MM **Privately Held**
SIC: 3423 1711 Plumbers' hand tools; carpenters' hand tools, except saws: levels, chisels, etc.; plumbing contractors

(G-819)
PAPERWORLD INC
3054 Lee Pl (11710-5034)
PHONE..............................516 221-2702
Carol Grubman, *President*
▲ EMP: 37
SALES (est): 7.3MM **Privately Held**
SIC: 2679 2675 Adding machine rolls, paper: made from purchased material; die-cut paper & board

(G-820)
RUSH GOLD MANUFACTURING LTD
Also Called: G R M
2400 Merrick Rd (11710-3821)
PHONE..............................516 781-3155
Harold Lazar, *President*
Shirley Lazar, *Admin Sec*
▲ EMP: 74
SQ FT: 10,000
SALES: 5MM **Privately Held**
SIC: 3499 3961 Novelties & giftware, including trophies; costume jewelry

(G-821)
SALISBURY SPORTSWEAR INC
2523 Marine Pl (11710-5107)
PHONE..............................516 221-9519
Herbert Margolis, *President*
EMP: 50
SALES (est): 3MM **Privately Held**
SIC: 2339 Sportswear, women's

(G-822)
SIGN UP NOW INC
2541 Merrick Rd (11710-5710)
PHONE..............................516 221-3394
Gail Palmieri, *President*
George Palmieri, *Admin Sec*
EMP: 9 EST: 1998
SQ FT: 4,000
SALES: 290K **Privately Held**
SIC: 3993 Signs & advertising specialties

(G-823)
SPEEDY SIGN A RAMA USA INC
Also Called: Sign-A-Rama
2956 Merrick Rd (11710-5760)
PHONE..............................516 783-1075
Fax: 516 783-4708
Michael Bolz, *President*
Stanley Swanson, *CFO*
EMP: 5
SALES (est): 389.3K **Privately Held**
SIC: 3993 Signs & advertising specialties

Bellport
Suffolk County

(G-824)
50+ LIFESTYLE
146 S Country Rd Ste 4 (11713-2530)
PHONE..............................631 286-0058
Hon Frank C Trotta, *President*
Frank C Trotta, *Owner*
Mary Alice Graham, *Finance*
Evelyn Aloisio, *Accounts Exec*
Tim Edwards, *Sales Executive*
EMP: 8
SALES: 750K **Privately Held**
SIC: 2711 Newspapers

(G-825)
ABLE ELECTRONICS INC
18 Sawgrass Dr (11713-1549)
PHONE..............................631 924-5386
Fax: 631 924-5389
Loraine Leverock, *CEO*
Elizabeth Padrazo, *Chairman*
Ann Konon, *Vice Pres*
Kenneth Levebrock, *Vice Pres*
Cody Valentin, *Sales Mgr*
EMP: 10
SQ FT: 995
SALES: 3.1MM **Privately Held**
SIC: 3674 Semiconductors & related devices

(G-826)
AVS LAMINATES INC
Also Called: Steigercraft
99 Bellport Ave (11713-2106)
PHONE..............................631 286-2136
Alan Steiger, *President*
John Manarte, *Vice Pres*
William Rufer, *Vice Pres*
Mark Harak, *Controller*
▲ EMP: 25
SQ FT: 20,800
SALES (est): 5.3MM **Privately Held**
WEB: www.steigercraft.com
SIC: 3732 Fishing boats: lobster, crab, oyster, etc.: small

(G-827)
C HOWARD COMPANY INC
1007 Station Rd (11713-1552)
PHONE..............................631 286-7940
Fax: 631 286-7947
EMP: 9 EST: 1934
SQ FT: 10,000
SALES (est): 520K **Privately Held**
SIC: 2064 Mfg Candy/Confectionery

(G-828)
CRAZ WOODWORKING ASSOC INC
24 Sawgrass Dr (11713-1549)
PHONE..............................631 205-1890
Peter Craz, *President*
Steve Lineberger, *Office Mgr*
EMP: 12
SQ FT: 12,000
SALES (est): 1.8MM **Privately Held**
SIC: 2499 Decorative wood & woodwork

(G-829)
EASTERN PRECISION MACHINING
11 Farber Dr Ste I (11713-1500)
PHONE..............................631 286-4758
Norbert G Schreiber, *President*
Annmarie Schreiber, *Vice Pres*
EMP: 5
SQ FT: 6,000
SALES (est): 653.8K **Privately Held**
WEB: www.easternprecisionmachining.com
SIC: 3728 3599 Aircraft parts & equipment; machine shop, jobbing & repair

▲ = Import ▼ = Export
◆ = Import/Export

(G-830)
EDGE DISPLAY GROUP ENTP INC
35 Sawgrass Dr Ste 2 (11713-1577)
PHONE..................................631 498-1373
Philip J Zellner, *President*
▼ **EMP:** 10
SALES (est): 1MM **Privately Held**
SIC: 3993 Displays & cutouts, window & lobby

(G-831)
FIREWORKS BY GRUCCI INC
20 Pinehurst Dr (11713-1573)
PHONE..................................631 286-0088
Phil Grucci, *President*
Felix Grucci Jr, *President*
Donna Butler, *Vice Pres*
Stephanie Seib, *Vice Pres*
Carol Drozdowski, *Manager*
◆ **EMP:** 30
SQ FT: 6,000
SALES (est): 7.1MM **Privately Held**
SIC: 2899 Flares, fireworks & similar preparations

(G-832)
HEINECK ASSOCIATES INC
28 Curtis Ave (11713-1120)
PHONE..................................631 207-2347
Andrew Heineck, *President*
EMP: 6 **EST:** 2000
SALES: 500K **Privately Held**
SIC: 7372 Prepackaged software

(G-833)
MAEHR INDUSTRIES INC
14 Sawgrass Dr (11713-1549)
PHONE..................................631 924-1661
Michael Maehr, *President*
EMP: 6
SQ FT: 5,000
SALES (est): 760K **Privately Held**
WEB: www.maehr.com
SIC: 3469 3599 Machine parts, stamped or pressed metal; machine shop, jobbing & repair

(G-834)
MCKEON ROLLING STL DOOR CO INC (PA)
44 Sawgrass Dr (11713-1549)
PHONE..................................631 803-3000
Joseph J McKeon, *Chairman*
Jean Elizer, *Purchasing*
Andrew Meyer, *Sales Staff*
▲ **EMP:** 48 **EST:** 1986
SALES (est): 7.5MM **Privately Held**
SIC: 3442 Metal doors; rolling doors for industrial buildings or warehouses, metal; fire doors, metal

(G-835)
OPTISOURCE INTERNATIONAL INC
Also Called: Nu-Chem Laboratories
40 Sawgrass Dr Ste 1 (11713-1564)
PHONE..................................631 924-8360
Daryl Squicciarini, *President*
Anthony Zanghi, *Project Mgr*
Wendy Schneider, *Sales Mgr*
Jose Cepeda Jr, *Sales Associate*
Josh Yenis, *Manager*
▲ **EMP:** 30
SQ FT: 30,000
SALES: 13MM
SALES (corp-wide): 88.1MM **Privately Held**
WEB: www.1-800-optisource.com
SIC: 3851 Lens coating, ophthalmic
HQ: Essilor Laboratories Of America, Inc.
13515 N Stemmons Fwy
Dallas TX 75234
972 241-4141

(G-836)
ORE-LUBE CORPORATION
Also Called: Orelube
20 Sawgrass Dr (11713-1549)
PHONE..................................631 205-0030
Fax: 631 205-9797
Robert Silverstein, *President*
Stan Steckler, *General Mgr*
Fritz Louif, *Warehouse Mgr*
Donna Klempka, *Office Mgr*
Debbie Desprel, *Manager*
▲ **EMP:** 15 **EST:** 1958
SQ FT: 15,000
SALES (est): 3.7MM **Privately Held**
WEB: www.orelube.com
SIC: 2992 Lubricating oils & greases

(G-837)
PALLETS R US INC
555 Woodside Ave (11713-1220)
PHONE..................................631 758-2360
Nicholas Sorge, *Ch of Bd*
Thomas Sorge, *Vice Pres*
EMP: 50
SQ FT: 10,000
SALES (est): 12.1MM **Privately Held**
SIC: 2448 Pallets, wood

(G-838)
PINPOINT SYSTEMS INTL INC (PA)
10 Pinehurst Dr (11713-1573)
PHONE..................................631 775-2100
William Silhan, *President*
Joe Reisinger, *Vice Pres*
Bruce Barlowe, *Buyer*
Tom Hicks, *Controller*
Michael McIntire, *Director*
EMP: 100
SALES (est): 8.5MM **Privately Held**
WEB: www.destdirect.com
SIC: 3699 Electrical equipment & supplies

(G-839)
POLYMAG INC
685 Station Rd Ste 2 (11713-1697)
PHONE..................................631 286-4111
Fax: 631 286-0607
Devineni Ratnam, *President*
Lou Gunn, *Manager*
Dev Ranam, *Manager*
▲ **EMP:** 20
SQ FT: 15,000
SALES (est): 3MM **Privately Held**
WEB: www.polymaginc.com
SIC: 3499 Magnets, permanent: metallic

(G-840)
PYROTECHNIQUE BY GRUCCI INC (PA)
Also Called: Starlight Properties
20 Pinehurst Dr (11713-1573)
PHONE..................................540 639-8800
Fax: 631 286-9036
Felix P Grucci, *President*
Donna Butler Grucci, *Vice Pres*
Felix J Grucci Jr, *CFO*
John Grennan, *Controller*
Scott Kern, *Persnl Dir*
▲ **EMP:** 30
SQ FT: 8,000
SALES (est): 17.1MM **Privately Held**
WEB: www.grucci.com
SIC: 2899 Flares, fireworks & similar preparations

(G-841)
THEGO CORPORATION
Also Called: Acme Marine Hoist
2 Mooring Dr (11713-2810)
PHONE..................................631 776-2472
EMP: 5 **EST:** 1948
SQ FT: 11,500
SALES: 1MM **Privately Held**
SIC: 3536 Mfg Marine Hoists

(G-842)
TORINO INDUSTRIAL INC
Also Called: Torino Industrial Fabrication
4 Pinehurst Dr (11713-1573)
PHONE..................................631 509-1640
Vincent Sette, *Ch of Bd*
Keith Passanante, *Vice Pres*
Maria Passanante, *Treasurer*
Palmina Sette, *Shareholder*
EMP: 13
SQ FT: 10,000
SALES (est): 2.4MM **Privately Held**
WEB: www.torinoindustrial.com
SIC: 3449 Bars, concrete reinforcing: fabricated steel

Belmont
Allegany County

(G-843)
SUIT-KOTE CORPORATION
5628 Tuckers Corners Rd (14813-9604)
PHONE..................................585 268-7127
EMP: 84
SALES (corp-wide): 278.7MM **Privately Held**
SIC: 2911 Asphalt or asphaltic materials, made in refineries
PA: Suit-Kote Corporation
1911 Lorings Crossing Rd
Cortland NY 13045
607 753-1100

Bemus Point
Chautauqua County

(G-844)
LAKESIDE INDUSTRIES INC
Also Called: Point Industrial
2 Lakeside Dr (14712-9310)
P.O. Box 9130 (14712-0913)
PHONE..................................716 386-3031
Fax: 716 386-5428
Roy Benson, *CEO*
Brad Benson, *President*
Greg Benson, *Marketing Staff*
EMP: 10
SQ FT: 2,000
SALES: 950K **Privately Held**
SIC: 3599 Amusement park equipment

Bergen
Genesee County

(G-845)
DIEHL DEVELOPMENT INC
Also Called: Diehl Sand & Gravel
5922 N Lake Rd (14416-9507)
PHONE..................................585 494-2920
Fax: 585 494-2920
Keith Diehl, *President*
EMP: 5
SQ FT: 500
SALES (est): 1.9MM **Privately Held**
SIC: 1442 Gravel mining

(G-846)
GUTHRIE HELI-ARC INC
6276 Clinton Street Rd (14416-9738)
PHONE..................................585 548-5053
Fax: 716 434-2662
Will Guthrie, *President*
EMP: 8
SQ FT: 4,500
SALES (est): 715K **Privately Held**
SIC: 7692 Welding repair

(G-847)
K2 PLASTICS INC
8210 Buffalo Rd (14416-9444)
PHONE..................................585 494-2727
Klaus Kremmin II, *President*
Carol Zaccour, *Manager*
EMP: 5
SALES (est): 754K **Privately Held**
WEB: www.k2plasticsinc.com
SIC: 3089 Molding primary plastic

(G-848)
LEWIS & MYERS INC (PA)
Also Called: LMI
7307 S Lake Rd (14416-9357)
PHONE..................................585 494-1410
Fax: 585 494-1436
Lawrence Lewis, *President*
Rebecca Taylor, *General Mgr*
EMP: 4
SQ FT: 33,000
SALES (est): 1.7MM **Privately Held**
WEB: www.lmipacking.com
SIC: 3086 Plastics foam products

(G-849)
LIBERTY PUMPS INC
7000 Appletree Ave (14416-9446)
PHONE..................................585 494-1817
Fax: 585 494-1839
Charles E Cook, *Ch of Bd*
Robyn Brookhart, *Business Mgr*
Allan Davis, *Vice Pres*
Rebecca Evangelista, *Vice Pres*
Gary Volk, *Vice Pres*
◆ **EMP:** 130 **EST:** 1965
SQ FT: 120,000
SALES: 86.1MM **Privately Held**
WEB: www.libertypumps.com
SIC: 3561 Pumps, domestic: water or sump

(G-850)
MILLERS MILLWORKS INC
Also Called: Millers Presentation Furniture
29 N Lake Ave (14416-9528)
P.O. Box 175 (14416-0175)
PHONE..................................585 494-1420
Greg Lumb, *President*
John Finch, *Sales Executive*
Kathleen Dunlap, *Office Mgr*
EMP: 20 **EST:** 1996
SQ FT: 6,192
SALES: 2.1MM **Privately Held**
WEB: www.millersmillwork.com
SIC: 2521 Wood office furniture

(G-851)
ODYSSEY CONTROLS INC
6256 Clinton Street Rd (14416-9738)
P.O. Box 613 (14416-0613)
PHONE..................................585 548-9800
Danie T Harmon Jr, *Ch of Bd*
EMP: 6
SALES (est): 974.7K **Privately Held**
SIC: 3613 Control panels, electric

(G-852)
SCOMAC INC
8629 Buffalo Rd (14416)
P.O. Box 455 (14416-0455)
PHONE..................................585 494-2200
Fax: 585 494-2300
Lawrence Scott, *President*
EMP: 12
SQ FT: 12,000
SALES (est): 1.9MM **Privately Held**
WEB: www.scomac.com
SIC: 3545 Diamond dressing & wheel crushing attachments

Berkshire
Tioga County

(G-853)
TIOGA HARDWOODS INC (PA)
12685 State Route 38 (13736-1930)
P.O. Box 195 (13736-0195)
PHONE..................................607 657-8686
Fax: 607 687-9439
Kevin Gillette, *President*
Randy Bowers, *Vice Pres*
Scott Snyder, *Vice Pres*
Chad Cotterill, *Sales Staff*
▼ **EMP:** 1
SQ FT: 20,000
SALES (est): 4.5MM **Privately Held**
WEB: www.tiogahardwoods.com
SIC: 2861 Hardwood distillates

(G-854)
TREIMAN PUBLICATIONS CORP
12724 State Route 38 (13736-1911)
PHONE..................................607 657-8473
Fax: 607 657-8505
Dov Trieman, *President*
EMP: 5
SALES (est): 287.1K **Privately Held**
SIC: 2741 Miscellaneous publishing

Berlin
Rensselaer County

(G-855)
COWEE FOREST PRODUCTS INC
28 Taylor Ave (12022-2431)
PHONE...............518 658-2233
William Stallkamp, *President*
Tara Fisher, *General Mgr*
Arthur Bogen, *Vice Pres*
▲ **EMP:** 20 **EST:** 1898
SQ FT: 100,000
SALES: 2MM **Privately Held**
WEB: www.cowee.com
SIC: 2499 Novelties, wood fiber; carved & turned wood

(G-856)
GREEN RENEWABLE INC
28 Taylor Ave (12022-2431)
PHONE...............518 658-2233
Sean M Gallivan, *President*
Todd Tierney, *General Mgr*
EMP: 40
SALES (est): 120.9K **Privately Held**
SIC: 2499 Clothespins, wood

(G-857)
MILANESE COMMERCIAL DOOR LLC
28 Taylor Ave (12022-2431)
P.O. Box 560 (12022-0560)
PHONE...............518 658-0398
Brian Milanese, *Principal*
EMP: 10 **EST:** 2007
SALES (est): 1.4MM **Privately Held**
SIC: 3442 5031 Metal doors; door frames, all materials

Bernhards Bay
Oswego County

(G-858)
MCINTOSH BOX & PALLET CO INC
741 State Route 49 (13028)
P.O. Box 76 (13028-0076)
PHONE...............315 675-8511
Fax: 315 675-3068
Brian Cole, *Opers Mgr*
Michael Milson, *Branch Mgr*
EMP: 60
SALES (corp-wide): 24.8MM **Privately Held**
WEB: www.mcintoshbox.com
SIC: 2448 2441 Pallets, wood; nailed wood boxes & shook
PA: Mcintosh Box & Pallet Co., Inc.
5864 Pyle Dr
East Syracuse NY 13057
315 446-9350

Bethel
Sullivan County

(G-859)
ALEXY ASSOCIATES INC
86 Jim Stephenson Rd (12720)
P.O. Box 70 (12720-0070)
PHONE...............845 482-3000
Fax: 845 482-3040
Cornelius Alexy, *President*
James Alexy, *Systems Mgr*
Sharon Alexy, *Admin Sec*
EMP: 20 **EST:** 1974
SALES: 200K **Privately Held**
WEB: www.aaultrasoniccleaners.com
SIC: 3699 7629 Cleaning equipment, ultrasonic, except medical & dental; electronic equipment repair

(G-860)
CAMPANELLIS POULTRY FARM INC
4 Perry Rd (12720)
PHONE...............845 482-2222
Anthony Campanelli, *Owner*
EMP: 5
SALES: 1.7MM **Privately Held**
SIC: 2015 Poultry slaughtering & processing

Bethpage
Nassau County

(G-861)
A & M LITHO INC
4 Hunt Pl (11714-6411)
PHONE...............516 342-9727
Anna Laperuta, *President*
EMP: 25
SALES: 2.5MM **Privately Held**
SIC: 2752 Commercial printing, offset

(G-862)
ABBLE AWNING CO INC
313 Broadway Ste 315 (11714-3003)
PHONE...............516 822-1200
Thomas Catalano, *President*
John Catalano, *Vice Pres*
EMP: 9
SQ FT: 2,400
SALES: 500K **Privately Held**
WEB: www.abbleawning.com
SIC: 2394 Awnings, fabric: made from purchased materials; canopies, fabric: made from purchased materials

(G-863)
AC MOORE INCORPORATED
3988 Hempstead Tpke (11714-5603)
PHONE...............516 796-5831
Fax: 516 796-5852
EMP: 5
SALES (corp-wide): 546.1MM **Privately Held**
SIC: 2499 5023 Mfg Wood Products Whol Homefurnishings
HQ: A.C. Moore Incorporated
130 A C Moore Dr
Berlin NJ 08009
856 768-4930

(G-864)
AGUA ENERVIVA LLC
15 Grumman Rd W Ste 1300 (11714-5029)
PHONE...............516 597-5440
Michael Venuti, *President*
Carol Dollard, *COO*
Thomas Reynolds, *Finance*
EMP: 12
SALES (est): 1.4MM **Privately Held**
SIC: 2087 Beverage bases, concentrates, syrups, powders & mixes

(G-865)
BRUNSCHWIG & FILS LLC (HQ)
245 Central Ave (11714-3922)
PHONE...............800 538-1880
Carlos Anderson, *Credit Mgr*
Peter Smith,
Brusnchwig Fils, *Representative*
▲ **EMP:** 13
SALES: 26.8MM
SALES (corp-wide): 494.9MM **Privately Held**
SIC: 2329 2211 Ski & snow clothing: men's & boys'; upholstery, tapestry & wall coverings: cotton
PA: Kravet Inc.
225 Cent Ave S
Bethpage NY 11714
516 293-2000

(G-866)
EVENT JOURNAL INC
700 Hicksville Rd (11714-3471)
PHONE...............516 470-1811
Dawn Strain, *President*
Marisa Kerby, *Opers Staff*
William Frank, *Client Mgr*
Lisa Smith, *Consultant*
Deborah Hudak, *Business Dir*
EMP: 8
SALES (est): 513.3K **Privately Held**
SIC: 2711 Newspapers, publishing & printing

(G-867)
GRUMMAN FIELD SUPPORT SERVICES
S Oyster Bay Rd (11714)
PHONE...............516 575-0574
Ed Sax, *Principal*
Brian Boyer, *Vice Pres*
Tony Miller, *Finance*
EMP: 70
SALES (est): 11.6MM **Publicly Held**
WEB: www.sperry.ngc.com
SIC: 3721 8731 Aircraft; commercial physical research
HQ: Northrop Grumman Systems Corporation
2980 Fairview Park Dr
Falls Church VA 22042
703 280-2900

(G-868)
HOWE MACHINE & TOOL CORP
236 Park Ave (11714-3709)
PHONE...............516 931-5687
Fax: 516 931-5717
Paul Howe, *President*
Ryan Howe, *Vice Pres*
Sue Howe, *Manager*
Jacquelin Castagna, *Admin Asst*
EMP: 11 **EST:** 1953
SQ FT: 11,500
SALES: 11.5MM **Privately Held**
WEB: www.howemachine.com
SIC: 3724 Aircraft engines & engine parts

(G-869)
KRAVET FABRICS INC (PA)
225 Central Ave S (11714-4990)
PHONE...............516 293-2000
Fax: 516 293-2158
Cary Kravet, *CEO*
Elliot Halem, *Opers Mgr*
Arnold Grodman, *VP Sales*
Mike Degroso, *Telecomm Mgr*
John Nora, *Database Admin*
▲ **EMP:** 66
SALES (est): 92.5MM **Privately Held**
SIC: 2392 Mattress pads

(G-870)
KREON INC
999 S Oyster Bay Rd # 105 (11714-1041)
PHONE...............516 470-9522
Thomas Mindt, *CEO*
Darin Fowler, *President*
Naresh Ramsaran, *Engineer*
Christina Sewkaran, *Administration*
EMP: 5
SALES (est): 1MM **Privately Held**
SIC: 3641 Electric lamps
HQ: Kreon Nv
Industrieweg-Noord 1152
Opglabbeek 3660
898 197-80

(G-871)
LDC
127 Brenner Ave (11714-4303)
P.O. Box 12 (11714-0012)
PHONE...............516 822-2499
Andrew Senior, *Principal*
EMP: 5
SALES: 100K **Privately Held**
SIC: 3842 Surgical appliances & supplies

(G-872)
LOGIC CONTROLS INC
Also Called: Bematech
999 S Oyster Bay Rd (11714-1038)
PHONE...............516 248-0400
Fax: 516 248-0443
Juliet Derby, *President*
Waldimir Alvarez, *Principal*
Breann Murray, *Business Mgr*
Paul Cagnard, *Controller*
Wladimir Alvarez, *VP Sales*
▲ **EMP:** 33
SQ FT: 10,000
SALES (est): 8.1MM
SALES (corp-wide): 447.6MM **Privately Held**
WEB: www.logiccontrols.com
SIC: 3578 Accounting machines & cash registers; cash registers; point-of-sale devices; registers, credit account
HQ: Bematech Industria E Comercio De Equipamentos Eletronicos S/A.
Av. Rui Barbosa 2.529
Sao Jose Dos Pinhais PR 83055
413 351-2700

(G-873)
MARK DRI PRODUCTS INC
999 S Oyster Bay Rd # 312 (11714-1042)
PHONE...............516 484-6200
Fax: 516 484-6279
Charles Reichmann, *CEO*
Andre Reichmann, *President*
Lynn Paugh, *COO*
Mickey Ciranni, *Purch Mgr*
Cathy Williams-Owen, *Controller*
▲ **EMP:** 200
SQ FT: 54,000
SALES (est): 24.8MM **Privately Held**
WEB: www.drimark.com
SIC: 3951 5112 Markers, soft tip (felt, fabric, plastic, etc.); pens &/or pencils

(G-874)
MELMONT FINE PRINGNG/GRAPHICS
6 Robert Ct Ste 24 (11714-1415)
P.O. Box 395, Old Bethpage (11804-0395)
PHONE...............516 939-2253
Angela Melledy, *President*
EMP: 6
SALES: 150K **Privately Held**
SIC: 2711 7389 Newspapers, publishing & printing; printing broker

(G-875)
MLS SALES
226 10th St (11714-1703)
PHONE...............516 681-2736
Mary Lafauci, *Owner*
EMP: 6
SALES: 120K **Privately Held**
SIC: 3679 Electronic components

(G-876)
NORTHROP GRUMMAN CORPORATION
660 Grumman Rd W (11714)
PHONE...............703 280-2900
Wesley G Bush, *Branch Mgr*
EMP: 702 **Publicly Held**
SIC: 3812 Search & navigation equipment
PA: Northrop Grumman Corporation
2980 Fairview Park Dr
Falls Church VA 22042

(G-877)
NORTHROP GRUMMAN SYSTEMS CORP
925 S Oyster Bay Rd (11714-3582)
PHONE...............516 575-0574
Michael Gross, *General Mgr*
Dominic Anton, *Project Mgr*
Shawn McCandless, *Facilities Mgr*
Kevin Witt, *Facilities Mgr*
John Munyak, *Technical Mgr*
EMP: 1659 **Publicly Held**
WEB: www.sperry.ngc.com
SIC: 3721 8731 Aircraft; commercial physical research
HQ: Northrop Grumman Systems Corporation
2980 Fairview Park Dr
Falls Church VA 22042
703 280-2900

(G-878)
RAIN CATCHERS SEAMLESS GUTTERS
39 Park Ln (11714-5226)
PHONE...............516 520-1956
Robert Dambrosio, *CEO*
EMP: 5
SALES (est): 433.2K **Privately Held**
SIC: 3272 Floor slabs & tiles, precast concrete

(G-879)
WILSONART INTL HOLDINGS LLC
999 S Oyster Bay Rd # 3305 (11714-1038)
PHONE...............516 935-6980
Fax: 516 935-6875
Greg Martino, *Manager*
EMP: 20

GEOGRAPHIC SECTION

SALES (corp-wide): 7.8B **Privately Held**
WEB: www.wilsonart.com
SIC: **2821** 2541 Plastics materials & resins; table or counter tops, plastic laminated
HQ: Wilsonart International Holdings Llc
2400 Wilson Pl
Temple TX 76504
254 207-7000

Big Flats
Chemung County

(G-880)
CORNING INCORPORATED
271 County Rt 64 (14814)
PHONE.................................607 974-0206
EMP: 48
SALES (corp-wide): 9.1B **Publicly Held**
SIC: **3229** Glass fiber products
PA: Corning Incorporated
1 Riverfront Plz
Corning NY 14831
607 974-9000

(G-881)
CORNING INCORPORATED
271 Rr 64 (14814)
PHONE.................................607 974-0206
Fax: 607 974-0292
EMP: 461
SALES (corp-wide): 9.1B **Publicly Held**
SIC: **3229** Glass fiber products; glass tubes & tubing; TV tube blanks, glass
PA: Corning Incorporated
1 Riverfront Plz
Corning NY 14831
607 974-9000

(G-882)
REYNOLDS MANUFACTURING INC
3298 State Rte 352 (14814)
PHONE.................................607 562-8936
Kasandra Reynolds, *Ch of Bd*
Terri Fitzpatrick, *Purchasing*
Paula White-Arcovio, *Accounts Mgr*
Kristi Hackrd, *Administration*
EMP: 17
SQ FT: 11,000
SALES (est): 4.1MM **Privately Held**
SIC: **3444** 3469 Sheet metalwork; machine parts, stamped or pressed metal

(G-883)
X-GEN PHARMACEUTICALS INC (PA)
300 Daniel Zenker Dr (14814)
P.O. Box 445 (14814-0445)
PHONE.................................607 562-2700
Fax: 607 562-2760
Susan E Badia, *Ch of Bd*
J R Liles, *Vice Pres*
Robin Liles, *Vice Pres*
Tony Dowd, *Safety Mgr*
Catherine Liles, *Treasurer*
EMP: 3
SQ FT: 53,000
SALES (est): 4.6MM **Privately Held**
SIC: **2834** Pharmaceutical preparations

Binghamton
Broome County

(G-884)
A-LINE TECHNOLOGIES INC
197 Corporate Dr (13904-3214)
PHONE.................................607 772-2439
Fax: 607 772-2439
Alex Boyce, *President*
Frank J Boyce, *Vice Pres*
Tucker Williams, *Manager*
EMP: 10
SQ FT: 10,000
SALES: 1.1MM **Privately Held**
SIC: **3714** 3599 Motor vehicle transmissions, drive assemblies & parts; machine shop, jobbing & repair

(G-885)
ALL AMERICAN BUILDING
109 Crestmont Rd (13905-3951)
PHONE.................................607 797-7123
Douglas E Hamm, *Owner*
EMP: 8
SALES (est): 360K **Privately Held**
SIC: **3448** Prefabricated metal buildings

(G-886)
ALL SPEC FINISHING INC
219 Clinton St (13905-2236)
PHONE.................................607 770-9174
Fax: 607 770-9174
Anthony Milasi, *President*
Dennis Smith, *President*
Seth Blood, *Finance Other*
Shirley Milasi, *Admin Sec*
EMP: 50
SQ FT: 80,000
SALES (est): 5.9MM **Privately Held**
WEB: www.allspecfinishing.com
SIC: **3479** 7699 Painting, coating & hot dipping; painting of metal products; plastics products repair

(G-887)
AMERICAN QUALITY TECHNOLOGY
6 Emma St (13905-2508)
PHONE.................................607 777-9488
Gary Crounse, *President*
Jerome Luchuk, *CFO*
EMP: 12
SALES: 980K **Privately Held**
SIC: **3672** 3679 3825 Printed circuit boards; electronic circuits; instruments to measure electricity

(G-888)
AMETEK INC
33 Lewis Rd Ste 6 (13905-1045)
PHONE.................................607 763-4700
Ed Scott, *Engineer*
Robert Glydon, *Finance Mgr*
Robert Hyland, *Branch Mgr*
Michael V Stoddard, *Technology*
EMP: 68
SALES (corp-wide): 3.9B **Publicly Held**
SIC: **3621** Motors & generators
PA: Ametek, Inc.
1100 Cassatt Rd
Berwyn PA 19312
610 647-2121

(G-889)
ARNOLD-DAVIS LLC
Also Called: Harris Assembly Group
187 Indl Pk Dr (13904)
PHONE.................................607 772-1201
Thomas Davis, *CEO*
David Arnold, *Treasurer*
David Martin, *VP Finance*
Susan Priestley, *Administration*
David D Arnold,
▲ EMP: 125
SQ FT: 30,000
SALES (est): 24.9MM **Privately Held**
WEB: www.harrisasm.com
SIC: **3679** Harness assemblies for electronic use: wire or cable

(G-890)
BARRETT PAVING MATERIALS INC
14 Brandywine St (13901-2203)
P.O. Box 2368 (13902-2368)
PHONE.................................607 723-5367
Bill Lallier, *Facilities Mgr*
Craig Scovell, *Facilities Mgr*
Gary Hoyt, *Manager*
Brad Balcom, *Director*
EMP: 6
SQ FT: 1,144
SALES (corp-wide): 84.5MM **Privately Held**
WEB: www.barrettpaving.com
SIC: **2951** 1442 Asphalt paving mixtures & blocks; construction sand & gravel
HQ: Barrett Paving Materials Inc.
3 Becker Farm Rd Ste 307
Roseland NJ 07068
973 533-1001

(G-891)
BINGHAMTON BURIAL VAULT CO INC
1114 Porter Ave (13901-1688)
PHONE.................................607 722-4931
Brian Abbey, *President*
Janet Evenson, *Vice Pres*
EMP: 14
SQ FT: 10,000
SALES (est): 2MM **Privately Held**
SIC: **3272** Steps, prefabricated concrete; burial vaults, concrete or precast terrazzo

(G-892)
BINGHAMTON KNITTING CO INC
11 Alice St (13904-1587)
P.O. Box 1646 (13902-1646)
PHONE.................................607 722-6941
Fax: 607 722-4621
Douglas W Hardler, *President*
Lee Sherwood, *Prdtn Mgr*
Craig Hardler, *Shareholder*
Julia Sherwood, *Admin Sec*
▲ EMP: 20
SQ FT: 23,200
SALES: 1.1MM **Privately Held**
WEB: www.brimwick.com
SIC: **2253** 2258 Knit outerwear mills; sweaters & sweater coats, knit; lace & warp knit fabric mills

(G-893)
BINGHAMTON PRECAST & SUP CORP
18 Phelps St (13901-1858)
PHONE.................................607 722-0334
Fax: 607 722-0496
Jay Abbey, *Ch of Bd*
John Sanford, *General Mgr*
Fred Harper, *Project Engr*
Lanny Tracey, *Project Engr*
Frank Falank, *Electrical Engi*
EMP: 50
SALES (est): 11.1MM **Privately Held**
WEB: www.binghamtonprecast.com
SIC: **3272** Pipe, concrete or lined with concrete; culvert pipe, concrete

(G-894)
BINGHAMTON PRECISION TOOL INC
Also Called: Plastic Techniques
10 Ballard St (13904-1309)
PHONE.................................607 772-6021
Fax: 607 723-8601
William Basos, *President*
Betty Ann Basos, *Treasurer*
EMP: 7 EST: 1965
SQ FT: 6,000
SALES (est): 982.1K **Privately Held**
SIC: **3599** 3544 3089 Machine shop, jobbing & repair; special dies, tools, jigs & fixtures; injection molding of plastics

(G-895)
BINGHAMTON SIMULATOR CO INC
Also Called: B S C
151 Court St (13901-3529)
PHONE.................................607 321-2980
Fax: 607 722-6504
John Matthews, *CEO*
E Terry Lewis, *President*
Robin Laabs, *Principal*
Greg Stanton, *COO*
Barbara Blincoe, *Treasurer*
▲ EMP: 40
SQ FT: 14,000
SALES (est): 5.9MM **Privately Held**
WEB: www.bsc.com
SIC: **3571** 3577 7699 7373 Electronic computers; graphic displays, except graphic terminals; aircraft & heavy equipment repair services; systems integration services; electrical equipment & supplies

(G-896)
BINGHAMTON UNIVERSITY
Also Called: School of Management
Vestal Pkwy E (13901)
P.O. Box 6000 (13902-6000)
PHONE.................................607 777-2316
Gary Roodman, *Dean*
EMP: 73 **Privately Held**

SIC: **2731** 8221 9411 Books: publishing only; university; administration of educational programs;
HQ: Binghamton University
4400 Vestal Pkwy
Binghamton NY 13902
607 777-2000

(G-897)
BOCES BUSINESS OFFICE
Also Called: Broom Tioga Boces
435 Glenwood Rd (13905-1699)
PHONE.................................607 763-3300
Sandra Ruffo, *President*
Callie Kavleski, *Engineer*
Donna Balles, *Accountant*
Alan Slocum, *Cust Mgr*
Valerie Vavra, *Manager*
EMP: 21
SALES (est): 2.4MM **Privately Held**
SIC: **2761** Continuous forms, office & business

(G-898)
BOKA PRINTING INC
12 Hall St (13903-2114)
PHONE.................................607 725-3235
Bob Carr, *Principal*
EMP: 6 EST: 2013
SALES (est): 847.2K **Privately Held**
SIC: **2752** Commercial printing, lithographic

(G-899)
BSC ASSOCIATES LLC
100 Eldredge St (13901-2631)
PHONE.................................607 321-2980
Greg Stanton, *Branch Mgr*
Barry Wolf, *Systs Prg Mgr*
Barbara Blincoe,
EMP: 19
SALES (est): 2.1MM **Privately Held**
SIC: **3699** Flight simulators (training aids), electronic

(G-900)
BW ELLIOTT MFG CO LLC
11 Beckwith Ave (13901-1726)
P.O. Box 773 (13902-0773)
PHONE.................................607 772-0404
Fax: 607 772-0431
Richard Allbritton, *CEO*
George Scherer, *President*
Cyril Macinka, *COO*
Frank Kappauf, *Buyer*
Ken Palmer, *Engineer*
▲ EMP: 295
SQ FT: 250,000
SALES (est): 94.7MM
SALES (corp-wide): 1.2B **Publicly Held**
WEB: www.elliottmfg.com
SIC: **3568** 3492 3531 Power transmission equipment; shafts, flexible; joints, swivel & universal, except aircraft & automotive; control valves, fluid power: hydraulic & pneumatic; construction machinery
PA: Actuant Corporation
N86w12500 Westbrook Xing
Menomonee Falls WI 53051
262 293-1500

(G-901)
C H THOMPSON COMPANY INC
69-93 Eldredge St (13902)
PHONE.................................607 724-1094
Fax: 607 724-6990
Stacy Cacialli, *President*
Thomas Talerico, *President*
Stacy Schraeder, *Vice Pres*
Joseph Talerico, *CFO*
Mary Ciatiak, *Office Mgr*
EMP: 65 EST: 1924
SQ FT: 75,000
SALES (est): 8.7MM **Privately Held**
SIC: **3471** 2396 3479 Anodizing (plating) of metals or formed products; automotive & apparel trimmings; painting, coating & hot dipping

(G-902)
CMP ADVNCED MECH SLTONS NY LLC
Also Called: Cmp New York
90 Bevier Ct (13901-2117)
PHONE.................................607 352-1712
Steven Zimmerman, *Mng Member*

Binghamton - Broome County (G-903) — GEOGRAPHIC SECTION

Scott McManus, *Maintence Staff*
EMP: 9
SALES (est): 1.6MM
SALES (corp-wide): 471.1K Privately Held
SIC: 3824 Mechanical & electromechanical counters & devices
PA: Cmp Ams (International) Limitee
1241 Rue Des Cascades
Chateauguay QC J6J 4
450 691-5510

(G-903)
CREATIVE ORTHOTICS PROSTHETICS
65 Pennsylvania Ave 207 (13903-1651)
PHONE..................................607 771-4672
Thomas Kirk PHD, *CEO*
David Sicklis, *Manager*
Sheryl Price, *Director*
EMP: 9
SALES (corp-wide): 51.9MM Privately Held
SIC: 3842 5999 Limbs, artificial; orthopedic & prosthesis applications
PA: Creative Orthotics & Prosthetics Inc
1300 College Ave Ste 1
Elmira NY 14901
607 734-7215

(G-904)
CROWLEY FOODS INC (HQ)
93 Pennsylvania Ave (13903-1645)
PHONE..................................800 637-0019
John Kaned, *President*
Lynn Wordsworth, *Manager*
▼ **EMP:** 31 EST: 1904
SALES (est): 214.3MM
SALES (corp-wide): 1.9B Privately Held
WEB: www.crowleyfoods.com
SIC: 2026 2024 Fluid milk; fermented & cultured milk products; yogurt; cottage cheese; ice cream & frozen desserts
PA: Hp Hood Llc
6 Kimball Ln Ste 400
Lynnfield MA 01940
617 887-8441

(G-905)
CRYSTA-LYN CHEMICAL COMPANY
Also Called: Clearweld
6 Emma St (13905-2508)
PHONE..................................607 296-4721
Frank Goreleski, *President*
Bradly Galusha, *Vice Pres*
▲ **EMP:** 8
SQ FT: 12,000
SALES (est): 1.6MM Privately Held
WEB: www.crystalyn.com
SIC: 3699 Laser welding, drilling & cutting equipment

(G-906)
D D & L INC
Also Called: E D I Window Systems
3 Alice St (13904-1502)
P.O. Box 2949 (13902-2949)
PHONE..................................607 729-9131
Fax: 607 772-1855
David P Smith, *President*
Richard Smith, *Vice Pres*
EMP: 17
SQ FT: 15,120
SALES (est): 1.8MM Privately Held
SIC: 3442 5211 Window & door frames; door & window products

(G-907)
DBASE LLC
31 Front St (13905-4703)
P.O. Box 917, Oxford (13830-0917)
PHONE..................................607 729-0234
Fax: 607 729-3830
Robert Thompson, *Principal*
Cheryl Thompson, *Controller*
Martin Kay, *CTO*
Michael Rozlog,
EMP: 8 EST: 2011
SALES (est): 748.9K Privately Held
SIC: 7372 Application computer software

(G-908)
DOT TOOL CO INC
131 Nowlan Rd (13901-1693)
PHONE..................................607 724-7001
Fax: 607 723-5767
Gary Braman, *President*
EMP: 5
SQ FT: 3,004
SALES (est): 695.2K Privately Held
WEB: www.dottoolco.com
SIC: 3544 3444 Special dies, tools, jigs & fixtures; sheet metalwork

(G-909)
ECK PLASTIC ARTS INC
87 Prospect Ave (13901-2616)
PHONE..................................607 722-3227
Fax: 607 722-3081
Robert L Eck Jr, *President*
Chris Figures, *Opers Mgr*
EMP: 25
SQ FT: 30,000
SALES (est): 5.9MM Privately Held
WEB: www.eckplastics.com
SIC: 3089 Plastic processing; injection molded finished plastic products

(G-910)
ELECTRO FORM CORP
128 Bevier St (13904-1094)
PHONE..................................607 722-6404
Fax: 607 724-5184
Auguste Mathey Jr, *President*
Donna Jadarondak, *Admin Sec*
Bonnie Johnson, *Admin Sec*
EMP: 11
SQ FT: 6,000
SALES (est): 760K Privately Held
SIC: 3544 Special dies & tools

(G-911)
EMERSON NETWORK POWER
100 Emerson Pkwy (13905-6600)
PHONE..................................607 724-2484
Ray Rickard, *Manager*
Dan Buchanan, *Director*
EMP: 16
SALES (est): 2.8MM Privately Held
SIC: 3613 Regulators, power

(G-912)
EMS TECHNOLOGIES INC
71 Frederick St (13901-2563)
PHONE..................................607 723-3676
Clarence Hotchkiss, *Ch of Bd*
Mark Hotchkiss, *President*
Tom Costello, *Principal*
Michael Conner, *Vice Pres*
Joanne Delanoy, *Engineer*
EMP: 40
SQ FT: 36,000
SALES (est): 10.2MM
SALES (corp-wide): 11.1MM Privately Held
WEB: www.emstech.com
SIC: 3629 Electronic generation equipment
PA: Nelson Holdings Ltd
71 Frederick St
Binghamton NY 13901
607 772-1794

(G-913)
ENJOY CITY NORTH INC
Also Called: Save Around
31 Front St (13905-4703)
P.O. Box 2399 (13902-2399)
PHONE..................................607 584-5061
Luke Stanton, *President*
Eric Hinkle, *Business Mgr*
Charles Wellman, *Production*
Wendy Hickin, *Accountant*
MEI McRae, *Sales Dir*
EMP: 64
SALES: 5.9MM Privately Held
SIC: 2741 Miscellaneous publishing

(G-914)
FELCHAR MANUFACTURING CORP (HQ)
Also Called: Norwich Manufacturing Division
196 Corporate Dr (13904-3295)
PHONE..................................607 723-3106
Fax: 607 723-4084
Jonathan Miller, *President*
Vince Bungo, *Vice Pres*
Steve Cole, *Vice Pres*
Mike Carr, *Plant Mgr*
Ron Sternberg, *Plant Mgr*
▲ **EMP:** 650
SQ FT: 40,000
SALES (est): 222.8MM
SALES (corp-wide): 418.9MM Privately Held
WEB: www.felchar.com
SIC: 3678 3089 3621 Electronic connectors; injection molding of plastics; motors & generators
PA: Shop Vac Corporation
2323 Reach Rd
Williamsport PA 17701
570 326-0502

(G-915)
FRATELLIS LLC
Also Called: New Horizons Bakery
20 Campbell Rd (13905-4304)
PHONE..................................607 722-5663
Anthony Roma, *Principal*
Mary Roma, *Mng Member*
EMP: 21
SQ FT: 23,000
SALES (est): 850K Privately Held
SIC: 2051 2053 5142 5149 Bread, cake & related products; frozen bakery products, except bread; croissants, frozen; bakery products, frozen; bakery products

(G-916)
FRITO-LAY NORTH AMERICA INC
10 Spud Ln (13904-3299)
PHONE..................................607 775-7000
Fax: 607 775-3567
Pat Zimmer, *Safety Mgr*
Frank Armetta, *Mfg Spvr*
Thomas Brown, *Mfg Staff*
Brian Stringer, *Opers-Prdtn-Mfg*
Kyle Kilmer, *QC Dir*
EMP: 85
SQ FT: 4,906
SALES (corp-wide): 63B Publicly Held
WEB: www.fritolay.com
SIC: 2096 2099 Potato chips & other potato-based snacks; food preparations
HQ: Frito-Lay North America, Inc.
7701 Legacy Dr
Plano TX 75024

(G-917)
G J C LTD INC
Also Called: Wilson Electroplating
6 Emma St (13905-2508)
PHONE..................................607 770-4500
Fax: 607 770-9117
Gary Crounse, *President*
Olin Russell, *Mng Officer*
EMP: 24
SQ FT: 30,000
SALES (est): 2.4MM Privately Held
SIC: 3471 Electroplating & plating

(G-918)
GEOWEB3D INC
45 Lewis St (13901-3000)
P.O. Box 2019 (13902-2019)
PHONE..................................607 323-1212
Robert Holicky, *CEO*
Vincent Autieri, *COO*
Christian Maire, *Vice Pres*
EMP: 5
SQ FT: 800
SALES (est): 284.8K Privately Held
WEB: www.geoweb3d.com
SIC: 7372 Prepackaged software

(G-919)
GLOWA MANUFACTURING INC
6 Emma St (13905-2508)
PHONE..................................607 770-0811
Fax: 607 770-0950
Jerry Glowa, *President*
Karen Glowa, *Vice Pres*
William Pomeroy, *Shareholder*
EMP: 47
SQ FT: 10,000
SALES (est): 5.3MM Privately Held
SIC: 3577 Computer peripheral equipment

(G-920)
GOLUB CORPORATION
Also Called: Price Chopper Pharmacy 234
33 Chenango Bridge Rd (13901-1233)
PHONE..................................607 235-7243
EMP: 104
SALES (corp-wide): 3.4B Privately Held
SIC: 3751 Motorcycles & related parts
PA: The Golub Corporation
461 Nott St
Schenectady NY 12308
518 355-5000

(G-921)
HANGER PRSTHETCS & ORTHO INC
65 Pennsylvania Ave (13903-1651)
PHONE..................................607 771-4672
EMP: 7
SALES (corp-wide): 500.5MM Privately Held
SIC: 3842 Limbs, artificial
HQ: Hanger Prosthetics & Orthotics, Inc.
10910 Main Dr
Austin TX 78758
512 777-3800

(G-922)
HP HOOD LLC
Also Called: Crowley Foods
93 Pennsylvania Ave (13903-1645)
PHONE..................................607 772-6580
Joe Cervantes, *Senior VP*
Jeff Wager, *Director*
EMP: 1660
SALES (corp-wide): 1.9B Privately Held
WEB: www.hphood.com
SIC: 2026 2024 Fluid milk; fermented & cultured milk products; yogurt; cottage cheese; ice cream & frozen desserts
PA: Hp Hood Llc
6 Kimball Ln Ste 400
Lynnfield MA 01940
617 887-8441

(G-923)
I3 ASSEMBLIES INC
100 Eldredge St (13901-2631)
PHONE..................................607 238-7077
James T Matthews, *President*
Paul Marra, *Controller*
EMP: 5
SALES (est): 216.8K Privately Held
SIC: 3672 Printed circuit boards

(G-924)
I3 CABLE & HARNESS LLC
100 Eldredge St (13901-2631)
P.O. Box 1830 (13902-1830)
PHONE..................................607 238-7077
James Matthews, *President*
Paul Marra, *Controller*
EMP: 70 EST: 2015
SQ FT: 185,000
SALES (est): 7MM Privately Held
SIC: 3679 Harness assemblies for electronic use: wire or cable

(G-925)
IHD MOTORSPORTS LLC
Also Called: Independence Harley-Davidson
1152 Upper Front St (13905-1119)
PHONE..................................979 690-1669
Fax: 979 690-1660
James E Booth, *Mng Member*
EMP: 15 EST: 2014
SQ FT: 15,000
SALES (est): 2.6MM Privately Held
SIC: 3751 2396 Motorcycles & related parts; motorcycle accessories; automotive & apparel trimmings

(G-926)
ILLINOIS TOOL WORKS INC
33 Lewis Rd (13905-1048)
PHONE..................................607 770-4945
Ron Skeeles, *General Mgr*
EMP: 20
SALES (corp-wide): 13.4B Publicly Held
SIC: 3444 Metal housings, enclosures, casings & other containers
PA: Illinois Tool Works Inc.
155 Harlem Ave
Glenview IL 60025
847 724-7500

(G-927)
INSULATING COATINGS CORP
27 Link Dr Ste D (13904-3208)
PHONE..................................607 723-1727
Tony Loup, *Manager*
EMP: 10

▲ = Import ▼=Export
◆ =Import/Export

GEOGRAPHIC SECTION

Binghamton - Broome County (G-952)

SALES (corp-wide): 8.4MM **Privately Held**
WEB: www.insulatingcoatings.com
SIC: 2851 Paints & allied products
PA: Insulating Coatings Corp.
956 S Us Highway 41
Inverness FL 34450
352 344-8741

(G-928)
IPP ENERGY LLC
Also Called: Transalta
22 Charles St (13905-2268)
PHONE..................................607 773-3307
Richard Langhammer, *President*
Doug Haglund, *Vice Pres*
Gary Hart, *Treasurer*
Elizabeth J Osler, *Admin Sec*
EMP: 5
SQ FT: 19,640
SALES (est): 353.9K **Privately Held**
WEB: www.transalta.com
SIC: 1311 Natural gas production

(G-929)
IVI SERVICES INC
Also Called: Indian Valley
5 Pine Camp Dr (13904)
PHONE..................................607 729-5111
Wayne A Rozen, *CEO*
Chuck Hutton, *Natl Sales Mgr*
◆ EMP: 72 EST: 1940
SQ FT: 250,000
SALES (est): 13.8MM **Privately Held**
WEB: www.iviindustries.com
SIC: 2299 4225 4953 2673 Bagging, jute; general warehousing; recycling, waste materials; bags: plastic, laminated & coated; textile bags; broadwoven fabric mills, manmade

(G-930)
JANE LEWIS
Also Called: Sun Valley Printing
82 Castle Creek Rd (13901-1004)
PHONE..................................607 722-0584
Fax: 607 723-7741
Jane Lewis, *Owner*
David A Lewis, *Co-Owner*
Janet Ingraham, *Office Mgr*
EMP: 6
SQ FT: 2,400
SALES: 250K **Privately Held**
SIC: 2752 2791 2789 Commercial printing, lithographic; typesetting; bookbinding & related work

(G-931)
JOHNSON OUTDOORS INC
Eureka Tents
625 Conklin Rd (13903-2700)
P.O. Box 966 (13902-0966)
PHONE..................................607 779-2200
Tom Poplawski, *Engineer*
William Kelly, *Branch Mgr*
Suzanne Lewis-Mott, *Manager*
EMP: 175
SALES (corp-wide): 430.4MM **Publicly Held**
SIC: 2394 2393 5091 5941 Tents: made from purchased materials; knapsacks, canvas: made from purchased materials; camping equipment & supplies; camping equipment; canoe & kayak dealers; sporting & athletic goods
PA: Johnson Outdoors Inc.
555 Main St
Racine WI 53403
262 631-6600

(G-932)
JONES HUMDINGER
204 Hayes Rd (13905-5918)
PHONE..................................607 771-6501
Steve Kallfelz, *Owner*
EMP: 15
SALES: 180K **Privately Held**
SIC: 2024 Ice cream & frozen desserts

(G-933)
LEO P CALLAHAN INC
229 Lwer Stlla Ireland Rd (13905)
PHONE..................................607 797-7314
Fax: 607 797-3538
James Callahan, *President*
EMP: 10 EST: 1960

SQ FT: 1,600
SALES (est): 980K **Privately Held**
SIC: 2796 Color separations for printing

(G-934)
MECHANICAL PWR CONVERSION LLC
Also Called: E&M Power
6 Emma St (13905-2508)
PHONE..................................607 766-9620
David Eddy, *President*
William Peterson, *Vice Pres*
EMP: 9
SQ FT: 10,000
SALES (est): 840K **Privately Held**
WEB: www.eandmpower.com
SIC: 3679 Electronic loads & power supplies

(G-935)
MELLEM CORPORATION
Also Called: Goldsmith
31 Lewis St Ste 1 (13901-3018)
PHONE..................................607 723-0001
Gina McHugh, *President*
▲ EMP: 10
SQ FT: 750
SALES (est): 1.1MM **Privately Held**
SIC: 3911 5944 Jewelry, precious metal; jewelry, precious stones & precious metals

(G-936)
METAL FAB LLC
13 Spud Ln (13904-3210)
PHONE..................................607 775-3200
Fax: 607 775-3233
Janet Beal, *Mng Member*
Rick Simon,
Eugene Taren,
EMP: 5
SQ FT: 9,500
SALES: 857K **Privately Held**
SIC: 3441 Fabricated structural metal

(G-937)
MORO CORPORATION
Also Called: Titchener Iron Works Division
23 Griswold St (13904-1511)
PHONE..................................607 724-4241
Fax: 607 724-3439
Wendy Coman, *Accountant*
Douglas Wilcox, *Branch Mgr*
EMP: 25
SQ FT: 7,368
SALES (corp-wide): 75.7MM **Publicly Held**
WEB: www.mcgregorindustries.com
SIC: 3446 Architectural metalwork
PA: Moro Corporation
994 Old Eagle School Rd # 1000
Wayne PA 19087
484 367-0300

(G-938)
MS MACHINING INC
Also Called: Mechanical Specialties Co
2 William St (13904-1418)
PHONE..................................607 723-1105
Fax: 607 772-6805
Eugene Mazza, *President*
Jo Ann Risley, *Office Mgr*
EMP: 9 EST: 1956
SQ FT: 10,000
SALES (est): 1.4MM **Privately Held**
SIC: 3544 3599 Special dies & tools; custom machinery; machine shop, jobbing & repair

(G-939)
NELSON HOLDINGS LTD (PA)
71 Frederick St (13901-2529)
PHONE..................................607 772-1794
Clarence Hotchkiss Jr, *Ch of Bd*
Mark Hotchkiss, *President*
Frederick Hotchkiss, *Vice Pres*
EMP: 1 EST: 1875
SQ FT: 180,000
SALES (est): 11.1MM **Privately Held**
SIC: 3679 5261 7699 Electronic circuits; lawn & garden equipment; lawn mower repair shop

(G-940)
NIELSEN HARDWARE CORPORATION (PA)
Also Called: Nielsen/Sessions
71 Frederick St (13901-2529)
P.O. Box 773 (13902-0773)
PHONE..................................607 821-1475
Don Conant, *Purchasing*
Sonia Pelletier Moore, *CFO*
Gail Oliveira, *Bookkeeper*
Candie Mirch, *Sales Staff*
Wassef Moukalled, *Director*
▲ EMP: 25
SQ FT: 40,000
SALES (est): 3.7MM **Privately Held**
WEB: www.nielsensessions.com
SIC: 3429 Manufactured hardware (general)

(G-941)
PARLOR CITY PAPER BOX CO INC
2 Eldredge St (13901-2600)
P.O. Box 756 (13902-0756)
PHONE..................................607 772-0600
Fax: 607 772-0806
David L Culver, *Ch of Bd*
Bruce Culver, *Vice Pres*
Maria Snyder, *Marketing Staff*
Maryanne Bebla, *Manager*
EMP: 56
SQ FT: 140,000
SALES (est): 14.4MM **Privately Held**
WEB: www.pghcitypaper.com
SIC: 2653 2652 Corrugated & solid fiber boxes; setup paperboard boxes

(G-942)
PETER PAPASTRAT
Also Called: A A P C O Screen Prntng/Sprtwr
193 Main St (13905-2619)
P.O. Box 285 (13905-0285)
PHONE..................................607 723-8112
Peter Papastrat, *Owner*
EMP: 5
SQ FT: 6,000
SALES (est): 303.9K **Privately Held**
SIC: 2759 5699 Screen printing; customized clothing & apparel

(G-943)
PIPE DREAM
Also Called: Student Association At The
4400 Vestal Pkwy (13902-4600)
PHONE..................................607 777-2515
Nicolas Vega, *President*
Rachel Bluth, *Editor*
Daphne Eidman, *Office Mgr*
Emma Siegel, *Manager*
William Sanders, *Web Dvlpr*
EMP: 30
SALES (est): 536.4K **Privately Held**
SIC: 2711 Newspapers

(G-944)
R M S MOTOR CORPORATION
41 Travis Dr (13904-2822)
PHONE..................................607 723-2323
Fax: 607 723-8165
Michael Jimenez, *President*
Ruth Rusiloski, *Vice Pres*
EMP: 13 EST: 1962
SQ FT: 10,000
SALES (est): 1.4MM **Privately Held**
SIC: 3621 Motors, electric

(G-945)
RB CONVERTING INC
28 Track Dr (13904-2717)
PHONE..................................607 777-1325
Paul Haslett, *Branch Mgr*
Tim Molliggi, *Manager*
EMP: 2
SALES (corp-wide): 10.6MM **Privately Held**
SIC: 2679 Paper products, converted
HQ: Rb Converting, Inc.
12855 Valley Branch Ln
Dallas TX 75234
972 866-0880

(G-946)
REYNOLDS BOOK BINDERY LLC
37 Milford St (13904-1615)
PHONE..................................607 772-8937

Fax: 607 772-0152
Dick Reynolds, *Owner*
Jody Reynolds, *CFO*
EMP: 11
SQ FT: 15,000
SALES (est): 720K **Privately Held**
SIC: 2789 Bookbinding & related work

(G-947)
ROCKWELL COLLINS SIMULATION
31 Lewis Rd (13905-1005)
PHONE..................................607 352-1298
Robert Wuestner, *Managing Dir*
Dale Pluss, *Engineer*
Tony Stenta, *Engineer*
Jim Mizerak, *Program Mgr*
Kemmeth Schreder, *Manager*
EMP: 67 **Publicly Held**
SIC: 3699 Electronic training devices
HQ: Rockwell Collins Simulation & Training Solutions Llc
400 Collins Rd Ne
Cedar Rapids IA 52498
319 295-1000

(G-948)
S L C INDUSTRIES INCORPORATED
63 Barlow Rd (13904-2722)
P.O. Box 116, Kirkwood (13795-0116)
PHONE..................................607 775-2299
Fax: 607 775-2785
Art Boyle, *President*
Adam Milligan, *General Mgr*
Michael Prozeralik, *Treasurer*
Thomas O Milligan, *Admin Sec*
EMP: 10
SQ FT: 20,000
SALES (est): 910K **Privately Held**
WEB: www.slcindustries.com
SIC: 2759 Commercial printing

(G-949)
SCORPION SECURITY PRODUCTS INC
1429 Upper Front St (13901-1151)
PHONE..................................607 724-9999
Pete Gulick, *President*
▲ EMP: 5
SQ FT: 4,700
SALES: 200K **Privately Held**
SIC: 3699 Security devices

(G-950)
SENSOR & DECONTAMINATION INC
Also Called: S D I
892 Powderhouse Rd (13903-7104)
P.O. Box 132 (13903-0132)
PHONE..................................301 526-8389
Barry R Jones, *President*
David Doetschman, *Corp Secy*
EMP: 10
SALES (est): 710K **Privately Held**
WEB: www.sensoranddecon.com
SIC: 2842 7389 Specialty cleaning preparations;

(G-951)
SHELTRED WKSHP FOR DSABLED INC
200 Court St (13901-3604)
PHONE..................................607 722-2364
Lou Harasymczuck, *CFO*
Louis Harasymczuck, *CFO*
Dennis Donovan, *Manager*
Barbara Kaminsky, *Manager*
EMP: 239
SQ FT: 200,000
SALES: 262.5K **Privately Held**
SIC: 3315 3672 Welded steel wire fabric; printed circuit boards

(G-952)
SOUTHERN TIER PLASTICS INC
Kirkwood Industrial Park (13902)
P.O. Box 2015 (13902-2015)
PHONE..................................607 723-2601
Fax: 607 772-9881
John Gwyn, *CEO*
Joyce Gray, *President*
Douglas Gray, *Treasurer*
Holly Geiser, *Controller*
Barbara Gwyn, *Admin Sec*

(PA)=Parent Co (HQ)=Headquarters (DH)=Div Headquarters
✪ = New Business established in last 2 years

2017 Harris
New York Manufacturers Directory

Binghamton - Broome County (G-953)

▲ EMP: 72
SQ FT: 30,000
SALES (est): 16.1MM Privately Held
WEB: www.southerntierplastics.com
SIC: 3089 Injection molding of plastics

(G-953)
SURESCAN CORPORATION
Also Called: X1000
100 Eldredge St (13901-2631)
PHONE..................607 321-0042
James J McNamara Jr, Ch of Bd
John Percival, President
Michael Hollenbeck, Engineer
EMP: 23
SALES (est): 4.7MM Privately Held
WEB: www.surescaneds.com
SIC: 3844 X-ray apparatus & tubes

(G-954)
TCMF INC
Also Called: C.H.thompson Finishing
85 Eldredge St (13901-2637)
PHONE..................607 724-1094
George Morgan, President
Charles Morgan, Vice Pres
Trevor Morgan, Admin Sec
EMP: 75
SALES (est): 3.7MM Privately Held
SIC: 3471 3479 2759 Plating & polishing; commercial printing

(G-955)
TJ POWDER COATERS LLC
24 Broad St (13904-1017)
PHONE..................607 724-4779
Fax: 607 724-4655
Jim Foran, Owner
EMP: 7
SQ FT: 7,500
SALES (est): 947.6K Privately Held
SIC: 3479 Coating of metals with plastic or resins

(G-956)
TOTAL DISPLAY SOLUTIONS INC
1429 Upper Front St (13901-1151)
PHONE..................607 724-9999
Pete Gulick, CFO
Richard Stahlman, Administration
EMP: 15
SQ FT: 18,000
SALES (est): 1.5MM Privately Held
SIC: 2541 Store & office display cases & fixtures

(G-957)
TRI CITY HIGHWAY PRODUCTS INC
111 Bevier St (13904-1013)
PHONE..................607 722-2967
Fax: 607 722-3469
Martin A Galasso Jr, CEO
Warner Hodydon, Opers Mgr
EMP: 30
SQ FT: 2,500
SALES (est): 5.2MM Privately Held
SIC: 2951 1442 Asphalt paving mixtures & blocks; construction sand & gravel

(G-958)
VIRTUSPHERE INC
2 Dewey Ave (13903-2639)
PHONE..................607 760-2207
Nourakhmed Latypov, CEO
Nurulla Latypov, President
EMP: 11
SALES: 150K Privately Held
SIC: 7372 Educational computer software

(G-959)
WESTCODE INCORPORATED
2226 Airport Rd (13905-5912)
PHONE..................607 766-9881
Fax: 607 766-9868
EMP: 25
SALES (corp-wide): 16.7MM Privately Held
WEB: www.westcodeus.com
SIC: 3743 Railroad equipment
PA: Westcode Incorporated
   1372 Enterprise Dr
   Chadds Ford PA 19317
   610 738-1200

Blasdell
Erie County

(G-960)
B F G ELCPLTG AND MFG CO
3949 Jeffrey Blvd (14219-2334)
P.O. Box 825, Hamburg (14075-0825)
PHONE..................716 362-0888
Fax: 716 649-5649
Minta Marie, CEO
EMP: 32
SALES (est): 174.1K Privately Held
SIC: 3999 Manufacturing industries

(G-961)
BUFFALO SPORTS INC
3840 Mckinley Pkwy (14219-3006)
PHONE..................716 826-7700
David Westfall, President
EMP: 6
SQ FT: 4,000
SALES (est): 450.4K Privately Held
SIC: 3949 Sporting & athletic goods

(G-962)
EVERLASTING MEMORIES
3701 Mckinley Pkwy # 210 (14219-2695)
PHONE..................716 833-1111
Dennis Field, Owner
EMP: 6
SALES (est): 302.2K Privately Held
SIC: 2335 Wedding gowns & dresses

(G-963)
GENERAL WELDING & FABG INC
3701 Mckinley Pkwy (14219-2695)
PHONE..................716 824-1572
EMP: 7
SALES (corp-wide): 5.3MM Privately Held
SIC: 7692 Welding repair
PA: General Welding & Fabricating, Inc.
   991 Maple Rd
   Elma NY 14059
   716 652-0033

(G-964)
RAPISTAK CORPORATION
2025 Electric Ave (14219-1045)
PHONE..................716 822-2804
Nathan Pautorek, CEO
EMP: 7
SALES (est): 1.6MM Privately Held
WEB: www.rapistak.com
SIC: 3531 Dozers, tractor mounted: material moving

(G-965)
REPUBLIC STEEL INC
Also Called: Lackawanna Hot Rolled Plant
3049 Lake Shore Rd (14219-1447)
PHONE..................716 827-2800
Tom Tyrrell, Branch Mgr
William Kilinskas, Technician
EMP: 360
SALES (corp-wide): 2.2B Privately Held
SIC: 3312 Blast furnaces & steel mills
HQ: Republic Steel Inc.
   2633 8th St Ne
   Canton OH 44704
   330 438-5435

(G-966)
SOTEK INC
3590 Jeffrey Blvd (14219-2390)
PHONE..................716 821-5961
Fax: 716 821-5965
John E Maurer, President
Michael Maurer, Vice Pres
Ann Skummer, Accounting Mgr
Ann Schumaer, Accountant
▲ EMP: 52
SQ FT: 45,000
SALES (est): 11MM Privately Held
WEB: www.sotek.com
SIC: 3599 Machine shop, jobbing & repair

(G-967)
TRANSCO RAILWAY PRODUCTS INC
Milestrip Rd (14219)
P.O. Box 1968, Buffalo (14219-0168)
PHONE..................716 824-1219
Fax: 716 825-1108
Tom Jakubowski, Manager
EMP: 23
SALES (corp-wide): 104.3MM Privately Held
SIC: 3743 Railroad equipment, except locomotives
HQ: Transco Railway Products Inc.
   200 N La Salle St # 1550
   Chicago IL 60601
   312 427-2818

(G-968)
VALENTI DISTRIBUTING
84 Maple Ave (14219-1624)
PHONE..................716 824-2304
John Valenti, Principal
EMP: 5
SALES (est): 16.1K Privately Held
SIC: 2064 Candy & other confectionery products

Blauvelt
Rockland County

(G-969)
AERCO INTERNATIONAL INC (HQ)
100 Oritani Dr (10913-1022)
PHONE..................845 580-8000
James F Dagley, President
Fred Depuy, Vice Pres
Bree McQuillan, Vice Pres
Lou Vorsteveld, Vice Pres
Karen Defranco, Opers Mgr
▲ EMP: 153
SQ FT: 150,000
SALES (est): 46.6MM
SALES (corp-wide): 1.4B Publicly Held
WEB: www.aerco.com
SIC: 3443 3492 Heat exchangers, plate type; heat exchangers: coolers (after, inter), condensers, etc.; boilers: industrial, power, or marine; control valves, fluid power: hydraulic & pneumatic
PA: Watts Water Technologies, Inc.
   815 Chestnut St
   North Andover MA 01845
   978 688-1811

(G-970)
CWS POWDER COATINGS COMPANY LP
2234 Bradley Hill Rd # 12 (10913-1014)
PHONE..................845 398-2911
Fax: 845 398-2912
Cws Powder Coatings, Partner
Victoria Phillips, Controller
Jonathan Abrams, Director
▲ EMP: 9
SQ FT: 2,500
SALES (est): 2.2MM
SALES (corp-wide): 81.6MM Privately Held
SIC: 3399 Powder, metal
HQ: Cws Powder Coatings Gmbh
   Katharinenstr. 61
   Duren 52353
   242 198-30

(G-971)
ERT SOFTWARE INC
4 Pine Glen Dr (10913-1150)
PHONE..................845 358-5721
Roman Tenenbaum, President
EMP: 5
SALES: 1.5MM Privately Held
WEB: www.alivest.com
SIC: 7372 Prepackaged software

(G-972)
K-BINET INC
624 Route 303 (10913-1170)
PHONE..................845 348-1149
Fax: 845 620-0666
Jay Kim, President
Ann Degli, Admin Sec

EMP: 8 EST: 2001
SALES (est): 680K Privately Held
SIC: 2434 Wood kitchen cabinets

(G-973)
RBHAMMERS CORP
Also Called: Heatherdell RB Hammers
500 Bradley Hill Rd (10913-1134)
PHONE..................845 353-5042
Richard Tegtmeier, President
Derrick Ternvillo, Accountant
Ann Glasthal, Office Mgr
EMP: 10
SQ FT: 1,500
SALES: 7.4MM Privately Held
SIC: 3546 Hammers, portable: electric or pneumatic, chipping, etc.

(G-974)
RYAN PRINTING INC
300 Corporate Dr Ste 6 (10913-1162)
PHONE..................845 535-3235
Fax: 845 353-8740
Al Ryan, President
Jeff Fay, Sales Mgr
Chuck Cash, Accounts Exec
Sal Fazzi, Accounts Exec
Mark Halpin, Accounts Exec
EMP: 26
SQ FT: 35,000
SALES (est): 5MM Privately Held
SIC: 2752 Commercial printing, lithographic

(G-975)
SWIVELIER COMPANY INC
Also Called: Point Electric Div
600 Bradley Hill Rd Ste 3 (10913-1171)
PHONE..................845 353-1455
Fax: 845 353-1512
Michael I Schwartz, President
I Schucker, Sales Staff
Carol Zane, Sales Staff
Louis M Cafarchio, Admin Sec
EMP: 70
SQ FT: 125,000
SALES (est): 10.3MM Privately Held
WEB: www.swivelier.com
SIC: 3646 3645 3643 Commercial indusl & institutional electric lighting fixtures; residential lighting fixtures; current-carrying wiring devices

(G-976)
TAPPAN WIRE & CABLE INC (HQ)
100 Bradley Pkwy (10913-1012)
P.O. Box 4000, Carrollton GA (30112-5050)
PHONE..................845 353-9000
Fax: 845 353-9315
Stuart W Thorn, Ch of Bd
Darren Krych, President
Mike Luterzo, Vice Pres
Jerry Rosen, CFO
Michael Dougher, Controller
▲ EMP: 189 EST: 1978
SQ FT: 180,000
SALES (est): 39MM
SALES (corp-wide): 1.9B Privately Held
WEB: www.tappanwire.com
SIC: 3315 3643 3357 Wire & fabricated wire products; current-carrying wiring devices; nonferrous wiredrawing & insulating
PA: Southwire Company, Llc
   1 Southwire Dr
   Carrollton GA 30119
   770 832-4242

(G-977)
TRI-SEAL HOLDINGS INC
900 Bradley Hill Rd (10913-1163)
PHONE..................845 353-3300
Paul Young, Ch of Bd
Diane Schweitzer, Owner
F Patrick Smith, Chairman
Shevman Smith, Accounts Mgr
Kevin Baker, Manager
EMP: 63 EST: 1946
SQ FT: 58,000
SALES (est): 11.3MM
SALES (corp-wide): 1.1B Privately Held
WEB: www.tri-seal.com
SIC: 3081 2821 Packing materials, plastic sheet; plastics materials & resins

PA: Tekni-Plex, Inc.
460 E Swedesford Rd # 3000
Wayne PA 19087
484 690-1520

(G-978)
TRI-SEAL INTERNATIONAL INC (HQ)
900 Bradley Hill Rd (10913-1163)
PHONE..................................845 353-3300
Fax: 845 353-3376
Anatoly Verdel, *President*
▲ EMP: 3
SALES (est): 1MM
SALES (corp-wide): 1.1B Privately Held
SIC: 2679 Egg cartons, molded pulp; made from purchased material
PA: Tekni-Plex, Inc.
460 E Swedesford Rd # 3000
Wayne PA 19087
484 690-1520

(G-979)
VITS INTERNATIONAL INC
200 Corporate Dr (10913-1142)
PHONE..................................845 353-5000
Fax: 845 353-7759
Deirdre Ryder, *President*
Nina Shapiro, *Office Mgr*
Kim Markovich, *Director*
▲ EMP: 40
SQ FT: 22,000
SALES: 20MM Privately Held
WEB: www.vitsamerica.com
SIC: 3555 Printing trades machinery

Bliss
Wyoming County

(G-980)
FIVE CORNERS REPAIR INC
6653 Hardys Rd (14024-9714)
PHONE..................................585 322-7369
Jason Sampson, *President*
Scott Lester, *Vice Pres*
EMP: 12
SALES: 950K Privately Held
SIC: 3441 Fabricated structural metal

Bloomfield
Ontario County

(G-981)
BENJAMIN SHERIDAN CORPORATION (DH)
7629 State Route 5 And 20 (14469-9210)
PHONE..................................585 657-6161
Ken D'Arcy, *President*
George Ribbert, *Div Sub Head*
Hal Parker, *Director*
EMP: 5
SQ FT: 224,000
SALES (est): 9.3MM
SALES (corp-wide): 287.8MM Privately Held
SIC: 3484 3482 Small arms; pellet & BB guns; pellets & BB's; pistol & air rifle ammunition
HQ: Crosman Corporation
7629 State Route 5 And 20
Bloomfield NY 14469
585 657-6161

(G-982)
BRISTOL METALS INC
7817 State Route 5 And 20 (14469-9352)
PHONE..................................585 657-7665
Edward Gilligan, *President*
Kelly Gilligan, *Corp Secy*
Kecia Donnelly, *Executive Asst*
EMP: 10
SQ FT: 15,000
SALES (est): 1.4MM Privately Held
SIC: 3441 Fabricated structural metal

(G-983)
CARVER CREEK ENTERPRISES INC
2524 Cannan Rd (14469-9655)
PHONE..................................585 657-7511
Fax: 585 657-1175
Donald Dean, *President*
Thomas Dean, *Vice Pres*
EMP: 5
SQ FT: 1,764
SALES (est): 647K Privately Held
WEB: www.carvercreekent.com
SIC: 2511 Wood household furniture

(G-984)
COMMODORE MACHINE CO INC
26 Maple Ave (14469-9228)
PHONE..................................585 657-6916
Fax: 585 657-6400
George Brandoon, *Ch of Bd*
EMP: 17 EST: 1970
SALES (est): 3MM Privately Held
SIC: 3089 Trays, plastic

(G-985)
COMMODORE PLASTICS LLC
26 Maple Ave (14469-9228)
PHONE..................................585 657-7777
George Braddon III, *President*
Jeff Braddon, *Vice Pres*
Ken Warner, *Safety Dir*
Fritz Seager, *Prdtn Mgr*
Lloyd Hynes, *Purchasing*
▲ EMP: 50
SQ FT: 35,000
SALES (est): 18.8MM Privately Held
SIC: 3089 Plastic processing
PA: 26-28 Maple Avenue, Inc.
26 Maple Ave
Bloomfield NY 14469
585 657-7777

(G-986)
CROSMAN CORPORATION (HQ)
7629 State Route 5 And 20 (14469-9210)
PHONE..................................585 657-6161
Fax: 585 657-5405
Lloyd Heise, *Vice Pres*
Dan Schultz, *Vice Pres*
David Swanson, *Vice Pres*
Wallace Malheiros, *Engineer*
Robert Beckwith, *CFO*
▲ EMP: 29
SQ FT: 224,000
SALES (est): 11.6MM
SALES (corp-wide): 287.8MM Privately Held
WEB: www.crosman.com
SIC: 3484 3482 3563 Pellet & BB guns; pellets & BB's, pistol & air rifle ammunition; shot, steel (ammunition); air & gas compressors
PA: Wellspring Capital Management Llc
390 Park Ave Fl 5
New York NY 10022
212 318-9800

(G-987)
ELAM SAND & GRAVEL CORP (PA)
8222 State Route 5 And 20 (14469-9567)
P.O. Box 65, West Bloomfield (14585-0065)
PHONE..................................585 657-8000
Fax: 585 657-6575
Joseph Spezio, *President*
Ritamarie Dreimiller, *Vice Pres*
EMP: 35 EST: 1892
SQ FT: 9,000
SALES (est): 7.4MM Privately Held
SIC: 1442 Construction sand mining

(G-988)
FURNITURE DOCTOR INC
7007 State Route 5 And 20 (14469-9322)
P.O. Box 519 (14469-0519)
PHONE..................................585 657-6941
Fax: 585 657-6751
Thomas Baker, *President*
Marfa Baker, *Corp Secy*
Stacey Conley, *Finance Mgr*
EMP: 9
SQ FT: 16,000
SALES (est): 770K Privately Held
WEB: www.thefurnituredoctoronline.com
SIC: 2511 2514 5712 5021 Wood household furniture; metal household furniture; furniture stores; furniture; reupholstery & furniture repair; interior decorating

(G-989)
GULLO MACHINE & TOOL INC
4 E Main St (14469-9334)
P.O. Box 273 (14469-0273)
PHONE..................................585 657-7318
Fax: 585 657-4463
Nancy Gullo, *President*
EMP: 10
SQ FT: 15,000
SALES: 500K Privately Held
SIC: 3599 Machine shop, jobbing & repair

(G-990)
TERPHANE HOLDINGS LLC (DH)
2754 W Park Dr (14469-9385)
PHONE..................................585 657-5800
Dan Roy, *General Mgr*
Frank J Shutter, *Maint Spvr*
Renan Bergmann,
▼ EMP: 7
SALES (est): 14.2MM
SALES (corp-wide): 876MM Publicly Held
SIC: 2821 5199 Plastics materials & resins; packaging materials
HQ: Tredegar Film Products Corporation
1100 Boulders Pkwy # 200
North Chesterfield VA 23225
804 330-1000

(G-991)
TERPHANE INC
2754 W Park Dr (14469-9385)
PHONE..................................585 657-5800
Renan Bergmann, *CEO*
Dan Roy, *General Mgr*
Frank Shutter, *COO*
Francisco Cavalcanti, *Plant Mgr*
Richard Compasto, *Plant Mgr*
◆ EMP: 52
SQ FT: 100,000
SALES (est): 14.2MM
SALES (corp-wide): 876MM Publicly Held
WEB: www.terphane.com
SIC: 2821 Polyesters
HQ: Terphane Holdings Llc
2754 W Park Dr
Bloomfield NY 14469
585 657-5800

(G-992)
VELMEX INC
7550 State Route 5 And 20 (14469-9389)
PHONE..................................585 657-6151
Fax: 585 657-6153
Mitchel Evans, *President*
Alan Lane, *Engineer*
Evans Mitchel, *Project Engr*
Alayne Evans, *Treasurer*
Joseph Mehring, *Controller*
EMP: 32
SQ FT: 15,500
SALES: 5.8MM Privately Held
WEB: www.velmex.com
SIC: 3545 Machine tool attachments & accessories

Bloomington
Ulster County

(G-993)
COBRA SYSTEMS INC
2669 New York 32 (12411)
P.O. Box 209 (12411-0209)
PHONE..................................845 338-6675
Michael V Pavlov, *President*
▼ EMP: 10
SQ FT: 2,400
SALES (est): 1.5MM Privately Held
WEB: www.cobracoil.com
SIC: 3496 Barbed wire, made from purchased wire

Bloomville
Delaware County

(G-994)
ED BEACH FOREST MANAGEMENT
2042 Scott Rd (13739-1203)
PHONE..................................607 538-1745
Edwin R Beach, *Principal*
EMP: 6
SALES (est): 512.3K Privately Held
SIC: 2411 Logging

(G-995)
G HAYNES HOLDINGS INC
Also Called: Catskill Castings Co
51971 State Highway 10 (13739-2242)
P.O. Box 752 (13739-0752)
PHONE..................................607 538-1160
George Haynes, *President*
Tracy Kinch, *Office Mgr*
EMP: 6
SQ FT: 3,500
SALES (est): 350K Privately Held
WEB: www.catskillcastings.com
SIC: 3543 Foundry patternmaking

(G-996)
GREENE BRASS & ALUM FNDRY LLC
51971 State Highway 10 (13739-2242)
P.O. Box 752 (13739-0752)
PHONE..................................607 656-4204
Thomas Dodd, *Mng Member*
George Heynes,
EMP: 7 EST: 2004
SALES: 1.1MM Privately Held
SIC: 3334 3363 7389 Primary aluminum; aluminum die-castings;

Blossvale
Oneida County

(G-997)
BLUEBAR OIL CO INC
8446 Mill Pond Way (13308-3424)
PHONE..................................315 245-4328
Fax: 315 245-2160
David Link, *President*
EMP: 11
SQ FT: 2,000
SALES (est): 1MM Privately Held
SIC: 1389 5983 5172 Oil field services; fuel oil dealers; gasoline; fuel oil

Blue Point
Suffolk County

(G-998)
DEER PK STAIR BLDG MLLWK INC
51 Kennedy Ave (11715-1009)
P.O. Box 107 (11715-0107)
PHONE..................................631 363-5000
Fax: 631 363-2167
Michael Souto, *President*
Annette Andriano, *Manager*
Leita Souto, *Admin Sec*
EMP: 45 EST: 1950
SQ FT: 30,000
SALES (est): 7.9MM Privately Held
WEB: www.deerparkstairs.com
SIC: 2431 5211 5031 Stair railings, wood; staircases & stairs, wood; lumber products; cabinets, kitchen; kitchen cabinets

(G-999)
NOCHEM PAINT STRIPPING INC
32 Bergen Ln (11715-2111)
PHONE..................................631 563-2750
Gilbert H Kelley, *President*
Stephen Kelley, *Vice Pres*
EMP: 5
SALES (est): 531.3K Privately Held
SIC: 2851 7699 7532 1799 Paint removers; boat repair; body shop, automotive; paint & wallpaper stripping

Blue Point - Suffolk County (G-1000)

(G-1000)
SPECIALTY INK CO INC (PA)
Also Called: Aero Brand Inks
40 Harbour Dr (11715-1421)
P.O. Box 778, Deer Park (11729-0778)
PHONE..................................631 586-3666
Fax: 631 586-3874
Gary Werwa, *President*
▲ **EMP:** 16 **EST:** 1934
SQ FT: 15,000
SALES (est): 1.7MM **Privately Held**
WEB: www.specialtyink.com
SIC: 2899 3953 2893 Ink or writing fluids; pads, inking & stamping; printing ink

Bohemia
Suffolk County

(G-1001)
A P MANUFACTURING
21 Floyds Run (11716-2155)
PHONE..................................909 228-3049
Jane P Sobota, *Owner*
EMP: 7
SALES (est): 379.8K **Privately Held**
SIC: 3599 Industrial machinery

(G-1002)
ABACO STEEL PRODUCTS INC
1560 Locust Ave (11716-2194)
PHONE..................................631 589-1800
Fax: 631 589-1197
Kenneth Podd, *President*
Jennifer Rivera, *Bookkeeper*
EMP: 4 **EST:** 1972
SQ FT: 9,500
SALES: 1.2MM **Privately Held**
WEB: www.abacosteel.com
SIC: 2542 2541 Shelving, office & store: except wood; partitions for floor attachment, prefabricated: except wood; cabinets, lockers & shelving

(G-1003)
ABLE ENVIRONMENTAL SERVICES
1599 Ocean Ave (11716-1947)
PHONE..................................631 567-6585
Fax: 631 567-9390
Faith Barnard, *President*
EMP: 5
SALES (est): 550K **Privately Held**
SIC: 1382 Oil & gas exploration services

(G-1004)
ABSOLUTE MANUFACTURING INC
Also Called: Absolute Engineering Company
210 Knickerbocker Ave (11716-3175)
PHONE..................................631 563-7466
Val Palzzynski, *President*
Helene Strafford, *Manager*
EMP: 8
SQ FT: 5,000
SALES: 1MM **Privately Held**
SIC: 3599 Machine shop, jobbing & repair

(G-1005)
ACCURATE MARINE SPECIALTIES
2200 Artic Ave (11716-2414)
PHONE..................................631 589-5502
Gary Lucas, *President*
Chip Watkins, *Corp Secy*
EMP: 6
SQ FT: 5,900
SALES (est): 959.8K **Privately Held**
SIC: 7694 5541 Motor repair services; marine service station

(G-1006)
ACE CNTRACTING CONSULTING CORP
Also Called: Island Chimney Service
515 Johnson Ave (11716-2671)
PHONE..................................631 567-4752
Marc Jagerman, *President*
EMP: 9
SALES (est): 753.8K **Privately Held**
SIC: 3271 Blocks, concrete: chimney or fireplace

(G-1007)
ACE MOLDING & TOOL INC
51 Floyds Run (11716-2155)
PHONE..................................631 567-2355
Americo Carnaxide, *President*
EMP: 5
SALES: 40K **Privately Held**
SIC: 3089 Molding primary plastic

(G-1008)
AEROSPACE LIGHTING CORPORATION (HQ)
355 Knickerbocker Ave (11716-3103)
PHONE..................................631 563-6400
Fax: 631 563-8781
Werner Lieberherr, *President*
Fred Buckholtz, *Exec VP*
Thomas P McCaffrey, *Senior VP*
Sean Cromie, *Vice Pres*
Wayne R Exton, *Vice Pres*
EMP: 100 **EST:** 1987
SQ FT: 60,000
SALES (est): 17MM
SALES (corp-wide): 2.7B **Publicly Held**
SIC: 3647 5063 Aircraft lighting fixtures; electrical apparatus & equipment
PA: B/E Aerospace, Inc.
    1400 Corporate Center Way
    Wellington FL 33414
    561 791-5000

(G-1009)
AGRIUM ADVANCED TECH US INC
165 Orville Dr (11716-2508)
PHONE..................................631 286-0598
Ada Dundon, *Branch Mgr*
EMP: 11
SALES (corp-wide): 2.4B **Privately Held**
SIC: 2873 Nitrogenous fertilizers
HQ: Agrium Advanced Technologies (U.S.) Inc.
    2915 Rocky Mountain Ave # 400
    Loveland CO 80538
    970 292-9000

(G-1010)
AID WOOD WORKING
1555 Ocean Ave Ste C (11716-1933)
PHONE..................................631 244-7768
Rick Olveri, *Owner*
EMP: 10
SALES (est): 830.8K **Privately Held**
SIC: 2499 Wood products

(G-1011)
ALL AMERICAN AWARDS INC
Also Called: All American Uniform
331 Knickerbocker Ave (11716-3134)
PHONE..................................631 567-2025
Fax: 631 567-3953
Frank Coppola, *President*
Jean Coppola, *Vice Pres*
Dominic Coppola, *Manager*
EMP: 11
SQ FT: 10,000
SALES (est): 830K **Privately Held**
SIC: 3914 5699 5199 2395 Trophies; uniforms & work clothing; advertising specialties; embroidery & art needlework

(G-1012)
ALL COUNTY BLOCK & SUPPLY CORP
899 Lincoln Ave (11716-4105)
P.O. Box 502 (11716-0502)
PHONE..................................631 589-3675
Fax: 631 567-3676
Robert Affenita, *Mktg Dir*
Ken Walker, *Mktg Dir*
EMP: 5
SALES (est): 1MM **Privately Held**
WEB: www.allcountyblock.com
SIC: 3271 Concrete block & brick

(G-1013)
ALL ISLAND BLOWER & SHTMTL
1585 Smithtown Ave Unit C (11716-2406)
PHONE..................................631 567-7070
Fax: 631 567-6505
Brian Levine, *President*
Brian Higgins, *President*
Micheal Higgins, *Opers Mgr*
EMP: 10

SQ FT: 4,000
SALES: 1MM **Privately Held**
SIC: 3444 Sheet metalwork

(G-1014)
AMPLITECH INC
620 Johnson Ave Ste 2 (11716-2658)
PHONE..................................631 521-7738
Fawad Maqbool, *CEO*
Don Sartorius, *QC Mgr*
Louisa Sanfratello, *CFO*
Carol Klemm, *Finance*
EMP: 8
SQ FT: 5,500
SALES: 1.2MM **Privately Held**
WEB: www.amplitechinc.com
SIC: 3663 Microwave communication equipment

(G-1015)
AMPLITECH GROUP INC
620 Johnson Ave (11716-2649)
PHONE..................................631 521-7831
Fawad Maqbool, *Ch of Bd*
Louisa Sanfratello, *CFO*
EMP: 8 **EST:** 2012
SALES: 1.4MM **Privately Held**
SIC: 3651 3663 Amplifiers: radio, public address or musical instrument; microwave communication equipment

(G-1016)
ANDREA ELECTRONICS CORPORATION (PA)
620 Johnson Ave Ste 1b (11716-2636)
PHONE..................................631 719-1800
Douglas J Andrea, *Ch of Bd*
Stephan Auguste, *Electrical Engi*
Corisa L Guiffre, *CFO*
▲ **EMP:** 11 **EST:** 1934
SQ FT: 11,000
SALES: 13.2MM **Publicly Held**
WEB: www.andreaelectronics.com
SIC: 3651 3663 3577 Microphones; mobile communication equipment; computer peripheral equipment

(G-1017)
APEX SIGNAL CORPORATION
110 Wilbur Pl (11716-2402)
PHONE..................................631 567-1100
Fax: 631 981-1823
William Forman, *President*
Wayne Grandner, *COO*
David Dayton, *Planning Mgr*
Patty Angelos, *Manager*
EMP: 90
SALES (est): 10.5MM
SALES (corp-wide): 43.9MM **Privately Held**
SIC: 3669 5065 Traffic signals, electric; electronic parts & equipment
PA: North Atlantic Industries, Inc.
    110 Wilbur Pl
    Bohemia NY 11716
    631 567-1100

(G-1018)
ARCHIMEDES PRODUCTS INC
21 Floyds Run (11716-2155)
PHONE..................................631 589-1215
Fax: 631 589-1216
Jane Sobota, *President*
Mike Kielccewski, *Supervisor*
EMP: 8
SQ FT: 6,000
SALES (est): 760K **Privately Held**
WEB: www.cncarch.com
SIC: 3599 Machine shop, jobbing & repair

(G-1019)
ARLAN DAMPER CORPORATION
1598 Lakeland Ave (11716-2198)
PHONE..................................631 589-7431
Fax: 631 589-7558
Albert A Sapio, *President*
Valerie Cooper, *Office Mgr*
Gina Marx, *Executive*
EMP: 25 **EST:** 1961
SQ FT: 6,400
SALES (est): 4.8MM **Privately Held**
SIC: 3444 Sheet metalwork

(G-1020)
AUTOMOTIVE FILTERS MFG INC
80a Keyland Ct A (11716-2656)
PHONE..................................631 435-1010
Manny Hadad, *General Mgr*
◆ **EMP:** 13
SQ FT: 14,000
SALES: 3.2MM **Privately Held**
SIC: 3714 7538 5013 3564 Filters: oil, fuel & air, motor vehicle; general automotive repair shops; automotive supplies & parts; filters, air: furnaces, air conditioning equipment, etc.

(G-1021)
B & H PRECISION FABRICATORS
95 Davinci Dr (11716-2601)
PHONE..................................631 563-9620
Fax: 631 563-9658
Dan Barthelomew, *President*
Deborah Barthelomew, *Vice Pres*
Jared Bartholomew, *VP Opers*
Kathy Ott, *Manager*
Debbie Bartholomew, *Officer*
EMP: 15
SQ FT: 5,000
SALES: 1MM **Privately Held**
SIC: 3444 Sheet metalwork

(G-1022)
B/E AEROSPACE INC
355 Knickerbocker Ave (11716-3103)
PHONE..................................631 563-6400
Amin J Khoury, *Ch of Bd*
EMP: 32
SALES (corp-wide): 2.7B **Publicly Held**
SIC: 2531 3728 3647 Seats, aircraft; aircraft parts & equipment; aircraft lighting fixtures
PA: B/E Aerospace, Inc.
    1400 Corporate Center Way
    Wellington FL 33414
    561 791-5000

(G-1023)
B/E AEROSPACE INC
355 Knickerbocker Ave (11716-3103)
PHONE..................................631 589-0877
Steve Scover, *Vice Pres*
Vincent Cipolla, *Electrical Engi*
Peggy Knapp, *Manager*
Elaine Frank, *Admin Asst*
Gail Reissig, *Admin Asst*
EMP: 230
SALES (corp-wide): 2.7B **Publicly Held**
SIC: 2531 Seats, aircraft
PA: B/E Aerospace, Inc.
    1400 Corporate Center Way
    Wellington FL 33414
    561 791-5000

(G-1024)
BETA TRANSFORMER TECH CORP (DH)
40 Orville Dr Ste 2 (11716-2529)
PHONE..................................631 244-7393
Fax: 631 244-8893
Clifford Lane, *CEO*
Vincent Buffa, *President*
Keith McDonald, *General Mgr*
Roy Torzullo, *Vice Pres*
Owen A Hayes Jr, *QC Mgr*
EMP: 41
SQ FT: 11,000
SALES (est): 5.3MM
SALES (corp-wide): 2.7B **Publicly Held**
WEB: www.bttc-beta.com
SIC: 3677 Electronic transformers
HQ: Data Device Corporation
    105 Wilbur Pl
    Bohemia NY 11716
    631 567-5600

(G-1025)
BGA TECHNOLOGY LLC
116 Wilbur Pl (11716-2402)
PHONE..................................631 750-4600
Michael Cody, *President*
Ralph Prescott, *Vice Pres*
Brent Kolar, *Sales Staff*
Bill Kaspar, *Director*
EMP: 17

▲ = Import ▼=Export ◆ =Import/Export

SALES (est): 3.2MM **Privately Held**
SIC: **3674** 8734 Semiconductors & related devices; testing laboratories

(G-1026)
BMG PRINTING AND PROMOTION LLC
170 Wilbur Pl Ste 700 (11716-2416)
PHONE..................................631 231-9200
Paulette Desimone, *Principal*
John L Melillo,
EMP: 8
SALES: 50K **Privately Held**
SIC: **2761** 3993 2732 2752 Manifold business forms; signs & advertising specialties; pamphlets: printing & binding, not published on site; commercial printing, offset; promotional printing, lithographic

(G-1027)
BROCKYN CORPORATION
Also Called: Amax Industrial Products
606 Johnson Ave Ste 31 (11716-2688)
P.O. Box 577, East Islip (11730-0577)
PHONE..................................631 244-2770
Glen Heller, *President*
Tony Englin, *Vice Pres*
Tony England, *Manager*
EMP: 10
SQ FT: 3,500
SALES (est): 860K **Privately Held**
WEB: www.amaxindustrial.com
SIC: **2869** Industrial organic chemicals

(G-1028)
BULLITT MOBILE LLC
Also Called: Bullitt Group
80 Orville Dr Ste 100 (11716-2505)
PHONE..................................631 424-1749
Theresa Cangialosi, *Vice Pres*
Adriene Ohare, *Accounts Mgr*
EMP: 56
SQ FT: 1,200
SALES (est): 6.7MM **Privately Held**
SIC: **3663** Cellular radio telephone

(G-1029)
C & C DUPLICATORS INC
220 Knickerbocker Ave # 1 (11716-3181)
PHONE..................................631 244-0800
Fax: 631 244-0807
Frank Carroll Jr, *President*
Frank Carroll Sr, *Vice Pres*
EMP: 30
SQ FT: 11,000
SALES (est): 3.7MM **Privately Held**
SIC: **3652** 7389 Magnetic tape (audio): prerecorded; printing broker

(G-1030)
C & H MACHINING INC
281 Knickerbocker Ave (11716-3103)
PHONE..................................631 582-6737
Cliff W Havel, *President*
Phillip A Russo, *Vice Pres*
EMP: 13
SQ FT: 6,000
SALES (est): 1.3MM **Privately Held**
SIC: **3599** Machine shop, jobbing & repair

(G-1031)
C & M CIRCUITS INC
50 Orville Dr (11716-2548)
PHONE..................................631 589-0208
Fax: 631 589-1247
Charles Gwynn, *Ch of Bd*
John Lindy, *Administration*
EMP: 24
SQ FT: 7,500
SALES: 1.7MM **Privately Held**
SIC: **3629** Electronic generation equipment

(G-1032)
CERTIFIED PRCSION MCHINING INC
70 Knickerbocker Ave # 4 (11716-3166)
PHONE..................................631 244-3671
Michael Staib, *President*
James Turano, *Vice Pres*
EMP: 6
SQ FT: 8,000
SALES (est): 784.2K **Privately Held**
SIC: **3599** Machine shop, jobbing & repair

(G-1033)
CLIMATRONICS CORP (HQ)
606 Johnson Ave Ste 28 (11716-2419)
PHONE..................................541 471-7111
Thomas Pottberg, *President*
Joann Pottberg, *Corp Secy*
David W Gilmore, *Vice Pres*
James Riley Loftin, *CFO*
EMP: 14
SQ FT: 16,500
SALES (est): 1.2MM
SALES (corp-wide): 26.9MM **Privately Held**
WEB: www.climatronics.com
SIC: **3829** Meteorological instruments
PA: Met One Instruments, Inc.
1600 Nw Washington Blvd
Grants Pass OR 97526
541 471-7111

(G-1034)
CLINTRAK CLINICAL LABELINGS (PA)
Also Called: Eagle Business Systems
2800 Veterans Mem Hwy (11716-1002)
PHONE..................................631 467-3900
Bob Scarth, *General Mgr*
Kevin Greenwood, *Mfg Dir*
Kristine Williams, *Project Mgr*
Steven Kearns, *Opers Staff*
Joe Macdougall, *Opers Staff*
▲ EMP: 55
SQ FT: 45,000
SALES (est): 8.3MM **Privately Held**
WEB: www.clintrak.com
SIC: **2754** Letter, circular & form: gravure printing

(G-1035)
CLIP CLOP INTERNATIONAL INC
Also Called: C.C.I. Industries
271 Knickerbocker Ave (11716-3103)
PHONE..................................631 392-1340
Laurie Frank, *President*
Elizabeth Michie, *Administration*
EMP: 15
SALES (est): 870K **Privately Held**
SIC: **3599** Crankshafts & camshafts, machining

(G-1036)
CMB WIRELESS GROUP LLC (PA)
116 Wilbur Pl (11716-2402)
PHONE..................................631 750-4700
Joseph Lucania, *CEO*
Rich Meigh, *Exec VP*
Vincent Vivolo Jr, *Exec VP*
James McGuirk, *Vice Pres*
Frank Pipolo, *Vice Pres*
▲ EMP: 204
SALES (est): 32.7MM **Privately Held**
SIC: **3663** Mobile communication equipment

(G-1037)
CMS HEAT TRANSFER DIVISION INC
273 Knickerbocker Ave (11716-3103)
PHONE..................................631 968-0084
Chris Mauro, *President*
Marek Dolat, *Vice Pres*
Steve White, *Vice Pres*
Lisa White, *Manager*
EMP: 20
SQ FT: 16,000
SALES (est): 5.9MM **Privately Held**
WEB: www.cmsheattransfer.com
SIC: **3443** Finned tubes, for heat transfer; heat exchangers, plate type

(G-1038)
COLOR CRAFT FINISHING CORP
30 Floyds Run Ste A (11716-2212)
PHONE..................................631 563-3230
Fax: 631 563-3298
Angelo Zegarelli, *President*
EMP: 10
SALES (est): 1.1MM **Privately Held**
SIC: **3479** 3089 Painting of metal products; coloring & finishing of plastic products

(G-1039)
COS TEC MANUFACTURING CORP
Also Called: K C Technical Services
390 Knickerbocker Ave # 1 (11716-3123)
PHONE..................................631 589-7170
Fax: 631 589-7196
Guy A Cosmo, *President*
Elizabeth Cosmo, *Vice Pres*
▲ EMP: 7
SQ FT: 11,000
SALES (est): 500K **Privately Held**
SIC: **2678** Stationery products

(G-1040)
COTTONWOOD METALS INC
1625 Sycamore Ave Ste A (11716-1728)
PHONE..................................646 807-8674
Christopher Smith, *Chairman*
Jim Carter, *Manager*
EMP: 20 EST: 2011
SQ FT: 15,000
SALES (est): 2.2MM **Privately Held**
SIC: **3441** Fabricated structural metal

(G-1041)
COVERGRIP CORPORATION
30 Aero Rd (11716-2902)
PHONE..................................855 268-3747
John Barry, *President*
▲ EMP: 5 EST: 2011
SALES (est): 800K **Privately Held**
WEB: www.covergrip.com
SIC: **2394** Canvas covers & drop cloths

(G-1042)
CRAFT-TECH MFG CORP
1750 Artic Ave (11716-2423)
PHONE..................................631 563-4949
Fax: 631 563-4711
Joseph Desantis, *CEO*
Ralph Desantis Jr, *Vice Pres*
Ralph Desantis Sr, *Treasurer*
Steve Taylor, *Office Mgr*
EMP: 7 EST: 1978
SQ FT: 19,500
SALES (est): 840K **Privately Held**
SIC: **3444** Casings, sheet metal

(G-1043)
CREATIVE METAL FABRICATORS
360 Knickerbocker Ave # 13 (11716-3124)
PHONE..................................631 567-2266
Fax: 631 589-3924
Richard W Donovan, *President*
Liz King, *Bookkeeper*
EMP: 7
SQ FT: 8,500
SALES (est): 600K **Privately Held**
SIC: **3446** Architectural metalwork

(G-1044)
CROWNLITE MFG CORP
1650 Sycamore Ave Ste 24 (11716-1900)
PHONE..................................631 589-9100
William Siegel, *President*
Lois Carbonaro, *Sales Executive*
EMP: 30 EST: 1948
SQ FT: 57,600
SALES (est): 3.8MM **Privately Held**
SIC: **3646** 3645 Commercial indusl & institutional electric lighting fixtures; residential lighting fixtures

(G-1045)
CUSTOM DESIGN METALS INC
1612 Locust Ave Ste C (11716-2100)
PHONE..................................631 563-2444
Fax: 631 589-9198
Robert Lyon, *President*
Richard Mellace, *Vice Pres*
EMP: 5
SQ FT: 7,500
SALES (est): 576.1K **Privately Held**
SIC: **3446** Railings, bannisters, guards, etc.: made from metal pipe

(G-1046)
CUSTOM HOUSE ENGRAVERS INC
Also Called: Village Plaquesmith, Ththe
104 Keyland Ct (11716-2656)
PHONE..................................631 567-3004
Fax: 631 567-3019

Terry McLean, *President*
Terry Mc Lean, *Principal*
Brian McLean, *Vice Pres*
▲ EMP: 6
SQ FT: 3,200
SALES: 1MM **Privately Held**
SIC: **2796** 3089 3479 Engraving platemaking services; engraving of plastic; etching & engraving

(G-1047)
CYGNUS AUTOMATION INC
1605 9th Ave (11716-1202)
PHONE..................................631 981-0909
Fax: 631 981-1294
Sharon Dietrich, *President*
John Alessandro, *Vice Pres*
Mark Salerno, *Vice Pres*
Christian Dietrich, *Admin Sec*
EMP: 20
SQ FT: 6,000
SALES (est): 2.8MM **Privately Held**
SIC: **3629** 3672 5063 Electronic generation equipment; printed circuit boards; wire & cable

(G-1048)
D & I FINISHING INC
1560 Ocean Ave Ste 7 (11716-1951)
PHONE..................................631 471-3034
Danny Guerrier, *President*
Barbara Guerrier, *General Mgr*
EMP: 6
SQ FT: 4,500
SALES: 400K **Privately Held**
SIC: **3479** 1721 3471 Painting of metal products; painting & paper hanging; finishing, metals or formed products

(G-1049)
DATA DEVICE CORPORATION (DH)
105 Wilbur Pl (11716-2426)
PHONE..................................631 567-5600
Fax: 631 567-6357
Vincent Buffa, *President*
Charles Frazer, *President*
Frank Bloomfield, *Vice Pres*
Tammy Huml, *Vice Pres*
Glenn Mullan, *Vice Pres*
▲ EMP: 320
SQ FT: 196,000
SALES (est): 147.8MM
SALES (corp-wide): 2.7B **Publicly Held**
WEB: www.ddc-web.com
SIC: **3577** 3674 3677 Data conversion equipment, media-to-media: computer; modules, solid state; electronic transformers
HQ: Ilc Industries, Llc
105 Wilbur Pl
Bohemia NY 11716
631 567-5600

(G-1050)
DAVIS AIRCRAFT PRODUCTS CO INC
1150 Walnut Ave Ste 1 (11716-2168)
P.O. Box 525 (11716-0525)
PHONE..................................631 563-1500
Fax: 631 563-1117
Bruce T Davis, *CEO*
Douglas Davis, *Vice Pres*
Jill Davis, *Vice Pres*
Judy Bender, *Purchasing*
Jason Kuhlken, *Purchasing*
▲ EMP: 143 EST: 1967
SQ FT: 30,000
SALES (est): 30.3MM **Privately Held**
WEB: www.davisaircraftproducts.com
SIC: **3724** 3728 Aircraft engines & engine parts; aircraft parts & equipment

(G-1051)
DAVIS RESTRAINT SYSTEMS INC
1150 Walnut Ave (11716-2196)
P.O. Box 525 (11716-0525)
PHONE..................................631 563-1500
Bruce Davis, *President*
EMP: 11
SQ FT: 2,000
SALES: 1.2MM **Privately Held**
SIC: **2399** Seat belts, automobile & aircraft

Bohemia - Suffolk County (G-1052)   GEOGRAPHIC SECTION

(G-1052)
DAYTON T BROWN INC (PA)
Also Called: D T B
1175 Church St (11716-5014)
PHONE.................................631 589-6300
Fax: 631 567-9045
Dayton T Brown Jr, *Ch of Bd*
Richard Dunne, *President*
Dan Malore, *General Mgr*
Dan Johnson, *Business Mgr*
Greg Monahan, *Business Mgr*
EMP: 277 EST: 1950
SQ FT: 250,000
SALES (est): 67.2MM **Privately Held**
WEB: www.daytontbrown.com
SIC: 3444 2741 8711 8734 Sheet metal specialties, not stamped; technical manuals: publishing only, not printed on site; technical papers: publishing only, not printed on site; engineering services; testing laboratories; measuring & controlling devices

(G-1053)
DEALER-PRESSCOM INC
1595 Smithtown Ave Ste A (11716-2418)
PHONE.................................631 589-0434
Fax: 631 589-4449
Michael Endelson, *Principal*
William Ronnan, *Principal*
EMP: 7
SALES (est): 710K **Privately Held**
SIC: 2752 7334 Commercial printing, offset; photocopying & duplicating services

(G-1054)
DELTA LOCK COMPANY LLC
366 Central Ave (11716-3105)
PHONE.................................631 238-7035
Bob Harrison, *Principal*
▲ EMP: 12
SALES (est): 2.1MM **Privately Held**
SIC: 3429 Locks or lock sets

(G-1055)
DENTON ADVERTISING INC
1650 Sycamore Ave Ste 28 (11716-1731)
PHONE.................................631 586-4333
Fax: 631 586-7851
Dennis Dornan, *President*
Robert Dornan, *Managing Dir*
Patty Lyons, *Admin Sec*
EMP: 12
SQ FT: 8,000
SALES: 1.4MM **Privately Held**
WEB: www.dentonadvertising.com
SIC: 2752 Lithographing on metal; advertising posters, lithographed

(G-1056)
DEROSA FABRICATIONS INC
250 Knickerbocker Ave (11716-3112)
PHONE.................................631 563-0640
Fax: 631 563-1070
Tony Derosa, *President*
Lorry Derosa, *Vice Pres*
EMP: 20
SQ FT: 12,500
SALES (est): 2.3MM **Privately Held**
SIC: 3599 Machine shop, jobbing & repair

(G-1057)
DESIGN WORKS CRAFT INC (PA)
70 Orville Dr Ste 1 (11716-2547)
PHONE.................................631 244-5749
Fax: 631 244-6138
Susan Goldsmith, *Ch of Bd*
Daniel Knopp, *President*
Mike Giuliano, *Human Resources*
▲ EMP: 8
SQ FT: 24,500
SALES (est): 5.6MM **Privately Held**
WEB: www.designworkscrafts.com
SIC: 3944 Craft & hobby kits & sets

(G-1058)
DIVERSIFIED ELECTRICAL PDTS
1430 Church St Unit H (11716-5028)
P.O. Box 390 (11716-0390)
PHONE.................................631 567-5710
Fax: 631 567-5083
John Tiano, *President*
Mary Ann Tiano, *Vice Pres*
EMP: 10
SQ FT: 6,500

SALES (est): 1.6MM **Privately Held**
WEB: www.depcorp.com
SIC: 3643 3823 Current-carrying wiring devices; industrial instrmnts msrmnt display/control process variable

(G-1059)
EAGLE TELEPHONICS INC
3880 Veterans Mem Hwy (11716-1038)
PHONE.................................631 471-3600
Fax: 631 471-6595
Richard J Riccoboni, *Ch of Bd*
Don H Coleman, *COO*
Alexander Wenger, *Exec VP*
Frederic H Chapus, *Vice Pres*
Paul Neumann, *Data Proc Exec*
EMP: 15
SQ FT: 10,000
SALES (est): 3.3MM **Privately Held**
WEB: www.eagletelephonics.com
SIC: 3661 6794 Telephones & telephone apparatus; patent owners & lessors

(G-1060)
EASTERN COLOR STRIPPING INC
Also Called: Eastern Color Imaging
1566 Ocean Ave Ste 8 (11716-1932)
PHONE.................................631 563-3700
Fax: 631 563-5085
Michael Catera, *President*
Laura Catera, *Admin Sec*
EMP: 10 EST: 1975
SQ FT: 3,000
SALES (est): 1MM **Privately Held**
WEB: www.easterncolor.com
SIC: 2796 7335 Color separations for printing; color separation, photographic & movie film

(G-1061)
EASTERN EXTERIOR WALL
869 Lincoln Ave (11716-4105)
PHONE.................................631 589-3880
Charlie Bona, *Manager*
EMP: 20
SALES (corp-wide): 121.3MM **Privately Held**
SIC: 2452 Prefabricated wood buildings
HQ: Wall Eastern Exterior Systems Inc
645 Hamilton St Ste 300
Allentown PA 18101
610 868-5522

(G-1062)
EDO LLC
Also Called: Edo Crprtion-Fiber Science Div
5852 Johnson Ave (11716)
PHONE.................................631 218-1413
Fax: 631 218-5505
Weily Tung, *Branch Mgr*
EMP: 22
SALES (corp-wide): 7.4B **Publicly Held**
SIC: 3825 Instruments to measure electricity
HQ: Edo Llc
1500 New Horizons Blvd
Amityville NY 11701
631 630-4000

(G-1063)
EELE LABORATORIES LLC
50 Orville Dr (11716-2548)
PHONE.................................631 244-0051
Fax: 631 244-0053
Karlheinz Strobl, *President*
N Wayne Bailey, *Vice Pres*
Kris Volven, *CFO*
Gina Sansivero, *Marketing Staff*
Paul Gasteiger, *Director*
EMP: 16
SQ FT: 14,000
SALES: 500K **Privately Held**
WEB: www.eele.com
SIC: 3827 Optical instruments & lenses

(G-1064)
EL-GEN LLC
7 Shirley St Unit 1 (11716-1735)
PHONE.................................631 218-3400
Gerard Verbiar, *Treasurer*
Roy J Mc Keen,
EMP: 5
SQ FT: 7,500

SALES (est): 400K **Privately Held**
WEB: www.elgenmfg.com
SIC: 2023 Dietary supplements, dairy & non-dairy based

(G-1065)
ELAN UPHOLSTERY INC
120b Wilbur Pl Ste B (11716-2404)
PHONE.................................631 563-0650
Fax: 631 563-0652
Alan Fogg, *President*
Ann Fogg, *President*
EMP: 10
SQ FT: 7,500
SALES (est): 1MM **Privately Held**
SIC: 2512 7641 Upholstered household furniture; upholstery work

(G-1066)
ELECTRONIC PRINTING INC
50 Keyland Ct (11716-2637)
PHONE.................................631 218-2200
John Kwiecinski, *President*
Eileen Abrams, *Office Mgr*
Paul Kwiecinski, *Shareholder*
EMP: 7
SQ FT: 9,000
SALES (est): 1MM **Privately Held**
WEB: www.epi-printing.com
SIC: 2732 Book printing

(G-1067)
FORERUNNER TECHNOLOGIES INC (PA)
1430 Church St Unit A (11716-5028)
PHONE.................................631 337-2100
Jim Wallace, *President*
Michael Viola, *Vice Pres*
▲ EMP: 45
SQ FT: 8,000
SALES (est): 14.1MM **Privately Held**
SIC: 3661 7371 4813 4899 Telephone & telegraph apparatus; computer software development & applications; telephone communication, except radio; data communication services; electronic parts & equipment; communication services

(G-1068)
FOSTER - GORDON MANUFACTURING
55 Knickerbocker Ave G (11716-3131)
PHONE.................................631 589-6776
Fax: 631 589-5353
Jonathan Gordon, *President*
Pat Sharp, *Manager*
EMP: 8
SQ FT: 9,000
SALES (est): 530K **Privately Held**
SIC: 2789 2782 Bookbinding & related work; blankbooks & looseleaf binders

(G-1069)
FURNITURE BY CRAFTMASTER LTD
1595 Ocean Ave Ste A9 (11716-1962)
PHONE.................................631 750-0658
Michael Ruggiero, *President*
Donna Agate, *Corp Secy*
EMP: 5
SQ FT: 3,600
SALES (est): 622.1K **Privately Held**
SIC: 2521 2512 Wood office furniture; upholstered household furniture

(G-1070)
GABRIELLA IMPORTERS INC (PA)
481 Johnson Ave Ste D (11716-2608)
PHONE.................................212 579-3945
Jacques Azoulay, *President*
▲ EMP: 4
SALES (est): 2.3MM **Privately Held**
SIC: 2084 Wines

(G-1071)
GE AVIATION SYSTEMS LLC
1000 Macarthur Mem Hwy (11716)
P.O. Box 1000 (11716-0999)
PHONE.................................631 467-5500
Fax: 631 467-5510
Brett Rowles, *Manager*
Frank Komornik, *Director*
William Collins,
EMP: 250

SALES (corp-wide): 117.3B **Publicly Held**
SIC: 3728 Aircraft parts & equipment
HQ: Ge Aviation Systems Llc
1 Neumann Way
Cincinnati OH 45215
513 243-2000

(G-1072)
GFH ORTHOTIC & PROSTHETIC LABS
Also Called: Hutnick Rehab
161 Keyland Ct (11716-2621)
PHONE.................................631 467-3725
Glenn F Hutnick, *Ch of Bd*
Kathleen Ciano, *Admin Sec*
EMP: 5 EST: 1979
SALES (est): 609.6K **Privately Held**
SIC: 3842 Limbs, artificial; braces, orthopedic

(G-1073)
GLENN WAYNE WHOLESALE BKY INC
Also Called: Glenn Wayne Bakery
1800 Artic Ave (11716-2443)
PHONE.................................631 289-9200
Glenn Alessi, *Ch of Bd*
Wayne Stelz, *President*
Coleen Goehle, *Manager*
Dominic Seruggio, *Manager*
EMP: 85
SQ FT: 15,000
SALES (est): 18.8MM **Privately Held**
WEB: www.glennwayne.com
SIC: 2051 Bread, cake & related products

(G-1074)
GLOBAL PAYMENT TECH INC (PA)
Also Called: Gpt
170 Wilbur Pl Ste 600 (11716-2433)
PHONE.................................631 563-2500
Fax: 631 563-2630
Andre Soussa, *Ch of Bd*
William McMahon, *President*
Hal Chayrch, *Vice Pres*
Richard Soussa, *Vice Pres*
Dennys Noriega, *Opers Staff*
▲ EMP: 25
SQ FT: 25,550
SALES (est): 11MM **Publicly Held**
WEB: www.gptx.com
SIC: 3581 Mechanisms & parts for automatic vending machines

(G-1075)
HW SPECIALTIES CO INC
210 Knickerbocker Ave B (11716-3175)
PHONE.................................631 589-0745
Fax: 631 589-0739
Kevin Anderson, *President*
Fred Wichelman, *Vice Pres*
EMP: 18
SQ FT: 2,500
SALES: 1.4MM **Privately Held**
SIC: 3599 Machine shop, jobbing & repair

(G-1076)
ILC HOLDINGS INC (HQ)
105 Wilbur Pl (11716-2426)
PHONE.................................631 567-5600
Clifford P Lane, *CEO*
EMP: 7 EST: 1966
SALES (est): 147.8MM
SALES (corp-wide): 2.7B **Publicly Held**
SIC: 3674 Semiconductors & related devices
PA: Transdigm Group Incorporated
1301 E 9th St Ste 3000
Cleveland OH 44114
216 706-2960

(G-1077)
ILC INDUSTRIES LLC (DH)
Also Called: I L C
105 Wilbur Pl (11716-2426)
PHONE.................................631 567-5600
Fax: 631 567-7358
Clifford P Lane, *CEO*
Ken Sheedy, *CFO*
Nancy Henzel, *Accountant*
Jerry Kessler, *Product Mgr*
Pat Bohlert, *Manager*
▲ EMP: 23 EST: 2010

SQ FT: 150,000
SALES (est): 147.8MM
SALES (corp-wide): 2.7B **Publicly Held**
WEB: www.ilcindustries.com
SIC: 3674 Semiconductors & related devices
HQ: Ilc Holdings, Inc.
105 Wilbur Pl
Bohemia NY 11716
631 567-5600

(G-1078)
INTELLIGENT TRAFFIC SYSTEMS
140 Keyland Ct Unit 1 (11716-2646)
PHONE..................................631 567-5994
Joseph Battista, *President*
Karen Battista, *Admin Sec*
EMP: 8
SQ FT: 3,200
SALES: 400K **Privately Held**
SIC: 3669 Signaling apparatus, electric

(G-1079)
J PERCOCO INDUSTRIES INC
Also Called: Mjs Woodworking
1546 Ocean Ave Ste 4 (11716-1938)
PHONE..................................631 312-4572
Jerolamo Percoco, *President*
EMP: 8 **EST:** 1990
SQ FT: 15,000
SALES: 1MM **Privately Held**
SIC: 2511 2434 2431 Wood household furniture; wood kitchen cabinets; millwork

(G-1080)
JAMES D RUBINO INC
20 Jules Ct Ste 5 (11716-4106)
PHONE..................................631 244-8730
James D Rubino, *President*
EMP: 24
SALES (est): 3MM **Privately Held**
SIC: 3499 Fabricated metal products

(G-1081)
JANCO PRESS INC
20 Floyds Run (11716-2154)
PHONE..................................631 563-3003
Fax: 631 563-9475
Maurice Janco, *President*
Florence Janco, *Vice Pres*
Seth Janco, *Vice Pres*
EMP: 15
SQ FT: 10,000
SALES: 4MM **Privately Held**
SIC: 2754 2759 Labels: gravure printing; labels & seals: printing; embossing on paper

(G-1082)
JEROME STVENS PHRMCUTICALS INC
Also Called: Jsp
60 Davinci Dr (11716-2633)
PHONE..................................631 567-1113
Fax: 631 567-1189
Ronald Steinlauf, *Chairman*
EMP: 15
SQ FT: 20,000
SALES (est): 4.8MM **Privately Held**
SIC: 2834 Pharmaceutical preparations

(G-1083)
JOKA INDUSTRIES INC
65 Knickerbocker Ave A (11716-3160)
PHONE..................................631 589-0444
Fax: 631 589-0817
Nick Prignano, *Chairman*
Roger Chabra, *Manager*
Bibi Latiff, *Manager*
▲ **EMP:** 22
SQ FT: 15,000
SALES (est): 4.9MM **Privately Held**
WEB: www.jokaindustries.com
SIC: 3721 Aircraft

(G-1084)
JOLIN MACHINING CORP
1561 Smithtown Ave (11716-2409)
PHONE..................................631 589-1305
Fax: 631 589-1318
John Lutjen, *President*
EMP: 12
SQ FT: 7,000
SALES (est): 1.9MM **Privately Held**
SIC: 3599 Machine shop, jobbing & repair

(G-1085)
JONATHAN LORD CORP
87 Carlough Rd Unit A (11716-2921)
PHONE..................................631 563-4445
Fax: 631 563-8505
Carole Kentrup, *Co-President*
Kathleen Dancik, *Co-President*
EMP: 12
SQ FT: 8,000
SALES (est): 970K **Privately Held**
WEB: www.jonathanlord.com
SIC: 2051 2052 Bread, cake & related products; cakes, bakery: except frozen; cookies & crackers

(G-1086)
K C TECHNICAL SERVICES INC
390 Knickerbocker Ave # 1 (11716-3123)
PHONE..................................631 589-7170
Guy Cosmo, *President*
Elizabeth Cosmo, *Vice Pres*
EMP: 7
SQ FT: 12,700
SALES: 800K **Privately Held**
WEB: www.kctecserv.com
SIC: 3565 Packaging machinery

(G-1087)
KENTRONICS INC
140 Keyland Ct Unit 1 (11716-2646)
PHONE..................................631 567-5994
Robert W Davis, *President*
Joseph Battista, *Vice Pres*
EMP: 5
SQ FT: 3,200
SALES (est): 441.9K **Privately Held**
WEB: www.kentronics.net
SIC: 3669 Highway signals, electric

(G-1088)
KOEHLER INSTRUMENT COMPANY INC
1595 Sycamore Ave (11716-1732)
PHONE..................................631 589-3800
Fax: 631 589-3815
Roy Westerhaus, *Ch of Bd*
Atul Gautama, *General Mgr*
Khalid Masrour, *Materials Mgr*
Chris Koenig, *Engineer*
Peter Brey, *Treasurer*
▲ **EMP:** 55
SQ FT: 28,500
SALES (est): 19.1MM **Privately Held**
WEB: www.koehlerinstrument.com
SIC: 3823 Industrial instrmnts msrmnt display/control process variable

(G-1089)
L & J INTERIORS INC
35 Orville Dr Ste 3 (11716-2533)
PHONE..................................631 218-0838
Fax: 631 218-0380
Jerry Esquibel, *President*
Leon Esquibel, *Vice Pres*
Liz Vanderbilt, *Manager*
EMP: 8
SALES (est): 870K **Privately Held*
WEB: www.ljinteriors.com
SIC: 2541 1742 Store fixtures, wood; drywall

(G-1090)
LABEL MAKERS INC
170 Wilbur Pl Ste 100 (11716-2451)
PHONE..................................631 319-6329
Craig Becker, *President*
Teri Nolan, *Credit Mgr*
Babra Michkana, *Office Mgr*
Adel Altman, *Systems Analyst*
EMP: 20
SQ FT: 8,000
SALES (est): 3.1MM **Privately Held**
WEB: www.labelmakersinc.com
SIC: 2672 Adhesive papers, labels or tapes: from purchased material

(G-1091)
LED LUMINA USA LLC
116 Wilbur Pl (11716-2402)
PHONE..................................631 750-4433
Christina Bonlarron, *CFO*
John Bonlarron, *Mng Member*
James McGuirk, *Manager*
EMP: 1
SALES: 1MM **Privately Held**
SIC: 3229 Bulbs for electric lights

(G-1092)
LEETECH MANUFACTURING INC
105 Carlough Ave Unit C (11716-2914)
PHONE..................................631 563-1442
Fred Vasta, *President*
Jolleen Ogallagher, *Administration*
EMP: 5
SALES (est): 480K **Privately Held**
SIC: 3599 Machine shop, jobbing & repair

(G-1093)
LEIDEL CORPORATION (PA)
Also Called: Pentaplastics
95 Orville Dr (11716-2501)
PHONE..................................631 244-0900
Fax: 631 694-7876
Warren H Leidel, *Ch of Bd*
Roger D Leidel, *President*
Susan Barrisich, *Manager*
Abe Weisfelner, *Director*
EMP: 26 **EST:** 1902
SQ FT: 14,000
SALES: 5.9MM **Privately Held**
WEB: www.leidelcorp.com
SIC: 3089 Injection molded finished plastic products; molding primary plastic

(G-1094)
LOGITEK INC
110 Wilbur Pl (11716-2402)
PHONE..................................631 567-1100
William Forman, *CEO*
Debby Klaus, *Controller*
Patty Angelos, *Administration*
EMP: 90 **EST:** 1969
SALES: 20MM
SALES (corp-wide): 43.9MM **Privately Held**
WEB: www.naii.com
SIC: 3679 3825 3812 3674 Electronic circuits; instruments to measure electricity; search & navigation equipment; semiconductors & related devices; relays & industrial controls
PA: North Atlantic Industries, Inc.
110 Wilbur Pl
Bohemia NY 11716
631 567-1100

(G-1095)
LOUGHLIN MANUFACTURING CORP
1601 9th Ave (11716-1202)
PHONE..................................631 585-4422
Fax: 631 585-4518
Martin Loughlin, *President*
Kathy Loughlin, *Manager*
EMP: 14 **EST:** 1970
SQ FT: 5,000
SALES (est): 2.2MM **Privately Held**
SIC: 3599 Machine shop, jobbing & repair

(G-1096)
LSC PERIPHERALS INCORPORATED
415 Central Ave Ste F (11716-3118)
PHONE..................................631 244-0707
Fax: 631 244-0794
Frank Villa, *President*
Roger Strolin, *Vice Pres*
EMP: 4
SQ FT: 4,000
SALES: 1.5MM **Privately Held**
SIC: 3577 Computer peripheral equipment

(G-1097)
LUCAS DENTAL EQUIPMENT CO INC
360 Knickerbocker Ave # 4 (11716-3124)
PHONE..................................631 244-2807
Fax: 718 789-3819
Richard Lucas, *Ch of Bd*
Joyce Lucas, *President*
David Lichtman, *Exec Dir*
EMP: 14 **EST:** 1930
SQ FT: 20,000
SALES (est): 1.9MM **Privately Held**
SIC: 3843 Dental equipment

(G-1098)
M&C ASSOCIATES LLC
3920 Vtrans Mem Hwy Ste 7 (11716-1074)
PHONE..................................631 467-8760
Fax: 631 467-8767
Kelly Palacios, *President*
Leanora Gordon, *Principal*
Dave Depietro, *Vice Pres*
Joseph Cutillo, *Engineer*
John Ridulfo, *Engineer*
EMP: 40
SALES (est): 6.7MM **Privately Held**
SIC: 3571 Electronic computers

(G-1099)
MAGELLAN AEROSPACE NY INC
25 Aero Rd (11716-2901)
PHONE..................................631 589-2440
Fax: 631 589-2767
David Grynberg, *Mfg Staff*
Lee Pappas, *Mfg Staff*
John Mansfield, *CFO*
Jerry Myszka, *Manager*
John Marcello, *Manager*
EMP: 250
SALES (corp-wide): 738.6MM **Privately Held**
SIC: 3599 3728 5088 Machine shop, jobbing & repair; aircraft parts & equipment; aircraft equipment & supplies
HQ: Magellan Aerospace, New York, Inc.
9711 50th Ave
Corona NY 11368
718 699-4000

(G-1100)
MAGNAWORKS TECHNOLOGY INC
36 Carlough Rd Unit H (11716-2905)
PHONE..................................631 218-3431
Stan Stromski, *Director*
EMP: 7
SALES (est): 700K **Privately Held**
WEB: www.magnaworkstechnology.com
SIC: 3499 Magnets, permanent: metallic

(G-1101)
MALHAME PUBLS & IMPORTERS INC
Also Called: Regina Press
180 Orville Dr Unit A (11716-2546)
PHONE..................................631 694-8600
Robert Malhame, *President*
George E Malhame, *President*
Robert E Malhame, *Treasurer*
Barbara Ryan, *Manager*
▲ **EMP:** 22
SALES (est): 3.9MM **Privately Held**
WEB: www.malhame.com
SIC: 2731 5049 Books: publishing only; religious supplies

(G-1102)
MASS MDSG SELF SELECTION EQP
35 Orville Dr Ste 2 (11716-2533)
PHONE..................................631 234-3300
Fax: 631 234-3676
Stephen D Jaha, *Ch of Bd*
Bob Panagos, *Vice Pres*
Richard Benardes, *Sales Executive*
Stephanie Friscia, *Manager*
▲ **EMP:** 20 **EST:** 1961
SQ FT: 4,000
SALES (est): 3.4MM **Privately Held**
WEB: www.masmerch.com
SIC: 2542 1751 Partitions & fixtures, except wood; store fixture installation

(G-1103)
MCGUIGAN INC
Also Called: Concept Components
210 Knickerbocker Ave (11716-3175)
PHONE..................................631 750-6222
Fax: 631 563-4675
James W McGuigan, *Ch of Bd*
Mike Potuczo, *Plant Mgr*
Mark Dellaragione, *QC Mgr*
Helene Stradford, *Manager*
EMP: 25
SQ FT: 9,000
SALES (est): 6.9MM **Privately Held**
WEB: www.mcguigan.com
SIC: 3566 3599 3724 Gears, power transmission, except automotive; custom machinery; aircraft engines & engine parts

(G-1104)
MED SERVICES INC
100 Knickerbocker Ave C (11716-3127)
PHONE..................................631 218-6450

Bohemia - Suffolk County (G-1105)

Steven Cortese, *President*
Stefani Katz, *Senior VP*
EMP: 55
SQ FT: 1,800
SALES: 155MM **Privately Held**
SIC: 3845 7699 Electromedical equipment; medical equipment repair, non-electric

(G-1105)
MONARCH METAL FABRICATION INC
1625 Sycamore Ave Ste A (11716-1728)
PHONE.................................631 563-8967
▼ EMP: 8
SQ FT: 17,000
SALES (est): 1.3MM **Privately Held**
WEB: www.monarchmetal.com
SIC: 3444 3441 Sheet metalwork; fabricated structural metal

(G-1106)
MPE GRAPHICS INC
Also Called: Milburn Printing
120 Wilbur Pl Ste A (11716-2440)
PHONE.................................631 582-8900
Fax: 631 582-8995
Keith Quinn, *President*
Lisa Quinn, *Manager*
EMP: 11 EST: 2004
SQ FT: 5,000
SALES (est): 2MM **Privately Held**
SIC: 2759 Commercial printing

(G-1107)
MUSCLE SPORTS PRODUCTS
80 Orville Dr Ste 112 (11716-2505)
PHONE.................................631 755-1388
Ahmad Mousa, *Owner*
EMP: 7 EST: 2013
SALES (est): 530.3K **Privately Held**
SIC: 3949 Sporting & athletic goods

(G-1108)
NATURES BOUNTY INC
90 Orville Dr (11716-2521)
PHONE.................................631 567-9500
Fax: 631 563-1180
Donna Friedman, *Vice Pres*
Michael Oliveri, *Purch Mgr*
EMP: 13
SALES (corp-wide): 3B **Publicly Held**
SIC: 2834 Vitamin preparations
HQ: Nature's Bounty, Inc.
  2100 Smithtown Ave
  Ronkonkoma NY 11779
  631 580-6137

(G-1109)
NEW KIT ON THE BLOCK
100 Knickerbocker Ave K (11716-3127)
PHONE.................................631 757-5655
Fax: 631 757-5680
Lee Holcomb, *President*
John Burke, *Managing Dir*
Margaret Courtemancke, *Office Mgr*
EMP: 5
SQ FT: 4,000
SALES (est): 378.6K **Privately Held**
WEB: www.thenewkitontheblock.com
SIC: 3993 5251 Signs & advertising specialties; hardware

(G-1110)
NEWPORT BUSINESS SOLUTIONS INC
61 Keyland Ct (11716-2654)
PHONE.................................631 319-6129
Gina Lanzillotta, *President*
Brendan Primus, *Manager*
Lynn Stillwell-Marks, *Manager*
Catherine Fairburn, *Director*
George Feinman, *Director*
EMP: 18 EST: 2010
SALES (est): 1.1MM **Privately Held**
SIC: 2759 3555 5045 Commercial printing; promotional printing; printing trades machinery; printers, computer

(G-1111)
NORTH ATLANTIC INDUSTRIES INC (PA)
110 Wilbur Pl (11716-2402)
PHONE.................................631 567-1100
William Forman, *President*

Lino Massafra, *Vice Pres*
Edward Doepp, *Plant Mgr*
Eddie Gonzalez, *Facilities Mgr*
Deborah L Klaus, *Controller*
EMP: 115
SQ FT: 30,000
SALES: 43.9MM **Privately Held**
SIC: 3825 Instruments to measure electricity

(G-1112)
NORTHROCK INDUSTRIES INC
31 Crossway E (11716-1204)
PHONE.................................631 924-6130
Brian F Robertson, *President*
Alan Browning, *Treasurer*
Joe Vibrators, *Sales Staff*
Eric Rueb, *Admin Sec*
▲ EMP: 21
SQ FT: 12,000
SALES (est): 3.2MM **Privately Held**
WEB: www.northrockindustries.com
SIC: 3559 Concrete products machinery

(G-1113)
OLD WORLD MOULDINGS INC
821 Lincoln Ave (11716-4103)
PHONE.................................631 563-8660
Fax: 631 563-8815
Alan D Havranek, *President*
EMP: 8
SQ FT: 20,000
SALES (est): 2.4MM **Privately Held**
WEB: www.oldworldmouldings.com
SIC: 2431 Moldings, wood: unfinished & prefinished

(G-1114)
PACKAGING DYNAMICS LTD
35 Carlough Rd Ste 2 (11716-2913)
PHONE.................................631 563-4499
Daniel Lehmann, *CEO*
Eric Lehmann, *President*
Ann Lange, *Office Mgr*
Pat Lehmann, *Admin Sec*
▲ EMP: 15
SALES (est): 3.5MM **Privately Held**
SIC: 3565 Packaging machinery

(G-1115)
PASSUR AEROSPACE INC
35 Orville Dr Ste 1 (11716-2533)
PHONE.................................631 589-6800
G S Beckwith Gilbert, *Ch of Bd*
James T Barry, *President*
Bruce N Whitman, *Chairman*
James A Cole, *Senior VP*
Richard C Scott, *Senior VP*
EMP: 6
SQ FT: 3,000
SALES (est): 1.8MM
SALES (corp-wide): 12.5MM **Publicly Held**
WEB: www.passur.com
SIC: 3671 Cathode ray tubes, including rebuilt
PA: Passur Aerospace, Inc.
  1 Landmark Sq Ste 1900
  Stamford CT 06901
  203 622-4086

(G-1116)
PDA PANACHE CORP
Also Called: P D A Panache
70 Knickerbocker Ave # 7 (11716-3151)
P.O. Box 577, Bellport (11713-0577)
PHONE.................................631 776-0523
Paul Schiller, *President*
Lynn Schiller, *Vice Pres*
EMP: 5
SALES (est): 580K **Privately Held**
WEB: www.pdapanache.com
SIC: 3577 5941 5112 Input/output equipment, computer; sporting goods & bicycle shops; pens &/or pencils

(G-1117)
PERVI PRECISION COMPANY
220 Knickerbocker Ave # 1 (11716-3181)
PHONE.................................631 589-5557
Fax: 631 589-7637
Carlos Perez, *Owner*
EMP: 6
SQ FT: 4,100

SALES (est): 807.3K **Privately Held**
SIC: 3469 3599 Machine parts, stamped or pressed metal; machine shop, jobbing & repair

(G-1118)
POWER CONNECTOR INC
140 Wilbur Pl Ste 4 (11716-2400)
PHONE.................................631 563-7878
Fax: 631 563-6482
Andrew S Linder, *President*
Arlene R Linder, *Vice Pres*
Peter Spadaro, *Opers Staff*
Joan Saracino, *Controller*
▲ EMP: 50
SQ FT: 32,000
SALES (est): 10.6MM **Privately Held**
SIC: 3678 Electronic connectors

(G-1119)
PRECISION ASSEMBLY TECH INC
Also Called: P.A.t
160 Wilbur Pl Ste 500 (11716-2437)
PHONE.................................631 699-9400
Lorraine Caruso, *Principal*
Russell Gulotta, *Chairman*
Thomas Gulotta, *Vice Pres*
Michael Kellwick, *Manager*
Lorraine Caurso, *Administration*
▲ EMP: 50
SQ FT: 25,000
SALES (est): 15.5MM **Privately Held**
WEB: www.pat-inc.com
SIC: 3679 Electronic circuits; harness assemblies for electronic use: wire or cable

(G-1120)
PRECISION CHARTS INC
Also Called: PCI
130 Wilbur Pl Dept Pc (11716-2404)
P.O. Box 456 (11716-0456)
PHONE.................................631 244-8295
Barry Spencer, *President*
Michael Lesh, *General Mgr*
Peggy Easparro, *Manager*
♦ EMP: 25
SQ FT: 30,000
SALES (est): 5.8MM **Privately Held**
WEB: www.pcicharts.com
SIC: 2621 Book, bond & printing papers

(G-1121)
PRIMOPLAST INC
1555 Ocean Ave Ste E (11716-1933)
PHONE.................................631 750-0680
Eugene Ruoff, *President*
William Hayes, *Admin Sec*
EMP: 12
SQ FT: 1,000
SALES: 950K **Privately Held**
SIC: 3089 3531 Injection molded finished plastic products; construction machinery attachments

(G-1122)
PRO TORQUE
Also Called: J Rivera
1440 Church St (11716-5027)
PHONE.................................631 218-8700
Joseph Rivera, *President*
Susan Rivera, *Vice Pres*
Lynn Dimino, *CFO*
Lorrie Rivera, *Manager*
EMP: 25
SQ FT: 165,000
SALES: 1.7MM **Privately Held**
WEB: www.jrivera.com
SIC: 3714 Motor vehicle transmissions, drive assemblies & parts

(G-1123)
PROJECTOR LAMP SERVICES LLC
120 Wilbur Pl Ste C (11716-2440)
PHONE.................................631 244-0051
Santa Maria Scalza, *Accounting Mgr*
Barbara Trezza, *Accounting Mgr*
Derek Chang, *Web Dvlpr*
Paul Gasteiger, *Mgr*
EMP: 15
SALES (est): 2.4MM **Privately Held**
SIC: 3648 Reflectors for lighting equipment: metal

(G-1124)
PROTEX INTERNATIONAL CORP
Also Called: Securax
366 Central Ave (11716-3105)
PHONE.................................631 563-4250
David Wachsman, *CEO*
William Azzoli, *Electrical Engi*
Kevin Boyle, *CFO*
Patricia Voigt, *Accounts Mgr*
Arthur Varga, *Mktg Dir*
▲ EMP: 75
SQ FT: 34,000
SALES (est): 13MM **Privately Held**
WEB: www.protex-intl.com
SIC: 3699 Security control equipment & systems

(G-1125)
QUEUE SOLUTIONS LLC
250 Knickerbocker Ave (11716-3112)
PHONE.................................631 750-6440
Richard Prigg, *President*
EMP: 10
SALES: 5MM **Privately Held**
SIC: 2387 Apparel belts

(G-1126)
ROAD CASES USA INC
1625 Sycamore Ave Ste A (11716-1728)
PHONE.................................631 563-0633
Lucille Maielna, *Office Mgr*
EMP: 20
SALES (est): 66K **Privately Held**
SIC: 3523 Farm machinery & equipment

(G-1127)
RY-LECIA INC
Also Called: American Recreational Products
1535 Locust Ave (11716-2184)
PHONE.................................631 244-0011
Kevin Brown, *President*
Robert Brown, *Corp Secy*
Danielle Strauch, *Manager*
EMP: 6
SALES: 3MM **Privately Held**
WEB: www.americanrecreational.com
SIC: 2531 Picnic tables or benches, park

(G-1128)
S G NEW YORK LLC (PA)
Also Called: Pennysaver News
2950 Vtrans Mem Hwy Ste 1 (11716-1030)
PHONE.................................631 665-4000
Fax: 631 580-7748
Richard Megenedy Jr,
Murray Rossby,
EMP: 33
SQ FT: 4,000
SALES (est): 5.9MM **Privately Held**
SIC: 2741 2711 Shopping news: publishing & printing; newspapers, publishing & printing

(G-1129)
SCIENTIFIC INDUSTRIES INC (PA)
80 Orville Dr Ste 102 (11716-2505)
PHONE.................................631 567-4700
Fax: 631 567-5896
Joseph G Cremonese, *Ch of Bd*
Helena R Santos, *President*
Stacy Palladino, *General Mgr*
Robert P Nichols, *Exec VP*
Marie Schindlar, *VP Human Res*
▲ EMP: 33 EST: 1954
SQ FT: 19,000
SALES: 9.6MM **Publicly Held**
WEB: www.scind.com
SIC: 3821 Shakers & stirrers

(G-1130)
SECURITY DYNAMICS INC
217 Knickerbocker Ave (11716-3132)
PHONE.................................631 392-1701
Huihua Wang, *Ch of Bd*
William Wang, *President*
Lillian Chen, *General Mgr*
▲ EMP: 12
SQ FT: 3,000
SALES (est): 2.2MM **Privately Held**
SIC: 3699 Security devices

▲ = Import ▼ = Export
♦ = Import/Export

GEOGRAPHIC SECTION
Bohemia - Suffolk County (G-1156)

(G-1131)
SELECT CONTROLS INC
45 Knickerbocker Ave # 3 (11716-3119)
PHONE.................................631 567-9010
Fax: 631 567-9013
Robert Ufer, *President*
Diane Morris, *Corp Secy*
Tom Morris, *Opers Mgr*
Joe Cardimone, *Opers Staff*
Art Nintsel, *Engineer*
EMP: 32
SQ FT: 2,500
SALES (est): 5.8MM **Privately Held**
WEB: www.select-controls.com
SIC: 3823 3625 8711 3613 Industrial flow & liquid measuring instruments; industrial electrical relays & switches; consulting engineer; switchgear & switchboard apparatus

(G-1132)
SHAR-MAR MACHINE COMPANY
1648 Locust Ave Ste F (11716-2156)
PHONE.................................631 567-8040
Fax: 631 567-8042
Myron Rubin, *Owner*
EMP: 5
SQ FT: 3,200
SALES (est): 340K **Privately Held**
SIC: 3599 Machine shop, jobbing & repair

(G-1133)
SHORT RUN FORMS INC
171 Keyland Ct (11716-2621)
PHONE.................................631 567-7171
Fax: 631 567-4550
Steven Looney, *President*
Andrew Boccio, *Senior VP*
Robert Stumpo, *Vice Pres*
Jan Merritt, *Accountant*
EMP: 60
SQ FT: 17,000
SALES (est): 9MM **Privately Held**
WEB: www.shortrunforms.com
SIC: 2759 5943 Business forms: printing; office forms & supplies

(G-1134)
SIEMENS INDUSTRY INC
50 Orville Dr Ste 2 (11716-2548)
PHONE.................................631 218-1000
Fax: 631 218-1009
Vincent Catalano, *Accounts Exec*
Tim Cox, *Accounts Exec*
Marcie Milnamow, *Sales Executive*
Robert Hayes, *Manager*
EMP: 115
SALES (corp-wide): 83.5B **Privately Held**
WEB: www.sibt.com
SIC: 3823 Temperature measurement instruments, industrial
HQ: Siemens Industry, Inc.
   1000 Deerfield Pkwy
   Buffalo Grove IL 60089
   847 215-1000

(G-1135)
SMART HIGH VOLTAGE SOLUTIONS
390 Knickerbocker Ave # 6 (11716-3123)
P.O. Box 5135, Hauppauge (11788-0001)
PHONE.................................631 563-6724
Kevin R Smith, *President*
Hersh Ochakovski, *Exec VP*
▼ **EMP**: 16
SQ FT: 1,825
SALES: 2.5MM **Privately Held**
SIC: 3542 High energy rate metal forming machines

(G-1136)
SPECTRUM CRAFTS INC
Also Called: Janlynn Corporation, The
70 Orville Dr Ste 1 (11716-2547)
PHONE.................................631 244-5749
Daniel Knopp, *President*
EMP: 27
SALES (est): 141.6K
SALES (corp-wide): 5.6MM **Privately Held**
SIC: 3944 Craft & hobby kits & sets
PA: Design Works Craft Inc.
   70 Orville Dr Ste 1
   Bohemia NY 11716
   631 244-5749

(G-1137)
STRUCTURAL INDUSTRIES INC
2950 Veterans Memorial Hw (11716-1030)
PHONE.................................631 471-5200
Stanley Hirsch, *CEO*
Jamie Hirsch, *President*
Cliff Burger, *Exec VP*
Judy Hirsch, *Vice Pres*
Judy Vietheer, *CFO*
▲ **EMP**: 180 **EST**: 1966
SQ FT: 70,000
SALES (est): 25.4MM **Privately Held**
WEB: www.structuralindustries.com
SIC: 2499 3089 3499 Picture & mirror frames, wood; plastic processing; picture frames, metal

(G-1138)
SURF-TECH MANUFACTURING CORP
80 Orville Dr Ste 115 (11716-2538)
PHONE.................................631 589-1194
Fax: 631 589-1629
Richard Eggert, *President*
Diana Small, *Purch Mgr*
EMP: 12
SQ FT: 8,000
SALES (est): 2.3MM **Privately Held**
WEB: www.surftechmfg.com
SIC: 3672 5045 Printed circuit boards; computers, peripherals & software

(G-1139)
SYMBOL TECHNOLOGIES LLC
110 Orville Dr (11716-2506)
PHONE.................................631 738-2400
Ron Goldman, *Branch Mgr*
EMP: 15
SALES (corp-wide): 3.6B **Publicly Held**
WEB: www.symbol.com
SIC: 3577 Computer peripheral equipment
HQ: Symbol Technologies, Llc
   1 Zebra Plz
   Holtsville NY 11742
   631 738-2400

(G-1140)
SYNCO CHEMICAL CORPORATION
24 Davinci Dr (11716-2631)
P.O. Box 405 (11716-0405)
PHONE.................................631 567-5300
Fax: 631 567-5359
Sal A Randisi, *President*
Bill Reilly, *General Mgr*
Patrick E Malloy II, *Vice Pres*
Angela Tomaselli, *Manager*
◆ **EMP**: 50
SQ FT: 18,000
SALES (est): 10.9MM **Privately Held**
WEB: www.super-lube.com
SIC: 2842 Specialty cleaning, polishes & sanitation goods

(G-1141)
T R P MACHINE INC
35 Davinci Dr Ste B (11716-2666)
PHONE.................................631 567-9620
Patrick Price, *President*
Roger Price, *Principal*
Thomas Price, *Vice Pres*
Michelle Weiss, *Controller*
EMP: 25
SQ FT: 8,500
SALES (est): 4.1MM **Privately Held**
WEB: www.trpmachine.com
SIC: 3599 Machine & other job shop work; machine shop, jobbing & repair

(G-1142)
TEMRICK INC
1605 Sycamore Ave Unit B (11716-1734)
PHONE.................................631 567-8860
Fax: 631 567-1361
Trevor Glausen Jr, *President*
Melissa Glausen, *Vice Pres*
EMP: 5
SQ FT: 5,000
SALES: 550K **Privately Held**
SIC: 3599 7389 Machine shop, jobbing & repair; grinding, precision: commercial or industrial

(G-1143)
TEXTURE PLUS INC
1611 Lakeland Ave (11716-2190)
PHONE.................................631 218-9200
Katrina Vassar, *Manager*
Paul Kampe,
Brian Kampe,
EMP: 40
SQ FT: 16,000
SALES (est): 7.7MM **Privately Held**
WEB: www.foamvisions.com
SIC: 2952 Siding materials

(G-1144)
TOUCH ADJUST CLIP CO INC
1687 Roosevelt Ave (11716-1428)
PHONE.................................631 589-3077
Fax: 631 589-7489
Richard Haug Sr, *President*
Richard C Haug, *President*
Frank Grande, *Plant Mgr*
▲ **EMP**: 12
SQ FT: 10,000
SALES: 1.3MM **Privately Held**
WEB: www.touchadjustclip.com
SIC: 3915 Jewelers' materials & lapidary work

(G-1145)
TREO INDUSTRIES INC
Also Called: Genie Fastener Mfg Co
35 Carlough Rd Ste 1 (11716-2913)
PHONE.................................631 737-4022
Thomas W Blank, *Ch of Bd*
Tim Blank, *President*
Donald Blank, *Vice Pres*
Eugenia Blank, *Treasurer*
Corine Duffy, *Bookkeeper*
EMP: 7
SQ FT: 8,000
SALES (est): 957.7K **Privately Held**
SIC: 3452 Bolts, nuts, rivets & washers

(G-1146)
TRIAD COUNTER CORP
1225 Church St (11716-5014)
PHONE.................................631 750-0615
Frank Simone, *President*
Peter Amari, *Vice Pres*
Kirk Ibsen, *Treasurer*
EMP: 20
SQ FT: 20,000
SALES: 2.8MM **Privately Held**
SIC: 2541 5031 1799 Counter & sink tops; kitchen cabinets; kitchen & bathroom remodeling

(G-1147)
TRIANGLE RUBBER CO INC
50 Aero Rd (11716-2909)
PHONE.................................631 589-9400
Fax: 631 589-9403
Thomas Barresi, *President*
Joseph Barresi Jr, *Vice Pres*
Ann Taylor, *Manager*
▲ **EMP**: 25 **EST**: 1930
SQ FT: 13,000
SALES (est): 4.1MM **Privately Held**
WEB: www.trianglerubber.com
SIC: 3069 5085 3061 Hard rubber & molded rubber products; rubber goods, mechanical; mechanical rubber goods

(G-1148)
TRIPAR MANUFACTURING CO INC
1620 Ocean Ave Ste 1 (11716-1930)
PHONE.................................631 563-0855
John M McNamara, *President*
EMP: 7
SQ FT: 8,000
SALES: 1.3MM **Privately Held**
SIC: 3444 3599 Sheet metalwork; machine shop, jobbing & repair

(G-1149)
TRIPLE POINT MANUFACTURING
1371 Church St Ste 6 (11716-5026)
PHONE.................................631 218-4988
Fax: 631 218-4999
Bernard Lichtenberger, *President*
Karl Zorn, *Vice Pres*
Paul Jessen, *Purchasing*
Erwin Stropagel, *Treasurer*
EMP: 7
SQ FT: 4,000
SALES: 671K **Privately Held**
WEB: www.tpmny.com
SIC: 3451 3599 Screw machine products; machine & other job shop work

(G-1150)
TUSK MANUFACTURING INC
1371 Church St Ste 1 (11716-5026)
PHONE.................................631 567-3349
Fax: 631 567-3348
Edmund F Zorn, *President*
Karl Zorn, *Vice Pres*
Kevin Zorn, *Vice Pres*
EMP: 21 **EST**: 1979
SQ FT: 8,000
SALES: 2.2MM **Privately Held**
WEB: www.tuskmfg.com
SIC: 3812 Search & navigation equipment

(G-1151)
UNITED DATA FORMS INC
500 Johnson Ave Ste B (11716-2709)
P.O. Box 363 (11716-0363)
PHONE.................................631 218-0104
Fax: 631 218-0209
Louis Giangaspro, *President*
Wayne Silverman, *Treasurer*
EMP: 12 **EST**: 1997
SQ FT: 10,000
SALES: 3MM **Privately Held**
SIC: 2621 Business form paper

(G-1152)
UNITED MACHINING INC
1595 Smithtown Ave Ste D (11716-2418)
PHONE.................................631 589-6751
Corey Vercellone, *President*
EMP: 6
SALES: 430K **Privately Held**
SIC: 3599 Machine shop, jobbing & repair

(G-1153)
UPTEK SOLUTIONS
130 Knickerbocker Ave A (11716-3171)
PHONE.................................631 256-5565
Lin Xu, *President*
EMP: 15
SALES (est): 2.4MM **Privately Held**
SIC: 3826 3699 Laser scientific & engineering instruments; laser systems & equipment

(G-1154)
VJ TECHNOLOGIES INC (PA)
Also Called: Vjt
89 Carlough Rd (11716-2903)
PHONE.................................631 589-8800
Fax: 631 589-8992
Vijay Alreia, *Chairman*
Shiva Kumar, *Purchasing*
Jeffrey Ackerman, *Engineer*
John Loen, *Engineer*
Boris Soyfer, *Engineer*
◆ **EMP**: 35
SQ FT: 30,000
SALES: 0 **Privately Held**
SIC: 3844 3812 3829 X-ray apparatus & tubes; search & detection systems & instruments; nuclear radiation & testing apparatus

(G-1155)
VYTEK INC
271 Knickerbocker Ave (11716-3103)
PHONE.................................631 750-1770
Joan Crisafulli, *President*
EMP: 10
SALES (est): 1.2MM **Privately Held**
SIC: 3599 7539 Machine shop, jobbing & repair; machine shop, automotive

(G-1156)
WEMCO CASTING LLC
20 Jules Ct Ste 2 (11716-4106)
PHONE.................................631 563-8050
Fax: 631 563-8054
Sharen Fenchel, *Owner*
EMP: 70
SQ FT: 2,000
SALES: 9.4MM **Privately Held**
WEB: www.wemcocastingllc.com
SIC: 3369 Nonferrous foundries

Bohemia - Suffolk County (G-1157)

(G-1157)
Z WORKS INC
1395 Lakeland Ave Ste 10 (11716-3318)
PHONE..................631 750-0612
Zoltan Mata, *Owner*
Katalin Gergely, *Owner*
EMP: 5 EST: 2001
SALES (est): 475.5K **Privately Held**
WEB: www.z-works.com
SIC: 3544 Special dies, tools, jigs & fixtures

Boiceville
Ulster County

(G-1158)
STUCKI EMBROIDERY WORKS INC (PA)
Also Called: Am-Best Emblems
Rr 28 Box W (12412)
PHONE..................845 657-2308
Fax: 845 657-2860
Murray Fenwick, *President*
Ilse Fenwick, *Corp Secy*
Arthur Stucki, *Vice Pres*
Emily Oppimitti, *Sales Staff*
EMP: 18 EST: 1924
SQ FT: 17,000
SALES (est): 2.3MM **Privately Held**
SIC: 2395 Swiss loom embroideries; emblems, embroidered

Bolivar
Allegany County

(G-1159)
KLEIN CUTLERY LLC
Also Called: Scissor Online
7971 Refinery Rd (14715-9605)
PHONE..................585 928-2500
Fax: 585 928-1101
Wayne J West,
▲ EMP: 60
SQ FT: 18,000
SALES (est): 8.4MM **Privately Held**
WEB: www.scissorsonline.com
SIC: 3421 Scissors, hand; shears, hand

(G-1160)
MONEYSAVER ADVERTISING INC
Also Called: Moneysaver Shopping News
218 N Main St (14715-1091)
P.O. Box I (14715-0509)
PHONE..................585 593-1275
Fax: 585 928-2191
William W Jones, *President*
Deborah J Jones, *Vice Pres*
Carol Perrin, *Sales Mgr*
EMP: 15
SALES (est): 590K **Privately Held**
SIC: 2711 Newspapers: publishing only, not printed on site

Boonville
Oneida County

(G-1161)
3B TIMBER COMPANY INC
8745 Industrial Dr (13309-4845)
P.O. Box 761 (13309-0761)
PHONE..................315 942-6580
Fax: 315 942-4332
Mark S Bourgeois, *President*
Gary S Bourgeois, *Vice Pres*
Janet F Bourgeois, *Treasurer*
EMP: 19
SQ FT: 5,400
SALES (est): 1.5MM **Privately Held**
SIC: 2411 Poles, wood: untreated; posts, wood: hewn, round or split; piling, wood: untreated; wood chips, produced in the field

(G-1162)
BAILEY BOONVILLE MILLS INC
123 Mill St (13309-1115)
P.O. Box 257 (13309-0257)
PHONE..................315 942-2131
Delbert C Bailey, *President*
Sue Cain, *Office Mgr*
EMP: 7 EST: 1968
SALES (est): 801.8K **Privately Held**
SIC: 2048 5999 Prepared feeds; feed & farm supply

(G-1163)
BAILLIE LUMBER CO LP
189 West St (13309-1000)
P.O. Box 154 (13309-0154)
PHONE..................315 942-5284
Don Meyer, *Vice Pres*
Arnold Levensailor, *Manager*
Lynn Langdon, *Manager*
Paul Santoro, *MIS Dir*
EMP: 40
SALES (corp-wide): 1.5MM **Privately Held**
WEB: www.baillie.com
SIC: 2421 Sawmills & planing mills, general
PA: Baillie Lumber Co., L.P.
 4002 Legion Dr
 Hamburg NY 14075
 800 950-2850

(G-1164)
BOONVILLE HERALD INC
Also Called: Boonvlle Hrald Adrndack Turist
105 E Schuyler St (13309-1103)
P.O. Box 372 (13309-0372)
PHONE..................315 942-4449
Joe Kelly, *President*
EMP: 7
SALES (est): 310K **Privately Held**
SIC: 2711 Newspapers: publishing only, not printed on site

(G-1165)
BOONVILLE MANUFACTURING CORP
13485 State Route 12 (13309-3530)
P.O. Box 301 (13309-0301)
PHONE..................315 942-4368
Fax: 315 942-4367
Randy Anderson, *President*
Cheryl Tarasek, *Bookkeeper*
EMP: 7 EST: 1940
SQ FT: 8,000
SALES (est): 951.5K **Privately Held**
SIC: 3053 Gaskets & sealing devices

(G-1166)
NORTHERN FOREST PDTS CO INC
9833 Crolius Dr (13309-5001)
PHONE..................315 942-6955
Jeffrey Crolius, *President*
Jay Crolius, *Vice Pres*
EMP: 7
SQ FT: 2,800
SALES (est): 530K **Privately Held**
SIC: 2431 2499 Millwork; decorative wood & woodwork

(G-1167)
PRESERVING CHRSTN PUBLICATIONS (PA)
12614 State Route 46 (13309-4353)
P.O. Box 221 (13309-0221)
PHONE..................315 942-6617
Gerard Maicher, *President*
James Reilly, *Marketing Mgr*
John Parrot, *Admin Sec*
EMP: 8
SQ FT: 6,300
SALES (est): 252.7K **Privately Held**
WEB: www.pcpbooks.com
SIC: 2731 Book publishing

(G-1168)
QUALITY DAIRY FARMS INC
Also Called: Mercer's Dairy
13584 State Route 12 (13309-3532)
PHONE..................315 942-2611
Dalton Givens, *President*
Jackie Karpinski, *Manager*
Ruth Mignerey, *Shareholder*
▼ EMP: 24

SQ FT: 9,600
SALES (est): 4.3MM **Privately Held**
SIC: 2024 Ice cream & frozen desserts

(G-1169)
S M S C INC
Also Called: Central Adirondack Textiles
101 Water St (13309-1327)
PHONE..................315 942-4394
Chad Shoemaker, *Principal*
EMP: 6 EST: 2008
SALES (est): 588.4K **Privately Held**
SIC: 3321 Cooking utensils, cast iron

Bowmansville
Erie County

(G-1170)
PRECISION DENTAL CERAMICS OF B
5204 Genesee St (14026-1038)
PHONE..................716 681-4133
James Mantzanis, *President*
EMP: 11
SQ FT: 2,298
SALES: 700K **Privately Held**
SIC: 3843 Dental equipment & supplies

Brainardsville
Franklin County

(G-1171)
JACKSON WOODWORKS INC
6340 State Route 374 (12915)
P.O. Box 96 (12915-0096)
PHONE..................518 651-2032
Christine Jackson, *President*
EMP: 5
SALES (est): 924K **Privately Held**
SIC: 2431 Millwork

Branchport
Yates County

(G-1172)
HUNT COUNTRY VINEYARDS
4021 Italy Hill Rd (14418-9615)
PHONE..................315 595-2812
Fax: 315 595-2835
Art Hunt, *Owner*
Joyce Hunt, *Owner*
James Alsina, *Sales Staff*
Bonnie Barney, *Manager*
David Mortensen, *Manager*
EMP: 25
SQ FT: 2,256
SALES (est): 800K **Privately Held**
WEB: www.huntcountryvineyards.com
SIC: 2084 Wines, brandy & brandy spirits

Brant Lake
Warren County

(G-1173)
GAR WOOD CUSTOM BOATS
20 Duell Hill Rd (12815-2026)
PHONE..................518 494-2966
Thomas Turcotte, *Mng Member*
EMP: 8
SALES (est): 740K **Privately Held**
WEB: www.garwoodcustomboats.com
SIC: 3732 Boat building & repairing

Brasher Falls
St. Lawrence County

(G-1174)
TRI-TOWN PACKING CORP
Helena Rd (13613)
P.O. Box 387, Winthrop (13697-0387)
PHONE..................315 389-5101
Fax: 315 389-5106
John Liberty, *President*

Thomas Liberty, *President*
Jeff Liberty, *Vice Pres*
EMP: 15
SQ FT: 5,300
SALES: 1MM **Privately Held**
WEB: www.adirondacksmokedmeats.com
SIC: 2011 5147 Meat packing plants; meats & meat products

Brentwood
Suffolk County

(G-1175)
ALLIED AERO SERVICES INC
506 Grand Blvd (11717-7902)
PHONE..................631 277-9368
Larry Soech, *President*
Steven Leonard, *Vice Pres*
EMP: 6
SALES (est): 449.2K **Privately Held**
SIC: 3295 Minerals, ground or treated

(G-1176)
APPLAUSE COATING LLC
8b Grand Blvd (11717-5117)
PHONE..................631 231-5223
Fax: 631 231-5565
Barbara Pinto,
EMP: 11
SALES: 750K **Privately Held**
SIC: 3479 Coating of metals & formed products

(G-1177)
B & J DELIVERS INC
70 Emjay Blvd Bldg D (11717-3327)
P.O. Box 634 (11717-0633)
PHONE..................631 524-5550
Linda Marquez, *Owner*
EMP: 5
SALES (est): 496.9K **Privately Held**
SIC: 3537 Industrial trucks & tractors

(G-1178)
BECKS CLASSIC MFG INC
50 Emjay Blvd Ste 7 (11717-3300)
PHONE..................631 435-3800
Fax: 631 868-8282
Warren Beck, *CEO*
Steven Beck, *President*
Mary Closen, *Manager*
EMP: 100
SQ FT: 60,000
SALES (est): 10.6MM **Privately Held**
SIC: 2399 2341 2322 2676 Diapers, except disposable: made from purchased materials; panties: women's, misses', children's & infants'; underwear, men's & boys': made from purchased materials; sanitary paper products

(G-1179)
CUBITEK INC
95 Emjay Blvd Ste 2 (11717-3330)
PHONE..................631 665-6900
Daniel Hartman, *President*
Peter Hartman, *Vice Pres*
Judy Hartman, *Treasurer*
▼ EMP: 15
SQ FT: 500
SALES: 3.1MM **Privately Held**
SIC: 3599 Machine shop, jobbing & repair

(G-1180)
DATAGRAPHIC BUSINESS SYSTEMS
79 Emjay Blvd (11717-3323)
PHONE..................516 485-9069
Fax: 516 485-0544
Glenn M Schuster, *President*
EMP: 6
SQ FT: 3,000
SALES (est): 1.2MM **Privately Held**
WEB: www.datagraphicdesign.com
SIC: 2621 5943 Business form paper; office forms & supplies

(G-1181)
DELSUR PARTS
112 Pheasant Cir (11717-5047)
PHONE..................631 630-1606
Carlos Fuentes, *Owner*
EMP: 5

SALES: 150K **Privately Held**
SIC: 3556 Food products machinery

(G-1182)
DORMITORY AUTHORITY - STATE NY
998 Crooked Hill Rd # 26 (11717-1019)
PHONE..................................631 434-1487
Fax: 631 434-1486
Terry McGowan, *Director*
EMP: 8
SALES (corp-wide): 2.1B **Privately Held**
SIC: 3599 Pump governors, for gas machines
PA: Dormitory Authority - State Of New York
515 Broadway Ste 100
Albany NY 12207
518 257-3000

(G-1183)
EXPRESS CONCRETE INC
1250 Suffolk Ave (11717-4507)
PHONE..................................631 273-4224
Bruno Palmieri, *President*
Mario Palmieri, *Office Mgr*
EMP: 6
SQ FT: 3,000
SALES (est): 706.5K **Privately Held**
SIC: 3272 Concrete products

(G-1184)
I MEGLIO CORP
151 Alkier St (11717-5135)
PHONE..................................631 617-6900
Barbara Khanat, *President*
David Suarez, *Vice Pres*
EMP: 30
SQ FT: 65,000
SALES: 67MM **Privately Held**
SIC: 2431 5031 Millwork; millwork

(G-1185)
INTERSTATE LITHO CORP
151 Alkier St (11717-5135)
PHONE..................................631 232-6025
Fax: 631 273-8504
Henry Becker, *President*
Richard Becker, *Vice Pres*
EMP: 100 EST: 1975
SQ FT: 100,000
SALES (est): 8.3MM **Privately Held**
SIC: 2752 2791 2789 Commercial printing, lithographic; typesetting; bookbinding & related work

(G-1186)
INTERSTATE WINDOW CORPORATION
Also Called: Mannix
345 Crooked Hill Rd Ste 1 (11717-1020)
PHONE..................................631 231-0800
Fax: 631 231-0571
Robert Salzer, *President*
Paul Greenstein, *Vice Pres*
Sue Hausner, *Vice Pres*
Daniel Monosson, *Vice Pres*
Maria Juarez, *Human Res Dir*
▲ EMP: 100
SQ FT: 51,000
SALES (est): 30.7MM **Privately Held**
WEB: www.mannixwindows.com
SIC: 3442 Metal doors, sash & trim

(G-1187)
J & A USA INC
335 Crooked Hill Rd (11717-1041)
PHONE..................................631 243-3336
Fax: 631 243-3339
Yunho Kim, *President*
Sidney Park, *CFO*
▲ EMP: 9
SQ FT: 15,000
SALES (est): 980K **Privately Held**
WEB: www.jausa.com
SIC: 3999 Barber & beauty shop equipment

(G-1188)
KENNEY MANUFACTURING DISPLAYS
Also Called: Kenny Mfg
12 Grand Blvd (11717-5117)
PHONE..................................631 231-5563
Fax: 631 231-5821
Robert Kenney Jr, *President*

Michael Kenney, *Vice Pres*
Carolann Kenney, *Admin Sec*
EMP: 11
SQ FT: 7,500
SALES (est): 1.7MM **Privately Held**
WEB: www.kenneydisplays.com
SIC: 3089 3578 Plastic containers, except foam; point-of-sale devices

(G-1189)
LAURICELLA PRESS INC
Also Called: Imperial Color
81 Emjay Blvd (11717-3329)
P.O. Box 443, New York (10014-0443)
PHONE..................................516 931-5906
Arthur Lauricella, *President*
Marc Lauricella, *Vice Pres*
EMP: 20
SALES: 500K **Privately Held**
SIC: 2759 Commercial printing

(G-1190)
LLOYDS FASHIONS INC (PA)
335 Crooked Hill Rd (11717-1041)
P.O. Box 1162, Syosset (11791-0489)
PHONE..................................631 435-3353
Lloyd Goldberg, *President*
Rita Goldberg, *Vice Pres*
▲ EMP: 58 **EST:** 1958
SQ FT: 22,000
SALES: 2.6MM **Privately Held**
SIC: 2353 2253 5137 Millinery; shawls, knit; women's & children's clothing

(G-1191)
MARKETSHARE LLC
90 Cain Dr (11717-1265)
PHONE..................................631 273-0598
Nancy Mantell, *Principal*
Steven Zaken, *Co-Owner*
Monique Greene, *Manager*
EMP: 5
SALES (est): 380K **Privately Held**
SIC: 2752 3991 Playing cards, lithographed; toothbrushes, except electric

(G-1192)
MICHBI DOORS INC
Also Called: Open & Shut Doors
75 Emjay Blvd (11717-3323)
PHONE..................................631 231-9050
Fax: 631 231-9040
Michelle Bianculli, *President*
Doug Hommel, *Vice Pres*
Suzanne Mutone, *Vice Pres*
Jeannette Cambridge, *Project Mgr*
Craig Gough, *Project Mgr*
EMP: 56 **EST:** 1981
SQ FT: 30,000
SALES (est): 8.6MM **Privately Held**
WEB: www.michbidoors.com
SIC: 2431 3231 3442 Millwork; products of purchased glass; metal doors, sash & trim

(G-1193)
PLASTIRUN CORPORATION
70 Emjay Blvd Bldg A (11717-3394)
PHONE..................................631 273-2626
Fax: 631 273-7644
Jack Elyahouzadeh, *President*
Jacob Y Lavi, *Treasurer*
◆ EMP: 35 **EST:** 1982
SQ FT: 51,000
SALES (est): 13MM **Privately Held**
WEB: www.plastirun.com
SIC: 2656 2621 Straws, drinking: made from purchased material; towels, tissues & napkins: paper & stock

(G-1194)
SLEEPY HOLLOW CHIMNEY SUP LTD
85 Emjay Blvd (11717-3323)
PHONE..................................631 231-2333
Fax: 631 231-2364
Fred Schukal, *President*
Jeff Steffensen, *Office Mgr*
▲ EMP: 14
SQ FT: 9,000
SALES (est): 4MM **Privately Held**
WEB: www.bellfiresusa.com
SIC: 3229 Chimneys, lamp: pressed or blown glass

(G-1195)
T S O GENERAL CORP
81 Emjay Blvd Unit 1 (11717-3329)
P.O. Box 552 (11717-0552)
PHONE..................................631 952-5320
Kirk Malandrakis, *President*
Monica Cura, *Manager*
EMP: 20
SQ FT: 30,000
SALES: 2MM **Privately Held**
WEB: www.tsogen.com
SIC: 2759 Commercial printing

(G-1196)
THURO METAL PRODUCTS INC (PA)
21-25 Grand Blvd N (11717)
PHONE..................................631 435-0444
Fax: 631 435-0293
Albert Thuro, *Ch of Bd*
David Thuro, *President*
Carolyn Thuro, *Corp Secy*
Sam Handle, *Vice Pres*
David Harrison, *Safety Mgr*
▲ EMP: 40 **EST:** 1971
SQ FT: 25,000
SALES (est): 12.5MM **Privately Held**
WEB: www.thurometal.com
SIC: 3451 3545 Screw machine products; machine tool attachments & accessories

(G-1197)
THURO METAL PRODUCTS INC
50 Alkier St (11717)
PHONE..................................631 435-0444
Albert Thuro, *President*
EMP: 15
SALES (corp-wide): 12.5MM **Privately Held**
WEB: www.thurometal.com
SIC: 3451 Screw machine products
PA: Thuro Metal Products, Inc.
21-25 Grand Blvd N
Brentwood NY 11717
631 435-0444

(G-1198)
UNIWARE HOUSEWARE CORP
120 Wilshire Blvd Ste B (11717-8333)
PHONE..................................631 242-7400
Lily Hsu, *President*
Roger Hsu, *Vice Pres*
▲ EMP: 18
SALES (est): 3.1MM **Privately Held**
SIC: 3634 Electric housewares & fans

(G-1199)
US NONWOVENS CORP (PA)
100 Emjay Blvd (11717-3322)
PHONE..................................631 952-0100
Fax: 631 952-0200
Shervin Mehdizadeh, *CEO*
Samuel Mehdizadeh, *Ch of Bd*
Rody Mehdizadeh, *COO*
Michael Pischel, *CFO*
Alan Wolsky, *Credit Mgr*
◆ EMP: 125
SALES (est): 197.5MM **Privately Held**
WEB: www.usnonwovens.com
SIC: 2842 Specialty cleaning, polishes & sanitation goods

(G-1200)
USA FOIL INC
70 Emjay Blvd Bldg C (11717-3327)
PHONE..................................631 234-5252
Joseph Phami, *President*
Akhtar Gadi, *President*
Kami Youssi, *Vice Pres*
Deborah Joseph, *Manager*
▲ EMP: 20
SQ FT: 12,000
SALES (est): 3.4MM **Privately Held**
SIC: 3353 Aluminum sheet, plate & foil

(G-1201)
V E POWER DOOR CO INC
140 Emjay Blvd (11717-3322)
P.O. Box 663, Commack (11725-0663)
PHONE..................................631 231-4500
Fax: 631 231-4274
James Lanzarone, *CEO*
Philip Lanzarone, *President*
Evelyn Semar, *Corp Secy*
Susan Cruz, *Vice Pres*
Edward Lanzarone, *Vice Pres*

▲ EMP: 40
SQ FT: 23,000
SALES (est): 12.8MM **Privately Held**
SIC: 3699 Door opening & closing devices, electrical

Brewerton
Onondaga County

(G-1202)
AE FUND INC
Also Called: Frigo Design
5860 Mckinley Rd (13029-9691)
PHONE..................................315 698-7650
Fax: 315 698-7859
Eric J Gantley, *President*
Anthony Verdi, *Exec VP*
Allan Issacs, *Vice Pres*
EMP: 30
SQ FT: 15,000
SALES (est): 6.6MM **Privately Held**
WEB: www.frigodesign.com
SIC: 3632 Refrigerator cabinets, household: metal & wood

(G-1203)
GEORDIE MAGEE UPHL & CANVAS
Also Called: Magee Canvas & Trailer Sales
Weber Rd (13029)
P.O. Box 656 (13029-0656)
PHONE..................................315 676-7679
Fax: 315 676-2655
Geordie H Magee, *President*
Patty Arnoel, *Bookkeeper*
EMP: 6
SQ FT: 4,400
SALES: 1.1MM **Privately Held**
WEB: www.mageetrailers.com
SIC: 2211 5999 Canvas; canvas products

(G-1204)
IRENE CERONE
Also Called: Brewerton Special Tee's
9600 Brewerton Rd (13029-8798)
P.O. Box 670 (13029-0670)
PHONE..................................315 668-2899
Fax: 315 676-3010
Michael Cerone, *Owner*
Irene Cerone, *Co-Owner*
Sue Finley, *Office Mgr*
EMP: 7
SALES (est): 594.8K **Privately Held**
SIC: 2396 Screen printing on fabric articles

(G-1205)
ROBINSON CONCRETE INC
7020 Corporate Park Dr (13029)
PHONE..................................315 676-4662
Michael J Vitale, *Principal*
EMP: 10
SALES (corp-wide): 24MM **Privately Held**
SIC: 3273 Ready-mixed concrete
PA: Robinson Concrete, Inc.
3486 Franklin Street Rd
Auburn NY 13021
315 253-6666

Brewster
Putnam County

(G-1206)
AAAAAR ORTHOPEDICS INC
141 Main St (10509-1476)
PHONE..................................845 278-4938
Fax: 845 838-0967
Elizabeth Hawkins, *President*
Richard Dipompo, *Vice Pres*
EMP: 5
SALES (est): 360K **Privately Held**
SIC: 3842 Limbs, artificial

(G-1207)
ADVANCED PRECISION TECHNOLOGY
577 N Main St Ste 7 (10509-1240)
PHONE..................................845 279-3540
Fax: 845 278-0754
Olaf Brauer, *President*

Christine Brauer, *Vice Pres*
EMP: 10
SQ FT: 6,800
SALES (est): 800K **Privately Held**
SIC: 3444 3341 Sheet metalwork; secondary nonferrous metals

(G-1208)
AKZO NOBEL FUNCTIONAL CHEM LLC
281 Fields Ln (10509-2676)
PHONE....................845 276-8200
Terry Busch, *HR Admin*
Ton B Chner, *Branch Mgr*
EMP: 88
SALES (corp-wide): 15.9B **Privately Held**
SIC: 2869 Industrial organic chemicals
HQ: Akzo Nobel Functional Chemical, Llc
   525 W Van Buren St # 1600
   Chicago IL 60607
   312 544-7000

(G-1209)
ALLIANCE CONTROL SYSTEMS INC
577 N Main St Ste 9 (10509-1240)
PHONE....................845 279-4430
Doug Homberg, *President*
▲ **EMP:** 8
SALES (est): 943.6K **Privately Held**
SIC: 3629 Electronic generation equipment

(G-1210)
AMPRO INTERNATIONAL INC
30 Coventry Ln (10509-4808)
PHONE....................845 278-4910
Fax: 845 279-9753
Floyd Pircio, *President*
Laura Arone, *Admin Sec*
EMP: 2
SQ FT: 1,000
SALES: 1MM **Privately Held**
SIC: 3679 Antennas, receiving

(G-1211)
BASE SYSTEMS INC
Also Called: Tower Computers
1606 Route 22 (10509-4014)
PHONE....................845 278-1991
Lee Seacord, *President*
Linda Seacord, *Vice Pres*
EMP: 2
SQ FT: 3,000
SALES: 2MM **Privately Held**
SIC: 7372 5045 Prepackaged software; computer software

(G-1212)
BLACK & DECKER (US) INC
Also Called: Powers Fasteners
2 Powers Ln (10509-3633)
PHONE....................914 235-6300
Matt Chamberlain, *Vice Pres*
Leonard Colasuonno, *Vice Pres*
Arthur Bernardon, *Purch Mgr*
Mark Ziegler, *Engineer*
William Taylor, *Branch Mgr*
EMP: 375
SALES (corp-wide): 11.1B **Publicly Held**
SIC: 3546 Power-driven handtools
HQ: Black & Decker (U.S.) Inc.
   1000 Stanley Dr
   New Britain CT 06053
   410 716-3900

(G-1213)
BREWSTER TRANSIT MIX CORP (PA)
31 Fields Ln (10509-3507)
P.O. Box 410 (10509-0410)
PHONE....................845 279-3738
Fax: 845 279-6506
Ted Petrillo, *President*
James Harahan, *Division Mgr*
Henry Paparazzo, *Vice Pres*
Curtis Mc Gann, *Admin Sec*
▲ **EMP:** 45
SQ FT: 1,000
SALES (est): 6.3MM **Privately Held**
SIC: 3273 5032 Ready-mixed concrete; gravel; sand, construction

(G-1214)
BREWSTER TRANSIT MIX CORP
Fields Ln (10509)
P.O. Box 410 (10509-0410)
PHONE....................845 279-3738
Jeff Chattin, *General Mgr*
EMP: 35
SALES (corp-wide): 6.3MM **Privately Held**
SIC: 3273 Ready-mixed concrete
PA: Brewster Transit Mix Corp
   31 Fields Ln
   Brewster NY 10509
   845 279-3738

(G-1215)
DAIRY CONVEYOR CORP (PA)
38 Mount Ebo Rd S (10509-4005)
P.O. Box 411 (10509-0411)
PHONE....................845 278-7878
Fax: 845 278-7305
Gary Freudenberg, *President*
Tony Gomez, *President*
Roland Debald, *Vice Pres*
Karl Horberg, *CFO*
Pete Debald, *Treasurer*
▲ **EMP:** 86 **EST:** 1954
SQ FT: 68,000
SALES (est): 36.9MM **Privately Held**
SIC: 3535 7699 Conveyors & conveying equipment; industrial machinery & equipment repair

(G-1216)
DESIGN A SIGN OF PUTNAM INC
Also Called: Design-A-Sign
1456 Route 22 Ste A102 (10509-4352)
PHONE....................845 279-5328
Pam Caesar, *President*
EMP: 6
SQ FT: 1,250
SALES (est): 460K **Privately Held**
SIC: 3993 Signs & advertising specialties

(G-1217)
DUNMORE CORPORATION
3633 Danbury Rd (10509-4516)
PHONE....................845 279-5061
Fax: 845 279-5231
Donald Cregar, *Prdtn Mgr*
John Finger, *Prdtn Mgr*
Jen King, *Personnel*
Terry Jones, *Manager*
Daniel Sullivan, *Manager*
EMP: 75
SQ FT: 49,432
SALES (corp-wide): 76.6MM **Privately Held**
WEB: www.dunmore.com
SIC: 2621 3081 2672 Paper mills; plastic film & sheet; coated & laminated paper
PA: Dunmore Corporation
   145 Wharton Rd
   Bristol PA 19007
   215 781-8895

(G-1218)
ELSAG NORTH AMERICA LLC
7 Sutton Pl Ste A (10509-3537)
PHONE....................877 773-5724
Pete Kontos, *Vice Pres*
EMP: 7
SALES (corp-wide): 6.2MM **Privately Held**
SIC: 3829 Photogrammetrical instruments
PA: Elsag North America Llc
   205 Creek Ridge Rd Ste H
   Greensboro NC 27406
   336 379-7135

(G-1219)
FEYEM USA INC
7 Sutton Pl (10509-3536)
PHONE....................845 363-6253
EMP: 5
SALES (est): 202.9K **Privately Held**
SIC: 2329 2331 Men's & boys' sportswear & athletic clothing; women's & misses' blouses & shirts

(G-1220)
HIPOTRONICS INC (HQ)
1650 Route 22 (10509-4013)
P.O. Box 414 (10509-0414)
PHONE....................845 279-8091
Fax: 845 279-2467
Timothy H Powers, *CEO*
Richard Davies, *President*
Jeff Brown, *Vice Pres*
Reinold Grob, *Vice Pres*
Charles Consalvo, *Opers Mgr*
◆ **EMP:** 115 **EST:** 1962
SQ FT: 90,000
SALES (est): 26.1MM
SALES (corp-wide): 3.3B **Publicly Held**
WEB: www.hipotronics.com
SIC: 3825 3679 3829 3677 Instruments to measure electricity; test equipment for electronic & electric measurement; power supplies, all types: static; measuring & controlling devices; electronic coils, transformers & other inductors; electronic capacitors; semiconductors & related devices
PA: Hubbell Incorporated
   40 Waterview Dr
   Shelton CT 06484
   475 882-4000

(G-1221)
HUDSON MACHINE WORKS INC
Also Called: H M W
30 Branch Rd (10509-4522)
PHONE....................845 279-1413
Fax: 845 279-7220
Daniel R Ferguson, *Ch of Bd*
Michael Ferguson, *General Mgr*
Jennifer Ferguson, *Vice Pres*
Glenn Moss, *CFO*
EMP: 110
SQ FT: 25,000
SALES (est): 18.8MM **Privately Held**
WEB: www.hudsonmachine.com
SIC: 3743 Railroad equipment

(G-1222)
LAMOTHERMIC CORP
391 Route 312 (10509-2328)
PHONE....................845 278-6118
Amos Noach, *Ch of Bd*
Gideon Noach, *Vice Pres*
Ed Calabrese, *QC Mgr*
Tom Eng, *Engineer*
Carol Smith, *Manager*
EMP: 97
SQ FT: 42,000
SALES (est): 12MM **Privately Held**
WEB: www.lamothermic.com
SIC: 3369 Castings, except die-castings, precision

(G-1223)
MATERION BREWSTER LLC
42 Mount Ebo Rd S (10509-4005)
P.O. Box 1950 (10509-8950)
PHONE....................845 279-0900
Robert Greco, *Controller*
Pamela Every, *Accountant*
Richard Fager, *Mng Member*
Matthew Willson,
▲ **EMP:** 75
SQ FT: 36,000
SALES (est): 26MM
SALES (corp-wide): 1B **Publicly Held**
WEB: www.puretechinc.com
SIC: 3499 3674 Friction material, made from powdered metal; semiconductors & related devices
HQ: Materion Advanced Materials Technologies And Services Inc.
   2978 Main St
   Buffalo NY 14214
   800 327-1355

(G-1224)
MIGGINS SCREW PRODUCTS INC
66 Putnam Ave (10509-1114)
PHONE....................845 279-2307
Fax: 845 279-2602
Merle Delfay, *President*
John H Miggins, *President*
Merle Delsay, *Post Master*
EMP: 9 **EST:** 1946
SQ FT: 2,500
SALES (est): 1MM **Privately Held**
SIC: 3451 Screw machine products

(G-1225)
PARACO GAS CORPORATION
4 Joes Hill Rd (10509-5323)
PHONE....................845 279-8414
Jim Mc Ginty, *Principal*
EMP: 5
SALES (corp-wide): 326.7MM **Privately Held**
SIC: 1321 Propane (natural) production
PA: Paraco Gas Corporation
   800 Westchester Ave S604
   Rye Brook NY 10573
   800 647-4427

(G-1226)
PEDIFIX INC
281 Fields Ln (10509-2676)
PHONE....................845 277-2850
Fax: 845 277-2851
Dennis Case, *President*
Jon Case, *Vice Pres*
Richard Ovadek, *Purchasing*
Caroline Bochnia, *Executive*
▲ **EMP:** 25
SQ FT: 15,000
SALES (est): 4.9MM **Privately Held**
WEB: www.pedifix.com
SIC: 3144 3143 Orthopedic shoes, women's; orthopedic shoes, men's

(G-1227)
PRE CYCLED INC
1689 Route 22 (10509-4022)
P.O. Box 341 (10509-0341)
PHONE....................845 278-7611
Daniel Horkan, *President*
Carol Horkan, *Vice Pres*
Erik Spletzer, *Sales Staff*
EMP: 5
SQ FT: 3,000
SALES (est): 807.2K **Privately Held**
WEB: www.pre-cycled.com
SIC: 2752 Commercial printing, lithographic

(G-1228)
TRAFFIC LANE CLOSURES LLC
3620 Danbury Rd (10509-4507)
P.O. Box 726 (10509-0726)
PHONE....................845 228-6100
Fax: 845 278-5450
Ralph M Rosenfeld, *General Mgr*
Teri Godfrey, *Mng Member*
Ralph Rosenfeld, *Mng Member*
Mellissa Erreich, *Manager*
EMP: 9
SQ FT: 3,800
SALES (est): 1.4MM **Privately Held**
WEB: www.trafficlaneclosures.com
SIC: 3669 Highway signals, electric

(G-1229)
UNILOCK NEW YORK INC (HQ)
51 International Blvd (10509-2343)
PHONE....................845 278-6700
Fax: 845 278-6788
Edward Bryant, *President*
Sean O' Lary, *General Mgr*
Lyle Selk, *General Mgr*
Glenn Wiley, *General Mgr*
Joseph Kerr, *Vice Pres*
▲ **EMP:** 8
SALES (est): 12.6MM **Privately Held**
WEB: www.unilock.com
SIC: 3281 5211 3272 3271 Paving blocks, cut stone; paving stones; concrete products; concrete block & brick; asphalt paving mixtures & blocks

(G-1230)
VISTALAB TECHNOLOGIES INC
2 Geneva Rd (10509-2340)
PHONE....................914 244-6226
Richard Scordato, *Ch of Bd*
Jeffrey E Calhoun, *Vice Pres*
Joe Lindfey, *Safety Mgr*
Keith Pagello, *Engineer*
Edward Flynn, *CFO*
▲ **EMP:** 34
SQ FT: 25,000
SALES (est): 7.3MM **Privately Held**
SIC: 3821 Pipettes, hemocytometer

Briarcliff Manor
Westchester County

(G-1231)
THALLE INDUSTRIES INC (PA)
51 Route 100 (10510-1441)
PHONE..................................914 762-3415
Gregg J Pacchiana, *Ch of Bd*
Glenn Pacchiana, *Principal*
George Pacchiana, *Corp Secy*
Jeff Manganello, *Vice Pres*
Marco Pereira, *Opers Staff*
EMP: 35
SQ FT: 720
SALES (est): 4.9MM **Privately Held**
SIC: 2951 3281 Asphalt paving mixtures & blocks; stone, quarrying & processing of own stone products

Bridgehampton
Suffolk County

(G-1232)
BRIDGEHAMPTON STEEL & WLDG INC
Also Called: Aand D Maintenance
27 Foster Ave (11932)
P.O. Box 19 (11932-0019)
PHONE..................................631 537-2486
John Parry, *President*
Suzanne Parry, *Vice Pres*
EMP: 10
SQ FT: 3,000
SALES (est): 1.2MM **Privately Held**
SIC: 3443 1799 Fabricated plate work (boiler shop); welding on site

(G-1233)
COMERFORD HENNESSY AT HOME INC
Also Called: Comerford Collection
2442 Main St (11932)
P.O. Box 44 (11932-0044)
PHONE..................................631 537-6200
Fax: 631 725-5226
Karen Comerford, *President*
Michael Hennessy, *Vice Pres*
EMP: 5
SQ FT: 1,500
SALES (est): 584.1K **Privately Held**
SIC: 2511 Wood household furniture

(G-1234)
IRON HORSE GRAPHICS LTD
112 Maple Ln (11932)
PHONE..................................631 537-3400
Fax: 631 537-3424
Grover Gatewood, *President*
EMP: 9
SQ FT: 2,200
SALES: 782.1K **Privately Held**
SIC: 2752 2759 Offset & photolithographic printing; commercial printing

Bridgeport
Onondaga County

(G-1235)
POWER GNERATION INDUS ENGS INC
8927 Tyler Rd (13030-9727)
PHONE..................................315 633-9389
Mike Verdow, *President*
EMP: 18
SALES (est): 2.4MM **Privately Held**
SIC: 3621 Power generators

(G-1236)
ROBERT M VAULT
1360 Lestina Beach Rd (13030-9722)
PHONE..................................315 243-1447
Robert M Vault, *Principal*
EMP: 5
SALES (est): 302.2K **Privately Held**
SIC: 3272 Burial vaults, concrete or precast terrazzo

(G-1237)
SYRACUSE LETTER COMPANY INC
Also Called: Lettergraphics
1179 Oak Ln (13030-9779)
PHONE..................................315 476-8328
Fax: 315 476-1818
Nancy Osborn, *President*
David L Osborn, *Chairman*
Bill Davidson, *Vice Pres*
Joh Davidson, *Controller*
▲ **EMP:** 15
SQ FT: 24,500
SALES (est): 1.7MM **Privately Held**
SIC: 2759 7331 7389 Promotional printing; direct mail advertising services; coupon redemption service

Brightwaters
Suffolk County

(G-1238)
ALLEN FIELD CO INC
256 Orinoco Dr Ste A (11718-1823)
PHONE..................................631 665-2782
Fax: 631 756-0436
Andrew Franzone, *CEO*
Andrew Franzone Jr, *Ch of Bd*
David Kassel, *Ch of Bd*
Harry Goodman, *Vice Pres*
▲ **EMP:** 12 **EST:** 1945
SQ FT: 20,000
SALES: 6MM **Privately Held**
WEB: www.allenfield.com
SIC: 3089 Handles, brush or tool: plastic; injection molded finished plastic products

(G-1239)
UNLIMITED INDUSTRIES INC
234 Orinoco Dr (11718-1804)
PHONE..................................631 666-9483
Joseph Leone, *President*
EMP: 8
SALES (est): 1MM **Privately Held**
SIC: 3999 Manufacturing industries

Broadalbin
Fulton County

(G-1240)
BROADALBIN MANUFACTURING CORP
Also Called: BMC
8 Pine St (12025-3128)
P.O. Box 398 (12025-0398)
PHONE..................................518 883-5313
Fax: 518 883-5320
James C Stark, *President*
Michael Deuel, *President*
Mike Deuel, *Vice Pres*
Karen Deuel, *Manager*
Beverly Reed, *Asst Mgr*
EMP: 23 **EST:** 1970
SQ FT: 8,000
SALES (est): 4.2MM **Privately Held**
SIC: 3599 7692 1761 Machine shop, jobbing & repair; welding repair; sheet metalwork

(G-1241)
EMVI INC
Also Called: Emvi Chocolate
111 Bellen Rd Ste 2 (12025-2101)
PHONE..................................518 883-5111
Irina Gelman, *Principal*
EMP: 5
SALES (est): 483.4K **Privately Held**
SIC: 2066 Chocolate

(G-1242)
GL & RL LOGGING INC
713 Union Mills Rd (12025-1988)
PHONE..................................518 883-3936
George Lee, *President*
EMP: 15
SALES (est): 1.2MM **Privately Held**
SIC: 2411 Logging; timber, cut at logging camp

Brockport
Monroe County

(G-1243)
CUSTOM SERVICE SOLUTIONS INC
1900 Transit Way (14420-3006)
PHONE..................................585 637-3760
Paul Guglielmi, *CEO*
Diana Petranek, *CFO*
EMP: 6
SQ FT: 4,200
SALES: 1.4MM **Privately Held**
WEB: www.customservicesolutions.com
SIC: 3545 Machine tool accessories

(G-1244)
HAMILTON MARKETING CORPORATION
5211 Lake Rd S (14420-9753)
PHONE..................................585 395-0678
Edward Hamilton, *President*
EMP: 5
SQ FT: 5,000
SALES (est): 513.6K **Privately Held**
SIC: 3825 Microwave test equipment

(G-1245)
JETS LEFROIS CORP
Also Called: Jets Lefrois Foods
56 High St (14420-2058)
PHONE..................................585 637-5003
Fax: 585 637-2855
Duncan Tsay, *President*
Rosalinc Tsay, *Vice Pres*
EMP: 6
SQ FT: 6,000
SALES (est): 626K **Privately Held**
SIC: 2033 2035 Barbecue sauce: packaged in cans, jars, etc.; relishes, vinegar

(G-1246)
RHEINWALD PRINTING CO INC
Also Called: Tri County Advertiser
15 Main St (14420-1901)
PHONE..................................585 637-5100
Fax: 585 637-0111
Sally Abrams Becht, *President*
EMP: 15 **EST:** 1956
SQ FT: 3,000
SALES (est): 1MM **Privately Held**
SIC: 2741 2752 2711 Shopping news: publishing & printing; commercial printing, lithographic; newspapers

(G-1247)
ROCK IROQUOIS PRODUCTS INC
5251 Sweden Walker Rd (14420-9716)
PHONE..................................585 637-6834
Fax: 585 637-4475
Chris Pangrizio, *Manager*
EMP: 20
SALES (corp-wide): 25.3B **Privately Held**
SIC: 1429 Dolomitic marble, crushed & broken-quarrying
HQ: Rock Iroquois Products Inc
1150 Penfield Rd
Rochester NY 14625
585 381-7010

Brocton
Chautauqua County

(G-1248)
CARBON GRAPHITE MATERIALS INC
Also Called: Cgm
115 Central Ave (14716-9771)
PHONE..................................716 792-7979
Ryan Walker, *President*
▲ **EMP:** 9
SALES (est): 2.5MM **Privately Held**
SIC: 3624 Carbon & graphite products

(G-1249)
JAMESTOWN PLASTICS INC (PA)
8806 Highland Ave (14716-9791)
P.O. Box U (14716-0680)
PHONE..................................716 792-4144
Fax: 716 792-4154
Jay J Baker, *Ch of Bd*
Brandy Smith, *QC Mgr*
Romaine Hohenstein, *Accountant*
Dale Akin, *Manager*
Kurk Holm, *Maintence Staff*
EMP: 50
SQ FT: 87,000
SALES (est): 14.5MM **Privately Held**
WEB: www.jamestownplastics.com
SIC: 3089 Plastic containers, except foam

Bronx
Bronx County

(G-1250)
527 FRANCO BAKERY CORPORATION
Also Called: Caribe Bakery
527 E 138th St (10454-4971)
PHONE..................................718 993-4200
Franco Guillermo, *President*
EMP: 5
SALES (est): 332.8K **Privately Held**
SIC: 2051 Bread, cake & related products

(G-1251)
872 HUNTS POINT PHARMACY INC
872 Hunts Point Ave (10474-5402)
PHONE..................................718 991-3519
EMP: 7
SALES (est): 631.6K **Privately Held**
SIC: 2834 Mfg Pharmaceutical Preparations

(G-1252)
A & L DOORS & HARDWARE LLC
375 E 163rd St Frnt 2 (10451-4391)
PHONE..................................718 585-8400
Pinches Herman, *Manager*
Leo Lichstein,
EMP: 14
SQ FT: 16,000
SALES (est): 2.3MM **Privately Held**
WEB: www.urban-architectural-interiors.com
SIC: 3442 3429 7699 Metal doors; window & door frames; locks or lock sets; locksmith shop

(G-1253)
A & L SHTMTL FABRICATIONS CORP
1243 Oakpoint Ave (10474-6803)
PHONE..................................718 842-1600
Fax: 718 842-2597
Anatoly Lekhter, *President*
Marat Golnick, *Vice Pres*
Scott Ellis, *Foreman/Supr*
Deanna Daniels, *Controller*
Howard Schultz, *Accountant*
EMP: 45
SQ FT: 37,500
SALES (est): 11.8MM **Privately Held**
WEB: www.aandlsheetmetal.com
SIC: 3444 Sheet metalwork

(G-1254)
A L EASTMOND & SONS INC (PA)
Also Called: Easco Boiler
1175 Leggett Ave (10474-6246)
PHONE..................................718 378-3000
Fax: 718 378-4560
Arlington Leon Eastmond, *Chairman*
EMP: 80 **EST:** 1914
SQ FT: 50,000
SALES (est): 14MM **Privately Held**
WEB: www.easco.tv
SIC: 3443 7699 7629 Boilers: industrial, power, or marine; boiler repair shop; electrical repair shops

Bronx - Bronx County (G-1255)

(G-1255)
A&S REFRIGERATION EQUIPMENT
557 Longfellow Ave (10474-6913)
PHONE.................................718 993-6030
Alexander Savinon, *President*
EMP: 5
SALES: 98K Privately Held
SIC: 3585 Refrigeration & heating equipment

(G-1256)
A-1 TRANSITMIX INC
431 E 165th St Frnt 1 (10456-6644)
PHONE.................................718 292-3200
Fax: 718 292-3255
Sal Gelso, *President*
Frankie Gentile, *Vice Pres*
EMP: 12
SQ FT: 25,000
SALES (est): 2MM Privately Held
SIC: 3273 Ready-mixed concrete

(G-1257)
A1 INTERNATIONAL HEAT TREATING
905 Brush Ave (10465-1810)
P.O. Box 93, Valhalla (10595-0093)
PHONE.................................718 863-5552
Fax: 718 792-6902
Peter Palmero, *President*
John Palmero, *Vice Pres*
Theresa Palmero, *Manager*
EMP: 5
SQ FT: 2,000
SALES (est): 480K Privately Held
SIC: 3398 Metal heat treating

(G-1258)
AC AIR COOLING CO INC
Also Called: Air Conditioning
1637 Stillwell Ave (10461-2216)
PHONE.................................718 933-1011
Cac Dong Bui, *President*
Deonarine Sooknarain, *Vice Pres*
Maritza Matos, *Manager*
EMP: 15
SALES (est): 1.9MM Privately Held
SIC: 3585 Air conditioning units, complete: domestic or industrial

(G-1259)
ACA QUALITY BUILDING PDTS LLC
1322 Garrison Ave (10474-4710)
PHONE.................................718 991-2423
Rubin Goldklang, *Manager*
EMP: 25
SALES (corp-wide): 4.3MM Privately Held
SIC: 3446 Partitions & supports/studs, including accoustical systems
PA: Aca Quality Building Products Llc
   920 Longfellow Ave
   Bronx NY 10474
   718 991-2423

(G-1260)
ACE DROP CLOTH CANVAS PDTS INC
Also Called: Ace Drop Cloth Co
4216 Park Ave (10457-4201)
PHONE.................................718 731-1550
Fax: 718 299-5122
Jerry Mathios, *President*
Adam Mathios, *Vice Pres*
David Mathios, *Vice Pres*
Marc Mathios, *Vice Pres*
▲ EMP: 31
SQ FT: 35,000
SALES (est): 4.3MM Privately Held
WEB: www.acedropcloth.com
SIC: 2299 2326 2394 2393 Fibers, textile: recovery from textile mill waste & rags; work pants; work shirts: men's, youths' & boys'; cloth, drop (fabric): made from purchased materials; textile bags; socks

(G-1261)
ACE FIRE DOOR CORP
4000 Park Ave (10457-7318)
PHONE.................................718 901-0001
Fax: 718 294-1304
Aharon Blum, *President*
Joseph Strulovich, *Vice Pres*
Irving Bauer, *Treasurer*
EMP: 20
SQ FT: 20,000
SALES (est): 4MM Privately Held
SIC: 3442 2431 Fire doors, metal; doors, wood

(G-1262)
ACME AWNING CO INC
435 Van Nest Ave (10460-2876)
PHONE.................................718 409-1881
Fax: 718 824-3571
Lawrence Loiacono, *President*
Jay Loiacono, *Vice Pres*
Peggy Zeaphey, *Bookkeeper*
EMP: 15 EST: 1924
SQ FT: 25,000
SALES: 1MM Privately Held
WEB: www.acmeawn.com
SIC: 2394 3089 5039 5999 Awnings, fabric: made from purchased materials; awnings, fiberglass & plastic combination; awnings; awnings

(G-1263)
ADDEO BAKERS INC
2372 Hughes Ave (10458-8148)
PHONE.................................718 367-8316
Fax: 718 295-8746
Lawrence Addeo, *President*
EMP: 12
SQ FT: 2,300
SALES (est): 730K Privately Held
SIC: 2051 5461 Bread, all types (white, wheat, rye, etc): fresh or frozen; bread

(G-1264)
ADVANCED CMPT SFTWR CONSULTING
2236 Pearsall Ave (10469-5436)
PHONE.................................718 300-3577
Mohammad Ziauddin, *President*
EMP: 5
SALES (est): 241.7K Privately Held
SIC: 7372 Prepackaged software

(G-1265)
AIR WAVE AIR CONDITIONING CO
Also Called: AC Air Cooling Company
1637 Stillwell Ave (10461-2216)
PHONE.................................212 545-1122
Fax: 212 365-4731
Cac Bui, *President*
William Saferstein, *President*
EMP: 20
SQ FT: 20,000
SALES (est): 4.8MM Privately Held
WEB: www.airwaveac.com
SIC: 3564 Filters, air: furnaces, air conditioning equipment, etc.

(G-1266)
ALBA FUEL CORP
2135 Wlmsbrdge Rd Fl 2 (10461)
PHONE.................................718 931-1700
Esad Kukaj, *President*
EMP: 5
SALES (est): 910.8K Privately Held
SIC: 1389 Oil field services

(G-1267)
ALBERT MENIN INTERIORS LTD
2417 3rd Ave Fl 3 (10451-6339)
PHONE.................................212 876-3041
Fax: 212 876-4536
Emil Shikh, *President*
Clara Silva, *Manager*
EMP: 12
SQ FT: 1,500
SALES (est): 1.2MM Privately Held
WEB: www.albertmenin.com
SIC: 2519 5023 5713 5714 Household furniture, except wood or metal: upholstered; carpets; draperies; carpets; draperies

(G-1268)
ALLIED METAL SPINNING CORP
1290 Viele Ave (10474-7133)
PHONE.................................718 893-3300
Fax: 718 589-5780
Arlene Saunders, *Ch of Bd*
▲ EMP: 60
SQ FT: 80,000
SALES (est): 10.7MM Privately Held
WEB: www.alliedmetalusa.com
SIC: 3469 Cooking ware, except porcelain enamelled

(G-1269)
ALLWAY TOOLS INC
1255 Seabury Ave (10454-5534)
P.O. Box 777 (10462-0565)
PHONE.................................718 792-3636
Fax: 718 823-9640
Evan Anderson, *President*
Tim Cheng, *President*
Donald Gringer, *Chairman*
Tosia Gringer, *Corp Secy*
Boxing Lu, *Network Mgr*
▲ EMP: 100 EST: 1935
SQ FT: 80,000
SALES (est): 22.5MM Privately Held
WEB: www.allwaytools.com
SIC: 3423 3425 Hand & edge tools; saw blades & handsaws

(G-1270)
ALSTROM CORPORATION
1408 Seabury Ave (10461-3691)
PHONE.................................718 824-4901
Fax: 718 409-3605
Decklan Power, *President*
Philip Larosa, *Vice Pres*
Philip Rosa, *Vice Pres*
Alex Fayershteyn, *Engineer*
Gregory Mayzelshteyn, *VP Sales*
▲ EMP: 20 EST: 1939
SQ FT: 10,000
SALES (est): 4.5MM Privately Held
WEB: www.alstromcorp.com
SIC: 3585 Evaporative condensers, heat transfer equipment

(G-1271)
ALTYPE FIRE DOOR CORP
9 Bruckner Blvd (10454-4411)
PHONE.................................718 292-3500
Harold Halman, *President*
Douglas Halamn, *Corp Secy*
Gary Halman, *Vice Pres*
Aneda Rivera, *Manager*
EMP: 5
SQ FT: 12,000
SALES (est): 707.8K Privately Held
WEB: www.altypefiredoor.com
SIC: 3442 Fire doors, metal

(G-1272)
AMERICAN BLVD AUTO SUPS INC
911 Jennings St (10460-6005)
PHONE.................................718 328-1984
EMP: 5
SALES (est): 276.8K Privately Held
SIC: 3465 Body parts, automobile: stamped metal

(G-1273)
AMERICAN REFUSE SUPPLY INC
Also Called: American Hose & Hydralics
521 Longfellow Ave (10474-6913)
PHONE.................................718 893-8157
Tim Butler, *Manager*
EMP: 7
SALES (corp-wide): 2.1MM Privately Held
SIC: 3714 3562 Motor vehicle parts & accessories; ball & roller bearings
PA: American Refuse Supply Inc
   700 21st Ave
   Paterson NJ 07513
   973 684-3225

(G-1274)
AMSTERDAM COLOR WORKS INC
3326 Merritt Ave (10475-1307)
PHONE.................................718 231-8626
Fax: 718 231-8631
Jeff Derman, *President*
Nadine Ilahi, *Vice Pres*
Victor Lerro, *Accountant*
Maria Harrow, *Office Mgr*
Steven Aufferman, *Administration*
EMP: 12 EST: 1927
SQ FT: 32,500
SALES: 1.7MM Privately Held
SIC: 2851 Paints & allied products; paints & paint additives; enamels; varnishes

(G-1275)
ANASIA INC
1175 Jerome Ave (10452-3331)
PHONE.................................718 588-1407
Victor Florencio, *President*
EMP: 5
SALES (est): 451.7K Privately Held
SIC: 2671 Packaging paper & plastics film, coated & laminated

(G-1276)
ANHEUSER-BUSCH COMPANIES LLC
510 Food Center Dr (10474-7047)
PHONE.................................718 589-2610
Liz Montenegro, *Financial Exec*
Dave Anderson, *VP Mktg*
Chris Curtis, *Marketing Mgr*
Ed Fitzmaurice, *Manager*
Bryan King, *IT/INT Sup*
EMP: 7
SALES (corp-wide): 1B Privately Held
SIC: 2082 3411 Beer (alcoholic beverage); aluminum cans
HQ: Anheuser-Busch Companies, Llc
   1 Busch Pl
   Saint Louis MO 63118
   314 632-6777

(G-1277)
ATLAS COATINGS CORP
820 E 140th St (10454-1904)
PHONE.................................718 402-2000
Michael Landau, *President*
Stephan Landau, *Vice Pres*
EMP: 64
SQ FT: 25,000
SALES (est): 5.9MM Privately Held
SIC: 2893 Printing ink

(G-1278)
AURA DETERGENT LLC (PA)
1811 Mayflower Ave (10461-4103)
PHONE.................................718 824-2162
John Poppola, *Mng Member*
EMP: 11
SALES (est): 4.6MM Privately Held
SIC: 2841 Soap & other detergents

(G-1279)
BACO ENTERPRISES INC (PA)
1190 Longwood Ave (10474-5714)
P.O. Box 740487 (10474-0009)
PHONE.................................718 589-6225
Fax: 718 991-6647
Barry L Cohen, *President*
Jeannette Origazano, *Office Mgr*
Scott Boyer, *Manager*
▲ EMP: 80
SQ FT: 60,000
SALES: 28MM Privately Held
WEB: www.bacoent.com
SIC: 3449 3452 Bars, concrete reinforcing: fabricated steel; bolts, metal

(G-1280)
BANDIT INTERNATIONAL LTD
600 E 132nd St (10454-4639)
PHONE.................................718 402-2100
Albert Berkner, *President*
Sophie Berkner, *Vice Pres*
EMP: 15
SQ FT: 50,000
SALES (est): 810K Privately Held
SIC: 2329 2339 5136 5137 Men's & boys' sportswear & athletic clothing; sportswear, women's; sportswear, men's & boys'; women's & children's sportswear & swimsuits

(G-1281)
BEEHIVE PRESS INC
3742 Boston Rd (10469-2633)
P.O. Box 409 (10469-0409)
PHONE.................................718 654-1200
Fax: 718 653-4272
Roger Denhoff, *President*
Peter Kirkel, *Vice Pres*
EMP: 7 EST: 1927
SQ FT: 4,500

SALES: 1.2MM **Privately Held**
WEB: www.beehivepress.com
SIC: 2752 2791 Commercial printing, offset; typesetting

(G-1282)
BEL ART INTERNATIONAL
Also Called: Scala Furniture Industries NY
600 E 132nd St (10454-4639)
PHONE.................................718 402-2100
Fax: 718 402-2351
Albert Berkner, *President*
Sophie Berkner, *Vice Pres*
EMP: 25 EST: 1964
SQ FT: 50,000
SALES (est): 1.9MM **Privately Held**
SIC: 2511 Wood household furniture

(G-1283)
BELMET PRODUCTS INC (PA)
1350 Garrison Ave (10474-4807)
PHONE.................................718 542-8220
Fred Collins, *President*
Angelo Demauro, *Vice Pres*
John Collins, *Opers Mgr*
Sal Monteleone, *Sales Mgr*
Paul Norton, *Business Dir*
EMP: 48 EST: 1919
SQ FT: 39,000
SALES (est): 2.8MM **Privately Held**
WEB: www.belmetproducts.com
SIC: 3469 3312 Stamping metal for the trade; blast furnaces & steel mills

(G-1284)
BIMBO BAKERIES USA INC
5625 Broadway Frnt 2 (10463-5548)
PHONE.................................718 601-1561
EMP: 5
SALES (corp-wide): 13.7B **Privately Held**
SIC: 2051 Mfg Bread/Related Products
HQ: Bimbo Bakeries Usa, Inc
255 Business Center Dr # 200
Horsham PA 19044
215 347-5500

(G-1285)
BMS DESIGNS INC
1385 Seabury Ave (10461-3629)
PHONE.................................718 828-5792
Henry Mazzoni, *President*
▲ EMP: 30
SALES (est): 2MM **Privately Held**
SIC: 2335 Bridal & formal gowns

(G-1286)
BONK SAM UNFORMS CIVILIAN CAP
Also Called: Sam Bonk Uniform
131 Rose Feiss Blvd Fl 2 (10454-3662)
PHONE.................................718 585-0665
Fax: 718 402-3498
Sarah Bonk, *President*
Harry Bonk, *General Mgr*
Rachel B Jones, *Vice Pres*
Robert Striedl, *Treasurer*
Judy Bonk, *Manager*
EMP: 50 EST: 1963
SQ FT: 18,000
SALES (est): 5.4MM **Privately Held**
SIC: 2353 Uniform hats & caps

(G-1287)
BORGATTIS RAVIOLI EGG NOODLES
632 E 187th St (10458)
PHONE.................................718 367-3799
Mario John Borgatti, *President*
Christopher Borgatti, *Vice Pres*
EMP: 5
SQ FT: 500
SALES: 500K **Privately Held**
WEB: www.borgattis.com
SIC: 2098 2032 Noodles (e.g. egg, plain & water), dry; ravioli: packaged in cans, jars, etc.

(G-1288)
BRANDT EQUIPMENT LLC
Also Called: Brandt Industries
4461 Bronx Blvd (10470-1407)
PHONE.................................718 994-0800
Fax: 718 325-7905
Abe Reich,
Kathleen Rice, *Admin Asst*
EMP: 9 EST: 1930

SQ FT: 10,000
SALES: 1.5MM **Privately Held**
WEB: www.brandtind.com
SIC: 2599 3843 Hospital furniture, except beds; dental equipment

(G-1289)
BRONX NEW WAY CORP
113 E Kingsbridge Rd (10468-7510)
PHONE.................................347 431-1385
Adel Maflahi, *Principal*
EMP: 5
SALES (est): 478K **Privately Held**
SIC: 3643 Outlets, electric: convenience

(G-1290)
BUILDING MANAGEMENT ASSOC INC
998 E 167th St Ofc (10459-2054)
PHONE.................................718 542-4779
Fax: 718 328-6850
Jaime Diaz, *Manager*
EMP: 36
SALES (corp-wide): 11.8MM **Privately Held**
SIC: 3822 Building services monitoring controls, automatic
PA: Building Management Associates, Inc.
885 Bruckner Blvd
Bronx NY 10459
718 617-2800

(G-1291)
CASA REDIMIX CONCRETE CORP
886 Edgewater Rd (10474-4906)
PHONE.................................718 589-1555
Fax: 718 842-0443
Lucy Figueroa, *Principal*
EMP: 14
SALES (est): 2.2MM **Privately Held**
SIC: 3273 Ready-mixed concrete

(G-1292)
CEC ELEVATOR CAB CORP
540 Manida St (10474-6818)
PHONE.................................718 328-3632
Carlos Vanga Sr, *President*
Rakesh Rampersaud, *Purch Agent*
Carlos Vanga Jr, *CFO*
Sonia Rivas, *Accountant*
Olga Melendez, *Manager*
EMP: 65
SQ FT: 30,000
SALES (est): 16MM **Privately Held**
WEB: www.cecelevator.com
SIC: 3534 7699 Elevators & equipment; elevators: inspection, service & repair

(G-1293)
CENTER SHEET METAL INC
1371 E Bay Ave (10474-7025)
PHONE.................................718 378-4476
Fax: 718 893-7223
Maureen O'Connor, *CEO*
Victor Gany, *President*
Peter Pappas Jr, *Exec VP*
John Solla, *Senior VP*
Dennis M Appel Jr,
EMP: 150
SQ FT: 45,000
SALES (est): 23.5MM **Privately Held**
SIC: 3444 Sheet metalwork

(G-1294)
CENTURY SYSTEMS LTD
485 W 246th St (10471-3331)
PHONE.................................718 543-5991
Jack Jakubowicz, *Owner*
EMP: 7
SQ FT: 500
SALES (est): 771.7K **Privately Held**
WEB: www.centurysystems.com
SIC: 3699 Security devices

(G-1295)
CFS ENTERPRISES INC
Also Called: CFS Steel Company
650 E 132nd St (10454-4603)
PHONE.................................718 585-0500
Fax: 718 993-8079
James R Melvin Jr, *Ch of Bd*
EMP: 20
SQ FT: 40,000

SALES (est): 4.6MM
SALES (corp-wide): 24.5MM **Privately Held**
WEB: www.cfssteel.com
SIC: 3315 Wire & fabricated wire products
PA: Re-Steel Supply Company, Inc.
2000 Eddystone Indus Park
Eddystone PA 19022
610 876-8216

(G-1296)
CGSI GROUP LLC
3835 Sedgwick Ave (10463-4452)
PHONE.................................516 986-5503
Shannon Herdricks, *Principal*
EMP: 12
SQ FT: 1,000
SALES (est): 623K **Privately Held**
SIC: 3731 Drilling & production platforms, floating (oil & gas)

(G-1297)
CHARLES H BECKLEY INC (PA)
749 E 137th St (10454-3402)
PHONE.................................718 665-2218
Fax: 718 402-3386
Theodore W Marschke, *President*
Charles L Beckley, *Principal*
Ken Marschke, *Sales Dir*
Roy Babb, *Manager*
▲ EMP: 18 EST: 1932
SQ FT: 12,000
SALES (est): 2.1MM **Privately Held**
WEB: www.chbeckley.com
SIC: 2515 2511 Box springs, assembled; mattresses & foundations; wood household furniture

(G-1298)
CIBAO MEAT PRODUCTS INC
630 Saint Anns Ave (10455-1404)
PHONE.................................718 993-5072
Fax: 718 993-5638
Heinz Vieluf, *CEO*
Lutzi V Isidor, *President*
Julio G Isidor, *General Mgr*
Edgar Soto, *Vice Pres*
Maria Sandner, *Manager*
▲ EMP: 55
SQ FT: 6,000
SALES (est): 12.4MM **Privately Held**
WEB: www.cibaomeat.com
SIC: 2013 Sausages from purchased meat

(G-1299)
CITY EVOLUTIONARY
336 Barretto St (10474-6718)
PHONE.................................718 861-7585
Matt Tan, *General Mgr*
EMP: 8
SALES (est): 503.5K **Privately Held**
SIC: 3449 Bars, concrete reinforcing: fabricated steel

(G-1300)
CITY JEANS INC
845 White Plins Rd Frnt 1 (10473)
PHONE.................................718 239-5353
Kyle Christianson, *Owner*
EMP: 7
SALES (corp-wide): 29.6MM **Privately Held**
SIC: 2329 Men's & boys' sportswear & athletic clothing
PA: City Jeans Inc
1515 132nd St Fl 2nd
College Point NY 11356
718 359-2489

(G-1301)
COCA-COLA REFRESHMENTS USA INC
977 E 149th St (10455-5090)
PHONE.................................718 401-5200
Fax: 718 292-1848
Tom Sagliano, *General Mgr*
Tom Druell, *Sales & Mktg St*
Gary Battaglya, *Manager*
EMP: 20
SALES (corp-wide): 44.2B **Publicly Held**
WEB: www.cokecce.com
SIC: 2086 5149 Bottled & canned soft drinks; groceries & related products

HQ: Coca-Cola Refreshments Usa, Inc.
2500 Windy Ridge Pkwy Se
Atlanta GA 30339
770 989-3000

(G-1302)
COLOR CARTON CORP
341 Canal Pl (10451-6091)
PHONE.................................718 665-0840
Nicholas F Loprinzi, *President*
Vincent Loprinzi, *Corp Secy*
Nicholas V Loprinzi, *Vice Pres*
Jimmy Martinelli, *Warehouse Mgr*
Debbie Loprinzi, *Manager*
▲ EMP: 60 EST: 1960
SQ FT: 90,000
SALES: 7.7MM **Privately Held**
WEB: www.colorcarton.com
SIC: 2752 2653 2657 Commercial printing, offset; corrugated & solid fiber boxes; folding paperboard boxes

(G-1303)
COLUMBIA POOL ACCESSORIES INC
111 Bruckner Blvd (10454-4514)
PHONE.................................718 993-0389
Fax: 718 993-8323
Richard L Cudney, *President*
Rich Medina, *Manager*
▲ EMP: 5
SALES (est): 504K **Privately Held**
SIC: 3585 Refrigeration & heating equipment

(G-1304)
CORAL MANAGEMENT CORP
Also Called: Total Machine and Welding
923 Bryant Ave (10474-4701)
PHONE.................................718 893-9286
EMP: 5
SALES: 320K **Privately Held**
SIC: 3449 Mfg Misc Structural Metalwork

(G-1305)
COVINGTON SOUND
2705 Kingsbridge Ter (10463-7456)
PHONE.................................646 256-7486
Velma Harris, *Owner*
EMP: 6
SALES: 570K **Privately Held**
SIC: 3651 Speaker systems

(G-1306)
CUMMINS INC
890 Zerega Ave (10473-1122)
PHONE.................................718 892-2400
Laura Rychlicki, *Human Resources*
Marshall Lomazow, *Branch Mgr*
EMP: 343
SALES (corp-wide): 19.1B **Publicly Held**
WEB: www.cummins.com
SIC: 3519 Internal combustion engines
PA: Cummins Inc.
500 Jackson St
Columbus IN 47201
812 377-5000

(G-1307)
D B F ASSOCIATES
Also Called: August Graphics
1150 E 156th St (10474-6227)
PHONE.................................718 328-0005
Fax: 718 328-1123
Bruce Feldman, *President*
Debra Bashore, *Assistant VP*
EMP: 8
SALES: 460K **Privately Held**
WEB: www.dbfassociates.com
SIC: 2759 Screen printing

(G-1308)
D W HABER & SON INC
825 E 140th St (10454-1930)
PHONE.................................718 993-6405
Fax: 718 585-0726
Robert H Haber, *President*
David Haber, *Vice Pres*
▲ EMP: 25
SQ FT: 40,000
SALES (est): 4.2MM **Privately Held**
WEB: www.habersilver.com
SIC: 3914 Silversmithing; hollowware, plated (all metals)

Bronx - Bronx County (G-1309)

(G-1309)
DA ELECTRIC
6 E Clarke Pl (10452-7501)
PHONE.....................347 270-3422
Damal Dudley, *Owner*
EMP: 45
SALES (est): 4MM **Privately Held**
SIC: 3699 Electrical equipment & supplies

(G-1310)
DALE PRESS INC
Also Called: Riverdale Press, The
5676 Riverdale Ave # 311 (10471-2138)
PHONE.....................718 543-6200
Fax: 718 548-4038
Bernard L Stein, *President*
Richard L Stein, *Vice Pres*
EMP: 25 **EST:** 1950
SQ FT: 2,500
SALES (est): 1.5MM **Privately Held**
WEB: www.riverdalepress.com
SIC: 2711 Newspapers: publishing only, not printed on site

(G-1311)
DAYTON INDUSTRIES INC
1350 Garrison Ave (10474-4807)
PHONE.....................718 542-8144
Fax: 718 793-2758
J Fred Collins, *CEO*
Barbara Agovino, *Human Resources*
Catherine Goetz, *Office Mgr*
Dwayne Tucker, *Manager*
Hector Medina, *Prgrmr*
EMP: 45 **EST:** 1980
SQ FT: 45,000
SALES (est): 11.8MM **Privately Held**
WEB: www.daytonind.com
SIC: 3469 3442 Stamping metal for the trade; metal doors, sash & trim

(G-1312)
DELBIA DO COMPANY INC (PA)
2550 Park Ave (10451-6014)
PHONE.....................718 585-2226
Fax: 718 665-7922
Daryl Do, *Vice Pres*
◆ **EMP:** 9
SQ FT: 8,000
SALES (est): 1.6MM **Privately Held**
SIC: 2087 2844 Flavoring extracts & syrups; perfumes, natural or synthetic

(G-1313)
DELBIA DO COMPANY INC
11 Canal Pl (10451-6009)
PHONE.....................718 585-2226
Delbia Do, *Branch Mgr*
EMP: 13
SALES (corp-wide): 1.6MM **Privately Held**
SIC: 2844 2087 Toilet preparations; flavoring extracts & syrups
PA: Delbia Do Company Inc.
  2550 Park Ave
  Bronx NY 10451
  718 585-2226

(G-1314)
DELICIOSO COCO HELADO INC
849 Saint Anns Ave (10456-7633)
PHONE.....................718 292-1930
Fax: 718 292-1243
Alfred Thiebaud, *President*
Lois Thiebaud, *Bookkeeper*
Sophia Thiebaud, *Admin Sec*
EMP: 15
SQ FT: 20,000
SALES (est): 2.1MM **Privately Held**
SIC: 2024 5451 Ice cream, bulk; ice cream (packaged)

(G-1315)
DOMENICK DENIGRIS INC (PA)
1485 Bassett Ave (10461-2309)
PHONE.....................718 823-2264
Fax: 718 823-5765
Donald Denigris, *President*
◆ **EMP:** 50
SQ FT: 4,000
SALES (est): 6.8MM **Privately Held**
SIC: 3281 Monument or burial stone, cut & shaped

(G-1316)
DOMINIC DE NIGRIS INC
3255 E Tremont Ave Frnt (10461-5790)
PHONE.....................718 597-4460
Dominic De Nigris, *President*
Dan A De Nigris, *Vice Pres*
Dan C De Nigris, *Admin Sec*
EMP: 30
SQ FT: 2,910
SALES (est): 2.7MM **Privately Held**
SIC: 3281 1411 Monuments, cut stone (not finishing or lettering only); dimension stone

(G-1317)
DOYLE-HILD SAILMAKERS
225 Fordham St (10464-1467)
PHONE.....................718 885-2255
Mark Ploch, *Owner*
EMP: 8
SALES (est): 360K **Privately Held**
SIC: 2394 Sails: made from purchased materials

(G-1318)
DUFOUR PASTRY KITCHENS INC
251 Locust Ave (10454-2004)
PHONE.....................718 402-8800
Fax: 718 402-7002
Judith Arnold, *Ch of Bd*
Carla Krasner, *Vice Pres*
Aida Puente, *Bookkeeper*
Craig Levison, *Business Dir*
EMP: 24
SALES (est): 3.7MM **Privately Held**
SIC: 2038 2053 Frozen specialties; frozen bakery products, except bread

(G-1319)
DUN-RITE SPCLIZED CARRIERS LLC
1561 Southern Blvd (10460-5602)
PHONE.....................718 991-1100
Brett Deutsch, *Vice Pres*
Dominick Conetta, *Opers Staff*
Anthony Conetta, *VP Finance*
Carl Panepinto, *VP Finance*
EMP: 12
SALES: 1MM **Privately Held**
SIC: 3536 Hoists, cranes & monorails

(G-1320)
E & J IRON WORKS INC
801 E 136th St (10454-3546)
PHONE.....................718 665-6040
Gerhard Teicht, *President*
Edmund Teicht, *General Mgr*
EMP: 20
SQ FT: 22,000
SALES (est): 3.7MM **Privately Held**
SIC: 3446 Architectural metalwork; gates, ornamental metal; railings, prefabricated metal; fire escapes, metal

(G-1321)
E H HURWITZ & ASSOCIATES
3000 Kingsbridge Ave (10463-5101)
PHONE.....................718 884-3766
EMP: 9 **EST:** 1978
SALES (est): 720K **Privately Held**
SIC: 7372 Prepackaged Software Services

(G-1322)
EASCO BOILER CORP
1175 Leggett Ave (10474-6294)
PHONE.....................718 378-3000
Arlington Leon Eastmond, *Ch of Bd*
Leon Eastmond, *President*
Emil Stranzl, *Plant Mgr*
Bequn Pong, *Engineer*
Ben Sosin, *Engineer*
EMP: 30
SQ FT: 15,000
SALES (est): 6.5MM **Privately Held**
SIC: 3567 Heating units & devices, industrial: electric

(G-1323)
EDWARD C LYONS COMPANY INC
Also Called: E C Lyons
3646 White Plains Rd Frnt (10467-5717)
PHONE.....................718 515-5361
Gary Owens, *President*
Cheryl Owens, *Vice Pres*
EMP: 7 **EST:** 1958
SQ FT: 5,000
SALES: 500K **Privately Held**
WEB: www.eclyons.com
SIC: 3423 Engravers' tools, hand

(G-1324)
EDWARD C MULLER CORP
Also Called: Edward C. Lyons
3646 White Plains Rd Frnt (10467-5717)
PHONE.....................718 881-7270
Fax: 718 515-7790
Gary Owens, *President*
Cheryl D Owens, *Vice Pres*
EMP: 15 **EST:** 1898
SQ FT: 3,600
SALES: 700K **Privately Held**
SIC: 3423 Engravers' tools, hand

(G-1325)
EDWARDS GRAPHIC CO INC
3801 Hudson Manor Ter 4s (10463-1105)
PHONE.....................718 548-6858
Fax: 718 796-2255
Jackie Ginsberg, *President*
Ed Edwards, *Vice Pres*
Paula Mack, *Sales Staff*
EMP: 5
SALES (est): 437.7K **Privately Held**
SIC: 2752 Commercial printing, lithographic

(G-1326)
ENDRES KNITWEAR CO INC
3020 Jerome Ave (10468-1333)
PHONE.....................718 933-8687
Adam Endres, *President*
Ann Endres, *Corp Secy*
EMP: 5
SQ FT: 10,000
SALES (est): 367.4K **Privately Held**
SIC: 2253 Sweaters & sweater coats, knit; skirts, knit

(G-1327)
ENTERPRISE METALWORKS INC
1162 Southern Blvd (10459-1902)
PHONE.....................718 328-9331
Paul Kirschner, *President*
EMP: 5 **EST:** 1944
SQ FT: 7,000
SALES (est): 457.3K **Privately Held**
SIC: 3446 Architectural metalwork

(G-1328)
EVE SALES CORP
945 Close Ave (10473-4906)
PHONE.....................718 589-6800
Irving Nadler, *President*
Stuart Gale, *Vice Pres*
◆ **EMP:** 13
SQ FT: 22,000
SALES (est): 3MM **Privately Held**
WEB: www.evesales.com
SIC: 2032 Mexican foods: packaged in cans, jars, etc.

(G-1329)
FELIX STORCH INC (PA)
Also Called: Summit Appliances
770 Garrison Ave (10474-5603)
PHONE.....................718 893-3900
Fax: 718 328-5069
Paul Storch, *President*
Susan Storch, *Corp Secy*
Stephen Ross, *Vice Pres*
Mark Weingarten, *Opers Mgr*
George Rejwan, *Senior Engr*
◆ **EMP:** 122 **EST:** 1969
SQ FT: 100,000
SALES (est): 32.9MM **Privately Held**
WEB: www.summitappliance.com
SIC: 3632 Household refrigerators & freezers

(G-1330)
FIDAZZEL INC
2280 Olinville Ave # 409 (10467-7806)
PHONE.....................917 557-3860
Erick Wright, *CEO*
Melissa Colbourne, *Admin Sec*
EMP: 6
SALES (est): 340K **Privately Held**
SIC: 2741 Miscellaneous publishing

(G-1331)
FINEST CC CORP
3111 E Tremont Ave (10461-5705)
PHONE.....................917 574-4525
Larry Derasmo, *President*
EMP: 6
SQ FT: 1,000
SALES (est): 227.1K **Privately Held**
SIC: 3471 Electroplating of metals or formed products

(G-1332)
FIVE ISLANDS PUBLISHING INC
Also Called: Fire Island News
8 Fort Charles Pl (10463-6705)
PHONE.....................631 583-5345
Shawn Beqaj, *President*
Nicole Pressly, *Treasurer*
EMP: 10
SQ FT: 1,000
SALES (est): 460K **Privately Held**
SIC: 2711 Newspapers

(G-1333)
FLAIR DISPLAY INC
3920 Merritt Ave (10466-2502)
PHONE.....................718 324-9330
Fax: 718 994-4174
Eugene Dilorenzo, *President*
Chris Dilorenzo, *Vice Pres*
Raymond Hand, *Vice Pres*
Betty Hood, *Assistant*
▲ **EMP:** 60 **EST:** 1953
SQ FT: 50,000
SALES (est): 8.5MM **Privately Held**
WEB: www.flairdisplay.com
SIC: 3993 Signs & advertising specialties; displays & cutouts, window & lobby; displays, paint process

(G-1334)
FOAM PRODUCTS INC
360 Southern Blvd (10454-1711)
PHONE.....................718 292-4830
Karen Ippolito, *President*
Frank Ippolito, *Vice Pres*
Jim Wink, *VP Sales*
EMP: 20
SQ FT: 32,000
SALES (est): 4.6MM **Privately Held**
SIC: 3069 3086 Foam rubber; insulation or cushioning material, foamed plastic

(G-1335)
FORDHAM UNIVERSITY
Also Called: Fordham University Press
2546 Belmont Ave (10458-5106)
P.O. Box L (10458)
PHONE.....................718 817-4795
Fax: 718 817-4785
Fredric Nachbaur, *Director*
Ian Pace, *Assistant*
EMP: 10
SALES (corp-wide): 566MM **Privately Held**
WEB: www.fordham.edu
SIC: 2741 8221 Miscellaneous publishing; university
PA: Fordham University
  441 E Fordham Rd
  Bronx NY 10458
  718 817-1000

(G-1336)
FOUR SASONS MULTI-SERVICES INC
3525 Decatur Ave Apt 2k (10467-1729)
PHONE.....................347 843-6262
Gabriel Gomez, *CEO*
Juan Carlos, *Office Mgr*
EMP: 5
SQ FT: 100
SALES (est): 389.2K **Privately Held**
SIC: 2842 Specialty cleaning preparations

(G-1337)
FRA-RIK FORMICA FABG CO INC
1464 Blondell Ave Fl 2 (10461-2688)
PHONE.....................718 597-3335
Philip De Candido, *President*
Frank Maiore, *Vice Pres*
EMP: 9 **EST:** 1965
SQ FT: 5,000
SALES (est): 962.5K **Privately Held**
SIC: 2434 3299 Wood kitchen cabinets; mica products

▲ = Import ▼ = Export
◆ = Import/Export

GEOGRAPHIC SECTION

Bronx - Bronx County (G-1363)

(G-1338)
FUEL WATCHMAN SALES & SERVICE
Also Called: Full Timer
364 Jackson Ave (10454-1698)
P.O. Box 202, Garden City (11530-0202)
PHONE.................................718 665-6100
Benjamin Strysko, *President*
Tom Strysco, *Vice Pres*
Joan Strysko, *Admin Sec*
EMP: 10 **EST:** 1944
SALES (est): 1.7MM **Privately Held**
SIC: 3822 3669 Auto controls regulating residntl & coml environmt & applncs; smoke detectors

(G-1339)
G & O EQUIPMENT CORP
1211 Oakpoint Ave (10474-6701)
PHONE.................................718 218-7844
Donato Sammarco, *President*
Phil Seltzer, *Exec VP*
EMP: 5
SQ FT: 1,000
SALES (est): 880.7K **Privately Held**
SIC: 3824 Fluid meters & counting devices

(G-1340)
G&J GRAPHICS INC
Also Called: Bronx Design Group, The
2914 Westchester Ave (10461-4504)
PHONE.................................718 409-9874
Fax: 718 931-0717
Geri Sciortino, *President*
John Sciortino, *Vice Pres*
Danielle Sciortino, *Manager*
Ann M Papanagnostou, *Graphic Designe*
EMP: 7
SQ FT: 3,100
SALES (est): 894.2K **Privately Held**
WEB: www.bronxdesign.com
SIC: 2759 Commercial printing

(G-1341)
GARY PLASTIC PACKAGING CORP (PA)
Also Called: Garyline
1340 Viele Ave (10474-7134)
PHONE.................................718 893-2200
Fax: 718 860-7002
Gary Hellinger, *Ch of Bd*
Richard Hellinger, *President*
Gustavo That, *Opers Mgr*
Gianna Morea, *Purchasing*
Harold King, *CFO*
▲ **EMP:** 395 **EST:** 1962
SQ FT: 300,000
SALES (est): 68.3MM **Privately Held**
WEB: www.plasticboxes.com
SIC: 3089 Plastic containers, except foam

(G-1342)
GENERAL FIRE-PROOF DOOR CORP
913 Edgewater Rd (10474-4930)
PHONE.................................718 893-5500
Fax: 718 893-1770
Aaron Szabo, *President*
Rubin Kuszel, *Vice Pres*
EMP: 50 **EST:** 1921
SALES (est): 7.5MM **Privately Held**
SIC: 3442 Fire doors, metal

(G-1343)
GENERAL GALVANIZING SUP CO INC (PA)
652 Whittier St Fl Mezz (10474-6194)
PHONE.................................718 589-4300
Fax: 718 589-4738
Anthony Visentin, *President*
Tarek Elgendy, *Engineer*
Edith Jenkins, *Bookkeeper*
Tony Visentin, *Personnel Exec*
EMP: 37 **EST:** 1935
SQ FT: 10,000
SALES (est): 5.4MM **Privately Held**
SIC: 3471 5085 Electroplating & plating; fasteners & fastening equipment

(G-1344)
GLOBUS CORK INC
741 E 136th St (10454-3410)
PHONE.................................347 963-4059
Fax: 718 742-7265
Jen Biscoe, *Vice Pres*
▲ **EMP:** 11
SALES (est): 1.5MM **Privately Held**
WEB: www.globuscork.com
SIC: 2499 Tiles, cork

(G-1345)
GOLDEN GLOW COOKIE CO INC
Also Called: Cookie Factory
1844 Givan Ave (10469-3155)
PHONE.................................718 379-6223
Fax: 718 379-4417
Rose Florio, *President*
Joan Florio, *Vice Pres*
Salvatore Florio Jr, *Vice Pres*
EMP: 20
SQ FT: 15,000
SALES (est): 3.4MM **Privately Held**
SIC: 2051 2052 Bread, cake & related products; cookies

(G-1346)
GOODO BEVERAGE COMPANY
Also Called: Coco Rico Southeast
1801 Boone Ave (10460-5101)
PHONE.................................347 226-9996
Fax: 718 328-7002
Kersia Corporation, *Partner*
Steven Kucerak, *Principal*
George Deyarca, *Manager*
Domiciano Diaz, *Manager*
Irving Mendelson, *Manager*
▲ **EMP:** 18 **EST:** 1942
SQ FT: 53,000
SALES (est): 4MM **Privately Held**
WEB: www.good-o.com
SIC: 2086 Carbonated soft drinks, bottled & canned

(G-1347)
GOURMET GURU INC
1123 Worthen St (10474-6223)
PHONE.................................718 842-2828
Fax: 718 425-9860
Jeff Lichtenstein, *President*
Brandon Lee, *Vice Pres*
Yisheng Liu, *Purchasing*
Kim Lichtenstein, *CFO*
Yang Yong, *Controller*
▲ **EMP:** 50
SALES (est): 19.8MM **Publicly Held**
WEB: www.gourmetguru.com
SIC: 2099 Food preparations
PA: United Natural Foods, Inc.
313 Iron Horse Way
Providence RI 02908

(G-1348)
GRAPHIC PRINTING
2376 Jerome Ave (10468-6401)
PHONE.................................718 701-4433
Joao Oliveira, *Owner*
EMP: 5
SALES (est): 218.7K **Privately Held**
SIC: 2759 Publication printing

(G-1349)
GRUBER DISPLAY CO INC
3920g Merritt Ave (10466-2502)
PHONE.................................718 882-8220
Fax: 718 392-0071
Jay Merkel, *President*
Ralph Merkel, *General Mgr*
EMP: 15
SQ FT: 10,000
SALES (est): 750K **Privately Held**
SIC: 2759 Screen printing

(G-1350)
H W WILSON COMPANY INC
950 University Ave (10452-4297)
P.O. Box 602, Ipswich MA (01938-0602)
PHONE.................................718 588-8635
Fax: 718 538-2716
F Dixon Brooke Jr, *President*
J David Walker, *President*
Clifford Thompson, *Editor*
Tim Collins, *Vice Pres*
Rose Fragola-Jones, *Manager*
EMP: 450
SQ FT: 150,000
SALES (est): 24.7MM
SALES (corp-wide): 2.1B **Privately Held**
WEB: www.hwwilson.com
SIC: 2721 2731 Periodicals: publishing & printing; books: publishing & printing
HQ: Ebsco Publishing, Inc.
10 Estes St
Ipswich MA 01938
978 356-6500

(G-1351)
HAT ATTACK INC (PA)
Also Called: Hat Attack I Bujibaja
4643 Bullard Ave Ste A (10470-1415)
PHONE.................................718 994-1000
Fax: 718 324-0519
William Gedney, *President*
Barbara J Gedney, *Vice Pres*
◆ **EMP:** 20
SQ FT: 11,000
SALES (est): 5MM **Privately Held**
WEB: www.hatattack.com
SIC: 3111 2353 Bag leather; hats, caps & millinery

(G-1352)
HB ARCHITECTURAL LIGHTING INC
862 E 139th St (10454-1909)
PHONE.................................347 851-4123
Howard Baldinger, *President*
Chris Hartmann, *Engineer*
Michele Sonsini, *Marketing Mgr*
Gloria Lendle, *Manager*
▲ **EMP:** 40
SQ FT: 7,000
SALES (est): 7.5MM **Privately Held**
WEB: www.hblightinginc.com
SIC: 3648 Lighting equipment

(G-1353)
HEALTHEE ENDEAVORS INC
3565c Boston Rd (10469-2500)
P.O. Box 690159 (10469-0761)
PHONE.................................718 653-5499
Junior Blake, *President*
Jennifer Blake, *Vice Pres*
Julian Reynolds, *Administration*
EMP: 7 **EST:** 1985
SALES (est): 400K **Privately Held**
SIC: 2833 Vitamins, natural or synthetic: bulk, uncompounded

(G-1354)
HEAT-TIMER CORPORATION
Also Called: Heat-Timer Service
79 Alexander Ave Ste 36a (10454-4428)
PHONE.................................212 481-2020
Fax: 212 684-5444
John Winston, *Manager*
EMP: 30
SALES (corp-wide): 7.5MM **Privately Held**
WEB: www.heat-timer.com
SIC: 3824 1711 7623 Controls, revolution & timing instruments; heating & air conditioning contractors; refrigeration service & repair
PA: Heat-Timer Corporation
20 New Dutch Ln
Fairfield NJ 07004
973 575-4004

(G-1355)
HEATING & BURNER SUPPLY INC
479 Walton Ave (10451-5337)
PHONE.................................718 665-0006
Bob Broker, *President*
Terrance Broker, *Vice Pres*
EMP: 7
SQ FT: 10,000
SALES (est): 890K **Privately Held**
WEB: www.heatingandburner.com
SIC: 3822 5063 Auto controls regulating residntl & coml environmt & applncs; motors, electric

(G-1356)
HENDRICKSON CUSTOM CABINETRY
132 Saint Anns Ave Fl 2 (10454-4600)
PHONE.................................718 401-0137
Fax: 718 401-0153
Felix Hendrickson, *President*
Mike Krall, *COO*
Lisa Hendrickson, *Vice Pres*
Gerry Remus, *Administration*
EMP: 10
SQ FT: 8,000
SALES (est): 697K **Privately Held**
WEB: www.hccco.com
SIC: 2434 Wood kitchen cabinets

(G-1357)
HIGH RIDGE NEWS LLC
5818 Broadway (10463-4105)
PHONE.................................718 548-7412
Atul Patel, *Owner*
EMP: 5
SALES (est): 268.4K **Privately Held**
SIC: 2711 Newspapers, publishing & printing

(G-1358)
HUB SURGICAL & ORTHOPEDIC SUPS (PA)
288 E 149th St Frnt A (10451-5630)
P.O. Box 6027 (10451-1702)
PHONE.................................718 585-5415
Oermila Harinandansingh, *CEO*
Mary Delgado, *Manager*
EMP: 5
SQ FT: 5,000
SALES (est): 718.6K **Privately Held**
WEB: www.hubsurgicalny.com
SIC: 3841 5047 Surgical instruments & apparatus; medical equipment & supplies

(G-1359)
IDEAL SIGNS INC
538 Wales Ave (10455-4510)
PHONE.................................718 292-9196
Fax: 718 292-9196
Yeudy Diaz, *President*
EMP: 5
SQ FT: 3,000
SALES (est): 396.1K **Privately Held**
SIC: 3993 Signs & advertising specialties

(G-1360)
IMPERIAL DAMPER & LOUVER CO
907 E 141st St (10454-2009)
PHONE.................................718 731-3800
Fax: 718 731-4920
Brad Mattes, *President*
Tom Tulley, *Vice Pres*
Myrna Garcia, *Prdtn Mgr*
Matt Kranz, *Engineer*
Aida Rivera, *Office Mgr*
EMP: 35
SQ FT: 16,500
SALES (est): 6.6MM **Privately Held**
WEB: www.imperialdamper.com
SIC: 3444 3446 Metal ventilating equipment; louvers, ventilating

(G-1361)
INDUSTRIAL PAPER TUBE INC
1335 E Bay Ave (10474-6992)
PHONE.................................718 893-5000
Fax: 718 378-0055
Howard Kramer, *President*
John Costello, *Vice Pres*
EMP: 19
SQ FT: 50,000
SALES (est): 3.2MM **Privately Held**
WEB: www.mailingtubes-ipt.com
SIC: 3089 2655 Closures, plastic; tubes, for chemical or electrical uses: paper or fiber

(G-1362)
INFORM STUDIO INC
480 Austin Pl Frnt E (10455-5023)
PHONE.................................718 401-6149
Patrick Eck, *President*
Emad Ebrahim, *Vice Pres*
EMP: 10
SQ FT: 7,000
SALES (est): 1.7MM **Privately Held**
SIC: 2431 Interior & ornamental woodwork & trim

(G-1363)
INNOVA INTERIORS INC
780 E 134th St Fl 2 (10454-3527)
PHONE.................................718 401-2122
Leon Mace Natenzon, *President*
EMP: 20
SALES (est): 1.2MM **Privately Held**
SIC: 2499 1751 Decorative wood & woodwork; carpentry work

Bronx - Bronx County (G-1364) GEOGRAPHIC SECTION

(G-1364)
JAB CONCRETE SUPPLY CORP
1465 Bronx River Ave (10472-1001)
P.O. Box 1223 (10472-0965)
PHONE..................718 842-5250
Carmine Valente, *President*
EMP: 30 **EST:** 1994
SALES (est): 2.4MM **Privately Held**
SIC: 3272 Concrete products

(G-1365)
JEM THREADING SPECIALTIES INC
1059 Washington Ave (10456-6636)
P.O. Box 491, Lake Peekskill (10537-0491)
PHONE..................718 665-3341
Fax: 718 292-0020
Michael Rottenkolber, *President*
John Rottenkolber, *Vice Pres*
Maria Vazqezi, *Manager*
EMP: 5
SQ FT: 17,500
SALES (est): 656.6K **Privately Held**
SIC: 3965 3354 3452 Fasteners; rods, extruded, aluminum; bolts, metal

(G-1366)
JENNA CONCRETE CORPORATION
1465 Bronx River Ave (10472-1001)
PHONE..................718 842-5250
Fax: 718 589-3446
Carmine Valente, *President*
Denny Lijlage, *Office Mgr*
Anthony Valente, *Manager*
EMP: 30
SQ FT: 1,000
SALES (est): 5.8MM **Privately Held**
SIC: 3272 3273 3271 Concrete products; ready-mixed concrete; concrete block & brick

(G-1367)
JENNA HARLEM RIVER INC
1465 Bronx River Ave (10472-1001)
PHONE..................718 842-5997
Carmine Valente, *President*
EMP: 5
SQ FT: 1,000
SALES (est): 454.9K **Privately Held**
SIC: 3272 3273 3271 Concrete products; ready-mixed concrete; concrete block & brick

(G-1368)
JOHN LANGENBACHER CO INC
888 Longfellow Ave (10474-4804)
PHONE..................718 328-0141
Fax: 718 542-2005
Harry Boyd, *President*
William Boyd, *President*
Larry Scherer, *Exec VP*
William Hudspeth, *CFO*
EMP: 50 **EST:** 1907
SQ FT: 100,000
SALES (est): 4.6MM **Privately Held**
SIC: 2431 5712 Millwork; custom made furniture, except cabinets

(G-1369)
KD DIDS INC (PA)
Also Called: K D Dance
140 E 144th St (10451-5434)
PHONE..................718 402-2012
Fax: 718 402-2013
David Lee, *President*
EMP: 2
SQ FT: 6,000
SALES (est): 4.5MM **Privately Held**
WEB: www.kddance.com
SIC: 2253 5961 Shirts (outerwear), knit; fitness & sporting goods, mail order

(G-1370)
KEMET PROPERTIES LLC
1179 E 224th St (10466-5834)
PHONE..................718 654-8079
Douglas Malcolm, *Principal*
EMP: 5
SALES (est): 588.5K **Privately Held**
SIC: 3675 Electronic capacitors

(G-1371)
KENMAR SHIRTS INC (PA)
1415 Blondell Ave (10461-2622)
PHONE..................718 824-3880
Fax: 718 823-4233
Mark Greene, *President*
Karen Greene, *Corp Secy*
Irwin Haberman, *Vice Pres*
EMP: 20
SQ FT: 8,000
SALES (est): 1.7MM **Privately Held**
WEB: www.kenmarshirts.com
SIC: 2759 5136 5137 2396 Screen printing; men's & boys' clothing; women's & children's clothing; automotive & apparel trimmings

(G-1372)
KICKS CLOSET SPORTSWEAR INC
1031 Southern Blvd Frnt 2 (10459-3435)
PHONE..................347 577-0857
Ismail Abadi, *President*
EMP: 6 **EST:** 2014
SQ FT: 1,800
SALES (est): 2.7MM **Privately Held**
SIC: 2329 3149 2339 Men's & boys' sportswear & athletic clothing; athletic shoes, except rubber or plastic; women's & misses' athletic clothing & sportswear

(G-1373)
KIRSCHNER BRUSH LLC
Also Called: Kbc
605 E 132nd St Frnt 3 (10454-4638)
PHONE..................718 292-1809
Fax: 718 292-1899
Israel Kirschner,
▲ **EMP:** 15 **EST:** 1939
SQ FT: 20,000
SALES: 900K **Privately Held**
SIC: 3991 Paint brushes

(G-1374)
KNJ FABRICATORS LLC
4341 Wickham Ave (10466-1809)
PHONE..................347 234-6985
Krishnadatt N Joe,
EMP: 10
SQ FT: 4,000
SALES: 500K **Privately Held**
SIC: 3441 Fabricated structural metal

(G-1375)
L & D MANUFACTURING CORP
Also Called: D & L Manufacturing
366 Canal Pl Frnt (10451-5911)
PHONE..................718 665-5226
Larry Weisel, *President*
Leon Weisel, *Vice Pres*
EMP: 6
SALES (est): 624.9K **Privately Held**
SIC: 2599 Restaurant furniture, wood or metal

(G-1376)
L A S REPLACEMENT PARTS INC
1645 Webster Ave (10457-8096)
P.O. Box 873 (10457-0873)
PHONE..................718 583-4700
Fax: 718 294-0661
Alan Siegel, *President*
Lloyd Siegel, *Corp Secy*
EMP: 10 **EST:** 1946
SQ FT: 10,000
SALES (est): 1.3MM **Privately Held**
WEB: www.lasparts.com
SIC: 3432 1711 Plumbing fixture fittings & trim; plumbing, heating, air-conditioning contractors

(G-1377)
LA PRIMA BAKERY INC (PA)
765 E 182nd St (10460-1140)
PHONE..................718 584-4442
Fax: 718 584-7521
Sal Attina, *President*
Rocco Attina, *Vice Pres*
EMP: 19
SQ FT: 18,000
SALES (est): 1.1MM **Privately Held**
SIC: 2051 Bread, all types (white, wheat, rye, etc): fresh or frozen

(G-1378)
LASALLE BRANDS INC
547 Manida St (10474-6821)
PHONE..................718 542-0900
Medhat Mohamed, *President*
Scott Campbell, *CFO*
EMP: 10
SALES (est): 617.8K **Privately Held**
SIC: 2024 Ice cream & frozen desserts

(G-1379)
LEADER SHEET METAL INC
759 E 133rd St 2 (10454-3425)
PHONE..................347 271-4961
Jenny Dashevsky, *President*
EMP: 17
SALES (est): 3.5MM **Privately Held**
SIC: 3444 Sheet metalwork

(G-1380)
LEMON BROTHERS FOUNDATION INC
23b Debs Pl (10475-2575)
PHONE..................347 920-2749
Mohammed Rahman, *Principal*
Pablo Narudha, *Director*
EMP: 15
SALES (est): 24K **Privately Held**
SIC: 3999 Education aids, devices & supplies

(G-1381)
LENS LAB
2124 Bartow Ave (10475-4615)
PHONE..................718 379-2020
Janet Bennis, *Manager*
Maria Ortiz, *Manager*
EMP: 6
SALES (est): 200K **Privately Held**
SIC: 3851 Ophthalmic goods

(G-1382)
LINDA CAMPBELL
Also Called: Campbell's Print Shop
4420 Richardson Ave (10470-1545)
PHONE..................718 994-4026
Linda Campbell, *Owner*
EMP: 7 **EST:** 1998
SALES (est): 349.4K **Privately Held**
SIC: 2759 Circulars: printing

(G-1383)
LINO PRESS INC
652 Southern Blvd (10455-3637)
PHONE..................718 665-2625
Franklin Nunez, *Owner*
EMP: 20
SALES (est): 1.2MM **Privately Held**
SIC: 2741 Miscellaneous publishing

(G-1384)
M J M TOOLING CORP
Also Called: Sutter Machine Tool and Die
1059 Washington Ave (10456-6636)
PHONE..................718 292-3590
John Rottenkolber, *President*
Michael Rottenkolber, *Treasurer*
EMP: 9
SALES (est): 660K **Privately Held**
SIC: 3544 Special dies & tools

(G-1385)
MARATHON ENTERPRISES INC
Also Called: House O'Weenies
787 E 138th St (10454-1989)
PHONE..................718 665-2560
Fax: 718 292-0610
Allan Thoreson, *Manager*
EMP: 60
SALES (corp-wide): 25.8MM **Privately Held**
WEB: www.sabrett.com
SIC: 2013 Frankfurters from purchased meat
PA: Marathon Enterprises, Inc.
9 Smith St
Englewood NJ 07631
201 935-3330

(G-1386)
MARINE BOILER & WELDING INC
1428 Sheridan Expy (10459-2106)
PHONE..................718 378-1900
William Falco, *President*
Thomas Falco, *Vice Pres*
EMP: 12
SQ FT: 5,000
SALES (est): 1MM **Privately Held**
SIC: 3443 1799 Boiler & boiler shop work; welding on site

(G-1387)
MARS FASHIONS INC
780 E 134th St Fl 5 (10454-3527)
PHONE..................718 402-2200
Rafael Sanchez, *President*
Sam Mann, *Treasurer*
Stuart Mann, *Admin Sec*
EMP: 50
SQ FT: 25,000
SALES: 756.9K **Privately Held**
SIC: 2339 2253 Women's & misses' athletic clothing & sportswear; knit outerwear mills

(G-1388)
MASON TRANSPARENT PACKAGE INC
1180 Commerce Ave (10462-5506)
PHONE..................718 792-6000
Fax: 718 823-7279
Richard Cole, *President*
Ellen Cole, *Vice Pres*
Kevin O'Connell, *Vice Pres*
Sylvia A Cole, *Admin Sec*
EMP: 30 **EST:** 1947
SQ FT: 25,000
SALES (est): 3.8MM **Privately Held**
WEB: www.masontransparent.com
SIC: 2671 2673 2759 Plastic film, coated or laminated for packaging; plastic bags: made from purchased materials; commercial printing

(G-1389)
MATERIALS DESIGN WORKSHOP
830 Barry St (10474-5707)
PHONE..................718 893-1954
Fax: 718 842-1122
Eugene Black, *President*
Avelin Rameiz, *Administration*
EMP: 14 **EST:** 1973
SQ FT: 11,000
SALES (est): 1.3MM **Privately Held**
SIC: 2521 Wood office furniture; cabinets, office: wood

(G-1390)
MELITA CORP
828 E 144th St (10454-1702)
PHONE..................718 392-7280
Emanuel Darmanin, *Ch of Bd*
Joann Atek, *COO*
Jack Darmanin, *VP Prdtn*
Michelle D' Oleivra, *Purchasing*
Michael Cassar, *CFO*
EMP: 201
SQ FT: 44,000
SALES (est): 44.7MM **Privately Held**
SIC: 2051 5411 Bread, cake & related products; grocery stores

(G-1391)
MENU SOLUTIONS INC
4510 White Plains Rd (10470-1609)
PHONE..................718 575-5160
Irwin Joel Borracas, *CEO*
Praful Pandya, *Controller*
▲ **EMP:** 75 **EST:** 1996
SALES: 3.2MM **Privately Held**
WEB: www.menucovers.biz
SIC: 2759 Commercial printing

(G-1392)
MERCURY LOCK AND DOOR SERVICE
529 C Wortham St (10474)
PHONE..................718 542-7048
Howard Levine, *President*
EMP: 29
SALES (est): 2.3MM **Privately Held**
SIC: 3442 Fire doors, metal

(G-1393)
METALLINE FIRE DOOR CO INC (PA)
4110 Park Ave (10457-6017)
PHONE..................718 583-2320

GEOGRAPHIC SECTION

Fax: 718 294-5681
Lydia Rodriguez, *President*
William Rodriguez, *Vice Pres*
EMP: 20
SQ FT: 12,500
SALES (est): 5.1MM **Privately Held**
SIC: 3442 5072 Fire doors, metal; window & door frames; hardware

(G-1394)
METALWORKS INC
1303 Herschell St (10461-3622)
PHONE.................................718 319-0011
Michael Josephs, *Ch of Bd*
Jeff Dynhas, *Vice Pres*
John Single, *Production*
Jeff Duvall, *CFO*
Denise Josephs, *Admin Sec*
EMP: 30
SQ FT: 15,000
SALES (est): 3.6MM **Privately Held**
SIC: 3446 Architectural metalwork

(G-1395)
METROPOLITAN SIGN & RIGGIN
330 Casanova St (10474-6708)
PHONE.................................718 231-0010
Dave Wehmeier, *President*
Tamara Kelly, *Manager*
EMP: 5
SALES (est): 523.9K **Privately Held**
SIC: 3993 Signs & advertising specialties

(G-1396)
MIL & MIR STEEL PRODUCTS CO
1210 Randall Ave (10474-6399)
PHONE.................................718 328-7596
Fax: 718 328-7913
William Miraglia, *President*
EMP: 6 **EST:** 1958
SQ FT: 5,000
SALES: 350K **Privately Held**
SIC: 3537 Lift trucks, industrial; fork, platform, straddle, etc.

(G-1397)
MILLENNIUM RMNFCTRED TONER INC
7 Bruckner Blvd (10454-4411)
PHONE.................................718 585-9887
Fax: 718 585-7445
Frank Garcia, *President*
Charles Baker, *Senior VP*
EMP: 11
SALES (est): 920K **Privately Held**
WEB: www.mrtoners.com
SIC: 2893 Printing ink

(G-1398)
MILLER BLAKER INC
620 E 132nd St (10454-4603)
PHONE.................................718 665-3930
Cliff Blaker, *Ch of Bd*
Lee Miller, *Senior VP*
Rabin Ramcharan, *Vice Pres*
Don Broas, *Project Mgr*
Rachel Lime, *Purch Agent*
▲ **EMP:** 100
SQ FT: 50,000
SALES (est): 17.3MM **Privately Held**
WEB: www.millerblaker.com
SIC: 2431 2521 Interior & ornamental woodwork & trim; wood office furniture

(G-1399)
MISS GRIMBLE ASSOCIATES INC
Also Called: Grimble Bakery
909 E 135th St (10454-3611)
PHONE.................................718 665-2253
Errol Bier, *President*
Craig Bier, *Sales Mgr*
EMP: 12
SQ FT: 15,000
SALES (est): 720K **Privately Held**
WEB: www.missgrimble.com
SIC: 2051 Bakery: wholesale or wholesale/retail combined

(G-1400)
MODULAR MEDICAL CORP
1513 Olmstead Ave (10462-4254)
PHONE.................................718 829-2626
Fax: 718 430-0914

Jeffery S Offner, *President*
Peter Wachs, *Vice Pres*
EMP: 30
SQ FT: 30,000
SALES (est): 1.6MM **Privately Held**
SIC: 3841 Surgical & medical instruments

(G-1401)
MONA SLIDE FASTENERS INC (PA)
Also Called: Mona Belts
4510 White Plains Rd (10470-1609)
PHONE.................................718 325-7700
Fax: 718 324-7222
Joel Barrocas, *President*
Mona Barrocas, *Vice Pres*
▲ **EMP:** 50 **EST:** 1944
SQ FT: 30,000
SALES (est): 10.8MM **Privately Held**
SIC: 3965 Buttons & parts

(G-1402)
MONARCH ELECTRIC PRODUCTS INC
Also Called: Vicron Electronic Mfg
4077 Park Ave Fl 5 (10457-7310)
PHONE.................................718 583-7996
Fax: 718 299-9121
▲ **EMP:** 6 **EST:** 1946
SQ FT: 5,000
SALES (est): 500K **Privately Held**
SIC: 3643 Mfg Fluorescent Starting Switches

(G-1403)
MONTE PRESS INC
4808 White Plains Rd (10470-1102)
PHONE.................................718 325-4999
Fax: 718 324-5017
Barbara Deangelo, *President*
EMP: 5
SQ FT: 2,400
SALES (est): 320K **Privately Held**
SIC: 2752 Commercial printing, offset

(G-1404)
N & L FUEL CORP
2014 Blackrock Ave (10472-6104)
PHONE.................................718 863-3538
Nick Leandro, *Principal*
EMP: 8
SALES (est): 947.5K **Privately Held**
SIC: 2869 Fuels

(G-1405)
NATIONAL EQUIPMENT CORPORATION (PA)
Also Called: Union Standard Eqp Co Div
801 E 141st St 825 (10454-1917)
PHONE.................................718 585-0200
Fax: 718 993-2650
Arthur A Greenberg, *Ch of Bd*
Andrew Greenberg, *President*
James Greenberg, *President*
John Greenberg, *President*
Charles Greenberg, *Exec VP*
◆ **EMP:** 18
SQ FT: 260,000
SALES (est): 10.3MM **Privately Held**
SIC: 3556 3559 3565 5084 Food products machinery; confectionery machinery; chemical machinery & equipment; pharmaceutical machinery; packaging machinery; processing & packaging equipment

(G-1406)
NATIONAL EQUIPMENT CORPORATION
Also Called: Union Standard & Un Conf McHy
801 E 141st St (10454-1917)
PHONE.................................718 585-0200
Eddie Greenberg, *Manager*
EMP: 30
SALES (corp-wide): 10.3MM **Privately Held**
SIC: 3556 3559 3565 5084 Food products machinery; confectionery machinery; chemical machinery & equipment; pharmaceutical machinery; packaging machinery; processing & packaging equipment
PA: National Equipment Corporation
801 E 141st St 825
Bronx NY 10454
718 585-0200

(G-1407)
NATIONAL STEEL RULE DIE INC
2407 3rd Ave (10451-6301)
PHONE.................................718 402-1396
Frank G Curatolo, *President*
Mark Sanders, *Manager*
Ray Farina, *Executive*
EMP: 14 **EST:** 1945
SQ FT: 5,000
SALES: 900K **Privately Held**
SIC: 3544 Dies, steel rule

(G-1408)
NEW YORK BOTTLING CO INC
Also Called: Mayim Chaim Beverages
626 Whittier St (10474-6121)
PHONE.................................718 963-3232
Zvi Hold, *President*
Joseph Hold, *Vice Pres*
Racheal Hold, *Admin Sec*
Esta Kohn, *Admin Sec*
EMP: 12 **EST:** 1967
SQ FT: 10,000
SALES (est): 2.2MM **Privately Held**
SIC: 2086 Soft drinks: packaged in cans, bottles, etc.

(G-1409)
NEW YORK INDUSTRIAL WORKS INC (PA)
796 E 140th St (10454-1915)
PHONE.................................718 292-0615
Gary Mahoni, *President*
Eve Polanco, *Admin Mgr*
EMP: 8 **EST:** 1979
SQ FT: 6,000
SALES (est): 2.4MM **Privately Held**
WEB: www.newdraulictools.com
SIC: 3546 Power-driven handtools; guns, pneumatic: chip removal

(G-1410)
NEX-GEN READY MIX CORP
334 Faile St (10474-7120)
PHONE.................................347 231-0073
Salvatore Bullaro, *Chairman*
EMP: 6
SALES (est): 792.1K **Privately Held**
SIC: 3273 Ready-mixed concrete

(G-1411)
NICHOLAS DFINE FURN DECORATORS
546 E 170th St 48 (10456-2302)
PHONE.................................914 245-8982
Fax: 718 538-1201
Helen Savastano, *President*
Frank Savastano, *Owner*
Vincent Savastano, *Corp Secy*
Nicholas Savastano, *Vice Pres*
EMP: 15
SQ FT: 6,600
SALES (est): 1.7MM **Privately Held**
SIC: 2511 2512 2521 7641 Wood household furniture; upholstered household furniture; wood office furniture; antique furniture repair & restoration

(G-1412)
NOROC ENTERPRISES INC (PA)
415 Concord Ave (10455-4801)
PHONE.................................718 585-3230
Fax: 718 292-2243
Elias Wexler, *CEO*
Jerry Heid, *Vice Pres*
Constantin Constantinide, *Research*
Steve Petko, *Sales Staff*
◆ **EMP:** 40 **EST:** 1928
SQ FT: 27,000
SALES (est): 17.8MM **Privately Held**
WEB: www.zerointernational.com
SIC: 3251 3053 Fireproofing tile, clay; gasket materials

(G-1413)
NORTH BRONX RETINAL & OPHTHLMI
3725 Henry Hudson Pkwy (10463-1527)
PHONE.................................347 535-4932
Daniel Chechik MD, *Ch of Bd*
EMP: 8
SALES (est): 1MM **Privately Held**
SIC: 3851 Ophthalmic goods

(G-1414)
NYBG
2900 Southern Blvd (10458-5126)
PHONE.................................718 817-8700
Gregory Long, *Principal*
EMP: 9
SALES (est): 754K **Privately Held**
SIC: 2741 Miscellaneous publishing

(G-1415)
NYSCO PRODUCTS LLC
2350 Lafayette Ave (10473-1104)
P.O. Box 725 (10473-0725)
PHONE.................................718 792-9000
Barry Kramer, *President*
Glenn Smith, *Vice Pres*
Stephen Yeh, *Design Engr*
Patricia Albright, *Human Res Dir*
Albert Lian, *VP Sales*
▲ **EMP:** 60 **EST:** 1935
SQ FT: 80,000
SALES (est): 11.9MM **Privately Held**
WEB: www.nysco.com
SIC: 3993 Signs & advertising specialties

(G-1416)
OMC INC
4010 Park Ave (10457-7397)
PHONE.................................718 731-5001
James O'Halpin, *President*
Mike Checci, *Corp Secy*
Robert Moteti, *Vice Pres*
Joe Checchi, *Manager*
EMP: 110
SQ FT: 25,000
SALES (est): 19.1MM **Privately Held**
WEB: www.omcdrafting.com
SIC: 3444 Sheet metalwork

(G-1417)
OPERATIVE CAKE CORP
Also Called: Lady Linda Cakes
711 Brush Ave (10465-1839)
P.O. Box 1017 (10465-0623)
PHONE.................................718 278-5600
Matthew Jacobson, *President*
Mark Jacobson, *President*
Sam Jacobson, *Vice Pres*
EMP: 50
SQ FT: 60,000
SALES (est): 6.8MM
SALES (corp-wide): 43.3MM **Privately Held**
WEB: www.groceryhaulers.com
SIC: 2051 5149 Bread, cake & related products; bakery products
PA: Grocery Haulers, Inc.
581 Main St Ste 510
Woodbridge NJ 07095
732 499-3745

(G-1418)
P & M SAFE AMERICA LLC
555 Longfellow Ave (10474-6913)
PHONE.................................718 292-6363
Prashant Parsram,
EMP: 15
SALES (est): 1.4MM **Privately Held**
WEB: www.safeamericaproducts.com
SIC: 3089 Automotive parts, plastic

(G-1419)
PACIFIC DESIGNS INTL INC
2743 Webster Ave (10458-3705)
PHONE.................................718 364-2867
Edward Nerenberg, *President*
Marisha Torres, *Assistant*
EMP: 5
SALES (est): 416.4K **Privately Held**
SIC: 3081 Floor or wall covering, unsupported plastic

(G-1420)
PARADIGM GROUP LLC
1357 Lafayette Ave Frnt 1 (10474-4847)
PHONE.................................718 860-1538
Vuac Heflaz, *Principal*
EMP: 5
SALES (est): 478.3K **Privately Held**
SIC: 3471 3479 Finishing, metals or formed products; hot dip coating of metals or formed products

Bronx - Bronx County (G-1421) GEOGRAPHIC SECTION

(G-1421)
PARKCHESTER DPS LLC
2000 E Tremont Ave (10462-5703)
PHONE.................................718 823-4411
Richard Vargas, *Manager*
EMP: 107
SALES (est): 9.1MM Privately Held
SIC: 3841 Surgical & medical instruments

(G-1422)
PATIENT-WEAR LLC
3940 Merritt Ave (10466-2502)
PHONE.................................914 740-7770
Thomas A Keith, *President*
EMP: 8
SALES: 950K Privately Held
SIC: 2389 Apparel & accessories

(G-1423)
PELICAN PRODUCTS CO INC (PA)
1049 Lowell St (10459-2608)
PHONE.................................718 860-3220
Fax: 718 860-4415
Kenneth Silver, *President*
David Silver, *Vice Pres*
Jan Pawelec, *Treasurer*
▲ EMP: 29 EST: 1946
SQ FT: 20,000
SALES (est): 2.5MM Privately Held
WEB: www.pelicanproducts.com
SIC: 3951 3089 Pens & mechanical pencils; novelties, plastic

(G-1424)
PEPSI-COLA BOTTLING CO NY INC
650 Brush Ave (10465-1804)
PHONE.................................718 892-1570
Jon Banner, *Exec VP*
Michael Moral, *Manager*
EMP: 75
SALES (corp-wide): 219.3MM Privately Held
SIC: 2086 Soft drinks: packaged in cans, bottles, etc.
PA: Pepsi-Cola Bottling Company Of New York, Inc.
11402 15th Ave Ste 5
College Point NY 11356
718 392-1000

(G-1425)
PERRIGO COMPANY
1625 Bathgate Ave (10457-8101)
PHONE.................................718 960-9900
Ange Francois, *Project Mgr*
Ori Gutwerg, *Natl Sales Mgr*
Joseph C Papa, *Branch Mgr*
Vikrant Bandekar, *Manager*
Michael Fissehaye, *Manager*
EMP: 34 Privately Held
SIC: 2834 Pharmaceutical preparations; analgesics; cold remedies; vitamin preparations
HQ: Perrigo Company
515 Eastern Ave
Allegan MI 49010
269 673-8451

(G-1426)
PERRIGO NEW YORK INC
455 Claremont Pkwy (10457-8301)
PHONE.................................718 901-2800
Oscar Camejo, *Manager*
EMP: 15 Privately Held
WEB: www.agis-group.com
SIC: 2834 Pharmaceutical preparations; ointments; dermatologicals
HQ: Perrigo New York, Inc.
1700 Bathgate Ave
Bronx NY 10457
718 960-9900

(G-1427)
PERRIGO NEW YORK INC (DH)
Also Called: Suppositoria Laboratory
1700 Bathgate Ave (10457-7512)
PHONE.................................718 960-9900
Joseph C Papa, *Ch of Bd*
Giora Carni, *President*
Raj Thota, *General Mgr*
Ofir Sova, *Vice Pres*
Mike Marcano, *Project Mgr*
▲ EMP: 500

SQ FT: 300,000
SALES (est): 108.3MM Privately Held
WEB: www.agis-group.com
SIC: 2834 Pharmaceutical preparations; ointments; dermatologicals
HQ: Perrigo Company
515 Eastern Ave
Allegan MI 49010
269 673-8451

(G-1428)
PLACE VENDOME HOLDING CO INC (PA)
Also Called: R & F Marketing
4238 Bronx Blvd Frnt 2 (10466-2671)
PHONE.................................212 696-0765
Rhonda Finkelstein, *Ch of Bd*
Jibreel Champion, *Project Mgr*
▲ EMP: 8
SQ FT: 3,500
SALES: 15MM Privately Held
WEB: www.rfmarketing.com
SIC: 2392 Household furnishings; pillows, bed: made from purchased materials

(G-1429)
POLYSEAL PACKAGING CORP
1178 E 180th St (10460-2401)
P.O. Box 1171, New York (10035-0807)
PHONE.................................718 792-5530
Fax: 718 792-5582
Lewis Matthews, *President*
Carol Smith, *Vice Pres*
EMP: 20
SQ FT: 20,000
SALES (est): 1.9MM Privately Held
SIC: 2673 2674 Plastic bags: made from purchased materials; paper bags: made from purchased materials

(G-1430)
PONCIO SIGNS
3007 Albany Cres (10463-5960)
PHONE.................................718 543-4851
Poncio Salcedo, *Owner*
EMP: 7 EST: 1962
SQ FT: 700
SALES (est): 290K Privately Held
SIC: 3993 Signs, not made in custom sign painting shops

(G-1431)
POORAN PALLET INC
319 Barretto St (10474-6722)
PHONE.................................718 938-7970
Zainool Pooran, *President*
EMP: 5
SQ FT: 5,000
SALES: 300K Privately Held
SIC: 2448 Pallets, wood & wood with metal

(G-1432)
PORK KING SAUSAGE INC
F22 Hunts Point Co Op Mkt (10474-7568)
PHONE.................................718 542-2810
Fax: 718 542-2847
Dominick Puntolillo, *President*
Frank Puntolillo, *Vice Pres*
Sean McGonigle, *Manager*
EMP: 25
SQ FT: 10,000
SALES (est): 5MM Privately Held
SIC: 2013 Sausages & other prepared meats

(G-1433)
PRECISION ORNA IR WORKS INC
Also Called: Precision Furniture
1838 Adee Ave (10469-3245)
PHONE.................................718 379-5200
Fax: 718 320-1270
Joseph Napolitano, *President*
Anthony Napolitano, *Vice Pres*
Philip Napolitano, *Admin Sec*
EMP: 9
SQ FT: 40,000
SALES: 700K Privately Held
WEB: www.precisionfurniture.com
SIC: 2514 Household furniture: upholstered on metal frames

(G-1434)
PRECISION TECHNIQUES INC
1169 E 156th St (10474-2206)
PHONE.................................718 991-1440

Fax: 718 991-1447
Paul Mangione, *President*
Joseph De Savage, *Corp Secy*
▲ EMP: 85
SQ FT: 70,000
SALES (est): 10.8MM Privately Held
WEB: www.precisiontechniquesinc.com
SIC: 3089 4783 Injection molding of plastics; packing & crating

(G-1435)
PREMIUM OCEAN LLC
1271 Ryawa Ave (10474-7114)
PHONE.................................917 231-1061
Marie Joseph, *Manager*
Esraim Basson,
Juliana Paparizou,
▲ EMP: 15
SALES (est): 4.5MM Privately Held
SIC: 2091 Seafood products: packaged in cans, jars, etc.

(G-1436)
PULSE PLASTICS PRODUCTS INC
1156 E 165th St (10459-2693)
P.O. Box 1228 (10459-1164)
PHONE.................................718 328-5224
Alan J Backelman, *President*
Mike Backelman, *General Mgr*
EMP: 25
SQ FT: 23,000
SALES (est): 1.5MM Privately Held
WEB: www.pulseplastics.com
SIC: 3089 Molding primary plastic

(G-1437)
QUALITY HM BRANDS HOLDINGS LLC (PA)
125 Rose Feiss Blvd (10454-3624)
PHONE.................................718 292-2024
Maurice Feiss, *Mng Member*
Thomas Bilbrough,
William J Haley,
▲ EMP: 3
SALES (est): 161.3MM Privately Held
SIC: 3645 5063 Residential lighting fixtures; lighting fixtures; lighting fixtures, residential

(G-1438)
QUALITY MILLWORK CORP
425 Devoe Ave (10460-2309)
P.O. Box 479 (10460-0241)
PHONE.................................718 892-2250
Anthony Guarino, *President*
▲ EMP: 28
SQ FT: 45,000
SALES (est): 3.6MM Privately Held
SIC: 2431 Doors, wood

(G-1439)
R GOLDSMITH
1974 Mayflower Ave (10461-4007)
PHONE.................................718 239-1396
Claudine Bryan, *Branch Mgr*
EMP: 10
SALES (est): 540.9K Privately Held
SIC: 3914 Silversmithing

(G-1440)
REEFER TEK LLC
885 E 149th St Fl 2a (10455-5010)
PHONE.................................347 590-1067
Michael Liedman, *Managing Dir*
▲ EMP: 12 EST: 2010
SQ FT: 12,000
SALES (est): 1.4MM Privately Held
SIC: 3559 Automotive related machinery

(G-1441)
ROANWELL CORPORATION
Also Called: Paramount Cords
2564 Park Ave (10451-6014)
PHONE.................................718 401-0288
Fax: 718 401-0663
Barbara Labarre, *CEO*
Jonathan Labarre, *President*
William Rathban, *Principal*
Marcelle Wahba, *Purch Mgr*
Lech Perdowski, *Chief Engr*
▼ EMP: 45
SQ FT: 28,000

SALES: 6MM Privately Held
WEB: www.roanwellcorp.com
SIC: 3669 Intercommunication systems, electric

(G-1442)
ROCKING THE BOAT INC
812 Edgewater Rd (10474-4902)
PHONE.................................718 466-5799
Amy Kantroitz, *President*
Victor Isayev, *Finance*
Adam Green, *Exec Dir*
Brian Bytnar, *Director*
Bryce Lefort, *Director*
EMP: 10
SALES: 2.1MM Privately Held
WEB: www.rockingtheboat.org
SIC: 3732 Non-motorized boat, building & repairing

(G-1443)
S & S FASHIONS INC
941 Longfellow Ave (10474-4810)
PHONE.................................718 328-0001
Sageev Mangal, *President*
EMP: 5
SQ FT: 18,000
SALES: 4MM Privately Held
SIC: 2329 Men's & boys' sportswear & athletic clothing

(G-1444)
S & S SOAP CO INC
815 E 135th St (10454-3584)
PHONE.................................718 585-2900
Fax: 718 585-2902
Zvi Sebrow, *President*
Joseph Sebrow, *Admin Sec*
EMP: 20 EST: 1930
SQ FT: 40,000
SALES (est): 4.2MM Privately Held
WEB: www.blutex.com
SIC: 2841 Detergents, synthetic organic or inorganic alkaline

(G-1445)
S & V RESTAURANT EQP MFRS INC
Also Called: Custom Cool
4320 Park Ave (10457-2442)
PHONE.................................718 220-1140
Fax: 718 364-1764
Sam Zeltser, *CEO*
Shlomo Zeltser, *President*
Vyacheslav Ulman, *Corp Secy*
Zelig Zeltser, *Vice Pres*
EMP: 46
SQ FT: 35,000
SALES (est): 9.7MM Privately Held
WEB: www.customcool.com
SIC: 3585 Refrigeration equipment, complete

(G-1446)
SACCOMIZE INC
1554 Stillwell Ave (10461-2212)
PHONE.................................818 287-3000
Fax: 718 918-0081
Anthony Saccommanno, *President*
Thomas Saccommanno, *Vice Pres*
EMP: 9
SQ FT: 5,000
SALES (est): 768K Privately Held
WEB: www.saccomize.com
SIC: 3471 7542 Finishing, metals or formed products; washing & polishing, automotive

(G-1447)
SANJAY PALLETS INC
424 Coster St (10474-6811)
PHONE.................................347 590-2485
Mohamed Salem Shaheed, *CEO*
EMP: 8
SALES (est): 1.1MM Privately Held
SIC: 2448 Pallets, wood & wood with metal

(G-1448)
SBK PRESERVES INC
Also Called: Sarabeth's Bakery
1161 E 156th St (10474-6226)
PHONE.................................800 773-7378
Fax: 718 589-8412
William Levine, *Ch of Bd*
Suzanne B Levine, *Vice Pres*
Jason Albucker, *Marketing Staff*

▲ = Import ▼ = Export
♦ = Import/Export

Sigal Seeber, *Marketing Staff*
▲ **EMP:** 40
SQ FT: 15,000
SALES (est): 7.1MM Privately Held
SIC: 2033 5149 5961 Jams, including imitation: packaged in cans, jars, etc.; preserves, including imitation: in cans, jars, etc.; pickles, preserves, jellies & jams; food, mail order

(G-1449)
SCACCIANOCE INC
Also Called: Daisy Brand Confectionery
1165 Burnett Pl (10474-5716)
PHONE..............................718 991-4462
Fax: 718 991-0154
Donald Beck, *President*
Anthony Scaccianoce, *Vice Pres*
Allen Gross, *CPA*
▲ **EMP:** 10 EST: 1904
SQ FT: 10,000
SALES (est): 964.8K Privately Held
SIC: 2064 2068 Candy & other confectionery products; salted & roasted nuts & seeds

(G-1450)
SENSORMATIC ELECTRONICS LLC
1575 Williamsbridge Rd 3c (10461-6209)
PHONE..............................718 597-6719
EMP: 15 Privately Held
WEB: www.sensormatic.com
SIC: 3812 Detection apparatus: electronic/magnetic field, light/heat
HQ: Sensormatic Electronics, Llc
6600 Congress Ave
Boca Raton FL 33487
561 912-6000

(G-1451)
SHARON METAL STAMPING CORP
Also Called: Aai Manufacturing Div
1457 Bassett Ave (10461-2393)
PHONE..............................718 828-4510
Hyman Kramer, *President*
Rhoda Kramer, *Corp Secy*
EMP: 5
SQ FT: 5,000
SALES (est): 390K Privately Held
SIC: 3469 3544 Metal stampings; special dies & tools

(G-1452)
SIDCO FOOD DISTRIBUTION CORP
2324 Webster Ave (10458-7506)
PHONE..............................718 733-3939
Fax: 718 584-1863
Jose Negron, *Ch of Bd*
Wilma Negron, *COO*
Lois Rodriguez, *Vice Pres*
Maria Marte, *Accounting Mgr*
EMP: 15
SQ FT: 10,000
SALES (est): 7.2MM Privately Held
SIC: 3556 1541 Food products machinery; food products manufacturing or packing plant construction

(G-1453)
SIDNEY A BUSH CO
728 E 136th St Ste 4 (10454-3431)
PHONE..............................718 742-9629
Fax: 718 563-7926
Michael Raske, *President*
Carol Warshaw, *Vice Pres*
EMP: 20 EST: 1946
SQ FT: 6,000
SALES (est): 916.4K Privately Held
SIC: 2341 Slips: women's, misses', children's & infants'

(G-1454)
SIGMA MANUFACTURING INDS INC
1361 E Bay Ave (10474-7025)
PHONE..............................718 842-9180
Fax: 718 991-4094
Apostolos Siantos, *President*
Yuri Reznik, *Corp Secy*
EMP: 13
SQ FT: 12,000

SALES (est): 3MM Privately Held
WEB: www.sigma-mfg.com
SIC: 3599 Machine shop, jobbing & repair

(G-1455)
SIGNATURE METAL MBL MAINT LLC
791 E 132nd St (10454-3512)
PHONE..............................718 292-8280
Howard Cheng, *Opers Staff*
Robert Brennan, *VP Sales*
Gary Swartz,
EMP: 100
SALES (est): 15.1MM Privately Held
SIC: 3449 Miscellaneous metalwork

(G-1456)
SKECHERS USA INC
Also Called: Skechers Factory Outlet 315
651 River Ave (10451-2113)
PHONE..............................718 585-3024
Daniel Lugo, *Branch Mgr*
EMP: 18
SALES (corp-wide): 3.1B Publicly Held
SIC: 3021 Rubber & plastics footwear
PA: Skechers U.S.A., Inc.
228 Manhattan Beach Blvd # 200
Manhattan Beach CA 90266
310 318-3100

(G-1457)
SML BROTHERS HOLDING CORP
820 E 140th St (10454-1904)
PHONE..............................718 402-2000
Michael Landau, *Vice Pres*
Jason Landau, *Research*
Mel Weinzimer, *Sales Staff*
Trish Brosnan, *MIS Dir*
Stephen Landau, *Admin Sec*
▲ **EMP:** 85 EST: 1976
SALES (est): 19MM Privately Held
WEB: www.polytexink.com
SIC: 3952 2851 2865 Ink, drawing: black & colored; paints & paint additives; color pigments, organic

(G-1458)
SOFA DOCTOR INC
Also Called: Dr Sofa
220 E 134th St Frnt 1b (10451-6410)
PHONE..............................718 292-6300
Shlomie Eini, *President*
EMP: 8 EST: 2004
SALES (est): 899K Privately Held
SIC: 2512 7641 Upholstered household furniture; furniture upholstery repair

(G-1459)
SPACE AGE PLSTC FBRCATORS INC
4519 White Plains Rd (10470-1680)
PHONE..............................718 324-4062
Fax: 212 994-0582
Arthur Barsky, *President*
Joel Barsky, *Vice Pres*
Loel Barsky, *Vice Pres*
Helena Barsky, *Human Res Mgr*
EMP: 15 EST: 1964
SQ FT: 12,000
SALES (est): 2.6MM Privately Held
WEB: www.plastic64.com
SIC: 3089 Plastic hardware & building products

(G-1460)
SPARROW MINING CO (PA)
3743 White Plains Rd (10467-5754)
PHONE..............................718 519-6600
Randolph Silverstein, *Partner*
David Silverstein, *Partner*
EMP: 7
SALES (est): 1.3MM Privately Held
SIC: 1442 Sand mining

(G-1461)
SPECIALTY STEEL FABG CORP
555 Longfellow Ave (10474-6913)
PHONE..............................718 893-6326
Fax: 718 861-5805
Gregory Burns, *President*
Warren Wilhelm, *Vice Pres*
EMP: 14
SQ FT: 12,000

SALES (est): 1.7MM Privately Held
WEB: www.specialtysteelinternational.com
SIC: 3441 5051 5084 Fabricated structural metal; metals service centers & offices; industrial machinery & equipment

(G-1462)
ST RAYMOND MONUMENT CO
2727 Lafayette Ave (10465-2228)
PHONE..............................718 824-3600
Raymond Carotenuto, *President*
Ethel Carotenuto, *Corp Secy*
EMP: 5
SQ FT: 1,200
SALES (est): 414.9K Privately Held
SIC: 3272 5999 Monuments, concrete; tombstones, precast terrazzo or concrete; monuments, finished to custom order

(G-1463)
STANDARD PAPER BOX MACHINE CO
347 Coster St Fl 2 (10474-6813)
PHONE..............................718 328-3300
Fax: 718 842-7772
Aaron Adams, *Ch of Bd*
Bruce Adams, *President*
Larry Wilson, *Vice Pres*
Vicki Adams, *Treasurer*
▲ **EMP:** 25
SQ FT: 35,000
SALES (est): 3.6MM Privately Held
SIC: 3554 3542 Box making machines, paper; die cutting & stamping machinery, paper converting; machine tools, metal forming type

(G-1464)
STARLITE PNT & VARNISH CO INC
Also Called: Starlight Paint Factory
724 E 140th St (10454-2405)
PHONE..............................718 292-6420
Peter J Gorynski Jr, *President*
Leo Gorynski, *Vice Pres*
EMP: 5 EST: 1938
SQ FT: 9,000
SALES (est): 2.5MM Privately Held
SIC: 2851 5231 Paints & paint additives; paint

(G-1465)
STEVEN JOHN OPTICIANS
5901 Riverdale Ave (10471-1602)
PHONE..............................718 543-3336
Steven John, *Owner*
EMP: 9
SALES (est): 670K Privately Held
SIC: 3827 Optical instruments & lenses

(G-1466)
STREAMLINE PLASTICS CO INC
2590 Park Ave (10451-6014)
PHONE..............................718 401-4000
Fax: 718 401-8540
Joseph Bartner, *President*
Stewart Bartner, *Vice Pres*
Beatrice Bartner, *Admin Sec*
EMP: 35 EST: 1939
SALES (est): 7.9MM Privately Held
SIC: 3089 Extruded finished plastic products; injection molded finished plastic products

(G-1467)
SUPERMARKET EQUIPMENT DEPO INC
1135 Bronx River Ave (10472-3101)
P.O. Box 368, Mountain Dale (12763-0368)
PHONE..............................718 665-6200
Daniel Resnick, *President*
Randy Resnick, *Sales Mgr*
EMP: 7
SALES: 2.5MM Privately Held
SIC: 3585 Refrigeration & heating equipment

(G-1468)
SUPREME FIRE-PROOF DOOR CO INC
391 Rider Ave (10451-5905)
PHONE..............................718 665-4224
Fax: 718 402-5807
Wazier Mahmood, *President*
Carla Kanglie, *Vice Pres*

Khan Fizul, *Manager*
EMP: 10 EST: 1942
SQ FT: 2,500
SALES (est): 1.2MM Privately Held
SIC: 3442 Fire doors, metal

(G-1469)
SVYZ TRADING CORP
4320 Park Ave (10457-2442)
PHONE..............................718 220-1140
Sam Zeltser, *Principal*
Zelk Zeltser, *Vice Pres*
Steve Ulman, *Admin Sec*
▲ **EMP:** 6
SQ FT: 5,000
SALES (est): 797.5K Privately Held
SIC: 3822 Refrigeration/air-conditioning defrost controls

(G-1470)
T J RONAN PAINT CORP
Also Called: Ronan Paints
749 E 135th St (10454-3408)
PHONE..............................718 292-1100
Fax: 718 292-0406
Dennis Doran, *Ch of Bd*
John A Doran Jr, *Corp Secy*
John Doran, *Treasurer*
John A Doran Jr, *Treasurer*
▼ **EMP:** 25 EST: 1984
SQ FT: 35,000
SALES (est): 5MM Privately Held
WEB: www.ronanpaints.com
SIC: 2851 Paints & paint additives

(G-1471)
T M INTERNATIONAL LLC
Also Called: Mazzella Blasting Mat Co
413 Faile St 15 (10474-6907)
P.O. Box 10930, Fairfield NJ (07004-6930)
PHONE..............................718 842-0949
Fax: 718 328-6021
Frank Stagnito, *President*
EMP: 7
SQ FT: 45,000
SALES (est): 1MM Privately Held
WEB: www.tmi2001.com
SIC: 2298 Blasting mats, rope

(G-1472)
TARA RIFIC SCREEN PRINTING INC
4197 Park Ave (10457-6033)
PHONE..............................718 583-6864
Sandy Stein, *President*
Jason Holden, *Manager*
EMP: 7
SALES: 170K Privately Held
SIC: 2759 Screen printing

(G-1473)
TOSCA BRICK OVEN PIZZA REAL
4038 E Tremont Ave (10465-3018)
PHONE..............................718 430-0026
Osa R Rref, *Owner*
EMP: 8
SALES (est): 443.8K Privately Held
SIC: 2045 5461 Pizza doughs, prepared: from purchased flour; bread

(G-1474)
TREMONT OFFSET INC
1500 Ericson Pl (10461-5414)
PHONE..............................718 892-7333
Robert Del Greco, *President*
Janet Del Greco, *Vice Pres*
EMP: 9
SQ FT: 2,000
SALES (est): 1.2MM Privately Held
SIC: 2752 Commercial printing, offset

(G-1475)
TRENCH & MARINE PUMP CO INC
3466 Park Ave (10456-4307)
P.O. Box 543 (10456-0525)
PHONE..............................212 423-9098
Fax: 212 423-0871
Herman Azia, *President*
Malcolm Azia, *Vice Pres*
Yvette Azia, *Treasurer*
EMP: 40 EST: 1918
SQ FT: 10,000

Bronx - Bronx County (G-1476)

SALES: 1.8MM **Privately Held**
SIC: 3561 3594 Pumps, domestic: water or sump; fluid power pumps & motors

(G-1476)
TRI-STATE BIODIESEL LLC
531 Barretto St (10474-6724)
PHONE..................718 860-6600
Brent Baker, *CEO*
Henry Dotson, *Opers Mgr*
Dehran Duckworth,
EMP: 63
SALES (est): 18.6MM **Privately Held**
SIC: 2911 Diesel fuels

(G-1477)
TRICEUTICAL INC
1652 Hering Ave (10461-2006)
PHONE..................631 249-0003
Richard Zhang, *President*
EMP: 12 **EST:** 2009
SALES (est): 1.1MM **Privately Held**
SIC: 2834 Druggists' preparations (pharmaceuticals)

(G-1478)
TRINE ROLLED MOULDING CORP
1421 Ferris Pl (10461-3610)
PHONE..................718 828-5200
Fax: 718 828-4052
Frank J Rella, *CEO*
Harry Jones, *Manager*
James Lange, *Director*
Blanca Cintron, *Administration*
EMP: 45 **EST:** 1942
SQ FT: 66,000
SALES: 6MM **Privately Held**
WEB: www.trinecorp.com
SIC: 3499 Metal ladders

(G-1479)
TROY SIGN & PRINTING
Also Called: Troy Sign Printing Center
4827 White Plains Rd (10470-1125)
PHONE..................718 994-4482
Leslie Peterson, *Owner*
EMP: 6
SALES (est): 475.2K **Privately Held**
SIC: 2752 Commercial printing, lithographic

(G-1480)
TRUXTON CORP
Also Called: Howard Formed Steel Pdts Div
1357 Lafayette Ave (10474-4846)
P.O. Box 225, Yonkers (10704-0225)
PHONE..................718 842-6000
Fax: 718 842-6001
Howard Schwartz, *President*
Steve Meier, *Sales Staff*
EMP: 5
SQ FT: 5,000
SALES (est): 809.3K **Privately Held**
WEB: www.mailcart.com
SIC: 3799 Pushcarts & wheelbarrows

(G-1481)
TRYLON WIRE & METAL WORKS INC
526 Tiffany St (10474-6614)
PHONE..................718 542-4472
Fax: 718 589-0177
Mark Herrmann, *President*
EMP: 25 **EST:** 1955
SQ FT: 20,000
SALES (est): 3.2MM **Privately Held**
SIC: 2542 3496 3444 Stands, merchandise display: except wood; miscellaneous fabricated wire products; sheet metalwork

(G-1482)
TWI-LAQ INDUSTRIES INC
Also Called: Stone Glo Products
1345 Seneca Ave (10474-4611)
PHONE..................718 638-5860
Lorin Wels, *President*
Robert Wels, *Vice Pres*
Steven Wels, *VP Sales*
Jon Wels, *Manager*
David Wels, *Director*
EMP: 30
SQ FT: 25,000
SALES (est): 7.1MM **Privately Held**
WEB: www.stoneglo.com
SIC: 2842 Sanitation preparations

(G-1483)
U S EMBROIDERY INC
Also Called: US Clothing Company
728 E 136th St Ste 1 (10454-3431)
PHONE..................718 585-9662
Fax: 718 292-6131
Muhammad Jahangir, *President*
EMP: 14
SQ FT: 20,000
SALES: 910K **Privately Held**
SIC: 2395 Embroidery & art needlework

(G-1484)
ULMER SALES LLC
Also Called: U K Sailmakers
175 City Island Ave (10464-1537)
PHONE..................718 885-1700
Fax: 718 885-1726
Charles Ulmer, *President*
Kerry Klinler, *Vice Pres*
EMP: 12
SQ FT: 6,500
SALES (est): 1.3MM **Privately Held**
SIC: 2394 Sails: made from purchased materials

(G-1485)
UNITED FARM PROCESSING CORP (PA)
4366 Park Ave (10457-2442)
PHONE..................718 933-6060
Marvin Weinhaus, *President*
Stephen Leibowitz, *Vice Pres*
EMP: 150
SQ FT: 31,000
SALES: 5.2MM **Privately Held**
SIC: 2035 Pickled fruits & vegetables

(G-1486)
UNITED PICKLE PRODUCTS CORP
4366 Park Ave (10457-2442)
PHONE..................718 933-6060
Fax: 718 367-8522
Marvin Weishaus, *President*
Stephen Leibowitz, *Vice Pres*
Marc Leibowitz, *Sales Mgr*
Gregg Smith, *Manager*
EMP: 49
SQ FT: 60,000
SALES: 25MM **Privately Held**
SIC: 2035 Vegetables, pickled

(G-1487)
VALENCIA BAKERY INC (PA)
801 Edgewater Rd (10474-4995)
PHONE..................718 991-6400
Fax: 718 991-6403
Roy List, *President*
Mike Eberle, *Vice Pres*
EMP: 20
SQ FT: 40,000
SALES: 2MM **Privately Held**
SIC: 2051 Bread, cake & related products

(G-1488)
VANITY FAIR BATHMART INC
2971 Webster Ave (10458-2424)
PHONE..................718 584-6700
John P O'Boyle, *President*
EMP: 10 **EST:** 1971
SQ FT: 3,500
SALES (est): 1MM **Privately Held**
WEB: www.vanityfairbathmart.com
SIC: 3431 3469 5023 5031 Bathroom fixtures, including sinks; kitchen fixtures & equipment: metal, except cast aluminum; kitchenware; lumber, plywood & millwork

(G-1489)
VICTORIA PLATING CO INC
650 Tiffany St (10474-6289)
P.O. Box 740486 (10474-0009)
PHONE..................718 589-1550
Fax: 718 378-0739
Charles Antmann, *President*
Jeffrey S Higdon, *Vice Pres*
▲**EMP:** 51
SQ FT: 45,000
SALES (est): 5.3MM **Privately Held**
WEB: www.victoriaplating.com
SIC: 3471 Electroplating of metals or formed products

(G-1490)
VIELE MANUFACTURING CORP
Also Called: Gary Plastic
1340 Viele Ave (10474-7134)
PHONE..................718 893-2200
Gary Hellinger, *CEO*
Marilyn Hellinger, *Vice Pres*
◆**EMP:** 500
SQ FT: 25,000
SALES (est): 54MM **Privately Held**
SIC: 3089 Plastic processing

(G-1491)
WACOAL AMERICA INC
1543 Saint Lawrence Ave (10460-3226)
PHONE..................718 794-1032
EMP: 115
SALES (corp-wide): 1.7B **Privately Held**
SIC: 2342 Brassieres
HQ: Wacoal America, Inc.
1 Wacoal Plz
Lyndhurst NJ 07071
201 933-8400

(G-1492)
WALDORF BAKERS INC
Also Called: Festival Bakers
909 E 135th St (10454-3611)
PHONE..................718 665-2253
Milton Bier, *Ch of Bd*
Errol M Bier, *President*
Nancy Bier, *Vice Pres*
EMP: 15
SQ FT: 13,328
SALES (est): 1MM **Privately Held**
SIC: 2051 Bread, cake & related products

(G-1493)
WENIG CORPORATION
230 Manida St Fl 2 (10474-7199)
PHONE..................718 542-3600
Fax: 718 542-3979
EMP: 30 **EST:** 1924
SQ FT: 50,000
SALES (est): 5.1MM **Privately Held**
SIC: 3444 Mfg Sheet Metalwork

(G-1494)
WEST AFRICAN MOVIES
1692 Webster Ave (10457-7307)
PHONE..................718 731-2190
EMP: 6
SALES (est): 664.9K **Privately Held**
SIC: 3695 Mfg Magnetic/Optical Recording Media

(G-1495)
YANKEE CORP
Also Called: Yankee Wiping Cloth
1180 Randall Ave (10474-6217)
PHONE..................718 589-1377
Fax: 718 589-9577
Todd W Hooper, *Chairman*
Richard Kocher, *Vice Pres*
▲**EMP:** 10
SQ FT: 16,250
SALES (est): 1.2MM **Privately Held**
SIC: 2299 5093 7218 Fabrics: linen, jute, hemp, ramie; waste rags; wiping towel supply

(G-1496)
YULA CORPORATION
330 Bryant Ave (10474-7197)
PHONE..................718 991-0900
Fax: 718 842-4239
Larry Feldman, *CEO*
Fred Feldman, *President*
Charles Robinson, *QC Mgr*
Raymond Levin, *Chief Engr*
Brigitte Wintner, *Director*
▲**EMP:** 40 **EST:** 1926
SQ FT: 20,000
SALES (est): 9.9MM **Privately Held**
WEB: www.yulacorp.com
SIC: 3443 Heat exchangers, plate type

(G-1497)
ZARO BAKE SHOP INC (PA)
Also Called: Zaro's Bread Basket
138 Bruckner Blvd (10454-4620)
PHONE..................718 993-7327
Fax: 718 292-9353
Stuart D Zaro, *Ch of Bd*
Philip Zaro, *Ch of Bd*
Stewart Zaro, *President*
Michael Zaro, *Exec VP*
Joseph Zaro, *Vice Pres*
EMP: 110
SQ FT: 40,000
SALES (est): 80.3MM **Privately Held**
WEB: www.zaro.com
SIC: 2051 2052 Bread, cake & related products; cookies & crackers

Bronxville
Westchester County

(G-1498)
ARTISANAL BRANDS INC
42 Forest Ln (10708-1936)
PHONE..................914 441-3591
Fax: 212 239-1476
Daniel W Dowe, *President*
James Lillis, *CFO*
EMP: 34
SQ FT: 10,000
SALES: 3.5MM **Privately Held**
SIC: 2022 5451 Cheese, natural & processed; cheese

(G-1499)
CLARK BOTANICALS INC
9 Paradise Rd (10708-2205)
P.O. Box 988 (10708-0988)
PHONE..................914 826-4319
Frangesco Clark, *President*
EMP: 10
SALES (est): 1.2MM **Privately Held**
SIC: 2844 Cosmetic preparations

(G-1500)
COIL-Q CORPORATION
340 Bronxville Rd (10708-2113)
PHONE..................914 779-7109
Fax: 914 779-7109
Larry Julie, *President*
EMP: 6
SALES (est): 1.1MM **Privately Held**
WEB: www.coilqcorp.com
SIC: 3677 Electronic coils, transformers & other inductors

(G-1501)
MNM SERVICE DISTRIBUTORS INC
1 Greystone Cir (10708-2314)
PHONE..................914 337-5268
Mitchell Camarda, *President*
EMP: 6
SALES: 3MM **Privately Held**
SIC: 2086 Fruit drinks (less than 100% juice): packaged in cans, etc.

(G-1502)
NOMAD EDITIONS LLC
123 Ellison Ave (10708-2728)
PHONE..................212 918-0992
Mark Edminston, *CEO*
Marjorie Martay, *Exec VP*
Samuel Spivy, *Vice Pres*
Cristine De Pedro, *CTO*
EMP: 18
SALES (est): 1MM **Privately Held**
SIC: 2759 Advertising literature: printing

(G-1503)
SOVEREIGN SERVICING SYSTEM LLC
1 Stone Pl Ste 200 (10708-3431)
PHONE..................914 779-1400
Stewart Alpert, *Principal*
EMP: 18
SALES (est): 1.2MM **Privately Held**
SIC: 1389 Roustabout service

(G-1504)
VIRTUAL URTH
80 Barrington Rd (10708-1013)
PHONE..................914 793-1269
Cezzane Huq, *President*
Tithi Malik, *Vice Pres*
EMP: 11
SALES (est): 542K **Privately Held**
WEB: www.virtualurth.com
SIC: 2721 Magazines: publishing only, not printed on site

▲ = Import ▼ = Export
◆ = Import/Export

GEOGRAPHIC SECTION

Brooklyn - Kings County (G-1533)

Brookhaven
Suffolk County

(G-1505)
AMNEAL PHARMACEUTICALS LLC
50 Horseblock Rd (11719-9509)
PHONE..................................908 231-1911
Chintu Patel, *Branch Mgr*
EMP: 50
SALES (corp-wide): 430MM **Privately Held**
SIC: 2834 Pharmaceutical preparations
PA: Amneal Pharmaceuticals, Llc
400 Crossing Blvd Fl 3
Bridgewater NJ 08807
631 952-0214

(G-1506)
AMNEAL PHARMACEUTICALS NY LLC (HQ)
50 Horseblock Rd (11719-9509)
PHONE..................................631 952-0214
Chintu Patel, *CEO*
Chirag Patel, *President*
Johnny Mikell, *Senior VP*
Sanjiv Patel, *Senior VP*
Shankar Hariharan, *Vice Pres*
▲ **EMP:** 50
SQ FT: 75,000
SALES (est): 110.3MM
SALES (corp-wide): 34.8MM **Privately Held**
WEB: www.amneal.com
SIC: 2834 5122 Pharmaceutical preparations; pharmaceuticals
PA: Amneal Pharmaceuticals Private Limited
882/1-871,
Ahmedabad GUJ 38222
866 525-7270

(G-1507)
GEOTECH ASSOCIATES LTD
20 Stiriz Rd (11719-9717)
PHONE..................................631 286-0251
Fax: 631 286-6313
Michael Verruto Jr, *President*
Linda Billski, *Bookkeeper*
EMP: 6
SQ FT: 1,500
SALES: 600K **Privately Held**
SIC: 3272 Concrete stuctural support & building material

(G-1508)
LONG ISLAND PRECAST INC
20 Stiriz Rd (11719-9717)
PHONE..................................631 286-0240
Fax: 631 286-6316
Michael Verruto, *Ch of Bd*
Michael Cetta, *Plant Mgr*
John Bilski, *Manager*
EMP: 30
SQ FT: 1,500
SALES (est): 6.2MM **Privately Held**
WEB: www.li-precast.com
SIC: 3272 Concrete products, precast

(G-1509)
POCKET SOLUTIONS INC
3 Andiron Ln (11719-9534)
PHONE..................................631 355-1073
Michael Dileo, *Principal*
EMP: 5
SALES (est): 370K **Privately Held**
WEB: www.thepocketsolution.com
SIC: 7372 Application computer software

(G-1510)
SALSBURG DIMENSIONAL STONE
18 Pine St (11719-9409)
PHONE..................................631 653-6790
Fax: 631 653-3317
Jay Salsburg, *President*
EMP: 11
SALES (est): 1MM **Privately Held**
SIC: 3281 Marble, building: cut & shaped; granite, cut & shaped

Brooklyn
Kings County

(G-1511)
16 TONS INC
27 Knickerbocker Ave (11237-1409)
PHONE..................................718 418-8446
Fax: 718 418-8447
David Goltl, *CEO*
EMP: 20
SQ FT: 16,000
SALES (est): 3.3MM **Privately Held**
WEB: www.16tons.net
SIC: 2541 Display fixtures, wood; store & office display cases & fixtures

(G-1512)
212KIDDISH INC
168 Spencer St (11205-3929)
PHONE..................................718 705-7227
Nachum Weberman, *President*
EMP: 5 **EST:** 2010
SALES (est): 270K **Privately Held**
SIC: 2099 5149 2052 Food preparations; cookies; cookies

(G-1513)
2P AGENCY USA INC
1674 E 22nd St Apt 3a (11229-1534)
PHONE..................................212 203-5586
Robert Azaryev, *CEO*
EMP: 2
SQ FT: 1,000
SALES (est): 45MM **Privately Held**
SIC: 3663 5999 4812 Mobile communication equipment; mobile telephones & equipment

(G-1514)
3 STAR PAPERS LIMITED
Also Called: Limited Papers
67 34th St Unit 4 (11232-2010)
PHONE..................................718 499-5481
Fax: 718 425-1718
Saul Rubin, *President*
Josh Kestenbaum, *Director*
EMP: 10
SQ FT: 13,000
SALES (est): 1.4MM **Privately Held**
WEB: www.limitedpapers.com
SIC: 2672 Coated & laminated paper

(G-1515)
3PHASE INDUSTRIES LLC
Also Called: Token
481 Van Buren St Unit 9a (11221-3046)
PHONE..................................347 763-2942
ABI Scholz, *Manager*
Will Kavesh,
Nicole Cornell,
EMP: 6
SQ FT: 4,000
SALES: 500K **Privately Held**
SIC: 2522 2519 Office furniture, except wood; household furniture, except wood or metal: upholstered

(G-1516)
3RD AVENUE DOUGHNUT INC
7111 3rd Ave (11209-1308)
PHONE..................................718 748-3294
Ahmesh Bratea, *President*
EMP: 10
SALES (est): 539K **Privately Held**
SIC: 2051 Doughnuts, except frozen

(G-1517)
3V COMPANY INC
Also Called: Three V
110 Bridge St Ste 3 (11201-1575)
PHONE..................................718 858-7333
Fax: 718 858-7371
Clara Crombo, *CEO*
Sam Gombo, *President*
Dan Gombo, *Vice Pres*
Tommy Marieno, *Production*
Harrison Gombo, *Manager*
EMP: 47
SQ FT: 22,000
SALES (est): 7.5MM **Privately Held**
WEB: www.threev.com
SIC: 2087 2834 2099 2086 Syrups, flavoring (except drink); pharmaceutical preparations; food preparations; bottled & canned soft drinks

(G-1518)
40 STREET BAKING INC
8617 17th Ave (11214-3601)
PHONE..................................212 683-4700
Mohammed Irfan,
EMP: 8
SALES (est): 465.8K **Privately Held**
SIC: 2051 Bread, cake & related products

(G-1519)
461 NEW LOTS AVENUE LLC
461 New Lots Ave (11207-6411)
P.O. Box 20540 (11202-0540)
PHONE..................................347 303-9305
Desmond R John Sr,
EMP: 6
SALES (est): 394.5K **Privately Held**
SIC: 2759 7991 Commercial printing; spas

(G-1520)
5TH AVENUE PHARMACY INC
4818 5th Ave Ste 1 (11220-1936)
PHONE..................................718 439-8585
Avraham Pudel, *President*
EMP: 9
SALES (est): 1.2MM **Privately Held**
SIC: 2834 Pharmaceutical preparations

(G-1521)
6727 11TH AVE CORP
Also Called: Prestige Printing Company
6727 11th Ave (11219-5904)
PHONE..................................718 837-8787
Vincent Costanza, *President*
Luke Spano, *Vice Pres*
EMP: 10 **EST:** 1973
SQ FT: 3,200
SALES (est): 1.4MM **Privately Held**
SIC: 2752 2759 Commercial printing, lithographic; offset & photolithographic printing; letterpress printing

(G-1522)
786 IRON WORKS CORP
50 Morgan Ave (11237-1605)
PHONE..................................718 418-4808
Fax: 718 418-4803
Baudin Canka, *President*
EMP: 5
SQ FT: 5,000
SALES (est): 736K **Privately Held**
SIC: 3446 Fences or posts, ornamental iron or steel

(G-1523)
888 PHARMACY INC
4821 8th Ave (11220-2213)
PHONE..................................718 871-8833
Larisa Golubets, *President*
EMP: 10 **EST:** 2012
SALES (est): 1.4MM **Privately Held**
SIC: 2834 Pharmaceutical preparations

(G-1524)
999 BAGELS INC
1410 86th St (11228-3408)
PHONE..................................718 915-0742
Stefano Mannino, *CEO*
Jaime Guli, *Manager*
Salvatore Mannino, *Director*
EMP: 8
SALES (est): 520K **Privately Held**
SIC: 2051 5461 Bagels, fresh or frozen; bagels

(G-1525)
A & B FINISHING INC
401 Park Ave (11205-1406)
PHONE..................................718 522-4702
Fax: 718 624-4916
EMP: 40
SQ FT: 20,000
SALES: 800K **Privately Held**
SIC: 2253 5199 2339 Knit Outerwear Mill Whol Nondurable Goods Mfg Women's/Misses' Outerwear

(G-1526)
A & L ASSET MANAGEMENT LTD
143 Alabama Ave (11207-2911)
PHONE..................................718 566-1500
Meir Akerman, *CEO*
Eugene Loevinger, *Admin Sec*
EMP: 150
SQ FT: 120,000
SALES (est): 12MM **Privately Held**
SIC: 3999 Candles

(G-1527)
A & L PEN MANUFACTURING CORP
145 12th St (11215-3818)
PHONE..................................718 499-8966
Fax: 718 499-5231
Angel L Martinez Sr, *President*
Felix Terrero, *Purch Agent*
Luz Martinez, *Treasurer*
Paul Richeer, *Controller*
Jeanette Terrero, *Human Res Dir*
▲ **EMP:** 100
SQ FT: 27,000
SALES (est): 13.7MM **Privately Held**
WEB: www.aandlpen.com
SIC: 3951 Pens & mechanical pencils

(G-1528)
A & MT REALTY GROUP LLC
1979 Pacific St Fl 1 (11233-3803)
PHONE..................................718 974-5871
Aboubacar Tounkara, *Mng Member*
EMP: 10
SALES (est): 1MM **Privately Held**
SIC: 1389 8741 Construction, repair & dismantling services; management services

(G-1529)
A & S ELECTRIC
952 Flushing Ave (11206-4720)
PHONE..................................212 228-2030
Jesus M Febus, *Principal*
Susan Burns, *CFO*
EMP: 7 **EST:** 2011
SALES (est): 1.1MM **Privately Held**
SIC: 3699 1731 Electrical equipment & supplies; electrical work

(G-1530)
A & S FINE JEWELRY CORP
777 Kent Ave Ste 244 (11205-1588)
PHONE..................................718 243-2201
Aron Schwartz, *President*
Virginia Schwartz, *Admin Sec*
EMP: 5
SALES (est): 470K **Privately Held**
SIC: 3911 Jewelry, precious metal

(G-1531)
A B C ELASTIC CORP
889 Metropolitan Ave (11211-2513)
PHONE..................................718 388-2953
Morris Freund, *President*
Herman Freund, *Admin Sec*
EMP: 8 **EST:** 1966
SQ FT: 10,000
SALES: 2MM **Privately Held**
SIC: 2221 Elastic fabrics, manmade fiber & silk

(G-1532)
A B S BRASS PRODUCTS INC
185 Moore St (11206-3707)
PHONE..................................718 497-2115
Mark Azerrad, *President*
EMP: 11
SQ FT: 6,000
SALES (est): 970K **Privately Held**
SIC: 3432 Plumbers' brass goods: drain cocks, faucets, spigots, etc.

(G-1533)
A G M DECO INC
305 Wallabout St 307 (11206-4325)
PHONE..................................718 624-6200
Leib Rosenberg, *Manager*
EMP: 15
SALES (corp-wide): 120MM **Privately Held**
SIC: 3442 Sash, door or window: metal

Brooklyn - Kings County (G-1534)

PA: A. G. M. Deco Inc.
741 Myrtle Ave
Brooklyn NY 11205
718 624-6200

(G-1534)
A G M DECO INC (PA)
Also Called: Steiner Doors
741 Myrtle Ave (11205-3924)
PHONE.................................718 624-6200
Gabrielle Steiner, *President*
Jole Steiner, *General Mgr*
Judy Friend, *Office Mgr*
Eli Frid, *Manager*
▲ **EMP:** 10
SQ FT: 2,000
SALES: 120MM **Privately Held**
SIC: 3442 Sash, door or window: metal

(G-1535)
A TO Z KOSHER MEAT PRODUCTS CO
Also Called: Empire National
123 Borinquen Pl (11211)
PHONE.................................718 384-7400
Fax: 718 384-7403
Edward Weinberg, *President*
Karen Weinberg, *Manager*
EMP: 20
SQ FT: 20,000
SALES (est): 2.6MM **Privately Held**
SIC: 2011 Meat packing plants

(G-1536)
A VAN HOEK WOODWORKING LIMITED
71 Montrose Ave (11206-2005)
PHONE.................................718 599-4388
Andre Van Hoek, *President*
EMP: 5
SALES: 300K **Privately Held**
SIC: 2499 5712 Decorative wood & woodwork; cabinet work, custom

(G-1537)
A-1 IRON WORKS INC
2413 Atlantic Ave (11233-3416)
PHONE.................................718 927-4766
Fax: 718 345-2958
Mario Palermo, *CEO*
Alberto Palermo, *President*
EMP: 6
SQ FT: 4,000
SALES (est): 1MM **Privately Held**
SIC: 3312 Hot-rolled iron & steel products

(G-1538)
A-1 PRODUCTS INC
165 Classon Ave (11205-2636)
PHONE.................................718 789-1818
Fax: 718 789-7522
Imre David Kaufman, *President*
EMP: 9
SQ FT: 7,000
SALES (est): 1.3MM **Privately Held**
WEB: www.a1prepaid.com
SIC: 3111 2789 3089 Cutting of leather; paper cutting; plastic processing

(G-1539)
A-1 SKULL CAP CORP
Also Called: A1 Skullcaps
1212 36th St (11218-2010)
PHONE.................................718 633-9333
Fax: 718 633-8028
Henny Blau, *President*
▲ **EMP:** 25
SALES (est): 1.3MM **Privately Held**
WEB: www.skullcap.com
SIC: 2353 5999 Hats & caps; religious goods

(G-1540)
A-ONE LAMINATING CORP
1636 Coney Island Ave 2b (11230-5808)
PHONE.................................718 266-6002
Fax: 718 265-2047
Sol Chaimovits, *CEO*
Reizel Chaimovits, *Admin Sec*
EMP: 6
SALES: 3MM **Privately Held**
SIC: 2295 2621 2672 Laminating of fabrics; asphalt paper, laminated; coated & laminated paper

(G-1541)
A-ONE MOVING & STORAGE INC
1725 Avenue M (11230-5303)
PHONE.................................718 266-6002
EMP: 25
SQ FT: 35,000
SALES (est): 3.5MM **Privately Held**
SIC: 2295 2257 Mfg Coated Fabrics Weft Knit Fabric Mill

(G-1542)
A-PLUS RESTAURANT EQUIPMENT
623 Sackett St (11217-3116)
PHONE.................................718 522-2656
Alex Picav, *Principal*
EMP: 10
SALES (est): 720K **Privately Held**
SIC: 2599 Carts, restaurant equipment

(G-1543)
A1 ORNAMENTAL IRON WORKS INC
61 Jefferson St (11206-6108)
PHONE.................................718 265-3055
Matt Barsily, *President*
EMP: 5
SALES (est): 350K **Privately Held**
SIC: 3446 Architectural metalwork

(G-1544)
AA USA TRADING INC
154 42nd St (11232-3317)
PHONE.................................917 586-2573
Yong Khu, *Owner*
EMP: 7
SQ FT: 6,000
SALES (est): 900K **Privately Held**
SIC: 2091 Canned & cured fish & seafoods

(G-1545)
AB FIRE INC
1554 61st St (11219-5431)
P.O. Box 230581 (11223-0581)
PHONE.................................917 416-6444
Ave Kay, *President*
EMP: 8
SALES (est): 500K **Privately Held**
SIC: 3711 Fire department vehicles (motor vehicles), assembly of

(G-1546)
ABC CHECK PRINTING CORP
544 Park Ave Ste 436 (11205-1793)
PHONE.................................718 855-4702
Joe Gold, *President*
EMP: 14
SQ FT: 3,000
SALES (est): 300K **Privately Held**
SIC: 2752 2782 Color lithography; bank checkbooks & passbooks

(G-1547)
ABETTER PROCESSING CORP
984 E 35th St (11210-3423)
PHONE.................................718 252-2223
Mary Di Nicola, *Owner*
EMP: 15
SALES (est): 919.1K **Privately Held**
SIC: 3471 Plating & polishing

(G-1548)
ABLE ANODIZING CORP
1767 Bay Ridge Ave (11204-5016)
PHONE.................................718 252-0660
Brenda Clark, *Vice Pres*
Mary Di Nicola, *Treasurer*
EMP: 13
SQ FT: 8,000
SALES (est): 2.3MM **Privately Held**
SIC: 3471 Anodizing (plating) of metals or formed products

(G-1549)
ABLE NATIONAL CORP
49 Wyckoff Ave Ste 1 (11237-2650)
PHONE.................................718 386-8801
Fax: 718 456-4583
Abraham Katz, *President*
EMP: 20
SQ FT: 150,000
SALES (est): 3.9MM **Privately Held**
WEB: www.ablenational.com
SIC: 2675 3469 2891 Paper die-cutting; metal stampings; adhesives & sealants

(G-1550)
ACCELIFY SOLUTIONS LLC
3611 14th Ave Ste 422 (11218-3787)
PHONE.................................888 922-2354
Alex Brecher, *CEO*
Joe Jacobs, *President*
David Thomas, *Vice Pres*
Natalie Roth, *Marketing Staff*
Leonid Shum, *CTO*
EMP: 25
SQ FT: 3,000
SALES (est): 2.4MM **Privately Held**
SIC: 7372 Educational computer software

(G-1551)
ACCURATE KNITTING CORP
1478 E 26th St (11210-5233)
PHONE.................................646 552-2216
Chajim Philip Franzos, *President*
EMP: 7
SQ FT: 5,800
SALES (est): 1.3MM **Privately Held**
SIC: 2253 Sweaters & sweater coats, knit

(G-1552)
ACCURATE PRECAST
1957 Pitkin Ave (11207-3305)
PHONE.................................718 345-2910
Fax: 718 345-2950
Fred Lermer, *Principal*
EMP: 18
SALES (est): 2MM **Privately Held**
SIC: 3272 Precast terrazo or concrete products

(G-1553)
ACCURATE SIGNS & AWNINGS INC
247 Prospect Ave Ste 2 (11215-8403)
PHONE.................................718 788-0302
Fax: 718 788-0315
Jim Coppersmith, *President*
EMP: 10
SQ FT: 4,000
SALES (est): 2MM **Privately Held**
SIC: 3993 Signs & advertising specialties

(G-1554)
ACME ARCHITECTURAL PRODUCTS
513 Porter Ave (11222-5312)
PHONE.................................718 360-0700
Jack Teich, *President*
Buddy Martin, *Treasurer*
Jeff Ackner, *Manager*
EMP: 500 **EST:** 1924
SQ FT: 15,000
SALES (est): 25.4MM **Privately Held**
WEB: www.acmesteel.com
SIC: 3469 Spinning metal for the trade; stamping metal for the trade

(G-1555)
ACME ARCHITECTURAL PDTS INC (PA)
Also Called: Acme Architectural Walls
251 Lombardy St (11222-5516)
PHONE.................................718 384-7800
Fax: 718 384-1062
Jack Teich, *President*
Joel Licari, *Vice Pres*
Michael Teich, *Vice Pres*
Mark Teich, *Treasurer*
▲ **EMP:** 58
SQ FT: 250,000
SALES (est): 60MM **Privately Held**
WEB: www.acmearchitecturalwalls.com
SIC: 3442 3444 3446 Metal doors; sheet metalwork; partitions & supports/studs, including accoustical systems

(G-1556)
ACME PARTS INC
901 Elton St (11208-5315)
PHONE.................................718 649-1750
Allan Rodolitz, *President*
EMP: 26
SQ FT: 20,000
SALES (est): 3.6MM **Privately Held**
WEB: www.acmeparts.com
SIC: 3432 Plumbers' brass goods: drain cocks, faucets, spigots, etc.

(G-1557)
ACME SMOKED FISH CORP (PA)
30 Gem St 56 (11222-2804)
PHONE.................................954 942-5598
Fax: 347 586-0310
Eric Caslow, *Ch of Bd*
Mark Brownstein, *Vice Pres*
Adam Caslow, *Vice Pres*
David Caslow, *Vice Pres*
Robert Caslow, *Vice Pres*
◆ **EMP:** 100
SQ FT: 70,000
SALES (est): 20.1MM **Privately Held**
WEB: www.acmesmokedfish.com
SIC: 2091 Fish, smoked; fish, cured

(G-1558)
ACTION RACK DISPLAY MFG
980 Alabama Ave (11207-8327)
PHONE.................................718 257-7111
Fax: 718 257-7171
Joseph Berkovitz, *President*
EMP: 12
SQ FT: 40,000
SALES (est): 1MM **Privately Held**
WEB: www.actionrack.com
SIC: 2653 5046 Corrugated & solid fiber boxes; store fixtures

(G-1559)
ACTIVE WORLD SOLUTIONS INC
Also Called: M/Wbe
609 Fountain Ave (11208-6006)
PHONE.................................718 922-9404
Fax: 718 922-9438
Alvaro Vazquez, *President*
Maria Vazquez, *Principal*
▲ **EMP:** 6
SALES (est): 696.9K **Privately Held**
SIC: 2759 2395 7389 Screen printing; embroidery & art needlework; advertising, promotional & trade show services

(G-1560)
ADAR MEDICAL UNIFORM LLC
307 Richardson St (11222-5709)
PHONE.................................718 935-1197
Mayer Teitelbaum, *Owner*
Rachel Jacobs, *VP Sales*
Dov Appel, *Sales Dir*
▲ **EMP:** 9
SALES (est): 810.4K **Privately Held**
SIC: 2337 2326 Uniforms, except athletic: women's, misses' & juniors'; medical & hospital uniforms, men's

(G-1561)
ADEL ROOTSTEIN (USA) INC
145 18th St (11215-5313)
PHONE.................................718 499-5650
Patty Marino, *Manager*
EMP: 42
SQ FT: 16,572
SALES (corp-wide): 133.1MM **Privately Held**
SIC: 3999 Mannequins
HQ: Adel Rootstein (Usa) Inc
205 W 19th St
New York NY
212 645-2020

(G-1562)
ADIR PUBLISHING CO
1212 36th St (11218-2010)
PHONE.................................718 633-9437
Matt Fef, *Owner*
EMP: 10
SALES: 910K **Privately Held**
WEB: www.a1skullcap.com
SIC: 2731 Books: publishing & printing

(G-1563)
ADRIATIC WOOD PRODUCTS INC
1994 Industrial Park Rd (11207-3335)
PHONE.................................718 922-4621
Fax: 718 922-4625
Anthony Grbic, *President*
John Grbic, *Vice Pres*
Paula Radushimsky, *Controller*
Miljenka Grbic, *Admin Sec*

▲ EMP: 38
SQ FT: 80,000
SALES (est): 4.8MM **Privately Held**
WEB: www.adriaticwood.com
SIC: 2431 Moldings, wood: unfinished & prefinished

(G-1564)
ADS-N-COLOR INC
20 Jay St Ste 530 (11201-8324)
PHONE...............................718 797-0900
Fax: 212 633-2743
Anthony Masi, *President*
Nicholas Masi, *Vice Pres*
EMP: 50
SQ FT: 5,000
SALES (est): 3.5MM **Privately Held**
SIC: 2752 Commercial printing, offset

(G-1565)
ADVANCE CHEMICALS USA INC
1230 57th St (11219-4523)
PHONE...............................718 633-1030
Heldon Eross, *President*
EMP: 4
SQ FT: 2,000
SALES (est): 1MM **Privately Held**
SIC: 3087 Custom compound purchased resins

(G-1566)
ADVANCED READY MIX CORP
239 Ingraham St (11237-1512)
PHONE...............................718 497-5020
Rocco Mancione, *President*
Maria Singh, *Manager*
EMP: 17
SALES (est): 2.8MM **Privately Held**
SIC: 3273 Ready-mixed concrete

(G-1567)
ADVANTAGE WHOLESALE SUPPLY LLC
172 Empire Blvd (11225-3401)
PHONE...............................718 839-3499
Shlomo Rosenfeld, *Principal*
David Smetana,
EMP: 55
SALES (est): 9.8MM **Privately Held**
SIC: 3429 Manufactured hardware (general)

(G-1568)
AFRO TIMES NEWSPAPER
Also Called: New American
1195 Atlantic Ave (11216-2709)
P.O. Box 160397 (11216-0397)
PHONE...............................718 636-9500
Tom Watkins, *Owner*
▲ EMP: 10
SQ FT: 7,500
SALES (est): 341.1K **Privately Held**
WEB: www.newamerican.com
SIC: 2711 Newspapers

(G-1569)
AGE MANUFACTURERS INC
10624 Avenue D (11236-1910)
PHONE...............................718 927-0048
Fax: 718 832-0696
Yosel Avtzon, *President*
▲ EMP: 65 EST: 1958
SQ FT: 43,000
SALES (est): 6.9MM **Privately Held**
SIC: 3999 3131 2339 2337 Hair & hair-based products; footwear cut stock; trimmings (leather), shoe; scarves, hoods, headbands, etc.: women's; women's & misses' suits & coats

(G-1570)
AGGRESSIVE ENERGY LLC
78 Rapelye St Ste A (11231-2654)
PHONE...............................718 836-9222
Bill Jebaily,
EMP: 40
SALES (est): 4.4MM **Privately Held**
SIC: 1321 Natural gas liquids

(G-1571)
AIR FLOW PUMP CORP
Also Called: Air Flow Pump Supply
8412 Foster Ave (11236-3205)
PHONE...............................718 241-2800
Joseph Weinstock, *President*
David Weinstock, *Vice Pres*

EMP: 8
SQ FT: 6,000
SALES (est): 1.5MM **Privately Held**
SIC: 3561 5084 Pumps & pumping equipment; water pumps (industrial)

(G-1572)
AIR SKATE & AIR JUMP CORP (PA)
Also Called: Solo
2208 E 5th St (11223-4827)
P.O. Box 7453, New York (10116-7453)
PHONE...............................212 967-1201
Morris Tawil, *CEO*
EMP: 13
SALES (est): 6.2MM **Privately Held**
SIC: 3143 5139 Men's footwear, except athletic; footwear, athletic

(G-1573)
AJMADISON CORP
3605 13th Ave (11218-3707)
PHONE...............................718 532-1800
Michael Gross, *Ch of Bd*
Robert Zuckerman, *CFO*
Shulamis Neuburger, *Accounts Mgr*
▼ EMP: 55
SALES (est): 18.9MM **Privately Held**
SIC: 3639 7389 Major kitchen appliances, except refrigerators & stoves;

(G-1574)
ALADDIN BAKERS INC (PA)
240 25th St (11232-1338)
PHONE...............................718 499-1818
Fax: 718 788-5174
Joseph Ayoub, *President*
Maria Andrzejewski, *Production*
Ed Curran, *Production*
Cosmo Locricchio, *Purch Mgr*
Don Guzzi, *Finance Dir*
EMP: 120
SALES (est): 22.8MM **Privately Held**
WEB: www.aladdinbakers.com
SIC: 2051 Bread, all types (white, wheat, rye, etc): fresh or frozen

(G-1575)
ALBERT KEMPERLE INC
890 E 51st St (11203-6736)
PHONE...............................718 629-1084
Albert Kemperle, *Owner*
EMP: 24
SALES (corp-wide): 279.2MM **Privately Held**
SIC: 3465 Body parts, automobile: stamped metal
PA: Albert Kemperle, Inc.
8400 New Horizons Blvd
Amityville NY 11701
631 841-1241

(G-1576)
ALBEST METAL STAMPING CORP
1 Kent Ave (11249-1000)
PHONE...............................718 388-6000
Alexander Fischer, *President*
Nathan Hirsch, *Corp Secy*
Yakov Fischer, *Vice Pres*
David Kleinbard, *Purch Agent*
Martin Nussbaum, *Engineer*
▲ EMP: 65 EST: 1959
SQ FT: 120,000
SALES (est): 12.6MM **Privately Held**
WEB: www.albest.com
SIC: 3469 3364 3089 3496 Stamping metal for the trade; nonferrous die-castings except aluminum; casting of plastic; miscellaneous fabricated wire products; aluminum die-castings

(G-1577)
ALBRIZIO INC
Also Called: Albrizio Couture
257 Varet St Ste Mgmt (11206-3859)
PHONE...............................212 719-5290
David Cicalese, *Chairman*
Ann Albrizio, *Executive*
EMP: 6
SALES (est): 657.5K **Privately Held**
SIC: 2353 Millinery

(G-1578)
ALDO FRUSTACCI IRON WORKS INC
165 27th St (11232-1624)
PHONE...............................718 768-0707
Aldo Frustaci, *President*
Connie Giglio, *Office Mgr*
EMP: 10
SQ FT: 8,000
SALES (est): 710K **Privately Held**
SIC: 3446 3444 3441 Architectural metalwork; stairs, staircases, stair treads: prefabricated metal; sheet metalwork; fabricated structural metal

(G-1579)
ALDOS IRON WORKS INC
75 Van Brunt St (11231-1428)
PHONE...............................718 834-0408
Fax: 718 243-2353
Enzo Frustaci, *President*
Fausto Frustaci, *Sales Mgr*
EMP: 7 EST: 1974
SQ FT: 2,700
SALES (est): 950K **Privately Held**
SIC: 3446 Architectural metalwork

(G-1580)
ALETA INDUSTRIES INC
40 Ash St (11222-1102)
PHONE...............................718 349-0040
Fax: 718 349-3247
Zinovy Malinov, *President*
Michael Guitonowitz, *Vice Pres*
Alex Sandler, *Treasurer*
EMP: 18
SQ FT: 15,000
SALES (est): 2.8MM **Privately Held**
WEB: www.aletastjames.com
SIC: 3444 Sheet metalwork

(G-1581)
ALEXANDRA FERGUSON LLC
34 35th St Unit 6 (11232-2212)
PHONE...............................718 788-7768
Alexandra Ferguson, *Mng Member*
EMP: 8
SALES (est): 626.6K **Privately Held**
SIC: 2392 Cushions & pillows

(G-1582)
ALEXIS BITTAR LLC (PA)
45 Main St Ste 725 (11201-1076)
PHONE...............................718 422-7580
Fax: 718 422-7584
Alexis Bittar, *President*
Tara Kurobe, *Principal*
Natasha Moench, *Principal*
Sandy Clarke, *COO*
Arlene Hildreth, *Vice Pres*
▲ EMP: 175
SQ FT: 11,000
SALES (est): 50.7MM **Privately Held**
SIC: 3961 Costume jewelry

(G-1583)
ALGEMEINER JOURNAL INC
508 Montgomery St (11225-3023)
P.O. Box 250746 (11225-0746)
PHONE...............................718 771-0400
Fax: 718 771-0308
Gershon Jacobson, *President*
Dovid Efune, *Managing Dir*
Sagy Braun, *Manager*
Astra Taylor, *Director*
EMP: 5
SALES (est): 300K **Privately Held**
WEB: www.algemeiner.com
SIC: 2711 Newspapers

(G-1584)
ALL AMERICAN CONCRETE CORP
239 Ingraham St (11237-1512)
PHONE...............................718 497-3301
Fax: 718 497-3197
Walter Charles, *President*
Anne Kresse, *Vice Pres*
EMP: 4
SALES: 2MM **Privately Held**
SIC: 3271 Concrete block & brick

(G-1585)
ALL AMERICAN TRANSIT MIX CORP
46 Knickerbocker Ave (11237-1410)
PHONE...............................718 417-3654
Catherine Manzione, *President*
Anne Kressi, *Office Mgr*
EMP: 9
SALES (est): 800K **Privately Held**
SIC: 3273 Ready-mixed concrete

(G-1586)
ALL IN AUDIO INC
5314 16th Ave Ste 83 (11204-1425)
P.O. Box 68, Monroe (10949-0068)
PHONE...............................718 506-0948
Joe Feder, *Ch of Bd*
Debbie Kastow, *General Mgr*
Steve Silver, *Info Tech Mgr*
EMP: 19
SALES: 6.5MM **Privately Held**
SIC: 3651 Household audio & video equipment

(G-1587)
ALL OUT DIE CUTTING INC
49 Wyckoff Ave Ste 1 (11237-2650)
PHONE...............................718 346-6666
Abraham Katc, *President*
EMP: 25 EST: 1980
SQ FT: 20,000
SALES (est): 2.1MM **Privately Held**
SIC: 3544 3469 2891 2675 Special dies & tools; metal stampings; adhesives & sealants; die-cut paper & board

(G-1588)
ALL UNITED WINDOW CORP
Also Called: ABC Showerdoors
85 Classon Ave 97 (11205-1401)
PHONE...............................718 624-0490
Fax: 718 624-3070
Tommy Eng, *President*
Sherry Ing, *President*
EMP: 21
SQ FT: 10,000
SALES (est): 3.4MM **Privately Held**
WEB: www.allunitedwindow.com
SIC: 3442 5211 Storm doors or windows, metal; windows, storm: wood or metal

(G-1589)
ALLIED DOWN PRODUCTS INC
84 Oak St (11222-2015)
PHONE...............................718 389-5454
Steve Belamut, *President*
EMP: 6
SQ FT: 6,000
SALES (est): 410K **Privately Held**
SIC: 2392 Cushions & pillows

(G-1590)
ALLIED FOOD PRODUCTS INC
251 Saint Marks Ave (11238-3503)
PHONE...............................718 230-4227
Ernest Stern, *President*
David Weill, *Marketing Mgr*
Laya Gross, *Manager*
▲ EMP: 10
SQ FT: 10,000
SALES (est): 1.1MM **Privately Held**
WEB: www.alliedfoodproducts.com
SIC: 2034 2024 Dried & dehydrated soup mixes; pudding pops, frozen; gelatin pops, frozen

(G-1591)
ALLIED SAMPLE CARD CO INC
140 58th St Ste 7a (11220-2524)
PHONE...............................718 238-0523
Fax: 718 238-0696
Marc Trager, *President*
Thomas Firavanti, *Vice Pres*
EMP: 30
SQ FT: 22,000
SALES: 1MM **Privately Held**
SIC: 2675 Cards, folders & mats: die-cut

(G-1592)
ALLIED TILE MFG CORP
2840 Atlantic Ave Ste 3 (11207-2635)
PHONE...............................718 647-2200
Fax: 718 647-2656
G Peter Gregor, *President*
▲ EMP: 9 EST: 1962

Brooklyn - Kings County (G-1593)   GEOGRAPHIC SECTION

SQ FT: 10,000
SALES (est): 1.2MM **Privately Held**
WEB: www.alliedtile.com
SIC: 3292 Tile, vinyl asbestos

(G-1593)
ALPHA INCORPORATED
265 80th St (11209-3611)
PHONE..................718 765-1614
Michael Gerovich, *Owner*
EMP: 5 **EST:** 2010
SALES (est): 377K **Privately Held**
SIC: 3089 Identification cards, plastic

(G-1594)
ALPHA KNITTING MILLS INC
41 Varick Ave Ste Mgmt (11237-1527)
PHONE..................718 628-6300
Fax: 718 628-0743
Rose Fuchs, *President*
Bernard Fried, *Corp Secy*
Alex Fried, *Vice Pres*
William Fried, *Vice Pres*
EMP: 15
SQ FT: 15,000
SALES (est): 1.2MM **Privately Held**
SIC: 2253 Knit outerwear mills

(G-1595)
ALPINE PAPER BOX CO INC
2246 Fulton St (11233-3306)
PHONE..................718 345-4040
Fax: 718 345-7039
Anthony Caggiano, *President*
EMP: 30 **EST:** 1953
SQ FT: 15,000
SALES (est): 5MM **Privately Held**
SIC: 3499 2631 Boxes for packing & shipping, metal; paperboard mills

(G-1596)
ALTRONIX CORP
140 58th St Bldg A3w (11220-2521)
PHONE..................718 567-8181
Fax: 718 567-9056
Jonathan Sohnis, *Ch of Bd*
Alan Forman, *President*
Jacqueline Joseph, *General Mgr*
Matt Doumitt, *Vice Pres*
Igor Volkov, *Foreman/Supr*
◆ **EMP:** 100
SQ FT: 52,000
SALES (est): 38MM **Privately Held**
SIC: 3699 3625 5063 Security control equipment & systems; control equipment, electric; burglar alarm systems

(G-1597)
AMBY INTERNATIONAL INC
1460 E 12th St (11230-6606)
PHONE..................718 645-0964
Ben Wallerstein, *President*
▲ **EMP:** 5
SALES (est): 740K **Privately Held**
SIC: 2673 Plastic bags: made from purchased materials

(G-1598)
AMCO INTL MFG & DESIGN INC
10 Conselyea St (11211-2202)
PHONE..................718 388-8668
Adam Milewski, *President*
Amanda Bey, *Manager*
EMP: 26
SALES (est): 950K **Privately Held**
SIC: 3691 Storage batteries

(G-1599)
AMERICAN ALMOND PDTS CO INC (PA)
103 Walworth St (11205-2898)
PHONE..................718 875-8310
Fax: 718 935-1505
Victor Frumolt, *President*
Patrick Holsgrove, *Plant Engr*
Warren Bendiner, *Manager*
◆ **EMP:** 30 **EST:** 1924
SQ FT: 23,000
SALES (est): 9.2MM **Privately Held**
SIC: 2087 2099 2068 Pastes, flavoring; almond pastes; salted & roasted nuts & seeds

(G-1600)
AMERICAN CRAFT JEWELERS INC (PA)
3611 14th Ave Ste 522 (11218-3750)
PHONE..................718 972-0945
Fax: 718 854-5727
Stanley Grimstein, *President*
EMP: 9
SQ FT: 2,000
SALES (est): 8MM **Privately Held**
SIC: 3911 Jewelry, precious metal

(G-1601)
AMERICAN DIES INC
37 Provost St (11222-1813)
PHONE..................718 387-1900
Fax: 718 387-1110
Joel Lefkowitz, *President*
EMP: 14
SALES (est): 1.5MM **Privately Held**
SIC: 3544 Dies & die holders for metal cutting, forming, die casting

(G-1602)
AMERICAN INTL TRIMMING
80 39th St (11232-2604)
PHONE..................718 369-9643
Fax: 718 369-9649
Tony Wu, *President*
▲ **EMP:** 6
SQ FT: 32,000
SALES (est): 642.3K **Privately Held**
WEB: www.aiglifeus.com
SIC: 3089 3496 Clothes hangers, plastic; garment hangers, made from purchased wire

(G-1603)
AMERICAN LEATHER SPECIALTIES
87 34th St Unit 1 (11232-2009)
PHONE..................800 556-6488
Fax: 718 499-2481
Paul Weinberg, *President*
Jeff Weinberg, *General Mgr*
Alan Weinberg, *Corp Secy*
George Schuman, *Vice Pres*
Joel Weinberg, *Vice Pres*
▲ **EMP:** 100 **EST:** 1931
SQ FT: 70,000
SALES (est): 7.9MM **Privately Held**
WEB: www.americanleatherspecialties.com
SIC: 2399 5199 Pet collars, leashes, etc.: non-leather; pet supplies

(G-1604)
AMERICAN MTAL STMPING SPINNING
1 Nassau Ave (11222-3115)
PHONE..................718 384-1500
Fax: 718 782-2359
Stephanie Eisenberg, *President*
EMP: 15
SALES (est): 1.5MM **Privately Held**
SIC: 3469 Stamping metal for the trade; spinning metal for the trade

(G-1605)
AMERICAN PACKAGE COMPANY INC
Also Called: Ampaco
226 Franklin St (11222-1382)
PHONE..................718 389-4444
Martin C Kofman, *President*
EMP: 40 **EST:** 1921
SQ FT: 120,000
SALES (est): 7.1MM **Privately Held**
SIC: 2652 3089 Setup paperboard boxes; boxes, plastic

(G-1606)
AMERICAN PRINT SOLUTIONS INC
561 President St (11215-1018)
PHONE..................718 246-7800
Fax: 718 246-7830
Steven Klein, *Branch Mgr*
EMP: 25
SALES (corp-wide): 3.9MM **Privately Held**
SIC: 2752 Commercial printing, lithographic

PA: American Print Solutions Inc.
2233 Nostrand Ave Ste 7
Brooklyn NY 11210
718 208-2309

(G-1607)
AMERICAN PRINT SOLUTIONS INC (PA)
2233 Nostrand Ave Ste 7 (11210-3029)
PHONE..................718 208-2309
Erica Braun, *President*
Isaac Braun, *Vice Pres*
Malki Lipshitz, *Treasurer*
Israel Izzy Braun, *Finance Dir*
Mark Lipshitz, *Admin Sec*
EMP: 5
SQ FT: 20,000
SALES (est): 3.9MM **Privately Held**
SIC: 2754 5112 Business forms: gravure printing; business forms

(G-1608)
AMERICAN SCIENTIFIC LTG CORP
Also Called: A S L
25 12th St Ste 4 (11215-8019)
PHONE..................718 369-1100
Yaakov Singer, *President*
Boris Aronbelg, *Engineer*
John Deola, *Manager*
Ben Leifer, *Manager*
Chaya Singer, *Manager*
▲ **EMP:** 25 **EST:** 1979
SQ FT: 25,000
SALES (est): 6.1MM **Privately Held**
WEB: www.asllighting.com
SIC: 3646 Commercial indusl & institutional electric lighting fixtures

(G-1609)
AMERICAN SHIP REPAIRS COMPANY
1011 38th St 13 (11219-1012)
PHONE..................718 435-5570
Fax: 718 871-9050
Peter Gianopulos, *President*
▲ **EMP:** 10 **EST:** 1952
SQ FT: 7,000
SALES (est): 1.7MM **Privately Held**
SIC: 3561 7699 Pumps & pumping equipment; industrial pumps & parts; pumps & pumping equipment repair

(G-1610)
AMERICAN WOOD COLUMN CORP
913 Grand St (11211-2785)
PHONE..................718 782-3163
Fax: 718 387-9099
Thomas Lupo, *President*
EMP: 8 **EST:** 1916
SQ FT: 12,000
SALES (est): 982.8K **Privately Held**
SIC: 2431 3299 Woodwork, interior & ornamental; ornamental & architectural plaster work

(G-1611)
AMIRAM DROR INC (PA)
Also Called: Black Hound
226 India St (11222-1804)
P.O. Box 170, Short Hills NJ (07078-0170)
PHONE..................212 979-9505
Amiram Dror, *President*
EMP: 16
SQ FT: 7,500
SALES: 1.8MM **Privately Held**
WEB: www.blackhoundny.com
SIC: 2051 2064 2066 2033 Bakery: wholesale or wholesale/retail combined; chocolate candy, except solid chocolate; chocolate bars, solid; chocolate candy, solid; fruits & fruit products in cans, jars, etc.; chocolate; canned goods: fruit, vegetables, seafood, meats, etc.; candy

(G-1612)
ANGEL-MADE IN HEAVEN INC
Also Called: 116 26 Street
116 26th St (11232-1405)
PHONE..................718 832-4778
Fax: 718 832-9768
Morris Dahan, *President*
EMP: 9
SQ FT: 29,800

SALES (corp-wide): 1.2MM **Privately Held**
WEB: www.angelmih.com
SIC: 2339 Women's & misses' outerwear
PA: Angel-Made In Heaven, Inc.
525 Fashion Ave Rm 1710
New York NY 10018
212 869-5678

(G-1613)
ANNE TAINTOR INC
Also Called: ATI
137 Montague St (11201-3548)
PHONE..................718 483-9312
Anne Taintor, *President*
Nathan Janoff, *Vice Pres*
▲ **EMP:** 6
SALES (est): 643K **Privately Held**
WEB: www.annetaintor.com
SIC: 2771 2752 2678 7389 Greeting cards; post cards, picture: lithographed; poster & decal printing, lithographic; notebooks: made from purchased paper;

(G-1614)
ANNOINTED BUTY MINISTRIES LLC
1697 E 54th St (11234-3921)
P.O. Box 340437 (11234-0437)
PHONE..................646 867-3796
Rachel Ineus, *CEO*
EMP: 5
SALES (est): 261.9K **Privately Held**
SIC: 2721 Periodicals

(G-1615)
AP&G CO INC
Also Called: Catchmaster
75 E 2nd St (11218-1407)
PHONE..................718 492-3648
Steven Frisch, *Ch of Bd*
Ilona Frisch, *President*
Jeffory Lawson, *Managing Dir*
Craig Martelle, *Vice Pres*
Michael Osterink, *Vice Pres*
◆ **EMP:** 80
SQ FT: 160,000
SALES (est): 30.8MM **Privately Held**
WEB: www.catchmaster.com
SIC: 2879 Pesticides, agricultural or household

(G-1616)
APEX AIRTRONICS INC (PA)
2465 Atlantic Ave (11207-2346)
PHONE..................718 485-8560
William Rosenblum, *President*
Helen Rosenblum, *Corp Secy*
▲ **EMP:** 20 **EST:** 1948
SQ FT: 14,000
SALES (est): 2.5MM **Privately Held**
SIC: 3663 Radio broadcasting & communications equipment

(G-1617)
APOLLO WINDOWS & DOORS INC
1003 Metropolitan Ave (11211-2605)
PHONE..................718 386-3326
Fax: 718 386-6060
Hang Hsin Cheng, *President*
Wen Tsui Ping, *Admin Sec*
EMP: 10
SQ FT: 20,000
SALES (est): 1MM **Privately Held**
WEB: www.apollowindows.com
SIC: 2431 Doors & door parts & trim, wood; windows & window parts & trim, wood

(G-1618)
APPLE CORE ELECTRONICS INC
991 Flushing Ave (11206-4721)
PHONE..................718 628-4068
Fax: 718 628-4082
Michael Arnold, *President*
Gregory Arnold, *Vice Pres*
EMP: 11
SQ FT: 4,000
SALES (est): 1.8MM **Privately Held**
SIC: 3669 5065 Intercommunication systems, electric; intercommunication equipment, electronic

GEOGRAPHIC SECTION

Brooklyn - Kings County (G-1648)

(G-1619)
APPSBIDDER INC
55 Clark St 772 (11201-2415)
PHONE..............................917 880-4269
Oladapo Ajayi, *CEO*
EMP: 5
SALES (est): 184.7K **Privately Held**
SIC: 7372 Prepackaged software

(G-1620)
APSCO SPORTS ENTERPRISES INC
Also Called: Abercrombie & Fitch
50th & 1st Ave Bldg 57 (11232)
PHONE..............................718 965-9500
Philip Livoti, *President*
Philip Di Pietro, *Vice Pres*
Vincent Dipietro, *Opers Mgr*
Christine De Chirico, *Controller*
Fran Di Pietro, *Accountant*
▲ **EMP:** 60 **EST:** 1968
SQ FT: 30,000
SALES (est): 7.2MM **Privately Held**
SIC: 2396 Screen printing on fabric articles

(G-1621)
ARCHITCTRAL DSIGN ELEMENTS LLC
52 Box St (11222-1150)
PHONE..............................718 218-7800
Alan Paulenoff, *Mng Member*
Tess Cross, *Manager*
EMP: 7
SALES (est): 850K **Privately Held**
SIC: 3083 Laminated plastics plate & sheet

(G-1622)
ARCHITECTURAL COATINGS INC
538 Johnson Ave (11237-1226)
PHONE..............................718 418-9584
Fax: 718 418-9587
Nick Comaianni, *President*
Daniel France, *Vice Pres*
Margaret Karnick, *Admin Sec*
EMP: 18
SALES (est): 1.2MM **Privately Held**
SIC: 3599 Machine & other job shop work

(G-1623)
ARCTIC GLACIER NEWBURGH INC
335 Moffat St (11237-6408)
PHONE..............................718 456-2013
Vincent Losquadro, *Branch Mgr*
EMP: 6
SALES (corp-wide): 310.9MM **Privately Held**
SIC: 2097 Manufactured ice
HQ: Arctic Glacier Newburgh Inc.
225 Lake St
Newburgh NY 12550
845 561-0549

(G-1624)
ARES BOX LLC
63 Flushing Ave Unit 224 (11205-1073)
PHONE..............................718 858-8760
Mary Filippidis,
EMP: 85
SALES (est): 6.3MM **Privately Held**
SIC: 2671 Packaging paper & plastics film, coated & laminated

(G-1625)
ARES PRINTING AND PACKG CORP
Brooklyn Navy Yard Bldg (11205)
PHONE..............................718 858-8760
Fax: 718 260-8692
Mary Filippidis, *President*
Bob Filippidis, *Vice Pres*
George Filippidis, *Vice Pres*
Jerry Filippidis, *Vice Pres*
EMP: 125
SQ FT: 150,000
SALES (est): 16.6MM **Privately Held**
WEB: www.aresny.com
SIC: 2752 2653 Commercial printing, offset; corrugated & solid fiber boxes; boxes, corrugated: made from purchased materials; display items, corrugated: made from purchased materials

(G-1626)
ARIMED ORTHOTICS PROSTHETICS P (PA)
302 Livingston St (11217-1002)
PHONE..............................718 875-8754
Steven Mirones, *President*
Gary E Korbel, *COO*
EMP: 14
SQ FT: 10,000
SALES (est): 3.7MM **Privately Held**
WEB: www.arimed.com
SIC: 3842 5661 5999 7251 Surgical appliances & supplies; shoes, orthopedic; orthopedic & prosthesis applications; shoe repair shop

(G-1627)
ARISTA STEEL DESIGNS CORP
788 3rd Ave (11232-1418)
PHONE..............................718 965-7077
Steve Viglis, *President*
Maria Holmeerg, *Office Mgr*
EMP: 5
SALES: 1,000K **Privately Held**
SIC: 3449 Bars, concrete reinforcing: fabricated steel

(G-1628)
ARISTOCRAT LIGHTING INC
104 Halleck St (11231-2100)
PHONE..............................718 522-0003
Leon Gross, *President*
Michael Gross, *Vice Pres*
EMP: 12 **EST:** 1983
SQ FT: 18,000
SALES (est): 1.2MM **Privately Held**
SIC: 3646 Commercial indusl & institutional electric lighting fixtures

(G-1629)
ARNOLDS MEAT FOOD PRODUCTS
274 Heyward St (11206-2994)
PHONE..............................718 384-8071
Fax: 718 963-2303
Sheldon Dosik, *President*
Jason Judd, *Vice Pres*
EMP: 25
SALES (est): 3.8MM **Privately Held**
SIC: 2013 Sausages from purchased meat

(G-1630)
AROMASONG USA INC
35 Frost St (11211-1202)
PHONE..............................718 838-9669
Sam Neustein, *President*
EMP: 10
SALES (est): 409.5K **Privately Held**
SIC: 2844 2099 Bath salts; seasonings & spices

(G-1631)
ART AND COOK INC
14 C 53rd St Fl 2 (11232)
PHONE..............................718 567-7778
Ester Harosh, *VP Opers*
Allan Ben, *Exec Dir*
▲ **EMP:** 15
SALES: 10MM **Privately Held**
SIC: 3229 Cooking utensils, glass or glass ceramic

(G-1632)
ART BEDI-MAKKY FOUNDRY CORP
227 India St Ste 31 (11222-1803)
PHONE..............................718 383-4191
Fax: 718 349-8998
Istvan Makky, *President*
EMP: 8
SQ FT: 7,500
SALES: 400K **Privately Held**
SIC: 3366 Castings (except die): bronze

(G-1633)
ART CRAFT LEATHER GOODS INC
1970 Pitkin Ave (11207-3329)
PHONE..............................718 257-7401
Bernard Kandler, *President*
Jo Kandler, *Sales Executive*
EMP: 15 **EST:** 1952
SQ FT: 15,000
SALES (est): 1.6MM **Privately Held**
SIC: 3199 Leather garments

(G-1634)
ART DIGITAL TECHNOLOGIES LLC
85 Debevoise Ave (11222-5608)
PHONE..............................646 649-4820
Fax: 646 861-6580
Meryl Adler, *Controller*
Dan Bright,
EMP: 11
SALES (est): 1.2MM **Privately Held**
WEB: www.artdigitaltech.com
SIC: 2752 7336 Commercial printing, lithographic; commercial art & graphic design

(G-1635)
ARTEMIS STUDIOS INC
Also Called: Diane Artemis Studios
34 35th St Ste 2b (11232-2212)
PHONE..............................718 788-6022
Martin Kurant, *President*
Valerie Hennessy, *Office Mgr*
EMP: 70 **EST:** 1964
SQ FT: 30,000
SALES (est): 5MM **Privately Held**
WEB: www.artemisstudios.com
SIC: 3999 3645 Shades, lamp or candle; residential lighting fixtures

(G-1636)
ARTHUR GLUCK SHIRTMAKERS INC
871 E 24th St (11210-2821)
PHONE..............................212 755-8165
Fax: 212 758-0627
Michael Spitzer, *President*
EMP: 10
SALES: 1.5MM **Privately Held**
WEB: www.shirtcreations.com
SIC: 2321 Men's & boys' dress shirts

(G-1637)
ASA MANUFACTURING INC
1352 39th St (11218-3616)
PHONE..............................718 853-3033
Fax: 718 435-8486
Alex Klein, *President*
Sam Hershkovich, *Vice Pres*
EMP: 20
SQ FT: 4,000
SALES: 3.8MM **Privately Held**
WEB: www.par4shelters.com
SIC: 3915 Jewelry parts, unassembled

(G-1638)
ASAP RACK RENTAL INC
33 35th St St5 (11232-2022)
PHONE..............................718 499-4495
David Fox, *President*
EMP: 7
SQ FT: 6,000
SALES: 969.3K **Privately Held**
SIC: 2542 3537 5051 5021 Garment racks: except wood; industrial trucks & tractors; pipe & tubing, steel; racks

(G-1639)
ASHLEY RESIN CORP
1171 59th St (11219-4909)
P.O. Box 190733 (11219-0733)
PHONE..............................718 851-8111
Nathan Freedman, *President*
Misem Moskobics, *Admin Sec*
▼ **EMP:** 5
SALES (est): 1.3MM **Privately Held**
WEB: www.ashleypoly.com
SIC: 2821 Plastics materials & resins

(G-1640)
ASPECT PRINTING INC
904 E 51st St (11203-6736)
PHONE..............................347 789-4284
Olga Belenkaya, *Ch of Bd*
Anatoly Fusman, *Manager*
EMP: 20
SALES (est): 3MM **Privately Held**
SIC: 2711 2759 Commercial printing & newspaper publishing combined; magazines: printing

(G-1641)
ASTRO LABEL & TAG LTD
5820 Fort Hamilton Pkwy (11219-4832)
PHONE..............................718 435-4474
Sheldon Kustin, *President*
Lew Kustin, *Vice Pres*
Ellis Amies, *Admin Sec*
EMP: 5
SQ FT: 5,000
SALES: 600K **Privately Held**
SIC: 2759 Flexographic printing; tags: printing; labels & seals: printing

(G-1642)
ATAIR AEROSPACE INC
63 Flushing Ave Unit 262 (11205-1077)
PHONE..............................718 923-1709
Fax: 718 923-1733
Paul Casner Jr, *President*
Vlad Kopman, *CTO*
EMP: 17
SALES (est): 3.2MM **Privately Held**
WEB: www.extremefly.com
SIC: 3812 Aircraft/aerospace flight instruments & guidance systems

(G-1643)
ATALLA HANDBAGS INC
117 57th St (11220-2513)
PHONE..............................718 965-5500
Sami Atalla, *President*
EMP: 4 **EST:** 1978
SQ FT: 1,300
SALES: 1.1MM **Privately Held**
SIC: 3171 Handbags, women's

(G-1644)
ATELIER VIOLLET CORP
505 Driggs Ave (11211-2020)
PHONE..............................718 782-1727
Jean Paul Viollet, *President*
EMP: 6
SQ FT: 7,500
SALES (est): 778.7K **Privately Held**
WEB: www.atelierviollet.com
SIC: 2511 5712 2499 Wood household furniture; custom made furniture, except cabinets; decorative wood & woodwork

(G-1645)
ATERES PUBLISHING & BK BINDERY
Also Called: Ateres Book Binding
845 Bedford Ave (11205-2801)
PHONE..............................718 935-9355
Fax: 718 935-9335
Sam Greenfield, *President*
Simon Pollak, *Sales Executive*
Joseph Greenfield, *Admin Sec*
▲ **EMP:** 14 **EST:** 1975
SQ FT: 20,000
SALES (est): 1.6MM **Privately Held**
SIC: 2789 2731 Bookbinding & repairing: trade, edition, library, etc.; book publishing

(G-1646)
ATLANTIC ELECTRONIC TECH LLC
Also Called: Atlantic Electronic Technology
285 5th Ave Apt 2b (11215-2421)
PHONE..............................800 296-2177
Absalam Ottafa,
▲ **EMP:** 5
SQ FT: 1,500
SALES: 500K **Privately Held**
SIC: 3699 Security control equipment & systems

(G-1647)
ATLANTIC STAIRS CORP
Also Called: Design Interiors
284a Meserole St (11206-2242)
PHONE..............................718 417-8818
Fax: 718 381-5501
Stanley Majkut, *President*
Elizabeth Wozniak, *Admin Sec*
EMP: 6
SQ FT: 3,000
SALES (est): 480K **Privately Held**
WEB: www.atlanticstairs.com
SIC: 2431 Doors & door parts & trim, wood; staircases, stairs & railings

(G-1648)
ATLAS COATINGS GROUP CORP (PA)
4808 Farragut Rd (11203-6612)
PHONE..............................718 469-8787
Ben Berman, *CEO*
Jeff Berman, *President*

(PA)=Parent Co (HQ)=Headquarters (DH)=Div Headquarters
✿ = New Business established in last 2 years

Brooklyn - Kings County (G-1649) GEOGRAPHIC SECTION

Lance Berman, *Vice Pres*
EMP: 75 **EST:** 2001
SALES (est): 4.2MM **Privately Held**
SIC: 2851 5231 Paints & paint additives; paint

(G-1649)
ATLAS SIGN
1544 Atlantic Ave (11213-1008)
PHONE.................................718 604-7446
Paul Kayken, *Owner*
EMP: 7 **EST:** 2007
SQ FT: 5,500
SALES (est): 609.5K **Privately Held**
SIC: 3444 Sheet metalwork

(G-1650)
ATTIAS OVEN CORP
Also Called: Cannon Co
926 3rd Ave (11232-2002)
PHONE.................................718 499-0145
Simon Attias, *President*
Carrie Gorelick, *Manager*
▲ **EMP:** 6
SQ FT: 5,000
SALES (est): 1MM **Privately Held**
WEB: www.attiasco.com
SIC: 3589 Commercial cooking & food-warming equipment

(G-1651)
AUDIBLE DIFFERENCE INC
193 6th St (11215-3104)
PHONE.................................212 662-4848
Erich R Bechtel, *President*
EMP: 15
SALES (corp-wide): 2.6MM **Privately Held**
SIC: 3699 Electric sound equipment
PA: Audible Difference, Inc.
 370 State St
 Brooklyn NY 11217
 212 662-4848

(G-1652)
AUDIBLE DIFFERENCE INC (PA)
Also Called: Audible Difference Lnc
370 State St (11217-1707)
PHONE.................................212 662-4848
Erich R Bechtel, *President*
Levy Vargas, *Director*
EMP: 2
SALES (est): 2.6MM **Privately Held**
WEB: www.adigroup.net
SIC: 3699 Electric sound equipment

(G-1653)
AUDIO TECHNOLOGY NEW YORK INC
Also Called: Audiology
129 31st St (11232-1824)
PHONE.................................718 369-7528
Alan Safdiah, *Senior VP*
Alison Goessling, *Engineer*
Charles Safdiah, *CFO*
Jamie Safdiah, *Director*
▲ **EMP:** 10
SQ FT: 30,000
SALES (est): 1.7MM **Privately Held**
SIC: 3651 Audio electronic systems

(G-1654)
AZURRX BIOPHARMA INC
760 Parkside Ave Ste 217 (11226-1785)
PHONE.................................646 699-7855
Edward J Borkowski, *Ch of Bd*
Johan M Spoor, *President*
Daniel Dupret, *Officer*
EMP: 12
SQ FT: 687
SALES (est): 1.2MM **Privately Held**
SIC: 2834 Pharmaceutical preparations

(G-1655)
B & B SWEATER MILLS INC (PA)
1160 Flushing Ave (11237-1747)
PHONE.................................718 456-8693
Fax: 718 821-3150
Berl Biderman, *President*
Sol Biderman, *Corp Secy*
Joseph Cohen, *Accountant*
▲ **EMP:** 10 **EST:** 1954
SQ FT: 42,000

SALES (est): 975.4K **Privately Held**
SIC: 2253 5137 Sweaters & sweater coats, knit; sweaters, women's & children's

(G-1656)
B & K DYE CUTTING INC
245 Varet St (11206-3823)
PHONE.................................718 497-5216
Nafrali Klagsbrun, *President*
EMP: 6
SQ FT: 5,000
SALES: 300K **Privately Held**
SIC: 2261 Dyeing cotton broadwoven fabrics

(G-1657)
B BARINE INC
145 18th St (11215-5313)
PHONE.................................718 499-5650
Fax: 718 499-5583
Barbara Marino, *President*
Dennis Rocillo, *Manager*
▲ **EMP:** 50
SQ FT: 15,000
SALES (est): 4.2MM **Privately Held**
SIC: 3999 3993 Mannequins; signs & advertising specialties

(G-1658)
B CAKE NY LLC
702 Washington Ave (11238-2264)
PHONE.................................347 787-7199
Miriam Milord, *Principal*
EMP: 8
SALES (est): 746.8K **Privately Held**
SIC: 2051 Cakes, pies & pastries

(G-1659)
B D B TYPEWRITER SUPPLY WORKS
6215 14th Ave (11219-5338)
PHONE.................................718 232-4800
Albert Brauner, *Owner*
EMP: 25 **EST:** 1948
SQ FT: 3,160
SALES (est): 1.4MM **Privately Held**
SIC: 2521 2752 Wood office furniture; commercial printing, lithographic

(G-1660)
BABY CENTRAL LLC
2436 Mcdonald Ave (11223-5231)
PHONE.................................718 372-2229
Mike Seda, *Principal*
EMP: 6 **EST:** 2007
SALES (est): 620K **Privately Held**
SIC: 2023 Baby formulas

(G-1661)
BABY UV/KIDS UV INC
Also Called: Kids Uv Suncare Products
50th St & 1st Bdg 57 Fl 5 (11232)
PHONE.................................917 301-9020
Chris Zanaty, *Branch Mgr*
EMP: 10 **Privately Held**
SIC: 2369 4225 Bathing suits & swimwear: girls', children's & infants'; general warehousing & storage
PA: Baby Uv/Kids Uv Inc
 11 Hawks Nest Rd
 Stony Brook NY 11790

(G-1662)
BACKSTAGE LLC (PA)
45 Main St Ste 416 (11201-1093)
PHONE.................................212 493-4243
James Reynolds, *President*
John Berkowitz, *Editor*
Pete Keeley, *Editor*
Melinda Loewenstein, *Editor*
Anna Paone, *Editor*
EMP: 21
SALES (est): 9.8MM **Privately Held**
SIC: 2721 Periodicals

(G-1663)
BAGELS BY BELL LTD
Also Called: B & S Bialy
10013 Foster Ave (11236-2117)
PHONE.................................718 272-2780
Fax: 718 272-2789
Warren Bell, *President*
Marvin Wolsy, *Manager*
▼ **EMP:** 34

SALES (est): 5.5MM **Privately Held**
SIC: 2051 Bagels, fresh or frozen

(G-1664)
BAGGU
109 Ingraham St (11237-1405)
PHONE.................................347 457-5266
Emily Sugihara, *Owner*
EMP: 5 **EST:** 2010
SALES (est): 464K **Privately Held**
SIC: 2673 Plastic bags: made from purchased materials

(G-1665)
BAKERLY LLC (PA)
81 Prospect St (11201-1473)
PHONE.................................212 220-3901
Julien Caron, *CEO*
Fabian Milon, *COO*
EMP: 3
SQ FT: 100
SALES: 4.5MM **Privately Held**
SIC: 2051 Bakery: wholesale or wholesale/retail combined

(G-1666)
BANNER SMOKED FISH INC
2715 W 15th St (11224-2705)
PHONE.................................718 449-1992
Abraham A Attias, *Ch of Bd*
Alan Levitz, *Admin Sec*
▲ **EMP:** 32
SQ FT: 20,000
SALES (est): 5.7MM **Privately Held**
SIC: 2091 Fish, smoked

(G-1667)
BAR FIELDS INC
2614 W 13th St (11223-5815)
PHONE.................................347 587-7795
Rose Ranna, *Ch of Bd*
Steve Jacobs, *General Mgr*
EMP: 10 **EST:** 2011
SALES (est): 590K **Privately Held**
SIC: 3728 Aircraft parts & equipment

(G-1668)
BARCLAY BROWN CORP
47 Lancaster Ave (11223-5533)
PHONE.................................718 376-7166
Gladys Hedaya, *President*
Maurice Hedaya, *Vice Pres*
EMP: 10
SALES (est): 630K **Privately Held**
WEB: www.barclaybrowncorp.com
SIC: 3161 Satchels

(G-1669)
BASE CONTAINER INC
Also Called: M. C. Container
180 Classon Ave (11205-2637)
PHONE.................................718 636-2004
Malka Katz, *President*
EMP: 12
SALES (est): 1MM **Privately Held**
SIC: 2631 5113 Container, packaging & boxboard; boxes & containers

(G-1670)
BASIC LTD
3611 14th Ave Ste B02 (11218-3750)
PHONE.................................718 438-5576
Fax: 718 871-3616
Harris Mermelstein, *President*
Paul Satoh, *Vice Pres*
▲ **EMP:** 25
SALES (est): 4.8MM **Privately Held**
WEB: www.basic.net
SIC: 2673 Garment & wardrobe bags, (plastic film)

(G-1671)
BASS OIL & CHEMICAL LLC
136 Morgan Ave (11237-1220)
PHONE.................................718 628-4444
Leonard Roz, *CEO*
EMP: 17
SALES (est): 1.4MM **Privately Held**
SIC: 1389 Oil & gas field services

(G-1672)
BASS OIL COMPANY INC
136 Morgan Ave (11237-1220)
PHONE.................................718 628-4444
Gregory Bass, *Ch of Bd*
EMP: 30

SQ FT: 28,000
SALES (est): 7MM **Privately Held**
SIC: 2899 5172 Antifreeze compounds; engine fuels & oils

(G-1673)
BATAMPTE PICKLE PRODUCTS INC (PA)
77 Brooklyn Terminal Mkt (11236-1511)
PHONE.................................718 251-2100
Fax: 718 531-9212
Barry Silberstein, *President*
Howard Silberstein, *Corp Secy*
Scott Silberstein, *Vice Pres*
Shimon Horowitz, *Office Mgr*
Mike Field, *Manager*
EMP: 60 **EST:** 1955
SQ FT: 12,000
SALES (est): 9.3MM **Privately Held**
SIC: 2035 5149 Pickles, vinegar; pickles, preserves, jellies & jams

(G-1674)
BATOR BINTOR INC
42 Delevan St (11231-1808)
PHONE.................................347 546-6503
Max Connolly, *President*
EMP: 10
SALES (est): 587.7K **Privately Held**
WEB: www.batorbintor.com
SIC: 2431 2541 1521 Windows & window parts & trim, wood; cabinets, lockers & shelving; general remodeling, single-family houses

(G-1675)
BDB TECHNOLOGIES LLC
Also Called: Fingertech USA
768 Bedford Ave (11205-1508)
PHONE.................................800 921-4270
Norana Johar, *COO*
Hershey Goldstein, *Manager*
Zvi Kohn, *Manager*
Joel Kohn,
▲ **EMP:** 8
SQ FT: 1,200
SALES: 1MM **Privately Held**
SIC: 3699 Security control equipment & systems; security devices

(G-1676)
BEDESSEE IMPORTS LTD
140 Varick Ave (11237-1219)
PHONE.................................718 272-1300
Fax: 718 628-7790
Andrew Bedessee, *VP Opers*
Verman Bedessee, *Branch Mgr*
EMP: 20
SALES (corp-wide): 13.5MM **Privately Held**
SIC: 2098 Noodles (e.g. egg, plain & water), dry
PA: Bedessee Imports Ltd
 2 Golden Gate Crt
 Scarborough ON
 416 292-2400

(G-1677)
BEDFORD DOWNING GLASS
220 Ingraham St Ste 2 (11237-1514)
P.O. Box 220015 (11222-0015)
PHONE.................................718 418-6409
Ingo Williams, *Owner*
▼ **EMP:** 9
SQ FT: 25,000
SALES: 605K **Privately Held**
SIC: 3229 5999 Glassware, art or decorative; art, picture frames & decorations

(G-1678)
BEDGEVANT INC
200 60th St (11220-3712)
PHONE.................................718 492-0297
▲ **EMP:** 5
SALES (est): 417.6K **Privately Held**
SIC: 3052 Cotton fabric, rubber lined hose

(G-1679)
BEIS MOSHIACH INC
744 Eastern Pkwy (11213-3409)
PHONE.................................718 778-8000
Menachem Hendel, *President*
Boruch Merkur, *Editor*
Naftoli Greenfield, *Admin Sec*
Rami Antian,
EMP: 35

▲ = Import ▼ = Export
◆ = Import/Export

SALES: 3.3MM **Privately Held**
SIC: 2759 Publication printing

(G-1680)
BELTRAN ASSOCIATES INC
1133 E 35th St Ste 1 (11210-4243)
PHONE...................................718 252-2996
Fax: 718 253-9028
Michael Beltran, *Ch of Bd*
Ichael Beltran, *Ch of Bd*
Michael R Beltran, *Ch of Bd*
Debbie Zarneski, *Manager*
EMP: 40
SQ FT: 10,000
SALES (est): 9.6MM **Privately Held**
WEB: www.beltranassociates.com
SIC: 3564 Air purification equipment

(G-1681)
BENCHMARK FURNITURE MFG
300 Dewitt Ave (11236-1912)
PHONE...................................718 257-4707
Fax: 718 257-4757
Sandy Marks, *President*
Russell Marks, *Treasurer*
Hal Levenstein, *Manager*
Arthur Dichiara, *Info Tech Mgr*
▲ **EMP:** 70
SQ FT: 50,000
SALES (est): 8.1MM **Privately Held**
WEB: www.benchmarkfurnituremfg.com
SIC: 2511 Wood household furniture

(G-1682)
BENNETT MULTIMEDIA INC
1087 Utica Ave (11203-5318)
PHONE...................................718 629-1454
David Newman, *President*
EMP: 10
SQ FT: 4,000
SALES (est): 870K **Privately Held**
SIC: 2752 Commercial printing, lithographic

(G-1683)
BENNETT PRINTING CORPORATION
1087 Utica Ave (11203-5390)
PHONE...................................718 629-1454
Fax: 718 451-1799
Lawrence Newman, *President*
David Newman, *Vice Pres*
Ellen Newman, *Treasurer*
EMP: 10
SQ FT: 5,800
SALES: 950K **Privately Held**
SIC: 2752 Commercial printing, lithographic

(G-1684)
BENSON MILLS INC
140 58th St Ste 7j (11220-2538)
PHONE...................................718 236-6743
Fax: 718 532-1406
Keith Levy, *CEO*
Gabriel Levy, *President*
Ralph Levy, *Vice Pres*
▲ **EMP:** 22
SQ FT: 5,000
SALES (est): 3.6MM **Privately Held**
SIC: 2299 Fabrics: linen, jute, hemp, ramie

(G-1685)
BENSON SALES CO INC
6813 20th Ave (11204-4504)
PHONE...................................718 236-6743
Fax: 718 236-6736
Gabriel Levy, *President*
Keith Levy, *Vice Pres*
EMP: 13 **EST:** 1962
SQ FT: 10,000
SALES: 2.9MM **Privately Held**
SIC: 2392 5023 5199 Tablecloths: made from purchased materials; linens, table; general merchandise, non-durable

(G-1686)
BERKMAN BROS INC
538 Johnson Ave (11237-1226)
PHONE...................................718 782-1827
Gerald R Berkman, *President*
▲ **EMP:** 21
SQ FT: 20,000

SALES (est): 1.7MM **Privately Held**
WEB: www.berkmanbrothers.com
SIC: 3471 3479 Electroplating of metals or formed products; lacquering of metal products

(G-1687)
BEST BOILERS INC
2402 Neptune Ave (11224-2316)
P.O. Box 240607 (11224-0607)
PHONE...................................718 372-4210
Aaron Ganguli, *President*
Raymond Miele, *Treasurer*
EMP: 10
SALES (est): 600K **Privately Held**
WEB: www.bestboilers.com
SIC: 3433 Boilers, low-pressure heating: steam or hot water

(G-1688)
BEST MEDICAL WEAR LTD
21 Hall St (11205-1315)
P.O. Box 50221 (11205-0221)
PHONE...................................718 858-5544
Fax: 718 858-5545
Herman Schwartz, *CEO*
Gittel Schwartz, *President*
Naftuli Schwartz, *Vice Pres*
Jack Schwartz, *Manager*
▲ **EMP:** 8 **EST:** 1997
SALES: 2.5MM **Privately Held**
WEB: www.bestmedicalwear.com
SIC: 2326 Work uniforms; medical & hospital uniforms, men's

(G-1689)
BEST TOY MANUFACTURING LTD
43 Hall St Ste B1 (11205-1395)
PHONE...................................718 855-9040
Fax: 718 875-5934
Abraham Hammer, *President*
Angie Rempersad, *Bookkeeper*
▲ **EMP:** 15
SQ FT: 22,500
SALES (est): 2.3MM **Privately Held**
SIC: 3942 Stuffed toys, including animals

(G-1690)
BETTER FRESH CORP
41 Varick Ave (11237-1521)
PHONE...................................718 628-3682
Hamish McCall, *Finance Dir*
EMP: 5
SQ FT: 600
SALES (est): 360K **Privately Held**
SIC: 2087 Beverage bases

(G-1691)
BEVERAGE WORKS INCORPORATED
70 Hamilton Ave 8 (11231-1305)
PHONE...................................718 834-0500
Fax: 914 961-0597
Pat Mezzatesta, *Office Mgr*
Steve Dimario, *Manager*
EMP: 7
SALES (est): 548.3K **Privately Held**
SIC: 2086 Carbonated beverages, nonalcoholic: bottled & canned

(G-1692)
BEVERAGE WORKS NY INC
70 Hamilton Ave 8 (11231-1305)
PHONE...................................718 812-2034
Fax: 718 834-9526
Gerald Ponfigslione, *Principal*
EMP: 20
SALES (corp-wide): 46.4MM **Privately Held**
WEB: www.beverageworks.com
SIC: 2086 Bottled & canned soft drinks
PA: The Beverage Works Nj Inc
1800 State Route 34 # 203
Wall Township NJ 07719
732 938-7600

(G-1693)
BIEN CUIT LLC
120 Smith St (11201-6217)
PHONE...................................718 852-0200
David Golper, *Principal*
EMP: 8 **EST:** 2011
SALES (est): 809.2K **Privately Held**
SIC: 2051 Bakery: wholesale or wholesale/retail combined

(G-1694)
BIG APPLE WELDING SUPPLY
236 47th St (11220-1010)
PHONE...................................718 439-3959
Vincent Pampillonia, *President*
EMP: 5
SALES (est): 691.7K **Privately Held**
SIC: 7692 Automotive welding

(G-1695)
BIGROW PAPER MFG CORP
Also Called: Bigrow Paper Product
930 Bedford Ave (11205-4502)
PHONE...................................718 624-4439
David Greenwald, *President*
▲ **EMP:** 10
SQ FT: 13,000
SALES (est): 1.4MM **Privately Held**
SIC: 2621 Business form paper; envelope paper

(G-1696)
BILLIE-ANN PLASTICS PKG CORP
360 Troutman St (11237-2614)
PHONE...................................718 497-3409
Toll Free:.......................................888 -
Fax: 718 497-6095
William Rubinstein, *President*
Joan Rubinstein, *Vice Pres*
▲ **EMP:** 30
SQ FT: 15,000
SALES (est): 5.4MM **Privately Held**
WEB: www.billieannplastics.com
SIC: 3089 Plastic containers, except foam

(G-1697)
BILLING CODING AND PRTG INC
455 Grant Ave (11208-3056)
PHONE...................................718 827-9409
Omirta Rickheeram, *President*
EMP: 7
SALES (est): 560K **Privately Held**
SIC: 2752 Commercial printing, lithographic

(G-1698)
BINAH MAGAZINES CORP
207 Foster Ave (11230-2195)
PHONE...................................718 305-5200
Sarah Kohn, *Editor*
Chanie Berger, *Marketing Staff*
Ruth Lichtenstein, *Manager*
EMP: 5
SALES (est): 544.1K **Privately Held**
SIC: 2721 Periodicals

(G-1699)
BINDLE AND KEEP
47 Hall St Ste 109 (11205-1315)
PHONE...................................917 740-5002
Daniel Friedman, *Owner*
EMP: 8 **EST:** 2013
SALES (est): 680K **Privately Held**
SIC: 2311 2337 Suits, men's & boys': made from purchased materials; women's & misses' suits & skirts

(G-1700)
BLACKBIRDS BROOKLYN LLC
Also Called: Four &TWenty Blackbirds
597 Sackett St (11217-3116)
PHONE...................................917 362-4080
Kathryn Morrissette, *Administration*
Emily Elsen,
Melissa Elsen,
EMP: 25
SALES (est): 809.2K **Privately Held**
SIC: 2051 Bakery: wholesale or wholesale/retail combined

(G-1701)
BLUE MARBLE ICE CREAM
220 36th St Unit 33 (11232-2405)
PHONE...................................718 858-5551
Jennie Dundas, *Owner*
Alexis Miesen, *Co-Owner*
Janaye Pohl, *Wholesale*
Sarah Green, *Social Dir*
EMP: 10
SALES (est): 1MM **Privately Held**
SIC: 2024 Ice cream, bulk

(G-1702)
BLUE OCEAN FOOD TRADING INC
5726 1st Ave Ste 12 (11220-2509)
PHONE...................................718 689-4290
EMP: 6
SALES (est): 500.4K **Privately Held**
SIC: 2091 Canned & cured fish & seafoods

(G-1703)
BLUE SKY PLASTIC PRODUCTION
305 Johnson Ave (11206-2804)
PHONE...................................718 366-3966
▲ **EMP:** 10
SALES (est): 1.4MM **Privately Held**
SIC: 3083 Plastic finished products, laminated

(G-1704)
BLUE STAR BEVERAGES CORP
1099 Flushing Ave (11237-1830)
PHONE...................................718 381-3535
Albert Shtainer, *Principal*
▲ **EMP:** 9
SALES (est): 837.5K **Privately Held**
SIC: 2086 Carbonated beverages, nonalcoholic: bottled & canned

(G-1705)
BLUEBERRY KNITTING INC (PA)
138 Ross St (11211-7705)
PHONE...................................718 599-6520
Phillip Werzberger, *President*
EMP: 2
SQ FT: 1,000
SALES (est): 2.2MM **Privately Held**
SIC: 2253 Sweaters & sweater coats, knit

(G-1706)
BNC INNOVATIVE WOODWORKING
555 Liberty Ave (11207-3109)
PHONE...................................718 277-2800
Hyman Cassuto, *Owner*
EMP: 11
SQ FT: 11,202
SALES (est): 1MM **Privately Held**
SIC: 2431 Millwork

(G-1707)
BNEI ARAM SOBA INC
Also Called: Community Magazine
1616 Ocean Pkwy (11223-2144)
PHONE...................................718 645-4460
Fax: 347 504-4246
Jack Cohen, *President*
Fayton Washington, *Publisher*
AVI Selvman, *Opers-Prdtn-Mfg*
David Sitt, *Treasurer*
Max Sharp, *Controller*
EMP: 11
SQ FT: 8,000
SALES (est): 1.1MM **Privately Held**
WEB: www.communitym.com
SIC: 2721 Periodicals

(G-1708)
BODY BUILDERS INC
Also Called: Red Line Networx Screen Prtg
5518 3rd Ave (11220-2609)
PHONE...................................718 492-7997
Richard Baez, *Ch of Bd*
EMP: 6
SALES (est): 565.7K **Privately Held**
SIC: 2759 Commercial printing

(G-1709)
BOOKLINKS PUBLISHING SVCS LLC
55 Washington St Ste 253c (11201-1073)
PHONE...................................718 852-2116
Maria Villela, *President*
Jose Schettino, *Bd of Directors*
EMP: 6
SQ FT: 5,000
SALES: 2MM **Privately Held**
SIC: 2731 Textbooks: publishing only, not printed on site

(G-1710)
BOOKLYN ARTISTS ALLIANCE
37 Greenpoint Ave Ste C4 (11222-1553)
PHONE...................................718 383-9621

Brooklyn - Kings County (G-1711)

GEOGRAPHIC SECTION

Bridget Elmer, *President*
Chris Wilde, *President*
Mark Wagner, *Treasurer*
EMP: 5
SALES: 319.1K **Privately Held**
WEB: www.booklyn.org
SIC: 2731 Books: publishing & printing

(G-1711)
BRACCI IRONWORKS INC
1440 Utica Ave (11203-6617)
PHONE.................................718 629-2374
Fax: 718 629-9101
Cory Bracci, *President*
Jonathan Bracci, *Vice Pres*
Vanessa Vargas, *Accounts Mgr*
Michael Bracci, *Admin Sec*
EMP: 10
SQ FT: 9,000
SALES: 1.6MM **Privately Held**
SIC: 3446 7692 Stairs, staircases, stair treads: prefabricated metal; welding repair

(G-1712)
BRAGLEY MFG CO INC
Also Called: Bragley Shipg Carrying Cases
924 Bergen St (11238-3301)
PHONE.................................718 622-7469
Neil Lurie, *President*
Vincent Lorello, *Vice Pres*
Leila Lurie, *Admin Sec*
Teabicha Jenkins, *Administration*
EMP: 50 **EST:** 1946
SQ FT: 20,000
SALES (est): 4.8MM **Privately Held**
WEB: www.bragleycases.com
SIC: 2441 3089 3161 Cases, wood; cases, plastic; luggage

(G-1713)
BRAZEN STREET LLC
734 Pennsylvania Ave (11207-6903)
PHONE.................................516 305-7951
Dr Ade Bushansky, *CEO*
Dr Tyrone Johnson, *CFO*
EMP: 50
SALES (est): 4.1MM **Privately Held**
SIC: 2082 Beer (alcoholic beverage)

(G-1714)
BRIDES INC
4817 New Utrecht Ave (11219-3042)
PHONE.................................718 435-6092
Hindy Werzberger, *Principal*
EMP: 5
SALES (est): 415.7K **Privately Held**
SIC: 2335 Bridal & formal gowns

(G-1715)
BRIDGE ENTERPRISES INC
544 Park Ave (11205-1600)
PHONE.................................718 625-6622
Sara Lev, *President*
EMP: 5
SALES (est): 415.9K **Privately Held**
SIC: 2732 Book music: printing & binding, not published on site

(G-1716)
BRIDGEWATER MDSG CONCEPTS
Also Called: BMC
924 Meeker Ave (11222-3805)
PHONE.................................718 383-5500
Fax: 718 963-1739
Mel Telzi, *President*
EMP: 15
SQ FT: 10,000
SALES (est): 770K **Privately Held**
SIC: 3993 Displays & cutouts, window & lobby

(G-1717)
BRIGHT WAY SUPPLY INC
6302 Fort Hamilton Pkwy (11219-5122)
PHONE.................................718 833-2882
Phillip Lee, *Ch of Bd*
▲ **EMP:** 15
SQ FT: 10,000
SALES (est): 1.8MM **Privately Held**
SIC: 3677 Transformers power supply, electronic type

(G-1718)
BRODER MFG INC
566 Johnson Ave (11237-1305)
P.O. Box 370182 (11237-0182)
PHONE.................................718 366-1667
Fax: 718 386-9671
Martin Broder, *President*
▲ **EMP:** 6
SQ FT: 6,000
SALES (est): 440K **Privately Held**
SIC: 2392 5162 Tablecloths & table settings; plastics products

(G-1719)
BROOK TELEPHONE MFG & SUP CO
Also Called: Brook-Tel
2338 Mcdonald Ave (11223-4740)
P.O. Box 230239 (11223-0239)
PHONE.................................718 449-4222
Fax: 718 372-3464
John Crescentini, *President*
Albert Nervegna, *Purchasing*
Robert Crescentini, *Admin Sec*
▲ **EMP:** 12 **EST:** 1950
SQ FT: 11,000
SALES (est): 1.1MM **Privately Held**
SIC: 3661 Telephones & telephone apparatus

(G-1720)
BROOKLYN BABY CAKES INC
411 Hancock St (11216-2414)
PHONE.................................917 334-2518
EMP: 5
SALES (est): 245.6K **Privately Held**
SIC: 2053 Frozen bakery products, except bread

(G-1721)
BROOKLYN BANGERS LLC
111 Atlantic Ave Ste 1r (11201-6726)
PHONE.................................718 875-3535
Joseph Del Prete, *Mng Member*
Saul Bolton,
EMP: 17
SQ FT: 1,800
SALES (est): 139.9K **Privately Held**
SIC: 2013 5147 Sausages & other prepared meats; meats & meat products

(G-1722)
BROOKLYN BREW SHOP LLC
20 Jay St Ste 410 (11201-8311)
PHONE.................................718 874-0119
Stephen Valand,
EMP: 12
SQ FT: 2,000
SALES: 3.5MM **Privately Held**
SIC: 3556 5084 Beverage machinery; industrial machinery & equipment

(G-1723)
BROOKLYN CASING CO INC
412 3rd St (11215-2882)
PHONE.................................718 522-0866
Morris Klasbole, *President*
EMP: 6
SALES (est): 410K **Privately Held**
SIC: 2013 Sausage casings, natural

(G-1724)
BROOKLYN CSTM MET FBRCTION INC
48 Prospect Park Sw (11215-5915)
PHONE.................................718 499-1573
David Stanavich, *President*
EMP: 5
SALES (est): 453.1K **Privately Held**
SIC: 3499 Fabricated metal products

(G-1725)
BROOKLYN DENIM CO
85 N 3rd St (11249-3944)
PHONE.................................718 782-2600
Frank Pizzurro, *Principal*
Marika Krudysz, *Manager*
EMP: 10
SALES (est): 980K **Privately Held**
SIC: 2211 2389 5651 Denims; apparel for handicapped; jeans stores

(G-1726)
BROOKLYN INDUSTRIES LLC
328 7th Ave (11215-4105)
PHONE.................................718 788-5250
Lindsey Stamps, *Manager*
EMP: 10
SALES (corp-wide): 20MM **Privately Held**
SIC: 3999 Barber & beauty shop equipment
PA: Brooklyn Industries Llc
  45 Main St Ste 413
  Brooklyn NY 11201
  718 801-8900

(G-1727)
BROOKLYN INDUSTRIES LLC
162 Bedford Ave Ste A (11249-1369)
PHONE.................................718 486-6464
Fax: 718 943-1278
Vahap Avsar, *Branch Mgr*
EMP: 10
SALES (corp-wide): 20MM **Privately Held**
SIC: 3999 Barber & beauty shop equipment
PA: Brooklyn Industries Llc
  45 Main St Ste 413
  Brooklyn NY 11201
  718 801-8900

(G-1728)
BROOKLYN INDUSTRIES LLC
206 5th Ave Ste 1 (11217-4431)
PHONE.................................718 789-2764
EMP: 10
SALES (corp-wide): 20MM **Privately Held**
SIC: 3999 Barber & beauty shop equipment
PA: Brooklyn Industries Llc
  45 Main St Ste 413
  Brooklyn NY 11201
  718 801-8900

(G-1729)
BROOKLYN JOURNAL PUBLICATIONS
Also Called: Brooklyn Heights Press
16 Court St 30 (11241-0102)
PHONE.................................718 422-7400
Fax: 718 857-3291
John Dozier Hasty, *President*
EMP: 20
SALES (est): 1MM **Privately Held**
WEB: www.brooklyneagle.net
SIC: 2711 Newspapers

(G-1730)
BROOKLYN RAIL INC
99 Commercial St Apt 15 (11222-1081)
PHONE.................................718 349-8427
Theodore Hann, *President*
Phong Bui, *Publisher*
Corina Larkin, *Editor*
Rachael Rakes, *Editor*
Chloe Wyma, *Assoc Editor*
EMP: 12
SALES (est): 563.2K **Privately Held**
WEB: www.brooklynrail.org
SIC: 2711 Newspapers

(G-1731)
BROOKLYN REMEMBERS INC
9201 4th Ave (11209-7065)
PHONE.................................718 491-1705
Patrick Condon, *Admin Sec*
Lisa Deljanin, *Administration*
EMP: 17
SALES (est): 847.7K **Privately Held**
SIC: 3299 Architectural sculptures: gypsum, clay, papier mache, etc.

(G-1732)
BROOKLYN STORE FRONT CO INC
62 Throop Ave (11206-4307)
PHONE.................................718 384-4372
Samuel Greenberg, *President*
EMP: 5
SQ FT: 5,000
SALES (est): 261.1K **Privately Held**
SIC: 3442 1542 Metal doors, sash & trim; store front construction

(G-1733)
BROOKLYN SWEET SPOT INC
366 Myrtle Ave (11205-2441)
PHONE.................................718 522-2577
EMP: 5 **EST:** 2013
SALES (est): 302.2K **Privately Held**
SIC: 2051 Cakes, pies & pastries

(G-1734)
BROOKLYN WINERY
213 N 8th St (11211-2007)
PHONE.................................347 763-1506
Bryan Leventhal, *Owner*
Pam Wroblewski, *Finance Mgr*
Rachel Schauman, *Sales Mgr*
Kara Taylor, *Sales Mgr*
Jessica Wittwer, *Social Dir*
EMP: 11
SALES (est): 1.9MM **Privately Held**
SIC: 2084 Wines, brandy & brandy spirits

(G-1735)
BSD ALUMINUM FOIL LLC
260 Hewest St (11211)
PHONE.................................347 689-3875
Esther Klein, *President*
EMP: 25 **EST:** 2009
SQ FT: 100,000
SALES (est): 1.8MM **Privately Held**
SIC: 2621 3421 3353 Towels, tissues & napkins: paper & stock; table & food cutlery, including butchers'; aluminum sheet, plate & foil

(G-1736)
BUDD WOODWORK INC
54 Franklin St (11222-2089)
PHONE.................................718 389-1110
Fax: 718 389-7712
Serafin Caamano, *President*
Belen Caamano, *Shareholder*
EMP: 15
SQ FT: 14,000
SALES (est): 2.3MM **Privately Held**
SIC: 2499 Decorative wood & woodwork

(G-1737)
BUNA BESTA TORTILLAS
219 Johnson Ave (11206-2713)
PHONE.................................347 987-3995
Francis Forgione, *Principal*
EMP: 6
SALES (est): 493.6K **Privately Held**
SIC: 2099 Tortillas, fresh or refrigerated

(G-1738)
BURT MILLWORK CORPORATION
1010 Stanley Ave (11208-5291)
PHONE.................................718 257-4601
Fax: 718 649-4398
Eli Gordon, *President*
Seymour Gordon, *Vice Pres*
Bruce Gordon, *Admin Sec*
▲ **EMP:** 22
SQ FT: 42,500
SALES (est): 6MM **Privately Held**
SIC: 2431 Doors, wood; door shutters, wood; windows, wood

(G-1739)
BUSHWICK KITCHEN LLC
630 Flushing Ave Fl 5 (11206-5026)
PHONE.................................917 297-1045
Casey Elsas, *Mng Member*
Ped Barbeau,
EMP: 5
SQ FT: 1,400
SALES: 500K **Privately Held**
SIC: 2035 Seasonings & sauces, except tomato & dry

(G-1740)
BUSINESS DIRECTORY INC
Also Called: Community Directory
137 Division Ave Ste A (11211-8270)
PHONE.................................718 486-8099
Shie Krausz, *President*
EMP: 10
SALES (est): 850K **Privately Held**
SIC: 2741 Telephone & other directory publishing

Brooklyn - Kings County (G-1770)

(G-1741)
BUST INC
Also Called: Bust Magazine
253 36th St Unit 3 (11232-2415)
P.O. Box 1016, New York (10276-1016)
PHONE.................................212 675-1707
Laura Henzel, *President*
Debbie Stoller, *Vice Pres*
EMP: 5
SALES (est): 601.7K Privately Held
WEB: www.bust.com
SIC: 2721 Periodicals

(G-1742)
BYFUSION INC
350 Manhattan Ave Apt 104 (11211-2446)
PHONE.................................347 563-5286
Gregory Gomory, *CEO*
Gregor Gomory, *CEO*
Heidi Kujawa, *COO*
Steve Rocco, *CFO*
EMP: 5
SALES (est): 207.2K Privately Held
SIC: 3559 Plastics working machinery

(G-1743)
C B S FOOD PRODUCTS CORP
770 Chauncey St (11207-1120)
PHONE.................................718 452-2500
Fax: 718 452-2516
Bernard Steinberg, *Ch of Bd*
Chaim Stein, *President*
Phillip Shapiro, *Vice Pres*
EMP: 15 EST: 1939
SQ FT: 34,000
SALES (est): 6.4MM Privately Held
SIC: 2079 Cooking oils, except corn: vegetable refined; shortening & other solid edible fats

(G-1744)
C K PRINTING
267 41st St (11232-2811)
PHONE.................................718 965-0388
Bo Chen, *Owner*
EMP: 6
SALES (est): 706.6K Privately Held
SIC: 2752 Commercial printing, lithographic

(G-1745)
CAB SIGNS INC
Also Called: Cab Plastics
38 Livonia Ave (11212-4011)
PHONE.................................718 479-2424
Fax: 718 385-1187
Christopher Bayer, *President*
Charles Bayer, *Vice Pres*
EMP: 26
SQ FT: 14,000
SALES (est): 3.2MM Privately Held
WEB: www.cabplastics.com
SIC: 3993 Signs & advertising specialties

(G-1746)
CABEZON DESIGN GROUP INC
197 Waverly Ave (11205-3605)
PHONE.................................718 488-9868
Kurt Lebeck, *President*
EMP: 7
SALES (est): 220K Privately Held
WEB: www.cabezondesign.com
SIC: 3446 7389 Architectural metalwork; business services

(G-1747)
CABINETS BY STANLEY INC
46 Hall St (11205-1304)
PHONE.................................718 222-5861
Stanley Stryszowski, *CEO*
Lukasz Stryszowski, *Exec VP*
Tom Stryszowski, *Project Mgr*
EMP: 7
SALES (est): 517.2K Privately Held
SIC: 2434 Wood kitchen cabinets

(G-1748)
CALIPER ARCHITECTURE PC
67 Metropolitan Ave Ste 2 (11249-4038)
PHONE.................................718 302-2427
Stephen Lynch, *President*
EMP: 6
SALES (est): 565.7K Privately Held
WEB: www.caliperstudio.com
SIC: 3446 Architectural metalwork

(G-1749)
CALIPERSTUDIO CO
75 Scott Ave (11237-1320)
PHONE.................................718 302-3504
Steve Lynch, *President*
Jonathan Taylor, *Vice Pres*
Maria Gonzalez, *Consultant*
EMP: 6
SALES (est): 1.3MM Privately Held
SIC: 3446 Architectural metalwork

(G-1750)
CAM FUEL INC
50 Commerce St (11231-1643)
PHONE.................................718 246-4306
Robert Petrillo, *Principal*
EMP: 6
SALES (est): 1.1MM Privately Held
SIC: 2869 Fuels

(G-1751)
CAMEO METAL PRODUCTS INC
127 12th St (11215-3891)
PHONE.................................718 788-1106
Fax: 718 788-3761
Vito Di Maio, *Ch of Bd*
Antonio D Maio, *President*
Anthony Di Maio, *Vice Pres*
Adolpho Polo, *Manager*
▲ EMP: 40
SQ FT: 48,988
SALES (est): 8.8MM Privately Held
WEB: www.cameometal.com
SIC: 3559 3469 Metal finishing equipment for plating, etc.; metal stampings

(G-1752)
CANARSIE COURIER INC
1142 E 92nd St 44 (11236-3698)
PHONE.................................718 257-0600
Fax: 718 272-0870
Donna Marra, *Publisher*
Sandra Greco, *Principal*
Catherine Rosa, *Business Mgr*
EMP: 10
SALES (est): 470K Privately Held
WEB: www.canarsiecourier.com
SIC: 2711 Newspapers

(G-1753)
CANDLE IN THE WINDOW INC
Also Called: Aura Essence
43 Hall St Ste C10 (11205-1393)
P.O. Box 230123, New York (10023-0003)
PHONE.................................718 852-5743
Marni Bouchardy, *Ch of Bd*
Barnard Bouchardy, *Manager*
▲ EMP: 16
SQ FT: 8,000
SALES (est): 1.1MM Privately Held
SIC: 3999 5199 Candles; candles

(G-1754)
CANNIZZARO SEAL & ENGRAVING CO
435 Avenue U (11223-4007)
P.O. Box 230304 (11223-0304)
PHONE.................................718 513-6125
Fax: 718 645-7296
Janet Cannizzaro, *President*
▲ EMP: 5
SQ FT: 1,200
SALES (est): 320K Privately Held
WEB: www.cannizzaroseal.com
SIC: 3953 5199 Embossing seals & hand stamps; gifts & novelties

(G-1755)
CAPITOL POLY CORP
101 Spencer St (11205-2805)
P.O. Box 270, Haverstraw (10927-0270)
PHONE.................................718 855-6000
Fax: 718 855-6800
Benny Green, *President*
EMP: 20
SALES (est): 1.8MM Privately Held
WEB: www.capitalpoly.com
SIC: 2673 Bags: plastic, laminated & coated

(G-1756)
CAPUTO BAKERY INC
Also Called: Caputo's Bake Shop
329 Court St Ste 1 (11231-4390)
PHONE.................................718 875-6871
John Caputo, *President*
Francis Tunzi, *Vice Pres*
EMP: 5
SQ FT: 2,000
SALES (est): 300K Privately Held
SIC: 2051 5461 Bakery: wholesale or wholesale/retail combined; bakeries

(G-1757)
CARDINAL TANK CORP
Also Called: Cardinal Boiler and Tank
700 Hicks St (11231-1823)
PHONE.................................718 625-4350
Fax: 718 852-4592
William J Weidmann, *President*
Eddie King, *Plant Supt*
Joe Snow, *Manager*
Patricia Helmer, *Admin Asst*
EMP: 50
SQ FT: 31,000
SALES (est): 9.5MM Privately Held
WEB: www.cardinal-detecto.centralcarolinascale.co
SIC: 3443 Fuel tanks (oil, gas, etc.): metal plate

(G-1758)
CARECONNECTOR
177 Concord St Apt 2a (11201-2091)
PHONE.................................919 360-2987
Sima Pendharkar, *Principal*
EMP: 5 EST: 2015
SALES (est): 181.5K Privately Held
SIC: 7372 Business oriented computer software

(G-1759)
CARRY-ALL CANVAS BAG CO INC
1983 Coney Island Ave (11223-2328)
PHONE.................................718 375-4230
Fax: 718 375-4230
Michel Kraut, *President*
▲ EMP: 7
SQ FT: 3,800
SALES: 500K Privately Held
WEB: www.carryallbag.com
SIC: 3161 Traveling bags

(G-1760)
CARTER ENTERPRISES LLC (PA)
Also Called: Mil-Spec. Enterprises
4610 12th Ave (11219-2556)
PHONE.................................718 853-5052
Chaim Wolf, *Mng Member*
Sarah Tannbm, *Executive Asst*
▲ EMP: 46
SALES (est): 55.6MM Privately Held
WEB: www.carterny.com
SIC: 2389 Men's miscellaneous accessories

(G-1761)
CARTS MOBILE FOOD EQP CORP
Also Called: Cfe
113 8th St (11215-3115)
PHONE.................................718 788-5540
Fax: 718 788-4962
Jeno Rosenberg, *President*
Florence Rosenberg, *Corp Secy*
Dave Nader, *Exec VP*
David Nadler, *Sales Mgr*
Michelle Burstein, *Manager*
EMP: 22
SQ FT: 15,000
SALES (est): 4MM Privately Held
WEB: www.cartsfoodeqp.com
SIC: 2599 3589 3556 Food wagons, restaurant; carts, restaurant equipment; commercial cooking & foodwarming equipment; food products machinery

(G-1762)
CASA COLLECTION INC
106 Ferris St (11231-1066)
PHONE.................................718 694-0272
Roberto Gil, *President*
EMP: 5
SALES (est): 480K Privately Held
WEB: www.casacollection.us
SIC: 2434 5712 Wood kitchen cabinets; juvenile furniture

(G-1763)
CASA INNOVATIONS INC
Also Called: Shredder Essentials
140 58th St Ste 5h-1 (11220-2525)
PHONE.................................718 965-6600
Aron Abramson, *CEO*
Charles Sued, *President*
▲ EMP: 6
SQ FT: 5,300
SALES (est): 810K Privately Held
SIC: 3678 Electronic connectors

(G-1764)
CATALINA PRODUCTS CORP (PA)
2455 Mcdonald Ave (11223-5232)
PHONE.................................718 336-8288
Fax: 718 375-9028
Victor Salama, *President*
Marie Mireille Salama, *Corp Secy*
Linda Reyzis, *Vice Pres*
Paul Yedin, *Vice Pres*
▲ EMP: 35
SQ FT: 75,000
SALES (est): 2.3MM Privately Held
WEB: www.catalinabath.com
SIC: 2392 Shower curtains: made from purchased materials

(G-1765)
CBC CUSTOM MILLWORK INC
232 42nd St (11232-2814)
PHONE.................................718 499-6742
Brian Colins, *President*
Hyman Cassuto, *Vice Pres*
EMP: 16
SQ FT: 5,000
SALES (est): 2.3MM Privately Held
SIC: 2434 Wood kitchen cabinets

(G-1766)
CC FAMILY LLC
146 Spencer St Ste 5015 (11205-5631)
PHONE.................................516 666-8116
Chana Noe, *President*
EMP: 10 EST: 2015
SALES (est): 443.8K Privately Held
SIC: 3499 Novelties & giftware, including trophies

(G-1767)
CCC PUBLICATIONS INC
12020 Flatlands Ave (11207-8203)
PHONE.................................718 306-1008
AR Bernard, *CEO*
Robin Hogan, *General Mgr*
Karen Bernard, *Vice Pres*
EMP: 7
SQ FT: 2,500
SALES: 600K
SALES (corp-wide): 7.7MM Privately Held
SIC: 2731 Book publishing
PA: Christian Cultural Center, Inc
  12020 Flatlands Ave
  Brooklyn NY 11207
  718 306-1000

(G-1768)
CELLULAR EMPIRE INC
Also Called: AB Aerospace
2614 W 13th St (11223-5815)
PHONE.................................347 587-7795
Doris Mosseri, *President*
Steve Jacobs, *President*
EMP: 10
SALES: 950K Privately Held
SIC: 3728 Electronic generation equipment

(G-1769)
CELONIS INC
1820 Avenue M Unit 544 (11230-5347)
PHONE.................................941 615-9670
Alexander Rinke, *CEO*
EMP: 5
SALES (est): 117.2K Privately Held
SIC: 7372 Prepackaged software

(G-1770)
CERTIFIED HEALTH PRODUCTS INC
67 35th St Unit 12 (11232-2200)
PHONE.................................718 339-7498
Fax: 718 946-6727
Gene Kisselman, *President*

Brooklyn - Kings County (G-1771) GEOGRAPHIC SECTION

Steve Zeltser, *Vice Pres*
EMP: 35
SQ FT: 12,000
SALES (est): 3.9MM **Privately Held**
SIC: **3069** Orthopedic sundries, molded rubber

(G-1771)
CHAIR FACTORY
1355 Atlantic Ave (11216-2810)
PHONE..................................718 363-2383
AB Bellsky, *Owner*
EMP: 50
SALES (est): 4.5MM **Privately Held**
WEB: www.thechairfactory.com
SIC: **2531** 5712 Chairs, table & arm; furniture stores

(G-1772)
CHAMBORD LLC
4302 Farragut Rd (11203-6520)
PHONE..................................718 859-1110
Daniel Faks, *President*
EMP: 20
SQ FT: 12,000
SALES (est): 1.3MM **Privately Held**
SIC: **2051** Bread, cake & related products

(G-1773)
CHAN & CHAN (USA) CORP
2 Rewe St (11211-1708)
PHONE..................................718 388-9633
EMP: 7
SALES (est): 517.8K **Privately Held**
SIC: **2099** 3999 Food preparations; atomizers, toiletry

(G-1774)
CHAN KEE DRIED BEAN CURD INC
71 Steuben St (11205-2608)
PHONE..................................718 622-0820
Alex Luk, *President*
Tan Muneng Sing, *Principal*
Tran Van Track, *Principal*
EMP: 6
SQ FT: 1,000
SALES: 500K **Privately Held**
SIC: **2099** Tofu, except frozen desserts

(G-1775)
CHARLOTTE NEUVILLE DESIGN LLC
Also Called: Fashion Chef, The
882 3rd Ave (11232-1904)
PHONE..................................646 530-4570
Charlotte Neuville, *President*
EMP: 6
SQ FT: 2,000
SALES (est): 492.6K **Privately Held**
SIC: **2051** Cakes, bakery: except frozen

(G-1776)
CHEFS DELIGHT PACKING CO
94 N 8th St (11249-2802)
PHONE..................................718 388-8581
Bradford Karroll, *President*
Doug Karroll, *Vice Pres*
EMP: 13 EST: 1956
SQ FT: 3,000
SALES (est): 1.1MM **Privately Held**
SIC: **2011** Meat packing plants

(G-1777)
CHERI MON BABY LLC
1562 E 4th St (11230-6319)
PHONE..................................212 354-5511
Ralph Kassin,
▲ EMP: 6
SQ FT: 400
SALES (est): 470K **Privately Held**
SIC: **2385** Bibs, waterproof: made from purchased materials

(G-1778)
CHROMOSENSE LLC
1 Metrotech Ctr Fl 19 (11201-3949)
PHONE..................................347 770-5421
Filip Mlekicki, *COO*
EMP: 6
SALES (est): 53.9K **Privately Held**
SIC: **3826** Analytical instruments

(G-1779)
CIC INTERNATIONAL LTD
1118 42nd St (11219-1213)
P.O. Box 533, New York (10011)
PHONE..................................212 213-0089
S G Fassoulis, *President*
David Ceva, *Exec VP*
James Chladek, *Vice Pres*
Robert Perry, *Vice Pres*
Larry Thompson, *Vice Pres*
EMP: 98
SQ FT: 14,656
SALES (est): 6.3MM **Privately Held**
SIC: **3812** 3711 3482 3483 Aircraft/aerospace flight instruments & guidance systems; military motor vehicle assembly; small arms ammunition; ammunition components; rocket launchers; helicopters

(G-1780)
CIDC CORP
Also Called: Ocs Industries
2015 Pitkin Ave (11207-3424)
PHONE..................................718 342-5820
Henry Gutman, *President*
▲ EMP: 15
SALES (est): 1.8MM **Privately Held**
SIC: **2514** 3433 Cabinets, radio & television: metal; heating equipment, except electric

(G-1781)
CITY COOLING ENTERPRISES INC
1624 61st St (11204-2109)
PHONE..................................718 331-7400
Fax: 718 331-5524
Derick Pearlin, *President*
Joel Zuller, *CPA*
EMP: 8
SQ FT: 5,000
SALES (est): 760K **Privately Held**
SIC: **3444** 1711 Sheet metalwork; heating & air conditioning contractors

(G-1782)
CITY OF NEW YORK
Also Called: HRA Poster Project
4014 1st Ave Fl 3 (11232-2700)
PHONE..................................718 965-8787
David Hall, *Branch Mgr*
EMP: 30 **Privately Held**
WEB: www.nyc.gov
SIC: **2741** 9199 Shopping news: publishing & printing; general government administration;
PA: City Of New York
City Hl
New York NY 10007
212 788-3000

(G-1783)
CITY OF NEW YORK
Also Called: Department of Sanitation
5602 19th Ave (11204-2049)
PHONE..................................718 236-2693
Jay Ryan, *Superintendent*
EMP: 117 **Privately Held**
WEB: www.nyc.gov
SIC: **2842** 9511 Sanitation preparations; waste management program administration, government;
PA: City Of New York
City Hl
New York NY 10007
212 788-3000

(G-1784)
CITY SIGNS INC
1940 Mcdonald Ave (11223-1829)
PHONE..................................718 375-5933
Fax: 718 382-0876
Yehuda Mizrahi, *President*
Eyal Mizrahi, *Vice Pres*
Smadar Mizrahi, *Treasurer*
EMP: 5
SQ FT: 12,000
SALES (est): 655.3K **Privately Held**
WEB: www.citysignsinc.com
SIC: **3993** 2399 5999 Signs & advertising specialties; neon signs; flags, fabric; awnings

(G-1785)
CITY SITES SPORTSWEAR INC (PA)
2421 Mcdonald Ave (11223-5230)
PHONE..................................718 375-2990
Fax: 718 998-4112
Sui Tong MA, *President*
David Schwitzer, *Corp Secy*
▲ EMP: 24
SQ FT: 8,000
SALES (est): 2.6MM **Privately Held**
SIC: **2339** Sportswear, women's

(G-1786)
CLASSIC ALBUM
343 Lorimer St (11206-1998)
PHONE..................................718 388-2818
Fax: 718 436-1650
Barry Himmel, *President*
EMP: 30
SQ FT: 12,500
SALES (est): 3.2MM **Privately Held**
SIC: **2782** 7221 2789 2759 Blankbooks & looseleaf binders; photographic studios, portrait; bookbinding & related work; commercial printing

(G-1787)
CLASSIC ALBUM LLC
343 Lorimer St (11206-1998)
PHONE..................................718 388-2818
Fax: 718 388-0214
Cindy Schwartz, *Manager*
Barry Himmel,
▲ EMP: 75 EST: 1952
SQ FT: 10,000
SALES (est): 9.3MM **Privately Held**
SIC: **2782** 7221 Albums; photographic studios, portrait

(G-1788)
CLEANSE TEC
1000 Linwood St (11208-5320)
PHONE..................................718 346-9111
Fax: 718 346-9133
Steven Feig, *President*
Bob Clark, *Senior VP*
Andy Feig, *Opers Staff*
Philip T Seng, *Controller*
Andrew Feig, *Director*
EMP: 29
SQ FT: 14,000
SALES (est): 7.2MM **Privately Held**
WEB: www.soapman.com
SIC: **2841** 2899 Detergents, synthetic organic or inorganic alkaline; specialty cleaning, polishes & sanitation goods

(G-1789)
CNV ARCHITECTURAL COATINGS INC
538 Johnson Ave (11237-1226)
PHONE..................................718 418-9584
Nicola Comaianni, *President*
EMP: 6 EST: 2015
SQ FT: 10,000
SALES (est): 297.5K **Privately Held**
SIC: **3479** Metal coating & allied service

(G-1790)
CODA RESOURCES LTD (PA)
Also Called: Cambridge Resources
960 Alabama Ave (11207-8327)
PHONE..................................718 649-1666
Hillel Tropper, *CEO*
Moshe Tropper, *Vice Pres*
Solomon Tropper, *Vice Pres*
Larry Bloom, *VP Opers*
Eytan Bayme, *Opers Mgr*
▲ EMP: 85
SQ FT: 100,000
SALES (est): 29.5MM **Privately Held**
WEB: www.codaresources.com
SIC: **3469** 2821 Metal stampings; molding compounds, plastics

(G-1791)
COLONIAL REDI RECORD CORP
1225 36th St (11218-2023)
PHONE..................................718 972-7433
Fax: 718 972-7438
Joe Berkobits, *President*
EMP: 25
SQ FT: 12,000
SALES: 2.5MM **Privately Held**
SIC: **3993** Signs & advertising specialties

(G-1792)
COLUMBIA BUTTON NAILHEAD CORP
306 Stagg St 316 (11206-1702)
PHONE..................................718 386-3414
Fax: 718 386-3881
Robert Matz, *President*
Charles J Matz Jr, *Corp Secy*
EMP: 17 EST: 1946
SQ FT: 20,000
SALES (est): 2.2MM **Privately Held**
SIC: **3965** Studs, shirt, except precious/semiprecious metal or stone; buttons & parts; buckles & buckle parts

(G-1793)
COMBOLAND PACKING CORP
2 Cumberland St (11205-1040)
PHONE..................................718 858-4200
Marvin Eisenstadt, *President*
Ira Eisenstadt, *Vice Pres*
Tony Buccola, *Executive*
EMP: 99
SALES (est): 8.8MM **Privately Held**
SIC: **2869** Perfumes, flavorings & food additives

(G-1794)
COMFORT BEDDING INC
13 Christopher Ave (11212-8038)
PHONE..................................718 485-7662
Fax: 718 485-7499
Mark Kohn, *President*
Moses Kohn, *Vice Pres*
Moses Weiner, *Sales Executive*
▲ EMP: 30 EST: 2000
SQ FT: 3,000
SALES (est): 4.9MM **Privately Held**
SIC: **2515** Mattresses & bedsprings

(G-1795)
COMMODORE MANUFACUTRING CORP
Also Called: Commodore Tool
3913 2nd Ave (11232-2707)
PHONE..................................718 788-2600
Abraham Damast, *Branch Mgr*
EMP: 50
SALES (corp-wide): 22.2MM **Privately Held**
SIC: **3542** Machine tools, metal forming type
PA: Commodore Manufacutring Corporation
4312 2nd Ave
Brooklyn NY 11232
718 788-2600

(G-1796)
COMMUNITY NEWS GROUP LLC (PA)
Also Called: Bronx Times Reporter
1 Metrotech Ctr Fl 10 (11201-3949)
PHONE..................................718 260-2500
Les Goodstein, *CEO*
Jennifer Goodstein, *President*
Eric Hercules, *Info Tech Dir*
EMP: 105
SQ FT: 14,000
SALES (est): 28.9MM **Privately Held**
SIC: **2711** Commercial printing & newspaper publishing combined

(G-1797)
CONFRTRNITY OF PRESCIOUS BLOOD
5300 Fort Hamilton Pkwy (11219)
PHONE..................................718 436-1120
Fax: 718 854-6058
Susan Pergolizzi, *Principal*
Austin Bennett, *Director*
EMP: 8
SALES (est): 690K **Privately Held**
WEB: www.confraternitypb.org
SIC: **2731** Books: publishing only

(G-1798)
CONSUMER FLAVORING EXTRACT CO
921 Mcdonald Ave (11218-5611)
PHONE..................................718 435-0201
Louis Fontana, *President*

Frank Biscello, *Executive*
EMP: 14 **EST:** 1962
SQ FT: 5,000
SALES (est): 1.9MM **Privately Held**
WEB: www.consumersflavoring.com
SIC: 2079 2087 Edible oil products, except corn oil; concentrates, flavoring (except drink)

(G-1799)
CONTINENTAL LATEX CORP
1489 Shore Pkwy Apt 1g (11214-6321)
PHONE 718 783-7883
George Miller, *President*
EMP: 10 **EST:** 1953
SALES (est): 800K **Privately Held**
SIC: 3069 3089 Air-supported rubber structures; plastic processing

(G-1800)
CONTINENTAL QUILTING CO INC
72 87th St (11209-4216)
PHONE 718 499-9100
Alfred G Sayegh, *President*
Stephen Sayegh, *Vice Pres*
Peter Jabara, *Controller*
▲ **EMP:** 50 **EST:** 1919
SQ FT: 40,000
SALES (est): 4.5MM **Privately Held**
SIC: 2392 Mattress pads; mattress protectors, except rubber; comforters & quilts: made from purchased materials

(G-1801)
CONTROL ELECTROPOLISHING CORP
109 Walworth St (11205-2897)
P.O. Box 50237 (11205-0237)
PHONE 718 858-6634
Fax: 718 596-6127
Nancy Zapata, *President*
Manuel Acosta, *Safety Mgr*
Lina De-La-Cruz, *Office Mgr*
EMP: 15 **EST:** 1959
SQ FT: 7,000
SALES: 1.2MM **Privately Held**
SIC: 3471 Polishing, metals or formed products

(G-1802)
CONVERGENT MED MGT SVCS LLC
7513 3rd Ave (11209-3103)
PHONE 718 921-6159
Anthony Pennacchio, *President*
EMP: 6
SALES (est): 614.7K **Privately Held**
SIC: 3674 Semiconductors & related devices

(G-1803)
COPY CORNER INC
200 Division Ave (11211-7108)
PHONE 718 388-4545
Fax: 718 388-4949
Zalman Eizikovits, *President*
EMP: 5
SQ FT: 1,500
SALES (est): 410K **Privately Held**
SIC: 2754 2789 Commercial printing, gravure; bookbinding & related work

(G-1804)
CORNELL BEVERAGES INC
105 Harrison Pl (11237-1403)
PHONE 718 381-3000
Helene Hoffman, *President*
Donna Hoffman, *Corp Secy*
Allen Hoffman, *Vice Pres*
EMP: 10
SALES (est): 890K **Privately Held**
WEB: www.cornellbev.com
SIC: 2086 Soft drinks: packaged in cans, bottles, etc.

(G-1805)
CORONET PARTS MFG CO INC (PA)
883 Elton St (11208-5315)
PHONE 718 649-1750
Fax: 718 272-2956
Allan Rodolitz, *President*
Jeffrey Rodolitz, *President*
Mark Silfen, *General Mgr*
Armand Salvati, *Sales Staff*

Joel Poretz, *Branch Mgr*
EMP: 20 **EST:** 1945
SQ FT: 15,000
SALES (est): 7.2MM **Privately Held**
WEB: www.coronetparts.com
SIC: 3432 5074 Plumbers' brass goods: drain cocks, faucets, spigots, etc.; plumbers' brass goods & fittings

(G-1806)
CORONET PARTS MFG CO INC
901 Elton St Fl 1 (11208-5315)
PHONE 718 649-1750
Joel Poretz, *Branch Mgr*
EMP: 20
SALES (corp-wide): 7.2MM **Privately Held**
WEB: www.coronetparts.com
SIC: 3432 Plumbers' brass goods: drain cocks, faucets, spigots, etc.
PA: Coronet Parts Mfg. Co. Inc.
883 Elton St
Brooklyn NY 11208
718 649-1750

(G-1807)
COSMIC ENTERPRISE
147 Rockaway Ave Ste A (11233-3289)
PHONE 718 342-6257
Marjorie Thorne, *Owner*
EMP: 6
SALES (est): 320K **Privately Held**
SIC: 2833 5499 Drugs & herbs: grading, grinding & milling; health & dietetic food stores

(G-1808)
COUNTY ENERGY CORP
65 S 11th St Apt 1e (11249-7003)
PHONE 718 626-7000
David Rosner, *President*
Theresa Goihman, *Executive Asst*
EMP: 4
SALES: 20MM **Privately Held**
SIC: 1311 4911 Natural gas production; electric services

(G-1809)
COURIER PACKAGING INC
220 West St (11222-1350)
PHONE 718 349-2390
Fax: 718 349-2394
Isaac Markstein, *President*
Peter Sanabria, *Executive*
EMP: 25
SQ FT: 20,000
SALES (est): 4.5MM **Privately Held**
SIC: 2673 Plastic bags: made from purchased materials

(G-1810)
COURIER-LIFE INC
Also Called: Courier Life Publications
1 Metrotech Ctr (11201-3948)
PHONE 718 260-2500
Fax: 718 260-2592
Les Goodstein, *CEO*
Jennifer Goodstein, *President*
EMP: 218
SQ FT: 11,300
SALES (est): 11MM
SALES (corp-wide): 28.9MM **Privately Held**
WEB: www.courierlife.net
SIC: 2711 Newspapers: publishing only, not printed on site
PA: Community News Group Llc
1 Metrotech Ctr Fl 10
Brooklyn NY 11201
718 260-2500

(G-1811)
CRAFT PACKAGING INC
1274 49th St Ste 350 (11219-3011)
PHONE 718 633-4045
Fax: 718 633-4046
Fhia Rothstein, *President*
Rothstein Shia, *Owner*
EMP: 5
SALES (est): 445K **Privately Held**
SIC: 2671 Packaging paper & plastics film, coated & laminated

(G-1812)
CRAFT-PAK INC
2771 Strickland Ave (11234-6428)
PHONE 718 763-0700
Anthony De Biasi, *President*
Vincent Tomaselli, *Vice Pres*
EMP: 16
SQ FT: 13,000
SALES (est): 2MM **Privately Held**
SIC: 2673 Plastic bags: made from purchased materials

(G-1813)
CREAM BEBE
694 Myrtle Ave Ste 220 (11205-3916)
PHONE 917 578-2088
Yossi Greenburg, *Owner*
EMP: 10 **EST:** 2012
SALES (est): 380K **Privately Held**
SIC: 2361 Shirts: girls', children's & infants'

(G-1814)
CREATIONS IN LUCITE INC
165 Franklin Ave Apt 5 (11205-2760)
PHONE 718 871-2000
Davin Rand, *President*
David Rand, *President*
Shaye Gross, *Vice Pres*
Brenda Gross, *Office Mgr*
EMP: 9
SALES (est): 150K **Privately Held**
WEB: www.creationsinlucite.com
SIC: 2821 Acrylic resins

(G-1815)
CREATIVE GOLD LLC
1425 37th St Ste 5 (11218-3771)
PHONE 718 686-2225
▲ **EMP:** 23 **EST:** 2003
SALES: 500K **Privately Held**
SIC: 3911 Manufacture Precious Metals

(G-1816)
CREATIVE SCENTS USA INC
183 Wilson St Ste 106 (11211-7578)
PHONE 718 522-5901
Adolf Kraus, *CEO*
EMP: 3
SALES: 2MM **Privately Held**
SIC: 2392 Household furnishings

(G-1817)
CREPINI LLC
Also Called: Crepe Team, The
5600 1st Ave (11220-2550)
PHONE 347 422-0829
Paula Rimer, *CEO*
Charles Rabinovich, *President*
Eric Shkolnik,
Sam Shkolnik,
▲ **EMP:** 30
SQ FT: 12,000
SALES: 12MM **Privately Held**
WEB: www.crepini.com
SIC: 2024 5084 Ice cream & frozen desserts; dairy based frozen desserts; food product manufacturing machinery

(G-1818)
CREST LOCK CO INC
342 Herzl St (11212-4442)
PHONE 718 345-9898
Samuel Sheiman, *President*
▲ **EMP:** 15 **EST:** 1938
SQ FT: 20,000
SALES (est): 1.4MM **Privately Held**
WEB: www.crestlock.net
SIC: 3429 Luggage hardware

(G-1819)
CRITERION BELL & SPECIALTY
4312 2nd Ave (11232-3306)
PHONE 718 788-2600
Fax: 718 788-4071
Abraham Damast, *President*
Donald Damast, *Corp Secy*
Gary Damast, *Vice Pres*
EMP: 40
SQ FT: 30,000
SALES (est): 3.6MM **Privately Held**
SIC: 3499 3999 Novelties & specialties, metal; Christmas tree ornaments, except electrical & glass

(G-1820)
CROWN WOODWORKING CORP
583 Montgomery St (11225-3009)
PHONE 718 974-6415
Mendel Barber, *President*
EMP: 9
SALES (est): 350K **Privately Held**
SIC: 2431 Millwork

(G-1821)
CRUSADER CANDLE CO INC
325 Nevins St Ste 327329 (11215-1084)
PHONE 718 625-0005
Fax: 718 855-7195
Paul J Morra, *President*
▼ **EMP:** 28 **EST:** 1946
SQ FT: 14,500
SALES: 4.7MM **Privately Held**
SIC: 3999 Candles

(G-1822)
CT INDUSTRIAL SUPPLY CO INC
305 Ten Eyck St (11206-1724)
P.O. Box 60338 (11206-0338)
PHONE 718 417-3226
Charles Tolkin, *President*
Addy Gonanzalez, *Manager*
EMP: 10
SALES (est): 1MM **Privately Held**
SIC: 3089 Garbage containers, plastic

(G-1823)
CTAC HOLDINGS LLC
68 35th Street Brooklyn (11232)
PHONE 212 924-2280
Anthony Cirone, *President*
EMP: 20
SALES (est): 2.1MM **Privately Held**
SIC: 2066 Chocolate

(G-1824)
CUMBERLAND PACKING CORP (PA)
2 Cumberland St (11205-1000)
PHONE 718 858-4200
Fax: 718 260-9017
Steven Eisenstadt, *CEO*
Jeffrey Eisenstadt, *Principal*
Michael Briskey, *Exec VP*
Ira Eisenstadt, *Senior VP*
Rob Bowen, *Vice Pres*
◆ **EMP:** 390
SQ FT: 13,000
SALES: 150MM **Privately Held**
WEB: www.cpack.com
SIC: 2869 Sweeteners, synthetic; flavors or flavoring materials, synthetic

(G-1825)
CUSTOM FIXTURES INC
129 13th St (11215-4603)
PHONE 718 965-1141
Fax: 718 832-0448
Michael Lerich, *President*
Joseph Waknine, *Manager*
EMP: 9
SQ FT: 8,000
SALES (est): 960K **Privately Held**
WEB: www.customfixturesonline.com
SIC: 2542 Fixtures: display, office or store: except wood

(G-1826)
CUSTOM LAMPSHADES INC
Also Called: Creative Custom Shades
544 Park Ave Ste 503 (11205-1788)
P.O. Box 50186 (11205-0186)
PHONE 718 254-0500
Nachman Heller, *President*
EMP: 16 **EST:** 1979
SALES (est): 1.7MM **Privately Held**
SIC: 3645 Lamp & light shades

(G-1827)
CUSTOM LUCITE CREATIONS INC
165 Franklin Ave Apt 5 (11205-2760)
PHONE 718 871-2000
David L Rand, *CEO*
EMP: 10
SALES (est): 816K **Privately Held**
SIC: 3089 Plastic processing

Brooklyn - Kings County (G-1828)

(G-1828)
CUSTOM WOOD INC
770 E 94th St (11236-1817)
PHONE..................................718 927-4700
Fax: 718 345-0341
James Campo, *President*
EMP: 8 **EST:** 1980
SQ FT: 3,200
SALES: 750K **Privately Held**
SIC: 2541 2431 Store fixtures, wood; woodwork, interior & ornamental

(G-1829)
D BEST SERVICE CO INC
Also Called: D Best Glass & Mirror
729 Church Ave (11218-3305)
PHONE..................................718 972-6133
William Omalley Jr, *President*
Grace Fradella O'Malley, *Admin Sec*
EMP: 7
SQ FT: 400
SALES (est): 947K **Privately Held**
SIC: 3429 1751 7699 Metal fasteners; window & door installation & erection; mirror repair shop

(G-1830)
D MALDARI & SONS INC
557 3rd Ave (11215-4600)
PHONE..................................718 499-3555
Fax: 718 499-6071
Chris Maldari, *President*
Daniel Maldari, *Vice Pres*
▲ **EMP:** 30 **EST:** 1902
SQ FT: 16,000
SALES (est): 5.3MM **Privately Held**
WEB: www.maldari.com
SIC: 3544 Extrusion dies

(G-1831)
D ORO ONOFRIO INC
1051 73rd St Apt 1 (11228-1939)
PHONE..................................718 491-2961
Onofrio Demattia, *President*
EMP: 5
SALES (est): 291.9K **Privately Held**
SIC: 3911 Jewelry, precious metal

(G-1832)
D V S IRON & ALUMINUM WORKS
117 14th St (11215-4607)
PHONE..................................718 768-7961
Fax: 718 369-6814
Louis Di Janic, *President*
Steve Janic, *Manager*
EMP: 9 **EST:** 1969
SQ FT: 1,000
SALES (est): 1.3MM **Privately Held**
SIC: 3446 Architectural metalwork; railings, prefabricated metal; fire escapes, metal; guards, made from pipe

(G-1833)
DAHILL DISTRIBUTORS INC
975 Dahill Rd (11204-1738)
PHONE..................................347 371-9453
Hirsch Stengel, *President*
Yitty Stengel, *Office Mgr*
EMP: 8
SQ FT: 500
SALES: 800K **Privately Held**
WEB: www.filmart.com
SIC: 3699 5199 Electrical equipment & supplies; general merchandise, nondurable

(G-1834)
DAILY WEAR SPORTSWEAR CORP (PA)
2308 Mcdonald Ave (11223-4739)
PHONE..................................718 972-0533
Isaac Abed, *President*
Joey Abed, *Vice Pres*
Michael Abed, *Vice Pres*
▲ **EMP:** 8
SQ FT: 20,000
SALES (est): 1MM **Privately Held**
SIC: 2339 Sportswear, women's

(G-1835)
DAIRY MAID RAVIOLO MFG (PA)
216 Avenue U Fl 1 (11223-3825)
PHONE..................................718 449-2620
Louis Ballarino, *President*
Salvatore Ballarino, *Vice Pres*
EMP: 10 **EST:** 1953
SQ FT: 4,000
SALES: 1.5MM **Privately Held**
WEB: www.dairymaidravioli.com
SIC: 2098 5499 Macaroni & spaghetti; macaroni products (e.g. alphabets, rings & shells), dry; spaghetti, dry; gourmet food stores

(G-1836)
DALY MEGHAN
78 5th Ave (11217-4647)
PHONE..................................347 699-3259
Meghan Daly, *Owner*
EMP: 10
SALES (est): 283.4K **Privately Held**
SIC: 2051 Bakery: wholesale or wholesale/retail combined

(G-1837)
DAMASCUS BAKERY INC
56 Gold St (11201-1297)
PHONE..................................718 855-1456
Fax: 718 403-0948
Edward Mafoud, *President*
David Mafoud, *Exec VP*
Donald Anerella, *Project Dir*
Rodolfo Toledo, *Safety Mgr*
Jose Lara, *Opers Staff*
EMP: 140 **EST:** 1930
SQ FT: 20,000
SALES (est): 29.5MM **Privately Held**
WEB: www.damascusbakery.com
SIC: 2051 5149 Bread, cake & related products; bread, all types (white, wheat, rye, etc): fresh or frozen; bakery products

(G-1838)
DANET INC
Also Called: Russian Bazaar
8518 17th Ave Fl 2 (11214-2810)
PHONE..................................718 266-4444
Nathasha Shapiro, *President*
Anatoli Shapiro, *Vice Pres*
Margarita Shapiro, *Director*
EMP: 12
SALES (est): 490K **Privately Held**
WEB: www.danet.com
SIC: 2711 7319 Newspapers: publishing only, not printed on site; transit advertising services

(G-1839)
DAPPER DADS INC
45 Rochester Ave (11233-3011)
PHONE..................................917 903-8045
Mario Daniels, *President*
Geayse Williams, *Vice Pres*
EMP: 5
SALES (est): 252.3K **Privately Held**
SIC: 2741 7389 Miscellaneous publishing;

(G-1840)
DAS YIDISHE LICHT INC
66 Middleton St Apt 1 (11206-5088)
PHONE..................................718 387-3166
Mike Kraus, *President*
EMP: 5
SQ FT: 1,500
SALES (est): 290K **Privately Held**
SIC: 2711 Newspapers: publishing only, not printed on site

(G-1841)
DAVEL SYSTEMS INC
1314 Avenue M (11230-5206)
PHONE..................................718 382-6024
Fax: 718 336-4420
David Liberman, *President*
EMP: 6
SALES (est): 495K **Privately Held**
SIC: 7372 Prepackaged software

(G-1842)
DAVID KING LINEN INC
523 E 82nd St (11236-3118)
PHONE..................................718 241-7298
Abraham Aosi, *Ch of Bd*
▲ **EMP:** 15
SQ FT: 8,000
SALES (est): 1.6MM **Privately Held**
SIC: 2299 5023 Linen fabrics; linens & towels

(G-1843)
DAVIDSON CORPORATION (DH)
5002 2nd Ave (11232-4320)
PHONE..................................718 439-6300
Peter Davidson, *Ch of Bd*
Bill Krueger, *President*
H Peter Davidson, *General Mgr*
◆ **EMP:** 2
SQ FT: 30,000
SALES (est): 15MM
SALES (corp-wide): 20.8B **Privately Held**
SIC: 3317 5085 5051 Pipes, seamless steel; tubes, seamless steel; valves & fittings; pipe & tubing, steel
HQ: Ferguson Enterprises, Inc.
12500 Jefferson Ave
Newport News VA 23602
757 874-7795

(G-1844)
DAWNEX INDUSTRIES INC
861 Park Ave (11206-7300)
PHONE..................................718 384-0199
Fax: 718 709-1331
EMP: 10
SALES (est): 600K **Privately Held**
SIC: 3089 Mfg Plastic Products

(G-1845)
DBG MEDIA
358 Classon Ave (11238-1306)
PHONE..................................718 599-6828
David Greaves, *Owner*
EMP: 8
SQ FT: 900
SALES (est): 230K **Privately Held**
WEB: www.ourtimepress.com
SIC: 2711 Newspapers: publishing only, not printed on site

(G-1846)
DE ANS PORK PRODUCTS INC (PA)
899 4th Ave (11232-2150)
PHONE..................................718 788-2464
Fax: 718 832-2817
Frank De Angelis, *President*
Anthony Gaglia, *Vice Pres*
Guy De Angelis, *Treasurer*
Guy Deangelis, *Treasurer*
Bernadette Petrella, *Office Mgr*
EMP: 20 **EST:** 1932
SQ FT: 13,000
SALES (est): 5MM **Privately Held**
SIC: 2013 Sausages from purchased meat

(G-1847)
DEAN TRADING CORP
200 Junius St (11212-8103)
PHONE..................................718 485-0600
Robert Clemente, *Ch of Bd*
EMP: 18 **EST:** 1966
SQ FT: 20,000
SALES (est): 7.5MM **Privately Held**
SIC: 2299 Textile mill waste & remnant processing

(G-1848)
DECOR BY DENE INC
2569 Mcdonald Ave (11223-5995)
PHONE..................................718 376-5566
Fax: 718 375-3822
Michael Dene, *President*
Maurice Dene, *Corp Secy*
Joe Pentangelo, *Manager*
EMP: 12
SQ FT: 10,000
SALES (est): 910K **Privately Held**
SIC: 3645 Residential lighting fixtures; wall lamps

(G-1849)
DECORATIVE NOVELTY CO INC
74 20th St (11232-1101)
PHONE..................................718 965-8600
Fax: 718 965-8600
Dr Leonard Feldman, *President*
Robert Notine, *Corp Secy*
Matt Notine, *Vice Pres*
Margret Hickey, *Manager*
EMP: 10
SQ FT: 10,000
SALES (est): 760K **Privately Held**
WEB: www.decorativenovelty.com
SIC: 2391 5947 Curtains & draperies; draperies, plastic & textile: from purchased materials; party favors

(G-1850)
DELLET INDUSTRIES INC
1 43rd St Ste L8 (11232-2621)
PHONE..................................718 965-0101
Mike Brown, *Regional Mgr*
EMP: 16
SALES (est): 1.4MM **Privately Held**
SIC: 2599 Furniture & fixtures

(G-1851)
DELLS MARASCHINO CHERRIES INC (PA)
175 Dikeman St Ste 177 (11231-1105)
PHONE..................................718 624-4380
Fax: 718 624-4381
Arthur Mondella, *CEO*
Steve Leffler, *General Mgr*
Joanne Capece, *Corp Secy*
Ann Mondella, *Vice Pres*
Urb Brinker, *Natl Sales Mgr*
◆ **EMP:** 30
SQ FT: 30,000
SALES (est): 6.4MM **Privately Held**
WEB: www.dellscherry.com
SIC: 2033 Maraschino cherries: packaged in cans, jars, etc.

(G-1852)
DELTA METAL PRODUCTS CO INC
476 Flushing Ave (11205-1614)
P.O. Box 50239 (11205-0239)
PHONE..................................718 855-4200
Fax: 718 237-0979
Mark Beer, *President*
Nathan Mazurek, *Vice Pres*
EMP: 50
SALES (est): 6.3MM **Privately Held**
SIC: 3644 3643 Noncurrent-carrying wiring services; switch boxes, electric; electric switches; sockets, electric

(G-1853)
DELUXE PAINT
605 4th Ave (11215-5342)
PHONE..................................718 768-9494
Fax: 718 369-0979
Leo Orgel, *Owner*
EMP: 12
SALES (est): 2.2MM **Privately Held**
SIC: 2851 2816 Paints & allied products; inorganic pigments

(G-1854)
DEN-JO WOODWORKING CORP
Also Called: Excellent Cabinet Works
415 Withers St (11222-5735)
PHONE..................................718 388-2287
Fax: 718 963-3831
John Fontana, *President*
Robert Fontana, *Vice Pres*
Joseph Fontana, *Manager*
EMP: 15 **EST:** 1977
SQ FT: 13,000
SALES: 1MM **Privately Held**
SIC: 2521 Wood office furniture

(G-1855)
DENVIN INC
6520 New Utrecht Ave (11219-5725)
PHONE..................................718 232-3389
Joseph Otranto, *President*
Vinny Mongelli, *Vice Pres*
Dennis Otranto, *Treasurer*
EMP: 50 **EST:** 1941
SQ FT: 16,000
SALES (est): 5MM **Privately Held**
WEB: www.empiresilver.com
SIC: 3914 Silversmithing

(G-1856)
DER YID INC
Also Called: DER YID PUBLICATION
84 Bay St (11231)
P.O. Box 110556 (11211-0556)
PHONE..................................718 797-3900
Fax: 718 797-1985
Moses Freidman, *Owner*
Aron Friedman, *Editor*
EMP: 35

▲ = Import ▼ = Export
◆ = Import/Export

SQ FT: 2,900
SALES: 1.7MM **Privately Held**
SIC: **2711** Newspapers

(G-1857)
DESIGNS BY ROBERT SCOTT INC
Also Called: Closet Systems Group, The
810 Humboldt St Ste 3 (11222-1913)
PHONE..................................718 609-2535
Fax: 718 609-2538
Robert S Feingold, *President*
Jason Kesselman, *Vice Pres*
EMP: 20
SQ FT: 16,000
SALES: 1.8MM **Privately Held**
WEB: www.robertscottinc.com
SIC: **2511** 2521 2499 Wood household furniture; wood office furniture; kitchen, bathroom & household ware: wood

(G-1858)
DESKU GROUP INC
7206 7th Ave (11209-2617)
PHONE..................................646 436-1464
Kriste Desku, *President*
EMP: 8 EST: 2010
SQ FT: 5,000
SALES: 30MM **Privately Held**
SIC: **1241** Coal mining services

(G-1859)
DIAMOND BRASS CORP
1231 Flushing Ave (11237-1504)
PHONE..................................718 418-3871
Charles Goldenberg, *CEO*
Shaindy Goldenberg, *Admin Sec*
EMP: 7
SQ FT: 7,000
SALES (est): 730K **Privately Held**
SIC: **3432** Plumbers' brass goods: drain cocks, faucets, spigots, etc.

(G-1860)
DIANA KANE INCORPORATED
229 5th Ave Ste B (11215-7708)
PHONE..................................718 638-6520
Diana Kane, *President*
Tanya Lewellyl, *Accounts Mgr*
EMP: 5
SQ FT: 600
SALES: 500K **Privately Held**
WEB: www.dianakane.com
SIC: **3911** 5094 Jewelry, precious metal; jewelry

(G-1861)
DIANE STUDIOS INC (PA)
34 35th St Ste 2b (11232-2212)
PHONE..................................718 788-6007
Fax: 718 499-7849
Martin Kurant, *President*
EMP: 55
SQ FT: 30,000
SALES (est): 4.9MM **Privately Held**
WEB: www.dianestudios.com
SIC: **3999** Shades, lamp or candle

(G-1862)
DIB MANAGMNT INC
Also Called: Airtech Lab
251 53rd St (11220-1716)
PHONE..................................718 439-8190
Rollads Dib, *President*
Ramona Luckert, *CFO*
EMP: 10
SALES (est): 1.1MM **Privately Held**
SIC: **2869** Fuels

(G-1863)
DICK BAILEY SERVICE INC
Also Called: Dick Bailey Printers
25 Chapel St Ste 602 (11201-1916)
PHONE..................................718 522-4363
Fax: 718 522-4024
Richard Bailey, *President*
William Bailey, *Vice Pres*
EMP: 14
SALES (est): 1.9MM **Privately Held**
SIC: **2752** 8111 Commercial printing, offset; legal services

(G-1864)
DIJIFI LLC
1166 Manhattan Ave # 100 (11222-1035)
PHONE..................................646 519-2447

Anthony Pinder, *Manager*
Jesse Crowder,
EMP: 11
SALES (est): 1.1MM **Privately Held**
SIC: **2754** Photogravure printing

(G-1865)
DINETTE DEPOT LTD
Also Called: Dining Furniture
350 Dewitt Ave (11207-6618)
P.O. Box 696, Bay Shore (11706-0845)
PHONE..................................516 515-9623
Walter Lustig, *Partner*
Barry Lustig, *Partner*
Salie Jagroop, *Bookkeeper*
▲ EMP: 75 EST: 1919
SQ FT: 60,000
SALES (est): 8.9MM **Privately Held**
SIC: **2511** Kitchen & dining room furniture

(G-1866)
DIVINE ART FURNITURE INC
43 Hall St Ste C9 (11205-1393)
PHONE..................................718 834-0111
David Masarsky, *President*
EMP: 8
SQ FT: 6,000
SALES: 100K **Privately Held**
WEB: www.davineartwood.com
SIC: **2521** Wood office furniture

(G-1867)
DIXIE FOAM LTD
Also Called: Dixiefoam Beds
1205 Manhattan Ave # 311 (11222-6155)
PHONE..................................212 645-8999
Fax: 212 691-3092
MD Taracido-Bram, *President*
Roger Wade, *Sales Dir*
EMP: 5 EST: 1971
SQ FT: 2,000
SALES: 600K **Privately Held**
WEB: www.dixiefoam.com
SIC: **2515** Mattresses, containing felt, foam rubber, urethane, etc.

(G-1868)
DLC COMPREHENSIVE MEDICAL PC
979 Fulton St (11238-2346)
P.O. Box 216, Old Westbury (11568-0216)
PHONE..................................718 857-1200
Fax: 718 857-1222
EMP: 10 EST: 1997
SALES (est): 692K **Privately Held**
SIC: **2741** 5961 Miscellaneous publishing; magazines, mail order

(G-1869)
DLX INDUSTRIES INC
Also Called: Columbia Seal N Sew
1970 Pitkin Ave (11207-3329)
PHONE..................................718 272-9420
Fax: 718 522-6636
Martin Prince, *President*
Marc Stewart, *Vice Pres*
Mark Stuart, *Manager*
◆ EMP: 100 EST: 1950
SQ FT: 70,000
SALES (est): 14.9MM **Privately Held**
SIC: **3161** Attache cases; briefcases; cases, carrying

(G-1870)
DOLCE VITE INTERNATIONAL LLC
386 12th St (11215-5002)
PHONE..................................713 962-5767
Christina Summers, *Mng Member*
EMP: 5 EST: 2015
SALES (est): 267.6K **Privately Held**
SIC: **2066** Chocolate

(G-1871)
DOMANI FASHIONS CORP
86 S 1st St (11249-4171)
PHONE..................................718 797-0505
Fax: 718 875-8028
Moses Rosenberg, *President*
Benjamin Schlesinger, *Vice Pres*
◆ EMP: 9
SQ FT: 3,000
SALES (est): 840K **Privately Held**
SIC: **2369** 2253 Girls' & children's outerwear; sweaters & sweater coats, knit

(G-1872)
DOMESTIC CASING CO
410 3rd Ave (11215-3179)
PHONE..................................718 522-1902
Fax: 718 260-8291
Morris Klagsbald, *Partner*
Harold Klagsbald, *Partner*
▲ EMP: 6 EST: 1956
SQ FT: 12,000
SALES (est): 1.9MM **Privately Held**
SIC: **2013** 2011 Sausage casings, natural; meat packing plants

(G-1873)
DOORTEC ARCHTCTURAL MET GL LLC
234 46th St (11220-1008)
PHONE..................................718 567-2730
Boris Barskiy,
EMP: 27
SALES (corp-wide): 4.8MM **Privately Held**
SIC: **3444** Sheet metalwork
PA: Doortec Architectural Metal & Glass, L.L.C.
303 Martin St
River Vale NJ 07675
201 497-5056

(G-1874)
DOUBLE STAR USA INC
307 Kingsland Ave (11222-3708)
PHONE..................................212 929-2210
Fax: 212 863-8901
Jean Chau, *President*
▲ EMP: 8
SQ FT: 4,500
SALES (est): 504.4K **Privately Held**
SIC: **1499** Gemstone & industrial diamond mining

(G-1875)
DOUBLE TAKE FASHIONS INC
68 34th St Unit 5 (11232-2000)
PHONE..................................718 832-9000
Fax: 718 832-6988
Michael Mizrahi, *President*
Jeanette Mizrahi, *Vice Pres*
Daniel Marchese, *Production*
Ralfh Mizrahi, *Manager*
EMP: 8
SQ FT: 5,000
SALES (est): 1.8MM **Privately Held**
WEB: www.doubletakefashions.com
SIC: **2339** Sportswear, women's

(G-1876)
DOVELIN PRINTING COMPANY INC
43 Hall St Ste C2 (11205-1393)
PHONE..................................718 302-3951
Fax: 718 599-4929
Stanley Darmachman, *President*
EMP: 12
SQ FT: 12,000
SALES (est): 970K **Privately Held**
SIC: **2752** Commercial printing, lithographic

(G-1877)
DR PEPPER SNAPPLE GROUP INC
212 Wolcott St (11231-1130)
PHONE..................................718 246-6200
Joseph Poli, *CEO*
EMP: 6
SALES (corp-wide): 6.2B **Publicly Held**
SIC: **2086** Bottled & canned soft drinks
PA: Dr Pepper Snapple Group, Inc.
5301 Legacy Dr
Plano TX 75024
972 673-7000

(G-1878)
DREAM STATUARY INC
Also Called: Original Dream Statuary
251 Cleveland St (11208-1004)
PHONE..................................718 647-2024
Kumar Budhu, *President*
EMP: 6
SALES: 100K **Privately Held**
SIC: **3299** Statuary: gypsum, clay, papier mache, metal, etc.; art goods: plaster of paris, papier mache & scagliola

(G-1879)
DREAMS TO PRINT
Also Called: Hard Ten
10101 Foster Ave (11236-2107)
PHONE..................................718 483-8020
Michael Azafrani, *Owner*
EMP: 1
SALES: 3MM **Privately Held**
SIC: **2731** Book clubs: publishing & printing

(G-1880)
DRESSER-ARGUS INC
36 Bridge St (11201-1170)
PHONE..................................718 643-1540
Warren Frank, *Ch of Bd*
Bonita Wetmore, *Admin Sec*
▲ EMP: 5
SQ FT: 6,000
SALES (est): 480K **Privately Held**
SIC: **3728** 3423 Military aircraft equipment & armament; hand & edge tools

(G-1881)
DRNS CORP
Also Called: Carousel ADS
140 58th St Ste 3f (11220-2561)
PHONE..................................718 369-4530
Fax: 718 265-3722
Mark Nacson, *President*
Robert Barber, *Manager*
Joan Kalmanowitz, *Admin Sec*
▲ EMP: 11
SQ FT: 3,500
SALES (est): 1.2MM **Privately Held**
WEB: www.directpromos.com
SIC: **2759** 7311 7514 8743 Letterpress & screen printing; screen printing; advertising agencies; hearse or limousine rental, without drivers; promotion service

(G-1882)
DUCTS WEBZINE ASSOCIATION
158 Noble St (11222-6342)
P.O. Box 3203, New York (10163-3203)
PHONE..................................718 383-6728
Anne Mironchik, *Manager*
EMP: 13
SALES (est): 633K **Privately Held**
SIC: **2721** Magazines: publishing only, not printed on site

(G-1883)
DURALL DOLLY LLC
48 Spencer St (11205-1737)
PHONE..................................802 728-7122
EMP: 15 EST: 1981
SQ FT: 14,000
SALES (est): 990K **Privately Held**
SIC: **2599** Mfg Harwood Dollies

(G-1884)
DWECK INDUSTRIES INC (PA)
Also Called: Stephen Dweck Industries
2455 Mcdonald Ave Fl 2 (11223-5232)
PHONE..................................718 615-1695
Edmond Dweck, *President*
Gregory Dweck, *Corp Secy*
Stephen Dweck, *Vice Pres*
EMP: 2
SQ FT: 8,000
SALES (est): 3.3MM **Privately Held**
WEB: www.stephendweck.com
SIC: **3911** Pearl jewelry, natural or cultured

(G-1885)
DWECK INDUSTRIES INC
2247 E 16th St Fl 2 (11229-4424)
PHONE..................................718 615-1695
Fax: 718 934-3303
Stephen Dweck, *Vice Pres*
Edmond Dweck, *Branch Mgr*
EMP: 36
SALES (corp-wide): 3.3MM **Privately Held**
WEB: www.stephendweck.com
SIC: **3915** Lapidary work, contract or other
PA: Dweck Industries, Inc.
2455 Mcdonald Ave Fl 2
Brooklyn NY 11223
718 615-1695

(G-1886)
DYNAMIC HEALTH LABS INC
Also Called: Pet Authority
110 Bridge St Ste 2 (11201-1575)
PHONE.....................718 858-0100
Bruce Burwick, *President*
Esther Troupe, *Bookkeeper*
▲ **EMP:** 33
SQ FT: 24,000
SALES (est): 11.7MM **Privately Held**
SIC: 2037 Fruit juices

(G-1887)
DYNAMIC PACKAGING INC
1825 65th St Ste 1 (11204-3801)
PHONE.....................718 388-0800
Fax: 718 388-7733
Stanley Freund, *Ch of Bd*
David Brown, *Manager*
EMP: 10
SALES (est): 760K **Privately Held**
WEB: www.dynamicpackaging.net
SIC: 2759 5113 Bags, plastic: printing; bags, paper & disposable plastic

(G-1888)
DYNATABS LLC
Also Called: Www.dynatabs.com
1933 E 12th St (11229-2703)
PHONE.....................718 376-6084
Harold Baum, *Managing Dir*
Setty Baum, *CFO*
EMP: 11
SQ FT: 3,900
SALES (est): 1.3MM **Privately Held**
WEB: www.dynatabs.com
SIC: 2023 Dietary supplements, dairy & non-dairy based

(G-1889)
E & G BEDDING CORP
1901 8th Ave (11215-6201)
P.O. Box 60978, Staten Island (10306-0978)
PHONE.....................718 369-1092
Walkiria Murphy, *President*
Wilmina Musto, *Vice Pres*
EMP: 30 **EST:** 1980
SALES (est): 3MM **Privately Held**
SIC: 2515 7699 Mattresses & foundations; mattress renovating & repair shop

(G-1890)
E CHABOT LTD
Also Called: Chabot Jewelry
1544 E 13th St Apt 1a (11230-7196)
PHONE.....................212 575-1026
Ezra Shabot, *President*
Bob Shabot, *Treasurer*
EMP: 50
SQ FT: 5,000
SALES: 5.5MM **Privately Held**
WEB: www.echabot.com
SIC: 3911 5094 Jewelry apparel; jewelry

(G-1891)
E G M RESTAURANT EQUIPMENT MFG
688 Flushing Ave (11206-5025)
PHONE.....................718 782-9800
Scott Michaels, *President*
EMP: 7
SQ FT: 2,500
SALES (est): 640K **Privately Held**
SIC: 3444 Restaurant sheet metalwork

(G-1892)
E GRAPHICS CORPORATION
160 Havemeyer St (11211-8772)
PHONE.....................718 486-9767
Esmeralda Lora, *President*
Daniel Beleski, *Manager*
EMP: 6
SALES (est): 450.6K **Privately Held**
SIC: 2732 Book printing

(G-1893)
E S P METAL CRAFTS INC
379 Harman St (11237-4071)
PHONE.....................718 381-2443
Fax: 718 381-1061
Edward Grancagnolo, *President*
▲ **EMP:** 9

SALES: 1MM **Privately Held**
SIC: 3446 Railings, bannisters, guards, etc.: made from metal pipe

(G-1894)
E-Z GLOBAL WHOLESALE INC
925 E 14th St (11230-3648)
PHONE.....................888 769-7888
Shakhim Mamedov, *President*
EMP: 5 **EST:** 2012
SALES (est): 190.2K **Privately Held**
SIC: 3999 Manufacturing industries

(G-1895)
E-Z WARE DISHES INC
1002 Quentin Rd (11223-2228)
PHONE.....................718 376-3244
Joseph Massry, *President*
▲ **EMP:** 3 **EST:** 2010
SQ FT: 2,000
SALES: 1MM **Privately Held**
SIC: 3089 Plastic kitchenware, tableware & houseware

(G-1896)
EAGLE FINISHING
Also Called: Eagle Fashions U S A
49 Wyckoff Ave (11237-8001)
PHONE.....................718 497-7875
Ariam Kurti, *Principal*
Ermir Kurti, *Manager*
EMP: 20
SALES (est): 672.7K **Privately Held**
SIC: 2396 Apparel findings & trimmings

(G-1897)
EAST WEST GLOBAL SOURCING INC
425 Neptune Ave Apt 22a (11224-4587)
PHONE.....................917 887-2286
Michael Zeidner, *CEO*
EMP: 8
SQ FT: 2,000
SALES (est): 306.6K **Privately Held**
SIC: 3199 Leather garments

(G-1898)
EASTERN FEATHER & DOWN CORP
Also Called: Yugo Landau
1027 Metropolitan Ave (11211-2710)
PHONE.....................718 387-4100
Fax: 718 387-2001
Joseph Landau, *President*
Yehoshua Weiner, *Vice Pres*
▲ **EMP:** 8
SQ FT: 45,000
SALES: 4MM **Privately Held**
SIC: 3999 Down (feathers)

(G-1899)
EASTERN SILVER OF BORO PARK
4901 16th Ave (11204-1115)
PHONE.....................718 854-5600
Bernard Gelbstein, *President*
EMP: 5
SQ FT: 4,500
SALES: 1MM **Privately Held**
SIC: 3479 Engraving jewelry silverware, or metal

(G-1900)
ECONOMY 24/7 INC
167 6th Ave (11217-3508)
PHONE.....................917 403-8876
Marius Meland, *President*
EMP: 20
SALES (est): 635.4K **Privately Held**
SIC: 2741 Miscellaneous publishing

(G-1901)
ECOPLAST & PACKAGING LLC
4619 Surf Ave (11224-1047)
PHONE.....................718 996-0800
Shifra Lefkowitz, *CEO*
Larry Lefkowitz,
EMP: 6 **EST:** 2009
SALES (est): 2.5MM **Privately Held**
SIC: 2673 2671 3081 2754 Bags: plastic, laminated & coated; plastic film, coated or laminated for packaging; unsupported plastics film & sheet; commercial printing, gravure

(G-1902)
ED NEGRON FINE WOODWORKING
43 Hall St Fl 5 (11205-1315)
PHONE.....................718 246-1016
Ed Negron, *President*
EMP: 8
SALES (est): 722.4K **Privately Held**
SIC: 2431 2499 Millwork; decorative wood & woodwork

(G-1903)
EDCO SUPPLY CORPORATION
323 36th St (11232-2599)
PHONE.....................718 788-8108
Fax: 718 788-7481
Carl Freyer, *CEO*
Howard Greenberg, *General Mgr*
Joaquin Celis, *Safety Mgr*
Arlene Amuso, *Human Res Mgr*
Louisa Susman, *Sales Staff*
EMP: 53 **EST:** 1955
SQ FT: 25,000
SALES (est): 9.5MM **Privately Held**
WEB: www.edcosupply.com
SIC: 3081 5113 2673 Packing materials, plastic sheet; pressure sensitive tape; bags: plastic, laminated & coated

(G-1904)
EDISON POWER & LIGHT CO INC
204 Van Dyke St Ste 207 (11231-1038)
PHONE.....................718 522-0002
Leon Gross, *President*
EMP: 14
SQ FT: 36,000
SALES (est): 1.3MM **Privately Held**
SIC: 3648 5719 Lighting equipment; lighting fixtures

(G-1905)
EDSAL MACHINE PRODUCTS INC (PA)
126 56th St (11220-2575)
PHONE.....................718 439-9163
Fax: 718 748-4984
Evangelos S Tsevdos, *Ch of Bd*
Steven Tsevdos, *President*
Dessie Tsevdos, *Admin Sec*
▲ **EMP:** 11
SQ FT: 20,000
SALES (est): 2.3MM **Privately Held**
SIC: 3599 Machine shop, jobbing & repair

(G-1906)
EFS DESIGNS
610 Smith St Ste 3 (11231-2113)
PHONE.....................718 852-9511
Robert Burns, *President*
EMP: 6
SQ FT: 20,000
SALES (est): 591.5K **Privately Held**
SIC: 2262 2759 Screen printing: man-made fiber & silk broadwoven fabrics; screen printing

(G-1907)
EKS MANUFACTURING INC
577 Wortman Ave (11208-5415)
P.O. Box 21325 (11202-1325)
PHONE.....................917 217-0784
William Socolov, *Owner*
Yoseph Moriah, *General Mgr*
EMP: 10
SALES (est): 1.1MM **Privately Held**
SIC: 3652 Phonograph records, prerecorded

(G-1908)
EL DIARIO LLC
1 Metrotech Ctr Fl 18 (11201-3949)
PHONE.....................212 807-4600
Rossana Rosado, *CEO*
Luis Caaarte, *Editor*
Pedro Frisneda, *Editor*
Ramon Vera, *Opers Staff*
Oscar Hernandez, *Accounts Exec*
EMP: 122
SQ FT: 28,000
SALES (est): 7.7MM **Privately Held**
WEB: www.eldiariony.com
SIC: 2711 Newspapers

(G-1909)
EL ERMAN INTERNATIONAL LTD
1205 E 29th St (11210-4630)
PHONE.....................212 444-9440
Shelley Cohen, *President*
Moshe Cohen, *Vice Pres*
David Elan, *Vice Pres*
◆ **EMP:** 3
SALES: 2MM **Privately Held**
SIC: 2844 5122 Face creams or lotions; hair preparations
PA: E.L. Erman Cosmetic Production Ltd
3 Haplada
Ashdod
525 200-877

(G-1910)
ELECTRIC MOTORS AND PUMPS INC
466 Carroll St (11215-1012)
PHONE.....................718 935-9118
Jorge Fraticelli, *President*
Maria Fraticelli, *Vice Pres*
EMP: 7
SQ FT: 4,500
SALES (est): 790K **Privately Held**
SIC: 3469 5999 5084 Machine parts, stamped or pressed metal; engine & motor equipment & supplies; motors, electric; plumbing & heating supplies; pumps & pumping equipment

(G-1911)
ELECTRONIC DIE CORP
19th St Fl 2 (11232)
PHONE.....................718 455-3200
Joseph Assenza, *President*
Michael Reiss, *Principal*
Alfred Torez, *Treasurer*
EMP: 10
SQ FT: 10,000
SALES (est): 650K **Privately Held**
WEB: www.electronicdiecorp.com
SIC: 3544 Special dies, tools, jigs & fixtures

(G-1912)
ELEGANT DESSERTS BY METRO INC
868 Kent Ave (11205-2702)
PHONE.....................718 388-1323
Martin Weisz, *President*
Benjamin Weisz, *Principal*
EMP: 12
SQ FT: 7,500
SALES (est): 830K **Privately Held**
SIC: 2024 Ices, flavored (frozen dessert)

(G-1913)
ELEGANT LINEN INC (PA)
5719 New Utrecht Ave (11219-4634)
PHONE.....................718 871-3535
Fax: 718 437-4160
Benjamin Barber, *President*
Richard Citron, *Vice Pres*
EMP: 25
SQ FT: 4,000
SALES (est): 3.1MM **Privately Held**
WEB: www.elegantlinen.com
SIC: 2392 Sheets, fabric: made from purchased materials

(G-1914)
ELEPATH INC
110 Kent Ave 9 (11249-2812)
PHONE.....................347 417-4975
Bryan Goldberg, *CFO*
EMP: 5
SALES (est): 344.7K **Privately Held**
SIC: 7372 Application computer software

(G-1915)
ELRAMIDA HOLDINGS INC
2555 E 29th St (11235-2020)
PHONE.....................646 280-0503
Mark Harris, *CEO*
Eldar Rakhamineev, *Ch of Bd*
EMP: 18
SALES (est): 3.7MM **Privately Held**
SIC: 3537 Trucks, tractors, loaders, carriers & similar equipment

Brooklyn - Kings County

(G-1916)
EMCO CHEMICAL (USA) CORP
334 Douglass St (11217-3114)
PHONE..................................718 797-3652
Andy Uchitel, *President*
Mary Ellen Limer, *Vice Pres*
EMP: 25
SQ FT: 6,000
SALES (est): 3.1MM Privately Held
SIC: 2819 Industrial inorganic chemicals

(G-1917)
EMERALD ELECTRONICS USA INC
Also Called: E and E USA
251 Avenue W Ste 2 (11223-5202)
PHONE..................................718 872-5544
Elliot Tobal, *CEO*
EMP: 9
SQ FT: 6,500
SALES: 400K Privately Held
SIC: 3634 Electric household cooking appliances

(G-1918)
EMERALD HOLDINGS INC
Also Called: Emerald Knitting
63 Flushing Ave Unit 201 (11205-1072)
PHONE..................................718 797-4404
Michael Engle, *President*
Arnold Shulman, *Vice Pres*
▲ EMP: 5
SALES (est): 890K Privately Held
SIC: 2339 2253 Women's & misses' outerwear; knit outerwear mills

(G-1919)
EMES MOTOR INC
876 Metropolitan Ave (11211-2515)
PHONE..................................718 387-2445
Abraham Mertz, *President*
EMP: 5
SALES (est): 600K Privately Held
SIC: 3621 5999 Motors & generators; motors, electric

(G-1920)
EMILIA INTERIORS INC (PA)
867 E 52nd St (11203-6701)
PHONE..................................718 629-4202
Nicholas Vignapiano, *President*
Jennie Vignapiano, *Corp Secy*
EMP: 19
SQ FT: 20,000
SALES (est): 1.4MM Privately Held
WEB: www.girardemilia.com
SIC: 2511 Wood household furniture

(G-1921)
EMPIRE PRESS CO (PA)
550 Empire Blvd (11225-3131)
PHONE..................................718 756-9500
Fax: 718 604-7633
Mordechai Chein, *Owner*
Joe Katz, *Office Mgr*
EMP: 5
SQ FT: 6,000
SALES (est): 606.5K Privately Held
WEB: www.empirepress.com
SIC: 2791 2752 Typesetting; commercial printing, offset

(G-1922)
EMPIRE TRANSIT MIX INC
430 Maspeth Ave (11211-1704)
PHONE..................................718 384-3000
Fax: 718 384-3113
Rocco Tomassetti, *President*
Dina Tammaro, *Office Mgr*
EMP: 40
SALES (est): 7.8MM Privately Held
SIC: 3273 Ready-mixed concrete

(G-1923)
ENCORE RETAIL SYSTEMS INC (PA)
138 Hinsdale St (11207-3302)
PHONE..................................718 385-3443
Fax: 718 385-3161
Louis Fusaro, *President*
Stephen Cain, *Vice Pres*
EMP: 10
SQ FT: 10,000

(G-1924)
SALES (est): 2.1MM Privately Held
SIC: 2499 2541 Display forms, boot & shoes; wood partitions & fixtures

(G-1924)
ENERGY CONSERVATION & SUP INC
Also Called: E C S
55 Washington St Ste 302a (11201-1077)
PHONE..................................718 855-5888
Luther Garcia, *President*
Ricky Dweck, *Vice Pres*
James Crespo, *Treasurer*
Ann Skinner, *Accounts Mgr*
David Fraser, *Exec Dir*
EMP: 15
SQ FT: 2,200
SALES: 8.1MM Privately Held
WEB: www.enerconsupply.com
SIC: 3646 Commercial indusl & institutional electric lighting fixtures

(G-1925)
ENTERPRISE NETWORK OF NEW YORK
1407 E 101st St Ste B (11236-5507)
PHONE..................................516 263-0641
Richmond Fox, *President*
Sanjay Fernandez, *Engineer*
EMP: 10 EST: 1997
SALES: 700K Privately Held
SIC: 7372 Operating systems computer software

(G-1926)
ENTERPRISE WOOD PRODUCTS INC
4712 18th Ave (11204-1260)
PHONE..................................718 853-9243
Fax: 718 470-0776
Jan Koegel, *President*
Leonard Rosenberg, *Treasurer*
EMP: 11 EST: 1961
SQ FT: 7,500
SALES (est): 1.1MM Privately Held
SIC: 2434 Wood kitchen cabinets

(G-1927)
ENTICING LINGERIE INC
166 Gravesend Neck Rd (11223-4707)
PHONE..................................718 998-8625
David Gindi, *President*
Arlette Gindi, *Corp Secy*
EMP: 20
SQ FT: 8,000
SALES: 5MM Privately Held
WEB: www.enticinglingerie.com
SIC: 2341 2342 Women's & children's underwear; bras, girdles & allied garments

(G-1928)
ENZO MANZONI LLC
2896 W 12th St (11224-2904)
PHONE..................................212 464-7000
Gene Isaac, *Director*
EMP: 5
SQ FT: 5,000
SALES (est): 230K Privately Held
SIC: 2326 5136 Work apparel, except uniforms; men's & boys' clothing; men's & boys' sportswear & work clothing

(G-1929)
EPNER TECHNOLOGY INCORPORATED (PA)
78 Kingsland Ave (11222-5603)
PHONE..................................718 782-5948
David Epner, *President*
Paul J Brancato, *General Mgr*
Stephen V Candiloro, *Corp Secy*
Steven A Candiloro Sr, *Vice Pres*
Michel Coury, *Exec Sec*
▼ EMP: 35
SQ FT: 40,000
SALES (est): 5.9MM Privately Held
WEB: www.epner.com
SIC: 3471 Electroplating of metals or formed products

(G-1930)
EPNER TECHNOLOGY INCORPORATED
78 Kingsland Ave (11222-5603)
PHONE..................................718 782-8722
Gerald Epner, *Enginr/R&D Mgr*
David Epner, *Marketing Staff*
Stephen V Candilaro, *Systems Mgr*
EMP: 35
SALES (corp-wide): 5.9MM Privately Held
WEB: www.epner.com
SIC: 3471 Plating & polishing
PA: Epner Technology Incorporated
78 Kingsland Ave
Brooklyn NY 11222
718 782-5948

(G-1931)
EQUITYARCADE LLC
33 Nassau Ave (11222-3132)
PHONE..................................678 232-1301
Aaron Kaplan, *CEO*
Ponsius Odaga, *Manager*
EMP: 5
SALES (est): 133K Privately Held
SIC: 2741

(G-1932)
ERCOLE NYC INC (PA)
142 26th St (11232-1405)
PHONE..................................212 675-2218
Fax: 718 797-4291
Ornella Pisano, *President*
▲ EMP: 18
SQ FT: 15,000
SALES (est): 1.8MM Privately Held
WEB: www.ercolehome.com
SIC: 3253 2511 Ceramic wall & floor tile; tables, household: wood

(G-1933)
ERNEX CORPORATION INC
Also Called: Ernex Chocolate
5518 Avenue N (11234-4006)
PHONE..................................718 951-2251
Fax: 718 951-2254
Carl Grunhut, *President*
Ernest Grunhut, *Vice Pres*
Jack Grunhut, *Vice Pres*
Lenny Grunhut, *Opers Staff*
Alia Calderon, *Admin Sec*
▲ EMP: 35
SQ FT: 15,000
SALES (est): 5.3MM Privately Held
WEB: www.empresschocolate.com
SIC: 2066 Chocolate

(G-1934)
ESER REALTY CORP (PA)
62 Greenpoint Ave 64 (11222-2057)
PHONE..................................718 383-0565
Robert Frenkel, *Ch of Bd*
Morton Frenkel, *President*
◆ EMP: 50
SQ FT: 30,000
SALES (est): 5.4MM Privately Held
SIC: 3999 Feathers, renovating

(G-1935)
ESQUIRE MECHANICAL CORP
79 Sandford St (11205-2829)
PHONE..................................718 625-4006
EMP: 7
SQ FT: 5,000
SALES: 1.2MM Privately Held
WEB: www.dunhill-esquire.com
SIC: 3556 Food products machinery

(G-1936)
ESS BEE INDUSTRIES INC
95 Evergreen Ave (11206-6124)
PHONE..................................718 894-5202
Alex Stein, *President*
Iza Stein, *Vice Pres*
EMP: 30
SQ FT: 40,000
SALES (est): 1.8MM Privately Held
SIC: 2221 2392 5023 Comforters & quilts, manmade fiber & silk; household furnishings; bedspreads

(G-1937)
ESSEX WORKS LTD
446 Riverdale Ave (11207-6121)
PHONE..................................718 495-4575
Fax: 718 218-8048
Douglas Schickler, *President*
EMP: 19

SALES (est): 1.8MM Privately Held
WEB: www.essexworks.com
SIC: 3299 Architectural sculptures: gypsum, clay, papier mache, etc.

(G-1938)
EURO WOODWORKING INC
303 Park Ave Fl 8 (11205-1307)
PHONE..................................718 246-9172
Wolfgang Michelitsch, *President*
EMP: 6
SALES (est): 619.4K Privately Held
SIC: 3089 Prefabricated plastic buildings

(G-1939)
EVER-NU-METAL PRODUCTS INC
471 20th St (11215-6294)
PHONE..................................646 423-5833
Fax: 718 788-0656
Frank Gagliardi Jr, *President*
Rocco Gagliardi, *Corp Secy*
▲ EMP: 12 EST: 1949
SQ FT: 14,000
SALES (est): 1.4MM Privately Held
WEB: www.evernumetal.com
SIC: 3471 Finishing, metals or formed products

(G-1940)
EVERFLOW SUPPLIES INC
1457 58th St (11219-4647)
PHONE..................................908 436-1100
Fax: 718 438-1304
Lazar Templar, *President*
▲ EMP: 20
SALES (est): 3.5MM Privately Held
WEB: www.everflow.com
SIC: 3494 5074 Plumbing & heating valves; plumbing fittings & supplies

(G-1941)
EVERLAST SEALS AND SUPPLY LLC
41 Montrose Ave (11206-2381)
PHONE..................................718 388-7373
Joshua Benjamin, *Managing Prtnr*
Barry Himmel,
▲ EMP: 10
SQ FT: 15,000
SALES: 1MM Privately Held
SIC: 3053 Gaskets & sealing devices

(G-1942)
EXCALBUR BRNZE SCULPTURE FNDRY
309 Starr St (11237-2611)
PHONE..................................718 366-3444
William R Gold, *President*
Rachel Gold, *Vice Pres*
Eleanor Brown, *Office Mgr*
EMP: 28
SQ FT: 13,500
SALES: 1MM Privately Held
WEB: www.excaliburbronze.com
SIC: 3366 8711 3645 Bronze foundry; engineering services; residential lighting fixtures

(G-1943)
EXCELLENT POLY INC
820 4th Ave (11232-1612)
PHONE..................................718 768-6555
Joshua Silber, *CEO*
Isaac Stern, *President*
Harry Weingarten, *Exec VP*
EMP: 15 EST: 1959
SQ FT: 55,000
SALES (est): 3.3MM Privately Held
WEB: www.excellentpoly.com
SIC: 2673 3081 Plastic bags: made from purchased materials; unsupported plastics film & sheet

(G-1944)
EXCELLENT PRINTING INC
Also Called: Excellent Photocopies
165 Hooper St (11211-7911)
PHONE..................................718 384-7272
Fax: 718 384-7366
Gubor Rubin, *President*
Joseph Weinburger, *Vice Pres*
EMP: 6

Brooklyn - Kings County (G-1945)
GEOGRAPHIC SECTION

SALES (est): 540K **Privately Held**
WEB: www.yeshivanet.com
SIC: **2759** Commercial printing

(G-1945)
EXECUTIVE MACHINES INC
Also Called: Jeam Imports
882 3rd Ave Fl 10-1 (11232-1904)
P.O. Box 320150 (11232-0150)
PHONE...................................718 965-6600
Aron Abramson, *CEO*
Charles Sued, *President*
▲ EMP: 30
SQ FT: 20,000
SALES: 20K **Privately Held**
WEB: www.executivemachines.com
SIC: **3678** Electronic connectors

(G-1946)
EXPERT INDUSTRIES INC
848 E 43rd St (11210-3502)
PHONE...................................718 434-6060
Cynthia Rubinberg, *President*
Martin Sterling, *General Mgr*
Michael Rubinberg, *Vice Pres*
Erenst Senatore, *Sales Staff*
EMP: 25
SQ FT: 25,000
SALES (est): 4.5MM **Privately Held**
SIC: **3443** 3556 3444 Fabricated plate work (boiler shop); vessels, process or storage (from boiler shops): metal plate; mixers, commercial, food; sheet metal-work

(G-1947)
EY INDUSTRIES INC
Also Called: Ruckel Manufacturing Co
63 Flushing Ave Unit 331 (11205-1083)
PHONE...................................718 624-9122
Fax: 718 643-8008
Joseph Friedman, *President*
Sam Friedman, *General Mgr*
Aaron Parnes, *COO*
EMP: 15 EST: 1937
SQ FT: 15,000
SALES (est): 980K **Privately Held**
WEB: www.yarmulka.com
SIC: **2392** Comforters & quilts: made from purchased materials; pillowcases: made from purchased materials; mattress protectors, except rubber; sheets, fabric: made from purchased materials

(G-1948)
EYE GRAPHICS & PRINTING INC
499 Van Brunt St Ste 3a (11231-1051)
P.O. Box 110314 (11211-0314)
PHONE...................................718 488-0606
Faisal Iqbal, *Ch of Bd*
Mohamad Ikhmies, *Vice Pres*
EMP: 15
SALES (est): 1.9MM **Privately Held**
WEB: www.eyeprinters.com
SIC: **2759** 7336 7311 Commercial printing; commercial art & graphic design; advertising consultant

(G-1949)
EZ NEWSLETTER LLC
1449 Bay Ridge Ave 2 (11219-6232)
PHONE...................................412 943-7777
Eric V Hileman, *Mng Member*
EMP: 10
SALES (est): 890K **Privately Held**
SIC: **7372** Prepackaged software

(G-1950)
EZ SYSTEMS US INC
Also Called: EZ CMS Systems US
35 Meadow St 103 (11206-1710)
PHONE...................................212 634-6899
Gabriele Viebach, *CEO*
Tom Jergensen, *Ch of Bd*
Bard Farstad, *Co-Founder*
Svein Arne Gusland, *CFO*
Dylan Williams, *Manager*
EMP: 105 EST: 2011
SALES (est): 3.4MM
SALES (corp-wide): 7.4MM **Privately Held**
SIC: **7372** Business oriented computer software

PA: Ez Systems As
Porselensvegen 18
Porsgrunn 3920
355 870-20

(G-1951)
F R A M TECHNOLOGIES INC
3048 Bedford Ave (11210-3714)
PHONE...................................718 338-6230
Mordechai Plotsker, *President*
EMP: 6
SALES (est): 50.2K **Privately Held**
WEB: www.framtech.com
SIC: **7372** Prepackaged software

(G-1952)
FACTORY EAST
Also Called: Factory Nyc
723 Kent Ave (11249-7807)
PHONE...................................718 280-1558
Paul Outlaw, *Owner*
EMP: 20
SALES (est): 1.4MM **Privately Held**
SIC: **3499** Fabricated metal products

(G-1953)
FAIRVIEW BELL AND INTERCOM
502 Gravesend Neck Rd B (11223-4800)
PHONE...................................718 627-8621
Grzegorz Butny, *President*
Florence Kachman, *Manager*
David Rozenblyum, *Manager*
EMP: 5
SQ FT: 600
SALES (est): 200K **Privately Held**
SIC: **3699** Security devices

(G-1954)
FAL COFFEE INC
Also Called: Novetree Coffee
240 Kent Ave Ste A8 (11249-4121)
PHONE...................................718 305-4255
John Moore, *CEO*
EMP: 10
SQ FT: 7,500
SALES: 2MM **Privately Held**
SIC: **2095** Roasted coffee

(G-1955)
FALCONES COOKIE LAND LTD (PA)
Also Called: Falcone Food Distribution
1648 61st St (11204-2109)
PHONE...................................718 236-4200
Fax: 718 259-6133
Carmine Falcone Jr, *Ch of Bd*
Angelo Falcone, *President*
Francis Falcone, *Vice Pres*
EMP: 6
SQ FT: 24,000
SALES (est): 5.8MM **Privately Held**
SIC: **2052** Cookies

(G-1956)
FAMILY FUEL CO INC
1571 W 10th St (11204-6302)
PHONE...................................718 232-2009
Carol Maiden, *Chairman*
EMP: 5
SALES (est): 499.7K **Privately Held**
SIC: **2869** Fuels

(G-1957)
FANCY WINDOWS & DOORS MFG CORP
Also Called: Fancy Window & Door
100 Morgan Ave (11237-1220)
PHONE...................................718 366-7800
Jin Hu Ye, *Ch of Bd*
Jackson Ye, *President*
Jian Xu Chong, *Shareholder*
▲ EMP: 7
SQ FT: 4,000
SALES (est): 868.1K **Privately Held**
SIC: **2431** Doors & door parts & trim, wood; windows & window parts & trim, wood

(G-1958)
FANTASY HOME IMPROVEMENT CORP
2731 Atlantic Ave (11207-2803)
PHONE...................................718 277-4021
Fax: 718 277-4022
Dominic Trimarchi, *President*

Lucy Trimarchi, *Admin Sec*
EMP: 5 EST: 1974
SALES: 300K **Privately Held**
SIC: **2434** 1521 Wood kitchen cabinets; single-family housing construction

(G-1959)
FAO PRINTING
5107 Avenue H (11234-1630)
PHONE...................................718 282-3310
Fax: 718 732-2523
Philip Fisher, *Owner*
EMP: 10
SALES (est): 500K **Privately Held**
SIC: **2752** Commercial printing, lithographic

(G-1960)
FASTENERS DEPOT LLC
5308 13th Ave (11219-3804)
PHONE...................................718 622-4222
Mandle Sandle, *Office Mgr*
▲ EMP: 12
SALES (est): 1.7MM **Privately Held**
SIC: **3965** Fasteners

(G-1961)
FAVORITE PLASTIC CORP
1465 Utica Ave (11234-1108)
PHONE...................................718 253-7000
Fax: 718 377-1918
Hershey Friedman, *President*
Mitch Kirschner, *Vice Pres*
▲ EMP: 110 EST: 1956
SQ FT: 75,000
SALES (est): 16.8MM **Privately Held**
WEB: www.favoriteplastics.com
SIC: **3081** 3083 Plastic film & sheet; laminated plastics plate & sheet

(G-1962)
FAYE BERNARD LOUNGEWEAR
2604 Avenue M (11210-4611)
PHONE...................................718 951-7245
Faye Zola, *Partner*
Bernard Zola, *Partner*
EMP: 8
SQ FT: 2,000
SALES (est): 600K **Privately Held**
SIC: **2341** Nightgowns & negligees: women's & children's

(G-1963)
FEDERAL PUMP CORPORATION (PA)
1144 Utica Ave (11203-5319)
PHONE...................................718 451-2000
Fax: 718 629-0367
John Marr, *President*
Jeff Mayzus, *General Mgr*
Annette Appelbaum, *Purchasing*
Annette Appelbaum, *Accountant*
Robert Rosen, *Manager*
▲ EMP: 45 EST: 1935
SQ FT: 53,000
SALES (est): 9.2MM **Privately Held**
SIC: **3561** Pumps & pumping equipment

(G-1964)
FELDMAN JEWELRY CREATIONS INC
4821 16th Ave (11204-1109)
PHONE...................................718 438-8895
Fax: 718 438-8895
Susan Feldman, *President*
Mordecai Feldman, *Vice Pres*
EMP: 5
SQ FT: 650
SALES (est): 490K **Privately Held**
SIC: **3911** Necklaces, precious metal; rings, finger: precious metal

(G-1965)
FELDWARE INC
250 Avenue W (11223-5288)
PHONE...................................718 372-0486
Fax: 718 372-3421
Sidney Feldman, *President*
Charles Feldman, *Vice Pres*
Sam Farrell, *Manager*
▼ EMP: 25 EST: 1959
SQ FT: 15,000
SALES (est): 4MM **Privately Held**
SIC: **3469** Stamping metal for the trade

(G-1966)
FENCE PLAZA CORP
1020 Rogers Ave (11226-5417)
PHONE...................................718 469-2200
Fax: 718 469-3735
George Prince, *President*
EMP: 6
SQ FT: 300
SALES (est): 520K **Privately Held**
WEB: www.fenceplaza.com
SIC: **3446** 1799 5211 3441 Fences or posts, ornamental iron or steel; fence construction; fencing; fabricated structural metal

(G-1967)
FERRO FABRICATORS INC
1119 38th St (11218-1926)
PHONE...................................718 851-4027
Gregory Dec, *President*
EMP: 13 EST: 2003
SQ FT: 10,000
SALES (est): 2MM **Privately Held**
SIC: **3449** Bars, concrete reinforcing: fabricated steel

(G-1968)
FIBERWAVE CORPORATION
Also Called: Fiberwave Technologies
140 58th St Ste 6e (11220-2524)
PHONE...................................718 802-9011
Fax: 718 802-0116
John Romeo, *President*
Ed Kirchgessner, *CFO*
Sal Agnello, *Controller*
▲ EMP: 200
SALES (est): 26.2MM **Privately Held**
WEB: www.fiberwave.com
SIC: **3661** Fiber optics communications equipment

(G-1969)
FIL DOUX INC
227 5th Ave (11215-1202)
PHONE...................................212 202-1459
Leonardo Novik, *Ch of Bd*
Crystal Henry, *Director*
EMP: 10
SALES: 3MM **Privately Held**
SIC: **2299** Broadwoven fabrics: linen, jute, hemp & ramie

(G-1970)
FILTA CLEAN CO INC
Also Called: Belton Industries
107 Georgia Ave (11207-2489)
PHONE...................................718 495-3800
Tommy Weber, *President*
Ron Weber, *Vice Pres*
EMP: 35
SQ FT: 10,000
SALES (est): 8.1MM **Privately Held**
WEB: www.multidisplayandpanel.com
SIC: **3564** 7349 Filters, air: furnaces, air conditioning equipment, etc.; air duct cleaning

(G-1971)
FINE AND RAW CHOCOLATE
288 Seigel St (11206-3813)
PHONE...................................718 366-3633
Daniel Sklaar, *Owner*
EMP: 5
SALES (est): 150K **Privately Held**
SIC: **2064** Candy bars, including chocolate covered bars

(G-1972)
FINELINE THERMOGRAPHERS INC
544 Park Ave Ste 308 (11205-1647)
PHONE...................................718 643-1100
Fax: 718 643-6952
Samuel Fried, *President*
Themmy Sixler, *Admin Sec*
EMP: 7
SQ FT: 7,000
SALES (est): 610K **Privately Held**
SIC: **2759** Thermography

(G-1973)
FINESSE CREATIONS INC
3004 Avenue J (11210-3838)
PHONE...................................718 692-2100
Fax: 718 692-3303

Esther Machlis, *President*
Daniel Machlis, *Manager*
▲ **EMP:** 10
SQ FT: 2,500
SALES (est): 2.4MM **Privately Held**
WEB: www.finessecreations.com
SIC: 3599 5044 3569 Custom machinery; office equipment; baling machines, for scrap metal, paper or similar material

(G-1974)
FIRE FOX SECURITY CORP
2070 72nd St Apt B1 (11204-5823)
PHONE 917 981-9280
John Mansi, *President*
EMP: 5
SQ FT: 800
SALES: 250K **Privately Held**
SIC: 3699 5045 Security control equipment & systems; computers, peripherals & software

(G-1975)
FIRST INTERNATIONAL USA LTD
768 39th St (11232-3210)
PHONE 718 854-0181
Solomon Pavel, *President*
EMP: 35
SQ FT: 4,000
SALES: 800K **Privately Held**
SIC: 3961 Costume jewelry

(G-1976)
FIST INC
20 Jay St Ste 212 (11201-8319)
PHONE 718 643-3478
Fax: 718 858-6878
Jim Murnak, *President*
Bruce Nichol, *Vice Pres*
EMP: 6
SQ FT: 10,700
SALES (est): 540K **Privately Held**
SIC: 3949 3842 Protective sporting equipment; personal safety equipment

(G-1977)
FIVE BORO HOLDING LLC
1425 37th St Ste 3 (11218-3771)
PHONE 718 431-9500
Monique Cohen, *Office Mgr*
Joey Cohen, *Mng Member*
EMP: 10
SQ FT: 18,000
SALES (est): 860K **Privately Held**
WEB: www.fiveboroughprinting.com
SIC: 2761 Computer forms, manifold or continuous

(G-1978)
FIVE STAR FIELD SERVICES
Also Called: Five Star Measurement
584 Carroll St Fl 1 (11215-1118)
PHONE 347 446-6816
Douglas Asch, *Mng Member*
William Cook,
Keith Stone,
EMP: 7
SQ FT: 1,000
SALES (est): 668.6K **Privately Held**
SIC: 1389 Measurement of well flow rates, oil & gas

(G-1979)
FIVEBORO PRINTING & SUPPLIES
1425 37th St Ste 5 (11218-3771)
PHONE 718 431-9500
Bernard Eisdorfer, *Principal*
EMP: 6
SALES (est): 633.3K **Privately Held**
WEB: www.goldh.com
SIC: 2752 Commercial printing, lithographic

(G-1980)
FIXTURE HARDWARE MFG CORP
4116 1st Ave Ste 13 (11232-3389)
PHONE 718 499-9422
Fax: 718 768-5605
Kenneth Weiss, *President*
Luis Lagman, *Controller*
Victor Cardona, *Office Mgr*
▲ **EMP:** 28 **EST:** 1947
SQ FT: 30,000
SALES (est): 4.1MM **Privately Held**
WEB: www.fixturehardwaremfg.com
SIC: 2542 3446 3498 3429 Fixtures, store: except wood; architectural metalwork; fabricated pipe & fittings; manufactured hardware (general)

(G-1981)
FJS INDUSTRIES INC
Also Called: S & T Machine
970 E 92nd St (11236-1720)
PHONE 917 428-3797
Sam Accardi, *President*
EMP: 10
SALES (est): 1MM **Privately Held**
SIC: 3446 Gratings, tread: fabricated metal

(G-1982)
FLARE MULTICOPY CORP
Also Called: Flare Multi Copy
1840 Flatbush Ave (11210-4831)
PHONE 718 258-8860
Fax: 718 252-5568
Steven Zeller, *President*
Sam Stempler, *Treasurer*
EMP: 22
SALES (est): 3.2MM **Privately Held**
SIC: 2752 2791 2789 2732 Commercial printing, offset; typesetting; bookbinding & related work; book printing

(G-1983)
FLATCUT LLC
68 Jay St Ste 901 (11201-8364)
PHONE 212 542-5732
Tomer Ben-Gal, *Principal*
Jay Schainholz, *Principal*
Daniel Ramirez, *Research*
Deven Pravin Shah, *Marketing Staff*
EMP: 5 **EST:** 2010
SALES (est): 360K **Privately Held**
SIC: 3532 3496 3498 Mining machinery; miscellaneous fabricated wire products; fabricated pipe & fittings

(G-1984)
FLAUM APPETIZING CORP
288 Scholes St (11206-1728)
PHONE 718 821-1970
Fax: 718 821-9051
Moshe Grunhut, *Ch of Bd*
▲ **EMP:** 20
SQ FT: 20,000
SALES (est): 4.5MM **Privately Held**
SIC: 2099 5145 Food preparations; snack foods

(G-1985)
FLAVOR PAPER LTD
Also Called: Flavor League
216 Pacific St (11201-5713)
PHONE 718 422-0230
Emily Cangie, *COO*
Jon Sherman, *Administration*
EMP: 13
SQ FT: 3,500
SALES (est): 1.4MM **Privately Held**
WEB: www.flavorleague.com
SIC: 2679 Wallpaper

(G-1986)
FLEETWOOD CABINET CO INC (PA)
673 Livonia Ave (11207-5407)
PHONE 516 379-2139
Fax: 718 345-7164
Eric Belgraier, *President*
EMP: 8 **EST:** 1948
SQ FT: 12,000
SALES: 1MM **Privately Held**
SIC: 2541 Cabinets, except refrigerated: show, display, etc.: wood; counters or counter display cases, wood; table or counter tops, plastic laminated; sink tops, plastic laminated

(G-1987)
FLICKINGER GLASSWORKS INC
204 Van Dyke St Ste 207 (11231-1038)
PHONE 718 875-1531
Fax: 718 875-4264
Charles Flickinger, *President*
EMP: 8
SQ FT: 7,000
SALES (est): 1.3MM **Privately Held**
WEB: www.flickingerglassworks.com
SIC: 3231 5231 Glass sheet, bent: made from purchased glass; glass, leaded or stained

(G-1988)
FLUSHING BOILER & WELDING CO
8720 Ditmas Ave (11236-1606)
PHONE 718 463-1266
EMP: 7
SALES (est): 470K **Privately Held**
SIC: 7692 7699 5074 1799 Welding Repair Services Whol Plumbing Equip/Supp Special Trade Contractor

(G-1989)
FLUSHING PHARMACY INC
414 Flushing Ave Ste 1 (11205-1548)
PHONE 718 260-8999
Michell Wifemen, *President*
EMP: 250
SALES (est): 245K **Privately Held**
SIC: 2834 5813 Druggists' preparations (pharmaceuticals); night clubs

(G-1990)
FOCUS CAMERA INC (PA)
Also Called: Asavings.com
895 Mcdonald Ave (11218-5611)
PHONE 718 437-8800
Fax: 718 437-8811
Anthony Z Berkowitz, *Ch of Bd*
Ernest Berkowitz, *President*
Abe Berkowitz, *Vice Pres*
Barry Plaut, *Senior Buyer*
Esty Lebowitz, *Buyer*
▲ **EMP:** 145
SQ FT: 30,000
SALES (est): 76.2MM **Privately Held**
WEB: www.focus-camera.com
SIC: 3861 Cameras & related equipment

(G-1991)
FODERA GUITARS INC
68 34th St Unit 3 (11232-2000)
PHONE 718 832-3455
Vincent Fodera, *President*
Jason Desalvo, *Principal*
Joseph Lauricella, *Principal*
Mika Goines, *Manager*
EMP: 15
SQ FT: 6,800
SALES (est): 2.1MM **Privately Held**
WEB: www.fodera.ssl-central.com
SIC: 3931 7699 5736 Musical instruments; guitars & parts, electric & nonelectric; musical instrument repair services; musical instrument stores

(G-1992)
FOLENE PACKAGING LLC
2509 Avenue M (11210-4544)
P.O. Box 300965 (11230-0965)
PHONE 917 626-6740
Edward Weiss,
▲ **EMP:** 5
SALES (est): 586.6K **Privately Held**
SIC: 2671 Plastic film, coated or laminated for packaging

(G-1993)
FOLIO GRAPHICS CO INC
2759 E 66th St (11234-6806)
PHONE 718 763-2076
Stanley Drate, *President*
Rochelle Drate, *Vice Pres*
EMP: 6
SQ FT: 780
SALES (est): 420K **Privately Held**
SIC: 2731 7335 Books: publishing only; commercial photography

(G-1994)
FOOD52 INC
116 Willow St Apt 2 (11201-2202)
PHONE 718 596-5560
Amanda Hesser, *CEO*
Allison B Buford, *Manager*
Haley Sonneland, *Director*
Bridget Williams, *Advisor*
EMP: 7
SALES (est): 300K **Privately Held**
SIC: 2741 Miscellaneous publishing

(G-1995)
FORD REGULATOR VALVE CORP
199 Varet St (11206-3704)
PHONE 718 497-3255
Joseph Tuzzolo, *President*
Paula Tuzollo, *Treasurer*
EMP: 5 **EST:** 1889
SQ FT: 5,000
SALES (est): 520K **Privately Held**
WEB: www.fordregulatorvalve.com
SIC: 3494 5085 Valves & pipe fittings; industrial supplies

(G-1996)
FORO MARBLE CO INC
166 2nd Ave (11215-4619)
PHONE 718 852-2322
Fax: 718 802-0143
Joseph P Guido, *President*
Joseph A Guido Jr, *Exec VP*
Joan Foro, *Vice Pres*
John Addarino, *Controller*
EMP: 25
SQ FT: 25,000
SALES (est): 4.3MM **Privately Held**
WEB: www.foromarble.com
SIC: 3272 5032 Tile, precast terrazzo or concrete; slabs, crossing: concrete; tile, clay or other ceramic, excluding refractory

(G-1997)
FORTUNE SIGN
1334 39th St (11218-3616)
PHONE 646 383-8682
Fax: 646 383-5913
Anatoliy Kreychmar, *Principal*
EMP: 5 **EST:** 2011
SALES (est): 320K **Privately Held**
SIC: 3993 Signs & advertising specialties

(G-1998)
FOSTER REEVE & ASSOCIATES INC (PA)
1155 Manhattan Ave # 1011 (11222-6161)
PHONE 718 609-0090
Foster Reeve, *CFO*
Cathy Reilly, *CFO*
Heidi Hulse, *Bookkeeper*
Nancy Roscoe, *Office Mgr*
▲ **EMP:** 6
SQ FT: 4,000
SALES (est): 3.4MM **Privately Held**
WEB: www.fraplaster.com
SIC: 3299 1742 Moldings, architectural: plaster of paris; plastering, plain or ornamental

(G-1999)
FOUNTAIN TILE OUTLET INC
609 Fountain Ave Ste A (11208-6007)
PHONE 718 927-4555
Frank Lapetina, *Principal*
EMP: 6
SALES (est): 420K **Privately Held**
SIC: 2426 Flooring, hardwood

(G-2000)
FOUR DEE INC
2247 E 16th St (11229-4424)
PHONE 718 615-1695
Edmond Dweck, *President*
EMP: 62
SQ FT: 10,000
SALES: 750K **Privately Held**
SIC: 2339 Women's & misses' accessories

(G-2001)
FOUR S SHOWCASE MANUFACTURING
1044 Linwood St (11208-5422)
PHONE 718 649-4900
Tony Razi, *President*
Isabel Razi, *Vice Pres*
EMP: 8
SQ FT: 12,000
SALES (est): 770K **Privately Held**
WEB: www.4sshowcase.com
SIC: 2542 Office & store showcases & display fixtures

(G-2002)
FRANKLIN POLY FILM INC
1149 56th St (11219-4504)
PHONE 718 492-3523

Brooklyn - Kings County (G-2003)

GEOGRAPHIC SECTION

Fax: 718 492-1149
Isidore Handler, *President*
Rose Frankel, *Principal*
Israel Kahan, *Corp Secy*
Angela Rice, *Plant Mgr*
Mory Eigner, *Manager*
▼ **EMP:** 39
SQ FT: 26,000
SALES (est): 5.4MM **Privately Held**
SIC: 2673 3082 3081 Plastic bags: made from purchased materials; unsupported plastics profile shapes; unsupported plastics film & sheet

(G-2003)
FRANZ FISCHER INC
1267 Flushing Ave (11237-2302)
P.O. Box 370715 (11237-0715)
PHONE................................718 821-1300
Franz Fischer, *President*
EMP: 10
SQ FT: 14,000
SALES (est): 1.5MM **Privately Held**
WEB: www.franzfischer.com
SIC: 2511 Wood household furniture

(G-2004)
FRENCH & ITLN FURN CRAFTSMEN
Also Called: French Itln Furn Craftsmen Cor
999 Grand St (11211-2704)
PHONE................................718 599-5000
Patrick F Molloy, *President*
EMP: 7
SQ FT: 6,000
SALES (est): 490K **Privately Held**
WEB: www.frenchanditalian.com
SIC: 2511 5712 Wood household furniture; furniture stores

(G-2005)
FRESH FANATIC INC
88 Washington Ave (11205-1202)
PHONE................................516 521-6574
Andrew Goldin, *CEO*
David Goldin, *President*
EMP: 9
SALES (est): 1.3MM **Privately Held**
SIC: 2033 5146 5149 Fruit juices: fresh; fish, fresh; sandwiches

(G-2006)
FRESH ICE CREAM COMPANY LLC
630 Flushing Ave 4 (11206-5026)
PHONE................................347 603-6021
Gerard Tucci, *Manager*
EMP: 10 **Privately Held**
SIC: 2024 5143 Ice cream & frozen desserts; ice cream & ices
PA: The Fresh Ice Cream Company Llc
  630 Flushing Ave
  Brooklyn NY 11206

(G-2007)
FRIENDLY STAR FUEL INC
889 3rd Ave (11232-1907)
PHONE................................718 369-8801
Gurpal Cheema, *Principal*
EMP: 6
SALES (est): 622.5K **Privately Held**
SIC: 2869 Fuels

(G-2008)
FUTURE STAR DIGATECH
713 Monroe St (11221-2813)
PHONE................................718 666-0350
Kertena Seabrook, *Owner*
EMP: 10
SALES (est): 760.6K **Privately Held**
SIC: 3577 Printers, computer

(G-2009)
FWC NETWORKS INC
1615 Carroll St (11213-5409)
PHONE................................718 408-1558
Boruch Lowenbein, *CEO*
Barbara Nowha, *Ch of Bd*
Shlomo Oved, *President*
Bashie Lowenbein, *CFO*
EMP: 18
SQ FT: 6,000
SALES (est): 2.1MM **Privately Held**
SIC: 3699 Electrical welding equipment

(G-2010)
G S COMMUNICATIONS USA INC
Also Called: Gs Communications USA
179 Greenpoint Ave (11222-7088)
PHONE................................718 389-7371
Helen Juszczak, *President*
David Pasirstein, *Vice Pres*
Louis Makowski, *Network Mgr*
EMP: 22
SQ FT: 11,250
SALES (est): 2MM **Privately Held**
WEB: www.gscomm.com
SIC: 3571 5734 Personal computers (microcomputers); computer & software stores

(G-2011)
G Z G REST & KIT MET WORKS
120 13th St (11215-4604)
PHONE................................718 788-8621
Fax: 718 788-0482
Gregory Uchatel, *President*
Alex Blyustein, *Vice Pres*
EMP: 15
SQ FT: 5,500
SALES (est): 920K **Privately Held**
SIC: 2599 Bar, restaurant & cafeteria furniture; carts, restaurant equipment

(G-2012)
GALIVA INC
236 Broadway Ste 214 (11211-6289)
PHONE................................903 600-5755
Joel Gelb, *COO*
EMP: 4
SQ FT: 10,000
SALES: 1.4MM **Privately Held**
SIC: 2252 Socks

(G-2013)
GARCO MANUFACTURING CORP INC
4802 Farragut Rd (11203-6612)
PHONE................................718 287-3330
EMP: 7 **EST:** 1960
SQ FT: 4,000
SALES (est): 64.5K **Privately Held**
SIC: 2851 Mfg Paints/Allied Products

(G-2014)
GARY GELBFISH MD
2502 Avenue I (11210-2830)
PHONE................................718 258-3004
Fax: 718 421-0628
Gary Gelbfish, *Owner*
Chana E Gelbfish, *Med Doctor*
Abigail Falk, *Manager*
EMP: 8
SALES (est): 690K **Privately Held**
SIC: 3845 Surgical support systems: heart-lung machine, exc. iron lung

(G-2015)
GCM METAL INDUSTRIES INC
454 Troutman St (11237-2604)
PHONE................................718 386-4059
Baldo Ciaravino, *President*
EMP: 15
SALES (est): 1.4MM **Privately Held**
SIC: 3449 1791 5051 1799 Bars, concrete reinforcing: fabricated steel; structural steel erection; structural shapes, iron or steel; ornamental metal work

(G-2016)
GCM STEEL PRODUCTS INC
454 Troutman St (11237-2604)
PHONE................................718 386-3346
Giovanna Mattarella, *President*
Josephine Dolce, *General Mgr*
EMP: 10
SALES (est): 1.1MM **Privately Held**
SIC: 3499 Metal household articles

(G-2017)
GCNS TECHNOLOGY GROUP INC
597 Rutland Rd (11203-1703)
PHONE................................347 713-8160
Joann Henry, *President*
EMP: 15
SALES (est): 605K **Privately Held**
SIC: 3825 Network analyzers

(G-2018)
GDI CUSTOM MARBLE & GRANITE
134 Avenue T (11223-3624)
PHONE................................718 996-9100
Fax: 718 996-9104
Peter Desantis, *President*
▲ **EMP:** 10
SQ FT: 8,500
SALES (est): 1.1MM **Privately Held**
SIC: 3281 1743 Marble, building: cut & shaped; granite, cut & shaped; tile installation, ceramic

(G-2019)
GENERAL VY-COAT LLC
1636 Coney Island Ave 2b (11230-5808)
PHONE................................718 266-6002
Allen Gottfried, *General Mgr*
Sol Chaimovits,
EMP: 40
SQ FT: 80,000
SALES (est): 5.2MM **Privately Held**
SIC: 2851 3086 2821 Vinyl coatings, strippable; plastics foam products; plastics materials & resins

(G-2020)
GENIUS MEDIA GROUP INC
Also Called: Rap Genius
92 3rd St (11231-4808)
PHONE................................509 670-7502
Thomas Lehman, *President*
EMP: 15
SALES (est): 880K **Privately Held**
SIC: 2741 Miscellaneous publishing

(G-2021)
GERI-GENTLE CORPORATION (PA)
3841 Ocean View Ave (11224-1343)
PHONE................................917 804-7807
Joseph Grun, *CEO*
Harold Rubin, *President*
EMP: 2
SQ FT: 5,000
SALES (est): 2MM **Privately Held**
SIC: 3069 Medical & laboratory rubber sundries & related products

(G-2022)
GFL USA INC
Also Called: Gfl Amenities
81 Prospect St (11201-1473)
PHONE................................917 297-8701
Guido Bonadonna, *CEO*
Anna Childs, *Sales Mgr*
EMP: 2
SQ FT: 100
SALES (est): 1.2MM **Privately Held**
SIC: 2841 2844 Soap & other detergents; shampoos, rinses, conditioners: hair; towelettes, premoistened
PA: Gfl Sa
  Via Per Sorengo 1
  Lugano TI
  919 607-500

(G-2023)
GHANI TEXTILES INC
2459 Coyle St Fl 2 (11235-1207)
PHONE................................718 859-4561
Muhammad Aslam, *CEO*
EMP: 1
SALES (est): 1MM **Privately Held**
SIC: 2299 Acoustic felts

(G-2024)
GILLIES COFFEE COMPANY
150 19th St (11232-1005)
PHONE................................718 499-7766
Fax: 718 499-7771
Donald N Schoenholt, *President*
Hy Chabbott, *Treasurer*
EMP: 25
SQ FT: 14,000
SALES: 3.3MM **Privately Held**
WEB: www.gilliescoffee.com
SIC: 2095 2099 Coffee roasting (except by wholesale grocers); tea blending

(G-2025)
GIUMENTA CORP (PA)
Also Called: Utility Brass & Bronze Div
42 2nd Ave (11215-3102)
PHONE................................718 832-1200
Fax: 718 832-1390
Anthony J Giumenta, *President*
Anthony F Giumenta, *Vice Pres*
Stephen Giumenta, *Treasurer*
▲ **EMP:** 46
SQ FT: 55,000
SALES (est): 12.9MM **Privately Held**
SIC: 3446 Architectural metalwork; ornamental metalwork; grillwork, ornamental metal

(G-2026)
GLENNYS INC
1960 59th St (11204-2340)
PHONE................................516 377-1400
Mendel Fischer, *Vice Pres*
EMP: 8
SQ FT: 15,000
SALES (est): 770.5K **Privately Held**
SIC: 2064 2096 Breakfast bars; corn chips & other corn-based snacks

(G-2027)
GLENWOOD CAST STONE INC
Also Called: Glenwood Mason Supply
4106 Glenwood Rd (11210-2025)
PHONE................................718 859-6500
Constance M Cincotta, *President*
EMP: 5
SALES (est): 445.2K **Privately Held**
SIC: 3272 Concrete products, precast

(G-2028)
GLISSEN CHEMICAL CO INC (PA)
1321 58th St (11219-4594)
P.O. Box 190034 (11219-0034)
PHONE................................718 436-4200
Fax: 718 851-2938
Joseph W Lehr, *President*
Barbara Lehr, *Exec VP*
Rosita Barca, *Administration*
EMP: 27 **EST:** 1930
SQ FT: 25,000
SALES (est): 8.1MM **Privately Held**
SIC: 2841 Detergents, synthetic organic or inorganic alkaline

(G-2029)
GLOBEX KOSHER FOODS INC
Also Called: Interntonal Glatt Kosher Meats
5600 1st Ave Ste 19 (11220-2551)
PHONE................................718 630-5555
Fax: 718 921-1542
Abraham Chaimovitz, *Ch of Bd*
Leib Chaimovitz, *President*
♦ **EMP:** 23
SALES (est): 4.3MM **Privately Held**
SIC: 2011 Meat packing plants

(G-2030)
GLOBMARBLE LLC
2201 Neptune Ave Ste 5 (11224-2362)
PHONE................................347 717-4088
Iryna Semenenko, *Mng Member*
EMP: 6 **EST:** 2010
SALES (est): 316.8K **Privately Held**
SIC: 3544 5031 Industrial molds; molding, all materials

(G-2031)
GM SHEET METAL INC
193 Newell St (11222-2421)
PHONE................................718 349-2830
Fax: 718 349-2968
Michael Flatley, *President*
EMP: 16
SALES (est): 1.5MM **Privately Held**
SIC: 3444 Metal ventilating equipment

(G-2032)
GMS HICKS STREET CORPORATION
214 Hicks St (11201-4110)
PHONE................................718 858-1010
Greg Markman, *Principal*
EMP: 40
SALES (est): 2.4MM **Privately Held**
SIC: 3088 Plastics plumbing fixtures

▲ = Import ▼ = Export
♦ = Import/Export

Brooklyn - Kings County (G-2061)

(G-2033)
GNI COMMERCE INC
Also Called: Yourhealth911.com
458 Neptune Ave Apt 11f (11224-4319)
PHONE.................................347 275-1155
Vladimir Gouliaev, *President*
Bella Bomze, *Vice Pres*
▼ **EMP:** 7
SQ FT: 3,500
SALES: 3.1MM **Privately Held**
WEB: www.gnicommerce.com
SIC: 2023 Dietary supplements, dairy & non-dairy based

(G-2034)
GODDARD DESIGN CO
51 Nassau Ave Ste 1b (11222-3171)
PHONE.................................718 599-0170
Robert Goddard, *Owner*
Rosemary Heath, *Office Mgr*
EMP: 7
SQ FT: 2,000
SALES: 500K **Privately Held**
WEB: www.goddarddesign.com
SIC: 3648 3625 3669 Lighting equipment; control equipment, electric; intercommunication systems, electric

(G-2035)
GODFREY PRPELLER ADJUSTING SVC
Also Called: Jnc Repair
155 25th St (11232-1408)
PHONE.................................718 768-3744
John Boutsikakis, *President*
Michael Papaderos, *President*
EMP: 5
SQ FT: 2,200
SALES (est): 530K **Privately Held**
SIC: 3731 Shipbuilding & repairing

(G-2036)
GODIVA CHOCOLATIER INC
5378 Kings Plz (11234-5216)
PHONE.................................718 677-1452
Osbert James, *Branch Mgr*
EMP: 24 **Privately Held**
SIC: 2066 Chocolate
HQ: Godiva Chocolatier, Inc.
  333 W 34th St Fl 6
  New York NY 10001
  212 984-5900

(G-2037)
GOLD & DIAMONDS WHOLESALE OUTL
4417 5th Ave (11220-6834)
PHONE.................................718 438-7888
Alex Gatfif, *President*
EMP: 4
SALES: 2MM **Privately Held**
SIC: 3911 5094 Jewel settings & mountings, precious metal; diamonds (gems)

(G-2038)
GOLDEN LEAVES KNITWEAR INC
43 Hall St Ste B3 (11205-1395)
PHONE.................................718 875-8235
Cheskel Gluck, *President*
▲ **EMP:** 40
SQ FT: 25,000
SALES: 2.3MM **Privately Held**
SIC: 2253 2339 Sweaters & sweater coats, knit; women's & misses' outerwear

(G-2039)
GOLDMARK INC
Also Called: Gold Mark Mfg Co
3611 14th Ave Ste B01 (11218-3750)
PHONE.................................718 438-0295
Fax: 718 438-1274
Shimson Jalas, *President*
EMP: 20
SQ FT: 20,000
SALES (est): 3.3MM **Privately Held**
WEB: www.goldmark.com
SIC: 3915 Jewelers' findings & materials

(G-2040)
GOODLITE PRODUCTS INC
2042 Pitkin Ave (11207-3430)
PHONE.................................718 697-7502
Nathan Meisels, *President*
▲ **EMP:** 10
SQ FT: 20,000
SALES: Privately Held
SIC: 3229 Bulbs for electric lights

(G-2041)
GORILLA COFFEE INC (PA)
97 5th Ave (11217-3201)
PHONE.................................718 230-3244
Darleen Scherer, *Ch of Bd*
EMP: 5
SALES (est): 605.7K **Privately Held**
WEB: www.gorillacoffee.com
SIC: 2095 Coffee roasting (except by wholesale grocers)

(G-2042)
GOTENNA INC
81 Willoughby St Fl 3 (11201-5232)
PHONE.................................415 894-2616
Daniela Perdomo, *President*
John Levy, *Principal*
Jorge Perdomo, *Chief Engr*
EMP: 13
SALES (est): 1MM **Privately Held**
SIC: 3679 Headphones, radio

(G-2043)
GOURMET CRAFTS INC
152 Highlawn Ave (11223-2636)
P.O. Box 200006 (11220-0006)
PHONE.................................718 372-0505
Borris Tulman, *President*
Eugene Tulman, *Vice Pres*
Eric Shkolnik, *CFO*
EMP: 16
SQ FT: 4,000
SALES: 925K **Privately Held**
WEB: www.thecrepeteam.com
SIC: 2099 Food preparations

(G-2044)
GOURMET TOAST CORP
345 Park Ave (11205-1389)
PHONE.................................718 852-4536
Jack Feld, *President*
EMP: 8 **EST:** 1958
SQ FT: 8,000
SALES: 600K **Privately Held**
SIC: 2099 2051 Bread crumbs, not made in bakeries; bread, cake & related products

(G-2045)
GOVERNMENT DATA PUBLICATION
1661 Mcdonald Ave (11230-6312)
PHONE.................................347 789-8719
Fax: 718 998-5960
Siegfried Lobel, *President*
Barbara Calabrese, *Director*
EMP: 35 **EST:** 1959
SQ FT: 10,000
SALES (est): 3.1MM **Privately Held**
WEB: www.govdata.com
SIC: 2731 2741 2721 2752 Books: publishing only; miscellaneous publishing; directories: publishing only, not printed on site; periodicals: publishing only; commercial printing, lithographic

(G-2046)
GRADO LABORATORIES INC
4614 7th Ave Ste 1 (11220-1499)
PHONE.................................718 435-5340
Fax: 718 633-6941
John A Grado, *President*
John Chen, *Vice Pres*
Todd Green, *Manager*
▲ **EMP:** 10 **EST:** 1953
SQ FT: 10,000
SALES (est): 1.6MM **Privately Held**
SIC: 3679 Phonograph needles; headphones, radio

(G-2047)
GRANADA ELECTRONICS INC
485 Kent Ave (11249-5927)
PHONE.................................718 387-1157
Fax: 718 486-6995
Nachman Brach, *President*
EMP: 6
SQ FT: 55,000
SALES (est): 540K **Privately Held**
SIC: 3651 Audio electronic systems; television receiving sets

(G-2048)
GRAND PROCESSING INC
1050 Grand St (11211-1701)
PHONE.................................718 388-0600
Iggy Panadora, *President*
EMP: 30
SQ FT: 30,000
SALES (est): 1.3MM **Privately Held**
SIC: 2253 Dyeing & finishing knit outerwear, excl. hosiery & glove

(G-2049)
GRAPHIC DIMENSIONS PRESS INC
Also Called: Bell Press
3502 Quentin Rd (11234-4231)
PHONE.................................718 252-4003
Fax: 718 692-0659
J Zuller, *President*
Sue Kassierer, *Bookkeeper*
EMP: 12
SQ FT: 3,500
SALES: 850K **Privately Held**
SIC: 2752 7338 Commercial printing, offset; resume writing service

(G-2050)
GRECO BROS RDYMX CON CO INC
381 Hamilton Ave (11231-3943)
PHONE.................................718 855-6271
Joseph Greco, *President*
EMP: 8
SALES (corp-wide): 10.1MM **Privately Held**
SIC: 3273 Ready-mixed concrete
PA: Greco Bros. Ready Mix Concrete Co. Inc.
  8713 Rockaway Blvd
  Ozone Park NY 11416
  718 849-5200

(G-2051)
GREEN WAVE INTERNATIONAL INC
5423 1st Ave (11220-2503)
P.O. Box 90288 (11209-0288)
PHONE.................................718 499-3371
Kay Dan Wong, *President*
Gerry Callaghan, *Sales Mgr*
Garret Fong, *Manager*
Ivan Hui, *Manager*
Abel Leung, *Technical Staff*
▲ **EMP:** 7
SQ FT: 12,000
SALES (est): 964.4K **Privately Held**
SIC: 3263 Commercial tableware or kitchen articles, fine earthenware

(G-2052)
GREENBUDS LLC
1434 57th St (11219-4619)
PHONE.................................718 483-9212
Miriam Mandel,
EMP: 5 **EST:** 2010
SQ FT: 1,000
SALES: 500K **Privately Held**
SIC: 2221 Bedding, manmade or silk fabric

(G-2053)
GREENEBUILD LLC
390a Lafayette Ave (11238-1406)
PHONE.................................917 562-0556
Winston Greene,
EMP: 12
SALES (est): 755.8K **Privately Held**
SIC: 1442 Construction sand & gravel

(G-2054)
GREENTREE PHARMACY INC
291 7th Ave (11215-7263)
PHONE.................................718 768-2700
Julia Nudelman, *Owner*
EMP: 10 **EST:** 2013
SALES (est): 1.8MM **Privately Held**
SIC: 2834 5961 Pharmaceutical preparations; pharmaceuticals, mail order

(G-2055)
GUERNICA
Also Called: Guernica Magazine
63 3rd Pl Apt 4r (11231-4047)
PHONE.................................914 414-7318
Joel Whitney, *Principal*
Elizabeth Onusko, *Principal*
EMP: 15
SALES: 20K **Privately Held**
SIC: 2721 Periodicals

(G-2056)
GUMBUSTERS (PA)
1424 74th St (11228-2208)
PHONE.................................866 846-8486
Anthony Mule, *Owner*
Andrea Mule, *Co-Owner*
EMP: 6
SQ FT: 5,000
SALES (est): 1.1MM **Privately Held**
SIC: 2861 Gum & wood chemicals

(G-2057)
H & H LABORATORIES INC (PA)
61 4th St (11231-4809)
PHONE.................................718 624-8041
Fax: 718 246-2738
George Hoffmann, *President*
Trina Moslih, *Assistant*
▲ **EMP:** 14
SQ FT: 5,000
SALES (est): 1.6MM **Privately Held**
WEB: www.hhlabs.com
SIC: 2844 2841 Toilet preparations; soap & other detergents

(G-2058)
H & H LABORATORIES INC
409 Hoyt St (11231-4858)
PHONE.................................718 624-8041
George Hoffman, *Branch Mgr*
EMP: 5
SALES (corp-wide): 1.6MM **Privately Held**
SIC: 2844 2841 Toilet preparations; soap & other detergents
PA: H & H Laboratories Inc.
  61 4th St
  Brooklyn NY 11231
  718 624-8041

(G-2059)
H FOX & CO INC
Also Called: Fox's U-Bet Syrups
416 Thatford Ave (11212-5895)
PHONE.................................718 385-4600
Fax: 718 345-4283
David Fox, *Ch of Bd*
Karen Fox, *Corp Secy*
Susan Frank, *Office Mgr*
EMP: 30 **EST:** 1900
SQ FT: 36,000
SALES (est): 6.3MM **Privately Held**
WEB: www.foxs-u-bet.com
SIC: 2087 2066 Syrups, flavoring (except drink); chocolate coatings & syrup

(G-2060)
H T L & S LTD
Also Called: Peerless Envelopes & Prtg Co
5820 Fort Hamilton Pkwy (11219-4832)
PHONE.................................718 435-4474
Fax: 718 438-1750
Sheldon Kustin, *Partner*
Lewis Kustin, *Partner*
EMP: 11 **EST:** 1933
SQ FT: 20,000
SALES: 700K **Privately Held**
SIC: 2752 2759 Commercial printing, offset; letterpress printing; flexographic printing

(G-2061)
HADDAD BROS INC
1200 Mcdonald Ave (11230-3321)
PHONE.................................718 377-5505
Fax: 718 252-2426
John Isseco, *Executive*
EMP: 50
SALES (corp-wide): 7.2MM **Privately Held**
WEB: www.haddadbros.com
SIC: 2361 2369 2335 Girls' & children's dresses, blouses & shirts; girls' & children's outerwear; women's, juniors' & misses' dresses
PA: Haddad Bros. Inc.
  28 W 36th St Rm 1026
  New York NY 10018
  212 563-2117

(G-2062)
HAGADAH PASSOVER BAKERY
814 Bergen St (11238-3702)
PHONE................718 638-1589
Fax: 718 623-6681
P Woodsberger, *Owner*
Joe Castri, *Manager*
EMP: 8
SALES (est): 453.6K **Privately Held**
SIC: 2051 Bread, cake & related products

(G-2063)
HALMARK ARCHITECTURAL FINSHG
353 Stanley Ave (11207-7601)
PHONE................718 272-1831
Fax: 718 272-1835
Hal Spergel, *President*
EMP: 24
SQ FT: 10,000
SALES (est): 2.9MM **Privately Held**
SIC: 3471 2843 3449 Finishing, metals or formed products; surface active agents; miscellaneous metalwork

(G-2064)
HAMODIA CORP
Also Called: Daily Newsppr For Torah Jewry
207 Foster Ave (11230-2195)
PHONE................718 853-9094
Fax: 718 853-9103
Ruth Lichtenstein, *CEO*
Moshe Vatalion, *Controller*
EMP: 14 EST: 1998
SALES (est): 861K **Privately Held**
SIC: 2711 Newspapers

(G-2065)
HANA PASTRIES INC
34 35th St Unit 9 (11232-2212)
P.O. Box 320154 (11232-0154)
PHONE................718 369-7593
Michael Schwartz, *Principal*
Michael Hu, *Mng Member*
EMP: 6
SALES (est): 757.2K **Privately Held**
SIC: 2051 5411 Bread, cake & related products; supermarkets

(G-2066)
HANCO METAL PRODUCTS INC
25 Jay St (11201-1139)
PHONE................212 787-5992
Fax: 718 243-2915
Mark Meyer Hantman, *President*
Myles Hantman, *General Mgr*
Debra Hantman, *Corp Secy*
EMP: 10 EST: 1934
SQ FT: 2,000
SALES (est): 800K **Privately Held**
SIC: 3451 3432 Screw machine products; faucets & spigots, metal & plastic

(G-2067)
HANDMADE FRAMES INC
1013 Grand St Ste 2 (11211-1720)
PHONE................718 782-8364
Fax: 212 782-6146
Paul Baumann, *President*
Marilyn Gold, *Vice Pres*
EMP: 14
SQ FT: 9,000
SALES (est): 983.6K **Privately Held**
SIC: 3999 3952 Framed artwork; frames for artists' canvases

(G-2068)
HANDY TOOL & MFG CO INC
1205 Rockaway Ave (11236-2132)
P.O. Box 360524 (11236-0524)
PHONE................718 478-9203
Fax: 718 429-5062
Rochelle Sherman, *Treasurer*
Raquel Genao, *Admin Asst*
EMP: 22 EST: 1948
SQ FT: 13,600
SALES (est): 5.9MM **Privately Held**
SIC: 3728 Aircraft assemblies, subassemblies & parts

(G-2069)
HEALTHONE PHARMACY INC
119 Pennsylvania Ave (11207-2428)
PHONE................718 495-9015
Mel Springer, *President*
EMP: 15
SALES (est): 3.5MM **Privately Held**
SIC: 2834 Pharmaceutical preparations

(G-2070)
HEALTHY WAY OF LIFE MAGAZINE
1529 Voorhies Ave (11235-3912)
PHONE................718 616-1681
Boris Zat, *President*
EMP: 5
SALES (est): 319.8K **Privately Held**
SIC: 2721 Periodicals

(G-2071)
HECHT & SOHN GLASS CO INC
406 Willoughby Ave (11205-4509)
PHONE................718 782-8295
Fax: 718 486-6414
Abe Sabel, *President*
▲ EMP: 6
SQ FT: 11,000
SALES (est): 685.4K **Privately Held**
WEB: www.entrances.com
SIC: 3211 3231 Flat glass; doors, glass: made from purchased glass

(G-2072)
HELLO AND HOLA MEDIA INC
1 Metrotech Ctr Fl 18 (11201-3949)
PHONE................212 807-4795
Eduardo Sanchez Perez, *CEO*
EMP: 22
SALES (est): 624K **Privately Held**
SIC: 2721 Magazines: publishing & printing

(G-2073)
HENRYS DEALS INC
Also Called: Allstateelectronics
1002 Quentin Rd Ste 2009 (11223-2248)
PHONE................347 821-4685
David Matts, *CEO*
Simon Sarweh, *CEO*
EMP: 20
SALES: 1MM **Privately Held**
SIC: 3861 Photographic equipment & supplies

(G-2074)
HERCULES HEAT TREATING CORP
101 Classon Ave 113 (11205-1401)
PHONE................718 625-1266
Anthony Rizzo Jr, *President*
Joseph Rizzo, *Vice Pres*
Gabriel Giraldo, *Engineer*
EMP: 27
SQ FT: 25,000
SALES (est): 6.1MM **Privately Held**
WEB: www.herculesht.com
SIC: 3398 Metal heat treating

(G-2075)
HERCULES INCORPORATED
Also Called: Ashland Hercules Water Tech
761 Humboldt St (11222-3001)
PHONE................718 383-1717
Peter Coster, *Branch Mgr*
EMP: 9
SALES (corp-wide): 5.3B **Publicly Held**
SIC: 2891 Adhesives
HQ: Hercules Incorporated
500 Hercules Rd
Wilmington DE 19808
302 594-5000

(G-2076)
HERMAN H STICHT COMPANY INC
Also Called: Megohmer Vbrating Reed Standco
45 Main St Ste 401 (11201-1084)
PHONE................718 852-7602
Fax: 718 852-7915
Paul H Plotkin, *President*
Glenn A Butterfield, *Vice Pres*
Edna E Brown, *Treasurer*
EMP: 6
SQ FT: 6,000
SALES (est): 1MM **Privately Held**
WEB: www.stichtco.com
SIC: 3825 3823 3829 Measuring instruments & meters, electric; industrial instrmnts msrmnt display/control process variable; measuring & controlling devices

(G-2077)
HERMAN HALL COMMUNICATIONS
Also Called: Everybodys Carribbean Magazine
1630 Nostrand Ave (11226-5516)
PHONE................718 941-1879
Fax: 718 941-1886
Herman Hall, *President*
Helen Lucas, *Treasurer*
EMP: 12
SQ FT: 5,000
SALES: 500K **Privately Held**
SIC: 2721 Magazines: publishing only, not printed on site

(G-2078)
HERRIS GOURMET INC
536 Grand St (11211-3503)
PHONE................917 578-2308
Herman Franczoz, *Vice Pres*
EMP: 5
SQ FT: 2,500
SALES (est): 270.2K **Privately Held**
SIC: 2051 5812 5499 Bread, cake & related products; contract food services; gourmet food stores

(G-2079)
HERTLING TROUSERS INC
236 Greenpoint Ave (11222-2493)
PHONE................718 784-6100
Fax: 718 784-7015
Julius Hertling, *President*
▲ EMP: 40
SQ FT: 8,000
SALES (est): 4.4MM **Privately Held**
SIC: 2325 2253 Men's & boys' trousers & slacks; pants, slacks or trousers, knit

(G-2080)
HIGHWAY BAGELS CORP
1921 Kings Hwy 1923 (11229-1313)
PHONE................347 350-6493
Fax: 718 382-9143
Alberto Pernicone, *President*
Luigi Curto, *Vice Pres*
EMP: 5
SQ FT: 2,000
SALES (est): 380K **Privately Held**
SIC: 2051 5461 Bagels, fresh or frozen; bakeries

(G-2081)
HMO BEVERAGE CORP
68 33rd St Unit 4 (11232-1912)
PHONE................917 371-6100
Georgios Papanastasatos, *Principal*
EMP: 5
SALES (est): 464.2K **Privately Held**
SIC: 2086 Carbonated beverages, nonalcoholic: bottled & canned

(G-2082)
HOFSET FABRICS LTD
445 Park Ave Bsmt (11205-2735)
PHONE................718 522-6228
Fax: 718 855-9352
Israel Hoffman, *President*
Chaim Fiund, *Accountant*
Sarah Freund, *Manager*
EMP: 5
SQ FT: 30,000
SALES (est): 380K **Privately Held**
SIC: 2259 Convertors, knit goods

(G-2083)
HOLLYWOOD SIGNS INC
388 3rd Ave (11215-2705)
PHONE................917 577-7333
Steve Kokonovich, *President*
EMP: 9
SALES (est): 690K **Privately Held**
SIC: 3993 Signs & advertising specialties

(G-2084)
HOME AND ABOVE LLC
199 Lee Ave Ste 895 (11211-8919)
PHONE................914 220-3451
Charles Kohn, *CEO*
Becca Gurkov, *Admin Asst*
EMP: 10
SALES (est): 393.6K **Privately Held**
SIC: 3089 3421 Kitchenware, plastic; knives: butchers', hunting, pocket, etc.; potato peelers, hand

(G-2085)
HOME REPORTER INC
Also Called: Home Reporter & Sunset News
8723 3rd Ave (11209-5103)
PHONE................718 238-6600
Fax: 718 238-6630
James F Griffin Jr, *President*
Alex Kalas, *Corp Secy*
Marvile Griffin, *Vice Pres*
Sara Otey, *Advt Staff*
EMP: 50 EST: 1956
SQ FT: 2,000
SALES (est): 2.3MM **Privately Held**
WEB: www.homereporter.net
SIC: 2711 Newspapers, publishing & printing

(G-2086)
HOME4U INC
152 Skillman St Apt 8 (11205-3906)
PHONE................347 262-7214
Abraham Goldstein, *CEO*
Joel Teitelbaum, *CFO*
EMP: 7
SQ FT: 2,000
SALES (est): 413.3K **Privately Held**
SIC: 2541 Cabinets, lockers & shelving

(G-2087)
HONEYBEE ROBOTICS LTD (PA)
Also Called: Honeybee Rbtics Cft Mechanisms
Suit Bldg 128 (11205)
PHONE................212 966-0661
Fax: 646 459-7898
Kiel Davis, *President*
Stephen Gorvan, *Chairman*
Jason Herman, *Vice Pres*
Erik Mumm, *Vice Pres*
Kris Zacny, *Vice Pres*
EMP: 44
SQ FT: 110,000
SALES (est): 9.1MM **Privately Held**
WEB: www.honeybeerobotics.com
SIC: 3569 Robots, assembly line: industrial & commercial

(G-2088)
HOSKIE CO INC
132 Harrison Pl (11237-1522)
PHONE................718 628-8672
Fax: 718 628-5545
Glenn Ho, *CEO*
◆ EMP: 80
SQ FT: 38,000
SALES (est): 17.4MM **Privately Held**
WEB: www.hoskiecompanyinc.com
SIC: 2015 3999 Poultry slaughtering & processing; atomizers, toiletry

(G-2089)
HPI CO INC (PA)
1656 41st St (11218-5512)
PHONE................718 851-2753
Moshe Kenner, *President*
Peggy Oberland, *Vice Pres*
▲ EMP: 5
SQ FT: 3,000
SALES: 100K **Privately Held**
WEB: www.hpico.net
SIC: 3567 Industrial furnaces & ovens

(G-2090)
HUDSON POWER TRANSMISSION CO
241 Halsey St (11216-2403)
PHONE................718 622-3869
Fax: 718 622-9396
Lawrence Saft, *President*
EMP: 5
SQ FT: 880
SALES (est): 440K **Privately Held**
SIC: 3568 Power transmission equipment

(G-2091)
HUNTINGTON ICE & CUBE CORP (PA)
335 Moffat St (11237-6408)
PHONE................718 456-2013
Gaspar Piccolo, *Vice Pres*
EMP: 10

▲ = Import ▼ = Export
◆ = Import/Export

GEOGRAPHIC SECTION

Brooklyn - Kings County (G-2118)

SALES (est): 1.1MM **Privately Held**
SIC: 2097 Block ice

(G-2092)
HYMAN PODRUSNICK CO INC
212 Foster Ave (11230-2197)
P.O. Box 300158 (11230-0158)
PHONE..................718 853-4502
David Binder, *President*
Mae Binder, *Vice Pres*
▲ EMP: 5
SQ FT: 5,000
SALES (est): 410K **Privately Held**
SIC: 3469 3821 Household cooking & kitchen utensils, porcelain enameled; laboratory apparatus & furniture

(G-2093)
IAM MALIAMILLS LLC
Also Called: Malia Mills Studio
32 33rd St Unit 13 (11232-1924)
PHONE..................805 845-2137
Malian Mills,
EMP: 6
SALES (est): 650K **Privately Held**
SIC: 2253 Bathing suits & swimwear, knit

(G-2094)
IBERIA FOODS CORP (HQ)
1900 Linden Blvd (11207-6806)
PHONE..................718 272-8900
Eric Miller, *President*
William Schneible, *CFO*
John Pierrard, *Controller*
Mario Casas, *Manager*
Stuart Streger, *Admin Sec*
▲ EMP: 80
SQ FT: 240
SALES (est): 35.5MM
SALES (corp-wide): 41.2MM **Privately Held**
SIC: 2032 Ethnic foods: canned, jarred, etc.
PA: Brooklyn Bottling Of Milton, New York, Inc.
643 South Rd
Milton NY 12547
845 795-2171

(G-2095)
ICESTONE LLC
63 Flushing Ave Unit 283b (11205-1079)
PHONE..................718 624-4900
Dal Lamagna, *CEO*
Jana Milcikova, *President*
Arti Bhatt, *Vice Pres*
Alison Tester, *Purch Dir*
Raymond Chen, *Research*
▲ EMP: 37
SQ FT: 55,000
SALES (est): 7.5MM **Privately Held**
SIC: 3281 2541 1752 3499 Building stone products; counter & sink tops; ceramic floor tile installation; furniture parts, metal

(G-2096)
IEH CORPORATION
140 58th St Ste 8e (11220-2525)
PHONE..................718 492-4440
Fax: 718 492-9898
Michael Offerman, *Ch of Bd*
Robert Knoth, *CFO*
Sam Ling, *Legal Staff*
EMP: 150 **EST**: 1937
SQ FT: 20,400
SALES: 19.3MM **Privately Held**
WEB: www.iehcorp.com
SIC: 3678 Electronic connectors

(G-2097)
IMPERIAL FRAMES & ALBUMS LLC
8200 21st Ave (11214-2506)
PHONE..................718 832-9793
Moshe Wigdder, *Mng Member*
▲ EMP: 5
SALES: 2.5MM **Privately Held**
WEB: www.imperialframes.com
SIC: 2499 Woodenware, kitchen & household

(G-2098)
IMPERIAL LAMINATORS CO INC
961 Elton St (11208-5417)
P.O. Box 7367, Hicksville (11802-7361)
PHONE..................718 272-9500
Fax: 718 649-1292
Bernard Brown, *President*
David Brown, *Treasurer*
▲ EMP: 10
SQ FT: 40,000
SALES (est): 740K **Privately Held**
SIC: 2295 2297 Laminating of fabrics; bonded-fiber fabrics, except felt

(G-2099)
IMPERIAL POLYMERS INC
534 Grand St (11211-3503)
PHONE..................718 387-4741
Joseph Freund, *President*
EMP: 6
SALES (est): 550K **Privately Held**
SIC: 2821 3089 Molding compounds, plastics; plastic processing

(G-2100)
IMPERIAL SWEATER MILLS INC
Also Called: Eagle Nesher
1365 38th St (11218-3634)
PHONE..................718 871-4414
Fax: 718 871-5463
Shalom Katz, *President*
Benjamin Katz, *Admin Sec*
EMP: 6 **EST**: 1955
SQ FT: 18,500
SALES (est): 707.1K **Privately Held**
SIC: 2253 Sweaters & sweater coats, knit

(G-2101)
IMPREMEDIA LLC (DH)
Also Called: La Raza
1 Metrotech Ctr Fl 18 (11201-3949)
PHONE..................212 807-4785
Carmen Villavicencio, *Editor*
Olga Casabona, *Vice Pres*
Maria Mendillo, *Accounts Exec*
John Paton, *Mng Member*
Vivian Chavez, *Manager*
▲ EMP: 99
SALES (est): 103.5MM **Privately Held**
WEB: www.impremedia.com
SIC: 2711 Newspapers: publishing only, not printed on site
HQ: Us Hispanic Media Inc
1 Metrotech Ctr Fl 18
Brooklyn NY 11201
212 885-8000

(G-2102)
INDIAN LARRY LEGACY
400 Union Ave (11211-3429)
PHONE..................718 609-9184
EMP: 5
SALES: 500K **Privately Held**
SIC: 3751 Mfg Motorcycles/Bicycles

(G-2103)
INDUSTRIAL ELECTRONIC HARDWARE
140 58th St Ste 8e (11220-2525)
PHONE..................718 492-4440
Fax: 718 492-9897
Bob Offman, *President*
Robert Romeo, *Vice Pres*
Reggie Johnson, *Manager*
Cindy Sciascia, *Manager*
Rolando Velez, *Manager*
EMP: 70
SALES (est): 6MM **Privately Held**
SIC: 3429 Manufactured hardware (general)

(G-2104)
INDUSTRIAL FINISHING PRODUCTS
820 Remsen Ave (11236-1611)
PHONE..................718 342-4871
Andrew Galgano, *Manager*
EMP: 12
SALES (corp-wide): 11.2MM **Privately Held**
WEB: www.industrialfinishings.com
SIC: 2851 Plastics base paints & varnishes

PA: Industrial Finishing Products Inc
465 Logan St
Brooklyn NY 11208
718 277-3333

(G-2105)
INFANT FORMULA LABORATORY SVC
711 Livonia Ave (11207-5497)
PHONE..................718 257-3000
Richard C Miller, *President*
EMP: 10 **EST**: 1947
SQ FT: 20,000
SALES (est): 1MM **Privately Held**
SIC: 2023 5149 Bottled baby formula; groceries & related products

(G-2106)
INK PUBLISHING CORPORATION
68 Jay St Ste 315 (11201-8360)
PHONE..................347 294-1220
Steve Oconnor, *Sales Dir*
Phyll Castle, *Branch Mgr*
Jacqueline Detwiler, *Assoc Editor*
EMP: 5
SALES (corp-wide): 19.5MM **Privately Held**
SIC: 2721 Periodicals
HQ: Ink Publishing Corporation
1375b Spring St Nw
Atlanta GA 30309
678 553-8080

(G-2107)
INK WELL
1440 Coney Island Ave (11230-4120)
PHONE..................718 253-9736
Yosef Oratz, *Owner*
EMP: 5
SQ FT: 4,000
SALES (est): 340K **Privately Held**
SIC: 2752 Commercial printing, lithographic

(G-2108)
INLAND PAPER PRODUCTS CORP
Also Called: Wew Container
444 Liberty Ave (11207)
P.O. Box 70137 (11207-0137)
PHONE..................718 827-8150
Daniel Weicher, *President*
Joel Einbinoer, *Corp Secy*
▲ EMP: 20
SQ FT: 30,000
SALES (est): 3.6MM **Privately Held**
SIC: 3083 Laminated plastics plate & sheet

(G-2109)
INTEGRA MICROSYSTEM 1988 INC
Also Called: All-Tech
61 Greenpoint Ave Ste 412 (11222-1526)
PHONE..................718 609-6099
Israel Haber, *Ch of Bd*
EMP: 5
SQ FT: 1,000
SALES (est): 826.8K **Privately Held**
SIC: 3575 Computer terminals, monitors & components

(G-2110)
INTERIOR METALS
Also Called: M&A Metals
255 48th St (11220-1011)
PHONE..................718 439-7324
Fax: 718 439-8723
Michael Tommasi, *President*
Antonella Tommasi, *Corp Secy*
Eric Ulmer, *Project Mgr*
Laura Lopez, *Assistant*
EMP: 27
SQ FT: 13,000
SALES (est): 4.9MM **Privately Held**
WEB: www.interiormetals.com
SIC: 3444 Radiator shields or enclosures, sheet metal

(G-2111)
INTERNATIONAL STONE ACCESSRS
703 Myrtle Ave (11205-3903)
PHONE..................718 522-5399
Fax: 718 596-6373

Abraham Levy, *President*
Sanny Levy, *Vice Pres*
▲ EMP: 6
SQ FT: 7,500
SALES (est): 907.4K **Privately Held**
WEB: www.stonecityexpo.com
SIC: 3281 Marble, building: cut & shaped

(G-2112)
INTERNTIONAL FIREPROF DOOR INC
1005 Greene Ave (11221-2910)
PHONE..................718 783-1310
Fax: 718 783-4308
Eric Arrow, *President*
EMP: 10
SQ FT: 7,500
SALES (est): 990K **Privately Held**
WEB: www.firedoor.com
SIC: 3442 Fire doors, metal; window & door frames

(G-2113)
INTERNTNAL STRPPING DIECUTTING
Also Called: Deslauriers
200 Franklin St (11222-1633)
PHONE..................718 383-7720
Fax: 718 349-2954
Jan Chielewski, *President*
EMP: 6 **EST**: 1955
SQ FT: 10,000
SALES (est): 460K **Privately Held**
SIC: 3554 7699 Paper industries machinery; box making machines, paper; printing trades machinery & equipment repair

(G-2114)
INTEX COMPANY INC (PA)
Also Called: Semtex Industrial
5317 Church Ave (11203-3614)
PHONE..................718 336-3491
Henrietta Rivman, *President*
EMP: 61
SQ FT: 20,000
SALES (est): 6MM **Privately Held**
SIC: 3674 5065 Semiconductors & related devices; electronic parts

(G-2115)
IQUIT CIG LLC
4014 13th Ave (11218-3502)
PHONE..................718 475-1422
Zelman Pollak,
EMP: 6
SQ FT: 250
SALES (est): 335.6K **Privately Held**
SIC: 3999 Cigarette & cigar products & accessories

(G-2116)
ISH PRECISION MACHINE CORP (PA)
786 Mcdonald Ave (11218-5606)
PHONE..................718 436-8858
Fax: 718 436-8858
Issac Sheran, *President*
Aleksandr Sherman, *Vice Pres*
EMP: 10
SALES: 1.5MM **Privately Held**
SIC: 3541 Machine tools, metal cutting type

(G-2117)
ISSACS YISROEL
Also Called: Benchers Unlimited
4424 18th Ave (11204-1201)
PHONE..................718 851-7430
Yisroel Issacs, *Owner*
Grant Gray, *Bd of Directors*
Karen Olsen, *Admin Sec*
EMP: 5
SALES: 600K **Privately Held**
WEB: www.benchers.com
SIC: 2759 5947 Imprinting; gifts & novelties

(G-2118)
IT COMMODITY SOURCING INC
Also Called: Federal Contract MGT Svcs
1640 E 22nd St (11210-5125)
PHONE..................718 677-1577
Aviva Tabak, *CEO*
Vevel Tabak, *President*
Peretz Charach, *Vice Pres*

Brooklyn - Kings County (G-2119)

EMP: 5
SALES (est): 370K Privately Held
SIC: 3663 Radio & TV communications equipment

(G-2119)
ITAC LABEL & TAG CORP
179 Lexington Ave (11216-1114)
PHONE 718 625-2148
Fax: 718 625-3806
ARI Adler, *President*
Rarzy Schwartz, *Manager*
EMP: 7
SQ FT: 17,500
SALES: 700K Privately Held
SIC: 2672 Labels (unprinted), gummed: made from purchased materials

(G-2120)
ITIN SCALE CO INC
4802 Glenwood Rd (11234-1106)
PHONE 718 336-5900
Samuel Racer, *President*
Philip Levinson, *Manager*
▲ **EMP:** 20 **EST:** 1970
SQ FT: 4,500
SALES (est): 5.1MM Privately Held
WEB: www.itinscales.com
SIC: 3829 3699 3596 3821 Measuring & controlling devices; electrical equipment & supplies; scales & balances, except laboratory; laboratory apparatus & furniture; scales, except laboratory; commercial cooking & food service equipment

(G-2121)
J & J BRONZE & ALUMINUM CAST
Also Called: All Cast Foundry
249 Huron St (11222-1801)
PHONE 718 383-2111
Fax: 718 383-3893
Vincent Grosso, *Vice Pres*
Robert Grosso, *Vice Pres*
EMP: 34
SQ FT: 23,000
SALES (est): 4.6MM Privately Held
SIC: 3366 3365 3369 Castings (except die): bronze; aluminum & aluminum-based alloy castings; nonferrous foundries

(G-2122)
J H C FABRICATIONS INC (PA)
Also Called: Jhc Labresin
595 Berriman St (11208-5203)
P.O. Box 80377 (11208-0377)
PHONE 718 649-0065
Henry L Calamari, *President*
John Calamari, *Corp Secy*
Christopher Delgrosso, *Marketing Staff*
Michael Manachevtz, *Manager*
▲ **EMP:** 20 **EST:** 1986
SQ FT: 16,000
SALES (est): 3MM Privately Held
WEB: www.jhclabresin.com
SIC: 3821 3644 Laboratory furniture; insulators & insulation materials, electrical

(G-2123)
J H M ENGINEERING
4014 8th Ave (11232-3706)
PHONE 718 871-1810
J H Maliga, *Owner*
Bud Hammen, *Sales/Mktg Mgr*
Carmen Martinez, *Bookkeeper*
EMP: 25 **EST:** 1966
SQ FT: 15,000
SALES (est): 2.3MM Privately Held
SIC: 3841 3843 3845 3699 Surgical & medical instruments; dental equipment; electromedical equipment; electrical equipment & supplies

(G-2124)
J LOWY CO
Also Called: J Lowy Lea Skullcaps Mfg Co
940 E 19th St (11230-3805)
PHONE 718 338-7324
Jerry Lowy, *Owner*
▲ **EMP:** 8
SALES: 1MM Privately Held
WEB: www.kippott.com
SIC: 2386 5999 Hats & caps, leather; religious goods

(G-2125)
J M C BOW CO INC
1271 39th St Ste 3 (11218-1981)
PHONE 718 686-8110
Bernard Kalisch, *President*
EMP: 15 **EST:** 1952
SQ FT: 7,500
SALES (est): 1.4MM Privately Held
SIC: 2323 2389 Bow ties, men's & boys': made from purchased materials; cummerbunds

(G-2126)
J M L PRODUCTIONS INC
162 Spencer St (11205-3929)
PHONE 718 643-1674
Jay Cohen, *President*
Michael Dymburt, *Admin Sec*
EMP: 60
SQ FT: 30,000
SALES (est): 2.3MM Privately Held
SIC: 2396 2759 Screen printing on fabric articles; screen printing

(G-2127)
J M P DISPLAY FIXTURE CO INC
760 E 96th St (11236-1821)
PHONE 718 649-0333
Fax: 718 485-4125
Joseph Cangelosi, *President*
Rosalie Angelosi, *Vice Pres*
EMP: 7
SQ FT: 7,200
SALES (est): 1MM Privately Held
SIC: 2541 Display fixtures, wood

(G-2128)
J ZELUCK INC (PA)
5300 Kings Hwy (11234-1016)
PHONE 718 251-8060
Roy Zeluck, *President*
Kevin Zeluck, *Vice Pres*
Michael Sincaglia, *Project Mgr*
◆ **EMP:** 50 **EST:** 1921
SALES (est): 8.9MM Privately Held
WEB: www.zeluck.com
SIC: 2431 Windows, wood; doors, wood

(G-2129)
JACKS GOURMET LLC
1000 Dean St Ste 214 (11238-3382)
PHONE 718 954-4681
Jack Silberstein, *CEO*
EMP: 12
SALES: 1.5MM Privately Held
SIC: 2013 Sausages & other prepared meats

(G-2130)
JACMAX INDUSTRIES LLC
Also Called: Expressive Scent
14a 53rd St Unit 501 (11232-2631)
PHONE 718 439-3743
Max Antar, *CEO*
Jack Eida, *President*
EMP: 5
SQ FT: 150,000
SALES: 455.6K Privately Held
SIC: 2677 Envelopes

(G-2131)
JACOB INC
287 Keap St (11211-7477)
PHONE 646 450-3067
Solomon Breuer, *CEO*
EMP: 40
SQ FT: 8,000
SALES (est): 20MM Privately Held
SIC: 3554 Paper industries machinery

(G-2132)
JACOBS JUICE CORP
388 Avenue X Apt 2h (11223-6025)
PHONE 646 255-2860
Jacob Prig, *President*
EMP: 5
SALES (est): 290K Privately Held
SIC: 3999 Novelties, bric-a-brac & hobby kits

(G-2133)
JACOBY ENTERPRISES LLC
1615 54th St (11204-1438)
PHONE 718 435-0289
Shraga F Jacobowitz, *Office Mgr*
Abraham Jacobowitz,
Karen Zheng, *Assoc Prof*
▲ **EMP:** 7
SQ FT: 1,500
SALES (est): 1.2MM Privately Held
WEB: www.jacobygems.com
SIC: 3911 5094 Bracelets, precious metal; cigarette lighters, precious metal; precious stones & metals; jewelry

(G-2134)
JAKES SNEAKERS INC
845 Classon Ave (11238-6103)
PHONE 718 233-1132
Jake Zebak, *President*
Beatrellia Francis, *Manager*
EMP: 1
SALES (est): 1.2MM Privately Held
SIC: 2393 5661 Cushions, except spring & carpet: purchased materials; children's shoes

(G-2135)
JAXIS INC (PA)
Also Called: Jaxi's Sportswear
1365 38th St (11218-3634)
PHONE 212 302-7611
Ezra Abed, *President*
Nathan Mann, *Vice Pres*
Eddy Mann, *Admin Sec*
EMP: 6
SQ FT: 1,100
SALES (est): 622.2K Privately Held
SIC: 2339 5137 Sportswear, women's; sportswear, women's & children's

(G-2136)
JAY TUROFF
Also Called: Jay-Art Nvelties/Tower Grafics
681 Coney Island Ave (11218-4306)
PHONE 718 856-7300
Jay Turoff, *Owner*
EMP: 11 **EST:** 1965
SQ FT: 3,500
SALES: 1.2MM Privately Held
SIC: 3993 7336 3961 Signs & advertising specialties; commercial art & graphic design; costume novelties

(G-2137)
JERRY TOMASELLI
Also Called: Express Tag & Label
141 32nd St (11232-1809)
PHONE 718 965-1400
Fax: 718 965-1648
Jerry Tomaselli, *Owner*
EMP: 10
SQ FT: 10,000
SALES: 500K Privately Held
SIC: 2679 Tags, paper (unprinted): made from purchased paper

(G-2138)
JEWELERS SOLDER SUPPLY INC
Also Called: Jewler's Solder Sheet & Wire
1362 54th St (11219-4219)
P.O. Box 190141 (11219-0141)
PHONE 718 637-1256
Michael Goldenberg, *Owner*
Connie Klinger, *Principal*
Rachel Goldenberg, *Vice Pres*
EMP: 11
SQ FT: 10,000
SALES: 145.2K Privately Held
SIC: 3356 Solder: wire, bar, acid core, & rosin core

(G-2139)
JEWISH HERITAGE FOR BLIND
1655 E 24th St (11229-2401)
PHONE 718 338-4999
Fax: 718 338-0653
Rabbi David Toiv, *President*
EMP: 8
SQ FT: 2,000
SALES (est): 470K Privately Held
WEB: www.jhftb.org
SIC: 2741 Miscellaneous publishing

(G-2140)
JEWISH JOURNAL
7014 13th Ave (11228-1604)
PHONE 718 630-9350
EMP: 5
SALES (est): 160K Privately Held
SIC: 2711 Newspapers-Publishing/Printing

(G-2141)
JEWISH PRESS INC
4915 16th Ave (11204-1115)
PHONE 718 330-1100
Fax: 718 935-1215
Sidney Klass, *President*
Shelia Abrams, *Editor*
Jerry Greenwald, *Vice Pres*
Harry Rosenthal, *Vice Pres*
Arthur Federman, *Controller*
EMP: 149 **EST:** 1949
SQ FT: 40,000
SALES (est): 9.6MM Privately Held
WEB: www.jewishpress.com
SIC: 2711 Newspapers: publishing only, not printed on site

(G-2142)
JILL FENICHELL INC
Also Called: Bongenre.com
169 Prospect Pl (11238-3801)
PHONE 718 237-2490
Jill Fenichell, *President*
▲ **EMP:** 6
SALES: 250K Privately Held
SIC: 3263 Tableware, household & commercial: semivitreous

(G-2143)
JO-MART CANDIES CORP
Also Called: Jo Mart Chocolates
2917 Avenue R (11229-2525)
PHONE 718 375-1277
Fax: 718 382-7144
Michael Rogak, *President*
EMP: 11 **EST:** 1946
SQ FT: 3,000
SALES (est): 1.4MM Privately Held
WEB: www.jomartchocolates.com
SIC: 2064 5441 2066 Candy & other confectionery products; candy; chocolate & cocoa products

(G-2144)
JOEL ZELCER
102 S 8th St (11249-8632)
P.O. Box 20102 (11202-0102)
PHONE 917 525-6790
Joel Zelcer, *Owner*
EMP: 10
SALES (est): 479.1K Privately Held
SIC: 3944 7389 Games, toys & children's vehicles;

(G-2145)
JOHN AUGULIARO PRINTING CO
Also Called: John V Agugliaro Printing
2533 Mcdonald Ave (11223-5232)
PHONE 718 382-5283
Fax: 718 382-5283
Justin Agugliaro, *President*
EMP: 8
SALES (est): 760K Privately Held
SIC: 2759 Commercial printing

(G-2146)
JOMAT NEW YORK INC
4100 1st Ave Ste 3 (11232-3303)
PHONE 718 369-7641
Marc Landman, *President*
EMP: 35
SQ FT: 12,000
SALES: 1MM Privately Held
SIC: 2339 2369 Women's & misses' outerwear; girls' & children's outerwear

(G-2147)
JORDACHE WOODWORKING CORP
276 Greenpoint Ave # 1303 (11222-2451)
PHONE 718 349-3373
Fax: 718 349-3372
Nicholas Jordache, *President*
EMP: 14
SALES: 500K Privately Held
SIC: 2434 2499 Wood kitchen cabinets; decorative wood & woodwork

(G-2148)
JOS H LOWENSTEIN AND SONS INC
420 Morgan Ave (11222-5705)
PHONE 718 218-8013
Fax: 718 387-3806

GEOGRAPHIC SECTION

Brooklyn - Kings County (G-2178)

Stephen J Lowenstein, *Ch of Bd*
David Lowenstein, *President*
Sue Papish, *Exec VP*
Richard Cahayla-Wynne, *Vice Pres*
Thomas Sowpel, *Vice Pres*
◆ **EMP:** 85 **EST:** 1897
SQ FT: 100,000
SALES (est): 30.1MM **Privately Held**
WEB: www.jhlowenstein.com
SIC: 2869 2865 Industrial organic chemicals; dyes, synthetic organic

(G-2149)
JOSEPH PAUL
Also Called: Perfect Publications
1064 Rogers Ave Apt 5 (11226-6234)
P.O. Box 1087, New York (10163-1087)
PHONE..............................718 693-4269
Joseph Paul, *Owner*
A Bourne, *Manager*
◆ **EMP:** 6
SALES (est): 340K **Privately Held**
SIC: 2752 Commercial printing, lithographic

(G-2150)
JOSEPH SHALHOUB & SON INC
1258 Prospect Ave (11218-1304)
PHONE..............................718 871-6300
Fax: 718 871-6300
Joseph Shalhoub Jr, *President*
Ray Shalhoub, *Vice Pres*
EMP: 14
SQ FT: 15,000
SALES (est): 710K **Privately Held**
SIC: 2064 Fruits: candied, crystallized, or glazed

(G-2151)
JOSEPH ZAKON WINERY LTD
Also Called: Kesser Wine
586 Montgomery St (11225-3130)
PHONE..............................718 604-1430
Joseph Zakon, *President*
EMP: 3
SQ FT: 5,000
SALES (est): 1.5MM **Privately Held**
SIC: 2084 Wines

(G-2152)
JOY OF LEARNING
992 Gates Ave (11221-3602)
PHONE..............................718 443-6463
C Clay Berry, *Owner*
EMP: 7
SALES: 200K **Privately Held**
SIC: 2211 Broadwoven fabric mills, cotton

(G-2153)
JOYA LLC
Also Called: Joya Studio
19 Vanderbilt Ave (11205-1113)
PHONE..............................718 852-6979
Bernard Bouchardy, *CEO*
Mayra Miranda, *Manager*
EMP: 15
SALES (est): 1.2MM **Privately Held**
SIC: 3999 Candles

(G-2154)
JOYVA CORP (PA)
53 Varick Ave (11237-1523)
PHONE..............................718 497-0170
Fax: 718 366-8504
Milton Radutzky, *President*
Sanford Wiener, *Treasurer*
Donna Dhanraj, *Accounts Mgr*
Sandy Wienner, *Manager*
Richard Radutzky, *Admin Sec*
▲ **EMP:** 60 **EST:** 1906
SQ FT: 26,370
SALES (est): 12.3MM **Privately Held**
WEB: www.joyva.com
SIC: 2064 2066 2099 Candy & other confectionery products; halvah (candy); chocolate & cocoa products; food preparations

(G-2155)
JTA USA INC
63 Flushing Ave Unit 339 (11205-1084)
PHONE..............................718 722-0902
Alex Rub, *President*
EMP: 7 **EST:** 2012
SQ FT: 2,000

SALES (est): 799.8K **Privately Held**
SIC: 3291 Wheels, abrasive

(G-2156)
JUDAICA PRESS INC
123 Ditmas Ave (11218-4930)
PHONE..............................718 972-6202
Fax: 718 972-6204
Gloria Goldman, *President*
▲ **EMP:** 8 **EST:** 1963
SQ FT: 2,325
SALES (est): 1MM **Privately Held**
WEB: www.judaicapress.com
SIC: 2731 Books: publishing only

(G-2157)
JUDIS LAMPSHADES INC
1495 E 22nd St (11210-5122)
PHONE..............................917 561-3921
Fax: 718 336-0416
Judith Sadan, *President*
Judi Sadan, *President*
EMP: 5 **EST:** 1998
SQ FT: 1,000
SALES (est): 310K **Privately Held**
WEB: www.judislampshades.com
SIC: 3645 Lamp shades, metal

(G-2158)
JUICES ENTERPRISES INC
1142 Nostrand Ave (11225-5414)
PHONE..............................718 953-1860
Juliet McNaughton, *President*
EMP: 6
SALES (est): 535.6K **Privately Held**
SIC: 2086 Carbonated beverages, nonalcoholic: bottled & canned

(G-2159)
JULIANS RECIPE LLC
128 Norman Ave (11222-3382)
PHONE..............................888 640-8880
Joe Cancilleri, *Controller*
Alexander Dzieduszycki, *Mng Member*
Tim Wike, *Director*
Roza Jacquez, *Administration*
▲ **EMP:** 8
SQ FT: 1,100
SALES: 9.2MM **Privately Held**
SIC: 2038 Frozen specialties

(G-2160)
JUNIORS CHEESECAKE INC
386 Flatbush Avenue Ext (11201-5331)
PHONE..............................718 852-5257
Alan Rosen, *President*
Walter Rosen, *Chairman*
Kevin Rosen, *Vice Pres*
Nancy Weinberger, *Mktg Dir*
Adriana Sims, *Office Mgr*
EMP: 7
SQ FT: 30,000
SALES (est): 450K **Privately Held**
WEB: www.juniorscheesecake.com
SIC: 2051 Cakes, pies & pastries

(G-2161)
K & R ALLIED INC
Also Called: Allied K & R Broom & Brush Co
39 Pearl St Fl 2 (11201-8302)
PHONE..............................718 625-6610
Fax: 718 643-3741
Karl Chang, *President*
Kam Lau, *Vice Pres*
EMP: 10
SQ FT: 18,000
SALES (est): 960K **Privately Held**
WEB: www.alliedkr.com
SIC: 3991 Brooms & brushes; brooms

(G-2162)
K & S CHILDRENS WEAR INC
Also Called: Elegant Sportswear
204 Wallabout St (11206-5418)
PHONE..............................718 624-0006
Fax: 718 596-8770
Thomas Klein, *President*
Jacob Klein, *Vice Pres*
EMP: 47
SQ FT: 20,000
SALES (est): 7.5MM **Privately Held**
SIC: 2253 2369 Sweaters & sweater coats, knit; jackets: girls', children's & infants'

(G-2163)
K DISPLAYS
1363 47th St (11219-2612)
PHONE..............................718 854-6045
Fax: 718 854-5983
Malvin Boehm, *President*
EMP: 10
SALES (est): 440K **Privately Held**
SIC: 3172 Cases, jewelry

(G-2164)
K M DRIVE LINE INC
966 Grand St (11211-2707)
PHONE..............................718 599-0628
Salvatore Bucchio Jr, *President*
John Smith, *Accounts Mgr*
EMP: 8
SQ FT: 5,000
SALES (est): 1.2MM **Privately Held**
WEB: www.kmdriveline.com
SIC: 3714 5013 5531 Drive shafts, motor vehicle; motor vehicle supplies & new parts; automobile & truck equipment & parts

(G-2165)
K T A V PUBLISHING HOUSE INC
527 Empire Blvd (11225-3121)
PHONE..............................201 963-9524
Sol Scharfstein, *President*
Bernard Scharfstein, *Corp Secy*
▲ **EMP:** 13
SQ FT: 25,000
SALES (est): 1.3MM **Privately Held**
WEB: www.ktav.com
SIC: 2731 Books: publishing only

(G-2166)
KALE FACTORY INC
790 Washington Ave (11238-7706)
PHONE..............................917 363-6361
EMP: 6
SALES (est): 504.4K **Privately Held**
SIC: 2099 Food preparations

(G-2167)
KAMMETAL INC
75 Huntington St (11231-1825)
PHONE..............................718 625-2628
Alastair Kusack, *Branch Mgr*
EMP: 10
SALES (corp-wide): 5.5MM **Privately Held**
SIC: 3446 Architectural metalwork
PA: Kammetal Inc.
 29 Imlay St
 Brooklyn NY 11231
 718 722-9991

(G-2168)
KAMMETAL INC (PA)
29 Imlay St (11231-1336)
PHONE..............................718 722-9991
Samuel Kusack, *President*
Alastair Kusack, *Vice Pres*
Kate Dubois, *Project Mgr*
David Weinstein, *Controller*
EMP: 18
SQ FT: 1,500
SALES (est): 5.5MM **Privately Held**
SIC: 3446 Architectural metalwork

(G-2169)
KARO SHEET METAL INC
Also Called: Karosheet Metal
229 Russell St (11222-3004)
PHONE..............................718 542-8420
Fax: 718 383-6145
Kathleen Portman, *President*
EMP: 40
SQ FT: 10,000
SALES (est): 5.7MM **Privately Held**
SIC: 3444 Ducts, sheet metal; ventilators, sheet metal

(G-2170)
KENDI IRON WORKS INC (PA)
236 Johnson Ave (11206-2819)
PHONE..............................718 821-2722
Fax: 718 456-8006
Zadok Zvi, *President*
Anna Zvi, *Vice Pres*
EMP: 8
SQ FT: 16,500
SALES (est): 680.6K **Privately Held**
SIC: 3446 Ornamental metalwork

(G-2171)
KINFOLK STUDIOS INC
90 Wythe Ave (11249-1923)
PHONE..............................347 799-2946
Ryan Carney, *President*
EMP: 30
SQ FT: 900
SALES: 950K **Privately Held**
SIC: 2599 Bar, restaurant & cafeteria furniture

(G-2172)
KING RESEARCH INC
114 12th St Ste 1 (11215-3892)
PHONE..............................718 788-0122
Fax: 718 788-0290
Bernard R King, *President*
Carol Ordyk, *Asst Sec*
◆ **EMP:** 23 **EST:** 1947
SQ FT: 23,500
SALES (est): 3.2MM **Privately Held**
SIC: 2842 2841 2844 3229 Disinfectants, household or industrial plant; detergents, synthetic organic or inorganic alkaline; toilet preparations; glassware, art or decorative

(G-2173)
KING SALES INC
284 Wallabout St (11206-4927)
PHONE..............................718 301-9862
David Schwimmer, *Owner*
▲ **EMP:** 4
SALES (est): 480.7K **Privately Held**
SIC: 2329 Athletic (warmup, sweat & jogging) suits: men's & boys'

(G-2174)
KING STEEL IRON WORK CORP
2 Seneca Ave (11237)
PHONE..............................718 384-7500
Fax: 718 384-8647
Eliran Galapo, *Vice Pres*
Jorge Fernandez, *Manager*
EMP: 15
SALES (est): 2.7MM **Privately Held**
SIC: 3441 Fabricated structural metal

(G-2175)
KINGS FILM & SHEET INC
Also Called: Kings Specialty Co
482 Baltic St (11217-2508)
P.O. Box 170144 (11217-0144)
PHONE..............................718 624-7510
Forrest T Weisburst, *President*
Joel Leonard, *General Mgr*
Paulette Anderson, *Purchasing*
Richard Blalock, *CTO*
EMP: 24
SQ FT: 15,000
SALES (est): 4.2MM **Privately Held**
WEB: www.kingsspecialty.com
SIC: 3081 Plastic film & sheet

(G-2176)
KMS CONTRACTING INC
Also Called: Sure Iron Works
86 Georgia Ave (11207-2402)
PHONE..............................718 495-6500
Fax: 718 495-6503
Steven Horn, *President*
EMP: 14
SQ FT: 11,500
SALES (est): 2.9MM **Privately Held**
WEB: www.sureiron.com
SIC: 3446 Architectural metalwork

(G-2177)
KO FRO FOODS INC
4418 18th Ave 4420 (11204-1201)
PHONE..............................718 972-6480
Kalman Mendelsohn, *President*
Abraham Mendelsohn, *Chairman*
Heshy Mendelsohn, *Treasurer*
EMP: 20
SQ FT: 4,300
SALES: 2MM **Privately Held**
WEB: www.mendelsohns.com
SIC: 2053 Frozen bakery products, except bread

(G-2178)
KODIAK STUDIOS INC
3030 Emmons Ave Apt 3t (11235-2226)
PHONE..............................718 769-5399
Alex Tish, *President*

Brooklyn - Kings County (G-2179) — GEOGRAPHIC SECTION

EMP: 5
SALES (est): 384.4K **Privately Held**
WEB: www.kodiakstudios.com
SIC: 3299 Architectural sculptures: gypsum, clay, papier mache, etc.

(G-2179)
KON TAT GROUP CORPORATION
Also Called: Ametal International
1491 E 34th St (11234-2601)
PHONE 718 207-5022
Kong Tat Yee, *CEO*
David Kong, *Exec VP*
▼ **EMP:** 8
SQ FT: 4,000
SALES (est): 179.7K **Privately Held**
SIC: 7692 Welding repair

(G-2180)
KONSTANTINOS FLORAL DECORATORS
1502 Avenue J (11230-3708)
PHONE 718 434-3603
Gus Vellios, *Owner*
EMP: 9
SQ FT: 3,800
SALES (est): 796.7K **Privately Held**
SIC: 3269 Pottery products

(G-2181)
KURRIER INC
145 Java St (11222-1602)
PHONE 718 389-3018
Wladyslaw Wawrzonek, *President*
EMP: 5
SALES (est): 310K **Privately Held**
WEB: www.kurrier.com
SIC: 2759 5813 Newspapers: printing; drinking places

(G-2182)
KWADAIR LLC
137 Kent St (11222-2127)
PHONE 646 824-2511
EMP: 5
SALES (est): 505.9K **Privately Held**
SIC: 3812 Aircraft/aerospace flight instruments & guidance systems

(G-2183)
KWIK TICKET INC (PA)
Also Called: Jon Barry Company Division
4101 Glenwood Rd (11210-2024)
PHONE 718 421-3800
Fax: 718 421-5328
Larry Spiewak, *CEO*
Brian Katz, *Sales Staff*
Malky Jacobovits, *Office Mgr*
Ike Betesh, *Manager*
Michelle Jacubovits, *Manager*
◆ **EMP:** 15
SQ FT: 30,000
SALES (est): 2.3MM **Privately Held**
WEB: www.kwikticket.com
SIC: 2752 Tags, lithographed; tickets, lithographed

(G-2184)
KWONG CHI METAL FABRICATION
166 41st St (11232-3320)
PHONE 718 369-6429
Larry Lang, *President*
EMP: 8
SALES (est): 400K **Privately Held**
SIC: 3479 3499 Metal coating & allied service; fabricated metal products

(G-2185)
L & M UNISERV CORP
4416 18th Ave Pmb 133 (11204-1201)
PHONE 718 854-3700
Morris Wizel, *President*
EMP: 6
SALES (est): 585.9K **Privately Held**
SIC: 2759 Magazines: printing; catalogs: printing

(G-2186)
L MAGAZINE LLC
45 Main St Ste 806 (11201-1076)
PHONE 212 807-1254
Nick Burry, *Publisher*
Scott Stedman, *Mng Member*
Daniel Stedman,
EMP: 18
SQ FT: 2,500
SALES (est): 1.2MM **Privately Held**
WEB: www.themagazine.com
SIC: 2721 Magazines: publishing & printing

(G-2187)
L Y Z CREATIONS LTD INC
78 18th St (11232-1010)
PHONE 718 768-2977
Fax: 718 768-3157
Amram Weinstock, *President*
EMP: 20
SQ FT: 10,000
SALES: 350K **Privately Held**
SIC: 3172 3993 Wallets; watch straps, except metal; leather money holders; signs & advertising specialties

(G-2188)
LA MART MANUFACTURING CORP
Also Called: Lamart Manufacturing Co
248 Flushing Ave Ste 1 (11205-1214)
PHONE 718 384-6917
Fax: 718 384-0235
Louis Spitzer, *President*
▲ **EMP:** 8 EST: 1989
SQ FT: 3,000
SALES (est): 1.4MM **Privately Held**
WEB: www.coverus.com
SIC: 3083 Plastic finished products, laminated

(G-2189)
LACE MARBLE & GRANITE INC
1465 39th St (11218-3617)
PHONE 718 854-9028
▲ **EMP:** 5
SQ FT: 5,000
SALES (est): 498.4K **Privately Held**
SIC: 3281 Mfg Cut Stone/Products

(G-2190)
LADYBIRD BAKERY INC
1112 8th Ave (11215-4314)
PHONE 718 499-8108
Mary L Clemens, *Ch of Bd*
Christy Jones, *Manager*
EMP: 6
SQ FT: 750
SALES (est): 630.2K **Privately Held**
WEB: www.twolittleredhens.com
SIC: 2051 2052 Bakery: wholesale or wholesale/retail combined; cookies & crackers

(G-2191)
LAGE INDUSTRIES CORPORATION
9814 Ditmas Ave (11236-1914)
PHONE 718 342-3400
Daniel Lage, *Owner*
EMP: 12
SALES (est): 2MM **Privately Held**
SIC: 3271 Blocks, concrete or cinder: standard

(G-2192)
LAKEVIEW SPORTSWEAR CORP
Also Called: All Weather Outerwear
1425 37th St Ste 607 (11218-3755)
PHONE 347 663-9519
▲ **EMP:** 8
SQ FT: 18,000
SALES (est): 1.2MM **Privately Held**
SIC: 2329 Men's & boys' sportswear & athletic clothing; hunting coats & vests, men's

(G-2193)
LAMM INDUSTRIES INC
Also Called: Lamm Audio Lab
2621 E 24th St Ste 1 (11235-2609)
PHONE 718 368-0181
Vladimir Lamm, *President*
EMP: 6
SALES (est): 580K **Privately Held**
WEB: www.lammindustries.com
SIC: 3651 5731 Audio electronic systems; radio, television & electronic stores

(G-2194)
LANCASTER QUALITY PORK INC
5600 1st Ave Ste 6 (11220-2558)
PHONE 718 439-8822
David Kaplan, *Owner*
EMP: 16
SALES (est): 2.3MM **Privately Held**
SIC: 2013 Prepared pork products from purchased pork

(G-2195)
LANOVES INC
72 Anthony St (11222-5329)
PHONE 718 384-1880
Sebastian Antoniuk, *President*
Maria Antoniuk, *Manager*
EMP: 8
SALES (est): 710K **Privately Held**
SIC: 2511 Wood household furniture

(G-2196)
LAYTON MANUFACTURING CORP (PA)
864 E 52nd St (11203-6702)
PHONE 718 498-6000
Fax: 718 498-6003
Steve Layton, *President*
Antonia Layton, *Vice Pres*
Marina Marshalova, *Bookkeeper*
Skip Straughter, *Sales Engr*
Colleen Meehan, *Office Mgr*
EMP: 24
SQ FT: 9,000
SALES (est): 3.2MM **Privately Held**
WEB: www.laytonmfg.com
SIC: 3585 1711 5075 Air conditioning equipment, complete; heating & air conditioning contractors; air conditioning & ventilation equipment & supplies

(G-2197)
LAZER MARBLE & GRANITE CORP
1053 Dahill Rd (11204-1741)
PHONE 718 859-9644
Lazer Mechlovitz, *CEO*
Nachman Mechlovitz, *President*
▲ **EMP:** 7
SQ FT: 4,200
SALES (est): 1MM **Privately Held**
SIC: 3211 3253 Building glass, flat; ceramic wall & floor tile

(G-2198)
LDI LIGHTING INC (PA)
240 Broadway Ste C (11211-8409)
PHONE 718 384-4490
Allen Mundle, *President*
EMP: 9
SQ FT: 5,000
SALES (est): 2.7MM **Privately Held**
SIC: 3646 Ornamental lighting fixtures, commercial

(G-2199)
LDI LIGHTING INC
193 Williamsburg St W A (11211-7984)
PHONE 718 384-4490
Alex Menzlowitz, *Branch Mgr*
EMP: 5
SALES (corp-wide): 2.7MM **Privately Held**
SIC: 3646 Commercial indusl & institutional electric lighting fixtures
PA: Ldi Lighting, Inc
  240 Broadway Ste C
  Brooklyn NY 11211
  718 384-4490

(G-2200)
LE HOOK ROUGE LLC
275 Conover St Ste 3q-3p (11231-1035)
PHONE 212 947-6272
Esther Chen, *President*
▲ **EMP:** 1 EST: 2014
SQ FT: 10,000
SALES: 8MM **Privately Held**
SIC: 3911 Jewelry apparel

(G-2201)
LE LABO INC
80 39th St Fl Ground (11232-2614)
PHONE 646 719-1740
Jean B Mondesir Jr, *Principal*
EMP: 25
SALES (corp-wide): 4.8MM **Privately Held**
SIC: 2844 Perfumes & colognes
PA: Le Labo Inc.
  584 Broadway Rm 1103
  New York NY 10012
  212 532-7206

(G-2202)
LEARNIMATION
55 Washington St Ste 454 (11201-1045)
PHONE 917 868-7261
Sarah Manning, *Owner*
EMP: 9
SALES (est): 429.7K **Privately Held**
SIC: 3999 Education aids, devices & supplies

(G-2203)
LEARNINGATEWAY LLC
106 Saint James Pl (11238-1831)
PHONE 212 920-7969
Catherine Gichenje, *Senior Mgr*
EMP: 5
SALES (est): 289.1K **Privately Held**
SIC: 7372 Educational computer software

(G-2204)
LED WAVES INC
4100 1st Ave Ste 3n (11232-3303)
PHONE 347 416-6182
Joel Slavis, *CEO*
Ayn Slavis, *COO*
Nancy Ahn, *Marketing Staff*
Kori Lozinski, *Manager*
Tiago Zeitoune, *Manager*
▲ **EMP:** 12
SALES (est): 2MM **Privately Held**
SIC: 3641 5063 Electric lamps; light bulbs & related supplies

(G-2205)
LEE PRINTING INC
188 Lee Ave (11211-8028)
PHONE 718 237-1651
Fax: 718 852-1862
Leo Wollner, *President*
EMP: 5 EST: 1976
SQ FT: 1,800
SALES: 800K **Privately Held**
SIC: 2752 Commercial printing, offset

(G-2206)
LEE SPRING COMPANY LLC (HQ)
140 58th St Ste 3c (11220-2560)
PHONE 718 362-5183
Al Mangels Jr, *President*
Ralph Mascolo, *Vice Pres*
Paul Ng, *Vice Pres*
Jorge Cortes, *Plant Mgr*
John Staskauskas, *Opers Mgr*
▲ **EMP:** 150
SQ FT: 33,000
SALES (est): 33.2MM
SALES (corp-wide): 33.4MM **Privately Held**
WEB: www.leespring.com
SIC: 3495 3493 3315 5085 Mechanical springs, precision; steel springs, except wire; wire & fabricated wire products; springs
PA: Unimex Corporation
  54 E 64th St
  New York NY 10065
  212 755-8800

(G-2207)
LEE SPRING LLC (PA)
140 58th St Ste 3c (11220-2560)
PHONE 718 236-2222
Al Amangels, *President*
Jenny Ceccacci, *Purch Mgr*
Carmela Papagni, *Purch Mgr*
Elvis Jarvis, *QC Mgr*
Kedar Muzumdar, *Engineer*
EMP: 34 EST: 1918
SALES (est): 7.1MM **Privately Held**
SIC: 3495 Wire springs

(G-2208)
LEGION LIGHTING CO INC
221 Glenmore Ave (11207-3307)
PHONE 718 498-1770
Sheldon Bellovin, *President*

Evan Bellovin, *Vice Pres*
Michael Bellovin, *Vice Pres*
Wayne Cowell, *Engineer*
▲ **EMP:** 30 **EST:** 1946
SQ FT: 75,000
SALES: 7.3MM **Privately Held**
WEB: www.legionlighting.com
SIC: 3646 Fluorescent lighting fixtures, commercial

(G-2209)
LEITER SUKKAHS INC
1346 39th St (11218-3616)
PHONE..................................718 436-0303
Gitel Goldman, *President*
▲ **EMP:** 7
SQ FT: 8,000
SALES (est): 989.2K **Privately Held**
WEB: www.leiterssukkah.com
SIC: 2394 5049 5999 Tents: made from purchased materials; religious supplies; tents; religious goods

(G-2210)
LEMRAL KNITWEAR INC
70 Franklin Ave (11205-1504)
PHONE..................................718 210-0175
Fax: 718 596-7601
Eva Freund, *President*
Andrew Freund, *Treasurer*
A Schon, *Admin Sec*
EMP: 60 **EST:** 1968
SQ FT: 30,000
SALES (est): 3.6MM **Privately Held**
SIC: 2257 2339 Weft knit fabric mills; women's & misses' outerwear

(G-2211)
LENS LAB EXPRESS
Also Called: Vision Quest
482 86th St (11209-4708)
PHONE..................................718 921-5488
Sherri Smith, *Owner*
EMP: 6
SALES (est): 420K **Privately Held**
SIC: 3851 5995 5049 Ophthalmic goods; opticians; optical goods

(G-2212)
LENS LAB EXPRESS OF GRAHAM AVE
28 Graham Ave (11206-4008)
PHONE..................................718 486-0117
Candido Diaz, *Principal*
EMP: 5
SQ FT: 7,600
SALES (est): 531.9K **Privately Held**
SIC: 3851 Ophthalmic goods

(G-2213)
LEO INTERNATIONAL INC
471 Sutter Ave (11207-3905)
PHONE..................................718 290-8005
Gary Stern, *President*
▲ **EMP:** 25
SQ FT: 65,000
SALES (est): 6.4MM **Privately Held**
WEB: www.leointernational.com
SIC: 3498 Fabricated pipe & fittings

(G-2214)
LEWIS MACHINE CO INC
Also Called: Lewis, S J Machine Co
209 Congress St (11201-6415)
PHONE..................................718 625-0799
Gene Wayda, *President*
EMP: 8 **EST:** 1933
SQ FT: 2,000
SALES: 750K **Privately Held**
SIC: 3599 Machine shop, jobbing & repair

(G-2215)
LIBERTY FABRICATION INC
226 Glenmore Ave (11207-3323)
PHONE..................................718 495-5735
Jimmy Hsu, *President*
EMP: 5
SALES (est): 650K **Privately Held**
SIC: 3315 Wire & fabricated wire products

(G-2216)
LIBERTY PANEL CENTER INC (PA)
Also Called: Liberty Panel & Home Center
1009 Liberty Ave (11208-2812)
PHONE..................................718 647-2763
Fax: 718 647-0450
Irwin Kandel, *President*
Cory Kandel, *Vice Pres*
Craig Kandel, *Vice Pres*
EMP: 19
SQ FT: 25,000
SALES (est): 2.6MM **Privately Held**
SIC: 2851 Paints & paint additives

(G-2217)
LIDDABIT SWEETS
330 Wythe Ave Apt 2g (11249-4153)
PHONE..................................917 912-1370
EMP: 5
SALES (est): 556.8K **Privately Held**
SIC: 2053 Buns, sweet; frozen

(G-2218)
LIDS CORPORATION
5385 Kings Plz (11234-5220)
PHONE..................................718 338-7790
Stephanie Marin, *Manager*
EMP: 37
SALES (corp-wide): 3B **Publicly Held**
WEB: www.hatworld.com
SIC: 2353 Hats & caps
HQ: Lids Corporation
    7555 Woodland Dr
    Indianapolis IN 46278

(G-2219)
LIFESTYLE-TRIMCO (PA)
Also Called: Lifestyle-Trimco Viaggo
323 Malta St (11207-8210)
PHONE..................................718 257-9101
Charles Rosenthal, *President*
Chuck Rosenthal, *Principal*
Lloyd Kielson, *Vice Pres*
Gary Jacob, *Controller*
Dianna Murphy, *Accounts Exec*
◆ **EMP:** 39
SQ FT: 12,000
SALES: 18MM **Privately Held**
SIC: 3999 2542 2541 5046 Mannequins; garment racks: except wood; garment racks, wood; mannequins; display equipment, except refrigerated; signs & advertising specialties

(G-2220)
LIFFEY SHEET METAL CORP
117 Hausman St (11222-3730)
PHONE..................................347 381-1134
Michael Freeman, *President*
Francisco Piscitelly, *Principal*
Priscilla Freeman, *Shareholder*
Bridgette Piscitelli, *Shareholder*
EMP: 14 **EST:** 2006
SALES (est): 3MM **Privately Held**
SIC: 3444 1711 Ducts, sheet metal; ventilation & duct work contractor

(G-2221)
LIGHT BLUE USA LLC
697 Mcdonald Ave (11218-4913)
PHONE..................................718 475-2515
Isaac Markowitz, *Director*
EMP: 5 **EST:** 2012
SALES (est): 389.1K **Privately Held**
SIC: 3674 3648 1731 Light emitting diodes; lighting equipment; lighting contractor

(G-2222)
LILLYS HOMESTYLE BAKESHOP INC
6210 9th Ave (11220-4726)
PHONE..................................718 491-2904
Ethan Lieberman, *Ch of Bd*
Mendel Brach, *President*
Giji Stern, *Accountant*
Diane Adams, *Manager*
EMP: 60 **EST:** 2003
SALES (est): 9.8MM **Privately Held**
SIC: 2051 Bakery: wholesale or wholesale/retail combined

(G-2223)
LIN JIN FENG
7718 18th Ave (11214-1110)
PHONE..................................718 232-3039
Lin Jinfeng, *Manager*
EMP: 5
SALES (est): 596.1K **Privately Held**
SIC: 2674 Grocers' bags: made from purchased materials

(G-2224)
LINDA TOOL & DIE CORPORATION
163 Dwight St (11231-1539)
PHONE..................................718 522-2066
Fax: 718 522-2075
Michael Di Marino, *President*
Linda Cataffo, *Vice Pres*
Arlene Di Marino, *Vice Pres*
▲ **EMP:** 23 **EST:** 1952
SQ FT: 17,500
SALES (est): 4.4MM **Privately Held**
WEB: www.lindatool.com
SIC: 3599 Machine shop, jobbing & repair

(G-2225)
LINDA WINE & SPIRIT
1219 Flatbush Ave (11226-7004)
PHONE..................................718 703-5707
Pierre Raoul, *Owner*
EMP: 6
SALES (est): 586.9K **Privately Held**
SIC: 2086 Bottled & canned soft drinks

(G-2226)
LINDEN FORMS & SYSTEMS INC
40 S 6th St (11249-5938)
PHONE..................................212 219-1100
Leo Green, *President*
EMP: 25 **EST:** 1975
SQ FT: 8,000
SALES (est): 2MM **Privately Held**
SIC: 2761 2759 Computer forms, manifold or continuous; commercial printing

(G-2227)
LINDSEY ADELMAN
27 Prospect Park W (11215-1706)
PHONE..................................718 623-3013
Lindsey Adelman, *Owner*
EMP: 28
SALES (est): 1.3MM **Privately Held**
SIC: 3648 Decorative area lighting fixtures

(G-2228)
LINK GROUP INC
Also Called: Carrier Hardware Building Pdts
6204 5th Ave (11220-4652)
PHONE..................................718 567-7082
EMP: 15
SALES (est): 3.3MM **Privately Held**
SIC: 3541 5963 Home workshop machine tools, metalworking; home related products, direct sales

(G-2229)
LION DIE-CUTTING CO INC
95 Dobbin St Ste 1 (11222-2851)
PHONE..................................718 383-8841
Fax: 718 383-7801
Leo Friedman, *President*
Moshe Lieberman, *Vice Pres*
Mendel Friedman, *Manager*
EMP: 27 **EST:** 1958
SQ FT: 40,000
SALES: 3MM **Privately Held**
SIC: 2675 2621 Cutouts, cardboard, die-cut: from purchased materials; card paper

(G-2230)
LION IN THE SUN PARK SLOPE LTD
232 7th Ave (11215-3041)
PHONE..................................718 369-4006
Melinda Greenberg, *CEO*
David Morris, *Vice Pres*
EMP: 9
SQ FT: 2,000
SALES (est): 1.1MM **Privately Held**
WEB: www.lioninthesuninvitations.com
SIC: 2759 Invitation & stationery printing & engraving; invitations: printing

(G-2231)
LITE BRITE MANUFACTURING INC
575 President St (11215)
PHONE..................................718 855-9797
David Kabasso, *President*
Shaul Kabasso, *Vice Pres*
EMP: 15
SQ FT: 20,000
SALES (est): 1.2MM **Privately Held**
SIC: 3646 3643 Fluorescent lighting fixtures, commercial; current-carrying wiring devices

(G-2232)
LLCS PUBLISHING CORP
2071 Flatbush Ave Ste 189 (11234-4340)
PHONE..................................718 569-2703
Matt Cunningham, *Owner*
Alex Englard, *Accounts Exec*
EMP: 10 **EST:** 2007
SALES (est): 632.6K **Privately Held**
WEB: www.llcpublishing.com
SIC: 2741 Miscellaneous publishing

(G-2233)
LO & SONS INC
20 Jay St Ste 840 (11201-8306)
PHONE..................................917 775-4025
Helen Lo, *CEO*
Jan Lo, *President*
EMP: 10
SALES (est): 131.2K **Privately Held**
SIC: 3161 Traveling bags

(G-2234)
LONDON PARIS LTD
4211 13th Ave (11219-1334)
PHONE..................................718 564-4793
Elias Brach, *President*
▲ **EMP:** 7
SALES: 1.4MM **Privately Held**
SIC: 2329 Men's & boys' sportswear & athletic clothing

(G-2235)
LOPEZ RESTORATIONS INC (PA)
394 Mcguinness Blvd Ste 4 (11222-1201)
PHONE..................................718 383-1555
Fax: 718 383-0908
Angel Lopez, *President*
EMP: 11
SQ FT: 3,500
SALES (est): 1MM **Privately Held**
SIC: 3952 Frames for artists' canvases

(G-2236)
LOPOPOLO IRON WORKS INC
2495 Mcdonald Ave (11223-5232)
PHONE..................................718 339-0572
Fax: 718 336-3073
Joseph Lopopolo, *President*
Mike Lopopolo, *Shareholder*
EMP: 7 **EST:** 1965
SQ FT: 4,000
SALES (est): 1.1MM **Privately Held**
SIC: 3446 Architectural metalwork; gates, ornamental metal; fences or posts, ornamental iron or steel; stairs, staircases, stair treads: prefabricated metal

(G-2237)
LOTUS AWNINGS ENTERPRISES INC
157 11th St (11215-3815)
PHONE..................................718 965-4824
Fax: 718 965-1166
Susana Merchan, *President*
EMP: 7
SQ FT: 5,000
SALES (est): 867K **Privately Held**
SIC: 3444 5999 Awnings & canopies; awnings

(G-2238)
LOWEL-LIGHT MANUFACTURING INC
140 58th St Ste 8c (11220-2524)
PHONE..................................718 921-0600
Fax: 718 921-0303
Marvin Seligman, *President*
Toni Pearl, *Administration*
▲ **EMP:** 40
SQ FT: 34,000

Brooklyn - Kings County (G-2239)

(G-2239)
LUCINAS GOURMET FOOD INC
825 E 21st St (11210-1041)
P.O. Box 36-46 37th St, Long Island City (11101)
PHONE.....................................646 835-9784
Desmond Morais, *President*
Pauline Morais, *Vice Pres*
EMP: 6
SQ FT: 500
SALES: 18.5K **Privately Held**
SIC: 2035 Pickles, sauces & salad dressings

(G-2240)
LYN JO KITCHENS INC
1679 Mcdonald Ave (11230-6312)
PHONE.....................................718 336-6060
Fax: 718 336-5238
Hal Grosshandler, *President*
EMP: 5 **EST:** 1964
SQ FT: 2,400
SALES: 260K **Privately Held**
SIC: 2434 Wood kitchen cabinets

(G-2241)
LYNCH KNITTING MILLS INC
538 Johnson Ave (11237-1226)
PHONE.....................................718 821-3436
Fax: 718 821-3461
Joseph Rotstein, *President*
EMP: 35 **EST:** 1965
SQ FT: 15,000
SALES (est): 3.2MM **Privately Held**
SIC: 2253 Knit outerwear mills

(G-2242)
M & C FURNITURE
Also Called: M C Kitchen & Bath
375 Park Ave (11205-2635)
PHONE.....................................718 422-2136
Moshe Chayun, *President*
Erez Chayun, *Vice Pres*
▲ **EMP:** 6
SQ FT: 9,000
SALES (est): 769.2K **Privately Held**
WEB: www.fintec-usa.com
SIC: 2511 5031 1751 Wood household furniture; kitchen cabinets; cabinet & finish carpentry

(G-2243)
M & D INSTALLERS INC (PA)
Also Called: M & D Fire Door
70 Flushing Ave (11205-1064)
PHONE.....................................718 782-6978
Fax: 718 782-6360
Moshe Deutsch, *Ch of Bd*
David Posner, *President*
Jay Posner, *CFO*
▼ **EMP:** 44
SQ FT: 50,000
SALES (est): 4.8MM **Privately Held**
WEB: www.mdfiredoor.com
SIC: 3442 5211 5031 Fire doors, metal; door & window products; metal doors, sash & trim

(G-2244)
M & M FOOD PRODUCTS INC
Also Called: Flaum Appetizing
286 Scholes St (11206-1728)
PHONE.....................................718 821-1970
Morris Grunhut, *Ch of Bd*
EMP: 14
SQ FT: 23,000
SALES (est): 940K **Privately Held**
WEB: www.flaumappetizing.com
SIC: 2099 Salads, fresh or refrigerated

(G-2245)
M & R WOODWORKING & FINISHING
49 Withers St (11211-6891)
PHONE.....................................718 486-5480
Fax: 718 486-5501
Robert Wieczorkowski, *President*
Milgorzata Wieczorkowski, *Vice Pres*
EMP: 7
SQ FT: 5,625

SALES: 500K **Privately Held**
SIC: 2499 Decorative wood & woodwork

(G-2246)
M A M KNITTING MILLS CORP
Also Called: Mam Knitg
43 Hall St (11205-1315)
PHONE.....................................800 570-0093
Fax: 718 237-1169
Michael Engel, *President*
Pinchas Brach, *Treasurer*
▲ **EMP:** 40
SQ FT: 32,000
SALES: 1.6MM **Privately Held**
SIC: 2253 2329 2339 Sweaters & sweater coats, knit; sweaters & sweater jackets: men's & boys'; women's & misses' outerwear

(G-2247)
M B C METAL INC
Also Called: Milgo Industrial
68 Lombardy St (11222-5207)
PHONE.....................................718 384-6713
Fax: 718 963-0614
Bruce Gitlin, *President*
EMP: 10
SQ FT: 5,000
SALES (est): 750K **Privately Held**
SIC: 3446 Architectural metalwork

(G-2248)
M B M MANUFACTURING INC
331 Rutledge St Ste 203 (11211-7546)
PHONE.....................................718 769-4148
David Goldstein, *President*
Susan Goldstein, *Vice Pres*
Eugene Goldstein, *Manager*
▲ **EMP:** 15 **EST:** 1978
SQ FT: 25,000
SALES (est): 1.2MM **Privately Held**
SIC: 2253 Sweaters & sweater coats, knit

(G-2249)
MAC ARTSPRAY FINISHING CORP
Also Called: Mac-Artspray Finshg
799 Sheffield Ave (11207-7797)
PHONE.....................................718 649-3800
Fax: 718 927-2389
Howard Moskowitz, *President*
EMP: 12
SQ FT: 10,000
SALES: 800K **Privately Held**
SIC: 3479 Painting of metal products

(G-2250)
MACEDONIA LTD
Also Called: Carlton Ice Cream Co
34 E 29th St (11226-5027)
PHONE.....................................718 462-3596
Fax: 718 469-3277
Aristides Saketos, *President*
Zeno Gianopoulos, *Vice Pres*
Belinda Turpitt, *Office Mgr*
▲ **EMP:** 12
SQ FT: 8,500
SALES (est): 2.1MM **Privately Held**
WEB: www.macedonia.com
SIC: 2024 5143 Ice cream & frozen desserts; ice cream & ices

(G-2251)
MAD SCNTSTS BRWING PRTNERS LLC
Also Called: Sixpoint Brewery
40 Van Dyke St (11231-1529)
PHONE.....................................347 766-2739
Shane Welch, *President*
▲ **EMP:** 26
SALES (est): 7.9MM **Privately Held**
SIC: 2082 Malt beverages

(G-2252)
MADE CLOSE LLC
141 Meserole Ave (11222-2744)
PHONE.....................................917 837-1357
David Mehlman, *CEO*
EMP: 6
SALES (est): 185.1K **Privately Held**
SIC: 2051 Bakery: wholesale or wholesale/retail combined

(G-2253)
MAJESTIC HOME IMPRVS DISTR
5902 Fort Hamilton Pkwy (11219-4834)
PHONE.....................................718 853-5079
Man L Wong, *President*
▲ **EMP:** 5
SALES (est): 399.3K **Privately Held**
WEB: www.majesticimprovements.com
SIC: 2514 1521 Kitchen cabinets: metal; single-family home remodeling, additions & repairs

(G-2254)
MAKERBOT INDUSTRIES LLC (DH)
1 Metrotech Ctr Fl 21 (11201-3949)
PHONE.....................................347 334-6800
Jenny Lawton, *CEO*
Russell Kummer, *Business Mgr*
Kathryn Hurley, *Counsel*
Carla Echevarria, *Vice Pres*
Brendan Rafferty, *Facilities Dir*
▲ **EMP:** 300
SQ FT: 15,000
SALES: 82MM
SALES (corp-wide): 699.1MM **Privately Held**
SIC: 3621 3625 5084 Motors & generators; actuators, industrial; industrial machinery & equipment
HQ: Stratasys, Inc.
  7665 Commerce Way
  Eden Prairie MN 55344
  952 937-3000

(G-2255)
MAKKOS OF BROOKLYN LTD
Also Called: New York Pretzel
200 Moore St (11206-3708)
PHONE.....................................718 366-9800
Fax: 718 821-4544
Thomas Makkos, *President*
Richard Berger, *Vice Pres*
Jack Eybas, *Controller*
Richard Berter, *Natl Sales Mgr*
EMP: 75
SQ FT: 25,000
SALES (est): 10.6MM
SALES (corp-wide): 976.2MM **Publicly Held**
WEB: www.nypretzel.com
SIC: 2052 Pretzels
PA: J & J Snack Foods Corp.
  6000 Central Hwy
  Pennsauken NJ 08109
  856 665-9533

(G-2256)
MALIA MILLS INC
32 33rd St Unit 13 (11232-1924)
PHONE.....................................212 354-4200
Malia Mills, *President*
EMP: 11
SALES (est): 654.2K **Privately Held**
SIC: 2339 5699 Bathing suits: women's, misses' & juniors'; bathing suits

(G-2257)
MANDALAY FOOD PRODUCTS INC
640 Dean St (11238-3021)
PHONE.....................................718 230-3370
U Han Kyu, *President*
EMP: 5
SQ FT: 300
SALES (est): 396.2K **Privately Held**
WEB: www.mandalay.org
SIC: 2099 5411 Food preparations; grocery stores, independent

(G-2258)
MANGO USA INC
5620 1st Ave Ste 1 (11220-2519)
PHONE.....................................718 998-6050
Kheder Fatiha, *CEO*
▲ **EMP:** 20
SALES (est): 4.2MM **Privately Held**
SIC: 3144 3021 3149 2339 Dress shoes, women's; canvas shoes, rubber soled; athletic shoes, except rubber or plastic; women's & misses' athletic clothing & sportswear; women's & children's clothing

(G-2259)
MANHATTAN COMFORT INC
1784 Atlantic Ave (11213-1208)
PHONE.....................................888 230-2225
Schneur Langsam, *President*
▲ **EMP:** 23
SQ FT: 18,000
SALES: 1.5MM **Privately Held**
SIC: 2521 5712 Wood office furniture; furniture stores

(G-2260)
MANHATTAN POLY BAG CORPORATION
1228 47th St (11219-2501)
PHONE.....................................917 689-7549
Fax: 718 326-1887
William Kaufman, *President*
Sylvia Kaufman, *Vice Pres*
Gary Kaufman, *Controller*
EMP: 32
SQ FT: 88,500
SALES (est): 4.1MM **Privately Held**
SIC: 2673 Plastic bags: made from purchased materials

(G-2261)
MANHATTAN SPECIAL BOTTLING
342 Manhattan Ave (11211-2404)
PHONE.....................................718 388-4144
Fax: 718 384-0244
Aurora Passaro, *President*
Louis Passaro, *Exec VP*
EMP: 10
SQ FT: 7,500
SALES (est): 930K **Privately Held**
WEB: www.manhattanspecial.com
SIC: 2086 Soft drinks: packaged in cans, bottles, etc.

(G-2262)
MANNING LEWIS DIV RUBICON INDS
848 E 43rd St (11210-3502)
PHONE.....................................908 687-2400
Michael Rubinberg, *President*
EMP: 25
SALES (est): 1.2MM **Privately Held**
SIC: 3585 Refrigeration & heating equipment

(G-2263)
MANOR ELECTRIC SUPPLY CORP
2737 Ocean Ave (11229-4700)
PHONE.....................................347 312-2521
Fax: 718 648-7351
Kenneth Rabinowitz, *Ch of Bd*
Christine Gandee, *Office Mgr*
EMP: 10
SQ FT: 10,000
SALES (est): 2.2MM **Privately Held**
SIC: 3699 Electrical equipment & supplies

(G-2264)
MANZIONE READY MIX CORP
Also Called: Manzione Enterprises
46 Knickerbocker Ave (11237-1410)
PHONE.....................................718 628-3837
Rocco Manzione, *President*
Gary Snolpava, *President*
EMP: 4 **EST:** 1999
SQ FT: 45,000
SALES (est): 3MM **Privately Held**
SIC: 3273 Ready-mixed concrete

(G-2265)
MARAMONT CORPORATION (PA)
5600 1st Ave (11220-2550)
PHONE.....................................718 439-8900
Fax: 718 238-0974
George Chivari, *President*
Celia Lyons, *Purchasing*
Linda Jannzzkowski, *CFO*
Warren Schmitgall, *Controller*
Barry Mittelmann, *MIS Dir*
▲ **EMP:** 420
SQ FT: 65,000

SALES (est): 108.9MM **Privately Held**
SIC: 2099 8322 Ready-to-eat meals, salads & sandwiches; salads, fresh or refrigerated; sandwiches, assembled & packaged: for wholesale market; individual & family services

(G-2266)
MARBLE KNITS INC
Also Called: Marble Knitting Mills
544 Park Ave Ste 3 (11205-1608)
PHONE..................................718 237-7990
Fax: 718 237-2781
Kalman Sinay, *President*
David Bark, *Vice Pres*
EMP: 20
SQ FT: 55,000
SALES (est): 2.6MM **Privately Held**
SIC: 2253 Sweaters & sweater coats, knit

(G-2267)
MARCY BUSINESS FORMS INC
1468 40th St (11218-3510)
PHONE..................................718 935-9100
Samuel Roth, *Ch of Bd*
EMP: 5
SALES (est): 550K **Privately Held**
WEB: www.marcybusinessforms.com
SIC: 2761 Manifold business forms

(G-2268)
MARCY PRINTING INC
777 Kent Ave Ste A (11205-1543)
P.O. Box 110199 (11211-0199)
PHONE..................................718 935-9100
Fax: 718 935-9349
Charles H Laufer, *President*
Jano Roth, *Manager*
EMP: 5
SQ FT: 12,000
SALES (est): 735.4K **Privately Held**
SIC: 2752 Commercial printing, offset; letters, circular or form: lithographed

(G-2269)
MARINA HOLDING CORP
Also Called: Venice Marina
3939 Emmons Ave (11235-1001)
PHONE..................................718 646-9283
Fax: 718 646-5889
Albert Levi, *Managing Dir*
Chuck Rondot, *Manager*
EMP: 15
SQ FT: 6,000
SALES (est): 1.3MM
SALES (corp-wide): 1.3B **Privately Held**
WEB: www.venicemarina.com
SIC: 2339 5551 5541 Women's & misses' outerwear; boat dealers; gasoline service stations
PA: Jordache Enterprises Inc.
  1400 Broadway Rm 1404b
  New York NY 10018
  212 643-8400

(G-2270)
MARINA ICE CREAM
888 Jamaica Ave (11208-1525)
PHONE..................................718 235-3000
Frank Birone, *Owner*
EMP: 5 EST: 2007
SALES (est): 368.8K **Privately Held**
SIC: 2024 5143 Ice cream & frozen desserts; ice cream & ices

(G-2271)
MARINE PARK APPLIANCES LLC
3412 Avenue N (11234-2607)
PHONE..................................718 513-1808
Issac Wizel, *President*
EMP: 1
SALES: 5MM **Privately Held**
SIC: 3639 Major kitchen appliances, except refrigerators & stoves

(G-2272)
MARK POSNER
1950 52nd St (11204-1731)
PHONE..................................718 258-6241
Mark Posner, *Owner*
EMP: 5
SALES (est): 218.2K **Privately Held**
SIC: 3432 Plastic plumbing fixture fittings, assembly

(G-2273)
MARLBOROUGH JEWELS INC
67 35th St Unit 2 (11232-2200)
P.O. Box 320673 (11232-0673)
PHONE..................................718 768-2000
Fax: 718 788-1653
Donald Calaman, *President*
EMP: 8
SALES (est): 1MM **Privately Held**
SIC: 3961 5094 3911 Costume jewelry, ex. precious metal & semiprecious stones; jewelry; jewelry, precious metal

(G-2274)
MARLOW PRINTING CO INC
Also Called: Nap Industries
667 Kent Ave (11249-7530)
PHONE..................................718 625-4949
Jack Freund, *President*
Morris Lowy, *Vice Pres*
EMP: 30 EST: 1977
SQ FT: 35,000
SALES (est): 3.6MM **Privately Held**
WEB: www.napind.com
SIC: 2759 2752 Flexographic printing; commercial printing, lithographic

(G-2275)
MAROVATO INDUSTRIES INC
100 Dobbin St (11222-2806)
PHONE..................................718 389-0800
Fax: 718 389-0258
Margaret Rotondi, *Ch of Bd*
Marty Pietanza, *Opers Mgr*
Gabriel Xu, *Engineer*
Rosemarie Rotondi, *Treasurer*
EMP: 15
SALES (est): 4.2MM **Privately Held**
WEB: www.marovato.com
SIC: 3441 8711 Building components, structural steel; structural engineering; mechanical engineering

(G-2276)
MARTIN CHAFKIN
Also Called: Perfection Electricks
1155 Manhattan Ave # 431 (11222-6102)
P.O. Box 6146, Astoria (11106-0146)
PHONE..................................718 383-1155
Martin Chafkin, *Owner*
Myles Ambrose, *Manager*
EMP: 7
SALES (est): 400K **Privately Held**
WEB: www.perfectionelectric.com
SIC: 3999 7922 3446 Stage hardware & equipment, except lighting; equipment rental, theatrical; architectural metalwork

(G-2277)
MARTIN GREENFIELD CLOTHIERS
Also Called: Greenfield Martin Clothiers
239 Varet St (11206-3823)
PHONE..................................718 497-5480
Fax: 718 456-3365
Martin Greenfield, *President*
Jay Greenfield, *Exec VP*
Todd Greenfield, *Vice Pres*
Michelle Guiseppone, *Manager*
▲ EMP: 140
SQ FT: 40,000
SALES (est): 15MM **Privately Held**
SIC: 2311 2325 Suits, men's & boys': made from purchased materials; jackets, tailored suit-type: men's & boys'; topcoats, men's & boys': made from purchased materials; slacks, dress: men's, youths' & boys'

(G-2278)
MARVEL EQUIPMENT CORP INC
215 Eagle St (11222-1210)
PHONE..................................718 383-6597
Carl Ungenheuer, *President*
Barbara Maxwell, *Vice Pres*
Emma Ungenheuer, *Admin Sec*
EMP: 7
SALES: 200K **Privately Held**
SIC: 3612 Generator voltage regulators

(G-2279)
MASS APPEAL MAGAZINE
261 Vandervoort Ave (11211-1718)
PHONE..................................718 858-0979
Adrian Moeller, *Partner*
Patrick Elasik, *Partner*

Owen Strock, *Vice Pres*
EMP: 7
SQ FT: 1,100
SALES (est): 790.3K **Privately Held**
SIC: 2721 Magazines: publishing only, not printed on site

(G-2280)
MAST BROTHERS INC
105 N 3rd St Apt A (11249-3927)
PHONE..................................718 388-2625
Rick Mast, *Principal*
EMP: 27
SALES (est): 4.6MM **Privately Held**
SIC: 2066 Chocolate & cocoa products

(G-2281)
MASTER WINDOW & DOOR CORP
199 Starr St (11237-2607)
PHONE..................................718 782-5407
Penn Ku, *President*
EMP: 12
SALES (est): 2MM **Privately Held**
SIC: 3442 Window & door frames

(G-2282)
MATCHABLES INC
Also Called: Bara Fashions
106 Green St Ste A (11222-1352)
PHONE..................................718 389-9318
Raphael Blumenstock, *President*
Ruth Malach, *Vice Pres*
EMP: 10
SQ FT: 8,000
SALES (est): 750K **Privately Held**
SIC: 2253 Sweaters & sweater coats, knit

(G-2283)
MATERIAL PROCESS SYSTEMS INC
87 Richardson St Ste 2 (11211-1319)
PHONE..................................718 302-3081
Fax: 718 302-9043
Steven Urbatsch, *President*
Matthew Josephs, *Vice Pres*
▲ EMP: 14
SALES (est): 1.2MM **Privately Held**
WEB: www.materialprocess.com
SIC: 2434 3446 Wood kitchen cabinets; architectural metalwork

(G-2284)
MATRIX STEEL COMPANY INC
50 Bogart St (11206-3818)
PHONE..................................718 381-6800
Francesca Montagna, *President*
Anna Pedri, *Bookkeeper*
EMP: 6
SALES: 1.5MM **Privately Held**
SIC: 3312 3321 Structural & rail mill products; gray & ductile iron foundries

(G-2285)
MATTHEWS HATS
99 Kenilworth Pl Fl 1 (11210-2423)
PHONE..................................718 859-4683
Fax: 212 704-0583
Larry S Matthews, *Partner*
Merrill Matthews, *Partner*
EMP: 7
SALES (est): 410K **Privately Held**
SIC: 2353 Hats, trimmed: women's, misses' & children's

(G-2286)
MAXWELL BAKERY INC
2700 Atlantic Ave (11207-2893)
PHONE..................................718 498-2200
George Jograj, *Owner*
Earl Wheelin, *General Mgr*
EMP: 25
SQ FT: 10,000
SALES (est): 1.2MM **Privately Held**
WEB: www.maxwellbakery.com
SIC: 2051 Bakery: wholesale or wholesale/retail combined

(G-2287)
MDCARE911 LLC
Also Called: Gocare247
30 Main St Apt 5c (11201-8213)
PHONE..................................917 640-4869
Anthony Schweinzer,
EMP: 5

SALES (est): 270K **Privately Held**
SIC: 7372 Home entertainment computer software

(G-2288)
MDEK INC
9728 3rd Ave (11209-7742)
P.O. Box 90318 (11209-0318)
PHONE..................................347 569-7318
Rick Manak, *President*
EMP: 1
SQ FT: 15,000
SALES: 3.5MM **Privately Held**
SIC: 3799 8711 Electrocars for transporting golfers; consulting engineer

(G-2289)
MDS HOT BAGELS DELI INC
127 Church Ave (11218-3917)
PHONE..................................718 438-5650
Alex Esalias, *Manager*
EMP: 7
SQ FT: 1,000
SALES (est): 483.3K **Privately Held**
SIC: 2051 5461 5411 Bagels, fresh or frozen; bagels; delicatessens

(G-2290)
MECHANICAL DISPLAYS INC
4420 Farragut Rd (11203-6522)
PHONE..................................718 258-5588
Fax: 718 258-6202
Hugo Paulucci, *President*
Lou Nasti, *Vice Pres*
▲ EMP: 7
SQ FT: 7,500
SALES: 1MM **Privately Held**
WEB: www.mechanicaldisplays.com
SIC: 3944 7389 Trains & equipment, toy: electric & mechanical; convention & show services

(G-2291)
MEDI-TECH INTERNATIONAL CORP (PA)
Also Called: Spandage
26 Court St Ste 1301 (11242-1113)
PHONE..................................800 333-0109
Fax: 718 855-1618
Jacqueline Fortunato, *CEO*
Marilyn Geiger, *Principal*
Derrick Brown, *Regional Mgr*
Mike Burr, *Regional Mgr*
Carol Callahan, *Regional Mgr*
▲ EMP: 4 EST: 1973
SQ FT: 1,000
SALES (est): 4MM **Privately Held**
WEB: www.medi-techintl.com
SIC: 3842 2339 Bandages: plastic, muslin, plaster of paris, etc.; dressings, surgical; maternity clothing

(G-2292)
MEDIA SIGNS LLC
6404 14th Ave (11219-5314)
PHONE..................................718 252-7575
EMP: 7
SALES (est): 248.7K **Privately Held**
SIC: 2759 Commercial printing

(G-2293)
MEEKER SALES CORP
551 Sutter Ave (11207-4001)
PHONE..................................718 384-5400
Harvey Worth, *President*
Jim Kaye, *Manager*
EMP: 1
SQ FT: 150
SALES: 1.2MM **Privately Held**
SIC: 2514 Metal household furniture

(G-2294)
MEGA VATIONS INC
3177 Coney Island Ave A (11235-6443)
PHONE..................................718 934-2192
Horace Bryan, *President*
Araceli Bryan, *Vice Pres*
EMP: 5 EST: 1977
SQ FT: 3,000
SALES (est): 440K **Privately Held**
SIC: 3647 Vehicular lighting equipment

Brooklyn - Kings County (G-2295)

(G-2295)
MEGA VISION INC
1274 Flushing Ave (11237-2303)
P.O. Box 370715 (11237-0715)
PHONE..................................718 228-1065
Michael Chiriac, *President*
Joe Baboola, *Sales Executive*
Katica Chiriac, *Admin Sec*
EMP: 35
SQ FT: 22,000
SALES (est): 7.7MM Privately Held
WEB: www.megavision.net
SIC: 3444 2542 Sheet metalwork; office & store showcases & display fixtures; fixtures: display, office or store: except wood

(G-2296)
MEISEL-PESKIN CO INC (PA)
349 Scholes St 353 (11206-1787)
PHONE..................................718 497-1840
Garry Meisel, *President*
▲ **EMP:** 78
SQ FT: 18,000
SALES (est): 4.9MM Privately Held
SIC: 3999 Furs, dressed: bleached, curried, scraped, tanned or dyed

(G-2297)
MEP ALASKA LLC
Also Called: Magnum Energy Partners
3619 Bedford Ave Apt 4e (11210-5206)
PHONE..................................646 535-9005
Mark Steinmetz, *Owner*
Terrence Manning, *COO*
EMP: 5
SALES (est): 380K Privately Held
SIC: 1389 3569 1382 Construction, repair & dismantling services; gas producers, generators & other gas related equipment; oil & gas exploration services

(G-2298)
MERCURY PAINT CORPORATION (PA)
4808 Farragut Rd (11203-6612)
PHONE..................................718 469-8787
Fax: 718 469-0858
Jeff Berman, *President*
Frank Corchia, *Controller*
Ronald Alli, *Sales Mgr*
John Van, *Manager*
EMP: 75 EST: 1961
SQ FT: 100,000
SALES (est): 25.1MM Privately Held
WEB: www.mercurypaintcorp.com
SIC: 2851 5231 Paints & paint additives; paint

(G-2299)
MERCURY PLASTICS CORP
989 Utica Ave 995 (11203-4399)
PHONE..................................718 498-5400
Fax: 718 498-1103
William Wright, *President*
George Wright Jr, *Corp Secy*
▲ **EMP:** 20 EST: 1945
SQ FT: 8,000
SALES (est): 3MM Privately Held
SIC: 3089 Molding primary plastic

(G-2300)
MERKOS LINYONEI CHINUCH INC
Also Called: Merkos Bookstore
291 Kingston Ave (11213-3402)
PHONE..................................718 778-0226
Fax: 718 778-4148
Malka Ahern, *Manager*
EMP: 20
SALES (corp-wide): 950K Privately Held
WEB: www.chabad.org
SIC: 2731 Book publishing
PA: Merkos L'inyonei Chinuch, Inc.
770 Eastern Pkwy
Brooklyn NY 11213
718 774-4000

(G-2301)
MERZON LEATHER CO INC
810 Humboldt St Ste 2 (11222-1913)
PHONE..................................718 782-6260
Richard Merzon, *President*
▲ **EMP:** 150
SQ FT: 50,000
SALES (est): 16.3MM Privately Held
SIC: 3161 3172 Cases, carrying; suitcases; camera carrying bags; personal leather goods

(G-2302)
MESORAH PUBLICATIONS LTD
4401 2nd Ave (11232-4212)
PHONE..................................718 921-9000
Fax: 718 680-1875
Martin Zlotowitz, *President*
Jacob Brander, *Vice Pres*
Efraim Perlowitz, *Marketing Staff*
Bernard Kempler, *MIS Dir*
Nosson Scherman, *Admin Sec*
▲ **EMP:** 43
SQ FT: 20,000
SALES (est): 7.6MM Privately Held
WEB: www.artscroll.com
SIC: 2731 Books: publishing only; pamphlets: publishing only, not printed on site

(G-2303)
METAL CRAFTS INC
Also Called: Metalcraft By N Barzel
650 Berriman St (11208-5304)
PHONE..................................718 443-3333
Norman Barzel, *President*
Norman Barsi, *President*
EMP: 6
SALES (est): 590K Privately Held
SIC: 3441 Fabricated structural metal

(G-2304)
METPAK INC
320 Roebling St Ste 601 (11211-6262)
PHONE..................................917 309-0196
Izzy Katz, *President*
EMP: 4
SALES: 1MM Privately Held
SIC: 2673 Bags: plastic, laminated & coated

(G-2305)
METRO KITCHENS CORP
1040 E 45th St (11203-6542)
PHONE..................................718 434-1166
Fax: 718 531-1374
John Ciavattoni, *President*
Kevin Taflin, *Vice Pres*
▲ **EMP:** 11
SQ FT: 10,000
SALES (est): 880K Privately Held
WEB: www.metro-kitchens.com
SIC: 2434 5031 1751 Wood kitchen cabinets; kitchen cabinets; cabinet & finish carpentry

(G-2306)
METRO LINING COMPANY
Also Called: Metropolitan Packaging
68 Java St (11222-1519)
P.O. Box 220149 (11222-0149)
PHONE..................................718 383-2700
Jack Schwartz, *President*
EMP: 5
SALES (est): 15.4K Privately Held
SIC: 2673 Plastic bags: made from purchased materials

(G-2307)
METROPOLITAN PACKG MFG CORP
68 Java St (11222-1519)
PHONE..................................718 383-2700
Fax: 718 383-7952
Malka Katz, *President*
Herman Katz, *Vice Pres*
▲ **EMP:** 35 EST: 1964
SQ FT: 20,000
SALES (est): 6.2MM Privately Held
WEB: www.metropack.com
SIC: 2673 Plastic bags: made from purchased materials

(G-2308)
MICHAEL BERNSTEIN DESIGN ASSOC
361 Stagg St Fl 4 (11206-1748)
PHONE..................................718 456-9277
Fax: 718 456-9284
Michael Bernstein, *President*
EMP: 20
SQ FT: 10,000
SALES (est): 1.7MM Privately Held
WEB: www.mbda.com
SIC: 2431 2434 Woodwork, interior & ornamental; wood kitchen cabinets

(G-2309)
MICHAEL STUART INC
199 Cook St (11206-3701)
P.O. Box 60267 (11206-0267)
PHONE..................................718 821-0704
Michael Stuart Fuchs, *President*
EMP: 20 EST: 1975
SQ FT: 20,000
SALES (est): 1.4MM Privately Held
SIC: 2369 2392 2211 2361 Girls' & children's outerwear; tablecloths: made from purchased materials; bathmats, cotton; girls' & children's dresses, blouses & shirts

(G-2310)
MICRO ESSENTIAL LABORATORY
4224 Avenue H (11210-3518)
P.O. Box 100824 (11210-0824)
PHONE..................................718 338-3618
Joel Florin, *President*
Evelyn La Nier, *Office Mgr*
Evelyn Lanier, *Office Mgr*
Mark Florin, *Executive*
EMP: 30
SQ FT: 7,500
SALES (est): 7.8MM Privately Held
WEB: www.microessentiallab.com
SIC: 2672 Chemically treated papers: made from purchased materials

(G-2311)
MICRON POWDER INDUSTRIES LLC
5114 Fort Hamilton Pkwy (11219-4006)
PHONE..................................718 851-0011
Barry Gottehrer,
EMP: 10
SALES (est): 580K Privately Held
SIC: 3089 Plastics products

(G-2312)
MIDWOOD SIGNS & DESIGN INC
202 28th St (11232-1604)
PHONE..................................718 499-9041
Ron Guercio, *President*
Maryanne Bowman, *Principal*
EMP: 3
SALES: 1.5MM Privately Held
SIC: 3993 2431 Signs & advertising specialties; awnings, wood

(G-2313)
MILGO INDUSTRIAL INC (PA)
Also Called: Milgo/Bufkin
68 Lombardy St (11222-5234)
PHONE..................................718 388-6476
Fax: 718 388-3154
Bruce J Gitlin, *President*
Rose Gitlin, *Vice Pres*
Gina Jordan, *Vice Pres*
Barbara Kanter, *CFO*
Michelle O'Donnell, *Controller*
EMP: 69 EST: 1918
SQ FT: 30,000
SALES (est): 11.6MM Privately Held
WEB: www.milgo-bufkin.com
SIC: 3446 3442 3398 Architectural metalwork; metal doors, sash & trim; store fronts, prefabricated, metal; brazing (hardening) of metal

(G-2314)
MILGO INDUSTRIAL INC
514 Varick Ave (11222-5400)
PHONE..................................718 387-0406
Alex Kveton, *Branch Mgr*
EMP: 6
SALES (corp-wide): 11.6MM Privately Held
WEB: www.milgo-bufkin.com
SIC: 3446 3442 3398 Architectural metalwork; metal doors, sash & trim; brazing (hardening) of metal
PA: Milgo Industrial Inc.
68 Lombardy St
Brooklyn NY 11222
718 388-6476

(G-2315)
MILLA GLOBAL INC
Also Called: Concepts New York, The
1301 Metropolitan Ave (11237-1102)
PHONE..................................516 488-3601
Glen Parprolff, *Director*
EMP: 4
SALES: 10MM Privately Held
SIC: 2673 3911 Bags: plastic, laminated & coated; jewelry, precious metal

(G-2316)
MILLENNIUM STL RACK RNTALS INC (PA)
253 Bond St (11217-2919)
PHONE..................................212 594-2190
Toll Free:..................................877 -
Fax: 718 868-1128
David Fox, *President*
Rachael Wilson, *Manager*
▲ **EMP:** 9 EST: 1999
SALES (est): 1.4MM Privately Held
WEB: www.millenniumsteelservice.com
SIC: 2542 7359 Garment racks: except wood; equipment rental & leasing

(G-2317)
MINDBODYGREEN LLC
45 Main St Ste 422 (11201-1093)
PHONE..................................347 529-6952
Jason Wacob,
Stephen Anderson,
EMP: 29
SQ FT: 2,500
SALES (est): 1.7MM Privately Held
SIC: 2741

(G-2318)
MINI-CIRCUITS FORT WAYNE LLC
13 Neptune Ave (11235-4404)
P.O. Box 350166 (11235-0166)
PHONE..................................718 934-4500
Jennifer Fogel, *Human Res Mgr*
Harvey Kaylie,
EMP: 500
SALES (est): 71.1MM Privately Held
WEB: www.matchingpad.com
SIC: 3679 3678 3677 3674 Attenuators; electronic connectors; electronic coils, transformers & other inductors; semiconductors & related devices; radio & TV communications equipment; current-carrying wiring devices

(G-2319)
MISHPACHA MAGAZINE INC
5809 16th Ave (11204-2112)
PHONE..................................718 686-9339
Eli Peli, *President*
Barbara Bensoussan, *Editor*
Yehuda Heimowitz, *Editor*
Nina Feiner, *Marketing Staff*
EMP: 5
SALES (est): 512.5K Privately Held
SIC: 2721 Magazines: publishing & printing

(G-2320)
MISS SPORTSWEAR INC
117 9th St (11215-3108)
PHONE..................................212 391-2535
EMP: 9
SALES (corp-wide): 15.4MM Privately Held
SIC: 2339 Women's & misses' athletic clothing & sportswear
PA: M.I.S.S. Sportswear, Inc.
1410 Broadway Rm 703
New York NY 10018
212 391-2535

(G-2321)
MISS SPORTSWEAR INC
Also Called: Miss Group, The
117 9th St (11215-3108)
PHONE..................................718 369-6012
Sammy Fallas, *Branch Mgr*
EMP: 21
SALES (corp-wide): 15.4MM Privately Held
SIC: 2339 Women's & misses' athletic clothing & sportswear

PA: M.I.S.S. Sportswear, Inc.
1410 Broadway Rm 703
New York NY 10018
212 391-2535

(G-2322)
MISSIONTEX INC
236 Greenpoint Ave Ste 12 (11222-2495)
PHONE..................................718 532-9053
Jay McLaughlin, *Principal*
EMP: 5
SALES (est): 320K **Privately Held**
SIC: 2281 5949 5632 5651 Yarn spinning mills; fabric stores piece goods; fur apparel; family clothing stores

(G-2323)
MJK CUTTING INC
Also Called: M J K
117 9th St (11215-3108)
PHONE..................................718 384-7613
Wing Lau, *President*
EMP: 10
SALES (est): 750K **Privately Held**
SIC: 3552 Jacquard card cutting machines

(G-2324)
MJK ENTERPRISES LLC
Also Called: M & J Custom Lampshade Company
34 35th St (11232-2021)
PHONE..................................917 653-9042
Martin Kuranc, *Managing Prtnr*
EMP: 8 **EST:** 2011
SALES: 50MM **Privately Held**
SIC: 3648 Lanterns: electric, gas, carbide, kerosene or gasoline

(G-2325)
MJM JEWELRY CORP
Also Called: Berry Jewelry Company
400 3rd Ave (11215-2738)
PHONE..................................718 596-1600
Percival S Mijares, *Branch Mgr*
EMP: 70
SALES (corp-wide): 14.6MM **Privately Held**
WEB: www.berryjewelry.com
SIC: 3911 Jewelry, precious metal
PA: Mjm Jewelry Corp.
29 W 38th St Rm 1601
New York NY 10018
212 354-5014

(G-2326)
MNN HOLDING COMPANY LLC
Also Called: Mother Nature & Partners
155 Water St Ste 616 (11201-1016)
PHONE..................................404 558-5251
Michael Jacobson, *CFO*
EMP: 15 **Privately Held**
SIC: 7372 8748 Publishers' computer software; publishing consultant
PA: Mnn Holding Company, Llc
191 Peachtree St Ne Ste 4
Atlanta GA 30303

(G-2327)
MODERN PLASTIC BAGS MFG INC
63 Flushing Ave Unit 303 (11205-1080)
PHONE..................................718 237-2985
Abrahm Stossel, *President*
EMP: 5
SQ FT: 3,000
SALES: 450K **Privately Held**
SIC: 2673 Plastic & pliofilm bags

(G-2328)
MOES WEAR APPAREL INC
1020 E 48th St Ste 8 (11203-6609)
PHONE..................................718 940-1597
Selly Nessry, *President*
Jeff Saad, *Vice Pres*
Morris Saad, *Vice Pres*
Mellisa Clark, *Office Mgr*
▲ **EMP:** 13
SQ FT: 50,000
SALES (est): 2.1MM **Privately Held**
SIC: 2339 Women's & misses' outerwear

(G-2329)
MOLDING DECOR INC
1946 50th St (11204-1312)
PHONE..................................718 377-2930
Nosson Berger, *CEO*

EMP: 5
SALES (est): 358.1K **Privately Held**
SIC: 3089 Molding primary plastic

(G-2330)
MOLDOVA PICKLES & SALADS INC
1060 E 46th St (11203-6516)
PHONE..................................718 284-2220
Naum Zozulya, *President*
Vitality Pinchev, *Vice Pres*
▲ **EMP:** 5
SALES (est): 420K **Privately Held**
SIC: 2035 Pickles, vinegar

(G-2331)
MONFEFO LLC ✪
630 Flushing Ave 5q (11206-5026)
PHONE..................................347 779-2600
Justin Monsul, *Mng Member*
EMP: 5 **EST:** 2016
SQ FT: 600
SALES: 300K **Privately Held**
SIC: 2086 Soft drinks: packaged in cans, bottles, etc.

(G-2332)
MONTROSE EQUIPMENT SALES INC
Also Called: Ace
202 N 10th St (11211-1109)
PHONE..................................718 388-7446
Fax: 718 218-8422
Emil Romotzki, *President*
Jack Pivovarov, *Corp Secy*
▲ **EMP:** 12
SQ FT: 8,000
SALES (est): 1.1MM **Privately Held**
SIC: 3541 Machine tools, metal cutting type

(G-2333)
MORCO PRODUCTS CORP
556 39th St (11232-3002)
PHONE..................................718 853-4005
Fax: 718 436-0692
Michael Morgan, *President*
Neil Falcone, *Vice Pres*
EMP: 15
SQ FT: 6,200
SALES (est): 1.1MM **Privately Held**
SIC: 3599 Machine shop, jobbing & repair

(G-2334)
MORRIS KITCHEN INC
30 Chester Ct (11225-5605)
PHONE..................................646 413-5186
Kari Morris, *Owner*
EMP: 15
SALES (est): 2.2MM **Privately Held**
SIC: 2099 2032 2033 Food preparations; chicken soup: packaged in cans, jars, etc.; tomato products: packaged in cans, jars, etc.

(G-2335)
MOTI INC
4118 13th Ave (11219-1333)
PHONE..................................718 436-4280
Mordechai Fleicher, *President*
▲ **EMP:** 16
SQ FT: 8,000
SALES (est): 1.2MM **Privately Held**
SIC: 3999 Wigs, including doll wigs, toupees or wiglets

(G-2336)
MOTOROLA SOLUTIONS INC
335 Adams St Fl 7 (11201-3754)
PHONE..................................718 330-2163
Tom Driscoll, *Manager*
Christopher Sparrow, *Senior Mgr*
EMP: 153
SALES (corp-wide): 5.7B **Publicly Held**
SIC: 3663 Radio & TV communications equipment
PA: Motorola Solutions, Inc.
1303 E Algonquin Rd
Schaumburg IL 60196
847 576-5000

(G-2337)
MOZNAIM PUBLISHING CO INC
Also Called: Moznaim Co
4304 12th Ave (11219-1301)
PHONE..................................718 853-0525
Fax: 718 438-1305
Menachem Wagshol, *President*
Monshe Sternlicht, *Vice Pres*
▲ **EMP:** 6
SALES (est): 360K **Privately Held**
WEB: www.moznaim.com
SIC: 2731 5192 5999 Books: publishing only; books; religious goods

(G-2338)
MPR MAGAZINE APP INC
Also Called: Soldi
2653 E 19th St Fl 2 (11235-3302)
PHONE..................................718 403-0303
Gady Kohanov, *President*
Gary Porat, *Vice Pres*
EMP: 20
SQ FT: 5,000
SALES (est): 1.3MM **Privately Held**
SIC: 7372 Application computer software

(G-2339)
MR DISPOSABLE INC
101 Richardson St Ste 2 (11211-1344)
PHONE..................................718 388-8574
Raymond Cora, *CEO*
Victor Morales, *Vice Pres*
Debbie Cora, *Admin Sec*
▲ **EMP:** 10
SALES (est): 400K **Privately Held**
WEB: www.mrdisposable.com
SIC: 2676 Diapers, paper (disposable): made from purchased paper

(G-2340)
MR SIGN USA INC
1920 Atlantic Ave (11233-3004)
PHONE..................................718 218-3321
Michael Leivowitz, *President*
Ester Atran, *Manager*
EMP: 15
SALES (est): 1.2MM **Privately Held**
SIC: 3993 Signs & advertising specialties

(G-2341)
MRCHOCOLATECOM LLC
Also Called: Jacques Torres Chocolate
66 Water St Ste 2 (11201-1048)
PHONE..................................718 875-9772
Fax: 718 875-2167
Jacques Torres, *Partner*
Keitaro Goto, *Partner*
Kris Kruid, *Partner*
Brittany Hall, *Asst Mgr*
▲ **EMP:** 18
SALES (est): 910K **Privately Held**
WEB: www.jacquestorres.com
SIC: 2064 5145 5441 Candy & other confectionery products; confectionery; candy, nut & confectionery stores

(G-2342)
MS PAPER PRODUCTS CO INC
930 Bedford Ave (11205-4502)
PHONE..................................718 624-0248
Fax: 718 625-4748
Solomon Schwimmer, *President*
Hirsh Krauss, *Empl Benefits*
EMP: 6 **EST:** 1970
SQ FT: 12,000
SALES: 500K **Privately Held**
SIC: 2631 Paperboard mills

(G-2343)
MUSICSKINS LLC
140 58th St Ste 197 (11220-2539)
PHONE..................................646 827-4271
Robert Scarcello, *Senior VP*
Vince Bartozzi, *Mng Member*
Jed Seifert,
EMP: 11
SQ FT: 4,000
SALES: 1.5MM **Privately Held**
SIC: 2851 5099 Vinyl coatings, strippable; musical instruments parts & accessories

(G-2344)
MY HANKY INC
680 81st St Apt 4d (11228-2833)
PHONE..................................646 321-0869
Frank Marino, *President*

EMP: 10
SQ FT: 500
SALES: 500K **Privately Held**
SIC: 2389 Handkerchiefs, except paper

(G-2345)
MYSTIC DISPLAY CO INC
909 Remsen Ave (11236-1624)
PHONE..................................718 485-2651
David Censi, *President*
Barry Censi, *Corp Secy*
Hank Lombardi, *Vice Pres*
Anthony Valentine, *Vice Pres*
Dorothy Sylvester, *Controller*
▼ **EMP:** 2
SQ FT: 47,000
SALES: 8MM **Privately Held**
WEB: www.mysticdisplay.com
SIC: 3993 7319 Displays & cutouts, window & lobby; display advertising service

(G-2346)
N C IRON WORKS INC
1117 60th St (11219-4925)
PHONE..................................718 633-4660
Fax: 718 436-0334
Nicholas Sorrentino, *President*
EMP: 5
SQ FT: 3,900
SALES (est): 1MM **Privately Held**
SIC: 3312 Hot-rolled iron & steel products

(G-2347)
NAGAD CABINETS INC
1039 Mcdonald Ave (11230-1020)
PHONE..................................718 382-7200
Naftali Grueberger, *President*
EMP: 5
SQ FT: 2,000
SALES (est): 704.4K **Privately Held**
SIC: 2434 Vanities, bathroom: wood

(G-2348)
NAP INDUSTRIES INC
Also Called: N A P
667 Kent Ave (11249-7500)
PHONE..................................718 625-4948
Fax: 718 596-4342
Leopold Lowy, *President*
Morris Lowy, *Chairman*
Jack Freund, *Vice Pres*
Ram Sirupurapu, *Exec Dir*
▲ **EMP:** 90 **EST:** 1961
SQ FT: 55,000
SALES (est): 18.7MM **Privately Held**
SIC: 2673 Plastic bags: made from purchased materials

(G-2349)
NARRATIVELY INC
221 Cumberland St Apt 4 (11205-4687)
PHONE..................................203 536-0332
Noah Rosenberg, *President*
EMP: 25 **EST:** 2012
SQ FT: 20,000
SALES (est): 929K **Privately Held**
SIC: 2741

(G-2350)
NATIONAL DIE & BUTTON MOULD CO
Also Called: Eisen Bros
1 Kent Ave (11249-1014)
PHONE..................................201 939-7800
Fax: 212 575-2153
Louis Eisenpresser, *Chairman*
George Eisenpresser, *Chairman*
EMP: 50 **EST:** 1911
SQ FT: 65,000
SALES (est): 5.1MM **Privately Held**
WEB: www.nailheads.com
SIC: 3965 3469 Buttons & parts; buckles & buckle parts; eyelets, metal: clothing, fabrics, boots or shoes; metal stampings

(G-2351)
NATIONAL PRFMCE SOLUTIONS INC
Also Called: Squeaky Clean
7106 13th Ave (11228-1606)
PHONE..................................718 833-4767
Lola Bizas, *Ch of Bd*
Jacob Kahle, *Principal*
Greg Bowman, *Co-Owner*
Michell Bowman, *Co-Owner*
EMP: 100

Brooklyn - Kings County (G-2352)

SQ FT: 400
SALES: 20.1MM **Privately Held**
SIC: 3993 Advertising artwork

(G-2352)
NATIONWIDE DAIRY INC
792 E 93rd St (11236-1831)
PHONE..................................347 689-8148
Eduard Magidov, *CEO*
◆ EMP: 5
SQ FT: 9,000
SALES (est): 423.4K **Privately Held**
SIC: 2023 Dry, condensed, evaporated dairy products

(G-2353)
NATURAL STONE & CABINET INC
1365 Halsey St (11237-6102)
PHONE..................................718 388-2988
Sally Lee, *Owner*
▲ EMP: 6
SALES (est): 470.1K **Privately Held**
SIC: 2522 Cabinets, office: except wood

(G-2354)
NAUTICAL MARINE PAINT CORP
Also Called: Nautical Paint
4802 Farragut Rd (11203-6690)
PHONE..................................718 462-7000
Fax: 718 462-4100
Michael Schnurr, *President*
EMP: 25
SQ FT: 4,000
SALES (corp-wide): 7.2MM **Privately Held**
SIC: 2851 5231 Paints & allied products; paint
PA: Nautical Marine Paint Corp
1999 Elizabeth St
North Brunswick NJ 08902
732 821-3200

(G-2355)
NCC NY LLC
140 58th St Ste A (11220-2539)
PHONE..................................718 943-7000
Michelle Cohen, *COO*
Liane Yee, *Manager*
Sharon Miller, *Executive*
Joey Haber,
Joe Nakash,
▲ EMP: 20 EST: 1999
SQ FT: 9,000
SALES (est): 4.9MM **Privately Held**
WEB: www.ehalacha.com
SIC: 3699 Extension cords
PA: Nakash Five Points Llc
1400 Broadway Fl 15
New York NY 10018

(G-2356)
NEO CABINETRY LLC
400 Liberty Ave (11207-3032)
PHONE..................................718 403-0456
Louis Doucet, *Owner*
EMP: 10
SALES (est): 900.9K **Privately Held**
SIC: 2434 Wood kitchen cabinets

(G-2357)
NEPTUNE MACHINE INC
521 Carroll St (11215-1011)
PHONE..................................718 852-4100
Fax: 718 797-5113
Nicholas G Karkas, *President*
John Karkas, *Vice Pres*
Camille Manzo, *Controller*
EMP: 20
SQ FT: 12,500
SALES (est): 3.9MM **Privately Held**
WEB: www.neptunemachine.com
SIC: 3599 Machine & other job shop work; machine shop, jobbing & repair

(G-2358)
NEW AGE IRONWORKS INC
183 Van Siclen Ave (11207-2605)
PHONE..................................718 277-1895
Fax: 718 277-1897
Yair Tapia, *President*
EMP: 14
SALES (est): 1.7MM **Privately Held**
SIC: 7692 Welding repair

(G-2359)
NEW ART PUBLICATIONS INC
Also Called: Bomb Magazine
80 Hanson Pl Ste 703 (11217-2998)
PHONE..................................718 636-9100
Fax: 718 636-9200
Betsy Sussler, *President*
Ryan Chapman, *Managing Dir*
Alexis Boehmler, *Principal*
Richard Goldstein, *Editor*
Clinton Krute, *Editor*
EMP: 10
SALES (est): 1.2MM **Privately Held**
WEB: www.bombsite.com
SIC: 2721 Magazines: publishing only, not printed on site

(G-2360)
NEW DIMENSION AWARDS INC (PA)
Also Called: New Dimension Trophies
6505 11th Ave (11219-5602)
PHONE..................................718 236-8200
Fax: 718 236-6979
Joseph S Cardinale, *President*
Michael S Fasano, *Vice Pres*
EMP: 9 EST: 1979
SQ FT: 16,000
SALES (est): 1MM **Privately Held**
WEB: www.newdimensioninc.com
SIC: 3499 Trophies, metal, except silver; novelties & specialties, metal

(G-2361)
NEW DIMENSIONS OFFICE GROUP
Also Called: Acme Office Group
540 Morgan Ave (11222-5227)
PHONE..................................718 387-0995
Fax: 718 387-1162
Ernest Eager, *President*
Bertran Teich, *Vice Pres*
Buddy Martin, *Treasurer*
Joseph Klinsky, *Controller*
Jack Teich, *Admin Sec*
EMP: 52
SQ FT: 20,000
SALES (est): 3.5MM **Privately Held**
SIC: 2521 3446 2541 2522 Wood office furniture; panel systems & partitions (free-standing), office: wood; architectural metalwork; wood partitions & fixtures; office furniture, except wood

(G-2362)
NEW PROJECT LLC
122 18th St (11215-5312)
PHONE..................................718 788-3444
Dennis Potami, *Principal*
EMP: 9
SALES (est): 1.2MM **Privately Held**
SIC: 3399 Primary metal products

(G-2363)
NEW YORK CHRISTAN TIMES INC
1061 Atlantic Ave (11238-2902)
PHONE..................................718 638-6397
Fax: 718 638-1810
Dennis Dillon, *President*
Karen Granger, *Vice Pres*
EMP: 6
SALES (est): 460K **Privately Held**
SIC: 2759 Publication printing

(G-2364)
NEW YORK DAILY CHALLENGE INC (PA)
1195 Atlantic Ave Fl 2 (11216-2709)
PHONE..................................718 636-9500
Fax: 718 857-9115
Thomas H Watkins Jr, *President*
Tatsianna Singleton, *Office Mgr*
Duwad Philip, *Manager*
EMP: 12
SQ FT: 1,000
SALES (est): 1.6MM **Privately Held**
SIC: 2711 Newspapers: publishing only, not printed on site

(G-2365)
NEW YORK HOSPITAL DISPOSABLE
101 Richardson St Ste 1 (11211-1344)
PHONE..................................718 384-1620
Fax: 718 599-1183
Rosa Ramos, *President*
Victor Cora, *President*
Ricardo Cora, *Vice Pres*
Zitzor Cora, *Admin Sec*
EMP: 20
SQ FT: 12,000
SALES (est): 1.1MM **Privately Held**
SIC: 2389 2326 Hospital gowns; men's & boys' work clothing

(G-2366)
NEW YORK POPLIN LLC
4611 1st Ave (11232-4200)
PHONE..................................718 768-3296
Wayne Yip,
▲ EMP: 8
SQ FT: 8,000
SALES (est): 4.5MM **Privately Held**
SIC: 2221 Apparel & outerwear fabric, manmade fiber or silk

(G-2367)
NEW YORK POPULAR INC
Also Called: Popularity Products
168 39th St Unit 3 (11232-2714)
PHONE..................................718 499-2020
Benjamin Tebele, *CEO*
Albert Tebele, *Ch of Bd*
Edward Tebele, *Admin Sec*
▲ EMP: 100
SQ FT: 50,000
SALES (est): 16.2MM **Privately Held**
WEB: www.popularityproducts.com
SIC: 2389 5136 5137 Men's miscellaneous accessories; men's & boys' clothing; women's & children's clothing

(G-2368)
NEW YORK QRTRLY FOUNDATION INC
322 76th St (11209-3106)
P.O. Box 2015, New York (10113-2015)
PHONE..................................917 843-8825
Raymond Hammond, *President*
Neil Smith, *Vice Pres*
Linda Tieber, *Treasurer*
Andrea Lockett, *Admin Sec*
EMP: 12
SALES (est): 52K **Privately Held**
SIC: 2731 7389 Book publishing;

(G-2369)
NEWCASTLE FABRICS CORP
Also Called: Newtown Finishing
86 Beadel St (11222-5232)
PHONE..................................718 388-6600
Daniel Aldalezo, *Manager*
EMP: 5
SALES (corp-wide): 5.6MM **Privately Held**
WEB: www.newcastlefabrics.com
SIC: 2269 7389 Finishing plants; textile & apparel services
PA: Newcastle Fabrics Corp.
140 58th St Ste 112
Brooklyn NY 11220
718 782-5560

(G-2370)
NEWS REPORT INC
Also Called: Diyzeitung
1281 49th St Ste 3 (11219-3055)
PHONE..................................718 851-6607
Albert Friedman, *Ch of Bd*
Rose Friedman, *Vice Pres*
EMP: 25
SALES (est): 1.1MM **Privately Held**
SIC: 2711 Newspapers: publishing only, not printed on site

(G-2371)
NEWYORK PEDORTHIC ASSOCIATES
Also Called: Rosenbaum Foot
2102 63rd St (11204-3058)
PHONE..................................718 236-7700
Mark Rosenbaum, *President*
EMP: 6

SALES (est): 480K **Privately Held**
SIC: 3069 Orthopedic sundries, molded rubber

(G-2372)
NITEL INC
199 Lee Ave Ste 119 (11211-8919)
PHONE..................................347 731-1558
Solomon Rubin, *President*
EMP: 5
SALES (est): 213.3K **Privately Held**
SIC: 7372 Application computer software

(G-2373)
NOBLE CHECKS INC
1682 43rd St Apt 2 (11204-1059)
PHONE..................................212 537-6241
Isaac Dresdner, *Ch of Bd*
EMP: 5
SALES (est): 564.8K **Privately Held**
WEB: www.noblechecks.com
SIC: 2759 Commercial printing

(G-2374)
NORTHERN ADHESIVES INC
97 Apollo St (11222-3893)
PHONE..................................718 388-5834
Fax: 718 388-6355
Herbert Rosen, *President*
Richard Rosen, *Vice Pres*
Elaine Rosen, *Admin Sec*
EMP: 30
SQ FT: 25,000
SALES (est): 5.3MM **Privately Held**
WEB: www.northernadhesives.com
SIC: 2891 Adhesives

(G-2375)
NORTHSIDE MEDIA GROUP LLC (HQ)
1 Metrotech Ctr Ste 1803 (11201-3949)
PHONE..................................917 318-6513
Jesse Smith, *Vice Pres*
Scott Stedman,
Daniel Stedman,
EMP: 10
SALES (est): 2.8MM
SALES (corp-wide): 9.4MM **Privately Held**
SIC: 2721 Magazines: publishing & printing
PA: Zealot Networks, Inc.
2114 Narcissus Ct
Venice CA 90291
310 821-3737

(G-2376)
NORTHSIDE MEDIA GROUP LLC
1 Metrotech Ctr Fl 18 (11201-3949)
PHONE..................................917 318-6513
Fax: 718 596-3662
Scott Stedman, *Branch Mgr*
Dana Keith, *Business Dir*
EMP: 25
SALES (corp-wide): 9.4MM **Privately Held**
SIC: 2721 Magazines: publishing & printing
HQ: Northside Media Group Llc
1 Metrotech Ctr Ste 1803
Brooklyn NY 11201
917 318-6513

(G-2377)
NOVEL BOX COMPANY LTD
659 Berriman St (11208-5303)
PHONE..................................718 965-2222
Moishe Sternhill, *President*
Abe Kwadrat, *Vice Pres*
▲ EMP: 25 EST: 1942
SQ FT: 41,000
SALES (est): 4.7MM **Privately Held**
WEB: www.novelbox.com
SIC: 2657 3469 3089 Folding paperboard boxes; boxes, stamped metal; boxes, plastic

(G-2378)
NOVOYE RSSKOYE SLOVO PUBG CORP
Also Called: Russian Daily
2614 Voorhies Ave (11235-2414)
PHONE..................................646 460-4566
Fax: 646 218-6951
Yuri Ivnitsky, *Ch of Bd*
Lawrence Weinberg, *President*
Michael German, *Business Mgr*
Alexander Goldfarb, *Controller*

▲ = Import ▼ = Export
◆ = Import/Export

GEOGRAPHIC SECTION — Brooklyn - Kings County (G-2408)

EMP: 52
SQ FT: 16,000
SALES (est): 2.9MM Privately Held
WEB: www.nrs.com
SIC: 2711 Newspapers: publishing only, not printed on site

(G-2379)
NUHART & CO INC
49 Dupont St (11222-1008)
P.O. Box 786, Deer Park (11729-0786)
PHONE..................................718 383-8484
Fax: 718 383-7215
Alex Folkman, *President*
Joseph Folkman, *Vice Pres*
David Rauch, *Vice Pres*
Roopriarane Dan, *Controller*
EMP: 76
SQ FT: 130,000
SALES (est): 9.2MM Privately Held
SIC: 3081 Vinyl film & sheet

(G-2380)
NUVITE CHEMICAL COMPOUNDS CORP
213 Freeman St 215 (11222-1400)
PHONE..................................718 383-8351
Fax: 718 383-0008
EMP: 11 EST: 1949
SQ FT: 7,000
SALES (est): 1MM Privately Held
SIC: 2842 Mfg Industrial Cleaning Specialties

(G-2381)
NY CABINET FACTORY INC
6901 14th Ave (11228-1701)
PHONE..................................718 256-6541
Vin Burratto, *President*
Frank Burratto, *Vice Pres*
EMP: 11 EST: 2015
SQ FT: 2,500
SALES: 2MM Privately Held
SIC: 2434 Wood kitchen cabinets

(G-2382)
NY ORTHOPEDIC USA INC
63 Flushing Ave Unit 333 (11205-1083)
PHONE..................................718 852-5330
Fax: 718 852-4095
Michael Rozenberg, *President*
Michael Blatt, *Vice Pres*
▲ EMP: 80
SQ FT: 24,000
SALES (est): 10.8MM Privately Held
WEB: www.nyorthousa.com
SIC: 3842 2389 5999 Personal safety equipment; uniforms & vestments; medical apparatus & supplies

(G-2383)
NY TILEMAKERS
331 Grand St (11211-4464)
PHONE..................................989 278-8353
Andru Eron, *Owner*
EMP: 5 EST: 2012
SALES: 80K Privately Held
SIC: 3253 Ceramic wall & floor tile

(G-2384)
NYC COMMUNITY MEDIA LLC
Also Called: Villager, The
1 Metrotech Ctr N Fl 10 (11201-3875)
PHONE..................................212 229-1890
Jennifer Goodstein,
EMP: 18 EST: 2012
SQ FT: 1,200
SALES (est): 1.1MM Privately Held
SIC: 2711 Newspapers: publishing only, not printed on site

(G-2385)
NYP HOLDINGS INC
Also Called: New York Post
1 Metrotech Ctr N Fl 10 (11201-3875)
PHONE..................................718 260-2500
Cliff Luster, *Principal*
EMP: 60
SALES (corp-wide): 8.2B Publicly Held
SIC: 2711 Newspapers
HQ: Nyp Holdings, Inc.
1211 Avenue Of The Amer
New York NY 10036
212 997-9272

(G-2386)
OFFICE GRABS NY INC
1303 53rd St 105 (11219-3823)
PHONE..................................212 444-1331
Meir Barminka, *CEO*
Moshe Rosenberg, *President*
EMP: 6
SALES (est): 695K Privately Held
SIC: 2752 Commercial printing, lithographic

(G-2387)
OGOSPORT LLC
63 Flushing Ave Unit 137 (11205-1070)
PHONE..................................718 554-0777
Jenie Fu,
Charlotte Kreitmann, *Admin Sec*
Kevin Williams,
▲ EMP: 5
SQ FT: 5,000
SALES (est): 580K Privately Held
WEB: www.ogosport.com
SIC: 3944 Games, toys & children's vehicles

(G-2388)
OLD POLAND FOODS LLC
Also Called: Pipkarnia Starodolska
149 N 8th St (11249-2001)
PHONE..................................718 486-7700
Richard Podedworny,
Teresa Kramer,
▲ EMP: 16
SALES (est): 1.9MM Privately Held
SIC: 2051 Pastries, e.g. danish: except frozen

(G-2389)
OLD WILLIAMSBURGH CANDLE CORP
143 Alabama Ave (11207-2911)
P.O. Box 6, Suffern (10901-0006)
PHONE..................................718 566-1500
Merav Gold, *CEO*
Shrage Marasow, *General Mgr*
Niv Zikdershtein, *Principal*
S H Fischer, *Vice Pres*
Joel Kaliroff, *Vice Pres*
▲ EMP: 150
SQ FT: 120,000
SALES (est): 27.9MM Privately Held
WEB: www.palacecandlesusa.com
SIC: 3999 Candles

(G-2390)
OLOLLO INC
43 Hall St Ste B8 (11205-1395)
PHONE..................................877 701-0110
Regan Chen, *President*
EMP: 7 EST: 2009
SQ FT: 10,000
SALES (est): 1MM Privately Held
SIC: 2519 Household furniture, except wood or metal: upholstered

(G-2391)
OMILK LLC
189 Schermerhorn St 14d (11201-6096)
PHONE..................................646 530-2908
Lawrence Swan, *Principal*
EMP: 5
SALES (est): 431.9K Privately Held
SIC: 2023 Dried & powdered milk & milk products

(G-2392)
ONE GIRL COOKIES LTD
68 Dean St Ste A (11201-7749)
PHONE..................................212 675-4996
Dawn Casale, *Ch of Bd*
Reymon Sinsay, *Director*
EMP: 10
SALES (est): 1.1MM Privately Held
WEB: www.onegirlcookies.com
SIC: 2052 Cookies

(G-2393)
ONE STORY INC
232 3rd St Ste A108 (11215-2708)
PHONE..................................917 816-3659
Maribeth Batcha, *President*
Will Allison, *Editor*
Ellie Kincaid, *Editor*
Hannah Tinti, *Vice Pres*
Lynn Beckenstein, *Manager*

EMP: 8
SALES: 322.5K Privately Held
SIC: 2741 Miscellaneous publishing

(G-2394)
ONE TECHNOLOGIES LLC
44 Court St Ste 1217 (11201-4410)
PHONE..................................718 509-0704
Yevhenii Lozovyi,
Polina Lozovyi,
EMP: 6
SALES: 2.2MM Privately Held
SIC: 3571 Electronic computers

(G-2395)
ORIGINAL CONVECTOR SPECIALIST
Also Called: Ocs
2015 Pitkin Ave (11207-3424)
PHONE..................................718 342-5820
Fax: 718 338-8529
Henry Gutman, *President*
Sol Breuer, *Vice Pres*
Shirley Fisher, *Bookkeeper*
Chaim Breuer, *Admin Sec*
▲ EMP: 8
SALES (est): 640K Privately Held
SIC: 3433 Radiators, except electric

(G-2396)
ORTHOCRAFT INC
1477 E 27th St (11210-5308)
PHONE..................................718 692-0113
Herschel Sauber, *President*
EMP: 6
SQ FT: 800
SALES (est): 530K Privately Held
SIC: 3842 5999 Prosthetic appliances; orthopedic appliances; orthopedic & prosthesis applications

(G-2397)
ORTHOPEDIC ARTS LABORATORY INC
141 Atlantic Ave Apt 1 (11201-5516)
PHONE..................................718 858-2400
Fax: 718 858-9258
Stephan Manucharian, *CEO*
EMP: 6
SQ FT: 850
SALES: 950K Privately Held
SIC: 3842 Prosthetic appliances

(G-2398)
OSO INDUSTRIES INC
647 Myrtle Ave Ste 1 (11205-3935)
PHONE..................................917 709-2050
Eric Weil, *Principal*
EMP: 6
SALES (est): 263.3K Privately Held
SIC: 3999 Manufacturing industries

(G-2399)
OUTREACH PUBLISHING CORP
546 Montgomery St (11225-3023)
PHONE..................................718 773-0525
Shlomo Lakein, *President*
Reuben Lakein, *Vice Pres*
EMP: 7
SALES (est): 660K Privately Held
WEB: www.outreach770.com
SIC: 2741 Miscellaneous publishing

(G-2400)
P B O E PWRED BY OUR ENVMT INC
Also Called: Retracase
419 Madison St Apt 2a (11221-1120)
PHONE..................................917 803-9474
Mike Roper, *President*
Arlene Williams, *Vice Pres*
EMP: 6
SALES: 950K Privately Held
SIC: 2389 Apparel & accessories

(G-2401)
P M BELTS USA INC
131 32nd St (11232-1809)
PHONE..................................800 762-3580
Fax: 718 369-9700
Gregory O'Neil, *President*
EMP: 45 EST: 1986
SQ FT: 12,500

SALES (est): 1.9MM Privately Held
WEB: www.pmbelt.com
SIC: 2387 Apparel belts

(G-2402)
PALAGONIA BAKERY CO INC
Also Called: Palagonia Italian Bread
508 Junius St (11212-7199)
PHONE..................................718 272-5400
Christopher Palagonia, *President*
Joseph A Palagonia, *General Mgr*
Steve Toto, *QC Dir*
Dennis Pizzer, *Research*
▲ EMP: 100
SQ FT: 25,000
SALES (est): 14.5MM Privately Held
SIC: 2051 Bread, cake & related products

(G-2403)
PAP CHAT INC
3105 Quentin Rd (11234-4234)
PHONE..................................516 350-1888
Justin Schwartz, *CEO*
EMP: 5 EST: 2015
SALES (est): 156K Privately Held
SIC: 7372 7389 Prepackaged software;

(G-2404)
PAPER SOLUTIONS INC
342 37th St (11232-2506)
PHONE..................................718 499-4226
Wing FAI Lam, *CEO*
Natalie Lam, *Manager*
▲ EMP: 12
SALES (est): 2.1MM Privately Held
SIC: 2621 Paper mills

(G-2405)
PARADISE PLASTICS LLC
116 39th St (11232-2712)
PHONE..................................718 788-3733
Max Berg,
Judith Berg,
Ernest Grossberger,
Gabriella Grossberger,
EMP: 25 EST: 1952
SQ FT: 40,000
SALES (est): 4.7MM Privately Held
WEB: www.paradiseplastics.com
SIC: 2673 Plastic bags: made from purchased materials

(G-2406)
PARAGON PUBLISHING INC
97 Harrison Ave (11206-2918)
PHONE..................................718 302-2093
Mendel Sicherman, *President*
Suzanne Holtman, *Controller*
EMP: 5
SALES (est): 440K Privately Held
SIC: 2741 Miscellaneous publishing

(G-2407)
PARK AVE BLDG & ROOFG SUPS LLC
2120 Atlantic Ave (11233-3162)
PHONE..................................718 403-0100
Fax: 718 403-0095
Bob Groeninger, *CEO*
Raymond Rivera, *President*
Tom Hussey, *CFO*
Margarita Ptaszek, *Controller*
Tim Keegan, *Accounts Mgr*
EMP: 40
SQ FT: 15,000
SALES (est): 40.2MM Privately Held
SIC: 3531 5033 Aerial work platforms: hydraulic/elec. truck/carrier mounted; roofing & siding materials

(G-2408)
PARK AVENUE SPORTSWEAR LTD (PA)
820 4th Ave (11232-1612)
PHONE..................................718 369-0520
Fax: 718 369-0521
EMP: 12 EST: 1962
SQ FT: 15,000
SALES (est): 1.8MM Privately Held
SIC: 2339 Sportswear, women's

Brooklyn - Kings County (G-2409)

(G-2409)
PATRICK MACKIN CUSTOM FURN
Also Called: Art Boards
612 Degraw St (11217-3112)
PHONE.................................718 237-2592
Patrick Mackin, *President*
▲ EMP: 7
SALES: 600K **Privately Held**
WEB: www.art-boards.com
SIC: 2511 Wood household furniture

(G-2410)
PAUL & FRANZA LLC
90 Junius St (11212-8029)
PHONE.................................718 342-8106
Hs Paul,
EMP: 10
SQ FT: 5,000
SALES (est): 588.2K **Privately Held**
SIC: 3462 Ornamental metal forgings, ferrous

(G-2411)
PECORARO DAIRY PRODUCTS INC (PA)
287 Leonard St (11211-3618)
PHONE.................................718 388-2379
Cesare Pecoraro, *President*
Ralph Parlato, *Vice Pres*
EMP: 6
SQ FT: 4,000
SALES (est): 959.9K **Privately Held**
SIC: 2022 Natural cheese

(G-2412)
PEELED INC
Also Called: Peeled Snack
65 15th St Ste 1 (11215-4653)
PHONE.................................212 706-2001
Noha Waibsnaider, *President*
Cassie Abrams, *Principal*
Jessica Aquila, *Principal*
Ian Kelleher, *Principal*
Dawn Techow, *COO*
▲ EMP: 8
SALES: 4.7MM **Privately Held**
SIC: 2068 2034 Nuts: dried, dehydrated, salted or roasted; dried & dehydrated fruits

(G-2413)
PEKING FOOD LLC
47 Stewart Ave (11237-1517)
PHONE.................................718 628-8080
Lawrence Wu, *Mng Member*
Teresa Wu,
EMP: 30
SQ FT: 28,000
SALES: 4MM **Privately Held**
SIC: 2051 Bread, cake & related products

(G-2414)
PENN SIGNS INC
Also Called: Mr Sign
1920 Atlantic Ave (11233-3004)
PHONE.................................718 797-1112
Fax: 718 797-1153
Shulm Miller, *President*
Leo Lew, *Manager*
EMP: 20
SALES (est): 2MM **Privately Held**
SIC: 3993 Signs & advertising specialties

(G-2415)
PENN STATE METAL FABRI
810 Humboldt St Ste 9 (11222-1913)
PHONE.................................718 786-8814
Herbert Engler, *President*
Ron Desena, *Manager*
EMP: 4
SQ FT: 7,500
SALES: 1MM **Privately Held**
SIC: 3531 3463 Construction machinery; pump & compressor forgings, nonferrous

(G-2416)
PERALTA METAL WORKS INC
602 Atkins Ave (11208-5202)
PHONE.................................718 649-8661
Fax: 718 384-5450
Omar Peralta, *President*
Yvette Peralta, *Vice Pres*
EMP: 8
SQ FT: 3,500
SALES (est): 1.5MM **Privately Held**
SIC: 3441 Fabricated structural metal

(G-2417)
PERFECT PRINT INC
220 36th St Unit 2a (11232-2413)
PHONE.................................718 832-5280
Fax: 718 832-5272
Orly Masry, *President*
Alla Goldenburg, *Prdtn Mgr*
EMP: 20
SALES: 250K **Privately Held**
SIC: 2211 Print cloths, cotton

(G-2418)
PICTURE PERFECT FRAMING
1758 50th St (11204-1220)
PHONE.................................718 851-1884
Harry Gruber, *Owner*
Chaya Gruber, *Owner*
EMP: 5
SALES: 30K **Privately Held**
SIC: 2499 3499 Picture & mirror frames, wood; picture frames, metal

(G-2419)
PILGRIM SURF & SUPPLY
68 N 3rd St (11249-3925)
PHONE.................................718 218-7456
Chris Gentile, *Owner*
Chelsea Burcz, *Editor*
EMP: 7
SALES (est): 527.5K **Privately Held**
SIC: 3949 Surfboards

(G-2420)
PILLOW PERFECTIONS LTD INC
252 Norman Ave Ste 101 (11222-6412)
PHONE.................................718 383-2259
Fax: 718 383-3151
Kenny Fried, *President*
▼ EMP: 8
SQ FT: 7,000
SALES: 700K **Privately Held**
SIC: 2511 5712 Wood household furniture; furniture stores

(G-2421)
PIN PRETTY INC
5415 14th Ave (11219-4218)
PHONE.................................718 887-5290
Joel Spitzer, *Chairman*
EMP: 5
SALES (est): 419.1K **Privately Held**
SIC: 3452 Pins

(G-2422)
PINK BOX ACCESSORIES LLC
Also Called: Blue Box
1170 72nd St (11228-1306)
PHONE.................................716 777-4477
Mariano Uy, *Mng Member*
Michael Uy,
◆ EMP: 5
SALES: 500K **Privately Held**
SIC: 3911 7389 Jewelry, precious metal;

(G-2423)
PIROKE TRADE INC
1430 35th St Fl 2 (11218-3706)
PHONE.................................646 515-1537
Keitaro Maruyama, *President*
EMP: 5
SALES (est): 280K **Privately Held**
SIC: 2789 Trade binding services

(G-2424)
PIVOT RECORDS LLC
600 Johnson Ave (11237-1318)
P.O. Box 70276 (11207-0276)
PHONE.................................718 417-1213
EMP: 11
SALES (est): 490K **Privately Held**
SIC: 3652 Mfg Prerecorded Records/Tapes

(G-2425)
PLACEMETER INC
865 President St (11215-1405)
PHONE.................................917 225-4579
Alexandre Winter, *CEO*
Florent Peyre, *COO*
Stanislav Parfenov, *Technology*
EMP: 5 EST: 2012
SQ FT: 100
SALES (est): 501.3K **Privately Held**
SIC: 3812 Air traffic control systems & equipment, electronic

(G-2426)
PLATFORM EXPERTS INC
2938 Quentin Rd (11229-1825)
PHONE.................................646 843-7100
Joshua Newman, *President*
Zev Graber, *Manager*
EMP: 8
SQ FT: 4,000
SALES: 1.1MM **Privately Held**
WEB: www.platformexperts.com
SIC: 7372 Prepackaged software

(G-2427)
PLURIBUS PRODUCTS INC
77 Washington Ave (11205-1294)
PHONE.................................718 852-1614
Fax: 718 852-4575
Peter V Martino, *President*
John V Martino, *Purchasing*
Michael Racconova, *Manager*
Sabrina Stabile, *Manager*
EMP: 32 EST: 1966
SQ FT: 50,000
SALES (est): 4.9MM **Privately Held**
SIC: 2531 2449 3341 Public building & related furniture; wood containers; secondary nonferrous metals

(G-2428)
POLYTECH POOL MFG INC
Also Called: Wet & Wild Pools & Spas
262 48th St 262 (11220-1012)
P.O. Box 544, Cedarhurst (11516-0544)
PHONE.................................718 492-8991
Fax: 718 439-1254
EMP: 10 EST: 1975
SQ FT: 60,000
SALES (est): 870K **Privately Held**
SIC: 3949 Mfg Sporting/Athletic Goods

(G-2429)
POP PRINTING INCORPORATED
288 Hamilton Ave (11231-3208)
PHONE.................................212 808-7800
Stephen Stein, *Ch of Bd*
EMP: 14
SALES (est): 1.8MM **Privately Held**
SIC: 2752 Commercial printing, lithographic

(G-2430)
POTENTIAL POLY BAG INC
1253 Coney Island Ave (11230-3520)
PHONE.................................718 258-0800
Mark Katz, *President*
Jerry Millman, *Vice Pres*
Chaya Freilich, *Manager*
▲ EMP: 9
SQ FT: 10,000
SALES (est): 1.6MM **Privately Held**
WEB: www.potentialpolybag.com
SIC: 3081 Polyethylene film

(G-2431)
POWERMATE CELLULAR
140 58th St Ste 1d (11220-2525)
PHONE.................................718 833-9400
Fax: 718 567-7020
▲ EMP: 7
SALES (est): 730.8K **Privately Held**
SIC: 3661 Mfg Telephone/Telegraph Apparatus

(G-2432)
PPR DIRECT INC
Also Called: Icommunicator
74 20th St Fl 2 (11232-1101)
PHONE.................................718 965-8600
Leonard Feldman, *President*
Larry Brown, *Vice Pres*
Steve Bruner, *Vice Pres*
Robert Notine, *Treasurer*
Richard Kirschner, *Controller*
▲ EMP: 15
SQ FT: 8,000
SALES (est): 2.2MM
SALES (corp-wide): 3.7MM **Privately Held**
WEB: www.pprdirect.com
SIC: 3089 Novelties, plastic

PA: Professional Product Research Co. Inc.
74 20th St
Brooklyn NY 11232
718 965-8600

(G-2433)
PPR DIRECT MARKETING LLC (PA)
74 20th St (11232-1101)
PHONE.................................718 965-8600
Robert Notine,
Richard Carvalho,
Margaret Hickey,
▲ EMP: 8
SALES (est): 3.6MM **Privately Held**
SIC: 2389 Men's miscellaneous accessories

(G-2434)
PR & STONE & TILE INC
Also Called: Stone Crafters International
17 Beadel St (11222-5110)
PHONE.................................718 383-1115
Edward Rynkosky, *President*
Arakdiusz Rakowski, *Vice Pres*
EMP: 5
SALES: 900K **Privately Held**
SIC: 3281 Granite, cut & shaped

(G-2435)
PRECISION MTAL FABRICATORS INC
Also Called: PMF
236 39th St (11232-2820)
PHONE.................................718 832-9805
Fax: 718 832-9405
Dimitrios Theodoru, *President*
EMP: 12
SQ FT: 8,000
SALES (est): 2.1MM **Privately Held**
SIC: 3444 Sheet metalwork

(G-2436)
PRECISION PRODUCT INC
18 Steuben St (11205-1306)
PHONE.................................718 852-7127
Sonny K Chan, *President*
▲ EMP: 5
SQ FT: 6,000
SALES (est): 470K **Privately Held**
SIC: 3531 Construction machinery

(G-2437)
PREEBRO PRINTING
5319 Fort Hamilton Pkwy (11219-4036)
PHONE.................................718 633-7300
Zur Getter, *Owner*
EMP: 5
SALES (est): 537.4K **Privately Held**
WEB: www.preebroprinting.com
SIC: 2752 Commercial printing, lithographic

(G-2438)
PREMIUM WOODWORKING LLC
78 Division Pl Fl 1 (11222-5230)
PHONE.................................718 782-7747
Bhevendra Persaud,
EMP: 5
SQ FT: 5,000
SALES: 2MM **Privately Held**
SIC: 2434 Wood kitchen cabinets

(G-2439)
PRESSER KOSHER BAKING CORP
1720 Avenue M (11230-5304)
PHONE.................................718 375-5088
Fax: 718 375-2050
Sam Klein, *President*
Judy Klein, *Human Res Dir*
EMP: 20
SQ FT: 2,500
SALES (est): 2.5MM **Privately Held**
SIC: 2051 5461 Bakery: wholesale or wholesale/retail combined; bakeries

(G-2440)
PRESTIGE HANGERS STR FIXS CORP
1026 55th St (11219-4024)
PHONE.................................718 522-6777
Abe Minkosf, *President*
Mozes Parnes, *Principal*
EMP: 5

GEOGRAPHIC SECTION
Brooklyn - Kings County (G-2468)

SQ FT: 5,000
SALES: 370K **Privately Held**
WEB: www.prestigestorefixtures.com
SIC: 3089 Clothes hangers, plastic

(G-2441)
PRIME FOOD PROCESSING CORP
300 Vandervoort Ave (11211-1715)
PHONE.................................718 963-2323
Albert Chan, *Ch of Bd*
Yee Hung Chan, *President*
Tommy Ng, *Accounting Mgr*
Raymond Leung, *Manager*
▲ EMP: 80
SQ FT: 35,000
SALES (est): 12.5MM **Privately Held**
SIC: 2013 2037 Frozen meats from purchased meat; vegetables, quick frozen & cold pack, excl. potato products

(G-2442)
PRIMO FROZEN DESSERTS INC
Also Called: Ices Queen
1633 Utica Ave (11234-1524)
PHONE.................................718 252-2312
Fax: 718 253-1202
Dan Lazzaro, *CEO*
Dominick Lazzaro, *Vice Pres*
EMP: 8
SQ FT: 4,500
SALES: 400K **Privately Held**
SIC: 2024 Ices, flavored (frozen dessert)

(G-2443)
PRIMO PLASTICS INC
162 Russell St (11222-3619)
P.O. Box 220187 (11222-0187)
PHONE.................................718 349-1000
Fax: 718 349-1036
John Primo, *President*
Pete Krutros, *Vice Pres*
Stanley Primo, *Vice Pres*
▲ EMP: 20
SQ FT: 7,800
SALES (est): 2.3MM **Privately Held**
SIC: 2673 5113 Plastic & pliofilm bags; bags, paper & disposable plastic

(G-2444)
PRINCE SEATING CORP
1355 Atlantic Ave (11216-2810)
PHONE.................................718 363-2300
Fax: 718 363-9800
Abe Belsky, *President*
Henry Bodner, *Vice Pres*
Bluma Staruss, *Controller*
▲ EMP: 25
SQ FT: 80,000
SALES (est): 3.5MM **Privately Held**
WEB: www.chairfactory.net
SIC: 2522 2521 Tables, office: except wood; chairs, office: padded or plain, except wood; stools, office: except wood; tables, office: wood; chairs, office: padded, upholstered or plain: wood; stools, office: wood

(G-2445)
PRINT HOUSE INC
Also Called: Printhouse, The
538 Johnson Ave (11237-1226)
PHONE.................................718 443-7500
Fax: 718 628-6900
Sholom Laine, *Ch of Bd*
Yousef Laine, *Manager*
Rebecca Laine, *Administration*
▲ EMP: 60
SQ FT: 71,000
SALES (est): 11MM **Privately Held**
SIC: 2759 Commercial printing

(G-2446)
PRINT MALL
4122 16th Ave (11204-1052)
PHONE.................................718 437-7700
Sara Olewski, *Owner*
EMP: 5 EST: 1997
SALES (est): 411.9K **Privately Held**
WEB: www.invitations123.com
SIC: 2759 Commercial printing

(G-2447)
PRINTING FACTORY LLC
1940 Utica Ave (11234-3214)
PHONE.................................718 451-0500

Lisa Blitman,
EMP: 12
SALES (est): 891K **Privately Held**
SIC: 2732 Book printing

(G-2448)
PRINTING MAX NEW YORK INC
2282 Flatbush Ave (11234-4518)
PHONE.................................718 692-1400
George Blair, *Principal*
EMP: 6
SALES (est): 490K **Privately Held**
SIC: 2759 Commercial printing

(G-2449)
PRINTING SALES GROUP LIMITED
Also Called: Flair Printers
1856 Flatbush Ave (11210-4831)
PHONE.................................718 258-8860
Steven Zuller, *President*
EMP: 20
SALES (est): 2.2MM **Privately Held**
SIC: 2752 Offset & photolithographic printing

(G-2450)
PRINTOUT COPY CORP
829 Bedford Ave (11205-2801)
PHONE.................................718 855-4040
Sinai Roth, *President*
Jacob Sabel, *Vice Pres*
EMP: 21
SQ FT: 3,500
SALES (est): 3.6MM **Privately Held**
SIC: 2759 Commercial printing

(G-2451)
PRINTUTOPIA
393 Prospect Ave (11215-5608)
PHONE.................................718 788-1545
Hamlet Villa, *General Mgr*
EMP: 10
SALES (est): 710K **Privately Held**
SIC: 2752 Commercial printing, lithographic

(G-2452)
PRODUCTAND DESIGN INC
63 Flushing Ave Unit 322 (11205-1082)
PHONE.................................718 858-2440
John Milich, *President*
▲ EMP: 10
SALES: 2MM **Privately Held**
SIC: 3441 8712 Fabricated structural metal; architectural services

(G-2453)
PROFOOT INC
74 20th St Fl 2 (11232-1101)
PHONE.................................718 965-8600
Leonard Feldman, *President*
Robert Notine, *Corp Secy*
Larry Brown, *Vice Pres*
Richard Carvalho, *Controller*
Richard Kirchner, *Controller*
◆ EMP: 45
SQ FT: 35,000
SALES (est): 7.9MM
SALES (corp-wide): 3.7MM **Privately Held**
WEB: www.profootcare.com
SIC: 3842 Orthopedic appliances; foot appliances, orthopedic
PA: Professional Product Research Co. Inc.
74 20th St
Brooklyn NY 11232
718 965-8600

(G-2454)
PROJECT ENERGY SAVERS LLC
Also Called: PES Group
68 Jay St Ste 516 (11201-8362)
PHONE.................................718 596-4231
Alexandra Preefer, *Project Mgr*
Joshua Wolfe, *Mng Member*
Marcy Rubenstein, *Manager*
Joshua F Wolfe, *Manager*
Mark Wolfe,
EMP: 14
SALES: 1.2MM **Privately Held**
SIC: 2731 8748 Textbooks: publishing only, not printed on site; energy conservation consultant

(G-2455)
PROMOTIONAL DEVELOPMENT INC
Also Called: P D I
909 Remsen Ave (11236-1624)
PHONE.................................718 485-8550
Henry Lombardi, *President*
Anthony Valentine, *Vice Pres*
David Censi, *CFO*
Barry Censi, *Treasurer*
▲ EMP: 80
SQ FT: 60,000
SALES (est): 17.8MM **Privately Held**
WEB: www.promotionaldevelopment.com
SIC: 3999 3993 Advertising display products; signs & advertising specialties

(G-2456)
PROTECTIVE LINING CORP
601 39th St (11232-3101)
PHONE.................................718 854-3838
Fax: 718 854-4658
Steven Howard, *President*
Morton Howard, *Vice Pres*
Mary Ann, *Finance*
▲ EMP: 65 EST: 1950
SQ FT: 28,000
SALES (est): 15.5MM **Privately Held**
WEB: www.prolining.com
SIC: 2673 Plastic bags: made from purchased materials

(G-2457)
PURE ACOUSTICS INC
18 Fuller Pl (11215-6007)
PHONE.................................718 788-4411
Rami Ezratty, *CEO*
EMP: 7 EST: 2003
SALES: 2MM **Privately Held**
SIC: 3651 Speaker systems

(G-2458)
PURE PLANET WATERS LLC
4809 Avenue N Ste 185 (11234-3711)
PHONE.................................718 676-7900
James Falce, *Manager*
Denise Piccolo,
Gary Cucuza,
EMP: 10
SQ FT: 2,000
SALES: 1MM **Privately Held**
SIC: 3589 Water filters & softeners, household type

(G-2459)
PUTNAM ROLLING LADDER CO INC
444 Jefferson St (11237-2326)
PHONE.................................718 381-8219
Fax: 718 497-1703
Henry Skiba, *Manager*
EMP: 17
SALES (corp-wide): 3.6MM **Privately Held**
WEB: www.putnamrollingladder.com
SIC: 2499 Ladders, wood
PA: Putnam Rolling Ladder Co Inc
32 Howard St
New York NY 10013
212 226-5147

(G-2460)
PYX INC
Also Called: Pyx Enterprise
143 E 29th St (11226-5505)
PHONE.................................718 469-4253
Omega Ashanti, *President*
EMP: 9
SALES: 250K **Privately Held**
SIC: 3993 Advertising artwork

(G-2461)
QUALITY FOAM INC
137 Gardner Ave (11237-1107)
PHONE.................................718 381-3644
Paul Minarsky, *President*
Kyle Minarsky, *Vice Pres*
◆ EMP: 12
SALES (est): 1.5MM **Privately Held**
WEB: www.qualityfoamproducts.com
SIC: 2515 Mattresses, containing felt, foam rubber, urethane, etc.

(G-2462)
QUALITY NATURE INC
8225 5th Ave Ste 215 (11209-4508)
PHONE.................................718 484-4666
Sagie Gernshteyn, *President*
EMP: 5
SQ FT: 300
SALES: 733.6K **Privately Held**
SIC: 2834 Vitamin, nutrient & hematinic preparations for human use

(G-2463)
QUALITY STRAPPING INC
55 Meadow St (11206-1700)
PHONE.................................718 418-1111
Fax: 718 418-1639
Imre Oberlander, *President*
Aharon L Grossman, *Vice Pres*
Abraham Stern, *CFO*
Mike Grossman, *Financial Exec*
Abe Gross, *Manager*
◆ EMP: 58
SQ FT: 60,000
SALES (est): 11.5MM **Privately Held**
WEB: www.qualitystrapping.com
SIC: 3559 Plastics working machinery

(G-2464)
QUALITY WOODWORKING CORP
260 Butler St (11217-3006)
PHONE.................................718 875-3437
Fax: 718 875-0036
Joseph Borruso Sr, *President*
Anthony Borruso, *Admin Sec*
EMP: 15 EST: 1943
SQ FT: 16,000
SALES (est): 2MM **Privately Held**
SIC: 2441 Nailed wood boxes & shook; boxes, wood

(G-2465)
QUEBRACHO INC
421 Troutman St (11237-2601)
PHONE.................................718 326-3605
Miguel Bavaro, *President*
Miguel Erich, *Mayor*
EMP: 5
SQ FT: 8,000
SALES (est): 460K **Privately Held**
SIC: 2499 Picture frame molding, finished

(G-2466)
QUEEN ANN MACARONI MFG CO INC
Also Called: Queen Ann Ravioli
7205 18th Ave (11204-5634)
PHONE.................................718 256-1061
Fax: 718 256-1189
Alfred Ferrara, *President*
Anna Ferrara, *Vice Pres*
EMP: 7
SQ FT: 4,000
SALES (est): 590K **Privately Held**
WEB: www.queenannravioliandmacaroni.com
SIC: 2098 5499 Macaroni products (e.g. alphabets, rings & shells), dry; gourmet food stores

(G-2467)
QUIP NYC INC
45 Main St Ste 628 (11201-1085)
PHONE.................................703 615-1076
Simon Enever, *President*
EMP: 5
SALES (est): 316.6K **Privately Held**
SIC: 2844 3634 Toothpastes or powders, dentifrices; toothbrushes, electric

(G-2468)
QUIST INDUSTRIES LTD
204 Van Dyke St Ste 320a (11231-1005)
P.O. Box 150083 (11215-0083)
PHONE.................................718 243-2800
Rebecca Steinman, *President*
Paul Steinman, *Controller*
EMP: 10
SQ FT: 3,500
SALES (est): 944K **Privately Held**
WEB: www.quistindustries.com
SIC: 2759 2395 Letterpress & screen printing; emblems, embroidered

Brooklyn - Kings County (G-2469)

(G-2469)
R & F BOARDS & DIVIDERS INC
1678 57th St (11204-1800)
PHONE................................718 331-1529
Regina Frankl, *Ch of Bd*
EMP: 5
SALES (est): 480K **Privately Held**
SIC: 3081 Unsupported plastics film & sheet

(G-2470)
R & H BAKING CO INC
19 5th St (11231-4514)
PHONE................................718 852-1768
Humayun Kabir, *Owner*
EMP: 25 **EST:** 2003
SQ FT: 15,000
SALES: 1.5MM **Privately Held**
WEB: www.kabirbakery.com
SIC: 2051 Bread, cake & related products

(G-2471)
R H GUEST INCORPORATED
Also Called: Guesthouse Division
1300 Church Ave (11226-2602)
PHONE................................718 675-7600
Fax: 718 675-7660
Robert Guest, *President*
Gloria Caprio, *Treasurer*
EMP: 8
SQ FT: 1,000
SALES: 1.7MM **Privately Held**
WEB: www.rhgexhibits.com
SIC: 2542 2541 Showcases (not refrigerated): except wood; showcases, except refrigerated: wood

(G-2472)
R HOCHMAN PAPERS INCORPORATED
1000 Dean St Ste 315 (11238-3384)
PHONE................................516 466-6414
Fax: 516 466-6535
Ronald Hochman, *President*
Erik Rimalovski, *COO*
▲ **EMP:** 11
SQ FT: 2,100
SALES (est): 15MM **Privately Held**
WEB: www.hochmanpapers.com
SIC: 2752 Commercial printing, lithographic

(G-2473)
RAGS KNITWEAR LTD
850 Metropolitan Ave (11211-2515)
P.O. Box 420, Lynbrook (11563-0420)
PHONE................................718 782-8417
Paul Gross, *President*
EMP: 10
SQ FT: 40,000
SALES (est): 980K **Privately Held**
SIC: 2253 Sweaters & sweater coats, knit

(G-2474)
RAILINGS BY NEW STAR BRASS
Also Called: J Ironwork
26 Cobeck Ct (11223-6147)
PHONE................................516 358-1153
Carlo Lopopolo, *President*
Al Grancagnolo, *President*
Mary Ann Harmon, *Purchasing*
EMP: 20 **EST:** 1917
SQ FT: 25,000
SALES (est): 3.8MM **Privately Held**
SIC: 3446 Architectural metalwork

(G-2475)
RAINBOW PLASTICS INC
371 Vandervoort Ave (11211-1712)
PHONE................................718 218-7288
Maggie Zheng, *Vice Pres*
▲ **EMP:** 13
SALES (est): 2MM **Privately Held**
SIC: 3089 Garbage containers, plastic

(G-2476)
RAINBOW POLY BAG CO INC
179 Morgan Ave (11237-1015)
PHONE................................718 386-3500
Fax: 718 386-2300
Gladys Harmanoglu, *President*
Hank Harmanoglu, *Vice Pres*
Hikmet Harmanoglu, *Vice Pres*
Sibel Harman, *Manager*
Susan Harmanoglu, *Manager*
EMP: 40
SQ FT: 50,000
SALES (est): 7.5MM **Privately Held**
WEB: www.rainbowpolybag.com
SIC: 2673 3081 Plastic bags: made from purchased materials; unsupported plastics film & sheet

(G-2477)
RALPH PAYNE
Also Called: A-R Payne Cabinet Comp
475 Van Buren St Ste 11c (11221-3009)
PHONE................................718 222-4200
Ralph Payne, *Owner*
EMP: 7
SQ FT: 5,000
SALES: 300K **Privately Held**
WEB: www.ralphpayne.com
SIC: 2434 5087 1751 Wood kitchen cabinets; beauty parlor equipment & supplies; cabinet & finish carpentry

(G-2478)
RAPID-LITE FIXTURE CORPORATION
249 Huron St (11222-1801)
PHONE................................347 599-2600
Fax: 718 292-6461
Joel Eskin, *Ch of Bd*
EMP: 10 **EST:** 1946
SQ FT: 4,500
SALES (est): 1MM **Privately Held**
WEB: www.rapidlite.com
SIC: 3645 3646 5063 5719 Residential lighting fixtures, commercial indusl & institutional electric lighting fixtures; lighting fixtures, residential; lighting fixtures, commercial & industrial; lighting fixtures

(G-2479)
RAWPOTHECARY INC
630 Flushing Ave (11206-5026)
PHONE................................917 783-7770
Stephanie Walzack, *President*
Dan Gollin, *Sales Dir*
EMP: 8
SALES (est): 722.5K **Privately Held**
SIC: 2099 5812 Ready-to-eat meals, salads & sandwiches; eating places

(G-2480)
RAY GOLD SHADE INC
16 Wellington Ct (11230-2424)
PHONE................................718 377-8892
Martin Rosenbaum, *President*
Sonia Rosenbaum, *Vice Pres*
EMP: 10
SQ FT: 18,000
SALES (est): 560K **Privately Held**
WEB: www.goldrayshades.com
SIC: 3999 Shades, lamp or candle

(G-2481)
RBW STUDIO LLC
Also Called: Rich Brilliant Willing
67 34th St Unit 5 (11232-2010)
PHONE................................212 388-1621
Theodore Richardson, *President*
Charles Brill, *Vice Pres*
Alex Williams, *Vice Pres*
Olivia Sholler, *Marketing Staff*
Emma Sullivan, *Manager*
EMP: 23 **EST:** 2009
SQ FT: 2,000
SALES: 750K **Privately Held**
SIC: 3699 Christmas tree lighting sets, electric

(G-2482)
REAR VIEW SAFETY INC
1797 Atlantic Ave (11233-3040)
PHONE................................855 815-3842
Gila Newman, *CEO*
EMP: 25
SQ FT: 6,000
SALES (est): 4.5MM
SALES (corp-wide): 11.7MM **Privately Held**
SIC: 3861 Cameras & related equipment
PA: Safe Fleet Investments Llc
6800 E 163rd St
Belton MO 64012
844 258-8178

(G-2483)
RECOM POWER INC
18 Bridge St Ste 3g (11201-1107)
PHONE................................718 855-9713
Karsten Bier, *CEO*
Robert Gerding, *General Mgr*
Jeff Heffner, *Sales Mgr*
Mical Anselmo, *Regl Sales Mgr*
Andrew Casterlin, *Marketing Staff*
▲ **EMP:** 7
SALES (est): 1MM **Privately Held**
SIC: 3679 Static power supply converters for electronic applications

(G-2484)
RECORDED ANTHLOGY OF AMRCN MUS
Also Called: New World Records
20 Jay St Ste 1001 (11201-8346)
PHONE................................212 290-1695
Fax: 212 290-1685
Herman E Krawitz, *President*
Auther Moorhaed, *Treasurer*
Mogi Oke, *Accounts Mgr*
Paul Herzman, *Manager*
Robert McNeill, *Manager*
▲ **EMP:** 12
SALES (est): 1.2MM **Privately Held**
WEB: www.newworldrecords.org
SIC: 3652 Pre-recorded records & tapes

(G-2485)
RECYCLED BROOKLYN GROUP LLC
84 Ferris St (11231-1116)
PHONE................................917 902-0662
Matthew Lostice,
Alberto Baudo,
Nilesh Dawda,
Andrea De Sanctis,
Marco Gentilucci,
EMP: 14
SQ FT: 8,000
SALES (est): 993.9K **Privately Held**
SIC: 2511 5712 Wood household furniture; furniture stores

(G-2486)
REDI RECORDS PAYROLL
1225 36th St (11218-2023)
PHONE................................718 854-6990
Joe Burke, *President*
EMP: 10
SALES (est): 800K **Privately Held**
SIC: 2752 Calendars, lithographed

(G-2487)
REGIONAL MGT & CONSULTING INC
79 Bridgewater St (11222-3818)
PHONE................................718 599-3718
Fax: 718 599-4454
Henryk Jarosz, *President*
Bogdan Szczurek, *Exec VP*
EMP: 10
SQ FT: 4,200
SALES (est): 1.4MM **Privately Held**
SIC: 3292 5033 Asbestos products; insulation materials

(G-2488)
REISMAN BROS BAKERY INC
Also Called: Reismans Bros. Bakery
110 Avenue O (11204-6501)
P.O. Box 40112 (11204-0112)
PHONE................................718 331-1975
Fax: 718 256-0833
Bernat Reisman, *Ch of Bd*
Larry Fisler, *Vice Pres*
Esther Friedman, *Admin Sec*
EMP: 15
SQ FT: 4,000
SALES (est): 3.8MM **Privately Held**
WEB: www.reismansbakery.com
SIC: 2051 5411 Bread, cake & related products; cakes, bakery: except frozen; supermarkets

(G-2489)
RELIABLE PRESS II INC
Also Called: Printing
148 39th St Unit 6 (11232-2713)
PHONE................................718 840-5812
Fax: 718 431-6843
Ira Cohen, *President*
Sam Kowlessar, *Manager*
EMP: 16
SALES (est): 1.1MM **Privately Held**
SIC: 2741 Miscellaneous publishing

(G-2490)
REMEDIES SURGICAL SUPPLIES
331 Rutledge St Ste 204 (11211-7546)
PHONE................................718 599-5301
Mordchai Hirsch, *President*
EMP: 7
SQ FT: 2,000
SALES: 5MM **Privately Held**
SIC: 3634 3069 Humidifiers, electric: household; medical & laboratory rubber sundries & related products

(G-2491)
REMSEN GRAPHICS CORP
52 Court St 2 (11201-4901)
PHONE................................718 643-7500
Greg Vellanti, *President*
Frank Vellanti, *Vice Pres*
Piero Galluzzo, *Admin Sec*
EMP: 5
SQ FT: 1,200
SALES: 1MM **Privately Held**
SIC: 2752 7389 Offset & photolithographic printing; brokers' services

(G-2492)
RENE PORTIER INC
3611 14th Ave Ste 6 (11218-3750)
PHONE................................718 853-7896
Charlotte Fixler, *President*
Aaron Fixler, *Vice Pres*
EMP: 9
SQ FT: 6,000
SALES (est): 1MM **Privately Held**
SIC: 2339 Sportswear, women's

(G-2493)
RICHARD MANUFACTURING CO INC
63 Flushing Ave Unit 327 (11205-1083)
PHONE................................718 254-0958
Fax: 718 254-0959
Solomon Mayer, *President*
Janet Mayer, *Admin Sec*
EMP: 8 **EST:** 1943
SALES: 200K **Privately Held**
SIC: 2326 2339 Aprons, work, except rubberized & plastic: men's; aprons, except rubber or plastic: women's, misses', juniors'

(G-2494)
RINI TANK & TRUCK SERVICE
327 Nassau Ave (11222-3811)
PHONE................................718 384-6606
Richard V Rini, *President*
EMP: 16
SQ FT: 10,000
SALES (est): 889.7K **Privately Held**
SIC: 7692 Welding repair

(G-2495)
RIOT NEW MEDIA GROUP INC
147 Prince St Ste 1 (11201-3011)
PHONE................................604 700-4896
Jeffrey O'Neal, *CEO*
Jeff Oneal, *Editor*
Clinton Kabler, *COO*
EMP: 6
SALES (est): 560.7K **Privately Held**
SIC: 2741

(G-2496)
RIVA JEWELRY MANUFACTURING INC
140 58th St Ste 8b (11220-2524)
PHONE................................718 361-3100
Ted Doudak, *President*
John Badee, *Engineer*
Alfonse Grace, *Controller*
Edgar Andrade, *Manager*
Naem Malki, *Manager*
▲ **EMP:** 125
SQ FT: 20,000
SALES (est): 19.6MM **Privately Held**
WEB: www.rivajewelry.com
SIC: 3911 Jewelry apparel

GEOGRAPHIC SECTION

Brooklyn - Kings County (G-2523)

(G-2497)
RIVERSIDE MACHINERY COMPANY (PA)
Also Called: Sns Machinery
140 53rd St (11232-4319)
PHONE.................................718 492-7400
Simon Srybnik, *President*
Louis Srybnik, *Vice Pres*
Saul Waller, *Treasurer*
Jay B Srybnik, *Admin Sec*
EMP: 5
SQ FT: 30,000
SALES (est): 4.3MM **Privately Held**
SIC: 3599 Machine shop, jobbing & repair

(G-2498)
RIVERSIDE MACHINERY COMPANY
132 54th St (11220-2506)
PHONE.................................718 492-7400
Simon Srybnik, *Manager*
EMP: 20
SQ FT: 35,060
SALES (corp-wide): 4.3MM **Privately Held**
SIC: 3549 5084 Metalworking machinery; industrial machinery & equipment
PA: Riverside Machinery Company Inc
140 53rd St
Brooklyn NY 11232
718 492-7400

(G-2499)
ROB HERSCHENFELD DESIGN INC
304 Boerum St (11206-3590)
PHONE.................................718 456-6801
Rob Herschenfeld, *President*
EMP: 10
SQ FT: 10,000
SALES (est): 1.2MM **Privately Held**
SIC: 2512 1522 Upholstered household furniture; remodeling, multi-family dwellings

(G-2500)
ROBERT PORTEGELLO GRAPHICS
2028 Utica Ave (11234-3216)
PHONE.................................718 241-8118
Fax: 718 241-3894
Robert Portegello, *President*
Grace Portegello, *Vice Pres*
EMP: 7
SQ FT: 9,000
SALES: 350K **Privately Held**
SIC: 2752 Commercial printing, lithographic

(G-2501)
ROBIN INDUSTRIES LTD
56 N 3rd St (11249-3925)
PHONE.................................718 218-9616
Fax: 718 218-8922
Monica Vega, *President*
Raul Sillau, *Manager*
EMP: 11
SQ FT: 10,000
SALES (est): 1.2MM **Privately Held**
WEB: www.robinindustries.com
SIC: 3632 1711 Household refrigerators & freezers; heating & air conditioning contractors

(G-2502)
ROGER MICHAEL PRESS INC (PA)
499 Van Brunt St Ste 6b (11231-1053)
P.O. Box 27176 (11202-7176)
PHONE.................................732 752-0800
Michael Held, *President*
Deborah Held, *Vice Pres*
Walter Kovac, *Plant Mgr*
Amy Neufeld, *Marketing Staff*
▲ **EMP:** 18
SQ FT: 20,000
SALES (est): 200K **Privately Held**
WEB: www.mrogerpress.com
SIC: 2782 2789 Blankbooks & looseleaf binders; looseleaf binders & devices; bookbinding & related work

(G-2503)
ROMANTIC TIMES INC
Also Called: Romantic Times Magazine
81 Willoughby St Ste 701 (11201-5233)
PHONE.................................718 237-1097
Fax: 718 624-4231
Kathryn Falk, *President*
Nancy Collaco, *Office Mgr*
EMP: 17
SQ FT: 6,000
SALES (est): 2.2MM **Privately Held**
WEB: www.romantictimes.com
SIC: 2721 5942 Magazines; publishing & printing; book stores

(G-2504)
ROODE HOEK & CO INC
55 Ferris St (11231-1194)
PHONE.................................718 522-5921
Edward R Butler, *President*
EMP: 13
SALES: 750K
SALES (corp-wide): 4.7MM **Privately Held**
WEB: www.erbutler.com
SIC: 2431 Millwork
PA: E.R. Butler & Co., Inc.
55 Prince St
New York NY 10012
212 925-3565

(G-2505)
ROOM AT THE TOP INC
Also Called: Hat Depot
632 Hegeman Ave (11207-7111)
PHONE.................................718 257-0766
Shellie McDowell, *President*
EMP: 5
SALES (est): 630.3K **Privately Held**
SIC: 2353 Hats, caps & millinery

(G-2506)
ROSE SOLOMON CO
63 Flushing Ave Unit 330 (11205-1083)
PHONE.................................718 855-1788
Fax: 718 855-1800
Mendel Reichman, *President*
▲ **EMP:** 21 **EST:** 1908
SQ FT: 7,000
SALES (est): 1.1MM **Privately Held**
SIC: 2389 5049 2869 Burial garments; religious supplies; industrial organic chemicals

(G-2507)
ROSENDAHL INDUSTRIES LTD INC
Also Called: Art Supply & Instruments
1449 37th St (11218-4380)
PHONE.................................718 436-2711
Fax: 718 436-2710
Leonard Rosendahl, *President*
EMP: 35
SQ FT: 22,000
SALES (est): 3MM **Privately Held**
SIC: 3952 Lead pencils & art goods

(G-2508)
ROTH CLOTHING CO INC (PA)
300 Penn St (11211-7405)
PHONE.................................718 384-4927
Fax: 718 486-7438
Mates Roth, *President*
▲ **EMP:** 3 **EST:** 1957
SQ FT: 30,000
SALES (est): 1.2MM **Privately Held**
SIC: 2389 2311 Clergymen's vestments; suits, men's & boys': made from purchased materials

(G-2509)
ROTH DESIGN & CONSULTING INC
Also Called: Roth's Metal Works
132 Bogart St (11206)
PHONE.................................718 209-0193
Arnold Roth, *President*
Jake Roth, *Vice Pres*
Abe Jaros, *Controller*
EMP: 40
SQ FT: 40,000

SALES (est): 7MM **Privately Held**
SIC: 3441 8711 1791 Fabricated structural metal; building construction consultant; structural engineering; structural steel erection

(G-2510)
ROYAL CLOTHING CORP
1316 48th St Apt 1 (11219-3167)
PHONE.................................718 436-5841
Fax: 718 436-5841
Abraham Sports, *President*
EMP: 6
SQ FT: 2,000
SALES: 2MM **Privately Held**
SIC: 2311 5611 Suits, men's & boys': made from purchased materials; suits, men's

(G-2511)
ROYAL INDUSTRIES INC (PA)
Also Called: Royal Line The
225 25th St (11232-1337)
PHONE.................................718 369-3046
Michael Rudensky, *President*
ARI Rudensky, *Vice Pres*
Marybeth Chichetti, *Marketing Staff*
◆ **EMP:** 36 **EST:** 1985
SQ FT: 75,000
SALES (est): 12.6MM **Privately Held**
WEB: www.royalindustries.com
SIC: 3089 3161 2631 Novelties, plastic; luggage; paperboard mills

(G-2512)
ROYAL MOLDS INC
1634 Marine Pkwy (11234-4217)
PHONE.................................718 382-7686
EMP: 15 **EST:** 1946
SQ FT: 10,000
SALES (est): 1.1MM **Privately Held**
SIC: 3544 3423 Mfg Dies/Tools/Jigs/Fixtures Mfg Hand/Edge Tools

(G-2513)
ROYAL PLASTICS CORP
2840 Atlantic Ave Ste 1 (11207-2692)
PHONE.................................718 647-7500
Fax: 718 647-7503
Donald Marchese, *President*
Joann Foster, *Controller*
▲ **EMP:** 19 **EST:** 1958
SQ FT: 40,000
SALES (est): 2.4MM **Privately Held**
WEB: www.royalplastics.com
SIC: 3081 Plastic film & sheet

(G-2514)
ROYAL SWEET BAKERY INC
119 49th St (11232-4229)
PHONE.................................718 567-7770
Fax: 718 567-7375
Mikhail Yusim, *President*
Joseph Dubinski, *Manager*
◆ **EMP:** 10
SALES (est): 1MM **Privately Held**
SIC: 2051 Bread, cake & related products

(G-2515)
RUBICON INDUSTRIES CORP (PA)
848 E 43rd St (11210-3500)
PHONE.................................718 434-4700
Michael Rubinberg, *President*
Mathew Rubinberg, *General Mgr*
Mathew Rubinberg, *General Mgr*
▲ **EMP:** 24
SQ FT: 20,000
SALES (est): 4.7MM **Privately Held**
WEB: www.rubiconhx.com
SIC: 3585 Evaporative condensers, heat transfer equipment

(G-2516)
RUBY ENGINEERING LLC
354 Sackett St (11231-4702)
PHONE.................................646 391-4600
Phillip Roach, *Vice Pres*
Dennis Roach,
EMP: 5
SQ FT: 1,000
SALES (est): 310K **Privately Held**
WEB: www.rubyengineering.com
SIC: 1442 Construction sand mining

(G-2517)
RUSSIAN MIX INC
2225 Benson Ave Apt 74 (11214-5245)
PHONE.................................347 385-7198
EMP: 5
SALES (est): 339.4K **Privately Held**
SIC: 3273 Ready-mixed concrete

(G-2518)
RUSSKAYA REKLAMA INC
2699 Coney Island Ave (11235-5004)
PHONE.................................718 769-3000
Fax: 718 769-4700
Paul Reklama, *President*
EMP: 20
SALES (est): 1MM **Privately Held**
SIC: 2711 Newspapers

(G-2519)
RYBA GENERAL MERCHANDISE INC
63 Flushing Ave Unit 332 (11205-1083)
PHONE.................................718 522-2028
Fax: 718 522-2476
Sam Ryba, *President*
Marvin Ryba, *Vice Pres*
Chaya Knopfler, *Admin Sec*
◆ **EMP:** 7
SQ FT: 25,000
SALES (est): 710K **Privately Held**
WEB: www.rybagen.com
SIC: 2325 5136 Slacks, dress: men's, youths' & boys'; men's & boys' clothing; shirts, men's & boys'

(G-2520)
S & S MACHINERY CORP (PA)
Also Called: CAM Machinery Co
140 53rd St (11232-4319)
PHONE.................................718 492-7400
Fax: 718 439-3930
Simon Srybnik, *President*
Louis Srybnik, *Vice Pres*
Spiros Dendrios, *Research*
Adam Zheng, *Engineer*
▲ **EMP:** 30
SQ FT: 100,000
SALES (est): 6.4MM **Privately Held**
WEB: www.sandsmachinery.com
SIC: 3541 3549 5084 3545 Machine tools, metal cutting type; metalworking machinery; metalworking machinery; machine tools & accessories; machine tool accessories

(G-2521)
S & S MACHINERY CORP
132 54th St (11220-2506)
PHONE.................................718 492-7400
Al Testa, *Branch Mgr*
EMP: 40
SALES (corp-wide): 6.4MM **Privately Held**
WEB: www.sandsmachinery.com
SIC: 3541 3549 5084 Machine tools, metal cutting type; metalworking machinery; machine tools & accessories; metalworking machinery
PA: S. & S. Machinery Corp.
140 53rd St
Brooklyn NY 11232
718 492-7400

(G-2522)
S & S PRTG DIE-CUTTING CO INC
488 Morgan Ave Ste A (11222-5703)
PHONE.................................718 388-8990
Fax: 718 388-0306
Felix Sikar, *President*
▲ **EMP:** 14
SQ FT: 21,000
SALES (est): 1.4MM **Privately Held**
WEB: www.printdiecut.com
SIC: 3469 7389 2759 2675 Stamping metal for the trade; metal cutting services; letterpress printing; die-cut paper & board; coated & laminated paper

(G-2523)
S & T MACHINE INC
970 E 92nd St Fl 1 (11236-1720)
PHONE.................................718 272-2484
Saverio Accardi, *President*
Tinal Accardi, *Vice Pres*

Brooklyn - Kings County (G-2524)

EMP: 15
SQ FT: 5,000
SALES (est): 1.4MM Privately Held
SIC: 3444 Sheet metalwork

(G-2524)
S & W KNITTING MILLS INC
703 Bedford Ave Fl 3 (11206)
PHONE.................................718 237-2416
Fax: 718 797-3710
Henry Weiss, *President*
Manachem Samuel, *Treasurer*
Mindy Friedlander, *Controller*
EMP: 50
SQ FT: 35,000
SALES (est): 3.6MM Privately Held
SIC: 2253 2329 2339 2257 Sweaters & sweater coats, knit; sweaters & sweater jackets: men's & boys'; women's & misses' outerwear; weft knit fabric mills

(G-2525)
S D Z METAL SPINNING STAMPING
1807 Pacific St (11233-3505)
PHONE.................................718 778-3600
Fax: 718 604-8481
Kenny Mersand, *President*
EMP: 15
SQ FT: 10,000
SALES: 971.2K Privately Held
SIC: 3469 Spinning metal for the trade; stamping metal for the trade

(G-2526)
S HELLERMAN INC (PA)
242 Green St (11222-1208)
PHONE.................................718 622-2995
Fax: 718 622-2916
Robert Hellerman, *President*
Joseph Hellerman, *Vice Pres*
EMP: 11
SQ FT: 20,000
SALES: 750K Privately Held
SIC: 2299 Textile mill waste & remnant processing

(G-2527)
S2 SPORTSWEAR INC
4100 1st Ave Ste 5n (11232-3303)
PHONE.................................347 335-0713
Saul Chakkall, *CEO*
Albert Zayat, *Vice Pres*
Ronnie Chakkall, *CFO*
EMP: 10
SQ FT: 6,000
SALES: 1.3MM Privately Held
SIC: 2339 5137 Sportswear, women's; sportswear, women's & children's

(G-2528)
SABBSONS INTERNATIONAL INC
Also Called: Simple Elegance New York
474 50th St (11220-1913)
PHONE.................................718 360-1947
Isaac Sabbagh, *CEO*
Victor Sabbagh, *CFO*
◆ EMP: 10
SALES (est): 492.2K Privately Held
SIC: 2299 Linen fabrics

(G-2529)
SAGA INTERNATIONAL RECYCL LLC
6623 13th Ave (11219-6122)
PHONE.................................718 621-5900
Akiva Klein, *Principal*
▲ EMP: 6
SQ FT: 3,000
SALES (est): 1MM Privately Held
SIC: 2821 Plastics materials & resins

(G-2530)
SAHADI FINE FOODS INC
4215 1st Ave (11232-3300)
PHONE.................................718 369-0100
Fax: 718 369-0800
Pat Whelan, *Managing Dir*
Audrey Sahadi, *Director*
Charles Sahadi, *Director*
Robert Sahadi, *Director*
Ron Sahadi, *Director*
◆ EMP: 22
SQ FT: 116,000

SALES (est): 5.2MM Privately Held
WEB: www.sahadifinefoods.com
SIC: 2068 2032 5149 5145 Nuts: dried, dehydrated, salted or roasted; seeds: dried, dehydrated, salted or roasted; beans & bean sprouts, canned, jarred, etc.; fruits, dried; nuts, salted or roasted

(G-2531)
SALTY ROAD INC
190 Bedford Ave 404 (11249-2904)
PHONE.................................347 673-3925
Marisa Wu, *President*
EMP: 8
SALES (est): 662.8K Privately Held
SIC: 2064 Candy & other confectionery products

(G-2532)
SANGSTER FOODS INC
225 Parkside Ave Apt 3p (11226-1352)
PHONE.................................212 993-9129
EMP: 10
SALES (est): 283.4K Privately Held
SIC: 2032 2043 2091 5149 Ethnic foods: canned, jarred, etc.; infants' foods, cereal type; canned & cured fish & seafoods; health foods; instant coffee

(G-2533)
SARES INTERNATIONAL INC
95 Evergreen Ave Ste 5 (11206-6129)
PHONE.................................718 366-8412
Fax: 718 366-8415
Manuel Barretto, *President*
EMP: 45
SQ FT: 15,000
SALES (est): 4.7MM Privately Held
SIC: 2253 Sweaters & sweater coats, knit

(G-2534)
SARUG INC
2055 Mcdonald Ave (11223-2821)
PHONE.................................718 339-2791
Henrik Zylberstein, *President*
EMP: 55 EST: 1979
SQ FT: 3,000
SALES (est): 3.3MM Privately Held
SIC: 2253 Sweaters & sweater coats, knit

(G-2535)
SAS MAINTENANCE SERVICES INC
8435 Bay 16th St Ste A (11214-2844)
PHONE.................................718 837-2124
Maria Locascio, *President*
EMP: 15
SALES: 1.6MM Privately Held
WEB: www.sasmaint.com
SIC: 3471 Cleaning, polishing & finishing

(G-2536)
SATELLITE NETWORK INC
2030 Mcdonald Ave (11223-2819)
PHONE.................................718 336-2698
Boris Demchenko, *Executive*
EMP: 14
SALES (est): 954.9K Privately Held
SIC: 2711 Newspapers

(G-2537)
SCHWARTZ TEXTILE CONVERTING CO
Also Called: Protege
160 7th St (11215-3107)
PHONE.................................718 499-8243
Mitchell Schwartz, *Partner*
Irving Schwartz, *Partner*
Marc Schwartz, *Partner*
Kewal Sukhoo, *Business Mgr*
▲ EMP: 25
SQ FT: 60,000
SALES (est): 1.5MM Privately Held
SIC: 2329 2321 Sweaters & sweater jackets: men's & boys'; men's & boys' furnishings

(G-2538)
SCIENTIFIC COMPONENTS CORP (PA)
Also Called: Mini-Circuits
13 Neptune Ave (11235-4404)
P.O. Box 350199 (11235-0199)
PHONE.................................718 934-4500
Fax: 718 332-4661

Harvey Kaylie, *President*
Gloria Kaylie, *Corp Secy*
Stephen Sherman, *Vice Pres*
Luis E Zambrano, *Production*
Anthony Blugh, *Purchasing*
▲ EMP: 475
SQ FT: 50,000
SALES (est): 110.9MM Privately Held
WEB: www.minicircuits.com
SIC: 3679 Electronic switches; electronic circuits

(G-2539)
SCIENTIFIC COMPONENTS CORP
Also Called: Mini Circuits
2450 Knapp St (11235-1006)
PHONE.................................718 368-2060
EMP: 264
SALES (corp-wide): 110.9MM Privately Held
SIC: 3679 Electronic circuits
PA: Scientific Components Corp
13 Neptune Ave
Brooklyn NY 11235
718 934-4500

(G-2540)
SCULPTGRAPHICZ INC
67 35th St Unit B520 (11232-2018)
PHONE.................................646 837-7302
Marvin Seligman, *President*
Robert Chiari, *VP Sales*
EMP: 5 EST: 2011
SALES (est): 370.4K Privately Held
SIC: 7372 Prepackaged software

(G-2541)
SEALCRAFT INDUSTRIES INC
5308 13th Ave Ste 251 (11219-3804)
PHONE.................................718 517-2000
Fax: 718 517-2020
Joshua Benjamin, *CEO*
EMP: 10
SALES (est): 850K Privately Held
SIC: 3053 Gaskets, packing & sealing devices

(G-2542)
SEASONS SOYFOOD INC
605 Degraw St (11217-3120)
PHONE.................................718 797-9896
Fax: 718 722-7922
Johnny Hong, *President*
▲ EMP: 8
SALES (est): 500K Privately Held
SIC: 2099 Tofu, except frozen desserts

(G-2543)
SEPHARDIC YELLOW PAGES
2150 E 4th St (11223-4037)
PHONE.................................718 998-0299
David Benhorren, *Owner*
EMP: 20 EST: 1998
SALES (est): 1.6MM Privately Held
SIC: 2759 2741 Publication printing; miscellaneous publishing

(G-2544)
SERGE DUCT DESIGNS INC
535 Dean St Apt 124 (11217-5207)
PHONE.................................718 783-7799
Fax: 718 783-9499
Serge Rozenbaum, *President*
Micha Rozenbaug, *Vice Pres*
EMP: 20
SALES (est): 3.2MM Privately Held
SIC: 3549 Metalworking machinery

(G-2545)
SETTEPANI INC (PA)
Also Called: Settepani Bakery
602 Lorimer St (11211-2220)
PHONE.................................718 349-6524
Fax: 718 349-2149
Nino Settepani, *President*
Biagio Settepani, *Vice Pres*
Antonio Settepani, *Admin Sec*
EMP: 28
SQ FT: 5,000
SALES: 700K Privately Held
WEB: www.settepani.com
SIC: 2051 5461 Bakery: wholesale or wholesale/retail combined; bakeries

(G-2546)
SFOGLINI LLC
630 Flushing Ave Fl 2 (11206-5026)
PHONE.................................646 872-1035
Steven Gonzalez, *Mng Member*
Scott Ketchum, *Mng Member*
EMP: 10
SQ FT: 4,000
SALES (est): 1.2MM Privately Held
SIC: 2099 Pasta, uncooked: packaged with other ingredients

(G-2547)
SH LEATHER NOVELTY COMPANY
123 Clymer St Bsmt (11249-6708)
PHONE.................................718 387-7742
Shiee Handler, *President*
Solmen Delowitz, *Vice Pres*
Feiga Handler, *Treasurer*
EMP: 3 EST: 1954
SQ FT: 4,000
SALES: 1MM Privately Held
SIC: 2387 Apparel belts

(G-2548)
SHALAM IMPORTS INC (PA)
Also Called: Shalamex
1552 Dahill Rd Ste B (11204-3572)
PHONE.................................718 686-6271
Sasson Shalam, *President*
Abraham Shalam, *Vice Pres*
EMP: 12 EST: 1955
SQ FT: 1,800
SALES (est): 1.2MM Privately Held
SIC: 2674 Shipping bags or sacks, including multiwall & heavy duty

(G-2549)
SHALOM TOY CO INC
128 32nd St Fl 4 (11232-1833)
PHONE.................................718 499-3770
Fax: 718 832-1232
Eva Weber, *President*
Martin Weber, *Vice Pres*
Shalom N Weber, *Treasurer*
▲ EMP: 15
SQ FT: 34,000
SALES (est): 1.3MM Privately Held
SIC: 3942 Stuffed toys, including animals

(G-2550)
SHANGHAI STOVE INC
78 Gerry St 82 (11206-4326)
PHONE.................................718 599-4583
Fax: 718 599-1250
James Wong, *President*
Sylvia Wong, *Admin Sec*
EMP: 15 EST: 1979
SALES (est): 1.6MM Privately Held
SIC: 3444 Restaurant sheet metalwork

(G-2551)
SHOWERAY CO (PA)
225 25th St (11232-1337)
P.O. Box 320141 (11232-0141)
PHONE.................................718 965-3633
Fax: 718 965-3647
Abraham Grazi, *President*
Jack Grazi, *Vice Pres*
Maurice Grazi, *Admin Sec*
EMP: 99 EST: 1938
SQ FT: 60,000
SALES (est): 4.6MM Privately Held
SIC: 2392 2391 Shower curtains: made from purchased materials; tablecloths: made from purchased materials; mattress protectors, except rubber; curtains & draperies

(G-2552)
SIGN & SIGNS
785 Coney Island Ave (11218-5309)
PHONE.................................718 941-6200
Ali Chashir, *Principal*
EMP: 6
SALES (est): 431.8K Privately Held
SIC: 3993 Signs & advertising specialties

(G-2553)
SIGN GROUP INC
Also Called: Boro Park Signs
5215 New Utrecht Ave (11219-3829)
PHONE.................................718 438-7103
Fax: 718 871-7446

▲ = Import ▼ = Export
◆ = Import/Export

Ushe Steinmetz, *President*
Jerry Greenberger, *Accounts Mgr*
Solomon Gutter, *Admin Sec*
EMP: 25
SQ FT: 9,000
SALES (est): 3.3MM **Privately Held**
WEB: www.signgroup.com
SIC: 3993 Signs & advertising specialties

(G-2554)
SIGN WORLD INC
1194 Utica Ave (11203-5997)
PHONE..............................212 619-9000
Herman Weiss, *President*
Carl Weiss, *Corp Secy*
EMP: 25 **EST:** 1964
SQ FT: 10,000
SALES (est): 1.9MM **Privately Held**
SIC: 3993 2752 Signs & advertising specialties; commercial printing, lithographic

(G-2555)
SIGNS & DECAL CORP
410 Morgan Ave (11211-1640)
PHONE..............................718 486-6400
Abdulrasul M Khalfan, *President*
Abdulrasul Khalfan, *President*
Oana Baciu, *Sales Staff*
Tazzim U Khalfan, *Technology*
Mohammad Khalfan, *Executive*
▲ **EMP:** 30
SQ FT: 25,000
SALES (est): 5.3MM **Privately Held**
WEB: www.signsanddecal.com
SIC: 3993 Displays & cutouts, window & lobby; signs, not made in custom sign painting shops

(G-2556)
SILLY PHILLIE CREATIONS INC
Also Called: Swisse Cheeks
140 58th St Ste 6f (11220-2526)
PHONE..............................718 492-6300
Fax: 718 492-3003
Richard S'Dao, *President*
Phyllis G S'Dao, *Vice Pres*
▲ **EMP:** 30
SQ FT: 30,000
SALES (est): 2.7MM **Privately Held**
WEB: www.sillyphillie.com
SIC: 2369 2392 2361 Girls' & children's outerwear; sun suits: girls', children's & infants'; bathrobes: girls', children's & infants'; household furnishings; girls' & children's dresses, blouses & shirts

(G-2557)
SILVER OAK PHARMACY INC
5105 Church Ave (11203-3511)
PHONE..............................718 922-3400
Axay B Joshi, *Principal*
EMP: 6
SALES (est): 536.7K **Privately Held**
SIC: 2834 Pharmaceutical preparations

(G-2558)
SILVERMAN & GORF INC
60 Franklin Ave (11205-1594)
PHONE..............................718 625-1309
Edward Gorf, *President*
Harry Moorer, *Vice Pres*
EMP: 6
SQ FT: 30,000
SALES (est): 490K **Privately Held**
SIC: 3471 Plating of metals or formed products

(G-2559)
SILVERSTONE SHTMTL FBRICATIONS
66 Huntington St (11231)
PHONE..............................718 422-0380
Rustem Duka, *President*
EMP: 5
SQ FT: 10,000
SALES (est): 1MM **Privately Held**
SIC: 3441 Fabricated structural metal

(G-2560)
SIMON LIU INC
5113 2nd Ave (11232-4308)
PHONE..............................718 567-2011
Fax: 718 567-2015
Simon Liu, *President*
▲ **EMP:** 12
SQ FT: 7,500
SALES (est): 750K **Privately Held**
WEB: www.simonliuinc.com
SIC: 3952 5999 Artists' equipment; artists' supplies & materials

(G-2561)
SIMON S DECORATING INC
1670 E 19th St (11229-1312)
PHONE..............................718 339-2931
Simon Poldanl, *President*
EMP: 5
SALES (est): 433.1K **Privately Held**
SIC: 2512 Upholstered household furniture

(G-2562)
SIMPLE ELEGANCE NEW YORK INC
474 50th St (11220-1913)
PHONE..............................718 360-1947
Isaac Sabbagh, *President*
Victor Sabbagh, *Vice Pres*
Abraham Sabbagh, *CFO*
EMP: 15
SQ FT: 6,000
SALES (est): 986.3K **Privately Held**
SIC: 2299 5131 Linen fabrics; linen piece goods, woven

(G-2563)
SINCERUS LLC
2478 Mcdonald Ave (11223-5233)
PHONE..............................800 419-2804
Marc Poirier,
EMP: 5
SQ FT: 5,000
SALES (est): 229.7K **Privately Held**
SIC: 2834 Pharmaceutical preparations

(G-2564)
SING AH POULTRY
114 Sackett St (11231-1414)
PHONE..............................718 625-7253
Fax: 718 260-9212
Perry Chen, *Owner*
EMP: 5
SQ FT: 2,400
SALES (est): 290.1K **Privately Held**
SIC: 2015 Poultry, slaughtered & dressed

(G-2565)
SING TAO NEWSPAPERS NY LTD
5317 8th Ave (11220-3259)
PHONE..............................212 431-9030
Rick Ho, *Manager*
EMP: 10 **Privately Held**
WEB: www.nysingtao.com
SIC: 2711 Newspapers
PA: Sing Tao Newspapers New York Ltd.
188 Lafayette St
New York NY 10013

(G-2566)
SING TAO NEWSPAPERS NY LTD
905 Flushing Ave Fl 2 (11206-4602)
PHONE..............................718 821-0123
Fax: 718 628-0121
Patrick Seto, *Manager*
EMP: 30
SQ FT: 20,900 **Privately Held**
WEB: www.nysingtao.com
SIC: 2711 Newspapers, publishing & printing
PA: Sing Tao Newspapers New York Ltd.
188 Lafayette St
New York NY 10013

(G-2567)
SITA FINISHING INC
Also Called: Sita Knitting
207 Starr St Ste 1 (11237-2639)
PHONE..............................718 417-5295
Fax: 718 417-5295
Loan Sita, *President*
Ioan Sita, *President*
George Sita, *Vice Pres*
▲ **EMP:** 10
SQ FT: 8,000
SALES (est): 1MM **Privately Held**
WEB: www.sitafashion.com
SIC: 2211 Canvas

(G-2568)
SLAVA INDUSTRIES INCORPORATED (PA)
Also Called: Nfk International
555 16th St (11215-5914)
PHONE..............................718 499-4850
Nevio Kovacevic, *Principal*
Ilaria Sialino, *CFO*
Gerard Barry, *Accounting Mgr*
▲ **EMP:** 2
SQ FT: 1,200
SALES: 38MM **Privately Held**
SIC: 2512 2514 Upholstered household furniture; metal household furniture

(G-2569)
SLEEPING PARTNERS INTL INC
Also Called: Sleeping Partners Home Fashion
140 58th St Ste 11 (11220-2522)
PHONE..............................212 254-1515
Fax: 718 254-5553
Salvo Stoch, *CEO*
Salvatore Stoch, *Ch of Bd*
Kathy Lander, *Opers Mgr*
Cathy Randa, *Manager*
▲ **EMP:** 15
SQ FT: 25,000
SALES: 5MM **Privately Held**
SIC: 2392 Household furnishings

(G-2570)
SLEEPY HEAD INC
230 3rd St (11215-2714)
PHONE..............................718 237-9655
Victor Daniels, *President*
Haim Zeitoune, *Vice Pres*
EMP: 10
SQ FT: 17,000
SALES (est): 720K **Privately Held**
WEB: www.sleepyheadinc.com
SIC: 2369 Pantsuits: girls', children's & infants'; shorts (outerwear): girls' & children's

(G-2571)
SLN GROUP INC
2172 E 26th St (11229-4955)
PHONE..............................718 677-5969
Luiza Shamilova, *Principal*
EMP: 5
SALES (est): 419.6K **Privately Held**
SIC: 3679 Electronic components

(G-2572)
SMARTONERS INC (PA)
289 Keap St Ste A (11211-7459)
PHONE..............................718 975-0197
Aidel Appel, *President*
EMP: 4
SQ FT: 3,000
SALES (est): 11MM **Privately Held**
SIC: 3955 Print cartridges for laser & other computer printers

(G-2573)
SMITH STREET BREAD CO LLC
17 5th St (11231-4514)
PHONE..............................718 797-9712
Mark Rubin, *Mng Member*
Humayun Kabir, *Manager*
▲ **EMP:** 12
SQ FT: 500
SALES: 1MM **Privately Held**
SIC: 2051 Bread, cake & related products

(G-2574)
SNACK INNOVATIONS INC
67 35th St Unit 3 (11232-2200)
PHONE..............................718 509-9366
Allen Benz, *CEO*
Jack Benz, *Sales Mgr*
▲ **EMP:** 20
SQ FT: 30,000
SALES (est): 5.3MM **Privately Held**
SIC: 2096 Potato chips & similar snacks

(G-2575)
SNACKS ON 48 INC
1960 59th St (11204-2340)
PHONE..............................347 663-1100
Chana Fischer, *Principal*
EMP: 5 **EST:** 2013
SALES (est): 464.6K **Privately Held**
SIC: 2096 Potato chips & similar snacks; potato chips & other potato-based snacks; corn chips & other corn-based snacks

(G-2576)
SOCIAL BICYCLES INC
Also Called: Sobi
47 Hall St Ste 414 (11205-1315)
P.O. Box F9 (11205)
PHONE..............................917 746-7624
Stephen Ryan Rzepecki, *CEO*
Edward Rayner, *CFO*
EMP: 25
SQ FT: 700
SALES (est): 4.6MM **Privately Held**
SIC: 3751 7372 Bicycles & related parts; prepackaged software

(G-2577)
SOCKS AND MORE OF NY INC
1605 Avenue Z Fl 1 (11235-3809)
PHONE..............................718 769-1785
Irene Dubrovsky, *Chairman*
EMP: 8
SALES (est): 824.3K **Privately Held**
SIC: 2252 Socks

(G-2578)
SOHO LETTERPRESS INC
68 35th St Unit 6 (11232-2211)
PHONE..............................718 788-2518
Fax: 212 334-4357
Anne Noonan, *President*
EMP: 12
SALES: 1MM **Privately Held**
WEB: www.soholetterpress.com
SIC: 2759 Commercial printing

(G-2579)
SOLA HOME EXPO INC
172 Neptune Ave (11235-5317)
PHONE..............................718 646-3383
Sergiy Orlov, *President*
▲ **EMP:** 6
SALES: 80K **Privately Held**
SIC: 3431 Bathroom fixtures, including sinks

(G-2580)
SOLAR ENERGY SYSTEMS LLC (PA)
1205 Manhattan Ave # 1210 (11222-6156)
PHONE..............................718 389-1545
Fax: 718 389-2820
David Buckner, *President*
John Salmon, *General Mgr*
Christopher Moustakis, *Vice Pres*
Nadja Bruder, *Admin Asst*
EMP: 14
SQ FT: 1,300
SALES (est): 2.5MM **Privately Held**
WEB: www.solaresystems.com
SIC: 3433 1711 Solar heaters & collectors; solar energy contractor

(G-2581)
SOLARWATERWAY
Also Called: Solarwaterstar
4703 Bay Pkwy (11230-3334)
PHONE..............................646 387-9346
Murray Sarway, *Owner*
▲ **EMP:** 20
SALES: 200K **Privately Held**
SIC: 3822 Auto controls regulating residntl & coml environmt & applncs

(G-2582)
SOLARZ BROS PRINTING CORP
231 Norman Ave Ste 105 (11222-1559)
PHONE..............................718 383-1330
Sbigniew Solarz, *Principal*
EMP: 5
SALES (est): 363.4K **Privately Held**
SIC: 2759 Commercial printing

(G-2583)
SOLOMON SCHWIMMER
65 Heyward St (11249-7806)
PHONE..............................718 625-5719
EMP: 8
SALES (est): 923.4K **Privately Held**
SIC: 2631 Paperboard mills

Brooklyn - Kings County (G-2584)

(G-2584)
SONAAL INDUSTRIES INC
210 Kingsland Ave (11222-4303)
PHONE..........................718 383-3860
Rana P Mukhopadhyay, *Principal*
EMP: 6
SALES (est): 228.3K **Privately Held**
SIC: 3999 Manufacturing industries

(G-2585)
SOURCE TECHNOLOGIES
9728 3rd Ave (11209-7742)
PHONE..........................718 708-0305
Nick Anthony, *Owner*
EMP: 12
SQ FT: 2,000
SALES: 1MM **Privately Held**
SIC: 3599 Machine & other job shop work

(G-2586)
SOUTH CENTRAL BOYZ
2568 Bedford Ave Apt 1a (11226-7071)
PHONE..........................718 496-7270
Keith Bessor, *President*
EMP: 5
SALES (est): 280K **Privately Held**
SIC: 2389 7389 Costumes;

(G-2587)
SPACE 150
20 Jay St Ste 928 (11201-8354)
PHONE..........................612 332-6458
EMP: 120 EST: 2003
SALES (est): 11.6MM **Privately Held**
SIC: 2741 Misc Publishing

(G-2588)
SPFM CORP (PA)
Also Called: Spray Market, The
162 2nd Ave (11215-4619)
PHONE..........................718 788-6800
Jacob Kloc, *President*
Ann Marie Wolf, *Administration*
EMP: 5
SALES: 500K **Privately Held**
SIC: 3563 Spraying & dusting equipment

(G-2589)
SPOT CERTIFIED INC
278 Van Brunt St (11231-1236)
PHONE..........................212 643-6770
Keith Smith, *President*
Jane Abutel, *President*
EMP: 6
SALES: 500K **Privately Held**
SIC: 2869 Fluorinated hydrocarbon gases

(G-2590)
SPRI CLINICAL TRIALS
3044 Coney Island Ave (11235-5660)
PHONE..........................718 616-2400
ARI Kiev, *President*
Alan Fainer, *Business Mgr*
Jamie Wajid, *Research Analys*
EMP: 10
SALES (est): 870K **Privately Held**
SIC: 2834 Pharmaceutical preparations

(G-2591)
SPRING PRINTING INC
489 Baltic St (11217-2507)
PHONE..........................718 797-2818
Steven Fung, *President*
▲ EMP: 10
SALES (est): 630K **Privately Held**
SIC: 2752 Commercial printing, lithographic

(G-2592)
SPRING PUBLISHING CORPORATION
Also Called: Polska Gazeta
419 Manhattan Ave (11222-4914)
PHONE..........................718 782-0881
Janus Czuj, *President*
EMP: 6
SALES (est): 439.5K **Privately Held**
WEB: www.polskagazeta.com
SIC: 2711 Newspapers

(G-2593)
SQUOND INC
185 Marcy Ave Ste 302 (11211-6261)
P.O. Box 110873 (11211-0873)
PHONE..........................718 778-6630

Moshe Teitelbaum, *Principal*
EMP: 25
SQ FT: 2,100
SALES (est): 861.6K **Privately Held**
SIC: 7372 4812 Business oriented computer software; cellular telephone services

(G-2594)
SSP WINDOW CLEANING CORP
2351 E 26th St (11229-4920)
PHONE..........................917 750-2619
Yuriy Karpinskyy, *President*
EMP: 14
SALES (est): 1.9MM **Privately Held**
SIC: 2431 Equipment rental & leasing

(G-2595)
ST JOHN
1700 Saint Johns Pl (11233-4906)
PHONE..........................718 771-4541
EMP: 5 EST: 2010
SALES (est): 363.4K **Privately Held**
SIC: 2339 Mfg Women's/Misses' Outerwear

(G-2596)
STAG BROTHERS CAST STONE CO
909 E 51st St (11203-6735)
PHONE..........................718 629-0975
Sal Stagliano, *President*
EMP: 8
SALES (est): 310K **Privately Held**
SIC: 3272 Concrete products

(G-2597)
STANLEY M INDIG
2173 E 38th St (11234-4929)
PHONE..........................718 692-0648
Fax: 718 692-0648
Stanley M Indig, *Owner*
EMP: 8
SQ FT: 10,000
SALES (est): 1.2MM **Privately Held**
SIC: 2731 Textbooks: publishing only, not printed on site

(G-2598)
STAPLEX COMPANY INC
777 5th Ave (11232-1695)
PHONE..........................718 768-3333
Fax: 718 965-0750
James J Cussani Jr, *President*
Gregory Cussani, *Vice Pres*
David Hill, *Vice Pres*
R Powers, *Vice Pres*
Harry Winters, *Mfg Staff*
▲ EMP: 20 EST: 1949
SQ FT: 20,000
SALES (est): 4.3MM **Privately Held**
SIC: 3579 3821 Stapling machines (hand or power); laboratory apparatus & furniture

(G-2599)
STAR POLY BAG INC (PA)
200 Liberty Ave (11207-2904)
PHONE..........................718 384-3130
Fax: 718 384-2342
Rachel Posen, *CEO*
Joel Posen, *Principal*
Jay Kaufman, *Manager*
EMP: 17 EST: 1961
SQ FT: 22,000
SALES (est): 3.6MM **Privately Held**
WEB: www.starpoly.com
SIC: 2673 Plastic bags: made from purchased materials

(G-2600)
STARLINER SHIPPING & TRAVEL
5305 Church Ave Ste 1 (11203-3638)
PHONE..........................718 385-1515
Fax: 718 385-2890
Rhea Murray, *President*
Leighton Murray, *Vice Pres*
Blueth Murray-Ogunnoiki, *Vice Pres*
Anthia Murray, *Treasurer*
▼ EMP: 7
SALES (est): 540K **Privately Held**
SIC: 2599 Ship furniture

(G-2601)
STEALTH ARCHTCTRAL WINDOWS INC
Also Called: Stealth Window
232 Varet St (11206-3822)
PHONE..........................718 821-6666
Barry Borgen, *President*
EMP: 19
SQ FT: 52,000
SALES (est): 2.1MM **Privately Held**
WEB: www.avantguards.com
SIC: 2431 Windows, wood

(G-2602)
STEALTH INC
1129 E 27th St (11210-4620)
PHONE..........................718 252-7900
Fax: 718 252-7935
Jack Edelstein, *President*
Alexandra Rowinski, *Marketing Staff*
Raphaelle Loren, *Consultant*
Sanjeev Gupta,
EMP: 16
SQ FT: 3,000
SALES: 1.7MM **Privately Held**
SIC: 2326 Industrial garments, men's & boys'

(G-2603)
STEELCRAFT MANUFACTURING CO
Also Called: Steel Craft
352 Pine St (11208-2807)
PHONE..........................718 277-2404
Fax: 718 277-0507
Louis Massa, *President*
David Massa, *Vice Pres*
EMP: 11 EST: 1945
SQ FT: 9,000
SALES (est): 790K **Privately Held**
SIC: 2514 3444 2541 Metal household furniture; kitchen cabinets: metal; radiator shields or enclosures, sheet metal; wood partitions & fixtures

(G-2604)
STEELDECK NY INC
141 Banker St (11222-3147)
PHONE..........................718 599-3700
Fax: 718 599-3800
Philip Parsons, *President*
Gail Moorcroft, *Vice Pres*
EMP: 15 EST: 2001
SQ FT: 20,000
SALES (est): 506.7K **Privately Held**
SIC: 3999 5049 2541 2531 Stage hardware & equipment, except lighting; theatrical equipment & supplies; partitions for floor attachment, prefabricated: wood; theater furniture

(G-2605)
STEELMASTERS INC
135 Liberty Ave (11212-8008)
PHONE..........................718 498-2854
Matthew Rosio, *President*
Anthony Masi, *Vice Pres*
EMP: 23 EST: 1994
SQ FT: 14,000
SALES (est): 3MM **Privately Held**
SIC: 3442 Rolling doors for industrial buildings or warehouses, metal

(G-2606)
STEINBOCK-BRAFF INC
Also Called: Kat Nap Products
3611 14th Ave (11218-3773)
PHONE..........................718 972-6500
Fax: 718 435-4202
Corey Steinbock, *President*
▲ EMP: 30 EST: 1933
SQ FT: 80,000
SALES (est): 3.8MM **Privately Held**
WEB: www.sleepmattress.com
SIC: 2515 5021 Mattresses & foundations; household furniture

(G-2607)
STEINWAY PASTA & GELATI INC
37 Grand Ave Ste 1 (11205-1309)
PHONE..........................718 246-5414
Fax: 718 246-5236
Vincenzo Arpaia, *President*
▲ EMP: 15

SALES (est): 2.3MM **Privately Held**
SIC: 2099 5149 Packaged combination products: pasta, rice & potato; pasta & rice

(G-2608)
STIEGELBAUER ASSOCIATES INC (PA)
Bldg 280 (11205)
PHONE..........................718 624-0835
Michael Stiegelbauer, *President*
Dawn Stiegelbauer, *Corp Secy*
Steven Paone, *Vice Pres*
Butch Huerta, *Project Mgr*
Kimberly Amato, *Mktg Dir*
EMP: 22
SQ FT: 180,000
SALES (est): 3MM **Privately Held**
SIC: 3999 Theatrical scenery

(G-2609)
STONE AND BATH GALLERY
856 39th St (11232-3230)
PHONE..........................718 438-4500
Samuel Stru, *Owner*
▲ EMP: 8
SALES (est): 185.4K **Privately Held**
SIC: 3261 3251 Bathroom accessories/fittings, vitreous china or earthenware; brick & structural clay tile

(G-2610)
STREET BEAT SPORTSWEAR INC (PA)
Also Called: Visual F-X
462 Kent Ave Fl 2 (11249-5922)
PHONE..........................718 302-1500
Fax: 718 387-8012
Albert Papouchado, *President*
Allen Smith, *CFO*
Micheal Amar, *Treasurer*
▲ EMP: 11
SQ FT: 66,000
SALES (est): 3.6MM **Privately Held**
SIC: 2339 Sportswear, women's

(G-2611)
STRONG TEMPERING GL INDUST LLC
530 63rd St Ste B (11220-4608)
PHONE..........................718 765-0007
Joy Huang, *Sales Staff*
Mark Chen,
EMP: 12
SALES (est): 919.3K **Privately Held**
SIC: 3211 Tempered glass

(G-2612)
STUDIO 21 LA INC
13 42nd St Fl 5 (11232-2616)
PHONE..........................718 965-6579
Leonid Tszang, *President*
▲ EMP: 20
SQ FT: 5,000
SALES (est): 1.7MM **Privately Held**
WEB: www.studio21usa.com
SIC: 2531 5399 5712 Picnic tables or benches, park; catalog showrooms; furniture stores

(G-2613)
STUDIO 40 INC
810 Humboldt St Ste 4 (11222-1913)
PHONE..........................212 420-8631
Richard Temerian, *President*
EMP: 6
SALES (corp-wide): 846.1K **Privately Held**
SIC: 3446 Architectural metalwork
PA: Studio 40 Inc
    40 Great Jones St Apt 1
    New York NY 10012
    212 420-8631

(G-2614)
STUDIO DELLARTE
74 Bayard St (11222-3905)
PHONE..........................718 599-3715
Fax: 718 599-4738
Jeremy Lebensohn, *Owner*
EMP: 5 EST: 1984
SALES (est): 320K **Privately Held**
WEB: www.studiodellarte.com
SIC: 3446 Architectural metalwork

(G-2615)
STUHRLING ORIGINAL LLC
449 20th St (11215-6247)
PHONE..................................718 840-5760
Barry Kaplan, *COO*
Jay Schiss, *CFO*
Israel Jacobson, *Controller*
Shifra Birnhack, *Accounts Mgr*
Tali Brach, *Accounts Mgr*
▲ **EMP:** 7
SQ FT: 20,000
SALES: 10MM **Privately Held**
SIC: 3873 5094 Watches, clocks, watchcases & parts; clocks, watches & parts; watches & parts

(G-2616)
STURDY STORE DISPLAYS INC
485 Johnson Ave (11237-1201)
PHONE..................................718 389-9919
Fax: 718 389-9929
Michael Fried, *President*
Sam Grossinger, *General Mgr*
Jacob Brauner, *Vice Pres*
Moshe Nathan Neuman, *Controller*
▲ **EMP:** 23
SQ FT: 35,000
SALES (est): 3MM **Privately Held**
WEB: www.sturdystoredisplays.com
SIC: 2542 Partitions & fixtures, except wood

(G-2617)
STYLIST PLEATING CORP
109 S 5th St (11249-5869)
PHONE..................................718 384-8181
Fax: 718 384-9108
Kenneth Stier, *President*
EMP: 18 **EST:** 1938
SQ FT: 11,000
SALES (est): 1.2MM **Privately Held**
SIC: 2395 Permanent pleating & pressing, for the trade

(G-2618)
SUE & SAM CO INC (PA)
Also Called: W & G Manufacturing
720 39th St 720 (11232-3200)
PHONE..................................718 436-1672
Fax: 718 436-7508
Howard Wollman, *President*
Martin Stern, *Controller*
▲ **EMP:** 25
SQ FT: 37,000
SALES (est): 5.2MM **Privately Held**
SIC: 2321 2361 Polo shirts, men's & boys': made from purchased materials; shirts: girls', children's & infants'

(G-2619)
SUN MING JAN INC
145 Noll St (11206-4714)
PHONE..................................718 418-8221
Ben Chen, *CEO*
▲ **EMP:** 10 **EST:** 1999
SALES (est): 940.8K **Privately Held**
SIC: 2013 Sausages & other prepared meats

(G-2620)
SUNBURST STUDIOS INC
584 3rd Ave (11215-4612)
PHONE..................................718 768-6360
Ihor Nykolak, *President*
Peter Friedman, *Treasurer*
EMP: 5 **EST:** 1976
SQ FT: 3,600
SALES: 400K **Privately Held**
WEB: www.sunburststudio.com
SIC: 3231 8999 Stained glass: made from purchased glass; cut & engraved glassware: made from purchased glass; art restoration

(G-2621)
SUNRISE BAKING CO LLC
4564 2nd Ave (11232-4215)
PHONE..................................718 499-0800
Frank S Laferlita, *Mng Member*
Michael Laferlita,
EMP: 115
SQ FT: 32,000
SALES (est): 11.3MM **Privately Held**
SIC: 2051 Bakery: wholesale or wholesale/retail combined

(G-2622)
SUNRISE BKG ACQUISITION CO LLC
4564 2nd Ave (11232-4215)
PHONE..................................718 499-0800
Frank Laferlita,
EMP: 99
SALES: 950K **Privately Held**
SIC: 2051 Bread, cake & related products

(G-2623)
SUNWIRE ELECTRIC CORP
70 Wyckoff Ave Apt 4h (11237-3385)
PHONE..................................718 456-7500
Chen Birbaul, *Vice Pres*
EMP: 6
SALES: 700K **Privately Held**
SIC: 3699 Electrical equipment & supplies

(G-2624)
SUPER NEON LIGHT CO INC
7813 16th Ave (11214-1003)
PHONE..................................718 236-5667
Fax: 718 236-6101
James Coccaro Jr, *President*
EMP: 8 **EST:** 1939
SQ FT: 1,600
SALES (est): 550K **Privately Held**
SIC: 3993 Neon signs

(G-2625)
SUPERFLEX LTD
152 44th St (11232-3310)
PHONE..................................718 768-1400
Fax: 718 768-5065
Shimon Elbaz, *Ch of Bd*
Yigal Elbaz, *President*
Adna Elbaz, *Admin Asst*
▲ **EMP:** 50
SQ FT: 60,000
SALES (est): 17.6MM **Privately Held**
WEB: www.superflex.com
SIC: 3644 3052 Electric conduits & fittings; plastic hose

(G-2626)
SUPERIOR BLOCK CORP
Also Called: Glenwood Masonry Products
4106 Glenwood Rd (11210-2025)
PHONE..................................718 421-0900
Constance Cincotta, *President*
EMP: 10
SQ FT: 75,000
SALES (est): 1.7MM **Privately Held**
SIC: 3271 Concrete block & brick

(G-2627)
SUPERIOR ELEC ENCLOSURE INC
16 Spencer St (11205-1605)
PHONE..................................718 797-9090
Harris Grant, *President*
EMP: 7
SALES (est): 933K **Privately Held**
SIC: 3444 Metal housings, enclosures, casings & other containers

(G-2628)
SUPERIOR FIBER MILLS INC
181 Lombardy St (11222-5417)
P.O. Box 306, East Norwich (11732-0306)
PHONE..................................718 782-7500
Helen Burney, *President*
Henry Burney, *Vice Pres*
EMP: 40
SQ FT: 125,000
SALES (est): 4.9MM **Privately Held**
WEB: www.superiorfibers.com
SIC: 2299 2221 Batts & batting: cotton mill waste & related material; broadwoven fabric mills, manmade

(G-2629)
SUPERLEAF LLC
Also Called: Detox Water
286 Flushing Ave (11205-1212)
PHONE..................................607 280-9198
Kenneth Park, *CEO*
Dennis Chen, *CFO*
EMP: 5
SQ FT: 1,300
SALES (est): 153.8K **Privately Held**
SIC: 2086 Water, pasteurized: packaged in cans, bottles, etc.

(G-2630)
SUPERSIL LLC
4750 Bedford Ave Apt 6l (11235-2624)
PHONE..................................347 266-9900
Vadim Tarnovskiy,
EMP: 94
SALES: 950K **Privately Held**
SIC: 3999 Manufacturing industries

(G-2631)
SUPREME BOILERS INC
9221 Ditmas Ave (11236-1711)
PHONE..................................718 342-2220
Aaron Ganguli, *President*
David Rakst, *Vice Pres*
EMP: 5 **EST:** 2007
SALES (est): 540K **Privately Held**
SIC: 3443 Boiler & boiler shop work

(G-2632)
SUPREME POLY PLASTICS INC
299 Meserole St (11206-1732)
PHONE..................................718 456-9300
Fax: 718 821-8170
Abe Eilander, *President*
Abe Wertaberger, *General Mgr*
EMP: 25
SQ FT: 45,000
SALES (est): 3.9MM **Privately Held**
WEB: www.supremepoly.com
SIC: 2673 Plastic bags: made from purchased materials

(G-2633)
SURE-KOL REFRIGERATOR CO INC
490 Flushing Ave (11205-1615)
PHONE..................................718 625-0601
Fax: 718 624-1719
Steven Waslin, *President*
David J Waslin, *Corp Secy*
EMP: 10 **EST:** 1947
SQ FT: 13,000
SALES (est): 1.5MM **Privately Held**
SIC: 3632 Household refrigerators & freezers

(G-2634)
SURPRISE PLASTICS INC
124 57th St (11220-2576)
PHONE..................................718 492-6355
Fax: 718 492-0258
Joseph M Tancredi, *President*
Kenneth Tancredi, *Corp Secy*
Christopher Tancredi, *Vice Pres*
Vincent Tancredi, *Vice Pres*
Raymond Tancredi, *Treasurer*
▲ **EMP:** 115 **EST:** 1946
SQ FT: 48,000
SALES (est): 16.8MM **Privately Held**
WEB: www.surpriseplastics.com
SIC: 3089 Injection molding of plastics

(G-2635)
SWEATER BRAND INC
Also Called: Domain
86 S 1st St (11249-4171)
PHONE..................................718 797-0505
Moshe Rosenberg, *Manager*
EMP: 6
SALES (corp-wide): 3.2MM **Privately Held**
SIC: 2253 Sweaters & sweater coats, knit
PA: Sweater Brand Inc.
22 Wallenberg Cir
Monsey NY
718 797-0505

(G-2636)
SYNERGY DIGITAL
43 Hall St (11205-1315)
PHONE..................................718 643-2742
Fax: 718 643-9212
EMP: 15
SALES (est): 720K **Privately Held**
SIC: 3691 Mfg Storage Batteries

(G-2637)
T & L TRADING CO
17 Meserole St (11206-1901)
PHONE..................................718 782-5550
Fax: 718 599-4342
David Tang, *Owner*
▲ **EMP:** 5
SQ FT: 5,000

(G-2638)
T M I PLASTICS INDUSTRIES INC
28 Wythe Ave (11249-1036)
PHONE..................................718 383-0363
Sam Yuen, *President*
▲ **EMP:** 15
SALES (est): 2.2MM **Privately Held**
SIC: 2673 Plastic bags: made from purchased materials

(G-2639)
T MIX INC
6217 5th Ave (11220-4611)
PHONE..................................646 379-6814
Lin Jian, *CEO*
EMP: 6
SALES (est): 523.7K **Privately Held**
SIC: 3273 Ready-mixed concrete

(G-2640)
T&K PRINTING INC
Also Called: T & K Printing
262 44th St (11232-2816)
PHONE..................................718 439-9454
Fax: 718 439-9455
Hien Khuu, *President*
Dianna SOO, *Administration*
EMP: 10
SALES (est): 1.3MM **Privately Held**
SIC: 3577 2759 Optical scanning devices; commercial printing

(G-2641)
TAAM-TOV FOODS INC
Also Called: Ko-Sure Food Distributors
196 28th St (11232-1604)
PHONE..................................718 788-8880
Meyer Thurm, *President*
Max Thurm, *Vice Pres*
Sam Sherer, *Treasurer*
Marvin Weinstein, *Intl Dir*
▲ **EMP:** 7
SALES (est): 420K **Privately Held**
SIC: 2022 Cheese, natural & processed; cheese spreads, dips, pastes & other cheese products

(G-2642)
TABLE TOPS PAPER CORP
43 Hall St Ste C2 (11205-1393)
P.O. Box 220443 (11222-0443)
PHONE..................................718 598-7832
Ben Ruiz, *President*
EMP: 8
SALES (est): 660K **Privately Held**
SIC: 2759 5111 5999 Financial note & certificate printing & engraving; printing & writing paper; alarm signal systems

(G-2643)
TABLET PUBLISHING COMPANY INC
Also Called: Tablet Newspaper, The
1712 10th Ave (11215-6215)
PHONE..................................718 965-7333
Monsignor Anthony Danna, *Publisher*
Ed Wilkinson, *Principal*
Leonard W Kaiser, *Business Mgr*
Kimberly Benn, *Sales Executive*
Steven Ettinger, *Manager*
EMP: 25
SQ FT: 18,000
SALES (est): 1.4MM **Privately Held**
SIC: 2711 2741 Newspapers: publishing only, not printed on site; miscellaneous publishing

(G-2644)
TAI SENG
106 Lexington Ave (11238-1412)
PHONE..................................718 399-6311
▲ **EMP:** 6
SALES (est): 330K **Privately Held**
SIC: 2673 Mfg Bags-Plastic/Coated Paper

(G-2645)
TANEN CAP CO
Also Called: Tanen & Co
397 Bridge St Fl 8 (11201-5238)
PHONE..................................212 254-7100
Fax: 212 581-0011
David Steinberg, *Partner*

Aaron Steinberg, *Partner*
EMP: 12 **EST:** 1975
SQ FT: 5,000
SALES (est): 1.1MM Privately Held
SIC: 2353 Uniform hats & caps

(G-2646)
TARGUM PRESS USA INC
Also Called: Horizons Magazine
1946 59th St (11204-2340)
PHONE..............................248 355-2266
Sydney Choncow, *President*
David Dombey, *Admin Sec*
EMP: 8
SALES (est): 499.4K Privately Held
SIC: 2731 Book publishing

(G-2647)
TAYLOR TANK COMPANY INC
848 E 43rd St (11210-3502)
PHONE..............................718 434-1300
Michael Rubinberg, *President*
Cynthia Rubinberg, *Admin Sec*
EMP: 30 **EST:** 1947
SQ FT: 20,000
SALES (est): 4.7MM Privately Held
WEB: www.rubiconhx.com
SIC: 3443 Tanks, standard or custom fabricated: metal plate
PA: Rubicon Industries Corp.
  848 E 43rd St
  Brooklyn NY 11210
  718 434-4700

(G-2648)
TEACUP SOFTWARE INC
661 Saint Johns Pl (11216-4112)
PHONE..............................212 563-9288
Lawrence Horwitz, *President*
EMP: 9
SALES (est): 526.6K Privately Held
WEB: www.teacupsoftware.com
SIC: 7372 7379 Prepackaged software; computer related consulting services

(G-2649)
TECHNICAL LIBRARY SERVICE INC
Also Called: Talas
330 Morgan Ave (11211-2716)
PHONE..............................212 219-0770
Jacob Salik, *Ch of Bd*
Marjorie Salik, *President*
Aaron Salik, *Vice Pres*
EMP: 11 **EST:** 1962
SQ FT: 25,000
SALES (est): 1.3MM Privately Held
WEB: www.talas-nyc.com
SIC: 2653 8231 5199 Corrugated boxes, partitions, display items, sheets & pad; boxes, corrugated: made from purchased materials; libraries; law library; packaging materials

(G-2650)
TECHNIPOLY MANUFACTURING INC
Also Called: T M I of New York
20 Wythe Ave (11249-1036)
PHONE..............................718 383-0363
Fax: 718 383-2769
Kam S Yuen, *Owner*
Lip Foo Yee, *Vice Pres*
Allen Yuen, *Admin Sec*
EMP: 28
SQ FT: 16,000
SALES (est): 4.4MM Privately Held
SIC: 2673 2752 Plastic bags: made from purchased materials; commercial printing, lithographic

(G-2651)
TECNOLUX INCORPORATED
103 14th St (11215-4607)
PHONE..............................718 369-3900
Fax: 718 369-2845
David Ablon, *President*
Robert Tinkelman, *CTO*
▲ **EMP:** 7
SQ FT: 10,000
SALES (est): 710K Privately Held
WEB: www.tecnolux.com
SIC: 3648 Lighting equipment

(G-2652)
TEKA FINE LINE BRUSHES INC
3691 Bedford Ave (11229-1703)
PHONE..............................718 692-2928
Terry Ettkins, *President*
EMP: 7
SALES (est): 580K Privately Held
WEB: www.tekabrush.com
SIC: 3991 Hair pencils (artists' brushes)

(G-2653)
TELLER PRINTING CORP
317 Division Ave (11211-7307)
PHONE..............................718 486-3662
James Teller, *President*
EMP: 6
SALES (est): 510K Privately Held
SIC: 2752 Commercial printing, lithographic

(G-2654)
TELTECH SECURITY CORP
5014 16th Ave Ste 478 (11204-1404)
PHONE..............................718 871-8800
David Katz, *Ch of Bd*
EMP: 6
SALES (est): 1MM Privately Held
SIC: 3699 1731 Security control equipment & systems; telephone & telephone equipment installation

(G-2655)
THATS MY GIRL INC (PA)
80 39th St Ste 501 (11232-2604)
P.O. Box 230317 (11223-0317)
PHONE..............................212 695-0020
Salomon Salem, *President*
Raymond Kassin, *Vice Pres*
Steven Salem, *Manager*
EMP: 2
SQ FT: 800
SALES (est): 1.9MM Privately Held
SIC: 2361 Girls' & children's dresses, blouses & shirts

(G-2656)
THE EARTH TIMES FOUNDATION
195 Adams St Apt 6j (11201-1808)
PHONE..............................718 297-0488
Pranay Gupte, *President*
Ranjit Sahni, *Treasurer*
Nandini Ansari, *Director*
Jon Quint, *Director*
EMP: 5
SALES (est): 984.9K Privately Held
SIC: 2711 Newspapers, publishing & printing

(G-2657)
THEMIS CHIMNEY INC
190 Morgan Ave (11237-1014)
PHONE..............................718 937-4716
Mark Papadimitriou, *President*
EMP: 12
SQ FT: 12,000
SALES (est): 2.3MM Privately Held
SIC: 3443 3444 Liners/lining; sheet metalwork

(G-2658)
THOMPSON OVERHEAD DOOR CO INC
47 16th St (11215-4613)
PHONE..............................718 788-2470
Fax: 718 788-3344
Olav M Thompson, *President*
Edward Thompson, *Corp Secy*
Robert Kligman, *Sales Mgr*
EMP: 15
SQ FT: 16,000
SALES (est): 2.8MM Privately Held
SIC: 3442 5211 Rolling doors for industrial buildings or warehouses, metal; door & window products

(G-2659)
TIE KING INC (PA)
Also Called: Jimmy Sales
243 44th St (11232-2815)
PHONE..............................718 768-8484
Fax: 718 768-0355
Jimmy Azizo, *President*
Solomon Azizo, *Treasurer*
David Azizo, *Controller*
Steven Azizo, *Manager*
Jack Azizo, *Admin Sec*
▲ **EMP:** 50
SQ FT: 20,000
SALES (est): 4.6MM Privately Held
WEB: www.thetieking.com
SIC: 2323 Men's & boys' neckties & bow ties

(G-2660)
TIE VIEW NECKWEAR CO INC
1559 58th St (11219-4748)
PHONE..............................718 853-4156
Irving Spierer, *President*
EMP: 7 **EST:** 1967
SQ FT: 2,000
SALES (est): 700K Privately Held
SIC: 2323 Men's & boys' neckwear

(G-2661)
TLI IMPORT INC
151 2nd Ave (11215-4615)
PHONE..............................917 578-4568
Nouri Arabi, *President*
EMP: 6 **EST:** 2010
SALES (est): 350K Privately Held
SIC: 2221 Textile warping, on a contract basis

(G-2662)
TONER-N-MORE INC
2220 65th St Ste 103 (11204-4035)
PHONE..............................718 232-6200
Yoni Glatzer, *President*
EMP: 5
SQ FT: 10,000
SALES (est): 591.2K Privately Held
WEB: www.tonernmore.com
SIC: 3861 Toners, prepared photographic (not made in chemical plants)

(G-2663)
TOOLS & STAMPING CORP
Also Called: Balint Tool
48 Eagle St (11222-1013)
P.O. Box 220375 (11222-0375)
PHONE..............................718 392-4040
Ernest Feldman, *President*
Judah Feldman, *Vice Pres*
M Feldman, *Admin Sec*
EMP: 5 **EST:** 1960
SALES (est): 390K Privately Held
WEB: www.jnet.com
SIC: 3469 3544 3429 Stamping metal for the trade; special dies & tools; luggage hardware

(G-2664)
TOOTTER INC
1470 Royce St (11234-5924)
PHONE..............................212 300-7489
Sade Metellus, *Vice Pres*
EMP: 25
SQ FT: 1,200
SALES (est): 541.2K Privately Held
SIC: 7372 Application computer software

(G-2665)
TOP RACE INC
531 Wortman Ave (11208-5411)
PHONE..............................347 424-5795
Mayer D Deutsch, *President*
EMP: 6 **EST:** 2014
SQ FT: 10,000
SALES (est): 390K Privately Held
SIC: 3944 Airplane models, toy & hobby

(G-2666)
TOPOO INDUSTRIES INCORPORATED
7815 16th Ave (11214-1003)
PHONE..............................718 331-3755
▲ **EMP:** 8
SALES (est): 777.8K Privately Held
SIC: 3999 Manufacturing industries

(G-2667)
TOPRINT LTD
6110 7th Ave (11220-4107)
PHONE..............................718 439-0469
Thomas Corey, *Principal*
EMP: 5
SALES (est): 340K Privately Held
SIC: 2759 Commercial printing

(G-2668)
TORTILLERIA CHINANTLA INC
975 Grand St (11211-2704)
PHONE..............................718 302-0101
Fax: 718 302-0608
Erasmo Ponce, *Manager*
EMP: 7
SALES (corp-wide): 2MM Privately Held
SIC: 2096 Tortilla chips
PA: Tortilleria Chinantla Inc
  86 Central Ave
  Brooklyn NY 11206
  718 456-2828

(G-2669)
TOTAL METAL RESOURCE
Also Called: Pmrnyc
175 Bogart St (11206-1720)
PHONE..............................718 384-7818
Scott Behr, *President*
EMP: 10
SALES (est): 1.4MM Privately Held
SIC: 3499 Fabricated metal products

(G-2670)
TOURA LLC
392 2nd St 2 (11215-2404)
PHONE..............................646 652-8668
Kathleen Schnoor, *Principal*
Aaron Radin,
EMP: 10
SALES (est): 730.4K Privately Held
SIC: 3663 Mobile communication equipment

(G-2671)
TOWER ISLES FROZEN FOODS LTD
Also Called: Tower Isles Patties
2025 Atlantic Ave (11233-3131)
P.O. Box 330625 (11233-0625)
PHONE..............................718 495-2626
Fax: 718 342-6437
Patrick Jolly, *President*
Johnr Lokhandwala, *General Mgr*
James Jobson, *Vice Pres*
Joel Bower, *Accounts Mgr*
EMP: 73 **EST:** 1969
SQ FT: 32,600
SALES: 20MM Privately Held
WEB: www.towerislespatties.com
SIC: 2013 Boneless meat, from purchased meat

(G-2672)
TOWN FOOD SERVICE EQP CO INC (PA)
72 Beadel St (11222-5232)
PHONE..............................718 388-5650
Fax: 718 388-5860
Robert Pavlovich, *President*
◆ **EMP:** 15 **EST:** 1929
SQ FT: 1,500
SALES (est): 5MM Privately Held
SIC: 3491 Industrial valves

(G-2673)
TRADE MARK GRAPHICS INC
2418 Ralph Ave (11234-5517)
PHONE..............................718 306-0001
Avery Marder, *President*
EMP: 7
SQ FT: 24,000
SALES (est): 873.3K Privately Held
SIC: 2752 Commercial printing, offset

(G-2674)
TRANSCNTINENTAL ULTRA FLEX INC
975 Essex St (11208-5419)
PHONE..............................718 272-9100
Fax: 718 272-5424
Eli Blatt, *CEO*
Dan B Kochba, *General Mgr*
Ben Jagarnath, *Opers Staff*
Alex Zirulnik, *Engineer*
Todd Addison, *Treasurer*
◆ **EMP:** 270
SQ FT: 115,000

GEOGRAPHIC SECTION
Brooklyn - Kings County (G-2701)

SALES (est): 71.8MM
SALES (corp-wide): 1.5B **Privately Held**
WEB: www.ultraflex.com
SIC: 2759 2671 2752 Flexographic printing; packaging paper & plastics film, coated & laminated; commercial printing, lithographic
PA: Transcontinental Inc
1 Place Ville-Marie Bureau 3315
Montreal QC H3B 3
514 954-4000

(G-2675)
TRANSLAND SOURCING LLC
5 Lynch St (11249-9223)
PHONE.................................718 596-5704
Jacob Frankl, *CEO*
EMP: 4
SALES: 5MM **Privately Held**
SIC: 3571 Electronic computers

(G-2676)
TRI MAR ENTERPRISES INC
36 Gardner Ave (11237-1509)
P.O. Box 370503 (11237-0503)
PHONE.................................718 418-3644
Fax: 718 418-3644
Marvin Siegel, *President*
EMP: 5
SALES (est): 549.5K **Privately Held**
SIC: 3952 Canvas board, artists'

(G-2677)
TRI STATE SHEARING BENDING INC
366 Herzl St (11212-4442)
P.O. Box 120002 (11212-0002)
PHONE.................................718 485-2200
Alan Blaier, *President*
Michele Blaier, *Vice Pres*
Ronald Blaier, *Manager*
EMP: 15
SQ FT: 12,000
SALES (est): 4.6MM **Privately Held**
SIC: 3446 Stairs, staircases, stair treads: prefabricated metal

(G-2678)
TRI-STATE FOOD JOBBERS INC
5600 1st Ave Unit A5 (11220-2550)
PHONE.................................718 921-1211
Maor Ohana, *President*
EMP: 6 **EST:** 2009
SALES: 2.6MM **Privately Held**
SIC: 3497 Foil containers for bakery goods & frozen foods

(G-2679)
TRIANGLE LABEL TAG INC
525 Dekalb Ave (11205-4818)
PHONE.................................718 875-3030
Fax: 718 875-9830
Joseph Kahan, *President*
Herman Frankel, *Vice Pres*
EMP: 8
SQ FT: 5,000
SALES: 1.3MM **Privately Held**
SIC: 2672 2759 5131 2241 Adhesive papers, labels or tapes: from purchased material; labels & seals: printing; piece goods & notions; labels; labels, woven

(G-2680)
TRICO MANUFACTURING CORP
196 Dupont St (11222-1241)
PHONE.................................718 349-6565
Elizabeth Fling, *President*
EMP: 6 **EST:** 2000
SQ FT: 7,000
SALES (est): 537.9K **Privately Held**
SIC: 3429 Door locks, bolts & checks; door opening & closing devices, except electrical

(G-2681)
TRIMET COAL LLC
1615 Avenue I Apt 420 (11230-3041)
PHONE.................................718 951-3654
EMP: 21
SALES (est): 1.3MM **Privately Held**
SIC: 1241 Coal Mining Services

(G-2682)
TRIPI ENGRAVING CO INC
Also Called: Royal Engraving
60 Meserole Ave (11222-2638)
PHONE.................................718 383-6500
Phil Tripi, *President*
EMP: 25
SQ FT: 10,000
SALES (est): 2.2MM **Privately Held**
SIC: 2759 5112 5943 2796 Engraving; stationery; stationery stores; platemaking services; typesetting; commercial printing, lithographic

(G-2683)
TRM LINEN INC
1546 59th St (11219-5028)
PHONE.................................718 686-6075
Chaim Cohen, *Ch of Bd*
▼ **EMP:** 5
SALES (est): 461.9K **Privately Held**
SIC: 2299 5961 Linen fabrics; mail order house

(G-2684)
TROVE INC
20 Jay St Ste 846 (11201-8306)
PHONE.................................212 268-2046
Jee Levin, *Principal*
Randall Buck, *Buyer*
EMP: 15
SALES (est): 1.6MM **Privately Held**
SIC: 3999 5199 Fire extinguishers, portable; gifts & novelties

(G-2685)
TROVVIT INC
445 7th St (11215-3614)
PHONE.................................718 908-5376
Torrance Robinson, *CEO*
EMP: 9
SALES (est): 271.8K **Privately Held**
SIC: 7372 7389 Educational computer software;

(G-2686)
TRU-TONE METAL PRODUCTS INC
1261 Willoughby Ave (11237-2904)
P.O. Box 370711 (11237-0711)
PHONE.................................718 386-5960
Fax: 718 386-1021
James P Murtha, *President*
Catherine Murtha, *Vice Pres*
Nick Murtha, *Director*
EMP: 20
SQ FT: 5,000
SALES (est): 2MM **Privately Held**
SIC: 3471 Anodizing (plating) of metals or formed products; coloring & finishing of aluminum or formed products

(G-2687)
TUNECORE INC (PA)
45 Main St Ste 705 (11201-1075)
P.O. Box 20256 (11202-0256)
PHONE.................................646 651-1060
Scott Ackerman, *CEO*
Troy Denkinger, *Vice Pres*
Elise Holzheimer, *Vice Pres*
Gillian Morris, *Vice Pres*
Matt Barrington, *Controller*
EMP: 32
SALES (est): 1.4MM **Privately Held**
SIC: 3651 Music distribution apparatus

(G-2688)
TUROFF TOWER GRAPHICS INC
Also Called: Tower Sales Co
681 Coney Island Ave (11218-4306)
PHONE.................................718 856-7300
Jay Turoff, *President*
Rose Turoff, *Corp Secy*
Georgina Snyder, *Vice Pres*
EMP: 14 **EST:** 1969
SQ FT: 1,000
SALES (est): 1.3MM **Privately Held**
SIC: 3993 Neon signs

(G-2689)
TUV TAAM CORP
502 Flushing Ave (11205-1616)
PHONE.................................718 855-2207
Aaron Nutovich, *President*
Rivka Nutovich, *Treasurer*
Lea Gold, *Admin Sec*
▲ **EMP:** 50
SQ FT: 10,000
SALES (est): 7.4MM **Privately Held**
SIC: 2099 2038 Food preparations; salads, fresh or refrigerated; frozen specialties

(G-2690)
TWI WATCHES LLC
Also Called: Akribos Watches
4014 1st Ave (11232-2606)
PHONE.................................718 663-3969
Ben Rosenbaum, *Sales Dir*
Chaim Sischer, *Mng Member*
▲ **EMP:** 35
SALES: 2MM **Privately Held**
SIC: 3873 Watches, clocks, watchcases & parts

(G-2691)
TWIN MARQUIS INC (HQ)
7 Bushwick Pl (11206-2815)
PHONE.................................718 386-6868
Fax: 718 386-0516
Hyung Kyun Kim, *Ch of Bd*
Jing Lin, *Engineer*
Flora Lin, *Office Mgr*
Chung Pun Tang, *Admin Sec*
▲ **EMP:** 65
SQ FT: 33,000
SALES (est): 10.5MM
SALES (corp-wide): 3.9B **Privately Held**
WEB: www.twinmarquis.com
SIC: 2098 2099 2035 Macaroni & spaghetti; noodles, fried (Chinese); pickles, sauces & salad dressings
PA: Cj Cheiljedang Corp.
Cj Jeiljedang Center
Seoul SEO 04560
272 681-14

(G-2692)
TWO SISTERS KIEV BAKERY INC (PA)
2737 W 15th St (11224-2705)
PHONE.................................718 769-2626
Rita Shoikhetman, *President*
Pauline Rusanovsky, *Vice Pres*
EMP: 4
SQ FT: 5,000
SALES (est): 1.3MM **Privately Held**
SIC: 2051 Bakery: wholesale or wholesale/retail combined

(G-2693)
TWO SISTERS KIEV BAKERY INC
1627 E 18th St (11229-1203)
PHONE.................................718 627-5438
Rita Shoikhetman, *Branch Mgr*
EMP: 11
SALES (corp-wide): 1.3MM **Privately Held**
SIC: 2051 Bakery: wholesale or wholesale/retail combined
PA: Two Sisters Kiev Bakery Inc
2737 W 15th St
Brooklyn NY 11224
718 769-2626

(G-2694)
TWO WORLDS ARTS LTD
307 Kingsland Ave (11222-3708)
PHONE.................................212 929-2210
Fax: 718 349-6420
Jean Chau, *Manager*
EMP: 6
SALES (corp-wide): 631.9K **Privately Held**
SIC: 2512 Upholstered household furniture
PA: Two Worlds Arts Ltd
122 W 18th St
New York NY 10011
212 929-2210

(G-2695)
ULANO PRODUCT INC
110 3rd Ave (11217-2397)
PHONE.................................718 622-5200
David Eisenbeiss, *Chairman*
Gary Gayton, *Sales Mgr*
John Burgher, *Manager*
EMP: 108
SQ FT: 20,000
SALES (est): 6.5MM **Privately Held**
SIC: 3953 Screens, textile printing

(G-2696)
ULTRAPEDICS LTD (PA)
355 Ovington Ave Ste 104 (11209-1457)
P.O. Box 90384 (11209-0384)
PHONE.................................718 748-4806
Eric Schwelke, *President*
EMP: 7
SQ FT: 3,400
SALES (est): 570.3K **Privately Held**
SIC: 3842 5999 Surgical appliances & supplies; artificial limbs

(G-2697)
UNIFIED SOLUTIONS FOR CLG INC
1829 Pacific St (11233-3505)
PHONE.................................718 782-8800
Fax: 718 782-8801
Mendel Jacobowitz, *President*
Lipa Jacobowitz, *Vice Pres*
EMP: 15
SALES (est): 2.3MM **Privately Held**
SIC: 2869 Butadiene (industrial organic chemical)

(G-2698)
UNIFORMS BY PARK COATS INC
790 3rd Ave (11232-1510)
PHONE.................................718 499-1182
Fax: 718 499-1646
Nick Haymandos, *President*
Despina Haymandos, *Vice Pres*
Mary Jane, *Manager*
EMP: 28
SQ FT: 8,000
SALES (est): 3MM **Privately Held**
WEB: www.uniformsbypark.com
SIC: 2311 2337 Men's & boys' uniforms; uniforms, except athletic: women's, misses' & juniors'

(G-2699)
UNIMEX CORPORATION
Lee Spring Company Division
1462 62nd St (11219-5413)
PHONE.................................718 236-2222
Albert Mangels, *President*
Carmela Papagni, *Chf Purch Ofc*
Richard Carpaino, *Sales Mgr*
John Salvaggio, *Manager*
EMP: 160
SALES (corp-wide): 33.4MM **Privately Held**
SIC: 3495 Mechanical springs, precision
PA: Unimex Corporation
54 E 64th St
New York NY 10065
212 755-8800

(G-2700)
UNITED GEMDIAM INC
Also Called: UGI
1537 52nd St (11219-3910)
PHONE.................................718 851-5083
Morris Friedman, *President*
Isaac Friedman, *Office Mgr*
EMP: 43
SQ FT: 5,000
SALES (est): 3.5MM **Privately Held**
WEB: www.ugi.com
SIC: 3915 5094 Diamond cutting & polishing; diamonds (gems)

(G-2701)
UNITED PLASTICS INC
640 Humboldt St Ste 1 (11222-4121)
P.O. Box 220363 (11222-0363)
PHONE.................................718 389-2255
Charles Smiley, *Sales Executive*
Gary Mayo, *Manager*
Kenneth Farina, *Manager*
EMP: 7
SALES (corp-wide): 1.6MM **Privately Held**
SIC: 2673 3089 Plastic bags: made from purchased materials; plastic processing
PA: United Plastics, Inc
219 Nassau Ave
Brooklyn NY
718 389-2255

Brooklyn - Kings County (G-2702)   GEOGRAPHIC SECTION

(G-2702)
UNITED SHIP REPAIR INC
54 Richards St (11231-1626)
PHONE 718 237-2800
Jim Tampakis, *President*
EMP: 10 **EST:** 1975
SALES (est): 890K **Privately Held**
SIC: 3731 Shipbuilding & repairing; military ships, building & repairing

(G-2703)
UNITED TRANSIT MIX INC
318 Boerum St (11206-3505)
P.O. Box 370647 (11237-0647)
PHONE 718 416-3400
Fax: 718 416-4329
Tony Mastronardi, *President*
EMP: 14
SALES (est): 4MM **Privately Held**
SIC: 3273 Ready-mixed concrete

(G-2704)
UNITED WIND INC
20 Jay St Ste 928 (11201-8354)
PHONE 800 268-9896
Russell Tencer, *CEO*
Aaron Lubowitz, *COO*
Jason Kaplan, *Counsel*
Joseph Yurcisin, *Vice Pres*
Kyle Andrucyk, *VP Finance*
EMP: 19 **EST:** 2013
SALES (est): 3.9MM **Privately Held**
SIC: 3443 Wind tunnels

(G-2705)
UNIVERSAL COOLERS INC
120 13th St (11215-4604)
PHONE 718 788-8621
Gregory Uchitel, *Ch of Bd*
▲ **EMP:** 6 **EST:** 1995
SALES (est): 1MM **Privately Held**
SIC: 3585 Parts for heating, cooling & refrigerating equipment

(G-2706)
UNIVERSAL FIRE PROOF DOOR
1171 Myrtle Ave (11206-6007)
PHONE 718 455-8442
Abelardo Galicia, *President*
Al Bender, *Finance Other*
Joseph Epstein, *Executive*
EMP: 25 **EST:** 1924
SQ FT: 24,000
SALES (est): 4.9MM **Privately Held**
SIC: 3442 Fire doors, metal

(G-2707)
UNIVERSAL PARENT AND YOUTH
Also Called: Upayori
1530 Pa Ave Apt 17e (11239-2620)
PHONE 917 754-2426
Vincent Riggins, *Exec Dir*
EMP: 10
SALES (est): 537.8K **Privately Held**
SIC: 3585 Refrigeration & heating equipment

(G-2708)
UNIVERSAL SCREENING ASSOCIATES
Also Called: USA Tees.com
6509 11th Ave (11219-5602)
PHONE 718 232-2744
Fax: 718 232-3793
David Cardinale, *President*
Eugene Polishchuk, *Graphic Designe*
▲ **EMP:** 12
SQ FT: 500
SALES: 500K **Privately Held**
SIC: 2759 Screen printing

(G-2709)
UNIVERSAL STEEL FABRICATORS
90 Junius St (11212-8029)
PHONE 718 342-0782
Fax: 718 342-0382
Harvinder Paul, *President*
Emilio Franza, *Treasurer*
EMP: 15
SQ FT: 3,500
SALES: 1MM **Privately Held**
SIC: 3446 5051 1799 Architectural metalwork; structural shapes, iron or steel; fence construction

(G-2710)
UPPER 90 SOCCER & SPORT
359 Atlantic Ave (11217-1701)
PHONE 718 643-0167
Zac Rubin,
EMP: 9
SALES (est): 729.7K **Privately Held**
SIC: 3131 Uppers

(G-2711)
URBAN WOODWORKS LTD
18 Crescent St (11208-1516)
PHONE 718 827-1570
Gewan Bharatlall, *President*
Gabriela Bharatlall, *Vice Pres*
Akela Etienne-Forbes, *Admin Mgr*
EMP: 5
SALES: 1.8MM **Privately Held**
SIC: 2431 Millwork

(G-2712)
US CONCRETE INC
Also Called: Kings Material
692 Mcdonald Ave (11218-4914)
PHONE 718 438-6800
Robert Bruzzese, *Branch Mgr*
EMP: 20
SALES (corp-wide): 974.7MM **Publicly Held**
SIC: 3273 Ready-mixed concrete
PA: U.S. Concrete, Inc.
331 N Main St
Euless TX 76039
817 835-4105

(G-2713)
US HISPANIC MEDIA INC (DH)
1 Metrotech Ctr Fl 18 (11201-3949)
PHONE 212 885-8000
Eduardo Lomanto, *President*
EMP: 7
SALES (est): 103.5MM **Privately Held**
SIC: 2711 Newspapers: publishing only, not printed on site

(G-2714)
US MILPACK & MFG CORP
1567 Bergen St (11213-1704)
PHONE 718 342-1307
Shams Ayub, *President*
EMP: 6
SQ FT: 4,000
SALES: 1MM **Privately Held**
SIC: 3728 Military aircraft equipment & armament

(G-2715)
VAAD LHAFOTZAS SICHOES
788 Eastern Pkwy (11213-3409)
PHONE 718 778-5436
Zalmen Chanin, *President*
Nachman Shapiro, *Treasurer*
Sholom Jacobson, *Admin Sec*
▲ **EMP:** 13
SQ FT: 10,000
SALES: 1MM **Privately Held**
SIC: 2731 Books: publishing only

(G-2716)
VALENTINE PRINTING CORP
509 E 79th St (11236-3134)
P.O. Box 940096, Rockaway Park (11694-0096)
PHONE 718 444-4400
Fax: 718 444-3722
Herb Villanueva, *President*
Raymond Villanueva, *Med Doctor*
EMP: 5
SQ FT: 2,200
SALES (est): 460K **Privately Held**
SIC: 2752 Commercial printing, offset

(G-2717)
VALI INDUSTRIES INC
285 Lombardy St (11222-5516)
PHONE 718 821-5555
Vincent Ali, *Owner*
EMP: 13
SALES (est): 1.4MM **Privately Held**
SIC: 3999 Manufacturing industries

(G-2718)
VAN BLARCOM CLOSURES INC (PA)
156 Sanford St (11205)
PHONE 718 855-3810
Vincent Scuderi Jr, *Ch of Bd*
Ron Camuto, *Vice Pres*
Paula Frey, *Opers Mgr*
Anthony Scuderi, *QC Mgr*
John Scuderi, *Treasurer*
▲ **EMP:** 195 **EST:** 1947
SQ FT: 160,000
SALES: 49.3MM **Privately Held**
WEB: www.vbcpkg.com
SIC: 3089 3466 3549 Closures, plastic; caps, plastic; closures, stamped metal; bottle caps & tops, stamped metal; jar tops & crowns, stamped metal; assembly machines, including robotic

(G-2719)
VAN LEEUWEN ARTISAN ICE CREAM
56 Dobbin St (11222-3110)
PHONE 718 701-1630
Ben Van Leeuwen, *Principal*
EMP: 6
SALES (est): 405.4K **Privately Held**
SIC: 2024 Ice cream & frozen desserts

(G-2720)
VANS INC
25 Franklin St (11222-2007)
PHONE 718 349-2311
EMP: 10
SALES (corp-wide): 12.3B **Publicly Held**
SIC: 3021 Canvas shoes, rubber soled
HQ: Vans, Inc.
6550 Katella Ave
Cypress CA 90630
714 889-6100

(G-2721)
VAULT WO
828 E 21st St (11210-1042)
PHONE 212 281-1723
EMP: 6
SALES (est): 722.2K **Privately Held**
SIC: 3272 Mfg Concrete Products

(G-2722)
VENTURE RESPIRATORY INC
1413 38th St (11218-3613)
PHONE 718 437-3633
Moshe Richard, *President*
EMP: 13
SQ FT: 5,000
SALES (est): 2.6MM **Privately Held**
WEB: www.ventrespiratory.com
SIC: 3842 Respiratory protection equipment, personal

(G-2723)
VERSO INC
20 Jay St Ste 1010 (11201-8346)
PHONE 718 246-8160
Jacob Stevens, *Director*
EMP: 8
SQ FT: 2,500
SALES: 959.9K **Privately Held**
SIC: 2731 Book publishing
PA: New Left Books Limited
6 Meard Street
London
207 437-3546

(G-2724)
VIAMEDIA CORPORATION
2610 Atlantic Ave (11207-2415)
PHONE 718 485-7792
James Underwood, *President*
Michael Underwood, *Vice Pres*
EMP: 5
SQ FT: 3,200
SALES (est): 280.4K **Privately Held**
WEB: www.via-indy.com
SIC: 2741 Miscellaneous publishing

(G-2725)
VICTORIA FINE FOODS LLC (PA)
Also Called: Corporate Offices & Plant
443 E 100th St (11236-2103)
PHONE 718 649-1635
Gerald Aquilina, *CEO*
Tim Shanley, *CEO*
Brian Dean, *President*
Jerry Aquilina, *Vice Pres*
Robert Haberman, *Vice Pres*
▲ **EMP:** 100 **EST:** 2011
SQ FT: 90,000
SALES (est): 54MM **Privately Held**
SIC: 2035 2099 5149 2033 Pickles, sauces & salad dressings; spices, including grinding; pasta & rice; canned fruits & specialties

(G-2726)
VICTORY VISION CARE INC
565 Atlantic Ave (11217-1913)
PHONE 718 622-2020
Fax: 718 622-5404
Viktor Kolesnyk, *President*
EMP: 9
SALES (est): 960K **Privately Held**
SIC: 3827 Optical instruments & lenses

(G-2727)
VIKING MAR WLDG SHIP REPR LLC
14 Raleigh Pl (11226-4218)
PHONE 718 758-4116
Floyd Ricketts,
EMP: 10
SALES (est): 520.5K **Privately Held**
SIC: 3731 Shipbuilding & repairing

(G-2728)
VINELAND KOSHER POULTRY INC
Also Called: Poultry Dist
5600 1st Ave A7 (11220-2550)
PHONE 718 921-1347
Fax: 718 921-8913
Armin Silberstein, *Finance Mgr*
David Lefkowitz, *Systems Mgr*
EMP: 10
SALES (corp-wide): 9.7MM **Privately Held**
WEB: www.vinelandkosherpoultry.com
SIC: 2015 5144 Poultry slaughtering & processing; poultry & poultry products
PA: Vineland Kosher Poultry Inc
1050 S Mill Rd
Vineland NJ 08360
856 692-1871

(G-2729)
VIRGINIA DARE EXTRACT CO INC
Also Called: V & E Kohnstamm & Co Div
882 3rd Ave Unit 2 (11232-1902)
PHONE 718 788-6320
Fax: 718 768-3978
Howard Smith Jr, *President*
Stephen Balter, *Vice Pres*
Laura McCord, *Purchasing*
◆ **EMP:** 175
SQ FT: 165,000
SALES (est): 52MM **Privately Held**
SIC: 2087 Flavoring extracts & syrups; extracts, flavoring

(G-2730)
VIRTUALAPT CORP
45 Main St Ste 408 (11201-1084)
PHONE 917 293-3173
Bryan Colin, *CEO*
EMP: 8
SALES (est): 300.6K **Privately Held**
SIC: 3812 Search & detection systems & instruments

(G-2731)
VISITAINER CORP
Also Called: Plastifold Industries Division
148 Classon Ave (11205-2637)
PHONE 718 636-0300
Fax: 718 636-0302
William Lefkovitz, *President*
William Leskowitz, *Manager*
EMP: 25 **EST:** 1962
SQ FT: 30,000
SALES (est): 2.2MM **Privately Held**
SIC: 2657 3089 Folding paperboard boxes; plastic containers, except foam

GEOGRAPHIC SECTION
Brooklyn - Kings County (G-2760)

(G-2732)
VISTA PACKAGING INC
1425 37th St Ste 6 (11218-3769)
PHONE..................................718 854-9200
William Schwartz, *President*
Judy Weinberg, *Accounts Mgr*
▲ **EMP:** 35 **EST:** 2000
SQ FT: 43,000
SALES (est): 5.6MM **Privately Held**
WEB: www.vistatubes.com
SIC: 3085 Plastics bottles

(G-2733)
VITAROSE CORP OF AMERICA
2615 Nostrand Ave Ste 1 (11210-4643)
PHONE..................................718 951-9700
Joe Derose, *President*
EMP: 6 **EST:** 1959
SQ FT: 2,625
SALES: 1MM **Privately Held**
SIC: 2541 3231 3089 3444 Window backs, store or lunchroom, prefabricated: wood; products of purchased glass; awnings, fiberglass & plastic combination; awnings & canopies

(G-2734)
VOILA SWEETS LLC
65 Porter Ave (11237-1415)
PHONE..................................718 366-1100
EMP: 350
SALES (est): 26.7MM
SALES (corp-wide): 143.5MM **Privately Held**
SIC: 2051 Mfg Bread/Related Products
PA: Rockland Bakery Inc.
   94 Demarest Mill Rd W
   Nanuet NY 10954
   845 623-5800

(G-2735)
VOLCKENING INC (PA)
6700 3rd Ave (11220-5296)
PHONE..................................718 748-0294
Fax: 718 748-2811
William J Schneider, *Ch of Bd*
Frederick C Schneider, *President*
Henry Schneider, *Vice Pres*
Michael Rutigliano, *Mfg Staff*
James Pelosis, *Engineer*
EMP: 45
SQ FT: 30,000
SALES (est): 6.6MM **Privately Held**
WEB: www.volckening.com
SIC: 3565 3991 Packaging machinery; brushes, household or industrial

(G-2736)
VOODOO MANUFACTURING INC
361 Stagg St Ste 408 (11206-1743)
PHONE..................................646 893-8366
Max Friefeld, *CEO*
EMP: 5
SALES: 100K **Privately Held**
SIC: 3555 Printing trades machinery

(G-2737)
VSG INTERNATIONAL LLC
Also Called: Kustom Collabo
196 Clinton Ave Apt A2 (11205-3411)
PHONE..................................718 300-8171
Yusef Sirius-El, *Mng Member*
Nicholas Vasilopoulos,
▲ **EMP:** 5 **EST:** 2012
SQ FT: 5,000
SALES (est): 311.8K **Privately Held**
SIC: 3149 Athletic shoes, except rubber or plastic

(G-2738)
VUS IS NEIAS LLC
5514 13th Ave (11219-4515)
P.O. Box 40188 (11204-0188)
PHONE..................................347 627-3999
EMP: 6
SALES (est): 302K **Privately Held**
SIC: 2711 Newspapers, publishing & printing

(G-2739)
W & M HEADWEAR CO INC
148 39th St Unit 8 (11232-2713)
PHONE..................................718 768-2222
Fax: 718 499-2641
Isaac Elias, *President*
Faye Urbach, *Manager*
▲ **EMP:** 30 **EST:** 1954
SQ FT: 27,000
SALES (est): 16.7MM **Privately Held**
SIC: 2353 5136 Hats & caps; hats, men's & boys'

(G-2740)
W E W CONTAINER CORPORATION
189 Wyona St (11207-3009)
PHONE..................................718 827-8150
Daniel Weicher, *Branch Mgr*
EMP: 20
SALES (corp-wide): 3.5MM **Privately Held**
SIC: 2673 2671 Bags: plastic, laminated & coated; plastic film, coated or laminated for packaging
PA: W E W Container Corporation
   200 Bradford St
   Brooklyn NY
   718 827-8150

(G-2741)
W&P DESIGN LLC (PA)
86 S 1st St Apt 4b (11249-4173)
PHONE..................................434 806-1443
Elizabeth Tilton, *Vice Pres*
Eric Prum,
EMP: 6
SALES: 1.2MM **Privately Held**
SIC: 2599 5942 5192 Food, mail order; book stores; books

(G-2742)
WALLY PACKAGING INC (HQ)
1168 E 21st St (11210-3618)
PHONE..................................718 377-5323
Fax: 718 258-2324
Ray Wallerstein, *President*
Chumie Wallerstein, *Vice Pres*
▲ **EMP:** 5
SQ FT: 15,000
SALES (est): 607.1K
SALES (corp-wide): 1.1MM **Privately Held**
SIC: 2673 Bags: plastic, laminated & coated
PA: Quest Packaging Llc
   525 E County Line Rd # 8
   Lakewood NJ 08701
   732 276-7767

(G-2743)
WALTER P SAUER LLC
Also Called: Morris Fine Furniture Workshop
276 Greenpoint Ave # 8400 (11222-2434)
PHONE..................................718 937-0600
Renee Tavares, *Accounts Mgr*
Andrew Dron, *Manager*
Anthony Morris,
Shanika Hudson, *Admin Sec*
EMP: 43
SQ FT: 2,100
SALES (est): 2MM **Privately Held**
WEB: www.walterpsauer.com
SIC: 2511 Wood household furniture

(G-2744)
WARNACO INC
70 Washington St Fl 10 (11201-1442)
PHONE..................................718 722-3000
Smitty Seelall, *Branch Mgr*
EMP: 10
SALES (corp-wide): 8B **Publicly Held**
WEB: www.warnaco.com
SIC: 2342 2341 2321 2253 Bras, girdles & allied garments; panties: women's, misses', children's & infants'; men's & boys' dress shirts; shirts (outerwear), knit; athletic (warmup, sweat & jogging) suits: men's & boys'; underwear, men's & boys': made from purchased materials
HQ: Warnaco Inc.
   501 Fashion Ave Fl 14
   New York NY 10018
   212 287-8000

(G-2745)
WATERMARK DESIGNS HOLDINGS LTD
350 Dewitt Ave (11207-6618)
PHONE..................................718 257-2800
AVI Abel, *President*
Jack Abel, *Vice Pres*
▲ **EMP:** 55
SQ FT: 20,000
SALES (est): 10.6MM **Privately Held**
SIC: 3431 3432 Bathroom fixtures, including sinks; plumbing fixture fittings & trim

(G-2746)
WG SHEET METAL CORP
341 Amber St (11208-5104)
PHONE..................................718 235-3093
Andy Tolta, *Admin Sec*
EMP: 5
SALES: 700K **Privately Held**
SIC: 3444 Sheet metalwork

(G-2747)
WHISPR GROUP INC
45 Main St Ste 1036 (11201-1032)
PHONE..................................212 924-3979
Joakim Leijon, *President*
John Studer, *Finance*
EMP: 13 **EST:** 2009
SQ FT: 4,000
SALES (est): 1.1MM **Privately Held**
SIC: 3993 5199 7389 7311 Advertising artwork; advertising specialties; ; advertising consultant

(G-2748)
WHITLEY EAST LLC
Brooklyn Navy Yd Bg 2 Fl (11205)
PHONE..................................718 403-0050
William McShane, *General Mgr*
EMP: 79
SALES (corp-wide): 115MM **Privately Held**
WEB: www.capsyscorp.com
SIC: 2452 Modular homes, prefabricated, wood
HQ: Whitley East, Llc
   64 Hess Rd
   Leola PA 17540
   717 656-2081

(G-2749)
WIDE FLANGE INC
176 27th St (11232-1625)
PHONE..................................718 492-8705
Joyce Cavagnaro, *President*
Blaze Bono, *Vice Pres*
Annette Opulente, *Manager*
EMP: 11
SQ FT: 5,500
SALES: 1.8MM **Privately Held**
SIC: 3449 Bars, concrete reinforcing; fabricated steel

(G-2750)
WIGGBY PRECISION MACHINE CORP
140 58th St Ste 56 (11220-2526)
PHONE..................................718 439-6900
Ronald Wiggberg, *CEO*
Robert G Wiggberg, *Corp Secy*
EMP: 30 **EST:** 1949
SALES (est): 4.4MM **Privately Held**
SIC: 3599 Machine shop, jobbing & repair

(G-2751)
WILCO FINISHING CORP
1288 Willoughby Ave (11237-2905)
P.O. Box 370708 (11237-0708)
PHONE..................................718 417-6405
Julius Medwin, *Principal*
Bob Augi, *Vice Pres*
EMP: 38
SQ FT: 20,000
SALES (est): 3.3MM **Privately Held**
WEB: www.wilcoplating.com
SIC: 3471 Plating & polishing

(G-2752)
WILLIAM BROOKS WOODWORKING
856 Saratoga Ave (11212-4350)
PHONE..................................718 495-9767
William Brooks, *Owner*
EMP: 10
SALES: 275K **Privately Held**
SIC: 2434 Wood kitchen cabinets

(G-2753)
WILLIAM HARVEY STUDIO INC
214 N 8th St (11211-2008)
PHONE..................................718 599-4343
William Harvey, *President*
Reed Harvey, *Admin Sec*
EMP: 5
SQ FT: 2,500
SALES (est): 290K **Privately Held**
WEB: www.williamharveydesign.com
SIC: 2392 Household furnishings

(G-2754)
WILLIAM KANES MFG CORP
23 Alabama Ave (11207-2303)
PHONE..................................718 346-1515
Fax: 718 346-1537
William Kanes, *President*
EMP: 7
SQ FT: 5,000
SALES: 500K **Privately Held**
SIC: 3444 3599 Sheet metalwork; machine shop, jobbing & repair

(G-2755)
WILLIAMSBURG BULLETIN
136 Ross St (11211-7705)
PHONE..................................718 387-0123
EMP: 6
SALES (est): 377.9K **Privately Held**
SIC: 2711 Newspapers, publishing & printing

(G-2756)
WIND PRODUCTS INC
20 Jay St Ste 936 (11201-8354)
PHONE..................................212 292-3135
Russell Tencer, *President*
William Jacoby, *Vice Pres*
EMP: 6
SALES (est): 500K **Privately Held**
SIC: 3511 Turbines & turbine generator sets

(G-2757)
WINDOW-FIX INC
331 37th St Fl 1 (11232-2505)
PHONE..................................718 854-3475
Ernesto Cappello, *President*
John Cappello, *Vice Pres*
Jose Sanchez, *Controller*
Louie Rinaldi, *Manager*
EMP: 20
SALES (est): 3.2MM **Privately Held**
SIC: 3211 1751 7699 Window glass, clear & colored; window & door installation & erection; window blind repair services

(G-2758)
WINDOWMAN INC (USA)
460 Kingsland Ave (11222-1906)
PHONE..................................718 246-2626
Fax: 718 246-2455
Bruce Schmutter, *President*
EMP: 6
SALES (est): 630K **Privately Held**
WEB: www.windowmanusa.com
SIC: 3442 3699 1796 1751 Metal doors, sash & trim; door opening & closing devices, electrical; installing building equipment; window & door installation & erection; safety & security specialization

(G-2759)
WINDOWS MEDIA PUBLISHING LLC
369 Remsen Ave (11212-1245)
PHONE..................................917 732-7892
Mark McLean,
EMP: 25
SALES (est): 627.2K **Privately Held**
SIC: 2731 Books: publishing & printing

(G-2760)
WINGHING 8 LTD
6215 6th Ave (11220-4704)
PHONE..................................718 439-0021
Jennifer Hui, *President*
Frank Wong, *Manager*
EMP: 6
SQ FT: 59,640
SALES (est): 780K **Privately Held**
SIC: 2679 Paperboard products, converted

Brooklyn - Kings County (G-2761)

(G-2761)
WINTER WATER FACTORY
191 33rd St (11232-2109)
PHONE.....................646 387-3247
Stefanie Lynen, *Owner*
EMP: 6
SALES (est): 250K **Privately Held**
SIC: 2253 Dresses, knit

(G-2762)
WIRELESS GENERATION INC
55 Washington St Ste 900 (11201-1071)
PHONE.....................212 213-8177
Larry Berger, *CEO*
Andrea Reibel, *Vice Pres*
Gary M Holloway Jr,
EMP: 5
SALES (est): 590K **Privately Held**
SIC: 7372 Educational computer software

(G-2763)
WONTON FOOD INC (PA)
220 Moore St 222 (11206-3708)
PHONE.....................718 628-6868
Norman Wong, *CEO*
Ching Sun Wong, *Ch of Bd*
Foo Kam Wong, *Vice Pres*
Ralph Chan, *Plant Mgr*
Ray Jou, *Plant Mgr*
▲ EMP: 160
SQ FT: 55,000
SALES (est): 63MM **Privately Held**
WEB: www.wontonfood.com
SIC: 2099 2052 5149 Noodles, fried (Chinese); cookies; canned goods: fruit, vegetables, seafood, meats, etc.

(G-2764)
WOODWARD/WHITE INC
45 Main St Ste 820 (11201-1076)
PHONE.....................718 509-6082
Bradley Silberberg, *Branch Mgr*
EMP: 10
SALES (corp-wide): 7.6MM **Privately Held**
SIC: 2731 Book publishing
PA: Woodward/White, Inc.
 237 Park Ave Sw
 Aiken SC 29801
 803 648-0300

(G-2765)
WORLD CHEESE CO INC
178 28th St (11232-1604)
PHONE.....................718 965-1700
Leo S Thurm, *President*
Meyer Thurm, *President*
Easter Swartz, *Controller*
Jay Sherer, *Sales Staff*
▼ EMP: 16
SQ FT: 25,000
SALES (est): 4.8MM **Privately Held**
SIC: 2022 Cheese, natural & processed; cheese spreads, dips, pastes & other cheese products

(G-2766)
WORLD JOURNAL LLC
6007 8th Ave (11220-4337)
PHONE.....................718 871-5000
Fax: 718 871-5024
Boby Chou, *CEO*
EMP: 12
SALES (corp-wide): 52.1MM **Privately Held**
WEB: www.wjnews.net
SIC: 2711 Newspapers, publishing & printing
HQ: World Journal Llc
 14107 20th Ave Fl 2
 Whitestone NY 11257
 718 746-8889

(G-2767)
WORLDS FINEST CHOCOLATE INC
73 Exeter St (11235-2703)
PHONE.....................718 332-2442
Edward Opler Jr, *CEO*
EMP: 150
SALES (corp-wide): 35MM **Privately Held**
SIC: 2064 Candy & other confectionery products
HQ: World's Finest Chocolate, Inc.
 4801 S Lawndale Ave
 Chicago IL 60632
 773 847-4600

(G-2768)
WORLDWIDE RESOURCES INC
1908 Avenue O (11230-6721)
PHONE.....................718 760-5000
David Pick, *President*
EMP: 16 EST: 2012
SQ FT: 1,200
SALES (est): 994.3K **Privately Held**
SIC: 3324 Aerospace investment castings, ferrous

(G-2769)
WP LAVORI USA INC
225 Smith St (11231-4719)
PHONE.....................718 855-4295
EMP: 5 **Privately Held**
SIC: 2311 5136 Men's & boys' suits & coats; men's & boys' clothing
HQ: Wp Lavori Usa Inc.
 597 Broadway Fl 2
 New York NY 10012
 212 244-6074

(G-2770)
X F INC
Also Called: Facilities Exchange
349 Arlington Ave (11208-1245)
PHONE.....................212 244-2240
Fax: 718 235-3156
Martin Friedman, *President*
Charles Valva, *Corp Secy*
EMP: 18
SQ FT: 15,000
SALES (est): 1.7MM **Privately Held**
SIC: 2522 7641 1799 5712 Office furniture, except wood; furniture refinishing; counter top installation; office furniture

(G-2771)
XSTATIC PRO INC
Proxcases
901 Essex St (11208-5317)
PHONE.....................718 237-2299
Gabriel Menashe, *Branch Mgr*
EMP: 11
SALES (corp-wide): 1.1MM **Privately Held**
SIC: 3161 Musical instrument cases
PA: Xstatic Pro, Inc.
 901 Essex St
 Brooklyn NY 11208
 718 237-2299

(G-2772)
Y & A TRADING INC
Also Called: Sukkah Center
1365 38th St (11218-3634)
PHONE.....................718 436-6333
Joe Biston, *President*
▲ EMP: 10
SALES (est): 570K **Privately Held**
WEB: www.sukkah.com
SIC: 2394 5999 Canvas & related products; religious goods

(G-2773)
YALOZ MOULD & DIE CO INC
Also Called: Yaloz Mold & Die
239 Java St Fl 2 (11222-1893)
PHONE.....................718 389-1131
Fax: 718 389-5997
Yehuda Leon Yaloz, *President*
EMP: 30
SQ FT: 45,000
SALES (est): 2.6MM **Privately Held**
SIC: 2542 3429 Fixtures, store: except wood; manufactured hardware (general)

(G-2774)
YEPES FINE FURNITURE
72 Van Dam St (11222-3807)
PHONE.....................718 383-0221
Tiberio Yepes, *Owner*
EMP: 20
SALES (est): 1.4MM **Privately Held**
SIC: 2512 5712 Upholstered household furniture; furniture stores

(G-2775)
YOFAH RELIGIOUS ARTICLES INC
2001 57th St Ste 1 (11204-2035)
PHONE.....................718 435-3288
Jacob Leser, *President*
▲ EMP: 13
SQ FT: 2,000
SALES (est): 1.4MM **Privately Held**
SIC: 3911 Rosaries or other small religious articles, precious metal

(G-2776)
YOLAND CORPORATION
253 36th St Unit 2 (11232-2415)
PHONE.....................718 499-4803
Ayal Adler, *President*
Roni Ginat, *General Mgr*
Tal Ganet, *Vice Pres*
ADI Ginat, *Manager*
EMP: 40
SQ FT: 8,000
SALES (est): 4.8MM **Privately Held**
WEB: www.yolandcorp.com
SIC: 2399 Parachutes
PA: D. Yoland Ltd.
 17 Hamasger
 Netanya
 522 456-041

(G-2777)
YORK FUEL INCORPORATED
1760 Flatbush Ave (11210-4203)
PHONE.....................718 951-0202
EMP: 6
SALES (est): 498.5K **Privately Held**
SIC: 2869 Fuels

(G-2778)
YS MARKETING INC
Also Called: Numed Pharmaceuticals
2004 Mcdonald Ave (11223-2819)
PHONE.....................718 778-6080
Joel Silberstein, *President*
Joy Azar, *Administration*
EMP: 10
SALES (est): 5MM **Privately Held**
SIC: 2834 Pharmaceutical preparations

(G-2779)
Z-STUDIOS DSIGN FBRICATION LLC
124 Noll St (11206-4713)
PHONE.....................347 512-4210
Zachary Zaus,
EMP: 5
SQ FT: 2,500
SALES (est): 200K **Privately Held**
SIC: 3446 Architectural metalwork

(G-2780)
ZAM BARRETT DIALOGUE INC
220 36th St Unit 62 (11232-2425)
PHONE.....................646 649-0140
Zam Barrett, *CEO*
EMP: 9
SQ FT: 2,000
SALES (est): 300K **Privately Held**
SIC: 2389 Men's miscellaneous accessories

(G-2781)
ZAN OPTICS PRODUCTS INC
982 39th St (11219-1035)
P.O. Box 110695, Lakewood Rch FL (34211-0009)
PHONE.....................718 435-0533
Fax: 718 435-8215
Walter Mazzanti, *President*
Kathy Mazzanti, *Vice Pres*
EMP: 25 EST: 1933
SQ FT: 10,000
SALES (est): 2MM **Privately Held**
WEB: www.zanenterprises.com
SIC: 2759 3089 2789 2396 Engraving; plastic processing; molding primary plastic; bookbinding & related work; automotive & apparel trimmings

(G-2782)
ZOOMERS INC (PA)
Also Called: Liz Lange
32 33rd St (11232-1901)
PHONE.....................718 369-2656
Fax: 212 244-1372
Gary Jay Schulman, *CEO*
Deborah Schulman, *President*
Wayne Sternberg, *Vice Pres*
▲ EMP: 30
SQ FT: 20,000
SALES (est): 5.1MM **Privately Held**
SIC: 2339 Maternity clothing; sportswear, women's

Brownville
Jefferson County

(G-2783)
FIBERMARK NORTH AMERICA INC
101 Bridge St (13615)
PHONE.....................315 782-5800
Joe Hurd, *Branch Mgr*
Larry Kiefer, *Manager*
EMP: 80
SALES (corp-wide): 887.7MM **Publicly Held**
SIC: 2631 2621 Pressboard; specialty papers
HQ: Fibermark North America
 70 Front St
 West Springfield MA 01089
 413 533-0699

(G-2784)
FLORELLE TISSUE CORPORATION
1 Bridge St (13615-7765)
PHONE.....................647 997-7405
Harry Minas, *President*
▲ EMP: 50
SALES (est): 950K **Privately Held**
SIC: 2676 Towels, napkins & tissue paper products

Buchanan
Westchester County

(G-2785)
CONTINENTAL BUCHANAN LLC
350 Broadway (10511-1000)
PHONE.....................703 480-3800
Ike Preston, *President*
Dennis Romps, *CFO*
Robbe Pearson, *Director*
▲ EMP: 100
SALES (est): 9.6MM **Privately Held**
SIC: 2493 3275 2891 Building board & wallboard, except gypsum; building board, gypsum; sealing compounds for pipe threads or joints

(G-2786)
LAFARGE NORTH AMERICA INC
350 Broadway (10511-1000)
PHONE.....................914 930-3027
Criss Fraley, *Opers-Prdtn-Mfg*
James Tierney, *Sales Mgr*
Christopher Conrad, *Maintence Staff*
EMP: 100
SALES (corp-wide): 23.4B **Privately Held**
SIC: 3241 3275 Cement, hydraulic; gypsum products
HQ: Lafarge North America Inc.
 8700 W Bryn Mawr Ave Ll
 Chicago IL 60631
 703 480-3600

(G-2787)
SILVA CABINETRY INC
12 White St Ste C (10511-1665)
PHONE.....................914 737-7697
Fax: 914 737-7553
Antonio Dasilva, *President*
Xiomara Machabo, *Admin Sec*
EMP: 25
SALES (est): 2.9MM **Privately Held**
SIC: 2434 Wood kitchen cabinets

Buffalo
Erie County

(G-2788)
260 OAK STREET INC
260 Oak St (14203-1626)
PHONE..................................877 852-4676
Glenn Snyder, *Ch of Bd*
EMP: 5
SQ FT: 6,233
SALES (est): 570K **Privately Held**
SIC: 2542 Cabinets: show, display or storage: except wood

(G-2789)
4695 MAIN STREET SNYDER INC
Also Called: Industrial Elec & Automtn
358 Walton Dr (14226-4846)
PHONE..................................716 833-3270
Herb Segiel, *President*
EMP: 6
SALES (corp-wide): 492.2K **Privately Held**
SIC: 3535 7699 Conveyors & conveying equipment; industrial machinery & equipment repair
PA: 4695 Main Street Snyder, Inc
4695 Main St
Amherst NY

(G-2790)
5TH & OCEAN CLOTHING INC
160 Delaware Ave (14202-2404)
PHONE..................................716 604-9000
Daisy Reyes, *Controller*
Robert Fonseca, *Sales Dir*
Luis Leiter Jr, *Mng Member*
Alex A Leiter, *Director*
Esther Fung-Pontiff, *Director*
◆ EMP: 115
SQ FT: 40,000
SALES (est): 12.3MM
SALES (corp-wide): 433.1MM **Privately Held**
WEB: www.5thocean.com
SIC: 2339 Women's & misses' outerwear; women's & misses' accessories
PA: New Era Cap Co., Inc.
160 Delaware Ave
Buffalo NY 14202
716 604-9000

(G-2791)
760 NL HOLDINGS
760 Northland Ave (14211-1041)
PHONE..................................716 821-1391
Fax: 716 821-1380
Timothy R George, *President*
Daryl Zurawski, *General Mgr*
EMP: 30
SQ FT: 20,000
SALES (est): 8.5MM **Privately Held**
WEB: www.nfcf.net
SIC: 3441 Fabricated structural metal

(G-2792)
A J M ENTERPRISES
348 Cayuga Rd (14225-1927)
PHONE..................................716 626-7294
Fax: 716 626-6717
Jarek Chelpinski, *Partner*
EMP: 10
SALES (est): 607.7K **Privately Held**
SIC: 3915 Jewelers' castings

(G-2793)
A-FAB INITIATIVES INC
99 Bud Mil Dr (14206-1801)
PHONE..................................716 877-5257
Edward Raimonde, *President*
◆ EMP: 7
SALES (est): 886.4K **Privately Held**
SIC: 3441 3354 Fabricated structural metal; aluminum extruded products

(G-2794)
ACCENTA INCORPORATED
150 Lawrence Bell Dr # 108 (14221-8403)
PHONE..................................716 565-6262
Ulf Ernetoft, *Owner*
EMP: 5 EST: 2012
SALES (est): 392.4K **Privately Held**
SIC: 3999 Advertising display products

(G-2795)
ACCESS PRODUCTS INC
241 Main St Ste 100 (14203-2703)
PHONE..................................800 679-4022
Kenneth E J Szekely, *President*
Sean Morrison, *Principal*
David Murray, *Vice Pres*
George Kozman, *Controller*
EMP: 6
SALES: 5.3MM **Privately Held**
SIC: 3272 Building materials, except block or brick: concrete

(G-2796)
ACME NIPPLE MFG CO INC
1930 Elmwood Ave (14207-1902)
PHONE..................................716 873-7491
John Hurley, *President*
EMP: 8 EST: 1945
SQ FT: 10,000
SALES (est): 1MM **Privately Held**
SIC: 3321 Pressure pipe & fittings, cast iron

(G-2797)
ADM MILLING CO
250 Ganson St (14203-3048)
P.O. Box 487 (14240-0487)
PHONE..................................716 849-7333
Charles Bayless, *Vice Pres*
Andreas Martin, *Vice Pres*
Brad Heald, *Plant Mgr*
Yvette Ceser, *Manager*
George Siradis, *Manager*
EMP: 75
SALES (corp-wide): 67.7B **Publicly Held**
WEB: www.admmilling.com
SIC: 2041 Flour & other grain mill products
HQ: Adm Milling Co.
8000 W 110th St Ste 300
Overland Park KS 66210
913 491-9400

(G-2798)
ADPRO SPORTS INC
55 Amherst Villa Rd (14225-1432)
PHONE..................................716 854-5116
Ron Raccuia, *President*
Thomas Naples, *Exec VP*
Jeffrey Diebel, *Senior VP*
Paul Schintzius, *Senior VP*
John Fabiano, *Sales Staff*
EMP: 76 EST: 2010
SALES (est): 714K **Privately Held**
SIC: 2329 2339 3949 Men's & boys' sportswear & athletic clothing; women's & misses' athletic clothing & sportswear; team sports equipment

(G-2799)
ADSCO MANUFACTURING CORP
4979 Lake Ave (14219-1398)
PHONE..................................716 827-5450
Fax: 716 827-5460
Gustav Linda, *President*
James Treantis, *Controller*
EMP: 60
SQ FT: 32,000
SALES (est): 14.3MM **Privately Held**
WEB: www.adscomfg.com
SIC: 3441 Expansion joints (structural shapes), iron or steel

(G-2800)
ADVANCED MACHINE DESIGN CO INC
45 Roberts Ave (14206-3130)
PHONE..................................716 826-2000
Fax: 716 826-2394
Heinrich Moelbert, *Ch of Bd*
Reiner Moelbert, *President*
Ursula Moelbert, *Corp Secy*
Trisha Bard, *Admin Sec*
EMP: 30
SQ FT: 102,000
SALES (est): 6.3MM **Privately Held**
WEB: www.amd-co.com
SIC: 3541 3542 8711 3549 Machine tools, metal cutting type; machine tools, metal forming type; presses: hydraulic & pneumatic, mechanical & manual; shearing machines, power; industrial engineers; metalworking machinery; cutlery

(G-2801)
AEP ENVIRONMENTAL LLC
2495 Main St Ste 230 (14214-2156)
PHONE..................................716 446-0739
Lynn Zier, *Mng Member*
Renee Larcom, *Manager*
Anthony Zier, *Admin Sec*
Scott Meacham,
Kenneth Pronti,
EMP: 10
SALES: 500K **Privately Held**
SIC: 3646 2844 5122 5047 Commercial indusl & institutional electric lighting fixtures; toilet preparations; drugs, proprietaries & sundries; medical & hospital equipment; household furnishings

(G-2802)
ALLEN BOAT CO INC
370 Babcock St Rear (14206-2802)
PHONE..................................716 842-0800
Fax: 716 842-0113
Thomas Allen Jr, *President*
Michael Huffman, *Vice Pres*
Sharon Hicok, *Controller*
EMP: 6 EST: 1961
SQ FT: 10,000
SALES (est): 920.2K **Privately Held**
WEB: www.allenboatco.com
SIC: 3732 2394 Sailboats, building & repairing; sails: made from purchased materials

(G-2803)
ALLIED CIRCUITS LLC
22 James E Casey Dr (14206-2367)
PHONE..................................716 551-0285
Carol Schreckengost, *Vice Pres*
Terrence Hayes, *Prdtn Mgr*
Tom Hoch, *Prdtn Mgr*
Chester Szewczyk, *Purch Agent*
Debbie Burgio, *Purchasing*
EMP: 50
SQ FT: 10,400
SALES: 9.6MM **Privately Held**
WEB: www.alliedcircuits.com
SIC: 3613 Panelboards & distribution boards, electric

(G-2804)
ALP STEEL CORP
650 Exchange St (14210-1303)
P.O. Box 1085 (14220-8085)
PHONE..................................716 854-3030
Fax: 716 854-3070
Robert W Waver Jr, *CEO*
Mike Fetes, *Safety Mgr*
Donna G Waver, *CFO*
Bill Miller, *Manager*
Kathy Richards, *Info Tech Mgr*
EMP: 39
SQ FT: 126,000
SALES (est): 11.6MM **Privately Held**
WEB: www.alpsteel.com
SIC: 3441 5051 Fabricated structural metal; building components, structural steel; structural shapes, iron or steel

(G-2805)
AMBIND CORP
Cheektowaga (14225)
P.O. Box 886 (14231-0886)
PHONE..................................716 836-4365
David Spiezer, *President*
EMP: 5
SALES (est): 660.1K **Privately Held**
SIC: 2241 Bindings, textile

(G-2806)
AMERICAN CITY BUS JOURNALS INC
465 Main St Ste 100 (14203-1717)
PHONE..................................716 541-1654
Jack Connors, *Principal*
Bo Sunshine, *Marketing Staff*
Donna Collins, *Senior Editor*
Sean Connors, *Graphic Designe*
EMP: 32
SALES (corp-wide): 322.5MM **Privately Held**
SIC: 2711 Newspapers: publishing only, not printed on site
HQ: American City Business Journals, Inc.
120 W Morehead St Ste 400
Charlotte NC 28202
704 973-1000

(G-2807)
AMERICAN DOUGLAS METALS INC
Also Called: Afab Initiative
99 Bud Mil Dr (14206-1801)
PHONE..................................716 856-3170
Edward Raimonde, *CEO*
Kevin Blake, *Branch Mgr*
EMP: 12
SQ FT: 29,700
SALES (corp-wide): 16.7MM **Privately Held**
WEB: www.americandouglasmetals.com
SIC: 1099 3353 3291 Aluminum ore mining; aluminum sheet, plate & foil; abrasive products
PA: American Douglas Metals, Inc.
783 Thorpe Rd
Orlando FL 32824
407 855-6590

(G-2808)
AMERICAN IMAGES INC
25 Imson St (14210-1615)
PHONE..................................716 825-8888
Fax: 716 821-7991
Steve Wojtkowiak, *President*
EMP: 10
SALES (est): 1.2MM **Privately Held**
SIC: 2397 Schiffli machine embroideries

(G-2809)
AMHERST MEDIA INC
175 Rano St Ste 200 (14207-2176)
P.O. Box 538 (14213-0538)
PHONE..................................716 874-4450
Fax: 716 874-4508
Craig Alesse, *President*
Kate Neaverth, *Sales Mgr*
Barbara Lynch-Johnt, *Assoc Editor*
EMP: 5
SALES (est): 705K **Privately Held**
WEB: www.amherstmedia.com
SIC: 2731 7812 Books: publishing only; video production

(G-2810)
AMHERST SYSTEMS INC (DH)
1740 Wehrle Dr (14221-7032)
PHONE..................................716 631-0610
Jeffrey D Palombo, *Ch of Bd*
John Stanfill, *President*
Glen Sharpe, *Managing Dir*
Andy Ryan, *Facilities Dir*
Richard Keenen, *Engineer*
EMP: 169
SQ FT: 150,000
SALES (est): 25.6MM **Publicly Held**
WEB: www.amherst-systems.com
SIC: 3812 8731 7373 Search & navigation equipment; radar systems & equipment; commercial physical research; value-added resellers, computer systems
HQ: Northrop Grumman Systems Corporation
2980 Fairview Park Dr
Falls Church VA 22042
703 280-2900

(G-2811)
AMSCO INC
925 Bailey Ave (14206-2338)
PHONE..................................716 823-4213
Norm Brodfuhrersin, *President*
Jack Kraus, *Vice Pres*
Maria Opoka, *Purchasing*
Linda Nowak, *Treasurer*
EMP: 16
SQ FT: 18,000
SALES (est): 1.3MM **Privately Held**
SIC: 3544 3444 Jigs & fixtures; sheet metalwork

(G-2812)
ANNESE & ASSOCIATES INC
500 Corporate Pkwy # 106 (14226-1263)
PHONE..................................716 972-0076
Ray Apy, *Branch Mgr*
EMP: 7
SALES (corp-wide): 54.9MM **Privately Held**
SIC: 3577 Data conversion equipment, media-to-media: computer

Buffalo - Erie County (G-2813) — GEOGRAPHIC SECTION

PA: Annese & Associates, Inc.
747 Pierce Rd Ste 2
Clifton Park NY 12065
518 877-7058

(G-2813)
ANTIQUES & COLLECTIBLE AUTOS
35 Dole St (14210-1603)
PHONE..................716 825-3990
Joseph Trombley, *President*
EMP: 3
SALES: 1.6MM **Privately Held**
WEB: www.acrods.com
SIC: 3711 Automobile bodies, passenger car, not including engine, etc.

(G-2814)
ANTONICELLI VITO RACE CAR
3883 Broadway St (14227-1105)
PHONE..................716 684-2205
Vito Antonicelli, *Owner*
EMP: 5
SQ FT: 6,000
SALES (est): 75K **Privately Held**
SIC: 3711 Motor vehicles & car bodies

(G-2815)
API HEAT TRANSF THERMASYS CORP (DH)
2777 Walden Ave (14225-4788)
PHONE..................716 901-8504
Joseph Cordosi, *President*
Ross Bratlee, *CFO*
Jeffrey Lennox, *Admin Sec*
◆ EMP: 35 EST: 2014
SQ FT: 6,000
SALES: 400MM
SALES (corp-wide): 411.7MM **Privately Held**
SIC: 3567 Heating units & devices, industrial: electric
HQ: Api Heat Transfer Inc.
2777 Walden Ave Ste 1
Buffalo NY 14225
716 684-6700

(G-2816)
API HEAT TRANSFER COMPANY (PA)
2777 Walden Ave Ste 1 (14225-4788)
PHONE..................716 684-6700
Joseph Cordosi, *President*
EMP: 9 EST: 2005
SALES: 411.7MM **Privately Held**
SIC: 3443 Heat exchangers: coolers (after, inter), condensers, etc.

(G-2817)
APPLE IMPRINTS APPAREL INC
2336 Bailey Ave (14211-1738)
PHONE..................716 893-1130
Fax: 716 893-7701
Jack Lipomi, *President*
Kevin Lipomi, *Vice Pres*
EMP: 22 EST: 1981
SQ FT: 15,000
SALES (est): 2.8MM **Privately Held**
WEB: www.appleimprints.com
SIC: 2396 7319 Screen printing on fabric articles; display advertising service

(G-2818)
APPLINCE INSTALLATION SVC CORP (PA)
3190 Genesee St (14225-2607)
PHONE..................716 884-7425
Fax: 716 884-0410
Paul Glowlacki, *CEO*
Wayne Stoutner, *President*
Kim Carney, *Warehouse Mgr*
Andrew Glowacki, *Manager*
Dave Glowacki, *Manager*
EMP: 24
SALES (est): 13.4MM **Privately Held**
SIC: 3631 5085 7699 Household cooking equipment; industrial supplies; restaurant equipment repair

(G-2819)
ARCHER-DANIELS-MIDLAND COMPANY
Also Called: ADM
250 Ganson St (14203-3048)
P.O. Box 487 (14240-0487)
PHONE..................716 849-7333
Brad Heald, *Branch Mgr*
David Brick, *Director*
EMP: 100
SALES (corp-wide): 67.7B **Publicly Held**
WEB: www.admworld.com
SIC: 2048 Prepared feeds
PA: Archer-Daniels-Midland Company
77 W Wacker Dr Ste 4600
Chicago IL 60601
312 634-8100

(G-2820)
ARTVOICE
810 Main St (14202-1501)
P.O. Box 695 (14205-0695)
PHONE..................716 881-6604
Fax: 716 881-6682
Jamie Moses, *Owner*
Agathi Georgiou, *Advt Staff*
Deborah Allis, *Manager*
EMP: 15
SQ FT: 3,000
SALES (est): 653.5K **Privately Held**
WEB: www.artvoice.com
SIC: 2711 Newspapers

(G-2821)
ATECH-SEH METAL FABRICATOR
330 Greene St (14206-1025)
PHONE..................716 895-8888
EMP: 20
SALES (est): 1.7MM **Privately Held**
SIC: 3499 Fabricated metal products

(G-2822)
AURUBIS BUFFALO INC
600 Military Rd (14207-1750)
PHONE..................716 879-6700
Raymond Mercer, *President*
EMP: 10
SALES (corp-wide): 12.1B **Privately Held**
SIC: 3351 Copper rolling & drawing
HQ: Aurubis Buffalo, Inc.
70 Sayre St
Buffalo NY 14207
716 879-6700

(G-2823)
AURUBIS BUFFALO INC (HQ)
70 Sayre St (14207-2225)
P.O. Box 981 (14240-0981)
PHONE..................716 879-6700
Fax: 716 879-6961
Raymond Mercer, *President*
Tod Heusner, *Vice Pres*
Peter Pavlovich, *Opers Staff*
Greg Thiesen, *Engineer*
Yumin Wang, *Engineer*
▲ EMP: 277
SQ FT: 1,214,500
SALES (est): 219MM
SALES (corp-wide): 12.1B **Privately Held**
WEB: www.luvata.com
SIC: 3351 Copper rolling & drawing
PA: Aurubis Ag
Hovestr. 50
Hamburg 20539
407 883-0

(G-2824)
AUSTIN AIR SYSTEMS LIMITED
500 Elk St (14210-2208)
PHONE..................716 856-3700
Fax: 716 856-6023
Richard Taylor, *President*
Joyce Taylor, *Vice Pres*
Brian Popovich, *Prdtn Mgr*
Jason Armstrong, *Mfg Staff*
Lauren Bert, *Sales Mgr*
▲ EMP: 60
SQ FT: 173,000
SALES (est): 17.3MM **Privately Held**
SIC: 3564 Air purification equipment

(G-2825)
AVALON COPY CENTERS AMER INC
Also Called: Avalon Document Services
741 Main St (14203-1321)
PHONE..................716 995-7777
Hilary Kleppe, *Branch Mgr*
EMP: 25
SALES (corp-wide): 23.5MM **Privately Held**
SIC: 2741 7375 7336 7334 Art copy: publishing & printing; information retrieval services; commercial art & graphic design; photocopying & duplicating services
PA: Avalon Copy Centers Of America, Inc.
901 N State St
Syracuse NY 13208
315 471-3333

(G-2826)
AVANTI ADVANCED MFG CORP
673 Ontario St (14207-1614)
PHONE..................716 541-8945
Jim WEI, *Ch of Bd*
▲ EMP: 9 EST: 2013
SALES (est): 736.9K **Privately Held**
SIC: 3999 Atomizers, toiletry

(G-2827)
AVF INC (PA)
2775 Broadway St Ste 200 (14227-1043)
PHONE..................951 360-7111
Jerry Jacobs, *President*
Brenda Gaines, *Sales Mgr*
◆ EMP: 14
SALES (est): 3.6MM **Privately Held**
WEB: www.avf.com
SIC: 2542 Partitions & fixtures, except wood

(G-2828)
AVON PRODUCTS INC
433 Thorncliff Rd (14223-1128)
PHONE..................716 572-4842
Kathy Gleason, *Principal*
EMP: 12
SALES (corp-wide): 6.1B **Publicly Held**
SIC: 2844 Toilet preparations
PA: Avon Products, Inc.
777 3rd Ave
New York NY 10017
212 282-5000

(G-2829)
B & K COMPONENTS LTD
2100 Old Union Rd (14227-2725)
PHONE..................323 776-4277
Fax: 716 656-1241
John L Beyer III, *President*
Dr Charles A Marchetta, *Admin Sec*
▲ EMP: 70 EST: 1981
SQ FT: 18,500
SALES (est): 9.6MM **Privately Held**
WEB: www.bkcomp.com
SIC: 3651 Audio electronic systems

(G-2830)
B & P JAYS INC
Also Called: Mecca Printing
19 N Hill Dr (14224-2582)
PHONE..................716 668-8408
Betty Mecca, *President*
Paul Mecca, *Vice Pres*
EMP: 5
SQ FT: 1,400
SALES: 200K **Privately Held**
SIC: 2752 Commercial printing, offset

(G-2831)
BAK USA TECHNOLOGIES CORP
425 Michigan Ave Ste 4 (14203-2240)
PHONE..................716 248-2704
J P Folsgaard Bak, *Ch of Bd*
Ulla Bak, *President*
Alan Jankowski, *Controller*
EMP: 32
SQ FT: 15,000
SALES (est): 1.5MM **Privately Held**
SIC: 2678 Stationery products

(G-2832)
BARRON GAMES INTL CO LLC
84 Aero Dr Ste 5 (14225-1435)
PHONE..................716 630-0054
Gregory Bacorn, *President*
Mike Tomashoff, *General Mgr*
Anna Zykina, *Vice Pres*
Alyssa Chawgo, *Office Mgr*
▲ EMP: 11
SQ FT: 4,500
SALES: 2MM **Privately Held**
WEB: www.barrongames.com/
SIC: 3944 5092 Electronic games & toys; video games

(G-2833)
BATAVIA PRECISION GLASS LLC
231 Currier Ave (14212-2262)
PHONE..................585 343-6050
Steve Barber,
EMP: 6
SQ FT: 9,000
SALES: 63K **Privately Held**
SIC: 3231 8748 Leaded glass; business consulting

(G-2834)
BATES JACKSON ENGRAVING CO INC
17 Elm St 21 (14203-2605)
PHONE..................716 854-3000
Fax: 716 847-1965
Rozanne Flammer, *CEO*
Edward Flammer, *President*
Gregory Flammer, *Controller*
EMP: 35
SQ FT: 19,000
SALES (est): 3.8MM **Privately Held**
SIC: 2759 2752 2791 Engraving; commercial printing, offset; typesetting

(G-2835)
BATTENFELD-AMERICAN INC
1575 Clinton St (14206-3064)
P.O. Box 728, North Tonawanda (14120-0728)
PHONE..................716 822-8410
Fax: 716 822-8410
John A Bellanti Sr, *CEO*
Barbara A Bellanti, *Ch of Bd*
Barbara Bellanti, *President*
Debbi Carpenter, *Vice Pres*
Sara Dumont, *Manager*
▼ EMP: 38
SQ FT: 110,000
SALES (est): 10.7MM
SALES (corp-wide): 63.2MM **Privately Held**
WEB: www.battenfeld-grease.com
SIC: 2992 Oils & greases, blending & compounding
PA: Battenfeld Management, Inc.
1174 Erie Ave
North Tonawanda NY 14120
716 695-2100

(G-2836)
BEAR METAL WORKS INC
144 Milton St (14210-1644)
P.O. Box 2528 (14240-2528)
PHONE..................716 824-4350
Barrett E Price, *Ch of Bd*
January Delaney, *Office Mgr*
Catherine Jasinski, *Admin Sec*
EMP: 10 EST: 1999
SALES (est): 2.1MM **Privately Held**
SIC: 3441 Fabricated structural metal

(G-2837)
BELRIX INDUSTRIES INC
3590 Jeffrey Blvd (14219-2390)
PHONE..................716 821-5964
Gail Maurer, *President*
Ann Skummer, *Manager*
EMP: 6
SQ FT: 15,000
SALES (est): 1.1MM **Privately Held**
WEB: www.belrix.com
SIC: 3469 Machine parts, stamped or pressed metal

(G-2838)
BEMCO OF WESTERN NY INC
122 Roberts Ave (14206-3120)
PHONE..................716 823-8400
Fax: 716 823-8441
Barry E Medwin, *President*
Paul Kunkes, *Vice Pres*
EMP: 6

▲ = Import ▼ = Export
◆ = Import/Export

GEOGRAPHIC SECTION

Buffalo - Erie County (G-2862)

SQ FT: 60,000
SALES (est): 780K **Privately Held**
SIC: 3625 Motor control accessories, including overload relays

(G-2839)
BENTON ANNOUNCEMENTS INC
3006 Bailey Ave 3010 (14215-2898)
PHONE.................................716 836-4100
Fax: 716 836-4161
Philip J Guerra, *President*
Michael J Guerra Jr, *Vice Pres*
EMP: 10 EST: 1935
SQ FT: 13,500
SALES (est): 920K **Privately Held**
SIC: 2754 5719 5944 Commercial printing, gravure; invitations: gravure printing; stationery: gravure printing; glassware; china; silverware

(G-2840)
BETTER WIRE PRODUCTS INC
1255 Niagara St (14213-1591)
PHONE.................................716 883-3377
Fax: 716 883-5075
William Breeser, *President*
Lynn Youngman, *Sales Associate*
Betty Breeser, *Manager*
Maria Dinezza, *Manager*
Dennis McCarthy, *Data Proc Exec*
▲ EMP: 35 EST: 1952
SQ FT: 30,000
SALES (est): 8.7MM **Privately Held**
SIC: 3496 Miscellaneous fabricated wire products

(G-2841)
BFG MANUFACTURING SERVICES INC
3949 Jeffrey Blvd (14219-2334)
P.O. Box 825, Hamburg (14075-0825)
PHONE.................................716 362-0888
Fax: 716 362-0835
Minta Marie, *Branch Mgr*
Joan Benzinger, *Manager*
EMP: 27
SALES (corp-wide): 12.6MM **Privately Held**
WEB: www.bfgelectroplating.com
SIC: 3471 Electroplating of metals or formed products
PA: Bfg Manufacturing Services, Inc.
   701 Martha St
   Punxsutawney PA 15767
   814 938-9164

(G-2842)
BIG HEART PET BRANDS
Del Monte Foods
243 Urban St (14211-1532)
PHONE.................................716 891-6566
Greg Pastore, *General Mgr*
Les Wagner, *Enginr/R&D Mgr*
Terry Wolcott, *Controller*
Joyce Lenda, *Human Res Dir*
Don Hartman, *Manager*
EMP: 36
SALES (corp-wide): 7.8B **Publicly Held**
WEB: www.kraftfoods.com
SIC: 2066 Chocolate & cocoa products
HQ: Big Heart Pet Brands
   1 Maritime Plz Fl 2
   San Francisco CA 94111
   415 247-3000

(G-2843)
BLACK & DECKER (US) INC
881 W Delavan Ave (14209-1297)
PHONE.................................716 884-6220
Mike Eaton, *Manager*
EMP: 5
SQ FT: 4,112
SALES (corp-wide): 11.1B **Publicly Held**
WEB: www.dewalt.com
SIC: 3546 Power-driven handtools
HQ: Black & Decker (U.S.) Inc.
   1000 Stanley Dr
   New Britain CT 06053
   410 716-3900

(G-2844)
BMC LLC
3155 Broadway St (14227-1034)
PHONE.................................716 681-7755
Richard Neal, *President*
▲ EMP: 24

SQ FT: 4,500
SALES (est): 2.5MM **Privately Held**
SIC: 3084 Plastics pipe

(G-2845)
BRYANT MACHINE & DEVELOPMENT
63 Stanley St (14206-1017)
PHONE.................................716 894-8282
Michael Denz, *President*
Matthew Bryant Jr, *Corp Secy*
Cindy White, *Office Mgr*
EMP: 10
SQ FT: 8,000
SALES (est): 200K **Privately Held**
SIC: 3599 Machine shop, jobbing & repair

(G-2846)
BRYANT MACHINE CO INC
63 Stanley St (14206-1017)
PHONE.................................716 894-8282
Fax: 716 894-8283
Kip Laviolette, *President*
Erica Laviolette, *Office Mgr*
EMP: 10 EST: 1946
SQ FT: 5,000
SALES (est): 1.1MM **Privately Held**
WEB: www.bryantmachine.com
SIC: 3469 Machine parts, stamped or pressed metal

(G-2847)
BRYANT MANUFACTURING WNY INC
63 Stanley St (14206-1017)
PHONE.................................716 894-8282
Kip A Laviolette, *CEO*
EMP: 6
SALES (est): 950K **Privately Held**
SIC: 3312 Stainless steel

(G-2848)
BUFFALO ARMORY LLC
1050 Military Rd (14217-2528)
PHONE.................................716 935-6346
John Bastiste, *President*
Brent Nicholson, *Manager*
EMP: 5
SALES (est): 815.6K **Privately Held**
SIC: 3398 Metal heat treating

(G-2849)
BUFFALO BLENDS INC (PA)
1400 William St (14206-1813)
PHONE.................................716 825-4422
Fax: 716 825-1505
Timothy Sheehy, *President*
Kevin Prise, *Corp Secy*
Liz Hichcock, *Manager*
▲ EMP: 22 EST: 1999
SQ FT: 35,000
SALES (est): 3.2MM **Privately Held**
WEB: www.buffaloblends.com
SIC: 2087 Beverage bases, concentrates, syrups, powders & mixes

(G-2850)
BUFFALO CRUSHED STONE INC (HQ)
500 Como Park Blvd (14227-1606)
PHONE.................................716 826-7310
Fax: 716 566-9614
Steven B Detwiler, *Ch of Bd*
Gary Blum, *Vice Pres*
David Firmstone, *Vice Pres*
Jamie Hypnarowski, *Vice Pres*
Richard Mirabelli, *Vice Pres*
EMP: 40
SQ FT: 25,000
SALES (est): 45.4MM
SALES (corp-wide): 651.9MM **Privately Held**
SIC: 3272 Concrete products
PA: New Enterprise Stone & Lime Co., Inc.
   3912 Brumbaugh Rd
   New Enterprise PA 16664
   814 224-6883

(G-2851)
BUFFALO FINISHING WORKS INC
1255 Niagara St (14213-1501)
PHONE.................................716 893-5266
John Warchocki, *President*
Ulrike Warchocki, *Vice Pres*

Duane Warchocki, *Manager*
EMP: 5
SQ FT: 7,000
SALES (est): 250K **Privately Held**
SIC: 3479 Painting of metal products; enameling, including porcelain, of metal products

(G-2852)
BUFFALO GAMES INC
Also Called: Buffalo Games & Puzzles
220 James E Casey Dr (14206-2362)
PHONE.................................716 827-8393
Fax: 716 827-8163
Paul A Dedrick, *CEO*
Jennifer Mengay, *President*
Nagendra Raina, *General Mgr*
Eden Dedrick, *Vice Pres*
Eden Scott-Dedrick, *Vice Pres*
▲ EMP: 70
SQ FT: 88,000
SALES (est): 11.6MM **Privately Held**
WEB: www.buffalogames.com
SIC: 3944 Puzzles

(G-2853)
BUFFALO LAW JOURNAL
465 Main St Ste 100 (14203-1717)
PHONE.................................716 541-1600
Fax: 716 854-3394
Kim Schaus, *General Mgr*
EMP: 6
SALES (est): 310K **Privately Held**
WEB: www.buffalolawjournal.com
SIC: 2711 Newspapers: publishing only, not printed on site

(G-2854)
BUFFALO LINING & FABRICATING
73 Gillette Ave (14214-2702)
PHONE.................................716 883-6500
Bruce F Meyers, *President*
James Meyers, *Vice Pres*
Robert Murray, *Vice Pres*
Charlotte Boorman, *Office Mgr*
EMP: 6 EST: 1956
SQ FT: 12,000
SALES (est): 688.4K **Privately Held**
SIC: 3069 Molded rubber products

(G-2855)
BUFFALO METAL CASTING CO INC
1875 Elmwood Ave (14207-1997)
PHONE.................................716 874-6211
Fax: 716 874-6213
John Klodzinski, *President*
Justin Klodzinski, *General Mgr*
Chris Chadbourne, *Supervisor*
Jennifer Patterson, *Admin Mgr*
EMP: 40
SQ FT: 80,000
SALES (est): 7.7MM **Privately Held**
WEB: www.buffalometalcasting.com
SIC: 3369 Castings, except die-castings, precision

(G-2856)
BUFFALO METAL FINISHING CO (PA)
135 Dart St (14213-1087)
P.O. Box 1012 (14213-7012)
PHONE.................................716 883-2751
Fax: 716 883-6177
Frank Bonare, *President*
EMP: 8 EST: 1941
SQ FT: 11,000
SALES (est): 500K **Privately Held**
SIC: 3471 3479 Plating of metals or formed products; polishing, metals or formed products; anodizing (plating) of metals or formed products; painting of metal products

(G-2857)
BUFFALO NEWS INC
1 News Plz (14203-2994)
P.O. Box 100 (14240-0100)
PHONE.................................716 849-4401
Fax: 716 849-3409
Stanford Lipsey, *CEO*
Karen Colville, *President*
Warren Colville, *President*
Bruce Andriatch, *Editor*

Mike Connelly, *Editor*
EMP: 900
SQ FT: 1,000
SALES: 176.1K
SALES (corp-wide): 210.8B **Publicly Held**
WEB: www.berkshirehathaway.com
SIC: 2711 Newspapers, publishing & printing
PA: Berkshire Hathaway Inc.
   3555 Farnam St Ste 1440
   Omaha NE 68131
   402 346-1400

(G-2858)
BUFFALO NEWSPRESS INC
200 Broadway St (14204-1439)
P.O. Box 648 (14240-0648)
PHONE.................................716 852-1600
Fax: 716 856-2017
Warren T Colville, *President*
Mark Korzelius, *President*
Michael A Kibler, *Chairman*
Joan Holzman, *Vice Pres*
Marcus Regoord, *Vice Pres*
EMP: 120
SQ FT: 80,000
SALES (est): 22.6MM **Privately Held**
WEB: www.buffalonewspress.com
SIC: 2759 Newspapers: printing; advertising literature: printing

(G-2859)
BUFFALO SPREE PUBLISHING INC (PA)
1738 Elmwood Ave Ste 103 (14207-2465)
PHONE.................................716 783-9119
Laurence Levite, *CEO*
Lucy Cieply, *Business Mgr*
Theresa Clair, *CFO*
Robin Kurss, *Accounts Exec*
Betty Tata, *Accounts Exec*
EMP: 25
SQ FT: 10,000
SALES (est): 2.3MM **Privately Held**
WEB: www.buffalospree.com
SIC: 2721 Magazines: publishing only, not printed on site

(G-2860)
BUFFALO STANDARD PRINTING CORP
Also Called: Am-Pol Eagle
3620 Harlem Rd Ste 5 (14215-2042)
PHONE.................................716 835-9454
Fax: 716 835-9457
Irene Harzewski, *President*
EMP: 10 EST: 1958
SALES (est): 752.5K **Privately Held**
SIC: 2711 Commercial printing & newspaper publishing combined; job printing & newspaper publishing combined

(G-2861)
BUFLOVAK LLC (PA)
750 E Ferry St (14211-1106)
PHONE.................................716 895-2100
Mike Durusky, *Plant Mgr*
Tami McNamara, *Materials Mgr*
Maliek Likely, *Engineer*
Dave Bielecki, *Controller*
Duncan Hemink, *Human Res Mgr*
▼ EMP: 28
SQ FT: 225,000
SALES (est): 10.8MM **Privately Held**
WEB: www.buffalotechnologies.com
SIC: 3556 5084 3567 3443 Food products machinery; industrial machinery & equipment; industrial furnaces & ovens; fabricated plate work (boiler shop)

(G-2862)
BUSINESS FIRST OF NEW YORK (DH)
465 Main St Ste 100 (14203-1793)
PHONE.................................716 854-5822
Jack Connors, *President*
Jeff Wright, *Editor*
Shelley Rohauer, *Advt Staff*
Larry Ponzi, *Manager*
Maureen R Twist, *Manager*
EMP: 44
SQ FT: 10,000

Buffalo - Erie County (G-2863) — GEOGRAPHIC SECTION

SALES (est): 4.1MM
SALES (corp-wide): 322.5MM **Privately Held**
SIC: 2711 Newspapers: publishing only, not printed on site
HQ: American City Business Journals, Inc.
120 W Morehead St Ste 400
Charlotte NC 28202
704 973-1000

(G-2863)
BUXTON MACHINE AND TOOL CO INC
2181 Elmwood Ave (14216-1002)
PHONE....................716 876-2312
Fax: 716 876-0161
James P Hettrick, *President*
Mildred Di Luca, *Admin Sec*
EMP: 12 EST: 1984
SQ FT: 12,000
SALES (est): 1.8MM **Privately Held**
SIC: 3599 Machine shop, jobbing & repair

(G-2864)
CALSPAN CORPORATION (PA)
4455 Genesee St (14225-1955)
P.O. Box 400 (14225)
PHONE....................716 631-6955
Fax: 716 631-6969
Louis H Knotts, *President*
Derek Garner, *General Mgr*
Peter Sauer, *COO*
Thomas Pleban, *Exec VP*
John Yurtchuk, *Exec VP*
▲ EMP: 129
SQ FT: 170,200
SALES (est): 41.1MM **Privately Held**
WEB: www.windtunnel.com
SIC: 3721 Research & development on aircraft by the manufacturer

(G-2865)
CAMELLIA GENERAL PROVISION CO
Also Called: Camellia Foods
1333 Genesee St (14211-2227)
PHONE....................716 893-5352
Fax: 716 895-7713
Peter J Cichocki, *Ch of Bd*
Edmund J Cichocki Jr, *President*
Eric Cichocki, *Vice Pres*
Patrick Cichocki, *Vice Pres*
Joell Gilley, *Manager*
EMP: 46 EST: 1937
SQ FT: 40,000
SALES: 10MM **Privately Held**
WEB: www.camelliafoods.com
SIC: 2013 5147 Sausage casings, natural; bologna from purchased meat; smoked meats from purchased meat; meats, fresh; meats, cured or smoked

(G-2866)
CANTINAFOODS INC
258 Amherst St (14207-2808)
PHONE....................716 602-3536
Sayed Elkhoury, *President*
Danny Elkhoury, *Director*
EMP: 5 EST: 2011
SQ FT: 3,000
SALES (est): 447.9K **Privately Held**
SIC: 3556 Meat processing machinery

(G-2867)
CARAUSTAR INDUSTRIES INC
25 Dewberry Ln (14227-2709)
PHONE....................716 874-0391
Lynn Ramsey, *Branch Mgr*
EMP: 8
SALES (corp-wide): 1.6B **Privately Held**
SIC: 2655 Tubes, fiber or paper: made from purchased material
PA: Caraustar Industries, Inc.
5000 Astell Pwdr Sprng Rd
Austell GA 30106
770 948-3101

(G-2868)
CCL LABEL INC
685 Howard St (14206-2210)
P.O. Box 550 (14240-0550)
PHONE....................716 852-2155
Fax: 716 852-2175
Joe Langan, *Plant Mgr*
Matt Piejda, *Buyer*
Blaine Jackson, *Engineer*
Peter Lowry, *Engineer*
Robert Wilson, *Design Engr*
EMP: 150
SQ FT: 25,883
SALES (corp-wide): 188.4K **Privately Held**
WEB: www.avery.com
SIC: 2672 2671 Coated & laminated paper; packaging paper & plastics film, coated & laminated
HQ: Ccl Label, Inc.
161 Worcester Rd Ste 504
Framingham MA 01701
508 872-4511

(G-2869)
CENO TECHNOLOGIES INC
1234 Delaware Ave (14209-1430)
PHONE....................716 885-5050
Scott Patrick, *President*
Alan Rowdon, *Vice Pres*
EMP: 5
SALES (est): 661.9K **Privately Held**
SIC: 3531 Construction machinery

(G-2870)
CERTAINTEED CORPORATION
Pipe and Plastic Div
231 Ship Canal Pkwy (14218-1026)
PHONE....................716 827-7560
Bob Kearful, *Branch Mgr*
Derrick Campbell, *Manager*
Tom Flaws, *Manager*
David Sence, *Manager*
Dave Senne, *Manager*
EMP: 400
SALES (corp-wide): 207.6MM **Privately Held**
WEB: www.certainteed.net
SIC: 3089 Extruded finished plastic products
HQ: Certainteed Corporation
20 Moores Rd
Malvern PA 19355
610 341-7000

(G-2871)
CHOCO PEANUTS INC
2495 Main St Ste 524 (14214-2135)
PHONE....................716 998-2353
EMP: 5
SALES (corp-wide): 15.5K **Privately Held**
SIC: 2066 2068 Chocolate coatings & syrup; nuts: dried, dehydrated, salted or roasted
HQ: Choco Peanuts, Inc.
11239 Ferina St
Norwalk CA 90650
647 786-7531

(G-2872)
CHOCOLATE DELIVERY SYSTEMS INC (PA)
Also Called: Tomric Plastic
85 River Rock Dr Ste 202 (14207-2170)
PHONE....................716 854-6050
Timothy M Thill, *Ch of Bd*
Anne Rosa, *Vice Pres*
Melissa Benzee, *Sales Mgr*
Thomas Elsinghorst, *Admin Sec*
▲ EMP: 55 EST: 1962
SQ FT: 30,000
SALES (est): 21.8MM **Privately Held**
WEB: www.tomric.com
SIC: 3089 5145 3086 Molding primary plastic; candy; packaging & shipping materials, foamed plastic

(G-2873)
CHOCOMAKER INC
85 River Rock Dr Ste 202 (14207-2170)
PHONE....................716 877-3146
Timothy Thill, *President*
Anne Rosa, *Vice Pres*
▲ EMP: 6
SALES (est): 249.8K
SALES (corp-wide): 21.8MM **Privately Held**
SIC: 2064 Candy bars, including chocolate covered bars
PA: Chocolate Delivery Systems, Inc.
85 River Rock Dr Ste 202
Buffalo NY 14207
716 854-6050

(G-2874)
CILYOX INC
Also Called: New Rosen Printing
345 Broadway St (14204-1541)
PHONE....................716 853-3809
Fax: 716 853-1075
Michael Cimato, *President*
Bryan Knox, *Vice Pres*
EMP: 10 EST: 1963
SQ FT: 43,000
SALES (est): 1.3MM **Privately Held**
SIC: 2752 Commercial printing, offset

(G-2875)
CLEARVIEW SOCIAL INC
640 Ellicott St Ste 108 (14203-1252)
PHONE....................801 414-7675
Adrian Dayton, *CEO*
EMP: 5 EST: 2013
SALES (est): 141.8K **Privately Held**
SIC: 7372 Business oriented computer software

(G-2876)
CLEVELAND BIOLABS INC (PA)
73 High St (14203-1149)
PHONE....................716 849-6810
Fax: 716 849-6820
Yakov Kogan, *CEO*
Debra Bowes, *President*
C Neil Lyons, *CFO*
Christopher Zosh, *Accountant*
John Szydlo, *Finance*
EMP: 33
SQ FT: 32,000
SALES (est): 2.7MM **Publicly Held**
WEB: www.cbiolabs.com
SIC: 2834 Pharmaceutical preparations

(G-2877)
COBEY INC (PA)
1 Ship Canal Pkwy (14218-1024)
PHONE....................716 362-9550
Fax: 716 362-9551
John J Obey, *Ch of Bd*
Robert J Castle, *Vice Pres*
Neil Ackerman, *Project Mgr*
Jonathan Gesicki, *Project Mgr*
Donna Hagerty, *Project Mgr*
▲ EMP: 99
SQ FT: 117,000
SALES (est): 26.7MM **Privately Held**
WEB: www.cobey.com
SIC: 3498 Fabricated pipe & fittings

(G-2878)
COGNIGEN CORPORATION
Also Called: Cognigen Acquisition
1780 Wehrle Dr Ste 110 (14221-7000)
PHONE....................716 633-3463
Ted Grasela, *President*
Cynthia Walawander, *Exec VP*
Jill Fiedler-Kelly, *Vice Pres*
Rebecca Humphrey, *Manager*
Andrew Rokitka, *Manager*
EMP: 65
SALES (est): 8.8MM **Publicly Held**
SIC: 2834 8999 Druggists' preparations (pharmaceuticals); scientific consulting
PA: Simulations Plus, Inc.
42505 10th St W Ste 103
Lancaster CA 93534

(G-2879)
COHENS BAKERY INC
Also Called: Al Cohens Famous Rye Bread Bky
1132 Broadway St (14212-1502)
PHONE....................716 892-8149
Fax: 716 892-8150
Mark Didomenico, *President*
John J Blando, *Vice Pres*
Gary East Abrook, *Accountant*
Mary Russo, *Admin Asst*
EMP: 45
SQ FT: 25,000
SALES (est): 5.7MM **Privately Held**
SIC: 2045 5149 2051 Doughs & batters: from purchased flour; groceries & related products; bread, cake & related products

(G-2880)
COLAD GROUP LLC (HQ)
693 Seneca St 5 (14210-1324)
PHONE....................716 961-1776
Fax: 716 961-1753
Judy Freitas, *Production*
Wayne Coverley, *Controller*
F Martin Anson, *Mng Member*
Cindy Flonrino, *Data Proc Dir*
J Todd Anson,
EMP: 81
SALES (est): 10.7MM
SALES (corp-wide): 20.5MM **Privately Held**
WEB: www.colad.com
SIC: 2782 2671 2752 2759 Blankbooks & looseleaf binders; packaging paper & plastics film, coated & laminated; commercial printing, lithographic; commercial printing; signs & advertising specialties
PA: Bindagraphics, Inc.
2701 Wilmarco Ave
Baltimore MD 21223
410 362-7200

(G-2881)
COMET FLASHER INC (PA)
1 Babcock St (14210-2253)
PHONE....................716 821-9595
James Casey, *President*
Jamie Rybij, *Admin Sec*
EMP: 9
SALES (est): 1.6MM **Privately Held**
SIC: 3669 Traffic signals, electric

(G-2882)
COMMERCIAL PRINT & IMAGING
4778 Main St (14226-4020)
PHONE....................716 597-0100
Fax: 716 597-0232
Kevin Preston, *President*
John A Polvino, *Vice Pres*
EMP: 25
SQ FT: 6,500
SALES (est): 4MM **Privately Held**
SIC: 2752 Commercial printing, lithographic

(G-2883)
COMMITMENT 2000 INC
Also Called: Father Sam's Bakery
105 Msgr Valente Dr (14206-1815)
PHONE....................716 439-1206
Fax: 716 853-1062
William A Sam, *Ch of Bd*
Nick Sam, *Plant Mgr*
Samuel A Sam II, *Treasurer*
Glenn Povitz, *VP Sales*
Catherine Galati, *Sales Staff*
EMP: 40
SQ FT: 40,000
SALES (est): 8.5MM **Privately Held**
WEB: www.fathersams.com
SIC: 2051 Bread, all types (white, wheat, rye, etc): fresh or frozen

(G-2884)
COMPLEMAR PRINT LLC
Also Called: Merrill Press
3034 Genesee St (14225-2641)
PHONE....................716 875-7238
Fax: 716 875-7189
Michael Gotthelf, *President*
Christine Gotthelf, *Vice Pres*
Joan Gotthelf, *Admin Sec*
EMP: 12
SQ FT: 7,000
SALES (est): 1.7MM
SALES (corp-wide): 33.2MM **Privately Held**
WEB: www.quickbizcards.com
SIC: 2752 Commercial printing, offset
PA: Complemar Partners, Inc.
500 Lee Rd Ste 200
Rochester NY 14606
585 647-5800

(G-2885)
CONAX TECHNOLOGIES LLC (PA)
2300 Walden Ave (14225-4765)
PHONE....................716 684-4500
Fax: 716 684-7133
Thomas Mech, *General Mgr*
Ed Wilson, *Mfg Mgr*
Greg Wittmann, *Mfg Staff*
Joe Kelly, *Purch Mgr*
Martin Mazurkiewizz, *Purch Agent*
EMP: 126
SQ FT: 83,000

▲ = Import ▼ = Export ◆ = Import/Export

GEOGRAPHIC SECTION — Buffalo - Erie County (G-2910)

SALES (est): 20.5MM Privately Held
WEB: www.conaxbuffalo.com
SIC: 3823 Industrial process control instruments

(G-2886)
CONNIES LAUNDRY
1494 S Park Ave (14220-1075)
PHONE..................................716 822-2800
Fax: 716 822-2800
Froncell Clifton, *Owner*
EMP: 5
SQ FT: 1,000
SALES: 500K Privately Held
SIC: 2842 Laundry cleaning preparations

(G-2887)
CONSUMERS BEVERAGES INC
3025 Sheridan Dr (14226-1910)
PHONE..................................716 837-3087
Fax: 716 837-3087
EMP: 25
SALES (corp-wide): 21.6MM Privately Held
WEB: www.consumersbeverage.com
SIC: 2086 Bottled & canned soft drinks
PA: Consumers Beverages, Inc.
    2230 S Park Ave
    Buffalo NY
    716 826-9200

(G-2888)
CONTRACT PHRMCTCALS LTD NAGARA
100 Forest Ave (14213-1032)
PHONE..................................716 887-3400
John Ross, *Branch Mgr*
Todd Burdick, *Manager*
Michele Miller, *Manager*
Dale Jacobs, *Info Tech Dir*
Rick Fairess, *Info Tech Mgr*
EMP: 200
SALES (corp-wide): 37.5MM Privately Held
WEB: www.cplltd.com
SIC: 2834 Pharmaceutical preparations
PA: Contract Pharmaceuticals Limited
    Canada
    7600 East Danbro Cres
    Mississauga ON L5N 6
    905 821-7600

(G-2889)
COOKIEBAKER LLC
1 Robert Rich Way (14213-1701)
PHONE..................................716 878-8000
Sam Stolbun, *President*
EMP: 6
SALES (est): 464.2K Privately Held
SIC: 2099 Food preparations

(G-2890)
COOPER TURBOCOMPRESSOR INC (DH)
3101 Broadway St (14227-1034)
P.O. Box 209 (14225-0209)
PHONE..................................716 896-6600
Fax: 716 896-1233
Jeff Altamari, *Vice Pres*
Frank Athearn, *Vice Pres*
Ron Flecknoe, *Vice Pres*
Ray Plachta, *Vice Pres*
Ed Roper, *Vice Pres*
▲ EMP: 485
SQ FT: 273,000
SALES (est): 79.6MM Privately Held
SIC: 3511 3563 Turbines & turbine generator sets; air & gas compressors
HQ: Cameron International Corporation
    4646 W Sam Houston Pkwy N
    Houston TX 77041
    713 513-3300

(G-2891)
COSTANZOS BAKERY INC
30 Innsbruck Dr (14227-2736)
PHONE..................................716 656-9093
Fax: 716 656-9218
Jeffrey A Costanzo, *CEO*
Michael Costanzo, *Vice Pres*
Laura McKenrick, *QC Mgr*
Bob Murray, *Finance*
Donna Ciulis, *Human Res Mgr*
EMP: 130 EST: 1933
SQ FT: 20,000
SALES (est): 28.2MM Privately Held
WEB: www.costanzosbakery.com
SIC: 2051 5461 5149 Bread, cake & related products; bakeries; bakery products

(G-2892)
CRANDALL FILLING MACHINERY INC
80 Gruner Rd (14227-1007)
PHONE..................................716 897-3486
Fax: 716 897-3488
David Reed, *President*
Heather Wood, *Corp Secy*
Charles Wood, *VP Sales*
Dian Reed, *Shareholder*
EMP: 6 EST: 1906
SQ FT: 7,000
SALES (est): 454.1K Privately Held
SIC: 3569 Liquid automation machinery & equipment

(G-2893)
CROSBY COMPANY
183 Pratt St (14204-1519)
PHONE..................................716 852-3522
Peter W Crosby, *CEO*
Leslie Richardson, *Vice Pres*
Jack Spencer, *Buyer*
Art Machuca, *Engineer*
Paul Marun, *Engineer*
EMP: 50
SQ FT: 300,000
SALES (est): 11.3MM Privately Held
WEB: www.crosbycompany.com
SIC: 3469 Metal stampings

(G-2894)
CRYSTAL ROCK LLC
100 Stradtman St Ste 1 (14206-2665)
PHONE..................................716 626-7460
Tom Gawel, *Division Mgr*
EMP: 25
SALES (corp-wide): 73.9MM Publicly Held
SIC: 2086 Water, pasteurized: packaged in cans, bottles, etc.
HQ: Crystal Rock Llc
    1050 Buckingham St
    Watertown CT 06795
    877 302-4241

(G-2895)
CURTIS L MACLEAN L C
Also Called: Maclean Curtis
50 Thielman Dr (14206-2364)
PHONE..................................716 898-7800
Duncan Mac Lean, *CEO*
Paul Hojnacki, *President*
Daryle Shaw, *CFO*
Barbara Bragg, *Admin Sec*
EMP: 300
SALES (est): 44.8MM
SALES (corp-wide): 1.3B Privately Held
SIC: 3714 Motor vehicle engines & parts
PA: Mac Lean-Fogg Company
    1000 Allanson Rd
    Mundelein IL 60060
    847 566-0010

(G-2896)
CURTIS SCREW CO INC
50 Thielman Dr (14206-2364)
PHONE..................................716 898-7800
John Hoskins, *Chairman*
EMP: 36
SALES (est): 7.9MM Privately Held
SIC: 3451 Screw machine products

(G-2897)
CUSTOM CANVAS MANUFACTURING CO
775 Seneca St (14210-1487)
PHONE..................................716 852-6372
Fax: 716 852-2328
Anthony L Guido Jr, *President*
Phyllis Guido, *Vice Pres*
William Sal Guido, *Prdtn Mgr*
▲ EMP: 28 EST: 1961
SQ FT: 32,000
SALES (est): 3.4MM Privately Held
SIC: 2394 7699 Canvas covers & drop cloths; liners & covers, fabric: made from purchased materials; tarpaulins, fabric: made from purchased materials; tents: made from purchased materials; tent repair shop

(G-2898)
CUSTOM SHEET METAL CONTG LLC
303 Central Ave (14206-1007)
PHONE..................................716 896-2122
Henry Van Mollenberg, *President*
EMP: 13
SQ FT: 25,000
SALES (est): 1.2MM
SALES (corp-wide): 48.1MM Privately Held
SIC: 3444 Sheet metalwork
HQ: Mollenberg-Betz, Inc.
    300 Scott St
    Buffalo NY 14204
    716 614-7473

(G-2899)
D & G WELDING INC
249 Hertel Ave (14207-2153)
PHONE..................................716 873-3088
Toll Free:........................888 -
Fax: 716 873-3088
David M Black, *President*
EMP: 5
SQ FT: 2,300
SALES (est): 387K Privately Held
SIC: 7692 3498 Welding repair; pipe fittings, fabricated from purchased pipe

(G-2900)
D-C THEATRICKS
747 Main St (14203-1321)
PHONE..................................716 847-0180
David Dejac, *Partner*
Douglas Caskey, *Partner*
EMP: 5
SQ FT: 4,600
SALES (est): 430K Privately Held
WEB: www.costume.com
SIC: 2389 5699 5136 5137 Theatrical costumes; costumes, masquerade or theatrical; men's & boys' clothing; women's & children's clothing

(G-2901)
DAN TRENT COMPANY INC
Also Called: D & D Printing
1728 Clinton St (14206-3151)
PHONE..................................716 822-1422
Fax: 716 822-3876
Daniel Trent, *President*
EMP: 8
SQ FT: 5,610
SALES (est): 820K Privately Held
SIC: 2752 Commercial printing, lithographic

(G-2902)
DATES WEISER FURNITURE CORP (PA)
1700 Broadway St (14212-2031)
PHONE..................................716 891-1700
Fax: 716 891-0399
Joseph Iannello, *Vice Pres*
Joseph S Iannello, *CFO*
EMP: 60
SQ FT: 90,000
SALES: 13MM Privately Held
WEB: www.datesweiser.com
SIC: 2521 Wood office furniture

(G-2903)
DAVIS
283 Minnesota Ave (14215-1013)
PHONE..................................716 833-4678
Arthur L Davis, *Principal*
EMP: 9
SALES (est): 668.9K Privately Held
SIC: 2389 Clergymen's vestments

(G-2904)
DECK BROS INC
222 Chicago St (14204-2249)
PHONE..................................716 852-0262
Ronald P Kellner, *President*
Karl J Kellner, *Vice Pres*
Randy Sanders, *Plt & Fclts Mgr*
Russell Reczek, *Engineer*
Hazel Weaver, *Controller*
EMP: 25 EST: 1952
SQ FT: 45,000
SALES: 3MM Privately Held
SIC: 3599 7692 Machine shop, jobbing & repair; welding repair

(G-2905)
DELAWARE VALLEY FORGE INC
241 Rano St (14207-2149)
P.O. Box 220, Kenmore (14217-0220)
PHONE..................................716 447-9140
Fax: 716 447-9122
Margaret Duggan, *President*
EMP: 20
SALES (est): 1.7MM Privately Held
SIC: 3462 Iron & steel forgings

(G-2906)
DELTACRAFT PAPER COMPANY LLC
Also Called: Nicraft
99 Bud Mil Dr (14206-1801)
PHONE..................................716 856-5135
Fax: 716 856-1113
Frank Kohl, *Purchasing*
James Lauck, *Director*
Charles Mlakar,
William Grubich,
Chuck Mlakar Jr,
▲ EMP: 190
SQ FT: 85,000
SALES (est): 20.7MM
SALES (corp-wide): 400.1MM Privately Held
WEB: www.millcraft.com
SIC: 2679 Paperboard products, converted
PA: The Millcraft Paper Company
    6800 Grant Ave
    Cleveland OH 44105
    216 441-5505

(G-2907)
DENNY MACHINE CO INC
20 Norris St (14207-2207)
PHONE..................................716 873-6865
Frank Deni, *President*
Joseph Deni, *Vice Pres*
Leonard Deni, *Vice Pres*
George Macholtz, *Manager*
Jennie Deni, *Admin Sec*
EMP: 65 EST: 1957
SQ FT: 10,000
SALES (est): 8.4MM Privately Held
WEB: www.deni.com
SIC: 3599 Machine shop, jobbing & repair

(G-2908)
DERONDE DOORS AND FRAMES INC
330 Greene St (14206-1025)
P.O. Box 686 (14240-0686)
PHONE..................................716 895-8888
Grace W Munschauer, *Ch of Bd*
EMP: 13 EST: 2008
SALES (est): 2.2MM Privately Held
SIC: 3442 Window & door frames

(G-2909)
DERRICK CORPORATION (PA)
Also Called: Derrick Equipment
590 Duke Rd (14225-5102)
PHONE..................................716 683-9010
Fax: 716 683-4991
James W Derrick, *Ch of Bd*
William W Derrick, *President*
John J Bakula, *Exec VP*
Robert G Derrick, *Exec VP*
Dan Carroll, *Vice Pres*
◆ EMP: 200 EST: 1951
SQ FT: 210,000
SALES (est): 215.5MM Privately Held
WEB: www.derrickcorp.com
SIC: 3533 Oil & gas field machinery

(G-2910)
DESIGNERS FOLDING BOX CORP
84 Tennessee St (14204-2797)
PHONE..................................716 853-5141
Fax: 716 853-5149
Jeffrey P Winney, *President*
James Winney, *Treasurer*
Teri McAndrews, *Admin Sec*
EMP: 25 EST: 1950
SQ FT: 38,000
SALES: 2.5MM Privately Held
WEB: www.designersfoldingbox.com
SIC: 2657 Folding paperboard boxes

(PA)=Parent Co (HQ)=Headquarters (DH)=Div Headquarters
✿ = New Business established in last 2 years

Buffalo - Erie County (G-2911)

(G-2911)
DEX MEDIA INC
6215 Sheridan Dr Ste 200 (14221-4837)
PHONE..................................603 263-2811
Michele Morgan, *Branch Mgr*
EMP: 40
SALES (corp-wide): 1.8B **Publicly Held**
SIC: 2741 Telephone & other directory publishing
HQ: Supermedia Inc.
2200 W Airfield Dr
Dfw Airport TX 75261
972 453-7000

(G-2912)
DEX MEDIA INC
6215 Sheridan Dr Ste 200 (14221-4837)
PHONE..................................315 251-3300
Lisa Miller, *Branch Mgr*
EMP: 42
SALES (corp-wide): 1.8B **Publicly Held**
SIC: 2741 Telephone & other directory publishing
PA: Dex Media, Inc.
2200 W Airfield Dr
Dfw Airport TX 75261
972 453-7000

(G-2913)
DIA-NIELSEN USA INCORPORATED (DH)
400 Exchange St (14204-2064)
PHONE..................................856 642-9700
Rick Tallinghast, *General Mgr*
Rick Tallinghast, *General Mgr*
▲ **EMP:** 6
SQ FT: 11,200
SALES (est): 801.6K
SALES (corp-wide): 1B **Privately Held**
WEB: www.dianielsen.com
SIC: 3577 Graphic displays, except graphic terminals
HQ: Dia-Nielsen Gmbh & Co. Kg Zubehor Fur MeB- Und Labortechnik
Industriestr. 8
Duren
242 159-010

(G-2914)
DIGITAL PRINT SERVICES
Also Called: Digital Print Svces
1057 Kensington Ave (14215-2737)
PHONE..................................877 832-1200
John Polvino, *Partner*
Kevin Preston, *Partner*
EMP: 7
SQ FT: 2,000
SALES (est): 300K **Privately Held**
SIC: 2759 Commercial printing

(G-2915)
DILESE INTERNATIONAL INC
Also Called: Choco-Logo
141 Broadway St (14203-1629)
PHONE..................................716 855-3500
Fax: 716 855-3501
Daniel Johnson, *President*
EMP: 10
SQ FT: 10,000
SALES (est): 1MM **Privately Held**
WEB: www.chocologo.com
SIC: 2066 2064 Chocolate; candy & other confectionery products

(G-2916)
DKM SALES LLC
Also Called: Dkm Ad Art
1352 Genesee St (14211-2296)
PHONE..................................716 893-7777
Ken Krzeminski, *Partner*
Ryan Carpenter, *Manager*
EMP: 40
SQ FT: 65,000
SALES (est): 5.2MM **Privately Held**
WEB: www.dkm-sales.com
SIC: 2759 3993 2399 Screen printing; advertising novelties; banners, made from fabric

(G-2917)
DORIC VAULT OF WNY INC
73 Gilbert St (14206-2948)
PHONE..................................716 828-1776
Fax: 716 828-9018
Dennis Schultz, *President*
Carol Schultz, *Vice Pres*
EMP: 12
SQ FT: 27,000
SALES: 1MM **Privately Held**
SIC: 3272 Burial vaults, concrete or pre-cast terrazzo

(G-2918)
DRESCHER PAPER BOX INC
459 Broadway St (14204-1634)
PHONE..................................716 854-0288
J Baird Langworthy, *President*
J Macleod, *Div Sub Head*
John Langworthy, *Exec VP*
EMP: 14 **EST:** 1867
SQ FT: 48,000
SALES (est): 1.2MM **Privately Held**
WEB: www.drescherpuzzle.com
SIC: 2652 3944 Setup paperboard boxes; games, toys & children's vehicles; puzzles

(G-2919)
DRS-ELECTRONIC WARFARE & NETWO
485 Cayuga Rd (14225-1368)
PHONE..................................716 631-6200
Joseph Tomasino, *General Mgr*
David Hagelberger, *Engineer*
Mark Dobosz, *Controller*
Phillip Sandmann, *Finance Dir*
EMP: 325
SQ FT: 300,000
SALES: 30.3MM
SALES (corp-wide): 79.5MM **Privately Held**
SIC: 3812 Search & navigation equipment; navigational systems & instruments; search & detection systems & instruments
HQ: Drs Technologies, Inc
2345 Crystal Dr Ste 1000
Arlington VA 22202
973 898-1500

(G-2920)
DUALL FINISHING INC
53 Hopkins St (14220-2130)
PHONE..................................716 827-1707
Fax: 716 827-5848
Richard Duman, *President*
EMP: 8
SALES: 325K **Privately Held**
SIC: 3549 Metalworking machinery

(G-2921)
DURO-SHED INC (PA)
721 Center Rd (14224-2181)
PHONE..................................585 344-0800
Dave Delagrange, *President*
Dawn Ulm, *Finance Mgr*
EMP: 33
SQ FT: 6,000
SALES (est): 2.6MM **Privately Held**
WEB: www.duro-shed.com
SIC: 2452 Prefabricated wood buildings

(G-2922)
E B ATLAS STEEL CORP
120 Tonawanda St (14207-3117)
PHONE..................................716 876-0900
Brian Hogle, *President*
Mary Gibbons, *Manager*
EMP: 16
SQ FT: 7,000
SALES (est): 3.2MM **Privately Held**
SIC: 3441 Fabricated structural metal

(G-2923)
E B IRON ART LLC
Also Called: Steel Crazy
70 Tonawanda St (14207-3117)
PHONE..................................716 876-7510
Edward Hogle, *Mng Member*
Bryan Hogle,
EMP: 10
SQ FT: 5,000
SALES (est): 1.3MM **Privately Held**
SIC: 3315 Steel wire & related products

(G-2924)
E I DU PONT DE NEMOURS & CO
Also Called: Dupont
3115 River Rd (14207-1059)
P.O. Box 88 (14207-0088)
PHONE..................................716 876-4420
Fax: 716 879-1899
Rich Gentilucci, *Safety Mgr*

Terri Singer, *Purch Mgr*
Jeffrey Rose, *Research*
James Blocho, *Engineer*
Charles Fisher, *Engineer*
EMP: 50
SALES (corp-wide): 25.1B **Publicly Held**
WEB: www.dupont.com
SIC: 2823 2253 2821 Cellulosic manmade fibers; knit outerwear mills; plastics materials & resins
PA: E. I. Du Pont De Nemours And Company
974 Centre Rd
Wilmington DE 19805
302 774-1000

(G-2925)
EAC HOLDINGS OF NY CORP
701 Willet Rd (14218-3756)
PHONE..................................716 822-2500
Kristine Ramming, *President*
Betty Ramming, *Chairman*
James Kintzel, *Corp Secy*
Brian Hauer, *Opers Mgr*
▼ **EMP:** 23
SQ FT: 70,000
SALES (est): 3MM **Privately Held**
WEB: www.electroabrasives.com
SIC: 3291 Abrasive grains

(G-2926)
EAST CAST ORTHTICS PROSTHETICS
505 Delaware Ave (14202-1309)
PHONE..................................716 856-5192
Vincent Benenati, *President*
Larry Benenati, *Vice Pres*
EMP: 12
SALES (est): 1.1MM **Privately Held**
SIC: 3842 Orthopedic appliances

(G-2927)
EAST COAST TOOL & MFG
1 Alliance Dr (14218-2529)
PHONE..................................716 826-5183
Fax: 716 827-0871
Richard R Stjohn, *President*
Robert Dewey, *Treasurer*
Bernie Pruchniewski, *Admin Sec*
Michael Bauer, *Administration*
Jeanine St John, *Administration*
EMP: 6
SQ FT: 5,000
SALES (est): 510K **Privately Held**
SIC: 3541 Machine tools, metal cutting type; grinding machines, metalworking

(G-2928)
EASTERN NIAGRA RADIOLOGY
899 Main St (14203-1109)
PHONE..................................716 882-6544
Joseph Serghany MD, *Partner*
Phillip J Silberberg, *Bd of Directors*
Cynithia Selmensburger, *Admin Sec*
EMP: 22
SALES: 300K **Privately Held**
SIC: 3829 Medical diagnostic systems, nuclear

(G-2929)
EASTMAN MACHINE COMPANY
779 Washington St (14203-1396)
PHONE..................................716 856-2200
Robert L Stevenson, *CEO*
Marla Coniglio, *Exec VP*
Wade Stevenson, *Vice Pres*
Michael Boniszewski, *Plant Mgr*
Mayme Egan, *Opers Mgr*
◆ **EMP:** 110 **EST:** 1888
SQ FT: 130,000
SALES (est): 38.1MM **Privately Held**
WEB: www.eastmancuts.com
SIC: 3552 Textile machinery

(G-2930)
EATON CORPORATION
55 Pineview Dr Ste 600 (14228-2170)
PHONE..................................716 691-0008
Brian Noble, *Sales Staff*
Bratt Nanna, *Manager*
EMP: 7 **Privately Held**
WEB: www.eaton.com
SIC: 3625 Relays & industrial controls

HQ: Eaton Corporation
1000 Eaton Blvd
Cleveland OH 44122
216 523-5000

(G-2931)
EAZY MOVEMENTS
337 Hoyt St (14213-1246)
PHONE..................................716 837-2083
Everard Shaw, *Owner*
EMP: 7
SALES (est): 297.4K **Privately Held**
SIC: 2542 Racks, merchandise display or storage: except wood

(G-2932)
EDWIN J MCKENICA & SONS INC
Also Called: E.J. McKenica & Sons Inc
1200 Clinton St (14206-2824)
PHONE..................................716 823-4646
Fax: 716 823-6253
Richard E McKenica, *Ch of Bd*
Glenn Milbrand, *President*
Bob Brigham, *General Mgr*
Glen Milbrand, *Senior VP*
Ronald K McKenica, *Vice Pres*
▲ **EMP:** 15 **EST:** 1974
SQ FT: 28,000
SALES (est): 4MM **Privately Held**
SIC: 3599 Machine shop, jobbing & repair

(G-2933)
ELECTRO ABRASIVES LLC
701 Willet Rd (14218-3798)
PHONE..................................716 822-2500
Fax: 716 822-2858
Kristine L Ramming, *President*
Leonardo Curimbaba, *General Mgr*
Robert A Mesanovic, *Superintendent*
James R Kintzel, *Plant Mgr*
Charles Hubbard, *QC Mgr*
◆ **EMP:** 20
SALES (est): 3.6MM **Privately Held**
SIC: 3291 Abrasive products

(G-2934)
ELWOOD SPECIALTY PRODUCTS INC
2180 Elmwood Ave (14216-1003)
PHONE..................................716 877-6622
Peter McGennis Jr, *President*
Bill Easton, *Mfg Staff*
EMP: 13
SQ FT: 20,000
SALES (est): 1.5MM **Privately Held**
WEB: www.coolsac.com
SIC: 3842 Clothing, fire resistant & protective

(G-2935)
EM-KAY MOLDS INC
398 Ludington St (14206-1446)
PHONE..................................716 895-6180
Richard Boehler, *President*
C F Boehler, *Vice Pres*
EMP: 6
SQ FT: 24,000
SALES: 400K **Privately Held**
SIC: 3089 Injection molding of plastics; molding primary plastic

(G-2936)
EMCOM INDUSTRIES INC
235 Genesee St (14204-1456)
PHONE..................................716 852-3711
Daniel A Higgins, *President*
EMP: 5
SQ FT: 40,000
SALES: 290K **Privately Held**
SIC: 3322 3599 Malleable iron foundries; machine shop, jobbing & repair

(G-2937)
EMPIRE INNOVATION GROUP LLC
410 Main St Ste 5 (14202-3735)
PHONE..................................716 852-5000
Nicolas Knab,
EMP: 10
SALES (est): 1MM **Privately Held**
SIC: 7372 Application computer software

GEOGRAPHIC SECTION

Buffalo - Erie County (G-2964)

(G-2938)
ENERTECH LABS INC
714 Northland Ave (14211-1045)
P.O. Box 732, Getzville (14068-0732)
PHONE..................................716 332-9074
Michael Hall, *President*
Ronald Greene, *Principal*
EMP: 6
SQ FT: 30,000
SALES (est): 1.1MM **Privately Held**
WEB: www.enertechlabs.com
SIC: 2911 Fuel additives

(G-2939)
ENGINEERED COMPOSITES INC
Also Called: Armor Tile
55 Roberts Ave (14206-3119)
PHONE..................................716 362-0295
Daniel Bolubash, *President*
Roman Bolubash, *Vice Pres*
David Holmes, *Manager*
▲ **EMP:** 30
SQ FT: 43,000
SALES (est): 12.3MM **Privately Held**
WEB: www.armortile.com
SIC: 3089 Floor coverings, plastic

(G-2940)
ENRG INC
155 Rano St Ste 300 (14207-2132)
PHONE..................................716 873-2939
Fax: 716 873-3196
John Olenick, *President*
Tim Curry, *Manager*
Viswanathan Venkateswaran, *Manager*
EMP: 15
SQ FT: 13,000
SALES: 1.5MM **Privately Held**
WEB: www.enrg-inc.com
SIC: 3299 3674 Ceramic fiber; solid state electronic devices

(G-2941)
ENTERPRISE FOLDING BOX CO INC
75 Isabelle St (14207-1739)
PHONE..................................716 876-6421
Fax: 716 876-7197
Andrew Baranyi, *CEO*
Lynette Ovitt, *President*
Tom Hartman, *Manager*
EMP: 24
SQ FT: 100,000
SALES (est): 8.9MM **Privately Held**
WEB: www.enterprisebox.com
SIC: 2631 Folding boxboard

(G-2942)
EXTEN II LLC
50 Stradtman St (14206-1908)
P.O. Box 875, Orchard Park (14127-0875)
PHONE..................................716 895-2214
Richard Swanson, *President*
EMP: 18
SALES (est): 1.9MM **Privately Held**
SIC: 3714 Motor vehicle parts & accessories

(G-2943)
F X GRAPHIX INC
3043 Delaware Ave (14217-2059)
PHONE..................................716 871-1511
Fax: 716 871-1232
Thomas Giambra, *President*
Pamela Gittins, *Partner*
EMP: 6
SQ FT: 1,600
SALES (est): 686.4K **Privately Held**
WEB: www.fxgraphix.com
SIC: 2395 7336 Embroidery products, except schiffli machine; commercial art & graphic design

(G-2944)
FAMOUS DOUGHNUTS INC
3043 Main St (14214-1333)
PHONE..................................716 834-6356
Richard Roehm Sr, *President*
EMP: 8 **EST:** 1945
SQ FT: 6,000
SALES (est): 791.7K **Privately Held**
SIC: 2051 Doughnuts, except frozen

(G-2945)
FARTHING PRESS INC
258 Oak St Ste 260 (14203-1626)
PHONE..................................716 852-4674
Fax: 716 852-4677
David W Snyder, *President*
Carolyn Snyder, *Vice Pres*
EMP: 9 **EST:** 1908
SQ FT: 6,800
SALES (est): 1.1MM **Privately Held**
SIC: 2752 2759 Commercial printing, offset; letterpress & screen printing; letterpress printing; screen printing

(G-2946)
FIBERGLASS REPLACEMENT PARTS
200 Colorado Ave (14215-4006)
PHONE..................................716 893-6471
Thomas E Hall, *President*
Roger Drew, *Mfg Staff*
EMP: 15
SQ FT: 37,500
SALES (est): 1.1MM **Privately Held**
WEB: www.speedwayone.com
SIC: 3713 3711 Truck bodies & parts; motor vehicles & car bodies

(G-2947)
FIBRON PRODUCTS INC
Also Called: Real Wood Tiles
170 Florida St (14208-1212)
PHONE..................................716 886-2378
Fax: 716 886-2394
Robert C Oshei Jr, *President*
Jack Oshei, *Purchasing*
EMP: 50 **EST:** 1949
SQ FT: 65,000
SALES (est): 3.5MM **Privately Held**
SIC: 2499 2426 Handles, wood; hardwood dimension & flooring mills

(G-2948)
FLASHFLO MANUFACTURING INC
88 Hopkins St (14220-2131)
PHONE..................................716 826-9500
Fax: 716 854-5585
Lawrence Speiser, *President*
EMP: 15
SALES (est): 1.6MM **Privately Held**
SIC: 3545 Machine tool accessories

(G-2949)
FLASHFLO MANUFACTURING INC
222 Chicago St (14204-2249)
PHONE..................................716 840-9594
Lawrence J Speiser, *President*
Susan A Speiser, *Office Mgr*
EMP: 5
SALES (est): 704K **Privately Held**
WEB: www.flashflomfg.com
SIC: 3545 Machine tool accessories

(G-2950)
FLEXLUME SIGN CORPORATION
1464 Main St (14209-1780)
P.O. Box 804 (14209-0804)
PHONE..................................716 884-2020
Fax: 716 881-0361
Alfred P Rowell Sr, *CEO*
Alfred P Rowell Jr, *President*
Shirley J Rowell, *Corp Secy*
EMP: 9 **EST:** 1904
SQ FT: 22,000
SALES (est): 1.2MM **Privately Held**
WEB: www.flexlume.com
SIC: 3993 1799 Electric signs; sign installation & maintenance

(G-2951)
FLEXO TRANSPARENT INC
28 Wasson St (14210-1544)
P.O. Box 128 (14240-0128)
PHONE..................................716 825-7710
Fax: 716 825-0139
Brian Marby, *President*
Candace Richardson, *General Mgr*
Ronald D Mabry, *Chairman*
Sharon Mabry, *Vice Pres*
◆ **EMP:** 115 **EST:** 1954
SQ FT: 120,000
SALES (est): 20.2MM **Privately Held**
WEB: www.flexotransparent.com
SIC: 2759 Bags, plastic: printing

(G-2952)
FORD MOTOR COMPANY
3663 Lake Shore Rd (14219-2397)
PHONE..................................716 821-4000
Fax: 716 821-4009
Mario Ciach, *Plant Mgr*
John Nowak, *Design Engr Mgr*
Mark McGiveron, *Sales Mgr*
David Buvo, *Manager*
Dan Sirica, *Manager*
EMP: 500
SQ FT: 2,446,347
SALES (corp-wide): 149.5B **Publicly Held**
WEB: www.ford.com
SIC: 3465 Body parts, automobile: stamped metal
PA: Ford Motor Company
1 American Rd
Dearborn MI 48126
313 322-3000

(G-2953)
FORSYTH INDUSTRIES INC
1195 Colvin Blvd (14223-1909)
PHONE..................................716 652-1070
Fax: 585 652-0414
Joseph Takats III, *President*
Daniel Grew, *General Mgr*
Ellen A Mormul, *Finance*
EMP: 29 **EST:** 1890
SQ FT: 50,000
SALES (est): 4.2MM **Privately Held**
SIC: 3469 3315 Metal stampings; wire products, ferrous/iron: made in wiredrawing plants

(G-2954)
FPPF CHEMICAL CO INC (PA)
117 W Tupper St Ste 1 (14201-2171)
PHONE..................................716 856-9607
Fax: 716 856-0750
Christopher Lory, *President*
Jim Thurston, *Buyer*
Peter Guerra, *VP Mktg*
Michael Gigliotti, *Marketing Staff*
EMP: 8
SQ FT: 4,000
SALES (est): 1.2MM **Privately Held**
WEB: www.fppf.com
SIC: 2911 2899 Fuel additives; antifreeze compounds

(G-2955)
FRANK WARDYNSKI & SONS INC
336 Peckham St (14206-1717)
P.O. Box 336 (14240-0336)
PHONE..................................716 854-6083
Fax: 716 854-4887
Raymond F Wardynski, *Ch of Bd*
Betsy Hooey, *Controller*
Edmund Wardynski, *Admin Sec*
EMP: 40
SQ FT: 24,000
SALES (est): 7.1MM **Privately Held**
WEB: www.wardynski.com
SIC: 2013 5149 2011 Sausage casings, natural; canned goods: fruit, vegetables, seafood, meats, etc.; meat packing plants

(G-2956)
FREDERICK MACHINE REPAIR INC
405 Ludington St (14206-1445)
PHONE..................................716 332-0104
Fax: 716 892-1426
Alan Frederick, *President*
EMP: 8 **EST:** 1945
SQ FT: 11,000
SALES (est): 1.3MM **Privately Held**
SIC: 3599 Machine shop, jobbing & repair

(G-2957)
FRONTIER HT-DIP GLVANIZING INC
1740 Elmwood Ave (14207-2410)
P.O. Box 199 (14207-0199)
PHONE..................................716 875-2091
Fax: 716 875-5435
Lewis G Pierce, *President*
James Abel, *Prdtn Mgr*
Diane Goodwin, *Office Mgr*
▲ **EMP:** 18 **EST:** 1971
SQ FT: 65,000
SALES (est): 3.2MM **Privately Held**
WEB: www.frontierhdgalvanizing.com
SIC: 3479 Galvanizing of iron, steel or endformed products

(G-2958)
FRONTIER HYDRAULICS CORP
1738 Elmwood Ave Ste 2 (14207-2465)
PHONE..................................716 694-2070
Fax: 716 874-0211
Steve M Jackson, *President*
EMP: 12
SQ FT: 10,000
SALES (est): 750K **Privately Held**
WEB: www.frontierhydraulics.com
SIC: 3511 Hydraulic turbines

(G-2959)
FRONTIER PLATING
Also Called: Frontier Plating Co
68 Dignity Cir (14211-1053)
PHONE..................................716 896-2811
Fax: 716 896-3430
Arnold Collier Jr, *Owner*
EMP: 6 **EST:** 1942
SALES (est): 480.2K **Privately Held**
SIC: 3471 Electroplating of metals or formed products; polishing, metals or formed products

(G-2960)
FULL CIRCLE STUDIOS LLC
710 Main St (14202-1915)
PHONE..................................716 875-7740
Fax: 716 875-7162
Kevin Crosby, *General Mgr*
Cole Bielecki, *Editor*
Terry Fisher,
Jim Phillips,
EMP: 7
SALES (est): 864.1K **Privately Held**
WEB: www.fullcirclestudios.com
SIC: 3699 Electronic training devices

(G-2961)
FUTURE MOBILITY PRODUCTS INC
1 Buffalo River Pl (14210-2153)
PHONE..................................716 783-9130
Abdul Samad Panchbhaya, *President*
Mohammed Aswat, *Supervisor*
EMP: 20
SALES (est): 732.9K **Privately Held**
SIC: 3842 Wheelchairs

(G-2962)
GALLAGHER PRINTING INC
Also Called: Rocket Communications
2518 Delaware Ave (14216-1702)
PHONE..................................716 873-2434
David Gallagher, *President*
Dean Gallagher, *Corp Secy*
Daryl Gallagher, *Vice Pres*
Dennis Gallagher, *Treasurer*
EMP: 30
SQ FT: 30,000
SALES (est): 3.6MM **Privately Held**
WEB: www.gallagherprinting.com
SIC: 2752 2711 6513 Commercial printing, offset; newspapers; apartment building operators

(G-2963)
GALLE & ZINTER INC
Also Called: Galle Memorial
3405 Harlem Rd (14225-2019)
PHONE..................................716 833-4212
Paul Zinter, *President*
Rick Zinter, *Principal*
Tina Zinter, *Admin Sec*
EMP: 7
SQ FT: 2,198
SALES (est): 594.1K **Privately Held**
SIC: 3272 Monuments & grave markers, except terrazo

(G-2964)
GARLAND TECHNOLOGY LLC
199 Delaware Ave (14202-2102)
P.O. Box 711 (14205-0711)
PHONE..................................716 242-8500
Christopher Bihary, *CEO*

Buffalo - Erie County (G-2965) — GEOGRAPHIC SECTION

Pam Makofski, *Finance*
Jennifer Hillman, *Mktg Dir*
Jerry Dillard, *CTO*
EMP: 20
SALES (est): 3.6MM **Privately Held**
SIC: 3572 Computer storage devices

(G-2965)
GAS TCHNLGY ENRGY CNCEPTS LLC
Also Called: G Tech Natureal Gasses Systems
401 William L Gaiter Pkwy (14215-2767)
PHONE 716 831-9695
David Reichard,
William Hess,
EMP: 8
SQ FT: 5,000
SALES (est): 1.2MM **Privately Held**
SIC: 3563 Air & gas compressors

(G-2966)
GAY SHEET METAL DIES INC
301 Hinman Ave (14216-1093)
PHONE 716 877-0208
Dolores Dewey, *President*
David Jaworski, *Executive*
EMP: 8 **EST:** 1936
SQ FT: 6,500
SALES (est): 1.3MM **Privately Held**
SIC: 3469 3544 Stamping metal for the trade; die sets for metal stamping (presses)

(G-2967)
GEAR MOTIONS INCORPORATED
Also Called: Oliver Gear
1120 Niagara St (14213-1714)
PHONE 716 885-1080
Mike Barron, *Branch Mgr*
Jamie McAllister, *Manager*
EMP: 22
SALES (corp-wide): 18.4MM **Privately Held**
WEB: www.gearmotions.com
SIC: 3462 Gears, forged steel
PA: Gear Motions Incorporated
 1750 Milton Ave
 Syracuse NY 13209
 315 488-0100

(G-2968)
GEMTROL INC
1800 Broadway St Bldg 1c (14212-2001)
PHONE 716 894-0716
Fax: 716 894-0717
Jeffrey Dombek, *President*
EMP: 8
SQ FT: 4,400
SALES (est): 900K **Privately Held**
WEB: www.gemtrol.com
SIC: 3625 Electric controls & control accessories, industrial

(G-2969)
GENERAL MILLS INC
54 S Michigan Ave (14203-3086)
PHONE 716 856-6060
Fax: 716 857-3689
Jon Blake, *Plant Mgr*
Michelle Brydalski, *Sales Staff*
Jerry Baty, *Manager*
Jeff Dils, *Manager*
Kevin McFeely, *Manager*
EMP: 50
SALES (corp-wide): 16.5B **Publicly Held**
WEB: www.generalmills.com
SIC: 2041 Flour: blended, prepared or self-rising; flour mixes
PA: General Mills, Inc.
 1 General Mills Blvd
 Minneapolis MN 55426
 763 764-7600

(G-2970)
GENERAL MILLS INC
315 Ship Canal Pkwy (14218-1018)
PHONE 716 856-6060
EMP: 58
SALES (corp-wide): 16.5B **Publicly Held**
SIC: 2043 Wheat flakes: prepared as cereal breakfast food
PA: General Mills, Inc.
 1 General Mills Blvd
 Minneapolis MN 55426
 763 764-7600

(G-2971)
GENERAL MOTORS LLC
2995 River Rd 2 (14207-1059)
PHONE 716 879-5000
Fax: 716 879-5425
Patrick Pellow, *General Mgr*
Joseph Felong, *Superintendent*
Kevin Hamilton, *VP Opers*
Lewis Campbell, *Prdtn Mgr*
Darla Flatt, *Mfg Mgr*
EMP: 900
SALES (corp-wide): 152.3B **Publicly Held**
SIC: 3462 Automotive & internal combustion engine forgings
HQ: General Motors Llc
 300 Renaissance Ctr L1
 Detroit MI 48243
 313 556-5000

(G-2972)
GENERAL WELDING & FABG INC
1 Walden Galleria (14225-5408)
PHONE 716 681-8200
EMP: 7
SALES (corp-wide): 5.3MM **Privately Held**
SIC: 7692 Welding repair
PA: General Welding & Fabricating, Inc.
 991 Maple Rd
 Elma NY 14059
 716 652-0033

(G-2973)
GENESEE RESERVE BUFFALO LLC
300 Bailey Ave (14210-2211)
P.O. Box 20619, Rochester (14602-0619)
PHONE 716 824-3116
Bob Victor,
EMP: 30
SALES (est): 2.5MM **Privately Held**
SIC: 2491 Structural lumber & timber, treated wood

(G-2974)
GIBRALTAR INDUSTRIES INC (PA)
3556 Lake Shore Rd # 100 (14219-1400)
P.O. Box 2028 (14219-0228)
PHONE 716 826-6500
Fax: 716 826-1592
Frank Heard, *President*
Andy Blanchard, *President*
Paul C Soucier, *President*
J A Rosenecker, *Exec VP*
Joseph A Rosenecker, *Exec VP*
◆ **EMP:** 82
SALES: 1B **Publicly Held**
WEB: www.gibraltar1.com
SIC: 3499 3316 3441 3398 Strapping, metal; cold finishing of steel shapes; strip steel, cold-rolled: from purchased hot-rolled; sheet, steel, cold-rolled: from purchased hot-rolled; bars, steel, cold finished, from purchased hot-rolled; fabricated structural metal; metal heat treating

(G-2975)
GLAXOSMITHKLINE LLC
17 Mahogany Dr (14221-2420)
PHONE 716 913-5679
EMP: 26
SALES (corp-wide): 36B **Privately Held**
SIC: 2834 Pharmaceutical preparations
HQ: Glaxosmithkline Llc
 5 Crescent Dr
 Philadelphia PA 19112
 215 751-4000

(G-2976)
GLOBAL EARTH ENERGY
534 Delaware Ave Ste 412 (14202-1340)
PHONE 716 332-7150
Sydney A Harland, *Owner*
EMP: 6
SALES: 20K **Privately Held**
SIC: 2911 Petroleum refining

(G-2977)
GOERGEN-MACKWIRTH CO INC
765 Hertel Ave (14207-1992)
P.O. Box 750 (14207-0750)
PHONE 716 874-4800
Fax: 716 874-4715
Jeffrey Mertz, *President*
Katherine Schreckenberger, *Vice Pres*
Katherine Schreckenberge, *Human Resources*
Katherine Smith, *Manager*
Gail Strassburg, *Executive Asst*
EMP: 45
SQ FT: 24,000
SALES (est): 11.4MM **Privately Held**
WEB: www.goergenmackwirth.com
SIC: 3444 1761 Sheet metalwork; sheet metalwork

(G-2978)
GRAPHIC CNTRLS ACQISITION CORP (DH)
400 Exchange St (14204-2064)
P.O. Box 1271 (14240-1271)
PHONE 716 853-7500
Fax: 716 847-7565
Sam Heleba, *CEO*
Sam Haleba, *General Mgr*
Jeffrey A Blair, *COO*
Jon Bollie, *Vice Pres*
Brandon Hoffman, *Vice Pres*
▲ **EMP:** 275
SQ FT: 235,000
SALES (est): 131.5MM
SALES (corp-wide): 1B **Privately Held**
WEB: www.graphiccontrols.com
SIC: 2752 2679 Tag, ticket & schedule printing: lithographic; paper products, converted
HQ: Graphic Controls Holdings, Inc.
 400 Exchange St
 Buffalo NY 14204
 716 853-7500

(G-2979)
GRAPHIC CONTROLS HOLDINGS INC (HQ)
400 Exchange St (14204-2064)
PHONE 716 853-7500
EMP: 14
SQ FT: 235,000
SALES (est): 131.5MM
SALES (corp-wide): 1B **Privately Held**
SIC: 2752 2679 6719 Tag, ticket & schedule printing: lithographic; paper products, converted; investment holding companies, except banks
PA: Nissha Printing Co.,Ltd.
 3, Hanaicho, Mibu, Nakagyo-Ku
 Kyoto KYO 604-8
 758 118-111

(G-2980)
GREAT LAKES ORTHOPEDIC LABS
219 Bryant St (14222-2006)
PHONE 716 878-7307
Fax: 716 878-1174
Blanche Daley, *Manager*
EMP: 5
SALES (corp-wide): 570.3K **Privately Held**
SIC: 3842 Prosthetic appliances; orthopedic appliances; braces, orthopedic
PA: Great Lakes Orthopedic Labs Inc
 2362 Genesee St
 Cheektowaga NY 14225
 716 893-4116

(G-2981)
GREAT LAKES PLASTICS CO INC
2371 Broadway St (14212-2313)
PHONE 716 896-3100
Fax: 716 896-3244
Thomas Barzycki, *CEO*
Curtis Rice, *President*
Phil Coleman, *General Mgr*
Amy Nelson, *Corp Secy*
Catherine Barzycki, *Vice Pres*
EMP: 28 **EST:** 1946
SQ FT: 28,000
SALES (est): 5.1MM **Privately Held**
WEB: www.greatlakesplastic.com
SIC: 3082 3081 Rods, unsupported plastic; unsupported plastics film & sheet

(G-2982)
GREAT LAKES PRESSED STEEL CORP
1400 Niagara St (14213-1302)
PHONE 716 885-4037
Fax: 716 885-4038
Timothy O Nichols, *President*
Maryjane Nichols, *Vice Pres*
Linda Ajdaj, *Manager*
Mary Jane Nichols, *Admin Sec*
EMP: 20
SQ FT: 21,000
SALES (est): 4.1MM **Privately Held**
WEB: www.glpscorp.com
SIC: 3469 3544 Metal stampings; dies, steel rule

(G-2983)
GREENBELT INDUSTRIES INC
45 Comet Ave (14216-1710)
PHONE 800 668-1114
Fax: 716 873-1728
Jim McFarlane, *President*
Sue King, *Plant Mgr*
Bryan Cormack, *CFO*
Mark Lewis, *Manager*
Gale Lipaka, *Manager*
▲ **EMP:** 40
SQ FT: 25,758
SALES: 12MM **Privately Held**
SIC: 3535 Belt conveyor systems, general industrial use
HQ: Ammeraal Beltech International Beheer B.V.
 Comeniusstraat 8
 Alkmaar
 725 751-212

(G-2984)
HABASIT AMERICA INC
1400 Clinton St (14206-2919)
PHONE 716 824-8484
Maureen Beecher, *Human Res Mgr*
Tim Eldridge, *Branch Mgr*
John Berdysiak, *Manager*
Vinod Chahal, *Manager*
Mike Berdysiak, *Info Tech Mgr*
EMP: 75
SQ FT: 50,000
SALES (corp-wide): 663.9MM **Privately Held**
WEB: www.habasit.com
SIC: 3496 3052 Conveyor belts; rubber & plastics hose & beltings
HQ: Habasit America, Inc.
 805 Satellite Blvd Nw
 Suwanee GA 30024
 678 288-3600

(G-2985)
HADLEY EXHIBITS INC (PA)
1700 Elmwood Ave (14207-2408)
PHONE 716 874-3666
Fax: 716 874-9994
Theodore K Johnson, *President*
Ralph Allen, *Vice Pres*
Greg Kerl, *Project Mgr*
Robert Riehle, *Project Mgr*
Scott Calhoun, *Sales Mgr*
EMP: 90
SQ FT: 180,000
SALES (est): 13.2MM **Privately Held**
WEB: www.hadleyexhibits.com
SIC: 3993 Displays & cutouts, window & lobby

(G-2986)
HAGNER INDUSTRIES INC
95 Botsford Pl (14216-2601)
PHONE 716 873-5720
Fax: 716 873-4250
Peter Hagner, *President*
EMP: 8
SQ FT: 3,800
SALES: 400K **Privately Held**
SIC: 3599 1799 Machine shop, jobbing & repair; welding on site

▲ = Import ▼ = Export
◆ = Import/Export

GEOGRAPHIC SECTION
Buffalo - Erie County (G-3011)

(G-2987)
HANKIN BROTHERS CAP CO
Also Called: Han-Kraft Uniform Headwear
1910 Genesee St (14211-1818)
PHONE.....................716 892-8840
Fax: 716 892-8840
Benjamin Hankin, *Partner*
Richard Hankin, *Partner*
EMP: 10 **EST:** 1938
SQ FT: 2,800
SALES (est): 1MM **Privately Held**
SIC: 2353 Uniform hats & caps

(G-2988)
HARD MANUFACTURING CO INC
230 Grider St (14215-3797)
PHONE.....................716 893-1800
Fax: 716 896-2579
William Godin, *Ch of Bd*
▼ **EMP:** 65
SQ FT: 180,000
SALES (est): 10.6MM **Privately Held**
WEB: www.hardmfg.com
SIC: 2514 2599 2515 2511 Cribs: metal; hospital beds; mattresses & bedsprings; wood household furniture

(G-2989)
HARMAC MEDICAL PRODUCTS INC (PA)
2201 Bailey Ave (14211-1797)
PHONE.....................716 897-4500
Fax: 716 897-0016
John F Somers, *President*
John Czamara, *Manager*
Lou Ann Digiacomo, *Manager*
Robert Moran, *Director*
Robert Evans,
▲ **EMP:** 187
SQ FT: 80,000
SALES (est): 72.3MM **Privately Held**
WEB: www.harmac.com
SIC: 3841 Surgical & medical instruments

(G-2990)
HAROLD WOOD CO INC
329 Hinman Ave (14216-1096)
PHONE.....................716 873-1535
Fax: 716 873-9974
Richard L Wood, *President*
Jane Wood, *Admin Sec*
EMP: 5 **EST:** 1927
SQ FT: 3,200
SALES (est): 607.9K **Privately Held**
WEB: www.haroldwood.com
SIC: 3479 Name plates: engraved, etched, etc.

(G-2991)
HARPER INTERNATIONAL CORP
4455 Genesee St Ste 123 (14225-1965)
PHONE.....................716 276-9900
Tom Kittell, *CEO*
Charles Miller, *President*
Waldron Bamford, *Chairman*
Ronald Vacek, *Project Dir*
John Pace, *Purch Mgr*
◆ **EMP:** 100 **EST:** 1988
SALES: 50MM **Privately Held**
WEB: www.harperintl.com
SIC: 3567 Industrial furnaces & ovens

(G-2992)
HEALTH MATTERS AMERICA INC
2501 Broadway St Unit 2 (14227-1042)
P.O. Box 1482 (14225-8482)
PHONE.....................716 235-8772
▲ **EMP:** 14
SALES (est): 1.7MM **Privately Held**
SIC: 2393 Tea bags, fabric: made from purchased materials

(G-2993)
HEINTZ & WEBER CO INC
150 Reading St (14220-2156)
PHONE.....................716 852-7171
Fax: 716 852-7173
Steven D Desmond, *CEO*
Suzanne M Desmond, *Exec VP*
EMP: 7 **EST:** 1922
SQ FT: 12,500
SALES (est): 921.4K **Privately Held**
WEB: www.webersmustard.com
SIC: 2035 Pickles, vinegar; mustard, prepared (wet); relishes, fruit & vegetable

(G-2994)
HERITAGE CONTRACT FLOORING LLC
29 Depot St (14206-2203)
PHONE.....................716 853-1555
William H Russell, *CEO*
Don Faltisio, *CEO*
Bill Russell, *CEO*
Jeff Friedman, *Vice Pres*
Todd Richter, *Vice Pres*
EMP: 45
SALES (est): 9MM **Privately Held**
SIC: 3996 Hard surface floor coverings

(G-2995)
HI-TEMP FABRICATION INC
79 Perry St Ste 2 (14203-3079)
PHONE.....................716 852-5655
Shelly Kent, *President*
Dave Schedlbauer, *Vice Pres*
John Lent, *Sales Mgr*
Bill Oreilly, *Manager*
EMP: 13
SQ FT: 40,000
SALES (est): 1.9MM **Privately Held**
WEB: www.hi-tempfab.com
SIC: 2493 Hardboard & fiberboard products

(G-2996)
HOHL MACHINE & CONVEYOR CO INC
Also Called: Hohlveyor
1580 Niagara St (14213-1199)
PHONE.....................716 882-7210
Fax: 716 882-9575
Richard Milazzo, *President*
EMP: 50 **EST:** 1945
SQ FT: 30,000
SALES (est): 14.9MM **Privately Held**
SIC: 3535 3599 Conveyors & conveying equipment; belt conveyor systems, general industrial use; robotic conveyors; machine & other job shop work

(G-2997)
HOSPIRA INC
2501 Walden Ave (14225-4737)
PHONE.....................716 684-9400
Carlos E Simon, *Opers Mgr*
Wayne Dreibelbis, *Mfg Spvr*
Paul Lesniak, *Opers Staff*
Steve Wisniewski, *Engineer*
Jane Jontz, *Human Res Dir*
EMP: 193
SALES (corp-wide): 48.8B **Publicly Held**
SIC: 2834 Pharmaceutical preparations
HQ: Hospira, Inc.
275 N Field Dr
Lake Forest IL 60045
224 212-2000

(G-2998)
HUTCHINSON INDUSTRIES INC
Rodgard
92 Msgr Valente Dr (14206-1822)
PHONE.....................716 852-1435
Joseph Duffy, *Sales Mgr*
Bill Barrett, *Branch Mgr*
EMP: 30
SALES (corp-wide): 471.6MM **Privately Held**
SIC: 2821 Elastomers, nonvulcanizable (plastics)
HQ: Hutchinson Industries, Inc.
460 Southard St
Trenton NJ 08638
609 394-1010

(G-2999)
HYDRA TECHNOLOGY CORP
179 Grider St (14215-3724)
PHONE.....................716 896-8316
Fax: 716 896-4629
Kenneth Brown, *President*
May Fehmer, *Manager*
EMP: 5
SQ FT: 24,000

SALES: 2MM **Privately Held**
WEB: www.hydra-tek.com
SIC: 3593 Fluid power cylinders, hydraulic or pneumatic; fluid power actuators, hydraulic or pneumatic

(G-3000)
HYDRO-AIR COMPONENTS INC
Also Called: Zehnder Rittling
100 Rittling Blvd (14220-1885)
PHONE.....................716 827-6510
Scott Pallotta, *CEO*
Tony Scime, *COO*
Robert Daigler, *Vice Pres*
Bill Putney, *Purchasing*
Jim Blount, *Engineer*
▲ **EMP:** 130
SQ FT: 80,000
SALES (est): 36.3MM
SALES (corp-wide): 572.5MM **Privately Held**
SIC: 3585 1711 Refrigeration & heating equipment; plumbing, heating, air-conditioning contractors
PA: Zehnder Group Ag
Moortalstrasse 1
GrAnichen AG
628 551-500

(G-3001)
I ON YOUTH
115 Godfrey St (14215-2361)
PHONE.....................716 832-6509
Marilyn Nixon, *President*
EMP: 5
SALES (est): 304.6K **Privately Held**
SIC: 2721 Periodicals

(G-3002)
IMAGE TECH
96 Donna Lea Blvd (14221-3104)
PHONE.....................716 635-0167
Joan Hudack, *Owner*
EMP: 15
SALES (est): 520K **Privately Held**
SIC: 3999 Pet supplies

(G-3003)
IMMCO DIAGNOSTICS INC
640 Ellicott St Fl 3 (14203-1245)
PHONE.....................716 691-6955
Thomas C Shanahan, *Branch Mgr*
EMP: 6 **Privately Held**
SIC: 3231 2835 8071 Medical & laboratory glassware: made from purchased glass; in vitro & in vivo diagnostic substances; medical laboratories
HQ: Immco Diagnostics, Inc.
60 Pineview Dr
Buffalo NY 14228
716 691-6911

(G-3004)
IMMCO DIAGNOSTICS INC (HQ)
60 Pineview Dr (14228-2120)
PHONE.....................716 691-6911
Fax: 716 691-0466
William Maggio, *CEO*
Thomas C Shanahan, *Senior VP*
Rajmish Mittal, *CFO*
Robert Greene, *Controller*
Alfredo Aguirre, *Director*
EMP: 63 **EST:** 1971
SQ FT: 20,000
SALES (est): 15.8MM **Privately Held**
WEB: www.immco.com
SIC: 3231 8071 2835 Medical & laboratory glassware: made from purchased glass; medical laboratories; in vitro & in vivo diagnostic substances

(G-3005)
IN ROOM PLUS INC
2495 Main St Ste 217 (14214-2154)
PHONE.....................716 838-9433
Fax: 716 838-9437
Mike Amrose, *CEO*
Wanda Jones, *President*
Madelyn George, *Purch Agent*
Kim Hamilton, *Director*
Elizabeth Jones, *Director*
▼ **EMP:** 32
SQ FT: 21,000

SALES (est): 6.3MM **Privately Held**
WEB: www.inroomplus.com
SIC: 2064 Candy & other confectionery products

(G-3006)
INDUSTRIAL SUPPORT INC
36 Depot St (14206-2204)
PHONE.....................716 662-2954
Fax: 716 827-2782
David P Sullivan, *President*
Yvonne Neal, *General Mgr*
Bill Liscavage, *Purchasing*
John Hess, *Manager*
▲ **EMP:** 75
SQ FT: 55,000
SALES (est): 19.4MM **Privately Held**
WEB: www.industrialsupportinc.com
SIC: 3441 5999 2541 Fabricated structural metal; electronic parts & equipment; wood partitions & fixtures

(G-3007)
INFINITY ARCHITECTUAL SYSTEMS
1555 Niagara St (14213-1101)
PHONE.....................716 882-2321
Gina Paigen, *President*
Cindy Gardo, *Office Mgr*
EMP: 15
SALES (est): 1.8MM **Privately Held**
SIC: 1422 Crushed & broken limestone

(G-3008)
INGERSOLL-RAND COMPANY
3101 Broadway St (14227-1034)
P.O. Box 209 (14217-0209)
PHONE.....................716 896-6600
Brian Flemming, *Project Mgr*
Joe Gross, *Project Mgr*
Ernie Pead, *Project Mgr*
Robert Zent, *Project Mgr*
Pauline Brownschele, *Buyer*
EMP: 40 **Privately Held**
SIC: 3511 Turbines & turbine generator set units, complete
HQ: Ingersoll-Rand Company
800 Beaty St Ste B
Davidson NC 28036
704 655-4000

(G-3009)
INHANCE TECHNOLOGIES LLC
Also Called: Fluoro Seal
1951 Hamburg Tpke Ste 5 (14218-1046)
PHONE.....................716 825-9031
Fax: 716 825-9036
Jim Doush, *Manager*
EMP: 21
SALES (corp-wide): 8.1MM **Privately Held**
WEB: www.fluoroseal.com
SIC: 3089 2851 Plastic processing; paints & allied products
PA: Inhance Technologies Llc
16223 Park Row Ste 100
Houston TX 77084
281 578-1440

(G-3010)
INSTANTWHIP OF BUFFALO INC
2117 Genesee St (14211-1907)
PHONE.....................716 892-7031
Fax: 716 892-2921
John Beck, *General Mgr*
EMP: 20
SALES (corp-wide): 48MM **Privately Held**
SIC: 2099 2035 2026 2022 Food preparations; pickles, sauces & salad dressings; fluid milk; cheese, natural & processed; sample distribution
HQ: Instantwhip Of Buffalo, Inc
2200 Cardigan Ave
Columbus OH 43215
614 488-2536

(G-3011)
INTERIOR SOLUTIONS OF WNY LLC
472 Franklin St (14202-1302)
PHONE.....................716 332-0372
Jan Malof,
EMP: 9

Buffalo - Erie County (G-3012) — GEOGRAPHIC SECTION

SALES (est): 982.6K **Privately Held**
SIC: 2521 Chairs, office: padded, upholstered or plain: wood

(G-3012)
INTERNATIONAL PAPER COMPANY
100 Bud Mil Dr (14206-1802)
PHONE...................................716 852-2144
Pam Regans, *Branch Mgr*
EMP: 15
SALES (corp-wide): 22.3B **Publicly Held**
WEB: www.tin.com
SIC: 2653 Corrugated & solid fiber boxes
PA: International Paper Company
6400 Poplar Ave
Memphis TN 38197
901 419-9000

(G-3013)
J D COUSINS INC
667 Tifft St (14220-1890)
PHONE...................................716 824-1098
Fax: 716 823-7745
Gregory N Pauly, *CEO*
Jim Howard, *Bookkeeper*
Mark Diefenbach, *Sales Staff*
EMP: 24 EST: 1904
SQ FT: 30,000
SALES (est): 5.3MM **Privately Held**
WEB: www.jdcousins.com
SIC: 3599 Machine shop, jobbing & repair

(G-3014)
JAMESTOWN INDUSTRIAL TRCKS INC
Also Called: Toyota Industrial Eqp Dlr
999 Harlem Rd (14224-1007)
P.O. Box 613, Frewsburg (14738-0613)
PHONE...................................716 893-6105
Fax: 716 893-1004
Joyce Schwob, *General Mgr*
EMP: 10
SALES (corp-wide): 15.3MM **Privately Held**
WEB: www.jitny.com
SIC: 3537 Automobiles, new & used
PA: Jamestown Industrial Trucks, Inc.
52 S Pearl St
Frewsburg NY 14738
716 569-2410

(G-3015)
JAYS FURNITURE PRODUCTS INC
321 Ramsdell Ave (14216-1030)
PHONE...................................716 876-8854
Fax: 716 876-1279
James Gianni, *President*
Dean Gianni, *Plant Mgr*
Janie Gianni, *Admin Sec*
EMP: 30
SQ FT: 25,000
SALES (est): 5.4MM **Privately Held**
WEB: www.jaysfurnitureproducts.com
SIC: 2531 2512 2431 Benches for public buildings; upholstered household furniture; millwork

(G-3016)
JENTSCH & CO INC
107 Dorothy St (14206-2939)
PHONE...................................716 852-4111
Fax: 716 852-4270
Christopher Jentsch, *President*
Walter Peters, *Corp Secy*
EMP: 6 EST: 1931
SQ FT: 28,500
SALES (est): 944.3K **Privately Held**
WEB: www.jentschandcompany.com
SIC: 3441 Fabricated structural metal

(G-3017)
JERRY MILLER MOLDED SHOES INC (PA)
Also Called: Jerry Miller I.D. Shoes
36 Mason St (14213-1505)
PHONE...................................716 881-3920
Fax: 716 881-0349
Hussain Syed, *President*
Sarah Syed, *Vice Pres*
Wayne Weisedel, *Sls & Mktg Exec*
Wayne Weisedel, *Sales Mgr*
◆ EMP: 11
SQ FT: 26,000
SALES (est): 1.2MM **Privately Held**
WEB: www.jerrymillershoes.com
SIC: 3143 3144 Orthopedic shoes, men's; orthopedic shoes, women's

(G-3018)
JERSEY EXPRESS INC
3080 Main St (14214-1304)
PHONE...................................716 834-6151
Nancy Miranda, *President*
Scott Simard, *Principal*
Michael Miranda, *Vice Pres*
EMP: 15
SALES (est): 1.4MM **Privately Held**
WEB: www.jerseyexpress.com
SIC: 2389 Footlets

(G-3019)
JET-BLACK SEALERS INC
555 Ludwig Ave (14227-1026)
P.O. Box 7257 (14240-7257)
PHONE...................................716 891-4197
Fax: 716 891-4244
William C Smith, *Ch of Bd*
Eric Moggaffin, *Sales Mgr*
John Smith, *Manager*
Rosemary Smith, *Admin Sec*
EMP: 6
SQ FT: 6,400
SALES (est): 1MM **Privately Held**
WEB: www.sealmasterbuffalo.com
SIC: 2951 Asphalt paving mixtures & blocks

(G-3020)
JOHNSON CONTROLS INC
130 John Muir Dr Ste 100 (14228-1139)
PHONE...................................716 688-7340
Fax: 716 688-7453
Harold Witschi, *Branch Mgr*
EMP: 50 **Privately Held**
SIC: 3822 Auto controls regulating residntl & coml environmt & applncs
HQ: Johnson Controls, Inc.
5757 N Green Bay Ave
Milwaukee WI 53209
414 524-1200

(G-3021)
JOHNSON MANUFACTURING COMPANY
Also Called: SA Day Buffalo Flux Facility
1489 Niagara St (14213-1103)
PHONE...................................716 881-3030
Jackson Bowling, *General Mgr*
EMP: 10
SALES (corp-wide): 3.2MM **Privately Held**
WEB: www.johnsonmfg.com
SIC: 2899 Fluxes: brazing, soldering, galvanizing & welding
PA: Johnson Manufacturing Company, Inc
114 Lost Grove Rd
Princeton IA 52768
563 289-5123

(G-3022)
JUST LAMPS OF NEW YORK INC
334 Harris Hill Rd Apt 1 (14221-7473)
PHONE...................................716 626-2240
Dave Bethell, *CEO*
Eric Lanham, *President*
Mark Murray, *CFO*
Melissa Cutway, *Manager*
EMP: 12
SALES (est): 2.2MM **Privately Held**
WEB: www.justlamps.us.com
SIC: 3861 Projectors, still or motion picture, silent or sound

(G-3023)
K & E FABRICATING CO INC
40 Stanley St (14206-1018)
PHONE...................................716 829-1829
Fax: 716 823-2183
Peter Fasolino, *President*
David Fasolino, *Manager*
EMP: 12
SQ FT: 10,000
SALES (est): 3MM **Privately Held**
SIC: 3441 Fabricated structural metal

(G-3024)
K D M DIE COMPANY INC
620 Elk St (14210-2237)
PHONE...................................716 828-9000
Fax: 716 828-9100
Gary Posluszny, *CEO*
Carl Posluszny, *Treasurer*
Linn Emser, *Finance*
EMP: 17
SQ FT: 32,000
SALES: 2.5MM **Privately Held**
SIC: 3544 3599 Special dies & tools; machine shop, jobbing & repair

(G-3025)
K-TECHNOLOGIES INC
4090 Jeffrey Blvd (14219-2338)
PHONE...................................716 828-4444
Jeffrey Kryszak, *President*
Reginald Hilton, *Manager*
Michael Murphy, *CTO*
EMP: 40
SQ FT: 5,400
SALES: 4MM **Privately Held**
WEB: www.k-technologies.net
SIC: 3824 Electromechanical counters

(G-3026)
KALNITZ KITCHENS INC
Also Called: K Kitchen
2620 Walden Ave (14225-4736)
PHONE...................................716 684-1700
Fax: 716 684-4733
Jamie Kalnitz, *President*
▲ EMP: 10 EST: 1980
SQ FT: 6,000
SALES (est): 970K **Privately Held**
WEB: www.kkitchen.com
SIC: 2434 5031 5211 Wood kitchen cabinets; kitchen cabinets; cabinets, kitchen

(G-3027)
KEHR-BUFFALO WIRE FRAME CO INC
Also Called: Rogers Industrial Spring
127 Kehr St (14211-1522)
P.O. Box 806, Grand Island (14072-0806)
PHONE...................................716 897-2288
George Rogers, *President*
James Rogers III, *Vice Pres*
EMP: 30
SQ FT: 27,000
SALES (est): 5.4MM **Privately Held**
WEB: www.kbwf.net
SIC: 3496 Miscellaneous fabricated wire products

(G-3028)
KELLER BROS & MILLER INC
401 Franklin St (14202-1586)
PHONE...................................716 854-2374
Fax: 716 856-7978
Ralph Salerno, *President*
Pat Sitek, *Office Mgr*
EMP: 9
SQ FT: 8,600
SALES (est): 1.5MM **Privately Held**
WEB: www.kbmprinting.com
SIC: 2752 Commercial printing, lithographic

(G-3029)
KEY TECH FINISHING
2929 Main St Ste 2 (14214-1760)
PHONE...................................716 832-1232
Fax: 716 832-1298
Jack Karet, *President*
Jennifer Masse, *General Mgr*
Joan Karet, *Corp Secy*
EMP: 30
SQ FT: 80,000
SALES (est): 3MM
SALES (corp-wide): 8.1MM **Privately Held**
WEB: www.keyfinishing.com
SIC: 3471 Electroplating of metals or formed products; electroplating & plating
PA: Keystone Corporation
2929 Main St
Buffalo NY 14214
716 832-1232

(G-3030)
KEYNOTE SYSTEMS CORPORATION
2810 Sweet Home Rd (14228-1347)
PHONE...................................716 564-1332
Leonard Gostowski, *President*
EMP: 5
SALES (est): 560.8K **Privately Held**
SIC: 7372 Prepackaged software

(G-3031)
KEYSTONE CORPORATION (PA)
2929 Main St (14214-1719)
PHONE...................................716 832-1232
Fax: 716 836-8885
Jack A Karet, *President*
Joan Karet, *Corp Secy*
Michael Karet, *Vice Pres*
Sam Goorevich, *Sales Mgr*
EMP: 40 EST: 1923
SQ FT: 45,000
SALES (est): 8.4MM **Privately Held**
WEB: www.keyfinishing.com
SIC: 3471 Electroplating of metals or formed products; electroplating & plating; anodizing (plating) of metals or formed products

(G-3032)
KINEQUIP INC
365 Old Niagara Fls Blvd (14228-1636)
PHONE...................................716 694-5000
Scott Fotheringham, *Marketing Staff*
John Mistreda, *Manager*
Eric Lee, *Consultant*
Jon Kreiss, *Executive Asst*
EMP: 13
SALES (corp-wide): 13.9MM **Privately Held**
WEB: www.buywika.com
SIC: 3563 5084 Vacuum pumps, except laboratory; industrial machinery & equipment
PA: Kinequip Inc.
365 Old Niagara Fls Blvd
Amherst NY 14228
716 694-5000

(G-3033)
KITTINGER COMPANY INC
4675 Transit Rd (14221-6022)
PHONE...................................716 876-1000
Raymond C Bialkowski, *CEO*
Karen Bialkowski, *Human Res Mgr*
EMP: 50
SQ FT: 60,000
SALES (est): 7MM **Privately Held**
WEB: www.kittingerfurniture.com
SIC: 2521 2512 2511 Wood office furniture; upholstered household furniture; wood household furniture

(G-3034)
KOCH METAL SPINNING CO INC
74 Jewett Ave (14214-2421)
PHONE...................................716 835-3631
Fax: 716 833-0834
Gregory C Koch, *Ch of Bd*
Eric Koch, *President*
Candace Farrell, *Bookkeeper*
McManigle Robert, *Manager*
▼ EMP: 52 EST: 1939
SQ FT: 25,000
SALES: 4MM **Privately Held**
WEB: www.kochmetalspinning.com
SIC: 3469 Spinning metal for the trade

(G-3035)
KOEHLR-GIBSON MKG GRAPHICS INC
Also Called: Koehler-Gibson Mkg & Graphics
875 Englewood Ave (14223-2334)
PHONE...................................716 838-5960
Fax: 716 835-5960
David Koehler, *President*
Roselyn Kieffer, *Purchasing*
EMP: 20 EST: 1958
SQ FT: 13,000
SALES (est): 2.8MM **Privately Held**
SIC: 3953 2796 Date stamps, hand: rubber or metal; postmark stamps, hand: rubber or metal; printing dies, rubber or plastic, for marking machines; photoengraving plates, linecuts or halftones

▲ = Import ▼ = Export
◆ = Import/Export

GEOGRAPHIC SECTION

Buffalo - Erie County (G-3059)

(G-3036)
KOHLER AWNING INC
2600 Walden Ave (14225-4736)
PHONE..................................716 685-3333
John M Kohler III, *President*
Craig Kohler, *Corp Secy*
Jesse W Kohler, *Vice Pres*
Patricia Kusz, *Office Mgr*
EMP: 30 **EST:** 1924
SQ FT: 2,182
SALES (est): 4.4MM **Privately Held**
WEB: www.kohlerawning.com
SIC: 2394 7699 Awnings, fabric: made from purchased materials; awning repair shop

(G-3037)
KREPE KRAFT INC
Also Called: Krepe-Kraft
1801 Elmwood Ave (14207-2463)
P.O. Box 1907 (14219-0107)
PHONE..................................716 826-7086
Daniel Keane, *President*
Leo Eckman, *President*
Kevin T Keane, *Principal*
Donna Eckman, *Vice Pres*
John M Yessa, *Treasurer*
EMP: 370
SQ FT: 47,300
SALES (est): 25.6MM
SALES (corp-wide): 59.2MM **Privately Held**
WEB: www.krepekraft.com
SIC: 2754 5947 Commercial printing, gravure; invitations: gravure printing; cards, except greeting: gravure printing; gift, novelty & souvenir shop
PA: Mod-Pac Corp.
1801 Elmwood Ave Ste 1
Buffalo NY 14207
716 873-0640

(G-3038)
KYNTEC CORPORATION
2100 Old Union Rd (14227-2725)
PHONE..................................716 810-6956
Patrick Lee, *Ch of Bd*
Scott Taylor, *President*
Gerald Spyche, *Vice Pres*
Rich Ryan, *Treasurer*
EMP: 6 **EST:** 2012
SALES (est): 1.2MM **Privately Held**
SIC: 3569 3484 3429 3531 Industrial shock absorbers; rifles or rifle parts, 30 mm. & below; aircraft hardware; marine related equipment

(G-3039)
L LLC
106 Soldiers Pl (14222-1261)
PHONE..................................716 885-3918
Mohsen Lachaal, *Mng Member*
EMP: 20 **EST:** 2001
SALES (est): 2MM **Privately Held**
SIC: 2079 Olive oil

(G-3040)
L LOY PRESS INC
Also Called: Insty-Prints
3959 Union Rd (14225-4253)
PHONE..................................716 634-5966
Fax: 716 634-0841
Richard Delong, *President*
Joyce S Delong, *Vice Pres*
EMP: 5
SQ FT: 1,894
SALES (est): 750.9K **Privately Held**
SIC: 2752 2791 2789 2759 Commercial printing, lithographic; typesetting; bookbinding & related work; commercial printing

(G-3041)
LABATT USA LLC
50 Fountain Plz Ste 900 (14202-2214)
PHONE..................................716 604-1050
Fax: 716 604-1055
Glen Walter, *President*
Thomas Cardella, *Vice Pres*
Frank Oostdyk, *Engineer*
Shari Keisow, *Manager*
Bruce McAuley, *Manager*
▲ **EMP:** 60
SALES (est): 10.1MM **Privately Held**
SIC: 2082 Beer (alcoholic beverage)

HQ: North American Breweries, Inc.
445 Saint Paul St
Rochester NY 14605
585 546-1030

(G-3042)
LACTALIS AMERICAN GROUP INC
2375 S Park Ave (14220-2653)
PHONE..................................716 827-2622
Sean Paul Quiblier, *Principal*
Donald Dixon, *Purch Mgr*
Sharon Pusateri, *Assistant*
EMP: 100
SALES (corp-wide): 19.2MM **Privately Held**
SIC: 2022 Cheese, natural & processed
HQ: Lactalis American Group, Inc.
2376 S Park Ave
Buffalo NY 14220
716 823-6262

(G-3043)
LACTALIS AMERICAN GROUP INC (DH)
Also Called: Sorrento Lactalis
2376 S Park Ave (14220-2670)
PHONE..................................716 823-6262
Frederick Bouisset, *CEO*
Paul Peterson, *Vice Pres*
Bill Senay, *Plant Mgr*
Jeffrey Pugliese, *Natl Sales Mgr*
Ed Sullivan, *Natl Sales Mgr*
◆ **EMP:** 500
SALES (est): 456.1MM
SALES (corp-wide): 19.2MM **Privately Held**
WEB: www.lactalisamericangroup.com
SIC: 2022 Cheese, natural & processed
HQ: Parmalat Spa
Via Delle Nazioni Unite 4
Collecchio PR 43044
052 180-81

(G-3044)
LAFARGE NORTH AMERICA INC
575 Ohio St (14203-3119)
PHONE..................................716 854-5791
Fax: 716 854-3112
Edward Hickey, *Manager*
Robert Hafner, *Manager*
Robert Lloyd, *Manager*
Matthew Pehler, *Manager*
Mark Joslin, *Traffic Dir*
EMP: 5
SALES (corp-wide): 23.4B **Privately Held**
WEB: www.lafargenorthamerica.com
SIC: 3241 Cement, hydraulic
HQ: Lafarge North America Inc.
8700 W Bryn Mawr Ave Ll
Chicago IL 60631
703 480-3600

(G-3045)
LAM WESTERN NEW YORK INC
Also Called: Final Cut Letterpress Spc
32 Cornelia St (14210-1202)
PHONE..................................716 856-0308
Fax: 716 856-0185
Lawrence N Wypior, *President*
Matthew Wypior, *Vice Pres*
EMP: 5
SQ FT: 8,000
SALES (est): 444.4K **Privately Held**
SIC: 2759 Commercial printing

(G-3046)
LANDIES CANDIES CO INC
2495 Main St Ste 350 (14214-2154)
PHONE..................................716 834-8212
Fax: 716 833-9113
Larry Szrama, *President*
Andrew Gaiek, *Vice Pres*
Alan Nowak, *Safety Dir*
Matthew Halizak, *Facilities Mgr*
Dennis Hussak, *Marketing Staff*
EMP: 10
SALES (est): 1.7MM **Privately Held**
WEB: www.landiescandies.com
SIC: 2066 Chocolate candy, solid

(G-3047)
LAURUS DEVELOPMENT INC
3556 Lake Shore Rd # 121 (14219-1460)
PHONE..................................716 823-1202
Vincent Coppola, *President*

John Feuerstein, *Vice Pres*
EMP: 14
SALES (est): 1MM **Privately Held**
WEB: www.laurusdevelopment.com
SIC: 7372 7371 8748 7379 Business oriented computer software; computer software systems analysis & design, custom; computer software development & applications; systems engineering consultant, ex. computer or professional; computer related maintenance services

(G-3048)
LINDE LLC
101 Katherine St (14210-2005)
PHONE..................................716 847-0748
Jack Pederson, *Opers-Prdtn-Mfg*
EMP: 40
SALES (corp-wide): 19.2B **Privately Held**
SIC: 2813 Nitrogen; oxygen, compressed or liquefied
HQ: Linde Llc
200 Somerset Corporate Bl
Bridgewater NJ 08807
908 464-8100

(G-3049)
LINE WARD CORPORATION
157 Seneca Creek Rd (14224-2347)
PHONE..................................716 675-7373
Fax: 716 674-5334
Cheryl Gustavel, *President*
Roger Gustavel, *Vice Pres*
Robert J Ward, *Plant Mgr*
EMP: 7
SQ FT: 3,000
SALES (est): 800K **Privately Held**
WEB: www.lineward.com
SIC: 3531 Construction machinery

(G-3050)
LITELAB CORP (PA)
251 Elm St (14203-1603)
PHONE..................................716 856-4300
Fax: 716 856-0156
Frederick A Spaulding, *CEO*
Jacob Levin, *President*
Ellen Conrad, *General Mgr*
Dawn M Casati, *Corp Secy*
Lawrence Christ, *COO*
▲ **EMP:** 135
SQ FT: 80,000
SALES (est): 27MM **Privately Held**
WEB: www.litelab.com
SIC: 3646 3645 Commercial indusl & institutional electric lighting fixtures; residential lighting fixtures

(G-3051)
LUVATA HEAT TRANSFER SOLUTIONS
70 Sayre St (14207-2225)
P.O. Box 1981 (14240-1981)
PHONE..................................716 879-6700
Dennis Appel, *President*
Rich Lyons, *Treasurer*
Corina Arroyo, *Finance*
EMP: 5
SALES (est): 412.4K **Privately Held**
SIC: 3351 Copper rolling & drawing; strip, copper & copper alloy; tubing, copper & copper alloy

(G-3052)
M A MOSLOW & BROS INC
375 Norfolk Ave (14215-3108)
PHONE..................................716 896-2950
Fax: 716 896-2699
David Moslow, *President*
Joe Moslow, *Vice Pres*
Laurie Keggins, *Office Mgr*
▲ **EMP:** 40
SQ FT: 21,000
SALES (est): 4.3MM **Privately Held**
WEB: www.moslowbros.com
SIC: 2499 Trophy bases, wood

(G-3053)
M K ULRICH CONSTRUCTION INC
Also Called: Bison Iron & Step
1601 Harlem Rd (14206-1923)
PHONE..................................716 893-5777
Fax: 716 893-1125
Don Ulrich, *President*
Marie Ulrich, *Vice Pres*

EMP: 12
SQ FT: 4,800
SALES: 900K **Privately Held**
SIC: 3272 1799 Concrete products; steps, prefabricated concrete; ornamental metal work

(G-3054)
MACNEIL POLYMERS INC (PA)
3155 Broadway St (14227-1034)
PHONE..................................716 681-7755
Richard Neil, *President*
EMP: 15
SQ FT: 35,097
SALES (est): 1MM **Privately Held**
WEB: www.macneilpolymers.com
SIC: 2821 Plastics materials & resins

(G-3055)
MAGTROL INC
70 Gardenville Pkwy W (14224-1394)
PHONE..................................716 668-5555
Fax: 716 668-8705
William A Mulroy III, *President*
Thomas Rymarczyk, *General Mgr*
▼ **EMP:** 50 **EST:** 1953
SQ FT: 35,000
SALES (est): 13.8MM **Privately Held**
WEB: www.magtrol.com
SIC: 3829 3625 3568 3825 Measuring & controlling devices; aircraft & motor vehicle measurement equipment; brakes, electromagnetic; clutches, except vehicular; instruments to measure electricity; industrial instrmnts msrmnt display/control process variable; motor vehicle parts & accessories

(G-3056)
MARKIN TUBING LP
Also Called: Markin Tubing Division
400 Ingham Ave (14218-2536)
PHONE..................................585 495-6211
Fax: 716 824-3525
Tom Stamper, *Manager*
EMP: 17
SALES (corp-wide): 18.1MM **Privately Held**
SIC: 3312 3317 Tubes, steel & iron; steel pipe & tubes
PA: Markin Tubing, Lp
1 Markin Ln
Wyoming NY 14591
585 495-6211

(G-3057)
MASSIMO FRIEDMAN INC
Also Called: Great Arrow Graphics
2495 Main St Ste 457 (14214-2154)
PHONE..................................716 836-0408
Fax: 716 736-0702
Alan Friedman, *President*
Donna M Massimo, *Corp Secy*
Lisa Samar, *Vice Pres*
EMP: 20
SALES (est): 2MM **Privately Held**
WEB: www.greatarrow.com
SIC: 2771 Greeting cards

(G-3058)
MATERION ADVANCED MATERIALS (DH)
2978 Main St (14214-1004)
PHONE..................................800 327-1355
Donald Klinkowicz, *President*
Amy Maundrell, *General Mgr*
Matthew Willson, *General Mgr*
Sally James, *Regional Mgr*
Mark Devillier, *Vice Pres*
▲ **EMP:** 198 **EST:** 1912
SQ FT: 150,000
SALES (est): 111.9MM
SALES (corp-wide): 1B **Publicly Held**
WEB: www.williams-adv.com
SIC: 3339 Primary nonferrous metals
HQ: Materion Brush Inc.
6070 Parkland Blvd Ste 1
Mayfield Heights OH 44124
216 486-4200

(G-3059)
MAXSECURE SYSTEMS INC
300 International Dr # 100 (14221-5781)
PHONE..................................800 657-4336
Ken Szekely, *President*
Ken Lawrence, *Admin Sec*

Buffalo - Erie County (G-3060) — GEOGRAPHIC SECTION

EMP: 3
SALES: 1.3MM Privately Held
WEB: www.max-secure.com
SIC: 2531 Public building & related furniture

(G-3060)
MC IVOR MANUFACTURING INC
400 Ingham Ave (14218-2536)
P.O. Box 13 (14220-0013)
PHONE.....................716 825-1808
Fax: 716 825-1809
Bruce Mc Ivor, *President*
EMP: 6
SQ FT: 13,000
SALES (est): 540K Privately Held
SIC: 3599 Machine shop, jobbing & repair

(G-3061)
MEDICAL ACOUSTICS LLC
640 Ellicott St Ste 407 (14203-1253)
PHONE.....................716 218-7353
Nicolaas Smith, *Vice Pres*
Frank Codella, *Mng Member*
Joel Castlevetere,
EMP: 12
SALES: 1MM Privately Held
SIC: 3842 Respirators

(G-3062)
MERZ METAL & MACHINE CORP
237 Chelsea Pl (14211-1003)
PHONE.....................716 893-7786
Fax: 716 893-8727
Dave Nieman, *President*
Joe Huefner, *Vice Pres*
Kathy Charczuk, *Human Resources*
EMP: 22 EST: 1948
SQ FT: 13,000
SALES (est): 5MM Privately Held
WEB: www.merzmetal.com
SIC: 3444 1711 Sheet metalwork; ventilators, sheet metal; ducts, sheet metal; ventilation & duct work contractor

(G-3063)
MGS MFG GROUP INC
Also Called: Mgs Buffalo
2400 Walden Ave (14225-4745)
PHONE.....................716 684-9400
Wayne Dreibelbis, *Mfg Staff*
Ed Hopkins, *QC Dir*
Kathy Hakala, *Controller*
James Hughes, *Controller*
Jane Jontz, *Human Res Dir*
EMP: 100
SQ FT: 41,395
SALES (corp-wide): 235.1MM Privately Held
WEB: www.abbotthpd.com
SIC: 3089 Plastic containers, except foam
PA: Mgs Mfg. Group, Inc.
    W188n11707 Maple Rd
    Germantown WI 53022
    262 255-5790

(G-3064)
MIBRO GROUP
Also Called: Allied
4039 Genesee St (14225-1904)
PHONE.....................716 631-5713
Fax: 716 837-9500
Leon Lapidus, *President*
Sharon McNutt, *COO*
Larry Lucyshyn, *Exec VP*
Barry J Smith, *CFO*
Elaine Cruise-Smith, *Human Res Dir*
▲ EMP: 75 EST: 1954
SQ FT: 100,000
SALES (est): 11.2MM
SALES (corp-wide): 34.2MM Privately Held
WEB: www.mibro.com
SIC: 3545 Drill bits, metalworking
PA: Mibro Partners
    111 Sinnott Rd
    Scarborough ON M1L 4
    416 285-9000

(G-3065)
MIKEN COMPANIES INC
75 Boxwood Ln (14227-2707)
P.O. Box 178 (14231-0178)
PHONE.....................716 668-6311
Fax: 716 668-7630
Walter J Jaworski, *CEO*
Michael Bolas, *President*
Pauline Jaworski, *Vice Pres*
Ralph Leskiw, *Purchasing*
Rick Brzezicki, *Manager*
EMP: 100 EST: 1929
SQ FT: 65,000
SALES (est): 13.5MM Privately Held
WEB: www.mikencompanies.com
SIC: 2752 2759 2675 2672 Commercial printing, lithographic; commercial printing; die-cut paper & board; coated & laminated paper

(G-3066)
MILLCRAFT PAPER COMPANY
Also Called: Deltacraft Paper Company
99 Bud Mil Dr (14206-1801)
PHONE.....................716 856-5135
Bill Grubich, *Branch Mgr*
EMP: 50
SALES (corp-wide): 400.1MM Privately Held
WEB: www.millcraft.com
SIC: 2679 Paper products, converted
PA: The Millcraft Paper Company
    6800 Grant Ave
    Cleveland OH 44105
    216 441-5505

(G-3067)
MINEO & SAPIO MEATS INC
Also Called: Minero & Sapio Sausage
410 Connecticut St (14213-2641)
PHONE.....................716 884-2398
Fax: 716 884-2515
Michael Pierro, *President*
Nadine Pierro, *Treasurer*
EMP: 6
SALES (est): 1.4MM Privately Held
WEB: www.mineosapio.com
SIC: 2013 5421 Sausages & other prepared meats; meat markets, including freezer provisioners

(G-3068)
MIRION TECH CONAX NUCLEAR INC
Also Called: Ist Conax Nuclear
402 Sonwil Dr (14225-5530)
PHONE.....................716 681-1973
Fax: 716 681-1139
Iain Wilson, *CEO*
Jukka Kahilainen, *Vice Pres*
Jack Pacheco, *CFO*
Seth B Rosen, *Admin Sec*
EMP: 23
SQ FT: 26,200
SALES (est): 4.8MM
SALES (corp-wide): 173.7MM Privately Held
WEB: www.mirion.com
SIC: 3829 Nuclear radiation & testing apparatus
HQ: Mirion Technologies (Ist) Corporation
    315 Daniel Zenker Dr # 204
    Horseheads NY 14845
    607 562-4300

(G-3069)
MM OF EAST AURORA LLC
Also Called: Buffalo Hardwood Floor Center
3801 Harlem Rd (14215-1907)
PHONE.....................716 651-9663
Greg Tramont, *CFO*
Marlena Maloney, *Mng Member*
James Maloney,
EMP: 10
SALES (est): 1.5MM Privately Held
SIC: 2426 Hardwood dimension & flooring mills

(G-3070)
MOBILEAPP SYSTEMS LLC
4 Grand View Trl (14217)
PHONE.....................716 667-2780
EMP: 5 EST: 2012
SALES (est): 310.6K Privately Held
SIC: 7372 Prepackaged software

(G-3071)
MOD-PAC CORP (PA)
1801 Elmwood Ave Ste 1 (14207-2496)
PHONE.....................716 873-6040
Fax: 716 873-6008
Kevin T Keane, *Ch of Bd*
Daniel G Keane, *President*
Robert J McKenna, *Principal*
Howard Zemsky, *Principal*
David B Lupp, *COO*
▼ EMP: 172
SQ FT: 333,000
SALES: 59.2MM Privately Held
WEB: www.modpac.com
SIC: 2657 2759 Folding paperboard boxes; commercial printing; invitations: printing; business forms: printing

(G-3072)
MOD-PAC CORP
1801 Elmwood Ave Ste 1 (14207-2496)
P.O. Box 1907, Blasdell (14219-0107)
PHONE.....................716 447-9013
Robert Heilman, *Vice Pres*
Leo Eckman, *Manager*
EMP: 100
SALES (corp-wide): 59.2MM Privately Held
WEB: www.modpac.com
SIC: 2754 2752 Commercial printing, gravure; commercial printing, lithographic
PA: Mod-Pac Corp.
    1801 Elmwood Ave Ste 1
    Buffalo NY 14207
    716 873-6040

(G-3073)
MODERN HEAT TRTING FORGING INC (PA)
1112 Niagara St (14213-1714)
PHONE.....................716 884-2176
Fax: 716 884-1419
Douglas Feind Sr, *President*
Scott Feind, *Vice Pres*
Pamela Feind, *Office Mgr*
EMP: 16 EST: 1929
SQ FT: 17,000
SALES (est): 2.1MM Privately Held
WEB: www.modernheattreat.com
SIC: 3398 Metal heat treating

(G-3074)
MONO-SYSTEMS INC
180 Hopkins St (14220-1854)
PHONE.....................716 821-1344
Fax: 716 821-1345
Bill Lignos, *Purchasing*
Jim Sutton, *Manager*
EMP: 30
SALES (corp-wide): 10.1MM Privately Held
WEB: www.monosystems.com
SIC: 3443 3643 3549 Cable trays, metal plate; current-carrying wiring devices; metalworking machinery
PA: Mono-Systems, Inc.
    4 International Dr # 280
    Rye Brook NY 10573
    914 934-2075

(G-3075)
MOOR ELECTRONICS INC
95 Dorothy St Ste 6 (14206-2900)
P.O. Box 765 (14240-0765)
PHONE.....................716 821-5304
Duane Simano, *President*
Henry Zagara, *Corp Secy*
▲ EMP: 6
SQ FT: 5,000
SALES: 274K Privately Held
SIC: 3812 7699 Nautical instruments; nautical & navigational instrument repair

(G-3076)
MRI NORTHTOWNS GROUP PC
Also Called: Northtown Imaging
199 Park Club Ln Ste 300 (14221-5269)
PHONE.....................716 836-4646
Fax: 716 836-4696
James Rinaldi, *Director*
Elizabeth M Sobieraj, *Diag Radio*
EMP: 11
SALES (corp-wide): 2.5MM Privately Held
WEB: www.lockportmri.com
SIC: 3231 Medical & laboratory glassware: made from purchased glass
PA: Mri Northtown's Group Pc
    1020 Youngs Rd Ste 120w
    Williamsville NY 14221
    716 689-4406

(G-3077)
MULLER TOOL INC
74 Anderson Rd (14225-4979)
PHONE.....................716 895-3658
Fax: 716 895-3972
Gary D Reisweber, *President*
Bruce Reisweber, *Vice Pres*
EMP: 20 EST: 1941
SQ FT: 12,000
SALES (est): 3.7MM Privately Held
WEB: www.mullertool.com
SIC: 3599 3451 Machine shop, jobbing & repair; screw machine products

(G-3078)
MULTISORB TECH INTL LLC (PA)
325 Harlem Rd (14224-1825)
PHONE.....................716 824-8900
James Renda, *President*
Laxmikant Khaitan, *Business Mgr*
Sarah Cook, *Opers Staff*
Laureen Shupe, *Purch Agent*
Deb Hasley, *Buyer*
EMP: 1
SALES (est): 31.4MM Privately Held
SIC: 2819 Industrial inorganic chemicals

(G-3079)
MULTISORB TECHNOLOGIES INC
Also Called: Ecto Tech Automation
10 French Rd (14227-2702)
PHONE.....................716 656-1402
Fax: 716 662-8281
John S Cullen, *CEO*
Andrew Zippiroli, *Engineer*
Mark Morelli, *Manager*
EMP: 30
SALES (corp-wide): 86.6MM Privately Held
SIC: 2819 Industrial inorganic chemicals
PA: Multisorb Technologies, Inc.
    325 Harlem Rd
    Buffalo NY 14224
    716 824-8900

(G-3080)
N MAKE MOLD INC
Also Called: Chocolate Delivery Systems
85 River Rock Dr Ste 202 (14207-2170)
PHONE.....................716 854-6050
Timothy Thill, *President*
Nancy Hnowski, *Credit Mgr*
▲ EMP: 50
SALES (est): 18.5MM
SALES (corp-wide): 21.8MM Privately Held
SIC: 2064 Candy bars, including chocolate covered bars
PA: Chocolate Delivery Systems, Inc.
    85 River Rock Dr Ste 202
    Buffalo NY 14207
    716 854-6050

(G-3081)
NAS QUICK SIGN INC
Also Called: North American Signs Buffalo
1628 Elmwood Ave (14207-3014)
PHONE.....................716 876-7599
Fax: 716 876-7729
Frank Strada, *President*
Mike Francano, *Prdtn Mgr*
Paul Strada, *Sales Mgr*
Agnes Strada, *Shareholder*
EMP: 9
SQ FT: 7,000
SALES (est): 1.3MM Privately Held
SIC: 3993 Signs, not made in custom sign painting shops; electric signs

(G-3082)
NC INDUSTRIES INC (PA)
Also Called: Niagara Cutter
200 John James Audubon (14228-1120)
P.O. Box 279, Reynoldsville PA (15851-0279)
PHONE.....................248 528-5200
Fax: 716 689-8485
Roger D Bollier, *Ch of Bd*
Sherwood L Bollier, *Vice Pres*
William C Szabo, *Treasurer*
William Rees, *Office Mgr*
Dan Wells, *Manager*
EMP: 15
SQ FT: 8,500

▲ = Import ▼ = Export ◆ = Import/Export

GEOGRAPHIC SECTION — Buffalo - Erie County (G-3107)

SALES (est): 52.8MM **Privately Held**
SIC: **3545** 3479 5084 Cutting tools for machine tools; coating of metals & formed products; machine tools & accessories

(G-3083)
NERVVE TECHNOLOGIES INC (PA)
500 Seneca St Ste 501 (14204-1963)
PHONE...........................716 800-2250
Thomas Slowe, *CEO*
Jose Cecin, *COO*
Jacob Goellner, *CTO*
Robert Robey, *Executive*
Darci Hosier, *Administration*
EMP: 22
SALES (est): 4.1MM **Privately Held**
SIC: **7372** 8711 Application computer software; electrical or electronic engineering

(G-3084)
NEW ERA CAP CO INC
160 Delaware Ave (14202-2404)
PHONE...........................716 604-9000
Michael Thorton, *Manager*
EMP: 300
SALES (corp-wide): 433.1MM **Privately Held**
WEB: www.neweracap.com
SIC: **2353** Uniform hats & caps; baseball caps
PA: New Era Cap Co., Inc.
   160 Delaware Ave
   Buffalo NY 14202
   716 604-9000

(G-3085)
NEW ERA CAP CO INC (PA)
160 Delaware Ave (14202-2404)
P.O. Box 208, Derby (14047-0208)
PHONE...........................716 604-9000
Fax: 716 604-9299
Christopher Koch, *Ch of Bd*
Peter M Augustine, *President*
Valerie Koch, *Corp Secy*
Jim Patterson, *COO*
Gerry Matos, *Senior VP*
▲ EMP: 200
SQ FT: 120,000
SALES (est): 433.1MM **Privately Held**
WEB: www.neweracap.com
SIC: **2353** Uniform hats & caps; baseball caps

(G-3086)
NIAGARA DISPENSING TECH INC
170 Northpointe Pkwy (14228-1991)
PHONE...........................716 636-9827
Glenn Kaufmann, *CEO*
Thomas Gagliano, *CEO*
Carlo Petermann, *COO*
Neil Fischer, *Sales Dir*
▲ EMP: 10
SQ FT: 3,000
SALES: 2MM **Privately Held**
SIC: **3585** Beer dispensing equipment

(G-3087)
NIAGARA FIBERGLASS INC
88 Okell St (14220-2133)
PHONE...........................716 822-3921
Fax: 716 822-0406
Stephen Gale, *President*
Philip O'Donnell, *Vice Pres*
Gordon Dickinson, *Sales Staff*
EMP: 45
SQ FT: 23,000
SALES: 2.3MM **Privately Held**
SIC: **3089** 3544 Molding primary plastic; special dies, tools, jigs & fixtures

(G-3088)
NIAGARA GEAR CORPORATION
941 Military Rd (14217-2590)
PHONE...........................716 874-3131
Fax: 716 874-9003
Matthew Babisz, *President*
Robert C Barden, *Vice Pres*
Marcia Iore, *Finance Mgr*
Marcia Fiore, *Persnl Dir*
EMP: 25 EST: 1952
SQ FT: 30,000
SALES: 4.2MM **Privately Held**
WEB: www.niagaragear.com
SIC: **3566** Gears, power transmission, except automotive

(G-3089)
NIAGARA LASALLE CORPORATION
110 Hopkins St (14220-2195)
P.O. Box 399 (14240-0399)
PHONE...........................716 827-7010
Margo Mack, *Sales Staff*
Craig Zito, *Sales Staff*
Mike Slood, *Manager*
EMP: 75
SALES (corp-wide): 590.8MM **Privately Held**
SIC: **3316** Bars, steel, cold finished, from purchased hot-rolled
HQ: Niagara Lasalle Corporation
   1412 150th St
   Hammond IN 46327
   219 853-6000

(G-3090)
NIAGARA PUNCH & DIE CORP
176 Gruner Rd (14227-1090)
PHONE...........................716 896-7619
Fax: 716 896-8958
Jay Czerniak, *President*
Jean Czerniak, *Admin Sec*
EMP: 8 EST: 1956
SQ FT: 5,000
SALES (est): 1.7MM **Privately Held**
WEB: www.npd123.com
SIC: **3544** Special dies & tools

(G-3091)
NIAGARA TRANSFORMER CORP
1747 Dale Rd (14225-4964)
P.O. Box 233 (14225-0233)
PHONE...........................716 896-6500
Fax: 716 896-8871
John F Darby, *President*
Robert Fishlock, *Vice Pres*
Sheldon Kennedy, *Vice Pres*
Stan Hatch, *Mfg Mgr*
Bob Murphy, *QC Mgr*
▲ EMP: 75 EST: 1928
SQ FT: 100,000
SALES (est): 27.7MM **Privately Held**
WEB: www.niagaratransformer.com
SIC: **3612** Power transformers, electric

(G-3092)
NIAGARA TYING SERVICE INC
176 Dingens St (14206-2308)
PHONE...........................716 825-0066
Fax: 716 825-0542
Albert J Barrato, *President*
James Smith, *Manager*
Antoinette Barrato, *Admin Sec*
▲ EMP: 38
SALES (est): 5.9MM **Privately Held**
WEB: www.niagaratyingservice.com
SIC: **2013** Sausage casings, natural

(G-3093)
NORAZZA INC (PA)
3938 Broadway St (14227-1104)
PHONE...........................716 706-1160
Thomas J Sperazza, *CEO*
Cindy Judd, *Accounting Mgr*
▲ EMP: 4
SALES (est): 1.6MM **Privately Held**
WEB: www.norazza.com
SIC: **3577** 3861 Computer peripheral equipment; photographic equipment & supplies

(G-3094)
NORSE ENERGY CORP USA
3556 Lake Shore Rd # 700 (14219-1445)
PHONE...........................716 568-2048
EMP: 5 EST: 1993
SALES (est): 690K **Privately Held**
SIC: **1382** Oil/Gas Exploration Services

(G-3095)
NORTHEAST METROLOGY CORP
2601 Genesee St (14225-2916)
PHONE...........................716 827-3770
Fax: 716 827-3775
Basil Korbut, *President*
Fred Miller, *Research*
EMP: 10
SQ FT: 6,120
SALES (est): 2MM **Privately Held**
WEB: www.vantek-nem.com
SIC: **3825** 8734 Test equipment for electronic & electric measurement; testing laboratories

(G-3096)
NORTHROP GRUMMAN INTL TRDG INC
Also Called: Land Self Prtction Systems Div
1740 Wehrle Dr (14221-7032)
PHONE...........................716 626-7233
Patrick Duffey, *General Mgr*
Michael Clark, *Senior Engr*
Brian Schmidt, *Marketing Staff*
Robert Britton, *Manager*
Joseph Downie, *Director*
EMP: 8
SALES (est): 785.8K **Publicly Held**
SIC: **3699** Flight simulators (training aids), electronic
HQ: Northrop Grumman Overseas Holding, Inc.
   2980 Fairview Park Dr
   Falls Church VA 22042
   703 280-4069

(G-3097)
NORTHROP GRUMMAN SYSTEMS CORP
1740 Wehrle Dr (14221-7032)
PHONE...........................716 626-4600
Tim Green, *Principal*
Roger Karlinski, *Purch Agent*
Kevin Ditondo, *Engineer*
Mary Gladhill, *Engineer*
James Heimbueger, *Engineer*
EMP: 99 **Publicly Held**
SIC: **3721** Aircraft
HQ: Northrop Grumman Systems Corporation
   2980 Fairview Park Dr
   Falls Church VA 22042
   703 280-2900

(G-3098)
OEHLERS WLDG & FABRICATION INC
242 Elk St (14210-2102)
PHONE...........................716 821-1800
Mark Appelbaum, *President*
EMP: 15
SQ FT: 45,000
SALES: 1.4MM **Privately Held**
SIC: **3441** Fabricated structural metal

(G-3099)
OERLIKON BALZERS COATING USA
375 N French Rd Ste 104 (14228-2009)
PHONE...........................716 564-8557
John Jesnowski, *Branch Mgr*
EMP: 30
SALES (corp-wide): 2.6B **Privately Held**
WEB: www.balzers.com
SIC: **3479** 3471 Coating of metals & formed products; finishing, metals or formed products
HQ: Oerlikon Balzers Coating Usa Inc.
   1475 E Wdfield Rd Ste 201
   Schaumburg IL 60173
   847 619-5541

(G-3100)
OLIVER GEAR INC
1120 Niagara St (14213-1790)
PHONE...........................716 885-1080
Fax: 716 885-1145
Sam Haines, *President*
Mike Barron, *Vice Pres*
Barbara Stone, *CFO*
EMP: 25
SQ FT: 21,000
SALES (est): 6.3MM
SALES (corp-wide): 18.4MM **Privately Held**
WEB: www.gearmotions.com
SIC: **3566** 7699 Speed changers, drives & gears; industrial equipment services
PA: Gear Motions Incorporated
   1750 Milton Ave
   Syracuse NY 13209
   315 488-0100

(G-3101)
ONEIDA SALES & SERVICE INC (PA)
Also Called: Oneida Concrete Products
155 Commerce Dr (14218-1041)
PHONE...........................716 822-8205
Frederick Saia, *President*
Jeff Kramer, *Controller*
EMP: 25
SALES (est): 5MM **Privately Held**
WEB: www.oneidagroup.com
SIC: **3531** 1799 3496 Concrete plants; fence construction; miscellaneous fabricated wire products

(G-3102)
ONY INC BAIRD RESEARCHPARK
1576 Sweet Home Rd (14228-2710)
PHONE...........................716 636-9096
Edmond Egan, *President*
EMP: 30
SALES (est): 1.9MM **Privately Held**
SIC: **2834** Druggists' preparations (pharmaceuticals)

(G-3103)
OPTA MINERALS
266 Elmwood Ave (14222-2202)
P.O. Box 818 (14222)
PHONE...........................905 689-7361
Bernie Rumbold, *CEO*
John Dietrich, *President*
▲ EMP: 16
SALES (est): 2.4MM **Privately Held**
SIC: **3295** Magnesite, crude: ground, calcined or dead-burned

(G-3104)
ORBITAL HOLDINGS INC
2775 Broadway St Ste 200 (14227-1043)
PHONE...........................951 360-7100
Fax: 951 823-9559
Jerry Jacobs, *Vice Pres*
▲ EMP: 20
SQ FT: 35,160
SALES (est): 3.6MM **Privately Held**
WEB: www.avf.com
SIC: **3449** 3429 Miscellaneous metalwork; manufactured hardware (general)
PA: Avf Inc.
   2775 Broadway St Ste 200
   Buffalo NY 14227
   951 360-7111

(G-3105)
OTIS BEDDING MFG CO INC (PA)
80 James E Casey Dr (14206-2367)
PHONE...........................716 825-2599
Fax: 716 824-2073
John Roma Sr, *President*
John Roma Jr, *Vice Pres*
Carol Roma, *Treasurer*
▲ EMP: 20 EST: 1882
SQ FT: 40,000
SALES (est): 2MM **Privately Held**
WEB: www.otisbed.com
SIC: **2515** 5712 Mattresses & bedsprings; mattresses

(G-3106)
P J R INDUSTRIES INC
Also Called: Southside Precast Products
1951 Hamburg Tpke Frnt (14218-1047)
PHONE...........................716 825-9300
Fax: 716 825-1155
Paul Rossi, *President*
Larry Gold, *Engineer*
Jerrell Bihm, *Info Tech Mgr*
Ron Hayden, *Info Tech Mgr*
Jody Tucker, *Administration*
EMP: 32
SQ FT: 18,500
SALES: 3.5MM **Privately Held**
WEB: www.southsideprecast.com
SIC: **3272** Concrete products, precast

(G-3107)
P P I BUSINESS FORMS INC
94 Spaulding St (14220-1238)
PHONE...........................716 825-1241
Fax: 716 685-4740
Frank Kalenda, *President*
EMP: 9
SQ FT: 9,500

Buffalo - Erie County (G-3108) — GEOGRAPHIC SECTION

SALES (est): 900K **Privately Held**
WEB: www.ppibusinessforms.com
SIC: 2761 Manifold business forms

(G-3108)
P&G METAL COMPONENTS CORP
54 Gruner Rd (14227-1007)
PHONE.................716 896-7900
Fax: 716 896-4129
Scott Bauer, *General Mgr*
David E Ponkow, *Chairman*
Andrew Ponkow, *Exec VP*
Thomas Brush, *CFO*
Gregory Ponkow, *Sales Mgr*
▲ EMP: 100 EST: 1955
SQ FT: 75,000
SALES (est): 31.6MM **Privately Held**
WEB: www.pgsteel.com
SIC: 3469 3544 Metal stampings; special dies, tools, jigs & fixtures

(G-3109)
P-HGH 2 CO INC
180 Cambridge Ave (14215-3702)
PHONE.................954 534-6058
Matthew Taylor, *President*
EMP: 6
SALES (est): 265.8K **Privately Held**
SIC: 2099 Food preparations

(G-3110)
PACKAGE PRINT TECHNOLOGIES
1831 Niagara St (14207-3112)
PHONE.................716 871-9905
Tracy Wettlaufer, *President*
Ward Wettlaufer, *General Mgr*
Tony Collini, *Admin Sec*
▲ EMP: 21
SQ FT: 5,000
SALES (est): 4.1MM **Privately Held**
WEB: www.packageprinttech.com
SIC: 3555 3069 Printing trades machinery; printers' rolls & blankets: rubber or rubberized fabric

(G-3111)
PACKSTAR GROUP INC
215 John Glenn Dr (14228-2227)
PHONE.................716 853-1688
Fax: 716 853-0974
Andrew Sharp, *Ch of Bd*
Todd Mann, *Prdtn Mgr*
Paul Johnson, *CFO*
Janice Bauer, *Cust Mgr*
Robert Enright, *Admin Sec*
▲ EMP: 95 EST: 1997
SQ FT: 50,000
SALES (est): 23.5MM **Privately Held**
WEB: www.packstargroup.com
SIC: 2671 4789 Plastic film, coated or laminated for packaging; cargo loading & unloading services
PA: Brook & Whittle Limited
    260 Branford Rd
    North Branford CT 06471

(G-3112)
PAR-FOAM PRODUCTS INC
239 Van Rensselaer St (14210-1345)
PHONE.................716 855-2066
Fax: 716 855-2119
Kaushik A Shah, *President*
Rolandd J Neuffer, *Vice Pres*
George Captain, *Engineer*
Larry Parker, *Sales Mgr*
EMP: 130
SQ FT: 64,000
SALES (est): 14.7MM **Privately Held**
SIC: 3069 3714 3086 Foam rubber; motor vehicle parts & accessories; plastics foam products

(G-3113)
PARK AVENUE IMPRINTS LLC (PA)
2955 S Park Ave (14218-2613)
PHONE.................716 822-5737
Fax: 716 822-5700
Josh Holtzman, *Sales Dir*
Cindy B Anticola, *Department Mgr*
James Roorda,
EMP: 6
SQ FT: 1,200
SALES (est): 456.5K **Privately Held**
SIC: 2396 Screen printing on fabric articles

(G-3114)
PARKSIDE CANDY CO INC (PA)
3208 Main St (14214-1379)
PHONE.................716 833-7540
Fax: 716 833-7560
Phillip J Buffamonte, *President*
EMP: 17 EST: 1978
SALES (est): 1.5MM **Privately Held**
WEB: www.parksidecandy.com
SIC: 2066 5441 Chocolate bars, solid; chocolate candy, solid; candy

(G-3115)
PARRINELLO PRINTING INC
84 Aero Dr (14225-1435)
PHONE.................716 633-7780
Colleen Parrinello, *President*
Renee Shone, *Manager*
EMP: 14
SALES (est): 2.1MM **Privately Held**
SIC: 2752 Commercial printing, lithographic

(G-3116)
PDI CONE CO INC
Also Called: Dutchtreat
69 Leddy St (14210-2134)
PHONE.................716 825-8750
Fax: 716 827-8615
Geoge Page, *Principal*
EMP: 67 EST: 2008
SALES (est): 11.2MM **Privately Held**
SIC: 2052 Cones, ice cream

(G-3117)
PELLICANO SPECIALTY FOODS INC
195 Reading St (14220-2157)
P.O. Box 34, Lake View (14085-0034)
PHONE.................716 822-2366
Mario Pellicano, *President*
EMP: 18 EST: 1996
SALES (est): 4MM **Privately Held**
SIC: 2099 Food preparations

(G-3118)
PENINSULA PLASTICS LTD
161 Marine Dr Apt 6e (14202-4214)
P.O. Box 1179 (14202)
PHONE.................716 854-3050
Craig Bolton, *Owner*
EMP: 54
SALES (est): 2.1MM **Privately Held**
WEB: www.penplast.com
SIC: 3089 Injection molding of plastics

(G-3119)
PEOPLES CHOICE M R I
125 Galileo Dr (14221-2776)
PHONE.................716 681-7377
Vafeem Iqbal, *President*
EMP: 10
SALES (est): 919K **Privately Held**
WEB: www.peoplesmri.com
SIC: 3577 Magnetic ink & optical scanning devices

(G-3120)
PERAFLEX HOSE INC
155 Great Arrow Ave Ste 4 (14207-3010)
PHONE.................716 876-8806
Fax: 716 876-8708
Newell Kraik, *President*
Mark Montgomery, *Sales Mgr*
James Nelson, *Manager*
▲ EMP: 15
SQ FT: 13,000
SALES (est): 3MM **Privately Held**
WEB: www.peraflex.com
SIC: 3052 5085 Rubber & plastics hose & beltings; industrial supplies

(G-3121)
PERKINS INTERNATIONAL INC (HQ)
672 Delaware Ave (14209-2202)
PHONE.................309 675-1000
Michael J Baunton, *CEO*
Dan Hagan, *Analyst*
EMP: 5
SALES (est): 3.4MM
SALES (corp-wide): 47B **Publicly Held**
WEB: www.tuckaway.com
SIC: 3519 Internal combustion engines
PA: Caterpillar Inc.
    100 Ne Adams St
    Peoria IL 61629
    309 675-1000

(G-3122)
PERMA TECH INC
363 Hamburg St (14204-2086)
PHONE.................716 854-0707
Fax: 716 854-0774
Richard E Lund Jr, *President*
EMP: 22
SQ FT: 45,000
SALES (est): 2.7MM **Privately Held**
WEB: www.permatechinc.com
SIC: 2394 3441 3089 Awnings, fabric: made from purchased materials; fabricated structural metal; doors, folding: plastic or plastic coated fabric

(G-3123)
PHILCOM LIMITED
1144 Military Rd (14217-2232)
PHONE.................716 875-8005
Bruce G Phillips, *Ch of Bd*
Karen Phillips, *Vice Pres*
EMP: 60
SALES (est): 4.3MM **Privately Held**
SIC: 3089 Boxes, plastic

(G-3124)
PHILPAC CORPORATION (PA)
1144 Military Rd (14217-2232)
PHONE.................716 875-8005
Fax: 716 875-9908
Bruce G Phillips, *President*
Karen Phillips, *Corp Secy*
Courtney Gorman, *Materials Mgr*
Stephen Dysert, *Sales Mgr*
Mike Bartz, *Sales Associate*
EMP: 50
SALES (est): 15.3MM **Privately Held**
SIC: 2653 5085 3086 2655 Boxes, corrugated: made from purchased materials; packing, industrial; padding, foamed plastic; fiber cans, drums & similar products; nailed wood boxes & shook
HQ: Berwind Consolidated Holdings, Inc.
    3000 Ctr Sq W 1500 Mkt St 1500 W
    Philadelphia PA 19102
    215 563-2800

(G-3125)
PIERCE ARROW DRAPERY MFG
Also Called: Pierce Arrow Draperies
1685 Elmwood Ave Ste 312 (14207-2435)
PHONE.................716 876-3023
Robert Merkel, *President*
EMP: 5
SQ FT: 2,000
SALES (est): 360K **Privately Held**
SIC: 2221 Draperies & drapery fabrics, manmade fiber & silk

(G-3126)
PII HOLDINGS INC (DH)
2150 Elmwood Ave (14207-1910)
PHONE.................716 876-9951
Mike McLelland, *CEO*
Ray Baran, *Treasurer*
EMP: 2
SALES (est): 220MM
SALES (corp-wide): 3.1B **Privately Held**
SIC: 3089 3822 6719 Molding primary plastic; temperature controls, automatic; investment holding companies, except banks

(G-3127)
PINE HILL FABRICATORS
2731 Seneca St (14224-1895)
PHONE.................716 823-2474
Fax: 716 823-2475
Joseph L Neuner, *Owner*
Liz Eichelberger, *Office Mgr*
EMP: 6
SQ FT: 4,000
SALES (est): 789.7K **Privately Held**
SIC: 2541 Counter & sink tops

(G-3128)
PLASLOK CORP
3155 Broadway St (14227-1034)
PHONE.................716 681-7755
Fax: 716 681-9142
Richard A Neil, *President*
Donald Bauman, *Research*
Gregory Maher, *Controller*
EMP: 43
SQ FT: 75,000
SALES: 7MM **Privately Held**
SIC: 2821 Molding compounds, plastics

(G-3129)
PLASTIC SYS/GR BFLO INC
465 Cornwall Ave (14215-3125)
PHONE.................716 835-7555
Daniel McNamara, *President*
Sean Lobue, *General Mgr*
EMP: 5
SQ FT: 9,200
SALES (est): 700K **Privately Held**
WEB: www.plasticsystems.com
SIC: 3089 Plastic containers, except foam; trays, plastic; thermoformed finished plastic products; cases, plastic

(G-3130)
POL-TEK INDUSTRIES LTD
2300 Clinton St (14227-1735)
PHONE.................716 823-1502
Fax: 716 823-5871
Martin Ostrowski, *CEO*
Wanda Ostrowski, *Corp Secy*
Natalie Handzlik, *Office Mgr*
EMP: 15
SQ FT: 11,000
SALES (est): 1.9MM **Privately Held**
WEB: www.pol-tek.com
SIC: 3599 Machine shop, jobbing & repair

(G-3131)
POWER UP MANUFACTURING INC
275 N Pointe Pkwy Ste 100 (14228-1895)
PHONE.................716 876-4890
Dean T Wright, *President*
Elizabeth Wright, *Admin Dir*
▲ EMP: 25
SQ FT: 15,000
SALES (est): 3.6MM **Privately Held**
WEB: www.powerupmfg.com
SIC: 3069 Battery boxes, jars or parts, hard rubber

(G-3132)
POWERFLOW INC
1714 Broadway St (14212-2090)
P.O. Box 905 (14240-0905)
PHONE.................716 892-1014
Douglas K Ward, *Ch of Bd*
Douglas Capps, *Vice Pres*
Robert Dilski, *Purchasing*
Donald R Halt, *VP Finance*
Bill Coles, *Supervisor*
▲ EMP: 66
SQ FT: 55,000
SALES (est): 21.9MM **Privately Held**
WEB: www.powerflowinc.com
SIC: 3714 Motor vehicle parts & accessories

(G-3133)
PRECISION PHOTO-FAB INC
Also Called: Switzer
4020 Jeffrey Blvd (14219-2393)
PHONE.................716 821-9393
Fax: 716 821-9399
Bernie Switzer, *Ch of Bd*
Dennis Switzer, *President*
Patrick Haefner, *Principal*
Joseph Dunlop, *VP Sales*
Kim Heimburg, *Representative*
EMP: 55
SQ FT: 20,000
SALES (est): 14MM **Privately Held**
WEB: www.precisionphotofab.com
SIC: 3469 Metal stampings

(G-3134)
PRECISION SPCLTY FBRCTIONS LLC
51 N Gates Ave (14218-1029)
PHONE.................716 824-2108
Fax: 716 827-1364

GEOGRAPHIC SECTION
Buffalo - Erie County (G-3159)

Dennis Switzer,
John Maher,
EMP: 20
SALES (est): 3.3MM **Privately Held**
SIC: 3499 Strapping, metal

(G-3135)
PREMIER MACHINING TECH INC
2100 Old Union Rd (14227-2725)
PHONE....................................716 608-1311
William G Belcher, *President*
Kimberly Belcher, *Admin Sec*
EMP: 8
SQ FT: 18,500
SALES: 1.2MM **Privately Held**
SIC: 3599 Machine shop, jobbing & repair

(G-3136)
PRINCE RUBBER & PLAS CO INC (PA)
137 Arthur St (14207-2098)
PHONE...............................225 272-1653
Fax: 716 877-0743
S Warren Prince Jr, *Ch of Bd*
Mary Churchman, *Controller*
Tom Hashar, *Marketing Staff*
Lary Terzian, *Manager*
John G Putnam, *Admin Sec*
▲ **EMP:** 25
SQ FT: 35,000
SALES (est): 6.9MM **Privately Held**
WEB: www.princerp.com
SIC: 3069 3089 3084 3053 Hard rubber & molded rubber products; plastic processing; plastics pipe; gaskets, packing & sealing devices

(G-3137)
PRINTED IMAGE
1906 Clinton St (14206-3206)
PHONE....................................716 821-1880
Richard Zavarella, *Owner*
EMP: 5
SQ FT: 3,000
SALES (est): 410.1K **Privately Held**
SIC: 2759 Commercial printing

(G-3138)
PRO-GEAR CO INC
1120 Niagara St (14213-1714)
PHONE....................................716 684-3811
Fax: 716 684-7717
Gary Rackley, *President*
Dolores Reidy, *Office Mgr*
Kevin Rackley, *Manager*
EMP: 5
SQ FT: 6,500
SALES: 377.2K
SALES (corp-wide): 18.4MM **Privately Held**
SIC: 3462 Gears, forged steel
PA: Gear Motions Incorporated
    1750 Milton Ave
    Syracuse NY 13209
    315 488-0100

(G-3139)
PROTECTIVE INDUSTRIES INC (DH)
Also Called: Caplugs
2150 Elmwood Ave (14207-1910)
PHONE....................................716 876-9951
Fax: 716 874-1680
Gregory J Tucholski, *President*
Steven Smith, *Senior VP*
Susan McElligott, *Vice Pres*
Kennery Rob, *Vice Pres*
Sharon Burke, *Plant Mgr*
◆ **EMP:** 250
SALES: 220MM
SALES (corp-wide): 3.1B **Privately Held**
WEB: www.mokon.com
SIC: 3089 3822 Molding primary plastic; temperature controls, automatic
HQ: Pii Holdings, Inc.
    2150 Elmwood Ave
    Buffalo NY 14207
    716 876-9951

(G-3140)
PROTECTIVE INDUSTRIES INC
Also Called: Caplugs
2150 Elmwood Ave (14207-1910)
PHONE....................................716 876-9855
Jeff Smith, *Branch Mgr*
EMP: 238

SALES (corp-wide): 3.1B **Privately Held**
WEB: www.mokon.com
SIC: 3089 Molding primary plastic
HQ: Protective Industries, Inc.
    2150 Elmwood Ave
    Buffalo NY 14207
    716 876-9951

(G-3141)
PROTECTIVE INDUSTRIES INC
Mokon
2510 Elmwood Ave (14217-2223)
PHONE....................................716 876-9951
Robert Kennery, *General Mgr*
EMP: 55
SALES (corp-wide): 3.1B **Privately Held**
WEB: www.mokon.com
SIC: 3822 Temperature controls, automatic
HQ: Protective Industries, Inc.
    2150 Elmwood Ave
    Buffalo NY 14207
    716 876-9951

(G-3142)
PVS CHEMICAL SOLUTIONS INC
55 Lee St (14210-2109)
PHONE....................................716 825-5762
Chris Cancilla, *Plant Mgr*
Patrick Murphy, *Opers Mgr*
Jane Lamanna, *Engineer*
EMP: 51
SALES (corp-wide): 549.3MM **Privately Held**
SIC: 2819 2899 Sulfur chloride; chemical preparations
HQ: Pvs Chemical Solutions, Inc.
    10900 Harper Ave
    Detroit MI 48213
    313 921-1200

(G-3143)
PVS TECHNOLOGIES INC
Also Called: PVS Chemical Solutions
55 Lee St (14210-2109)
PHONE....................................716 825-5762
William Decker, *Manager*
EMP: 48
SQ FT: 65,268
SALES (corp-wide): 549.3MM **Privately Held**
SIC: 2819 Metal salts & compounds, except sodium, potassium, aluminum
HQ: Pvs Technologies, Inc.
    10900 Harper Ave
    Detroit MI 48213
    313 571-1100

(G-3144)
QLS SOLUTIONS GROUP INC
701 Seneca St Ste 600 (14210-1361)
PHONE....................................716 852-2203
Fax: 716 852-2204
Gary Skalyo, *President*
EMP: 24
SQ FT: 30,000
SALES (est): 4.3MM **Privately Held**
WEB: www.qualitylaser.com
SIC: 3955 3861 Print cartridges for laser & other computer printers; reproduction machines & equipment

(G-3145)
QTA MACHINING INC
Also Called: Quick Turn Around Machining
876 Bailey Ave (14206-2300)
PHONE....................................716 862-8108
Fax: 716 837-5002
Suzanne M Pelczynski, *President*
Roxanne Pelczynski, *Vice Pres*
John Hake, *Materials Mgr*
Tom Pelczynski, *Manager*
EMP: 12
SQ FT: 10,000
SALES (est): 1.3MM **Privately Held**
WEB: www.qtanow.com
SIC: 3599 Machine shop, jobbing & repair

(G-3146)
QUAKER BONNET INC
54 Irving Pl (14201-1521)
PHONE....................................716 885-7208
Fax: 716 885-7245
Elizabeth Kolken, *President*
Ben Kolken, *Vice Pres*
EMP: 5 **EST:** 1930

SQ FT: 4,400
SALES (est): 494.2K **Privately Held**
WEB: www.quakerbonnet.com
SIC: 2051 2052 2024 Bakery: wholesale or wholesale/retail combined; cookies; ice cream & frozen desserts

(G-3147)
QUALITY BINDERY SERVICE INC
501 Amherst St (14207-2913)
PHONE....................................716 883-5185
Fax: 716 883-1598
Kathleen Hartmans, *President*
Cathy Rajca, *Mktg Dir*
EMP: 34
SQ FT: 4,000
SALES (est): 4.1MM **Privately Held**
SIC: 2789 Trade binding services

(G-3148)
QUANTUM ASSET RECOVERY
482 Niagara Falls Blvd (14223-2634)
PHONE....................................716 393-2712
EMP: 5
SALES (est): 270.1K **Privately Held**
SIC: 3572 Computer storage devices

(G-3149)
QUEEN CITY MANUFACTURING INC
333 Henderson Ave (14217-1538)
PHONE....................................716 877-1102
Fax: 716 773-7071
Robert Maranto, *President*
Joseph Mallare, *Vice Pres*
Steve Nappo, *Vice Pres*
Nancy Natto, *Manager*
▲ **EMP:** 5
SALES (est): 1.4MM **Privately Held**
WEB: www.queencitymanufacturing.com
SIC: 2821 Melamine resins, melamine-formaldehyde

(G-3150)
R & A INDUSTRIAL PRODUCTS
Also Called: R&A Prods
30 Cornelia St (14210-1202)
PHONE....................................716 823-4300
Fax: 716 825-2080
Tony Onello, *President*
EMP: 5
SQ FT: 2,600
SALES: 376.6K **Privately Held**
SIC: 3061 Mechanical rubber goods

(G-3151)
R & B MACHINERY CORP
400 Kennedy Rd Ste 3 (14227-1073)
PHONE....................................716 894-3332
Fax: 716 894-3335
James B Broman, *President*
EMP: 4
SQ FT: 28,000
SALES (est): 2.2MM **Privately Held**
WEB: www.dualwheel.com
SIC: 3559 Metal finishing equipment for plating, etc.

(G-3152)
R E RICH FAMILY HOLDING CORP
1 Robert Rich Way (14213-1701)
PHONE....................................716 878-8000
Christopher T Dunstan, *Principal*
◆ **EMP:** 75
SALES (est): 7.7MM **Privately Held**
SIC: 2053 Frozen bakery products, except bread

(G-3153)
RAPID RAYS PRINTING & COPYING
300 Broadway St (14204-1433)
P.O. Box 442 (14205-0442)
PHONE....................................716 852-0550
Fax: 716 852-5208
Raymond Wellence, *President*
Kathleen Wellence, *Vice Pres*
Victor Garrow, *Opers Mgr*
Jeffery Steinborn, *Manager*
EMP: 9
SQ FT: 4,100
SALES (est): 1.1MM **Privately Held**
WEB: www.rapidrays.com
SIC: 2752 Photo-offset printing

(G-3154)
RAPID SERVICE ENGRAVING CO
1593 Genesee St (14211-1634)
PHONE....................................716 896-4555
Fax: 716 896-4557
James F Egloff, *President*
Dolores Webb, *Manager*
John F Egloff, *Admin Sec*
EMP: 6
SQ FT: 6,000
SALES (est): 558.9K **Privately Held**
SIC: 2796 2752 Photoengraving plates, linecuts or halftones; commercial printing, lithographic

(G-3155)
REALTIMETRADERSCOM
1325 N Forest Rd Ste 350 (14221-2143)
PHONE....................................716 632-6600
Andrew Marthiasan, *President*
EMP: 33 **EST:** 1995
SQ FT: 2,000
SALES (est): 1.6MM **Privately Held**
SIC: 2711 7375 Newspapers; information retrieval services

(G-3156)
REIMANN & GEORGER CORPORATION
1849 Harlem Rd (14212-2401)
P.O. Box 681 (14240-0681)
PHONE....................................716 895-1156
Fax: 716 895-1547
Phil Ventura, *Purchasing*
John Stegner, *Marketing Staff*
EMP: 42
SQ FT: 38,000
SALES (est): 19.9MM **Privately Held**
WEB: www.rgcproducts.com
SIC: 3536 3546 Hoists; boat lifts; power-driven handtools

(G-3157)
RICH PRODUCTS CORPORATION (PA)
1 Robert Rich Way (14213-1701)
P.O. Box 245 (14240-0245)
PHONE....................................716 878-8422
Fax: 716 878-8008
William G Gisel, *CEO*
Melinda R Rich, *Vice Ch Bd*
Joel Bearfield, *General Mgr*
Robert Rich Jr, *Chairman*
Joyce Deskins, *Area Mgr*
◆ **EMP:** 1300 **EST:** 1993
SQ FT: 60,000
SALES (est): 3.5B **Privately Held**
WEB: www.richs.com
SIC: 2053 2092 2023 2099 Frozen bakery products, except bread; fresh or frozen packaged fish; shrimp, frozen: prepared; shellfish, frozen: prepared; dry, condensed, evaporated dairy products; whipped topping, dry mix; cream substitutes; dessert mixes & fillings

(G-3158)
RIGIDIZED METALS CORPORATION
Also Called: Rigidized-Metal
658 Ohio St (14203-3185)
PHONE....................................716 849-4703
Fax: 716 849-0401
Richard S Smith Jr, *Ch of Bd*
Richard S Smith III, *President*
Douglas F Lum, *Treasurer*
Patty Hammer, *Manager*
▲ **EMP:** 48 **EST:** 1940
SQ FT: 58,060
SALES (est): 22.4MM **Privately Held**
WEB: www.rigidized.com
SIC: 3469 3444 2796 Rigidizing metal; sheet metalwork; platemaking services

(G-3159)
RLP HOLDINGS INC
Also Called: Belt Maintenance Systems
1049 Military Rd (14217-2228)
PHONE....................................716 852-0832
Fax: 716 852-4198
Joe Hooley, *President*
Brian RE, *VP Sales*
▲ **EMP:** 8
SQ FT: 18,000

Buffalo - Erie County (G-3160) — GEOGRAPHIC SECTION

SALES (est): 1.1MM **Privately Held**
SIC: 3535 Conveyors & conveying equipment

(G-3160)
ROBERTS-GORDON LLC (HQ)
Also Called: RG
1250 William St (14206-1819)
P.O. Box 44 (14240-0044)
PHONE..............................716 852-4400
Mark J Dines, *President*
Mark Murdoch, *Vice Pres*
Kevin Shamrock, *Safety Mgr*
Richard G Jasiura, *CFO*
Sarah Kosprzewa, *Personnel Exec*
▲ EMP: 100 EST: 1998
SQ FT: 107,000
SALES (est): 98.1MM **Privately Held**
WEB: www.rg-inc.com
SIC: 3675 3433 Condensers, electronic; unit heaters, domestic

(G-3161)
ROBINSON KNIFE
2615 Walden Ave (14225-4735)
PHONE..............................716 685-6300
Fax: 716 685-4916
Robert Skerker, *CEO*
EMP: 12
SALES (est): 1.7MM **Privately Held**
SIC: 3089 Plastic kitchenware, tableware & houseware

(G-3162)
ROCKET COMMUNICATIONS INC
Also Called: Buffalo Rocket
2507 Delaware Ave (14216-1712)
PHONE..............................716 873-2594
David Gallagher, *CEO*
Dennis Gallagher, *Vice Pres*
Dean Gallagher, *Treasurer*
Daryl Gallagher, *Admin Sec*
EMP: 12 EST: 1996
SQ FT: 30,000
SALES (est): 657.7K **Privately Held**
WEB: www.buffalorocket.com
SIC: 2711 Newspapers

(G-3163)
RODGARD CORPORATION
92 Msgr Valente Dr (14206-1822)
PHONE..............................716 852-1435
Richard E Hauck, *Ch of Bd*
EMP: 30
SALES (est): 26.8K
SALES (corp-wide): 692.2MM **Publicly Held**
WEB: www.rodgard.com
SIC: 2821 Elastomers, nonvulcanizable (plastics)
PA: Astronics Corporation
130 Commerce Way
East Aurora NY 14052
716 805-1599

(G-3164)
ROLLERS INC
2495 Main St Ste 359 (14214-2154)
PHONE..............................716 837-0700
Frank Reppenhagen, *Owner*
Michelle Fritzius, *Bookkeeper*
EMP: 9
SALES (est): 640K **Privately Held**
WEB: www.rollers.com
SIC: 2515 3555 5085 Mattresses, containing felt, foam rubber, urethane, etc.; printing trade parts & attachments; industrial supplies

(G-3165)
ROSINA FOOD PRODUCTS INC (HQ)
Also Called: Ceoentano
170 French Rd (14227-2777)
PHONE..............................716 668-0123
Russell A Corigliano, *Ch of Bd*
James Corigliano, *Ch of Bd*
John Zimmerman, *President*
Frank Corigliano, *Vice Pres*
Tom Murphy, *Vice Pres*
EMP: 178
SQ FT: 60,000
SALES (est): 37.3MM
SALES (corp-wide): 48.4MM **Privately Held**
SIC: 2013 5812 Sausages & other prepared meats; eating places
PA: Rosina Holding, Inc.
170 French Rd
Buffalo NY 14227
716 668-0123

(G-3166)
ROSINA HOLDING INC (PA)
170 French Rd (14227-2717)
PHONE..............................716 668-0123
Fax: 716 656-0548
Russell A Corigliano, *Ch of Bd*
Todd Palczewski, *Research*
Frank Corigliano, *Treasurer*
James Corigliano Jr, *VP Human Res*
Chris Langdon, *Regl Sales Mgr*
EMP: 3
SQ FT: 40,000
SALES (est): 48.4MM **Privately Held**
SIC: 2013 Sausages & other prepared meats

(G-3167)
ROSS L SPORTS SCREENING INC
2756 Seneca St (14224-1866)
PHONE..............................716 824-5350
Dave Cellino, *Owner*
EMP: 15
SALES (est): 490K **Privately Held**
SIC: 2395 Embroidery & art needlework

(G-3168)
ROYAL BEDDING CO BUFFALO INC
Also Called: Restonic
201 James E Casey Dr (14206-2363)
PHONE..............................716 895-1414
Thomas Comer Jr, *President*
Judy Houlanhan, *Manager*
▲ EMP: 25
SQ FT: 110,000
SALES (est): 5.1MM **Privately Held**
SIC: 2515 Mattresses, innerspring or box spring; box springs, assembled

(G-3169)
RWB CONTROLS INC
471 Connecticut St (14213-2645)
PHONE..............................716 897-4341
Fax: 716 882-1575
EMP: 6
SQ FT: 4,000
SALES (est): 600K **Privately Held**
SIC: 3823 5063 Mfg Industrial Process Control Instruments & Displays

(G-3170)
S & H MACHINE COMPANY INC
83 Clyde Ave (14215-2237)
PHONE..............................716 834-1194
EMP: 5
SQ FT: 5,500
SALES: 400K **Privately Held**
SIC: 3599 Machine Shop

(G-3171)
S J B FABRICATION
430 Kennedy Rd (14227-1032)
PHONE..............................716 895-0281
Sean Brubckman, *Owner*
EMP: 10
SALES (est): 310.1K **Privately Held**
SIC: 7692 Welding repair

(G-3172)
S J MCCULLAGH INC (PA)
Also Called: McCullagh Coffee
245 Swan St (14204-2051)
PHONE..............................716 856-3473
Warren E Emblidge Jr, *President*
Dan Phillips, *CFO*
Mark Crotty, *Controller*
Rose Vohwinkel, *Executive Asst*
Carol Emblidge, *Admin Sec*
▲ EMP: 50
SQ FT: 16,000
SALES (est): 12.4MM **Privately Held**
SIC: 2095 5113 5149 Roasted coffee; cups, disposable plastic & paper; groceries & related products; dried or canned foods; sugar, refined; chocolate

(G-3173)
SAFETEC OF AMERICA INC
887 Kensington Ave (14215-2720)
PHONE..............................716 895-1822
Fax: 716 895-2969
Scott A Weinstein, *CEO*
Peter Weinstein, *Vice Pres*
Jeffrey Escott, *Prdtn Mgr*
Nadine Martz, *Research*
Dee Ciminelli, *Accountant*
▲ EMP: 60
SQ FT: 80,000
SALES: 10.3MM **Privately Held**
WEB: www.safetec.com
SIC: 2842 2834 Specialty cleaning, polishes & sanitation goods; drugs affecting parasitic & infective diseases

(G-3174)
SAFETY-KLEEN SYSTEMS INC
60 Katherine St (14210-2006)
PHONE..............................716 855-2212
James Drozdowski, *Branch Mgr*
EMP: 16
SQ FT: 24,259
SALES (corp-wide): 3.2B **Publicly Held**
SIC: 2992 Re-refining lubricating oils & greases
HQ: Safety-Kleen Systems, Inc.
2600 N Central Expy # 400
Richardson TX 75080
972 265-2000

(G-3175)
SAHLEN PACKING COMPANY INC
318 Howard St (14206-2760)
P.O. Box 280 (14240-0280)
PHONE..............................716 852-8677
Fax: 716 852-8684
Joseph E Sahlen, *Ch of Bd*
Christopher Cauley, *Vice Pres*
Deborah Howell, *Vice Pres*
Ed Colburn, *Controller*
James Bowen, *CPA*
▲ EMP: 85 EST: 1869
SQ FT: 53,789
SALES (est): 16.3MM **Privately Held**
WEB: www.sahlen.com
SIC: 2011 Sausages from meat slaughtered on site; hams & picnics from meat slaughtered on site; bacon, slab & sliced from meat slaughtered on site

(G-3176)
SANTORO SIGNS INC
3180 Genesee St Ste 1 (14225-2682)
PHONE..............................716 895-8875
Fax: 716 895-9931
Rocco Santoro, *President*
John Santoro, *Vice Pres*
EMP: 8
SALES (est): 1.2MM **Privately Held**
SIC: 3993 7389 Signs & advertising specialties; electric signs; neon signs; sign painting & lettering shop

(G-3177)
SCHULER-SUBRA INC
Also Called: Eskay Metal Fabricating
83 Doat St (14211-2048)
PHONE..............................716 893-3100
Fax: 716 893-0443
Jeff Subra, *President*
Ken White, *Sales Executive*
Kathy Bristol, *Manager*
EMP: 6 EST: 1944
SQ FT: 16,500
SALES (est): 589.9K **Privately Held**
WEB: www.specialtystainless.com
SIC: 3441 Fabricated structural metal

(G-3178)
SCHUTTE-BUFFALO HAMMERMILL LLC
Also Called: Schutte-Buffalo Hammer Mill
61 Depot St (14206-2203)
PHONE..............................716 855-1202
Fax: 716 855-3417
Thomas E Warne, *President*
Mark Podgorny, *Design Engr*
Cassie Brown, *Webmaster*
Linda Sperduti, *Admin Sec*
James Klopser,
▲ EMP: 25 EST: 1933
SQ FT: 22,500
SALES (est): 11.6MM **Privately Held**
WEB: www.hammermills.com
SIC: 3531 Hammer mills (rock & ore crushing machines), portable

(G-3179)
SCREW COMPRESSOR TECH INC
158 Ridge Rd (14218-1035)
PHONE..............................716 827-6600
John Zahner, *President*
EMP: 13
SALES (est): 2.4MM **Privately Held**
SIC: 3563 Air & gas compressors

(G-3180)
SECOND AMENDMENT FOUNDATION
Also Called: Gun Week
267 Linwood Ave Ste A (14209-1816)
PHONE..............................716 885-6408
Fax: 716 884-4471
Joseph Tartaro, *President*
Peggy Tartaro, *Editor*
EMP: 5
SALES (corp-wide): 4.4MM **Privately Held**
WEB: www.saf.org
SIC: 2711 Newspapers, publishing & printing
PA: Second Amendment Foundation Inc
12500 Ne 10th Pl
Bellevue WA 98005
425 454-7012

(G-3181)
SECONDARY SERVICES INC
757 E Ferry St (14211-1105)
PHONE..............................716 896-4000
Dan O'Connor, *CEO*
EMP: 12
SALES (est): 1.9MM **Privately Held**
WEB: www.secondaryservice.com
SIC: 3599 Machine shop, jobbing & repair

(G-3182)
SERVICE CANVAS CO INC
149 Swan St Unit 155 (14203-2624)
PHONE..............................716 853-0558
Fax: 716 845-6071
Jerald H Eron, *President*
EMP: 12 EST: 1946
SQ FT: 80,000
SALES (est): 1.2MM **Privately Held**
WEB: www.servicecanvas.com
SIC: 2394 Canvas & related products; canopies, fabric: made from purchased materials; tarpaulins, fabric: made from purchased materials; liners & covers, fabric: made from purchased materials
PA: Synthetic Textiles Inc
398 Broadway St
Buffalo NY 14204

(G-3183)
SERVICE MFG GROUP INC (PA)
400 Scajaquada St (14211-1722)
PHONE..............................716 893-1482
Linda Casoni, *CEO*
Vito Casoni, *President*
George Smith, *Sales Mgr*
Rounld Rusin, *Manager*
Bridget Kashmer, *Info Tech Mgr*
EMP: 12
SQ FT: 150,000
SALES (est): 8MM **Privately Held**
WEB: www.t-smg.com
SIC: 3625 3444 Relays & industrial controls; sheet metal specialties, not stamped

(G-3184)
SERVICE MFG GROUP INC
Also Called: Smg Control Systems
400 Scajaquada St (14211-1722)
PHONE..............................716 893-1482
Fax: 716 893-1495
Linda Casoni, *Vice Pres*
James Ochal, *Plant Mgr*
Carl Sellato, *Opers Mgr*
George W Leone, *Mfg Mgr*
Bob Kulp, *Mfg Staff*
EMP: 35
SALES (corp-wide): 8MM **Privately Held**
WEB: www.t-smg.com
SIC: 3444 Sheet metalwork

GEOGRAPHIC SECTION   Buffalo - Erie County (G-3210)

PA: The Service Manufacturing Group Inc
400 Scajaquada St
Buffalo NY 14211
716 893-1482

(G-3185)
SERVICE SPECIALTIES INC
127 Langner Rd (14224-3341)
PHONE.................................716 822-7706
Fax: 716 822-7707
Michael J Zilich, *President*
Wanda Zilich, *Vice Pres*
EMP: 8
SQ FT: 2,400
SALES (est): 730K **Privately Held**
SIC: 3535 Conveyors & conveying equipment

(G-3186)
SIEMENS CORPORATION
302 Sonwill Rd (14225)
PHONE.................................905 528-8811
EMP: 20
SALES (corp-wide): 83.5B **Privately Held**
SIC: 3661 Telephones & telephone apparatus
HQ: Siemens Corporation
300 New Jersey Ave Nw A
Washington DC 20001
202 434-4800

(G-3187)
SIEMENS INDUSTRY INC
85 Northpointe Pkwy Ste 8 (14228-1886)
PHONE.................................716 568-0983
Fax: 716 568-1449
Tom Strollo, *General Mgr*
Patrick Parlane, *Branch Mgr*
Jerry K Wilson, *Manager*
Nancy Gawron, *Supervisor*
EMP: 50
SALES (corp-wide): 83.5B **Privately Held**
WEB: www.sibt.com
SIC: 3585 7373 1541 Heating equipment, complete; computer integrated systems design; industrial buildings & warehouses
HQ: Siemens Industry, Inc.
1000 Deerfield Pkwy
Buffalo Grove IL 60089
847 215-1000

(G-3188)
SMARTPILL CORPORATION
847 Main St (14203-1109)
PHONE.................................716 882-0701
David Barthel, *President*
Broadhurst Austin, *Mng Member*
Laura Matott, *Director*
Austin Broadhurst, *Bd of Directors*
EMP: 31
SQ FT: 7,500
SALES (est): 4.1MM **Privately Held**
WEB: www.smartpill.com
SIC: 3826 Analytical instruments

(G-3189)
SOMERSET PRODUCTION CO LLC
338 Harris Hill Rd # 102 (14221-7470)
PHONE.................................716 932-6480
Thomas H O'Neil Jr, *Principal*
William A Ziegler,
EMP: 7
SQ FT: 6,000
SALES (est): 620K **Privately Held**
SIC: 1382 Oil & gas exploration services

(G-3190)
SOMMER AND SONS PRINTING INC
2222 S Park Ave (14220-2296)
PHONE.................................716 822-4311
Dennis Sommer, *President*
EMP: 11
SQ FT: 10,000
SALES (est): 1.3MM **Privately Held**
SIC: 2754 Job printing, gravure

(G-3191)
SOPARK CORP (PA)
3300 S Park Ave (14218-3530)
PHONE.................................716 822-0434
Fax: 716 822-5062
Gerald Murak, *Ch of Bd*
Kevin M Wyckoff, *Exec VP*
John Kasperek, *Controller*
EMP: 150
SQ FT: 28,000
SALES (est): 32.3MM **Privately Held**
WEB: www.sopark.com
SIC: 3672 3679 3621 3694 Printed circuit boards; electronic circuits; motors, electric; engine electrical equipment

(G-3192)
SOROC TECHNOLOGY CORP
1051 Clinton St (14206-2823)
PHONE.................................716 849-5913
Rudy Cheddie, *President*
EMP: 2
SALES (est): 1.7MM
SALES (corp-wide): 84.8MM **Privately Held**
WEB: www.soroc.com
SIC: 7372 Prepackaged software
PA: Soroc Technology Inc
607 Chrislea Rd
Woodbridge ON L4L 8
905 265-8000

(G-3193)
SORRENTO LACTALIS INCORPORATED
37 Franklin St (14202-4107)
PHONE.................................716 823-6262
James Binner, *Manager*
Victoire Visseaux, *Manager*
EMP: 6
SALES (est): 433.3K **Privately Held**
SIC: 2022 Cheese, natural & processed

(G-3194)
SOUND VIDEO SYSTEMS WNY LLC
1720 Military Rd (14217-1148)
PHONE.................................716 684-8200
Joseph Caprino,
▲ EMP: 10
SALES (est): 1.4MM **Privately Held**
SIC: 3651 Household audio & video equipment

(G-3195)
SPEEDWAYS CONVEYORS INC
1210 E Ferry St (14211-1615)
PHONE.................................716 893-2222
Fax: 716 893-3067
John T Thorn, *President*
John Jacobowitz, *Exec VP*
Donald Sauer, *VP Finance*
Dan Buckley, *Marketing Staff*
Debbie Doran, *Office Mgr*
EMP: 47 EST: 1945
SQ FT: 100,000
SALES (est): 4.3MM **Privately Held**
SIC: 3535 5084 3537 Conveyors & conveying equipment; industrial machinery & equipment; industrial trucks & tractors

(G-3196)
STEPHEN M KIERNAN
Also Called: Big Bear
701 Seneca St Ste 300 (14210-1351)
PHONE.................................716 836-6300
Stephen M Kiernan, *CEO*
David M Thiemecke, *COO*
EMP: 40
SALES (est): 1.7MM **Privately Held**
SIC: 2395 Embroidery & art needlework

(G-3197)
STETRON INTERNATIONAL INC (PA)
90 Broadway St Ste 1 (14203-1687)
PHONE.................................716 854-3443
Fax: 716 854-3448
Edward R Steger, *Ch of Bd*
Monique Steger, *President*
Caroline A Steger, *Exec VP*
Roy T Chao, *Senior VP*
R Hogwood, *Vice Pres*
▲ EMP: 14
SQ FT: 13,000
SALES (est): 3.3MM **Privately Held**
WEB: www.stetron.com
SIC: 3679 8734 3676 3674 Electronic circuits; electronic loads & power supplies; electronic switches; testing laboratories; electronic resistors; semiconductors & related devices; printed circuit boards; relays & industrial controls

(G-3198)
STORYBOOKS FOREVER
4 Magnolia Ave (14220-2005)
P.O. Box 1234 (14220-8234)
PHONE.................................716 822-7845
Dan Devlin, *Owner*
EMP: 14 EST: 2001
SALES (est): 530.2K **Privately Held**
SIC: 2731 Book publishing

(G-3199)
SUCCESSWARE REMOTE LLC
Also Called: Swremote
403 Main St Ste 200 (14203-2107)
PHONE.................................716 842-1439
Stephen Kiernan, *President*
Steven Raines, *Vice Pres*
EMP: 2
SQ FT: 18,000
SALES: 1.6MM **Privately Held**
SIC: 7372 5734 5045 Business oriented computer software; software, business & non-game; computer software

(G-3200)
SUIT-KOTE CORPORATION
505 Como Park Blvd (14227-1605)
PHONE.................................716 683-8850
Scott Harris, *Opers Staff*
Gary Thompson, *Branch Mgr*
EMP: 15
SALES (corp-wide): 278.7MM **Privately Held**
WEB: www.suit-kote.com
SIC: 2843 Surface active agents
PA: Suit-Kote Corporation
1911 Lorings Crossing Rd
Cortland NY 13045
607 753-1100

(G-3201)
SUNLIGHT US CO INC (HQ)
3556 Lake Shore Rd # 100 (14219-1445)
PHONE.................................716 826-6500
Frank Heard, *President*
Paul M Murray, *Senior VP*
Kenneth W Smith, *CFO*
Timothy F Murphy, *Treasurer*
EMP: 5
SALES (est): 87MM
SALES (corp-wide): 1B **Publicly Held**
SIC: 3499 3316 3441 3398 Strapping, metal; cold finishing of steel shapes; fabricated structural metal; metal heat treating
PA: Gibraltar Industries, Inc.
3556 Lake Shore Rd # 100
Buffalo NY 14219
716 826-6500

(G-3202)
SUPER PRICE CHOPPER INC
1580 Genesee St (14211-1635)
PHONE.................................716 893-3323
AK Kaid, *President*
EMP: 6
SALES (est): 274.2K **Privately Held**
SIC: 3751 Motorcycles & related parts

(G-3203)
SUPERIOR EXTERIORS OF BUFFALO
275 Vulcan St (14207-1237)
PHONE.................................716 873-1000
Salvatore Dinatale, *President*
Patty Parker, *Office Mgr*
EMP: 10
SQ FT: 15,000
SALES (est): 910K **Privately Held**
SIC: 3444 Awnings & canopies

(G-3204)
SURMET CERAMICS CORPORATION
699 Hertel Ave Ste 290 (14207-2341)
PHONE.................................716 875-4091
Timothy Davis, *CEO*
Terry McInerney, *Finance Mgr*
Tom Mroz, *Manager*
Mark Smith, *Manager*
Ashock Gunda, *MIS Dir*
EMP: 17
SALES (est): 1.7MM
SALES (corp-wide): 8.9MM **Privately Held**
SIC: 3297 Graphite refractories: carbon bond or ceramic bond
PA: Surmet, Corp.
31 B St
Burlington MA 01803
781 345-5731

(G-3205)
SWEETWORKS INC (PA)
Also Called: Niagara Chocolates
3500 Genesee St (14225-5015)
PHONE.................................716 634-4545
Philip Terranova, *CEO*
Sara Kelly, *Plant Mgr*
Drew Keller, *Mfg Mgr*
Matthew Orcutt, *QA Dir*
Daniel Wierzbicki, *Controller*
◆ EMP: 166
SQ FT: 115,000
SALES (est): 142.1MM **Privately Held**
WEB: www.sweetworks.net
SIC: 2066 2067 2064 Chocolate; chewing gum; candy & other confectionery products; chocolate candy, except solid chocolate; lollipops & other hard candy

(G-3206)
SYNTHETIC TEXTILES INC (PA)
398 Broadway St (14204-1546)
P.O. Box 1465 (14240-1465)
PHONE.................................716 842-2598
Jerald H Eron, *President*
Margaret Syracuse, *General Mgr*
EMP: 2
SQ FT: 88,000
SALES (est): 1.2MM **Privately Held**
WEB: www.synthetictextile.com
SIC: 3083 Plastic finished products, laminated

(G-3207)
SYSTEMS DRS C3 INC (DH)
485 Cayuga Rd (14225-1368)
PHONE.................................716 631-6200
Alan Dietrich, *President*
Robert Riordan, *Exec VP*
Bill Collins, *Vice Pres*
Keith Doucet, *Vice Pres*
Jason Rinsky, *Vice Pres*
EMP: 300
SQ FT: 300,000
SALES (est): 23.2MM
SALES (corp-wide): 57.7MM **Privately Held**
WEB: www.drs-ewns.com
SIC: 3812 8713 Radar systems & equipment;
HQ: Drs Technologies, Inc.
2345 Crystal Dr Ste 1000
Arlington VA 22202
973 898-1500

(G-3208)
T M MACHINE INC
176 Reading St (14220-2198)
PHONE.................................716 822-0817
Fax: 716 822-2340
Theodore S Michalski, *President*
Dennis Michalski, *Vice Pres*
EMP: 9
SQ FT: 7,000
SALES (est): 1.5MM **Privately Held**
SIC: 3599 Machine shop, jobbing & repair

(G-3209)
TAILORED COATINGS INC
1800 Brdwy St Bldg 2a (14212)
PHONE.................................716 893-4869
David R Mohamed, *Ch of Bd*
Fred Tafelski, *Principal*
EMP: 24
SALES (est): 4MM **Privately Held**
SIC: 3479 Painting of metal products

(G-3210)
TEACHSPIN INC
2495 Main St Ste 409 (14214-2157)
PHONE.................................716 725-6116
Fax: 716 836-1077
Jonathan Reichert, *President*
Barbara Wolff, *Marketing Staff*
Amanda Hughes, *Office Mgr*
EMP: 13 EST: 1994

Buffalo - Erie County (G-3211) — GEOGRAPHIC SECTION

SQ FT: 10,000
SALES (est): 1.7MM **Privately Held**
WEB: www.teachspin.com
SIC: 3999 Education aids, devices & supplies

(G-3211)
TECTRAN MFG INC (HQ)
2345 Walden Ave Ste 1 (14225-4770)
PHONE.................................800 776-5549
Bruce McKie, *Ch of Bd*
David Levan, *General Mgr*
Janet Heiderman, *Credit Mgr*
Janet Rodgers, *Accountant*
Paul Sage, *Manager*
▲ **EMP:** 100
SALES: 19.4MM
SALES (corp-wide): 43.4MM **Privately Held**
WEB: www.tectran.com
SIC: 3713 Truck bodies & parts
PA: Commonwealth Venture Funding Group, Inc
391 Totten Pond Rd # 402
Waltham MA 02451
781 684-0095

(G-3212)
TEGNA INC
Also Called: W G R Z - T V Channel 2
259 Delaware Ave (14202-2008)
PHONE.................................716 849-2222
Fax: 716 849-7602
Jim Toellner, *General Mgr*
Tim Bonk, *Business Mgr*
Mike Morano, *Engineer*
Boomer Connell, *Info Tech Dir*
Deanna Russo, *Exec Dir*
EMP: 130
SALES (corp-wide): 3B **Publicly Held**
WEB: www.gannett.com
SIC: 2711 4833 Newspapers; television broadcasting stations
PA: Tegna Inc,
7950 Jones Branch Dr
Mc Lean VA 22102
703 854-7000

(G-3213)
TENT AND TABLE COM LLC
2845 Bailey Ave (14215-3242)
PHONE.................................716 570-0258
▲ **EMP:** 15
SALES: 7MM **Privately Held**
SIC: 3999 Mfg Misc Products

(G-3214)
TERRAPIN STATION LTD
1172 Hertel Ave (14216-2704)
PHONE.................................716 874-6677
Barry Cohen, *President*
Robert Colsanti, *Vice Pres*
EMP: 13
SALES (est): 1.1MM **Privately Held**
WEB: www.terrapinstationbuffalo.com
SIC: 2337 Women's & misses' suits & coats

(G-3215)
THE CHOCOLATE SHOP
871 Niagara St (14213-2114)
PHONE.................................716 882-5055
Fax: 716 835-6008
Vincent Caruana, *Owner*
James Vincent, *Manager*
EMP: 6
SQ FT: 3,500
SALES (est): 200K **Privately Held**
WEB: www.chocolateshopandmore.com
SIC: 2066 5441 Chocolate & cocoa products; candy

(G-3216)
THERMAL FOAMS/SYRACUSE INC (PA)
2101 Kenmore Ave (14207-1695)
PHONE.................................716 874-6474
William F Wopperer, *Ch of Bd*
John P Jeffery, *President*
David Wopperer, *Vice Pres*
Larry Brady, *Treasurer*
▲ **EMP:** 2
SQ FT: 150,000
SALES (est): 6MM **Privately Held**
SIC: 3086 Insulation or cushioning material, foamed plastic

(G-3217)
THERMOTECH CORP
3 Bradford St (14210-1601)
PHONE.................................716 823-3311
Fred Muhitch, *President*
Bruce Smith, *Vice Pres*
EMP: 9
SQ FT: 18,000
SALES (est): 1.2MM **Privately Held**
WEB: www.thermalprecision.com
SIC: 3443 Air coolers, metal plate

(G-3218)
TIEDEMANN WALDEMAR INC
Also Called: Roofing Consultant
1720 Military Rd Ste 2 (14217-1148)
PHONE.................................716 875-5665
Waldemar Tiedemann, *President*
EMP: 11 **EST:** 1964
SALES (est): 1.3MM **Privately Held**
SIC: 2431 1761 Millwork; roofing contractor

(G-3219)
TIME RELEASE SCIENCES INC
Also Called: Trs Packaging
205 Dingens St (14206-2309)
PHONE.................................716 823-4580
Fax: 716 823-4625
Jeffrey Dorn, *Ch of Bd*
Jim Pasvek, *Controller*
Dennis McGee, *Supervisor*
▲ **EMP:** 20
SALES (est): 4.8MM **Privately Held**
SIC: 2671 Packaging paper & plastics film, coated & laminated

(G-3220)
TMP TECHNOLOGIES INC (PA)
Also Called: Advanced Foam Products Div
1200 Northland Ave (14215-3835)
PHONE.................................716 895-6100
Fax: 716 895-6396
Jeffrey T Doran, *Ch of Bd*
Gary R Ashe, *Vice Pres*
Don Phister, *Vice Pres*
Bob Schultz, *Safety Mgr*
David Glassman, *Engineer*
▼ **EMP:** 65 **EST:** 1993
SQ FT: 47,000
SALES (est): 21.8MM **Privately Held**
WEB: www.tmptech.com
SIC: 3069 3086 2834 2821 Sponge rubber & sponge rubber products; molded rubber products; foam rubber; plastics foam products; pharmaceutical preparations; plastics materials & resins

(G-3221)
TOMRIC SYSTEMS INC
85 River Rock Dr (14207-2178)
PHONE.................................716 854-6050
Timothy Thill, *Ch of Bd*
Anne Rosa, *Vice Pres*
Sean Tucci, *Sales Staff*
▲ **EMP:** 9
SALES (est): 302.6K
SALES (corp-wide): 21.8MM **Privately Held**
SIC: 2064 Candy & other confectionery products
PA: Chocolate Delivery Systems, Inc.
85 River Rock Dr Ste 202
Buffalo NY 14207
716 854-6050

(G-3222)
TOOLING ENTERPRISES INC
680 New Babcock St Ste 1 (14206-2285)
PHONE.................................716 842-0445
Fax: 716 842-0305
Eugene Joseph, *President*
Art Beyer, *General Mgr*
Thomas Deangelo, *Branch Mgr*
EMP: 10
SQ FT: 21,000
SALES (est): 1.2MM **Privately Held**
SIC: 3469 3544 Metal stampings; special dies, tools, jigs & fixtures

(G-3223)
TOVIE ASARESE ROYAL PRTG CO
351 Grant St (14213-1423)
PHONE.................................716 885-7692
Fax: 716 885-0533
Ottoviano Asarese, *President*
Grace Campanella, *Office Mgr*
EMP: 7 **EST:** 1952
SQ FT: 1,500
SALES (est): 915.1K **Privately Held**
SIC: 2752 2759 Commercial printing, offset; letterpress printing

(G-3224)
TRANE US INC
45 Earhart Dr Ste 103 (14221-7809)
PHONE.................................716 626-1260
Fax: 716 626-9412
Ronald Gerster, *Branch Mgr*
Bruce Siebert, *Data Proc Exec*
EMP: 50 **Privately Held**
SIC: 3585 Refrigeration & heating equipment
HQ: Trane U.S. Inc.
1 Centennial Ave Ste 101
Piscataway NJ 08854
732 652-7100

(G-3225)
TRIPP PLATING WORKS INC
1491 William St (14206-1807)
PHONE.................................716 894-2424
Fax: 716 893-9377
Steven E Jagielo, *President*
Cherie Jagielo, *Vice Pres*
EMP: 7 **EST:** 1922
SQ FT: 6,000
SALES (est): 752.4K **Privately Held**
SIC: 3471 Electroplating of metals or formed products; polishing, metals or formed products; buffing for the trade

(G-3226)
TRU MOLD SHOES INC
42 Breckenridge St (14213-1555)
PHONE.................................716 881-4484
Fax: 716 837-6663
Ahmed Syed, *President*
Wayne Weisedel, *General Mgr*
Andrea Syed, *Vice Pres*
Cheryl Garrow, *Office Mgr*
Sharon Huber, *Director*
EMP: 35
SQ FT: 11,000
SALES (est): 3.9MM **Privately Held**
WEB: www.trumold.com
SIC: 3143 3144 Orthopedic shoes, men's; orthopedic shoes, women's

(G-3227)
TWENTY-FIRST CENTURY PRESS INC
501 Cornwall Ave (14215-3125)
PHONE.................................716 837-0800
Tracy B Lach, *President*
Mary Crimmen, *Vice Pres*
▲ **EMP:** 18 **EST:** 1979
SQ FT: 40,000
SALES (est): 3.4MM **Privately Held**
SIC: 2752 2789 Commercial printing, offset; photo-offset printing; binding only: books, pamphlets, magazines, etc.

(G-3228)
TYSON DELI INC (HQ)
Also Called: MGM
665 Perry St (14210-1355)
PHONE.................................716 826-6400
Fax: 716 826-9186
Howard Zemsky, *Chairman*
Viren Sitwala, *Vice Pres*
Ken Murray, *Plant Mgr*
Robert Neely, *Plant Mgr*
Audey Mase, *Controller*
EMP: 450
SQ FT: 85,000
SALES (est): 44.6MM
SALES (corp-wide): 41.3B **Publicly Held**
SIC: 2013 Sausages & other prepared meats
PA: Tyson Foods, Inc.
2200 W Don Tyson Pkwy
Springdale AR 72762
479 290-4000

(G-3229)
U S SUGAR CO INC (PA)
692 Bailey Ave (14206-3003)
PHONE.................................716 828-1170
Fax: 716 828-1509
Tom Ferlito, *CEO*
Ed Jackson, *Senior VP*
Vern Miller, *Vice Pres*
Vernessa Roberts, *Vice Pres*
Steve Ward, *Vice Pres*
▲ **EMP:** 50
SQ FT: 300,000
SALES (est): 14.1MM **Privately Held**
SIC: 2099 Sugar

(G-3230)
UC COATINGS CORPORATION
2250 Fillmore Ave (14214-2119)
P.O. Box 1066 (14215-6066)
PHONE.................................716 833-9366
Fax: 716 833-0120
Norman E Murray, *CEO*
Thomas D Johel, *President*
Thuy N Murray, *Corp Secy*
Eleanor Murray, *Vice Pres*
Paulette Welker, *Cust Mgr*
▼ **EMP:** 23
SQ FT: 30,000
SALES (est): 6.2MM **Privately Held**
WEB: www.uccoatings.com
SIC: 2851 Wood fillers or sealers; lacquers, varnishes, enamels & other coatings

(G-3231)
UNICELL BODY COMPANY INC (PA)
571 Howard St (14206-2195)
PHONE.................................716 853-8628
Fax: 716 854-7208
Roger J Martin, *Ch of Bd*
Paul Martin, *Vice Pres*
Dale Wunsch, *Purch Mgr*
Tom Scheeler, *Engineer*
Ping Zu, *Engineer*
EMP: 45 **EST:** 1963
SQ FT: 67,000
SALES: 20MM **Privately Held**
WEB: www.unicell.com
SIC: 3713 5013 Truck bodies (motor vehicles); truck parts & accessories

(G-3232)
UNIFORM NAMEMAKERS INC
55 Amherst Villa Rd (14225-1432)
PHONE.................................716 626-5474
Warren Clark, *President*
EMP: 10
SQ FT: 7,000
SALES (est): 550K **Privately Held**
WEB: www.uniformnamemakers.com
SIC: 2395 Embroidery & art needlework

(G-3233)
UNILOCK LTD
510 Smith St (14210-1288)
PHONE.................................716 822-6074
David Mc Intyre, *Branch Mgr*
EMP: 20
SALES (corp-wide): 103.6MM **Privately Held**
SIC: 3271 Paving blocks, concrete
PA: Unilock Ltd
401 The West Mall Suite 610
Etobicoke ON M9C 5
905 453-1438

(G-3234)
UNITED GRAPHICS INC
100 River Rock Dr Ste 301 (14207-2163)
PHONE.................................716 871-2600
John Giblin, *President*
EMP: 30
SQ FT: 10,000
SALES (est): 3.4MM **Privately Held**
SIC: 2759 Commercial printing

(G-3235)
UNITED RICHTER ELECTRICAL MTRS
106 Michigan Ave (14204-2111)
PHONE.................................716 855-1945
Fax: 716 852-2589
Thomas Weiner, *President*
John Cook, *Vice Pres*
Judith Weiner, *Admin Sec*
EMP: 10
SQ FT: 10,000
SALES (est): 1.7MM **Privately Held**
SIC: 7694 5063 Electric motor repair; power transmission equipment, electric

GEOGRAPHIC SECTION
Buffalo - Erie County (G-3262)

(G-3236)
UPSTATE MEDICAL SOLUTIONS INC
25 Minnetonka Rd (14220-2411)
PHONE.................................716 799-3782
Brian Huck, *Director*
EMP: 5
SALES (est): 429.5K **Privately Held**
SIC: 3842 Surgical appliances & supplies

(G-3237)
UPSTATE NIAGARA COOP INC (PA)
Also Called: Bison Products
25 Anderson Rd (14225-4905)
P.O. Box 650 (14225-0650)
PHONE.................................716 892-3156
Fax: 716 768-2089
Larry Webster, *CEO*
Daniel Wolf, *President*
Ed Porter, *General Mgr*
Doug Ricketts, *General Mgr*
Penney J Arnone, *Business Mgr*
EMP: 55 **EST:** 1930
SALES: 775.5MM **Privately Held**
SIC: 2026 Fermented & cultured milk products

(G-3238)
UPSTATE NIAGARA COOP INC
Also Called: Upstate Milk Co-Operatives
1730 Dale Rd (14225-4921)
P.O. Box 650 (14225-0650)
PHONE.................................716 892-2121
Fax: 716 892-3158
Larry Darch, *Principal*
Sherrie Green, *Regl Sales Mgr*
Colleen Keller, *Executive*
EMP: 200
SQ FT: 53,690
SALES (corp-wide): 775.5MM **Privately Held**
SIC: 2023 2026 Ice cream mix, unfrozen: liquid or dry; fluid milk
PA: Upstate Niagara Cooperative, Inc.
25 Anderson Rd
Buffalo NY 14225
716 892-3156

(G-3239)
V LAKE INDUSTRIES INC
1555 Niagara St (14213-1101)
PHONE.................................716 885-9141
Keith McCoy, *President*
David Russell, *Project Mgr*
EMP: 8
SQ FT: 24,000
SALES (est): 1MM **Privately Held**
SIC: 3469 3599 Metal stampings; machine & other job shop work

(G-3240)
VENT-A-KILN CORPORATION
Also Called: Vent-A-Fume
51 Botsford Pl (14216-2601)
PHONE.................................716 876-2023
Fax: 716 876-4383
Susan Lee, *President*
Richard Smith Jr, *Opers-Prdtn-Mfg*
EMP: 5
SQ FT: 1,200
SALES (est): 871.7K **Privately Held**
WEB: www.ventakiln.com
SIC: 3567 Kilns

(G-3241)
VERMED INC
400 Exchange St (14204-2064)
PHONE.................................802 463-9976
Sam Heleba, *President*
Ayu Vitous, *Mfg Staff*
Abel Rich, *Purch Agent*
Colleen Mollica, *VP Human Res*
Mollica Colleen, *Personnel Exec*
▲ **EMP:** 85
SQ FT: 45,000
SALES (est): 6MM
SALES (corp-wide): 1B **Privately Held**
WEB: www.vermed.com
SIC: 3845 Electromedical equipment
HQ: Graphic Controls Acquisition Corp.
400 Exchange St
Buffalo NY 14204
716 853-7500

(G-3242)
VIDBOLT INC
4 Elam Pl (14214-1911)
PHONE.................................716 560-8944
John Hutchinson, *President*
Jerod Sikorskyj, *Admin Sec*
EMP: 6
SALES (est): 241.1K **Privately Held**
SIC: 2741

(G-3243)
VINCENT MARTINO DENTAL LAB
74 Ransier Dr (14224-2244)
PHONE.................................716 674-7800
Vincent Martino, *President*
Deborah Martino, *Admin Sec*
EMP: 10 **EST:** 1976
SQ FT: 800
SALES: 300K **Privately Held**
SIC: 3843 8072 Orthodontic appliances; orthodontic appliance production

(G-3244)
VISIMETRICS CORPORATION
2290 Kenmore Ave (14207-1312)
PHONE.................................716 871-7070
Fax: 716 871-1308
Kenneth Luczkiewicz, *President*
William Umiker, *Vice Pres*
EMP: 8
SQ FT: 22,000
SALES (est): 1MM **Privately Held**
WEB: www.visicnc.com
SIC: 3599 Machine shop, jobbing & repair

(G-3245)
VOYAGER EMBLEMS INC
Also Called: Voyager Custom Products
701 Seneca St Ste D (14210-1351)
PHONE.................................416 255-3421
Donald B Grant, *Ch of Bd*
Sally Grant, *President*
Henry Maurer, *Vice Pres*
James Klein, *Purch Mgr*
Peter Barker, *Controller*
EMP: 108
SQ FT: 38,000
SALES: 5.2MM
SALES (corp-wide): 433.1K **Privately Held**
WEB: www.voyager-emblems.com
SIC: 2395 Emblems, embroidered
HQ: Grant Emblems Limited
55 Fieldway Rd Suite A
Etobicoke ON M8Z 3
416 255-3421

(G-3246)
VULCAN STEAM FORGING CO
247 Rano St (14207-2189)
P.O. Box 87 (14207-0087)
PHONE.................................716 875-3680
Fax: 716 875-3226
Michael Duggan, *President*
Daniel Disinger, *Engineer*
Andrew Andersen, *Sales Mgr*
Mary Joe, *Manager*
▲ **EMP:** 27
SQ FT: 30,000
SALES (est): 5.6MM **Privately Held**
WEB: www.vulcansf.com
SIC: 3462 Iron & steel forgings; flange, valve & pipe fitting forgings, ferrous

(G-3247)
WARD INDUSTRIAL EQUIPMENT INC (PA)
Also Called: Ward Iron Works Limited
1051 Clinton St (14206-2823)
PHONE.................................716 856-6966
Guy Nelson, *President*
▲ **EMP:** 1 **EST:** 1980
SQ FT: 500
SALES (est): 4.3MM **Privately Held**
WEB: www.devansco.com
SIC: 3535 5084 Bulk handling conveyor systems; industrial machinery & equipment

(G-3248)
WARNER
84 Paige Ave (14223-2636)
PHONE.................................716 446-0663
Alan Warner, *Principal*
EMP: 9
SALES (est): 526.4K **Privately Held**
SIC: 2389 Clergymen's vestments

(G-3249)
WEB ASSOCIATES INC
1255 Niagara St (14213-1501)
PHONE.................................716 883-3377
William E Breeser, *President*
EMP: 6
SALES (est): 480.3K **Privately Held**
WEB: www.betterwire.com
SIC: 3315 3469 Wire & fabricated wire products; metal stampings

(G-3250)
WEBB-MASON INC
300 Airborne Pkwy Ste 210 (14225-1491)
PHONE.................................716 276-8792
Jon Webber, *Manager*
EMP: 23
SALES (corp-wide): 117MM **Privately Held**
SIC: 2752 Business form & card printing, lithographic
PA: Webb-Mason, Inc.
10830 Gilroy Rd
Hunt Valley MD 21031
410 785-1111

(G-3251)
WENDT CORPORATION
2555 Walden Ave (14225-4737)
PHONE.................................716 391-1200
Fax: 716 873-9309
Thomas A Wendt Sr, *CEO*
Joseph Bertozzi, *Vice Pres*
Michael Muench, *Plant Mgr*
Patrick Krzysiak, *Foreman/Supr*
Michael Woodward, *Opers Staff*
◆ **EMP:** 100
SQ FT: 66,000
SALES (est): 38.3MM **Privately Held**
SIC: 3599 Custom machinery

(G-3252)
WEST METAL WORKS INC
Also Called: W M W
68 Hayes Pl (14210-1614)
PHONE.................................716 895-4900
Fax: 716 895-4861
Matthew G Gehman, *Ch of Bd*
Melissa Gehman, *Vice Pres*
David Wojtkowiak, *Marketing Staff*
Gail Perona, *Office Mgr*
Gail Strassburg, *Manager*
EMP: 20 **EST:** 1946
SALES (est): 3.1MM **Privately Held**
WEB: www.westmetalworks.com
SIC: 7692 3559 Welding repair; chemical machinery & equipment

(G-3253)
WESTERN NEW YORK FAMILY MAG
3147 Delaware Ave Ste B (14217-2002)
PHONE.................................716 836-3486
Fax: 716 836-3680
Michelle J Miller, *Owner*
EMP: 5
SALES (est): 517.2K **Privately Held**
WEB: www.wnyfamilymagazine.com
SIC: 2721 Magazines: publishing only, not printed on site

(G-3254)
WILCRO INC
90 Earhart Dr Ste 19 (14221-7802)
PHONE.................................716 632-4204
Fax: 716 632-4263
Richard Crooks Sr, *President*
Richard Crooks Jr, *Vice Pres*
Robert Crooks, *Admin Sec*
EMP: 9
SALES (est): 351.6K **Privately Held**
WEB: www.wilcro.com
SIC: 3571 2796 Personal computers (microcomputers); engraving on copper, steel, wood or rubber: printing plates

(G-3255)
WILLARD MACHINE
73 Forest Ave (14213-1093)
PHONE.................................716 885-1630
Fax: 716 885-1632
Jeffrey Rathmann, *President*
EMP: 13
SQ FT: 10,000
SALES (est): 1.1MM **Privately Held**
WEB: www.willardmachine.com
SIC: 3599 Machine shop, jobbing & repair

(G-3256)
WILLIAM S HEIN & CO INC
Also Called: Metro Center Western New York
1575 Main St (14209-1513)
PHONE.................................716 882-2600
Kevin Marmion, *President*
EMP: 100
SALES (corp-wide): 15.2MM **Privately Held**
WEB: www.foreign-law.com
SIC: 2731 Books: publishing only
PA: William S. Hein & Co., Inc.
2350 N Forest Rd Ste 14a
Getzville NY 14068
716 882-2600

(G-3257)
WINDOW WORKSHOPS INC
6040 N Bailey Ave Ste 1 (14226-1061)
PHONE.................................716 876-9981
Kenneth Slomovitz, *President*
Michael Osika, *VP Finance*
EMP: 15
SALES (est): 1.6MM **Privately Held**
SIC: 2591 Drapery hardware & blinds & shades

(G-3258)
X-L ENVELOPE AND PRINTING INC
701 Seneca St Ste 100 (14210-1376)
PHONE.................................716 852-2135
Terry Allen, *CEO*
Bob Woollacott, *Treasurer*
EMP: 11
SQ FT: 20,000
SALES (est): 2.3MM **Privately Held**
SIC: 2677 2752 Envelopes; commercial printing, lithographic

(G-3259)
XEROX CORPORATION
450 Corporate Pkwy # 100 (14226-1268)
PHONE.................................716 831-3300
Susan Ready, *Manager*
Chris Santella, *Manager*
EMP: 75
SALES (corp-wide): 18B **Publicly Held**
WEB: www.xerox.com
SIC: 3861 Photographic equipment & supplies
PA: Xerox Corporation
45 Glover Ave Ste 700
Norwalk CT 06850
203 968-3000

(G-3260)
YOUNG & SWARTZ INC
39 Cherry St (14204-1298)
PHONE.................................716 852-2171
Fax: 716 852-5652
Raphael Winzig, *President*
EMP: 10 **EST:** 1886
SQ FT: 15,000
SALES (est): 1.2MM **Privately Held**
SIC: 3991 5198 Brushes, household or industrial; paint brushes, rollers, sprayers

(G-3261)
YR BLANC & CO LLC
Also Called: Renovatio Med & Surgical Sups
1275 Main St Ste 120 (14209-1911)
PHONE.................................716 800-3999
Yves-Richard Blanc, *CEO*
EMP: 5
SALES (est): 839K **Privately Held**
SIC: 2899 3589 1781 5078   ; sewage & water treatment equipment; water well servicing; drinking water coolers, mechanical

(G-3262)
ZEPTOMETRIX CORPORATION (PA)
872 Main St (14202-1403)
PHONE.................................716 882-0920
Gregory Chiklis, *President*
Chris Collins, *Vice Pres*
John Paul, *Vice Pres*
Jaclyn Gross, *QA Dir*

Bullville - Orange County (G-3263)

GEOGRAPHIC SECTION

Ronald Urmson, *CFO*
▼ **EMP:** 30
SQ FT: 20,000
SALES (est): 11.1MM **Privately Held**
WEB: www.zeptometrix.com
SIC: 2836 Biological products, except diagnostic

Bullville
Orange County

(G-3263)
WOODARDS CONCRETE PRODUCTS INC
629 Lybolt Rd (10915)
P.O. Box 8 (10915-0008)
PHONE 845 361-3471
Fax: 845 361-1050
Robert Zwart, *President*
Gayle Cortright, *Corp Secy*
Allen Zwart, *Vice Pres*
Steve Zwart, *Vice Pres*
EMP: 25 **EST:** 1955
SQ FT: 14,000
SALES (est): 4.2MM **Privately Held**
WEB: www.woodardsconcrete.com
SIC: 3272 Concrete products; septic tanks, concrete; steps, prefabricated concrete

Burdett
Schuyler County

(G-3264)
ATWATER ESTATE VINEYARDS LLC
5055 State Route 414 (14818-9816)
PHONE 607 546-8463
Fax: 607 535-4692
Ted Marks, *Partner*
Stacy Yeater, *Accountant*
Denise Clappier, *Manager*
Katie Marks, *Manager*
EMP: 20 **EST:** 2000
SQ FT: 672
SALES (est): 2.3MM **Privately Held**
WEB: www.atwatervineyards.com
SIC: 2084 Wines

(G-3265)
FINGER LAKES DISTILLING
4676 State Route 414 (14818-9730)
PHONE 607 546-5510
Brian McKenzie, *President*
Thomas McKenzie, *Master*
EMP: 15
SALES (est): 2.1MM **Privately Held**
SIC: 2085 Distilled & blended liquors

Burke
Franklin County

(G-3266)
CREST HAVEN PRECAST INC
4925 State Route 11 (12917-2410)
PHONE 518 483-4750
Fax: 518 483-7577
Gary Boileau, *President*
Eva Boileau, *Vice Pres*
EMP: 7
SALES: 800K **Privately Held**
SIC: 3271 Concrete block & brick

Burnt Hills
Saratoga County

(G-3267)
MAMAS
119 Lake Hill Rd (12027-9519)
PHONE 518 399-2828
Panayiotis J Menagias, *Principal*
EMP: 5 **EST:** 2007
SALES (est): 314.1K **Privately Held**
SIC: 2024 Ice cream, bulk

Burt
Niagara County

(G-3268)
AKZO NOBEL CHEMICALS LLC
2153 Lockport Olcott Rd (14028-9788)
PHONE 716 778-8554
Fax: 716 778-7930
Gordon Martens, *Manager*
EMP: 8
SALES (corp-wide): 15.9B **Privately Held**
WEB: www.akzo-nobel.com
SIC: 2869 2899 Industrial organic chemicals; chemical preparations
HQ: Akzo Nobel Chemicals Llc
525 W Van Buren St # 1600
Chicago IL 60607
312 544-7000

Byron
Genesee County

(G-3269)
OXBO INTERNATIONAL CORPORATION (HQ)
7275 Batavia Byron Rd (14422-9599)
PHONE 585 548-2665
Gary C Stich, *CEO*
Richard Glazier, *Ch of Bd*
Paul Dow, *Vice Pres*
Andrew Talbott, *Vice Pres*
John Borrelli, *Senior Buyer*
▲ **EMP:** 100
SQ FT: 43,500
SALES (est): 42.9MM
SALES (corp-wide): 175.2MM **Privately Held**
WEB: www.oxbocorp.com
SIC: 3523 5083 Farm machinery & equipment; farm & garden machinery
PA: Ploeger Oxbo Group B.V.
Electronweg 5
Roosendaal
165 319-333

Cairo
Greene County

(G-3270)
B & B FOREST PRODUCTS LTD
251 Route 145 (12413-2659)
P.O. Box 907 (12413-0907)
PHONE 518 622-0811
William Fabian, *President*
▼ **EMP:** 13 **EST:** 1993
SALES (est): 1.3MM **Privately Held**
SIC: 2411 Logging

(G-3271)
BILBEE CONTROLS INC
628 Main St (12413-2806)
PHONE 518 622-3033
Fax: 518 622-3163
Robert Levinn, *President*
Barbara Powell, *Owner*
EMP: 12 **EST:** 1975
SQ FT: 12,000
SALES (est): 1.5MM **Privately Held**
WEB: www.bilbeecontrols.com
SIC: 3822 Thermostats, except built-in

(G-3272)
HIGHLAND MUSEUM & LIGHTHOUSE
111 M Simons Rd (12413-3135)
PHONE 508 487-1121
Dan Sanders, *President*
Gordon S Russell, *President*
Francine Webster, *Treasurer*
EMP: 15 **EST:** 1997
SALES: 180.5K **Privately Held**
SIC: 3731 Lighthouse tenders, building & repairing

(G-3273)
JRS FUELS INC
8037 Route 32 (12413-2526)
PHONE 518 622-9939
John Vandenburgh, *Principal*
EMP: 5 **EST:** 2009
SALES (est): 641.3K **Privately Held**
SIC: 2869 Fuels

(G-3274)
K & B WOODWORKING INC
133 Rolling Meadow Rd (12413-2201)
PHONE 518 634-7253
Fax: 518 634-7863
Peter Vogel, *President*
Richard Vogel, *Corp Secy*
Melissa Hulbert, *Office Mgr*
EMP: 7
SQ FT: 10,000
SALES (est): 726K **Privately Held**
WEB: www.kbwoodworking.com
SIC: 2511 2499 Wood household furniture; decorative wood & woodwork

Caledonia
Livingston County

(G-3275)
ADVIS INC
2218 River Rd (14423-9518)
PHONE 585 568-0100
Mark F Bocko, *CEO*
Donna REA, *Business Mgr*
Stephen Glaser, *Sales Staff*
Scott Housel, *Director*
EMP: 9
SALES: 950K **Privately Held**
SIC: 3674 Semiconductors & related devices

(G-3276)
ALLEN-BAILEY TAG & LABEL INC (PA)
3177 Lehigh St (14423-1053)
P.O. Box 123 (14423-0123)
PHONE 585 538-2324
Fax: 585 538-2800
Eugene S Tonucci, *Ch of Bd*
Ken Flasburg, *General Mgr*
Mark Eagle, *Plant Mgr*
Dennis Buckley, *Purch Agent*
Jody Bailey, *Accountant*
▲ **EMP:** 86 **EST:** 1911
SQ FT: 60,000
SALES (est): 16.9MM **Privately Held**
WEB: www.abtl.com
SIC: 2679 2672 2671 Tags, paper (unprinted): made from purchased paper; labels, paper: made from purchased material; labels (unprinted), gummed: made from purchased materials; packaging paper & plastics film, coated & laminated

(G-3277)
APPLIED ENERGY SOLUTIONS LLC
1 Technology Pl (14423-1246)
PHONE 585 538-3270
Peter Morris, *Engineer*
Vern Fleming,
EMP: 44
SQ FT: 60,000
SALES (est): 11.7MM **Privately Held**
WEB: www.appliedenergysol.com
SIC: 3629 Battery chargers, rectifying or nonrotating

(G-3278)
COMMODITY RESOURCE CORPORATION
2773 Caledonia Leroy Rd (14423-9538)
P.O. Box 576, Lakeville (14480-0576)
PHONE 585 538-9500
Fax: 585 538-9511
Leslie Cole, *President*
EMP: 12
SALES (est): 1.3MM **Privately Held**
WEB: www.crcconnect.com
SIC: 2875 2048 Fertilizers, mixing only; feed premixes

(G-3279)
GROWMARK FS LLC
2936 Telephone Rd (14423-9708)
PHONE 585 538-2186
Dale Bartholomew, *Manager*
EMP: 10
SALES (corp-wide): 8.7B **Privately Held**
WEB: www.growmarkfs.com
SIC: 2875 Fertilizers, mixing only
HQ: Growmark Fs, Llc
308 Ne Front St
Milford DE 19963
302 422-3001

(G-3280)
GULDENSCHUH LOGGING & LBR LLC
143 Wheatland Center Rd (14423-9750)
P.O. Box 191 (14423-0191)
PHONE 585 538-4750
Fax: 585 538-6993
Don Guldenschuh, *Mng Member*
Garrett Guldenschuh,
EMP: 9
SQ FT: 50,000
SALES (est): 1.3MM **Privately Held**
SIC: 2426 2411 5099 5211 Furniture stock & parts, hardwood; logging; timber products, rough; lumber products

(G-3281)
RHETT M CLARK INC
Also Called: Gregson-Clark
3213 Lehigh St (14423-1073)
PHONE 585 538-9570
Rhett M Clark, *President*
EMP: 6
SQ FT: 5,000
SALES (est): 860K **Privately Held**
SIC: 3524 5083 Lawn & garden equipment; lawn & garden machinery & equipment

(G-3282)
SPECIALIZED PRINTED FORMS INC
Also Called: Spforms
352 Center St (14423-1202)
P.O. Box 118 (14423-0118)
PHONE 585 538-2381
Fax: 585 538-4922
Kevin Johnston, *General Mgr*
Russell Shepard, *Plant Mgr*
Jody Bailey, *Accountant*
Mary J Randall, *Sales Staff*
▲ **EMP:** 20 **EST:** 1951
SQ FT: 135,000
SALES (est): 1.8MM
SALES (corp-wide): 568.9MM **Publicly Held**
WEB: www.spforms.com
SIC: 2761 Continuous forms, office & business
PA: Ennis, Inc.
2441 Presidential Pkwy
Midlothian TX 76065
972 775-9801

(G-3283)
TSS FOAM INDUSTRIES CORP
2770 W Main St (14423-9560)
P.O. Box 119 (14423-0119)
PHONE 585 538-2321
Fax: 585 538-2876
Samuel Di Liberto, *Ch of Bd*
EMP: 15
SQ FT: 60,000
SALES (est): 2.9MM **Privately Held**
SIC: 3086 5047 7389 Plastics foam products; medical & hospital equipment; sewing contractor

Callicoon
Sullivan County

(G-3284)
CATSKILL DELAWARE PUBLICATIONS (PA)
Also Called: Sullivan County Democrat
5 Lower Main St (12723-5000)
P.O. Box 308 (12723-0308)
PHONE 845 887-5200
Fax: 845 887-5386

Frederick W Stabbert III, *President*
Frank Rizzo, *Editor*
Dan Hust, *Advt Staff*
Susan Owens, *Office Mgr*
Christine Nappi, *Manager*
EMP: 19 **EST:** 1900
SQ FT: 5,704
SALES: 1MM **Privately Held**
WEB: www.sc-democrat.com
SIC: 2711 2752 Commercial printing & newspaper publishing combined; commercial printing, lithographic

(G-3285)
ELECTRO-KINETICS INC
51 Creamery Rd (12723-7710)
P.O. Box 188 (12723-0188)
PHONE 845 887-4930
Fax: 845 887-4745
Eric Andkjar, *President*
Jesse Ballew, *Marketing Staff*
EMP: 13
SQ FT: 8,000
SALES (est): 2.6MM **Privately Held**
WEB: www.electro-kinetics.com
SIC: 3625 Motor controls & accessories

Calverton
Suffolk County

(G-3286)
BONSAL AMERICAN INC
931 Burman Blvd (11933-3027)
PHONE 631 208-8073
John Cardona, *Principal*
EMP: 20
SALES (corp-wide): 25.3B **Privately Held**
WEB: www.bonsalamerican.com
SIC: 1442 Construction sand & gravel
HQ: Bonsal American, Inc.
625 Griffith Rd Ste 100
Charlotte NC 28217
704 525-1621

(G-3287)
BUNCEE LLC
4603 Middle Country Rd (11933-4104)
PHONE 631 591-1390
Bonpreet Sethi, *CTO*
Marie Arturi,
EMP: 10
SALES (est): 730K **Privately Held**
SIC: 7372 Prepackaged software

(G-3288)
COASTAL PIPELINE PRODUCTS CORP
55 Twomey Ave (11933-1374)
P.O. Box 575 (11933-0575)
PHONE 631 369-4000
Fax: 631 369-4006
Alexander Koke, *President*
▲ **EMP:** 50
SQ FT: 32,000
SALES (est): 10.9MM **Privately Held**
WEB: www.coastalpipeline.com
SIC: 3272 Precast terrazo or concrete products

(G-3289)
COOKING WITH CHEF MICHELLE LLC
Also Called: Ms. Michelles
4603 Middle Country Rd (11933-4104)
PHONE 516 662-2324
Michelle Gilette-Kelly, *President*
Michelle Marie Gilette-Kelly, *President*
Christopher Kelly, *CFO*
EMP: 6
SQ FT: 8,400
SALES: 229.6K **Privately Held**
SIC: 2052 5149 Cookies; crackers, cookies & bakery products

(G-3290)
EAST END COUNTRY KITCHENS INC
Also Called: Pezera Associates
121 Edwards Ave (11933-1602)
PHONE 631 727-2258
Fax: 631 727-0771
Henry Pazera, *President*
EMP: 10

SALES (est): 740K **Privately Held**
SIC: 2511 Kitchen & dining room furniture

(G-3291)
GLOBAL MARINE POWER INC
Also Called: Hustler Powerboats
221 Scott Ave (11933-3039)
PHONE 631 208-2933
Fax: 631 208-2942
Joe Logiudice, *Owner*
Richard Logiudice, *Vice Pres*
Linda Shrine, *Manager*
EMP: 40
SQ FT: 32,000
SALES (est): 8.3MM **Privately Held**
WEB: www.hustlerpowerboats.com
SIC: 3089 3732 5551 Plastic boats & other marine equipment; boat building & repairing; boat dealers

(G-3292)
LONG ISLAND SPIRITS INC
2182 Sound Ave (11933-1280)
PHONE 631 630-9322
Richard Stabile, *President*
EMP: 10
SALES (est): 426.9K **Privately Held**
SIC: 2085 Distilled & blended liquors

(G-3293)
LUMINATI AEROSPACE LLC
400 David Ct (11933-3007)
PHONE 631 574-2616
Daniel Preston, *CEO*
April Chapple, *Vice Pres*
EMP: 16
SALES (est): 682K **Privately Held**
SIC: 3721 Research & development on aircraft by the manufacturer

(G-3294)
PELLA CORPORATION
Also Called: Reilly Windows & Doors
901 Burman Blvd (11933-3027)
PHONE 631 208-0710
EMP: 126
SALES (corp-wide): 1.9B **Privately Held**
SIC: 2431 5211 5031 2499 Millwork; millwork & lumber; doors & windows; decorative wood & woodwork; window & door (prefabricated) installation
PA: Pella Corporation
102 Main St
Pella IA 50219
641 621-1000

(G-3295)
PORTABLE TECH SOLUTIONS LLC
221 David Ct (11933-3053)
PHONE 631 727-8084
Sharon Taylor, *Accountant*
Dan Peluso, *Human Res Dir*
Bradley Horn,
Daniel Peluso,
EMP: 10
SALES (est): 980K **Privately Held**
WEB: www.ptshome.com
SIC: 7372 Prepackaged software

(G-3296)
RACING INDUSTRIES INC
901 Scott Ave (11933-3033)
PHONE 631 905-0100
Ameet Bambami, *President*
▲ **EMP:** 20
SQ FT: 20,000
SALES (est): 4.5MM **Privately Held**
WEB: www.racingindustries.com
SIC: 3465 Body parts, automobile; stamped metal

(G-3297)
ROAR BIOMEDICAL INC
4603 Middle Country Rd (11933-4104)
PHONE 631 591-2749
Robert Brocia, *Branch Mgr*
EMP: 5
SALES (corp-wide): 2.4MM **Privately Held**
SIC: 2836 5122 Biological products, except diagnostic; biologicals & allied products

PA: Roar Biomedical Inc
3960 Broadway
New York NY 10032
212 280-2983

(G-3298)
STONY BROOK MFG CO INC (PA)
652 Scott Ave (11933-3046)
PHONE 631 369-9530
Fax: 631 369-9513
Ella Scaife, *President*
Graham Scaife, *Vice Pres*
Peter Day, *Project Mgr*
Peter Candela, *Engineer*
EMP: 30
SQ FT: 11,000
SALES (est): 4.6MM **Privately Held**
WEB: www.stonybrookmfg.com
SIC: 3317 Steel pipe & tubes

(G-3299)
SUFFOLK CEMENT PRECAST INC (PA)
1813 Middle Rd (11933-1450)
P.O. Box 261 (11933-0261)
PHONE 631 727-4432
Kenneth Lohr, *President*
Sherrill Meshel, *Bookkeeper*
EMP: 9
SQ FT: 500
SALES (est): 1.1MM **Privately Held**
SIC: 3272 Septic tanks, concrete

(G-3300)
SUFFOLK CEMENT PRODUCTS INC
1843 Middle Rd (11933-1450)
PHONE 631 727-2317
Fax: 631 727-6211
Mark A Lohr, *Ch of Bd*
Linda Hagen, *Vice Pres*
EMP: 29
SQ FT: 4,500
SALES (est): 10.2MM **Privately Held**
WEB: www.suffolkcement.com
SIC: 3273 3271 Ready-mixed concrete; blocks, concrete or cinder: standard

(G-3301)
TEBBENS STEEL LLC
800 Burman Blvd (11933-3024)
PHONE 631 208-8330
Louis Vito, *Engineer*
Thomas A Tebbens II, *Mng Member*
Elsie Tebbens,
EMP: 18 **EST:** 2001
SQ FT: 9,000
SALES (est): 5.9MM **Privately Held**
SIC: 3449 8711 Miscellaneous metalwork; structural engineering

(G-3302)
US HOISTS CORP
Also Called: Acme Marine
800 Burman Blvd (11933-3024)
PHONE 631 472-3030
Thomas A Tebbens II, *President*
Kelly Tebbens, *Vice Pres*
Norman Marcioch, *Sales Staff*
Michael Bonner, *Manager*
▼ **EMP:** 7
SALES (est): 870K **Privately Held**
SIC: 3536 Hoists, cranes & monorails

Cambria Heights
Queens County

(G-3303)
MADISON ELECTRIC
21916 Linden Blvd (11411-1619)
PHONE 718 358-4121
Pete Danielsson, *Owner*
Larry Zassman, *Office Mgr*
EMP: 18
SQ FT: 2,000
SALES: 300K **Privately Held**
SIC: 3699 Electrical equipment & supplies

Cambridge
Washington County

(G-3304)
B & J LUMBER CO INC
1075 State Route 22 (12816-2501)
P.O. Box 40 (12816-0040)
PHONE 518 677-3845
John Merriman, *President*
Barbara Merriman, *Vice Pres*
EMP: 5 **EST:** 1955
SALES: 100K **Privately Held**
SIC: 2421 5989 0115 Sawmills & planing mills, general; wood (fuel); corn

(G-3305)
CAMBRIDGE-PACIFIC INC
Also Called: CTX Printing
891 State Rd 22 (12816)
P.O. Box 159 (12816-0159)
PHONE 518 677-5988
Chris Belnap, *President*
▲ **EMP:** 33 **EST:** 1986
SQ FT: 12,000
SALES (est): 6.7MM **Privately Held**
WEB: www.cpacific.com
SIC: 2677 Envelopes

(G-3306)
COMMON SENSE NATURAL SOAP
7 Pearl St (12816-1127)
PHONE 518 677-0224
Robert Racine, *Owner*
David Woodward, *Info Tech Dir*
EMP: 30 **EST:** 2014
SALES (est): 5.5MM **Privately Held**
SIC: 2844 Toilet preparations

(G-3307)
EASTERN CASTINGS CO
2 Pearl St (12816-1107)
P.O. Box 129 (12816-0129)
PHONE 518 677-5610
Fax: 518 677-5610
Anthony McDonald, *President*
Andrew Nolan, *Treasurer*
EMP: 15
SQ FT: 25,000
SALES (est): 1.5MM **Privately Held**
SIC: 3365 Aluminum & aluminum-based alloy castings

(G-3308)
ED LEVIN INC
Also Called: Ed Levin Jewelry
52 W Main St (12816-1158)
PHONE 518 677-8595
Fax: 518 677-8597
Peter Tonjes, *President*
Ed Levin, *Chairman*
Marianne Dallaird, *Purchasing*
Leslie Resio, *Controller*
EMP: 25
SQ FT: 10,000
SALES: 2MM **Privately Held**
WEB: www.edlevinjewelry.com
SIC: 3911 Jewelry, precious metal

(G-3309)
ROBERT RACINE (PA)
Also Called: Common Sense Natural Soap
41 N Union St (12816-1025)
PHONE 518 677-0224
Robert Racine, *Owner*
Andre Mathieu, *Manager*
▲ **EMP:** 41
SALES (est): 7MM **Privately Held**
WEB: www.commonsensefarm.com
SIC: 2841 2844 Soap & other detergents; toilet preparations

(G-3310)
WAYMOR1 INC (PA)
879 State Rte 22 (12816)
P.O. Box 302 (12816-0302)
PHONE 518 677-8511
Fax: 518 677-5984
Joseph F Raccuia, *President*
▲ **EMP:** 54
SQ FT: 50,000
SALES (est): 32MM **Privately Held**
SIC: 2679 Paper products, converted

Cambridge - Washington County (G-3311)

(G-3311)
WAYMOR1 INC
Hc 22 (12816)
P.O. Box 302 (12816-0302)
PHONE..................518 677-8511
Susan H Morris, *Owner*
Wayne R Morris, *Owner*
EMP: 50
SALES (corp-wide): 32MM **Privately Held**
SIC: **2679** 2676 Paper products, converted; sanitary paper products
PA: Waymor1, Inc.
  879 State Rte 22
  Cambridge NY 12816
  518 677-8511

Camden
Oneida County

(G-3312)
CAMDEN NEWS INC
Also Called: Queens Central News
39 Main St (13316-1301)
P.O. Box 117 (13316-0117)
PHONE..................315 245-1849
Fax: 315 245-1880
James Van Winkle, *President*
James Winkle, *Editor*
EMP: 5 EST: 1974
SQ FT: 7,000
SALES (est): 270K **Privately Held**
SIC: **2711** Newspapers

(G-3313)
CAMDEN WIRE CO INC
Also Called: International Wire Group
12 Masonic Ave (13316-1294)
PHONE..................315 245-3800
Rodney Kent, *President*
Charles Knapp, *General Mgr*
Vince Donaldson, *Vice Pres*
Chuck Lovengoth, *Vice Pres*
Ken Suits, *Plant Mgr*
EMP: 700 EST: 1929
SQ FT: 400,000
SALES (est): 116.9MM
SALES (corp-wide): 442.1MM **Privately Held**
SIC: **3351** 3357 Wire, copper & copper alloy; nonferrous wiredrawing & insulating
HQ: International Wire Group, Inc.
  12 Masonic Ave
  Camden NY 13316
  315 245-2000

(G-3314)
DAVIS LOGGING & LUMBER
1450 Curtiss Rd (13316-5006)
PHONE..................315 245-1040
Leonard Davis, *Principal*
EMP: 6
SALES (est): 340K **Privately Held**
SIC: **2411** Logging

(G-3315)
INTERNATIONAL WIRE GROUP (PA)
12 Masonic Ave (13316-1202)
PHONE..................315 245-3800
Rodney Kent, *CEO*
Donald Dekay, *CFO*
Peter Blum, *Director*
Peter Reed, *Director*
Hugh Steven Wilson, *Director*
EMP: 9
SALES (est): 442.1MM **Privately Held**
SIC: **3351** Wire, copper & copper alloy

(G-3316)
INTERNATIONAL WIRE GROUP INC (HQ)
Also Called: Bare Wire Division
12 Masonic Ave (13316-1202)
PHONE..................315 245-2000
Fax: 315 245-4014
Rodney D Kent, *Ch of Bd*
William L Pennington, *Vice Chairman*
Geoff Kent, *Vice Pres*
Charles Lovenguth, *Vice Pres*
James Mills, *Vice Pres*
▲ EMP: 300
SALES (est): 442.1MM **Privately Held**
SIC: **3357** Nonferrous wiredrawing & insulating
PA: International Wire Group
  12 Masonic Ave
  Camden NY 13316
  315 245-3800

(G-3317)
KEVIN REGAN LOGGING LTD
1011 Hillsboro Rd (13316-4518)
P.O. Box 439 (13316-0439)
PHONE..................315 245-3890
Kevin Regan, *President*
Sharlene Regan, *Office Mgr*
EMP: 5
SALES (est): 585.6K **Privately Held**
SIC: **2411** 1629 Logging; land clearing contractor

(G-3318)
OMEGA WIRE INC (DH)
Also Called: Bare Wire Div
12 Masonic Ave (13316-1202)
P.O. Box 131 (13316-0131)
PHONE..................315 245-3800
Fax: 315 964-2148
Rodney D Kent, *President*
Peter Ernenwein, *Vice Pres*
Matthew Dolansky, *Controller*
Donald De Kay, *VP Finance*
Jim Stoughton, *Manager*
▲ EMP: 325
SQ FT: 200,000
SALES (est): 96.9MM
SALES (corp-wide): 442.1MM **Privately Held**
WEB: www.omegawire.com
SIC: **3351** Wire, copper & copper alloy
HQ: International Wire Group, Inc.
  12 Masonic Ave
  Camden NY 13316
  315 245-2000

(G-3319)
OWI CORPORATION
Also Called: Bare Wire Division
12 Masonic Ave (13316-1202)
P.O. Box 131 (13316-0131)
PHONE..................315 245-4305
Fax: 315 245-0750
Rodney Kent, *President*
Donald De Kay, *VP Finance*
▲ EMP: 7
SALES (est): 960.9K
SALES (corp-wide): 442.1MM **Privately Held**
SIC: **3351** Wire, copper & copper alloy
HQ: International Wire Group, Inc.
  12 Masonic Ave
  Camden NY 13316
  315 245-2000

(G-3320)
PERFORMANCE WIRE & CABLE INC
9482 State Route 13 (13316-4947)
P.O. Box 126 (13316-0126)
PHONE..................315 245-2594
Steven Benjamin, *President*
Eddie Edwards, *VP Sales*
EMP: 13
SQ FT: 37,500
SALES (est): 2.5MM **Privately Held**
WEB: www.performancewire.com
SIC: **3351** Wire, copper & copper alloy

Camillus
Onondaga County

(G-3321)
AQUARII INC
17 Genesee St (13031-1126)
PHONE..................315 672-8807
Ray Carrock, *President*
Hannah Carrock, *Marketing Mgr*
EMP: 8 **Privately Held**
SIC: **3646** Commercial indusl & institutional electric lighting fixtures

(G-3322)
CLEARSTEP TECHNOLOGIES LLC
213 Emann Dr (13031-2009)
PHONE..................315 952-3628
Scott Buehler, *General Mgr*
EMP: 7 EST: 2007
SQ FT: 2,000
SALES: 1.8MM **Privately Held**
WEB: www.clearsteptech.com
SIC: **2741** Technical manual & paper publishing

(G-3323)
KSA MANUFACTURING LLC
5050 Smoral Rd (13031-9726)
PHONE..................315 488-0809
Fax: 315 488-5142
Tyler Hudlick, *Prdtn Mgr*
Adam Kudlick,
Jane Kudlick,
▲ EMP: 12
SQ FT: 8,500
SALES (est): 1.4MM **Privately Held**
WEB: www.ksamanufacturing.com
SIC: **3492** Hose & tube fittings & assemblies, hydraulic/pneumatic

(G-3324)
STEVE POLI SALES
Also Called: Imprinted Sportswear
102 Farmington Dr (13031-2113)
PHONE..................315 487-0394
Steve Poli, *Owner*
EMP: 5
SALES (est): 283.6K **Privately Held**
SIC: **2261** Screen printing of cotton broadwoven fabrics

(G-3325)
TOSCH PRODUCTS LTD
25 Main St (13031-1126)
PHONE..................315 672-3040
Fax: 315 672-3318
Todd Oudemool, *President*
Liz Fkllon, *Office Mgr*
Dirk J Oudemool,
EMP: 6
SQ FT: 12,000
SALES: 500K **Privately Held**
WEB: www.toschltd.com
SIC: **3949** Lacrosse equipment & supplies, general

(G-3326)
UPSTATE TUBE INC
5050 Smoral Rd (13031-9726)
PHONE..................315 488-5636
Michael Kudlick, *President*
Kristy Kudlick, *Principal*
Tyler Kudlick, *Vice Pres*
EMP: 5
SALES (est): 350.8K **Privately Held**
SIC: **3492** Fluid power valves & hose fittings

(G-3327)
WESTROCK - SOUTHERN CONT LLC
100 Southern Dr (13031-1578)
PHONE..................315 487-6111
Fax: 315 488-4310
Sandy Lewek, *Office Mgr*
Dave Atkwell, *Manager*
EMP: 120
SALES (corp-wide): 11.3B **Publicly Held**
WEB: www.southerncontainer.com
SIC: **2653** 3412 Boxes, corrugated: made from purchased materials; metal barrels, drums & pails
HQ: Westrock - Southern Container, Llc
  133 River Rd
  Cos Cob CT 06807
  631 232-5704

(G-3328)
WESTROCK RKT COMPANY
4914 W Genesee St (13031-2374)
PHONE..................770 448-2193
Mark Van Der Kloet, *Director*
EMP: 161
SALES (corp-wide): 11.3B **Publicly Held**
WEB: www.rocktenn.com
SIC: **2653** Partitions, solid fiber: made from purchased materials
HQ: Westrock Rkt Company
  504 Thrasher St
  Norcross GA 30071
  770 448-2193

Campbell
Steuben County

(G-3329)
KRAFT HEINZ FOODS COMPANY
8600 Main St (14821)
PHONE..................607 527-4584
EMP: 210
SALES (corp-wide): 210.8B **Publicly Held**
SIC: **2022** Processed cheese
HQ: Heinz Kraft Foods Company
  1 Ppg Pl Ste 3200
  Pittsburgh PA 15222
  412 456-5700

(G-3330)
KRAFT HEINZ FOODS COMPANY
8596 Main St (14821-9636)
PHONE..................607 527-4584
Fax: 607 527-8060
Kenneth Blake, *Principal*
Henry Mapes, *Branch Mgr*
EMP: 350
SALES (corp-wide): 210.8B **Publicly Held**
WEB: www.kraftfoods.com
SIC: **2022** 2026 Cheese, natural & processed; fluid milk
HQ: Heinz Kraft Foods Company
  1 Ppg Pl Ste 3200
  Pittsburgh PA 15222
  412 456-5700

Canaan
Columbia County

(G-3331)
HILLTOWN PORK INC (PA)
12948 State Route 22 (12029-2118)
PHONE..................518 781-4050
Fax: 518 781-4139
Richard A Beckwith, *President*
Edwin S Beckwith, *Vice Pres*
Paula Beckwith, *Office Mgr*
Robert A Beckwith, *Admin Sec*
EMP: 16 EST: 1973
SALES (est): 1.6MM **Privately Held**
SIC: **2011** 2013 Pork products from pork slaughtered on site; sausages & other prepared meats

Canajoharie
Montgomery County

(G-3332)
GRAVYMASTER INC
Also Called: Dryden & Palmer Co
101 Erie Blvd (13317-1148)
PHONE..................203 453-1893
Stephen A Besse, *President*
John M Mills, *Treasurer*
EMP: 44
SQ FT: 31,000
SALES (est): 4.6MM **Privately Held**
WEB: www.gravy.com
SIC: **2064** 2035 2099 Candy & other confectionery products; seasonings & sauces, except tomato & dry; food preparations

(G-3333)
RICHARDSON BRANDS COMPANY (HQ)
Also Called: Richardson Foods
101 Erie Blvd (13317-1148)
PHONE..................518 673-3553
Fax: 518 673-2451
Arnold J D'Angelo, *CEO*
Kathy Hiserodt, *Vice Pres*
Tracey Burton, *VP Opers*
Richard Hersey, *Plant Mgr*
Tom Shellooe, *Plant Mgr*

◆ EMP: 150
SQ FT: 180,000
SALES (est): 25.9MM
SALES (corp-wide): 358.4MM Privately Held
WEB: www.richardsonbrands.com
SIC: 2064 Candy & other confectionery products
PA: Founders Equity, Inc.
711 5th Ave Ste 501
New York NY 10022
212 829-0900

(G-3334)
W W CUSTOM CLAD INC
75 Creek St (13317-1446)
PHONE.............................518 673-3322
Fax: 518 673-3343
April Chamberlain, Human Res Dir
EMP: 62
SQ FT: 23,804
SALES (corp-wide): 5.2MM Privately Held
WEB: www.wwcustomclad.com
SIC: 3479 Coating of metals & formed products
PA: W. W. Custom Clad, Inc.
337 E Main St
Canajoharie NY

Canandaigua
Ontario County

(G-3335)
BADGE MACHINE PRODUCTS INC
2491 Brickyard Rd (14424-7969)
PHONE.............................585 394-0330
Fax: 585 394-0446
Gail Flugel, President
Christian Flugel, Vice Pres
Cindy Baxter, Materials Mgr
Francis Flugel, Treasurer
Debi Ellis, Manager
EMP: 30
SQ FT: 24,000
SALES (est): 5.2MM Privately Held
WEB: www.badgemachine.com
SIC: 3599 Machine shop, jobbing & repair

(G-3336)
BRISTOL CORE INC
5310 North St (14424-7965)
P.O. Box 507 (14424-0507)
PHONE.............................585 919-0302
Morgan Curtice, President
EMP: 19
SALES (est): 3.4MM Privately Held
SIC: 2621 Bristols

(G-3337)
CANANDAIGUA MSGNR INCORPORATED (PA)
Also Called: Daily Messenger
73 Buffalo St (14424-1001)
PHONE.............................585 394-0770
Fax: 585 394-1675
George Ewing Jr, President
George Ewing Sr, Chairman
Andrew Kavulich, Vice Pres
Joy Daggett, Purchasing
Lynn Brown, Sls & Mktg Exec
EMP: 100 EST: 1910
SALES (est): 12.2MM Privately Held
SIC: 2711 2752 Newspapers; commercial printing, lithographic

(G-3338)
CARGES ENTPS OF CANANDAIGUA
Also Called: Canandaigua Quick Print
330 S Main St (14424-2117)
PHONE.............................585 394-2600
Fax: 585 394-2616
Elizabeth Carges, President
Kevin Carges, Vice Pres
Robert Carges, Vice Pres
Jeremy Luke, Graphic Designe
EMP: 6
SQ FT: 2,000

SALES (est): 1.4MM Privately Held
WEB: www.quickprintny.com
SIC: 2752 7334 Commercial printing, offset; photocopying & duplicating services

(G-3339)
CONSTELLATION BRANDS INC
3325 Marvin Sands Dr (14424-8405)
PHONE.............................585 393-4880
EMP: 31
SALES (corp-wide): 6.5B Publicly Held
WEB: www.cbrands.com
SIC: 2084 Wines, brandy & brandy spirits
PA: Constellation Brands, Inc.
207 High Point Dr # 100
Victor NY 14564
585 678-7100

(G-3340)
CONSTELLATION BRANDS US OPRS
116 Buffalo St (14424-1012)
PHONE.............................585 396-7600
Christopher Benziger, Branch Mgr
EMP: 773
SALES (corp-wide): 6.5B Publicly Held
SIC: 2084 Wines
HQ: Constellation Brands U.S. Operations, Inc.
235 N Bloomfield Rd
Canandaigua NY 14424
585 396-7600

(G-3341)
CONSTELLATION BRANDS US OPRS (HQ)
Also Called: Centerra Wine Company
235 N Bloomfield Rd (14424-1059)
PHONE.............................585 396-7600
John Wright, CEO
William F Hackett, President
Scott McCain, District Mgr
Jim Debonis, COO
Kocoloski Jim, Senior VP
◆ EMP: 277
SALES (est): 495.7MM
SALES (corp-wide): 6.5B Publicly Held
SIC: 2084 Wines
PA: Constellation Brands, Inc.
207 High Point Dr # 100
Victor NY 14564
585 678-7100

(G-3342)
DENNIES MANUFACTURING INC
2543 State Route 21 (14424-8718)
PHONE.............................585 393-4646
Fax: 585 396-9693
Richard Warkentin, President
Norma Vanderwall, Accountant
Dina Bennett, Manager
EMP: 27
SQ FT: 10,000
SALES (est): 4.8MM Privately Held
SIC: 3599 3441 7692 Machine shop, jobbing & repair; fabricated structural metal; welding repair

(G-3343)
DOUGS MACHINE SHOP INC
5300 North St (14424-7965)
P.O. Box 699 (14424-0699)
PHONE.............................585 905-0004
Douglas Leonard, Ch of Bd
EMP: 9
SALES (est): 1.2MM Privately Held
SIC: 3599 Machine shop, jobbing & repair

(G-3344)
EATON CORPORATION
2375 State Route 332 # 250 (14424-7517)
PHONE.............................585 394-1780
EMP: 217 Privately Held
SIC: 3625 Motor controls & accessories
HQ: Eaton Corporation
1000 Eaton Blvd
Cleveland OH 44122
216 523-5000

(G-3345)
EXFO BURLEIGH PDTS GROUP INC
181 S Main St Ste 10 (14424-1911)
PHONE.............................585 301-1530
Germain Lamonde, Ch of Bd

Sue Yoffee, Principal
Pierre Plamondon, Vice Pres
Jim Bluett, Opers Mgr
Peter Battisti, VP Finance
EMP: 87
SQ FT: 20,000
SALES (est): 11.9MM Privately Held
WEB: www.burleigh.com
SIC: 3625 3827 3699 3826 Relays & industrial controls; optical instruments & lenses; laser systems & equipment; analytical optical instruments

(G-3346)
FINGER LAKES EXTRUSION CORP
Also Called: Flex Tubing
2437 State Route 21 (14424-8716)
PHONE.............................585 905-0632
Fax: 315 889-7708
William Scott, President
Erica Wright, VP Finance
▲ EMP: 21 EST: 1998
SQ FT: 56,000
SALES: 5.6MM Privately Held
WEB: www.flextubing.com
SIC: 3089 3082 Extruded finished plastic products; tubes, unsupported plastic

(G-3347)
GATEHOUSE MEDIA LLC
Mpnnow
73 Buffalo St (14424-1001)
PHONE.............................585 394-0770
James Marotta, Vice Pres
Carl Helbig, Branch Mgr
Beth Kesel, Manager
Dan Goldman, Relations
EMP: 100
SALES (corp-wide): 1.2B Publicly Held
WEB: www.gatehousemedia.com
SIC: 2711 2752 Newspapers; commercial printing, lithographic
HQ: Gatehouse Media, Llc
175 Sullys Trl Ste 300
Pittsford NY 14534
585 598-0030

(G-3348)
JUST RIGHT CARBINES LLC
231 Saltonstall St (14424-8301)
PHONE.............................585 261-5331
Richard J Cutri,
EMP: 6
SALES: 900K Privately Held
SIC: 3999 Manufacturing industries

(G-3349)
MOORE PRINTING COMPANY INC
9 Coy St (14424-1595)
PHONE.............................585 394-1533
Donna Miller, President
Burton Moore, President
EMP: 8
SQ FT: 3,500
SALES (est): 670K Privately Held
SIC: 2752 2759 Commercial printing, offset; letterpress printing

(G-3350)
NUPRO TECHNOLOGIES LLC
23 Coach St Ste 2a (14424-1529)
P.O. Box 182 (14424-0182)
PHONE.............................412 422-5922
Greg Novack, Controller
Patty Sim, Bookkeeper
Sam Altman, Mng Member
Marro Vidal,
▲ EMP: 15
SQ FT: 2,500
SALES (est): 2.7MM Privately Held
SIC: 3315 Wire & fabricated wire products

(G-3351)
PACTIV LLC
2480 Sommers Dr (14424-5250)
PHONE.............................585 394-1525
Richard Wambold, Chairman
Dave Klas, Plant Mgr
Bill Howard, Engineer
Tom Morscheimer, Engineer
Scott Snyder, Engineer
EMP: 9 Privately Held
WEB: www.pactiv.com

SIC: 2621 Pressed & molded pulp & fiber products
HQ: Pactiv Llc
1900 W Field Ct
Lake Forest IL 60045
847 482-2000

(G-3352)
PACTIV LLC
5310 North St (14424-7965)
PHONE.............................847 482-2000
Phil Korenscra, Manager
David Chung, Technology
EMP: 7 Privately Held
WEB: www.pactiv.com
SIC: 3089 Plastic containers, except foam
HQ: Pactiv Llc
1900 W Field Ct
Lake Forest IL 60045
847 482-2000

(G-3353)
PACTIV LLC
5250 North St (14424-1026)
PHONE.............................585 393-3229
Richard Wambold, CEO
David C Jones, Facilities Mgr
Bob D'Ottavio, Manager
Bruce Goerss, Manager
Allan Rickett, Info Tech Dir
EMP: 207 Privately Held
WEB: www.pactiv.com
SIC: 3089 Plates, plastic
HQ: Pactiv Llc
1900 W Field Ct
Lake Forest IL 60045
847 482-2000

(G-3354)
PACTIV LLC
Also Called: Canandaigua Technology Center
5250 North St (14424-1026)
PHONE.............................585 393-3149
David Class, Branch Mgr
EMP: 800 Privately Held
WEB: www.pactiv.com
SIC: 3089 Tableware, plastic; composition stone, plastic; doors, folding: plastic or plastic coated fabric
HQ: Pactiv Llc
1900 W Field Ct
Lake Forest IL 60045
847 482-2000

(G-3355)
PLURES TECHNOLOGIES INC (PA)
4070 County Road 16 (14424-8314)
PHONE.............................585 905-0554
Aaron Dobrinsky, President
EMP: 1
SALES: 5.5MM Privately Held
SIC: 3674 Integrated circuits, semiconductor networks, etc.

(G-3356)
QUICKPRINT
330 S Main St (14424-2117)
PHONE.............................585 394-2600
Kevin Carges, CEO
Robert Carges, Vice Pres
Dawn Miles, Manager
EMP: 5
SALES (est): 356K Privately Held
SIC: 2752 Commercial printing, offset

(G-3357)
SELECT FABRICATORS INC
5310 North St Bldg 5 (14424-7965)
P.O. Box 119 (14424-0119)
PHONE.............................585 393-0650
Fax: 585 393-1378
David A Yearsley, President
Eleanor Yearsley, Vice Pres
Kristin Lupien, Production
Gary W Winch, CFO
Brian Smith, Sales Associate
▼ EMP: 15 EST: 2000
SQ FT: 19,728

Canandaigua - Ontario County (G-3358) GEOGRAPHIC SECTION

SALES (est): 2.4MM **Privately Held**
WEB: www.selectfabricatorsinc.com
SIC: **2393** 3812 2673 2394 Duffle bags, canvas; made from purchased materials; aircraft/aerospace flight instruments & guidance systems; bags: plastic, laminated & coated; tents: made from purchased materials

(G-3358)
T & G WHOLESALE ELECTRIC CORP
200 Saltonstall St (14424-8301)
PHONE..................................585 396-9690
Steve Guererri, *President*
EMP: 7
SALES (est): 807.6K **Privately Held**
SIC: **3699** Electrical equipment & supplies

(G-3359)
TIMBER FRAMES INC
5557 State Route 64 (14424-9382)
PHONE..................................585 374-6405
Alan R Milanette, *President*
Brenda Milanette, *Office Mgr*
EMP: 7
SQ FT: 800
SALES (est): 1.3MM **Privately Held**
WEB: www.timberframesinc.com
SIC: **2439** 1751 Structural wood members; framing contractor

(G-3360)
WOLFE PUBLICATIONS INC (PA)
Also Called: Messenger Post Media
73 Buffalo St (14424-1001)
PHONE..................................585 394-0770
Kathy Hammond, *President*
Rick Jensen, *Editor*
Marie Ewing, *Vice Pres*
Lorrie Helling, *Purchasing*
Martha Hagerman, *Bookkeeper*
EMP: 104 **EST:** 1956
SQ FT: 17,500
SALES (est): 11.3MM **Privately Held**
WEB: www.mpnewspapers.com
SIC: **2711** Commercial printing & newspaper publishing combined

(G-3361)
YOUNG EXPLOSIVES CORP
Also Called: Display Fireworks
2165 New Michigan Rd (14424-7918)
P.O. Box 18653, Rochester (14618-0653)
PHONE..................................585 394-1783
James R Young, *President*
Nancy Calvey, *Corp Comm Staff*
▲ **EMP:** 70
SQ FT: 400
SALES (est): 11.6MM **Privately Held**
WEB: www.youngexplosives.com
SIC: **2899** 7999 Fireworks; fireworks display service

Canaseraga
Allegany County

(G-3362)
BEAVER CREEK INDUSTRIES INC
11530 White Rd (14822-9607)
PHONE..................................607 545-6382
Fax: 607 545-6383
Gary Bajus, *President*
Ethan Flint, *Publisher*
Gary Bajus II, *Vice Pres*
Mary Bajus, *Treasurer*
EMP: 9
SQ FT: 8,000
SALES: 1MM **Privately Held**
SIC: **2431** Interior & ornamental woodwork & trim

Canastota
Madison County

(G-3363)
BLADING SERVICES UNLIMITED LLC
40 Madison Blvd (13032-3500)
PHONE..................................315 875-5313
Stephen Stevens,
EMP: 13
SALES (est): 2.1MM **Privately Held**
SIC: **3599** Machine shop, jobbing & repair

(G-3364)
CALLANAN INDUSTRIES INC
6375 Tuttle Rd (13032-4168)
PHONE..................................315 697-9569
Fax: 315 697-7501
Tim Hauck, *Principal*
EMP: 25
SALES (corp-wide): 25.3B **Privately Held**
SIC: **3272** Concrete products, precast
HQ: Callanan Industries, Inc.
1245 Kings Rd Ste 1
Schenectady NY 12303
518 374-2222

(G-3365)
CANASTOTA PUBLISHING CO INC
130 E Center St (13032-1307)
PHONE..................................315 697-9010
Fax: 315 697-8496
Patrick Milmoe, *President*
EMP: 5
SQ FT: 3,200
SALES (est): 530K **Privately Held**
SIC: **2752** Commercial printing, offset

(G-3366)
DEBRUCQUE CLEVELAND TRAMRAIL S
3 Technology Blvd (13032-3517)
PHONE..................................315 697-5160
Ron Debrucque, *Mng Member*
EMP: 6
SQ FT: 4,500
SALES (est): 670K **Privately Held**
SIC: **3536** Cranes & monorail systems

(G-3367)
DIEMOLDING CORPORATION (PA)
125 Rasbach St (13032-1429)
P.O. Box 26, Wampsville (13163-0026)
PHONE..................................315 697-2221
Donald R Dew, *CEO*
Mark Vanderveen, *Ch of Bd*
Dennis O'Brien, *President*
Jim Morin, *General Mgr*
Christopher Beehner, *CFO*
◆ **EMP:** 6 **EST:** 1920
SQ FT: 50,000
SALES (est): 19MM **Privately Held**
WEB: www.diemolding.com
SIC: **2655** Containers, laminated phenolic & vulcanized fiber

(G-3368)
DIEMOLDING CORPORATION
7887 Rt 13 N (13032)
PHONE..................................315 697-2221
Bruce, *Branch Mgr*
EMP: 5
SALES (corp-wide): 19MM **Privately Held**
SIC: **2655** Containers, laminated phenolic & vulcanized fiber
PA: Diemolding Corporation
125 Rasbach St
Canastota NY 13032
315 697-2221

(G-3369)
METAL FINISHING SUPPLY INC
6032 Nelson Rd (13032-4807)
P.O. Box 37, East Syracuse (13057-0037)
PHONE..................................315 655-8068
Fax: 315 437-5841
James Shanahan, *President*
William Walch, *Vice Pres*
Katherine Shanahan, *Admin Sec*

EMP: 5 **EST:** 1955
SQ FT: 5,000
SALES: 500K **Privately Held**
SIC: **3479** 5084 Coating of metals with plastic or resins; metal refining machinery & equipment

(G-3370)
OWL WIRE & CABLE LLC
3127 Seneca Tpke (13032-3514)
PHONE..................................315 697-2011
Fax: 315 697-2123
Philip J Kemper, *President*
Robert J Ratti, *Chairman*
Benjamin Norris, *Plant Mgr*
Josh Levesque, *Opers Mgr*
Emily Sorbello, *Purch Agent*
▲ **EMP:** 180 **EST:** 1951
SQ FT: 400,000
SALES (est): 78.8MM
SALES (corp-wide): 210.8B **Publicly Held**
WEB: www.owlwire.com
SIC: **3315** Wire & fabricated wire products
HQ: The Marmon Group Llc
181 W Madison St Ste 2600
Chicago IL 60602
312 372-9500

(G-3371)
PRIME MATERIALS RECOVERY INC
51 Madison Blvd (13032-3501)
PHONE..................................315 697-5251
Francis Pratt, *Branch Mgr*
EMP: 8
SALES (corp-wide): 181.4MM **Privately Held**
SIC: **3441** Fabricated structural metal
PA: Prime Materials Recovery Inc.
99 E River Dr
East Hartford CT 06108
860 622-7626

(G-3372)
SALARINOS ITALIAN FOODS INC
Also Called: Basilio's
110 James St (13032-1410)
PHONE..................................315 697-9766
Fax: 315 697-2551
Vincent Salamone Jr, *President*
Debra Salamone, *Vice Pres*
EMP: 10
SQ FT: 4,050
SALES (est): 997K **Privately Held**
SIC: **2013** 2038 Sausages from purchased meat; pizza, frozen

(G-3373)
SIDE HILL FARMERS COOP INC
8275 State Route 13 (13032-4470)
PHONE..................................315 447-4693
Paul O'Mara, *President*
Kirsten Tolman, *Treasurer*
EMP: 6
SALES: 1MM **Privately Held**
SIC: **2011** Meat packing plants

(G-3374)
THERMOLD CORPORATION
7059 Harp Rd (13032-4583)
PHONE..................................315 697-3924
Fax: 315 697-7177
Jeremy Schwimmer, *Ch of Bd*
Dan Emmons, *President*
Jerry Rath, *President*
Michael Dunn, *Vice Pres*
Ashish Mare, *Project Mgr*
▲ **EMP:** 106 **EST:** 1945
SQ FT: 35,000
SALES (est): 30.5MM **Privately Held**
WEB: www.thermold.com
SIC: **3089** Molding primary plastic

(G-3375)
TRICON PIPING SYSTEMS INC
2 Technology Blvd (13032-3520)
P.O. Box 361 (13032-0361)
PHONE..................................315 655-4178
Hugh Roszel, *President*
Sara Jeffris, *Manager*
▼ **EMP:** 12 **EST:** 1999
SALES (est): 2.8MM **Privately Held**
WEB: www.triconpiping.com
SIC: **3317** Steel pipe & tubes

(G-3376)
VICTORY SIGNS INC
8915 Old State Route 13 (13032-5417)
PHONE..................................315 762-0220
Anthony Deperno, *President*
Jennifer Deperno, *Vice Pres*
EMP: 8
SQ FT: 2,000
SALES (est): 1MM **Privately Held**
SIC: **3993** Signs & advertising specialties

Candor
Tioga County

(G-3377)
H L ROBINSON SAND & GRAVEL (PA)
535 Ithaca Rd (13743)
P.O. Box 121 (13743-0121)
PHONE..................................607 659-5153
Hannah L Robinson, *President*
Shane Reeves, *Sales Mgr*
Brad Robinson, *Manager*
Raymond Dailey, *Director*
EMP: 18
SQ FT: 5,000
SALES: 2.6MM **Privately Held**
SIC: **1442** Sand mining; gravel mining

(G-3378)
MARCELLUS ENERGY SERVICES LLC
3 Mill St Ste 6 (13743-1400)
PHONE..................................607 236-0038
Gloria Tubbs, *Mng Member*
EMP: 20
SALES (est): 1.3MM **Privately Held**
SIC: **1389** Oil field services

Canisteo
Steuben County

(G-3379)
SIVKO FURS INC
3089 County Route 119 (14823-9681)
PHONE..................................607 698-4827
Fax: 607 698-4827
Ann Farkas, *President*
EMP: 9
SQ FT: 3,675
SALES (est): 1MM **Privately Held**
SIC: **2299** Grease, wool

Canton
St. Lawrence County

(G-3380)
BIMBO BAKERIES USA INC
19 Miner St Ste D (13617-1231)
PHONE..................................315 379-9069
EMP: 18
SALES (corp-wide): 13B **Privately Held**
SIC: **2051** Bread, cake & related products
HQ: Bimbo Bakeries Usa, Inc
255 Business Center Dr # 200
Horsham PA 19044
215 347-5500

(G-3381)
COMMERCIAL PRESS INC
6589 Us Highway 11 (13617-3980)
PHONE..................................315 274-0028
Fax: 315 386-5259
David Charleson, *President*
Tracy Charleson, *Vice Pres*
EMP: 6
SQ FT: 1,200
SALES (est): 620K **Privately Held**
SIC: **2752** 2759 Commercial printing, offset; commercial printing

(G-3382)
CORNING INCORPORATED
334 County Route 16 (13617-3135)
PHONE..................................315 379-3200
Fax: 315 379-3211
Joseph Neubert, *Plant Mgr*

David Navan, *Engineer*
Joe Neubert, *Manager*
Mark Randall, *Senior Mgr*
Joseph A Miller Jr, *CTO*
EMP: 86
SALES (corp-wide): 9.1B **Publicly Held**
WEB: www.corning.com
SIC: 3229 3211 Pressed & blown glass; flat glass
PA: Corning Incorporated
1 Riverfront Plz
Corning NY 14831
607 974-9000

(G-3383)
FRAZER COMPUTING INC
6196 Us Highway 11 (13617-3967)
P.O. Box 569 (13617-0569)
PHONE...............................315 379-3500
Michael Frazer, *Owner*
EMP: 26
SALES (est): 3.9MM **Privately Held**
WEB: www.frazercomputing.com
SIC: 7372 Prepackaged software

Cape Vincent
Jefferson County

(G-3384)
METALCRAFT MARINE US INC
583 E Broadway St (13618-4152)
PHONE...............................315 501-4015
Tom Wroe, *President*
Michael Allen, *General Mgr*
Paul Cooledge, *Project Mgr*
Rob Phippen, *Controller*
Bob Clark, *Admin Sec*
▼ **EMP:** 17
SQ FT: 4,000
SALES: 547K
SALES (corp-wide): 5MM **Privately Held**
SIC: 3732 3731 Boat building & repairing; shipbuilding & repairing; barges, building & repairing; combat vessels, building & repairing; fireboats, building & repairing
PA: Metal Craft Marine Incorporated
347 Wellington St
Kingston ON K7K 6
613 549-7747

Carle Place
Nassau County

(G-3385)
AMERICAN ENGNRED CMPONENTS INC
Also Called: A E C Electrotech
40 Voice Rd (11514-1513)
P.O. Box 343 (11514-0343)
PHONE...............................516 742-8386
Bincent Rozen, *Principal*
EMP: 53
SALES (corp-wide): 35MM **Privately Held**
SIC: 3714 8711 Motor vehicle parts & accessories; engineering services
PA: American Engineered Components Inc, 17951 W Austin Rd
Manchester MI 48158
734 428-8301

(G-3386)
BEE GREEN INDUSTRIES INC
322 Westbury Ave (11514-1607)
PHONE...............................516 334-3525
Harold Livine, *President*
EMP: 6
SALES (est): 283.7K **Privately Held**
SIC: 3999 Manufacturing industries

(G-3387)
BIOTEMPER
Also Called: Biotemper Plus
516 Mineola Ave (11514-1716)
PHONE...............................516 302-7985
Nadeem Khan, *Administration*
EMP: 5 **EST:** 2015
SALES (est): 229.7K **Privately Held**
SIC: 2833 Medicinal chemicals

(G-3388)
FORMED PLASTICS INC
207 Stonehinge Ln (11514-1743)
P.O. Box 347 (11514-0347)
PHONE...............................516 334-2300
Fax: 516 334-2679
Patrick K Long, *President*
Steve Zamprelli, *President*
David Long, *Exec VP*
Matthew Desmond, *Vice Pres*
Ron Joannou, *VP Mfg*
EMP: 80 **EST:** 1946
SQ FT: 74,000
SALES (est): 21.1MM **Privately Held**
WEB: www.formedplastics.com
SIC: 3089 Plastic processing

(G-3389)
GENNARIS ITLN FRENCH BKY INC
Also Called: Cardinali Bakery
465 Westbury Ave (11514-1401)
PHONE...............................516 997-8968
Giuseppe A Mauro, *President*
Joe Mauro, *Sales Executive*
Mary Lou Makelski, *Admin Sec*
EMP: 6 **EST:** 1935
SALES (est): 500K **Privately Held**
SIC: 2051 5461 Bread, cake & related products; bakeries

(G-3390)
GOOD TIMES MAGAZINE
346 Westbury Ave Ste LI (11514-1654)
PHONE...............................516 280-2100
Rich Braciforte, *Owner*
EMP: 8 **EST:** 1969
SALES (est): 648.2K **Privately Held**
WEB: www.goodtimesmag.com
SIC: 2721 Periodicals

(G-3391)
JEFF COOPER INC
288 Westbury Ave (11514-1605)
P.O. Box 361 (11514-0361)
PHONE...............................516 333-8200
Fax: 516 333-0620
Jeff Cooper, *President*
Laurie Cooper, *Vice Pres*
David Cooper, *Manager*
EMP: 12 **EST:** 1978
SALES (est): 1.7MM **Privately Held**
WEB: www.jcplatinum.com
SIC: 3911 Jewelry, precious metal; rings, finger; precious metal; pins (jewelry), precious metal; bracelets, precious metal

(G-3392)
JOHNSON & HOFFMAN LLC
40 Voice Rd (11514-1511)
P.O. Box 343 (11514-0343)
PHONE...............................516 742-3333
Brad Ansary, *President*
Larry Zettwoch, *VP Opers*
Drew Taormina, *Plant Mgr*
Barry Trontz, *Purch Mgr*
Albert Costabile, *Human Res Mgr*
EMP: 90
SQ FT: 65,000
SALES (est): 19.6MM **Privately Held**
WEB: www.aecjh.com
SIC: 3469 Metal stampings
PA: Ansaco, Llc
56 E 13th St Apt 4
New York NY 10003
602 323-0653

(G-3393)
LOW-COST MFG CO INC
318 Westbury Ave (11514-1607)
P.O. Box 147 (11514-0147)
PHONE...............................516 627-3282
Fax: 516 997-9890
Harold Rothlin, *President*
Freddy Malamud, *General Mgr*
▲ **EMP:** 6
SQ FT: 4,000
SALES (est): 1MM **Privately Held**
WEB: www.lowcostmfg.com
SIC: 3564 5087 Purification & dust collection equipment; laundry equipment & supplies

(G-3394)
M&M PRINTING INC
Also Called: MARsid-M&m Group, The
245 Westbury Ave (11514-1604)
PHONE...............................516 796-3020
Barry Caputo, *President*
Sidney Halpern, *Vice Pres*
Jeff Sanderoff, *Accounts Exec*
Giovanni Jaramillo, *Marketing Staff*
EMP: 15
SALES (est): 1.4MM **Privately Held**
SIC: 2731 Book publishing

(G-3395)
MARKET PLACE PUBLICATIONS
Also Called: J & F Advertising
234 Silverlake Blvd Ste 2 (11514-1644)
PHONE...............................516 997-7909
Fax: 516 997-7906
Gonzalez Jose, *Principal*
EMP: 40
SALES (est): 1.5MM **Privately Held**
SIC: 2711 7313 Newspapers; newspaper advertising representative

(G-3396)
MARSID GROUP LTD
Also Called: Marsid Press
245 Westbury Ave (11514-1604)
PHONE...............................516 334-1603
Sidney Halpern, *President*
Mike Halpern, *Vice Pres*
▼ **EMP:** 9
SALES (est): 940K **Privately Held**
WEB: www.mmprint.com
SIC: 2752 Commercial printing, offset

(G-3397)
VINCENTS FOOD CORP
179 Old Country Rd (11514-1907)
PHONE...............................516 481-3544
Anthony Marisi, *President*
Robert Marisi, *Treasurer*
EMP: 12
SALES (est): 720K **Privately Held**
SIC: 2033 Tomato sauce: packaged in cans, jars, etc.

Carmel
Putnam County

(G-3398)
BIODESIGN INC OF NEW YORK (PA)
1 Sunset Rdg (10512-1118)
P.O. Box 1050 (10512-8050)
PHONE...............................845 454-6610
Fax: 845 454-6077
Susanne Ruddnick PHD, *President*
Michael Payne PHD, *Vice Pres*
Suzanne Payne, *Manager*
EMP: 18
SQ FT: 26,000
SALES (est): 1MM **Privately Held**
WEB: www.biodesignofny.com
SIC: 3821 3829 Laboratory apparatus & furniture; measuring & controlling devices

(G-3399)
EASTERN JUNGLE GYM INC (PA)
30 Commerce Dr (10512-3026)
PHONE...............................845 878-9800
Fax: 845 878-1088
Scott Honigsberg, *President*
Rolf Zimmerman, *President*
Mark Honigsberg, *Vice Pres*
Janice Borowy, *Manager*
EMP: 30
SQ FT: 30,000
SALES (est): 6MM **Privately Held**
WEB: www.playsystem.com
SIC: 3949 5941 Playground equipment; playground equipment

(G-3400)
J & J TL DIE MFG & STAMPG CORP
594 Horsepound Rd (10512-4703)
PHONE...............................845 228-0242
Ronald C Johnson, *President*
EMP: 5 **EST:** 1981

SQ FT: 4,800
SALES (est): 531.7K **Privately Held**
SIC: 3599 Machine & other job shop work

(G-3401)
JAMES A STALEY CO INC
5 Bowen Ct (10512-4535)
PHONE...............................845 878-3344
Fax: 845 878-3429
James A Staley, *President*
J David Mori, *Vice Pres*
Chris Staley, *Foreman/Supr*
Kevin Loffredo, *Engineer*
Boris Shnitser, *Engineer*
EMP: 18
SQ FT: 15,800
SALES (est): 5.2MM **Privately Held**
WEB: www.staleyco.com
SIC: 3829 7699 Aircraft & motor vehicle measurement equipment; testers for checking hydraulic controls on aircraft; fuel system instruments, aircraft; aircraft & heavy equipment repair services; hydraulic equipment repair

(G-3402)
NORTHEAST MESA LLC (PA)
10 Commerce Dr (10512-3026)
PHONE...............................845 878-9344
Fax: 845 878-9351
Denise Persek, *Sales Staff*
Giulio Burra,
Phil Waylonis,
EMP: 6 **EST:** 1995
SQ FT: 8,400
SALES (est): 1.2MM **Privately Held**
WEB: www.northeastmesa.com
SIC: 3271 Blocks, concrete: landscape or retaining wall

(G-3403)
PATTERSON BLACKTOP CORP
Also Called: Peckham Materials
1181 Route 6 (10512-1645)
PHONE...............................845 628-3425
Kurt Gabrielson, *Branch Mgr*
EMP: 6
SALES (corp-wide): 192MM **Privately Held**
SIC: 3531 Asphalt plant, including gravel-mix type
HQ: Patterson Blacktop Corp
20 Haarlem Ave
White Plains NY 10603
914 949-2000

(G-3404)
PRECISION ARMS INC
Also Called: Time Precision
421 Route 52 (10512-6063)
PHONE...............................845 225-1130
Art Cocchia, *President*
Steven Cocchia, *Vice Pres*
Josephine Cocchia, *Admin Sec*
EMP: 6
SQ FT: 3,500
SALES (est): 524.2K **Privately Held**
WEB: www.precisionarms.com
SIC: 3599 7699 Machine shop, jobbing & repair; gunsmith shop

(G-3405)
SILARX PHARMACEUTICALS INC
1033 Stoneleigh Ave (10512-2414)
P.O. Box 449, Spring Valley (10977-0449)
PHONE...............................845 352-4020
Fax: 845 352-4037
Rohit Desai, *President*
Vipin Patel, *Vice Pres*
Nayan Raval, *Vice Pres*
Rashmi Gandhi, *Research*
John Mathews, *Engineer*
▲ **EMP:** 49
SQ FT: 30,000
SALES (est): 9.9MM
SALES (corp-wide): 542.4MM **Publicly Held**
SIC: 2834 Pharmaceutical preparations
PA: Lannett Company, Inc.
9000 State Rd
Philadelphia PA 19136
215 333-9000

Carmel - Putnam County (G-3406) — GEOGRAPHIC SECTION

(G-3406)
TPA COMPUTER CORP
531 Route 52 Apt 4 (10512-6073)
PHONE.................877 866-6044
Steven Barnes, *President*
EMP: 10
SQ FT: 1,000
SALES: 1.2MM **Privately Held**
WEB: www.tpacomputer.com
SIC: 7372 5734 Application computer software; computer & software stores

Carthage
Jefferson County

(G-3407)
A B C MC CLEARY SIGN CO INC
40230 State Route 3 (13619-9727)
PHONE.................315 493-3550
Fax: 315 493-3573
Ronald Moore, *President*
Jo Anne Moore, *Corp Secy*
EMP: 11
SQ FT: 15,000
SALES (est): 730K **Privately Held**
SIC: 3993 Signs & advertising specialties; electric signs

(G-3408)
CARTHAGE FIBRE DRUM INC (PA)
14 Hewitt Dr (13619-1101)
P.O. Box 109 (13619-0109)
PHONE.................315 493-2730
Fax: 315 493-6818
Timothy Wright, *President*
Cathy Wright, *Corp Secy*
Ford Wright Sr, *Vice Pres*
EMP: 15 EST: 1915
SQ FT: 1,509
SALES (est): 1.9MM **Privately Held**
SIC: 2655 Fiber cans, drums & similar products

(G-3409)
CEM MACHINE INC (PA)
571 W End Ave (13619-1038)
PHONE.................315 493-4258
Fax: 315 493-4236
Mark Robinson, *President*
Roxanne Robinson, *Corp Secy*
Jason Flint, *Engineer*
Timothy Nettles, *Treasurer*
Richard Mayo, *Director*
▲ EMP: 48
SQ FT: 80,000
SALES (est): 9.5MM **Privately Held**
WEB: www.cem-machine.com
SIC: 3553 Woodworking machinery

(G-3410)
CHAMPION MATERIALS INC (PA)
502 S Washington St (13619-1533)
P.O. Box 127 (13619-0127)
PHONE.................315 493-2654
Fax: 315 493-2672
James D Uhlinger Jr, *Ch of Bd*
Turnbull Zoay, *Manager*
Corina Houppert, *Admin Asst*
Arrianne Turnbell, *Administration*
EMP: 6
SALES (est): 6.3MM **Privately Held**
WEB: www.championmaterials.com
SIC: 3273 5211 Ready-mixed concrete; sand & gravel

(G-3411)
CHAMPION MATERIALS INC
21721 Cole Rd (13619-9559)
PHONE.................315 493-2654
James Uhlinger, *Branch Mgr*
EMP: 44
SALES (corp-wide): 6.3MM **Privately Held**
SIC: 3273 5211 Ready-mixed concrete; sand & gravel
PA: Champion Materials, Inc.
502 S Washington St
Carthage NY 13619
315 493-2654

(G-3412)
CLIMAX MANUFACTURING COMPANY (PA)
Also Called: Climax Packaging
30 Champion St (13619-1190)
PHONE.................315 376-8000
Fax: 315 376-6534
Patrick Purdy, *CEO*
Lizbeth Hirschey, *President*
Donald Schnackel, *General Mgr*
Sarah Miller, *Exec VP*
Michael Lambert, *Vice Pres*
▲ EMP: 180
SALES (est): 74.2MM **Privately Held**
WEB: www.climaxpkg.com
SIC: 2657 Folding paperboard boxes

(G-3413)
DAVID JOHNSON
Also Called: Poly Can
Deer River Rd (13619)
PHONE.................315 493-4735
Fax: 315 493-4735
David Johnson, *Owner*
EMP: 12
SQ FT: 12,000
SALES: 2MM **Privately Held**
SIC: 3085 Plastics bottles

Cassadaga
Chautauqua County

(G-3414)
CASSADAGA DESIGNS INC
309 Maple Ave (14718-9723)
P.O. Box 289 (14718-0289)
PHONE.................716 595-3030
Fax: 716 595-2312
Harold Hawkins, *President*
Daniel Hicks, *Vice Pres*
EMP: 6
SQ FT: 25,000
SALES: 500K **Privately Held**
SIC: 2426 2511 Frames for upholstered furniture, wood; chairs, household, except upholstered: wood

(G-3415)
WRIGHTS HARDWOODS INC
Also Called: Livermoore Logging
6868 Route 60 (14718-9706)
P.O. Box 1021, Sinclairville (14782-1021)
PHONE.................716 595-2345
Fax: 716 595-2585
Michael A Livermore, *President*
L Phillip Wright, *Vice Pres*
EMP: 22
SQ FT: 2,832
SALES (est): 1.6MM **Privately Held**
SIC: 2426 Dimension, hardwood

Castile
Wyoming County

(G-3416)
DON BECK INC
5249 State Route 39 (14427-9518)
PHONE.................585 493-3040
Fax: 585 493-2256
Richard T Beck, *President*
EMP: 7
SALES (est): 1.1MM **Privately Held**
SIC: 3523 Farm machinery & equipment

Castle Creek
Broome County

(G-3417)
A D BOWMAN & SON LUMBER CO
1737 Us Highway 11 (13744-1107)
PHONE.................607 692-2595
Fax: 607 692-4176
Melvin Bowman, *Ch of Bd*
Joanne Bowman, *President*
Joel Bowman, *Vice Pres*
EMP: 28
SALES (est): 4.3MM **Privately Held**
SIC: 2426 2448 2421 Lumber, hardwood dimension; pallets, wood & wood with metal; sawmills & planing mills, general

Castleton On Hudson
Rensselaer County

(G-3418)
IN NORTHEAST PRECISION WELDING
1177 Route 9 (12033-1910)
P.O. Box 109, East Greenbush (12061-0109)
PHONE.................518 441-2260
Christine W Dwileski, *Principal*
EMP: 5 EST: 2008
SALES (est): 547K **Privately Held**
SIC: 7692 Automotive welding

(G-3419)
MOORADIAN HYDRAULICS & EQP CO (PA)
1190 Route 9 (12033-9686)
PHONE.................518 766-3866
Fax: 518 766-3183
Richard Mooradian, *President*
Thomas Mooradian, *Vice Pres*
EMP: 10
SQ FT: 17,200
SALES (est): 1.9MM **Privately Held**
SIC: 7692 7699 5085 Welding repair; hydraulic equipment repair; hose, belting & packing

(G-3420)
SAXTON CORPORATION
1320 Route 9 (12033-9686)
PHONE.................518 732-7705
Fax: 518 732-7716
Mike Kellog, *President*
EMP: 30
SALES (est): 2.7MM **Privately Held**
SIC: 3993 Signs & advertising specialties

Castorland
Lewis County

(G-3421)
BLACK RIVER VALLEY WDWKG LLC
4773 State Route 410 (13620-2301)
PHONE.................315 376-8405
Melvin Hess, *Partner*
Brian Ball, *Partner*
Ronald Hess, *Partner*
EMP: 5 EST: 1993
SQ FT: 6,000
SALES: 500K **Privately Held**
SIC: 2511 Wood household furniture

(G-3422)
CLIMAX MANUFACTURING COMPANY
5204 Climax St (13620-7706)
PHONE.................315 376-8000
Fax: 315 376-2034
Patrick Purdy, *CEO*
EMP: 200
SALES (corp-wide): 74.2MM **Privately Held**
SIC: 2657 Folding paperboard boxes
PA: Climax Manufacturing Company Inc
30 Champion St
Carthage NY 13619
315 376-8000

(G-3423)
DANIEL & LOIS LYNDAKER LOGGING
10460 Monnat School Rd (13620-1270)
PHONE.................315 346-6527
Lois Lyndaker, *Principal*
EMP: 7 EST: 2010
SALES (est): 732.7K **Privately Held**
SIC: 2411 Logging

(G-3424)
LYNDAKER TIMBER HARVESTING LLC
10204 State Route 812 (13620-1268)
PHONE.................315 346-1328
David R Lyndaker,
Anita Lyndaker,
EMP: 11
SALES (est): 970K **Privately Held**
SIC: 2411 Timber, cut at logging camp

Cato
Cayuga County

(G-3425)
ZAPPALA FARMS AG SYSTEMS INC
11404 Schuler Rd (13033-4276)
PHONE.................315 626-6293
James R Zappala, *President*
Samuel Zappala, *Vice Pres*
Mark Ferlito, *Treasurer*
John R Zappala, *Admin Sec*
EMP: 30
SALES (est): 2.5MM **Privately Held**
SIC: 3523 5531 Farm machinery & equipment; automotive accessories

Catskill
Greene County

(G-3426)
CIMENT ST-LAURENT INC
Also Called: St Lawrence Cement Co
6446 Route 9w (12414-5322)
P.O. Box 31 (12414-0031)
PHONE.................518 943-4040
Fax: 518 943-6894
Clifford Graves, *Site Mgr*
Ken Dewitt, *Purchasing*
Georges Hubin, *Branch Mgr*
EMP: 140
SALES (corp-wide): 25.3B **Privately Held**
SIC: 3241 Masonry cement
HQ: Crh Canada Group Inc
2300 Steeles Ave W Suite 300
Concord ON L4K 5
905 532-3000

(G-3427)
DAILY MAIL & GREENE CNTY NEWS (HQ)
414 Main St (12414-1303)
P.O. Box 484 (12414-0484)
PHONE.................518 943-2100
Roger Coleman, *President*
Raymond Pignone, *Principal*
Sara Tully, *Editor*
Michael Higgins, *Vice Pres*
Brenda Nickles, *Exec Dir*
EMP: 15 EST: 1951
SQ FT: 5,000
SALES (est): 3.1MM
SALES (corp-wide): 32MM **Privately Held**
WEB: www.thedailymail.org
SIC: 2711 Newspapers, publishing & printing
PA: Johnson Newspaper Corporation
260 Washington St
Watertown NY
315 782-1000

(G-3428)
GOLUB CORPORATION
Also Called: Price Chopper Pharmacy
320 W Bridge St (12414-1730)
PHONE.................518 943-3903
EMP: 78
SALES (corp-wide): 3.4B **Privately Held**
SIC: 3751 Motorcycles & related parts
PA: The Golub Corporation
461 Nott St
Schenectady NY 12308
518 355-5000

GEOGRAPHIC SECTION

Cazenovia - Madison County (G-3452)

(G-3429)
HILL CREST PRESS
Also Called: E & G Press
138 Grandview Ave (12414-1934)
PHONE....................................518 943-0671
Christine French, *Principal*
EMP: 8 **EST:** 1965
SQ FT: 1,500
SALES (est): 1.1MM **Privately Held**
SIC: 2752 2759 Commercial printing, off-set; letterpress printing

(G-3430)
LEHIGH CEMENT COMPANY
120 Alpha Rd (12414-6902)
PHONE....................................518 943-5940
Jeff Fetty, *Opers Staff*
Cheryl McElroy, *Manager*
Al Austin, *Manager*
EMP: 20
SALES (corp-wide): 271.5MM **Privately Held**
WEB: www.gfcement.com
SIC: 3273 5032 Ready-mixed concrete; cement
HQ: Lehigh Cement Company
313 Warren St
Glens Falls NY 12801
518 792-1137

(G-3431)
MARK T WESTINGHOUSE
Also Called: Pro Printers of Greene County
138 Grandview Ave (12414-1934)
PHONE....................................518 678-3262
Mark T Westinghouse, *Owner*
EMP: 6
SQ FT: 2,000
SALES: 600K **Privately Held**
SIC: 2752 2759 Commercial printing, off-set; letterpress printing

(G-3432)
MOUNTAIN T-SHIRTS INC
Also Called: Mountain T-Shirts & Sign Works
8 W Bridge St (12414-1620)
PHONE....................................518 943-4533
Fax: 518 943-4577
Craig Remaley, *President*
Daniel Webster, *Corp Secy*
Michael Marciante, *Treasurer*
EMP: 6 **EST:** 1984
SALES (est): 380K **Privately Held**
WEB: www.mountaintshirts.com
SIC: 2396 2261 5136 5199 Printing & embossing on plastics fabric articles; printing of cotton broadwoven fabrics; men's & boys' clothing; gifts & novelties

(G-3433)
PECKHAM INDUSTRIES INC
7065 Us Highway 9w (12414-5311)
P.O. Box 146, Ashland (12407-0146)
PHONE....................................518 943-0155
Fax: 518 943-6956
Gary Metcalf, *Principal*
EMP: 18
SALES (corp-wide): 192MM **Privately Held**
SIC: 2951 Concrete, asphaltic (not from refineries)
PA: Peckham Industries, Inc.
20 Haarlem Ave Ste 200
White Plains NY 10603
914 949-2000

(G-3434)
WILLIAM MOON IRON WORKS INC
Also Called: Moon, Wm
80 Main St (12414-1805)
PHONE....................................518 943-3861
Fax: 518 943-3135
Paul Moon, *President*
Shelly Moon, *Bookkeeper*
EMP: 10
SQ FT: 6,000
SALES: 450K **Privately Held**
SIC: 3599 Machine shop, jobbing & repair

(G-3435)
WOLFGANG B GOURMET FOODS INC
117 Cauterskill Ave (12414-1748)
PHONE....................................518 719-1727
Wolfgang Brandl, *President*
Penelope Queen, *Vice Pres*
Bruce Johnson, *Executive*
Dr Fereidoon Behin, *Shareholder*
EMP: 14
SQ FT: 10,000
SALES (est): 2.3MM **Privately Held**
SIC: 2033 Spaghetti & other pasta sauce: packaged in cans, jars, etc.

Cattaraugus
Cattaraugus County

(G-3436)
ADAMS LUMBER CO INC
6052 Adams Rd (14719-9567)
PHONE....................................716 358-2815
Fax: 716 358-2220
Leona Adams, *President*
Robert Adams, *Vice Pres*
Dennis Adams, *Treasurer*
EMP: 16 **EST:** 1961
SQ FT: 10,000
SALES (est): 2.2MM **Privately Held**
SIC: 2421 Lumber: rough, sawed or planed

(G-3437)
CHESTER-JENSEN COMPANY
124 S Main St (14719-1240)
PHONE....................................610 876-6276
Fax: 716 357-3764
Steven Miller, *Vice Pres*
Albert Gimbrone, *Opers-Prdtn-Mfg*
Larry Barr, *Engineer*
EMP: 40
SQ FT: 52,232
SALES (corp-wide): 6.9MM **Privately Held**
WEB: www.chester-jensen.com
SIC: 3556 Food products machinery
PA: Chester-Jensen Company
345 Tilghman St
Chester PA 19013
610 876-6276

(G-3438)
P & C GAS MEASUREMENTS SERVICE
Also Called: P & C Service
9505 Tannery Rd (14719-9761)
PHONE....................................716 257-3412
Fax: 716 257-5253
James Perkins, *CEO*
Marie Robbons, *Manager*
EMP: 11
SQ FT: 5,000
SALES (est): 826.6K **Privately Held**
SIC: 1389 Oil sampling service for oil companies

(G-3439)
PKK INC
Also Called: Setterstix Corporation
261 S Main St (14719-1312)
PHONE....................................716 257-3451
Fax: 716 257-9818
Frederick Rossetti, *CEO*
Christopher Cadigan, *President*
Jeffrey B Gaynor, *Exec VP*
▼ **EMP:** 44
SQ FT: 59,000
SALES (est): 14MM
SALES (corp-wide): 550.4MM **Privately Held**
WEB: www.setterstix.com
SIC: 2679 Paper products, converted
HQ: Setter International Gmbh
Reeser Str. 87
Emmerich Am Rhein
282 291-4580

Cayuta
Schuyler County

(G-3440)
WAGNER HARDWOODS LLC
6307 St Route 224 (14824)
P.O. Box 68 (14824-0068)
PHONE....................................607 594-3321
Les Wagner, *Manager*
Roy L Hanville, *Manager*
▼ **EMP:** 41
SALES (est): 7.5MM **Privately Held**
SIC: 2426 Hardwood dimension & flooring mills

(G-3441)
WAGNER HARDWOODS LLC
6307 St Route 224 (14824)
P.O. Box 68 (14824-0068)
PHONE....................................607 594-3321
Les Wagner, *Branch Mgr*
EMP: 200 **Privately Held**
WEB: www.wagner-hardwoods.com
SIC: 2426 Hardwood dimension & flooring mills
PA: Wagner Hardwoods Llc
6052 County Road 20
Friendship NY 14739

Cazenovia
Madison County

(G-3442)
BYS PUBLISHING LLC
118 Albany St (13035-1257)
PHONE....................................315 655-9431
Brent Selleck,
◆ **EMP:** 5
SALES (est): 317.6K **Privately Held**
SIC: 2741 Miscellaneous publishing

(G-3443)
CONTINENTAL CORDAGE CORP (DH)
75 Burton St (13035-1156)
P.O. Box 623 (13035-0623)
PHONE....................................315 655-9800
Fax: 315 655-9686
Rodney D Kent, *President*
Jim Murphy, *Division Mgr*
Jeff Wood, *Plant Mgr*
Bruce Ball, *Human Res Dir*
▲ **EMP:** 100
SQ FT: 60,000
SALES (est): 4.8MM
SALES (corp-wide): 442.1MM **Privately Held**
WEB: www.iwgbwd.com
SIC: 2298 3357 3496 3356 Cordage: abaca, sisal, henequen, hemp, jute or other fiber; nonferrous wiredrawing & insulating; miscellaneous fabricated wire products; nonferrous rolling & drawing; copper rolling & drawing; steel wire & related products
HQ: International Wire Group, Inc.
12 Masonic Ave
Camden NY 13316
315 245-2000

(G-3444)
D R CORNUE WOODWORKS
3206 Us Route 20 (13035-8408)
PHONE....................................315 655-9463
Dale R Cornue, *Owner*
EMP: 6
SQ FT: 6,000
SALES (est): 600K **Privately Held**
SIC: 2431 Doors, wood; woodwork, interior & ornamental; windows, wood

(G-3445)
FITZSIMMONS SYSTEMS INC
53 Nelson St (13035-1306)
PHONE....................................315 214-7010
Fax: 315 708-5424
Lowell Todd Fitzsimmons, *President*
Lucy McClaine, *Accountant*
▼ **EMP:** 13 **EST:** 1998
SQ FT: 1,500
SALES (est): 1.3MM **Privately Held**
WEB: www.fuelstoragetank.com
SIC: 2899 Chemical preparations

(G-3446)
JBF STAINLESS LLC
4905 E Lake Rd (13035-9346)
P.O. Box 632 (13035-0632)
PHONE....................................315 569-2800
John Feldmeier, *President*
Margaret Feldmeier, *Principal*
EMP: 26
SQ FT: 4,500
SALES (est): 5.9MM **Privately Held**
SIC: 3324 Steel investment foundries

(G-3447)
KNOWLES CAZENOVIA INC (HQ)
Also Called: Dli
2777 Us Route 20 (13035-8444)
PHONE....................................315 655-8710
Fax: 315 655-0445
Michael P Busse, *Ch of Bd*
David Wightman, *President*
Howard Ingleson, *Managing Dir*
Amy Pierce, *Purch Mgr*
Christopher Carney, *Engineer*
▲ **EMP:** 179
SQ FT: 120,000
SALES: 34MM
SALES (corp-wide): 1B **Publicly Held**
WEB: www.dilabs.com
SIC: 3675 Electronic capacitors
PA: Knowles Corporation
1151 Maplewood Dr
Itasca IL 60143
630 250-5100

(G-3448)
MADISON COUNTY DISTILLERY LLC
2420 Rte 20 (13035-8438)
PHONE....................................315 391-6070
Patrick Ruddy,
EMP: 5
SALES (est): 169.5K **Privately Held**
SIC: 2085 Gin (alcoholic beverage); vodka (alcoholic beverage)

(G-3449)
MARQUARDT SWITCHES INC (DH)
2711 Us Route 20 (13035-9405)
PHONE....................................315 655-8050
Fax: 315 655-8042
Harold Marquardt, *Ch of Bd*
Jochen Becker, *President*
John Jelfo, *CFO*
Christine Dillingham, *Accounts Mgr*
Peter Mitchell, *Admin Sec*
▲ **EMP:** 200 **EST:** 1975
SQ FT: 98,000
SALES: 219.7MM **Privately Held**
WEB: www.switches.com
SIC: 3625 3613 Switches, electric power; switchgear & switchboard apparatus
HQ: Marquardt Gmbh
SchloBstr. 16
Rietheim-Weilheim 78604
742 499-0

(G-3450)
PDJ INC
Also Called: Johnson Bros Lumber
2550 E Ballina Rd (13035-8475)
PHONE....................................315 655-8824
Fax: 315 655-4449
Paul Johnson, *President*
Judith Johnson, *Vice Pres*
Kara Connellan, *Office Spvr*
Heather Johnson, *Admin Sec*
EMP: 30
SQ FT: 39,400
SALES (est): 5.3MM **Privately Held**
SIC: 2421 Sawmills & planing mills, general

(G-3451)
PRICET PRINTING
3852 Charles Rd (13035-4505)
PHONE....................................315 655-0369
Nathan Hoak, *President*
EMP: 6
SALES (est): 726.3K **Privately Held**
SIC: 2752 Commercial printing, lithographic

(G-3452)
STK ELECTRONICS INC
Also Called: Air-O-Tronics
2747 Rte 20 (13035-8444)
PHONE....................................315 655-8476
Fax: 800 634-0285
Bill Merlini, *Ch of Bd*
Peter M Kip, *Principal*
Peter Mitchell, *Principal*
William Merlini, *CFO*

Dan Koehl, *Manager*
▲ **EMP:** 40
SQ FT: 20,000
SALES (est): 9.4MM **Privately Held**
WEB: www.stkelectronics.com
SIC: 3675 5063 Electronic capacitors; electrical apparatus & equipment; circuit breakers

(G-3453)
TRONSER INC
3066 John Trush Jr Blvd (13035-9541)
PHONE.................................315 655-9528
Michael Tronser, *President*
Mike Beckett, *General Mgr*
James Dowd, *Vice Pres*
James Biando, *Mfg Mgr*
Peter Mitchell, *Admin Sec*
▲ **EMP:** 6
SQ FT: 7,000
SALES (est): 1.3MM
SALES (corp-wide): 18MM **Privately Held**
WEB: www.tronser.com
SIC: 3675 Electronic capacitors
PA: Alfred Tronser Gmbh
  Quellenweg 14
  Engelsbrand 75331
  708 279-80

(G-3454)
VOLTRONICS LLC
Also Called: Trimmer Capacitor Company, The
2777 Us Route 20 (13035-8444)
PHONE.................................410 749-2424
Aaron Goldberg, *General Mgr*
Mary Finkelstein, *Manager*
EMP: 48 **EST:** 1963
SQ FT: 200,000
SALES (est): 8.5MM
SALES (corp-wide): 6.9B **Publicly Held**
WEB: www.variablecap.com
SIC: 3675 Electronic capacitors
PA: Dover Corporation
  3005 Highland Pkwy # 200
  Downers Grove IL 60515
  630 541-1540

Cedarhurst
Nassau County

(G-3455)
ABLE KITCHEN
Also Called: Able Kitchen Supplies
540 Willow Ave Unit B (11516-2211)
PHONE.................................877 268-1264
Schulman Joseph, *Owner*
Joseph Schulman, *Mng Member*
EMP: 15
SALES (est): 994.2K **Privately Held**
SIC: 2434 Wood kitchen cabinets

(G-3456)
ELMAT QUALITY PRINTING LTD
79 Columbia Ave (11516-2011)
PHONE.................................516 569-5722
Fax: 516 569-5913
Matt Friedman, *President*
Ellen Friedman, *Treasurer*
EMP: 16
SQ FT: 4,000
SALES: 1.5MM **Privately Held**
SIC: 2752 Commercial printing, offset

(G-3457)
FRANKLIN PRINTING GROUP LTD
Also Called: Fpg
140 Washington Ave Unit A (11516-1921)
PHONE.................................516 569-1248
Gerald Stulberger, *President*
▼ **EMP:** 3
SALES: 3.3MM **Privately Held**
SIC: 2752 Commercial printing, lithographic

(G-3458)
LAVISH LAYETTE INC
406 Central Ave (11516-1907)
PHONE.................................516 256-9130
EMP: 5

SALES (corp-wide): 844.3K **Privately Held**
SIC: 2339 2335 Women's & misses' athletic clothing & sportswear; women's, juniors' & misses' dresses
PA: Lavish Layette Inc.
  876 Woodmere Pl
  Woodmere NY 11598
  347 962-9955

(G-3459)
M & M BAGEL CORP
Also Called: Bagelry
507 Central Ave (11516-2010)
PHONE.................................516 295-1222
Vincent Matuozzi, *President*
Robert Madorsky, *Vice Pres*
EMP: 12
SALES (est): 1MM **Privately Held**
SIC: 2051 5461 Bagels, fresh or frozen; bagels

(G-3460)
MARK F ROSENHAFT N A O
538 Central Ave (11516-2127)
PHONE.................................516 374-1010
Mark F Rosenhaft, *Owner*
EMP: 8
SALES (est): 423.7K **Privately Held**
SIC: 3851 5999 Eyes, glass & plastic; miscellaneous retail stores

(G-3461)
NANO VIBRONIX INC
601 Chestnut St (11516-2228)
PHONE.................................516 374-8330
Harold Jacobs, *President*
EMP: 17
SALES: 16K **Privately Held**
SIC: 3841 Surgical & medical instruments

(G-3462)
NJR MEDICAL DEVICES
390 Oak Ave (11516-1824)
P.O. Box 582, New York (10021-0034)
PHONE.................................440 258-8204
Nicholas Pastron, *CEO*
EMP: 20
SALES (est): 1.9MM **Privately Held**
SIC: 3841 Suction therapy apparatus

(G-3463)
STJ ENTERPRISES
540 Willow Ave (11516-2211)
PHONE.................................516 612-0110
Joseph Schulman, *CEO*
Spencer Silverstein, *CFO*
EMP: 65
SALES (est): 4.4MM **Privately Held**
SIC: 3845 3841 Ultrasonic medical equipment, except cleaning; surgical & medical instruments

Center Moriches
Suffolk County

(G-3464)
DIAMOND PRECAST PRODUCTS INC
170 Railroad Ave (11934-1906)
PHONE.................................631 874-3777
Rick Cerrone, *President*
Dominic Iannuci, *Treasurer*
Steven Cerrone, *Manager*
Jeff Lashley, *Manager*
Ronald Notaranonio, *Admin Sec*
EMP: 15 **EST:** 1999
SALES (est): 1.6MM **Privately Held**
SIC: 3272 Concrete products

(G-3465)
EASTEND ENFORCEMENT PRODUCTS
24 Chichester Ave (11934-2402)
P.O. Box 309 (11934-0309)
PHONE.................................631 878-8424
John Koenig, *Owner*
Edithy Koenig, *Manager*
EMP: 5
SALES (est): 359.4K **Privately Held**
SIC: 3559 Ammunition & explosives, loading machinery

(G-3466)
GLASS STAR AMERICA INC
15 Frowein Rd Bldg E2 (11934-1609)
PHONE.................................631 291-9432
Fax: 631 951-0676
Anthony Jacino, *President*
Joseph Jacino, *Vice Pres*
▲ **EMP:** 11
SQ FT: 15,000
SALES (est): 2.1MM **Privately Held**
SIC: 3559 Automotive maintenance equipment

(G-3467)
ISLAND READY MIX INC
170 Railroad Ave (11934-1906)
PHONE.................................631 874-3777
Fax: 631 874-2860
Rice Cerrone, *President*
Dominic Iannuci, *Treasurer*
Ronald Notarantonio, *Admin Sec*
EMP: 25 **EST:** 1961
SALES (est): 4.3MM **Privately Held**
WEB: www.islandreadymix.com
SIC: 3273 3272 Ready-mixed concrete; concrete products, precast

(G-3468)
RED TAIL MOULDING & MLLWK LLC
23 Frowein Rd Ste 1 (11934-1606)
PHONE.................................516 852-4613
Tom Smith,
EMP: 3
SALES (est): 1.2MM **Privately Held**
SIC: 2431 Doors & door parts & trim, wood

Centereach
Suffolk County

(G-3469)
A M S SIGN DESIGNS
2360 Middle Country Rd (11720-3523)
PHONE.................................631 467-7722
Mark Saccone, *Owner*
Suzanne Saccone, *Co-Owner*
EMP: 5
SALES (est): 415.3K **Privately Held**
SIC: 3993 Signs & advertising specialties

(G-3470)
CALIBRATION TECHNOLOGIES INC
30 Woodland Blvd (11720-3636)
PHONE.................................631 676-6133
Thomas J Accardi, *President*
EMP: 5
SALES (est): 526K **Privately Held**
SIC: 3629 Electrical industrial apparatus

(G-3471)
I FIX SCREEN
203 Centereach Mall (11720-2751)
PHONE.................................631 421-1938
Alberto Cruz, *Principal*
EMP: 6
SALES (est): 316.5K **Privately Held**
SIC: 3442 Screen & storm doors & windows

(G-3472)
QUANTA ELECTRONICS INC
48 Fran Ln (11720-4441)
PHONE.................................631 961-9953
Martin Czerniewski, *President*
Carolina Zuniga, *Info Tech Mgr*
EMP: 12
SALES (est): 1.5MM **Privately Held**
SIC: 3663 Radio & TV communications equipment

(G-3473)
SPIRIT PHARMACEUTICALS LLC
1919 Middle Country Rd (11720-5601)
PHONE.................................215 943-4000
Ajoy Joshi, *CEO*
EMP: 5
SALES (est): 99K **Privately Held**
SIC: 2834 Analgesics; laxatives; cough medicines

(G-3474)
WIN SET TECHNOLOGIES LLC
2364 Middle Country Rd (11720-3502)
P.O. Box 2007, Miller Place (11764-8786)
PHONE.................................631 234-7077
Fax: 631 582-5777
Philip Settepani,
Frederick Winter III,
▼ **EMP:** 10
SQ FT: 3,000
SALES: 750K **Privately Held**
WEB: www.winset.net
SIC: 3542 Presses: forming, stamping, punching, sizing (machine tools)

Centerport
Suffolk County

(G-3475)
BLONDIE S BAKESHOP INC
90 Washington Dr (11721-1831)
PHONE.................................631 424-4545
Jeff Kennaugh, *President*
EMP: 8
SALES (est): 592.2K **Privately Held**
SIC: 2051 Bakery: wholesale or wholesale/retail combined

(G-3476)
FORUM PUBLISHING CO
Also Called: Marketer's Forum Magazine
383 E Main St (11721-1538)
PHONE.................................631 754-5000
Fax: 631 754-0630
Martin B Stevens, *Owner*
EMP: 9
SQ FT: 3,000
SALES: 1.4MM **Privately Held**
WEB: www.forum123.com
SIC: 2721 Trade journals: publishing & printing

(G-3477)
FUEL TANK ENVIRONMENTAL
674 Washington Dr (11721-1809)
PHONE.................................631 902-1408
Murad Sevinch, *Principal*
EMP: 8
SALES (est): 1.2MM **Privately Held**
SIC: 2869 Fuels

(G-3478)
LEESA DESIGNS LTD
31 Glenn Cres (11721-1715)
P.O. Box 488 (11721-0488)
PHONE.................................631 261-3991
Helen L Dello-Iacona, *President*
Helen L Dello-Iacora, *President*
Sara Mazzola, *Treasurer*
EMP: 5 **EST:** 1997
SALES: 200K **Privately Held**
SIC: 2339 Neckwear & ties: women's, misses' & juniors'

(G-3479)
LIBERTY INSTALL INC
100 Centershore Rd (11721-1527)
PHONE.................................631 651-5655
Sheri Stevens, *President*
EMP: 11 **EST:** 2014
SALES (est): 423.3K **Privately Held**
SIC: 3841 Surgical & medical instruments

(G-3480)
MSP TECHNOLOGYCOM LLC
77 Bankside Dr (11721-1738)
PHONE.................................631 424-7542
Walter Stark, *CEO*
Jeanne Connor-Stark,
EMP: 3
SQ FT: 1,200
SALES (est): 1.3MM **Privately Held**
WEB: www.msptechnology.com
SIC: 3585 5075 Humidifiers & dehumidifiers; dehumidifiers, except portable

(G-3481)
SURVIVAL INC
90 Washington Dr Ste C (11721-1831)
PHONE.................................631 385-5060
Sanjay Lakhani, *President*
Rebecca Lakhani, *Vice Pres*
▲ **EMP:** 8

GEOGRAPHIC SECTION

Central Islip - Suffolk County (G-3506)

SALES (est): 1.1MM **Privately Held**
WEB: www.survivalrules.com
SIC: 2339 Women's & misses' outerwear

Central Bridge
Schoharie County

(G-3482)
AMERICAN STANDARD MFG INC
Also Called: Asm
106 Industrial Park Ln (12035)
P.O. Box 164 (12035-0164)
PHONE..................518 868-2512
Coleman Vickary, *Chairman*
David Dane, *Manager*
William Cleveland, *Director*
Connie Vickary, *Admin Sec*
EMP: 25
SQ FT: 28,000
SALES (est): 6.2MM **Privately Held**
WEB: www.amrstd.com
SIC: 3499 2542 Machine bases, metal; partitions & fixtures, except wood

Central Islip
Suffolk County

(G-3483)
ABK ENTERPRISES INC
Also Called: Beval Engine & Machine
403 E Suffolk Ave (11749-2352)
PHONE..................631 348-0555
Beverly Kaiser, *Vice Pres*
EMP: 5
SQ FT: 8,500
SALES (est): 43.8K **Privately Held**
SIC: 3599 Machine shop, jobbing & repair

(G-3484)
AH ELCTRONIC TEST EQP REPR CTR
7 Olive St (11722-4017)
PHONE..................631 234-8979
Audley Haynes, *Principal*
EMP: 12
SALES (corp-wide): 1.7MM **Privately Held**
WEB: www.ahelectronics.com
SIC: 1389 3825 7629 Testing, measuring, surveying & analysis services; standards & calibration equipment for electrical measuring; electronic equipment repair
PA: Ah Electronic Test Equipment Repair Center Inc
374 Islip Ave Ste 201
Islip NY 11751
631 277-6282

(G-3485)
AUTRONIC PLASTICS INC (PA)
Also Called: API
1150 Motor Pkwy (11722-1217)
PHONE..................516 333-7577
Fax: 516 333-7695
Michael Lax, *President*
Tim Keuning, *President*
Phil Tjimos, *Project Mgr*
Agjah I Libohova, *Research*
Agjah Libohova, *Research*
▲ **EMP:** 70 **EST:** 1961
SQ FT: 55,000
SALES (est): 29.5MM **Privately Held**
WEB: www.apisolution.com
SIC: 3089 5162 Injection molding of plastics; plastics products

(G-3486)
AVCO INDUSTRIES INC
120 Windsor Pl (11722-3331)
P.O. Box 416, Huntington Station (11746-0338)
PHONE..................631 851-1555
Fax: 631 232-9504
Gil Korine, *Ch of Bd*
Marcela Lazo, *Accountant*
▼ **EMP:** 15
SQ FT: 40,000
SALES (est): 9.3MM **Privately Held**
SIC: 2679 Pressed fiber & molded pulp products except food products

(G-3487)
BERKSHIRE TRANSFORMER (PA)
Also Called: Custom Power Systems
77 Windsor Pl Ste 18 (11722-3334)
PHONE..................631 467-5328
Paul Alessandrini, *Owner*
EMP: 5
SALES (est): 916.7K **Privately Held**
SIC: 3679 3612 Electronic loads & power supplies; transformers, except electric

(G-3488)
BI NUTRACEUTICALS INC
120 Hoffman Ln (11749-5008)
PHONE..................631 232-1105
Fax: 631 232-0369
Sandra Lako, *Human Res Dir*
Deanne Dolnick, *Regl Sales Mgr*
Bob Harvey, *Manager*
EMP: 52 **Privately Held**
WEB: www.botanicals.com
SIC: 2834 Vitamin preparations
HQ: Bi Nutraceuticals, Inc.
2384 E Pacifica Pl
Rancho Dominguez CA 90220
310 669-2100

(G-3489)
CELLU TISSUE - LONG ISLAND LLC
555 N Research Pl (11722-4417)
PHONE..................631 232-2626
Russell C Taylor,
▲ **EMP:** 210
SALES (est): 24.2MM
SALES (corp-wide): 1.7B **Publicly Held**
SIC: 2676 Sanitary paper products
HQ: Cellu Tissue Holdings, Inc.
12725 Morris Road Ext # 210
Alpharetta GA 30004

(G-3490)
CENTRAL ISLIP PHARMACY INC
1629 Islip Ave (11722-2701)
PHONE..................631 234-6039
Ronald Goodstadt, *Principal*
EMP: 7
SALES (est): 847.4K **Privately Held**
SIC: 2834 Adrenal pharmaceutical preparations

(G-3491)
COLOR CARD LLC
Also Called: Limo-Print.com
1065 Islip Ave (11722-4203)
PHONE..................631 232-1300
Robert Haller Sr, *President*
Marilyn Haller, *Vice Pres*
EMP: 18
SQ FT: 110,000
SALES (est): 1.6MM **Privately Held**
SIC: 2752 5961 2759 Business form & card printing, lithographic; cards, mail order; invitations: printing

(G-3492)
CREATIVE HOME FURNISHINGS (PA)
Also Called: Dakotah
250 Creative Dr (11722-4404)
PHONE..................631 582-8000
Gunther Bartsch, *President*
▲ **EMP:** 3
SALES (est): 9MM **Privately Held**
WEB: www.dakotah.com
SIC: 2392 Household furnishings; cushions & pillows; blankets, comforters & beddings; slip covers & pads

(G-3493)
CVD EQUIPMENT CORPORATION (PA)
355 S Technology Dr (11722-4416)
PHONE..................631 981-7081
Fax: 631 360-2132
Leonard A Rosenbaum, *Ch of Bd*
Steven Aragon, *COO*
Kevin R Collins, *Vice Pres*
William S Linss, *Vice Pres*
Karlheinz Strobl, *Vice Pres*
▲ **EMP:** 192
SQ FT: 130,000
SALES: 38.9MM **Publicly Held**
WEB: www.cvdequipment.com
SIC: 3559 Semiconductor manufacturing machinery

(G-3494)
D & R SILK SCREENING LTD
201 Creative Dr (11722-4405)
PHONE..................631 234-7464
Dominick De Ricco, *President*
Rose De Ricco, *Admin Sec*
EMP: 15
SQ FT: 4,000
SALES (est): 1.2MM **Privately Held**
SIC: 2261 2396 Screen printing of cotton broadwoven fabrics; automotive & apparel trimmings

(G-3495)
EUGENE G DANNER MFG INC
Also Called: Danner, Eg Mfg
160 Oval Dr (11749-1403)
PHONE..................631 234-5261
Fax: 631 234-4778
Eugene G Danner, *President*
Bill Minnick, *General Mgr*
Josephine Danner, *Corp Secy*
Michael Danner, *Vice Pres*
▲ **EMP:** 38 **EST:** 1948
SQ FT: 31,000
SALES (est): 7.9MM **Privately Held**
WEB: www.dannermfg.com
SIC: 3089 Aquarium accessories, plastic

(G-3496)
FAR EASTERN COCONUT COMPANY
200 Corporate Plz 201a (11749-1552)
PHONE..................631 851-8800
Fax: 631 851-7950
Richard Martino, *President*
Mitchell Bauman, *Treasurer*
Anthony Armen, *Sales Staff*
▲ **EMP:** 10
SQ FT: 2,000
SALES (est): 640K **Privately Held**
SIC: 2099 Coconut, desiccated & shredded

(G-3497)
FREEPORT PAPER INDUSTRIES INC
120 Windsor Pl (11722-3331)
PHONE..................631 851-1555
Gil Korine, *Ch of Bd*
Debby Steiner, *Controller*
Marcela Lazo, *Accountant*
Linda Franca, *Bookkeeper*
▲ **EMP:** 60
SQ FT: 40,000
SALES (est): 15.6MM **Privately Held**
SIC: 2621 Paper mills

(G-3498)
GMR MANUFACTURING INC
Also Called: George Raum Manufacturing
101 Windsor Pl Unit D (11722-3329)
PHONE..................631 582-2600
Fax: 631 582-0548
George Raum, *President*
EMP: 6 **EST:** 1976
SQ FT: 2,300
SALES (est): 520.4K **Privately Held**
SIC: 3599 Machine shop, jobbing & repair

(G-3499)
INVAGEN PHARMACEUTICALS INC
550 S Research Pl (11722-4415)
PHONE..................631 949-6367
Fakiha Rana, *Branch Mgr*
EMP: 150 **Privately Held**
SIC: 2834 Tablets, pharmaceutical
HQ: Invagen Pharmaceuticals Inc.
7 Oser Ave Ste 4
Hauppauge NY 11788
631 231-3233

(G-3500)
ISLAND RECYCLING CORP
228 Blydenburg Rd (11749-5006)
PHONE..................631 234-6688
Fax: 631 234-4201
Mary Dimatteo, *President*
EMP: 5
SQ FT: 10,000
SALES (est): 572.3K **Privately Held**
SIC: 3341 Recovery & refining of nonferrous metals

(G-3501)
ISLANDIA MRI ASSOCIATES PC
200 Corporate Plz Ste 203 (11749-1507)
PHONE..................631 234-2828
Joel Reiter, *President*
Maggie Hernandez, *Office Mgr*
EMP: 15
SALES (est): 1.5MM **Privately Held**
SIC: 3826 Magnetic resonance imaging apparatus

(G-3502)
LENARO PAPER CO INC
31 Windsor Pl (11722-3301)
P.O. Box 9024 (11722-9024)
PHONE..................631 439-8800
Fax: 631 439-8801
Leonard Aronica, *Ch of Bd*
Anthony J Aronica, *Vice Pres*
John McClung, *Controller*
Isabel Friedlander, *MIS Dir*
◆ **EMP:** 18
SQ FT: 143,000
SALES (est): 10.3MM **Privately Held**
WEB: www.lenaropaper.com
SIC: 2621 5111 Paper mills; fine paper

(G-3503)
M & M MOLDING CORP
250 Creative Dr (11722-4404)
PHONE..................631 582-1900
Mathias Meinzinger, *President*
John McLaughlin, *CFO*
Gunther Bartsch, *Treasurer*
EMP: 200 **EST:** 1977
SQ FT: 50,000
SALES (est): 27.2MM **Privately Held**
SIC: 3089 Injection molded finished plastic products

(G-3504)
MONARCH GRAPHICS INC
1065 Islip Ave (11722-4203)
PHONE..................631 232-1300
Fax: 631 232-1392
Marilyn Haller, *President*
Robert Haller, *Vice Pres*
EMP: 18
SQ FT: 11,000
SALES (est): 2.8MM **Privately Held**
WEB: www.monarchgraphics.com
SIC: 2752 Commercial printing, lithographic

(G-3505)
NATIONWIDE EXHIBITOR SVCS INC
Also Called: Nationwide Displays
110 Windsor Pl (11722-3331)
PHONE..................631 467-2034
Steven Griffith, *President*
William Griffith, *Vice Pres*
Jim Reardon, *Project Mgr*
Robin Matthews, *Bookkeeper*
John Griffith, *Manager*
EMP: 10
SQ FT: 20,000
SALES (est): 2.2MM **Privately Held**
SIC: 3993 3999 2542 Displays & cutouts, window & lobby; advertising display products; fixtures: display, office or store: except wood

(G-3506)
NETEGRITY INC (HQ)
1 Ca Plz (11749-5305)
PHONE..................631 342-6000
Barry N Bycoff, *President*
Erik Hansen, *General Mgr*
William C Bartow, *Vice Pres*
Steve McLaughlin, *Vice Pres*
James Rosen, *Vice Pres*
EMP: 160
SALES (est): 20.2MM
SALES (corp-wide): 4B **Publicly Held**
WEB: www.netegrity.com
SIC: 7372 Prepackaged software
PA: Ca, Inc.
520 Madison Ave Fl 22
New York NY 10022
800 225-5224

Central Islip - Suffolk County (G-3507)

(G-3507)
NORTH AMERICAN ENCLOSURES INC (PA)
Also Called: Nae
85 Jetson Ln Ste B (11722-1202)
P.O. Box 913, Westbury (11590-0126)
PHONE..................................631 234-9500
Fax: 631 234-9504
Richard Schwartz, Ch of Bd
Norman S Grafstein, President
Marie Neubert, Corp Secy
Nick Dibeneditto, Purchasing
Alan Streisfeld, Credit Mgr
▲ EMP: 40 EST: 1962
SQ FT: 55,000
SALES (est): 64.9MM Privately Held
WEB: www.naeframes.com
SIC: 2499 3827 Picture & mirror frames, wood; mirrors, optical

(G-3508)
QUALITY ENCLOSURES INC (PA)
101 Windsor Pl Unit H (11722-3339)
PHONE..................................631 234-0115
Manny Schwartz, Ch of Bd
Michael Schwartz, President
▲ EMP: 23
SQ FT: 27,000
SALES (est): 5.9MM Privately Held
WEB: www.qualityenclosures.com
SIC: 3088 3231 Plastics plumbing fixtures; products of purchased glass

(G-3509)
RICHARD RUFFNER
Also Called: Dynamic Printing
69 Carleton Ave (11722-3018)
PHONE..................................631 234-4600
Richard Ruffner, Owner
Rosie Dejesus, Exec Dir
EMP: 15
SQ FT: 6,000
SALES (est): 1.1MM Privately Held
SIC: 2759 7349 5943 2789 Commercial printing; building maintenance services; office forms & supplies; bookbinding & related work; manifold business forms; commercial printing, lithographic

(G-3510)
SONOTEC US INC
15 2nd Ave (11722-3011)
PHONE..................................631 404-7497
Christopher Portelli, President
EMP: 120 EST: 2013
SALES (est): 9.8MM
SALES (corp-wide): 17.5MM Privately Held
SIC: 3674 Solid state electronic devices
PA: Sonotec Ultraschallsensorik Halle Gmbh
  Nauendorfer Str. 2
  Halle (Saale) 06112
  345 133-170

(G-3511)
SPECTRUM CATALYSTS INC
69 Windsor Pl (11722-3300)
P.O. Box 472, Smithtown (11787-0472)
PHONE..................................631 560-3683
John Plunkett, President
Michael Plunkett, Senior VP
EMP: 5
SQ FT: 100,000
SALES: 1MM Privately Held
SIC: 3559 Chemical machinery & equipment

(G-3512)
SYSTEM OF AME BINDING
95 Hoffman Ln (11749-5020)
PHONE..................................631 390-8560
Fax: 631 390-8559
William Stross, Vice Pres
EMP: 11
SALES (est): 1.8MM Privately Held
SIC: 3111 Bookbinders' leather

(G-3513)
UNITED BAKING CO INC
16 Bronx Ave (11722-2406)
PHONE..................................631 413-5116
EMP: 17 Privately Held
SIC: 2052 Cookies & crackers
PA: United Baking Co., Inc.
  41 Natcon Dr
  Shirley NY 11967

(G-3514)
VANGUARD METALS INC
135 Brightside Ave (11722-2709)
PHONE..................................631 234-6500
Fax: 631 234-5304
Joel Frank, President
Helene Frank, Vice Pres
EMP: 15
SQ FT: 6,000
SALES: 1.6MM Privately Held
WEB: www.vanguardmetals.com
SIC: 3451 3599 Screw machine products; machine shop, jobbing & repair

Central Square — Oswego County

(G-3515)
ALLOY METAL PRODUCTS LLC
193 Us Route 11 (13036-9760)
P.O. Box 2 (13036-0002)
PHONE..................................315 676-2405
James Thayer, Mng Member
▲ EMP: 10
SQ FT: 14,000
SALES: 1MM Privately Held
WEB: www.alloymetalproducts.com
SIC: 3714 Motor vehicle parts & accessories

(G-3516)
AMERITOOL MFG INC
64 Corporate Park Dr (13036-9595)
P.O. Box 213 (13036-0213)
PHONE..................................315 668-2172
Fax: 315 668-6853
Jerome E Beck, President
Cheryl Joyce, Vice Pres
▲ EMP: 20
SALES (est): 3.9MM Privately Held
SIC: 3593 Fluid power cylinders & actuators

(G-3517)
NASIFF ASSOCIATES INC
841 County Route 37 (13036-2133)
P.O. Box 88, Brewerton (13029-0088)
PHONE..................................315 676-2346
Fax: 315 676-4711
Roger Nasiff, President
Anita Bourdeau, Marketing Mgr
Anita M Bourdeau, Corp Comm Staff
EMP: 6
SALES (est): 1MM Privately Held
WEB: www.nasiff.com
SIC: 3841 8711 Surgical & medical instruments; professional engineer

(G-3518)
TORRINGTON INDUSTRIES INC
Also Called: Mid-State Ready Mix
90 Corporate Park Dr (13036-9595)
PHONE..................................315 676-4662
Fax: 315 676-5006
Theodore Zoli, President
EMP: 6
SALES (corp-wide): 1.9MM Privately Held
SIC: 3273 Ready-mixed concrete
PA: Torrington Industries Inc
  112 Wall St
  Torrington CT 06790
  860 489-9261

(G-3519)
UPSTATE INSULATED GLASS INC
47 Weber Rd (13036-2109)
PHONE..................................315 475-4960
Fax: 315 423-7189
James R Markert, President
EMP: 6
SQ FT: 3,100
SALES: 800K Privately Held
SIC: 3231 1793 5231 Insulating units, multiple-glazed; made from purchased glass; glass & glazing work; glass

Central Valley — Orange County

(G-3520)
AG ADRIANO GOLDSCHMIED INC
216 Red Apple Ct (10917-6605)
PHONE..................................845 928-8616
Nicole Linda, Principal
EMP: 8
SALES (corp-wide): 49.1MM Privately Held
SIC: 3663 Television closed circuit equipment
PA: Ag Adriano Goldschmied, Inc.
  2741 Seminole Ave
  South Gate CA 90280
  323 357-1111

(G-3521)
CROCS INC
498 Red Apple Ct (10917-6619)
PHONE..................................845 928-3002
Debbie Heffern, Manager
EMP: 14
SALES (corp-wide): 1.2B Publicly Held
SIC: 3021 Shoes, rubber or rubber soled fabric uppers
PA: Crocs, Inc.
  7477 Dry Creek Pkwy
  Niwot CO 80503
  303 848-7000

(G-3522)
DAVID YURMAN ENTERPRISES LLC
484 Evergreen Ct (10917-6716)
PHONE..................................845 928-8660
EMP: 9
SALES (corp-wide): 46.9MM Privately Held
SIC: 3911 Mfg Precious Metal Jewelry
PA: David Yurman Enterprises Llc
  24 Vestry St
  New York NY 10013
  212 896-1550

(G-3523)
FRAGRANCE OUTLET INC
404 Evergreen Ct (10917-6702)
PHONE..................................845 928-1408
Fax: 845 928-1408
Kerry Donbrowski, Manager
EMP: 10
SALES (corp-wide): 34.3MM Privately Held
SIC: 2844 Perfumes & colognes
PA: The Fragrance Outlet Inc
  11920 Miramar Pkwy
  Miramar FL 33025
  888 919-6613

(G-3524)
GUESS INC
498 Red Apple Ct (10917-6619)
PHONE..................................845 928-3930
EMP: 25
SALES (corp-wide): 2.2B Publicly Held
SIC: 2325 Men's & boys' jeans & dungarees
PA: Guess , Inc.
  1444 S Alameda St
  Los Angeles CA 90021
  213 765-3100

(G-3525)
MAX LEON INC
825 Grapevine Ct (10917-6901)
PHONE..................................845 928-8201
Fax: 845 928-2601
Kristen Osbourne, Branch Mgr
EMP: 11
SALES (corp-wide): 124MM Privately Held
SIC: 2339 Sportswear, women's
PA: Max Leon Inc
  3100 New York Dr
  Pasadena CA 91107
  626 797-6886

(G-3526)
SARAR USA INC
Also Called: Woodbury Cmmon Premium Outlets
873 Grapevine Ct (10917-6902)
PHONE..................................845 928-8874
Tufan Aksahin, Opers Mgr
Zafer Zere, Branch Mgr
Jim Riley, Manager
EMP: 5
SALES (corp-wide): 30.9MM Privately Held
WEB: www.sararusa.com
SIC: 2326 Men's & boys' work clothing
PA: Sarar Usa, Inc.
  1585 Us Highway 46
  Little Falls NJ 07424
  973 837-8600

(G-3527)
SCHILLER STORES INC
Also Called: Lecreuset of America
869 Grapevine Ct (10917-6902)
PHONE..................................845 928-4316
Marcia York, Branch Mgr
EMP: 5
SALES (corp-wide): 491K Privately Held
WEB: www.lecreusetofamerica.com
SIC: 3269 Cookware: stoneware, coarse earthenware & pottery
PA: Schiller Stores Inc
  509 Tanger Mall Dr
  Riverhead NY 11901
  631 208-9400

(G-3528)
VF OUTDOOR LLC
Also Called: North Face
461 Evergreen Ct (10917-6716)
PHONE..................................845 928-4900
Fax: 845 928-4940
Justin Dobson, Manager
Justin Dodson, Manager
EMP: 25
SALES (corp-wide): 12.3B Publicly Held
WEB: www.thenorthface.com
SIC: 2329 2339 Men's & boys' leather, wool & down-filled outerwear; women's & misses' outerwear
HQ: Vf Outdoor, Llc
  2701 Harbor Bay Pkwy
  Alameda CA 94502
  510 618-3500

(G-3529)
WOODBURY PRINTING PLUS + INC
96 Turner Rd (10917-4001)
PHONE..................................845 928-6610
Frank Collins, President
EMP: 7
SQ FT: 3,800
SALES (est): 832.4K Privately Held
WEB: www.wprintingplus.com
SIC: 2752 7334 2791 3993 Commercial printing, offset; photocopying & duplicating services; typesetting; signs & advertising specialties

Chadwicks — Oneida County

(G-3530)
NEW YORK STATE TOOL CO INC
3343 Oneida St (13319-3403)
PHONE..................................315 737-8985
Fax: 315 737-7784
David Wilsey, President
Matthew Wilsey, President
EMP: 11
SQ FT: 6,000
SALES (est): 1.6MM Privately Held
WEB: www.nystool.com
SIC: 3599 Machine shop, jobbing & repair

(G-3531)
WILLIAMS TOOL INC
9372 Elm St (13319-3515)
P.O. Box 430 (13319-0430)
PHONE..................................315 737-7226
Ray Williams, President
Jeffery Gerling, Managing Dir
Bob Prichard, Prdtn Mgr

GEOGRAPHIC SECTION

Frances Gerling, *Manager*
Dan Petrie, *Manager*
EMP: 38 **EST:** 1957
SQ FT: 17,000
SALES: 3.3MM **Privately Held**
WEB: www.wmstool.com
SIC: 3599 Machine shop, jobbing & repair

Chaffee
Erie County

(G-3532)
DIAMOND SAW WORKS INC (PA)
12290 Olean Rd (14030-9767)
PHONE...............................716 496-7417
Fax: 585 496-6057
James Ziemer, *President*
James M Ziemer, *President*
Robert Gust, *Opers Staff*
Ed Duschen, *Engineer*
Charles Lafonte, *Engineer*
▲ **EMP:** 50
SQ FT: 55,000
SALES (est): 5MM **Privately Held**
WEB: www.diamondsaw.com
SIC: 3425 Saw blades & handsaws

(G-3533)
DONALD STEFAN
Also Called: Stefan & Sons Welding
3428 W Yorkshire Rd (14030-9619)
PHONE...............................716 492-1110
Donald Stefan, *Owner*
EMP: 5
SALES (est): 140.3K **Privately Held**
SIC: 7692 3441 Welding repair; fabricated structural metal

(G-3534)
HART TO HART INDUSTRIES INC
Also Called: Arcade Glass Works
13520 Chaffee Curriers Rd (14030-9701)
PHONE...............................716 492-2709
Bill Harter, *President*
EMP: 5
SQ FT: 3,500
SALES: 516.1K **Privately Held**
SIC: 3444 3089 Awnings & canopies; window frames & sash, plastic

(G-3535)
P & R TRUSS CO
Also Called: Uft New York
13989 E Schutt Rd (14030-9763)
PHONE...............................716 496-5484
Fax: 585 496-5490
Steven Slowick, *Manager*
EMP: 20
SALES (est): 1.6MM **Privately Held**
SIC: 2439 Trusses, wooden roof

(G-3536)
UFP NEW YORK LLC
Also Called: Universal Forest Products
13989 E Schutt Rd (14030-9763)
PHONE...............................716 496-5484
Fax: 716 496-5490
Jim Howard, *Sales Staff*
Steve Slowik, *Branch Mgr*
EMP: 40
SQ FT: 18,720
SALES (corp-wide): 10.1MM **Privately Held**
WEB: www.ufpinc.com
SIC: 2439 Trusses, wooden roof
PA: Ufp New York, Llc
  13 Winkler Rd
  Sidney NY 13838
  607 563-1556

Champlain
Clinton County

(G-3537)
AWAKEN LED COMPANY
477 State Route 11 # 1050 (12919-4819)
PHONE...............................802 338-5971
Douglas Schwartz, *President*
EMP: 15

SALES (est): 1.6MM **Privately Held**
SIC: 3646 Commercial indusl & institutional electric lighting fixtures

(G-3538)
BOW INDUSTRIAL CORPORATION
178 W Service Rd (12919-4440)
PHONE...............................518 561-0190
Samuel Bern, *President*
John Coney, *Controller*
EMP: 96
SQ FT: 60,000
SALES (est): 901.8K **Privately Held**
SIC: 3088 Plastics plumbing fixtures

(G-3539)
BURTON CORPORATION
Also Called: Burton Snowboards
21 Lawrence Paquette Dr (12919-4857)
PHONE...............................802 862-4500
EMP: 100
SALES (corp-wide): 136.9MM **Privately Held**
WEB: www.burton.com
SIC: 3949 Sporting & athletic goods
PA: The Burton Corporation
  80 Industrial Pkwy
  Burlington VT 05401
  802 862-4500

(G-3540)
ELEGANCE COATING LTD
33 W Service Rd 100 (12919-4438)
PHONE...............................386 668-8379
Mario Morin, *CEO*
Emilie Morin, *Business Mgr*
Yoland Cloutier, *Finance Mgr*
Stephene Polequein, *Shareholder*
EMP: 25 **EST:** 2007
SALES (est): 2.2MM **Privately Held**
SIC: 3479 Painting, coating & hot dipping

(G-3541)
GREAT WESTERN MALTING CO
16 Beeman Way (12919-4965)
PHONE...............................800 496-7732
▲ **EMP:** 9
SALES (est): 365K **Privately Held**
SIC: 2083 Malt

(G-3542)
HUMANWARE USA INC (PA)
1 Ups Way (12919-4569)
P.O. Box 800 (12919-0800)
PHONE...............................800 722-3393
Phillip Rance, *President*
Lou Lipschultz, *Vice Pres*
Vincent Rappa, *Vice Pres*
Greg Brown, *CFO*
Dan Brown, *Sales Staff*
EMP: 21
SQ FT: 3,800
SALES (est): 5.5MM **Privately Held**
SIC: 3851 Eyeglasses, lenses & frames

(G-3543)
KOREGON ENTERPRISES INC
Also Called: Nite Train R
102 W Service Rd (12919-4440)
PHONE...............................450 218-6836
Fax: 503 644-1366
H J Park, *President*
▲ **EMP:** 5
SQ FT: 3,300
SALES (est): 655.4K **Privately Held**
WEB: www.nitetrain-r.com
SIC: 3699 5047 Electrical equipment & supplies; incontinent care products & supplies

(G-3544)
MODERN MECHANICAL FAB INC
100 Walnut St Ste 7 (12919-5337)
PHONE...............................518 298-5177
Fax: 518 298-2336
Heather Trombly, *President*
John Trombly, *Corp Secy*
▲ **EMP:** 9
SALES (est): 1.3MM **Privately Held**
WEB: www.modmechfab.com
SIC: 7692 Welding repair

(G-3545)
NORTH COUNTRY MALT SUPPLY LLC
16 Beeman Way (12919-4965)
PHONE...............................518 298-2300
Fax: 518 298-8901
Bryan Bechard, *General Mgr*
Robin Couture, *Principal*
Shannon Rabideau, *Principal*
Kelly Kuehl, *Director*
▲ **EMP:** 7
SALES (est): 1.1MM **Privately Held**
WEB: www.northcountrymalt.com
SIC: 2082 Malt beverage products

(G-3546)
TESTORI INTERIORS INC
107 Lwrnce Paqtte Indstrl (12919)
PHONE...............................518 298-4400
Lindo Lapegna, *CEO*
Peter George, *Principal*
Ajay Thakker, *CFO*
◆ **EMP:** 43 **EST:** 2000
SQ FT: 100,000
SALES (est): 9.4MM
SALES (corp-wide): 71MM **Privately Held**
SIC: 2531 Public building & related furniture
PA: Testori Americas Corporation
  45 Cannon Dr
  Slemon Park PE C0B 2
  902 888-3200

(G-3547)
UNI SOURCE TECHNOLOGY
1320 Rt 9 (12919)
PHONE...............................514 748-8888
Lawrence Rutenberg, *Branch Mgr*
EMP: 10
SALES (corp-wide): 3.1MM **Privately Held**
SIC: 3812 Defense systems & equipment
PA: Unisource Technologie Inc
  9010 Av Ryan
  Dorval QC H9P 2
  514 636-0000

(G-3548)
UNIQUE PACKAGING CORPORATION
1320 State Route 9 # 3807 (12919-5007)
P.O. Box 219, Plattsburgh (12901-0219)
PHONE...............................514 341-5872
Fax: 518 561-2242
Fred Povitz, *President*
Earl Povitz, *Opers Staff*
EMP: 5
SALES (est): 440K **Privately Held**
SIC: 3053 3172 Packing materials; cases, jewelry

(G-3549)
WATER SPLASH INC
25 Locust St Ste 421 (12919-5001)
PHONE...............................800 936-3430
Gokhan Celik, *CEO*
Susie Cirillo, *Sales Staff*
Tara Menon, *Manager*
▲ **EMP:** 5
SALES (est): 320K **Privately Held**
SIC: 3999 Manufacturing industries

Chappaqua
Westchester County

(G-3550)
AIR ENGINEERING FILTERS INC
17 Memorial Dr (10514-3528)
P.O. Box 174 (10514-0174)
PHONE...............................914 238-5945
Pam Rubin, *President*
EMP: 9
SQ FT: 2,000
SALES (est): 1.3MM **Privately Held**
SIC: 3564 Filters, air: furnaces, air conditioning equipment, etc.

(G-3551)
DECORATIVE HARDEWARE
180 Hunts Ln (10514-2602)
P.O. Box 627 (10514-0627)
PHONE...............................914 238-5251

Ronald Lawrence Prezener, *President*
Marie Anne Prezener, *Vice Pres*
▲ **EMP:** 10
SQ FT: 2,000
SALES (est): 970K **Privately Held**
WEB: www.decorative-hardware.com
SIC: 3429 Furniture builders' & other household hardware; furniture hardware

(G-3552)
INSIGHT UNLIMITED INC
660 Quaker Rd (10514-1505)
PHONE...............................914 861-2090
Shmuel Kliger, *President*
EMP: 6
SALES (est): 282K **Privately Held**
SIC: 7372 Prepackaged software

(G-3553)
NANORX INC
6 Devoe Pl (10514-3601)
PHONE...............................914 671-0224
Palayakopai Raghavan, *President*
EMP: 2
SALES: 1MM **Privately Held**
SIC: 2834 Medicines, capsuled or ampuled

(G-3554)
PROFESSIONAL ACCESS LLC
88 Old Farm Rd N (10514-3706)
PHONE...............................212 432-2844
Radhika Venkatesh,
EMP: 5
SALES (est): 326.8K **Privately Held**
SIC: 7372 Prepackaged software

Charlotteville
Schoharie County

(G-3555)
FLY-TYERS CARRY-ALL LLC
Also Called: Folstaf Company, The
112 Meade Rd (12036-1612)
PHONE...............................607 821-1460
Lee Stoliar,
EMP: 5
SQ FT: 850
SALES (est): 300K **Privately Held**
WEB: www.folstaf.com
SIC: 3949 5091 Fishing equipment; fishing tackle, general; fishing equipment & supplies; fishing tackle

Chateaugay
Franklin County

(G-3556)
AGRI-MARK INC
39 Mccadam Ln (12920-4306)
P.O. Box 900 (12920-0900)
PHONE...............................518 497-6644
Matt Helm, *Safety Mgr*
Pat Dragon, *Warehouse Mgr*
Jerry Bessette, *Purch Mgr*
David McNiece, *Treasurer*
Jerry Besette, *Personnel*
EMP: 100
SALES (corp-wide): 239.8MM **Privately Held**
WEB: www.agrimark.net
SIC: 2022 Cheese, natural & processed
PA: Agri-Mark, Inc.
  100 Milk St Ste 5
  Methuen MA 01844
  978 689-4442

Chatham
Columbia County

(G-3557)
CRAFTECH
5 Dock St (12037)
PHONE...............................518 828-5011
Linda Geblanski, *CEO*
Erwin Gerard, *Owner*
EMP: 55

Chatham - Columbia County (G-3558)

SALES (est): 2.6MM **Privately Held**
SIC: 2821 3089 Molding compounds, plastics; molding primary plastic

(G-3558)
KLING MAGNETICS INC
343 State Route 295 (12037-3713)
P.O. Box 348 (12037-0248)
PHONE..................................518 392-4000
Jody Rael, *President*
▲ EMP: 20
SQ FT: 20,000
SALES (est): 2.2MM **Privately Held**
SIC: 3993 3089 2752 3944 Advertising novelties; novelties, plastic; commercial printing, lithographic; games, toys & children's vehicles

(G-3559)
RAPID INTELLECT GROUP INC
77b Church St (12037-1319)
P.O. Box 131, Stuyvesant Falls (12174-0131)
PHONE..................................518 929-3210
Steve Grzeskow, *President*
Peter Grzeskow, *Vice Pres*
EMP: 12 EST: 1997
SALES (est): 888.4K **Privately Held**
SIC: 2731 Book publishing

(G-3560)
SONOCO-CRELLIN INC (DH)
87 Center St (12037-1032)
PHONE..................................518 392-2000
Fax: 518 392-2022
Bob Puechl, *Ch of Bd*
Leslie Lak, *Exec VP*
Dennis Norman, *Manager*
▲ EMP: 132
SQ FT: 60,000
SALES (est): 64.1MM
SALES (corp-wide): 4.9B **Publicly Held**
SIC: 3089 Injection molding of plastics
HQ: Sonoco-Crellin International, Inc.
    87 Center St
    Chatham NY 12037
    518 392-2000

(G-3561)
SONOCO-CRELLIN INTL INC (HQ)
87 Center St (12037-1032)
PHONE..................................518 392-2000
Fax: 518 392-6213
Bob Puechl, *Vice Pres*
David Marche, *Vice Pres*
Michael Tucker, *Vice Pres*
Angela Hamm, *Purch Agent*
Ralph Tassone, *CFO*
▲ EMP: 500
SQ FT: 70,000
SALES (est): 119.6MM
SALES (corp-wide): 4.9B **Publicly Held**
SIC: 3089 Molding primary plastic
PA: Sonoco Products Company
    1 N 2nd St
    Hartsville SC 29550
    843 383-7000

Chazy
Clinton County

(G-3562)
JP SIGNS
9592 State Route 9 (12921-3102)
PHONE..................................518 569-3907
Jessica Macnerland, *Owner*
EMP: 5
SALES: 150K **Privately Held**
SIC: 3993 7389 5699 Signs & advertising specialties; printers' services: folding, collating; T-shirts, custom printed

Cheektowaga
Erie County

(G-3563)
BUFFALO COMPRESSED AIR INC
2727 Broadway St Ste 3a (14227-1070)
P.O. Box 468, Lancaster (14086-0468)
PHONE..................................716 783-8673
Greg Fuer, *Principal*
EMP: 6
SALES (est): 320K **Privately Held**
SIC: 3563 Air & gas compressors

(G-3564)
COMAIRCO EQUIPMENT INC (DH)
3250 Union Rd (14227-1044)
PHONE..................................716 656-0211
Roland Nadeau, *President*
Edward Murphy, *Vice Pres*
Donna Wolfley, *Controller*
Judy Cook, *Manager*
EMP: 7
SQ FT: 6,000
SALES (est): 6.3MM
SALES (corp-wide): 5.7MM **Privately Held**
WEB: www.comairco.com
SIC: 3563 Air & gas compressors
HQ: Equipement Comairco Ltee
    5535 Rue Ernest-Cormier
    Laval QC H7C 2
    450 665-8780

(G-3565)
CRS NUCLEAR SERVICES LLC
840 Aero Dr Ste 150 (14225-1451)
PHONE..................................716 810-0688
Daniel Guarasci, *Director*
Kevin Connor,
▲ EMP: 12
SALES: 5.4MM **Privately Held**
SIC: 2834 Pharmaceutical preparations

(G-3566)
CULINARY ARTS SPECIALTIES INC
Also Called: Cas
2268 Union Rd (14227-2726)
PHONE..................................716 656-8943
Fax: 716 656-8945
Arthur L Keller, *Ch of Bd*
Andrew P Keller, *Vice Pres*
Jonathan Polly, *Purch Mgr*
Thomas Dagonese, *Controller*
Nancy Keller, *Financial Exec*
EMP: 85
SQ FT: 50,000
SALES (est): 23.2MM **Privately Held**
SIC: 2053 Cakes, bakery; frozen

(G-3567)
DERRICK CORPORATION
2540 Walden Ave (14225-4744)
PHONE..................................716 685-4892
EMP: 189
SALES (corp-wide): 215.5MM **Privately Held**
SIC: 3533 Derricks, oil or gas field
PA: Derrick Corporation
    590 Duke Rd
    Buffalo NY 14225
    716 683-9010

(G-3568)
DUAL PRINT & MAIL LLC
340 Nagel Dr (14225-4731)
PHONE..................................716 684-3825
Fax: 716 684-3828
Thomas Salisbury, *Ch of Bd*
EMP: 73
SALES (corp-wide): 18.4MM **Privately Held**
SIC: 2752 Commercial printing, lithographic
HQ: Dual Print & Mail, Llc
    3235 Grand Island Blvd
    Grand Island NY 14072
    716 775-8001

(G-3569)
ECOLAB INC
3719 Union Rd Ste 121 (14225-4250)
PHONE..................................716 683-6298
Fax: 716 683-0679
Dave Beckwith, *Branch Mgr*
EMP: 17
SALES (corp-wide): 13.5B **Publicly Held**
WEB: www.ecolab.com
SIC: 2841 Soap & other detergents
PA: Ecolab Inc.
    370 Wabasha St N
    Saint Paul MN 55102
    800 232-6522

(G-3570)
FLUID HANDLING LLC
Standard Xchange
175 Standard Pkwy (14227-1233)
PHONE..................................716 897-2800
Daniel Leschuitta, *Regl Sales Mgr*
Tony Scioli, *Regl Sales Mgr*
William Blankemeier, *Marketing Staff*
Joseph McMara, *Branch Mgr*
Nick Baker, *Systems Mgr*
EMP: 240 **Publicly Held**
WEB: www.ittind.com
SIC: 3443 Industrial vessels, tanks & containers
HQ: Fluid Handling, Llc
    175 Standard Pkwy
    Cheektowaga NY 14227
    716 897-2800

(G-3571)
FLUID HANDLING LLC (HQ)
Also Called: Xylem
175 Standard Pkwy (14227-1233)
PHONE..................................716 897-2800
Ken Napolitano, *President*
Scott Alford,
Mike Romance, *Assistant*
▲ EMP: 1
SALES (est): 250.2MM **Publicly Held**
SIC: 3561 Pumps & pumping equipment

(G-3572)
GEMINI MANUFACTURES
160 Holtz Dr (14225-1418)
PHONE..................................716 633-0306
Fax: 716 633-2564
Todd Lehmann, *Partner*
Irene Turski, *Partner*
EMP: 14
SQ FT: 4,200
SALES: 860K **Privately Held**
SIC: 3915 Jewelers' materials & lapidary work

(G-3573)
HAMMOND MANUFACTURING CO INC
475 Cayuga Rd (14225-1309)
PHONE..................................716 630-7030
Fax: 716 630-7042
Robert F Hammond, *CEO*
Marc A Dube, *Principal*
Kevin Bond, *COO*
Ray Schatzel, *Vice Pres*
Doug Hutt, *Engineer*
▲ EMP: 14
SQ FT: 17,000
SALES (est): 3.6MM
SALES (corp-wide): 92.2MM **Privately Held**
WEB: www.hammfg.com
SIC: 3677 5063 Transformers power supply, electronic type; electrical apparatus & equipment; transformers, electric
PA: Hammond Manufacturing Company Limited
    394 Edinburgh Rd N
    Guelph ON N1H 1
    519 822-2960

(G-3574)
HANZLIAN SAUSAGE INCORPORATED
Also Called: Hanzlian Sausage Deli
2351 Genesee St (14225-2839)
PHONE..................................716 891-5247
David Hanzlian, *President*
George J Hanzlian Jr, *Vice Pres*
EMP: 8
SQ FT: 7,800
SALES (est): 950.7K **Privately Held**
SIC: 2013 Sausages from purchased meat

(G-3575)
HUGH F MCPHERSON INC
Also Called: Franklin's Printing
70 Innsbruck Dr (14227-2735)
PHONE..................................716 668-6107
Hugh F McPherson, *President*
Barbara L McPherson, *Vice Pres*
EMP: 7
SALES (est): 764.4K **Privately Held**
SIC: 2752 2791 Commercial printing, lithographic; typesetting

(G-3576)
HVR ADVNCED PWR COMPONENTS INC
2090 Old Union Rd (14227-2770)
PHONE..................................716 693-4700
Richard Arndt, *Principal*
Eugene Feind, *Principal*
David M Yanko, *Principal*
William Glodzik II, *Vice Pres*
Ronald Wills, *QC Mgr*
EMP: 10
SQ FT: 4,000
SALES (est): 1.3MM **Privately Held**
WEB: www.hvrapc.com
SIC: 3676 Electronic resistors

(G-3577)
LEO SCHULTZ
Also Called: Cuore Technology
1144 Maryvale Dr (14225-2312)
PHONE..................................716 969-0945
Kevin Ryan, *Branch Mgr*
EMP: 5
SALES (corp-wide): 1.5MM **Privately Held**
SIC: 3822 Auto controls regulating residntl & coml environmt & applncs
PA: Leo Rue Schultz
    821 Panelli Pl
    Santa Clara CA 95050
    716 969-0945

(G-3578)
LINDE GAS NORTH AMERICA LLC
Also Called: Lifegas
45 Boxwood Ln (14227-2707)
PHONE..................................866 543-3427
Jerry Pompeo, *Branch Mgr*
EMP: 19
SALES (corp-wide): 19.2B **Privately Held**
SIC: 2813 Nitrogen; oxygen, compressed or liquefied
HQ: Linde Gas North America Llc
    575 Mountain Ave
    New Providence NJ 07974
    908 464-8100

(G-3579)
MP CAROLL INC
4822 Genesee St (14225-2494)
PHONE..................................716 683-8520
Fax: 716 683-8510
Michael Carrol, *President*
Brian Murphy, *Sales Staff*
Amy Huntingcon, *Office Mgr*
◆ EMP: 12
SALES (est): 2MM **Privately Held**
SIC: 2426 Flooring, hardwood

(G-3580)
MULTI-HEALTH SYSTEMS INC
Indus Pkwy Ste 70660 60 (14227)
P.O. Box 950, North Tonawanda (14120-0950)
PHONE..................................800 456-3003
Steven J Stein, *Branch Mgr*
Steven Stein, *Security Mgr*
Alasdair Maclean, *Information Mgr*
Brian Boutilier, *Systems Analyst*
Theresa Murray, *Software Dev*
EMP: 90
SALES (corp-wide): 13.6MM **Privately Held**
WEB: www.mhs.com
SIC: 3695 2741 Computer software tape & disks: blank, rigid & floppy; miscellaneous publishing

PA: Multi-Health Systems Inc
3770 Victoria Park Ave
North York ON M2H 3
416 492-2627

(G-3581)
MULTISORB TECHNOLOGIES INC
20 French Rd (14227-2702)
PHONE.................................716 668-4191
John Cullen, *Branch Mgr*
EMP: 5
SALES (corp-wide): 78.8MM **Privately Held**
SIC: 2819 Industrial inorganic chemicals
PA: Multisorb Technologies, Inc.
325 Harlem Rd
Buffalo NY 14224
716 824-8900

(G-3582)
NEVILLE MFG SVC & DIST INC (PA)
2320 Clinton St (14227-1735)
PHONE.................................716 834-3038
Patrick Crowe, *President*
Erica Druzbik, *Admin Sec*
EMP: 10 **EST:** 1951
SQ FT: 4,000
SALES (est): 2.6MM **Privately Held**
SIC: 2448 Pallets, wood; skids, wood

(G-3583)
NOVATECH INC
190 Gruner Rd (14227-1022)
PHONE.................................716 892-6682
Fax: 716 892-1403
John Popovich Sr, *President*
John Popovich Jr, *Vice Pres*
EMP: 20
SQ FT: 8,000
SALES (est): 3.4MM **Privately Held**
WEB: www.novatechmachining.com
SIC: 3545 Precision tools, machinists'

(G-3584)
ORIGINAL FOWLERS CHOCLAT INC
2563 Union Rd Ste 101 (14227-2275)
PHONE.................................716 668-2113
Fax: 716 668-1009
Sue Ortman, *Manager*
Judy Almond, *Manager*
EMP: 5
SALES (corp-wide): 17.8MM **Privately Held**
WEB: www.fowlerschocolate.com
SIC: 2024 Ice cream & frozen desserts
PA: Original Fowler's Chocolate Co., Inc.
100 River Rock Dr
Buffalo NY
716 877-9983

(G-3585)
PEPSI COLA BUFFALO BTLG CORP
2770 Walden Ave (14225-4747)
PHONE.................................716 684-2800
Fax: 716 684-0408
John Cahill, *Ch of Bd*
Frank Cooper, *Vice Pres*
Daniel Tantalo Sr, *Vice Pres*
Ed Bennett, *Safety Mgr*
Jason Cartwright, *Accounts Mgr*
EMP: 350 **EST:** 1955
SQ FT: 180,000
SALES (est): 41.3MM
SALES (corp-wide): 63B **Publicly Held**
WEB: www.pbg.com
SIC: 2086 Soft drinks: packaged in cans, bottles, etc.; fruit drinks (less than 100% juice): packaged in cans, etc.
HQ: Pepsi-Cola Metropolitan Bottling Company, Inc.
1111 Westchester Ave
White Plains NY 10604
914 767-6000

(G-3586)
POLE POSITION RACEWAY
1 Walden Galleria (14225-5408)
PHONE.................................716 683-7223
EMP: 5
SALES (est): 378.1K **Privately Held**
SIC: 3644 Raceways

(G-3587)
PROSTHETICS BY NELSON INC (PA)
Also Called: Nelson Prsthtics Orthotics Lab
2959 Genesee St (14225-2653)
PHONE.................................716 894-6666
Christopher Vandusen, *President*
EMP: 13
SQ FT: 8,500
SALES (est): 1.2MM **Privately Held**
SIC: 3842 5999 Prosthetic appliances; orthopedic appliances; orthopedic & prosthesis applications

(G-3588)
QUALITY GRAPHICS WEST SENECA
2460 Union Rd (14227-2238)
PHONE.................................716 668-4528
Fax: 716 668-3502
Charles Lauck, *President*
Barbara Lauck, *Vice Pres*
EMP: 5
SQ FT: 3,500
SALES: 750K **Privately Held**
SIC: 2759 Commercial printing

(G-3589)
REDLAND FOODS CORP
40 Sonwil Dr (14225-2425)
PHONE.................................716 288-9061
Eva Mounsteven, *Director*
EMP: 12
SALES (est): 892.7K **Privately Held**
SIC: 2099 Emulsifiers, food

(G-3590)
STEREO ADVANTAGE INC
Also Called: Advantage Wood Shop
45 Boxwood Ln (14227-2707)
PHONE.................................716 656-7161
Fax: 716 656-7166
Anthony Ragusa Jr, *Partner*
EMP: 10
SALES (corp-wide): 47.7MM **Privately Held**
SIC: 2541 Store & office display cases & fixtures
PA: Stereo Advantage, Inc.
1955 Wehrle Dr Ste B
Williamsville NY 14221
716 204-2346

(G-3591)
TECTRAN INC
2345 Walden Ave Ste 1 (14225-4770)
PHONE.................................800 776-5549
Bruce McKie, *President*
EMP: 8
SALES (est): 956.3K **Privately Held**
SIC: 3699 3799 Cleaning equipment, ultrasonic, except medical & dental; carriages, horse drawn

(G-3592)
USA SEALING INC
356 Sonwil Dr (14225-5520)
PHONE.................................716 288-9952
David Cassert, *President*
EMP: 50
SALES (est): 1.5MM **Privately Held**
SIC: 3053 Gaskets & sealing devices

Chemung
Chemung County

(G-3593)
CUSTOM MIX CONCRETE INC
Chemung Flat Rd (14825)
PHONE.................................607 737-0281
EMP: 8
SALES (corp-wide): 8MM **Privately Held**
SIC: 3273 Ready-mixed concrete
PA: Custom Mix Concrete, Inc.
1229 Lowman Rd
Lowman NY
607 737-0281

(G-3594)
DALRYMPLE GRAV & CONTG CO INC
Chemung Flats Rd (14825)
P.O. Box 278 (14825-0278)
PHONE.................................607 529-3235
Fax: 607 529-3434
Hank Dalrymple, *President*
EMP: 30
SALES (corp-wide): 98.5MM **Privately Held**
SIC: 1442 5032 Gravel mining; stone, crushed or broken
HQ: Dalrymple Gravel And Contracting Company, Inc.
2105 S Broadway
Pine City NY 14871
607 739-0391

(G-3595)
VULCRAFT OF NEW YORK INC (HQ)
621 M St (14825)
P.O. Box 280 (14825-0280)
PHONE.................................607 529-9000
Fax: 607 529-9001
Peggy Peters, *Principal*
Ray Napolitan, *Exec VP*
John Giovenco, *Traffic Mgr*
Doreen Yackel, *Production*
Greg Crooker, *Sales Mgr*
EMP: 122
SQ FT: 300,000
SALES (est): 53MM
SALES (corp-wide): 16.4B **Publicly Held**
WEB: www.nucor.com
SIC: 3441 Expansion joints (structural shapes), iron or steel
PA: Nucor Corporation
1915 Rexford Rd Ste 400
Charlotte NC 28211
704 366-7000

Chenango Bridge
Broome County

(G-3596)
ATWOOD TOOL & MACHINE INC
39 Kattelville Rd (13745)
P.O. Box 609 (13745-0609)
PHONE.................................607 648-6543
Fax: 607 648-6300
H Blair Atwood, *President*
Brent Atwood, *Vice Pres*
Danny Winchester, *Purchasing*
Laurie Atwood, *Treasurer*
Cindy Hood, *Admin Sec*
EMP: 22 **EST:** 1963
SQ FT: 23,000
SALES (est): 4.3MM **Privately Held**
WEB: www.atwoodknives.com
SIC: 3545 Tools & accessories for machine tools

Cherry Valley
Otsego County

(G-3597)
THISTLE HILL WEAVERS
101 Chestnut Ridge Rd (13320-2405)
PHONE.................................518 284-2729
Fax: 518 284-2729
Rabbit Goody, *Owner*
Jill Maney, *Manager*
EMP: 5
SALES (est): 240K **Privately Held**
WEB: www.thistlehillweavers.com
SIC: 2299 7219 Hand woven fabrics; reweaving textiles (mending service)

Chester
Orange County

(G-3598)
ADVERTISER PUBLICATIONS INC
Also Called: Marketplace, The
148 State Route 17m (10918-1412)
PHONE.................................845 783-1111
Howard Kaplan, *President*
Seth Kaplan, *Vice Pres*
Marc M Hennion, *Personnel Exec*
Steve Herman, *Manager*
EMP: 13
SQ FT: 2,200
SALES: 1.9MM **Privately Held**
SIC: 2711 7331 7313 Newspapers; direct mail advertising services; newspaper advertising representative

(G-3599)
AMSCAN INC
47 Elizabeth Dr (10918-1367)
PHONE.................................845 469-9116
Karen M Kenzie, *General Mgr*
EMP: 58
SALES (corp-wide): 2.2B **Publicly Held**
SIC: 2656 Plates, paper: made from purchased material
HQ: Amscan Inc.
80 Grasslands Rd Ste 3
Elmsford NY 10523
914 345-2020

(G-3600)
B J S ELECTRIC
1000 Craigville Rd (10918-4116)
PHONE.................................845 774-8166
Jack Sherry, *Partner*
Elizabeth Sherry, *Partner*
EMP: 9
SALES (est): 968.4K **Privately Held**
SIC: 7694 1731 Electric motor repair; electrical work

(G-3601)
BRAKEWELL STL FABRICATORS INC
55 Leone Ln (10918-1363)
PHONE.................................845 469-9131
Fax: 845 469-7618
Dan Doyle, *President*
Dave Bendlin, *Project Mgr*
Robert McGrath, *Project Mgr*
William Valentin, *Project Mgr*
Carol Vandemark, *Project Mgr*
EMP: 45
SQ FT: 26,000
SALES: 7MM **Privately Held**
WEB: www.brakewell.com
SIC: 3411 3499 Metal cans; metal ladders

(G-3602)
BYK USA INC
48 Leone Ln (10918-1362)
PHONE.................................845 469-5800
Stephan Glander, *Branch Mgr*
EMP: 29 **Privately Held**
SIC: 2819 Industrial inorganic chemicals
HQ: Byk Usa Inc.
524 S Cherry St
Wallingford CT 06492
203 265-2086

(G-3603)
COMMUNITY PRODUCTS LLC
Also Called: Community Playthings
359 Gibson Hill Rd (10918-2321)
PHONE.................................845 658-7720
Andy Keiderling, *Marketing Staff*
John Rhodes, *Branch Mgr*
EMP: 25
SALES (corp-wide): 88.5MM **Privately Held**
SIC: 3842 Surgical appliances & supplies
PA: Community Products, Llc
2032 Route 213 St
Rifton NY 12471
845 658-8799

Chester - Orange County (G-3604)

GEOGRAPHIC SECTION

(G-3604)
COMMUNITY PRODUCTS LLC
24 Elizabeth Dr (10918-1366)
PHONE...........................845 572-3433
Ben Maendel, *Branch Mgr*
EMP: 18
SALES (corp-wide): 88.5MM **Privately Held**
SIC: 3842 Orthopedic appliances
PA: Community Products, Llc
    2032 Route 213 St
    Rifton NY 12471
    845 658-8799

(G-3605)
DURASOL SYSTEMS INC (HQ)
445 Bellvale Rd (10918-3115)
PHONE...........................845 610-1100
Fax: 845 610-1100
Vince Best, *President*
Paolo Galliani, *President*
Frank Dorr, *Vice Pres*
Trace Feinstein, *Vice Pres*
Tim Robinson, *Vice Pres*
▲ EMP: 51
SQ FT: 65,000
SALES (est): 26.3MM
SALES (corp-wide): 24.2MM **Privately Held**
WEB: www.durasol.com
SIC: 2394 Awnings, fabric: made from purchased materials
PA: Bat Spa
    Via H. Ford 2
    Noventa Di Piave VE 30020
    042 165-672

(G-3606)
F A ALPINE WINDOWS MFG
1683 State Route 17m (10918-1020)
PHONE...........................845 469-5700
Larry Maddaloni, *President*
John Maddaloni, *Opers Mgr*
EMP: 10
SALES (est): 1.5MM **Privately Held**
WEB: www.faalpinewindowmfg.com
SIC: 3442 Metal doors, sash & trim

(G-3607)
G SCHIRMER INC
Also Called: Music Sales
2 Old Rt 17 (10918)
P.O. Box 572 (10918-0572)
PHONE...........................845 469-4699
Ella Winfield, *Manager*
EMP: 50
SALES (corp-wide): 13.6MM **Privately Held**
WEB: www.schirmer.com
SIC: 2741 Music books: publishing only, not printed on site
HQ: G Schirmer Inc
    180 Madison Ave Ste 2400
    New York NY 10016
    212 254-2100

(G-3608)
GREEN ENERGY CONCEPTS INC
37 Elkay Dr Ste 51 (10918-3025)
P.O. Box 1023, Harriman (10926-1023)
PHONE...........................845 238-2574
Richard Mueller, *President*
▲ EMP: 6
SALES: 950K **Privately Held**
SIC: 3646 Commercial indusl & institutional electric lighting fixtures

(G-3609)
KE DURASOL AWNINGS INC
445 Bellvale Rd (10918-3115)
PHONE...........................845 610-1100
Paolo Galliani, *President*
Vince Best, *Principal*
EMP: 8
SALES (est): 960.1K **Privately Held**
SIC: 3444 Awnings & canopies

(G-3610)
NEXANS ENERGY USA INC
Also Called: Industrial Cables
25 Oakland Ave (10918-1011)
PHONE...........................845 469-2141
Steve Hall, *Ch of Bd*
Gordon Thursfield, *President*
Sande Aivaliotis, *Vice Pres*
Julie Land, *CFO*
Al Blazy, *Manager*
◆ EMP: 160
SQ FT: 350,000
SALES (est): 63.6MM
SALES (corp-wide): 24.5MM **Privately Held**
SIC: 3496 Cable, uninsulated wire: made from purchased wire
HQ: Nexans Canada Inc
    140 Allstate Pky Suite 300
    Markham ON L3R 0
    905 944-4300

(G-3611)
PDJ COMPONENTS INC
35 Brookside Ave (10918-1409)
PHONE...........................845 469-9191
George W Ketchum, *CEO*
Taft Ketchum, *General Mgr*
Pamela Ketchum, *Vice Pres*
David Crandall, *Buyer*
Tony Salvagno, *Sales Executive*
EMP: 40
SQ FT: 30,000
SALES (est): 7.2MM **Privately Held**
WEB: www.pdjtruss.com
SIC: 2439 2499 Trusses, wooden roof; trusses, except roof: laminated lumber; decorative wood & woodwork

(G-3612)
REPRO MED SYSTEMS INC
Also Called: RMS MEDICAL PRODUCTS
24 Carpenter Rd Ste 1 (10918-1065)
PHONE...........................845 469-2042
Andrew I Sealfon, *Ch of Bd*
Barry Volaski, *Purch Mgr*
Karen Fisher, *CFO*
Justyn Okoniewski, *Mktg Dir*
EMP: 55
SALES: 12.2MM **Privately Held**
SIC: 3841 Surgical & medical instruments; suction therapy apparatus

(G-3613)
RIC-LO PRODUCTIONS LTD
Also Called: Lycian Stage Lighting
1144 Kings Hwy (10918-3100)
P.O. Box 214, Sugar Loaf (10981-0214)
PHONE...........................845 469-2285
Fax: 845 469-5355
Richard F Logothetis, *Chairman*
▲ EMP: 43
SQ FT: 17,400
SALES (est): 8.3MM **Privately Held**
SIC: 3648 3641 Stage lighting equipment; electric lamps

(G-3614)
S A BAXTER LLC (PA)
37 Elkay Dr Ste 33 (10918-3025)
PHONE...........................845 469-7995
Colin Gentle, *Manager*
Scott Baxter,
▲ EMP: 2
SALES: 2MM **Privately Held**
SIC: 3446 5072 Architectural metalwork; builders' hardware

(G-3615)
SATIN FINE FOODS INC
32 Leone Ln (10918-1362)
PHONE...........................845 469-1034
Kevin O' Reilly, *Ch of Bd*
Alan Standish, *General Mgr*
Maria D Laboy, *Export Mgr*
Danielle Giaquinto, *QA Dir*
Susan Gillinder, *Finance*
◆ EMP: 15
SQ FT: 3,000
SALES (est): 5MM **Privately Held**
SIC: 2064 Candy & other confectionery products

(G-3616)
STRAUS COMMUNICATIONS
Also Called: Straus Newspaper
20 West Ave Ste 201 (10918-1053)
PHONE...........................845 782-4000
Stan Martin, *Manager*
EMP: 15
SALES (corp-wide): 2.5MM **Privately Held**
WEB: www.strausnews.com
SIC: 2711 Newspapers, publishing & printing
PA: Straus Communications
    57 W 57th St Ste 1204
    New York NY
    212 751-0400

(G-3617)
STRAUS NEWSPAPERS INC
20 West Ave (10918-1032)
PHONE...........................845 782-4000
Fax: 845 469-9001
Jeanne Straus, *President*
Juan Ayala, *Principal*
Heidi Robertson, *Accounts Exec*
Rick Sophia, *Director*
EMP: 24 EST: 1991
SALES (est): 1.7MM **Privately Held**
SIC: 2711 Newspapers

(G-3618)
SYMRISE INC
45 Leone Ln (10918-1363)
PHONE...........................845 469-7675
Wayne Millazo, *Director*
EMP: 45
SALES (corp-wide): 2.7B **Privately Held**
WEB: www.belmay.com
SIC: 2869 2844 5122 Perfumes, flavorings & food additives; toilet preparations; perfumes
HQ: Symrise Inc,
    300 North St
    Teterboro NJ 07608
    201 462-5559

(G-3619)
TELE-VUE OPTICS INC
32 Elkay Dr (10918-3001)
PHONE...........................845 469-4551
Albert Nagler, *CEO*
David Nagler, *President*
Sandy Nagler, *Vice Pres*
▲ EMP: 20
SQ FT: 14,000
SALES (est): 4.1MM **Privately Held**
WEB: www.televue.com
SIC: 3827 Optical instruments & lenses

(G-3620)
THEODORE A RAPP ASSOCIATES
728 Craigville Rd (10918-4014)
PHONE...........................845 469-2100
Theodore A Rapp, *President*
EMP: 7
SALES (est): 718.8K **Privately Held**
SIC: 3651 Microphones

Chestertown
Warren County

(G-3621)
CETTEL STUDIO OF NEW YORK INC
636 Atateka Dr (12817-2010)
PHONE...........................518 494-3622
Peter Heonis, *President*
EMP: 6
SALES: 350K **Privately Held**
SIC: 3843 Orthodontic appliances

(G-3622)
PECKHAM MATERIALS CORP
5983 State Route 9 (12817-2513)
PHONE...........................518 494-2313
Fax: 518 494-2065
John McClure, *Opers-Prdtn-Mfg*
EMP: 10
SQ FT: 208
SALES (corp-wide): 192MM **Privately Held**
SIC: 2951 5032 Asphalt paving mixtures & blocks; brick, stone & related material
HQ: Peckham Materials Corp
    20 Haarlem Ave Ste 200
    White Plains NY 10603
    914 686-2045

Chestnut Ridge
Rockland County

(G-3623)
MEHRON INC
Also Called: Lechler Labs
100 Red Schoolhouse Rd C2 (10977-7056)
PHONE...........................845 426-1700
Martin Melik, *President*
Gene Flaharty, *Sales Mgr*
Mary Cavallini, *Marketing Staff*
Elizabeth Simmons, *Office Mgr*
Shelly Farber, *Manager*
▲ EMP: 35 EST: 1932
SQ FT: 15,000
SALES (est): 12MM **Privately Held**
WEB: www.mehron.com
SIC: 2844 Cosmetic preparations

(G-3624)
PAR PHRMCEUTICAL COMPANIES INC (DH)
1 Ram Ridge Rd (10977-6714)
PHONE...........................845 573-5500
Paul V Campanelli, *CEO*
Terrance J Coughlin, *COO*
Michael Tropiano, *CFO*
Thomas J Haughey,
EMP: 23 EST: 2012
SALES (est): 278.9MM **Privately Held**
SIC: 2834 Pharmaceutical preparations
HQ: Endo Health Solutions Inc.
    1400 Atwater Dr
    Malvern PA 19355
    484 216-0000

(G-3625)
PAR STERILE PRODUCTS LLC (DH)
1 Ram Ridge Rd (10977-6714)
PHONE...........................845 573-5500
Fax: 973 658-3582
Paul V Campanelli, *CEO*
Eric Bruce, *Opers Staff*
Michael Tropiano, *CFO*
Melissa Williams, *Controller*
Valerie Luczak, *Sales Mgr*
EMP: 32
SALES (est): 118.9MM **Privately Held**
WEB: www.jhppharma.com
SIC: 2834 Pharmaceutical preparations
HQ: Par Pharmaceutical, Inc.
    1 Ram Ridge Rd
    Spring Valley NY 10977
    845 425-7100

(G-3626)
TELEDYNE LECROY INC (HQ)
700 Chestnut Ridge Rd (10977-6435)
PHONE...........................845 425-2000
Fax: 845 425-8967
Thomas H Reslewic, *Ch of Bd*
Sui LI, *General Mgr*
Martina Rogan, *General Mgr*
Fernando Gomez, *Business Mgr*
Eric Bogatin, *Dean*
▲ EMP: 204 EST: 1964
SQ FT: 95,000
SALES (est): 181.5MM
SALES (corp-wide): 2.3B **Publicly Held**
WEB: www.lecroy.com
SIC: 3825 3829 Oscillographs & oscilloscopes; measuring & controlling devices
PA: Teledyne Technologies Inc
    1049 Camino Dos Rios
    Thousand Oaks CA 91360
    805 373-4545

(G-3627)
U S PLYCHMICAL OVERSEAS CORP
584 Chestnut Ridge Rd # 586 (10977-5646)
PHONE...........................845 356-5530
David Cherry, *President*
Bruce W Gebhardt, *General Mgr*
Ralph Almonte, *Controller*
Richard E Knipe Jr, *VP Sales*
Mark Paul, *Director*
EMP: 20
SQ FT: 20,000

▲ = Import ▼=Export
◆ =Import/Export

SALES (est): 3.3MM **Privately Held**
WEB: www.uspoly.com
SIC: **2842** Cleaning or polishing preparations; sanitation preparations

Childwold
St. Lawrence County

(G-3628)
LEATHER ARTISAN
Also Called: Artisan Bags
Rr 3 (12922)
PHONE.................................518 359-3102
Thomas Amoroso, *Partner*
EMP: 5
SQ FT: 7,000
SALES (est): 585.6K **Privately Held**
WEB: www.leatherartisan.com
SIC: **3172** 5699 5199 Personal leather goods; leather garments; leather, leather goods & furs

Chittenango
Madison County

(G-3629)
A L SEALING
2280 Osborne Rd (13037-8791)
PHONE.................................315 699-6900
John C Thomas, *Ch of Bd*
EMP: 5
SALES (est): 312.3K **Privately Held**
SIC: **3053** Gaskets & sealing devices

(G-3630)
CONSOLDTED PRECISION PDTS CORP
901 E Genesee St (13037-1325)
PHONE.................................315 687-0014
Mark Gaspari, *Manager*
EMP: 350
SALES (corp-wide): 6.7B **Privately Held**
SIC: **3365** 3324 Aluminum foundries; steel investment foundries
HQ: Consolidated Precision Products Corp.
     1621 Euclid Ave Ste 1850
     Cleveland OH 44115
     909 595-2252

(G-3631)
CPP - GUAYMAS
901 E Genesee St (13037-1325)
PHONE.................................315 687-0014
Carl Bratt, *General Mgr*
Catherine Renfer, *Engineer*
Dale Vibbert, *Engineer*
Bill Kehoe, *Plant Engr*
John Derosia, *Controller*
EMP: 200
SQ FT: 1,000
SALES (est): 28.6MM
SALES (corp-wide): 6.7B **Privately Held**
WEB: www.escocorp.com
SIC: **3321** Cast iron pipe & fittings
HQ: Cpp-Syracuse, Inc.
     901 E Genesee St
     Chittenango NY 13037
     315 687-0014

(G-3632)
CPP-SYRACUSE INC (DH)
901 E Genesee St (13037-1325)
PHONE.................................315 687-0014
James Stewart, *CEO*
Francois R Baril, *President*
Tom Cacace, *Mfg Dir*
Barry Weary, *Opers Mgr*
Joe Perechinsky, *Finance*
EMP: 30
SQ FT: 95,000
SALES (est): 101.9MM
SALES (corp-wide): 6.7B **Privately Held**
SIC: **3324** 3369 3356 Aerospace investment castings, ferrous; nonferrous foundries; nonferrous rolling & drawing
HQ: Consolidated Precision Products Corp.
     1621 Euclid Ave Ste 1850
     Cleveland OH 44115
     909 595-2252

Churchville
Monroe County

(G-3633)
AMA PRECISION SCREENING INC
456 Sanford Rd N (14428-9503)
PHONE.................................585 293-0820
Fax: 585 293-0822
George Pietropaolo, *President*
Robert Hubbard, *Human Res Dir*
Kelley Copani, *Manager*
EMP: 18
SALES (est): 1.7MM **Privately Held**
WEB: www.amatech.com
SIC: **2759** Commercial printing

(G-3634)
BURNT MILL SMITHING
127 Burnt Mill Rd (14428-9405)
PHONE.................................585 293-2380
Fax: 585 293-1372
Dennis Schrieber, *Owner*
Dennis Schriber, *Owner*
EMP: 5
SALES (est): 295K **Privately Held**
WEB: www.burnt-mill.com
SIC: **3949** 5941 Sporting & athletic goods; sporting goods & bicycle shops

(G-3635)
CUSTOM MOLDING SOLUTIONS INC
456 Sanford Rd N (14428-9503)
PHONE.................................585 293-1702
Dwight Campbell, *President*
EMP: 21
SALES (est): 4.4MM **Privately Held**
SIC: **3544** Industrial molds

(G-3636)
DYNAK INC
530 Savage Rd (14428-9614)
PHONE.................................585 271-2255
Fax: 585 271-6048
Bob Vorndran, *President*
Barbara Klink, *Vice Pres*
Michael R Petes, *Engineer*
Michael Allen, *Manager*
EMP: 13
SQ FT: 25,000
SALES: 2MM **Privately Held**
WEB: www.dynak.com
SIC: **3599** Custom machinery

(G-3637)
GT INNOVATIONS LLC
116 Bridgeman Rd (14428-9509)
PHONE.................................585 739-7659
Fax: 585 293-2826
Daniel Grastorf, *Owner*
EMP: 5
SALES (est): 622.3K **Privately Held**
SIC: **3444** Concrete forms, sheet metal

(G-3638)
INLAND VACUUM INDUSTRIES INC (PA)
35 Howard Ave (14428-8008)
P.O. Box 373 (14428-0373)
PHONE.................................585 293-3330
Fax: 585 293-3093
Peter C Yu, *Ch of Bd*
Lusanne Lam, *Vice Pres*
Carol Taylor, *Manager*
Cindy Oliver, *CIO*
▲ EMP: 12
SQ FT: 1,000
SALES (est): 1.8MM **Privately Held**
WEB: www.inlandvacuum.com
SIC: **2992** Lubricating oils & greases

(G-3639)
INTEK PRECISION
539 Attridge Rd (14428-9712)
PHONE.................................585 293-0853
Susan Kurucz, *Partner*
Paul Kurucz, *Partner*
EMP: 8
SQ FT: 3,000
SALES: 200K **Privately Held**
WEB: www.intekprecision.com
SIC: **3544** Special dies, tools, jigs & fixtures

(G-3640)
QUALICOAT INC
14 Sanford Rd N (14428-9503)
PHONE.......................585 293-2650
Michael Pontarelli, *Ch of Bd*
Don Lawson, *Plant Mgr*
Ross Mazzola, *QC Dir*
Debbie Ray, *Human Res Mgr*
Sharon Cubitt, *Manager*
▲ EMP: 80
SQ FT: 48,000
SALES (est): 10.7MM **Privately Held**
WEB: www.qualicoat.com
SIC: **3479** Coating of metals & formed products; painting of metal products

Cicero
Onondaga County

(G-3641)
ADD ASSOCIATES INC
Also Called: Image Press, The
6333 Daedalus Rd (13039-8889)
PHONE.................................315 449-3474
Toll Free:.................................888   -
Fax: 315 449-3480
Chris Arnone, *President*
Lonnie Dahl, *Vice Pres*
Christine Staniec, *Senior Buyer*
Bill Brokhoff, *Purchasing*
Stan Patte, *Manager*
EMP: 8
SQ FT: 10,000
SALES (est): 1.3MM **Privately Held**
SIC: **2741** Miscellaneous publishing

(G-3642)
AWNING MART INC
5665 State Route 31 (13039-8513)
PHONE.................................315 699-5928
Doug Loguidice, *President*
Tina Loguidice, *General Mgr*
EMP: 7
SQ FT: 4,400
SALES (est): 749.3K **Privately Held**
SIC: **2394** 1799 5199 5999 Awnings, fabric: made from purchased materials; awning installation; canvas products; awnings; canvas products

(G-3643)
CLINTONS DITCH COOP CO INC
8478 Pardee Rd (13039-8531)
PHONE.................................315 699-2695
Ronald Anania, *President*
Michael Moehringer, *General Mgr*
Bill Fitzgerald, *Vice Pres*
Tim Tenney, *Vice Pres*
Thomas Millert, *Plant Mgr*
EMP: 155
SQ FT: 250,000
SALES: 62.6MM **Privately Held**
WEB: www.clintonsditch.com
SIC: **2086** Carbonated soft drinks, bottled & canned

(G-3644)
DAF OFFICE NETWORKS INC
6121 Jemola Runne (13039-8238)
PHONE.................................315 699-7070
David A Farabee, *President*
EMP: 10
SALES (est): 1.3MM **Privately Held**
SIC: **2521** 5112 5044 Wood office furniture; office supplies; office equipment

(G-3645)
EJ GROUP INC
6177 S Bay Rd (13039-9303)
PHONE.................................315 699-2601
EMP: 8 **Privately Held**
SIC: **3446** Architectural metalwork
PA: Ej Group, Inc.
     301 Spring St
     East Jordan MI 49727

(G-3646)
GIBAR INC
7838 Brewerton Rd (13039-9536)
PHONE.................................315 452-5656
EMP: 244
SALES (corp-wide): 9MM **Privately Held**
SIC: **3421** Table & food cutlery, including butchers'
PA: Gibar, Inc
     1 Technology Pl
     East Syracuse NY 13057
     315 432-4546

(G-3647)
LIBERTY MACHINE & TOOL
7908 Ontario Ave (13039-9759)
PHONE.................................315 699-3242
Fax: 315 699-1314
Thomas Burgmeier, *Owner*
EMP: 1
SQ FT: 2,500
SALES: 1MM **Privately Held**
SIC: **3599** Machine shop, jobbing & repair

(G-3648)
MACHINE TOOL SPECIALTY
8125 Thompson Rd (13039-9454)
P.O. Box 2398, Syracuse (13220-2398)
PHONE.................................315 699-5287
Fax: 315 699-7604
David Carrington, *Owner*
EMP: 5
SQ FT: 1,000
SALES (est): 486.3K **Privately Held**
SIC: **3544** Special dies & tools

(G-3649)
NATIONAL PARTS PEDDLER NEWSPPR
Also Called: National Parts Peddler, The
7408 Lakeshore Rd (13039-9729)
P.O. Box 486, Bridgeport (13030-0486)
PHONE.................................315 699-7583
Fax: 315 699-8712
Carlton D Stockham, *President*
EMP: 6
SALES (est): 240K **Privately Held**
SIC: **2711** Newspapers: publishing only, not printed on site

(G-3650)
PAUL DE LIMA COMPANY INC
8550 Pardee Rd (13039-8519)
PHONE.................................315 457-3725
Fax: 315 457-3730
Steve Zaremba, *CFO*
Peter Sansone, *Human Res Dir*
Karen Huntley, *Mktg Dir*
W Drescher, *Branch Mgr*
EMP: 23
SALES (corp-wide): 15.3MM **Privately Held**
SIC: **2095** Roasted coffee
PA: Paul De Lima Company, Inc.
     7546 Morgan Rd Ste 1
     Liverpool NY 13090
     315 457-3725

(G-3651)
PAUL DELIMA COFFEE COMPANY
8550 Pardee Rd (13039-8519)
PHONE.................................315 457-3725
Paul De Lima, *Principal*
Don Hughes, *Senior VP*
Steve Janeosik, *Info Tech Mgr*
▲ EMP: 9
SALES (est): 1.1MM **Privately Held**
SIC: **2095** Roasted coffee

(G-3652)
THERMAL FOAMS/SYRACUSE INC
6173 S Bay Rd (13039-9303)
P.O. Box 1981 (13039-1981)
PHONE.................................315 699-8734
Fax: 315 699-4969
Charlie Wopperer, *Sales Staff*
John Jeffery, *Branch Mgr*
EMP: 25
SALES (corp-wide): 6MM **Privately Held**
SIC: **3053** Packing materials

Cincinnatus - Cortland County (G-3653) GEOGRAPHIC SECTION

PA: Thermal Foams/Syracuse, Inc.
2101 Kenmore Ave
Buffalo NY 14207
716 874-6474

Cincinnatus
Cortland County

(G-3653)
DAVID CHRISTY
Also Called: Uniform Professionals
2810 Cincinnatus Rd (13040)
P.O. Box 180 (13040-0180)
PHONE..................607 863-4610
David Christy, *Owner*
Janice Livermore, *Manager*
EMP: 9
SALES (est): 878.7K **Privately Held**
WEB: www.uniformpro.com
SIC: 2326 Work uniforms

Clarence
Erie County

(G-3654)
A C T ASSOCIATES
10100 Main St (14031-2049)
P.O. Box 510 (14031-0510)
PHONE..................716 759-8348
William Thalmann, *Principal*
EMP: 11 **EST:** 2010
SALES (est): 1.8MM **Privately Held**
SIC: 3823 Water quality monitoring & control systems

(G-3655)
ANABEC INC
9393 Main St (14031-1912)
P.O. Box 433 (14031-0433)
PHONE..................716 759-1674
Fax: 716 759-7829
Stephen Meyers, *President*
Nancy Ewing, *Vice Pres*
Michael Whipple, *Natl Sales Mgr*
Lisa Pawlowski, *Manager*
EMP: 5 **EST:** 1995
SQ FT: 3,200
SALES (est): 757.7K **Privately Held**
WEB: www.anabec.com
SIC: 2899 Chemical preparations

(G-3656)
DIMAR MANUFACTURING CORP
10123 Main St (14031-2164)
P.O. Box 597 (14031-0597)
PHONE..................716 759-0351
Fax: 716 759-0389
Gregory A Fry, *President*
David Kostelich, *General Mgr*
Beverly Rehwaldt, *COO*
Edward Clark, *Project Mgr*
Thomas J Kowalski, *CFO*
EMP: 140
SQ FT: 93,000
SALES: 15.3MM **Privately Held**
WEB: www.dimarmfg.com
SIC: 3499 3444 Furniture parts, metal; sheet metalwork

(G-3657)
DORM COMPANY CORPORATION
Also Called: Dorm Co.
9150 Hillview Dr (14031-1415)
P.O. Box 485, Clarence Center (14032-0485)
PHONE..................502 551-6195
Jeff Gawronski, *Ch of Bd*
EMP: 5
SQ FT: 6,000
SALES (est): 979.8K **Privately Held**
SIC: 2431 Dormers, wood

(G-3658)
DYNABRADE INC (PA)
8989 Sheridan Dr (14031-1490)
PHONE..................716 631-0100
Fax: 716 631-2073
Walter N Welsch, *Ch of Bd*
Ned T Librock, *President*
Dave Stuhler, *Production*
John Sgroi, *Purch Mgr*
Clyde Tulowitzki, *Purch Mgr*
▲ **EMP:** 175
SQ FT: 95,000
SALES (est): 31.4MM **Privately Held**
WEB: www.dynabrade.com
SIC: 3546 Power-driven handtools

(G-3659)
EASTERN HILLS PRINTING (PA)
9195 Main St (14031-1931)
PHONE..................716 741-3300
Fax: 716 741-4225
Geoffrey Mohring, *CEO*
EMP: 9
SQ FT: 400
SALES (est): 867.5K **Privately Held**
SIC: 2752 Commercial printing, offset

(G-3660)
ELECTROCHEM SOLUTIONS INC (HQ)
10000 Wehrle Dr (14031-2086)
PHONE..................716 759-5800
Thomas J Hook, *Ch of Bd*
Steven Towne, *Senior Buyer*
Arden Johnson, *Research*
Alvin Chow, *Engineer*
Marius Ghita, *Engineer*
EMP: 27
SALES (est): 8MM
SALES (corp-wide): 800.4MM **Publicly Held**
WEB: www.electrochemsolutions.com
SIC: 3692 Primary batteries, dry & wet
PA: Greatbatch, Inc.
2595 Dallas Pkwy Ste 310
Frisco TX 75034
716 759-5800

(G-3661)
EXCEL INDUSTRIES INC
11737 Main St (14031)
P.O. Box 409 (14031-0409)
PHONE..................716 542-5468
Fax: 716 542-5820
Francis Nicholas, *President*
Mark Steck, *General Mgr*
Donald Nicholas, *Vice Pres*
Diana Fiske, *Treasurer*
Craig Nicholas, *Office Mgr*
EMP: 40 **EST:** 1947
SQ FT: 35,000
SALES (est): 6.3MM **Privately Held**
WEB: www.excelindustriesinc.com
SIC: 3599 3441 Machine shop, jobbing & repair; fabricated structural metal

(G-3662)
GILDAN APPAREL USA INC
4055 Casillio Pkwy (14031-2047)
PHONE..................716 759-6273
EMP: 7
SALES (corp-wide): 2.1B **Privately Held**
SIC: 2395 7336 Embroidery & art needlework; silk screen design
HQ: Gildan Apparel Usa Inc.
48 W 38th St Fl 8
New York NY 10018
212 476-0341

(G-3663)
GREATBATCH INC
Engineered Components Division
4098 Barton Rd (14031-1814)
PHONE..................716 759-5200
Fax: 716 634-0306
Jerry Hale, *Draft/Design*
Mike Okeefe, *Engineer*
Ralph Bendlin, *Marketing Staff*
Charles Wemhoff, *Manager*
EMP: 100
SALES (corp-wide): 800.4MM **Publicly Held**
WEB: www.greatbatch.com
SIC: 3841 3842 Surgical & medical instruments; surgical appliances & supplies
PA: Greatbatch, Inc.
2595 Dallas Pkwy Ste 310
Frisco TX 75034
716 759-5800

(G-3664)
MCDUFFIES OF SCOTLAND INC
Also Called: Mc Duffies Bakery
9920 Main St (14031-2043)
P.O. Box 427 (14031-0427)
PHONE..................716 759-8510
Fax: 716 759-6082
David Thomas, *President*
Brian Thomas, *Vice Pres*
EMP: 20
SQ FT: 10,000
SALES (est): 2.7MM **Privately Held**
WEB: www.mcduffies.com
SIC: 2052 Cookies

(G-3665)
MCHUGH PAINTING CO INC
10335 Clarence Center Rd (14031-1003)
PHONE..................716 741-8077
Michael McHugh, *President*
Michael Mc Hugh, *President*
Rosalie McHugh, *Admin Sec*
EMP: 14
SALES (est): 1.4MM **Privately Held**
SIC: 3479 Painting of metal products

(G-3666)
MEDIMA LLC
5727 Strickler Rd (14031-1372)
PHONE..................716 741-0400
Barry Lazar, *Mng Member*
▲ **EMP:** 250
SALES: 425MM **Privately Held**
SIC: 3339 3313 Silicon & chromium; ferroalloys

(G-3667)
OEM SOLUTIONS INC
4995 Rockhaven Dr (14031-2438)
PHONE..................716 864-9324
Michael King, *CEO*
▲ **EMP:** 4
SQ FT: 3,000
SALES: 1MM **Privately Held**
SIC: 3469 3699 Metal stampings; electrical equipment & supplies

(G-3668)
PEAK MOTION INC
11190 Main St (14031-1702)
PHONE..................716 534-4925
Douglas Webster, *President*
EMP: 7
SALES (est): 2.3MM **Privately Held**
WEB: www.peakmotion.com
SIC: 3499 3544 Aerosol valves, metal; special dies, tools, jigs & fixtures

(G-3669)
PRECIMED INC
Also Called: Greatbatch Medical
10000 Wehrle Dr (14031-2086)
PHONE..................716 759-5600
Patrick White, *CEO*
Patrick Berdoz, *President*
Alan Booker, *Opers Mgr*
Charles Andrews, *Treasurer*
Barbara Lyons, *Director*
EMP: 46
SQ FT: 2,000
SALES (est): 4.1MM
SALES (corp-wide): 800.4MM **Publicly Held**
WEB: www.precimed.com
SIC: 3841 5047 Surgical & medical instruments; medical & hospital equipment
HQ: Greatbatch Ltd.
10000 Wehrle Dr
Clarence NY 14031
612 331-6750

(G-3670)
QUADPHARMA LLC
11342 Main St (14031-1718)
PHONE..................877 463-7823
Stephen A Panaro, *CEO*
Nicholas Bidwell, *Project Mgr*
Mark Czopp, *Project Mgr*
Mica Downey, *QC Mgr*
Ryan Downey, *Director*
EMP: 7 **EST:** 2012
SQ FT: 18,000
SALES (est): 2MM
SALES (corp-wide): 5.2MM **Privately Held**
SIC: 2834 Pharmaceutical preparations

PA: Athenex, Inc.
1001 Main St Ste 600
Buffalo NY 14203
716 898-8626

(G-3671)
RLS HOLDINGS INC
11342 Main St (14031-1718)
PHONE..................716 418-7274
Stephen A Panaro PHD, *President*
Ryan Downey, *QA Dir*
Leanna Kisicki, *Director*
EMP: 5 **EST:** 2010
SALES (est): 617.5K **Privately Held**
SIC: 2834 Pharmaceutical preparations

(G-3672)
RODAC USA CORP
5605 Kraus Rd (14031-1342)
PHONE..................716 741-3931
Daniel Primeau, *CEO*
EMP: 25
SALES (est): 2.4MM **Privately Held**
SIC: 3648 Lighting equipment

Clarence Center
Erie County

(G-3673)
CLARENCE RESINS AND CHEMICALS
9585 Keller Rd (14032-9230)
PHONE..................716 406-9804
James G Lawrence, *President*
EMP: 8
SQ FT: 800
SALES (est): 1.4MM **Privately Held**
SIC: 2821 5169 Plastics materials & resins; synthetic resins, rubber & plastic materials

(G-3674)
EASTERN MANUFACTURING INC
9760 County Rd (14032-9651)
P.O. Box 379 (14032-0379)
PHONE..................716 741-4572
Fax: 716 741-4572
Barbara Gomlar, *President*
EMP: 10
SQ FT: 8,000
SALES: 1.6MM **Privately Held**
SIC: 3441 Fabricated structural metal

(G-3675)
EXACTA LLC
8955 Williams Ct (14032-9414)
PHONE..................716 406-2303
Peter Buchbinder, *Owner*
James B Schleer, *Mng Member*
EMP: 9
SQ FT: 1,200
SALES (est): 640K **Privately Held**
WEB: www.exacta.com
SIC: 3555 Copy holders, printers'

(G-3676)
ITALIAN MARBLE & GRANITE INC
8526 Roll Rd (14032-9761)
PHONE..................716 741-1800
Mark K Zografos, *President*
Virginia Sorrentino, *Office Mgr*
▲ **EMP:** 16
SQ FT: 21,000
SALES (est): 2.1MM **Privately Held**
SIC: 3281 Marble, building: cut & shaped

(G-3677)
J R PRODUCTS INC
9680 County Rd (14032-9240)
PHONE..................716 633-7565
Doug Rouba, *President*
▲ **EMP:** 9
SALES (est): 730K **Privately Held**
WEB: www.jrpvinc.com
SIC: 3949 Camping equipment & supplies

GEOGRAPHIC SECTION

Cohoes - Albany County (G-3750)

(G-3727)
FUEL EFFICIENCY LLC
101 Davis Pkwy (14433)
PHONE.....................315 923-2511
Karl Simon, *Sales Staff*
Joseph Connelly,
Karen Connelly,
EMP: 8
SQ FT: 12,700
SALES (est) 1.3MM **Privately Held**
WEB: www.fuelefficiency.com
SIC: 3443 Boilers: industrial, power, or marine; boiler shop products: boilers, smokestacks, steel tanks

(G-3728)
MEADE MACHINE CO INC
31 Ford St (14433-1306)
PHONE.....................315 923-1703
Fax: 315 923-2811
Mark Clinton Meade, *President*
Elizabeth Meade, *Vice Pres*
EMP: 6 EST: 1943
SQ FT: 8,000
SALES: 800K **Privately Held**
SIC: 3599 7539 Machine shop, jobbing & repair; machine shop, automotive

(G-3729)
MODERN BLOCK LLC
2440 Wyne Zandra Rose Vly (14433)
PHONE.....................315 923-7443
Andy Martin,
Glen S Martin,
EMP: 8
SALES: 600K **Privately Held**
SIC: 3271 Concrete block & brick

(G-3730)
PARKER-HANNIFIN CORPORATION
Also Called: Parker-Hannifin Aerospace
124 Columbia St (14433-1049)
PHONE.....................631 231-3737
Fax: 315 923-7759
Horace Bassaragh, *Engineer*
Brian Cario, *Engineer*
AVI Korenshtein, *Engineer*
David Wright, *Manager*
EMP: 248
SALES (corp-wide): 11.3B **Publicly Held**
SIC: 3728 Aircraft parts & equipment
PA: Parker-Hannifin Corporation
6035 Parkland Blvd
Cleveland OH 44124
216 896-3000

(G-3731)
PRODUCTS SUPERB INC
231 Clyde Marengo Rd (14433-9528)
PHONE.....................315 923-7057
Fax: 315 923-1593
Ellen Bellizzi, *President*
EMP: 7
SQ FT: 8,000
SALES (est): 670.9K **Privately Held**
SIC: 3471 7389 Finishing, metals or formed products; packaging & labeling services

(G-3732)
THOMAS ELECTRONICS INC (PA)
208 Davis Pkwy (14433-9550)
PHONE.....................315 923-2051
Fax: 315 923-4401
David A Ketchum, *President*
Jeff Culmo, *General Mgr*
Douglas Ketchum, *Exec VP*
Fred Cornelius, *Mfg Dir*
Steve Clark, *Prdtn Mgr*
▲ **EMP:** 160
SQ FT: 71,180
SALES (est): 23.1MM **Privately Held**
SIC: 3671 Cathode ray tubes, including rebuilt

Clymer
Chautauqua County

(G-3733)
CUSTOM SHIPPING PRODUCTS INC
8661 Knowlton Rd (14724-9706)
P.O. Box 245 (14724-0245)
PHONE.....................716 355-4437
Fax: 716 355-4439
John Holthouse, *President*
Shelly Schenck, *Corp Secy*
Mike Schenck, *Vice Pres*
EMP: 10
SQ FT: 3,000
SALES: 890K **Privately Held**
SIC: 2448 Pallets, wood

Cobleskill
Schoharie County

(G-3734)
CLAPPER HOLLOW DESIGNS INC
369 N Grand St (12043-4140)
PHONE.....................518 234-9561
Michael Lambert, *President*
Brigette Belka, *Vice Pres*
Tony Lee, *Vice Pres*
EMP: 20
SQ FT: 10,000
SALES (est): 1.6MM **Privately Held**
SIC: 3952 Frames for artists' canvases

(G-3735)
COBLESKILL STONE PRODUCTS INC (PA)
112 Rock Rd (12043-5738)
P.O. Box 220 (12043-0220)
PHONE.....................518 234-0221
Fax: 518 234-0226
Emil Galasso, *Chairman*
Michael Galasso, *Vice Pres*
Daniel Kleeschulte, *Vice Pres*
Michael Moore, *Vice Pres*
Craig Watson, *Admin Sec*
EMP: 15 EST: 1954
SQ FT: 5,000
SALES (est): 114.3MM **Privately Held**
WEB: www.cobleskillstone.com
SIC: 1422 Crushed & broken limestone

(G-3736)
DIVISION STREET NEWS CORP
Also Called: Time Journal
108 Division St Apt 7 (12043-4606)
PHONE.....................518 234-2515
Fax: 518 234-7898
James Poole, *President*
Patsy Nicosia, *Manager*
EMP: 18
SALES (est): 1.9MM **Privately Held**
WEB: www.schohariechamber.com
SIC: 2752 5994 2711 Commercial printing, lithographic; newsstand; newspapers

(G-3737)
EFJ INC
Also Called: Mill Services
128 Macarthur Ave (12043-3603)
P.O. Box 577 (12043-0577)
PHONE.....................518 234-4799
Daniel W Holt, *President*
James Place, *Vice Pres*
James Bender, *Manager*
Vickie McDonald, *Manager*
Randall Betts, *Supervisor*
EMP: 60 EST: 1993
SQ FT: 80,000
SALES: 10.6MM **Privately Held**
WEB: www.millservices.com
SIC: 2431 Millwork

(G-3738)
KELLEY FARM & GARDEN INC
Also Called: Agway
239 W Main St (12043-1713)
P.O. Box 37 (12043-0037)
PHONE.....................518 234-2332
Fax: 518 234-2017
Scott F Kelley, *President*
Kathy Kelley, *Corp Secy*
Scott Kelly, *Plant Mgr*
Barbara Robarge, *Manager*
EMP: 20
SQ FT: 3,700
SALES (est): 6.7MM **Privately Held**
SIC: 3546 5191 5261 Saws & sawing equipment; animal feeds; lawnmowers & tractors

(G-3739)
T A S SALES SERVICE LLC
105 Kenyon Rd (12043-5713)
PHONE.....................518 234-4919
Thomas Sachs, *Principal*
EMP: 9
SALES (est): 1.1MM **Privately Held**
SIC: 1389 Gas field services

Cochecton
Sullivan County

(G-3740)
COCHECTON MILLS INC (PA)
30 Depot Rd (12726-5221)
PHONE.....................845 932-8282
Fax: 570 932-8865
Dennis E Nearing, *President*
Robert Nearing Jr, *Treasurer*
Sean Nearing, *Manager*
EMP: 20
SQ FT: 8,500
SALES (est): 2.1MM **Privately Held**
SIC: 2048 2041 Poultry feeds; livestock feeds; flour & other grain mill products

(G-3741)
JML QUARRIES INC
420 Bernas Rd (12726-5423)
PHONE.....................845 932-8206
Fax: 845 888-4198
Rodney Cornelius, *President*
EMP: 25
SQ FT: 2,000
SALES (est): 4MM **Privately Held**
SIC: 1422 Crushed & broken limestone

(G-3742)
MASTEN ENTERPRISES LLC (PA)
420 Bernas Rd (12726-5423)
PHONE.....................845 932-8206
John Bernas, *Principal*
Mauren Cowger, *Manager*
EMP: 75
SQ FT: 2,000
SALES (est): 22.1MM **Privately Held**
SIC: 1429 Grits mining (crushed stone)

(G-3743)
MORLYN ASPHALT CORP
420 Bernas Rd (12726-5423)
PHONE.....................845 888-2695
John Bernas, *President*
Bob Burgio, *CFO*
Warrien Cowger, *Manager*
EMP: 6
SQ FT: 2,000
SALES (est): 885.8K
SALES (corp-wide): 24.4MM **Privately Held**
SIC: 2951 Asphalt paving mixtures & blocks
PA: Masten Enterprises Llc
420 Bernas Rd
Cochecton NY 12726
845 932-8206

(G-3744)
SULLIVAN CONCRETE INC
Also Called: Sullivan Structures
420 Bernas Rd (12726-5423)
PHONE.....................845 888-2235
Fax: 845 932-8139
John Bernas, *President*
Bob Burgio, *CFO*
EMP: 12 EST: 1954
SQ FT: 2,000
SALES (est): 2.3MM **Privately Held**
WEB: www.sullivanstructures.com
SIC: 3273 Ready-mixed concrete

Coeymans
Albany County

(G-3745)
FCA LLC
149 Coeymans Ind Pk Ln (12045)
PHONE.....................518 756-9655
David Wilsted, *President*
EMP: 18
SALES (corp-wide): 155.5MM **Privately Held**
SIC: 2441 Cases, wood
PA: Fca, Llc
7601 John Deere Pkwy
Moline IL 61265
309 792-3444

(G-3746)
TRACEY WELDING CO INC
29 Riverview Dr (12045-7719)
P.O. Box 799 (12045-0799)
PHONE.....................518 756-6309
Richard Tracey, *President*
Richard J Tracey, *Vice Pres*
EMP: 8
SQ FT: 15,200
SALES (est): 1.3MM **Privately Held**
WEB: www.traceywelding.com
SIC: 7692 Welding repair

Cohoes
Albany County

(G-3747)
ELECTRONIC COATING TECH INC (PA)
1 Mustang Dr Ste 4 (12047-4856)
PHONE.....................518 688-2048
Tom Charlton, *President*
Michelle Hughes, *Controller*
▲ **EMP:** 12
SALES (est): 1.2MM **Privately Held**
SIC: 3479 Coating of metals & formed products; coating of metals with silicon

(G-3748)
JAY MOULDING CORPORATION
7 Bridge Ave Ste 1 (12047-4799)
PHONE.....................518 237-4200
Fax: 518 237-6576
Christy Smagala, *President*
Nancy Uvin, *Office Mgr*
Richard Smagala, *Shareholder*
EMP: 10
SQ FT: 9,000
SALES: 1MM **Privately Held**
WEB: www.jaymoulding.com
SIC: 3083 Thermosetting laminates: rods, tubes, plates & sheet; thermoplastic laminates: rods, tubes, plates & sheet

(G-3749)
LINDE GAS NORTH AMERICA LLC
Also Called: Lifegas
10 Arrowhead Ln (12047-4812)
Fax: 518 713-2019
EMP: 40
SALES (corp-wide): 19.2B **Privately Held**
SIC: 2813 Mfg Nitrogen/ Oxygen
HQ: Linde Gas North America Llc
575 Mountain Ave
New Providence NJ 07974
908 464-8100

(G-3750)
MATHESON TRI-GAS INC
15 Green Mountain Dr (12047-4807)
PHONE.....................518 203-5003
Scott Kallman, *Branch Mgr*
EMP: 6
SALES (corp-wide): 5.4B **Privately Held**
SIC: 2813 Industrial gases; nitrogen; oxygen, compressed or liquefied; argon
HQ: Matheson Tri-Gas, Inc.
150 Allen Rd Ste 302
Basking Ridge NJ 07920
908 991-9200

Cohoes - Albany County (G-3751)

(G-3751)
MOHAWK FINE PAPERS INC (PA)
465 Saratoga St (12047-4626)
P.O. Box 497 (12047-0497)
PHONE..................518 237-1740
Fax: 518 233-7102
Thomas D O'Connor, *Ch of Bd*
Walter Duignan, *Vice Ch Bd*
John F Haren, *President*
Thomas Maddock, *Business Mgr*
Kevin P Richard, *COO*
▲ EMP: 300 EST: 1876
SQ FT: 207,000
SALES (est): 251.1MM Privately Held
WEB: www.mohawkpaper.com
SIC: 2672 2621 Coated & laminated paper; paper mills; uncoated paper

(G-3752)
MOHAWK FINE PAPERS INC
465 Saratoga St (12047-4626)
PHONE..................518 237-1741
Dave Raley, *Manager*
EMP: 30
SALES (corp-wide): 251.1MM Privately Held
WEB: www.mohawkpaper.com
SIC: 2621 Paper mills
PA: Mohawk Fine Papers Inc.
  465 Saratoga St
  Cohoes NY 12047
  518 237-1740

(G-3753)
NIS MANUFACTURING INC
Also Called: Northern Indus Svces Mech Div
1 Mustang Dr Ste 5 (12047-4856)
PHONE..................518 456-2566
William Nattress, *Branch Mgr*
EMP: 9
SALES (corp-wide): 4.8MM Privately Held
WEB: www.northernindustrial.com
SIC: 3829 Testing equipment: abrasion, shearing strength, etc.
PA: Nis Manufacturing, Inc.
  1 Mustang Dr Ste 5
  Cohoes NY 12047
  518 456-2566

(G-3754)
NORLITE CORPORATION
628 Saratoga St (12047-4697)
P.O. Box 694 (12047-0694)
PHONE..................518 235-0030
Fax: 518 235-0233
Robert O'Brien, *President*
Michael Ferraro, *Corp Secy*
Brian Abely, *Vice Pres*
Ed Whalen, *Marketing Staff*
Becky Mc-Clellam, *Manager*
EMP: 325 EST: 1973
SQ FT: 5,000
SALES (est): 44.5MM
SALES (corp-wide): 580.8K Privately Held
WEB: www.norliteagg.com
SIC: 3295 Shale, expanded
HQ: Tradebe Environmental Services, Llc
  1301 W 22nd St Ste 500
  Oak Brook IL 60523

(G-3755)
PRECISION VALVE & AUTOMTN INC (PA)
Also Called: PVA
1 Mustang Dr Ste 3 (12047-4856)
PHONE..................518 371-2684
Anthony J Hynes, *Ch of Bd*
Craig Tuttle, *Mfg Dir*
Jeremy Prusky, *Opers Mgr*
Rich Degonza, *Mfg Mgr*
Peter Howe, *Facilities Mgr*
◆ EMP: 185
SQ FT: 115,000
SALES (est): 35.6MM Privately Held
WEB: www.pva.net
SIC: 3491 Industrial valves

(G-3756)
REO WELDING INC
5 New Cortland St (12047-2628)
PHONE..................518 238-1022
Fax: 518 238-9004
Robert J REO Jr, *President*
Michael REO, *Vice Pres*
Janet Hems, *Office Mgr*
EMP: 17
SQ FT: 6,000
SALES (est): 4.5MM Privately Held
WEB: www.reowelding.com
SIC: 3441 7692 Fabricated structural metal; welding repair

(G-3757)
SCHONWETTER ENTERPRISES INC
Also Called: Bilinski Sausage Mfg Co
41 Lark St (12047-4618)
PHONE..................518 237-0171
Fax: 518 237-0205
Steven M Schonwetter, *Ch of Bd*
Stacie Waters, *COO*
Catherine Schonwetter, *Admin Sec*
EMP: 25
SQ FT: 20,000
SALES (est): 5.8MM Privately Held
WEB: www.bilinski.com
SIC: 2013 Sausages & related products, from purchased meat

(G-3758)
SHELTER ENTERPRISES INC
8 Saratoga St (12047-3109)
P.O. Box 618 (12047-0618)
PHONE..................518 237-4100
Jeffory J Myers, *President*
Don Bartolucci, *General Mgr*
Dan Bartolucci, *Plant Mgr*
Robert Lang, *Sales Staff*
Dan Oconnor, *Manager*
◆ EMP: 60
SQ FT: 110,000
SALES (est): 13.7MM Privately Held
WEB: www.shelter-ent.com
SIC: 3086 2452 Insulation or cushioning material, foamed plastic; prefabricated buildings, wood

(G-3759)
TROS LANSCAPING SUPPLY COMPANY
1266 Loudon Rd (12047-5150)
PHONE..................518 783-6954
Troy Miller, *President*
Monica Mickman, *Vice Pres*
EMP: 11
SQ FT: 2,520
SALES (est): 940.8K Privately Held
SIC: 3271 Blocks, concrete: landscape or retaining wall

(G-3760)
VITAL SIGNS & GRAPHICS CO INC
251 Saratoga St (12047-3120)
PHONE..................518 237-8372
Fax: 518 237-0607
Alexander Coloruotolo, *President*
EMP: 5
SQ FT: 1,200
SALES (est): 496.4K Privately Held
SIC: 3993 7336 Signs & advertising specialties; graphic arts & related design

(G-3761)
W N VANALSTINE & SONS INC (PA)
Also Called: Macaran Printed Products
18 New Cortland St (12047-2628)
P.O. Box 380 (12047-0380)
PHONE..................518 237-1436
Fax: 518 237-0194
Nicholas V Alstine, *President*
William N Van Astine III, *Chairman*
Edward Wixted, *CFO*
Patrick Degnan, *Accounts Exec*
Joan Godzik, *Manager*
EMP: 65 EST: 1952
SQ FT: 52,000
SALES (est): 17.2MM Privately Held
WEB: www.printandapply.com
SIC: 2759 5199 Flexographic printing; packaging materials

Cold Spring
Putnam County

(G-3762)
DI VICO CRAFT PRODUCTS LTD
Also Called: Divico Products
3441 Route 9 (10516-3851)
PHONE..................845 265-9390
Fax: 845 265-9390
David Di Vico Jr, *President*
EMP: 5
SQ FT: 5,500
SALES: 700K Privately Held
SIC: 2499 Fencing, docks & other outdoor wood structural products

(G-3763)
MID-HUDSON CONCRETE PDTS INC
3504 Route 9 (10516-3862)
PHONE..................845 265-3141
Fax: 845 265-3741
Joe Giachinta, *President*
Katie Demarco, *Marketing Staff*
EMP: 7
SQ FT: 3,000
SALES (est): 650K Privately Held
WEB: www.midhudsonconcreteproducts.com
SIC: 3272 Concrete products; septic tanks, concrete

(G-3764)
PUTNAM CNTY NEWS RECORDER LLC
144 Main St Ste 1 (10516-2854)
P.O. Box 185 (10516-0185)
PHONE..................845 265-2468
Joseph P Lindsley Jr, *Editor*
Brian Odonnell, *Network Mgr*
Elizabeth Ailes,
EMP: 12 EST: 1939
SALES (est): 631.2K Privately Held
WEB: www.pcnr.com
SIC: 2711 Newspapers

(G-3765)
RIVERVIEW INDUSTRIES INC
3012 Route 9 Ste 1 (10516-3675)
PHONE..................845 265-5284
Kevin Reichard, *President*
Paul Reichard, *Vice Pres*
EMP: 7
SALES (est): 949.4K Privately Held
SIC: 3548 7538 7549 Welding apparatus; general truck repair; high performance auto repair & service

(G-3766)
SCANGA WOODWORKING CORP
22 Corporate Park W (10516)
PHONE..................845 265-9115
Laura Hammond, *Ch of Bd*
Hugo Scanga, *President*
John Scagna, *Vice Pres*
Mark Scanga, *Vice Pres*
Laura Hammond, *Controller*
EMP: 38
SQ FT: 9,000
SALES (est): 7.1MM Privately Held
SIC: 2431 Moldings, wood: unfinished & prefinished; interior & ornamental woodwork & trim; panel work, wood

Cold Spring Harbor
Suffolk County

(G-3767)
ACCUVEIN INC (PA)
40 Goose Hill Rd (11724-1308)
P.O. Box 1303, Huntington (11743-0657)
PHONE..................816 997-9400
Ron Goldman, *Ch of Bd*
Daniel Delaney, *COO*
Heidi Siegel, *COO*
Jeff Schou, *Vice Pres*
Fred Wood, *Engineer*
EMP: 6
SQ FT: 5,000
SALES (est): 6.9MM Privately Held
SIC: 3829 Thermometers, including digital: clinical

(G-3768)
CIRRUS HEALTHCARE PRODUCTS LLC (PA)
60 Main St (11724-1433)
P.O. Box 220 (11724-0220)
PHONE..................631 692-7600
Joanne Calabria, *VP Opers*
Drew O'Connell,
▲ EMP: 28
SALES (est): 6.5MM Privately Held
WEB: www.cirrushealthcare.com
SIC: 3842 Ear plugs

(G-3769)
INFOSERVICES INTERNATIONAL
Also Called: Itelinso
1 Saint Marks Pl (11724-1825)
PHONE..................631 549-1805
Michael Dohan, *President*
Akademika Skryabina, *General Mgr*
Deirdre Bluemer, *Vice Pres*
Keith Andersen, *Manager*
EMP: 15
SALES (est): 840K Privately Held
WEB: www.infoservices.com
SIC: 2741 Telephone & other directory publishing

(G-3770)
PRINT CENTER INC
3 Harbor Rd Ste 21 (11724-1514)
PHONE..................718 643-9559
Robert Hershon, *President*
EMP: 6
SALES (est): 479K Privately Held
WEB: www.rhinography.com
SIC: 2752 Commercial printing, lithographic

(G-3771)
WATER RESOURCES GROUP LLC
Also Called: Ice Box Water
84 Main St (11724-1441)
P.O. Box 178 (11724-0178)
PHONE..................631 824-9088
Andrew Reynolds, *President*
EMP: 9
SALES (est): 877.6K Privately Held
SIC: 2086 Pasteurized & mineral waters, bottled & canned

Colden
Erie County

(G-3772)
O & S MACHINE & TOOL CO INC
8143 State Rd (14033-9713)
P.O. Box 303 (14033-0303)
PHONE..................716 941-5542
Fax: 716 941-5553
Philip J Schueler, *President*
Connie Caruso, *Manager*
EMP: 9 EST: 1977
SQ FT: 5,000
SALES (est): 1.1MM Privately Held
SIC: 3599 Machine shop, jobbing & repair

College Point
Queens County

(G-3773)
A ANGONOA INC (PA)
11505 15th Ave (11356-1597)
P.O. Box 560089 (11356-0089)
PHONE..................718 762-4466
Fax: 718 359-1013
Peter Zampieri, *President*
John Armao, *Plant Mgr*
Gregg Desantis, *Natl Sales Mgr*
Christopher Desantis, *Sales Staff*
Eileen Rapp, *Manager*
EMP: 77
SQ FT: 60,000

GEOGRAPHIC SECTION

College Point - Queens County (G-3799)

SALES (est): 9.2MM **Privately Held**
WEB: www.angonoa.com
SIC: **2051** Bread, cake & related products

(G-3774)
AABACS GROUP INC
1509 132nd St (11356-2441)
PHONE 718 961-3577
Michael Shin, *Principal*
Tom Park, *Manager*
EMP: 10
SALES (est): 1.1MM **Privately Held**
SIC: **3699** Security control equipment & systems

(G-3775)
ABC WINDOWS AND SIGNS CORP
12606 18th Ave (11356-2326)
PHONE 718 353-6210
Lin Yang, *Ch of Bd*
EMP: 11
SALES (est): 1.1MM **Privately Held**
SIC: **3993** Signs & advertising specialties

(G-3776)
AEROSPACE WIRE & CABLE INC
12909 18th Ave (11356-2407)
PHONE 718 358-2345
Fax: 718 358-2522
Richard Chen, *President*
Leo Tong, *Sales Mgr*
Devin Rosenberg, *Marketing Staff*
Al Lee, *Manager*
CHI Chung Chen, *Shareholder*
▲ EMP: 30
SQ FT: 3,500
SALES (est): 7.3MM **Privately Held**
WEB: www.aerospacewire.com
SIC: **3315** Wire, steel: insulated or armored; cable, steel: insulated or armored

(G-3777)
AFC INDUSTRIES INC
1316 133rd Pl Ste 1 (11356-2024)
PHONE 347 532-1200
Fax: 718 747-0726
Avner Farkash, *General Mgr*
Anat Barnes, *Chairman*
Curt Robertson, *VP Finance*
Joe Cusack, *Sales Dir*
Scott Schneider, *Regl Sales Mgr*
▲ EMP: 100
SQ FT: 20,000
SALES (est): 22.1MM **Privately Held**
WEB: www.afcindustries.com
SIC: **2599** Hospital furniture, except beds

(G-3778)
AMERICAN ORTHOTIC LAB CO INC
924 118th St (11356-1557)
PHONE 718 961-6487
Kevin John Renart, *President*
Kathleen Dodson, *Manager*
EMP: 7
SQ FT: 1,080
SALES (est): 917.5K **Privately Held**
SIC: **3544** Industrial molds

(G-3779)
CAPITAL KIT CAB & DOOR MFRS
Also Called: Capital Ktchens Cab Doors Mfrs
1425 128th St (11356-2335)
PHONE 718 886-0303
Fax: 718 445-4630
Tom Catalanotto Sr, *President*
Steven Catalanotto, *Corp Secy*
Tom Catalanotto Jr, *Vice Pres*
EMP: 7
SQ FT: 10,000
SALES (est): 700K **Privately Held**
WEB: www.capitalkitchens.com
SIC: **2434** 2431 5031 1751 Wood kitchen cabinets; doors, wood; kitchen cabinets; cabinet & finish carpentry

(G-3780)
CENTURY TOM INC
12214 18th Ave (11356-2202)
PHONE 347 654-3179
Yanru Lin, *CEO*
EMP: 4 **EST:** 2012

SQ FT: 1,800
SALES: 1.7MM **Privately Held**
SIC: **2023** Dietary supplements, dairy & non-dairy based

(G-3781)
CITY STORE GATES MFG CORP
Also Called: None
1520 129th St (11356-2400)
PHONE 718 939-9700
Fax: 212 353-0724
Vincent Greco Jr, *Ch of Bd*
Darlene Leavens, *Manager*
Red Leavens, *Manager*
Steve Morisco, *Manager*
▲ EMP: 25
SQ FT: 35,000
SALES (est): 5.6MM **Privately Held**
SIC: **3446** 5211 1799 3429 Gates, ornamental metal; door & window products; fence construction; manufactured hardware (general); millwork

(G-3782)
EAST COAST THERMOGRAPHERS INC
1558 127th St Ste 1 (11356-2347)
PHONE 718 321-3211
Fax: 718 321-3222
Barry Schwartz, *President*
EMP: 30
SQ FT: 6,000
SALES (est): 2MM **Privately Held**
SIC: **2759** 3953 2752 Thermography; marking devices; commercial printing, lithographic

(G-3783)
FILLING EQUIPMENT CO INC
1539 130th St (11356-2481)
PHONE 718 445-2111
Fax: 718 463-6034
Robert A Hampton, *President*
George Hite, *Admin Mgr*
EMP: 11 **EST:** 1959
SQ FT: 6,800
SALES (est): 2.8MM **Privately Held**
WEB: www.fillingequipment.com
SIC: **3565** 5084 Bottling machinery: filling, capping, labeling; industrial machinery & equipment

(G-3784)
GLOPAK USA CORP (PA)
1816 127th St 2 (11356-2334)
PHONE 347 869-9252
Kenneth Wang, *CEO*
▲ EMP: 19
SALES (est): 10.3MM **Privately Held**
SIC: **3221** Bottles for packing, bottling & canning: glass

(G-3785)
GMD INDUSTRIES INC
Also Called: Designer Glass
12920 18th Ave (11356-2408)
PHONE 718 445-8779
Fax: 718 358-8614
Jorge Rodriguez, *President*
Maria Rodriguez, *Vice Pres*
Greg Macpherson, *Engineer*
▲ EMP: 8
SQ FT: 1,500
SALES (est): 1.1MM **Privately Held**
WEB: www.gmdindustries.com
SIC: **3231** Decorated glassware: chipped, engraved, etched, etc.; mirrored glass

(G-3786)
HEAT USA II LLC (PA)
11902 23rd Ave (11356-2506)
P.O. Box 560240 (11356-0240)
PHONE 212 254-4328
Mark Kohan, *General Mgr*
EMP: 11
SALES (est): 2.4MM **Privately Held**
SIC: **2911** Oils, fuel

(G-3787)
IN-HOUSE INC
1535 126th St Ste 3 (11356-2346)
PHONE 718 445-9007
Fax: 718 445-9043
Joseph Passarella, *President*
EMP: 10
SQ FT: 5,000

SALES: 1.5MM **Privately Held**
SIC: **2752** 2791 2789 2732 Commercial printing, offset; typesetting; bookbinding & related work; book printing

(G-3788)
INK-IT PRINTING INC
Also Called: Ink-It Prtg Inc/Angle Offset
1535 126th St Ste 1 (11356-2346)
PHONE 718 229-5590
Fax: 718 631-5530
Michael Igoe, *President*
EMP: 8
SQ FT: 750
SALES (est): 638K **Privately Held**
SIC: **2752** Commercial printing, offset

(G-3789)
INTER-FENCE CO INC
1520 129th St (11356-2400)
PHONE 718 939-9700
Vincent Greco Sr, *President*
Vincent Greco Jr, *Vice Pres*
Thomas A Greco, *Treasurer*
Angela Greco, *Admin Sec*
EMP: 40
SQ FT: 35,000
SALES (est): 6.3MM **Privately Held**
SIC: **3442** 3446 Metal doors; gates, ornamental metal

(G-3790)
INTERPLEX INDUSTRIES INC (HQ)
1434 110th St Ste 301 (11356-1448)
PHONE 718 961-6212
Jack Seidler, *Ch of Bd*
Sanjiv Chhahira, *President*
Peter Salvas, *Opers Mgr*
David Derose, *Engineer*
Tom Labeau, *Design Engr*
▲ EMP: 10
SQ FT: 40,000
SALES (est): 132.9MM
SALES (corp-wide): 969.5MM **Privately Held**
WEB: www.interplex.com
SIC: **3471** 3825 3674 3469 Electroplating of metals or formed products; instruments to measure electricity; semiconductor circuit networks; stamping metal for the trade
PA: Interplex Holdings Pte. Ltd.
298 Tiong Bahru Raod
Singapore 16873
666 398-45

(G-3791)
ISLAND CIRCUITS INTERNATIONAL
1318 130th St Fl 2 (11356-1917)
PHONE 516 625-5555
Maurizio Lanza, *Branch Mgr*
EMP: 7
SALES (corp-wide): 1.8MM **Privately Held**
SIC: **3679** Electronic circuits
PA: Island Circuits International
100 E 2nd St Ste 201
Mineola NY 11501
516 625-5555

(G-3792)
JAD CORP OF AMERICA
2048 119th St (11356-2123)
PHONE 718 762-8900
Fax: 718 762-7320
Joseph A Dussich Jr, *President*
David Newell, *Business Mgr*
James Jozkowski, *Purchasing*
Henry Schaeffer, *CFO*
Trina Laxa, *Controller*
EMP: 50
SQ FT: 45,000
SALES (est): 25.7MM **Privately Held**
WEB: www.jad.com
SIC: **2673** 5087 5169 Trash bags (plastic film): made from purchased materials; cleaning & maintenance equipment & supplies; chemicals & allied products

(G-3793)
JPMORGAN CHASE BANK NAT ASSN
13207 14th Ave (11356-2001)
PHONE 718 767-3592
EMP: 6
SALES (corp-wide): 101B **Publicly Held**
SIC: **3578** Automatic teller machines (ATM)
HQ: Jpmorgan Chase Bank, National Association
1111 Polaris Pkwy
Columbus OH 43240
614 436-3055

(G-3794)
LAHOYA ENTERPRISE INC
Also Called: Kouroush
1842 College Point Blvd (11356-2221)
PHONE 718 886-8799
Kourosh Tehrani, *Ch of Bd*
Daphne Hwang, *Manager*
▲ EMP: 30
SALES (est): 2MM **Privately Held**
SIC: **2339** Women's & misses' outerwear

(G-3795)
LIBERTY CONTROLS INC
1505 132nd St Fl 2 (11356-2441)
PHONE 718 461-0600
Fax: 718 461-3613
Charles Papalcure, *President*
David Derose, *Project Mgr*
EMP: 7 **EST:** 1998
SALES (est): 660K **Privately Held**
WEB: www.liberty-controls.com
SIC: **3829** Measuring & controlling devices

(G-3796)
M T M PRINTING CO INC
2321 College Point Blvd (11356-2596)
PHONE 718 353-3297
Fax: 718 353-4500
Steven Kolman, *President*
Tracy Kolman, *Vice Pres*
Tracy K Silverman, *Manager*
EMP: 14 **EST:** 1940
SQ FT: 5,500
SALES (est): 2.4MM **Privately Held**
WEB: www.mtmprinting.com
SIC: **2752** 2759 Commercial printing, offset; letterpress printing

(G-3797)
MATIC INDUSTRIES INC
1540 127th St (11356-2332)
PHONE 718 886-5470
Fax: 718 886-5132
Roland Tatzel, *President*
EMP: 7
SALES (est): 580K **Privately Held**
SIC: **3599** Machine shop, jobbing & repair

(G-3798)
MINT-X PRODUCTS CORPORATION
2048 119th St (11356-2123)
PHONE 877 646-8224
Joseph Dussich, *President*
Frank Fernandez, *Opers Mgr*
EMP: 10
SALES: 10MM **Privately Held**
SIC: **2673** Food storage & trash bags (plastic)

(G-3799)
NAS CP CORP (DH)
Also Called: Interplex Nas Electronics
1434 110th St Apt 4a (11356-1445)
PHONE 718 961-6757
Jack Seidler, *President*
John Pease, *Exec VP*
Irving Klein, *Treasurer*
▲ EMP: 84 **EST:** 1958
SQ FT: 41,000
SALES (est): 15.3MM
SALES (corp-wide): 969.5MM **Privately Held**
SIC: **3544** 3471 3825 Dies & die holders for metal cutting, forming, die casting; plating of metals or formed products; test equipment for electronic & electric measurement

College Point - Queens County (G-3800)

HQ: Interplex Industries, Inc.
1434 110th St Ste 301
College Point NY 11356
718 961-6212

(G-3800) PEPSI-COLA BOTTLING CO NY INC
11202 15th Ave (11356-1496)
PHONE 718 649-2465
Fax: 718 649-9154
Stephen Del Priore, *General Mgr*
Stephen Delpriore, *General Mgr*
Harold Honickman, *Chairman*
Charlie Zimmerman, *Plant Mgr*
EMP: 300
SALES (corp-wide): 219.3MM **Privately Held**
PA: Pepsi-Cola Bottling Company Of New York, Inc.
11402 15th Ave Ste 5
College Point NY 11356
718 392-1000
SIC: 2086 Soft drinks: packaged in cans, bottles, etc.

(G-3801) PEPSI-COLA BOTTLING CO NY INC (PA)
11402 15th Ave Ste 5 (11356-1402)
PHONE 718 392-1000
William Wilson, *Ch of Bd*
Richard Goodman, *Exec VP*
Jim Wilkinson, *Exec VP*
Umran Beba, *Vice Pres*
Santo Bonanno, *Vice Pres*
EMP: 318 EST: 1987
SQ FT: 400,000
SALES (est): 219.3MM **Privately Held**
SIC: 2086 Soft drinks: packaged in cans, bottles, etc.

(G-3802) PRECISION GEAR INCORPORATED
11207 14th Ave (11356-1407)
PHONE 718 321-7200
Mathew S Forelli, *Ch of Bd*
M Briggs Forelli, *President*
Jack Rockstad, *Vice Pres*
Viviana Rosa, *Purchasing*
Edmundo Castillo, *QC Mgr*
▲ EMP: 147 EST: 1936
SQ FT: 56,000
SALES (est): 39.9MM **Privately Held**
WEB: www.precisiongearinc.com
SIC: 3728 Aircraft power transmission equipment; beaching gear, aircraft

(G-3803) QUALITY LIFE INC
2047 129th St (11356-2725)
PHONE 718 939-5787
Fax: 718 939-7393
Ping Ping Huang, *Ch of Bd*
▲ EMP: 15
SALES (est): 1.1MM **Privately Held**
SIC: 3634 Massage machines, electric, except for beauty/barber shops

(G-3804) RAINBOW LEATHER INC
1415 112th St (11356-1435)
PHONE 718 939-8762
Fax: 718 461-7908
Richard Lipson, *President*
Nax Pierrot, *General Mgr*
Danny Pilpe, *Prdtn Dir*
Maria LI, *Prdtn Mgr*
▲ EMP: 10 EST: 1981
SQ FT: 8,000
SALES (est): 1.5MM **Privately Held**
WEB: www.rainbowleather.com
SIC: 3111 Embossing of leather

(G-3805) RKL BUILDING SPC CO INC
1530 131st St (11356-2423)
PHONE 718 728-7788
Joseph Kucich, *President*
Claire Kucich, *Corp Secy*
Gary Kucich, *Vice Pres*
Steve Walters, *Sales Staff*
Judith Walker, *Admin Asst*
▲ EMP: 5 EST: 1953
SQ FT: 5,000
SALES (est): 880.3K
SALES (corp-wide): 210.8B **Publicly Held**
SIC: 3429 Builders' hardware
HQ: Hohmann & Barnard, Inc.
30 Rasons Ct
Hauppauge NY 11788
631 234-0600

(G-3806) SCHUSTER & RICHARD LABORTORIES
Also Called: Schuster & Richard Lab
1420 130th St (11356-2416)
PHONE 718 358-8607
Fax: 718 358-8764
Charles Boudiette, *President*
EMP: 6
SQ FT: 1,500
SALES (est): 540K **Privately Held**
SIC: 3842 Foot appliances, orthopedic

(G-3807) SESCO INDUSTRIES INC
11019 15th Ave (11356-1425)
P.O. Box 560242 (11356-0242)
PHONE 718 939-5137
Fax: 718 461-0553
Steven Shulman, *President*
Colleen Valerio, *Sales Mgr*
EMP: 11 EST: 1976
SQ FT: 4,000
SALES: 1.8MM **Privately Held**
WEB: www.sescoindustries.com
SIC: 3452 Bolts, nuts, rivets & washers

(G-3808) SPACE SIGN
1525 132nd St (11356-2441)
PHONE 718 961-1112
Fax: 718 961-5577
Chang Kon Hahn, *President*
Joyce Hahn, *Vice Pres*
EMP: 11
SQ FT: 5,000
SALES (est): 770K **Privately Held**
WEB: www.spacesign.com
SIC: 3993 3089 3444 1799 Signs & advertising specialties; awnings, fiberglass & plastic combination; awnings, sheet metal; awning installation; awnings

(G-3809) TAG ENVELOPE CO INC
1419 128th St (11356-2335)
P.O. Box 220372, Brooklyn (11222-0372)
PHONE 718 389-6844
Fax: 718 383-6188
Geraldine Wald, *President*
Eric Wald, *Vice Pres*
Ian Wald, *Vice Pres*
EMP: 22 EST: 1919
SQ FT: 10,000
SALES: 3MM **Privately Held**
SIC: 2621 2679 Envelope paper; tags, paper (unprinted): made from purchased paper

(G-3810) WEDCO FABRICATIONS INC
2016 130th St (11356-2732)
PHONE 718 852-6330
Dan Gordon, *President*
EMP: 7
SALES (est): 700K **Privately Held**
WEB: www.wedcofab.com
SIC: 3498 Fabricated pipe & fittings

(G-3811) YOGA IN DAILY LIFE - NY INC
1438 132nd St (11356-2020)
PHONE 718 539-8548
Denis Licul, *Principal*
EMP: 5 EST: 2010
SALES (est): 287.4K **Privately Held**
SIC: 2711 Newspapers, publishing & printing

(G-3812) YOURS TRADING INC
1521 132nd St (11356-2441)
PHONE 718 539-0088
Ji Yu, *President*
Eunkyung Yu, *Vice Pres*
▲ EMP: 3
SALES (est): 1MM **Privately Held**
SIC: 2844 5131 Hair preparations, including shampoos; hair accessories

(G-3813) ZERED INC (PA)
12717 20th Ave (11356-2317)
PHONE 718 353-7464
Fax: 718 353-7149
Hakjin Han, *President*
James Han, *Director*
▲ EMP: 11
SALES (est): 1.5MM **Privately Held**
SIC: 3211 Plate glass, polished & rough

Colliersville
Otsego County

(G-3814) C & F FABRICATORS & ERECTORS
Rr 7 (13747)
PHONE 607 432-3520
Fax: 607 432-6435
Matthew Centofante, *President*
EMP: 6
SQ FT: 2,000
SALES (est): 580K **Privately Held**
SIC: 3443 Fabricated plate work (boiler shop)

Collins
Erie County

(G-3815) COUNTRY SIDE SAND & GRAVEL (HQ)
Taylor Hollow Rd (14034)
PHONE 716 988-3271
Daniel Gernatt Jr, *President*
EMP: 1
SQ FT: 10,000
SALES (est): 1.2MM
SALES (corp-wide): 33.7MM **Privately Held**
SIC: 1442 Sand mining; gravel mining
PA: Gernatt Asphalt Products, Inc.
13870 Taylor Hollow Rd
Collins NY 14034
716 532-3371

(G-3816) EAST END
1995 Lenox Rd (14034-9785)
PHONE 716 532-2622
Cheryl Whiteparker, *Owner*
EMP: 10
SALES (est): 1.1MM **Privately Held**
WEB: www.eastend.com
SIC: 2111 Cigarettes

(G-3817) GERNATT ASPHALT PRODUCTS INC (PA)
Also Called: Gernatt Companies
13870 Taylor Hollow Rd (14034-9713)
P.O. Box 400 (14034-0400)
PHONE 716 532-3371
Daniel R Gernatt Jr, *Ch of Bd*
Randall Best, *Vice Pres*
Bill Schmitz, *Vice Pres*
Ken Ziccarelli, *Vice Pres*
John Redman, *Safety Mgr*
EMP: 20 EST: 1961
SQ FT: 10,000
SALES (est): 33.7MM **Privately Held**
WEB: www.gernatt.com
SIC: 2951 Asphalt paving mixtures & blocks

(G-3818) ZEBROWSKI INDUSTRIES INC
4345 Route 39 (14034-9765)
PHONE 716 532-3911
Peter Zebrowski, *Chairman*
EMP: 8
SALES (est): 690K **Privately Held**
SIC: 3999 Chairs, hydraulic, barber & beauty shop

Colonie
Albany County

(G-3819) COLONIE BLOCK AND SUPPLY CO
124 Lincoln Ave (12205-4917)
PHONE 518 869-8411
Fax: 518 456-6209
Thomas Gentile, *President*
Donald Countermine, *Vice Pres*
Marlene Countermine, *Treasurer*
EMP: 5
SQ FT: 5,000
SALES (est): 693.3K **Privately Held**
SIC: 3271 5032 Blocks, concrete or cinder: standard; masons' materials

(G-3820) GERALD MCGLONE
17 Zoar Ave (12205-3531)
PHONE 518 482-2613
Gerald McGlone, *Owner*
EMP: 5
SALES (est): 423.6K **Privately Held**
SIC: 2679 Wallpaper

(G-3821) SNYDERS NEON DISPLAYS INC
Also Called: Snyder Neon & Plastic Signs
5 Highland Ave (12205-5458)
PHONE 518 857-4100
Fax: 518 437-9285
Mary Elizabeth Orminski, *President*
Mark Orminski, *Vice Pres*
EMP: 6 EST: 1931
SQ FT: 5,800
SALES: 230K **Privately Held**
SIC: 3993 7389 Signs & advertising specialties; crane & aerial lift service

Commack
Suffolk County

(G-3822) AVENTURA TECHNOLOGIES INC (PA)
48 Mall Dr (11725-5704)
PHONE 631 300-4000
Frances Cabasso, *CEO*
Boris Katzenberg, *Vice Pres*
Lavonne Lazarus, *Vice Pres*
Kevin A Lichtman, *Vice Pres*
Kevin Lichtman, *Vice Pres*
EMP: 40
SQ FT: 40,000
SALES (est): 16.6MM **Privately Held**
WEB: www.ati247.com
SIC: 3577 3812 1731 Computer peripheral equipment; search & navigation equipment; voice, data & video wiring contractor; closed circuit television installation

(G-3823) AVERY BIOMEDICAL DEVICES INC
61 Mall Dr Ste 1 (11725-5725)
PHONE 631 864-1600
Martin Dobelle, *CEO*
Antonio Martins, *CEO*
Claire Dobelle, *President*
Linda Towler, *CFO*
Willem Kolff, *Manager*
EMP: 16
SQ FT: 4,000
SALES (est): 1.7MM **Privately Held**
WEB: www.dobelle.com
SIC: 3841 Surgical instruments & apparatus

(G-3824) BEYER GRAPHICS INC
30 Austin Blvd Ste A (11725-5747)
PHONE 631 543-3900
Fax: 631 543-3916
Jose Beyer, *CEO*
William Beyer Sr, *Ch of Bd*
Daniel Byer, *CFO*
Dan Beyer, *Webmaster*

GEOGRAPHIC SECTION

Commack - Suffolk County (G-3848)

▲ EMP: 99
SQ FT: 40,000
SALES (est): 36MM Privately Held
SIC: 2752 2791 2789 7374 Commercial printing, offset; typesetting; bookbinding & related work; computer graphics service

(G-3825)
BREN-TRNICS BATTERIES INTL INC
10 Brayton Ct (11725-3104)
PHONE 631 499-5155
Leo A Brenna, *President*
Kathleen Menikos, *VP Finance*
EMP: 7
SALES (est): 620K Privately Held
SIC: 3691 Batteries, rechargeable

(G-3826)
BREN-TRNICS BATTERIES INTL LLC
10 Brayton Ct (11725-3104)
PHONE 631 499-5155
Leo Brenna,
EMP: 20
SQ FT: 94,000
SALES (est): 2.2MM Privately Held
SIC: 3691 Alkaline cell storage batteries

(G-3827)
BREN-TRONICS INC
10 Brayton Ct (11725-3104)
PHONE 631 499-5155
Fax: 631 499-5504
SAI W Fung, *President*
Gregor Ritchie, *President*
Bokhari Bilal, *Managing Prtnr*
Sylvain Lhuissier, *Vice Pres*
Leigh Straub, *Opers Mgr*
▲ EMP: 200
SQ FT: 80,000
SALES (est): 59.6MM Privately Held
WEB: www.bren-tronics.com
SIC: 3691 3692 3699 Storage batteries; primary batteries, dry & wet; electrical equipment & supplies

(G-3828)
COMFORT CARE TEXTILES INC (HQ)
368 Veterans Memorial Hwy # 5 (11725-4322)
PHONE 631 543-0531
Scott Janicola, *Chairman*
Cynthia Langhauser, *Finance Dir*
▲ EMP: 40
SQ FT: 26,000
SALES (est): 6.5MM
SALES (corp-wide): 20MM Privately Held
SIC: 2295 Coated fabrics, not rubberized
PA: Jan Lew Textile Corp
   368 Veterans Memorial Hwy # 5
   Commack NY 11725
   631 543-0531

(G-3829)
CORAL COLOR PROCESS LTD
50 Mall Dr (11725-5704)
PHONE 631 543-5200
Fax: 631 543-0264
Edward Aiello, *President*
Edie Dinapoli, *Managing Dir*
Ediedie D Npolis, *Vice Pres*
EMP: 37
SQ FT: 20,000
SALES (est): 14.8MM Privately Held
SIC: 2752 Commercial printing, lithographic

(G-3830)
DREAMSEATS LLC
60 Austin Blvd (11725-5702)
PHONE 631 656-1066
Dave Fibo, *Accountant*
Scott Suprina, *Mng Member*
Desiree Cain, *Info Tech Mgr*
▲ EMP: 27
SQ FT: 10,000
SALES: 3.8MM Privately Held
SIC: 3429 Furniture hardware

(G-3831)
FOREST LABORATORIES LLC
500 Commack Rd (11725-5020)
P.O. Box 9025 (11725)
PHONE 631 858-6010
Fax: 631 462-2794
Richard Overt, *Vice Pres*
Lori J Nuckols, *Project Mgr*
Darby Galletta, *Opers Mgr*
Vito Ryder, *Facilities Mgr*
James Hamilton, *Opers Staff*
EMP: 130 Privately Held
WEB: www.frx.com
SIC: 2834 Pharmaceutical preparations; antibiotics, packaged; drugs acting on the respiratory system; thyroid preparations
HQ: Forest Laboratories, Llc
   909 3rd Ave Fl 23
   New York NY 10022
   212 421-7850

(G-3832)
GASSER & SONS INC (PA)
440 Moreland Rd (11725-5778)
PHONE 631 543-6600
Fax: 631 543-6649
Richard F Gasser, *Chairman*
Jack Gasser, *Vice Pres*
Christine Valenti, *Finance Mgr*
Jaymee Karabin, *Mktg Coord*
Rod Bush, *Manager*
▲ EMP: 125 EST: 1916
SQ FT: 30,000
SALES (est): 23.6MM Privately Held
WEB: www.gasser.com
SIC: 3469 Metal stampings

(G-3833)
GEMINI PHARMACEUTICALS INC
87 Modular Ave Ste 1 (11725-5718)
PHONE 631 543-3334
Andrew Finamore, *President*
Joni Foley, *Senior VP*
Bianca Eulloqui, *Vice Pres*
Michael Finamore, *Vice Pres*
Jeremy Maceno, *Opers Mgr*
▲ EMP: 150
SALES (est): 36.4MM Privately Held
WEB: www.geminipharm.com
SIC: 2833 Vitamins, natural or synthetic: bulk, uncompounded

(G-3834)
HAROME DESIGNS LLC
75 Modular Ave (11725-5705)
PHONE 631 864-1900
Alan J Cohen, *Mng Member*
EMP: 22
SALES (est): 1.2MM Privately Held
SIC: 2519 Household furniture, except wood or metal: upholstered

(G-3835)
HOBART CORPORATION
71 Mall Dr Ste 1 (11725-5728)
PHONE 631 864-3440
Fax: 631 864-4042
Paul Todoro, *Manager*
EMP: 24
SALES (corp-wide): 13.4B Publicly Held
WEB: www.hobartcorp.com
SIC: 3639 5084 7629 7699 Major kitchen appliances, except refrigerators & stoves; food product manufacturing machinery; electrical repair shops; restaurant equipment repair
HQ: Hobart Corporation
   701 S Ridge Ave
   Troy OH 45374
   937 332-3000

(G-3836)
ISLAND AUDIO ENGINEERING
7 Glenmere Ct (11725-5607)
PHONE 631 543-2372
George Alexandrovich, *Owner*
EMP: 5 EST: 1972
SALES (est): 387.9K Privately Held
SIC: 3677 Inductors, electronic

(G-3837)
MALOYA LASER INC
65a Mall Dr Ste 1 (11725-5726)
PHONE 631 543-2327
Fax: 631 543-2374
Reto Hug, *President*
Marc Anderes, *Vice Pres*
Paul H Ug, *Human Res Dir*
Roger Hug, *VP Sales*
Michael Boccio, *Sales Executive*
EMP: 27
SQ FT: 22,500
SALES (est): 6.4MM Privately Held
WEB: www.maloyalaser.com
SIC: 3444 Mail (post office) collection or storage boxes, sheet metal

(G-3838)
MOBILE MINI INC
1158 Jericho Tpke (11725-3020)
PHONE 631 543-4900
Ryan Catarelli, *Branch Mgr*
EMP: 20
SALES (corp-wide): 530.7MM Publicly Held
WEB: www.mobilemini.com
SIC: 3448 Buildings, portable: prefabricated metal
PA: Mobile Mini, Inc.
   4646 E Van Buren St # 400
   Phoenix AZ 85008
   480 894-6311

(G-3839)
RCE MANUFACTURING LLC
10 Brayton Ct (11725-3104)
PHONE 631 856-9005
Kathleen Menikos, *VP Finance*
SAI Fung, *Mng Member*
EMP: 5 EST: 2015
SQ FT: 5,000
SALES (est): 262.3K Privately Held
SIC: 3672 Printed circuit boards

(G-3840)
ROPACK USA INC
49 Mall Dr (11725-5722)
PHONE 631 482-7777
Yves Massicotta, *CEO*
EMP: 10 EST: 2015
SALES (est): 1.8MM Privately Held
SIC: 2834 Pharmaceutical preparations

(G-3841)
RPF ASSOCIATES INC
Also Called: Signs By Tomorrow
2155 Jericho Tpke Ste A (11725-2919)
PHONE 631 462-7446
Fax: 631 462-5330
Ron Facchiano, *President*
Patricia Facchiano, *Controller*
EMP: 5
SQ FT: 1,250
SALES (est): 605K Privately Held
SIC: 3993 Signs & advertising specialties

(G-3842)
SETTONS INTL FOODS INC (PA)
Also Called: Setton Farms
85 Austin Blvd (11725-5701)
PHONE 631 543-8090
Fax: 631 543-8070
Joshua Setton, *CEO*
Morris Setton, *Exec VP*
Jeff Gibbons, *Plant Mgr*
Steward Fellner, *CFO*
Stewart Felner, *CFO*
◆ EMP: 50
SQ FT: 55,000
SALES (est): 63.9MM Privately Held
WEB: www.settonfarms.com
SIC: 2034 2068 2099 2066 Dried & dehydrated fruits; nuts: dried, dehydrated, salted or roasted; food preparations; chocolate & cocoa products; candy & other confectionery products

(G-3843)
SIMPLY NATURAL FOODS LLC
Also Called: Simply Lite Foods
74 Mall Dr (11725-5711)
PHONE 631 543-9600
Pat Buechler, *Purch Agent*
Norman Gross, *CFO*
Solomon Gluck, *Controller*
Abe Brach,
Russ Asaro,
▲ EMP: 50
SQ FT: 55,000
SALES (est): 18.9MM Privately Held
WEB: www.simplylite.com
SIC: 3556 2064 2066 Food products machinery; candy & other confectionery products; chocolate & cocoa products

(G-3844)
TWINS ENTERPRISE INC
Also Called: Nu Image
2171 Jericho Tpke (11725-2937)
PHONE 631 368-4702
Ray Coppola, *Manager*
EMP: 5
SALES (corp-wide): 54.3MM Privately Held
WEB: www.twins.com
SIC: 2353 Baseball caps
PA: Twins Enterprise, Inc.
   19 Yawkey Way
   Boston MA 02215
   617 437-1384

(G-3845)
UNIVERSAL PACKG SYSTEMS INC (PA)
Also Called: Paklab
6080 Jericho Tpke (11725-2850)
PHONE 631 543-2277
Andrew Young III, *Ch of Bd*
Alan Kristel, *COO*
Peter Belinsky, *Exec VP*
Nancy Weinmaster, *Vice Pres*
Rita Arellano, *Project Mgr*
▲ EMP: 750
SQ FT: 115,000
SALES (est): 127MM Privately Held
SIC: 2844 7389 3565 2671 Cosmetic preparations; packaging & labeling services; bottling machinery: filling, capping, labeling; plastic film, coated or laminated for packaging

(G-3846)
VEHICLE TRACKING SOLUTIONS LLC
152 Veterans Memorial Hwy (11725-3634)
PHONE 631 586-7400
John Cunningham, *President*
Glenn Reed, *COO*
Karen Cunningham, *CFO*
Adam Ross, *Manager*
Ryan Wilkinson, *CTO*
EMP: 50
SQ FT: 17,000
SALES (est): 17.1MM Privately Held
WEB: www.vehicletrackingsolutions.com
SIC: 7372 Prepackaged software

(G-3847)
VITAMIX LABORATORIES INC
69 Mall Dr (11725-5727)
PHONE 631 465-9245
Michael Koschitz, *President*
John Greenough, *Facilities Dir*
Angelica Rodriguez, *Human Resources*
Amelia Connelly, *Manager*
Eric Haller, *Manager*
EMP: 25
SALES (est): 1MM Privately Held
SIC: 2833 Vitamins, natural or synthetic: bulk, uncompounded

(G-3848)
WICKERS SPORTSWEAR INC (PA)
Also Called: Wickers Performance Wear
340 Veterans Memorial Hwy # 1 (11725-4368)
PHONE 631 543-1700
Fax: 631 543-1378
Anthony Mazzenga, *CEO*
Diane Basso, *President*
Carol Mazzenga, *Principal*
Maryann D'Erario, *Treasurer*
▲ EMP: 7
SQ FT: 2,000
SALES (est): 1.4MM Privately Held
WEB: www.wickers.com
SIC: 2322 2341 Underwear, men's & boys': made from purchased materials; women's & children's underwear

Commack - Suffolk County (G-3849) — GEOGRAPHIC SECTION

(G-3849)
WINDOW RAMA ENTERPRISES INC
6333 Jericho Tpke Ste 11 (11725-2824)
PHONE...................................631 462-9054
John Wood, *Manager*
EMP: 5
SALES (corp-wide): 36.4MM **Privately Held**
WEB: www.windowrama.com
SIC: 3442 Window & door frames
PA: Window Rama Enterprises, Inc.
 71 Heartland Blvd
 Edgewood NY 11717
 631 667-2555

Conesus
Livingston County

(G-3850)
EAGLE CREST VINEYARD LLC
Also Called: O-Neh-Da Vineyard
7107 Vineyard Rd (14435-9521)
PHONE...................................585 346-5760
Fax: 585 346-2322
Sally Brown, *Manager*
Bob Quinn, *Manager*
Elizabeth Goldstone,
▲ EMP: 5
SQ FT: 20,000
SALES (est): 380K **Privately Held**
SIC: 2084 0172 Wines; grapes

Congers
Rockland County

(G-3851)
ANKA TOOL & DIE INC
150 Wells Ave (10920-2096)
PHONE...................................845 268-4116
Fax: 845 268-2159
Agnes Karl, *Corp Secy*
Anton Karl Jr, *Vice Pres*
Anthony Pisello, *Engineer*
Patricia McCoy, *Manager*
EMP: 35 EST: 1970
SQ FT: 6,400
SALES (est): 6.5MM **Privately Held**
WEB: www.ankatool.com
SIC: 3544 3089 Special dies & tools; injection molding of plastics

(G-3852)
APTARGROUP INC
Also Called: Aptar Congers
250 N Route 303 (10920-1450)
PHONE...................................845 639-3700
Stephen Scott, *Facilities Mgr*
Kevin Hoover, *Engineer*
Cedric Hugo, *Engineer*
Zouhir Tammam, *Engineer*
Sylvia Gonzalez, *Human Res Mgr*
EMP: 150
SALES (corp-wide): 2.3B **Publicly Held**
SIC: 3586 Measuring & dispensing pumps
PA: Aptargroup, Inc.
 475 W Terra Cotta Ave E
 Crystal Lake IL 60014
 815 477-0424

(G-3853)
BOURGHOL BROTHERS INC
73 Lake Rd (10920-2323)
P.O. Box 80 (10920-0080)
PHONE...................................845 268-9752
Fax: 845 268-4562
Charles Bourghol, *President*
Alexander Bourghol, *Treasurer*
EMP: 7
SQ FT: 1,200
SALES (est): 1.2MM **Privately Held**
WEB: www.bourgholbrosjewelers.com
SIC: 3911 5944 Jewelry, precious metal; jewelry, precious stones & precious metals

(G-3854)
CHARTWELL PHARMA NDA B2 HOLDIN
77 Brenner Dr (10920-1307)
PHONE...................................845 268-5000
EMP: 5
SALES (est): 229.7K **Privately Held**
SIC: 2834 Tablets, pharmaceutical

(G-3855)
CHARTWELL PHARMACEUTICALS LLC
77 Brenner Dr (10920-1307)
PHONE...................................845 268-5000
David I Chipkin, *COO*
Francis Ezdebski, *Vice Pres*
EMP: 75
SALES (est): 19.3MM **Privately Held**
SIC: 2834 Pharmaceutical preparations

(G-3856)
F M GROUP INC
100 Wells Ave (10920-2037)
PHONE...................................845 589-0102
Josef Feldman, *President*
EMP: 10
SALES (est): 1.7MM **Privately Held**
WEB: www.functionalmaterials.com
SIC: 2899 2865 Ink or writing fluids; dyes & pigments

(G-3857)
HUDSON VALLEY COATINGS LLC
175 N Route 9w Ste 12 (10920-1780)
PHONE...................................845 398-1778
Joseph Montana,
EMP: 5
SALES (est): 504.3K **Privately Held**
SIC: 3479 Coating of metals with plastic or resins

(G-3858)
KERRY INC
225 New York Hwy 303 N St (10920)
PHONE...................................845 584-3080
EMP: 25 **Privately Held**
SIC: 2099 Food preparations
HQ: Kerry Inc.
 3330 Millington Rd
 Beloit WI 53511
 608 363-1200

(G-3859)
LINDEN COOKIES INC
25 Brenner Dr (10920-1307)
PHONE...................................845 268-5050
Fax: 845 268-5055
Paul L Sturz, *President*
Patricia Neuenhoff, *Vice Pres*
Pat Nevenhoff, *Vice Pres*
C Ronald Sturz, *Vice Pres*
EMP: 50 EST: 1960
SQ FT: 33,000
SALES (est): 10.9MM **Privately Held**
WEB: www.lindencookies.com
SIC: 2052 Cookies

(G-3860)
STAR KAY WHITE INC (PA)
151 Wells Ave (10920-1398)
PHONE...................................845 268-2600
Benjamin Katzenstein, *Vice Pres*
James Katzenstein, *Treasurer*
Mark Hetzel, *Accounts Mgr*
Tracy Herb, *Manager*
George Granada, *Officer*
◆ EMP: 65
SQ FT: 45,000
SALES (est): 13MM **Privately Held**
WEB: www.starkaywhite.com
SIC: 2087 Flavoring extracts & syrups

(G-3861)
VALOIS OF AMERICA INC
250 N Route 303 (10920-1450)
PHONE...................................845 639-3700
Fax: 845 639-3900
Alex Thoedorakis, *President*
Pamela Moran, *Sales Associate*
Jennifer Diaz, *Office Mgr*
Lidiette Celado, *Manager*
▲ EMP: 150
SQ FT: 3,500
SALES (est): 18.7MM
SALES (corp-wide): 2.3B **Publicly Held**
WEB: www.aptargroup.com
SIC: 3586 Measuring & dispensing pumps
PA: Aptargroup, Inc.
 475 W Terra Cotta Ave E
 Crystal Lake IL 60014
 815 477-0424

(G-3862)
VITANE PHARMACEUTICALS INC
125 Wells Ave (10920-2036)
PHONE...................................845 267-6700
Mohammed Hassan, *CEO*
Ezz Hamza, *President*
Deepali Bhole, *Manager*
◆ EMP: 24
SQ FT: 15,000
SALES: 7.4MM **Privately Held**
SIC: 2834 Pharmaceutical preparations

(G-3863)
WYNN STARR FLAVORS INC (PA)
225 N Route 303 Ste 109 (10920-3001)
PHONE...................................845 584-3080
Steven B Zavagli, *Chairman*
Roland Abate, *Vice Pres*
Mark Laslo, *Vice Pres*
Barry Friedson, *VP Mfg*
Gary Raff, *VP Finance*
EMP: 25
SQ FT: 12,000
SALES (est): 13.1MM **Privately Held**
WEB: www.wynnstarr.com
SIC: 2087 Flavoring extracts & syrups

Conklin
Broome County

(G-3864)
ALL READY INC
Also Called: All Ready Printing
39 Carol Ct (13748-1435)
PHONE...................................607 722-0826
Fax: 607 722-2105
Ernest Kensey, *President*
Valerie Kensey, *Vice Pres*
EMP: 9
SQ FT: 3,500
SALES (est): 870K **Privately Held**
WEB: www.allready.com
SIC: 2752 7334 2791 Commercial printing, offset; photocopying & duplicating services; typesetting

(G-3865)
ARDAGH METAL PACKAGING USA INC
379 Broome Corporate Pkwy (13748)
PHONE...................................607 584-3300
EMP: 126
SALES (corp-wide): 12K **Privately Held**
SIC: 3411 Metal cans
HQ: Ardagh Metal Packaging Usa Inc.
 600 N Bell Ave Ste 200
 Carnegie PA 15106
 412 923-1080

(G-3866)
CADMUS JOURNAL SERVICES INC
Also Called: Digital Printing
136 Carlin Rd (13748-1533)
PHONE...................................607 762-5365
Gordie Gottlieb, *Branch Mgr*
Gordon Gottlieb, *Manager*
EMP: 75
SALES (corp-wide): 1.7B **Publicly Held**
SIC: 2752 Commercial printing, lithographic
HQ: Cadmus Journal Services, Inc.
 2901 Byrdhill Rd
 Richmond VA 23228
 804 287-5680

(G-3867)
DOLMEN
216 Broome Corporate Pkwy (13748-1506)
PHONE...................................912 596-1537
Steve Hanratty, *Principal*
EMP: 10
SALES (est): 400K **Privately Held**
SIC: 3999 Manufacturing industries

(G-3868)
E-SYSTEMS GROUP LLC (HQ)
Also Called: SMC
100 Progress Pkwy (13748-1320)
PHONE...................................607 775-1100
Diana Smith, *Transportation*
Francisco Rodriguez, *Production*
John Lion, *Buyer*
Richard Bullers, *Engineer*
Ken Overby, *Design Engr*
▲ EMP: 44 EST: 1952
SQ FT: 30,000
SALES (est): 6.4MM
SALES (corp-wide): 48.4MM **Privately Held**
WEB: www.smcplus.com
SIC: 2521 2522 5045 3571 Wood office furniture; office furniture, except wood; computers, peripherals & software; computer peripheral equipment; electronic computers; partitions & fixtures, except wood
PA: Celeritas Group, Llc
 6800 W 117th Ave
 Broomfield CO 80020
 303 465-2800

(G-3869)
INTERNATIONAL PAPER COMPANY
1240 Conklin Rd (13748-1407)
PHONE...................................607 775-1550
Don Bonualas, *Engineer*
Edward Badyna, *Manager*
EMP: 150
SALES (corp-wide): 22.3B **Publicly Held**
SIC: 2621 2653 2656 2631 Paper mills; printing paper; text paper; bristols; boxes, corrugated: made from purchased materials; food containers (liquid tight), including milk cartons; cartons, milk: made from purchased material; container, packaging & boxboard; container board; packaging board; pulp mills
PA: International Paper Company
 6400 Poplar Ave
 Memphis TN 38197
 901 419-9000

(G-3870)
IRVING WOODLANDS LLC
53 Shaw Rd (13748-1007)
PHONE...................................607 723-4862
Michael Senneway, *General Mgr*
Graham Smith, *QC Mgr*
Paul G Sherrard, *Treasurer*
EMP: 28
SQ FT: 63,350
SALES (corp-wide): 1.5B **Privately Held**
WEB: www.jdirving.com
SIC: 3441 Fabricated structural metal
HQ: Irving Woodlands Llc
 1798 St John Rd
 St John Plt ME 04743
 207 834-5767

(G-3871)
NEWSPAPER PUBLISHER LLC
Also Called: Independent Baptist Voice
1035 Conklin Rd (13748-1102)
P.O. Box 208 (13748-0208)
PHONE...................................607 775-0472
Fax: 607 775-8563
Don Einstein, *President*
EMP: 10
SQ FT: 15,000
SALES (est): 540.1K **Privately Held**
WEB: www.automarketpaper.com
SIC: 2711 2791 7011 Newspapers: publishing only, not printed on site; typesetting; bed & breakfast inn

(G-3872)
PERFORATED SCREEN SURFACES
216 Broome Corporate Pkwy (13748-1506)
PHONE...................................866 866-8690
Davis Fleming, *President*
Kurt Behrenfeld, *Info Tech Dir*
EMP: 20
SALES (est): 3.2MM **Privately Held**
SIC: 3443 Perforating on heavy metal

GEOGRAPHIC SECTION

Copiague - Suffolk County (G-3896)

(G-3873)
RELX INC
Also Called: Lexisnexis
136 Carlin Rd (13748-1533)
PHONE.....................607 772-2600
Les Howard, *Vice Pres*
James Davern, *Senior Mgr*
EMP: 110
SALES (corp-wide): 9B **Privately Held**
SIC: 2731 Book publishing
HQ: Relx Inc.
230 Park Ave
New York NY 10169
212 309-8100

(G-3874)
S & T KNITTING CO INC (PA)
Also Called: Derby Fashion Center
1010 Conklin Rd (13748-1004)
P.O. Box 1512, Binghamton (13902-1512)
PHONE.....................607 722-7558
Richard Horner, *President*
Bridgette Harvey, *Admin Sec*
EMP: 27 **EST:** 1958
SQ FT: 65,000
SALES (est): 1.9MM **Privately Held**
SIC: 2253 5651 Sweaters & sweater coats, knit; family clothing stores

(G-3875)
SAMSCREEN INC
216 Broome Corporate Pkwy (13748-1506)
PHONE.....................607 722-3979
Fax: 607 722-7128
Fintan D Fleming, *CEO*
Bobby Barry, *Production*
Ryan McCann, *Engineer*
Tony Yajko, *Cust Mgr*
Roger Doane, *Information Mgr*
◆ **EMP:** 28
SQ FT: 30,000
SALES (est): 6.7MM **Privately Held**
WEB: www.samscreen.com
SIC: 3429 Piano hardware

(G-3876)
TOOLROOM EXPRESS INC
Also Called: Four Square Tool
1010 Conklin Rd (13748-1004)
PHONE.....................607 723-5373
Richard Haddock, *President*
Shelly Haddock, *Manager*
▲ **EMP:** 55
SQ FT: 20,000
SALES (est): 11.9MM **Privately Held**
WEB: www.toolroomexpress.com
SIC: 3089 3599 Injection molding of plastics; machine shop, jobbing & repair

(G-3877)
UI ACQUISITION HOLDING CO (PA)
33 Broome Corporate Pkwy (13748-1510)
PHONE.....................607 779-7522
Jean-Luc Pelissier, *President*
Keith O'Leary, *Vice Pres*
EMP: 2
SALES (est): 145.4MM **Privately Held**
SIC: 3559 Electronic component making machinery

(G-3878)
UI HOLDING COMPANY (HQ)
33 Broome Corporate Pkwy (13748-1510)
PHONE.....................607 779-7522
Jeroen Schmits, *President*
Koen A Gieskes, *Vice Pres*
Patrick J Gillard, *CFO*
EMP: 3
SALES (est): 145.4MM **Privately Held**
SIC: 3559 Electronic component making machinery
PA: Ui Acquisition Holding Co.
33 Broome Corporate Pkwy
Conklin NY 13748
607 779-7522

(G-3879)
UNIVERSAL INSTRUMENTS CORP (DH)
33 Broome Corporate Pkwy (13748-1510)
PHONE.....................800 842-9732
Jean-Luc Pelissier, *CEO*
Lynn Tilton, *CEO*
Keith O'Leary, *CFO*

Lisa D'Angelo, *Treasurer*
Jay Smith, *Controller*
▲ **EMP:** 200 **EST:** 1919
SALES (est): 129.8MM
SALES (corp-wide): 145.4MM **Privately Held**
WEB: www3.uic.com
SIC: 3559 Electronic component making machinery
HQ: Ui Holding Company
33 Broome Corporate Pkwy
Conklin NY 13748
607 779-7522

Constantia
Oswego County

(G-3880)
BRIDGEPORT METALCRAFT INC
567 County Route 23 (13044-2737)
P.O. Box 470 (13044-0470)
PHONE.....................315 623-9597
Fax: 315 623-9145
Donald Deitz Jr, *President*
Cristy Deitz, *Vice Pres*
EMP: 5 **EST:** 1965
SQ FT: 5,000
SALES (est): 550K **Privately Held**
WEB: www.bridgeportmetalcraft.com
SIC: 3469 Spinning metal for the trade

(G-3881)
MICHAEL P MMARR
Also Called: Mike's Custom Cabinets
1358 State Route 49 (13044-2769)
P.O. Box 91 (13044-0091)
PHONE.....................315 623-9380
Fax: 315 623-7416
Michael Marr, *Owner*
Michael P Marr, *Owner*
EMP: 9
SALES (est): 325K **Privately Held**
SIC: 2434 5211 2541 Wood kitchen cabinets; cabinets, kitchen; wood partitions & fixtures

---
Coopers Plains
Steuben County

(G-3882)
CUSTOM MIX CONCRETE INC
Smith Hill Rd (14827)
PHONE.....................607 737-0281
EMP: 8
SALES (corp-wide): 8MM **Privately Held**
SIC: 3273 Ready-mixed concrete
PA: Custom Mix Concrete, Inc.
1229 Lowman Rd
Lowman NY
607 737-0281

Cooperstown
Otsego County

(G-3883)
BREWERY OMMEGANG LTD
656 County Highway 33 (13326-4737)
PHONE.....................607 286-4144
Simon Thorpe, *President*
Sean Bolger, *Store Mgr*
Phil Leinhart, *Opers Staff*
Bobbie Boehler, *QC Mgr*
Rick Debar, *Technical Mgr*
▲ **EMP:** 30
SQ FT: 35,000
SALES (est): 7.6MM **Privately Held**
WEB: www.ommegang.com
SIC: 2082 Malt beverages

(G-3884)
COOPERSTOWN BAT CO INC
118 Main St (13326-1225)
PHONE.....................607 547-2415
Fax: 607 547-6156
Timothy Haney, *Owner*
EMP: 5

SALES (corp-wide): 1.2MM **Privately Held**
WEB: www.cooperstownbat.com
SIC: 3949 5941 Sporting & athletic goods; sporting goods & bicycle shops
PA: Cooperstown Bat Co Inc
Rr 28
Fly Creek NY 13337
607 547-2415

(G-3885)
DUVEL MORTGAGE USA INC
656 County Highway 33 (13326-4737)
PHONE.....................607 267-6121
Fax: 607 544-1801
Tom Gardner, *Executive*
EMP: 5
SALES (est): 197K **Privately Held**
SIC: 2082 Malt beverages

(G-3886)
VANBERG & DEWULF CO INC
52 Pioneer St Ste 4 (13326-1231)
PHONE.....................607 547-8184
Fax: 607 547-8374
Don Feinberg, *Principal*
EMP: 8
SALES (est): 436.6K **Privately Held**
SIC: 2082 Beer (alcoholic beverage)

Copake
Columbia County

(G-3887)
HIGH VOLTAGE INC
31 County Route 7a (12516-1214)
PHONE.....................518 329-3275
Fax: 518 329-3271
Stephen S Peschel, *Ch of Bd*
Michael Peschel, *Chairman*
James Grayson, *Vice Pres*
Jim Grayson, *VP Opers*
Diane Ham, *Purch Agent*
EMP: 37
SQ FT: 23,760
SALES (est): 10MM **Privately Held**
WEB: www.hvinc.com
SIC: 3826 Analytical instruments

Copake Falls
Columbia County

(G-3888)
ALUMISEAL CORP
Also Called: C T Hogan
118 N Mountain Rd (12517-5329)
P.O. Box 60 (12517-0060)
PHONE.....................518 329-2820
Fax: 518 329-2822
James J Golden, *President*
Robert Callahan, *General Mgr*
Mary C Golden, *Corp Secy*
Gregg Miller, *Admin Sec*
EMP: 23 **EST:** 1951
SQ FT: 2,000
SALES (est): 2.1MM **Privately Held**
SIC: 3644 1711 5169 Insulators & insulation materials, electrical; refrigeration contractor; chemicals & allied products

---
Copiague
Suffolk County

(G-3889)
ACTAVIS LABORATORIES NY INC
33 Ralph Ave (11726-1532)
PHONE.....................631 693-8000
Brenton Saunders, *CEO*
EMP: 80
SALES (est): 6.6MM **Privately Held**
SIC: 2834 Pharmaceutical preparations; druggists' preparations (pharmaceuticals); medicines, capsuled or ampuled
HQ: Actavis Llc
400 Interpace Pkwy
Parsippany NJ 07054
862 261-7000

(G-3890)
ACTION MACHINED PRODUCTS INC
1355 Bangor St (11726-2911)
PHONE.....................631 842-2333
Fax: 516 842-5902
Edward G Korndoerfer, *President*
Chris Derrig, *Sales & Mktg St*
Nancy Gallagher, *Controller*
EMP: 13 **EST:** 1967
SQ FT: 8,750
SALES (est): 1.6MM **Privately Held**
SIC: 3469 Machine parts, stamped or pressed metal

(G-3891)
AJES PHARMACEUTICALS LLC
11a Lincoln St (11726-1530)
PHONE.....................631 608-1728
Cheatan Patel, *Controller*
Asha Patel,
Jatendra Patel,
▼ **EMP:** 20
SQ FT: 25,000
SALES (est): 4.6MM **Privately Held**
SIC: 2833 5499 Vitamins, natural or synthetic: bulk, uncompounded; health & dietetic food stores

(G-3892)
ARCHITECTURAL FIBERGLASS CORP
1395 Marconi Blvd (11726-2814)
P.O. Box 116 (11726-0116)
PHONE.....................631 842-4772
Fax: 516 842-4790
Charles Wittman, *President*
Aileen Carroll, *Manager*
EMP: 22
SALES (est): 2.1MM **Privately Held**
WEB: www.afcornice.com
SIC: 2295 5999 Varnished glass & coated fiberglass fabrics; fiberglass materials, except insulation

(G-3893)
ARGENCORD MACHINE CORP INC
10 Reith St (11726-1414)
PHONE.....................631 842-8990
Emilio Benenati, *Ch of Bd*
Gustavo Sanchez, *COO*
Steven Peltier, *CFO*
EMP: 7 **EST:** 1967
SQ FT: 10,000
SALES: 300K **Privately Held**
SIC: 3599 Machine shop, jobbing & repair

(G-3894)
ART PRECISION METAL PRODUCTS
1465 S Strong Ave (11726-3253)
PHONE.....................631 842-8889
Fax: 516 842-8897
Steven Triola, *President*
Sam Levine, *Business Mgr*
EMP: 10
SQ FT: 13,500
SALES (est): 1.8MM **Privately Held**
SIC: 3599 3469 3444 3544 Machine shop, jobbing & repair; spinning metal for the trade; sheet metalwork; special dies & tools

(G-3895)
ASTRA PRODUCTS INC
6 Bethpage Rd (11726-1413)
P.O. Box 479, Baldwin (11510-0479)
PHONE.....................631 464-4747
Fax: 516 868-2371
Mark Bogin, *President*
Jeffrey Bogin, *Vice Pres*
▲ **EMP:** 6 **EST:** 1979
SQ FT: 4,000
SALES: 3MM **Privately Held**
SIC: 3081 5162 Plastic film & sheet; plastics sheets & rods

(G-3896)
BALDWIN MACHINE WORKS INC
20 Grant Ave 2040 (11726-3817)
PHONE.....................631 842-9110
Kenneth Roblin, *President*
John Comporato, *Manager*
▲ **EMP:** 6

Copiague - Suffolk County (G-3897)

SQ FT: 6,000
SALES (est): 788.3K **Privately Held**
SIC: 3541 3545 Drill presses; machine tool accessories; drills (machine tool accessories); drilling machine attachments & accessories

(G-3897)
CHIVVIS ENTERPRISES INC
10 Grant St (11726-1504)
PHONE.................................631 842-9055
Fax: 516 842-7624
Floyd G Chivvis, *President*
Douglas J Chivvis, *Treasurer*
Yolanda Cudrado, *Office Mgr*
EMP: 10
SQ FT: 10,000
SALES (est): 1.6MM **Privately Held**
WEB: www.chivvisent.com
SIC: 3469 Metal stampings

(G-3898)
D & C CLEANING INC
1095 Campagnoli Ave (11726-2309)
PHONE.................................631 789-5659
Fax: 631 842-1114
Joan Estrella, *President*
EMP: 12
SALES (est): 946.3K **Privately Held**
SIC: 3635 Household vacuum cleaners

(G-3899)
ELWOOD INTERNATIONAL INC
Also Called: Elwood, William J
89 Hudson St (11726-1505)
P.O. Box 180 (11726-0180)
PHONE.................................631 842-6600
Fax: 631 842-6603
Stuart Roll, *Ch of Bd*
Richard Roll, *President*
EMP: 18
SQ FT: 37,000
SALES (est): 4.7MM **Privately Held**
WEB: www.elwoodintl.com
SIC: 2035 Seasonings & sauces, except tomato & dry

(G-3900)
ENGINEERED METAL PRODUCTS INC
10 Reith St (11726-1414)
PHONE.................................631 842-3780
Gustavo Sanchez, *President*
Michael Dantona, *Opers Mgr*
EMP: 9
SALES (est): 511.3K **Privately Held**
SIC: 3728 Aircraft parts & equipment; aircraft assemblies, subassemblies & parts

(G-3901)
GABILA & SONS MFG INC
Also Called: Gabila's Knishes
100 Wartburg Ave (11726-2919)
PHONE.................................631 789-2220
Fax: 718 384-8621
Elliott Gabay, *President*
Sophie Levy, *Chairman*
Pauline Santiago, *Controller*
EMP: 50 EST: 1921
SQ FT: 20,000
SALES (est): 8.2MM **Privately Held**
SIC: 2051 Bread, cake & related products; knishes, except frozen

(G-3902)
GABILA FOOD PRODUCTS INC
100 Wartburg Ave (11726-2919)
PHONE.................................631 789-2220
Elliot Gabay, *President*
EMP: 50
SALES: 7MM **Privately Held**
SIC: 2043 Cereal breakfast foods

(G-3903)
GLOBE GRINDING CORP
1365 Akron St (11726-2909)
PHONE.................................631 694-1970
Fax: 631 694-1886
Jeffrey Rapisarda, *President*
Robert Rapisarda, *Vice Pres*
Janette Rapisarda, *Office Mgr*
EMP: 10
SQ FT: 10,000
SALES: 2MM **Privately Held**
SIC: 3599 Machine shop, jobbing & repair

(G-3904)
H & M LEASING CORP
1245 Marconi Blvd (11726-2815)
PHONE.................................631 225-5246
Fax: 631 225-5293
Mark Field, *President*
Marc B Field, *President*
EMP: 6 EST: 1997
SALES (est): 670K **Privately Held**
SIC: 3444 Bins, prefabricated sheet metal

(G-3905)
HERMANN GERDENS INC
1725 N Strongs Rd (11726-2926)
PHONE.................................631 841-3132
Joseph Gerdens, *President*
EMP: 6
SALES (est): 772.9K **Privately Held**
SIC: 3444 Sheet metalwork

(G-3906)
HOLLYWOOD ADVERTISING BANNERS
Also Called: Hollywood Banners
539 Oak St (11726-3215)
PHONE.................................631 842-3000
Timothy Cox, *President*
EMP: 24
SALES (est): 1.1MM **Privately Held**
SIC: 2396 Fabric printing & stamping

(G-3907)
HOLLYWOOD BANNERS INC
539 Oak St (11726-3261)
PHONE.................................631 842-3000
Fax: 516 842-3148
Daniel F Mahoney, *Ch of Bd*
Carmen Laren, *Manager*
EMP: 30
SQ FT: 22,000
SALES (est): 3.4MM **Privately Held**
WEB: www.hollywoodbanners.com
SIC: 2399 Banners, made from fabric

(G-3908)
JAF CONVERTERS INC
60 Marconi Blvd (11726-2098)
PHONE.................................631 842-3131
Fax: 516 842-3185
John Flandina, *CEO*
Rudy Ruiss, *Engineer*
Claudia Ruiz, *Human Resources*
Emily Flandina, *Admin Sec*
▲ EMP: 45
SQ FT: 10,000
SALES (est): 6MM **Privately Held**
WEB: www.jafstamp.com
SIC: 3993 Signs & advertising specialties

(G-3909)
KREFAB CORPORATION
240 N Oak St (11726-1224)
PHONE.................................631 842-5151
Fax: 631 842-5156
Robert S Krenn, *President*
James Krenn, *Vice Pres*
Thomas Krenn, *Vice Pres*
EMP: 16 EST: 1959
SQ FT: 12,500
SALES: 1.5MM **Privately Held**
SIC: 2431 2521 Millwork; wood office furniture

(G-3910)
LONG ISLAND TOOL & DIE INC
1445 S Strong Ave (11726-3227)
PHONE.................................631 225-0600
Fax: 631 225-0608
Richard Cohen, *Principal*
EMP: 5
SALES (est): 396.8K **Privately Held**
SIC: 3544 Special dies & tools

(G-3911)
LUBOW MACHINE CORP
1700 N Strongs Rd (11726-2930)
PHONE.................................631 226-1700
Fax: 631 226-8701
Myron J Lubow, *President*
▲ EMP: 19 EST: 1952
SQ FT: 20,000

SALES (est): 3.5MM **Privately Held**
SIC: 3569 5084 3548 3542 Assembly machines, non-metalworking; industrial machinery & equipment; welding apparatus; machine tools, metal forming type; machine tools, metal cutting type; miscellaneous fabricated wire products

(G-3912)
MALISA BRANKO INC
95 Garfield Ave (11726-3222)
PHONE.................................631 225-9741
Fax: 631 225-2437
Branko Malisa, *President*
Regina Malisa, *Corp Secy*
EMP: 12
SQ FT: 5,600
SALES (est): 1.3MM **Privately Held**
SIC: 3599 Machine shop, jobbing & repair

(G-3913)
MARK - 10 CORPORATION
11 Dixon Ave (11726-1902)
PHONE.................................631 842-9200
Fax: 631 822-5301
William Fridman, *President*
Vera Sabov, *Manager*
EMP: 20
SQ FT: 12,000
SALES (est): 5.3MM **Privately Held**
WEB: www.mark-10.com
SIC: 3823 5084 8731 Electrolytic conductivity instruments, industrial process; industrial process control instruments; industrial machinery & equipment; electronic research

(G-3914)
METRO DYNMC SCNTIFIC INSTR LAB
80 Ralph Ave (11726-1508)
PHONE.................................631 842-4300
Steve Plaener, *President*
EMP: 15
SQ FT: 6,000
SALES (est): 1.5MM **Privately Held**
SIC: 3812 Search & navigation equipment

(G-3915)
NELL-JOY INDUSTRIES INC (PA)
8 Reith St Ste 10 (11726-1414)
PHONE.................................631 842-8989
Fax: 631 842-8040
Emilio L Benenati, *CEO*
Steven Peltier, *President*
Regina Booker, *General Mgr*
Melissa Gavin, *Controller*
Sandra Origoni, *Sales Mgr*
EMP: 32
SQ FT: 35,000
SALES (est): 3.7MM **Privately Held**
SIC: 3724 5088 Aircraft engines & engine parts; aircraft & space vehicle supplies & parts; aeronautical equipment & supplies

(G-3916)
NORJAC BOXES INC
Also Called: PATCO PACKAGING
570 Oak St (11726-3216)
PHONE.................................631 842-1300
Robert Reilly, *President*
William Mc Elwain, *Vice Pres*
Lenore Mc Knight, *Office Mgr*
EMP: 25
SQ FT: 30,000
SALES (est): 188.7K **Privately Held**
SIC: 2441 Boxes, wood

(G-3917)
NORTH EAST FINISHING CO INC
Also Called: Nefco
245 Ralph Ave (11726-1514)
PHONE.................................631 789-8000
Fax: 631 789-8094
Bill Dechirico, *President*
Donna Ward, *Corp Secy*
Joseph Ricchetti, *Vice Pres*
Chris Deangelo, *Manager*
EMP: 11
SQ FT: 7,500
SALES (est): 1.1MM **Privately Held**
SIC: 3471 Plating & polishing

(G-3918)
PIPER PLASTICS CORP
102 Ralph Ave (11726-1510)
PHONE.................................631 842-6889
Fax: 631 842-6870
Andrew Weiss, *President*
Charles Weiss, *Vice Pres*
EMP: 29
SQ FT: 16,000
SALES (est): 4.1MM **Privately Held**
WEB: www.piper-plastics.com
SIC: 3089 3479 Molding primary plastic; coating of metals with plastic or resins

(G-3919)
PRECISION ELECTRONICS INC
1 Di Tomas Ct (11726-1943)
PHONE.................................631 842-4900
Fax: 516 842-4904
Dominick Scaringella, *President*
Joseph Corrigan, *Vice Pres*
Joseph A Whalen Jr, *Treasurer*
Rita Scaringella, *Admin Sec*
EMP: 15 EST: 1955
SQ FT: 13,000
SALES: 3.5MM **Privately Held**
WEB: www.precisionelect.com
SIC: 3677 3625 3612 Coil windings, electronic; electronic transformers; relays, for electronic use; voltage regulators, transmission & distribution

(G-3920)
PROTOFAST HOLDING CORP
182 N Oak St (11726-1223)
PHONE.................................631 753-2549
Fax: 631 753-2553
Marco Gil, *President*
EMP: 6
SQ FT: 5,600
SALES (est): 700K **Privately Held**
SIC: 3444 Sheet metalwork

(G-3921)
QUALITY CANDLE MFG CO INC
121 Cedar St (11726-1201)
PHONE.................................631 842-8475
Joseph Arnone, *President*
EMP: 10 EST: 1955
SQ FT: 6,000
SALES (est): 870K **Privately Held**
WEB: www.qualitycandlecompany.com
SIC: 3999 Candles

(G-3922)
REESE MANUFACTURING INC
16 Reith St (11726-1414)
PHONE.................................631 842-3780
Emilio Benenati, *President*
Terri Martin, *Vice Pres*
EMP: 8
SALES (est): 367.8K **Privately Held**
SIC: 3728 Aircraft body assemblies & parts

(G-3923)
RIVER & SOUND PUBLICATION LLC
620 Montauk Hwy (11726-4918)
PHONE.................................631 225-7100
Bill Sherman, *Mng Member*
Linda Sherman,
EMP: 5
SALES (est): 310K **Privately Held**
WEB: www.liboating.net
SIC: 2759 Publication printing

(G-3924)
RMW FILTRATION PRODUCTS CO LLC
230 Lambert Ave (11726-3207)
P.O. Box 573, Lindenhurst (11757-0573)
PHONE.................................631 226-9412
Michael Ryan,
Lowell Ryan,
EMP: 3
SQ FT: 4,000
SALES: 2MM **Privately Held**
SIC: 3599 Machine shop, jobbing & repair

(G-3925)
SCAN-A-CHROME COLOR INC
555 Oak St (11726-3215)
PHONE.................................631 532-6146
Brian Geiger, *President*
EMP: 6

▲ = Import ▼ = Export
◆ = Import/Export

SALES (est): 698.8K **Privately Held**
SIC: 2759 7336 7389 Commercial printing; commercial art & graphic design;

(G-3926)
SEAL REINFORCED FIBERGLASS INC (PA)
19 Bethpage Rd (11726-1421)
PHONE..................................631 842-2230
Fax: 516 842-2276
Patrick Kaler, *President*
Kevin Kaler, *Vice Pres*
Timothy Kaler, *Shareholder*
Helen Kaler, *Admin Sec*
Laura Kaler, *Admin Asst*
EMP: 28 EST: 1961
SQ FT: 20,000
SALES: 3MM **Privately Held**
WEB: www.sealfiberglass.com
SIC: 3089 Plastic processing

(G-3927)
SEAL REINFORCED FIBERGLASS INC
23 Bethpage Rd (11726-1421)
PHONE..................................631 842-2230
Thomas Kaler, *Branch Mgr*
EMP: 9
SQ FT: 11,000
SALES (corp-wide): 3MM **Privately Held**
WEB: www.sealfiberglass.com
SIC: 3089 Plastic processing
PA: Seal Reinforced Fiberglass, Inc.
19 Bethpage Rd
Copiague NY 11726
631 842-2230

(G-3928)
SIGN SHOP INC
1272 Montauk Hwy (11726-4908)
PHONE..................................631 226-4145
Fax: 631 957-9338
John Prete, *President*
EMP: 6
SQ FT: 6,500
SALES: 500K **Privately Held**
WEB: www.thesignshopinc.com
SIC: 2759 7389 Screen printing; lettering & sign painting services

(G-3929)
STEEL CRAFT ROLLING DOOR
5 Di Tomas Ct (11726-1943)
PHONE..................................631 608-8662
Joan Palmieri, *General Mgr*
EMP: 10
SALES (est): 1.5MM **Privately Held**
SIC: 3325 Steel foundries

(G-3930)
SUNRISE DOOR SOLUTIONS
Also Called: Sunrise Installation
1215 Sunrise Hwy (11726-1405)
PHONE..................................631 464-4139
EMP: 5
SALES (est): 466.7K **Privately Held**
SIC: 3442 Mfg Metal Doors/Sash/Trim

(G-3931)
SWISS TOOL CORPORATION
100 Court St (11726-1287)
PHONE..................................631 842-2766
Fax: 516 842-7743
Anton Croenlein, *President*
Anna Croenlein, *Corp Secy*
EMP: 40
SQ FT: 20,000
SALES (est): 7.5MM **Privately Held**
WEB: www.swisstoolcorp.com
SIC: 3354 Aluminum extruded products

(G-3932)
TATRA MFG CORPORATION
30 Railroad Ave (11726-2717)
PHONE..................................631 691-1184
Fax: 631 691-1187
Joseph Tyminski, *President*
Lana Tyminski, *Corp Secy*
EMP: 15
SQ FT: 10,000
SALES (est): 2.5MM **Privately Held**
SIC: 3444 Sheet metalwork

(G-3933)
TII INDUSTRIES INC
1385 Akron St (11726-2932)
PHONE..................................631 789-5000
Fax: 516 789-5063
Thomas Smith, *President*
T Roach, *Principal*
Maribel Rivera, *Sales Associate*
EMP: 13
SALES (est): 992.5K **Privately Held**
SIC: 3999 Manufacturing industries

(G-3934)
TOBAY PRINTING CO INC
1361 Marconi Blvd (11726-2898)
PHONE..................................631 842-3300
Fax: 516 842-3305
Robert Rogers, *President*
Chuck Williams Jr, *General Mgr*
Jean Rogers, *Vice Pres*
Bob Rogers, *Financial Exec*
Anthony Martino, *Supervisor*
EMP: 40
SALES (est): 6.1MM **Privately Held**
WEB: www.tobayprinting.com
SIC: 2732 2752 2796 2791 Book printing; commercial printing, lithographic; platemaking services; typesetting; bookbinding & related work

(G-3935)
TRIL INC
320 Pioxi St (11726-2132)
PHONE..................................631 645-7989
Sushe Zhang, *Principal*
Xiaoling Wang, *Vice Pres*
EMP: 9
SALES (est): 770K **Privately Held**
SIC: 3841 Surgical & medical instruments

(G-3936)
VIBRATION ELIMINATOR CO INC (PA)
15 Dixon Ave (11726-1902)
PHONE..................................631 841-4000
Fax: 631 841-0020
Stuart Levy, *President*
Pat Gagliano, *Vice Pres*
Don Warick Jr, *Vice Pres*
Kevin Tur, *Manager*
▲ EMP: 17 EST: 1933
SQ FT: 13,000
SALES (est): 4.1MM **Privately Held**
WEB: www.veco-ny.com
SIC: 3625 Noise control equipment

(G-3937)
VIN MAR PRECISION METAL INC
1465 S Strong Ave (11726-3210)
PHONE..................................631 563-6608
Catherine Leo, *President*
Anthony Leo, *Vice Pres*
EMP: 15
SQ FT: 6,000
SALES (est): 1.5MM **Privately Held**
WEB: www.vin-mar.com
SIC: 3444 Sheet metalwork

(G-3938)
W A BAUM CO INC
620 Oak St (11726-3217)
P.O. Box 209 (11726-0209)
PHONE..................................631 226-3940
Fax: 631 226-3969
William A Baum Jr, *Ch of Bd*
John C Baum Sr, *President*
James M Baum, *Vice Pres*
Michael Hayes, *Vice Pres*
Margaret Faber, *Export Mgr*
▲ EMP: 80 EST: 1916
SQ FT: 31,000
SALES (est): 11.7MM **Privately Held**
WEB: www.wabaum.com
SIC: 3841 Blood pressure apparatus

(G-3939)
WORLDWIDE ARNTCAL CMPNENTS INC (PA)
10 Reith St (11726-1414)
PHONE..................................631 842-3780
Fax: 516 842-8040
Emilio L Benenati, *President*
Jacob Weingarten, *Accountant*
Selwin Mohan, *Bookkeeper*
Henry Deutsch, *Sales Mgr*
EMP: 19 EST: 1965
SQ FT: 10,000
SALES (est): 1MM **Privately Held**
WEB: www.aeronauticalcomponents.com
SIC: 3812 5088 Search & navigation equipment; aircraft equipment & supplies

(G-3940)
WORLDWIDE ARNTCAL CMPNENTS INC
Also Called: Beryllium Manufacturing
10 Reith St (11726-1414)
P.O. Box 407, Lindenhurst (11757-0407)
PHONE..................................631 842-3780
Steve Paltier, *CFO*
EMP: 6
SALES (corp-wide): 1MM **Privately Held**
WEB: www.aeronauticalcomponents.com
SIC: 3812 5088 Search & navigation equipment; transportation equipment & supplies
PA: Worldwide Aeronautical Components Inc.
10 Reith St
Copiague NY 11726
631 842-3780

Coram
Suffolk County

(G-3941)
BAYSHORE WIRE PRODUCTS CORP
480 Mill Rd (11727-4108)
PHONE..................................631 451-8825
Socratis Stavropoulos, *President*
EMP: 11
SQ FT: 11,000
SALES (est): 1.1MM **Privately Held**
SIC: 3496 Miscellaneous fabricated wire products

(G-3942)
G L 7 SALES PLUS LTD
Also Called: Land and Sea Trailer Shop
125 Middle Country Rd F (11727-4474)
PHONE..................................631 696-8290
George Applescott, *Owner*
EMP: 6
SALES (est): 532.2K **Privately Held**
SIC: 3715 Truck trailers

(G-3943)
HAMPTON TRANSPORT INC
3655 Route 112 (11727-4123)
PHONE..................................631 716-4445
Keith Lewin, *President*
EMP: 12 EST: 1993
SALES (est): 100K **Privately Held**
SIC: 2399 4119 Horse harnesses & riding crops, etc.: non-leather; local passenger transportation

(G-3944)
HUNT GRAPHICS INC
43 Pineview Ln (11727-5105)
PHONE..................................631 751-5349
Jeffrey Homire, *President*
EMP: 6
SALES (est): 1.5MM **Privately Held**
WEB: www.huntgraphics.com
SIC: 2752 7336 Commercial printing, lithographic; business form & card printing, lithographic; commercial art & graphic design

(G-3945)
ISLAND INDUSTRIES CORP
480 Mill Rd (11727-4108)
PHONE..................................631 451-8825
Fax: 631 451-8829
Socratis Stavropoulos, *President*
▲ EMP: 7
SALES (est): 920K **Privately Held**
SIC: 3315 Wire & fabricated wire products

(G-3946)
NATURES VALUE INC (PA)
468 Mill Rd (11727-4108)
PHONE..................................631 846-2500
Oscar Ramjeet, *CEO*
Carl Ramjeet, *COO*
Sharon Madramuthu, *Purchasing*
Richie Persaud, *Purchasing*
Joe Kramer, *CFO*
▲ EMP: 167
SQ FT: 224,000
SALES (est): 76.1MM **Privately Held**
WEB: www.naturesvalue.com
SIC: 2834 Vitamin preparations

(G-3947)
NEW YORK FAN COIL LLC
7 Chesapeake Bay Rd (11727-2004)
PHONE..................................646 580-1344
EMP: 5
SALES (est): 663.4K **Privately Held**
SIC: 3677 Electronic coils, transformers & other inductors

(G-3948)
NOTO INDUSTRIAL CORP
11 Thomas St (11727-3153)
PHONE..................................631 736-7600
John Noto, *President*
EMP: 7
SALES (est): 1.1MM **Privately Held**
SIC: 3535 Conveyors & conveying equipment

(G-3949)
PREMIUM MULCH & MATERIALS INC
482 Mill Rd (11727-4108)
PHONE..................................631 320-3666
Nicholas Sorge, *President*
EMP: 10
SALES (est): 68.3K **Privately Held**
SIC: 2499 Mulch or sawdust products, wood

(G-3950)
SHARONANA ENTERPRISES INC
52 Sharon Dr (11727-1923)
PHONE..................................631 875-5619
Orlando Vizcaino, *Principal*
EMP: 20
SALES: 1MM **Privately Held**
SIC: 2541 Store & office display cases & fixtures

(G-3951)
SUFFOLK INDUS RECOVERY CORP
Also Called: Pk Metals
3542 Route 112 (11727-4101)
PHONE..................................631 732-6403
Fax: 631 732-6917
Philip L Fava, *CEO*
Richard Smith, *Vice Pres*
Louis Fava, *Human Resources*
Cathy Finn, *Payroll Mgr*
EMP: 65
SALES (est): 18.3MM **Privately Held**
WEB: www.pkmetals.com
SIC: 2611 4212 Pulp mills, mechanical & recycling processing; garbage collection & transport, no disposal

---
Corfu
Genesee County

(G-3952)
BAILEY ELECTRIC MOTOR REPAIR
2186 Main Rd (14036-9650)
PHONE..................................585 542-5902
Glen Bailey, *Owner*
EMP: 8
SQ FT: 3,000
SALES (est): 540K **Privately Held**
SIC: 7694 Electric motor repair

(G-3953)
CORFU MACHINE INC (PA)
1977 Genesee St (14036-9656)
PHONE..................................585 418-4083
David Johnson, *President*
Dale Choate, *General Mgr*
Elaine Johnson, *Vice Pres*
Cary Dixson, *Director*
▲ EMP: 20 EST: 1978
SQ FT: 20,000

SALES (est): 2.9MM **Privately Held**
WEB: www.corfumachine.com
SIC: 3511 Hydraulic turbines

(G-3954)
DELAVAL INC
Also Called: Beck, Don
850 Main Rd (14036-9753)
PHONE.................................585 599-4696
Fax: 585 599-4698
Donald M Beck, *Branch Mgr*
EMP: 18
SQ FT: 8,100
SALES (corp-wide): 7.1B **Privately Held**
WEB: www.donbeckinc.com
SIC: 3556 Milk processing machinery
HQ: Delaval Inc.
   11100 N Congress Ave
   Kansas City MO 64153
   816 891-7700

(G-3955)
IDEAL BURIAL VAULT COMPANY
1166 Vision Pkwy (14036-9794)
PHONE.................................585 599-2242
George Tilley, *President*
EMP: 8 EST: 1953
SQ FT: 4,500
SALES (est): 1.2MM **Privately Held**
SIC: 3272 Burial vaults, concrete or pre-cast terrazzo

(G-3956)
KUTTERS CHEESE FACTORY INC
857 Main Rd (14036-9709)
PHONE.................................585 599-3693
Richard Kutter, *Ch of Bd*
EMP: 30 EST: 1971
SALES (est): 3.2MM **Privately Held**
SIC: 2022 Natural cheese

Corinth
Saratoga County

(G-3957)
CURTIS/PALMER HYDROELECTRIC LP
15 Pine St (12822-1319)
PHONE.................................518 654-6297
David Liebetreu, *Plant Mgr*
EMP: 7
SALES (est): 1.4MM
SALES (corp-wide): 420.2MM **Publicly Held**
SIC: 3629 Power conversion units, a.c. to d.c.: static-electric
PA: Atlantic Power Corporation
   3 Allied Dr Ste 220
   Dedham MA 02026
   617 977-2400

(G-3958)
EVERGREEN BLEACHERS INC
122 Maple St (12822-1026)
PHONE.................................518 654-9084
Louis R McArthur Jr, *Principal*
EMP: 9
SALES (est): 1.2MM **Privately Held**
SIC: 3827 Telescopic sights

(G-3959)
MANUF APPLD RENOVA SYS
Also Called: Mars
105 Mill St (12822-1090)
PHONE.................................518 654-9084
Fax: 518 654-2232
Louis McArthur, *President*
Sharon J Komsa, *Treasurer*
Doris Lohfink, *Admin Sec*
EMP: 9
SQ FT: 8,868
SALES (est): 630K **Privately Held**
WEB: www.bleacherman.com
SIC: 3599 7699 Machine shop, jobbing & repair; miscellaneous building item repair services

Corning
Steuben County

(G-3960)
CORNING CABLE SYSTEMS CR UN
1 Riverfront Plz (14831-0002)
PHONE.................................607 974-9000
Clay Franklin, *Marketing Staff*
Clark S Kinlin, *Manager*
Donna Gotshall, *Programmer Anys*
Gail Baity, *Director*
EMP: 7
SALES (corp-wide): 9.1B **Publicly Held**
SIC: 3357 Nonferrous wiredrawing & insulating
HQ: Corning Cable Systems Credit Union
   800 17th St Nw
   Hickory NC 28601
   828 327-5290

(G-3961)
CORNING INC
1 Riverfront Plz (14831-0002)
PHONE.................................607 974-9000
James R Houghton, *Ch of Bd*
Wendell P Weeks, *President*
Daiping MA, *Director*
EMP: 50
SALES (est): 5.1MM
SALES (corp-wide): 9.1B **Publicly Held**
WEB: www.corning.com
SIC: 3357 Fiber optic cable (insulated)
PA: Corning Incorporated
   1 Riverfront Plz
   Corning NY 14831
   607 974-9000

(G-3962)
CORNING INCORPORATED (PA)
1 Riverfront Plz (14831-0002)
PHONE.................................607 974-9000
Fax: 607 974-2063
Wendell P Weeks, *Ch of Bd*
James P Clappin, *President*
John Geniviva, *President*
Ann Nicholson, *Business Mgr*
Rob Vanni, *Business Mgr*
◆ EMP: 6300 EST: 1851
SALES: 9.1B **Publicly Held**
WEB: www.corning.com
SIC: 3229 3357 3661 3674 Glass fiber products; glass tubes & tubing; TV tube blanks, glass; fiber optic cable (insulated); telephone & telegraph apparatus; semiconductors & related devices

(G-3963)
CORNING INCORPORATED
Decker Bldg (14831-0001)
PHONE.................................607 974-9000
Jamie Houghton, *Branch Mgr*
EMP: 51
SALES (corp-wide): 9.1B **Publicly Held**
WEB: www.corning.com
SIC: 3229 Pressed & blown glass
PA: Corning Incorporated
   1 Riverfront Plz
   Corning NY 14831
   607 974-9000

(G-3964)
CORNING INCORPORATED
1 Riverfront Plz (14831-0002)
PHONE.................................607 974-9000
Fax: 607 974-2065
Dick Jack, *General Mgr*
EMP: 45
SALES (corp-wide): 9.1B **Publicly Held**
WEB: www.corning.com
SIC: 3229 Pressed & blown glass
PA: Corning Incorporated
   1 Riverfront Plz
   Corning NY 14831
   607 974-9000

(G-3965)
CORNING INCORPORATED
Hp-Ab-01-A9b (14831-0001)
PHONE.................................607 248-1200
Kirk Gregg, *Officer*
EMP: 48

SALES (corp-wide): 9.1B **Publicly Held**
SIC: 3229 3661 3674 3357 Glass fiber products; glass tubes & tubing; TV tube blanks, glass; telephone & telegraph apparatus; semiconductors & related devices; fiber optic cable (insulated)
PA: Corning Incorporated
   1 Riverfront Plz
   Corning NY 14831
   607 974-9000

(G-3966)
CORNING INCORPORATED
1 W Market St Ste 601 (14830-2673)
PHONE.................................607 974-4488
John Holliday, *Branch Mgr*
Katherine Funk, *Exec Dir*
Sheree Vail, *Bd of Directors*
EMP: 6
SALES (corp-wide): 9.1B **Publicly Held**
WEB: www.corning.com
SIC: 3229 Pressed & blown glass
PA: Corning Incorporated
   1 Riverfront Plz
   Corning NY 14831
   607 974-9000

(G-3967)
CORNING INCORPORATED
1 Museum Way (14830-2253)
PHONE.................................607 974-8496
Sean Keenan, *Engineer*
Rashid Rahman, *Engineer*
Bryan Cole, *Electrical Engi*
Pete Knott, *Manager*
Jon Chester, *Manager*
EMP: 20
SQ FT: 7,500
SALES (corp-wide): 9.1B **Publicly Held**
WEB: www.corning.com
SIC: 3211 Flat glass
PA: Corning Incorporated
   1 Riverfront Plz
   Corning NY 14831
   607 974-9000

(G-3968)
CORNING INTERNATIONAL CORP (HQ)
1 Riverfront Plz (14831-0002)
PHONE.................................607 974-9000
Wendell P Weeks, *CEO*
John W Loose, *Ch of Bd*
James W Wheat, *President*
Kirk P Gregg, *Vice Pres*
Kenneth C KAO, *Vice Pres*
▼ EMP: 7
SQ FT: 15,000
SALES (est): 786.3MM
SALES (corp-wide): 9.1B **Publicly Held**
WEB: www.corningware.com
SIC: 3229 Pressed & blown glass
PA: Corning Incorporated
   1 Riverfront Plz
   Corning NY 14831
   607 974-9000

(G-3969)
CORNING OPTCAL CMMNCATIONS LLC
22 W 3rd St (14830-3114)
P.O. Box 2306, Hickory NC (28603-2306)
PHONE.................................607 974-7543
Tony Tripeny, *Manager*
Sherry Derose, *Manager*
EMP: 12
SALES (corp-wide): 9.1B **Publicly Held**
WEB: www.corningcablesystems.com
SIC: 3357 Communication wire
HQ: Corning Optical Communications Llc
   800 17th St Nw
   Hickory NC 28601
   828 901-5000

(G-3970)
CORNING SPECIALTY MTLS INC
1 Riverfront Plz (14831-0002)
PHONE.................................607 974-9000
Wendell P Weeks, *Ch of Bd*
Jim Dennison, *Credit Mgr*
EMP: 8

SALES (est): 2.9MM
SALES (corp-wide): 9.1B **Publicly Held**
SIC: 3357 3229 3674 Fiber optic cable (insulated); glass fiber products; glass tubes & tubing; TV tube blanks, glass; semiconductors & related devices
PA: Corning Incorporated
   1 Riverfront Plz
   Corning NY 14831
   607 974-9000

(G-3971)
CORNING VITRO CORPORATION
Also Called: Corning Consumer Products Co
1 Riverfront Plz (14830-2556)
PHONE.................................607 974-8605
Peter Campanella, *President*
John W Loose, *President*
Hayward R Gipson, *Senior VP*
Thomas E Blumer, *Vice Pres*
Dawn M Cross, *Vice Pres*
◆ EMP: 7000
SALES (est): 228.8MM
SALES (corp-wide): 9.1B **Publicly Held**
WEB: www.corning.com
SIC: 3229 3469 Pressed & blown glass; household cooking & kitchen utensils, metal
PA: Corning Incorporated
   1 Riverfront Plz
   Corning NY 14831
   607 974-9000

(G-3972)
FT SEISMIC SUPPORT INC
70 E 1st St Ste 101 (14830-2716)
PHONE.................................607 527-8595
Melinda A Comstock, *President*
Michael Comstock, *Opers Mgr*
EMP: 130
SALES (est): 21.4MM **Privately Held**
SIC: 1382 Oil & gas exploration services

(G-3973)
GATEHOUSE MEDIA LLC
Also Called: Leader, The
34 W Pulteney St (14830-2211)
P.O. Box 1017 (14830-0817)
PHONE.................................607 936-4651
Fax: 607 936-9939
Denny Bruen, *Principal*
Jeff Kovaleski, *Editor*
Becky Jenkins, *Bookkeeper*
Bill Blake, *Manager*
Breenna Hilton, *Manager*
EMP: 85
SALES (corp-wide): 1.2B **Publicly Held**
WEB: www.the-leader.com
SIC: 2711 Newspapers
HQ: Gatehouse Media, Llc
   175 Sullys Trl Ste 300
   Pittsford NY 14534
   585 598-0030

(G-3974)
JOSEPH H NAVAIE
Also Called: Soul Full Cup
81 W Market St (14830-2526)
PHONE.................................607 936-9030
Joseph H Navaie, *Owner*
EMP: 11
SALES (est): 420K **Privately Held**
SIC: 2095 Roasted coffee

(G-3975)
KABRICS
2737 Forest Hill Dr (14830-3690)
PHONE.................................607 962-6344
Kathy Wilson, *Owner*
EMP: 8 EST: 2001
SALES: 300K **Privately Held**
SIC: 2395 Embroidery & art needlework

(G-3976)
MULTIMEDIA SERVICES INC
11136 River Rd 40 (14830-9324)
PHONE.................................607 936-3186
Fax: 607 936-3187
Richard Bartholomew, *President*
Daniel Flatt, *Vice Pres*
Rose Flatt, *Vice Pres*
Belinda Wilcox, *VP Finance*
Ralph Begeal, *Marketing Staff*
EMP: 21
SQ FT: 13,000

SALES (est): 5.4MM **Privately Held**
SIC: 2752 Commercial printing, lithographic

(G-3977)
OFFI & COMPANY
Also Called: Pure Design
60 E Market St Ste 101 (14830-2743)
PHONE.................................800 958-6334
Phillip Kirk Hobbs, *President*
Barry Nicholson, *CFO*
▲ **EMP:** 7
SQ FT: 5,600
SALES (est): 540K **Privately Held**
SIC: 2511 Children's wood furniture

(G-3978)
PANELOGIC INC
366 Baker Street Ext (14830-1639)
PHONE.................................607 962-6319
Fax: 607 936-0619
George Welch, *CEO*
Douglas Brown, *President*
Jim Cunnigham, *Engineer*
Moza Kealec, *Office Mgr*
Rich Pavlick, *Network Mgr*
EMP: 32
SQ FT: 14,500
SALES (est): 9.3MM **Privately Held**
WEB: www.panelogic.com
SIC: 3625 Relays & industrial controls; control equipment, electric; electric controls & control accessories, industrial

(G-3979)
RISING SONS 6 BREWING CO INC
Also Called: Iron Flamingo Brewery
196 Baker St (14830-2074)
P.O. Box 1064 (14830-0864)
PHONE.................................607 368-4836
Nadia Mauer, *Principal*
Mark Mauer, *Principal*
EMP: 5
SQ FT: 5,400
SALES (est): 289K **Privately Held**
SIC: 2082 Malt beverages; ale (alcoholic beverage); porter (alcoholic beverage); stout (alcoholic beverage)

(G-3980)
RYERS CREEK CORP
Also Called: Mill, The
1330 Mill Dr (14830-9020)
PHONE.................................607 523-6617
Fax: 607 523-8260
Graham Howard, *Manager*
EMP: 20
SQ FT: 7,500
SALES (est): 2.2MM **Privately Held**
WEB: www.gotothemill.com
SIC: 2499 3999 Novelties, wood fiber; tobacco pipes, pipestems & bits

(G-3981)
SIEMENS INDUSTRIES INC
23 W Market St Ste 3 (14830-2600)
PHONE.................................607 936-9512
Fax: 607 936-9551
EMP: 6
SALES (est): 585.3K **Privately Held**
SIC: 3661 Telephones & telephone apparatus

(G-3982)
STORFLEX HOLDINGS INC
Also Called: Storflex Fixture
392 Pulteney St (14830-2134)
PHONE.................................607 962-2137
Fax: 607 962-7655
Timothy Purdie, *Ch of Bd*
Ralph Santell, *Production*
Connie Santell, *Treasurer*
EMP: 152
SQ FT: 160,000
SALES (est): 41.2MM **Privately Held**
WEB: www.storflex.com
SIC: 3585 Lockers, refrigerated

(G-3983)
TOBEYCO MANUFACTURING CO INC
165 Cedar St (14830-2603)
PHONE.................................607 962-2446
Stephen Tobey, *President*
EMP: 12

SQ FT: 16,000
SALES (est): 800K **Privately Held**
SIC: 3599 Machine & other job shop work; machine shop, jobbing & repair

(G-3984)
VITRIX INC
Also Called: Vitrix Hot Glass and Crafts
77 W Market St (14830-2526)
PHONE.................................607 936-8707
Fax: 607 936-2488
Thomas Kelly, *President*
EMP: 6
SALES (est): 651K **Privately Held**
WEB: www.vitrixhotglass.com
SIC: 3231 5719 Products of purchased glass; glassware

Cornwall
Orange County

(G-3985)
ADVANCE D TECH INC
2 Mill St Stop 19 (12518-1265)
P.O. Box 38 (12518-0038)
PHONE.................................845 534-8248
Fax: 845 534-8255
Samuel Brach, *President*
Matty Wolner, *Office Mgr*
EMP: 10
SQ FT: 6,000
SALES (est): 1.5MM **Privately Held**
SIC: 3545 Diamond cutting tools for turning, boring, burnishing, etc.

(G-3986)
ASPIRE ONE COMMUNICATIONS LLC
245 Main St Ste 8 (12518-1564)
PHONE.................................201 281-2998
Steven Mandel,
EMP: 12
SQ FT: 20,000
SALES (est): 4MM **Privately Held**
SIC: 2721 8999 Magazines: publishing & printing; communication services

(G-3987)
COSTUME ARMOUR INC
Also Called: Christo-Vac
2 Mill St Stop 4 (12518-1265)
P.O. Box 85 (12518-0085)
PHONE.................................845 534-9120
Fax: 845 534-8602
Nino Novellino, *President*
Susan Truncale, *Admin Asst*
Susan Truncale, *Admin Asst*
EMP: 16 **EST:** 1962
SQ FT: 20,000
SALES (est): 1.8MM **Privately Held**
WEB: www.costumearmour.com
SIC: 2389 3999 Theatrical costumes; theatrical scenery

(G-3988)
MOMN POPS INC
13 Orr Hatch (12518-1727)
PHONE.................................845 567-0640
EMP: 25
SALES (est): 3.6MM **Privately Held**
SIC: 2064 2066 Mfg Candy/Confectionery & Chocolate/Cocoa Products

(G-3989)
NEW YORK STATE FOAM ENRGY LLC
2 Commercial Dr (12518-1484)
P.O. Box 175 (12518-0175)
PHONE.................................845 534-4656
Dennis Bender,
EMP: 8
SALES (est): 1.2MM **Privately Held**
SIC: 3086 1742 Insulation or cushioning material, foamed plastic; acoustical & insulation work

(G-3990)
NEWS OF THE HIGHLANDS INC (PA)
Also Called: Cornwall Local
35 Hasbrouck Ave (12518-1603)
P.O. Box 518 (12518-0518)
PHONE.................................845 534-7771

Fax: 845 534-3855
Constantine Eristoff, *President*
Anne Phipps Sidamon-Eristoff, *Vice Pres*
Henry J Sylvestri, *Treasurer*
EMP: 14
SALES (est): 936.7K **Privately Held**
WEB: www.newsofthehighlands.com
SIC: 2711 Newspapers, publishing & printing

(G-3991)
RANDOB LABS LTD
45 Quaker Ave Ste 207 (12518-2146)
P.O. Box 440 (12518-0440)
PHONE.................................845 534-2197
James Creagan, *President*
Daniel Creagan, *President*
Barbara Creagan, *Corp Secy*
EMP: 3
SALES (est): 2MM **Privately Held**
SIC: 2834 Pharmaceutical preparations

Cornwall On Hudson
Orange County

(G-3992)
EXECUTIVE SIGN CORP
43 Boulevard (12520-1809)
PHONE.................................212 397-4050
Isaac Goldman, *Owner*
EMP: 6
SALES (est): 250K **Privately Held**
WEB: www.executivesigncorp.com
SIC: 3993 Signs & advertising specialties

Corona
Queens County

(G-3993)
BONO SAWDUST SUPPLY CO INC
Also Called: Bono Sawdust Co
3330 127th Pl (11368-1508)
PHONE.................................718 446-1374
Fax: 718 446-6715
EMP: 6 **EST:** 1931
SQ FT: 12,000
SALES (est): 750K **Privately Held**
SIC: 2421 2842 Mfg Sawdust & Shavings

(G-3994)
CAZAR PRINTING & ADVERTISING
4215 102nd St (11368-2460)
PHONE.................................718 446-4606
Herman Cazar, *Owner*
▲ **EMP:** 5
SALES (est): 320K **Privately Held**
SIC: 2752 Commercial printing, lithographic

(G-3995)
CORONA READY MIX INC
5025 97th Pl (11368-3028)
PHONE.................................718 271-5940
Fax: 718 592-2650
Paul Melis, *President*
John Vasilantonakis, *Vice Pres*
Tommy Phillips, *Plant Mgr*
Lisa Kuchinski, *Office Mgr*
EMP: 10
SQ FT: 6,500
SALES (est): 1.5MM **Privately Held**
SIC: 3273 Ready-mixed concrete

(G-3996)
CT PUBLICATIONS CO
Also Called: Queens Times
4808 111th St (11368-2920)
PHONE.................................718 592-2196
James Lisa, *President*
EMP: 7
SALES: 240K **Privately Held**
WEB: www.queenstimes.com
SIC: 2711 Newspapers

(G-3997)
DELICIOUS FOODS INC
11202 Roosevelt Ave (11368-2624)
PHONE.................................718 446-9352

Berminder Chahal, *President*
EMP: 11
SALES (est): 1MM **Privately Held**
WEB: www.deliciousasianfood.com
SIC: 2038 2032 5812 Ethnic foods, frozen; ethnic foods: canned, jarred, etc.; caterers

(G-3998)
IMAGE IRON WORKS INC
5050 98th St (11368-3023)
PHONE.................................718 592-8276
Fax: 718 592-8786
Sigi Fredo Gomez, *President*
EMP: 8
SALES (est): 720K **Privately Held**
SIC: 3312 Hot-rolled iron & steel products

(G-3999)
JASON & JEAN PRODUCTS INC
104 Corona Ave (11368)
PHONE.................................718 271-8300
Chin Ho Kim, *President*
EMP: 10
SQ FT: 6,000
SALES (est): 710K **Privately Held**
SIC: 3999 Hair & hair-based products

(G-4000)
KENAN INTERNATIONAL TRADING
Also Called: Moo Goong Hwa
10713 Northern Blvd (11368-1235)
PHONE.................................718 672-4922
Fax: 718 672-1501
Young Kim, *Owner*
▲ **EMP:** 5
SQ FT: 6,720
SALES (est): 535.6K **Privately Held**
WEB: www.kenandigital.com
SIC: 3444 3993 2759 5999 Awnings, sheet metal; signs & advertising specialties; commercial printing; awnings

(G-4001)
MAGELLAN AEROSPACE NY INC (HQ)
9711 50th Ave (11368-2740)
P.O. Box 847256, Boston MA (02284-7256)
PHONE.................................718 699-4000
Fax: 718 592-0722
N Murray Edwards, *Ch of Bd*
John Marcello, *Ch of Bd*
James S Butyniec, *President*
Henry David, *General Mgr*
Jo-Ann Ball, *Vice Pres*
EMP: 200 **EST:** 1939
SQ FT: 205,000
SALES (est): 34.2MM
SALES (corp-wide): 738.6MM **Privately Held**
WEB: www.magellan.aero
SIC: 3728 3812 3769 3489 Aircraft parts & equipment; aircraft assemblies, sub-assemblies & parts; wing assemblies & parts, aircraft; gears, aircraft power transmission; search & navigation equipment; guided missile & space vehicle parts & auxiliary equipment; ordnance & accessories
PA: Magellan Aerospace Corporation
3160 Derry Rd E
Mississauga ON L4T 1
905 677-1889

(G-4002)
MATTRESS FACTORY
5312 104th St (11368-3222)
PHONE.................................718 760-4202
Fax: 718 760-3664
Kaston Etal, *President*
EMP: 5
SALES (est): 390K **Privately Held**
SIC: 2515 Mattresses & bedsprings

(G-4003)
MILAN PROVISION CO INC
10815 Roosevelt Ave (11368-2538)
PHONE.................................718 899-7678
Fax: 718 335-3354
Sal Laurita, *President*
EMP: 20
SQ FT: 3,000
SALES (est): 2.3MM **Privately Held**
SIC: 2013 Sausages & other prepared meats

Corona - Queens County (G-4004)

(G-4004)
MOGA TRADING COMPANY INC
57 Granger St (11368)
PHONE................................718 760-2966
Paul Cheng, *President*
EMP: 7
SALES (est): 531.4K **Privately Held**
SIC: 2392 Household furnishings

(G-4005)
RUTCARELE INC
3449 110th St (11368-1333)
PHONE................................347 830-5353
Alex Rovira, *CEO*
EMP: 8
SALES: 950K **Privately Held**
SIC: 3999 Manufacturing industries

(G-4006)
S S PRECISION GEAR & INSTR
4512 104th St (11368-2890)
PHONE................................718 457-7474
Salvatore Silvestri, *President*
Michael Silvestri, *General Mgr*
EMP: 7
SQ FT: 2,500
SALES: 500K **Privately Held**
SIC: 3545 Machine tool accessories

(G-4007)
SOLAR SCREEN CO INC
5311 105th St (11368-3297)
PHONE................................718 592-8222
Fax: 718 271-0891
Miles Joseph, *President*
Michelle Rubin, *Manager*
Gia Spencer, *Manager*
EMP: 9 EST: 1955
SQ FT: 10,000
SALES: 2MM **Privately Held**
WEB: www.solar-screen.com
SIC: 2591 Window shades

(G-4008)
TWINNY PRODUCTS INC
11145 44th Ave (11368-2640)
PHONE................................718 592-7500
Fax: 718 592-7502
Marvin Friedman, *President*
▲ EMP: 15 EST: 1955
SQ FT: 7,000
SALES (est): 500K **Privately Held**
WEB: www.twinny.com
SIC: 2392 2393 Pillows, bed: made from purchased materials; cushions, except spring & carpet: purchased materials

(G-4009)
UNITED STEEL PRODUCTS INC
3340 127th Pl (11368-1508)
PHONE................................718 478-5330
Fax: 516 779-3202
Fred Budetti, *President*
Alfred Franza, *Vice Pres*
▲ EMP: 80
SQ FT: 22,000
SALES: 9.1MM **Privately Held**
WEB: www.unitedsteelproducts.com
SIC: 3442 1542 7699 Metal doors; commercial & office building contractors; door & window repair

(G-4010)
YONG JI PRODUCTIONS INC
10219 44th Ave (11368-2430)
PHONE................................917 559-4616
Wanchang Yin, *President*
EMP: 20
SALES (est): 1.2MM **Privately Held**
SIC: 2311 Men's & boys' suits & coats

Cortland
Cortland County

(G-4011)
ACTUANT CORPORATION
Also Called: Cortland
44 River St (13045-2311)
PHONE................................607 753-8276
John Stidd, *CEO*
EMP: 47
SALES (corp-wide): 1.2B **Publicly Held**
SIC: 3593 Fluid power cylinders, hydraulic or pneumatic
PA: Actuant Corporation
N86w12500 Westbrook Xing
Menomonee Falls WI 53051
262 293-1500

(G-4012)
BESTWAY ENTERPRISES INC (PA)
3877 Luker Rd (13045-9339)
PHONE................................607 753-8261
Fax: 607 753-9948
Karl D Ochs, *CEO*
David Hayes, *Sales Mgr*
Cindy Johnson, *Office Mgr*
Michelle Kinney, *Manager*
Mark Plouffe, *Director*
EMP: 50
SQ FT: 200,000
SALES (est): 59.8MM **Privately Held**
SIC: 2491 5031 Structural lumber & timber, treated wood; building materials, exterior

(G-4013)
BESTWAY OF NEW YORK INC
3877 Luker Rd (13045-9385)
PHONE................................607 753-8261
Karl D Ochs, *President*
EMP: 1
SALES (est): 7.5MM
SALES (corp-wide): 59.8MM **Privately Held**
SIC: 2491 Structural lumber & timber, treated wood
PA: Bestway Enterprises Inc.
3877 Luker Rd
Cortland NY 13045
607 753-8261

(G-4014)
BFMA HOLDING CORPORATION
37 Huntington St (13045-3096)
PHONE................................607 753-6746
Barry W Florescue, *Ch of Bd*
Sue Vanbuskirk, *Executive Asst*
EMP: 9
SQ FT: 3,000
SALES (est): 1.1MM **Privately Held**
SIC: 2841 5122 5131 5139 Soap: granulated, liquid, cake, flaked or chip; toiletries; sewing accessories; shoe accessories; display equipment, except refrigerated; packaging & labeling services

(G-4015)
BORGWARNER MORSE TEC INC
3690 Luker Rd (13045-9397)
PHONE................................607 257-6700
Roger Wood, *Branch Mgr*
EMP: 90
SALES (corp-wide): 8B **Publicly Held**
WEB: www.borgwarnermorsetec.com
SIC: 3714 Motor vehicle parts & accessories
HQ: Borgwarner Morse Tec Inc.
800 Warren Rd
Ithaca NY 14850
607 257-6700

(G-4016)
BP DIGITAL IMAGING LLC
Also Called: Carbon Copies
87 Main St (13045-2610)
P.O. Box 5396 (13045-5396)
PHONE................................607 753-0022
Fax: 607 753-0026
Betsy Allen, *Mng Member*
Jeff Czimmer, *Technology*
Jim Coon, *Graphic Designe*
Paul Allen,
▼ EMP: 8
SQ FT: 1,800
SALES: 500K **Privately Held**
SIC: 2752 Photolithographic printing

(G-4017)
CORTLAND COMPANY INC (HQ)
44 River St (13045-2311)
P.O. Box 330 (13045-0330)
PHONE................................607 753-8276
Fax: 607 753-3183
John A Stidd, *CEO*

John Thomas, *President*
Sam Bull, *Vice Pres*
John G Greco, *Vice Pres*
Steve Davis, *Plant Mgr*
EMP: 134
SALES (est): 41.5MM
SALES (corp-wide): 1.2B **Publicly Held**
WEB: www.actuant.com
SIC: 2298 5063 Ropes & fiber cables; wire & cable; electronic wire & cable
PA: Actuant Corporation
N86w12500 Westbrook Xing
Menomonee Falls WI 53051
262 293-1500

(G-4018)
CORTLAND LINE MFG LLC
3736 Kellogg Rd (13045-8818)
PHONE................................607 756-2851
Randy Brown, *President*
Ralph Canfield, *CFO*
EMP: 30
SALES (est): 2MM **Privately Held**
SIC: 3949 Fishing equipment

(G-4019)
CORTLAND MACHINE AND TOOL CO
60 Grant St (13045-2173)
P.O. Box 27 (13045-0027)
PHONE................................607 756-5852
Fax: 607 756-5985
Stan Pierce, *President*
Debbie Hoyt, *Human Res Mgr*
Scott Rogers, *Technology*
EMP: 11 EST: 1913
SQ FT: 10,000
SALES: 900K **Privately Held**
SIC: 3599 Machine shop, jobbing & repair

(G-4020)
CORTLAND PLASTICS INTL LLC
211 S Main St (13045-3284)
PHONE................................607 662-0120
David Kievit, *General Mgr*
Harlen Desotell, *Prdtn Mgr*
Fritz Kern, *Engineer*
Kay Breed, *Controller*
Christine Leyburn, *Office Mgr*
EMP: 26
SALES (est): 5.6MM **Privately Held**
SIC: 3085 Plastics bottles

(G-4021)
CORTLAND READY MIX INC
6 Locust Ave Ofc Rte 13 (13045-1412)
PHONE................................607 753-3063
Fax: 607 753-8719
Michael Saunders, *President*
Jim Giddings, *Plant Mgr*
Dick Maloney, *Controller*
EMP: 12 EST: 1944
SQ FT: 4,000
SALES: 200K
SALES (corp-wide): 8.7MM **Privately Held**
WEB: www.saundersconcrete.com
SIC: 3273 Ready-mixed concrete
PA: Saunders Concrete Co. Inc.
5126 S Onondaga Rd
Nedrow NY 13120
315 469-3217

(G-4022)
CORTLAND STANDARD PRINTING CO
110 Main St (13045-6607)
P.O. Box 5548 (13045-5548)
PHONE................................607 756-5665
Fax: 607 756-5665
Kevin R Howe, *President*
Kevin Conlon, *Editor*
Scott Conroe, *Editor*
Katie Hall, *Editor*
F M Catalano, *Chief*
EMP: 65 EST: 1867
SQ FT: 15,000
SALES (est): 4.3MM **Privately Held**
WEB: www.cortlandstandard.com
SIC: 2711 2791 Newspapers; typesetting

(G-4023)
COUTURE LOGGING INC
3060 State Route 13 (13045-9743)
PHONE................................607 753-6445
Lisa Couture, *President*

Bruno Couture, *Vice Pres*
EMP: 9
SQ FT: 5,100
SALES (est): 728.8K **Privately Held**
SIC: 2411 Logging camps & contractors

(G-4024)
CROWN INDUSTRIAL
839 State Route 13 (13045-8997)
PHONE................................607 745-8709
Kevin Patterson, *General Mgr*
▲ EMP: 7
SALES (est): 1MM **Privately Held**
SIC: 3462 Gear & chain forgings

(G-4025)
EATON ELECTRIC HOLDINGS LLC
45 Cleveland St (13045-2399)
PHONE................................607 756-2821
William Cain, *Engineer*
John F Englebrecht, *Engineer*
Kathie O'Mara, *Branch Mgr*
Lyn Bethea, *Manager*
Dan Gretsch, *Manager*
EMP: 125 **Privately Held**
WEB: www.cooperus.com
SIC: 3462 3494 3469 3429 Iron & steel forgings; valves & pipe fittings; metal stampings; manufactured hardware (general); galvanizing lines (rolling mill equipment)
HQ: Eaton Electric Holdings Llc
600 Travis St Ste 5600
Houston TX 77002
713 209-8400

(G-4026)
FORKEY CONSTRUCTION & FABG INC
3690 Luker Rd (13045-9397)
PHONE................................607 849-4879
Fax: 607 849-4882
Charles Forkey, *President*
Borey Bliss, *Manager*
EMP: 30
SQ FT: 27,000
SALES (est): 9MM **Privately Held**
SIC: 3469 Machine parts, stamped or pressed metal

(G-4027)
GRAPH-TEX INC
46 Elm St (13045-2225)
P.O. Box 109 (13045-0109)
PHONE................................607 756-7791
Brent Riley, *President*
Donna Lee, *General Mgr*
Shawn Riley, *Director*
EMP: 10
SALES (corp-wide): 3.1MM **Privately Held**
WEB: www.graph-tex.com
SIC: 2759 Screen printing
PA: Graph-Tex, Inc.
24 Court St
Cortland NY 13045
607 756-1875

(G-4028)
GRAPH-TEX INC (PA)
24 Court St (13045-2685)
P.O. Box 109 (13045-0109)
PHONE................................607 756-1875
Fax: 607 756-5479
Brent Riley, *President*
Mindy Myers, *Store Mgr*
Donna Lee, *Office Mgr*
EMP: 8
SQ FT: 3,600
SALES (est): 3.1MM **Privately Held**
WEB: www.graph-tex.com
SIC: 2759 5941 5091 Screen printing; sporting goods & bicycle shops; sporting & recreation goods

(G-4029)
GRAPHICS PLUS PRINTING INC
215 S Main St (13045-3266)
PHONE................................607 299-0500
Fax: 607 753-0115
Robert Eckard, *President*
Patty Batsford, *Marketing Staff*
EMP: 24
SQ FT: 47,000

SALES (est): 5.6MM **Privately Held**
SIC: 2752 2759 7336 Commercial printing, offset; screen printing; art design services

(G-4030)
GUTCHESS LUMBER CO INC (PA)
890 Mclean Rd (13045-9393)
PHONE..................................607 753-3393
Fax: 607 753-6234
Gary H Gutchess, *Ch of Bd*
Matthew F Gutchess, *Vice Pres*
Andrew Middleton, *Plant Mgr*
Jeffrey D Breed, *Treasurer*
Linda Luther, *Manager*
▼ **EMP:** 250 **EST:** 1904
SQ FT: 3,500
SALES (est): 72.5MM **Privately Held**
WEB: www.gutchess.com
SIC: 2421 2426 Building & structural materials, wood; lumber, hardwood dimension

(G-4031)
JM MURRAY CENTER INC (PA)
823 State Route 13 Ste 1 (13045-8731)
PHONE..................................607 756-9913
Floyd Moon, *President*
Jerry Gebhard, *General Mgr*
Judy O Brien, *Vice Pres*
Dale Davis, *Vice Pres*
Gerald Gebhard, *Vice Pres*
▲ **EMP:** 110
SQ FT: 110,000
SALES: 17.8MM **Privately Held**
WEB: www.jmmurray.com
SIC: 2673 3843 7349 Bags: plastic, laminated & coated; dental equipment & supplies; building maintenance services

(G-4032)
JM MURRAY CENTER INC
4057 West Rd (13045-1637)
PHONE..................................607 756-0246
Judy O'Brien, *Branch Mgr*
EMP: 110
SALES (corp-wide): 17.8MM **Privately Held**
WEB: www.jmmurray.com
SIC: 2673 3843 7349 Bags: plastic, laminated & coated; dental equipment & supplies; building maintenance services
PA: J.M. Murray Center, Inc.
823 State Route 13 Ste 1
Cortland NY 13045
607 756-9913

(G-4033)
MARIETTA CORPORATION (HQ)
37 Huntington St (13045-3098)
P.O. Box 5250 (13045-5250)
PHONE..................................607 753-6746
Fax: 607 756-0648
Donald W Sturdivant, *CEO*
Eileen Anderson, *COO*
Chris Calhoun, *Senior VP*
Beth Corl, *Senior VP*
Ray Ferretti, *Senior VP*
♦ **EMP:** 500
SQ FT: 550,000
SALES (est): 334MM
SALES (corp-wide): 340MM **Privately Held**
SIC: 2844 2834 2541 Cosmetic preparations; toilet preparations; druggists' preparations (pharmaceuticals); store & office display cases & fixtures
PA: Marietta Holding Corporation, Inc.
37 Huntington St
Cortland NY 13045
607 753-6746

(G-4034)
MARIETTA CORPORATION
106 Central Ave (13045)
PHONE..................................607 753-0982
Greg Rudy, *Branch Mgr*
EMP: 350
SALES (corp-wide): 340MM **Privately Held**
SIC: 2841 7389 Soap: granulated, liquid, cake, flaked or chip; packaging & labeling services

HQ: Marietta Corporation
37 Huntington St
Cortland NY 13045
607 753-6746

(G-4035)
PALL CORPORATION
Also Called: Pall Trinity Micro
3643 State Route 281 (13045-3591)
P.O. Box 2030 (13045-0930)
PHONE..................................607 753-6041
Fax: 607 753-9653
David Berger, *President*
Steven Chisolm, *Vice Pres*
Douglas Conn, *Vice Pres*
Carl Boise, *Opers Staff*
Bob Connor, *Engineer*
EMP: 750
SALES (corp-wide): 20.5B **Publicly Held**
WEB: www.pall.com
SIC: 3842 3841 3569 3599 Surgical appliances & supplies; surgical & medical instruments; IV transfusion apparatus; filters; filters, general line: industrial; filter elements, fluid, hydraulic line; air intake filters, internal combustion engine, except auto; gasoline filters, internal combustion engine, except auto; oil filters, internal combustion engine, except automotive; filters: oil, fuel & air, motor vehicle; perforated metal, stamped
HQ: Pall Corporation
25 Harbor Park Dr
Port Washington NY 11050
516 484-5400

(G-4036)
PALL CORPORATION
3669 State Route 281 (13045-8957)
PHONE..................................607 753-6041
Jim Bair, *Research*
Angela Griffin, *Engineer*
Ruth A Wood, *Engineer*
Brian Palermo, *Design Engr*
Jacques Joseph, *Branch Mgr*
EMP: 750
SALES (corp-wide): 20.5B **Publicly Held**
WEB: www.pall.com
SIC: 3842 Surgical appliances & supplies
HQ: Pall Corporation
25 Harbor Park Dr
Port Washington NY 11050
516 484-5400

(G-4037)
PALL CORPORATION
Also Called: Pall's Advnced Sprtons Systems
839 State Route 13 Ste 12 (13045-8998)
P.O. Box 2030 (13045-0930)
PHONE..................................607 753-6041
Carl Boise, *Opers Staff*
Lance Benjamin, *Engineer*
Brian Keefer, *Manager*
Nile Stocum, *Technical Staff*
Pam Wright,
EMP: 750
SALES (corp-wide): 20.5B **Publicly Held**
SIC: 3842 Surgical appliances & supplies
HQ: Pall Corporation
25 Harbor Park Dr
Port Washington NY 11050
516 484-5400

(G-4038)
PALL TRINITY MICRO CORPORATION
Also Called: Pall Well Technology Div
3643 State Route 281 (13045-3591)
P.O. Box 2030 (13045-0930)
PHONE..................................607 753-6041
Fax: 607 756-5559
Glen Petaja, *Senior VP*
Dean Johnson, *Engineer*
Chris Montreuil, *Engineer*
Jonas Rodriguez, *Electrical Engi*
Don Bordoni, *Controller*
▲ **EMP:** 600 **EST:** 1961
SALES (est): 150.5MM
SALES (corp-wide): 20.5B **Publicly Held**
WEB: www.pall.com
SIC: 3677 Filtration devices, electronic
HQ: Pall Corporation
25 Harbor Park Dr
Port Washington NY 11050
516 484-5400

(G-4039)
PAUL BUNYAN PRODUCTS INC
890 Mclean Rd (13045-9393)
PHONE..................................315 696-6164
Fax: 315 696-6649
Judith Greene, *President*
Margaret Hudson, *Corp Secy*
William Oustad, *Vice Pres*
EMP: 20
SQ FT: 36,000
SALES (est): 3.8MM **Privately Held**
SIC: 2448 Pallets, wood

(G-4040)
PRECISION EFORMING LLC
839 State Route 13 Ste 1 (13045-8999)
PHONE..................................607 753-7730
Jodi Marie, *Export Mgr*
Scott Selbach,
Doug Ondrack,
EMP: 13
SQ FT: 7,000
SALES (est): 1.8MM **Privately Held**
WEB: www.precisioneforming.com
SIC: 3542 Electroforming machines

(G-4041)
PYROTEK INCORPORATED
641 State Route 13 (13045-8836)
PHONE..................................607 756-3050
Thomas Howard, *Manager*
Dave Quilter, *Manager*
EMP: 97
SALES (corp-wide): 632.7MM **Privately Held**
SIC: 3365 Aluminum foundries
PA: Pyrotek Incorporated
705 W 1st Ave
Spokane WA 99201
509 926-6212

(G-4042)
QUADRA FLEX CORP
Also Called: Quadra Flex Quality Labels
1955 State Route 13 (13045-9619)
P.O. Box 286 (13045-0286)
PHONE..................................607 758-7066
Fax: 607 758-4943
David Masri, *President*
Christopher Meddaugh, *General Mgr*
Thresa Meddaugh, *Treasurer*
Ben Masri, *Director*
Elizabeth Masri, *Admin Sec*
EMP: 5
SQ FT: 2,500
SALES: 700K **Privately Held**
WEB: www.quadraflex.com
SIC: 2759 2679 Commercial printing; labels, paper: made from purchased material

(G-4043)
REDDING-HUNTER INC
Also Called: Redding Reloading Equipment
1089 Starr Rd (13045-8806)
PHONE..................................607 753-3331
Fax: 607 756-8445
Richard W Beebe, *President*
Robin Sharpless, *VP Sales*
EMP: 25 **EST:** 1946
SQ FT: 15,000
SALES (est): 5MM **Privately Held**
WEB: www.redding-reloading.com
SIC: 3484 3599 Small arms; machine shop, jobbing & repair

(G-4044)
SAUNDERS CONCRETE CO INC
Also Called: Cortland Ready Mix
6 Locust Ave (13045-1412)
PHONE..................................607 756-7905
Wilbur Hayes, *Manager*
EMP: 15
SALES (corp-wide): 8.7MM **Privately Held**
SIC: 3273 Ready-mixed concrete
PA: Saunders Concrete Co. Inc.
5126 S Onondaga Rd
Nedrow NY 13120
315 469-3217

(G-4045)
SELLCO INDUSTRIES INC
58 Grant St (13045-2174)
P.O. Box 70 (13045-0070)
PHONE..................................607 756-7594

Fax: 607 756-7511
George Delorenzo Jr, *President*
Marilyn De Lorenzo, *Vice Pres*
EMP: 20
SQ FT: 19,000
SALES (est): 2.3MM **Privately Held**
WEB: www.sellcoinc.com
SIC: 3993 2782 2399 2396 Signs & advertising specialties; looseleaf binders & devices; banners, made from fabric; automotive & apparel trimmings

(G-4046)
SUIT-KOTE CORPORATION (PA)
1911 Lorings Crossing Rd (13045-9775)
PHONE..................................607 753-1100
Fax: 607 756-8611
Frank H Suits Jr, *President*
Steve Sanfilippo, *Regional Mgr*
Scott Harris, *Vice Pres*
Dan Quinlan, *Vice Pres*
Steve Rebman, *Vice Pres*
▲ **EMP:** 200
SQ FT: 10,000
SALES (est): 278.7MM **Privately Held**
WEB: www.suit-kote.com
SIC: 2951 1611 Asphalt & asphaltic paving mixtures (not from refineries); highway & street paving contractor

(G-4047)
WILBEDONE INC
1133 State Route 222 (13045-9352)
PHONE..................................607 756-8813
Fax: 607 756-8818
Thomas L Beames, *President*
Diana Simpson, *Human Resources*
David Motyl, *Manager*
EMP: 33
SQ FT: 18,000
SALES (est): 4.8MM **Privately Held**
WEB: www.wilbedone.com
SIC: 2541 Counter & sink tops

Cortlandt Manor
Westchester County

(G-4048)
ABLE INDUSTRIES INC
Also Called: Able Wire Co
18 Brook Ln (10567-6502)
PHONE..................................914 739-5685
Warren Button, *President*
Louis Malano, *Sales Staff*
Patricia Button, *Admin Sec*
▲ **EMP:** 12 **EST:** 1980
SQ FT: 18,000
SALES (est): 1.1MM **Privately Held**
WEB: www.ablewire.com
SIC: 3315 Wire, steel: insulated or armored

(G-4049)
DURANM INC
101 Dale Ave (10567-1617)
PHONE..................................914 774-3367
Martin F Duran, *CEO*
EMP: 5
SALES (est): 633.3K **Privately Held**
SIC: 3272 Floor slabs & tiles, precast concrete

(G-4050)
ELMSFORD SHEET METAL WORKS INC
23 Arlo Ln (10567-2631)
PHONE..................................914 739-6300
Donald J Trier, *President*
Mark Dipasquale, *Vice Pres*
EMP: 75 **EST:** 1950
SQ FT: 24,000
SALES: 14MM
SALES (corp-wide): 4.4B **Publicly Held**
WEB: www.elmsfordsheetmetal.com
SIC: 3444 Sheet metalwork
HQ: Talen Energy Services Northeast, Inc
50 Inwood Rd Ste 3
Rocky Hill CT 06067
860 513-1036

Cortlandt Manor - Westchester County (G-4051)

(G-4051)
GC MOBILE SERVICES INC
Also Called: G C Mobile Svces
32 William Puckey Dr (10567-6216)
PHONE..................914 736-9730
Garth Cooperman, *President*
EMP: 6
SALES: 250K **Privately Held**
SIC: 7692 Welding repair

(G-4052)
MINES PRESS INC
231 Croton Ave (10567-5284)
PHONE..................914 788-1800
Fax: 914 788-1698
Steven Mines, *Ch of Bd*
Daniel Mines, *Ch of Bd*
Cynthia Mines, *Corp Secy*
Carl Hutt, *CFO*
Bernadetta Depinna, *Bookkeeper*
▲ EMP: 115 EST: 1933
SQ FT: 100,000
SALES (est): 34.1MM **Privately Held**
WEB: www.minespress.com
SIC: 2752 2759 2789 2791 Commercial printing, offset; letterpress printing; gold stamping on books; typesetting

(G-4053)
PRONTO PRINTER
2085 E Main St Ste 3 (10567-2616)
PHONE..................914 737-0800
Fax: 914 737-4921
John P Marvin, *Owner*
EMP: 6 EST: 1974
SQ FT: 7,000
SALES: 650K **Privately Held**
SIC: 2752 Photo-offset printing

(G-4054)
TERRACE MANAGEMENT INC
Also Called: Colonial Terrace Hotel
119 Oregon Rd (10567-1200)
P.O. Box 142, Peekskill (10566-0142)
PHONE..................914 737-0400
Sheila Drogy, *President*
Alan Drogy, *Vice Pres*
EMP: 25
SALES (est): 3.4MM **Privately Held**
SIC: 2099 Food preparations

Cossayuna
Washington County

(G-4055)
FRONHOFER TOOL COMPANY INC
4197 County Rd 48 (12823)
P.O. Box 84 (12823-0084)
PHONE..................518 692-2496
Fax: 518 692-2450
Paul Fronhofer II, *Ch of Bd*
Kyle Fronhofer, *Vice Pres*
Heidi Grissin, *Manager*
EMP: 30
SQ FT: 10,000
SALES: 5MM **Privately Held**
WEB: www.fronhofertool.com
SIC: 3545 Tools & accessories for machine tools

Coxsackie
Greene County

(G-4056)
DUCOMMUN AEROSTRUCTURES NY INC
171 Stacey Rd (12051-2613)
PHONE..................518 731-2791
Michael D Grosso, *CEO*
Anthony J Reardon, *Ch of Bd*
Hugh J Quigley, *President*
Paul Burton, *Vice Pres*
Rose Rogers, *VP Human Res*
EMP: 270
SQ FT: 65,000
SALES (est): 60.8MM
SALES (corp-wide): 666MM **Publicly Held**
WEB: www.dynabil.com
SIC: 3728 Aircraft parts & equipment
HQ: Ducommun Aerostructures, Inc.
268 E Gardena Blvd
Gardena CA 90248
310 380-5390

Cranberry Lake
St. Lawrence County

(G-4057)
FORM A ROCKLAND PLASTICS INC
7152 Main St (12927)
P.O. Box 670 (12927-0670)
PHONE..................315 848-3300
Donald Lashomb II, *President*
Cynthia Whitmore Lashomb, *Treasurer*
EMP: 5 EST: 1963
SQ FT: 6,000
SALES (est): 623.7K **Privately Held**
SIC: 3089 3172 Plastic containers, except foam; key cases

Croghan
Lewis County

(G-4058)
FARNEY TREE & EXCAVATION LLC
7610 Yousey Rd (13327-2705)
P.O. Box 6597, Watertown (13601-6597)
PHONE..................315 783-1161
John Farney, *Principal*
EMP: 8
SALES (est): 807.5K **Privately Held**
SIC: 2411 Logging

(G-4059)
GRAND SLAM SAFETY LLC
9793 S Bridge St (13327-2329)
P.O. Box 35 (13327-0035)
PHONE..................315 766-7008
Robert K Lyndaker, *President*
Robert Chamberlain,
Mick Lehman,
David Moore,
EMP: 6
SALES: 300K **Privately Held**
SIC: 3949 Sporting & athletic goods

Cropseyville
Rensselaer County

(G-4060)
R J VALENTE GRAVEL INC
3349 Rte 2 (12052)
PHONE..................518 279-1001
Tim Banks, *Branch Mgr*
EMP: 29
SALES (corp-wide): 26.2MM **Privately Held**
SIC: 1442 Construction sand & gravel
PA: R. J. Valente Gravel, Inc.
118 Button Rd
Waterford NY 12188
518 432-4470

Croton Falls
Westchester County

(G-4061)
GARY STOCK CORPORATION
597 Rte 22 (10519)
P.O. Box 609 (10519-0609)
PHONE..................914 276-2700
Fax: 914 276-2941
Gary Stock, *President*
EMP: 7
SALES (est): 630K **Privately Held**
WEB: www.gstockco.com
SIC: 2759 Promotional printing

Croton On Hudson
Westchester County

(G-4062)
BLUE PIG ICE CREAM FACTORY
121 Maple St (10520-2538)
PHONE..................914 271-3850
Julia Horowitz, *Owner*
EMP: 5
SALES: 250K **Privately Held**
SIC: 2024 5812 Ice cream & frozen desserts; ice cream stands or dairy bars

(G-4063)
GENERAL SPLICE CORPORATION
Hwy 129 (10520)
PHONE..................914 271-5131
Fax: 914 271-2665
Ralph Milano, *President*
Nicole Milano, *Treasurer*
EMP: 6
SQ FT: 7,000
SALES (est): 878.8K **Privately Held**
SIC: 3535 Conveyors & conveying equipment

(G-4064)
HEALTHY N FIT INTL INC
435 Yorktown Rd (10520-3703)
PHONE..................914 271-6040
Fax: 914 271-6042
Robert Sepe Jr, *Ch of Bd*
Irene Sepe, *Vice Pres*
EMP: 13 EST: 1976
SALES (est): 4.4MM **Privately Held**
SIC: 2833 5122 Vitamins, natural or synthetic: bulk, uncompounded; vitamins & minerals

(G-4065)
NK ELECTRIC LLC
22 Scenic Dr (10520-1848)
P.O. Box 171 (10520-0171)
PHONE..................914 271-0222
Fax: 914 271-0223
James Brophy, *Principal*
EMP: 7
SALES (est): 1MM **Privately Held**
SIC: 3699 Electrical equipment & supplies

(G-4066)
VERY BEST IRTJ
435 Yorktown Rd (10520-3703)
PHONE..................914 271-6585
Robert Supe, *President*
EMP: 15
SALES (est): 1.3MM **Privately Held**
SIC: 2834 Vitamin preparations

Crown Point
Essex County

(G-4067)
MOUNTAIN FOREST PRODUCTS INC
3281 Nys Route 9n (12928-2405)
PHONE..................518 597-3674
Kevin Mero, *President*
Vicki Mero, *Corp Secy*
EMP: 6
SQ FT: 1,152
SALES (est): 733.8K **Privately Held**
SIC: 2411 Logging

Cuba
Allegany County

(G-4068)
D F STAUFFER BISCUIT CO INC
8670 Farnsworth Rd (14727-9720)
PHONE..................585 968-2700
Fax: 716 968-2722
Jim Clubine, *Senior Engr*
Maria Defaria, *Human Res Mgr*
Jeff Howard, *Manager*
Dawn Snyder, *Manager*
Larry Chandler, *Maintence Staff*
EMP: 50
SALES (corp-wide): 10.4B **Privately Held**
WEB: www.stauffers.net
SIC: 2052 Cookies
HQ: D F Stauffer Biscuit Co Inc
360 S Belmont St
York PA 17403
717 815-4600

(G-4069)
EMPIRE CHEESE INC
4520 County Road 6 (14727-9598)
PHONE..................585 968-1552
Fax: 585 968-2660
Gary Vanic, *CEO*
John Epprecht, *Corp Secy*
Russell Mullins, *Vice Pres*
Loren Sweet, *Transptn Dir*
Thomas Eastham, *Plant Mgr*
EMP: 175
SQ FT: 100,000
SALES (est): 92.8MM
SALES (corp-wide): 1.3B **Privately Held**
WEB: www.empirecheese.com
SIC: 2022 Cheese, natural & processed
PA: Great Lakes Cheese Co., Inc.
17825 Great Lakes Pkwy
Hiram OH 44234
440 834-2500

(G-4070)
SPS MEDICAL SUPPLY CORP
Also Called: Sterilator Company
31 Water St Ste 1 (14727-1030)
PHONE..................585 968-2377
Fax: 585 359-0167
Shawn Doyle, *Branch Mgr*
EMP: 10
SALES (corp-wide): 664.7MM **Publicly Held**
SIC: 3842 3821 Sterilizers, hospital & surgical; autoclaves, laboratory
HQ: Sps Medical Supply Corp.
6789 W Henrietta Rd
Rush NY 14543
585 359-0130

Cutchogue
Suffolk County

(G-4071)
DI BORGHESE CASTELLO LLC
17150 County Road 48 (11935-1041)
P.O. Box 957 (11935-0957)
PHONE..................631 734-5111
Marco Borghese, *Mng Member*
EMP: 10
SALES (est): 780.6K **Privately Held**
WEB: www.castellodiborghese.com
SIC: 2084 Wines, brandy & brandy spirits

(G-4072)
PELLEGRINI VINEYARDS LLC
23005 Main Rd (11935-1331)
PHONE..................631 734-4111
Fax: 631 734-4159
Rita Pellegrini, *Partner*
Robert Pellegrini, *Partner*
Joyce Pellegrini, *Vice Pres*
EMP: 5
SALES (est): 555.8K **Privately Held**
WEB: www.pellegrinivineyards.com
SIC: 2084 Wines

(G-4073)
PUGLIESE VINEYARDS INC
34515 Main Rd Rr 25 (11935)
P.O. Box 467 (11935-0467)
PHONE..................631 734-4057
Patricia Pugliese, *President*
EMP: 5
SALES (est): 460K **Privately Held**
WEB: www.pugliesevineyards.com
SIC: 2084 Wines

(G-4074)
VEDELL NORTH FORK LLC
Also Called: Corey Creek Vineyards
36225 Main Rd (11935-1346)
PHONE..................631 323-3526
Peggy Lauber,
Jean Partridge,
EMP: 7

SALES (est): 590K **Privately Held**
SIC: **2084** Wines

Dansville
Livingston County

(G-4075)
AMERICAN MOTIVE POWER INC
9431 Foster Wheeler Rd (14437-9178)
PHONE...................................585 335-3132
Lawrence Mehlenbacher, *CEO*
Richard Tamborski, *President*
Fred Olinger, *General Mgr*
Richard Rizzieri, *General Mgr*
Frank Larkin, *Exec VP*
EMP: 20
SALES (est): 4MM **Privately Held**
WEB: www.magnetech.com
SIC: **3743** Lubrication systems, locomotive

(G-4076)
DANSVILLE LOGGING & LUMBER
10903 State Route 36 (14437-9444)
PHONE...................................585 335-5879
Fax: 585 335-8089
Timothy Rauber, *President*
EMP: 23
SQ FT: 900
SALES (est): 1.4MM **Privately Held**
SIC: **2421** Lumber: rough, sawed or planed

(G-4077)
GPM ASSOCIATES LLC
Also Called: Forbes Products
10 Forbes St (14437-9268)
PHONE...................................585 335-3940
Fax: 585 335-7285
Ron Van Duyne, *Engineer*
Nancy Barrett, *Human Res Mgr*
Elroy Power, *Manager*
Mark McDermott,
EMP: 20
SALES (corp-wide): 15.8MM **Privately Held**
SIC: **2782** 3089 2752 2393 Blankbooks & looseleaf binders; novelties, plastic; commercial printing, lithographic; textile bags
PA: Gpm Associates Llc
45 High Tech Dr
Rush NY 14543
585 334-4800

(G-4078)
JUST IN TIME CNC MACHINING
88 Ossian St (14437-9101)
PHONE...................................585 335-2010
Kelly Alexander, *President*
EMP: 14
SQ FT: 10,000
SALES (est): 1.6MM **Privately Held**
SIC: **3599** Machine shop, jobbing & repair

(G-4079)
SHAPES ETC INC
9094 Rte 36 (14437)
PHONE...................................585 335-6619
Fax: 585 335-6070
Susan Demuth, *President*
Susan De Muth, *President*
EMP: 15
SQ FT: 7,000
SALES (est): 960K **Privately Held**
WEB: www.shapesetc.com
SIC: **3999** Education aids, devices & supplies

Davenport
Delaware County

(G-4080)
GREENE LUMBER CO LP
16991 State Highway 23 (13750-8304)
PHONE...................................607 278-6101
Fax: 607 278-6919
Jeffrey Meyer,
EMP: 35
SQ FT: 13,888

SALES (est): 5.6MM
SALES (corp-wide): 1.5MM **Privately Held**
SIC: **2421** Sawmills & planing mills, general
PA: Baillie Lumber Co., L.P.
4002 Legion Dr
Hamburg NY 14075
800 950-2850

De Ruyter
Madison County

(G-4081)
KELLEY BROS LLC
1714 Albany St (13052-6566)
PHONE...................................315 852-3302
EMP: 5
SALES (corp-wide): 37.6MM **Privately Held**
SIC: **3429** Builders' hardware
HQ: Kelley Bros. Hardware Corp
317 E Brighton Ave
Syracuse NY 13210
315 478-2151

(G-4082)
USA BODY INC
994 Middle Lake Rd (13052-1244)
PHONE...................................315 852-6123
Fax: 315 852-9514
Bruce Macrae, *President*
Kristine Macrae, *Admin Sec*
EMP: 8
SALES (est): 1.7MM **Privately Held**
SIC: **3713** Truck bodies (motor vehicles)

De Witt
Onondaga County

(G-4083)
MAXI COMPANIES INC
4317 E Genesee St (13214-2114)
PHONE...................................315 446-1002
Charles C Giancola, *President*
▼ EMP: 6
SALES (est): 532.9K **Privately Held**
SIC: **3582** Dryers, laundry: commercial, including coin-operated

Deansboro
Oneida County

(G-4084)
BUELL FUEL LLC
2676 State Route 12b (13328-1128)
PHONE...................................315 841-3000
Michael Buell, *Principal*
EMP: 12
SALES (est): 2.5MM **Privately Held**
SIC: **2869** Fuels

Deer Park
Suffolk County

(G-4085)
ABLE WELDBUILT INDUSTRIES INC
1050 Grand Blvd (11729-5710)
PHONE...................................631 643-9700
Steve Laganas, *President*
EMP: 15
SALES (est): 3.2MM **Privately Held**
SIC: **3713** Truck & bus bodies

(G-4086)
ABRA-KA-DATA SYSTEMS LTD
39 W Jefryn Blvd Ste 1 (11729-5792)
PHONE...................................631 667-5550
Fax: 631 667-5572
Robert A Berding, *Ch of Bd*
Kenneth Berding, *President*
Dorothy Berding, *Admin Sec*
▲ EMP: 22
SQ FT: 15,000

SALES (est): 2.8MM **Privately Held**
SIC: **2761** Manifold business forms

(G-4087)
AD MAKERS LONG ISLAND INC
60 E Jefryn Blvd Ste 3 (11729-5798)
PHONE...................................631 595-9100
Fax: 631 595-1975
Arthur Lituchy, *President*
Evan Navarret, *General Mgr*
Henry Houston, *Vice Pres*
EMP: 10
SQ FT: 1,500
SALES (est): 930K **Privately Held**
WEB: www.admadvertising.com
SIC: **3993** 7311 Signs & advertising specialties; advertising agencies

(G-4088)
ADVANCED STRUCTURES CORP (PA)
235 W Industry Ct (11729-4688)
PHONE...................................631 667-5015
Fax: 631 667-5015
James Henderson, *President*
Eloise Foot, *Corp Secy*
Thomas Findlayson, *Vice Pres*
Dennis Shipman, *Manager*
EMP: 14
SQ FT: 22,000
SALES (est): 4.5MM **Privately Held**
WEB: www.advancedstructurescorp.com
SIC: **3469** 3083 Metal stampings; laminated plastic sheets

(G-4089)
AERO SPECIALTIES MANUFACTURING
20 Burt Dr (11729-5770)
PHONE...................................631 242-7200
Donald Carter, *President*
Elizabeth A Smith, *Vice Pres*
EMP: 12 EST: 1999
SQ FT: 1,400
SALES (est): 1.7MM **Privately Held**
SIC: **3599** Machine shop, jobbing & repair

(G-4090)
ALARM CONTROLS CORPORATION
19 Brandywine Dr (11729-5721)
P.O. Box 280 (11729-0280)
PHONE...................................631 586-4220
Fax: 631 586-6500
Howard Berger, *President*
John Benedetto, *General Mgr*
Arlene Berger, *Corp Secy*
▲ EMP: 20 EST: 1971
SQ FT: 8,000
SALES (est): 3.1MM **Privately Held**
WEB: www.alarmcontrols.com
SIC: **3669** 3625 3613 Burglar alarm apparatus, electric; relays & industrial controls; switchgear & switchboard apparatus

(G-4091)
ALL COLOR BUSINESS SPC LTD
305 Suburban Ave (11729-6806)
PHONE...................................516 420-0649
Fax: 516 753-2506
William Bogue, *Ch of Bd*
EMP: 6
SALES (est): 760K **Privately Held**
SIC: **2752** Commercial printing, lithographic

(G-4092)
ALLSTATE GASKET & PACKING INC
31 Prospect Pl (11729-3713)
PHONE...................................631 254-4050
Fax: 516 254-4330
Angelo Romano, *President*
Rosanne Kelly, *Manager*
▲ EMP: 17
SQ FT: 2,000
SALES (est): 1.7MM **Privately Held**
WEB: www.allstategasket.com
SIC: **3053** 5085 3443 Gaskets, all materials; industrial supplies; fabricated plate work (boiler shop)

(G-4093)
ALLSTATE SIGN & PLAQUE CORP
70 Burt Dr (11729-5702)
P.O. Box 725 (11729-0725)
PHONE...................................631 242-2828
Fax: 631 242-2433
David Fick, *President*
Mark Fick, *Vice Pres*
Peter Fick, *Treasurer*
EMP: 15 EST: 1956
SQ FT: 15,000
SALES (est): 2.6MM **Privately Held**
WEB: www.allstatesign.com
SIC: **3993** 2796 Signs, not made in custom sign painting shops; engraving platemaking services

(G-4094)
ALNEY GROUP LTD
Also Called: Mend All
435 Brook Ave Unit 16 (11729-6826)
PHONE...................................631 242-9100
Fax: 631 242-1734
Sheldon Schiffman, *President*
EMP: 5
SQ FT: 5,000
SALES (est): 602.3K **Privately Held**
WEB: www.mendallproducts.com
SIC: **2891** Glue

(G-4095)
AMALFI INGREDIENTS LLC
94 E Jefryn Blvd Ste H (11729-5728)
PHONE...................................631 392-1526
Serge Jean Charles, *Principal*
▲ EMP: 5
SALES (est): 618.8K **Privately Held**
SIC: **2099** Molasses, mixed or blended: from purchased ingredients

(G-4096)
AMERICAN RACING HEADERS INC
Also Called: Arh
880 Grand Blvd (11729-5708)
PHONE...................................631 608-1427
Nick Filippides, *CEO*
Jose Cruz, *Principal*
EMP: 30 EST: 2011
SALES (est): 6.8MM **Privately Held**
SIC: **3542** Headers

(G-4097)
AMERICAN SEALING TECHNOLOGY
31 Prospect Pl (11729-3713)
P.O. Box 545, Levittown (11756-0545)
PHONE...................................631 254-0019
Angelo Romano, *President*
Dominico Bono, *Purch Mgr*
EMP: 12
SQ FT: 10,000
SALES (est): 960K **Privately Held**
SIC: **3053** Gaskets, packing & sealing devices

(G-4098)
ANAND PRINTING MACHINERY INC
188 W 16th St (11729-4909)
PHONE...................................631 667-3079
Amand Kumar, *President*
EMP: 1
SALES (est): 8MM **Privately Held**
SIC: **3555** Printing trades machinery

(G-4099)
ANTHONY MANNO & CO INC
307 Skidmores Rd Ste 2 (11729-7117)
P.O. Box 32, Freeport (11520-0032)
PHONE...................................631 445-1834
Anthony Manno, *President*
Russell Fragala, *Senior VP*
EMP: 7
SQ FT: 5,000
SALES (est): 644.2K **Privately Held**
SIC: **3452** Screws, metal

(G-4100)
APOGEE TRANSLITE INC
593 Acorn St Ste B (11729-3613)
PHONE...................................631 254-6975
Lynn Nicoali, *President*
Marty Gaon, *Exec VP*

Deer Park - Suffolk County (G-4101) **GEOGRAPHIC SECTION**

Dominick Persichilli, *Production*
Ted Rykowski, *Senior Engr*
Nicole Enlow, *CFO*
EMP: 25
SQ FT: 30,000
SALES (est): 6.6MM **Privately Held**
WEB: www.apogeetranslite.com
SIC: 3548 3646 Welding apparatus; commercial indusl & institutional electric lighting fixtures

(G-4101)
ARMA CONTAINER CORP
65 N Industry Ct (11729-4601)
PHONE..................................631 254-1200
Fax: 631 254-3600
Bruce Margolis, *CEO*
Howard Gottfried, *Vice Pres*
Jack Hausman, *Treasurer*
Kim Geraci, *Controller*
Rob Golove, *VP Sales*
▼ **EMP:** 50 **EST:** 1946
SQ FT: 70,000
SALES (est): 12.7MM **Privately Held**
WEB: www.armacontainer.com
SIC: 2653 Boxes, corrugated: made from purchased materials

(G-4102)
ARTHUR BROWN W MFG CO
49 E Industry Ct Ste I (11729-4711)
PHONE..................................631 243-5594
Fax: 631 243-5596
Philip Sabatino, *President*
Anthony Sabatino, *Vice Pres*
EMP: 15
SQ FT: 8,000
SALES (est): 1.8MM **Privately Held**
WEB: www.arthurwbrown.com
SIC: 2511 Wood household furniture

(G-4103)
ARTSAICS STUDIOS INC
1006 Grand Blvd (11729-5710)
PHONE..................................631 254-2558
Fax: 631 254-2451
Nelson Londono, *President*
EMP: 6
SALES (est): 649.3K **Privately Held**
WEB: www.artsaics.com
SIC: 3253 Mosaic tile, glazed & unglazed: ceramic

(G-4104)
AUTO DATA SYSTEMS INC (PA)
Also Called: Auto Data Labels
2000 Deer Park Ave (11729-2730)
PHONE..................................631 831-7427
Scott Saal, *President*
▼ **EMP:** 14
SQ FT: 3,000
SALES: 1.9MM **Privately Held**
SIC: 2679 5131 Tags & labels, paper; labels

(G-4105)
AUTO MARKET PUBLICATIONS INC
1641 Deer Park Ave Ste 5 (11729-5209)
PHONE..................................631 667-0500
Corey Franklin, *President*
EMP: 8
SALES (est): 640.2K **Privately Held**
SIC: 2741 Telephone & other directory publishing

(G-4106)
BEST WAY TOOLS BY ANDERSON INC
171 Brook Ave (11729-7204)
PHONE..................................631 586-4702
Arleen Anderson CPA, *CEO*
Wayne Anderson, *President*
Warren Anderson, *Vice Pres*
Paul Cassutti, *Vice Pres*
EMP: 4
SQ FT: 15,000
SALES: 8MM **Privately Held**
WEB: www.bestwaytools.com
SIC: 3423 5072 Hand & edge tools; hardware

(G-4107)
BICON PHARMACEUTICAL INC
75 N Industry Ct (11729-4601)
PHONE..................................631 593-4199
Brian Li, *Director*
EMP: 10
SALES (est): 630K **Privately Held**
SIC: 2834 Pharmaceutical preparations

(G-4108)
BIMBO BAKERIES
955 Grand Blvd (11729-5707)
PHONE..................................631 274-4906
EMP: 8
SALES (est): 622.7K **Privately Held**
SIC: 2051 Bread, cake & related products

(G-4109)
BLI INTERNATIONAL INC
Also Called: Allegiant Health
75 N Industry Ct (11729-4601)
PHONE..................................631 940-9000
Brian Li, *President*
Lee Rudibaugh, *Senior VP*
Jerry Maleh, *Vice Pres*
John Zhong, *Vice Pres*
Jianshi Yang, *Assistant*
EMP: 130
SALES (est): 29.2MM **Privately Held**
SIC: 2834 Tablets, pharmaceutical

(G-4110)
BLUE SKIES
859 Long Island Ave (11729-3426)
PHONE..................................631 392-1140
Lisa Delvecchio, *Owner*
EMP: 5
SALES (est): 419.4K **Privately Held**
SIC: 3577 Printers & plotters

(G-4111)
BRENSEKE GEORGE WLDG IR WORKS
Also Called: Brenseke's
915 Long Island Ave Ste A (11729-3731)
PHONE..................................631 271-4870
Carol Brenseke, *President*
George Brenseke, *Vice Pres*
EMP: 6 **EST:** 1974
SALES: 800K **Privately Held**
SIC: 7692 Welding repair

(G-4112)
BROOKS LITHO DIGITAL GROUP INC
35 W Jefryn Blvd Ste A (11729-5784)
PHONE..................................631 789-4500
Fax: 631 789-4505
David Brooks, *President*
Linda Brooks, *Vice Pres*
Tina Simonella, *Production*
EMP: 5
SQ FT: 500
SALES (est): 530K **Privately Held**
WEB: www.brookslitho.com
SIC: 2752 2791 2789 2759 Commercial printing, lithographic; typesetting; bookbinding & related work; commercial printing

(G-4113)
C F PRINT LTD INC
35 W Jefryn Blvd Ste 2 (11729-5784)
PHONE..................................631 567-2110
Fax: 631 567-2695
Steve Scelfo, *President*
EMP: 10
SALES (est): 1MM **Privately Held**
WEB: www.cfprintltd.com
SIC: 2759 Commercial printing

(G-4114)
CAL BLEN ELECTRONIC INDUSTRIES
44 W Jefryn Blvd Ste H (11729-4721)
PHONE..................................631 242-6243
Fax: 631 242-1937
Rod Staehlin, *President*
EMP: 12 **EST:** 1961
SQ FT: 7,500
SALES (est): 2.2MM **Privately Held**
SIC: 3577 3823 Optical scanning devices; computer interface equipment for industrial process control

(G-4115)
CHALLENGE GRAPHICS SVCS INC (PA)
22 Connor Ln (11729-7234)
PHONE..................................631 586-0171
Fax: 631 586-0174
Anthony Brancato, *Ch of Bd*
Jim McLoone, *General Mgr*
William Boublik, *Sr Corp Ofcr*
Joseph Brancato, *Vice Pres*
Kurt Hochreiter, *Prdtn Mgr*
EMP: 42
SQ FT: 32,000
SALES (est): 6MM **Privately Held**
SIC: 2752 2791 2789 Lithographing on metal; typesetting; bookbinding & related work

(G-4116)
CHAPMAN SKATEBOARD CO INC
Also Called: New York Skateboards
87 N Industry Ct Ste A (11729-4607)
PHONE..................................631 321-4773
Greg Chapman, *President*
Christine Chapman, *Vice Pres*
Glenn Chapman, *Administration*
▲ **EMP:** 5
SQ FT: 2,000
SALES (est): 582.4K **Privately Held**
WEB: www.chapmanskateboards.com
SIC: 3949 5941 Skates & parts, roller; skateboarding equipment

(G-4117)
CHASE CORPORATION
1948 Deer Park Ave (11729-2798)
PHONE..................................631 243-6380
Virginia O'Brien, *Branch Mgr*
EMP: 11
SALES (corp-wide): 238MM **Publicly Held**
SIC: 3644 Noncurrent-carrying wiring services
PA: Chase Corporation
   26 Summer St
   Bridgewater MA 02324
   508 819-4200

(G-4118)
CHEMARK INTERNATIONAL USA INC
729 Acorn St (11729-3234)
PHONE..................................631 593-4566
Wayne Chao, *President*
EMP: 6
SALES (est): 707.5K **Privately Held**
SIC: 3621 Electric motor & generator parts

(G-4119)
COLUMBIA SPORTSWEAR COMPANY
152 The Arches Cir (11729-7057)
PHONE..................................631 274-6091
EMP: 250
SALES (corp-wide): 2.3B **Publicly Held**
SIC: 2329 Men's & boys' sportswear & athletic clothing
PA: Columbia Sportswear Company
   14375 Nw Science Park Dr
   Portland OR 97229
   503 985-4000

(G-4120)
CONTINENTAL KNITTING MILLS
Also Called: La-Mar Fashions
156 Brook Ave (11729-7251)
PHONE..................................631 242-5330
Pat Marini, *President*
Jennifer Marini, *Vice Pres*
EMP: 5
SQ FT: 4,000
SALES: 300K **Privately Held**
SIC: 2329 2339 5131 Men's & boys' sportswear & athletic clothing; women's & misses' athletic clothing & sportswear; sportswear, women's; knit fabrics

(G-4121)
COUSINS FURNITURE & HM IMPRVS
Also Called: Cousin's Furniture
515 Acorn St (11729-3601)
PHONE..................................631 254-3752
Fax: 631 254-3752
Joaquim L Rodrigues, *President*
Ilidio Rodrigues, *Vice Pres*
Maria Mejia, *Bookkeeper*
EMP: 42
SQ FT: 10,200
SALES (est): 5.2MM **Privately Held**
SIC: 2511 2431 Wood household furniture; millwork

(G-4122)
CROSLEY MEDICAL PRODUCTS INC
Also Called: Cmp Adaptive Equipment Supply
60 S 2nd St Ste E (11729-4717)
PHONE..................................631 595-2547
Fax: 631 595-1732
Gary Kornberg, *President*
Anthony Potenzone, *Mfg Staff*
EMP: 10
SQ FT: 4,000
SALES: 1.5MM **Privately Held**
SIC: 3842 Wheelchairs

(G-4123)
CTI SOFTWARE INC
44 W Jefryn Blvd Ste P (11729-4721)
PHONE..................................631 253-3550
Eric Meyn, *Ch of Bd*
EMP: 13
SALES (est): 1MM **Privately Held**
WEB: www.ctisoftware.com
SIC: 7372 Prepackaged software

(G-4124)
CUBBIES UNLIMITED CORPORATION
74 N Industry Ct (11729-4602)
PHONE..................................631 586-8572
Stefanie Stein, *President*
Joel Fromkin, *Treasurer*
Cyrus J Fromkin, *Admin Sec*
Chrysatll Tellacani, *Admin Sec*
▲ **EMP:** 15
SQ FT: 7,000
SALES (est): 1.2MM **Privately Held**
WEB: www.cubbiesunlimited.com
SIC: 3089 5211 Organizers for closets, drawers, etc.: plastic; stock shapes, plastic; closets, interiors & accessories

(G-4125)
D W S ASSOCIATES INC
Also Called: D W S Printing
89 N Industry Ct (11729-4601)
PHONE..................................631 667-6616
Thomas Staib, *President*
Andrew Staib, *Vice Pres*
Sal Addotta, *Project Mgr*
Courtney Casey, *Asst Controller*
Craig Smith, *Financial Exec*
EMP: 36
SQ FT: 20,000
SALES (est): 11.8MM **Privately Held**
WEB: www.dwsprinting.com
SIC: 2672 Labels (unprinted), gummed: made from purchased materials

(G-4126)
DAVINCI DESIGNS INC
Also Called: Davinci Dsgns Distinctive Furn
899 Long Island Ave (11729-3709)
PHONE..................................631 595-1095
Ralph Vinci, *CEO*
Chris Vinci, *Vice Pres*
Patricia Kennedy, *Manager*
EMP: 15
SQ FT: 3,000
SALES (est): 1.2MM **Privately Held**
WEB: www.davincidesigns.com
SIC: 2522 2521 Office furniture, except wood; wood office furniture

(G-4127)
DEER PARK DRIVESHAFT & HOSE
Also Called: Deer Park Drv Shaft & Hose Co
85 Brook Ave Ste C (11729-7202)
PHONE..................................631 667-4091
Fax: 631 242-6814
Nick Monastero, *President*
Richard Desena, *Vice Pres*
EMP: 4

GEOGRAPHIC SECTION
Deer Park - Suffolk County (G-4153)

SALES: 1MM **Privately Held**
SIC: 3714 3052 5013 Drive shafts, motor vehicle; axles, motor vehicle; automobile hose, plastic; automotive supplies & parts

(G-4128)
DEER PARK MACARONI CO INC (PA)
Also Called: Dpr Food Service
1882 Deer Park Ave (11729-4318)
PHONE 631 667-4600
Ernest Oliviero, *President*
Tom McDonald, *Vice Pres*
Phil Litrel, *Human Res Mgr*
Christopher Litrel, *Admin Sec*
EMP: 5 **EST:** 1949
SQ FT: 5,000
SALES (est): 1MM **Privately Held**
WEB: www.deerparkravioli.com
SIC: 2098 Macaroni & spaghetti

(G-4129)
DEER PARK MACARONI CO INC
Also Called: Deer Park Ravioli & Macaroni
1882 Deer Park Ave (11729-4318)
PHONE 631 667-4600
Fax: 631 667-4741
Earnest Olivero, *Manager*
EMP: 10
SALES (corp-wide): 1MM **Privately Held**
WEB: www.deerparkravioli.com
SIC: 2098 5149 Macaroni & spaghetti; pasta & rice
PA: Deer Park Macaroni Co Inc
   1882 Deer Park Ave
   Deer Park NY 11729
   631 667-4600

(G-4130)
DESIGN DISTRIBUTORS INC
300 Marcus Blvd (11729-4500)
PHONE 631 242-2000
Fax: 631 242-7367
Stuart J Avrick, *Ch of Bd*
Adam G Avrick, *President*
Mark F Rice, *Vice Pres*
Vincent Granberg, *Plant Mgr*
Phil Gerry, *Prdtn Mgr*
EMP: 85 **EST:** 1962
SQ FT: 80,000
SALES (est): 19.1MM **Privately Held**
SIC: 2759 2752 7331 Envelopes: printing; commercial printing, lithographic; direct mail advertising services

(G-4131)
DOVER MARINE MFG & SUP CO INC
98 N Industry Ct (11729-4602)
PHONE 631 667-4300
Fax: 718 899-6876
Theodore Cerrito, *President*
Lisa Cerrito, *Treasurer*
EMP: 5 **EST:** 1958
SQ FT: 5,000
SALES (est): 480K **Privately Held**
WEB: www.dovermfg.com
SIC: 3429 Marine hardware

(G-4132)
DP MURPHY CO INC
945 Grand Blvd (11729-5707)
PHONE 631 673-9400
Timothy M Schratwieser, *President*
John Van, *Opers Mgr*
Adriane Gray, *Opers Staff*
Mary Peters, *Sales Mgr*
EMP: 66 **EST:** 1873
SQ FT: 20,000
SALES (est): 10.4MM **Privately Held**
WEB: www.dpmurphy.com
SIC: 2752 7374 7331 2791 Commercial printing, offset; data processing service; mailing service; typesetting; bookbinding & related work

(G-4133)
EAST COAST EMBROIDERY LTD
74 Brook Ave Ste 1 (11729-7227)
PHONE 631 254-3878
Susan Simione, *President*
EMP: 7
SALES: 750K **Privately Held**
SIC: 2395 Embroidery products, except schiffli machine

(G-4134)
EAST COAST ORTHOIC & PROS COR (PA)
75 Burt Dr (11729-5701)
PHONE 516 248-5566
Vincent A Benenati, *CEO*
Lawrence J Benenati, *President*
John Fernandez, *Opers Mgr*
George Mitchell, *Controller*
Lola Menghi, *Human Res Mgr*
▲ **EMP:** 61
SALES (est): 9.8MM **Privately Held**
WEB: www.ec-op.com
SIC: 3841 Medical instruments & equipment, blood & bone work

(G-4135)
EC WOOD & COMPANY INC
110 E Industry Ct (11729-4706)
PHONE 718 388-2287
Joseph Fontana, *President*
Crystal Corcez, *Office Mgr*
EMP: 15
SQ FT: 13,000
SALES (est): 1.4MM **Privately Held**
SIC: 2434 Wood kitchen cabinets

(G-4136)
ELITE CELLULAR ACCESSORIES INC
61 E Industry Ct (11729-4725)
PHONE 877 390-2502
John Nordstrom, *President*
Stephen Conlon, *Exec VP*
EMP: 30
SQ FT: 10,000
SALES (est): 2.2MM **Privately Held**
SIC: 3663 5065 5731 Mobile communication equipment; intercommunication equipment, electronic; video cameras, recorders & accessories

(G-4137)
ELSENER ORGAN WORKS INC
120 E Jefryn Blvd Ste A (11729-5723)
PHONE 631 254-2744
Fax: 631 254-8723
Josephine Elsener, *President*
EMP: 7
SQ FT: 5,000
SALES: 500K **Privately Held**
WEB: www.elsenerorganworks.com
SIC: 3931 Blowers, pipe organ

(G-4138)
EMBASSY DINETTES INC
70 N Industry Ct (11729-4602)
PHONE 631 253-2292
Michael Walman, *Vice Pres*
◆ **EMP:** 5
SQ FT: 15,000
SALES (est): 498.7K **Privately Held**
SIC: 2514 Dinette sets: metal

(G-4139)
EMPIRE INDUSTRIAL BURNER SVC
550 Brook Ave (11729-6802)
PHONE 631 242-4619
Edward Roufberg, *President*
Rose Marie Price, *Administration*
EMP: 10
SQ FT: 37,000
SALES (est): 1.1MM **Privately Held**
SIC: 3433 1711 Burners, furnaces, boilers & stokers; boiler maintenance contractor; heating systems repair & maintenance
PA: Empire Industrial Systems Corp.
   40 Corbin Ave
   Bay Shore NY 11706
   631 242-4619

(G-4140)
EMPIRE SCIENTIFIC
Also Called: Empire Central
151 E Industry Ct (11729-4705)
PHONE 630 510-8636
Jeff English, *Owner*
EMP: 5
SALES (est): 250K **Privately Held**
WEB: www.empirescientific.com
SIC: 3692 Primary batteries, dry & wet

(G-4141)
FABRICATION SPECIALTIES CORP
2 Saxwood St Ste G (11729-4790)
PHONE 631 242-0326
Fax: 631 242-0344
David Conroy, *President*
Joseph W Schneider, *President*
Natale Marcellino, *Vice Pres*
EMP: 5 **EST:** 1972
SQ FT: 5,000
SALES (est): 750K **Privately Held**
SIC: 3469 Electronic enclosures, stamped or pressed metal

(G-4142)
FLOW X RAY CORPORATION
Also Called: Flow Dental
100 W Industry Ct (11729-4604)
PHONE 631 242-9729
Fax: 631 242-1001
Howard Wolf, *President*
Martin B Wolf, *Chairman*
Arlene Wolf, *Vice Pres*
Hugo Burbano, *Purch Mgr*
Carolyn Price, *CFO*
▲ **EMP:** 96 **EST:** 1974
SQ FT: 70,000
SALES (est): 14.8MM **Privately Held**
SIC: 3844 X-ray apparatus & tubes

(G-4143)
FORCE DIGITAL MEDIA INC
39 W Jefryn Blvd Ste 2 (11729-5792)
PHONE 631 243-0243
John Mazzio, *President*
EMP: 5
SALES (est): 156.9K **Privately Held**
SIC: 2759 7336 Commercial printing; package design

(G-4144)
FORMATS UNLIMITED INC
Also Called: Mf Digital
19 W Jefryn Blvd Ste 2 (11729-5749)
PHONE 631 249-9200
Fax: 516 249-9273
Anthony Cosentino, *Ch of Bd*
Joyce Cosentino, *Vice Pres*
John McGrath, *Manager*
EMP: 10
SQ FT: 2,500
SALES (est): 1.3MM **Privately Held**
WEB: www.formats-unlimited.com
SIC: 7372 5045 3572 5065 Prepackaged software; disk drives; disk drives, computer; diskettes, computer

(G-4145)
FOSSIL INDUSTRIES INC
44 W Jefryn Blvd Ste A (11729-4721)
PHONE 631 254-9200
Howard Decesare, *President*
Mark Decesare, *Vice Pres*
Steve Melisi, *VP Opers*
Rhiannon Cesare, *Project Mgr*
Pam Brandsema, *Production*
▼ **EMP:** 25
SQ FT: 25,000
SALES (est): 3MM **Privately Held**
WEB: www.fossilinc.com
SIC: 3993 Signs & advertising specialties

(G-4146)
FUTURE SPRAY FINISHING CO
78 Brook Ave Ste A (11729-7226)
PHONE 631 242-6252
Fax: 631 242-6252
Josephine Galea, *Owner*
EMP: 5
SQ FT: 4,500
SALES (est): 320K **Privately Held**
SIC: 3479 Coating of metals & formed products

(G-4147)
GLOBAL STEEL PRODUCTS CORP (HQ)
95 Marcus Blvd (11729-4501)
PHONE 631 586-3455
Peter Rolla, *President*
Max Moore, *General Mgr*
Adrienne Rolla, *Treasurer*
Mike Ramzey, *Controller*
Dana Patient, *Manager*
◆ **EMP:** 150
SQ FT: 85,000
SALES (est): 22.6MM
SALES (corp-wide): 169.4MM **Privately Held**
WEB: www.globalpartitions.com
SIC: 2542 3446 3443 3442 Partitions for floor attachment, prefabricated: except wood; architectural metalwork; fabricated plate work (boiler shop); metal doors, sash & trim
PA: ltr Industries, Inc
   441 Saw Mill River Rd
   Yonkers NY 10701
   914 964-7063

(G-4148)
HI-TEMP BRAZING INC
539 Acorn St (11729-3601)
PHONE 631 491-4917
Raymond M Gentner, *President*
Raymond M Gentner III, *Opers Mgr*
EMP: 30
SQ FT: 7,500
SALES (est): 5.2MM **Privately Held**
WEB: www.hitempbrazing.com
SIC: 3398 Brazing (hardening) of metal

(G-4149)
HIGH FREQUENCY TECH CO INC
172 Brook Ave Ste D (11729-7243)
PHONE 631 242-3020
Fax: 631 242-4823
Andrew Amabile, *President*
Mary Ann Amabile, *Shareholder*
▲ **EMP:** 12
SQ FT: 10,000
SALES (est): 2.2MM **Privately Held**
WEB: www.hftinc.com
SIC: 3559 5065 5084 Plastics working machinery; electronic parts & equipment; materials handling machinery

(G-4150)
HIGHLAND ORGANIZATION CORP
435 Unit 23 Brook Ave (11729)
PHONE 631 991-3240
Marc Piacenti, *President*
John Holland, *Project Mgr*
Jennifer McGee, *Comptroller*
EMP: 35 **EST:** 1999
SQ FT: 3,200
SALES: 5MM **Privately Held**
SIC: 2431 Millwork

(G-4151)
HRD METAL PRODUCTS INC
120 E Jefryn Blvd Ste A (11729-5723)
PHONE 631 243-6700
Fax: 631 243-2585
Hector Lasalle, *President*
Martin Michie, *Vice Pres*
EMP: 8
SQ FT: 4,000
SALES: 800K **Privately Held**
SIC: 3444 Sheet metalwork

(G-4152)
INTERNTONAL TELECOM COMPONENTS
Also Called: Itc
94 E Jefryn Blvd Ste B (11729-5728)
PHONE 631 243-1444
Robert Smith, *President*
John Williams, *Sales Staff*
EMP: 10
SQ FT: 5,000
SALES: 900K **Privately Held**
WEB: www.itcincorporated.com
SIC: 3679 5065 Microwave components; electronic parts & equipment

(G-4153)
ISLAND INSTRUMENT CORP
65 Burt Dr (11729-5701)
PHONE 631 243-0550
Patrick McKeever, *President*
Candice McLellan, *Manager*
EMP: 9
SQ FT: 12,500
SALES (est): 750K **Privately Held**
WEB: www.sonnart.com
SIC: 3599 Machine shop, jobbing & repair

Deer Park - Suffolk County (G-4154)   GEOGRAPHIC SECTION

(G-4154)
J & J SWISS PRECISION INC
160 W Industry Ct Ste F (11729-4677)
P.O. Box 408 (11729-0408)
PHONE 631 243-5584
Fax: 631 243-5583
John Dojlidko, *President*
Tom Mak, *QC Mgr*
John Mroz, *Treasurer*
EMP: 30
SQ FT: 10,000
SALES (est): 4.7MM **Privately Held**
SIC: **3599** 3451 Machine shop, jobbing & repair; screw machine products

(G-4155)
JAMAR PRECISION PRODUCTS CO
5 Lucon Dr (11729-5711)
PHONE 631 254-0234
Fax: 631 254-0284
James Lewandoski, *President*
Joy Lewandoski, *Vice Pres*
EMP: 12
SQ FT: 10,500
SALES (est): 600K **Privately Held**
SIC: **3599** Machine shop, jobbing & repair

(G-4156)
JAMCO AEROSPACE INC
121a E Industry Ct (11729-4705)
PHONE 631 586-7900
Fax: 631 586-7505
Jack Lee, *CEO*
Linette Lee, *President*
Ronald Lee, *Project Engr*
Nigel Yeo, *Controller*
Hanna LI, *Admin Sec*
EMP: 50
SQ FT: 30,000
SALES (est): 10MM **Privately Held**
WEB: www.jamco-aerospace.com
SIC: **3728** Aircraft parts & equipment

(G-4157)
JAVCON MACHINE INC
255 Skidmores Rd (11729-7102)
PHONE 631 586-1890
Fax: 631 586-1868
Eric Clauss, *President*
Debra Fetsch, *Manager*
EMP: 9 EST: 1977
SALES: 1.5MM **Privately Held**
SIC: **3599** Machine shop, jobbing & repair

(G-4158)
JOHN J MAZUR INC
94 E Jefryn Blvd Ste K (11729-5728)
PHONE 631 242-4554
Fax: 631 242-4093
John J Mazur Jr, *President*
Peter Strouse, *QC Mgr*
Alice Mazur, *Admin Sec*
EMP: 15 EST: 1957
SQ FT: 15,000
SALES: 2.3MM **Privately Held**
SIC: **3599** Machine shop, jobbing & repair

(G-4159)
KONAR PRECISION MFG INC
62 S 2nd St Ste F (11729-4716)
PHONE 631 242-4466
Fax: 631 242-4467
Daruisz Konarski, *President*
Slawomir Konarski, *Vice Pres*
Karol Konarski, *Office Mgr*
EMP: 5
SQ FT: 2,000
SALES: 500K **Privately Held**
SIC: **3599** Machine shop, jobbing & repair

(G-4160)
KTD SCREW MACHINE INC
70 E Jefryn Blvd Ste D (11729-5754)
PHONE 631 243-6861
Fax: 631 243-6862
Kevin Dorman, *President*
Michael Dorman, *Vice Pres*
EMP: 8
SQ FT: 3,700
SALES (est): 1.1MM **Privately Held**
SIC: **3451** Screw machine products

(G-4161)
L & K GRAPHICS INC
Also Called: Minuteman Press
1917 Deer Park Ave (11729-3302)
PHONE 631 667-2269
Fax: 631 667-2346
Richard Crockett, *Ch of Bd*
Robert Mason, *President*
EMP: 6 EST: 1975
SQ FT: 2,000
SALES (est): 1MM **Privately Held**
SIC: **2752** Commercial printing, lithographic

(G-4162)
L MILLER DESIGN INC
Also Called: Bank Displays.com
100 E Jefryn Blvd Ste F (11729-5729)
PHONE 631 242-1163
Fax: 631 242-7308
Robert L Miller, *President*
Lisa Melloni, *General Mgr*
Leena Miller, *Corp Secy*
Mike Malone, *Vice Pres*
Michele Melloni, *Manager*
EMP: 7
SALES (est): 650K **Privately Held**
WEB: www.lmillerdesign.com
SIC: **3993** 7319 Signs & advertising specialties; display advertising service

(G-4163)
LA STRADA DANCE FOOTWEAR INC
770 Grand Blvd Ste 1 (11729-5725)
PHONE 631 242-1401
Daniel Cerasuolo, *President*
Linda O'Shea, *Corp Secy*
EMP: 6
SQ FT: 3,300
SALES (est): 350K **Privately Held**
SIC: **3149** 2252 Ballet slippers; socks

(G-4164)
LEADING EDGE FABRICATION
699 Acorn St Ste B (11729-4235)
PHONE 631 274-9797
Mitch Bard, *Owner*
EMP: 6
SALES (est): 666.1K **Privately Held**
SIC: **3441** Fabricated structural metal

(G-4165)
LESLY ENTERPRISE & ASSOCIATES
29 Columbo Dr (11729-1808)
P.O. Box 190 (11729-0190)
PHONE 631 988-1301
Lesly Senat, *Principal*
EMP: 5
SALES: 50K **Privately Held**
SIC: **3721** Aircraft

(G-4166)
LIGHTING SCULPTURES INC
Also Called: Versaponents
66 N Industry Ct (11729-4602)
PHONE 631 242-3387
Chet Yaswen, *President*
Laura Yaswen, *Vice Pres*
EMP: 10
SALES: 2.3MM **Privately Held**
SIC: **3648** Lighting equipment

(G-4167)
LONG ISLAND METALFORM INC
12 Lucon Dr (11729-5712)
PHONE 631 242-9088
Fax: 631 586-4711
George Seitz Jr, *President*
Tom McCormack, *Vice Pres*
EMP: 14
SQ FT: 14,000
SALES (est): 2.8MM **Privately Held**
WEB: www.longislandmetalform.com
SIC: **3469** Spinning metal for the trade

(G-4168)
LUCIA GROUP INC
45 W Jefryn Blvd Ste 108 (11729-5722)
PHONE 631 392-4900
Craig Lucia, *President*
Lieve Spiegel, *Sr Project Mgr*
▲ EMP: 5
SQ FT: 1,000
SALES (est): 610K **Privately Held**
WEB: www.theluciagroup.com
SIC: **2522** 2542 Office furniture, except wood; shelving, office & store: except wood

(G-4169)
M H STRYKE CO INC
181 E Industry Ct Ste A (11729-4718)
PHONE 631 242-2660
Kenneth Winter, *President*
EMP: 10 EST: 1931
SQ FT: 3,000
SALES (est): 812.3K **Privately Held**
SIC: **3965** Fasteners, snap

(G-4170)
MARKSMEN MANUFACTURING CORP
355 Marcus Blvd (11729-4509)
PHONE 800 305-6942
Peter Guttieri, *President*
▲ EMP: 48
SQ FT: 14,800
SALES (est): 11.7MM **Privately Held**
WEB: www.marksmenmfg.com
SIC: **3452** 3599 Bolts, nuts, rivets & washers; machine shop, jobbing & repair

(G-4171)
MASTER CRAFT FINISHERS INC
30 W Jefryn Blvd Ste 1 (11729-4730)
PHONE 631 586-0540
Fax: 631 586-0180
Roger J Fox, *President*
EMP: 40
SQ FT: 15,000
SALES (est): 4.5MM **Privately Held**
SIC: **3479** 3471 2396 Coating of metals & formed products; finishing, metals or formed products; automotive & apparel trimmings

(G-4172)
MCG ELECTRONICS INC
Also Called: McG Surge Protection
12 Burt Dr (11729-5778)
PHONE 631 586-5125
Fax: 631 586-5120
Michael Coyle, *President*
Suzanne Baron, *General Mgr*
Cecilia Coyle, *Vice Pres*
Kim Connors, *Purch Mgr*
Glenn Clifford, *Engineer*
▼ EMP: 50
SQ FT: 10,000
SALES (est): 8.6MM **Privately Held**
WEB: www.mcgsurge.com
SIC: **3674** Semiconductors & related devices

(G-4173)
MD INTERNATIONAL INDUSTRIES
Also Called: M D I Industries
120 E Jefryn Blvd Ste Aa (11729-5739)
PHONE 631 254-3100
Fax: 631 254-3325
Martin Michie, *President*
Blanche Michie, *Shareholder*
EMP: 24
SQ FT: 10,000
SALES (est): 4.4MM **Privately Held**
WEB: www.mdiindustries.com
SIC: **3728** 3444 Aircraft parts & equipment; sheet metalwork

(G-4174)
MINI-MAX DNTL REPR EQPMNTS INC
25 W Jefryn Blvd Ste B (11729-5740)
PHONE 631 242-0322
Brad Vollmer, *Principal*
Michael Gavris, *Principal*
Bill Smith, *Service Mgr*
EMP: 7
SALES: 1.2MM **Privately Held**
SIC: **3843** Dental equipment & supplies

(G-4175)
MODERN PACKAGING INC
505 Acorn St (11729-3601)
PHONE 631 595-2437
Fax: 631 595-2742
Syed Zaki Hossai, *Ch of Bd*
Syed Zaki Hossain, *Ch of Bd*
Towhidul Islam, *General Mgr*
Jaroslaw Dabek, *Vice Pres*
Mohammed Hossain, *Research*
EMP: 62
SQ FT: 20,000
SALES (est): 15.9MM **Privately Held**
WEB: www.modernpackaginginc.com
SIC: **3599** 3565 5084 Custom machinery; packaging machinery; packaging machinery & equipment

(G-4176)
NANZ CUSTOM HARDWARE INC
105 E Jefryn Blvd (11729-5713)
PHONE 212 367-7000
Kristen Ricci, *Project Mgr*
EMP: 52
SALES (corp-wide): 25.2MM **Privately Held**
WEB: www.nanz.com
SIC: **3429** 5031 Door opening & closing devices, except electrical; building materials, interior
PA: Nanz Custom Hardware, Inc.
20 Vandam St Fl 5l
New York NY 10013
212 367-7000

(G-4177)
NATIONAL COMPUTER & ELECTRONIC
Also Called: Nceec
367 Bay Shore Rd Ste D (11729-7244)
PHONE 631 242-7222
Neal Morofsky, *Chairman*
Lynn Nicolai, *Vice Pres*
Ruth Morofsky, *Manager*
EMP: 8
SQ FT: 5,000
SALES (est): 859K **Privately Held**
WEB: www.ncee.com
SIC: **3469** Electronic enclosures, stamped or pressed metal

(G-4178)
NELCO LABORATORIES INC
154 Brook Ave (11729-7251)
P.O. Box 58 (11729-0058)
PHONE 631 242-0082
Fax: 631 242-3290
April Catanzaro, *President*
Noelle Park, *Vice Pres*
Holly Mangieri, *Bookkeeper*
Fabio Cipolla, *Lab Dir*
EMP: 22
SQ FT: 6,800
SALES (est): 3.6MM **Privately Held**
WEB: www.nelcolabs.com
SIC: **2836** Allergens, allergenic extracts

(G-4179)
NEW WOP RECORDS
Also Called: Artists, Doo Wop
317 W 14th St (11729-6301)
PHONE 631 617-9732
Giro Manuele, *Owner*
EMP: 5
SALES (est): 210K **Privately Held**
SIC: **3651** Household audio & video equipment

(G-4180)
NIJON TOOL CO INC
12 Evergreen Pl 12 (11729-3708)
PHONE 631 242-3434
Franklin Trama, *President*
John Burns, *Vice Pres*
EMP: 10
SQ FT: 12,500
SALES (est): 870K **Privately Held**
SIC: **3544** Special dies & tools

(G-4181)
NIKE INC
102 The Arches Cir (11729-7057)
PHONE 631 242-3014
EMP: 38
SALES (corp-wide): 32.3B **Publicly Held**
SIC: **3021** Rubber & plastics footwear
PA: Nike, Inc.
1 Sw Bowerman Dr
Beaverton OR 97005
503 671-6453

▲ = Import ▼ = Export
◆ = Import/Export

GEOGRAPHIC SECTION   **Deer Park - Suffolk County (G-4210)**

(G-4182)
NUTEC COMPONENTS INC
81 E Jefryn Blvd Ste A (11729-5733)
PHONE..................................631 242-1224
Fax: 631 242-1310
Rene H Schnetzler, *President*
Glenn Stanley, *Vice Pres*
Ruth Ketay, *Director*
EMP: 15
SQ FT: 10,500
SALES (est): 3.6MM **Privately Held**
WEB: www.nutec1.com
SIC: 3823 Industrial instrmnts msrmnt display/control process variable

(G-4183)
NUTRA SOLUTIONS USA INC
Also Called: Nsusa
1019 Grand Blvd (11729-5709)
PHONE..................................631 392-1900
Latiful Hakue, *CEO*
EMP: 25
SALES: 9.5MM **Privately Held**
SIC: 2023 7389 Baby formulas; packaging & labeling services

(G-4184)
NY FROYO LLC
324 W 19th St (11729-6342)
PHONE..................................516 312-4588
EMP: 5
SALES (est): 255.4K **Privately Held**
SIC: 2024 Yogurt desserts, frozen

(G-4185)
OCEAN CARDIAC MONITORING
38 W 17th St (11729-3902)
PHONE..................................631 777-3700
Roberto Garcia, *Owner*
EMP: 5
SALES (est): 500K **Privately Held**
SIC: 3845 Patient monitoring apparatus

(G-4186)
OVERNIGHT LABELS INC
151 W Industry Ct Ste 15 (11729-4600)
PHONE..................................631 242-4240
Fax: 631 242-4385
Donald Earl, *President*
Maria Bordonarl, *Accountant*
Maureen Earl, *Human Resources*
Diane Tennezol, *Sales Mgr*
▲ **EMP:** 20
SQ FT: 3,400
SALES (est): 5.4MM **Privately Held**
WEB: www.overnightlabels.com
SIC: 2672 Coated & laminated paper

(G-4187)
PAULS RODS & RESTOS INC
131 Brook Ave Ste 13 (11729-7221)
PHONE..................................631 665-7637
Paul R Dimauro, *Principal*
EMP: 6
SALES (est): 830.5K **Privately Held**
SIC: 3531 Automobile wrecker hoists

(G-4188)
PDF SEAL INCORPORATED
503 Acorn St (11729-3601)
PHONE..................................631 595-7035
Jaroslaw Dabek, *Ch of Bd*
Syed Zaki Hossain, *Vice Pres*
Jeremy Bank, *Opers Mgr*
Adeeb Hakim, *Prdtn Mgr*
EMP: 25
SQ FT: 16,000
SALES (est): 6.5MM **Privately Held**
SIC: 2631 Container, packaging & boxboard

(G-4189)
PLX INC (PA)
Also Called: P L X
25 W Jefryn Blvd Ste A (11729-5740)
PHONE..................................631 586-4190
Jack Lipkins, *President*
Zvi Bleier, *Vice Pres*
Doinel Blaj, *Engineer*
Mary Youssef, *Bookkeeper*
Kevin Cavanagh, *Applctn Conslt*
EMP: 40 **EST:** 1953
SQ FT: 15,000
SALES: 6.7MM **Privately Held**
WEB: www.plxinc.com
SIC: 3827 Optical instruments & apparatus

(G-4190)
PNC SPORTS
1880 Deer Park Ave (11729-4318)
PHONE..................................516 665-2244
Richard Knowles, *Principal*
EMP: 6
SALES (est): 625.5K **Privately Held**
SIC: 3949 Sporting & athletic goods

(G-4191)
PRECISION CNC
71 E Jefryn Blvd (11729-5713)
PHONE..................................631 847-3999
Sal Napolitano, *Owner*
EMP: 6
SALES (est): 711.3K **Privately Held**
SIC: 3728 Aircraft parts & equipment

(G-4192)
PRIME ELECTRONIC COMPONENTS
Also Called: Prime Components
150 W Industry Ct (11729-4604)
PHONE..................................631 254-0101
Fax: 631 242-8896
Daniel Martin, *President*
EMP: 12
SALES (est): 1.1MM **Privately Held**
WEB: www.primecomponents.com
SIC: 3679 Electronic loads & power supplies

(G-4193)
PRINT MARKET INC
66 E Jefryn Blvd Ste 1 (11729-5760)
PHONE..................................631 940-8181
EMP: 8
SALES (est): 62.8K **Privately Held**
SIC: 2752 Lithographic Commercial Printing

(G-4194)
PROFESSIONAL MANUFACTURERS
475 Brook Ave (11729-7208)
P.O. Box 282 (11729-0282)
PHONE..................................631 586-2440
Fax: 631 586-2443
Richard Lizio, *President*
EMP: 10
SALES (est): 960K **Privately Held**
SIC: 3843 Dental equipment & supplies

(G-4195)
PVH CORP
Also Called: Van Heusen
1358 The Arches Cir (11729-7069)
PHONE..................................631 254-8200
Shannon Wright, *Branch Mgr*
EMP: 9
SALES (corp-wide): 8B **Publicly Held**
SIC: 2321 Men's & boys' dress shirts
PA: Pvh Corp.
    200 Madison Ave Bsmt 1
    New York NY 10016
    212 381-3500

(G-4196)
R E F PRECISION PRODUCTS
517 Acorn St Ste A (11729-3610)
PHONE..................................631 242-4471
Robert Fleece, *Partner*
Raymond Crisafulli, *Partner*
EMP: 17
SQ FT: 3,600
SALES (est): 1.5MM **Privately Held**
WEB: www.refprecisionproducts.com
SIC: 3599 Custom machinery

(G-4197)
R J S DIRECT MARKETING INC
561 Acorn St Ste E (11729-3600)
PHONE..................................631 667-5768
Micheal Manfre, *President*
EMP: 15
SALES: 1.5MM **Privately Held**
WEB: www.rjsmarketingonline.com
SIC: 2834 Solutions, pharmaceutical

(G-4198)
RAINBOW POWDER COATING CORP
86 E Industry Ct (11729-4704)
PHONE..................................631 586-4019
Fax: 631 586-4118
Ron Vincent, *President*
EMP: 5
SQ FT: 5,800
SALES (est): 496.4K **Privately Held**
SIC: 3471 Finishing, metals or formed products

(G-4199)
REFLEX OFFSET INC
305 Suburban Ave (11729-6806)
PHONE..................................516 746-4142
Fax: 516 746-4750
John Banks, *President*
Richard Banks, *Vice Pres*
EMP: 8
SQ FT: 5,400
SALES (est): 1MM **Privately Held**
WEB: www.reflexoffset.com
SIC: 2752 Commercial printing, offset

(G-4200)
ROCKPORT COMPANY LLC
1288 The Arches Cir (11729-7068)
PHONE..................................631 243-0418
EMP: 54
SALES (corp-wide): 51.8MM **Privately Held**
SIC: 3143 Men's footwear, except athletic
HQ: The Rockport Company Llc
    1895 J W Foster Blvd
    Canton MA 02021
    781 401-5000

(G-4201)
ROSEMONT PRESS INCORPORATED
35 W Jefryn Blvd Ste A (11729-5784)
PHONE..................................212 239-4770
Czarina Anif, *Branch Mgr*
EMP: 5
SALES (corp-wide): 9.6MM **Privately Held**
WEB: www.rosemontpress.com
SIC: 2741 Miscellaneous publishing
PA: Rosemont Press Incorporated
    253 Church St Apt 2
    New York NY 10013
    212 239-4770

(G-4202)
ROSS METAL FABRICATORS INC
225 Marcus Blvd (11729-4503)
P.O. Box 12308, Hauppauge (11788-0615)
PHONE..................................631 586-7000
Fax: 631 586-7006
Richard Ross, *President*
Ron Reid, *Vice Pres*
Lawrence Perez, *Treasurer*
EMP: 40
SQ FT: 30,000
SALES (est): 6.7MM
SALES (corp-wide): 37MM **Privately Held**
SIC: 3443 Metal parts
PA: Charles Ross & Son Company
    710 Old Willets Path
    Hauppauge NY 11788
    631 234-0500

(G-4203)
RSM ELECTRON POWER INC (PA)
Also Called: Sensitron Semiconductor
221 W Industry Ct (11729-4605)
PHONE..................................631 586-7600
Fax: 631 242-9798
Steve Saunders, *President*
Susan Saunders, *Accounts Mgr*
Kristie White, *Manager*
Mary Saunders, *Admin Sec*
▲ **EMP:** 90 **EST:** 1969
SQ FT: 20,000
SALES (est): 18.5MM **Privately Held**
WEB: www.sensitron.com
SIC: 3674 Semiconductors & related devices

(G-4204)
SAL MA INSTRUMENT CORP
2 Saxwood St Ste F (11729-4793)
PHONE..................................631 242-2227
Alfred Mahany, *President*
EMP: 9 **EST:** 1963
SQ FT: 7,500
SALES (est): 1.3MM **Privately Held**
SIC: 3599 Machine shop, jobbing & repair

(G-4205)
SCHENCK CORPORATION (DH)
535 Acorn St (11729-3698)
PHONE..................................631 242-4010
Bertram Dittmar, *President*
Peter Brooks, *Corp Secy*
Michele Bornholdt, *Personnel*
Ronald Green, *Manager*
Jan Dittmar, *Technology*
EMP: 70
SQ FT: 40,000
SALES (est): 62.5MM
SALES (corp-wide): 4B **Privately Held**
SIC: 3545 3829 Balancing machines (machine tool accessories); measuring & controlling devices
HQ: Schenck Industrie-Beteiligungen Ag
    C/O Dr. Thomas Hefti
    Glarus GL
    556 402-544

(G-4206)
SCHENCK TREBEL CORP (DH)
535 Acorn St (11729-3616)
PHONE..................................631 242-4397
Fax: 631 242-4147
Bertram Dittmar, *President*
Judith Foddy, *Accountant*
Michele Bornholdt, *Personnel Exec*
Rich Mason, *Branch Mgr*
Gary Kaufmann, *Manager*
▲ **EMP:** 60
SQ FT: 44,000
SALES (est): 16.3MM
SALES (corp-wide): 4B **Privately Held**
WEB: www.schenck-usa.com
SIC: 3545 3829 Balancing machines (machine tool accessories); measuring & controlling devices
HQ: Schenck Corporation
    535 Acorn St
    Deer Park NY 11729
    631 242-4010

(G-4207)
SCIENTIFIC COMPONENTS CORP
Also Called: Mini Circuits Lab
161 E Industry Ct (11729-4705)
PHONE..................................631 243-4901
Al Chasinov, *Branch Mgr*
EMP: 40
SALES (corp-wide): 110.9MM **Privately Held**
SIC: 3825 Instruments to measure electricity
PA: Scientific Components Corp
    13 Neptune Ave
    Brooklyn NY 11235
    718 934-4500

(G-4208)
SECTOR MICROWAVE INDS INC
999 Grand Blvd (11729-5799)
PHONE..................................631 242-2245
Fax: 631 242-8158
Victor Hnelson, *President*
Thomas J Nelson, *Vice Pres*
Patricia Nelson, *Admin Sec*
▼ **EMP:** 60
SQ FT: 28,000
SALES: 8.4MM **Privately Held**
SIC: 3643 Electric switches

(G-4209)
SHANKER INDUSTRIES INC (PA)
301 Suburban Ave (11729-6806)
PHONE..................................631 940-9889
Fax: 516 437-8866
John Shanker, *President*
Frances Shanker, *Vice Pres*
David Shanker, *Sales Mgr*
▲ **EMP:** 5
SQ FT: 5,700
SALES (est): 1.4MM **Privately Held**
WEB: www.shanko.com
SIC: 3446 Ornamental metalwork

(G-4210)
SHARON MANUFACTURING CO INC
540 Brook Ave (11729-6802)
PHONE..................................631 242-8870

Deer Park - Suffolk County (G-4211)

Robert Stamm, *President*
John Zaikowski, *Purch Agent*
EMP: 8
SQ FT: 7,500
SALES (est): 1.2MM **Privately Held**
SIC: 3565 3469 Packaging machinery; bag opening, filling & closing machines; machine parts, stamped or pressed metal

(G-4211)
SOMERS STAIN GLASS INC
108 Brook Ave Ste A (11729-7238)
PHONE..................................631 586-7772
Ronald Somers, *President*
Tricia Somers, *Office Mgr*
Tricia Franqueiro, *Manager*
EMP: 10
SQ FT: 10,000
SALES: 700K **Privately Held**
SIC: 3231 3229 Stained glass: made from purchased glass; lamp parts & shades, glass

(G-4212)
SOUNDCOAT COMPANY INC (DH)
1 Burt Dr (11729-5756)
PHONE..................................631 242-2200
Fax: 631 242-2246
Louis Nenninger, *CEO*
C Mayo, *Site Mgr*
Joe Antal, *Production*
John Duckworth, *Purch Mgr*
Elizabeth Orlando, *Treasurer*
▲ **EMP:** 65 **EST:** 1963
SQ FT: 70,000
SALES (est): 16.6MM
SALES (corp-wide): 326.2MM **Privately Held**
WEB: www.soundcoat.com
SIC: 3086 2299 3625 3296 Insulation or cushioning material, foamed plastic; acoustic felts; noise control equipment; mineral wool
HQ: Recticel Foam Corporation
5600 Bow Pointe Dr
Clarkston MI 48346
248 241-9100

(G-4213)
SPEAQUA CORP
46 W Jefryn Blvd (11729-4736)
PHONE..................................516 380-5008
Steven Patsis, *President*
Steve Patsis, *Vice Pres*
EMP: 40
SQ FT: 20,000
SALES (est): 3.9MM **Privately Held**
SIC: 3651 Loudspeakers, electrodynamic or magnetic

(G-4214)
SUFFOLK COMMUNITY COUNCIL INC (PA)
819 Grand Blvd Ste 1 (11729-5780)
PHONE..................................631 434-9277
Tom Williams, *Exec Dir*
Judith Pannullo, *Director*
Robert E Detor Jr,
EMP: 9
SQ FT: 2,000
SALES: 194.3K **Privately Held**
WEB: www.suffolkcommunitycouncil.org
SIC: 2721 8322 Periodicals: publishing only; individual & family services

(G-4215)
SUPER STEELWORKS CORPORATION
12 Lucon Dr (11729-5712)
PHONE..................................718 386-4770
Carlos Mery, *Principal*
▲ **EMP:** 5
SALES (est): 411K **Privately Held**
SIC: 3317 Steel pipe & tubes

(G-4216)
TAE TRANS ATLANTIC ELEC INC (PA)
Also Called: Empire Scientific
151 E Industry Ct (11729-4705)
P.O. Box 817 (11729-0981)
PHONE..................................631 595-9206
Fax: 631 595-9384
Janet English, *President*

Jeffrey English, *Vice Pres*
Spencer Slipko, *Vice Pres*
Moe Michael, *Sales Staff*
▲ **EMP:** 23 **EST:** 1965
SQ FT: 1,500
SALES (est): 4MM **Privately Held**
WEB: www.empirebat.com
SIC: 3692 5063 Primary batteries, dry & wet; batteries

(G-4217)
TEK PRECISION CO LTD
205 W Industry Ct (11729-4613)
PHONE..................................631 242-0330
Fax: 631 242-1481
John Krause, *CEO*
Steve Longobardi, *President*
Randall Strauss, *Vice Pres*
John A Kruse, *Project Dir*
Pat Sweeney, *Production*
EMP: 24
SQ FT: 21,000
SALES: 11MM **Privately Held**
WEB: www.tekprecision.com
SIC: 3728 Aircraft assemblies, subassemblies & parts

(G-4218)
TRI-STATE WINDOW FACTORY CORP
360 Marcus Blvd (11729-4504)
PHONE..................................631 667-8600
John Kypreos, *President*
Nichole Oberst, *Accountant*
David McMahon, *CPA*
EMP: 75
SQ FT: 31,000
SALES (est): 13.8MM **Privately Held**
SIC: 3089 1761 1751 Windows, plastic; siding contractor; window & door (prefabricated) installation

(G-4219)
UNIVERSAL SHIELDING CORP
20 W Jefryn Blvd (11729-5769)
PHONE..................................631 667-7900
Fax: 631 667-7912
Irwin Newman, *Ch of Bd*
Lois Newman, *Vice Pres*
Ruth Quiles, *Manager*
Daniel Driesman, *Council Mbr*
EMP: 50
SQ FT: 20,000
SALES (est): 13.5MM **Privately Held**
WEB: www.universalshielding.com
SIC: 3448 3469 3444 Buildings, portable: prefabricated metal; metal stampings; sheet metalwork

(G-4220)
UNIVERSAL SIGNS AND SVC INC
435 Brook Ave Unit 2 (11729-6826)
PHONE..................................631 446-1121
Marcos Marmol, *President*
EMP: 27
SQ FT: 20,000
SALES (est): 3MM **Privately Held**
SIC: 3993 Signs & advertising specialties

(G-4221)
USA SIGNS OF AMERICA INC
172 E Industry Ct (11729-4706)
PHONE..................................631 254-6900
John Prahalis, *President*
Lynn Loder, *Vice Pres*
EMP: 75
SALES (est): 7.3MM **Privately Held**
WEB: www.usasignsofamerica.com
SIC: 3993 Signs & advertising specialties

(G-4222)
VEJA ELECTRONICS INC (PA)
Also Called: Stack Electronics
46 W Jefryn Blvd Ste A (11729-4736)
PHONE..................................631 321-6086
Fax: 631 321-5662
Steven Patsis, *CEO*
Steve Patsis, *President*
EMP: 100
SQ FT: 40,000
SALES (est): 32.6MM **Privately Held**
WEB: www.stackny.com
SIC: 3644 5063 5065 Terminal boards; electrical fittings & construction materials; electronic parts

(G-4223)
VERSAPONENTS INC
Also Called: Writing Sculptures
66 N Industry Ct (11729-4602)
PHONE..................................631 242-3387
Fax: 631 242-3461
Chet Yaswen, *President*
Laura Yaswen, *Vice Pres*
EMP: 16
SQ FT: 4,500
SALES (est): 2.7MM **Privately Held**
SIC: 3646 Commercial indusl & institutional electric lighting fixtures

(G-4224)
VINYL MATERIALS INC
365 Bay Shore Rd (11729-7201)
PHONE..................................631 586-9444
Alex Folkman, *President*
Joseph Folkman, *Vice Pres*
Roop Narine Dhanrag, *Controller*
EMP: 50
SQ FT: 65,000
SALES (est): 9MM **Privately Held**
SIC: 3081 5162 3089 Vinyl film & sheet; plastics products; plastic processing

(G-4225)
W & W MANUFACTURING CO
151 E Industry Ct (11729-4705)
P.O. Box 817 (11729-0981)
PHONE..................................516 942-0011
Jeffrey Weitzman, *President*
Ronie Rosenbaum, *Vice Pres*
Saundrice Lucas, *Administration*
▲ **EMP:** 35
SALES (est): 2.1MM **Privately Held**
WEB: www.ww-manufacturing.com
SIC: 3691 3825 3663 Storage batteries; instruments to measure electricity; radio & TV communications equipment

(G-4226)
WESTROCK RKT COMPANY
140 W Industry Ct (11729-4604)
PHONE..................................330 296-5155
Ron Byers, *General Mgr*
Bennett Rossanda, *Purch Mgr*
Kathy Telesca, *Purchasing*
Noelle Pastore, *Human Res Dir*
EMP: 130
SQ FT: 120,000
SALES (corp-wide): 11.3B **Publicly Held**
WEB: www.rocktenn.com
SIC: 2653 5113 Boxes, corrugated: made from purchased materials; bags, paper & disposable plastic
HQ: Westrock Rkt Company
504 Thrasher St
Norcross GA 30071
770 448-2193

(G-4227)
WOLF X-RAY CORPORATION
100 W Industry Ct (11729-4604)
PHONE..................................631 242-9729
Martin Wolf, *President*
Carol Price, *Credit Mgr*
Howard Wolf, *Sales Mgr*
Ruth De La Rosa, *Manager*
William Winters, *Director*
▲ **EMP:** 60 **EST:** 1931
SQ FT: 80,000
SALES (est): 10.4MM **Privately Held**
WEB: www.wolfxray.com
SIC: 3844 X-ray apparatus & tubes

(G-4228)
WOLO MFG CORP
1 Saxwood St Ste 1 (11729-4779)
PHONE..................................631 242-0333
Fax: 631 242-0720
Stanley Solow, *President*
▲ **EMP:** 21
SQ FT: 10,000
SALES (est): 3.8MM **Privately Held**
SIC: 3429 3714 3647 Motor vehicle hardware; motor vehicle parts & accessories; vehiclular lighting equipment

(G-4229)
WORLD LLC
Also Called: Wmw Machinery Company
513 Acorn St Ste B (11729-3611)
PHONE..................................631 940-9121
Fax: 845 358-2378

Cornel Circiumaru, *Mng Member*
Lester White, *Info Tech Mgr*
▼ **EMP:** 15
SQ FT: 8,000
SALES (est): 1.5MM **Privately Held**
SIC: 3541 Machine tools, metal cutting type

(G-4230)
Z BEST PRINTING INC
699 Acorn St Ste B (11729-4235)
PHONE..................................631 595-1400
Fax: 516 845-1439
Ronald S Bard, *President*
Craig Bard, *Vice Pres*
Gayle Bard, *Admin Sec*
EMP: 10
SQ FT: 5,000
SALES: 1.5MM **Privately Held**
SIC: 2252 2261 Leg warmers; screen printing of cotton broadwoven fabrics

Delanson
Schenectady County

(G-4231)
BENZSAY & HARRISON INC
Railroad Ave (12053)
P.O. Box 459 (12053-0459)
PHONE..................................518 895-2311
Fax: 518 895-8475
Rudolph Benzsay, *President*
Sema Benzsay, *Admin Sec*
EMP: 6
SQ FT: 25,000
SALES: 900.1K **Privately Held**
WEB: www.bh-inc.com
SIC: 2819 Aluminum compounds

(G-4232)
ELECTRCAL INSTRUMENTATION CTRL
208 Hillman Rd (12053-4500)
P.O. Box 24, Duanesburg (12056-0024)
PHONE..................................518 861-5789
Michael Weiss, *President*
EMP: 11
SALES: 2MM **Privately Held**
SIC: 3823 Industrial process control instruments

(G-4233)
HARVEST HOMES INC
1331 Cole Rd (12053-3109)
PHONE..................................518 895-2341
Fax: 518 895-2287
Timothy O Brien, *Ch of Bd*
Robert A Guay, *Vice Pres*
Christian Guay, *Sales Mgr*
Dan Steiner, *Office Mgr*
Gary Shufelt, *Info Tech Mgr*
EMP: 26
SQ FT: 27,000
SALES: 4.9MM **Privately Held**
SIC: 2452 2439 Panels & sections, prefabricated, wood; structural wood members

Delevan
Cattaraugus County

(G-4234)
HALEY CONCRETE INC (PA)
10413 Delevan Elton Rd (14042-9613)
PHONE..................................716 492-0849
Fax: 585 492-0884
Lawrence Haley II, *President*
Lawrence Haley III, *Admin Sec*
EMP: 15
SQ FT: 1,250
SALES (est): 2MM **Privately Held**
SIC: 3273 4212 Ready-mixed concrete; local trucking, without storage

(G-4235)
KENDOR MUSIC INC
21 Grove St (14042-9682)
P.O. Box 278 (14042-0278)
PHONE..................................716 492-1254
Fax: 716 492-5124
Craig Cornwall, *President*

Jackie Cornwall, *Controller*
EMP: 12
SQ FT: 10,000
SALES (est): 1MM **Privately Held**
WEB: www.kendormusic.com
SIC: 2741 Music, sheet: publishing & printing

Delhi
Delaware County

(G-4236)
BIRCHBROOK PRESS
Also Called: Birchbrook Impressions
2309 County Highway 16 (13753-3159)
P.O. Box 81 (13753-0081)
PHONE..................607 746-7453
Tom Tolnay, *Manager*
EMP: 9
SALES (corp-wide): 699.3K **Privately Held**
SIC: 2731 Book publishing
PA: Birchbrook Press
    77 Bleecker St
    New York NY

(G-4237)
DELAWARE COUNTY TIMES INC
56 Main St (13753-1121)
PHONE..................607 746-2176
Fax: 607 746-3135
Donald F Bishop II, *President*
David Ketchum, *Sls & Mktg Exec*
Thomas Briggs, *Exec Dir*
EMP: 6
SALES (est): 250K **Privately Held**
SIC: 2711 2721 Newspapers; periodicals

(G-4238)
EXCELSIOR PUBLICATIONS
133 Main St (13753-1219)
PHONE..................607 746-7600
Fax: 607 746-2750
Francis P Ruggiero, *President*
EMP: 5 **EST:** 1999
SALES (est): 441K **Privately Held**
SIC: 2721 Magazines: publishing & printing

(G-4239)
FRIESLNDCMPINA INGRDNTS N AMER
40196 State Hwy 10 Delhi (13753)
PHONE..................607 746-0196
Don Combs, *Principal*
Irene Oerlemans, *Human Res Dir*
Maryalice Butler, *Human Res Mgr*
Joann Schreurs, *Office Mgr*
Marian Diepman, *Manager*
EMP: 35
SALES (corp-wide): 12.1B **Privately Held**
SIC: 2023 Dry, condensed, evaporated dairy products
HQ: Frieslandcampina Ingredients North America, Inc
    61 S Paramus Rd Ste 535
    Paramus NJ 07652
    201 655-7780

(G-4240)
MARTIN D WHITBECK
68 Meredith St (13753-1034)
PHONE..................607 746-7642
EMP: 6
SALES (est): 185.1K **Privately Held**
SIC: 2011 Variety meats, fresh edible organs

(G-4241)
PROMATS ATHLETICS LLC (PA)
41155 State Highway 10 (13753-3213)
P.O. Box 231 (13753-0231)
PHONE..................607 746-8911
Edward Rosa, *Vice Pres*
Liam Miller, *Sales Staff*
Danny Nance, *Sales Staff*
Dave Rama, *Sales Staff*
Wayne Oliver, *Manager*
EMP: 36
SALES (est): 5.4MM **Privately Held**
WEB: www.promats.com
SIC: 3949 Sporting & athletic goods

(G-4242)
SAPUTO DAIRY FOODS USA LLC
Also Called: Morningstar Foods
40236 State Highway 10 (13753-3207)
P.O. Box 1 (13753-0001)
PHONE..................607 746-2141
Elizabeth Banburen, *Manager*
EMP: 100
SALES (corp-wide): 86.6K **Privately Held**
WEB: www.morningstarfoods.com
SIC: 2026 Fluid milk
HQ: Saputo Dairy Foods Usa, Llc
    2711 N Haske Ave Ste 3700
    Dallas TX 75204
    214 863-2300

(G-4243)
SPORTSFIELD SPECIALTIES INC
41155 State Highway 10 (13753-3213)
P.O. Box 231 (13753-0231)
PHONE..................607 746-8911
Fax: 607 746-8481
Wayne Oliver, *President*
Ed Rosa, *Vice Pres*
Lynn Pickett, *Credit Mgr*
Savannah Wake, *Credit Mgr*
Sean Clark, *Sales Dir*
EMP: 45
SQ FT: 46,000
SALES (est): 15.3MM **Privately Held**
WEB: www.sportsfieldspecialties.com
SIC: 3949 Sporting & athletic goods

Delmar
Albany County

(G-4244)
COMMUNITY MEDIA GROUP LLC (PA)
Also Called: Spotlight Newspaper
125 Adams St (12054-3211)
PHONE..................518 439-4949
John McLntyre Jr, *Vice Pres*
John A McIntyre Jr,
Daniel E Alexander,
David B Tyler Jr,
EMP: 11
SALES (est): 1.7MM **Privately Held**
SIC: 2711 Newspapers

(G-4245)
NEWSGRAPHICS OF DELMAR INC
Also Called: The Spotlight
125 Adams St (12054-3211)
P.O. Box 100 (12054-0100)
PHONE..................518 439-5363
Richard Ahlstrom, *President*
Mary Ahlstrom, *Admin Sec*
EMP: 25
SQ FT: 2,500
SALES (est): 2.2MM **Privately Held**
SIC: 2721 2752 Magazines: publishing only, not printed on site; commercial printing, offset

(G-4246)
SANZDRANZ LLC (PA)
Also Called: Gatherer's Gourmet Granola
83 Dumbarton Dr (12054-4418)
PHONE..................518 894-8625
Sandro Gerbini, *President*
EMP: 5 **EST:** 2010
SQ FT: 3,700
SALES (est): 210K **Privately Held**
SIC: 2043 Cereal breakfast foods

Depew
Erie County

(G-4247)
AUBURN-WATSON CORP (PA)
3295 Walden Ave (14043-2313)
PHONE..................716 876-8000
Fax: 716 206-0799
Wayne Watson, *President*
Natalie Watson, *Vice Pres*
Laszlo Szlabonyi, *Prdtn Mgr*
EMP: 10 **EST:** 1946
SQ FT: 8,000
SALES (est): 754.5K **Privately Held**
SIC: 2434 1751 Wood kitchen cabinets; cabinet building & installation

(G-4248)
BISON STEEL INCORPORATED
2 Main St Ste 103 (14043-3323)
P.O. Box 454 (14043-0454)
PHONE..................716 683-0900
Fax: 716 683-3529
Edwin C Bailey, *President*
Gus Schiralli, *Admin Sec*
▲ **EMP:** 5
SQ FT: 27,000
SALES (est): 714.7K **Privately Held**
SIC: 3442 Screens, window, metal

(G-4249)
BUFFALO ENVELOPE INC
Also Called: Buffalo Envelope Company
2914 Walden Ave Ste 300 (14043-2694)
PHONE..................716 686-0100
Fax: 716 686-9005
Lorne Hill, *Managing Dir*
Dany Paradis, *Principal*
EMP: 12
SQ FT: 12,800
SALES (est): 2.7MM
SALES (corp-wide): 115.5MM **Privately Held**
SIC: 2677 5112 Envelopes; envelopes
PA: Supremex Inc
    7213 Rue Cordner
    Lasalle QC H8N 2
    514 595-0555

(G-4250)
BUFFALO POWER ELEC CTR DE
166 Taylor Dr Ste 1 (14043-2021)
PHONE..................716 651-1600
William Gates, *Ch of Bd*
Dennis M Cascio, *President*
Frank Stasio, *Vice Pres*
Mel Davis, *Mfg Mgr*
Jim Tokasz, *Sales Engr*
EMP: 45
SQ FT: 38,000
SALES (est): 6MM **Privately Held**
WEB: www.buffalopower.com
SIC: 3612 5065 3566 Transformers, except electric; transformers, electronic; speed changers, drives & gears

(G-4251)
BUFFALO TUNGSTEN INC
2 Main St (14043-3323)
P.O. Box 397 (14043-0397)
PHONE..................716 759-6353
Ralph V Shopwalter, *Ch of Bd*
Roger Showlte, *Prdtn Mgr*
Tlbed Showalte, *Accountant*
Jason Lahti, *Finance*
Nancy Meier, *Manager*
◆ **EMP:** 60
SQ FT: 500,000
SALES (est): 19.4MM **Privately Held**
WEB: www.buffalotungsten.com
SIC: 3399 2819 Powder, metal; tungsten carbide powder, except abrasive or metallurgical

(G-4252)
CENVEO INC
Also Called: Buffalo Envelope
2914 Walden Ave Ste 300 (14043-2609)
PHONE..................716 686-0100
Brian North, *Branch Mgr*
EMP: 18
SALES (corp-wide): 1.7B **Publicly Held**
WEB: www.mail-well.com
SIC: 2677 2752 2759 Envelopes; commercial printing, lithographic; color lithography; promotional printing, lithographic; catalogs, lithographed; labels & seals: printing
PA: Cenveo, Inc.
    200 First Stamford Pl # 200
    Stamford CT 06902
    203 595-3000

(G-4253)
CUSTOM COUNTERTOPS INC (PA)
3192 Walden Ave (14043-2846)
PHONE..................716 685-2871
Gloria Marino, *President*
EMP: 8
SALES: 750K **Privately Held**
WEB: www.customcountertops.com
SIC: 3131 2541 Counters; wood partitions & fixtures

(G-4254)
D R M MANAGEMENT INC (PA)
Also Called: Fresh Bake Pizza Co
3430 Transit Rd (14043-4853)
PHONE..................716 668-0333
Ronald Digiore, *President*
Daniel J Digiore, *Vice Pres*
Colleen Tranquilli, *Manager*
Mark Digiore, *Admin Sec*
EMP: 25
SQ FT: 1,200
SALES (est): 5.3MM **Privately Held**
WEB: www.drminc.us
SIC: 2099 2038 8741 Food preparations; pizza, refrigerated: except frozen; pizza, frozen; restaurant management

(G-4255)
DESU MACHINERY CORPORATION
200 Gould Ave (14043-3134)
P.O. Box 245 (14043-0245)
PHONE..................716 681-5798
Martin W Golden II, *CEO*
Mark L Dalquist, *President*
William Livingston, *Purchasing*
Tom Russles, *Human Res Dir*
Jim Dahlquist, *Marketing Mgr*
EMP: 85
SALES (est): 8MM **Privately Held**
SIC: 3556 3565 Packing house machinery; bottling machinery: filling, capping, labeling

(G-4256)
ELMAR INDUSTRIES INC
200 Gould Ave (14043-3138)
P.O. Box 245 (14043-0245)
PHONE..................716 681-5650
Fax: 716 681-4660
Martin W Golden II, *Ch of Bd*
Mark L Dahlquist, *Ch of Bd*
Mark Vaughn, *Engineer*
Linda Gregorio, *Finance*
▲ **EMP:** 62
SQ FT: 21,000
SALES (est): 19.3MM **Privately Held**
WEB: www.elmarworldwide.com
SIC: 3556 Food products machinery

(G-4257)
FIBRIX LLC
Buffalo Batt A Div of Polyeste
3307 Walden Ave (14043-2347)
PHONE..................716 683-4100
Bob Heilman, *Manager*
Chuck Bushsmer, *Manager*
Chuck Ramen, *Administration*
EMP: 50
SQ FT: 43,000
SALES (corp-wide): 74MM **Privately Held**
WEB: www.leggett.com
SIC: 2299 2824 2221 Batting, wadding, padding & fillings; pillow fillings: curled hair, cotton waste, moss, hemp tow; organic fibers, noncellulosic; broadwoven fabric mills, manmade
HQ: Fibrix, Llc
    1820 Evans St Ne
    Conover NC 28613
    828 459-7064

(G-4258)
FLADO ENTERPRISES INC
Also Called: Quality Quick Signs
1380 French Rd Ste 6 (14043-4800)
PHONE..................716 668-6400
Christopher R Flejtuch, *President*
EMP: 7
SQ FT: 7,000

Depew - ERIE COUNTY (G-4259)   GEOGRAPHIC SECTION

SALES (est): 798.2K Privately Held
WEB: www.qualityquicksigns.com
SIC: 3993 Signs & advertising specialties

(G-4259)
HOWDEN NORTH AMERICA INC (DH)
Also Called: Howdens
2475 George Urban Blvd # 100
(14043-2022)
PHONE.................803 741-2700
Matthew Ingle, CEO
Karl Kimmerling, President
Will Samuel, Chairman
Grahame Gurney, Vice Pres
David Smith, Plant Mgr
▲ EMP: 85 EST: 1980
SALES (est): 268.5MM
SALES (corp-wide): 3.9B Publicly Held
WEB: www.howdenbuffalo.com
SIC: 3564 3568 Exhaust fans: industrial or commercial; couplings, shaft: rigid, flexible, universal joint, etc.
HQ: Anderson Group Inc.
3411 Silverside Rd # 103
Wilmington DE 19810
302 478-6160

(G-4260)
HOWDEN NORTH AMERICA INC
Also Called: Howden Fan Company
2475 George Urban Blvd # 100
(14043-2022)
PHONE.................716 817-6900
Fax: 716 817-6901
Joe Okoniewski, Accountant
Robert Pheil, Human Res Dir
Greg Brill, Accounts Mgr
Sandy Henry, Sales Staff
John Auringer, Manager
EMP: 60
SALES (corp-wide): 3.9B Publicly Held
WEB: www.howdenbuffalo.com
SIC: 3564 8711 Ventilating fans: industrial or commercial; engineering services
HQ: Howden North America Inc.
2475 George Urban Blvd # 100
Depew NY 14043
803 741-2700

(G-4261)
LEGNO VENETO USA
3283 Walden Ave (14043-2311)
PHONE.................716 651-9169
James Carol II, Owner
James Caroll, Owner
Jerrie Janis, Bookkeeper
▲ EMP: 9
SQ FT: 26,000
SALES (est): 1MM Privately Held
WEB: www.lvwoodfloors.com
SIC: 2426 Flooring, hardwood

(G-4262)
LEICA MICROSYSTEMS INC
Also Called: Opd
3362 Walden Ave (14043-2475)
P.O. Box 123, Cragsmoor (12420-0123)
PHONE.................716 686-3000
Fax: 716 686-3085
Tom Tonner, QC Mgr
Mark Wood, Personnel Exec
John Burgess, Branch Mgr
EMP: 8
SALES (corp-wide): 20.5B Publicly Held
SIC: 3827 Optical instruments & apparatus; microscopes, except electron, proton & corneal
HQ: Leica Microsystems Inc.
1700 Leider Ln
Buffalo Grove IL 60089
847 405-0123

(G-4263)
LIFEFORMS PRINTING
786 Terrace Blvd Ste 2 (14043-3729)
PHONE.................716 685-4500
Nick Sanders, Principal
EMP: 5
SQ FT: 7,500
SALES (est): 570.8K Privately Held
SIC: 2759 Business forms: printing

(G-4264)
MAKE-WAVES INSTRUMENT CORP (PA)
4444 Broadway (14043-2915)
PHONE.................716 681-7524
Fax: 716 681-3412
John R Patterson, President
Brian Cory, Vice Pres
Richard Rang, Controller
▲ EMP: 25
SQ FT: 36,000
SALES (est): 2.4MM Privately Held
WEB: www.makewavesinstrumentcorp.com
SIC: 3825 3829 3641 3545 Tachometer generators; gauges, motor vehicle: oil pressure, water temperature; electric lamps; machine tool accessories; valves & pipe fittings; gaskets, packing & sealing devices

(G-4265)
MOLDCRAFT INC
240 Gould Ave (14043-3130)
PHONE.................716 684-1126
Fax: 716 684-0932
John Chase, President
Henry Lewandowski, Treasurer
Sharon Winkler, Manager
Jimmy Gray, Admin Sec
EMP: 20
SQ FT: 8,000
SALES: 3.8MM Privately Held
WEB: www.moldcraftinc.com
SIC: 3544 Forms (molds), for foundry & plastics working machinery

(G-4266)
NIAGARA REFINING LLC
5661 Transit Rd (14043-3227)
P.O. Box 398 (14043-0398)
PHONE.................716 706-1400
EMP: 30
SALES (est): 7.9MM Privately Held
SIC: 2819 Tungsten carbide powder, except abrasive or metallurgical

(G-4267)
OSMOSE HOLDINGS INC
2475 George Urban Blvd (14043-2022)
PHONE.................716 882-5905
Fax: 716 882-7822
James R Spengler Jr, President
Joe Dobyns, District Mgr
David L Bradley, Vice Pres
Jim McGiffert, Vice Pres
Christopher Macauley, Opers Mgr
◆ EMP: 1335
SALES (est): 228.8MM
SALES (corp-wide): 201.9MM Publicly Held
WEB: www.fireretardanttreatedwood.com
SIC: 2491 Preserving (creosoting) of wood
HQ: Oaktree Capital Management, L.P.
333 S Grand Ave Ste 2800
Los Angeles CA 90071
213 830-6300

(G-4268)
PCB GROUP INC (HQ)
Also Called: ICP
3425 Walden Ave (14043-2417)
PHONE.................716 684-0001
Mike Lally, CEO
James F Lally, Ch of Bd
Graham Turgoose, Managing Dir
John Betzig, Opers Mgr
Larry Dick, Opers Mgr
EMP: 50
SQ FT: 64,000
SALES (est): 224.9MM
SALES (corp-wide): 563.9MM Publicly Held
SIC: 3679 3823 Transducers, electrical; industrial instrmnts msrmnt display/control process variable
PA: Mts Systems Corporation
14000 Technology Dr
Eden Prairie MN 55344
952 937-4000

(G-4269)
PCB PIEZOTRONICS INC
Larson Davis
3425 Walden Ave (14043-2495)
PHONE.................716 684-0001
Fax: 716 926-8215
Jeff Williams, Sales Dir
EMP: 6
SALES (corp-wide): 563.9MM Publicly Held
SIC: 3829 Measuring & controlling devices
HQ: Pcb Piezotronics, Inc.
3425 Walden Ave
Depew NY 14043
716 684-0001

(G-4270)
PCB PIEZOTRONICS INC
Industrl Mntrng Instrmntatn Dv
3425 Walden Ave (14043-2495)
PHONE.................716 684-0003
John Cornaccio, Vice Pres
Sue Wood, Purchasing
Steve Boisvert, Engineer
Eric Vogel, Engineer
Susan Ruhland, Human Res Dir
EMP: 400
SALES (corp-wide): 233.2MM Privately Held
WEB: www.pcb.com
SIC: 3679 5063 Electronic circuits; electrical apparatus & equipment
HQ: Pcb Piezotronics, Inc.
3425 Walden Ave
Depew NY 14043
716 684-0001

(G-4271)
QMC TECHNOLOGIES INC
4388 Broadway (14043-2998)
PHONE.................716 681-0810
Fax: 716 681-0881
James A Serafin, President
Bob Serafin, Vice Pres
▲ EMP: 16
SQ FT: 5,500
SALES (est): 4.8MM Privately Held
WEB: www.qmctechnologies.com
SIC: 3315 Fence gates posts & fittings: steel

(G-4272)
REICHERT INC
Also Called: Reichert Technologies
3362 Walden Ave (14043-2437)
PHONE.................716 686-4500
Bruce Wilson, Ch of Bd
Timothy Levindofske, President
Jerry C Cirino, Vice Pres
Bruce Schneider, Project Engr
Brett Himes, CFO
▲ EMP: 147
SQ FT: 48,000
SALES (est): 42.4MM
SALES (corp-wide): 3.9B Publicly Held
WEB: www.leicams.com
SIC: 3841 Surgical & medical instruments
PA: Ametek, Inc.
1100 Cassatt Rd
Berwyn PA 19312
610 647-2121

(G-4273)
RMF PRINT MANAGEMENT GROUP
786 Terrace Blvd Ste 3 (14043-3729)
P.O. Box 329, Lancaster (14086-0329)
PHONE.................716 683-4351
Sharon Doherty, Manager
EMP: 12
SALES (est): 1.8MM Privately Held
SIC: 2752 Commercial printing, lithographic

(G-4274)
STANDARD ASCNSION TOWERS GROUP
5136 Transit Rd (14043-4439)
PHONE.................716 681-2222
Larry Jordan, CEO
Walt Pryzbal, Vice Pres
Robert Weig, Vice Pres
EMP: 60
SALES (est): 2.1MM Privately Held
SIC: 3441 1623 3731 3559 Fabricated structural metal for ships; communication line & transmission tower construction; transmitting tower (telecommunication) construction; radar towers, floating; semiconductor manufacturing machinery

(G-4275)
STERLING BUILDING SYSTEMS
2 Main St (14043-3323)
PHONE.................716 685-0505
Jason Drew, Partner
EMP: 5
SALES (est): 440K Privately Held
WEB: www.sterlingbuildingsystems.com
SIC: 2451 Mobile homes

Deposit
Broome County

(G-4276)
CANNONSVILLE LUMBER INC
199 Old Route 10 (13754-2100)
PHONE.................607 467-3380
Fax: 607 467-3376
Adolf Schaffer Jr, President
EMP: 5 EST: 1998
SALES (est): 781.9K Privately Held
SIC: 3553 Sawmill machines

(G-4277)
COURIER PRINTING CORP
24 Laurel Bank Ave Ste 2 (13754-1244)
PHONE.................607 467-2191
Hilton Evans, President
Brenda Degraw, Manager
Alice Martin, Manager
Sarah Evans, Admin Sec
EMP: 30 EST: 1848
SQ FT: 55,000
SALES: 2MM Privately Held
WEB: www.courierprintingcorp.com
SIC: 2752 Commercial printing, lithographic

(G-4278)
INTEGRATED WOOD COMPONENTS INC
Also Called: Iwci
791 Airport Rd (13754-1277)
P.O. Box 145 (13754-0145)
PHONE.................607 467-1739
Fax: 607 467-2035
John Kamp, President
Tom Stobert, Corp Secy
Gerard Kamp, Vice Pres
Melissa Decker, Administration
EMP: 49
SQ FT: 2,800
SALES (est): 4.8MM Privately Held
SIC: 2541 Wood partitions & fixtures

(G-4279)
SANFORD STONE LLC
185 Latham Rd (13754-1271)
PHONE.................607 467-1313
George W Sanford,
EMP: 21
SALES (est): 2.2MM Privately Held
SIC: 3281 Cut stone & stone products

(G-4280)
SCHAEFER ENTPS OF DEPOSIT
315 Old Route 10 (13754-2106)
PHONE.................607 467-4990
Larry Schaefer, President
EMP: 30
SALES (est): 3.3MM Privately Held
SIC: 1422 Cement rock, crushed & broken-quarrying

(G-4281)
SCHAEFER LOGGING INC
315 Old Route 10 (13754-2106)
PHONE.................607 467-4990
Larry Schaefer, President
EMP: 10
SALES (est): 983.9K Privately Held
SIC: 2411 5411 Logging; convenience stores

(G-4282)
WALTER R TUCKER ENTPS LTD
Also Called: E-Z Red Co
8 Leonard Way (13754-1240)
P.O. Box 80 (13754-0080)
PHONE.................607 467-2866
Fax: 607 467-2323
Mark Tucker, President
Bob Cacciabeve, Exec VP

▲ = Import ▼ = Export
◆ = Import/Export

GEOGRAPHIC SECTION

Schayne Bowen, *Foreman/Supr*
Luke Tucker, *Sales Mgr*
▲ **EMP:** 25 **EST:** 1966
SQ FT: 13,000
SALES (est): 5.8MM **Privately Held**
WEB: www.ezred.com
SIC: 3825 3824 3991 3629 Battery testers, electrical; test equipment for electronic & electric measurement; liquid meters; brushes, except paint & varnish; battery chargers, rectifying or nonrotating; motor vehicle supplies & new parts; testing equipment, electrical: automotive

Derby
Erie County

(G-4283)
GREYLINE SIGNS INC
6681 Schuyler Dr (14047-9644)
PHONE.................................716 947-4526
Linda Scritchfield, *President*
Everett Scritchfield, *Vice Pres*
EMP: 5
SALES (est): 430K **Privately Held**
SIC: 3993 Signs & advertising specialties

(G-4284)
NEW ERA CAP CO INC
8061 Erie Rd (14047-9503)
PHONE.................................716 549-0445
Roni Brown, *VP Human Res*
EMP: 7
SALES (corp-wide): 433.1MM **Privately Held**
SIC: 2353 Uniform hats & caps; baseball caps
PA: New Era Cap Co., Inc.
160 Delaware Ave
Buffalo NY 14202
716 604-9000

Dexter
Jefferson County

(G-4285)
HANA SPORTSWEAR INC
321 Lakeview Dr (13634)
P.O. Box 564 (13634-0564)
PHONE.................................315 639-6332
Fax: 315 639-6136
Robert Hartz, *President*
Beth Laster, *Treasurer*
Hartz Robert, *Manager*
▲ **EMP:** 20
SQ FT: 13,000
SALES (est): 1.9MM **Privately Held**
SIC: 3949 2339 2311 Sporting & athletic goods; women's & misses' outerwear; men's & boys' suits & coats

(G-4286)
I ABC CORPORATION
349 Lakeview Dr (13634)
PHONE.................................315 639-3100
Gretchen Young, *General Mgr*
▲ **EMP:** 30
SALES (est): 2.5MM **Privately Held**
SIC: 2339 Bathing suits: women's, misses' & juniors'

(G-4287)
VENUS MANUFACTURING CO INC (PA)
349 Lakeview Dr (13634)
P.O. Box 551 (13634-0551)
PHONE.................................315 639-3100
Fax: 315 639-3101
Roger Reifensnyder, *CEO*
Michael J Hennegan, *President*
▲ **EMP:** 90
SQ FT: 14,000
SALES (est): 6.2MM **Privately Held**
WEB: www.venusswimwear.com
SIC: 2339 Bathing suits: women's, misses' & juniors'

Dix Hills
Suffolk County

(G-4288)
A & D TOOL INC
30 Pashen Pl (11746-6600)
PHONE.................................631 243-4339
Dimitrios Margiellos, *President*
Tatiana Labate, *Corp Secy*
EMP: 7
SALES (est): 360K **Privately Held**
WEB: www.adtool.com
SIC: 3544 Forms (molds), for foundry & plastics working machinery

(G-4289)
AKA SPORT INC
16 Princeton Dr (11746-4826)
P.O. Box 1088, Commack (11725-0942)
PHONE.................................631 858-9888
Jon Bihn, *President*
Xiping Bihn, *Corp Secy*
▲ **EMP:** 11
SALES (est): 1.3MM **Privately Held**
SIC: 2393 3161 7389 Canvas bags; traveling bags;

(G-4290)
ALTERNATIVES FOR CHILDREN
600 S Service Rd (11746-6015)
PHONE.................................631 271-0777
Vivienne Viera, *Director*
EMP: 31
SALES (corp-wide): 10.5MM **Privately Held**
SIC: 3949 Windsurfing boards (sailboards) & equipment
PA: Alternatives For Children
14 Research Way
East Setauket NY 11733
631 331-6400

(G-4291)
AUTHORITY TRANSPORTATION INC
Also Called: Authority On Transportation
167 Oakfield Ave (11746-6327)
PHONE.................................888 933-1268
Jinya Kato, *Principal*
David Lipsky, *Principal*
EMP: 7
SQ FT: 40,000
SALES (est): 1MM **Privately Held**
SIC: 3716 Motor homes

(G-4292)
KENT ELECTRO-PLATING CORP
5 Dupont Ct (11746-6258)
PHONE.................................718 358-9599
Fax: 718 358-9799
Anthony Galluccio, *President*
Anthony Galluccio Jr, *Vice Pres*
Michael Galluccio, *Vice Pres*
Vera Galluccio, *Treasurer*
EMP: 10 **EST:** 1954
SQ FT: 7,500
SALES (est): 1.5MM **Privately Held**
SIC: 3471 Electroplating of metals or formed products

(G-4293)
MAYFLOWER SPLINT CO
16 Arbor Ln (11746-5127)
P.O. Box 381, Huntington Station (11746-0309)
PHONE.................................631 549-5131
Fax: 631 424-6451
Inge Krueger, *Owner*
EMP: 25
SALES (est): 1.6MM **Privately Held**
SIC: 3842 Surgical appliances & supplies

(G-4294)
MCG GRAPHICS INC
101 Village Hill Dr (11746-8335)
PHONE.................................631 499-0730
Fax: 631 493-0982
Michael Goldsmith, *President*
EMP: 6
SQ FT: 800
SALES (est): 763.7K **Privately Held**
SIC: 2752 2754 Commercial printing, lithographic; commercial printing, gravure

(G-4295)
PREMIERE LIVING PRODUCTS LLC
22 Branwood Dr (11746-5710)
PHONE.................................631 873-4337
Sandy Cohen, *Mng Member*
◆ **EMP:** 10
SALES (est): 477.2K **Privately Held**
SIC: 2511 Storage chests, household: wood

(G-4296)
PRINTING X PRESS IONS
5 Dix Cir (11746-6033)
PHONE.................................631 242-1992
Fax: 631 254-8911
Christine Sigel, *Owner*
EMP: 7
SALES (est): 1.5MM **Privately Held**
WEB: www.printingxpresns.com
SIC: 2752 Commercial printing, lithographic

(G-4297)
SAFE CIRCUITS INC
15 Shoreham Dr W (11746-6580)
PHONE.................................631 586-3682
James Ptucha, *Principal*
EMP: 7
SALES (est): 712.8K **Privately Held**
SIC: 3679 Electronic circuits

(G-4298)
SENTRY DEVICES CORP
33 Rustic Gate Ln (11746-6136)
PHONE.................................631 491-3191
Alex Feibush, *President*
EMP: 5
SALES (est): 400K **Privately Held**
SIC: 3669 1731 Burglar alarm apparatus, electric; marine horns, electric; fire detection & burglar alarm systems specialization

(G-4299)
TREBOR INSTRUMENT CORP
39 Balsam Dr (11746-7724)
PHONE.................................631 423-7026
Fax: 516 293-2065
Zygmunt Grzesiak, *President*
EMP: 8
SQ FT: 2,200
SALES (est): 913.2K **Privately Held**
WEB: www.treborinst.com
SIC: 3599 Machine shop, jobbing & repair

Dobbs Ferry
Westchester County

(G-4300)
AKZO NOBEL CHEMICALS LLC
Also Called: Akzo Nobel Central Research
7 Livingstone Ave (10522-3401)
PHONE.................................914 674-5008
Richard Fennelly, *Counsel*
Louis Morris, *Counsel*
Richard Lendecky, *Controller*
Al Williams, *Human Res Mgr*
Mark Buczek, *Marketing Staff*
EMP: 250
SALES (corp-wide): 15.9B **Privately Held**
WEB: www.akzo-nobel.com
SIC: 2819 8731 2899 Industrial inorganic chemicals; commercial physical research; chemical preparations
HQ: Akzo Nobel Chemicals Llc
525 W Van Buren St # 1600
Chicago IL 60607
312 544-7000

(G-4301)
AKZO NOBEL CHEMICALS LLC
Also Called: Manufacturing Engineering Svcs
9 Livingstone Ave (10522-3401)
PHONE.................................914 674-5432
Fax: 914 693-1059
Richard Lendecky, *Controller*
Jim La Mar, *Manager*
EMP: 10
SALES (corp-wide): 15.9B **Privately Held**
WEB: www.akzo-nobel.com
SIC: 2869 Industrial organic chemicals
HQ: Akzo Nobel Chemicals Llc
525 W Van Buren St # 1600
Chicago IL 60607
312 544-7000

(G-4302)
REMBAR COMPANY LLC
67 Main St (10522-2152)
P.O. Box 67 (10522-0067)
PHONE.................................914 693-2620
Fax: 914 693-2247
Frank H Firor, *CEO*
Walter Pastor, *President*
Audra Haase, *Vice Pres*
Tom Derentiis, *Manager*
▼ **EMP:** 23 **EST:** 1950
SQ FT: 8,000
SALES (est): 2.7MM **Privately Held**
WEB: www.rembar.com
SIC: 3297 3399 Nonclay refractories; metal powders, pastes & flakes

(G-4303)
SUN SCIENTIFIC INC
88 Ashford Ave (10522-1812)
PHONE.................................914 479-5108
Sundram Ravikumar, *President*
Shridhar Shanmugam, *COO*
Arti Ravikumar, *Vice Pres*
EMP: 7
SQ FT: 1,500
SALES (est): 674.8K **Privately Held**
SIC: 3845 Electromedical equipment

(G-4304)
W H WHITE PUBLICATIONS INC
Also Called: Rivertowns Enterprise
95 Main St (10522-1673)
PHONE.................................914 725-2500
Deborah White, *President*
EMP: 8 **EST:** 1981
SALES (est): 370K **Privately Held**
SIC: 2711 Newspapers

Dolgeville
Herkimer County

(G-4305)
GEHRING TRICOT CORPORATION
68 Ransom St Ste 272 (13329-1461)
PHONE.................................315 429-8551
Robert Lumley, *Vice Pres*
Ray Moissonnier, *QC Dir*
Paul Gutowski, *Controller*
Richard Patrick, *Data Proc Dir*
EMP: 125
SALES (corp-wide): 60.2MM **Privately Held**
SIC: 2257 2258 Dyeing & finishing circular knit fabrics; warp & flat knit products
PA: Gehring Tricot Corporation
1225 Franklin Ave Ste 300
Garden City NY 11530
315 429-8551

(G-4306)
NORTH HUDSON WOODCRAFT CORP
152 N Helmer Ave (13329-2826)
P.O. Box 192 (13329-0192)
PHONE.................................315 429-3105
Fax: 315 429-3479
Jeffrey C Slifka, *Ch of Bd*
William Slifka, *Treasurer*
Michael Jorrey, *Controller*
EMP: 50 **EST:** 1871
SQ FT: 100,000
SALES (est): 7.4MM **Privately Held**
WEB: www.northhudsonwoodcraft.com
SIC: 2426 3995 Furniture dimension stock, hardwood; burial caskets

(G-4307)
RAWLINGS SPORTING GOODS CO INC
52 Mckinley Ave (13329-1139)
PHONE.................................315 429-8511
Fax: 315 429-8507
Ronald Van Dergroef, *Principal*
Allen Mosier, *Purchasing*
EMP: 52
SQ FT: 62,884

Dolgeville - Herkimer County (G-4308)

SALES (corp-wide): 5.9B **Publicly Held**
SIC: **3949** Sporting & athletic goods
HQ: Rawlings Sporting Goods Company, Inc.
510 Maryville University
Saint Louis MO 63141
866 678-4327

(G-4308)
REAL DESIGN INC
187 S Main St (13329-1455)
PHONE..................................315 429-3071
Sam Camardello, *President*
EMP: 10
SALES: 400K **Privately Held**
WEB: www.realdesigninc.com
SIC: **3429** Furniture hardware

(G-4309)
TUMBLE FORMS INC (PA)
1013 Barker Rd (13329-2401)
PHONE..................................315 429-3101
Fax: 315 429-9739
Dave Faulchner, *General Mgr*
EMP: 20
SQ FT: 25,200
SALES (est): 8.9MM **Privately Held**
SIC: **3842** Surgical appliances & supplies

Douglaston
Queens County

(G-4310)
SALVADOR COLLETTI BLANK
25141 Van Zandt Ave (11362-1735)
PHONE..................................718 217-6725
Salvador Colletti, *Principal*
EMP: 5
SALES (est): 248.2K **Privately Held**
SIC: **2099** Food preparations

(G-4311)
SOLID-LOOK CORPORATION
4628 243rd St (11362-1129)
PHONE..................................917 683-1780
Raffaello Galli, *CEO*
EMP: 2
SQ FT: 2,000
SALES: 1MM **Privately Held**
SIC: **3841** Surgical & medical instruments

(G-4312)
SPRINGFIELD CONTROL SYSTEMS
4056 Douglaston Pkwy (11363-1507)
PHONE..................................718 631-0870
William Boettjer, *President*
EMP: 8
SALES (est): 680K **Privately Held**
SIC: **3823** Temperature measurement instruments, industrial

(G-4313)
TAMKA SPORT LLC
225 Beverly Rd (11363-1122)
PHONE..................................718 224-7820
Kathleen Derienzo, *Mng Member*
EMP: 8
SALES: 90K **Privately Held**
SIC: **2329** 2339 Men's & boys' athletic uniforms; uniforms, athletic: women's, misses' & juniors'

Dover Plains
Dutchess County

(G-4314)
CENTRAL DOVER DEVELOPMENT
247 Dover Furnace Rd (12522-5773)
PHONE..................................917 709-3266
Wayne Tanner, *President*
Elaine Tanner, *Vice Pres*
EMP: 4
SALES: 1MM **Privately Held**
SIC: **1442** 0191 Gravel mining; general farms, primarily crop

(G-4315)
J & J LOG & LUMBER CORP
528 Old State Route 22 (12522-5821)
P.O. Box 1139 (12522-1139)
PHONE..................................845 832-6535
Fax: 845 832-3757
Randolph L Williams, *CEO*
Julie Tuz, *VP Human Res*
Mil Oltman, *Technology*
▼ EMP: 80
SQ FT: 10,200
SALES (est): 15.6MM **Privately Held**
SIC: **2421** 2426 Sawmills & planing mills, general; hardwood dimension & flooring mills

(G-4316)
PALUMBO BLOCK CO INC
365 Dover Furnace Rd (12522-5775)
P.O. Box 810 (12522-0810)
PHONE..................................845 832-6100
Fax: 845 832-6431
Fortunato Palumbo, *President*
Anthony Palumbo, *Vice Pres*
Mary Palumbo, *Vice Pres*
Tony Palumbo, *Vice Pres*
Mary Palumbo Sprong, *Vice Pres*
EMP: 25
SQ FT: 28,000
SALES (est): 4.8MM **Privately Held**
SIC: **3271** 5082 5211 Concrete block & brick; masonry equipment & supplies; masonry materials & supplies

(G-4317)
PALUMBO SAND & GRAVEL COMPANY
Also Called: Palumbo Block
155 Sherman Hill Rd (12522-5625)
P.O. Box 810 (12522-0810)
PHONE..................................845 832-3356
Fortunato Palumbo, *President*
EMP: 45 EST: 1968
SQ FT: 20,000
SALES (est): 4MM **Privately Held**
SIC: **1442** Construction sand mining; gravel mining

Dresden
Yates County

(G-4318)
ABTEX CORPORATION
89 Main St (14441-9708)
P.O. Box 188 (14441-0188)
PHONE..................................315 536-7403
Fax: 315 536-0280
D Mark Fultz, *President*
John Roman, *Engineer*
Frank Sweet, *Engineer*
Brandon Boyd, *Project Engr*
David Burlew, *Project Engr*
EMP: 21
SQ FT: 20,000
SALES (est): 4.6MM **Privately Held**
WEB: www.abtex.com
SIC: **3991** 3541 Brushes, household or industrial; machine tools, metal cutting type

(G-4319)
FAULKNER TRUSS COMPANY INC
1830 King Hill Rd (14441)
P.O. Box 407, Hammondsport (14840-0407)
PHONE..................................315 536-8894
Richard C Faulkner, *Ch of Bd*
EMP: 5
SALES (est): 573.2K **Privately Held**
SIC: **2439** Structural wood members

Dryden
Tompkins County

(G-4320)
BAGELOVERS INC
42 Elm St (13053-9623)
P.O. Box 62 (13053-0062)
PHONE..................................607 844-3683
Fax: 607 844-5269

Charles Tallman, *President*
Gary Westphal, *Vice Pres*
EMP: 18
SQ FT: 12,500
SALES (est): 2.2MM **Privately Held**
SIC: **2051** 5142 Bagels, fresh or frozen; packaged frozen goods

(G-4321)
INTEGRATED WATER MANAGEMENT
Also Called: I W M
289 Cortland Rd (13053-9517)
P.O. Box 523 (13053-0523)
PHONE..................................607 844-4276
David Duffett, *President*
EMP: 5
SQ FT: 3,700
SALES (est): 1MM **Privately Held**
SIC: **3589** Water treatment equipment, industrial

(G-4322)
ROSCOE BROTHERS INC
15 Freeville Rd (13053-9537)
PHONE..................................607 844-3750
Chris Roscoe, *President*
Nick Roscoe, *Vice Pres*
EMP: 13 EST: 2014
SALES: 1MM **Privately Held**
SIC: **2452** 7389 Prefabricated buildings, wood;

(G-4323)
STURGES ELEC PDTS CO INC
Also Called: Sepco-Sturges Electronics
23 North St (13053)
P.O. Box 532 (13053-0532)
PHONE..................................607 844-8604
Fax: 607 844-8416
James Koch, *President*
Dick Biviano, *Manager*
EMP: 45
SQ FT: 15,000
SALES (est): 6.6MM **Privately Held**
WEB: www.sturgeselectronics.com
SIC: **3679** Harness assemblies for electronic use: wire or cable

Duanesburg
Schenectady County

(G-4324)
AMERICAN CAR SIGNS INC
1483 W Duane Lake Rd (12056-2713)
PHONE..................................518 227-1173
Eulaila Kulikoff, *CEO*
EMP: 6
SALES: 50K **Privately Held**
SIC: **3993** Signs & advertising specialties

(G-4325)
CUSTOM DESIGN KITCHENS INC
1700 Duanesburg Rd (12056-4310)
PHONE..................................518 355-4446
Fax: 518 355-4325
Terry Zarrillo, *President*
Dawn Zarrillo, *Corp Secy*
EMP: 10
SQ FT: 10,000
SALES (est): 920K **Privately Held**
SIC: **2541** 5031 5211 3131 Cabinets, except refrigerated: show, display, etc.: wood; kitchen cabinets; cabinets, kitchen; counter tops; counters

Dundee
Yates County

(G-4326)
EAST BRANCH WINERY INC (PA)
Also Called: Mc Gregor Vineyard Winery
5503 Dutch St (14837-9746)
PHONE..................................607 292-3999
Fax: 607 292-6929
Robert Mc Gregor, *President*
David Payne, *Shareholder*
Marge Mc Gregor, *Admin Sec*
EMP: 8
SQ FT: 2,000

SALES: 402K **Privately Held**
SIC: **2084** 0172 Wines, brandy & brandy spirits; wines; grapes

(G-4327)
FINGER LAKES MEDIA INC
Also Called: The Observer
45 Water St (14837-1029)
P.O. Box 127 (14837-0127)
PHONE..................................607 243-7600
Fax: 607 243-5833
George Lawson, *President*
EMP: 12
SALES (est): 558.1K **Privately Held**
WEB: www.fingerlakesmedia.com
SIC: **2711** Newspapers

(G-4328)
GLENORA WINE CELLARS INC
5435 State Route 14 (14837-8804)
PHONE..................................607 243-9500
Fax: 607 243-5514
Eugene Pierce, *President*
Scott Welliver, *Treasurer*
Tracey Dwyer, *Controller*
John Terry, *Controller*
Barbara Stone, *Human Res Mgr*
EMP: 34 EST: 1977
SQ FT: 18,000
SALES (est): 5.9MM **Privately Held**
WEB: www.glenora.com
SIC: **2084** Wines

(G-4329)
HERMANN J WIEMER VINEYARD
3962 Rte 14 (14837)
P.O. Box 38 (14837-0038)
PHONE..................................607 243-7971
Fax: 607 243-7983
Hermann J Wiemer, *President*
Osker Bynke, *Mktg Dir*
Tracey K Stritto, *Corp Comm Staff*
▲ EMP: 5
SALES (est): 467.9K **Privately Held**
WEB: www.wiemer.com
SIC: **2084** 0172 Wines; grapes

(G-4330)
HICKORY ROAD LAND CO LLC
Also Called: Hickory Hollow Wind Cellars
5289 Route 14 (14837-8800)
P.O. Box 37 (14837-0037)
PHONE..................................607 243-9114
Edward Woodland, *Mng Member*
Suzanne Kendall, *Manager*
EMP: 5
SALES (est): 363.2K **Privately Held**
SIC: **2084** Wine cellars, bonded: engaged in blending wines

Dunkirk
Chautauqua County

(G-4331)
AMCOR RIGID PLASTICS USA LLC
1 Cliffstar Ave (14048-2800)
PHONE..................................716 366-2440
Fax: 716 366-2707
Jan Szymanski, *VP Mktg*
Bryan Cotton, *Branch Mgr*
EMP: 50 **Privately Held**
WEB: www.slpcamericas.com
SIC: **3089** Plastic containers, except foam
HQ: Amcor Rigid Plastics Usa, Llc
10521 M 52
Manchester MI 48158

(G-4332)
BERRY PLASTICS GROUP INC
3565 Chadwick Dr (14048-9652)
PHONE..................................716 366-2112
EMP: 11
SALES (corp-wide): 4.8B **Publicly Held**
SIC: **3089** Air mattresses, plastic
PA: Berry Plastics Group, Inc.
101 Oakley St
Evansville IN 47710
812 424-2904

GEOGRAPHIC SECTION

Durham - Greene County (G-4355)

(G-4333)
CAPTIVE PLASTICS LLC
3565 Chadwick Dr (14048-9652)
PHONE.................................716 366-2112
Bob Humberger, *Branch Mgr*
EMP: 97
SALES (corp-wide): 4.8B **Publicly Held**
WEB: www.captiveplastics.com
SIC: 3089 Bottle caps, molded plastic
HQ: Captive Plastics, Inc.
    101 Oakley St
    Evansville IN 47710
    812 424-2904

(G-4334)
CARRIAGE HOUSE COMPANIES INC
26 E Talcott St (14048-2854)
PHONE.................................716 673-1000
Fax: 716 366-7715
Dick Scriven, *Manager*
EMP: 200
SALES (corp-wide): 3.2B **Publicly Held**
WEB: www.carriagehousecos.com
SIC: 2035 Spreads, sandwich: salad dressing base
HQ: The Carriage House Companies Inc
    196 Newton St
    Fredonia NY 14063
    716 672-4321

(G-4335)
CHAUTAUQUA CIRCUITS INC
855 Main St (14048-3505)
PHONE.................................716 366-5771
William E Wragge, *President*
EMP: 6
SALES: 250K **Privately Held**
SIC: 3672 Printed circuit boards

(G-4336)
CHAUTAUQUA WOODS CORP
134 Franklin Ave (14048-2806)
P.O. Box 130 (14048-0130)
PHONE.................................716 366-3808
Fax: 716 366-3814
Khalid Khan, *President*
Steve Dean, *Vice Pres*
Bia Khan, *Treasurer*
Donna Bolling, *Office Mgr*
Bia Kahn, *Manager*
EMP: 40
SQ FT: 50,000
SALES: 2.3MM **Privately Held**
WEB: www.chautauquawoods.com
SIC: 2431 Doors, wood

(G-4337)
CLIFFSTAR LLC (HQ)
Also Called: Cott Beverages
1 Cliffstar Dr (14048-2800)
PHONE.................................716 366-6100
Fax: 716 366-6161
Monica Consonery, *Exec VP*
Kevin Sanvidge, *Exec VP*
Richard Star, *Exec VP*
Kevin M Sanvidge, *VP Admin*
Mark Obrien, *Vice Pres*
◆ EMP: 700
SALES (est): 394MM
SALES (corp-wide): 2.9B **Privately Held**
SIC: 2033 2086 Fruit juices: fresh; bottled & canned soft drinks; pasteurized & mineral waters, bottled & canned
PA: Cott Corporation
    6525 Viscount Rd
    Mississauga ON L4V 1
    905 672-1900

(G-4338)
DUNKIRK CONSTRUCTION PRODUCTS
852 Main St (14048-3506)
P.O. Box 149 (14048-0149)
PHONE.................................716 366-5220
Patrick Pacos, *President*
James Pacos, *Vice Pres*
Dorothy Pacos, *Treasurer*
EMP: 5
SQ FT: 3,800
SALES (est): 643.3K **Privately Held**
SIC: 3273 Ready-mixed concrete

(G-4339)
DUNKIRK METAL PRODUCTS WNY LLC (PA)
3575 Chadwick Dr (14048-9652)
PHONE.................................716 366-2555
Fax: 716 366-4726
Joe Shull, *President*
▼ EMP: 22 EST: 1946
SQ FT: 50,000
SALES (est): 6.4MM **Privately Held**
SIC: 3469 Metal stampings

(G-4340)
DUNKIRK SPECIALTY STEEL LLC
830 Brigham Rd (14048-3473)
P.O. Box 319 (14048-0319)
PHONE.................................716 366-1000
Dennis Oates, *President*
Connie Carlson, *COO*
William W Beible Jr, *Senior VP*
Paul A McGrath, *VP Admin*
Paul Jess, *Project Mgr*
▲ EMP: 166
SALES (est): 43MM
SALES (corp-wide): 180.6MM **Publicly Held**
WEB: www.dunkirkspecialtysteel.com
SIC: 3312 Blast furnaces & steel mills
PA: Universal Stainless & Alloy Products, Inc.
    600 Mayer St Ste 2
    Bridgeville PA 15017
    412 257-7600

(G-4341)
ECR INTERNATIONAL INC
Dunkirk Division
85 Middle Rd (14048-1311)
P.O. Box 32 (14048-0032)
PHONE.................................716 366-5500
Fax: 716 366-1209
Steve Lilly, *Plant Mgr*
Warren Welka, *Site Mgr*
Todd Eggleston, *Buyer*
Dennis Keppel, *Engineer*
Phil Kleeberger, *Human Res Dir*
EMP: 130
SQ FT: 17,087
SALES (corp-wide): 119MM **Privately Held**
WEB: www.ecrinternational.com
SIC: 3433 3443 Boilers, low-pressure heating: steam or hot water; fabricated plate work (boiler shop)
PA: Ecr International, Inc.
    2201 Dwyer Ave
    Utica NY 13501
    315 797-1310

(G-4342)
FFC HOLDING CORP SUBSIDIARIES (PA)
1 Ice Cream Dr (14048-3300)
PHONE.................................716 366-5400
Kenneth A Johnson, *President*
Ron Odebralski, *Controller*
EMP: 12
SQ FT: 280,000
SALES (est): 102.3MM **Privately Held**
SIC: 2024 Ice cream & frozen desserts

(G-4343)
FIELDBROOK FOODS CORPORATION (HQ)
1 Ice Cream Dr (14048-3300)
P.O. Box 1318 (14048-6318)
PHONE.................................716 366-5400
Fax: 716 366-3588
Kenneth A Johnson, *CEO*
Robert Griewisch, *President*
Mary Lind, *Editor*
James Masood, *Senior VP*
Ronald Odebralski, *Vice Pres*
▼ EMP: 236
SQ FT: 280,000
SALES (est): 101.8MM **Privately Held**
SIC: 2024 Ice cream & frozen desserts
PA: Ffc Holding Corporation And Subsidiaries
    1 Ice Cream Dr
    Dunkirk NY 14048
    716 366-5400

(G-4344)
LAKESIDE PRECISION INC
208 Dove St (14048-1598)
PHONE.................................716 366-5030
Fax: 716 366-5041
James E Anson, *President*
Christopher Anson, *Opers Staff*
Phil Nosek, *QC Mgr*
Patty Dechart, *Controller*
Mary Barbknecht, *Office Mgr*
EMP: 22 EST: 1963
SQ FT: 11,300
SALES: 1.7MM **Privately Held**
WEB: www.lakesideprecision.com
SIC: 3599 Machine shop, jobbing & repair; custom machinery

(G-4345)
NESTLE PURINA PETCARE COMPANY
Also Called: Nestle Purina Factory
3800 Middle Rd (14048-9750)
PHONE.................................716 366-8080
Ron Krystofiak, *Purch Mgr*
Ron Bowers, *Branch Mgr*
Jay Ondus, *Manager*
John Palmer, *Systems Staff*
Stacey Olsen, *Training Super*
EMP: 300
SALES (corp-wide): 88.3B **Privately Held**
WEB: www.purina.com
SIC: 2047 Dog & cat food; dog food
HQ: Nestle Purina Petcare Company
    901 Chouteau Ave
    Saint Louis MO 63102
    314 982-1000

(G-4346)
OBSERVER DAILY SUNDAY NEWSPPR
Also Called: The Observer
10 E 2nd St (14048-1602)
P.O. Box 391 (14048-0391)
PHONE.................................716 366-3000
Fax: 716 366-3005
Karl T Davis, *General Mgr*
Craig Harvey, *Editor*
Gib Snyder, *Editor*
James Austin, *Plant Mgr*
Jerry Reilly, *Loan Officer*
EMP: 100
SALES (est): 13.8MM **Privately Held**
WEB: www.observertoday.com
SIC: 2752 2711 Commercial printing, lithographic; newspapers

(G-4347)
PERSCH SERVICE PRINT INC (PA)
11 W 3rd St (14048-2060)
PHONE.................................716 366-2677
Fax: 716 366-3626
Robert H Persch, *President*
Margaret T Persch, *Treasurer*
Margaret P Triaga, *Admin Sec*
EMP: 9 EST: 1911
SALES (est): 1MM **Privately Held**
SIC: 2752 7334 Commercial printing, lithographic; photocopying & duplicating services

(G-4348)
REM-TRONICS INC
659 Brigham Rd (14048-2361)
PHONE.................................716 934-2697
Fax: 716 934-9538
Abe M Kadis, *President*
Mathew Karalunas, *General Mgr*
Clayton Spaeth, *General Mgr*
Patricia Karalunas, *Purchasing*
Michael Kadis, *Controller*
EMP: 58
SQ FT: 20,000
SALES (est): 9.9MM **Privately Held**
WEB: www.rem-tronics.com
SIC: 3679 Electronic circuits

(G-4349)
REXFORD SERVICES INC
4849 W Lake Rd (14048-9613)
PHONE.................................716 366-6671
William Rexford, *President*
Trisha Rexford, *Vice Pres*
EMP: 5

SALES (est): 666.8K **Privately Held**
SIC: 3713 Specialty motor vehicle bodies

(G-4350)
SHAANT INDUSTRIES INC
134 Franklin Ave (14048-2806)
P.O. Box 130 (14048-0130)
PHONE.................................716 366-3654
Fax: 716 366-0041
Khalid Khan, *President*
Rebecca Berger, *Manager*
▲ EMP: 40
SQ FT: 50,000
SALES (est): 7.6MM **Privately Held**
WEB: www.ultrapak.net
SIC: 3081 2671 Polyvinyl film & sheet; packaging paper & plastics film, coated & laminated

(G-4351)
SPECIAL METALS CORPORATION
100 Willowbrook Ave (14048-3479)
P.O. Box 304 (14048-0304)
PHONE.................................716 366-5663
Fax: 716 366-7436
Fred A Schweizer, *Opers Staff*
Peter Eckman, *Production*
Greg Caserta, *Technical Mgr*
Don Borowski, *Manager*
George Gaston, *Manager*
EMP: 60
SALES (corp-wide): 210.8B **Publicly Held**
SIC: 3542 3463 3462 3341 Forging machinery & hammers; extruding machines (machine tools), metal; die casting machines; nonferrous forgings; iron & steel forgings; secondary nonferrous metals
HQ: Special Metals Corporation
    4832 Richmond Rd Ste 100
    Warrensville Heights OH 44128
    216 755-3030

(G-4352)
UNIVERSAL STAINLESS & ALLOY
830 Brigham Rd (14048-3473)
PHONE.................................716 366-1000
EMP: 142
SALES (corp-wide): 180.6MM **Publicly Held**
SIC: 3312 Blast furnaces & steel mills
PA: Universal Stainless & Alloy Products, Inc.
    600 Mayer St Ste 2
    Bridgeville PA 15017
    412 257-7600

(G-4353)
X PRESS SCREEN PRINTING
4867 W Lake Rd (14048-9613)
PHONE.................................716 679-7788
Chad Rizzo, *President*
EMP: 7
SALES (est): 584.7K **Privately Held**
SIC: 2759 Commercial printing

Durham
Greene County

(G-4354)
ADVANCED YARN TECHNOLOGIES INC
Also Called: Cidega American Trim
4750 State Hwy 145 (12422-5306)
PHONE.................................518 239-6600
Fax: 518 239-8153
Richard Gangi, *President*
Daniel Gangi, *Vice Pres*
Sebastian Gangi, *Vice Pres*
EMP: 50
SALES (est): 5.3MM **Privately Held**
SIC: 2281 5199 Yarn spinning mills; fabrics, yarns & knit goods

(G-4355)
AMERICAN TRIM MFG INC
4750 State Hwy 145 (12422-5306)
PHONE.................................518 239-8151
Richard Gangi, *President*
Daniel Gangi, *Vice Pres*
Sabastian Gangi, *Vice Pres*

▲ EMP: 50
SQ FT: 30,000
SALES (est): 12.5MM Privately Held
SIC: 2241 Trimmings, textile

Eagle Bridge
Rensselaer County

(G-4356)
EAGLE BRIDGE MACHINE & TL INC
135 State Route 67 (12057-2446)
PHONE..................518 686-4541
Fax: 518 686-3125
Robert Farrara, *President*
Raymond Farrara, *Corp Secy*
Peter Gardner, *Manager*
▲ EMP: 35 EST: 1965
SQ FT: 12,000
SALES (est): 4.3MM Privately Held
WEB: www.eaglebridgemachine.com
SIC: 3599 3743 Machine shop, jobbing & repair; railroad equipment

(G-4357)
PROFESSIONAL PACKG SVCS INC
Also Called: Pro Pack
62 Owlkill Rd (12057-2609)
PHONE..................518 677-5100
Ronald Dooley, *President*
Lorraine Dooley, *Corp Secy*
Donald E Pacher Sr, *Sales Mgr*
EMP: 30
SQ FT: 25,000
SALES (est): 5.6MM Privately Held
SIC: 2653 2631 3086 Boxes, corrugated: made from purchased materials; paperboard mills; plastics foam products

(G-4358)
PROPAK INC
70 Owlkill Rd (12057-2609)
PHONE..................518 677-5100
Fax: 518 677-5933
Jack Baratta, *Principal*
Frank Bowles, *Controller*
EMP: 6
SALES (est): 534.9K Privately Held
SIC: 2652 Setup paperboard boxes

(G-4359)
STRATO TRANSIT COMPONENTS LLC
155 State Route 67 (12057-2446)
PHONE..................518 686-4541
Michael Foxx,
Michael Corridon,
Steven Foxx,
▲ EMP: 8
SALES (est): 1MM Privately Held
SIC: 3743 Railroad equipment

Earlville
Chenango County

(G-4360)
EARLVILLE PAPER BOX CO INC
19 Clyde St (13332-2902)
PHONE..................315 691-2131
Fax: 315 691-2050
Richard T Upton, *President*
Marilyn J Upton, *Treasurer*
Steve Upton, *Sales Staff*
EMP: 20
SQ FT: 7,200
SALES (est): 3.8MM Privately Held
WEB: www.earlvillepaperbox.com
SIC: 2652 Setup paperboard boxes

East Amherst
Erie County

(G-4361)
INTEGRTED WORK ENVRONMENTS LLC
Also Called: Iwe
6346 Everwood Ct N (14051-2032)
P.O. Box 1514, Williamsville (14231-1514)
PHONE..................716 725-5088
Evan M Casey, *Mng Member*
EMP: 7
SALES (est): 1MM Privately Held
SIC: 3821 5047 5049 Laboratory apparatus & furniture; medical laboratory equipment; laboratory equipment, except medical or dental

(G-4362)
SWEET MELODYS LLC
8485 Transit Rd (14051-1059)
PHONE..................716 580-3227
Chuck Incorvia,
▲ EMP: 20
SALES (est): 2MM Privately Held
SIC: 2024 Dairy based frozen desserts

(G-4363)
VADER SYSTEMS LLC
179 Roxbury Park (14051-1775)
P.O. Box 179 (14051-0179)
PHONE..................716 636-1742
Scott Vader, *Mng Member*
EMP: 1
SALES: 8MM Privately Held
SIC: 3599 3542 3577 3549 Machine & other job shop work; metal deposit forming machines; computer peripheral equipment; metalworking machinery;

East Aurora
Erie County

(G-4364)
ADCO INNVTIVE PRMTNAL PDTS INC
574 Main St Ste 301 (14052-1751)
PHONE..................716 805-1076
Fax: 716 805-1228
Antoinette Dugas, *President*
EMP: 5
SALES: 850K Privately Held
SIC: 2759 Screen printing

(G-4365)
AMERICAN PRECISION INDS INC
API Delevan
270 Quaker Rd (14052-2192)
P.O. Box 449 (14052-0449)
PHONE..................716 652-3600
Fax: 716 652-4814
Daniel A Raskas, *President*
Steve Chandler, *Production*
James Cadwallader, *Engrg Mgr*
Brad Feltz, *Engineer*
George Ellis, *Sales Staff*
EMP: 100
SALES (corp-wide): 20.5B Publicly Held
WEB: www.apischmidtbretten.com
SIC: 3677 Coil windings, electronic; inductors, electronic
HQ: American Precision Industries Inc.
45 Hazelwood Dr
Amherst NY 14228
716 691-9100

(G-4366)
ASTRONICS CORPORATION (PA)
130 Commerce Way (14052-2164)
PHONE..................716 805-1599
Fax: 716 655-0309
Kevin T Keane, *Ch of Bd*
Peter J Gundermann, *President*
James S Kramer, *Exec VP*
Mark A Peabody, *Exec VP*
Martha Piedrahita, *Mfg Spvr*
▲ EMP: 212
SQ FT: 125,000
SALES: 692.2MM Publicly Held
SIC: 3728 3647 Aircraft parts & equipment; aircraft lighting fixtures

(G-4367)
AURORA TECHNICAL SERVICES LTD
11970 Parker Rd (14052-9533)
P.O. Box 103 (14052-0103)
PHONE..................716 652-1463
Karen Wright, *President*
Steven Wright, *Vice Pres*
Richard Ceier, *Manager*
EMP: 5
SQ FT: 1,100
SALES (est): 674.1K Privately Held
WEB: www.auroratechserv.com
SIC: 3829 3825 Ultrasonic testing equipment; meters: electric, pocket, portable, panelboard, etc.

(G-4368)
COLDEN CLOSET LLC
1375 Boies Rd (14052-9726)
PHONE..................716 713-6125
Kevin Lindberg, *Owner*
EMP: 9
SALES (est): 1MM Privately Held
SIC: 2673 Wardrobe bags (closet accessories): from purchased materials

(G-4369)
DIREKT FORCE LLC
455 Olean Rd Ste 3 (14052-9791)
PHONE..................716 652-3022
Kurt Knolle, *Mng Member*
EMP: 25 EST: 2001
SQ FT: 7,000
SALES (est): 5.2MM Privately Held
WEB: www.direktforce.com
SIC: 3492 3593 3443 Control valves, fluid power: hydraulic & pneumatic; fluid power cylinders, hydraulic or pneumatic; fabricated plate work (boiler shop)

(G-4370)
EVERFAB INC
12928 Big Tree Rd (14052-9524)
PHONE..................716 655-1550
Fax: 716 655-4398
Alan L Everett, *Ch of Bd*
Kirk Everett, *Vice Pres*
Lee Everett, *Vice Pres*
Scott Everett, *Vice Pres*
Mike Spink, *Purch Mgr*
EMP: 55
SQ FT: 45,000
SALES (est): 12.8MM Privately Held
WEB: www.everfab.com
SIC: 2821 3441 3545 3544 Elastomers, nonvulcanizable (plastics); molding compounds, plastics; fabricated structural metal; machine tool accessories; special dies, tools, jigs & fixtures; machine & other job shop work

(G-4371)
GRANT HAMILTON (PA)
Also Called: East Aurora Advertiser
710 Main St (14052-2406)
P.O. Box 5 (14052-0005)
PHONE..................716 652-0320
Fax: 716 652-8383
Grant Hamilton, *Owner*
Roger Leblanc, *Fire Chief*
Shane Krieger, *Chief*
Sandra Cunningham, *Office Mgr*
Bonnie Cecala, *Manager*
EMP: 15 EST: 1872
SQ FT: 2,850
SALES (est): 1MM Privately Held
WEB: www.eastaurorany.com
SIC: 2741 5943 Newsletter publishing; office forms & supplies

(G-4372)
GUARDIAN SYSTEMS TECH INC
659 Oakwood Ave (14052-2511)
PHONE..................716 481-5597
Edward Seebald, *CEO*
Meighan Lloyd, *Principal*
EMP: 10
SALES (est): 710.6K Privately Held
SIC: 3699 Electrical equipment & supplies

(G-4373)
LUMINESCENT SYSTEMS INC (HQ)
Also Called: L S I
130 Commerce Way (14052-2191)
PHONE..................716 655-0800
Peter Gundermann, *President*
Frank Johns, *Vice Pres*
James Kramer, *Vice Pres*
Richard Miller, *Vice Pres*
Richard Glinski, *Engineer*
EMP: 300
SALES (est): 68.6MM
SALES (corp-wide): 692.2MM Publicly Held
SIC: 3647 3646 3648 3577 Aircraft lighting fixtures; commercial indusl & institutional electric lighting fixtures; lighting equipment; computer peripheral equipment
PA: Astronics Corporation
130 Commerce Way
East Aurora NY 14052
716 805-1599

(G-4374)
MATTEL INC
609 Girard Ave (14052-1822)
P.O. Box 609 (14052-0609)
PHONE..................716 714-8514
Chris Schaden, *Senior VP*
Robynn Rich, *Opers Staff*
Regis Oconnor, *Engng Exec*
Teresa G Ruiz, *VP Mktg*
Lisa McKnight, *Mktg Dir*
EMP: 15
SALES (corp-wide): 5.7B Publicly Held
WEB: www.mattel.com
SIC: 3944 3942 3949 Games, toys & children's vehicles; dolls, except stuffed toy animals; stuffed toys, including animals; sporting & athletic goods
PA: Mattel, Inc.
333 Continental Blvd
El Segundo CA 90245
310 252-2000

(G-4375)
MOOG INC
Industrial Controls Division
300 Jamison Rd (14052)
P.O. Box 18 (14052-0018)
PHONE..................716 655-3000
Donna Ward, *Mktg Coord*
Rae Perrott, *Branch Mgr*
Sylvia Wright, *Program Mgr*
EMP: 300
SALES (corp-wide): 2.5B Publicly Held
WEB: www.moog.com
SIC: 3492 3721 Fluid power valves & hose fittings; aircraft
PA: Moog Inc.
400 Jamison Rd Plant26
Elma NY 14059
716 652-2000

(G-4376)
MOOG INC
Moog Systems Group
7021 Sneca St At Jmson Rd (14052)
PHONE..................716 805-8100
Fax: 716 687-4467
Sandra Reczek, *Buyer*
Emmanuel Jeanlouis, *Engineer*
Paul Bogucki, *Senior Engr*
Kristine Karnath, *Human Resources*
Doug Gallen, *Branch Mgr*
EMP: 225
SALES (corp-wide): 2.5B Publicly Held
WEB: www.moog.com
SIC: 3625 Relays & industrial controls
PA: Moog Inc.
400 Jamison Rd Plant26
Elma NY 14059
716 652-2000

(G-4377)
MOOG INC
Also Called: Moog Space and Defense Group
500 Jamison Rd (14052)
PHONE..................716 687-5486
David Schabel, *Design Engr*
Bill Watt, *Electrical Engi*
Eileen Tighe, *Human Resources*
Bryan Stinocher, *Sales Mgr*
EMP: 453

SALES (corp-wide): 2.5B **Publicly Held**
SIC: 3812 Aircraft control systems, electronic
PA: Moog Inc.
400 Jamison Rd
East Aurora NY 14059
716 652-2000

(G-4378)
NORTHERN DESIGN INC
12990 Old Big Tree Rd (14052-9525)
PHONE..716 652-7071
Robert Lippert, *President*
Gabor Bertalan, *Vice Pres*
EMP: 6
SQ FT: 550
SALES: 500K **Privately Held**
WEB: www.northerndesign.com
SIC: 3544 Forms (molds), for foundry & plastics working machinery; dies & die holders for metal cutting, forming, die casting

(G-4379)
SLOSSON EDCTL PUBLICATIONS INC
538 Buffalo Rd (14052-9456)
P.O. Box 280 (14052-0280)
PHONE..716 652-0930
Fax: 585 655-3840
Steven Slosson, *President*
Janet Slosson, *Chairman*
EMP: 12
SQ FT: 2,400
SALES (est): 1MM **Privately Held**
WEB: www.slosson.com
SIC: 2741 8748 Miscellaneous publishing; business consulting

(G-4380)
WEST FALLS MACHINE CO INC
Also Called: West Falls Machine Co 1
11692 E Main Rd (14052-9597)
PHONE..716 655-0440
Fax: 585 655-4048
Matthew Creps, *CEO*
Mary Ann George, *Vice Pres*
EMP: 15
SQ FT: 15,000
SALES (est): 2.7MM **Privately Held**
SIC: 3599 3471 Machine shop, jobbing & repair; chromium plating of metals or formed products

East Berne
Albany County

(G-4381)
RUDY STEMPEL & FAMILY SAWMILL
73 Stemple Rd (12059-2843)
PHONE..518 872-0431
Rudolph Stempel, *President*
EMP: 6
SALES (est): 510K **Privately Held**
SIC: 2421 Sawmills & planing mills, general

East Bethany
Genesee County

(G-4382)
EMERALD MODELS INC
10204 Transit Rd (14054-9757)
PHONE..585 584-3739
Fax: 585 584-3789
Edward E Stringham, *President*
EMP: 6
SQ FT: 6,200
SALES (est): 480K **Privately Held**
WEB: www.emeraldmodels.com
SIC: 3999 Models, general, except toy

(G-4383)
SANDVOSS FARMS LLC
Also Called: First Light Farm & Creamery
10198 East Rd (14054-9754)
PHONE..585 297-7044
Peter Sandvoss,
Stephen Sandvoss,
EMP: 8
SALES (est): 235.3K **Privately Held**
SIC: 2022 Natural cheese

East Branch
Delaware County

(G-4384)
JOHNSTON FOREST PRODUCTS INC
O And W Rd (13756)
P.O. Box 179 (13756-0179)
PHONE..607 363-2947
Charles N Johnston, *President*
C Johnston, *Vice Pres*
EMP: 9 **EST:** 1999
SALES (est): 710.8K **Privately Held**
SIC: 2421 Sawmills & planing mills, general

East Concord
Erie County

(G-4385)
MCEWAN TRUCKING & GRAV PRODUC
11696 Route 240 (14055-9717)
PHONE..716 609-1828
Mary McEwan, *Principal*
EMP: 6
SALES (est): 545.1K **Privately Held**
SIC: 1442 Construction sand & gravel

(G-4386)
WENDELS POULTRY FARM
12466 Vaughn St (14055-9747)
PHONE..716 592-2299
Martin Wendel, *Partner*
Denise Wandel, *Partner*
David Wendel, *Partner*
EMP: 8
SQ FT: 12,000
SALES (est): 881.6K **Privately Held**
SIC: 2015 0254 Poultry, processed; poultry hatcheries

East Durham
Greene County

(G-4387)
GLAXOSMITHKLINE LLC
Also Called: Glaxosmthkline Cnsmr Heathcare
3169 Route 145 (12423-1416)
PHONE..518 239-6901
Max Van Veem, *Vice Pres*
Mark Matlosz, *Plant Supt*
Ron Pelak, *QC Dir*
Max Van Vessem, *Branch Mgr*
EMP: 75
SALES (corp-wide): 36B **Privately Held**
SIC: 2834 3843 Pharmaceutical preparations; procaine pharmaceutical preparations; dental equipment & supplies
HQ: Glaxosmithkline Llc
5 Crescent Dr
Philadelphia PA 19112
215 751-4000

East Elmhurst
Queens County

(G-4388)
ARM CONSTRUCTION COMPANY INC
10001 27th Ave (11369-1647)
PHONE..646 235-6520
Abdul Motaleb, *President*
EMP: 5
SALES: 383K **Privately Held**
SIC: 1389 7389 Construction, repair & dismantling services;

(G-4389)
BROTHERS ROOFING SUPPLIES CO
10514 Astoria Blvd (11369-2097)
PHONE..718 779-0280
Fax: 718 446-8069
Robert Kersch, *Ch of Bd*
Michael Kersch, *Vice Pres*
EMP: 20 **EST:** 1969
SQ FT: 16,000
SALES (est): 4.3MM **Privately Held**
WEB: www.brothersroofingsupply.com
SIC: 3444 Metal roofing & roof drainage equipment

(G-4390)
CITROS BUILDING MATERIALS CO
10514 Astoria Blvd (11369-2027)
PHONE..718 779-0727
Bobby Kersh, *President*
EMP: 40
SQ FT: 1,600
SALES (est): 5.2MM **Privately Held**
SIC: 3444 Skylights, sheet metal

(G-4391)
DOROSE NOVELTY CO INC
Also Called: Dorose Albums
3107 103rd St (11369-2013)
PHONE..718 451-3088
Fax: 718 451-3089
Sam Krauthamer, *President*
Alex Brodsky, *Vice Pres*
Regina Krauthamer, *Treasurer*
EMP: 14 **EST:** 1958
SALES (est): 1.1MM **Privately Held**
SIC: 2782 Albums

(G-4392)
I RAUCHS SONS INC
3220 112th St (11369-2590)
PHONE..718 507-8844
Fax: 718 565-6018
Milton Levine, *President*
Joel Levine, *Corp Secy*
EMP: 21
SQ FT: 12,000
SALES (est): 3.5MM **Privately Held**
SIC: 3444 Sheet metalwork

(G-4393)
KESSO FOODS INC
Also Called: Mediterranean Thick Yogurt
7720 21st Ave (11370-1219)
PHONE..718 777-5303
Fax: 718 777-5303
Fotini Kessissoglou, *President*
EMP: 5
SALES: 100K **Privately Held**
SIC: 2026 5143 Fluid milk; yogurt

(G-4394)
LIBERTY AWNINGS & SIGNS INC
Also Called: Empire Signs
7705 21st Ave (11370-1250)
PHONE..347 203-1470
Panayiotis Panayi, *CEO*
Spiro Avlonitis, *Manager*
EMP: 2
SQ FT: 5,000
SALES: 2.3MM **Privately Held**
SIC: 3993 Advertising artwork

(G-4395)
MOON GATES COMPANY
3243 104th St (11369-2515)
PHONE..718 426-0023
Stephen Vieira, *Principal*
EMP: 6
SQ FT: 2,000
SALES (est): 400K **Privately Held**
SIC: 3446 1791 Gates, ornamental metal; iron work, structural

(G-4396)
PROGRAMATIC PLATERS INC
4925 20th Ave (11370-1196)
PHONE..718 721-4330
Fax: 718 274-1693
Arnold Abbey, *President*
Martin Adams, *Purchasing*
David Lieberman, *Sales Staff*
EMP: 12
SQ FT: 15,000
SALES (est): 1MM **Privately Held**
SIC: 3471 Plating of metals or formed products

(G-4397)
STANDARD GROUP (PA)
Also Called: Southern Standard Cartons
7520 Astoria Blvd Ste 100 (11370-1135)
PHONE..718 335-5500
Louis Cortes, *President*
Steven D Levkoff, *Chairman*
Tony Pallini, *Info Tech Dir*
Ed Stichweh, *Art Dir*
▲ **EMP:** 45
SQ FT: 115,000
SALES (est): 61.5MM **Privately Held**
SIC: 2657 Folding paperboard boxes

(G-4398)
STANDARD GROUP LLC (HQ)
Also Called: Southern Standard Cartoons
7520 Astoria Blvd Ste 100 (11370-1135)
PHONE..718 507-6430
Louis Cortes, *Vice Pres*
Tom Selmani, *Controller*
Cynthia Sapp, *Human Res Mgr*
Denise Barr, *Manager*
Joseph Rebecca,
▲ **EMP:** 235 **EST:** 2009
SQ FT: 115,000
SALES (est): 48.1MM **Privately Held**
WEB: www.thestandardgroup.com
SIC: 2657 Folding paperboard boxes

(G-4399)
T RJ SHIRTS INC
3050 90th St (11369-1706)
PHONE..347 642-3071
Femd Rocky, *Principal*
EMP: 6
SALES (est): 478.2K **Privately Held**
SIC: 2331 T-shirts & tops, women's: made from purchased materials

(G-4400)
WESTCHSTR CRNKSHFT GRNDNG
Also Called: Westchster Crankshaft Grinding
3263 110th St (11369-2525)
PHONE..718 651-3900
Fax: 718 651-3035
Marco Albanese, *Vice Pres*
▲ **EMP:** 9
SALES (est): 1.1MM **Privately Held**
SIC: 3599 Crankshafts & camshafts, machining

East Greenbush
Rensselaer County

(G-4401)
AUTOMATED & MGT SOLUTIONS LLC
743 Columbia Tpke (12061-2266)
PHONE..518 283-5352
Russ Streifert, *Programmer Anys*
Francis Clifford,
EMP: 5
SALES (est): 117.2K **Privately Held**
SIC: 7372 Application computer software; operating systems computer software

(G-4402)
CURTIS PRTG CO THE DEL PRESS
711 Columbia Tpke (12061-2212)
PHONE..518 477-4820
Fax: 518 689-0224
Richard Lieberman, *President*
EMP: 5
SQ FT: 4,000
SALES (est): 578.8K **Privately Held**
WEB: www.curtisprinting.com
SIC: 2759 Commercial printing; letterpress printing

(G-4403)
LEONARD CARLSON
Also Called: Carlson, L A Co
90 Waters Rd (12061-3422)
PHONE..518 477-4710
Leonard Carlson, *Owner*

East Greenbush - Rensselaer County (G-4404)

GEOGRAPHIC SECTION

▲ EMP: 6 EST: 1956
SQ FT: 6,000
SALES: 425K Privately Held
SIC: 3931 Organs, all types: pipe, reed, hand, electronic, etc.

(G-4404)
SABIC INNOVATIVE PLASTICS
1 Gail Ct (12061-1750)
PHONE.................713 448-7474
Narendra Mansharamani, Principal
Shelia Naab, Vice Pres
Jason Fuller, Project Mgr
Dominic Bruno, Safety Mgr
Mark Eckman, Production
EMP: 35 EST: 2012
SALES (est): 5.9MM Privately Held
SIC: 3089 Plastics products

East Hampton
Suffolk County

(G-4405)
BISTRIAN CEMENT CORPORATION
225 Springs Fireplace Rd (11937-4823)
P.O. Box 5048 (11937-6079)
PHONE.................631 324-1123
Barry Bistrian, President
Betsy Avallone, Shareholder
Bruce Bistrian, Shareholder
Pat Bistrian, Shareholder
Barbara Borg, Shareholder
EMP: 12
SQ FT: 20,000
SALES: 1.7MM Privately Held
SIC: 3272 3259 Septic tanks, concrete; drain tile, clay

(G-4406)
C E KING & SONS INC
10 Saint Francis Pl (11937-4330)
PHONE.................631 324-4944
Fax: 631 329-3669
Clarence E King III, President
David King, Treasurer
Deanna Tikkanen, Admin Sec
EMP: 7
SQ FT: 1,650
SALES: 600K Privately Held
WEB: www.kingsawnings.com
SIC: 2394 5999 Awnings, fabric: made from purchased materials; fire extinguishers

(G-4407)
CHESU INC
81 Newtown Ln (11937-2323)
PHONE.................239 564-2803
Chet Borgida, President
Susan Borgida, Vice Pres
EMP: 10 EST: 2012
SALES (est): 1MM Privately Held
SIC: 3086 5111 7389 Packaging & shipping materials, foamed plastic; printing paper; notary publics

(G-4408)
EAST HAMPTON IND NEWS INC
Also Called: East Hampton Independent The
74 Montauk Hwy Unit 19 (11937-3268)
PHONE.................631 324-2500
Fax: 631 324-2351
James Mackim, President
Jodi Della Femina, Vice Pres
Lee Minitree, Treasurer
Joanna Froschl, Sales Associate
Jerry Della Femina, Admin Sec
EMP: 28
SQ FT: 1,400
SALES (est): 1.7MM Privately Held
WEB: www.indyeastend.com
SIC: 2711 Newspapers

(G-4409)
EAST HAMPTON STAR INC
153 Main St (11937-2716)
P.O. Box 5002 (11937-6005)
PHONE.................631 324-0002
Helen Rattray, President
Angie Carpenter, Treasurer
Min Spear, Advt Staff
EMP: 40 EST: 1886
SQ FT: 6,400
SALES (est): 2.6MM Privately Held
WEB: www.easthamptonstar.com
SIC: 2711 Newspapers, publishing & printing

(G-4410)
ELIE TAHARI LTD
1 Main St (11937)
PHONE.................631 329-8883
Brenda Bolin, Branch Mgr
EMP: 75
SALES (corp-wide): 241.7MM Privately Held
SIC: 2337 Suits: women's, misses' & juniors'
PA: Elie Tahari Ltd.
16 Bleeker St
Millburn NJ 07041
973 671-6300

(G-4411)
IRONY LIMITED INC (PA)
Also Called: Hedges and Gardens
53 Sag Harbor Tpke (11937-4905)
PHONE.................631 329-4065
Robert Linker, President
Elizabeth Linker, Vice Pres
EMP: 2
SQ FT: 2,200
SALES (est): 1.2MM Privately Held
SIC: 3441 7641 3446 1799 Fabricated structural metal; antique furniture repair & restoration; stairs, staircases, stair treads: prefabricated metal; ornamental metal work

(G-4412)
KEENERS EAST END LITHO INC
10 Prospect Blvd (11937-5800)
PHONE.................631 324-8565
Charles Keener, President
Lynn Keener, Corp Secy
Greg Keener, Vice Pres
EMP: 8
SALES (est): 783.3K Privately Held
SIC: 2752 Commercial printing, lithographic

(G-4413)
LURIA COMMUNICATIONS INC
Also Called: Card Pak Start Up
31 Shorewood Dr Fl 1 (11937-3402)
PHONE.................631 329-4922
Jay Blatt, President
Vicki Luria, Vice Pres
EMP: 8
SALES: 500K Privately Held
SIC: 2721 7311 7331 Trade journals: publishing only, not printed on site; advertising agencies; mailing list brokers

(G-4414)
NATURPATHICA HOLISTIC HLTH INC
74 Montauk Hwy Unit 23 (11937-3268)
PHONE.................631 329-8792
Barbara Close, CEO
Jonathan Keattch, COO
Sharon Del Valle, CFO
Becky Discipio, Finance
EMP: 100
SQ FT: 750
SALES (est): 3.7MM Privately Held
SIC: 2844 Cosmetic preparations

(G-4415)
SABIN METAL CORPORATION (PA)
300 Pantigo Pl Ste 102 (11937-2630)
PHONE.................631 329-1695
Fax: 631 329-1985
Andrew Sabin, President
Jonathan Sabin, Exec VP
Kevin Beirne, Vice Pres
Yanan Sui, Opers Mgr
Scott Yarnes, Opers Staff
▲ EMP: 14 EST: 1945
SQ FT: 4,000
SALES (est): 56.6MM Privately Held
WEB: www.sabinmetal.com
SIC: 3341 Secondary precious metals

(G-4416)
STAR READY MIX EAST INC
225 Springs Fireplace Rd (11937-4823)
P.O. Box 371, Medford (11763-0371)
PHONE.................631 289-8787
Fax: 631 324-2258
Thomas Hess, President
Frank Otero, Vice Pres
EMP: 15
SALES (est): 1.1MM Privately Held
SIC: 3273 Ready-mixed concrete

East Islip
Suffolk County

(G-4417)
KEY CONTAINER CORP
135 Hollins Ln (11730-3006)
PHONE.................631 582-3847
Frank Giaquinko, President
EMP: 6 EST: 2010
SALES: 800K Privately Held
SIC: 2653 Corrugated & solid fiber boxes

East Meadow
Nassau County

(G-4418)
ARTYS SPRNKLR SVC INSTLLATION
448 Cedar Ln (11554-3710)
PHONE.................516 538-4371
Arthur R Wolf, President
Helen Wolf, Treasurer
EMP: 13
SALES: 700K Privately Held
SIC: 3432 Lawn hose nozzles & sprinklers

(G-4419)
CHV PRINTED COMPANY
1905 Hempstead Tpke B (11554-1047)
PHONE.................516 997-1101
Andrew Mazzone, Principal
EMP: 19
SALES (est): 1.4MM Privately Held
SIC: 2759 Commercial printing

(G-4420)
COMPLETE ORTHOPEDIC SVCS INC
2094 Front St (11554-1709)
PHONE.................516 357-9113
Fax: 516 357-9186
Noreen Diaz, Ch of Bd
Alexandra Divito, Sales Staff
Anne Genovese, Manager
EMP: 20 EST: 1999
SALES (est): 3.3MM Privately Held
SIC: 3842 Braces, orthopedic

(G-4421)
DATASONIC INC
1413 Cleveland Ave (11554-4405)
PHONE.................516 248-7330
Richard Mintz, President
EMP: 5
SALES (est): 320K Privately Held
SIC: 3669 Burglar alarm apparatus, electric

(G-4422)
E M T MANUFACTURING INC
Also Called: Engineering Mfg & Tech
273 Cherry Pl (11554-2936)
PHONE.................516 333-1917
Ernest Hippner, President
Marion Hippner, Corp Secy
EMP: 12
SQ FT: 10,000
SALES (est): 1.7MM Privately Held
SIC: 3599 3365 Machine shop, jobbing & repair; aerospace castings, aluminum

(G-4423)
EATON CORPORATION
280 Bellmore Rd (11554-3538)
PHONE.................516 353-3017
John Pierro, Principal
EMP: 222 Privately Held
SIC: 3625 Motor controls & accessories
HQ: Eaton Corporation
1000 Eaton Blvd
Cleveland OH 44122
216 523-5000

(G-4424)
HI TECH SIGNS OF NY INC
415 E Meadow Ave (11554-1975)
PHONE.................516 794-7880
Fax: 516 794-0410
Scott Abrecht, President
EMP: 5
SQ FT: 2,000
SALES (est): 430K Privately Held
SIC: 3993 5999 Signs & advertising specialties; banners, flags, decals & posters

(G-4425)
HIBU INC (DH)
90 Merrick Ave Ste 530 (11554-1575)
PHONE.................516 730-1900
Fax: 516 730-1950
Mike Pocock, CEO
John Condron, Ch of Bd
Joseph Walsh, President
Dan Perti, General Mgr
Bob Wigley, Chairman
▲ EMP: 200
SQ FT: 30,000
SALES (est): 1.8B
SALES (corp-wide): 1.1B Privately Held
SIC: 2741 Directories: publishing & printing
HQ: Hibu (Uk) Limited
One Reading Central, 23 Forbury Road
Reading BERKS RG1 3
800 838-200

(G-4426)
JOHN PRIOR
2545 Hempstead Tpke # 402 (11554-2144)
PHONE.................516 520-9801
John Prior, Principal
Barbara Gordon, Human Resources
Maria Lawrence, Sales Staff
Ronald Prior, Sales Executive
Jeffrey Arway, Info Tech Mgr
EMP: 8 EST: 2007
SALES (est): 746.6K Privately Held
SIC: 3999 Manufacturing industries

(G-4427)
PJ DECORATORS INC
257 Pontiac Pl (11554-1231)
PHONE.................516 735-9693
David Brill, President
EMP: 25
SALES (est): 2MM Privately Held
SIC: 2591 5023 5719 Drapery hardware & blinds & shades; vertical blinds; vertical blinds

(G-4428)
TRIPLE H CONSTRUCTION INC
832 Bethlynn Ct (11554-4911)
PHONE.................516 280-8252
Hesham Hassane, President
Venaal Hassane, Vice Pres
EMP: 22
SQ FT: 1,600
SALES: 700K Privately Held
SIC: 3446 1751 Fences or posts, ornamental iron or steel; window & door installation & erection

East Moriches
Suffolk County

(G-4429)
KEY SIGNALS
47 Tuthill Point Rd (11940-1216)
PHONE.................631 433-2962
Mark Gartung, Principal
EMP: 6
SALES (est): 500K Privately Held
SIC: 3629 Electrical industrial apparatus

(G-4430)
RINGHOFF FUEL INC
72 Atlantic Ave (11940-1324)
P.O. Box 510 (11940-0510)
PHONE.................631 878-0663
William J Ringhoff, Principal

EMP: 5
SALES (est): 370.5K **Privately Held**
SIC: 2911 Oils, fuel

(G-4431)
TATES WHOLESALE LLC
Also Called: Tate's Bake Shop
62 Pine St (11940-1117)
PHONE.................................631 780-6511
Kathleen King, *President*
Michel Dobbs, *Opers Mgr*
Robert Panarella, *Warehouse Mgr*
Margaret Brock, *Accounting Mgr*
EMP: 130
SALES (est): 25.6MM **Privately Held**
SIC: 2051 Bakery: wholesale or wholesale/retail combined

East Northport
Suffolk County

(G-4432)
ADVANTAGE ORTHOTICS INC
337 Larkfield Rd (11731-2904)
PHONE.................................631 368-1754
Claire Ann Ketcham, *Principal*
EMP: 9
SALES (est): 1.1MM **Privately Held**
SIC: 3842 Orthopedic appliances

(G-4433)
ARCHITCTRAL MLLWK INSTALLATION
590 Elwood Rd (11731-5629)
PHONE.................................631 499-0755
Shaun Hanley, *President*
EMP: 23
SALES: 2MM **Privately Held**
SIC: 2431 2439 Millwork; structural wood members

(G-4434)
COMPUTER CONVERSIONS CORP
6 Dunton Ct (11731-1704)
PHONE.................................631 261-3300
Fax: 631 261-3308
Stephen Renard, *President*
Paul Waldman, *Vice Pres*
Les Levy, *Project Engr*
Margaret Librizzi, *Human Res Mgr*
Craig J Hughes, *Sales Mgr*
EMP: 32
SQ FT: 5,000
SALES (est): 7.3MM **Privately Held**
WEB: www.computer-conversions.com
SIC: 3571 Electronic computers

(G-4435)
EAST TO WEST ARCHITECTRAL PDTS
103 Tinton Pl Ste 1a (11731-5330)
PHONE.................................631 433-9690
Dean Nichol, *President*
EMP: 1
SALES: 3MM **Privately Held**
WEB: www.easttowestsales.com
SIC: 3996 Hard surface floor coverings

(G-4436)
FORTE NETWORK
Also Called: Forte Security Group
75 Lockfield Rd (11731)
PHONE.................................631 390-9050
Richard Allen, *President*
EMP: 40
SALES (est): 4.3MM **Privately Held**
SIC: 3699 Security control equipment & systems

(G-4437)
ISLAND SILKSCREEN INC
Also Called: Connie's T Shirt Shop
328 Larkfield Rd (11731-2945)
PHONE.................................631 757-4567
Fax: 631 757-5080
Mike Sambur, *President*
EMP: 5
SALES (est): 453.4K **Privately Held**
SIC: 2759 Screen printing

(G-4438)
JOERGER ENTERPRISES INC
166 Laurel Rd Ste 214 (11731-1435)
PHONE.................................631 239-5579
Fax: 631 757-6201
Frederick Joerger, *President*
Kathleen Joerger, *Admin Sec*
EMP: 6
SQ FT: 2,000
SALES: 500K **Privately Held**
WEB: www.joergerinc.com
SIC: 3829 Nuclear radiation & testing apparatus

(G-4439)
JORDAN PANEL SYSTEMS CORP (PA)
196 Laurel Rd Unit 2 (11731-1441)
PHONE.................................631 754-4900
Fax: 631 754-4643
John A Finamore Sr, *President*
Monique Green, *Controller*
Monique Greene, *Controller*
Kathi Benjes, *Accounts Mgr*
Dianna Gannon, *Administration*
▼ **EMP:** 25
SQ FT: 5,000
SALES (est): 11MM **Privately Held**
WEB: www.jordanpanel.com
SIC: 3499 1761 1793 5033 Aerosol valves, metal; roofing, siding & sheet metal work; glass & glazing work; roofing, asphalt & sheet metal

(G-4440)
L & L PRECISION MACHINING
35 Doyle Ct Ste 3 (11731-6412)
PHONE.................................631 462-9587
Fax: 631 462-9491
Lawrence Giovanniello, *President*
EMP: 12
SQ FT: 20,000
SALES: 800K **Privately Held**
SIC: 3599 3581 Machine & other job shop work; mechanisms & parts for automatic vending machines

(G-4441)
LOUDON LTD
Also Called: Minuteman Press
281 Larkfield Rd (11731-2417)
PHONE.................................631 757-4447
Kathy Loudon, *President*
David Loudon, *General Mgr*
EMP: 5
SQ FT: 1,800
SALES (est): 699.7K **Privately Held**
SIC: 2752 2791 Commercial printing, lithographic; typesetting

(G-4442)
MONASANI SIGNS INC
Also Called: Mr Sign
22 Compton St (11731-5510)
PHONE.................................631 266-2635
Fax: 631 689-7039
William Monahan, *President*
EMP: 5
SQ FT: 1,500
SALES: 400K **Privately Held**
SIC: 3993 7532 Signs & advertising specialties; truck painting & lettering

(G-4443)
PROGRESSIVE HARDWARE CO INC
63 Brightside Ave (11731-1903)
PHONE.................................631 445-1826
Fax: 631 757-8870
William Zilz, *President*
▲ **EMP:** 9
SQ FT: 11,000
SALES (est): 960K **Privately Held**
WEB: www.progressive-hardware.com
SIC: 3429 Builders' hardware

(G-4444)
READY CHECK GLO INC
23 Bruce Ln Ste E (11731-2701)
PHONE.................................516 547-1849
Celestina Pugliese, *CEO*
EMP: 5 **EST:** 2010
SALES: 175K **Privately Held**
SIC: 2752 7389 Menus, lithographed;

East Norwich
Nassau County

(G-4445)
CATHAY RESOURCES INC
38 Cord Pl (11732-1155)
P.O. Box 314 (11732-0314)
PHONE.................................516 922-2839
Walter Belous, *President*
EMP: 3
SQ FT: 3,000
SALES: 10MM **Privately Held**
SIC: 3356 Tin & tin alloy bars, pipe, sheets, etc.

(G-4446)
GOLDEN EGRET LLC
38 Cord Pl (11732-1155)
P.O. Box 314 (11732-0314)
PHONE.................................516 922-2839
Walter Belous, *Mng Member*
▲ **EMP:** 6
SALES (est): 764.1K **Privately Held**
SIC: 3313 Tungsten carbide powder

East Patchogue
Suffolk County

(G-4447)
G & M DEGE INC
250 Orchard Rd Bldg 1 (11772-5535)
PHONE.................................631 475-1450
Fax: 631 475-1238
Nick Gallipoli, *President*
EMP: 14
SQ FT: 3,000
SALES (est): 3.5MM **Privately Held**
SIC: 2851 Removers & cleaners

(G-4448)
HUNTER METAL INDUSTRIES INC
Also Called: Hunter Displays
14 Hewlett Ave (11772-5499)
PHONE.................................631 475-5900
Fax: 631 475-5950
Harry Stoll, *CEO*
Sandy Stoll, *Senior VP*
Ken Kasper, *Vice Pres*
Renee Heuer, *Purch Mgr*
Linda Roesch, *Purch Mgr*
EMP: 100 **EST:** 1951
SQ FT: 75,000
SALES (est): 17.3MM **Privately Held**
WEB: www.hunterdisplays.com
SIC: 2542 2541 Fixtures: display, office or store: except wood; display fixtures, wood

(G-4449)
PROGRESSIVE ORTHOTICS LTD
285 Sills Rd Bldg 8c (11772-8800)
PHONE.................................631 447-3860
Bruce Goodman, *Branch Mgr*
EMP: 12
SALES (corp-wide): 905.9K **Privately Held**
WEB: www.progressiveorthotics.com
SIC: 3842 5999 Orthopedic appliances; orthopedic & prosthesis applications
PA: Progressive Orthotics Ltd
280 Middle Country Rd G
Selden NY 11784
631 732-5556

East Quogue
Suffolk County

(G-4450)
EAST COAST MINES LTD
Also Called: East Coast Mines & Material
2 Lewis Rd (11942)
PHONE.................................631 653-5445
Fax: 631 653-5743
William Tintle, *President*
EMP: 20
SQ FT: 5,000
SALES (est): 2.9MM **Privately Held**
SIC: 1442 5261 5032 Construction sand & gravel; top soil; brick, stone & related material

(G-4451)
HAMPTON SHIPYARDS INC
7 Carter Ln (11942-4334)
P.O. Box 3007 (11942-2008)
PHONE.................................631 653-6777
Fax: 631 653-6801
Fred Scopinich, *President*
Doris Scopinich, *Vice Pres*
EMP: 10 **EST:** 1956
SQ FT: 21,000
SALES (est): 1.1MM **Privately Held**
SIC: 3732 Boat building & repairing

(G-4452)
SITEWATCH TECHNOLOGY LLC
22 Sunset Ave (11942-4200)
PHONE.................................207 778-3246
Fax: 207 684-3207
Fred York, *Principal*
David B Horn,
EMP: 6
SALES (est): 645K **Privately Held**
SIC: 3678 Electronic connectors

East Rochester
Monroe County

(G-4453)
ART PARTS SIGNS INC
100 Lincoln Pkwy (14445-1450)
PHONE.................................585 381-2134
Patricia Ransco, *President*
EMP: 7
SQ FT: 8,000
SALES: 500K **Privately Held**
SIC: 3993 Signs, not made in custom sign painting shops

(G-4454)
CARDIAC LIFE PRODUCTS INC
349 W Coml St Ste 1400 (14445)
P.O. Box 25755, Rochester (14625-0755)
PHONE.................................585 267-7775
Mary Wynne, *President*
Robert Wynne, *Vice Pres*
Tom Masseth, *Accounting Mgr*
Justin Moore, *Manager*
Robin Vogt, *Director*
EMP: 3
SALES: 3MM **Privately Held**
SIC: 3845 Electromedical equipment

(G-4455)
CARPENTIER INDUSTRIES LLC
Also Called: Rochester Magnet
119 Despatch Dr (14445-1447)
PHONE.................................585 385-5550
Fax: 585 288-7925
Andrew Carpentier, *President*
Melissa Winslow, *Manager*
▲ **EMP:** 15
SQ FT: 10,000
SALES (est): 2.2MM **Privately Held**
WEB: www.rochestermagnet.com
SIC: 3499 Magnets, permanent: metallic

(G-4456)
CONNOVER PACKAGING INC
119 Despatch Dr (14445-1447)
PHONE.................................585 377-2510
Fax: 585 377-2604
Andrew Carpentier, *President*
Judy Stephens, *Office Mgr*
EMP: 6
SQ FT: 15,000
SALES (est): 1.2MM **Privately Held**
WEB: www.connoverpackaging.com
SIC: 2673 Plastic bags: made from purchased materials

(G-4457)
EMC CORPORATION
Also Called: Emc2
105 Despatch Dr (14445-1447)
PHONE.................................585 387-9505
Fax: 585 387-9070
Larry Koch, *Vice Pres*
Kyra Phegley, *Manager*

East Rochester - Monroe County (G-4458)

Michael Napieralski, *IT/INT Sup*
EMP: 32
SALES (corp-wide): 72.7B **Publicly Held**
WEB: www.emc.com
SIC: 3572 7372 Computer storage devices; prepackaged software
HQ: Emc Corporation
176 South St
Hopkinton MA 01748
508 435-1000

(G-4458)
FERRO CORPORATION
603 W Commercial St (14445-2253)
P.O. Box 389 (14445-0389)
PHONE.................................585 586-8770
Richard Veeder, *Branch Mgr*
EMP: 35
SQ FT: 30,000
SALES (corp-wide): 1B **Publicly Held**
WEB: www.ferro.com
SIC: 2819 Industrial inorganic chemicals
PA: Ferro Corporation
6060 Parkland Blvd # 250
Mayfield Heights OH 44124
216 875-5600

(G-4459)
FILTROS LTD
Also Called: Filtros Plant
603 W Commercial St (14445-2253)
P.O. Box 389 (14445-0389)
PHONE.................................585 586-8770
Fax: 585 586-7154
Byron Anderson, *CEO*
Allan Schilling, *Vice Pres*
Bob Ayers, *Plant Mgr*
Linda Wendt, *Accountant*
George Goeller, *Sales Mgr*
EMP: 35 **EST:** 1999
SQ FT: 45,000
SALES (est): 5.5MM **Privately Held**
WEB: www.filtrosltd.com
SIC: 3255 3564 3297 3264 Clay refractories; blowers & fans; nonclay refractories; porcelain electrical supplies

(G-4460)
GREATER RCHSTER ADVERTISER INC
Also Called: Shopping Bag, The
201 Main St (14445-1703)
P.O. Box 760 (14445-0760)
PHONE.................................585 385-1974
Fax: 585 385-3507
Peter John Stahlbrodt, *President*
Kay C Kolb, *General Mgr*
Betty Stahlbrodt, *Vice Pres*
Brenda Pitoni, *Info Tech Mgr*
EMP: 26
SQ FT: 6,600
SALES (est): 1.5MM **Privately Held**
WEB: www.rochesteradvertiser.com
SIC: 2741 Shopping news: publishing only, not printed on site

(G-4461)
HOERCHER INDUSTRIES INC
A1 Country Club Rd Ste 1 (14445-2230)
PHONE.................................585 398-2982
Fax: 585 383-1608
Lawrence Hoercher, *President*
EMP: 5
SQ FT: 3,500
SALES (est): 360K **Privately Held**
SIC: 3599 Electrical discharge machining (EDM)

(G-4462)
IDEAL MANUFACTURING INC
80 Bluff Dr (14445-1300)
PHONE.................................585 872-7190
Ben Stroyer, *President*
Arthur Stroyer, *Vice Pres*
Bruce Stroyer, *Accountant*
▼ **EMP:** 32
SQ FT: 7,000
SALES (est): 10MM **Privately Held**
SIC: 2515 Foundations & platforms

(G-4463)
KEMCO SALES LLC
119 Despatch Dr (14445-1447)
PHONE.................................203 762-1902
Fax: 203 762-2548
Andrew Carpentier, *President*

EMP: 15
SQ FT: 15,000
SALES (est): 2.8MM **Privately Held**
WEB: www.securpak.com
SIC: 2673 Bags: plastic, laminated & coated

(G-4464)
KRONENBERGER MFG CORP
115 Despatch Dr (14445-1447)
PHONE.................................585 385-2340
Gunter Kronenberger, *President*
Eric Kronenberger, *Vice Pres*
Kevin Kronenberger, *Vice Pres*
Bertha Parnusie, *Office Mgr*
John Girvin, *Manager*
EMP: 45
SQ FT: 40,000
SALES (est): 8.3MM **Privately Held**
SIC: 3599 Machine shop, jobbing & repair

(G-4465)
LINCDOC LLC
Also Called: Lincware
401 Main St (14445-1707)
PHONE.................................585 563-1669
Darren Mathis, *CEO*
Donna Moss, *Sales Staff*
Eileen Gaisser, *Business Anlyst*
David Kilmer, *Software Dev*
EMP: 7
SALES (est): 680K **Privately Held**
SIC: 7372 Prepackaged software

(G-4466)
RICHARDS & WEST INC
Also Called: Rw Manufacturing Company
501 W Commercial St Ste 1 (14445-2258)
PHONE.................................585 461-4088
Fax: 585 461-0716
John R Keim, *Ch of Bd*
Gary Keim, *Vice Pres*
John E Miner, *Vice Pres*
Gene Rozewski, *Purchasing*
EMP: 54 **EST:** 1982
SQ FT: 10,000
SALES (est): 8.5MM **Privately Held**
WEB: www.rwmfg.com
SIC: 3911 7631 5944 Jewelry, precious metal; jewelry repair services; jewelry, precious stones & precious metals

East Rockaway
Nassau County

(G-4467)
ADULTS AND CHILDREN WITH LEARN
22 Alice Ct (11518-1902)
PHONE.................................516 593-8230
EMP: 29
SALES (corp-wide): 64.8MM **Privately Held**
SIC: 3999 Barber & beauty shop equipment
PA: Adults And Children With Learning And Developmental Disabilities, Inc.
807 S Oyster Bay Rd
Bethpage NY 11714
516 681-4500

(G-4468)
CIRCUITS & SYSTEMS INC
Also Called: Arlyn Scales
59 2nd St (11518-1236)
PHONE.................................516 593-4301
Arnold Gordon, *President*
Lynne Gordon, *Corp Secy*
Helen Berwind, *Plant Mgr*
Robert Hirsch, *Sales Staff*
EMP: 22 **EST:** 1977
SQ FT: 6,000
SALES (est): 5.4MM **Privately Held**
WEB: www.chaverware.com
SIC: 3596 7373 Scales & balances, except laboratory; computer-aided design (CAD) systems service

(G-4469)
DAWN PAPER CO INC (PA)
Also Called: Dawn Printing Company
4 Leonard Dr (11518-1609)
PHONE.................................516 596-9110

Fax: 516 596-0167
Stephen Kucker, *President*
Jonathan Greenberg, *Vice Pres*
Marla Perrino, *Vice Pres*
EMP: 12
SQ FT: 5,000
SALES (est): 2.7MM **Privately Held**
SIC: 2752 5113 5085 Commercial printing, lithographic; bags, paper & disposable plastic; boxes, crates, etc., other than paper

(G-4470)
SEXTET FABRICS INC
21 Ryder Pl Ste 4 (11518-1200)
P.O. Box 10 (11518-0010)
PHONE.................................516 593-0608
Fax: 516 593-0430
Gordon Stern, *CEO*
Barbara Ross, *President*
Ronald Ross, *Principal*
Adam Ackerman, *Vice Pres*
Gail Koppel, *Treasurer*
EMP: 12 **EST:** 1971
SQ FT: 8,500
SALES (est): 1.4MM **Privately Held**
SIC: 2259 Convertors, knit goods

(G-4471)
STERLING PIERCE COMPANY INC
395 Atlantic Ave (11518-1423)
PHONE.................................516 593-1170
William Burke, *President*
Isabel Burke, *Vice Pres*
▼ **EMP:** 29
SQ FT: 5,000
SALES (est): 3.7MM **Privately Held**
WEB: www.sterlingpierce.com
SIC: 2789 2732 2752 Binding only: books, pamphlets, magazines, etc.; book printing; commercial printing, lithographic

(G-4472)
STYLEBUILT ACCESSORIES INC (PA)
Also Called: Stylebuilt Acesries
45 Rose Ln (11518-2126)
PHONE.................................917 439-0578
Jonathan Greenfield, *President*
Jerome Greenfield, *Vice Pres*
Jackie Greenfield, *Treasurer*
Carla Polizzi, *Comptroller*
Lois Kreiner, *Intl Dir*
▲ **EMP:** 12 **EST:** 1946
SQ FT: 65,000
SALES: 950K **Privately Held**
WEB: www.stylebuilt.com
SIC: 3499 Novelties & specialties, metal

East Schodack
Rensselaer County

(G-4473)
NORTHEAST PAVING CONCEPTS LLC
33 Brookside Dr (12063-1712)
PHONE.................................518 477-1338
Patrick Weber, *Managing Prtnr*
EMP: 5
SALES (est): 260K **Privately Held**
SIC: 3471 Decorative plating & finishing of formed products

East Setauket
Suffolk County

(G-4474)
ADVANCED RESEARCH MEDIA INC
21 Bennetts Rd Ste 101 (11733-1243)
PHONE.................................631 751-9696
Fax: 631 751-9699
Steve Blechman, *CEO*
Elyse Blechman, *President*
Benise Gehring, *Controller*
Kery Mirabile, *Manager*
Gail Nabbalsky, *Manager*
EMP: 17

SALES (est): 4.8MM **Privately Held**
SIC: 2721 Magazines: publishing only, not printed on site

(G-4475)
ALPINE OVERHEAD DOORS INC
8 Hulse Rd Ste 1 (11733-3649)
PHONE.................................631 456-7800
Sebastian Nagro, *Owner*
EMP: 30
SALES (corp-wide): 17.1MM **Privately Held**
WEB: www.alpinedoors.com
SIC: 3442 Metal doors
PA: Alpine Overhead Doors, Inc.
8 Hulse Rd Ste 1
East Setauket NY 11733
631 473-9300

(G-4476)
ANORAD CORPORATION
41 Research Way (11733-3454)
PHONE.................................631 380-2100
Fax: 631 344-6601
Marco H Wishart, *Ch of Bd*
Geoffrey Storms, *President*
Theodore D Crandall, *Senior VP*
John Callahan, *Vice Pres*
Thomas Derosa, *CFO*
▲ **EMP:** 102
SALES (est): 21.8MM **Publicly Held**
WEB: www.anorad.com
SIC: 3577 3827 Computer peripheral equipment; optical instruments & lenses
PA: Rockwell Automation, Inc.
1201 S 2nd St
Milwaukee WI 53204

(G-4477)
B & Z TECHNOLOGIES LLC
Also Called: Bnz Tech
7 Technology Dr (11733-4000)
PHONE.................................631 675-9666
Javed Siddiqui, *President*
David Hlinka, *General Mgr*
Asma Siddiqui, *CFO*
EMP: 7
SQ FT: 2,000
SALES: 2MM **Privately Held**
WEB: www.bnztech.com
SIC: 3812 Antennas, radar or communications; radar systems & equipment

(G-4478)
BASF CORPORATION
Also Called: BASF The Chemical Company
361 Sheep Pasture Rd (11733-3614)
PHONE.................................631 689-0200
Meredith Culver, *Branch Mgr*
Anthony Asselta, *Manager*
EMP: 157
SALES (corp-wide): 75.6B **Privately Held**
SIC: 2819 Industrial inorganic chemicals
HQ: Basf Corporation
100 Park Ave
Florham Park NJ 07932
973 245-6000

(G-4479)
COLLABORATIVE LABORATORIES (DH)
3 Technology Dr Ste 400 (11733-4078)
PHONE.................................631 689-0200
James Hayward PHD, *President*
Joseph Ceccoli, *COO*
EMP: 60
SQ FT: 25,000
SALES (est): 3.6MM
SALES (corp-wide): 75.6B **Privately Held**
WEB: www.collabo.com
SIC: 2844 2869 2833 8731 Toilet preparations; industrial organic chemicals; medicinals & botanicals; biotechnical research, commercial
HQ: Basf Catalysts Llc
25 Middlesex Tpke
Iselin NJ 08830
732 205-5000

(G-4480)
EATING EVOLVED INC
10 Technology Dr Unit 5 (11733-4063)
PHONE.................................516 510-2601
EMP: 7 **EST:** 2015
SALES (est): 573.4K **Privately Held**
SIC: 2066 Chocolate & cocoa products

GEOGRAPHIC SECTION

East Syracuse - Onondaga County (G-4505)

(G-4481)
EMPRESAS DE MANUFACTURA INC (PA)
7 S Jersey Ave Ste 3 (11733-2065)
PHONE.................................631 240-9251
Martin Higgins, *CEO*
Manuel Riveria, *President*
Nicolas Vitarelli, *Vice Pres*
EMP: 180
SQ FT: 157,000
SALES: 7MM **Privately Held**
SIC: 3679 3824 Electronic circuits; mechanical & electromechanical counters & devices

(G-4482)
FEDDERS ISLANDAIRE INC
Also Called: Fedders Islandaire Company
22 Research Way (11733-3453)
PHONE.................................631 471-2900
Robert Hansen, *President*
EMP: 85
SQ FT: 32,000
SALES (est): 23.7K
SALES (corp-wide): 141.1MM **Privately Held**
SIC: 3585 3822 3433 5722 Air conditioning equipment, complete; heat pumps, electric; auto controls regulating residntl & coml environmt & applncs; heating equipment, except electric; air conditioning room units, self-contained; heating & air conditioning contractors
PA: Fedders Corporation
13455 Noel Rd Ste 2200
Dallas TX 75240
604 908-8686

(G-4483)
FLAGPOLES INCORPORATED
95 Gnarled Hollow Rd (11733-1934)
P.O. Box 833 (11733-0643)
PHONE.................................631 751-5500
Fax: 631 751-7955
Jack Seferian, *CEO*
Haig Seferian, *Principal*
Gregory Seferian, *Vice Pres*
▼ **EMP:** 90
SQ FT: 96,000
SALES (est): 19.9MM **Privately Held**
WEB: www.flagpole.net
SIC: 3446 3441 3354 Flagpoles, metal; lamp posts, metal; fabricated structural metal; aluminum extruded products

(G-4484)
GOLDBERG PROSTHETIC & ORTHOTIC
9 Technology Dr (11733-4000)
PHONE.................................631 689-6606
Mark E Goldberg, *President*
Lisa Wilson, *Accountant*
EMP: 14
SALES (est): 2.3MM **Privately Held**
SIC: 3842 8021 5999 Limbs, artificial; prosthodontist; artificial limbs

(G-4485)
ICS PENETRON INTERNATIONAL LTD
45 Research Way Ste 203 (11733-6401)
PHONE.................................631 928-8282
Fax: 631 941-9777
Robert G Reuera, *CEO*
Sue Yi, *Info Tech Mgr*
Robert Revera, *Technology*
Jozef Van Beeck, *Director*
Ann Martucci, *Executive Asst*
▼ **EMP:** 14
SQ FT: 60,000
SALES (est): 5.4MM **Privately Held**
WEB: www.penetron.com
SIC: 2899 Waterproofing compounds

(G-4486)
MEDICINE RULES INC
2 Constance Ct (11733-3730)
PHONE.................................631 334-5395
Joseph Agartner, *President*
EMP: 5
SALES (est): 344.1K **Privately Held**
SIC: 3695 Computer software tape & disks: blank, rigid & floppy

(G-4487)
MILLER MOHR DISPLAY INC
12 Technology Dr Unit 6 (11733-4049)
PHONE.................................631 941-2769
Fax: 631 941-1147
Marilyn Mohr, *President*
Miller Mohr, *Principal*
EMP: 5
SALES: 950K **Privately Held**
SIC: 3993 Signs & advertising specialties

(G-4488)
MML SOFTWARE LTD
Also Called: Finance Manager
45 Research Way Ste 207 (11733-6401)
PHONE.................................631 941-1313
Ron Bovich, *President*
Andrew Miller, *President*
EMP: 20
SQ FT: 5,000
SALES (est): 2MM **Privately Held**
WEB: www.financemgr.com
SIC: 7372 6163 Prepackaged software; loan brokers

(G-4489)
POLE-TECH CO INC
Also Called: Poletech Flagpole Manufaturer
97 Gnarled Hollow Rd (11733-1980)
P.O. Box 715 (11733-0770)
PHONE.................................631 689-5525
Fax: 631 689-5528
Karnik M Seferian, *Ch of Bd*
Ralph Barbarite, *Vice Pres*
Nigg Pappu, *Manager*
Lori Jane, *Admin Sec*
▲ **EMP:** 17
SQ FT: 20,000
SALES (est): 4.5MM **Privately Held**
WEB: www.poletech.com
SIC: 3446 Flagpoles, metal

(G-4490)
PRINTING SPECTRUM INC
12 Research Way Ste 1 (11733-3531)
PHONE.................................631 689-1010
Fax: 631 689-7030
James Altebrando, *Ch of Bd*
John Visconti, *Sales Mgr*
EMP: 12
SQ FT: 10,000
SALES (est): 2MM **Privately Held**
WEB: www.printingspectrum.com
SIC: 2752 Commercial printing, lithographic

(G-4491)
RE HANSEN INDUSTRIES INC (PA)
Also Called: Islandaire
22 Research Way (11733-3453)
PHONE.................................631 471-2900
Robert Hansen Jr, *Ch of Bd*
Robert Altner, *Prdtn Mgr*
Bob Bissinger, *Design Engr*
Florin Mirica, *Design Engr*
Donna Thompson, *Controller*
▲ **EMP:** 118
SALES (est): 25.7MM **Privately Held**
SIC: 3585 3822 3433 5722 Air conditioning equipment, complete; heat pumps, electric; auto controls regulating residntl & coml environmt & applncs; heating equipment, except electric; air conditioning room units, self-contained; plumbing, heating, air-conditioning contractors

(G-4492)
SKYLINE LLC
16 Hulse Rd Ste 1 (11733-3645)
PHONE.................................631 403-4131
Erin Argyris, *Controller*
Louis Bove, *Mng Member*
Lawrence Schreiber,
EMP: 20
SALES: 3.5MM **Privately Held**
SIC: 3295 Perlite, aggregate or expanded

(G-4493)
TECHNOMAG INC
12 Technology Dr Unit 5 (11733-4000)
PHONE.................................631 246-6142
Vujay Katukota, *President*
▲ **EMP:** 5

SALES (est): 605K **Privately Held**
SIC: 3499 3577 7319 Magnets, permanent: metallic; computer peripheral equipment; distribution of advertising material or sample services

(G-4494)
TIMES BEACON RECORD NEWSPAPERS (PA)
Also Called: Village Times, The
185 Route 25a Ste 4 (11733-2870)
P.O. Box 707 (11733-0769)
PHONE.................................631 331-1154
Fax: 631 751-7744
Leah E Dunaeif, *President*
Leah Dunaief, *Owner*
Elana Glowatz, *Editor*
Marie Murtagh, *Advt Staff*
Ellen Segal, *Manager*
EMP: 17
SALES (est): 1.6MM **Privately Held**
SIC: 2711 Newspapers: publishing only, not printed on site

(G-4495)
TUCKER JONES HOUSE INC
1 Enterprise Dr (11733-4086)
P.O. Box 231 (11733-0231)
PHONE.................................631 642-9092
Donna Sucilsky, *President*
EMP: 20
SQ FT: 8,000
SALES (est): 2.3MM **Privately Held**
WEB: www.tavernpuzzle.com
SIC: 3944 Puzzles

(G-4496)
VISUAL LISTING SYSTEMS INC
19 Technology Dr (11733-4000)
P.O. Box 856, Stony Brook (11790-0856)
PHONE.................................631 689-7222
Dale Robins, *President*
Paul Singer, *Vice Pres*
EMP: 5
SALES (est): 419.4K **Privately Held**
WEB: www.vlshomes.com
SIC: 7372 8742 Prepackaged software; real estate consultant

(G-4497)
ZEPPELIN ELECTRIC COMPANY INC
26 Deer Ln (11733-3407)
PHONE.................................631 928-9467
William Zeppelin, *President*
EMP: 7
SQ FT: 1,250
SALES: 525.4K **Privately Held**
SIC: 3625 1731 Relays & industrial controls; electronic controls installation

East Syracuse
Onondaga County

(G-4498)
A NUCLIMATE QULTY SYSTEMS INC
6295 E Molloy Rd (13057-1072)
PHONE.................................315 431-0226
Edward Campagna Jr, *President*
John Dimillo, *Vice Pres*
James Miller, *VP Engrg*
EMP: 19
SALES (est): 2.8MM **Privately Held**
SIC: 3585 3433 Heating equipment, complete; heating & air conditioning combination units; heating equipment, except electric

(G-4499)
AEROSEAL LLC
6838 Ellicott Dr (13057-1039)
PHONE.................................315 373-0765
Amit Gupta, *CEO*
Vijay Kollepara, *VP Opers*
EMP: 15
SQ FT: 11,000
SALES (est): 1.5MM **Privately Held**
SIC: 3585 Refrigeration & heating equipment

(G-4500)
ALEXSCOE LLC
Also Called: Atlas Fence
6852 Manlius Center Rd (13057-9522)
PHONE.................................315 463-9207
Fax: 315 433-8561
Christopher Polimino, *President*
Gwen Umsted, *Executive*
EMP: 40 **EST:** 2012
SALES (est): 9.7MM **Privately Held**
SIC: 3315 Fence gates posts & fittings: steel

(G-4501)
ALLEN TOOL PHOENIX INC
6821 Ellicott Dr (13057-1148)
P.O. Box 3024, Liverpool (13089-3024)
PHONE.................................315 463-7533
Fax: 315 463-0303
Cheryl Maines, *President*
Jack Quartier, *Engineer*
Heath Severn, *Engineer*
Ed McCarthy, *Manager*
EMP: 20
SQ FT: 18,000
SALES (est): 4MM **Privately Held**
WEB: www.allentoolphoenix.com
SIC: 3599 7692 Machine shop, jobbing & repair; welding repair

(G-4502)
ANAREN INC (HQ)
6635 Kirkville Rd (13057-9672)
PHONE.................................315 432-8909
Lawrence A Sala, *CEO*
David E Kopf, *President*
David Whitaker, *General Mgr*
Carl W Gerst Jr, *Vice Chairman*
Mark P Burdick, *Senior VP*
▲ **EMP:** 300
SQ FT: 159,000
SALES (est): 232.2MM **Privately Held**
WEB: www.anaren.com
SIC: 3679 Electronic circuits; microwave components
PA: Anaren Holding Corp.
590 Madison Ave Fl 41
New York NY 10022
212 415-6700

(G-4503)
ANAREN MICROWAVE INC
6635 Kirkville Rd (13057-9600)
PHONE.................................315 432-8909
Fax: 315 432-9121
Lawrence A Sala, *CEO*
George Blanton, *Senior VP*
Brian Buyea, *Project Mgr*
Doreen R Barney, *Buyer*
Jim Budd, *Engineer*
EMP: 182
SALES (est): 75.1MM
SALES (corp-wide): 232.2MM **Privately Held**
SIC: 3821 Micromanipulator
HQ: Anaren, Inc.
6635 Kirkville Rd
East Syracuse NY 13057
315 432-8909

(G-4504)
ARMSTRONG MOLD CORPORATION (PA)
6910 Manlius Center Rd (13057-8507)
PHONE.................................315 437-1517
John Alfred Armstrong, *CEO*
Peter Armstrong, *President*
Mark Garofano, *President*
John Matthews, *General Mgr*
Christopher Tiffault, *General Mgr*
▼ **EMP:** 50
SQ FT: 90,000
SALES (est): 20.6MM **Privately Held**
WEB: www.armstrongmold.com
SIC: 3365 3089 3543 Aluminum & aluminum-based alloy castings; injection molding of plastics; industrial patterns

(G-4505)
ARMSTRONG MOLD CORPORATION
5860 Fisher Rd (13057-2962)
PHONE.................................315 437-1517
John Alfred Armstrong, *Principal*
Greg Mork, *Engineer*

East Syracuse - Onondaga County (G-4506)

EMP: 75
SQ FT: 31,060
SALES (corp-wide): 20.6MM **Privately Held**
WEB: www.armstrongmold.com
SIC: 3599 3365 3089 3543 Custom machinery; machine shop, jobbing & repair; aluminum & aluminum-based alloy castings; injection molding of plastics; industrial patterns
PA: Armstrong Mold Corporation
6910 Manlius Center Rd
East Syracuse NY 13057
315 437-1517

(G-4506)
ARTISTRY IN WOOD OF SYRACUSE
6804 Manlius Center Rd # 2 (13057-1394)
PHONE 315 431-4022
Fax: 315 431-0887
Gregory W McCartney, *President*
Kim Fanke, *Controller*
EMP: 17
SALES (est): 3.6MM **Privately Held**
SIC: 2599 2531 5046 Factory furniture & fixtures; public building & related furniture; library furniture; store fixtures

(G-4507)
ASSA ABLOY ENTRANCE SYSTEMS US
Also Called: Besam Entrance Solutions
28 Corporate Cir Ste 1 (13057-1283)
PHONE 315 492-6600
Shane Stone, *Branch Mgr*
EMP: 22
SALES (corp-wide): 7.8B **Privately Held**
SIC: 3699 1796 3442 Door opening & closing devices, electrical; installing building equipment; metal doors
HQ: Assa Abloy Entrance Systems Us Inc.
1900 Airport Rd
Monroe NC 28110
704 290-5520

(G-4508)
AURORA STONE GROUP LLC
114 Marcy St (13057-2143)
PHONE 315 471-6869
Sandra Murphy,
EMP: 10
SALES (est): 900K **Privately Held**
SIC: 3281 1743 Granite, cut & shaped; marble installation, interior

(G-4509)
B P NASH CO INC
5841 Butternut Dr (13057-9514)
PHONE 315 445-1310
Fax: 315 449-1003
Barry Nash, *President*
EMP: 15
SQ FT: 12,000
SALES (est): 1.5MM **Privately Held**
SIC: 3441 Fabricated structural metal

(G-4510)
BELLOTTI PACKAGING INC
Also Called: Bell-Pac
6881 Schuyler Rd (13057-9752)
PHONE 315 433-0131
Fax: 315 433-8514
Louis Bellotti Jr, *President*
Kathlyn Bellotti, *Vice Pres*
Kathleen Belotti, *Director*
EMP: 13
SQ FT: 26,100
SALES (est): 2.2MM **Privately Held**
WEB: www.bell-pak.com
SIC: 2653 Corrugated & solid fiber boxes

(G-4511)
BK PRINTING INC
Also Called: Speedpro Imaging
6507 Basile Rowe (13057-2928)
PHONE 315 565-5396
Robert Kelleher, *Principal*
EMP: 7 EST: 2010
SALES: 700K **Privately Held**
SIC: 2752 Commercial printing, lithographic

(G-4512)
BRISTOL-MYERS SQUIBB COMPANY
6000 Thompson Rd (13057-5050)
P.O. Box 4755, Syracuse (13221-4755)
PHONE 315 432-2000
Fax: 315 432-2202
John Baumes, *Project Mgr*
Kirk Wolfgang, *Engineer*
Steven Lee, *Branch Mgr*
John Sharak, *Security Mgr*
Jeff Axline, *Manager*
EMP: 40
SALES (corp-wide): 16.5B **Publicly Held**
WEB: www.bms.com
SIC: 2834 Druggists' preparations (pharmaceuticals)
PA: Bristol-Myers Squibb Company
345 Park Ave Bsmt Lc3
New York NY 10154
212 546-4000

(G-4513)
CARRIER CORPORATION
6390 Fly Rd (13057-9349)
PHONE 315 463-5744
Ralph Bott, *Branch Mgr*
Leslie Franklin, *Manager*
EMP: 293
SALES (corp-wide): 56.1B **Publicly Held**
WEB: www.carrier.com
SIC: 3585 Air conditioning equipment, complete
HQ: Carrier Corporation
17900 Bee Line Hwy
Jupiter FL 33478
561 796-2000

(G-4514)
CARRIER CORPORATION
Carrier Transicold
Kinne St (13057)
P.O. Box 4805, Syracuse (13221-4805)
PHONE 315 432-6000
Fax: 315 432-3099
Paul Chen, *Engineer*
Nick Pinchuk, *Manager*
Ben Ferguson, *Project Leader*
Robert Chopko, *Senior Mgr*
EMP: 293
SALES (corp-wide): 56.1B **Publicly Held**
WEB: www.carrier.com
SIC: 3585 Air conditioning equipment, complete
HQ: Carrier Corporation
17900 Bee Line Hwy
Jupiter FL 33478
561 796-2000

(G-4515)
CARRIER CORPORATION
Transicold
Carrier Pkwy Bldg Tr 20 (13057)
P.O. Box 4805, Syracuse (13221-4805)
PHONE 315 432-3844
Nick Pinchuk, *President*
Scott Lindsay, *Design Engr*
EMP: 293
SALES (corp-wide): 56.1B **Publicly Held**
WEB: www.carrier.com
SIC: 3585 Lockers, refrigerated
HQ: Carrier Corporation
17900 Bee Line Hwy
Jupiter FL 33478
561 796-2000

(G-4516)
CAYUGA PRESS CORTLAND INC
5795 Bridge St (13057-2920)
PHONE 888 229-8421
Thomas Quartier, *President*
Barney Schug, *Vice Pres*
Mark Binkowski, *Info Tech Mgr*
EMP: 32 EST: 2011
SALES (est): 233.6K **Privately Held**
SIC: 2752 2741 Commercial printing, offset; miscellaneous publishing

(G-4517)
CENTRAL NEW YORK GOLF CENTER
310 E 1st St (13057-2927)
PHONE 315 463-1200
Fax: 315 463-1213
Judith A Conger, *President*
Jack Conger, *Vice Pres*
EMP: 6
SQ FT: 6,000
SALES (est): 643.7K **Privately Held**
SIC: 3949 7999 Golf equipment; golf driving range; tennis club, non-membership

(G-4518)
CLEARWOOD CUSTOM CARPENTRY AND
617 W Manlius St Ste 1 (13057-2276)
PHONE 315 432-8422
Fax: 315 432-8469
Kyle Latray, *Mng Member*
Kathy Stay, *Manager*
Andrew McDonald,
EMP: 30
SQ FT: 33,856
SALES (est): 5.1MM **Privately Held**
WEB: www.clearwoodccm.com
SIC: 2431 2434 Millwork; wood kitchen cabinets

(G-4519)
CONSTRUCTION PARTS WHSE INC
5841 Butternut Dr (13057-9514)
PHONE 315 445-1310
Bruce P Nash Jr, *President*
Dale Spuches, *Vice Pres*
EMP: 6
SALES (est): 1MM **Privately Held**
SIC: 3444 Sheet metal specialties, not stamped

(G-4520)
CURBELL INCORPORATED
6805 Crossbow Dr (13057-4007)
PHONE 315 434-7240
Fax: 315 463-4165
Chet Wisniewski, *Manager*
EMP: 6
SALES (est): 529.9K **Privately Held**
SIC: 3081 Plastic film & sheet

(G-4521)
CWR MANUFACTURING CORPORATION
7000 Fly Rd (13057-9475)
PHONE 315 437-1032
Fax: 315 437-1493
James A Murphy, *President*
James Tilton, *Opers Mgr*
Clara Bolton, *Purchasing*
David Migliacco, *Controller*
Ernest Colella, *Human Resources*
EMP: 100
SQ FT: 62,000
SALES (est): 15.6MM **Privately Held**
WEB: www.cwronline.com
SIC: 3452 3498 Bolts, metal; nuts, metal; fabricated pipe & fittings

(G-4522)
DAIRY FARMERS AMERICA INC
5001 Brittonfield Pkwy (13057-9201)
P.O. Box 4844, Syracuse (13221-4844)
PHONE 816 801-6440
Diana Cordes, *Human Res Mgr*
Michelle Hart, *Business Anlyst*
David Geisler, *Manager*
Matt Tobia, *Manager*
Dave Nouza, *Sr Software Eng*
EMP: 41
SALES (corp-wide): 13.8B **Privately Held**
WEB: www.dfamilk.com
SIC: 2026 Fluid milk
PA: Dairy Farmers Of America, Inc.
10220 N Ambassador Dr
Kansas City MO 64153
816 801-6455

(G-4523)
DANCKER SELLEW & DOUGLAS INC
6067 Corporate Dr (13057-1082)
PHONE 908 231-1600
EMP: 6
SALES (corp-wide): 181.7MM **Privately Held**
SIC: 2869 Industrial organic chemicals
PA: Dancker, Sellew & Douglas, Inc.
291 Evans Way
Branchburg NJ 08876
908 429-1200

(G-4524)
DATACOM SYSTEMS INC
9 Adler Dr (13057-1201)
PHONE 315 463-9541
Fax: 315 463-9557
Kevin Formby, *President*
Timothy Crofton, *President*
Sam Lanzafane, *Chairman*
Peter Oconnell, *Vice Chairman*
Gilbert Kaufman, *Vice Pres*
EMP: 33
SQ FT: 16,000
SALES (est): 7.8MM **Privately Held**
WEB: www.datacomsystems.com
SIC: 3571 Electronic computers

(G-4525)
DEAN FOODS COMPANY
6867 Schuyler Rd (13057-9752)
PHONE 315 452-5001
Fax: 315 452-3238
Leah Curcio, *Principal*
EMP: 87 **Publicly Held**
SIC: 2026 Fluid milk; milk processing (pasteurizing, homogenizing, bottling)
PA: Dean Foods Company
2711 N Haskell Ave
Dallas TX 75204

(G-4526)
E F THRESH INC
6000 Galster Rd (13057-2917)
PHONE 315 437-7301
Eric F Thresh, *President*
Janet Thresh, *Corp Secy*
William Thresh, *Vice Pres*
EMP: 6 EST: 1955
SQ FT: 35,000
SALES: 728K **Privately Held**
SIC: 2541 6512 Cabinets, except refrigerated: show, display, etc.: wood; commercial & industrial building operation

(G-4527)
EASTSIDE PRINTERS
Also Called: East Side Printers
6163 E Molloy Rd (13057-1067)
PHONE 315 437-6515
Matthew Brennan, *Owner*
Cinthia Brennan, *Systems Mgr*
EMP: 12
SQ FT: 4,000
SALES (est): 1.7MM **Privately Held**
SIC: 2752 2789 Commercial printing, offset; bookbinding & related work

(G-4528)
EUCHNER USA INC
6723 Lyons St (13057-9332)
PHONE 315 701-0315
Michael Ladd, *President*
Catherine Cross, *Cust Mgr*
Ricardo Davalos, *Manager*
▲ **EMP:** 18 EST: 2000
SQ FT: 3,136
SALES (est): 3.2MM **Privately Held**
WEB: www.euchner-usa.com
SIC: 3699 Electrical equipment & supplies

(G-4529)
FIBERONE LLC
5 Technology Pl Ste 4 (13057-9738)
PHONE 315 434-8877
Liz Castaneda, *General Mgr*
Rich Brown, *Manager*
Craig Mead,
EMP: 15 EST: 2000
SALES (est): 1.8MM **Privately Held**
SIC: 2298 Cable, fiber

(G-4530)
FLEX-HOSE COMPANY INC
6801 Crossbow Dr (13057-1026)
PHONE 315 437-1903
Fax: 315 437-1903
Philip Argersinger, *President*
Joanna Carter, *Vice Pres*
Chuck Phillips, *Vice Pres*
David Rauch, *Vice Pres*
Chuck Phillips, *VP Mfg*
▲ **EMP:** 28 EST: 1968

SQ FT: 15,000
SALES (est): 8.5MM **Privately Held**
SIC: 3599 Hose, flexible metallic

(G-4531)
FOREST MEDICAL LLC
6700 Old Collamer Rd # 114 (13057-1167)
PHONE.................................315 434-9000
Fax: 315 432-8064
Donald Greenfield, *Finance*
Dick Bowman, *Technology*
Raymond Lichorobiec,
EMP: 9
SQ FT: 4,000
SALES (est): 1.1MM **Privately Held**
WEB: www.forestmedical.com
SIC: 3845 Electromedical equipment

(G-4532)
GAREY MFG & DESIGN CORP
4411 James St (13057-2111)
PHONE.................................315 463-5306
Michael Garrey, *President*
EMP: 5
SALES: 250K **Privately Held**
SIC: 3545 Precision tools, machinists'

(G-4533)
GEI INTERNATIONAL INC (PA)
Also Called: Gaebel Enterprises
100 Ball St (13057-2359)
P.O. Box 6849, Syracuse (13217-6849)
PHONE.................................315 463-9261
Fax: 315 463-9034
Peter Anderson, *President*
Maureen Anderson, *Vice Pres*
William Parker, *Sales Staff*
EMP: 20 EST: 1960
SALES (est): 1.8MM **Privately Held**
WEB: www.geionline.com
SIC: 3423 3531 5199 3829 Rules or rulers, metal; scrapers (construction machinery); art goods & supplies; measuring & controlling devices

(G-4534)
GREENWOOD WINERY LLC
6475 Collamer Rd (13057-1031)
P.O. Box 2949, Syracuse (13220-2949)
PHONE.................................315 432-8132
Tom Greenwood, *Owner*
Robyn Bombard, *Sales Mgr*
EMP: 30
SALES: 800K **Privately Held**
SIC: 2084 2066 Wines; chocolate

(G-4535)
H F W COMMUNICATIONS INC (HQ)
Also Called: Holstein World
6437 Collamer Rd Ste 1 (13057-1559)
PHONE.................................315 703-7979
Scott Smith, *CEO*
Joel Hastings, *President*
John Montandon, *President*
Eleanor Jacobs, *Editor*
Art Sweum, *Vice Pres*
EMP: 15
SALES (est): 6.5MM
SALES (corp-wide): 5.9MM **Privately Held**
SIC: 2721 Trade journals: publishing & printing
PA: Multi-Ag Media L.L.C.
6437 Collamer Rd
East Syracuse NY
315 703-7979

(G-4536)
HENRY SCHEIN INC
6057 Corporate Dr Ste 2 (13057-1068)
PHONE.................................315 431-0340
Fax: 315 431-0971
Kristen Esler, *Branch Mgr*
EMP: 24
SALES (corp-wide): 10.6B **Publicly Held**
SIC: 3843 Dental equipment & supplies
PA: Henry Schein, Inc.
135 Duryea Rd
Melville NY 11747
631 843-5500

(G-4537)
HERCULES CANDY CO
Also Called: Hercules Gift & Gormet
209 W Heman St (13057-2258)
PHONE.................................315 463-4339
Fax: 315 463-2796
Terry L Andrianos, *Partner*
EMP: 10
SALES (est): 232K **Privately Held**
WEB: www.herculescandy.com
SIC: 2064 5441 Candy & other confectionery products; candy

(G-4538)
ILLUMINATION TECHNOLOGIES INC
5 Adler Dr (13057-1262)
P.O. Box 1153, Elbridge (13060-1153)
PHONE.................................315 463-4673
Fax: 315 463-1401
Michael Muehlemann, *President*
EMP: 10
SQ FT: 6,000
SALES (est): 2MM **Privately Held**
WEB: www.illuminationtech.com
SIC: 3648 Lighting equipment

(G-4539)
INDUSTRIAL FABRICATING CORP (PA)
6201 E Molloy Rd (13057-1021)
PHONE.................................315 437-3353
Fax: 315 437-4075
Myron R Kocan, *President*
Jim McVicar, *Manager*
EMP: 33
SQ FT: 60,000
SALES (est): 13.1MM **Privately Held**
WEB: www.industrialfabricating.com
SIC: 3441 3444 Fabricated structural metal; sheet metalwork

(G-4540)
INDUSTRIAL FABRICATING CORP
4 Collamer Cir (13057-1102)
PHONE.................................315 437-8234
Fax: 315 432-1669
Gary Cristal, *Manager*
EMP: 29
SQ FT: 32,886
SALES (corp-wide): 13.1MM **Privately Held**
WEB: www.industrialfabricating.com
SIC: 3443 Weldments
PA: Industrial Fabricating Corp
6201 E Molloy Rd
East Syracuse NY 13057
315 437-3353

(G-4541)
INFICON INC (HQ)
2 Technology Pl (13057-9714)
PHONE.................................315 434-1149
Fax: 315 437-3803
Peter Maier, *President*
Hoang Cao, *Vice Pres*
Stephen Chabot, *Vice Pres*
Ulrich Doebler, *Vice Pres*
Terry Perkins, *Vice Pres*
▲ **EMP:** 250 EST: 1970
SQ FT: 135,000
SALES (est): 137.3MM
SALES (corp-wide): 305.4MM **Privately Held**
WEB: www.inficon.com
SIC: 3823 3812 Industrial process control instruments; search & navigation equipment
PA: Inficon Holding Ag
Hintergasse 15b
Bad Ragaz SG 7310
813 004-980

(G-4542)
INFICON HOLDING AG
2 Technology Pl (13057-9714)
PHONE.................................315 434-1100
William Busher, *QC Mgr*
Paul Mahunik, *Engineer*
Peter G Maier, *CFO*
Peter Maeir, *CFO*
Janice Smeall, *VP Finance*
EMP: 5

SALES (est): 370.3K **Privately Held**
SIC: 3823 Industrial instrmnts msrmnt display/control process variable

(G-4543)
INFITEC INC
6500 Badgley Rd (13057-9667)
P.O. Box 2956, Syracuse (13220-2956)
PHONE.................................315 433-1150
Fax: 315 433-1521
George W Ehegartner, *Ch of Bd*
David Lawrie, *Vice Pres*
Bob Eichenlaub, *Purch Mgr*
Kathy Ehegartner, *Purchasing*
Tom Kissmer, *Engineer*
▲ **EMP:** 60
SQ FT: 22,000
SALES (est): 3.9MM **Privately Held**
WEB: www.infitec.com
SIC: 3625 3822 Timing devices, electronic; auto controls regulating residntl & coml environmt & applncs

(G-4544)
INTERSURGICAL INCORPORATED (PA)
6757 Kinne St (13057-1215)
PHONE.................................315 451-2900
Howard Bellm, *Chairman*
Kristin Purdy, *Vice Pres*
Mary Sweeney, *Vice Pres*
Susan Jaeger, *Accountant*
Rhonda Steward, *Accountant*
EMP: 11
SQ FT: 7,000
SALES (est): 2.5MM **Privately Held**
SIC: 3841 Surgical & medical instruments; anesthesia apparatus

(G-4545)
J W STEVENS CO INC
6059 Corporate Dr (13057-1040)
PHONE.................................315 472-6311
Jeff Salanger, *Vice Pres*
EMP: 7
SALES (est): 734.3K **Privately Held**
SIC: 3443 Boiler shop products: boilers, smokestacks, steel tanks

(G-4546)
JE MILLER INC
747 W Manlius St (13057-2177)
PHONE.................................315 437-6811
Fax: 315 463-4597
Dennis J Hile, *President*
Barbara Hile, *Vice Pres*
Audrey More, *Manager*
EMP: 16 EST: 1951
SQ FT: 15,000
SALES (est): 3.6MM **Privately Held**
WEB: www.jemiller.com
SIC: 3625 3585 Relays & industrial controls; air conditioning units, complete: domestic or industrial

(G-4547)
JOY EDWARD COMPANY
Also Called: Joy Process Mechanical
6747 W Benedict Rd (13057-9391)
P.O. Box 338 (13057-0338)
PHONE.................................315 474-3360
Fax: 315 474-2416
Leonard P Markert III, *CEO*
Gerald Carhart, *Vice Pres*
Lyn Markert Hathaway, *Admin Sec*
EMP: 40 EST: 1875
SQ FT: 40,000
SALES (est): 17.5MM **Privately Held**
SIC: 3441 1711 Fabricated structural metal; mechanical contractor

(G-4548)
KERNER AND MERCHANT
104 Johnson St (13057-2840)
PHONE.................................315 463-8023
Benjamin R Merchant, *President*
Albert H Arnold, *Corp Secy*
Andrea Martin, *Bookkeeper*
EMP: 7 EST: 1978
SQ FT: 3,600
SALES: 300K **Privately Held**
SIC: 3931 7699 Pipes, organ; organ tuning & repair

(G-4549)
MD4 HOLDINGS INC
Also Called: Design Prototyping Tech Inc
6713 Collamer Rd (13057-9759)
PHONE.................................315 434-1869
Mike Rufo, *President*
Dan Simmons, *Treasurer*
EMP: 17
SQ FT: 17,000
SALES (est): 1.6MM
SALES (corp-wide): 666.1MM **Publicly Held**
WEB: www.dpt-fast.com
SIC: 3089 Plastic processing
PA: 3d Systems Corporation
333 Three D Systems Cir
Rock Hill SC 29730
803 326-3900

(G-4550)
MICROWAVE FILTER COMPANY INC (PA)
6743 Kinne St (13057-1269)
PHONE.................................315 438-4700
Fax: 315 463-1467
Paul W Mears, *CEO*
Carl F Fahrenkrug Jr, *Exec VP*
David Barnello, *Purch Dir*
Paul Mears, *VP Engrg*
Richard L Jones, *CFO*
EMP: 44
SQ FT: 40,000
SALES: 3.5MM **Publicly Held**
WEB: www.microwavefilter.com
SIC: 3677 3679 Filtration devices, electronic; microwave components

(G-4551)
MUTUAL LIBRARY BINDERY INC
6295 E Molloy Rd Ste 3 (13057-1104)
P.O. Box 6026, Syracuse (13217-6026)
PHONE.................................315 455-6638
Otto E Rausch, *President*
Robert Rausch, *Vice Pres*
Stephen Rausch, *Vice Pres*
EMP: 25 EST: 1915
SALES (est): 2.6MM **Privately Held**
SIC: 2789 Bookbinding & repairing: trade, edition, library, etc.

(G-4552)
NIAGARA SCIENTIFIC INC
Also Called: Schroeder Machine Div
6743 Kinne St (13057-1215)
P.O. Box 146 (13057-0146)
PHONE.................................315 437-0821
Fax: 315 437-0242
Carl Fahrenkrug, *President*
Milo Peterson, *Exec VP*
Dave Barnello, *Purchasing*
Robert Hamister, *VP Engrg*
Richard Jones, *CFO*
EMP: 54
SQ FT: 16,000
SALES (est): 4.3MM
SALES (corp-wide): 3.5MM **Publicly Held**
WEB: www.microwavefilter.com
SIC: 3565 3826 Carton packing machines; environmental testing equipment
PA: Microwave Filter Company, Inc.
6743 Kinne St
East Syracuse NY 13057
315 438-4700

(G-4553)
NIDEC MOTOR CORPORATION
Advanced Motors & Drives
6268 E Molloy Rd (13057-1047)
PHONE.................................315 434-9303
EMP: 10
SALES (corp-wide): 10B **Privately Held**
SIC: 3621 Motors & generators
HQ: Nidec Motor Corporation
8050 W Florissant Ave
Saint Louis MO 63136

(G-4554)
PEI LIQUIDATION COMPANY
6515 Basile Rowe (13057-2928)
PHONE.................................315 431-4697
Toll Free:.................................888 -
Fax: 315 431-9643
Steve Carey, *Manager*
EMP: 12
SQ FT: 7,500

East Syracuse - Onondaga County (G-4555)

SALES (corp-wide): 14.1MM **Privately Held**
WEB: www.patioenc.com
SIC: 3448 5712 5719 1542 Sunrooms, prefabricated metal; outdoor & garden furniture; wicker, rattan or reed home furnishings; greenhouse construction; patio & deck construction & repair
PA: Pei Liquidation Company
700 Highland Rd E
Macedonia OH 44056
330 467-4267

(G-4555)
RAYMOND CORPORATION
Also Called: Raymond Leasing
6650 Kirkville Rd (13057-9355)
PHONE.................607 656-2311
Fax: 315 463-0053
Jim Schaefer, *General Mgr*
Andre Buytaert, *Plant Mgr*
William Kosina, *Facilities Mgr*
Beryl Baldwin, *Warehouse Mgr*
Janet Sexton, *Buyer*
EMP: 137
SQ FT: 51,584
SALES (corp-wide): 19B **Privately Held**
WEB: www.raymondcorp.com
SIC: 3537 Forklift trucks
HQ: The Raymond Corporation
22 S Canal St
Greene NY 13778
607 656-2311

(G-4556)
RAYMOND CORPORATION
6517 Chrysler Ln (13057-1228)
PHONE.................315 463-5000
Leon A Eccleston, *Branch Mgr*
EMP: 469
SALES (corp-wide): 19B **Privately Held**
SIC: 3537 Forklift trucks
HQ: The Raymond Corporation
22 S Canal St
Greene NY 13778
607 656-2311

(G-4557)
RAYMOND CORPORATION
6533 Chrysler Ln (13057-1375)
PHONE.................315 643-5000
Jim Schaefer, *Branch Mgr*
EMP: 30
SALES (corp-wide): 18.2B **Privately Held**
SIC: 3535 3537 7359 Conveyors & conveying equipment; industrial trucks & tractors; equipment rental & leasing
HQ: The Raymond Corporation
22 S Canal St
Greene NY 13778
607 656-2311

(G-4558)
REYNOLDS TECH FABRICATORS INC
6895 Kinne St (13057-1217)
PHONE.................315 437-0532
Fax: 315 437-1390
Joan J Reynolds, *CEO*
Michael Nakoski, *Vice Pres*
Raoma Stevenson, *Manager*
EMP: 37
SQ FT: 35,000
SALES (est): 7.3MM **Privately Held**
SIC: 3559 3471 Refinery, chemical processing & similar machinery; plating of metals or formed products

(G-4559)
RICHLAR INDUSTRIES INC
Also Called: Richlar Custom Foam Div
6741 Old Collamer Rd (13057-1119)
PHONE.................315 463-5144
Fax: 315 463-0362
Richard Bruntarger, *President*
Dawn Popenfuss, *Vice Pres*
John Hakes, *Opers Mgr*
Bob Taldage, *Purch Mgr*
EMP: 18
SQ FT: 32,000
SALES (est): 2.4MM **Privately Held**
SIC: 3089 3296 3554 Plastic processing; fiberglass insulation; die cutting & stamping machinery, paper converting

(G-4560)
SAAB DEFENSE AND SEC USA LLC
5717 Enterprise Pkwy (13057-2905)
PHONE.................315 445-5009
Laurence Harris, *Principal*
EMP: 10
SALES (corp-wide): 3.1B **Privately Held**
SIC: 3812 Search & detection systems & instruments
HQ: Saab Defense And Security Usa Llc
20700 Loudoun County Pkwy
Ashburn VA 20147
703 406-7200

(G-4561)
SAAB SENSIS CORPORATION
5717 Enterprise Pkwy (13057-2905)
PHONE.................315 445-0550
Jason Anderson, *Branch Mgr*
EMP: 228
SALES (corp-wide): 3.1B **Privately Held**
SIC: 3577 Computer peripheral equipment
HQ: Saab Sensis Corporation
85 Collamer Crossings
East Syracuse NY 13057
315 445-0550

(G-4562)
SBB INC
6500 New Venture Gear Dr # 1000 (13057-1131)
PHONE.................315 422-2376
Fax: 315 437-6501
Robert McKenty, *Principal*
Tony Meehl, *Project Mgr*
EMP: 5
SALES (est): 1.2MM **Privately Held**
SIC: 3564 Air purification equipment

(G-4563)
SHAKO INC
6191 E Molloy Rd (13057-1038)
PHONE.................315 437-1294
Fax: 315 437-0351
Brian Mayfield, *Principal*
EMP: 8
SALES (est): 892.9K **Privately Held**
SIC: 3535 Pneumatic tube conveyor systems

(G-4564)
SIMPLEXGRINNELL LP
6731 Collamer Rd Ste 4 (13057-8704)
PHONE.................315 437-4660
Fred Rossborough, *Marketing Staff*
William Knodel, *Manager*
EMP: 29 **Privately Held**
WEB: www.simplexgrinnell.com
SIC: 3669 Emergency alarms
HQ: Simplexgrinnell Lp
4700 Exchange Ct
Boca Raton FL 33431
561 988-7200

(G-4565)
SIMPLEXGRINNELL LP
6731 Collamer Rd Ste 4 (13057-8704)
PHONE.................607 338-5100
Mike Delsanto, *Manager*
EMP: 10 **Privately Held**
WEB: www.simplexgrinnell.com
SIC: 3669 Emergency alarms
HQ: Simplexgrinnell Lp
4700 Exchange Ct
Boca Raton FL 33431
561 988-7200

(G-4566)
SOUTHERN STATES COOP INC
6701 Manlius Center Rd # 240 (13057-3086)
PHONE.................315 438-4500
Sall McGarraty, *Manager*
EMP: 12
SALES (corp-wide): 2B **Privately Held**
SIC: 2048 Prepared feeds
PA: Southern States Cooperative, Incorporated
6606 W Broad St Ste B
Richmond VA 23230
804 281-1000

(G-4567)
STF SERVICES INC
26 Corporate Cir Ste 2 (13057-1105)
PHONE.................315 463-8506
Fax: 315 437-8244
Michael Smith, *President*
John Siedlicki, *COO*
Therese Pearce, *Accounting Mgr*
Sam Froio, *Technology*
EMP: 50
SQ FT: 20,000
SALES (est): 4.6MM
SALES (corp-wide): 3.6B **Privately Held**
WEB: www.superforms.com
SIC: 2731 2741 Books: publishing only; miscellaneous publishing
HQ: The Bureau Of National Affairs Inc
1801 S Bell St Ste Cn110
Arlington VA 22202
703 341-3000

(G-4568)
SULLIVAN BAZINET BONGIO INC
Also Called: S B B
6500 New Venture Gear Dr (13057-1076)
PHONE.................315 437-6500
John Bazinet, *Partner*
Vincent Bongio, *Partner*
Mike Sullivan, *Partner*
Sheila Cooperider, *Manager*
EMP: 30
SQ FT: 9,000
SALES (est): 7.3MM **Privately Held**
WEB: www.sbbinc.com
SIC: 3564 Air purification equipment

(G-4569)
SUPERIOR PLUS CNSTR PDTS CORP
6741 Old Collamer Rd (13057-1119)
PHONE.................315 463-5144
Glen Markam, *Manager*
Danny Parella, *Senior Mgr*
EMP: 18
SALES (corp-wide): 2.4B **Privately Held**
WEB: www.spi-co.com
SIC: 3089 3296 3554 Plastic processing; fiberglass insulation; die cutting & stamping machinery, paper converting
HQ: Superior Plus Construction Products Corp.
1650 Manheim Pike Ste 202
Lancaster PA 17601
717 569-3900

(G-4570)
SYRACUSE CORRUGATED BOX CORP
302 Stoutenger St (13057-2841)
P.O. Box 126 (13057-0126)
PHONE.................315 437-9901
Fax: 315 437-6131
David R Wilde, *President*
Charles Wilde, *Vice Pres*
John Wilde, *Admin Sec*
EMP: 14 EST: 1969
SQ FT: 24,000
SALES (est): 2.3MM **Privately Held**
SIC: 2653 Boxes, corrugated: made from purchased materials

(G-4571)
THE PRS GROUP INC (PA)
Also Called: Political Risk Services, The
5800 Hrtge Lndng Dr Ste E (13057)
PHONE.................315 431-0511
Fax: 315 431-0200
Christopher McKee, *CEO*
Dianna Spinner, *Treasurer*
Patricia Davis, *Admin Sec*
EMP: 10 EST: 2000
SQ FT: 2,100
SALES (est): 737.4K **Privately Held**
WEB: www.prsgroup.com
SIC: 2721 Periodicals: publishing & printing; statistical reports (periodicals): publishing & printing

(G-4572)
TPC INC
6780 Nthrn Blvd Ste 401 (13057)
P.O. Box 2581, Syracuse (13220-2581)
PHONE.................315 438-8605
Fax: 315 438-8605
Max Bablok, *President*
EMP: 6
SALES: 24.3MM **Privately Held**
SIC: 3728 Aircraft parts & equipment

(G-4573)
TRANE US INC
15 Technology Pl (13057-9713)
PHONE.................315 234-1500
Mike Carey, *Branch Mgr*
EMP: 36
SQ FT: 4,500 **Privately Held**
SIC: 3585 Refrigeration & heating equipment
HQ: Trane U.S. Inc.
1 Centennial Ave Ste 101
Piscataway NJ 08854
732 652-7100

(G-4574)
TYCO SIMPLEXGRINNELL
6731 Collamer Rd Ste 4 (13057-9715)
PHONE.................315 437-9664
Kevin Hache, *Branch Mgr*
EMP: 40
SALES (corp-wide): 954.1MM **Privately Held**
SIC: 3569 3491 Sprinkler systems, fire: automatic; automatic regulating & control valves
PA: Tyco Simplexgrinnell
1501 Nw 51st St
Boca Raton FL 33431
561 988-3658

(G-4575)
U S TECH CORPORATION
6511 Basile Rowe (13057-2928)
P.O. Box 816, Skaneateles (13152-0816)
PHONE.................315 437-7207
Fax: 315 432-0225
Alexander E Gelston II, *President*
Janis J Soule, *Vice Pres*
EMP: 12
SALES: 6MM **Privately Held**
SIC: 3812 Search & detection systems & instruments

(G-4576)
UNITED TECHNOLOGIES CORP
6304 Carrier Pkwy (13057-6300)
PHONE.................315 432-7849
EMP: 7
SALES (corp-wide): 56.1B **Publicly Held**
SIC: 3724 Aircraft engines & engine parts
PA: United Technologies Corporation
10 Farm Springs Rd
Farmington CT 06032
860 728-7000

(G-4577)
UNIVERSAL STEP INC
5970 Butternut Dr (13057-8526)
PHONE.................315 437-7611
David Smith, *President*
EMP: 5 EST: 2009
SALES (est): 542.9K **Privately Held**
SIC: 3272 Steps, prefabricated concrete

(G-4578)
US OPTICAL LLC
6848 Ellicott Dr (13057-1046)
PHONE.................315 463-4800
Ronald Cotran, *Vice Pres*
Tim Wooster, *Sales Mgr*
Ronald Potran, *Mng Member*
Robert Potran, *Manager*
EMP: 50
SALES (est): 9.1MM **Privately Held**
SIC: 3827 Optical instruments & lenses

(G-4579)
VILLAGE DECORATION LTD
20 Corporate Cir (13057-1015)
PHONE.................315 437-2522
Michael Robinson, *President*
Shawn Robinson, *Plant Mgr*
EMP: 30
SQ FT: 13,500
SALES: 1.5MM **Privately Held**
SIC: 3599 Machine & other job shop work

(G-4580)
WERMA (USA) INC
6731 Collamer Rd Ste 1 (13057-9793)
PHONE.................315 414-0200

Michael Oneill, *President*
▲ **EMP:** 4
SQ FT: 4,500
SALES (est): 3MM
SALES (corp-wide): 48.8MM **Privately Held**
SIC: 3669 Signaling apparatus, electric
PA: Werma Signaltechnik Gmbh + Co. Kg
Durbheimer Str. 15
Rietheim-Weilheim 78604
742 495-570

East Yaphank
Suffolk County

(G-4581)
FIREMATIC SUPPLY CO INC (PA)
10 Ramsey Rd (11967-4704)
P.O. Box 187, Yaphank (11980-0187)
PHONE.................................631 924-3181
Fax: 631 924-5202
Michael Hanratty, *Ch of Bd*
Peter Hanratty, *President*
Barbara Hanratty, *Corp Secy*
George Barbieri, *Prdtn Mgr*
Marcel Rosenfeld, *Director*
EMP: 46
SQ FT: 22,000
SALES (est): 25.1MM **Privately Held**
WEB: www.firematic.com
SIC: 3569 Firefighting apparatus

Eastchester
Westchester County

(G-4582)
EASTCHESTER PHOTO SERVICES
Also Called: Eastchester Photo Svce
132 Fisher Ave (10709-2602)
P.O. Box 86 (10709-0086)
PHONE.................................914 961-6596
Fax: 914 961-6684
George Longobardo, *President*
Lorinda Longobardo, *Corp Secy*
EMP: 5
SQ FT: 2,400
SALES (est): 599.6K **Privately Held**
WEB: www.eastchesterphoto.com
SIC: 3861 5946 Developers, photographic (not made in chemical plants); camera & photographic supply stores

(G-4583)
W D TECHNOLOGY INC
42 Water St Ste B (10709-5502)
PHONE.................................914 779-8738
Vincent Rende, *President*
Joe Beard, *Sales Staff*
EMP: 6
SQ FT: 1,000
SALES: 1.5MM **Privately Held**
SIC: 3679 3825 Liquid crystal displays (LCD); radio frequency measuring equipment

Eastport
Suffolk County

(G-4584)
MEDIA TECHNOLOGIES LTD
220 Sonata Ct (11941-1617)
PHONE.................................631 467-7900
Rainer Zopfy, *President*
EMP: 12
SQ FT: 6,800
SALES (est): 3MM **Privately Held**
WEB: www.mediatechmail.com
SIC: 3652 5044 Compact laser discs, pre-recorded; duplicating machines

Eden
Erie County

(G-4585)
AARFID LLC (PA)
3780 Yochum Rd (14057-9519)
PHONE.................................716 992-3999
Chad Carpenter, *President*
EMP: 5
SALES (est): 880.7K **Privately Held**
SIC: 7372 3695 Business oriented computer software; magnetic & optical recording media

(G-4586)
EDEN TOOL & DIE INC
2721 Hemlock Rd (14057-1390)
P.O. Box 296 (14057-0296)
PHONE.................................716 992-4240
Fax: 716 992-4785
James Rettig, *President*
Gary Rettig, *Vice Pres*
Raymond Rettig, *Admin Sec*
▼ **EMP:** 8
SALES (est): 1.1MM **Privately Held**
SIC: 3544 Special dies & tools

(G-4587)
JOHN F RAFTER INC
Also Called: Jf Rafter The Lexington Co
2746 W Church St (14057-1011)
P.O. Box 300 (14057-0300)
PHONE.................................716 992-3425
Fax: 716 992-3426
John Rafter Jr, *President*
EMP: 5
SQ FT: 2,500
SALES (est): 480K **Privately Held**
SIC: 3452 Screws, metal

(G-4588)
MUSTANG-MAJOR TOOL & DIE CO
3243 N Boston Rd (14057-9500)
PHONE.................................716 992-9200
Fax: 716 992-9257
David Kolodczak, *President*
EMP: 6 **EST:** 1965
SQ FT: 8,200
SALES (est): 800K **Privately Held**
WEB: www.mmtooldie.com
SIC: 3544 Special dies & tools

Edgewood
Suffolk County

(G-4589)
ABH NATURES PRODUCTS INC
131 Heartland Blvd (11717-8315)
PHONE.................................631 249-5783
Fax: 631 249-3574
Jahirul Islam, *President*
Harsh Vyas, *CFO*
Sahina Islam, *Director*
David Rabinowit, *Director*
EMP: 28
SQ FT: 40,000
SALES (est): 10MM **Privately Held**
WEB: www.abhnature.com
SIC: 2833 Vitamins, natural or synthetic: bulk, uncompounded

(G-4590)
ADVANCE FOOD SERVICE CO INC
200 Heartland Blvd (11717-8380)
PHONE.................................631 242-4800
Fax: 631 242-6900
Milton Schwartz, *Corp Secy*
Daniel Schwartz, *Vice Pres*
Jerry Nolan, *Purchasing*
EMP: 200 **EST:** 1955
SQ FT: 60,000
SALES (est): 27.7MM **Privately Held**
SIC: 3589 Cooking equipment, commercial

(G-4591)
ADVANCE TABCO INC (HQ)
200 Heartland Blvd (11717-8379)
PHONE.................................631 242-8270
Fax: 631 242-6900
Penny Schwartz-Hutner, *President*
Alice Schwartz, *Chairman*
Daniel Schwartz, *Vice Pres*
Chris Pacicca, *Warehouse Mgr*
Ryan Fee, *Purch Mgr*
▼ **EMP:** 85
SQ FT: 70,000
SALES (est): 29.1MM
SALES (corp-wide): 93.5MM **Privately Held**
SIC: 3589 3431 Commercial cooking & foodwarming equipment; metal sanitary ware
PA: Kinplex Corp.
200 Heartland Blvd
Edgewood NY 11717
631 242-4800

(G-4592)
ALL ISLAND MEDIA INC (PA)
Also Called: Pennysaver/Town Crier
1 Rodeo Dr (11717-8318)
PHONE.................................631 698-8400
Ronald Rudolph, *President*
Katrina Innamorato, *Editor*
Robert Sussi, *Vice Pres*
Brenda Colonna, *Prdtn Dir*
Paul E Gregory, *CFO*
EMP: 110
SQ FT: 20,000
SALES (est): 13MM **Privately Held**
WEB: www.allislandmedia.com
SIC: 2711 Newspapers, publishing & printing

(G-4593)
AZTEC TOOL CO INC
180 Rodeo Dr (11717-8340)
PHONE.................................631 243-1144
Fax: 631 243-1149
Stewart Swiss, *President*
James Evarts, *Vice Pres*
Harry Herz, *Sales Dir*
EMP: 20
SQ FT: 24,000
SALES (est): 4.5MM **Privately Held**
WEB: www.aztectool.com
SIC: 3089 Injection molded finished plastic products; injection molding of plastics

(G-4594)
BEMIS COMPANY INC
Also Called: Bemis North America
100 Wilshire Blvd (11717-8302)
PHONE.................................631 794-2900
Igor Rakhmanskiy, *Engineer*
EMP: 171
SALES (corp-wide): 4B **Publicly Held**
SIC: 2671 Packaging paper & plastics film, coated & laminated
PA: Bemis Company, Inc.
1 Neenah Ctr Fl 4
Neenah WI 54956
920 527-5000

(G-4595)
BIOCHEMICAL DIAGNOSTICS INC
180 Heartland Blvd (11717-8314)
PHONE.................................631 595-9200
Fax: 631 595-9204
Allen Panetz, *President*
Maria Hunt, *General Mgr*
Amir Forooqi, *Corp Secy*
Rich Gordon, *Vice Pres*
EMP: 25
SQ FT: 30,000
SALES (est): 4.1MM **Privately Held**
WEB: www.biochemicaldiagnostics.com
SIC: 3841 2835 Diagnostic apparatus, medical; in vitro & in vivo diagnostic substances

(G-4596)
CPI AEROSTRUCTURES INC
91 Heartland Blvd (11717-8330)
PHONE.................................631 586-5200
Fax: 631 586-5840
Eric S Rosenfeld, *Ch of Bd*
Douglas McCrosson, *President*
Vincent Palazzolo, *CFO*
EMP: 280 **EST:** 1980
SQ FT: 171,000
SALES: 100.2MM **Privately Held**
WEB: www.cpiaero.com
SIC: 3728 Aircraft parts & equipment

(G-4597)
EMDA INC
250 Executive Dr Ste J (11717-8354)
P.O. Box 378, Plainview (11803-0378)
PHONE.................................631 243-6363
Alan Steinbok, *President*
EMP: 10
SALES: 1MM **Privately Held**
WEB: www.emdainc.com
SIC: 3861 Photographic equipment & supplies

(G-4598)
FLEXIM AMERICAS CORPORATION (HQ)
250 Executive Dr Ste V (11717-8354)
PHONE.................................631 492-2300
Jens Hilpert, *President*
John Obrien, *Vice Pres*
Sherry Stanley, *Manager*
EMP: 12
SQ FT: 7,250
SALES (est): 2.8MM
SALES (corp-wide): 26.7MM **Privately Held**
SIC: 3824 Impeller & counter driven flow meters
PA: Flexim Flexible IndustriemeBtechnik Gmbh
Wolfener Str. 36
Berlin 12681
309 366-7660

(G-4599)
GLOBAL MARKET DEVELOPMENT INC
Also Called: Accusonic Products
200 Executive Dr Ste G (11717-8322)
PHONE.................................631 667-1002
Fax: 631 667-1001
Anthony Mazzeo, *President*
Phillip Glickman, *Vice Pres*
Chris Scocco, *VP Opers*
Johanna Morales, *Production*
Daniel Pizarro, *QC Mgr*
▲ **EMP:** 30
SQ FT: 4,200
SALES (est): 5.9MM **Privately Held**
WEB: www.accusonicproducts.com
SIC: 3651 Loudspeakers, electrodynamic or magnetic

(G-4600)
IBA INDUSTRIAL INC
Also Called: Rdi
151 Heartland Blvd (11717-8315)
PHONE.................................631 254-6800
Richard A Galloway, *Ch of Bd*
Frederic Genin, *President*
Rick Galloway, *Vice Pres*
Vincent Ruelle, *Plant Mgr*
Joseph Giovagnoni, *Engineer*
▲ **EMP:** 41 **EST:** 1958
SQ FT: 42,000
SALES (est): 17.3MM
SALES (corp-wide): 61.4MM **Privately Held**
WEB: www.e-beam-rdi.com
SIC: 3699 5065 Electron linear accelerators; electronic parts & equipment
PA: Ion Beam Applications Sa
Chemin Du Cyclotron 3
Ottignies-Louvain-La-Neuve 1348
104 758-11

(G-4601)
INTERNATIONAL LEISURE PDTS INC
191 Rodeo Dr (11717-8319)
PHONE.................................631 254-2155
Larry Schwimmer, *President*
▲ **EMP:** 20
SALES (est): 2MM
SALES (corp-wide): 20.3MM **Privately Held**
SIC: 3949 Billiard & pool equipment & supplies, general
PA: Swimline Corp.
191 Rodeo Dr
Edgewood NY 11717
631 254-2155

Edgewood - Suffolk County (G-4602)

(G-4602)
KELTA INC (PA)
141 Rodeo Dr (11717-8378)
PHONE.....................631 789-5000
Parag Mehta, *President*
Jyotindra Mehta, *Admin Sec*
▲ **EMP:** 24
SQ FT: 25,000
SALES (est): 112.7MM **Privately Held**
SIC: 3089 3643 3661 Plastic hardware & building products; current-carrying wiring devices; telephone & telegraph apparatus

(G-4603)
KINPLEX CORP (PA)
200 Heartland Blvd (11717-8380)
PHONE.....................631 242-4800
Penny Hunter, *President*
Penny S Hunter, *President*
Daniel Schwartz, *Vice Pres*
Regina Dombal, *Credit Mgr*
▲ **EMP:** 50
SQ FT: 70,000
SALES (est): 93.5MM **Privately Held**
SIC: 3589 Commercial cooking & food-warming equipment

(G-4604)
KINPLEX CORP
Also Called: Tables Manufacturing
200 Heartland Blvd (11717-8380)
PHONE.....................631 242-4800
Maragret Ramsey, *Manager*
EMP: 50
SALES (corp-wide): 93.5MM **Privately Held**
SIC: 3589 2599 3556 Commercial cooking & foodwarming equipment; food wagons, restaurant; food products machinery
PA: Kinplex Corp.
 200 Heartland Blvd
 Edgewood NY 11717
 631 242-4800

(G-4605)
KNR FRAGRANCES & COSMETICS INC
250 Executive Dr Ste M (11717-8354)
PHONE.....................631 586-8500
Fax: 631 586-8501
Nauman Yousaf Butt, *President*
Rizwan Yousaf, *Vice Pres*
Shoaib M Sabir, *Marketing Staff*
♦ **EMP:** 13
SALES (est): 1.7MM **Privately Held**
WEB: www.knrfragrances.com
SIC: 3993 Signs & advertising specialties

(G-4606)
MERIT ELECTRONIC DESIGN CO INC
Also Called: Medco
190 Rodeo Dr (11717-8317)
PHONE.....................631 667-9699
Fax: 631 667-9853
Guy Intoci, *President*
Tony Petroccione, *Purchasing*
Cheryl Sickles, *CFO*
▲ **EMP:** 115
SQ FT: 20,000
SALES (est): 45.2MM **Privately Held**
WEB: www.medcomfg.com
SIC: 3679 Electronic circuits

(G-4607)
POLY-FLEX CORP (PA)
250 Executive Dr Ste S (11717-8354)
PHONE.....................631 586-9500
Barry Neustein, *President*
Roland Razon, *General Mgr*
Talbert Paola, *Principal*
▲ **EMP:** 10 EST: 1977
SQ FT: 8,000
SALES (est): 1.9MM **Privately Held**
WEB: www.poly-flexcorp.com
SIC: 2759 Envelopes: printing

(G-4608)
POLYGEN PHARMACEUTICALS INC
41 Mercedes Way Unit 17 (11717-8334)
PHONE.....................631 392-4044
Mallikarjun Desireddy, *Vice Pres*
Albert Assa, *Controller*
Andrew Fischman, *Marketing Staff*
EMP: 42
SQ FT: 32,000
SALES: 4.5MM **Privately Held**
SIC: 2834 5122 Pharmaceutical preparations; pharmaceuticals

(G-4609)
RSQUARED NY INC
100 Heartland Blvd (11717-8313)
P.O. Box 807, Deer Park (11729-0971)
PHONE.....................631 521-8700
Fax: 631 274-0005
Altaf Hirji, *President*
Lisa Candurard, *Manager*
♦ **EMP:** 98
SQ FT: 30,000
SALES (est): 15.2MM **Privately Held**
WEB: www.redvisuals.com
SIC: 3993 Signs & advertising specialties; advertising artwork

(G-4610)
S G NEW YORK LLC
Also Called: Penny Saver News
1 Rodeo Dr (11717-8318)
PHONE.....................631 698-8400
Bob Sussy, *Manager*
EMP: 17
SALES (corp-wide): 5.9MM **Privately Held**
SIC: 2711 Newspapers, publishing & printing
PA: S G New York Llc
 2950 Vtrans Mem Hwy Ste 1
 Bohemia NY 11716
 631 665-4000

(G-4611)
SATCO PRODUCTS INC (PA)
Also Called: Satco Lighting
110 Heartland Blvd (11717-8303)
PHONE.....................631 243-2022
Fax: 631 243-2027
Herbert Gildin, *CEO*
William Gildin, *Ch of Bd*
Raul Street, *Vice Pres*
Louis Kaufman, *CFO*
Jeff Martin, *Sales Mgr*
♦ **EMP:** 63
SQ FT: 80,000
SALES (est): 31.6MM **Privately Held**
WEB: www.satco.com
SIC: 3641 3645 5063 Electric lamps; residential lighting fixtures; lighting fixtures; light bulbs & related supplies

(G-4612)
SPACE-CRAFT WORLDWIDE INC
91 Rodeo Dr (11717-8318)
PHONE.....................631 603-3000
Mazher Khalfan, *President*
▲ **EMP:** 40
SALES (est): 8.2MM **Privately Held**
SIC: 2541 Store & office display cases & fixtures

(G-4613)
SWIMLINE CORP (PA)
191 Rodeo Dr (11717-8319)
PHONE.....................631 254-2155
Fax: 631 254-2363
Herman Schwimmer, *Ch of Bd*
Larry Schwimmer, *President*
Dennis Smith, *General Mgr*
David Schwartz, *Opers Mgr*
Adrienne Hellman, *Technology*
♦ **EMP:** 41
SALES (est): 20.3MM **Privately Held**
SIC: 3949 3081 Swimming pools, plastic; unsupported plastics film & sheet

(G-4614)
SWIMLINE INTERNATIONAL CORP
191 Rodeo Dr (11717-8319)
PHONE.....................631 254-2155
Larry Schwimmer, *President*
Cynthia Schwimmer, *Vice Pres*
Lisa Melnick, *Manager*
♦ **EMP:** 125
SALES (est): 9.7MM
SALES (corp-wide): 20.3MM **Privately Held**
SIC: 3423 Leaf skimmers or swimming pool rakes
PA: Swimline Corp.
 191 Rodeo Dr
 Edgewood NY 11717
 631 254-2155

(G-4615)
SYLHAN LLC (PA)
210 Rodeo Dr (11717-8317)
PHONE.....................631 243-6600
Fax: 631 243-2800
Steven Pasco, *COO*
Steven H Paskoff, *Sales Executive*
Ronald Manganiello,
Maria Gruner, *Admin Asst*
Edward N Epstein,
▲ **EMP:** 20
SQ FT: 20,000
SALES (est): 1.8MM **Privately Held**
WEB: www.sylhan.com
SIC: 3599 Machine shop, jobbing & repair

(G-4616)
TII TECHNOLOGIES INC (HQ)
141 Rodeo Dr (11717-8378)
PHONE.....................516 364-9300
Parag Mehta, *President*
Adnan Abrahim, *Counsel*
Bruce C Barksdale, *Exec VP*
Albert Rosenthaler, *Senior VP*
Gini Hall, *VP Admin*
▲ **EMP:** 29
SQ FT: 25,000
SALES (est): 12.9MM
SALES (corp-wide): 112.7MM **Privately Held**
WEB: www.tiinettech.com
SIC: 3089 3643 3661 Plastic hardware & building products; lightning protection equipment; telephone & telegraph apparatus
PA: Kelta, Inc.
 141 Rodeo Dr
 Edgewood NY 11717
 631 789-5000

(G-4617)
TIME BASE CORPORATION (PA)
Also Called: Time Base Consoles
170 Rodeo Dr (11717-8317)
PHONE.....................631 293-4068
Jerry Hahn, *President*
Jansen Hahn, *General Mgr*
Frank Lapallo, *Vice Pres*
Steve Struhs, *Accounts Mgr*
Bill Shea, *Sr Project Mgr*
EMP: 47
SQ FT: 20,000
SALES (est): 30.9MM **Privately Held**
SIC: 2517 5712 Wood television & radio cabinets; cabinet work, custom

(G-4618)
TOGA MANUFACTURING INC (HQ)
200 Heartland Blvd (11717-8379)
PHONE.....................631 242-4800
Alice Schwartz, *President*
Penny Schwartz Hutner, *Vice Pres*
Daniel Schwartz, *Vice Pres*
▲ **EMP:** 4
SQ FT: 40,000
SALES (est): 11.4MM
SALES (corp-wide): 93.5MM **Privately Held**
SIC: 3589 Commercial cooking & food-warming equipment
PA: Kinplex Corp.
 200 Heartland Blvd
 Edgewood NY 11717
 631 242-4800

(G-4619)
US ALLIANCE PAPER INC
101 Heartland Blvd (11717-8315)
PHONE.....................631 254-3030
Fax: 631 254-8697
John Sarraf, *President*
Steve Sarrafzadeh, *Vice Pres*
Bogdan Sujka, *Site Mgr*
Franklin Dejesus, *Accounts Mgr*
Jeff Leaf, *Director*
▲ **EMP:** 220
SQ FT: 250,000
SALES (est): 76MM **Privately Held**
WEB: www.usalliancepaper.com
SIC: 2676 Towels, napkins & tissue paper products

(G-4620)
WAYNE INTEGRATED TECH CORP
160 Rodeo Dr (11717-8317)
PHONE.....................631 242-0213
Helen Moks, *CEO*
Joseph V Moks Jr, *Vice Pres*
Joseph Moks, *VP Opers*
Karen Moks, *Office Mgr*
EMP: 38
SQ FT: 15,000
SALES (est): 7.7MM **Privately Held**
WEB: www.gowayne.com
SIC: 3443 3444 3599 Containers, shipping (bombs, etc.): metal plate; metal housings, enclosures, casings & other containers; machine shop, jobbing & repair

(G-4621)
WEICO WIRE & CABLE INC
Also Called: Magnet Wire Division
161 Rodeo Dr (11717-8359)
PHONE.....................631 254-2970
Fax: 631 254-2099
Theodore Weill, *President*
Ellen Moore, *Controller*
Susan Smith, *Administration*
▲ **EMP:** 28
SQ FT: 35,000
SALES: 12.5K **Privately Held**
SIC: 3496 Cable, uninsulated wire: made from purchased wire

Edmeston
Otsego County

(G-4622)
BISHOP PRINT SHOP INC
Also Called: Ecclesiastical Press
9 East St (13335-2428)
PHONE.....................607 965-8155
Fax: 607 965-2007
Michael Lampron, *President*
Walter Flores, *Manager*
EMP: 9 EST: 1949
SALES (est): 1.2MM **Privately Held**
WEB: www.bishopprintshop.com
SIC: 2752 2893 Commercial printing, offset; letterpress or offset ink

---

Elbridge
Onondaga County

(G-4623)
ACCURATE MCHNING INCORPORATION
Also Called: Acrolite
251 State Route 5 (13060-9640)
P.O. Box 1010 (13060-1010)
PHONE.....................315 689-1428
Fax: 315 689-1482
Ronald E Drake Sr, *President*
Karen Coleman, *Manager*
Matthew Dake, *Manager*
Matthew R Drake, *Admin Sec*
EMP: 19
SQ FT: 13,600
SALES (est): 4.9MM **Privately Held**
WEB: www.acrolite.com
SIC: 3559 Fiber optics strand coating machinery

(G-4624)
ALLRED & ASSOCIATES INC
321 Rte 5 W (13060)
PHONE.....................315 252-2559
Jimmie B Allred III, *President*
Cherie R Allred, *Exec VP*
Cherie R Alled, *Marketing Staff*
Andy Morabito, *Info Tech Dir*
EMP: 40

SALES (est): 7.2MM **Privately Held**
WEB: www.evi-inc.com
SIC: 3083 Laminated plastics plate & sheet; laminated plastic sheets; plastic finished products, laminated; retroreflective sheeting, plastic

(G-4625)
DUCK FLATS PHARMA
245 E Main St (13060-8706)
P.O. Box 101 (13060-0101)
PHONE...................315 689-3407
Luana Pescokoplowitz, *Owner*
Karen Ralston, *Manager*
EMP: 9
SALES (est): 570K **Privately Held**
SIC: 2678 Tablets & pads, book & writing: from purchased materials

Elizabethtown
Essex County

(G-4626)
DENTON PUBLICATIONS INC (PA)
Also Called: Free Trader
14 Hand Ave (12932)
P.O. Box 338 (12932-0338)
PHONE...................518 873-6368
Fax: 518 873-6360
Daniel Alexander, *President*
Gayle Alexander, *Vice Pres*
Jeff Davey, *Manager*
Cheryl Mitchell, *Manager*
Jennifer Valenze, *Manager*
EMP: 75 EST: 1948
SQ FT: 11,000
SALES (est): 9.5MM **Privately Held**
WEB: www.denpubs.com
SIC: 2711 2752 Commercial printing & newspaper publishing combined; commercial printing, lithographic

(G-4627)
E C C CORP
7 Church St (12932)
P.O. Box 567 (12932-0567)
PHONE...................518 873-6494
Fax: 518 873-2355
Peter Belzer, *President*
▲ EMP: 6
SQ FT: 5,304
SALES: 1MM **Privately Held**
SIC: 3944 Banks, toy

(G-4628)
HALFWAY HOUSE LLC
7158 Us Route 9 (12932-1712)
P.O. Box 171 (12932-0171)
PHONE...................518 873-2198
Tina Croff, *Partner*
Gifford Croff, *Partner*
EMP: 7
SALES (est): 611.8K **Privately Held**
SIC: 2599 Bar, restaurant & cafeteria furniture

Elka Park
Greene County

(G-4629)
CHURCH COMMUNITIES NY INC
Also Called: Community Playthings
2255 Platte Clove Rd (12427-1014)
PHONE...................518 589-5103
Martin Mathis, *Branch Mgr*
Peter Alexander, *Manager*
EMP: 40
SALES (corp-wide): 10.7MM **Privately Held**
WEB: www.churchcommunitiesfoundation.org
SIC: 3944 3842 Games, toys & children's vehicles; orthopedic appliances
PA: Church Communities Ny Inc.
2032 Route 213 St
Rifton NY 12471
845 658-7700

(G-4630)
CHURCH COMMUNITIES NY INC
Also Called: Community Playthings
Platte Clove Rd (12427)
PHONE...................518 589-5103
Martin Mathis, *Branch Mgr*
EMP: 40
SALES (corp-wide): 10.7MM **Privately Held**
WEB: www.churchcommunitiesfoundation.org
SIC: 3944 3842 Games, toys & children's vehicles; orthopedic appliances
PA: Church Communities Ny Inc.
2032 Route 213 St
Rifton NY 12471
845 658-7700

(G-4631)
COMMUNITY PRODUCTS LLC
2255 Platte Clove Rd (12427-1014)
PHONE...................518 589-5103
EMP: 25
SALES (corp-wide): 88.5MM **Privately Held**
WEB: www.communityplaythings.com
SIC: 3842 3942 Surgical appliances & supplies; dolls & stuffed toys
PA: Community Products, Llc
2032 Route 213 St
Rifton NY 12471
845 658-8799

Ellenville
Ulster County

(G-4632)
BROSS QUALITY PAVING
4 Kossar Pl (12428-2414)
PHONE...................845 532-7116
Julio Moya, *Partner*
EMP: 6
SALES (est): 479.2K **Privately Held**
SIC: 2951 Asphalt paving mixtures & blocks

(G-4633)
DEVIL DOG MANUFACTURING CO INC (PA)
23 Market St (12428-2107)
P.O. Box 588 (12428-0588)
PHONE...................845 647-4411
Carl J Rosenstock, *President*
Richard Rosenstock, *Vice Pres*
Herbert Rosenstock, *Treasurer*
Karen Rosselli, *Manager*
Tony Shananhan, *Manager*
▲ EMP: 6 EST: 1952
SQ FT: 30,000
SALES (est): 24MM **Privately Held**
WEB: www.sportwear.com
SIC: 2369 Girls' & children's outerwear; jeans: girls', children's & infants'

(G-4634)
JM ORIGINALS INC
Also Called: Sbi Enterprises
70 Berme Rd (12428-5605)
P.O. Box 563 (12428-0563)
PHONE...................845 647-3003
Fax: 845 647-1059
Martha Arginsky, *President*
Myrna Jargowsky, *Vice Pres*
Robert Rue, *Purchasing*
Miriam Lyons, *Manager*
Jenifer Weed, *MIS Dir*
▲ EMP: 140 EST: 1976
SQ FT: 35,000
SALES (est): 11.2MM **Privately Held**
WEB: www.jmoriginals.com
SIC: 2361 5137 5641 2369 Girls' & children's dresses, blouses & shirts; women's & children's clothing; children's wear; girls' & children's outerwear

(G-4635)
MASTER JUVENILE PRODUCTS INC
Also Called: Sbi Enterprises
70 Berme Rd (12428-5605)
P.O. Box 563 (12428-0563)
PHONE...................845 647-8400
Irwin Arginsky, *President*

EMP: 10
SQ FT: 40,000
SALES (est): 690K **Privately Held**
WEB: www.pogosticks.com
SIC: 3944 Games, toys & children's vehicles

(G-4636)
OPTIMUM WINDOW MFG CORP
28 Canal St (12428-1226)
PHONE...................845 647-1900
Fax: 845 647-1494
Candido Perez, *Ch of Bd*
Maria E Perez, *Corp Secy*
▲ EMP: 37
SALES (est): 10MM **Privately Held**
WEB: www.optimumwindow.com
SIC: 3442 Screen & storm doors & windows

(G-4637)
REED SYSTEMS LTD
17 Edwards Pl (12428-1601)
P.O. Box 209 (12428-0209)
PHONE...................845 647-3660
Fax: 845 647-5651
James Reed, *President*
Joan E Reed, *Vice Pres*
EMP: 15
SQ FT: 1,600
SALES (est): 4.1MM **Privately Held**
WEB: www.reedsystemsltd.com
SIC: 3399 Powder, metal

(G-4638)
ROCK MOUNTAIN FARMS INC
11 Spring St (12428-1329)
PHONE...................845 647-9084
Karen Osterhoudt, *President*
Howard Osterhoudt, *Vice Pres*
EMP: 5
SALES (est): 540K **Privately Held**
SIC: 1442 6519 Gravel mining; landholding office

(G-4639)
TOP SHELF JEWELRY INC
Also Called: Touch By A Memory
206 Canal St (12428-1600)
PHONE...................845 647-4661
Fax: 845 647-3314
Barbara Hoff, *President*
Michael Atcheson, *Manager*
EMP: 14
SQ FT: 6,000
SALES: 550K **Privately Held**
SIC: 3961 Costume jewelry, ex. precious metal & semiprecious stones

Ellicottville
Cattaraugus County

(G-4640)
AMERICAN LCKR SEC SYSTEMS INC
12 Martha St (14731-9714)
PHONE...................716 699-2773
Fax: 716 699-2775
EMP: 25
SQ FT: 4,800
SALES (corp-wide): 30.1MM **Privately Held**
SIC: 3581 Mfg Vending Machines
PA: American Locker Security Systems, Inc.
700 Freeport Pkwy Ste 300
Coppell TX 75019
817 329-1600

(G-4641)
FITZPATRICK AND WELLER INC
12 Mill St (14731-9614)
P.O. Box 490 (14731-0490)
PHONE...................716 699-2393
Gregory J Fitzpatrick, *Ch of Bd*
Dana G Fitzpatrick, *Chairman*
Daniel Fitzpatrick, *Vice Pres*
Greg Fitzpatrick, *Vice Pres*
Ryan Andrew, *Asst Controller*
▼ EMP: 85 EST: 1892
SQ FT: 220,000

SALES (est): 16.2MM **Privately Held**
WEB: www.fitzweller.com
SIC: 2426 Hardwood dimension & flooring mills; furniture dimension stock, hardwood

(G-4642)
MERITOOL LLC
5 Park Ave Ste 1 (14731-9705)
P.O. Box 148, Salamanca (14779-0148)
PHONE...................716 699-6005
Fax: 716 699-6337
Timm Herman,
John Bares,
Donna Finegan,
▲ EMP: 15 EST: 1939
SQ FT: 20,000
SALES (est): 2.6MM **Privately Held**
WEB: www.meritool.com
SIC: 3546 Power-driven handtools

(G-4643)
NORTH PK INNOVATIONS GROUP INC (PA)
6442 Route 242 E (14731-9742)
P.O. Box 900 (14731-0900)
PHONE...................716 699-2031
Fax: 440 498-6171
William Northrup, *CEO*
Lorie Northrup, *President*
Hugh Graham, *Buyer*
Geoff Kroeger, *Controller*
Greg Lain, *Sales Mgr*
▲ EMP: 5
SQ FT: 13,000
SALES: 20MM **Privately Held**
SIC: 3423 Hand & edge tools

Ellington
Chautauqua County

(G-4644)
ELLIOT INDUSTRIES INC
Leach Rd (14732)
PHONE...................716 287-3100
Fax: 716 287-2005
Thomas A Elliot, *President*
Ann Elliot, *Treasurer*
EMP: 8 EST: 1977
SQ FT: 5,000
SALES: 500K **Privately Held**
SIC: 3296 Fiberglass insulation

Elma
Erie County

(G-4645)
CLUB PROTECTOR INC
191 Buffalo Creek Rd (14059-9021)
PHONE...................716 652-4787
William T Held, *President*
Carol Held, *Vice Pres*
▲ EMP: 2
SQ FT: 3,500
SALES: 1MM **Privately Held**
WEB: www.clubprotectorinc.com
SIC: 3799 Golf carts, powered

(G-4646)
COMGRAPH SALES SERVICE
7491 Clinton St (14059-8807)
PHONE...................716 601-7243
Brian Schiemant, *Owner*
EMP: 5
SALES (est): 407.7K **Privately Held**
SIC: 2759 Commercial printing

(G-4647)
CONLEY CASEWORKS INC
580 Conley Rd (14059-9515)
P.O. Box 449 (14059-0449)
PHONE...................716 655-5830
Fred Boeheim, *CEO*
Matt Wendelboe, *Purchasing*
EMP: 5
SALES (est): 561.9K **Privately Held**
WEB: www.conleycaseworks.com
SIC: 2431 Millwork

Elma - Erie County (G-4648)

(G-4648)
FREDERICK COON INC
Also Called: Elma Press
5751 Clinton St (14059-9424)
PHONE................................716 683-6812
Fax: 716 683-5037
Frederick H Coon Jr, *President*
Douglas Coon, *Vice Pres*
Joel Coon, *Vice Pres*
Betty Coon, *Treasurer*
EMP: 23
SQ FT: 2,708
SALES: 900K **Privately Held**
SIC: **2752** 2759 Commercial printing, offset; letterpress printing

(G-4649)
GENERAL WELDING & FABG INC (PA)
991 Maple Rd (14059-9530)
PHONE................................716 652-0033
Fax: 585 652-0746
Mark S Andol, *President*
Steve Mayer, *General Mgr*
Edwin Pierrot, *Manager*
EMP: 3
SQ FT: 14,000
SALES (est): 5.3MM **Privately Held**
SIC: **7692** 3715 5531 Welding repair; truck trailers; truck equipment & parts

(G-4650)
KENS SERVICE & SALES INC
11500 Clinton St (14059-8830)
PHONE................................716 683-1155
Kenneth Kelchlin Jr, *President*
Matt Kelchlin, *Vice Pres*
EMP: 14 EST: 1955
SQ FT: 25,000
SALES (est): 2.6MM **Privately Held**
SIC: **3799** All terrain vehicles (ATV)

(G-4651)
MOOG INC (PA)
400 Jamison Rd Plant26 (14059-9497)
P.O. Box 18, East Aurora (14052-0018)
PHONE................................716 652-2000
Fax: 585 687-4457
John R Scannell, *Ch of Bd*
Richard A Aubrecht, *Vice Ch Bd*
Dave Fijas, *General Mgr*
Joseph Bell, *Vice Pres*
Gary A Szakmary, *Vice Pres*
◆ EMP: 2100 EST: 1951
SQ FT: 22,000
SALES: 2.5B **Publicly Held**
WEB: www.moog.com
SIC: **3812** 3492 3625 3769 Aircraft control systems, electronic; fluid power valves for aircraft; relays & industrial controls; actuators, industrial; guided missile & space vehicle parts & auxiliary equipment; aircraft parts & equipment; surgical & medical instruments

(G-4652)
MOOG INC
160 Jamison Rd (14059-9526)
PHONE................................716 687-4778
Dave Golda, *Manager*
EMP: 25
SALES (corp-wide): 2.5B **Publicly Held**
SIC: **3812** Aircraft control systems, electronic
PA: Moog Inc.
  400 Jamison Rd Plant26
  Elma NY 14059
  716 652-2000

(G-4653)
R W PUBLICATIONS DIV OF WTRHS (PA)
Also Called: Akron-Corfu Pennysaver
6091 Seneca St Bldg C (14059-9807)
PHONE................................716 714-5620
Fax: 716 662-0740
Robert Rozeski Sr, *President*
Thomas Rybczynski, *Vice Pres*
Cheryl Kowalski, *Treasurer*
EMP: 30 EST: 1961
SQ FT: 5,800
SALES (est): 12.9MM **Privately Held**
WEB: www.rwpennysaver.com
SIC: **2711** 2741 Newspapers, publishing & printing; miscellaneous publishing

(G-4654)
R W PUBLICATIONS DIV OF WTRHS
Also Called: Pennysavers Rw Publications
6091 Seneca St Bldg C (14059-9807)
PHONE................................716 714-5620
Fax: 716 675-3044
Meg Bourdette, *General Mgr*
Tom Rybczynski, *Sales Mgr*
EMP: 20
SALES (corp-wide): 12.9MM **Privately Held**
WEB: www.rwpennysaver.com
SIC: **2711** Newspapers, publishing & printing
PA: R W Publications Div Of Waterhouse Publication Inc
  6091 Seneca St Bldg C
  Elma NY 14059
  716 714-5620

(G-4655)
SERVOTRONICS INC (PA)
1110 Maple Rd (14059-9573)
PHONE................................716 655-5990
Fax: 585 655-6012
Nicholas D Trbovich Jr, *Ch of Bd*
Kenneth D Trbovich, *President*
Salvatore San Filippo, *Senior VP*
James C Takacs, *Vice Pres*
Dave Robert, *Facilities Mgr*
EMP: 156 EST: 1959
SQ FT: 83,000
SALES: 36.7MM **Publicly Held**
WEB: www.servotronics.com
SIC: **3492** 3728 3769 3421 Fluid power valves & hose fittings; electrohydraulic servo valves, metal; control valves, aircraft: hydraulic & pneumatic; aircraft parts & equipment; guided missile & space vehicle parts & auxiliary equipment; cutlery

(G-4656)
STEUBEN FOODS INCORPORATED
1150 Maple Rd (14059-9597)
PHONE................................716 655-4000
Tom Taggart, *VP Engrg*
Al Tokar, *QC Mgr*
Norman Bower, *Branch Mgr*
EMP: 200
SALES (corp-wide): 114.1MM **Privately Held**
SIC: **2026** Milk processing (pasteurizing, homogenizing, bottling)
PA: Steuben Foods, Incorporated
  15504 Liberty Ave
  Jamaica NY 11433
  718 291-3333

(G-4657)
STONY MANUFACTURING INC
591 Pound Rd (14059-9602)
PHONE................................716 652-6730
Fax: 585 652-9601
James A Wyzykiewicz, *President*
Michael C Wyzykiewicz, *Vice Pres*
Ronald P Wyzykiewicz, *Vice Pres*
EMP: 9
SQ FT: 12,500
SALES (est): 1MM **Privately Held**
SIC: **3599** Machine shop, jobbing & repair

Elmhurst
Queens County

(G-4658)
BUFFALO PROVISIONS CO INC
4009 76th St (11373-1033)
PHONE................................718 292-4300
Rene Armendariz, *President*
Staci Armendariz, *Vice Pres*
Andres Mendez, *Manager*
EMP: 15
SQ FT: 10,000
SALES (est): 1.6MM **Privately Held**
SIC: **2013** Sausages from purchased meat

(G-4659)
COACH INC
90 Queens Blvd (11373)
PHONE................................718 760-0624
EMP: 14
SALES (corp-wide): 4.1B **Publicly Held**
SIC: **3171** Mfg Women's Handbags/Purses
PA: Coach, Inc.
  516 W 34th St Bsmt 5
  New York NY 10001
  212 594-1850

(G-4660)
FEDERAL SAMPLE CARD CORP
4520 83rd St (11373-3599)
PHONE................................718 458-1344
Michael Cronin, *President*
EMP: 100
SQ FT: 40,000
SALES (est): 7.4MM **Privately Held**
SIC: **2782** 3999 Sample books; advertising display products

(G-4661)
GODIVA CHOCOLATIER INC
9015 Queens Blvd Ste 2045 (11373-4923)
PHONE................................718 271-3603
Nicole Keaton, *Manager*
EMP: 24 **Privately Held**
SIC: **2066** Chocolate candy, solid
HQ: Godiva Chocolatier, Inc.
  333 W 34th St Fl 6
  New York NY 10001
  212 984-5900

(G-4662)
GOLDEN BRIDGE GROUP INC
7416 Grand Ave (11373-4127)
PHONE................................718 335-8882
Roger Yang, *President*
▲ EMP: 6
SALES (est): 107.8K **Privately Held**
SIC: **3161** Luggage

(G-4663)
LA CALENITA BAKERY & CAFETERIA
4008 83rd St (11373-1307)
PHONE................................718 205-8273
Dilia Lindo, *Owner*
EMP: 8
SALES (est): 377.1K **Privately Held**
SIC: **2051** Bread, cake & related products

(G-4664)
MAJESTIC CURTAINS LLC
4410 Ketcham St Apt 2g (11373-3686)
PHONE................................718 898-0774
Fax: 718 505-4011
Robert Connor,
Barbara Tisdale,
EMP: 7
SALES: 660K **Privately Held**
SIC: **2391** 1799 Curtains & draperies; window treatment installation

(G-4665)
PENNER ELBOW COMPANY INC
4700 76th St (11373-2946)
PHONE................................718 526-9000
Fax: 718 235-6112
Sheldon Flatow, *President*
EMP: 12
SQ FT: 10,000
SALES (est): 1.4MM **Privately Held**
SIC: **3444** 3321 Elbows, for air ducts, stovepipes, etc.: sheet metal; pressure pipe & fittings, cast iron

(G-4666)
ROCKPORT COMPANY LLC
9015 Queens Blvd Ste 1025 (11373-4923)
PHONE................................718 271-3627
Miguel Mendez, *District Mgr*
EMP: 8
SALES (corp-wide): 51.8MM **Privately Held**
SIC: **3143** Men's footwear, except athletic
HQ: The Rockport Company Llc
  1895 J W Foster Blvd
  Canton MA 02021
  781 401-5000

(G-4667)
ROKON TECH LLC
5223 74th St (11373-4108)
PHONE................................718 429-0729
Manfred Konrad, *Mng Member*
EMP: 5
SALES (est): 657.2K **Privately Held**
SIC: **3534** Elevators & moving stairways

Elmira
Chemung County

(G-4668)
AFI CYBERNETICS CORPORATION
713 Batavia St (14904-2011)
PHONE................................607 732-3244
Fax: 607 732-1542
Kenneth Doyle, *President*
Todd Allen, *COO*
Mike Walls, *Supervisor*
Jerry Windows, *Info Tech Mgr*
EMP: 28
SQ FT: 25,000
SALES (est): 6.8MM **Privately Held**
WEB: www.aficybernetics.com
SIC: **3625** Relays & industrial controls

(G-4669)
AIR FLOW MANUFACTURING
365 Upper Oakwood Ave (14903-1127)
PHONE................................607 733-8284
Tom Musso, *Manager*
EMP: 10
SALES (est): 2.4MM **Privately Held**
SIC: **3999** 3711 Manufacturing industries; truck & tractor truck assembly

(G-4670)
AIR-FLO MFG CO INC
365 Upper Oakwood Ave (14903-1127)
PHONE................................607 733-8284
Fax: 607 522-4412
Charles Musso Jr, *President*
Tom Musso, *Vice Pres*
Kevin Foster, *Opers Mgr*
Lisa Brady, *Purchasing*
Christina Staight, *Admin Asst*
EMP: 75 EST: 1950
SQ FT: 60,000
SALES (est): 37.9MM **Privately Held**
WEB: www.air-flo.com
SIC: **3531** Construction machinery

(G-4671)
BEECHER EMSSN SLTN TCHNLGS LLC (PA)
Also Called: Ward Diesel Filter Systems
1580 Lake St (14901-1248)
PHONE................................607 796-0149
Fax: 607 739-7092
Scott Beecher, *President*
Henry E Kaeser, *Principal*
Theresa Kaeser, *Principal*
John Meier, *Principal*
Tim Rolls, *Warehouse Mgr*
EMP: 17
SQ FT: 12,000
SALES (est): 2.2MM **Privately Held**
WEB: www.warddiesel.com
SIC: **3564** Air purification equipment

(G-4672)
CAMERON BRIDGE WORKS LLC
1051 S Main St (14904-2713)
PHONE................................607 734-9456
Christopher Goll, *President*
EMP: 20
SQ FT: 85,000
SALES (est): 3.7MM **Privately Held**
SIC: **3441** Fabricated structural metal for bridges

(G-4673)
CARBAUGH TOOL COMPANY INC
126 Philo Rd W (14903-9755)
PHONE................................607 739-3293
Fax: 607 739-3274
Harold Dota, *President*
Terry Catlin, *Manager*
EMP: 30 EST: 1966
SQ FT: 10,600
SALES (est): 4.6MM **Privately Held**
SIC: **3599** 3544 Machine & other job shop work; special dies & tools

GEOGRAPHIC SECTION

Elmira - Chemung County (G-4697)

(G-4674)
CARBIDE-USA LLC
100 Home St (14901-1859)
P.O. Box 4005 (14904-0005)
PHONE.....................................607 331-9353
EMP: 8
SALES (est): 1.1MM **Privately Held**
SIC: 2819 Carbides

(G-4675)
CHEMUNG CTY ASSC RETRD CTZNS (HQ)
Also Called: Southern Tier Industries
711 Sullivan St (14901-2322)
PHONE.....................................607 734-6151
Fax: 607 734-2943
Peter Honsberger, *Division Mgr*
Jim Scott, *Sr Corp Ofcr*
Sandra Helman, *Accounting Mgr*
Joanne Conely, *Human Res Dir*
Joanne Conely, *Human Res Dir*
EMP: 150
SQ FT: 33,000
SALES: 17.3MM
SALES (corp-wide): 1.3B **Privately Held**
WEB: www.chemungarc.org
SIC: 3861 2448 8331 3577 Photographic equipment & supplies; home for the mentally retarded; wood pallets & skids; computer peripheral equipment; job training & vocational rehabilitation services
PA: Nysarc, Inc.
29 British American Blvd
Latham NY 12110
518 439-8311

(G-4676)
COMMUNITY GLASS INC
139 W 17th St (14903-1215)
PHONE.....................................607 737-8860
Fax: 607 737-8890
Patrick M Crouse, *President*
EMP: 6
SALES (est): 574.8K **Privately Held**
SIC: 3231 Scientific & technical glassware: from purchased glass

(G-4677)
COURSER INC
802 County Road 64 # 100 (14903-7984)
PHONE.....................................607 739-3861
Daniel Herman, *Ch of Bd*
Christophe Seeley, *Engineer*
Steve Seeley, *Finance*
Bob Cleveland, *Manager*
Tina McGrane, *Manager*
EMP: 25
SQ FT: 50,000
SALES (est): 5.5MM **Privately Held**
WEB: www.courser.com
SIC: 3599 Machine & other job shop work

(G-4678)
CREATIVE ORTHOTICS PROSTHETICS (PA)
1300 College Ave Ste 1 (14901-1154)
PHONE.....................................607 734-7215
Fax: 607 733-5281
John Renz, *President*
EMP: 16
SALES (est): 51.9MM **Privately Held**
WEB: www.creativeoandp.com
SIC: 3842 5999 5047 Limbs, artificial; artificial limbs; hospital equipment & furniture

(G-4679)
EASTERN METAL OF ELMIRA INC (PA)
1430 Sullivan St (14901-1698)
PHONE.....................................607 734-2295
Kevin Harrison, *Ch of Bd*
Sue Jones, *Managing Dir*
John Pendleton, *Vice Pres*
Kevin Burdick, *Purch Mgr*
Tom Aber, *VP Sales*
▼ EMP: 80 EST: 1947
SALES (est): 20MM **Privately Held**
WEB: www.usa-sign.com
SIC: 3993 7336 Signs & advertising specialties; graphic arts & related design

(G-4680)
EASTSIDE OXIDE CO
211 Judson St (14901-3308)
PHONE.....................................607 734-1253
Greg Wheeler, *Principal*
John Short, *Principal*
EMP: 40
SALES (est): 1.8MM **Privately Held**
WEB: www.eastsiderailnow.org
SIC: 3471 Finishing, metals or formed products

(G-4681)
ELMIRA COUNTRY CLUB INC
1538 W Church St (14905-1993)
PHONE.....................................607 734-6251
Fax: 607 734-6253
Tom Newkirk, *Superintendent*
Joe Steigerwald, *Manager*
EMP: 4
SALES (est): 2.7MM **Privately Held**
WEB: www.elmiracountryclub.com
SIC: 3949 Shafts, golf club

(G-4682)
ELMIRA HEAT TREATING INC
407 S Kinyon St (14904-2398)
PHONE.....................................607 734-1577
Fax: 607 732-2572
Terry Youngs, *CEO*
Richard Youngs, *President*
Mark Youngs, *Sales Mgr*
Ann Borden, *Manager*
EMP: 40 EST: 1962
SQ FT: 20,000
SALES (est): 9.9MM **Privately Held**
WEB: www.elmiraht.com
SIC: 3398 Tempering of metal

(G-4683)
ELMIRA METAL WORKS INC
1493 Cedar St (14904-2932)
P.O. Box 4110 (14904-0110)
PHONE.....................................607 734-9813
Jim Biggs, *President*
EMP: 6
SALES (est): 441.1K **Privately Held**
WEB: www.snowhog.com
SIC: 3441 Fabricated structural metal

(G-4684)
F M HOWELL & COMPANY (PA)
Also Called: Howell Packaging
79 Pennsylvania Ave (14904-1455)
P.O. Box 286 (14902-0286)
PHONE.....................................607 734-6291
Fax: 607 734-6759
Katherine H Roehlke, *President*
James Haley, *Division Mgr*
Pam Bryaton, *General Mgr*
Susan Kennedy, *Senior VP*
Keith Baumann, *Vice Pres*
▲ EMP: 74 EST: 1883
SQ FT: 168,000
SALES: 36.1MM **Privately Held**
WEB: www.howellpkg.com
SIC: 2657 2671 7389 2652 Folding paperboard boxes; thermoplastic coated paper for packaging; packaging & labeling services; setup paperboard boxes

(G-4685)
FENNELL INDUSTRIES LLC (PA)
Also Called: United Dividers
108 Stephens Pl (14901-1539)
PHONE.....................................607 733-6693
Fax: 607 733-0340
Tom Fennell, *Owner*
Patrick Sullivan, *Engineer*
Martin Fennell, *Mng Member*
Thomas Fennell,
EMP: 30
SQ FT: 13,500
SALES (est): 3.8MM **Privately Held**
SIC: 2653 Corrugated & solid fiber boxes; partitions, corrugated: made from purchased materials

(G-4686)
GEORGE CHILSON LOGGING
54 Franklin St (14904-1738)
PHONE.....................................607 732-1558
George Chilson, *Owner*
EMP: 1
SALES: 1.6MM **Privately Held**
SIC: 2411 Logging

(G-4687)
HANGER PRSTHETCS & ORTHO INC
1300 College Ave Ste 1 (14901-1154)
PHONE.....................................607 795-1220
Sheryl Price, *Manager*
Vickie Preston, *Manager*
EMP: 99
SALES (corp-wide): 500.5MM **Privately Held**
SIC: 3842 Braces, orthopedic
HQ: Hanger Prosthetics & Orthotics, Inc.
10910 Main Dr
Austin TX 78758
512 777-3800

(G-4688)
HARDINGE INC (PA)
1 Hardinge Dr (14902)
PHONE.....................................607 734-2281
Fax: 607 734-8819
John J Perrotti, *Ch of Bd*
Richard L Simons, *President*
Tom Mitchell, *General Mgr*
James P Langa, *Senior VP*
Douglas C Tifft, *Senior VP*
◆ EMP: 249 EST: 1890
SALES: 315.2MM **Publicly Held**
WEB: www.hardinge.com
SIC: 3541 3545 3553 3549 Machine tools, metal cutting type; lathes; grinding, polishing, buffing, lapping & honing machines; collets (machine tool accessories); lathes, wood turning: including accessories; metalworking machinery

(G-4689)
HAUN WELDING SUPPLY INC
1100 Sullivan St (14901-1640)
PHONE.....................................607 846-2289
Fax: 607 846-2292
Mike Cesaro, *Manager*
EMP: 10
SALES (corp-wide): 78.3MM **Privately Held**
SIC: 7692 5999 5169 Welding repair; welding supplies; industrial gases
PA: Haun Welding Supply, Inc.
5921 Court Street Rd
Syracuse NY 13206
315 463-5241

(G-4690)
HILLIARD CORPORATION (PA)
100 W 4th St (14901-2190)
P.O. Box 866 (14902-0866)
PHONE.....................................607 733-7121
Fax: 607 733-3009
Arie J Van Den Blink, *Ch of Bd*
Gene A Ebbrecht, *President*
Steven J Chesebro, *Exec VP*
Douglas Canfield, *Vice Pres*
Lindsey Canfield, *Vice Pres*
▲ EMP: 277 EST: 1905
SQ FT: 326,000
SALES: 106.5MM **Privately Held**
SIC: 3564 3569 3823 Purification & dust collection equipment; filters; industrial instrmnts msrmnt display/control process variable

(G-4691)
HILLIARD CORPORATION
1420 College Ave (14901-1153)
PHONE.....................................607 733-7121
Arie J Van Den Blink, *Branch Mgr*
James Graham, *Manager*
Liz Stage, *Admin Sec*
Michael Girardi, *Administration*
Mark Rose, *Administration*
EMP: 10
SALES (corp-wide): 106.5MM **Privately Held**
SIC: 3564 3569 3823 Purification & dust collection equipment; filters; industrial instrmnts msrmnt display/control process variable
PA: The Hilliard Corporation
100 W 4th St
Elmira NY 14901
607 733-7121

(G-4692)
I D MACHINE INC
Also Called: I Do Machining
1580 Lake St (14901-1248)
PHONE.....................................607 796-2549
Fax: 607 796-9024
John Meier, *Ch of Bd*
EMP: 7
SALES (est): 1.1MM **Privately Held**
WEB: www.idomachining.com
SIC: 3599 Machine shop, jobbing & repair

(G-4693)
KITCHEN SPECIALTY CRAFTSMEN
2366 Corning Rd (14903-1045)
PHONE.....................................607 739-0833
Fax: 607 739-5902
Douglas Wells, *President*
Kenneth Wells, *Vice Pres*
Phillis Wells, *Treasurer*
EMP: 9 EST: 1968
SALES (est): 1.1MM **Privately Held**
SIC: 2541 Table or counter tops, plastic laminated

(G-4694)
MCWANE INC
Also Called: Kennedy Valve Division
1021 E Water St (14901-3332)
P.O. Box 931 (14902-0931)
PHONE.....................................607 734-2211
Fax: 607 734-1003
Arne Feyling, *General Mgr*
Doug Bond, *Plant Mgr*
Matt Hicks, *Safety Mgr*
Thomas Shaw, *Safety Mgr*
Tim Decker, *Purch Mgr*
EMP: 376
SALES (corp-wide): 1.2B **Privately Held**
WEB: www.mcwane.com
SIC: 3491 3561 3321 5085 Industrial valves; pumps & pumping equipment; gray & ductile iron foundries; valves & fittings
PA: Mcwane, Inc.
2900 Highway 280 S # 300
Birmingham AL 35223
205 414-3100

(G-4695)
MEGA TOOL & MFG CORP
1023 Caton Ave (14904-2620)
PHONE.....................................607 734-8398
Fax: 607 734-8549
Craig Spencer, *President*
Nancy Ellison, *Controller*
Larry Lovell, *Executive*
Mary Lou Spencer, *Admin Sec*
EMP: 25
SQ FT: 18,000
SALES (est): 4MM **Privately Held**
WEB: www.megatool-mfg.com
SIC: 3599 3469 7692 3544 Machine shop, jobbing & repair; machine parts, stamped or pressed metal; welding repair; special dies, tools, jigs & fixtures

(G-4696)
NARDE PAVING COMPANY INC
400 E 14th St (14903-1817)
PHONE.....................................607 737-7177
Fax: 607 733-7887
Ann Narde, *CEO*
Donald A Narde Sr, *President*
Daniel Narde, *Vice Pres*
Donal Narde Jr, *Admin Sec*
EMP: 30
SQ FT: 7,000
SALES (est): 4.4MM **Privately Held**
SIC: 2951 Asphalt paving mixtures & blocks

(G-4697)
PC SOLUTIONS & CONSULTING
407 S Walnut St (14904-1637)
PHONE.....................................607 735-0466
Roy Brotherhood, *President*
Katherine Brotherhood, *Vice Pres*
EMP: 5
SQ FT: 1,800
SALES: 720K **Privately Held**
WEB: www.powerpcs.com
SIC: 3575 7371 Computer terminals, monitors & components; custom computer programming services

Elmira - Chemung County (G-4698)

(G-4698)
QUICKER PRINTER INC
210 W Gray St (14901-2907)
P.O. Box 1257 (14902-1257)
PHONE..................................607 734-8622
Fax: 607 737-0648
Robert Lavarnway Jr, *President*
Lorrie Lavarnway, *Office Mgr*
EMP: 7
SQ FT: 5,500
SALES (est): 950.1K Privately Held
WEB: www.quickerprinter.com
SIC: 2752 2791 Commercial printing, offset; typesetting

(G-4699)
RAINBOW LETTERING
1329 College Ave (14901-1133)
PHONE..................................607 732-5751
Tom Wolfe, *Owner*
EMP: 5
SALES: 150K Privately Held
SIC: 2396 2759 Screen printing on fabric articles; screen printing

(G-4700)
SEPAC INC
1580 Lake St (14901-1248)
PHONE..................................607 732-2030
Fax: 607 732-0273
John H Meier, *President*
Matthew Laser, *General Mgr*
Nancy Boise, *Purchasing*
Jeffrey Ryan, *Engineer*
Mike Vieira, *Engineer*
▲ EMP: 35
SQ FT: 17,352
SALES (est): 8.5MM Privately Held
SIC: 3568 Power transmission equipment

(G-4701)
SOUTHERN TIER PATTERNS
608 Chester St (14904-1640)
P.O. Box 313 (14902-0313)
PHONE..................................607 734-1265
Fax: 607 734-8872
David Pealer, *Owner*
Pauline Pealer, *Co-Owner*
EMP: 6
SQ FT: 26,000
SALES: 600K Privately Held
SIC: 3543 Foundry patternmaking

(G-4702)
STAR-GAZETTE FUND INC
Also Called: Elmira Star-Gazette
310 E Church St (14901-2704)
PHONE..................................607 734-5151
Fax: 607 733-4408
Monte I Trammer, *President*
Rose Cooper, *Editor*
Linda Rockwell, *Manager*
Lois Wilson, *Manager*
Jay Keller, *Info Tech Mgr*
EMP: 150
SALES: 20MM
SALES (corp-wide): 5.7B Publicly Held
SIC: 2711 Newspapers
HQ: Gannett Satellite Information Network, Llc
7950 Jones Branch Dr
Mc Lean VA 22102
703 854-6000

(G-4703)
SURFACE FINISH TECHNOLOGY
215 Judson St (14901-3308)
PHONE..................................607 732-2909
Fax: 607 733-6119
John Short, *President*
Linda Short, *Corp Secy*
Jack Slocum, *Engineer*
Carrie Roadarmel, *CFO*
Dan Goodwin, *Manager*
EMP: 35
SQ FT: 18,000
SALES (est): 4.3MM Privately Held
WEB: www.surfacefinishtech.com
SIC: 3471 Finishing, metals or formed products

(G-4704)
TDS FITNESS EQUIPMENT
160 Home St (14904-1811)
P.O. Box 4189 (14904-0189)
PHONE..................................607 733-6789
Thugginni D Seethapathy, *President*
▲ EMP: 45
SQ FT: 100,000
SALES (est): 4.6MM Privately Held
WEB: www.tdsfitnessequipment.com
SIC: 3949 3842 Dumbbells & other weightlifting equipment; exercise equipment; surgical appliances & supplies

(G-4705)
WINCHESTER OPTICAL COMPANY (DH)
1935 Lake St (14901-1239)
P.O. Box 1515 (14902-1515)
PHONE..................................607 734-4251
Fax: 607 732-0901
Ben E Lynch, *President*
Karla Lynch, *General Mgr*
Michael P Lynch, *Vice Pres*
Deborah Lynch, *Treasurer*
Art Waite, *Loan Officer*
EMP: 50 EST: 1902
SQ FT: 32,500
SALES (est): 12.3MM
SALES (corp-wide): 88.1MM Privately Held
WEB: www.winoptical.com
SIC: 3851 5048 Frames, lenses & parts, eyeglass & spectacle; ophthalmic goods
HQ: Essilor Of America, Inc.
13555 N Stemmons Fwy
Dallas TX 75234
214 496-4000

(G-4706)
WRIGHTCUT EDM & MACHINE INC
951 Carl St (14904-2662)
PHONE..................................607 733-5018
Fax: 607 735-0126
Byron Wright, *President*
Michelle Wright, *Vice Pres*
EMP: 9
SQ FT: 3,500
SALES (est): 1.3MM Privately Held
WEB: www.wrightcutedm.com
SIC: 3599 Machine shop, jobbing & repair

(G-4707)
X-GEN PHARMACEUTICALS INC
744 Baldwin St (14901-2226)
P.O. Box 150, Northport (11768-0150)
PHONE..................................631 261-8188
Susan Badia, *Branch Mgr*
EMP: 30
SALES (corp-wide): 4.6MM Privately Held
SIC: 2834 Pharmaceutical preparations
PA: X-Gen Pharmaceuticals, Inc
300 Daniel Zenker Dr
Big Flats NY 14814
607 562-2700

Elmira Heights
Chemung County

(G-4708)
ANCHOR GLASS CONTAINER CORP
151 E Mccanns Blvd (14903-1955)
PHONE..................................607 737-1933
Bill Butler, *Purchasing*
Michael Sopp, *Manager*
Jim Housworth, *Manager*
EMP: 370
SALES (corp-wide): 2.1B Privately Held
WEB: www.anchorglass.com
SIC: 3221 Glass containers
HQ: Anchor Glass Container Corporation
401 E Jackson St Ste 1100
Tampa FL 33602

(G-4709)
CAF USA INC
300 E 18th St (14903-1333)
PHONE..................................607 737-3004
Teresa Machado, *General Mgr*
Hoyos V Manuel, *General Mgr*
Rebeca Mellado, *General Mgr*
Juneldy Salazar, *General Mgr*
Octavio Rosselli, *Vice Pres*
EMP: 100
SALES (corp-wide): 840.3MM Privately Held
SIC: 3743 Railroad equipment
HQ: Caf Usa, Inc.
1401 K St Nw Ste 1003
Washington DC 20005
202 898-4848

(G-4710)
GOLOS PRINTING INC
110 E 9th St (14903-1733)
PHONE..................................607 732-1896
Fax: 607 732-2356
Thomas L Golos Sr, *President*
Thomas L Corp Sr, *President*
Hank Corp, *Vice Pres*
EMP: 6 EST: 1921
SQ FT: 10,000
SALES: 300K Privately Held
SIC: 2752 2759 Commercial printing, offset; letterpress printing

(G-4711)
MOTOR COMPONENTS LLC
2243 Corning Rd (14903-1031)
PHONE..................................607 737-8011
Reeve Howland, *Facilities Mgr*
Dave Demarco, *Controller*
Anita Mawhir, *HR Admin*
Kris Miller, *Manager*
Chris Miller, *Info Tech Mgr*
▲ EMP: 68
SQ FT: 300,000
SALES (est): 22.2MM
SALES (corp-wide): 43.6MM Privately Held
WEB: www.motorcomponents.com
SIC: 3714 Motor vehicle wheels & parts
PA: Bam Enterprises, Inc.
2243 Corning Rd
Grand Island NY 14072
716 773-7634

(G-4712)
SERVICE MACHINE & TOOL COMPANY
206 E Mccanns Blvd (14903-1958)
P.O. Box 2118 (14903-0118)
PHONE..................................607 732-0413
Fax: 607 734-9872
Keith Knowlden, *President*
Axieann Knowlden, *Corp Secy*
Marilyn Smith, *Manager*
Hal Fitzsimmons, *Tech/Comp Coord*
▲ EMP: 25
SALES (est): 5MM Privately Held
WEB: www.servicemachinetool.com
SIC: 3599 Machine shop, jobbing & repair

(G-4713)
STAMPED FITTINGS INC
217 Lenox Ave (14903-1118)
PHONE..................................607 733-9988
Shana Graham, *President*
Mike Graham, *Vice Pres*
▲ EMP: 25 EST: 1997
SQ FT: 25,000
SALES (est): 4.8MM Privately Held
WEB: www.stampedfittings.com
SIC: 3469 Metal stampings

(G-4714)
SWIFT GLASS CO INC
131 22nd St (14903-1329)
P.O. Box 879, Elmira (14902-0879)
PHONE..................................607 733-7166
Fax: 607 732-5829
Daniel J Burke, *President*
Gary Palmowski, *Plant Mgr*
Kevin Wheeler, *Opers Mgr*
Carlotta Munson, *Opers Staff*
Mary Owens, *Purch Agent*
▲ EMP: 85 EST: 1882
SQ FT: 80,000
SALES (est): 19.6MM Privately Held
WEB: www.swiftglass.com
SIC: 3231 Products of purchased glass; scientific & technical glassware: from purchased glass; tempered glass: made from purchased glass; industrial glassware: made from purchased glass

Elmont
Nassau County

(G-4715)
ANDREW SAPIENZA BAKERY INC
553 Meacham Ave (11003-3807)
PHONE..................................516 437-1715
Fax: 516 775-5719
Paul Tolomeo, *President*
Ronald Luisi, *Vice Pres*
Jack Tolomeo, *Treasurer*
EMP: 40
SQ FT: 6,000
SALES (est): 4.8MM Privately Held
SIC: 2051 Bread, cake & related products

(G-4716)
ARCHITECTURAL SIGN GROUP INC
145 Meacham Ave (11003-2633)
PHONE..................................516 326-1800
Abbas Jaffer, *President*
Rehana Jaffer, *Vice Pres*
EMP: 5
SQ FT: 4,000
SALES (est): 440K Privately Held
WEB: www.archsigngroup.com
SIC: 3993 Signs & advertising specialties

(G-4717)
AWT SUPPLY CORP
Also Called: American Printing Eqp & Sup
153 Meacham Ave (11003-2633)
PHONE..................................516 437-9105
Fax: 516 437-9107
Greg Mandel, *President*
Josh Solomon, *Vice Pres*
Max Mandel, *Admin Sec*
▲ EMP: 8
SQ FT: 45,000
SALES (est): 790K Privately Held
WEB: www.americanprintingequipment.com
SIC: 3555 5051 3546 Printing trades machinery; wire; power-driven handtools

(G-4718)
DOCTOR BRONZE SOLAR POTIONS
104 Hillsboro Ave (11003-1724)
PHONE..................................516 775-4974
Anthony Tesoriero Jr, *President*
Anthony Russo, *Master*
EMP: 20 EST: 1992
SQ FT: 1,500
SALES (est): 1MM Privately Held
WEB: www.drbronze.com
SIC: 2844 Suntan lotions & oils; cosmetic preparations

(G-4719)
ELMONT NORTH LITTLE LEAGUE
1532 Clay St (11003-1046)
PHONE..................................516 775-8210
Ronald Levin, *Owner*
Tom Laietta, *Vice Pres*
EMP: 7
SALES (est): 462.1K Privately Held
SIC: 2721 Trade journals: publishing only, not printed on site

(G-4720)
FLATBUSH SURGICAL SUPPLY CO
174 Meacham Ave Ste C (11003-2632)
PHONE..................................516 775-0507
Fax: 516 775-0605
Jim Brennon, *President*
EMP: 5
SALES (est): 410K Privately Held
SIC: 3841 Surgical & medical instruments

(G-4721)
GM INSULATION CORP
1345 Rosser Ave (11003-3244)
P.O. Box 2188, New Hyde Park (11040-8188)
PHONE..................................516 354-6000
Izabel Skugor, *President*
EMP: 13

GEOGRAPHIC SECTION

Elmsford - Westchester County (G-4748)

SALES (est): 2.4MM **Privately Held**
SIC: 2295 Sealing or insulating tape for pipe: coated fiberglass

(G-4722)
HOLLYWOOD CABINETS CO
182 Hendrickson Ave (11003-1255)
PHONE 516 354-0857
Mike Howie, *Owner*
EMP: 6
SALES: 500K **Privately Held**
SIC: 2434 Wood kitchen cabinets

(G-4723)
MARTIN ORNA IR WORKS II INC
266 Elmont Rd (11003-1600)
PHONE 516 354-3923
Martin Boventre, *President*
Charles Cascio, *Principal*
EMP: 5 **EST:** 1962
SQ FT: 5,000
SALES (est): 635.2K **Privately Held**
SIC: 3446 Architectural metalwork

(G-4724)
MERIDIAN TECHNOLOGIES INC
700 Elmont Rd (11003-4027)
PHONE 516 285-1000
Fax: 516 285-6300
Denise Shay, *CEO*
Alex Lebedev, *President*
Rachel Shifrin, *Vice Pres*
Michael Barry, *CFO*
Tim Medved, *Regl Sales Mgr*
EMP: 22
SQ FT: 10,000
SALES: 2.2MM **Privately Held**
WEB: www.meridian-tech.com
SIC: 3679 Electronic circuits

(G-4725)
OMNIUMEDIA LLC
77 Freeman Ave (11003-4107)
PHONE 516 593-2735
Joseph Regis,
EMP: 6
SALES (est): 410K **Privately Held**
SIC: 2731 Book publishing

(G-4726)
PROFESSNAL SPT PBLICATIONS INC
570 Elmont Rd (11003-3535)
PHONE 516 327-9500
Michael Shabsels, *Ch of Bd*
Patrick Kennedy, *Director*
EMP: 18
SALES (est): 1.8MM **Privately Held**
SIC: 2741 Miscellaneous publishing

(G-4727)
PROFESSNAL SPT PBLICATIONS INC
Also Called: Pspi
570 Elmont Rd Ste 202 (11003-3535)
PHONE 516 327-9500
EMP: 100
SALES (corp-wide): 31.3MM **Privately Held**
WEB: www.pspsports.com
SIC: 2721 Periodicals
PA: Professional Sports Publications Inc.
519 8th Ave
New York NY 10018
212 697-1460

(G-4728)
RPC INC
Also Called: RPC Car Service
165 Emporia Ave (11003-1837)
PHONE 347 873-3935
Michelle Franklin, *Branch Mgr*
EMP: 39
SALES (corp-wide): 1.2B **Publicly Held**
SIC: 1389 Oil field services
PA: Rpc, Inc.
2801 Buford Hwy Ne # 520
Brookhaven GA 30329
404 321-2140

(G-4729)
SAPIENZA PASTRY INC
Also Called: Sapienza Bake Shop
1376 Hempstead Tpke (11003-2539)
PHONE 516 352-5232
Fax: 516 352-2459
Paul Sapienza, *President*
EMP: 25
SQ FT: 3,600
SALES (est): 3.3MM **Privately Held**
SIC: 2051 5461 2099 2052 Bakery: wholesale or wholesale/retail combined; bakeries; food preparations; cookies & crackers

(G-4730)
TIMELY SIGNS INC
2135 Linden Blvd (11003-3901)
PHONE 516 285-5339
Fax: 516 285-9637
Eugene Goldsmith, *President*
EMP: 6
SQ FT: 2,000
SALES: 600K **Privately Held**
SIC: 3993 Displays & cutouts, window & lobby

Elmsford
Westchester County

(G-4731)
A GATTY PRODUCTS INC
Also Called: A Gatty Svce
1 Warehouse Ln (10523-1538)
P.O. Box 725 (10523-0725)
PHONE 914 592-3903
Andy Gattyan, *President*
Eva Gattyan, *Vice Pres*
EMP: 6
SQ FT: 5,000
SALES (est): 396K **Privately Held**
SIC: 3639 1799 Trash compactors, household; hydraulic equipment, installation & service

(G-4732)
AMSCAN INC (DH)
Also Called: Deco Division
80 Grasslands Rd Ste 3 (10523-1100)
PHONE 914 345-2020
Fax: 914 345-8145
Gerald C Rittenberg, *Ch of Bd*
Raoph Fink, *President*
James Harrison, *President*
Michael Correale, *CFO*
John Conlon, *Controller*
◆ **EMP:** 250 **EST:** 1947
SQ FT: 45,000
SALES (est): 579.3MM
SALES (corp-wide): 2.2B **Publicly Held**
SIC: 2656 3089 5113 2676 Cups, paper: made from purchased material; dishes, paper: made from purchased material; utensils, paper: made from purchased material; cups, plastic, except foam; dishes, plastic, except foam; cups, disposable plastic & paper; dishes, disposable plastic & paper; eating utensils, disposable plastic; sanitary paper products

(G-4733)
ANCHOR TECH PRODUCTS CORP
4 Vernon Ln Ste 2 (10523-1947)
PHONE 914 592-0240
Dan Esposito, *President*
Phyllis Loomis, *Treasurer*
Steve Ebanks, *Manager*
▲ **EMP:** 20
SQ FT: 3,000
SALES (est): 2MM **Privately Held**
SIC: 3052 Vacuum cleaner hose, rubber; vacuum cleaner hose, plastic; v-belts, rubber

(G-4734)
ARTINA GROUP INC
250 Clearbrook Rd Ste 245 (10523-1332)
P.O. Box 681, Tarrytown (10591-0681)
PHONE 914 592-1850
INA Shapiro, *President*
Rick Horn, *Vice Pres*
Adrienne Karlson, *Purch Agent*
Mark Spinozza, *Controller*
Gene Tedrow, *Natl Sales Mgr*
EMP: 34
SQ FT: 25,000
SALES (est): 6.1MM **Privately Held**
SIC: 2752 Commercial printing, lithographic; business forms, lithographed

(G-4735)
BEST PRICED PRODUCTS INC
250 Clearbrook Rd Ste 240 (10523-1332)
P.O. Box 1174, White Plains (10602-1174)
PHONE 914 345-3800
Linda Goldberg, *President*
EMP: 5
SQ FT: 30,000
SALES (est): 290K **Privately Held**
WEB: www.bpp2.com
SIC: 3999 Novelties, bric-a-brac & hobby kits

(G-4736)
BH COFFEE COMPANY LLC (PA)
Also Called: Barrie House Coffee & Tea
4 Warehouse Ln Ste 121 (10523-1541)
PHONE 914 377-2500
David Goldstein, *CEO*
Paul Goldstein, *President*
Miles Lewis, *Business Mgr*
Ronald Goldstein, *Vice Pres*
Karan Hennessy, *Vice Pres*
▲ **EMP:** 75 **EST:** 1934
SQ FT: 35,000
SALES (est): 18.8MM **Privately Held**
WEB: www.barriehouse.com
SIC: 2095 Coffee roasting (except by wholesale grocers)

(G-4737)
BLINDTEK DESIGNER SYSTEMS INC
1 Hayes St (10523-2531)
PHONE 914 347-7100
Lee Miller, *President*
Anthony Ash, *Vice Pres*
Steve Beamand, *Vice Pres*
▲ **EMP:** 18
SALES (est): 2.5MM **Privately Held**
SIC: 2591 Blinds vertical

(G-4738)
C & F IRON WORKS INC
14 N Payne St Ste 1 (10523-1839)
PHONE 914 592-2450
Fax: 914 592-2718
Fernando Pastilha, *President*
Michael Boino, *Manager*
EMP: 15
SQ FT: 1,600
SALES (est): 800K **Privately Held**
SIC: 3446 Railings, bannisters, guards, etc.: made from metal pipe

(G-4739)
C & F STEEL CORP
14 N Payne St Ste 2 (10523-1841)
PHONE 914 592-3928
Arthur Boino, *CEO*
EMP: 18 **EST:** 2000
SALES (est): 2.3MM **Privately Held**
SIC: 3446 Fences, gates, posts & flagpoles

(G-4740)
CHAMART EXCLUSIVES INC
68 Williams St (10523-2515)
PHONE 914 345-3870
Lenny Davidson, *President*
Gaines Davidson, *Vice Pres*
▲ **EMP:** 8
SALES (est): 560K **Privately Held**
SIC: 3469 Porcelain enameled products & utensils

(G-4741)
COCA-COLA BTLG CO OF NY INC
111 Fairview Pk Dr Ste 1 (10523-1536)
PHONE 914 592-4574
Fax: 914 592-3219
Kevin Stewart, *Safety Mgr*
Edward Bryan, *Branch Mgr*
EMP: 18
SALES (corp-wide): 44.2B **Publicly Held**
SIC: 2086 Bottled & canned soft drinks
HQ: The Coca-Cola Bottling Company Of New York Inc
2500 Windy Ridge Pkwy Se
Atlanta GA 30339
770 989-3000

(G-4742)
COCA-COLA BTLG CO OF NY INC
115 Fairview Pk Dr Ste 1 (10523-1535)
PHONE 914 789-1580
Margerite Lopiccollo, *Principal*
John Lacey, *Manager*
Frank Cllen, *Technical Staff*
EMP: 10
SALES (corp-wide): 44.2B **Publicly Held**
SIC: 2086 Bottled & canned soft drinks
HQ: The Coca-Cola Bottling Company Of New York Inc
2500 Windy Ridge Pkwy Se
Atlanta GA 30339
770 989-3000

(G-4743)
CORAL BLOOD SERVICE
525 Executive Blvd # 285 (10523-1240)
PHONE 800 483-4888
Fax: 914 872-6007
Rose Shaw, *Vice Pres*
EMP: 15
SALES (est): 1.7MM **Privately Held**
SIC: 2836 Plasmas

(G-4744)
CRAFTERS WORKSHOP INC
116 S Central Ave Ste 1 (10523-3503)
PHONE 914 345-2838
Fax: 914 345-0575
Jaime Echt, *President*
▼ **EMP:** 9
SQ FT: 3,000
SALES (est): 385K **Privately Held**
WEB: www.thecraftersworkshop.com
SIC: 3953 Stencils, painting & marking

(G-4745)
CRONIN ENTERPRISES INC
Also Called: Minuteman Press
120 E Main St (10523-3225)
PHONE 914 345-9600
Fax: 914 347-2563
Gary Cronin, *President*
Jacquiline Cronin, *Vice Pres*
Christina Sabbia, *Vice Pres*
Tom Hughes, *Mktg Dir*
EMP: 9
SQ FT: 4,000
SALES (est): 900K **Privately Held**
SIC: 2752 Commercial printing, lithographic

(G-4746)
CUSTOM PINS INC
150 Clearbrook Rd Ste 139 (10523-1148)
PHONE 914 690-9378
James Zendman, *President*
EMP: 6
SALES (est): 511.2K **Privately Held**
WEB: www.custompins.com
SIC: 3961 Pins (jewelry), except precious metal

(G-4747)
DR PEPPER SNAPPLE GROUP INC
55 Hunter Ln (10523-1334)
PHONE 914 846-2300
John Romano, *Warehouse Mgr*
Sam Suleiman, *Warehouse Mgr*
Ellen Morgan, *Sales Mgr*
Bill Byron, *Manager*
Marcus Pucci, *Manager*
EMP: 100
SALES (corp-wide): 6.2B **Publicly Held**
SIC: 2086 Bottled & canned soft drinks
PA: Dr Pepper Snapple Group, Inc.
5301 Legacy Dr
Plano TX 75024
972 673-7000

(G-4748)
EMKAY TRADING CORP (PA)
250 Clearbrook Rd Ste 127 (10523-1332)
P.O. Box 504 (10523-0504)
PHONE 914 592-9000
Fax: 914 592-9000
Howard Kravitz, *President*
Ruth Kravitz, *Vice Pres*
EMP: 2
SQ FT: 2,500

Elmsford - Westchester County (G-4749)

SALES (est): 1.9MM **Privately Held**
WEB: www.emkaytrading.org
SIC: 2022 Cheese, natural & processed

(G-4749)
EMPIRE GYPSUM PDTS & SUP CORP
25 Haven St (10523-1831)
P.O. Box 779 (10523-0779)
PHONE...................914 592-8141
Carl Nicolosi, *President*
EMP: 5
SALES (est): 1.1MM **Privately Held**
SIC: 3275 Gypsum products

(G-4750)
ENGAGEMENT TECHNOLOGY LLC
33 W Main St Ste 303 (10523-2413)
PHONE...................914 591-7600
Glen Holden, *General Mgr*
Andrea Lightman, *Vice Pres*
Bruce Bolger,
EMP: 10
SALES (est): 1.5MM **Privately Held**
SIC: 3679 Electronic loads & power supplies

(G-4751)
ERGOTECH GROUP INC
8 Westchester Plz Ste 184 (10523-1604)
PHONE...................914 347-3800
Fax: 914 347-2519
Christopher Malisse, *President*
Steve Solomon, *Exec VP*
Deborah Pizzella, *Controller*
▲ **EMP:** 20
SQ FT: 6,500
SALES (est): 4.1MM **Privately Held**
WEB: www.ergotechgroup.com
SIC: 3679 Liquid crystal displays (LCD)

(G-4752)
EXECUTIVE PRTG & DIRECT MAIL
8 Westchester Plz Ste 117 (10523-1604)
PHONE...................914 592-3200
Fax: 914 592-3103
Gary Dieckman, *President*
Andrew Dieckman, *General Mgr*
EMP: 9
SQ FT: 5,200
SALES (est): 1MM **Privately Held**
WEB: www.exprint.com
SIC: 2752 Commercial printing, lithographic

(G-4753)
FABRICATION ENTERPRISES INC
250 Clearbrook Rd Ste 240 (10523-1332)
P.O. Box 1500, White Plains (10602-1500)
PHONE...................914 591-9300
Fax: 914 345-9800
Elliott Goldberg, *President*
Andrew Goldberg, *VP Opers*
Jason Drucker, *VP Sales*
Joseph Cardone, *Sales Mgr*
Greg Guerci, *Accounts Mgr*
▲ **EMP:** 45
SQ FT: 30,000
SALES: 50MM **Privately Held**
WEB: www.fabricationenterprises.com
SIC: 3841 2297 Physiotherapy equipment, electrical; nonwoven fabrics

(G-4754)
G C D M IRONWORKS INC
Also Called: G C Ironworks
55 N Evarts Ave (10523-3215)
PHONE...................914 347-2058
Fax: 914 347-4916
Arrel Gordon, *President*
Michael Creegan, *Vice Pres*
Blondell Hill, *Manager*
EMP: 20
SQ FT: 650
SALES (est): 3.5MM **Privately Held**
SIC: 3446 Stairs, fire escapes, balconies, railings & ladders

(G-4755)
HUDSON SOFTWARE CORPORATION
3 W Main St Ste 106 (10523-2414)
PHONE...................914 773-0400
Ralph Santoni, *Manager*
EMP: 35
SQ FT: 6,000
SALES (est): 2.5MM **Privately Held**
WEB: www.hudsonsoft.com
SIC: 7372 7371 7374 Prepackaged software; custom computer programming services; service bureau, computer

(G-4756)
HYPRES INC
175 Clearbrook Rd (10523-1109)
PHONE...................914 592-1190
Fax: 914 347-2239
Richard E Hitt Jr, *Ch of Bd*
Richard Hitt, *President*
Dr Oleg Mukhanov, *Senior VP*
Dr Deepnarayan Gupta, *Vice Pres*
Jia Tang, *Engineer*
EMP: 37
SQ FT: 17,250
SALES: 8MM **Privately Held**
WEB: www.hypres.com
SIC: 3679 3565 Electronic circuits; packaging machinery

(G-4757)
IRON ART INC
14 N Payne St (10523-1835)
PHONE...................914 592-7977
Fernando Pastilha, *President*
EMP: 5
SALES: 200K **Privately Held**
SIC: 3446 Ornamental metalwork

(G-4758)
JAM PRINTING PUBLISHING INC
11 Clearbrook Rd Ste 133 (10523-1126)
PHONE...................914 345-8400
Fax: 914 345-6767
Judith Millman, *President*
Mitch Schilkraut, *General Mgr*
EMP: 7
SALES (est): 949.8K **Privately Held**
WEB: www.jamprinting.com
SIC: 2752 Commercial printing, lithographic

(G-4759)
JUDSCOTT HANDPRINTS LTD (PA)
2269 Saw Mill River Rd 4d (10523-3832)
PHONE...................914 347-5515
Fax: 914 347-3192
Sally Lefkowitz, *President*
Stephen Rabin, *Opers Staff*
EMP: 12
SQ FT: 8,000
SALES (est): 2.8MM **Privately Held**
WEB: www.judscott.com
SIC: 2262 2261 2221 Screen printing: manmade fiber & silk broadwoven fabrics; screen printing of cotton broadwoven fabrics; wall covering fabrics, manmade fiber & silk

(G-4760)
KIMBER MFG INC
555 Taxter Rd Ste 235 (10523-2314)
PHONE...................406 758-2222
Carmen Montenegro, *Production*
George Hawthorn, *Engineer*
Elliot Orenstein, *Engineer*
Brigit Salgado, *Engineer*
John Sanzo, *Engineer*
EMP: 85
SALES (corp-wide): 92.3MM **Privately Held**
WEB: www.kimbermfg.com
SIC: 3599 Machine shop, jobbing & repair
PA: Kimber Mfg. Inc.
  1 Lawton St
  Yonkers NY 10705
  914 964-0771

(G-4761)
LUXO CORPORATION
5 Westchester Plz Ste 110 (10523-1613)
PHONE...................914 345-0067
Fax: 914 345-0068
Sam Gumins, *President*
Michael Vuolo, *Opers Mgr*
Lynn Green, *Production*
Bob Grinnell, *CFO*
Robert Grinnell, *CFO*
▲ **EMP:** 19 **EST:** 1953
SALES: 7.5MM
SALES (corp-wide): 702.2MM **Privately Held**
WEB: www.luxous.com
SIC: 3646 Commercial indusl & institutional electric lighting fixtures
HQ: Glamox As
  Birger Hatlebakks Veg 15
  Molde 6415
  712 460-00

(G-4762)
MAGNETIC ANALYSIS CORPORATION (PA)
Also Called: M A C
103 Fairview Pk Dr Ste 2 (10523-1544)
PHONE...................914 530-2000
JI Vitulli, *Ch of Bd*
Billy Beasley, *General Mgr*
William S Gould III, *Chairman*
Robert Gould, *Vice Chairman*
Fred Fundy, *District Mgr*
▲ **EMP:** 90 **EST:** 1928
SQ FT: 26,000
SALES (est): 34.9MM **Privately Held**
WEB: www.mac-ndt.com
SIC: 3829 3825 Testing equipment: abrasion, shearing strength, etc.; instruments to measure electricity

(G-4763)
MASTER IMAGE PRINTING INC
75 N Central Ave Ste 202 (10523-2548)
PHONE...................914 347-4400
Fax: 914 347-4955
John Sabatino, *President*
Mary Jane Yollen, *Vice Pres*
EMP: 5
SQ FT: 5,000
SALES: 1MM **Privately Held**
WEB: www.masterimage.com
SIC: 2759 2752 2396 2679 Commercial printing; commercial printing, lithographic; automotive & apparel trimmings; labels, paper: made from purchased material

(G-4764)
MASTERDISK CORPORATION
134 S Central Ave Ste C (10523-3539)
PHONE...................212 541-5022
Douglas Levine, *CEO*
Graham Goldman, *Engineer*
Laksham Fernando, *Treasurer*
EMP: 15
SQ FT: 10,000
SALES: 981K **Privately Held**
WEB: www.masterdisk.com
SIC: 3652 3651 2851 Master records or tapes, preparation of; household audio & video equipment; vinyl coatings, strippable

(G-4765)
METHODSOURCING CORP
9 W Main St (10523-2464)
PHONE...................914 217-7276
Steven Greenstein, *CEO*
Avishai Greenstein, *Vice Pres*
Valerie Greenstein, *Director*
Nissen Isakova, *Director*
EMP: 11
SQ FT: 1,800
SALES: 2.7MM **Privately Held**
SIC: 3089 5023 Plastic kitchenware, tableware & houseware; kitchenware; decorative home furnishings & supplies

(G-4766)
MMO MUSIC GROUP INC
Also Called: Music Minus One
50 Executive Blvd Ste 236 (10523-1341)
PHONE...................914 592-1188
Fax: 914 592-3116
Irving Kratka, *CEO*
Patricia Dichek, *Office Mgr*
EMP: 9
SQ FT: 35,000
SALES (est): 1.9MM **Privately Held**
WEB: www.musicminusone.com
SIC: 3652 Compact laser discs, prerecorded; magnetic tape (audio): prerecorded

(G-4767)
MOTTS LLP (HQ)
Also Called: Motts
55 Hunter Ln (10523-1334)
P.O. Box 869077, Plano TX (75086-9077)
PHONE...................972 673-8088
Angela Stephens, *Controller*
Jeff Morgan, *MIS Dir*
Jim Baldwin, *General Counsel*
Larry D Young,
◆ **EMP:** 250
SQ FT: 160,000
SALES (est): 228.8MM
SALES (corp-wide): 6.2B **Publicly Held**
WEB: www.maunalai.com
SIC: 2033 5149 2087 Fruit juices: packaged in cans, jars, etc.; apple sauce: packaged in cans, jars, etc.; beverage concentrates; cocktail mixes, nonalcoholic
PA: Dr Pepper Snapple Group, Inc.
  5301 Legacy Dr
  Plano TX 75024
  972 673-7000

(G-4768)
MYPUBLISHER INC (PA)
8 Westchester Plz Ste 145 (10523-1604)
PHONE...................914 773-4312
Jeffrey T Housenbold, *Ch of Bd*
Lisa Heck, *Accountant*
Igor Karpov, *Software Engr*
Jude Niles, *Administration*
▲ **EMP:** 19
SALES (est): 3.9MM **Privately Held**
WEB: www.mypublisher.com
SIC: 2782 Albums

(G-4769)
NANOVIBRONIX INC
525 Executive Blvd (10523-1240)
PHONE...................914 233-3004
William Stern, *CEO*
EMP: 12
SQ FT: 5,000
SALES (est): 439K **Privately Held**
SIC: 3845 Ultrasonic medical equipment, except cleaning

(G-4770)
NANTUCKET ALLSERVE INC
Also Called: Nantucket Nectars
55 Hunter Ln (10523-1334)
PHONE...................914 612-4000
Mark Hellendrung, *President*
Thomas First, *Co-COB*
Thomas Scott, *Co-COB*
Tim Chan, *Treasurer*
Ellen Ludwig, *Human Resources*
EMP: 400
SALES (est): 17.9MM **Privately Held**
SIC: 2086 5499 Fruit drinks (less than 100% juice): packaged in cans, etc.; juices, fruit or vegetable

(G-4771)
NOVAMED-USA INC
4 Westchester Plz Ste 137 (10523-1612)
PHONE...................914 789-2100
Robert Gates, *General Mgr*
Carol Schuler, *Exec VP*
▲ **EMP:** 40
SQ FT: 30,000
SALES (est): 5.4MM **Privately Held**
SIC: 3841 3845 Catheters; patient monitoring apparatus

(G-4772)
OLYMPIA SPORTS COMPANY INC
Also Called: Olympia Company
500 Executive Blvd # 170 (10523-1239)
PHONE...................914 347-4737
Roger Heumann, *President*
Ed Brodsky, *Vice Pres*
▲ **EMP:** 10
SQ FT: 7,200
SALES (est): 920K **Privately Held**
WEB: www.olympiagloves.com
SIC: 3949 Gloves, sport & athletic: boxing, handball, etc.

GEOGRAPHIC SECTION
Endicott - Broome County (G-4797)

(G-4773)
PRESS EXPRESS
400 Executive Blvd # 146 (10523-1243)
PHONE..................................914 592-3790
Al Tiso, *President*
EMP: 5
SALES (est): 333.5K **Privately Held**
SIC: 2741 7313 Miscellaneous publishing; printed media advertising representatives

(G-4774)
RADON TESTING CORP OF AMERICA (PA)
Also Called: R T C A
2 Hayes St (10523-2502)
PHONE..................................914 345-3380
Michael Osterer, *CEO*
Nancy Bredhoff, *President*
Alan S Bande, *Vice Pres*
Alan S Bandes, *Vice Pres*
Mark A Goodman, *Vice Pres*
EMP: 12
SQ FT: 4,500
SALES (est): 1.9MM **Privately Held**
WEB: www.rtca.com
SIC: 3821 Laboratory apparatus & furniture

(G-4775)
RALPH MARTINELLI
Also Called: Suburban Marketing Assoc
100 Clearbrook Rd Ste 170 (10523-1135)
PHONE..................................914 345-3055
Fax: 914 345-3515
Ralph Martinelli, *Owner*
EMP: 30
SALES (est): 1.5MM **Privately Held**
WEB: www.sub-pub.com
SIC: 2721 Periodicals

(G-4776)
RELIABLE AUTMTC SPRNKLR CO INC (PA)
103 Fairview Pk Dr Ste 1 (10523-1523)
PHONE..................................914 829-2042
Fax: 914 592-3676
Frank J Fee III, *President*
Candida M Fee, *Vice Pres*
Kevin T Fee, *Vice Pres*
Michael R Fee, *Vice Pres*
Robert C Hultgren, *Vice Pres*
▲ EMP: 350 EST: 1920
SQ FT: 64,000
SALES (est): 382.9MM **Privately Held**
SIC: 3569 Sprinkler systems, fire: automatic

(G-4777)
SAVE O SEAL CORPORATION INC
90 E Main St (10523-3218)
P.O. Box 553 (10523-0553)
PHONE..................................914 592-3031
Fax: 914 592-4511
Tullio Muscariello, *President*
Rose Muscariello, *Vice Pres*
EMP: 7
SQ FT: 3,000
SALES (est): 1.2MM **Privately Held**
SIC: 3565 5085 Packaging machinery; knives, industrial

(G-4778)
SCHOTT CORPORATION (DH)
555 Taxter Rd Ste 470 (10523-2363)
PHONE..................................914 831-2200
Linda S Mayer, *Ch of Bd*
Greg Wolters, *Ch of Bd*
Dr Andreas F Liebenberg, *President*
Robert Galante, *General Mgr*
Joe Hale, *General Mgr*
▲ EMP: 70
SQ FT: 70,000
SALES (est): 987.4MM **Privately Held**
SIC: 3211 3829 3221 3229 Flat glass; measuring & controlling devices; glass containers; vials, glass; glass fiber products
HQ: Schott Ag
Hattenbergstr. 10
Mainz 55122
613 166-0

(G-4779)
SCHOTT GEMTRON CORPORATION
555 Taxter Rd Ste 470 (10523-2352)
PHONE..................................423 337-3522
Linda S Mayer, *President*
Robert Galante, *General Mgr*
EMP: 194 **Privately Held**
SIC: 3211 Flat glass
HQ: Schott Gemtron Corporation
615 New Highway 68
Sweetwater TN 37874
423 337-3522

(G-4780)
SCHOTT GOVERNMENT SERVICES LLC
Also Called: Schott Defense
555 Taxter Rd Ste 470 (10523-2352)
PHONE..................................703 418-1409
Scott Custer, *President*
Mona Roche, *Business Mgr*
EMP: 7 EST: 2007
SALES (est): 690.4K **Privately Held**
SIC: 3211 Flat glass
HQ: Schott North America, Inc.
555 Taxter Rd Ste 470
Elmsford NY 10523
914 831-2200

(G-4781)
SCHOTT LITHOTEC USA CORP
555 Taxter Rd Ste 470 (10523-2352)
PHONE..................................845 463-5300
Patrick Markschlaeger, *President*
EMP: 80
SQ FT: 36,115
SALES (est): 7.1MM **Privately Held**
SIC: 3674 Semiconductors & related devices

(G-4782)
SCHOTT SOLAR PV INC
555 Taxter Rd Ste 470 (10523-2352)
PHONE..................................888 457-6527
Mark Finocchario, *President*
Hans-Juergen Gebel, *Vice Pres*
Doug Jenks, *CFO*
Lauren Lake, *Human Resources*
Manfred Jaeckel, *Admin Sec*
▲ EMP: 7
SALES (est): 762.6K **Privately Held**
SIC: 3674 3211 Solar cells; flat glass
HQ: Schott Solar Ag
Hattenbergstr. 10
Mainz 55122
613 166-0

(G-4783)
SEQUENTIAL ELECTRONICS SYSTEMS
399 Executive Blvd (10523-1205)
PHONE..................................914 592-1345
Fax: 914 592-6014
Lewis S Schiller, *Ch of Bd*
Norman Wheatcroft, *Vice Pres*
Elliott Laitman, *CFO*
EMP: 22
SQ FT: 15,000
SALES (est): 1.9MM
SALES (corp-wide): 2.5MM **Privately Held**
SIC: 3577 3625 3823 3663 Encoders, computer peripheral equipment; positioning controls, electric; industrial instrmnts msrmnt display/control process variable; radio & TV communications equipment
PA: Trinity Group Acquisition Corp
249 Saw Mill River Rd
Elmsford NY

(G-4784)
SIGN WORKS INCORPORATED
150 Clearbrook Rd Ste 118 (10523-1142)
PHONE..................................914 592-0700
Fax: 914 592-4971
Lynn Feiner, *President*
Roseanne Bocknik, *Manager*
EMP: 25
SQ FT: 11,000
SALES (est): 2.5MM **Privately Held**
SIC: 3993 1799 Signs & advertising specialties; sign installation & maintenance

(G-4785)
SML ACQUISITION LLC
33 W Main St Ste 505 (10523-2453)
PHONE..................................914 592-3130
Robert B Wetzel, *President*
Laura Hutter, *Controller*
EMP: 179 EST: 2011
SQ FT: 35,000
SALES (est): 12.5MM **Privately Held**
SIC: 2844 Toilet preparations

(G-4786)
SNAPPLE
55 Hunter Ln (10523-1334)
PHONE..................................914 846-2300
Bill Byron, *Manager*
Carmen Bracho, *Director*
EMP: 5
SALES (est): 442.6K **Privately Held**
SIC: 2086 Bottled & canned soft drinks

(G-4787)
SPOTLIGHT PUBLICATIONS LLC
100 Clearbrook Rd Ste 170 (10523-1135)
PHONE..................................914 345-9473
John Jordan, *Principal*
EMP: 5
SALES (est): 470K **Privately Held**
SIC: 2721 Magazines: publishing only, not printed on site

(G-4788)
TRANE US INC
3 Westchester Plz Ste 198 (10523-1623)
PHONE..................................914 593-0303
Terry Connor, *Manager*
EMP: 5 **Privately Held**
SIC: 3585 Refrigeration & heating equipment
HQ: Trane U.S. Inc.
1 Centennial Ave Ste 101
Piscataway NJ 08854
732 652-7100

(G-4789)
TRI-STATE METALS LLC
Also Called: Tsm
41 N Lawn Ave (10523-2632)
PHONE..................................914 347-8157
Patti Carone, *Manager*
Ray Ayerbe, *Webmaster*
EMP: 10
SQ FT: 10,000
SALES (est): 1.8MM **Privately Held**
SIC: 3444 Culverts, flumes & pipes

(G-4790)
U E SYSTEMS INCORPORATED (PA)
14 Hayes St (10523-2536)
PHONE..................................914 592-1220
Fax: 914 347-2181
Michael Osterer, *Ch of Bd*
Blake Canham, *Regional Mgr*
Greg Inverso, *Regional Mgr*
Mike Naro, *Regional Mgr*
Mike Pierce, *Regional Mgr*
EMP: 30
SALES (est): 4.8MM **Privately Held**
WEB: www.uesystems.com
SIC: 3829 3812 3699 Ultrasonic testing equipment; search & navigation equipment; electrical equipment & supplies

(G-4791)
VISIPLEX INSTRUMENTS CORP
250 Clearbrook Rd (10523-1305)
PHONE..................................845 365-0190
David Vozick, *Ch of Bd*
Donald Rabinovitch, *President*
Elise Nissen, *CFO*
Thalia Rosales, *Controller*
EMP: 62
SALES: 20MM **Privately Held**
WEB: www.afpimaging.com
SIC: 3845 Electromedical equipment
HQ: Afp Imaging Corporation
185 Kisco Ave Ste 202
Mount Kisco NY 10549
914 592-6665

(G-4792)
VITERION CORPORATION
565 Taxter Rd Ste 175 (10523-2371)
PHONE..................................914 333-6033

Hernani Castro, *QA Dir*
Pramod Gaur, *CFO*
Elizabeth Olis, *Manager*
Daren Watson, *Technical Staff*
EMP: 16 EST: 2012
SALES (est): 2.5MM **Privately Held**
SIC: 3841 Surgical & medical instruments

(G-4793)
WESTINGHOUSE A BRAKE TECH CORP
Also Called: Metro Service Center
4 Warehouse Ln Ste 144 (10523-1556)
PHONE..................................914 347-8650
Doug Cavallo, *Manager*
EMP: 13
SALES (corp-wide): 3.3B **Publicly Held**
WEB: www.wabco-rail.com
SIC: 3743 Rapid transit cars & equipment
PA: Westinghouse Air Brake Technologies Corporation
1001 Airbrake Ave
Wilmerding PA 15148
412 825-1000

(G-4794)
WHITE PLAINS MARBLE INC
186 E Main St (10523-3302)
PHONE..................................914 347-6000
John Bargellini, *President*
Judy Birdsall, *Manager*
EMP: 7
SQ FT: 5,000
SALES (est): 700K **Privately Held**
SIC: 3281 1743 Marble, building: cut & shaped; statuary, marble; terrazzo, tile, marble, mosaic work

Endicott
Broome County

(G-4795)
AMPHENOL INTRCONNECT PDTS CORP (HQ)
20 Valley St (13760-3600)
PHONE..................................607 754-4444
Fax: 607 786-4234
Richard Adam Norwitt, *CEO*
Martin H Loeffler, *President*
Craig Lampo, *Vice Pres*
Sue Dodge, *Purch Agent*
Sue Thompson, *Buyer*
▲ EMP: 5
SQ FT: 140,000
SALES (est): 90.4MM
SALES (corp-wide): 5.5B **Publicly Held**
WEB: www.amphenol-aipc.com
SIC: 3679 Harness assemblies for electronic use: wire or cable
PA: Amphenol Corporation
358 Hall Ave
Wallingford CT 06492
203 265-8900

(G-4796)
BAE SYSTEMS CONTROLS INC (DH)
1098 Clark St (13760-2815)
PHONE..................................607 770-2000
Thomas A Asrseneault, *President*
Thomas A Arseneault, *President*
Katelyn Warren, *General Mgr*
Thomas Lipko, *Superintendent*
Joyce Sherwood, *Principal*
▲ EMP: 1400 EST: 2000
SALES (est): 397.2MM
SALES (corp-wide): 25.3B **Privately Held**
WEB: www.baesystemscontrols.com
SIC: 3812 Aircraft/aerospace flight instruments & guidance systems
HQ: Bae Systems, Inc.
1101 Wilson Blvd Ste 2000
Arlington VA 22209
703 312-6100

(G-4797)
BROOME COUNTY
Central Foods & Nutrition Svcs
2001 E Main St (13760-5622)
P.O. Box 1766, Binghamton (13902-1766)
PHONE..................................607 785-9567
Fax: 607 748-0268
Michelle Hauf, *Director*

Endicott - Broome County (G-4798) — GEOGRAPHIC SECTION

Michelle L Haus, *Director*
EMP: 20
SQ FT: 11,076 **Privately Held**
WEB: www.bcstopdwi.com
SIC: 2099 Emulsifiers, food
PA: Broome County
  60 Hawley St
  Binghamton NY 13901
  607 778-2452

(G-4798)
CHAKRA COMMUNICATIONS INC
32 Washington Ave (13760-5305)
PHONE.....................607 748-7491
Gregory Hennessey, *Mktg Dir*
Jim Arnold, *Branch Mgr*
EMP: 20 **Privately Held**
WEB: www.chakracentral.com
SIC: 2752 7334 2791 2789 Commercial printing, offset; photocopying & duplicating services; typesetting; bookbinding & related work; commercial printing
HQ: Chakra Communications, Inc.
  80 W Drullard Ave
  Lancaster NY 14086
  716 505-7300

(G-4799)
CROWLEY FABG MACHINING CO INC (PA)
403 N Nanticoke Ave (13760-4138)
PHONE.....................607 484-0299
Thomas Crowley, *President*
Mike Crowley, *General Mgr*
Mike Newfrock, *Info Tech Mgr*
EMP: 4
SQ FT: 30,000
SALES (est): 4.2MM **Privately Held**
WEB: www.crowleyfab.com
SIC: 3541 Machine tools, metal cutting type

(G-4800)
DATUM ALLOYS INC
407 Airport Rd (13760-4405)
PHONE.....................607 239-6274
Ben Scott, *President*
Kevin Graham, *General Mgr*
Duncan Watey, *Vice Pres*
Pete Anniss, *Sales Dir*
Daniel Jin, *Sales Mgr*
▲ **EMP:** 6
SQ FT: 800
SALES (est): 737.4K **Privately Held**
SIC: 3291 Abrasive metal & steel products

(G-4801)
ELTEE TOOL & DIE CO
404 E Franklin St (13760-4124)
PHONE.....................607 748-4301
William Andrew Keeler, *Owner*
EMP: 10
SQ FT: 10,000
SALES (est): 1.2MM **Privately Held**
SIC: 3559 Automotive related machinery

(G-4802)
ENDICOTT INTERCONNECT TECH INC
Also Called: Ei
1701 North St (13760-5553)
P.O. Box 5250, Binghamton (13902-5250)
PHONE.....................866 820-4820
James J Mc Namara Jr, *Ch of Bd*
Jeff Knight, *General Mgr*
Frank Egitto, *Research*
Douglas Chrzanowski, *Engineer*
Marybeth Perrino, *Engineer*
▲ **EMP:** 600
SQ FT: 1,400,000
SALES (est): 61.6K **Privately Held**
WEB: www.endicottinterconnect.com
SIC: 3674 Semiconductors & related devices

(G-4803)
ENDICOTT PRECISION INC
1328-30 Campville Rd (13760-4414)
PHONE.....................607 754-7076
Fax: 607 754-7150
Ronald Oliveira, *General Mgr*
Douglas Walters, *General Mgr*
Manuel Oliveira, *Chairman*
Dolores Oliveira, *Vice Pres*

Lee Warner, *Facilities Mgr*
EMP: 125 **EST:** 1959
SQ FT: 85,000
SALES: 19.1MM **Privately Held**
WEB: www.endicottprecision.com
SIC: 3444 3443 3599 3469 Sheet metalwork; fabricated plate work (boiler shop); weldments; custom machinery; metal stampings

(G-4804)
ENDICOTT RESEARCH GROUP INC
2601 Wayne St (13760-3207)
PHONE.....................607 754-9187
Fax: 607 754-9255
Nathan Burd, *President*
Dean Barnes, *Regional Mgr*
Scott Barney, *Vice Pres*
Anna Quick, *Mfg Staff*
Scott Dittrich, *Buyer*
EMP: 64
SQ FT: 30,000
SALES (est): 14.8MM **Privately Held**
WEB: www.ergpower.com
SIC: 3629 Power conversion units, a.c. to d.c.: static-electric; inverters, nonrotating; electrical

(G-4805)
ENGINEERING MFG TECH LLC
101 Delaware Ave (13760-6106)
PHONE.....................607 754-7111
Fax: 607 754-2237
Patricia Marconi, *President*
Wyoma Chambala, *Vice Pres*
Michael Nowalk, *Vice Pres*
Cary Simon, *Manager*
EMP: 90 **EST:** 1946
SQ FT: 80,000
SALES (est): 23.3MM **Privately Held**
WEB: www.endicottmachine.com
SIC: 3444 3599 3496 3469 Sheet metalwork; machine & other job shop work; miscellaneous fabricated wire products; metal stampings

(G-4806)
EVERLASTING IMAGES
504 Shady Dr (13760-5918)
PHONE.....................607 785-8743
John C Kupiec, *Principal*
EMP: 7
SALES (est): 477.1K **Privately Held**
SIC: 3479 Etching & engraving

(G-4807)
FAMBUS INC
Also Called: Village Printing
2800 Watson Blvd (13760-3512)
PHONE.....................607 785-3700
David Labelle, *President*
Frank Labelle, *Consultant*
EMP: 6
SQ FT: 2,100
SALES (est): 590K **Privately Held**
WEB: www.fambus.com
SIC: 2752 7334 Commercial printing, offset; photocopying & duplicating services

(G-4808)
FELIX ROMA & SONS INC
2 S Page Ave (13760-4693)
P.O. Box 5547 (13763-5547)
PHONE.....................607 748-3336
Fax: 607 748-3607
Eugene F Roma, *President*
Eugene Romask, *Vice Pres*
Lucille Fetsko, *Bookkeeper*
EMP: 60
SQ FT: 43,000
SALES (est): 8.1MM **Privately Held**
WEB: www.felixroma.com
SIC: 2051 Bread, cake & related products; bread, all types (white, wheat, rye, etc): fresh or frozen; rolls, bread type: fresh or frozen

(G-4809)
G B INTERNATIONAL TRDG CO LTD
408 Airport Rd (13760-4494)
PHONE.....................607 785-0938
Fax: 607 785-1109
August Garufy, *President*
Ben Winn, *Senior Buyer*

Cherie Cudo, *Financial Exec*
◆ **EMP:** 250
SQ FT: 30,000
SALES (est): 40.9MM **Privately Held**
WEB: www.gbint.com
SIC: 3629 5065 5999 Power conversion units, a.c. to d.c.: static-electric; electronic parts & equipment; electronic parts & equipment

(G-4810)
GEORGE INDUSTRIES LLC
1 S Page Ave (13760-4695)
PHONE.....................607 748-3371
Fax: 607 754-9883
W Mark Ciaravino, *President*
Daniel T Ciaravino, *Vice Pres*
John Ferro, *Purch Mgr*
Kellen Kafka, *Engineer*
Marilyn Cline, *Manager*
EMP: 117 **EST:** 1951
SQ FT: 100,000
SALES (est): 20.4MM **Privately Held**
WEB: www.georgeindustries.com
SIC: 3441 Fabricated structural metal

(G-4811)
I3 ELECTRONICS INC (PA)
1701 North St (13760-5553)
P.O. Box 149 (13761-0149)
PHONE.....................866 820-4820
Jim Matthews Jr, *President*
Voya Markovich, *Senior VP*
Matthew Coppola, *Production*
Janet Hernandez, *Controller*
Jim Harding, *Manager*
EMP: 134 **EST:** 2013
SALES (est): 102.4MM **Privately Held**
SIC: 3672 Printed circuit boards

(G-4812)
I3 ELECTRONICS INC
Mdc Bldg 48 Odell Ave (13760)
PHONE.....................866 820-4820
EMP: 286
SALES (corp-wide): 102.4MM **Privately Held**
SIC: 3674 Semiconductors & related devices
PA: I3 Electronics, Inc.
  1701 North St
  Endicott NY 13760
  866 820-4820

(G-4813)
INTERNATIONAL BUS MCHS CORP
Also Called: IBM
1701 North St (13760-5553)
PHONE.....................607 754-9558
Fax: 607 755-3527
Mike Cadigan, *Vice Pres*
Ed Cervantes, *Vice Pres*
John Spalik, *Project Mgr*
Thomas Forsberg, *Production*
Mario Monaco, *Production*
EMP: 2000
SALES (corp-wide): 81.7B **Publicly Held**
WEB: www.ibm.com
SIC: 3571 Electronic computers
PA: International Business Machines Corporation
  1 New Orchard Rd Ste 1
  Armonk NY 10504
  914 499-1900

(G-4814)
JARETS STUFFED CUPCAKES
116 Oak Hill Ave (13760-2810)
PHONE.....................607 658-9096
EMP: 8 **EST:** 2015
SALES (est): 386.7K **Privately Held**
SIC: 2051 Bread, cake & related products

(G-4815)
JAX SIGNS AND NEON INC
108 Odell Ave (13760-2817)
PHONE.....................607 727-3420
James E Taber, *Ch of Bd*
EMP: 7
SALES (est): 847.6K **Privately Held**
SIC: 3993 Signs & advertising specialties

(G-4816)
JD TOOL INC
521 E Main St (13760-5023)
PHONE.....................607 786-3129
Jeffrey Dibble, *President*
Mandy Esposito, *Office Mgr*
Mandy Hill, *Manager*
EMP: 3
SALES: 1.8MM **Privately Held**
WEB: www.jdtool.net
SIC: 3545 Tools & accessories for machine tools

(G-4817)
JIM ROMAS BAKERY INC
202 N Nanticoke Ave (13760-4135)
PHONE.....................607 748-7425
James Roma, *President*
Carl Roma, *Vice Pres*
EMP: 30
SQ FT: 5,200
SALES: 800K **Privately Held**
SIC: 2051 5411 Bakery: wholesale or wholesale/retail combined; delicatessens

(G-4818)
MEDSIM-EAGLE SIMULATION INC
811 North St (13760-5127)
PHONE.....................607 658-9354
Nimrod Goor, *President*
Christopher Paulsen, *Vice Pres*
EMP: 12
SALES (est): 760.4K **Privately Held**
WEB: www.medsim.com
SIC: 3571 3577 7373 Electronic computers; graphic displays, except graphic terminals; systems integration services
HQ: Medsim Inc
  741 Curlew Rd
  Delray Beach FL 33444

(G-4819)
MICROCHIP TECHNOLOGY INC
3301 Country Club Rd (13760-3401)
PHONE.....................607 785-5992
Steve Sanghi, *Branch Mgr*
EMP: 166
SALES (corp-wide): 2.1B **Publicly Held**
SIC: 3674 Semiconductors & related devices
PA: Microchip Technology Inc
  2355 W Chandler Blvd
  Chandler AZ 85224
  480 792-7200

(G-4820)
NEW VISION INDUSTRIES INC
1239 Campville Rd (13760-4424)
P.O. Box 570, Apalachin (13732-0570)
PHONE.....................607 687-7700
Michael R Copt, *President*
Betsy Copt, *Vice Pres*
Diane Horne, *Assistant*
EMP: 18
SQ FT: 4,100
SALES (est): 4.6MM **Privately Held**
WEB: www.newvisionindustries.com
SIC: 3569 3441 Assembly machines, non-metalworking; fabricated structural metal

(G-4821)
NORTH POINT TECHNOLOGY LLC
816 Buffalo St (13760-1780)
PHONE.....................866 885-3377
Ryan Kane, *Engineer*
Robert P Lee,
EMP: 10
SALES: 600K **Privately Held**
WEB: www.northpointusa.com
SIC: 3625 Relays & industrial controls

(G-4822)
PALMER INDUSTRIES INC
2320 Lewis St (13760-6157)
PHONE.....................607 754-8741
Jeck Palmer Jr, *Manager*
EMP: 7
SALES (corp-wide): 2.2MM **Privately Held**
WEB: www.palmerind.com
SIC: 3842 3534 Wheelchairs; elevators & moving stairways

▲ = Import ▼ = Export
◆ = Import/Export

GEOGRAPHIC SECTION

Fairport - Monroe County (G-4849)

PA: Palmer Industries Inc
509 Paden St
Endicott NY 13760
607 754-2957

(G-4823)
PALMER INDUSTRIES INC (PA)
509 Paden St (13760-4631)
P.O. Box 5707 (13763-5707)
PHONE...................................607 754-2957
Fax: 607 754-1954
Jack Palmer Sr, *President*
Jack Palmer Jr, *General Mgr*
EMP: 22
SALES (est): 2.2MM **Privately Held**
WEB: www.palmerind.com
SIC: 3842 Wheelchairs

(G-4824)
PALMER INDUSTRIES INC
1 Heath St (13760-6110)
P.O. Box 5707 (13763-5707)
PHONE...................................607 754-1954
Jack Palmer Jr, *Manager*
EMP: 6
SALES (corp-wide): 2.2MM **Privately Held**
WEB: www.palmerind.com
SIC: 3751 3842 Motorcycles, bicycles & parts; wheelchairs
PA: Palmer Industries Inc
509 Paden St
Endicott NY 13760
607 754-2957

(G-4825)
PHOTONIX TECHNOLOGIES INC
48 Washington Ave (13760-5305)
PHONE...................................607 786-4600
John Urban, *President*
Sam Cucci, *Vice Pres*
EMP: 12
SQ FT: 2,500
SALES: 1,000K **Privately Held**
WEB: www.photonixtechnologies.com
SIC: 3825 Test equipment for electronic & electric measurement

(G-4826)
PRO LETTERING LLC
127 W Main St (13760-4773)
P.O. Box 5727 (13763-5727)
PHONE...................................607 484-0255
Fax: 607 484-0257
Jim Emery,
EMP: 9
SQ FT: 6,000
SALES: 450K **Privately Held**
SIC: 2395 Embroidery & art needlework

(G-4827)
R SPOOR FINISHING CORP
3006 Wayne St (13760-3541)
PHONE...................................607 748-5905
Rick Spoor, *President*
Joette Amaro, *Office Mgr*
EMP: 13
SALES (est): 1.1MM **Privately Held**
SIC: 3479 Coating of metals & formed products

(G-4828)
SAM A LUPO & SONS INC (PA)
1219 Campville Rd (13760-4411)
P.O. Box 5721 (13763-5721)
PHONE...................................607 748-1141
Sam A Lupo Jr, *President*
Stephen J Lupo, *Vice Pres*
Diane Peris, *Manager*
Jennifer Perkins, *Admin Sec*
EMP: 3
SALES (est): 9.9MM **Privately Held**
WEB: www.spiedies.com
SIC: 2011 5411 Meat by-products from meat slaughtered on site; delicatessens

(G-4829)
SMARTYS CORNER
501 W Main St (13760-4621)
PHONE...................................607 239-5276
Laura Cla, *Principal*
EMP: 6 EST: 2008
SALES (est): 423.7K **Privately Held**
SIC: 2024 Ice cream, bulk

(G-4830)
TIOGA TOOL INC (PA)
160 Glendale Dr (13760-3704)
PHONE...................................607 785-6005
Fax: 607 625-2155
Jeff Rudler, *President*
Jeff Koprevich, *Sales Mgr*
EMP: 12 EST: 1965
SQ FT: 5,500
SALES (est): 1.7MM **Privately Held**
WEB: www.tiogatool.com
SIC: 3599 1799 Machine & other job shop work; welding on site

(G-4831)
TNTPAVING
1077 Taft Ave (13760-7201)
PHONE...................................607 372-4911
Dale Thomas, *Owner*
EMP: 5
SALES (est): 140K **Privately Held**
SIC: 2952 Asphalt felts & coatings

(G-4832)
TRUEBITE INC
129 Squires Ave (13760-2936)
PHONE...................................607 786-3184
Ed Calafut, *President*
▲ **EMP:** 12
SALES (est): 750K **Privately Held**
WEB: www.fotofiles.com
SIC: 3545 Drills (machine tool accessories)

(G-4833)
VESTAL ELECTRONIC DEVICES LLC
635 Dickson St (13760-4527)
PHONE...................................607 773-8461
Fax: 607 772-8184
Joel Osborne, *Manager*
Walter H Kintner Jr,
▲ **EMP:** 15
SQ FT: 110,000
SALES (est): 2.2MM **Privately Held**
WEB: www.vestalelectronics.com
SIC: 3679 Electronic circuits

(G-4834)
WEDDING GOWN PRESERVATION CO
707 North St (13760-5011)
PHONE...................................607 748-7999
Fax: 607 754-9863
Michael Schapiro, *Owner*
Susan Schapiro, *Vice Pres*
Mary Roberts, *CFO*
Colby Schapiro, *Manager*
Vicki Raposo, *Data Proc Staff*
EMP: 60
SALES (est): 7.3MM **Privately Held**
WEB: www.gownpreservation.com
SIC: 2842 Drycleaning preparations

Endwell
Broome County

(G-4835)
EMPIRE PLASTICS INC
2011 E Main St (13760-5622)
PHONE...................................607 754-9132
Fax: 607 748-0391
John Witinski Sr, *President*
John Witinski Jr, *Vice Pres*
Shirley Westover, *Data Proc Dir*
EMP: 33 EST: 1958
SQ FT: 11,000
SALES (est): 6MM **Privately Held**
SIC: 3599 3699 2821 Machine shop, jobbing & repair; laser welding, drilling & cutting equipment; thermosetting materials; acrylic resins; nylon resins; polytetrafluoroethylene resins (teflon)

(G-4836)
J T SYSTEMATIC
Also Called: Just In Time Company
39 Valley St (13760-3659)
PHONE...................................607 754-0929
Fax: 607 754-7509
Roger Carr, *Owner*
EMP: 5
SQ FT: 6,000
SALES: 350K **Privately Held**
SIC: 3544 3999 3089 3599 Industrial molds; models, general, except toy; injection molded finished plastic products; machine shop, jobbing & repair

(G-4837)
LIGHTSPIN TECHNOLOGIES INC
616 Lowell Dr (13760-2525)
PHONE...................................301 656-7600
Jared Bowling, *President*
Richard Clayton, *Chairman*
EMP: 6
SALES: 1MM **Privately Held**
WEB: www.polychip.com
SIC: 3674 Semiconductors & related devices

(G-4838)
PROGRESSIVE TOOL COMPANY INC
3221 Lawndale St (13760-3593)
PHONE...................................607 748-8294
Fax: 607 748-5683
Gordon E Markoff, *CEO*
Ronald G Markoff, *President*
Sandra J Roloson, *Corp Secy*
Lorraine Markoff, *Vice Pres*
Pat Crowley, *Plant Mgr*
EMP: 35 EST: 1956
SQ FT: 15,900
SALES (est): 5MM **Privately Held**
SIC: 3599 Machine shop, jobbing & repair

Esperance
Montgomery County

(G-4839)
US SANDER LLC
4131 Rte 20 (12066)
P.O. Box 335 (12066-0335)
PHONE...................................518 875-9157
Gary Rudolph, *Mng Member*
David Rudolph,
Peggy Rudolph,
EMP: 9
SQ FT: 10,000
SALES (est): 790K **Privately Held**
WEB: www.ussander.com
SIC: 3553 Sanding machines, except portable floor sanders: woodworking

(G-4840)
WIND SOLUTIONS LLC
251 County Road 156 (12066)
P.O. Box 57, Sanford NC (27331-0057)
PHONE...................................518 813-8029
Christopher Winslow, *Principal*
▲ **EMP:** 7
SALES (est): 825.1K **Privately Held**
SIC: 3621 Windmills, electric generating

Fabius
Onondaga County

(G-4841)
VILLAGE WROUGHT IRON INC
7756 Main St (13063-9749)
PHONE...................................315 683-5589
Gary Host, *President*
Adam Host, *Vice Pres*
EMP: 12
SQ FT: 15,000
SALES (est): 1.1MM **Privately Held**
SIC: 3446 Architectural metalwork

Fairport
Monroe County

(G-4842)
ARCTIC GLACIER MINNESOTA INC
900 Turk Hill Rd (14450-8747)
PHONE...................................585 388-0080
EMP: 39
SALES (corp-wide): 310.9MM **Privately Held**
SIC: 2097 Manufactured ice

HQ: Arctic Glacier Minnesota Inc.
1601 Halbur Rd
Marshall MN 56258
507 532-5411

(G-4843)
ARCTIC GLACIER PA INC
900 Turk Hill Rd (14450-8747)
PHONE...................................610 494-8200
John Stratman, *Executive*
EMP: 50
SALES (est): 4.7MM
SALES (corp-wide): 1.3MM **Privately Held**
SIC: 2097 Manufactured ice
PA: Arctic Glacier Income Fund
625 Henry Ave
Winnipeg MB R3A 0
204 772-2473

(G-4844)
ARCTIC GLACIER TEXAS INC
900 Turk Hill Rd (14450-8747)
PHONE...................................215 283-0326
EMP: 38
SALES (corp-wide): 310.9MM **Privately Held**
SIC: 2097 Block ice
HQ: Arctic Glacier Texas Inc.
130 E 42nd St
Lubbock TX

(G-4845)
ARCTIC GLACIER USA
900 Turk Hill Rd (14450-8747)
PHONE...................................215 283-0326
Peter Stack, *President*
Arne Zipkin, *Manager*
EMP: 25
SALES (est): 5MM **Privately Held**
SIC: 2097 Ice cubes

(G-4846)
BARS PRECISION INC
15 Wind Loft Cir (14450-4415)
PHONE...................................585 742-6380
Robert Born, *President*
Marc Ramsperger, *Manager*
Jana Born, *Admin Sec*
EMP: 11
SALES (est): 1.7MM **Privately Held**
WEB: www.toolingonline.com
SIC: 3542 Presses: forming, stamping, punching, sizing (machine tools)

(G-4847)
BASELINE GRAPHICS INC
148 Selborne Chase (14450-3240)
PHONE...................................585 223-0153
David B Finger, *President*
EMP: 12
SALES (est): 670K **Privately Held**
WEB: www.graphicsolutionsny.com
SIC: 2759 2675 Commercial printing; paper die-cutting

(G-4848)
BERNARD HALL
Also Called: Minuteman Press
10 Perinton Hills Mall (14450-3621)
PHONE...................................585 425-3340
Fax: 585 425-4924
Bernard Hall, *Owner*
EMP: 5
SALES (est): 482.4K **Privately Held**
SIC: 2752 2791 2789 Commercial printing, lithographic; typesetting; bookbinding & related work

(G-4849)
BREED ENTERPRISES INC
34 Water St (14450-1549)
PHONE...................................585 388-0126
Fax: 585 388-0125
Ronald Reding, *President*
Bruce Caruana, *Vice Pres*
Dave Kirsher, *Manager*
EMP: 5
SALES: 1.1MM **Privately Held**
WEB: www.bullittmansparts.com
SIC: 3599 Machine shop, jobbing & repair

Fairport - Monroe County (G-4850)

(G-4850)
CASA LARGA VINEYARDS (PA)
27 Emerald Hill Cir (14450-9504)
P.O. Box 400 (14450-0400)
PHONE..................585 223-4210
Ann Colaruotolo, *President*
Andrew Colaruotolo, *President*
John Colaruotolo, *Vice Pres*
Maria Digiambattista, *Financial Analy*
EMP: 3
SALES (est): 1.4MM **Privately Held**
WEB: www.casalarga.com
SIC: 2084 5921 7299 Wines; wine; banquet hall facilities

(G-4851)
CASA LARGA VINEYARDS
2287 Turk Hill Rd (14450-9579)
P.O. Box 400 (14450-0400)
PHONE..................585 223-4210
Fax: 585 223-8899
John Colaruotolo, *Facilities Mgr*
Ann Lloyd, *Opers Staff*
Andrea Oneill, *Opers Staff*
Ann Colaruottolo, *Manager*
EMP: 7
SALES (corp-wide): 1.6MM **Privately Held**
WEB: www.casalarga.com
SIC: 2084 Wines
PA: Casa Larga Vineyards
27 Emerald Hill Cir
Fairport NY 14450
585 223-4210

(G-4852)
CORNING TROPEL CORPORATION
60 Oconnor Rd (14450-1328)
PHONE..................585 377-3200
Fax: 585 377-1966
Curt Weinstein, *Ch of Bd*
John Burning, *President*
Dan Gales, *Mfg Mgr*
James Platten, *Mfg Mgr*
Kelly Scott, *Purchasing*
EMP: 195
SQ FT: 100,000
SALES (est): 30.8MM
SALES (corp-wide): 9.1B **Publicly Held**
WEB: www.tropel.com
SIC: 3841 3827 3229 Ophthalmic instruments & apparatus; optical instruments & lenses; pressed & blown glass
PA: Corning Incorporated
1 Riverfront Plz
Corning NY 14831
607 974-9000

(G-4853)
D BAG LADY INC
183 Perinton Pkwy (14450-9104)
PHONE..................585 425-8095
Debra Perry, *President*
Rick Perry, *QC Mgr*
EMP: 8
SQ FT: 8,500
SALES (est): 1MM **Privately Held**
WEB: www.dbaglady.com
SIC: 3081 Unsupported plastics film & sheet

(G-4854)
DAVIS INTERNATIONAL INC
388 Mason Rd (14450-9561)
PHONE..................585 421-8175
Timothy M McGraw, *President*
James R Davis, *Principal*
EMP: 7
SQ FT: 5,000
SALES (est): 770K **Privately Held**
WEB: www.davisinternational.net
SIC: 3555 5084 Printing trades machinery; printing trades machinery, equipment & supplies

(G-4855)
DUNDEE FOODS LLC (PA)
Also Called: Dundeespirits
815 Whitney Rd W (14450-1030)
PHONE..................585 377-7700
Fax: 607 243-3877
Giovanni Lidestri, *CEO*
Holly Feily, *Accounts Mgr*
Keith Silsbee, *Manager*
▲ EMP: 19

SALES (est): 2.9MM **Privately Held**
SIC: 2099 Food preparations

(G-4856)
EAST PATTERN & MODEL CORP (PA)
75 N Main St (14450-1544)
PHONE..................585 461-3240
Fax: 585 461-0798
Warren H Kellogg, *President*
Mark Landers, *General Mgr*
Rosario Gaglianese, *Plant Mgr*
Michelle E Kellogg, *Treasurer*
Carl Sudore, *Sales Staff*
EMP: 26
SQ FT: 15,000
SALES: 3MM **Privately Held**
SIC: 3544 3089 3365 3275 Industrial molds; injection molding of plastics; aluminum foundries; gypsum products

(G-4857)
HANDONE STUDIOS INC
388 Mason Rd (14450-9561)
PHONE..................585 421-8175
Fax: 585 421-8707
Jim Davis, *President*
Chris Stewart, *Opers Mgr*
Anatol Topolewski, *Purch Mgr*
Lynn Davis, *Office Mgr*
EMP: 9
SQ FT: 6,000
SALES: 300K **Privately Held**
SIC: 2759 Screen printing

(G-4858)
J & N COMPUTER SERVICES INC
1387 Fairport Rd Ste 900j (14450-2087)
PHONE..................585 388-8780
Fax: 585 388-8783
Nancy E Jacobsen, *Ch of Bd*
Jonathon Hull, *Opers Mgr*
Matt Jacobus, *Manager*
EMP: 11
SQ FT: 3,000
SALES (est): 3.7MM **Privately Held**
SIC: 3571 5734 Electronic computers; computer & software stores

(G-4859)
JASCO HEAT TREATING INC
75 Macedon Center Rd (14450-9763)
P.O. Box 60620, Rochester (14606-0620)
PHONE..................585 388-0071
Eugine W Baldino, *CEO*
Diane Simons, *CFO*
Ed Bessette, *Human Resources*
Bryan Jerman, *Marketing Staff*
Rick Hook, *Supervisor*
EMP: 23
SQ FT: 50,000
SALES (est): 5.7MM **Privately Held**
WEB: www.jascotools.com
SIC: 3398 Metal heat treating

(G-4860)
LAHR RECYCLING & RESINS INC
Also Called: Lahr Plastics
164 Daley Rd (14450-9524)
PHONE..................585 425-8608
Fax: 585 425-2849
Craig A Lahr, *President*
EMP: 15
SQ FT: 20,000
SALES (est): 1.3MM **Privately Held**
SIC: 3087 Custom compound purchased resins

(G-4861)
LIDESTRI FOODS INC (PA)
Also Called: Lidestri Food and Drink
815 Whitney Rd W (14450-1030)
PHONE..................585 377-7700
John Lidestri, *CEO*
Jeff Lalonde, *Managing Dir*
Joe Ferrigno, *Principal*
Robert Schiefer, *Principal*
Tony Bash, *Vice Pres*
▲ EMP: 400
SQ FT: 260,000

SALES (est): 271.6MM **Privately Held**
WEB: www.francescorinaldi.com
SIC: 3221 2033 Bottles for packing, bottling & canning: glass; spaghetti & other pasta sauce: packaged in cans, jars, etc.

(G-4862)
LMG NATIONAL PUBLISHING INC (HQ)
350 Willowbrook Office Pa (14450-4222)
P.O. Box 580, Middletown (10940-0580)
PHONE..................585 598-6874
Leslie Hinton, *Ch of Bd*
EMP: 32
SALES (est): 11.3MM
SALES (corp-wide): 1.2B **Publicly Held**
SIC: 2711 2752 Newspapers; commercial printing, lithographic
PA: New Media Investment Group Inc.
1345 Avenue Of The Americ
New York NY 10105
212 479-3160

(G-4863)
MASTERCRAFT DECORATORS INC
Also Called: Caldwell Cor
320 Macedon Center Rd (14450-9759)
PHONE..................585 223-5150
James Yonosko, *President*
Rosemary Smith, *Vice Pres*
Christine Pollock, *Controller*
Tim Bayer, *Credit Mgr*
Ben McAllister, *CTO*
▲ EMP: 40
SQ FT: 6,000
SALES (est): 6.2MM
SALES (corp-wide): 4.7MM **Privately Held**
WEB: www.guildlines.com
SIC: 2759 Screen printing
PA: Zenan Custom Cresting Inc
430 Flint Rd
North York ON M3J 2
416 736-6652

(G-4864)
MOONLIGHT CREAMERY
36 West Ave (14450-2158)
PHONE..................585 223-0880
Hiedi Grenik, *Owner*
EMP: 6
SALES (est): 572.1K **Privately Held**
SIC: 2024 Ice cream & frozen desserts

(G-4865)
MURPHY MANUFACTURING CO INC
38 West Ave (14450-2159)
P.O. Box 119 (14450-0119)
PHONE..................585 223-0100
Fax: 585 223-0101
Gordon D Murphy Sr, *President*
Donna Faust, *Database Admin*
▲ EMP: 5 EST: 1946
SQ FT: 6,500
SALES (est): 360K **Privately Held**
WEB: www.murphymanufacturing.com
SIC: 3451 3491 Screw machine products; industrial valves

(G-4866)
ORACLE AMERICA INC
Sun Microsystems
345 Woodcliff Dr Ste 1 (14450-4210)
PHONE..................585 317-4648
Fax: 585 385-5078
Otis Harper, *Engineer*
Fritz Rupp, *Engineer*
Kevin Regan, *Manager*
Jeff Barteld, *Director*
EMP: 55
SALES (corp-wide): 37B **Publicly Held**
SIC: 3571 Minicomputers
HQ: Oracle America, Inc.
500 Oracle Pkwy
Redwood City CA 94065
650 506-7000

(G-4867)
PARKER-HANNIFIN CORPORATION
Also Called: Chomerics Div
83 Estates Dr W (14450-8425)
PHONE..................585 425-7000

Patrick Malone, *CEO*
Brian Smith, *QC Mgr*
EMP: 126
SALES (corp-wide): 11.3B **Publicly Held**
SIC: 3594 Fluid power pumps & motors
PA: Parker-Hannifin Corporation
6035 Parkland Blvd
Cleveland OH 44124
216 896-3000

(G-4868)
PARLEC INC (PA)
101 Perinton Pkwy (14450-9182)
PHONE..................585 425-4400
Fax: 585 425-7542
Michael R Nuccitelli, *CEO*
Mark Higgins, *Vice Pres*
Jay Nuccitelli, *Vice Pres*
Ronald S Ricotta, *Vice Pres*
Jeff Sweedler, *Vice Pres*
▲ EMP: 130
SQ FT: 100,000
SALES (est): 24MM **Privately Held**
WEB: www.parlec.com
SIC: 3541 3545 Numerically controlled metal cutting machine tools; machine tool accessories

(G-4869)
PENNSAUKEN PACKING COMPANY LLC
815 Whitney Rd W (14450-1030)
PHONE..................585 377-7700
EMP: 11
SALES (est): 350.2K
SALES (corp-wide): 271.6MM **Privately Held**
SIC: 3221 Food containers, glass
PA: Lidestri Foods, Inc.
815 Whitney Rd W
Fairport NY 14450
585 377-7700

(G-4870)
PERFORMANCE DESIGNED BY PETERS
Also Called: Poerformance Design
7 Duxbury Hts (14450-3331)
PHONE..................585 223-9062
Peter R Geib, *President*
Todd Geib, *Vice Pres*
EMP: 19
SALES: 5MM **Privately Held**
SIC: 3714 Motor vehicle parts & accessories

(G-4871)
PRINTER COMPONENTS INC (HQ)
100 Photikon Dr Ste 2 (14450-8430)
PHONE..................585 924-5190
Richard Dipasquale, *Vice Pres*
◆ EMP: 9
SQ FT: 16,000
SALES (est): 1.5MM
SALES (corp-wide): 93MM **Privately Held**
WEB: www.pcivictor.com
SIC: 3861 5112 3955 5999 Printing equipment, photographic; laserjet supplies; print cartridges for laser & other computer printers; photocopy machines; printers, computer
PA: Floturn, Inc.
4236 Thunderbird Ln
West Chester OH 45014
513 860-8040

(G-4872)
QUALITROL COMPANY LLC (HQ)
Also Called: Otiwti
1385 Fairport Rd (14450-1399)
PHONE..................586 643-3717
Fax: 585 377-0220
Ronald Meyer, *President*
John Piper, *President*
Jay Cunningham, *Vice Pres*
Brian English, *Vice Pres*
Bill Savino, *Buyer*
▲ EMP: 111
SQ FT: 50,000
SALES (est): 138.8MM
SALES (corp-wide): 5B **Publicly Held**
WEB: www.qualitrolcorp.com
SIC: 3825 Instruments for measuring electrical quantities

PA: Fortive Corporation
6920 Seaway Blvd
Everett WA 98203
425 446-5000

(G-4873)
QUALITROL FINANCE CORP
1385 Fairport Rd (14450-1399)
PHONE.....................................585 586-1515
Ronald Meyer, *President*
Karen Howe, *Controller*
EMP: 5
SALES (est): 357.9K
SALES (corp-wide): 20.5B **Publicly Held**
SIC: 3825 Instruments to measure electricity
PA: Danaher Corporation
2200 Penn Ave Nw Ste 800w
Washington DC 20037
202 828-0850

(G-4874)
QUALTECH TOOL & MACHINE INC
1000 Turk Hill Rd Ste 292 (14450-8755)
P.O. Box 356 (14450-0356)
PHONE.....................................585 223-9227
Fax: 585 223-4348
Anita Palmer, *President*
Richard T Palmer III, *Vice Pres*
EMP: 10
SQ FT: 10,500
SALES (est): 1.3MM **Privately Held**
SIC: 3599 Machine shop, jobbing & repair

(G-4875)
R STEINER TECHNOLOGIES INC
180 Perinton Pkwy (14450-9107)
PHONE.....................................585 425-5912
Rudolph Steiner, *CEO*
Andy Nolan, *President*
EMP: 20
SQ FT: 12,000
SALES: 1.5MM **Privately Held**
WEB: www.steinertechnologies.com
SIC: 3541 Machine tools, metal cutting type

(G-4876)
SELBY MARKETING ASSOCIATES INC (PA)
Also Called: Direct 2 Market Solutions
1387 Fairport Rd Ste 800 (14450-2002)
PHONE.....................................585 377-0750
Fax: 585 377-0763
Richard L Selby, *President*
Trina Selby, *Manager*
EMP: 15
SQ FT: 6,000
SALES: 3MM **Privately Held**
SIC: 2741 7319 Miscellaneous publishing; media buying service

(G-4877)
SENDEC CORP (DH)
Also Called: API Technologies
72 Perinton Pkwy (14450-9107)
PHONE.....................................585 425-3390
Fax: 585 425-3392
Kenton W Fiske, *President*
Jay Soper, *General Mgr*
Tom Tette, *CFO*
Mike Campoli, *Manager*
▲ EMP: 140
SQ FT: 86,000
SALES (est): 19.1MM
SALES (corp-wide): 232.2MM **Privately Held**
WEB: www.sendec.com
SIC: 3679 Electronic circuits
HQ: Api Technologies Corp.
400 Nickerson Rd
Marlborough MA 01752
855 294-3800

(G-4878)
SENECA TEC INC
73 Country Corner Ln (14450-3034)
PHONE.....................................585 381-2645
Fax: 585 381-6308
John Kidd, *President*
James Kidd, *Vice Pres*
Art Trimble, *Vice Pres*
EMP: 9
SQ FT: 1,500

SALES (est): 746.3K **Privately Held**
WEB: www.senecatec.com
SIC: 3861 3841 Photographic processing equipment & chemicals; surgical & medical instruments

(G-4879)
SIEMENS PRODUCT LIFE MGMT SFTW
345 Woodcliff Dr (14450-4210)
PHONE.....................................585 389-8699
EMP: 34
SALES (corp-wide): 83.5B **Privately Held**
SIC: 7372 Business oriented computer software
HQ: Siemens Product Lifecycle Management Software Inc.
5800 Granite Pkwy Ste 600
Plano TX 75024
972 987-3000

(G-4880)
STEINER TECHNOLOGIES INC
180 Perinton Pkwy (14450-9107)
PHONE.....................................585 425-5910
Fax: 585 425-5913
Andrew Nolan, *President*
Ryan Nolan, *Opers Mgr*
Tyler Nolan, *Marketing Staff*
EMP: 19 EST: 2008
SALES (est): 3.6MM **Privately Held**
SIC: 3545 Cutting tools for machine tools

(G-4881)
STREAMLINE PRECISION INC
205 Turk Hill Park (14450-8728)
PHONE.....................................585 421-9050
Kelly Palladino, *President*
Robert Levitsky, *Vice Pres*
Tom Gore, *Engineer*
EMP: 8
SQ FT: 1,000
SALES (est): 878.9K **Privately Held**
SIC: 3545 Precision tools, machinists'

(G-4882)
STREAMLINE PRECISION INC
Also Called: Steamline Machine
1000 Turk Hill Rd Ste 205 (14450-8755)
PHONE.....................................585 421-9050
Fax: 585 421-9198
Kelly Palladino, *President*
Robert Levitsky, *Vice Pres*
EMP: 6
SALES: 650K **Privately Held**
SIC: 3545 Machine tool accessories

(G-4883)
SUHOR INDUSTRIES INC (PA)
Also Called: Si Funeral Services
72 Oconnor Rd (14450-1328)
PHONE.....................................585 377-5100
Joe Suhor, *President*
▲ EMP: 14
SQ FT: 4,250
SALES (est): 2.2MM **Privately Held**
WEB: www.wilbertservices.com
SIC: 3272 Burial vaults, concrete or pre-cast terrazzo

(G-4884)
THALES LASER SA
78 Schuyler Baldwin Dr (14450-9100)
PHONE.....................................585 223-2370
Ariane Andreani, *General Mgr*
EMP: 65
SALES (est): 3.4MM **Privately Held**
SIC: 3674 Semiconductors & related devices

(G-4885)
VIDEK INC
1387 Fairport Rd 1000c (14450-2004)
PHONE.....................................585 377-0377
Thomas Slechta, *President*
Moreen Jorjensen, *Controller*
Chris Haidvogel, *Manager*
EMP: 25
SQ FT: 14,861
SALES (est): 5.5MM **Privately Held**
WEB: www.videk.com/
SIC: 3827 3829 Optical test & inspection equipment; measuring & controlling devices

(G-4886)
VOLT TEK INC
111 Parce Ave (14450-1467)
PHONE.....................................585 377-2050
Fax: 585 377-2654
Steve Holland, *President*
Mike Buczko, *Manager*
▲ EMP: 15
SALES (est): 1.4MM **Privately Held**
WEB: www.volttek.com
SIC: 3644 Insulators & insulation materials, electrical

(G-4887)
WORKPLACE INTERIORS LLC
400 Packetts Lndg (14450-1576)
PHONE.....................................585 425-7420
Liz Kiefer, *Opers Mgr*
Scott Maccaull, *Mng Member*
EMP: 13 EST: 2015
SQ FT: 6,000
SALES: 5MM **Privately Held**
SIC: 2522 5021 Office furniture, except wood; office furniture

(G-4888)
XEROX CORPORATION
1387 Fairport Rd Ste 200 (14450-2003)
PHONE.....................................585 425-6100
Fax: 585 383-7517
Tim Conlin, *Principal*
Chris Snyder, *Manager*
Delynn Boyd, *Info Tech Mgr*
Don Wegeng, *Associate*
EMP: 75
SQ FT: 1,485
SALES (corp-wide): 18B **Publicly Held**
WEB: www.xerox.com
SIC: 3861 Photographic equipment & supplies
PA: Xerox Corporation
45 Glover Ave Ste 700
Norwalk CT 06850
203 968-3000

Falconer
Chautauqua County

(G-4889)
AJ GENCO MCH SP MCHY RDOUT SVC
Also Called: A J Gnco Mch Shp/Mchnery Rdout
235 Carter St (14733-1409)
PHONE.....................................716 664-4925
Anthony J Genco, *President*
EMP: 10
SQ FT: 23,940
SALES: 610K **Privately Held**
SIC: 3599 7692 3444 Machine shop, jobbing & repair; welding repair; sheet metalwork

(G-4890)
ALCOA INC
2632 S Work St Ste 24 (14733-1705)
PHONE.....................................716 358-6451
Dave Groetsch, *Branch Mgr*
EMP: 11
SALES (corp-wide): 22.5B **Publicly Held**
SIC: 3542 High energy rate metal forming machines
PA: Alcoa Inc.
390 Park Ave Fl 12
New York NY 10022
212 836-2674

(G-4891)
ALLIED INSPECTION SERVICES LLC
2020 Allen Street Ext # 120 (14733-1706)
PHONE.....................................716 489-3199
Scott M Lynn, *Director*
EMP: 10
SALES (est): 1.5MM **Privately Held**
SIC: 3569 Sprinkler systems, fire: automatic

(G-4892)
BARTON TOOL INC
1864 Lyndon Blvd (14733-1735)
P.O. Box 17 (14733-0017)
PHONE.....................................716 665-2801

Fax: 716 665-4713
Jo Anne Barton, *President*
John Barton, *Vice Pres*
Joanne Barton, *Admin Sec*
EMP: 7
SQ FT: 20,000
SALES (est): 1.1MM **Privately Held**
WEB: www.bartontool.com
SIC: 3089 3599 Injection molding of plastics; machine shop, jobbing & repair

(G-4893)
CHAUTAUQUA SIGN CO INC
2164 Allen Street Ext (14733-1703)
PHONE.....................................716 665-2222
Gregory J Winter, *President*
EMP: 8
SALES (est): 796.2K **Privately Held**
WEB: www.chautauquasportshalloffame.org
SIC: 3993 Signs & advertising specialties

(G-4894)
CPI OF FALCONER INC
1890 Lyndon Blvd (14733-1731)
PHONE.....................................716 664-4444
EMP: 22
SQ FT: 20,000
SALES (est): 266.7K **Privately Held**
SIC: 3089 3965 Mfg Plastic Products Mfg Fasteners/Buttons/Pins

(G-4895)
ELLISON BRONZE INC
125 W Main St (14733-1698)
PHONE.....................................716 665-6522
Fax: 716 665-5552
Peter Stark, *Ch of Bd*
Mark Graves, *President*
Billy Emerson, *Vice Pres*
Roger Overend, *Vice Pres*
Kent Brown, *Plant Mgr*
◆ EMP: 59
SQ FT: 65,000
SALES (est): 12.7MM **Privately Held**
WEB: www.ellisonbronze.com
SIC: 3442 Metal doors, sash & trim

(G-4896)
EMC FINTECH
1984 Allen Street Ext (14733-1717)
PHONE.....................................716 488-9071
Eric Corey, *Vice Pres*
EMP: 11
SALES (est): 900K **Privately Held**
SIC: 3552 3585 Dyeing, drying & finishing machinery & equipment; air conditioning equipment, complete

(G-4897)
FALCON CHAIR AND TABLE INC
121 S Work St (14733-1433)
P.O. Box 8 (14733-0008)
PHONE.....................................716 664-7136
Fax: 716 664-3157
Peter Scheira, *President*
Gary Henry, *Vice Pres*
Sue Freeburg, *Bookkeeper*
Joan Erickson, *Admin Sec*
EMP: 49
SQ FT: 23,000
SALES (est): 4.7MM **Privately Held**
SIC: 2511 Dining room furniture: wood

(G-4898)
FALCONER ELECTRONICS INC (PA)
421 W Everett St (14733-1647)
PHONE.....................................716 665-4176
Fax: 716 665-2017
Roger E Hall, *President*
Janine Hall, *Vice Pres*
EMP: 68
SQ FT: 20,000
SALES (est): 11.8MM **Privately Held**
WEB: www.falconer-electronics.com
SIC: 3672 5065 Printed circuit boards; electronic parts

(G-4899)
FALCONER PRINTING & DESIGN INC
Also Called: Jamestown Envelope
66 E Main St (14733-1390)
P.O. Box 262 (14733-0262)
PHONE.....................................716 665-2121

Falconer - Chautauqua County (G-4900)

Fax: 716 665-6328
Stephen E Roach, *President*
James M Roach, *Vice Pres*
Karen Mazzu, *Bookkeeper*
Julie Norblund, *Product Mgr*
Misty Johnson, *Marketing Staff*
EMP: 17
SQ FT: 12,000
SALES: 2.1MM **Privately Held**
WEB: www.falconerprinting.com
SIC: 2752 7335 5112 2791 Commercial printing, lithographic; commercial printing, offset; photo-offset printing; photographic studio, commercial; office supplies; type-setting; commercial printing

(G-4900)
HANSON AGGREGATES EAST LLC
4419 S 9 Mile Rd (14733)
PHONE.................................716 372-1574
Mike Shumack, *Manager*
Robert Wilson, *Supervisor*
EMP: 17
SALES (corp-wide): 14.4B **Privately Held**
SIC: 3273 Ready-mixed concrete
HQ: Hanson Aggregates East Llc
3131 Rdu Center Dr
Morrisville NC 27560
919 380-2500

(G-4901)
HANSON SIGN & SCREEN PROCESS
Also Called: Hanson Sign Companies
82 Carter St (14733-1406)
PHONE.................................716 484-8564
Gene M Aversa, *President*
Shelly Cooper, *Business Mgr*
Brett Aversa, *Vice Pres*
Patricia Reynolds, *Purch Mgr*
EMP: 40 **EST:** 1949
SQ FT: 25,000
SALES (est): 5.5MM **Privately Held**
WEB: www.hansonsign.com
SIC: 3993 2759 Signs, not made in custom sign painting shops; screen printing

(G-4902)
INSCAPE (NEW YORK) INC (HQ)
Also Called: Inscape Archtectural Interiors
221 Lister Ave 1 (14733-1459)
PHONE.................................716 665-6210
Rod Turgeon, *CEO*
Craig Dunlop, *Ch of Bd*
Nic Balderi, *Vice Pres*
Gwen Keanary, *Safety Mgr*
Stephen Holland, *Purch Mgr*
▲ **EMP:** 82
SALES (est): 17.1MM
SALES (corp-wide): 54.2K **Privately Held**
SIC: 2542 3442 3441 3449 Partitions for floor attachment, prefabricated: except wood; metal doors; fabricated structural metal; custom roll formed products;
PA: Inscape Corporation
67 Toll Rd
Holland Landing ON L9N 1
905 836-7676

(G-4903)
JAMES TOWN MACADAM INC
1946 New York Ave (14733-1739)
PHONE.................................716 665-4504
Fax: 716 665-6040
Jim Ells, *Principal*
Mike Wellman, *Manager*
EMP: 56
SQ FT: 2,000
SALES (est): 5.2MM **Privately Held**
SIC: 3273 Ready-mixed concrete

(G-4904)
JAMESTOWN CONTAINER CORP (PA)
14 Deming Dr (14733-1697)
P.O. Box 8, Jamestown (14702-0008)
PHONE.................................716 665-4623
Fax: 716 665-2954
Bruce Janowsky, *Ch of Bd*
Larry Hudson, *General Mgr*
Dick Weimer, *Corp Secy*
Richards Emmerick, *Vice Pres*
Joseph R Palmeri, *Vice Pres*
▼ **EMP:** 90 **EST:** 1956
SQ FT: 100,000
SALES (est): 116MM **Privately Held**
WEB: www.jamestowncontainer.com
SIC: 2653 3086 Corrugated & solid fiber boxes; packaging & shipping materials, foamed plastic

(G-4905)
JAMESTOWN IRON WORKS INC
2022 Allen Street Ext (14733-1793)
PHONE.................................716 665-2818
Fax: 716 665-2851
David W Maher, *President*
Michelle Maher, *Manager*
EMP: 16 **EST:** 1881
SQ FT: 3,600
SALES (est): 4.3MM **Privately Held**
SIC: 3321 3599 Ductile iron castings; machine shop, jobbing & repair

(G-4906)
JAMESTOWN MVP LLC
Also Called: Mvp Plastics
2061 Allen Street Ext (14733-1710)
PHONE.................................716 846-1418
Danielle Huber, *Marketing Staff*
Moshe Rosenvosser,
Amanda Eyring, *Admin Asst*
Jacob Deutsch,
EMP: 3
SALES (est): 1MM **Privately Held**
SIC: 3089 Plastic processing

(G-4907)
MONOFRAX LLC
1870 New York Ave (14733-1797)
PHONE.................................716 483-7200
Bill Andrews, *President*
Darin Fidurko, *Engineer*
Rowland Crosby, *Executive*
◆ **EMP:** 250
SQ FT: 300,000
SALES (est): 60.6MM **Privately Held**
WEB: www.monofrax.com
SIC: 3297 Nonclay refractories
PA: Callista Holdings Gmbh & Co. Kg
Steinstr. 48
Munchen
892 070-4243

(G-4908)
RAND MACHINE PRODUCTS INC (PA)
2072 Allen Street Ext (14733-1709)
P.O. Box 72 (14733-0072)
PHONE.................................716 665-5217
Fax: 716 665-3374
Herman C Ruhlman Jr, *President*
Chad Ruhlman, *Exec VP*
Jason Ruhlman, *Vice Pres*
Carl Hornstrom, *Plant Mgr*
Tim Lyon, *Purch Mgr*
EMP: 51 **EST:** 1964
SQ FT: 15,000
SALES (est): 29.6MM **Privately Held**
WEB: www.randmachine.com
SIC: 3544 3494 3743 3599 Special dies, tools, jigs & fixtures; special dies & tools; valves & pipe fittings; industrial locomotives & parts; custom machinery

(G-4909)
RAPID REMOVAL LLC
1599 Route 394 (14733-9716)
P.O. Box 498 (14733-0498)
PHONE.................................716 665-4663
Brian Hasson,
EMP: 10
SALES (est): 385K **Privately Held**
SIC: 2851 Removers & cleaners

(G-4910)
REYNOLDS PACKAGING MCHY INC
Also Called: Csi
2632 S Work St Ste 24 (14733-1705)
PHONE.................................716 358-6451
Fax: 716 358-6459
Rochard Kelson, *Exec VP*
Valeria Muka, *Purch Mgr*
Joe Schrecengost, *Purch Mgr*
Angela Hymen, *Engineer*
Pat Depas, *Design Engr*
EMP: 55 **Privately Held**
SIC: 3565 3643 3466 Canning machinery, food; current-carrying wiring devices; crowns & closures
HQ: Reynolds Packaging Machinery Inc.
2632 S Work St Ste 24
Falconer NY 14733
716 358-6451

(G-4911)
RHI US LTD (DH)
1870 New York Ave (14733-1740)
PHONE.................................716 483-7200
Phil Poulin, *President*
Hans Joerg Junger, *Vice Pres*
Friedrich Schweighofer, *Vice Pres*
Erica Soller, *Admin Sec*
◆ **EMP:** 20
SALES (est): 6.2MM
SALES (corp-wide): 1.8B **Privately Held**
SIC: 3823 Refractometers, industrial process type

(G-4912)
SKF USA INC
Also Called: SKF Aeroengine North America
1 Maroco St (14733-9705)
P.O. Box 263 (14733-0263)
PHONE.................................716 661-2869
Steve Koehler, *Branch Mgr*
EMP: 61
SALES (corp-wide): 8.7B **Privately Held**
WEB: www.skfusa.com
SIC: 3562 3769 Ball bearings & parts; guided missile & space vehicle parts & auxiliary equipment
HQ: Skf Usa Inc.
890 Forty Foot Rd
Lansdale PA 19446
267 436-6000

(G-4913)
SKF USA INC
1 Maroco St (14733-9705)
PHONE.................................716 661-2600
Pierre Chagnon, *Branch Mgr*
EMP: 61
SALES (corp-wide): 8.7B **Privately Held**
SIC: 3562 Ball bearings & parts
HQ: Skf Usa Inc.
890 Forty Foot Rd
Lansdale PA 19446
267 436-6000

(G-4914)
STUART MOLD & MANUFACTURING
560 N Work St (14733-1115)
PHONE.................................716 488-9765
Fax: 716 488-9767
Randall Stuart, *President*
Charles Stuart, *Vice Pres*
Mike Malinoski, *Opers Mgr*
Tina Himes, *Office Mgr*
EMP: 12
SQ FT: 10,000
SALES (est): 1.3MM **Privately Held**
WEB: www.stumold.com
SIC: 3089 Injection molding of plastics

(G-4915)
STUART TOOL & DIE INC
600 N Work St (14733-1117)
P.O. Box 152 (14733-0152)
PHONE.................................716 488-1975
Fax: 716 488-1977
Randy Stuart, *President*
Patrick J Degnan, *Owner*
Ronald Rothleder, *Owner*
Eric Kilbourn, *Design Engr*
EMP: 34
SQ FT: 10,000
SALES: 9.1MM **Privately Held**
WEB: www.stu-t-d.com
SIC: 3544 Industrial molds

(G-4916)
TRUCK-LITE CO LLC
2640 1st Ave (14733-1727)
PHONE.................................716 661-1235
EMP: 55 **Privately Held**
SIC: 3647 3648 Vehicular lighting equipment; lighting equipment
PA: Truck-Lite Co., Llc
310 E Elmwood Ave
Falconer NY 14733

(G-4917)
TRUCK-LITE CO LLC
310 E Elmwood Ave (14733-1421)
PHONE.................................716 665-2614
Chris Richardson, *Regional Mgr*
Greg Pond, *Materials Mgr*
Cindy Franklin, *Hum Res Coord*
Greg Certo, *Manager*
Brian Melquist, *MIS Mgr*
EMP: 20 **Privately Held**
WEB: www.truck-lite.com
SIC: 3647 3648 Vehicular lighting equipment; lighting equipment
PA: Truck-Lite Co., Llc
310 E Elmwood Ave
Falconer NY 14733

(G-4918)
TRUCK-LITE CO LLC (PA)
310 E Elmwood Ave (14733-1421)
PHONE.................................716 665-6214
Fax: 716 665-4825
Brian Kupchella, *President*
Jeff Church, *COO*
Chris Ross, *Project Engr*
Robert Reed, *Manager*
Donald Alexander, *CIO*
◆ **EMP:** 273
SALES: 500MM **Privately Held**
SIC: 3647 Vehicular lighting equipment

Far Rockaway
Queens County

(G-4919)
BUSINESS ADVISORY SERVICES
Also Called: Universal Water Technology
1104 Bay 25th St (11691-1749)
PHONE.................................718 337-3740
Michael Walfish, *President*
EMP: 5
SALES: 750K **Privately Held**
SIC: 3589 Water treatment equipment, industrial

(G-4920)
EAZY LOCKS LLC
1914 Mott Ave (11691-4102)
PHONE.................................718 327-7770
Carl Roberts, *CEO*
EMP: 6
SQ FT: 1,000
SALES: 304.2K **Privately Held**
SIC: 3429 Locks or lock sets

(G-4921)
EMPIRE PUBLISHING INC
Also Called: West End Journal
1525 Central Ave Ste 1 (11691-4020)
PHONE.................................516 829-4000
Fax: 516 829-4776
Jerome Lippman, *President*
EMP: 15
SQ FT: 2,000
SALES (est): 870.4K **Privately Held**
SIC: 2711 Newspapers: publishing only, not printed on site

(G-4922)
FAR ROCKAWAY DRUGS INC
Also Called: Ocean Park Drugs & Surgical
1727 Seagirt Blvd (11691-4513)
PHONE.................................718 471-2500
Fax: 718 471-0840
Russell Shvartsshteyn, *President*
Steven Blick, *Vice Pres*
EMP: 16
SQ FT: 4,000
SALES (est): 2.9MM **Privately Held**
WEB: www.mynucare.com
SIC: 3842 5912 Surgical appliances & supplies; drug stores & proprietary stores

(G-4923)
J P R PHARMACY INC
Also Called: Vista Pharmacy & Surgical
529 Beach 20th St (11691-3645)
PHONE.................................718 327-0600
Fax: 718 327-8019
Jeffrey Rosenberg, *President*
Russell Shvartsshteyn, *Vice Pres*
EMP: 11
SQ FT: 800

▲ = Import ▼ = Export
◆ = Import/Export

GEOGRAPHIC SECTION

Farmingdale - Nassau County (G-4949)

SALES: 4.6MM **Privately Held**
SIC: **3842** 5912 Surgical appliances & supplies; drug stores & proprietary stores

(G-4924)
ROCKAWAY STAIRS LTD
1011 Bay 24th St (11691-1801)
PHONE..................718 945-0047
Nollah Pastor, *President*
EMP: 5
SALES (est): 304.3K **Privately Held**
SIC: **2431** Stair railings, wood

Farmingdale
Nassau County

(G-4925)
A & J MACHINE & WELDING INC
6040 New Hwy (11735)
PHONE..................631 845-7586
Ahalya Narine, *Manager*
EMP: 15
SALES (corp-wide): 536.3K **Privately Held**
SIC: **7692** Welding repair
PA: A & J Machine & Welding Inc.
8776 130th St
Jamaica NY
718 815-5757

(G-4926)
A C ENVELOPE INC
51 Heisser Ln Ste B (11735-3321)
PHONE..................516 420-0646
Bob Kuhlmann, *President*
William Bogue, *Corp Secy*
EMP: 5
SALES: 500K **Privately Held**
SIC: **3555** 5112 2759 2752 Presses, envelope, printing; envelopes; commercial printing; commercial printing, lithographic

(G-4927)
A R V PRECISION MFG INC
60 Baiting Place Rd Ste B (11735-6228)
PHONE..................631 293-9643
Fax: 631 293-9166
Fred Freyre, *President*
EMP: 5
SQ FT: 2,000
SALES (est): 480K **Privately Held**
SIC: **3679** 3599 3089 Electronic circuits; machine shop, jobbing & repair; injection molded finished plastic products

(G-4928)
AAA CATALYTIC RECYCLING INC
345 Eastern Pkwy (11735-2713)
PHONE..................631 920-7944
Drew Vecchionem, *CEO*
▲ EMP: 10 EST: 2011
SALES: 10MM **Privately Held**
SIC: **3339** Platinum group metal refining (primary)

(G-4929)
ABBE LABORATORIES INC
1095 Broadhollow Rd Ste E (11735-4815)
PHONE..................631 756-2223
Eleanor Posner, *President*
Robert Posner, *Corp Secy*
Denise Rogan, *Admin Asst*
EMP: 10
SALES (est): 1.8MM **Privately Held**
WEB: www.abbelabs.com
SIC: **2844** 5122 Cosmetic preparations; cosmetics

(G-4930)
ADVANCED AEROSPACE MACHINING
154 Rome St (11735-6609)
PHONE..................631 694-7745
Bruce Hambrecht, *President*
EMP: 6
SQ FT: 4,000
SALES (est): 655.9K **Privately Held**
SIC: **3599** Custom machinery

(G-4931)
AFCO SYSTEMS INC
Also Called: Afco Modular Enclosure Systems
200 Finn Ct Ste 1 (11735-1119)
PHONE..................631 424-3935
Fax: 516 249-9450
Vincent Mallia, *Ch of Bd*
Michael Mallia, *President*
Gerard Becker, *President*
Joji Joseph, *COO*
Lawrence Mallia, *Exec VP*
EMP: 102
SQ FT: 65,000
SALES (est): 19.2MM **Privately Held**
WEB: www.afcosystems.com
SIC: **2522** 3469 3444 Panel systems & partitions, office: except wood; metal stampings; sheet metalwork
PA: Ultimate Precision Metal Products Inc.
200 Finn Ct
Farmingdale NY 11735
631 249-9441

(G-4932)
AIRFLEX CORP
965 Conklin St (11735-2412)
PHONE..................631 752-1219
Jonathan Fogelman, *President*
Lorraine Mazzella, *Manager*
EMP: 89
SQ FT: 10,000
SALES (est): 14.6MM **Privately Held**
SIC: **3441** Fabricated structural metal

(G-4933)
AIRFLEX INDUSTRIAL INC (PA)
965 Conklin St (11735-2412)
PHONE..................631 752-1234
Jonathan Fogelman, *Ch of Bd*
Lorraine Mazzella, *Manager*
EMP: 42
SQ FT: 10,000
SALES (est): 15.6MM **Privately Held**
WEB: www.airflexind.com
SIC: **3446** 3822 3365 Louvers, ventilating; damper operators: pneumatic, thermostatic, electric; aluminum & aluminum-based alloy castings

(G-4934)
AIRFLEX INDUSTRIAL INC
937 Conklin St (11735-2412)
PHONE..................631 752-1234
Jonathan Fogelman, *Branch Mgr*
EMP: 58
SALES (corp-wide): 15.6MM **Privately Held**
SIC: **3446** Louvers, ventilating
PA: Airflex Industrial, Inc.
965 Conklin St
Farmingdale NY 11735
631 752-1234

(G-4935)
ALA SCIENTIFIC INSTRUMENTS INC
60 Marine St Ste 1 (11735-5660)
PHONE..................631 393-6401
Alan Kriegstein, *President*
Andrew Pomerantz, *Vice Pres*
Christena Lopez, *Manager*
Irene Pomerantz, *Manager*
EMP: 13
SQ FT: 6,000
SALES: 2.5MM **Privately Held**
WEB: www.alascience.com
SIC: **3841** 5047 Surgical & medical instruments; medical equipment & supplies

(G-4936)
ALL COLOR OFFSET PRINTERS INC
Also Called: All Color Business Specialties
51 Henry St Ste A (11735-4111)
PHONE..................516 420-0649
Fax: 631 753-2506
William Bogue, *President*
Tim Dorman, *Vice Pres*
Donald Romano, *Vice Pres*
Louis Divito, *Sales Executive*
Paul Currao, *Manager*
EMP: 5
SQ FT: 2,500
SALES (est): 912.2K **Privately Held**
SIC: **2752** Commercial printing, offset

(G-4937)
ALLOY METAL WORKS INC
146 Verdi St (11735-6324)
PHONE..................631 694-8163
Fax: 516 293-1134
Phillip Rajotte Jr, *President*
EMP: 5
SQ FT: 2,500
SALES: 250K **Privately Held**
SIC: **7692** Welding repair

(G-4938)
ALPHA MANUFACTURING CORP
152 Verdi St (11735-6324)
PHONE..................631 249-3700
Fax: 516 249-3705
George Sparacio, *President*
EMP: 10
SQ FT: 6,000
SALES: 1MM **Privately Held**
SIC: **3599** Machine shop, jobbing & repair

(G-4939)
AMANA TOOL CORP
Also Called: Age Timberline Mamba
120 Carolyn Blvd (11735-1525)
PHONE..................631 752-1300
Fax: 631 752-1674
Eitan Spiegel, *CEO*
Aaron Einstein, *Chairman*
John P McInerney, *Vice Pres*
Zygmunt L Miewski, *Vice Pres*
Zygmunt L Milewski, *Vice Pres*
◆ EMP: 52
SQ FT: 80,000
SALES (est): 10.3MM **Privately Held**
WEB: www.amanatool.com
SIC: **3425** Saw blades & handsaws

(G-4940)
AMERICAN AEROSPACE CONTRLS INC
Also Called: A A C
570 Smith St (11735-1115)
PHONE..................631 694-5100
Fax: 516 694-6739
Ruth Gitlin, *CEO*
Philip Koch, *Opers Mgr*
Cindy Legendre, *Purchasing*
Celeste Morrissey, *QC Mgr*
Peter Pacholski, *Engineer*
EMP: 47
SQ FT: 16,000
SALES (est): 10.2MM **Privately Held**
WEB: www.a-a-c.com
SIC: **3679** Transducers, electrical

(G-4941)
AMERICAN VISUALS INC
Also Called: American Visual Display
90 Gazza Blvd (11735-1402)
PHONE..................631 694-6104
Morris Charnow, *President*
EMP: 7
SQ FT: 8,200
SALES (est): 825.6K **Privately Held**
WEB: www.americanvisuals.com
SIC: **3993** 3089 Displays & cutouts, window & lobby; plastic processing

(G-4942)
ANDREA SYSTEMS LLC
140 Finn Ct (11735-1107)
PHONE..................631 390-3140
Tony Macri, *Engineer*
Luis Rivera, *Electrical Engi*
Robert J Carton, *Sales Mgr*
Frank Randazzo, *Mng Member*
Robert Carton, *Manager*
EMP: 23
SQ FT: 15,000
SALES (est): 4.5MM **Privately Held**
WEB: www.andreasystems.com
SIC: **3669** Intercommunication systems, electric

(G-4943)
APEX PACKING & RUBBER CO INC
1855 New Hwy Ste D (11735-1557)
PHONE..................631 420-8150
Fax: 631 756-9639
Ralph Oppenheim, *President*
EMP: 13 EST: 1940
SQ FT: 8,000

SALES (est): 2.1MM **Privately Held**
WEB: www.apexgaskets.com
SIC: **3053** Gaskets & sealing devices

(G-4944)
APSIS USA INC
1855 New Hwy Ste B (11735-1557)
PHONE..................631 421-6800
Jersey Wu, *President*
Terry Wu, *Vice Pres*
EMP: 15
SQ FT: 5,000
SALES: 4MM **Privately Held**
WEB: www.apsisusa.com
SIC: **3714** 7532 Motor vehicle parts & accessories; motor vehicle body components & frame; customizing services, non-factory basis

(G-4945)
ARBE MACHINERY INC
54 Allen Blvd (11735-5623)
PHONE..................631 756-2477
Fax: 516 756-2485
Artin Karakaya, *President*
Burc Karakaya, *Vice Pres*
◆ EMP: 10
SQ FT: 30,000
SALES (est): 1.3MM **Privately Held**
SIC: **3559** 5084 3599 Jewelers' machines; industrial machinery & equipment; machine shop, jobbing & repair

(G-4946)
ATI MODEL PRODUCTS INC (PA)
Also Called: Model Power
180 Smith St (11735-1023)
PHONE..................631 694-7022
Fax: 516 694-7133
Michael Tager, *Ch of Bd*
Matthew Tager, *President*
Joshua Tager, *Vice Pres*
Ida Yonenson, *Treasurer*
William Larkin, *Manager*
▲ EMP: 45
SQ FT: 44,000
SALES (est): 3.2MM **Privately Held**
SIC: **3944** Trains & equipment, toy: electric & mechanical

(G-4947)
AUSCO INC
425 Smith St Ste 1 (11735-1124)
PHONE..................516 944-9882
Fax: 516 944-8522
Kenneth Bram, *Ch of Bd*
Jackie Gregus, *General Mgr*
Marguerite Fenech, *Vice Pres*
Thai Tong, *Vice Pres*
Glenn Davis, *Mfg Mgr*
EMP: 100
SQ FT: 11,000
SALES (est): 25.8MM **Privately Held**
WEB: www.auscoinc.com
SIC: **3728** Aircraft parts & equipment

(G-4948)
AUTEL US INC (HQ)
Also Called: Autel North America
175 Central Ave Ste 200 (11735-6917)
PHONE..................631 923-2620
Arthur Jacobsen, *CEO*
▲ EMP: 5
SQ FT: 20,000
SALES (est): 1.8MM **Privately Held**
SIC: **3694** Automotive electrical equipment
PA: Autel Intelligent Technology Corp., Ltd.
6-10f,Block B1, Zhiyuan,Xueyuan Ave., Xili, Nanshan Dist.
Shenzhen
755 226-7227

(G-4949)
AVANTI FURNITURE CORP
497 Main St (11735-3579)
PHONE..................516 293-8220
Fax: 631 293-9335
Joan Bagnasco, *President*
Kevin Bagnasco, *Treasurer*
▲ EMP: 12
SQ FT: 10,000
SALES (est): 1.6MM **Privately Held**
SIC: **2512** Chairs: upholstered on wood frames

Farmingdale - Nassau County (G-4950) GEOGRAPHIC SECTION

(G-4950)
B & R ELECTRIC MOTOR INC
5919 Central Ave (11735)
PHONE...................................631 752-7533
Ellen M McQuade, *President*
Roy A Mack, *Vice Pres*
EMP: 5
SQ FT: 3,000
SALES (est): 602.5K **Privately Held**
SIC: 7694 7629 Electric motor repair; electrical equipment repair services

(G-4951)
BDR CREATIVE CONCEPTS INC
141 Central Ave Ste B (11735-6903)
PHONE...................................516 942-7768
Fax: 516 938-7302
Ronald Cohen, *President*
Pearl Cohen, *Vice Pres*
Judie Seaton, *Office Mgr*
Bruce Beckerman, *Shareholder*
Debra Beckerman, *Shareholder*
EMP: 14
SQ FT: 7,000
SALES (est): 1.4MM **Privately Held**
WEB: www.bdrcc.com
SIC: 2759 Poster & decal printing & engraving; posters, including billboards; printing

(G-4952)
BESCOR VIDEO ACCESSORIES LTD
244 Route 109 (11735-1503)
PHONE...................................631 420-1717
Fax: 516 420-0106
Douglas Brandwin, *President*
David Issacs, *Sales Mgr*
▲ **EMP:** 16
SQ FT: 8,000
SALES (est): 3.1MM **Privately Held**
SIC: 3861 5065 5043 Cameras & related equipment; video equipment, electronic; photographic cameras, projectors, equipment & supplies

(G-4953)
BEVERAGE WORKS NJ INC
16 Dubon Ct (11735-1008)
PHONE...................................631 293-3501
Fax: 631 293-3505
Jeffrey Brown, *VP Opers*
Iies Hantman, *Manager*
EMP: 20
SALES (corp-wide): 46.4MM **Privately Held**
WEB: www.beverageworks.com
SIC: 2086 Bottled & canned soft drinks
PA: The Beverage Works Nj Inc
1800 State Route 34 # 203
Wall Township NJ 07719
732 938-7600

(G-4954)
C & C BINDERY CO INC
Also Called: C&C Diecuts
25 Central Ave Unit B (11735-6920)
PHONE...................................631 752-7078
Joe Spalone, *President*
Mitch Holsborg, *Vice Pres*
EMP: 30
SQ FT: 11,000
SALES (est): 4.1MM **Privately Held**
SIC: 2789 Bookbinding & related work

(G-4955)
C A M GRAPHICS CO INC
24 Central Dr (11735-1202)
PHONE...................................631 842-3400
Emanuel Cardinale, *President*
Jorge Reyes, *Vice Pres*
Jose Vargas, *Mfg Mgr*
Elizabeth Heiser, *Admin Sec*
EMP: 27
SQ FT: 20,000
SALES (est): 4.6MM **Privately Held**
WEB: www.camgraphics.com
SIC: 3672 3679 3643 3613 Printed circuit boards; electronic switches; current-carrying wiring devices; switchgear & switchboard apparatus

(G-4956)
CAM TOUCHVIEW PRODUCTS INC
24 Central Dr (11735-1202)
P.O. Box 1980, Sag Harbor (11963-0067)
PHONE...................................631 842-3400
Emanuel Cardinale, *President*
EMP: 15 **EST:** 2013
SQ FT: 4,000
SALES (est): 1.3MM **Privately Held**
SIC: 3674 Semiconductors & related devices

(G-4957)
CEMTREX INC (PA)
19 Engineers Ln (11735-1207)
PHONE...................................631 756-9116
Fax: 631 845-0541
Saagar Govil, *Ch of Bd*
Ravi Narayan, *Vice Pres*
Renato Dela Rama, *CFO*
Ronald Monte, *Marketing Staff*
EMP: 37
SQ FT: 4,000
SALES (est): 56.8MM **Publicly Held**
SIC: 3823 7389 Industrial instrmnts msrmnt display/control process variable; controllers for process variables, all types; air pollution measuring service

(G-4958)
CHIM-CAP CORP
120 Schmitt Blvd (11735-1424)
PHONE...................................631 454-7576
Fax: 631 454-7535
Fred Giumenta Jr, *President*
EMP: 20
SQ FT: 40,000
SALES (est): 3.5MM **Privately Held**
WEB: www.chimcapcorp.com
SIC: 3272 Fireplace & chimney material: concrete; chimney caps, concrete

(G-4959)
CIGAR OASIS INC
79 Heisser Ct (11735-3310)
PHONE...................................516 520-5258
Albert P Foundos, *President*
Christine Beno, *Vice Pres*
Donna Oswald, *Vice Pres*
Philip Foundos, *Treasurer*
▲ **EMP:** 7
SQ FT: 2,000
SALES (est): 510K **Privately Held**
SIC: 3911 Cigar & cigarette accessories

(G-4960)
COLONIAL PRECISION MACHINERY
Also Called: Colonial Electric
134 Rome St (11735-6607)
PHONE...................................631 249-0738
James Tormey, *President*
Scott Tormey, *Vice Pres*
EMP: 7
SQ FT: 15,000
SALES (est): 650K **Privately Held**
SIC: 3469 Machine parts, stamped or pressed metal

(G-4961)
COMMERCE SPRING CORP
143 Allen Blvd (11735-5616)
PHONE...................................631 293-4844
Fax: 516 293-4859
Bruno Rotellini, *President*
Janet Halleran, *Office Mgr*
EMP: 12
SQ FT: 10,000
SALES (est): 1.2MM **Privately Held**
WEB: www.commercespring.com
SIC: 3495 Wire springs

(G-4962)
COSMO ELECTRONIC MACHINE CORP
Also Called: D & L Electronic Die
113 Gazza Blvd (11735-1421)
PHONE...................................631 249-2535
Fax: 631 694-2349
Kenneth Arutt, *President*
Bruce Mc Kee, *Vice Pres*
Vladimir Lipkin, *Manager*
EMP: 50
SQ FT: 3,000
SALES (est): 4.5MM **Privately Held**
SIC: 3544 Special dies, tools, jigs & fixtures

(G-4963)
COSMOS ELECTRONIC MACHINE CORP (PA)
140 Schmitt Blvd (11735-1461)
PHONE...................................631 249-2535
Kenneth Arutt, *President*
Bruce McKee, *Vice Pres*
Wayne Nelson, *Purch Mgr*
Paul Abriola, *Sales Mgr*
Linda Allen, *Chief Mktg Ofcr*
EMP: 43
SQ FT: 20,000
SALES (est): 7.9MM **Privately Held**
SIC: 3567 Industrial furnaces & ovens

(G-4964)
CPW DIRECT MAIL GROUP LLC
110 Schmitt Blvd (11735-1424)
P.O. Box 216, Bohemia (11716-0216)
PHONE...................................631 588-6565
Fax: 631 588-6502
John Plate, *Mng Member*
Loraine Chaudhry Ekinci, *Mng Member*
Mark Krevitski, *Mng Member*
Todd Meties, *Mng Member*
Dave Swanson, *Mng Member*
EMP: 28
SQ FT: 42,000
SALES (est): 2.9MM **Privately Held**
SIC: 2759 2677 3577 Laser printing; envelopes: printing; envelopes; bar code (magnetic ink) printers

(G-4965)
CRISRAY PRINTING CORP
50 Executive Blvd Ste A (11735-4712)
PHONE...................................631 293-3770
Fax: 631 249-1954
Raymond J Marro, *President*
Anthony Conti, *Vice Pres*
Patricia Marro, *Vice Pres*
Cris Ray, *Accounts Mgr*
Terry Brown, *Manager*
EMP: 30 **EST:** 1971
SQ FT: 10,000
SALES (est): 4.7MM **Privately Held**
WEB: www.crisray.com
SIC: 2759 Labels & seals: printing

(G-4966)
CRYSTAL FUSION TECH INC
25 Dubon Ct (11735-1016)
PHONE...................................631 253-9800
Ray Doran, *President*
Gary Locicero, *Manager*
EMP: 17
SALES (est): 2.9MM **Privately Held**
SIC: 2899 Water treating compounds

(G-4967)
CURTISS-WRIGHT CONTROLS
Also Called: Curtiss-Wrght Intgrted Sensing
175 Central Ave Ste 100 (11735-6917)
P.O. Box 7751, Philadelphia PA (19101-7751)
PHONE...................................631 756-4740
Thomas P Quinly, *COO*
Christopher Kelly, *Engineer*
Dora Pinones, *Manager*
EMP: 7
SALES (corp-wide): 2.2B **Publicly Held**
SIC: 3674 Semiconductors & related devices
HQ: Curtiss-Wright Controls Integrated Sensing, Inc.
1150 N Fiesta Blvd # 101
Gilbert AZ 85233
626 851-3100

(G-4968)
CURTISS-WRIGHT FLOW CTRL CORP (HQ)
Also Called: Target Rock
1966 Broadhollow Rd Ste E (11735-1726)
PHONE...................................631 293-3800
Fax: 516 293-6144
Martin Benante, *Ch of Bd*
David Linton, *President*
David C Adams, *COO*
Joseph Callaghan, *Vice Pres*
Greg Hempfling, *Vice Pres*
◆ **EMP:** 236 **EST:** 1950
SQ FT: 100,000
SALES (est): 445.7MM
SALES (corp-wide): 2.2B **Publicly Held**
SIC: 3491 3494 Industrial valves; valves & pipe fittings
PA: Curtiss-Wright Corporation
13925 Balntyn Corp Pl
Charlotte NC 28277
704 869-4600

(G-4969)
CURTISS-WRIGHT FLOW CTRL CORP
1966 Broadhollow Rd Ste E (11735-1726)
P.O. Box 379 (11735-0379)
PHONE...................................631 293-3800
Richard Langseder, *Vice Pres*
William Hughes, *Purch Dir*
Bill Hughes, *Purch Agent*
Pedro Estrada, *QA Dir*
John Debonis, *QC Mgr*
EMP: 160
SALES (corp-wide): 2.2B **Publicly Held**
SIC: 3491 Industrial valves
HQ: Curtiss-Wright Flow Control Corporation
1966 Broadhollow Rd Ste E
Farmingdale NY 11735
631 293-3800

(G-4970)
CUSTOM DOOR & MIRROR INC
Also Called: Flex Supply
148 Milbar Blvd (11735-1425)
PHONE...................................631 414-7725
Angelo Sciubba, *Ch of Bd*
Philip Sciubba, *Vice Pres*
Vincent Barbagallo, *Project Mgr*
▲ **EMP:** 20 **EST:** 1996
SQ FT: 17,000
SALES: 3MM **Privately Held**
WEB: www.paniflex.com
SIC: 3089 2431 Doors, folding: plastic or plastic coated fabric; millwork

(G-4971)
CUSTOM SITECOM LLC
Also Called: Buckle Down
470 Smith St (11735-1105)
PHONE...................................631 420-4238
Eric Swope, *COO*
Jason Dorf,
▲ **EMP:** 11
SALES (est): 2.1MM **Privately Held**
SIC: 3714 Motor vehicle parts & accessories

(G-4972)
DADDARIO & COMPANY INC (PA)
595 Smith St (11735-1120)
P.O. Box 290 (11735-0290)
PHONE...................................631 439-3300
Fax: 631 439-3336
James D'Addario, *Ch of Bd*
Rick Drumm, *President*
John D'Addario III, *Exec VP*
John D'Addario Jr, *Vice Pres*
David Via, *Vice Pres*
◆ **EMP:** 700
SQ FT: 110,000
SALES (est): 220.3MM **Privately Held**
WEB: www.daddario.com
SIC: 3931 String instruments & parts; strings, musical instrument

(G-4973)
DAKOTA SYSTEMS MFG CORP
Also Called: Dakota Wall
1885 New Hwy Ste 2 (11735-1518)
PHONE...................................631 249-5811
Fax: 631 249-5819
Edward Owsinski, *President*
Jimmy Eowinski, *Bookkeeper*
EMP: 6
SQ FT: 3,000
SALES: 1.3MM **Privately Held**
SIC: 2542 3312 Partitions & fixtures, except wood; stainless steel

(G-4974)
DANBURY PHARMA LLC
220 Smith St (11735-1024)
PHONE...................................631 393-6333
Lou Ferreira, *Manager*
Carmen Martinez, *Manager*

▲ = Import ▼ = Export ◆ = Import/Export

GEOGRAPHIC SECTION

BJ Harid,
▲ **EMP:** 33 **EST:** 2008
SQ FT: 19,000
SALES (est): 9.7MM **Privately Held**
SIC: 2834 Vitamin preparations

(G-4975)
DESIGN PRINTING CORP
101 Verdi St Ste 3 (11735-6344)
PHONE..................631 753-9801
Fax: 516 753-9803
Gunther Roth, *President*
EMP: 8
SALES (est): 680K **Privately Held**
WEB: www.designprintingcorp.com
SIC: 2752 2759 2789 Commercial printing, offset; letterpress printing; binding & repair of books, magazines & pamphlets

(G-4976)
DESKTOP PUBLISHING CONCEPTS
Also Called: Toledo Graphics Group
855 Conklin St Ste T (11735-2409)
P.O. Box 34 (11735-0034)
PHONE..................631 752-1934
Fax: 631 752-1423
Nicholas Sachs, *President*
Jennifer Plattman, *Graphic Designe*
EMP: 12
SQ FT: 2,500
SALES (est): 1.4MM **Privately Held**
WEB: www.toledogroup.com
SIC: 2791 7336 Typesetting; graphic arts & related design

(G-4977)
DIGICOM INTERNATIONAL INC
155 Rome St (11735-6610)
PHONE..................631 249-8999
Fax: 631 249-5536
Chia I Chen, *CEO*
Linn Grieshaber, *Controller*
Jammy Chen, *Executive*
▲ **EMP:** 15
SQ FT: 20,000
SALES (est): 3MM **Privately Held**
SIC: 3571 5045 Electronic computers; computer peripheral equipment

(G-4978)
DIGITAL MATRIX CORP
34 Sarah Dr Ste B (11735-1218)
PHONE..................516 481-7990
Fax: 516 481-7320
Alex Greenspan, *President*
Freeman Peng, *Managing Prtnr*
Jan Berman, *Vice Pres*
Alexsandr Davelman, *Engineer*
Boris Lopantnikov, *Engineer*
EMP: 21
SQ FT: 20,000
SALES (est): 3.7MM **Privately Held**
WEB: www.galvanics.com
SIC: 3559 Electroplating machinery & equipment

(G-4979)
DUCON TECHNOLOGIES INC
19 Engineers Ln (11735-1207)
PHONE..................631 420-4900
Aron Govil, *Branch Mgr*
EMP: 45
SALES (corp-wide): 479.4MM **Privately Held**
SIC: 3564 3537 Blowers & fans; industrial trucks & tractors
PA: Ducon Technologies Inc.
5 Penn Plz Ste 2403
New York NY 10001
631 694-1700

(G-4980)
DURO DYNE CORPORATION (HQ)
130 Broadhollow Rd (11735-4828)
P.O. Box 9117, Bay Shore (11706-9117)
PHONE..................631 249-9000
Fax: 631 249-8346
Randall Hinden, *President*
Joe Auriemmo, *Purchasing*
Paul Thompson, *VP Sales*
Alyssa Irish, *Network Analyst*
Stephen Trant, *Admin Asst*
◆ **EMP:** 150 **EST:** 1952
SQ FT: 130,000
SALES (est): 33.2MM
SALES (corp-wide): 120.9MM **Privately Held**
SIC: 3585 Air conditioning equipment, complete; heating equipment, complete
PA: Dyne Duro National Corp
81 Spence St
Bay Shore NY 11706
631 249-9000

(G-4981)
E B INDUSTRIES LLC (PA)
90 Carolyn Blvd (11735-1525)
PHONE..................631 293-8565
Fax: 631 752-7866
Thaddeus Woskowiak, *Technology*
Steven M Delalio,
Jerry Bianco,
EMP: 25 **EST:** 1965
SQ FT: 16,000
SALES (est): 3.3MM **Privately Held**
WEB: www.ebindustries.com
SIC: 3599 Machine shop, jobbing & repair

(G-4982)
E B INDUSTRIES LLC
90 Carolyn Blvd (11735-1525)
PHONE..................631 293-8565
Steven Delalio, *Mng Member*
EMP: 25
SALES (est): 440.7K
SALES (corp-wide): 3.3MM **Privately Held**
WEB: www.ebindustries.com
SIC: 7692 Welding repair
PA: E B Industries, Llc
90 Carolyn Blvd
Farmingdale NY 11735
631 293-8565

(G-4983)
EAST COAST CYCLE LLC
80 Smith St Ste 1 (11735-1011)
PHONE..................631 780-5360
Joshua Kohn, *Manager*
Jeffrey Bruno,
▲ **EMP:** 9
SQ FT: 2,500
SALES (est): 900K **Privately Held**
SIC: 3751 5091 Bicycles & related parts; bicycles

(G-4984)
EAST COAST ENVMTL GROUP INC
136 Allen Blvd (11735-5659)
PHONE..................516 352-1946
Edwin Rincon, *President*
Jennifer Mosquera, *Manager*
EMP: 5
SQ FT: 15,000
SALES: 1MM **Privately Held**
SIC: 3826 Differential thermal analysis instruments

(G-4985)
EDLAW PHARMACEUTICALS INC
195 Central Ave Ste B (11735-6904)
PHONE..................631 454-6888
Fax: 516 454-4846
Scott Giroux, *General Mgr*
Bonnie Hilton Green, *Principal*
▼ **EMP:** 20
SQ FT: 6,500
SALES (est): 3.8MM **Privately Held**
SIC: 2834 Pharmaceutical preparations

(G-4986)
EEG ENTERPRISES INC
586 Main St (11735-3546)
PHONE..................516 293-7472
Fax: 516 293-7417
Philip McLaughlin, *President*
William Jorden, *Vice Pres*
Frank Zovko, *Design Engr*
Eric McErlain, *Sales Dir*
Jerlin Boccio, *Manager*
EMP: 12
SQ FT: 5,000
SALES (est): 1.4MM **Privately Held**
WEB: www.eegent.com
SIC: 3663 Cable television equipment; television antennas (transmitting) & ground equipment

(G-4987)
ELLIOT GANTZ & COMPANY INC
115 Schmitt Blvd (11735-1403)
P.O. Box 756, Commack (11725-0756)
PHONE..................631 249-0680
Elliot Gantz, *President*
Barbara Yacker, *Controller*
Elliot Guntz, *Personnel Exec*
Rachel Allgood, *CTO*
EMP: 40
SQ FT: 20,000
SALES (est): 4.2MM **Privately Held**
WEB: www.elliotgantz.com
SIC: 3299 Architectural sculptures: gypsum, clay, papier mache, etc.

(G-4988)
ENZO LIFE SCIENCES INC (HQ)
Also Called: Enzo Diagnostics
10 Executive Blvd (11735-4710)
PHONE..................631 694-7070
Fax: 516 694-7501
Elazar Rabbani, *Ch of Bd*
Norman Kelker, *General Mgr*
Jennifer Norman, *Business Mgr*
Barry W Weiner, *Exec VP*
Herbert Bass, *Vice Pres*
EMP: 30
SQ FT: 40,000
SALES (est): 14.8MM
SALES (corp-wide): 102.7MM **Publicly Held**
SIC: 2835 2834 5049 In vitro & in vivo diagnostic substances; pharmaceutical preparations; laboratory equipment, except medical or dental
PA: Enzo Biochem, Inc.
527 Madison Ave Rm 901
New York NY 10022
212 583-0100

(G-4989)
ENZO LIFE SCIENCES INTL INC
10 Executive Blvd (11735-4710)
PHONE..................610 941-0430
Robert Zipkin, *President*
Ira Taffer, *Vice Pres*
Debbie Dejzak, *Credit Mgr*
Debbie Lilley, *Accountant*
◆ **EMP:** 28
SQ FT: 20,000
SALES (est): 3.4MM
SALES (corp-wide): 102.7MM **Publicly Held**
WEB: www.biomol.com
SIC: 2834 Pharmaceutical preparations
HQ: Enzo Life Sciences, Inc.
10 Executive Blvd
Farmingdale NY 11735
631 694-7070

(G-4990)
EVANS MANUFACTURING LLC
595 Smith St (11735-1116)
P.O. Box 290 (11735-0290)
PHONE..................631 439-3300
James D'Addario,
John D'Addario Jr,
Robert Dodaro,
Michael Russo,
Domenick Scarfogliero,
▲ **EMP:** 75 **EST:** 1995
SQ FT: 110,000
SALES (est): 6MM **Privately Held**
WEB: www.dadario.com
SIC: 3931 Musical instruments; heads, drum

(G-4991)
FARMINGDALE IRON WORKS INC
105 Florida St (11735-6305)
PHONE..................631 249-5995
John Cardullo, *President*
Vita Cardullo, *Corp Secy*
EMP: 6 **EST:** 1959
SQ FT: 4,500
SALES: 642.4K **Privately Held**
SIC: 3441 Fabricated structural metal

(G-4992)
FERRARO MANUFACTURING COMPANY
150 Central Ave (11735-6900)
PHONE..................631 752-1509
Fax: 631 752-2233
Joseph Ferraro, *President*
Sharon Allocco, *Admin Sec*
EMP: 6
SALES (est): 800.9K **Privately Held**
WEB: www.ferrarofirm.com
SIC: 3599 Machine shop, jobbing & repair

(G-4993)
FIBER FOOT APPLIANCES INC
34 Sarah Dr Ste A (11735-1218)
PHONE..................631 465-9199
Jeffrey Fiber, *President*
Allan Fiber, *Treasurer*
Helene Fiber, *Admin Sec*
EMP: 13
SQ FT: 6,500
SALES (est): 1MM **Privately Held**
SIC: 3842 Foot appliances, orthopedic

(G-4994)
FRUITCROWN PRODUCTS CORP (PA)
250 Adams Blvd (11735-6615)
PHONE..................631 694-5800
Fax: 516 694-6467
Robert E Jagenburg, *President*
Bruce Jagenburg, *Vice Pres*
Frank Poma, *VP Opers*
Nick Mendola, *Warehouse Mgr*
Peter Pace, *Purchasing*
▼ **EMP:** 45
SQ FT: 40,000
SALES (est): 23.2MM **Privately Held**
WEB: www.fruitcrown.com
SIC: 2033 Fruits: packaged in cans, jars, etc.

(G-4995)
FUN INDUSTRIES OF NY
111 Milbar Blvd (11735-1426)
PHONE..................631 845-3805
Bryan Spodek, *Principal*
EMP: 13
SALES (est): 1.4MM **Privately Held**
SIC: 3999 Manufacturing industries

(G-4996)
GANTZ-NEWMAN LLC
115 Schmitt Blvd (11735-1403)
PHONE..................631 249-0680
Tara G Newman, *CEO*
Elliott Gantz,
John Newman,
EMP: 10
SQ FT: 1,500
SALES (est): 968.7K **Privately Held**
WEB: www.gantznewman.com
SIC: 3089 Plastic processing; injection molded finished plastic products

(G-4997)
GAVIN MFG CORP
25 Central Ave Unit A (11735-6920)
PHONE..................631 467-0040
Christopher Gavin, *President*
Brian Gavin, *Vice Pres*
Michael Gavin, *Vice Pres*
Ryan Gavin, *Vice Pres*
EMP: 45 **EST:** 1953
SQ FT: 15,000
SALES (est): 7.7MM **Privately Held**
WEB: www.gavinmfgcorp.com
SIC: 2679 2653 2657 Paper products, converted; paperboard products, converted; corrugated & solid fiber boxes; folding paperboard boxes

(G-4998)
GILD-RITE INC
51 Carolyn Blvd (11735-1527)
PHONE..................631 752-9000
Howard Schneider, *President*
Morris D Schneider, *Chairman*
Roert Schneider, *Vice Pres*
Sylvia K Zang, *Treasurer*
EMP: 5
SQ FT: 7,000
SALES: 250K
SALES (corp-wide): 15.1MM **Privately Held**
SIC: 2789 Gilding books, cards or paper
PA: Leather Craftsmen, Inc.
160a Marine St
Farmingdale NY 11735
631 752-9000

Farmingdale - Nassau County (G-4999)

(G-4999)
GLISSADE NEW YORK LLC
399 Smith St (11735-1106)
PHONE..................................631 756-4800
Jed Leadman,
▲ EMP: 25
SQ FT: 30,000
SALES (est): 2.5MM Privately Held
WEB: www.glissade.com
SIC: 2434 2514 Wood kitchen cabinets; vanities, bathroom: wood; medicine cabinets & vanities: metal

(G-5000)
GMS DRUM CO INC
330 Conklin St (11735-2609)
PHONE..................................516 586-8820
Fax: 631 293-4246
Anthony Gallino, *President*
Robert Mazzella, *Vice Pres*
▲ EMP: 6
SQ FT: 3,000
SALES (est): 480K Privately Held
SIC: 3931 Drums, parts & accessories (musical instruments)

(G-5001)
GOLDMARK PRODUCTS INC
855 Conklin St Ste D (11735-2409)
PHONE..................................631 777-3343
Stanley Dabrowski, *President*
Matthew Paliwoda, *Treasurer*
EMP: 30
SQ FT: 5,000
SALES (est): 3.2MM Privately Held
SIC: 3911 3339 Jewelry, precious metal; primary nonferrous metals

(G-5002)
GREENMAKER INDUSTRIES LLC
885 Conklin St (11735-2400)
PHONE..................................866 684-7800
Bruce Respler, *Principal*
Aj Rego, *Buyer*
▲ EMP: 11 EST: 2005
SALES (est): 2MM Privately Held
SIC: 2841 2842 Soap & other detergents; rug, upholstery, or dry cleaning detergents or spotters; sanitation preparations, disinfectants & deodorants; degreasing solvent; window cleaning preparations

(G-5003)
GUSTBUSTER LTD
Also Called: Sunbuster
855 Conklin St Ste O (11735-2409)
PHONE..................................631 391-9000
Steven Asman, *President*
Cathy Hamel, *Manager*
▲ EMP: 8
SQ FT: 17,000
SALES: 2MM Privately Held
WEB: www.gustbuster.com
SIC: 3999 Umbrellas, canes & parts

(G-5004)
HADES MANUFACTURING CORP
135 Florida St (11735-6307)
PHONE..................................631 249-4244
Fax: 516 249-1618
Eugene L Brand, *President*
Ken Norris, *Vice Pres*
EMP: 10 EST: 1966
SQ FT: 3,000
SALES (est): 1.9MM Privately Held
WEB: www.hadesmfgcorp.com
SIC: 3823 5084 Industrial instrmnts msrmnt display/control process variable; temperature instruments: industrial process type; industrial machinery & equipment

(G-5005)
HAHNS OLD FASHIONED CAKE CO
75 Allen Blvd (11735-5614)
PHONE..................................631 249-3456
Fax: 516 492-3492
Regina C Hahn, *President*
Andrew M Hahn, *Corp Secy*
EMP: 12
SQ FT: 4,550
SALES: 1MM Privately Held
WEB: www.crumbcake.net
SIC: 2051 5149 Cakes, bakery: except frozen; bakery products

(G-5006)
HIRSCH OPTICAL CORP
91 Carolyn Blvd (11735-1409)
PHONE..................................516 752-2211
Fax: 516 752-0104
Harold M Rothstein, *President*
Fernando Buitrago, *Exec VP*
Kenneth Mitel, *Vice Pres*
Michael Weinstein, *Vice Pres*
Joanne Rosalia, *Comptroller*
EMP: 60 EST: 1978
SQ FT: 12,000
SALES (est): 6.8MM Privately Held
WEB: www.hirschoptical.com
SIC: 3851 Eyeglasses, lenses & frames

(G-5007)
HORNE PRODUCTS INC
144 Verdi St (11735-6324)
PHONE..................................631 293-0773
John Hind, *President*
Joanne Incalcatera, *Corp Secy*
Patricia A O'Neill, *Vice Pres*
EMP: 6
SQ FT: 2,200
SALES (est): 630K Privately Held
WEB: www.horneproducts.com
SIC: 3743 5088 Railroad equipment; railroad equipment & supplies

(G-5008)
HURON TL & CUTTER GRINDING CO
2045 Wellwood Ave (11735-1212)
PHONE..................................631 420-7000
Fax: 631 420-7007
James Cosenza, *President*
Richard Cosenza, *Vice Pres*
Robert Gooch, *Manager*
Blanche Silbert, *Admin Sec*
EMP: 30 EST: 1955
SQ FT: 25,000
SALES: 4MM Privately Held
WEB: www.hurontool.com
SIC: 3545 3841 3842 3568 Tools & accessories for machine tools; knives, surgical; surgical appliances & supplies; power transmission equipment; hand & edge tools

(G-5009)
I J WHITE CORPORATION
20 Executive Blvd (11735-4710)
PHONE..................................631 293-3788
Fax: 516 293-3788
Peter J White, *Ch of Bd*
Niv Eldor, *COO*
Andy Cohn, *Vice Pres*
Roy Berntsen, *Plant Mgr*
Joyce Bridges, *Controller*
▼ EMP: 70 EST: 1919
SQ FT: 42,500
SALES (est): 23.1MM Privately Held
WEB: www.ijwhite.com
SIC: 3556 3535 Food products machinery; conveyors & conveying equipment

(G-5010)
IMPRESSIVE IMPRINTS INC
195 Central Ave Ste N (11735-6904)
PHONE..................................631 293-6161
Howard Lang, *President*
EMP: 5
SQ FT: 3,000
SALES (est): 506.4K Privately Held
SIC: 3993 Signs & advertising specialties

(G-5011)
INNOVATIVE AUTOMATION INC
595 Smith St (11735-1116)
P.O. Box 290 (11735-0290)
PHONE..................................631 439-3300
Fax: 631 391-5410
James D'Addario, *President*
Michael Russo, *Exec VP*
John D'Addario Jr, *Vice Pres*
EMP: 12
SQ FT: 25,000
SALES (est): 1.6MM Privately Held
WEB: www.innovativeautomation.net
SIC: 3545 Machine tool attachments & accessories

(G-5012)
INSTANT VERTICALS INC
330 Broadhollow Rd (11735-4807)
PHONE..................................631 501-0001
Fax: 631 501-0952
Michael Moran, *President*
John Joy, *Vice Pres*
EMP: 10
SALES (est): 1.2MM Privately Held
WEB: www.instantverticals.com
SIC: 2591 1799 Window blinds; window treatment installation

(G-5013)
J M HALEY CORP
151 Toledo St Ste 1 (11735-6640)
PHONE..................................631 845-5200
Fax: 516 334-8382
John Ackerson, *President*
Jerry Iavarone, *CFO*
Julia Giangrasso, *HR Admin*
Terri Carson, *Office Mgr*
Daniel Pagliarulo, *Assistant*
EMP: 60
SQ FT: 5,000
SALES (est): 13.8MM Privately Held
WEB: www.jmhaleycorp.com
SIC: 3441 Fabricated structural metal

(G-5014)
J P MACHINE PRODUCTS INC
144 Rome St (11735-6609)
PHONE..................................631 249-9229
Fax: 631 249-1619
Joseph Piliero, *President*
Yoland Coulaz, *Principal*
Frank Piliero, *Treasurer*
EMP: 11
SQ FT: 7,600
SALES: 500K Privately Held
SIC: 3469 Machine parts, stamped or pressed metal

(G-5015)
J P PRINTING INC (PA)
Also Called: Minuteman Press
331 Main St (11735-3508)
PHONE..................................516 293-6110
Fax: 516 293-7692
Jeff Miller, *President*
Susan Miller, *Vice Pres*
EMP: 5
SQ FT: 1,200
SALES: 385K Privately Held
SIC: 2752 5943 Commercial printing, lithographic; office forms & supplies

(G-5016)
JAMES WOERNER INC
130 Allen Blvd (11735-5617)
PHONE..................................631 454-9330
James Woerner, *President*
Barbara Woerner, *Vice Pres*
EMP: 6 EST: 1972
SQ FT: 7,000
SALES (est): 790K Privately Held
SIC: 3498 3441 7538 Fabricated pipe & fittings; fabricated structural metal; general automotive repair shops

(G-5017)
JANED ENTERPRISES
48 Allen Blvd Unit B (11735-5642)
PHONE..................................631 694-4494
Joseph Pileri, *CEO*
Claudia Montuori, *President*
EMP: 15
SQ FT: 14,000
SALES (est): 2.8MM Privately Held
WEB: www.janed.net
SIC: 3449 Miscellaneous metalwork

(G-5018)
JOE P INDUSTRIES INC
Also Called: Carrmet Industries
6 Commerce Dr (11735-1206)
PHONE..................................631 293-7889
Fax: 516 293-2160
Joseph Parente, *President*
Maryann Young, *Bookkeeper*
EMP: 17
SQ FT: 3,500
SALES: 1MM Privately Held
SIC: 3444 Sheet metalwork; metal housings, enclosures, casings & other containers

(G-5019)
JUNK IN MY TRUNK INC
266 Route 109 (11735-1503)
PHONE..................................631 420-5865
Tomasz Myszke, *Principal*
EMP: 5
SALES (est): 611.7K Privately Held
SIC: 3161 Trunks

(G-5020)
JUSTIN GREGORY INC
6 Banfi Plz W (11735-1532)
PHONE..................................631 249-5187
Justin Gregory, *CEO*
Renee Levin, *President*
EMP: 6
SALES (est): 505.6K Privately Held
SIC: 3111 Accessory products, leather

(G-5021)
K SIDRANE INC
24 Baiting Place Rd (11735-6227)
PHONE..................................631 393-6974
Fax: 516 378-3580
Michael Liff, *General Mgr*
Neil Sidrane, *Chairman*
Andrew Hersh, *Accounts Mgr*
▲ EMP: 45 EST: 1948
SQ FT: 10,000
SALES (est): 12.6MM Privately Held
SIC: 2679 2671 2672 Tags & labels, paper; packaging paper & plastics film, coated & laminated; coated & laminated paper; adhesive papers, labels or tapes: from purchased material

(G-5022)
KABAR MANUFACTURING CORP (HQ)
140 Schmitt Blvd (11735-1461)
PHONE..................................631 694-6857
Fax: 516 694-6846
Bruce Mc Kee, *President*
Richard Czach, *Vice Pres*
Ken Arutt, *Treasurer*
Paul Abriola, *Sales Mgr*
Sarah Squillace, *Admin Asst*
▲ EMP: 31 EST: 1945
SQ FT: 12,000
SALES (est): 6.8MM
SALES (corp-wide): 8.3MM Privately Held
WEB: www.cosmos-kabar.com
SIC: 3565 3559 Packaging machinery; plastics working machinery
PA: Cosmos Electronic Machine Corp.
140 Schmitt Blvd
Farmingdale NY 11735
631 249-2535

(G-5023)
KABAR MANUFACTURING CORP
113 Gazza Blvd (11735-1421)
PHONE..................................631 694-1036
Bruce Mc Kee, *President*
EMP: 30
SALES (corp-wide): 7.9MM Privately Held
WEB: www.cosmos-kabar.com
SIC: 3559 Plastics working machinery
HQ: Kabar Manufacturing Corp.
140 Schmitt Blvd
Farmingdale NY 11735
631 694-6857

(G-5024)
KAZAC INC
Also Called: Corzane Cabinets
55 Allen Blvd Ste C (11735-5643)
PHONE..................................631 249-7299
Fax: 631 249-1454
EMP: 5
SQ FT: 4,200
SALES: 450K Privately Held
SIC: 2511 2521 Mfg Wood Household Furniture Mfg Wood Office Furniture

GEOGRAPHIC SECTION
Farmingdale - Nassau County (G-5049)

(G-5025)
KEDCO INC
Also Called: Kedco Wine Storage Systems
564 Smith St (11735-1115)
PHONE...................................516 454-7800
Fax: 631 454-4876
Helene Windt, *President*
David Windt, *Corp Secy*
Ken Windt, *Vice Pres*
EMP: 12 **EST:** 1970
SQ FT: 20,000
SALES (est): 1.2MM **Privately Held**
SIC: 3585 2599 3556 Refrigeration & heating equipment; bar, restaurant & cafeteria furniture; beverage machinery

(G-5026)
KELLY WINDOW SYSTEMS INC
460 Smith St (11735-1105)
PHONE...................................631 420-8500
Fax: 516 420-8628
Carl J Giugliano, *President*
Frank Giugliano, *Vice Pres*
Pat Giugliano, *Vice Pres*
EMP: 32
SQ FT: 20,000
SALES (est): 4.6MM **Privately Held**
WEB: www.kellywindows.com
SIC: 2431 3442 Windows, wood; metal doors, sash & trim

(G-5027)
KEM MEDICAL PRODUCTS CORP (PA)
400 Broadhollow Rd Ste 2 (11735-4824)
PHONE...................................631 454-6565
Fax: 631 454-8083
Douglas A Kruger, *President*
Joseph Ebenstein, *Vice Pres*
EMP: 3
SQ FT: 2,500
SALES (est): 1.5MM **Privately Held**
WEB: www.kemmed.com
SIC: 3842 3829 Personal safety equipment; measuring & controlling devices

(G-5028)
KINEMOTIVE CORPORATION
222 Central Ave Ste 1 (11735-6958)
PHONE...................................631 249-6440
Fax: 516 249-6482
Arthur Szeglin, *Ch of Bd*
William Niedzwiecki, *President*
Charles Szeglin, *Principal*
Chuck Szeglin, *Principal*
Engin Oge, *Vice Pres*
EMP: 48 **EST:** 1959
SQ FT: 20,000
SALES (est): 11.7MM **Privately Held**
WEB: www.kinemotive.com
SIC: 3492 3452 3599 3568 Fluid power valves & hose fittings; screws, metal; bellows, industrial: metal; couplings, shaft: rigid, flexible, universal joint, etc.; pivots, power transmission; precision springs; pressure transducers

(G-5029)
KROGER PACKAGING INC
215 Central Ave Ste M (11735-6905)
PHONE...................................631 249-6690
Fax: 631 249-8492
Alfred Knapp, *President*
Joseph Deangelo, *CFO*
Terri Brennan, *Bookkeeper*
EMP: 33
SQ FT: 15,000
SALES: 8MM **Privately Held**
WEB: www.krogerpackaging.com
SIC: 2759 Labels & seals: printing

(G-5030)
L AND S PACKING CO
Also Called: Paesana
101 Central Ave (11735-6915)
P.O. Box 709 (11735-0709)
PHONE...................................631 845-1717
Fax: 631 420-7309
Louis J Scaramelli III, *Ch of Bd*
Louis Scarmelli IV, *President*
Stan Staszewski, *General Mgr*
Jacqueline Massaro, *Exec VP*
Lorraine Scaramelli, *Exec VP*
▲ **EMP:** 72 **EST:** 1946
SQ FT: 73,000
SALES (est): 18.2MM **Privately Held**
WEB: www.paesana.com
SIC: 2033 2035 Olives: packaged in cans, jars, etc.; vegetables: packaged in cans, jars, etc.; maraschino cherries: packaged in cans, jars, etc.; spaghetti & other pasta sauce: packaged in cans, jars, etc.; pickles, sauces & salad dressings

(G-5031)
L P R PRECISION PARTS & TLS CO
108 Rome St Ste 1 (11735-6637)
PHONE...................................631 293-7334
Tarquin Rattotti Jr, *President*
Tarquin Rattotti Sr, *Principal*
Lucy Rattotti, *Corp Secy*
Clarke Mizuk, *Foreman/Supr*
EMP: 10
SQ FT: 5,000
SALES (est): 2.2MM **Privately Held**
WEB: www.lprprecision.com
SIC: 3599 Machine shop, jobbing & repair

(G-5032)
LA MAR LIGHTING CO INC
485 Smith St (11735-1106)
P.O. Box 9013 (11735-9013)
PHONE...................................631 777-7700
Fax: 516 777-7705
Jeffrey Goldstein, *CEO*
Barry Kugel, *Ch of Bd*
Bill Phillips, *Vice Pres*
Keith Briggs, *Purch Mgr*
Don Dimino, *Engineer*
▲ **EMP:** 65 **EST:** 1957
SQ FT: 40,000
SALES (est): 15.5MM **Privately Held**
WEB: www.lamarlighting.com
SIC: 3646 3648 3641 2542 Fluorescent lighting fixtures, commercial; lighting equipment; electric lamps; partitions & fixtures, except wood

(G-5033)
LADY BURD EXCLUSIVE COSMT INC (PA)
Also Called: Lady Burd Private Label Cosmt
44 Executive Blvd Ste 1 (11735-4706)
PHONE...................................631 454-0444
Fax: 631 454-0445
Roberta Burd, *Chairman*
Allan Burd, *Vice Pres*
Christina Burd, *Vice Pres*
Lawrence Burd, *Vice Pres*
Tina Burd, *Vice Pres*
▲ **EMP:** 109
SQ FT: 40,000
SALES (est): 20MM **Privately Held**
WEB: www.ladyburd.com
SIC: 2844 Cosmetic preparations

(G-5034)
LEATHER CRAFTSMEN INC (PA)
160a Marine St (11735-5608)
PHONE...................................631 752-9000
Fax: 516 752-9220
Howard Schneider, *President*
Joseph Fiore, *Vice Pres*
Dan Hammel, *Director*
Robert Schneider, *Admin Sec*
EMP: 70
SQ FT: 18,000
SALES (est): 15.1MM **Privately Held**
WEB: www.leathercraftsmen.com
SIC: 2782 Albums

(G-5035)
LEVON GRAPHICS CORP
210 Route 109 (11735-1503)
P.O. Box 9073 (11735-9073)
PHONE...................................631 753-2022
Donna A Dickran, *Ch of Bd*
Harry L Dickran, *President*
Mario Devita, *Director*
Debbie Kubler, *Admin Asst*
Elizabeth Meisser, *Admin Asst*
EMP: 80
SQ FT: 42,000
SALES (est): 18MM **Privately Held**
WEB: www.levongraphics.com
SIC: 2752 2759 Commercial printing, offset; commercial printing

(G-5036)
LOGOMAX INC
242 Route 109 Ste B (11735-1500)
PHONE...................................631 420-0484
Victor Rouse, *President*
EMP: 4 **EST:** 1998
SALES (est): 1.1MM **Privately Held**
WEB: www.logomaxusa.com
SIC: 2759 Screen printing

(G-5037)
LOS OLIVOS LTD
105 Bi County Blvd (11735-3919)
PHONE...................................631 773-6439
Ester Alvarado, *Principal*
EMP: 12
SALES (est): 2.2MM **Privately Held**
SIC: 3556 Smokers, food processing equipment

(G-5038)
M C PACKAGING CORPORATION (PA)
200 Adams Blvd (11735-6615)
P.O. Box 1031, Melville (11747-0031)
PHONE...................................631 414-7840
Fax: 631 694-6135
Robert M Silverberg, *Ch of Bd*
Marc Silverberg, *President*
Jennifer Penney, *Accounts Mgr*
Kerstein Carter, *Manager*
▲ **EMP:** 21
SQ FT: 9,000
SALES (est): 23.2MM **Privately Held**
WEB: www.mcpkg.com
SIC: 2679 Cardboard products, except die-cut

(G-5039)
MACHINIT INC
400 Smith St (11735-1105)
PHONE...................................631 454-9297
Tony Kusturic, *Ch of Bd*
Tony Kustics, *Controller*
EMP: 4
SALES (est): 1.2MM **Privately Held**
SIC: 2339 2253 Women's & misses' outerwear; sweaters & sweater coats, knit

(G-5040)
MAN PRODUCTS INC
99 Milbar Blvd Unit 1 (11735-1407)
PHONE...................................631 789-6500
Fax: 631 789-1313
Attilio Mancusi, *President*
Corrain Bar, *General Mgr*
EMP: 30
SALES (est): 5.3MM **Privately Held**
WEB: www.manproducts.com
SIC: 3448 Prefabricated metal buildings

(G-5041)
MARKEN LLP
123 Smith St (11735-1004)
PHONE...................................631 396-7454
Steve Roese, *Partner*
Steve Menzies, *CFO*
Joseph Perricone, *Manager*
James Schaitel, *Manager*
EMP: 6
SQ FT: 10,000 **Privately Held**
SIC: 2834 4731 Tablets, pharmaceutical; freight forwarding
HQ: Marken Llp
 4307 Emperor Blvd Ste 210
 Durham NC 27703
 919 472-0403

(G-5042)
MAROTTA DENTAL STUDIO INC
130 Finn Ct (11735-1107)
PHONE...................................631 249-7520
Fax: 631 249-2343
Leonard Marotta, *President*
Steven Pigliacelli, *Vice Pres*
Justin Hayes, *Opers Mgr*
Chris Marotta, *Treasurer*
Joshua Marotta, *Manager*
EMP: 40
SQ FT: 15,000
SALES (est): 7.4MM **Privately Held**
WEB: www.marottadental.com
SIC: 3843 8021 8072 Dental materials; offices & clinics of dentists; dental laboratories

(G-5043)
MART-TEX ATHLETICS INC
180 Allen Blvd (11735-5617)
PHONE...................................631 454-9583
Fax: 516 454-1604
Richard Marte, *President*
Raymond Marte Jr, *Corp Secy*
EMP: 35
SQ FT: 15,000
SALES (est): 3.9MM **Privately Held**
WEB: www.mart-tex.com
SIC: 2396 Screen printing on fabric articles

(G-5044)
MASTER MOLDING INC
97 Gazza Blvd (11735-1401)
PHONE...................................631 694-1444
Fax: 631 694-6230
Peter Innvar, *President*
Kristen Reinke, *Office Mgr*
Ronald Valino, *Supervisor*
EMP: 15
SQ FT: 11,000
SALES (est): 2.2MM **Privately Held**
SIC: 3089 Injection molding of plastics

(G-5045)
MAXUS PHARMACEUTICALS INC
Also Called: Island Vitamin
50 Executive Blvd Ste B (11735-4712)
PHONE...................................631 249-0003
Bob Kathuria, *President*
Survir Salaria, *Vice Pres*
EMP: 12
SALES: 1MM **Privately Held**
SIC: 2834 Pharmaceutical preparations

(G-5046)
MAZZA CLASSICS INCORPORATED
117 Gazza Blvd (11735-1415)
PHONE...................................631 390-9060
Jim Rivera, *President*
Esther Rivera, *Office Mgr*
EMP: 7
SQ FT: 5,000
SALES: 500K **Privately Held**
SIC: 2512 Upholstered household furniture

(G-5047)
MEMORY PROTECTION DEVICES INC
200 Broadhollow Rd Ste 4 (11735-4814)
PHONE...................................631 293-5891
Fax: 631 249-0002
Thomas Blaha, *President*
Charles Engelstein, *Chairman*
Daniel Lynch, *Vice Pres*
Dan Lynch, *Info Tech Mgr*
Letitia Dicicco, *Admin Asst*
EMP: 10
SQ FT: 3,000
SALES: 7MM **Privately Held**
WEB: www.memoryprotectiondevices.com
SIC: 3089 Battery cases, plastic or plastic combination

(G-5048)
MERB LLC
Also Called: BELGIAN BOYS USA
140 Carolyn Blvd (11735-1525)
PHONE...................................631 393-3621
Michael Berro, *President*
Ricardo Dellajiovanna, *Vice Pres*
EMP: 5 **EST:** 2013
SQ FT: 2,000
SALES (est): 14MM **Privately Held**
SIC: 2099 Food preparations

(G-5049)
METADURE DEFENSE & SEC LLC
165 Gazza Blvd (11735-1415)
PHONE...................................631 249-2141
Gary Templeton, *President*
Nickos Chatzis, *Vice Pres*
George Strouzakis, *Vice Pres*
EMP: 12
SALES (est): 870K **Privately Held**
SIC: 3448 9711 Prefabricated metal buildings; national security

Farmingdale - Nassau County (G-5050)

(G-5050)
METADURE PARTS & SALES INC
Also Called: Sbcontract.com
165 Gazza Blvd (11735-1415)
PHONE..................................631 249-2141
Gary Templeton, *Ch of Bd*
Mike Foster, *QA Dir*
Cristine Tesimone, *Manager*
EMP: 12
SQ FT: 10,000
SALES: 2MM **Privately Held**
SIC: 3728 Military aircraft equipment & armament

(G-5051)
METROPLTAN DATA SLTONS MGT INC
279 Conklin St (11735-2608)
P.O. Box 11394, Newark NJ (07101-4394)
PHONE..................................516 586-5520
John Dankowitz, *President*
Patricia Dankowitz, *Administration*
EMP: 11
SQ FT: 1,500
SALES (est): 2MM **Privately Held**
SIC: 3089 Identification cards, plastic

(G-5052)
MICROWAVE CIRCUIT TECH INC
45 Central Dr (11735-1201)
PHONE..................................631 845-1041
Brit Andresen, *CEO*
Edward Frankoski, *President*
Leif Andresen, *Vice Pres*
Elsie Andresen, *CFO*
Kariann Hunter, *Director*
EMP: 30
SQ FT: 5,700
SALES (est): 5.5MM **Privately Held**
WEB: www.mct-rf.com
SIC: 3679 Microwave components

(G-5053)
MID ISLAND DIE CUTTING CORP
77 Schmitt Blvd (11735-1403)
PHONE..................................631 293-0180
Robert Geier, *President*
Ruth Geier, *Admin Sec*
EMP: 200
SQ FT: 12,000
SALES (est): 33.8MM **Privately Held**
SIC: 2675 Die-cut paper & board

(G-5054)
MID ISLAND GROUP
Also Called: Geier Bindery Co
77 Schmitt Blvd (11735-1403)
PHONE..................................631 293-0180
Ruth Geier, *Partner*
Robert Geier, *Partner*
EMP: 25
SALES (est): 4.5MM **Privately Held**
WEB: www.midislandgroup.com
SIC: 2789 Binding only: books, pamphlets, magazines, etc.

(G-5055)
MID-ISLAND BINDERY INC
77 Schmitt Blvd (11735-1403)
PHONE..................................631 293-0180
Robert Geier, *CEO*
EMP: 48
SQ FT: 30,000
SALES (est): 6.4MM **Privately Held**
SIC: 2789 Pamphlets, binding

(G-5056)
MILLER TECHNOLOGY INC
61 Gazza Blvd (11735-1401)
PHONE..................................631 694-2224
Walter Miller Jr, *President*
Joane Miller, *Treasurer*
EMP: 5 **EST:** 1954
SQ FT: 3,000
SALES: 250K **Privately Held**
SIC: 3089 3369 3599 Casting of plastic; castings, except die-castings, precision; machine shop, jobbing & repair

(G-5057)
MIRAGE MOULDING MFG INC
Also Called: Mirage Moulding & Supply
160 Milbar Blvd (11735-1425)
PHONE..................................631 843-6168
Hashim Ismailzadah, *Ch of Bd*
▲ **EMP:** 10
SALES (est): 1.3MM **Privately Held**
SIC: 3089 Molding primary plastic

(G-5058)
MISONIX INC (PA)
1938 New Hwy (11735-1214)
PHONE..................................631 694-9555
Fax: 516 694-9412
Stavros Vizirgianakis, *CEO*
Stavros G Vizirgianakis, *CEO*
Robert Vose, *Regional Mgr*
Jeff Thompson, *Business Mgr*
Robert S Ludecker, *Senior VP*
▲ **EMP:** 80
SQ FT: 34,400
SALES: 22.2MM **Publicly Held**
WEB: www.misonix.com
SIC: 3841 3845 3677 Surgical & medical instruments; electromedical equipment; electronic coils, transformers & other inductors

(G-5059)
MKT329 INC
Also Called: Superior Packaging
565 Broadhollow Rd Ste 5 (11735-4826)
P.O. Box 667, North Bellmore (11710-0667)
PHONE..................................631 249-5500
Marlene Tallon, *President*
EMP: 14 **EST:** 2014
SQ FT: 121
SALES (est): 2.4MM **Privately Held**
SIC: 2653 Corrugated & solid fiber boxes

(G-5060)
MOREY PUBLISHING
Also Called: Long Island Press
20 Hempstead Tpke Unit B (11735-2043)
PHONE..................................516 284-3300
Fax: 516 284-3310
Jed Morey, *Ch of Bd*
Beverly Fortune, *Publisher*
Amanda Kollmer, *Publisher*
Tom Butcher, *Editor*
Jamie Castagna, *Editor*
EMP: 30
SALES (est): 4.4MM **Privately Held**
SIC: 2741 Miscellaneous publishing

(G-5061)
NAMEPLATE MFRS OF AMER
65 Toledo St (11735-6620)
PHONE..................................631 752-0055
Bill Williams, *CEO*
Darren Cash, *COO*
Connie Case, *Office Mgr*
EMP: 40
SQ FT: 8,000
SALES (est): 4.9MM **Privately Held**
WEB: www.nameplateamerica.com
SIC: 3479 3993 2752 2671 Name plates: engraved, etched, etc.; signs & advertising specialties; commercial printing, lithographic; packaging paper & plastics film, coated & laminated

(G-5062)
NATIONWIDE SALES AND SERVICE
303 Smith St Ste 4 (11735-1110)
PHONE..................................631 491-6625
Mark Genoa, *Ch of Bd*
Scott Genoa, *Vice Pres*
▲ **EMP:** 10
SQ FT: 10,000
SALES (est): 1.6MM **Privately Held**
WEB: www.shopnss.com
SIC: 3635 5087 5722 Household vacuum cleaners; janitors' supplies; vacuum cleaning systems; vacuum cleaners

(G-5063)
NEIGHBOR NEWSPAPERS
565 Broadhollow Rd Ste 3 (11735-4826)
PHONE..................................631 226-2636
Richard A Freedman, *Principal*
EMP: 7
SALES (est): 348.1K **Privately Held**
SIC: 2711 Newspapers, publishing & printing

(G-5064)
NEILSON INTERNATIONAL INC
144 Allen Blvd Ste B (11735-5644)
P.O. Box 784, Hicksville (11802-0784)
PHONE..................................631 454-0400
Kamlesh Mehta, *President*
▲ **EMP:** 3
SQ FT: 8,000
SALES: 1MM **Privately Held**
WEB: www.neilsoninc.com
SIC: 2211 Print cloths, cotton

(G-5065)
NETECH CORPORATION
110 Toledo St (11735-6623)
PHONE..................................631 531-0100
Fax: 631 433-7458
Mohan Das, *President*
Nicolc Nipp, *Opers Staff*
Amelia Voccola, *Opers Staff*
Jessica Roush, *Engineer*
Ginger Spray, *Engineer*
EMP: 11
SQ FT: 4,500
SALES (est): 1.9MM **Privately Held**
WEB: www.gonetech.com
SIC: 3845 Electromedical equipment

(G-5066)
NOGA DAIRIES INC
Also Called: Dairy Delite
175 Price Pkwy (11735-1318)
PHONE..................................516 293-5448
Eli Paz, *CEO*
Zami Leinson, *President*
▲ **EMP:** 10
SQ FT: 22,000
SALES (est): 1.3MM **Privately Held**
SIC: 2026 2022 Yogurt; spreads, cheese

(G-5067)
NORTECH LABORATORIES INC
125 Sherwood Ave (11735-1717)
PHONE..................................631 501-1452
Fax: 631 501-1453
Caryn Nazarieh, *President*
David Nazarieh, *Vice Pres*
Jonathan Nazarieh, *VP Sales*
Daniel Dunleavy, *Mktg Dir*
Sandra Spencer, *Admin Sec*
EMP: 17
SQ FT: 16,200
SALES (est): 3.4MM **Privately Held**
WEB: www.nortechlabs.com
SIC: 3842 Surgical appliances & supplies

(G-5068)
NUTRASCIENCE LABS INC
70 Carolyn Blvd (11735-1525)
PHONE..................................631 247-0660
Steve Rolfes, *CEO*
EMP: 27 **EST:** 2014
SALES (est): 848.5K
SALES (corp-wide): 61.4MM **Privately Held**
SIC: 2834 2833 Pharmaceutical preparations; druggists' preparations (pharmaceuticals); botanical products, medicinal: ground, graded or milled
PA: Twinlab Consolidated Holdings Inc.
2255 Glades Rd Ste 342w
Boca Raton FL 33431
212 651-8500

(G-5069)
O C P INC
Also Called: Morania Oil of Long Island
500 Bi County Blvd # 209 (11735-3931)
PHONE..................................516 679-2000
Ronald I Shields, *President*
EMP: 40
SQ FT: 6,000
SALES (est): 5.6MM **Privately Held**
SIC: 3433 Heaters, swimming pool: oil or gas

(G-5070)
ORICS INDUSTRIES INC
240 Smith St (11735-1113)
PHONE..................................718 461-8613
Ori Cohen, *Ch of Bd*
Suzi Oneill, *Executive Asst*
▲ **EMP:** 50
SQ FT: 15,000
SALES (est): 22MM **Privately Held**
WEB: www.orics.com
SIC: 3565 3841 Packaging machinery; surgical & medical instruments

(G-5071)
ORLANDI INC (PA)
Also Called: Orlandi Scented Products
131 Executive Blvd (11735-4719)
PHONE..................................631 756-0110
Sven Dobler, *Ch of Bd*
Kenneth Kane, *Senior VP*
Per Dobler, *Vice Pres*
Henri Liesenfelt, *Vice Pres*
Julio Caraballo, *Warehouse Mgr*
▲ **EMP:** 100
SQ FT: 80,000
SALES: 34.2MM **Privately Held**
WEB: www.orlandi-usa.com
SIC: 3993 3999 7389 2752 Signs & advertising specialties; novelties, bric-a-brac & hobby kits; packaging & labeling services; commercial printing, lithographic

(G-5072)
ORLANDI INC
121 Executive Blvd (11735-4719)
PHONE..................................631 756-0110
Sven Dobler, *President*
Kevin O'Leary, *Controller*
EMP: 50
SQ FT: 45,500
SALES (corp-wide): 34.2MM **Privately Held**
SIC: 3993 3999 7389 2752 Signs & advertising specialties; novelties, bric-a-brac & hobby kits; packaging & labeling services; commercial printing, lithographic
PA: Orlandi, Inc.
131 Executive Blvd
Farmingdale NY 11735
631 756-0110

(G-5073)
OSI PHARMACEUTICALS LLC
500 Bi County Blvd # 118 (11735-3959)
PHONE..................................631 847-0175
EMP: 84
SALES (corp-wide): 10.4B **Privately Held**
SIC: 2834 Mfg Pharmaceutical Preparations
HQ: Osi Pharmaceuticals, Llc
1 Bioscience Way Dr
Farmingdale NY 11735
631 962-2000

(G-5074)
OSI PHARMACEUTICALS LLC (DH)
1 Bioscience Way Dr (11735)
PHONE..................................631 962-2000
Fax: 631 845-5671
Colin Goddard PHD, *CEO*
Gabriel Leung, *President*
Anker Lundemose MD PHD, *President*
Robert L Simon, *Exec VP*
Linda E Amper PHD, *Senior VP*
▼ **EMP:** 2
SALES (est): 69.9MM
SALES (corp-wide): 11.7B **Privately Held**
WEB: www.osip.com
SIC: 2834 8731 Drugs affecting neoplasms & endrocrine systems; drugs acting on the central nervous system & sense organs; commercial physical research
HQ: Astellas Us Holding, Inc.
1 Astellas Way
Northbrook IL 60062
224 205-8800

(G-5075)
PCX AEROSTRUCTURES LLC
60 Milbar Blvd (11735-1406)
PHONE..................................631 467-2632
Mike Iannotta, *Branch Mgr*
EMP: 25
SALES (corp-wide): 100MM **Privately Held**
SIC: 3441 Fabricated structural metal
PA: Pcx Aerostructures, Llc
300 Fenn Rd
Newington CT 06111
860 666-2471

GEOGRAPHIC SECTION

Farmingdale - Nassau County (G-5102)

(G-5076)
PEERLESS INSTRUMENT CO INC
1966 Broadhollow Rd Ste D (11735-1726)
PHONE..................................631 396-6500
Fax: 631 243-5408
Martin R Benante, *CEO*
David Linton, *President*
Frederic Borah, *General Mgr*
Klaus Steinmeyer, *Vice Pres*
Fran Vargas, *Buyer*
EMP: 109 **EST:** 1938
SQ FT: 55,000
SALES (est): 26MM
SALES (corp-wide): 2.2B **Publicly Held**
WEB: www.peerlessny.com
SIC: 3829 7389 3825 3625 Measuring & controlling devices; design services; instruments to measure electricity; relays & industrial controls
PA: Curtiss-Wright Corporation
13925 Balntyn Corp Pl
Charlotte NC 28277
704 869-4600

(G-5077)
PHARBEST PHARMACEUTICALS INC
14 Engineers Ln Ste 1 (11735-1219)
PHONE..................................631 249-5130
Munir Islam, *President*
Ravi Dalwadi, *Research*
Nishant Parikh, *Manager*
EMP: 35
SQ FT: 22,000
SALES (est): 7.3MM **Privately Held**
WEB: www.pharbestusa.com
SIC: 2834 Druggists' preparations (pharmaceuticals)

(G-5078)
PHARMALIFE INC
130 Gazza Blvd (11735-1420)
PHONE..................................631 249-4040
Larry Sayage, *President*
EMP: 5
SQ FT: 4,300
SALES (est): 440K **Privately Held**
SIC: 2834 Vitamin, nutrient & hematinic preparations for human use

(G-5079)
PHOENIX LABORATORIES INC
200 Adams Blvd (11735-6615)
PHONE..................................516 822-1230
Melvin Rich, *President*
Stephen R Stern, *Exec VP*
Al Assa, *Controller*
Steven Tuohey, *Director*
Charlotte Rich, *Admin Sec*
EMP: 180 **EST:** 1966
SQ FT: 40,000
SALES (est): 24.9MM **Privately Held**
WEB: www.phoenixlaboratories.com
SIC: 2834 Vitamin, nutrient & hematinic preparations for human use; vitamin preparations

(G-5080)
PIRNAT PRECISE METALS INC
Also Called: F & M Precise Metals Co
127 Marine St (11735-5609)
PHONE..................................631 293-9169
Frank Pirnat, *President*
Mark Pirnat, *Vice Pres*
EMP: 7 **EST:** 1967
SQ FT: 10,000
SALES (est): 1MM **Privately Held**
SIC: 3444 Sheet metalwork

(G-5081)
PLASCAL CORP
361 Eastern Pkwy (11735-2713)
P.O. Box 590 (11735-0590)
PHONE..................................516 249-2200
Fax: 516 249-2256
Mark Hurd, *CEO*
Fred Hurd, *President*
Sheldon Eskowitz, *Corp Secy*
Thomas Blackler, *Vice Pres*
Raymond Brown, *Vice Pres*
▲ **EMP:** 4 **EST:** 1975
SQ FT: 75,000

SALES: 6MM **Privately Held**
WEB: www.plascal.com
SIC: 3081 Vinyl film & sheet

(G-5082)
PLATINUM PRINTING & GRAPHICS
70 Carolyn Blvd Ste C (11735-1525)
PHONE..................................631 249-3325
Fax: 516 249-3318
Paul Currao, *President*
EMP: 5 **EST:** 1996
SALES (est): 474.8K **Privately Held**
SIC: 2752 Commercial printing, lithographic

(G-5083)
POLYPLASTIC FORMS INC
49 Gazza Blvd (11735-1401)
PHONE..................................631 249-5011
Fax: 516 249-8504
Thomas Garrett, *President*
Diane Garrett, *Corp Secy*
Richard Garrett, *Vice Pres*
Nancy Behrens, *Sls & Mktg Exec*
EMP: 35
SQ FT: 10,000
SALES (est): 5.2MM **Privately Held**
WEB: www.polyplasticforms.com
SIC: 3993 Displays & cutouts, window & lobby; signs, not made in custom sign painting shops

(G-5084)
POSILLICO MATERIALS LLC
1750 New Hwy (11735-1562)
PHONE..................................631 249-1872
Joseph K Posillico, *CEO*
Michael J Posillico, *President*
Mario A Posillico, *Chairman*
Joseph D Posillico, *Senior VP*
Paul F Posillico, *Senior VP*
EMP: 11 **EST:** 1971
SQ FT: 2,500
SALES (est): 16.8MM **Privately Held**
SIC: 2951 Asphalt & asphaltic paving mixtures (not from refineries)

(G-5085)
PRECIPART CORPORATION
120 Finn Ct (11735-1121)
PHONE..................................631 777-8727
Fax: 631 694-4016
John P Walter, *President*
Lloyd W Miller, *Chairman*
Georges Assimilalo, *COO*
Karl Walter, *Vice Pres*
Donald Weinzimer, *Vice Pres*
EMP: 216
SQ FT: 16,200
SALES (est): 46.1MM
SALES (corp-wide): 52.4MM **Privately Held**
WEB: www.precipart.com
SIC: 3566 Speed changers, drives & gears
PA: Precipart Group, Inc.
100 Finn Ct
Farmingdale NY 11735
631 694-5900

(G-5086)
PRECISION ENVELOPE CO INC
Also Called: H & R Precision
110 Schmitt Blvd 7a (11735-6961)
PHONE..................................631 694-3990
Fax: 516 694-3998
Gilbert M Colombo Jr, *President*
Jane Colombo, *Corp Secy*
EMP: 9
SQ FT: 7,000
SALES (est): 1.3MM **Privately Held**
SIC: 2759 2752 Envelopes: printing; stationery: printing; business forms, lithographed

(G-5087)
PRECISION LABEL CORPORATION
175 Marine St (11735-5609)
PHONE..................................631 270-4490
Bradley A Cohn, *CEO*
EMP: 12
SQ FT: 4,000

SALES (est): 1.2MM **Privately Held**
SIC: 2759 2679 Labels & seals: printing; labels, paper: made from purchased material

(G-5088)
PRINT PACK INC (DH)
70 Schmitt Blvd (11735-1404)
PHONE..................................404 460-7000
Barbara Drillings, *Marketing Staff*
Rob George, *Manager*
◆ **EMP:** 150
SQ FT: 100,000
SALES (est): 26.5MM
SALES (corp-wide): 1.3B **Privately Held**
WEB: www.sealitinc.com
SIC: 2671 2759 Packaging paper & plastics film, coated & laminated; labels & seals: printing
HQ: Printpack, Inc.
2800 Overlook Pkwy Ne
Atlanta GA 30339
404 460-7000

(G-5089)
PROMPT PRINTING INC
160 Rome St (11735-6609)
PHONE..................................631 454-6524
Fax: 631 454-6370
John Probst, *President*
EMP: 6 **EST:** 1980
SQ FT: 2,000
SALES (est): 370K **Privately Held**
SIC: 2752 Commercial printing, offset

(G-5090)
PROOF INDUSTRIES INC
125 Rome St (11735-6606)
PHONE..................................631 694-7663
Vincent Cacioppo, *President*
Christie Cacioppo, *Office Mgr*
EMP: 9
SQ FT: 3,000
SALES (est): 1.3MM **Privately Held**
WEB: www.proofroof.com
SIC: 2439 5999 1751 Trusses, wooden roof; awnings; window & door (prefabricated) installation

(G-5091)
PROPER CHEMICAL LTD
280 Smith St (11735-1113)
PHONE..................................631 420-8000
Emil Backstrom, *President*
EMP: 5
SQ FT: 20,000
SALES (est): 400K **Privately Held**
SIC: 2833 Medicinal chemicals

(G-5092)
QUALIFIED MANUFACTURING CORP
134 Toledo St (11735-6625)
PHONE..................................631 249-4440
Donald Wojnar, *President*
EMP: 11 **EST:** 1970
SQ FT: 7,000
SALES (est): 1.5MM **Privately Held**
SIC: 3599 Machine shop, jobbing & repair

(G-5093)
QUALITY STAIR BUILDERS INC
95 Schmitt Blvd (11735-1403)
PHONE..................................631 694-0711
Fax: 516 694-0712
Esta Topal, *President*
Sherri Sugar, *Corp Secy*
EMP: 16 **EST:** 1955
SQ FT: 10,000
SALES (est): 2.2MM **Privately Held**
SIC: 2431 Staircases & stairs, wood

(G-5094)
QUICK SIGN F X
6 Powell St (11735-4019)
PHONE..................................516 249-6531
Steve Levine, *President*
EMP: 13
SALES (est): 825.7K **Privately Held**
SIC: 3993 Signs & advertising specialties

(G-5095)
R & J GRAPHICS INC
45 Central Ave (11735-6901)
PHONE..................................631 293-6611
Fax: 516 293-0303

John Merendino, *President*
Vinnie Farrell, *Sales Staff*
Ann Merendino, *Admin Sec*
EMP: 16
SQ FT: 15,000
SALES (est): 2.9MM **Privately Held**
SIC: 2752 Commercial printing, offset

(G-5096)
R D PRINTING ASSOCIATES INC
1865 New Hwy Ste 1 (11735-1501)
PHONE..................................631 390-5964
Fax: 516 694-8489
Ralph Demartino Jr, *President*
EMP: 14
SQ FT: 10,000
SALES (est): 1.4MM **Privately Held**
SIC: 2752 Commercial printing, offset

(G-5097)
RASON ASPHALT INC (PA)
Rr 110 (11735)
P.O. Box 530, Old Bethpage (11804-0530)
PHONE..................................631 293-6210
Fax: 631 293-6849
Anthony J Shakesby, *President*
Tony Shakesby, *Vice Pres*
Donna Bryan, *Manager*
Kim Hartley, *Manager*
John F Hendrickson, *Admin Sec*
EMP: 7 **EST:** 1950
SALES (est): 9.3MM **Privately Held**
WEB: www.rason1.com
SIC: 2951 Asphalt paving mixtures & blocks

(G-5098)
RENEWAL BY ANDERSEN LLC
Also Called: Renewal By Andrsen Long Island
2029 New Hwy (11735-1103)
PHONE..................................631 843-1716
EMP: 43
SALES (corp-wide): 3.4B **Privately Held**
SIC: 3442 Screens, window, metal
HQ: Renewal By Andersen Llc
9900 Jamaica Ave S
Cottage Grove MN 55016
855 871-7377

(G-5099)
RICO INTERNATIONAL
8484 San Fernando Rd (11735)
P.O. Box 290 (11735-0290)
PHONE..................................818 767-7711
Dan Fasani, *General Mgr*
EMP: 5 **EST:** 2009
SALES (est): 616.9K **Privately Held**
SIC: 3931 Reeds for musical instruments

(G-5100)
RIPI PRECISION CO INC (PA)
92 Toledo St (11735-6623)
PHONE..................................631 694-2453
Fax: 631 694-2458
Michael Perciballi, *President*
EMP: 12 **EST:** 1976
SQ FT: 12,000
SALES (est): 2.2MM **Privately Held**
SIC: 3728 Aircraft parts & equipment

(G-5101)
ROBOCOM US LLC (PA)
Also Called: Robocom Systems International
1111 Broadhollow Rd # 100 (11735-4819)
PHONE..................................631 861-2045
Fred Radcliffe, *President*
Richard Adamo, *Vice Pres*
Raymond Oconnor, *Vice Pres*
Steve Pharo, *Purchasing*
Elias Jubran, *Engineer*
EMP: 13
SQ FT: 4,000
SALES: 7MM **Privately Held**
WEB: www.avantce.com
SIC: 7372 Prepackaged software

(G-5102)
ROLI RETREADS INC
Also Called: Roli Tire and Auto Repair
212 E Carmans Rd Unit A (11735-4722)
PHONE..................................631 694-7670
Fax: 631 694-7625
Richard Bucci, *President*
EMP: 20
SQ FT: 6,500

(PA)=Parent Co (HQ)=Headquarters (DH)=Div Headquarters
✿ = New Business established in last 2 years

2017 Harris
New York Manufacturers Directory

Farmingdale - Nassau County (G-5103)

SALES (est): 3.9MM **Privately Held**
WEB: www.rolitire.com
SIC: **3011** 7549 Tire & inner tube materials & related products; automotive maintenance services

(G-5103)
ROTA PACK INC
34 Sarah Dr Ste B (11735-1218)
PHONE.....................................631 274-1037
Adrian Spirea, *Ch of Bd*
EMP: 11
SALES: 525K **Privately Held**
WEB: www.rotaindustries.com
SIC: **3565** 3535 Packaging machinery; conveyors & conveying equipment

(G-5104)
ROZAL INDUSTRIES INC
151 Marine St (11735-5609)
PHONE.....................................631 420-4277
Brian Casio, *President*
Gary Grieber, *Vice Pres*
EMP: 47
SALES (est): 3.8MM **Privately Held**
SIC: **3599** Machine shop, jobbing & repair

(G-5105)
RS PRECISION INDUSTRIES INC
295 Adams Blvd (11735-6632)
PHONE.....................................631 420-0424
Fax: 516 249-2624
Robert Savitzky, *President*
George Macy, *Engineer*
Thomas Shelby, *Engineer*
Eileen Levine, *Manager*
Lily Savitzky, *Admin Sec*
EMP: 24
SQ FT: 6,700
SALES (est): 6.6MM **Privately Held**
WEB: www.rsprecision.com
SIC: **3339** Primary nonferrous metals

(G-5106)
S & V KNITS INC
117 Marine St (11735-5607)
PHONE.....................................631 752-1595
Steve Sustrean, *President*
Virginia Sustrean, *Vice Pres*
Doris Alfson, *Accountant*
EMP: 30
SQ FT: 14,000
SALES (est): 3MM **Privately Held**
SIC: **2253** 2339 Knit outerwear mills; sweaters & sweater coats, knit; women's & misses' outerwear

(G-5107)
SABRA DIPPING COMPANY LLC
535 Smith St (11735-1116)
PHONE.....................................516 249-0151
Abner Hornick, *Exec Dir*
EMP: 11 **Privately Held**
SIC: **2099** 5148 Food preparations; fresh fruits & vegetables
HQ: Sabra Dipping Company, Llc
    777 Westchester Ave Fl 3
    White Plains NY 10604
    914 372-3900

(G-5108)
SEANAIR MACHINE CO INC
95 Verdi St (11735-6320)
PHONE.....................................631 694-2820
Fax: 631 694-2859
Laura Abel Nawrocki, *Ch of Bd*
Dorothy Abel, *President*
Thomas J Nawrochi, *Vice Pres*
EMP: 18 EST: 1955
SQ FT: 16,000
SALES (est): 3.3MM **Privately Held**
SIC: **3599** Machine shop, jobbing & repair

(G-5109)
SIMTEC INDUSTRIES CORPORATION
65 Marine St Ste A (11735-5638)
PHONE.....................................631 293-0080
Jean J Simon, *President*
EMP: 6
SALES: 1MM **Privately Held**
SIC: **3552** Textile machinery

(G-5110)
SMITH GRAPHICS INC
40 Florida St (11735-6301)
PHONE.....................................631 420-4180
Rick Smith, *President*
Beryl Smith, *Vice Pres*
EMP: 8
SQ FT: 2,500
SALES: 1.2MM **Privately Held**
WEB: www.smithgraphicsinc.com
SIC: **3993** Signs & advertising specialties

(G-5111)
SOURCE ENVELOPE INC
104 Allen Blvd Ste I (11735-5627)
PHONE.....................................866 284-0707
Fred Blustein, *President*
Alan Blustein, *Vice Pres*
David Blustein, *Treasurer*
EMP: 9
SQ FT: 2,000
SALES (est): 1MM **Privately Held**
WEB: www.source-envelope.com
SIC: **2752** 2759 Commercial printing, lithographic; letterpress printing

(G-5112)
SPACE COAST SEMICONDUCTOR INC
1111 Broadhollow Rd Fl 3 (11735-4881)
PHONE.....................................631 414-7131
Anthony Tamborrino, *Director*
EMP: 10
SALES (est): 682.4K **Privately Held**
WEB: www.spacecoastsemi.com
SIC: **3679** Electronic components

(G-5113)
STANDWILL PACKAGING INC
220 Sherwood Ave (11735-1718)
PHONE.....................................631 752-1236
Fax: 516 752-8036
William Standwill Jr, *President*
Stacy Bardavid, *Opers Mgr*
Randy Hallam, *Prdtn Mgr*
▲ EMP: 25 EST: 1976
SQ FT: 15,000
SALES (est): 4.5MM **Privately Held**
WEB: www.standwill.com
SIC: **2752** 2759 Commercial printing, offset; commercial printing

(G-5114)
STAR DRAPERIES INC
24 Florida St (11735-6301)
PHONE.....................................631 756-7121
Fax: 631 756-7121
Jacqueline Stolberg, *CEO*
EMP: 10
SQ FT: 3,200
SALES (est): 1.1MM **Privately Held**
SIC: **2211** 5023 Draperies & drapery fabrics, cotton; draperies

(G-5115)
STAR MOLD CO INC
125 Florida St (11735-6307)
PHONE.....................................631 694-2283
Fax: 516 694-2283
Guenther Merz, *President*
EMP: 6
SQ FT: 2,400
SALES: 320K **Privately Held**
SIC: **3544** Industrial molds

(G-5116)
STEPHEN J LIPKINS INC
855 Conklin St Ste A (11735-2409)
PHONE.....................................631 249-8866
Fax: 631 420-0862
Jonathan Lipkins, *President*
EMP: 5
SQ FT: 2,800
SALES (est): 420K **Privately Held**
SIC: **3915** Jewel cutting, drilling, polishing, recutting or setting; jewelry polishing for the trade

(G-5117)
STERLING INDUSTRIES INC
410 Eastern Pkwy (11735-2431)
PHONE.....................................631 753-3070
Fax: 631 753-3075
Brian Lewis, *President*
EMP: 25

SALES (est): 4.4MM **Privately Held**
SIC: **3444** Sheet metalwork

(G-5118)
SUNDIAL GROUP LLC
Also Called: Sundial Creations
100 Adams Blvd (11735-6633)
PHONE.....................................631 842-8800
Marry Dennis, *CEO*
Dennis Richelieu, *CEO*
Richard Gallucci, *Senior VP*
Dennis Layer, *Purch Agent*
EMP: 40
SQ FT: 50,000
SALES (est): 18.7MM **Privately Held**
SIC: **2844** Toilet preparations; perfumes & colognes

(G-5119)
SUPERIOR METAL & WOODWORK INC
70 Central Ave (11735-6906)
PHONE.....................................631 465-9004
John Cipri, *President*
George Castrillon, *Vice Pres*
Joseph Cipri, *Vice Pres*
EMP: 25
SQ FT: 12,500
SALES: 6.5MM **Privately Held**
SIC: **3446** Architectural metalwork

(G-5120)
SUPERIOR MOTION CONTROLS INC
40 Smith St (11735-1005)
PHONE.....................................516 420-2921
Frank Grieco, *CEO*
Tony Reda, *Engineer*
EMP: 35
SQ FT: 25,000
SALES (est): 9.9MM **Privately Held**
WEB: www.superior-ny.com
SIC: **3593** 3728 3679 3541 Fluid power cylinders & actuators; aircraft assemblies, subassemblies & parts; electronic loads & power supplies; machine tools, metal cutting type; iron & steel forgings

(G-5121)
SWIMWEAR ANYWHERE INC (PA)
Also Called: Liz Claiborne Swimwear
85 Sherwood Ave (11735-1717)
PHONE.....................................631 420-1400
Rosemarie Dilorenzo, *Chairman*
Joseph Dilorenzo, *COO*
Joseph Roehrig, *CFO*
James Lamanna, *Accounting Mgr*
Pam Olliver, *Human Resources*
◆ EMP: 75 EST: 1998
SALES (est): 45.5MM **Privately Held**
SIC: **2339** Bathing suits: women's, misses' & juniors'

(G-5122)
SYNTHO PHARMACEUTICALS INC
230 Sherwood Ave (11735-1718)
PHONE.....................................631 755-9898
Hosneara Malik, *President*
EMP: 7
SALES: 2.1MM **Privately Held**
WEB: www.synthopharmaceutical.com
SIC: **2834** Pharmaceutical preparations

(G-5123)
T A TOOL & MOLDING INC
Also Called: Konrad Design
185 Marine St (11735-5609)
PHONE.....................................631 293-0172
Fax: 631 293-2647
Ludwig Konrad, *President*
Maryann Konrad, *Vice Pres*
EMP: 18
SALES (est): 1.9MM **Privately Held**
SIC: **3089** 3544 Injection molding of plastics; industrial molds

(G-5124)
TANGENT MACHINE & TOOL CORP
108 Gazza Blvd (11735-1489)
PHONE.....................................631 249-3088
Fax: 631 249-5503
Joseph A Scafidi, *President*

Charles C Piola, *CFO*
EMP: 20 EST: 1953
SQ FT: 30,000
SALES (est): 3.6MM **Privately Held**
SIC: **3599** 7692 3728 Machine shop, jobbing & repair; welding repair; aircraft parts & equipment

(G-5125)
TAPE PRINTERS INC
155 Allen Blvd Ste A (11735-5640)
PHONE.....................................631 249-5585
Alexander J Kruk, *President*
▲ EMP: 15
SQ FT: 10,000
SALES (est): 2.9MM **Privately Held**
WEB: www.tapeprinters.com
SIC: **2759** Bag, wrapper & seal printing & engraving; labels & seals: printing

(G-5126)
TELEPHONICS CORPORATION
Also Called: Communications Systems Div
815 Broadhollow Rd (11735-3937)
PHONE.....................................631 755-7659
EMP: 99
SALES (corp-wide): 2B **Publicly Held**
SIC: **3661** Telephone & telegraph apparatus
HQ: Telephonics Corporation
    815 Broadhollow Rd
    Farmingdale NY 11735
    631 755-7000

(G-5127)
TELEPHONICS CORPORATION (HQ)
815 Broadhollow Rd (11735-3937)
PHONE.....................................631 755-7000
Fax: 631 755-7046
Joseph Battaglia, *President*
Alan Bryan, *Principal*
John Depace, *Editor*
Joseph M Beck, *Vice Pres*
Joseph Beck, *Vice Pres*
▲ EMP: 667
SQ FT: 160,000
SALES (est): 348.2MM
SALES (corp-wide): 2B **Publicly Held**
SIC: **3669** 3661 3679 3812 Intercommunication systems, electric; telephone & telegraph apparatus; electronic circuits; radar systems & equipment; air traffic control systems & equipment, electronic; radio & TV communications equipment
PA: Griffon Corporation
    712 5th Ave Fl 18
    New York NY 10019
    212 957-5000

(G-5128)
TELEPHONICS CORPORATION
Also Called: Command Systems Division
815 Broadhollow Rd (11735-3937)
PHONE.....................................631 755-7000
Joseph Battaglia, *CEO*
EMP: 99
SALES (corp-wide): 2B **Publicly Held**
SIC: **3699** Electronic training devices
HQ: Telephonics Corporation
    815 Broadhollow Rd
    Farmingdale NY 11735
    631 755-7000

(G-5129)
THERMAL PROCESS CNSTR CO
19 Engineers Ln (11735-1207)
PHONE.....................................631 293-6400
Al Gupta, *President*
EMP: 22
SQ FT: 10,000
SALES (est): 1.5MM **Privately Held**
SIC: **3567** 3497 Incinerators, metal: domestic or commercial; metal foil & leaf

(G-5130)
TIGER SUPPLY INC
99 Sherwood Ave (11735-1717)
PHONE.....................................631 293-2700
Fax: 631 293-2707
Anthony Davanzo, *President*
Anthony Devanzo, *Human Res Dir*
EMP: 5
SALES (est): 789.4K **Privately Held**
WEB: www.tigersupplyinc.com
SIC: **3843** Dental equipment & supplies

▲ = Import ▼=Export
◆ =Import/Export

GEOGRAPHIC SECTION

Farmington - Ontario County (G-5155)

(G-5131)
TIME-CAP LABORATORIES INC
Also Called: Custom Coatings
7 Michael Ave (11735-3921)
PHONE.....................................631 753-9090
Fax: 516 753-2220
Mark Saldanha, *Ch of Bd*
Irene McGregor, *Principal*
Robert Azzara, *COO*
Conrad Petersohn, *Prdtn Mgr*
Alex Martinez, *Production*
▲ EMP: 145
SQ FT: 45,000
SALES (est): 40.1MM
SALES (corp-wide): 54.1MM **Privately Held**
SIC: 2834 Proprietary drug products
PA: Marksans Pharma Limited
  11th Floor, Grandeur,
  Mumbai MH 40005
  224 001-2000

(G-5132)
TIN BOX COMPANY OF AMERICA INC (PA)
216 Sherwood Ave (11735-1718)
P.O. Box 9068 (11735)
PHONE.....................................631 845-1600
Lloyd Roth, *President*
Lloyd Ross, *Sr Corp Ofcr*
Andy Siegel, *Vice Pres*
Michael Siegel, *Vice Pres*
Stephanie Terry, *Vice Pres*
▲ EMP: 25
SQ FT: 20,000
SALES (est): 2.9MM **Privately Held**
SIC: 2631 5051 Container, packaging & boxboard; tin & tin base metals, shapes, forms, etc.

(G-5133)
TRI-FLEX LABEL CORP
48 Allen Blvd Unit A (11735-5642)
PHONE.....................................631 293-0411
Fax: 631 293-1496
Kevin Duckman, *President*
Kevin Duckham, *President*
Denise Duckham, *Office Mgr*
Gene Saraniero, *Manager*
Kayla Kerbs, *Graphic Designe*
▲ EMP: 20
SQ FT: 6,000
SALES (est): 4.4MM **Privately Held**
WEB: www.triflexlabel.com
SIC: 2672 2679 Labels (unprinted), gummed: made from purchased materials; labels, paper: made from purchased material

(G-5134)
TRI-SUPREME OPTICAL LLC
Also Called: Tri Supreme Optical
91 Carolyn Blvd (11735-1527)
PHONE.....................................631 249-2020
Fax: 516 249-0577
Michael Cooper, *General Mgr*
Robert Grecco, *Purchasing*
Eileen Lewis, *Personnel*
Myrna Eng, *VP Sales*
Richard Salberg, *Sales Mgr*
▲ EMP: 95
SQ FT: 18,000
SALES (est): 12.3MM
SALES (corp-wide): 88.1MM **Privately Held**
WEB: www.essilor.com
SIC: 3851 5049 Lenses, ophthalmic; optical goods
HQ: Essilor Of America, Inc.
  13555 N Stemmons Fwy
  Dallas TX 75234
  214 496-4000

(G-5135)
TRONIC PLATING CO INC
37 Potter St (11735-4200)
PHONE.....................................516 293-7883
Herbert Buckstone, *President*
Gerald Alletto, *President*
Stanley J Buckstone, *Vice Pres*
EMP: 11 EST: 1955
SQ FT: 6,000
SALES: 629.2K **Privately Held**
SIC: 3471 Electroplating of metals or formed products; finishing, metals or formed products

(G-5136)
ULTIMATE PRCISION MET PDTS INC (PA)
200 Finn Ct (11735-1119)
PHONE.....................................631 249-9441
Fax: 631 777-1828
Michael Mallia, *CEO*
Vincent Mallia, *President*
Paul Mallia, *Principal*
Larry Mallia, *Vice Pres*
Joseph Reid, *Vice Pres*
▼ EMP: 84
SQ FT: 70,000
SALES (est): 19.2MM **Privately Held**
WEB: www.ultimateprecision.com
SIC: 3469 3544 3444 Stamping metal for the trade; special dies & tools; sheet metalwork

(G-5137)
VELOCITY PHARMA LLC
226 Sherwood Ave Unit B (11735-1732)
PHONE.....................................631 393-2905
Ankur Shah, *President*
Nicholas Monte, *Director*
▲ EMP: 8
SQ FT: 20,000
SALES (est): 1.9MM **Privately Held**
SIC: 2834 Vitamin, nutrient & hematinic preparations for human use

(G-5138)
VITA-NAT INC
298 Adams Blvd (11735-6615)
PHONE.....................................631 293-6000
Mohd M Alam, *President*
Khurshid Anwar, *Vice Pres*
Anwar Khurshid, *Vice Pres*
▲ EMP: 6
SQ FT: 7,000
SALES: 861.1K **Privately Held**
SIC: 2834 Vitamin, nutrient & hematinic preparations for human use

(G-5139)
W R P WELDING LTD
Also Called: Ramick Welding
126 Toledo St (11735-6625)
PHONE.....................................631 249-8859
William R Pontecorvo, *President*
EMP: 6
SQ FT: 3,500
SALES (est): 410K **Privately Held**
SIC: 7692 Brazing

(G-5140)
WALNUT PACKAGING INC
450 Smith St (11735-1105)
PHONE.....................................631 293-3836
Fax: 631 293-3878
Jose Alvarado, *President*
Sheila Haile, *Vice Pres*
Leslee Marin, *Controller*
Elba Radriguez, *Office Mgr*
EMP: 21
SQ FT: 14,000
SALES (est): 3.3MM **Privately Held**
WEB: www.wpiplasticbags.com
SIC: 3086 Packaging & shipping materials, foamed plastic

(G-5141)
WEL MADE ENTERPRISES INC
1630 New Hwy (11735-1510)
PHONE.....................................631 752-1238
EMP: 14 EST: 1950
SQ FT: 1,800
SALES: 1.1MM **Privately Held**
SIC: 3272 Mfg Concrete Products

(G-5142)
WELLMILL LLC
Also Called: Vitamix Laboratories
141 Central Ave Ste B (11735-6903)
PHONE.....................................631 465-9245
Michael Kochitz, *Mng Member*
EMP: 17
SALES: 750K **Privately Held**
SIC: 2834 Vitamin preparations

(G-5143)
WESTSEA PUBLISHING CO INC
149d Allen Blvd Ste D (11735-5616)
PHONE.....................................631 420-1110
Anthony Nigro, *President*

Anthony Negro, *President*
Joan Mallon, *Admin Sec*
EMP: 7
SALES (est): 540K **Privately Held**
SIC: 2731 Books: publishing only

(G-5144)
XYLON INDUSTRIES INC
79 Florida St (11735-6305)
PHONE.....................................631 293-4717
Fax: 631 293-4748
Joseph Jones, *President*
EMP: 5
SQ FT: 4,200
SALES: 850K **Privately Held**
SIC: 3842 2431 Radiation shielding aprons, gloves, sheeting, etc.; millwork

(G-5145)
ZINGS COMPANY LLC
250 Adams Blvd (11735-6615)
PHONE.....................................631 454-0339
Fax: 631 694-2326
Robert Jagenburg,
EMP: 5
SALES (est): 385.1K **Privately Held**
WEB: www.zingsco.com
SIC: 2024 Juice pops, frozen

Farmington
Ontario County

(G-5146)
BADGER TECHNOLOGIES INC
5829 County Road 41 (14425-9103)
PHONE.....................................585 869-7101
Fax: 315 531-9883
Dave Bronger, *Vice Pres*
Lauren Moran, *Personnel Exec*
Gary Gray, *Manager*
EMP: 45
SALES (corp-wide): 10MM **Privately Held**
WEB: www.badgertech.com
SIC: 3679 Harness assemblies for electronic use: wire or cable
PA: Badger Technologies, Inc.
  5829 County Road 41
  Farmington NY 14425
  585 869-7101

(G-5147)
BADGER TECHNOLOGIES INC (PA)
5829 County Road 41 (14425-9103)
PHONE.....................................585 869-7101
Fax: 585 869-7199
Manoj Shekar, *President*
Jim Harris, *General Mgr*
Jeremy Jumper, *Engineer*
Jeff Sullivan, *CFO*
Barbara Jensen, *Accounts Mgr*
▲ EMP: 51
SQ FT: 15,000
SALES (est): 10MM **Privately Held**
WEB: www.badgertech.com
SIC: 3679 Harness assemblies for electronic use: wire or cable

(G-5148)
CROSMAN CORPORATION
1360 Rural Rte 8 (14425)
PHONE.....................................585 398-3920
Steve Burley, *Branch Mgr*
EMP: 30
SALES (corp-wide): 287.8MM **Privately Held**
SIC: 3484 3482 3563 Pellet & BB guns; pellets & BB's, pistol & air rifle ammunition; shot, steel (ammunition); air & gas compressors
HQ: Crosman Corporation
  7629 State Route 5 And 20
  Bloomfield NY 14469
  585 657-6161

(G-5149)
EBSCO INDUSTRIES INC
Global Point Products
5815 County Road 41 (14425-9103)
PHONE.....................................585 398-2000
David Testa, *Vice Pres*
EMP: 5

SALES (corp-wide): 2.1B **Privately Held**
WEB: www.ebscoind.com
SIC: 3861 Photographic equipment & supplies
PA: Ebsco Industries, Inc.
  5724 Highway 280 E
  Birmingham AL 35242
  205 991-6600

(G-5150)
EMORY MACHINE & TOOL CO INC
6176 Hunters Dr (14425-1122)
PHONE.....................................585 436-9610
James Fowler Jr, *President*
Rob Roney, *Manager*
EMP: 45
SQ FT: 30,000
SALES (est): 4.4MM **Privately Held**
WEB: www.emory-rockwood.com
SIC: 3599 3451 Machine shop, jobbing & repair; screw machine products

(G-5151)
GANNETT CO INC
Also Called: Democrat & Chronicle
6300 Collett Rd (14425-1075)
PHONE.....................................585 924-3406
Karen Beach, *Manager*
EMP: 8
SALES (corp-wide): 5.7B **Publicly Held**
WEB: www.gannett.com
SIC: 2711 Newspapers
PA: Gannett Co., Inc.
  7950 Jones Branch Dr
  Mc Lean VA 22102
  703 854-6000

(G-5152)
HANSEN STEEL
Also Called: Hansen Metal Fabrications
6021 County Road 41 (14425-8938)
PHONE.....................................585 398-2020
Fax: 585 398-3138
Thomas Hansen, *Owner*
Mike Hansen, *Sales Executive*
EMP: 25
SQ FT: 13,500
SALES (est): 4MM **Privately Held**
SIC: 3441 7692 3444 Fabricated structural metal; welding repair; sheet metalwork

(G-5153)
INGLESIDE MACHINE CO INC
1120 Hook Rd (14425-8956)
PHONE.....................................585 924-4363
Fax: 585 924-7904
Jan Marie Veomett, *Ch of Bd*
Gary Voemett, *Plant Mgr*
EMP: 80
SQ FT: 40,000
SALES (est): 12MM **Privately Held**
WEB: www.inglesidemachine.com
SIC: 7692 3599 Welding repair; machine shop, jobbing & repair

(G-5154)
ROCHESTER ASPHALT MATERIALS
5929 Loomis Rd (14425-9526)
PHONE.....................................585 924-7360
Daniel Coe, *Branch Mgr*
EMP: 60
SALES (corp-wide): 23.5B **Privately Held**
SIC: 3273 Ready-mixed concrete
HQ: Rochester Asphalt Materials Inc
  1150 Penfield Rd
  Rochester NY 14625
  585 381-7010

(G-5155)
ROCHESTER LUMBER COMPANY
Also Called: Trusses & Trim Division
6080 Collett Rd (14425-9531)
PHONE.....................................585 924-7171
Fax: 585 924-7173
Paul Rickner, *Branch Mgr*
EMP: 30
SALES (corp-wide): 10.2MM **Privately Held**
SIC: 2439 2431 3442 Trusses, wooden roof; doors, wood; staircases & stairs, wood; metal doors, sash & trim

Farmington - Ontario County (G-5156)

PA: Rochester Lumber Company
2040 East Ave
Rochester NY 14610
585 473-8080

(G-5156)
TCS ELECTRONICS INC
1124 Corporate Dr (14425-9570)
PHONE..................................585 337-4301
Jim Harris, *General Mgr*
Renee Strong, *Manager*
EMP: 27
SALES (est): 6.6MM Privately Held
SIC: 3672 3679 Circuit boards, television & radio printed; harness assemblies for electronic use: wire or cable

(G-5157)
TURNOMAT COMPANY LLC
1118 Mertensia Rd (14425-1008)
PHONE..................................585 924-1630
Fax: 585 924-2421
Nancy Role, *Owner*
EMP: 5
SALES (est): 409.8K Privately Held
WEB: www.turnomat.com
SIC: 3568 Bearings, plain

(G-5158)
ULTRAFAB INC (PA)
1050 Hook Rd (14425-9537)
PHONE..................................585 924-2186
Fax: 585 924-7680
◆ EMP: 200
SQ FT: 121,000
SALES (est): 43.3MM Privately Held
WEB: www.ultrafab.com
SIC: 2281 3089 Yarn Spinning Mill Mfg Plastic Products

Farmingville
Suffolk County

(G-5159)
BUD BARGER ASSOC INC
Also Called: Carduner Sales Company
3 Mount Mckinley Ave (11738-2107)
PHONE..................................631 696-6703
Bud Barger, *President*
EMP: 5
SALES (est): 609.7K Privately Held
SIC: 3679 Electronic components

(G-5160)
MIND DESIGNS INC (PA)
5 Gregory Ct (11738-4202)
PHONE..................................631 563-3644
Anibal Rodriguez, *President*
Joshua Rodriguez, *COO*
Dorothea Rodriguez, *CFO*
EMP: 8
SQ FT: 8,800
SALES (est): 1.5MM Privately Held
WEB: www.mindglow.com
SIC: 2431 5211 Planing mill, millwork; cabinets, kitchen

(G-5161)
PEI/GENESIS INC
2410 N Ocean Ave Ste 401 (11738-2917)
PHONE..................................631 256-1747
Donald Wood, *Branch Mgr*
EMP: 5
SALES (corp-wide): 317.2MM Privately Held
SIC: 3643 Electric connectors
PA: Pei/Genesis, Inc.
2180 Hornig Rd Ste 2
Philadelphia PA 19116
215 464-1410

Fayette
Seneca County

(G-5162)
SENECA STONE CORPORATION
Cty Rd 121 Hoster Cors Rd (13065)
P.O. Box 76 (13065-0076)
PHONE..................................315 549-8253
Fax: 315 549-7156
Tom Cleare, *Manager*
EMP: 15
SALES (corp-wide): 98.5MM Privately Held
SIC: 3281 5032 Cut stone & stone products; stone, crushed or broken
HQ: Seneca Stone Corporation
2105 S Broadway
Pine City NY 14871
607 737-6200

Fayetteville
Onondaga County

(G-5163)
CARTERS INC
537 Towne Dr (13066-1331)
PHONE..................................315 637-3128
EMP: 9
SALES (corp-wide): 3B Publicly Held
SIC: 2361 Girls' & children's dresses, blouses & shirts
PA: Carter's, Inc.
3438 Peachtree Rd Ne # 1800
Atlanta GA 30326
678 791-1000

(G-5164)
DATA KEY COMMUNICATION LLC
7573 Hunt Ln (13066-2560)
PHONE..................................315 445-2347
Fax: 315 445-9336
Judy Flannagan, *Mng Member*
Meocha Belle, *Director*
EMP: 15
SALES (est): 1.5MM Privately Held
WEB: www.datakeyllc.com
SIC: 2721 7375 7371 Magazines: publishing only, not printed on site; information retrieval services; custom computer programming services

(G-5165)
JENLOR LTD
523 E Genesee St (13066-1536)
PHONE..................................315 637-9080
Joseph Ophir, *President*
Ron Darby, *Manager*
▲ EMP: 10
SQ FT: 5,000
SALES (est): 1.3MM Privately Held
WEB: www.jenlor-samatic.com
SIC: 3679 Electronic circuits

(G-5166)
P B & H MOULDING CORPORATION
7121 Woodchuck Hill Rd (13066-9714)
PHONE..................................315 455-1756
Fax: 315 455-8748
Timothy Orcutt, *President*
Douglas Hatch, *Vice Pres*
Jo Dean Hall Orcutt, *Vice Pres*
EMP: 22
SQ FT: 33,000
SALES (est): 2.5MM Privately Held
WEB: www.pbhmoulding.com
SIC: 2499 Picture frame molding, finished

Felts Mills
Jefferson County

(G-5167)
CRANESVILLE BLOCK CO INC
Also Called: Drum Ready-Mix
23903 Cemetery Rd (13638-3113)
P.O. Box 210 (13638-0210)
PHONE..................................315 773-2296
Edward Bailey, *Regional Mgr*
Robert Vancoughnett, *Opers Mgr*
EMP: 35
SALES (corp-wide): 41.2MM Privately Held
SIC: 3271 3273 Blocks, concrete or cinder: standard; ready-mixed concrete
PA: Cranesville Block Co., Inc.
1250 Riverfront Ctr
Amsterdam NY 12010
518 684-6000

Ferndale
Sullivan County

(G-5168)
CHIPITA AMERICA INC
Also Called: Mamma Says
1243 Old Route 17 (12734-5422)
PHONE..................................845 292-2540
Norm Gallagher, *Plant Engr*
Ed McDermott, *Manager*
EMP: 50
SALES (corp-wide): 111.1MM Privately Held
SIC: 2052 Cookies
HQ: Chipita America, Inc.
1 Westbrook Corporate Ctr
Westchester IL 60154
708 731-2434

(G-5169)
DC FABRICATION & WELDING INC
17 Radcliff Rd (12734-5300)
PHONE..................................845 295-0215
Dan Coutermash, *President*
Bill Fredrick, *Treasurer*
EMP: 6
SQ FT: 8,000
SALES: 600K Privately Held
SIC: 2296 Cord & fabric for reinforcing industrial belting

(G-5170)
GETEC INC
624 Harris Rd (12734-5135)
P.O. Box 583 (12734-0583)
PHONE..................................845 292-0800
Jean Bader, *President*
Hans Bader Jr, *Vice Pres*
▲ EMP: 15
SQ FT: 10,000
SALES: 3.1MM Privately Held
WEB: www.getec.com
SIC: 3621 Generators & sets, electric

(G-5171)
HUDSON VALLEY FOIE GRAS LLC
80 Brooks Rd (12734-5101)
PHONE..................................845 292-2500
EMP: 11 EST: 2008
SALES (est): 2MM Privately Held
SIC: 2015 Ducks, processed; ducks, processed: canned; ducks, processed: fresh; ducks, processed: frozen

Feura Bush
Albany County

(G-5172)
LINDE LLC
76 W Yard Rd (12067-9739)
PHONE..................................518 439-8187
John Cox, *Branch Mgr*
Paul Marton, *Manager*
Bruce Toohey, *Manager*
Debbi Lacey, *Administration*
EMP: 55
SALES (corp-wide): 19.2B Privately Held
SIC: 2813 Nitrogen; oxygen, compressed or liquefied
HQ: Linde Llc
200 Somerset Corporate Bl
Bridgewater NJ 08807
908 464-8100

(G-5173)
MATHESON TRI-GAS INC
1297 Feura Bush Rd (12067-1719)
PHONE..................................518 439-0362
Fax: 518 439-3871
Roger Corvasce, *Manager*
Roger Corbasce, *Manager*
Jim Vincent, *Manager*
EMP: 19
SALES (corp-wide): 5.4B Privately Held
WEB: www.mgindustries.com
SIC: 2813 5084 Industrial gases; nitrogen; oxygen, compressed or liquefied; argon; welding machinery & equipment; safety equipment
HQ: Matheson Tri-Gas, Inc.
150 Allen Rd Ste 302
Basking Ridge NJ 07920
908 991-9200

(G-5174)
OWENS CORNING SALES LLC
1277 Feura Bush Rd (12067-1719)
P.O. Box 98, Delmar (12054-0098)
PHONE..................................518 475-3600
Craig Burroughs, *Branch Mgr*
Donna Baumann, *Director*
Anthony Williams, *Director*
EMP: 465
SQ FT: 1,860
SALES (corp-wide): 5.3B Publicly Held
WEB: www.owenscorning.com
SIC: 3229 3296 Pressed & blown glass; mineral wool
HQ: Owens Corning Sales, Llc
1 Owens Corning Pkwy
Toledo OH 43659
419 248-8000

Fillmore
Allegany County

(G-5175)
CUBA SPECIALTY MFG CO INC
Also Called: Tackle Factory
81 S Genesee St (14735-8700)
P.O. Box 195 (14735-0195)
PHONE..................................585 567-4176
Fax: 585 567-2366
Dana R Pickup, *President*
Stephen Fentz, *President*
Edward Fox, *President*
Michelle Popovice, *Controller*
▲ EMP: 10 EST: 1931
SQ FT: 23,000
SALES (est): 1.6MM Privately Held
SIC: 3496 Traps, animal & fish

(G-5176)
PRIMESOUTH INC
11537 Route 19 (14735-8667)
PHONE..................................585 567-4191
John Kingston, *Manager*
EMP: 10 EST: 1991
SALES (est): 740K Privately Held
SIC: 3825 Electrical power measuring equipment

Findley Lake
Chautauqua County

(G-5177)
OUR OWN CANDLE COMPANY INC (PA)
10349 Main St (14736-9722)
P.O. Box 99 (14736-0099)
PHONE..................................716 769-5000
Lawrence S Gross, *President*
Kurt M Duska, *Vice Pres*
EMP: 12
SALES (est): 2.1MM Privately Held
SIC: 3999 Shades, lamp or candle

Fishers
Ontario County

(G-5178)
GORBEL INC (PA)
600 Fishers Run (14453)
P.O. Box 593 (14453-0593)
PHONE..................................585 924-6262
Fax: 585 924-6273
David Reh, *CEO*
Brian D Reh, *Ch of Bd*
David Butwid, *Vice Pres*
Alex Chernyak, *Engineer*
Brian Peets, *Plant Engr*

GEOGRAPHIC SECTION

Floral Park - Nassau County (G-5206)

▲ EMP: 130 EST: 1977
SQ FT: 64,000
SALES (est): 76MM **Privately Held**
WEB: www.gorbel.com
SIC: 3536 Hoists, cranes & monorails; cranes, industrial plant

(G-5179)
GORBEL INC
590 Fishers Run (14453)
PHONE.................585 924-6262
EMP: 85
SALES (corp-wide): 76MM **Privately Held**
SIC: 3536 Hoists, cranes & monorails; cranes, industrial plant
PA: Gorbel, Inc.
 600 Fishers Run
 Fishers NY 14453
 585 924-6262

Fishkill
Dutchess County

(G-5180)
ACADIA STAIRS
73 Route 9 Ste 3 (12524-2944)
PHONE.................845 765-8600
EMP: 8
SALES (est): 650K **Privately Held**
SIC: 3441 Fabricated structural metal

(G-5181)
BIONIC EYE TECHNOLOGIES INC
4 Willow Lake Dr (12524-2952)
PHONE.................845 505-5254
Richard Birney, *CEO*
EMP: 7
SALES (est): 410K **Privately Held**
SIC: 3842 Implants, surgical

(G-5182)
CRANESVILLE BLOCK CO INC
70 Route 9 (12524-2962)
PHONE.................845 896-5687
John Tesrro, *CEO*
EMP: 20
SQ FT: 3,960
SALES (corp-wide): 41.2MM **Privately Held**
SIC: 3273 Ready-mixed concrete
PA: Cranesville Block Co., Inc.
 1250 Riverfront Ctr
 Amsterdam NY 12010
 518 684-6000

(G-5183)
ENTERPRISE BAGELS INC
Also Called: Bagel Shoppe, The
986 Main St Ste 3 (12524-3508)
PHONE.................845 896-3823
Joe Raffele, *CEO*
EMP: 12
SALES (est): 1.3MM **Privately Held**
SIC: 2051 Bagels, fresh or frozen

(G-5184)
FAMILY HEARING CENTER
18 Westage Dr Ste 16 (12524-2289)
PHONE.................845 897-3059
Lori Biasotti, *Owner*
EMP: 5
SALES (est): 459.5K **Privately Held**
SIC: 3842 8049 Hearing aids; audiologist

(G-5185)
LAM RESEARCH CORPORATION
300 Westage Bus Ctr Dr # 190 (12524-4201)
PHONE.................845 896-0606
Fax: 845 896-4151
Craig Bitzell, *Manager*
Dean Turnbaugh, *Manager*
EMP: 50
SALES (corp-wide): 5.8B **Publicly Held**
WEB: www.lamrc.com
SIC: 3559 Semiconductor manufacturing machinery
PA: Lam Research Corporation
 4650 Cushing Pkwy
 Fremont CA 94538
 510 572-0200

(G-5186)
MONTFORT BROTHERS INC
44 Elm St (12524-1804)
PHONE.................845 896-6694
Fax: 845 896-4456
Jacqueline Montfort, *President*
Melissa Oberle, *Controller*
EMP: 30
SQ FT: 15,000
SALES (est): 6.4MM **Privately Held**
WEB: www.montfortgroup.com
SIC: 3271 Blocks, concrete or cinder: standard

(G-5187)
N SKETCH BUILD INC
982 Main St Ste 4-130 (12524-3506)
PHONE.................800 975-0597
Jacqueline Ellison, *Ch of Bd*
▲ EMP: 8
SALES (est): 570K **Privately Held**
SIC: 2499 Decorative wood & woodwork

(G-5188)
UFN LLC
Also Called: United Florist Network
1399 Route 52 Ste 100 (12524-3250)
PHONE.................800 533-1787
Joseph Vega, *COO*
Mahima Kurian, *QA Dir*
Edward Castillo, *Sales Dir*
Ken Garland, *Mng Member*
Ryan Lowe, *Software Engr*
EMP: 8
SALES: 379.6K **Privately Held**
WEB: www.unitedfloristnetwork.com
SIC: 7372 Application computer software

Floral Park
Nassau County

(G-5189)
A D MFG CORP
24844 Jericho Tpke (11001-4002)
PHONE.................516 352-6161
Fax: 516 352-8502
Howard Karmitz, *President*
Ronald Karmitz, *Vice Pres*
EMP: 15
SQ FT: 6,000
SALES (est): 2.1MM **Privately Held**
WEB: www.adtrophy.com
SIC: 3499 Trophies, metal, except silver

(G-5190)
ALLIANCE SERVICES CORP
23 Van Siclen Ave (11001-2012)
PHONE.................516 775-7600
Frank De Oliveira, *President*
Peter Smith, *General Mgr*
Victor De Oliveira, *Vice Pres*
EMP: 14
SQ FT: 18,000
SALES (est): 1.6MM **Privately Held**
WEB: www.alliancewelding.com
SIC: 7692 Welding repair

(G-5191)
ALLIANCE WELDING & STEEL FABG
15 Van Siclen Ave (11001-2012)
PHONE.................516 775-7600
Fax: 516 775-5955
Victor De Oliveira, *President*
Frank De Oliveira, *Corp Secy*
Joe King, *Sales Mgr*
EMP: 18
SQ FT: 18,000
SALES (est): 1.8MM **Privately Held**
SIC: 3444 7692 Sheet metalwork; welding repair

(G-5192)
ALLOMATIC PRODUCTS COMPANY
Also Called: Sales Department
102 Jericho Tpke Ste 104 (11001-2004)
PHONE.................516 775-0330
Fax: 516 775-5543
Bob Clark, *Vice Pres*
Bob Tichy, *Marketing Mgr*
Israel Tabaksblat, *Marketing Staff*
John Butz, *Manager*
EMP: 5
SALES (corp-wide): 117.3MM **Privately Held**
WEB: www.allomatic.com
SIC: 3714 Motor vehicle parts & accessories
HQ: Allomatic Products Company Inc
 609 E Chaney St
 Sullivan IN 47882
 812 268-0322

(G-5193)
ART DENTAL LABORATORY INC
199 Jericho Tpke Ste 402 (11001-2190)
PHONE.................516 437-1882
Fax: 516 437-1887
James Pratap, *President*
Janice Schlin, *Exec Dir*
EMP: 8
SQ FT: 800
SALES (est): 1.2MM **Privately Held**
SIC: 3843 Dental equipment & supplies

(G-5194)
AUTOMATED BLDG MGT SYSTEMS INC (PA)
54 Cherry Ln (11001-1611)
PHONE.................516 216-5603
Alkesh Amin, *President*
Aika Patel, *Manager*
EMP: 33
SQ FT: 2,000
SALES (est): 5.9MM **Privately Held**
WEB: www.abmsys.com
SIC: 3822 Temperature controls, automatic

(G-5195)
BARCLAY TAGG RACING
86 Geranium Ave (11001-3035)
PHONE.................631 404-8269
Barclay Tagg, *Owner*
EMP: 30
SALES (est): 1.1MM **Privately Held**
SIC: 3721 Aircraft

(G-5196)
BUTTER COOKY BAKERY
217 Jericho Tpke (11001-2143)
PHONE.................516 354-3831
Ben Borgognone, *President*
EMP: 8
SALES (est): 605.5K **Privately Held**
SIC: 2051 Cakes, bakery: except frozen

(G-5197)
C & A SERVICE INC (PA)
Also Called: Citrus and Allied Essences
65 S Tyson Ave (11001-1821)
PHONE.................516 354-1200
Richard Pisano Jr, *President*
Marie Taormina, *Purchasing*
Nancy McDonald, *Controller*
▲ EMP: 5
SALES (est): 1MM **Privately Held**
SIC: 2899 2911 Chemical preparations; aromatic chemical products

(G-5198)
CANOPY BOOKS LLC (PA)
50 Carnation Ave Bldg 2-1 (11001-1741)
P.O. Box 280, New Hyde Park (11040-0280)
PHONE.................516 354-4888
Clifford Brechner, *CEO*
Sarah Panik, *Product Mgr*
EMP: 2
SALES (est): 1.5MM **Privately Held**
SIC: 2731 Book publishing

(G-5199)
CB PUBLISHING LLC
Also Called: CB Products
50 Carnation Ave Bldg 2-1 (11001-1741)
P.O. Box 280, New Hyde Park (11040-0280)
PHONE.................516 354-4888
Fax: 516 354-4889
Clifford Brechner, *President*
EMP: 7
SQ FT: 1,400
SALES (est): 577.4K **Privately Held**
WEB: www.cbproducts.com
SIC: 2731 Books: publishing only

(G-5200)
CITRUS AND ALLIED ESSENCES LTD (PA)
Also Called: C&A Aromatics
65 S Tyson Ave (11001-1898)
PHONE.................516 354-1200
Fax: 516 354-1262
Richard C Pisano Jr, *CEO*
Stephen Pisano, *Exec VP*
Christopher Pisano, *Vice Pres*
Carl Lembo, *Plant Mgr*
Rob Haedrich, *Purch Dir*
▲ EMP: 29
SQ FT: 11,000
SALES (est): 27.1MM **Privately Held**
WEB: www.citrusandallied.com
SIC: 2087 2899 2911 Flavoring extracts & syrups; chemical preparations; aromatic chemical products

(G-5201)
CREATRON SERVICES INC
Also Called: Lanel
504 Cherry Ln (11001-1646)
PHONE.................516 437-5119
Fax: 516 352-0465
Isidore Epstein, *President*
Alan Rosen, *Vice Pres*
EMP: 20
SQ FT: 10,000
SALES (est): 1.5MM **Privately Held**
SIC: 3861 Photographic equipment & supplies

(G-5202)
DECREE SIGNS & GRAPHICS INC
Also Called: Manhattan Signs
91 Tulip Ave Apt Kd1 (11001-1983)
PHONE.................973 278-3603
Anthony Decrescenzo, *President*
Jeff Taborda, *Asst Controller*
EMP: 15
SALES (est): 1.3MM **Privately Held**
SIC: 3993 Signs & advertising specialties

(G-5203)
EASTERN UNIT EXCH RMNFACTURING
186 Beech St (11001-3318)
P.O. Box 180346, Richmond Hill (11418-0346)
PHONE.................718 739-7113
Fax: 718 739-9005
Chester Brown, *President*
Mehendra Sarwan, *Manager*
EMP: 15 EST: 1976
SQ FT: 5,000
SALES (est): 1.8MM **Privately Held**
SIC: 3694 Alternators, automotive; generators, automotive & aircraft; motors, starting: automotive & aircraft

(G-5204)
FULL SERVICE AUTO BODY INC
Also Called: Lakeville Service Station
25601 Jericho Tpke (11001-1707)
PHONE.................718 831-9300
Anthony Coppolino, *President*
Steven Coppolino Jr, *Vice Pres*
EMP: 12
SQ FT: 25,000
SALES: 3MM **Privately Held**
SIC: 3715 Bus trailers, tractor type

(G-5205)
LANEL INC
504 Cherry Ln Ste 3 (11001-1643)
PHONE.................516 437-5119
Fax: 516 354-2194
Isidore Epstein, *President*
ARI Rosenberg, *Manager*
▲ EMP: 12
SALES (est): 1.3MM **Privately Held**
SIC: 3861 5099 Photographic equipment & supplies; video & audio equipment

(G-5206)
P T E INC
36 Ontario Rd (11001-4113)
PHONE.................516 775-3839
Fax: 516 842-5227
Gustave Loos, *President*
EMP: 19 EST: 1957
SQ FT: 10,125

Floral Park - Nassau County (G-5207)

SALES (est): 1.8MM **Privately Held**
SIC: **3599** Machine shop, jobbing & repair

(G-5207)
TWO BILLS MACHINE & TOOL CO
17 Concord St (11001-2819)
PHONE..................................516 437-2585
Wilhelm Sangen, *President*
Frederick Sangen, *Vice Pres*
EMP: 11
SQ FT: 7,000
SALES (est): 1.3MM **Privately Held**
SIC: **3599** Machine shop, jobbing & repair

Floral Park
Queens County

(G-5208)
INDIRA FOODS INC
25503 Hillside Ave # 255 (11004-1615)
PHONE..................................718 343-1500
Indira Mathur, *President*
EMP: 10
SALES (est): 820K **Privately Held**
SIC: **2032** Italian foods: packaged in cans, jars, etc.

(G-5209)
S & J TRADING INC
8030 263rd St (11004-1517)
P.O. Box 40337, Glen Oaks (11004-0337)
PHONE..................................718 347-1323
Surinder Chawla, *President*
▲ EMP: 8
SALES: 800K **Privately Held**
SIC: **3299** 5063 5033 Mica products; electrical apparatus & equipment; roofing, siding & insulation

Florida
Orange County

(G-5210)
BRACH KNITTING MILLS INC
12 Roosevelt Ave (10921-1808)
P.O. Box 13 (10921-0013)
PHONE..................................845 651-4450
Fax: 845 651-1068
Shea Brach, *President*
Joseph Fried, *Manager*
EMP: 15 EST: 1965
SQ FT: 32,000
SALES: 500K **Privately Held**
SIC: **2251** 2331 Panty hose; tights, women's; shirts, women's & juniors': made from purchased materials

(G-5211)
CONVERGENT CNNCTIVITY TECH INC
1751 State Route 17a (10921-1061)
P.O. Box 454 (10921-0454)
PHONE..................................845 651-5250
Joseph T Moore, *Ch of Bd*
Mary L Van Sise, *Info Tech Mgr*
▲ EMP: 5
SALES (est): 813K **Privately Held**
SIC: **3357** Nonferrous wiredrawing & insulating

(G-5212)
EMPIRE VENTILATION EQP CO INC (PA)
9 Industrial Dr (10921-1000)
PHONE..................................718 728-2143
Fax: 718 267-0143
George R Taylor, *President*
Linda L Taylor, *Vice Pres*
Robert E Warnken, *Treasurer*
Brian G Taylor, *Admin Sec*
EMP: 12 EST: 1936
SQ FT: 15,000
SALES: 1.5MM **Privately Held**
WEB: www.empirevent.com
SIC: **3444** Ventilators, sheet metal

(G-5213)
ISLAND NAMEPLATE INC
124 S Main St (10921-1818)
P.O. Box 548 (10921-0548)
PHONE..................................845 651-4005
Fax: 845 651-0609
Joseph C Sicina III, *President*
EMP: 5
SQ FT: 1,860
SALES: 260K **Privately Held**
SIC: **3993** Name plates: except engraved, etched, etc.: metal

(G-5214)
NEW ENGLAND TOOL CO LTD
Also Called: Fine Architectural Met Smiths
44 Jayne St (10921-1109)
P.O. Box 30, Chester (10918-0030)
PHONE..................................845 651-7550
Fax: 845 651-7857
Rhoda Mack, *President*
EMP: 6
SQ FT: 4,000
SALES: 250K **Privately Held**
WEB: www.iceforge.com
SIC: **3446** Architectural metalwork

(G-5215)
STAUBER PRFMCE INGREDIENTS INC
Also Called: Pharmline
41 Bridge St (10921-1323)
PHONE..................................845 651-4443
EMP: 9
SALES (corp-wide): 413.9MM **Publicly Held**
SIC: **2833** Medicinals & botanicals
HQ: Stauber Performance Ingredients, Inc.
4120 N Palm St
Fullerton CA 92835
714 441-3900

(G-5216)
ZIRCAR CERAMICS INC (PA)
100 N Main St Ste 2 (10921-1329)
P.O. Box 519 (10921-0519)
PHONE..................................845 651-6600
Phil Hamling, *President*
David Hamling, *Vice Pres*
Jay Magnelli, *Prdtn Mgr*
Jessica Tan, *Sales Engr*
Marilyn Sweeney, *Manager*
▲ EMP: 34
SQ FT: 30,000
SALES (est): 4.5MM **Privately Held**
WEB: www.zircarceramics.com
SIC: **2899** Insulating compounds

(G-5217)
ZIRCAR REFR COMPOSITES INC
14 Golden Hill Ter (10921-1116)
PHONE..................................845 651-2200
Julie Sterns, *Branch Mgr*
EMP: 12
SALES (corp-wide): 3.3MM **Privately Held**
WEB: www.zrci.com
SIC: **2493** Reconstituted wood products
PA: Zircar Refractory Composites, Inc.
46 Jayne St
Florida NY 10921
845 651-4481

(G-5218)
ZIRCAR REFR COMPOSITES INC (PA)
46 Jayne St (10921-1109)
P.O. Box 489 (10921-0489)
PHONE..................................845 651-4481
Tom Hamling, *Ch of Bd*
Peter Hamling, *President*
Michael Cauda, *Sales Engr*
Julie Stern, *Manager*
▲ EMP: 8
SQ FT: 4,000
SALES (est): 3.3MM **Privately Held**
WEB: www.zrci.com
SIC: **3297** Nonclay refractories

(G-5219)
ZIRCAR ZIRCONIA INC
87 Meadow Rd (10921-1112)
P.O. Box 287 (10921-0287)
PHONE..................................845 651-3040
Craig Hamling, *President*

Clare Hamling, *Vice Pres*
John Koar, *Engineer*
David Hoskins, *Sales Mgr*
EMP: 24
SQ FT: 20,800
SALES (est): 4MM **Privately Held**
WEB: www.zircarzirconia.com
SIC: **3297** Nonclay refractories

Flushing
Queens County

(G-5220)
5 STARS PRINTING CORP
13330 32nd Ave (11354-1921)
PHONE..................................718 461-4612
Fax: 718 461-4612
S K Han, *President*
EMP: 10
SALES (est): 894.5K **Privately Held**
WEB: www.bocasoccer.com
SIC: **2759** Commercial printing

(G-5221)
ACE PRINTING & PUBLISHING INC
Also Called: Ace Printing Co
14951 Roosevelt Ave (11354-4939)
PHONE..................................718 939-0040
Sung N Kang, *CEO*
EMP: 10
SQ FT: 3,000
SALES (est): 800K **Privately Held**
SIC: **2752** Offset & photolithographic printing

(G-5222)
AIR EXPORT MECHANICAL
4108 Parsons Blvd Apt 4r (11355-1940)
PHONE..................................917 709-5310
Gricelio Nosquera, *President*
EMP: 5
SALES (est): 480K **Privately Held**
SIC: **3564** Filters, air: furnaces, air conditioning equipment, etc.

(G-5223)
AJ GREENTECH HOLDINGS LTD
13620 38th Ave Ste 3g (11354-4232)
PHONE..................................718 395-8706
Chu LI An, *CEO*
EMP: 5 EST: 2013
SALES: 3.4MM **Privately Held**
SIC: **2869** 1711 5065 8742 Fuels; solar energy contractor; electronic parts & equipment; management consulting services

(G-5224)
ALBERT SIY
Also Called: Avant Garde Screen Printing Co
13508 Booth Memorial Ave (11355-5009)
PHONE..................................718 359-0389
Albert Siy, *Owner*
EMP: 8
SALES: 1MM **Privately Held**
SIC: **2752** 2759 2396 Commercial printing, lithographic; screen printing; automotive & apparel trimmings

(G-5225)
ALL ABOUT ART INC
4128 Murray St (11355-1055)
PHONE..................................718 321-0755
Gee Book Jeung, *President*
EMP: 11
SALES (est): 900K **Privately Held**
WEB: www.myallaboutart.com
SIC: **2395** 2261 Embroidery products, except schiffli machine; finishing plants, cotton

(G-5226)
AMERICAN AUTO ACC INCRPORATION (PA)
3506 Leavitt St Apt Cfc (11354-2967)
PHONE..................................718 886-6600
Henry Hsu, *President*
Betty L Hsu, *Vice Pres*
Nina Sung, *Accountant*
EMP: 20
SQ FT: 50,000

SALES (est): 1.4MM **Privately Held**
WEB: www.3aracing.com
SIC: **3714** 5013 Motor vehicle parts & accessories; motor vehicle supplies & new parts

(G-5227)
ARRINGEMENT INTERNATIONAL INC
16015 45th Ave (11358-3135)
PHONE..................................347 323-7974
WEI Huang, *President*
EMP: 6 EST: 2013
SQ FT: 1,500
SALES: 200K **Privately Held**
SIC: **3911** Jewelry, precious metal

(G-5228)
ATI TRADING INC
13631 41st Ave Ste 5a (11355-2446)
PHONE..................................718 888-7918
EMP: 16
SALES (est): 3.8MM **Privately Held**
SIC: **3823** Computer interface equipment for industrial process control

(G-5229)
BEL AIRE OFFSET CORP
Also Called: Bel Aire Printing
1853 College Point Blvd (11356-2220)
PHONE..................................718 539-8333
Fax: 718 321-9800
Carmine Nicoletti, *President*
Michael Vogell, *Manager*
EMP: 5 EST: 1973
SQ FT: 5,000
SALES (est): 680.7K **Privately Held**
WEB: www.belaireprintingcorp.com
SIC: **2752** Commercial printing, offset

(G-5230)
BEST CONCRETE MIX CORP
3510 College Point Blvd (11354-2719)
PHONE..................................718 463-5500
Fax: 718 762-0804
Michael Emanuele, *President*
EMP: 35
SQ FT: 20,000
SALES (est): 6.2MM **Privately Held**
SIC: **3273** Ready-mixed concrete

(G-5231)
CFP PURCHASING INC
4760 197th St (11358-3937)
PHONE..................................705 806-0383
Robert Mantrop, *President*
▼ EMP: 2 EST: 2014
SALES: 3MM **Privately Held**
SIC: **2499** 7389 Yard sticks, wood;

(G-5232)
CHINESE MEDICAL REPORT INC
3907 Prince St Ste 5b (11354-5308)
PHONE..................................718 359-5676
Fax: 718 359-3816
Ava Lee, *President*
▲ EMP: 5
SALES (est): 210K **Privately Held**
WEB: www.chinesemedical.com
SIC: **2711** Newspapers

(G-5233)
CHRISTIAN PRESS INC
14317 Franklin Ave (11355-2116)
PHONE..................................718 886-4400
Fax: 718 886-0074
Young-Choon Chang, *President*
EMP: 5
SQ FT: 1,200
SALES: 250K **Privately Held**
SIC: **2711** 8661 Newspapers, publishing & printing; miscellaneous denomination church

(G-5234)
COFIRE PAVING CORPORATION
12030 28th Ave (11354-1049)
PHONE..................................718 463-1403
Fax: 718 358-8522
Ross J Holland, *President*
John D Ficarelli, *Treasurer*
Linda Myer, *Office Mgr*
Robert Ficarelli, *Admin Sec*
EMP: 30 EST: 1946
SQ FT: 29,000

SALES (est): 4.6MM **Privately Held**
SIC: **2951** 1611 Asphalt paving mixtures & blocks; surfacing & paving

(G-5235)
COURTLANDT BOOT JACK CO INC
3334 Prince St (11354-2731)
PHONE..................................718 445-6200
Fax: 718 353-1524
John K Parlante Jr, *President*
▲ EMP: 35 EST: 1940
SQ FT: 30,000
SALES (est): 3.9MM **Privately Held**
SIC: **3199** 2387 Holsters, leather; apparel belts

(G-5236)
DAHUA ELECTRONICS CORPORATION
13412 59th Ave (11355-5244)
PHONE..................................718 886-2188
Gomita Junkiji, *President*
Scott Russel, *Manager*
EMP: 20
SALES: 156MM **Privately Held**
SIC: **3676** Electronic resistors

(G-5237)
DELICIAS ANDINAS FOOD CORP
5750 Maspeth Ave (11378-2212)
PHONE..................................718 416-2922
Fax: 718 416-2929
Manuel Midonda, *President*
Juanita Midonda, *Vice Pres*
Maritza Sanchez, *Manager*
EMP: 33
SALES (est): 5.6MM **Privately Held**
SIC: **2051** Bread, cake & related products

(G-5238)
DIGITAL ONE USA INC
Also Called: Akhon Samoy Weekly
7230 Roosevelt Ave (11372-6335)
PHONE..................................718 396-4890
Fax: 718 396-4810
Kazi S Hoque, *President*
EMP: 15
SALES (est): 735.5K **Privately Held**
SIC: **2711** Newspapers

(G-5239)
EXCELSIOR MLT-CLTURAL INST INC
13340 Roosevelt Ave 7g (11354-5263)
P.O. Box 14332, Augusta GA (30919-0332)
PHONE..................................706 627-4285
Rhonda Jackson, *CEO*
Ronald Nurse, *Director*
EMP: 14
SALES (est): 704.3K **Privately Held**
SIC: **3812** Cabin environment indicators

(G-5240)
FERRARA BROS BLDG MTLS CORP (PA)
12005 31st Ave (11354-2516)
PHONE..................................718 939-3030
Fax: 718 939-7286
Joseph Ferrara, *Chairman*
Leonard Ferrara, *Vice Pres*
Donna Ninocco, *CFO*
EMP: 20
SQ FT: 16,000
SALES: 15MM **Privately Held**
WEB: www.ferraraconcrete.com
SIC: **3273** 5211 5033 Ready-mixed concrete; masonry materials & supplies; roofing, siding & insulation

(G-5241)
FIBER USA CORP
13620 38th Ave Ste 11f (11354-4352)
PHONE..................................718 888-1512
Pengyu Zhu, *President*
EMP: 8
SQ FT: 3,000
SALES (est): 1.7MM **Privately Held**
SIC: **2653** 5093 Corrugated & solid fiber boxes; plastics scrap
PA: Jiangyin Mighty Chemical Fiber Co., Ltd.
Mazhen Industrial Park
Wuxi
510 827-1150

(G-5242)
FLUSHING IRON WELD INC
13125 Maple Ave (11355-4224)
PHONE..................................718 359-2208
Fax: 718 461-6376
Dario Toro, *President*
Hector Munoz, *Vice Pres*
Paula Munoz, *Manager*
EMP: 20
SQ FT: 5,000
SALES: 2.5MM **Privately Held**
SIC: **3446** Architectural metalwork

(G-5243)
GILDAN MEDIA CORP
6631 Wetherole St (11374-4640)
PHONE..................................718 459-6299
Fax: 718 459-6299
Gilles Dana, *President*
▲ EMP: 12
SALES (est): 1.2MM **Privately Held**
WEB: www.gildanmedia.com
SIC: **2731** Books: publishing only

(G-5244)
GLOBAL GRAPHICS INC
Also Called: Wen Hwa Printing
3711 Prince St Ste D (11354-4428)
PHONE..................................718 939-4967
Rong Fang, *President*
Chen Wang, *Manager*
EMP: 10
SALES: 500K **Privately Held**
SIC: **2752** Commercial printing, lithographic

(G-5245)
GROUP INTERNATIONAL LLC
14711 34th Ave (11354-3755)
PHONE..................................718 475-8805
John Liriano, *CEO*
EMP: 5 EST: 2013
SALES (est): 153.8K **Privately Held**
SIC: **2043** Infants' foods, cereal type

(G-5246)
H H B BAKERY OF LITTLE NECK
Also Called: Richer's Bakery
24914 Horace Harding Expy (11362-2050)
PHONE..................................718 631-7004
Eugene Stanko, *President*
EMP: 5
SALES (est): 230K **Privately Held**
SIC: **2051** Bakery: wholesale or wholesale/retail combined

(G-5247)
H&L COMPUTERS INC
13523 Northern Blvd (11354-4006)
PHONE..................................516 873-8088
Bothen Lin, *President*
EMP: 20
SQ FT: 5,000
SALES (est): 1.6MM **Privately Held**
SIC: **3571** Electronic computers

(G-5248)
HAIR COLOR RESEARCH GROUP INC
13320 Whitestone Expy (11354-2509)
PHONE..................................718 445-6026
Armando Petruccelli, *President*
EMP: 26
SALES: 2.5MM **Privately Held**
SIC: **3999** Hair & hair-based products

(G-5249)
HARVY SURGICAL SUPPLY CORP
Also Called: Harvy Canes
3435 Collins Pl (11354-2720)
PHONE..................................718 939-1122
Fax: 718 939-1222
Harvey Murtha, *President*
Paul Murtha, *Vice Pres*
Sara Moss, *Finance Other*
Judith Murtha, *Sales Mgr*
▲ EMP: 30 EST: 1897
SALES (est): 5.2MM **Privately Held**
SIC: **3842** Surgical appliances & supplies; canes, orthopedic

(G-5250)
HISUN OPTOELECTRONICS CO LTD
Also Called: Hisun Led
4109 College Point Blvd (11355-4226)
PHONE..................................718 886-6966
Eugene L Yu, *President*
Jane Wen, *Manager*
Daniel Wen, *Webmaster*
EMP: 15
SALES (est): 1.8MM **Privately Held**
SIC: **3674** Light emitting diodes

(G-5251)
HOME IDEAL INC
4528 159th St (11358-3148)
PHONE..................................718 762-8998
Fax: 718 353-3507
Henry Chin, *President*
Cheryl Lyn, *Corp Secy*
Winston Lyn, *Vice Pres*
EMP: 7
SALES: 300K **Privately Held**
SIC: **2434** 5712 1751 2541 Wood kitchen cabinets; cabinets, except custom made: kitchen; cabinet building & installation; wood partitions & fixtures

(G-5252)
INTER PACIFIC CONSULTING CORP
Also Called: Ipcc
14055 34th Ave Apt 3n (11354-3038)
PHONE..................................718 460-2787
Fax: 718 460-9433
John Tsao, *President*
▲ EMP: 5
SALES: 1MM **Privately Held**
SIC: **3499** 5023 Picture frames, metal; frames & framing, picture & mirror

(G-5253)
INTERCULTURAL ALLIANCE ARTISTS
Also Called: Iaas , The
4510 165th St (11358-3229)
P.O. Box 4378, New York (10163-4378)
PHONE..................................917 406-1202
Gabrielle David, *President*
Stephanie Agosto, *Vice Pres*
Michelle Aragon, *Vice Pres*
Joan Edmonds Ashman, *Vice Pres*
Naydene Brickus, *Vice Pres*
EMP: 5
SALES: 11.8K **Privately Held**
SIC: **2721** Magazines: publishing & printing

(G-5254)
INTREPID CONTROL SERVICE INC
29 Francis Lewis Blvd (11351)
PHONE..................................718 886-8771
William Varrone, *President*
James Colleran, *Corp Secy*
Andrew Manesis, *Vice Pres*
Dean Pecoraro, *Vice Pres*
EMP: 5
SQ FT: 750
SALES (est): 824.7K **Privately Held**
SIC: **3822** Temperature controls, automatic

(G-5255)
IVER PRINTING INC
6703 Main St (11367-1394)
PHONE..................................718 275-2070
Fax: 718 275-9149
William Iverson, *President*
Ann Iverson, *Vice Pres*
Martin Iverson, *Treasurer*
John Iverson, *Admin Sec*
EMP: 5 EST: 1979
SQ FT: 900
SALES: 400K **Privately Held**
WEB: www.iverprinting.com
SIC: **2752** Commercial printing, offset

(G-5256)
J D STEWARD INC
4537 162nd St (11358-3157)
PHONE..................................718 358-0169
Dominick Savino, *President*
Jean Stephens, *Vice Pres*
Joseph Savino, *Treasurer*
EMP: 5

SALES: 900K **Privately Held**
WEB: www.jdsteward.com
SIC: **3498** Fabricated pipe & fittings

(G-5257)
JOHN A VASSILAROS & SON INC
Also Called: Vassilaros Coffee
2905 120th St (11354-2505)
PHONE..................................718 886-4140
John Vassilaros, *President*
Irene Vassilaros, *Vice Pres*
Maria Peterson, *Manager*
EMP: 42
SQ FT: 25,000
SALES: 11MM **Privately Held**
WEB: www.vassilaroscoffee.com
SIC: **2095** Coffee roasting (except by wholesale grocers)

(G-5258)
KALEL PARTNERS LLC
7012 170th St Ste 101 (11365-3332)
PHONE..................................347 561-7804
Todd Friedman, *CEO*
EMP: 15
SALES (est): 493.8K **Privately Held**
SIC: **2741** Miscellaneous publishing

(G-5259)
KEPCO INC (PA)
13138 Sanford Ave (11355-4245)
PHONE..................................718 461-7000
Fax: 718 767-1102
Martin Kupferberg, *President*
Max Kupferberg, *Chairman*
Saul Kupferberg, *Vice Pres*
Seth Kupferberg, *Vice Pres*
Mark Kupferberg, *VP Mfg*
EMP: 40 EST: 1946
SQ FT: 145,000
SALES (est): 21.8MM **Privately Held**
SIC: **3612** Power & distribution transformers

(G-5260)
KEPCO INC
13140 Maple Ave (11355-4225)
PHONE..................................718 461-7000
Martin Kupferberg, *President*
EMP: 90
SALES (corp-wide): 21.8MM **Privately Held**
SIC: **3612** Power & distribution transformers
PA: Kepco, Inc.
13138 Sanford Ave
Flushing NY 11355
718 461-7000

(G-5261)
KEPCO INC
13138 Sanford Ave (11355-4245)
PHONE..................................718 461-7000
EMP: 50
SALES (corp-wide): 21.8MM **Privately Held**
SIC: **3612** Power & distribution transformers
PA: Kepco, Inc.
13138 Sanford Ave
Flushing NY 11355
718 461-7000

(G-5262)
KOREA TIMES NEW YORK INC
15408 Nthrn Blvd Ste 2b (11354)
PHONE..................................718 961-7979
Jae Chang, *President*
EMP: 7
SALES (corp-wide): 63.4MM **Privately Held**
SIC: **2711** Newspapers: publishing only, not printed on site
HQ: The Korea Times New York Inc
3710 Skillman Ave
Long Island City NY 11101
718 784-4526

(G-5263)
KOREAN YELLOW PAGES
14809 Northern Blvd (11354-4346)
PHONE..................................718 461-0073
Gwanseo Pak, *Owner*
EMP: 10

Flushing - Queens County (G-5264)

SALES: 300K **Privately Held**
SIC: 2741 Telephone & other directory publishing

(G-5264)
LB LAUNDRY INC
4431 Kissena Blvd (11355-3055)
PHONE...................347 399-8030
LI Xinli, *Owner*
EMP: 3
SQ FT: 700
SALES: 2MM **Privately Held**
SIC: 2842 3582 Laundry cleaning preparations; commercial laundry equipment

(G-5265)
LEVI STRAUSS & CO
13432 Blossom Ave (11355-4639)
PHONE...................917 213-6263
Chip Bergh, *Branch Mgr*
EMP: 19
SALES (corp-wide): 4.4B **Privately Held**
SIC: 2325 Jeans: men's, youths' & boys'
PA: Levi Strauss & Co.
   1155 Battery St
   San Francisco CA 94111
   415 501-6000

(G-5266)
LIFE WATCH TECHNOLOGY INC
Also Called: My Life My Health
42-10 Polen St Ste 412 (11355)
PHONE...................917 669-2428
Jiping Zhu, *CEO*
EMP: 56
SQ FT: 1,200
SALES (est): 1.6MM **Privately Held**
SIC: 3873 Watches & parts, except crystals & jewels

(G-5267)
LONG ISLAND PIPE SUPPLY INC
5858 56th St (11378-3106)
PHONE...................718 456-7877
David Pargon, *Manager*
EMP: 6
SALES (corp-wide): 59.7MM **Privately Held**
WEB: www.lipipe.com
SIC: 3498 Fabricated pipe & fittings
PA: Long Island Pipe Supply Inc
   586 Commercial Ave
   Garden City NY 11530
   516 222-8008

(G-5268)
LOOSELEAF LAW PUBLICATIONS INC
4308 162nd St (11358-3131)
P.O. Box 650042, Fresh Meadows (11365-0042)
PHONE...................718 359-5559
Fax: 718 539-0941
Warren Taylor, *President*
Michael Loughrey, *Vice Pres*
Hilliary McKeon, *Manager*
Hilary McKeon, *Manager*
Lynette Piper, *Admin Sec*
EMP: 10
SQ FT: 5,000
SALES: 1MM **Privately Held**
WEB: www.looseleaflaw.com
SIC: 2731 5961 Books: publishing only; books, mail order (except book clubs)

(G-5269)
MDS USA INC
13244 Booth Memorial Ave (11355-5128)
PHONE...................718 358-5588
Kim Jong Hag, *President*
EMP: 20
SALES (est): 1.6MM **Privately Held**
SIC: 3993 Neon signs

(G-5270)
NATURAL LAB INC
13538 39th Ave Ste 4 (11354-4423)
PHONE...................718 321-8848
Michael Chang, *Manager*
▲EMP: 6
SALES (est): 543.2K **Privately Held**
SIC: 2099 5149 Food preparations; organic & diet foods

(G-5271)
NEW STAR BAKERY
4121a Kissena Blvd (11355-3138)
PHONE...................718 961-8868
Huantang Liang, *Owner*
EMP: 20
SALES (est): 1.2MM **Privately Held**
SIC: 2051 Bread, cake & related products

(G-5272)
NEW YORK IL BO INC
Also Called: Korean New York Daily, The
4522 162nd St Fl 2 (11358-3280)
PHONE...................718 961-1538
Fax: 718 358-7243
Grace Chung, *CEO*
▲EMP: 15
SALES: 120K **Privately Held**
SIC: 2711 Newspapers

(G-5273)
NEW YORK TIMES COMPANY
1 New York Times Plz (11354-1200)
PHONE...................718 281-7000
Fax: 718 281-7219
Thomas P Lombardo, *Plant Mgr*
Mike Joyce, *Foreman/Supr*
EMP: 12
SALES (corp-wide): 1.5B **Publicly Held**
WEB: www.nytco.com
SIC: 2711 Newspapers, publishing & printing
PA: The New York Times Company
   620 8th Ave
   New York NY 10018
   212 556-1234

(G-5274)
NORTH AMERICA PASTEL ARTISTS
13303 41st Ave Apt 1a (11355-5840)
PHONE...................718 463-4701
Jason Chang, *President*
EMP: 8
SALES: 4.5K **Privately Held**
SIC: 3952 Pastels, artists'

(G-5275)
NORTH SHORE NEON SIGN CO INC
4649 54th Ave (11378-1011)
PHONE...................718 937-0569
Fax: 718 937-4848
Tom Brown, *Manager*
EMP: 30
SALES (corp-wide): 15.4MM **Privately Held**
WEB: www.northshoreneon.com
SIC: 3993 1799 Signs & advertising specialties; sign installation & maintenance
PA: North Shore Neon Sign Co. Inc.
   295 Skidmores Rd
   Deer Park NY 11729
   631 667-2500

(G-5276)
OLIVE LED LIGHTING INC
2819 119th St (11354-1068)
PHONE...................718 746-0830
Junho Lee, *President*
Alex Kang, *Manager*
▲EMP: 7
SQ FT: 4,000
SALES (est): 640K **Privately Held**
SIC: 3648 5063 Lighting equipment; light bulbs & related supplies

(G-5277)
PALADINO PRTG & GRAPHICS INC
20009 32nd Ave (11361-1037)
PHONE...................718 279-6000
Fax: 718 352-2745
Vincent Paladino, *President*
EMP: 9
SQ FT: 1,000
SALES (est): 1.2MM **Privately Held**
SIC: 2752 Commercial printing, lithographic

(G-5278)
PARIS BAGUETTE
15624 Northern Blvd (11354-5034)
PHONE...................718 961-0404
K Kang, *Manager*
EMP: 8
SALES (est): 723K **Privately Held**
SIC: 2051 Cakes, bakery: except frozen

(G-5279)
PARIS WEDDING CENTER CORP (PA)
42-53 42 55 Main St (11355)
PHONE...................347 368-4085
Yuki Lin, *President*
▲EMP: 9
SALES (est): 1.5MM **Privately Held**
SIC: 2335 Wedding gowns & dresses

(G-5280)
PEACE TIMES WEEKLY INC
14527 33rd Ave (11354-3145)
PHONE...................718 762-6500
Yongil Park, *President*
Joseph Aahn, *President*
▲EMP: 5
SALES: 368.8K **Privately Held**
SIC: 2711 Newspapers

(G-5281)
PERRY PLASTICS INC
3050 Whitestone Expy # 300 (11354-1964)
PHONE...................718 747-5600
Irwing Laub, *President*
Aaron Laub, *Vice Pres*
▼EMP: 10
SALES (est): 936K **Privately Held**
SIC: 2295 Chemically coated & treated fabrics

(G-5282)
PLASTI-VUE CORP
4130 Murray St (11355-1055)
PHONE...................718 463-2300
Fax: 718 358-1903
Gary Fischer, *President*
Bill Olveari, *General Mgr*
EMP: 6
SQ FT: 12,800
SALES (est): 410K **Privately Held**
SIC: 3993 Displays & cutouts, window & lobby

(G-5283)
PORCELAIN REFINISHING CORP
19905 32nd Ave (11358-1205)
PHONE...................516 352-4841
Fax: 718 352-3324
Paula Weinstock, *President*
EMP: 15
SQ FT: 700
SALES (est): 2.1MM **Privately Held**
SIC: 3431 5074 Bathtubs: enameled iron, cast iron or pressed metal; sanitary ware, china or enameled iron

(G-5284)
PS PIBBS INC (PA)
Also Called: Pibbs Industries
13315 32nd Ave (11354-1909)
PHONE...................718 445-8046
Fax: 718 461-3910
Damiano Petruccelli, *CEO*
Biagio Petruccelli, *President*
Sunny Thomas, *President*
Giulio Pertruccelli, *Vice Pres*
Antonio Petruccelli, *Vice Pres*
▲EMP: 50
SQ FT: 30,000
SALES (est): 10.1MM **Privately Held**
WEB: www.pibbs.com
SIC: 3999 2844 Barber & beauty shop equipment; shampoos, rinses, conditioners: hair; hair preparations, including shampoos; face creams or lotions

(G-5285)
PURE GHEE INC (PA)
5701 225th St (11364-2042)
PHONE...................718 224-7399
Mahesh K Maheshwari, *President*
Sucheta Maheshwari, *Senior VP*
EMP: 6 EST: 1988
SQ FT: 9,700
SALES: 1.5MM **Privately Held**
SIC: 2021 Creamery butter

(G-5286)
PURE KEMIKA LLC
6228 136th St Apt 2 (11367-1021)
PHONE...................718 745-2200

Luis F Becker, *Mng Member*
EMP: 6 EST: 2013
SQ FT: 1,000
SALES: 1.5MM **Privately Held**
SIC: 2899 Chemical preparations

(G-5287)
RAJBHOG FOODS INC
4123 Murray St (11355-1048)
PHONE...................718 358-5105
Fax: 718 358-5123
Ajit M Mody, *CEO*
Suzy Mody, *Vice Pres*
Sachin Mody, *Treasurer*
Cherry Rajbhog, *Sales Dir*
Lalita Mody, *Sales Mgr*
▲EMP: 30
SQ FT: 12,000
SALES (est): 4.4MM **Privately Held**
WEB: www.rajbhog.com
SIC: 2064 Candy & other confectionery products

(G-5288)
RIVERA
3330 109th St (11368-1216)
PHONE...................718 458-1488
EMP: 5
SALES (est): 214.2K **Privately Held**
SIC: 3281 Cut stone & stone products

(G-5289)
S & L AEROSPACE METALS LLC
12012 28th Ave (11354-1049)
PHONE...................718 326-1821
Fax: 718 894-5843
Jerry Wang, *President*
Carlos Quintana, *Vice Pres*
Ted Varvatsas, *Vice Pres*
Alan Wang, *Vice Pres*
Angelo Borgia, *Program Mgr*
EMP: 100 EST: 1946
SQ FT: 50,000
SALES (est): 28.1MM **Privately Held**
WEB: www.slaerospace.com
SIC: 3728 Aircraft parts & equipment

(G-5290)
SANFORD PRINTING INC
13335 41st Rd (11355-3667)
PHONE...................718 461-1202
Fax: 718 886-4258
Paul Peng, *President*
▲EMP: 5
SALES (est): 671.9K **Privately Held**
SIC: 2752 Commercial printing, offset

(G-5291)
SEO RYUNG INC
4128 Murray St (11355-1055)
PHONE...................718 321-0755
Gee Book Jeung, *President*
▲EMP: 11
SQ FT: 9,200
SALES (est): 1MM **Privately Held**
SIC: 2261 2395 Screen printing of cotton broadwoven fabrics; embroidery & art needlework

(G-5292)
SH IRONWORKS INC
15142 17th Ave (11357-3119)
PHONE...................917 907-0507
Therasa Sieve, *President*
EMP: 5 EST: 1998
SALES (est): 420K **Privately Held**
SIC: 3446 Architectural metalwork

(G-5293)
SNAPP TOO ENTERPRISE
3312 211th St (11361-1523)
PHONE...................718 224-5252
Edward Porzelt, *Owner*
EMP: 6
SALES (est): 330K **Privately Held**
SIC: 2086 Bottled & canned soft drinks

(G-5294)
SOPHIEXX CORPORATION
14715 33rd Ave (11354-3227)
PHONE...................917 963-5339
Jong Howard Lee, *President*
Kevin Kim, *Vice Pres*
EMP: 5

GEOGRAPHIC SECTION

Forest Hills - Queens County (G-5321)

SALES: 3.5MM **Privately Held**
SIC: **2339** Athletic clothing: women's, misses' & juniors'

(G-5295)
SPEEDY ENTERPRISE OF USA CORP
4120 162nd St (11358-4123)
PHONE.................................718 463-3000
Harolyn Paik, *Principal*
EMP: 6
SALES (est): 648.1K **Privately Held**
SIC: **2759** Commercial printing

(G-5296)
STAR CORRUGATED BOX CO INC
5515 Grand Ave (11378-3186)
PHONE.................................718 386-3200
Robert Karlin, *Chairman*
Richard H Etra, *Vice Pres*
EMP: 9
SALES (est): 1.6MM **Privately Held**
SIC: **2653** Boxes, corrugated: made from purchased materials

(G-5297)
STARK AQUARIUM PRODUCTS CO INC
Also Called: Stark Fish
2914 122nd St (11354-2530)
PHONE.................................718 445-5357
Edith Starkman, *President*
Omiros Gioroukos, *Vice Pres*
▲ EMP: 29 EST: 1977
SQ FT: 20,000
SALES (est): 3.8MM **Privately Held**
WEB: www.starkproducts.com
SIC: **3231** Products of purchased glass; aquariums & reflectors, glass

(G-5298)
STEVE ZINN
Also Called: Cotton Tail Shop
16111 29th Ave (11358-1049)
PHONE.................................718 746-8551
Fax: 718 746-8564
Steve Zinn, *Owner*
Ellen Zinn, *Vice Pres*
EMP: 15
SALES: 1MM **Privately Held**
SIC: **2361** Girls' & children's dresses, blouses & shirts

(G-5299)
SUNRISE TILE INC
13309 35th Ave (11354-2712)
PHONE.................................718 939-0538
▲ EMP: 8
SALES (est): 808.7K **Privately Held**
SIC: **2273** 1752 Carpets & rugs; wood floor installation & refinishing

(G-5300)
TEMPCO GLASS FABRICATION LLC
13110 Maple Ave (11355-4223)
PHONE.................................718 461-6888
Steven Powell, *General Mgr*
EMP: 9
SALES (est): 920K **Privately Held**
SIC: **3211** Building glass, flat

(G-5301)
TILCON NEW YORK INC
Also Called: Flushing Terminal
3466 College Point Blvd (11354-2717)
PHONE.................................845 480-3249
EMP: 63
SALES (corp-wide): 25.3B **Privately Held**
SIC: **1429** Dolomitic marble, crushed & broken-quarrying
HQ: Tilcon New York Inc.
162 Old Mill Rd
West Nyack NY 10994
845 358-4500

(G-5302)
TONGLI PHARMACEUTICALS USA INC (PA)
4260 Main St Apt 6f (11355-4737)
PHONE.................................212 842-8337
Mingli Yao, *Ch of Bd*
Ailing Zhao, *Admin Sec*
EMP: 11

SALES: 11.1MM **Publicly Held**
SIC: **2834** Pharmaceutical preparations

(G-5303)
TRIBORO BAGEL CO INC
Also Called: Bagel Oasis
18312 Horace Harding Expy (11365-2123)
PHONE.................................718 359-9245
Fax: 718 539-8484
Abe Moskowitz, *President*
Mike Edelstein, *Corp Secy*
Mike Donovan, *Controller*
EMP: 20 EST: 1961
SQ FT: 1,200
SALES: 1MM **Privately Held**
WEB: www.bageloasis.com
SIC: **2051** Bakery: wholesale or wholesale/retail combined; bagels, fresh or frozen

(G-5304)
TWINKLE LIGHTING INC
13114 40th Rd (11354-5137)
PHONE.................................718 225-0939
Fuchun Lin, *President*
Cheng Zhi Lai, *Sales Mgr*
EMP: 5
SALES (est): 389.7K **Privately Held**
SIC: **3646** Commercial indusl & institutional electric lighting fixtures

(G-5305)
UNIQUE PRINTING COMPANY LLC
5900 Decatur St Ste 6 (11385-5900)
PHONE.................................718 386-2519
Edward Kowlessar,
Dennis Kowlessar,
Reuben Sukhraj,
EMP: 5
SQ FT: 5,500
SALES: 340K **Privately Held**
SIC: **2752** Commercial printing, lithographic

(G-5306)
UNITED SATCOM INC
4555 Robinson St (11355-3444)
PHONE.................................718 359-4100
Ted Park, *President*
EMP: 7
SQ FT: 3,500
SALES: 1.5MM **Privately Held**
SIC: **3663** Microwave communication equipment

(G-5307)
WARODEAN CORPORATION
Also Called: Loosesleeve Law Publications
4308 162nd St (11358-3131)
P.O. Box 650042, Fresh Meadows (11365-0042)
PHONE.................................718 359-5559
Michael Loughrey, *President*
EMP: 8
SQ FT: 1,750
SALES (est): 690K **Privately Held**
SIC: **2731** Textbooks: publishing & printing

(G-5308)
WOLSKI WOOD WORKS INC
14134 78th Rd Apt 3c (11367-3331)
PHONE.................................718 577-9816
Tadeusz Wolski, *President*
EMP: 7
SALES (est): 121K **Privately Held**
SIC: **2421** Outdoor wood structural products

(G-5309)
WORLD COMPANY
3533 149th St 119 (11354-3740)
PHONE.................................718 551-8282
Yeon Hee Jeong, *Principal*
EMP: 5
SALES (est): 221.3K **Privately Held**
SIC: **3085** Plastics bottles

(G-5310)
WORLD JOURNAL LLC
Also Called: World Journal Book Store
13619 39th Ave (11354-5504)
PHONE.................................718 445-2277
Fax: 718 445-5157
Bob Chow, *Principal*
EMP: 20

SALES (corp-wide): 52.1MM **Privately Held**
WEB: www.wjnews.net
SIC: **2711** Newspapers: publishing only, not printed on site
HQ: World Journal Llc
14107 20th Ave Fl 2
Whitestone NY 11357
718 746-8889

(G-5311)
YELLOW E HOUSE INC
Also Called: GATECOMUSA
18812 Northern Blvd (11358-2811)
PHONE.................................718 888-2000
Stephan Cho, *CEO*
EMP: 7 EST: 2013
SQ FT: 3,000
SALES (est): 720K **Privately Held**
SIC: **3571** 5045 7629 Electronic computers; computers, peripherals & software; business machine repair, electric

(G-5312)
ZENITH SOLUTIONS
6922 Manse St (11375-5850)
PHONE.................................718 575-8570
P Bilello, *Principal*
EMP: 7
SALES (est): 631.8K **Privately Held**
SIC: **2834** Intravenous solutions

Fly Creek
Otsego County

(G-5313)
ADIRONDACK LEATHER PDTS INC
196 Cemetery Rd (13337-2102)
P.O. Box 180 (13337-0180)
PHONE.................................607 547-5798
Gregory M O Neil, *CEO*
Darlene O Neil, *Vice Pres*
EMP: 10
SALES (est): 1.4MM **Privately Held**
WEB: www.adirondackleatherproducts.com
SIC: **3199** 7389 Holsters, leather; leggings or chaps, canvas or leather; leather belting & strapping;

(G-5314)
COOPERSTOWN BAT CO INC (PA)
Rr 28 (13337)
PHONE.................................607 547-2415
Sharon Oberriter, *President*
Don Oberriter, *Vice Pres*
EMP: 15
SQ FT: 4,000
SALES (est): 1.2MM **Privately Held**
WEB: www.cooperstownbat.com
SIC: **3949** 5941 Sporting & athletic goods; sporting goods & bicycle shops

---

Fonda
Montgomery County

(G-5315)
KASSON & KELLER INC
Also Called: Kas-Kel
60 School St (12068-4809)
P.O. Box 777 (12068-0777)
PHONE.................................518 853-3421
Fax: 518 853-3929
William Keller III, *Ch of Bd*
Matthew Sullivan Jr, *General Mgr*
James P Keller, *Exec VP*
Linda Kilmartin, *Credit Mgr*
Mark Empie, *Sales Mgr*
▲ EMP: 900 EST: 1946
SQ FT: 60,000
SALES (est): 173.8MM **Privately Held**
WEB: www.kas-kel.com
SIC: **3442** 3089 1521 3231 Window & door frames; windows, plastic; single-family housing construction; products of purchased glass

(G-5316)
KEYMARK CORPORATION
1188 Cayadutta St (12068)
P.O. Box 626 (12068-0626)
PHONE.................................518 853-3421
Fax: 518 853-3130
William L Keller III, *Ch of Bd*
Kelly Fernet, *General Mgr*
Tony Maiolo, *COO*
James P Keller, *Exec VP*
Bob Channell, *VP Opers*
▲ EMP: 600 EST: 1964
SQ FT: 250,000
SALES (est): 228.8MM **Privately Held**
WEB: www.keymarkcorp.com
SIC: **3354** 3479 3471 Aluminum extruded products; painting of metal products; anodizing (plating) of metals or formed products

(G-5317)
TEMPER CORPORATION (PA)
544 Persse Rd (12068-7700)
P.O. Box 1127 (12068-1127)
PHONE.................................518 853-3467
Fax: 518 853-4092
John Rode, *President*
Bob Francisco, *Production*
Nancy S Chmaeh, *Office Mgr*
Alice Stanawich, *Office Mgr*
Ruth Browen, *Info Tech Mgr*
EMP: 25
SQ FT: 30,000
SALES (est): 3.9MM **Privately Held**
WEB: www.tempercorp.com
SIC: **3493** 3053 Steel springs, except wire; gaskets & sealing devices

(G-5318)
TEMPER CORPORATION
Temper Axle Products
544 Persse Rd (12068-7700)
PHONE.................................518 853-3467
John Rhode, *President*
EMP: 5
SALES (corp-wide): 3.9MM **Privately Held**
WEB: www.tempercorp.com
SIC: **3714** Axles, motor vehicle
PA: Temper Corporation
544 Persse Rd
Fonda NY 12068
518 853-3467

Forest Hills
Queens County

(G-5319)
2H INTERNATIONAL CORP
6766 108th St Apt D1 (11375-2904)
PHONE.................................347 623-9380
June Ll, *Manager*
EMP: 5
SALES: 300K **Privately Held**
SIC: **2337** Women's & misses' suits & coats

(G-5320)
AIGNER CHOCOLATES INC (PA)
10302 Metropolitan Ave (11375-6734)
PHONE.................................718 544-1850
Peter Aigner, *Ch of Bd*
Christopher Aigner, *Vice Pres*
EMP: 6
SQ FT: 2,000
SALES (est): 879.7K **Privately Held**
WEB: www.aignerchocolates.com
SIC: **2064** 2066 Chocolate candy, except solid chocolate; chocolate candy, solid

(G-5321)
ALLROUND LOGISTICS INC (PA)
Also Called: Allround Maritime Services
7240 Ingram St (11375-5927)
PHONE.................................718 544-8945
Roland Meier, *President*
Ellen Meier, *Vice Pres*
Charlie Boon, *Treasurer*
Jody Barton, *Asst Sec*
◆ EMP: 5
SQ FT: 3,600

Forest Hills - Queens County (G-5322)

GEOGRAPHIC SECTION

SALES (est): 864.1K **Privately Held**
WEB: www.allroundlogistics.com
SIC: 3534 Escalators, passenger & freight

(G-5322)
COMBINE GRAPHICS CORP
10714 Queens Blvd (11375-4249)
PHONE................................212 695-4044
Fax: 212 633-0352
Charles Caminiti, *President*
Louis Zafonte, *Vice Pres*
EMP: 5
SQ FT: 2,300
SALES (est): 590.6K **Privately Held**
SIC: 2752 Commercial printing, offset

(G-5323)
HANGER INC
Also Called: Hanger Prosthectics Orthotics
11835 Queens Blvd Ste Ll3 (11375-7205)
PHONE................................718 575-5504
Joe Nieto, *Manager*
EMP: 8
SALES (corp-wide): 500.5MM **Privately Held**
SIC: 3842 5999 Surgical appliances & supplies; artificial limbs
PA: Hanger, Inc.
10910 Domain Dr Ste 300
Austin TX 78758
512 777-3800

(G-5324)
HI-TECH ADVANCED SOLUTIONS INC
10525 65th Ave Apt 4h (11375-1802)
PHONE................................718 926-3488
Nison B Isaak, *President*
EMP: 10
SALES: 100K **Privately Held**
SIC: 3571 Electronic computers

(G-5325)
NATIVE AMERCN ENRGY GROUP INC (PA)
7211 Austin St Ste 288 (11375-5354)
PHONE................................718 408-2323
Fax: 718 793-4034
Raj Nanvaan, *Principal*
EMP: 2
SALES (est): 1.2MM **Privately Held**
SIC: 1382 Oil & gas exploration services

(G-5326)
NATURE ONLY INC
10420 Queens Blvd Apt 3b (11375-3602)
PHONE................................917 922-6539
EMP: 9
SALES (est): 780K **Privately Held**
SIC: 2844 Mfg Natural Rash Creams For Kids & Facial Creams

(G-5327)
NEW YORK TYPING & PRINTING CO
10816 72nd Ave (11375-5653)
PHONE................................718 268-7900
Jay Goldstin, *President*
EMP: 5 EST: 1981
SALES (est): 380K **Privately Held**
SIC: 2752 7338 Commercial printing, offset; secretarial & typing service

(G-5328)
PRESTON GLASS INDUSTRIES INC
Also Called: P G I
10420 Queens Blvd Apt 17a (11375-3610)
PHONE................................718 997-8888
Ashish Karnavat, *President*
EMP: 20
SALES (est): 1.3MM **Privately Held**
SIC: 3641 Electrodes, cold cathode fluorescent lamp

(G-5329)
VONN LLC
Also Called: Vonn Lighting
6945 108th St Apt 10b (11375-3832)
PHONE................................917 572-5000
Sergio Magarik, *CEO*
Lenny Valdberg, *President*
EMP: 18
SQ FT: 7,000

SALES (est): 5MM **Privately Held**
SIC: 3645 3646 Residential lighting fixtures; commercial indusl & institutional electric lighting fixtures

(G-5330)
WILSON & WILSON GROUP
Also Called: Wilson N Wilson Group & RES
6514 110th St (11375-1424)
PHONE................................212 729-4736
Pius Wilson, *Principal*
EMP: 5
SALES: 25K **Privately Held**
SIC: 3577 Computer peripheral equipment

Forestport
Oneida County

(G-5331)
NIRVANA INC
1 Nirvana Plz (13338)
P.O. Box 200 (13338-0200)
PHONE................................315 942-4900
Fax: 315 942-5013
Mozafar Rafizadeh, *President*
Mansur Rafizadeh, *Vice Pres*
MO Rafizadeh, *Vice Pres*
Edward Wiehl, *Vice Pres*
Darya Rafizadeh, *Sales Mgr*
▲ EMP: 160
SQ FT: 250,000
SALES (est): 83.7MM **Privately Held**
WEB: www.nirvanaspring.com
SIC: 2086 Mineral water, carbonated: packaged in cans, bottles, etc.; water, pasteurized: packaged in cans, bottles, etc.

(G-5332)
TOWN OF OHIO
Also Called: Town of Ohio Highway Garage
N Lake Rd (13338)
PHONE................................315 392-2055
Fred Reuter, *Manager*
EMP: 24
SQ FT: 2,066 **Privately Held**
SIC: 3531 Snow plow attachments
PA: Town Of Ohio
234 Nellis Rd
Cold Brook NY 13324
315 826-7912

Forestville
Chautauqua County

(G-5333)
BAILEY MANUFACTURING CO LLC
10987 Bennett State Rd (14062-9714)
P.O. Box 356 (14062-0356)
PHONE................................716 965-2731
Fax: 716 965-2764
John Hines, *President*
Dona Hines,
EMP: 50 EST: 2002
SQ FT: 40,000
SALES (est): 10.9MM **Privately Held**
SIC: 3469 Metal stampings

(G-5334)
MERRITT ESTATE WINERY INC
2264 King Rd (14062-9703)
PHONE................................716 965-4800
Fax: 716 965-4800
William T Merritt, *President*
Jason Merritt, *Corp Secy*
Lynette Aldrich, *Sales Staff*
EMP: 15
SQ FT: 20,000
SALES (est): 2.4MM **Privately Held**
WEB: www.merrittestatewinery.com
SIC: 2084 Wines

(G-5335)
P S M GROUP INC
Also Called: Pit Stop Motorsports
17 Main St (14062-9998)
P.O. Box 500 (14062-0500)
PHONE................................716 532-6686
Jeffrey A Furash, *President*
EMP: 20

SALES (est): 1.7MM **Privately Held**
WEB: www.burningasphalt.com
SIC: 2842 7948 Specialty cleaning, polishes & sanitation goods; race track operation

(G-5336)
SHYKAT PROMOTIONS
10561 Creek Rd (14062-9607)
PHONE................................866 574-2757
Krista Miller, *Owner*
EMP: 7
SALES (est): 372.9K **Privately Held**
SIC: 2759 2395 8743 Screen printing; embroidery & art needlework; promotion service

Fort Ann
Washington County

(G-5337)
PETTEYS LUMBER
Also Called: A Petteys Lumber
10247 State Route 149 (12827-1804)
PHONE................................518 792-5943
Alvin Petteys, *Owner*
EMP: 7
SALES: 370K **Privately Held**
SIC: 2421 2426 Lumber: rough, sawed or planed; hardwood dimension & flooring mills

Fort Drum
Jefferson County

(G-5338)
BLACK RIVER GENERATIONS LLC
Also Called: Reenergy Black River
4515 2nd St (13602)
P.O. Box 849 (13602-0849)
PHONE................................315 773-2314
Peter Lister, *Maintence Staff*
EMP: 23 EST: 2010
SALES (est): 9.8MM **Privately Held**
SIC: 3822 Energy cutoff controls, residential or commercial types

Fort Edward
Washington County

(G-5339)
A HYATT BALL CO LTD
School St (12828)
P.O. Box 342 (12828-0342)
PHONE................................518 747-0272
Fax: 518 747-2619
Robert Simpson, *President*
EMP: 7
SQ FT: 12,000
SALES (est): 640K **Privately Held**
SIC: 3562 3949 Ball bearings & parts; billiard & pool equipment & supplies, general

(G-5340)
BURNHAM POLYMERIC INC
Also Called: Burnhams, The
1408 Route 9 (12828-2459)
P.O. Box 317, Glens Falls (12801-0317)
PHONE................................518 792-3040
Fax: 518 792-4680
Warren Burnham Jr, *President*
Eileen Jensen, *Bookkeeper*
EMP: 7
SQ FT: 8,400
SALES (est): 670K **Privately Held**
WEB: www.burnhams.com
SIC: 3089 Extruded finished plastic products

(G-5341)
D K MACHINE INC
48 Sullivan Pkwy (12828-1027)
PHONE................................518 747-0626
Fax: 518 747-0889
Daniel Komarony, *President*
Jim Glacy, *Purchasing*

Theresa Komarony, *Admin Sec*
EMP: 10
SQ FT: 8,500
SALES (est): 1.7MM **Privately Held**
WEB: www.dkmachine.com
SIC: 3599 5085 Machine shop, jobbing & repair; industrial supplies

(G-5342)
IRVING CONSUMER PRODUCTS INC (DH)
Also Called: Irving Tissue Div
1 Eddy St (12828-1711)
PHONE................................518 747-4151
Fax: 518 747-2746
J K Irving, *Principal*
Arthur L Irving, *Vice Pres*
Bo B Lam, *Vice Pres*
Rachel Roy, *Vice Pres*
Bernice Wall, *Vice Pres*
▲ EMP: 300
SQ FT: 700,000
SALES (est): 98.4MM
SALES (corp-wide): 160.2K **Privately Held**
SIC: 2621 Towels, tissues & napkins: paper & stock
HQ: Irving Consumer Products Limited
100 Prom Midland
Dieppe NB E1A 6
506 858-7777

(G-5343)
PALLETS INC
99 1/2 East St (12828-1813)
P.O. Box 326 (12828-0326)
PHONE................................518 747-4177
Fax: 518 747-3757
Clinton Binley, *President*
Arthur Binley III, *Chairman*
Marvin Horowitz, *Admin Sec*
EMP: 45 EST: 1942
SQ FT: 100,000
SALES (est): 6MM **Privately Held**
WEB: www.palletsincorporated.com
SIC: 2448 2421 Pallets, wood; sawmills & planing mills, general; lumber: rough, sawed or planed

(G-5344)
PARKER MACHINE COMPANY INC
28 Sullivan Pkwy (12828-1027)
PHONE................................518 747-0675
Fax: 518 747-2930
Tammy Aust, *President*
Patrick A Whaley, *Vice Pres*
EMP: 17
SQ FT: 17,400
SALES: 3.1MM **Privately Held**
WEB: www.parkermachine.com
SIC: 3599 5251 Machine shop, jobbing & repair; tools

(G-5345)
REAL BARK MULCH LLC
1380 Towpath Ln (12828-1757)
PHONE................................518 747-3650
Patrick Gulsha,
Patrick Bulsha,
EMP: 9
SALES (est): 1.6MM **Privately Held**
SIC: 3524 Lawn & garden equipment

(G-5346)
STONEGATE STABLESS
106 Reynolds Rd (12828-9244)
PHONE................................518 746-7133
William Johnson, *Owner*
EMP: 8
SALES (est): 540.6K **Privately Held**
SIC: 2399 Horse harnesses & riding crops, etc.: non-leather

Fort Plain
Montgomery County

(G-5347)
ELITE PRECISE MANUFACTURER LLC
55 Willett St (13339-1134)
PHONE................................518 993-3040
Ross Stevenson, *Principal*

EMP: 8
SQ FT: 10,000
SALES (est): 600K **Privately Held**
SIC: 3599 Machine & other job shop work

(G-5348)
PERFORMANCE PRECISION MFG LLC
55 Willett St (13339-1134)
PHONE 518 993-3033
Joeseph Stevenson, *Owner*
EMP: 8
SALES (est): 952.2K **Privately Held**
SIC: 3999 Manufacturing industries

Frankfort
Herkimer County

(G-5349)
ABDO SHTMTL & FABRICATION INC
4293 Acme Rd (13340-3505)
P.O. Box 4071, Utica (13504-4071)
PHONE 315 894-4664
Michael Abdo, *President*
Trish McGowan, *Manager*
Laurie Rose, *Admin Sec*
EMP: 7
SQ FT: 8,000
SALES (est): 1.7MM **Privately Held**
WEB: www.abdosheetmetal.com
SIC: 3444 1721 1799 Sheet metalwork; painting & paper hanging; welding on site

(G-5350)
C-FLEX BEARING CO INC
104 Industrial Dr (13340-1139)
PHONE 315 895-7454
D Joanne Willcox, *President*
Wayne Smith, *Vice Pres*
Susan Cialdone, *Manager*
EMP: 10
SQ FT: 6,200
SALES: 1.4MM **Privately Held**
WEB: www.c-flex.com
SIC: 3568 3812 3556 3825 Bearings, bushings & blocks; search & navigation equipment; food products machinery; instruments to measure electricity

(G-5351)
DI SANOS CREATIVE CANVAS INC
113 W Main St (13340-1007)
PHONE 315 894-3137
Fax: 315 894-0210
John Di Sano, *President*
EMP: 5
SQ FT: 2,400
SALES (est): 425.3K **Privately Held**
WEB: www.disanoscreativecanvas.com
SIC: 2394 5999 5091 Awnings, fabric: made from purchased materials; canvas covers & drop cloths; awnings; canvas products; boat accessories & parts

(G-5352)
F E HALE MFG CO
120 Benson Pl (13340-3752)
P.O. Box 186 (13340-0186)
PHONE 315 894-5490
Fax: 315 894-5046
Jim Benson, *President*
Jon Benson, *Vice Pres*
Mark Macrina, *Plant Mgr*
Cindy Cole, *Credit Mgr*
Michelle Keib, *Natl Sales Mgr*
EMP: 65 **EST:** 1907
SQ FT: 80,000
SALES: 12.6MM **Privately Held**
WEB: www.halebookcases.com
SIC: 2521 Bookcases, office: wood

(G-5353)
FIBERDYNE LABS INC
127 Business Park Dr (13340-3700)
PHONE 315 895-8470
Fax: 315 895-8436
A Peter Polus III, *CEO*
Carl Fredlund, *President*
Chad A Polus, *President*
Eric Grossman, *Managing Prtnr*
Jeffrey Sperl, *General Mgr*

▲ **EMP:** 96
SQ FT: 20,000
SALES: 10.5MM **Privately Held**
WEB: www.fiberdyne.com
SIC: 3357 4822 4899 Fiber optic cable (insulated); telegraph & other communications; communication signal enhancement network system

(G-5354)
GRANNYS KITCHENS LLC
178 Industrial Park Dr (13340-4798)
PHONE 315 735-5000
Fax: 315 735-3200
Kevin McDonough, *President*
Barry J Thaler, *Vice Pres*
Francis Kauth, *Prdtn Mgr*
Thomas Kopa, *QC Mgr*
David Ivey, *VP Finance*
EMP: 280
SQ FT: 165,000
SALES (est): 62.4MM
SALES (corp-wide): 35.2B **Privately Held**
WEB: www.grannyskitchens.com
SIC: 2053 2051 Doughnuts, frozen; bread, cake & related products
HQ: Keystone Bakery Holdings, Llc
520 Lake Cook Rd
Deerfield IL 60015
603 792-3113

(G-5355)
MOHAWK VALLEY MANUFACTURING
2237 Broad St (13340-5101)
PHONE 315 797-0851
Joseph Smith, *President*
John Cronk, *Vice Pres*
Betty Montana, *Manager*
Timothy Savoy, *Admin Sec*
EMP: 7
SALES (est): 630K **Privately Held**
SIC: 3556 Ovens, bakery

(G-5356)
PRECISION POLISH LLC
144 Adams St (13340-3751)
PHONE 315 894-3792
Nial Williams, *President*
Jack Dunderdale, *Vice Pres*
Michelle Williams, *Manager*
EMP: 25
SALES (est): 1.4MM **Privately Held**
SIC: 3441 Fabricated structural metal

(G-5357)
SOFT-NOZE USA INC
2216 Broad St (13340-5100)
PHONE 315 732-2726
Fax: 315 732-2963
Brett Truett, *President*
Krista Petrowski, *Finance Mgr*
Haris Dervisevic, *Technology*
▲ **EMP:** 5
SQ FT: 4,500
SALES (est): 510K **Privately Held**
WEB: www.softnoze.com
SIC: 3625 Electric controls & control accessories, industrial

(G-5358)
TURBO MACHINED PRODUCTS LLC
102 Industrial Dr (13340-1139)
PHONE 315 895-3010
Fax: 315 895-3011
John A Kabot Jr, *President*
Robert Cartmell, *Vice Pres*
Robert Partmell, *Vice Pres*
Brett Brewer, *QC Mgr*
Gordy Black, *Engineer*
EMP: 35
SQ FT: 20,000
SALES (est): 8.7MM **Privately Held**
WEB: www.turbomp.com
SIC: 3824 3511 Impeller & counter driven flow meters; turbines & turbine generator sets & parts

Franklin Square
Nassau County

(G-5359)
514 ADAMS CORPORATION
Also Called: Adams Press
781 Hempstead Tpke (11010-4328)
PHONE 516 352-6948
Daniel Rummo, *President*
Chris Rummo, *Vice Pres*
Theresa Rummo, *Admin Sec*
EMP: 7
SQ FT: 3,000
SALES (est): 1MM **Privately Held**
SIC: 2752 2791 2789 Commercial printing, offset; typesetting; bookbinding & related work

(G-5360)
ARTISTICS PRINTING CORP
746 Franklin Ave Ste 2 (11010-1101)
PHONE 516 561-2121
Richard Farruggia, *President*
EMP: 5
SQ FT: 1,200
SALES (est): 400K **Privately Held**
SIC: 2759 Commercial printing

(G-5361)
BONURA AND SONS IRON WORKS
957 Lorraine Dr (11010-1812)
PHONE 718 381-4100
Frank Bonura, *Principal*
Enzo Bonuro, *Principal*
EMP: 15
SALES (est): 1.2MM **Privately Held**
SIC: 3312 1799 Fence posts, iron & steel; ornamental metal work

(G-5362)
D C I TECHNICAL INC
475 Franklin Ave Fl 2 (11010-1228)
PHONE 516 355-0464
Fax: 516 355-0467
Andrea Mannheim, *President*
Harold Adler, *Vice Pres*
Merideth Hilton, *Vice Pres*
Sidney Platt, *Vice Pres*
EMP: 12
SQ FT: 2,700
SALES (est): 882.8K **Privately Held**
SIC: 2731 2741 Books: publishing & printing; miscellaneous publishing

(G-5363)
FEMTECH WOMEN POWERED SOFTWARE
1230 Hempstead Tpke (11010-1534)
PHONE 516 328-2631
Colleen Simeone, *President*
EMP: 99
SALES (est): 2.6MM **Privately Held**
WEB: www.femtech.at
SIC: 7372 Prepackaged software

(G-5364)
LESSOILCOM
672 Dogwood Ave (11010-3247)
PHONE 516 319-5052
Mike Gregoretti, *Principal*
EMP: 6
SALES (est): 363K **Privately Held**
SIC: 1241 Bituminous coal mining services, contract basis

(G-5365)
MOVIN ON SOUNDS AND SEC INC
Also Called: M O S S Communications
636 Hempstead Tpke (11010-4326)
PHONE 516 489-2350
Fax: 516 489-9536
Bruce Cirillo, *President*
Paul Cirillo, *Vice Pres*
Jean Ulsheimer, *Manager*
EMP: 35
SALES (est): 5.8MM **Privately Held**
WEB: www.movinon.com
SIC: 3663 Radio & TV communications equipment

(G-5366)
NYCOM BUSINESS SOLUTIONS INC
804 Hempstead Tpke (11010-4321)
PHONE 516 345-6000
Jerry Sperduto, *President*
EMP: 3
SQ FT: 800
SALES: 1.2MM **Privately Held**
SIC: 3663 Cellular radio telephone

(G-5367)
STUDENT LIFELINE INC
Also Called: Student Safety Books
922 Hempstead Tpke (11010-3628)
P.O. Box 570200, Whitestone (11357-0200)
PHONE 516 327-0800
Richard Signarino, *President*
Bonnie Meehan, *Sales Mgr*
Jennifer Tores-Ebert, *Manager*
EMP: 42
SQ FT: 2,200
SALES (est): 4.1MM **Privately Held**
WEB: www.studentlifeline.com
SIC: 2741 Miscellaneous publishing

Franklinville
Cattaraugus County

(G-5368)
BUFFALO CRUSHED STONE INC
Rr 16 (14737)
P.O. Box 106 (14737-0106)
PHONE 716 566-9636
John Lentz, *Manager*
EMP: 11
SALES (corp-wide): 651.9MM **Privately Held**
SIC: 1442 5032 Gravel mining; stone, crushed or broken
HQ: Buffalo Crushed Stone, Inc.
500 Como Park Blvd
Buffalo NY 14227
716 826-7310

(G-5369)
CATTARAUGUS CONTAINERS INC
21 Elm St 23 (14737-1052)
P.O. Box 174 (14737-0174)
PHONE 716 676-2000
Fax: 585 676-3552
Jane Lemke, *President*
Paul Wagner, *Vice Pres*
Tammy Mooney, *Controller*
Tammy Webster, *Controller*
EMP: 33
SQ FT: 33,000
SALES: 3.8MM **Privately Held**
SIC: 2653 2657 5113 Boxes, corrugated: made from purchased materials; folding paperboard boxes; corrugated & solid fiber boxes

(G-5370)
ONTARIO KNIFE COMPANY
26 Empire St Ste 1 (14737-1099)
P.O. Box 145 (14737-0145)
PHONE 716 676-5527
Fax: 716 676-5535
Nicholas D Trbovich Jr, *CEO*
Kenneth Trbovich, *Ch of Bd*
Nicholas D Trbovich, *Chairman*
Robert J Breton, *Vice Pres*
John O'Brien, *Vice Pres*
◆ **EMP:** 63
SQ FT: 10,000
SALES: 6.5MM
SALES (corp-wide): 36.7MM **Publicly Held**
WEB: www.ontarioknife.com
SIC: 3421 Cutlery
PA: Servotronics, Inc.
1110 Maple Rd
Elma NY 14059
716 655-5990

Fredonia - Chautauqua County (G-5371)

GEOGRAPHIC SECTION

Fredonia
Chautauqua County

(G-5371)
CARRIAGE HOUSE COMPANIES INC (DH)
196 Newton St (14063-1354)
PHONE..................716 672-4321
Fax: 716 679-3444
Kevin Hunt, *CEO*
Mark Chamberlain, *Vice Pres*
Mary Jane Knight, *Vice Pres*
Rich Koulouris, *Vice Pres*
Marsha Schneibwind, *Vice Pres*
▼ **EMP:** 900 **EST:** 1986
SALES (est): 388.4MM
SALES (corp-wide): 3.2B **Publicly Held**
WEB: www.carriagehousecos.com
SIC: 2099 2033 2035 2087 Syrups; canned fruits & specialties; dressings, salad: raw & cooked (except dry mixes); concentrates, drink
HQ: Treehouse Private Brands, Inc.
   800 Market St
   Saint Louis MO 63101
   314 877-7300

(G-5372)
D & F PALLET INC
134 Clinton Ave (14063-1406)
PHONE..................716 672-2984
Fax: 716 679-3525
Jospeh J Ivory, *President*
Thomas A Ivory, *President*
Richard Ivory, *Vice Pres*
Vickie Ivory, *Treasurer*
Mary Ivory, *Admin Sec*
EMP: 18
SQ FT: 26,000
SALES (est): 2.8MM **Privately Held**
SIC: 2448 Pallets, wood

(G-5373)
FREDONIA PENNYSAVER INC (PA)
Also Called: Lakeshore Pennysaver
276 W Main St Ste 1 (14063-2099)
P.O. Box 493 (14063-0493)
PHONE..................716 679-1509
Fax: 716 672-2626
Thomas K Webb Jr, *President*
Maureen Webb, *Vice Pres*
EMP: 5
SQ FT: 1,000
SALES (est): 813.9K **Privately Held**
WEB: www.fredoniapennysaver.com
SIC: 2741 2711 Guides: publishing only, not printed on site; newspapers, publishing & printing

(G-5374)
GREAT LAKES SPECIALITES
9491 Route 60 (14063-9729)
P.O. Box 351 (14063-0351)
PHONE..................716 672-4622
Fax: 716 672-4620
Michael J Gloss, *Owner*
EMP: 20
SQ FT: 10,000
SALES (est): 1.8MM **Privately Held**
SIC: 2448 2449 2441 Pallets, wood; wood containers; nailed wood boxes & shook

(G-5375)
TUBE FABRICATION COMPANY INC
183 E Main St Ste 10 (14063-1435)
PHONE..................716 673-1871
Daniel Sturniolo, *President*
Charles Sturniolo, *Purchasing*
EMP: 12
SALES (est): 2MM **Privately Held**
SIC: 3498 5051 Tube fabricating (contract bending & shaping); tubing, metal

(G-5376)
URBAN TECHNOLOGIES INC
3451 Stone Quarry Rd (14063-9722)
PHONE..................716 672-2709
John Urbanik, *President*
EMP: 5

SALES (est): 656.5K **Privately Held**
SIC: 3677 Electronic transformers; inductors, electronic

(G-5377)
WOODBURY VINEYARDS INC
Also Called: Noble Vintages
3215 S Roberts Rd (14063-9417)
PHONE..................716 679-9463
Joseph Carney, *Branch Mgr*
EMP: 5
SALES (corp-wide): 1.5MM **Privately Held**
WEB: www.woodburyvineyards.com
SIC: 2084 Wines
PA: Woodbury Vineyards, Inc.
   2001 Crocker Rd Ste 440
   Westlake OH 44145
   440 835-2828

Freedom
Cattaraugus County

(G-5378)
GUTCHESS FREEDOM INC
10699 Maple Grove Rd (14065-9774)
PHONE..................716 492-2824
Larry Lines, *Manager*
EMP: 70 **EST:** 2007
SALES (est): 9.3MM
SALES (corp-wide): 72.5MM **Privately Held**
SIC: 2421 Custom sawmill
PA: Gutchess Lumber Co., Inc.
   890 Mclean Rd
   Cortland NY 13045
   607 753-3393

Freeport
Nassau County

(G-5379)
5TH AVENUE CHOCOLATIERE LTD (PA)
114 Church St (11520-3833)
PHONE..................212 935-5454
Joseph E Whaley, *President*
John Whaley, *Vice Pres*
▲ **EMP:** 4
SQ FT: 4,500
SALES: 1.6MM **Privately Held**
SIC: 2064 2066 5441 Candy & other confectionery products; chocolate & cocoa products; candy

(G-5380)
ACCESS DISPLAY GROUP INC
Also Called: Swing Frame
151 S Main St (11520-3845)
PHONE..................516 678-7772
Fax: 516 867-7073
Charles Abrams, *President*
Barbara Abrams, *Vice Pres*
Brian McAley, *Info Tech Mgr*
Brian McAuley, *Info Tech Mgr*
Craig R Abrams, *Exec Dir*
▲ **EMP:** 14
SQ FT: 6,000
SALES (est): 2.7MM **Privately Held**
WEB: www.swingframe.com
SIC: 3499 Picture frames, metal

(G-5381)
AIRMARINE ELECTROPLATING CORP
388 Woodcleft Ave (11520-6379)
PHONE..................516 623-4406
Fax: 516 623-6215
Ernest Rieger III, *President*
EMP: 6
SALES (est): 658.6K **Privately Held**
WEB: www.airmarine.com
SIC: 3471 Electroplating of metals or formed products

(G-5382)
ALABASTER GROUP INC
188 N Main St (11520-2232)
PHONE..................516 867-8223
Orna Alabaster, *President*

Zeev Alabaster, *Vice Pres*
EMP: 5
SQ FT: 7,300
SALES (est): 396K **Privately Held**
SIC: 2791 7336 7389 Typesetting; graphic arts & related design; printing broker

(G-5383)
ALL AMERICAN METAL CORPORATION (PA)
200 Buffalo Ave (11520-4732)
P.O. Box 108 (11520-0108)
PHONE..................516 223-1760
Fax: 516 378-0638
Bernard Pechter, *President*
Melissa Jaffe, *Vice Pres*
Laury Ryan, *Clerk*
EMP: 8
SQ FT: 50,000
SALES (est): 5.8MM **Privately Held**
WEB: www.allamericanmetal.com
SIC: 2542 Partitions for floor attachment, prefabricated: except wood

(G-5384)
ALL AMERICAN METAL CORPORATION
200 Buffalo Ave (11520-4732)
P.O. Box 108 (11520-0108)
PHONE..................516 623-0222
Bernard Pechter, *Manager*
EMP: 32
SALES (corp-wide): 5.8MM **Privately Held**
WEB: www.allamericanmetal.com
SIC: 2542 3446 Partitions & fixtures, except wood; architectural metalwork
PA: All American Metal Corporation
   200 Buffalo Ave
   Freeport NY 11520
   516 223-1760

(G-5385)
ALPHA FASTENERS CORP
154 E Merrick Rd (11520-4020)
PHONE..................516 867-6188
Fax: 516 867-6189
Koula Perdios, *President*
Archie Perdios, *Vice Pres*
Michael Perdios, *Vice Pres*
▲ **EMP:** 5
SQ FT: 3,000
SALES (est): 657.3K **Privately Held**
SIC: 3599 Machine shop, jobbing & repair

(G-5386)
AMADEO SERRANO
36 Frankel Ave (11520-4846)
PHONE..................516 608-8359
Amaeeo Serrano, *Owner*
EMP: 7
SALES (est): 674.8K **Privately Held**
SIC: 3089 Fences, gates & accessories: plastic

(G-5387)
AMERICAN PUFF CORP
225 Buffalo Ave (11520-4794)
PHONE..................516 379-1300
Fax: 516 378-2844
William Ostrower, *President*
EMP: 100
SQ FT: 70,000
SALES (est): 7.4MM **Privately Held**
SIC: 3172 2399 Personal leather goods; powder puffs & mitts

(G-5388)
ANNA YOUNG ASSOC LTD
Also Called: Lombardi Design & Mfg
100 Doxsee Dr (11520-4716)
PHONE..................516 546-4400
Fax: 516 546-4413
Carl M Lombardi, *President*
Jodi Stern, *Purchasing*
Steve Ash, *CFO*
Alice Weiber, *Accountant*
▲ **EMP:** 150
SQ FT: 50,000
SALES (est): 52.9MM **Privately Held**
WEB: www.lombardi.cc
SIC: 3089 Injection molded finished plastic products

(G-5389)
ARROW CHEMICAL CORP
28 Rider Pl (11520-4612)
PHONE..................516 377-7770
Sherry Bernstein, *CEO*
EMP: 17 **EST:** 1960
SQ FT: 8,000
SALES (est): 4.5MM **Privately Held**
WEB: www.arrowchemical.net
SIC: 2842 Cleaning or polishing preparations

(G-5390)
BRAMSON HOUSE INC
151 Albany Ave (11520-4710)
PHONE..................516 764-5006
Jules Abramson, *CEO*
Ellis Abramson, *President*
Betty Abramson, *Vice Pres*
Patty Abramson, *Vice Pres*
Mark Hecht, *Sales Dir*
▲ **EMP:** 120
SQ FT: 80,000
SALES (est): 17MM **Privately Held**
WEB: www.bramsonhouse.com
SIC: 2392 2391 Bedspreads & bed sets: made from purchased materials; curtains & draperies

(G-5391)
BRUETON INDUSTRIES INC (PA)
146 Hanse Ave Ste 1 (11520-4636)
PHONE..................516 379-3400
Ralph Somma, *President*
Daniel Dayao, *Controller*
R Power, *Programmer Anys*
EMP: 60 **EST:** 1920
SQ FT: 55,000
SALES (est): 6.9MM **Privately Held**
WEB: www.brueton.com
SIC: 2522 2514 2511 2521 Office furniture, except wood; metal household furniture; wood household furniture; wood office furniture

(G-5392)
CASTLEREAGH PRINTCRAFT INC
Also Called: Castle Reagh Print Craft
320 Buffalo Ave (11520-4711)
PHONE..................516 623-1728
Fax: 516 379-2386
James Vollaro, *President*
Robert Quadrino, *Vice Pres*
Steven Quadrino, *Vice Pres*
Donna Vollaro, *CFO*
EMP: 70
SQ FT: 35,000
SALES (est): 10.5MM **Privately Held**
WEB: www.printcraftonline.com
SIC: 3555 2791 2789 2752 Printing trades machinery; typesetting; bookbinding & related work; commercial printing, lithographic

(G-5393)
DART AWNING INC
365 S Main St (11520-5114)
PHONE..................718 945-4224
Thomas Hart, *President*
Richard Hart, *Admin Sec*
EMP: 12
SQ FT: 5,000
SALES (est): 1.6MM **Privately Held**
WEB: www.dartawnings.com
SIC: 3444 5999 1799 Awnings, sheet metal; awnings; fence construction

(G-5394)
DORAL REFINING CORP
533 Atlantic Ave (11520-5211)
PHONE..................516 223-3684
Fax: 516 223-3936
Stephen Faliks, *President*
Alan Zaret, *Vice Pres*
EMP: 20 **EST:** 1973
SQ FT: 10,000
SALES: 6MM **Privately Held**
WEB: www.doralcorp.com
SIC: 3339 Precious metals

(G-5395)
EDR INDUSTRIES INC
Also Called: Wil-Nic
100 Commercial St (11520-2832)
PHONE..................516 868-1928

▲ = Import ▼ = Export
◆ = Import/Export

Don Capriglione, *President*
Christopher Cullinan, *Vice Pres*
EMP: 19
SQ FT: 10,000
SALES (est): 3.4MM **Privately Held**
SIC: 3599 Machine shop, jobbing & repair

(G-5396)
EXCLUSIVE DESIGNS
84 Albany Ave (11520-4011)
PHONE.................................516 378-5258
Bob Mazzella, *Owner*
EMP: 10
SALES (est): 864.6K **Privately Held**
SIC: 2542 Stands, merchandise display: except wood

(G-5397)
FARBER PLASTICS INC
162 Hanse Ave (11520-4644)
PHONE.................................516 378-4860
Fax: 516 378-4312
Lewis Farber, *President*
Janet Hunn, *Bookkeeper*
David Garfinkel, *Sales Mgr*
Tracy Calderone, *Office Mgr*
EMP: 23
SALES (est): 4.5MM **Privately Held**
SIC: 3081 Plastic film & sheet

(G-5398)
FARBER TRUCKING CORP
162 Hanse Ave (11520-4644)
PHONE.................................516 378-4860
Lewis Farber, *President*
Kasey Calderone, *Manager*
EMP: 23
SQ FT: 35,000
SALES (est): 2.7MM **Privately Held**
SIC: 3081 Plastic film & sheet

(G-5399)
FORM-TEC INC
216 N Main St Ste E (11520-2200)
PHONE.................................516 867-0200
Fax: 516 867-7724
Howard Lebow, *President*
EMP: 20
SQ FT: 10,000
SALES (est): 3.5MM **Privately Held**
WEB: www.form-tec.com
SIC: 3089 Molding primary plastic

(G-5400)
FORSYTHE COSMETIC GROUP LTD
Also Called: Forsythe Licensing
10 Niagara Ave (11520-4704)
P.O. Box 431, Lawrence (11559-0431)
PHONE.................................516 239-4200
Harriet Rose, *Ch of Bd*
Michael Rose, *President*
Beth Friedman, *Vice Pres*
Whitney Matza, *Vice Pres*
David Zhou, *Info Tech Mgr*
▲ EMP: 75
SQ FT: 20,000
SALES: 15MM **Privately Held**
WEB: www.cosmeticgroup.com
SIC: 2844 Cosmetic preparations

(G-5401)
FREEPORT SCREEN & STAMPING
31 Hanse Ave (11520-4601)
PHONE.................................516 379-0330
Stan Papot, *President*
▲ EMP: 20
SQ FT: 13,250
SALES (est): 2.4MM **Privately Held**
SIC: 3469 2759 2396 Metal stampings; screen printing; automotive & apparel trimmings

(G-5402)
GLENN FOODS INC (PA)
Also Called: Glenny's
371 S Main St Ste 119-405 (11520-5114)
PHONE.................................516 377-1400
Glenn Schacher, *President*
Philip Fruchter, *Vice Pres*
Steven Fruchter, *Treasurer*
Demress Stockman, *Manager*
▼ EMP: 10

SALES (est): 880K **Privately Held**
WEB: www.glennys.com
SIC: 2099 Food preparations

(G-5403)
GREENFIELD DIE CASTING CORP
99 Doxsee Dr (11520-4717)
PHONE.................................516 623-9230
Fax: 516 623-6275
Peter Greenfield, *President*
Michael Greenfield, *Vice Pres*
Douglas Greenfield, *Admin Sec*
EMP: 50
SQ FT: 56,000
SALES (est): 7.3MM **Privately Held**
SIC: 3364 3369 Zinc & zinc-base alloy die-castings; nonferrous foundries

(G-5404)
GREENFIELD INDUSTRIES INC
99 Doxsee Dr (11520-4717)
PHONE.................................516 623-9230
Peter Greenfield, *President*
Douglas Greenfield, *Vice Pres*
Michael Greenfield, *Vice Pres*
Barry Krompier, *Controller*
Linda Teti, *Manager*
▲ EMP: 75
SQ FT: 70,000
SALES (est): 15.1MM **Privately Held**
WEB: www.greenfieldny.com
SIC: 3363 Aluminum die-castings

(G-5405)
HARWITT INDUSTRIES INC
61 S Main St Unit A (11520-3864)
PHONE.................................516 623-9787
Louis Harwitt, *President*
EMP: 13
SALES (est): 920K **Privately Held**
SIC: 3599 Machine & other job shop work

(G-5406)
KNICKERBOCKER PARTITION CORP (PA)
193 Hanse Ave (11520-4633)
P.O. Box 690 (11520-0690)
PHONE.................................516 546-0550
Fax: 516 546-0549
Stewart Markbreiter, *President*
Albert Giorgianni, *Vice Pres*
Mark Reiss, *VP Opers*
Andrew Kennedy, *Treasurer*
Brian Baird, *Info Tech Mgr*
▲ EMP: 90
SQ FT: 60,000
SALES (est): 15.1MM **Privately Held**
WEB: www.knickerbockerpartition.com
SIC: 2542 Partitions for floor attachment, prefabricated: except wood

(G-5407)
L & M WELDING LLC
10 Taylor St Unit A (11520-4726)
PHONE.................................516 220-1722
Aida Sanchez, *Principal*
EMP: 7 EST: 2010
SALES (est): 1MM **Privately Held**
SIC: 3669 Visual communication systems

(G-5408)
LAMAR PLASTICS PACKAGING LTD
216 N Main St Ste F (11520-2200)
PHONE.................................516 378-2500
Fax: 516 378-6192
Lawrence Aronson, *Ch of Bd*
Marc Aronson, *President*
Karen Persico, *Purchasing*
EMP: 60 EST: 1966
SQ FT: 60,000
SALES (est): 11.3MM **Privately Held**
SIC: 3086 3993 Packaging & shipping materials, foamed plastic; displays & cutouts, window & lobby

(G-5409)
LOVE & QUICHES LTD
Also Called: Love & Quiches Desserts
178 Hanse Ave (11520-4698)
PHONE.................................516 623-8800
Fax: 516 623-8817
Irwin Axelrod, *CEO*
Andrew Axelrod, *President*

Susan Axelrod, *Chairman*
Michael J Goldstein, *Vice Pres*
Aaron Heisler, *Vice Pres*
▼ EMP: 250
SALES (est): 73.6MM **Privately Held**
WEB: www.loveandquiches.com
SIC: 2053 Frozen bakery products, except bread

(G-5410)
MARCON ELECTRONIC SYSTEMS LLC
152 Westend Ave (11520-5245)
PHONE.................................516 633-6396
Grace Connelly,
EMP: 6
SALES: 750K **Privately Held**
SIC: 3679 Electronic components

(G-5411)
MARCON SERVICES
152 Westend Ave (11520-5245)
PHONE.................................516 223-8019
Grace Connelly, *Owner*
EMP: 6
SALES: 50K **Privately Held**
WEB: www.graceconnelly.com
SIC: 3674 Semiconductors & related devices

(G-5412)
MELTO METAL PRODUCTS CO INC
37 Hanse Ave (11520-4696)
PHONE.................................516 546-8866
Fax: 516 867-4339
Bernard Liebman, *Ch of Bd*
Juan Costa, *Project Mgr*
Elaine Rezny, *Manager*
▲ EMP: 35
SQ FT: 15,000
SALES (est): 7.5MM **Privately Held**
WEB: www.meltometalproducts.com
SIC: 3446 Architectural metalwork

(G-5413)
MICA INTERNATIONAL LTD
126 Albany Ave (11520-4702)
PHONE.................................516 378-3400
Fax: 516 379-0560
EMP: 12
SQ FT: 5,500
SALES (est): 820K **Privately Held**
SIC: 2511 Mfg Wood Household Furniture

(G-5414)
MIDBURY INDUSTRIES INC
86 E Merrick Rd (11520-4034)
PHONE.................................516 868-0600
Fax: 516 868-0659
Diane Jones, *President*
Michael Natilli Jr, *Vice Pres*
EMP: 15
SQ FT: 10,000
SALES: 900K **Privately Held**
WEB: www.midbury.com
SIC: 3089 Injection molding of plastics

(G-5415)
NEW YORK VANITY AND MFG CO
10 Henry St (11520-3910)
PHONE.................................718 417-1010
Teddy Foukalas, *President*
Helen Samaklis, *Bookkeeper*
George Mantikas, *Manager*
Tony Fotou, *Shareholder*
▲ EMP: 25
SQ FT: 30,000
SALES (est): 3.6MM **Privately Held**
WEB: www.nyvanity.com
SIC: 2434 Vanities, bathroom: wood

(G-5416)
ONDRIVESUS CORP
Also Called: Rino
216 N Main St Bldg B2 (11520-2200)
PHONE.................................516 771-6777
Fax: 516 867-5656
Dennis G Berg, *CEO*
D Lee Berg, *President*
Jayne Berg, *Vice Pres*
◆ EMP: 35
SQ FT: 11,000

SALES (est): 9MM **Privately Held**
WEB: www.ondrives.us
SIC: 3566 Speed changers, drives & gears

(G-5417)
ORAMAAX DENTAL PRODUCTS INC
216 N Main St Ste A (11520-2200)
PHONE.................................516 771-8514
Fax: 516 771-8518
Robert Endelson, *President*
Gary Galluzzo, *Engineer*
EMP: 15
SQ FT: 12,500
SALES (est): 1.4MM **Privately Held**
WEB: www.flosscard.com
SIC: 3843 5047 Dental equipment & supplies; dental equipment & supplies

(G-5418)
PENTHOUSE MANUFACTURING CO INC
Also Called: Penthouse Group, The
225 Buffalo Ave (11520-4709)
PHONE.................................516 379-1300
William Ostrower, *President*
Chris Gannotta, *Sales Staff*
David Ramos, *Manager*
▲ EMP: 350 EST: 1952
SALES (est): 36.4MM **Privately Held**
SIC: 3172 2399 Cosmetic bags; powder puffs & mitts

(G-5419)
PRESTI READY MIX CONCRETE INC
Also Called: Presti Stone and Mason
210 E Merrick Rd (11520-4029)
PHONE.................................516 378-6006
Joseph Prestigiacomo, *President*
EMP: 7
SQ FT: 2,500
SALES: 1.2MM **Privately Held**
SIC: 3273 3531 Ready-mixed concrete; bituminous, cement & concrete related products & equipment

(G-5420)
PRIMELITE MANUFACTURING CORP
Also Called: Prime Lite Mfg
407 S Main St (11520-5194)
PHONE.................................516 868-4411
Fax: 516 868-4609
Benjamin Heit, *President*
Emma Warren, *Office Mgr*
EMP: 9 EST: 1962
SQ FT: 12,000
SALES (est): 1.4MM **Privately Held**
WEB: www.primelite-mfg.com
SIC: 3646 Commercial indusl & institutional electric lighting fixtures

(G-5421)
QUALITY LINEALS USA INC
105 Bennington Ave Ste 1 (11520-3946)
PHONE.................................516 378-6577
Jill Kaiserman, *President*
EMP: 43
SQ FT: 40,000
SALES (corp-wide): 7.5MM **Privately Held**
SIC: 3544 Dies, plastics forming
PA: Quality Lineals Usa, Inc.
  1 Kees Pl
  Merrick NY 11566
  516 378-6577

(G-5422)
RAND & PASEKA MFG CO INC
10 Hanse Ave (11520-4602)
PHONE.................................516 867-1500
Fax: 516 867-0230
Marc Schwab, *President*
Andrea Schwab, *Senior VP*
Bogdan Chojnacki, *Manager*
EMP: 22
SQ FT: 19,000
SALES (est): 3.3MM **Privately Held**
SIC: 3911 Rosaries or other small religious articles, precious metal

Freeport - Nassau County (G-5423)

(G-5423)
ROSE FENCE INC (PA)
345 W Sunrise Hwy (11520-3120)
PHONE..................................516 223-0777
Fax: 516 223-0791
Janice Rosenzeig, *Ch of Bd*
Kevin Kaughfield, *Manager*
Dorrie Lobe, *Manager*
▲ EMP: 42
SQ FT: 2,000
SALES (est): 20.2MM Privately Held
WEB: www.rosefence.com
SIC: 3496 Fencing, made from purchased wire

(G-5424)
SEA ISLE CUSTOM ROD BUILDERS
495 Guy Lombardo Ave (11520-6293)
PHONE..................................516 868-8855
Fax: 516 546-2983
Robert Feuring, *President*
EMP: 7
SQ FT: 1,710
SALES (est): 900K Privately Held
SIC: 3949 5941 Fishing tackle, general; fishing equipment

(G-5425)
SEMITRONICS CORP (HQ)
80 Commercial St (11520-2832)
PHONE..................................516 223-0200
Fax: 516 623-6954
Henrietta Rivman, *President*
Brian Jipp, *Manager*
Roz Sollinger, *Manager*
EMP: 45
SQ FT: 10,000
SALES (est): 5.6MM
SALES (corp-wide): 6MM Privately Held
WEB: www.semitronics.com
SIC: 3674 5065 Semiconductors & related devices; electronic parts & equipment
PA: Intex Company Inc
  5317 Church Ave
  Brooklyn NY 11203
  718 336-3491

(G-5426)
SEVILLE CENTRAL MIX CORP (PA)
157 Albany Ave (11520-4710)
PHONE..................................516 868-3000
Fax: 516 293-9088
Peter Scalamandre, *Ch of Bd*
Joseph L Scalamandre, *Vice Pres*
Marty McCarthy, *Controller*
Christine Demacy, *Manager*
EMP: 5
SQ FT: 8,000
SALES (est): 13.6MM Privately Held
WEB: www.sevillecentralmix.com
SIC: 3273 Ready-mixed concrete

(G-5427)
SIGNATURE INDUSTRIES INC
32 Saint Johns Pl (11520-4618)
PHONE..................................516 679-5177
Fax: 516 771-8186
Emil Petschauer, *President*
Ante Vulin, *Vice Pres*
James Calderon, *Treasurer*
EMP: 15
SALES (est): 1.6MM Privately Held
WEB: www.signatureindustries.com
SIC: 3993 Signs & advertising specialties

(G-5428)
SPARTAN PRECISION MACHINING
9 Niagara Ave (11520-4728)
PHONE..................................516 546-5171
Fax: 516 546-8359
George Pappas, *President*
Mabel Pappas, *Bookkeeper*
William Draffen, *Sales Staff*
EMP: 35 EST: 1966
SQ FT: 5,000
SALES (est): 4MM Privately Held
SIC: 3599 Machine shop, jobbing & repair

(G-5429)
TEENA CREATIONS INC
10 Hanse Ave (11520-4628)
PHONE..................................516 867-1500
Jules Rand, *President*
Michael Rand, *Treasurer*
Mark Schwab, *Admin Sec*
EMP: 5
SQ FT: 19,000
SALES (est): 520K Privately Held
SIC: 3911 Jewelry, precious metal

(G-5430)
TEMREX CORPORATION (PA)
300 Buffalo Ave (11520-4720)
P.O. Box 182 (11520-0182)
PHONE..................................516 868-6221
Fax: 516 868-5700
Alda Levander, *CEO*
Ethan Levander, *President*
Jackie Prather, *Sales Executive*
Hubert Levander, *Executive*
Ruth Fusci, *Admin Sec*
EMP: 37
SQ FT: 5,000
SALES (est): 4.5MM Privately Held
WEB: www.temrex.com
SIC: 3843 Dental equipment & supplies

(G-5431)
THREE STAR OFFSET PRINTING
188 N Main St (11520-2232)
PHONE..................................516 867-8223
Fax: 516 867-8227
Zeev Alabaster, *President*
Orna Alabaster, *Corp Secy*
EMP: 10 EST: 1958
SQ FT: 7,300
SALES (est): 1.7MM Privately Held
SIC: 2752 Photo-offset printing

(G-5432)
TRIUMPH ACTUATION SYSTEMS LLC
417 S Main St (11520-5144)
PHONE..................................516 378-0162
EMP: 55
SALES (corp-wide): 3.8B Publicly Held
SIC: 3593 3728 3724 3594 Mfg Fluid Power Cylinder Mfg Aircraft Parts/Equip Mfg Aircraft Engine/Part Mfg Fluid Power Pump/Mtr Whol Industrial Equip
HQ: Triumph Actuation Systems, Llc
  4520 Hampton Rd
  Clemmons NC 27012
  336 766-9036

(G-5433)
UNIQUE DISPLAY MFG CORP (PA)
216 N Main St Ste D (11520-2200)
PHONE..................................516 546-3800
Philip Boxer, *President*
Eleanor Boxer, *Corp Secy*
EMP: 8 EST: 1976
SQ FT: 50,000
SALES (est): 1MM Privately Held
SIC: 3993 Displays & cutouts, window & lobby

(G-5434)
WL CONCEPTS & PRODUCTION INC
1 Bennington Ave (11520-3953)
PHONE..................................516 538-5300
Fax: 516 565-5115
William Levine, *President*
Marian Keilson, *Director*
EMP: 7
SQ FT: 4,500
SALES (est): 660K Privately Held
WEB: www.wlconcepts.com
SIC: 3993 Signs & advertising specialties

Freeville
Tompkins County

(G-5435)
FREEVILLE PUBLISHING CO INC
Also Called: Cortland-Ithaca Subn Shopper
9 Main St (13068-9599)
P.O. Box 210 (13068-0210)
PHONE..................................607 844-9119
Fax: 607 844-3381
Michael Down, *President*
EMP: 10 EST: 1949
SQ FT: 1,998
SALES (est): 913.7K Privately Held
SIC: 2741 2752 2759 Shopping news: publishing only, not printed on site; commercial printing, offset; commercial printing

(G-5436)
GENOA SAND & GRAVEL LNSG
390 Peruville Rd (13068-9732)
PHONE..................................607 533-4551
Tracy Pinney, *Owner*
EMP: 5
SALES (est): 210K Privately Held
SIC: 1442 Construction sand & gravel

(G-5437)
WEAVER WIND ENERGY LLC
7 Union St (13068-3201)
PHONE..................................607 379-9463
Alex Hagen, *President*
Art Weaver, *Vice Pres*
EMP: 5
SQ FT: 5,000
SALES (est): 310K Privately Held
SIC: 3511 Turbines & turbine generator sets

Fresh Meadows
Queens County

(G-5438)
AMERICAN CIGAR
6940 Fresh Meadow Ln (11365-3422)
PHONE..................................718 969-0008
Allen Schuster, *President*
EMP: 6
SALES (est): 450K Privately Held
WEB: www.smokeyscigars.com
SIC: 2121 Cigars

(G-5439)
CDML COMPUTER SERVICES LTD
5343 198th St (11365-1719)
PHONE..................................718 428-9063
Leonard Kaplan, *President*
EMP: 6
SALES (est): 281.3K Privately Held
WEB: www.cdml.com
SIC: 7372 7371 Prepackaged software; custom computer programming services

(G-5440)
FRENCH ASSOCIATES INC
Also Called: French Pdts Frnch Pickle Works
7339 172nd St (11366-1420)
PHONE..................................718 387-9880
Seymour Rosen, *President*
Jerry Rosen, *Vice Pres*
EMP: 10 EST: 1919
SQ FT: 20,000
SALES (est): 650K Privately Held
WEB: www.frenchassociates.com
SIC: 2035 5199 5149 Pickles, vinegar; general merchandise, non-durable; groceries & related products

(G-5441)
HACULLA NYC INC
6805 Fresh Meadow Ln (11365-3438)
PHONE..................................718 886-3163
Jonathan Koon, *Principal*
EMP: 10 EST: 2014
SALES (est): 530K Privately Held
SIC: 2329 Men's & boys' sportswear & athletic clothing

(G-5442)
KOON ENTERPRISES LLC
6805 Fresh Madow Ln Ste B (11365)
PHONE..................................718 886-3163
Jonathan M Koon, *Mng Member*
Katherine Koon,
EMP: 5
SALES (est): 1.2MM Privately Held
SIC: 2389 Costumes

(G-5443)
KOONICHI INC
6805 Fresh Madow Ln Ste B (11365)
PHONE..................................718 886-8338
Jonathan Koon, *President*
Katherine Koon, *Vice Pres*
Raymond Koon, *CFO*
▲ EMP: 7
SQ FT: 2,500
SALES (est): 590K Privately Held
WEB: www.koonichi.com
SIC: 3089 Automotive parts, plastic

(G-5444)
MANIFESTATION-GLOW PRESS INC
7740 164th St (11366-1227)
PHONE..................................718 380-5259
Fax: 718 380-7651
IA Konopiaty, *Ch of Bd*
Abakash Konopiaty, *President*
EMP: 5
SQ FT: 1,800
SALES (est): 540K Privately Held
WEB: www.heart-light.com
SIC: 2752 Commercial printing, offset

(G-5445)
SOCKS FOR EVERYONE INC
18415 58th Ave (11365-2209)
PHONE..................................347 754-0210
Perminder Chhabra, *Principal*
EMP: 5
SALES (est): 332.8K Privately Held
SIC: 2252 Socks

(G-5446)
TOROTRON CORPORATION
18508 Union Tpke Ste 101 (11366-1700)
PHONE..................................718 428-6992
Oscar Zanger, *President*
Donny Korblit, *Engineer*
Steve Bortnicker, *Controller*
Miriam Zanger, *Admin Sec*
EMP: 8
SQ FT: 3,000
SALES: 350K Privately Held
SIC: 3679 Electronic circuits

(G-5447)
VR CONTAINMENT LLC
17625 Union Tpke Ste 175 (11366-1515)
PHONE..................................917 972-3441
EMP: 5
SALES (est): 585.5K Privately Held
SIC: 3442 3446 Metal doors; gates, ornamental metal

Frewsburg
Chautauqua County

(G-5448)
ARTISAN MANAGEMENT GROUP INC
39 Venman St (14738-9565)
PHONE..................................716 569-4094
Kevin Delong, *President*
Matt Delong, *Parts Mgr*
EMP: 7
SALES (est): 950K Privately Held
SIC: 3544 3599 Special dies, tools, jigs & fixtures; machine shop, jobbing & repair

(G-5449)
COLBURNS AC RFRGN
17 White Dr (14738-9553)
P.O. Box 9430 (14738-1443)
PHONE..................................716 569-3695
Fax: 716 569-6362
George M Colburn, *President*
EMP: 10
SQ FT: 3,600
SALES (est): 1.7MM Privately Held
SIC: 3585 7623 Heating & air conditioning combination units; refrigeration repair service

(G-5450)
FREW RUN GRAVEL PRODUCTS INC
984 Frew Run Rd (14738-9746)
PHONE..................................716 569-4712
Michael Nelson, *President*
EMP: 6
SALES (est): 441.4K Privately Held
SIC: 1442 Construction sand & gravel

Fulton - Oswego County (G-5474)

(G-5451)
MONARCH PLASTICS INC
225 Falconer St (14738-9506)
P.O. Box 648 (14738-0648)
PHONE....................................716 569-2175
Donald Olander, *President*
Steve Luzzi, *Sales Mgr*
Bamry Muro, *Manager*
Rebecca Chase, *Clerk*
▲ **EMP:** 30 **EST:** 1960
SQ FT: 16,000
SALES (est): 5.7MM **Privately Held**
WEB: www.monarchplastic.com
SIC: 3089 Molding primary plastic

Friendship
Allegany County

(G-5452)
FRIENDSHIP DAIRIES LLC
6701 County Road 20 (14739-8660)
PHONE....................................585 973-3031
Fax: 585 973-2401
Ron Klein, *President*
Greg Knapp, *General Mgr*
John Albanese, *Vice Pres*
Jeffrey Rakers, *Plant Mgr*
Sherry Crawford, *Buyer*
EMP: 250
SQ FT: 15,000
SALES (est): 54.7MM
SALES (corp-wide): 86.6K **Privately Held**
WEB: www.deanfoods.com
SIC: 2023 2022 Dry, condensed, evaporated dairy products; cheese, natural & processed
HQ: Saputo Dairy Foods Usa, Llc
2711 N Haske Ave Ste 3700
Dallas TX 75204
214 863-2300

Fulton
Oswego County

(G-5453)
C & C METAL FABRICATIONS INC
159 Hubbard St (13069-1247)
PHONE....................................315 598-7607
Fax: 315 598-7613
Judy Davis, *Manager*
John F Sharkey IV,
EMP: 19
SQ FT: 32,000
SALES (est): 3.5MM **Privately Held**
WEB: www.candcfabrication.com
SIC: 3441 Fabricated structural metal

(G-5454)
CANFIELD MACHINE & TOOL LLC
121 Howard Rd (13069-4278)
PHONE....................................315 593-8062
Fax: 315 592-5963
Chris Canfield, *CIO*
Debra Canfield, *Director*
EMP: 41
SQ FT: 24,000
SALES (est): 5.7MM **Privately Held**
SIC: 3599 Machine shop, jobbing & repair

(G-5455)
D-K MANUFACTURING CORP
Also Called: DK
551 W 3rd St S (13069-2824)
P.O. Box 600 (13069-0600)
PHONE....................................315 592-4327
Fax: 315 593-2252
Norman W Kesterke, *President*
Donald L Kesterke, *General Mgr*
Pam Kesterke, *Human Resources*
Lorry Bailey, *Manager*
Sue Kesterke, *CIO*
EMP: 20
SQ FT: 30,000
SALES: 2MM **Privately Held**
WEB: www.d-kmfg.com
SIC: 3469 3599 Stamping metal for the trade; machine shop, jobbing & repair

(G-5456)
DOT PUBLISHING
Also Called: Fulton Daily News
117 Cayuga St (13069-1709)
PHONE....................................315 593-2510
Fax: 315 593-2515
Monica Mackenzie, *President*
EMP: 10
SQ FT: 2,048
SALES (est): 573K **Privately Held**
SIC: 2711 Newspapers, publishing & printing

(G-5457)
FULTON NEWSPAPERS INC
Also Called: Fulton Patriot
67 S 2nd St (13069-1725)
PHONE....................................315 598-6397
Vincent R Caravan, *President*
Ronald Caravan, *Vice Pres*
EMP: 20
SQ FT: 8,000
SALES (est): 810K **Privately Held**
SIC: 2711 2752 2791 2789 Newspapers: publishing only, not printed on site; commercial printing, offset; typesetting; bookbinding & related work

(G-5458)
FULTON TOOL CO INC
802 W Broadway Ste 1 (13069-1522)
PHONE....................................315 598-2900
Fax: 315 598-4210
Bruce Phelps, *President*
Barbara Phelps, *Corp Secy*
Peter Russell, *Vice Pres*
Jim Bowers, *QC Mgr*
Peter Russells, *Sales Mgr*
EMP: 21 **EST:** 1959
SQ FT: 32,000
SALES (est): 4.3MM **Privately Held**
WEB: www.fultontool.com
SIC: 3599 Machine shop, jobbing & repair

(G-5459)
GONE SOUTH CONCRETE BLOCK INC
Also Called: John Deere Authorized Dealer
2809 State Route 3 (13069-5805)
P.O. Box 420 (13069-0420)
PHONE....................................315 598-2141
Thomas S Venezia, *President*
Desire Descastalzo, *Controller*
Melissa Gentile, *Human Res Dir*
EMP: 30
SQ FT: 2,000
SALES (est): 9.2MM **Privately Held**
SIC: 3271 5211 5082 Blocks, concrete or cinder: standard; lumber & other building materials; construction & mining machinery

(G-5460)
HAUN WELDING SUPPLY INC
214 N 4th St (13069-1216)
PHONE....................................315 592-5012
Fax: 315 592-2447
Patty Sasso, *Manager*
EMP: 7
SQ FT: 1,938
SALES (corp-wide): 71.2MM **Privately Held**
SIC: 7692 5084 Welding repair; welding machinery & equipment
PA: Haun Welding Supply, Inc.
5921 Court Street Rd
Syracuse NY 13206
315 463-5241

(G-5461)
HUHTAMAKI INC
Huhtamaki Consumer Packaging
100 State St (13069-2518)
PHONE....................................315 593-5311
Fax: 315 593-5378
Dietmar Johann, *Opers Mgr*
Rick Davis, *Engineer*
Anne Scruton, *Financial Exec*
Jim Carroll, *Manager*
Stephen Horth, *Manager*
EMP: 585
SALES (corp-wide): 2.9B **Privately Held**
SIC: 2621 Pressed pulp products
HQ: Huhtamaki, Inc.
9201 Packaging Dr
De Soto KS 66018
913 583-3025

(G-5462)
INTERFACE PERFORMANCE MTLS INC
2885 State Route 481 (13069-4221)
PHONE....................................315 592-8100
Richard Isbell, *QC Dir*
Dave Meritech, *Marketing Mgr*
Debra Morris, *Technology*
EMP: 219 **Privately Held**
WEB: www.sealinfo.com
SIC: 3053 Gaskets, packing & sealing devices
PA: Interface Performance Materials, Inc.
216 Wohlsen Way
Lancaster PA 17603

(G-5463)
IVES FARM MARKET
Also Called: Ives Slaughterhouse
2652 Rr 176 (13069)
PHONE....................................315 592-4880
Ronald Ives, *Owner*
Jean Ives, *Partner*
EMP: 5
SALES (est): 360K **Privately Held**
SIC: 2011 5411 5421 Meat packing plants; grocery stores; meat markets, including freezer provisioniers

(G-5464)
JOHN CRANE INC
2314 County Route 4 (13069-3659)
PHONE....................................315 593-6237
John Crane, *Branch Mgr*
EMP: 64
SALES (corp-wide): 4.5B **Privately Held**
SIC: 3053 Gaskets & sealing devices
HQ: John Crane Inc.
227 W Monroe St Ste 1800
Chicago IL 60606
312 605-7800

(G-5465)
K&NS FOODS USA LLC
607 Phillips St (13069-1520)
PHONE....................................315 598-8080
Jimmy Koid, *Mng Member*
▲ **EMP:** 30 **EST:** 2012
SALES (est): 7.9MM **Privately Held**
SIC: 2015 Chicken, processed: frozen
PA: K&N's Foods (Private) Limited
Business Centre, Shadman Second Floor
Lahore
423 742-1710

(G-5466)
KENWELL CORPORATION
871 Hannibal St (13069-4186)
P.O. Box 207 (13069-0207)
PHONE....................................315 592-4263
Fax: 315 593-2063
Roger Horning Jr, *President*
Bruce Horning, *Vice Pres*
Douglas Horning, *Finance*
Bob Flack, *Manager*
EMP: 52
SQ FT: 13,000
SALES (est): 12MM **Privately Held**
WEB: www.kenwellcorp.com
SIC: 3599 Machine shop, jobbing & repair

(G-5467)
KRENGEL MANUFACTURING CO INC
Also Called: American Marking Systems
121 Fulton Ave Fl 2 (13069)
PHONE....................................212 227-1901
EMP: 18
SALES (est): 980K **Privately Held**
SIC: 3953 Mfg Marking Devices

(G-5468)
LE ROI INC
21 S 2nd St (13069-1706)
PHONE....................................315 342-3681
Fax: 315 343-0388
Terry Leroy, *President*
Julie Symons, *Office Mgr*
EMP: 12 **EST:** 1997
SQ FT: 3,400
SALES (est): 1.7MM **Privately Held**
WEB: www.leroi.com
SIC: 3911 Jewelry, precious metal

(G-5469)
LINDE MERCHANT PRODUCTION INC
370 Owen Rd (13069)
PHONE....................................315 593-1360
Richard Olinger, *Principal*
Randy Draving, *Opers Staff*
EMP: 8
SALES (corp-wide): 19.2B **Privately Held**
SIC: 2813 Carbon dioxide
HQ: Linde Merchant Production, Inc.
575 Mountain Ave
New Providence NJ 07974
908 464-8100

(G-5470)
NET & DIE INC
24 Foster St (13069)
P.O. Box 240 (13069-0240)
PHONE....................................315 592-4311
Fax: 315 598-1232
Richard N Shatrau, *President*
Helena Rockwood, *Corp Secy*
EMP: 38 **EST:** 1963
SQ FT: 30,000
SALES (est): 6.7MM **Privately Held**
SIC: 3599 Machine shop, jobbing & repair

(G-5471)
NORTH END PAPER CO INC
702 Hannibal St (13069-1020)
PHONE....................................315 593-8100
William F Shafer III, *President*
Sam Gabriele, *Manager*
EMP: 7
SQ FT: 40,000
SALES (est): 1.1MM
SALES (corp-wide): 8.7MM **Privately Held**
WEB: www.flowercitytissue.com
SIC: 2621 Tissue paper
PA: Flower City Tissue Mills Company, Inc.
700 Driving Park Ave
Rochester NY 14613
585 458-9200

(G-5472)
NORTHERN BITUMINOUS MIX INC
32 Silk Rd (13069-4862)
P.O. Box 420 (13069-0420)
PHONE....................................315 598-2141
Thomas Venezia Sr, *President*
EMP: 6
SQ FT: 2,000
SALES (est): 773.5K **Privately Held**
SIC: 2951 Asphalt & asphaltic paving mixtures (not from refineries)

(G-5473)
NORTHERN READY-MIX INC (PA)
32 Silk Rd (13069-4862)
P.O. Box 420 (13069-0420)
PHONE....................................315 598-2141
Fax: 315 593-8252
Thomas S Venezia, *President*
Desiree Capousis, *Controller*
Cris Yates, *Credit Mgr*
Melissa Gentile, *Human Res Mgr*
EMP: 15
SQ FT: 2,000
SALES (est): 5.4MM **Privately Held**
WEB: www.northerncompanies.com
SIC: 3273 Ready-mixed concrete

(G-5474)
PATHFINDER INDUSTRIES INC
117 N 3rd St (13069-1256)
PHONE....................................315 593-2483
Fax: 315 593-3311
Marsha Ives, *President*
Maribeth Myers, *Vice Pres*
Wally Corzett, *Prgrmr*
Audrey Williams, *Admin Asst*
EMP: 21
SQ FT: 22,000
SALES (est): 4.6MM **Privately Held**
WEB: www.pathfinderind.com
SIC: 3444 Sheet metalwork

(G-5475)
SYRACUSE SAND & GRAVEL LLC
1902 County Route 57 (13069-4909)
PHONE...............................315 548-8207
EMP: 6
SALES (est): 580K **Privately Held**
SIC: 1442 Construction sand & gravel

(G-5476)
UNIVERSAL METAL WORKS LLC
159 Hubbard St (13069-1247)
PHONE...............................315 598-7607
John F Sharkey IV,
EMP: 19
SALES (est): 4.5MM **Privately Held**
SIC: 3441 Fabricated structural metal

Fultonville
Montgomery County

(G-5477)
ANDERSON INSTRUMENT CO INC (HQ)
156 Auriesville Rd (12072-2031)
PHONE...............................518 922-5315
Fax: 518 922-8997
Andrew Hider, *CEO*
David Chatt, *VP Finance*
Icole Demagistris, *Human Res Mgr*
Gaddiel Garcia, *Regl Sales Mgr*
Seth Hanson, *Regl Sales Mgr*
▲ EMP: 70
SQ FT: 40,000
SALES (est): 21.7MM
SALES (corp-wide): 5B **Publicly Held**
WEB: www.andinst.com
SIC: 3823 5084 3822 3625 Controllers for process variables, all types; industrial machinery & equipment; auto controls regulating residntl & coml environmt & applncs; relays & industrial controls
PA: Fortive Corporation
   6920 Seaway Blvd
   Everett WA 98203
   425 446-5000

(G-5478)
CONSOLIDATED BARRICADES INC
179 Dillenbeck Rd (12072-3311)
PHONE...............................518 922-7944
Joseph Melideo, *President*
EMP: 8
SQ FT: 7,000
SALES (est): 780K **Privately Held**
WEB: www.consolidatedbarricades.com
SIC: 3499 Barricades, metal

(G-5479)
FULTONVILLE MACHINE & TOOL CO
73 Union St (12072-1836)
P.O. Box 426 (12072-0426)
PHONE...............................518 853-4441
Fax: 518 853-3445
Randolf C Snyder, *President*
Patricia Snyder, *Corp Secy*
EMP: 11 EST: 1945
SQ FT: 18,000
SALES (est): 1.2MM **Privately Held**
SIC: 3599 Machine shop, jobbing & repair

(G-5480)
MOHAWK RIVER LEATHER WORKS
32 Broad St (12072)
P.O. Box 425 (12072-0425)
PHONE...............................518 853-3900
Fax: 518 853-3729
Joseph H Sicilia, *President*
Robert Hojohn, *Vice Pres*
Tammy Plantt, *Bookkeeper*
EMP: 17
SQ FT: 3,534
SALES (est): 2.9MM **Privately Held**
SIC: 3111 Coloring of leather

(G-5481)
PARTLOW CORPORATION
Also Called: Partlow West
156 Auriesville Rd (12072-2031)
PHONE...............................518 922-5315
Craig Purse, *President*
Donald D'Amico, *Vice Pres*
Frank Stagliano, *Vice Pres*
Dominick Caracas, *Engineer*
Carol Bennett, *Human Res Mgr*
EMP: 175
SQ FT: 60,000
SALES: 34.8MM **Privately Held**
SIC: 3823 Industrial process control instruments

(G-5482)
PERRONE LEATHER LLC (PA)
Also Called: Perrone Aerospace
182a Riverside Dr (12072-1750)
PHONE...............................518 853-4300
Bartle Avery, *CEO*
William T Perrone Jr, *President*
Kevin Shea, *Vice Pres*
Brenda McInnis, *Buyer*
Patrick Champion, *CFO*
▲ EMP: 60
SQ FT: 69,221
SALES (est): 14.7MM **Privately Held**
WEB: www.perroneleather.com
SIC: 3199 5611 Leather garments; men's & boys' clothing stores

Gainesville
Wyoming County

(G-5483)
DRASGOW INC
4150 Poplar Tree Rd (14066-9723)
PHONE...............................585 786-3603
Karl Drasgow, *President*
Crystal Hilton, *Info Tech Mgr*
EMP: 21
SQ FT: 17,946
SALES: 1.7MM **Privately Held**
SIC: 3569 Filters

Galway
Saratoga County

(G-5484)
WHALENS HORSERADISH PRODUCTS
1710 Route 29 (12074-2213)
PHONE...............................518 587-6404
Kim Bibens, *President*
EMP: 5
SALES (est): 451.9K **Privately Held**
SIC: 2035 Horseradish, prepared

Gansevoort
Saratoga County

(G-5485)
AUREONIC
13 Whispering Pines Rd (12831-1443)
PHONE...............................518 791-9331
Shawn Lescault, *CEO*
Nicholas Karker, *Co-Owner*
Patrick Roden, *Co-Owner*
Robert Schramm, *Co-Owner*
Ian Tucker, *CFO*
EMP: 5
SALES (est): 350K **Privately Held**
SIC: 3823 7389 Combustion control instruments;

(G-5486)
GRANITE & MARBLE WORKS INC
8 Commerce Park Dr (12831-2240)
PHONE...............................518 584-2800
Margaret P Roohan, *President*
▲ EMP: 20
SALES (est): 3.2MM **Privately Held**
SIC: 3281 Granite, cut & shaped

(G-5487)
PALLETTE STONE CORPORATION
269 Ballard Rd (12831-1597)
PHONE...............................518 584-2421
Thomas Longe, *President*
D Alan Collins, *Corp Secy*
Rob Montague, *Project Mgr*
Dennis Cenci, *Sales Staff*
Christopher Weed, *Manager*
EMP: 40
SQ FT: 3,000
SALES (est): 6.9MM
SALES (corp-wide): 43.3MM **Privately Held**
SIC: 3281 2951 3241 5032 Cut stone & stone products; concrete, bituminous; portland cement; stone, crushed or broken; asphalt mixture; concrete & cinder block; paving stones; concrete & cinder block
PA: D. A. Collins Construction Co., Inc.
   269 Ballard Rd
   Gansevoort NY 12831
   518 664-9855

(G-5488)
RASP INCORPORATED
8 Dukes Way (12831-1668)
PHONE...............................518 747-8020
Fax: 518 747-8729
Ronald Richards, *Vice Pres*
Jeff Bruno, *Engineer*
Michael Close, *Treasurer*
EMP: 27
SQ FT: 8,000
SALES (est): 6.4MM **Privately Held**
WEB: www.rasp-controls.com
SIC: 3625 Industrial controls: push button, selector switches, pilot

(G-5489)
ROCK HILL BAKEHOUSE LTD
21 Saratoga Rd (12831-1554)
PHONE...............................518 743-1627
Fax: 518 743-9623
Matthew Funiciello, *President*
Michael London, *Vice Pres*
Adam Witt, *Treasurer*
Wendy London, *Admin Sec*
EMP: 30
SALES (est): 2.7MM **Privately Held**
WEB: www.rockhillbakehouse.com
SIC: 2051 5461 Bread, all types (white, wheat, rye, etc); fresh or frozen; bread

(G-5490)
STONE BRIDGE IRON AND STL INC
426 Purinton Rd (12831-2193)
PHONE...............................518 695-3752
Fax: 518 695-3056
Brian B Carmer, *CEO*
Ron Carmer, *Principal*
Britt Carmer, *Exec VP*
Mark Hutchinson, *Vice Pres*
Jeff Poland, *Project Mgr*
▲ EMP: 60
SQ FT: 45,000
SALES (est): 21.4MM **Privately Held**
WEB: www.stonebridgeiron.com
SIC: 3441 Building components, structural steel

(G-5491)
TRUARC FABRICATION
1 Commerce Park Dr (12831-2239)
PHONE...............................518 691-0430
Cris Edgerly, *President*
EMP: 9
SALES (est): 956.8K **Privately Held**
SIC: 3599 Flexible metal hose, tubing & bellows

Garden City
Nassau County

(G-5492)
A G MASTER CRAFTS LTD
5 South St Ste A (11530-4926)
PHONE...............................516 745-6262
Fax: 516 745-6276
Tom Gardianos, *President*
Diana Gardianos, *Vice Pres*
Cynthia Herman, *Manager*
▲ EMP: 15
SALES (est): 1.9MM **Privately Held**
WEB: www.agmastercrafts.com
SIC: 2521 Wood office furniture; cabinets, office: wood

(G-5493)
AAR ALLEN SERVICES INC
AAR Aircraft Component
747 Zeckendorf Blvd (11530-2188)
PHONE...............................516 222-9000
Fax: 516 222-0987
Rob Bruinsna, *General Mgr*
Michael Amilov, *Sales Mgr*
EMP: 46
SALES (corp-wide): 1.6B **Publicly Held**
SIC: 3679 Electronic circuits
HQ: Aar Allen Services, Inc.
   1100 N Wood Dale Rd
   Wood Dale IL 60191
   630 227-2410

(G-5494)
AMETEK INC
Also Called: Hughes-Treitler
300 Endo Blvd (11530-6708)
PHONE...............................516 832-7710
Fax: 516 832-8054
Colleen Maloney, *Principal*
Ronald Brasser, *Vice Pres*
Michael Denicola, *Vice Pres*
Anthony Salucci, *Mfg Staff*
Fabrizio Coduri, *Production*
EMP: 175
SALES (corp-wide): 3.9B **Publicly Held**
SIC: 3443 Fabricated plate work (boiler shop)
PA: Ametek, Inc.
   1100 Cassatt Rd
   Berwyn PA 19312
   610 647-2121

(G-5495)
ATLAS SWITCH CO INC
969 Stewart Ave (11530-4816)
PHONE...............................516 222-6280
Fax: 516 222-6287
Gina Paradise, *President*
Javier Castagnola, *Engineer*
Fred Creda, *Engineer*
Billy Falcone, *Engineer*
John Paradise, *Engineer*
EMP: 33
SQ FT: 30,000
SALES (est): 12.4MM **Privately Held**
WEB: www.atlasswitch.com
SIC: 3613 3699 Switches, electric power except snap, push button, etc.; electrical equipment & supplies

(G-5496)
BHARAT ELECTRONICS LIMITED
53 Hilton Ave (11530-2806)
PHONE...............................516 248-4021
Fax: 516 741-5894
Siva Muthuswamy, *Manager*
EMP: 7
SALES (corp-wide): 1B **Privately Held**
WEB: www.bel-india.com
SIC: 3674 Solid state electronic devices
PA: Bharat Electronics Limited
   Outer Ring Road, Nagavara,
   Bengaluru KAR 56004
   802 503-9266

(G-5497)
BRISTOL-MYERS SQUIBB COMPANY
1000 Stewart Ave (11530-4814)
PHONE...............................516 832-2191
Richard Serafin, *Branch Mgr*
Patrick McFarland, *Associate Dir*
Leacy Pryor, *Associate Dir*
EMP: 225
SALES (corp-wide): 16.5B **Publicly Held**
WEB: www.bms.com
SIC: 2834 Pharmaceutical preparations
PA: Bristol-Myers Squibb Company
   345 Park Ave Bsmt Lc3
   New York NY 10154
   212 546-4000

▲ = Import ▼ = Export
◆ = Import/Export

Garden City - Nassau County (G-5524)

(G-5498)
BUSINESS TECH COMMUNICATIONS
18 Hudson Rd (11530-1020)
PHONE..................................516 354-5205
Paul Beatty, *Owner*
EMP: 11
SALES: 2.3MM **Privately Held**
SIC: 2721 Periodicals

(G-5499)
CAMPUS COURSE PAKS INC
1 South Ave Fl 1 (11530-4213)
PHONE..................................516 877-3967
Wayne Piskin, *President*
Stanley Rosenfeld, *Financial Exec*
Sabine Dorcean, *Manager*
EMP: 5
SQ FT: 1,500
SALES: 237.4MM **Privately Held**
WEB: www.ccpaks.com
SIC: 2731 Books: publishing only

(G-5500)
DYNA-EMPIRE INC
1075 Stewart Ave (11530-4871)
PHONE..................................516 222-2700
Fax: 516 222-1896
G Patrick Mc Carthy, *President*
Richard Shaper, *Vice Pres*
Syd Crossley, *Opers Staff*
John Sallami, *Opers Staff*
Dennis Harty, *Purch Agent*
▲ EMP: 145 EST: 1941
SQ FT: 52,000
SALES (est): 34.3MM **Privately Held**
WEB: www.dyna-empire.com
SIC: 3724 3728 3829 3823 Aircraft engines & engine parts; aircraft landing assemblies & brakes; measuring & controlling devices; industrial instrmnts msrmnt display/control process variable; search & navigation equipment

(G-5501)
EDGEWOOD INDUSTRIES INC
635 Commercial Ave (11530-6409)
PHONE..................................516 227-2447
Frank Suppa, *President*
EMP: 6
SALES (est): 551.9K **Privately Held**
SIC: 3271 Concrete block & brick

(G-5502)
ELEVATOR SYSTEMS INC
465 Endo Blvd Unit 1 (11530-4924)
PHONE..................................516 239-4044
Fax: 516 239-5793
Ignatius Alcamo Jr, *President*
Annie-Marie Alcamo, *Corp Secy*
James Sullivan, *Sales Mgr*
Alma Ignites, *Shareholder*
▲ EMP: 25
SQ FT: 10,000
SALES (est): 4.9MM **Privately Held**
SIC: 3625 Relays & industrial controls

(G-5503)
EURO FINE PAPER INC
220 Nassau Blvd (11530-5500)
PHONE..................................516 238-5253
Tom McShea Sr, *President*
EMP: 8
SALES (est): 640K **Privately Held**
SIC: 2621 Paper mills

(G-5504)
EUROPEAN MARBLE WORKS CO INC
Also Called: Puccio Marble and Onyx
54 Nassau Blvd (11530-4139)
PHONE..................................718 387-9778
Paul Puccio, *President*
John Puccio, *Vice Pres*
▲ EMP: 12 EST: 1956
SQ FT: 70,000
SALES (est): 1.2MM **Privately Held**
SIC: 3281 Cut stone & stone products

(G-5505)
EXERGY LLC
320 Endo Blvd Unit 1 (11530-6747)
PHONE..................................516 832-9300
Jordan Finkelstein, *President*
Bob Scott, *President*
Edward Loring, *General Mgr*
Robert Scott, *Vice Pres*
EMP: 37
SQ FT: 20,000
SALES (est): 6MM **Privately Held**
WEB: www.exergyllc.com
SIC: 3443 8711 Heat exchangers, condensers & components; consulting engineer

(G-5506)
GAFFNEY KROESE SUPPLY CORP
Also Called: Gaffney Kroese Electrial
377 Oak St Ste 202 (11530-6542)
PHONE..................................516 228-5091
Fax: 516 334-2794
John Kroese, *President*
Gregory Poli, *Opers Staff*
Robert Jouas, *Controller*
Ilene Paulvin, *Accounting Mgr*
Iris Pinnaro, *Accounts Exec*
▼ EMP: 14 EST: 2012
SALES (est): 1.6MM **Privately Held**
SIC: 3621 Motors & generators

(G-5507)
GEHRING TRICOT CORPORATION (PA)
Also Called: Gehring Textiles
1225 Franklin Ave Ste 300 (11530-1659)
P.O. Box 272, Dolgeville (13329-0272)
PHONE..................................315 429-8551
Fax: 315 429-8469
George G Gehring Jr, *President*
Brenda Gehring, *Principal*
Marie Bevilaqua, *Vice Pres*
Martin Callahan, *Vice Pres*
Paul Gutowski, *Vice Pres*
▲ EMP: 71 EST: 1952
SQ FT: 50,000
SALES (est): 60.2MM **Privately Held**
SIC: 2258 2262 Dyeing & finishing lace goods & warp knit fabric; tricot fabrics; finishing plants, manmade fiber & silk fabrics

(G-5508)
GEM FABRICATION OF NC
586 Commercial Ave (11530-6418)
PHONE..................................704 278-6713
Greg Smith, *Branch Mgr*
EMP: 7
SALES (est): 1.8MM **Privately Held**
SIC: 3569 Sprinkler systems, fire: automatic

(G-5509)
IMACOR INC
821 Franklin Ave Ste 301 (11530-4519)
PHONE..................................516 393-0970
Fax: 516 393-0969
Peter Pellerito, *President*
Jenn Kujawski, *Exec VP*
Scott Roth, *Vice Pres*
Dipak Rajhansa, *Sales Staff*
Sheila McGarrigle, *Manager*
EMP: 20
SALES (est): 3.6MM **Privately Held**
SIC: 3845 Ultrasonic scanning devices, medical

(G-5510)
INCORPORATED VILLAGE GARDEN CY
103 11th St (11530-1605)
PHONE..................................516 465-4020
Domenick Stanco, *Superintendent*
EMP: 150 **Privately Held**
WEB: www.fop911.com
SIC: 3589 9511 Sewage & water treatment equipment;
PA: Incorporated Village Of Garden City
351 Stewart Ave
Garden City NY 11530
516 742-5800

(G-5511)
INFORMA SOLUTIONS INC
Also Called: Analytics Intell
237 Ellington Ave W (11530-5068)
PHONE..................................516 543-3733
David Bissainthe, *President*
EMP: 48 EST: 2015
SQ FT: 200
SALES (est): 3MM **Privately Held**
SIC: 7372 7373 7374 Prepackaged software; computer integrated systems design; data processing & preparation; data processing service

(G-5512)
ISSCO CORPORATION (PA)
Also Called: Industrial SEC Systems Contrls
111 Cherry Valley Ave # 410 (11530-1573)
PHONE..................................212 732-8748
Fax: 516 334-7064
Arthur R Katon, *President*
Marsha Katon, *Corp Secy*
Flavie Aronowicz, *Persnl Dir*
EMP: 20
SQ FT: 14,000
SALES (est): 1.6MM **Privately Held**
SIC: 3699 Security control equipment & systems

(G-5513)
L & M PUBLICATIONS INC
Also Called: Freeport Baldwin Leader
2 Endo Blvd (11530-6707)
PHONE..................................516 378-3133
Linda Laursen Toscano, *President*
Paul Laursen, *Vice Pres*
John Laursen, *Shareholder*
EMP: 33
SALES (est): 1.6MM **Privately Held**
WEB: www.merricklife.com
SIC: 2711 7313 Newspapers; newspaper advertising representative

(G-5514)
LIFETIME BRANDS INC (PA)
1000 Stewart Ave (11530-4814)
PHONE..................................516 683-6000
Fax: 516 555-0101
Jeffrey Siegel, *Ch of Bd*
Daniel Siegel, *President*
Ronald Shiftan, *COO*
Paul Kanter, *Senior VP*
Carolyn Lefavour, *Senior VP*
▼ EMP: 277
SQ FT: 159,000
SALES (est): 587.6MM **Publicly Held**
WEB: www.lifetimebrands.com
SIC: 3421 5023 5719 Cutlery; home furnishings; kitchen tools & utensils; stainless steel flatware; kitchenware; cutlery; glassware

(G-5515)
LONG ISLAND PIPE SUPPLY INC (PA)
Also Called: LI Pipe Supply
586 Commercial Ave (11530-6418)
PHONE..................................516 222-8008
Robert Moss, *CEO*
Kim Smith, *Controller*
Paul Badejo, *Manager*
EMP: 40
SQ FT: 35,000
SALES (est): 23.4MM **Privately Held**
SIC: 3569 Sprinkler systems, fire: automatic

(G-5516)
LONG ISLAND PIPE SUPPLY INC (PA)
586 Commercial Ave (11530-6418)
PHONE..................................516 222-8008
Fax: 516 222-9234
Robert Moss, *President*
Kim Smith, *Manager*
EMP: 28
SQ FT: 35,000
SALES (est): 59.7MM **Privately Held**
WEB: www.lipipe.com
SIC: 3498 5074 Fabricated pipe & fittings; plumbing fittings & supplies

(G-5517)
LORD & BERRY NORTH AMERICA LTD
585 Stewart Ave Fl 5 (11530-4783)
PHONE..................................516 745-0088
Paolo Blayer, *President*
EMP: 4
SQ FT: 400
SALES: 2MM
SALES (corp-wide): 1.5MM **Privately Held**
SIC: 2844 5122 Cosmetic preparations; cosmetics
PA: Lord & Berry Europe Srl
Via Mose' Bianchi 19
Milano MI 20149
029 379-6836

(G-5518)
M AND J HAIR CENTER INC
Also Called: Natural Image Hair Concepts
1103 Stewart Ave Ste 100 (11530-4886)
PHONE..................................516 872-1010
Jean Dreyfuss, *President*
EMP: 15
SQ FT: 1,600
SALES (est): 1.4MM **Privately Held**
WEB: www.mjhair.com
SIC: 3999 Wigs, including doll wigs, toupees or wiglets

(G-5519)
MCQUILLING PARTNERS INC (PA)
1035 Stewart Ave Ste 100 (11530-4825)
PHONE..................................516 227-5718
John F Desantes, *Ch of Bd*
Angelos Meimeteas, *Managing Dir*
Peter Neave, *Managing Dir*
Christopher Desantis, *Vice Pres*
Matthew E Ellison, *Broker*
EMP: 27 EST: 1964
SALES (est): 3.1MM **Privately Held**
WEB: www.mcquilling.com
SIC: 3731 Tankers, building & repairing

(G-5520)
MEADOWBROOK DISTRIBUTING CORP
95 Jefferson St (11530-3931)
PHONE..................................516 226-9000
Patrick O'Conner, *Branch Mgr*
EMP: 60
SALES (corp-wide): 64.4MM **Privately Held**
SIC: 2086 Carbonated soft drinks, bottled & canned
HQ: Meadowbrook Distributing Corp
550 New Horizons Blvd
Amityville NY 11701
631 226-9000

(G-5521)
MELWOOD PARTNERS INC (PA)
100 Qentin Roosevelt Blvd (11530-4874)
PHONE..................................516 307-8030
Brian Wasserman, *Ch of Bd*
EMP: 4
SALES (est): 2.1MM **Privately Held**
SIC: 2331 2335 Women's & misses' blouses & shirts; blouses, women's & juniors': made from purchased material; shirts, women's & juniors': made from purchased materials; women's, juniors' & misses' dresses

(G-5522)
META PHARMACY SYSTEMS INC
401 Franklin Ave Ste 106 (11530-5942)
PHONE..................................516 488-6189
Fax: 516 488-6647
Salvatore M Barcia, *President*
EMP: 25
SALES (est): 1.8MM **Privately Held**
WEB: www.metapharmacy.com
SIC: 7372 Prepackaged software

(G-5523)
NEW YORK PACKAGING II LLC
Also Called: Redi Bag Brand
135 Fulton Ave (11530)
P.O. Box 1039, New Hyde Park (11040-7039)
PHONE..................................516 746-0600
Jeffrey Rabiea, *President*
▲ EMP: 249
SALES (est): 32.9MM **Privately Held**
SIC: 2673 Plastic bags: made from purchased materials

(G-5524)
NORCATEC LLC (PA)
100 Garden Cy Plz Ste 530 (11530)
PHONE..................................516 222-7070

Garden City - Nassau County (G-5525)

Fax: 516 222-8811
Eytan Erez, *President*
Doreen Romanello, *Editor*
Carmen Hornsby, *Vice Pres*
Danny Vinluan, *Purch Dir*
Theresa Hurley, *Purchasing*
▼ **EMP:** 25
SQ FT: 65,000
SALES (est): 22.7MM **Privately Held**
WEB: www.norcatec.com
SIC: 3714 Motor vehicle parts & accessories

(G-5525)
PINCHARMING INC
215 Brixton Rd (11530-1339)
PHONE..............................516 663-5115
Susan Smith, *President*
Barry Smith, *Vice Pres*
EMP: 12
SALES (est): 1MM **Privately Held**
SIC: 3961 Costume jewelry

(G-5526)
PRACTICEPRO SOFTWARE SYSTEMS
666 Old Country Rd Bsmt (11530-2079)
PHONE..............................516 222-0010
Gary J Balsamo, *President*
EMP: 5
SALES: 313.6K **Privately Held**
WEB: www.practicepro.com
SIC: 7372 Prepackaged software

(G-5527)
PROGINET CORPORATION
200 Garden Cy Plz Ste 220 (11530)
PHONE..............................516 535-3600
Fax: 516 248-3360
Sandison E Weil, *President*
Stephen M Flynn, *COO*
John W Gazzola, *Senior VP*
Jennifer Mundy, *Vice Pres*
Joe Christel, *CFO*
EMP: 37
SALES: 9.3MM **Privately Held**
WEB: www.proginet.com
SIC: 7372 Application computer software; business oriented computer software; operating systems computer software

(G-5528)
PUCCIO DESIGN INTERNATIONAL
Also Called: Puccio European Marble & Onyx
54 Nassau Blvd (11530-4139)
PHONE..............................516 248-6426
Paul Puccio, *President*
EMP: 15 **EST:** 1968
SQ FT: 4,000
SALES (est): 128.3K **Privately Held**
WEB: www.puccio.info
SIC: 3281 Furniture, cut stone

(G-5529)
RICHNER COMMUNICATIONS INC (PA)
Also Called: Prime Time
2 Endo Blvd (11530-6707)
PHONE..............................516 569-4000
Stuart Richner, *CEO*
Tony Bellissimo, *Editor*
Scott Brinton, *Editor*
John Connell, *Editor*
Mary Malloy, *Editor*
EMP: 130
SQ FT: 90,000
SALES (est): 16.3MM **Privately Held**
SIC: 2711 Commercial printing & newspaper publishing combined

(G-5530)
ROBECO/ASCOT PRODUCTS INC
100 Ring Rd W (11530-3219)
PHONE..............................516 248-1521
EMP: 0
SALES (est): 1.2MM **Privately Held**
SIC: 3081 Vinyl film & sheet; plastic film & sheet

(G-5531)
SAVENERGY INC
645 South St Unit A (11530-4928)
PHONE..............................516 239-1958
John Hyung Choi, *President*
Turab Syed, *General Mgr*
Raaed Junaid, *Project Mgr*
▲ **EMP:** 9 **EST:** 2010
SALES (est): 1.1MM **Privately Held**
SIC: 3646 Commercial indusl & institutional electric lighting fixtures

(G-5532)
SEVIROLI FOODS INC (PA)
601 Brook St (11530-6431)
PHONE..............................516 222-6220
Fax: 516 222-0534
Joseph Seviroli Jr, *Ch of Bd*
Paul Vertullo, *COO*
Alan Bronstein, *VP Opers*
John Stancek, *Project Mgr*
Bert Singh, *Purch Mgr*
▲ **EMP:** 167
SQ FT: 80,000
SALES (est): 71.9MM **Privately Held**
WEB: www.seviroli.com
SIC: 2038 Frozen specialties

(G-5533)
STANDARD WEDDING BAND CO
951 Franklin Ave (11530-2909)
PHONE..............................516 294-0954
Walter E Soderlund, *President*
Mabel T Soderlund, *Treasurer*
EMP: 6
SALES: 500K **Privately Held**
SIC: 3911 Rings, finger: precious metal

(G-5534)
THERMAL TECH DOORS INC (PA)
576 Brook St (11530-6416)
PHONE..............................516 745-0100
Emanuel Karavas, *President*
Stephanos Kourtis, *Vice Pres*
George Gregory, *Comptroller*
EMP: 28
SQ FT: 25,000
SALES (est): 4.3MM **Privately Held**
SIC: 3442 Sash, door or window: metal

(G-5535)
VIRAJ - USA INC (DH)
100 Quentin Roosevelt Blv (11530-4848)
PHONE..............................516 280-8380
Dhruv Kochhar, *President*
Daulat Tannan, *Vice Pres*
Imran Hassan, *Admin Asst*
▲ **EMP:** 6
SALES (est): 899.3K **Privately Held**
SIC: 3312 Stainless steel
HQ: Viraj Profiles Limited
1st Floor, 10, Imperial Chambers,
Mumbai MH
222 261-4327

(G-5536)
WILDER MANUFACTURING CO INC
439 Oak St (11530-6453)
PHONE..............................516 222-0433
Jonathan J Holtz, *President*
Richard Leads, *General Mgr*
Dominick Scarfogliero, *COO*
John Jameson, *Vice Pres*
John McLaughlin, *Vice Pres*
EMP: 55
SQ FT: 37,500
SALES (est): 3.1MM **Privately Held**
SIC: 3589 3556 Commercial cooking & foodwarming equipment; food products machinery

(G-5537)
WIN-HOLT EQUIPMENT CORP
439 Oak St Ste 1 (11530-6453)
PHONE..............................516 222-0433
Ed Campbell, *Branch Mgr*
Milton Perez, *Manager*
EMP: 120
SQ FT: 45,000
SALES (corp-wide): 88.1MM **Privately Held**
WEB: www.winholt.com
SIC: 3499 3556 3537 Machine bases, metal; food products machinery; industrial trucks & tractors
PA: Win-Holt Equipment Corp.
20 Crossways Park Dr N # 205
Woodbury NY 11797
516 222-0335

(G-5538)
WON & LEE INC
Also Called: Unicorn Graphics
971 Stewart Ave (11530-4816)
PHONE..............................516 222-0712
Jong Suk Lee, *President*
Jong Hoon Lee, *Vice Pres*
Jeffrey Chun, *Marketing Staff*
Jason Lee, *Manager*
Michael Park, *Director*
▲ **EMP:** 30
SQ FT: 30,000
SALES (est): 6.9MM **Privately Held**
WEB: www.unicorngraphics.com
SIC: 2759 2789 2752 2741 Calendars: printing; bookbinding & related work; commercial printing, lithographic; miscellaneous publishing; ink, printers'

Garden City Park
Nassau County

(G-5539)
DENTON STONEWORKS INC
94 Denton Ave (11040-4036)
PHONE..............................516 746-1500
Fax: 516 746-6776
Boguslaw Kaczor, *CEO*
Monika Krasuska, *Manager*
EMP: 14
SQ FT: 15,000
SALES (est): 1.8MM **Privately Held**
SIC: 3281 Cut stone & stone products

(G-5540)
JED LIGHTS INC
4 3rd St (11040-4410)
PHONE..............................516 812-5001
John Jones, *President*
Frank Wess, *Bookkeeper*
EMP: 7
SQ FT: 10,000
SALES (est): 931.1K **Privately Held**
SIC: 3648 5063 Lighting equipment; lighting fittings & accessories

(G-5541)
PERFECT GEAR & INSTRUMENT
125 Railroad Ave (11040-5016)
PHONE..............................516 873-6122
Karen Hearne, *Principal*
EMP: 24
SALES (corp-wide): 110.2MM **Privately Held**
SIC: 3462 Gears, forged steel
HQ: Perfect Gear & Instrument Corp
55 Denton Ave S
New Hyde Park NY 11040
516 328-3330

(G-5542)
SQUARE ONE PUBLISHERS INC
115 Herricks Rd (11040-5341)
PHONE..............................516 535-2010
Rudy Shur, *President*
Bob Love, *Finance*
Ariel Colletti, *Manager*
Rob Benson, *Director*
▲ **EMP:** 12
SQ FT: 8,000
SALES (est): 3.5MM **Privately Held**
SIC: 2731 Book publishing

(G-5543)
STRIANO ELECTRIC CO INC
246 Park Ave (11040-5318)
PHONE..............................516 408-4969
Vincent T Striano, *Ch of Bd*
Salvatore Lomonaco, *Project Mgr*
Lynn Gallagher, *Opers Staff*
Victoria Caballero, *Controller*
Patrick Hickey, *Assistant*
EMP: 42
SALES (est): 11.7MM **Privately Held**
SIC: 3699 Electrical equipment & supplies

(G-5544)
WINDOWCRAFT INC
77 2nd Ave (11040-5030)
PHONE..............................516 294-3580
Fax: 516 294-0444
Joseph Daniels, *President*
Ellen Caro, *Accountant*
◆ **EMP:** 18
SQ FT: 6,000
SALES (est): 2.5MM **Privately Held**
SIC: 2591 Window shades

(G-5545)
WINDOWTEX INC
77 2nd Ave (11040-5030)
PHONE..............................877 294-3580
Dara Centonze, *Business Mgr*
David Lin, *Opers Mgr*
Fang Lin, *Design Engr*
Faith Daniels, *Accounting Mgr*
Eric Dudley, *Cust Mgr*
EMP: 7
SALES (est): 82.9K **Privately Held**
SIC: 2591 Window shade rollers & fittings

(G-5546)
YORK INDUSTRIES INC
303 Nassau Blvd (11040-5213)
PHONE..............................516 746-3736
Fax: 516 746-3741
Lee E Smith, *Ch of Bd*
Paul Byers, *Vice Pres*
Janne Allen, *Purchasing*
Frank Filadelfo, *Engineer*
Maria Maqueda, *VP Sales*
EMP: 50 **EST:** 1942
SQ FT: 9,000
SALES (est): 11.1MM **Privately Held**
WEB: www.york-ind.com
SIC: 3829 3568 3462 3429 Measuring & controlling devices; ball joints, except aircraft & automotive; iron & steel forgings; manufactured hardware (general); hand & edge tools; tire cord & fabrics

Gardiner
Ulster County

(G-5547)
ARTHUR LAUER INC
47 Steves Ln (12525-5322)
P.O. Box 745, Dublin OH (43017-0845)
PHONE..............................845 255-7871
Jeremy Smith, *President*
Joyce Salimeno, *Partner*
Kathleen Martin, *Controller*
▲ **EMP:** 29
SALES (est): 3MM **Privately Held**
WEB: www.arthurlauer.com
SIC: 2511 2512 Wood household furniture; upholstered household furniture

(G-5548)
BYCMAC CORP
Also Called: Kiss My Face
144 Main St (12525-5245)
P.O. Box 224 (12525-0224)
PHONE..............................845 255-0884
Robert Macleod, *President*
Steve Byckiewicz, *Exec VP*
Betty Jordan, *Vice Pres*
Christine Croce, *Production*
Renee Smitherman, *Research*
▲ **EMP:** 45
SQ FT: 20,000
SALES (est): 10.4MM **Privately Held**
WEB: www.kissmyface.com
SIC: 2844 Cosmetic preparations

(G-5549)
DAVID KUCERA INC
42 Steves Ln (12525-5319)
PHONE..............................845 255-1044
Fax: 845 255-1597
David Kucera, *President*
Ted Fair, *Project Mgr*
Melanie Prouty, *Project Mgr*
Ann Kramer, *Purchasing*
Dan Couse, *Sales Staff*
EMP: 35
SQ FT: 15,000

SALES (est): 6.6MM Privately Held
WEB: www.davidkucerainc.com
SIC: 3272 Concrete products, precast

(G-5550)
S P INDUSTRIES INC
Also Called: Sp Scientific
815 Rte 208 (12525)
PHONE.................................845 255-5000
Fax: 845 255-5338
David T Sutherland, *Vice Pres*
Duane Richards, *Production*
Drli Mylie, *Purchasing*
Kenneth Tenedini, *Sales Mgr*
Dan De Beau, *Branch Mgr*
EMP: 82
SQ FT: 7,200
SALES (corp-wide): 1.6B Privately Held
WEB: www.virtis.com
SIC: 3829 3821 Measuring & controlling devices; laboratory apparatus & furniture
HQ: S P Industries, Inc.
 935 Mearns Rd
 Warminster PA 18974
 215 672-7800

(G-5551)
TUTHILLTOWN SPIRITS LLC
14 Gristmill Ln (12525-5528)
P.O. Box 320 (12525-0320)
PHONE.................................845 255-1527
Cathy Erenzo, *Opers Mgr*
Gable Lnd, *Manager*
Brian Lee,
Ralph Erenzo,
▲ EMP: 15
SALES (est): 3.4MM Privately Held
SIC: 2085 Distilled & blended liquors

(G-5552)
UTILITY CANVAS INC (PA)
2686 Route 44 55 (12525-5125)
P.O. Box 217 (12525-0217)
PHONE.................................845 255-9290
Fax: 845 255-9293
Hal Grano, *President*
Jillian Kaufman, *Vice Pres*
EMP: 4
SQ FT: 4,000
SALES: 1MM Privately Held
SIC: 2394 Canvas & related products

Garnerville
Rockland County

(G-5553)
AM ARCHITECTURAL METAL & GLASS
5 Bridge St (10923-1201)
PHONE.................................845 942-8848
Paula Maunsell, *CEO*
Philip Gordon, *Sales Executive*
EMP: 35
SALES: 1.5MM Privately Held
SIC: 3449 Curtain walls for buildings, steel

Garrison
Putnam County

(G-5554)
ELEANORS BEST
15 Peacock Way (10524-3107)
P.O. Box 9 (10524-0009)
PHONE.................................845 809-5621
Jennifer Mercurio, *Mng Member*
EMP: 10
SALES (est): 596.6K Privately Held
SIC: 2033 Jams, jellies & preserves: packaged in cans, jars, etc.

Gasport
Niagara County

(G-5555)
AG-PAK INC
8416 Telegraph Rd (14067-9246)
P.O. Box 304 (14067-0304)
PHONE.................................716 772-2651
Fax: 716 772-2555
James W Currie, *CEO*
Andy Currie, *President*
Warren Farewell, *Foreman/Supr*
Greg Lureman, *Sales Mgr*
Phil Fowler, *Sales Staff*
◆ EMP: 15
SQ FT: 14,000
SALES (est): 3.5MM Privately Held
WEB: www.agpak.com
SIC: 3556 Food products machinery

(G-5556)
COSMICOAT OF WNY INC
Also Called: Star Seal of New York
8419 East Ave (14067-9102)
P.O. Box 376 (14067-0376)
PHONE.................................716 772-2644
Fax: 716 772-2648
John Rouch, *President*
EMP: 4
SQ FT: 10,000
SALES (est): 2.2MM Privately Held
WEB: www.starsealny.com
SIC: 2951 Asphalt & asphaltic paving mixtures (not from refineries)

(G-5557)
GASPORT WELDING & FABG INC
8430 Telegraph Rd (14067-9246)
P.O. Box 410 (14067-0410)
PHONE.................................716 772-7205
Fax: 716 772-7388
Edward J Wojtkowski Jr, *President*
Beverly Wojtkowski, *Corp Secy*
Edward J Wotkowski, *Marketing Staff*
Christine Pittler, *Office Mgr*
EMP: 10
SQ FT: 14,000
SALES (est): 990K Privately Held
SIC: 3443 7692 3441 Tanks, standard or custom fabricated: metal plate; hoppers, metal plate; containers, shipping (bombs, etc.): metal plate; welding repair; fabricated structural metal

(G-5558)
MAKIPLASTIC
4904 Gasport Rd (14067-9506)
P.O. Box 2 (14067-0002)
PHONE.................................716 772-2222
Scott Brauer, *Owner*
EMP: 5
SALES (est): 170K Privately Held
SIC: 3949 Bait, artificial: fishing

(G-5559)
MILNE MFG INC
8411 State St (14067-9246)
P.O. Box 159 (14067-0159)
PHONE.................................716 772-2536
Janet Filipovich, *Human Res Mgr*
Ann Cain, *Branch Mgr*
EMP: 11
SALES (corp-wide): 3.5MM Privately Held
WEB: www.mmplastics.com
SIC: 3089 7389 Injection molding of plastics; telephone answering service
PA: M M Plastic (Mfg) Company, Inc
 1301 Blundell Rd
 Mississauga ON L4Y 1
 905 277-5514

(G-5560)
WOLFE LUMBER MILL INC
8416 Ridge Rd (14067-9415)
PHONE.................................716 772-7750
Fax: 716 772-7750
David C Caldwell, *President*
Sandy Lawrence, *Admin Sec*
EMP: 7
SQ FT: 11,000
SALES: 800K Privately Held
SIC: 2449 2448 2431 Fruit crates, wood: wirebound; pallets, wood; millwork

Gates
Monroe County

(G-5561)
KEYES MACHINE WORKS INC
147 Park Ave (14606-3818)
PHONE.................................585 426-5059
Fax: 585 426-5063
John Ritchie, *President*
Fraser Ritchie, *Vice Pres*
EMP: 5
SQ FT: 2,500
SALES: 490K Privately Held
SIC: 3544 3599 7699 Special dies & tools; custom machinery; industrial equipment services

(G-5562)
QSF INC
Also Called: Quality Stainless Fabrication
140 Cherry Rd (14624-2510)
PHONE.................................585 247-6200
Fax: 585 247-7093
Clyde Wingate, *President*
Gail Craig, *Office Mgr*
EMP: 7
SQ FT: 10,000
SALES (est): 1MM Privately Held
WEB: www.qsfportal.com
SIC: 3312 1731 7692 Stainless steel; electronic controls installation; welding repair

(G-5563)
R D A CONTAINER CORPORATION
70 Cherry Rd (14624-2592)
PHONE.................................585 247-2323
Fax: 585 247-5680
Alan P Brant, *Ch of Bd*
Steve Douglass, *Dept Chairman*
Michael Mangione, *QC Mgr*
Theodre Brant, *Treasurer*
Brian Burger, *Marketing Staff*
EMP: 42
SQ FT: 103,000
SALES (est): 9.3MM Privately Held
WEB: www.rdacontainer.com
SIC: 2653 3086 2449 Boxes, corrugated: made from purchased materials; packaging & shipping materials, foamed plastic; rectangular boxes & crates, wood

Geneseo
Livingston County

(G-5564)
CLARION PUBLICATIONS INC
38 Main St (14454-1216)
P.O. Box 236 (14454-0236)
PHONE.................................585 243-3530
Fax: 585 243-3764
M Corrin Strong, *President*
Howard Appell, *Editor*
Phil Livingston, *Editor*
EMP: 12
SQ FT: 1,600
SALES (est): 570K Privately Held
WEB: www.clarioncall.com
SIC: 2711 2721 2754 7334 Newspapers: publishing only, not printed on site; magazines: publishing & printing; color printing, gravure; photocopying & duplicating services

(G-5565)
DEER RUN ENTERPRISES INC
Also Called: Deer Run Winery
3772 W Lake Rd (14454-9743)
PHONE.................................585 346-0850
George Kuyon, *President*
Joan Kuyon, *Vice Pres*
Scott Kuyon, *Manager*
EMP: 6
SQ FT: 4,000
SALES (est): 520K Privately Held
WEB: www.deerrunwinery.com
SIC: 2084 Wines

(G-5566)
LIVINGSTON COUNTY NEWS
122 Main St (14454-1230)
PHONE.................................585 243-1234
Tom Turanvull, *President*
Tina Hancy, *Editor*
Howard Aggell, *Manager*
EMP: 7
SALES (est): 442.3K
SALES (corp-wide): 32MM Privately Held
WEB: www.ogd.com
SIC: 2711 Newspapers, publishing & printing
PA: Johnson Newspaper Corporation
 260 Washington St
 Watertown NY
 315 782-1000

(G-5567)
PPI CORP
Also Called: Ftt Automation
112 Riverside Dr (14454-1010)
PHONE.................................585 880-7277
John Longuil, *President*
Darrell Gibson, *Mfg Mgr*
Mike Cianciola, *Purch Mgr*
Paul Opela, *Controller*
Janet Oliviari, *Human Resources*
EMP: 42
SALES (est): 203.9K Privately Held
SIC: 3541 3449 3599 3544 Numerically controlled metal cutting machine tools; miscellaneous metalwork; machine shop, jobbing & repair; special dies, tools, jigs & fixtures

(G-5568)
PPI CORP
Also Called: Ftt Mfg
112 Riverside Dr (14454-1010)
PHONE.................................585 243-0300
Fax: 585 243-1520
John Longuil, *CEO*
Mike Cianciola, *Purch Mgr*
Lynn Rowling, *Purch Mgr*
John Gunn, *QC Mgr*
Tim Witherell, *Engineer*
▲ EMP: 60
SQ FT: 47,000
SALES (est): 14.7MM Privately Held
WEB: www.fttmfg.com
SIC: 3545 Precision tools, machinists'

Geneva
Ontario County

(G-5569)
ALLESON OF ROCHESTER INC
Also Called: Don Alleson Athletic
833 Canandaigua Rd Ste 40 (14456-2015)
PHONE.................................315 789-8464
Fax: 315 789-8762
Lyla Bousfiou, *Opers-Prdtn-Mfg*
Robert Ruditis, *Engrg Mgr*
Michael Kretovic, *Controller*
Lila Bouffiou, *Personnel*
EMP: 40
SQ FT: 53,685
SALES (corp-wide): 52.7MM Privately Held
SIC: 2329 2339 Athletic (warmup, sweat & jogging) suits: men's & boys'; athletic clothing: women's, misses' & juniors'
PA: Alleson Of Rochester, Inc.
 2921 Brighton Henrietta
 Rochester NY 14623
 585 272-0630

(G-5570)
BILLSBORO WINERY
4760 State Route 14 (14456-9746)
PHONE.................................315 789-9538
Kim Aliberti, *President*
Evan Pierce, *Sales Associate*
Jessica McGuigan, *Manager*
EMP: 6 EST: 1999
SALES (est): 559.4K Privately Held
SIC: 2084 Wines

Geneva - Ontario County (G-5571)

(G-5571)
CCMI INC
88 Middle St (14456-1836)
PHONE.................................315 781-3270
Fax: 315 781-3271
Wells C Lewis, *CEO*
Anthony Lewis, *President*
James Hartman, *Treasurer*
Rose Hammond-Hoose, *Office Mgr*
Rose Hammond Hoose, *Manager*
EMP: 8
SQ FT: 7,500
SALES (est): 700K Privately Held
WEB: www.ccmi-reedco.com
SIC: 2821 7389 Plastics materials & resins; packaging & labeling services

(G-5572)
CCN INTERNATIONAL INC
200 Lehigh St (14456-1096)
PHONE.................................315 789-4400
Fax: 315 789-0376
Charles Richard Conoyer, *President*
Anne Nenneau, *Exec VP*
Timothy Ceniceros, *Vice Pres*
Michael Hryzak, *Vice Pres*
Timothy Lesslie, *Vice Pres*
▼ EMP: 74 EST: 1970
SQ FT: 85,000
SALES (est): 8.8MM Privately Held
WEB: www.ccnintl.com
SIC: 2521 Wood office furniture; desks, office; wood; tables, office; wood; bookcases, office; wood

(G-5573)
CHERIBUNDI INC (PA)
500 Technology Farm Dr (14456-1325)
PHONE.................................800 699-0460
Steve Pear, *President*
Ed Maguire, *Vice Pres*
Mary Sterling, *QC Mgr*
Carol Langdon, *Controller*
EMP: 21
SQ FT: 8,300
SALES (est): 4.5MM Privately Held
SIC: 2037 2033 2086 Fruit juices; fruit juice concentrates, frozen; fruit juices: fresh; fruit drinks (less than 100% juice): packaged in cans, etc.

(G-5574)
ENVIROFORM RECYCLED PDTS INC
287 Gambee Rd (14456-1025)
P.O. Box 553 (14456-0553)
PHONE.................................315 789-1810
Robert L Bates, *President*
Joe Bates, *Project Mgr*
Amanda Wright, *Office Mgr*
EMP: 9
SQ FT: 5,000
SALES: 2.5MM Privately Held
WEB: www.enviroform.com
SIC: 3069 Molded rubber products; rubber automotive products

(G-5575)
FAHY-WILLIAMS PUBLISHING INC
171 Reed St (14456-2137)
P.O. Box 1080 (14456-8080)
PHONE.................................315 781-6820
Fax: 315 789-4263
Kevin Fahy, *President*
Tim Braden, *Vice Pres*
Trisha McKenna, *Office Mgr*
Jenn Bergin, *Assoc Editor*
Danielle Valente, *Assoc Editor*
EMP: 13
SQ FT: 3,200
SALES (est): 1.8MM Privately Held
WEB: www.fwpi.com
SIC: 2721 Periodicals: publishing only

(G-5576)
FINGER LAKES PRINTING CO INC (HQ)
218 Genesee St (14456-2323)
P.O. Box 393 (14456-0393)
PHONE.................................315 789-3333
Fax: 315 789-4077
William L McLean III, *President*
Leslie Sutterby, *Sales Staff*
EMP: 50
SQ FT: 20,000
SALES (est): 8.1MM
SALES (corp-wide): 77.1MM Privately Held
WEB: www.fltimes.com
SIC: 2711 Newspapers
PA: Independent Publications, Inc.
945 E Haverford Rd Ste 5
Bryn Mawr PA
610 527-6330

(G-5577)
FINGER LAKES RADIOLOGY LLC
196 North St (14456-1651)
PHONE.................................315 787-5399
John Oates, *Information Mgr*
Leza Hassett, *Director*
Rich Laurenzo, *Director*
Andre Forcier,
EMP: 6
SALES (est): 1.2MM Privately Held
SIC: 3826 Magnetic resonance imaging apparatus

(G-5578)
GENEVA GRANITE CO INC (PA)
272 Border City Rd (14456-1988)
P.O. Box 834 (14456-0834)
PHONE.................................315 789-8142
Fax: 315 781-2900
Ralph Fratto Jr, *President*
Joseph Fratto, *Corp Secy*
Jean Fratto, *Vice Pres*
EMP: 15
SQ FT: 1,200
SALES (est): 3MM Privately Held
SIC: 3281 1771 Curbing, paving & walkway stone; concrete work; curb construction

(G-5579)
GENEVA PRINTING COMPANY INC
40 Castle St (14456-2679)
PHONE.................................315 789-8191
Fax: 315 789-1618
Ronald Alcock, *President*
Jo Ellen Alcock, *Vice Pres*
EMP: 8
SQ FT: 7,500
SALES (est): 820K Privately Held
WEB: www.genevaprinting.com
SIC: 2752 Commercial printing, offset

(G-5580)
GUARDIAN INDUSTRIES CORP
50 Forge Ave (14456-1281)
PHONE.................................315 787-7000
Fax: 315 787-7065
Christopher Housman, *General Mgr*
Dean Cambell, *Principal*
Cheryl Hess, *Human Resources*
Janet Humphrey, *Sales Mgr*
Mark Bennett, *Manager*
EMP: 332
SALES (corp-wide): 5B Privately Held
WEB: www.guardian.com
SIC: 3211 Flat glass
PA: Guardian Industries Corp.
2300 Harmon Rd
Auburn Hills MI 48326
248 340-1800

(G-5581)
HANGER PRSTHETCS & ORTHO INC
787 State Route 5 And 20 (14456-2001)
PHONE.................................315 789-4810
Thomas Kirk PHD, *CEO*
Sheryl Price, *Director*
EMP: 5
SALES (corp-wide): 500.5MM Privately Held
SIC: 3842 Limbs, artificial; braces, orthopedic
HQ: Hanger Prosthetics & Orthotics, Inc.
10910 Main Dr
Austin TX 78758
512 777-3800

(G-5582)
MCINTOSH BOX & PALLET CO INC
40 Doran Ave (14456-1224)
PHONE.................................315 789-8750
Fax: 315 789-8820
Robert Randall, *Facilities Mgr*
William Wester, *Opers Staff*
Joshua Stasik, *Sales Staff*
Vayeli Rivera, *Manager*
Danielle Wester, *Manager*
EMP: 18
SQ FT: 14,400
SALES (corp-wide): 24.8MM Privately Held
WEB: www.mcintoshbox.com
SIC: 2441 2448 Shipping cases, wood: nailed or lock corner; wood pallets & skids
PA: Mcintosh Box & Pallet Co., Inc.
5864 Pyle Dr
East Syracuse NY 13057
315 446-9350

(G-5583)
NEGYS NEW LAND VINYRD WINERY
Also Called: Three Brothers Winery
623 Lerch Rd Ste 1 (14456-9295)
PHONE.................................315 585-4432
Nancy Burdick, *President*
Dave Mansfield, *Owner*
Erica Ridley, *General Mgr*
EMP: 7
SALES: 100K Privately Held
SIC: 2084 5921 Wines; wine

(G-5584)
R M REYNOLDS (PA)
Also Called: Point of Sale Outfitters
504 Exchange St (14456-3407)
PHONE.................................315 789-7365
R M Reynolds, *Owner*
EMP: 5
SQ FT: 5,500
SALES (est): 583.8K Privately Held
SIC: 3911 5094 Jewelry, precious metal; jewelry

(G-5585)
SENECA FOODS CORPORATION
Also Called: Vegetable Operations
100 Gambee Rd (14456-1099)
PHONE.................................315 781-8733
Fax: 315 789-1586
Warren Fredericksen, *Plant Mgr*
Gary Hadyk, *Plant Mgr*
Mark Forsting, *Opers-Prdtn-Mfg*
Katie Gushlaw, *Human Res Mgr*
Jeff Johnson, *Manager*
EMP: 150
SALES (corp-wide): 1.2B Publicly Held
SIC: 2033 Sauerkraut: packaged in cans, jars, etc.; vegetables: packaged in cans, jars, etc.
PA: Seneca Foods Corporation
3736 S Main St
Marion NY 14505
315 926-8100

(G-5586)
SENECA TRUCK & TRAILER INC
2200 State Route 14 (14456-9511)
PHONE.................................315 781-1100
Patrick O'Connor, *President*
Patrick O Connor, *President*
EMP: 6
SALES (est): 350K Privately Held
WEB: www.senecatruck.com
SIC: 3715 Truck trailers

(G-5587)
TRAMWELL INC
Also Called: Graphic Connections
70 State St (14456-1760)
PHONE.................................315 789-2762
Fax: 315 789-2910
William D Whitwell, *President*
Nancy F Whitwell, *Vice Pres*
EMP: 5
SQ FT: 4,000
SALES: 300K Privately Held
SIC: 2261 Screen printing of cotton broadwoven fabrics

(G-5588)
VANCE METAL FABRICATORS INC
251 Gambee Rd (14456-1025)
PHONE.................................315 789-5626
Fax: 315 789-1848
Joseph A Hennessy, *Ch of Bd*
William Dobbin Jr, *Chairman*
Len Visco, *Opers Mgr*
John Sabin, *Foreman/Supr*
Ryan Shane, *Opers Staff*
▲ EMP: 85 EST: 1880
SQ FT: 36,000
SALES (est): 45.5MM Privately Held
WEB: www.vancemetal.com
SIC: 3441 3444 Fabricated structural metal; sheet metalwork

(G-5589)
ZOTOS INTERNATIONAL INC
Joico Laboritoriies
300 Forge Ave (14456-1294)
PHONE.................................315 781-3207
Fax: 315 789-0744
Herb Nieporent, *Principal*
John Mahon, *Research*
Debi Jones, *Human Res Dir*
Jeffrey Doyle, *Manager*
EMP: 289
SALES (corp-wide): 6.2B Privately Held
WEB: www.zotos.com
SIC: 2844 Hair preparations, including shampoos; cosmetic preparations
HQ: Zotos International, Inc.
100 Tokeneke Rd
Darien CT 06820
203 655-8911

Genoa
Cayuga County

(G-5590)
STONE WELL BODIES & MCH INC
625 Sill Rd (13071-4182)
PHONE.................................315 497-3512
Fax: 315 497-1550
Luigi Sposito, *CEO*
Robert Todd Mix, *Vice Pres*
Steve Becraft, *Purchasing*
▼ EMP: 15
SQ FT: 12,000
SALES (est): 3.6MM Privately Held
WEB: www.stonewellbodies.com
SIC: 3715 3441 8711 Truck trailers; fabricated structural metal; engineering services

Germantown
Columbia County

(G-5591)
ON THE DOUBLE INC
Also Called: John Patrick
178 Viewmont Rd (12526-5808)
PHONE.................................518 431-3571
Walter Fleming, *Ch of Bd*
EMP: 5
SALES (est): 423.6K Privately Held
SIC: 2339 2329 Women's & misses' athletic clothing & sportswear; men's & boys' sportswear & athletic clothing

Gerry
Chautauqua County

(G-5592)
COBBE INDUSTRIES INC
Also Called: Valley Industries
1397 Harris Hollow Rd (14740-9515)
PHONE.................................716 287-2661
Fax: 716 287-2663
Daniel W Cobbe, *President*
Tad Henderson, *Engineer*
Tina Godfrey, *Manager*
EMP: 30 EST: 1976
SQ FT: 22,000

SALES (est): 4MM **Privately Held**
WEB: www.valleyindustries.com
SIC: 3469 3441 Metal stampings; fabricated structural metal

(G-5593)
SWANSON LUMBER
5273 N Hill Rd (14740-9521)
PHONE..........................716 499-1726
Charles Swanson, *Owner*
EMP: 5
SQ FT: 2,688
SALES (est): 311.2K **Privately Held**
SIC: 2421 Sawmills & planing mills, general

(G-5594)
UNIVERSAL TOOLING CORPORATION
4533 Route 60 (14740-9540)
P.O. Box 364 (14740-0364)
PHONE..........................716 985-4691
Fax: 716 985-4430
Nichole Segrue, *CEO*
Warren Piazza, *President*
Scott Sando, *Manager*
EMP: 13 EST: 1981
SQ FT: 10,630
SALES (est): 1.4MM **Privately Held**
WEB: www.u-t-c.com
SIC: 3544 3545 Forms (molds), for foundry & plastics working machinery; dies, plastics forming; machine tool accessories

Getzville
Erie County

(G-5595)
COLUMBUS MCKINNON CORPORATION (PA)
205 Crosspoint Pkwy (14068-1605)
PHONE..........................716 689-5400
Fax: 716 689-5598
Ernest R Verebelyi, *Ch of Bd*
Timothy T Tevens, *President*
Gene P Buer, *Vice Pres*
Ivo Celi, *Vice Pres*
Richard Knoffloch, *Vice Pres*
◆ EMP: 145 EST: 1875
SALES: 597.1MM **Publicly Held**
WEB: www.cmworks.com
SIC: 3536 3496 3535 3537 Hoists; cranes, industrial plant; cranes, overhead traveling; chain, welded; conveyor belts; conveyors & conveying equipment; tables, lift: hydraulic

(G-5596)
COLUMBUS MCKINNON CORPORATION
Also Called: Columbus McKnnon- Lift TEC Div
205 Crosspoint Pkwy (14068-1605)
PHONE..........................716 689-5400
Maureen Strimple, *Business Anlyst*
Linda Riggi, *Manager*
EMP: 100
SALES (corp-wide): 597.1MM **Publicly Held**
WEB: www.cmworks.com
SIC: 3462 Iron & steel forgings
PA: Columbus Mckinnon Corporation
205 Crosspoint Pkwy
Getzville NY 14068
716 689-5400

(G-5597)
COLUMBUS MCKINNON CORPORATION
Also Called: Coffing
205 Crosspoint Pkwy (14068-1605)
PHONE..........................716 689-5400
EMP: 134
SALES (corp-wide): 597.1MM **Publicly Held**
WEB: www.cmworks.com
SIC: 3536 3496 3535 3537 Hoists; cranes, industrial plant; cranes, overhead traveling; chain, welded; conveyor belts; conveyors & conveying equipment; tables, lift: hydraulic

PA: Columbus Mckinnon Corporation
205 Crosspoint Pkwy
Getzville NY 14068
716 689-5400

(G-5598)
COLUMBUS MCKINNON CORPORATION
Also Called: Yale
205 Crosspoint Pkwy (14068-1605)
PHONE..........................716 689-5400
EMP: 134
SALES (corp-wide): 597.1MM **Publicly Held**
WEB: www.cmworks.com
SIC: 3536 3496 3535 3537 Hoists; cranes, industrial plant; cranes, overhead traveling; chain, welded; conveyor belts; conveyors & conveying equipment; tables, lift: hydraulic
PA: Columbus Mckinnon Corporation
205 Crosspoint Pkwy
Getzville NY 14068
716 689-5400

(G-5599)
INTEL CORPORATION
55 Dodge Rd (14068-1205)
PHONE..........................408 765-8080
Victor Arabagian, *Sales Staff*
Mike Brunner, *Branch Mgr*
EMP: 60
SALES (corp-wide): 55.3B **Publicly Held**
WEB: www.intel.com
SIC: 3674 7372 Microprocessors; application computer software
PA: Intel Corporation
2200 Mission College Blvd
Santa Clara CA 95054
408 765-8080

(G-5600)
MISSION CRITICAL ENERGY INC
Also Called: Starboard Sun
1801 N French Rd (14068-1032)
PHONE..........................716 276-8465
Mark Dettmer, *President*
EMP: 5 EST: 2012
SALES (est): 395.7K **Privately Held**
SIC: 3511 Turbines & turbine generator sets

(G-5601)
NINAS CUSTARD
2577 Millersport Hwy (14068-1445)
PHONE..........................716 636-0345
Fax: 716 689-2258
Merry Scioli, *Partner*
EMP: 30
SALES (est): 3.5MM **Privately Held**
SIC: 2024 Ice cream & frozen desserts

(G-5602)
OLD DUTCHMANS WROUGH IRON INC
2800 Millersport Hwy (14068-1449)
P.O. Box 632 (14068-0632)
PHONE..........................716 688-2034
Keith Deck, *Principal*
▲ EMP: 6
SQ FT: 2,416
SALES: 100K **Privately Held**
WEB: www.oldutchman.com
SIC: 3446 Architectural metalwork

(G-5603)
PETIT PRINTING CORP
42 Hunters Gln (14068-1264)
PHONE..........................716 871-9490
Fax: 716 871-0760
Richard Petit, *President*
EMP: 8
SQ FT: 14,000
SALES: 540K **Privately Held**
WEB: www.petitprinting.com
SIC: 2752 Commercial printing, offset

(G-5604)
SPX FLOW TECH SYSTEMS INC (HQ)
Also Called: APV Crepaco
105 Crosspoint Pkwy (14068-1603)
PHONE..........................716 692-3000
Christopher J Kearney, *CEO*

Marc Michael, *President*
Patrick J O'Leary, *President*
Katie Masters, *Safety Mgr*
Brian Goff, *CFO*
▲ EMP: 80
SALES (est): 342.5MM
SALES (corp-wide): 2.3B **Publicly Held**
SIC: 3556 8742 Food products machinery; food & beverage consultant
PA: Spx Flow, Inc.
13320 Balntyn Corp Pl
Charlotte NC 28277
704 752-4400

(G-5605)
U S ENERGY DEVELOPMENT CORP (PA)
2350 N Forest Rd (14068-1296)
PHONE..........................716 636-0401
Fax: 716 636-0418
Joseph M Jayson, *Ch of Bd*
Douglas Walch, *President*
Jerry Jones, *Opers Mgr*
Cyndi Stonebraker, *Investment Ofcr*
Richard Walton, *Investment Ofcr*
EMP: 53
SQ FT: 5,000
SALES (est): 56.4MM **Privately Held**
WEB: www.usenergydevcorp.com
SIC: 1382 1381 1389 Oil & gas exploration services; drilling oil & gas wells; oil field services

(G-5606)
WILLIAM S HEIN & CO INC (PA)
Also Called: Metro Storage Center
2350 N Forest Rd Ste 14a (14068-1296)
PHONE..........................716 882-2600
Fax: 716 883-8100
William S Hein Sr, *Ch of Bd*
Kevin Marmion, *President*
Richard Spinnelli, *Senior VP*
Len Grieco, *Vice Pres*
Susan H Mc Clinton, *Vice Pres*
EMP: 100
SQ FT: 140,000
SALES: 53.7K **Privately Held**
WEB: www.foreign-law.com
SIC: 2731 5942 3572 Books: publishing only; book stores; computer storage devices

Ghent
Columbia County

(G-5607)
J D HANDLING SYSTEMS INC
1346 State Route 9h (12075-3415)
PHONE..........................518 828-9676
Fax: 518 828-9629
Joseph Cardinale Jr, *President*
Joseph Cardinale Sr, *Shareholder*
Diane Cardinale, *Admin Sec*
▲ EMP: 12
SQ FT: 53,000
SALES: 1.5MM **Privately Held**
WEB: www.jdhand.com
SIC: 3535 5599 Conveyors & conveying equipment; utility trailers

Glen Cove
Nassau County

(G-5608)
A LOSEE & SONS
68 Landing Rd (11542-1844)
PHONE..........................516 676-3060
Fax: 516 676-1520
Allan Losee, *President*
Mark Losee, *Treasurer*
EMP: 7 EST: 1963
SQ FT: 3,000
SALES: 500K **Privately Held**
SIC: 2431 Woodwork, interior & ornamental

(G-5609)
ALESSI INTERNATIONAL LIMITED
51 Buckeye Rd (11542-1416)
PHONE..........................516 676-8841

Lynn Alessi, *President*
EMP: 10
SALES (est): 516.2K **Privately Held**
WEB: www.alessi.com
SIC: 2211 Card roll fabrics, cotton

(G-5610)
ALLEN PICKLE WORKS INC
36 Garvies Point Rd (11542-2821)
PHONE..........................516 676-0640
Fax: 516 759-5780
Ronald Horman, *President*
Nick Horman, *Vice Pres*
EMP: 19
SQ FT: 20,000
SALES (est): 9MM **Privately Held**
SIC: 2035 Pickles, vinegar

(G-5611)
AUGUST THOMSEN CORP
36 Sea Cliff Ave (11542-3635)
PHONE..........................516 676-7100
Fax: 516 676-7108
Jeffrey G Schneider, *President*
Douglas J Schneider, *Vice Pres*
Douglass Schnieder, *Sales Dir*
Ingrid Schneider, *Shareholder*
◆ EMP: 40
SQ FT: 25,000
SALES (est): 8.1MM **Privately Held**
WEB: www.atecousa.com
SIC: 3365 Cooking/kitchen utensils, cast aluminum

(G-5612)
AVALONBAY COMMUNITIES INC
1100 Avalon Sq (11542-2877)
PHONE..........................516 484-7766
Fax: 516 484-7801
Karen Griemsmann, *Vice Pres*
EMP: 25
SALES (corp-wide): 1.8B **Publicly Held**
SIC: 3843 Dental equipment & supplies
PA: Avalonbay Communities, Inc.
671 N Glebe Rd Ste 800
Arlington VA 22203
703 329-6300

(G-5613)
COMMUNITY CPONS FRNCHISING INC
100 Carney St Ste 2 (11542-3687)
PHONE..........................516 277-1968
Fax: 516 671-6399
Matthew Rosencrans, *President*
Dennis Coupons, *Sales Mgr*
Stu Golden, *Regl Sales Mgr*
EMP: 25
SQ FT: 3,200
SALES: 3.5MM **Privately Held**
SIC: 2741 7313 Miscellaneous publishing; newspaper advertising representative

(G-5614)
COMPS INC
3 School St Ste 101b (11542-2548)
P.O. Box 255, Sea Cliff (11579-0255)
PHONE..........................516 676-0400
Keith Larson, *President*
EMP: 12
SALES (est): 887.8K **Privately Held**
WEB: www.compsny.com
SIC: 2741 Miscellaneous publishing

(G-5615)
EXPO FURNITURE DESIGNS INC
Also Called: Expo Lighting Design
1 Garvies Point Rd (11542-2821)
PHONE..........................516 674-1420
Fax: 516 674-6778
Brian Landau, *President*
Mary Miluso, *Sales Mgr*
Maria Landau, *Admin Sec*
▲ EMP: 10
SQ FT: 5,000
SALES: 900K **Privately Held**
WEB: www.expodesigninc.com
SIC: 3648 5063 5072 Lighting fixtures, except electric; residential; lighting fixtures; hardware

(G-5616)
G SICURANZA LTD
4 East Ave (11542-3917)
PHONE..........................516 759-0259
Gaetano Sicuranza, *Ch of Bd*

Glen Cove - Nassau County (G-5617)

EMP: 5
SALES (est): 510.4K Privately Held
SIC: 3432 Plumbing fixture fittings & trim

(G-5617)
GLEN PLAZA MARBLE & GRAN INC
75 Glen Cove Ave Ste A (11542-3261)
PHONE..................................516 671-1100
Fax: 516 759-0970
Frank Caruso, President
Joe Caruso, Corp Secy
Angelo Caruso, Vice Pres
▲ EMP: 7
SQ FT: 7,500
SALES (est): 702.1K Privately Held
SIC: 3281 5032 5999 5211 Granite, cut & shaped; marble, building: cut & shaped; granite building stone; marble building stone; monuments & tombstones; tile, ceramic

(G-5618)
HORIZON POWER SOURCE LLC
50 Glen St (11542-4304)
PHONE..................................877 240-0580
David Shaoulpour,
Derrick Shaoulpour,
EMP: 20
SALES (est): 1.4MM Privately Held
SIC: 2899 Battery acid

(G-5619)
KCH PUBLICATIONS INC
Also Called: Gold Coast Gazette
57 Glen St Ste 1 (11542-2785)
PHONE..................................516 671-2360
Fax: 516 671-2361
Kevin Horton, President
EMP: 20
SALES (est): 960.7K Privately Held
WEB: www.goldcoastgazette.net
SIC: 2711 Newspapers, publishing & printing

(G-5620)
KORE INFRASTRUCTURE LLC (PA)
4 High Pine (11542-1422)
PHONE..................................646 532-9060
Cornelius Shields, Mng Member
David Harding, Officer
EMP: 3
SQ FT: 3,000
SALES (est): 3.5MM Privately Held
SIC: 2869 4953 Fuels; recycling, waste materials

(G-5621)
MIL-SPEC INDUSTRIES CORP
42 Herb Hill Rd (11542-2817)
PHONE..................................516 625-5787
Fax: 516 625-0988
Ron Nanne, President
Jin Park, Finance Dir
Bill Morris, Accounts Exec
Hardik Patel, Marketing Staff
Ayse Erguner, Manager
◆ EMP: 7
SALES (est): 1.6MM Privately Held
WEB: www.mil-spec-industries.com
SIC: 3489 Ordnance & accessories

(G-5622)
NORESCO INDUSTRIAL GROUP INC
3 School St Ste 103 (11542-2548)
PHONE..................................516 759-3355
Fax: 516 759-3497
Daan Hu, President
Julie Lee, Exec VP
▲ EMP: 40
SALES (est): 9.1MM Privately Held
WEB: www.norescoindustrial.com
SIC: 3321 5013 5084 3322 Ductile iron castings; automotive supplies & parts; industrial machinery & equipment; malleable iron foundries

(G-5623)
NOVITA FABRICS FURNISHING CORP
1 Brewster St (11542-2571)
PHONE..................................516 299-4500
David Rahimi, President

EMP: 12 EST: 2014
SQ FT: 12,000
SALES (est): 2.5MM Privately Held
SIC: 2299 Linen fabrics

(G-5624)
PLEATCO LLC
28 Garvies Point Rd (11542-2821)
PHONE..................................516 609-0200
Fax: 516 609-0204
Howard Smith, President
John Antretter, Vice Pres
Scott Bittner, Vice Pres
Richard Medina, Vice Pres
Mary Bethray, VP Opers
▲ EMP: 80
SQ FT: 21,000
SALES (est): 34.5MM Privately Held
SIC: 3589 Swimming pool filter & water conditioning systems

(G-5625)
PROFESSIONAL TAPE CORPORATION
100 Pratt Oval (11542-1482)
P.O. Box 234271, Great Neck (11023-4271)
PHONE..................................516 656-5519
Fax: 516 656-5519
Morris Kamkar, President
Jeff Levigne, Warehouse Mgr
▲ EMP: 4
SQ FT: 10,000
SALES (est): 7MM Privately Held
WEB: www.proftapeco.com
SIC: 3695 7819 5099 Magnetic tape; video tape or disk reproduction; video & audio equipment

(G-5626)
RASON ASPHALT INC
44 Morris Ave (11542-2816)
PHONE..................................516 671-1500
Fax: 516 671-0234
Gene Sullivan, Manager
EMP: 5
SALES (corp-wide): 9.3MM Privately Held
WEB: www.rason1.com
SIC: 2951 Asphalt paving mixtures & blocks
PA: Rason Asphalt Inc.
   Rr 110
   Farmingdale NY 11735
   631 293-6210

(G-5627)
SHERCO SERVICES LLC
2 Park Pl Ste A (11542-2566)
PHONE..................................516 676-3028
Shawn Sheridan,
EMP: 10
SALES (est): 1.2MM Privately Held
SIC: 3441 Fabricated structural metal

(G-5628)
SLANTO MANUFACTURING INC
40 Garvies Point Rd (11542-2887)
PHONE..................................516 759-5721
Mel Dubin, President
EMP: 25
SALES (est): 1.6MM Privately Held
SIC: 3442 Baseboards, metal

(G-5629)
STEVENSON PRINTING CO INC
1 Brewster St Ste 2 (11542-2556)
PHONE..................................516 676-1233
Fax: 516 676-1250
Anthony Messineo, President
Cindy Messineo Hawxhurst, Vice Pres
Glenn Messineo, Vice Pres
EMP: 6 EST: 1909
SQ FT: 12,800
SALES (est): 800.8K Privately Held
WEB: www.printingedgemarketing.com
SIC: 2752 Commercial printing, offset

(G-5630)
SUNNYSIDE DECORATIVE PRINTS CO
Also Called: Etcetera Wallpapers
67 Robinson Ave (11542-2944)
PHONE..................................516 671-1935
Douglas Fletcher Jr, President
Melissa Wolf, Manager

EMP: 9
SQ FT: 12,000
SALES (est): 1.2MM Privately Held
SIC: 2679 Wallpaper

(G-5631)
WELLS RUGS INC
Also Called: Wells, George Ruggery
44 Sea Cliff Ave (11542-3627)
PHONE..................................516 676-2056
Joseph Misiak, President
EMP: 6
SALES (est): 404.7K Privately Held
SIC: 2273 Carpets & rugs

Glen Head
Nassau County

(G-5632)
HALM INDUSTRIES CO INC (PA)
180 Glen Head Rd (11545-1995)
PHONE..................................516 676-6700
Donald Lyon, President
Donald Schanck, Vice Pres
John Lampitz, Opers Staff
Mark Winkler, Purch Mgr
Joe Puma, CFO
▲ EMP: 90
SQ FT: 32,000
SALES (est): 16.4MM Privately Held
SIC: 3555 Printing trades machinery

(G-5633)
HALM INSTRUMENT CO INC
180 Glen Head Rd (11545-1924)
PHONE..................................516 676-6700
Fax: 516 676-6751
Floyd A Lyon, President
Steven Lyon, Vice Pres
Donald Schanck, Vice Pres
EMP: 76 EST: 1945
SQ FT: 32,000
SALES (est): 5MM Privately Held
SIC: 3555 Printing trades machinery

(G-5634)
INCREDIBLE SCENTS INC
1009 Glen Cove Ave Ste 6 (11545-1592)
PHONE..................................516 656-3300
Howard Rabinowitz, President
Richard Davi, Exec VP
EMP: 5
SQ FT: 1,500
SALES (est): 10MM Privately Held
WEB: www.incrediblescents.com
SIC: 3841 Surgical & medical instruments

(G-5635)
INTERNATIONAL NEWSPPR PRTG CO
Also Called: International Newspaper Prntng
18 Carlisle Dr (11545-2120)
PHONE..................................516 626-6095
Fax: 718 392-4777
Richard Schwartz, Vice Pres
Gilda Schwartz, Admin Sec
EMP: 25 EST: 1932
SQ FT: 12,500
SALES (est): 3.1MM Privately Held
SIC: 2752 Commercial printing, offset

(G-5636)
LOMIN CONSTRUCTION COMPANY
Also Called: O'Neil Construction
328 Glen Cove Rd (11545-2273)
PHONE..................................516 759-5734
Steven O'Neil, Partner
EMP: 6
SALES (est): 490K Privately Held
SIC: 3531 1629 1611 Pavers; tennis court construction; surfacing & paving

(G-5637)
NEW ART SIGNS CO INC
78 Plymouth Dr N (11545-1127)
PHONE..................................718 443-0900
Fax: 718 455-2340
Steven Weiss, President
EMP: 5
SALES (est): 350K Privately Held
SIC: 3993 2759 Signs & advertising specialties; screen printing

(G-5638)
NIRX MEDICAL TECHNOLOGIES LLC
15 Cherry Ln (11545-2215)
PHONE..................................516 676-6479
Doug Maxwell, Branch Mgr
EMP: 15
SALES (corp-wide): 1.8MM Privately Held
WEB: www.nirx.net
SIC: 3845 Position emission tomography (PET scanner)
PA: Nirx Medical Technologies, Llc
   7083 Hollywood Blvd Fl 4
   Los Angeles CA 90028
   424 264-0556

(G-5639)
NORTH SHORE MONUMENTS INC
667 Cedar Swamp Rd Ste 5 (11545-2267)
PHONE..................................516 759-2156
Fax: 516 671-2885
Hugh A Tanchuck, President
Maggie L Tanchuck, President
EMP: 6
SQ FT: 3,100
SALES: 734.4K Privately Held
WEB: www.northshoremonuments.com
SIC: 3281 5999 1799 Cut stone & stone products; monuments & tombstones; sandblasting of building exteriors

Glen Oaks
Queens County

(G-5640)
BAYSIDE BEEPERS & CELLULAR
25607 Hillside Ave (11004-1617)
PHONE..................................718 343-3888
Albert Castro, Owner
EMP: 5 EST: 2013
SALES (est): 313.9K Privately Held
SIC: 3663 4812 Pagers (one-way); cellular telephone services

(G-5641)
WYNCO PRESS ONE INC
Also Called: Minuteman Press
7839 268th St (11004-1330)
PHONE..................................516 354-6145
Fax: 516 354-6145
Jeff Wheeler, President
EMP: 6
SQ FT: 1,000
SALES: 750K Privately Held
SIC: 2752 2791 2789 Commercial printing, lithographic; typesetting; bookbinding & related work

Glendale
Queens County

(G-5642)
A & S WINDOW ASSOCIATES INC
8819 76th Ave (11385-7992)
PHONE..................................718 275-7900
Fax: 718 997-7683
Alan Herman, President
▲ EMP: 20 EST: 1952
SQ FT: 14,000
SALES (est): 3.8MM Privately Held
WEB: www.aswindowassociates.com
SIC: 3442 Storm doors or windows, metal

(G-5643)
ALFA CARD INC
7915 Cooper Ave (11385-7528)
PHONE..................................718 326-7107
Fax: 718 326-7532
George Chase, President
Judy Chase, Vice Pres
EMP: 8
SQ FT: 1,400
SALES (est): 385K Privately Held
WEB: www.alfacard.com
SIC: 2754 Business form & card printing, gravure

Glens Falls - Warren County

(G-5644)
ALLEN WILLIAM & COMPANY INC
Also Called: Alvin J Bart
7119 80th St Ste 8315 (11385-7733)
PHONE.................212 675-6461
Fax: 718 821-2486
Alvin J Bart, *President*
Ed Rovera, *Vice Pres*
Jose Villalba, *Marketing Mgr*
Patrick Snodgrass, *Art Dir*
EMP: 200 **EST:** 1884
SALES (est): 24MM **Privately Held**
SIC: 2678 2752 Stationery: made from purchased materials; commercial printing, offset

(G-5645)
ALVIN J BART & SONS INC
7119 80th St Ste 8315 (11385-7733)
PHONE.................718 417-1300
Fax: 718 366-7940
Richard Bart, *Ch of Bd*
Alvin J Bart, *President*
Ira Bart, *Vice Pres*
Denise Crafa, *Vice Pres*
Bob Stein, *Plant Mgr*
▲ **EMP:** 150 **EST:** 1956
SQ FT: 170,000
SALES (est): 26.4MM **Privately Held**
WEB: www.ajbartny.com
SIC: 2759 Commercial printing; bank notes: engraved

(G-5646)
BOWE INDUSTRIES INC (PA)
Also Called: Changes
8836 77th Ave (11385-7826)
PHONE.................718 441-6464
Fax: 718 441-8624
Daniel Barasch, *CEO*
Marek Kiyashka, *Co-President*
Michael Ohlstein, *Senior VP*
Michael Olsten, *Human Res Dir*
Angelo Digiorgio, *Mktg Dir*
▲ **EMP:** 100
SQ FT: 62,000
SALES (est): 61MM **Privately Held**
SIC: 2321 2331 2361 Men's & boys' furnishings; T-shirts & tops, women's: made from purchased materials; shirts, women's & juniors': made from purchased materials; t-shirts & tops: girls', children's & infants'; shirts: girls', children's & infants'

(G-5647)
BOWE INDUSTRIES INC
8836 77th Ave (11385-7826)
PHONE.................718 441-6464
Michael Ohlsten, *Branch Mgr*
EMP: 75
SALES (corp-wide): 61MM **Privately Held**
SIC: 2321 Men's & boys' furnishings
PA: Bowe Industries Inc.
  8836 77th Ave
  Glendale NY 11385
  718 441-6464

(G-5648)
C F PETERS CORP
7030 80th St Ste 2 (11385-7735)
PHONE.................718 416-7800
Dr Don Gillespie, *Vice Pres*
Richie Anichiarico, *Warehouse Mgr*
Shili Uddin, *Finance*
Frank Billack, *Sales Dir*
Martin Gonzalez, *Sales Staff*
▲ **EMP:** 27 **EST:** 1948
SQ FT: 7,200
SALES (est): 3.3MM **Privately Held**
WEB: www.petersedition.com
SIC: 2741 Music book & sheet music publishing

(G-5649)
COSTUME CULTURE BY FRANCO LLC
7030 80th St (11385-7737)
PHONE.................718 821-7100
EMP: 10
SALES (est): 1.2MM **Privately Held**
SIC: 2389 Costumes

(G-5650)
COTTON EMPORIUM INC (PA)
8000 Cooper Ave (11385-7739)
PHONE.................718 894-3365
Josef Moshevili, *President*
Nana Moshevili, *Vice Pres*
Mzia Krikhely, *Bookkeeper*
▲ **EMP:** 8
SQ FT: 8,500
SALES (est): 2.6MM **Privately Held**
SIC: 2329 Sweaters & sweater jackets: men's & boys'

(G-5651)
DISPLAYS & BEYOND INC
8816 77th Ave (11385-7826)
PHONE.................718 805-7786
Dilawar Syed, *President*
EMP: 12
SALES (est): 2MM **Privately Held**
SIC: 2653 3993 5999 Display items, corrugated: made from purchased materials; signs & advertising specialties; trophies & plaques; banners, flags, decals & posters

(G-5652)
FM BRUSH CO INC
7002 72nd Pl (11385-7307)
PHONE.................718 821-5939
Fred J Mink Jr, *Ch of Bd*
Beatrice Mink, *Corp Secy*
Jeffrey A Mink, *Vice Pres*
Carolyn Koster, *Traffic Mgr*
Linda Mayer, *Human Res Mgr*
▲ **EMP:** 120 **EST:** 1929
SQ FT: 20,000
SALES (est): 16.2MM **Privately Held**
WEB: www.fmbrush.com
SIC: 3991 Brushes, household or industrial

(G-5653)
FRED M VELEPEC CO INC
7172 70th St (11385-7246)
PHONE.................718 821-6636
Fax: 718 821-5874
Fredric A Velepec, *President*
Gerda Velepec, *Vice Pres*
Dolores Quigley, *Office Mgr*
Terry Reilly, *Manager*
▲ **EMP:** 21 **EST:** 1942
SQ FT: 6,000
SALES (est): 1.8MM **Privately Held**
SIC: 3545 Tools & accessories for machine tools

(G-5654)
GLENDALE ARCHITECTURAL WD PDTS
Also Called: Glendale Products
7102 80th St (11385-7715)
PHONE.................718 326-2700
Fax: 718 894-2528
Vincenzo Alcamo, *President*
Ben Alcamo, *Purchasing*
Ben Larocca, *CTO*
EMP: 30
SALES (est): 4.2MM **Privately Held**
WEB: www.glendalecustomfurniture.com
SIC: 2521 2511 Wood office furniture; wood household furniture

(G-5655)
GLENRIDGE FABRICATORS INC
7945 77th Ave (11385-7522)
PHONE.................718 456-2297
Fax: 718 386-1286
Albert Putre, *Ch of Bd*
Kampta Persaud, *Vice Pres*
Marilyn White, *Manager*
EMP: 10
SQ FT: 36,000
SALES (est): 1.9MM **Privately Held**
SIC: 3441 3443 1799 Fabricated structural metal; weldments; welding on site

(G-5656)
HANSEL N GRETEL BRAND INC
7936 Cooper Ave (11385-7530)
P.O. Box 60452, Florence MA (01062-0452)
PHONE.................718 326-0041
Fax: 718 326-2069
Milton Rattner, *President*
Ruth Rattner, *Exec VP*
Eddie Olkano, *Manager*
Jim Rowe, *Officer*
Robert Shapiro, *Admin Sec*
▲ **EMP:** 150
SQ FT: 30,000
SALES (est): 19.6MM **Privately Held**
SIC: 2013 2015 Prepared pork products from purchased pork; prepared beef products from purchased beef; turkey processing & slaughtering

(G-5657)
LEA APPAREL INC
6126 Cooper Ave (11385-6115)
PHONE.................718 418-2800
Fax: 718 418-2805
Leonard Novick, *President*
Ellen Novick, *Vice Pres*
Andrew Porter, *Manager*
EMP: 5
SQ FT: 8,000
SALES (est): 5MM **Privately Held**
SIC: 2339 Sportswear, women's

(G-5658)
MEROLA SALES COMPANY INC
7308 88th St (11385-7950)
PHONE.................800 963-7652
Kevin Merola, *Principal*
EMP: 20
SALES (corp-wide): 31.1MM **Privately Held**
SIC: 3253 Ceramic wall & floor tile
PA: Merola Sales Company, Inc.
  20 Reed Pl
  Amityville NY 11701
  631 464-4444

(G-5659)
NEW DAY WOODWORK INC
Also Called: John Bossone
8861 76th Ave (11385-7910)
PHONE.................718 275-1721
Fax: 718 275-3220
Jay Levtow, *President*
Ross Levtow, *Vice Pres*
EMP: 30
SQ FT: 14,000
SALES (est): 2.5MM **Privately Held**
WEB: www.newdaywoodwork.com
SIC: 2511 Wood household furniture

(G-5660)
NORTH STAR KNITTING MILLS INC
7030 80th St (11385-7737)
PHONE.................718 894-4848
Fax: 718 894-4884
Todor Stefan, *President*
Marian Stefan, *Admin Sec*
EMP: 7
SQ FT: 12,500
SALES: 900K **Privately Held**
SIC: 2253 5199 Knit outerwear mills; knit goods

(G-5661)
ROLLING GATE SUPPLY CORP
7919 Cypress Ave (11385-6038)
PHONE.................718 366-5258
Miguel Molinare, *President*
▲ **EMP:** 9 **EST:** 2009
SALES (est): 970K **Privately Held**
SIC: 3315 Steel wire & related products

(G-5662)
SCHINDLER ELEVATOR CORPORATION
8400 72nd Dr Ste 2 (11385-7900)
PHONE.................718 417-3131
Linda Marchese, *Manager*
EMP: 110
SALES (corp-wide): 9.3B **Privately Held**
WEB: www.us.schindler.com
SIC: 3534 Elevators & equipment
HQ: Schindler Elevator Corporation
  20 Whippany Rd
  Morristown NJ 07960
  973 397-6500

(G-5663)
SMART USA INC
6907 69th Pl (11385-6639)
PHONE.................718 416-4400
Jim Soleiman, *Ch of Bd*
Yosi Soleimany, *Vice Pres*
EMP: 20
SALES (est): 5MM **Privately Held**
SIC: 2671 3365 Thermoplastic coated paper for packaging; cooking/kitchen utensils, cast aluminum

(G-5664)
SUPERIOR DECORATORS INC
Also Called: Superior Plastic Slipcovers
7416 Cypress Hills St (11385-6946)
PHONE.................718 381-4793
Fax: 718 381-2500
Peter Cassar, *Owner*
Charlie Heavens, *Manager*
EMP: 16
SQ FT: 3,500
SALES (est): 710K **Privately Held**
SIC: 2392 Slipcovers: made of fabric, plastic etc.

(G-5665)
T & R KNITTING MILLS INC (PA)
8000 Cooper Ave Ste 6 (11385-7734)
PHONE.................718 497-4017
Rocco Marini, *President*
Christine Fumei, *Prdtn Mgr*
Carol Schultz, *CFO*
▲ **EMP:** 24
SQ FT: 100,000
SALES: 20MM **Privately Held**
SIC: 2253 Sweaters & sweater coats, knit

Glenmont
Albany County

(G-5666)
AIR PRODUCTS AND CHEMICALS INC
461 River Rd (12077-4307)
PHONE.................518 463-4273
Micheal Joczak, *Branch Mgr*
Scott Loupe, *Manager*
EMP: 53
SQ FT: 8,624
SALES (corp-wide): 9.8B **Publicly Held**
WEB: www.airproducts.com
SIC: 2813 Oxygen, compressed or liquefied
PA: Air Products And Chemicals, Inc.
  7201 Hamilton Blvd
  Allentown PA 18195
  610 481-4911

(G-5667)
DEMARTINI OIL EQUIPMENT SVC
214 River Rd (12077-4604)
P.O. Box 9 (12077-0009)
PHONE.................518 463-5752
Fax: 518 426-4240
James Demartini, *President*
James De Martini, *President*
Marianne Carner, *Vice Pres*
Mathew Carner, *Treasurer*
EMP: 6 **EST:** 1945
SQ FT: 4,000
SALES (est): 977.1K **Privately Held**
SIC: 3713 7699 Truck bodies (motor vehicles); industrial machinery & equipment repair

(G-5668)
INNOVATIVE MUNICIPAL PDTS US
Also Called: Innovative Surface Solutions
454 River Rd (12077-4306)
PHONE.................800 387-5777
Greg Baun, *President*
Mark Pooler, *Vice Pres*
Don Horan, *Opers Staff*
EMP: 30
SALES: 20MM **Privately Held**
SIC: 2819 Industrial inorganic chemicals

Glens Falls
Warren County

(G-5669)
AMES GOLDSMITH CORP
21 Rogers St (12801-3803)
PHONE.................518 792-7435

Glens Falls - Warren County (G-5670)

Fax: 518 792-1034
Bill Hamelin, *President*
Mike Delsignore, *General Mgr*
Michael Herman, *Vice Pres*
Michelle Sellick, *Purchasing*
Lisa Davis, *Controller*
EMP: 20
SALES (corp-wide): 44.9MM **Privately Held**
SIC: 3399 2819 3339 2869 Silver powder; flakes, metal; catalysts, chemical; primary nonferrous metals; industrial organic chemicals
PA: Ames Goldsmith Corp.
50 Harrison Ave
South Glens Falls NY 12803
518 792-5808

(G-5670)
ANDRITZ INC
Also Called: Ahlstrom Kamyr
13 Pruyns Island Dr (12801-4706)
PHONE 518 745-2988
Michael Kingsley, *Manager*
EMP: 20
SALES (corp-wide): 6.8B **Privately Held**
SIC: 2611 Pulp manufactured from waste or recycled paper
HQ: Andritz Inc.
500 Technology Dr
Canonsburg PA 15317
724 597-7801

(G-5671)
ANGIODYNAMICS INC
10 Glens Fls Technical Pa (12801)
PHONE 518 792-4112
Fax: 518 798-3625
Mark Frost, *President*
Myles Donnelly, *Info Tech Mgr*
EMP: 275
SALES (corp-wide): 353.8MM **Publicly Held**
SIC: 3841 Surgical & medical instruments
PA: Angiodynamics, Inc.
14 Plaza Dr
Latham NY 12110
518 795-1400

(G-5672)
BARTON MINES COMPANY LLC (PA)
Also Called: Barton International
6 Warren St (12801-4531)
PHONE 518 798-5462
Fax: 518 798-5728
Charles Bracken Jr, *Ch of Bd*
John Swertner, *Sls & Mktg Exec*
Barton Mines, *CFO*
Todd Agans, *Finance Dir*
Michael Cortese, *Human Res Dir*
◆ **EMP:** 150 **EST:** 1996
SQ FT: 5,000
SALES (est): 175.2MM **Privately Held**
WEB: www.barton.com
SIC: 1499 3291 5085 Garnet mining; coated abrasive products; abrasives

(G-5673)
BRENNANS QUICK PRINT INC
Also Called: Bqp
6 Collins Dr (12804-1493)
P.O. Box 4221, Queensbury (12804-0221)
PHONE 518 793-4999
Fax: 518 793-5075
Sue Brennan, *President*
EMP: 6
SALES (est): 820.2K **Privately Held**
WEB: www.bqprinting.com
SIC: 2752 Commercial printing, offset

(G-5674)
C R BARD INC
Glens Falls Manufacturing
289 Bay Rd (12804-2015)
PHONE 518 793-2531
Ron Green, *Safety Mgr*
Tammy Monahan, *Purchasing*
Anne Linehan, *Engineer*
Mike Lockhart, *Engineer*
Marna Moore, *Human Res Dir*
EMP: 960
SALES (corp-wide): 3.4B **Publicly Held**
WEB: www.crbard.com
SIC: 3841 3845 Surgical & medical instruments; electromedical equipment

PA: C. R. Bard, Inc.
730 Central Ave
New Providence NJ 07974
908 277-8000

(G-5675)
CONVERTER DESIGN INC (PA)
25 Murdock Ave (12801-2456)
PHONE 518 745-7138
Jim Wood, *President*
EMP: 1
SALES: 1.2MM **Privately Held**
SIC: 3599 Custom machinery

(G-5676)
COOPERS CAVE ALE CO S-CORP
2 Sagamore St (12801-3179)
PHONE 518 792-0007
Edward Bethel, *Partner*
Patricia Bethel, *Partner*
EMP: 15 **EST:** 1999
SALES (est): 1.3MM **Privately Held**
WEB: www.cooperscaveale.com
SIC: 2082 Malt beverages

(G-5677)
DOHENY NICE AND EASY
Also Called: Doheny's Mobil
150 Broad St (12801-4253)
PHONE 518 793-1733
EMP: 8
SALES (est): 380K **Privately Held**
SIC: 2086 Mfg Bottled/Canned Soft Drinks

(G-5678)
FLOMATIC CORPORATION
Also Called: Flomatic Valves
15 Pruyns Island Dr (12801-4706)
PHONE 518 761-9797
Fax: 518 761-9798
Bo Andersson, *President*
Nick Farrrara, *Vice Pres*
George Swenson, *Research*
Chris Bauder, *Engineer*
Nick Farrara, *VP Sales*
▲ **EMP:** 50 **EST:** 1959
SQ FT: 50,000
SALES (est): 13.4MM
SALES (corp-wide): 16.3MM **Privately Held**
WEB: www.flomatic.com
SIC: 3494 3491 Valves & pipe fittings; water works valves
HQ: Boshart Industries Inc
25 Whaley Ave
Milverton ON N0K 1
519 595-4444

(G-5679)
GENPAK LLC (DH)
68 Warren St (12801-4530)
P.O. Box 727 (12801-0727)
PHONE 518 798-9511
Fax: 518 798-1730
James Allen Pattison, *CEO*
Kevin Kelly, *President*
Edward Rider, *President*
Amanda Masterson, *Safety Mgr*
Ron Hinton, *Warehouse Mgr*
◆ **EMP:** 45
SQ FT: 30,000
SALES (est): 650MM
SALES (corp-wide): 14.2B **Privately Held**
WEB: www.genpak.com
SIC: 3411 5113 Food & beverage containers; sanitary food containers
HQ: Great Pacific Enterprises (U.S.) Inc.
68 Warren St
Glens Falls NY 12801
518 761-2593

(G-5680)
GLENS FALLS NEWSPAPERS INC
76 Lawrence St (12801-3741)
P.O. Box 2157 (12801-2157)
PHONE 518 792-3131
James Marshall, *Principal*
EMP: 6
SALES (est): 358K **Privately Held**
SIC: 2711 Newspapers, publishing & printing

(G-5681)
GLENS FALLS PRINTING LLC
51 Hudson Ave (12801-4347)
PHONE 518 793-0555
Fax: 518 793-8624
Tom Harrington, *Sales Staff*
George Beyerbach,
Barbara Beyerbach,
Robert Beyerbach,
EMP: 12 **EST:** 1966
SQ FT: 4,800
SALES (est): 2.3MM **Privately Held**
SIC: 2752 Commercial printing, offset

(G-5682)
GREAT PACIFIC ENTPS US INC (DH)
Also Called: Genpak
68 Warren St (12801-4530)
P.O. Box 727 (12801-0727)
PHONE 518 761-2593
Michael Korenberg, *CEO*
James Pattison, *Ch of Bd*
James Reilly, *Chairman*
Nick Geer, *Vice Pres*
Mike Linacre, *Controller*
▲ **EMP:** 45
SQ FT: 36,000
SALES (est): 650MM
SALES (corp-wide): 14.2B **Privately Held**
SIC: 3089 Plastic containers, except foam
HQ: Great Pacific Enterprises Inc
1067 Cordova St W Unit 1800
Vancouver BC V6C 1
604 688-6764

(G-5683)
JUST BEVERAGES LLC
31 Broad St (12801-4301)
P.O. Box 4392, Queensbury (12804-0392)
PHONE 480 388-1133
EMP: 9 **EST:** 2014
SALES (est): 1MM **Privately Held**
SIC: 2086 Mineral water, carbonated: packaged in cans, bottles, etc.

(G-5684)
KADANT INC
436 Quaker Rd (12801-1535)
PHONE 518 793-8801
Jeff Bachand, *Branch Mgr*
EMP: 11
SALES (corp-wide): 390.1MM **Publicly Held**
SIC: 3554 Paper industries machinery
PA: Kadant Inc.
1 Technology Park Dr # 210
Westford MA 01886
978 776-2000

(G-5685)
KMA CORPORATION
153 Maple St Ste 5 (12801-3796)
PHONE 518 743-1330
Fax: 518 743-9450
Eric Ukauf, *President*
Joe Congel, *Office Mgr*
▲ **EMP:** 9
SALES (est): 1.1MM **Privately Held**
SIC: 3599 Machine & other job shop work

(G-5686)
LEE ENTERPRISES INCORPORATED
Also Called: Post Star
76 Lawrence St (12801-3741)
P.O. Box 2157 (12801-2157)
PHONE 518 792-3131
Fax: 518 761-1255
Terry Doomes, *President*
Greg Brownell, *Editor*
Adam Colver, *Editor*
Bob Condon, *Editor*
Brian J Corcoran, *Editor*
EMP: 160
SQ FT: 5,000
SALES (est): 11.4MM
SALES (corp-wide): 648.5MM **Publicly Held**
SIC: 2711 Newspapers: publishing only, not printed on site
HQ: Lee Publications, Inc.
201 N Harrison St Ste 600
Davenport IA 52801
563 383-2100

(G-5687)
LEHIGH CEMENT COMPANY (DH)
Also Called: Lehigh Northeast Cement
313 Warren St (12801-3820)
P.O. Box 440 (12801-0440)
PHONE 518 792-1137
Dan Harrington, *President*
Vince Fischer, *Foreman/Supr*
Karen Tooorop, *Buyer*
Mark Trybendis, *QC Mgr*
Nancy Stevens, *Research*
▲ **EMP:** 122
SQ FT: 20,000
SALES (est): 30.8MM
SALES (corp-wide): 271.5MM **Privately Held**
WEB: www.gfcement.com
SIC: 3241 Portland cement; masonry cement
HQ: Dyckerhoff Gmbh
Biebricher Str. 68
Wiesbaden 65203
611 676-0

(G-5688)
LEHIGH CEMENT COMPANY LLC
313 Lower Warren St (12804-3822)
PHONE 518 792-1137
EMP: 35
SALES (corp-wide): 14.4B **Privately Held**
WEB: www.lehighcement.com
SIC: 3241 Portland cement
HQ: Lehigh Cement Company Llc
300 E John Carpenter Fwy
Irving TX 75062
877 534-4442

(G-5689)
MEDTEK LIGHTING CORPORATION (PA)
Also Called: Phototherapeutix
206 Glen St Ste 5 (12801-3585)
PHONE 518 745-7264
Fax: 518 745-1402
Jack Springer, *President*
Anthony Ianniello, *Vice Pres*
Emmett Haydel, *Sales Mgr*
Jerri Corlew, *Executive Asst*
EMP: 4
SQ FT: 9,000
SALES (est): 3.3MM **Privately Held**
WEB: www.uvbiotek.com
SIC: 3648 Sun tanning equipment, incl. tanning beds

(G-5690)
MILLER MECHANICAL SERVICES INC
55-57 Walnut St (12801)
P.O. Box 504 (12801-0504)
PHONE 518 792-0430
Fax: 518 792-2956
Elizabeth Miller, *President*
Ken Lofton, *Superintendent*
Ken Pagels, *Opers Staff*
Ted Schfelt, *Manager*
Elaine Lambert, *Administration*
EMP: 20
SQ FT: 2,240
SALES (est): 5.7MM **Privately Held**
WEB: www.millermech.com
SIC: 3542 Machine tools, metal forming type

(G-5691)
NATIONAL VAC ENVMTL SVCS CORP
80 Park Rd (12804-7614)
PHONE 518 743-0563
Fax: 518 743-0463
Roger Letendre, *Branch Mgr*
EMP: 20
SALES (corp-wide): 9.6MM **Privately Held**
SIC: 3589 Vacuum cleaners & sweepers, electric; industrial
PA: National Vacuum Environmental Services Corp.
408 47th St
Niagara Falls NY 14304
716 773-1167

▲ = Import ▼ = Export ◆ = Import/Export

GEOGRAPHIC SECTION

Gloversville - Fulton County (G-5714)

(G-5692)
NAVILYST MEDICAL INC
10 Glens Fls Technical Pa (12801)
PHONE..................................800 833-9973
Fax: 518 742-4397
Renee Berg, *Purch Mgr*
Kim Seabury, *Director*
▲ **EMP:** 670
SALES (est): 188.6MM
SALES (corp-wide): 353.8MM **Publicly Held**
SIC: 3841 Surgical & medical instruments
PA: Angiodynamics, Inc.
   14 Plaza Dr
   Latham NY 12110
   518 795-1400

(G-5693)
OAK LONE PUBLISHING CO INC
Also Called: Chronicle, The
15 Ridge St (12801-3608)
P.O. Box 153 (12801-0153)
PHONE..................................518 792-1126
Fax: 518 793-1587
Mark Frost, *President*
Gordon Woodworth, *Editor*
Patricia Maddock, *Vice Pres*
Teresa Hackett, *Office Mgr*
EMP: 27
SQ FT: 5,280
SALES (est): 1.3MM **Privately Held**
WEB: www.loneoak.com
SIC: 2711 Newspapers: publishing only, not printed on site

(G-5694)
PACTIV CORPORATION
6 Haskell Ave (12801-3854)
P.O. Box 148 (12801-0148)
PHONE..................................518 743-3100
Christopher G Angus, *Vice Pres*
Gene Tomczak, *CTO*
Stan Lucas, *Info Tech Dir*
EMP: 207 **Privately Held**
WEB: www.pactiv.com
SIC: 3089 Thermoformed finished plastic products
HQ: Pactiv Llc
   1900 W Field Ct
   Lake Forest IL 60045
   847 482-2000

(G-5695)
PACTIV LLC
18 Peck Ave (12801-3833)
PHONE..................................518 793-2524
Gene Tomzzac, *Plant Mgr*
Mitch Brehm, *Plant Mgr*
Brian Williams, *MIS Dir*
EMP: 110 **Privately Held**
WEB: www.pactiv.com
SIC: 2673 3497 3089 Food storage & trash bags (plastic); trash bags (plastic film): made from purchased materials; food storage & frozen food bags, plastic; metal foil & leaf; plastic containers, except foam; plastic kitchenware, tableware & houseware
HQ: Pactiv Llc
   1900 W Field Ct
   Lake Forest IL 60045
   847 482-2000

(G-5696)
PEXCO LLC
Also Called: Precision Extrusion
12 Glens Fls Technical Pa (12801)
PHONE..................................518 792-1199
Ann Morrill, *Purch Mgr*
Barbara Samiley, *Human Resources*
Michael J Badera, *Manager*
EMP: 35
SALES (corp-wide): 1.6B **Privately Held**
SIC: 3061 Medical & surgical rubber tubing (extruded & lathe-cut)
HQ: Pexco Llc
   2500 Northwinds Pkwy # 472
   Alpharetta GA 30009
   404 564-8560

(G-5697)
PREGIS LLC
18 Peck Ave (12801-3833)
P.O. Box 148 (12801-0148)
PHONE..................................518 743-3100
Barbara Blanchette, *Opers Mgr*

David Stiller, *Opers Mgr*
Heidi Geroux, *QC Mgr*
Mark Riel, *Engineer*
Sharon Pugh, *Sales Associate*
EMP: 65
SALES (corp-wide): 5.7B **Privately Held**
SIC: 2671 Plastic film, coated or laminated for packaging
HQ: Pregis Llc
   1650 Lake Cook Rd Ste 400
   Deerfield IL 60015
   847 597-9330

(G-5698)
R BRUCE MAPES
15 E Washington St (12801-3065)
PHONE..................................518 761-2020
Franklin Westfalle, *Principal*
EMP: 11
SALES (est): 508.8K **Privately Held**
SIC: 3229 Optical glass

(G-5699)
UMICORE TECHNICAL MATERIALS
9 Pruyns Island Dr (12801-4706)
PHONE..................................518 792-7700
Marc Grynberg, *CEO*
Jens-Uwe Heitsch, *General Mgr*
Martin Boarder, *Chairman*
Stephan Csoma, *Exec VP*
Filip Platteeuw, *CFO*
▲ **EMP:** 110
SALES (est): 27MM
SALES (corp-wide): 3B **Privately Held**
SIC: 3339 Silver refining (primary)
PA: Umicore Sa
   Rue Du Marais 31
   Bruxelles 1000
   222 771-11

(G-5700)
UMICORE USA INC
9 Pruyns Island Dr (12801-4706)
PHONE..................................919 874-7171
Allen Molvar, *Branch Mgr*
EMP: 25
SALES (corp-wide): 3B **Privately Held**
SIC: 3339 5051 5052 5169 Cobalt refining (primary); nonferrous metal sheets, bars, rods, etc.; metallic ores; industrial chemicals; metal scrap & waste materials
HQ: Umicore Usa Inc.
   3600 Glenwood Ave Ste 250
   Raleigh NC 27612
   919 874-7171

Glenville
Schenectady County

(G-5701)
DSM NUTRITIONAL PRODUCTS LLC
Fortitech
300 Tech Park (12302-7107)
PHONE..................................518 372-5155
Chris Nulmerrick, *Manager*
EMP: 152
SALES (corp-wide): 11.5B **Privately Held**
SIC: 2834 3295 2087 Vitamin, nutrient & hematinic preparations for human use; vitamin preparations; minerals, ground or treated; flavoring extracts & syrups
HQ: Dsm Nutritional Products, Llc
   2105 Technology Dr
   Schenectady NY 12308
   518 372-5155

(G-5702)
INTERNATIONAL PAPER COMPANY
803 Corporation Park (12302-1057)
PHONE..................................518 372-6461
EMP: 92
SALES (corp-wide): 22.3B **Publicly Held**
WEB: www.tin.com
SIC: 2653 Corrugated & solid fiber boxes
PA: International Paper Company
   6400 Poplar Ave
   Memphis TN 38197
   901 419-9000

Glenwood
Erie County

(G-5703)
LK INDUSTRIES INC
9731 Center St (14069-9611)
PHONE..................................716 941-9202
Larry Krzeminski, *President*
John Brennan, *Manager*
EMP: 5
SQ FT: 3,000
SALES: 600K **Privately Held**
SIC: 3541 Machine tools, metal cutting type

Gloversville
Fulton County

(G-5704)
ADIRONDACK STAINED GLASS WORKS
29 W Fulton St Ste 6 (12078-2937)
PHONE..................................518 725-0387
Fax: 518 725-0384
Donald Dwyer, *President*
Brenda Dwyer, *Treasurer*
Patrick Duell, *Admin Sec*
EMP: 6
SQ FT: 9,600
SALES: 275K **Privately Held**
SIC: 3231 Stained glass: made from purchased glass

(G-5705)
AMERICAN TARGET MARKETING INC
11 Cayadutta St (12078-3816)
PHONE..................................518 725-4369
Richard Denero, *President*
Al Parillo, *Treasurer*
EMP: 31
SQ FT: 18,000
SALES: 700K **Privately Held**
SIC: 3151 Leather gloves & mittens

(G-5706)
ANDROME LEATHER INC
21 Foster St (12078-1600)
P.O. Box 826 (12078-0826)
PHONE..................................518 773-7945
Fax: 518 773-7942
Frank A Garguilo, *President*
Christopher Garguilo, *Vice Pres*
Richard Mancini, *Executive*
Lisa Garguilo, *Admin Sec*
▲ **EMP:** 15
SQ FT: 10,000
SALES (est): 1.1MM **Privately Held**
SIC: 3111 2843 Finishing of leather; leather finishing agents

(G-5707)
AVANTI CONTROL SYSTEMS INC
1 Hamilton St Fl 2 (12078-2321)
P.O. Box 113 (12078-0113)
PHONE..................................518 921-4368
Timothy M Tesiero, *President*
Annette Greg, *Manager*
EMP: 6
SALES (est): 1.3MM **Privately Held**
SIC: 3613 8711 Control panels, electric; engineering services

(G-5708)
BEEBIE PRINTING & ART AGCY INC
40 E Pine St (12078-4339)
P.O. Box 1277 (12078-0011)
PHONE..................................518 725-4528
Fax: 518 773-3855
Craig J Beebie, *President*
EMP: 7
SQ FT: 10,000
SALES (est): 560K **Privately Held**
SIC: 2759 7336 Commercial printing; graphic arts & related design

(G-5709)
COLONIAL TANNING CORPORATION (PA)
8 Wilson St 810 (12078-1500)
P.O. Box 1068 (12078-0009)
PHONE..................................518 725-7171
Fax: 518 773-8195
William Studenic, *President*
Matthew Smrtic, *General Mgr*
George Bradt, *Opers Mgr*
Leslie Smrtic, *Controller*
▲ **EMP:** 7 **EST:** 1971
SQ FT: 50,000
SALES (est): 1.1MM **Privately Held**
SIC: 3111 Tanneries, leather

(G-5710)
CURTIN-HEBERT CO INC
Also Called: Curtin-Hebert Machines
11 Forest St (12078-3999)
P.O. Box 511 (12078-0005)
PHONE..................................518 725-7157
Fax: 518 773-3805
James Curtin, *Ch of Bd*
George Wells, *Office Mgr*
Bruce Anderson, *Director*
EMP: 11 **EST:** 1908
SQ FT: 11,000
SALES (est): 1.3MM **Privately Held**
WEB: www.curtinhebert.com
SIC: 3559 Rubber working machinery, including tires; leather working machinery; metal pickling equipment

(G-5711)
FOWNES BROTHERS & CO INC
204 County Highway 157 (12078-6043)
PHONE..................................518 752-4411
Rennie Sanges, *Branch Mgr*
EMP: 30
SALES (corp-wide): 59.8MM **Privately Held**
SIC: 3151 2381 5136 5137 Gloves, leather: dress or semidress; gloves, woven or knit: made from purchased materials; gloves, men's & boys'; gloves, women's & children's; gloves, sport & athletic: boxing, handball, etc.
PA: Fownes Brothers & Co Inc
   16 E 34th St Fl 5
   New York NY 10016
   212 683-0150

(G-5712)
GREENFIBER ALBANY INC
Also Called: US Greenfiber
210 County Highway 102 (12078-7023)
PHONE..................................518 842-1470
Dennis Barrineau, *Ch of Bd*
Richard Linek, *Plant Mgr*
EMP: 49 **EST:** 1986
SALES (est): 19.2MM **Privately Held**
SIC: 2679 Building, insulating & packaging paperboard
HQ: Us Greenfiber, Llc
   5500 77 Center Dr Ste 100
   Charlotte NC 28217
   704 379-0640

(G-5713)
HALO OPTICAL PRODUCTS INC
9 Phair St Ste 1 (12078-4398)
P.O. Box 1369 (12078-0011)
PHONE..................................518 773-4256
Fax: 518 773-8992
Peter Leonardi, *President*
EMP: 65 **EST:** 1964
SQ FT: 32,000
SALES (est): 8MM **Privately Held**
SIC: 3827 Optical instruments & apparatus

(G-5714)
HAWKINS FABRICS INC (PA)
111 Woodside Ave Ste 1 (12078-2744)
P.O. Box 351 (12078-0351)
PHONE..................................518 773-9550
James Batty, *President*
Ted Sweet, *Controller*
EMP: 38
SQ FT: 50,000
SALES (est): 14.9MM **Privately Held**
WEB: www.safeind.com
SIC: 2259 2231 Gloves, knit, except dress & semidress gloves; mittens, knit; work gloves, knit; broadwoven fabric mills, wool

Gloversville - Fulton County (G-5715)

(G-5715)
HOHENFORST SPLITTING CO INC
152 W Fulton St (12078-2799)
PHONE.................................518 725-0012
Robert Hohenforst, *President*
Loretta Hohenforst, *Vice Pres*
Richard Hohenforst, *Manager*
EMP: 6
SQ FT: 6,000
SALES (est): 704.4K **Privately Held**
SIC: 3111 Cutting of leather

(G-5716)
HUDSON DYING & FINISHING LLC
68 Harrison St (12078-4732)
PHONE.................................518 752-4389
Mark Shore,
EMP: 30 EST: 2009
SALES (est): 1.8MM **Privately Held**
SIC: 2389 Men's miscellaneous accessories

(G-5717)
LITCHFIELD FABRICS OF NC (PA)
111 Woodside Ave (12078-2741)
PHONE.................................518 773-9500
William Conroy, *President*
Dale Steenburgh, *CFO*
Morris Evans, *Treasurer*
EMP: 3
SQ FT: 2,000
SALES (est): 3.2MM **Privately Held**
SIC: 2258 Tricot fabrics

(G-5718)
MOHAWK CABINET COMPANY INC
137 E State St (12078-1200)
PHONE.................................518 725-0645
James Law, *President*
EMP: 12
SALES (est): 2.1MM **Privately Held**
SIC: 3585 Cabinets, show & display, refrigerated

(G-5719)
PROTECH (LLC)
Also Called: Pro-TEC V I P
11 Cayadutta St (12078-3816)
PHONE.................................518 725-7785
Fax: 518 725-7783
Al Parillo, *Mng Member*
Richard Denero,
EMP: 26
SALES (est): 2.3MM **Privately Held**
SIC: 3151 5699 Gloves, leather: work; work clothing

(G-5720)
SOMERSET DYEING & FINISHING
68 Harrison St (12078-4732)
P.O. Box 1189 (12078-0010)
PHONE.................................518 773-7383
Edward Falk, *Corp Secy*
EMP: 42
SQ FT: 24,000
SALES (est): 5.5MM **Privately Held**
SIC: 2258 Dyeing & finishing lace goods & warp knit fabric

(G-5721)
SOMERSET INDUSTRIES INC (PA)
Also Called: CJ Indstries A Div Smrset Inds
68 Harrison St (12078-4732)
P.O. Box 1189 (12078-0010)
PHONE.................................518 773-7383
Fax: 518 773-7383
Ed Falk, *CEO*
Bruce Dingman, *Controller*
▲ EMP: 36
SQ FT: 35,000
SALES (est): 14MM **Privately Held**
WEB: www.somersetindustries.com
SIC: 2258 Lace & warp knit fabric mills

(G-5722)
ST REGIS SPORTSWEAR LTD
51 Beaver St (12078-4214)
PHONE.................................518 725-6767
Fax: 518 725-5715
Martin Krieger, *President*
Ellen Gillen, *Manager*
Priscilla Blood, *Admin Sec*
EMP: 9
SALES (est): 1.2MM **Privately Held**
SIC: 2281 Yarn spinning mills

(G-5723)
STEPHEN MILLER GEN CONTRS INC
Also Called: Miller's Ready Mix
301 Riceville Rd (12078-6958)
P.O. Box 291, Mayfield (12117-0291)
PHONE.................................518 661-5601
Fax: 518 661-6264
Stephen Miller, *CEO*
Lynn Holland, *Bookkeeper*
Patricia Miller, *Manager*
Trish Miller, *Officer*
EMP: 25 EST: 1971
SQ FT: 640
SALES (est): 6.4MM **Privately Held**
SIC: 3273 1541 1761 1542 Ready-mixed concrete; industrial buildings, new construction; roofing, siding & sheet metal work; nonresidential construction

(G-5724)
TAYLOR MADE GROUP LLC (HQ)
66 Kingsboro Ave (12078-3415)
PHONE.................................518 725-0681
Brian Castleman, *Plant Engr*
Mark Kenyon, *Controller*
Mike Oathout, *Marketing Mgr*
John Taylor, *Mng Member*
EMP: 54
SQ FT: 5,000
SALES: 135.9MM
SALES (corp-wide): 182MM **Privately Held**
SIC: 3429 3231 Marine hardware; windshields, glass: made from purchased glass
PA: Taylor Made Group Holdings, Inc.
66 Kingsboro Ave
Gloversville NY 12078
518 725-0681

(G-5725)
TAYLOR PRODUCTS INC (PA)
66 Kingsboro Ave (12078-3415)
P.O. Box 1190 (12078-0190)
PHONE.................................518 773-9312
James W Taylor, *Ch of Bd*
Dennis F Flint, *President*
Cindy Walsh, *Manager*
▲ EMP: 2
SQ FT: 20,000
SALES (est): 5.4MM **Privately Held**
SIC: 3231 Tempered glass: made from purchased glass; safety glass: made from purchased glass

(G-5726)
TIC TAC TOES MFG CORP
1 Hamilton St (12078-2321)
P.O. Box 953 (12078-0953)
PHONE.................................518 773-8187
Fax: 518 725-8116
Robert Winig, *President*
Ed Wager, *Human Res Dir*
Edward Wagar, *Office Mgr*
▲ EMP: 75
SQ FT: 75,000
SALES (est): 9.5MM **Privately Held**
WEB: www.tictactoes.com
SIC: 3143 3144 Men's footwear, except athletic; women's footwear, except athletic

(G-5727)
WADSWORTH LOGGING INC
3095 State Highway 30 (12078-7601)
P.O. Box 177, Northville (12134-0177)
PHONE.................................518 863-6870
Stephen S Wadsworth, *President*
EMP: 10
SALES (est): 910K **Privately Held**
SIC: 2411 Logging camps & contractors

(G-5728)
WASHBURNS DAIRY INC
145 N Main St (12078-3078)
P.O. Box 551 (12078-0005)
PHONE.................................518 725-0629
Fax: 518 725-0098
Richard J Washburn, *President*
Alfred J Washburn, *Corp Secy*
Bill Washburn, *Vice Pres*
William Washburn, *Vice Pres*
EMP: 45
SQ FT: 6,000
SALES (est): 5.7MM **Privately Held**
SIC: 2024 5143 Ice cream & ice milk; ice cream & ices

(G-5729)
WILLIAM B COLLINS COMPANY (HQ)
Also Called: Leader Herald, The
8 E Fulton St (12078-3227)
PHONE.................................518 773-8272
Fax: 518 725-3556
George Ogden Nutting, *President*
Tim Fonda, *Editor*
Brenda Anich, *District Mgr*
Robert M Nutting, *Vice Pres*
William C Nutting, *Vice Pres*
EMP: 70 EST: 1961
SQ FT: 15,000
SALES: 8.9MM
SALES (corp-wide): 553.9MM **Privately Held**
WEB: www.lhprint.com
SIC: 2711 Newspapers, publishing & printing
PA: The Ogden Newspapers Inc
1500 Main St
Wheeling WV 26003
304 233-0100

(G-5730)
WOOD & HYDE LEATHER CO INC
68 Wood St (12078-1695)
P.O. Box 786 (12078-0007)
PHONE.................................518 725-7105
Fax: 518 725-5158
Randall Doerter, *CEO*
James Keiffer, *President*
Thomas Porter, *CFO*
Greg Patterson, *Executive*
◆ EMP: 30
SQ FT: 266,000
SALES (est): 3.5MM **Privately Held**
WEB: www.woodandhyde.com
SIC: 3111 Tanneries, leather

Goshen
Orange County

(G-5731)
BIMBO BAKERIES USA INC
Also Called: Stroehmann Bakeries 72
9 Police Dr (10924-6730)
PHONE.................................845 294-5282
Phil Tobin, *Manager*
EMP: 19
SALES (corp-wide): 13B **Privately Held**
SIC: 2051 5149 Breads, rolls & buns; groceries & related products
HQ: Bimbo Bakeries Usa, Inc
255 Business Center Dr # 200
Horsham PA 19044
215 347-5500

(G-5732)
BLASER PRODUCTION INC
31 Hatfield Ln (10924-6712)
PHONE.................................845 294-3200
Peter Blaser, *Ch of Bd*
Nick Blaser, *Vice Pres*
Doris Martini, *Vice Pres*
Judy Villiers, *Accountant*
▲ EMP: 11
SALES (est): 18.7MM **Privately Held**
WEB: www.blaser.com
SIC: 2992 Lubricating oils
HQ: Blaser Swisslube Holding Corp
31 Hatfield Ln
Goshen NY 10924
845 294-3200

(G-5733)
BLASER SWISSLUBE HOLDING CORP (HQ)
31 Hatfield Ln (10924-6712)
PHONE.................................845 294-3200
Fax: 914 428-1914
Peter Blaser, *CEO*
Ulrich Krahenbuhl, *President*
Bob Green, *Area Mgr*
Richard Surico, *Vice Pres*
Linda Aldorasi, *Controller*
◆ EMP: 17
SQ FT: 40,000
SALES (est): 84.3MM **Privately Held**
SIC: 2992 Lubricating oils & greases
PA: Koras Ag
Winterseistrasse 22
Hasle-RUegsau BE
344 600-101

(G-5734)
FG GALASSI MOULDING CO INC
699 Pulaski Hwy (10924-6009)
P.O. Box 700, Pine Island (10969-0700)
PHONE.................................845 258-2100
John Petromilli, *President*
Linda Petromilli, *Sales Staff*
Alice Hicks, *Manager*
▲ EMP: 9
SQ FT: 11,000
SALES (est): 890K **Privately Held**
WEB: www.fggalassi.com
SIC: 2499 Picture & mirror frames, wood

(G-5735)
JUNO CHEFS
Also Called: Milmar Food Group
1 6 1/2 Station Rd (10924-6723)
PHONE.................................845 294-5400
Julius Spessot, *President*
Luisa Spessot, *President*
Rita Oconnor, *Vice Pres*
Barry Werk, *Purch Dir*
Bruce Wiegand, *Plant Engr Mgr*
EMP: 65
SQ FT: 25,000
SALES (est): 13.9MM **Privately Held**
WEB: www.junofoundation.org
SIC: 2038 Breakfasts, frozen & packaged

(G-5736)
KONICA MNOLTA SUPS MFG USA INC
51 Hatfield Ln (10924-6712)
PHONE.................................845 294-8400
Fax: 845 294-2689
Miyako Asai, *President*
Gene Rachelski, *Engineer*
Patricia Miranda, *Accounts Exec*
Mike Ikeda, *Manager*
Joanne Krueger, *Producer*
▲ EMP: 75
SQ FT: 88,039
SALES: 100MM
SALES (corp-wide): 8.8B **Privately Held**
WEB: www.konicabt.com
SIC: 3861 Toners, prepared photographic (not made in chemical plants)
HQ: Konica Minolta Holdings U.S.A. Inc.
100 Williams Dr
Ramsey NJ 07446
201 825-4000

(G-5737)
MAX THERMO CORPORATION
5 Reservoir Rd (10924-5854)
PHONE.................................845 294-3640
Russell W Anderson, *President*
EMP: 10
SALES (est): 905.4K **Privately Held**
SIC: 3585 Heating equipment, complete

(G-5738)
MILMAR FOOD GROUP II LLC
1 6 1/2 Station Rd (10924-6777)
PHONE.................................845 294-5400
Roy Makinen, *Exec VP*
Judah Koolyk, *MIS Dir*
Martin Hoffman,
Marie Triantafillou, *Executive Asst*
Debbie Manfordonia, *Admin Sec*
▲ EMP: 250
SQ FT: 66,000

SALES (est): 69.3MM **Privately Held**
WEB: www.milmarfoodgroup.com
SIC: **2038** 8748 Frozen specialties; business consulting

(G-5739)
SKIN ATELIER INC
Also Called: Skinprint
1997 Route 17m (10924-5229)
PHONE..................................845 294-1202
Robert P Manzo, *President*
James Hannan, *Vice Pres*
▼ EMP: 10
SQ FT: 4,000
SALES (est): 1.9MM **Privately Held**
WEB: www.skinprint.com
SIC: **2844** Toilet preparations

(G-5740)
TILCON NEW YORK INC
Also Called: Goshen Quarry
2 Quarry Rd (10924-6045)
PHONE..................................845 615-0216
EMP: 63
SALES (corp-wide): 25.3B **Privately Held**
SIC: **1429** Dolomitic marble, crushed & broken-quarrying
HQ: Tilcon New York Inc.
   162 Old Mill Rd
   West Nyack NY 10994
   845 358-4500

(G-5741)
VALUE FRAGRANCES INC
Also Called: Value Fragrances & Flavors
7 Musket Ct (10924)
P.O. Box 550 (10924-0550)
PHONE..................................845 294-5726
Fax: 845 294-7230
Debra Mitzner, *President*
B Mitzner, *Network Mgr*
▼ EMP: 9
SQ FT: 8,268
SALES (est): 1.7MM **Privately Held**
SIC: **2844** 5122 Perfumes & colognes; perfumes

Gouverneur
St. Lawrence County

(G-5742)
BAKERY & COFFEE SHOP
274 W Main St (13642-1333)
PHONE..................................315 287-1829
John Yerdon, *Owner*
EMP: 5
SALES: 230K **Privately Held**
SIC: **2051** Bakery: wholesale or wholesale/retail combined

(G-5743)
CIVES CORPORATION
Also Called: Cives Steel Company Nthrn Div
8 Church St (13642-1416)
PHONE..................................315 287-2200
Fax: 315 287-4569
Richard Cowles, *Plant Supt*
Bill Mayers, *Plant Supt*
Tyler Estabrooks, *Project Mgr*
Norm Newvine, *Purchasing*
Thomas M Farr, *Engineer*
EMP: 150
SALES (corp-wide): 453.1MM **Privately Held**
WEB: www.cives.com
SIC: **3441** 1791 Fabricated structural metal; structural steel erection
PA: Cives Corporation
   3700 Mansell Rd Ste 500
   Alpharetta GA 30022
   770 993-4424

(G-5744)
CLEARWATER PAPER CORPORATION
4921 State Highway 58 (13642-3207)
PHONE..................................315 287-1200
John E Keel, *Human Resources*
Jeremery Bartholomew, *Branch Mgr*
EMP: 85
SALES (corp-wide): 1.7B **Publicly Held**
SIC: **2621** Paper mills

PA: Clearwater Paper Corporation
   601 W Riverside Ave # 1100
   Spokane WA 99201
   509 344-5900

(G-5745)
DUNN PAPER - NATURAL DAM INC
4921 St Rt 58 (13642-3207)
PHONE..................................315 287-1200
Brent Earnshaw, *President*
Greg Howe, *Vice Pres*
Darzy Fehnekenburger, *VP Sls/Mktg*
Al Magnan, *CFO*
EMP: 88
SALES: 48MM
SALES (corp-wide): 254.8MM **Privately Held**
SIC: **2621** Specialty papers
HQ: Dunn Paper, Inc.
   218 Riverview St
   Port Huron MI 48060
   810 984-5521

(G-5746)
IMERYS USA INC
16a Main St Hailesboro Rd (13642-3360)
P.O. Box 479 (13642-0479)
PHONE..................................315 287-0780
Bob Snyder, *Branch Mgr*
EMP: 17
SQ FT: 30,000
SALES (corp-wide): 1.2MM **Privately Held**
SIC: **1411** Granite, dimension-quarrying; marble, dimension-quarrying
HQ: Imerys Usa, Inc.
   100 Mansell Ct E Ste 300
   Roswell GA 30076
   770 645-3300

(G-5747)
RIVERSIDE IRON LLC
26 Water St (13642-1438)
PHONE..................................315 535-4864
Eric Tessmer, *President*
EMP: 12
SALES (est): 531.2K **Privately Held**
SIC: **3441** 3446 3449 Dam gates, metal plate; architectural metalwork; miscellaneous metalwork

Gowanda
Cattaraugus County

(G-5748)
HAR-SON MFG INC
7 Palmer St (14070-1520)
PHONE..................................716 532-2641
R Michael Harris, *President*
EMP: 16
SQ FT: 20,000
SALES (est): 1.9MM **Privately Held**
WEB: www.har-son.com
SIC: **3599** 3365 Machine shop, jobbing & repair; aluminum foundries

(G-5749)
TTE FILTERS LLC (HQ)
1 Magnetic Pkwy (14070-1526)
P.O. Box 111 (14070-0111)
PHONE..................................716 532-2234
Claude Badawy, *President*
Thomas Norsen, *CFO*
EMP: 8
SALES: 1.5MM
SALES (corp-wide): 15.3MM **Privately Held**
SIC: **3677** Filtration devices, electronic
PA: Gowanda Holdings, Llc
   1 Magnetic Pkwy
   Gowanda NY 14070
   716 532-2234

Grand Island
Erie County

(G-5750)
ABRAXIS BIOSCIENCE LLC
3159 Staley Rd (14072-2028)
PHONE..................................716 773-0800

Mark Forell, *Manager*
EMP: 6
SALES (corp-wide): 9.2B **Publicly Held**
SIC: **2834** Pharmaceutical preparations
HQ: Abraxis Bioscience, Llc
   11755 Wilshire Blvd Fl 20
   Los Angeles CA 90025
   800 564-0216

(G-5751)
ASI SIGN SYSTEMS INC
2957 Alt Blvd (14072-1220)
PHONE..................................716 775-0104
Fax: 716 775-3329
Bethany Bernatovicz, *Human Res Mgr*
Andy Bernatovicz, *Branch Mgr*
Laura Thorne, *Info Tech Mgr*
EMP: 7
SALES (corp-wide): 16.9MM **Privately Held**
SIC: **3993** Signs & advertising specialties
PA: Asi Sign Systems, Inc.
   8181 Jetstar Dr Ste 110
   Irving TX 75063
   214 352-9140

(G-5752)
BAKED CUPCAKERY
1879 Whitehaven Rd (14072-1803)
PHONE..................................716 773-2050
EMP: 8
SALES (est): 649.3K **Privately Held**
SIC: **2051** Bread, cake & related products

(G-5753)
BAM ENTERPRISES INC (PA)
2243 Corning Rd (14072)
PHONE..................................716 773-7634
Gary Moose, *CEO*
Victor Alfiero, *CFO*
Linda Smth, *Administration*
EMP: 2
SQ FT: 310,000
SALES (est): 43.6MM **Privately Held**
SIC: **3714** Motor vehicle wheels & parts

(G-5754)
DUAL PRINT & MAIL LLC (HQ)
3235 Grand Island Blvd (14072-1284)
PHONE..................................716 775-8001
Michael Vitch, *CEO*
Thomas Salisbury, *Ch of Bd*
EMP: 3
SALES (est): 18.2MM
SALES (corp-wide): 18.4MM **Privately Held**
SIC: **2752** Commercial printing, lithographic
PA: Compu-Mail, Llc
   3235 Grand Island Blvd
   Grand Island NY 14072
   716 775-8001

(G-5755)
DYLIX CORPORATION
347 Lang Blvd (14072-3123)
PHONE..................................719 773-2985
Nathaniel G Bargar, *President*
Bryan Barrett, *General Mgr*
Will Bargar, *VP Sales*
Tom Glynn, *Sales Staff*
Kenneth Lenz, *Manager*
EMP: 25
SALES (est): 4.9MM **Privately Held**
WEB: www.dylixcorp.com
SIC: **3829** Pressure transducers

(G-5756)
EMERSON INDUS AUTOMTN USA LLC
Also Called: Emerson Control Techniques
359 Lang Blvd Bldg B (14072-3123)
PHONE..................................716 774-1193
Fax: 716 774-8327
Jim Hovey, *Technical Mgr*
Diane Thompson, *Branch Mgr*
John Johnson, *Manager*
Ken Siddall, *Manager*
Don Hubbard, *IT/INT Sup*
EMP: 30
SALES (corp-wide): 22.3B **Publicly Held**
SIC: **3566** 3823 Drives, high speed industrial, except hydrostatic; industrial process control instruments

HQ: Emerson Industrial Automation Usa Llc
   7078 Shady Oak Rd
   Eden Prairie MN 55344
   952 995-8000

(G-5757)
FAST BY GAST INC
120 Industrial Dr (14072-1270)
PHONE..................................716 773-1536
Fax: 716 773-7509
Paul Gast, *President*
Dana Gast, *Vice Pres*
Kevin Gilham, *Sales Staff*
▲ EMP: 9
SQ FT: 4,240
SALES (est): 1.2MM **Privately Held**
WEB: www.fastbygast.com
SIC: **3714** Motor vehicle parts & accessories

(G-5758)
FRESENIUS KABI USA LLC
3159 Staley Rd (14072-2028)
PHONE..................................716 773-0053
Peter Martinez, *Vice Pres*
Bob Brockman, *Project Mgr*
David Marzec, *Engineer*
Richard J Tajak, *CFO*
Justine Budowski, *Supervisor*
EMP: 450
SALES (corp-wide): 30B **Privately Held**
WEB: www.appdrugs.com
SIC: **2834** Pharmaceutical preparations
HQ: Fresenius Kabi Usa, Inc.
   3 Corporate Dr Ste 300
   Lake Zurich IL 60047
   847 969-2700

(G-5759)
FRESENIUS KABI USA LLC
3159 Staley Rd (14072-2028)
PHONE..................................716 773-0800
Fax: 716 773-0878
Nicholas Bateman, *Opers Staff*
Rich Rowles, *QA Dir*
Frank Harmon, *Branch Mgr*
David Conrad, *Manager*
Peggy Dryburgh, *Manager*
EMP: 35
SALES (corp-wide): 29.1B **Privately Held**
SIC: **2834** Pharmaceutical preparations
HQ: Fresenius Kabi Usa Llc
   3 Corporate Dr Ste 300
   Lake Zurich IL 60047
   847 550-2300

(G-5760)
GRAND ISLAND ANIMAL HOSPITAL
Also Called: Grand Island Research & Dev
2323 Whitehaven Rd (14072-1505)
PHONE..................................716 773-7645
Robert Harper, *President*
Lysa P Posner Dvm, *Principal*
EMP: 20
SALES (est): 1.4MM **Privately Held**
SIC: **3999** 0742 Pet supplies; veterinary services, specialties

(G-5761)
ISLECHEM LLC
2801 Long Rd (14072-1244)
PHONE..................................716 773-8618
Fax: 716 773-8517
Daniel Canavan, *Vice Pres*
Dave Ernst, *Manager*
Kevin Rader, *Manager*
Vivian Hoffman, *Analyst*
Richard Morlok, *Analyst*
▲ EMP: 25
SALES (est): 11.6MM **Privately Held**
WEB: www.islechem.com
SIC: **2869** 8731 Industrial organic chemicals; commercial physical research

(G-5762)
LIFE TECHNOLOGIES CORPORATION
3175 Staley Rd (14072-2028)
PHONE..................................716 774-6700
Fax: 716 774-6694
Lyle Turner, *Vice Pres*
Drew Burch, *Vice Pres*
Kelli A Richard, *Vice Pres*
Doug Evans, *Opers Staff*
Carl Bennett, *Mfg Staff*

Grand Island - Erie County (G-5763)

EMP: 100
SALES (corp-wide): 16.9B **Publicly Held**
SIC: 2836 Biological products, except diagnostic
HQ: Life Technologies Corporation
5791 Van Allen Way
Carlsbad CA 92008
760 603-7200

(G-5763)
LINDE LLC
3279 Grand Island Blvd (14072-1216)
PHONE 716 773-7552
Jeffrey Schutrum, *Division Mgr*
Darin Hippner, *Engineer*
Glen Murray, *VP Mktg*
Jeff Schutrum, *Manager*
David Kryszak, *Agent*
EMP: 60
SALES (corp-wide): 19.2B **Privately Held**
SIC: 3825 3625 3567 3561 Instruments to measure electricity; relays & industrial controls; industrial furnaces & ovens; pumps & pumping equipment; machine tool accessories
HQ: Linde Llc
200 Somerset Corporate Bl
Bridgewater NJ 08807
908 464-8100

(G-5764)
NRD LLC
2937 Alt Blvd (14072-1292)
P.O. Box 310 (14072-0310)
PHONE 716 773-7634
Fax: 716 773-7744
Douglas J Fiegel, *President*
Chandana Desilva, *Project Mgr*
Mark Contardi, *Engineer*
Brian Diffenderfer, *Engineer*
Kristin Garza, *Engineer*
▲ **EMP:** 50
SQ FT: 32,000
SALES (est): 12.2MM
SALES (corp-wide): 43.6MM **Privately Held**
WEB: www.nrdstaticcontrol.com
SIC: 3629 3669 3499 Static elimination equipment, industrial; smoke detectors; fire- or burglary-resistive products
PA: Bam Enterprises, Inc.
2243 Corning Rd
Grand Island NY 14072
716 773-7634

(G-5765)
OCCIDENTAL CHEMICAL CORP
2801 Long Rd (14072-1244)
PHONE 716 773-8100
Fax: 716 773-8110
Charles G Radar, *Branch Mgr*
EMP: 30
SALES (corp-wide): 12.7B **Publicly Held**
WEB: www.oxychem.com
SIC: 2812 Alkalies & chlorine
HQ: Occidental Chemical Corporation
5005 Lyndon B Johnson Fwy # 2200
Dallas TX 75244
972 404-3800

(G-5766)
RR DONNELLEY & SONS COMPANY
Also Called: Moore Business Forms
300 Lang Blvd (14072-3122)
PHONE 716 773-0647
Thomas Johnson, *VP Mktg*
Jeffrey Gebhart, *Branch Mgr*
Ted Cyman, *Manager*
EMP: 56
SALES (corp-wide): 11.2B **Publicly Held**
WEB: www.moore.com
SIC: 2761 Manifold business forms
PA: R.R. Donnelley & Sons Company
35 W Wacker Dr Ste 3650
Chicago IL 60601
312 326-8000

(G-5767)
RR DONNELLEY & SONS COMPANY
Also Called: Moore Research Center
300 Lang Blvd (14072-3122)
PHONE 716 773-0300
Fax: 716 773-1091
Anthony D Joseph, *Vice Pres*
Edward J Zurbugh Jr, *Librarian*
EMP: 65
SALES (corp-wide): 11.2B **Publicly Held**
WEB: www.moore.com
SIC: 2761 Manifold business forms
PA: R.R. Donnelley & Sons Company
35 W Wacker Dr Ste 3650
Chicago IL 60601
312 326-8000

(G-5768)
SAINT-GOBAIN ADFORS AMER INC (DH)
Also Called: Saint-Gobain-Paris France
1795 Baseline Rd (14072-2010)
PHONE 716 775-3900
Fax: 716 775-3901
John Bedell, *CEO*
Rudy Coetzee, *General Mgr*
Marilyn Woomer, *Credit Mgr*
▲ **EMP:** 55
SALES (est): 146.9MM
SALES (corp-wide): 189MM **Privately Held**
WEB: www.sgtf.com
SIC: 2297 Nonwoven fabrics
HQ: Saint-Gobain Corporation
20 Moores Rd
Malvern PA 19355
610 893-6000

(G-5769)
SIHI PUMPS INC (DH)
303 Industrial Dr (14072-1293)
P.O. Box 460 (14072-0460)
PHONE 716 773-6450
Fax: 716 773-2330
David P Moran, *Ch of Bd*
Ian Reynolds, *Business Mgr*
Frank Papp, *Vice Pres*
Mike Pastore, *Vice Pres*
▲ **EMP:** 47
SQ FT: 37,500
SALES (est): 12.7MM **Privately Held**
WEB: www.sihi.com
SIC: 3561 Pumps & pumping equipment
HQ: S.F. Americas Inc
303 Industrial Dr
Grand Island NY
716 773-6450

(G-5770)
STARLINE USA INC
3036 Alt Blvd (14072-1274)
PHONE 716 773-0100
Fax: 716 773-2332
Joshua Lapsker, *CEO*
Dennis Mincks, *President*
Daniel Norris, *President*
Ron Lapsker, *Chairman*
Tony Brasconio, *VP Mfg*
EMP: 120
SQ FT: 80,000
SALES (est): 15.5MM **Privately Held**
SIC: 2396 Printing & embossing on plastics fabric articles

(G-5771)
TULLY PRODUCTS INC
2065 Baseline Rd (14072-2060)
PHONE 716 773-3166
Fax: 716 773-7894
Richard Ray, *President*
EMP: 5
SQ FT: 8,000
SALES: 500K **Privately Held**
SIC: 3089 Trays, plastic

(G-5772)
US PEROXIDE
1815 Love Rd Ste 1 (14072-2248)
PHONE 716 775-5585
EMP: 9
SALES (est): 1.5MM **Privately Held**
SIC: 2819 Peroxides, hydrogen peroxide

Granville
Washington County

(G-5773)
CENTRAL TIMBER CO INC
Also Called: Central Timber Research/Devt
9088 State Route 22 (12832-4805)
PHONE 518 638-6338
Fax: 518 638-6121
Ralph Jameson II, *President*
EMP: 5
SQ FT: 52,704
SALES (est): 322K **Privately Held**
SIC: 2411 Logging

(G-5774)
LOCKER MASTERS INC
10329 State Route 22 (12832-5024)
PHONE 518 288-3203
Martha Lyng, *President*
William Lyng, *Treasurer*
Carmen Dodge, *Bookkeeper*
Allan Lyng, *Admin Sec*
EMP: 12
SQ FT: 12,000
SALES: 600K **Privately Held**
SIC: 2542 7699 Lockers (not refrigerated): except wood; industrial machinery & equipment repair

(G-5775)
MANCHESTER NEWSPAPER INC (PA)
Also Called: Whitehall Times
14 E Main St (12832-1334)
P.O. Box 330 (12832-0330)
PHONE 518 642-1234
Fax: 518 642-1344
John Manchester, *President*
Darell Beebe, *Editor*
John Manchester, *Editor*
Bill Toscano, *Editor*
Lisa Manchester, *Vice Pres*
EMP: 33 **EST:** 1875
SQ FT: 10,000
SALES (est): 3.4MM **Privately Held**
WEB: www.manchesternewspapers.com
SIC: 2711 Newspapers: publishing only, not printed on site

(G-5776)
MANCHESTER WOOD INC
1159 County Route 24 (12832-9438)
P.O. Box 180 (12832-0180)
PHONE 518 642-9518
Fax: 518 642-9682
Edward Eriksen, *President*
Priscilla Eriksen, *Treasurer*
Laurie Grottoli, *Accountant*
EMP: 148 **EST:** 1976
SQ FT: 54,000
SALES (est): 19.2MM **Privately Held**
WEB: www.manchesterwood.com
SIC: 2511 Wood household furniture; chairs, household, except upholstered: wood; tables, household: wood

(G-5777)
METTOWEE LUMBER & PLASTICS CO
82 Church St (12832-1662)
PHONE 518 642-1100
Henry V Derminden Jr, *President*
Robert Vanderminden Jr, *Vice Pres*
Paul Parker, *Purch Agent*
Rick Doyle, *Manager*
EMP: 250 **EST:** 1936
SQ FT: 20,000
SALES (est): 19.4MM
SALES (corp-wide): 36.6MM **Privately Held**
SIC: 2421 0811 3089 Sawmills & planing mills, general; timber tracts; plastic processing
PA: Telescope Casual Furniture, Inc.
82 Church St
Granville NY 12832
518 642-1100

(G-5778)
NORTH AMERICAN SLATE INC
50 Columbus St (12832-1024)
PHONE 518 642-1702
Robert Tatko, *President*
EMP: 7 **EST:** 1998
SQ FT: 3,500
SALES (est): 502.6K **Privately Held**
SIC: 3281 Slate products

(G-5779)
NORTON PERFORMANCE PLAS CORP
1 Sealants Park (12832-1652)
PHONE 518 642-2200
Fax: 518 642-1792
Robert C Ayotte, *President*
Dean Mason, *Purchasing*
Trish Tulenko, *Controller*
Edward Canning, *Manager*
Mark Godfrey, *CTO*
EMP: 6
SALES (est): 500.5K **Privately Held**
SIC: 3083 Laminated plastics plate & sheet

(G-5780)
QUANTUM PERFORMANCE COMPANY
31 County Route 28 (12832-4400)
PHONE 518 642-3111
Drew Rozell, *Principal*
EMP: 5
SALES (est): 456.3K **Privately Held**
SIC: 3572 Computer storage devices

(G-5781)
SAINT-GOBAIN PRFMCE PLAS CORP
1 Sealants Park (12832-1652)
PHONE 518 642-2200
Dave Williams, *General Mgr*
Robert J Lewandusky, *Purch Mgr*
Bryan W Harrison, *Engineer*
Edward K Prunier, *Engineer*
Dean Waldenberger, *Enginr/R&D Mgr*
EMP: 150
SALES (corp-wide): 189MM **Privately Held**
SIC: 2891 3086 2821 2671 Sealants; plastics foam products; plastics materials & resins; packaging paper & plastics film, coated & laminated
HQ: Saint-Gobain Performance Plastics Corporation
31500 Solon Rd
Solon OH 44139
440 836-6900

(G-5782)
WINN MANUFACTURING INC
12 Burtis Ave (12832-1341)
P.O. Box 308 (12832-0308)
PHONE 518 642-3515
Steve Winn, *President*
Sandra Winn, *Vice Pres*
EMP: 6 **EST:** 1995
SQ FT: 4,500
SALES: 500K **Privately Held**
SIC: 3599 Machine shop, jobbing & repair

Great Bend
Jefferson County

(G-5783)
HANSON AGGREGATES EAST LLC
County Rt 47 (13643)
P.O. Box 130, Watertown (13601-0130)
PHONE 315 493-3721
Fax: 315 493-3539
Dan Oconnor, *Superintendent*
EMP: 15
SQ FT: 910
SALES (corp-wide): 14.4B **Privately Held**
SIC: 3281 Limestone, cut & shaped
HQ: Hanson Aggregates East Llc
2300 Gateway Centre Blvd
Morrisville NC 27560
919 380-2500

▲ = Import ▼ = Export
◆ = Import/Export

GEOGRAPHIC SECTION

Great Neck
Nassau County

(G-5784)
ADVANCED BARCODE TECHNOLOGY
Also Called: ABT
175 E Shore Rd Ste 228 (11023-2430)
PHONE.................................516 570-8100
Fax: 516 829-2955
Charles Bibas, *President*
Stephen A Bauman, *President*
Dafna Bibas, *Vice Pres*
EMP: 16
SQ FT: 7,500
SALES: 3.8MM **Privately Held**
WEB: www.abtworld.com
SIC: 3577 7371 Bar code (magnetic ink) printers; computer software development

(G-5785)
AFP MANUFACTURING CORP
9 Park Pl (11021-5034)
PHONE.................................516 466-6464
Attilio F Petrocelli, *Principal*
EMP: 18
SALES (est): 3.6MM **Privately Held**
SIC: 3999 Manufacturing industries

(G-5786)
ALFRED BUTLER INC
107 Grace Ave (11021-1608)
PHONE.................................516 829-7460
Jerome Butler, *President*
Diana Schavaria, *Manager*
▲ **EMP:** 16
SQ FT: 8,000
SALES (est): 1.8MM **Privately Held**
WEB: www.alfredbutler.com
SIC: 3911 Rings, finger: precious metal

(G-5787)
ALFRED KHALILY INC
Also Called: Alfa Chem
2 Harbor Way (11024-2117)
PHONE.................................516 504-0059
Alfred Khalily, *President*
Farry Khalily, *Vice Pres*
Freshteh Khalily, *Treasurer*
▲ **EMP:** 14
SQ FT: 5,000
SALES (est): 2.7MM **Privately Held**
WEB: www.alfachem1.com
SIC: 2834 Pharmaceutical preparations

(G-5788)
ALL NET LTD
15 Cuttermill Rd Ste 145 (11021-3252)
PHONE.................................516 504-4559
Fax: 212 760-2710
Kishore Hemrajani, *President*
Priya Najrani, *Corp Secy*
EMP: 12
SQ FT: 1,500
SALES (est): 987.5K **Privately Held**
SIC: 2329 5136 Basketball uniforms: men's, youths' & boys'; men's & boys' clothing

(G-5789)
ALLURE FASHIONS INC
8 Barstow Rd Apt 2e (11021-3543)
PHONE.................................516 829-2470
Jay Confino, *President*
Abdool S Ali, *Vice Pres*
EMP: 2
SQ FT: 800
SALES: 1.5MM **Privately Held**
SIC: 2341 Women's & children's nightwear

(G-5790)
AMERICAN APPAREL LTD
15 Cuttermill Rd Ste 145 (11021-3252)
PHONE.................................516 504-4559
Kishore Hemrajani, *President*
EMP: 8
SQ FT: 1,000
SALES (est): 611.7K **Privately Held**
SIC: 2326 Men's & boys' work clothing

(G-5791)
ARCADIA CHEM PRESERVATIVE LLC
100 Great Neck Rd Apt 5b (11021-3349)
PHONE.................................516 466-5258
Richard Rofe, *Mng Member*
EMP: 5
SQ FT: 3,000
SALES: 6.5MM **Privately Held**
SIC: 2869 5169 Industrial organic chemicals; alkalines & chlorine; drilling mud; industrial chemicals; silicon lubricants

(G-5792)
ARGON CORP (PA)
160 Great Neck Rd (11021-3304)
PHONE.................................516 487-5314
Fax: 516 487-5121
Moshe Albaum, *CEO*
Mike Forde, *COO*
Steve Wilkinson, *Vice Pres*
Scott Teicher, *Purchasing*
Cynthia Panter, *QC Mgr*
▲ **EMP:** 14
SQ FT: 10,000
SALES (est): 8.6MM **Privately Held**
WEB: www.argoncorp.com
SIC: 3571 8731 Electronic computers; computer (hardware) development

(G-5793)
AVANTE
35 Hicks Ln (11024-2026)
PHONE.................................516 782-4888
Arash Ouriel, *Partner*
Albert Alishahi, *Partner*
John Haskin, *Manager*
EMP: 6
SALES (est): 430K **Privately Held**
WEB: www.avante.net
SIC: 2371 Fur goods

(G-5794)
BEAUTY AMERICA LLC
10 Bond St Ste 296 (11021-2454)
PHONE.................................917 744-1430
AVI Sivan,
EMP: 30
SALES: 1.9MM **Privately Held**
SIC: 3823 4813 Viscosimeters, industrial process type;

(G-5795)
CADDY CONCEPTS INC
15 Cuttermill Rd (11021-3252)
PHONE.................................516 570-6279
Kishore Hemrajani, *President*
▲ **EMP:** 10
SALES (est): 1.2MM **Privately Held**
SIC: 2392 Household furnishings

(G-5796)
CARDONA INDUSTRIES USA LTD (PA)
505 Northern Blvd Ste 213 (11021-5112)
P.O. Box 7778, Delray Beach FL (33482-7778)
PHONE.................................516 466-5200
Ben Feinsod, *President*
Edward Streim, *Chairman*
Douglas Knapp, *Vice Pres*
Joyce Campisi, *Manager*
▲ **EMP:** 4
SQ FT: 2,500
SALES (est): 1.6MM **Privately Held**
SIC: 3369 5094 White metal castings (lead, tin, antimony), except die; jewelers' findings

(G-5797)
CHAMELEON GEMS INC
98 Cuttermill Rd Ste 398n (11021-3009)
PHONE.................................516 829-3333
Aaron Hakimian, *CEO*
Abraham Hakimian, *President*
EMP: 12
SALES (est): 1.1MM **Privately Held**
SIC: 3911 Jewelry, precious metal

(G-5798)
CLASSIC CREATIONS INC
Also Called: Viducci
1 Linden Pl Ste 409 (11021-2640)
PHONE.................................516 498-1991
Tony Nemati, *Owner*
EMP: 5
SALES (est): 412.2K **Privately Held**
SIC: 3915 Jewel cutting, drilling, polishing, recutting or setting

(G-5799)
COLONIAL TAG & LABEL CO INC
425 Northern Blvd Ste 36 (11021-4803)
PHONE.................................516 482-0508
Eric Kono, *President*
Marc Kono, *Sales Associate*
Peggy Esterman, *Systems Staff*
▲ **EMP:** 13
SQ FT: 10,000
SALES (est): 9.7MM **Privately Held**
WEB: www.cdscds.com
SIC: 2759 2241 Commercial printing; tags: printing; labels & seals: printing; business forms: printing; labels, woven

(G-5800)
CONFORMER PRODUCTS INC
60 Cuttermill Rd Ste 411 (11021-3104)
PHONE.................................516 504-6300
Marvin Makofsky, *CEO*
EMP: 14
SALES (est): 2.4MM **Privately Held**
SIC: 2677 Envelopes

(G-5801)
CONNIE FRENCH CLEANERS INC
Also Called: Connie Cleaners
801 Middle Neck Rd (11024-1932)
PHONE.................................516 487-1343
Michael Estivo, *President*
EMP: 9 **EST:** 1938
SQ FT: 2,000
SALES (est): 1.2MM **Privately Held**
SIC: 2842 7219 Drycleaning preparations; garment alteration & repair shop

(G-5802)
DALCOM USA LTD
Also Called: Dalfon
11 Middle Neck Rd Ste 301 (11021-2301)
PHONE.................................516 466-7733
Fred Hakim, *President*
EMP: 11
SQ FT: 4,000
SALES: 2.5MM **Privately Held**
WEB: www.dalfon.com
SIC: 2326 Men's & boys' work clothing

(G-5803)
DSR INTERNATIONAL CORP
107 Northern Blvd Ste 401 (11021-4312)
PHONE.................................631 427-2600
Thil NA, *President*
Harvey Drill, *Sales Staff*
▲ **EMP:** 6
SALES (est): 705.4K **Privately Held**
SIC: 3315 5063 Cable, steel: insulated or armored; electronic wire & cable

(G-5804)
EDUCA PUBLISHING INC
391 Great Neck Rd Unit C (11021-4221)
PHONE.................................516 472-0678
Jongsung Kim, *CEO*
EMP: 6
SALES (est): 511.2K
SALES (corp-wide): 4.7MM **Privately Held**
SIC: 2741 Miscellaneous publishing
PA: Educa Korea Co., Ltd.
3/F Wonil Bldg., Daechi-Dong
Seoul SEO 06194
255 745-42

(G-5805)
ELITE UNIFORMS LTD
310 Northern Blvd Ste A (11021-4806)
PHONE.................................516 487-5481
Fax: 516 487-5483
Corey Greenberg, *President*
EMP: 8 **EST:** 2009
SALES (est): 812.7K **Privately Held**
SIC: 2311 Men's & boys' uniforms

(G-5806)
EUROPEAN CRAFT INC
48 Rose Ave (11021-1524)
PHONE.................................516 313-2243

EMP: 5 **EST:** 2002
SQ FT: 4,000
SALES: 400K **Privately Held**
SIC: 2434 Wood kitchen cabinets

(G-5807)
EXPEDI-PRINTING INC
41 Red Brook Rd (11024-1437)
PHONE.................................516 513-0919
Fax: 718 417-8096
Shiann Jong Chen, *Chairman*
Tom Sheng, *COO*
▲ **EMP:** 145
SQ FT: 130,000
SALES (est): 15.7MM **Privately Held**
WEB: www.expedi.com
SIC: 2759 Newspapers: printing; periodicals: printing

(G-5808)
F L DEMETER INC
12 N Gate Rd (11023-1313)
PHONE.................................516 487-5187
Fax: 516 487-1027
Debra Janke, *President*
Mark Crames, *Vice Pres*
Seth Crames, *Assistant*
▲ **EMP:** 25
SQ FT: 3,000
SALES (est): 5.3MM **Privately Held**
SIC: 2844 5122 Perfumes & colognes; cosmetics, perfumes & hair products

(G-5809)
FAB INDUSTRIES CORP (HQ)
98 Cuttermill Rd Ste 412 (11021-3006)
PHONE.................................516 498-3200
Fax: 516 829-0783
Steven Myers, *President*
Sam Hiatt, *Vice Pres*
Beth Myers, *Vice Pres*
Jerry Deese, *CFO*
David A Miller, *CFO*
EMP: 33
SQ FT: 2,409
SALES (est): 58.4MM **Privately Held**
WEB: www.fab-industries.com
SIC: 2258 2211 Warp & flat knit products; lace & lace products; bedspreads, lace: made on lace machines; bed sets, lace; sheets, bedding & table cloths: cotton

(G-5810)
FABRIC RESOURCES INTL LTD (PA)
9 Park Pl (11021-5034)
PHONE.................................516 829-4550
Steven Richman, *President*
Stephen Gold, *COO*
◆ **EMP:** 16 **EST:** 1939
SQ FT: 5,500
SALES (est): 2.7MM **Privately Held**
SIC: 2221 2262 2231 2295 Broadwoven fabric mills, manmade; finishing plants, manmade fiber & silk fabrics; broadwoven fabric mills, wool; coated fabrics, not rubberized

(G-5811)
FIRST QLTY PACKG SOLUTIONS LLC (PA)
80 Cuttermill Rd Ste 500 (11021-3108)
PHONE.................................516 829-3030
EMP: 11
SALES (est): 5.2MM **Privately Held**
SIC: 3086 Packaging & shipping materials, foamed plastic

(G-5812)
FIRST QUALITY PRODUCTS INC (HQ)
80 Cuttermill Rd Ste 500 (11021-3108)
P.O. Box 270, Mc Elhattan PA (17748-0270)
PHONE.................................516 829-4949
Fax: 516 829-4949
Kambiz Damaghi, *Ch of Bd*
Nasser Damaghi, *Ch of Bd*
Noam Yarimi, *Business Mgr*
Kambiz Damagh, *Vice Pres*
Bob Damaghi, *Vice Pres*
◆ **EMP:** 11
SQ FT: 6,000

Great Neck - Nassau County (G-5813)

SALES (est): 359.6MM
SALES (corp-wide): 4.6B Privately Held
SIC: 2676 Sanitary paper products
PA: First Quality Enterprises Inc
80 Cuttermill Rd Ste 500
Great Neck NY 11021
516 829-3030

(G-5813)
FLEXTRADE SYSTEMS INC (PA)
111 Great Neck Rd Ste 314 (11021-5403)
PHONE..................................516 627-8993
Fax: 516 627-8994
Vijay Kedia, *President*
Phyllis Emmanuel, *President*
Scott Moynihan, *President*
Christopher Vandenbrande, *President*
Vikas Kedia, *Managing Dir*
EMP: 140
SALES (est): 96.2MM Privately Held
WEB: www.flextrade.com
SIC: 7372 Prepackaged software

(G-5814)
FULLER SPORTSWEAR CO INC
10 Grenfell Dr (11020-1429)
PHONE..................................516 773-3353
Robert Feinerman, *President*
Aaron Feinerman, *Corp Secy*
Robin Feinerman, *Vice Pres*
EMP: 6 **EST:** 1960
SQ FT: 50,000
SALES (est): 550K Privately Held
SIC: 2331 Blouses, women's & juniors': made from purchased material

(G-5815)
ILICO JEWELRY INC
98 Cuttermill Rd Ste 396 (11021-3008)
PHONE..................................516 482-0201
Michael Ilian, *President*
Rodney Ilian, *Vice Pres*
Mirai Bechara, *Manager*
Rebecca Ilian, *Admin Sec*
EMP: 5
SQ FT: 1,200
SALES (est): 505.2K Privately Held
SIC: 3911 Jewelry, precious metal

(G-5816)
INTERNATIONAL CASEIN CORP CAL
111 Great Neck Rd Ste 218 (11021-5408)
PHONE..................................516 466-4363
Marvin Match, *President*
Vance Perry, *Vice Pres*
EMP: 5
SQ FT: 1,500
SALES (est): 459.3K Privately Held
SIC: 2821 Plastics materials & resins

(G-5817)
IRIDIUM INDUSTRIES INC
Also Called: Artube
17 Barstow Rd Ste 302 (11021-2213)
PHONE..................................516 504-9700
Fax: 516 504-9800
Jacques Sassouni, *Principal*
EMP: 50
SALES (corp-wide): 34.2MM Privately Held
SIC: 3089 3083 Plastic containers, except foam; laminated plastics plate & sheet
PA: Iridium Industries, Inc.
147 Forge Rd
East Stroudsburg PA 18301
570 476-8800

(G-5818)
ISABELLA PRODUCTS INC
Also Called: Starwalk Kids Media
15 Cuttermill Rd Ste 242 (11021-3252)
PHONE..................................516 699-8404
John Benfield, *General Mgr*
EMP: 18
SALES (corp-wide): 4.4MM Privately Held
SIC: 7372 7389 Educational computer software;
PA: Isabella Products Inc.
23 Bradford St Ste 2
Concord MA 01742
978 287-0007

(G-5819)
KAMALI GROUP INC
Also Called: Automotive Leather Group
17 Barstow Rd Ste 206 (11021-2213)
PHONE..................................516 627-4000
Bahman Kamali, *Ch of Bd*
Bob Kamali, *Principal*
Ruth Kamali, *Vice Pres*
Selena Lau, *Vice Pres*
EMP: 5
SQ FT: 3,000
SALES (est): 533.5K Privately Held
SIC: 2399 3111 Automotive covers, except seat & tire covers; accessory products, leather

(G-5820)
LE VIAN CORP (PA)
Also Called: Arusha Tanzanite
235 Great Neck Rd (11021-3301)
PHONE..................................516 466-7200
Moosa Levian, *President*
Fanny Louie, *Production*
Abtin Etessami, *Buyer*
Joseph Elbaz, *Auditing Mgr*
Mathew Banilivi, *Sales Staff*
▲ **EMP:** 78
SQ FT: 7,000
SALES (est): 21.9MM Privately Held
WEB: www.levian.com
SIC: 3911 Jewelry, precious metal

(G-5821)
LINO INTERNATIONAL INC
Also Called: Lino Metal
111 Great Neck Rd 300a (11021-5403)
PHONE..................................516 482-7100
Ling Hong LI, *President*
Aisan Kim, *Manager*
EMP: 7
SALES: 5MM Privately Held
SIC: 3312 Pipes, iron & steel

(G-5822)
MARCO MOORE INC
825 Northern Blvd Ste 201 (11021-5323)
PHONE..................................212 575-2090
David Zar, *President*
EMP: 60
SQ FT: 11,000
SALES: 4MM
SALES (corp-wide): 5.8MM Privately Held
SIC: 3911 3873 Jewelry, precious metal; watches, clocks, watchcases & parts
PA: Royal Jewelry Manufacturing Inc.
825 Northern Blvd Fl 2
Great Neck NY 11021
212 302-2500

(G-5823)
NIBMOR PROJECT LLC
11 Middle Neck Rd (11021-2312)
PHONE..................................718 374-5091
Jennifer Love, *CEO*
Heather Terry, *Director*
EMP: 14
SALES (est): 2.3MM Privately Held
SIC: 2066 Chocolate

(G-5824)
OAKWOOD PUBLISHING CO
14 Bond St Ste 386 (11021-2045)
PHONE..................................516 482-7720
Richard Weiss, *President*
Lisa Whitney, *CFO*
EMP: 7
SQ FT: 3,000
SALES: 100K Privately Held
SIC: 2741 Miscellaneous publishing

(G-5825)
OLD DUTCH MUSTARD CO INC (PA)
Also Called: Pilgrim Foods Co
98 Cuttermill Rd Ste 260s (11021-3033)
PHONE..................................516 466-0522
Fax: 516 466-0762
Charles R Santich, *Ch of Bd*
Paul Santich, *President*
Renate Santich, *Vice Pres*
Evan Dobkins, *Sales Dir*
▼ **EMP:** 6 **EST:** 1915
SQ FT: 3,000
SALES (est): 13.3MM Privately Held
SIC: 2099 2033 2035 Vinegar; fruit juices: concentrated, hot pack; fruit juices: fresh; fruit juices: packaged in cans, jars, etc.; mustard, prepared (wet)

(G-5826)
ORO AVANTI INC (PA)
250 Kings Point Rd (11024-1022)
PHONE..................................516 487-5185
Fax: 516 482-4369
Hersel Sarraf, *President*
Gidion Sarraf, *Vice Pres*
EMP: 7
SALES (est): 1.7MM Privately Held
SIC: 3295 Minerals, ground or treated

(G-5827)
OZ BAKING COMPANY LTD
114 Middle Neck Rd (11021-1245)
PHONE..................................516 466-5114
Ofer Zur, *Ch of Bd*
EMP: 8
SALES (est): 568.7K Privately Held
SIC: 2051 Bread, cake & related products

(G-5828)
PAMA ENTERPRISES INC
60 Cuttermill Rd Ste 411 (11021-3104)
PHONE..................................516 504-6300
Fax: 516 504-6363
Marvin A Makofsky, *President*
Wilner Merrill, *Finance Mgr*
Merrill Wilner, *CPA*
Alison Hickerson, *Manager*
EMP: 5
SALES (est): 330K Privately Held
SIC: 3993 2752 Advertising novelties; commercial printing, lithographic

(G-5829)
PEARL LEATHER GROUP LLC
17 Barstow Rd Ste 206 (11021-2213)
PHONE..................................516 627-4047
Selena Lau, *Sales Staff*
Bob Kamali,
John Ruggeiro,
▲ **EMP:** 50
SQ FT: 4,000
SALES: 10MM Privately Held
SIC: 3111 Leather processing

(G-5830)
PENFLI INDUSTRIES INC
11 Woodland Pl (11021-1035)
PHONE..................................212 947-6080
Anton Fischman, *President*
Joe Fischman, *Vice Pres*
▲ **EMP:** 15
SALES (est): 1.6MM Privately Held
WEB: www.penfliusa.com
SIC: 2326 5136 2339 5137 Men's & boys' work clothing; men's & boys' clothing; women's & misses' athletic clothing & sportswear; women's & children's clothing

(G-5831)
PRECISION BIOLOGICS INC
445 Northern Blvd Ste 24 (11021-4804)
PHONE..................................516 482-1200
Philip M Arlen MD, *President*
EMP: 7
SALES (est): 560K Privately Held
SIC: 3829 3841 Medical diagnostic systems, nuclear; diagnostic apparatus, medical

(G-5832)
PREMIER INGRIDIENTS INC
3 Johnstone Rd (11021-1507)
PHONE..................................516 641-6763
Dennis Provda, *CEO*
▲ **EMP:** 4 **EST:** 2010
SALES: 1.3MM Privately Held
SIC: 2999 Waxes, petroleum: not produced in petroleum refineries

(G-5833)
PRESTIGE BOX CORPORATION (PA)
115 Cuttermill Rd (11021-3101)
P.O. Box 220428 (11022-0428)
PHONE..................................516 773-3115
Fax: 516 773-3612
Sherry Warren, *President*
Ray Turin, *Vice Pres*
EMP: 37 **EST:** 1963
SQ FT: 12,000
SALES (est): 45.2MM Privately Held
SIC: 2657 2653 2631 2652 Folding paperboard boxes; boxes, corrugated: made from purchased materials; boxboard; setup paperboard boxes

(G-5834)
PROGRESSIVE COLOR GRAPHICS
122 Station Rd (11023-1723)
PHONE..................................212 292-8787
Hugo Saltini, *President*
Stuart Linzer, *Vice Pres*
EMP: 41
SQ FT: 28,000
SALES (est): 4.2MM Privately Held
SIC: 2752 Offset & photolithographic printing

(G-5835)
ROSECORE DIVISION
Also Called: Corey Rugs
11 Grace Ave Ste 100 (11021-2417)
P.O. Box 855, Plainview (11803-0855)
PHONE..................................516 504-4530
Fax: 516 504-4542
Irwin Corey, *President*
EMP: 10
SALES (est): 820K Privately Held
SIC: 2273 Carpets & rugs

(G-5836)
ROYAL JEWELRY MFG INC (PA)
825 Northern Blvd Fl 2 (11021-5321)
PHONE..................................212 302-2500
Fax: 212 768-0601
Parviz Hakimian, *President*
Ben Hakimian, *Vice Pres*
Sammy Hakimian, *Sales Staff*
Martin Ghodsi, *VP Mktg*
Mojgan Hakimian, *Manager*
▲ **EMP:** 38
SQ FT: 9,000
SALES (est): 5.8MM Privately Held
WEB: www.royaljewelrymfg.com
SIC: 3911 5094 5944 Jewelry, precious metal; jewelry; jewelry stores

(G-5837)
S KASHI & SONS INC
175 Great Neck Rd Ste 204 (11021-3313)
PHONE..................................212 869-9393
Fax: 212 869-9467
Sarah Kashi, *President*
Eley Kashi, *Vice Pres*
Ronen Kashi, *Admin Sec*
EMP: 15
SQ FT: 1,300
SALES (est): 1.9MM Privately Held
WEB: www.skashi.com
SIC: 3911 5094 Jewelry, precious metal; precious stones & metals

(G-5838)
SAMUEL B COLLECTION INC
98 Cuttermill Rd (11021-3036)
PHONE..................................516 466-1826
Neda Behnam, *President*
▲ **EMP:** 3
SALES: 3MM Privately Held
SIC: 3911 Jewelry, precious metal

(G-5839)
SCARGUARD LABS LLC
15 Barstow Rd (11021-2211)
PHONE..................................516 482-8050
Joel Studin, *CEO*
Jim Dun, *President*
James Dunns, *Exec VP*
Alan Graham, *Exec V*
Steve Levinson, *VP Opers*
EMP: 12
SQ FT: 5,000
SALES (est): 2.8MM Privately Held
SIC: 2834 Pharmaceutical preparations

(G-5840)
SEYMOUR SCIENCE LLC
4 Sheffield Rd (11021-2728)
PHONE..................................516 699-8404
Liz Nealon, *CEO*
EMP: 7
SALES (est): 365.2K Privately Held
SIC: 2741 7389 ;

GEOGRAPHIC SECTION

(G-5841)
SPRINGFIELD OIL SERVICES INC
40 Cuttermill Rd Ste 201 (11021-3213)
PHONE..................................516 482-5995
Bentley Blum, *Manager*
EMP: 5
SALES (corp-wide): 1.8MM **Privately Held**
SIC: 1382 Oil & gas exploration services
PA: Springfield Oil Services, Inc.
    550 Mmaroneck Ave Ste 503
    Harrison NY 10528
    914 315-6812

(G-5842)
STAR SPORTS CORP
Also Called: American Turf Monthly
747 Middle Neck Rd # 103 (11024-1950)
PHONE..................................516 773-4075
Allen Hakim, *President*
Diane Karron, *Publisher*
Scott Romick, *Manager*
EMP: 20
SQ FT: 2,500
SALES (est): 900K **Privately Held**
WEB: www.carteriley.com
SIC: 2711 Newspapers

(G-5843)
STYLECRAFT INTERIORS INC
22 Watermill Ln (11021-4235)
PHONE..................................516 487-2133
Fred Reindl, *President*
Matthew Reindl, *Treasurer*
EMP: 10
SQ FT: 5,000
SALES: 600K **Privately Held**
WEB: www.stylecraftinteriors.com
SIC: 3843 2521 Cabinets, dental; cabinets, office: wood

(G-5844)
TODD ENTERPRISES INC
747 Middle Neck Rd # 103 (11024-1955)
PHONE..................................516 773-8087
Alan Sarfaty, *President*
EMP: 100
SQ FT: 16,000
SALES (est): 10.6MM **Privately Held**
WEB: www.scinetcorp.com
SIC: 3571 5045 3577 3572 Electronic computers; computers; computer peripheral equipment; computer storage devices

(G-5845)
TONI INDUSTRIES INC
Also Called: Hbs
111 Great Neck Rd Ste 305 (11021-5403)
PHONE..................................212 921-0700
Ophelia Chung, *President*
Neil Blumstein, *Vice Pres*
EMP: 14 EST: 2002
SALES: 18MM **Privately Held**
SIC: 2339 Athletic clothing: women's, misses' & juniors'

(G-5846)
UNIQUE OVERSEAS INC
425 Northern Blvd Ste 22 (11021-4803)
PHONE..................................516 466-9792
Raju Shewakramani, *President*
Ragu Ramani, *Principal*
◆ EMP: 8
SALES (est): 894K **Privately Held**
WEB: www.uniqueoverseas.com
SIC: 3199 Equestrian related leather articles

(G-5847)
UNIVERSAL METALS INC
98 Cuttermill Rd Ste 428 (11021-3006)
PHONE..................................516 829-0896
Pushpa Kochar, *CEO*
Hira Kochar, *Vice Pres*
◆ EMP: 5
SALES (est): 1.6MM **Privately Held**
SIC: 3399 Metal fasteners

(G-5848)
VARIETY GEM CO INC (PA)
295 Northern Blvd Ste 208 (11021-4701)
PHONE..................................212 921-1820
Effie Bezalel, *President*
Yehuda Bezalel, *VP Mfg*
▲ EMP: 10
SQ FT: 2,000
SALES: 3.5MM **Privately Held**
WEB: www.varietygem.com
SIC: 3911 Jewelry, precious metal

(G-5849)
WEGO INTERNATIONAL FLOORS LLC
239 Great Neck Rd (11021-3301)
PHONE..................................516 487-3510
Bert Eshaghpour, *CEO*
Barry Okun, *CFO*
EMP: 11 EST: 2015
SALES (est): 549.7K
SALES (corp-wide): 6.4MM **Privately Held**
SIC: 2491 5023 Flooring, treated wood block; wood flooring
PA: Wego Chemical Group Inc
    239 Great Neck Rd
    Great Neck NY 11021
    516 487-3510

Great River
Suffolk County

(G-5850)
HEARST BUSINESS MEDIA CORP
3500 Sunrise Hwy Ste 100 (11739-1001)
PHONE..................................631 650-6151
Peter Olsen, *Principal*
EMP: 9
SALES (corp-wide): 4.9B **Privately Held**
SIC: 2721 Magazines: publishing only, not printed on site
HQ: Hearst Business Media Corp
    2620 Barrett Rd
    Gainesville GA 30507
    770 532-4111

(G-5851)
HEARST BUSINESS MEDIA CORP
3500 Sunrise Hwy (11739-1001)
PHONE..................................631 650-4441
Richard P Malloch, *President*
Gregory Dorn MD MPH, *Exec VP*
Steven A Hobbs, *Exec VP*
Donna Yeager, *Manager*
Jim Wood, *Director*
EMP: 14
SALES (est): 167.3K
SALES (corp-wide): 4.9B **Privately Held**
SIC: 2721 2731 2711 4832 Magazines: publishing only, not printed on site; books: publishing only; newspapers, publishing & printing; newspapers: publishing only, not printed on site; radio broadcasting stations; television broadcasting stations; news feature syndicate
PA: The Hearst Corporation
    300 W 57th St Fl 42
    New York NY 10019
    212 649-2000

(G-5852)
METRO DOOR INC (DH)
Also Called: Metro Door A Cintas Company
3500 Sunrise Hwy (11739-1001)
PHONE..................................631 277-6490
Scott McDermott, *President*
Jeff Chevalier, *General Mgr*
Jim Karcher, *Co-Founder*
Brian Wilmhoff, *Project Mgr*
Ellen Kraus, *Opers Mgr*
▼ EMP: 80
SQ FT: 17,200
SALES (est): 25.1MM
SALES (corp-wide): 4.9B **Publicly Held**
WEB: www.metrodoor.com
SIC: 3446 1799 Fences, gates, posts & flagpoles; fence construction

Green Island
Albany County

(G-5853)
ARCADIA MFG GROUP INC (PA)
80 Cohoes Ave (12183-1505)
PHONE..................................518 434-6213
William T Sumner, *Ch of Bd*
Michael Werner, *President*
George Quigley, *Vice Pres*
Jen Canone, *Purch Mgr*
Charlie Schuffert, *Purch Mgr*
▲ EMP: 44
SQ FT: 20,000
SALES (est): 11.4MM **Privately Held**
WEB: www.arcadiasupply.com
SIC: 3498 3446 3444 3999 Fabricated pipe & fittings; ornamental metalwork; sheet metalwork; cigar lighters, except precious metal

(G-5854)
CASE GROUP LLC
Also Called: Case Window and Door
195 Cohoes Ave (12183-1501)
PHONE..................................518 720-3100
Russell Brooks, *Mng Member*
Mike Wright, *Director*
Gerhard Loeffel,
◆ EMP: 36
SQ FT: 50,000
SALES (est): 5MM **Privately Held**
WEB: www.casewindow.com
SIC: 2431 Doors & door parts & trim, wood; windows & window parts & trim, wood

(G-5855)
GENERAL CONTROL SYSTEMS INC
60 Cohoes Ave Ste 101 (12183-1553)
PHONE..................................518 270-8045
Fax: 518 270-8042
Clay Robinson, *President*
Gregory Pacifico, *General Mgr*
Daniel Robens, *Prdtn Mgr*
Bill Powers, *Purchasing*
Jason Baniak, *Engineer*
EMP: 50
SQ FT: 24,000
SALES (est): 12.9MM
SALES (corp-wide): 4.4B **Publicly Held**
WEB: www.gcontrol.net
SIC: 3625 Industrial controls: push button, selector switches, pilot
PA: Talen Energy Corporation
    835 Hamilton St Ste 150
    Allentown PA 18101
    888 211-6011

(G-5856)
GREEN ISLAND POWER AUTHORITY
20 Clinton St (12183-1117)
PHONE..................................518 273-0661
John J Brown, *Chairman*
Robert Bourgeois, *Fire Chief*
Micheal Cocca, *Vice Chairman*
Dave Filieau, *Supervisor*
Matthew Lansing, *Assistant*
EMP: 11
SQ FT: 8,400
SALES: 5.8MM **Privately Held**
WEB: www.villageofgreenisland.com
SIC: 3699 Electrical equipment & supplies

(G-5857)
HUERSCH MARKETING GROUP LLC
70 Cohoes Ave Ste 4 (12183-1533)
PHONE..................................518 874-1045
Thomas R Huerter, *CEO*
EMP: 8
SALES (est): 529.4K **Privately Held**
SIC: 2711 Commercial printing & newspaper publishing combined

(G-5858)
LAI INTERNATIONAL INC
1 Tibbits Ave (12183-1430)
PHONE..................................763 780-0060
Rici Smentek, *Credit Mgr*
Michael Bagel, *Manager*
EMP: 60
SALES (corp-wide): 60MM **Privately Held**
SIC: 3728 Aircraft assemblies, subassemblies & parts
PA: Lai International, Inc.
    7645 Baker St Ne
    Minneapolis MN 55432
    763 780-0060

(G-5859)
LYDALL PERFORMANCE MTL INC
68 George St (12183-1113)
PHONE..................................518 273-6320
John Minnick, *Engineer*
Joanne Roscoe, *Engineer*
Tim Reilly, *Controller*
Timothy Reilly, *VP Finance*
Susan Pratt, *Human Resources*
◆ EMP: 115
SQ FT: 300,000
SALES (est): 21.4MM
SALES (corp-wide): 524.5MM **Publicly Held**
WEB: www.lydall.com
SIC: 2211 Cotton broad woven goods
PA: Lydall, Inc.
    1 Colonial Rd
    Manchester CT 06042
    860 646-1233

(G-5860)
LYDALL PERFORMANCE MTLS INC
68 George St (12183-1113)
PHONE..................................518 273-6320
EMP: 14
SALES (corp-wide): 524.5MM **Publicly Held**
SIC: 3569 Filters
HQ: Lydall Performance Materials, Inc.
    134 Chestnut Hill Rd
    Rochester NH 03867
    603 332-4600

(G-5861)
RELIABLE BROTHERS INC
185 Cohoes Ave (12183-1501)
PHONE..................................518 273-6732
Fax: 518 273-6784
Kyle Buchakjiar, *Ch of Bd*
Vahan Buchakjian, *President*
Douglas Waldmann, *Accounts Mgr*
EMP: 30
SALES (est): 5.9MM **Privately Held**
SIC: 2013 5147 Meat extracts from purchased meat; meats, fresh

Greene
Chenango County

(G-5862)
CHARLES LAY
Also Called: Greene Brass & Aluminum Fndry
47 Birdsall St (13778-1053)
PHONE..................................607 656-4204
Fax: 607 656-4245
Tom Todd, *Manager*
EMP: 8
SALES (corp-wide): 1MM **Privately Held**
WEB: www.charleslay.com
SIC: 3366 3365 Bronze foundry; aluminum foundries
PA: Charles Lay
    138 Roundhouse Rd
    Oneonta NY 13820
    607 432-4518

(G-5863)
CROSS COUNTRY MFG INC
2355 Rte 206 (13778)
P.O. Box 565 (13778-0565)
PHONE..................................607 656-4103
Frank M Hanrahan, *Branch Mgr*
EMP: 15
SALES (corp-wide): 3.4MM **Privately Held**
WEB: www.crosscountrymfg.com
SIC: 3715 Truck trailers

Greene - Chenango County (G-5864)   GEOGRAPHIC SECTION

PA: Cross Country Manufacturing, Inc.
2355 State Highway 206
Greene NY 13778
607 656-4103

(G-5864)
CROSS COUNTRY MFG INC (PA)
2355 State Highway 206 (13778-2367)
P.O. Box 565 (13778-0565)
PHONE....................607 656-4103
Fax: 607 656-7188
Frank M Hanrahan, *President*
Catherine Hanrahan, *Vice Pres*
Ruth Smith, *Manager*
Leslie Haddad, *Admin Asst*
EMP: 18
SQ FT: 2,544
SALES (est): 3.4MM **Privately Held**
WEB: www.crosscountrymfg.com
SIC: 3715 Truck trailers

(G-5865)
G C CONTROLS INC
1408 County Road 2 (13778-2257)
PHONE....................607 656-4117
Fax: 607 656-7452
Mert Gilbert, *Ch of Bd*
Steven Gilbert, *Principal*
Dan Snowberger, *Vice Pres*
Peggy Clark, *Manager*
EMP: 40
SQ FT: 12,000
SALES (est): 8.6MM **Privately Held**
WEB: www.gccontrols.com
SIC: 3625 Relays & industrial controls; control equipment, electric; timing devices, electronic

(G-5866)
GREENE TECHNOLOGIES INC
Grand & Clinton St (13778)
PHONE....................607 656-4166
Carol M Rosenkrantz, *Chairman*
Robert Lindridge, *Vice Pres*
George Howe, *Plant Mgr*
Douglas Ramsay, *Engineer*
Ron Gaska, *Sales Staff*
EMP: 100
SQ FT: 49,000
SALES (est): 17.2MM **Privately Held**
WEB: www.greenetech.biz
SIC: 3444 3479 3471 3469 Sheet metalwork; coating of metals & formed products; electroplating of metals or formed products; polishing, metals or formed products; metal stampings; miscellaneous fabricated wire products; fabricated pipe & fittings

(G-5867)
RAPP SIGNS INC
3979 State Route 206 (13778-2134)
PHONE....................607 656-8167
Fax: 607 656-8677
Ronald J Rapp, *President*
David Rapp, *Principal*
Darlene Wilkins, *Manager*
EMP: 13
SALES (est): 1.3MM **Privately Held**
SIC: 3993 1799 Signs, not made in custom sign painting shops; sign installation & maintenance

(G-5868)
RAYMOND CONSOLIDATED CORP (DH)
22 S Canal St (13778-1244)
PHONE....................800 235-7200
Jim Malvaso, *President*
Timothy Combs, *Exec VP*
John Everts, *Vice Pres*
Ryan Delaney, *QC Mgr*
Edward J Rompala, *CFO*
◆ **EMP:** 200
SQ FT: 180,000
SALES (est): 888MM
SALES (corp-wide): 19B **Privately Held**
SIC: 3537 Industrial trucks & tractors
HQ: Toyota Material Handling Europe Ab
Svarvargatan 8
Mjolby 595 3
142 860-00

(G-5869)
RAYMOND CORPORATION (DH)
22 S Canal St (13778-1244)
P.O. Box 130 (13778-0130)
PHONE....................607 656-2311
Fax: 607 656-9005
Michael G Field, *President*
Louis J Callea, *Counsel*
Arthur A Goodell, *Counsel*
Timothy Combs, *Exec VP*
Rick Harrington, *Senior VP*
◆ **EMP:** 800 **EST:** 1987
SQ FT: 325,000
SALES (est): 888MM
SALES (corp-wide): 19B **Privately Held**
WEB: www.raymondcorp.com
SIC: 3537 3535 7359 Industrial trucks & tractors; lift trucks, industrial: fork, platform, straddle, etc.; forklift trucks; straddle carriers, mobile; conveyors & conveying equipment; belt conveyor systems, general industrial use; pneumatic tube conveyor systems; equipment rental & leasing; aircraft & industrial truck rental services
HQ: Raymond Consolidated Corporation
22 S Canal St
Greene NY 13778
800 235-7200

(G-5870)
RAYMOND SALES CORPORATION (DH)
22 S Canal St (13778-1244)
P.O. Box 130 (13778-0130)
PHONE....................607 656-2311
James Malvaso, *President*
Diana Gurney, *Office Mgr*
EMP: 2
SQ FT: 325,000
SALES (est): 125.9MM
SALES (corp-wide): 19B **Privately Held**
SIC: 3537 5084 Forklift trucks; materials handling machinery
HQ: The Raymond Corporation
22 S Canal St
Greene NY 13778
607 656-2311

Greenfield Center
Saratoga County

(G-5871)
PECKHAM INDUSTRIES INC
430 Coy Rd (12833-1042)
PHONE....................518 893-2176
William H Peckham, *Branch Mgr*
EMP: 18
SALES (corp-wide): 192MM **Privately Held**
SIC: 2951 Concrete, asphaltic (not from refineries)
PA: Peckham Industries, Inc.
20 Haarlem Ave Ste 200
White Plains NY 10603
914 949-2000

Greenlawn
Suffolk County

(G-5872)
ALL CULTURES INC
Also Called: American Culture
12 Gates St (11740-1427)
PHONE....................631 293-3143
Louis Guaneri, *CEO*
◆ **EMP:** 35
SQ FT: 30,000
SALES (est): 6.7MM **Privately Held**
WEB: www.americanculturehair.com
SIC: 2844 Hair preparations, including shampoos; shampoos, rinses, conditioners: hair

(G-5873)
BAE SYSTEMS INFO & ELEC SYS
450 Pulaski Rd (11740-1606)
PHONE....................631 912-1525
Anthony Boniciolli, *Engineer*
Richard F Brofka, *Engineer*
Steve Fischetti, *Engineer*
Robert Lafferty, *Project Engr*
Arin Lanis, *Senior Engr*
EMP: 10
SALES (corp-wide): 25.3B **Privately Held**
WEB: www.iesi.na.baesystems.com
SIC: 3823 Digital displays of process variables
HQ: Bae Systems Information And Electronic Systems Integration Inc.
65 Spit Brook Rd
Nashua NH 03060
603 885-4321

(G-5874)
MB PLASTICS INC (PA)
130 Stony Hollow Rd (11740-1511)
PHONE....................718 523-1180
Fax: 718 526-4002
Milton Bassin, *President*
Sandra Benton, *Personnel*
Eddy Megerne, *Manager*
▲ **EMP:** 14 **EST:** 1964
SQ FT: 15,000
SALES (est): 1.5MM **Privately Held**
SIC: 2821 3911 Plastics materials & resins; jewelry apparel

(G-5875)
MEDICAL TECHNOLOGY PRODUCTS
33a Smith St (11740-1219)
PHONE....................631 285-6640
Fax: 631 285-6641
Thomas J Hartnett Jr, *Ch of Bd*
David Hawkins, *Admin Sec*
EMP: 8
SQ FT: 5,000
SALES (est): 1MM **Privately Held**
SIC: 3841 Surgical & medical instruments

Greenport
Suffolk County

(G-5876)
125-127 MAIN STREET CORP
Also Called: Mills, William J & Company
125 Main St 127 (11944-1421)
P.O. Box 2126 (11944-0978)
PHONE....................631 477-1500
Fax: 631 477-1504
William J Mills III, *President*
Robert Hills, *Vice Pres*
EMP: 18 **EST:** 1880
SQ FT: 25,000
SALES (est): 2MM **Privately Held**
WEB: www.millscanvas.com
SIC: 2394 Awnings, fabric: made from purchased materials; sails: made from purchased materials

(G-5877)
STIDD SYSTEMS INC
220 Carpenter St (11944-1406)
P.O. Box 87 (11944-0087)
PHONE....................631 477-2400
Fax: 631 477-1095
Walter A Gezari, *President*
Robert J Digregorio, *Vice Pres*
David J Wilberding, *Vice Pres*
Abbey Boskoff, *Accountant*
Richard Wagner, *Program Mgr*
▼ **EMP:** 41
SQ FT: 62,000
SALES (est): 22.5MM **Privately Held**
WEB: www.stidd.com
SIC: 2399 3429 3731 3732 Seat covers, automobile; manufactured hardware (general); shipbuilding & repairing; boats, fiberglass: building & repairing; transportation equipment & supplies

(G-5878)
WOODEN BOATWORKS
190 Sterling St Unit 2 (11944-1454)
PHONE....................631 477-6507
Robert Wahl, *Principal*
EMP: 6
SALES (est): 737.8K **Privately Held**
SIC: 3732 Boat building & repairing

Greenvale
Nassau County

(G-5879)
CALL FORWARDING TECHNOLOGIES
55 Northern Blvd Ste 3b (11548-1301)
PHONE....................516 621-3600
Charles Hart, *President*
EMP: 7
SQ FT: 600
SALES: 900K **Privately Held**
SIC: 3661 Telephones & telephone apparatus

(G-5880)
DALMA DRESS MFG CO INC
3 Carman Rd (11548-1123)
PHONE....................212 391-8296
Fax: 212 391-0076
Madalin Dipalma, *President*
Madalina Dipalma, *Owner*
Giovanna Darmiani, *Vice Pres*
EMP: 25
SQ FT: 5,500
SALES (est): 1.7MM **Privately Held**
SIC: 2335 2339 Women's, juniors' & misses' dresses; women's & misses' outerwear

(G-5881)
SLANT/FIN CORPORATION (PA)
100 Forest Dr (11548-1295)
P.O. Box 416 (11548-0416)
PHONE....................516 484-2600
Fax: 516 484-2694
Melvin Dubin, *Ch of Bd*
Adam Dubin, *Chairman*
Gary Golden, *Plant Mgr*
Neil Segal, *Plant Mgr*
Robert Viets, *Buyer*
▲ **EMP:** 374 **EST:** 1949
SQ FT: 200,000
SALES (est): 102.8MM **Privately Held**
WEB: www.slantfin.com
SIC: 3433 3443 Heating equipment, except electric; fabricated plate work (boiler shop)

(G-5882)
SLANTCO MANUFACTURING INC (HQ)
100 Forest Dr (11548-1205)
PHONE....................516 484-2600
Melvin Dubin, *President*
Selwyn Steinberg, *Senior VP*
John Sweiteck, *Vice Pres*
Shah Mahfuz, *Engineer*
Donald Brown, *Treasurer*
EMP: 7 **EST:** 1976
SQ FT: 150,000
SALES (est): 1.1MM
SALES (corp-wide): 102.8MM **Privately Held**
SIC: 3443 Heat exchangers: coolers (after, inter), condensers, etc.
PA: Slant/Fin Corporation
100 Forest Dr
Greenvale NY 11548
516 484-2600

(G-5883)
WIN WOOD CABINETRY INC
200 Forest Dr Ste 7 (11548-1216)
PHONE....................516 304-2216
Frank Lin, *President*
▲ **EMP:** 8
SALES (est): 413K **Privately Held**
SIC: 2434 Wood kitchen cabinets

Greenville
Greene County

(G-5884)
CLASSIC AUTO CRAFTS INC
Also Called: Town Line Auto
6501 State Route 32 (12083-2212)
P.O. Box 10 (12083-0010)
PHONE....................518 966-8003
John Dolce, *President*

▲ = Import ▼ = Export
◆ = Import/Export

EMP: 8
SALES (est): 1MM Privately Held
WEB: www.townlineauto.com
SIC: 3599 Machine shop, jobbing & repair

(G-5885)
HAWKENCATSKILLS LLC
Also Called: Catskill Boiler Co.
18 Shultes Rd (12083-2032)
PHONE.................................518 966-8900
Bert Tobin,
Holly Tobin,
▲ EMP: 6 EST: 2006
SALES (est): 767.5K Privately Held
SIC: 3433 Burners, furnaces, boilers & stokers

Greenwich
Washington County

(G-5886)
BDP INDUSTRIES INC (PA)
Also Called: Belt Dewatering Press
354 State Route 29 (12834-4518)
P.O. Box 118 (12834-0118)
PHONE.................................518 695-6851
Fax: 518 695-5417
Albert J Schmidt, President
Scott Enflinger, Regional Mgr
Dickey Liu, Regional Mgr
Socrates Fronhofer, Vice Pres
Kelly Falk, Purchasing
EMP: 49 EST: 1978
SALES: 14.3MM Privately Held
WEB: www.bdpindustries.com
SIC: 3523 3545 3542 Turf & grounds equipment; turf equipment, commercial; machine tool accessories; machine tools, metal forming type

(G-5887)
FORT MILLER GROUP INC
688 Wilbur Ave (12834-4413)
P.O. Box 98, Schuylerville (12871-0098)
PHONE.................................518 695-5000
Fax: 518 695-4970
John T Hedbring, Ch of Bd
John Marcelle, Exec VP
Robert Mann, Engineer
Richard Schumaker, CFO
John Gonyea, Manager
▲ EMP: 420
SQ FT: 160,000
SALES (est): 115.1MM
SALES (corp-wide): 144.9MM Privately Held
WEB: www.fortmiller.com
SIC: 3272 3441 Concrete products, precast; fabricated structural metal
PA: The Fort Miller Service Corp
    688 Wilbur Ave
    Greenwich NY 12834
    518 695-5000

(G-5888)
FORT MILLER SERVICE CORP (PA)
688 Wilbur Ave (12834-4413)
P.O. Box 98, Schuylerville (12871-0098)
PHONE.................................518 695-5000
John T Hedbring, Ch of Bd
Mary Ann Spiezio, Vice Pres
Richard Schumaker, CFO
▼ EMP: 12
SQ FT: 10,000
SALES (est): 144.9MM Privately Held
SIC: 3272 3271 5211 1799 Concrete products, precast; burial vaults, concrete or precast terrazzo; concrete block & brick; concrete & cinder block; fence construction

(G-5889)
HOLLINGSWORTH & VOSE COMPANY
3235 County Rte 113 (12834)
PHONE.................................518 695-8000
Donald Wagner, Opers-Prdtn-Mfg
David Graham, Engineer
Ed Dunavin, Human Res Mgr
Paul Blinn, Manager
Laurie Moore, Admin Asst
EMP: 160

SQ FT: 3,594
SALES (corp-wide): 754.7MM Privately Held
WEB: www.hovo.com
SIC: 2621 3053 Filter paper; gasket materials
PA: Hollingsworth & Vose Company
    112 Washington St
    East Walpole MA 02032
    508 850-2000

(G-5890)
ICE CREAM MAN INC
417 State Route 29 (12834-4233)
PHONE.................................518 692-8382
Fax: 518 692-1298
Julia Reynolds, President
EMP: 20
SALES: 200K Privately Held
WEB: www.the-ice-cream-man.com
SIC: 2024 Ice cream, bulk

(G-5891)
PHANTOM LABORATORY INC
Also Called: Phantom Laboratory, The
2727 State Route 29 (12834-3212)
P.O. Box 511, Salem (12865-0511)
PHONE.................................518 692-1190
Fax: 518 692-3329
Joshua Levy, President
Julie Simms, Vice Pres
Bonnie Hanlon, VP Opers
Megan Stalter, Cust Mgr
Ariel Dickson, Manager
EMP: 15
SQ FT: 65,000
SALES: 750K Privately Held
WEB: www.phantomlab.com
SIC: 3844 X-ray apparatus & tubes

(G-5892)
SCA TISSUE NORTH AMERICA LLC
72 County Route 53 (12834-2233)
PHONE.................................518 692-8434
Fax: 518 692-8451
Michael Bell, Safety Mgr
Kathleen Hockenberry, Safety Mgr
Dale Long, Safety Mgr
Cathy Crimmins, Purch Agent
Glenn Jones, Branch Mgr
EMP: 50
SALES (corp-wide): 14B Privately Held
WEB: www.scatissue.com
SIC: 2621 Paper mills; napkin stock, paper; facial tissue stock; toilet tissue stock
HQ: Sca Tissue North America, Llc
    1451 Mcmahon Rd
    Neenah WI 54956
    920 725-7031

(G-5893)
SOUTHERN ADRNDCK FBR PRDCRS CP
2532 State Route 40 (12834-2300)
PHONE.................................518 692-2700
Mary Jeanne Packer, President
EMP: 5
SALES: 50K Privately Held
SIC: 2299 Textile goods

(G-5894)
TEFFT PUBLISHERS INC
Also Called: Journal Stationers
35 Salem St (12834-1320)
PHONE.................................518 692-9290
Sally Tefft, President
Culver Tefft, Vice Pres
EMP: 9 EST: 1980
SQ FT: 2,766
SALES (est): 421.5K Privately Held
SIC: 2711 5943 Newspapers: publishing only, not printed on site; writing supplies

(G-5895)
TYMETAL CORP (HQ)
678 Wilbur Ave (12834-4413)
P.O. Box 139, Schuylerville (12871-0139)
PHONE.................................518 692-9930
Fax: 518 692-9404
John T Hedbring, President
Rob Douglas, President
Chuck Alexander, Vice Pres
Douglas Blanchard, Opers Mgr
Peg Harrington, Opers Staff

EMP: 30
SQ FT: 25,000
SALES: 15MM
SALES (corp-wide): 144.9MM Privately Held
WEB: www.tymetal.com
SIC: 3446 3441 Fences, gates, posts & flagpoles; fabricated structural metal
PA: The Fort Miller Service Corp
    688 Wilbur Ave
    Greenwich NY 12834
    518 695-5000

Greenwood Lake
Orange County

(G-5896)
BARNABY PRINTS INC (PA)
673 Jersey Ave (10925-2014)
P.O. Box 98 (10925-0098)
PHONE.................................845 477-2501
Fax: 845 477-2739
Robert Brodhurst, President
William Neuhaus, Treasurer
Diane Eccher, Office Mgr
EMP: 15
SQ FT: 12,000
SALES (est): 1.1MM Privately Held
SIC: 2759 2396 Screen printing; automotive & apparel trimmings

Groton
Tompkins County

(G-5897)
C & D ASSEMBLY INC
107 Corona Ave (13073-1206)
PHONE.................................607 898-4275
Fax: 607 898-4685
Jeffrey Cronk, President
Michael Hammond, Vice Pres
John Wolff, Prdtn Mgr
Dale Harris, Purchasing
Jason Adams, Engineer
▲ EMP: 42
SQ FT: 10,600
SALES (est): 8.7MM Privately Held
WEB: www.cdassembly.com
SIC: 3672 8731 Printed circuit boards; electronic research

(G-5898)
CAYUGA TOOL AND DIE INC
182 Newman Rd (13073-8712)
PHONE.................................607 533-7400
Fax: 607 533-7401
Judson Bailey, President
Becky Bailey, Treasurer
EMP: 9
SQ FT: 3,680
SALES: 664.9K Privately Held
SIC: 3599 Machine shop, jobbing & repair

(G-5899)
LEWBRO READY MIX INC (PA)
502 Locke Rd (13073-9494)
PHONE.................................315 497-0498
Mitchell Metzgar, President
EMP: 6
SQ FT: 5,000
SALES (est): 833.3K Privately Held
SIC: 3273 Ready-mixed concrete

(G-5900)
MARTINEZ SPECIALTIES INC
205 Bossard Rd (13073-9779)
PHONE.................................607 898-3053
Philip Martinez, President
Dorothy Martinez, Vice Pres
EMP: 8
SALES (est): 1.1MM Privately Held
SIC: 3694 Ignition apparatus & distributors

(G-5901)
PYLANTIS NEW YORK LLC
102 E Cortland St (13073-1108)
PHONE.................................310 429-5911
Jeff Toolan, CEO
Eli Gill, COO
Matt Ruttenberg,
EMP: 5 EST: 2012

SALES (est): 348.9K Privately Held
SIC: 3089 Injection molding of plastics

Guilderland
Albany County

(G-5902)
CUSTOM PRTRS GUILDERLAND INC
Also Called: Guilderland Printing
2210 Western Ave (12084-9701)
PHONE.................................518 456-2811
Fax: 518 456-1093
Joyce Ragone, President
Thomas Ragone, Vice Pres
Kathleen Szesnat, Manager
EMP: 15
SQ FT: 4,000
SALES (est): 2.5MM Privately Held
SIC: 2759 Commercial printing

Hadley
Saratoga County

(G-5903)
NORTHEASTERN ELECTRIC MOTORS
34 Hollow Rd (12835-2822)
PHONE.................................518 793-5939
Walter R Burnham, President
EMP: 5
SQ FT: 6,500
SALES (est): 380K Privately Held
SIC: 7694 5063 Electric motor repair; rewinding services; motors, electric

Halcottsville
Delaware County

(G-5904)
ALTA INDUSTRIES LTD
Also Called: Alta Log Homes
46966 State Hwy 30 (12438)
PHONE.................................845 586-3336
Fax: 845 586-2582
Frank Mann, President
David S Mann, Vice Pres
Ken Castle, Plant Mgr
Franscine Ladenheim, Purch Mgr
EMP: 16
SQ FT: 7,000
SALES (est): 2.2MM Privately Held
WEB: www.altaloghomes.com
SIC: 2452 Log cabins, prefabricated, wood

Halesite
Suffolk County

(G-5905)
MANUFACTURERS INDEXING PDTS
Also Called: Mip
53 Gristmill Ln (11743-2134)
PHONE.................................631 271-0956
Charles Busk Jr, President
Janet Boone, Bookkeeper
EMP: 9 EST: 1964
SQ FT: 12,000
SALES (est): 920K Privately Held
SIC: 2821 2675 Vinyl resins; die-cut paper & board

(G-5906)
ROSE FENCE INC
356 Bay Ave (11743-1141)
PHONE.................................516 790-2308
EMP: 88
SALES (corp-wide): 20.2MM Privately Held
SIC: 3496 Fencing, made from purchased wire
PA: Rose Fence, Inc.
    345 W Sunrise Hwy
    Freeport NY 11520
    516 223-0777

Halfmoon
Saratoga County

(G-5907)
6N SYSTEMS INC
3 Corporate Dr Ste 202 (12065-8635)
PHONE..................................518 583-6400
Arthur Webb, *President*
David Finkelstein, *Treasurer*
Christopher Titterton, *Admin Sec*
EMP: 7 **EST:** 2001
SALES (est): 544.1K
SALES (corp-wide): 39.6MM **Privately Held**
WEB: www.6nsystems.com
SIC: 7372 7371 Prepackaged software; custom computer programming services
PA: Ehealth Solutions Inc.
    575 8th Ave Fl 15
    New York NY 10018
    212 268-4242

(G-5908)
ADVANCE ENERGY TECH INC
1 Solar Dr (12065-3402)
PHONE..................................518 371-2140
Timothy K Carlo, *Ch of Bd*
EMP: 27 **EST:** 1965
SQ FT: 30,000
SALES (est): 6.4MM **Privately Held**
WEB: www.advanceet.com
SIC: 3585 Parts for heating, cooling & refrigerating equipment

(G-5909)
CAPITAL DISTRICT STAIRS INC
45 Dunsbach Rd (12065-7906)
PHONE..................................518 383-2449
Fax: 518 371-9655
Alex Nikiforov, *President*
EMP: 7
SALES (est): 1MM **Privately Held**
WEB: www.capitaldistrictstairs.com
SIC: 2431 Staircases & stairs, wood; stair railings, wood

(G-5910)
EBELING ASSOCIATES INC (PA)
Also Called: Control Global Solutions
9 Corporate Dr Ste 1 (12065-8636)
PHONE..................................518 688-8700
Allan Robison, *President*
James Colunio, *CIO*
Scott Ebeling, *Systems Analyst*
EMP: 17
SQ FT: 5,500
SALES (est): 2.8MM **Privately Held**
WEB: www.execontrol.com
SIC: 7372 Prepackaged software

(G-5911)
INFO LABEL INC
12 Enterprise Ave (12065-3424)
PHONE..................................518 664-0791
Mark Dufort, *President*
EMP: 15
SQ FT: 7,000
SALES (est): 2MM **Privately Held**
WEB: www.infolabel.net
SIC: 2759 5084 Labels & seals: printing; printing trades machinery, equipment & supplies

(G-5912)
MOTOROLA SOLUTIONS INC
7 Deer Run Holw (12065-5664)
PHONE..................................518 348-0833
Carolely Urgenson, *Principal*
Thomas Lee, *Electrical Engi*
Harvey Edelman, *Manager*
EMP: 148
SALES (corp-wide): 5.7B **Publicly Held**
WEB: www.motorola.com
SIC: 3663 Radio broadcasting & communications equipment
PA: Motorola Solutions, Inc.
    1303 E Algonquin Rd
    Schaumburg IL 60196
    847 576-5000

(G-5913)
MOVINADS & SIGNS LLC
1771 Route 9 (12065-2413)
PHONE..................................518 378-3000
Fax: 518 937-9022
Rob Potter, *President*
EMP: 5
SQ FT: 4,000
SALES: 300K **Privately Held**
SIC: 3993 Signs & advertising specialties

(G-5914)
REQUEST INC
Also Called: Request Multimedia
14 Corporate Dr Ste 6 (12065-8607)
PHONE..................................518 899-1254
Fax: 518 899-1251
Peter M Cholnoky, *President*
Andy Lopez, *Sales Dir*
Susan Zelensky, *Accounts Mgr*
Scott Bartgis, *Director*
EMP: 30
SQ FT: 8,100
SALES: 5MM **Privately Held**
WEB: www.request.com
SIC: 3651 Home entertainment equipment, electronic

(G-5915)
REQUEST SERIOUS PLAY LLC
14 Corporate Dr (12065-8607)
PHONE..................................518 899-1254
Barry Evans, *Principal*
EMP: 7
SALES (est): 680K **Privately Held**
SIC: 3651 Home entertainment equipment, electronic

(G-5916)
SAVE MORE BEVERAGE CORP
Also Called: Uptown
1512 Route 9 Ste 1 (12065-8664)
PHONE..................................518 371-2520
Fax: 518 371-1764
Harold Rockowitz, *President*
Donald Morin, *Vice Pres*
Robert Popp, *Treasurer*
EMP: 8
SALES: 2.5MM **Privately Held**
SIC: 2086 5921 5149 5181 Carbonated beverages, nonalcoholic: bottled & canned; beer (packaged); soft drinks; beer & other fermented malt liquors

Hall
Ontario County

(G-5917)
MILLCO WOODWORKING LLC
1710 Railroad Pl (14463-9005)
P.O. Box 38 (14463-0038)
PHONE..................................585 526-6844
Fax: 585 526-5664
Kent Bingham, *Project Mgr*
Charles L Millerd,
Mark M Millerd,
EMP: 11
SQ FT: 6,290
SALES (est): 1.6MM **Privately Held**
WEB: www.millcowoodworking.com
SIC: 2434 2431 Wood kitchen cabinets; millwork

Hamburg
Erie County

(G-5918)
ABASCO INC
5225 Southwestern Blvd (14075-3524)
P.O. Box 247 (14075-0247)
PHONE..................................716 649-4790
Fax: 716 649-4791
Frank A Saeli Jr, *President*
Michael Saeli, *Vice Pres*
Bill Seipel, *Vice Pres*
Michael Hitt, *Purch Mgr*
William G Seipel, *Marketing Mgr*
▲ **EMP:** 30 **EST:** 1962
SALES (est): 8.8MM **Privately Held**
WEB: www.abasco.net
SIC: 3613 3713 3714 3449 Control panels, electric; specialty motor vehicle bodies; motor vehicle parts & accessories; axles, motor vehicle; steering mechanisms, motor vehicle; miscellaneous metalwork

(G-5919)
CAPITAL CONCRETE INC
5690 Camp Rd (14075-3706)
PHONE..................................716 648-8001
Rosanne Lettieri, *President*
EMP: 6
SALES (est): 912.9K **Privately Held**
SIC: 3273 Ready-mixed concrete

(G-5920)
CLASSIC AWNINGS INC
Also Called: Classic Awnings & Party Tents
1 Elmview Ave (14075-3761)
PHONE..................................716 649-0390
David Vesneske, *President*
EMP: 12
SQ FT: 5,000
SALES (est): 750K **Privately Held**
WEB: www.classicawnings.com
SIC: 2394 7359 Awnings, fabric: made from purchased materials; tent & tarpaulin rental

(G-5921)
E-ONE INC
4760 Camp Rd (14075-2604)
PHONE..................................716 646-6790
Kevin Nunn, *Regl Sales Mgr*
Gerard Stockmeyer, *Branch Mgr*
EMP: 70
SALES (corp-wide): 1.5B **Privately Held**
SIC: 2511 3537 Wood household furniture; industrial trucks & tractors
HQ: E-One, Inc.
    1601 Sw 37th Ave
    Ocala FL 34474
    352 237-1122

(G-5922)
EATON BROTHERS CORP
3530 Lakeview Rd (14075-6160)
P.O. Box 60 (14075-0060)
PHONE..................................716 649-8250
Fax: 716 649-9466
Ralph D Allen, *President*
Gary Allen, *Exec VP*
Christopher Allen, *Shareholder*
▲ **EMP:** 9
SQ FT: 21,000
SALES (est): 2MM **Privately Held**
WEB: www.eatonbrothers.com
SIC: 3524 3272 Lawn & garden tractors & equipment; tombstones, precast terrazzo or concrete

(G-5923)
EL-DON BATTERY POST INC
4109 Saint Francis Dr (14075-1722)
PHONE..................................716 627-3697
Fax: 716 896-0406
Gary K Logsdon, *Principal*
Cindy Logsdon, *Manager*
EMP: 5
SALES (est): 833.7K **Privately Held**
SIC: 3691 5063 Storage batteries; batteries

(G-5924)
EMCS LLC
4414 Manor Ln (14075-1117)
PHONE..................................716 523-2002
Ed Monacelli, *President*
Rob Haefner, *Vice Pres*
EMP: 8
SALES (est): 933.4K **Privately Held**
SIC: 3572 Computer storage devices

(G-5925)
EVENHOUSE PRINTING
4783 Southwestern Blvd (14075-1926)
PHONE..................................716 649-2666
Fax: 716 640-0266
Robin L Evenhouse, *Partner*
EMP: 7
SALES (est): 550K **Privately Held**
WEB: www.evenhouseprinting.com
SIC: 2759 Commercial printing

(G-5926)
GATEWAY PRTG & GRAPHICS INC
3970 Big Tree Rd (14075-1320)
PHONE..................................716 823-3873
Jeffery Donner, *President*
Eugene Donner, *Corp Secy*
Brian Lattimore, *Production*
Dennis Oddi, *Accounts Exec*
Colleen Cavanaugh, *Sales Staff*
EMP: 22
SQ FT: 20,000
SALES (est): 4.9MM **Privately Held**
WEB: www.gatewayprints.com
SIC: 2752 2791 2789 2761 Commercial printing, offset; typesetting; bookbinding & related work; manifold business forms

(G-5927)
GREAT AMERICAN TOOL CO INC
7223 Boston State Rd (14075-6932)
P.O. Box 600, Getzville (14068-0600)
PHONE..................................716 646-5700
Fax: 716 877-2591
John Anthon, *President*
▲ **EMP:** 6
SALES (est): 1MM **Privately Held**
WEB: www.timberlineknives.com
SIC: 3546 3421 Power-driven handtools; table & food cutlery, including butchers'

(G-5928)
HAWKEYE FOREST PRODUCTS LP (PA)
Also Called: Hawkeye Forest Products
4002 Legion Dr (14075-4508)
PHONE..................................608 534-6156
Jeffrey Meyer, *President*
Andrew Lander, *Credit Mgr*
Karen Long, *Executive*
EMP: 15
SALES (est): 3MM **Privately Held**
SIC: 2421 Sawmills & planing mills, general

(G-5929)
JOBS WEEKLY INC
Also Called: Wny Jobs.com
31 Buffalo St Ste 2 (14075-5000)
PHONE..................................716 648-5627
Fax: 716 648-5658
Thomas Kluckhohn, *President*
Carl Kluckhohn, *Vice Pres*
Steve Kluckhohn, *Treasurer*
Susan O'Connor, *Manager*
Joe Rindfuss, *Admin Sec*
EMP: 11
SALES: 1MM **Privately Held**
WEB: www.wnyjobs.com
SIC: 2711 Newspapers

(G-5930)
K & H INDUSTRIES INC (PA)
160 Elmview Ave (14075-3763)
PHONE..................................716 312-0088
Fax: 716 312-0028
Joseph Pinker Jr, *Ch of Bd*
Karl A Baake, *President*
John Herc, *Vice Pres*
Joe Panker Jr, *Vice Pres*
Tim Cooke, *Purchasing*
EMP: 17 **EST:** 1960
SQ FT: 100,000
SALES (est): 6.4MM **Privately Held**
WEB: www.khindustries.com
SIC: 3641 3643 3599 3089 Lamps, fluorescent, electric; plugs, electric; connectors & terminals for electrical devices; electrical discharge machining (EDM); injection molding of plastics

(G-5931)
K & H INDUSTRIES INC
160 Elmview Ave (14075-3763)
PHONE..................................716 312-0088
Robert KickbusIt, *Sales Dir*
Klaus Baake, *Branch Mgr*
EMP: 20
SALES (corp-wide): 6.4MM **Privately Held**
WEB: www.khindustries.com
SIC: 3089 3641 Injection molding of plastics; lamps, fluorescent, electric

PA: K & H Industries, Inc.
160 Elmview Ave
Hamburg NY 14075
716 312-0088

(G-5932)
KRAGEL CO INC
Also Called: Custom Bags Unlimited
23 Lake St (14075-4940)
P.O. Box 71 (14075-0071)
PHONE 716 648-1344
Fax: 716 648-6833
Jim Bednasz, *President*
EMP: 7
SQ FT: 4,980
SALES (est): 150K **Privately Held**
SIC: 2394 2221 2393 Canvas & related products; liners & covers, fabric: made from purchased materials; nylon broadwoven fabrics; textile bags

(G-5933)
KUSTOM KORNER
Also Called: West Herr Automotive Group
5140 Camp Rd (14075-2704)
PHONE 716 646-0173
Scott Beiler, *President*
Eric Zimmerman, *General Mgr*
Ruby Ocasio, *Marketing Staff*
Mark Boland, *Manager*
EMP: 13
SALES (est): 1.1MM **Privately Held**
SIC: 3465 Body parts, automobile: stamped metal

(G-5934)
NITRO MANUFACTURING LLC
106 Evans St Ste E (14075-6169)
PHONE 716 646-9900
Bill Frascella, *Manager*
EMP: 10
SALES (est): 246.8K **Privately Held**
SIC: 3999 Barber & beauty shop equipment

(G-5935)
ON THE MARK DIGITAL PRINTING &
5758 S Park Ave (14075-3739)
PHONE 716 823-3373
Mark Poydock, *President*
EMP: 5
SALES (est): 626.7K **Privately Held**
SIC: 3993 Signs & advertising specialties

(G-5936)
POTTER LUMBER CO LLC
4002 Legion Dr (14075-4508)
P.O. Box 9001 (14075-9091)
PHONE 814 438-7888
Andrew Lander, *Credit Mgr*
Jeffrey Meyer, *Mng Member*
▼ **EMP:** 100 **EST:** 2013
SALES (est): 7.1MM **Privately Held**
SIC: 2426 Lumber, hardwood dimension

(G-5937)
PRAXAIR INC
5322 Scranton Rd (14075-2935)
PHONE 716 649-1600
Jim Hodgson, *Manager*
EMP: 20
SALES (corp-wide): 10.7B **Publicly Held**
SIC: 2813 Industrial gases
PA: Praxair, Inc.
39 Old Ridgebury Rd
Danbury CT 06810
203 837-2000

(G-5938)
QUEST MANUFACTURING INC
5600 Camp Rd (14075-3706)
PHONE 716 312-8000
Kimberly M Leach, *Principal*
Dennis Crissy, *Sales Staff*
John Kennedy, *Sales Staff*
Matt Sharpless, *Sales Staff*
Gloria Obrien, *Manager*
EMP: 20
SALES (est): 2.8MM **Privately Held**
SIC: 3999 Manufacturing industries

(G-5939)
QUO VADIS EDITIONS INC
120 Elmview Ave (14075-3770)
PHONE 716 648-2602
Oliver Beltrami, *CEO*
Jerome Malavoy, *Ch of Bd*
Richard T Lydo, *General Mgr*
Keith Porter, *Senior VP*
Jean-Pierre Bermond, *Asst Treas*
▲ **EMP:** 34
SQ FT: 45,000
SALES (est): 3.9MM
SALES (corp-wide): 1.3MM **Privately Held**
SIC: 2782 Diaries
HQ: Editions Quo Vadis
Zone Industrielle
Carquefou
240 304-812

(G-5940)
RIEFLER CONCRETE PRODUCTS LLC
5690 Camp Rd (14075-3706)
PHONE 716 649-3260
Michael Sheehan, *President*
Echarles Cotten, *Vice Pres*
David J Lichner, *VP Opers*
Thomas Noonan, *Treasurer*
William C Haas, *VP Sales*
EMP: 170
SQ FT: 6,700
SALES (est): 20.1MM **Privately Held**
SIC: 3273 5999 3271 3272 Ready-mixed concrete; concrete products, pre-cast; blocks, concrete or cinder: standard; concrete products

(G-5941)
ROLY DOOR SALES INC
5659 Herman Hill Rd (14075-6909)
PHONE 716 877-1515
Frank Sowa, *President*
EMP: 5 **EST:** 1952
SALES (est): 340.3K **Privately Held**
SIC: 3442 Garage doors, overhead: metal

(G-5942)
SINCLAIR TECHNOLOGIES INC (DH)
5811 S Park Ave 3 (14075-3738)
PHONE 716 874-3682
Valerie Sinclair, *Ch of Bd*
David Ralston, *President*
David Grinstead, *Vice Pres*
David Savel, *CFO*
Andrea Sinclair, *Treasurer*
EMP: 25 **EST:** 1960
SQ FT: 36,000
SALES (est): 1.9MM
SALES (corp-wide): 36.1MM **Privately Held**
WEB: www.sinctech.com
SIC: 3663 5065 3674 3643 Antennas, transmitting & communications; communication equipment; amateur radio communications equipment; semiconductors & related devices; current-carrying wiring devices; switchgear & switchboard apparatus; nonferrous wiredrawing & insulating
HQ: Sinclair Technologies Inc
85 Mary St
Aurora ON L4G 6
905 727-0165

(G-5943)
SOLOWAVE DESIGN CORP
4625 Clark St (14075-3903)
PHONE 716 646-3103
Richard Boyer, *CEO*
Frederic Rieber, *Vice Pres*
Mat Wolf, *CFO*
EMP: 3
SQ FT: 500
SALES: 62.5MM
SALES (corp-wide): 9.6MM **Privately Held**
SIC: 3944 Structural toy sets
HQ: Solowave Design Inc
103 Bauer Pl Suite 5
Waterloo ON N2L 6
519 323-3833

(G-5944)
STAUB MACHINE COMPANY INC
Also Called: Staub Square
206 Lake St (14075-4471)
PHONE 716 649-4211
Anthony J Staub, *Ch of Bd*
Tony Staub, *President*
Jim Staub, *Opers Mgr*
Erik Bauerlein, *Marketing Mgr*
Jennifer Staub, *Manager*
EMP: 20
SQ FT: 1,500
SALES (est): 4.3MM **Privately Held**
WEB: www.staubmachine.com
SIC: 3599 Machine shop, jobbing & repair

(G-5945)
WILLIAM R SHOEMAKER INC
399 Pleasant Ave (14075-4719)
PHONE 716 649-0511
Fax: 716 649-2750
William R Shoemaker, *President*
EMP: 5
SQ FT: 1,800
SALES (est): 470K **Privately Held**
SIC: 3569 Firefighting apparatus

(G-5946)
WORLDWIDE PROTECTIVE PDTS LLC
4255 Mckinley Pkwy (14075-1005)
PHONE 877 678-4568
Fax: 716 332-9280
Matt Stucke, *Managing Prtnr*
Fred Driver, *General Mgr*
Al Williams, *Business Mgr*
Albert Bowman, *Project Dir*
Alex Byrd, *Regl Sales Mgr*
▲ **EMP:** 200
SALES (est): 67.5MM **Privately Held**
WEB: www.wwprotective.com
SIC: 3151 Gloves, leather: work

Hamilton
Madison County

(G-5947)
COSSITT CONCRETE PRODUCTS INC
6543 Middleport Rd (13346-2275)
P.O. Box 379 (13346-0379)
PHONE 315 824-2700
Fax: 315 824-2823
Lance Kenyon, *President*
Lance Cenyon, *Vice Pres*
Jeniffer Tfardakas, *Accounts Mgr*
EMP: 10 **EST:** 1947
SQ FT: 1,500
SALES (est): 2MM **Privately Held**
SIC: 3271 3272 3273 5211 Concrete block & brick; architectural concrete: block, split, fluted, screen, etc.; concrete stuctural support & building material; ready-mixed concrete; lumber & other building materials

(G-5948)
JAMES MORRIS
Also Called: Madison Manufacturing
6697 Airport Rd (13346-2118)
PHONE 315 824-8519
James Morris, *Owner*
Bob Britton, *General Mgr*
EMP: 30
SQ FT: 6,000
SALES (est): 2.8MM **Privately Held**
WEB: www.jamesmorris.net
SIC: 3559 Electronic component making machinery

(G-5949)
PARRYS
100 Utica St (13346-2009)
PHONE 315 824-0002
Fax: 315 824-0086
Bill Parry, *Partner*
Rebecca Parry, *Partner*
EMP: 11
SQ FT: 9,000
SALES (est): 1.8MM **Privately Held**
WEB: www.morrisvilleny.com
SIC: 3663 7378 5731 Cellular radio telephone; computer maintenance & repair; consumer electronic equipment

Hamlin
Monroe County

(G-5950)
HF TECHNOLOGIES LLC
810 Martin Rd (14464-9743)
PHONE 585 254-5030
David Fletcher,
Angela Fletcher,
EMP: 20 **EST:** 2001
SQ FT: 25,000
SALES (est): 2.3MM **Privately Held**
WEB: www.hftechnologies.com
SIC: 3577 3955 Printers, computer; print cartridges for laser & other computer printers

(G-5951)
SPEER EQUIPMENT INC
832 Moscow Rd (14464-9711)
P.O. Box 40, Brockport (14420-0040)
PHONE 585 964-2700
Fax: 585 964-7685
EMP: 5
SQ FT: 10,000
SALES (est): 2MM **Privately Held**
SIC: 3625 Electric controls & control accessories, industrial

Hammond
St. Lawrence County

(G-5952)
YESTERYEARS VINTAGE DOORS LLC
66 S Main St (13646-3201)
PHONE 315 324-5250
Fax: 315 324-5250
Howard Demick,
EMP: 9
SQ FT: 5,760
SALES (est): 930K **Privately Held**
WEB: www.vintagedoors.com
SIC: 2431 Doors, wood

Hammondsport
Steuben County

(G-5953)
ATLAS METAL INDUSTRIES INC
17 Wheeler Ave (14840-9566)
PHONE 607 776-2048
EMP: 1 **EST:** 2012
SALES (est): 3.4MM
SALES (corp-wide): 118.8MM **Privately Held**
SIC: 3999 Manufacturing industries
PA: Mercury Aircraft Inc.
8126 County Route 88
Hammondsport NY 14840
607 569-4200

(G-5954)
CUSTOM MANUFACTURING INC
10034 E Lake Rd (14840-7015)
PHONE 607 569-2738
Carmen J Waters, *President*
Michael Waters, *Vice Pres*
▲ **EMP:** 5
SALES: 700K **Privately Held**
WEB: www.archivalboxes.com
SIC: 2655 Containers, liquid tight fiber: from purchased material

(G-5955)
HEARTWOOD SPECIALTIES INC
10249 Gibson Rd (14840-9431)
PHONE 607 654-0102
Bruce G Bozman, *President*
EMP: 7
SQ FT: 5,000
SALES (est): 680K **Privately Held**
SIC: 2521 2541 Wood office furniture; wood partitions & fixtures

Hammondsport - Steuben County (G-5956)

GEOGRAPHIC SECTION

(G-5956)
HERON HILL VINEYARDS INC (PA)
Also Called: Heron Hill Winery
9301 County Route 76 (14840-9685)
PHONE..................607 868-4241
Fax: 607 868-3435
John Engle Jr, *CEO*
Chuck Oyler, *General Mgr*
Paul Wilson, *Opers Mgr*
Christy Dann, *CFO*
Robert Wojnar, *Mktg Dir*
EMP: 36
SQ FT: 8,640
SALES (est): 2.6MM Privately Held
WEB: www.heronhill.com
SIC: 2084 5812 0172 Wines; eating places; grapes

(G-5957)
KEUKA BREWING CO LLC
8572 Briglin Rd (14840-9633)
PHONE..................607 868-4648
Mark Goodwin, *Manager*
EMP: 7
SALES (est): 616.4K Privately Held
SIC: 2082 Malt beverages

(G-5958)
KONSTANTIN D FRANK& SONS VINI
Also Called: Vinifera Wine Cellard
9749 Middle Rd (14840-9612)
PHONE..................607 868-4884
Fax: 607 868-4888
Fred Frank, *President*
Susan Eisenhart, *Marketing Staff*
Karen Smolos, *Manager*
Hilda Volz, *Admin Sec*
▲ EMP: 30
SALES (est): 3.9MM Privately Held
WEB: www.drfrankwines.com
SIC: 2084 0172 Wines; grapes

Hampton
Washington County

(G-5959)
HADEKA STONE CORP (PA)
115 Staso Ln (12837-2214)
P.O. Box 108 (12837-0108)
PHONE..................518 282-9605
Eileen Hadeka, *President*
Raymond Hadeka, *Vice Pres*
William Hadeka, *Treasurer*
Gerald Hadeka, *Admin Sec*
EMP: 8 EST: 1946
SQ FT: 640
SALES (est): 1.5MM Privately Held
WEB: www.hadekastone.com
SIC: 1411 Slate, dimension-quarrying

Hampton Bays
Suffolk County

(G-5960)
BROCK AWNINGS LTD
211 E Montauk Hwy Ste 1 (11946-2035)
PHONE..................631 765-5200
Fax: 631 728-0134
Earl Brock, *President*
EMP: 10 EST: 1975
SQ FT: 8,000
SALES: 693.1K Privately Held
WEB: www.brockawnings.com
SIC: 2394 5999 5199 5091 Canvas & related products; canvas products; canvas products; boat accessories & parts

(G-5961)
NEW YORK MARINE ELEC INC
124 Springville Rd Ste 1 (11946-3043)
P.O. Box 2131, Aquebogue (11931-2131)
PHONE..................631 734-6050
Sean York, *Ch of Bd*
John Lamendola, *Principal*
Danette Carroll, *Office Mgr*
Candice York, *Executive Asst*
EMP: 9
SALES (est): 1MM Privately Held
SIC: 3845 Electromedical equipment

Hancock
Delaware County

(G-5962)
COBLESKILL STONE PRODUCTS INC
Also Called: Hancock Quarry/Asphalt
1565 Green Flats Rd (13783)
PHONE..................607 637-4271
Fax: 607 637-4470
Ray Althiser, *Branch Mgr*
EMP: 10
SALES (corp-wide): 103.9MM Privately Held
WEB: www.cobleskillstone.com
SIC: 1422 2951 Crushed & broken limestone; asphalt & asphaltic paving mixtures (not from refineries)
PA: Cobleskill Stone Products, Inc.
112 Rock Rd
Cobleskill NY 12043
518 234-0221

(G-5963)
COMPREHENSIVE DENTAL TECH
Rr 1 Box 69 (13783)
PHONE..................607 467-4456
Marie Benjamin, *President*
Mike Archer, *Vice Pres*
EMP: 4
SQ FT: 2,700
SALES (est): 1.3MM Privately Held
SIC: 7372 8021 Prepackaged software; offices & clinics of dentists

(G-5964)
K TOOLING LLC
396 E Front St (13783-1169)
PHONE..................607 637-3781
George Willis, *Sales Associate*
Perry Kuehn, *Mng Member*
EMP: 10
SQ FT: 10,000
SALES (est): 1.2MM Privately Held
WEB: www.ktooling.com
SIC: 3469 Machine parts, stamped or pressed metal

(G-5965)
MALLERY LUMBER LLC
158 Labarre St (13783)
Rural Route 4060 Gaskill Rd, Owego (13827)
PHONE..................607 637-2236
Les Wagner, *President*
Lori Moore, *Controller*
EMP: 7
SQ FT: 2,000
SALES (est): 43K Privately Held
SIC: 2421 Kiln drying of lumber

(G-5966)
PETERS LLC
5259 Peas Eddy Rd (13783-4237)
PHONE..................607 637-5470
Jennie Moshure, *Buyer*
Van Peters,
Beverly Peters,
EMP: 5
SALES (est): 360K Privately Held
SIC: 2411 Logging

(G-5967)
RUSSELL BASS
Also Called: Russell Bass & Son Lumber
59 Saw Mill Rd (13783)
P.O. Box 718 (13783-0718)
PHONE..................607 637-5253
Russell Bass, *Partner*
EMP: 15
SALES (est): 1.3MM Privately Held
SIC: 2421 2411 Sawmills & planing mills, general; logging

(G-5968)
VAN CPETERS LOGGING INC
4480 Peas Eddy Rd (13783-4232)
PHONE..................607 637-3574
Van Peters, *Principal*
EMP: 6
SALES (est): 573K Privately Held
SIC: 2411 Logging

Hannibal
Oswego County

(G-5969)
ACRO-FAB LTD
55 Rochester St (13074-3139)
P.O. Box 184 (13074-0184)
PHONE..................315 564-6688
Fax: 315 564-5599
Mike Combes, *Ch of Bd*
Martin Victory, *Corp Secy*
Darrell Baker, *Vice Pres*
EMP: 23
SQ FT: 12,000
SALES (est): 3.9MM Privately Held
WEB: www.acro-fab.com
SIC: 7692 3444 3599 Welding repair; sheet metalwork; machine shop, jobbing & repair

Harriman
Orange County

(G-5970)
AMSCAN INC
Kookaburra
2 Commerce Dr S (10926-3101)
PHONE..................845 782-0490
Fax: 845 782-7442
Walter Thompson, *Manager*
EMP: 60
SALES (corp-wide): 2.2B Publicly Held
SIC: 2656 Plates, paper: made from purchased material
HQ: Amscan Inc.
80 Grasslands Rd Ste 3
Elmsford NY 10523
914 345-2020

(G-5971)
EXQUIS LLC
16 Berwynn Rd (10926-3815)
PHONE..................845 537-5380
Kalidas Kale, *Mng Member*
EMP: 10
SALES (est): 730K Privately Held
SIC: 2844 5122 5999 7389 Toilet preparations; cosmetics; cosmetics;

(G-5972)
HOME MAIDE INC
1 Short St (10926-3311)
PHONE..................845 837-1700
Edward Fennessy, *President*
EMP: 14
SALES (est): 2.8MM Privately Held
SIC: 3556 Ovens, bakery

(G-5973)
PREMIER INK SYSTEMS INC
2 Commerce Dr S (10926-3101)
PHONE..................845 782-5802
Fax: 845 782-5041
EMP: 48
SALES (corp-wide): 14.3MM Privately Held
SIC: 2759 Commercial printing
PA: Premier Ink Systems, Inc.
10420 N State St
Harrison OH 45030
513 367-4700

(G-5974)
SIMPLEXGRINNELL LP
4 Commerce Dr S Ste 3 (10926-3101)
PHONE..................845 774-4120
Fax: 845 566-8608
Steve Walsh, *Manager*
Melissa Degiglio, *Manager*
EMP: 5 Privately Held
WEB: www.simplexgrinnell.com
SIC: 3669 5087 1731 1711 Emergency alarms; firefighting equipment; fire detection & burglar alarm systems specialization; fire sprinkler system installation
HQ: Simplexgrinnell Lp
4700 Exchange Ct
Boca Raton FL 33431
561 988-7200

(G-5975)
TAKASAGO INTL CORP USA
114 Commerce Dr S (10926-3101)
PHONE..................845 751-0799
Dana Drevitson, *Branch Mgr*
EMP: 100
SALES (corp-wide): 1.2B Privately Held
SIC: 2844 Concentrates, perfume
HQ: Takasago International Corporation (U.S.A)
4 Volvo Dr
Rockleigh NJ 07647
201 767-9001

Harris
Sullivan County

(G-5976)
JUS-SAR FUEL INC
Also Called: Black Bear Fuels Oil
884 Old Route 17 (12742-5016)
P.O. Box 289 (12742-0289)
PHONE..................845 791-8900
Darren Mapes, *President*
Tina Mapes, *Admin Sec*
EMP: 5
SALES (est): 788K Privately Held
SIC: 3433 Heaters, swimming pool: oil or gas

Harrison
Westchester County

(G-5977)
CASTLE FUELS CORPORATION
440 Mamaroneck Ave (10528-2418)
PHONE..................914 381-6600
Michael Romita, *CEO*
EMP: 39
SALES (est): 4.6MM Privately Held
SIC: 2869 Fuels

(G-5978)
CEMAC FOODS CORP
8 Cayuga Trl (10528-1820)
PHONE..................914 835-0526
Thomas May, *President*
Helen Nash May, *Corp Secy*
Mel Persily, *Vice Pres*
Mildred Nash, *CFO*
EMP: 16
SQ FT: 3,000
SALES (est): 1.7MM Privately Held
WEB: www.cemacfoods.com
SIC: 2022 Natural cheese; imitation cheese

(G-5979)
CHEMLUBE INTERNATIONAL LLC (PA)
500 Mmaroneck Ave Ste 306 (10528)
PHONE..................914 381-5800
Fax: 914 381-8988
Robert Nobel, *CEO*
Rob Kress, *Vice Pres*
Fernando Walters, *Manager*
EMP: 13 EST: 2012
SQ FT: 5,300
SALES (est): 6.4MM Privately Held
SIC: 2992 5172 5169 Lubricating oils & greases; lubricating oils & greases; chemicals & allied products

(G-5980)
CHEMLUBE MARKETING INC
500 Mmaroneck Ave Ste 308 (10528)
PHONE..................914 381-5800
Robert Nobel, *Ch of Bd*
Beverly Walter, *Finance Mgr*
◆ EMP: 13
SQ FT: 5,300
SALES (est): 5.1MM Privately Held
WEB: www.sopetra.com
SIC: 2992 5172 5169 Lubricating oils & greases; lubricating oils & greases; chemicals & allied products

▲ = Import ▼=Export
◆ =Import/Export

GEOGRAPHIC SECTION

(G-5981)
COUNTY WASTE MANAGEMENT INC
565 Harrison Ave (10528-1431)
P.O. Box 548 (10528-0548)
PHONE 914 592-5007
Ralph Mancini, *President*
EMP: 5
SQ FT: 2,500
SALES (est): 819.1K Privately Held
SIC: 2842 Sanitation preparations

(G-5982)
DAL-TILE CORPORATION
31 Oakland Ave (10528-3709)
PHONE 914 835-1801
Brian Scocio, *Manager*
EMP: 7
SALES (corp-wide): 8B Publicly Held
WEB: www.mohawk.com
SIC: 3253 5032 Ceramic wall & floor tile; ceramic wall & floor tile
HQ: Dal-Tile Corporation
    7834 C F Hawn Fwy
    Dallas TX 75217
    214 398-1411

(G-5983)
DATA TRANSMISSION ESSENTIALS
83 Calvert St Ste 3 (10528-3243)
PHONE 516 378-8820
Theodore A Granata, *President*
EMP: 12 EST: 1979
SQ FT: 13,000
SALES (est): 970K Privately Held
SIC: 3661 5065 Telephone & telegraph apparatus; telephone & telegraphic equipment

(G-5984)
GGP PUBLISHING INC
105 Calvert St Ste 201 (10528-3138)
PHONE 914 834-8896
Generosa Gina Protano, *President*
EMP: 10
SALES: 1MM Privately Held
WEB: www.ggppublishing.com
SIC: 2731 Book publishing

(G-5985)
GLOBEOP FINANCIAL SERVICES LLC (DH)
1 South Rd (10528-3309)
PHONE 914 670-3600
Fax: 914 670-3601
William Stone, *CEO*
Hans Hufschmid, *Principal*
Vernon Barback, *COO*
Peter Robillard, *Opers Mgr*
Simon Behan, *Sls & Mktg Exec*
EMP: 148
SQ FT: 24,000
SALES (est): 59.1MM
SALES (corp-wide): 1B Publicly Held
WEB: www.globeop.com
SIC: 7372 Prepackaged software
HQ: Ss&C Technologies, Inc.
    80 Lamberton Rd
    Windsor CT 06095
    860 298-4500

(G-5986)
GRACE ASSOCIATES INC
470 West St (10528-2510)
PHONE 718 767-9000
Anthony Grace, *President*
Richard Grace, *Vice Pres*
Steven Marano, *Plant Mgr*
William Urig, *Manager*
Sweeney Aleli, *Director*
EMP: 5
SQ FT: 1,500
SALES (est): 639.3K Privately Held
SIC: 3271 3272 2951 Concrete block & brick; concrete products; asphalt paving mixtures & blocks

(G-5987)
LIFE TIME FITNESS INC
1 Westchester Park Dr (10528)
PHONE 914 290-5100
EMP: 9

SALES (corp-wide): 773.5MM Privately Held
SIC: 2711 Newspapers
HQ: Life Time Fitness, Inc.
    2902 Corporate Pl
    Chanhassen MN 55317
    952 229-7543

(G-5988)
PACE POLYETHYLENE MFG CO INC (PA)
46 Calvert St (10528-3238)
P.O. Box 385 (10528-0385)
PHONE 914 381-3000
Fax: 914 381-3062
Stan Nathanson, *President*
Marc Lawrence, *Vice Pres*
EMP: 20
SQ FT: 1,500
SALES (est): 5.9MM Privately Held
SIC: 3081 Unsupported plastics film & sheet; polyethylene film

(G-5989)
PROFESSIONAL MEDICAL DEVICES
10 Century Trl (10528-1702)
PHONE 914 835-0614
Mark Waldman, *President*
EMP: 10
SALES: 500K Privately Held
SIC: 3841 Surgical & medical instruments

(G-5990)
SOAVEDRA MASONRY INC
77 Batavia Pl (10528-2925)
PHONE 347 695-5254
Gaodeceo Soavedra, *President*
EMP: 6
SALES: 200K Privately Held
SIC: 2679 Wall tile, enameled masonite: made from purchased material

(G-5991)
SPRINGFIELD OIL SERVICES INC (PA)
550 Mmaroneck Ave Ste 503 (10528)
PHONE 914 315-6812
Bentley Blum, *President*
Mary Irwin, *Vice Pres*
▲ EMP: 10
SQ FT: 1,000
SALES (est): 1.8MM Privately Held
SIC: 1382 Oil & gas exploration services

(G-5992)
TREO BRANDS LLC
106 Calvert St (10528-3131)
PHONE 914 341-1850
Robert Golten, *CEO*
Brian O'Byrne, *President*
EMP: 8
SQ FT: 3,800
SALES (est): 235.3K Privately Held
SIC: 2086 Carbonated beverages, nonalcoholic: bottled & canned

(G-5993)
UNIVERSAL REMOTE CONTROL INC (PA)
500 Mmaroneck Ave Ste 502 (10528)
PHONE 914 630-4343
Chang Park, *Chairman*
Ed Thibault, *Vice Pres*
Glenn Gentilin, *Natl Sales Mgr*
Lars Granoe, *VP Sales*
Debra Sharker, *Sales Dir*
▲ EMP: 57
SQ FT: 11,000
SALES (est): 12.8MM Privately Held
WEB: www.universalremote.com
SIC: 3678 Electronic connectors

(G-5994)
VALUE SPRING TECHNOLOGY INC
521 Harrison Ave (10528-1431)
PHONE 917 705-4658
William Doyle, *President*
EMP: 15
SALES (est): 305.2K Privately Held
SIC: 7372 Prepackaged software

Harrisville
Lewis County

(G-5995)
CIVES CORPORATION
Also Called: Viking-Cives
14331 Mill St (13648-3331)
PHONE 315 543-2321
Fax: 315 543-2366
Larry Jeroscko, *General Mgr*
Steve Rider, *General Mgr*
Steve Chartrand, *Prdtn Mgr*
Aj Macdonald, *Prdtn Mgr*
John Miller, *Safety Mgr*
EMP: 75
SQ FT: 46,000
SALES (corp-wide): 453.1MM Privately Held
WEB: www.cives.com
SIC: 3531 Snow plow attachments
PA: Cives Corporation
    3700 Mansell Rd Ste 500
    Alpharetta GA 30022
    770 993-4424

Hartford
Washington County

(G-5996)
RICHARD STEWART
4495 State Rte 149 (12838)
P.O. Box 18 (12838-0018)
PHONE 518 632-5363
Richard Stewart, *Owner*
Mary Stewart, *Owner*
EMP: 5
SALES (est): 480K Privately Held
SIC: 3523 Dairy equipment (farm)

Hartsdale
Westchester County

(G-5997)
APOGEE POWER USA INC
7 Verne Pl (10530-1026)
PHONE 202 746-2890
Michael Harper, *CEO*
John Hollins, *President*
Dr Kc Tsai, *Mfg Mgr*
EMP: 10
SALES (est): 11K Privately Held
SIC: 3825 3621 Electrical energy measuring equipment; storage battery chargers, motor & engine generator type

(G-5998)
FRISCH PLASTICS CORP
7 Joyce Rd (10530-2929)
PHONE 973 685-5936
Ruth Lefkowitz, *President*
Irwin Lefkowitz, *Vice Pres*
Eve Lefkowitz, *Manager*
EMP: 20
SALES (est): 500K Privately Held
WEB: www.frischplastics.com
SIC: 3089 Novelties, plastic

(G-5999)
RICHARD EDELSON
Also Called: Pinewood Marketing
80 Pinewood Rd (10530-1672)
PHONE 914 428-7573
Richard Edelson, *Owner*
EMP: 1
SALES: 2MM Privately Held
SIC: 2252 Hosiery

(G-6000)
SIGN HERE ENTERPRISES LLC
Also Called: Sign-A-Rama
28 N Central Ave Rear (10530-2430)
PHONE 914 328-3111
Fax: 914 682-8610
David Reichenberg,
EMP: 5
SALES (est): 350K Privately Held
SIC: 3993 Signs & advertising specialties

(G-6001)
TAPEMAKER SUPPLY COMPANY LLC
22 Sherbrooke Rd (10530-2938)
PHONE 914 693-3407
Ronald Huppert, *Mng Member*
EMP: 7
SALES (est): 453.1K Privately Held
WEB: www.tapemakersupply.com
SIC: 2759 Commercial printing

Hastings On Hudson
Westchester County

(G-6002)
ALTERNATIVE TECHNOLOGY CORP
Also Called: Marketfax Information Services
1 North St Ste 1 (10706-1542)
P.O. Box 357 (10706-0357)
PHONE 914 478-5900
Fax: 914 478-5908
Tom Kadala, *CEO*
EMP: 5
SQ FT: 3,000
SALES: 1.2MM Privately Held
WEB: www.marketfax.com
SIC: 3661 5065 4822 7375 Facsimile equipment; facsimile equipment; facsimile transmission services; information retrieval services

(G-6003)
FLOGIC INC
Also Called: F Logic
25 Chestnut Dr (10706-1901)
PHONE 914 478-1352
Julius Funaro, *President*
Michael Piscatelli, *Vice Pres*
Michael Piscitelli, *Opers Mgr*
Elle Lang, *Sales Staff*
Angela Vargas, *Office Mgr*
EMP: 13
SALES (est): 1.3MM Privately Held
WEB: www.flinc.com
SIC: 7372 Prepackaged software

(G-6004)
JAMES RICHARD SPECIALTY CHEM
24 Ridge St (10706-2702)
PHONE 914 478-7500
Katrine Barth, *President*
EMP: 6
SQ FT: 1,300
SALES: 3MM Privately Held
WEB: www.rjsconline.com
SIC: 2842 Specialty cleaning, polishes & sanitation goods

(G-6005)
LORENA CANALS USA INC
104 Burnside Dr (10706-3013)
PHONE 844 567-3622
Delia Elbaum, *General Mgr*
EMP: 3
SQ FT: 3,000
SALES: 1MM
SALES (corp-wide): 2.7MM Privately Held
SIC: 2273 5023 Carpets & rugs; rugs
PA: Lorena Canals Sl.
    Calle Alexandre Goicoechea, 6 - Loc 8
    Sant Just Desvern 08960

Hauppauge
Suffolk County

(G-6006)
A & Z PHARMACEUTICAL INC
350 Wireless Blvd (11788-3947)
PHONE 631 952-3802
Frank Berstler, *Vice Pres*
EMP: 90 Privately Held
SIC: 2834 8734 Pills, pharmaceutical; testing laboratories
PA: A & Z Pharmaceutical Inc.
    180 Oser Ave
    Hauppauge NY 11788

Hauppauge - Suffolk County (G-6007)

(G-6007)
A & Z PHARMACEUTICAL INC (PA)
180 Oser Ave (11788-3736)
PHONE 631 952-3800
Fax: 631 952-3900
Emma Li, *CEO*
Glenn Wilson, *Project Mgr*
Marian Vija, *Research*
Xian Chen, *Engineer*
Tony Lin, *Engineer*
◆ **EMP:** 102
SQ FT: 73,000
SALES: 60MM **Privately Held**
SIC: 2834 Pharmaceutical preparations

(G-6008)
AD NOTAM LLC
135 Ricefield Ln (11788-2046)
PHONE 631 951-2020
Nurdan Citamak, *Treasurer*
Isaac Fattal, *Mng Member*
▲ **EMP:** 15
SALES (est): 1.8MM **Privately Held**
SIC: 3231 5023 Mirrored glass; mirrors & pictures, framed & unframed

(G-6009)
ADVANCED BACK TECHNOLOGIES
89 Ste F Cabot Ct (11788)
PHONE 631 231-0076
David F Cuccia, *President*
Mohamed Mostafa, *Marketing Staff*
EMP: 5 **EST:** 1997
SALES (est): 669.5K **Privately Held**
SIC: 3069 Orthopedic sundries, molded rubber

(G-6010)
ADVANCED PLSTIC FBRCTIONS CORP
Also Called: Apf Marine Co
99 Marcus Blvd (11788-3712)
PHONE 631 231-4466
Christopher Clark, *President*
Jeffrey Lingner, *Vice Pres*
EMP: 5
SQ FT: 7,720
SALES (est): 845.6K **Privately Held**
WEB: www.adplasfab.com
SIC: 3086 4493 Plastics foam products; marinas

(G-6011)
AEROFLEX PLAINVIEW INC
Aeroflex Motion Control Div
350 Kennedy Dr (11788-4014)
PHONE 631 231-9100
Fax: 631 231-8375
Jim Smith, *Division Mgr*
Bill Brown, *Vice Pres*
Richard Casper, *Vice Pres*
Boz Sharif, *Chief Engr*
Harsad Shah, *Engineer*
EMP: 120
SALES (corp-wide): 3.1B **Privately Held**
SIC: 3679 3621 3674 3577 Electronic circuits; motors & generators; semiconductors & related devices; computer peripheral equipment
HQ: Aeroflex Plainview, Inc.
35 S Service Rd
Plainview NY 11803
516 694-6700

(G-6012)
AIPING PHARMACEUTICAL INC
350w Wireless Blvd (11788-3959)
PHONE 631 952-3802
Jing Zou, *Principal*
Frank Berstler, *Vice Pres*
EMP: 5 **EST:** 2015
SALES (est): 371.4K **Privately Held**
SIC: 2834 2899 Tablets, pharmaceutical; gelatin: edible, technical, photographic or pharmaceutical

(G-6013)
AIR INDUSTRIES GROUP (PA)
360 Motor Pkwy Ste 100 (11788-5182)
PHONE 631 881-4920
Fax: 631 968-5377
Michael N Taglich, *Ch of Bd*
Daniel R Godin, *President*
Gary Settoducato, *President*
Marianne Giglio,
EMP: 63
SALES: 80.4MM **Publicly Held**
SIC: 3728 Aircraft body assemblies & parts; aircraft landing assemblies & brakes; aircraft assemblies, subassemblies & parts

(G-6014)
ALADDIN PACKAGING LLC
115 Engineers Rd (11788-4005)
PHONE 631 273-4747
Bill Dowd, *Plant Mgr*
Moshe Wortzberger, *Sales Associate*
Abraham Mandell, *Mng Member*
Joel Endzweig,
▲ **EMP:** 60
SQ FT: 40,000
SALES (est): 18MM **Privately Held**
SIC: 2673 Cellophane bags, unprinted: made from purchased materials

(G-6015)
ALLCRAFT FABRICATORS INC
150 Wireless Blvd (11788-3955)
PHONE 631 951-4100
Fax: 631 951-4040
Douglas Donaldson, *President*
Darren J Winter, *Exec VP*
Raymond Melendez, *Project Mgr*
Renier Schepers, *Project Mgr*
Mike Donovan, *Facilities Mgr*
EMP: 75 **EST:** 1964
SALES (est): 12.7MM **Privately Held**
SIC: 2522 Office furniture, except wood

(G-6016)
ALLEN MACHINE PRODUCTS INC
120 Ricefield Ln Ste 100 (11788-2033)
PHONE 631 630-8800
Fax: 631 630-8801
Peter Allen, *Ch of Bd*
Richard Pettenato, *Vice Pres*
Robert Renz, *Vice Pres*
Una Scheriff, *Vice Pres*
Chris Bonadonna, *Mfg Dir*
▲ **EMP:** 50
SQ FT: 30,000
SALES (est): 5.9MM **Privately Held**
WEB: www.allenmachine.com
SIC: 3469 3444 Machine parts, stamped or pressed metal; sheet metalwork

(G-6017)
ALPHAMED BOTTLES INC
360 Oser Ave (11788-3608)
PHONE 631 275-5042
Subhakar Viyala, *President*
Pavan Vemula, *Opers Mgr*
▲ **EMP:** 17
SALES: 4MM **Privately Held**
SIC: 3085 Plastics bottles

(G-6018)
ALUFOIL PRODUCTS CO INC
135 Oser Ave Ste 3 (11788-3722)
PHONE 631 231-4141
Fax: 631 231-1435
Howard Lent, *Ch of Bd*
Elliot Lent, *Vice Pres*
Cornelius Nagel, *Vice Pres*
Duke Simms, *Vice Pres*
Estelle Lent, *Shareholder*
◆ **EMP:** 18 **EST:** 1945
SQ FT: 45,000
SALES: 4MM **Privately Held**
WEB: www.alufoil.com
SIC: 3497 3353 Foil, laminated to paper or other materials; foil, aluminum

(G-6019)
AMERICAN ACCESS CARE LLC
32 Central Ave (11788-4734)
PHONE 631 582-9729
Thea Hemback, *Manager*
Phea Hemback, *Manager*
EMP: 11
SALES (corp-wide): 16.6B **Privately Held**
WEB: www.americanaccesscare.com
SIC: 3844 X-ray apparatus & tubes
HQ: American Access Care, Llc
182 Industrial Rd
Glen Rock PA 17327
717 235-0181

(G-6020)
AMERICAN CHIMNEY SUPPLIES INC
129 Oser Ave Ste B (11788-3813)
PHONE 631 434-2020
Fax: 631 434-2010
Chris Arbucci, *President*
▲ **EMP:** 6 **EST:** 1993
SQ FT: 21,000
SALES (est): 910.5K **Privately Held**
SIC: 3312 3272 3259 Stainless steel; chimney caps, concrete; clay chimney products

(G-6021)
AMERICAN DIAGNOSTIC CORP
Also Called: A D C
55 Commerce Dr (11788-3931)
PHONE 631 273-6155
Fax: 631 273-9659
Marc Blitstein, *President*
Neal Weingart, *Vice Pres*
Thelma Valle, *Sales Staff*
Charles McRae, *Manager*
Mike Falco, *Director*
◆ **EMP:** 81
SALES (est): 15.8MM **Privately Held**
WEB: www.adctoday.com
SIC: 3841 Blood pressure apparatus; stethoscopes & stethographs

(G-6022)
AMERICAN INTRMDAL CONT MFG LLC
Also Called: Aicm
150 Motor Pkwy Ste 401 (11788-5108)
PHONE 631 774-6790
Pat Marron, *President*
EMP: 8
SQ FT: 200
SALES (est): 807.7K **Privately Held**
SIC: 2655 Fiber shipping & mailing containers

(G-6023)
ARC SYSTEMS INC
2090 Joshuas Path (11788-4764)
PHONE 631 582-8020
Fax: 631 582-8038
Robert Miller, *President*
Kathleen Mooney, *General Mgr*
Clifford Miller, *Treasurer*
▲ **EMP:** 33 **EST:** 1967
SQ FT: 12,000
SALES (est): 6.5MM **Privately Held**
WEB: www.arcsystemsinc.com
SIC: 3621 3694 3724 Motors & generators; electric motor & generator parts; battery charging alternators & generators; aircraft engines & engine parts

(G-6024)
ARKAY PACKAGING CORPORATION (PA)
100 Marcus Blvd Ste 2 (11788-3749)
PHONE 631 273-2000
Fax: 631 273-2478
Mitchell Kaneff, *Chairman*
Craig Bradley, *Plant Mgr*
Brian Hopkins, *Plant Mgr*
Richard Legler, *Plant Mgr*
Bob Hodgdon, *QC Mgr*
▲ **EMP:** 40
SQ FT: 5,000
SALES (est): 44.2MM **Privately Held**
WEB: www.arkay.com
SIC: 2657 Folding paperboard boxes

(G-6025)
ARTEMIS INC
36 Central Ave (11788-4734)
PHONE 631 232-2424
Yuly Margulis, *CEO*
Jeffrey Dunn, *COO*
Alex Margulis, *Vice Pres*
William Roe, *Design Engr*
Joseph Campagna, *Info Tech Mgr*
▲ **EMP:** 7
SQ FT: 9,000
SALES (est): 1.4MM **Privately Held**
WEB: www.artemis.com
SIC: 3674 3812 Integrated circuits, semiconductor networks, etc.; radar systems & equipment

(G-6026)
ARTISTIC PRODUCTS LLC
125 Commerce Dr (11788-3932)
PHONE 631 435-0200
Richard Leifer, *CEO*
Bradley Brighton, *President*
Norma Friedman, *Accountant*
▲ **EMP:** 45
SQ FT: 50,000
SALES (est): 4.7MM **Privately Held**
WEB: www.artistic-products.com
SIC: 2521 5044 Wood office furniture; office equipment

(G-6027)
ATLANTIC ESSENTIAL PDTS INC
7 Oser Ave Ste 1 (11788-3811)
PHONE 631 434-8333
Fax: 631 434-8222
Maxim G Uvarov, *Ch of Bd*
Pailla Rebby, *Vice Pres*
Selven Sam, *Vice Pres*
EMP: 57
SQ FT: 22,000
SALES (est): 10.3MM **Privately Held**
WEB: www.atlanticep.com
SIC: 2834 7389 Pharmaceutical preparations; packaging & labeling services

(G-6028)
ATLANTIC ULTRAVIOLET CORP
375 Marcus Blvd (11788-2026)
PHONE 631 234-3275
Fax: 631 273-0771
Hilary Boehme, *President*
Thomas Dituro, *Vice Pres*
Celeste Kopp, *Treasurer*
Ronald Henderson, *Director*
Anne Wysocki, *Admin Sec*
◆ **EMP:** 30 **EST:** 1963
SALES (est): 8MM **Privately Held**
WEB: www.ultraviolet.com
SIC: 3589 3641 Water purification equipment, household type; ultraviolet lamps

(G-6029)
AUTOMATIC CONNECTOR INC
375 Oser Ave (11788-3607)
PHONE 631 543-5000
David Lax, *President*
EMP: 19
SALES (est): 3.1MM **Privately Held**
WEB: www.automaticconnector.com
SIC: 3678 3643 Electronic connectors; electric connectors

(G-6030)
AVM PRINTING INC
Also Called: Printers 3
43 Corporate Dr (11788-2048)
PHONE 631 351-1331
Anthony Viscuso, *President*
EMP: 13
SQ FT: 6,000
SALES: 2MM **Privately Held**
SIC: 2752 Commercial printing, lithographic

(G-6031)
AVON REPRODUCTIONS INC
Also Called: Avon Press
175 Engineers Rd (11788-4020)
PHONE 631 273-2400
Fax: 631 420-0930
Brad Peters, *President*
James Gibb, *Vice Pres*
▲ **EMP:** 35 **EST:** 1958
SQ FT: 10,000
SALES (est): 3.7MM **Privately Held**
WEB: www.avonpress.com
SIC: 2752 Lithographing on metal

(G-6032)
BARRONS EDUCATIONAL SERIES INC (PA)
Also Called: Barrons Educational
250 Wireless Blvd (11788-3924)
PHONE 631 434-3311
Fax: 631 434-3217
Manuel H Barron, *Chairman*
Ellen Sibley, *Exec VP*
Mary E Owens, *Production*
Debbie Bacek, *Purchasing*
Jackie Raab, *Sales Staff*
◆ **EMP:** 94
SQ FT: 75,000

SALES (est): 20.7MM **Privately Held**
WEB: www.barronseduc.com
SIC: **2731** 5942 Book publishing; book stores

(G-6033)
BEHLMAN ELECTRONICS INC (HQ)
80 Cabot Ct (11788-3729)
PHONE..................................631 435-0410
Fax: 631 951-4341
Mitchell Binder, *CEO*
Mitchell Buder, *Ch of Bd*
Mark Tublisky, *President*
Barry Nolan, *Mfg Mgr*
Joseph Belmonte, *Engineer*
▲ EMP: 3
SQ FT: 25,000
SALES (est): 5MM
SALES (corp-wide): 19.1MM **Publicly Held**
WEB: www.behlman.com
SIC: **3679** Power supplies, all types: static
PA: Orbit International Corp.
80 Cabot Ct
Hauppauge NY 11788
631 435-8300

(G-6034)
BIO-BOTANICA INC (PA)
75 Commerce Dr (11788-3943)
PHONE..................................631 231-0987
Fax: 631 231-7332
Frank D'Amelio Sr, *CEO*
Josephine Perricone, *President*
Frank D'Amelio Jr, *Vice Pres*
Jonathan Selzer, *Vice Pres*
Kurt Rettig, *Opers Mgr*
◆ EMP: 100
SQ FT: 100,000
SALES (est): 19.6MM **Privately Held**
SIC: **2833** 2834 2844 Alkaloids & other botanical based products; drugs & herbs: grading, grinding & milling; botanical products, medicinal: ground, graded or milled; extracts of botanicals: powdered, pilular, solid or fluid; toilet preparations

(G-6035)
BLACK & DECKER (US) INC
180 Oser Ave Ste 100 (11788-3709)
PHONE..................................631 952-2008
Joe Rufino, *Branch Mgr*
EMP: 7
SALES (corp-wide): 11.1B **Publicly Held**
WEB: www.dewalt.com
SIC: **3546** Power-driven handtools
HQ: Black & Decker (U.S.) Inc.
1000 Stanley Dr
New Britain CT 06053
410 716-3900

(G-6036)
BLUE STAR PRODUCTS INC
355 Marcus Blvd Ste 2 (11788-2027)
PHONE..................................631 952-3204
Gerald Jacino Sr, *President*
Marie Dydland, *Manager*
EMP: 12
SQ FT: 15,000
SALES (est): 1.3MM **Privately Held**
WEB: www.bluestar-products.com
SIC: **3559** Automotive maintenance equipment

(G-6037)
BRICKIT
17 Central Ave (11788-4733)
PHONE..................................631 727-8977
Fax: 631 348-0400
Oscar Hernandez, *Marketing Staff*
Robert Dolinsk,
Robert Dolinsky,
EMP: 20
SALES (est): 3.4MM **Privately Held**
SIC: **3271** Brick, concrete

(G-6038)
BRONSON NUTRITIONALS LLC (PA)
Also Called: Bronson Labrotaries
70 Commerce Dr (11788-3962)
PHONE..................................631 750-0000
Steven Kane, *Warehouse Mgr*
Michelle Coscia, *Controller*
Cindy Warsaw, *Financial Exec*

Sheri Taubes, *Mktg Dir*
Marcin Gora, *Info Tech Dir*
EMP: 20
SALES (est): 5.9MM **Privately Held**
SIC: **2834** Vitamin preparations

(G-6039)
C & C CUSTOM METAL FABRICATORS
2 N Hoffman Ln (11788-2735)
PHONE..................................631 235-9646
Chris Drago, *President*
EMP: 6
SQ FT: 1,500
SALES (est): 537.5K **Privately Held**
SIC: **3441** Fabricated structural metal

(G-6040)
CASTELLA IMPORTS INC
60 Davids Dr (11788-2041)
PHONE..................................631 231-5500
Vasilios Valsamos, *Ch of Bd*
Chris Valsamos, *Vice Pres*
Gina Berezny, *Purch Agent*
John Roumbos, *CFO*
Tara Franco, *Art Dir*
◆ EMP: 185
SQ FT: 110,000
SALES (est): 65MM **Privately Held**
WEB: www.castellaimports.com
SIC: **2099** 5149 Food preparations; specialty food items

(G-6041)
CENTRAL SEMICONDUCTOR CORP
145 Adams Ave (11788-3603)
PHONE..................................631 435-1110
Fax: 631 435-1824
W S Radgowski, *CEO*
Susan M Ryan, *President*
T Radgowski, *General Mgr*
Tom Hambel, *Vice Pres*
Steven Radgowski, *Vice Pres*
▲ EMP: 80
SQ FT: 30,000
SALES (est): 21.5MM **Privately Held**
WEB: www.centralsemi.com
SIC: **3674** Semiconductors & related devices

(G-6042)
CHAMPION ALUMINUM CORP
Also Called: Champion Window and Door
250 Kennedy Dr (11788-4002)
PHONE..................................631 656-3424
Anthony Muraco, *CEO*
Mike Piltoff, *President*
James Trupiano, *Treasurer*
Stephanie Bellotto, *Controller*
Anthony Arcati, *Shareholder*
▲ EMP: 140 EST: 1952
SQ FT: 80,000
SALES (est): 23.4MM **Privately Held**
WEB: www.championwindows.com
SIC: **3442** Metal doors, sash & trim

(G-6043)
CHARL INDUSTRIES INC
225 Engineers Rd (11788-4020)
PHONE..................................631 234-0100
Fax: 631 234-5544
Richard Coronato Sr, *President*
Linda Stence, *Controller*
Kitt Tyson, *Manager*
Charlotte Coronato, *Admin Sec*
EMP: 40
SQ FT: 44,000
SALES (est): 8.1MM **Privately Held**
WEB: www.charlco.com
SIC: **3599** Machine shop, jobbing & repair

(G-6044)
CHARLES ROSS & SON COMPANY (PA)
Also Called: Ross Metal Fabricators Div
710 Old Willets Path (11788-4193)
P.O. Box 12308 (11788-0615)
PHONE..................................631 234-0500
Fax: 631 234-0691
Richard Ross, *President*
Joseph Martorana, *Vice Pres*
Heinz Feibert, *Mfg Dir*
Dave Almeida, *Purch Mgr*
Tom Dee-G-Norio, *Engineer*

▲ EMP: 60 EST: 1840
SQ FT: 50,000
SALES (est): 37MM **Privately Held**
WEB: www.cosmeticmixers.com
SIC: **3443** 3586 3559 5084 Fabricated plate work (boiler shop); measuring & dispensing pumps; chemical machinery & equipment; pharmaceutical machinery; industrial machinery & equipment

(G-6045)
CIRCOR AEROSPACE INC
Aerodyne Controls
425 Rabro Dr Ste 1 (11788-4245)
PHONE..................................631 737-1900
Daniel R Godin, *Division Mgr*
Dave Hohf, *Engineer*
Cory Jordan, *Project Engr*
Jeff Horning, *Design Engr*
Melody Pagotto, *Marketing Staff*
EMP: 70
SALES (corp-wide): 656.2MM **Publicly Held**
SIC: **3483** 3829 3728 Ammunition, except for small arms; measuring & controlling devices; aircraft parts & equipment
HQ: Circor Aerospace, Inc.
2301 Wardlow Cir
Corona CA 92880
951 270-6200

(G-6046)
CLEAN GAS SYSTEMS INC
380 Townline Rd Ste 120 (11788-2842)
PHONE..................................631 467-1600
Anil M Shah, *President*
EMP: 20
SQ FT: 4,000
SALES (est): 4.8MM **Privately Held**
WEB: www.cgscgs.com
SIC: **3564** 8711 7389 Air purification equipment; pollution control engineering; air pollution measuring service

(G-6047)
CLICK IT INC
85 Corporate Dr (11788-2021)
PHONE..................................631 686-2900
James J Carey, *CEO*
Diane Jutting, *Cust Mgr*
Michael Simco, *Manager*
Vincent Pastore, *Technical Staff*
Bradford Dillon, *Analyst*
EMP: 60
SALES (est): 11.1MM **Privately Held**
WEB: www.clickitinc.com
SIC: **3663** Television closed circuit equipment

(G-6048)
COCA-COLA BTLG CO OF NY INC
375 Wireless Blvd (11788-3940)
PHONE..................................631 434-3535
Mike Chidester, *Manager*
Mike Taroli, *Manager*
Joanne Harms, *Executive*
EMP: 50
SALES (corp-wide): 44.2B **Publicly Held**
SIC: **2086** Bottled & canned soft drinks
HQ: The Coca-Cola Bottling Company Of New York Inc
2500 Windy Ridge Pkwy Se
Atlanta GA 30339
770 989-3000

(G-6049)
COLONIAL WIRE & CABLE CO INC (PA)
40 Engineers Rd (11788-4079)
PHONE..................................631 234-8500
Fax: 631 234-8544
Thomas J Walsh III, *President*
Thomas J Walsh Jr, *Chairman*
George Stubbs, *Corp Secy*
Tony Affrunti, *Plant Mgr*
Michael Rossi, *Accountant*
EMP: 55 EST: 1944
SQ FT: 100,000
SALES (est): 10.4MM **Privately Held**
WEB: www.colonialwire.com
SIC: **3357** Nonferrous wiredrawing & insulating

(G-6050)
COMME-CI COMME-CA AP GROUP
Also Called: Male Power Apparel
380 Rabo Dr (11788)
PHONE..................................631 300-1035
Fax: 631 300-1039
Sam Baker, *President*
Marybeth Healy, *Vice Pres*
Marybeth Onken, *Vice Pres*
Elizabeth Tracey, *Manager*
▲ EMP: 21
SQ FT: 12,000
SALES (est): 3.5MM **Privately Held**
WEB: www.malepower.com
SIC: **2322** 2329 2339 2341 Underwear, men's & boys': made from purchased materials; bathing suits & swimwear: men's & boys'; bathing suits: women's, misses' & juniors'; panties: women's, misses, children's & infants'

(G-6051)
COMMUNICATION POWER CORP
80 Davids Dr Ste 3 (11788-2002)
PHONE..................................631 434-7306
Daniel P Myer, *President*
Tuna Djemil, *Manager*
Walter Bonilla, *Technology*
▲ EMP: 36
SQ FT: 11,000
SALES (est): 10.2MM **Privately Held**
WEB: www.cpcamps.com
SIC: **3663** 3651 5065 Amplifiers, RF power & IF; household audio & video equipment; communication equipment

(G-6052)
CONTRACT PHARMACAL CORP
110 Plant Ave (11788-3830)
PHONE..................................631 231-4610
Mark Wolf, *Manager*
Joe Lubrano, *Manager*
EMP: 20
SQ FT: 48,000
SALES (corp-wide): 282.2MM **Privately Held**
SIC: **2834** Pharmaceutical preparations
PA: Contract Pharmacal Corp.
135 Adams Ave
Hauppauge NY 11788
631 231-4610

(G-6053)
CONTRACT PHARMACAL CORP
1324 Motor Pkwy (11749-5262)
PHONE..................................631 231-4610
Mark Wolf, *Manager*
EMP: 125
SALES (corp-wide): 282.2MM **Privately Held**
SIC: **2834** Pharmaceutical preparations
PA: Contract Pharmacal Corp.
135 Adams Ave
Hauppauge NY 11788
631 231-4610

(G-6054)
CONTRACT PHARMACAL CORP
250 Kennedy Dr (11788-4002)
PHONE..................................631 231-4610
Matt Wolf, *CEO*
EMP: 50
SALES (corp-wide): 282.2MM **Privately Held**
SIC: **2834** Pharmaceutical preparations
PA: Contract Pharmacal Corp.
135 Adams Ave
Hauppauge NY 11788
631 231-4610

(G-6055)
CONTRACT PHARMACAL CORP
145 Oser Ave (11788-3725)
PHONE..................................631 231-4610
Mark Wolf, *President*
EMP: 79
SALES (corp-wide): 282.2MM **Privately Held**
SIC: **2834** Pharmaceutical preparations
PA: Contract Pharmacal Corp.
135 Adams Ave
Hauppauge NY 11788
631 231-4610

Hauppauge - Suffolk County (G-6056)

(G-6056)
CONTRACT PHARMACAL CORP
160 Commerce Dr (11788-3944)
PHONE..................................631 231-4610
Fax: 631 231-4156
Mark Wolf, Manager
EMP: 181
SALES (corp-wide): 282.2MM **Privately Held**
SIC: 2834 Pharmaceutical preparations
PA: Contract Pharmacal Corp.
   135 Adams Ave
   Hauppauge NY 11788
   631 231-4610

(G-6057)
CONTRACT PHARMACAL CORP
150 Commerce Dr (11788-3930)
PHONE..................................631 231-4610
Mark Wolf, Manager
EMP: 19
SALES (corp-wide): 282.2MM **Privately Held**
SIC: 2834 Pharmaceutical preparations
PA: Contract Pharmacal Corp.
   135 Adams Ave
   Hauppauge NY 11788
   631 231-4610

(G-6058)
CROSSTEX INTERNATIONAL INC (HQ)
10 Ranick Rd (11788-4209)
PHONE..................................631 582-6777
Gary Steinberg, CEO
Mitchell Steinberg, Exec VP
Ken Plunkett, Senior VP
Sheldon Fisher, Vice Pres
Dan Pitkowsky, Vice Pres
▲ EMP: 75
SQ FT: 63,000
SALES (est): 48.3MM
SALES (corp-wide): 664.7MM **Publicly Held**
WEB: www.crosstex.com
SIC: 3843 2621 5047 2842 Dental equipment & supplies; toweling tissue, paper; dentists' professional supplies; specialty cleaning, polishes & sanitation goods; soap & other detergents; sanitary paper products
PA: Cantel Medical Corp.
   150 Clove Rd Ste 36
   Little Falls NJ 07424
   973 890-7220

(G-6059)
CURRAN MANUFACTURING CORP (PA)
Also Called: Royal Products
200 Oser Ave (11788-3724)
PHONE..................................631 273-1010
Fax: 631 273-1066
F Allan Curran, President
Lynn Telis, Director
▲ EMP: 49 EST: 1946
SALES (est): 10.2MM **Privately Held**
WEB: www.airchucks.com
SIC: 3545 5084 Machine tool attachments & accessories; machine tools & accessories

(G-6060)
CURRAN MANUFACTURING CORP
Also Called: Royal Products
210 Oser Ave (11788-3724)
PHONE..................................631 273-1010
Allan Curran, President
EMP: 50
SALES (corp-wide): 10.2MM **Privately Held**
WEB: www.airchucks.com
SIC: 3545 Machine tool attachments & accessories
PA: Curran Manufacturing Corp
   200 Oser Ave
   Hauppauge NY 11788
   631 273-1010

(G-6061)
DEPCO INC
20 Newton Pl (11788-4752)
PHONE..................................631 582-1995
Fax: 631 582-2015
Greg Minuto, CEO
David W Bean, President
▲ EMP: 10
SQ FT: 20,000
SALES (est): 1.7MM **Privately Held**
SIC: 2822 Silicone rubbers

(G-6062)
DEUTSCH RELAYS
55 Engineers Rd (11788-4007)
PHONE..................................631 342-1700
Fax: 631 342-9455
Thomas M Sadusky, President
Varin Parker, Vice Pres
Rich Stadalik, Opers Mgr
Jim Bedell, Manager
Agnes Lebel, Manager
EMP: 14
SALES (est): 1.8MM **Privately Held**
SIC: 3625 Relays & industrial controls

(G-6063)
DISC GRAPHICS INC
30 Gilpin Ave (11788-4724)
PHONE..................................631 300-1129
Margaret Krumholz, President
EMP: 150
SALES (corp-wide): 61.5MM **Privately Held**
SIC: 2657 Folding paperboard boxes
PA: Disc Graphics, Inc.
   10 Gilpin Ave
   Hauppauge NY 11788
   631 234-1400

(G-6064)
DISC GRAPHICS INC (PA)
10 Gilpin Ave (11788-4770)
PHONE..................................631 234-1400
Fax: 631 234-1460
Donald Sinkin, Ch of Bd
Margaret Krumholz, President
Stephen Frey, Senior VP
John A Rebecchi, Senior VP
John Rebecchi, Senior VP
▲ EMP: 266
SALES (est): 61.5MM **Privately Held**
WEB: www.discgraphics.com
SIC: 2657 Folding paperboard boxes

(G-6065)
DISPLAY PRESENTATIONS LTD
104 Parkway Dr S (11788-2012)
PHONE..................................631 951-4050
Fax: 631 951-4015
Fabian Zaneski, President
Stan Zaneski, Vice Pres
Debbie Rampulla, Mktg Dir
Mike Fabian, Marketing Staff
Lillian Mancuso, Manager
EMP: 52
SQ FT: 56,000
SALES (est): 7.6MM **Privately Held**
WEB: www.displaypresentations.net
SIC: 3993 Displays & cutouts, window & lobby

(G-6066)
DOCTOR PRINT INC (PA)
Also Called: Dr Print
18 Commerce Dr Ste 1 (11788-3975)
PHONE..................................631 873-4560
Mitch Cohen, CEO
EMP: 20 EST: 2011
SQ FT: 4,000
SALES (est): 3.3MM **Privately Held**
SIC: 2759 Laser printing

(G-6067)
DRI RELAYS INC (HQ)
60 Commerce Dr (11788-3929)
PHONE..................................631 342-1700
Michel Nespoulous, President
Diane Goerz, Vice Pres
Steve Byun, Project Mgr
Tracy Gu, Production
Gary Smith, Purch Mgr
▲ EMP: 100
SALES (est): 17.8MM **Privately Held**
SIC: 3625 Relays, for electronic use
PA: Financiere De Societes Techniques
   17 Rue Vicq D Azir
   Paris
   142 039-420

(G-6068)
DRIVE SHAFT SHOP INC
210 Blydenburg Rd Unit A (11749-5022)
PHONE..................................631 348-1818
Frank J Rehak III, President
Mike Smith, Manager
EMP: 10
SQ FT: 1,600
SALES (est): 840K **Privately Held**
WEB: www.driveshaftshop.com
SIC: 3714 Drive shafts, motor vehicle; axle housings & shafts, motor vehicle; axles, motor vehicle; hydraulic fluid power pumps for auto steering mechanism

(G-6069)
EHRLICH ENTERPRISES INC
Also Called: Floymar Manufacturing
91 Marcus Blvd (11788-3712)
PHONE..................................631 956-0690
Don Ehrlich, President
Al Schneider, General Mgr
EMP: 16
SQ FT: 18,000
SALES (est): 1.3MM **Privately Held**
SIC: 3599 Machine shop, jobbing & repair

(G-6070)
ELECTRONIC MACHINE PARTS LLC
Also Called: Emp
400 Oser Ave Ste 2000 (11788-3658)
PHONE..................................631 434-3700
Fax: 631 434-3718
Tim McAdam, Vice Pres
Ryan McAdam, Engineer
Maureen McAdam, Mng Member
Tetal Scantlebury, Manager
Maureen Ramert,
EMP: 13
SQ FT: 2,100
SALES (est): 3.1MM **Privately Held**
WEB: www.empregister.com
SIC: 3625 3823 3714 Control equipment, electric; industrial instrmnts msrmnt display/control process variable; motor vehicle parts & accessories

(G-6071)
EMBASSY INDUSTRIES INC
Also Called: Franklin Manufacturing Div
315 Oser Ave Ste 1 (11788-3680)
PHONE..................................631 435-0209
Fax: 631 694-1832
Robert Ramistella, President
Richard Horowitz, Chairman
Richard Cisek, COO
Joe Krowl, Sls & Mktg Exec
Jamie Nella, Natl Sales Mgr
▲ EMP: 170 EST: 1950
SQ FT: 75,000
SALES (est): 19.3MM
SALES (corp-wide): 81.7MM **Publicly Held**
WEB: www.embassyind.com
SIC: 3433 1711 3567 Heating equipment, except electric; plumbing, heating, air-conditioning contractors; industrial furnaces & ovens
PA: P & F Industries, Inc.
   445 Broadhollow Rd # 100
   Melville NY 11747
   631 694-9800

(G-6072)
ERA-CONTACT USA LLC
55 Cabot Ct Ste B (11788-3717)
PHONE..................................631 524-5530
Claudio Meier, President
EMP: 17 EST: 2011
SALES (est): 2.7MM **Privately Held**
SIC: 3743 Railroad equipment

(G-6073)
ES BETA INC ◆
110 Nicon Ct (11788-4212)
PHONE..................................631 582-6740
Robert James, Treasurer
EMP: 43 EST: 2016
SALES (est): 1.3MM **Privately Held**
SIC: 3677 Electronic coils, transformers & other inductors

(G-6074)
ET OAKES CORPORATION
686 Old Willets Path (11788-4102)
PHONE..................................631 630-9837
Fax: 631 232-0170
W Peter Oakes, Ch of Bd
Noel Oakes, Corp Secy
Robert Peck, Vice Pres
EMP: 20
SQ FT: 25,000
SALES (est): 5.8MM **Privately Held**
WEB: www.oakes.com
SIC: 3556 3531 5084 3599 Cutting, chopping, grinding, mixing & similar machinery; construction machinery; food product manufacturing machinery; machine shop, jobbing & repair

(G-6075)
F & T GRAPHICS INC
690 Old Willets Path (11788-4102)
PHONE..................................631 643-1000
Fax: 631 643-1098
John M Leone, President
Debbie Lioni, Manager
EMP: 17
SQ FT: 15,000
SALES (est): 4.3MM **Privately Held**
SIC: 2752 Commercial printing, offset

(G-6076)
FB LABORATORIES INC
Also Called: Futurebiotics
70 Commerce Dr (11788-3962)
PHONE..................................631 750-0000
Saiful Kibria, President
Kerilee Crennan, Purch Mgr
Elizabeth Brynes, Admin Asst
▲ EMP: 50 EST: 2010
SALES (est): 10MM **Privately Held**
SIC: 2834 Vitamin preparations

(G-6077)
FINISH LINE TECHNOLOGIES INC (PA)
50 Wireless Blvd (11788-3954)
PHONE..................................631 666-7300
Fax: 631 666-7391
Henry J Krause, President
David Clopton, Director
◆ EMP: 28
SQ FT: 60,000
SALES (est): 13MM **Privately Held**
SIC: 2992 Lubricating oils & greases

(G-6078)
FLUID MECHANISMS HAUPPAUGE INC
225 Engineers Rd (11788-4020)
PHONE..................................631 234-0100
Richard Coronato, President
Charlotte Coronato, Corp Secy
EMP: 35 EST: 1962
SQ FT: 44,000
SALES (est): 9.8MM **Privately Held**
SIC: 3728 Aircraft parts & equipment

(G-6079)
FORECAST CONSOLES INC
681 Old Willets Path (11788-4109)
PHONE..................................631 253-9000
William Haberman, President
Ryan Haberman, General Mgr
V Decesare, Prdtn Mgr
Steven Cirone, Engineer
Janet Haberman, CFO
▲ EMP: 24
SQ FT: 21,000
SALES (est): 3.7MM **Privately Held**
WEB: www.forecast-consoles.com
SIC: 2511 2531 2521 2541 Console tables: wood; public building & related furniture; wood office furniture; shelving, office & store, wood; office furniture, except wood

(G-6080)
FOREST LABORATORIES LLC
45 Adams Ave (11788-3605)
PHONE..................................212 421-7850
Warren Zaugg, Project Mgr
Christine Stone, Office Mgr
Elaine Hochberg, Branch Mgr
EMP: 54 **Privately Held**
WEB: www.frx.com

▲ = Import ▼ = Export ◆ = Import/Export

GEOGRAPHIC SECTION

Hauppauge - Suffolk County (G-6103)

SIC: 2834 Pharmaceutical preparations
HQ: Forest Laboratories, Llc
909 3rd Ave Fl 23
New York NY 10022
212 421-7850

(G-6081)
FUNGILAB INC
89 Cabot Ct Ste K (11788-3719)
PHONE.................................631 750-6361
Ernest Buira, *CEO*
Joan Buira, *President*
Giovanni Capella, *Sales Mgr*
◆ EMP: 5
SQ FT: 10,000
SALES: 1MM
SALES (corp-wide): 2.2MM **Privately Held**
SIC: 3821 Laboratory apparatus & furniture
PA: Fungi Lab Sa
Calle Constitucio (Pg Ind Les Grases),
64 - Nave 15
Sant Feliu De Llobregat 08980
936 853-500

(G-6082)
FUTUREBIOTICS LLC
70 Commerce Dr (11788-3936)
PHONE.................................631 273-6300
Fax: 631 273-1165
John Waine, *General Mgr*
Steve Welling, *COO*
Jay Patel, *Prdtn Mgr*
Steve Tuohey, *Research*
Michellle Cofcia, *Controller*
▲ EMP: 25
SALES (est): 5.8MM **Privately Held**
WEB: www.futurebiotics.com
SIC: 2834 Medicines, capsuled or ampuled

(G-6083)
GENERAL SEMICONDUCTOR INC
150 Motor Pkwy Ste 101 (11788-5167)
PHONE.................................631 300-3818
Linda Perry, *Executive*
EMP: 5
SALES (est): 258.9K **Privately Held**
SIC: 3674 Semiconductors & related devices

(G-6084)
GEOSYNC MICROWAVE INC
320 Oser Ave (11788-3608)
PHONE.................................631 760-5567
Arthur Faverio, *President*
Stephen Philips, *Vice Pres*
Timothy Jahn, *Engineer*
M Zahidi, *Engineer*
Richard Bova, *Consultant*
EMP: 5
SQ FT: 4,000
SALES (est): 950K **Privately Held**
WEB: www.geosyncmicrowave.com
SIC: 3663 Satellites, communications

(G-6085)
GLARO INC
735 Calebs Path Ste 1 (11788-4201)
PHONE.................................631 234-1717
Fax: 631 234-9510
Neal Glass, *President*
Robert Glass, *Division Mgr*
Kane Kessler, *Counsel*
Sherman Lawrence, *Counsel*
Robert Betensky, *Exec VP*
▲ EMP: 60 EST: 1945
SQ FT: 50,000
SALES (est): 9.6MM **Privately Held**
WEB: www.glaro.com
SIC: 2542 Office & store showcases & display fixtures

(G-6086)
GLOBECOMM SYSTEMS INC (HQ)
45 Oser Ave (11788-3808)
PHONE.................................631 231-9800
Fax: 631 231-1557
Keith A Hall, *CEO*
Nick Governale, *Dean*
Thomas C Coyle, *Exec VP*
Julia Hanft, *Senior VP*
Paul J Johnson, *Senior VP*
◆ EMP: 250
SQ FT: 122,000
SALES: 319.6MM **Privately Held**
WEB: www.globecommsystems.com
SIC: 3663 4813 Satellites, communications; telephone communication, except radio
PA: Wasserstein Cosmos Co-Invest, L.P.
1301 Ave Of The Americas
New York NY 10019
212 702-5600

(G-6087)
GSE COMPOSITES INC
110 Oser Ave (11788-3820)
P.O. Box 13248 (11788-0593)
PHONE.................................631 389-1300
Anne D Shybunko, *President*
EMP: 14
SALES (est): 1.8MM **Privately Held**
SIC: 3089 Plastic containers, except foam

(G-6088)
HAIG PRESS INC
Also Called: Haig Graphic Communications
690 Old Willets Path (11788-4102)
PHONE.................................631 582-5800
Fax: 631 582-2806
James Kalousdian, *Ch of Bd*
Steve Kalousdian, *Vice Pres*
EMP: 44
SQ FT: 30,000
SALES: 7.5MM **Privately Held**
WEB: www.haiggraphic.com
SIC: 2752 2789 2759 Commercial printing, lithographic; bookbinding & related work; commercial printing

(G-6089)
HARMONIC DRIVE LLC
89 Cabot Ct Ste A (11788-3719)
PHONE.................................631 231-6630
Douglas Olson, *President*
Brian Stdenis, *Sls & Mktg Exec*
EMP: 5
SALES (corp-wide): 241.6MM **Privately Held**
WEB: www.harmonic-drive.com
SIC: 3566 Speed changers, drives & gears
HQ: Harmonic Drive L.L.C.
247 Lynnfield St
Peabody MA 01960
978 532-1800

(G-6090)
HAUPPAUGE COMPUTER WORKS INC (HQ)
Also Called: Hauppuge Cmpt Dgtal Erope Sarl
91 Cabot Ct (11788-3706)
PHONE.................................631 434-1600
Fax: 631 434-3198
Kenneth Plotkin, *Ch of Bd*
John Casey, *Vice Pres*
Sheila Easop, *Prdtn Mgr*
Steve Sullivan, *Mfg Staff*
Gerald Tucciarone, *CFO*
▲ EMP: 50
SQ FT: 25,000
SALES (est): 20.6MM
SALES (corp-wide): 34MM **Publicly Held**
WEB: www.happage.com
SIC: 3577 7371 Computer peripheral equipment; custom computer programming services
PA: Hauppauge Digital, Inc.
91 Cabot Ct
Hauppauge NY 11788
631 434-1600

(G-6091)
HAUPPAUGE DIGITAL INC (PA)
91 Cabot Ct (11788-3717)
PHONE.................................631 434-1600
Kenneth Plotkin, *Ch of Bd*
John Casey, *Vice Pres*
Ron Petralia, *Vice Pres*
Steve Sullivan, *Opers Mgr*
Yehia Oweiss, *VP Sls/Mktg*
▲ EMP: 35
SALES: 34MM **Publicly Held**
WEB: www.hauppauge.com
SIC: 3577 Computer peripheral equipment

(G-6092)
HAWK-I SECURITY INC
355 Oser Ave (11788-3607)
P.O. Box 13297 (11788-0723)
PHONE.................................631 656-1056
Joseph Smith, *CEO*
Eric Foreman, *Vice Pres*
Doug Miller, *CFO*
Anthony Matyszczyk, *Consultant*
◆ EMP: 5
SQ FT: 1,000
SALES (est): 498.7K **Privately Held**
WEB: www.hawkisecurity.com
SIC: 3699 Security devices

(G-6093)
HI-TRON SEMICONDUCTOR CORP
85 Engineers Rd (11788-4003)
PHONE.................................631 231-1500
Mel Lax, *President*
Barry Grossman, *Sales Staff*
Mindy Lax, *Admin Sec*
EMP: 20
SQ FT: 42,000
SALES (est): 1.4MM **Privately Held**
SIC: 3674 Semiconductors & related devices

(G-6094)
HILORD CHEMICAL CORPORATION
70 Engineers Rd (11788-4076)
PHONE.................................631 234-7373
Donald Balbinder, *President*
Cody Sickle, *Vice Pres*
Shawnee Sicke, *Treasurer*
Rommel Gloria, *Manager*
Terry Sickle, *Admin Sec*
EMP: 26
SQ FT: 37,000
SALES (est): 6.8MM **Privately Held**
WEB: www.hilord.com
SIC: 3861 2822 3479 Toners, prepared photographic (not made in chemical plants); ethylene-propylene rubbers, EPDM polymers; coating electrodes

(G-6095)
HOHMANN & BARNARD INC (DH)
Also Called: HB
30 Rasons Ct (11788-4206)
P.O. Box 5270 (11788-0270)
PHONE.................................631 234-0600
Fax: 631 234-0683
Ronald P Hohmann, *Ch of Bd*
Bob Hohmann, *Vice Pres*
Winfred Freeman, *Plant Mgr*
Christopher Hohmann, *Treasurer*
Saverio Minucci, *VP Sales*
◆ EMP: 25
SQ FT: 55,000
SALES (est): 39.5MM
SALES (corp-wide): 210.8B **Publicly Held**
WEB: www.foamfiller.com
SIC: 3496 3462 3315 Clips & fasteners, made from purchased wire; iron & steel forgings; steel wire & related products
HQ: Mitek Industries, Inc.
16023 Swinly Rdg
Chesterfield MO 63017
314 434-1200

(G-6096)
HUCKLEBERRY INC
Also Called: Minuteman Press
655 Old Willets Path (11788-4105)
PHONE.................................631 630-5450
Robin Eschenberg, *President*
Hayley Eschenberg, *VP Sales*
EMP: 6
SALES (est): 1MM **Privately Held**
SIC: 2752 Commercial printing, lithographic

(G-6097)
INNOVATIVE LABS LLC
85 Commerce Dr (11788-3902)
PHONE.................................631 231-5522
Frank Amelio Sr, *CEO*
Frank D Amelio Jr, *President*
Dean Lafemina, *Vice Pres*
Ahsanul Aziz, *Purch Mgr*
EMP: 60
SQ FT: 25,000
SALES: 10MM **Privately Held**
WEB: www.innovativelabsny.com
SIC: 2834 Tablets, pharmaceutical; medicines, capsuled or ampuled

(G-6098)
INNOVATIVE VIDEO TECH INC
Also Called: Invid Tech
355 Oser Ave (11788-3607)
PHONE.................................516 840-2587
Joe Troiano, *President*
EMP: 13
SALES (est): 598.1K **Privately Held**
SIC: 3699 Security control equipment & systems

(G-6099)
INVAGEN PHARMACEUTICALS INC (DH)
7 Oser Ave Ste 4 (11788-3811)
PHONE.................................631 231-3233
Sudhakar Vidiyala, *President*
Madhava U Reddy, *COO*
Praveen Ale, *Mfg Staff*
Taralynn Manja, *Purchasing*
RAO Prahallada, *Purchasing*
▲ EMP: 330
SQ FT: 150,000
SALES: 129MM **Privately Held**
SIC: 2834 5122 Pharmaceutical preparations; pharmaceuticals

(G-6100)
JACK MERKEL INC
1720 Express Dr S (11788-5302)
PHONE.................................631 234-2600
Jack Merkel, *President*
EMP: 5
SQ FT: 6,000
SALES: 800K **Privately Held**
SIC: 3599 7538 Machine shop, jobbing & repair; engine repair; engine rebuilding: automotive

(G-6101)
JACKNOB INTERNATIONAL LTD
Also Called: Omega Die Casting Co
290 Oser Ave (11788-3610)
P.O. Box 18032 (11788-8832)
PHONE.................................631 546-6560
Jerry M Loveless, *President*
Brendan Omalley, *Vice Pres*
Carole Termini, *Vice Pres*
Susan Marsh, *Info Tech Mgr*
Ron Reitz, *Info Tech Mgr*
▲ EMP: 90 EST: 1931
SQ FT: 20,000
SALES (est): 11.5MM **Privately Held**
WEB: www.jacknob.com
SIC: 3432 Plumbers' brass goods: drain cocks, faucets, spigots, etc.

(G-6102)
JOSH PACKAGING INC
245 Marcus Blvd Ste 1 (11788-2000)
PHONE.................................631 822-1660
Abraham Golshirazian, *Ch of Bd*
Abe Gulsh, *President*
Nejat Rahmani, *Vice Pres*
▲ EMP: 20
SQ FT: 30,000
SALES (est): 5MM **Privately Held**
SIC: 2673 5113 5162 Plastic bags: made from purchased materials; industrial & personal service paper; plastics materials

(G-6103)
KEEBLER COMPANY
55 Gilpin Ave (11788-4723)
PHONE.................................631 234-3700
Fax: 631 582-3570
Jean Meigl, *Manager*
EMP: 40
SALES (corp-wide): 13.5B **Publicly Held**
WEB: www.keebler.com
SIC: 2052 Cookies
HQ: Keebler Company
1 Kellogg Sq
Battle Creek MI 49017
269 961-2000

Hauppauge - Suffolk County (G-6104)

(G-6104)
KILTRONX ENVIRO SYSTEMS LLC
330 Motor Pkwy Ste 201 (11788-5118)
PHONE.................................917 971-7177
Gabriel Kasvoitz, *CEO*
Arlen Cabale, *COO*
EMP: 120
SQ FT: 2,500
SALES: 10MM **Privately Held**
SIC: 2299 Batting, wadding, padding & fillings

(G-6105)
KINGS PARK ASPHALT CORPORATION
201 Moreland Rd Ste 2 (11788-3922)
PHONE.................................631 269-9774
Michael Farino, *President*
James Farino, *Corp Secy*
Paul Farino, *Vice Pres*
EMP: 5
SQ FT: 1,000
SALES (est): 850K **Privately Held**
SIC: 2951 Asphalt paving mixtures & blocks; asphalt paving blocks (not from refineries); paving mixtures; asphalt & asphaltic paving mixtures (not from refineries)

(G-6106)
KLD LABS INC
55 Cabot Ct (11788-3717)
PHONE.................................631 549-4222
Steven Magnus, *President*
Daniel L Magnus, *Vice Pres*
Yury Malyarov, *Design Engr*
Ryan Danziger, *Electrical Engi*
Patricia Anwander, *Controller*
EMP: 40
SQ FT: 20,000
SALES (est): 12.2MM **Privately Held**
WEB: www.kldlabs.com
SIC: 3829 7373 Measuring & controlling devices; computer integrated systems design

(G-6107)
L-3 COMMUNICATIONS CORPORATION
Narda Microwave East
435 Moreland Rd (11788-3926)
PHONE.................................631 231-1700
Joe Merenda, *President*
John Mega, *Division Pres*
Tim Fowler, *Vice Pres*
Robert Koelzer, *Vice Pres*
Michael J Sanator, *Vice Pres*
EMP: 300
SALES (corp-wide): 10.4B **Publicly Held**
SIC: 3663 Telemetering equipment, electronic
HQ: L-3 Communications Corporation
600 3rd Ave
New York NY 10016
212 697-1111

(G-6108)
L-3 COMMUNICATIONS CORPORATION
Also Called: L-3 Narda-Miteq
100 Davids Dr (11788-2043)
PHONE.................................631 436-7400
Steven Skpock, *President*
Wendy U Ringhiser, *Executive*
EMP: 700
SALES (corp-wide): 10.4B **Publicly Held**
SIC: 3663 3769 3661 3651 Radio & TV communications equipment; guided missile & space vehicle parts & auxiliary equipment; telephone & telegraph apparatus; household audio & video equipment; current-carrying wiring devices
HQ: L-3 Communications Corporation
600 3rd Ave
New York NY 10016
212 697-1111

(G-6109)
L-3 COMMUNICATIONS CORPORATION
Also Called: Narda Satellite Networks
435 Moreland Rd (11788-3926)
PHONE.................................631 231-1700
Fax: 631 231-1485
Jeff Czworniak, *Opers Mgr*
Frank Sepulveda, *Facilities Mgr*
Charles Okon, *Engineer*
Mike Callegari, *Controller*
Sherry Dowe, *Human Res Dir*
EMP: 100
SQ FT: 60,000
SALES (corp-wide): 10.4B **Publicly Held**
SIC: 3663 8748 5731 Telemetering equipment, electronic; communications consulting; antennas, satellite dish
HQ: L-3 Communications Corporation
600 3rd Ave
New York NY 10016
212 697-1111

(G-6110)
L-3 COMMUNICATIONS CORPORATION
Also Called: L-3 Narda-Miteq
330 Oser Ave (11788-3630)
PHONE.................................631 436-7400
Aksel Kliss, *Manager*
EMP: 100
SALES (corp-wide): 10.4B **Publicly Held**
SIC: 3663 Radio broadcasting & communications equipment
HQ: L-3 Communications Corporation
600 3rd Ave
New York NY 10016
212 697-1111

(G-6111)
LA FLOR PRODUCTS COMPANY INC (PA)
Also Called: La Flor Spices
25 Hoffman Ave (11788-4717)
PHONE.................................631 851-9601
Ruben La Torre Sr, *President*
Dan La Torre, *Exec VP*
Justin Latorre, *Exec VP*
Ruben La Torre Jr, *Vice Pres*
Chris Pappas, *Vice Pres*
▲ **EMP:** 44
SQ FT: 90,000
SALES: 9MM **Privately Held**
WEB: www.laflor.com
SIC: 2099 Seasonings & spices; seasonings: dry mixes

(G-6112)
LEHNEIS ORTHOTICS PROSTHETIC
517 Route 111 Ste 300 (11788-4338)
PHONE.................................631 360-3859
Alfred Lehneis, *President*
EMP: 9
SALES (corp-wide): 5MM **Privately Held**
WEB: www.lehneis.com
SIC: 3842 5047 5999 Limbs, artificial; medical equipment & supplies; artificial limbs
PA: Lehneis Orthotics & Prosthetic Associates Ltd
13 Bedells Landing Rd
Roslyn NY
516 621-7277

(G-6113)
LIVING WELL INNOVATIONS INC
115 Engineers Rd (11788-4005)
PHONE.................................646 517-3200
Arthur Danziger, *President*
EMP: 6
SQ FT: 4,000
SALES: 5MM **Privately Held**
SIC: 2731 5192 Book publishing; books

(G-6114)
LNK INTERNATIONAL INC
22 Arkay Dr (11788-3708)
PHONE.................................631 435-3500
EMP: 100
SALES (corp-wide): 53.5MM **Privately Held**
SIC: 2834 Pharmaceutical preparations
PA: L.N.K. International Inc.
60 Arkay Dr
Hauppauge NY 11788
631 435-3500

(G-6115)
LNK INTERNATIONAL INC
100 Ricefield Ln (11788-2008)
PHONE.................................631 435-3500
Fax: 631 435-3542
Hajee Mohamed, *QC Dir*
Chudgar Pk, *Manager*
EMP: 100
SALES (corp-wide): 53.5MM **Privately Held**
SIC: 2834 Pharmaceutical preparations
PA: L.N.K. International Inc.
60 Arkay Dr
Hauppauge NY 11788
631 435-3500

(G-6116)
LNK INTERNATIONAL INC
325 Kennedy Dr (11788-4006)
PHONE.................................631 435-3500
Joseph J Mollica, *President*
EMP: 100
SALES (corp-wide): 53.5MM **Privately Held**
SIC: 2834 Pharmaceutical preparations
PA: L.N.K. International Inc.
60 Arkay Dr
Hauppauge NY 11788
631 435-3500

(G-6117)
LNK INTERNATIONAL INC
145 Ricefield Ln (11788-2007)
PHONE.................................631 543-3787
Fax: 631 543-2040
Dave Bergen, *Prdtn Mgr*
Pk Chudgar, *Manager*
EMP: 100
SALES (corp-wide): 53.5MM **Privately Held**
SIC: 2834 Pharmaceutical preparations
PA: L.N.K. International Inc.
60 Arkay Dr
Hauppauge NY 11788
631 435-3500

(G-6118)
LNK INTERNATIONAL INC
40 Arkay Dr (11788-3708)
PHONE.................................631 435-3500
Shaji Kumar Varghese, *Branch Mgr*
EMP: 100
SALES (corp-wide): 53.5MM **Privately Held**
SIC: 2834 Pharmaceutical preparations
PA: L.N.K. International Inc.
60 Arkay Dr
Hauppauge NY 11788
631 435-3500

(G-6119)
LNK INTERNATIONAL INC
60 Oscer Ave (11788)
PHONE.................................631 231-3415
Joseph J Mollica, *President*
EMP: 100
SALES (corp-wide): 53.5MM **Privately Held**
SIC: 2834 Pharmaceutical preparations
PA: L.N.K. International Inc.
60 Arkay Dr
Hauppauge NY 11788
631 435-3500

(G-6120)
LNK INTERNATIONAL INC
55 Arkay Dr (11788-3707)
PHONE.................................631 231-4020
Joseph J Mollica Sr, *Branch Mgr*
EMP: 100
SALES (corp-wide): 53.5MM **Privately Held**
SIC: 2834 Pharmaceutical preparations
PA: L.N.K. International Inc.
60 Arkay Dr
Hauppauge NY 11788
631 435-3500

(G-6121)
LOURDES INDUSTRIES INC (PA)
65 Hoffman Ave (11788-4798)
PHONE.................................631 234-6600
Fax: 631 234-7595
William J Jakobsen, *Ch of Bd*
Peter McKenna, *Vice Pres*
Paul Vaughan, *Opers Mgr*
Dave Hertling, *Engineer*
Rich Stevens, *Senior Engr*
EMP: 90 **EST:** 1954
SQ FT: 26,000
SALES (est): 18.9MM **Privately Held**
SIC: 3795 3492 3643 3724 Tanks & tank components; fluid power valves & hose fittings; current-carrying wiring devices; aircraft engines & engine parts; engineering services

(G-6122)
LOURDES SYSTEMS INC
21 Newton Pl (11788-4815)
PHONE.................................631 234-7077
George Powell, *Ch of Bd*
Peter Maguire, *President*
George Meyerle, *Vice Pres*
Peter McKenna, *Treasurer*
Jeff Jordan, *MIS Dir*
EMP: 12
SQ FT: 5,000
SALES (est): 1.3MM **Privately Held**
SIC: 3542 Machine tools, metal forming type

(G-6123)
MACHINERY MOUNTINGS INC
41 Sarah Dr (11788-2633)
PHONE.................................631 851-0480
Bernard H Kass, *President*
Steven Kass, *Vice Pres*
Wayne Kass, *Vice Pres*
EMP: 14
SALES (est): 1.6MM **Privately Held**
SIC: 3499 Machine bases, metal

(G-6124)
MAGGIO DATA FORMS PRINTING LTD
1735 Express Dr N (11788-5312)
PHONE.................................631 348-0343
Fax: 631 348-4422
Robert Maggio, *President*
James Maggio, *Vice Pres*
Mary Maggio, *Treasurer*
Charlie Johnson, *Sales Staff*
Charles Maggio, *Admin Sec*
EMP: 110
SQ FT: 30,000
SALES (est): 13.8MM **Privately Held**
WEB: www.maggio.com
SIC: 2761 Manifold business forms

(G-6125)
MAKERS NUTRITION LLC (PA)
315 Oser Ave (11788-3680)
PHONE.................................631 456-5397
Stephen Finnegan, *General Mgr*
Rosa Ciaccio, *Manager*
EMP: 25 **EST:** 2014
SALES: 12MM **Privately Held**
SIC: 2023 Dietary supplements, dairy & non-dairy based

(G-6126)
MASON INDUSTRIES INC (PA)
Also Called: M I
350 Rabro Dr (11788-4237)
P.O. Box 410, Smithtown (11787-0410)
PHONE.................................631 348-0282
Fax: 631 348-0279
Norm Mason, *Ch of Bd*
Patrick Lama, *Vice Pres*
Armando Gamble, *Safety Mgr*
Yuewei Chang, *Purchasing*
G Reddy, *Chief Engr*
▲ **EMP:** 165 **EST:** 1958
SQ FT: 60,000
SALES (est): 49.3MM **Privately Held**
WEB: www.mercer-rubber.com
SIC: 3625 3829 3052 3069 Noise control equipment; measuring & controlling devices; rubber hose; hard rubber & molded rubber products; fabricated structural metal; electronic connectors

(G-6127)
MASON INDUSTRIES INC
33 Ranick Rd Ste 1 (11788-4250)
PHONE.................................631 348-0282
Patricia Gowicki, *Manager*
EMP: 7
SALES (corp-wide): 49.3MM **Privately Held**
SIC: 3625 Noise control equipment
PA: Mason Industries, Inc.
350 Rabro Dr
Hauppauge NY 11788
631 348-0282

Hauppauge - Suffolk County

(G-6128)
MCKEE FOODS CORPORATION
111 Serene Pl (11788-3534)
PHONE 631 979-9364
John Meyer, *Branch Mgr*
EMP: 609
SALES (corp-wide): 1.7B **Privately Held**
WEB: www.mckeefoods.com
SIC: 2051 Cakes, bakery: except frozen
PA: Mckee Foods Corporation
    10260 Mckee Rd
    Collegedale TN 37315
    423 238-7111

(G-6129)
MEDICAL ACTION INDUSTRIES INC
150 Motor Pkwy Ste 205 (11788-5180)
PHONE 631 231-4600
Fax: 631 231-3075
Rick Setian, *Assistant VP*
Carmine Morello, *Vice Pres*
Paul Meringola, *Manager*
Chad Ellis, *CIO*
Blain Hoye, *Network Tech*
EMP: 215
SALES (corp-wide): 9.7B **Publicly Held**
WEB: www.medical-action.com
SIC: 3842 4226 5999 5047 Sponges, surgical; sterilizers, hospital & surgical; surgical appliances & supplies; special warehousing & storage; medical apparatus & supplies; hospital equipment & furniture
HQ: Medical Action Industries Inc.
    25 Heywood Rd
    Arden NC 28704
    631 231-4600

(G-6130)
MELLAND GEAR INSTR OF HUPPAUGE
225 Engineers Rd (11788-4020)
PHONE 631 234-0100
Richard C Coronato, *CEO*
Richard Coronato Sr, *President*
Oscar Duarte, *Purchasing*
Charlotte Coronato, *Admin Sec*
EMP: 35 **EST:** 1959
SQ FT: 44,000
SALES (est): 4.9MM **Privately Held**
SIC: 3824 3545 Mechanical counters; precision tools, machinists'

(G-6131)
MEOPTA USA INC
Also Called: Tyrolit Company
50 Davids Dr (11788-2040)
PHONE 631 436-5900
Fax: 631 436-5920
Gerald J Rausnitz, *President*
Reinhard Seipp, *General Mgr*
David Rausnitz, *COO*
Marcel Kappeler, *Vice Pres*
Carlos Arango, *Purch Mgr*
▲ **EMP:** 140 **EST:** 1957
SQ FT: 41,500
SALES (est): 43.7MM
SALES (corp-wide): 93.2MM **Privately Held**
WEB: www.meopta.com
SIC: 3827 Lenses, optical: all types except ophthalmic
PA: Meopta - Optika, S.R.O.
    Kabelikova 2682/1
    Prerov I-Mesto 75002
    581 241-111

(G-6132)
MERCER RUBBER CO
350 Rabro Dr (11788-4257)
PHONE 631 348-0282
Norman J Mason, *President*
Mary P Ryan, *Corp Secy*
Pat Lama, *Vice Pres*
▲ **EMP:** 150 **EST:** 1866
SQ FT: 60,000
SALES (est): 18.8MM
SALES (corp-wide): 49.3MM **Privately Held**
WEB: www.mercer-rubber.com
SIC: 3069 3052 Expansion joints, rubber; rubber hose
PA: Mason Industries, Inc.
    350 Rabro Dr
    Hauppauge NY 11788
    631 348-0282

(G-6133)
MERGENCE STUDIOS LTD
135 Ricefield Ln (11788-2046)
PHONE 212 288-5616
Douglas Schulman, *CEO*
▲ **EMP:** 10
SALES (est): 1.2MM **Privately Held**
SIC: 2241 Glass narrow fabrics

(G-6134)
METAL DYNAMICS INTL CORP
Also Called: Mdi
25 Corporate Dr (11788-2021)
P.O. Box 13248 (11788-0593)
PHONE 631 231-1153
Daniel Shybunko, *President*
Anne D Shybunko-Moore, *President*
Tim Austin, *Vice Pres*
Amy Pitarra, *Purchasing*
Ann Curran, *Controller*
◆ **EMP:** 25
SQ FT: 28,600
SALES (est): 991.9K **Privately Held**
WEB: www.metaldynamicsintl.com
SIC: 3728 Aircraft parts & equipment

(G-6135)
MICROCAD TRNING CONSULTING INC
77 Arkay Dr Ste C2 (11788-3742)
PHONE 631 291-9484
Michael F Frey, *Branch Mgr*
EMP: 7
SALES (corp-wide): 9.7MM **Privately Held**
SIC: 7372 Prepackaged software
PA: Microcad Training & Consulting, Inc.
    440 Arsenal St Ste 3
    Watertown MA 02472
    617 923-0500

(G-6136)
MICROCHIP TECHNOLOGY INC
80 Arkay Dr (11788-3705)
PHONE 631 233-3280
Fax: 631 249-8178
Kenneth Smalley, *Engineer*
Daniel Thornton, *Engineer*
Dan Levesser, *Manager*
Andrew Odlivak, *Manager*
Dean Steiding, *Manager*
EMP: 6
SALES (corp-wide): 2.1B **Publicly Held**
WEB: www.microchip.com
SIC: 3674 Microcircuits, integrated (semiconductor)
PA: Microchip Technology Inc
    2355 W Chandler Blvd
    Chandler AZ 85224
    480 792-7200

(G-6137)
MICROSOFT CORPORATION
2929 Expressway Dr N # 300 (11749-5302)
PHONE 516 380-1531
Fax: 631 630-8521
Wilhelm Gerbert, *General Mgr*
Charles Baker, *Project Mgr*
John Reumann, *Human Res Mgr*
Tom Marsh, *Sales Mgr*
Matt Destefano, *Accounts Mgr*
EMP: 100
SALES (corp-wide): 85.3B **Publicly Held**
WEB: www.microsoft.com
SIC: 7372 Prepackaged software
PA: Microsoft Corporation
    1 Microsoft Way
    Redmond WA 98052
    425 882-8080

(G-6138)
MILSO INDUSTRIES INC
25 Engineers Rd (11788-4019)
PHONE 631 234-1133
Al Orsi, *Branch Mgr*
EMP: 12
SQ FT: 10,000
SALES (corp-wide): 1.4B **Publicly Held**
SIC: 3995 5087 Burial caskets; caskets

HQ: Milso Industries Inc.
    534 Union St
    Brooklyn NY 11215
    718 624-4593

(G-6139)
MINI GRAPHICS INC
Also Called: Mgi
140 Commerce Dr (11788-3948)
PHONE 516 223-6464
James Delise, *CEO*
Charles J Delise, *Principal*
Steven Delise, *Principal*
Rob Diekroger, *Technical Mgr*
Jimmy Delise, *Controller*
EMP: 100
SALES (est): 24.5MM **Privately Held**
WEB: www.minigraphics.net
SIC: 2759 Commercial printing

(G-6140)
MMC ENTERPRISES CORP
175 Commerce Dr Ste E (11788-3920)
PHONE 800 435-1088
Jin Sun, *President*
▲ **EMP:** 8
SALES (est): 972.6K **Privately Held**
SIC: 3826 Instruments measuring magnetic & electrical properties

(G-6141)
MMC MAGNETICS CORP
175 Commerce Dr Ste E (11788-3920)
PHONE 631 435-9888
Huai Sheu Zhou, *Ch of Bd*
EMP: 17
SALES (est): 1.4MM **Privately Held**
SIC: 3674 3499 Photoelectric magnetic devices; magnets, permanent: metallic

(G-6142)
MOBILE FLEET INC (PA)
10 Commerce Dr (11788-3968)
P.O. Box 1240, Farmingdale (11735-0855)
PHONE 631 206-2920
Robert E Squicciarini Sr, *CEO*
Jeff Beutel, *General Mgr*
Jennifer Clark, *Purchasing*
Kevin Walker, *Vice Pres*
Matt Tannenbaum, *CFO*
▼ **EMP:** 7
SQ FT: 16,500
SALES: 15MM **Privately Held**
SIC: 3647 Automotive lighting fixtures

(G-6143)
MONITOR ELEVATOR PRODUCTS LLC
Also Called: Monitor Controls
125 Ricefield Ln (11788-2007)
PHONE 631 543-4334
Fax: 631 543-4372
Paul Horney, *President*
Steve Goldberg, *General Mgr*
Kathryn Byszewski, *Vice Pres*
Kevin White, *Production*
Louise Russo, *Purchasing*
▲ **EMP:** 65 **EST:** 2011
SQ FT: 30,000
SALES (est): 18.4MM
SALES (corp-wide): 22.4MM **Privately Held**
WEB: www.mcontrols.com
SIC: 3534 Elevators & equipment
PA: Innovation Industries, Inc.
    3500 E Main St
    Russellville AR 72802
    479 968-2232

(G-6144)
MULTIFOLD DIE CTNG FINSHG CORP
120 Ricefield Ln Ste B (11788-2033)
PHONE 631 232-1235
William Collins, *Ch of Bd*
Christine Collins, *President*
EMP: 5
SALES (est): 561.8K **Privately Held**
SIC: 3544 Special dies & tools

(G-6145)
NATUS MEDICAL INCORPORATED
Also Called: Neometrics
150 Motor Pkwy Ste 106 (11788-5167)
PHONE 631 457-4430
Fax: 631 457-4444
Joe Amato, *Principal*
Dwight Porter, *Materials Mgr*
EMP: 8
SALES (corp-wide): 375.8MM **Publicly Held**
SIC: 3845 Electromedical equipment
PA: Natus Medical Incorporated
    6701 Koll Center Pkwy # 150
    Pleasanton CA 94566
    925 223-6700

(G-6146)
NEOPOST USA INC
415 Oser Ave Ste K (11788-3637)
PHONE 631 435-9100
Joanne Lafrance, *Branch Mgr*
EMP: 50
SALES (corp-wide): 38.3MM **Privately Held**
SIC: 3579 7359 7629 Postage meters; business machine & electronic equipment rental services; business machine repair, electric
HQ: Neopost Usa Inc.
    478 Wheelers Farms Rd
    Milford CT 06461
    203 301-3400

(G-6147)
NEW HORIZON GRAPHICS INC
1200 Prime Pl (11788-4761)
PHONE 631 231-8055
Fax: 516 249-2127
Anthony Guida, *Chairman*
Annette Guida, *Corp Secy*
Rachel Guida, *Office Mgr*
Steve Guida, *Manager*
EMP: 45
SQ FT: 25,000
SALES (est): 10.5MM **Privately Held**
WEB: www.newhorizongraphic.com
SIC: 2752 2675 Commercial printing, offset; cards, folders & mats: die-cut

(G-6148)
NIKISH SOFTWARE CORP
801 Motor Pkwy (11788-5256)
PHONE 631 754-1618
Kishin Bharwani, *President*
Nitsha Bharwani, *Vice Pres*
Donald Quick, *Project Mgr*
Catherine Kraemer, *Administration*
EMP: 6
SALES (est): 700K **Privately Held**
WEB: www.nikish.com
SIC: 7372 Prepackaged software

(G-6149)
NOVA SCIENCE PUBLISHERS INC
400 Oser Ave Ste 1600 (11788-3667)
PHONE 631 231-7269
Frank Columbus, *President*
Alexandra Columbus, *Editor*
Nadezhda Columbus, *Vice Pres*
Melissa Nau, *Marketing Staff*
Angela Pontillo, *Marketing Staff*
EMP: 12
SQ FT: 1,500
SALES (est): 1.6MM **Privately Held**
SIC: 2721 2731 Periodicals; book publishing

(G-6150)
NUBIAN HERITAGE
367 Old Willets Path (11788-1217)
PHONE 631 265-3551
Edwin McCray, *Owner*
EMP: 5
SALES (est): 249.3K **Privately Held**
SIC: 3999 5199 Fire extinguishers, portable; gifts & novelties

(G-6151)
OLAN LABORATORIES INC
Also Called: Prolocksusa
20 Newton Pl (11788-4752)
PHONE 631 582-2006

Hauppauge - Suffolk County (G-6152)

EMP: 9
SQ FT: 20,000
SALES: 1.7MM Privately Held
SIC: 2844 Mfg Toilet Preparations

(G-6152)
OLDCASTLE BUILDINGENVELOPE INC
895 Motor Pkwy (11788-5232)
P.O. Box 18039 (11788-8839)
PHONE..................................631 234-2200
Lou Mangiaracina, *VP Mktg*
Daniel Dahill, *Branch Mgr*
Eric Arntsen, *Manager*
EMP: 125
SALES (corp-wide): 25.3B Privately Held
WEB: www.crh.ie
SIC: 3231 5231 Tempered glass: made from purchased glass; insulating glass: made from purchased glass; glass
HQ: Oldcastle Buildingenvelope, Inc.
5005 Lndn B Jnsn Fwy 10 Ste 1050
Dallas TX 75244
214 273-3400

(G-6153)
OLYMPIC MANUFACTURING INC
195 Marcus Blvd (11788-3702)
PHONE..................................631 231-8900
Donald Molloy Jr, *President*
EMP: 20
SQ FT: 6,000
SALES (est): 2.2MM Privately Held
SIC: 3444 Sheet metalwork

(G-6154)
ORBIT INTERNATIONAL CORP (PA)
80 Cabot Ct (11788-3771)
PHONE..................................631 435-8300
Mitchell Binder, *President*
Bruce Reissman, *COO*
David Goldman, *CFO*
Donna Holzeis, *Human Res Mgr*
Michael Anderson, *Manager*
EMP: 122 **EST:** 1957
SQ FT: 60,000
SALES: 19.1MM Publicly Held
WEB: www.orbitintl.com
SIC: 3679 3674 3643 3577 Power supplies, all types: static; solid state electronic devices; current-carrying wiring devices; computer peripheral equipment; computer terminals

(G-6155)
ORBIT INTERNATIONAL CORP
Tulip Development Laboratory
80 Cabot Ct (11788-3771)
PHONE..................................631 435-8300
Mitchell Binder, *Branch Mgr*
EMP: 53
SALES (corp-wide): 19.1MM Publicly Held
SIC: 3679 Static power supply converters for electronic applications
PA: Orbit International Corp.
80 Cabot Ct
Hauppauge NY 11788
631 435-8300

(G-6156)
ORGANIC FROG INC
Also Called: Frog International
85 Commerce Dr (11788-3902)
PHONE..................................516 897-0369
Ellen Piernick, *President*
EMP: 8
SQ FT: 2,200
SALES: 1.5MM Privately Held
SIC: 2834 5122 Vitamin, nutrient & hematinic preparations for human use; drugs, proprietaries & sundries

(G-6157)
P & H INC
Also Called: Valmont Site Pro 1
15 Oser Ave (11788-3808)
PHONE..................................631 231-7660
Joe Catapano, *General Mgr*
Joseph Cadapano, *Branch Mgr*
EMP: 33
SALES (corp-wide): 2.6B Publicly Held
SIC: 3441 Fabricated structural metal

HQ: P & H, Inc.
1545 Pidco Dr
Plymouth IN 46563
574 277-0670

(G-6158)
PARKER-HANNIFIN CORPORATION
Also Called: Electronics Systems Division
300 Marcus Blvd (11788-2044)
PHONE..................................631 231-3737
Fax: 631 231-3699
Donald Washkewicz, *President*
Lee Banks, *Vice Pres*
Jon Marten, *Vice Pres*
Thomas A Piraino Jr, *Vice Pres*
Daniel Serbin, *Vice Pres*
EMP: 335
SQ FT: 150,000
SALES (corp-wide): 11.3B Publicly Held
WEB: www.parker.com
SIC: 3829 Instrument board gauges, automotive: computerized
PA: Parker-Hannifin Corporation
6035 Parkland Blvd
Cleveland OH 44124
216 896-3000

(G-6159)
PEELLE COMPANY (PA)
373 Smithtown Byp 311 (11788-2516)
PHONE..................................631 231-6000
R B Peelle Jr, *Ch of Bd*
Henry E Peelle III, *President*
Michael J Ryan, *Vice Pres*
Dan Nieves, *Engineer*
Brad Hunt, *Sales Mgr*
▲ **EMP:** 7
SQ FT: 6,000
SALES (est): 12.5MM Privately Held
SIC: 3499 Aerosol valves, metal

(G-6160)
PEER SOFTWARE INCORPORATED (PA)
1363 Veterans Hwy Ste 44 (11788-3046)
PHONE..................................631 979-1770
Paul J Marsala, *Principal*
EMP: 6
SALES (est): 2MM Privately Held
SIC: 7372 Prepackaged software

(G-6161)
PETER KWASNY INC
400 Oser Ave Ste 1650 (11788-3669)
PHONE..................................727 641-1462
Hans Peter Kwasny, *President*
▲ **EMP:** 6
SALES (est): 811.1K
SALES (corp-wide): 61.3MM Privately Held
SIC: 2851 Paints & allied products
PA: Peter Kwasny Gmbh
Heilbronner Str. 96
Gundelsheim 74831
626 995-0

(G-6162)
PETS N PEOPLE INC
2100 Pacific St (11788-4737)
PHONE..................................631 232-1200
Fax: 631 232-1206
Mindy D Weiss Lasman, *President*
Marcia Weiss, *Corp Secy*
Mark Stern, *Personnel Exec*
▲ **EMP:** 8
SALES (est): 520K Privately Held
SIC: 3999 Pet supplies

(G-6163)
PHOENIX MCH PDTS OF HAUPPAUGE
225 Engineers Rd (11788-4020)
PHONE..................................631 234-0100
Richard F Coronato Sr, *President*
EMP: 5
SQ FT: 15,000
SALES (est): 392.5K Privately Held
SIC: 3599 Machine shop, jobbing & repair

(G-6164)
PINDER INTERNATIONAL INC (PA)
1140 Motor Pkwy Ste A (11788-5255)
PHONE..................................631 273-0324

Jatinder Dhall, *Ch of Bd*
▲ **EMP:** 5 **EST:** 2011
SQ FT: 15,000
SALES (est): 769.4K Privately Held
SIC: 2231 Apparel & outerwear broadwoven fabrics

(G-6165)
PNEUMERCATOR COMPANY INC
1785 Express Dr N (11788-5303)
PHONE..................................631 293-8450
Fax: 631 293-8533
Jonathan Levy, *President*
Agnes Amundsen, *Manager*
Peter Pietzyk, *Director*
EMP: 35 **EST:** 1914
SQ FT: 11,500
SALES (est): 8.4MM Privately Held
WEB: www.pneumercator.com
SIC: 3823 Gas flow computers, industrial process type; pressure gauges, dial & digital

(G-6166)
POLY CRAFT INDUSTRIES CORP
40 Ranick Rd (11788-4209)
PHONE..................................631 630-6731
Fax: 718 392-4044
Samuel Brach, *President*
Sylvia Brach, *Admin Sec*
▲ **EMP:** 25
SQ FT: 13,000
SALES (est): 5.4MM Privately Held
SIC: 2673 5113 Plastic bags: made from purchased materials; bags, paper & disposable plastic

(G-6167)
PRECARE CORP
Also Called: Premier Care Industries
400 Wireless Blvd (11788-3938)
PHONE..................................631 524-5171
Fax: 631 952-7478
Abraham Micheal, *Branch Mgr*
EMP: 5
SALES (corp-wide): 12.3MM Privately Held
SIC: 2676 Sanitary paper products
PA: Precare Corp.
100 Oser Ave
Hauppauge NY 11788
631 667-1055

(G-6168)
PRECARE CORP (PA)
Also Called: PREMIER CARE INDUSTRIES
100 Oser Ave (11788-3809)
PHONE..................................631 667-1055
Matthew Neman, *COO*
Ouri Neman, *Vice Pres*
Bill Lutz, *VP Sales*
▲ **EMP:** 5
SQ FT: 35,000
SALES: 12.3MM Privately Held
SIC: 2621 2676 Tissue paper; napkins, sanitary: made from purchased paper; diapers, paper (disposable): made from purchased paper; tampons, sanitary: made from purchased paper

(G-6169)
PRELOAD CONCRETE STRUCTURES
60 Commerce Dr (11788-3929)
PHONE..................................631 231-8100
Andrew E Tripp Jr, *President*
Nancy Coll, *Corp Secy*
Jack Hornstein, *Vice Pres*
Stephen G Kravitz, *Network Mgr*
EMP: 42
SQ FT: 29,000
SALES (est): 6.9MM Privately Held
WEB: www.preload.com
SIC: 3272 Tanks, concrete

(G-6170)
PREMIER FIXTURES LLC (PA)
Also Called: Premier Store Fixtures
400 Oser Ave Ste 350 (11788-3632)
PHONE..................................631 236-4100
Nelson Goodman, *President*
William Leun, *Accountant*
EMP: 93 **EST:** 2013
SQ FT: 500,000

SALES: 80.7MM Privately Held
SIC: 3053 6512 5962 2541 Gaskets, packing & sealing devices; shopping center, property operation only; merchandising machine operators; store fixtures, wood; design services

(G-6171)
PREMIER WOODWORKING INC
400 Oser Ave (11788-3619)
P.O. Box 14177 (11788-0401)
PHONE..................................631 236-4100
Jose Tellez, *President*
Carlos Zurita, *Vice Pres*
Jasmin Gonzalez, *Administration*
▲ **EMP:** 35
SQ FT: 230,000
SALES: 2.5MM Privately Held
SIC: 2541 Wood partitions & fixtures

(G-6172)
PRINTERS 3 INC
43 Corporate Dr Ste 2 (11788-2048)
PHONE..................................631 351-1331
Fax: 631 351-1384
Sal Viscuso, *Ch of Bd*
Anthony Viscuso, *President*
Christal Viscuso, *Corp Secy*
EMP: 10
SQ FT: 4,200
SALES (est): 1.1MM Privately Held
SIC: 2752 Commercial printing, lithographic

(G-6173)
PROFESSIONAL BUTY HOLDINGS INC
150 Motor Pkwy Ste 401 (11788-5108)
PHONE..................................631 787-8576
EMP: 10
SQ FT: 100,000
SALES: 10MM Privately Held
SIC: 2844 Mfg Toilet Preparations

(G-6174)
PROFESSIONAL SOLUTIONS PRINT
125 Wireless Blvd Ste E (11788-3937)
PHONE..................................631 231-9300
Karl Snyder, *President*
EMP: 6
SALES: 750K Privately Held
SIC: 2752 Commercial printing, lithographic

(G-6175)
PROFILE PRINTING & GRAPHICS (PA)
275 Marcus Blvd (11788-2022)
PHONE..................................631 273-2727
Michael Munda, *President*
EMP: 7
SQ FT: 3,000
SALES (est): 508.8K Privately Held
WEB: www.profileprinting.com
SIC: 2752 Commercial printing, lithographic

(G-6176)
QUOIZEL INC
590 Old Willets Path # 1 (11788-4119)
PHONE..................................631 436-4402
Manny Yniesta, *Project Mgr*
Sandy Stone, *Accounting Mgr*
Howard Greenberg, *Natl Sales Mgr*
Patrick Slater, *Marketing Staff*
Toni Phillips, *Branch Mgr*
EMP: 27
SALES (corp-wide): 76.9MM Privately Held
WEB: www.quoizel.com
SIC: 3645 5063 8741 Residential lighting fixtures; lighting fixtures; management services
PA: Quoizel, Inc.
6 Corporate Pkwy
Goose Creek SC 29445
843 553-6700

(G-6177)
RENTSCHLER BIOTECHNOLOGIE GMBH
400 Oser Ave Ste 1650 (11788-3669)
PHONE..................................631 656-7137
Nikolaus F Rentschler, *CEO*

GEOGRAPHIC SECTION

Hauppauge - Suffolk County (G-6198)

Daniela Ceixeira, *Accountant*
EMP: 5
SALES (est): 470K **Privately Held**
SIC: 2836 Biological products, except diagnostic

(G-6178)
ROBERT BUSSE & CO INC
Also Called: Busse Hospital Disposables
75 Arkay Dr (11788-3707)
P.O. Box 11067 (11788)
PHONE..................................631 435-4711
Fax: 631 435-4721
Jane Cardinale, *CEO*
Raymond O'Hara, *President*
Dean Cardinale, *Plant Mgr*
Ruth Ripley, *Traffic Mgr*
Mary Sherman, *Purch Agent*
▲ **EMP:** 280 **EST:** 1953
SQ FT: 78,000
SALES (est): 60.7MM **Privately Held**
WEB: www.busseinc.com
SIC: 3842 Sterilizers, hospital & surgical

(G-6179)
RODALE WIRELESS INC
Also Called: Rodale Electronics
20 Oser Ave Ste 2 (11788-3815)
PHONE..................................631 231-0044
John B Clement, *President*
Vince Maida, *Vice Pres*
Mary Licciardi, *Purch Dir*
Robert Ponzio, *Buyer*
Don Ellison, *Electrical Engi*
EMP: 25
SQ FT: 10,000
SALES: 4.7MM **Privately Held**
SIC: 3699 3825 3812 3663 Electrical equipment & supplies; countermeasure simulators, electric; instruments to measure electricity; search & navigation equipment; radio & TV communications equipment; current-carrying wiring devices; computer peripheral equipment

(G-6180)
ROTRONIC INSTRUMENT CORP (HQ)
135 Engineers Rd Ste 150 (11788-4018)
P.O. Box 11241 (11788-0703)
PHONE..................................631 348-6844
Patrick J Lafarie, *Senior VP*
David P Love, *Vice Pres*
Rose Mannarino, *Sales Mgr*
Jay Crum, *Regl Sales Mgr*
Mike McGinn, *Regl Sales Mgr*
▲ **EMP:** 18
SALES (est): 2.6MM
SALES (corp-wide): 49.2MM **Privately Held**
WEB: www.rotronic-usa.com
SIC: 3823 Temperature measurement instruments, industrial; temperature instruments: industrial process type; humidity instruments, industrial process type
PA: Rotronic Ag
Grindelstrasse 6
Bassersdorf ZH 8303
448 381-111

(G-6181)
RSM ELECTRON POWER INC
Also Called: Sensitron Semiconductor
100 Engineers Rd (11788-4023)
PHONE..................................631 586-7600
Bryan Rogers, *Vice Pres*
Susan Panagopoulos, *Opers Staff*
Steve Saunders, *Branch Mgr*
EMP: 90
SALES (corp-wide): 18.5MM **Privately Held**
SIC: 3674 Semiconductors & related devices
PA: Rsm Electron Power, Inc.
221 W Industry Ct
Deer Park NY 11729
631 586-7600

(G-6182)
SAMSON TECHNOLOGIES CORP (HQ)
45 Gilpin Ave Ste 100 (11788-4755)
PHONE..................................631 784-2200
Fax: 516 784-2201
Richard Ash, *Ch of Bd*
Scott Goodman, *President*
David Hakim, *General Mgr*
David Ash, *COO*
Douglas Bryant, *Vice Pres*
◆ **EMP:** 70
SALES (est): 9.4MM
SALES (corp-wide): 293.8MM **Privately Held**
WEB: www.samsontech.com
SIC: 3651 3931 5099 5065 Sound reproducing equipment; musical instruments; musical instruments; sound equipment, electronic
PA: Sam Ash Music Corporation
278 Duffy Ave Unit A
Hicksville NY 11801
516 932-6400

(G-6183)
SANTA FE MANUFACTURING CORP
225 Engineers Rd (11788-4020)
PHONE..................................631 234-0100
Richard Coronato Sr, *President*
Charlotte Coronato, *Vice Pres*
EMP: 5
SQ FT: 44,000
SALES (est): 605.2K **Privately Held**
SIC: 3728 3827 Aircraft parts & equipment; optical instruments & lenses

(G-6184)
SAPTALIS PHARMACEUTICALS LLC
45 Davids Dr (11788-2038)
PHONE..................................631 231-2751
Polireddy Dondeti, *President*
Tatiana Akimova, *Exec VP*
EMP: 17
SQ FT: 10,000
SALES (est): 739.5K **Privately Held**
SIC: 2834 Pharmaceutical preparations

(G-6185)
SCALAMANDRE WALLPAPER INC
Also Called: Scalamandre Silks
350 Wireless Blvd (11788-3947)
PHONE..................................631 467-8800
Edwin Bitter, *Ch of Bd*
Adrianne Bitter, *President*
Mark J Bitter, *Vice Pres*
Robert Bitter, *Vice Pres*
▲ **EMP:** 401
SQ FT: 30,000
SALES (est): 43.8MM **Privately Held**
SIC: 2621 5198 2231 2221 Kraft paper; wallcoverings; broadwoven fabric mills, wool; broadwoven fabric mills, manmade; broadwoven fabric mills, cotton

(G-6186)
SCIEGEN PHARMACEUTICALS INC
89 Arkay Dr (11788-3727)
PHONE..................................631 434-2723
EMP: 30
SQ FT: 89,000
SALES (corp-wide): 19.4MM **Privately Held**
SIC: 2834 Mfg Pharmaceutical Preparations
PA: Sciegen Pharmaceuticals, Inc.
20 Davids Dr
Hauppauge NY 11788
631 434-2723

(G-6187)
SCIEGEN PHARMACEUTICALS INC
89 Arkay Dr (11788-3727)
PHONE..................................631 434-2723
Pailla Malla Reddy, *CEO*
Siva Reddy, *Vice Pres*
Venkata Reddy, *Vice Pres*
Renee Reynolds, *CFO*
Krishna Mohan Chilakamarthy, *Director*
▲ **EMP:** 150
SQ FT: 89,000
SALES: 15MM **Privately Held**
SIC: 2834 Pharmaceutical preparations

(G-6188)
SCOTTS COMPANY LLC
65 Engineers Rd (11788-4003)
PHONE..................................631 478-6843
Peter Pirro, *Principal*
EMP: 8
SALES (corp-wide): 3B **Publicly Held**
SIC: 2873 Fertilizers: natural (organic), except compost
HQ: The Scotts Company Llc
14111 Scottslawn Rd
Marysville OH 43040
937 644-0011

(G-6189)
SIEMENS INDUSTRY INC
Process Instrmntation Bus Unit
155 Plant Ave (11788-3801)
PHONE..................................631 231-3600
Joseph Chilleme, *Engineer*
Frank Fromm, *Engineer*
Allan Cottrell, *Manager*
John Cochran, *Executive*
Robert Musano, *Associate*
EMP: 120
SALES (corp-wide): 83.5B **Privately Held**
WEB: www.sea.siemens.com
SIC: 3824 Totalizing meters, consumption registering
HQ: Siemens Industry, Inc.
1000 Deerfield Pkwy
Buffalo Grove IL 60089
847 215-1000

(G-6190)
SIGN A RAMA INC
Also Called: Sign-A-Rama
663 Old Willets Path C (11788-4117)
PHONE..................................631 952-3324
Fax: 631 952-3259
Jim Reardon, *Manager*
EMP: 5
SALES (corp-wide): 28.2MM **Privately Held**
WEB: www.franchisemart.com
SIC: 3993 Signs & advertising specialties
PA: Sign A Rama Inc.
2121 Vista Pkwy
West Palm Beach FL 33411
561 640-5570

(G-6191)
SIMA TECHNOLOGIES LLC
125 Commerce Dr (11788-3932)
PHONE..................................412 828-9130
George Simolin, *CFO*
Storm Orion, *Director*
Richard Leifer,
Bob Pennington, *Products*
Robert S Leifer,
▲ **EMP:** 7
SQ FT: 27,000
SALES (est): 1MM **Privately Held**
WEB: www.simacorp.com
SIC: 3651 3861 5999 3577 Household audio & video equipment; photographic processing equipment & chemicals; mobile telephones & equipment; computer peripheral equipment; electrical equipment & supplies; motors & generators

(G-6192)
SIR INDUSTRIES INC
208 Blydenburg Rd Unit C (11749-5023)
PHONE..................................631 234-2444
Fax: 631 234-5063
Stanley Rabinowitz, *President*
▲ **EMP:** 6
SQ FT: 7,000
SALES (est): 35.7K **Privately Held**
SIC: 3648 5063 5719 Stage lighting equipment; light bulbs & related supplies; lighting fixtures

(G-6193)
SPECTRON GLASS & ELECTRONICS
595 Old Willets Path A (11788-4112)
P.O. Box 13368 (11788-0744)
PHONE..................................631 582-5600
Fax: 631 582-5671
Robert S Marshall, *Ch of Bd*
Pastall Lemarie, *Vice Pres*
Norman Goldsobel, *VP Mfg*
Jennifer Marshall, *Human Res Mgr*
Danny Dalfonso, *Human Resources*
▲ **EMP:** 16 **EST:** 1946
SQ FT: 16,000
SALES (est): 2.9MM
SALES (corp-wide): 3.2MM **Privately Held**
WEB: www.spectronsensors.com
SIC: 3679 3674 Electronic switches; semiconductors & related devices
PA: Spectron Systems Technology Inc
595 Old Willets Path A
Hauppauge NY 11788
631 582-5600

(G-6194)
SPECTRON SYSTEMS TECHNOLOGY (PA)
595 Old Willets Path A (11788-4113)
P.O. Box 13368 (11788-0744)
PHONE..................................631 582-5600
Robert Marshall, *President*
Pascal Lemarie, *Exec VP*
Nancy Chereb, *Treasurer*
Bruce Smart, *Natl Sales Mgr*
EMP: 14
SQ FT: 14,000
SALES (est): 3.2MM **Privately Held**
WEB: www.tiltsensors.com
SIC: 3679 Electronic switches

(G-6195)
SPECTRUM BRANDS INC
Also Called: United Pet Group
2100 Pacific St (11788-4737)
PHONE..................................631 232-1200
Mark Stern, *Branch Mgr*
EMP: 275
SALES (corp-wide): 5.8B **Publicly Held**
SIC: 3999 Pet supplies
HQ: Spectrum Brands, Inc.
3001 Deming Way
Middleton WI 53562
608 275-3340

(G-6196)
SPECTRUM THIN FILMS INC
135 Marcus Blvd (11788-3702)
PHONE..................................631 901-1010
Anthony Pirera, *President*
Bruce Miao, *COO*
Carlos Penalbert, *Opers Staff*
Maricela Baksh, *QC Mgr*
Maria Pirera, *VP Sales*
EMP: 35
SQ FT: 3,400
SALES (est): 12.6MM **Privately Held**
WEB: www.spectrumthinfilms.com
SIC: 3827 5049 Lenses, optical: all types except ophthalmic; optical goods

(G-6197)
SPELLMAN HIGH VLTAGE ELEC CORP (PA)
475 Wireless Blvd (11788-3951)
PHONE..................................631 630-3000
Loren Skeist, *President*
Dennis Bay, *Managing Dir*
Robert Barone, *Vice Pres*
David Gillispie, *VP Opers*
Godrej Mehta, *VP Opers*
▲ **EMP:** 500
SQ FT: 100,000
SALES (est): 289.9MM **Privately Held**
SIC: 3612 Transformers, except electric

(G-6198)
SPOTLESS PLASTICS (USA) INC (DH)
100 Motor Pkwy Ste 155 (11788-5165)
PHONE..................................631 951-9000
Peter Wilson, *President*
Sophie Brading, *Business Mgr*
Stanley Gouldson, *Vice Pres*
Nancy Schoedler, *Manager*
Chuck Kelly, *Admin Sec*
EMP: 40
SQ FT: 10,000
SALES (est): 111.8MM
SALES (corp-wide): 2.3B **Privately Held**
SIC: 3089 Clothes hangers, plastic
HQ: Spotless Group Limited
549 St Kilda Rd
Melbourne VIC 3000
130 085-0505

Hauppauge - Suffolk County (G-6199)

(G-6199)
STANDARD MICROSYSTEMS CORP (HQ)
Also Called: Smsc
80 Arkay Dr Ste 100 (11788-3774)
PHONE..................................631 435-6000
Fax: 631 435-6110
Christine King, *President*
Ian Harris, *President*
David Coller, *Senior VP*
Aaron L Fisher, *Senior VP*
Walter Siegel, *Senior VP*
▲ EMP: 114
SQ FT: 200,000
SALES (est): 100.8MM
SALES (corp-wide): 2.1B **Publicly Held**
SIC: 3674 Integrated circuits, semiconductor networks, etc.
PA: Microchip Technology Inc
   2355 W Chandler Blvd
   Chandler AZ 85224
   480 792-7200

(G-6200)
STAR QUALITY PRINTING INC
Also Called: Star Communications
270 Oser Ave (11788-3610)
PHONE..................................631 273-1900
Alka Parikh, *Ch of Bd*
Kalpesh Parikh, *President*
James Gibb, *Vice Pres*
Adhish Parikh, *Vice Pres*
Kevin P Murphy, *Accounts Exec*
▲ EMP: 12
SQ FT: 7,500
SALES (est): 2.6MM **Privately Held**
WEB: www.sqprinting.com
SIC: 2752 Commercial printing, offset

(G-6201)
STERLING NORTH AMERICA INC
270 Oser Ave (11788-3610)
PHONE..................................631 243-6933
Ed McAllister, *President*
EMP: 28
SQ FT: 40,000
SALES: 7.2MM **Privately Held**
SIC: 2752 Commercial printing, lithographic

(G-6202)
SUMMIT APPAREL INC (PA)
65 Commerce Dr (11788-3902)
PHONE..................................631 213-8299
Morad Mayeri, *Ch of Bd*
Abraham Mayeri, *Vice Pres*
▲ EMP: 18
SQ FT: 25,000
SALES (est): 1.9MM **Privately Held**
WEB: www.summitapparel.com
SIC: 2253 Dresses, knit

(G-6203)
SUPERIOR WASHER & GASKET CORP (PA)
170 Adams Ave (11788-3612)
P.O. Box 5407 (11788-0407)
PHONE..................................631 273-8282
Fax: 631 273-8088
Allan Lippolis, *CEO*
Robert Lippolis, *Purchasing*
Jason Garrick, *QC Mgr*
Marie Panfilio, *VP Sales*
Luann Racca, *Sales Mgr*
EMP: 65
SQ FT: 42,000
SALES (est): 19.4MM **Privately Held**
WEB: www.superiorwasher.com
SIC: 3452 3469 Washers, metal; washers; metal stampings

(G-6204)
SUPERITE GEAR INSTR OF HPPAUGE (PA)
225 Engineers Rd (11788-4020)
PHONE..................................631 234-0100
Richard Coronato Sr, *President*
Barbara Knox, *Human Res Mgr*
Charlotte Coronato, *Admin Sec*
EMP: 8 EST: 1955
SQ FT: 44,000
SALES (est): 2.4MM **Privately Held**
SIC: 3462 Gears, forged steel

(G-6205)
SYMWAVE INC (DH)
80 Arkay Dr (11788-3705)
PHONE..................................949 542-4400
Yossi Cohen, *President*
Jun Ye, *Vice Pres*
Adam Spice, *CFO*
Wanda Knight, *Manager*
Christopher Thomas, *CTO*
EMP: 7
SALES (est): 669.6K
SALES (corp-wide): 2.1B **Publicly Held**
WEB: www.symwave.com
SIC: 3674 Semiconductors & related devices
HQ: Standard Microsystems Corporation
   80 Arkay Dr Ste 100
   Hauppauge NY 11788
   631 435-6000

(G-6206)
TARSIA TECHNICAL INDUSTRIES
Also Called: TTI
93 Marcus Blvd (11788-3712)
PHONE..................................631 231-8322
Joe Tarsia, *President*
EMP: 7
SALES (est): 664.2K **Privately Held**
WEB: www.ttind.com
SIC: 3599 Machine shop, jobbing & repair

(G-6207)
TDK-LAMBDA AMERICAS INC
145 Marcus Blvd Ste 3 (11788-3760)
PHONE..................................631 967-3000
Fax: 631 967-3022
Hiroshi Osawa, *President*
EMP: 15
SALES (corp-wide): 9.8B **Privately Held**
WEB: www.lambdapower.com
SIC: 3677 Transformers power supply, electronic type
HQ: Tdk-Lambda Americas Inc.
   405 Essex Rd
   Tinton Falls NJ 07753
   732 922-9300

(G-6208)
TDL MANUFACTURING INC
Also Called: Tulip Development Labs
80 Cabot Ct (11788-3729)
PHONE..................................215 538-8820
Dennis Sunshine, *Chairman*
Bruce Reissman, *Exec VP*
Mitch Binder, *CFO*
Edward Rusin, *Accounts Mgr*
EMP: 19
SQ FT: 9,000
SALES (est): 2MM
SALES (corp-wide): 19.1MM **Publicly Held**
WEB: www.orbitintl.com
SIC: 3728 Aircraft parts & equipment
PA: Orbit International Corp.
   80 Cabot Ct
   Hauppauge NY 11788
   631 435-8300

(G-6209)
TECHNAPULSE LLC
400 Oser Ave Ste 1950 (11788-3639)
PHONE..................................631 234-8700
Bernard Rachowitz, *President*
Joseph Schneider, *Plant Mgr*
▲ EMP: 17 EST: 1999
SALES (est): 376.5K **Privately Held**
SIC: 7692 Welding repair

(G-6210)
TECHNIMETAL PRECISION INDS
195 Marcus Blvd (11788-3796)
PHONE..................................631 231-8900
Fax: 631 231-8928
Donald T Molloy, *President*
Stephen J Miller, *Exec VP*
EMP: 50 EST: 1967
SQ FT: 27,000
SALES (est): 9.2MM **Privately Held**
WEB: www.tpimetals.com
SIC: 3444 Sheet metalwork

(G-6211)
TEK WELD
45 Rabro Dr Unit 1 (11788-4260)
PHONE..................................631 694-5503
Maryanne Coopersmith, *Principal*
Stacy Reiter, *Accounting Mgr*
Patrick Hale, *Credit Mgr*
Gregg Szpicek, *VP Sales*
Claire Ashford, *Sales Mgr*
▲ EMP: 16
SALES (est): 1.7MM **Privately Held**
SIC: 7692 Welding repair

(G-6212)
TELEBYTE INC (PA)
355 Marcus Blvd Ste 2 (11788-2027)
PHONE..................................631 423-3232
Dr Kenneth S Schneider, *CEO*
Michael Breneisen, *President*
Kenneth Schneicer, *Vice Pres*
Rein Holt, *Controller*
Abraham Weber, *Manager*
EMP: 25
SQ FT: 3,500
SALES (est): 4MM **Privately Held**
WEB: www.telebyteusa.com
SIC: 3669 Intercommunication systems, electric

(G-6213)
TELESITE USA INC
89 Arkay Dr (11788-3727)
PHONE..................................631 952-2288
Larry Greenwald, *President*
EMP: 11
SQ FT: 7,000
SALES (est): 782.8K
SALES (corp-wide): 44.8MM **Publicly Held**
WEB: www.viconindustries.com
SIC: 3669 Intercommunication systems, electric
PA: Vicon Industries, Inc.
   135 Fell Ct
   Hauppauge NY 11788
   631 952-2288

(G-6214)
THREAD CHECK INC
390 Oser Ave Ste 2 (11788-3682)
PHONE..................................631 231-1515
Hyman Jack Kipnes, *President*
Irving Kipnes, *Vice Pres*
EMP: 99
SQ FT: 74,000
SALES (est): 11.8MM **Privately Held**
WEB: www.threadcheck.com
SIC: 3552 5084 3823 Thread making machines, spinning machinery; industrial machinery & equipment; industrial instrmnts msrmnt display/control process variable

(G-6215)
TIFFEN ACQUISITION LLC
Also Called: Tiffen Co, The
80 Oser Ave (11788-3809)
PHONE..................................631 273-2500
EMP: 10
SALES (corp-wide): 25.3MM **Privately Held**
SIC: 3861 Photographic equipment & supplies
PA: Tiffen Acquisition Llc
   90 Oser Ave
   Hauppauge NY 11788
   631 273-2500

(G-6216)
TIFFEN ACQUISITION LLC (PA)
Also Called: Tiffen Company, The
90 Oser Ave (11788-3809)
PHONE..................................631 273-2500
Michael Cannata, *COO*
Russ Abelein, *Vice Pres*
Eric Jackson, *Engineer*
Joseph Yu, *Engineer*
Stacy Gonzalez, *Controller*
▲ EMP: 60
SALES (est): 25.3MM **Privately Held**
WEB: www.tiffen.com
SIC: 3861 Photographic equipment & supplies

(G-6217)
TIFFEN COMPANY LLC
90 Oser Ave (11788-3809)
PHONE..................................631 273-2500
Jim Long, *COO*
Richard Bonacrm, *Vice Pres*
Michael Crooks, *Vice Pres*
Ira Tiffen, *Vice Pres*
Jeffrey Cohen, *Mfg Staff*
EMP: 6
SALES (est): 560K **Privately Held**
SIC: 3861 Photographic equipment & supplies

(G-6218)
TUNAVERSE MEDIA INC
750 Veterans Hwy Ste 200 (11788-2943)
PHONE..................................631 778-8350
Ross Pirtle, *President*
Hal Denton, *Vice Pres*
Tom Diemidil, *Vice Pres*
Barbara Pirtle, *Bookkeeper*
EMP: 8
SALES: 500K **Privately Held**
SIC: 7372 Prepackaged software

(G-6219)
TWINCO MFG CO INC
30 Commerce Dr (11788-3904)
PHONE..................................631 231-0022
Fax: 631 231-0314
John A Schatz, *President*
Ellen Wilcken, *Vice Pres*
Veronica Broome, *Manager*
▲ EMP: 44 EST: 1965
SQ FT: 50,000
SALES: 8.4MM **Privately Held**
WEB: www.twincomfg.com
SIC: 3669 3469 3599 3743 Railroad signaling devices, electric; machine parts, stamped or pressed metal; machine & other job shop work; railroad equipment

(G-6220)
UNITED-GUARDIAN INC (PA)
230 Marcus Blvd (11788-3731)
P.O. Box 18050 (11788-8850)
PHONE..................................631 273-0900
Kenneth H Globus, *Ch of Bd*
Roseann La Corte, *General Mgr*
Peter A Hiltunen, *Vice Pres*
Peter Hiltunen, *Vice Pres*
Joseph J Vernice, *Vice Pres*
◆ EMP: 36
SQ FT: 50,000
SALES: 13.4MM **Publicly Held**
WEB: www.u-g.com
SIC: 2844 2834 Toilet preparations; cosmetic preparations; pharmaceutical preparations

(G-6221)
UNLIMITED INK INC
595 Old Willets Path B (11788-4114)
PHONE..................................631 582-0696
Josh Disamone, *President*
EMP: 20
SALES (est): 1MM **Privately Held**
SIC: 2759 5699 Screen printing; sports apparel

(G-6222)
VEHICLE MANUFACTURERS INC
Also Called: Skyguard
400 Oser Ave Ste 100 (11788-3600)
PHONE..................................631 851-1700
George J Wafer, *CEO*
Scott Wafer, *President*
Angelo Addesso, *COO*
Brent Depeppe, *Vice Pres*
Alex Keller, *Vice Pres*
EMP: 22
SQ FT: 3,000
SALES: 10MM **Privately Held**
SIC: 3069 Rubber automotive products

(G-6223)
VENUS PHARMACEUTICALS INTL INC
55a Kennedy Dr (11788-4038)
PHONE..................................631 249-4140
Bharat Kakumanu, *CEO*
Survir Singh Salaria, *President*
▼ EMP: 15
SQ FT: 25,000
SALES (est): 3.5MM **Privately Held**
WEB: www.venuspharmaceuticals.com
SIC: 2834 Pharmaceutical preparations

GEOGRAPHIC SECTION

Hawthorne - Westchester County (G-6247)

(G-6224)
VETRA SYSTEMS CORPORATION
275 Marcus Blvd Unit J (11788-2022)
PHONE.................................631 434-3185
Fax: 631 434-3516
Jonas Ulenas, *President*
Paul Sabatino, *Vice Pres*
George Zahn, *QC Dir*
Paul Wieties, *CIO*
Valdas Douba, *Shareholder*
EMP: 8
SALES (est): 1.1MM **Privately Held**
WEB: www.vetra.com
SIC: 3823 5084 Computer interface equipment for industrial process control; controllers for process variables, all types; conveyor systems

(G-6225)
VICON INDUSTRIES INC (PA)
135 Fell Ct (11788-4351)
PHONE.................................631 952-2288
Fax: 631 951-2288
Eric S Fullerton, *CEO*
Julian A Tiedemann, *Ch of Bd*
Frank Jacovino, *President*
Bret M McGowan, *Senior VP*
Peter A Horn, *Vice Pres*
◆ **EMP:** 148
SQ FT: 30,000
SALES: 44.8MM **Publicly Held**
WEB: www.viconindustries.com
SIC: 3663 3669 Television closed circuit equipment; visual communication systems; transportation signaling devices

(G-6226)
VIRTUE PAINTBALL LLC (PA)
40 Oser Ave Ste 14 (11788-3807)
PHONE.................................631 617-5560
Tom Conde, *Opers Mgr*
Michael Newman,
▲ **EMP:** 8
SQ FT: 4,000
SALES (est): 740.3K **Privately Held**
SIC: 3675 3676 3678 Electronic capacitors; electronic resistors; electronic connectors

(G-6227)
VISIONTRON CORP
720 Old Willets Path (11788-4102)
PHONE.................................631 582-8600
Lisa Torsiello, *President*
Donna Goroshko, *General Mgr*
Joseph Torsiello, *Vice Pres*
Laurence Torsiello, *Vice Pres*
Charles Hansen, *Mfg Dir*
▼ **EMP:** 25
SQ FT: 20,000
SALES (est): 6.4MM **Privately Held**
WEB: www.visiontron.com
SIC: 3669 Intercommunication systems, electric

(G-6228)
VITAMIN POWER INCORORATED
75 Commerce Dr (11788-3902)
PHONE.................................631 676-5790
David Friedlander, *President*
Edward Friedlander, *Chairman*
Robert Edwards, *Marketing Staff*
EMP: 7
SQ FT: 20,000
SALES: 1.2MM **Privately Held**
WEB: www.vitaminpower.com
SIC: 2023 Dietary supplements, dairy & non-dairy based

(G-6229)
W & H STAMPINGS INC
45 Engineers Rd (11788-4019)
PHONE.................................631 234-6161
Fax: 631 582-1540
Ernest E Hoffmann, *President*
Ron Marcisak, *General Mgr*
Al Toepfer, *Purchasing*
Maria Alfieri, *Bookkeeper*
EMP: 28 **EST:** 1956
SQ FT: 33,000
SALES: 1MM **Privately Held**
WEB: www.whstamp.com
SIC: 3469 Metal stampings

(G-6230)
WATSON PRODUCTIONS LLC
Also Called: Skyline New York
740 Old Willets Path # 400 (11788-4121)
PHONE.................................516 334-9766
Liz Kasavana, *Manager*
Robert Watson,
Robert T Watson,
▲ **EMP:** 12
SALES (est): 1.6MM **Privately Held**
WEB: www.watsonproductions.com
SIC: 3577 Graphic displays, except graphic terminals

(G-6231)
WELDING METALLURGY INC (HQ)
110 Plant Ave (11788-3830)
PHONE.................................631 253-0500
Fax: 631 231-4970
Gary Settoducato, *Ch of Bd*
Scott Glassman, *CFO*
Chuck Layne, *Manager*
Robert Makaw, *Officer*
EMP: 50
SQ FT: 35,000
SALES (est): 10.9MM
SALES (corp-wide): 80.4MM **Publicly Held**
WEB: www.weldingmet.com
SIC: 3441 Fabricated structural metal
PA: Air Industries Group
360 Motor Pkwy Ste 100
Hauppauge NY 11788
631 881-4920

(G-6232)
WELDING METALLURGY INC
110 Plant Ave (11788-3830)
PHONE.................................631 253-0500
Dan Godin, *CEO*
John Canova, *General Mgr*
Kristie Petersen, *Vice Pres*
EMP: 85
SQ FT: 84,000
SALES (est): 18.6MM
SALES (corp-wide): 80.4MM **Publicly Held**
WEB: www.compac-rf.com
SIC: 3469 Electronic enclosures, stamped or pressed metal
PA: Air Industries Group
360 Motor Pkwy Ste 100
Hauppauge NY 11788
631 881-4920

(G-6233)
WEST GLUERS
120 Ricefield Ln Ste 200 (11788-2033)
PHONE.................................631 232-1235
Michael Collins, *Owner*
EMP: 5
SALES (est): 750.6K **Privately Held**
SIC: 2652 Setup paperboard boxes

(G-6234)
WIDEX USA INC (DH)
Also Called: Widex International
185 Commerce Dr (11788-3916)
P.O. Box 6077, Long Island City (11106-0077)
PHONE.................................718 360-1000
Jake Haycock, *President*
Peter Schaade, *Managing Dir*
Sren Westermann, *Exec VP*
Francesca Dinota, *VP Finance*
Edward Searson, *Credit Mgr*
▲ **EMP:** 94
SALES (est): 19MM
SALES (corp-wide): 460.9MM **Privately Held**
SIC: 3842 Hearing aids
HQ: Widex A/S
Nymollevej 6
Lynge 3540
443 556-00

(G-6235)
WILBAR INTERNATIONAL INC
50 Cabot Ct (11788-3716)
PHONE.................................631 951-9800
Steven Cohen, *President*
Peter Rizzo, *Plant Mgr*
Bill Bezanson, *Controller*
Brian Kelley, *CIO*
▲ **EMP:** 100
SQ FT: 20,000
SALES (est): 22.8MM **Privately Held**
SIC: 3949 Swimming pools, plastic; swimming pools, except plastic

(G-6236)
WOODBINE PRODUCTS INC
110 Plant Ave (11788-3830)
PHONE.................................631 586-3770
Fax: 631 586-3777
Vincent J Conforti, *President*
Johanna Conforti, *Admin Sec*
EMP: 20
SQ FT: 20,000
SALES (est): 2.5MM
SALES (corp-wide): 80.4MM **Publicly Held**
WEB: www.woodbineproducts.com
SIC: 3812 Acceleration indicators & systems components, aerospace
HQ: Welding Metallurgy, Inc.
110 Plant Ave
Hauppauge NY 11788
631 253-0500

Haverstraw
Rockland County

(G-6237)
JAGUAR INDUSTRIES INC
89 Broadway (10927-1144)
P.O. Box 385 (10927-0385)
PHONE.................................845 947-1800
Marvin Kigler, *President*
EMP: 15
SQ FT: 15,000
SALES (est): 2.7MM **Privately Held**
SIC: 3679 5065 3643 3357 Electronic circuits; electronic parts & equipment; current-carrying wiring devices; nonferrous wiredrawing & insulating; laminated plastics plate & sheet

(G-6238)
LEXSTAR INC (PA)
Also Called: Lites On West Soho
25 Lincoln St (10927-1106)
PHONE.................................845 947-1415
Fax: 845 818-9627
Uri Redlich, *President*
David Regezv, *Vice Pres*
▲ **EMP:** 15
SQ FT: 15,000
SALES (est): 1.6MM **Privately Held**
WEB: www.lexstar.com
SIC: 3645 Residential lighting fixtures

(G-6239)
ROCKLAND INSULATED WIRE CABLE
87 Broadway (10927-1144)
P.O. Box 111 (10927-0111)
PHONE.................................845 429-3103
Fax: 845 947-1712
Lawrence Kigler, *President*
EMP: 7 **EST:** 1956
SQ FT: 10,000
SALES (est): 1.2MM **Privately Held**
SIC: 3357 Nonferrous wiredrawing & insulating

(G-6240)
ROSS ELECTRONICS LTD
12 Maple Ave (10927-1824)
PHONE.................................718 569-6643
Reuven Lakein, *President*
EMP: 20 **EST:** 2010
SALES: 12MM **Privately Held**
SIC: 3699 5999 Electrical equipment & supplies; electronic parts & equipment

(G-6241)
TILCON NEW YORK INC
Also Called: Haverstraw Quarry
66 Scratchup Rd (10927)
PHONE.................................845 638-3594
EMP: 63
SALES (corp-wide): 25.3B **Privately Held**
SIC: 1429 Dolomitic marble, crushed & broken-quarrying
HQ: Tilcon New York Inc.
162 Old Mill Rd
West Nyack NY 10994
845 358-4500

Hawthorne
Westchester County

(G-6242)
ACE ELECTRONICS INC
140 Old Saw Mill Riv Rd (10532-1515)
PHONE.................................914 773-2000
Fax: 914 773-2005
Mati Ben-AVI, *President*
Marie Ben-AVI, *Vice Pres*
EMP: 13
SQ FT: 12,000
SALES (est): 1.3MM **Privately Held**
SIC: 3679 3672 Electronic circuits; printed circuit boards

(G-6243)
ADL DATA SYSTEMS INC
9 Skyline Dr Ste 4 (10532-2146)
PHONE.................................914 591-1800
Fax: 914 591-1818
David Pollack, *President*
Aaron Weg, *Vice Pres*
Shelley Pollack, *Human Res Mgr*
Fila Kolodny, *Prgrmr*
Leslie Siegel, *Exec Dir*
EMP: 40
SQ FT: 13,000
SALES: 4.4MM **Privately Held**
WEB: www.adldata.com
SIC: 7372 Prepackaged software

(G-6244)
ASTRA TOOL & INSTR MFG CORP
369 Bradhurst Ave (10532-1141)
PHONE.................................914 747-3863
Fax: 914 747-3925
Greg Unmann, *President*
Greg Unman, *President*
Anthony Posco, *Controller*
EMP: 22 **EST:** 1950
SQ FT: 10,000
SALES: 2.9MM **Privately Held**
WEB: www.astratool.com
SIC: 3841 3599 Surgical & medical instruments; machine shop, jobbing & repair

(G-6245)
COCA-COLA REFRESHMENTS USA INC
3 Skyline Dr (10532-2174)
PHONE.................................914 592-0806
Fax: 914 789-1153
William Highberger, *Project Mgr*
John Krause, *Project Mgr*
Jeff Lumberg, *Human Res Mgr*
Brian Winn, *Branch Mgr*
EMP: 8
SALES (corp-wide): 44.2B **Publicly Held**
SIC: 2086 Bottled & canned soft drinks
HQ: Coca-Cola Refreshments Usa, Inc.
2500 Windy Ridge Pkwy Se
Atlanta GA 30339
770 989-3000

(G-6246)
FOUR BROTHERS ITALIAN BAKERY
Also Called: Sinapi's Italian Ice
332 Elwood Ave (10532-1217)
PHONE.................................914 741-5434
Pat Sinapi, *President*
Angelo Sinapi, *Vice Pres*
Anthony Sinapi, *Treasurer*
Luigi Sinapi, *Admin Sec*
EMP: 5
SALES (est): 426.9K **Privately Held**
SIC: 2024 5143 Ices, flavored (frozen dessert); ice cream & ices

(G-6247)
GAS TURBINE CONTROLS CORP
6 Skyline Dr Ste 150 (10532-8102)
P.O. Box 104, Ardsley (10502-0104)
PHONE.................................914 693-0830

Peter Zinman, *Ch of Bd*
Caroline Preece, *Marketing Mgr*
Robyn Howal, *Manager*
▲ EMP: 8
SALES (est): 2.1MM **Privately Held**
SIC: 3511 Turbines & turbine generator sets

(G-6248)
JOHNSON CONTROLS INC
8 Skyline Dr Ste 115 (10532-2151)
PHONE..................................914 593-5200
Rick Salon, *Manager*
EMP: 20 **Privately Held**
SIC: 3822 Energy cutoff controls, residential or commercial types
HQ: Johnson Controls, Inc.
5757 N Green Bay Ave
Milwaukee WI 53209
414 524-1200

(G-6249)
KRYTEN IRON WORKS INC
3 Browns Ln Ste 201 (10532-1546)
PHONE..................................914 345-0990
Peter Lavelli, *President*
Stephen Winiarski, *Accountant*
EMP: 8
SALES (est): 1.4MM **Privately Held**
SIC: 3441 3446 Fabricated structural metal; ornamental metalwork

(G-6250)
LUDL ELECTRONIC PRODUCTS LTD
Also Called: Lep
171 Brady Ave (10532-2216)
PHONE..................................914 769-6111
Fax: 914 769-4759
Helmut Ludl, *Ch of Bd*
Dirk Ludl, *President*
Mark Ludl, *President*
Petra H Ludl, *Corp Secy*
Nicholas Kucharik, *Mfg Staff*
▼ EMP: 25
SQ FT: 23,000
SALES: 2K **Privately Held**
WEB: www.ludl.com
SIC: 3825 Instruments to measure electricity

(G-6251)
MWSI INC (PA)
12 Skyline Dr Ste 230 (10532-2138)
PHONE..................................914 347-4200
Mark Wasserman, *President*
David Saily, *Vice Pres*
EMP: 70
SQ FT: 12,160
SALES (est): 3.9MM **Privately Held**
SIC: 3961 5094 3911 Costume jewelry, ex. precious metal & semiprecious stones; jewelry; jewelry, precious metal

(G-6252)
PEPSICO
3 Skyline Dr (10532-2174)
PHONE..................................419 252-0247
EMP: 17
SALES (est): 2.7MM **Privately Held**
SIC: 2086 Carbonated soft drinks, bottled & canned

(G-6253)
RAW INDULGENCE LTD
Also Called: Raw Revolution
200 Saw Mill River Rd (10532-1523)
P.O. Box 359 (10532-0359)
PHONE..................................866 498-4671
David Friedman, *CEO*
Alice Benedetto, *President*
▲ EMP: 14
SQ FT: 3,000
SALES (est): 3.1MM **Privately Held**
SIC: 2099 Food preparations

(G-6254)
SCHMERSAL INC
15 Skyline Dr Ste 230 (10532-2152)
PHONE..................................914 347-4775
Gary Ferguson, *Managing Dir*
David Upton, *Business Mgr*
Mario Tucci, *CFO*
Tushar Bachal, *Human Resources*
Lynn Higgins, *Sales Mgr*
◆ EMP: 26
SQ FT: 10,000
SALES (est): 5.3MM
SALES (corp-wide): 258.4MM **Privately Held**
WEB: www.schmersal.com
SIC: 3625 Motor control accessories, including overload relays
HQ: K. A. Schmersal Gmbh & Co. Kg
Moddinghofe 30
Wuppertal 42279
202 647-40

(G-6255)
U X WORLD INC
245 Saw Mill River Rd # 106 (10532-1547)
PHONE..................................914 375-6167
Vinod Pulkayath, *President*
EMP: 5
SQ FT: 300
SALES (est): 140K **Privately Held**
SIC: 7372 Prepackaged software

(G-6256)
WILLEMIN MACODEL INCORPORATED
10 Skyline Dr Ste 132 (10532-2160)
PHONE..................................914 345-3504
Melissa Dorsey, *Principal*
▲ EMP: 16 EST: 2011
SALES (est): 2.3MM **Privately Held**
SIC: 3545 Machine tool attachments & accessories

Hector
Schuyler County

(G-6257)
HAZLITTS 1852 VINEYARDS INC
Also Called: Hazlitt 1852 Vineyards
5712 State Route 414 (14841-9714)
P.O. Box 53 (14841-0053)
PHONE..................................607 546-9463
Fax: 607 546-5712
Doug Hazlitt, *CEO*
Elaine Hazlitt, *President*
Jerome Hazlitt, *President*
Fred Wickham, *Vice Pres*
Leigh Triner, *Treasurer*
EMP: 48
SQ FT: 4,500
SALES (est): 8.2MM **Privately Held**
WEB: www.hazlitt1852.com
SIC: 2084 0172 Wines, brandy & brandy spirits; grapes

(G-6258)
LAFAYETTE CHATEAU
Also Called: Chateau La Fayette Reneau
Rr 414 (14841)
PHONE..................................607 546-2062
Fax: 607 546-2069
Richard Reno, *Owner*
Heather Lodge, *General Mgr*
EMP: 25
SQ FT: 5,000
SALES (est): 2MM **Privately Held**
WEB: www.clrwine.com
SIC: 2084 Wines

(G-6259)
ONEH2 INC
3870 Dugue Rd (14841-9644)
PHONE..................................703 862-9656
Paul Dawson, *CEO*
Franklin Lomax, *CFO*
EMP: 6 EST: 2015
SQ FT: 1,000
SALES (est): 356K **Privately Held**
SIC: 2819 7389 Industrial inorganic chemicals;

(G-6260)
RED NEWT CELLARS INC
3675 Tichenor Rd (14841-9675)
PHONE..................................607 546-4100
Fax: 607 546-4101
David Whiting, *President*
Terri Myers, *Business Mgr*
Katie Goodwin, *Manager*
Katie Tasting, *Manager*
Greg Tumbarello, *Manager*
EMP: 10
SQ FT: 13,000
SALES (est): 2.8MM **Privately Held**
WEB: www.rednewt.com
SIC: 2084 Wines

(G-6261)
STANDING STONE VINEYARDS
9934 State Route 414 (14841-9727)
PHONE..................................607 582-6051
Martha Macinski, *Owner*
Tom Macinski, *Co-Owner*
EMP: 6
SALES (est): 416.1K **Privately Held**
WEB: www.standingstonewines.com
SIC: 2084 5921 Wines; wine

(G-6262)
TICKLE HILL WINERY
3831 Ball Diamond Rd (14841-9629)
PHONE..................................607 546-7740
Valerie Rosbaugh, *Owner*
EMP: 5
SALES (est): 283.8K **Privately Held**
SIC: 2084 Wine cellars, bonded: engaged in blending wines

Hemlock
Livingston County

(G-6263)
ITT CORPORATION
4847 Main St (14466-9714)
PHONE..................................585 269-7109
Rosario Pitta, *Branch Mgr*
EMP: 46
SALES (corp-wide): 2.4B **Publicly Held**
WEB: www.ittind.com
SIC: 3625 Control equipment, electric
HQ: Itt, Llc
1133 Westchester Ave N-100
White Plains NY 10604
914 641-2000

Hempstead
Nassau County

(G-6264)
ANHUI SKYWORTH LLC
44 Kensington Ct (11550-2126)
PHONE..................................917 940-6903
Fuzhen Ang, *Mng Member*
Fuzhen Wang, *Mng Member*
EMP: 65
SALES (est): 1.7MM **Privately Held**
SIC: 2392 5023 Cushions & pillows; pillowcases

(G-6265)
ARNELL INC
73 High St (11550-3817)
PHONE..................................516 486-7098
Fax: 516 292-0697
Doug Riebl, *President*
Ron Riebl, *Vice Pres*
EMP: 6 EST: 1956
SQ FT: 4,300
SALES (est): 924.3K **Privately Held**
SIC: 3469 3544 Metal stampings; special dies, tools, jigs & fixtures

(G-6266)
BP BEYOND PRINTING INC
117 Fulton Ave (11550-3706)
PHONE..................................516 328-2700
Christine Persaud, *Ch of Bd*
Bryan Prasad, *Asst Mgr*
EMP: 6
SALES (est): 790.3K **Privately Held**
SIC: 2752 2759 Commercial printing, lithographic; commercial printing

(G-6267)
CENTURY-TECH INC
32 Intersection St (11550-1306)
PHONE..................................718 326-9400
Peter Terranova, *Branch Mgr*
EMP: 15 **Privately Held**
SIC: 3561 Industrial pumps & parts
PA: Century-Tech Inc.
5825 63rd St
Hempstead NY 11550

(G-6268)
CENTURY-TECH INC (PA)
5825 63rd St (11550)
PHONE..................................718 326-9400
Peter Terranova, *President*
Jack Terranova, *Corp Secy*
Ronald Wiggberg, *Corp Secy*
Louis Mastrangelo, *Vice Pres*
▲ EMP: 3
SQ FT: 4,500
SALES: 5MM **Privately Held**
WEB: www.century-techinc.com
SIC: 3559 Plastics working machinery

(G-6269)
GAMMA INSTRUMENT CO INC
52 Chasner St (11550-4820)
PHONE..................................516 486-5526
Fax: 516 486-4905
John Schurr, *President*
William Hansen, *Vice Pres*
EMP: 7
SQ FT: 4,400
SALES: 500K **Privately Held**
SIC: 3599 Machine shop, jobbing & repair

(G-6270)
GENERAL REFINING & SMELTING
Also Called: Grc
106 Taft Ave (11550-4887)
PHONE..................................516 538-4747
Fax: 516 538-4767
Richard Spera, *President*
Andrea Poveromo, *Bookkeeper*
Carol Spera, *Office Mgr*
EMP: 7
SQ FT: 10,000
SALES (est): 810K **Privately Held**
SIC: 3339 3341 Gold refining (primary); silver refining (primary); platinum group metal refining (primary); secondary non-ferrous metals

(G-6271)
GENERAL REFINING CORPORATION
59 Madison Ave (11550-4813)
PHONE..................................516 538-4747
Peter Spera, *Principal*
EMP: 8
SALES (est): 850K **Privately Held**
SIC: 3339 Gold refining (primary)

(G-6272)
GOLD PURE FOOD PRODUCTS CO INC
1 Brooklyn Rd (11550-6619)
PHONE..................................516 483-5600
Fax: 516 483-5798
Steven Gold, *Ch of Bd*
Howard Gold, *Vice Pres*
Marc Gold, *Vice Pres*
Neil Gold, *CFO*
Jeff Turow, *Info Tech Mgr*
▲ EMP: 75 EST: 1932
SQ FT: 75,000
SALES (est): 15.2MM **Privately Held**
WEB: www.goldshoreradish.com
SIC: 2035 2099 Seasonings & sauces, except tomato & dry; horseradish, prepared; Worcestershire sauce; mustard, prepared (wet); food preparations

(G-6273)
HEMPSTEAD SENTINEL INC
Also Called: Sentinel Printing
55 Chasner St (11550-4807)
P.O. Box 305 (11551-0305)
PHONE..................................516 486-5000
Fax: 516 486-1966
Glenn Boehmer, *President*
Joan Boehmer, *Admin Sec*
EMP: 13
SQ FT: 7,000
SALES (est): 2.8MM **Privately Held**
SIC: 2752 Commercial printing, lithographic

(G-6274)
ICELL INC
133 Fulton Ave (11550-3710)
PHONE..................................516 590-0007
Arpreet Sanhi, *President*
EMP: 127

SQ FT: 4,000
SALES: 10MM *Privately Held*
SIC: 3663 Mobile communication equipment

(G-6275)
JEM SIGN CORP (PA)
Also Called: Tee Pee Signs
470 S Franklin St (11550-7419)
PHONE....................................516 867-4466
Jeraldine Eid, *President*
Teddy Eid, *Vice Pres*
EMP: 5
SQ FT: 3,700
SALES (est): 622.4K *Privately Held*
WEB: www.teepeesigns.com
SIC: 3993 7532 5999 1799 Signs & advertising specialties; truck painting & lettering; trophies & plaques; sign installation & maintenance

(G-6276)
JONICE INDUSTIRES
95 Angevine Ave (11550-5618)
PHONE....................................516 640-4283
EMP: 5
SALES (est): 232.3K *Privately Held*
SIC: 2299 Broadwoven fabrics: linen, jute, hemp & ramie

(G-6277)
KING CRACKER CORP
Also Called: Cristina
307 Peninsula Blvd (11550-4912)
PHONE....................................516 539-9251
Leonard Morales, *President*
EMP: 15
SALES (est): 450K *Privately Held*
SIC: 2051 5149 Bread, cake & related products; bakery products

(G-6278)
MAGER & GOUGELMAN INC
230 Hilton Ave Ste 112 (11550-8116)
PHONE....................................212 661-3939
Henry P Gougleman, *President*
EMP: 8
SALES (corp-wide): 855.4K *Privately Held*
WEB: www.artificial-eyes.com
SIC: 3851 Eyes, glass & plastic
PA: Mager & Gougelman Inc
   345 E 37th St Rm 316
   New York NY 10016
   212 661-3939

(G-6279)
MAGER & GOUGELMAN INC
230 Hilton Ave Ste 112 (11550-8116)
PHONE....................................516 489-0202
Denise Gougelmann, *Manager*
EMP: 9
SALES (corp-wide): 855.4K *Privately Held*
WEB: www.artificial-eyes.com
SIC: 3851 Eyes, glass & plastic
PA: Mager & Gougelman Inc
   345 E 37th St Rm 316
   New York NY 10016
   212 661-3939

(G-6280)
MILLENNIUM SIGNS & DISPLAY INC
90 W Graham Ave (11550-6102)
PHONE....................................516 292-8000
Sajjad Khalfan, *President*
Richard Seider, *Sales Staff*
◆ EMP: 25
SQ FT: 35,000
SALES (est): 4MM *Privately Held*
WEB: www.msdny.com
SIC: 3993 Signs & advertising specialties

(G-6281)
MYRTLE LEOLA INC
Also Called: AlphaGraphics
73 Sealey Ave (11550-1240)
PHONE....................................516 228-2312
Clifford Johnson, *President*
EMP: 6
SQ FT: 2,300
SALES (est): 590K *Privately Held*
SIC: 2752 Commercial printing, lithographic

(G-6282)
NASSAU AUTO REMANUFACTURER
Also Called: Nassau Auto Remanufacturers
25 Chasner St (11550-4807)
PHONE....................................516 485-4500
Fax: 516 485-1124
Dorothy Pontrelli, *President*
EMP: 8
SQ FT: 9,000
SALES: 500K *Privately Held*
SIC: 3714 Motor vehicle electrical equipment

(G-6283)
NASSAU COUNTY PUBLICATIONS
Also Called: Beacon Newspapers
5 Centre St (11550-2422)
PHONE....................................516 481-5400
Peter Hoegl, *President*
EMP: 5
SALES (est): 367.9K *Privately Held*
SIC: 2711 Newspapers

(G-6284)
ORTHOTIC & PROSTHETIC IMAGES
500 Front St (11550-4445)
PHONE....................................516 292-8726
Louis Scotti, *President*
Donna Scotti, *Treasurer*
EMP: 6
SALES (est): 586.1K *Privately Held*
SIC: 3842 5999 Prosthetic appliances; artificial limbs

(G-6285)
PLANT-TECH2O INC
30 Chasner St (11550-4808)
P.O. Box 520 (11551-0520)
PHONE....................................516 483-7845
William Lyon, *President*
EMP: 5
SQ FT: 5,000
SALES: 500K *Privately Held*
SIC: 3523 7359 7389 1791 Farm machinery & equipment; live plant rental; plant care service; exterior wall system installation

(G-6286)
ROYAL PRESTIGE LASTING CO
198 Jerusalem Ave (11550-6332)
PHONE....................................516 280-5148
Kevin Ramos, *General Mgr*
EMP: 15
SALES (est): 871.2K *Privately Held*
SIC: 3589 Water filters & softeners, household type

(G-6287)
SHANE TEX INC
Also Called: Henry Segal Co
50 Polk Ave (11550-5416)
PHONE....................................516 486-7522
Fax: 516 486-7534
Martin Segal, *Ch of Bd*
Robert Segal, *President*
▲ EMP: 18 EST: 1926
SQ FT: 30,000
SALES: 4MM *Privately Held*
WEB: www.henrysegal.com
SIC: 2311 2337 2335 Tailored suits & formal jackets; men's & boys' uniforms; uniforms, except athletic: women's, misses' & juniors'; women's & misses' suits & skirts; bridal & formal gowns

(G-6288)
ULTIMATE SIGNS & DESIGNS INC
86 Sewell St (11550-5432)
PHONE....................................516 481-0800
Fax: 516 481-7480
Michael Peras, *President*
Chris Hays, *General Mgr*
Shanna Peras, *Vice Pres*
Arlene Meli, *Project Mgr*
Marguerite Martinek, *Accounting Mgr*
EMP: 26
SQ FT: 10,000
SALES (est): 3.8MM *Privately Held*
WEB: www.ultimatesigns.com
SIC: 3993 Signs & advertising specialties

(G-6289)
WOODMOTIF INC
Also Called: Woodmotif Cabinetry
42 Chasner St (11550-4820)
PHONE....................................516 564-8325
George Dimitriadis, *President*
Lisa Louberel, *Manager*
EMP: 10
SALES (est): 1.3MM *Privately Held*
SIC: 2521 2511 2499 Wood office furniture; wood household furniture; decorative wood & woodwork

Henderson
Jefferson County

(G-6290)
VISHAY AMERICAS INC
14992 Snowshoe Rd (13650-2234)
PHONE....................................315 938-7575
Rich Mangan, *Branch Mgr*
EMP: 127
SALES (corp-wide): 2.3B *Publicly Held*
SIC: 3676 Electronic resistors
HQ: Vishay Americas, Inc.
   1 Greenwich Pl
   Shelton CT 06484
   203 445-5100

Henderson Harbor
Jefferson County

(G-6291)
HENDERSON HBR PRFRMG ARTS ASSN
12459 County Route 123 (13651)
PHONE....................................315 938-7333
Eunice Wescot, *Director*
EMP: 11
SALES (est): 590K *Privately Held*
SIC: 3275 Gypsum products

Henrietta
Monroe County

(G-6292)
ANGIOTECH BIOCOATINGS CORP
336 Summit Point Dr (14467-9607)
PHONE....................................585 321-1130
Richard Whitbourne, *Ch of Bd*
Richard Richmond, *President*
John F Lanzafame, *President*
Carolyn Eastman, *Vice Pres*
Gerard Whitbourne, *Vice Pres*
▲ EMP: 45
SQ FT: 13,000
SALES (est): 4.2MM
SALES (corp-wide): 88.6MM *Privately Held*
WEB: www.angiotech.com
SIC: 3479 2891 2851 Painting, coating & hot dipping; adhesives & sealants; paints & allied products
PA: Angiotech Pharmaceuticals, Inc
   355 Burrard St Suite 1100
   Vancouver BC V6C 2
   604 221-7676

(G-6293)
ARGON MEDICAL DEVICES INC
336 Summit Point Dr (14467-9607)
PHONE....................................585 321-1130
EMP: 6
SALES (corp-wide): 377.9MM *Privately Held*
SIC: 3841 3845 3842 Surgical & medical instruments; electromedical equipment; surgical appliances & supplies
HQ: Argon Medical Devices, Inc.
   5151 Hdqtr Dr Ste 210
   Plano TX 75024
   903 675-9321

(G-6294)
HYDROACOUSTICS INC
999 Lehigh Station Rd # 100 (14467-9389)
PHONE....................................585 359-1000
John V Bouyoucos, *Ch of Bd*
Michael J Czora, *President*
Marshall W Lesser, *Vice Pres*
James Rall, *Mfg Staff*
Mark Ozimek, *Design Engr*
EMP: 17
SQ FT: 45,000
SALES (est): 4MM *Privately Held*
WEB: www.hydroacoustics.com
SIC: 3594 Fluid power pumps & motors

(G-6295)
KONECRANES INC
1020 Lehigh Station Rd # 4 (14467-9369)
PHONE....................................585 359-4450
Christina Moss, *Manager*
Aaron Boutwelo, *Manager*
EMP: 12
SALES (corp-wide): 2.2B *Privately Held*
WEB: www.kciusa.com
SIC: 3536 7699 Cranes, industrial plant; industrial machinery & equipment repair
HQ: Konecranes, Inc.
   4401 Gateway Blvd
   Springfield OH 45502
   937 525-5533

(G-6296)
LAKE IMAGE SYSTEMS INC
205 Summit Point Dr Ste 2 (14467-9631)
PHONE....................................585 321-3630
Fax: 585 321-3788
Scott Stevens, *President*
Martin Keats, *President*
Paul Stinson, *Exec VP*
Paul Smith, *Senior VP*
Jim Miller, *Vice Pres*
EMP: 17
SQ FT: 7,500
SALES: 5.5MM *Privately Held*
WEB: www.lakeimage.com
SIC: 3554 3861 7371 Paper industries machinery; cameras & related equipment; computer software development
PA: Lake Image Systems Limited
   1 The Forum Icknield Way Industrial Estate
   Tring HERTS
   144 289-2700

(G-6297)
ORAFOL AMERICAS INC
Also Called: Reflexite Precision Tech Ctr
200 Park Centre Dr (14467)
PHONE....................................585 272-0309
Stephen Meissner, *Engineer*
Steven Scott, *Branch Mgr*
EMP: 25
SALES (corp-wide): 573MM *Privately Held*
WEB: www.reflexite.com
SIC: 3081 Vinyl film & sheet
HQ: Orafol Americas Inc.
   120 Darling Dr
   Avon CT 06001
   860 223-9297

(G-6298)
TUCKER PRINTERS INC
270 Middle Rd (14467-9312)
PHONE....................................585 359-3030
Fax: 585 359-3053
Joe R Davis, *CEO*
Daniel A Tucker, *President*
Glenn Marino, *Vice Pres*
Mary Fornataro, *Purchasing*
Deno Sfikas, *Finance Dir*
EMP: 82 EST: 1997
SQ FT: 60,000
SALES (est): 14.1MM
SALES (corp-wide): 11.2B *Publicly Held*
WEB: www.tuckerprinters.com
SIC: 2752 Commercial printing, offset
HQ: Consolidated Graphics, Inc.
   5858 Westheimer Rd # 200
   Houston TX 77057
   713 787-0977

Herkimer
Herkimer County

(G-6299)
ELG UTICA ALLOYS INC (DH)
378 Gros Blvd Ste 3 (13350-1446)
PHONE.................................315 733-0475
Fax: 315 733-2228
Dimitaij Orlov, *Ch of Bd*
Anthony Moreno, *President*
Joseph Jiampietro, *Vice Pres*
Fredrick Schweizer, *Vice Pres*
Lynn Claus, *Controller*
▲ EMP: 50 EST: 1965
SQ FT: 40,000
SALES (est): 35MM
SALES (corp-wide): 4B **Privately Held**
WEB: www.uticaalloys.com
SIC: 3599 Machine shop, jobbing & repair
HQ: Elg Utica Alloys International Gmbh
Kremerskamp 16
Duisburg
203 450-10

(G-6300)
GATEHOUSE MEDIA LLC
Also Called: Evening Telegram
111 Green St (13350-1914)
P.O. Box 551 (13350-0551)
PHONE.................................315 866-2220
Fax: 315 866-5913
Beth Brewer, *Manager*
EMP: 10
SALES (corp-wide): 1.2B **Publicly Held**
WEB: www.gatehousemedia.com
SIC: 2711 Newspapers, publishing & printing
HQ: Gatehouse Media, Llc
175 Sullys Trl Ste 300
Pittsford NY 14534
585 598-0030

(G-6301)
HEIDELBERG GROUP INC
3056 State Hwy Rte 28 N (13350)
P.O. Box 787 (13350-0787)
PHONE.................................315 866-0999
Boyd Bissell, *President*
Cheryl Phillips, *Opers Staff*
▲ EMP: 40
SQ FT: 8,000
SALES (est): 6.1MM **Privately Held**
WEB: www.heidelbergbakingco.com
SIC: 2051 Bread, cake & related products

(G-6302)
HERKIMER DIAMOND MINES INC
800 Mohawk St (13350-2261)
PHONE.................................315 891-7355
Fax: 516 867-1552
Renee Scialdo Schevat, *Ch of Bd*
EMP: 25
SALES (est): 3.2MM **Privately Held**
WEB: www.herkimerdiamond.com
SIC: 1499 5094 Gemstone & industrial diamond mining; diamonds (gems)

(G-6303)
HERKIMER TOOL & MACHINING CORP
Also Called: Herkimer Tool & Equipment Co
125 Marginal Rd (13350-2305)
PHONE.................................315 866-2110
Fax: 315 866-7129
F Ellis Green Jr, *President*
Francis E Green III, *Vice Pres*
Nancy J Green, *Admin Sec*
EMP: 10
SQ FT: 14,000
SALES (est): 1.2MM **Privately Held**
SIC: 3599 Machine shop, jobbing & repair

(G-6304)
LENNONS LITHO INC
Also Called: Mohawk Valley Printing Co
234 Kast Hill Rd (13350-4402)
PHONE.................................315 866-3156
Robert J Lennon, *Ch of Bd*
Elfrieda Lennon, *Treasurer*
EMP: 10
SQ FT: 6,400
SALES (est): 730K **Privately Held**
WEB: www.mohawkvalleyprinting.com
SIC: 2752 2759 Commercial printing, offset; commercial printing; letterpress printing

Heuvelton
St. Lawrence County

(G-6305)
LOSURDO FOODS INC
Also Called: Losurdo Creamery
34 Union St (13654-2200)
PHONE.................................315 344-2444
Fax: 315 344-2362
Michael Losurdo Sr, *President*
Antonio Fazzino, *Vice Pres*
Marc Losurdo, *Vice Pres*
Michael Losurdo Jr, *Vice Pres*
Maria Losurdo, *Treasurer*
EMP: 150
SQ FT: 75,000
SALES (est): 18.9MM
SALES (corp-wide): 100.9MM **Privately Held**
WEB: www.losurdofoods.com
SIC: 2022 Natural cheese
PA: Losurdo Foods, Inc.
20 Owens Rd
Hackensack NJ 07601
201 343-6680

Hewlett
Nassau County

(G-6306)
ABS METAL CORP
58 Holly Rd (11557-1411)
PHONE.................................646 302-9018
Alan Minchenberg, *Principal*
EMP: 5 EST: 2012
SALES (est): 475.4K **Privately Held**
SIC: 3471 Finishing, metals or formed products

(G-6307)
ALGAFUEL AMERICA
289 Meadowview Ave (11557-2106)
PHONE.................................516 295-2257
Allan Roffe, *Principal*
EMP: 7
SALES (est): 464.7K **Privately Held**
SIC: 2911 Diesel fuels

(G-6308)
LADY BRASS CO INC
1717 Broadway Unit 2 (11557-1682)
PHONE.................................516 887-8040
Fax: 516 887-8025
Lauren Brasco, *President*
EMP: 6
SALES (est): 919K **Privately Held**
SIC: 2337 2326 Uniforms, except athletic: women's, misses' & juniors'; work uniforms

(G-6309)
LIFESCIENCES TECHNOLOGY INC
906 Wateredge Pl (11557-2612)
PHONE.................................516 569-0085
Jon Garito, *CEO*
EMP: 7 EST: 2010
SALES (est): 812.5K **Privately Held**
SIC: 3845 Ultrasonic scanning devices, medical

(G-6310)
LIFEWATCH INC
Also Called: Lifewatch Personal Mergency
1344 Broadway Ste 106 (11557-1356)
PHONE.................................800 716-1433
Fax: 516 837-3852
Evan Sirlin, *President*
Art Sirlin, *Vice Pres*
Sarai Baker, *Opers Staff*
Art Mitchell, *Treasurer*
Mitchell Evan, *Manager*
EMP: 10
SALES (est): 700K **Privately Held**
WEB: www.lifewatch.net
SIC: 3669 5063 5999 Emergency alarms; alarm systems; alarm signal systems

(G-6311)
PETLAND DISCOUNTS INC
1340 Peninsula Blvd (11557-1226)
PHONE.................................516 821-3194
EMP: 6
SALES (corp-wide): 139.6MM **Privately Held**
SIC: 3999 Pet supplies
PA: Petland Discounts, Inc.
355 Crooked Hill Rd
Brentwood NY 11717
631 273-6363

(G-6312)
S & M RING CORP
1080 Channel Dr (11557-2638)
PHONE.................................212 382-0900
Fax: 212 398-1963
Wally Schafran, *President*
▲ EMP: 12
SALES (est): 622K **Privately Held**
SIC: 3911 Jewelry, precious metal; rings, finger: precious metal

(G-6313)
SKY BOUNCE BALL COMPANY INC
301 Mill Rd Ste U4 (11557-1232)
PHONE.................................516 305-4883
Martin Gevarter, *President*
Eileen Gevarter, *Vice Pres*
▲ EMP: 4
SALES (est): 1MM **Privately Held**
SIC: 3949 Balls: baseball, football, basketball, etc.; sticks: hockey, lacrosse, etc.

(G-6314)
TORSAF PRINTERS INC
Also Called: Minuteman Press
1315 Broadway Unit B (11557-2104)
PHONE.................................516 569-5577
Fax: 516 569-4740
David Toron, *President*
Michael Toron, *Corp Secy*
EMP: 6
SQ FT: 4,800
SALES (est): 876.7K **Privately Held**
SIC: 2752 2791 Commercial printing, lithographic; typesetting

(G-6315)
UNITED PIPE NIPPLE CO INC
1602 Lakeview Dr (11557-1818)
PHONE.................................516 295-2468
Fax: 718 756-3016
Roger Desimone, *CEO*
Selma Dolgov, *President*
▲ EMP: 15
SQ FT: 25,000
SALES (est): 5MM **Privately Held**
WEB: www.unitedpipenipple.com
SIC: 3494 Pipe fittings

(G-6316)
VENUS PRINTING COMPANY
1420 Kew Ave (11557-1413)
PHONE.................................212 967-8900
Fax: 516 967-8992
Erwin Goodman, *President*
Carol Goodman, *Treasurer*
Tom Shields, *Manager*
EMP: 15
SALES (est): 1MM **Privately Held**
SIC: 2759 Commercial printing

(G-6317)
YES WERE NUTS LTD
Also Called: I'M Nuts
1215 Broadway (11557-2001)
PHONE.................................516 374-1940
Fax: 516 374-2643
Catherine Davi, *President*
EMP: 6
SQ FT: 2,500
SALES (est): 530K **Privately Held**
SIC: 2066 Chocolate

Hicksville
Nassau County

(G-6318)
AJAX WIRE SPECIALTY CO INC
119 Bloomingdale Rd (11801-6508)
PHONE.................................516 935-2333
Fax: 516 935-2334
Patricia Ellner, *CEO*
David Ellner, *President*
EMP: 15
SQ FT: 5,000
SALES (est): 1MM **Privately Held**
SIC: 3495 Wire springs

(G-6319)
ALL ISLAND MEDIA INC
Also Called: Carrier News
325 Duffy Ave Unit 2 (11801-3644)
PHONE.................................516 942-8400
Fax: 516 942-3730
Bob Sussi, *Publisher*
Daniel Mikos, *Sales Staff*
Robert Sussi, *Branch Mgr*
EMP: 26
SALES (corp-wide): 13MM **Privately Held**
WEB: www.allislandmedia.com
SIC: 2711 Newspapers, publishing & printing
PA: All Island Media, Inc.
1 Rodeo Dr
Edgewood NY 11717
631 698-8400

(G-6320)
ALL THE RAGE INC
147 W Cherry St Unit 1 (11801-3885)
PHONE.................................516 605-2001
Michael J Demarco, *President*
Sridat Rambarren, *Manager*
EMP: 7
SQ FT: 3,000
SALES (est): 5MM **Privately Held**
SIC: 3911 Jewelry apparel

(G-6321)
ALLIES GF GOODIES LLC
1b W Village Grn (11801-3911)
PHONE.................................516 216-1719
Donna Miller,
EMP: 10
SALES (est): 570K **Privately Held**
SIC: 2051 Bakery: wholesale or wholesale/retail combined

(G-6322)
APPLIED POWER SYSTEMS INC
Also Called: A P S
124 Charlotte Ave (11801-2620)
PHONE.................................516 935-2230
Fax: 516 935-2603
James Murphy, *CEO*
Les Doti, *Vice Pres*
Andres Romay, *Vice Pres*
Paul Kowal, *Engineer*
Tom Murray, *Engineer*
▲ EMP: 25
SALES (est): 5.3MM **Privately Held**
WEB: www.appliedps.com
SIC: 3679 3677 3629 3823 Power supplies, all types: static; transformers power supply, electronic type; inverters, nonrotating: electrical; controllers for process variables, all types; frequency converters (electric generators)

(G-6323)
APX TECHNOLOGIES INC
264 Duffy Ave (11801-3605)
PHONE.................................516 433-1313
Yuval Ofek, *President*
Tony Nicotra, *Engineer*
Roberto Paniccia, *Engineer*
David Baum, *Sales Staff*
Jeanette Kahn, *Office Mgr*
▲ EMP: 20
SQ FT: 3,500
SALES (est): 2.9MM **Privately Held**
SIC: 3679 Harness assemblies for electronic use: wire or cable; electronic loads & power supplies

Hicksville - Nassau County (G-6350)

(G-6324)
ARSTAN PRODUCTS INTERNATIONAL
Also Called: Apx Arstan Products
264 Duffy Ave (11801-3605)
PHONE..................516 433-1313
Fax: 516 433-1457
Yuval Ofek, *President*
EMP: 15
SQ FT: 3,500
SALES (est): 1.2MM **Privately Held**
WEB: www.apxonline.com
SIC: 3679 3612 Power supplies, all types: static; transformers, except electric

(G-6325)
AUTO-MAT COMPANY INC
69 Hazel St (11801-5340)
PHONE..................516 938-7373
Fax: 516 931-8438
Timothy S Browner, *President*
Marilyn Browner, *Corp Secy*
Roger Browner, *Vice Pres*
EMP: 21 **EST:** 1956
SQ FT: 12,000
SALES (est): 1.5MM **Privately Held**
SIC: 2273 5013 7532 Automobile floor coverings, except rubber or plastic; automotive supplies & parts; interior repair services

(G-6326)
BALANCE ENTERPRISES INC
12 W Cherry St (11801-3802)
PHONE..................516 822-3183
Robert Philips, *President*
EMP: 8
SALES (est): 446.3K **Privately Held**
SIC: 3999 Education aids, devices & supplies

(G-6327)
BATTSCO LLC
190 Lauman Ln Unit A (11801-6570)
PHONE..................516 586-6544
Fred Hentschel, *Managing Prtnr*
John R Garnett, *Mng Member*
▲ **EMP:** 5
SQ FT: 2,500
SALES: 2MM **Privately Held**
SIC: 3691 Storage batteries

(G-6328)
C Q COMMUNICATIONS INC
Also Called: Cq Magazine
17 W John St Unit 1 (11801-1004)
PHONE..................516 681-2922
Richard Ross, *President*
Joe Lynch, *Editor*
Irwin Math, *Editor*
Wayne Yoshida, *Editor*
Dorothy Kehrwieder, *Prdtn Dir*
EMP: 22
SQ FT: 10,000
SALES (est): 3.3MM **Privately Held**
WEB: www.cq-vhf.com
SIC: 2721 Magazines: publishing only, not printed on site

(G-6329)
CAMBRIDGE KITCHENS MFG INC
280 Duffy Ave Unit 1 (11801-3656)
PHONE..................516 935-5100
Neoklis Vasiliades, *President*
Barbara Narene, *Admin Sec*
EMP: 15
SQ FT: 32,000
SALES: 2.6MM **Privately Held**
WEB: www.cambridgekitchens.com
SIC: 2434 Wood kitchen cabinets

(G-6330)
CLASSIC COLOR GRAPHICS INC (PA)
268 N Broadway Unit 8 (11801-2923)
P.O. Box 599, Jericho (11753-0599)
PHONE..................516 822-9090
Daniel Fischer, *President*
Meryl Fischer, *Treasurer*
EMP: 7
SALES (est): 508.8K **Privately Held**
SIC: 2752 Commercial printing, lithographic

(G-6331)
CLASSIC COLOR GRAPHICS INC
87 Broadway (11801-4272)
PHONE..................516 822-9090
Dan Fisher, *President*
Barry Moscowitz, *Accountant*
EMP: 5
SALES (corp-wide): 508.8K **Privately Held**
SIC: 2752 Commercial printing, lithographic
PA: Classic Color Graphics, Inc
268 N Broadway Unit 8
Hicksville NY 11801
516 822-9090

(G-6332)
CLASSIC CONCRETE CORP
29a Midland Ave (11801-1509)
PHONE..................516 822-1800
Saverio Potente Jr, *President*
EMP: 10
SQ FT: 700
SALES (est): 910K **Privately Held**
SIC: 3273 5032 Ready-mixed concrete; paving materials

(G-6333)
CLEARY CUSTOM CABINETS INC
794 S Broadway (11801-5017)
PHONE..................516 939-2475
Tom Cleary, *President*
Lora Cleary, *Vice Pres*
EMP: 15
SALES (est): 1.3MM **Privately Held**
WEB: www.clearycustomcabinets.com
SIC: 2517 Home entertainment unit cabinets, wood

(G-6334)
COOPER LIGHTING LLC
Also Called: Neo Ray Lighting Products
100 Andrews Rd Ste 1 (11801-1725)
PHONE..................516 470-1000
Harry Mangru, *Buyer*
Aida Rivera, *Design Engr*
Dennis Detore, *Controller*
Lisa Goodman,
▲ **EMP:** 110 **EST:** 2007
SALES (est): 21.5MM **Privately Held**
WEB: www.neoray-lighting.com
SIC: 3646 3645 Commercial indusl & institutional electric lighting fixtures; residential lighting fixtures
HQ: Cooper Industries Unlimited Company
41 A B Drury Street
Dublin

(G-6335)
CORAL GRAPHIC SERVICES INC (DH)
Also Called: Coral Graphic Svce
840 S Broadway (11801-5066)
PHONE..................516 576-2100
David Liess, *Ch of Bd*
Frank Cappo, *President*
Robert Vitale, *Exec VP*
Bob Vitale, *Vice Pres*
Walter Keane, *VP Opers*
▲ **EMP:** 106
SQ FT: 56,000
SALES (est): 82.2MM
SALES (corp-wide): 18.4B **Privately Held**
SIC: 2752 Commercial printing, offset
HQ: Dynamic Graphic Finishing, Inc.
945 Horsham Rd
Horsham PA 19044
215 441-8880

(G-6336)
CORAL GRAPHIC SERVICES INC
840 S Broadway (11801-5066)
PHONE..................516 576-2100
Dave Lieff, *President*
EMP: 102
SALES (corp-wide): 18.4B **Privately Held**
SIC: 2752 Commercial printing, lithographic
HQ: Coral Graphic Services, Inc.
840 S Broadway
Hicksville NY 11801
516 576-2100

(G-6337)
CREATIVE MODELS & PROTOTYPES
160 Lauman Ln Unit A (11801-6557)
PHONE..................516 433-6828
Deborah Dinoia, *President*
Brian Allbin, *Prdtn Mgr*
William Dinoia, *Manager*
EMP: 8
SALES: 40K **Privately Held**
SIC: 3999 Models, except toy

(G-6338)
CROWN EQUIPMENT CORPORATION
Also Called: Crown Lift Trucks
5 Charlotte Ave Ste 1 (11801-3607)
PHONE..................516 822-5100
Fax: 516 822-0205
Jim Casey, *Site Mgr*
Rob Forrier, *Manager*
EMP: 68
SALES (corp-wide): 4.8B **Privately Held**
SIC: 3537 Lift trucks, industrial: fork, platform, straddle, etc.
PA: Crown Equipment Corporation
44 S Washington St
New Bremen OH 45869
419 629-2311

(G-6339)
CULICOVER & SHAPIRO INC
270 Duffy Ave Ste K (11801-3600)
PHONE..................516 597-4888
Fax: 631 918-4561
Richard Shapiro, *President*
David Shapiro, *Treasurer*
▲ **EMP:** 4
SALES (est): 1.2MM **Privately Held**
SIC: 3991 Brushes, household or industrial

(G-6340)
CYNOSURE INC
Also Called: Ellman International
400 Karin Ln (11801-5352)
PHONE..................516 594-3333
Tom Oliveri, *VP Opers*
EMP: 8
SALES (corp-wide): 339.4MM **Publicly Held**
SIC: 3841 3843 Surgical & medical instruments; dental equipment & supplies
PA: Cynosure, Inc.
5 Carlisle Rd
Westford MA 01886
978 256-4200

(G-6341)
E-BEAM SERVICES INC (PA)
270 Duffy Ave Ste H (11801-3600)
PHONE..................516 622-1422
Fax: 516 622-1425
Paul R Minbiole, *President*
Bill Crilley, *President*
Mary C Daly, *Vice Pres*
Greg Shavzian, *Info Tech Mgr*
Shannon Wayne, *Technical Staff*
▲ **EMP:** 4
SQ FT: 2,000
SALES: 5MM **Privately Held**
WEB: www.e-beamservices.com
SIC: 3671 Electron beam (beta ray) generator tubes

(G-6342)
EDGIAN PRESS INC
10 Bethpage Rd (11801-1512)
PHONE..................516 931-2114
Fax: 516 931-7989
Edward E Giannelli, *President*
Ian R Fuller, *Principal*
Edward C Giannelli, *Principal*
EMP: 8
SQ FT: 6,000
SALES (est): 1.1MM **Privately Held**
SIC: 2752 2759 Commercial printing, offset; letterpress printing

(G-6343)
EISEMAN-LUDMAR CO INC
56 Bethpage Dr (11801-1502)
PHONE..................516 932-6990
Andrew Ludmar, *President*
Carol Ludmar, *Vice Pres*
David Ludmar, *Vice Pres*
Delores Becker, *Bookkeeper*
EMP: 10
SQ FT: 4,200
SALES (est): 810K **Privately Held**
WEB: www.elcaccessories.com
SIC: 2395 2241 Embroidery & art needlework; lace & decorative trim, narrow fabric

(G-6344)
FLEXFIT LLC
350 Karin Ln Unit A (11801-5360)
PHONE..................516 932-8800
Alan Schneidman, *General Mgr*
Leslie Umphrey, *General Mgr*
Mike Son, *Design Engr*
John Micheal, *Credit Mgr*
Austin OH, *Sales Dir*
▲ **EMP:** 60
SALES (est): 97MM **Privately Held**
SIC: 2353 Hats, caps & millinery

(G-6345)
FOOT LOCKER RETAIL INC
Also Called: Champs Sports
358 Broadway Mall (11801-2709)
PHONE..................516 827-5306
Jamie Blas, *Manager*
EMP: 5
SALES (corp-wide): 7.4B **Publicly Held**
WEB: www.venatorgroup.com
SIC: 2389 5611 Men's miscellaneous accessories; clothing, sportswear, men's & boys'
HQ: Foot Locker Retail, Inc.
112 W 34th St Frnt 1
New York NY 10120
212 465-9041

(G-6346)
FOUGERA PHARMACEUTICALS INC
55 Cantiague Rock Rd (11801-1126)
P.O. Box 2006, Melville (11747-0103)
PHONE..................631 454-7677
Robert Faivre, *Managing Dir*
EMP: 158
SALES (corp-wide): 49.4B **Privately Held**
SIC: 2834 Druggists' preparations (pharmaceuticals)
HQ: Fougera Pharmaceuticals Inc.
60 Baylis Rd
Melville NY 11747
631 454-7677

(G-6347)
GE POLYMERSHAPES
120 Andrews Rd (11801-1704)
PHONE..................516 433-4092
Mike Grimm, *Manager*
◆ **EMP:** 10
SALES (est): 929K **Privately Held**
SIC: 2295 Resin or plastic coated fabrics

(G-6348)
GENETCLLY ENHNCED ATHC RES INC
Also Called: Gear
960 S Broadway Ste 120 (11801-5028)
PHONE..................631 750-3195
Kristy Delaney, *Principal*
▲ **EMP:** 5 **EST:** 2011
SALES (est): 529.3K **Privately Held**
SIC: 3949 5941 Sporting & athletic goods; specialty sport supplies

(G-6349)
GIM ELECTRONICS CORP
270 Duffy Ave Ste H (11801-3600)
PHONE..................516 942-3382
Fax: 516 942-3389
Mark Douenias, *President*
William Cardenas, *Vice Pres*
Mac E Fetner, *Plant Mgr*
Mike Morand, *Rsch/Dvlpt Dir*
EMP: 15
SQ FT: 7,800
SALES: 10MM **Privately Held**
WEB: www.gimelectronics.com
SIC: 3572 5961 Computer storage devices; computer equipment & electronics, mail order

(G-6350)
GLOBAL GLASS CORP
134 Woodbury Rd (11801-3025)
PHONE..................516 681-2309

Hicksville - Nassau County (G-6351)

Fax: 516 937-0389
Jack Flax, *President*
▲ EMP: 6
SQ FT: 2,000
SALES (est): 662.4K **Privately Held**
SIC: 3211 3231 5231 5719 Flat glass; products of purchased glass; glass; mirrors; glass & glazing work

(G-6351)
GLOPAK USA CORP
35 Engel St Ste B (11801-2648)
PHONE.................................516 433-3214
EMP: 58
SALES (corp-wide): 10.3MM **Privately Held**
SIC: 3221 Bottles for packing, bottling & canning: glass
PA: Glopak Usa Corp
    1816 127th St 2
    College Point NY 11356
    347 869-9252

(G-6352)
GOLFING MAGAZINE
Also Called: Long Island Golfer Magazine
22 W Nicholai St Ste 200 (11801-3881)
PHONE.................................516 822-5446
Fax: 516 822-5446
John Glozek Jr, *President*
▲ EMP: 8
SALES (est): 411K **Privately Held**
WEB: www.ligolfer.com
SIC: 2721 5736 Magazines: publishing only, not printed on site; sheet music

(G-6353)
GREENWOOD GRAPHICS INC
960 S Broadway Ste 106 (11801-5028)
PHONE.................................516 822-4856
Michael Boker, *President*
EMP: 12
SALES: 1MM **Privately Held**
WEB: www.greenwoodgraphics.com
SIC: 2752 7336 7319 Commercial printing, offset; graphic arts & related design; display advertising service

(G-6354)
HANAN PRODUCTS COMPANY INC
196 Miller Pl (11801-1826)
PHONE.................................516 938-1000
Fax: 516 938-1925
Stuart M Hanan, *President*
Francis Hanan, *Vice Pres*
Bruce Meyerhoff, *Vice Pres*
Ryan Hanan, *Accounts Mgr*
Bruce Meyeroff, *Director*
▼ EMP: 20 EST: 1950
SQ FT: 23,000
SALES (est): 4MM **Privately Held**
WEB: www.hananproducts.com
SIC: 2026 Whipped topping, except frozen or dry mix

(G-6355)
HICKSVILLE MACHINE WORKS CORP
761 S Broadway (11801-5098)
PHONE.................................516 931-1524
Fax: 516 931-2308
Gioachino Jack Spiezio, *Ch of Bd*
John Spiezio, *General Mgr*
Holly Pasquarella, *Purchasing*
Debby Snyder, *Manager*
Betty Spiezio, *Admin Sec*
EMP: 18 EST: 1946
SQ FT: 35,000
SALES (est): 4MM **Privately Held**
WEB: www.hicksvillemachine.com
SIC: 3728 Aircraft parts & equipment

(G-6356)
JAY-AIMEE DESIGNS INC
99 Railroad Station Plz # 200 (11801-2850)
PHONE.................................718 609-0333
Isaac Matalon, *CEO*
Shlomi Matalon, *President*
Diana Maldimado, *Bookkeeper*
EMP: 175
SQ FT: 4,000

SALES (est): 21.8MM **Privately Held**
WEB: www.jayaimee.com
SIC: 3911 Jewelry, precious metal; earrings, precious metal; bracelets, precious metal

(G-6357)
JOHN E POTENTE & SONS INC
114 Woodbury Rd Unit 1 (11801-3047)
PHONE.................................516 935-8585
Fax: 516 935-8546
Eugene Potente, *CEO*
Ralph J Potente, *President*
Saverio Potente, *Vice Pres*
EMP: 6 EST: 1925
SQ FT: 5,000
SALES (est): 929.9K **Privately Held**
SIC: 3272 Concrete products

(G-6358)
KINGFORM CAP COMPANY INC
121 New South Rd (11801-5230)
PHONE.................................516 822-2501
Fax: 516 822-2536
Leonard Ochs, *President*
▲ EMP: 60 EST: 1955
SQ FT: 33,000
SALES (est): 6.7MM **Privately Held**
WEB: www.kingformcap.com
SIC: 2353 Uniform hats & caps

(G-6359)
KOZY SHACK ENTERPRISES LLC (HQ)
83 Ludy St (11801-5114)
PHONE.................................516 870-3000
Robert Striano, *CEO*
Paul Barbuzza, *Project Mgr*
Sally Olivero, *CFO*
Nancy Roberts, *Manager*
Joanne Caridi, *Admin Sec*
▲ EMP: 250 EST: 1967
SQ FT: 70,000
SALES (est): 81.4MM
SALES (corp-wide): 14.9B **Privately Held**
WEB: www.kozyshack.com
SIC: 2099 5149 Desserts, ready-to-mix; gelatin dessert preparations; groceries & related products
PA: Land O'lakes, Inc.
    4001 Lexington Ave N
    Arden Hills MN 55126
    651 375-2222

(G-6360)
KOZY SHACK ENTERPRISES LLC
Also Called: Freshway Distributors
50 Ludy St (11801-5115)
PHONE.................................516 870-3000
Frank Gilmartin, *Mfg Spvr*
Marina Pleitez, *Opers Staff*
Brian Duffy, *QC Mgr*
Roy Kasenchak, *Engineer*
Joe Anderson, *VP Sales*
EMP: 200
SALES (corp-wide): 14.9B **Privately Held**
WEB: www.kozyshack.com
SIC: 2099 5149 2024 Desserts, ready-to-mix; gelatin dessert preparations; groceries & related products; ice cream & frozen desserts
HQ: Kozy Shack Enterprises, Llc
    83 Ludy St
    Hicksville NY 11801
    516 870-3000

(G-6361)
KUNO STEEL PRODUCTS CORP
132 Duffy Ave (11801-3640)
PHONE.................................516 938-8500
Fax: 516 938-8516
Kuno Weckenmann, *President*
Irmgard Weckenmann, *Corp Secy*
W Weckenmann, *Vice Pres*
EMP: 10 EST: 1964
SQ FT: 1,500
SALES: 1.2MM **Privately Held**
WEB: www.kunosteel.com
SIC: 3441 Building components, structural steel

(G-6362)
LAND OLAKES INC
50 Ludy St (11801-5115)
PHONE.................................516 681-2980

EMP: 8
SALES (corp-wide): 14.9B **Privately Held**
SIC: 2099 Food preparations
PA: Land O'lakes, Inc.
    4001 Lexington Ave N
    Arden Hills MN 55126
    651 375-2222

(G-6363)
LEATHER INDEXES CORP
174a Miller Pl (11801-1826)
P.O. Box 1350, Port Washington (11050-7350)
PHONE.................................516 827-1900
Fax: 516 827-9300
Paul Ellenberg, *President*
Kay Ellenberg, *Vice Pres*
EMP: 60
SQ FT: 15,000
SALES: 1.5MM **Privately Held**
SIC: 2678 2782 2675 Stationery products; blankbooks & looseleaf binders; die-cut paper & board

(G-6364)
LITMOR PUBLISHING CORP (PA)
Also Called: Litmor Publications
81 E Barclay St (11801-1356)
PHONE.................................516 931-0012
Fax: 516 931-0027
Margaret Norris, *Publisher*
Edward Norris, *General Mgr*
EMP: 15 EST: 1953
SQ FT: 3,000
SALES (est): 1.3MM **Privately Held**
SIC: 2711 2791 2752 Newspapers, publishing & printing; typesetting, commercial printing, lithographic

(G-6365)
LONG ISLAND ICED TEA CORP (PA)
116 Charlotte Ave Ste 1 (11801-2626)
PHONE.................................855 542-2832
Philip J Thomas, *CEO*
Julian Davidson, *Ch of Bd*
Peter Dydensborg, *COO*
Richard B Allen, *CFO*
James Meehan,
EMP: 29
SQ FT: 5,000
SALES: 1.9MM **Publicly Held**
SIC: 2086 Iced tea & fruit drinks, bottled & canned

(G-6366)
M F MANUFACTURING ENTERPRISES
2 Ballad Ln (11801-4529)
PHONE.................................516 822-5135
Michael Funk, *CEO*
Fern Funk, *Vice Pres*
EMP: 5
SALES (est): 325K **Privately Held**
SIC: 3469 Machine parts, stamped or pressed metal

(G-6367)
MARCAL PRINTING INC
Also Called: PIP Printing
85 N Broadway (11801-2948)
PHONE.................................516 942-9500
Fax: 516 942-9502
Marc Saltzman, *President*
Alan Smith, *Vice Pres*
EMP: 6
SQ FT: 3,000
SALES (est): 720K **Privately Held**
SIC: 2752 Commercial printing, offset

(G-6368)
MARIAH METAL PRODUCTS INC
89 Tec St (11801-3618)
PHONE.................................516 938-9783
Fax: 516 938-9784
Raymond O Leary, *President*
EMP: 5
SQ FT: 2,000
SALES (est): 676.2K **Privately Held**
SIC: 3444 Sheet metalwork

(G-6369)
MARIGOLD SIGNS INC
Also Called: Sign-A-Rama
485 S Broadway Ste 34 (11801-5071)
PHONE.................................516 433-7446

Fax: 516 433-8023
Vincent Marino, *President*
Robert Goldaber, *Vice Pres*
Benjamin Lichtiger, *Consultant*
Mark Lifshitz, *Director*
Michael Eaton,
EMP: 10
SALES (est): 790K **Privately Held**
SIC: 3993 Signs & advertising specialties

(G-6370)
MARKWIK CORP
309 W John St (11801-1024)
PHONE.................................516 470-1990
Jane A Groene, *President*
Taylor Groene, *General Mgr*
EMP: 18 EST: 1949
SQ FT: 9,000
SALES (est): 2.3MM **Privately Held**
WEB: www.markwik.com
SIC: 3089 Plastic hardware & building products

(G-6371)
MICRO CONTACTS INC (PA)
1 Enterprise Pl Unit E (11801-2694)
PHONE.................................516 433-4830
Fax: 516 433-6379
Gerald F Tucci, *Ch of Bd*
Michael F Tucci, *President*
Robert Stinson, *General Mgr*
Steven Klekman, *Vice Pres*
Philip Uruburu, *Vice Pres*
▲ EMP: 50 EST: 1963
SQ FT: 40,000
SALES (est): 6.3MM **Privately Held**
WEB: www.microcontacts.com
SIC: 3643 Contacts, electrical

(G-6372)
MILES ALEXANDER LLC
485 S Broadway Ste 11 (11801-5071)
PHONE.................................516 937-5262
Arnold Goldstein, *CEO*
EMP: 14
SALES (est): 492.6K
SALES (corp-wide): 112.6MM **Privately Held**
SIC: 2389 Men's miscellaneous accessories
PA: Authentic Lifestyle Products Llc
    485 S Broadway Ste 11
    Hicksville NY 11801
    212 354-2170

(G-6373)
MISON CONCEPTS INC
485 S Broadway Ste 33 (11801-5071)
PHONE.................................516 933-8000
Fax: 516 933-8000
Joseph Jaroff, *President*
Bhavani Morganstern, *Vice Pres*
JP Proskauer, *Project Mgr*
Sandra Fiore, *Administration*
▲ EMP: 8
SQ FT: 2,000
SALES (est): 690K **Privately Held**
WEB: www.mison.com
SIC: 3446 Architectural metalwork

(G-6374)
MOD-A-CAN INC (PA)
178 Miller Pl (11801-1890)
PHONE.................................516 931-8545
Fax: 516 931-8545
Stan Buoninfante, *President*
Stan L Buoninfante, *President*
Roberta Wolfe, *General Mgr*
Michael Iannotta, *VP Opers*
Rick Schuetz, *Plant Mgr*
EMP: 20 EST: 1966
SQ FT: 19,400
SALES (est): 8MM **Privately Held**
WEB: www.modacan.com
SIC: 3812 Aircraft flight instruments

(G-6375)
MULTI PACKAGING SOLUTIONS INC
325 Duffy Ave Unit 1 (11801-3644)
PHONE.................................516 488-2000
Michael Greenberg, *Branch Mgr*
EMP: 113
SALES (corp-wide): 1.6B **Publicly Held**
SIC: 2671 Packaging paper & plastics film, coated & laminated

HQ: Multi Packaging Solutions, Inc.
150 E 52nd St Ste 2800
New York NY 10022
646 885-0157

(G-6376)
MULTI PACKAGING SOLUTIONS INC
325 Duffy Ave Unit 5 (11801-3644)
PHONE.................................812 422-4104
John Miles, *Plant Mgr*
EMP: 70
SALES (corp-wide): 1.6B **Publicly Held**
SIC: 2631 Paperboard mills
HQ: Multi Packaging Solutions, Inc.
150 E 52nd St Ste 2800
New York NY 10022
646 885-0157

(G-6377)
NU - COMMUNITEK LLC
108 New South Rd Ste A (11801-5262)
PHONE.................................516 433-3553
Allison Waserman, *Controller*
Gary Calmenson,
Jarret Calmenson,
EMP: 10
SQ FT: 1,500
SALES (est): 2.3MM **Privately Held**
WEB: www.loyaltykiosk.com
SIC: 3575 Computer terminals

(G-6378)
NY EMBROIDERY INC
Also Called: New York Embroidery & Monogram
25 Midland Ave (11801-1509)
PHONE.................................516 822-6456
Fax: 516 822-6461
John La Rocca, *President*
Annette Snow, *Vice Pres*
▲ **EMP:** 20
SALES (est): 1.5MM **Privately Held**
WEB: www.nyembroidery.com
SIC: 2395 Embroidery products, except schiffli machine

(G-6379)
OLMSTEAD PRODUCTS CORP
1 Jefry Ln (11801-5394)
PHONE.................................516 681-3700
Fax: 516 681-3702
Jack Tepper, *President*
Nicholas Lucarello, *Vice Pres*
▲ **EMP:** 12 **EST:** 1954
SQ FT: 7,000
SALES (est): 1.9MM **Privately Held**
SIC: 3556 Food products machinery

(G-6380)
OXYGEN INC (PA)
Also Called: Rodan
6 Midland Ave (11801-1510)
PHONE.................................516 433-1144
Fax: 516 433-8450
Daniel Joory, *President*
Ronnie Zubli, *CFO*
Kenny Miller, *Manager*
◆ **EMP:** 8
SQ FT: 2,000
SALES (est): 955.8K **Privately Held**
SIC: 2369 Bathing suits & swimwear: girls', children's & infants'; leggings: girls', children's & infants'

(G-6381)
OYSTER BAY PUMP WORKS INC
78 Midland Ave Unit 1 (11801-1537)
P.O. Box 725 (11802-0725)
PHONE.................................516 922-3789
Fax: 516 933-4501
Patrick Gaillard, *CEO*
EMP: 18
SALES (est): 4.8MM **Privately Held**
WEB: www.obpw.com
SIC: 3561 3829 3589 Pumps & pumping equipment; medical diagnostic systems, nuclear; liquor dispensing equipment & systems

(G-6382)
P & F BAKERS INC
640 S Broadway (11801-5016)
PHONE.................................516 931-6821
P Zamparelli, *CEO*
EMP: 5
SALES (est): 364.4K **Privately Held**
SIC: 2026 Bakers' cheese

(G-6383)
PAL ALUMINUM INC (PA)
Also Called: Pal Industries
230 Duffy Ave Unit B (11801-3641)
PHONE.................................516 937-1990
Pana Giotis Mar Neris, *President*
Laurel Marneris, *Vice Pres*
EMP: 2
SQ FT: 70,000
SALES (est): 4.3MM **Privately Held**
SIC: 3444 5033 5031 Metal roofing & roof drainage equipment; gutters, sheet metal; roof deck, sheet metal; siding, except wood; doors

(G-6384)
PAL MANUFACTURING CORP
230 Duffy Ave Unit B (11801-3641)
PHONE.................................516 937-1990
Laurel Marneris, *President*
Panagiotis Marneris, *Vice Pres*
Paul Baricelli, *Controller*
Victor Masterco, *Mktg Dir*
EMP: 28
SQ FT: 70,000
SALES (est): 4.4MM **Privately Held**
WEB: www.palwindows.com
SIC: 3442 3231 Screen & storm doors & windows; products of purchased glass

(G-6385)
PB08 INC
40 Bloomingdale Rd (11801-6507)
PHONE.................................347 866-7353
Jajtar Kular, *Owner*
Neeraj Sherma, *Principal*
EMP: 2
SALES: 3MM **Privately Held**
SIC: 3537 Trucks: freight, baggage, etc.: industrial, except mining

(G-6386)
PEDRE CORP (PA)
Also Called: Pedre Watch
270 Duffy Ave Ste G (11801-3600)
PHONE.................................212 868-2935
Fax: 212 868-3646
R Peter Gunshor, *President*
Jill Kiviat, *Vice Pres*
Cornelia Bourne, *Credit Mgr*
◆ **EMP:** 22
SQ FT: 10,000
SALES (est): 3.4MM **Privately Held**
WEB: www.pedrewatch.com
SIC: 3873 Watches, clocks, watchcases & parts

(G-6387)
PETRO INC
477 W John St (11801-1029)
PHONE.................................516 686-1900
Rodney Roberts, *Branch Mgr*
EMP: 7 **Publicly Held**
SIC: 1389 Oil field services
HQ: Petro, Inc.
9 W Broad St Ste 3
Stamford CT 06902
203 325-5400

(G-6388)
PIONEER WINDOW HOLDINGS INC (PA)
Also Called: Pioneer Windows Manufacturing
15 Frederick Pl (11801-4205)
PHONE.................................516 822-7000
Fax: 516 933-3607
Vincent Amato, *Ch of Bd*
Anthony J Ross, *President*
EMP: 12
SALES (est): 15.1MM **Privately Held**
WEB: www.pwindows.com
SIC: 3442 Storm doors or windows, metal

(G-6389)
PITNEY BOWES INC
220 Miller Pl (11801-1826)
PHONE.................................516 822-0900
Jim Sartory, *General Mgr*
Dan Hindman, *Branch Mgr*
EMP: 35
SALES (corp-wide): 3.5B **Publicly Held**
SIC: 3579 7359 Postage meters; business machine & electronic equipment rental services
PA: Pitney Bowes Inc.
3001 Summer St
Stamford CT 06905
203 356-5000

(G-6390)
PORTA DECOR
290 Duffy Ave Unit 3 (11801-3638)
PHONE.................................516 826-6900
Andrew Zaino, *Owner*
▼ **EMP:** 7
SALES (est): 805.7K **Privately Held**
SIC: 2599 Furniture & fixtures

(G-6391)
RUI XING INTERNATIONAL TRDG CO
89 Jerusalem Ave (11801-4950)
PHONE.................................516 298-2667
Ke Yi Sun, *Ch of Bd*
Katie Huang, *Manager*
▲ **EMP:** 5
SALES: 500K **Privately Held**
SIC: 3089 Boxes, plastic

(G-6392)
SCHINDLER ELEVATOR CORPORATION
7 Midland Ave (11801-1509)
PHONE.................................516 860-1321
Fax: 516 860-1350
Bob Delaney, *Branch Mgr*
EMP: 58
SALES (corp-wide): 9.3B **Privately Held**
WEB: www.us.schindler.com
SIC: 3534 Elevators & equipment
HQ: Schindler Elevator Corporation
20 Whippany Rd
Morristown NJ 07960
973 397-6500

(G-6393)
SCIARRA LABORATORIES INC
48509 S Broadway (11801)
PHONE.................................516 933-7853
Fax: 516 933-7807
John J Sciarra, *President*
Christopher J Sciarra, *Vice Pres*
Caroline Laregina, *Office Mgr*
EMP: 6
SALES (est): 1.2MM **Privately Held**
WEB: www.sciarralabs.com
SIC: 2834 Pharmaceutical preparations

(G-6394)
SI PARTNERS INC
15 E Carl St Unit 1 (11801-4290)
PHONE.................................516 433-1415
Amit Singhvi, *President*
Aj Shaah, *Manager*
▲ **EMP:** 8
SALES (est): 930.9K **Privately Held**
SIC: 3355 Aluminum wire & cable

(G-6395)
STS REFILL AMERICA LLC
399 W John St Unit A (11801-1043)
PHONE.................................516 934-8008
Shahar Turgeman,
Mark Freedman,
Uri Hason,
Scott Robert,
▲ **EMP:** 6
SQ FT: 2,500
SALES (est): 501.1K **Privately Held**
WEB: www.stsrefill.com
SIC: 3951 Cartridges, refill: ball point pens

(G-6396)
SUMMIT INSTRUMENT CORP
99 Engineers Dr (11801-6594)
PHONE.................................516 433-0140
Fax: 516 433-0281
Arthur Petschauer, *CEO*
Tom Petschauer, *President*
Stefanie Petschauer, *Corp Secy*
EMP: 8
SQ FT: 7,500
SALES: 750K **Privately Held**
SIC: 3599 Machine shop, jobbing & repair

(G-6397)
TAMPERPROOF SCREW COMPANY INC
30 Laurel St (11801-2641)
PHONE.................................516 931-1616
Fax: 516 931-1654
Lewis Friedman, *President*
George Friedman, *Corp Secy*
Alaina Picitelli, *Vice Pres*
Mary Paddock, *Office Mgr*
▲ **EMP:** 12
SQ FT: 5,000
SALES (est): 2.3MM **Privately Held**
WEB: www.tamperproof.com
SIC: 3452 Screws, metal

(G-6398)
VINDAGRA USA INCORPORATED
50 Bethpage Rd Ste 6 (11801-1500)
PHONE.................................516 605-1960
Karen McMahon, *President*
Steve Kunz, *Sales Mgr*
▲ **EMP:** 5 **EST:** 2010
SALES (est): 1MM **Privately Held**
SIC: 2084 Wines, brandy & brandy spirits
PA: Vindagra Usa Inc.
433 Plaza Real Ste 275
Boca Raton FL 33432
561 962-4162

High Falls
Ulster County

(G-6399)
ALE-TECHNIQUES INC
2452b Lucas Tpke (12440-5920)
PHONE.................................845 687-7200
Daniel Ale, *CEO*
Richard Kodnia, *Vice Pres*
EMP: 15
SQ FT: 35,000
SALES (est): 1.3MM **Privately Held**
SIC: 3545 Machine tool accessories

(G-6400)
DELTA PRESS INC
2426 Lucas Tpke (12440-5920)
PHONE.................................212 989-3445
Fax: 212 989-3668
Joel Sachs, *President*
EMP: 30 **EST:** 1959
SALES (est): 2.5MM **Privately Held**
WEB: www.deltapress.com
SIC: 2752 Commercial printing, offset

(G-6401)
OTTO-TECH MACHINE CO INC
2452b Lucas Tpke (12440-5920)
P.O. Box 467 (12440-0467)
PHONE.................................845 687-8800
Otto Scherrieble, *President*
Shawn Matthews, *Vice Pres*
Elisa Scherrieble, *Vice Pres*
EMP: 9
SQ FT: 7,000
SALES (est): 1.2MM **Privately Held**
WEB: www.otto-tech.com
SIC: 3599 Machine shop, jobbing & repair

(G-6402)
ULSTER COUNTY PRESS OFFICE
Also Called: Blue Stone Press
1209 State Route 213 (12440-5714)
P.O. Box 149, Stone Ridge (12484-0149)
PHONE.................................845 687-4480
Fax: 845 691-1424
Lori Childerss, *President*
Gregory Childress, *Principal*
EMP: 5
SALES (est): 635.8K **Privately Held**
WEB: www.ulstercountypress.com
SIC: 2711 Newspapers, publishing & printing

Highland
Ulster County

(G-6403)
BORABORA FRUIT JUICES INC
255 Milton (12528-2256)
P.O. Box 383, Pound Ridge (10576-0383)
PHONE.................................845 795-1027
Fax: 914 470-5940
EMP: 8
SQ FT: 10,000
SALES: 1MM **Privately Held**
SIC: 2086 Mfg Bottled/Canned Soft Drinks

(G-6404)
GORDON FIRE EQUIPMENT LLC
3199 Us Highway 9w (12528-2633)
PHONE.................................845 691-5700
Fax: 845 691-8700
Mary Anne Hein, *Mng Member*
EMP: 5
SALES (est): 450K **Privately Held**
SIC: 2899 Fire retardant chemicals

(G-6405)
M M TOOL AND MANUFACTURING
175 Chapel Hill Rd (12528-2105)
PHONE.................................845 691-4140
Fax: 845 691-4911
Matt Mc Cluskey, *President*
Kenneth P Castelo, *Director*
EMP: 8
SQ FT: 10,000
SALES: 1.2MM **Privately Held**
SIC: 3585 Air conditioning equipment, complete; air conditioning units, complete: domestic or industrial

(G-6406)
PHOENIX CABLES CORPORATION
131 Tillson Avenue Ext (12528-1828)
PHONE.................................845 691-6253
Fax: 845 691-7989
Frank Roberto, *President*
Jonathan Heptinstall, *Vice Pres*
Dorothy Roberto, *Treasurer*
EMP: 135
SQ FT: 26,000
SALES (est): 12.5MM **Privately Held**
SIC: 3679 Harness assemblies for electronic use: wire or cable

(G-6407)
PRISM SOLAR TECHNOLOGIES INC (PA)
180 South St (12528-2439)
PHONE.................................845 883-4200
Kevin R Stewart, *CEO*
David Waserstein, *Ch of Bd*
Carolyn Lewandowski, *Corp Secy*
Jeff Rosenberg, *Opers Mgr*
John Neidhardt, *Facilities Mgr*
▲ EMP: 38
SQ FT: 93,000
SALES (est): 4.2MM **Privately Held**
SIC: 3433 Solar heaters & collectors

(G-6408)
SELUX CORPORATION
5 Lumen Ln (12528-1903)
P.O. Box 1060 (12528-8060)
PHONE.................................845 691-7723
Fax: 845 691-6749
Felix Groenwaldt, *Ch of Bd*
Peter Stanway, *President*
Thomas Mindt, *Managing Dir*
Mike Seckler, *VP Mfg*
Randy Adams, *Plant Mgr*
▲ EMP: 164
SQ FT: 85,000
SALES: 42.5MM
SALES (corp-wide): 1.9MM **Privately Held**
WEB: www.selux.com
SIC: 3646 Commercial indusl & institutional electric lighting fixtures
PA: Selux Benelux Nv
    Grotesteenweg 50
    Kontich 2550

(G-6409)
ZUMTOBEL LIGHTING INC (DH)
3300 Us Highway 9w (12528-2630)
PHONE.................................845 691-6262
Kevin Maddy, *CEO*
Ferdinand Eberle, *Project Mgr*
Daniela Kraus, *Project Mgr*
Ron Moson, *Chief Engr*
Claus Kinder, *Engineer*
▲ EMP: 130
SQ FT: 80,000
SALES: 44MM
SALES (corp-wide): 46.5MM **Privately Held**
WEB: www.zumtobel.com
SIC: 3646 Commercial indusl & institutional electric lighting fixtures
HQ: Zumtobel Lighting Gmbh
    SchweizerstraBe 30
    Dornbirn 6850
    557 239-00

Highland Falls
Orange County

(G-6410)
SKD TACTICAL INC
291 Main St (10928-1803)
PHONE.................................845 897-2889
Dani Seuk, *CEO*
Joe Seuk, *Vice Pres*
EMP: 6 EST: 1999
SALES: 1.5MM **Privately Held**
SIC: 2399 Military insignia, textile

Highland Mills
Orange County

(G-6411)
ALL MERCHANDISE DISPLAY CORP
Also Called: AM Display
4 Pheasant Run (10930-2140)
PHONE.................................718 257-2221
Eddie Minkoff, *President*
Abraham J Minkoff, *Vice Pres*
EMP: 7
SALES (est): 627.8K **Privately Held**
SIC: 2541 Display fixtures, wood

(G-6412)
HIGHLAND SAND & GRAVEL INC
Also Called: Highland Stone
911 State Route 32 (10930-2309)
P.O. Box 1007 (10930-1007)
PHONE.................................845 928-2221
Fax: 845 928-6504
William G Desrosiers, *President*
Joan Squicciarini, *Chairman*
William Derosiers, *Manager*
Robin A Desrosiers, *Admin Sec*
EMP: 13
SQ FT: 6,000
SALES (est): 1.9MM **Privately Held**
SIC: 1429 Igneous rock, crushed & broken-quarrying; sandstone, crushed & broken-quarrying; slate, crushed & broken-quarrying

(G-6413)
M &L INDUSTRY OF NY INC
583 State Route 32 Ste 1u (10930-5229)
PHONE.................................845 827-6255
Melech Krauf, *CEO*
Tiffany Vesley, *Office Mgr*
EMP: 9
SALES (est): 700K **Privately Held**
SIC: 2441 Boxes, wood

(G-6414)
SPEYSIDE HOLDINGS LLC
911 State Route 32 (10930-2309)
P.O. Box 1007 (10930-1007)
PHONE.................................845 928-2221
Anthony Williams, *Chairman*
EMP: 25
SALES (est): 584.2K **Privately Held**
SIC: 1442 Construction sand & gravel

Hillburn
Rockland County

(G-6415)
HILLBURN GRANITE COMPANY INC
166 Sixth St (10931-1100)
P.O. Box 832, Tuxedo Park (10987-0832)
PHONE.................................845 357-8900
Leeann Matthews, *Info Tech Mgr*
EMP: 5
SQ FT: 1,000
SALES (est): 259.4K **Privately Held**
SIC: 1411 Dimension stone; granite dimension stone

(G-6416)
MERCO HACKENSACK INC
Also Called: MERCO TAPE
201 Route 59 Ste D2 (10931-1189)
P.O. Box 875 (10931-0875)
PHONE.................................845 357-3699
David Rose, *President*
Susan Hofmann, *General Mgr*
Adam Riskin, *Vice Pres*
Eleanor Rose, *Sales Staff*
Joshua Rose, *Sales Staff*
◆ EMP: 6 EST: 1972
SQ FT: 18,000
SALES: 4.7MM **Privately Held**
WEB: www.maskingtape.com
SIC: 2672 Tape, pressure sensitive: made from purchased materials

Hilton
Monroe County

(G-6417)
CUDDEBACK MACHINING INC
18 Draffin Rd (14468-9708)
PHONE.................................585 392-5889
Fax: 585 392-5888
Lawrence Cuddeback, *President*
Michael Ahl, *Managing Dir*
Sandra Cuddeback, *Admin Sec*
EMP: 7
SQ FT: 4,200
SALES (est): 1MM **Privately Held**
WEB: www.cuddebackmachining.com
SIC: 3496 3544 Miscellaneous fabricated wire products; special dies & tools

(G-6418)
MONROE FLUID TECHNOLOGY INC
36 Draffin Rd (14468-9717)
PHONE.................................585 392-3434
Alan Christodaro, *President*
Jeff Cliff, *VP Mfg*
Paul Silloway, *Prdtn Mgr*
Tim Kelley, *Sales Mgr*
Alan Eckard, *Director*
EMP: 25
SALES: 10MM **Privately Held**
SIC: 2992 2899 2841 Lubricating oils; cutting oils, blending: made from purchased materials; chemical preparations; soap & other detergents

(G-6419)
OMEGA CONSOLIDATED CORPORATION
101 Heinz St (14468-1226)
PHONE.................................585 392-9262
Fax: 585 392-4868
Martin Hunte, *President*
Robert Hunte, *Vice Pres*
Thomas Hunte, *Vice Pres*
Linda Kokorotsis, *Manager*
▼ EMP: 20 EST: 1981
SQ FT: 30,000
SALES (est): 3.1MM **Privately Held**
WEB: www.omegacon.com
SIC: 3541 Machine tools, metal cutting type

(G-6420)
RC IMAGING INC
50 Old Hojack Ln (14468-1147)
PHONE.................................585 392-4336
Eric Bostley, *President*
Claudia Eichas, *General Mgr*
Harry Bostley, *Vice Pres*
Michelle Rose, *Office Mgr*
Kim Manuel, *Manager*
▼ EMP: 9
SQ FT: 7,900
SALES (est): 1.7MM **Privately Held**
WEB: www.rochestercassette.com
SIC: 3844 7699 X-ray apparatus & tubes; X-ray equipment repair

(G-6421)
WILLIAM J RYAN
Also Called: Ryan Printing
1365 Hamlin Parma Townline (14468-9749)
PHONE.................................585 392-6200
Fax: 585 392-5229
William Ryan, *Owner*
EMP: 5
SQ FT: 3,000
SALES: 200K **Privately Held**
WEB: www.ryanprinting.com
SIC: 2752 7334 2759 Commercial printing, lithographic; photocopying & duplicating services; commercial printing

Himrod
Yates County

(G-6422)
LAPP MANAGEMENT CORP
Also Called: Wood-Tex Products
3700 Route 14 (14842-9802)
PHONE.................................607 243-5141
Barbara Lapp, *President*
EMP: 7
SQ FT: 12,000
SALES (est): 1.2MM **Privately Held**
WEB: www.woodtexproducts.com
SIC: 2452 Prefabricated buildings, wood

(G-6423)
WOOD TEX PRODUCTS LLC
3700 Route 14 (14842-9802)
PHONE.................................607 243-5141
Fax: 607 243-5767
Ben Lapp, *Exec VP*
Myron Glick, *Vice Pres*
Amy Coon, *Sales Staff*
Rebecca Lepp, *Sales Staff*
Chris Neu, *Sales Staff*
EMP: 54
SALES: 7.2MM **Privately Held**
SIC: 2452 Prefabricated wood buildings

Hinsdale
Cattaraugus County

(G-6424)
SIMPLICITY BANDSAW INC
3674 Main St (14743-9817)
PHONE.................................716 557-8805
Norbert J Witzigman, *Principal*
EMP: 8
SALES (est): 796.9K **Privately Held**
SIC: 2421 Sawmills & planing mills, general

Hobart
Delaware County

(G-6425)
HATHERLEIGH COMPANY LTD
62545 State Highway 10 (13788-3019)
PHONE.................................607 538-1092
Frederic Flach, *Ch of Bd*
Anna Krusinski, *Editor*
EMP: 9
SALES: 8.7K **Privately Held**
WEB: www.bodysculptingbible.com
SIC: 2721 7812 Trade journals: publishing only, not printed on site; audio-visual program production

GEOGRAPHIC SECTION

(G-6426)
MALLINCKRODT LLC
Also Called: Covidien
172 Railroad Ave (13788)
P.O. Box P (13788-0416)
PHONE..................................607 538-9124
Fax: 607 538-2501
Jacqueline Murphy, *Project Mgr*
Seth Merwin, *Opers Mgr*
Rick West, *Opers Mgr*
Tammi Tully, *Purch Agent*
Paul Dibble, *Engineer*
EMP: 630 Privately Held
WEB: www.mallinckrodt.com
SIC: 2834 Pharmaceutical preparations
HQ: Mallinckrodt Llc
    675 Jmes S Mcdonnell Blvd
    Hazelwood MO 63042
    314 654-2000

Hogansburg
Franklin County

(G-6427)
INDIAN TIME
1 Hilltop Dr (13655)
PHONE..................................518 358-9531
Mark Narfisian, *General Mgr*
Narsisian Mark, *Manager*
EMP: 15
SALES (est): 630K Privately Held
SIC: 2711 Newspapers

(G-6428)
JACOBS TOBACCO COMPANY
Also Called: Jacobs Manufacturing
344 Frogtown Rd (13655-3137)
PHONE..................................518 358-4948
Roseley Jacobs, *Owner*
Stiifny Codroy, *Accountant*
EMP: 24
SALES (est): 4.7MM Privately Held
SIC: 2111 Cigarettes

Holbrook
Suffolk County

(G-6429)
ACCENT SPEAKER TECHNOLOGY LTD
Also Called: Nola Speaker
1511 Lincoln Ave (11741-2216)
PHONE..................................631 738-2540
Carl Marchisotto, *CEO*
▲ **EMP: 7**
SALES (est): 939.5K Privately Held
SIC: 3651 Household audio & video equipment

(G-6430)
ACCURATE INDUSTRIAL MACHINING
1711 Church St (11741-5921)
PHONE..................................631 242-0566
Fax: 631 242-6469
Jerome Bricker, *President*
Marguerite Bricker, *Corp Secy*
▲ **EMP: 20**
SQ FT: 30,000
SALES (est): 2.7MM Privately Held
SIC: 3599 5084 Machine shop, jobbing & repair; industrial machinery & equipment

(G-6431)
ALWAYS BAKED FRESH
331 Dante Ct Ste F (11741-3800)
PHONE..................................631 648-0811
Victoria Kim, *Principal*
EMP: 8 EST: 2009
SALES (est): 460.2K Privately Held
SIC: 2051 Cakes, bakery: except frozen

(G-6432)
BNM PRODUCT SERVICE
1561 Lincoln Ave (11741-2217)
PHONE..................................631 750-1586
Sergio Lorenzo, *President*
EMP: 5
SALES (est): 626.8K Privately Held
SIC: 3545 Machine tool accessories

(G-6433)
BRYIT GROUP LLC
Also Called: Jentronics
1724 Church St (11741-5918)
PHONE..................................631 563-6603
Fax: 631 563-6509
Ira Obermeister, *General Mgr*
Larry Boas, *Vice Pres*
Laura Erwig, *Bookkeeper*
Barbara Weiss, *Mng Member*
EMP: 16
SQ FT: 4,000
SALES (est): 1.6MM Privately Held
WEB: www.jentronics.com
SIC: 3672 Printed circuit boards; harness assemblies for electronic use: wire or cable

(G-6434)
BRZOZKA INDUSTRIES INC
Also Called: Felber Metal Fabricators
790 Broadway Ave (11741-4906)
PHONE..................................631 588-8164
Waldmar Brazozka, *CEO*
Hans Felber, *President*
EMP: 10
SQ FT: 3,600
SALES (est): 1.5MM Privately Held
SIC: 3499 Machine bases, metal

(G-6435)
CALMETRICS INC
1340 Lincoln Ave Ste 6 (11741-2255)
PHONE..................................631 580-2522
Frank Ferrandino, *President*
David Cernese, *Vice Pres*
Tina Korpus, *Manager*
Justina Kortus, *Manager*
Justina Corpus, *Admin Sec*
EMP: 6
SQ FT: 1,650
SALES (est): 440K Privately Held
SIC: 3825 Standards & calibrating equipment, laboratory

(G-6436)
CAREFREE KITCHENS INC
925 Lincoln Ave Ste 1 (11741-2200)
PHONE..................................631 567-2120
Leonard Daino, *President*
Carolina Daino, *Vice Pres*
Mike Nikel, *Manager*
EMP: 5
SALES (est): 440K Privately Held
SIC: 2434 5031 5211 Wood kitchen cabinets; kitchen cabinets; cabinets, kitchen

(G-6437)
CJN MACHINERY CORP
917 Lincoln Ave Ste 13 (11741-2250)
PHONE..................................631 244-8030
Fax: 631 563-9850
Josephine Chillemi, *President*
Josephine Chllemi, *President*
Vivian Chillemi, *General Mgr*
EMP: 7
SQ FT: 4,000
SALES (est): 2MM Privately Held
SIC: 3599 Machine shop, jobbing & repair

(G-6438)
CLEAN ROOM DEPOT INC
1730 Church St (11741-5918)
PHONE..................................631 589-3033
Ken Lorello, *President*
Alexis Lorello, *Vice Pres*
Frank Vandeplanck, *Engineer*
EMP: 10
SQ FT: 3,600
SALES (est): 1MM Privately Held
WEB: www.cleanroomdepot.com
SIC: 3822 Auto controls regulating residntl & coml environmt & applncs

(G-6439)
COIL STAMPING INC
1340 Lincoln Ave Ste 1 (11741-2255)
PHONE..................................631 588-3040
Fax: 631 588-8912
Edward Kiss, *President*
EMP: 15
SALES (est): 1.5MM Privately Held
WEB: www.coilstamping.com
SIC: 3544 Special dies & tools

(G-6440)
COLORSPEC COATINGS INTL INC
1716 Church St (11741-5918)
P.O. Box 493, Bohemia (11716-0493)
PHONE..................................631 472-8251
Lisa Bancalari, *President*
Robert Bein, *Vice Pres*
Robert Pein, *Vice Pres*
Tim Strohsnitter, *Office Mgr*
Bincent Rotondi, *Manager*
▲ **EMP: 10**
SQ FT: 5,200
SALES (est): 1.4MM Privately Held
WEB: www.colorspeccoatings.com
SIC: 2491 Preserving (creosoting) of wood

(G-6441)
CRYSTALIZATIONS SYSTEMS INC
1401 Lincoln Ave (11741-2215)
PHONE..................................631 467-0090
Patricia Ellenwood, *President*
Kim Torregrosa, *Bookkeeper*
Nelson Young, *Admin Sec*
EMP: 15
SQ FT: 12,000
SALES (est): 2.3MM Privately Held
SIC: 3499 Fire- or burglary-resistive products

(G-6442)
CTB ENTERPRISE LLC
1170 Lincoln Ave Unit 7 (11741-2286)
PHONE..................................631 563-0088
Tom Passaro, *Mng Member*
Thomas Passaro Jr, *Mng Member*
EMP: 10
SALES (est): 774.2K Privately Held
WEB: www.ctbenterprise.com
SIC: 3826 Instruments measuring magnetic & electrical properties

(G-6443)
DATA DISPLAY USA INC
1330 Lincoln Ave Ste 2 (11741-2268)
P.O. Box 5135, Brookings SD (57006-5135)
PHONE..................................631 218-2130
Fax: 631 218-2140
Marie Neville, *CEO*
Kevin Neville, *President*
Staci Shannon, *Sls & Mktg Exec*
Robert Giglio, *Accounts Mgr*
Kathy Lawson, *Manager*
▲ **EMP: 120**
SQ FT: 5,000
SALES (est): 14MM
SALES (corp-wide): 570.1MM Publicly Held
WEB: www.data-display.com
SIC: 3674 Light emitting diodes
HQ: Daktronics Ireland Co. Limited
    Deerpark Industrial Estate
    Ennis

(G-6444)
DYNOCOAT INC
1738 Church St (11741-5918)
PHONE..................................631 244-9344
Fax: 631 244-9436
Patrick Dimaio, *President*
Donald Cowdell, *Vice Pres*
Terry Dimaio, *Bookkeeper*
Matt Dienna, *Director*
EMP: 10
SQ FT: 6,500
SALES: 850K Privately Held
WEB: www.dynocoat.com
SIC: 3479 Coating of metals & formed products

(G-6445)
ELECTRONIC SYSTEMS INC
Also Called: Esi
1742 Church St (11741-5918)
PHONE..................................631 589-4389
Gregory Quirk, *President*
EMP: 4 EST: 1997
SALES: 1.2MM Privately Held
SIC: 3571 Electronic computers

(G-6446)
ENCORE REFINING AND RECYCLEING
1120 Lincoln Ave (11741-2260)
PHONE..................................631 319-1910
Joseph Crisera, *Partner*
Robert Gaslindo, *Partner*
EMP: 9
SALES (est): 393K Privately Held
SIC: 3341 Secondary precious metals

(G-6447)
ENERAC INC
1320 Lincoln Ave Ste 1 (11741-2267)
PHONE..................................516 997-1554
Bill Dascal Sr, *President*
Russell Drago, *Plant Mgr*
Kevin Sullivan, *Mfg Staff*
Fred Dascal, *Purch Mgr*
Mary Kearney, *Financial Exec*
EMP: 14
SALES (est): 1.4MM Privately Held
WEB: www.enerac.com
SIC: 3823 3829 Analyzers, industrial process type; measuring & controlling devices

(G-6448)
GEOMETRIC CIRCUITS INC
920 Lincoln Ave Unit 1 (11741-2257)
PHONE..................................631 249-0230
Fax: 516 249-0286
John Pollina, *President*
Kurt J Meyer, *Corp Secy*
Kathy Whittaker, *Manager*
EMP: 60
SQ FT: 36,000
SALES (est): 8.1MM Privately Held
WEB: www.geometriccircuits.com
SIC: 3672 Printed circuit boards

(G-6449)
GRAND PRIX LITHO INC
101 Colin Dr Unit 5 (11741-4332)
PHONE..................................631 242-4182
Craig Lennon, *President*
EMP: 25 EST: 1968
SQ FT: 6,000
SALES: 4MM Privately Held
WEB: www.grandprixlitho.com
SIC: 2752 Commercial printing, lithographic

(G-6450)
IMAGE TYPOGRAPHY INC
Also Called: Starfire Printing
751 Coates Ave Ste 31 (11741-6039)
P.O. Box 5250, Miller Place (11764-7901)
PHONE..................................631 218-6932
Fax: 631 218-6935
James Bryant, *President*
EMP: 5 EST: 2001
SALES (est): 409.8K Privately Held
WEB: www.starfireprinting.com
SIC: 2759 Commercial printing

(G-6451)
INGHAM INDUSTRIES INC
Also Called: Authentic Parts
1363 Lincoln Ave Ste 1 (11741-2274)
PHONE..................................631 242-2493
Fax: 631 563-5853
Donna Miller, *President*
EMP: 3
SQ FT: 2,500
SALES: 1MM Privately Held
WEB: www.authelectric.com
SIC: 3699 5065 5251 3429 Chimes, electric; intercommunication equipment, electronic; builders' hardware; manufactured hardware (general)

(G-6452)
INNOVATIVE POWER PRODUCTS INC
1170 Lincoln Ave Unit 7 (11741-2286)
PHONE..................................631 563-0088
Thomas Passaro Jr, *President*
Thomas Dowling, *Vice Pres*
Dan Guiffre, *Engineer*
EMP: 22
SQ FT: 5,200
SALES: 3.1MM Privately Held
SIC: 3679 Passive repeaters

Holbrook - Suffolk County (G-6453)

(G-6453)
ISLAND COMPONENTS GROUP INC
101 Colin Dr Unit 4 (11741-4332)
PHONE................................631 563-4224
Fax: 631 563-4363
Demetris Agrotis, *CEO*
Ali Ghanbarian, *Vice Pres*
Edith Powers, *Manager*
Fran Close, *Admin Asst*
EMP: 17
SQ FT: 5,000
SALES: 2MM **Privately Held**
WEB: www.islandcomponents.com
SIC: 3621 Motors & generators; electric motor & generator parts; electric motor & generator auxillary parts

(G-6454)
JAGS MANUFACTURING NETWORK INC
13403 Lincoln Ave (11741)
PHONE................................631 750-6367
Ubalco Filippetti, *CEO*
Pat Filippetti, *General Mgr*
EMP: 6 EST: 2010
SQ FT: 3,200
SALES (est): 618.2K **Privately Held**
SIC: 3999 Barber & beauty shop equipment

(G-6455)
LATIUM USA TRADING LLC (PA)
Also Called: Four Seasons Sunrooms
5005 Veterans Mem Hwy (11741-4506)
PHONE................................631 563-4000
Shaun Kennedy, *President*
EMP: 70
SALES (est): 43.3MM **Privately Held**
SIC: 3448 Sunrooms, prefabricated metal

(G-6456)
LAWN ELEMENTS INC
1150 Lincoln Ave Ste 4 (11741-2251)
PHONE................................631 656-9711
Veronica Concilio, *Principal*
EMP: 8
SALES (est): 1.1MM **Privately Held**
SIC: 2819 Industrial inorganic chemicals

(G-6457)
LIBERTY LABEL MFG INC
21 Peachtree Ct (11741-4615)
PHONE................................631 737-2365
Fax: 631 737-2366
Mike Fernandez, *President*
Lawrence Fernandez, *Vice Pres*
Sandra Iannuzzi, *Office Mgr*
EMP: 15
SALES (est): 1.8MM **Privately Held**
WEB: www.libertylabel.com
SIC: 2754 2752 2672 Labels: gravure printing; commercial printing, lithographic; coated & laminated paper

(G-6458)
LONG ISLAND ANALYTICAL LABS
110 Colin Dr (11741-4306)
PHONE................................631 472-3400
Fax: 631 472-8505
Mike Veraldi, *President*
Domenik Veraldi Jr, *Vice Pres*
EMP: 18 EST: 1998
SQ FT: 6,000
SALES (est): 3.5MM **Privately Held**
WEB: www.lialinc.com
SIC: 3822 Auto controls regulating residntl & coml environmt & applncs

(G-6459)
M C PRODUCTS
Also Called: Division of Emergency Services
1330 Lincoln Ave Ste 2 (11741-2268)
P.O. Box 821 (11741-0821)
PHONE................................631 471-4070
Fax: 631 471-4254
William Barnes, *President*
Jennifer Riccobono, *Office Mgr*
Steve Walter, *Director*
EMP: 25
SALES (est): 4.5MM **Privately Held**
WEB: www.mcproducts.com
SIC: 3674 Semiconductors & related devices

(G-6460)
MACHINE TOOL REPAIR & SALES
1537 Lincoln Ave (11741-2263)
PHONE................................631 580-2550
Michael Cohen, *President*
EMP: 5
SALES: 1MM **Privately Held**
WEB: www.machineryselection.com
SIC: 3569 Assembly machines, non-metal-working

(G-6461)
MARKETPLACE SLUTIONS GROUP LLC
48 Nimbus Rd Ste 303 (11741-4417)
PHONE................................631 868-0111
Paul Pensabene, *Mng Member*
EMP: 25
SQ FT: 30,000
SALES: 4MM **Privately Held**
SIC: 2032 8742 8748 Italian foods: packaged in cans, jars, etc.; management consulting services; business consulting

(G-6462)
METALS BUILDING PRODUCTS
5005 Veterans Mem Hwy (11741-4506)
PHONE................................844 638-2527
Shaun Kennedy, *President*
EMP: 40
SALES (est): 8.1MM
SALES (corp-wide): 43.3MM **Privately Held**
SIC: 3448 Prefabricated metal buildings
PA: Latium Usa Trading Llc
    5005 Veterans Mem Hwy
    Holbrook NY 11741
    631 563-4000

(G-6463)
METALSMITH INC
1340 Lincoln Ave Ste 13 (11741-2255)
PHONE................................631 467-1500
Fax: 631 467-1504
Jeff Smith, *President*
EMP: 5
SQ FT: 3,500
SALES (est): 420K **Privately Held**
SIC: 3444 Sheet metalwork

(G-6464)
NBTY INC
4320 Veterans Mem Hwy (11741-4504)
PHONE................................631 588-3492
Donald Dust, *VP Sales*
Denise Roman, *Marketing Staff*
Albert Anastafi, *Manager*
Kristi Latuso, *Manager*
Dawn Lombardi, *Manager*
EMP: 19
SALES (corp-wide): 3B **Publicly Held**
SIC: 2833 Vitamins, natural or synthetic: bulk, uncompounded
HQ: Nbty, Inc.
    2100 Smithtown Ave
    Ronkonkoma NY 11779
    631 200-2000

(G-6465)
OMICRON TECHNOLOGIES INC
1736 Church St (11741-5918)
PHONE................................631 434-7697
Fax: 631 434-7699
Bob Levine, *President*
John Kennedy, *Vice Pres*
EMP: 20
SALES (est): 901.2K **Privately Held**
SIC: 3999 Manufacturing industries

(G-6466)
PERCEPTION IMAGING INC
90 Colin Dr Unit 11 (11741-4333)
PHONE................................631 676-5262
Jeanine A Segall, *President*
Douglas Segall, *Exec VP*
EMP: 10
SQ FT: 5,000
SALES: 2MM **Privately Held**
SIC: 2752 7311 7331 Commercial printing, offset; advertising agencies; direct mail advertising services

(G-6467)
READ MANUFACTURING COMPANY INC
330 Dante Ct (11741-3845)
PHONE................................631 567-4487
Fax: 631 580-4830
Ronald H Read Sr, *CEO*
Heather Read-Connor, *President*
Joanne Gacho, *Controller*
EMP: 21
SQ FT: 10,000
SALES: 2.6MM **Privately Held**
WEB: www.readmfg.com
SIC: 3444 3479 Sheet metalwork; painting, coating & hot dipping

(G-6468)
ROADIE PRODUCTS INC
Also Called: Hybrid Cases
1121 Lincoln Ave Unit 20 (11741-2264)
P.O. Box 98, Oakdale (11769-0098)
PHONE................................631 567-8588
Fax: 631 563-1390
Frank Maiella, *President*
Jennifer Moran, *Manager*
▲ EMP: 25
SQ FT: 15,000
SALES (est): 5MM **Privately Held**
WEB: www.islandcases.com
SIC: 3161 3171 Musical instrument cases; handbags, women's

(G-6469)
RV PRINTING
39 Portside Dr (11741-5814)
PHONE................................631 567-8658
Robert Viola, *Owner*
EMP: 7
SALES: 1.4MM **Privately Held**
SIC: 2752 Commercial printing, lithographic

(G-6470)
SELECT-A-FORM INC
4717 Veterans Mem Hwy (11741-4515)
PHONE................................631 981-3076
Fax: 631 981-3073
Dave Walters, *President*
John Candia, *Vice Pres*
Gwen Little, *Office Mgr*
EMP: 52
SQ FT: 17,000
SALES (est): 4.2MM **Privately Held**
SIC: 2759 2761 2752 Business forms: printing; manifold business forms; color lithography

(G-6471)
SOLAR METROLOGY LLC
1340 Lincoln Ave Ste 6 (11741-2255)
PHONE................................845 247-4701
Francis Reilly,
EMP: 9
SALES (est): 686.9K **Privately Held**
SIC: 3823 Industrial instrmnts msrmnt display/control process variable

(G-6472)
SPECTRA COLOR CORP
45 Knickerbocker Ave 4 (11741-1725)
P.O. Box 447 (11741-0447)
PHONE................................631 563-4828
Jay Desilva, *Manager*
EMP: 15
SALES (est): 2.2MM **Privately Held**
SIC: 2899 Ink or writing fluids

(G-6473)
SPEEDCARD INC
Also Called: B C T
133 Glenmere Way (11741-5013)
PHONE................................631 472-1904
Jeffery Lewis, *President*
Sharon Lewis, *Manager*
EMP: 8
SQ FT: 3,000
SALES: 320K **Privately Held**
WEB: www.speedcard.com
SIC: 2752 Commercial printing, lithographic

(G-6474)
STICKERSHOPCOM INC
Also Called: Labels, Stickers & More
10 Ferraro Dr (11741-5320)
PHONE................................631 563-4323
Stacy Ianson, *CEO*
EMP: 5
SALES (est): 590K **Privately Held**
SIC: 2679 Tags & labels, paper

(G-6475)
SUMMIT TECHNOLOGIES LLC
Also Called: Summit Laser Products
723 Broadway Ave (11741-4955)
PHONE................................631 590-1040
Steven Hecht, *Mng Member*
Mike Kosiah,
▲ EMP: 38
SQ FT: 25,300
SALES (est): 3.7MM **Privately Held**
WEB: www.uninetimaging.com
SIC: 3955 Print cartridges for laser & other computer printers
PA: Uninet Imaging, Inc.
    3232 W El Segundo Blvd
    Hawthorne CA 90250

(G-6476)
SUPERIOR WELDING
331 Dante Ct Ste G (11741-3800)
PHONE................................631 676-2751
Steve Takats, *Executive*
EMP: 7
SALES (est): 802.6K **Privately Held**
SIC: 3599 Machine shop, jobbing & repair

(G-6477)
SYMBOL TECHNOLOGIES LLC
25 Andrea Rd (11741-4310)
PHONE................................631 218-3907
James Rawson, *Manager*
EMP: 16
SALES (corp-wide): 3.6B **Publicly Held**
WEB: www.symbol.com
SIC: 3577 Magnetic ink & optical scanning devices
HQ: Symbol Technologies, Llc
    1 Zebra Plz
    Holtsville NY 11742
    631 738-2400

(G-6478)
TENS MACHINE COMPANY INC
800 Grundy Ave (11741-2606)
PHONE................................631 981-0490
Fax: 631 981-3372
Salvatore Berlingieri, *President*
Fabio Berlingieri, *Vice Pres*
Mike Berlingieri, *Vice Pres*
Diane Terrell, *Purchasing*
Tom Crescenzo, *Manager*
EMP: 28
SQ FT: 9,620
SALES: 5.4MM **Privately Held**
WEB: www.tensmachine.com
SIC: 3728 Aircraft parts & equipment

(G-6479)
UNISOURCE FOOD EQP SYSTEMS INC
1505 Lincoln Ave (11741-2216)
PHONE................................516 681-0537
Ronald Mondello, *President*
Rita Tenaglia, *Manager*
▲ EMP: 9
SALES (est): 896.7K **Privately Held**
SIC: 3556 2499 Bakery machinery; bakers' equipment, wood

Holland
Erie County

(G-6480)
BUFFALO POLYMER PROCESSORS INC
42 Edgewood Dr (14080-9784)
PHONE................................716 537-3153
Miro O Staroba, *Ch of Bd*
Barbara Staroba, *Manager*
EMP: 40
SQ FT: 180,000
SALES (est): 7.8MM **Privately Held**
SIC: 3089 Plastic processing

(G-6481)
INEX INC
9229 Olean Rd (14080-9773)
PHONE..................................716 537-2270
Fax: 716 537-3218
Michael Kasprzyk, *President*
Curt Colopy, *Vice Pres*
EMP: 9
SALES (est): 1.6MM **Privately Held**
WEB: www.schunk-inex.com
SIC: 3443 Heat exchangers, plate type

(G-6482)
MULLICAN FLOORING LP
209 Vermont St (14080-9735)
P.O. Box 342 (14080-0342)
PHONE..................................716 537-2642
Rick Tyburski, *Manager*
EMP: 45
SALES (corp-wide): 1.5MM **Privately Held**
WEB: www.mullicanlumberco.com
SIC: 2426 Flooring, hardwood
HQ: Mullican Flooring, L.P.
655 Woodlyn Rd
Johnson City TN 37601
423 262-8440

(G-6483)
PRO-TECK COATING INC
7785 Olean Rd (14080-9709)
P.O. Box 372 (14080-0372)
PHONE..................................716 537-2619
Fax: 716 537-2083
Wayne Rutkowski Sr, *President*
Jeff Weber, *Vice Pres*
EMP: 13
SQ FT: 22,000
SALES (est): 1MM **Privately Held**
WEB: www.proteckcoating.com
SIC: 3479 Coating of metals with plastic or resins

(G-6484)
STAROBA PLASTICS INC
42 Edgewood Dr (14080-9784)
PHONE..................................716 537-3153
Fax: 716 537-9536
Miro Staroba, *CEO*
Barbara Staroba, *Vice Pres*
Ed Staroba, *Manager*
EMP: 125
SALES (est): 20.3MM **Privately Held**
SIC: 3089 Injection molding of plastics

(G-6485)
UHMAC INC
136 N Main St (14080-9704)
PHONE..................................716 537-2343
Fax: 716 537-2955
James McBride, *President*
Rhonda B Juhasz, *Corp Secy*
EMP: 10
SQ FT: 9,973
SALES (est): 1.6MM **Privately Held**
WEB: www.uhmac.com
SIC: 3542 Rebuilt machine tools, metal forming types

(G-6486)
ZAHM & NAGEL CO INC
210 Vermont St (14080-9735)
P.O. Box 400 (14080-0400)
PHONE..................................716 833-1532
Fax: 716 537-2106
David C Koch, *Ch of Bd*
EMP: 7
SQ FT: 9,000
SALES (est): 1MM **Privately Held**
WEB: www.zahmnagel.com
SIC: 3556 Brewers' & maltsters' machinery

Holland Patent
Oneida County

(G-6487)
CUSTOM KLEAN CORP
Also Called: Pressure Washer Sales
8890 Boak Rd E (13354-3608)
PHONE..................................315 865-8101
Fax: 315 865-8101
Paul Sears, *President*
EMP: 15

SQ FT: 30,000
SALES (est): 1.8MM **Privately Held**
WEB: www.pressurewashersales.com
SIC: 3589 7363 High pressure cleaning equipment; domestic help service

(G-6488)
STEFFEN PUBLISHING INC
Also Called: Adirondack Home News
9584 Main St (13354-3819)
P.O. Box 403 (13354-0403)
PHONE..................................315 865-4100
Fax: 315 865-4000
Sally M Steffen, *President*
Preston P Steffen Jr, *Publisher*
G Mann, *Division Mgr*
Jack Behrens, *Manager*
Pam Kulig, *Manager*
EMP: 100
SQ FT: 20,000
SALES (est): 4.4MM **Privately Held**
SIC: 2711 2752 2732 2731 Newspapers: publishing only, not printed on site; commercial printing, lithographic; book printing; book publishing; periodicals

Holley
Orleans County

(G-6489)
AMY PAK PUBLISHING INC
3997 Roosevelt Hwy (14470-9201)
PHONE..................................585 964-8188
Amy Pak, *Principal*
EMP: 9 **EST:** 2008
SALES (est): 784.5K **Privately Held**
SIC: 2741 Miscellaneous publishing

(G-6490)
ORLEANS CUSTOM PACKING INC
101 Cadbury Way (14470-1079)
PHONE..................................585 314-8227
Donald Ward, *Ch of Bd*
EMP: 6
SALES (est): 624.9K **Privately Held**
SIC: 2011 Meat packing plants

(G-6491)
PRECISION PACKAGING PDTS INC
88 Nesbitt Dr (14470-1078)
PHONE..................................585 638-8200
Fax: 585 638-4600
Michael Evans, *CEO*
Steve Langdon, *Vice Pres*
Mike Bankes, *Plant Mgr*
Kerry Kyle, *Plant Mgr*
Robert Kyle, *Buyer*
▲ **EMP:** 110
SQ FT: 68,000
SALES (est): 24.8MM
SALES (corp-wide): 5.9B **Publicly Held**
WEB: www.prepackpro.com
SIC: 3081 Packing materials, plastic sheet
HQ: Waddington North America, Inc
50 E Rivercenter Blvd # 650
Covington KY 41011
859 292-8028

(G-6492)
SEAWARD CANDIES
3588 N Main Street Rd (14470-9305)
PHONE..................................585 638-6761
Donna Seaward,
EMP: 6
SALES (est): 75K **Privately Held**
SIC: 2064 5441 Candy & other confectionery products; candy

(G-6493)
SHEPARDS SAWMILL
15547 Brown Scholhouse Rd (14470-9048)
PHONE..................................585 638-5664
James Stymus, *Partner*
EMP: 6 **EST:** 1933
SQ FT: 3,000
SALES (est): 310K **Privately Held**
SIC: 2435 2448 Hardwood veneer & plywood; pallets, wood

Hollis
Queens County

(G-6494)
BORDEN & RILEY PAPER CO INC
18410 Jamaica Ave Ste W3 (11423-2434)
PHONE..................................718 454-9494
Fax: 718 454-0791
Zoila P Woodward, *President*
Juan Guerra, *Vice Pres*
▲ **EMP:** 25
SQ FT: 31,500
SALES (est): 4.9MM **Privately Held**
WEB: www.bordenandriley.com
SIC: 2675 Die-cut paper & board

(G-6495)
CHINA RUITAI INTL HOLDINGS LTD
8710 Clover Pl (11423-1252)
PHONE..................................718 740-2278
James Herbst, *Principal*
EMP: 3
SALES (est): 43.1MM **Privately Held**
SIC: 2869 Industrial organic chemicals

(G-6496)
CRUMBRUBBER TECHNOLOGY INC
18740 Hollis Ave (11423-2808)
PHONE..................................718 468-3988
Angelo Reali, *President*
Michael Reali, *Vice Pres*
EMP: 10
SQ FT: 60,000
SALES (est): 5MM **Privately Held**
SIC: 3559 4953 Recycling machinery; recycling, waste materials

(G-6497)
G & J RDYMX & MASNRY SUP INC
18330 Jamaica Ave (11423-2302)
PHONE..................................718 454-0800
John Cervoni, *President*
John Cerzoni, *President*
Mark Blankson, *Office Mgr*
EMP: 12
SQ FT: 80,000
SALES (est): 1.2MM **Privately Held**
SIC: 3273 Ready-mixed concrete

(G-6498)
NEW ATLANTIC READY MIX CORP
18330 Jamaica Ave (11423-2302)
PHONE..................................718 812-0739
John Cervoni, *President*
EMP: 7
SALES (est): 1MM **Privately Held**
SIC: 3273 Ready-mixed concrete

(G-6499)
UNIFY360 LLC
9914 203rd St (11423-3423)
PHONE..................................718 213-7687
Mosis Gregoire, *Partner*
EMP: 5
SALES (est): 300K **Privately Held**
SIC: 2741 Miscellaneous publishing

Holtsville
Suffolk County

(G-6500)
ADVANCE PHARMACEUTICAL INC (PA)
895 Waverly Ave (11742-1109)
PHONE..................................631 981-4600
Fax: 631 981-4112
Tasrin Hossain, *President*
Liaquat Hossain, *Vice Pres*
EMP: 30
SQ FT: 80,000
SALES: 9MM **Privately Held**
SIC: 2834 Pharmaceutical preparations

(G-6501)
BROOKHAVEN INSTRUMENTS CORP
750 Blue Point Rd (11742-1896)
PHONE..................................631 758-3200
Fax: 631 758-3255
Walther Tscharnuter, *CEO*
Joe Pozzolano, *Ch of Bd*
Bruce Weiner, *President*
Eric Farrell, *Sales Staff*
Zachary Weiner, *Corp Comm Staff*
EMP: 24
SQ FT: 15,000
SALES (est): 5.9MM **Privately Held**
WEB: www.bic.com
SIC: 3826 Analytical instruments

(G-6502)
C & H PRECISION TOOLS INC
194 Morris Ave Ste 20 (11742-1451)
PHONE..................................631 758-3806
Fax: 631 758-3539
Donald Schwabe, *President*
EMP: 20
SALES (est): 1.9MM **Privately Held**
SIC: 3469 Metal stampings

(G-6503)
CUTTING EDGE METAL WORKS
12 Long Island Ave (11742-1803)
PHONE..................................631 981-8333
Tom Richards, *Owner*
Lou Tancredi, *Vice Pres*
EMP: 24
SALES (est): 3.1MM **Privately Held**
SIC: 3444 Sheet metalwork

(G-6504)
METAVAC LLC
4000 Point St (11742-2008)
PHONE..................................631 207-2344
Fax: 631 447-7715
Samuel E Fox, *Controller*
Louise Adler, *Finance*
Richard Vinkiewicz, *Manager*
Michael J Kessler,
Robert Longo,
EMP: 46
SQ FT: 33,000
SALES (est): 7.9MM
SALES (corp-wide): 16.9B **Publicly Held**
WEB: www.medavac.com
SIC: 3827 Optical elements & assemblies, except ophthalmic
HQ: Fisher Scientific International Llc
81 Wyman St
Waltham MA 02451
781 622-1000

(G-6505)
OASIS COSMETIC LABS INC
182 Long Island Ave (11742-1815)
PHONE..................................631 758-0038
Thomas Murray, *CEO*
EMP: 12
SALES (est): 1.2MM **Privately Held**
SIC: 2844 Cosmetic preparations

(G-6506)
PAVCO ASPHALT INC
615 Furrows Rd (11742-2001)
PHONE..................................631 289-3223
Ronald Marone, *President*
Ronald Fehr, *Treasurer*
Sally Marone, *Admin Sec*
EMP: 20
SQ FT: 2,000
SALES (est): 2MM **Privately Held**
SIC: 2951 1611 Asphalt paving mixtures & blocks; highway & street paving contractor

(G-6507)
PRIMA ASPHALT AND CONCRETE
615 Furrows Rd (11742-2099)
PHONE..................................631 289-3223
Fax: 631 758-3958
William Fehr, *Vice Pres*
Ronald Fehr, *Treasurer*
Kathy Stanley, *Controller*
Sally Marone, *Admin Sec*
EMP: 11
SQ FT: 2,000

Holtsville - Suffolk County (G-6508)

SALES (est): 3.3MM **Privately Held**
SIC: 2951 Asphalt paving mixtures & blocks

(G-6508)
SCREEN THE WORLD INC
Also Called: Crazy Hatter
658 Blue Point Rd (11742-1848)
PHONE..................................631 475-0023
Jeff Liebowitz, *President*
Jeffery Leibowitz, *Sr Corp Ofcr*
EMP: 12
SQ FT: 5,000
SALES (est): 890K **Privately Held**
WEB: www.crazyhatter.com
SIC: 2759 2395 Screen printing; art needlework: made from purchased materials

(G-6509)
STARFIRE PRINTING INC
28 Washington Ave (11742-1027)
PHONE..................................631 736-1495
EMP: 5
SALES (est): 230K **Privately Held**
SIC: 2759 Commercial Printing

(G-6510)
SYMBOL TECHNOLOGIES LLC
1 Zebra Plz (11742-1300)
PHONE..................................631 738-3346
EMP: 5
SALES (corp-wide): 3.6B **Publicly Held**
SIC: 3577 Magnetic ink & optical scanning devices
HQ: Symbol Technologies, Llc
  1 Zebra Plz
  Holtsville NY 11742
  631 738-2400

(G-6511)
TANGRAM COMPANY LLC
125 Corporate Dr (11742-2007)
PHONE..................................631 758-0460
Sheila Mandl, *Manager*
Philip Gillette,
John Takakjian,
▼ **EMP:** 25
SQ FT: 32,000
SALES (est): 6.4MM **Privately Held**
WEB: www.tangramco.com
SIC: 2819 2899 Industrial inorganic chemicals; chemical preparations

(G-6512)
TELXON CORPORATION (DH)
1 Zebra Plz (11742-1300)
PHONE..................................631 738-2400
John W Paxton, *Ch of Bd*
Kenneth A Cassady, *President*
David H Briggs, *Vice Pres*
Laurel Meissner, *Vice Pres*
Woody M McGee, *CFO*
▲ **EMP:** 35
SALES (est): 63MM
SALES (corp-wide): 3.6B **Publicly Held**
WEB: www.telxon.com
SIC: 3571 7373 3663 Personal computers (microcomputers); systems integration services; radio & TV communications equipment
HQ: Symbol Technologies, Llc
  1 Zebra Plz
  Holtsville NY 11742
  631 738-2400

(G-6513)
TOPAZ INDUSTRIES INC
130 Corporate Dr (11742-2005)
PHONE..................................631 207-0700
Fax: 631 207-0705
Craig Stowell, *President*
EMP: 10
SQ FT: 3,000
SALES (est): 1.4MM **Privately Held**
SIC: 2899 Salt

(G-6514)
WEISS INSTRUMENTS INC
905 Waverly Ave (11742-1109)
PHONE..................................631 207-1200
Fax: 631 207-0900
William Weiss, *CEO*
John Weiss, *President*
Phillip J Weiss, *Chairman*
John A Carnival, *Vice Pres*

Kenneth Weiss, *Plant Mgr*
▲ **EMP:** 100 **EST:** 1882
SQ FT: 50,000
SALES (est): 30.2MM **Privately Held**
WEB: www.weissinstruments.com
SIC: 3823 3829 Temperature instruments: industrial process type; pressure gauges, dial & digital; measuring & controlling devices

Homer
Cortland County

(G-6515)
ALBANY INTERNATIONAL CORP
156 S Main St (13077-1600)
PHONE..................................607 749-7226
Fax: 607 749-7216
Tim Stevens, *Safety Mgr*
Gary R Seales, *Manager*
Kevin Cook, *Associate*
Jay Jandris, *Associate*
EMP: 115
SALES (corp-wide): 709.8MM **Publicly Held**
WEB: www.albint.com
SIC: 2298 3089 2284 Cordage & twine; extruded finished plastic products; thread mills
PA: Albany International Corp.
  216 Airport Dr
  Rochester NH 03867
  518 445-2200

(G-6516)
DEWEY MACHINE & TOOL INC
49 James St (13077-1221)
PHONE..................................607 749-3930
Chris Dewey, *President*
Sandra Dewey, *Vice Pres*
EMP: 6
SQ FT: 2,000
SALES (est): 480K **Privately Held**
SIC: 3599 Machine shop, jobbing & repair

(G-6517)
F M L INDUSTRIES INC
10 Hudson St (13077-1043)
P.O. Box 398 (13077-0398)
PHONE..................................607 749-7273
Fax: 607 749-7520
Paul Dries, *President*
Paul Drief, *Manager*
EMP: 9
SQ FT: 12,000
SALES (est): 1.2MM **Privately Held**
SIC: 7692 3444 3599 Welding repair; sheet metalwork; machine shop, jobbing & repair

(G-6518)
HASKELL MACHINE & TOOL INC
5 S Fulton St (13077-1232)
PHONE..................................607 749-2421
Fax: 607 749-7386
James E Harris, *President*
Roberta J Harris, *Vice Pres*
EMP: 10 **EST:** 1947
SQ FT: 7,000
SALES: 1.2MM **Privately Held**
WEB: www.haskellmachine.com
SIC: 3599 7692 Machine shop, jobbing & repair; welding repair

(G-6519)
HOMER IRON WORKS LLC
5130 Us Route 11 (13077-9528)
PHONE..................................607 749-3963
Dan Gustasson, *General Mgr*
Mike Park,
EMP: 7
SQ FT: 2,100
SALES: 700K **Privately Held**
SIC: 3441 7692 7538 Fabricated structural metal; welding repair; general automotive repair shops

(G-6520)
HOMER LOGGING CONTRACTOR
6176 Sunnyside Dr (13077-9321)
PHONE..................................607 753-8553
Steve Hubbard, *Principal*

EMP: 5
SALES (est): 336.1K **Privately Held**
SIC: 2411 Logging camps & contractors

(G-6521)
PHOTON VISION SYSTEMS INC (PA)
1 Technology Pl (13077-1526)
PHONE..................................607 749-2689
Thomas L Vogelsong, *President*
Jeffrey J Zarnowski, *COO*
EMP: 15 **EST:** 1997
SALES (est): 1.6MM **Privately Held**
SIC: 3571 Electronic computers

(G-6522)
SOLIDUS INDUSTRIES INC
Also Called: Pb Industries
6849 N Glen Haven Rd (13077-9522)
PHONE..................................607 749-4540
Frank Girardi, *President*
Steve Tak, *Opers Mgr*
Chris Figures, *Controller*
EMP: 96
SQ FT: 28,000
SALES (est): 14.3MM **Privately Held**
WEB: www.pb-industries.com
SIC: 3444 3469 3479 2396 Sheet metalwork; machine parts, stamped or pressed metal; coating of metals & formed products; automotive & apparel trimmings

Honeoye
Ontario County

(G-6523)
CY PLASTICS WORKS INC
8601 Main St (14471-9603)
P.O. Box 560 (14471-0560)
PHONE..................................585 229-2555
Fax: 585 229-5520
Andy Molodetz, *President*
Edgar White, *Prdtn Mgr*
Eric Kunisch, *QC Mgr*
Julie Molodetz, *Controller*
Stephen Craine, *Sales Mgr*
▲ **EMP:** 40
SQ FT: 35,000
SALES (est): 11.5MM **Privately Held**
SIC: 3089 3544 3842 3949 Injection molding of plastics; special dies, tools, jigs & fixtures; industrial molds; surgical appliances & supplies; sporting & athletic goods

(G-6524)
ROOME TECHNOLOGIES INC
4796 Honeoye Business Par (14471-8808)
P.O. Box 742 (14471-0742)
PHONE..................................585 229-4437
David Roome, *President*
EMP: 7
SQ FT: 8,500
SALES: 2MM **Privately Held**
WEB: www.roometechnologies.com
SIC: 3564 Filters, air: furnaces, air conditioning equipment, etc.

Honeoye Falls
Monroe County

(G-6525)
BRANSON ULTRASONICS CORP
475 Quaker Meeting Hse Rd (14472-9754)
PHONE..................................585 624-8000
Fax: 585 359-1189
Nancy Parmeter, *Opers Staff*
Scott Lazeronni, *Electrical Engi*
Craig Birrittella, *Manager*
Scott Latona, *Manager*
Paul Rooney, *Manager*
EMP: 20
SQ FT: 78,580
SALES (corp-wide): 22.3B **Publicly Held**
WEB: www.bransonic.com
SIC: 3699 Welding machines & equipment, ultrasonic
HQ: Branson Ultrasonics Corporation
  41 Eagle Rd Ste 1
  Danbury CT 06810
  203 796-0400

(G-6526)
CUSTOM BREWCRAFTERS INC
300 Village Square Blvd (14472-1180)
PHONE..................................585 624-4386
Fax: 585 624-5756
Walter Alcorn, *President*
EMP: 12 **EST:** 1997
SQ FT: 4,800
SALES (est): 1.7MM **Privately Held**
WEB: www.custombrewcrafters.com
SIC: 2082 Malt beverages

(G-6527)
EQUICENTER INC
3247 Rush Mendon Rd (14472-9333)
PHONE..................................585 742-2522
Jonathan Friedlander, *President*
EMP: 30 **Privately Held**
SIC: 3199 Equestrian related leather articles

(G-6528)
GRAVER TECHNOLOGIES LLC
300 W Main St (14472-1197)
PHONE..................................585 624-1330
Herbert J Ego, *General Mgr*
William Bellingham, *Plant Mgr*
Bob Simpson, *Plant Mgr*
Jack Schultz, *Mfg Staff*
Gary Clements, *Purch Mgr*
EMP: 40
SQ FT: 34,000
SALES (est): 11.5MM
SALES (corp-wide): 210.8B **Publicly Held**
SIC: 3569 Filters, general line: industrial
HQ: Graver Technologies Llc
  200 Lake Dr
  Newark DE 19702
  302 731-1700

(G-6529)
HANSON AGGREGATES PA LLC
2049 County Rd 6 (14472)
P.O. Box 151 (14472-0151)
PHONE..................................585 624-3800
Bob Lange, *Sales Staff*
Douglas Fuess, *Manager*
Larry Clark, *Manager*
EMP: 35
SALES (corp-wide): 14.4B **Privately Held**
SIC: 2951 1442 5032 Asphalt & asphaltic paving mixtures (not from refineries); gravel mining; brick, stone & related material
HQ: Hanson Aggregates Pennsylvania, Llc
  7660 Imperial Way
  Allentown PA 18195
  610 366-4626

(G-6530)
HANSON AGGREGATES PA LLC
2049 Honeoye Falls 6 Rd (14472-8913)
P.O. Box 151 (14472-0151)
PHONE..................................585 624-1220
Mike Clark, *Branch Mgr*
Larry Clark, *Manager*
EMP: 30
SALES (corp-wide): 14.4B **Privately Held**
SIC: 1442 5999 1422 5032 Gravel mining; stones, crystalline: rough; crushed & broken limestone; asphalt mixture
HQ: Hanson Aggregates Pennsylvania, Llc
  7660 Imperial Way
  Allentown PA 18195
  610 366-4626

(G-6531)
HONEOYE FALLS DISTILLERY LLC (PA)
168 W Main St (14472-1135)
PHONE..................................201 780-4618
Scott M Stanton, *Mng Member*
John D Marshall,
Robert Teal Schlegel,
EMP: 11 **EST:** 2014
SQ FT: 7,000
SALES: 200K **Privately Held**
SIC: 2085 Applejack (alcoholic beverage)

(G-6532)
K & H PRECISION PRODUCTS INC
45 Norton St (14472-1032)
PHONE..................................585 624-4894

Fax: 585 624-1553
Steven Hogarth, *President*
Alex Ferguson, *Vice Pres*
Richard Parham, *QA Dir*
George Reeners, *CFO*
Colin Hogarth, *Manager*
EMP: 40
SQ FT: 20,000
SALES (est): 8.3MM **Privately Held**
WEB: www.kandhprecision.com
SIC: 3543 3089 3599 3544 Industrial patterns; injection molded finished plastic products; machine shop, jobbing & repair; special dies, tools, jigs & fixtures; nonferrous foundries

(G-6533)
KADDIS MANUFACTURING CORP
Enerco Plant
1175 Bragg St (14472-8602)
P.O. Box 92985, Rochester (14692-9085)
PHONE.................................585 624-3070
Bruce Whitmore, *Manager*
Robert Dardenne, *Supervisor*
EMP: 8
SALES (corp-wide): 8.4MM **Privately Held**
WEB: www.kaddis.com
SIC: 3451 3621 3568 Screw machine products; motors & generators; power transmission equipment
PA: Kaddis Manufacturing Corp.
293 Patriot Way
Rochester NY 14624
585 464-9000

(G-6534)
MENDON HNOYE FLS LIMA SENTINEL
Also Called: Sentinel Publishing
201 N Main St (14472-1056)
PHONE.................................585 624-5470
Fax: 585 624-7913
Michael Shelman, *CEO*
EMP: 5
SALES: 120K **Privately Held**
SIC: 2711 Newspapers

(G-6535)
MICROPEN TECHNOLOGIES CORP
Also Called: Micropen Division
93 Papermill St (14472-1252)
PHONE.................................585 624-2610
Fax: 585 624-2692
Edwin P Petrazzolo, *CEO*
William Grande, *Vice Pres*
Eric Van Wormer, *Vice Pres*
Eric Wormer, *Vice Pres*
Don Hamilton, *Safety Mgr*
▼ **EMP:** 75
SQ FT: 38,000
SALES: 11.4MM **Privately Held**
WEB: www.ohmcraft.com
SIC: 3676 3625 Electronic resistors; resistors & resistor units

(G-6536)
RUSH GRAVEL CORP
130 Kavanaugh Rd (14472-9599)
PHONE.................................585 533-1740
Marie Schillinger, *Treasurer*
David Schillinger Jr, *Shareholder*
Timothy Schillinger, *Shareholder*
EMP: 8
SALES (est): 770K **Privately Held**
WEB: www.rushgravel.com
SIC: 1442 Sand mining; gravel mining

(G-6537)
SOUTHCO INC
Honeoye Falls Div
250 East St (14472-1298)
PHONE.................................585 624-2545
Fax: 585 624-4635
Eric Cook, *Engineer*
Matt Frame, *Engineer*
Terry Graham, *Engineer*
Pradeep Jayanna, *Engineer*
David Milne, *Engineer*
EMP: 400
SQ FT: 40,000

SALES (corp-wide): 547.2MM **Privately Held**
WEB: www.southco.com
SIC: 3429 3452 Metal fasteners; bolts, nuts, rivets & washers
HQ: Southco, Inc.
210 N Brinton Lake Rd
Concordville PA 19331
610 459-4000

(G-6538)
STEVER-LOCKE INDUSTRIES INC
Also Called: Metal Stampings
179 N Main St (14472-1056)
PHONE.................................585 624-3450
Fax: 585 624-3146
Elaine R Davin, *President*
Phil Owens, *Opers Mgr*
Bruce Rose, *Design Engr*
▲ **EMP:** 9
SQ FT: 33,000
SALES (est): 6.9MM **Privately Held**
WEB: www.steverlocke.com
SIC: 3469 3672 3643 Metal stampings; wiring boards; current-carrying wiring devices

Hoosick Falls
Rensselaer County

(G-6539)
GRAPHITEK INC
4883 State Route 67 (12090-4829)
PHONE.................................518 686-5966
Al Randle, *President*
Thierry Guerlain, *Vice Pres*
EMP: 18
SQ FT: 8,500
SALES: 3.5MM **Privately Held**
WEB: www.graphitek.com
SIC: 3993 Signs & advertising specialties

(G-6540)
INTERFACE PERFORMANCE MTLS INC
12 Davis St (12090-1006)
PHONE.................................518 686-3400
Daniel Collett, *Treasurer*
Ann Fort, *Personnel*
James Lynch, *Branch Mgr*
EMP: 60 **Privately Held**
WEB: www.sealinfo.com
SIC: 2631 3053 Paperboard mills; gaskets, packing & sealing devices
PA: Interface Performance Materials, Inc.
216 Wohlsen Way
Lancaster PA 17603

(G-6541)
LOVEJOY CHAPLET CORPORATION
12 River St (12090-1815)
P.O. Box 66 (12090-0066)
PHONE.................................518 686-5232
Fax: 518 686-4919
Peter McGuire, *President*
Lisa McGuire, *Vice Pres*
Mark Harrison, *Engineer*
James Smith, *Controller*
Mallory McGuire, *Sales Mgr*
EMP: 28 **EST:** 1911
SQ FT: 20,000
SALES (est): 5.6MM **Privately Held**
WEB: www.lovejoychaplet.com
SIC: 3545 Precision tools, machinists'

(G-6542)
OAK-MITSUI INC
1 Mechanic St Bldg 2 (12090-1011)
PHONE.................................518 686-8060
Fax: 803 425-7982
EMP: 54
SALES (corp-wide): 3.8B **Privately Held**
SIC: 3497 Copper foil
HQ: Oak-Mitsui Inc.
29 Battleship Road Ext
Camden SC 29020
518 686-4961

(G-6543)
OAK-MITSUI TECHNOLOGIES LLC
80 1st St (12090-1631)
P.O. Box 501 (12090-0501)
PHONE.................................518 686-4961
William Hall, *QA Dir*
Fujio Kuwako,
▲ **EMP:** 30
SALES (est): 3.8MM
SALES (corp-wide): 3.8B **Privately Held**
WEB: www.oakmitsui.com
SIC: 3497 Copper foil
HQ: Oak-Mitsui Inc.
29 Battleship Road Ext
Camden SC 29020
518 686-4961

(G-6544)
SAINT-GOBAIN PRFMCE PLAS CORP
14 Mccaffrey St (12090-1819)
PHONE.................................518 686-7301
Amanda Rawson, *Purchasing*
Chris Lower, *Manager*
EMP: 177
SALES (corp-wide): 207.6MM **Privately Held**
SIC: 3229 Pressed & blown glass
HQ: Saint-Gobain Performance Plastics Corporation
31500 Solon Rd
Solon OH 44139
440 836-6900

(G-6545)
SAINT-GOBAIN PRFMCE PLAS CORP
1 Liberty St (12090-1019)
P.O. Box 320 (12090)
PHONE.................................518 686-7301
Chris Lower, *Prdtn Mgr*
Pat Traynor, *Branch Mgr*
Ed Yankas, *MIS Mgr*
EMP: 190
SALES (corp-wide): 207.6MM **Privately Held**
SIC: 2821 Polytetrafluoroethylene resins (teflon)
HQ: Saint-Gobain Performance Plastics Corporation
31500 Solon Rd
Solon OH 44139
440 836-6900

(G-6546)
TROJAN STEEL
48 Factory Hill Rd (12090-4405)
P.O. Box 59, North Hoosick (12133-0059)
PHONE.................................518 686-7426
Ray Revenoic, *Owner*
EMP: 5
SQ FT: 2,000
SALES (est): 622.6K **Privately Held**
SIC: 3462 Armor plate, forged iron or steel

Hopewell Junction
Dutchess County

(G-6547)
BEECH GROVE TECHNOLOGY INC
11 Sandy Pines Blvd (12533-8211)
P.O. Box 406, Stormville (12582-0406)
PHONE.................................845 223-6844
Carol Petvai, *President*
Steve Petvai, *Vice Pres*
EMP: 5
SQ FT: 1,500
SALES (est): 480K **Privately Held**
SIC: 3674 Semiconductors & related devices

(G-6548)
EBARA TECHNOLOGIES INC
20 Corporate Park Rd B (12533-6557)
PHONE.................................845 896-1370
EMP: 52
SALES (corp-wide): 4.1B **Privately Held**
SIC: 3563 Vacuum pumps, except laboratory

HQ: Ebara Technologies Incorporated
51 Main Ave
Sacramento CA 95838
916 920-5451

(G-6549)
EMAGIN CORPORATION (PA)
2070 Route 52 (12533-3507)
PHONE.................................845 838-7900
Fax: 425 284-5201
Jill J Wittels, *Ch of Bd*
Andrew G Sculley, *President*
Jerome T Carollo, *Senior VP*
Amalkumar Ghosh, *Senior VP*
Margaret Kohin, *Senior VP*
EMP: 90
SQ FT: 37,000
SALES: 25.1MM **Publicly Held**
WEB: www.emagin.com
SIC: 3674 Light emitting diodes

(G-6550)
FRITTERS & BUNS INC
236 Blue Hill Rd (12533-6659)
PHONE.................................845 227-6609
Fred Fonzie, *President*
Fran Fonzie, *Vice Pres*
EMP: 8 **EST:** 1985
SALES (est): 400K **Privately Held**
SIC: 2051 Cakes, pies & pastries

(G-6551)
GLOBALFOUNDRIES US INC
2070 Route 52 (12533-3507)
PHONE.................................512 457-3900
EMP: 12 **Privately Held**
SIC: 3559 3674 Semiconductor manufacturing machinery; semiconductors & related devices
HQ: Globalfoundries U.S. Inc.
2600 Great America Way
Santa Clara CA 95054
408 462-3900

(G-6552)
HOPEWELL PRECISION INC
19 Ryan Rd (12533-8322)
P.O. Box 551 (12533-0551)
PHONE.................................845 221-2737
Fax: 845 226-7285
Richard Skeen, *President*
Sangeeta Dev, *Accounts Mgr*
Donna Cznarty, *Admin Sec*
EMP: 22
SQ FT: 25,000
SALES (est): 3.8MM **Privately Held**
WEB: www.hopewell-precision.com
SIC: 3663 Studio equipment, radio & television broadcasting

(G-6553)
INTERNATIONAL BUS MCHS CORP
IBM
2070 State Rte 52 (12533)
PHONE.................................845 894-2121
Fax: 845 892-5541
Bob Curran, *Vice Pres*
Tom Reeves, *Vice Pres*
Rose Ulanmo, *Research*
Michael Baldwin, *Engineer*
Gary Behm, *Engineer*
EMP: 5000
SALES (corp-wide): 81.7B **Publicly Held**
WEB: www.ibm.com
SIC: 3674 Semiconductors & related devices
PA: International Business Machines Corporation
1 New Orchard Rd Ste 1
Armonk NY 10504
914 499-1900

(G-6554)
INTERNATIONAL BUS MCHS CORP
Also Called: IBM
10 North Dr (12533)
PHONE.................................800 426-4968
Michel Mayer, *General Mgr*
Jonathan Morris, *Vice Pres*
Tom Reeves, *Vice Pres*
Anand RAO, *Opers Staff*
Manuel Fusco, *Production*
EMP: 170

Hopewell Junction - Dutchess County (G-6555)

SALES (corp-wide): 81.7B **Publicly Held**
WEB: www.ibm.com
SIC: 3674 Semiconductors & related devices
PA: International Business Machines Corporation
  1 New Orchard Rd Ste 1
  Armonk NY 10504
  914 499-1900

(G-6555)
KENT OPTRONICS INC
40 Corporate Park Rd (12533-6557)
PHONE.....................845 897-0138
Le LI, *CEO*
Deng Ke Yang, *President*
Jack Lippert, *Manager*
EMP: 10
SALES (est): 1.2MM **Privately Held**
WEB: www.kentoptronics.com
SIC: 3661 Fiber optics communications equipment

(G-6556)
LIFE MEDICAL TECHNOLOGIES LLC
2070 Rte 52 21a Bldg 320a (12533)
PHONE.....................845 894-2121
EMP: 10
SALES (est): 660K **Privately Held**
SIC: 3069 Mfg Fabricated Rubber Products

(G-6557)
PHILLIP J ORTIZ MANUFACTURING
44 Railroad Ave (12533-7318)
P.O. Box 116 (12533-0116)
PHONE.....................845 226-7030
Fax: 845 226-8775
Barry Ortiz, *President*
EMP: 6 EST: 1946
SQ FT: 10,000
SALES (est): 440K **Privately Held**
SIC: 7692 3714 Welding repair; motor vehicle parts & accessories

(G-6558)
PURESPICE LLC
173 Shagbark Ln (12533-5281)
PHONE.....................617 549-8400
Robert Wilder, *Mng Member*
Brian Benko,
EMP: 5
SQ FT: 2,000
SALES: 1MM **Privately Held**
SIC: 2099 Seasonings & spices

(G-6559)
SPECTRAL SYSTEMS LLC (PA)
35 Corporate Park Rd (12533-6558)
PHONE.....................845 896-2200
Fax: 845 896-2203
Scott Little, *President*
Laura Francomano, *Human Resources*
Carlos Guajardo, *Sales Executive*
Bruce Capuano,
EMP: 47
SALES: 11MM **Privately Held**
SIC: 3827 Optical instruments & lenses

Hornell
Steuben County

(G-6560)
BOMBARDIER TRANSPORTATION
1 William K Jackson Ln (14843-1457)
PHONE.....................607 324-0216
Dave Sharma, *Branch Mgr*
EMP: 60
SALES (corp-wide): 18.1B **Privately Held**
SIC: 3441 3743 Fabricated structural metal; railroad equipment, except locomotives
HQ: Bombardier Transportation (Holdings) Usa Inc.
  1501 Lebanon Church Rd
  Pittsburgh PA 15236
  412 655-5700

(G-6561)
DOLOMITE PRODUCTS COMPANY INC
Also Called: A.L. Blades
7610 County Road 65 (14843-9626)
P.O. Box 590 (14843-0590)
PHONE.....................607 324-3636
Robert Blades, *Branch Mgr*
EMP: 16
SALES (corp-wide): 25.3B **Privately Held**
SIC: 2951 Paving mixtures
HQ: Dolomite Products Company Inc.
  1150 Penfield Rd
  Rochester NY 14625
  315 524-1998

(G-6562)
DYCO ELECTRONICS INC
7775 Industrial Park Rd (14843-9673)
PHONE.....................607 324-2036
Fax: 607 324-2030
Gregory D Georgek, *President*
Roque Santiago, *General Mgr*
Jeffrey Wilkins, *Opers Mgr*
Allan Klus, *Engineer*
Karla Dungan, *Manager*
EMP: 80
SQ FT: 30,000
SALES (est): 17.1MM **Privately Held**
WEB: www.dycoelectronics.com
SIC: 3612 Specialty transformers

(G-6563)
FORTITUDE INDUSTRIES
Also Called: A T M
7200 County Route 70a (14843-9303)
PHONE.....................607 324-1500
Fax: 607 698-4851
Margaret E Walsh, *President*
Randy Harkenrider, *President*
Barry Walsh, *Vice Pres*
Gina Bixby, *Buyer*
James Green, *QC Mgr*
EMP: 65
SQ FT: 13,500
SALES: 11MM **Privately Held**
SIC: 3625 Electromagnetic clutches or brakes

(G-6564)
GATEHOUSE MEDIA LLC
Also Called: Evening Tribune
32 Broadway Mall (14843-1920)
PHONE.....................607 324-1425
Dave Broderick, *Sales Staff*
Bonnie Willey, *Sales Staff*
Kelly Luvinson, *Manager*
EMP: 101
SALES (corp-wide): 1.2B **Publicly Held**
WEB: www.gatehousemedia.com
SIC: 2711 Newspapers
HQ: Gatehouse Media, Llc
  175 Sullys Trl Ste 300
  Pittsford NY 14534
  585 598-0030

(G-6565)
GRAY MANUFACTURING INDS LLC
Also Called: G M I
6258 Ice House Rd (14843-9739)
P.O. Box 126 (14843-0126)
PHONE.....................607 281-1325
Fax: 607 281-1327
David Gray, *CEO*
Marie Stewart, *Administration*
Richard Head,
Dennis Mullikin,
EMP: 17
SQ FT: 15,000
SALES (est): 7MM **Privately Held**
SIC: 3743 Railroad equipment

(G-6566)
SENECA MEDIA INC (PA)
Also Called: Genesee County Express
32 Broadway Mall (14843-1920)
PHONE.....................607 324-1425
Fax: 607 324-1462
George Sample, *President*
Micheal Wnek, *President*
Cindy Giglio, *Clerk*
EMP: 75

SALES (est): 6.2MM **Privately Held**
WEB: www.eveningtribune.com
SIC: 2711 8661 Newspapers; religious organizations

(G-6567)
STERN & STERN INDUSTRIES INC
188 Thacher St (14843-1293)
P.O. Box 556 (14843-0556)
PHONE.....................607 324-4485
Fax: 607 324-6274
Peter B Thornton, *Ch of Bd*
Stanley Cone, *Vice Pres*
Lee Kessler, *Vice Pres*
Joanne Prouty, *Vice Pres*
Terry Bartel, *Credit Mgr*
EMP: 100
SALES (est): 27.2MM **Privately Held**
WEB: www.sternandstern.com
SIC: 2221 Manmade & synthetic broadwoven fabrics

(G-6568)
TRANSIT AIR INC
Also Called: Transitair Systems
1 William K Jackson Ln (14843-1693)
PHONE.....................607 324-0216
Fax: 607 324-2930
Dave Sharma, *President*
Thomas J Martin, *Vice Pres*
Allen Wright, *Vice Pres*
Robert Smith, *Purchasing*
Karen Nisbet, *Personnel*
▲ EMP: 25 EST: 1991
SQ FT: 50,000
SALES (est): 9.7MM **Privately Held**
SIC: 3585 3822 3613 Air conditioning equipment, complete; auto controls regulating residntl & coml environmt & applncs; control panels, electric

Horseheads
Chemung County

(G-6569)
BELDEN INC
Also Called: Lrc Electronics
224 N Main St Ste 4 (14845-1766)
PHONE.....................607 796-5600
Greg Hamilton, *Engineer*
Larry Zuber, *Branch Mgr*
Paul Corter, *Manager*
Stanley Cullen, *Manager*
EMP: 400
SALES (corp-wide): 2.3B **Publicly Held**
WEB: www.tnb.com
SIC: 3663 3678 3643 Cable television equipment; electronic connectors; current-carrying wiring devices
PA: Belden Inc.
  1 N Brentwood Blvd # 1500
  Saint Louis MO 63105
  314 854-8000

(G-6570)
BENNETT DIE & TOOL INC
130 Wygant Rd (14845-1564)
PHONE.....................607 739-5629
Fax: 607 739-3471
Jim Mc Millen, *President*
Brian Bennett, *Vice Pres*
Jim Pittman, *Plant Mgr*
Jane Mc Millen, *Manager*
Jim McMillen, *Executive*
EMP: 40
SQ FT: 25,000
SALES (est): 7.4MM **Privately Held**
WEB: www.bdandt.com
SIC: 3544 Special dies & tools; jigs & fixtures

(G-6571)
CAMERON MFG & DESIGN INC
727 Blostein Blvd (14845-2739)
P.O. Box 478 (14845-0478)
PHONE.....................607 739-3606
Fax: 607 739-3786
Christopher Goll, *President*
Ronald Johnson, *President*
Guy Loomis, *Plant Mgr*
Joshua Roloson, *Plant Mgr*
Michael Chevalier, *Project Mgr*

▲ EMP: 205
SQ FT: 106,000
SALES (est): 80.4MM **Privately Held**
WEB: www.camfab.com
SIC: 3441 Fabricated structural metal

(G-6572)
CROWN TANK COMPANY LLC
60 Electric Pkwy (14845-1424)
PHONE.....................855 276-9682
EMP: 9
SALES (est): 1.5MM **Privately Held**
SIC: 3443 Fuel tanks (oil, gas, etc.): metal plate

(G-6573)
DAVID HELSING
Also Called: Horseheads Printing
2077 Grand Central Ave (14845-2893)
PHONE.....................607 796-2681
Fax: 607 796-4127
David Helsing, *Owner*
EMP: 5
SQ FT: 3,200
SALES (est): 320K **Privately Held**
SIC: 2752 7336 2789 Lithographing on metal; commercial art & graphic design; bookbinding & related work

(G-6574)
DEPUY SYNTHES INC
Also Called: Synthes USA
35 Airport Rd (14845-1067)
PHONE.....................607 271-2500
Kyle Amberg, *Buyer*
Sandra Graham, *Buyer*
Eric Nelson, *Buyer*
Joel Buice, *QC Mgr*
Becky Lucas, *QC Mgr*
EMP: 150
SALES (corp-wide): 70B **Publicly Held**
SIC: 3842 Surgical appliances & supplies
HQ: Depuy Synthes, Inc.
  1302 Wrights Ln E
  West Chester PA 19380
  610 719-5000

(G-6575)
EM PFAFF & SON INC
204 E Franklin St (14845-2425)
PHONE.....................607 739-3691
Fax: 607 739-2844
Susan Alexander, *President*
John Alexander, *Vice Pres*
Tracey Stermer, *Office Mgr*
EMP: 19 EST: 1944
SQ FT: 21,000
SALES (est): 2.7MM **Privately Held**
SIC: 2431 2434 Millwork; wood kitchen cabinets

(G-6576)
EMHART GLASS MANUFACTURING INC
74 Kahler Rd (14845-1022)
PHONE.....................607 734-3671
C Mobayad, *Div Sub Head*
William Gruninger, *Vice Pres*
Scott Briggs, *Engineer*
M Claypool, *Engineer*
David Passmore, *Engineer*
EMP: 150
SALES (corp-wide): 2.4B **Privately Held**
WEB: www.emhartglass.com
SIC: 3559 Glass making machinery: blowing, molding, forming, etc.
HQ: Emhart Glass Manufacturing Inc.
  123 Great Pond Dr
  Windsor CT 06095
  860 298-7340

(G-6577)
FENNELL SPRING COMPANY LLC
295 Hemlock St (14845-2721)
PHONE.....................607 739-3541
Thomas Fennell, *Mng Member*
Suzanne Sandore, *Manager*
Martin Fennell,
EMP: 60
SQ FT: 75,000
SALES: 10MM **Privately Held**
SIC: 3495 Precision springs

GEOGRAPHIC SECTION

(G-6578)
FUEL ENERGY SERVICES USA LTD
250 Industrial Park Rd (14845-9024)
PHONE 607 846-2650
Mitch Liivam, *Manager*
EMP: 24
SALES (est): 7.4MM **Privately Held**
SIC: 2869 Fuels

(G-6579)
GAS FIELD SPECIALISTS INC
224 N Main St (14845-1766)
PHONE 716 378-6422
Brad West, *Branch Mgr*
EMP: 51
SALES (corp-wide): 43.1MM **Privately Held**
SIC: 1389 Oil field services; gas field services
PA: Gas Field Specialists, Inc.
2107 State Route 44 S
Shinglehouse PA 16748
814 698-2122

(G-6580)
HEADS & TAILS LURE CO
283 Hibbard Rd (14845-7930)
PHONE 607 739-7900
Clint Kellar, *Owner*
EMP: 5 **EST:** 2007
SQ FT: 4,000
SALES (est): 238.3K **Privately Held**
SIC: 3949 Lures, fishing; artificial

(G-6581)
ISCO INDUSTRIES
50 Electric Pkwy (14845-1424)
PHONE 502 714-5306
EMP: 17
SALES (est): 1.1MM **Privately Held**
SIC: 3999 Manufacturing industries

(G-6582)
MICATU INC
315 Daniel Zenker Dr # 202 (14845-1008)
PHONE 888 705-8836
Michael Oshetski, *CEO*
Michael Jagielski, *General Mgr*
Atul Pradhan, *Manager*
EMP: 5
SALES (est): 1.2MM **Privately Held**
SIC: 3827 Optical instruments & lenses

(G-6583)
MIRION TECH IMAGING LLC
Also Called: Mirion Tech Imging Systems Div
315 Daniel Zenker Dr (14845-1008)
PHONE 607 562-4300
David Stewart, *President*
Seth Rosen, *Admin Sec*
Emmanuelle Lee, *Asst Sec*
EMP: 23 **EST:** 2015
SQ FT: 15,000
SALES (est): 2.7MM
SALES (corp-wide): 173.7MM **Privately Held**
SIC: 3663 Radio & TV communications equipment
PA: Mirion Technologies, Inc.
3000 Executive Pkwy # 518
San Ramon CA 94583
925 543-0800

(G-6584)
MIRION TECHNOLOGIES IST CORP (HQ)
Also Called: Imaging and Sensing Technology
315 Daniel Zenker Dr # 204 (14845-1008)
PHONE 607 562-4300
Fax: 607 796-4482
Thomas Logan, *CEO*
David Stewart, *President*
Tim Pelot, *Vice Pres*
Hilton Harrell, *Project Dir*
Jeffery Schott, *Purch Agent*
EMP: 70
SQ FT: 105,000
SALES (est): 38.2MM
SALES (corp-wide): 173.7MM **Privately Held**
WEB: www.mirion.com
SIC: 3679 3861 3829 3812 Electronic circuits; photographic equipment & supplies; nuclear radiation & testing apparatus; search & navigation equipment; computer peripheral equipment
PA: Mirion Technologies, Inc.
3000 Executive Pkwy # 518
San Ramon CA 94583
925 543-0800

(G-6585)
MRC GLOBAL (US) INC
224 N Main St (14845-1766)
PHONE 607 739-8575
James Griffith, *Branch Mgr*
EMP: 11
SALES (corp-wide): 4.5B **Publicly Held**
SIC: 1311 Crude petroleum & natural gas
HQ: Mrc Global (Us) Inc.
1301 Mckinney St Ste 2300
Houston TX 77010
877 294-7574

(G-6586)
ORTHSTAR ENTERPRISES INC
119 Sing Sing Rd (14845-1073)
P.O. Box 459, Big Flats (14814-0459)
PHONE 607 562-2100
Fax: 607 562-2110
James E Orsillo, *Ch of Bd*
Joseph E Strykowski, *President*
EMP: 65
SALES (est): 3.7MM **Privately Held**
WEB: www.orthstar.com
SIC: 7372 7379 3812 3823 Business oriented computer software; ; search & navigation equipment; industrial instrmnts msrmnt display/control process variable

(G-6587)
PEPSI-COLA METRO BTLG CO INC
Also Called: Pepsico
140 Wygant Rd (14845-9126)
PHONE 607 795-1399
Chuck Dunn, *General Mgr*
Drew White, *Facilities Mgr*
Brian Morgan, *Manager*
EMP: 85
SALES (corp-wide): 63B **Publicly Held**
WEB: www.pbg.com
SIC: 2086 Carbonated soft drinks, bottled & canned
HQ: Pepsi-Cola Metropolitan Bottling Company, Inc.
1111 Westchester Ave
White Plains NY 10604
914 767-6000

(G-6588)
PHOTONIC CONTROLS LLC
500 1st Ctr Ste 2 (14845)
PHONE 607 562-4585
Fax: 607 562-4704
Ronald S Karfelt, *President*
EMP: 14
SQ FT: 6,250
SALES (est): 1.8MM **Privately Held**
WEB: www.photoniccontrols.com
SIC: 3229 Fiber optics strands

(G-6589)
PRINT SHOP
3153 Lake Rd (14845-3117)
PHONE 607 734-4937
Deb Dupey, *Superintendent*
Kathy Grave, *Superintendent*
Tony Micha, *Superintendent*
EMP: 7
SALES (est): 606.7K **Privately Held**
SIC: 2752 Commercial printing, lithographic

(G-6590)
RIMCO PLASTICS CORP
316 Colonial Dr (14845-9034)
PHONE 607 739-3864
Fax: 607 739-3577
Robert Reimsnyder, *President*
Nancy Kosalek, *Corp Secy*
Lester W Reimsnyder III, *Vice Pres*
EMP: 25 **EST:** 1966
SQ FT: 36,000
SALES (est): 4.7MM **Privately Held**
WEB: www.rimcoplastics.com
SIC: 3089 3086 Plastic processing; plastics foam products

(G-6591)
ROCHESTER COCA COLA BOTTLING
Also Called: Coca-Cola
210 Industrial Park Rd (14845-9024)
PHONE 607 739-5678
Robert Carney, *Safety Dir*
Sue Capalupo, *Manager*
George Keim, *Manager*
EMP: 35
SQ FT: 23,000
SALES (corp-wide): 44.2B **Publicly Held**
SIC: 2086 Bottled & canned soft drinks
HQ: Rochester Coca Cola Bottling Corp
300 Oak St
Pittston PA 18640
570 655-2874

(G-6592)
SCHLUMBERGER TECHNOLOGY CORP
224 N Main St Bldg S (14845-1766)
PHONE 607 378-0200
EMP: 200 **Privately Held**
SIC: 1382 1389 3825 3824 Geophysical exploration, oil & gas field; geological exploration, oil & gas field; well logging; cementing oil & gas well casings; pumping of oil & gas wells; oil field services; measuring instruments & meters, electric; meters: electric, pocket, portable, panelboard, etc.; controls, revolution & timing instruments; counters, revolution; oil & gas field machinery; measuring & dispensing pumps
HQ: Schlumberger Technology Corp
100 Gillingham Ln
Sugar Land TX 77478
281 285-8500

(G-6593)
SILICON CARBIDE PRODUCTS INC
361 Daniel Zenker Dr (14845-1008)
PHONE 607 562-8599
Fax: 607 562-7585
Martin Metzger, *President*
Mark Whitmer, *Vice Pres*
Rick Cleveland, *Sales Mgr*
Margaret Johnson, *Office Mgr*
▲ **EMP:** 30
SALES (est): 4.8MM **Privately Held**
WEB: www.siliconcarbideproducts.com
SIC: 3297 Nonclay refractories; cement: high temperature, refractory (nonclay); castable refractories, nonclay

(G-6594)
SIMPLYCULTIVATED GROUP LLC
110 N Main St Ste 103 (14845-2121)
PHONE 646 389-0682
Khadijat Olanrewaju, *President*
◆ **EMP:** 6
SQ FT: 1,000
SALES (est): 390K **Privately Held**
SIC: 2096 5149 2066 Potato chips & similar snacks; coffee & tea; cocoa & cocoa products

(G-6595)
TALISMAN ENERGY USA INC
337 Daniel Zenker Dr (14845-1008)
PHONE 607 562-4000
Todd Normane, *Vice Pres*
Woody Pace, *Vice Pres*
Pat Minor, *Plant Mgr*
Donald McCarty, *Engineer*
Arturo Santillan, *Accountant*
EMP: 5
SALES (corp-wide): 1.2B **Privately Held**
SIC: 1311 Natural gas production
HQ: Talisman Energy Usa Inc.
2445 Tech Forest Blvd # 1200
Spring TX 77381
281 210-2100

(G-6596)
X-GEN PHARMACEUTICALS INC
300 Daniel Zenker Dr (14845-1014)
P.O. Box 445, Big Flats (14814-0445)
PHONE 607 562-2700
Robin Liles, *Vice Pres*
RC Park, *QC Dir*
James Baileys, *Mktg Dir*
J Robin Liles, *Branch Mgr*
Rob Liles, *Senior Mgr*
EMP: 30
SALES (corp-wide): 4.6MM **Privately Held**
SIC: 2834 Pharmaceutical preparations
PA: X-Gen Pharmaceuticals, Inc
300 Daniel Zenker Dr
Big Flats NY 14814
607 562-2700

Howard Beach
Queens County

(G-6597)
GRILLMASTER INC
15314 83rd St (11414-1826)
PHONE 718 272-9191
Fax: 718 272-2268
Anne Cohen, *CEO*
Sherman Moss, *President*
Evelyn Kelly, *Manager*
Luis Marin, *Manager*
EMP: 50
SQ FT: 20,000
SALES (est): 7.8MM **Privately Held**
SIC: 3585 3822 3446 Parts for heating, cooling & refrigerating equipment; auto controls regulating residntl & coml environmt & applncs; architectural metalwork

(G-6598)
RAK FINISHING CORP
15934 83rd St (11414-2933)
PHONE 718 416-4242
Fax: 718 386-6166
John Muncan, *CEO*
Jon Muncan, *CEO*
Julianna Muncan, *President*
EMP: 48
SQ FT: 7,000
SALES (est): 3MM **Privately Held**
SIC: 2339 7389 Service apparel, washable: women's; textile & apparel services

(G-6599)
VIP PRINTING
16040 95th St (11414-3801)
PHONE 718 641-9361
Victor Ingrassia, *Owner*
EMP: 5
SALES: 150K **Privately Held**
SIC: 2752 Commercial printing, lithographic

(G-6600)
VPJ PUBLICATION INC
Also Called: Forum South, The
15519 Lahn St (11414-2858)
PHONE 718 845-3221
Patricia Adams, *President*
EMP: 25
SQ FT: 1,000
SALES (est): 1.3MM **Privately Held**
SIC: 2711 Newspapers, publishing & printing

Howes Cave
Schoharie County

(G-6601)
W KINTZ PLASTICS INC (PA)
Also Called: K P I Plastics
165 Caverns Rd (12092-1907)
PHONE 518 296-8513
Fax: 518 296-8309
Edwin Kintz, *Ch of Bd*
Laurie Dent, *Plant Mgr*
Roger Cusano, *Engineer*
Lawrence Kath, *CFO*
Elly Hill, *Human Res Dir*
▲ **EMP:** 122 **EST:** 1976
SQ FT: 60,000

Hudson
Columbia County

(G-6602)
A & S WOODWORKING INC
9 Partition St (12534-3111)
PHONE..................................518 821-0832
Arthur Cincotti, *CEO*
EMP: 7
SQ FT: 900
SALES: 5MM **Privately Held**
SIC: 2511 Wood household furniture
SALES (est): 19.3MM **Privately Held**
WEB: www.kintz.com
SIC: 3089 Plastic processing

(G-6603)
A COLARUSSO AND SON INC (PA)
Also Called: Colarusso Blacktop Co
91 Newman Rd (12534-4040)
P.O. Box 302 (12534-0302)
PHONE..................................518 828-3218
Fax: 518 828-0546
Peter G Colarusso Jr, *President*
David Laspada, *President*
Robert Colarusso, *Corp Secy*
Larry Gregory, *Safety Dir*
Jason Arrick, *Controller*
EMP: 20 **EST:** 1912
SQ FT: 10,000
SALES (est): 20.7MM **Privately Held**
WEB: www.acolarusso.com
SIC: 2951 5032 1611 1771 Asphalt & asphaltic paving mixtures (not from refineries); asphalt mixture; stone, crushed or broken; highway & street construction; concrete work; construction sand & gravel

(G-6604)
ACME KITCHENETTES CORP
4269 Us Route 9 (12534-4031)
PHONE..................................518 828-4191
Nick Peros, *President*
Mike Pavlovich, *Vice Pres*
EMP: 20
SALES (est): 3.4MM **Privately Held**
WEB: www.acme3in1.com
SIC: 3469 3632 2434 5064 Kitchen fixtures & equipment: metal, except cast aluminum; household refrigerators & freezers; wood kitchen cabinets; refrigerators & freezers

(G-6605)
ARCHER-DANIELS-MIDLAND COMPANY
201 State Route 23b (12534-4009)
P.O. Box 398 (12534-0398)
PHONE..................................518 828-4691
Fax: 518 828-7736
Andy Spirek, *Branch Mgr*
EMP: 50
SALES (corp-wide): 67.B **Publicly Held**
SIC: 2041 Bread & bread-type roll mixes
PA: Archer-Daniels-Midland Company
77 W Wacker Dr Ste 4600
Chicago IL 60601
312 634-8100

(G-6606)
ARCHER-DANIELS-MIDLAND COMPANY
Also Called: ADM
Ste B Rr 23 (12534)
P.O. Box 398 (12534-0398)
PHONE..................................518 828-4691
Mark Eisler, *Manager*
EMP: 52
SALES (corp-wide): 67.B **Publicly Held**
WEB: www.admworld.com
SIC: 2041 5149 Flour: blended, prepared or self-rising; flour
PA: Archer-Daniels-Midland Company
77 W Wacker Dr Ste 4600
Chicago IL 60601
312 634-8100

(G-6607)
ATLANTIC ENGINEER PRODUCTS LLC
239 State Route 23b (12534-4009)
P.O. Box 639, Kinderhook (12106-0639)
PHONE..................................518 822-1800
Robert Peloke,
Thomas Smith Sr,
Tucker Smith,
EMP: 25
SALES (est): 2.7MM **Privately Held**
SIC: 3537 Loading docks: portable, adjustable & hydraulic

(G-6608)
ATMOST REFRIGERATION CO INC (PA)
Also Called: R T F Manufacturing
793 Route 66 (12534-3410)
PHONE..................................518 828-2180
Fax: 518 828-2257
Thomas Finck, *President*
Bob Walsh, *Sls & Mktg Exec*
Ashley Finck, *Sales Mgr*
▲ **EMP:** 5
SQ FT: 25,000
SALES (est): 3.5MM **Privately Held**
WEB: www.rtfmanufacturing.com
SIC: 3585 Refrigeration equipment, complete

(G-6609)
BENNERS GARDENS LLC
1 Hudson City Ctr (12534-2354)
PHONE..................................518 828-1055
John Tonelli, *Partner*
EMP: 10
SALES (est): 1.3MM **Privately Held**
SIC: 3089 Fences, gates & accessories: plastic

(G-6610)
BERKSHIRE BUSINESS FORMS INC
829 Route 66 (12534-3406)
P.O. Box 118, Troy (12181-0118)
PHONE..................................518 828-2600
Fax: 518 828-3582
Nancy Linton, *President*
Jeffrey C Linton, *Vice Pres*
John S Linton, *VP Mfg*
EMP: 12 **EST:** 1960
SQ FT: 15,000
SALES: 1.2MM **Privately Held**
SIC: 2759 Commercial printing

(G-6611)
CRAFTECH INDUSTRIES INC
8 Dock St (12534-2003)
P.O. Box 636 (12534-0636)
PHONE..................................518 828-5001
Fax: 518 828-9468
Barbara Gerard, *President*
Tara Sterritt, *General Mgr*
Irving Gerard, *Vice Pres*
Linda Jablanski, *Accounts Mgr*
Katie Gerard, *Mktg Dir*
EMP: 55 **EST:** 1966
SQ FT: 18,500
SALES (est): 13.8MM **Privately Held**
WEB: www.craftechind.com
SIC: 3451 3089 3452 Screw machine products; injection molding of plastics; bolts, nuts, rivets & washers

(G-6612)
DINOSAW INC (PA)
340 Power Ave (12534-2442)
PHONE..................................518 828-9942
Fax: 518 828-6610
Henry J Warchol Jr, *CEO*
Gregg S Warchol, *President*
Franklin Winkler, *Plant Mgr*
Allison Coon, *Admin Sec*
EMP: 25
SQ FT: 14,000
SALES (est): 3.6MM **Privately Held**
WEB: www.dinosaw.com
SIC: 3425 3545 5085 3541 Saw blades & handsaws; machine tool accessories; industrial tools; machine tools, metal cutting type

(G-6613)
EMSIG MANUFACTURING CORP
160 Fairview Ave Ste 202 (12534-1267)
PHONE..................................518 828-7301
Fax: 518 828-0026
James Feane, *Manager*
EMP: 11
SALES (corp-wide): 22.5MM **Privately Held**
SIC: 3965 5131 Buttons & parts; buttons
PA: Emsig Manufacturing Corp.
263 W 38th St Fl 5
New York NY 10018
718 784-7717

(G-6614)
FOSTER REFRIGERATORS ENTP
300 Fairview Ave (12534-1214)
PHONE..................................518 671-6036
James Dinardi, *President*
Mir Pyson, *Accounting Mgr*
Robert E Walsh, *Sales Staff*
EMP: 10
SALES (est): 1.1MM **Privately Held**
SIC: 3585 7623 Refrigeration equipment, complete; refrigeration service & repair

(G-6615)
GOLUB CORPORATION
Also Called: Price Chopper Pharmacy
351 Fairview Ave Ste 3 (12534-1259)
PHONE..................................518 822-0075
Fax: 518 822-0075
Stacey McGovern, *Branch Mgr*
EMP: 78
SALES (corp-wide): 3.4B **Privately Held**
SIC: 3751 Motorcycles & related parts
PA: The Golub Corporation
461 Nott St
Schenectady NY 12308
518 355-5000

(G-6616)
H & H HULLS INC
35 Industrial Tract Anx (12534-1505)
PHONE..................................518 828-1339
Fax: 518 828-5208
Thomas Halpin, *President*
EMP: 5
SQ FT: 2,604
SALES (est): 290K **Privately Held**
SIC: 3089 Injection molded finished plastic products

(G-6617)
HUDSON FABRICS LLC
128 2nd Street Ext (12534-1626)
PHONE..................................518 671-6100
Mark Schur,
EMP: 15
SALES (est): 1.6MM **Privately Held**
SIC: 2258 Tricot fabrics

(G-6618)
HUDSON VALLEY CREAMERY LLC
2986 Us Route 9 (12534-4407)
PHONE..................................518 851-2570
Veronica Madey,
EMP: 10 **EST:** 2010
SALES (est): 1.1MM **Privately Held**
SIC: 2022 Cheese, natural & processed

(G-6619)
J V PRECISION INC
3031 Us Route 9 (12534-4320)
PHONE..................................518 851-3200
Dorothy Jahns, *President*
Scott Valentine, *Vice Pres*
Lisa Valentine, *Treasurer*
EMP: 6
SQ FT: 5,400
SALES (est): 908.4K **Privately Held**
WEB: www.jvprecision.com
SIC: 3624 Electrodes, thermal & electrolytic uses: carbon, graphite

(G-6620)
JEM WDWKG & CABINETS INC
250 Falls Rd (12534-3323)
PHONE..................................518 828-5361
Neil Schnelwar, *Chairman*
EMP: 13 **EST:** 2007
SALES (est): 1.7MM **Privately Held**
SIC: 2431 Millwork

(G-6621)
JOHNNYS IDEAL PRINTING CO
Also Called: Johnny's Ideal Prntng Co
352 Warren St (12534-2419)
PHONE..................................518 828-6666
Fax: 518 828-6970
John Brodowski, *President*
Virginia Brodowski, *Treasurer*
EMP: 5 **EST:** 1946
SQ FT: 5,000
SALES (est): 460K **Privately Held**
SIC: 2752 2759 2791 2789 Commercial printing, offset; letterpress printing; typesetting; bookbinding & related work

(G-6622)
JOHNSON ACQUISITION CORP (HQ)
Also Called: Chatham Courier, The
364 Warren St (12534-2419)
PHONE..................................518 828-1616
Roger Coleman, *President*
Karrie Allen, *Editor*
Lori Anander, *Editor*
Mike Labuff, *Editor*
William Lundquest, *Div Sub Head*
EMP: 17 **EST:** 1895
SQ FT: 35,000
SALES: 401.9K
SALES (corp-wide): 32MM **Privately Held**
WEB: www.registerstar.com
SIC: 2711 Newspapers, publishing & printing
PA: Johnson Newspaper Corporation
260 Washington St
Watertown NY
315 782-1000

(G-6623)
JONAS LOUIS PAUL STUDIOS INC
304 Miller Rd (12534-4522)
PHONE..................................518 851-2211
David Merritt, *President*
Pam Merritt, *Admin Sec*
EMP: 6 **EST:** 1942
SQ FT: 10,000
SALES (est): 454.9K **Privately Held**
WEB: www.jonasstudios.com
SIC: 3299 Statuary: gypsum, clay, papier mache, metal, etc.

(G-6624)
LB FURNITURE INDUSTRIES LLC
99 S 3rd St (12534-2172)
PHONE..................................518 828-1501
Fax: 518 828-3219
Amy Mecabe, *Sr Corp Ofcr*
Jenny Decker, *Cust Svc Dir*
Mark Zelinger, *Sales Mgr*
Simon F Segal,
Baruch Singer,
▲ **EMP:** 150
SQ FT: 300,000
SALES (est): 13.2MM **Privately Held**
WEB: www.lbempire.com
SIC: 2599 3469 Restaurant furniture, wood or metal; household cooking & kitchen utensils, metal

(G-6625)
MCCARROLL UPHL DESIGNS LLC
Also Called: Upholstery Unlimited
743 Columbia St (12534-2509)
PHONE..................................518 828-0500
Debbie Whelan, *Owner*
EMP: 8
SQ FT: 2,300
SALES: 250K **Privately Held**
SIC: 2591 5023 2512 2392 Drapery hardware & blinds & shades; window shades; window covering parts & accessories; window shades; decorative home furnishings & supplies; upholstered household furniture; household furnishings; curtains & draperies; slip covers

(G-6626)
MELTZ LUMBER CO OF MELLENVILLE
483 Route 217 (12534-3640)
PHONE..................................518 672-7021

Fax: 518 672-4492
Emil Meltz Jr, *President*
Jeffory Meltz, *Vice Pres*
Mary Stard, *Finance Mgr*
Betty Lou Meltz, *Admin Sec*
EMP: 20
SALES (est): 1.9MM **Privately Held**
SIC: 2421 5211 Sawmills & planing mills, general; millwork & lumber

(G-6627)
MICOSTA ENTERPRISES INC
Also Called: Easy H2b
3007 County Route 20 (12534-3384)
PHONE.................................518 822-9708
Steven A McKay, *President*
EMP: 8
SQ FT: 350
SALES (est): 811.4K **Privately Held**
WEB: www.micostaent.com
SIC: 2053 2066 Pies, bakery: frozen; chocolate bars, solid

(G-6628)
MODERN FARMER MEDIA INC
403 Warren St (12534-2414)
PHONE.................................518 828-7447
Ann M Gardner, *CEO*
EMP: 10
SALES (est): 972.4K **Privately Held**
SIC: 2721 7371 Periodicals: publishing only; custom computer programming services

(G-6629)
OVERHEAD DOOR CORPORATION
W McGuire Co
1 Hudson Ave (12534-2807)
PHONE.................................518 828-7652
Fax: 518 828-1262
Brad Knable, *Vice Pres*
Kevin Hoyt, *Mfg Staff*
Charlie Klotz, *Human Res Mgr*
Jennifer Noblin, *Sales Staff*
Rich Moore, *Manager*
EMP: 100
SALES (corp-wide): 3.1B **Privately Held**
WEB: www.overheaddoor.com
SIC: 3442 2431 5084 3842 Garage doors, overhead: metal; doors, wood; materials handling machinery; surgical appliances & supplies; packaging machinery; prefabricated metal buildings
HQ: Overhead Door Corporation
2501 S State Hwy 121 Ste
Lewisville TX 75067
469 549-7100

(G-6630)
PERIODICAL SERVICES CO INC
351 Fairview Ave Ste 300 (12534-1259)
PHONE.................................518 822-9300
Marcia Scneider, *President*
Rob Koskey, *Vice Pres*
EMP: 15 **EST:** 2013
SALES: 3MM **Privately Held**
SIC: 2721 Periodicals

(G-6631)
PHOENIX SERVICES GROUP LLC
1 Hudson City Ctr (12534-2354)
PHONE.................................518 828-6611
John Tonelli,
Dimitri Rakopoulos,
Peter Stavropoulos,
EMP: 25 **EST:** 2011
SQ FT: 70,000
SALES (est): 2.5MM **Privately Held**
SIC: 3089 Extruded finished plastic products

(G-6632)
SATURN INDUSTRIES INC (PA)
157 Union Tpke (12534-1524)
P.O. Box 367 (12534-0367)
PHONE.................................518 828-9956
Fax: 518 828-9868
Maryanne Lee, *President*
John Lee, *Vice Pres*
EMP: 40 **EST:** 1959
SQ FT: 25,000

SALES: 3.5MM **Privately Held**
SIC: 3624 3599 3544 3769 Electrodes, thermal & electrolytic uses: carbon, graphite; machine & other job shop work; special dies, tools, jigs & fixtures; guided missile & space vehicle parts & auxiliary equipment; current-carrying wiring devices

(G-6633)
SAUSBIERS AWNING SHOP INC
43 8th St (12534-2901)
PHONE.................................518 828-3748
Fax: 518 751-1033
William M Harp, *President*
Robert Stalker, *Business Mgr*
EMP: 8 **EST:** 1902
SQ FT: 4,000
SALES: 700K **Privately Held**
SIC: 2394 5999 7532 Awnings, fabric: made from purchased materials; fire extinguishers; upholstery & trim shop, automotive; tops (canvas or plastic), installation or repair: automotive

(G-6634)
SERVOTEC USA LLC
1 Industrial Tract Anx # 3 (12534-1517)
PHONE.................................518 671-6120
Theresa Pigott, *Cust Mgr*
Thomas Tanguay,
EMP: 6
SALES (est): 833.1K **Privately Held**
WEB: www.servotecusa.com
SIC: 3542 Presses: hydraulic & pneumatic, mechanical & manual

(G-6635)
SMITH CONTROL SYSTEMS INC
1839 Route 9h (12534-3374)
PHONE.................................518 828-7646
Fax: 518 828-2845
Thomas H Smith Sr, *President*
Marjorie Gallagher, *General Mgr*
Jim Dodd, *Business Mgr*
Kirt Coonradt, *Vice Pres*
Michael Keating, *Vice Pres*
EMP: 17
SQ FT: 10,000
SALES (est): 4.7MM **Privately Held**
WEB: www.smithcontrol.com
SIC: 3613 Control panels, electric

(G-6636)
TWIN COUNTIES PRO PRINTERS INC
59 Fairview Ave (12534-2334)
PHONE.................................518 828-3278
Fax: 518 828-4375
David Scott, *President*
Linda D Scott, *CFO*
Ryan Scott, *Sales Mgr*
EMP: 10
SQ FT: 3,500
SALES (est): 1.1MM **Privately Held**
WEB: www.pro-printers.com
SIC: 2752 7334 Commercial printing, offset; photocopying & duplicating services

(G-6637)
UFP NEW YORK LLC
Also Called: Universal Forest Products
11 Falls Industrial Pk Rd (12534-3377)
PHONE.................................518 828-2888
Rich Flinn, *General Mgr*
EMP: 35
SALES (corp-wide): 10.1MM **Privately Held**
WEB: www.ufpinc.com
SIC: 2439 Trusses, wooden roof
PA: Ufp New York, Llc
13 Winkler Rd
Sidney NY 13838
607 563-1556

Hudson Falls
Washington County

(G-6638)
ADIRONDACK MACHINE CORPORATION
84 Boulevard St (12839-1026)
PHONE.................................518 792-2258

Fax: 518 792-2274
Tom Ferari, *President*
EMP: 5 **EST:** 1963
SQ FT: 6,000
SALES: 750K **Privately Held**
WEB: www.adirondackmachine.com
SIC: 3821 Laboratory apparatus & furniture

(G-6639)
COLOR-AID CORPORATION
38 La Fayette St Ste 2 (12839-1247)
PHONE.................................212 673-5500
Fax: 518 475-0315
Richard O'Brien, *President*
Raymond O'Brien, *Vice Pres*
EMP: 8
SQ FT: 8,500
SALES (est): 1.2MM **Privately Held**
WEB: www.coloraid.com
SIC: 2752 Commercial printing, lithographic

(G-6640)
DIMENSIONAL MILLS INC
337 Main St (12839-1513)
PHONE.................................518 746-1047
David Lafountain, *President*
EMP: 5 **EST:** 1992
SALES: 600K **Privately Held**
SIC: 2448 Wood pallets & skids

(G-6641)
DWA PALLET INC
Also Called: Dimensional Mills
337 Main St (12839-1513)
PHONE.................................518 746-1047
Daniel Ellsworth, *President*
EMP: 9
SALES (est): 720K **Privately Held**
SIC: 2448 Pallets, wood & wood with metal

(G-6642)
GENERAL ELECTRIC COMPANY
446 Lock 8 Way 8th (12839)
PHONE.................................518 746-5750
Fax: 518 746-5447
Benjamin Heineman, *Senior VP*
Timothy Kilpeck, *Safety Mgr*
Rich Young, *Engineer*
Wendy Dangelo, *Controller*
Lou Kowalski, *Personnel*
EMP: 425
SALES (corp-wide): 117.3B **Publicly Held**
SIC: 3629 Capacitors, fixed or variable
PA: General Electric Company
41 Farnsworth St
Boston MA 02210
617 443-3000

(G-6643)
GL&V USA INC
27 Allen St (12839-1901)
PHONE.................................518 747-2444
Eve Lacroix, *General Mgr*
Valere Morissette, *General Mgr*
Jim Wilson, *Manager*
Brian Stringham, *Info Tech Mgr*
EMP: 83
SALES (corp-wide): 94.2K **Privately Held**
WEB: www.glv.com
SIC: 3554 Paper industries machinery
HQ: GL&V Usa Inc.
1 Cellu Dr Ste 200
Nashua NH 03063
603 882-2711

(G-6644)
GL&V USA INC (DH)
27 Allen St (12839-1901)
PHONE.................................518 747-2444
Fax: 518 747-1334
Laurent Verreault, *CEO*
Richard Verrault, *President*
Bob Burns, *Purchasing*
Kirk Bramer, *Marketing Staff*
▲ **EMP:** 65
SQ FT: 215,000
SALES (est): 17.1MM
SALES (corp-wide): 2.8B **Privately Held**
SIC: 3554 Paper industries machinery
HQ: 9189-6175 Quebec Inc
174 West St S
Orillia ON L3V 6
705 325-6181

(G-6645)
GRANVILLE GLASS & GRANITE
131 Revere Rd (12839)
PHONE.................................518 812-0492
Kyle Suchan, *President*
Scott Suchan, *Vice Pres*
EMP: 5
SALES (est): 514.4K **Privately Held**
SIC: 3231 Products of purchased glass

(G-6646)
HAANEN PACKARD MACHINERY INC (PA)
16 Allen St (12839-1941)
PHONE.................................518 747-2330
Fax: 518 747-2315
Michael Haanen, *President*
Grace Packard, *Corp Secy*
Tony Rouleau, *Prgrmr*
EMP: 2
SQ FT: 3,500
SALES (est): 1.1MM **Privately Held**
SIC: 3554 3559 Paper industries machinery; plastics working machinery

(G-6647)
HALL CONSTRUCTION PDTS & SVCS
31 Allen St (12839-1974)
P.O. Box 1392, South Glens Falls (12803-1392)
PHONE.................................518 747-7047
David Hall, *Owner*
EMP: 5
SQ FT: 7,000
SALES (est): 522.6K **Privately Held**
WEB: www.duraslot.com
SIC: 3089 Plastic hardware & building products

(G-6648)
NORTH-EAST MACHINE INC
4160 State Route 4 (12839-3716)
PHONE.................................518 746-1837
Tracy Stevenson, *President*
EMP: 7
SQ FT: 4,000
SALES: 450K **Privately Held**
SIC: 3599 Machine shop, jobbing & repair

(G-6649)
PECKHAM MATERIALS CORP
438 Vaughn Rd (12839-9644)
PHONE.................................518 747-3353
Fax: 518 747-4006
John R Peckham, *President*
EMP: 30
SALES (corp-wide): 192MM **Privately Held**
SIC: 1429 3531 2952 2951 Igneous rock, crushed & broken-quarrying; asphalt plant, including gravel-mix type; asphalt felts & coatings; asphalt paving mixtures & blocks; highway & street construction
HQ: Peckham Materials Corp
20 Haarlem Ave Ste 200
White Plains NY 10603
914 686-2045

(G-6650)
THE KINGSBURY PRINTING CO INC
110 Franklin St (12839-1256)
PHONE.................................518 747-6606
Fax: 518 747-8852
Robert Bombard Jr, *Ch of Bd*
Robert L Bombard Jr, *Ch of Bd*
Janette Bombard, *Vice Pres*
EMP: 8
SQ FT: 2,070
SALES (est): 1.1MM **Privately Held**
SIC: 2752 Commercial printing, lithographic

Huguenot
Orange County

(G-6651)
SOMERVILLE ACQUISITIONS CO INC
Also Called: Summit Research Laboratories
15 Big Pond Rd (12746-5003)
P.O. Box F (12746-0626)
PHONE.................................845 856-5261
Fran Baxter, *Branch Mgr*
EMP: 10
SALES (corp-wide): 27.3MM **Privately Held**
SIC: 2819 Aluminum compounds
PA: Somerville Acquisitions Co., Inc.
  45 River Rd Ste 300
  Flemington NJ 08822
  908 782-9500

(G-6652)
SOMERVILLE TECH GROUP INC
15 Big Pond Rd (12746-5003)
P.O. Box F (12746-0626)
PHONE.................................908 782-9500
Piyush J Patel, *CEO*
EMP: 100
SALES (est): 7.2MM **Privately Held**
SIC: 2819 Aluminum compounds

(G-6653)
SUMMIT RESEARCH LABS INC (PA)
Also Called: Summitreheis
15 Big Pond Rd (12746-5003)
P.O. Box 626 (12746-0626)
PHONE.................................845 856-5261
Fax: 845 856-6516
Piyush J Patel, *Ch of Bd*
Suresh Patel, *President*
Tony Buzzelli, *Plant Mgr*
Joe Gallo, *Warehouse Mgr*
Ernie Edwards, *Purch Mgr*
◆ EMP: 110
SQ FT: 106,000
SALES (est): 25.2MM **Privately Held**
SIC: 2819 Industrial inorganic chemicals

Huntington
Suffolk County

(G-6654)
APS ENTERPRISE SOFTWARE INC
775 Park Ave (11743-3976)
PHONE.................................631 784-7720
Peter Thiermann, *President*
Michael Jankowski, *Managing Dir*
Michael Sullivan, *Principal*
Steffen Heinke, *Treasurer*
EMP: 22
SALES (est): 1.2MM **Privately Held**
SIC: 7372 Prepackaged software

(G-6655)
AXLE TEKNOLOGY LLC (PA)
113 Woodbury Rd (11743-4135)
PHONE.................................631 423-3044
▲ EMP: 9
SALES (est): 1.3MM **Privately Held**
SIC: 3714 5013 Axles, motor vehicle; automotive supplies & parts

(G-6656)
BERJEN METAL INDUSTRIES LTD
645 New York Ave Ste 1 (11743-4266)
PHONE.................................631 673-7979
Robert Sentura, *President*
Barbara Santoro, *Vice Pres*
Robert J Santoro, *Admin Sec*
EMP: 6
SALES (est): 935.8K **Privately Held**
WEB: www.berjen.com
SIC: 3444 1761 Sheet metalwork; sheet metalwork

(G-6657)
BLUE CAST DENIM CO INC
10 Blue Grass Ct (11743-2512)
PHONE.................................212 719-1182
Fax: 212 719-1521
Steve Brandis, *Ch of Bd*
Joseph Rosenheck, *President*
Sal Romo, *Vice Pres*
EMP: 34
SQ FT: 3,000
SALES (est): 3.2MM **Privately Held**
WEB: www.bluecastdenim.com
SIC: 2339 Slacks: women's, misses' & juniors'; jeans: women's, misses' & juniors'

(G-6658)
BOA SECURITY TECHNOLOGIES CORP
586 New York Ave Unit 3 (11743-4269)
PHONE.................................516 576-0295
Alan Lurie, *President*
EMP: 6
SQ FT: 4,000
SALES (est): 560K **Privately Held**
WEB: www.cuffmaxx.com
SIC: 3429 Handcuffs & leg irons

(G-6659)
COOCOO SMS INC
356 New York Ave Ste 1 (11743-3304)
PHONE.................................646 459-4260
John J Tunney III, *Mng Member*
Larry Prager,
Ryan Thompson,
EMP: 11
SALES: 500K **Privately Held**
SIC: 7372 Prepackaged software

(G-6660)
DEJANA TRCK UTILITY EQP CO LLC
Also Called: Dejana Truck & Utility Eqp Co
743 Park Ave (11743-3912)
PHONE.................................631 549-0944
Fax: 631 549-0945
Richard Nieves, *Sales Staff*
Andrew Dejana, *Manager*
EMP: 25 **Publicly Held**
WEB: www.dejana.com
SIC: 3711 Trucks, pickup, assembly of
HQ: Dejana Truck & Utility Equipment Company, Llc
  490 Pulaski Rd
  Kings Park NY 11754
  631 544-9000

(G-6661)
FAD INC
Also Called: FAD TREASURES
630 New York Ave Ste B (11743-4289)
PHONE.................................631 385-2460
Fax: 631 385-4540
Allan Axelowitz, *President*
Donna Axelowitz, *Admin Sec*
▲ EMP: 27
SQ FT: 6,000
SALES: 3.3MM **Privately Held**
WEB: www.fad-treasures.com
SIC: 2339 5137 5632 Women's & misses' accessories; women's & children's accessories; women's accessory & specialty stores

(G-6662)
INTEGRATED CONTROL CORP
748 Park Ave (11743-3900)
PHONE.................................631 673-5100
Fax: 631 673-6756
Roberta Vaccaro Salerno, *President*
Roberta Salerno, *President*
John Patti, *Opers Staff*
Nat Cauldwell, *Engineer*
Jason Amian, *Project Engr*
▲ EMP: 34
SQ FT: 5,000
SALES (est): 8.4MM **Privately Held**
WEB: www.integratedcontrol.com
SIC: 3823 Industrial instrmnts msrmnt display/control process variable

(G-6663)
INTERNATIONAL LIFE SCIENCE
23 Gloria Ln (11743-2229)
PHONE.................................631 549-0471
Roy Chavarcode, *President*
EMP: 3
SALES: 1.5MM **Privately Held**
SIC: 2834 Pharmaceutical preparations

(G-6664)
J A T PRINTING INC
Also Called: Minuteman Press
46 Gerard St Unit 2 (11743-6944)
PHONE.................................631 427-1155
Fax: 631 427-1183
John Titus, *President*
Gina Titus, *Vice Pres*
EMP: 6
SALES (est): 630K **Privately Held**
SIC: 2752 Commercial printing, lithographic

(G-6665)
JURIS PUBLISHING INC
71 New St Ste 1 (11743-3397)
PHONE.................................631 351-5430
Charles Kitzen, *President*
Kristen Standfast, *Editor*
Michael Kitzen, *Vice Pres*
Benetta Pearson, *Prdtn Mgr*
Christopher Infantino, *Marketing Staff*
▲ EMP: 20 **EST:** 1994
SALES (est): 2.5MM **Privately Held**
WEB: www.jurispub.com
SIC: 2731 Book publishing

(G-6666)
LADY-N-TH-WNDOW CHOCOLATES INC
Also Called: Bon Bons Chocolatier
319 Main St (11743-6914)
PHONE.................................631 549-1059
Mary Alice Meinersman, *President*
Susanna Fasolino, *Vice Pres*
EMP: 10
SQ FT: 4,200
SALES (est): 1.3MM **Privately Held**
WEB: www.bonbonschocolatier.com
SIC: 2066 2064 5441 5947 Chocolate; candy & other confectionery products; candy; gift, novelty & souvenir shop

(G-6667)
LASER CONSULTANTS INC
344 W Hills Rd (11743-6343)
PHONE.................................631 423-4905
William T Walter, *President*
Susan Walter, *Vice Pres*
John W Walter, *Treasurer*
EMP: 5
SALES: 20K **Privately Held**
WEB: www.laser-consult.com
SIC: 3699 Laser systems & equipment

(G-6668)
LONG ISLAND CMNTY NWSPPERS INC
Also Called: Long Islndr Nrth/Sth Pblctns
322 Main St (11743-6923)
PHONE.................................631 427-7000
Fax: 631 427-5820
Sloggatt Peter, *Editor*
Peter Sloggatt, *Manager*
EMP: 12
SALES (corp-wide): 10.7MM **Privately Held**
WEB: www.antonnews.com
SIC: 2711 Newspapers, publishing & printing
PA: Long Island Community Newspapers Inc.
  132 E 2nd St
  Mineola NY 11501
  516 482-4490

(G-6669)
LONG ISLANDER NEWSPAPERS LLC
14 Wall St Ste A (11743-7622)
PHONE.................................631 427-7000
Luann Dallojacono, *Editor*
Linda Gilbert, *Advt Staff*
Peter Sloggatt, *Manager*
Michael Schenkler,
EMP: 7
SALES (est): 366.1K **Privately Held**
SIC: 2711 Newspapers

(G-6670)
NORTHEASTERN PAPER CORP
2 Lilac Ct (11743-6050)
PHONE.................................631 659-3634
Jeff Singer, *President*
Scott Zelen, *Vice Pres*
EMP: 8
SQ FT: 30,000
SALES (est): 1MM **Privately Held**
SIC: 2679 Paper products, converted

(G-6671)
NORTHROP GRUMMAN SYSTEMS CORP
70 Dewey St (11743-7126)
PHONE.................................631 423-1014
Ray Schubnel, *Manager*
Mary Westerling, *Administration*
EMP: 7 **Publicly Held**
WEB: www.sperry.ngc.com
SIC: 3721 Aircraft
HQ: Northrop Grumman Systems Corporation
  2980 Fairview Park Dr
  Falls Church VA 22042
  703 280-2900

(G-6672)
OUTDOOR LIGHTNING PERSPECTIVES
1 Warner Ct (11743-5829)
PHONE.................................631 266-6200
Dennis Dowling, *President*
Amy Dowling, *Principal*
EMP: 6
SALES (est): 869.2K **Privately Held**
SIC: 3648 Outdoor lighting equipment

(G-6673)
PASSIVE-PLUS INC
48 Elm St (11743-3402)
PHONE.................................631 425-0938
Lisa Beyel, *President*
Steve Beyel, *Vice Pres*
Jessica Magnano, *Accountant*
Erin Hannigan, *Sales Staff*
Joan Bender, *Sales Associate*
▲ EMP: 12
SALES (est): 1.9MM **Privately Held**
SIC: 3679 3675 3676 3674 Microwave components; electronic capacitors; electronic resistors; magnetohydrodynamic (MHD) devices

(G-6674)
PHOTO AGENTS LTD
Also Called: Country Printer, The
716 New York Ave (11743-4413)
PHONE.................................631 421-0258
Fax: 631 421-0308
Gary Lerman, *President*
EMP: 5
SALES (est): 488K **Privately Held**
WEB: www.thecountryprinter.com
SIC: 2759 2752 Commercial printing; commercial printing, lithographic

(G-6675)
PUPA TEK INC
Also Called: Test Cloud
6 Queens St (11743-3725)
PHONE.................................631 664-7817
Ryan Katz, *CEO*
Arnold Katz, *Principal*
EMP: 5 **EST:** 2011
SALES (est): 198.2K **Privately Held**
SIC: 7372 Prepackaged software

(G-6676)
RINGLEAD INC ✪
205 E Main St Ste 2-3a (11743-7944)
PHONE.................................310 906-0545
Jaime Muirhead, *Senior VP*
Joe Kosturos, *Sales Staff*
EMP: 10 **EST:** 2016
SALES (est): 221.8K **Privately Held**
SIC: 7372 Business oriented computer software

(G-6677)
ROBOT FRUIT INC
40 Radcliff Dr (11743-2649)
PHONE.................................631 423-7250
Thomas Vieweg, *CEO*
EMP: 12 **EST:** 2012

SALES (est): 712.6K **Privately Held**
SIC: 7372 Application computer software

(G-6678)
ROLLSON INC
10 Smugglers Cv (11743-1616)
PHONE.................................631 423-9578
Rudolph Creteur, *President*
Tom Perry, *Vice Pres*
EMP: 25 EST: 1938
SQ FT: 15,000
SALES (est): 2.8MM **Privately Held**
WEB: www.rollson.com
SIC: 3429 3444 3446 Marine hardware; sheet metalwork; architectural metalwork

(G-6679)
SC TEXTILES INC
Also Called: Affiliated Services Group
434 New York Ave (11743-3438)
PHONE.................................631 944-6262
Stephen S Cohen, *President*
EMP: 2
SQ FT: 3,500
SALES: 4MM **Privately Held**
SIC: 3679 Electronic loads & power supplies

(G-6680)
SECURITY OFFSET SERVICES INC
11 Grandview St (11743-3534)
PHONE.................................631 944-6031
Fax: 631 944-6034
George Hirsch, *President*
EMP: 9
SQ FT: 10,000
SALES (est): 939.4K **Privately Held**
SIC: 2752 Commercial printing, offset

(G-6681)
SELECT PRODUCTS HOLDINGS LLC
1 Arnold Dr Unit 3 (11743-3981)
P.O. Box 707 (11743-0707)
PHONE.................................855 777-3532
Simon Roozrokh, *CEO*
David Darouvar, *CFO*
▲ **EMP:** 49
SQ FT: 80,000
SALES: 30MM **Privately Held**
SIC: 2676 Towels, napkins & tissue paper products

(G-6682)
STEVEN KRAUS ASSOCIATES INC
9 Private Rd (11743-2243)
PHONE.................................631 923-2033
Steven Kraus, *President*
EMP: 5
SQ FT: 2,500
SALES: 475K **Privately Held**
SIC: 2542 Office & store showcases & display fixtures

(G-6683)
TELEPHONICS CORPORATION
Tlsi Division
770 Park Ave (11743-3974)
PHONE.................................631 549-6000
Fax: 631 549-6114
Mark Supko, *President*
Peter A Wolfe, *Senior VP*
Barry Eckstein, *Vice Pres*
Siedlewicz Russell, *Facilities Dir*
Jerry Golden, *Purch Agent*
EMP: 30
SALES (corp-wide): 2B **Publicly Held**
SIC: 3679 3674 Electronic circuits; semiconductors & related devices
HQ: Telephonics Corporation
815 Broadhollow Rd
Farmingdale NY 11735
631 755-7000

(G-6684)
TELEPHONICS CORPORATION
7820 Park Ave (11743)
PHONE.................................631 470-8838
Linda Monaco, *Manager*
EMP: 5
SALES (corp-wide): 2B **Publicly Held**
SIC: 3699 Electronic training devices

HQ: Telephonics Corporation
815 Broadhollow Rd
Farmingdale NY 11735
631 755-7000

(G-6685)
TELEPHONICS CORPORATION
770 Park Ave (11743-3974)
PHONE.................................631 755-7000
Fax: 631 549-6100
Dominic Nocera, *Controller*
Donald Pastor, *VP Finance*
Ken Hoffman, *Manager*
Christina Radzewsky, *Admin Asst*
EMP: 16
SALES (corp-wide): 2B **Publicly Held**
SIC: 3669 Emergency alarms
HQ: Telephonics Corporation
815 Broadhollow Rd
Farmingdale NY 11735
631 755-7000

(G-6686)
TELEPHONICS CORPORATION
780 Park Ave (11743-4516)
PHONE.................................631 470-8800
Stephen Maroney, *Director*
EMP: 99
SALES (corp-wide): 2B **Publicly Held**
SIC: 3699 Electronic training devices
HQ: Telephonics Corporation
815 Broadhollow Rd
Farmingdale NY 11735
631 755-7000

(G-6687)
TELEPHONICS TLSI CORP
780 Park Ave (11743-4516)
PHONE.................................631 470-8854
Zhigang MA, *President*
Marshall Lacoff, *Senior VP*
Dan McGovern, *Engineer*
Rudy Rupe, *Engineer*
Dominic Nocera, *CFO*
EMP: 200
SQ FT: 20,000
SALES (est): 3.8MM
SALES (corp-wide): 2B **Publicly Held**
SIC: 3674 Microcircuits, integrated (semiconductor)
HQ: Telephonics Corporation
815 Broadhollow Rd
Farmingdale NY 11735
631 755-7000

(G-6688)
TLSI INCORPORATED
780 Park Ave (11743-4516)
PHONE.................................631 470-8880
Fax: 631 470-8858
Kevin McSweeney, *COO*
Zhigang MA, *Vice Pres*
Kerry Ebbecke, *Purchasing*
Pawel Janczykowski, *Design Engr*
Mike Perry, *Manager*
EMP: 65
SALES (est): 9.1MM
SALES (corp-wide): 2B **Publicly Held**
SIC: 3674 3679 Semiconductors & related devices; electronic circuits
HQ: Telephonics Corporation
815 Broadhollow Rd
Farmingdale NY 11735
631 755-7000

(G-6689)
VALLEY INDUSTRIAL PRODUCTS INC
152 New York Ave (11743-2185)
PHONE.................................631 385-9300
Fax: 631 385-9340
Laurel B Phelan, *CEO*
Laurel Phelan, *Ch of Bd*
Alberta Barth Dwyer, *Treasurer*
EMP: 35 EST: 1965
SQ FT: 14,000
SALES (est): 12.2MM **Privately Held**
WEB: www.valleyindustrialtape.com
SIC: 2672 2671 2241 Tape, pressure sensitive: made from purchased materials; packaging paper & plastics film, coated & laminated; narrow fabric mills

(G-6690)
VDC ELECTRONICS INC
155 W Carver St Ste 2 (11743-3376)
PHONE.................................631 683-5850
Sheryl Ross, *Ch of Bd*
▲ **EMP:** 14
SALES (est): 2.1MM **Privately Held**
SIC: 3621 Storage battery chargers, motor & engine generator type

(G-6691)
VENCO SALES INC
755 Park Ave Ste 300 (11743-3979)
PHONE.................................631 754-0782
Fax: 631 754-4659
John Venini, *President*
Gary Bosma, *Sales Staff*
Frank Brecher, *Sales Staff*
Rob Morrision, *Sales Staff*
EMP: 20
SALES (est): 2.5MM **Privately Held**
SIC: 3494 Plumbing & heating valves

(G-6692)
ZACMEL GRAPHICS LLC
11 Grandview St (11743-3534)
PHONE.................................631 944-6031
David Warheit,
EMP: 7 EST: 2003
SALES (est): 955.3K **Privately Held**
SIC: 2752 7336 Commercial printing, lithographic; commercial art & graphic design

Huntington Station
Suffolk County

(G-6693)
AEROBIC WEAR INC
16 Depot Rd (11746-1737)
PHONE.................................631 673-1830
Fax: 631 673-1834
Bradley Rosen, *President*
EMP: 5
SQ FT: 6,200
SALES: 527.8K **Privately Held**
WEB: www.aerobicwear.com
SIC: 2339 2369 Athletic clothing: women's, misses' & juniors'; girls' & children's outerwear

(G-6694)
AMERICAN CULTURE HAIR INC
159 E 2nd St (11746-1430)
PHONE.................................631 242-3142
Louis Guarneri, *President*
Becky Oswald, *Opers Mgr*
Alicyn McDermott, *Advisor*
▲ **EMP:** 22
SALES (est): 2.1MM **Privately Held**
SIC: 3999 Hair & hair-based products

(G-6695)
AMERICAN TECHNICAL CERAMICS (DH)
Also Called: Atc
1 Norden Ln (11746-2140)
PHONE.................................631 622-4700
John Lawing, *CEO*
John S Gilbertson, *Principal*
Richard Monsorno, *Senior VP*
David B Ott, *Senior VP*
Bill Johnson, *Vice Pres*
◆ **EMP:** 440
SQ FT: 18,000
SALES (est): 147.7MM
SALES (corp-wide): 12.6B **Publicly Held**
WEB: www.atceramics.com
SIC: 3672 3675 Printed circuit boards; electronic capacitors
HQ: Avx Corporation
1 Avx Blvd
Fountain Inn SC 29644
864 967-2150

(G-6696)
AMERICAN TECHNICAL CERAMICS
17 Stepar Pl (11746-2141)
PHONE.................................631 622-4700
Fax: 631 622-4748
Michael Giacalone, *Vice Pres*
Frank Bennett, *Prdtn Mgr*
James Navas, *Foreman/Supr*

Yardley Cornet, *Purch Agent*
Robert Clark, *QC Mgr*
EMP: 400
SALES (corp-wide): 12.6B **Publicly Held**
WEB: www.atceramics.com
SIC: 3675 Electronic capacitors
HQ: American Technical Ceramics Corp
1 Norden Ln
Huntington Station NY 11746
631 622-4700

(G-6697)
AUTO SPORT DESIGNS INC
203 W Hills Rd (11746-3147)
PHONE.................................631 425-1555
Fax: 631 425-6185
Tom Papadopoulos, *President*
Tomas Papadopoulos, *President*
Beveroy Higgins, *Manager*
▲ **EMP:** 11
SQ FT: 30,000
SALES (est): 2.1MM **Privately Held**
WEB: www.autosportdesigns.com
SIC: 3711 5511 5531 Automobile assembly, including specialty automobiles; new & used car dealers; speed shops, including race car supplies

(G-6698)
CALIFORNIA FRAGRANCE COMPANY
Also Called: Aromafloria
171 E 2nd St (11746-1430)
PHONE.................................631 424-4023
Fax: 516 424-0219
Sharon Christie, *President*
Tracy Gunther, *Purch Agent*
Mark Manno, *Webmaster*
▲ **EMP:** 30
SQ FT: 30,000
SALES (est): 7.4MM **Privately Held**
SIC: 2844 Toilet preparations

(G-6699)
CARTERS INC
350 Walt Whitman Rd (11746-8704)
PHONE.................................631 549-6781
EMP: 9
SALES (corp-wide): 3B **Publicly Held**
SIC: 2361 Girls' & children's dresses, blouses & shirts
PA: Carter's, Inc.
3438 Peachtree Rd Ne # 1800
Atlanta GA 30326
678 791-1000

(G-6700)
COMPLETE SEC & CONTRLS INC
100 Hillwood Dr (11746-1345)
PHONE.................................631 421-7200
Steve Krishnayah, *President*
EMP: 18
SQ FT: 7,000
SALES (est): 131.7K **Privately Held**
WEB: www.completesecuritycorp.com
SIC: 3644 Noncurrent-carrying wiring services

(G-6701)
DC CONTRACTING & BUILDING CORP
136 Railroad St (11746-1540)
PHONE.................................631 385-1117
Fax: 631 385-4430
Dean Confessore, *President*
Frank Carollo, *Accountant*
Kristy Shoclin, *Manager*
EMP: 13
SQ FT: 5,000
SALES (est): 1.7MM **Privately Held**
SIC: 2431 Woodwork, interior & ornamental

(G-6702)
DILLNER PRECAST INC
200 W 9th St (11746-1667)
PHONE.................................631 421-9130
John Dillner, *President*
EMP: 5
SQ FT: 4,000
SALES (corp-wide): 1MM **Privately Held**
SIC: 3272 Concrete products, precast

Huntington Station - Suffolk County (G-6703)

PA: Dillner Precast Inc
14 Meadow Ln
Lloyd Harbor NY 11743
631 421-9130

(G-6703)
EXIMUS CONNECTIONS CORPORATION
Also Called: Herbal Destination
2387 New York Ave Unit 3 (11746-4270)
PHONE.................................631 421-1700
Sharvani Srinivas, *President*
Bharathi Nemanuthala, *Vice Pres*
Julie Solomon, *Vice Pres*
EMP: 6
SQ FT: 1,800
SALES (est): 490.9K **Privately Held**
SIC: 2023 5149 Dietary supplements, dairy & non-dairy based; diet foods

(G-6704)
FERACO INDUSTRIES
3 Plumb Ct (11746-1128)
PHONE.................................631 547-8120
Ray Albini, *Owner*
EMP: 8
SALES (est): 734.4K **Privately Held**
SIC: 3999 Manufacturing industries

(G-6705)
FORMAC WELDING INC
42 W Hills Rd (11746-2304)
PHONE.................................631 421-5525
Fax: 631 421-2023
Joel Mc Elearney, *President*
Maureen Mc Elearney, *Admin Sec*
EMP: 7
SQ FT: 3,800
SALES (est): 470K **Privately Held**
SIC: 7692 Welding repair

(G-6706)
FOUR-WAY PALLET CORP
191 E 2nd St (11746-1430)
PHONE.................................631 351-3401
Fax: 631 673-7345
Leonard Koppelman, *President*
Jay Koppelman, *Manager*
EMP: 28
SALES (est): 3.3MM **Privately Held**
SIC: 2448 7699 5084 Wood pallets & skids; pallet repair; materials handling machinery

(G-6707)
HART SPORTS INC
4 Roxanne Ct (11746-1122)
PHONE.................................631 385-1805
James Hart, *President*
EMP: 6
SALES (est): 560K **Privately Held**
SIC: 3949 Hockey equipment & supplies, general

(G-6708)
HERCULES INTERNATIONAL INC
95 W Hills Rd (11746-3119)
PHONE.................................631 423-6900
Michael Flaxman, *President*
EMP: 20
SALES (est): 2.2MM **Privately Held**
WEB: www.herculesintlcorp.com
SIC: 3589 Car washing machinery

(G-6709)
HUNTINGTON WELDING & IRON
139 W Pulaski Rd (11746-1693)
PHONE.................................631 423-3331
Fax: 631 423-3318
Andrew Blondrage, *Owner*
EMP: 5
SALES (est): 301.5K **Privately Held**
SIC: 7692 Welding repair

(G-6710)
I A S NATIONAL INC
Also Called: Hercules
95 W Hills Rd (11746-3197)
PHONE.................................631 423-6900
Fax: 631 385-3222
Michael Flaxman, *President*
Lynn Kramer, *Manager*
▼ **EMP:** 20

SALES (est): 3MM **Privately Held**
WEB: www.hercules.com
SIC: 3589 2899 Car washing machinery; chemical preparations

(G-6711)
ISLAND AUTOMATED GATE CO LLC
125 W Hills Rd (11746-3144)
PHONE.................................631 425-0196
Stan Osowski,
EMP: 3
SALES: 1MM **Privately Held**
SIC: 3569 Bridge or gate machinery, hydraulic

(G-6712)
JOHN LAROCCA & SON INC
Also Called: E C Sumereau & Sons
290 Broadway (11746-1403)
PHONE.................................631 423-5256
Fax: 631 423-5271
John Larocca, *President*
EMP: 6 **EST:** 1856
SQ FT: 10,000
SALES (est): 741.9K **Privately Held**
WEB: www.ecsumereau.com
SIC: 3471 Electroplating of metals or formed products

(G-6713)
JOSEPH CORCORAN MARBLE INC
50 W Hills Rd Unit B (11746-2356)
PHONE.................................631 423-8712
Fax: 631 423-8708
Joseph Corcoran Sr, *President*
Helen Corcoran, *Vice Pres*
Joseph Corcoran Jr, *Treasurer*
Robert Corcoran, *Admin Sec*
▲ **EMP:** 8 **EST:** 1946
SALES (est): 791.3K **Privately Held**
SIC: 3281 Marble, building: cut & shaped

(G-6714)
KELMAR SYSTEMS INC
284 Broadway (11746-1497)
PHONE.................................631 421-1230
Fax: 631 421-1274
Andrew Marglin, *President*
Thomas Mohr, *President*
Laurie Franz, *Vice Pres*
Raymond Matthews, *Engineer*
Joan Marglin, *Admin Sec*
EMP: 16
SQ FT: 4,500
SALES: 1.4MM **Privately Held**
WEB: www.kelmarsystems.com
SIC: 3861 Sound recording & reproducing equipment, motion picture

(G-6715)
LUCKY BRAND DUNGAREES LLC
100 Walt Whitman Rd 1090b (11746-4100)
PHONE.................................631 350-7358
EMP: 36
SALES (corp-wide): 479.8MM **Privately Held**
SIC: 2325 Men's & boys' trousers & slacks
PA: Lucky Brand Dungarees, Llc
540 S Santa Fe Ave
Los Angeles CA 90013
213 443-5700

(G-6716)
MELBOURNE C FISHER YACHT SAILS
Also Called: Doyle Sails
1345 New York Ave Ste 2 (11746-1751)
PHONE.................................631 673-5055
Fax: 631 673-6736
Mark Washeim, *President*
Diana Malkin'washeim, *Vice Pres*
▼ **EMP:** 6
SALES (est): 614.2K **Privately Held**
SIC: 2394 Sails: made from purchased materials

(G-6717)
MODERN SETTINGS LLC
1540 New York Ave (11746-1727)
PHONE.................................631 351-1212
Fax: 631 351-1261
EMP: 21 **EST:** 1951

SQ FT: 22,000
SALES (est): 1.7MM **Privately Held**
SIC: 3915 Manufacturer Of Jewelry Findings & Materials

(G-6718)
NEW YORK DIGITAL CORPORATION
33 Walt Whitman Rd # 117 (11746-3678)
PHONE.................................631 630-9798
Salil Bandy, *President*
John Tully, *Sales Mgr*
EMP: 11
SQ FT: 30,000
SALES (est): 830K **Privately Held**
SIC: 3679 Electronic loads & power supplies

(G-6719)
NORTH SHORE PALLET INC
191 E 2nd St (11746-1430)
PHONE.................................631 673-4700
EMP: 8
SALES (est): 1.3MM **Privately Held**
SIC: 2448 Pallets, wood & wood with metal

(G-6720)
ROTTKAMP TENNIS INC
100 Broadway (11746-1448)
PHONE.................................631 421-0040
Richard Rottkamp, *President*
EMP: 25
SALES (est): 1.9MM **Privately Held**
SIC: 3949 Tennis equipment & supplies

(G-6721)
RUBBER STAMP X PRESS
7 Bradford Pl (11747-1043)
PHONE.................................631 423-1322
Ilene Schleichkorn, *Chairman*
EMP: 5
SALES (est): 380.4K **Privately Held**
SIC: 3953 Embossing seals & hand stamps

(G-6722)
SCENT-A-VISION INC
171 E 2nd St (11746-1430)
PHONE.................................631 424-4905
Fax: 631 424-0219
Sharon Christie, *President*
Mark Christie, *Admin Director*
EMP: 23
SQ FT: 5,000
SALES (est): 3.7MM **Privately Held**
WEB: www.aromafloria.com
SIC: 2844 5122 Toilet preparations; perfumes

(G-6723)
SELECTRODE INDUSTRIES INC
230 Broadway (11746-1403)
PHONE.................................631 547-5470
Fax: 631 547-5475
Joe Paternoster, *Ch of Bd*
Paul Paternoster, *President*
Rich Oliveri, *Manager*
Randy Bruckner, *Technology*
▼ **EMP:** 95
SQ FT: 26,000
SALES (est): 20.4MM **Privately Held**
WEB: www.selectrode.com
SIC: 3356 3496 Nonferrous rolling & drawing; miscellaneous fabricated wire products

(G-6724)
SWISSWAY INC
123 W Hills Rd (11746-3155)
PHONE.................................631 351-5350
Fax: 631 351-1662
Gerard Cavalier Jr, *President*
Jody Cavalier, *Controller*
EMP: 25 **EST:** 1963
SQ FT: 10,000
SALES (est): 3.7MM **Privately Held**
WEB: www.swisswayinc.com
SIC: 3599 Machine shop, jobbing & repair

(G-6725)
TECHNOPAVING NEW YORK INC
270 Broadway (11746-1561)
PHONE.................................631 351-6472
Christine Brown, *President*

EMP: 7
SALES (est): 600K **Privately Held**
SIC: 3531 Pavers

(G-6726)
TEQUIPMENT INC
Also Called: T E Q
7 Norden Ln (11746-2102)
PHONE.................................516 922-3508
Fax: 516 922-6385
Robert Sugarman, *President*
Christine Sugarman, *Corp Secy*
Frank Falconeri, *Warehouse Mgr*
Vincent Chiarelli, *Accounts Exec*
David Cooper, *Accounts Exec*
EMP: 100
SQ FT: 40,000
SALES (est): 24.2MM **Privately Held**
WEB: www.tequipment.com
SIC: 7372 Educational computer software

(G-6727)
VAIRE LLC
200 E 2nd St Ste 34 (11746-1464)
PHONE.................................631 271-4933
Fax: 631 424-1128
Robert Pearl,
EMP: 8
SQ FT: 23,000
SALES (est): 1.1MM **Privately Held**
SIC: 3652 5211 Compact laser discs, prerecorded; bathroom fixtures, equipment & supplies

(G-6728)
WALSH & HUGHES INC (PA)
Also Called: Velvetop Products
1455 New York Ave (11746-1706)
PHONE.................................631 427-5904
Fax: 631 673-3301
John B Walsh, *President*
Linda J Walsh, *Corp Secy*
EMP: 8
SQ FT: 3,800
SALES (est): 1.9MM **Privately Held**
WEB: www.velvetop.com
SIC: 2891 5941 5032 5091 Sealants; tennis goods & equipment; clay construction materials, except refractory; sporting & recreation goods

(G-6729)
WTBI INC
Also Called: Whats The Big Idea
200 E 2nd St Ste 12 (11746-1462)
PHONE.................................631 547-1993
Jeff Vogel, *President*
▲ **EMP:** 7
SQ FT: 6,000
SALES (est): 710K **Privately Held**
WEB: www.wtbi.com
SIC: 3499 Magnets, permanent: metallic

(G-6730)
Z-CAR-D CORP
Also Called: Sign-A-Rama
403 Oakwood Rd (11746-7207)
PHONE.................................631 424-2077
Fax: 631 424-2078
Dawn M Tiritter-Bent, *Ch of Bd*
Michael Ziccardi, *Vice Pres*
Krystal Eichler, *Assistant*
EMP: 28
SQ FT: 15,000
SALES (est): 3.1MM **Privately Held**
WEB: www.ssar.com
SIC: 3993 Signs & advertising specialties

Hurleyville
Sullivan County

(G-6731)
MONGIELLO SALES INC
250 Hilldale Rd (12747-5301)
P.O. Box 320 (12747-0320)
PHONE.................................845 436-4200
Anthony Mongiello, *President*
Gary Kudrowitz, *Manager*
▼ **EMP:** 40
SALES (est): 4.1MM **Privately Held**
SIC: 2022 Natural cheese

GEOGRAPHIC SECTION

Inwood - Nassau County (G-6757)

(G-6732)
MONGIELLOS ITLN CHEESE SPC LLC
Also Called: Formaggio Italian Cheese
250 Hilldale Rd (12747-5301)
P.O. Box 320 (12747-0320)
PHONE..................845 436-4200
Fax: 845 436-7076
Anthony Mongiello, *CEO*
John Jmongiello, *COO*
Sal Maccarello, *Buyer*
Stuart Parsons, *Controller*
Gary Kudrowitz, *Manager*
EMP: 150
SQ FT: 65,000
SALES: 25.6MM **Privately Held**
SIC: 2022 Natural cheese

Hyde Park
Dutchess County

(G-6733)
ABE POOL SERVICE
793 Violet Ave (12538-1952)
PHONE..................845 473-7730
Fax: 845 229-2378
Abraham Stewart, *President*
EMP: 5
SALES (est): 618.4K **Privately Held**
SIC: 3589 Swimming pool filter & water conditioning systems

(G-6734)
HYDE PARK BREWING CO INC
4076 Albany Post Rd (12538-1934)
PHONE..................845 229-8277
Fax: 845 229-6146
Carmelo Decicco, *President*
EMP: 20
SQ FT: 4,000
SALES (est): 2.2MM **Privately Held**
WEB: www.hydeparkbrewing.com
SIC: 2082 5812 Malt beverages; eating places

(G-6735)
NEW CITY PRESS INC
202 Cardinal Rd (12538-2903)
PHONE..................845 229-0335
Fax: 845 229-0351
Patrick Markey, *General Mgr*
Gary Brandal, *Manager*
Robert Cummings, *Administration*
EMP: 5
SALES (est): 444.4K **Privately Held**
WEB: www.newcitypress.com
SIC: 2731 Books: publishing only

(G-6736)
RICHARD R CAIN INC
50 Scenic Dr (12538-1313)
PHONE..................845 229-7410
Fax: 845 229-6538
Richard R Cain, *President*
EMP: 11
SQ FT: 1,200
SALES (est): 1.1MM **Privately Held**
SIC: 3589 1629 Sewage treatment equipment; waste water & sewage treatment plant construction

(G-6737)
RIVERWOOD SGNS BY DNDEV DSIGNS
3 Terwilliger Rd (12538-1710)
PHONE..................845 229-0282
Kathleen Hinz-Shaffer, *President*
EMP: 5
SALES: 100K **Privately Held**
SIC: 3993 7336 7389 Signs & advertising specialties; commercial art & graphic design; design, commercial & industrial

(G-6738)
VICTORIA PRECISION INC
78 Travis Rd (12538-2753)
PHONE..................845 473-9309
Vincent Slaninka, *President*
EMP: 5
SQ FT: 3,000
SALES: 270K **Privately Held**
WEB: www.victoriaprecisioninc.com
SIC: 3599 Machine shop, jobbing & repair

Ilion
Herkimer County

(G-6739)
ACORN PRODUCTS CORP
27 Pleasant Ave (13357-1115)
PHONE..................315 894-4868
John Thayer, *President*
EMP: 15
SALES (est): 1.1MM **Privately Held**
SIC: 2396 Printing & embossing on plastics fabric articles

(G-6740)
FERMER PRECISION INC
114 Johnson Rd (13357-3899)
PHONE..................315 822-6371
Fax: 315 822-6300
Stewart Bunce, *President*
Mark Cushman, *Exec VP*
John Tofani, *Vice Pres*
Chad Bernier, *Production*
Tina Lafountain, *Purchasing*
EMP: 72
SQ FT: 60,000
SALES: 8MM **Privately Held**
WEB: www.fermerprecision.com
SIC: 3599 Electrical discharge machining (EDM)

(G-6741)
ILION PLASTICS INC
27 Pleasant Ave (13357-1115)
PHONE..................315 894-4868
Fax: 315 894-4890
Steve Quinn, *President*
Kathy Quinn, *President*
EMP: 16
SQ FT: 10,000
SALES: 800K **Privately Held**
SIC: 3089 Injection molding of plastics

(G-6742)
JAMES WIRE DIE CO
138 West St (13357-2250)
PHONE..................315 894-3233
R B Roux, *President*
Alex Roux, *Vice Pres*
EMP: 5
SALES: 100K **Privately Held**
SIC: 3544 Special dies & tools

(G-6743)
ORIGINAL HRKMER CNTY CHESE INC
Also Called: Herkimer Cheese
2745 State Route 51 (13357-4299)
P.O. Box 310, Herkimer (13350-0310)
PHONE..................315 895-7428
Sheldon Basloe, *President*
Norma Basloe, *Corp Secy*
Robert Basloe, *Vice Pres*
Nora Ray, *Safety Mgr*
Jacob Basloe, *Purch Mgr*
EMP: 60 **EST:** 1949
SQ FT: 22,913
SALES (est): 8.6MM **Privately Held**
WEB: www.herkimerfoods.com
SIC: 2022 2099 Cheese, natural & processed; gelatin dessert preparations; dessert mixes & fillings

(G-6744)
REMINGTON ARMS COMPANY LLC
14 Hoefler Ave (13357-1888)
PHONE..................315 895-3482
Fax: 315 895-3237
Laird G Williams, *Principal*
Steven Taylor, *Safety Dir*
Robert Skinner, *Purch Mgr*
Eric Hamblin, *Engineer*
Frank Ogrodnik, *Engineer*
EMP: 850
SALES (corp-wide): 33.1B **Publicly Held**
WEB: www.remington.com
SIC: 3484 8711 Small arms; engineering services
HQ: Remington Arms Company, Llc
870 Remington Dr
Madison NC 27025
336 548-8700

(G-6745)
REVIVAL INDUSTRIES INC
126 Old Forge Rd (13357-4200)
PHONE..................315 868-1085
Richard Jackson, *President*
Edward R Jackson, *Vice Pres*
EMP: 17
SQ FT: 16,000
SALES (est): 1MM **Privately Held**
WEB: www.revivalindustries.com
SIC: 2426 2499 Gun stocks, wood; handles, poles, dowels & stakes: wood; novelties, wood fiber

Interlaken
Seneca County

(G-6746)
AMERICANA VINEYARDS & WINERY
4367 E Covert Rd (14847-9720)
PHONE..................607 387-6801
Fax: 607 387-3852
Joseph Gober, *President*
EMP: 15
SALES: 750K **Privately Held**
SIC: 2084 Wines

(G-6747)
HIPSHOT PRODUCTS INC
Also Called: Melissa
8248 State Route 96 (14847-9655)
PHONE..................607 532-9404
Fax: 607 532-9503
David Borisoff, *President*
▲ **EMP:** 15
SALES (est): 1.1MM **Privately Held**
WEB: www.hipshotproducts.com
SIC: 3931 5736 Guitars & parts, electric & nonelectric; musical instrument stores

(G-6748)
LUCAS VINEYARDS & WINERY
3862 County Road 150 (14847-9805)
PHONE..................607 532-4825
Fax: 607 532-8580
Ruth Lucas, *President*
EMP: 12
SALES (est): 2MM **Privately Held**
WEB: www.lucasvineyards.com
SIC: 2084 0172 5921 Wines; grapes; liquor stores

(G-6749)
PINE TREE FARMS INC
3714 Cayuga St (14847-9607)
P.O. Box 254 (14847-0254)
PHONE..................607 532-4312
Fax: 607 532-4311
Mark Stillions, *President*
Joelle Stillions, *Corp Secy*
Neal Stillions, *Vice Pres*
Michelle Griego-Stillions, *Sales Mgr*
EMP: 30
SQ FT: 14,000
SALES (est): 5.6MM **Privately Held**
WEB: www.pinetreefarmsinc.com
SIC: 2048 Bird food, prepared

Inwood
Nassau County

(G-6750)
APEX ARIDYNE CORP
168 Doughty Blvd (11096-2010)
P.O. Box 960670 (11096-0670)
PHONE..................516 239-4400
Edward Schlussel, *President*
EMP: 5
SALES (corp-wide): 8.6MM **Privately Held**
SIC: 2258 2257 Lace & warp knit fabric mills; weft knit fabric mills
PA: Apex Aridyne Corp.
2350 Long Dairy Rd
Graham NC
516 239-4400

(G-6751)
ARLEE LIGHTING CORP
125 Doughty Blvd (11096-2003)
PHONE..................516 595-8558
Pinchaf Gralla, *President*
▲ **EMP:** 4
SQ FT: 10,000
SALES: 3MM **Privately Held**
SIC: 3646 Commercial indusl & institutional electric lighting fixtures

(G-6752)
AUDIOSAVINGS INC
Also Called: Rockville Pro
600 Bayview Ave Ste 200 (11096-1625)
PHONE..................888 445-1555
▼ **EMP:** 14
SALES (est): 2.5MM **Privately Held**
SIC: 3651 Mfg Home Audio/Video Equipment

(G-6753)
BEL TRANSFORMER INC (HQ)
Also Called: Signal Transformer
500 Bayview Ave (11096-1702)
P.O. Box 36129, Newark NJ (07188-6106)
PHONE..................516 239-5777
Fax: 516 239-7208
Daniel Bernstein, *President*
Sandy Axelrad, *General Mgr*
Colin Dunn, *Vice Pres*
Mohammad Siddiqui, *Accountant*
▲ **EMP:** 60
SQ FT: 40,000
SALES: 17MM
SALES (corp-wide): 567MM **Publicly Held**
WEB: www.signaltransformer.com
SIC: 3677 Electronic coils, transformers & other inductors
PA: Bel Fuse Inc.
206 Van Vorst St
Jersey City NJ 07302
201 432-0463

(G-6754)
CUSTOM CANDY CONCEPTS INC
50 Inip Dr (11096-1011)
PHONE..................516 824-3228
Barry J Bass, *President*
Leonid Kaufman, *Treasurer*
EMP: 7
SALES (est): 530K **Privately Held**
WEB: www.customcandyconcepts.com
SIC: 2064 Candy & other confectionery products

(G-6755)
EXCEL PAINT APPLICATORS INC
555 Doughty Blvd (11096-1031)
PHONE..................347 221-1968
Fax: 718 927-3662
P C Sekar, *President*
Georgio Lee, *Manager*
▲ **EMP:** 45 **EST:** 1995
SQ FT: 48,000
SALES (est): 6MM **Privately Held**
SIC: 2851 Paints & allied products

(G-6756)
EXCELLENT ART MFG CORP
Also Called: Neva Slip
531 Bayview Ave (11096-1703)
PHONE..................718 388-7075
Fax: 718 388-9404
Marshall Korn, *President*
David Korn, *Vice Pres*
▲ **EMP:** 16 **EST:** 1929
SQ FT: 25,000
SALES (est): 1.3MM **Privately Held**
SIC: 2392 3949 2273 Household furnishings; mattress pads; sporting & athletic goods; carpets & rugs

(G-6757)
FIBERALL CORP
449 Sheridan Blvd (11096-1203)
PHONE..................516 371-5200
Fax: 516 371-2509
Isaac Zilber, *President*
Sophie Zilber, *Vice Pres*
▲ **EMP:** 25
SQ FT: 8,000

Inwood - Nassau County (G-6758)

GEOGRAPHIC SECTION

SALES (est): 6MM **Privately Held**
WEB: www.fiberall.com
SIC: 3661 Multiplex equipment, telephone & telegraph

(G-6758)
GENERAL DIARIES CORPORATION
56 John St (11096-1353)
PHONE.....................516 371-2244
Fax: 516 239-0851
Mark Lebo, *President*
▲ EMP: 15 EST: 1953
SALES (est): 1.9MM **Privately Held**
WEB: www.dallasnews.com
SIC: 2782 2678 Memorandum books, printed; diaries; desk pads, paper: made from purchased materials

(G-6759)
INWOOD MATERIAL
1 Sheridan Blvd (11096-1807)
PHONE.....................516 371-1842
Fax: 516 671-5273
Frank Sciarrino, *President*
EMP: 11
SALES (est): 1.7MM **Privately Held**
SIC: 3273 5082 Ready-mixed concrete; masonry equipment & supplies

(G-6760)
LES CHATEAUX DE FRANCE INC
1 Craft Ave (11096-1609)
PHONE.....................516 239-6795
Fax: 516 239-6215
Gerald Shapiro, *President*
Marie Cuscianna, *Vice Pres*
EMP: 28 EST: 1950
SQ FT: 7,000
SALES (est): 3.5MM **Privately Held**
SIC: 2038 Snacks, including onion rings, cheese sticks, etc.

(G-6761)
MGR EQUIPMENT CORP
22 Gates Ave (11096-1612)
PHONE.....................516 239-3030
Fax: 516 239-3602
Gerald Ross, *President*
Robert Ross, *Corp Secy*
George Mauder, *Vice Pres*
▼ EMP: 25
SQ FT: 40,000
SALES (est): 4.6MM **Privately Held**
WEB: www.mgrequip.com
SIC: 3585 Refrigeration & heating equipment; ice making machinery

(G-6762)
N3A CORPORATION
345 Doughty Blvd (11096-1348)
PHONE.....................516 284-6799
Niall Alli, *CEO*
Adrienne Alli, *CFO*
▲ EMP: 100 EST: 2007
SQ FT: 100,000
SALES (est): 11.4MM **Privately Held**
SIC: 2676 2599 Towels, napkins & tissue paper products; hotel furniture

(G-6763)
NEA MANUFACTURING CORP
345 Doughty Blvd (11096-1348)
PHONE.....................516 371-4200
Fax: 516 239-0239
Sheik Alli, *President*
Niall Alli, *Senior VP*
Justin Alli, *CFO*
▲ EMP: 37
SQ FT: 4,000
SALES (est): 5MM **Privately Held**
SIC: 3672 3679 3677 3678 Printed circuit boards; electronic switches; electronic transformers; electronic connectors; household audio & video equipment; current-carrying wiring devices

(G-6764)
NOEL ASSOC
114 Henry St Ste A (11096-2350)
PHONE.....................516 371-5420
EMP: 5
SALES (est): 300K **Privately Held**
SIC: 3993 Mfg Signs/Advertising Specialties

Irving
Chautauqua County

(G-6765)
SENECA NATION ENTERPRISE
Also Called: This Business Is Tribaly Owned
11482 Route 20 (14081-9539)
PHONE.....................716 934-7430
Fax: 716 934-3255
Seneca Nation, *Owner*
Julie Carry, *Exec Dir*
EMP: 12
SALES (est): 1.3MM **Privately Held**
SIC: 2111 5172 Cigarettes; gasoline

Irvington
Westchester County

(G-6766)
ABYRX INC
1 Bridge St Ste 121 (10533-1553)
PHONE.....................914 357-2600
John Pacifico, *President*
David Hart, *Vice Pres*
Richard Kronenthal, *Officer*
EMP: 11 EST: 2013
SALES (est): 1.4MM **Privately Held**
SIC: 3841 Surgical instruments & apparatus

(G-6767)
CITY GEAR INC
213 Taxter Rd (10533-1111)
PHONE.....................914 450-4746
John Clark, *President*
Ingred Roberg, *Vice Pres*
▼ EMP: 6
SQ FT: 3,000
SALES (est): 510K **Privately Held**
SIC: 3599 Machine shop, jobbing & repair

(G-6768)
EILEEN FISHER INC (PA)
Also Called: Eileen Fisher Womens Apparel
2 Bridge St Ste 230 (10533-3500)
PHONE.....................914 591-5700
Fax: 914 591-8824
Eileen Fisher, *Ch of Bd*
Christine Beisiegel, *General Mgr*
Hillary Old, *Vice Pres*
Mariclare Vanbergen, *Vice Pres*
Loretta Torcicello, *Prdtn Dir*
▲ EMP: 125
SQ FT: 20,000
SALES: 350MM **Privately Held**
WEB: www.eileenfisher.com
SIC: 2339 Sportswear, women's

(G-6769)
FEINKIND INC
Also Called: REFINEDKIND PET PRODUCTS
17 Algonquin Dr (10533-1007)
PHONE.....................800 289-6136
Josh Feinkind, *CEO*
EMP: 1
SQ FT: 65,000
SALES: 1MM **Privately Held**
SIC: 2511 Novelty furniture: wood

(G-6770)
GUTTZ CORPORATION OF AMERICA
Also Called: Gutts Corporation of America
50 S Buckhout St Ste 104 (10533-2217)
PHONE.....................914 591-9600
Robert H Cohen, *President*
Ronald Roemer, *Vice Pres*
Jane Berger, *Manager*
EMP: 13
SQ FT: 7,000
SALES (est): 1.5MM **Privately Held**
WEB: www.marketvis.com
SIC: 3955 Print cartridges for laser & other computer printers

---

(G-6771)
HAIR VENTURES LLC
Also Called: Hairstory
94 Fargo Ln (10533-1202)
PHONE.....................718 664-7689
Eli Halliwell, *CEO*
EMP: 13
SALES (est): 650.4K **Privately Held**
SIC: 2844 7389 Hair preparations, including shampoos;

(G-6772)
ILEX CONSUMER PDTS GROUP LLC
Also Called: Healing Garden Calgon, The
323 W Camden St Ste 700 (10533)
PHONE.....................410 897-0701
Bradley Brommer, *CFO*
Joseph Matthews, *Mng Member*
Robert Bailey,
Rick Foster,
Bernard Kropfeldrr,
▲ EMP: 14
SALES (est): 1.9MM **Privately Held**
SIC: 2841 Detergents, synthetic organic or inorganic alkaline

(G-6773)
ISP OPTICS CORPORATION (PA)
50 S Buckhout St (10533-2203)
PHONE.....................914 591-3070
Mark Lifshotz, *CEO*
Joseph Menaker, *President*
Joseph Washer, *Business Mgr*
Rasvana Popescu, *VP Opers*
Devaunshi Sampat, *Treasurer*
▲ EMP: 63
SQ FT: 22,000
SALES: 8.7MM **Privately Held**
WEB: www.ispoptics.com
SIC: 3827 Optical instruments & lenses

(G-6774)
NEUROTROPE INC
60 Hampden Ln (10533-2424)
PHONE.....................973 242-0005
Joshua Silverman, *Ch of Bd*
William S Singer, *Vice Ch Bd*
Charles S Ramat, *President*
Paula T Trzepacz, *Exec VP*
Robert Weinstein, *CFO*
EMP: 6 EST: 2013
SQ FT: 4,000
SALES (est): 565.9K **Privately Held**
SIC: 2834 8731 Pharmaceutical preparations; biological research

(G-6775)
ORTHOCON INC
1 Bridge St Ste 121 (10533-1553)
PHONE.....................914 357-2600
John J Pacifico, *President*
David J Hart, *Vice Pres*
Christine Moley, *Vice Pres*
Stephen Hall, *CFO*
EMP: 23 EST: 2006
SALES (est): 2.8MM **Privately Held**
SIC: 3841 Surgical & medical instruments

(G-6776)
PECO PALLET INC (HQ)
2 Bridge St Ste 210 (10533-1594)
PHONE.....................914 376-5444
Fax: 914 376-7376
Joseph Dagnese, *CEO*
Jeff Euritt, *Vice Pres*
Roberto Sobrino, *Vice Pres*
Manasvi Tindall, *Vice Pres*
Vince Panfil, *Opers Staff*
EMP: 24
SQ FT: 5,000
SALES (est): 31.4MM
SALES (corp-wide): 249MM **Privately Held**
WEB: www.pecopallet.com
SIC: 2448 7359 Pallets, wood; pallet rental services
PA: The Pritzker Group- Chicago Llc
111 S Wacker Dr Ste 4000
Chicago IL 60606
312 447-6000

Island Park
Nassau County

(G-6777)
A-1 MANHATTAN CUSTOM FURN INC
Also Called: Manhattan Cabinets
4315 Austin Blvd (11558-1627)
PHONE.....................212 750-9800
Eric Heim, *Manager*
EMP: 5
SALES (corp-wide): 9.4MM **Privately Held**
WEB: www.manhattancabinetry.com
SIC: 2511 Wood household furniture
PA: A-1 Manhattan Custom Furniture Inc.
4315 Austin Blvd
Island Park NY 11558
718 937-4780

(G-6778)
BHI ELEVATOR CABS INC
74 Alabama Ave (11558-1116)
PHONE.....................516 431-5665
Rick Hart, *President*
Brian Holodar, *Principal*
EMP: 15
SALES (est): 3.2MM **Privately Held**
SIC: 3534 Elevators & equipment

(G-6779)
F & B PHOTO OFFSET CO INC (PA)
4 California Pl N (11558-2215)
P.O. Box 366 (11558-0366)
PHONE.....................516 431-5433
Frank Naudus, *President*
EMP: 7
SQ FT: 6,000
SALES: 1MM **Privately Held**
SIC: 2752 2759 Commercial printing, offset; letterpress printing

(G-6780)
H D M LABS INC
153 Kingston Blvd (11558-1926)
PHONE.....................516 431-8357
Hardat Singh, *President*
EMP: 5
SQ FT: 1,600
SALES (est): 799.9K **Privately Held**
WEB: www.hdmlabsinc.com
SIC: 3829 Medical diagnostic systems, nuclear

(G-6781)
NATHAN BERRIE & SONS INC
Also Called: Naomi Manufacturing
3956 Long Beach Rd (11558-1146)
P.O. Box 240 (11558-0240)
PHONE.....................516 432-8500
Fax: 516 432-8544
Stanley Berrie, *President*
Suzanne Berrie, *Admin Sec*
EMP: 9 EST: 1944
SQ FT: 4,000
SALES (est): 1.1MM **Privately Held**
SIC: 3915 Jewelers' findings & materials

(G-6782)
NORTHFELD PRECISION INSTR CORP
Also Called: NORTH FIELD
4400 Austin Blvd (11558-1621)
P.O. Box 550 (11558-0550)
PHONE.....................516 431-1112
Fax: 516 431-1928
Donald Freedman, *Ch of Bd*
Paul Defeo, *COO*
Linda Vassallo, *Accounting Mgr*
Ken Sprenger, *VP Sales*
Charles Florio, *Sales Staff*
EMP: 32 EST: 1953
SQ FT: 15,000
SALES: 5.1MM **Privately Held**
WEB: www.northfield.com
SIC: 3545 Chucks: drill, lathe or magnetic (machine tool accessories)

GEOGRAPHIC SECTION

Islip - Suffolk County (G-6807)

(G-6783)
ONLY NATURAL INC
Also Called: Bio Nutrition
31 Saratoga Blvd (11558-1117)
PHONE.................................516 897-7001
Fax: 516 897-9332
Robert Lomaccio, *President*
EMP: 15
SQ FT: 3,600
SALES (est): 2.3MM Privately Held
WEB: www.onlynaturalinc.com
SIC: 2833 5499 Vitamins, natural or synthetic; bulk, uncompounded; health & dietetic food stores

(G-6784)
SOUTH SHORE TRIBUNE INC
4 California Pl N (11558-2215)
P.O. Box 366 (11558-0366)
PHONE.................................516 431-5628
Fax: 516 431-5990
Frank Naudus, *President*
EMP: 8
SQ FT: 6,000
SALES (est): 249.7K
SALES (corp-wide): 1MM Privately Held
SIC: 2711 Newspapers, publishing & printing
PA: F & B Photo Offset Co Inc
4 California Pl N
Island Park NY 11558
516 431-5433

Islandia
Suffolk County

(G-6785)
A & L MACHINE COMPANY INC
200 Blydenburg Rd Ste 9 (11749-5011)
PHONE.................................631 463-3111
Fax: 631 778-8071
Horst Ehinger, *President*
George Ramos, *Principal*
EMP: 7 EST: 1963
SQ FT: 4,000
SALES (est): 966.7K Privately Held
WEB: www.anlmachine.com
SIC: 3599 Machine shop, jobbing & repair

(G-6786)
ARCSERVE (USA) LLC
1 Ca Plz (11749-5305)
PHONE.................................866 576-9742
Michael Crest, *CEO*
Cristophe Bertrand, *Vice Pres*
Steve Fairbanks, *Vice Pres*
Louis Lautin, *Vice Pres*
Chris Ross, *Vice Pres*
EMP: 20
SQ FT: 6,000
SALES: 103MM
SALES (corp-wide): 2.6B Privately Held
SIC: 7372 Business oriented computer software
PA: Marlin Equity Partners, Llc
338 Pier Ave
Hermosa Beach CA 90354
310 364-0100

(G-6787)
ARK SCIENCES INC
1601 Veterans Hwy Ste 315 (11749-1543)
PHONE.................................646 943-1520
Joseph Tosini, *President*
EMP: 6
SALES (est): 690.3K Privately Held
SIC: 2834 Veterinary pharmaceutical preparations

(G-6788)
BIG APPLE SIGN CORP
Also Called: Big Apple Visual Group
3 Oval Dr (11749-1402)
PHONE.................................631 342-0303
Amir Khalfan, *Branch Mgr*
Ahmedali Ahalsan, *Manager*
EMP: 35

SALES (corp-wide): 12.7MM Privately Held
WEB: www.bigapplegroup.com
SIC: 3993 2399 3552 Signs, not made in custom sign painting shops; displays & cutouts, window & lobby; banners, made from fabric; silk screens for textile industry
PA: Big Apple Sign Corp.
247 W 35th St Frnt 1
New York NY 10001
212 629-3650

(G-6789)
CENTURY DIRECT LLC
15 Enter Ln (11749-4811)
PHONE.................................212 763-0600
Eric Seid, *COO*
Martin Rego, *Vice Pres*
Chris Calahan, *Plant Mgr*
Richard Skolnick, *VP Sales*
Lisa Fuchs, *Accounts Exec*
▲ EMP: 200
SQ FT: 80,000
SALES (est): 44.3MM Privately Held
WEB: www.centltr.com
SIC: 2759 7331 7379 Commercial printing; direct mail advertising services; computer related maintenance services

(G-6790)
CES INDUSTRIES INC
95 Hoffman Ln Ste S (11749-5020)
PHONE.................................631 782-7088
Fax: 516 293-8556
Mitchell B Nesenoff, *CEO*
Edward J Ermler, *Vice Pres*
Frank Ellis, *Manager*
William Smith, *Technical Staff*
EMP: 40
SQ FT: 20,000
SALES (est): 6.7MM Privately Held
WEB: www.cesindustries.com
SIC: 3699 Electronic training devices

(G-6791)
DISPLAY MARKETING GROUP INC
170 Oval Dr Ste B (11749-1419)
PHONE.................................631 348-4450
Steven Larit, *President*
EMP: 35
SQ FT: 24,000
SALES (est): 5.3MM Privately Held
SIC: 3993 Displays & cutouts, window & lobby

(G-6792)
DUETTO INTEGRATED SYSTEMS INC
Also Called: Dis
85 Hoffman Ln Ste Q (11749-5019)
PHONE.................................631 851-0102
Carmela Faraci, *Office Mgr*
Gary Sortino, *Manager*
Michael Faraci, *Technician*
EMP: 10
SQ FT: 2,000
SALES (est): 1.5MM Privately Held
SIC: 3599 Custom machinery

(G-6793)
FLEXBAR MACHINE CORPORATION
Also Called: Mediflex
250 Gibbs Rd (11749-2697)
PHONE.................................631 582-8440
Jon Adler, *President*
Juanita Adler, *Corp Secy*
Robert Adler, *Vice Pres*
Lance Larkin, *Vice Pres*
Anthony Vite, *Plant Mgr*
▲ EMP: 27
SQ FT: 10,500
SALES (est): 6.3MM Privately Held
WEB: www.flexbar.com
SIC: 3545 3841 Machine tool attachments & accessories; surgical & medical instruments

(G-6794)
GAC
1 Ca Plz Ste 100 (11749-5303)
PHONE.................................631 357-8600
Pedro Duarte, *Principal*
EMP: 5

SALES (est): 602.9K Privately Held
SIC: 3843 Dental equipment & supplies

(G-6795)
I E D CORP
88 Bridge Rd (11749)
PHONE.................................631 348-0424
Fax: 631 348-0425
Martin Ramage, *President*
Robert Jaffe, *Engineer*
EMP: 10
SQ FT: 5,000
SALES (est): 1.4MM Privately Held
SIC: 3674 3625 Microprocessors; relays & industrial controls

(G-6796)
ICD PUBLICATIONS INC (PA)
Also Called: Hotel Business
1377 Motor Pkwy Ste 410 (11749-5258)
PHONE.................................631 246-9300
Fax: 516 246-9496
Ian Gittlitz, *President*
James Schultz, *Publisher*
Dennis Nessler, *Editor*
Adam Perkowsky, *Editor*
Christina Trauthwein, *Editor*
EMP: 25
SQ FT: 10,000
SALES (est): 3.5MM Privately Held
WEB: www.icdnet.com
SIC: 2721 7313 Magazines: publishing only, not printed on site; magazine advertising representative

(G-6797)
JET COMPONENTS INC
62 Bridge Rd (11749-1411)
PHONE.................................631 436-7300
Fax: 631 436-7342
Gina Pedroli, *President*
Charles Scarborough, *General Mgr*
Ken Pedroli, *Vice Pres*
▲ EMP: 6
SQ FT: 6,000
SALES (est): 1.3MM Privately Held
WEB: www.jet-components.com
SIC: 3679 Electronic circuits

(G-6798)
JOMART ASSOCIATES INC
170 Oval Dr Ste A (11749-1419)
PHONE.................................212 627-2153
Walter Waltman, *President*
Peter Batterson, *Vice Pres*
Steve Perry, *Manager*
Walter Woltmann, *Exec Dir*
Evelyn Giman, *Admin Sec*
EMP: 30
SQ FT: 1,200
SALES (est): 2.8MM Privately Held
WEB: www.jomartassociates.com
SIC: 2759 Commercial printing

(G-6799)
LIF DISTRIBUTING INC
155 Oval Dr (11749-1402)
PHONE.................................631 630-6900
Steven Frielander, *President*
Gerard Mach, *Vice Pres*
EMP: 13
SQ FT: 8,000
SALES (est): 1.9MM Privately Held
SIC: 2541 Table or counter tops, plastic laminated

(G-6800)
M & M CANVAS & AWNINGS INC
Also Called: M & M Signs & Awnings
180 Oval Dr (11749-1403)
PHONE.................................631 424-5370
Fax: 631 424-5375
Mike Mere, *President*
EMP: 7
SALES (est): 660K Privately Held
WEB: www.mmawning.com
SIC: 2394 Canvas & related products

(G-6801)
PRINTEX PACKAGING CORPORATION
555 Raymond Dr (11749-4844)
PHONE.................................631 234-4300
Fax: 631 234-4840
David Heller, *President*
Joel Heller, *President*

Carol Heller, *Vice Pres*
Tom Vollmuth, *Vice Pres*
Barbara Colangelo, *Accounting Mgr*
▲ EMP: 70
SQ FT: 40,000
SALES (est): 27.2MM Privately Held
WEB: www.printexpackaging.com
SIC: 3089 3086 2671 Boxes, plastic; packaging & shipping materials, foamed plastic; packaging paper & plastics film, coated & laminated

(G-6802)
REPELLEM CONSUMER PDTS CORP
Also Called: Ecosmartplastics
10 Oval Dr (11749-1403)
PHONE.................................631 273-3992
Terry Feinberg, *President*
EMP: 10
SALES (est): 1.2MM Privately Held
SIC: 2673 2392 Trash bags (plastic film): made from purchased materials; tablecloths: made from purchased materials

(G-6803)
SOCKET PRODUCTS MFG CORP
175 Bridge Rd (11749-5202)
PHONE.................................631 232-9870
Fax: 631 232-3215
Sol Kellner, *President*
EMP: 5
SQ FT: 5,000
SALES (est): 663.8K Privately Held
SIC: 3452 3545 Screws, metal; nuts, metal; bolts, metal; sockets (machine tool accessories)

(G-6804)
WHITSONS FOOD SVC BRONX CORP
1800 Motor Pkwy (11749-5216)
PHONE.................................631 424-2700
Robert Whitcomb, *President*
Beth Bunster, *Corp Secy*
Douglas Whitcomb, *Vice Pres*
John Whitcomb, *Vice Pres*
Andrew Whitcomb, *Shareholder*
EMP: 350
SQ FT: 65,000
SALES (est): 47.7MM Privately Held
SIC: 2068 2099 Salted & roasted nuts & seeds; food preparations; peanut butter

(G-6805)
ZAHK SALES INC
Also Called: Project Visual
75 Hoffman Ln Ste A (11749-5027)
PHONE.................................631 348-9300
Husein Kermalli, *President*
Nick Kermalli, *Manager*
▲ EMP: 7
SALES (est): 566.3K Privately Held
WEB: www.zahk.com
SIC: 3444 1752 Sheet metalwork; wood floor installation & refinishing

Islip
Suffolk County

(G-6806)
AINES MANUFACTURING CORP
96 E Bayberry Rd (11751-4903)
PHONE.................................631 471-3900
▼ EMP: 30
SQ FT: 10,000
SALES (est): 4.3MM Privately Held
SIC: 3661 Mfg Telephone/Telegraph Apparatus

(G-6807)
COOKIES UNITED LLC
141 Freeman Ave (11751-1428)
PHONE.................................631 581-4000
Louis Avignone, *Mng Member*
EMP: 120
SQ FT: 80,000
SALES (est): 4.8MM Privately Held
SIC: 2052 Cookies & crackers
PA: United Baking Co., Inc.
41 Natcon Dr
Shirley NY 11967

Islip - Suffolk County (G-6808)

(G-6808)
EUGENIA SELECTIVE LIVING INC
122 Freeman Ave (11751-1417)
PHONE..................................631 277-1361
Fax: 631 277-1536
Edward Smith, *President*
Mary Schlichting, *Office Mgr*
Eugenia Smith, *Admin Sec*
EMP: 10
SQ FT: 5,000
SALES (est): 1.2MM **Privately Held**
WEB: www.selectiveliving.com
SIC: 2511 2519 2521 2522 Wood household furniture; furniture, household: glass, fiberglass & plastic; wood office furniture; office furniture, except wood; laboratory equipment, except medical or dental; cabinet & finish carpentry

(G-6809)
IAHCP INC
Also Called: International Association
181 Freeman Ave Unit C (11751-1400)
PHONE..................................631 650-2499
Anthony Casimano, *President*
▲ EMP: 50 EST: 2009
SALES (est): 3.7MM **Privately Held**
SIC: 2741 Miscellaneous publishing

(G-6810)
MEADES WELDING AND FABRICATING
331 Islip Ave (11751-2800)
PHONE..................................631 581-1555
Michelle Mede, *President*
EMP: 5
SALES (est): 217K **Privately Held**
SIC: 7692 5046 Welding repair; commercial cooking & food service equipment

(G-6811)
MJB PRINTING CORP
Also Called: Mod Printing
280 Islip Ave (11751-2818)
PHONE..................................631 581-0177
Fax: 631 581-0137
Jeanine Bazata, *President*
Michael Bazata, *Treasurer*
EMP: 5
SQ FT: 2,800
SALES (est): 666.5K **Privately Held**
SIC: 2752 Commercial printing, offset

(G-6812)
RIKE ENTERPRISES INC
Also Called: Corpkit Legal Supplies
46 Taft Ave (11751-2112)
PHONE..................................631 277-8338
Fax: 631 277-8448
Richard Jansen, *President*
Hongtao Liao, *Prgrmr*
▼ EMP: 15
SALES (est): 1.6MM **Privately Held**
WEB: www.corpkit.com
SIC: 2759 5112 Commercial printing; office supplies

(G-6813)
T J SIGNS UNLIMITED LLC (PA)
Also Called: American Signcrafters
171 Freeman Ave (11751-1430)
PHONE..................................631 273-4800
Jeff Petersen, *President*
Jonathan Bell, *Vice Pres*
Anthony Lipari, *Vice Pres*
Valerie Mayer, *VP Finance*
Debra Russe, *Manager*
EMP: 50
SQ FT: 20,000
SALES: 25MM **Privately Held**
WEB: www.americansigncrafters.com
SIC: 3993 1799 7389 Electric signs; neon signs; sign installation & maintenance; personal service agents, brokers & bureaus

Islip Terrace
Suffolk County

(G-6814)
BARRASSO & SONS TRUCKING INC
160 Floral Park St (11752-1399)
PHONE..................................631 581-0360
Fax: 631 581-0902
Michael Barrasso, *President*
Joseph Longo, *Corp Secy*
Anthony Barrasso Jr, *Bd of Directors*
EMP: 30 EST: 1996
SQ FT: 2,500
SALES (est): 8.1MM **Privately Held**
SIC: 3271 5211 5032 Concrete block & brick; brick; brick, stone & related material

(G-6815)
NIKE INC
2675 Sunrise Hwy (11752-2119)
PHONE..................................631 960-0184
John Grasselino, *Branch Mgr*
EMP: 38
SALES (corp-wide): 32.3B **Publicly Held**
SIC: 3021 Rubber & plastics footwear
PA: Nike, Inc.
1 Sw Bowerman Dr
Beaverton OR 97005
503 671-6453

Ithaca
Tompkins County

(G-6816)
ADVANCED DIGITAL INFO CORP
10 Brown Rd (14850-1287)
PHONE..................................607 266-4000
James H Watson Jr, *Principal*
EMP: 50
SALES (corp-wide): 475.9MM **Publicly Held**
SIC: 3672 Printed circuit boards
HQ: Advanced Digital Information Corporation
11431 Willows Rd Ne
Redmond WA 98052
425 881-8004

(G-6817)
ADVION INC (PA)
10 Brown Rd Ste 101 (14850-1287)
PHONE..................................607 266-9162
David Patterson, *President*
Thomas R Kurz, *President*
Rosemary French, *General Mgr*
Mark Allen PH, *Vice Pres*
John Ackerman, *Mfg Staff*
EMP: 20
SQ FT: 16,500
SALES (est): 10.5MM **Privately Held**
SIC: 3826 Analytical instruments; mass spectrometers; spectrometers

(G-6818)
ALPINE MACHINE INC
1616 Trumansburg Rd (14850-9213)
PHONE..................................607 272-1344
Fax: 607 272-0935
Richard Hoffman, *President*
David Osburn, *Corp Secy*
William Osburn, *Vice Pres*
Russell Timblin, *Vice Pres*
EMP: 15
SQ FT: 6,000
SALES (est): 2MM **Privately Held**
WEB: www.alpinemachine.com
SIC: 3599 7692 3541 3444 Machine shop, jobbing & repair; welding repair; machine tools, metal cutting type; sheet metalwork

(G-6819)
ARNOLD PRINTING CORP
604 W Green St (14850-5250)
PHONE..................................607 272-7800
Fax: 607 272-2607
Robert Becker Jr, *President*
Christian J Becker, *Vice Pres*
EMP: 18 EST: 1963
SQ FT: 8,000
SALES (est): 2.6MM **Privately Held**
SIC: 2752 Commercial printing, offset

(G-6820)
AUTODESK INC
2353 N Triphammer Rd (14850-1011)
PHONE..................................607 257-4280
Henry Smith, *Sales Staff*
Rebekah Personius, *Manager*
Jin Wang, *Senior Mgr*
William L Myers, *Sr Software Eng*
EMP: 45
SALES (corp-wide): 2.5B **Publicly Held**
WEB: www.autodesk.com
SIC: 7372 7371 Prepackaged software; custom computer programming services
PA: Autodesk, Inc.
111 Mcinnis Pkwy
San Rafael CA 94903
415 507-5000

(G-6821)
BENNETT DIE & TOOL INC
113 Brewery Ln (14850-8814)
PHONE..................................607 273-2836
James McMillen, *President*
Brian Bennett, *Vice Pres*
EMP: 16
SALES (est): 1.2MM **Privately Held**
SIC: 3544 Special dies & tools

(G-6822)
BIGWOOD SYSTEMS INC
35 Thornwood Dr Ste 400 (14850-1284)
PHONE..................................607 257-0915
Hsiao-Dong Chiang, *President*
Pat Causgrove, *General Mgr*
Bin Wang, *Engineer*
EMP: 7
SALES (est): 590K **Privately Held**
WEB: www.bigwood-systems.com
SIC: 7372 Prepackaged software

(G-6823)
BINOPTICS LLC (DH)
9 Brown Rd (14850-1247)
PHONE..................................607 257-3200
Fax: 607 257-9753
Alex Behfar, *CEO*
William Fritz, *COO*
Norman Kwong, *Exec VP*
Christopher Smith, *CFO*
Prascilla Walter, *Manager*
▼ EMP: 59
SQ FT: 28,600
SALES (est): 26.8MM **Publicly Held**
WEB: www.binoptics.com
SIC: 3827 Optical instruments & lenses
HQ: Macom Technology Solutions Inc.
100 Chelmsford St
Lowell MA 01851
978 656-2500

(G-6824)
BORGWARNER INC
780 Warren Rd (14850-1242)
PHONE..................................607 257-1800
Roger Wood, *President*
Steven Leung, *Buyer*
Dustin Bordonaro, *Engineer*
Adam Kellerson, *Engineer*
Jay Stearns, *Manager*
EMP: 30
SALES (corp-wide): 8B **Publicly Held**
SIC: 3714 Motor vehicle parts & accessories
PA: Borgwarner Inc.
3850 Hamlin Rd
Auburn Hills MI 48326
248 754-9200

(G-6825)
BORGWARNER ITHACA LLC
Also Called: Morse Systems
800 Warren Rd (14850-1266)
PHONE..................................607 257-6700
James R Verrier, *President*
Steven G Carlson, *Vice Pres*
John J Gasparovic, *Vice Pres*
Alexandra Harvey, *Vice Pres*
Kathy Dickenson, *Purchasing*
EMP: 300
SQ FT: 100,000
SALES (est): 29MM **Privately Held**
SIC: 3462 Iron & steel forgings

(G-6826)
BORGWARNER MORSE TEC INC (HQ)
800 Warren Rd (14850-1266)
PHONE..................................607 257-6700
Fax: 607 257-3337
James R Verrier, *President*
Ronald M Ruzic, *President*
Timothy M Manganello, *Chairman*
Steve G Carlson, *Vice Pres*
Tony Hensel, *Vice Pres*
▲ EMP: 267
SALES (est): 246.7MM
SALES (corp-wide): 8B **Publicly Held**
WEB: www.borgwarnermorsetec.com
SIC: 3714 3462 3568 Motor vehicle parts & accessories; iron & steel forgings; power transmission equipment
PA: Borgwarner Inc.
3850 Hamlin Rd
Auburn Hills MI 48326
248 754-9200

(G-6827)
BORGWARNER MORSE TEC INC
780 Warren Rd (14850-1242)
PHONE..................................607 266-5111
Timothy M Manganello, *CEO*
Donald Freyburger, *Chief Engr*
Jason Moss, *Engineer*
Nick Stolten, *Technology*
EMP: 90
SALES (corp-wide): 8B **Publicly Held**
WEB: www.borgwarnermorsetec.com
SIC: 3714 Motor vehicle parts & accessories
HQ: Borgwarner Morse Tec Inc.
800 Warren Rd
Ithaca NY 14850
607 257-6700

(G-6828)
BORGWARNER MORSE TEC INC
781 Warner Rd (14850)
PHONE..................................607 257-6700
EMP: 90
SALES (corp-wide): 8B **Publicly Held**
SIC: 3714 3568 3462 Motor vehicle parts & accessories; power transmission equipment; iron & steel forgings
HQ: Borgwarner Morse Tec Inc.
800 Warren Rd
Ithaca NY 14850
607 257-6700

(G-6829)
BSU INC
445 E State St (14850-4409)
PHONE..................................607 272-8100
Christine Houseworth, *Chairman*
Denver Jones, *Vice Pres*
Richard Stillwaggon, *Purch Agent*
Dottie Highfield, *Accounts Mgr*
EMP: 42
SQ FT: 17,000
SALES (est): 7.7MM **Privately Held**
WEB: www.bsuinc.com
SIC: 3672 8711 Printed circuit boards; engineering services

(G-6830)
CAYUGA WOODEN BOATWORKS INC
381 Enfield Main Rd (14850-9346)
P.O. Box 301, Cayuga (13034-0301)
PHONE..................................315 253-7447
Fax: 607 272-1601
Phil Walker, *General Mgr*
Ken Anderson, *Principal*
EMP: 21
SQ FT: 10,000
SALES (est): 1.5MM **Privately Held**
WEB: www.cwbw.com
SIC: 3732 7699 Boat building & repairing; boat repair

(G-6831)
CBORD GROUP INC (HQ)
950 Danby Rd Ste 100c (14850-5795)
PHONE..................................607 257-2410
Fax: 607 257-1902
Max Steinhardt, *President*
Tim Tighe, *President*
Rich Imlay, *General Mgr*
Bruce Lane, *Exec VP*

Randy Eckels, *Senior VP*
EMP: 250
SQ FT: 40,000
SALES (est): 99.8MM
SALES (corp-wide): 3.5B **Publicly Held**
WEB: www.cbord.com
SIC: 7372 5045 Application computer software; computer peripheral equipment; computers
PA: Roper Technologies, Inc.
6901 Prof Pkwy E Ste 200
Sarasota FL 34240
941 556-2601

(G-6832)
CHARLES A HONES INC
222 S Albany St Ste 3 (14850-5480)
PHONE.................607 273-5720
EMP: 5 **EST:** 2013
SALES (est): 300.9K **Privately Held**
SIC: 3291 Hones

(G-6833)
CORNELL UNIVERSITY
Also Called: Cornell University Press
512 E State St (14850-4412)
PHONE.................607 277-2338
Fax: 607 277-2374
Susan Specter, *Editor*
Roger Hubbs, *Controller*
Bonnie Bailey, *HR Admin*
Mahinder Kingra, *Marketing Mgr*
Susan M Kuc, *Marketing Mgr*
EMP: 51
SALES (corp-wide): 2.3B **Privately Held**
SIC: 2731 8221 Textbooks: publishing only, not printed on site; university
PA: Cornell University
308 Duffield Hall
Ithaca NY 14853
607 254-4636

(G-6834)
CORNELL UNIVERSITY
Also Called: Cornell Laboratory Ornithology
159 Sapsucker Woods Rd (14850-1923)
PHONE.................607 254-2473
Fax: 607 254-2415
Richard Adie, *General Mgr*
Todd Pfeiffer, *Facilities Dir*
Michael Mott, *Purch Agent*
Nick Polato, *Research*
Carol Terrizzi, *Comms Dir*
EMP: 20
SALES (corp-wide): 2.3B **Privately Held**
SIC: 2721 8221 Periodicals; university
PA: Cornell University
308 Duffield Hall
Ithaca NY 14853
607 254-4636

(G-6835)
CORNELL UNIVERSITY
Also Called: Agricultrure Biological Engrg
152 Riley Robb Hall (14853-5701)
PHONE.................607 255-0897
Marty Sailuf, *President*
EMP: 5
SALES (corp-wide): 2.3B **Privately Held**
SIC: 2741 2731 Miscellaneous publishing; book publishing
PA: Cornell University
308 Duffield Hall
Ithaca NY 14853
607 254-4636

(G-6836)
DAILY CORNELL SUN
Also Called: Dail Cornell Sun, The
139 W State St (14850-5427)
PHONE.................607 273-0746
Fax: 607 273-0746
John Marcham, *President*
Annie Bui, *Editor*
Nicole Hamilton, *Editor*
Anushka Mehrotra, *Editor*
Maegan Nevins, *Editor*
EMP: 25
SQ FT: 7,020
SALES (est): 1.8MM **Privately Held**
WEB: www.cornellsun.com
SIC: 2711 Newspapers: publishing only, not printed on site

(G-6837)
DNANO INC
Weill Hall 526 Campus 4 (14853)
PHONE.................607 316-3694
Al Biloski,
James P Bailey,
Dan Luo,
Bryan MI,
EMP: 5
SQ FT: 2,500
SALES (est): 250K **Privately Held**
SIC: 2835 8731 In vitro & in vivo diagnostic substances; biotechnical research, commercial

(G-6838)
DOREEN CHRYSLER
Also Called: Auntie Anne's
40 Catherwood Rd (14850-1056)
PHONE.................607 257-2241
Fax: 607 257-2241
Doreen Chrysler, *Owner*
EMP: 12
SALES (est): 577.4K **Privately Held**
SIC: 2052 Pretzels

(G-6839)
F M ABDULKY INC (PA)
527 W Seneca St (14850-4033)
PHONE.................607 272-7373
Fax: 607 277-7106
Fareed M Abdulky, *President*
Fareed Abdulky, *President*
Lamia Abdulky, *Vice Pres*
Don Covert, *Manager*
EMP: 13
SQ FT: 4,000
SALES (est): 1.2MM **Privately Held**
WEB: www.abdulky.com
SIC: 3911 Jewelry, precious metal

(G-6840)
F M ABDULKY INC
Also Called: Buffalo Finishing Company
527 W Seneca St (14850-4033)
PHONE.................607 272-7373
Don Covert, *Manager*
EMP: 6
SQ FT: 2,616
SALES (corp-wide): 1.2MM **Privately Held**
WEB: www.abdulky.com
SIC: 3911 Jewelry, precious metal
PA: F M Abdulky Inc
527 W Seneca St
Ithaca NY 14850
607 272-7373

(G-6841)
FINGER LAKES MASSAGE GROUP (PA)
Also Called: Finger Lakes School of Massage
215 E State St Ste 2 (14850-5547)
PHONE.................607 272-9024
Fax: 607 272-4271
John Robinson, *Ch of Bd*
David Merwin, *President*
Alicia Marshall, *Director*
Angela Neivert, *Director*
Linda Van Almelo, *Director*
EMP: 15
SQ FT: 8,000
SALES (est): 189K **Privately Held**
WEB: www.flsm.com
SIC: 2741 Music books: publishing & printing

(G-6842)
FINGER LAKES STONE CO INC
33 Quarry Rd (14850-8726)
PHONE.................607 273-4646
Fax: 607 273-4692
James Hobart, *President*
Ann Hobart, *Vice Pres*
EMP: 16
SQ FT: 1,000
SALES (est): 1.8MM **Privately Held**
WEB: www.fingerlakesstone.net
SIC: 1411 Dimension stone

(G-6843)
GLOBA PHONI COMPU TECHN SOLUT (PA)
21 Dutch Mill Rd (14850-9785)
P.O. Box 3959 (14852-3959)
PHONE.................607 257-7279
Fax: 607 257-3450
Danqing Kong, *Ch of Bd*
Kelly Smith, *Office Mgr*
Kevin Kong, *Info Tech Mgr*
◆ **EMP:** 29 **EST:** 2013
SALES (est): 7.3MM **Privately Held**
SIC: 3651 Home entertainment equipment, electronic

(G-6844)
GOULD J PERFECT SCREEN PRTRS
Also Called: Psp Unlimited
245 Cherry St (14850-5024)
PHONE.................607 272-0099
Fax: 607 272-0317
Jonathan E Gould, *President*
Jeff Frey, *Vice Pres*
Chris Bilyk, *Sales Associate*
Eric Nichols, *Marketing Staff*
▲ **EMP:** 12
SQ FT: 4,000
SALES (est): 1MM **Privately Held**
WEB: www.pspunlimited.com
SIC: 2759 7389 Screen printing; textile & apparel services

(G-6845)
GRATITUDE & COMPANY INC
215 N Cayuga St Ste 71 (14850-4323)
PHONE.................607 277-3188
Julie Umbach, *President*
Kimberly Griffghs, *Admin Sec*
EMP: 6
SALES (est): 902.4K **Privately Held**
WEB: www.giftsofgratitude.com
SIC: 2621 Specialty papers

(G-6846)
HANGER PRSTHETCS & ORTHO INC
Also Called: Creative Orthotics Prosthetics
310 Taughannock Blvd 1a (14850-3251)
PHONE.................607 277-6620
Fax: 607 257-1802
Thomas Kirk PHD, *CEO*
Robert Frank, *Manager*
Christopher Lange, *Manager*
Sheryl S Price, *Director*
EMP: 10
SALES (corp-wide): 500.5MM **Privately Held**
SIC: 3842 Surgical appliances & supplies
HQ: Hanger Prosthetics & Orthotics, Inc.
10910 Main Dr
Austin TX 78758
512 777-3800

(G-6847)
HENRY NEWMAN LLC
Also Called: Ithaca Ice Company, The
312 4th St (14850-3481)
PHONE.................607 273-8512
EMP: 10
SQ FT: 8,000
SALES (est): 284.7K **Privately Held**
SIC: 2097 5999 Ice cubes; ice

(G-6848)
INCODEMA INC
407 Cliff St (14850-2009)
PHONE.................607 277-7070
Sean Whittaker, *CEO*
James Hockey, *Business Mgr*
Mike Wargo, *Opers Mgr*
Chris Hern, *Engineer*
Andy Jaye, *Engineer*
▼ **EMP:** 47
SQ FT: 30,000
SALES (est): 12.2MM **Privately Held**
SIC: 3444 Sheet metalwork

(G-6849)
INCODEMA3D LLC
407 Cliff St (14850-2009)
PHONE.................607 269-4390
Illa Burbank, *CFO*
Scott Volk, *Director*
EMP: 15
SALES (est): 1.2MM **Privately Held**
SIC: 2759 Commercial printing

(G-6850)
INDUSTRIAL MACHINE REPAIR
1144 Taughannock Blvd (14850-9573)
PHONE.................607 272-0717
Martin J Sullivan, *Owner*
EMP: 6
SALES (est): 150K **Privately Held**
SIC: 3823 Computer interface equipment for industrial process control

(G-6851)
INTERNATIONAL CENTER FOR POSTG
Also Called: Icpme-Ithaca Center
179 Graham Rd Ste E (14850-1141)
PHONE.................607 257-5860
Fax: 607 257-5891
John Leyendecker, *Director*
Kenneth Zeserson,
EMP: 9
SALES (est): 858.6K
SALES (corp-wide): 120MM **Privately Held**
WEB: www.radinfonet.com
SIC: 2721 8741 Periodicals: publishing only; management services
PA: Jobson Medical Information Llc
100 Ave Of Amer Fl 9
New York NY 10013
212 274-7000

(G-6852)
INTERNATIONAL CLIMBING MCHS
630 Elmira Rd (14850-8745)
PHONE.................607 288-4001
Samuel J Maggio, *President*
Carolina Osorio Gil, *Manager*
EMP: 5
SALES (est): 644.5K **Privately Held**
SIC: 3599 Custom machinery

(G-6853)
ITHACA BEER COMPANY INC
122 Ithaca Beer Dr (14850-8813)
PHONE.................607 272-1305
Fax: 607 273-0766
Dan Mitchell, *President*
Pete Browning, *Vice Pres*
Chris Marriott, *Marketing Staff*
Amanda McGonigal, *Office Mgr*
Paul Wagner, *Admin Sec*
EMP: 30
SQ FT: 6,100
SALES (est): 5.8MM **Privately Held**
WEB: www.ithacabeer.com
SIC: 2082 Beer (alcoholic beverage)

(G-6854)
ITHACA JOURNAL NEWS CO INC
123 W State St Ste 1 (14850-5479)
PHONE.................607 272-2321
Fax: 607 272-4248
Sherman Bodner, *President*
John Semo, *Production*
Tad Kilgore, *Manager*
Stephen Miller, *Manager*
Steve Miller, *Manager*
EMP: 50 **EST:** 1815
SQ FT: 6,000
SALES (est): 3.9MM
SALES (corp-wide): 5.7B **Publicly Held**
WEB: www.ithaca.gannett.com
SIC: 2711 Commercial printing & newspaper publishing combined
PA: Gannett Co., Inc.
7950 Jones Branch Dr
Mc Lean VA 22102
703 854-6000

(G-6855)
JOE MORO
Also Called: Moro Design
214 Fayette St (14850-5263)
PHONE.................607 272-0591
Fax: 607 272-0591
Joe Moro, *Owner*
EMP: 5
SALES (est): 170K **Privately Held**
SIC: 3949 Bowling equipment & supplies

Ithaca - Tompkins County (G-6856) — GEOGRAPHIC SECTION

(G-6856)
KIONIX INC
36 Thornwood Dr (14850-1263)
PHONE.................................607 257-1080
Fax: 607 257-1146
Nader Sadrzadeh, *President*
Paul Bryan, *Exec VP*
Timothy J Davis, *Exec VP*
Kenneth N Salky, *Exec VP*
Kenneth Hager, *Vice Pres*
▲ **EMP:** 185
SQ FT: 60,000
SALES (est): 72MM
SALES (corp-wide): 3B **Privately Held**
WEB: www.kionix.com
SIC: 3676 Electronic resistors
PA: Rohm Company Limited
  21, Mizosakicho, Saiin, Ukyo-Ku
  Kyoto KYO 615-0
  753 112-121

(G-6857)
MADISON PRINTING CORP
Also Called: Instant Printing Service
704 W Buffalo St (14850-3300)
PHONE.................................607 273-3535
Angelo Digiacomo, *President*
Molly Digiacomo, *Vice Pres*
EMP: 5 **EST:** 1972
SQ FT: 1,600
SALES (est): 576.9K **Privately Held**
SIC: 2752 Commercial printing, offset

(G-6858)
MAG INC
Also Called: Momentummedia Sports Pubg
20 Eastlake Rd (14850-9786)
PHONE.................................607 257-6970
Mark Goldberg, *President*
Mike Gruppe, *General Mgr*
Eleanor Frankel, *Chief*
Pennie Small, *Business Mgr*
Mike Townsend, *Sales Staff*
EMP: 25
SQ FT: 3,600
SALES (est): 3.6MM **Privately Held**
WEB: www.momentummedia.com
SIC: 2721 Magazines: publishing only, not printed on site

(G-6859)
MCBOOKS PRESS INC
520 N Meadow St 2 (14850-3229)
PHONE.................................607 272-2114
Fax: 607 273-6068
Alexander G Skutt, *President*
Chris Carey, *Vice Pres*
▲ **EMP:** 5
SQ FT: 750
SALES (est): 1.2MM **Privately Held**
WEB: www.mcbooks.com
SIC: 2731 Book publishing

(G-6860)
METTLER-TOLEDO INC
5 Barr Rd (14850-9117)
PHONE.................................607 257-6000
Olivier Filliol, *CEO*
William P Donnelly, *Ch of Bd*
Gerald Liswoski, *General Mgr*
Tom Dorward, *Production*
Carlos Karam, *Research*
EMP: 135 **EST:** 1987
SQ FT: 45,000
SALES (est): 39MM
SALES (corp-wide): 2.4B **Publicly Held**
WEB: www.hispeedcheckweigher.com
SIC: 3596 3537 Weighing machines & apparatus; industrial trucks & tractors
HQ: Mettler-Toledo, Llc
  1900 Polaris Pkwy Fl 6
  Columbus OH 43240
  614 438-4511

(G-6861)
MEZMERIZ INC
33 Thornwood Dr Ste 100 (14850-1275)
PHONE.................................607 216-8140
Bradley N Treat, *President*
Shahyaan Desai, *CTO*
Cliff Lardin, *Director*
EMP: 5
SALES (est): 935K **Privately Held**
SIC: 3679 Electronic components

(G-6862)
MITEGEN LLC
95 Brown Rd Ste 1034 (14850-1277)
P.O. Box 3867 (14852-3867)
PHONE.................................607 266-8877
Robert Newman, *General Mgr*
Benjamin Apker, *Opers Staff*
Stephen Hollabaugh, *Research*
Ben Apker, *Engineer*
Robert E Thorne,
EMP: 5
SALES: 200K **Privately Held**
WEB: www.mitegen.com
SIC: 3844 X-ray apparatus & tubes

(G-6863)
MOTION INTELLIGENCE INC
95 Brown Rd Ste 208 (14850-1294)
PHONE.................................607 227-4400
Richard Uhlig, *CEO*
EMP: 7
SALES (est): 317.8K **Privately Held**
SIC: 3845 Patient monitoring apparatus

(G-6864)
MPL INC
41 Dutch Mill Rd (14850-9785)
PHONE.................................607 266-0480
Fax: 607 266-0482
Shane French, *CEO*
Michelle French, *Ch of Bd*
Bill Lanigan, *Engineer*
Betty Ford, *Manager*
Joanne Underhill, *Admin Sec*
EMP: 39
SQ FT: 7,500
SALES (est): 14.3MM **Privately Held**
WEB: www.mplinc.com
SIC: 3672 Printed circuit boards

(G-6865)
MULTIWIRE LABORATORIES LTD
95 Brown Rd 1018266a (14850-1294)
PHONE.................................607 257-3378
Fax: 607 257-3201
Donald Bilderback, *President*
Bill Hawley, *Business Mgr*
Owen Vajk, *Business Mgr*
Becky Bilderback, *Vice Pres*
▼ **EMP:** 6
SQ FT: 2,668
SALES (est): 855.4K **Privately Held**
WEB: www.multiwire.com
SIC: 3844 3826 X-ray apparatus & tubes; analytical instruments

(G-6866)
NCR CORPORATION
950 Danby Rd (14850-5778)
PHONE.................................607 273-5310
Donald J Moses, *Opers Staff*
Paul Gardner, *Human Res Dir*
Malcom Unsworth, *Branch Mgr*
EMP: 247
SALES (corp-wide): 6.3B **Publicly Held**
WEB: www.ncr.com
SIC: 2752 3577 Commercial printing, lithographic; computer peripheral equipment
PA: Ncr Corporation
  3097 Satellite Blvd # 100
  Duluth GA 30096
  937 445-5000

(G-6867)
NEW SKI INC
Also Called: Ithaca Times
109 N Cayuga St Ste A (14850-4340)
P.O. Box 27 (14851-0027)
PHONE.................................607 277-7000
Fax: 607 277-1012
James Belinski, *President*
Glynis Hart, *Editor*
Andre Hafner, *Prdtn Mgr*
EMP: 30
SQ FT: 2,000
SALES (est): 1.3MM **Privately Held**
WEB: www.ithacatimes.com
SIC: 2711 Newspapers: publishing only, not printed on site

(G-6868)
PERFORMANCE SYSTEMS CONTG INC
124 Brindley St (14850-5002)
PHONE.................................607 277-6240
Greg Thomas, *President*
Jody Schwan, *Finance*
EMP: 50
SQ FT: 20,000
SALES (est): 4.6MM **Privately Held**
WEB: www.pscontracting.com
SIC: 3825 Energy measuring equipment, electrical

(G-6869)
PETRUNIA LLC
Also Called: Petrune
126 E State St (14850-5542)
PHONE.................................607 277-1930
Dominica Brookman, *Mng Member*
EMP: 5
SALES (est): 571.4K **Privately Held**
SIC: 2339 Women's & misses' outerwear; women's & misses' accessories; service apparel, washable: women's

(G-6870)
POROUS MATERIALS INC (PA)
Also Called: Advance Pressure Products
20 Dutch Mill Rd (14850-9199)
PHONE.................................607 257-5544
Krishna M Gupta, *President*
Divya Bajpai, *Engineer*
John Wanagel, *VP Mktg*
Evan Sorel, *Lab Dir*
Sudha Gupta, *Admin Sec*
EMP: 25
SQ FT: 10,000
SALES (est): 4MM **Privately Held**
WEB: www.pmiapp.com
SIC: 3826 Laser scientific & engineering instruments

(G-6871)
PRECISION FILTERS INC (PA)
240 Cherry St (14850-5099)
PHONE.................................607 277-3550
Fax: 607 277-4466
Douglas Firth, *Ch of Bd*
Donald Chandler, *President*
John Morris, *General Mgr*
Paul Costantini, *Vice Pres*
Mike Potter, *Opers Staff*
EMP: 35
SQ FT: 15,500
SALES (est): 6.1MM **Privately Held**
WEB: www.pfinc.com
SIC: 3825 Test equipment for electronic & electric measurement

(G-6872)
PURITY ICE CREAM CO INC (PA)
700 Cascadilla St Ste A (14850-3255)
PHONE.................................607 272-1545
Fax: 607 272-1546
Bruce Lane, *President*
Heather Lane, *Vice Pres*
EMP: 16 **EST:** 1936
SQ FT: 10,000
SALES (est): 1.2MM **Privately Held**
WEB: www.purityicecream.com
SIC: 2024 5143 5812 2026 Ice cream & ice milk; ice cream & ices; ice cream stands or dairy bars; fluid milk

(G-6873)
RHEONIX INC (PA)
10 Brown Rd Ste 103 (14850-1287)
PHONE.................................607 257-1242
Gregory J Galvin PHD, *Ch of Bd*
Richard A Montagna PHD, *Senior VP*
Peng Zhou PHD, *Senior VP*
John Brenner Ms, *Vice Pres*
Tom Karpen, *VP Opers*
EMP: 60
SALES (est): 3.6MM **Privately Held**
WEB: www.rheonix.com
SIC: 3826 Analytical instruments

(G-6874)
RPS HOLDINGS INC
2415 N Triphammer Rd # 2 (14850-1093)
PHONE.................................607 257-7778
David Johnson, *President*
EMP: 22

SALES (est): 2.6MM **Privately Held**
WEB: www.rpsolutions.com
SIC: 7372 Business oriented computer software

(G-6875)
SCHENECTADY STEEL CO INC
234 Durfee Hill Rd (14850-9424)
PHONE.................................607 275-0086
Glenn Phelps, *President*
EMP: 45
SALES (est): 2.3MM **Privately Held**
WEB: www.ssfd.net
SIC: 3441 Fabricated structural metal

(G-6876)
STORK H & E TURBO BLADING INC
334 Comfort Rd (14850-8626)
P.O. Box 177 (14851-0177)
PHONE.................................607 277-4968
Fax: 607 277-1193
John Slocum, *Ch of Bd*
Joseph Walker, *General Mgr*
Ben Tepeek, *CFO*
John Paige, *Accountant*
Debbie M Chadwick, *Human Res Mgr*
▲ **EMP:** 170
SQ FT: 49,046
SALES (est): 44.3MM **Privately Held**
WEB: www.he-machinery.com
SIC: 3511 Turbines & turbine generator sets
HQ: Stork Turbo Blading B.V.
  Kamerlingh Onnesstraat 21
  Sneek
  880 891-290

(G-6877)
THERM INCORPORATED
1000 Hudson Street Ext (14850-5999)
PHONE.................................607 272-8500
Fax: 607 277-5799
Robert R Sprole III, *Ch of Bd*
Rodney Ross, *Purch Agent*
Tim Sullivan, *Engineer*
Valerie Talcott, *Manager*
Richard Grossman, *Admin Sec*
▲ **EMP:** 200
SQ FT: 130,000
SALES (est): 45.2MM **Privately Held**
WEB: www.therm.com
SIC: 3724 Aircraft engines & engine parts

(G-6878)
TOMPKINS WEEKLY INC
36 Besemer Rd (14850-9638)
P.O. Box 6404 (14851-6404)
PHONE.................................607 539-7100
James Graney, *Principal*
EMP: 6
SALES (est): 296.5K **Privately Held**
SIC: 2711 Newspapers

(G-6879)
TPG PRINTERS INC
950 Danby Rd (14850-5778)
PHONE.................................607 273-5310
Stuart Groom, *CEO*
Keith Burlingame, *COO*
Malcolm Unsworth, *Vice Pres*
Rick George, *Dir Ops-Prd-Mfg*
Jim Andres, *CFO*
EMP: 350
SQ FT: 244,000
SALES: 34.5MM
SALES (corp-wide): 34.8MM **Privately Held**
SIC: 3577 Printers, computer
HQ: Tpg Ipb Inc.
  25 Tri State Intl
  Lincolnshire IL 60069
  847 383-7900

(G-6880)
TRANSACT TECHNOLOGIES INC
Also Called: Ithaca Peripherals
20 Bomax Dr (14850-1200)
PHONE.................................607 257-8901
Fax: 607 257-8922
Andy Hoffman, *Exec VP*
Donald Brooks, *Vice Pres*
John Hays, *Vice Pres*
Michael Kachala, *Vice Pres*
Dave Ritchie, *Vice Pres*
EMP: 94

▲ = Import ▼ = Export
◆ = Import/Export

SQ FT: 70,000 **Publicly Held**
WEB: www.transact-tech.com
SIC: 3577 Printers, computer
PA: Transact Technologies Incorporated
2319 Whitney Ave Ste 3b
Hamden CT 06518

(G-6881)
TRANSACTION PRINTER GROUP
108 Woodcrest Ter (14850-6224)
PHONE..................................607 274-2500
Dana Wardlaw, *Principal*
Barry Shaw, *Info Tech Dir*
EMP: 6 **EST:** 2009
SALES (est): 550.7K **Privately Held**
SIC: 2752 Commercial printing, lithographic

(G-6882)
VANGUARD GRAPHICS LLC
Also Called: Vanguard Printing
17 Hallwoods Rd (14850-8787)
PHONE..................................607 272-1212
Steve Rossi, *President*
William Post, *Vice Pres*
Bill Post, *Plant Mgr*
Lynn Hickey, *Purch Agent*
Sophia Darling, *CFO*
EMP: 140
SALES (est): 3.4MM
SALES (corp-wide): 6.4MM **Privately Held**
SIC: 2752 Commercial printing, lithographic
PA: Kappa Media, Llc
40 Skippack Pike
Fort Washington PA 19034
215 643-5800

(G-6883)
VECTOR MAGNETICS LLC
236 Cherry St (14850-5023)
PHONE..................................607 273-8351
Arthur Kuckes, *CEO*
Rahn Pitzer, *President*
Alex Specker, *Engineer*
EMP: 25
SQ FT: 12,000
SALES (est): 4.7MM **Privately Held**
SIC: 3829 Magnetometers

(G-6884)
VYBION INC
33 Thornwood Dr Ste 104 (14850-1275)
P.O. Box 4030 (14852-4030)
PHONE..................................607 266-0860
Lee A Henderson, *Ch of Bd*
Rick Hendrick, *Manager*
EMP: 16
SQ FT: 2,500
SALES (est): 2.6MM **Privately Held**
WEB: www.vybion.com
SIC: 2824 Protein fibers

(G-6885)
WIDETRONIX INC
950 Danby Rd Ste 139 (14850-5714)
PHONE..................................607 330-4752
Jonathan Greene, *President*
Samuel Portnoff, *Engineer*
Chris Thomas, *CTO*
EMP: 5
SQ FT: 300
SALES (est): 762.8K **Privately Held**
SIC: 3674 Semiconductors & related devices

(G-6886)
ZYMTRNIX CATALYTIC SYSTEMS INC
405 Will Hall Crnell Univ (14850)
PHONE..................................918 694-8206
Juan Alonso Succar, *President*
Stephane Corgie, *COO*
EMP: 6 **EST:** 2013
SALES (est): 663K **Privately Held**
SIC: 2869 Enzymes

Jackson Heights
Queens County

(G-6887)
BORNOMALA USA INC
Also Called: Weekly Bornomal
3766 72nd St Fl 3 (11372-6143)
PHONE..................................347 753-2355
Mahfuzur Rahman, *President*
EMP: 5 **EST:** 2015
SALES (est): 83.8K **Privately Held**
SIC: 2711 Newspapers, publishing & printing; newspapers: publishing only, not printed on site

(G-6888)
KARISHMA FASHIONS INC
Also Called: Lavanya
3708 74th St (11372-6338)
PHONE..................................718 565-5404
Shiv Dass, *President*
EMP: 5
SQ FT: 1,500
SALES: 300K **Privately Held**
SIC: 2395 Embroidery & art needlework

(G-6889)
WEEKLY AJKAL
3707 74th St Ste 8 (11372-6308)
PHONE..................................718 565-2100
Jakaria Masud, *Owner*
EMP: 10
SALES (est): 372.1K **Privately Held**
SIC: 2711 Newspapers

Jamaica
Queens County

(G-6890)
A & D ENTRANCES LLC
11090 Dunkirk St (11412-1950)
Rural Route 213-37 39th Ave, Bayside (11361)
PHONE..................................718 989-2441
David L Viteri, *President*
Kimberly Matos, *Manager*
◆ **EMP:** 15
SALES (est): 3.5MM **Privately Held**
SIC: 3534 Elevators & equipment

(G-6891)
ABBOTT INDUSTRIES INC (PA)
Also Called: Woodmaster Industries
9525 149th St (11435-4511)
PHONE..................................718 291-0800
Fax: 718 739-0937
Leonard Grossman, *Ch of Bd*
Jeffrey Grossman, *Vice Pres*
Robert Candea, *Engineer*
Pat Iaonne, *Manager*
Mark Murray, *Executive*
▲ **EMP:** 26 **EST:** 1958
SQ FT: 225,000
SALES (est): 30MM **Privately Held**
SIC: 2499 2541 3089 2542 Woodenware, kitchen & household; store fixtures, wood; plastic hardware & building products; office & store showcases & display fixtures; fryers, electric: household; heating units, for electric appliances; can openers, electric; food mixers, electric: household; miscellaneous fabricated wire products

(G-6892)
ACCORD PIPE FABRICATORS INC
9226 180th St (11433-1427)
PHONE..................................718 657-3900
Fax: 718 657-3549
Harry Schwarz, *President*
Thomas S Bloom, *Vice Pres*
EMP: 35
SQ FT: 40,000
SALES (est): 5.5MM **Privately Held**
SIC: 3498 5051 Fabricated pipe & fittings; pipe & tubing, steel

(G-6893)
AMERICAN STEEL GATE CORP
10510 150th St (11435-5018)
PHONE..................................718 291-4050
Tony Lohay, *President*
Anthony Lohay, *President*
EMP: 6
SQ FT: 3,000
SALES (est): 663K **Privately Held**
WEB: www.americansteelgate.com
SIC: 3442 Rolling doors for industrial buildings or warehouses, metal

(G-6894)
AMERICAN TORQUE INC
10522 150th St (11435-5018)
PHONE..................................718 526-2433
Marsha McCarthy, *President*
EMP: 10
SQ FT: 4,000
SALES (est): 1MM **Privately Held**
SIC: 3566 Torque converters, except automotive

(G-6895)
ATLANTIC PORK & PROVISIONS INC
14707 94th Ave (11435-4513)
PHONE..................................718 272-9550
Jack Antinori, *President*
Ronald Romeo, *Vice Pres*
Susan Antinori, *Treasurer*
Acevedo Genis, *Manager*
EMP: 40 **EST:** 1948
SQ FT: 30,000
SALES (est): 4.3MM **Privately Held**
SIC: 2013 Bologna from purchased meat; ham, boiled: from purchased meat; ham, roasted: from purchased meat; ham, smoked: from purchased meat

(G-6896)
ATLAS CONCRETE BATCHING CORP
9511 147th Pl (11435-4507)
PHONE..................................718 523-3000
Thomas Polsinelli, *Principal*
EMP: 100
SQ FT: 12,000
SALES (est): 9MM **Privately Held**
SIC: 3273 Ready-mixed concrete

(G-6897)
ATLAS TRANSIT MIX CORP
9511 147th Pl (11435-4507)
PHONE..................................718 523-3000
Fax: 718 658-2293
Mary Polsinelli, *President*
Vincent Polsinelli, *Corp Secy*
Tom Polsinelli, *Vice Pres*
EMP: 150
SQ FT: 12,000
SALES: 900K **Privately Held**
SIC: 3273 Ready-mixed concrete

(G-6898)
BAUERSCHMIDT & SONS INC
11920 Merrick Blvd (11434-2296)
PHONE..................................718 528-3500
Fax: 718 276-9021
Fred Bauerschmidt, *Ch of Bd*
Robert Bauerschmidt, *Treasurer*
Patricia Bauerschmidt, *Manager*
Douglas Wefer, *Admin Asst*
EMP: 70 **EST:** 1948
SQ FT: 28,000
SALES (est): 10.7MM **Privately Held**
WEB: www.bauerschmidtandsons.com
SIC: 2541 2431 2521 2434 Office fixtures, wood; cabinets, except refrigerated: show, display, etc.: wood; woodwork, interior & ornamental; wood office furniture; wood kitchen cabinets

(G-6899)
C T M INDUSTRIES LTD (HQ)
22005 97th Ave (11429-1398)
PHONE..................................718 479-3300
Fax: 718 217-4451
Perry Ciarletta, *President*
Martin Silver, *Vice Pres*
Howard Cherry, *Admin Director*
EMP: 30
SQ FT: 1,000

SALES (est): 7.8MM
SALES (corp-wide): 13.6MM **Privately Held**
SIC: 2836 5122 Plasmas; blood plasma
PA: Life Resources Llc
71 S Bedford Rd
Mount Kisco NY
914 241-1646

(G-6900)
CAPITOL AWNING CO INC
Also Called: Capitol Awning & Shade Co
10515 180th St (11433-1818)
PHONE..................................212 505-1717
Fred Catalano Jr, *President*
Steven Rubino, *General Mgr*
Phil Catalano, *Vice Pres*
Ryan Catalano, *Treasurer*
Mike Grosso, *Accounts Exec*
EMP: 18
SQ FT: 8,000
SALES (est): 1.4MM **Privately Held**
WEB: www.capitolawning.com
SIC: 2394 Awnings, fabric: made from purchased materials

(G-6901)
CHEMCLEAN CORPORATION
13045 180th St (11434-4107)
PHONE..................................718 525-4500
Fax: 718 481-6470
Bernard Esquenet, *President*
Marc Esquenet, *Research*
Brian Alexander, *Sales Executive*
Miriam Ramos, *Manager*
Crispin Paul, *Supervisor*
▲ **EMP:** 28 **EST:** 1943
SQ FT: 30,000
SALES (est): 5.9MM **Privately Held**
WEB: www.chemclean.com
SIC: 2842 Specialty cleaning preparations

(G-6902)
CIRCLE 5 DELI CORP
13440 Guy R Brewer Blvd (11434-3728)
PHONE..................................718 525-5687
Yahya Alsaidi, *Principal*
EMP: 8
SALES (est): 455.7K **Privately Held**
SIC: 2051 Bakery, for home service delivery

(G-6903)
CITY MASON CORP
Also Called: Three Star Supply
10417 148th St (11435-4921)
PHONE..................................718 658-3796
Fax: 718 658-6878
Anthony Scaccia, *Ch of Bd*
Frank Landen Jr, *President*
EMP: 15
SQ FT: 20,000
SALES (est): 1.1MM **Privately Held**
SIC: 3272 Concrete products

(G-6904)
CITY POST EXPRESS INC
17518 147th Ave (11434-5402)
PHONE..................................718 995-8690
Robert Swords, *Principal*
▲ **EMP:** 9
SALES (est): 875.4K **Privately Held**
SIC: 2741 Miscellaneous publishing

(G-6905)
CLASSIC COOKING LLC
16535 145th Dr (11434-5108)
PHONE..................................718 439-0200
Andy Reichgut, *President*
Peg Lowell, *Sales Dir*
Julie Gould, *Marketing Staff*
Karen Velazquez, *Office Mgr*
Elliott Huss, *Mng Member*
▲ **EMP:** 100
SQ FT: 40,000
SALES: 15.8MM **Privately Held**
SIC: 2035 2037 2038 Pickles, sauces & salad dressings; vegetables, quick frozen & cold pack, excl. potato products; soups, frozen

(G-6906)
CONCORD EXPRESS CARGO INC
17214 119th Ave (11434-2260)
PHONE..................................718 276-7200

Jamaica - Queens County (G-6907)

Chris Okafor, *CEO*
Maggie Burnes, *Manager*
Margaret Jones, *Admin Sec*
▼ **EMP:** 5
SALES (est): 642.5K **Privately Held**
SIC: 2448 Cargo containers, wood & wood with metal

(G-6907)
CORKHILL MANUFACTURING CO INC
Also Called: Corkhill Grp
13121 Merrick Blvd (11434-4133)
PHONE.................................718 528-7413
Dennis Wugaller, *President*
EMP: 8 **EST:** 1947
SQ FT: 7,000
SALES (est): 1.3MM **Privately Held**
SIC: 3442 Storm doors or windows, metal

(G-6908)
CRS REMANUFACTURING CO INC
9440 158th St (11433-1017)
PHONE.................................718 739-1720
Pratab Angira, *President*
Balkrishna Angira, *Vice Pres*
▲ **EMP:** 10
SALES (est): 920K **Privately Held**
SIC: 3714 Power steering equipment, motor vehicle

(G-6909)
D AND D SHEET METAL CORP
9510 218th St Ste 4 (11429-1216)
PHONE.................................718 465-7585
Jeff Novair, *President*
EMP: 12
SALES (est): 960K **Privately Held**
SIC: 3444 Ducts, sheet metal

(G-6910)
ELMHURST DAIRY INC
15525 Styler Rd (11433-1500)
PHONE.................................718 526-3442
Fax: 718 291-0919
Henry Schwartz, *President*
Joe Kranz, *Vice Pres*
Jay Valentine, *Vice Pres*
Sam Chadwick, *Opers Staff*
Bob Giurco, *QC Dir*
EMP: 208
SALES (est): 67.1MM **Privately Held**
WEB: www.elmhurstdairy.net
SIC: 2026 5143 Milk processing (pasteurizing, homogenizing, bottling); milk & cream, fluid

(G-6911)
EXPRESSIONS PUNCHING & DIGITIZ
Also Called: Expression Embroidery
9315 179th Pl (11433-1425)
PHONE.................................718 291-1177
George Hanakis, *President*
Evelyn Hanakis, *Vice Pres*
Alicia Clarke, *Office Mgr*
EMP: 9
SQ FT: 7,000
SALES (est): 980K **Privately Held**
SIC: 2395 Embroidery & art needlework

(G-6912)
FORTUNE POLY PRODUCTS INC
17910 93rd Ave (11433-1406)
PHONE.................................718 361-0767
Fax: 718 361-1756
Roger Truong, *President*
▲ **EMP:** 14
SQ FT: 25,000
SALES (est): 2.8MM **Privately Held**
SIC: 2673 Plastic bags: made from purchased materials

(G-6913)
FRANCHET METAL CRAFT INC
17832 93rd Ave (11433-1489)
PHONE.................................718 658-6400
Fax: 718 658-5627
Frank Grodio, *President*
EMP: 6 **EST:** 1947
SQ FT: 4,000
SALES (est): 700K **Privately Held**
SIC: 3444 Sheet metal specialties, not stamped

(G-6914)
FRANKLIN ELECTRIC CO INC
17501 Rockaway Blvd # 309 (11434-5502)
PHONE.................................718 244-7744
EMP: 563
SALES (corp-wide): 924.9MM **Publicly Held**
SIC: 3621 Motors, electric
PA: Franklin Electric Co., Inc.
9255 Coverdale Rd
Fort Wayne IN 46809
260 824-2900

(G-6915)
GLEANER COMPANY LTD
Also Called: Jamaican Weekly Gleaner
9205 172nd St Fl 2 (11433-1218)
PHONE.................................718 657-0788
Fax: 718 657-0857
Lolita Long, *Manager*
Sheila Alexander, *Director*
EMP: 13
SALES (est): 754.1K
SALES (corp-wide): 29.5MM **Privately Held**
WEB: www.gleaner-classifieds.com
SIC: 2711 Newspapers
HQ: Gleaner Company (Canada) Inc, The
1390 Eglinton Ave W Suite 2
Toronto ON M6C 2
416 784-3002

(G-6916)
GOURMET BOUTIQUE LLC (PA)
14402 158th St (11434-4214)
PHONE.................................718 977-1200
Fax: 718 977-0200
David Andersen, *General Mgr*
Robert Liberto, *COO*
Robert Stewart, *Opers Mgr*
Hugh Anderson, *Maint Spvr*
Helen Stampfl, *Opers Staff*
▲ **EMP:** 217
SQ FT: 60,000
SALES: 64MM **Privately Held**
WEB: www.gourmetboutique.com
SIC: 2099 Food preparations

(G-6917)
H & H FURNITURE CO
11420 101st Ave (11419-1139)
PHONE.................................718 850-5252
John Hassan, *Manager*
EMP: 5
SALES (est): 330K **Privately Held**
SIC: 2512 Upholstered household furniture

(G-6918)
H G MAYBECK CO INC
17930 93rd Ave Ste 2 (11433-1405)
PHONE.................................718 297-4410
Fax: 718 297-4213
John Arapis, *President*
Chris Arapis, *Vice Pres*
▲ **EMP:** 30
SQ FT: 26,000
SALES (est): 4.2MM **Privately Held**
SIC: 2393 2673 Canvas bags; bags: plastic, laminated & coated

(G-6919)
HILLSIDE PRINTING INC
Also Called: Printing Express
16013 Hillside Ave (11432-3982)
PHONE.................................718 658-6719
Fax: 718 658-4892
Joseph Randazzo, *President*
EMP: 10
SQ FT: 2,000
SALES (est): 1MM **Privately Held**
WEB: www.hillsideprinting.com
SIC: 2752 Commercial printing, offset

(G-6920)
HUDA KAWSHAI LLC ◆
8514 168th St Ste 3 (11432-2624)
PHONE.................................929 255-7009
EMP: 5 **EST:** 2016
SALES (est): 139.9K **Privately Held**
SIC: 2011 Meat by-products from meat slaughtered on site

(G-6921)
IMPLADENT LTD (PA)
19845 Foothill Ave (11423-1611)
PHONE.................................718 465-1810

Fax: 718 464-9620
Maurice Valen, *President*
Virginia Valen, *Vice Pres*
Stephanie Georgi, *Executive*
Gisele Sasson, *Admin Sec*
EMP: 8
SALES: 2MM **Privately Held**
WEB: www.impladentltd.com
SIC: 3843 3069 5047 Dental equipment & supplies; medical & laboratory rubber sundries & related products; dental equipment & supplies

(G-6922)
J SUSSMAN INC
10910 180th St (11433-2622)
PHONE.................................718 297-0228
Fax: 718 297-3090
David Sussman, *President*
Steve Sussman, *Vice Pres*
Robin Sussman, *Manager*
▼ **EMP:** 45 **EST:** 1906
SQ FT: 55,000
SALES (est): 11.4MM **Privately Held**
WEB: www.jsussmaninc.com
SIC: 3442 3354 Window & door frames; aluminum extruded products

(G-6923)
JAMAICA IRON WORKS INC
10847 Merrick Blvd (11433-2992)
PHONE.................................718 657-4849
Fax: 718 526-3450
Robert Pape, *President*
EMP: 10 **EST:** 1927
SQ FT: 2,000
SALES (est): 830K **Privately Held**
SIC: 3446 Fences or posts, ornamental iron or steel

(G-6924)
JONATHAN METAL & GLASS LTD
17818 107th Ave (11433-1802)
PHONE.................................718 846-8000
Fax: 718 847-9397
Wilfred Smith, *President*
Efrain Torres, *Purch Agent*
▲ **EMP:** 70
SQ FT: 6,000
SALES: 47.3MM **Privately Held**
SIC: 3446 Bank fixtures, ornamental metal; brasswork, ornamental: structural; grillwork, ornamental metal

(G-6925)
LITE-MAKERS INC
10715 180th St (11433-2617)
PHONE.................................718 739-9300
John Iorio, *President*
Priya Bery, *Research*
Gary Iorio, *Treasurer*
Paul Davis, *Director*
▲ **EMP:** 30 **EST:** 1974
SQ FT: 12,000
SALES (est): 4.9MM **Privately Held**
WEB: www.litemakers.com
SIC: 3646 Commercial indusl & institutional electric lighting fixtures; chandeliers, commercial

(G-6926)
MACHINA DEUS LEX INC
15921 Grand Central Pkwy (11432-1128)
PHONE.................................917 577-0972
Glen Kieser, *President*
EMP: 6
SALES: 150K **Privately Held**
SIC: 2421 Silo stock, wood: sawed

(G-6927)
MAIA SYSTEMS LLC
8344 Parsons Blvd Ste 101 (11432-1642)
PHONE.................................718 206-0100
Jack Najyb, *President*
EMP: 6
SALES (est): 846.4K **Privately Held**
SIC: 3661 3577 5734 Telephone sets, all types except cellular radio; computer peripheral equipment; computer & software stores

(G-6928)
MARTIN BRASS WORKS INC
17544 Liberty Ave (11433-1391)
PHONE.................................718 523-3146

Fax: 718 523-6631
Aloysia Carl, *President*
Joseph Carl III, *Engineer*
EMP: 7 **EST:** 1954
SQ FT: 2,500
SALES (est): 700K **Privately Held**
WEB: www.martinbrassworks.com
SIC: 3494 3432 Pipe fittings; plumbing fixture fittings & trim

(G-6929)
MAUCERI SIGN INC
Also Called: Mauceri Sign & Awning Co
16725 Rockaway Blvd (11434-5222)
PHONE.................................718 656-7700
James V Mauceri, *President*
Carol Caruso, *General Mgr*
EMP: 18
SQ FT: 14,000
SALES (est): 2.6MM **Privately Held**
SIC: 3993 2394 5999 Signs, not made in custom sign painting shops; awnings, fabric: made from purchased materials; awnings

(G-6930)
METAL WORKS OF NY INC
11603 Merrick Blvd (11434-1825)
PHONE.................................718 525-9440
Fax: 718 525-9462
Vincent Sabatino, *President*
Danny Sabatino, *Treasurer*
EMP: 5
SALES (est): 520K **Privately Held**
SIC: 3441 Fabricated structural metal

(G-6931)
METEOR EXPRESS INC
16801 Rockaway Blvd # 202 (11434-5247)
PHONE.................................718 551-9177
Ning Fang, *CEO*
EMP: 15
SALES (est): 1.2MM **Privately Held**
SIC: 3537 Trucks: freight, baggage, etc.: industrial, except mining

(G-6932)
MINUTEMAN PRESS INTL INC
24814 Union Tpke (11426-1837)
PHONE.................................718 343-5440
Rob Schiffman, *Manager*
EMP: 5
SALES (corp-wide): 22.2MM **Privately Held**
SIC: 2752 Commercial printing, lithographic
PA: Minuteman Press International, Inc.
61 Executive Blvd
Farmingdale NY 11735
631 249-1370

(G-6933)
MONTANA GLOBAL LLC
9048 160th St (11432-6124)
PHONE.................................212 213-1572
Mathieu Goldenberg, *President*
EMP: 5 **EST:** 2013
SALES: 1.4MM **Privately Held**
SIC: 3172 Cases, glasses
PA: Duval, Llc
15929 Jamaica Ave 2
Jamaica NY 11432
718 324-0011

(G-6934)
NEW CLASSIC TRADE INC
17211 93rd Ave (11433-1210)
PHONE.................................347 822-9052
Mustafo Masik, *CEO*
EMP: 6
SQ FT: 1,200
SALES: 1MM **Privately Held**
SIC: 2241 Trimmings, textile

(G-6935)
NEW YORK STEEL SERVICES CO
18009 Liberty Ave (11433-1434)
PHONE.................................718 291-7770
Fax: 718 291-8609
George Cromwell, *Owner*
EMP: 5
SALES (est): 390K **Privately Held**
SIC: 3449 Bars, concrete reinforcing: fabricated steel

(G-6936)
OLYMPIC ICE CREAM CO INC
Also Called: Marion's Italian Ices
12910 91st Ave (11418-3317)
PHONE..................718 849-6200
Michael Barone, *President*
EMP: 50
SALES (corp-wide): 12MM **Privately Held**
WEB: www.marinositalianices.com
SIC: 2024 Ices, flavored (frozen dessert)
PA: Olympic Ice Cream Co., Inc.
12910 91st Ave
Richmond Hill NY 11418
718 849-6200

(G-6937)
PAL ALUMINUM INC
Also Called: Pal Industries
10620 180th St (11433-1828)
PHONE..................718 262-0091
Pana Giotis Mar Neris, *Branch Mgr*
EMP: 23
SALES (corp-wide): 4.3MM **Privately Held**
SIC: 3444 Metal roofing & roof drainage equipment
PA: Pal Aluminum, Inc.
230 Duffy Ave Unit B
Hicksville NY 11801
516 937-1990

(G-6938)
PATI INC
Also Called: Airport Press, The
Jfk Intl Airprt Hngar 16 (11430)
PHONE..................718 244-6788
Fax: 718 895-3432
William Puckhaber, *President*
Thomas Smith, *General Mgr*
Ruben Cruz, *Sales Staff*
EMP: 10
SQ FT: 1,000
SALES (est): 790K **Privately Held**
SIC: 2721 Periodicals: publishing only

(G-6939)
PRECISION READY MIX INC
14707 Liberty Ave (11435-4727)
PHONE..................718 658-5600
Frank Scaccia, *President*
EMP: 6
SQ FT: 700
SALES (est): 500K **Privately Held**
SIC: 3273 Ready-mixed concrete

(G-6940)
PREMIUM SWEETS USA INC
16803 Hillside Ave (11432-4340)
PHONE..................718 739-6000
Babu Khan, *CEO*
EMP: 8
SALES (est): 370K **Privately Held**
SIC: 2064 5145 Candy & other confectionery products; candy

(G-6941)
PREMIUMBAG LLC
14550 Liberty Ave (11435-4828)
PHONE..................718 657-6219
Fax: 718 657-4433
Evelyn Diaz, *Vice Pres*
Richard Schwartz, *Mng Member*
Greta Rubin, *Director*
▲ **EMP:** 8
SQ FT: 15,000
SALES (est): 975K **Privately Held**
SIC: 3949 Bags, golf

(G-6942)
QUEENS READY MIX INC
14901 95th Ave (11435-4521)
PHONE..................718 526-4919
Tony Mastronardi, *President*
Jerry Mastronardi, *Vice Pres*
EMP: 7
SALES (est): 1MM **Privately Held**
SIC: 3273 Ready-mixed concrete

(G-6943)
R & M THERMOFOIL DOORS INC
14830 94th Ave (11435-4516)
PHONE..................718 206-4991
Robby Moyal, *Ch of Bd*
Robbert Moy, *Manager*
Alison Pucorte, *Admin Asst*
EMP: 5
SALES (est): 643.2K **Privately Held**
SIC: 2434 Wood kitchen cabinets

(G-6944)
RAYCO MANUFACTURING CO INC
Also Called: Rayco Manufacturing Div
10715 180th St (11433-2617)
PHONE..................516 431-2006
Fax: 718 626-1163
Sidney L Friedman, *President*
John Iannuzzo, *Treasurer*
EMP: 12
SQ FT: 15,000
SALES (est): 970K **Privately Held**
SIC: 3444 3469 Sheet metalwork; machine parts, stamped or pressed metal

(G-6945)
RAYS RESTAURANT & BAKERY INC
12325 Jamaica Ave (11418-2640)
PHONE..................718 441-7707
Ray Manharalall, *CEO*
▲ **EMP:** 6
SQ FT: 3,100
SALES (est): 320K **Privately Held**
SIC: 2051 Bakery: wholesale or wholesale/retail combined

(G-6946)
REHABILITATION INTERNATIONAL
15350 89th Ave Apt 1101 (11432-3977)
PHONE..................212 420-1500
Fax: 212 505-0871
Tomas Lagerwall, *President*
Leonor Coello, *Office Mgr*
Venus Ilagan, *Manager*
EMP: 5
SQ FT: 4,000
SALES (est): 497.1K **Privately Held**
SIC: 3663

(G-6947)
RENT-A-CENTER INC
11211 Liberty Ave (11419-1813)
PHONE..................718 322-2400
Fax: 718 322-2404
Derrick Williams, *Manager*
EMP: 6
SALES (corp-wide): 3.2B **Publicly Held**
WEB: www.rentacenter.com
SIC: 2519 Furniture, household: glass, fiberglass & plastic
PA: Rent-A-Center, Inc.
5501 Headquarters Dr
Plano TX 75024
972 801-1100

(G-6948)
ROSCO INC (PA)
9021 144th Pl (11435-4227)
PHONE..................718 526-2601
Sol Englander, *Chairman*
Gertrude Englander, *Corp Secy*
Ben Englander, *Vice Pres*
Danny Englander, *Vice Pres*
Joe Ippolito, *Plant Mgr*
▲ **EMP:** 180
SQ FT: 85,000
SALES (est): 44MM **Privately Held*
WEB: www.roscomirrors.com
SIC: 3231 3714 3429 Mirrors, truck & automobile: made from purchased glass; motor vehicle parts & accessories; manufactured hardware (general)

(G-6949)
SKY LAUNDROMAT INC
8615 Ava Pl Apt 4e (11432-2954)
PHONE..................718 639-7070
David Mendoza, *President*
Jay Wright, *Vice Pres*
Herman Mendoza, *Chief Mktg Ofcr*
EMP: 13
SQ FT: 5,000
SALES (est): 660K **Privately Held**
SIC: 2211 7215 Laundry nets; laundry, coin-operated

(G-6950)
SSRJA LLC
Also Called: Five Star Printing
10729 180th St (11433-2617)
PHONE..................718 725-7020
Savithri Somwaru,
Anand Jagessar,
Seelochini S Liriano,
Javier Rojas,
Sandy Shivnarayan, *Assistant*
EMP: 11
SQ FT: 10,000
SALES (est): 3MM **Privately Held**
SIC: 2711 Newspapers, publishing & printing

(G-6951)
STAR MOUNTAIN JFK INC
Also Called: Star Mountain Coffee
Federal Cir Bldg 141 (11430)
PHONE..................718 553-6787
Carmen Ham, *President*
EMP: 5
SALES (est): 350K **Privately Held**
SIC: 2095 Roasted coffee

(G-6952)
STEUBEN FOODS INCORPORATED (PA)
15504 Liberty Ave (11433-1000)
PHONE..................718 291-3333
Len Carruthers, *President*
Kenneth Schlossberg, *President*
Jeffrey Sokal, *Principal*
Bruce Budinoff, *Vice Pres*
David Cantor, *Vice Pres*
EMP: 17
SQ FT: 10,000
SALES (est): 114.1MM **Privately Held**
SIC: 2032 2026 Puddings, except meat: packaged in cans, jars, etc.; yogurt; milk drinks, flavored

(G-6953)
SUGARBEAR CUPCAKES
14552 159th St (11434-4220)
PHONE..................917 698-9005
Louise Torbert, *Principal*
EMP: 8
SALES (est): 315K **Privately Held**
SIC: 2051 Bread, cake & related products

(G-6954)
SUNBILT SOLAR PDTS BY SUSSMAN
10910 180th St (11433-2622)
PHONE..................718 297-0228
Steven Sussman, *President*
David Sussman, *Vice Pres*
EMP: 55
SQ FT: 80,000
SALES (est): 5.7MM **Privately Held**
SIC: 3448 Sunrooms, prefabricated metal

(G-6955)
TEASUREBOX PUBLISHING LLC
11730 Sutphin Blvd (11434-1541)
PHONE..................718 506-4354
Tiffany Johnson, *Partner*
EMP: 5
SALES (est): 380K **Privately Held**
SIC: 2731 Books: publishing only

(G-6956)
TECHNICAL SERVICE INDUSTRIES
Also Called: ABC Casting
17506 Devonshire Rd 5n (11432-2949)
PHONE..................212 719-9800
Mitch Altman, *President*
Michael Hooks, *Vice Pres*
EMP: 27
SQ FT: 3,500
SALES (est): 3.3MM **Privately Held**
SIC: 3911 Jewelry, precious metal

(G-6957)
TEE PEE FENCE AND RAILING
Also Called: Tee Pee Fence & Rail
9312 179th Pl (11433-1426)
PHONE..................718 658-8323
Fax: 718 297-1174
Tom Pendergast, *President*
Jim Pendergast, *Office Mgr*
EMP: 15
SQ FT: 15,000
SALES: 1.3MM **Privately Held**
SIC: 3446 Fences or posts, ornamental iron or steel; railings, prefabricated metal

(G-6958)
THE SANDHAR CORP
16427 Highland Ave (11432-3555)
PHONE..................718 523-0819
Hardev Sandhu, *President*
Shawinder Sandhu, *Vice Pres*
Shyamal N Bastola DDS, *Fmly & Gen Dent*
EMP: 7 **EST:** 1990
SALES (est): 453K **Privately Held**
SIC: 2711 Newspapers

(G-6959)
TRU-ART SIGN CO INC
Also Called: Signs By Sunrise
10515 180th St (11433-1818)
PHONE..................718 658-5068
Lawrence Amatulli, *President*
EMP: 12
SALES (corp-wide): 1.3MM **Privately Held**
SIC: 3993 Signs & advertising specialties
PA: Tru-Art Sign Co. Inc.
187 N Main St
Freeport NY
516 378-0066

(G-6960)
TURBO EXPRESS INC
16019 Rockaway Blvd Ste D (11434-5100)
PHONE..................718 723-3686
Fax: 718 723-5270
Gilberto Rosario, *Principal*
Gilbert Rosaio, *Manager*
EMP: 5
SALES (est): 239.2K **Privately Held**
SIC: 2741 Miscellaneous publishing

(G-6961)
URDU TIMES
16920 Hillside Ave (11435-4435)
PHONE..................718 297-8700
Fax: 718 297-8700
Khalil Ur Rehman, *President*
EMP: 5
SALES (est): 180.5K **Privately Held**
SIC: 2711 Newspapers

(G-6962)
VISUAL EFFECTS INC
15929 Jamaica Ave 2 (11432-6002)
PHONE..................718 324-0011
Thomas Murphy, *President*
Henry Kwitel, *Vice Pres*
Evelyn Viera, *Office Mgr*
▲ **EMP:** 10 **EST:** 1968
SALES (est): 1.5MM **Privately Held**
SIC: 3648 5063 3993 Lighting equipment; lighting fixtures; electric signs; displays & cutouts, window & lobby

(G-6963)
WAYNE DECORATORS INC
14409 Rockaway Blvd Apt 1 (11436-1602)
PHONE..................718 529-4200
Louis Sapodin, *President*
Alex Greenberg, *Vice Pres*
EMP: 8
SQ FT: 2,000
SALES (est): 617.1K **Privately Held**
SIC: 2391 2392 2393 Draperies, plastic & textile: from purchased materials; bedspreads & bed sets: made from purchased materials; pillows, bed: made from purchased materials; cushions, except spring & carpet: purchased materials

(G-6964)
WHITNEY FOODS INC
Also Called: Kissle
15504 Liberty Ave (11433-1038)
PHONE..................718 291-3333
Fax: 718 291-0560
Henry Schwartz, *Ch of Bd*
Kenneth Schlossberg, *Vice Ch Bd*
D Bruce Budinoff, *Vice Pres*
Robert E Braks, *Treasurer*
EMP: 16
SALES (est): 1.3MM
SALES (corp-wide): 114.1MM **Privately Held**
SIC: 2026 Yogurt

Jamaica - Queens County (G-6965)
GEOGRAPHIC SECTION

PA: Steuben Foods, Incorporated
15504 Liberty Ave
Jamaica NY 11433
718 291-3333

(G-6965)
X-TREME READY MIX INC
17801 Liberty Ave (11433-1432)
PHONE.................................718 739-3384
Michael Falco, *Ch of Bd*
EMP: 7
SALES (est): 1MM **Privately Held**
SIC: 3531 Mixers, concrete

Jamesport
Suffolk County

(G-6966)
NORTH HOUSE VINEYARDS INC
Also Called: Jamesport Vineyards
1216 Main Rd Rr 25 (11947)
P.O. Box 842 (11947-0842)
PHONE.................................631 779-2817
Fax: 631 722-5256
Ronald B Goerler, *President*
Ann Marie Goerler, *Treasurer*
▲ EMP: 5
SALES (est): 431.7K **Privately Held**
WEB: www.jamesportvineyards.com
SIC: 2084 Wines

Jamestown
Chautauqua County

(G-6967)
ACCESS ELEVATOR & LIFT INC (PA)
1209 E 2nd St (14701-1952)
PHONE.................................716 483-3696
Sean Fenton, *President*
Michelle Butman, *General Mgr*
Debra Fagerstrom, *Office Mgr*
Norm Klein, *Manager*
EMP: 1
SALES: 1.8MM **Privately Held**
SIC: 3534 Elevators & moving stairways

(G-6968)
ACU RITE COMPANIES INC
1 Precision Way (14701-9630)
PHONE.................................716 661-1700
Fax: 716 661-1888
Thomas Wright, *CEO*
Kenneth Cramer, *Software Engr*
Bob Medsker, *Technical Staff*
◆ EMP: 5
SALES (est): 384.5K **Privately Held**
SIC: 1389 Testing, measuring, surveying & analysis services

(G-6969)
ALL METAL SPECIALTIES INC
300 Livingston Ave (14701-2665)
PHONE.................................716 664-6009
Fax: 716 483-0575
Raymond Anderson, *President*
EMP: 21 EST: 1953
SQ FT: 18,500
SALES: 3MM **Privately Held**
WEB: www.allmetalspecialties.com
SIC: 3446 Architectural metalwork

(G-6970)
ALLIED INDUSTRIAL PRODUCTS CO
Also Called: Allied Industries
880 E 2nd St (14701-3824)
PHONE.................................716 664-3893
Greg Bender, *Manager*
EMP: 6
SALES (corp-wide): 90K **Privately Held**
SIC: 3599 Machine & other job shop work
PA: Allied Industrial Products Co
180 W Olive St
Long Beach NY

(G-6971)
ANDERSON PRECISION INC
20 Livingston Ave (14701-2844)
PHONE.................................716 484-1148

Steven Godfrey, *President*
Jason Carlson, *Prdtn Mgr*
Gene Byrd, *Engineer*
Mike Potter, *Engineer*
Tracy Nelson, *Human Res Mgr*
▲ EMP: 83
SQ FT: 80,000
SALES (est): 22.1MM **Privately Held**
WEB: www.andersonprecision.com
SIC: 3451 3494 Screw machine products; valves & pipe fittings

(G-6972)
ARTONE LLC
Also Called: Artone Furniture By Design
1089 Allen St (14701-2327)
PHONE.................................716 664-2232
Fax: 716 664-1511
Michael Calimeri, *President*
Sebastion Calimeri, *Vice Pres*
Sally Donisi, *Controller*
Victorian Doucette, *Info Tech Mgr*
Lori Crowell, *Admin Asst*
▲ EMP: 85
SQ FT: 240,000
SALES: 9.8MM **Privately Held**
WEB: www.artonemfg.com
SIC: 2521 2522 2531 2541 Wood office furniture; office furniture, except wood; public building & related furniture; wood partitions & fixtures; wood kitchen cabinets; upholstered household furniture

(G-6973)
BELLA INTERNATIONAL INC
111 W 2nd St Ste 4000 (14701-5207)
PHONE.................................716 484-0102
Stephen Pownell, *Principal*
EMP: 5
SALES (est): 536.1K **Privately Held**
WEB: www.bellayre.com
SIC: 2835 In vitro & in vivo diagnostic substances

(G-6974)
BIOPOOL US INC
Also Called: Trinity Biotech Distribution
2823 Girts Rd (14701-9666)
P.O. Box 1059 (14702-1059)
PHONE.................................716 483-3851
Ian Woodwards, *CEO*
Sharon Bell, *Production*
Bonnie D Joy, *QA Dir*
Brendan Fitzpatrick, *Auditor*
Teresa Pirog, *Marketing Staff*
▲ EMP: 48
SALES (est): 8.6MM **Privately Held**
SIC: 2835 In vitro & in vivo diagnostic substances
HQ: Trinity Biotech, Inc.
2823 Girts Rd
Jamestown NY 14701
800 325-3424

(G-6975)
BLACKSTONE ADVANCED TECH LLC
86 Blackstone Ave (14701-2202)
PHONE.................................716 665-5410
Richard Turner, *CEO*
Charles Swanson, *Production*
EMP: 101
SALES (est): 24.7MM **Privately Held**
SIC: 3444 3441 3443 Sheet metalwork; fabricated structural metal; fabricated plate work (boiler shop)

(G-6976)
BLACKSTONE BUSINESS ENTPS INC
100 Blackstone Ave (14701-2202)
PHONE.................................716 665-5410
Fax: 716 665-5152
EMP: 150
SQ FT: 285,000
SALES (est): 28.8MM **Privately Held**
WEB: www.bbei.com
SIC: 3444 Sheet Metalwork, Nsk

(G-6977)
BNO INTL TRDG CO INC
505 Chautauqua Ave (14701-7615)
P.O. Box 97 (14702-0097)
PHONE.................................716 487-1900
Benjamin Okwumabua, *President*
Constance Okwumabua, *Vice Pres*

EMP: 4 EST: 1997
SQ FT: 100,000
SALES: 2.5MM **Privately Held**
WEB: www.bnointl.com
SIC: 3669 5063 Highway signals, electric; signaling equipment, electrical

(G-6978)
BUSH INDUSTRIES INC (PA)
1 Mason Dr (14701-9200)
P.O. Box 460 (14702-0460)
PHONE.................................716 665-2000
Fax: 716 665-2510
Jim Garde, *CEO*
Mike Evans, *Exec VP*
Jerry Green, *Exec VP*
Stephen Phelan, *Exec VP*
Steve Phelan, *Exec VP*
◆ EMP: 234 EST: 1959
SQ FT: 440,000
SALES (est): 187.9MM **Privately Held**
WEB: www.bushindustries.com
SIC: 2511 2521 Wood household furniture; desks, office: wood; cabinets, office: wood; bookcases, office: wood; panel systems & partitions (free-standing), office: wood

(G-6979)
CLARK LABORATORIES INC (DH)
Also Called: Trinity Biotech USA
2823 Girts Rd (14701-9666)
P.O. Box 1059 (14702-1059)
PHONE.................................716 483-3851
Fax: 716 488-1990
Ian M Woodwards, *CEO*
Joe Vacante, *General Mgr*
▲ EMP: 8
SQ FT: 25,000
SALES (est): 14.6MM **Privately Held**
SIC: 2835 In vitro & in vivo diagnostic substances
HQ: Trinity Biotech, Inc.
2823 Girts Rd
Jamestown NY 14701
800 325-3424

(G-6980)
CLARKE-BOXIT CORPORATION
45 Norwood Ave (14701-6564)
PHONE.................................716 487-1950
Donald Zaas, *Ch of Bd*
Joel Zaas, *President*
Mark Cassese, *COO*
John Asimakopoulos, *CFO*
EMP: 5
SALES (est): 223.5K
SALES (corp-wide): 65MM **Privately Held**
WEB: www.boxit.com
SIC: 2652 Setup paperboard boxes
PA: The Apex Paper Box Company
5601 Walworth Ave
Cleveland OH 44102
216 631-4000

(G-6981)
CLEANING TECH GROUP LLC
Blackstone-Ney Ultrasonics
9 N Main St (14701-5213)
P.O. Box 220 (14702-0220)
PHONE.................................716 665-2340
Timothy Piazza, *President*
Alan Atcheson, *General Mgr*
Tony Chapman, *Purch Agent*
William Puskas, *Research*
Dan Limbert, *Engineer*
EMP: 50
SALES (corp-wide): 23MM **Privately Held**
SIC: 3569 3559 Blast cleaning equipment, dustless; degreasing machines, automotive & industrial
HQ: Cleaning Technologies Group, Llc
4933 Provident Dr
West Chester OH 45246
513 870-0100

(G-6982)
CNTRY CROSS COMMUNICATIONS LLC
Also Called: W K Z A 106.9 K I S S-F M
106 W 3rd St Ste 106 (14701-5105)
PHONE.................................386 758-9696
Fax: 716 488-2169

John Newman, *Mng Member*
EMP: 10
SALES (est): 1MM **Privately Held**
WEB: www.1069kissfm.com
SIC: 3663 Radio receiver networks

(G-6983)
CONTAINER TSTG SOLUTIONS LLC
17 Tiffany Ave (14701-1953)
PHONE.................................716 487-3300
Ron Barrett, *Electrical Engi*
Brian Johnson, *Branch Mgr*
EMP: 12
SALES (corp-wide): 1.7MM **Privately Held**
SIC: 2834 Solutions, pharmaceutical
PA: Container Testing Solutions Llc
17 Lester St
Sinclairville NY 14782
716 487-3300

(G-6984)
COPPER RIDGE OIL INC
111 W 2nd St Ste 404 (14701-5229)
P.O. Box 626, Olean (14760-0626)
PHONE.................................716 372-4021
Greg Thropp, *President*
EMP: 8
SALES (est): 950K **Privately Held**
SIC: 1381 Drilling oil & gas wells

(G-6985)
CRAWFORD FURNITURE MFG CORP
347 Broadhead Ave (14701-8163)
P.O. Box 668 (14702-0668)
PHONE.................................716 483-2102
Fax: 716 483-2634
Michael Cappa, *Ch of Bd*
Peter Cardinale, *Manager*
Catherine Cappa, *Director*
Edward Wright, *Admin Sec*
EMP: 250 EST: 1883
SQ FT: 130,000
SALES (est): 24.1MM **Privately Held**
WEB: www.crawfordfurniture.com
SIC: 2511 2421 2448 Wood household furniture; wood bedroom furniture; chairs, household, except upholstered: wood; dining room furniture: wood; sawmills & planing mills, general; pallets, wood

(G-6986)
CUMMINS INC
101-133 Jackson Ave (14701)
PHONE.................................812 377-5000
EMP: 319
SALES (corp-wide): 19.1B **Publicly Held**
SIC: 3519 3714 3694 3621 Internal combustion engines; engines, diesel & semi-diesel or dual-fuel; diesel engine rebuilding; motor vehicle parts & accessories; motor vehicle engines & parts; crankshaft assemblies, motor vehicle; filters: oil, fuel & air, motor vehicle; engine electrical equipment; generator sets: gasoline, diesel or dual-fuel
PA: Cummins Inc.
500 Jackson St
Columbus IN 47201
812 377-5000

(G-6987)
DAWSON METAL COMPANY INC
Also Called: Dawson Doors
825 Allen St (14701-3998)
P.O. Box 278 (14702-0278)
PHONE.................................716 664-3811
Fax: 716 664-3485
Chad Morrison, *General Mgr*
Rick Carlson, *Vice Pres*
Mike Restivo, *Vice Pres*
Dennis Ewing, *Mfg Staff*
Tom Greene, *Mfg Staff*
EMP: 110 EST: 1945
SQ FT: 100,000
SALES: 13.1MM **Privately Held**
WEB: www.dawsondoors.com
SIC: 3444 3442 Sheet metalwork; metal doors, sash & trim; sash, door or window: metal; moldings & trim, except automobile: metal

GEOGRAPHIC SECTION
Jamestown - Chautauqua County (G-7011)

(G-6988)
DOMINION VOTING SYSTEMS INC
221 Hopkins Ave (14701-2252)
PHONE.....................................404 955-9799
John Poulos, *President*
Tonya Rice, *Regional Mgr*
Robert H Cook, *Vice Pres*
Ian Macvicar, *CFO*
Steven Bennett, *Regl Sales Mgr*
EMP: 18
SALES (est): 1.2MM **Privately Held**
SIC: 3579 Voting machines

(G-6989)
EAGLESOME GRAPHICS INC
Also Called: Kwik Kopy Printing
20 W 3rd St Ste 10 (14701-5150)
PHONE...716 665-1116
Fax: 716 661-3329
Melissa Uber, *President*
Sheila Eaglesome, *Vice Pres*
Michelle Camarata, *Treasurer*
EMP: 15
SALES (est): 1.8MM **Privately Held**
SIC: 2759 Thermography

(G-6990)
ECKO FIN & TOOLING INC
221 Hopkins Ave Ste 2 (14701-2252)
PHONE...716 487-0200
Steve Rauschenberger, *CEO*
Lance Rauschenberger, *Vice Pres*
Walter Dunmore, *Manager*
Brenda Nelson, *Admin Sec*
◆ **EMP:** 11
SALES: 1.3MM **Privately Held**
SIC: 3542 Machine tools, metal forming type

(G-6991)
EL GRECO WOODWORKING INC (PA)
106 E 1st St Ste 1 (14701-5499)
PHONE...716 483-0315
Fax: 716 661-3131
George Theofilactidis, *President*
Constantina Kathleen Theofilac, *Corp Secy*
Dimitri Theofilactidis, *Vice Pres*
EMP: 20
SQ FT: 100,000
SALES (est): 1.7MM **Privately Held**
WEB: www.elgrecofurniture.com
SIC: 2511 Wood household furniture; chairs, household, except upholstered: wood; tables, household: wood; dressers, household: wood

(G-6992)
ELECTRIC MOTOR SPECIALTY INC
Also Called: Electric Motor Specialties
490 Crescent St (14701-3828)
PHONE...716 487-1458
Fax: 716 483-2895
William L Allen, *President*
EMP: 6
SALES (est): 645.1K **Privately Held**
SIC: 7694 5063 Electric motor repair; motors, electric

(G-6993)
EMCO FINISHING PRODUCTS INC
470 Crescent St (14701-3897)
PHONE...716 483-1176
Fax: 716 664-6680
Daniel S Alexander, *President*
Barbara L Sheldon, *Admin Sec*
▲ **EMP:** 9 **EST:** 1999
SQ FT: 14,000
SALES (est): 2.1MM **Privately Held**
SIC: 2851 Lacquer: bases, dopes, thinner

(G-6994)
GENCO JOHN
Also Called: S & S Enterprises
71 River St (14701-3806)
PHONE...716 483-5446
Fax: 716 664-6269
John Genco, *Owner*
Jon Scherzinger, *Sales Mgr*
EMP: 6
SQ FT: 21,000
SALES (est): 543.7K **Privately Held**
SIC: 3599 1541 7692 3541 Machine shop, jobbing & repair; dry cleaning plant construction; welding repair; machine tools, metal cutting type

(G-6995)
GRACE WHEELER
Also Called: Superior Bat Company
118 E 1st St (14701-5430)
P.O. Box 3331 (14702-3331)
PHONE...716 664-6501
Grace Wheeler, *Owner*
EMP: 6
SQ FT: 26,000
SALES (est): 513.6K **Privately Held**
SIC: 3949 Baseball equipment & supplies, general; softball equipment & supplies

(G-6996)
GREEN PROSTHETICS & ORTHOTICS
1290 E 2nd St (14701-1915)
PHONE...716 484-1088
Michelle Lohrke, *Opers-Prdtn-Mfg*
EMP: 7
SALES (corp-wide): 1.9MM **Privately Held**
SIC: 3842 5999 Limbs, artificial; artificial limbs
PA: Green Prosthetics & Orthotics, Inc
2241 Peninsula Dr
Erie PA 16506
814 833-2311

(G-6997)
H & H METAL SPECIALTY INC
153 Hopkins Ave (14701-2289)
PHONE...716 665-2110
Fax: 716 665-3481
Paul W Harris Jr, *President*
Bruce W Harris, *Vice Pres*
Donna Bakewell, *Manager*
Thomas Harris, *Executive*
EMP: 21 **EST:** 1953
SQ FT: 15,000
SALES (est): 2.4MM **Privately Held**
WEB: www.hhmetalspecialty.com
SIC: 3498 Fabricated pipe & fittings

(G-6998)
HANSON AGGREGATES NEW YORK LLC
2237 Allen Street Ext (14701-9632)
PHONE...716 665-4620
Scott Wheaton, *Manager*
EMP: 15
SALES (corp-wide): 14.4B **Privately Held**
SIC: 3273 Ready-mixed concrete
HQ: Hanson Aggregates New York Llc
8505 Freport Pkwy Ste 500
Irving TX 75063

(G-6999)
HEIDENHAIN INTERNATIONAL INC (DH)
1 Precision Way (14701-9630)
PHONE...716 661-1700
Michael D Metzger, *CEO*
Gerhard Hagenau, *Vice Pres*
Charles Yeskey, *Purch Mgr*
Chris Bartkowiak, *Engineer*
Jerry Reynolds, *Controller*
▲ **EMP:** 130
SQ FT: 118,000
SALES (est): 11.6MM **Privately Held**
SIC: 3545 3953 3823 3272 Machine tool accessories; marking devices; industrial instrmnts msrmnt display/control process variable; solid containing units, concrete
HQ: Heidenhain Holding Inc
333 E State Pkwy
Schaumburg IL 60173
716 661-1700

(G-7000)
HOPES WINDOWS INC
84 Hopkins Ave (14701-2223)
P.O. Box 580 (14702-0580)
PHONE...716 665-5124
Frank A Farrell Jr, *Ch of Bd*
Brian Whalen, *General Mgr*
John Brown, *Vice Pres*
Mary C Lausterer, *Vice Pres*
Randall P Manitta, *Vice Pres*
▲ **EMP:** 250
SQ FT: 228,000
SALES (est): 62.4MM **Privately Held**
SIC: 3442 Sash, door or window: metal

(G-7001)
HYTECH TOOL & DIE INC
2202 Washington St (14701-2028)
PHONE...716 488-2796
Fax: 716 488-2797
William Swanson, *President*
▲ **EMP:** 8
SQ FT: 6,625
SALES (est): 1.3MM
SALES (corp-wide): 4.8MM **Privately Held**
WEB: www.hytechmold.com
SIC: 3544 Special dies & tools; industrial molds
PA: Hytech Tool & Design Co
12076 Edinboro Rd
Edinboro PA 16412
814 734-6000

(G-7002)
IDT ENERGY INC
315 N Main St Ste 300 (14701-5124)
P.O. Box 400 (14702-0400)
PHONE...877 887-6866
Geoffrey Rochwarger, *CEO*
Alan Schwab, *COO*
Wayne Stoughton, *Vice Pres*
Terrence P Stronz, *CFO*
EMP: 32 **EST:** 2004
SALES (est): 3.1MM **Publicly Held**
SIC: 3679 Power supplies, all types: static
PA: Genie Energy Ltd.
550 Broad St Ste 1700
Newark NJ 07102

(G-7003)
INTERNATIONAL ORD TECH INC
101 Harrison St (14701-6614)
PHONE...716 664-1100
Fax: 716 664-1115
Tammy H Snyder, *President*
Fred Callahan, *Vice Pres*
John Hedman, *Vice Pres*
EMP: 90
SALES (est): 14.1MM **Privately Held**
WEB: www.iotusa.net
SIC: 3469 3398 2874 Metal stampings; metal heat treating; phosphates

(G-7004)
JAMESTOWN ADVANCED PDTS CORP
2855 Girts Rd (14701-9666)
PHONE...716 483-3406
Fax: 716 483-5398
Wendi Lodestro, *Ch of Bd*
Wendi A Lodestro, *Ch of Bd*
Beth Woodward, *General Mgr*
Lee Lodestro, *Vice Pres*
Jon Wehrenberg, *Manager*
EMP: 46
SALES (est): 17.9MM **Privately Held**
WEB: www.jamestownadvanced.com
SIC: 3444 Sheet metalwork

(G-7005)
JAMESTOWN AWNING INC
313 Steele St (14701-6287)
PHONE...716 483-1435
Fax: 716 483-3995
Mark Saxton, *President*
EMP: 9 **EST:** 1964
SQ FT: 5,000
SALES (est): 896.4K **Privately Held**
SIC: 2394 Awnings, fabric: made from purchased materials

(G-7006)
JAMESTOWN BRONZE WORKS INC
174 Hopkins Ave (14701-2290)
PHONE...716 665-2302
Fax: 716 665-2980
Robert R Knobloch, *President*
Wolfgang Michael Dunker, *Vice Pres*
Rexford Knapp, *Foreman/Supr*
▼ **EMP:** 9
SQ FT: 10,000
SALES: 500K **Privately Held**
WEB: www.jamestownbronze.com
SIC: 3369 3363 3479 Nonferrous foundries; aluminum die-castings; etching on metals

(G-7007)
JAMESTOWN FAB STL & SUP INC
1034 Allen St (14701-2302)
PHONE...716 665-2227
Fax: 716 665-5361
Mel Duggan, *President*
Malachai Ives, *Vice Pres*
Dee Higley, *Manager*
EMP: 6 **EST:** 1946
SQ FT: 20,000
SALES (est): 1.2MM **Privately Held**
SIC: 3446 Fire escapes, metal; railings, bannisters, guards, etc.: made from metal pipe; stairs, staircases, stair treads: prefabricated metal; fences or posts, ornamental iron or steel

(G-7008)
JAMESTOWN KITCHEN & BATH INC
1085 E 2nd St (14701-2243)
PHONE...716 665-2299
Fax: 716 665-1178
Donald Proctor, *President*
Andy Proctor, *Vice Pres*
Lora Proctor, *Admin Sec*
EMP: 7
SQ FT: 15,000
SALES (est): 1.2MM **Privately Held**
SIC: 3281 5712 Bathroom fixtures, cut stone; cabinet work, custom

(G-7009)
JAMESTOWN MACADAM INC (PA)
Also Called: Corbett Hill Gravel Products
74 Walden Ave (14701-2751)
P.O. Box 518, Celoron (14720-0518)
PHONE...716 664-5108
Fax: 716 267-7827
Michael Wellman, *Ch of Bd*
Roger R Olson, *President*
Tim Sickles, *Managing Dir*
Thomas Olson, *Vice Pres*
Steve Russo, *Mktg Dir*
EMP: 15
SQ FT: 3,000
SALES (est): 9MM **Privately Held**
WEB: www.jamestownmacadam.com
SIC: 2951 5032 Asphalt paving mixtures & blocks; gravel

(G-7010)
JAMESTOWN MATTRESS CO
150 Blackstone Ave (14701-2204)
PHONE...716 665-2247
James L Pullan Sr, *President*
EMP: 35
SALES: 950K **Privately Held**
SIC: 2515 Mattresses & bedsprings

(G-7011)
JAMESTOWN METAL PRODUCTS LLC
178 Blackstone Ave (14701-2297)
PHONE...716 665-5313
Fax: 716 665-5121
Richard McLeod, *President*
Joanne Cowan, *COO*
Jim Difonzo, *Engineer*
Sam Lamancuso, *Engineer*
Lori Dumaine, *Controller*
▲ **EMP:** 105
SQ FT: 165,000
SALES (est): 30.4MM
SALES (corp-wide): 57.5MM **Privately Held**
SIC: 3821 Laboratory apparatus & furniture; laboratory equipment: fume hoods, distillation racks, etc.; laboratory furniture
PA: Institutional Casework, Incorporated
1865 Hwy 641 North Paris
Paris TN 38242
731 642-4251

Jamestown - Chautauqua County (G-7012)

(G-7012) JAMESTOWN SCIENTIFIC INDS LLC
1300 E 2nd St (14701-1915)
PHONE..................716 665-3224
Bob Trusler, *Safety Mgr*
Kelly Haight, *Facilities Mgr*
Shannon Miller, *Facilities Mgr*
Richard O'Neill, *Sales Mgr*
Duane Smith, *Prgrmr*
EMP: 12
SALES (est): 1.9MM **Privately Held**
WEB: www.jamestownscientific.com
SIC: 3069 Medical & laboratory rubber sundries & related products

(G-7013) JEFFREY D MENOFF
785 Fairmount Ave (14701-2608)
PHONE..................716 665-1468
Jeffrey D Menoff, *Owner*
EMP: 7
SALES (est): 619.4K **Privately Held**
SIC: 3843 Enamels, dentists'

(G-7014) JOHNSON MCH & FIBR PDTS CO INC
142 Hopkins Ave (14701-2208)
PHONE..................716 665-2003
Fax: 716 665-6516
Michael Marshall, *President*
Richard Thorpe, *General Mgr*
Dale L Marshall, *Principal*
Brian Maloy, *Site Mgr*
Joyce Workens, *Manager*
EMP: 15
SQ FT: 11,000
SALES (est): 2.4MM **Privately Held**
SIC: 3599 3541 Machine shop, jobbing & repair; screw machines, automatic

(G-7015) LAKESIDE CAPITAL CORPORATION
Also Called: Dahlstrom Roll Form
402 Chandler St Ste 2 (14701-3890)
P.O. Box 446 (14702-0446)
PHONE..................716 664-2555
Fax: 716 661-3992
Robert G White, *Ch of Bd*
Tom Heppeler, *VP Opers*
Mike Richner, *Mfg Mgr*
Peggy Ambrose, *Manager*
Jessica Keefer, *Admin Asst*
▲ EMP: 21
SQ FT: 73,800
SALES (est): 5.9MM **Privately Held**
WEB: www.dahlstromrollform.com
SIC: 3449 Custom roll formed products

(G-7016) LARSON METAL MANUFACTURING CO
Also Called: Design Craft Division
1831 Mason Dr (14701-9290)
P.O. Box 1182 (14702-1182)
PHONE..................716 665-6807
Fax: 716 665-6007
Melda W Larson, *President*
William E Larson, *Vice Pres*
EMP: 6
SQ FT: 31,000
SALES: 1MM **Privately Held**
SIC: 2522 Office furniture, except wood

(G-7017) MASON CARVINGS INC
101 Water St (14701-6934)
P.O. Box 637 (14702-0637)
PHONE..................716 664-9402
Fax: 716 664-9403
EMP: 8
SQ FT: 18,000
SALES: 350K **Privately Held**
SIC: 2426 Mfg Wood Furniture Carvings

(G-7018) MASTER MACHINE INCORPORATED
155 Blackstone Ave (14701-2203)
PHONE..................716 487-2555
Fax: 716 488-2668
Steven Carolus, *President*
Jean Carolus, *Info Tech Mgr*
▲ EMP: 14
SQ FT: 15,000
SALES (est): 1.4MM **Privately Held**
SIC: 3599 Machine shop, jobbing & repair

(G-7019) MD ELECTRONICS OF ILLINOIS
33 Precision Way (14701-9630)
PHONE..................716 488-0300
Bruce Dudgeon, *President*
Debbie Kennelley, *Manager*
▲ EMP: 77
SALES (est): 15.2MM **Privately Held**
SIC: 3643 Current-carrying wiring devices
HQ: Md Elektronik Gmbh
   Neutraublinger Str. 4
   Waldkraiburg 84478
   863 860-40

(G-7020) MILES MACHINE INC
85 Jones And Gifford Ave (14701-2826)
PHONE..................716 484-6026
Richard Page, *President*
Michael Page, *Vice Pres*
Diane Start, *Office Mgr*
EMP: 6
SQ FT: 5,000
SALES: 588.5K **Privately Held**
SIC: 3599 Machine shop, jobbing & repair

(G-7021) NATIONAL WIRE & METAL TECH INC
200 Harrison St Ste 10 (14701-6969)
PHONE..................716 661-9180
Fax: 716 661-9189
Bump Hedman, *President*
John Hedman, *Vice Pres*
Tammy Snyder, *Vice Pres*
Lucy Hedman, *Treasurer*
Brenda Goodwill, *Manager*
▲ EMP: 25
SQ FT: 80,000
SALES (est): 4.2MM **Privately Held**
SIC: 3469 2392 Perforated metal, stamped; mops, floor & dust

(G-7022) OGDEN NEWSPAPERS INC
Also Called: Post-Journal, The
15 W 2nd St (14701-5215)
P.O. Box 190 (14702-0190)
PHONE..................716 487-1111
Fax: 716 664-3119
Michael Bird, *President*
Chris Murphy, *Editor*
Jamie Hewson, *Business Mgr*
Jim Funcell, *Prdtn Mgr*
Michael Warren, *Mfg Staff*
EMP: 200
SALES (corp-wide): 553.9MM **Privately Held**
SIC: 2711 Commercial printing & newspaper publishing combined
PA: The Ogden Newspapers Inc
   1500 Main St
   Wheeling WV 26003
   304 233-0100

(G-7023) POST JOURNAL
412 Murray Ave (14701-4742)
PHONE..................716 487-1111
Debra Brunner, *Principal*
Adam C Glasier, *Editor*
Scott Kindberg, *Editor*
Matt Spielman, *Editor*
Natalie King, *Cust Mgr*
EMP: 17
SALES (est): 1.4MM **Privately Held**
SIC: 2711 Newspapers, publishing & printing

(G-7024) PRODUCTO CORPORATION
Also Called: Ring Division Producto Machine
2980 Turner Rd (14701-9024)
P.O. Box 490 (14702-0490)
PHONE..................716 484-7131
Newman Marsilius, *President*
Jack Kelly, *COO*
Gregory Timko, *Plant Mgr*
Ron Jorgenson, *Safety Mgr*
John O'Neil, *Purchasing*
EMP: 113
SQ FT: 40,800
SALES (corp-wide): 79.1MM **Privately Held**
WEB: www.ringprecision.com
SIC: 3541 3542 3544 Machine tools, metal cutting type; machine tools, metal forming type; special dies, tools, jigs & fixtures
HQ: The Producto Corporation
   800 Union Ave
   Bridgeport CT 06607
   203 366-3224

(G-7025) ROLLFORM OF JAMESTOWN INC
Also Called: Precision Locker
181 Blackstone Ave (14701-2203)
PHONE..................716 665-5310
Fax: 716 665-4479
Edward F Ruttenberg, *President*
Pat Traniello, *Opers Mgr*
Debby Walsh, *Accountant*
▲ EMP: 17
SQ FT: 43,000
SALES (est): 4.4MM **Privately Held**
WEB: www.rollform.com
SIC: 3449 Miscellaneous metalwork; custom roll formed products

(G-7026) ROYAL JAMESTOWN FURNITURE INC
Also Called: Jamestown Royal
300 Crescent St (14701-3819)
PHONE..................716 664-5260
Peter Johnson, *President*
Kathleen Johnson, *Vice Pres*
Betty Sweet, *Office Mgr*
▲ EMP: 20 EST: 1913
SALES: 1.5MM **Privately Held**
SIC: 2512 5712 2511 Living room furniture: upholstered on wood frames; furniture stores; wood household furniture

(G-7027) SHRED CENTER
428 Livingston Ave (14701-2665)
PHONE..................716 664-3052
Ronald Mazonie, *Owner*
Monica Mazany, *Vice Pres*
EMP: 6 EST: 2008
SALES (est): 525K **Privately Held**
SIC: 3559 Tire shredding machinery

(G-7028) SKF USA INC
402 Chandler St (14701-3890)
P.O. Box 263, Falconer (14733-0263)
PHONE..................716 661-2600
Rolf Jacobson, *Branch Mgr*
EMP: 61
SALES (corp-wide): 8.7B **Privately Held**
WEB: www.skfusa.com
SIC: 3562 3053 3829 Ball & roller bearings; ball bearings & parts; roller bearings & parts; gaskets & sealing devices; oil seals, rubber; vibration meters, analyzers & calibrators
HQ: Skf Usa Inc.
   890 Forty Foot Rd
   Lansdale PA 19446
   267 436-6000

(G-7029) SPARTAN PUBLISHING INC
Also Called: Southern Tier Pennysaver
2 Harding Ave (14701-4778)
PHONE..................716 664-7373
Fax: 716 664-7377
Robert V Stanley, *President*
Sandra Stanley, *Treasurer*
EMP: 12
SQ FT: 4,000
SALES (est): 530K **Privately Held**
SIC: 2711 Newspapers, publishing & printing

(G-7030) SPRAY-TECH FINISHING INC
443 Buffalo St (14701-2262)
P.O. Box 278 (14702-0278)
PHONE..................716 664-6317
Fax: 716 664-6318
David Dawson, *President*
George Fuller, *Vice Pres*
Guy Lombardo, *Treasurer*
Harold Andersen, *Admin Sec*
EMP: 11
SQ FT: 80,000
SALES: 1.1MM **Privately Held**
WEB: www.spraytechfinishing.com
SIC: 2952 Coating compounds, tar

(G-7031) STAR TUBING CORP
53 River St (14701-3806)
P.O. Box 904 (14702-0904)
PHONE..................716 483-1703
Fax: 716 484-8894
Gary F Johnson, *President*
Gary Johnson, *President*
Sandra Johnson, *Vice Pres*
Charles A Lawson, *Shareholder*
EMP: 6
SQ FT: 46,000
SALES: 1.3MM **Privately Held**
WEB: www.startubing.com
SIC: 3498 Tube fabricating (contract bending & shaping)

(G-7032) SUHOR INDUSTRIES INC
Also Called: GM Pre Cast Products
584 Buffalo St (14701-2307)
PHONE..................716 483-6818
Joel Suhor, *President*
EMP: 5
SALES (corp-wide): 2.2MM **Privately Held**
WEB: www.wilbertservices.com
SIC: 3272 Concrete products
PA: Suhor Industries, Inc.
   72 Oconnor Rd
   Fairport NY 14450
   585 377-5100

(G-7033) SUIT-KOTE CORPORATION
57 Lister St (14701-2701)
PHONE..................716 664-3750
Fax: 716 664-3752
George Ginter, *Branch Mgr*
EMP: 35
SALES (corp-wide): 278.7MM **Privately Held**
WEB: www.suit-kote.com
SIC: 2951 1611 Asphalt & asphaltic paving mixtures (not from refineries); highway & street paving contractor
PA: Suit-Kote Corporation
   1911 Lorings Crossing Rd
   Cortland NY 13045
   607 753-1100

(G-7034) SUNSET RIDGE HOLDINGS INC
Also Called: Electric Motor Specialty
490-496 Crescent St (14701)
PHONE..................716 487-1458
Rebecca Ames, *President*
EMP: 5
SALES: 230K **Privately Held**
SIC: 7694 7699 Armature rewinding shops; pumps & pumping equipment repair

(G-7035) SUPERIOR ENERGY SERVICES INC
1720 Foote Avenue Ext (14701-9385)
PHONE..................716 483-0100
EMP: 5 **Publicly Held**
SIC: 1389 Servicing oil & gas wells
PA: Superior Energy Services, Inc.
   1001 La St Ste 2900
   Houston TX 77002

(G-7036) SUPERIOR STL DOOR TRIM CO INC
154 Fairmount Ave (14701-2866)
PHONE..................716 665-3256
Fax: 716 665-3230
Ellen Connell, *President*
Bevan Connell, *Vice Pres*
Tammy Ryder, *Manager*
EMP: 15
SALES: 5MM **Privately Held**
SIC: 3442 Metal doors, sash & trim

(G-7037)
SUPERIOR WOOD TURNINGS
118 E 1st St (14701-5430)
P.O. Box 3341 (14702-3341)
PHONE..................................716 483-1254
Fax: 716 483-1264
Shane Goodwill, *Partner*
Doug Wheeler, *Partner*
EMP: 16
SQ FT: 30,000
SALES (est): 2MM **Privately Held**
WEB: www.superiorwoodturnings.com
SIC: 2499 Carved & turned wood

(G-7038)
TILAROS BAKERY INC
32 Willard St Ste 34 (14701-6937)
PHONE..................................716 488-3209
Robert Tilaro, *President*
Donald Sholl, *Treasurer*
EMP: 7
SQ FT: 1,250
SALES (est): 420K **Privately Held**
SIC: 2051 Bakery: wholesale or whole-sale/retail combined

(G-7039)
TITANX ENGINE COOLING INC
2258 Allen Street Ext (14701-2330)
PHONE..................................716 665-7129
Stefan Nordstrm, *CEO*
Matthew Moore, *President*
Ulf Hellgesson, *Vice Pres*
Mats Hman, *Vice Pres*
Jonas Nilsson, *Vice Pres*
▲ **EMP:** 320
SALES (est): 153.4MM
SALES (corp-wide): 687.3K **Privately Held**
SIC: 3714 Air conditioner parts, motor vehicle
HQ: Titanx Engine Cooling Ab
Klockskogsvagen 9
Solvesborg 294 7
456 550-00

(G-7040)
TYCO SIMPLEXGRINNELL
527 Foote Ave (14701-8206)
PHONE..................................716 483-0079
Michael Vito, *Principal*
EMP: 40
SALES (corp-wide): 954.1MM **Privately Held**
SIC: 3569 Sprinkler systems, fire: automatic
PA: Tyco Simplexgrinnell
1501 Nw 51st St
Boca Raton FL 33431
561 988-3658

(G-7041)
UPSTATE NIAGARA COOP INC
223 Fluvanna Ave (14701-2050)
PHONE..................................716 484-7178
Fax: 716 484-7142
Michael Conklin, *Manager*
EMP: 20
SALES (corp-wide): 775.5MM **Privately Held**
SIC: 2026 0241 5143 Milk processing (pasteurizing, homogenizing, bottling); milk production; dairy products, except dried or canned
PA: Upstate Niagara Cooperative, Inc.
25 Anderson Rd
Buffalo NY 14225
716 892-3156

(G-7042)
VAC AIR SERVICE INC
Also Called: Ameri Serv South
1295 E 2nd St (14701-1914)
P.O. Box 940 (14702-0940)
PHONE..................................716 665-2206
George Carlson, *President*
Tom Beichner, *Vice Pres*
EMP: 11
SQ FT: 4,000
SALES (est): 1.1MM **Privately Held**
SIC: 3563 Tire inflators, hand or compressor operated

(G-7043)
WEBER-KNAPP COMPANY (PA)
441 Chandler St (14701-3895)
PHONE..................................716 484-9135
Fax: 716 484-9142
Rex Mc Cray, *Ch of Bd*
Donald Pangborn, *Senior VP*
Rhonda Johnson, *Opers Mgr*
Ginny Sweet, *Traffic Mgr*
Kory Slye, *Engineer*
▲ **EMP:** 102 **EST:** 2002
SQ FT: 146,000
SALES (est): 20.4MM **Privately Held**
WEB: www.weberknapp.com
SIC: 3429 Furniture hardware

(G-7044)
WILSTON ENTERPRISES INC
Also Called: Industrial Welding & Fabg Co
121 Jackson Ave (14701-2441)
PHONE..................................716 483-1411
Susan L Nilston, *Principal*
EMP: 18 **EST:** 2007
SALES (est): 1.6MM **Privately Held**
SIC: 3441 Building components, structural steel

Jamesville
Onondaga County

(G-7045)
B & B LUMBER COMPANY INC (PA)
4800 Solvay Rd (13078-9530)
P.O. Box 420 (13078-0420)
PHONE..................................315 492-1786
Fax: 315 469-4946
Jeffrey H Booher, *Ch of Bd*
Brent Booher, *Principal*
Brigham Booher, *Principal*
Pat Buff, *Principal*
Gary R Booher, *Vice Pres*
EMP: 80
SQ FT: 300,000
SALES (est): 19.8MM **Privately Held**
SIC: 2448 2421 2426 Pallets, wood; lumber: rough, sawed or planed; hardwood dimension & flooring mills

(G-7046)
CHRISTIANA MILLWORK INC (PA)
4755 Jamesville Rd (13078)
PHONE..................................315 492-9099
Fax: 315 492-6863
Lawrence J Christiana, *President*
Ross Tuzzo Lino, *President*
EMP: 26
SQ FT: 26,000
SALES: 2.5MM **Privately Held**
SIC: 2431 Millwork

(G-7047)
HANSON AGGREGATES NEW YORK LLC
2237 Allen St (13078)
PHONE..................................716 665-4620
Scott Wheaton, *Manager*
EMP: 10
SALES (corp-wide): 14.4B **Privately Held**
SIC: 3241 Natural cement
HQ: Hanson Aggregates New York Llc
8505 Freport Pkwy Ste 500
Irving TX 75063

(G-7048)
HANSON AGGREGATES NEW YORK LLC
4800 Jamesville Rd (13078)
P.O. Box 513 (13078-0513)
PHONE..................................315 469-5501
Dan Meehan, *Vice Pres*
Daniel Meeham, *Vice Pres*
Liz Simmons, *Office Mgr*
EMP: 120
SALES (corp-wide): 14.4B **Privately Held**
SIC: 3273 Ready-mixed concrete
HQ: Hanson Aggregates New York Llc
8505 Freport Pkwy Ste 500
Irving TX 75063

(G-7049)
HANSON AGGREGATES PA LLC
4800 Jamesville Rd (13078)
P.O. Box 310 (13078-0310)
PHONE..................................315 469-5501
Dan Meehan, *Vice Pres*
Mike Cornell, *Purch Agent*
Roger Hutchinson, *Sales Mgr*
Liz Simmons, *Office Mgr*
Gary Eno, *Branch Mgr*
EMP: 20
SALES (corp-wide): 14.4B **Privately Held**
SIC: 1442 1422 Common sand mining; crushed & broken limestone
HQ: Hanson Aggregates Pennsylvania, Llc
7660 Imperial Way
Allentown PA 18195
610 366-4626

(G-7050)
PREMIER HARDWOOD PRODUCTS INC
4800 Solvay Rd (13078-9530)
P.O. Box 434 (13078-0434)
PHONE..................................315 492-1786
Brigham Booher, *Ch of Bd*
Lawrence G English, *President*
Anna Lamb, *Corp Secy*
Jeffrey Booher, *Vice Pres*
Gary Booher, *Treasurer*
EMP: 50
SQ FT: 80,000
SALES (est): 9.5MM **Privately Held**
WEB: www.premierhardwood.com
SIC: 2426 Hardwood dimension & flooring mills

(G-7051)
ROBINSON CONCRETE INC
3537 Apulia Rd (13078-9663)
PHONE..................................315 492-6200
Micheal Vitale, *President*
EMP: 12
SALES (corp-wide): 24MM **Privately Held**
SIC: 3273 Ready-mixed concrete
PA: Robinson Concrete, Inc.
3486 Franklin Street Rd
Auburn NY 13021
315 253-6666

(G-7052)
U-CUT ENTERPRISES INC
4800 Solvay Rd (13078-9530)
P.O. Box 420 (13078-0420)
PHONE..................................315 492-9316
Fax: 315 492-1586
John R Storrier Jr, *President*
Nanette Hildreth, *Admin Sec*
EMP: 22
SQ FT: 8,000
SALES: 2.5MM **Privately Held**
WEB: www.u-cut.com
SIC: 3599 Machine shop, jobbing & repair

Java Village
Wyoming County

(G-7053)
FARRANT SCREW MACHINE PRODUCTS
Gulf Rd (14083)
PHONE..................................585 457-3213
Fax: 585 457-3297
Thomas Farrant, *President*
EMP: 7
SQ FT: 13,000
SALES: 1MM **Privately Held**
SIC: 3599 Machine shop, jobbing & repair

Jay
Essex County

(G-7054)
ADIRONDACK LIFE INC (PA)
Also Called: Adirondack Life Magazine
Rr 9 Box North (12941)
P.O. Box 410 (12941-0410)
PHONE..................................518 946-2191
Fax: 518 946-7461
Barry Silverstein, *President*
Tom Hughes, *Publisher*
Tim S Pierre, *Info Tech Dir*
EMP: 17
SALES (est): 1MM **Privately Held**
WEB: www.adirondacklife.com
SIC: 2721 Magazines: publishing only, not printed on site

(G-7055)
WILLIAM WARD LOGGING
Valley Rd (12941)
P.O. Box 300 (12941-0300)
PHONE..................................518 946-7826
William L Ward Sr, *Owner*
Kathy Ward, *Finance Other*
EMP: 17
SALES (est): 1.2MM **Privately Held**
SIC: 2411 Logging

Jefferson Valley
Westchester County

(G-7056)
GEORGE PONTE INC
Also Called: Gpi Equipment Company
500 E Main St (10535-1100)
PHONE..................................914 243-4202
Fax: 914 243-2380
George Ponte, *President*
EMP: 5
SQ FT: 4,000
SALES (est): 630K **Privately Held**
WEB: www.gpiusa.com
SIC: 3559 5084 Pharmaceutical machinery; materials handling machinery

(G-7057)
LONGSTEM ORGANIZERS INC
380 E Main St (10535-1200)
P.O. Box 22 (10535-0022)
PHONE..................................914 777-2174
Alison Albanese, *President*
Gregery Alabnese, *Vice Pres*
▲ **EMP:** 6
SQ FT: 4,500
SALES (est): 600K **Privately Held**
SIC: 3449 Miscellaneous metalwork

Jeffersonville
Sullivan County

(G-7058)
A S A PRECISION CO INC
295 Jffersonville N Br Rd (12748-5825)
PHONE..................................845 482-4870
Fax: 845 482-4721
Steve Schmidt, *President*
Rich Schmidt, *Vice Pres*
EMP: 6 **EST:** 1961
SQ FT: 6,400
SALES (est): 780K **Privately Held**
SIC: 3826 Analytical instruments

(G-7059)
JEFFERSONVILLE VOLUNTEER
49 Callicoon Center Rd (12748)
P.O. Box 396 (12748-0396)
PHONE..................................845 482-3110
Dawnrenee Hauschild, *Chairman*
EMP: 50
SALES: 498.2K **Privately Held**
SIC: 3713 Ambulance bodies

Jericho
Nassau County

(G-7060)
BAMBERGER POLYMERS INTL CORP
2 Jericho Plz Ste 109 (11753-1681)
PHONE..................................516 622-3600
Steven Goldberg, *President*
Dennis Don, *Exec VP*
Alfonso Garcia, *Vice Pres*
Christine Levy, *Vice Pres*
Paul Coco, *CFO*
EMP: 10

Jericho - Nassau County (G-7061)

GEOGRAPHIC SECTION

SQ FT: 11,000
SALES (est): 963.3K
SALES (corp-wide): 291.2MM Privately Held
WEB: www.bambergerpolymers.com
SIC: 2821 Plasticizer/additive based plastic materials
PA: Bamberger Polymers Corp.
2 Jericho Plz Ste 109
Jericho NY 11753
516 622-3600

(G-7061)
CFFCO USA INC
55 Jericho Tpke Ste 302 (11753-1013)
PHONE 718 747-1118
Fax: 718 747-1119
James Yan, CEO
David Xu, Vice Pres
Juan Lopez, Manager
▲ EMP: 7
SQ FT: 1,800
SALES: 15.8MM Privately Held
WEB: www.cffco.com
SIC: 2499 Fencing, docks & other outdoor wood structural products

(G-7062)
CLOPAY AMES TRUE TMPER HLDNG (HQ)
100 Jericho Quadrangle # 224 (11753-2708)
PHONE 516 938-5544
Ronald J Kramer, CEO
Linda Broering, Administration
EMP: 10
SALES (est): 359.5MM
SALES (corp-wide): 2B Publicly Held
SIC: 3423 3799 3524 Garden & farm tools, including shovels; shovels, spades (hand tools); wheelbarrows; lawn & garden equipment
PA: Griffon Corporation
712 5th Ave Fl 18
New York NY 10019
212 957-5000

(G-7063)
CONTINENTAL KRAFT CORP
100 Jericho Quadrangle # 219 (11753-2702)
PHONE 516 681-9090
Peter J Bogan, Ch of Bd
David Landau, President
Steve Roth, Treasurer
Darlene Moseen, Manager
▼ EMP: 6
SQ FT: 2,264
SALES (est): 998.3K Privately Held
WEB: www.continentalkraft.com
SIC: 2631 Kraft linerboard

(G-7064)
D SQUARED TECHNOLOGIES INC
71 Birchwood Park Dr (11753-2238)
PHONE 516 932-7319
David Delman, President
EMP: 5
SALES (est): 255.5K Privately Held
WEB: www.d2tech.net
SIC: 3949 Exercise equipment

(G-7065)
DARBY DENTAL SUPPLY
105 Executive Ct (11753)
PHONE 516 688-6421
Gary Rosenberg, Principal
Anthony Ricigilano, Vice Pres
John Ostipwko, Associate
EMP: 9
SALES (est): 1.7MM Privately Held
SIC: 3843 Dental equipment & supplies

(G-7066)
ELARA FDSRVICE DISPOSABLES LLC
420 Jericho Tpke Ste 320 (11753-1319)
Rural Route R 28089 Ne, Chicago IL (60673-0001)
PHONE 516 470-1523
Daniel Girnderg, President
Ernesto Grinberg, Chairman
Donna Cherulnik, Vice Pres
Fran Laudicina, Vice Pres

Darci Rodriguez, Vice Pres
▲ EMP: 7
SALES: 10MM Privately Held
SIC: 3089 5113 Work gloves, plastic; bags, paper & disposable plastic

(G-7067)
ELECTRIC LIGHTING AGENCIES
500 N Broadway (11753-2127)
PHONE 212 645-4580
Drew Cohen, Sales Associate
Kim Daley, Sales Associate
Haseena Correia, Branch Mgr
EMP: 28
SALES (corp-wide): 3.8MM Privately Held
SIC: 3646 Commercial indusl & institutional electric lighting fixtures
PA: Electric Lighting Agencies Inc
36 W 25th St Fl 6
New York NY 10010
212 645-4580

(G-7068)
EXCHANGE MY MAIL INC
30 Jericho Executive Plz 100c (11753-1025)
PHONE 516 605-1835
Sal Dipiazza, CEO
Steven Daneshgar, Exec VP
EMP: 15
SQ FT: 2,500
SALES (est): 1.6MM Privately Held
WEB: www.exchangemymail.com
SIC: 7372 Application computer software

(G-7069)
FIRETRONICS INC (PA)
50 Jericho Tpke (11753-1014)
PHONE 516 997-5151
Gail Miller, President
John Moreno, Accountant
EMP: 6
SALES (est): 1.9MM Privately Held
SIC: 3669 Fire detection systems, electric

(G-7070)
HEALTH CARE COMPLIANCE (HQ)
30 Jericho Executive Plz 400c (11753-1098)
PHONE 516 478-4100
Fax: 516 478-6773
Mitchell Diamond, CEO
Benjamin Diamond, President
Sheryl Imada, Counsel
Diamond Benjamin, Vice Pres
Lise Rauzi Chc, Vice Pres
EMP: 21
SQ FT: 5,350
SALES (est): 3.9MM
SALES (corp-wide): 209MM Publicly Held
WEB: www.hccsonline.com
SIC: 7372 Educational computer software
PA: Healthstream, Inc.
209 10th Ave S Ste 450
Nashville TN 37203
615 301-3100

(G-7071)
HS ASSOCIATES CORP
290 Vista Dr (11753-2807)
PHONE 516 496-2940
Harry Sussman, President
▲ EMP: 9
SQ FT: 2,000
SALES (est): 850K Privately Held
WEB: www.cxam.net
SIC: 3679 Electronic circuits

(G-7072)
INTELLICHECK MOBILISA INC (PA)
100 Jericho Quadrangle # 202 (11753-2702)
PHONE 360 344-3233
William H Roof, CEO
John W Paxton, Vice Chairman
Mark Armstrong, Senior VP
Russell T Embry, Senior VP
Lou Gryga, Senior VP
EMP: 31
SQ FT: 5,840

SALES: 7MM Publicly Held
WEB: www.intellicheck.com
SIC: 7372 7373 Prepackaged software; systems software development services

(G-7073)
INTERNATIONAL TIME PRODUCTS
410 Jericho Tpke Ste 110 (11753-1318)
PHONE 516 931-0005
Raymond T D'Alessio, Owner
EMP: 6
SALES (est): 240K Privately Held
SIC: 3172 Watch straps, except metal

(G-7074)
JPM FINE WOODWORKING LLC
103 Estate Dr (11753-2829)
PHONE 516 236-7605
Mitchell Kahn,
EMP: 6
SALES (est): 340K Privately Held
SIC: 3999 Novelties, bric-a-brac & hobby kits

(G-7075)
LIGHTRON CORPORATION
Also Called: Western Synthetic Felt
100 Jericho Quadrangle (11753-2708)
PHONE 516 938-5544
Robert Balemian, President
Allen R Kaden, Vice Pres
Edward Kramer, Admin Sec
EMP: 3
SQ FT: 2,500
SALES: 40.2MM
SALES (corp-wide): 2B Publicly Held
SIC: 3429 3585 Manufactured hardware (general); cold drink dispensing equipment (not coin-operated)
PA: Griffon Corporation
712 5th Ave Fl 18
New York NY 10019
212 957-5000

(G-7076)
LUMIA ENERGY SOLUTIONS LLC
48 Jericho Tpke (11753-1004)
PHONE 516 478-5795
John Lee, CEO
Turab Syed, COO
Syed Turab, COO
EMP: 7
SQ FT: 14,000
SALES (est): 421.5K Privately Held
SIC: 3641 Electric lamps; electric light bulbs, complete; tubes, electric light

(G-7077)
N F & M INTERNATIONAL INC (PA)
131 Jericho Tpke Ste 204 (11753-1017)
PHONE 516 997-4212
Fax: 516 997-4599
Allan Seligson, President
Dean Musi, Vice Pres
▲ EMP: 58 EST: 1965
SALES (est): 15.2MM Privately Held
SIC: 3463 Nonferrous forgings

(G-7078)
NCR CORPORATION
30 Jericho Executive Plz (11753-1057)
PHONE 516 876-7200
Paul Buscemi, Manager
EMP: 200
SALES (corp-wide): 6.3B Publicly Held
WEB: www.ncr.com
SIC: 3571 7622 Electronic computers; radio & television repair
PA: Ncr Corporation
3097 Satellite Blvd # 100
Duluth GA 30096
937 445-5000

(G-7079)
NORTH AMERICAN PIPE CORP
Also Called: Jekerda Sales
420 Jericho Tpke Ste 222 (11753-1319)
PHONE 516 338-2863
Jamie Hebert, Manager
EMP: 10

SALES (corp-wide): 4.4B Publicly Held
SIC: 3354 3084 Pipe, extruded, aluminum; plastics pipe
HQ: North American Pipe Corporation
2801 Post Oak Blvd # 600
Houston TX 77056
855 624-7473

(G-7080)
ORCAM INC
99 Jericho Tpke Ste 2013 (11753-1073)
PHONE 800 713-3741
AVI Gabay, Controller
Rhys Filmer, Sales Mgr
EMP: 10
SALES (est): 468.2K Privately Held
SIC: 3842 Technical aids for the handicapped

(G-7081)
PARKSIDE PRINTING CO INC
4 Tompkins Ave (11753-1920)
PHONE 516 933-5423
William Goldstein, President
Ellen Goldstein, Corp Secy
EMP: 10
SQ FT: 10,000
SALES (est): 1MM Privately Held
SIC: 2752 Commercial printing, lithographic

(G-7082)
PRODUCT STATION INC
366 N Broadway Ste 410 (11753-2000)
PHONE 516 942-4220
Scott Roberts, President
Peter Oliveto, Vice Pres
EMP: 11
SALES (est): 1.1MM Privately Held
SIC: 3613 Distribution cutouts

(G-7083)
ROYCE ASSOCIATES A LTD PARTNR
366 N Broadway Ste 400 (11753-2000)
PHONE 516 367-6298
Joanna Moskowitz, Manager
EMP: 5
SALES (corp-wide): 16.8MM Privately Held
SIC: 2869 3089 2851 2842 Industrial organic chemicals; plastic processing; varnishes; polishing preparations & related products; chemical preparations
PA: Royce Associates, A Limited Partnership
35 Carlton Ave
East Rutherford NJ 07073
201 438-5200

(G-7084)
SATNAM DISTRIBUTORS LLC
Also Called: Lion & Bear Distributors
200 Robbins Ln Unit B (11753-2341)
PHONE 516 802-0600
Bila Singh, Office Mgr
Ann Goerler, Exec Dir
Rachna Sachdev,
EMP: 3
SQ FT: 6,000
SALES: 4.5MM Privately Held
SIC: 2834 Tablets, pharmaceutical

(G-7085)
SC MEDICAL OVERSEAS INC
Also Called: Orfit Industries America
350 Jericho Tpke Ste 302 (11753-1317)
PHONE 516 935-8500
Steven A Cuypres, President
Martin Ratner, Vice Pres
Mark Graniero, Sales Mgr
America Orfit, Executive
▲ EMP: 9
SQ FT: 3,000
SALES (est): 780K Privately Held
WEB: www.orfit.com
SIC: 2821 Plastics materials & resins

(G-7086)
SD EAGLE GLOBAL INC
2 Kay St (11753-2648)
PHONE 516 822-1778
Shaojun Liu, President
EMP: 7
SALES (est): 500K Privately Held
SIC: 2211 Denims

▲ = Import ▼ = Export
◆ = Import/Export

GEOGRAPHIC SECTION

Johnstown - Fulton County (G-7110)

(G-7087)
SJ ASSOCIATES INC (PA)
500 N Broadway Ste 159 (11753-2111)
PHONE.................................516 942-3232
Fax: 516 216-4943
Bruce Joseph, *President*
Owen Drugan, *Controller*
Mark Wachtel, *Manager*
EMP: 25
SQ FT: 3,000
SALES (est): 6.7MM **Privately Held**
SIC: 3559 5065 Electronic component making machinery; electronic parts

(G-7088)
SKD DISTRIBUTION CORP
28 Westchester Ave (11753-1442)
PHONE.................................718 525-6000
Richard Marks, *President*
Bill Stephan, *General Mgr*
Harold Marks, *Vice Pres*
Stanley AST, *Controller*
Richard Mark, *Manager*
▲ **EMP:** 30
SQ FT: 45,000
SALES (est): 4.9MM **Privately Held**
SIC: 3089 3086 Novelties, plastic; plastics foam products

(G-7089)
SPRINGFIELD LLC (PA)
100 Jericho Quadrangle # 340 (11753-2710)
PHONE.................................516 861-6250
Ed Shogan, *CEO*
James C Tennyson, *President*
Lenard Fishman, *Vice Pres*
Aby Snyder, *CFO*
James Tennyson, *CFO*
◆ **EMP:** 25 **EST:** 1998
SQ FT: 5,000
SALES (est): 114.4MM **Privately Held**
WEB: www.springfieldllc.com
SIC: 2221 Broadwoven fabric mills, man-made

(G-7090)
WAGNERS LLC (PA)
366 N Broadway Ste 402 (11753-2027)
PHONE.................................516 933-6580
Harry Tyre, *President*
Donald P Corr, *Senior VP*
Danielle Traietta, *Engineer*
Margaret Keller, *VP Finance*
EMP: 6
SQ FT: 1,500
SALES: 50MM **Privately Held**
WEB: www.wagnerproducts.com
SIC: 2048 Bird food, prepared

Johnson City
Broome County

(G-7091)
DONALD R HUSBAND INC
Also Called: Maine Coil & Transformer Co
1140 E Maine Rd (13790-4002)
PHONE.................................607 770-1990
Fax: 607 729-3019
Don Husband, *President*
Donald Husband, *President*
Edward E Paden, *Principal*
EMP: 8
SQ FT: 10,000
SALES (est): 770K **Privately Held**
WEB: www.mainecoil.com
SIC: 3629 Electronic generation equipment

(G-7092)
GAGNE ASSOCIATES INC
41 Commercial Dr (13790-4111)
P.O. Box 487 (13790-0487)
PHONE.................................800 800-5954
Fax: 607 729-7644
Mary Ann Holland, *Ch of Bd*
William Coak, *Vice Pres*
Michelle Clark, *VP Mfg*
Kim Prentice, *Natl Sales Mgr*
Anthony Burshnick, *Accounts Mgr*
▲ **EMP:** 25 **EST:** 1961
SQ FT: 37,250

SALES (est): 5.3MM **Privately Held**
WEB: www.gagneinc.com
SIC: 3089 5063 Plastic hardware & building products; lighting fittings & accessories

(G-7093)
GANNETT CO INC
Also Called: Gannett NY Production Facility
10 Gannett Dr (13790-2260)
PHONE.................................607 352-2702
Kevin Crane, *Manager*
EMP: 100
SALES (corp-wide): 5.7B **Publicly Held**
WEB: www.gannett.com
SIC: 2741 Miscellaneous publishing
PA: Gannett Co., Inc.
 7950 Jones Branch Dr
 Mc Lean VA 22102
 703 854-6000

(G-7094)
HI-TECH INDUSTRIES NY INC
23 Ozalid Rd (13790-2306)
PHONE.................................607 217-7361
Douglas Gardner, *Ch of Bd*
Douglas P Sterns, *President*
Rob George, *Human Res Dir*
EMP: 28 **EST:** 1999
SQ FT: 8,900
SALES (est): 3.7MM **Privately Held**
SIC: 3444 3599 Sheet metalwork; machine shop, jobbing & repair

(G-7095)
INNOVATION ASSOCIATES INC
530 Columbia Dr Ste 101 (13790-1096)
PHONE.................................607 798-9376
Fax: 607 729-5008
Mary Reno, *CEO*
Joseph Harry Boyer, *Chairman*
Thomas Boyer, *COO*
Joseph Galati, *COO*
Doyle Jensen, *Exec VP*
▲ **EMP:** 150
SQ FT: 18,700
SALES (est): 76.6MM **Privately Held**
WEB: www.innovat.com
SIC: 3559 8711 Pharmaceutical machinery; consulting engineer

(G-7096)
J H ROBOTICS INC
109 Main St (13790-2482)
PHONE.................................607 729-3758
Fax: 607 797-6941
John F Hartman, *Ch of Bd*
Jamie Micha, *Engineer*
Gerald Sensenig, *Engineer*
Clifford Solowiej, *Engineer*
Cindy Warner, *Manager*
EMP: 35
SQ FT: 41,000
SALES (est): 8.8MM **Privately Held**
WEB: www.jhrobotics.com
SIC: 3494 3569 3545 Valves & pipe fittings; robots, assembly line: industrial & commercial; machine tool accessories

(G-7097)
KLEMMT ORTHOTICS & PROSTHETICS
Also Called: Klemmt Orthopaedic Services
130 Oakdale Rd (13790-1758)
PHONE.................................607 770-4400
Marcus Klemmt, *President*
Julie Klemmt, *Principal*
EMP: 8 **EST:** 1965
SQ FT: 3,000
SALES (est): 680K **Privately Held**
SIC: 3842 5999 Orthopedic appliances; prosthetic appliances; orthopedic & prosthesis applications

(G-7098)
KNUCKLEHEAD EMBROIDERY INC
800 Valley Plz Ste 4 (13790-1046)
PHONE.................................607 797-2725
Fax: 607 766-9554
Dave Cobb, *President*
Diane Cobb, *Vice Pres*
Matt Heier, *Treasurer*
Bridget Heier, *Admin Sec*
EMP: 5
SQ FT: 1,500

SALES: 500K **Privately Held**
WEB: www.knuckleheadinc.com
SIC: 2262 5699 2759 2395 Embossing: manmade fiber & silk broadwoven fabrics; customized clothing & apparel; screen printing; art needlework: made from purchased materials

(G-7099)
NORTH POINT TECHNOLOGIES
530 Columbia Dr (13790-3301)
PHONE.................................607 238-1114
Lisa Lee, *Co-Owner*
Richard Wrobleski, *Administration*
EMP: 32
SALES (est): 4.9MM **Privately Held**
SIC: 3625 Industrial controls: push button, selector switches, pilot

(G-7100)
PELLA CORPORATION
Also Called: Pella Window Door
800 Valley Plz Ste 5 (13790-1046)
PHONE.................................607 223-2023
Chris Ward, *Branch Mgr*
EMP: 316
SALES (corp-wide): 1.9B **Privately Held**
SIC: 2431 Windows, wood
PA: Pella Corporation
 102 Main St
 Pella IA 50219
 641 621-1000

(G-7101)
PELLA CORPORATION
Also Called: Pella Window Door
800 Valley Plz Ste 5 (13790-1046)
PHONE.................................607 231-8550
Fax: 607 231-8584
Chris Ward, *Branch Mgr*
EMP: 316
SALES (corp-wide): 1.9B **Privately Held**
SIC: 2431 Windows, wood
PA: Pella Corporation
 102 Main St
 Pella IA 50219
 641 621-1000

(G-7102)
PELLA CORPORATION
Also Called: Pella Window Door
800 Valley Plz Ste 5 (13790-1046)
PHONE.................................607 231-8550
Chris Ward, *Branch Mgr*
EMP: 316
SALES (corp-wide): 1.9B **Privately Held**
SIC: 2431 Windows, wood
PA: Pella Corporation
 102 Main St
 Pella IA 50219
 641 621-1000

(G-7103)
PELLA CORPORATION
Also Called: Pella Window Door
800 Valley Plz Ste 5 (13790-1046)
PHONE.................................607 238-2812
Chris Ward, *Branch Mgr*
EMP: 316
SALES (corp-wide): 1.9B **Privately Held**
SIC: 2431 Windows, wood
PA: Pella Corporation
 102 Main St
 Pella IA 50219
 641 621-1000

(G-7104)
PELLA CORPORATION
Also Called: Pella Window Door
800 Valley Plz Ste 5 (13790-1046)
PHONE.................................607 238-2812
Chris Ward, *Branch Mgr*
EMP: 316
SALES (corp-wide): 1.9B **Privately Held**
SIC: 2431 Windows, wood
PA: Pella Corporation
 102 Main St
 Pella IA 50219
 641 621-1000

(G-7105)
ROB SALAMIDA COMPANY INC
71 Pratt Ave Ste 1 (13790-2255)
PHONE.................................607 729-4868
Robert A Salamida, *President*
▲ **EMP:** 19 **EST:** 1975

SQ FT: 9,136
SALES (est): 4.3MM **Privately Held**
WEB: www.spiedie.com
SIC: 2035 2099 Seasonings & sauces, except tomato & dry; food preparations

(G-7106)
UPSTATE OFFICE LIQUIDATORS INC
Also Called: Upstate Office Furniture
718 Azon Rd (13790-1725)
PHONE.................................607 722-9234
Fax: 607 722-3148
Sylvia J Kerber, *President*
Wayne Kerber Jr, *Vice Pres*
Judy Sarr, *Manager*
▲ **EMP:** 11
SQ FT: 45,000
SALES (est): 1.9MM **Privately Held**
WEB: www.upstateofficefurniture.com
SIC: 2521 Wood office furniture

Johnstown
Fulton County

(G-7107)
ARROW LEATHER FINISHING INC
12 W State St (12095-2104)
P.O. Box 542 (12095-0542)
PHONE.................................518 762-3121
Fax: 518 762-2203
Joseph De Cristofaro, *President*
▲ **EMP:** 50
SQ FT: 18,000
SALES (est): 6.1MM **Privately Held**
SIC: 3111 Finishing of leather

(G-7108)
BENJAMIN MOORE & CO
Union Ave Ext (12095)
P.O. Box 220 (12095-0220)
PHONE.................................518 736-1723
Fax: 518 736-1722
Bob Nowicki, *Plant Mgr*
Denise Hulsaver, *Purch Agent*
Robert Nowicki, *Manager*
Perry Cimo, *Mng Officer*
Ed Vozna, *Maintence Staff*
EMP: 40
SQ FT: 2,403
SALES (corp-wide): 210.8B **Publicly Held**
WEB: www.benjaminmoore.com
SIC: 2851 5198 Paints & allied products; paints
HQ: Benjamin Moore & Co.
 101 Paragon Dr
 Montvale NJ 07645
 201 573-9600

(G-7109)
ELECTRO-METRICS CORPORATION
231 Enterprise Rd (12095-3340)
PHONE.................................518 762-2600
Fax: 518 762-2812
Kenneth Bach, *CEO*
John Fallone, *CEO*
▼ **EMP:** 34
SQ FT: 42,500
SALES (est): 8.3MM **Privately Held**
WEB: www.emihq.com
SIC: 3663 Radio & TV communications equipment

(G-7110)
EMPIRE ARCHTCTURAL SYSTEMS INC
125 Belzano Rd (12095-9755)
PHONE.................................518 773-5109
Paul Lusenhop, *President*
Mike Richards, *General Mgr*
EMP: 35
SQ FT: 40,000
SALES (est): 4.1MM **Privately Held**
SIC: 2541 3442 Store fronts, prefabricated: wood; store fronts, prefabricated, metal

Johnstown - Fulton County (G-7111)

(G-7111)
EUPHRATES INC
230 Enterprise Rd (12095-3338)
P.O. Box 977 (12095-0977)
PHONE.................................518 762-3488
Hamdi Ulukaya, *President*
Besnik Fetoski, *Controller*
Peter Averell, *Maintence Staff*
▲ **EMP:** 87
SQ FT: 44,000
SALES: 34MM **Privately Held**
WEB: www.euphrates.com
SIC: 2022 Cheese, natural & processed

(G-7112)
FAGE USA DAIRY INDUSTRY INC
Also Called: Fage USA Yogurt Mfg Plant
1 Opportunity Dr (12095-3349)
PHONE.................................518 762-5912
Athanasios Filippou, *CEO*
Robert Shea, *Corp Secy*
Spyridon Giantatas, *Vice Pres*
Ioannis Ravanis, *Vice Pres*
Jeffrey Scipione, *Vice Pres*
◆ **EMP:** 265
SALES (est): 100.8MM
SALES (corp-wide): 196MM **Privately Held**
WEB: www.fageusa.com
SIC: 2026 Yogurt
HQ: Fage Usa Holdings
  1 Opportunity Dr
  Johnstown NY 12095
  518 762-5912

(G-7113)
FAGE USA HOLDINGS (HQ)
1 Opportunity Dr (12095-3349)
PHONE.................................518 762-5912
Anthanasios Filippou, *CEO*
David Marino, *Business Mgr*
Ioannis Ravanis, *Exec VP*
Christos Koloventzos, *Treasurer*
Charlotte Gross, *Accounts Mgr*
◆ **EMP:** 5 EST: 2000
SALES (est): 100.8MM
SALES (corp-wide): 196MM **Privately Held**
SIC: 2026 5143 Yogurt; yogurt
PA: Fage Dairy Industry S.A.
  35 Ermou
  Metamorfosi 14452
  210 289-2555

(G-7114)
FALK INDUSTRIES INC
179 Corporate Dr (12095-4062)
P.O. Box 946 (12095-0946)
PHONE.................................518 725-2777
Fax: 518 725-6849
Paul Levine, *Principal*
Kathy Lobel, *Sr Corp Ofcr*
Kathy Loebel, *Director*
▼ **EMP:** 12
SQ FT: 6,000
SALES (est): 1.4MM **Privately Held**
SIC: 3999 Manufacturing industries

(G-7115)
HUDSON INDUSTRIES CORPORATION
Also Called: Milligan & Higgins Div
100 Maple Ave (12095-1041)
P.O. Box 506 (12095-0506)
PHONE.................................518 762-4638
Fax: 518 762-7039
Ron Kormanek, *Branch Mgr*
EMP: 40
SQ FT: 36,025
SALES (corp-wide): 7.2MM **Privately Held**
WEB: www.milligan1868.com
SIC: 2891 Glue
HQ: Hudson Industries Corporation
  271 Us Highway 46 F204
  Fairfield NJ 07004
  973 402-0100

(G-7116)
JAG MANUFACTURING INC
26 Grecco Dr (12095-1067)
P.O. Box 957 (12095-0957)
PHONE.................................518 762-9558
Fax: 518 762-2807

Joseph A Galea, *President*
Kelly L Galea, *Vice Pres*
Christopher Wiltey, *Marketing Staff*
▲ **EMP:** 45
SQ FT: 10,000
SALES (est): 5.2MM **Privately Held**
SIC: 3949 3732 2394 2393 Sporting & athletic goods; boat building & repairing; canvas & related products; textile bags; broadwoven fabric mills, manmade

(G-7117)
KAMALI LEATHER CORP
204 Harrison St (12095-4072)
PHONE.................................518 762-2522
Fax: 518 762-2526
Mark Towne, *Manager*
EMP: 5
SALES (corp-wide): 4.5MM **Privately Held**
SIC: 3199 Boxes, leather
PA: Kamali Leather Corp.
  44 Hillside Ave
  Manhasset NY 11030
  516 627-6505

(G-7118)
LEE DYEING COMPANY NC INC
Also Called: Merrimac Leasing
328 N Perry St (12095-1210)
P.O. Box 100 (12095-0100)
PHONE.................................518 736-5232
Morris Evans, *President*
John Henley, *Manager*
EMP: 10
SQ FT: 76,063
SALES (est): 1.3MM **Privately Held**
WEB: www.leedyeing.com
SIC: 2261 Embossing cotton broadwoven fabrics

(G-7119)
PEACEFUL VALLEY MAPLE FARM (PA)
116 Lagrange Rd (12095-4031)
PHONE.................................518 762-0491
Stephen M Savage, *Owner*
Barbara Kirk, *Manager*
EMP: 5
SALES: 100K **Privately Held**
SIC: 2099 Maple syrup

(G-7120)
PEARL LEATHER FINISHERS INC
11 Industrial Pkwy 21 (12095-1046)
PHONE.................................518 762-4543
Fax: 518 762-2898
Carmen F Ruggiero, *CEO*
Chuck Frascatore, *Plant Mgr*
Harry Downing, *Associate*
▲ **EMP:** 95
SQ FT: 20,000
SALES (est): 12.3MM **Privately Held**
WEB: www.pearlleather.com
SIC: 3111 Leather tanning & finishing

(G-7121)
PEARL MEADOW STABLES INC
11 Industrial Pkwy 21 (12095-1046)
P.O. Box 709 (12095-0709)
PHONE.................................518 762-7733
Carmen Ruggiero, *CEO*
John Ruggiero, *President*
Susan Johnson, *Vice Pres*
▲ **EMP:** 150
SQ FT: 120,000
SALES (est): 11.8MM **Privately Held**
SIC: 3111 Finishing of leather; upholstery leather

(G-7122)
PIONEER WINDOW HOLDINGS INC
200 Union Ave Ext (12095-3336)
P.O. Box 70 (12095-0070)
PHONE.................................518 762-5526
Fax: 518 762-5527
Vincent Amato, *President*
Barbara Amato, *Vice Pres*
Robert Bridge, *Purchasing*
Joseph Boltzer, *Manager*
Ian Chan, *Manager*
EMP: 50

SALES (corp-wide): 15.1MM **Privately Held**
WEB: www.pwindows.com
SIC: 3442 3354 Storm doors or windows, metal; aluminum extruded products
PA: Pioneer Window Holdings, Inc.
  15 Frederick Pl
  Hicksville NY 11801
  516 822-7000

(G-7123)
R H CROWN CO INC
100 N Market St (12095-2126)
PHONE.................................518 762-4589
Fax: 518 762-4478
Michael Gray, *President*
Richard Reynolds, *Exec VP*
EMP: 30
SQ FT: 58,000
SALES (est): 9.6MM **Privately Held**
SIC: 2911 7349 Oils, lubricating; janitorial service, contract basis

(G-7124)
READYJET TECHNICAL SVCS INC
1 Warren St (12095-2009)
PHONE.................................518 705-4019
Mark Farrington, *CEO*
EMP: 15
SQ FT: 13,000
SALES (est): 200K **Privately Held**
SIC: 2531 Seats, aircraft

(G-7125)
SAMCO LLC
308 W Main St (12095-2303)
PHONE.................................518 725-4705
Fax: 518 725-4705
Tobin Cash, *Accountant*
Richard Warner,
EMP: 50
SQ FT: 30,000
SALES (est): 4MM **Privately Held**
SIC: 3151 Leather gloves & mittens; gloves, leather: dress or semidress; gloves, leather: work

(G-7126)
SILK SCREEN ART INC
1 School St (12095-2198)
PHONE.................................518 762-8423
Fax: 518 736-1110
David P Sponenberg, *President*
Guy B Sponenberg, *Vice Pres*
EMP: 12
SQ FT: 20,000
SALES (est): 870K **Privately Held**
SIC: 2759 Screen printing

(G-7127)
SIMCO LEATHER CORPORATION
99 Pleasant Ave (12095-1720)
P.O. Box 509 (12095-0509)
PHONE.................................518 762-7100
Fax: 518 762-1514
Gerald Simek, *President*
▲ **EMP:** 20
SQ FT: 45,000
SALES (est): 3MM **Privately Held**
SIC: 3111 Tanneries, leather

(G-7128)
SPRAY NINE CORPORATION
309 W Montgomery St (12095-2435)
PHONE.................................800 477-7299
Greg Mostooler, *General Mgr*
Mary Shippee, *Asst Controller*
Amy Yackbucci, *Accounting Mgr*
Stanley Banovic, *Manager*
Jack Case, *MIS Mgr*
EMP: 80
SQ FT: 82,000
SALES (est): 13.1MM **Privately Held**
WEB: www.spraynine.com
SIC: 2842 Specialty cleaning preparations

(G-7129)
STEPHEN A MANOOGIAN INC
Also Called: Pioneer Tanning Equipment
12 Industrial Pkwy (12095-1045)
PHONE.................................518 762-2525
Fax: 518 762-2935
Stephen Manoogian, *President*
Patricia Arata, *Vice Pres*

James Senzio, *Treasurer*
EMP: 5
SQ FT: 14,000
SALES (est): 470K **Privately Held**
SIC: 3559 3599 Leather working machinery; machine shop, jobbing & repair

Jordan
Onondaga County

(G-7130)
OMEGA WIRE INC
Also Called: Bare Wire Div
24 N Beaver St (13080-9531)
PHONE.................................315 689-7115
Fax: 315 689-1080
C Knapp, *Manager*
EMP: 90
SALES (corp-wide): 442.1MM **Privately Held**
WEB: www.omegawire.com
SIC: 3351 3366 3315 Wire, copper & copper alloy; copper foundries; steel wire & related products
HQ: Omega Wire Inc,
  12 Masonic Ave
  Camden NY 13316
  315 245-3800

(G-7131)
WECARE ORGANICS LLC
9293 Bonta Bridge Rd (13080-9430)
PHONE.................................315 689-1937
Jeffrey Leblanc, *President*
Brad Leyburn, *Sales Staff*
EMP: 33
SALES (est): 12.7MM **Privately Held**
SIC: 2869 Plasticizers, organic: cyclic & acyclic

Jordanville
Herkimer County

(G-7132)
HANSON AGGREGATES PA INC
237 Kingdom Rd (13361-2603)
PHONE.................................315 858-1100
Kevin Smith, *Superintendent*
William Scherer, *Plant Mgr*
EMP: 30
SQ FT: 2,944
SALES (corp-wide): 14.4B **Privately Held**
SIC: 1442 1422 Common sand mining; crushed & broken limestone
HQ: Hanson Aggregates Pennsylvania, Llc
  7660 Imperial Way
  Allentown PA 18195
  610 366-4626

Katonah
Westchester County

(G-7133)
NOVA PACKAGING LTD INC
7 Sunrise Ave (10536-2301)
P.O. Box 785, Goldens Bridge (10526-0785)
PHONE.................................914 232-8406
Fax: 914 232-8968
Greg Scott, *President*
EMP: 37
SALES (est): 5.5MM **Privately Held**
SIC: 2671 3081 2673 Packaging paper & plastics film, coated & laminated; unsupported plastics film & sheet; bags: plastic, laminated & coated

(G-7134)
US AUTHENTIC LLC
11 Mt Holly Rd E (10536-2400)
PHONE.................................914 767-0295
Shaul Dover, *Mng Member*
▲ **EMP:** 6 EST: 2000
SQ FT: 4,000
SALES (est): 639.8K **Privately Held**
WEB: www.flightjacket.com
SIC: 2386 Garments, sheep-lined

▲ = Import ▼ = Export
◆ = Import/Export

(G-7135)
WORDWISE INC
1 Brady Ln (10536-2503)
PHONE..................................914 232-5366
Karen Gotimer, *CEO*
EMP: 3
SALES (est): 1.8MM **Privately Held**
WEB: www.wordwiseinc.com
SIC: 2731 Textbooks: publishing only, not printed on site

Kauneonga Lake
Sullivan County

(G-7136)
B H M METAL PRODUCTS CO
Horseshoe Lake Rd (12749)
P.O. Box 76, Mongaup Valley (12762-0076)
PHONE..................................845 292-5297
Robert Gordon, *Owner*
EMP: 6 EST: 1947
SQ FT: 15,000
SALES: 100K **Privately Held**
SIC: 3469 3441 3312 3679 Metal stampings; fabricated structural metal; tool & die steel & alloys; electronic circuits

Keeseville
Clinton County

(G-7137)
ESSEX BOX & PALLET CO INC
49 Industrial Park Rd (12944-2936)
PHONE..................................518 834-7279
Fax: 518 834-9156
Michael Lemza, *President*
EMP: 22
SQ FT: 19,000
SALES (est): 3MM **Privately Held**
WEB: www.essexboxandpallet.com
SIC: 2449 2448 2499 Wood containers; pallets, wood; handles, poles, dowels & stakes: wood

(G-7138)
INTERNATIONAL MTLS & SUPS INC
56 Industrial Park Rd (12944-2937)
PHONE..................................518 834-9899
David Kruse, *President*
John Burns, *Vice Pres*
Martin Caouette, *Vice Pres*
Jeffrey Kinblom, *Vice Pres*
David Rumble, *Vice Pres*
▼ **EMP:** 5 EST: 2001
SALES (est): 661.6K
SALES (corp-wide): 1.2B **Privately Held**
SIC: 2869 Industrial organic chemicals
HQ: Virginia Materials Inc.
3306 Peterson St
Norfolk VA 23509

(G-7139)
LOREMANSS EMBROIDERY ENGRAV
Also Called: Loreman's
1599 Route 9 (12944-2848)
P.O. Box 546 (12944-0546)
PHONE..................................518 834-9205
Fax: 518 834-9001
Jim Reisdorf, *Sales Staff*
Thomas H Loreman, *Mng Member*
Donald Loreman Sr,
EMP: 12
SQ FT: 7,000
SALES: 1.7MM **Privately Held**
WEB: www.loremans.com
SIC: 2261 2759 7389 2395 Screen printing of cotton broadwoven fabrics; screen printing; engraving service; embroidery & art needlework; automotive & apparel trimmings

(G-7140)
MURRAY LOGGING LLC
1535 Route 9 (12944-2848)
PHONE..................................518 834-7372
Fax: 518 834-7768
Robert Murray,
James Murray,
EMP: 5
SALES (est): 400.7K **Privately Held**
SIC: 2411 Logging

(G-7141)
P H GUCKER INC
419 Frontage Rd (12944-2809)
PHONE..................................518 834-9501
Peter H Gucker, *President*
EMP: 8
SQ FT: 3,000
SALES: 2.2MM **Privately Held**
SIC: 2411 Logging camps & contractors

(G-7142)
UPSTATE RECORDS MANAGEMENT LLC
1729 Front St (12944-3620)
PHONE..................................518 834-1144
Barbara Davidson,
Barbara M Davidson,
EMP: 5
SALES: 125K **Privately Held**
SIC: 7372 Prepackaged software

Kendall
Orleans County

(G-7143)
DMD MACHINING TECHNOLOGY INC
17231 Roosevelt Hwy (14476-9762)
PHONE..................................585 659-8180
David Hofer, *President*
EMP: 5
SALES: 250K **Privately Held**
SIC: 3599 Machine & other job shop work

(G-7144)
NORTHEAST WATER SYSTEMS LLC
2338 W Kendall Rd (14476-9786)
PHONE..................................585 943-9225
Daniel Halling, *Owner*
EMP: 6
SALES (est): 500K **Privately Held**
WEB: www.northeastwatersystems.com
SIC: 3589 Sewage & water treatment equipment

Kenmore
Erie County

(G-7145)
ARMENTO INCORPORATED
Also Called: Armento Architectural Arts
1011 Military Rd (14217-2225)
P.O. Box 39, Buffalo (14217-0039)
PHONE..................................716 875-2423
Fax: 716 875-8010
Robert W Pierce, *President*
Douglas Knox, *Exec Dir*
EMP: 6 EST: 1946
SQ FT: 5,000
SALES (est): 1MM **Privately Held**
SIC: 3446 Architectural metalwork; ornamental metalwork

(G-7146)
DENNYS DRIVE SHAFT SERVICE
1189 Military Rd (14217-1845)
PHONE..................................716 875-6640
Dennis Bringhurst, *President*
Mary Bringhurst, *Vice Pres*
EMP: 8
SALES (est): 1MM **Privately Held**
WEB: www.dennysdriveshaft.com
SIC: 3714 7538 Drive shafts, motor vehicle; general automotive repair shops

(G-7147)
HARGRAVE DEVELOPMENT
Also Called: Hargraves Bus MGT Consulting
84 Shepard Ave (14217-1914)
PHONE..................................716 877-7880
Lawrence Tanner, *Owner*
Lloyd Tanner, *Principal*
EMP: 15

SALES (est): 597.2K **Privately Held**
SIC: 1499 8742 Miscellaneous nonmetallic minerals; business consultant

(G-7148)
HERRMANN GROUP LLC
Also Called: Identity Ink & Custom Tee
2320 Elmwood Ave (14217-2645)
PHONE..................................716 876-9798
Fax: 716 876-9684
William Herrmann,
EMP: 5
SALES (est): 355.8K **Privately Held**
SIC: 2759 3552 3949 5136 Screen printing; embroidery machines; sporting & athletic goods; men's & boys' clothing; clothing, sportswear, men's & boys'

(G-7149)
HORACE J METZ
Also Called: Insty Trints
2385 Elmwood Ave (14217-2648)
PHONE..................................716 873-9103
Horace J Metz, *Owner*
Jim Metz, *Manager*
EMP: 7 EST: 1976
SALES (est): 311.4K **Privately Held**
SIC: 2759 Commercial printing

(G-7150)
KEN-TON OPEN MRI PC
2882 Elmwood Ave (14217-1325)
PHONE..................................716 876-7000
Fax: 716 876-7447
Joseph Serghany, *Ch of Bd*
Dr H Chen Park, *Principal*
EMP: 7
SALES (est): 670K **Privately Held**
SIC: 3841 8071 2835 Diagnostic apparatus, medical; testing laboratories; in vivo diagnostics

(G-7151)
W H JONES & SON INC
1208 Military Rd (14217-1833)
PHONE..................................716 875-8233
Elizabeth Jones, *Ch of Bd*
W Todd Jones, *President*
Kevin B Jones, *Vice Pres*
Peter W Jones, *Vice Pres*
EMP: 10 EST: 1941
SQ FT: 6,800
SALES: 737.7K **Privately Held**
SIC: 3599 Custom machinery

(G-7152)
ZENGER PARTNERS LLC
1881 Kenmore Ave (14217-2523)
PHONE..................................716 876-2284
George Zenger, *Vice Pres*
Donna Benzel, *Manager*
Joseph Zenger,
EMP: 37 EST: 1947
SQ FT: 12,000
SALES: 3.1MM **Privately Held**
SIC: 2752 2791 2789 Commercial printing, offset; typesetting; bookbinding & related work

Kennedy
Chautauqua County

(G-7153)
CARGILL INCORPORATED
1029 Poland Center Rd (14747-9708)
PHONE..................................716 665-6570
Al Johnson, *General Mgr*
Tim Decker, *Branch Mgr*
EMP: 7
SALES (corp-wide): 107.1B **Privately Held**
WEB: www.growmarkfs.com
SIC: 2041 Grain cereals, cracked
PA: Cargill, Incorporated
15407 Mcginty Rd W
Wayzata MN 55391
952 742-7575

Kerhonkson
Ulster County

(G-7154)
BARRA & TRUMBORE INC
40 Old Mine Rd (12446-2641)
PHONE..................................845 626-5442
Fax: 845 626-5476
David Barra, *President*
Martin Trumbore, *Vice Pres*
▲ **EMP:** 8
SALES (est): 805.8K **Privately Held**
WEB: www.barratrumbore.com
SIC: 3281 Cut stone & stone products

(G-7155)
DAVES PRECISION MACHINE SHOP
56 Webster Ave (12446-2672)
PHONE..................................845 626-7263
Fax: 845 626-7263
David Seymour, *Owner*
EMP: 12
SQ FT: 1,500
SALES (est): 540K **Privately Held**
SIC: 3599 Machine shop, jobbing & repair

(G-7156)
MORGAN FUEL & HEATING CO INC
5 Webster Ave (12446-2669)
PHONE..................................845 626-7766
EMP: 28
SALES (corp-wide): 53.3MM **Privately Held**
SIC: 2869 Fuels
PA: Morgan Fuel & Heating Co., Inc.
2785 W Main St
Wappingers Falls NY 12590
845 297-5580

Kew Gardens
Queens County

(G-7157)
A & B COLOR CORP (DEL) (PA)
Also Called: Soho Guilds
8204 Lefferts Blvd # 356 (11415-1731)
PHONE..................................718 441-5482
William Rabinowitz, *President*
EMP: 6
SQ FT: 2,500
SALES (est): 180K **Privately Held**
SIC: 2851 5198 Paints & allied products; paints

(G-7158)
ADVANTAGE PRINTING INC
12034 Queens Blvd Ste 310 (11415-1231)
PHONE..................................718 820-0688
Francene Biderman, *President*
Ruth Sommer, *Production*
Derrek Lyons, *Manager*
EMP: 11
SALES (est): 2.3MM **Privately Held**
WEB: www.advantages.net
SIC: 2752 5199 7336 Commercial printing, offset; advertising specialties; graphic arts & related design

(G-7159)
CUMMINS - ALLISON CORP
8002 Kew Gardens Rd # 402 (11415-3613)
PHONE..................................718 263-2482
EMP: 64
SALES (corp-wide): 388.1MM **Privately Held**
SIC: 3579 3519 Perforators (office machines); internal combustion engines
PA: Cummins - Allison Corp.
852 Feehanville Dr
Mount Prospect IL 60056
847 759-6403

(G-7160)
CUZINS DUZIN CORP
8420 Austin St Apt 3a (11415-2213)
P.O. Box 313073, Jamaica (11431-3073)
PHONE..................................347 724-6200
Todd Jones, *Manager*

Kew Gardens - Queens County (G-7161)

EMP: 8
SALES: 76K Privately Held
SIC: 2051 Doughnuts, except frozen

(G-7161)
I D E PROCESSES CORPORATION (PA)
106 81st Ave (11415-1108)
PHONE 718 544-1177
Fax: 718 575-8050
Zdenek A Capek, President
Lilly Capek, Corp Secy
Paul T Weirich, Vice Pres
▲ EMP: 17
SQ FT: 500
SALES: 2.1MM Privately Held
SIC: 3625 Noise control equipment

(G-7162)
ISRAELI YELLOW PAGES
12510 Queens Blvd Ste 14 (11415-1522)
PHONE 718 520-1000
Assaf Ran, CEO
EMP: 20
SALES (est): 782.1K Privately Held
SIC: 2741 Telephone & other directory publishing

(G-7163)
JACK L POPKIN & CO INC
12510 84th Rd (11415-2202)
PHONE 718 361-6700
Leonard F Popkin, President
Kyle Popkin, Office Mgr
Debra Z Popkin, Admin Sec
EMP: 8 EST: 1947
SQ FT: 6,000
SALES: 1.6MM Privately Held
SIC: 3861 7699 Printing equipment, photographic; printing trades machinery & equipment repair

(G-7164)
JG INNOVATIVE INDUSTRIES INC
8002 Kew Gardens Rd (11415-3600)
PHONE 718 784-7300
Joseph Gottlieb, Ch of Bd
EMP: 8
SALES (est): 710K Privately Held
SIC: 3999 Advertising display products

(G-7165)
MANHOLE BRRIER SEC SYSTEMS INC
Also Called: Mbss
8002 Kew Gardens Rd # 901 (11415-3600)
PHONE 516 741-1032
Michael Manoussos, CEO
John Messer, President
EMP: 22 EST: 2001
SQ FT: 5,000
SALES (est): 3.6MM Privately Held
SIC: 3699 Security devices

Kill Buck
Cattaraugus County

(G-7166)
DONVER INCORPORATED
4185 Killbuck Rd (14748)
P.O. Box 181 (14748-0181)
PHONE 716 945-1910
Fax: 716 945-4047
Donald A Vershay, President
Patricia B Vershay, Vice Pres
Merry Lankow, Office Mgr
Donald A Vershy, Manager
EMP: 18
SQ FT: 900
SALES: 4.3MM Privately Held
SIC: 2421 3713 2491 2426 Sawmills & planing mills, general; truck & bus bodies; wood preserving; hardwood dimension & flooring mills

Kinderhook
Columbia County

(G-7167)
AMERICAN BIO MEDICA CORP (PA)
122 Smith Rd (12106-2819)
PHONE 518 758-8158
Fax: 518 758-8171
Melissa A Waterhouse, CEO
Richard P Koskey, Ch of Bd
Edmund M Jaskiewicz, President
Douglas Casterlin, Vice Pres
Melissa Waterhouse, Vice Pres
EMP: 61
SQ FT: 30,000
SALES: 6.3MM Publicly Held
WEB: www.americanbiomedica.com
SIC: 2834 3841 Pharmaceutical preparations; diagnostic apparatus, medical

King Ferry
Cayuga County

(G-7168)
LAKE VIEW MANUFACTURING LLC
Also Called: Aurora Shoe Company
1690 State Route 90 N (13081-9713)
P.O. Box 430, Aurora (13026-0430)
PHONE 315 364-7892
David Binns, President
EMP: 10
SQ FT: 5,000
SALES (est): 1.4MM Privately Held
SIC: 3143 3144 Men's footwear, except athletic; women's footwear, except athletic

Kings Park
Suffolk County

(G-7169)
AMFAR ASPHALT CORP
Also Called: Farino & Sons Asphalt
137 Old Northport Rd (11754-4200)
PHONE 631 269-9660
Anthony Farino, President
EMP: 5 EST: 1955
SQ FT: 7,500
SALES (est): 474K Privately Held
SIC: 2951 Asphalt & asphaltic paving mixtures (not from refineries)

(G-7170)
DEJANA TRCK UTILITY EQP CO LLC (HQ)
490 Pulaski Rd (11754-1317)
PHONE 631 544-9000
Peter Dejana, President
Andrew Dejana, Vice Pres
Jerry Dresel, CFO
EMP: 150
SQ FT: 25,000
SALES: 24.6MM Publicly Held
SIC: 3711 5531 Truck & tractor truck assembly; truck equipment & parts

(G-7171)
HANSA PLASTICS INC
8 Meadow Glen Rd (11754-1312)
PHONE 631 269-9050
Fax: 631 269-9143
Harold Schmidt, President
Nellie Schmidt, Corp Secy
Peter Schmidt Jr, Vice Pres
▲ EMP: 10 EST: 1961
SQ FT: 5,000
SALES (est): 1.6MM Privately Held
WEB: www.hansasystemsusa.com
SIC: 3089 Injection molding of plastics

(G-7172)
KINGS PARK READY MIX CORP
140 Old Northport Rd E (11754-4211)
PHONE 631 269-4330
Fax: 631 269-4639
Claudio Valente, President
Jason Berchoff, General Mgr
EMP: 15
SALES: 2MM Privately Held
SIC: 3273 Ready-mixed concrete

(G-7173)
PELKOWSKI PRECAST CORP
294a Old Northport Rd (11754-4200)
PHONE 631 269-5727
Fax: 631 269-2100
Tom Pelkowski, President
Bob Pelkowski, Vice Pres
Bryan Pelkowski, Treasurer
Bill Pelkowski, Admin Sec
EMP: 17
SQ FT: 400
SALES (est): 2.7MM Privately Held
SIC: 3272 Concrete products, precast; septic tanks, concrete; manhole covers or frames, concrete; covers, catch basin: concrete

(G-7174)
R SCHLEIDER CONTRACTING CORP
135 Old Northport Rd (11754-4200)
PHONE 631 269-4249
Fax: 631 269-1534
Ray Schleider, President
Loretta Schleider, Vice Pres
EMP: 5
SQ FT: 2,500
SALES (est): 797.8K Privately Held
SIC: 2951 5169 Road materials, bituminous (not from refineries); industrial salts & polishes

Kingston
Ulster County

(G-7175)
ALCOA FASTENING SYSTEMS
1 Corporate Dr (12401-5536)
PHONE 845 334-7203
Klaus Kleinfeld, Principal
▲ EMP: 130
SQ FT: 40,000
SALES (est): 23.9MM Privately Held
SIC: 3728 Mfg Aircraft Parts/Equipment

(G-7176)
ALMANAC
Also Called: Ulster Publishing
322 Wall St (12401-3820)
P.O. Box 3329 (12402-3329)
PHONE 845 334-8206
George Vogel, Principal
Paul Leclerc, Manager
EMP: 5
SALES (est): 241.9K Privately Held
SIC: 2711 Newspapers

(G-7177)
AMERIBAG OUTDOORS
5 Ameribag Dr (12401-6975)
PHONE 845 339-4082
Jerry Michelson, President
▲ EMP: 33 EST: 2010
SALES (est): 1.5MM
SALES (corp-wide): 27.2MM Privately Held
SIC: 3161 Traveling bags
PA: Ameribag, Inc.
5 Ameribag Dr
Kingston NY 12401
845 339-1292

(G-7178)
ARMOR DYNAMICS INC
138 Maple Hill Rd (12401-8616)
PHONE 845 658-9200
Bernard C Schaeffer, President
EMP: 15
SALES: 1.5MM Privately Held
SIC: 3711 Cars, armored, assembly of

(G-7179)
BESICORP LTD (PA)
1151 Flatbush Rd (12401-7011)
PHONE 845 336-7700
William Seils, President
Frederic M Zinn Sr, President
Michael F Zinn, Chairman
Jim Waleur, Plant Mgr
EMP: 16 EST: 1998
SQ FT: 8,000
SALES (est): 4.2MM Privately Held
SIC: 3674 4911 3585 Photovoltaic devices, solid state; electric services; refrigeration & heating equipment

(G-7180)
C & G OF KINGSTON INC
25 Cornell St (12401-3625)
P.O. Box 1458 (12402-1458)
PHONE 845 331-0148
Fax: 845 331-6218
Clyde E Wonderly, CEO
Patricia Schweikart, Controller
Drew Wonderly, Manager
Gloria M Wonderly, Admin Sec
EMP: 60
SQ FT: 20,000
SALES (est): 5.7MM Privately Held
WEB: www.wonderlys.com
SIC: 2391 2392 Curtains & draperies; bedspreads & bed sets: made from purchased materials

(G-7181)
C S I G INC
721 Broadway 270 (12401-3449)
PHONE 845 383-3800
Jonathan Peck, CEO
Tim Peck, Vice Pres
Andrew Peck, CFO
Andy Peck, Human Res Mgr
EMP: 9
SQ FT: 1,450
SALES: 650K Privately Held
WEB: www.csiginc.com
SIC: 7372 Application computer software

(G-7182)
CALLANAN INDUSTRIES INC
Salem St (12401)
P.O. Box 1220 (12402-1220)
PHONE 845 331-6868
Fax: 845 331-1740
Randy Anson, Manager
EMP: 25
SALES (corp-wide): 25.3B Privately Held
WEB: www.callanan.com
SIC: 3272 3281 2951 1442 Concrete products, precast; stone, quarrying & processing of own stone products; asphalt paving mixtures & blocks; construction sand & gravel
HQ: Callanan Industries, Inc.
1245 Kings Rd Ste 1
Schenectady NY 12303
518 374-2222

(G-7183)
CHARLTON PRECISION PDTS INC
461 Sawkill Rd (12401-1229)
P.O. Box 500, Mount Marion (12456-0500)
PHONE 845 338-2351
Fax: 845 338-9202
Robert Charlton, President
Bonnie Charlton, Vice Pres
Nancy Charlton, Shareholder
Katherine Charlton, Admin Sec
EMP: 9 EST: 1962
SQ FT: 4,000
SALES: 1.2MM Privately Held
WEB: www.charltonprecision.com
SIC: 3643 Current-carrying wiring devices

(G-7184)
CITY OF KINGSTON
Also Called: Kingston Wste Wtr Trment Plant
91 E Strand St (12401-6001)
PHONE 845 331-2490
Fax: 845 331-4648
Allen Winchell, Director
Dan Heitzmam, Director
EMP: 11 Privately Held
WEB: www.kingstonez.com
SIC: 3589 9511 Sewage & water treatment equipment;
PA: City Of Kingston
420 Broadway
Kingston NY 12401
845 334-3935

Kingston - Ulster County (G-7211)

(G-7185)
CRANESVILLE BLOCK CO INC
637 E Chester St (12401-1738)
PHONE............................845 331-1775
Will Longto, *Principal*
EMP: 25
SQ FT: 4,262
SALES (corp-wide): 41.2MM **Privately Held**
SIC: 3273 Ready-mixed concrete
PA: Cranesville Block Co., Inc.
1250 Riverfront Ctr
Amsterdam NY 12010
518 684-6000

(G-7186)
DAILY FREEMAN
79 Hurley Ave (12401-2898)
PHONE............................845 331-5000
Fax: 845 331-3557
Ira Fusfeld, *Publisher*
Jan Dewey, *Principal*
Sam Daleo, *Principal*
Darryl Gangloff, *Editor*
Sarah Gantz, *Correspondent*
EMP: 11
SALES (est): 486K **Privately Held**
SIC: 2711 Newspapers

(G-7187)
DIRT T SHIRTS INC
444 Old Neighborhood Rd (12401-1508)
PHONE............................845 336-4230
Fax: 845 336-6127
John Stote, *President*
Scott Winter, *Vice Pres*
William Stote, *Treasurer*
Daryl Morrrell, *Credit Mgr*
John Stote III, *Admin Sec*
EMP: 40
SQ FT: 25,000
SALES (est): 3.5MM **Privately Held**
SIC: 2396 2395 Screen printing on fabric articles; art goods for embroidering, stamped: purchased materials

(G-7188)
EAST COAST CULTURES LLC
906 State Route 28 (12401-7264)
P.O. Box 220147, Brooklyn (11222-0147)
PHONE............................917 261-3010
EMP: 10
SALES (est): 932K **Privately Held**
SIC: 2086 Mfg Bottled/Canned Soft Drinks

(G-7189)
FALA TECHNOLOGIES INC
430 Old Neighborhood Rd (12401-1508)
PHONE............................845 336-4000
Fax: 845 336-4030
Frank Falatyn, *Ch of Bd*
Henry Dimarco, *President*
Gerry Dimarco, *General Mgr*
John Falatyn, *Senior VP*
James Dewitt, *Vice Pres*
EMP: 38 **EST:** 1946
SQ FT: 48,000
SALES: 7MM **Privately Held**
WEB: www.falatech.com
SIC: 3449 Miscellaneous metalwork

(G-7190)
HEALTHALLIANCE HOSPITAL
Also Called: Benedictine Hospital
105 Marys Ave (12401-5848)
PHONE............................845 338-2500
Jeffrey Murphy, *Manager*
EMP: 7
SALES (corp-wide): 3.8MM **Privately Held**
SIC: 3821 Laboratory apparatus & furniture
HQ: Healthalliance Hospital Mary's Avenue Campus
105 Marys Ave
Kingston NY 12401
845 338-2500

(G-7191)
HUCK INTERNATIONAL INC
Also Called: Alcoa Fastening Systems Rings
1 Corporate Dr (12401-5536)
PHONE............................845 331-7300
Fax: 845 334-7214
Steven Boderck, *Branch Mgr*
Kim Ball, *Info Tech Mgr*
Tim Barkman, *Maintence Staff*
EMP: 203
SALES (corp-wide): 22.5B **Publicly Held**
WEB: www.huck.com
SIC: 3452 3594 3546 Bolts, nuts, rivets & washers; fluid power pumps & motors; power-driven handtools
HQ: Huck International, Inc.
3724 E Columbia St
Tucson AZ 85714
520 519-7400

(G-7192)
KEEGAN ALES LLC
20 Saint James St (12401-4534)
PHONE............................845 331-2739
Tommy Keegan, *Mng Member*
Toni Roser, *Manager*
EMP: 13
SALES (est): 1.1MM **Privately Held**
WEB: www.keeganales.com
SIC: 2082 Beer (alcoholic beverage)

(G-7193)
KINGSTON HOOPS SUMMER
68 Glen St (12401-6406)
P.O. Box 2606 (12402-2606)
PHONE............................845 401-6830
Charlene Laday Hill, *Owner*
EMP: 8
SALES: 24K **Privately Held**
SIC: 3494 Valves & pipe fittings

(G-7194)
KNIGHTLY ENDEAVORS
319 Wall St Ste 2 (12401-3884)
PHONE............................845 340-0949
John Reeder, *Owner*
EMP: 11 **EST:** 1996
SALES (est): 789.1K **Privately Held**
WEB: www.knightly.com
SIC: 2211 Apparel & outerwear fabrics, cotton

(G-7195)
LABELLA PASTA INC
906 State Route 28 (12401-7264)
PHONE............................845 331-9130
Nancy Covello, *President*
Dennis Covello, *President*
EMP: 7
SQ FT: 4,800
SALES (est): 709.5K **Privately Held**
WEB: www.labellapasta.com
SIC: 2099 Pasta, uncooked: packaged with other ingredients

(G-7196)
LHV PRECAST INC
540 Ulster Landing Rd (12401-6963)
PHONE............................845 336-8880
Fax: 845 336-8962
Henry Killian, *CEO*
Robert Willis, *President*
James Willis, *Vice Pres*
Kathy Hayman, *Safety Mgr*
Mike Venett, *Plant Engr*
EMP: 50
SQ FT: 30,000
SALES (est): 10.4MM **Privately Held**
WEB: www.lhvprecast.com
SIC: 3272 Concrete products, precast

(G-7197)
LOCAL MEDIA GROUP INC
Also Called: Times Herald-Record
34 John St (12401-3822)
PHONE............................845 340-4910
EMP: 12
SALES (corp-wide): 1.2B **Publicly Held**
SIC: 2711 Newspapers-Publishing/Printing
HQ: Local Media Group, Inc.
40 Mulberry St
Middletown NY 10940
845 341-1100

(G-7198)
LUDWIG HOLDINGS CORP
Also Called: Wolf-TEC
20 Kieffer Ln (12401-2209)
PHONE............................845 340-9727
Fax: 845 340-9732
Ralf Ludwig, *CEO*
Peter Ludwig, *Owner*
Matthew Dellaventura, *Project Mgr*
Kelli Ingersoll, *Buyer*
Steve Shemella, *Engineer*
◆ **EMP:** 85
SQ FT: 47,500
SALES (est): 20.8MM **Privately Held**
WEB: www.wolf-tec.com
SIC: 3556 8742 Food products machinery; meat, poultry & seafood processing machinery; industry specialist consultants; food & beverage consultant

(G-7199)
LUMINARY PUBLISHING INC
314 Wall St (12401-3820)
PHONE............................845 334-8600
Jason Stern, *President*
Amara Projansky, *Vice Pres*
Ralph Jenkins, *Accounts Exec*
Mathew Watzka, *Manager*
EMP: 15
SQ FT: 1,000
SALES (est): 2MM **Privately Held**
WEB: www.chronogram.com
SIC: 2721 2741 Magazines: publishing & printing; art copy & poster publishing

(G-7200)
M & E MFG CO INC
19 Progress St (12401-3611)
P.O. Box 1548 (12402-1548)
PHONE............................845 331-7890
Fax: 845 331-7898
Jeffrey Weinberger, *Ch of Bd*
Don Hall, *COO*
Pam Bailey, *Purch Agent*
Mary Blauvelt, *Cust Mgr*
Jim Akin, *Info Tech Mgr*
EMP: 55
SQ FT: 54,000
SALES: 6.1MM **Privately Held**
WEB: www.zframerack.com
SIC: 3556 Food products machinery

(G-7201)
MILLROCK TECHNOLOGY INC
39 Kieffer Ln Ste 2 (12401-2210)
PHONE............................845 339-5700
Mary A Whitman, *General Mgr*
Taylor Thompson, *Chairman*
Mary Anne Whitnas, *Accounts Mgr*
▲ **EMP:** 20
SQ FT: 12,000
SALES (est): 4.9MM **Privately Held**
WEB: www.millrocktech.com
SIC: 3585 Refrigeration equipment, complete

(G-7202)
MONKEY JOE ROASTING COMPANY
478 Broadway Ste A (12401-4623)
PHONE............................845 331-4598
Gabriel Cicale, *CEO*
EMP: 8
SALES (est): 733.5K **Privately Held**
SIC: 2095 Coffee roasting (except by wholesale grocers)

(G-7203)
NORTHAST COML WIN TRTMENTS INC
Also Called: Wonderly Company, The
25 Cornell St (12401-3625)
PHONE............................845 331-0148
Al Parsons, *CEO*
Pat Schweikart, *CFO*
EMP: 65
SALES: 6MM **Privately Held**
SIC: 2391 Cottage sets (curtains): made from purchased materials

(G-7204)
NORTHEAST DATA DESTRUCTION & R
619 State Route 28 (12401-7466)
P.O. Box 316, West Hurley (12491-0316)
PHONE............................845 331-5554
Mark Wachtel, *Owner*
EMP: 7
SALES (est): 1.1MM **Privately Held**
SIC: 3559 Tire shredding machinery

(G-7205)
NORTHEAST PANEL & TRUSS LLC
2 Kieffer Ln (12401-2206)
PHONE............................845 339-3656
Fax: 845 339-5096
Ed Collins,
Bruce Hutchins,
EMP: 40
SQ FT: 50,000
SALES (est): 3.3MM **Privately Held**
WEB: www.northeastpanel.com
SIC: 2439 2435 Trusses, wooden roof; trusses, except roof: laminated lumber; panels, hardwood plywood

(G-7206)
PEARSON EDUCATION INC
317 Wall St (12401-3819)
PHONE............................845 340-8700
EMP: 27
SALES (corp-wide): 6.7B **Privately Held**
WEB: www.phgenit.com
SIC: 2731 Book publishing
HQ: Pearson Education, Inc.
1 Lake St
Upper Saddle River NJ 07458
201 236-7000

(G-7207)
R & F HANDMADE PAINTS INC
84 Ten Broeck Ave (12401-3921)
PHONE............................845 331-3112
Richard Frumess, *President*
Darin Seim, *Opers Staff*
Jim Haskin, *Treasurer*
Cynthia Winika, *Instructor*
▲ **EMP:** 12
SQ FT: 5,000
SALES (est): 875.1K **Privately Held**
SIC: 3952 5199 Lead pencils & art goods; artists' materials

(G-7208)
RAMSEY CHARLES COMPANY
401 Sawkill Rd (12401-1229)
P.O. Box 2264 (12402-2264)
PHONE............................845 338-1464
Fax: 845 338-5751
Richard Trout, *President*
Vincent Hart, *Vice Pres*
▲ **EMP:** 12
SQ FT: 12,000
SALES (est): 1.5MM **Privately Held**
SIC: 3441 Fabricated structural metal

(G-7209)
ROBERT TABATZNIK ASSOC INC (PA)
Also Called: American Printing and Off Sups
867 Flatbush Rd (12401-7315)
PHONE............................845 336-4555
Fax: 845 336-7717
Patricia Tabatznik, *Ch of Bd*
Sarah Sprague, *Manager*
EMP: 10
SQ FT: 7,300
SALES (est): 1.6MM **Privately Held**
WEB: www.rtachicago.com
SIC: 2752 5112 Commercial printing, lithographic; office supplies

(G-7210)
SOLVENTS COMPANY INC
9 Cornell St (12401-3623)
P.O. Box 231015, Great Neck (11023-0015)
PHONE............................631 595-9300
Batia Shellef, *President*
EMP: 10 **EST:** 2013
SALES (est): 1.8MM **Privately Held**
SIC: 2911 2869 2899 2842 Solvents; non-aromatic chemical products; industrial organic chemicals; chlorinated solvents; orange oil; degreasing solvent

(G-7211)
SPIEGEL WOODWORKS INC
Also Called: S A W
418 Old Neighborhood Rd (12401-1508)
PHONE............................845 336-8090
Fax: 845 336-8087
Gary Spiegel, *President*
EMP: 10
SQ FT: 12,000
SALES: 1.6MM **Privately Held**
WEB: www.sawmoulding.com
SIC: 2431 2421 Moldings, wood: unfinished & prefinished; doors, wood; sawmills & planing mills, general

Kingston - Ulster County (G-7212)

(G-7212)
STATEBOOK LLC
185 Fair St Ste 2 (12401-0503)
P.O. Box 3659 (12402-3659)
PHONE 845 383-1991
Calandra Cruickshank, *Principal*
Ira Schuman, *Manager*
EMP: 5
SALES (est): 292.6K **Privately Held**
SIC: 2741

(G-7213)
STAVO INDUSTRIES INC (PA)
Also Called: Ertel Alsop
132 Flatbush Ave (12401-2202)
PHONE 845 331-4552
George T Quigley, *Vice Pres*
Bianca Quigley, *Vice Pres*
David Thompson, *Research*
Jean Winter, *Human Res Mgr*
Bill Kearney, *VP Sales*
▲ **EMP:** 17 **EST:** 1966
SQ FT: 15,000
SALES (est): 11.2MM **Privately Held**
WEB: www.ertelalsop.com
SIC: 3569 3561 3443 Filters, general line: industrial; industrial pumps & parts; tanks, standard or custom fabricated: metal plate

(G-7214)
STAVO INDUSTRIES INC
Also Called: Ertel Engineering Co
132 Flatbush Ave (12401-2202)
PHONE 845 331-5389
Fax: 845 339-1063
George Quigley, *Vice Pres*
EMP: 45
SALES (corp-wide): 11.2MM **Privately Held**
WEB: www.ertelalsop.com
SIC: 3569 Filters
PA: Stavo Industries, Inc.
132 Flatbush Ave
Kingston NY 12401
845 331-4552

(G-7215)
TIMELY SIGNS OF KINGSTON INC
154 Clinton Ave Fl 1 (12401-4922)
PHONE 845 331-8710
Gerard Beichert, *President*
Jeff Zduniak, *Principal*
Joe Beichert, *Vice Pres*
EMP: 12
SQ FT: 15,000
SALES (est): 1.5MM **Privately Held**
WEB: www.timelysigns.com
SIC: 3993 Signs & advertising specialties

(G-7216)
TONNER DOLL COMPANY INC (PA)
301 Wall St (12401-3819)
P.O. Box 4410 (12402-4410)
PHONE 845 339-9537
Fax: 845 339-1259
Robert Tonner, *CEO*
Jack Kralik, *Vice Pres*
Lorri Booth, *Manager*
Noreen Morris, *Manager*
▲ **EMP:** 24
SQ FT: 8,500
SALES (est): 2.1MM **Privately Held**
WEB: www.tonnerdoll.com
SIC: 3942 Miniature dolls, collectors'

(G-7217)
TORTILLA HEAVEN INC
Also Called: Armadillo Bar & Grill
97 Abeel St (12401-6009)
PHONE 845 339-1550
Fax: 845 657-2261
Merle Borenstein, *Owner*
EMP: 20
SQ FT: 3,200
SALES (est): 2.3MM **Privately Held**
SIC: 2099 5812 Tortillas, fresh or refrigerated; eating places

(G-7218)
ULSTER PRECISION INC
57 Teller St (12401-2600)
P.O. Box 1668 (12402-1668)
PHONE 845 338-0995
Fax: 845 338-3045
Selma Boris, *President*
Harold Hill, *Exec VP*
Lenore Eckhardt, *Vice Pres*
Christopher Eckhardt, *Foreman/Supr*
Anthony Rivas, *Purch Mgr*
EMP: 20
SQ FT: 16,000
SALES (est): 5.1MM **Privately Held**
SIC: 3444 3441 3645 Sheet metalwork; fabricated structural metal; residential lighting fixtures

(G-7219)
ULSTER PUBLISHING CO INC (PA)
Also Called: Woodstock Times
322 Wall St Fl 1 (12401-3820)
P.O. Box 3329 (12402-3329)
PHONE 845 334-8205
Fax: 845 334-8202
Geddy Sveikauskas, *President*
Debbie Alexsa, *Editor*
Geddy Sveikauskass, *Sales Mgr*
Genia Wiskwire, *Sales Mgr*
Terry Breitenstein, *Director*
EMP: 20
SQ FT: 2,500
SALES (est): 3.6MM **Privately Held**
WEB: www.ulsterpublishing.com
SIC: 2711 2721 Newspapers: publishing only, not printed on site; magazines: publishing only, not printed on site

(G-7220)
ULSTER-GREENE COUNTY A R C
307 Washington Ave (12401-4469)
PHONE 845 331-8451
Maureen Tank, *Branch Mgr*
EMP: 7
SALES (corp-wide): 1.3B **Privately Held**
SIC: 3652 Phonograph records, prerecorded
HQ: Ulster-Greene County A R C
471 Albany Ave
Kingston NY 12401
845 331-4300

(G-7221)
UNIVERSAL METAL FABRICATORS
Also Called: Reliance Gayco
27 Emerick St (12401-3009)
PHONE 845 331-8248
James Hassett, *President*
EMP: 10
SQ FT: 50,000
SALES (est): 2MM **Privately Held**
WEB: www.urminc.com
SIC: 3555 3599 3569 3532 Printing trades machinery; machine shop, jobbing & repair; separators for steam, gas, vapor or air (machinery); mining machinery

(G-7222)
US HEALTH EQUIPMENT COMPANY
138 Maple Hill Rd (12401-8616)
PHONE 845 658-7576
Bernard Schaeffer, *President*
Wayne Schaeffer, *President*
EMP: 20 **EST:** 1961
SALES (est): 2.2MM **Privately Held**
WEB: www.saunex.com
SIC: 3634 Sauna heaters, electric

(G-7223)
USHECO INC
138 Maple Hill Rd (12401-8616)
PHONE 845 658-9200
Fax: 845 658-7224
Bernarr C Schaeffer, *CEO*
Wayne M Schaeffer, *President*
Lorene Schaeffer, *Vice Pres*
Cynthia Marketti, *Bookkeeper*
EMP: 16
SQ FT: 40,000
SALES: 1.3MM **Privately Held**
WEB: www.usheco.com
SIC: 3089 Plastic processing

(G-7224)
VINCENT CONIGLIARO
Also Called: Salvin Company
308 State Route 28 (12401-7445)
PHONE 845 340-0489
Fax: 845 334-9618
Vincent Conigliaro, *Owner*
EMP: 15
SQ FT: 12,000
SALES (est): 860K **Privately Held**
SIC: 3648 5719 1731 5731 Lighting equipment; lighting, lamps & accessories; lighting contractor; radio, television & electronic stores; audio electronic systems

(G-7225)
WORKSHOP ART FABRICATION
117 Tremper Ave (12401-3619)
P.O. Box 1009 (12402-1009)
PHONE 845 331-0385
Vincent Didonato, *President*
Andrew Tharmer, *President*
EMP: 12
SALES: 1MM **Privately Held**
SIC: 3562 Casters

(G-7226)
YUM YUM NOODLE BAR
275 Fair St Ste 17 (12401-3882)
PHONE 845 679-7992
Dorothy Lee, *Owner*
EMP: 8
SALES (est): 665.8K **Privately Held**
SIC: 2098 Noodles (e.g. egg, plain & water), dry

Kirkville
Onondaga County

(G-7227)
MANTH-BROWNELL INC
1120 Fyler Rd (13082-9445)
PHONE 315 687-7263
Fax: 315 687-6856
Wesley R Skinner Jr, *Ch of Bd*
Rob Pike, *Vice Pres*
James Wilsey, *Opers Mgr*
Pat Hachey, *Purchasing*
Glenn Spaarling, *CFO*
EMP: 180 **EST:** 1951
SQ FT: 140,000
SALES (est): 50.3MM **Privately Held**
WEB: www.manth.com
SIC: 3451 Screw machine products

(G-7228)
STANLEY INDUSTRIAL EQP LLC
8094 Saintsville Rd (13082-9325)
PHONE 315 656-8733
Thomas Stanley, *Mng Member*
EMP: 6
SQ FT: 5,200
SALES (est): 1.2MM **Privately Held**
SIC: 3537 Forklift trucks

(G-7229)
TITAN STEEL CORP
6333 N Kirkville Rd (13082-3300)
P.O. Box 10 (13082-0010)
PHONE 315 656-7046
Gretchen K Conway, *President*
Jeff Kealin, *Vice Pres*
Dave Carbone, *Project Mgr*
Micheal Conway, *Controller*
EMP: 12
SALES (est): 2.2MM **Privately Held**
SIC: 3441 Fabricated structural metal

Kirkwood
Broome County

(G-7230)
ACTIVE MANUFACTURING INC
32 Laughlin Rd (13795)
P.O. Box 332 (13795-0332)
PHONE 607 775-3162
Fax: 607 775-5086
Frank Sweetay, *President*
EMP: 12
SQ FT: 2,000
SALES (est): 1.4MM **Privately Held**
SIC: 3599 3999 Machine shop, jobbing & repair; models, general, except toy

(G-7231)
AKRATURN MFG INC
1743 Us Route 11 (13795-1637)
PHONE 607 775-2802
Fax: 607 775-2227
Douglas Gardner, *President*
Douglas Sterns, *Corp Secy*
David Gardner, *Vice Pres*
Kimberly Reger, *Manager*
EMP: 51
SQ FT: 60,000
SALES (est): 5.2MM **Privately Held**
WEB: www.akraturn.com
SIC: 3599 Machine shop, jobbing & repair

(G-7232)
BELDEN MANUFACTURING INC
Also Called: Dan Ann Associates
1813 Us Route 11 (13795-1608)
PHONE 607 238-0998
Fax: 607 238-0996
Gerry Wilson, *CEO*
Jerry Wilson, *President*
Thomas Davis, *Admin Sec*
EMP: 20
SQ FT: 6,000
SALES: 3MM **Privately Held**
SIC: 3599 Machine shop, jobbing & repair

(G-7233)
FUSE ELECTRONICS INC
1223 Us Route 11 (13795-1641)
PHONE 607 352-3222
Susane Lewis, *CEO*
Patricia Mancinelli, *Ch of Bd*
EMP: 7
SALES (est): 972.6K **Privately Held**
SIC: 3677 Electronic coils, transformers & other inductors

(G-7234)
L-3 COMMUNICATIONS CORPORATION
265 Industrial Park Dr (13795)
P.O. Box 1237, Binghamton (13902-1237)
PHONE 607 721-5465
Fax: 607 721-5458
Donald Ulmer, *Purch Agent*
Bob Hansen, *Manager*
Todd Cundey, *Info Tech Mgr*
EMP: 100
SALES (corp-wide): 10.4B **Publicly Held**
SIC: 3663 7371 3699 Telemetering equipment, electronic; custom computer programming services; electrical equipment & supplies
HQ: L-3 Communications Corporation
600 3rd Ave
New York NY 10016
212 697-1111

La Fargeville
Jefferson County

(G-7235)
GLOBAL TOWER LLC
23696 Bacon Rd (13656-2256)
PHONE 561 995-0320
EMP: 5
SALES (est): 395.9K **Privately Held**
SIC: 3663 Radio broadcasting & communications equipment

(G-7236)
HP HOOD LLC
20700 State Route 411 (13656-3228)
PHONE 315 656-2132
David Flanders, *Plant Engr*
Daniel Langkabel, *Personnel*
Rich Miles, *Supervisor*
EMP: 300
SALES (corp-wide): 1.9B **Privately Held**
SIC: 2026 Fluid milk

PA: Hp Hood Llc
6 Kimball Ln Ste 400
Lynnfield MA 01940
617 887-8441

(G-7237)
JOHNSON S SAND GRAVEL INC
23284 County Route 3 (13656-3111)
PHONE................................315 771-1450
Fax: 315 482-7632
Rusty Johnson, *Principal*
EMP: 6
SALES (est): 547.9K **Privately Held**
SIC: 1442 Construction sand & gravel

(G-7238)
THOUSAND ISLAND READY MIX CON
38760 State Route 180 (13656-3108)
PHONE................................315 686-3203
Fax: 315 686-1107
Thomas Dillenbeck, *President*
Steven Dillenbeck, *Vice Pres*
EMP: 8 **EST:** 1964
SQ FT: 2,988
SALES (est): 1.2MM **Privately Held**
WEB: www.thousandislandsconcrete.com
SIC: 3273 Ready-mixed concrete

La Fayette
Onondaga County

(G-7239)
BEAK & SKIFF CIDER MILL INC
4472 Us Route 20 (13084-9729)
PHONE................................315 677-5105
David Pittard, *President*
Stephen F Morse, *Treasurer*
Timothy Beak, *Shareholder*
Mark Fleckenstein, *Shareholder*
Marshall Skiff, *Shareholder*
EMP: 9
SQ FT: 9,800
SALES: 1.1MM **Privately Held**
SIC: 2099 Cider, nonalcoholic

(G-7240)
BOULAY FABRICATION INC
Rr 20 Box West (13084)
P.O. Box 508 (13084-0508)
PHONE................................315 677-5247
Fax: 315 677-5325
Timothy Foody, *President*
Daniel Foody, *Vice Pres*
Connie Foody, *Admin Sec*
EMP: 12
SQ FT: 14,000
SALES (est): 3MM **Privately Held**
WEB: www.boulayfab.com
SIC: 3613 Control panels, electric

(G-7241)
BYRNE DAIRY INC (PA)
2394 Us Route 11 (13084-9583)
P.O. Box 176 (13084-0176)
PHONE................................315 475-2121
Fax: 315 471-0930
Carl Byrne, *Ch of Bd*
Kingsley Irobunda, *General Mgr*
James Obrist, *General Mgr*
William M Byrne Jr, *Principal*
James Kehoe, *Regional Mgr*
EMP: 300 **EST:** 1932
SQ FT: 32,000
SALES (est): 287.4MM **Privately Held**
WEB: www.byrnedairy.com
SIC: 2026 2024 Milk processing (pasteurizing, homogenizing, bottling); ice cream, packaged; molded, on sticks, etc.; ice cream, bulk

Lackawanna
Erie County

(G-7242)
ALLIANCE INNOVATIVE MFG INC
1 Alliance Dr (14218-2529)
PHONE................................716 822-1626
Richard St John, *President*

Jeanine Zaleski, *Controller*
Jeanine Stjohn, *Manager*
EMP: 34 **EST:** 2007
SQ FT: 35,000
SALES: 7MM **Privately Held**
SIC: 3443 Metal parts

(G-7243)
CERTAINTEED CORPORATION
231 Ship Canal Pkwy (14218-1026)
PHONE................................716 823-3684
EMP: 226
SALES (corp-wide): 189MM **Privately Held**
SIC: 3221 Glass containers
HQ: Certainteed Corporation
20 Moores Rd
Malvern PA 19355
610 341-7000

(G-7244)
LINITA DESIGN & MFG CORP
1951 Hamburg Tpke Ste 24 (14218-1047)
P.O. Box 1101, Buffalo (14201-6101)
PHONE................................716 566-7753
Carlos Vera, *President*
Sean Greenhouse, *General Mgr*
Chris Macrides, *Manager*
Andrea Vera, *Manager*
Eva Vera, *Shareholder*
EMP: 50
SQ FT: 80,000
SALES: 10.6MM **Privately Held**
SIC: 3441 7389 7692 8711 Dam gates, metal plate; design services; welding repair; engineering services

(G-7245)
ONEIDA SALES & SERVICE INC
Also Called: Oneida Concrete Products
155 Commerce Dr (14218-1041)
PHONE................................716 270-0433
Fax: 716 822-1740
Frederick Saia, *President*
EMP: 15
SALES (corp-wide): 5MM **Privately Held**
WEB: www.oneidagroup.com
SIC: 3531 3272 3273 Concrete plants; building materials, except block or brick; concrete; ready-mixed concrete
PA: Oneida Sales & Service, Inc.
155 Commerce Dr
Buffalo NY 14218
716 822-8205

(G-7246)
PAGE FRONT GROUP INC
2703 S Park Ave (14218-1511)
PHONE................................716 823-8222
Fax: 716 821-0550
William Delmont, *President*
Beverly Mazur, *Corp Secy*
EMP: 6
SQ FT: 1,500
SALES (est): 290K **Privately Held**
SIC: 2711 Newspapers: publishing only, not printed on site

(G-7247)
QUIKRETE COMPANIES INC
Also Called: Quikrete-Buffalo
11 N Steelawanna Ave (14218-1114)
PHONE................................716 213-2027
Fax: 716 824-3902
Chuck Morell, *Regional Mgr*
John Kosar, *Sales Staff*
Chuck Olgin, *Manager*
EMP: 30
SQ FT: 26,293 **Privately Held**
WEB: www.quikrete.com
SIC: 3272 Concrete products
HQ: Quikrete Companies, Inc.
3490 Piedmont Rd Ne
Atlanta GA 30305
404 634-9100

(G-7248)
RJS MACHINE WORKS INC
1611 Electric Ave (14218-3021)
PHONE................................716 826-1778
Ronald J Szewczyk, *President*
Lori Szewczyk, *Vice Pres*
EMP: 6
SQ FT: 9,000
SALES (est): 470K **Privately Held**
SIC: 3599 Machine shop, jobbing & repair

(G-7249)
SAMPLA BELTING NORTH AMER LLC
61 N Gates Ave (14218-1029)
PHONE................................716 667-7450
Fax: 716 667-7428
Gary Dombrowski, *Accountant*
Steven Beecher, *Sales Staff*
Lucio Depaoli, *Mng Member*
Cris Balint, *Manager*
Stefan Cristian Balint,
▲ **EMP:** 20
SQ FT: 40,000
SALES (est): 4.1MM **Privately Held**
SIC: 3199 3052 Transmission belting, leather; transmission belting, rubber

(G-7250)
WELDED TUBE USA INC
2537 Hamburg Tpke (14218)
PHONE................................716 828-1111
Robert Mandel, *CEO*
▲ **EMP:** 60 **EST:** 2013
SALES (est): 18.6MM
SALES (corp-wide): 467.6MM **Privately Held**
SIC: 3317 Steel pipe & tubes
PA: Welded Tube Of Canada Corp
111 Rayette Rd
Concord ON L4K 2
905 669-1111

Lacona
Oswego County

(G-7251)
PINE RIDGE LOG HM RESTORATIONS
Also Called: Pine Ridge Log HM Restoration
1866 County Route 48 (13083-3132)
PHONE................................315 387-3360
Richard Trump, *President*
EMP: 10
SALES (est): 762.3K **Privately Held**
SIC: 2452 Log cabins, prefabricated, wood

(G-7252)
VANHOUTEN MOTORSPORTS
27 Center Rd (13083-4127)
PHONE................................315 387-6312
Henry E Van Houten, *Principal*
EMP: 6
SALES (est): 626.3K **Privately Held**
SIC: 3531 Automobile wrecker hoists

Lagrangeville
Dutchess County

(G-7253)
GRAPHICS SLUTION PROVIDERS INC (PA)
Also Called: Brewster Coachworks
115 Barmore Rd (12540-6601)
P.O. Box 159 (12540-0159)
PHONE................................845 677-5088
Theresa Brewster, *President*
Alexander S Brewster, *Vice Pres*
Jack Brewster, *Vice Pres*
EMP: 8 **EST:** 1977
SQ FT: 2,500
SALES: 2.5MM **Privately Held**
WEB: www.graphics-solutions.com
SIC: 2499 7373 Novelties, wood fiber; value-added resellers, computer systems

(G-7254)
INTENTIONS JEWELRY LLC
83 Miller Hill Dr (12540-5641)
PHONE................................845 226-4650
Bob Baff,
Shareane Baff,
EMP: 5
SALES (est): 430K **Privately Held**
SIC: 3911 Jewelry, precious metal

(G-7255)
MACRO TOOL & MACHINE COMPANY
1397 Route 55 (12540-5118)
PHONE................................845 223-3824
Fax: 845 223-7304
Daniel Siegel, *President*
Gisela Siegel, *Corp Secy*
Roland Siegel, *Vice Pres*
Linda Petandrea, *Manager*
EMP: 8
SQ FT: 30,000
SALES: 500K **Privately Held**
WEB: www.macrotool.com
SIC: 3599 Amusement park equipment

(G-7256)
MICROCAD TRNING CONSULTING INC
1110 Route 55 Ste 209 (12540-5048)
PHONE................................617 923-0500
Agustin Fernandez, *Principal*
Jesse Battaglia, *Accounts Exec*
Jonathan Martell, *Accounts Exec*
John Christensen, *Technical Staff*
EMP: 7
SALES (corp-wide): 9.7MM **Privately Held**
SIC: 7372 8243 Prepackaged software; software training, computer
PA: Microcad Training & Consulting, Inc.
440 Arsenal St Ste 3
Watertown MA 02472
617 923-0500

(G-7257)
PARAGON AQUATICS
Also Called: KDI Paragon
1351 Route 55 Unit 1 (12540-5128)
PHONE................................845 452-5500
Fax: 845 452-5426
Thomas A Saldarelli, *Principal*
Devin Hare, *Safety Mgr*
▲ **EMP:** 50 **EST:** 1969
SQ FT: 38,000
SALES (est): 8.4MM **Privately Held**
WEB: www.paragonaquatics.com
SIC: 3449 3446 Miscellaneous metalwork; railings, prefabricated metal
HQ: Pentair Water Pool And Spa, Inc.
1620 Hawkins Ave
Sanford NC 27330
919 774-4151

(G-7258)
PENTAIR WATER POOL AND SPA INC
Paragon Aquatics
341 Route 55 (12540-5105)
PHONE................................845 452-5500
Thomas Saldarelli, *President*
EMP: 45 **Privately Held**
WEB: www.pentairpool.com
SIC: 3589 3561 Swimming pool filter & water conditioning systems; pumps, domestic: water or sump
HQ: Pentair Water Pool And Spa, Inc.
1620 Hawkins Ave
Sanford NC 27330
919 774-4151

(G-7259)
STYLES AVIATION INC (PA)
Also Called: Sky Geek
30 Airway Dr Ste 2 (12540-5254)
PHONE................................845 677-8185
Fax: 845 677-6252
Steven T Styles, *CEO*
Virginia R Styles, *Vice Pres*
Sherri Palm, *Treasurer*
Jeffery Cross, *Manager*
Robert Rose, *Web Dvlpr*
▲ **EMP:** 5
SQ FT: 5,000
SALES (est): 4.5MM **Privately Held**
SIC: 3728 5088 Aircraft parts & equipment; aircraft equipment & supplies

(G-7260)
TYMOR PARK
249 Duncan Rd (12540-5845)
PHONE................................845 724-5691
Fax: 845 724-5692
Robert Mattes, *Director*
EMP: 5

Lake George - Warren County (G-7261) — GEOGRAPHIC SECTION

SALES (est): 370.8K Privately Held
WEB: www.unionvaleny.us
SIC: 2531 Picnic tables or benches, park

Lake George
Warren County

(G-7261)
JOCKEY INTERNATIONAL INC
1439 State Route 9 Ste 10 (12845-3447)
P.O. Box 5 (12845-0005)
PHONE.................................518 761-0965
Beverly Schult, *Manager*
EMP: 20
SALES (corp-wide): 1.4B Privately Held
SIC: 2254 Underwear, knit
PA: Jockey International, Inc.
  2300 60th St
  Kenosha WI 53140
  262 658-8111

(G-7262)
LEATHER OUTLET
1656 State Route 9 (12845-3440)
PHONE.................................518 668-0328
Fax: 518 381-3827
Kevin Clint, *Owner*
EMP: 8
SALES (est): 788.8K Privately Held
SIC: 3199 Leather garments

(G-7263)
PERFORMANCE CUSTOM TRAILER
230 Lockhart Mountain Rd (12845-4904)
P.O. Box 408, Warrensburg (12885-0408)
PHONE.................................518 504-4021
William Bunting, *President*
Diane Bunting, *Treasurer*
EMP: 7
SQ FT: 3,000
SALES (est): 1MM Privately Held
SIC: 3799 Boat trailers

(G-7264)
UNDER ARMOUR INC
1444 State Route 9 (12845-3480)
PHONE.................................518 761-6787
EMP: 29
SALES (corp-wide): 3.9B Publicly Held
SIC: 2329 Men's & boys' sportswear & athletic clothing
PA: Under Armour, Inc.
  1020 Hull St Ste 300
  Baltimore MD 21230
  410 454-6428

Lake Grove
Suffolk County

(G-7265)
S&B ALTERNATIVE FUELS INC
1232 Stony Brook Rd (11755-1624)
PHONE.................................631 585-6637
Scott Kunz, *Principal*
EMP: 5 EST: 2009
SALES (est): 464.7K Privately Held
SIC: 2869 Fuels

(G-7266)
SPEEDWAY LLC
2825 Middle Country Rd (11755-2105)
PHONE.................................631 738-2536
Jaswante Kor, *Branch Mgr*
EMP: 15 Publicly Held
SIC: 1311 Crude petroleum production
HQ: Speedway Llc
  500 Speedway Dr
  Enon OH 45323
  937 864-3000

(G-7267)
SUNDOWN SKI & SPORT SHOP INC (PA)
3060 Middle Country Rd (11755-2106)
PHONE.................................631 737-8600
Fax: 631 737-5985
Winfred Breuer, *President*
Michael Rahatigan, *Vice Pres*
▲ EMP: 20

SQ FT: 13,000
SALES (est): 9.9M Privately Held
SIC: 2511 5091 Wood lawn & garden furniture; skiing equipment

(G-7268)
VANS INC
313 Smith Haven Mall (11755-1201)
PHONE.................................631 724-1011
EMP: 10
SALES (corp-wide): 12.3B Publicly Held
SIC: 3021 Canvas shoes, rubber soled
HQ: Vans, Inc.
  6550 Katella Ave
  Cypress CA 90630
  714 889-6100

Lake Katrine
Ulster County

(G-7269)
COBRA MANUFACTURING CORP
68 Leggs Mills Rd (12449-5145)
P.O. Box 209, Bloomington (12411-0209)
PHONE.................................845 514-2505
Michael V Pavlov, *President*
Hillarie Pavlov, *Treasurer*
▲ EMP: 9
SALES (est): 970K Privately Held
SIC: 3315 Barbed & twisted wire

(G-7270)
CURTISS-WRIGHT FLOW CONTROL
Also Called: Qualtech NP
731 Grant Ave (12449-5350)
PHONE.................................845 382-6918
Matt Eyre, *Branch Mgr*
EMP: 6
SQ FT: 4,500
SALES (corp-wide): 2.2B Publicly Held
SIC: 3443 8734 Fabricated plate work (boiler shop); testing laboratories
HQ: Curtiss-Wright Flow Control Service Corporation
  2950 E Birch St
  Brea CA 92821
  714 982-1898

(G-7271)
WCD WINDOW COVERINGS INC
1711 Ulster Ave (12449-5426)
P.O. Box 723 (12449-0723)
PHONE.................................845 336-4511
Fax: 845 336-2071
Drew Wonderly, *President*
Vicky Delavan, *Accounting Mgr*
EMP: 50
SQ FT: 14,000
SALES (est): 1.3MM Privately Held
WEB: www.wcd-drapery.com
SIC: 2391 5021 2591 Draperies, plastic & textile: from purchased materials; beds & bedding; drapery hardware & blinds & shades

Lake Luzerne
Warren County

(G-7272)
KETCHUM MANUFACTURING CO INC
11 Town Shed Rd (12846)
P.O. Box 10 (12846-0010)
PHONE.................................518 696-3331
Fax: 518 696-4048
Gary Powers, *President*
Lisa Podwirny, *Vice Pres*
Helen A Powers, *Admin Sec*
EMP: 13 EST: 1964
SQ FT: 8,000
SALES: 1.2MM Privately Held
WEB: www.ketchummfg.com
SIC: 3999 2652 Identification tags, except paper; setup paperboard boxes

Lake Placid
Essex County

(G-7273)
COMSEC VENTURES INTERNATIONAL
17 Tamarack Ave (12946-1607)
PHONE.................................518 523-1600
Fax: 518 523-1971
William H Borland, *President*
Tina Preston, *Manager*
EMP: 6
SQ FT: 1,700
SALES (est): 458.2K Privately Held
SIC: 3699 4822 4215 7929 Security control equipment & systems; telegraph & other communications; courier services, except by air; entertainers & entertainment groups

(G-7274)
EVERGREEN HIGH VOLTAGE LLC
140 Peninsula Way (12946-4402)
PHONE.................................281 814-9973
Carlos Delgado,
William Larzeler,
EMP: 5 EST: 2013
SALES: 2MM Privately Held
SIC: 3699 3825 7629 Particle accelerators, high voltage; test equipment for electronic & electric measurement; electrical equipment repair, high voltage

(G-7275)
LAKE PLACID ADVERTISERS WKSHP
Also Called: Sir Speedy
Cold Brook Plz (12946)
PHONE.................................518 523-3359
Tom Connors, *President*
Adele Pierce, *Vice Pres*
EMP: 20
SQ FT: 2,000
SALES: 4.5MM Privately Held
SIC: 2752 2759 2791 Commercial printing, lithographic; commercial printing; typesetting

(G-7276)
SUGAR SHACK DESERT COMPANY INC
2567 Main St (12946-3305)
PHONE.................................518 523-7540
Gina D Cimaglia, *CEO*
EMP: 6
SALES (est): 290K Privately Held
SIC: 2099 Sugar

Lake Pleasant
Hamilton County

(G-7277)
WILT INDUSTRIES INC
2452 State Route 8 (12108-4416)
PHONE.................................518 548-4961
Daniel Wilt, *President*
Richard Wilt, *Vice Pres*
Donna Mandon, *Bookkeeper*
EMP: 6 EST: 1949
SQ FT: 10,000
SALES (est): 1MM Privately Held
WEB: www.wiltindustries.com
SIC: 3559 Glass making machinery: blowing, molding, forming, etc.

Lake Ronkonkoma
Suffolk County

(G-7278)
J F B & SONS LITHOGRAPHERS
1700 Ocean Ave (11779-6570)
PHONE.................................631 467-1444
Fax: 631 467-2174
Joseph Brown, *President*
Randall Brown, *Corp Secy*
Gary Brown, *Vice Pres*

Dennis Ganzak, *CFO*
EMP: 75
SQ FT: 43,000
SALES (est): 5.1MM
SALES (corp-wide): 1B Publicly Held
SIC: 2752 Commercial printing, lithographic
HQ: Earth Color New York, Inc.
  249 Pomeroy Rd
  Parsippany NJ 07054
  973 884-1300

Lake View
Erie County

(G-7279)
DEEDEE DESSERTS LLC
6969 Southwestern Blvd (14085-9644)
P.O. Box 353 (14085-0353)
PHONE.................................716 627-2330
Dawn Davis,
EMP: 7
SALES (est): 330K Privately Held
SIC: 2099 Dessert mixes & fillings

(G-7280)
DELAWARE GRAPHICS LLC
Also Called: AlphaGraphics
1934 Crescent Ter (14085-9718)
PHONE.................................716 627-7582
Fax: 716 884-1262
Leroy Osborn,
EMP: 8
SQ FT: 5,400
SALES (est): 560K Privately Held
SIC: 2752 Commercial printing, lithographic

(G-7281)
LAKESHORE CARBIDE INC
5696 Minerva Dr (14085-9633)
PHONE.................................716 462-4349
Carl Ciesla, *Chairman*
EMP: 5
SALES (est): 763K Privately Held
SIC: 2819 Carbides

Lakeville
Livingston County

(G-7282)
ARCHER-DANIELS-MIDLAND COMPANY
Also Called: ADM
3401 Rochester Rd (14480-9762)
PHONE.................................585 346-2311
Lee Robinson, *Branch Mgr*
Tim Calway, *Manager*
EMP: 7
SALES (corp-wide): 67.7B Publicly Held
WEB: www.admworld.com
SIC: 2046 Corn sugars & syrups
PA: Archer-Daniels-Midland Company
  77 W Wacker Dr Ste 4600
  Chicago IL 60601
  312 634-8100

(G-7283)
CONESUS LAKE ASSOCIATION INC
5828 Big Tree Rd (14480-9737)
P.O. Box 637 (14480-0637)
PHONE.................................585 346-6864
Greg Foust, *Ch of Bd*
George Coolbaugh, *President*
Burt Lyon, *Treasurer*
EMP: 30
SALES: 51.3K Privately Held
SIC: 3599 2511 Machine & other job shop work; wood household furniture

(G-7284)
GANNETT CO INC
Also Called: Democrat & Chronicle
3155 Rochester Rd Bldg E (14480-9713)
PHONE.................................585 346-4150
Fax: 585 346-4146
Perry Van Dunk, *Manager*
Tom Callahan, *Manager*
EMP: 6

▲ = Import ▼ = Export
◆ = Import/Export

GEOGRAPHIC SECTION

Lancaster - Erie County (G-7308)

SALES (corp-wide): 5.7B **Publicly Held**
WEB: www.gannett.com
SIC: 2711 Newspapers
PA: Gannett Co., Inc.
7950 Jones Branch Dr
Mc Lean VA 22102
703 854-6000

(G-7285)
S & R TOOL INC
6066 Stone Hill Rd (14480-9712)
PHONE.................................585 346-2029
Fax: 585 346-5865
Samuel Dandrea, *President*
Richard Panipinto, *Vice Pres*
EMP: 6
SQ FT: 10,428
SALES (est): 936.1K **Privately Held**
SIC: 3545 Precision tools, machinists'

(G-7286)
SWEETENERS PLUS INC
5768 Sweeteners Blvd (14480-9741)
P.O. Box 520 (14480-0520)
PHONE.................................585 728-3770
Carlton Myers, *President*
Mark Rudolph, *QC Mgr*
Kyle Whitford, *Marketing Staff*
Ann Coffey, *Admin Sec*
▲ EMP: 70
SQ FT: 30,000
SALES (est): 37.6MM **Privately Held**
WEB: www.sweetenersplus.com
SIC: 2062 Cane sugar refining

Lakewood
Chautauqua County

(G-7287)
ARRO TOOL & DIE INC
4687 Gleason Rd (14750)
P.O. Box 7 (14750-0007)
PHONE.................................716 763-6203
Fax: 716 763-8511
James R Lindell, *President*
Eric Corey, *Vice Pres*
Jeff A Lindell, *Vice Pres*
Richard Morris, *Vice Pres*
Timothy Raynor, *Engineer*
▼ EMP: 19 EST: 1952
SQ FT: 23,000
SALES (est): 3.2MM **Privately Held**
WEB: www.arrotool.com
SIC: 3544 3469 Special dies & tools; metal stampings

(G-7288)
CLASSIC BRASS INC
2051 Stoneman Cir (14750-9779)
P.O. Box 3563, Jamestown (14702-3563)
PHONE.................................716 763-1400
Fax: 716 664-3281
J Christopher Creighton, *President*
▲ EMP: 56
SQ FT: 30,050
SALES (est): 9.2MM **Privately Held**
SIC: 3429 Furniture builders' & other household hardware

(G-7289)
CUMMINS INC
Also Called: Jamestown Engine Plant
4720 Baker St (14750-9772)
PHONE.................................716 456-2676
Karine Ramsey, *Principal*
Dan Nelson, *Purch Mgr*
Howard Bryan, *Engineer*
William Herrick, *Engineer*
Scott Lord, *Engineer*
◆ EMP: 62
SALES (est): 14.1MM **Privately Held**
SIC: 3519 Internal combustion engines

(G-7290)
CUMMINS INC
Also Called: Cummins Eng Company/James Town
4720 Baker St (14750-9772)
PHONE.................................716 456-2111
Fax: 716 456-2316
Ian Ramsay, *Managing Dir*
Maria Jones, *Opers Mgr*
Dan Nelson, *Purchasing*
Howard M Bryan, *Engineer*
Cecil Rhoades, *Engineer*
EMP: 800
SQ FT: 1,733
SALES (corp-wide): 19.1B **Publicly Held**
WEB: www.cummins.com
SIC: 3519 3714 Internal combustion engines; motor vehicle parts & accessories
PA: Cummins Inc.
500 Jackson St
Columbus IN 47201
812 377-5000

(G-7291)
DLH ENERGY SERVICE LLC
4422 W Fairmount Ave (14750-9705)
P.O. Box 40, Ashville (14710-0040)
PHONE.................................716 410-0028
Kim Helffrich, *Manager*
Charles Dubose,
EMP: 3
SQ FT: 1,000
SALES: 5MM **Privately Held**
SIC: 1311 Crude petroleum & natural gas

(G-7292)
QUALITY MANUFACTURING SYS LLC
1995 Stoneman Cir (14750-9776)
PHONE.................................716 763-0988
Patsy Jo Kosinski, *Partner*
EMP: 6
SQ FT: 12,000
SALES (est): 1.1MM **Privately Held**
SIC: 3569 Assembly machines, non-metalworking

(G-7293)
R-CO PRODUCTS CORPORATION
1855 Big Tree Rd (14750-9759)
PHONE.................................800 854-7657
Fax: 716 763-0080
Edward Roemer Jr, *President*
Erika Roemer, *Treasurer*
Katy Lord, *Admin Sec*
EMP: 13
SQ FT: 30,000
SALES (est): 1.6MM **Privately Held**
SIC: 2891 Sealants

(G-7294)
RR DONNELLEY & SONS COMPANY
Also Called: Moore Business Forms
112 Winchester Rd (14750-1739)
P.O. Box 137 (14750-0137)
PHONE.................................716 763-2613
Fax: 716 763-5948
Kevin Diluca, *Manager*
Dan Caruso, *Manager*
EMP: 12
SALES (corp-wide): 11.2B **Publicly Held**
WEB: www.moore.com
SIC: 2759 Commercial printing
PA: R.R. Donnelley & Sons Company
35 W Wacker Dr Ste 3650
Chicago IL 60601
312 326-8000

(G-7295)
ULRICH PLANFILING EQP CORP
2120 4th Ave (14750-9727)
P.O. Box 135 (14750-0135)
PHONE.................................716 763-1815
Fax: 716 763-1818
Daniel Berry, *President*
Jamie Carlson, *Vice Pres*
Reid Van Every, *Plant Mgr*
Barbara Sauer, *Purch Mgr*
Joni Drocy, *Engineer*
▼ EMP: 40
SQ FT: 42,400
SALES (est): 8.8MM **Privately Held**
WEB: www.ulrichcorp.com
SIC: 2522 Office cabinets & filing drawers: except wood

(G-7296)
WATER STREET BRASS CORPORATION
4515 Gleason Rd (14750-9748)
P.O. Box 463 (14750-0463)
PHONE.................................716 763-0059
Mathew Churchill, *President*
EMP: 22
SALES (est): 2.7MM **Privately Held**
SIC: 3429 Furniture hardware

Lancaster
Erie County

(G-7297)
A & T TOOLING LLC
91 Beach Ave (14086-1658)
PHONE.................................716 601-7299
Maureen Hassenbohler,
EMP: 5
SALES: 250K **Privately Held**
SIC: 3543 Industrial patterns

(G-7298)
ADVANCED THERMAL SYSTEMS INC
15 Enterprise Dr (14086-9773)
PHONE.................................716 681-1800
Fax: 716 681-0228
Edward W Patnode, *Ch of Bd*
Eugene Miliczky, *President*
Edward Patnode, *General Mgr*
EMP: 40
SQ FT: 31,000
SALES (est): 8.5MM **Privately Held**
WEB: www.advancedthermal.net
SIC: 3494 3568 3498 3441 Expansion joints pipe; ball joints, except aircraft & automotive; fabricated pipe & fittings; fabricated structural metal

(G-7299)
AFTER 50 INC
5 W Main St Rear (14086-2109)
PHONE.................................716 832-9300
Bonnie Degweck, *President*
Phyllis Goasiti, *Vice Pres*
EMP: 5
SALES: 500K **Privately Held**
SIC: 2711 Newspapers

(G-7300)
AIR SYSTEM PRODUCTS INC
Also Called: AFP Industries
51 Beach Ave (14086-1658)
PHONE.................................716 683-0435
Fax: 716 683-7128
Patrick Scanlon, *President*
Henry Bourg, *President*
Bill Niblock, *Vice Pres*
Mike Zacharko, *Accounts Mgr*
▲ EMP: 12
SQ FT: 17,000
SALES (est): 1.7MM **Privately Held**
WEB: www.airsyspro.com
SIC: 3491 Industrial valves

(G-7301)
ALCO PLASTICS INC
35 Ward Rd (14086-9779)
PHONE.................................716 683-3020
Fax: 716 683-3739
Raymond Mazurczyk, *President*
EMP: 20
SQ FT: 25,000
SALES (est): 3.1MM **Privately Held**
SIC: 2673 Plastic bags: made from purchased materials

(G-7302)
ALDEN OPTICAL LABORATORY INC
6 Lancaster Pkwy (14086-9713)
PHONE.................................716 937-9181
Fax: 585 937-3303
Charles H Creighton, *President*
Helen Creighton, *Treasurer*
Lisa Kaminski, *Bookkeeper*
Ann Townsend, *Lab Dir*
EMP: 16
SQ FT: 8,000
SALES: 2.4MM **Privately Held**
WEB: www.aldenoptical.com
SIC: 3851 Contact lenses

(G-7303)
APPLE RUBBER PRODUCTS INC (PA)
Also Called: Express Seal Div
310 Erie St (14086-9504)
PHONE.................................716 684-6560
Fax: 716 684-1678
Steven L Apple, *President*
Carol Malaney, *Vice Pres*
Chris Chiodo, *Engineer*
Romel Ner, *Project Engr*
Daniel Friol, *Info Tech Mgr*
▲ EMP: 25
SQ FT: 11,000
SALES (est): 23.9MM **Privately Held**
WEB: www.applerubber.com
SIC: 3069 Hard rubber & molded rubber products; molded rubber products

(G-7304)
APPLE RUBBER PRODUCTS INC
Also Called: Expresseal
204 Cemetery Rd (14086-9798)
PHONE.................................716 684-7649
Fax: 716 683-7053
Steven Apple, *President*
Craig Ross, *Executive*
EMP: 110
SQ FT: 49,668
SALES (corp-wide): 23.9MM **Privately Held**
WEB: www.applerubber.com
SIC: 3069 3061 3053 Hard rubber & molded rubber products; molded rubber products; mechanical rubber goods; gaskets, packing & sealing devices
PA: Apple Rubber Products, Inc.
310 Erie St
Lancaster NY 14086
716 684-6560

(G-7305)
BABULA CONSTRUCTION INC
5136 William St (14086-9447)
PHONE.................................716 681-0886
Stanley Babula, *President*
Janet Babula, *Vice Pres*
EMP: 7
SALES: 300K **Privately Held**
SIC: 1389 Construction, repair & dismantling services

(G-7306)
BIMBO BAKERIES USA INC
2900 Commerce Pkwy (14086-1741)
PHONE.................................716 706-0450
George Weston, *Owner*
EMP: 18
SALES (corp-wide): 13B **Privately Held**
WEB: www.gwbakeries.com
SIC: 2051 Bread, cake & related products
HQ: Bimbo Bakeries Usa, Inc
255 Business Center Dr # 200
Horsham PA 19044
215 347-5500

(G-7307)
BUFFALO FILTER LLC
5900 Genesee St (14086-9024)
PHONE.................................716 835-7000
Samantha Bonano, *CEO*
Greg Pepe, *Vice Pres*
David McKay, *Opers Staff*
Cathy Carson, *Purch Mgr*
Pamela Netzel, *QA Dir*
▲ EMP: 85
SQ FT: 15,000
SALES (est): 18.5MM **Privately Held**
WEB: www.buffalofilter.com
SIC: 3841 3845 3699 3564 Surgical & medical instruments; laser systems & equipment, medical; electrical equipment & supplies; blowers & fans

(G-7308)
CASEY MACHINE CO INC
74 Ward Rd (14086-9779)
PHONE.................................716 651-0150
Fax: 716 651-4614
Thomas Radziwon, *Ch of Bd*
Ronald C Radziwon, *President*
Peter Szulc, *Vice Pres*
Dawn Delzer, *Purch Agent*
Bill Gillan, *Purch Agent*
EMP: 95 EST: 1976
SQ FT: 15,000
SALES (est): 17.2MM **Privately Held**
WEB: www.caseymachine.com
SIC: 3599 Machine shop, jobbing & repair

Lancaster - Erie County (G-7309) GEOGRAPHIC SECTION

(G-7309)
CHAKRA COMMUNICATIONS INC
80 W Drullard Ave (14086-1649)
PHONE.............................716 505-7300
Terry Sember, *Vice Pres*
Sharique Ansari, *Branch Mgr*
EMP: 50 **Privately Held**
WEB: www.chakracentral.com
SIC: 2796 2791 7812 7375 Lithographic plates, positives or negatives; typesetting; motion picture & video production; information retrieval services; color lithography
HQ: Chakra Communications, Inc.
    80 W Drullard Ave
    Lancaster NY 14086
    716 505-7300

(G-7310)
CLASSIC & PERFORMANCE SPC
Also Called: Classic Tube
80 Rotech Dr (14086-9755)
PHONE.............................716 759-1800
Fax: 716 759-1014
Paul Fix, *President*
Lauren J Fix, *Vice Pres*
Jane Fix, *Manager*
Pam Ladue, *Exec Dir*
EMP: 24
SQ FT: 20,000
SALES (est): 4.5MM **Privately Held**
WEB: www.classictube.com
SIC: 3714 Motor vehicle parts & accessories

(G-7311)
DELFT PRINTING INC
4401 Walden Ave Ste 8 (14086-9013)
PHONE.............................716 683-1100
Fax: 716 683-1101
Kamal C Jowdy, *President*
EMP: 7
SQ FT: 2,200
SALES: 800K **Privately Held**
WEB: www.delftprinting.com
SIC: 2759 Commercial printing

(G-7312)
DIVERSIFIED MANUFACTURING INC
4401 Walden Ave (14086-9013)
PHONE.............................716 681-7670
Walt Kempa, *Branch Mgr*
EMP: 15
SALES (corp-wide): 18.6MM **Privately Held**
WEB: www.dmimfg.com
SIC: 3441 Fabricated structural metal
PA: Diversified Manufacturing Inc.
    410 Ohio St
    Lockport NY 14094
    716 434-5585

(G-7313)
EASTERN AIR PRODUCTS LLC
Also Called: Engineered Air Products
41 Ward Rd (14086-9779)
PHONE.............................716 391-1866
Jeffrey Browne, *President*
Peter Baran, *Vice Pres*
Michael Arno, *CFO*
EMP: 18
SQ FT: 12,500
SALES: 3.2MM **Privately Held**
SIC: 3563 Air & gas compressors including vacuum pumps

(G-7314)
ERIE ENGINEERED PRODUCTS INC
3949 Walden Ave (14086-1472)
PHONE.............................716 206-0204
Barry Newman, *Ch of Bd*
Ron Korczynski, *Vice Pres*
David Vystup, *Vice Pres*
Thomas Kilpatrick, *Manager*
Sandra Whiteford, *Manager*
EMP: 45
SQ FT: 88,000
SALES (est): 12.3MM **Privately Held**
WEB: www.containers-cases.com
SIC: 3443 3441 3412 3411 Containers, shipping (bombs, etc.): metal plate; fabricated structural metal; metal barrels, drums & pails; metal cans

(G-7315)
FBC CHEMICAL CORPORATION
4111 Walden Ave (14086-1599)
PHONE.............................716 681-1581
Fax: 716 681-1512
Joe Villafranca, *Manager*
Rick Hewitt, *Assistant*
EMP: 5
SQ FT: 4,000
SALES (corp-wide): 60MM **Privately Held**
WEB: www.fbcchem.com
SIC: 2842 5169 Cleaning or polishing preparations; chemicals & allied products
PA: Fbc Chemical Corporation
    634 Route 228
    Mars PA 16046
    724 625-3116

(G-7316)
FLOWNET LLC
580 Lake Ave (14086-9627)
PHONE.............................716 685-4036
EMP: 6 EST: 2012
SALES (est): 305.2K **Privately Held**
SIC: 1311 Natural gas production

(G-7317)
GOOD EARTH INC
5960 Broadway St (14086-9531)
PHONE.............................716 684-8111
Gunter Burkhardt, *President*
Cornelia Orffeo, *Vice Pres*
EMP: 6 EST: 1999
SALES (est): 844.9K **Privately Held**
WEB: www.goodearth.net
SIC: 2833 Organic medicinal chemicals: bulk, uncompounded

(G-7318)
GOOD EARTH ORGANICS CORP (PA)
5960 Broadway St (14086-9531)
PHONE.............................716 684-8111
Fax: 716 684-3722
Guenter H Burkhardt, *Ch of Bd*
Eva Burkhardt, *Exec VP*
Andreas G Burkhardt, *Vice Pres*
Bernhard G Burkhardt, *Vice Pres*
Cornelia Orffeo, *Purchasing*
EMP: 20
SQ FT: 180,000
SALES: 17MM **Privately Held**
WEB: www.goodearth.org
SIC: 3523 Planting machines, agricultural

(G-7319)
HC BRILL CO INC
3765 Walden Ave (14086-1405)
PHONE.............................716 685-4000
Bob Craiglow, *Vice Pres*
Melissa Price, *Telecom Exec*
EMP: 9
SALES (est): 1.4MM **Privately Held**
SIC: 2033 Canned fruits & specialties

(G-7320)
ILLINOIS TOOL WORKS INC
United Silicone Div
4471 Walden Ave (14086-9754)
PHONE.............................716 681-8222
Diane Genco, *Mktg Coord*
Joseph Wukovits, *Branch Mgr*
Patrick Smith, *Manager*
EMP: 155
SALES (corp-wide): 13.4B **Publicly Held**
SIC: 3559 Plastics working machinery
PA: Illinois Tool Works Inc.
    155 Harlem Ave
    Glenview IL 60025
    847 724-7500

(G-7321)
KZ PRECISION INC
Also Called: K Z Precision
1 Mason Pl (14086-1615)
PHONE.............................716 683-3202
Kenneth Zwara, *President*
Jerome Zwara, *Manager*
EMP: 15
SQ FT: 7,500
SALES (est): 700K **Privately Held**
WEB: www.kzprecision.com
SIC: 3599 Machine shop, jobbing & repair

(G-7322)
LAFARGE NORTH AMERICA INC
6125 Genesee St (14086-9722)
PHONE.............................716 651-9235
Fax: 716 651-9580
Ron Morgan, *Manager*
EMP: 25
SALES (corp-wide): 23.4B **Privately Held**
WEB: www.lafargenorthamerica.com
SIC: 3241 1442 Cement, hydraulic; construction sand & gravel
HQ: Lafarge North America Inc.
    8700 W Bryn Mawr Ave Ll
    Chicago IL 60631
    703 480-3600

(G-7323)
LANCASTER KNIVES INC (PA)
165 Court St (14086-2399)
PHONE.............................716 683-5050
Fax: 716 683-5068
Scott C Cant, *President*
Ray Gangloff, *Mfg Mgr*
Allen A Turton, *Engineer*
Franes M Cant, *Accounting Mgr*
Harold Landahl, *Mktg Dir*
▲ **EMP:** 45 EST: 1896
SQ FT: 46,000
SALES (est): 5.5MM **Privately Held**
WEB: www.lancasterknives.com
SIC: 3423 3545 3469 3541 Knives, agricultural or industrial; shear knives; machine parts, stamped or pressed metal; machine tools, metal cutting type

(G-7324)
LANCE VALVES
15 Enterprise Dr (14086-9749)
PHONE.............................716 681-5825
Eugene Miliczky, *Vice Pres*
Geoffrey Schrott, *Manager*
EMP: 8
SQ FT: 6,000
SALES (est): 740K **Privately Held**
WEB: www.lancevalves.com
SIC: 3494 Valves & pipe fittings

(G-7325)
MANHASSET TOOL & DIE CO INC
4270 Walden Ave (14086-9770)
PHONE.............................716 684-6066
Fax: 716 684-6067
Mark Fenimore, *President*
EMP: 10 EST: 1955
SALES (est): 1MM **Privately Held**
WEB: www.manhassettool.com
SIC: 3544 3542 Jigs & fixtures; jigs: inspection, gauging & checking; die sets for metal stamping (presses); dies & die holders for metal cutting, forming, die casting; punching & shearing machines; bending machines

(G-7326)
MARKAR ARCHITECTURAL PRODUCTS
Also Called: Adams Ridge
68 Ward Rd (14086-9779)
PHONE.............................716 685-4104
Fax: 716 685-3919
EMP: 8 **Privately Held**
SIC: 3442 Mfg Metal Doors/Sash/Trim

(G-7327)
MOLDTECH INC
1900 Commerce Pkwy (14086-1735)
PHONE.............................716 685-3344
H Wayne Gerhart, *Ch of Bd*
Rob Paladichuk, *Vice Pres*
James H Wittman, *CFO*
James Wittman, *CFO*
Lisa Govenettio, *Administration*
▲ **EMP:** 45
SQ FT: 35,000
SALES (est): 15.6MM **Privately Held**
SIC: 3069 3061 Molded rubber products; mechanical rubber goods

(G-7328)
ORFFEO PRINTING & IMAGING INC
99 Cambria St (14086-1952)
P.O. Box 426 (14086-0426)
PHONE.............................716 681-5757
Fax: 716 684-0444
Gregory Orffeo, *Ch of Bd*
EMP: 5
SQ FT: 27,000
SALES (est): 3MM **Privately Held**
SIC: 2752 7331 Commercial printing, offset; direct mail advertising services

(G-7329)
PALMA TOOL & DIE COMPANY INC
40 Ward Rd (14086-9779)
PHONE.............................716 681-4685
Fax: 716 681-4785
William D Tate Sr, *President*
Jeff Parks, *General Mgr*
Thomas Owczarak, *Vice Pres*
William Cocklin, *Manager*
Ron Federice, *Manager*
EMP: 42 EST: 1962
SQ FT: 23,000
SALES (est): 8MM **Privately Held**
WEB: www.palmatool.com
SIC: 3544 Special dies & tools

(G-7330)
PARKER-HANNIFIN CORPORATION
Finite Airtek Filtration
4087 Walden Ave (14086-1512)
PHONE.............................248 628-6017
John Carpenter, *Facilities Mgr*
Judy Ryan, *Mfg Staff*
Dan Ryan, *Research*
Gary Stack, *Chief Engr*
Thomas Comstock, *Product Mgr*
EMP: 82
SALES (corp-wide): 11.3B **Publicly Held**
WEB: www.parker.com
SIC: 3569 3714 3564 Filters; motor vehicle parts & accessories; blowers & fans
PA: Parker-Hannifin Corporation
    6035 Parkland Blvd
    Cleveland OH 44124
    216 896-3000

(G-7331)
PARKER-HANNIFIN CORPORATION
Purification, Dehydration
4087 Walden Ave (14086-1512)
PHONE.............................716 685-4040
Adam Hoot, *Purch Agent*
Mark Harvey, *Electrical Engi*
Johanne Ipperciel, *Human Res Mgr*
David Peters, *VP Sales*
Jon Hilberg, *Branch Mgr*
EMP: 85
SALES (corp-wide): 11.3B **Publicly Held**
WEB: www.parker.com
SIC: 3585 3567 Refrigeration & heating equipment; industrial furnaces & ovens
PA: Parker-Hannifin Corporation
    6035 Parkland Blvd
    Cleveland OH 44124
    216 896-3000

(G-7332)
PERFORMANCE ADVANTAGE CO INC
6 W Main St Lowr Rear (14086-2110)
PHONE.............................716 683-7413
Richard Young, *President*
James Everett, *General Mgr*
Mike McGuire, *Executive*
EMP: 15
SQ FT: 13,000
SALES (est): 2.2MM **Privately Held**
WEB: www.pactoolmounts.com
SIC: 3089 Plastic hardware & building products

(G-7333)
PFANNENBERG INC
68 Ward Rd (14086-9779)
PHONE.............................716 685-6866
Fax: 716 681-1521
Andreas Pfannenberg, *President*
Meyer ISA-Bianka, *Senior VP*

▲ = Import ▼ = Export
◆ = Import/Export

GEOGRAPHIC SECTION

Latham - Albany County (G-7357)

William Baron, *Vice Pres*
Laura Chasalow, *Vice Pres*
George McNamara, *Vice Pres*
◆ **EMP:** 43
SQ FT: 65,000
SALES (est): 14MM
SALES (corp-wide): 528.6K **Privately Held**
WEB: www.pfannenbergusa.com
SIC: 3585 Air conditioning units, complete: domestic or industrial
PA: Pfannenberg Group Holding Gmbh
  Werner-Witt-Str. 1
  Hamburg 21035
  407 341-20

(G-7334)
PRZ TECHNOLOGIES INC
5490 Broadway St (14086-2220)
P.O. Box 369 (14086-0369)
PHONE...........................716 683-1300
Walt Przybyl, *President*
Karan Andrea, *Accountant*
EMP: 15
SALES (est): 3.4MM **Privately Held**
SIC: 3599 Machine & other job shop work

(G-7335)
QUICK CUT GASKET & RUBBER
192 Erie St (14086-9532)
P.O. Box 330 (14086-0330)
PHONE...........................716 684-8628
Fax: 716 684-0169
Norman J Steinbruckner, *Ch of Bd*
Scott Steinbruckner, *Vice Pres*
EMP: 13
SQ FT: 10,000
SALES (est): 1.9MM **Privately Held**
WEB: www.quickcutgasket.com
SIC: 3053 Gaskets, all materials

(G-7336)
RAM PRECISION TOOL INC
139 Gunnville Rd (14086-9017)
PHONE...........................716 759-8722
Fax: 716 759-8747
Joseph Walter, *President*
Barbara M Walter, *Vice Pres*
EMP: 6
SQ FT: 6,000
SALES (est): 760K **Privately Held**
WEB: www.ramprecisiontool.com
SIC: 3544 Special dies & tools

(G-7337)
RAYCO ENTERPRISES INC
Also Called: Airtek
4087 Walden Ave (14086-1512)
PHONE...........................716 685-6860
Fax: 716 685-1010
Raymond Arno, *President*
Dale Zimmerman, *Regional Mgr*
Sandy Goldsmith, *Controller*
Bob Besant, *Human Res Dir*
Jeff Browne, *Manager*
▲ **EMP:** 85
SQ FT: 125,000
SALES (est): 14.4MM **Privately Held**
SIC: 3585 3567 Refrigeration & heating equipment; industrial furnaces & ovens

(G-7338)
RICHARDS MACHINE TOOL CO INC
3753 Walden Ave (14086-1496)
PHONE...........................716 683-3380
Fax: 716 683-3408
Dennis Richards, *President*
Betsy Richards, *Vice Pres*
Peter Valenti, *QC Mgr*
Jeanne Walkowski, *Manager*
EMP: 23
SQ FT: 18,000
SALES (est): 2.4MM **Privately Held**
SIC: 3599 Machine shop, jobbing & repair

(G-7339)
RMF PRINTING TECHNOLOGIES INC
Also Called: Ogilvie Press
50 Pearl St (14086-1922)
PHONE...........................716 683-7500
Monica Castano, *Ch of Bd*
Keith Makey, *Maint Spvr*
Juan Carlos Yanez, *CFO*
▲ **EMP:** 50

SQ FT: 140,000
SALES (est): 17.1MM **Privately Held**
WEB: www.rmfprinttechnology.com
SIC: 2761 Manifold business forms

(G-7340)
ROLITE MFG INC
10 Wendling Ct (14086-9766)
PHONE...........................716 683-0259
Fax: 716 683-5406
Ron Roberts, *President*
Ronald Roberts, *President*
Thomas Debbins, *Vice Pres*
Frank Gurgol, *Director*
William Yeager, *Director*
▲ **EMP:** 25
SQ FT: 65,000
SALES (est): 7MM **Privately Held**
WEB: www.rolitemfg.com
SIC: 3469 3449 Stamping metal for the trade; custom roll formed products

(G-7341)
S3J ELECTRONICS LLC
2000 Commerce Pkwy (14086-1733)
PHONE...........................716 206-1309
EMP: 20
SALES (est): 4.2MM **Privately Held**
SIC: 3674 Mfg Semiconductors/Related Devices

(G-7342)
SEIBEL MODERN MFG & WLDG CORP
38 Palmer Pl (14086-2144)
PHONE...........................716 683-1536
Fax: 716 683-2552
Leon A Seibel, *Ch of Bd*
Mark Seibel, *Vice Pres*
Jeff Heath, *Engineer*
Lynne M Sobkowiak, *Manager*
▲ **EMP:** 85 **EST:** 1945
SQ FT: 70,000
SALES (est): 20.9MM **Privately Held**
WEB: www.seibelmodern.com
SIC: 3441 3443 Fabricated structural metal; fabricated plate work (boiler shop)

(G-7343)
SILICONE PRODUCTS & TECHNOLOGY
4471 Walden Ave (14086-9754)
PHONE...........................716 684-1155
Fax: 716 684-0310
Kim Jackson, *President*
Bill Boquard, *Vice Pres*
Michael Robinson, *Treasurer*
Jeannine Smolarek, *VP Finance*
Paul Schneeberger, *Sales Dir*
EMP: 150
SALES (est): 13.2MM
SALES (corp-wide): 13.4B **Publicly Held**
SIC: 2822 3544 Silicone rubbers; special dies, tools, jigs & fixtures
PA: Illinois Tool Works Inc.
  155 Harlem Ave
  Glenview IL 60025
  847 724-7500

(G-7344)
STUTZMAN MANAGEMENT CORP
11 Saint Joseph St (14086-1800)
PHONE...........................800 735-2013
Gerard Sheldon, *President*
EMP: 15
SQ FT: 32,000
SALES (est): 1.8MM **Privately Held**
SIC: 3443 Fuel tanks (oil, gas, etc.): metal plate

(G-7345)
UNITED SILICONE INC
4471 Walden Ave (14086-9778)
PHONE...........................716 681-8222
Fax: 716 681-8789
Donato Curcio, *President*
Karla Dearstyne, *Business Mgr*
Robert Le Posa, *Vice Pres*
Kevin Vincent, *Accounting Mgr*
▲ **EMP:** 81
SQ FT: 80,000
SALES (est): 16.1MM
SALES (corp-wide): 13.4B **Publicly Held**
SIC: 3953 Pads, inking & stamping

PA: Illinois Tool Works Inc.
  155 Harlem Ave
  Glenview IL 60025
  847 724-7500

(G-7346)
W N R PATTERN & TOOL INC
21 Pavement Rd (14086-9595)
PHONE...........................716 681-9334
Fax: 716 681-3520
Gary Machniak, *President*
Jeffrey Tucker, *Vice Pres*
EMP: 6
SQ FT: 6,000
SALES (est): 360K **Privately Held**
SIC: 3544 3543 Industrial molds; forms (molds), for foundry & plastics working machinery; industrial patterns

(G-7347)
WEB-TECH PACKAGING INC
500 Commerce Pkwy (14086-1793)
PHONE...........................716 684-4520
Fax: 716 684-6433
David C Rost, *President*
Kevin Kelly, *Shareholder*
William Rost, *Shareholder*
Kathleen Visciano, *Shareholder*
EMP: 16
SQ FT: 10,000
SALES (est): 3MM **Privately Held**
SIC: 2679 Tags & labels, paper

Lansing
Tompkins County

(G-7348)
CAYUGA CRUSHED STONE INC
87 Portland Point Rd (14882-9013)
P.O. Box 41 (14882-0041)
PHONE...........................607 533-4273
Fax: 607 533-7581
Thomas Besemer, *President*
Matthew Besemer, *Vice Pres*
Ruth Teeter, *Bd of Directors*
EMP: 20 **EST:** 1959
SQ FT: 1,200
SALES (est): 4.1MM **Privately Held**
SIC: 1429 Igneous rock, crushed & broken-quarrying

(G-7349)
METAL IMPROVEMENT COMPANY LLC
Also Called: IMR Test Labs
131 Woodsedge Dr (14882-8940)
PHONE...........................607 533-7000
Don Shuman, *Branch Mgr*
EMP: 69
SALES (corp-wide): 2.2B **Publicly Held**
SIC: 3398 Shot peening (treating steel to reduce fatigue)
HQ: Metal Improvement Company, Llc
  80 E State Rt 4 Ste 310
  Paramus NJ 07652
  201 843-7800

Larchmont
Westchester County

(G-7350)
INTERNATIONAL ROBOTICS INC
2001 Palmer Ave Ste Ll1 (10538-2420)
P.O. Box 11474, Naples FL (34101-1474)
PHONE...........................914 630-1060
Robert Doornic, *CEO*
EMP: 10
SALES (est): 978.9K **Privately Held**
SIC: 3535 Robotic conveyors

Latham
Albany County

(G-7351)
AB ENGINE
4a Northway Ln (12110-4809)
PHONE...........................518 557-3510

Alexander Bakharev, *Principal*
EMP: 8
SALES (est): 370K **Privately Held**
SIC: 3519 Internal combustion engines

(G-7352)
ACCUMETRICS INC
6 British American Blvd # 100 (12110-1476)
PHONE...........................716 684-0002
John Lally, *President*
EMP: 10
SALES (est): 1.3MM
SALES (corp-wide): 563.9MM **Publicly Held**
SIC: 3674 Semiconductors & related devices
HQ: Pcb Piezotronics, Inc.
  3425 Walden Ave
  Depew NY 14043
  716 684-0001

(G-7353)
ACCUMETRICS ASSOCIATES INC
6 British American Blvd # 100 (12110-1476)
PHONE...........................518 393-2200
Fax: 518 393-3622
John M Reschovsky, *President*
Tom Russell, *Engineer*
Svetlana Ushkina, *Design Engr*
Sandra Reschovsky, *Director*
EMP: 17
SQ FT: 5,000
SALES (est): 3MM **Privately Held**
WEB: www.accumetrix.com
SIC: 3674 Semiconductors & related devices

(G-7354)
ANGIODYNAMICS INC (PA)
14 Plaza Dr (12110-2166)
PHONE...........................518 795-1400
Howard W Donnelly, *Ch of Bd*
James C Clemmer, *President*
Gary Barrett, *Senior VP*
Ben Davis, *Senior VP*
Barbara Kucharczyk, *Senior VP*
EMP: 277
SQ FT: 55,000
SALES: 353.8MM **Publicly Held**
WEB: www.angiodynamics.com
SIC: 3841 Surgical & medical instruments

(G-7355)
BAJAN GROUP INC
950 New Loudon Rd Ste 280 (12110-2111)
PHONE...........................518 464-2884
Anthony Lombordo, *President*
EMP: 8
SALES (corp-wide): 5MM **Privately Held**
WEB: www.bajangroup.com
SIC: 2752 Commercial printing, offset
PA: The Bajan Group Inc
  950 New Loudon Rd Ste 280
  Latham NY 12110
  518 464-2884

(G-7356)
BRITISH AMERICAN PUBLISHING
19 British American Blvd (12110-6405)
PHONE...........................518 786-6000
Fax: 518 786-6001
Bernard F Conners, *Chairman*
Francis Coughlin, *Treasurer*
John T De Graff, *Admin Sec*
EMP: 60
SALES: 17MM **Privately Held**
WEB: www.bapublish.com
SIC: 2731 Books: publishing only

(G-7357)
BUSINESS FIRST OF NEW YORK
Also Called: Business Review
40 British American Blvd (12110-1421)
PHONE...........................518 640-6800
Caroline Jones, *General Mgr*
Mike Hendricks, *Editor*
Sarah Egan, *Opers Mgr*
Todd Kehoe, *Engineer*
Kristina Feigel, *Graphic Designe*
EMP: 23

Latham - Albany County (G-7358)

SALES (corp-wide): 322.5MM **Privately Held**
SIC: 2711 Newspapers: publishing only, not printed on site
HQ: Business First Of New York Inc
465 Main St Ste 100
Buffalo NY 14203
716 854-5822

(G-7358)
CARR MANUFACTURING JEWELERS
Also Called: Carr Jewelers
22 West Ln (12110-5320)
PHONE 518 783-6093
Fax: 518 783-3376
W James Dix, *President*
James E Dix, *Vice Pres*
Gloria Dix, *Treasurer*
EMP: 5
SALES (est): 351.2K **Privately Held**
SIC: 3911 7631 5944 Jewelry, precious metal; jewelry repair services; jewelry stores

(G-7359)
D & W DIESEL INC
51 Sicker Rd Ste 3 (12110-1505)
PHONE 518 437-1300
Jeffrey Hartgraves, *Manager*
EMP: 12
SALES (corp-wide): 96.6MM **Privately Held**
WEB: www.dwdiesel.com
SIC: 3519 Diesel engine rebuilding
PA: D & W Diesel, Inc.
1503 Clark Street Rd
Auburn NY 13021
315 253-5300

(G-7360)
DANI LU INC
601 New Loudon Rd Ste 4 (12110-4071)
PHONE 518 782-5411
Danielle Volpe, *President*
EMP: 22
SQ FT: 3,500
SALES (est): 2.1MM **Privately Held**
SIC: 2752 Commercial printing, offset

(G-7361)
EAZYLIFT ALBANY LLC
836 Troy Schenectady Rd (12110-2424)
P.O. Box 340 (12110-0340)
PHONE 518 452-6929
Theresa Farrigan,
EMP: 5
SALES: 950K **Privately Held**
SIC: 3534 Elevators & moving stairways

(G-7362)
EMERGENT POWER INC (HQ)
968 Albany Shaker Rd (12110-1401)
PHONE 201 441-3590
Andrew Marsh, *President*
EMP: 5
SALES (est): 21.9MM
SALES (corp-wide): 103.2MM **Publicly Held**
SIC: 2679 Fuel cell forms, cardboard: made from purchased material
PA: Plug Power Inc.
968 Albany Shaker Rd
Latham NY 12110
518 782-7700

(G-7363)
G AND G SERVICE
21 Nelson Ave (12110-1805)
PHONE 518 785-9247
Greg Gilbert,
EMP: 5
SALES (est): 336.9K **Privately Held**
SIC: 3089 8999 Plastics products; services

(G-7364)
HOWMEDICA OSTEONICS CORP
2 Northway Ln (12110-4820)
PHONE 518 783-1880
Steve Bulger, *Branch Mgr*
EMP: 9
SALES (corp-wide): 9.9B **Publicly Held**
SIC: 3842 Surgical appliances & supplies

HQ: Howmedica Osteonics Corp.
325 Corporate Dr
Mahwah NJ 07430
201 831-5000

(G-7365)
IMPERIAL POOLS INC (PA)
33 Wade Rd (12110-2613)
PHONE 518 786-1200
Fax: 518 786-0954
William Churchman, *CEO*
John V Maiuccoro, *President*
Katie Maiuccoro, *Principal*
Robert Burke, *Vice Pres*
Gary Maiuccoro, *Vice Pres*
◆ EMP: 123 EST: 1966
SQ FT: 100,000
SALES (est): 69.1MM **Privately Held**
WEB: www.imperialpools.com
SIC: 3949 5091 Swimming pools, except plastic; swimming pools, equipment & supplies

(G-7366)
JUNIOR ACHEVEMENT OF EASTRN NY
8 Stanley Cir Ste 8 (12110-2606)
PHONE 518 783-4336
Fax: 518 783-4346
Ed Murray, *President*
Tovah Lisky, *Marketing Staff*
EMP: 5
SALES: 635K **Privately Held**
SIC: 3613 Distribution cutouts

(G-7367)
KAFKO (US) CORP
787 Watervliet Shaker Rd (12110-2211)
PHONE 877 721-7665
Mark Laven, *President*
EMP: 5
SALES (est): 447.8K
SALES (corp-wide): 218.9MM **Privately Held**
SIC: 3999 Manufacturing industries
PA: Latham International, Inc.
787 Watervliet Shaker Rd
Latham NY 12110
518 783-7776

(G-7368)
LATHAM INTERNATIONAL INC (PA)
787 Watervliet Shaker Rd (12110-2211)
PHONE 518 783-7776
Mark Laven, *President*
Gary Whitcher, *VP Opers*
Tom Correll, *Plant Mgr*
Lynn Hyatt, *Safety Mgr*
Ryan Legere, *QA Dir*
◆ EMP: 1 EST: 2004
SQ FT: 90,000
SALES (est): 218.9MM **Privately Held**
WEB: www.pacificpools.com
SIC: 3086 3081 Plastics foam products; vinyl film & sheet

(G-7369)
LATHAM POOL PRODUCTS INC (PA)
787 Watervliet Shaker Rd (12110-2211)
P.O. Box 550, Jane Lew WV (26378-0550)
PHONE 518 951-1000
Fax: 518 785-0004
Mark Laven, *President*
John McGough, *Vice Pres*
Harold A Brooks, *Engineer*
Jennifer Lyons, *HR Admin*
Richard Piontkowski, *VP Sales*
▼ EMP: 129
SQ FT: 25,000
SALES (est): 119.9MM **Privately Held**
SIC: 3949 Swimming pools, except plastic

(G-7370)
LATHAM POOL PRODUCTS INC
Also Called: Latham Manufacturing
787 Watervliet Shaker Rd (12110-2211)
PHONE 260 432-8731
Fax: 260 432-0500
Richard Piontkowski, *VP Sales*
Matt Geyman, *Branch Mgr*
Rob Fuess, *Technology*
EMP: 44 **Privately Held**
SIC: 3086 Plastics foam products

PA: Latham Pool Products, Inc.
787 Watervliet Shaker Rd
Latham NY 12110

(G-7371)
LATHAM SOFTWARE SCIENCES INC
678 Troy Schenectady Rd # 104 (12110-2502)
PHONE 518 785-1100
Michael Dellavilla, *President*
John D Miller, *Vice Pres*
EMP: 12
SALES (est): 840K **Privately Held**
SIC: 7372 Prepackaged software

(G-7372)
LATORRE ORTHOPEDIC LABORATORY
960 Troy Schenectady Rd (12110-1609)
PHONE 518 786-8655
Timothy Lacy, *President*
EMP: 15
SALES (est): 930K **Privately Held**
SIC: 3842 Orthopedic appliances; prosthetic appliances

(G-7373)
MARKTECH INTERNATIONAL CORP (PA)
Also Called: Marktech Optoelectronics
3 Northway Ln N (12110-2232)
PHONE 518 956-2980
Mark G Campito, *Ch of Bd*
Clive A Sofe, *President*
Joseph Andrascik, *Vice Pres*
Han CHI, *Engineer*
Vincent Forte, *Engineer*
▲ EMP: 25
SALES (est): 3.6MM **Privately Held**
WEB: www.marktechopto.com
SIC: 3674 Semiconductors & related devices

(G-7374)
PEPSI BEVERAGES CO
Also Called: Pepsico
421 Old Niskayuna Rd (12110-1566)
PHONE 518 782-2150
EMP: 7
SALES (est): 506.6K **Privately Held**
SIC: 2086 Carbonated soft drinks, bottled & canned

(G-7375)
PEPSI-COLA ALLIED BOTTLERS
1 Pepsi Cola Dr (12110-2306)
PHONE 518 783-8811
John R Strachan, *Ch of Bd*
Mac McIlverid, *General Mgr*
Darren Silveria, *General Mgr*
Kathy Cary, *Vice Pres*
Carlton Endemann, *Vice Pres*
▲ EMP: 850
SQ FT: 180,000
SALES (est): 94.4MM
SALES (corp-wide): 63B **Publicly Held**
WEB: www.pbg.com
SIC: 2086 Soft drinks: packaged in cans, bottles, etc.
HQ: Pepsi-Cola Metropolitan Bottling Company, Inc.
1111 Westchester Ave
White Plains NY 10604
914 767-6000

(G-7376)
PHILIPS MEDICAL SYSTEMS MR (DH)
Also Called: Philips Healthcare
450 Old Niskayuna Rd (12110-1569)
PHONE 518 782-1122
Stephen H Rusckowski, *CEO*
Leo Blecher, *President*
Richard Stevens, *President*
Thomas J O'Brien, *Exec VP*
Thomas J Obrien, *Exec VP*
◆ EMP: 400
SQ FT: 146,000

SALES (est): 152.5MM
SALES (corp-wide): 26B **Privately Held**
SIC: 3845 3674 3679 Electromedical equipment; magnetic resonance imaging device, nuclear; integrated circuits, semiconductor networks, etc.; cryogenic cooling devices for infrared detectors, masers; cores, magnetic

(G-7377)
PLUG POWER INC (PA)
968 Albany Shaker Rd (12110-1428)
PHONE 518 782-7700
Fax: 518 782-7914
George C McNamee, *Ch of Bd*
Andrew J Marsh, *President*
Keith C Schmid, *COO*
Gerard L Conway Jr, *Senior VP*
Jose Luis Crespo, *Vice Pres*
▲ EMP: 277 EST: 1997
SQ FT: 140,000
SALES: 103.2MM **Publicly Held**
WEB: www.plugpower.com
SIC: 2679 Fuel cell forms, cardboard: made from purchased material

(G-7378)
RESPONSELINK INC
Also Called: Responselink of Albany
31 Dussault Dr (12110-2303)
PHONE 518 424-7776
Jason Kutey, *President*
EMP: 6
SALES (est): 365.1K **Privately Held**
SIC: 3841 Surgical & medical instruments

(G-7379)
TIRE CONVERSION TECH INC
874 Albany Shaker Rd (12110-1416)
PHONE 518 372-1600
Fax: 518 372-5505
Garen Szablewski, *CEO*
Jeff Henry, *Vice Pres*
Robert Donohue, *Controller*
Jack Hout, *Accounts Mgr*
EMP: 25
SQ FT: 10,000
SALES (est): 4.2MM **Privately Held**
WEB: www.tire-conversion.com
SIC: 3069 Custom compounding of rubber materials

(G-7380)
TRANE US INC
301 Old Niskayuna Rd # 1 (12110-2276)
PHONE 518 785-1315
Fax: 518 785-4359
William Seward, *Branch Mgr*
EMP: 35 **Privately Held**
SIC: 3585 Refrigeration & heating equipment
HQ: Trane U.S. Inc.
1 Centennial Ave Ste 101
Piscataway NJ 08854
732 652-7100

(G-7381)
TRANSTECH SYSTEMS INC (PA)
900 Albany Shaker Rd (12110-1416)
PHONE 518 370-5558
Fax: 518 370-5538
David Apkarian, *CEO*
Mike Debrino, *Vice Pres*
Jaret C Morse, *Vice Pres*
Donald Colosimo, *Treasurer*
David Dussault, *Director*
▼ EMP: 20
SQ FT: 16,000
SALES: 4.2MM **Privately Held**
WEB: www.transtechsys.com
SIC: 3823 8731 Industrial instrmnts msrmnt display/control process variable; commercial physical research

(G-7382)
VAN ALPHEN & DORAN CORP
1050 Troy Schenectady Rd (12110-1008)
PHONE 518 782-9242
Teresa M Van Alphen, *Principal*
EMP: 5
SALES (est): 306K **Privately Held**
SIC: 2024 Ice cream & frozen desserts

▲ = Import ▼ = Export
◆ = Import/Export

GEOGRAPHIC SECTION

(G-7383)
VINYL WORKS INC
33 Wade Rd (12110-2613)
PHONE..................................518 786-1200
John Maiuccoro, *President*
EMP: 50
SALES (est): 3.7MM **Privately Held**
WEB: www.thevinylworks.com
SIC: 2394 Liners & covers, fabric: made from purchased materials

(G-7384)
WERCS LTD
23 British American Blvd # 2 (12110-1426)
PHONE..................................518 640-9200
Lou Desorbo, *President*
Laura Campbell, *Vice Pres*
Tom Carter, *Vice Pres*
Gabriel Guzman, *Project Mgr*
Crystal Nussbaumer, *Project Mgr*
EMP: 46
SALES (est): 9.3MM
SALES (corp-wide): 1.8B **Privately Held**
WEB: www.thewercs.com
SIC: 7372 8748 Business oriented computer software; business consulting
PA: Underwriters Laboratories Inc.
333 Pfingsten Rd
Northbrook IL 60062
847 272-8800

(G-7385)
WILLIAM BOYD PRINTING CO INC
Also Called: Boyd Printing Company
4 Weed Rd Ste 1 (12110-2939)
PHONE..................................518 339-5832
Henry R Bosselman, *Ch of Bd*
Jane Q Carey, *President*
Stacey Dunning, *Principal*
James Blaauboer, *Vice Pres*
Carl R Johnson, *Vice Pres*
EMP: 120 EST: 1889
SQ FT: 81,000
SALES (est): 4.9MM **Privately Held**
SIC: 2711 2752 Commercial printing & newspaper publishing combined; commercial printing, lithographic

Laurelton
Queens County

(G-7386)
CLINTON CREAMERY INC
13221 220th St (11413-1547)
PHONE..................................917 324-9699
Robyn Clinton, *President*
Cedrizk Clinton, *Vice Pres*
EMP: 14
SALES (est): 690K **Privately Held**
SIC: 2024 5451 Ice cream & frozen desserts; ice cream (packaged)

(G-7387)
EPIC PHARMA LLC
22715 N Conduit Ave (11413-3134)
PHONE..................................718 276-8600
Jai Narine, *Exec VP*
Christopher Aupperlee, *Vice Pres*
Marcus Taylor, *Research*
Paul Cook, *Engineer*
John J Smith, *Controller*
▲ EMP: 160
SQ FT: 110,000
SALES (est): 62.3MM **Privately Held**
SIC: 2834 Pharmaceutical preparations

(G-7388)
NOVARTIS CORPORATION
22715 N Conduit Ave (11413-3134)
PHONE..................................718 276-8600
Kumar Rathnam, *Vice Pres*
EMP: 56
SALES (corp-wide): 49.4B **Privately Held**
WEB: www.novartis.com
SIC: 2834 Pharmaceutical preparations
HQ: Novartis Corporation
608 5th Ave
New York NY 10020
212 307-1122

(G-7389)
NOVARTIS PHARMACEUTICALS CORP
22715 N Conduit Ave (11413-3134)
PHONE..................................718 276-8600
EMP: 8
SALES (est): 2.2MM
SALES (corp-wide): 49.4B **Privately Held**
SIC: 2834 Pharmaceutical Preparations
PA: Novartis Ag
Lichtstrasse 35
Basel BS 4056
613 241-111

Lawrence
Nassau County

(G-7390)
ATLAZ INTERNATIONAL LTD
298 Lawrence Ave Unit 1 (11559-1268)
PHONE..................................516 239-1854
Fax: 516 239-1939
Loretta Zalta, *President*
Adam Zalta, *Vice Pres*
Andre Zalta, *Vice Pres*
EMP: 11
SQ FT: 3,000
SALES (est): 2.5MM **Privately Held**
WEB: www.atlaz.com
SIC: 3577 5045 5112 Computer peripheral equipment; computer peripheral equipment; stationery & office supplies

(G-7391)
HASTINGS HIDE INC
Also Called: A J Hollander Enterprises
335 Central Ave Ste 4 (11559-1621)
PHONE..................................516 295-2400
Howard Ganz, *President*
EMP: 6
SALES (corp-wide): 1.7MM **Privately Held**
SIC: 3111 5159 4731 Leather tanning & finishing; hides; agents, shipping
PA: Hastings Hide, Inc.
231 Road 3168
Hastings NE 68901
402 463-5308

(G-7392)
JOHN J RICHARDSON
Also Called: Gad Systems
12 Bernard St (11559-1245)
PHONE..................................516 538-6339
John J Richardson, *Owner*
EMP: 15
SQ FT: 4,000
SALES: 900K **Privately Held**
SIC: 3695 Computer software tape & disks: blank, rigid & floppy

(G-7393)
LAST STRAW INC
Also Called: Zenith Promotions
22 Lawrence Ln Unit 1 (11559-1137)
P.O. Box 960177, Inwood (11096-0177)
PHONE..................................516 371-2727
Fax: 516 371-2442
Sharon Hecht, *President*
Maria Lafichi, *Shareholder*
▲ EMP: 40 EST: 1995
SQ FT: 9,000
SALES (est): 8MM **Privately Held**
WEB: www.zenithpromotions.com
SIC: 2656 5092 Straws, drinking: made from purchased material; toys & games

(G-7394)
M W MICROWAVE CORP
45 Auerbach Ln (11559-2529)
PHONE..................................516 295-1814
Fax: 631 420-0621
Mariam Wiesenfeld, *President*
EMP: 12 EST: 1970
SQ FT: 10,000
SALES (est): 1MM **Privately Held**
SIC: 3679 Waveguides & fittings; microwave components

(G-7395)
MEDITUB INCORPORATED
11 Wedgewood Ln (11559-1427)
P.O. Box 668 (11559-0668)
PHONE..................................866 633-4882
Joseph Swartz, *President*
Mark Barnathan, *Sales Staff*
EMP: 14
SALES (est): 513.7K
SALES (corp-wide): 15.7MM **Privately Held**
SIC: 3272 Bathtubs, concrete
PA: Spa World Corporation
1 Oakwood Blvd Ste 200
Hollywood FL 33020
866 588-8008

(G-7396)
NEW YORK RHBILITATIVE SVCS LLC
135 Rockaway Tpke Ste 107 (11559-1023)
PHONE..................................516 239-0990
Michael Nadata, *Owner*
EMP: 14
SALES (est): 1.6MM **Privately Held**
SIC: 3842 Prosthetic appliances

(G-7397)
PREMIER SKIRTING PRODUCTS INC
Also Called: Premier Skrting Tblecloths Too
241 Mill St (11559-1209)
PHONE..................................516 239-6581
Fax: 516 239-6810
Ross Yudin, *CEO*
Beth Yudin, *President*
Linda Ehrlich, *Corp Secy*
EMP: 16
SQ FT: 8,500
SALES (est): 1.5MM **Privately Held**
WEB: www.premierskirting.com
SIC: 2392 Tablecloths: made from purchased materials; napkins, fabric & nonwoven: made from purchased materials

(G-7398)
RASON ASPHALT INC
4 Johnson Rd (11559-1036)
PHONE..................................516 239-7880
Fax: 516 239-7621
Fred Wallenquest, *Manager*
EMP: 6
SALES (corp-wide): 9.3MM **Privately Held**
WEB: www.rason1.com
SIC: 2951 Asphalt & asphaltic paving mixtures (not from refineries)
PA: Rason Asphalt Inc.
Rr 110
Farmingdale NY 11735
631 293-6210

(G-7399)
RICHNER COMMUNICATIONS INC
Also Called: Oceanside-Island Park Herald
379 Central Ave (11559-1607)
PHONE..................................516 569-4000
Rhonda Glickman, *Vice Pres*
Karen Mengel, *Prdtn Mgr*
Ellen Frisch, *Accounts Exec*
Vicki Kaplan, *Accounts Exec*
Cliff Richner, *Branch Mgr*
EMP: 5
SALES (corp-wide): 16.3MM **Privately Held**
SIC: 2711 Newspapers: publishing only, not printed on site
PA: Richner Communications, Inc.
2 Endo Blvd
Garden City NY 11530
516 569-4000

(G-7400)
SEVILLE CENTRAL MIX CORP
101 Johnson Rd (11559)
PHONE..................................516 239-8333
Fax: 516 239-7496
Peter Buck, *Manager*
EMP: 30
SALES (corp-wide): 13.6MM **Privately Held**
WEB: www.sevillecentralmix.com
SIC: 3273 Ready-mixed concrete
PA: Seville Central Mix Corp.
157 Albany Ave
Freeport NY 11520
516 868-3000

(G-7401)
TG PEPPE INC
Also Called: Doery Awning Co
299 Rockaway Tpke Unit B (11559-1269)
PHONE..................................516 239-7852
Fax: 516 239-0696
Thomas Peppe, *President*
Gregory Peppe, *Vice Pres*
Sabrina Peppe, *Office Mgr*
EMP: 8
SQ FT: 6,000
SALES (est): 490K **Privately Held**
SIC: 2394 7699 Awnings, fabric: made from purchased materials; awning repair shop

Le Roy
Genesee County

(G-7402)
ALUMINUM INJECTION MOLD CO LLC
8741 Lake Street Rd Ste 4 (14482-9381)
PHONE..................................585 502-6087
Gerald Ayers, *Vice Pres*
Russ Bailey, *Admin Asst*
Tom Bergman,
EMP: 8
SQ FT: 12,000
SALES (est): 1.2MM **Privately Held**
WEB: www.aluminuminjectionmold.com
SIC: 3089 Injection molded finished plastic products

(G-7403)
BATAVIA LEGAL PRINTING INC
7 Bank St (14482-1413)
PHONE..................................585 768-2100
Susan Duyssen, *President*
Pat Maher, *Manager*
EMP: 5
SQ FT: 6,111
SALES (est): 725K **Privately Held**
WEB: www.batavialegal.com
SIC: 2621 Printing paper

(G-7404)
CK COATINGS
57 North St Ste 150 (14482-1143)
PHONE..................................585 502-0425
Linda Wright, *Owner*
EMP: 5
SALES (est): 482.3K **Privately Held**
SIC: 3827 Optical instruments & lenses

(G-7405)
DOLOMITE PRODUCTS COMPANY INC
8250 Golf Rd (14482)
PHONE..................................585 768-7295
Fax: 585 768-7246
Susan Langfeld, *Human Res Mgr*
Matt McCormick, *Manager*
Matt M Cormick, *Manager*
EMP: 12
SQ FT: 9,122
SALES (corp-wide): 25.3B **Privately Held**
WEB: www.dolomitegroup.com
SIC: 2951 Paving mixtures
HQ: Dolomite Products Company Inc.
1150 Penfield Rd
Rochester NY 14625
315 524-1998

(G-7406)
DRAY ENTERPRISES INC
Also Called: Le Roy Pennysaver
1 Church St (14482-1017)
P.O. Box 190 (14482-0190)
PHONE..................................585 768-2201
Fax: 585 768-2201
David J Grayson Jr, *President*
Danette L Grayson, *Admin Sec*
EMP: 14 EST: 1963
SQ FT: 16,000

Le Roy - Genesee County (G-7407)

SALES (est): 1.1MM **Privately Held**
WEB: www.leroyny.com
SIC: 2711 7389 Newspapers; embroidering of advertising on shirts, etc.

(G-7407)
DUZMOR PAINTING INC
Also Called: Finishing Line, The
7959 E Main Rd (14482-9726)
P.O. Box 135 (14482-0135)
PHONE..............................585 768-4760
Fax: 585 768-2296
Peter Mc Quillen, *President*
Judy Mc Quillen, *Vice Pres*
EMP: 6
SQ FT: 10,000
SALES (est): 757.8K **Privately Held**
WEB: www.thefinishinglineco.com
SIC: 3479 Painting of metal products

(G-7408)
HELIOJET CLEANING TECH INC
57 North St Ste 120 (14482-1143)
PHONE..............................585 768-8710
Russell Knisel Jr, *President*
Scott Meurer, *Vice Pres*
Lee Nicodemus, *Marketing Mgr*
EMP: 12 EST: 1980
SQ FT: 11,640
SALES (est): 1.1MM **Privately Held**
WEB: www.heliojet.com
SIC: 3589 High pressure cleaning equipment

(G-7409)
ICON DESIGN LLC
9 Lent Ave (14482-1009)
PHONE..............................585 768-6040
Fax: 585 768-7558
Wendell Castle,
EMP: 25
SALES (est): 3MM **Privately Held**
WEB: www.icondesign.com
SIC: 2511 Wood household furniture

(G-7410)
J & L PRECISION CO INC
9222 Summit Street Rd (14482-8950)
PHONE..............................585 768-6388
James Lytle, *President*
Laurita Lytle, *Corp Secy*
EMP: 8 EST: 1977
SQ FT: 6,500
SALES (est): 720K **Privately Held**
SIC: 3599 Machine shop, jobbing & repair; electrical discharge machining (EDM)

(G-7411)
LAPP INSULATOR COMPANY LLC
130 Gilbert St (14482-1392)
PHONE..............................585 768-6221
Ing Bernhard Kahl, *CEO*
Rob Johnson, *COO*
Veronika Capek, *CFO*
Cindy Bishop, *Human Resources*
EMP: 14 EST: 1998
SALES (est): 15MM **Privately Held**
SIC: 3264 3644 Insulators, electrical: porcelain; noncurrent-carrying wiring services; insulators & insulation materials, electrical

(G-7412)
LAPP INSULATORS LLC
130 Gilbert St (14482-1392)
PHONE..............................585 768-6221
Fax: 585 768-5768
Ing Bernhard Kahl, *CEO*
Rob Johnson, *President*
Wayne Subject, *Plant Mgr*
Gordon Prince, *Purch Mgr*
Eric Kress, *QA Dir*
▲ EMP: 125
SQ FT: 651,000
SALES (est): 25MM **Privately Held**
WEB: www.lappinsulator.com
SIC: 3264 3644 Insulators, electrical: porcelain; noncurrent-carrying wiring services; insulators & insulation materials, electrical

(G-7413)
LEROY PLASTICS INC
20 Lent Ave (14482-1010)
PHONE..............................585 768-8158
Fax: 585 768-4283
Ernest Truax, *President*
George Jinks, *QC Mgr*
Kay Miggins, *Office Mgr*
◆ EMP: 61
SQ FT: 62,305
SALES: 7MM **Privately Held**
WEB: www.leroyplastics.com
SIC: 3498 Fabricated pipe & fittings

(G-7414)
MARMACH MACHINE INC
11 Lent Ave (14482-1009)
PHONE..............................585 768-8800
Fax: 585 768-4809
John M Lynch, *President*
J P Lynch, *Business Mgr*
EMP: 6
SALES (est): 873.7K **Privately Held**
SIC: 3451 Screw machine products

(G-7415)
MOFFITT CORPORATION INC
Also Called: Moffit Fan
54 Church St (14482-1037)
PHONE..............................585 768-7010
Terence R Wirth II, *President*
EMP: 22
SALES (corp-wide): 10.6MM **Privately Held**
SIC: 3564 Blowers & fans; blowers & fans
PA: Moffitt Corporation, Inc.
 1351 13th Ave S Ste 130
 Jacksonville Beach FL 32250
 904 241-9944

(G-7416)
MOFFITT FAN CORPORATION
54 Church St (14482-1037)
PHONE..............................585 768-7010
John Moffitt, *Ch of Bd*
Terence R Wirth II, *President*
Michael Andorka, *Plant Mgr*
Barbara Snell, *Office Mgr*
EMP: 40
SQ FT: 50,000
SALES (est): 10MM **Privately Held**
SIC: 3564 Blowers & fans; blowers & fans

(G-7417)
ORCON INDUSTRIES CORP (PA)
8715 Lake Rd (14482-9396)
PHONE..............................585 768-7000
Fax: 585 768-6999
Bruce E Olson, *Ch of Bd*
Gale Hastings, *Exec VP*
Cheryl Le Blanc, *Vice Pres*
Cheryl Hastings, *Prdtn Mgr*
Randy Vink, *Marketing Staff*
▲ EMP: 75
SQ FT: 98,000
SALES (est): 21.8MM **Privately Held**
WEB: www.orconind.com
SIC: 2653 3086 7336 Corrugated & solid fiber boxes; packaging & shipping materials, foamed plastic; chart & graph design

(G-7418)
PCORE ELECTRIC COMPANY INC
135 Gilbert St (14482-1353)
PHONE..............................585 768-1200
Fax: 585 768-1235
Timothy Powers, *President*
Andrew McNulty, *Engineer*
Eric Weatherbee, *Senior Engr*
Zachary Hopkins, *Marketing Staff*
Peter G Schulpz, *Director*
▲ EMP: 64
SQ FT: 100,000
SALES (est): 15.1MM
SALES (corp-wide): 3.3B **Publicly Held**
WEB: www.pcoreelectric.com
SIC: 3325 Bushings, cast steel: except investment
PA: Hubbell Incorporated
 40 Waterview Dr
 Shelton CT 06484
 475 882-4000

(G-7419)
T S P CORP
Also Called: Thom McGinnes Excavating Plbg
78 One Half Lake St (14482)
P.O. Box 126 (14482-0126)
PHONE..............................585 768-6769
Thomas W McGinnis, *President*
EMP: 10
SQ FT: 1,000
SALES: 550K **Privately Held**
SIC: 3531 Plows: construction, excavating & grading

Leicester
Livingston County

(G-7420)
CPAC INC (DH)
Also Called: Stanley Home Products
2364 State Route 20a (14481-9734)
P.O. Box 175 (14481-0175)
PHONE..............................585 382-3223
Fax: 585 382-3031
Thomas N Hendrickson, *Principal*
David P Biehn, *Senior VP*
Thomas N Hedrickso, *Project Mgr*
Sue Doerflinger, *Opers Mgr*
Tish Johnson, *Purchasing*
▼ EMP: 50
SQ FT: 31,262
SALES (est): 55.4MM
SALES (corp-wide): 74MM **Privately Held**
SIC: 2842 3991 2392 2841 Specialty cleaning, polishes & sanitation goods; specialty cleaning preparations; sanitation preparations, disinfectants & deodorants; brooms & brushes; mops, floor & dust; soap & other detergents; shampoos, rinses, conditioners: hair; cosmetic preparations; photographic equipment & supplies; sensitized film, cloth & paper; photographic processing chemicals
HQ: Buckingham Cpac Inc
 2364 State Route 20a
 Leicester NY 14481
 585 382-3223

(G-7421)
CPAC EQUIPMENT INC
2364 State Route 20a (14481-9734)
P.O. Box 175 (14481-0175)
PHONE..............................585 382-3223
Thomas Weldgen, *CEO*
Natalie Gayton, *Controller*
EMP: 16
SQ FT: 15,000
SALES (est): 2.1MM **Privately Held**
WEB: www.cpacequipment.com
SIC: 3843 Sterilizers, dental; dental equipment; glue, dental
PA: Integrated Medical Technologies, Inc.
 2422 E Washington St # 103
 Bloomington IL 61704
 309 662-3614

(G-7422)
SENECA FOODS CORPORATION
Also Called: Comstock Food
5705 Rte 36 (14481)
P.O. Box 278 (14481-0278)
PHONE..............................585 658-2211
Fax: 585 658-3848
Cameron Ellis, *Warehouse Mgr*
Flo Mullen, *QC Mgr*
Mike Hanchette, *Manager*
EMP: 40
SALES (corp-wide): 1.2B **Publicly Held**
SIC: 2033 Vegetables: packaged in cans, jars, etc.
PA: Seneca Foods Corporation
 3736 S Main St
 Marion NY 14505
 315 926-8100

Levittown
Nassau County

(G-7423)
APOGEE RETAIL NY
3041 Hempstead Tpke (11756-1332)
PHONE..............................516 731-1727
EMP: 5 EST: 2010
SALES (est): 379.5K **Privately Held**
SIC: 2329 Men's & boys' clothing

(G-7424)
AVALONICS INC
94 Gardiners Ave Ste 164 (11756-3705)
PHONE..............................516 238-7074
Sharjeel Ansari, *CEO*
Raheel Ansari, *President*
Chris Papas, *Manager*
EMP: 7
SALES (est): 1.3MM **Privately Held**
WEB: www.security-cameras-cctv.com
SIC: 3699 Security devices

(G-7425)
BEYOND BEAUTY BASICS LLC
3359 Hempstead Tpke (11756-1310)
PHONE..............................516 731-7100
Claudie Oslian,
EMP: 17
SALES (est): 1.8MM **Privately Held**
SIC: 2899 Core wash or wax

(G-7426)
CCZ READY MIX CONCRETE CORP
2 Loring Rd (11756-1516)
PHONE..............................516 579-7352
Michael Zampini, *President*
EMP: 6
SALES (est): 616.5K **Privately Held**
SIC: 3273 Ready-mixed concrete

(G-7427)
DEUNALL CORPORATION
147 Blacksmith Rd E (11756-3127)
PHONE..............................516 667-8875
Kevin Park, *President*
Steve Yoon, *Vice Pres*
Myeoan Kim, *Shareholder*
Russell Lin, *Shareholder*
Hugh Thung, *Shareholder*
EMP: 205
SQ FT: 2,800
SALES: 4MM **Privately Held**
SIC: 2342 Foundation garments, women's

(G-7428)
GLITNIR TICKETING INC
Also Called: Glitner Ticketing
3 Snapdragon Ln (11756-3315)
PHONE..............................516 390-5168
Gordon Krstacic, *CEO*
Mike Hasl, *Marketing Staff*
EMP: 5
SALES (est): 488.9K **Privately Held**
WEB: www.glitnir.com
SIC: 7372 Prepackaged software

(G-7429)
KB MILLWORK INC
36 Grey Ln (11756-4411)
P.O. Box 395 (11756-0395)
PHONE..............................516 280-2183
Kenneth Wright, *President*
EMP: 5
SQ FT: 1,200
SALES: 1.5MM **Privately Held**
SIC: 2431 Millwork

(G-7430)
PAGE DEVICES INC
11 Sunny Ln (11756-3819)
P.O. Box 7003, Wantagh (11793-0603)
PHONE..............................516 735-8376
Fax: 516 694-3017
Terry Page, *President*
EMP: 10 EST: 1963
SQ FT: 5,000
SALES: 500K **Privately Held**
SIC: 3599 Machine shop, jobbing & repair

▲ = Import ▼ = Export
◆ = Import/Export

GEOGRAPHIC SECTION

Lewis
Essex County

(G-7431)
GRAYMONT MATERIALS (NY) INC
Also Called: Lewis Sand & Gravel
Rr 9 (12950)
PHONE..................518 873-2275
Ron Haugh, *Manager*
EMP: 9
SALES (corp-wide): 260.9MM **Privately Held**
WEB: www.graymont-ab.com
SIC: 2951 3273 3272 3241 Asphalt paving mixtures & blocks; ready-mixed concrete; concrete products; cement, hydraulic
HQ: Graymont Materials (Ny) Inc.
111 Quarry Rd
Plattsburgh NY 12901
518 561-5321

Lewiston
Niagara County

(G-7432)
450 RIDGE ST INC
Also Called: Mellen Pressroom & Bindery
450 Ridge St (14092-1206)
P.O. Box 450 (14092-0450)
PHONE..................716 754-2789
Ruth Koheil, *President*
Dick Cessna, *Controller*
EMP: 7
SQ FT: 1,488
SALES (est): 1MM **Privately Held**
SIC: 2731 2752 2732 Books: publishing & printing; commercial printing, lithographic; book printing

(G-7433)
ALTA GROUP INC
Also Called: Chateau Royal
210 S 8th St (14092-1702)
PHONE..................905 262-5707
Robert Allen, *CEO*
EMP: 10
SALES: 1.2MM **Privately Held**
SIC: 2015 Poultry sausage, luncheon meats & other poultry products

(G-7434)
EDWIN MELLEN PRESS INC
442 Center St (14092-1604)
PHONE..................716 754-2796
Herbert Richardson, *President*
EMP: 38
SALES (est): 1.5MM **Privately Held**
SIC: 2731 Book publishing

(G-7435)
PSR PRESS LTD
Also Called: Mellen Press, The
415 Ridge St (14092-1205)
P.O. Box 450 (14092-0450)
PHONE..................716 754-2266
Fax: 716 754-4056
Herbert Richardson, *CEO*
Dick Cessna, *Finance Mgr*
John Rupnow, *Director*
EMP: 12
SQ FT: 2,000
SALES (est): 1.1MM **Privately Held**
WEB: www.mellenpress.com
SIC: 2731 Book publishing

Liberty
Sullivan County

(G-7436)
CRANESVILLE BLOCK CO INC
Also Called: Cranesville Concrete Co
1794 State Route 52 (12754-8304)
PHONE..................845 292-1585
Fax: 845 292-2083
Stephen Miller, *Manager*
EMP: 10
SALES (corp-wide): 41.2MM **Privately Held**
SIC: 3273 Ready-mixed concrete
PA: Cranesville Block Co., Inc.
1250 Riverfront Ctr
Amsterdam NY 12010
518 684-6000

(G-7437)
IDEAL SNACKS CORPORATION
89 Mill St (12754-2038)
PHONE..................845 292-7000
Fax: 845 292-3100
Zeke Alenick, *President*
Miriam Ehrenberg, *Vice Pres*
Steven Van Poucke, *Vice Pres*
Steven Vanpoucke, *Engineer*
Jim Pietro, *Sls & Mktg Exec*
◆ EMP: 200
SQ FT: 250,000
SALES (est): 49.6MM **Privately Held**
WEB: www.idealsnacks.com
SIC: 2096 Potato chips & similar snacks

(G-7438)
MAJOR-IPC INC
53 Webster Ave (12754-2005)
P.O. Box 350 (12754-0350)
PHONE..................845 292-2200
David Feldman, *President*
Elizabeth McCalister, *Office Mgr*
▲ EMP: 5 EST: 1976
SQ FT: 9,800
SALES (est): 825.3K **Privately Held**
SIC: 3089 3441 Plastic processing; fabricated structural metal

Lido Beach
Nassau County

(G-7439)
AIRLINE CONTAINER SERVICES
Also Called: Airline Container Svces
354 Harbor Dr (11561-4907)
PHONE..................516 371-4125
R Dino Persaud, *President*
Gomattie Persaud, *Vice Pres*
Isherwin Glabman, *Manager*
▲ EMP: 7
SALES (est): 1.1MM **Privately Held**
SIC: 2448 Cargo containers, wood & wood with metal

(G-7440)
BRODCO INC
67 Woodhail St (11561-5115)
PHONE..................631 842-4477
Jonathan Brodsky, *President*
EMP: 20
SQ FT: 8,000
SALES (est): 2.7MM **Privately Held**
WEB: www.brodco.com
SIC: 3564 5072 5074 5031 Ventilating fans: industrial or commercial; hardware; plumbing fittings & supplies; building materials, exterior; building materials, interior

(G-7441)
JFB PRINT SOLUTIONS INC
21 Park Dr (11561-4920)
PHONE..................631 694-8300
Randy Brown, *President*
Gary Brown, *Vice Pres*
EMP: 2
SQ FT: 2,000
SALES (est): 1.6MM **Privately Held**
SIC: 2752 Commercial printing, lithographic

(G-7442)
MARVEL DAIRY WHIP INC
258 Lido Blvd (11561-5024)
PHONE..................516 889-4232
Pauline Seremetis, *President*
EMP: 5
SALES (est): 312.6K **Privately Held**
SIC: 2024 5451 Ice cream, bulk; ice cream (packaged)

Lima
Livingston County

(G-7443)
BEARS MANAGEMENT GROUP INC
Also Called: Bears Playgrounds
7577 E Main St (14485-9735)
PHONE..................585 624-5694
Fax: 585 624-5694
C Daniel Bears, *President*
Marcie Bears, *Vice Pres*
EMP: 9
SQ FT: 2,000
SALES: 1.4MM **Privately Held**
WEB: www.bearsplaygrounds.com
SIC: 3949 Playground equipment

(G-7444)
EAST MAIN ASSOCIATES
Also Called: Lakelands Concrete
7520 E Main St (14485-9731)
PHONE..................585 624-1990
Todd Clarke, *President*
EMP: 60
SQ FT: 28,720
SALES: 270K **Privately Held**
SIC: 3272 Concrete products

(G-7445)
LAKELANDS CONCRETE PDTS INC
7520 E Main St (14485-9731)
PHONE..................585 624-1990
Fax: 585 624-2102
Todd Clarke, *President*
Scott S Smith, *Engineer*
Chad Bond, *Sales Dir*
Gina Lathan, *Sales Mgr*
Nathan Reiner, *Sales Staff*
EMP: 49 EST: 1951
SQ FT: 40,000
SALES (est): 9.7MM **Privately Held**
WEB: www.lakelandsconcrete.com
SIC: 3272 Concrete products, precast

(G-7446)
NORTHEAST CONVEYORS INC
7620 Evergreen St (14485-9727)
P.O. Box 55, Le Roy (14482-0055)
PHONE..................585 768-8912
Fax: 585 624-8015
Paul Hastings, *Ch of Bd*
Guy Bianchi, *Vice Pres*
Michael Shaffer, *Vice Pres*
Michael Shaffer, *Vice Pres*
Beth Bartz, *Treasurer*
EMP: 17
SQ FT: 8,024
SALES (est): 4.9MM
SALES (corp-wide): 57.6MM **Privately Held**
WEB: www.neind.com
SIC: 3535 Conveyors & conveying equipment
PA: Northeast Industrial Technologies, Inc.
7115 W Main Rd Ste 2
Le Roy NY 14482
585 768-8912

(G-7447)
P & H THERMOTECH INC
1883 Heath Markham Rd (14485-9529)
PHONE..................585 624-1310
Dave Howes, *CEO*
Ray Platt, *President*
EMP: 5
SALES (est): 463.7K **Privately Held**
SIC: 2796 Platemaking services

(G-7448)
SMIDGENS INC
7336 Community Dr (14485-9772)
PHONE..................585 624-1486
Rita Villa, *President*
Gary Villa, *Vice Pres*
EMP: 8
SQ FT: 3,000
SALES (est): 1.1MM **Privately Held**
WEB: www.smidgens.com
SIC: 3599 Machine shop, jobbing & repair

(G-7449)
SUPERIOR WALLS UPSTATE NY INC
7574 E Main St (14485-9731)
PHONE..................585 624-9390
Fax: 585 624-9572
Gary T Hess, *President*
Liza Gfeller, *Manager*
EMP: 90
SQ FT: 200,000
SALES (est): 17.9MM **Privately Held**
SIC: 3272 Precast terrazo or concrete products

Limestone
Cattaraugus County

(G-7450)
CASE BROTHERS INC
370 Quinn Rd (14753-9713)
P.O. Box 181 (14753-0181)
PHONE..................716 925-7172
Thomas A Case, *President*
EMP: 9
SALES (est): 949.7K **Privately Held**
SIC: 1389 Oil & gas field services

(G-7451)
JAY LITTLE OIL WELL SERVI
5460 Nichols Run (14753-9774)
PHONE..................716 925-8905
Jay Little, *Principal*
EMP: 5
SALES (est): 333.2K **Privately Held**
SIC: 1389 Well logging

Lindenhurst
Suffolk County

(G-7452)
ALRAJS INC (PA)
Also Called: Yohay Baking Company
146 Albany Ave (11757-3628)
PHONE..................631 225-0300
Fax: 631 225-4277
Mike Solomon, *President*
Lew Solomon, *Chairman*
Mitch Margolis, *Vice Pres*
▲ EMP: 27 EST: 1948
SQ FT: 15,000
SALES (est): 6.4MM **Privately Held**
WEB: www.yohay.com
SIC: 2051 2052 2064 Pastries, e.g. danish: except frozen; cones, ice cream; fudge (candy)

(G-7453)
ALRO MACHINE TOOL & DIE CO INC
585 W Hoffman Ave (11757-4032)
PHONE..................631 226-5020
Fax: 631 226-5026
Ronald Young, *President*
Elizabeth Young, *Corp Secy*
Steven Young, *Vice Pres*
Maya Young, *Administration*
EMP: 15 EST: 1960
SQ FT: 22,000
SALES (est): 3.1MM **Privately Held**
SIC: 3728 Aircraft assemblies, subassemblies & parts

(G-7454)
ANTHONY MANUFACTURING INC
34 Gear Ave (11757-1005)
PHONE..................631 957-9424
Jon Hatz, *President*
Benjamin Hatz, *Shareholder*
Melanie Hatz, *Shareholder*
Sandy Hatz, *Shareholder*
Kevin Jampolis, *Shareholder*
EMP: 9
SQ FT: 12,000
SALES (est): 780K **Privately Held**
WEB: www.keithmachinery.com
SIC: 3547 5084 Rolling mill machinery; industrial machinery & equipment

Lindenhurst - Suffolk County (G-7455)

(G-7455)
AUTO BODY SERVICES LLC
400 W Hoffman Ave (11757-4038)
PHONE..................631 431-4640
Michael Moretti, *Officer*
EMP: 12
SALES: 5MM **Privately Held**
SIC: 3563 3444 5013 Spraying outfits: metals, paints & chemicals (compressor); booths, spray: prefabricated sheet metal; body repair or paint shop supplies, automotive

(G-7456)
AUTODYNE MANUFACTURING CO INC
200 N Strong Ave (11757-3629)
PHONE..................631 957-5858
Lindsay Howe, *Ch of Bd*
Shari Kramberg, *Treasurer*
Jose Lino, *Manager*
Linsy Marino, *Manager*
EMP: 10
SALES: 2MM **Privately Held**
WEB: www.autodyne.com
SIC: 3674 Solid state electronic devices

(G-7457)
BUXTON MEDICAL EQUIPMENT CORP
1178 Route 109 (11757-1004)
PHONE..................631 957-4500
Fax: 631 957-3884
Carl Newman, *President*
Phillip McCann, *Vice Pres*
EMP: 30
SALES (est): 5.2MM **Privately Held**
WEB: www.buxtonmed.com
SIC: 3841 Surgical & medical instruments

(G-7458)
CANFIELD ELECTRONICS INC (PA)
6 Burton Pl (11757-1812)
PHONE..................631 585-4100
Fax: 631 585-4200
Lynn Zaun, *President*
Charles Crawford, *Sales Staff*
Laura Holme, *Manager*
▼ EMP: 18
SQ FT: 15,000
SALES (est): 3.1MM **Privately Held**
WEB: www.canfieldelectronics.com
SIC: 3679 5065 Electronic circuits; electronic parts & equipment

(G-7459)
CAROB INDUSTRIES INC
215 W Hoffman Ave (11757-4096)
PHONE..................631 225-0900
Robert A Levey, *President*
EMP: 10
SQ FT: 8,000
SALES: 1.2MM **Privately Held**
SIC: 2431 Millwork

(G-7460)
DELANEY MACHINE PRODUCTS LTD
150 S Alleghany Ave Ste A (11757-5062)
PHONE..................631 225-1032
Fax: 516 225-5723
Bob Delaney, *President*
Sharon Delaney, *Vice Pres*
EMP: 6
SQ FT: 10,000
SALES: 850K **Privately Held**
SIC: 3599 Machine shop, jobbing & repair

(G-7461)
DERMATECH LABS INC
165 S 10th St (11757-4505)
PHONE..................631 225-1700
Dan Bryle, *President*
Ava Abbati, *Manager*
▲ EMP: 10
SQ FT: 11,000
SALES (est): 940K **Privately Held**
SIC: 2844 5122 Cosmetic preparations; cosmetics

(G-7462)
DINE RITE SEATING PRODUCTS INC
165 E Hoffman Ave Unit 3 (11757-5036)
PHONE..................631 592-8126
Fax: 631 225-2399
Phil Driesen, *President*
EMP: 20
SALES (est): 3.5MM **Privately Held**
SIC: 2599 7641 Restaurant furniture, wood or metal; upholstery work

(G-7463)
ELITE SEMI CONDUCTOR PRODUCTS
860 N Richmond Ave (11757-3007)
PHONE..................631 884-8400
Fax: 631 884-8427
Robert Kravitz, *President*
Edward Kravitz, *Vice Pres*
Joan Kravitz, *Vice Pres*
EMP: 8
SQ FT: 5,000
SALES (est): 790K **Privately Held**
WEB: www.elitesemi.com
SIC: 3674 Semiconductors & related devices

(G-7464)
EXCEL COMMERCIAL SEATING
Also Called: Dine Right Seating
165 E Hoffman Ave Unit 2 (11757-5036)
PHONE..................828 428-8338
Phil Breisen, *Owner*
EMP: 50
SALES (est): 2.7MM **Privately Held**
SIC: 2599 Restaurant furniture, wood or metal

(G-7465)
GABRIELA SYSTEMS LTD
135 Bangor St (11757-3632)
PHONE..................631 225-7952
John Russo, *Owner*
EMP: 5 EST: 1999
SALES (est): 363.8K **Privately Held**
WEB: www.blendexindustrial.com
SIC: 2851 Polyurethane coatings

(G-7466)
JOHNNY MICA INC
116 E Hoffman Ave (11757-5029)
PHONE..................631 225-5213
John Desimini, *President*
Karla Desimini, *Corp Secy*
EMP: 5
SALES (est): 590K **Privately Held**
WEB: www.johnnymica.com
SIC: 2541 5031 1799 1751 Cabinets, except refrigerated: show, display, etc.: wood; kitchen cabinets; counter top installation; cabinet & finish carpentry

(G-7467)
LINDENHURST FABRICATORS INC
117 S 13th St (11757-4546)
PHONE..................631 226-3737
Fax: 631 226-3867
Charles Rogers, *President*
EMP: 8
SQ FT: 17,500
SALES (est): 1.6MM **Privately Held**
SIC: 3441 Fabricated structural metal

(G-7468)
LINEAR SIGNS INC
Also Called: Vista Visual Group
275 W Hoffman Ave Ste 1 (11757-4081)
PHONE..................631 532-5330
Fax: 631 532-5331
Mike Shroff, *President*
Sohel Vakil, *Vice Pres*
EMP: 15
SQ FT: 7,000
SALES (est): 2.3MM **Privately Held**
SIC: 3993 Signs & advertising specialties

(G-7469)
LONGO COMMERCIAL CABINETS INC
Also Called: Longo Cabinets
829 N Richmond Ave (11757-3008)
PHONE..................631 225-4290
Robert Longo, *President*
Clarke Ganshaw, *Legal Staff*
EMP: 50
SQ FT: 22,000
SALES (est): 6.1MM **Privately Held**
SIC: 2541 2521 2434 Store fixtures, wood; wood office furniture; wood kitchen cabinets

(G-7470)
MAR-A-THON FILTERS INC
369 41st St (11757-2713)
PHONE..................631 957-4774
Fax: 631 957-1181
John Reinbold, *President*
Thomas Cornell, *Corp Secy*
EMP: 6
SQ FT: 7,000
SALES (est): 769.7K **Privately Held**
SIC: 3364 3599 5046 Nonferrous die-castings except aluminum; machine & other job shop work; commercial cooking & food service equipment

(G-7471)
MATTHEW-LEE CORPORATION
149 Pennsylvania Ave (11757-5052)
PHONE..................631 226-0100
Fax: 631 226-0226
John Ferrigno, *President*
Matthew Ferrigno, *Corp Secy*
EMP: 10
SQ FT: 13,000
SALES (est): 830K **Privately Held**
WEB: www.mattlee.com
SIC: 2759 Screen printing

(G-7472)
MIDDLEBY CORPORATION
Also Called: Marsal & Sons
175 E Hoffman Ave (11757-5013)
PHONE..................631 226-6688
Fax: 631 226-6890
Rosemarie Ferrara, *Bookkeeper*
Joseph Ferrera, *Branch Mgr*
EMP: 33
SALES (corp-wide): 1.8B **Publicly Held**
SIC: 3444 Sheet metalwork; restaurant sheet metalwork
PA: The Middleby Corporation
1400 Toastmaster Dr
Elgin IL 60120
847 741-3300

(G-7473)
MODERN CRAFT BAR REST EQUIP
Also Called: Modern Craft Bar Rest Equip
165 E Hoffman Ave Unit 3 (11757-5036)
PHONE..................631 226-5647
John Venticinque, *President*
Heidee Venticinque, *Admin Sec*
EMP: 7
SALES (est): 959.7K **Privately Held**
WEB: www.moderncraft.com
SIC: 2599 5046 2542 Bar, restaurant & cafeteria furniture; commercial cooking & food service equipment; bar fixtures, except wood

(G-7474)
NAS-TRA AUTOMOTIVE INDS INC
Also Called: Nastra Automotive
3 Sidney Ct (11757-1011)
PHONE..................631 225-1225
James Lambert, *Ch of Bd*
Americo De Rocchis, *President*
Antonio Abbatiello, *Corp Secy*
Mary Smith, *Office Mgr*
▲ EMP: 150 EST: 1978
SQ FT: 60,000
SALES (est): 24.1MM **Privately Held**
WEB: www.nastra.com
SIC: 3714 3694 3625 Motor vehicle parts & accessories; engine electrical equipment; relays & industrial controls

(G-7475)
NEXGEN ENVIRO SYSTEMS INC
190 E Hoffman Ave Ste D (11757-5017)
PHONE..................631 226-2930
Michael Robbins, *President*
Jason Robbins, *Vice Pres*
▲ EMP: 3
SALES: 1.1MM **Privately Held**
WEB: www.nexgenenviro.com
SIC: 3826 Environmental testing equipment

(G-7476)
NICOLIA CONCRETE PRODUCTS INC
Also Called: Nicolia of Long Island
640 Muncy St (11757-4318)
P.O. Box 1120, West Babylon (11704-0120)
PHONE..................631 669-0700
R Glenn Schroeder, *Principal*
Robert Nicolia, *Chairman*
Antonio Nicolia, *Vice Pres*
Gian Nicolia, *Vice Pres*
Franco Nicolia, *Treasurer*
▲ EMP: 53
SQ FT: 22,000
SALES (est): 6.4MM **Privately Held**
SIC: 3271 3272 2951 5211 Paving blocks, concrete; concrete products; asphalt paving mixtures & blocks; masonry materials & supplies

(G-7477)
NICOLIA READY MIX INC
615 Cord Ave (11757-4314)
PHONE..................631 669-7000
Antonio L Nicolia, *President*
EMP: 30
SALES (corp-wide): 17.8MM **Privately Held**
WEB: www.nicoliareadymix.com
SIC: 3273 Ready-mixed concrete
PA: Nicolia Ready Mix, Inc.
615 Cord Ave
Lindenhurst NY 11757
631 669-7000

(G-7478)
PACE UP PHARMACEUTICALS LLC
200 Bangor St (11757-3644)
PHONE..................631 450-4495
Ming Yang,
EMP: 9
SALES (est): 1.6MM **Privately Held**
SIC: 2834 Druggists' preparations (pharmaceuticals)

(G-7479)
PRIDE LINES LTD
651 W Hoffman Ave (11757-4034)
PHONE..................631 225-0033
Fax: 631 225-0099
EMP: 8
SQ FT: 8,000
SALES (est): 720K **Privately Held**
SIC: 3944 Manufactures Toy Trains

(G-7480)
RAPACKI & SONS (PA)
Also Called: Rapacki & Sons Kielbasa
633 N Queens Ave (11757-3004)
PHONE..................516 538-3939
Frank Rapacki, *Partner*
Frances Rapacki, *Partner*
Raymond Rapacki, *Partner*
EMP: 11
SQ FT: 2,800
SALES (est): 1.5MM **Privately Held**
SIC: 2013 2051 Sausages & other prepared meats; bread, cake & related products

(G-7481)
RUSSELL PLASTICS TECH CO INC
521 W Hoffman Ave (11757-4052)
PHONE..................631 963-8602
Fax: 631 226-3707
Alexander Bozza, *Ch of Bd*
EMP: 110
SQ FT: 58,000
SALES (est): 25.8MM
SALES (corp-wide): 1.7B **Privately Held**
WEB: www.russellplastics.com
SIC: 3089 Plastic processing
HQ: Vaupell Holdings, Inc.
1144 Nw 53rd St
Seattle WA 98107

GEOGRAPHIC SECTION

Little Falls - Herkimer County (G-7506)

(G-7482)
SIMS STEEL CORPORATION
650 Muncy St (11757-4396)
PHONE.................................631 587-8670
Fax: 631 587-2077
William Sims, *President*
David Geremenko, *Vice Pres*
David Jeremenko, *Vice Pres*
EMP: 25
SQ FT: 4,000
SALES (est): 6.3MM **Privately Held**
WEB: www.simssteel.com
SIC: 3449 Miscellaneous metalwork

(G-7483)
STEELFLEX ELECTRO CORP
145 S 13th St (11757-4546)
P.O. Box 515 (11757-0515)
PHONE.................................516 226-4466
Fax: 631 226-4321
Philip Rine, *President*
Anthony Rine, *Vice Pres*
EMP: 60
SQ FT: 25,000
SALES (est): 7.9MM **Privately Held**
SIC: 3357 Nonferrous wiredrawing & insulating

(G-7484)
STJ ORTHOTIC SERVICES INC (PA)
Also Called: S T J Orthotic Svces
920 Wellwood Ave Ste B (11757-1246)
PHONE.................................631 956-0181
James De Francisco, *President*
Steve Goldring, *General Mgr*
Steven Levitz, *Vice Pres*
EMP: 12
SQ FT: 14,000
SALES: 3.5MM **Privately Held**
WEB: www.stjorthotic.com
SIC: 3842 Orthopedic appliances

(G-7485)
STRUX CORP
Also Called: Art Foam
100 Montauk Hwy (11757-5835)
PHONE.................................516 768-3969
Fax: 631 957-7203
Robert Kjeldsen, *President*
EMP: 25 **EST:** 1970
SQ FT: 30,000
SALES (est): 2.1MM **Privately Held**
WEB: www.strux.com
SIC: 3083 3675 3086 Laminated plastics plate & sheet; electronic capacitors; plastics foam products

(G-7486)
SUFFOLK GRANITE MANUFACTURING
Also Called: Suffolk Monument Mfg
25 Gear Ave (11757-1006)
PHONE.................................631 226-4774
Martin Solomon, *President*
Pat Leavy, *Bookkeeper*
EMP: 20
SQ FT: 17,500
SALES (est): 2.1MM **Privately Held**
WEB: www.uk-engineering.net
SIC: 3281 1423 1411 Monuments, cut stone (not finishing or lettering only); crushed & broken granite; dimension stone

(G-7487)
SUPERBOATS INC
694 Roosevelt Ave (11757-5820)
PHONE.................................631 226-1761
John H Coen, *President*
EMP: 6
SQ FT: 10,000
SALES: 600K **Privately Held**
SIC: 3732 5551 7699 Boats, fiberglass: building & repairing; boat dealers; boat repair

(G-7488)
SUPERIOR AGGRAGATES SUPPLY LLC
612 Muncy St (11757-4318)
PHONE.................................516 333-2923
Robert Nicolia,
Antonio L Nicolia,
Franco A Nicolia,
Gian P Nicolia,
Sandy H Nicolia,
EMP: 30
SALES: 2.9MM **Privately Held**
SIC: 3272 Precast terrazo or concrete products

(G-7489)
SUPREME STEEL INC
690 N Jefferson Ave (11757-2902)
PHONE.................................631 884-1320
Fax: 718 346-3711
Jay Shikora, *President*
Vincent Caravana, *Vice Pres*
EMP: 12
SQ FT: 10,000
SALES (est): 1.1MM **Privately Held**
WEB: www.supremesteelinc.com
SIC: 3441 5051 Fabricated structural metal; structural shapes, iron or steel

(G-7490)
TENTINA WINDOW FASHIONS INC
1186 Route 109 (11757-1088)
P.O. Box 617 (11757-0617)
PHONE.................................631 957-9585
Fax: 631 957-9588
Frank J Miritello, *CEO*
Andrea Miritello, *President*
Jeffery Miritello, *Vice Pres*
Neil Miritello, *Treasurer*
Barbara Guill, *Office Mgr*
EMP: 105
SQ FT: 40,000
SALES (est): 11.1MM **Privately Held**
WEB: www.tentina.com
SIC: 2591 Window blinds; window shades

(G-7491)
VELIS ASSOCIATES INC (PA)
151 S 14th St (11757-4432)
PHONE.................................631 225-4220
Fax: 631 777-3127
Glenn Mastoberti, *General Mgr*
Suriya Khan, *Chairman*
Rafael Croissiert, *Vice Pres*
Brian Mastoberti, *Vice Pres*
Susanna Bryson, *Production*
EMP: 3
SALES (est): 6.7MM **Privately Held**
SIC: 3534 Elevators & moving stairways

(G-7492)
VIKING ATHLETICS LTD
80 Montauk Hwy Ste 1 (11757-5800)
PHONE.................................631 957-8000
David C Kjeldsen, *CEO*
EMP: 40 **EST:** 1995
SQ FT: 28,000
SALES (est): 3.7MM **Privately Held**
WEB: www.vikingathletics.com
SIC: 3949 5949 2759 Sporting & athletic goods; needlework goods & supplies; screen printing

(G-7493)
VIKING TECHNOLOGIES LTD
80 E Montauk Hwy (11757)
PHONE.................................631 957-8000
David Kjeldsen, *President*
Hugh R Foster, *Manager*
EMP: 45 **EST:** 1959
SQ FT: 35,000
SALES: 10MM **Privately Held**
WEB: www.cardwellcondenser.com
SIC: 3629 3674 3675 Condensers, fixed or variable; semiconductors & related devices; electronic capacitors

(G-7494)
VILLAGE LANTERN BAKING CORP
155 N Wellwood Ave (11757-4085)
PHONE.................................631 225-1690
EMP: 8
SALES (est): 586.6K **Privately Held**
SIC: 2051 Bread, cake & related products

(G-7495)
VISUAL CITI INC (PA)
305 Henry St (11757-4315)
PHONE.................................631 482-3030
Abbas Devji, *President*
Fazle Abbas Deyjiyani, *Chairman*
Samina Devji, *Vice Pres*
Zahirabbas Merchant, *Project Mgr*
Deloar Khan, *Prdtn Mgr*
▲ **EMP:** 125
SQ FT: 28,000
SALES (est): 40.1MM **Privately Held**
WEB: www.visualciti.com
SIC: 3993 Displays & cutouts, window & lobby

Lindley
Steuben County

(G-7496)
LINDLEY WOOD WORKS INC
9625 Morgan Creek Rd (14858-9780)
P.O. Box 5 (14858-0005)
PHONE.................................607 523-7786
Fax: 607 523-6697
Peter McIntosh, *President*
Peter Mc Intosh, *President*
Keith Mc Intosh, *Vice Pres*
Mary Mc Intosh, *Admin Sec*
EMP: 15
SQ FT: 10,000
SALES (est): 1.5MM **Privately Held**
SIC: 2448 Pallets, wood

Little Falls
Herkimer County

(G-7497)
BURROWS PAPER CORPORATION
Also Called: Burrows Paper Mill
730 E Mill St (13365)
PHONE.................................315 823-2300
Fax: 315 823-0614
Fred Scarano, *Manager*
EMP: 70
SALES (corp-wide): 178.2MM **Privately Held**
WEB: www.burrowspaper.com
SIC: 2621 Paper mills
PA: Burrows Paper Corporation
501 W Main St Ste 1
Little Falls NY 13365
315 823-2300

(G-7498)
BURROWS PAPER CORPORATION
Also Called: Mohawk Valley Mill
489 W Main St (13365-1815)
PHONE.................................315 823-2300
Fax: 315 823-1032
Duane Judd, *Manager*
EMP: 66
SALES (corp-wide): 178.2MM **Privately Held**
WEB: www.burrowspaper.com
SIC: 2621 Tissue paper; specialty papers
PA: Burrows Paper Corporation
501 W Main St Ste 1
Little Falls NY 13365
315 823-2300

(G-7499)
FELDMEIER EQUIPMENT INC
245 Riverside Ind Park (13365)
PHONE.................................315 823-2000
EMP: 65
SALES (corp-wide): 90.5MM **Privately Held**
SIC: 3443 Fabricated plate work (boiler shop)
PA: Feldmeier Equipment, Inc.
6800 Townline Rd
Syracuse NY 13211
315 823-2000

(G-7500)
FELDMEIER EQUIPMENT INC
575 E Mill St (13365-2099)
PHONE.................................315 823-2000
Fax: 315 823-5012
Robert Feldmeier, *Vice Pres*
Elroy Moore, *Plant Mgr*
Rocco D Scarano, *Prdtn Mgr*
Ed Ashton, *Opers Staff*
Craig Wright, *Purch Mgr*
EMP: 135
SALES (corp-wide): 90.5MM **Privately Held**
WEB: www.feldmeier.com
SIC: 3556 3443 3565 Food products machinery; fabricated plate work (boiler shop); packaging machinery
PA: Feldmeier Equipment, Inc.
6800 Townline Rd
Syracuse NY 13211
315 823-2000

(G-7501)
IDEAL WOOD PRODUCTS INC
Also Called: Ideal Stair Parts
225 W Main St (13365-1800)
PHONE.................................315 823-1124
Fax: 315 823-1127
Bruce Mang, *President*
Doug Plourde, *Controller*
▲ **EMP:** 40
SQ FT: 14,000
SALES (est): 6.3MM **Privately Held**
WEB: www.idealstairparts.com
SIC: 2431 Staircases, stairs & railings

(G-7502)
PEMS TOOL & MACHINE INC
125 Southern Ave (13365-1906)
PHONE.................................315 823-3595
Fax: 315 823-4116
Isabella Stone, *Ch of Bd*
Roger Schulze, *Engineer*
Larry Laporta, *Manager*
EMP: 48
SQ FT: 17,500
SALES (est): 8.4MM **Privately Held**
WEB: www.pemstoolandmachine.com
SIC: 3599 3549 Machine shop, jobbing & repair; metalworking machinery

(G-7503)
R D S MOUNTAIN VIEW TRUCKING
Also Called: R D Drive and Shop
1600 State Route 5s (13365-5405)
P.O. Box 924 (13365-0924)
PHONE.................................315 823-4265
Randall Dawley, *Owner*
EMP: 7
SALES (est): 745.9K **Privately Held**
SIC: 2611 Soda pulp

(G-7504)
REDCO FOODS INC
1 Hansen Is (13365-1997)
PHONE.................................315 823-1300
Gordon Boggis, *CEO*
Sarah Collins, *Manager*
Chris Recchia, *Manager*
Justin Izzo, *Planning*
EMP: 75
SALES (corp-wide): 266.1MM **Privately Held**
SIC: 2393 Textile bags
HQ: Redco Foods, Inc.
3893 Adler Pl Ste 130
Bethlehem PA 18017
315 823-1300

(G-7505)
SUNBELT INDUSTRIES INC (PA)
540 E Mill St (13365-2027)
P.O. Box 584 (13365-0584)
PHONE.................................315 823-2947
Fax: 315 823-4458
Earl Mannion, *President*
EMP: 10
SQ FT: 36,000
SALES (est): 1MM **Privately Held**
SIC: 3291 5085 Abrasive grains; abrasives

(G-7506)
VINCENT MANUFACTURING CO INC
560 E Mill St (13365-2027)
P.O. Box 306 (13365-0306)
PHONE.................................315 823-0280
Fax: 315 823-0928
Todd R Vincent, *President*
Alan N Vincent, *President*
Todd Vincent, *President*
Linda B Vincent, *Vice Pres*
EMP: 11 **EST:** 1892
SQ FT: 50,000

Little Neck - Queens County (G-7507) — GEOGRAPHIC SECTION

SALES: 800K **Privately Held**
SIC: **2299** 5169 Batts & batting: cotton mill waste & related material; polyurethane products

Little Neck
Queens County

(G-7507)
BRAVE CHEFS INCORPORATED
4130 249th St Ste 2 (11363-1655)
PHONE.....................347 956-5905
Michael Kim, *President*
EMP: 5 EST: 2013
SALES (est): 289.6K **Privately Held**
SIC: **2086** Carbonated beverages, nonalcoholic: bottled & canned

(G-7508)
E GLUCK CORPORATION (PA)
Also Called: Armitron Watch Div
6015 Little Neck Pkwy (11362-2500)
PHONE.....................718 784-0700
Fax: 718 482-2700
Eugen Gluck, *President*
Stanislav Kravets, *Editor*
Jerry Dikowitz, *Vice Pres*
Michael Feagan, *Vice Pres*
Michael Feagan, *Vice Pres*
◆ EMP: 160 EST: 1957
SQ FT: 200,000
SALES (est): 94.5MM **Privately Held**
WEB: www.egluck.com
SIC: **3873** 5094 Watches & parts, except crystals & jewels; clocks, assembly of; watches & parts; clocks

(G-7509)
RECON CONSTRUCTION CORP
1108 Shore Rd (11363-1054)
PHONE.....................718 939-1305
Fax: 718 463-6263
Gloria Kemper, *President*
EMP: 30
SQ FT: 5,000
SALES: 3.5MM **Privately Held**
SIC: **3312** Stainless steel

(G-7510)
RENEWABLE ENERGY INC
6 Cornell Ln (11363-1939)
PHONE.....................718 690-2691
EMP: 6
SALES (est): 518.5K **Privately Held**
SIC: **3674** Mfg Semiconductors/Related Devices

Little Valley
Cattaraugus County

(G-7511)
LITTLE VALLEY SAND & GRAVEL
8984 New Albion Rd (14755-9771)
P.O. Box 164 (14755-0164)
PHONE.....................716 938-6676
John R Charlesworth, *President*
Jay Charlesworth, *Treasurer*
Mary Charlesworth, *Admin Sec*
EMP: 7
SQ FT: 5,000
SALES (est): 622.3K **Privately Held**
SIC: **1442** 4212 Construction sand mining; gravel mining; local trucking, without storage

Liverpool
Onondaga County

(G-7512)
BRANNOCK DEVICE CO INC
116 Luther Ave (13088-6726)
PHONE.....................315 475-9862
Fax: 315 475-2723
Salvatore A Leonardi Jr, *President*
Tim Follett, *Vice Pres*
Garrison Davis, *Treasurer*
James Hanley, *Director*
EMP: 20 EST: 1929
SQ FT: 10,000
SALES (est): 2.5MM **Privately Held**
WEB: www.brannock.com
SIC: **3842** Foot appliances, orthopedic

(G-7513)
C & G VIDEO SYSTEMS INC (PA)
7778 Tirrell Hill Cir (13090-2508)
P.O. Box 2476, Syracuse (13220-2476)
PHONE.....................315 452-1490
Fax: 315 343-1623
Charles F Bisesi, *President*
Gail Bisesi, *Vice Pres*
EMP: 5 EST: 1964
SQ FT: 3,600
SALES: 1MM **Privately Held**
SIC: **3699** 1731 Security control equipment & systems; electrical welding equipment; electrical work

(G-7514)
C SPEED LLC
316 Commerce Blvd (13088-4511)
PHONE.....................315 453-1043
David Lysack, *President*
Michael Lesmerises, *Project Mgr*
Matt Ryan, *QC Mgr*
Brian D Sherry -, *Engineer*
Kevin Francis -, *Engineer*
EMP: 32
SQ FT: 5,000
SALES (est): 6.7MM **Privately Held**
WEB: www.cspeed.com
SIC: **3812** 8711 3825 Search & navigation equipment; electrical or electronic engineering; instruments to measure electricity

(G-7515)
CARGILL INCORPORATED
7700 Maltage Dr (13090-2513)
PHONE.....................315 622-3533
Fax: 315 652-1043
Hugh Fordyce, *Sales/Mktg Mgr*
Brians Parham, *Manager*
Luke Reynolds, *Manager*
EMP: 25
SQ FT: 27,466
SALES (corp-wide): 107.1B **Privately Held**
WEB: www.cargill.com
SIC: **2048** Prepared feeds
PA: Cargill, Incorporated
15407 Mcginty Rd W
Wayzata MN 55391
952 742-7575

(G-7516)
CASCADE HELMETS HOLDINGS INC
4697 Crssrads Pk Dr Ste 1 (13088)
PHONE.....................315 453-3073
Bill Brine, *CEO*
Steve Moore, *COO*
EMP: 1
SALES (est): 3MM **Privately Held**
SIC: **3949** Helmets, athletic
PA: Performance Sports Group Ltd.
100 Domain Dr
Exeter NH 03833

(G-7517)
COMPLEX BIOSYSTEMS INC
8266 Warbler Way Apt C6 (13090-1053)
PHONE.....................315 464-8007
Jacques Beaumont, *Owner*
EMP: 7
SQ FT: 600
SALES (est): 350K **Privately Held**
SIC: **3845** 7371 7373 8711 Electrotherapeutic apparatus; computer software systems analysis & design, custom; computer-aided engineering (CAE) systems service; consulting engineer

(G-7518)
EAGLE COMTRONICS INC
7665 Henry Clay Blvd (13088-3507)
P.O. Box 2457, Syracuse (13220-2457)
PHONE.....................315 451-3313
Fax: 315 451-4362
William Devendorf, *CEO*
Timothy Devendorf, *President*
Ron Barry, *Purch Mgr*
Ted Jewett, *Purch Mgr*
Rob Sgarlata, *Design Engr*
▲ EMP: 200 EST: 1975
SQ FT: 100,000
SALES (est): 42.8MM **Privately Held**
WEB: www.eaglecomtronics.com
SIC: **3663** Cable television equipment

(G-7519)
FAYETTE STREET COATINGS INC
1 Burr Dr (13088)
PHONE.....................315 488-5401
Bill Udovich, *Branch Mgr*
EMP: 11
SALES (corp-wide): 9.1MM **Publicly Held**
SIC: **2851** Paints & allied products
HQ: Fayette Street Coatings, Inc.
1970 W Fayette St
Syracuse NY 13204
315 488-5401

(G-7520)
GENERAL ELECTRIC COMPANY
443 Electronics Pkwy (13088-6056)
PHONE.....................315 456-7901
EMP: 12
SALES (corp-wide): 117.3B **Publicly Held**
SIC: **3511** Turbines & turbine generator sets
PA: General Electric Company
41 Farnsworth St
Boston MA 02210
617 443-3000

(G-7521)
HEARTH CABINETS AND MORE LTD
4483 Buckley Rd (13088-2506)
P.O. Box 2700 (13089-2700)
PHONE.....................315 641-1197
Richard D Hovey, *President*
Kim Hovey, *Manager*
Chris Yager, *Consultant*
EMP: 2
SALES: 2.3MM **Privately Held**
SIC: **2434** Wood kitchen cabinets

(G-7522)
HERCULES INCORPORATED
Also Called: Ashland Hercules Water Tech
911 Old Liverpool Rd (13088-1504)
PHONE.....................315 461-4730
EMP: 9
SALES (corp-wide): 5.3B **Publicly Held**
SIC: **2891** Adhesives
HQ: Hercules Incorporated
500 Hercules Rd
Wilmington DE 19808
302 594-5000

(G-7523)
HSM PACKAGING CORPORATION
4529 Crown Rd (13090-3541)
PHONE.....................315 476-7996
Fax: 315 476-7998
Sheila M Martin, *CEO*
Homer S Martin III, *COO*
Jessica T Pletka, *CFO*
Joan Brady, *Admin Sec*
▲ EMP: 58
SQ FT: 30,000
SALES (est): 15MM **Privately Held**
WEB: www.hsmpackaging.com
SIC: **2657** Folding paperboard boxes

(G-7524)
INFIMED INC (PA)
Also Called: Varian Medical Systems
121 Metropolitan Park Dr (13088-5335)
PHONE.....................315 453-4545
Fax: 315 453-4550
Robert Kluge, *CEO*
Norman Shoenfeld, *Ch of Bd*
Amy L Ryan, *President*
Bruce Perry, *Engineer*
Carrie Murphy, *Controller*
▲ EMP: 64
SQ FT: 26,000
SALES (est): 8.3MM **Privately Held**
WEB: www.digitalxrayimages.com
SIC: **3845** Electromedical equipment

(G-7525)
INFO QUICK SOLUTIONS
7460 Morgan Rd (13090-3979)
PHONE.....................315 463-1400
Bernie Owens, *President*
Brian Owens, *VP Sales*
EMP: 50
SALES (est): 5.8MM **Privately Held**
SIC: **7372** Prepackaged software

(G-7526)
INTEGRATED MEDICAL DEVICES
549 Electronics Pkwy # 200 (13088-4391)
PHONE.....................315 457-4200
Stephen L Esposito, *President*
EMP: 7
SQ FT: 4,400
SALES (est): 650K **Privately Held**
WEB: www.qrstech.com
SIC: **3845** Electrocardiographs

(G-7527)
IRONSHORE HOLDINGS INC
Also Called: Lipe Automation
290 Elwood Davis Rd (13088-2100)
PHONE.....................315 457-1052
Fax: 315 457-1678
Robert Offley, *CEO*
Jay Lacey, *President*
Bill Wagner, *Engineer*
Jeff Purdy, *Controller*
Ann Buerkle, *Manager*
EMP: 16
SQ FT: 27,000
SALES (est): 1.3MM **Privately Held**
SIC: **3599** Machine shop, jobbing & repair

(G-7528)
JOHN MEZZALINGUA ASSOC LLC (PA)
Also Called: Jma Wireless
7645 Henry Clay Blvd # 678 (13088-3512)
P.O. Box 678 (13088-0678)
PHONE.....................315 431-7100
Christian Barb, *Vice Pres*
Dan Cassinelli, *Vice Pres*
Todd Landry, *Vice Pres*
Andrew Klamm, *Production*
Matthew Lawrence, *Accountant*
▲ EMP: 150
SALES (est): 10MM **Privately Held**
SIC: **3663** Antennas, transmitting & communications; airborne radio communications equipment

(G-7529)
JT SYSTEMS INC
8132 Oswego Rd (13090-1500)
P.O. Box 2575 (13089-2575)
PHONE.....................315 622-1980
Jit Turakhia, *Ch of Bd*
Manda Turakhia, *Corp Secy*
EMP: 10
SQ FT: 1,700
SALES (est): 1.3MM **Privately Held**
WEB: www.jtsystemsinc.com
SIC: **3564** Air purification equipment; ventilating fans: industrial or commercial

(G-7530)
LOCKHEED MARTIN CORPORATION
497 Electronics Pkwy (13088-5394)
PHONE.....................315 456-1548
Steven Montagne, *General Mgr*
Peter Morin, *Principal*
Christopher Gregoire, *Vice Pres*
Anthony Stagnitta, *Project Mgr*
Gregory Anderson, *Opers Mgr*
EMP: 25
SALES (corp-wide): 46.1B **Publicly Held**
SIC: **3721** Aircraft
PA: Lockheed Martin Corporation
6801 Rockledge Dr
Bethesda MD 20817
301 897-6000

(G-7531)
LOCKHEED MARTIN CORPORATION
497 Electronics Pkwy # 5 (13088-5394)
P.O. Box 4840, Syracuse (13221-4840)
PHONE.....................315 456-0123
T S Kires, *Principal*

▲ = Import ▼ = Export
◆ = Import/Export

Marc Heller, *Business Mgr*
Carl Bannar, *Vice Pres*
Keith Speidel, *Vice Pres*
Robert Tucker, *Vice Pres*
EMP: 2200
SALES (corp-wide): 46.1B **Publicly Held**
WEB: www.lockheedmartin.com
SIC: 3761 3812 Rockets, space & military, complete; navigational systems & instruments
PA: Lockheed Martin Corporation
6801 Rockledge Dr
Bethesda MD 20817
301 897-6000

(G-7532)
LOCKHEED MARTIN GLOBAL INC (HQ)
Also Called: Lmgi
497 Electronics Pkwy # 5 (13088-5394)
PHONE...................................315 456-2982
Dale M Johnson, *President*
Christopher Gregoire, *Vice Pres*
Kenneth Possenriede, *Vice Pres*
Karen Barrett, *Admin Sec*
EMP: 65
SALES (est): 352.3MM
SALES (corp-wide): 46.1B **Publicly Held**
SIC: 3812 Search & navigation equipment
PA: Lockheed Martin Corporation
6801 Rockledge Dr
Bethesda MD 20817
301 897-6000

(G-7533)
LOCKHEED MARTIN OVERSEAS
497 Electronics Pkwy # 7 (13088-5394)
P.O. Box 4840, Syracuse (13221-4840)
PHONE...................................315 456-0123
Fax: 315 456-3881
Kwame Otieku, *Principal*
Ralph Heath, *Exec VP*
Andrew Yeman, *Engineer*
Linda Raymond, *Branch Mgr*
John Donahue, *Manager*
EMP: 27
SALES (corp-wide): 46.1B **Publicly Held**
SIC: 3812 Sonar systems & equipment; radar systems & equipment
HQ: Lockheed Martin Overseas Services Corporation
6801 Rockledge Dr
Bethesda MD 20817
301 897-6000

(G-7534)
MCAULIFFE PAPER INC
100 Commerce Blvd (13088-4500)
PHONE...................................315 453-2222
Fax: 315 453-2225
Charles Thiaville, *President*
Mary Y Maltbie, *Vice Pres*
Amy Caldeira, *VP Sales*
EMP: 35 **EST:** 1920
SQ FT: 40,000
SALES (est): 3.5MM **Privately Held**
WEB: www.mcauliffepad.com
SIC: 2759 Business forms: printing

(G-7535)
MERCER MILLING CO
4698 Crossroads Park Dr (13088-3598)
PHONE...................................315 701-1334
Fax: 315 701-4987
Bill Colten, *President*
Rene Lavoie II, *General Mgr*
Rick Langtry, *Production*
▲ **EMP:** 36 **EST:** 1829
SQ FT: 60,000
SALES (est): 17.6MM **Privately Held**
SIC: 2834 2833 Intravenous solutions; botanical products, medicinal: ground, graded or milled

(G-7536)
NANOPV CORPORATION
7526 Morgan Rd (13090-3502)
PHONE...................................609 851-3666
Anna Selvan John, *President*
EMP: 187
SALES (corp-wide): 10.4MM **Privately Held**
SIC: 3433 Solar heaters & collectors

PA: Nanopv Corporation
122 Mountainview Rd
Ewing NJ 08560
609 851-3666

(G-7537)
O BRIEN GERE MFG INC
7600 Morgan Rd Ste 1 (13090-4128)
PHONE...................................315 437-6100
Terry Brown, *Owner*
EMP: 8
SALES (est): 765.5K **Privately Held**
SIC: 3999 Manufacturing industries

(G-7538)
PACKAGING CORPORATION AMERICA
Also Called: Pca/Syracuse, 384
4471 Steelway Blvd S (13090-3508)
P.O. Box 584 (13088-0584)
PHONE...................................315 457-6780
Fax: 315 457-0630
Mike Hodges, *General Mgr*
Sharon Wilbur, *Safety Mgr*
Kevin Ryan, *Sales Mgr*
Robert Lombardi, *Sales Staff*
Teresa Bashore, *Branch Mgr*
EMP: 130
SQ FT: 144,672
SALES (corp-wide): 5.7B **Publicly Held**
WEB: www.packagingcorp.com
SIC: 2653 Corrugated & solid fiber boxes
PA: Packaging Corporation Of America
1955 W Field Ct
Lake Forest IL 60045
847 482-3000

(G-7539)
PACTIV LLC
4471 Steelway Blvd S (13090-3517)
P.O. Box 584 (13088-0584)
PHONE...................................315 457-6780
Teresa J Bashore, *Manager*
EMP: 130 **Privately Held**
WEB: www.pactiv.com
SIC: 2653 Boxes, corrugated: made from purchased materials; boxes, solid fiber: made from purchased materials
HQ: Pactiv Llc
1900 W Field Ct
Lake Forest IL 60045
847 482-2000

(G-7540)
PAUL DE LIMA COMPANY INC (PA)
Also Called: Paul De Lima Coffee Company
7546 Morgan Rd Ste 1 (13090-3532)
PHONE...................................315 457-3725
Paul W Delima Jr, *CEO*
William J Drescher Jr, *Ch of Bd*
Peter Miller, *Vice Pres*
Bill Kukula, *Manager*
Samantha Murphy, *Manager*
▲ **EMP:** 55
SQ FT: 15,000
SALES (est): 15.3MM **Privately Held**
WEB: www.delimacoffee.com
SIC: 2095 5149 Roasted coffee; coffee, green or roasted

(G-7541)
PERFORMANCE LACROSSE GROUP INC (DH)
Also Called: Sport Helmets, Inc.
4697 Crossroads Park Dr (13088-3515)
PHONE...................................315 453-3073
Stephen Moore, *President*
EMP: 8
SALES (est): 1.1MM **Privately Held**
WEB: www.sporthelmets.com
SIC: 3949 Helmets, athletic
HQ: Bauer Hockey, Inc.
100 Domain Dr Ste 1
Exeter NH 03833
603 430-2111

(G-7542)
POINTWISE INFORMATION SERVICE
223 1st St (13088-5140)
P.O. Box 11457, Syracuse (13218-1457)
PHONE...................................315 457-4111
Richard C Jaquin, *Owner*
EMP: 10

SQ FT: 1,000
SALES (est): 824.7K **Privately Held**
SIC: 2721 Periodicals: publishing only

(G-7543)
PRAXAIR DISTRIBUTION INC
4560 Morgan Pl (13090-3522)
PHONE...................................315 457-5821
Todd Saumier, *Principal*
Donna Kline, *Office Mgr*
EMP: 7
SALES (corp-wide): 10.7B **Publicly Held**
SIC: 2813 5984 5169 Oxygen, compressed or liquefied; nitrogen; liquefied petroleum gas dealers; oxygen; industrial gases; acetylene
HQ: Praxair Distribution, Inc.
39 Old Ridgebury Rd
Danbury CT 06810
203 837-2000

(G-7544)
PRECISION SYSTEMS MFG INC
4855 Executive Dr (13088-5378)
PHONE...................................315 451-3480
Theodore Jeske, *President*
Michael Parsley, *QA Dir*
Tom Anderson, *QC Mgr*
Tom Sivalia, *Engineer*
Gary S Price, *Controller*
EMP: 48
SQ FT: 40,000
SALES (est): 10.8MM **Privately Held**
WEB: www.psmi.org
SIC: 3599 3444 7389 3549 Machine & other job shop work; sheet metalwork: design, commercial & industrial; metalworking machinery; special dies, tools, jigs & fixtures

(G-7545)
PRINT SOLUTIONS PLUS INC
7325 Oswego Rd (13090-3717)
PHONE...................................315 234-3801
Darren Petragnani, *President*
EMP: 6
SALES (est): 788.9K **Privately Held**
SIC: 2752 Commercial printing, lithographic

(G-7546)
SCAPA NORTH AMERICA
Also Called: Great Lakes Technologies
1111 Vine St (13088-5301)
PHONE...................................315 413-1111
Fax: 315 413-1112
Duane Gordan, *Plant Mgr*
Edward Liscio, *Treasurer*
Kevin Toomey, *Human Res Dir*
Stuart Ganslaw,
Angelo Labbadia,
▲ **EMP:** 20
SQ FT: 70,000
SALES (est): 16MM
SALES (corp-wide): 357.3MM **Privately Held**
WEB: www.greatlakestechnologies.com
SIC: 3081 Unsupported plastics film & sheet
HQ: Scapa Tapes North America Llc
111 Great Pond Dr
Windsor CT 06095
860 688-8000

(G-7547)
SEABOARD GRAPHIC SERVICES LLC
Also Called: Minuteman Press
7570 Oswego Rd (13090-2928)
PHONE...................................315 652-4200
Melinda Kuhn, *Financial Exec*
Lawrence Kuhn, *Mng Member*
Sean Chenery, *Graphic Designe*
Cristin Quatman, *Graphic Designe*
Michael Siczynski, *Graphic Designe*
EMP: 25
SALES: 4.2MM **Privately Held**
WEB: www.seaboardgraphics.com
SIC: 2752 Commercial printing, lithographic

(G-7548)
STALLION TECHNOLOGIES INC
4324 Loveland Dr (13090-6862)
PHONE...................................315 622-1176
Marshall MA, *President*

EMP: 8
SALES (est): 520K **Privately Held**
WEB: www.stalliontech.com
SIC: 3861 Photographic equipment & supplies

(G-7549)
STAMPCRETE INTERNATIONAL LTD
Also Called: Stampcrete Decorative Concrete
325 Commerce Blvd (13088-4595)
PHONE...................................315 451-2837
Fax: 315 451-2290
Karen Reith, *President*
Bob Williams, *Vice Pres*
Michael Stevens, *Plant Mgr*
Amy Michales, *Accountant*
▼ **EMP:** 20
SQ FT: 10,000
SALES (est): 7MM **Privately Held**
SIC: 3469 Metal stampings

(G-7550)
SYRACUSE LABEL CO INC
Also Called: Syracuse Label & Surround Prtg
110 Luther Ave (13088-6726)
PHONE...................................315 422-1037
Fax: 315 422-6763
Peter Rhodes, *Ch of Bd*
Kathy Alaimo, *President*
Mark Howard, *Vice Pres*
Paul Roux, *Vice Pres*
Kevin Gagnon, *VP Prdtn*
EMP: 86
SQ FT: 35,000
SALES (est): 22.8MM **Privately Held**
WEB: www.syrlabel.com
SIC: 2672 2759 Labels (unprinted), gummed: made from purchased materials; commercial printing

(G-7551)
SYRACUSE PLASTICS LLC
7400 Morgan Rd (13090-3902)
PHONE...................................315 637-9881
Fax: 315 637-9260
Rick Gigon, *Manager*
David Nason, *Manager*
Bill Criss, *Supervisor*
Thomas Falcone,
Joseph R Falcone Sr,
▲ **EMP:** 150 **EST:** 1953
SQ FT: 55,000
SALES (est): 34.7MM **Privately Held**
SIC: 3089 Injection molding of plastics

(G-7552)
TACTAIR FLUID CONTROLS INC
4806 W Taft Rd (13088-4810)
PHONE...................................315 451-3928
Fax: 315 451-8919
Dudley D Johnson, *Ch of Bd*
Peter Kaido, *President*
Michael Yates, *President*
Bob Powell, *Superintendent*
Brian McMonagle, *Vice Pres*
EMP: 240
SQ FT: 70,000
SALES (est): 64.8MM
SALES (corp-wide): 2.7B **Publicly Held**
WEB: www.tactair.com
SIC: 3492 3593 Fluid power valves for aircraft; fluid power actuators, hydraulic or pneumatic
HQ: Young & Franklin, Inc.
942 Old Liverpool Rd
Liverpool NY 13088
315 457-3110

(G-7553)
THERMO CIDTEC INC
Also Called: Cid Technologies
101 Commerce Blvd (13088-4507)
PHONE...................................315 451-9410
Fax: 315 451-9421
Seth H Hoogasian, *Ch of Bd*
Mike Pilon, *General Mgr*
Jon Miles, *Mfg Mgr*
Mark Ptaszek, *Purchasing*
Robert Gorczynski, *Engineer*
EMP: 30
SQ FT: 14,000
SALES (est): 10.5MM
SALES (corp-wide): 16.9B **Publicly Held**
SIC: 3861 3674 Photographic equipment & supplies; solid state electronic devices

Liverpool - Onondaga County (G-7554)

HQ: Thermo Vision Corp
8 Forge Pkwy Ste 4
Franklin MA 02038

(G-7554)
VANSANTIS DEVELOPMENT INC
4595 Morgan Pl (13090-3521)
PHONE..................................315 461-0113
Fax: 315 461-0346
Bill Vanauken, *President*
EMP: 40
SQ FT: 16,356
SALES (est): 5.6MM **Privately Held**
SIC: 2448 Pallets, wood

(G-7555)
WARD STEEL COMPANY INC
4591 Morgan Pl (13090-3511)
P.O. Box 628 (13088-0628)
PHONE..................................315 451-4566
John E Ward, *President*
Terrance Ward, *Vice Pres*
Al Parisi, *Plant Mgr*
EMP: 25
SQ FT: 28,000
SALES (est): 7.1MM **Privately Held**
SIC: 3441 Fabricated structural metal

(G-7556)
WHITACRE ENGINEERING COMPANY
4522 Wetzel Rd (13090-2548)
PHONE..................................315 622-1075
Fax: 315 622-1076
Samuel Conley, *Branch Mgr*
Jeff Andrews, *Manager*
Yan Bukowy, *Manager*
Sam Poon, *Comp Tech*
EMP: 7
SQ FT: 48,359
SALES (corp-wide): 8.3MM **Privately Held**
SIC: 3441 Fabricated structural metal
PA: Whitacre Engineering Company
4645 Rebar Ave Ne
Canton OH 44705
330 455-8505

(G-7557)
WT MOTTO BUILDING PRODUCTS
4591 Morgan Pl (13090-3521)
PHONE..................................315 457-2211
Fax: 315 457-2363
William Motto, *Principal*
EMP: 13
SALES (est): 750K **Privately Held**
SIC: 2439 Structural wood members

(G-7558)
XTO INCORPORATED (PA)
110 Wrentham Dr (13088-4503)
PHONE..................................315 451-7807
Fax: 315 451-2687
Donald G Kreiger, *CEO*
Ric Sill, *President*
Bryon Hoffman, *Business Mgr*
D Keith Krieger, *Vice Pres*
Keith Hughes, *VP Sales*
EMP: 65
SQ FT: 38,000
SALES (est): 12.8MM **Privately Held**
WEB: www.xtoinc.com
SIC: 3053 5085 3549 Gaskets & sealing devices; adhesives, tape & plasters; seals, industrial; metalworking machinery

(G-7559)
YOUNG & FRANKLIN INC (HQ)
942 Old Liverpool Rd (13088-5596)
PHONE..................................315 457-3110
Dudley Johnson, *Ch of Bd*
Joe Lopez, *Vice Pres*
Lawrence Mitter, *Vice Pres*
Chuck Roberts, *Purch Mgr*
Richard Passero, *Engineer*
EMP: 100 EST: 1918
SQ FT: 70,000
SALES: 73MM
SALES (corp-wide): 2.7B **Publicly Held**
SIC: 3492 3625 3728 3593 Control valves, aircraft: hydraulic & pneumatic; control valves, fluid power; hydraulic & pneumatic; actuators, industrial; aircraft parts & equipment; fluid power cylinders & actuators
PA: Transdigm Group Incorporated
1301 E 9th St Ste 3000
Cleveland OH 44114
216 706-2960

Livingston
Columbia County

(G-7560)
F H STICKLES & SON INC
2590 Rr 9 (12541)
PHONE..................................518 851-9048
Bernard F Stickles Jr, *President*
EMP: 15 EST: 1928
SQ FT: 1,000
SALES (est): 1.8MM **Privately Held**
SIC: 3273 5032 Ready-mixed concrete; sand, construction; gravel

Livingston Manor
Sullivan County

(G-7561)
FLOUR POWER BAKERY CAFE
87 Debruce Rd (12758-2001)
PHONE..................................917 747-6895
Rowley, *President*
Denise Rowley, *Admin Sec*
EMP: 5
SALES: 250K **Privately Held**
SIC: 2051 Bakery: wholesale or wholesale/retail combined

(G-7562)
GLOBAL NATURAL FOODS INC
672 Old Route 17 Rear Ofc (12758-5031)
P.O. Box 276 (12758-0276)
PHONE..................................845 439-3292
Randy Lewis, *President*
Melissa Holden, *Vice Pres*
Trish Rampe, *Food Svc Dir*
◆ EMP: 30
SQ FT: 2,500
SALES (est): 7.3MM **Privately Held**
WEB: www.globalnaturalfoods.com
SIC: 2037 2033 Fruit juices; fruit juice concentrates, frozen; fruit purees: packaged in cans, jars, etc.

Livonia
Livingston County

(G-7563)
AG BIOTECH INC
3578 Shoreline Dr (14487-9645)
P.O. Box 636, Lakeville (14480-0636)
PHONE..................................585 346-0020
Fax: 585 346-0048
◆ EMP: 8
SALES: 2MM **Privately Held**
SIC: 2836 Biological products, except diagnostic

(G-7564)
FINGER LAKES TIMBER CO INC
6274 Decker Rd (14487-9528)
PHONE..................................585 346-2990
Ronald Munson, *President*
Aaron Munson, *Vice Pres*
EMP: 6
SQ FT: 1,000
SALES (est): 844.6K **Privately Held**
SIC: 2411 Logging

(G-7565)
TWISTERS
13 Commercial St (14487-9113)
P.O. Box 604 (14487-0604)
PHONE..................................585 346-3730
Jeffery Helwig, *Owner*
EMP: 6
SALES (est): 531.2K **Privately Held**
SIC: 2024 Ice cream & frozen desserts

Lloyd Harbor
Suffolk County

(G-7566)
DILLNER PRECAST INC (PA)
14 Meadow Ln (11743-9721)
PHONE..................................631 421-9130
John Dillner, *President*
Maureen Dillner, *Corp Secy*
EMP: 5
SALES: 1MM **Privately Held**
SIC: 3272 Concrete products, precast

(G-7567)
KANNALIFE SCIENCES INC
4 Knoll Ct (11743-9731)
PHONE..................................516 669-3219
EMP: 5
SALES (est): 514.4K **Privately Held**
SIC: 2834 2833 2835 Mfg Pharmaceutical Preparations Mfg Medicinal/Botanical Products Mfg Diagnostic Substances

Locke
Cayuga County

(G-7568)
COTE HARDWOOD PRODUCTS INC (PA)
Also Called: Cote Wood Products
4725 Cat Path Rd (13092-4135)
PHONE..................................607 898-5737
Fax: 315 497-3108
Pierre Cote, *President*
Carl Cote, *Vice Pres*
Paulette Cote, *Treasurer*
EMP: 11
SALES: 950K **Privately Held**
SIC: 2421 Sawmills & planing mills, general

Lockport
Niagara County

(G-7569)
ALLVAC
695 Ohio St (14094-4221)
PHONE..................................716 433-4411
Reginald C Buri, *Principal*
Beth Newton, *Manager*
Joe Gardner, *Director*
Mike Wilson, *Executive*
▲ EMP: 14
SALES (est): 2.8MM **Privately Held**
SIC: 3312 Blast furnaces & steel mills; stainless steel; rods, iron & steel: made in steel mills

(G-7570)
ARROWHEAD SPRING VINEYARDS LLC
4746 Townline Rd (14094-9604)
PHONE..................................716 434-8030
Duncan Ross,
EMP: 5
SALES (est): 441K **Privately Held**
WEB: www.duncanrossphoto.com
SIC: 2084 Wines

(G-7571)
BARRY STEEL FABRICATION INC (PA)
30 Simonds St (14094-4111)
P.O. Box 579 (14095-0579)
PHONE..................................716 433-2144
Fax: 716 433-7742
Steven R Barry, *President*
Jody Barry, *Vice Pres*
Randy Allen, *Project Mgr*
Kathryn Barry, *Marketing Mgr*
EMP: 15
SQ FT: 8,400
SALES (est): 6.8MM **Privately Held**
WEB: www.barrysteel.com
SIC: 3441 1791 Fabricated structural metal; structural steel erection

(G-7572)
BISON BAG CO INC
5404 Crown Dr (14094-1850)
PHONE..................................716 434-4380
Fax: 716 434-4546
James Streacher, *Ch of Bd*
Scott J Zgoda, *Ch of Bd*
Bruce Zgoda, *President*
Jim Streicher, *President*
James Streacher Jr, *Vice Pres*
▲ EMP: 55
SQ FT: 50,000
SALES (est): 14.1MM **Privately Held**
WEB: www.bisonbag.com
SIC: 2673 Plastic bags: made from purchased materials

(G-7573)
BUFFALO BIOBLOWER TECH LLC
6100 Donner Rd (14094-9227)
PHONE..................................716 625-8618
Dr John A Lordi, *CEO*
EMP: 8
SALES (est): 1.1MM **Privately Held**
SIC: 3564 Purification & dust collection equipment

(G-7574)
BUFFALO MACHINE TLS OF NIAGARA
4935 Lockport Rd (14094-9630)
PHONE..................................716 201-1310
Fax: 716 625-9850
Theresa Silva, *President*
Joseph Silva, *Vice Pres*
Karen Nuggent, *Manager*
Dara Clark, *Administration*
EMP: 11
SQ FT: 25,000
SALES: 500K **Privately Held**
WEB: www.bmt-usa.com
SIC: 3542 Machine tools, metal forming type

(G-7575)
CANDLELIGHT CABINETRY INC
Also Called: Renaissance Import
24 Michigan St (14094-2628)
PHONE..................................716 434-2114
Fax: 716 434-6748
Robert Sanderson, *Ch of Bd*
John Yakich, *President*
EMP: 210
SQ FT: 40,000
SALES (est): 26.6MM **Privately Held**
WEB: www.candlelightcab.com
SIC: 2434 Wood kitchen cabinets

(G-7576)
CHAMELEON COLOR CARDS LTD
6530 S Transit Rd (14094-6334)
PHONE..................................716 625-9452
Fax: 716 625-8580
Phyllis Duha, *President*
Emeric J Duha, *Corp Secy*
Bill Salverberger, *Finance*
Cathleen Lattanzio, *Manager*
Sherrie Campbell, *MIS Dir*
◆ EMP: 55
SQ FT: 16,000
SALES (est): 8.6MM
SALES (corp-wide): 32.9MM **Privately Held**
WEB: www.duhagroup.com
SIC: 3993 Displays, paint process
PA: Duha Color Services Limited
750 Bradford St
Winnipeg MB R3H 0
204 786-8961

(G-7577)
COMMUNITY NEWSPPR HOLDINGS INC
Also Called: Union Sun & Journal
135 Main St Ste 1 (14094-3728)
P.O. Box 503 (14095-0503)
PHONE..................................716 439-9222
Fax: 716 439-9239

▲ = Import ▼ = Export
◆ = Import/Export

GEOGRAPHIC SECTION
Lockport - Niagara County (G-7602)

Denise Young, *Branch Mgr*
Scott Moreland, *Manager*
EMP: 33 **Privately Held**
SIC: 2711 Newspapers: publishing only, not printed on site
PA: Community Newspaper Holdings, Inc.
445 Dexter Ave Ste 7000
Montgomery AL 36104

(G-7578)
CUSTOM LASER INC
6747 Akron Rd (14094-5316)
P.O. Box 962 (14095-0962)
PHONE.................................716 434-8600
Fax: 716 439-4805
Gary Brockman, *President*
Ken Hammond, *Opers Mgr*
Jason Walling, *Opers Staff*
Erin Berbhese, *Manager*
EMP: 30
SQ FT: 9,000
SALES (est): 6MM **Privately Held**
WEB: www.customlaserinc.com
SIC: 3479 7692 Etching & engraving; welding repair

(G-7579)
DELPHI THERMAL SYSTEMS
350 Upper Mountain Rd (14094-1861)
PHONE.................................716 439-2454
Andrew Minarcin, *Principal*
EMP: 11 **EST:** 2014
SALES (est): 1.6MM **Privately Held**
SIC: 3714 Motor vehicle parts & accessories

(G-7580)
DERN MOORE MACHINE COMPANY INC
151 S Niagara St (14094-1907)
PHONE.................................716 433-6243
Fax: 716 433-7018
Ken Moore, *President*
Sally J Moore, *Vice Pres*
EMP: 9
SQ FT: 10,000
SALES (est): 840K **Privately Held**
WEB: www.moorewashsystems.com
SIC: 3599 Machine shop, jobbing & repair

(G-7581)
DOBRIN INDUSTRIES INC (PA)
210 Walnut St Ste 22 (14094-3713)
PHONE.................................800 353-2229
Fax: 716 438-5000
Paul Dobrin, *President*
EMP: 5
SQ FT: 5,000
SALES (est): 483.5K **Privately Held**
WEB: www.time-frames.com
SIC: 3499 Picture frames, metal

(G-7582)
E & R MACHINE INC
211 Grand St (14094-2198)
P.O. Box 499 (14095-0499)
PHONE.................................716 434-6639
Fax: 716 434-9857
Garry E Sauls, *Ch of Bd*
Robert Swierczynski, *Plant Mgr*
Linda Penwright, *Office Mgr*
James Gaylord, *Manager*
EMP: 30 **EST:** 1961
SALES (est): 5.5MM **Privately Held**
WEB: www.er-machine.com
SIC: 3599 Machine shop, jobbing & repair

(G-7583)
E Z ENTRY DOORS INC
5299 Enterprise Dr (14094-1853)
PHONE.................................716 434-3440
Fax: 716 434-0197
Roger W Grear, *President*
Patricia R Grear, *Vice Pres*
EMP: 12
SQ FT: 5,000
SALES (est): 2.2MM **Privately Held**
WEB: www.ezentrydoors.com
SIC: 3534 Elevators & equipment

(G-7584)
EMPRO NIAGARA INC
5027 Ridge Rd (14094-8948)
PHONE.................................716 433-2769
Fax: 716 433-3353
Willa L Hand, *President*
Willa Hand, *President*
Will Hand, *Principal*
Melissa Hand, *Vice Pres*
EMP: 6
SALES: 500K **Privately Held**
WEB: www.emproniagara.com
SIC: 3599 Machine shop, jobbing & repair

(G-7585)
F W ROBERTS MFG CO INC
73 Lock St (14094-2891)
P.O. Box 497 (14095-0497)
PHONE.................................716 434-3555
Fax: 716 439-4603
Sherri Sczepczenski, *Admin Sec*
▲ **EMP:** 13
SQ FT: 13,363
SALES (est): 2.4MM **Privately Held**
SIC: 3554 3545 Paper mill machinery: plating, slitting, waxing, etc.; machine tool accessories

(G-7586)
FISHING VALLEY LLC
7217 N Canal Rd (14094-9411)
PHONE.................................716 523-6158
Anna Zhalyalotdinova,
EMP: 5
SALES (est): 159.6K **Privately Held**
SIC: 3949 Bait, artificial: fishing

(G-7587)
FREEDOM RUN WINERY INC
5138 Lower Mountain Rd (14094-9767)
PHONE.................................716 433-4136
Larry Manning, *Manager*
EMP: 7
SALES (est): 712.3K **Privately Held**
SIC: 2084 Wines

(G-7588)
GLOBAL ABRASIVE PRODUCTS INC (PA)
62 Mill St (14094-2460)
PHONE.................................716 438-0047
John T Sidebottom, *President*
Laurie J Sidebottom, *Vice Pres*
EMP: 20
SALES (est): 4.4MM **Privately Held**
WEB: www.preson.com
SIC: 3291 Coated abrasive products; sandpaper

(G-7589)
GM COMPONENTS HOLDINGS LLC
Also Called: Gmch Lockport Ptc
200 Upper Mountain Rd (14094-1819)
PHONE.................................716 439-2011
Jerry Griffin, *Purchasing*
Pat Murtha, *Branch Mgr*
Rich Thunhorst, *Manager*
EMP: 209
SALES (corp-wide): 152.3B **Publicly Held**
SIC: 3714 Air conditioner parts, motor vehicle; defrosters, motor vehicle; heaters, motor vehicle; radiators & radiator shells & cores, motor vehicle
HQ: Gm Components Holdings, Llc
300 Renaissance Ctr
Detroit MI 48243
313 556-5000

(G-7590)
GM COMPONENTS HOLDINGS LLC
Also Called: Gmch Lockport
200 Upper Mountain Rd (14094-1819)
PHONE.................................716 439-2463
Jeremy Cummins, *Engineer*
Ronald Pirtle, *Branch Mgr*
EMP: 350
SALES (corp-wide): 152.3B **Publicly Held**
SIC: 3629 3714 3585 3563 Condensers, for motors or generators; motor vehicle parts & accessories; refrigeration & heating equipment; air & gas compressors
HQ: Gm Components Holdings, Llc
300 Renaissance Ctr
Detroit MI 48243
313 556-5000

(G-7591)
GM COMPONENTS HOLDINGS LLC
Also Called: Integrated Indus Resources
200 Upper Mountain Rd # 10 (14094-1819)
PHONE.................................716 439-2402
Steven Kendall, *Engineer*
R Westby, *Engineer*
Mark Inchiosa, *Branch Mgr*
EMP: 75
SALES (corp-wide): 152.3B **Publicly Held**
WEB: www.delphiauto.com
SIC: 3053 Gaskets & sealing devices
HQ: Gm Components Holdings, Llc
300 Renaissance Ctr
Detroit MI 48243
313 556-5000

(G-7592)
GOODING CO INC
Also Called: Insert Outsert Experts, The
5568 Davison Rd (14094-9090)
PHONE.................................716 434-5501
Fax: 716 434-9778
Gerald J Hace, *President*
David Carver, *Vice Pres*
▼ **EMP:** 34
SQ FT: 16,500
SALES (est): 6.4MM **Privately Held**
WEB: www.goodingcoinc.com
SIC: 2754 Wrappers: gravure printing

(G-7593)
J M CANTY INC
6100 Donner Rd (14094-9227)
PHONE.................................716 625-4227
Thomas Canty, *Ch of Bd*
Jean Canty, *Vice Pres*
Adam Mattle, *Purchasing*
Jessica Gladysz, *Research*
Brittney Canty, *Engineer*
EMP: 30
SQ FT: 38,000
SALES (est): 8MM **Privately Held**
WEB: www.jmcanty.com
SIC: 3443 3648 2891 Vessels, process or storage (from boiler shops): metal plate; lighting equipment; sealants

(G-7594)
J T ENTERPRISES LLC
6602 Mulligan Dr (14094-1169)
P.O. Box 1213 (14095-1213)
PHONE.................................716 433-9368
David Strassburg, *Executive*
Terry A Strassburg,
Carol Strassburg,
EMP: 4
SALES: 1.3MM **Privately Held**
WEB: www.thesock.com
SIC: 2252 Socks

(G-7595)
JACK J FLORIO JR
Also Called: Micro Graphics
36b Main St (14094-3607)
PHONE.................................716 434-9123
Fax: 716 434-9152
Jack J Florio Jr, *Owner*
Rebecca Kelley, *Vice Pres*
EMP: 5
SALES (est): 370K **Privately Held**
SIC: 2752 2754 2759 2791 Commercial printing, lithographic; commercial printing, gravure; commercial printing; typesetting; bookbinding & related work; automotive & apparel trimmings

(G-7596)
LAFARGE NORTH AMERICA INC
400 Hinman Rd (14094-9276)
PHONE.................................716 772-2621
Courtland Hess, *Plant Mgr*
Len Studley, *Safety Mgr*
Harry McCormick, *Manager*
Rebecca Hartford, *Manager*
Todd Watson, *Manager*
EMP: 30
SQ FT: 47,480
SALES (corp-wide): 23.4B **Privately Held**
WEB: www.lafargenorthamerica.com
SIC: 3241 Cement, hydraulic
HQ: Lafarge North America Inc.
8700 W Bryn Mawr Ave Ll
Chicago IL 60631
703 480-3600

(G-7597)
LIBERTY TIRE RECYCLING LLC
490 Ohio St (14094-4220)
PHONE.................................716 433-7370
Rick Johnson, *Branch Mgr*
EMP: 30
SALES (corp-wide): 53.8MM **Privately Held**
SIC: 2822 Synthetic rubber
HQ: Liberty Tire Recycling, Llc
625 Liberty Ave Ste 3100
Pittsburgh PA 15222
412 562-1700

(G-7598)
MAHLE BEHR USA INC
Also Called: Delphi Thrmal Lckport Model Sp
350 Upper Mountain Rd (14094-1861)
PHONE.................................716 439-2011
Daniel L Martin, *Engineer*
Dave Patterson, *Branch Mgr*
Celia Paulin, *Info Tech Mgr*
EMP: 450 **Privately Held**
SIC: 3714 Motor vehicle parts & accessories
HQ: Mahle Behr Usa Inc.
2700 Daley Dr
Troy MI 48083
248 743-3700

(G-7599)
MERRITT MACHINERY LLC
10 Simonds St (14094-4111)
PHONE.................................716 434-5558
Micheal Smith, *Purchasing*
Anna McCann,
▲ **EMP:** 20 **EST:** 1977
SQ FT: 30,000
SALES (est): 4.1MM **Privately Held**
WEB: www.merrittpmi.com
SIC: 3553 Woodworking machinery

(G-7600)
METAL CLADDING INC
230 S Niagara St (14094-1927)
PHONE.................................716 434-5513
Fax: 716 439-4010
Alexander F Robb, *CEO*
Raymond S Adornetto, *CFO*
Deborah Reimer, *Admin Sec*
▲ **EMP:** 87 **EST:** 1945
SQ FT: 70,000
SALES (est): 13.6MM **Privately Held**
WEB: www.metalcladding.com
SIC: 3479 3089 Coating of metals with plastic or resins; coating, rust preventive; plastic hardware & building products; plastic & fiberglass tanks

(G-7601)
METRO GROUP INC
Also Called: Retailer
8 South St (14094-4412)
PHONE.................................716 434-4055
Fax: 716 434-6022
Bernard Bradpiece, *President*
David Smith, *Supervisor*
EMP: 5 **EST:** 1948
SQ FT: 1,500
SALES (est): 330K **Privately Held**
SIC: 2741 Guides: publishing only, not printed on site; shopping news: publishing only, not printed on site

(G-7602)
MILWARD ALLOYS INC
500 Mill St (14094-1712)
PHONE.................................716 434-5536
Fax: 716 434-3257
Johanna Van De Mark, *President*
Allen Van De Mark, *Vice Pres*
Johanna V Mark, *Plant Mgr*
David Summerlee, *Plant Mgr*
Tim Kosto, *Controller*
◆ **EMP:** 37 **EST:** 1948
SQ FT: 60,000
SALES: 5MM **Privately Held**
WEB: www.milward.com
SIC: 3351 3365 Bands, copper & copper alloy; aluminum & aluminum-based alloy castings

Lockport - Niagara County (G-7603)

(G-7603)
MODERN-TEC MANUFACTURING INC
4935 Lockport Rd (14094-9630)
PHONE..................716 625-8700
Christopher Matyas, *President*
EMP: 5
SQ FT: 11,000
SALES (est): 594.5K **Privately Held**
SIC: 3599 Air intake filters, internal combustion engine, except auto

(G-7604)
NIAGARA COOLER INC
6605 Slyton Settlement Rd (14094-1144)
PHONE..................716 434-1235
Fax: 716 434-1739
Joseph Loiacano, *President*
EMP: 7
SQ FT: 5,000
SALES: 1MM **Privately Held**
WEB: www.niagaracooler.com
SIC: 3743 Industrial locomotives & parts

(G-7605)
NIAGARA FIBERBOARD INC
140 Van Buren St (14094-2437)
P.O. Box 520 (14095-0520)
PHONE..................716 434-8881
Fax: 716 434-8884
Stephen W Halas, *Ch of Bd*
Kevin Cain, *Vice Pres*
EMP: 23
SQ FT: 60,000
SALES (est): 3.9MM **Privately Held**
WEB: www.niagarafiberboard.com
SIC: 2493 2631 Fiberboard, other vegetable pulp; paperboard mills

(G-7606)
NIAGARA PRECISION INC
233 Market St (14094-2917)
PHONE..................716 439-0956
Fax: 716 439-0117
Roger Hood, *President*
Dennis Hood, *Vice Pres*
Barbara Hood, *Admin Sec*
EMP: 24
SQ FT: 12,000
SALES (est): 4MM **Privately Held**
WEB: www.niagaraprecision.net
SIC: 3599 Machine shop, jobbing & repair

(G-7607)
NIAGARA TRUSS & PALLET LLC
5626 Old Saunders Settle (14094-4100)
PHONE..................716 433-5400
Fax: 716 433-8400
Gary Clark, *Marketing Staff*
EMP: 18
SQ FT: 12,000
SALES (est): 2.2MM **Privately Held**
SIC: 2439 Trusses, except roof: laminated lumber

(G-7608)
NORTON PULPSTONES INCORPORATED
53 Caledonia St (14094-2829)
P.O. Box 547 (14095-0547)
PHONE..................716 433-9400
Glen Smith, *Branch Mgr*
EMP: 8
SALES (corp-wide): 1.2MM **Privately Held**
SIC: 2611 Mechanical pulp, including groundwood & thermomechanical
PA: Norton Pulpstones Incorporated
   604 Lindsay Cir
   Villanova PA 19085
   610 964-0544

(G-7609)
ONTARIO LABEL GRAPHICS INC
6444 Ridge Rd (14094-1015)
PHONE..................716 434-8505
Fax: 716 434-8515
Richard E Verheyn, *President*
Rose M Verheyn, *Vice Pres*
EMP: 12
SQ FT: 9,000
SALES (est): 1.1MM **Privately Held**
SIC: 2759 Commercial printing; labels & seals: printing

(G-7610)
PIVOT PUNCH CORPORATION
6550 Campbell Blvd (14094-9228)
PHONE..................716 625-8000
Fax: 716 625-6995
Robert H King Jr, *CEO*
Christopher C King, *President*
Robert H King, *Chairman*
Richard Chapman, *Vice Pres*
Christopher King, *Vice Pres*
EMP: 97 EST: 1945
SQ FT: 32,500
SALES: 7.2MM **Privately Held**
WEB: www.pivotpunch.com
SIC: 3544 Punches, forming & stamping

(G-7611)
PRECISE PUNCH CORPORATION
6550 Campbell Blvd (14094-9210)
PHONE..................716 625-8000
Robert H King Jr, *President*
Christopher King, *Vice Pres*
Joseph La Monto, *Accounting Mgr*
EMP: 11
SQ FT: 3,000
SALES (est): 960K **Privately Held**
SIC: 3544 Punches, forming & stamping

(G-7612)
ROSS JC INC
6722 Lincoln Ave (14094-6220)
PHONE..................716 439-1161
John Ross, *President*
Natalie Ross, *Vice Pres*
EMP: 5
SQ FT: 5,452
SALES: 400K **Privately Held**
SIC: 3545 Machine tool accessories

(G-7613)
ROYALTON MILLWORK & DESIGN
7526 Tonawanda Creek Rd (14094-9350)
PHONE..................716 439-4092
Thomas Herberger, *President*
Cathy Fimbel, *Office Mgr*
EMP: 5
SQ FT: 10,000
SALES (est): 743.3K **Privately Held**
SIC: 2431 Doors & door parts & trim, wood; windows & window parts & trim, wood; moldings & baseboards, ornamental & trim; staircases, stairs & railings

(G-7614)
RUBBERFORM RECYCLED PDTS LLC
75 Michigan St (14094-2629)
PHONE..................716 478-0404
Bill Robbins, *CEO*
Kim Bunce, *Purchasing*
Roberta Callaghan, *Accounts Mgr*
Susie Robbins, *Accounts Mgr*
Susie Robins, *Manager*
▼ EMP: 14
SQ FT: 30,000
SALES (est): 3.5MM **Privately Held**
WEB: www.rubberform.com
SIC: 3069 Reclaimed rubber (reworked by manufacturing processes)

(G-7615)
SUMMIT GRAPHICS
6042 Old Beattie Rd (14094-7943)
PHONE..................716 433-1014
Fax: 716 433-1054
John Butcher, *Partner*
Rose Butcher, *Partner*
EMP: 8
SQ FT: 1,500
SALES (est): 720K **Privately Held**
SIC: 2752 Commercial printing, offset

(G-7616)
SUMMIT PRINT & MAIL LLC
6042 Old Beattie Rd (14094-7943)
PHONE..................716 433-1014
J Butcher, *Mng Member*
John Butcher, *Mng Member*
Cookie Butcher,
EMP: 7

SALES (est): 841.1K **Privately Held**
WEB: www.summitprintmail.com
SIC: 2752 Commercial printing, lithographic

(G-7617)
TDY INDUSTRIES LLC
Also Called: ATI Specialty Materials
695 Ohio St (14094-4221)
PHONE..................716 433-4411
H Dalton, *Branch Mgr*
Gordie Martin, *Sr Sys Analyst*
Sara Newton, *Systems Staff*
EMP: 35
SQ FT: 438 **Publicly Held**
WEB: www.alleghenyludlum.com
SIC: 3312 3339 Stainless steel; primary nonferrous metals
HQ: Tdy Industries, Llc
   1000 Six Ppg Pl
   Pittsburgh PA 15222
   412 394-2896

(G-7618)
TED WESTBROOK
Also Called: Westbrook Machinery
4736 Mapleton Rd (14094-9621)
PHONE..................716 625-4443
Ted Westbrook, *Owner*
EMP: 1 EST: 1995
SALES: 1MM **Privately Held**
SIC: 3599 Machine shop, jobbing & repair

(G-7619)
TITANIUM DEM REMEDIATION GROUP
4907 I D A Park Dr (14094-1833)
P.O. Box 471 (14095-0471)
PHONE..................716 433-4100
Angela M Bodami, *Principal*
EMP: 13
SALES (est): 5.2MM **Privately Held**
SIC: 3356 Titanium

(G-7620)
TORRENT EMS LLC
190 Walnut St (14094-3710)
PHONE..................716 312-4099
Michael Dehn, *CEO*
Louise Cadwalader, *Treasurer*
EMP: 16
SALES (est): 4.5MM
SALES (corp-wide): 14MM **Privately Held**
SIC: 3577 Computer peripheral equipment
PA: Trek, Inc.
   190 Walnut St
   Lockport NY 14094
   716 438-7555

(G-7621)
TREK INC (PA)
190 Walnut St (14094-3710)
PHONE..................716 438-7555
Toshio Uehara, *CEO*
Mike Dehn, *President*
Nathan Duxbury, *Project Mgr*
Audrey Edwards, *Purch Agent*
John Obrien, *Engineer*
EMP: 16
SQ FT: 30,330
SALES: 14MM **Privately Held**
SIC: 3825 Instruments to measure electricity

(G-7622)
TWIN LAKE CHEMICAL INC
520 Mill St (14094-1794)
P.O. Box 411 (14095-0411)
PHONE..................716 433-3824
Fax: 716 433-7271
James J Hodan, *President*
William Caswell, *Engineer*
▲ EMP: 18
SQ FT: 10,000
SALES (est): 3.9MM **Privately Held**
WEB: www.twinlakechemical.com
SIC: 2869 Industrial organic chemicals

(G-7623)
ULRICH SIGN CO INC
250 State Rd (14094-4824)
PHONE..................716 434-0167
Fax: 716 434-0226
C McCaffrey, *President*
Christopher McCaffrey, *President*

Joe Reinhart, *General Mgr*
Val Cox, *Office Mgr*
EMP: 21 EST: 1939
SQ FT: 6,000
SALES (est): 1.8MM **Privately Held**
WEB: www.ulrichsigns.com
SIC: 3993 Neon signs; signs, not made in custom sign painting shops

(G-7624)
VANCHLOR COMPANY INC (PA)
45 Main St (14094-2838)
PHONE..................716 434-2624
Richard G Shotell, *Ch of Bd*
Dirk A Van De Mark, *Vice Pres*
Judy Samuel, *Manager*
Richard White, *Manager*
◆ EMP: 12 EST: 1960
SALES (est): 2.7MM **Privately Held**
WEB: www.vanchlor.com
SIC: 2819 Aluminum chloride

(G-7625)
VANCHLOR COMPANY INC
555 W Jackson St (14094-1744)
PHONE..................716 434-2624
Richard Shotell, *Branch Mgr*
EMP: 16
SQ FT: 30,839
SALES (corp-wide): 2.7MM **Privately Held**
WEB: www.vanchlor.com
SIC: 2819 Aluminum chloride
PA: Vanchlor Company, Inc.
   45 Main St
   Lockport NY 14094
   716 434-2624

(G-7626)
VANDEMARK CHEMICAL INC (PA)
1 N Transit Rd (14094-2323)
PHONE..................716 433-6764
Fax: 716 433-2850
Michael Kucharski, *CEO*
Paul Ameis, *COO*
Brian Law, *Senior VP*
Chris Banach, *Safety Mgr*
Angela Muir, *Safety Mgr*
◆ EMP: 85 EST: 1951
SQ FT: 13,770
SALES (est): 28.9MM **Privately Held**
WEB: www.vdmchemical.com
SIC: 2819 Industrial inorganic chemicals

Lockwood
Tioga County

(G-7627)
H F CARY & SONS
70 Reniff Rd (14859-9753)
PHONE..................607 598-2563
Lewis A Cary, *Owner*
EMP: 5
SALES: 250K **Privately Held**
SIC: 3272 Septic tanks, concrete

Locust Valley
Nassau County

(G-7628)
ALPHA 6 DISTRIBUTIONS LLC
Also Called: Arctix
11 Oyster Bay Rd (11560-2322)
PHONE..................516 801-8290
Matthew Bruderman, *CEO*
Judy Ward, *CFO*
Courtney Adel, *Manager*
Adam Smith, *Executive Asst*
▲ EMP: 12
SQ FT: 3,000
SALES: 20MM **Privately Held**
SIC: 2329 2385 5136 2369 Athletic (warmup, sweat & jogging) suits: men's & boys'; waterproof outerwear; men's & boys' clothing; women's & misses' athletic clothing & sportswear; women's & children's clothing

▲ = Import ▼ = Export
◆ = Import/Export

(G-7629)
FILESTREAM INC
257 Buckram Rd (11560-1906)
P.O. Box 93, Glen Head (11545-0093)
PHONE..................................516 759-4100
Fax: 516 759-3011
Yao Chu, *President*
Marcus Hill, *Manager*
Tan-NA Lee, *CTO*
EMP: 10
SQ FT: 1,200
SALES: 2MM **Privately Held**
WEB: www.filestream.com
SIC: 7372 Prepackaged software; business oriented computer software; educational computer software

(G-7630)
FOREST IRON WORKS INC
3 Elm St Ste A (11560-2149)
PHONE..................................516 671-4229
Fax: 516 671-8613
Mario Gallo, *President*
EMP: 8
SQ FT: 13,000
SALES (est): 760K **Privately Held**
SIC: 3446 Architectural metalwork

(G-7631)
GADDIS INDUSTRIAL EQUIPMENT
Also Called: Gaddis Engineering
168 Forest Ave (11560-2131)
P.O. Box 915 (11560-0915)
PHONE..................................516 759-3100
Fax: 516 759-3175
M Francis Gaddis, *President*
Marie B Gaddis, *Treasurer*
Paul Gaddis, *Asst Treas*
L C Hills, *Admin Sec*
EMP: 12
SALES (est): 1.1MM **Privately Held**
SIC: 3053 Packing materials

(G-7632)
HENRY DESIGN STUDIOS INC
129 Birch Hill Rd Ste 2 (11560-1841)
PHONE..................................516 801-2760
Henry Perlstein, *President*
Henri Rayski, *Vice Pres*
Elka Perlstein, *Treasurer*
EMP: 7
SQ FT: 1,400
SALES: 1MM **Privately Held**
SIC: 3911 Jewelry, precious metal

(G-7633)
JK MANUFACTURING INC
115 Forest Ave Unit 22 (11560-4001)
PHONE..................................212 683-3535
Joe Rubens, *Owner*
EMP: 9
SALES (est): 809K **Privately Held**
SIC: 3911 Jewelry, precious metal

(G-7634)
T G S INC
6 Wildwood Ct (11560-1108)
PHONE..................................516 629-6905
Rajesh Raichoudhury, *CEO*
EMP: 5
SALES (est): 370K **Privately Held**
WEB: www.tgs.com
SIC: 2731 Books: publishing & printing

Lodi
Seneca County

(G-7635)
LAMOREAUX LANDING WI
Also Called: Wagner Farms
9224 State Route 414 (14860-9641)
PHONE..................................607 582-6162
Fax: 607 582-6010
Linsey Wig, *Sales Dir*
Mario Delrosso, *Sales Staff*
Mark Wagner,
EMP: 70
SQ FT: 4,070
SALES (est): 5.2MM **Privately Held**
WEB: www.lamoreauxwine.com
SIC: 2084 Wines

(G-7636)
WAGNER VINEYARDS & BREWING CO
Also Called: Ginny Lee Cafe
9322 State Route 414 (14860-9641)
PHONE..................................607 582-6574
Stanley Wagner, *Owner*
Kim Greenier, *Bookkeeper*
John Wagner, *Owner*
Brent Wojnowski, *Manager*
EMP: 30
SQ FT: 1,200
SALES (est): 2.6MM **Privately Held**
WEB: www.wagnervineyards.com
SIC: 2084 0172 2082 Wines; grapes; malt beverages

Long Beach
Nassau County

(G-7637)
AIR TITE MANUFACTURING INC
Also Called: Focus Point Windows & Doors
724 Park Pl Ste B (11561-2158)
P.O. Box 149 (11561-0149)
PHONE..................................516 897-0295
Robert Freedman, *President*
EMP: 120
SQ FT: 40,000
SALES (est): 1.3MM **Privately Held**
SIC: 3442 Storm doors or windows, metal

(G-7638)
BARRIER BREWING COMPANY LLC
612 W Walnut St (11561-2919)
PHONE..................................516 316-4429
Evan Klein, *Administration*
EMP: 5 **EST:** 2012
SALES (est): 262.8K **Privately Held**
SIC: 2082 Malt beverages

(G-7639)
DESIGNERS TOUCH INC (PA)
Also Called: Diamond Venetian Blind Shade
750 Shore Rd Apt 6b (11561-4734)
PHONE..................................718 641-3718
Marvin Kotin, *President*
Elaine Kotin, *Vice Pres*
EMP: 7 **EST:** 1952
SQ FT: 5,000
SALES (est): 654K **Privately Held**
SIC: 2591 5719 Blinds vertical; vertical blinds

(G-7640)
ECHO APPELLATE PRESS INC
30 W Park Ave Ste 200 (11561-2018)
PHONE..................................516 432-3601
Stuart Davis, *President*
Joyce Davis, *Corp Secy*
EMP: 7
SQ FT: 4,500
SALES (est): 763K **Privately Held**
WEB: www.echoappellate.com
SIC: 2752 Commercial printing, lithographic

(G-7641)
KIKLORD LLC
10 W Broadway Apt 5l (11561-4051)
PHONE..................................917 859-1700
Joseph Caruso III,
Roger Marion,
EMP: 7
SALES (est): 440K **Privately Held**
SIC: 3069 Boot or shoe products, rubber

Long Eddy
Sullivan County

(G-7642)
DEDECO INTERNATIONAL SALES INC (PA)
11617 State Route 97 (12760-5603)
PHONE..................................845 887-4840
Fax: 845 887-5281
Steven M Antler, *President*
Joseph Lancellotti, *Mktg Dir*
▲ **EMP:** 35
SALES (est): 7.5MM **Privately Held**
WEB: www.dedeco.com
SIC: 3291 3843 Abrasive products; dental equipment & supplies

Long Island City
Queens County

(G-7643)
21ST CENTURY OPTICS INC (DH)
Also Called: S&G Optical
4700 33rd St Ste 1r (11101-2401)
PHONE..................................347 527-1079
Fax: 718 685-0404
Ralph Woythaler, *President*
Bernard Woythaler, *Vice Pres*
Michael Woythaler, *Vice Pres*
Anthony Fulco, *VP Sales*
Nicholas Cacace, *Sales Mgr*
EMP: 34
SQ FT: 22,000
SALES (est): 8.3MM
SALES (corp-wide): 88.1MM **Privately Held**
WEB: www.21stcenturyoptics.com
SIC: 3827 3851 5048 Optical instruments & lenses; lenses, optical: all types except ophthalmic; ophthalmic goods; ophthalmic goods; lenses, ophthalmic
HQ: Essilor Of America, Inc.
   13555 N Stemmons Fwy
   Dallas TX 75234
   214 496-4000

(G-7644)
A W R GROUP INC
3715 Hunters Point Ave (11101-1913)
PHONE..................................718 729-0412
Mark Schinderman, *President*
Mia Coppala, *Accountant*
EMP: 10
SALES (est): 1.1MM **Privately Held**
SIC: 2385 7699 Waterproof outerwear; antique repair & restoration, except furniture, automobiles

(G-7645)
AAAA YORK INC
Also Called: York Ladders
3720 12th St (11101-6009)
PHONE..................................718 784-6666
Kenneth Buettner, *President*
▲ **EMP:** 10
SQ FT: 5,000
SALES (est): 1.3MM **Privately Held**
SIC: 3531 Construction machinery

(G-7646)
ABBOT & ABBOT BOX CORP
Also Called: Abbot & Abbot Packing Service
3711 10th St (11101-6043)
PHONE..................................888 930-5972
Fax: 718 392-8439
Stuart Gleiber, *President*
Douglas Gleiber, *Vice Pres*
Lee Schogel, *Sales Mgr*
Carol Maiorella, *Manager*
EMP: 17
SQ FT: 40,000
SALES (est): 3.3MM **Privately Held**
WEB: www.abbotbox.com
SIC: 2441 2448 2449 3412 Boxes, wood; pallets, wood; skids, wood; wood containers; metal barrels, drums & pails; folding paperboard boxes

(G-7647)
ABLE STEEL EQUIPMENT CO INC
5002 23rd St (11101-4595)
PHONE..................................718 361-9240
Fax: 718 937-5742
Bonnie S Tarkenton, *President*
William Tarkenton, *Mfg Staff*
Ed Morgan, *Treasurer*
Harris Singer, *Director*
EMP: 15 **EST:** 1935
SQ FT: 30,000
SALES (est): 1.5MM **Privately Held**
WEB: www.ablesteelequipment.com
SIC: 2542 1799 2531 2522 Cabinets: show, display or storage: except wood; partitions for floor attachment, prefabricated: except wood; shelving, office & store: except wood; demountable partition installation; public building & related furniture; office furniture, except wood

(G-7648)
ACTION TECHNOLOGIES INC
Also Called: Active Business Systems
3809 33rd St Apt 1 (11101-2230)
PHONE..................................718 278-1000
Francine Amendola, *President*
EMP: 5
SALES (est): 175K **Privately Held**
SIC: 3579 Canceling machinery, post office

(G-7649)
AIR LOUVER & DAMPER INC (PA)
2121 44th Rd (11101-5010)
PHONE..................................718 392-3232
Joseph Chalpin, *President*
Harold Blake, *Div Sub Head*
EMP: 12
SQ FT: 20,000
SALES (est): 3MM **Privately Held**
SIC: 3822 3444 Damper operators: pneumatic, thermostatic, electric; metal ventilating equipment

(G-7650)
ALFRED MAINZER INC (PA)
2708 40th Ave (11101-3725)
PHONE..................................718 392-4200
Fax: 718 392-2681
Ronald Mainzer, *President*
Barry Mainzer, *Vice Pres*
Brad Packer, *Treasurer*
Sari Mainzer, *Admin Sec*
▼ **EMP:** 25 **EST:** 1938
SQ FT: 40,000
SALES (est): 4.1MM **Privately Held**
WEB: www.alfredmainzer.com
SIC: 2741 Miscellaneous publishing

(G-7651)
ALL CITY SWITCHBOARD CORP
3541 11th St (11106-5013)
PHONE..................................718 956-7244
Peter Tsimoyianis, *President*
Efstratios Kountouris, *Treasurer*
Joan Wittlinder, *Controller*
EMP: 26
SALES (est): 8.9MM **Privately Held**
WEB: www.allcitywbd.com
SIC: 3613 Switchgear & switchboard apparatus

(G-7652)
ALLSTATEBANNERSCOM CORPORATION
Also Called: Allstate Banners
3511 9th St (11106-5103)
PHONE..................................718 300-1256
Panagiotis Panagi, *President*
Alexander Phioukas, *Vice Pres*
EMP: 9
SQ FT: 2,000
SALES (est): 1.5MM **Privately Held**
SIC: 2752 Commercial printing, offset

(G-7653)
ALP STONE INC
2520 50th Ave Fl 2 (11101-4421)
PHONE..................................718 706-6166
Yunus Bickici, *President*
Hakton Bor, *Vice Pres*
Ghiridhar Khurana, *Accountant*
▲ **EMP:** 15
SALES: 4MM **Privately Held**
WEB: www.alpstone.com
SIC: 3272 1743 Stone, cast concrete; tile installation, ceramic

(G-7654)
ALPHA PACKAGING INDUSTRIES INC
2004 33rd St (11105-2010)
PHONE..................................718 267-4115
Fax: 718 932-9549
David Zaret, *President*

Long Island City - Queens County (G-7655) — GEOGRAPHIC SECTION

Steven Zaret, *Corp Secy*
Michael Zaret, *Vice Pres*
EMP: 35
SQ FT: 25,000
SALES (est): 11.7MM **Privately Held**
SIC: 2657 Folding paperboard boxes

(G-7655)
AMBRAS FINE JEWELRY INC
Also Called: Ambras Fjc
3100 47th Ave Unit 3 (11101-3010)
PHONE 718 784-5252
Fax: 212 268-1546
Morris Dweck, *Ch of Bd*
EMP: 50
SQ FT: 9,000
SALES (est): 5.7MM **Privately Held**
SIC: 3911 Jewelry, precious metal

(G-7656)
AMCI LTD
3302 48th Ave (11101-2418)
PHONE 718 937-5858
Fax: 718 937-5867
Justo Lorenzotti, *President*
Luis Lorenzotti, *Vice Pres*
Beatriz Arroyave, *Manager*
▲ **EMP:** 60
SQ FT: 25,000
SALES (est): 7MM **Privately Held**
SIC: 2499 Picture & mirror frames, wood

(G-7657)
AMERICAN VINTAGE WINE BISCUIT
4003 27th St (11101-3814)
PHONE 718 361-1003
Fax: 718 361-0204
Mary-Lynn Mondich, *President*
EMP: 7
SQ FT: 2,500
SALES (est): 464.5K **Privately Held**
WEB: www.americanvintage.com
SIC: 2051 Bread, cake & related products

(G-7658)
AMERICAN WAX COMPANY INC
Also Called: American Cleaning Solutions
3930 Review Ave (11101-2020)
P.O. Box 1943 (11101-0943)
PHONE 718 392-8080
Fax: 718 482-9366
Alan Winik, *CEO*
Ronald Ingber, *President*
Michelle Devito, *Opers Staff*
EMP: 50
SQ FT: 65,000
SALES (est): 10.4MM **Privately Held**
WEB: www.cleaning-solutions.com
SIC: 2842 Specialty cleaning, polishes & sanitation goods; specialty cleaning preparations; polishing preparations & related products; cleaning or polishing preparations

(G-7659)
AMERICAN WOODS & VENEERS WORKS
4735 27th St (11101-4410)
PHONE 718 937-2195
Chingyu Peng, *President*
Dianna Serro, *Manager*
EMP: 30
SQ FT: 11,000
SALES (est): 4.7MM **Privately Held**
SIC: 2499 Furniture inlays (veneers); veneer work, inlaid

(G-7660)
ANIMA MUNDI HERBALS LLC
Also Called: Rainforest Apothecary
2323 Borden Ave (11101-4508)
PHONE 415 279-5727
Adriana Ayales, *CEO*
EMP: 6
SQ FT: 1,000
SALES (est): 556K **Privately Held**
SIC: 2834 Vitamin, nutrient & hematinic preparations for human use

(G-7661)
ANTHONY LAWRENCE OF NEW YORK
Also Called: Belfair Draperies
3233 47th Ave (11101-2426)
PHONE 212 206-8820
Joseph Calagna, *Ch of Bd*
Anthony Lawrence, *Owner*
Michael Giambattista, *Vice Pres*
EMP: 20
SALES (est): 3.1MM **Privately Held**
WEB: www.anthonylawrence.com
SIC: 2391 7641 2511 Draperies, plastic & textile: from purchased materials; re-upholstery; wood household furniture

(G-7662)
APPLE ENTERPRISES INC
Also Called: Apple Digital Printing
1308 43rd Ave (11101-6833)
PHONE 718 361-2200
Howard N Sturm, *CEO*
Howard Sturm, *CEO*
Adam Sturm, *President*
Alexandra Rosner, *Accounts Mgr*
Louis Stemkowski, *Accounts Mgr*
EMP: 30 **EST:** 1995
SALES (est): 5.7MM **Privately Held**
WEB: www.applevisualgraphics.com
SIC: 2759 7389 Commercial printing; advertising, promotional & trade show services

(G-7663)
APPLE HEALING & RELAXATION
3114 Broadway (11106-2585)
PHONE 718 278-1089
EMP: 5
SALES (est): 387.2K **Privately Held**
SIC: 3571 Personal computers (microcomputers)

(G-7664)
APPLIED SAFETY LLC
4349 10th St Ste 311 (11101-6941)
PHONE 718 608-6292
Jose Hernandez,
EMP: 8
SALES: 200K **Privately Held**
SIC: 3564 Blowers & fans

(G-7665)
ARC REMANUFACTURING INC
1940 42nd St (11105-1113)
PHONE 718 728-0701
Fax: 718 274-4348
William P Hayes, *President*
John Hayes, *Site Mgr*
▲ **EMP:** 60
SQ FT: 150,000
SALES (est): 9.4MM **Privately Held**
WEB: www.arcparts.com
SIC: 3714 Motor vehicle engines & parts; power steering equipment, motor vehicle; windshield wiper systems, motor vehicle; motor vehicle brake systems & parts

(G-7666)
ARCHAELOGY MAGAZINE
3636 33rd St Ste 301 (11106-2329)
PHONE 718 472-3050
Fax: 718 472-3751
Phyliss Katz, *President*
Zachary Zorich, *General Mgr*
EMP: 20
SALES (est): 1.4MM **Privately Held**
WEB: www.archaeology.org
SIC: 2721 Periodicals

(G-7667)
ARGO ENVELOPE CORP
4310 21st St (11101-5002)
PHONE 718 729-2700
Fax: 718 361-8950
Lawrence Chait, *President*
Eric Chait, *Vice Pres*
EMP: 60 **EST:** 1946
SQ FT: 50,000
SALES (est): 7MM **Privately Held**
SIC: 2759 2752 Envelopes: printing; commercial printing, lithographic

(G-7668)
ARGO GENERAL MACHINE WORK INC
3816 11th St (11101-6114)
PHONE 718 392-4605
Fax: 718 204-1985
Frank Scaduto, *President*
Ignazio Scaduto, *Vice Pres*
EMP: 7
SQ FT: 2,400
SALES (est): 862.6K **Privately Held**
SIC: 3599 Machine shop, jobbing & repair

(G-7669)
ARGO LITHOGRAPHERS INC
4310 21st St (11101-5002)
PHONE 718 729-2700
Lawrence Chait, *President*
Eric Chait, *Vice Pres*
EMP: 25
SQ FT: 5,000
SALES: 4MM **Privately Held**
WEB: www.argoenvelope.com
SIC: 2752 5112 5111 2789 Commercial printing, lithographic; stationery & office supplies; printing & writing paper; bookbinding & related work; commercial printing

(G-7670)
ART FORM SHEET METAL FABRICATO
2120 45th Rd (11101-4707)
PHONE 718 728-0111
George Panousopoulos, *President*
EMP: 5
SQ FT: 5,000
SALES (est): 400K **Privately Held**
SIC: 3444 Sheet metalwork

(G-7671)
ASCO CASTINGS INC (PA)
3100 47th Ave Ste G (11101-3013)
PHONE 212 719-9800
Barry Smith, *General Mgr*
EMP: 6
SQ FT: 4,000
SALES (est): 1.1MM **Privately Held**
WEB: www.ascocasting.com
SIC: 3915 Jewelers' castings

(G-7672)
ASIAN GLOBAL TRADING CORP
3613 36th Ave Ste 2 (11106-1306)
PHONE 718 786-0998
Fax: 718 786-0971
Chau Pei Hsu, *President*
▲ **EMP:** 10
SALES (est): 1MM **Privately Held**
SIC: 2253 Knit outerwear mills

(G-7673)
ASTRON CANDLE MANUFACTURING CO
1125 30th Ave (11102-4098)
PHONE 718 728-3330
Fax: 718 956-9583
Menelaos G Tzelios, *President*
◆ **EMP:** 7
SQ FT: 7,000
SALES (est): 811.5K **Privately Held**
SIC: 3999 Candles

(G-7674)
ASTUCCI US LTD
4369 9th St (11101-6907)
PHONE 718 752-9700
Dan Benmoshe, *Branch Mgr*
EMP: 18
SALES (corp-wide): 15MM **Privately Held**
SIC: 3172 Personal leather goods
PA: Astucci, U.S., Ltd.
385 5th Ave Rm 1100
New York NY 10016
212 725-3171

(G-7675)
ASUR JEWELRY INC
4709 30th St Ste 403 (11101-3400)
PHONE 718 472-1687
Aydin Barka, *President*
EMP: 6
SQ FT: 2,500
SALES: 700K **Privately Held**
SIC: 3915 Jewelers' castings

(G-7676)
ATLANTIC PRECIOUS METAL CAST
4132 27th St (11101-3825)
PHONE 718 937-7100
Fax: 718 937-6544
Ricky Barbieri, *Principal*
EMP: 9
SALES (est): 630K **Privately Held**
SIC: 3911 Jewelry, precious metal

(G-7677)
ATLANTIC STEINWAY AWNG II LLC
4230 24th St (11101-4608)
PHONE 718 729-2965
Zuzina Popp, *President*
EMP: 6
SALES (est): 410K **Privately Held**
SIC: 3993 5999 Signs & advertising specialties; awnings

(G-7678)
AUGUST STUDIOS
Also Called: Augusta Studios
4008 22nd St Fl 3 (11101-4826)
PHONE 718 706-6487
August Helbling, *Owner*
EMP: 8
SALES (est): 390K **Privately Held**
SIC: 2512 7641 Upholstered household furniture; upholstery work

(G-7679)
B & B SHEET METAL INC
2540 50th Ave (11101-4421)
PHONE 718 433-2501
Fax: 718 433-2709
Robert Baschnagel, *President*
Robert Baschnagel III, *President*
Daniela Espinoza, *Project Mgr*
Peter Barry, *Research*
Christopher Andreone, *Sales Mgr*
◆ **EMP:** 50
SALES (est): 11.6MM **Privately Held**
SIC: 3444 Sheet metalwork

(G-7680)
BAGEL LITES LLC
Also Called: Big City Bagel Lites
240 51st Ave Apt 1f (11101-5865)
PHONE 855 813-7888
Raquel Salas,
EMP: 2 **EST:** 2015
SQ FT: 2,000
SALES: 1MM **Privately Held**
SIC: 2051 5461 Bagels, fresh or frozen; bagels

(G-7681)
BANGLA PATRIKA INC
3806 31st St 2 (11101-2719)
PHONE 718 482-9923
Mahabubur Rahman, *President*
EMP: 9
SQ FT: 1,250
SALES: 32K **Privately Held**
SIC: 2711 Newspapers

(G-7682)
BARGOLD STORAGE SYSTEMS LLC
4141 38th St (11101-1708)
PHONE 718 247-7000
Fax: 212 247-7007
Gerald Goldman, *Mng Member*
Alan Goldman, *Mng Member*
Jordan Goldman, *Mng Member*
Joshua Goldman, *Mng Member*
EMP: 40
SQ FT: 3,000
SALES (est): 9.1MM **Privately Held**
WEB: www.bargoldstorage.com
SIC: 3444 1796 Sheet metalwork; installing building equipment

(G-7683)
BESTEC CONCEPT INC
Also Called: Maxivision
4310 23rd St Lbby 4 (11101-5020)
PHONE 718 937-5848
Fax: 718 937-5825

▲ = Import ▼ = Export ◆ = Import/Export

GEOGRAPHIC SECTION — Long Island City - Queens County (G-7711)

Helen M Han, *President*
EMP: 6
SALES (est): 792.7K **Privately Held**
SIC: 2326 2311 2337 2339 Work uniforms; men's & boys' uniforms; military uniforms, men's & youths': purchased materials; policemen's uniforms: made from purchased materials; uniforms, except athletic: women's, misses' & juniors'; service apparel, washable: women's

(G-7684)
BG BINDERY INC
3002 48th Ave (11101-3432)
PHONE 631 767-4242
Barbara Michael, *CEO*
EMP: 5 **EST:** 2011
SALES (est): 490.5K **Privately Held**
SIC: 2789 Bookbinding & related work

(G-7685)
BIMBO BAKERIES USA INC
4011 34th Ave (11101-1105)
PHONE 718 545-0291
Al Larocca, *Branch Mgr*
EMP: 5
SALES (corp-wide): 13B **Privately Held**
SIC: 2051 Cakes, pies & pastries
HQ: Bimbo Bakeries Usa, Inc
255 Business Center Dr # 200
Horsham PA 19044
215 347-5500

(G-7686)
BIRCH GUYS LLC
Also Called: Birch Coffee
4035 23rd St (11101-4818)
P.O. Box 287507, New York (10128-0026)
PHONE 917 763-0751
Paul Schlader,
EMP: 8
SALES (est): 360K **Privately Held**
SIC: 2095 Roasted coffee

(G-7687)
BLACK BEAR COMPANY INC
2710 49th Ave (11101-4408)
PHONE 718 784-7330
Barret T Schleicher, *President*
Jennifer Trubia, *Corp Secy*
▲ **EMP:** 20
SQ FT: 25,000
SALES (est): 4.5MM **Privately Held**
WEB: www.blackbearoil.com
SIC: 2992 Lubricating oils & greases

(G-7688)
BLATT SEARLE & COMPANY LTD (PA)
4121 28th St (11101-3718)
PHONE 212 730-7717
Fax: 212 764-4524
Searle Blatt, *President*
Alice Blatt, *Exec VP*
▲ **EMP:** 20
SALES (est): 4.3MM **Privately Held**
WEB: www.momao.com
SIC: 2337 Suits: women's, misses' & juniors'; skirts, separate: women's, misses' & juniors'; women's & misses' capes & jackets

(G-7689)
BLEECKER PASTRY TARTUFO INC
3722 13th St (11101-6025)
PHONE 718 937-9830
Fax: 718 392-5965
Lucy Di Saverio, *President*
Donato Di Saverio, *Principal*
EMP: 7
SQ FT: 7,500
SALES (est): 400K **Privately Held**
WEB: www.bleeckerpastrytartufo.com
SIC: 2024 5451 Ice cream, bulk; ice cream (packaged)

(G-7690)
BRIDGE PRINTING INC
4710 32nd Pl Fl 2 (11101-2415)
PHONE 212 243-5390
Fax: 718 361-9123
EMP: 5
SQ FT: 8,000
SALES: 1MM **Privately Held**
SIC: 2752 Lithographic Commercial Printing

(G-7691)
CABINET SHAPES CORP
3721 12th St (11101-6008)
PHONE 718 784-6255
Fax: 718 392-4282
John Seretis, *President*
EMP: 15
SALES: 1.2MM **Privately Held**
WEB: www.info-s.com
SIC: 2434 2499 1751 Wood kitchen cabinets; decorative wood & woodwork; cabinet & finish carpentry

(G-7692)
CAMA GRAPHICS INC
Also Called: Altum Press
3200 Skillman Ave Ste B (11101-2308)
PHONE 718 707-9747
Fax: 718 707-9751
Anthony Cappuccio, *President*
EMP: 12
SQ FT: 4,800
SALES (est): 830K **Privately Held**
WEB: www.camagraphics.com
SIC: 2759 Commercial printing

(G-7693)
CANDID LITHO PRINTING LTD
2511 Hunters Point Ave (11101-4429)
PHONE 212 431-3800
Howard Weinstein, *President*
Scott Weinstein, *Corp Secy*
Lewis Rosenberg, *Vice Pres*
Jhamar Brown, *Controller*
Kim Steefel, *CIO*
EMP: 60 **EST:** 1964
SQ FT: 109,285
SALES (est): 16.4MM **Privately Held**
WEB: www.candidlitho.com
SIC: 2752 Commercial printing, lithographic; commercial printing, offset

(G-7694)
CANDID WORLDWIDE LLC (PA)
2511 Hunters Point Ave # 2 (11101-4429)
PHONE 212 799-5300
David Stadler, *CEO*
Howard Weinstein, *President*
Rob Jamison, *General Mgr*
Brian Stephens, *Plant Mgr*
Jhamar Brown, *Controller*
EMP: 4
SALES (est): 6.2MM **Privately Held**
SIC: 2759 Posters, including billboards: printing

(G-7695)
CASSINELLI FOOD PRODUCTS INC
3112 23rd Ave (11105-2407)
PHONE 718 274-4881
Anthony Bonfigli, *President*
Nella Costella, *Treasurer*
EMP: 6
SQ FT: 3,000
SALES: 700K **Privately Held**
SIC: 2098 5411 Macaroni & spaghetti; delicatessens

(G-7696)
CENTRAL TIME CLOCK INC
Also Called: Discountclocks.com
523 50th Ave (11101-5711)
PHONE 718 784-4900
Fax: 718 472-9491
Sheldon Reinhardt, *President*
JP Altenau, *Managing Dir*
Hal Reinhardt, *Vice Pres*
Mathew Reinhardt, *Vice Pres*
Andrew Papadeas, *Sales Associate*
EMP: 10
SQ FT: 4,000
SALES: 1.4MM **Privately Held**
WEB: www.centraltimeclock.com
SIC: 3579 Time clocks & time recording devices

(G-7697)
CHOCOMIZE INC
3010 41st Ave (11101-2814)
PHONE 718 729-3264
Fabian Kaempfer, *CEO*
▲ **EMP:** 10
SQ FT: 5,000
SALES (est): 760K **Privately Held**
SIC: 2066 Chocolate & cocoa products; chocolate bars, solid

(G-7698)
CITY BAKING LLC
1041 45th Ave (11101-7017)
PHONE 718 392-8514
Fax: 718 392-1818
Barry Blaine, *Mng Member*
Fernando Lopez,
EMP: 7
SQ FT: 2,500
SALES: 765K **Privately Held**
SIC: 2052 Bakery products, dry

(G-7699)
CIVIL SVC RTRED EMPLOYEES ASSN
Also Called: Csrea
3427 Steinway St Ste 1 (11101-8602)
PHONE 718 937-0290
Kjell Kjellberg, *Editor*
EMP: 12
SALES (est): 560K **Privately Held**
SIC: 2721 Magazines: publishing & printing

(G-7700)
CLADDAGH ELECTRONICS LTD
1032 47th Rd (11101-5514)
PHONE 718 784-0571
Fax: 718 482-9471
William J Casey, *President*
Angelo Mottola, *Vice Pres*
Arthur Zagari, *Accounts Mgr*
Joanne Guidici, *Manager*
EMP: 20
SQ FT: 3,000
SALES (est): 3.6MM **Privately Held**
WEB: www.claddaghelectronics.com
SIC: 3613 5065 Panelboards & distribution boards, electric; electronic parts & equipment

(G-7701)
CNC MANUFACTURING CORP
Also Called: Gt Machine & Tool
3214 49th St (11103-1403)
PHONE 718 728-6800
Dean Theotos, *President*
EMP: 25
SALES (est): 105.6K **Privately Held**
SIC: 3469 Machine parts, stamped or pressed metal

(G-7702)
COE DISPLAYS INC
4301 22nd St Ste 603 (11101-5031)
PHONE 718 937-5658
Fax: 212 707-3207
Joel Sgroe, *CEO*
Masimo Russo, *Co-Owner*
EMP: 5 **EST:** 1960
SQ FT: 10,000
SALES (est): 641.1K **Privately Held**
SIC: 2752 3993 2396 Commercial printing, lithographic; signs & advertising specialties; automotive & apparel trimmings

(G-7703)
COLOR INDUSTRIES LLC
3002 48th Ave Ste H (11101-3401)
PHONE 718 392-8301
Edward Tikkanen, *Mng Member*
Meida Costanzo, *Manager*
EMP: 8
SALES (est): 1MM **Privately Held**
SIC: 2754 Commercial printing, gravure

(G-7704)
COOPERFRIEDMAN ELC SUP CO INC
2219 41st Ave (11101-4835)
PHONE 718 269-4906
EMP: 5
SALES (corp-wide): 9.8MM **Privately Held**
SIC: 3699 1731 Electrical equipment & supplies; electrical work
HQ: Cooperfriedman Electric Supply Co., Inc.
1 Matrix Dr
Monroe Township NJ 08831
732 747-2233

(G-7705)
COSMOS COMMUNICATIONS INC
1105 44th Dr (11101-7027)
PHONE 718 482-1800
Jack Weiss, *Ch of Bd*
Arnold Weiss, *President*
Gerald Weiss, *Corp Secy*
Joe Cashman, *COO*
Richard Quarto, *Vice Pres*
EMP: 105 **EST:** 1933
SQ FT: 54,000
SALES (est): 25.8MM **Privately Held**
WEB: www.cosmosinc.net
SIC: 2752 2791 2789 Commercial printing, lithographic; typesetting; bookbinding & related work

(G-7706)
CRAIG ENVELOPE CORP
1201 44th Ave (11101-6998)
PHONE 718 786-4277
Fax: 718 937-8178
Lawrence Aaronson, *President*
Susan Aaronson, *Corp Secy*
Robert Aaronson, *VP Opers*
Manny Ramos, *Prdtn Mgr*
John Lundgren, *Human Res Mgr*
EMP: 39
SQ FT: 20,000
SALES (est): 6.3MM **Privately Held**
SIC: 2752 2759 Commercial printing, offset; letterpress printing

(G-7707)
CRISADA INC
3913 23rd St (11101-4816)
PHONE 718 729-9730
Fax: 718 729-9740
Chris Kole, *President*
EMP: 5
SALES: 1.2MM **Privately Held**
WEB: www.crisada.com
SIC: 2335 2311 Gowns, formal; tailored suits & formal jackets

(G-7708)
CUSTOM CAS INC
2631 1st St (11102-4124)
PHONE 718 726-3575
Fax: 718 721-8814
Yiota Yerolemuo, *President*
Tasos Yerolemuo, *Vice Pres*
EMP: 20
SQ FT: 10,000
SALES (est): 2.1MM **Privately Held**
WEB: www.customcas.com
SIC: 2434 Wood kitchen cabinets

(G-7709)
CW METALS INC
3421 Greenpoint Ave (11101-2013)
PHONE 917 416-7906
Caesar Witek, *President*
EMP: 6
SALES: 1MM **Privately Held**
SIC: 3444 Sheet metalwork

(G-7710)
DAVID FLATT FURNITURE LTD
3842 Review Ave Ste 2 (11101-2045)
PHONE 718 937-7944
David Flatt, *President*
▲ **EMP:** 10
SQ FT: 11,000
SALES (est): 943.2K **Privately Held**
SIC: 2541 Display fixtures, wood

(G-7711)
DELTA SHEET METAL CORP
3935 Skillman Ave (11104-3706)
PHONE 718 429-5805
Peter J Pappas, *President*
Eva Georgopoulos, *Vice Pres*
EMP: 202
SQ FT: 25,000
SALES (est): 29.9MM **Privately Held**
SIC: 3444 Ducts, sheet metal

Long Island City - Queens County (G-7712)

(G-7712)
DEPENDABLE LITHOGRAPHERS INC
3200 Skillman Ave (11101-2309)
PHONE.....................718 472-4200
Fax: 718 472-4707
David Hananel, *President*
EMP: 15
SQ FT: 15,000
SALES (est): 1.5MM **Privately Held**
SIC: **2752** 2789 Commercial printing, lithographic; bookbinding & related work

(G-7713)
DEPP GLASS INC
4140 38th St (11101-1709)
PHONE.....................718 784-8500
Fax: 718 784-9018
Wesley R Depp, *President*
Judy Depp, *Admin Sec*
◆ EMP: 12 EST: 1923
SQ FT: 14,000
SALES (est): 1.9MM **Privately Held**
WEB: www.deppglass.com
SIC: **3229** 3231 Lamp parts & shades, glass; mirrored glass

(G-7714)
DEWES GUMBS DIE CO INC
3833 24th St (11101-3689)
PHONE.....................718 784-9755
Fax: 718 784-9755
Robert Salerni, *President*
EMP: 7 EST: 1906
SQ FT: 5,000
SALES (est): 490K **Privately Held**
SIC: **3544** Dies & die holders for metal cutting, forming, die casting

(G-7715)
DI FIORE AND SONS CUSTOM WDWKG
4202 Astoria Blvd (11103-2504)
PHONE.....................718 278-1663
Fax: 718 274-6848
Santino Di Fiore, *President*
Maria T Di Fiore, *Vice Pres*
Joseph Mazzola, *Manager*
EMP: 5
SQ FT: 8,000
SALES (est): 596.4K **Privately Held**
SIC: **2434** 5712 5031 2499 Wood kitchen cabinets; cabinet work, custom; kitchen cabinets; decorative wood & woodwork; kitchen & bathroom remodeling; single-family home remodeling, additions & repairs

(G-7716)
DIMENSION DEVELOPMENT CORP
3630 37th St Fl 1 (11101-1606)
PHONE.....................718 361-8825
Wiston A Williams, *President*
Jeanette M Pineda, *Administration*
EMP: 9
SALES: 256K **Privately Held**
SIC: **1389** Testing, measuring, surveying & analysis services

(G-7717)
DRILLCO EQUIPMENT CO INC
3452 11th St (11106-5012)
PHONE.....................718 777-5986
Gus Neos, *Treasurer*
Angelo Neos, *Treasurer*
▲ EMP: 25
SALES (est): 4.6MM **Privately Held**
SIC: **3532** Drills, bits & similar equipment

(G-7718)
DRILLCO NATIONAL GROUP INC (PA)
2432 44th St (11103-2002)
P.O. Box 2182 (11102-0182)
PHONE.....................718 726-9801
Patrick Lacey, *President*
Jim Wieder, *Corp Secy*
Nicholas Lacey, *Vice Pres*
Bill McGarry, *Project Mgr*
EMP: 36
SALES (est): 5.7MM **Privately Held**
SIC: **3531** Drags, road (construction & road maintenance equipment)

(G-7719)
DURA ENGRAVING CORPORATION
Also Called: Dura Architectural Signage
4815 32nd Pl (11101-2538)
PHONE.....................718 706-6400
Fax: 718 786-2863
Eva Forst, *CEO*
Ark Forst, *President*
Dan Forst, *Accountant*
Myra Hyman, *Assistant*
EMP: 25 EST: 1941
SQ FT: 20,000
SALES: 2MM **Privately Held**
WEB: www.duracorp.com
SIC: **3993** Signs, not made in custom sign painting shops; name plates: except engraved, etched, etc.: metal

(G-7720)
DURAL DOOR COMPANY INC
3128 Greenpoint Ave (11101-2006)
PHONE.....................718 729-1333
Fax: 718 729-1761
Peter Macari, *President*
Louis Vella, *Vice Pres*
EMP: 13 EST: 1945
SQ FT: 2,500
SALES (est): 1.2MM **Privately Held**
SIC: **3534** 3442 Elevators & equipment; metal doors, sash & trim

(G-7721)
DWM INTERNATIONAL INC
Also Called: Society Awards
37-18 Nthrn Blvd Ste 516 (11101)
PHONE.....................646 290-7448
David Moritz, *President*
Jason Garcia, *Accounts Mgr*
▲ EMP: 15
SQ FT: 3,000
SALES (est): 1.2MM **Privately Held**
SIC: **3914** 7336 Trophies; art design services

(G-7722)
E & T PLASTIC MFG CO INC (PA)
Also Called: E&T Plastics
4545 37th St (11101-1801)
PHONE.....................718 729-6226
Fax: 718 392-6277
Gary Thal, *President*
Mark Elowsky, *Vice Pres*
Sean Clowe, *Sales Staff*
Samuel Allen, *Sales Associate*
Robert Nachimson, *Marketing Staff*
◆ EMP: 80 EST: 1946
SQ FT: 60,000
SALES (est): 25.4MM **Privately Held**
SIC: **3089** Extruded finished plastic products

(G-7723)
EDISON PRICE LIGHTING INC (PA)
Also Called: Epl
4150 22nd St (11101-4815)
PHONE.....................718 685-0700
Fax: 718 392-6648
Emma Price, *President*
Gregory Mortman, *Vice Pres*
Mary Romano, *Vice Pres*
Richard Shaver, *Vice Pres*
Joel R Siegel, *Vice Pres*
EMP: 119 EST: 1952
SQ FT: 40,000
SALES (est): 22.2MM **Privately Held**
SIC: **3646** Commercial indusl & institutional electric lighting fixtures

(G-7724)
EDISON PRICE LIGHTING INC
4105 21st St (11101-6102)
PHONE.....................718 685-0700
Fulgencio Bengochea, *Branch Mgr*
EMP: 80
SALES (corp-wide): 22.2MM **Privately Held**
SIC: **3646** 5063 Commercial indusl & institutional electric lighting fixtures; electrical apparatus & equipment
PA: Edison Price Lighting, Inc.
4150 22nd St
Long Island City NY 11101
718 685-0700

(G-7725)
EFAM ENTERPRISES LLC
Also Called: Finestar
2919 39th Ave (11101-2707)
PHONE.....................718 204-1760
Toll Free:.....................888
Jeff Aronowitz, *Accounting Mgr*
Michael Ehrlich,
Shai Bivas,
Sandra Ehrlich,
EMP: 20
SQ FT: 12,000
SALES: 3MM **Privately Held**
SIC: **3861** 5045 Toners, prepared photographic (not made in chemical plants); computers, peripherals & software

(G-7726)
EFFANJAY PENS INC
2109 Borden Ave Fl 2 (11101-4531)
PHONE.....................212 316-9565
Carlos Evering, *President*
EMP: 40 EST: 1953
SQ FT: 26,000
SALES (est): 3.4MM **Privately Held**
SIC: **3951** 3953 3952 Ball point pens & parts; pencils & pencil parts, mechanical; markers, soft tip (felt, fabric, plastic, etc.); marking devices; lead pencils & art goods

(G-7727)
EFFICIENT AUTOMATED MCH CORP
Also Called: Efficient Mach Shop
3913 23rd St Fl 1 (11101-4887)
PHONE.....................718 937-9393
Fax: 718 786-6849
Vasilious Vasiadis, *President*
Edward Calleja, *Vice Pres*
Robert Calleja, *Vice Pres*
EMP: 10 EST: 1938
SQ FT: 7,500
SALES (est): 1.5MM **Privately Held**
SIC: **3599** Machine shop, jobbing & repair

(G-7728)
EFRON DESIGNS LTD
2121 41st Ave Ste 5b (11101-4828)
PHONE.....................718 482-8440
Daniel Efron, *President*
Jill Efron, *Vice Pres*
EMP: 8
SALES (est): 1MM **Privately Held**
SIC: **3911** Jewelry apparel

(G-7729)
ELENIS NYC INC (PA)
Also Called: Eleni's Cookies
4725 34th St Ste 305 (11101-2442)
PHONE.....................718 361-8136
Eleni Gianopulos, *CEO*
Randall Gianopulos, *President*
Ron Levine, *Opers Staff*
Matthew Gilson, *Controller*
▲ EMP: 32
SQ FT: 4,000
SALES (est): 4.3MM **Privately Held**
SIC: **2052** Cookies

(G-7730)
EMPIRE BIAS BINDING CO INC
Also Called: Karter Bias Binding
3439 31st St (11106-2301)
P.O. Box 6058 (11106-0058)
PHONE.....................718 545-0300
Darryl S Goldberg, *President*
Seymour Goldberg, *Shareholder*
▲ EMP: 15 EST: 1923
SQ FT: 8,000
SALES: 914K **Privately Held**
WEB: www.empiregrouponline.com
SIC: **2396** 5131 Bindings, bias: made from purchased materials; lace fabrics

(G-7731)
ENDEAVOR PRINTING LLC
3704 29th St (11101-2612)
PHONE.....................718 570-2720
Brian Baltes,
EMP: 5
SQ FT: 2,000
SALES: 650K **Privately Held**
SIC: **2759** Business forms; printing

(G-7732)
EUROCRAFT CUSTOM FURNITURE
3425 11th St (11106-5011)
PHONE.....................718 956-0600
Tsambikos Mahramas, *President*
EMP: 5
SQ FT: 6,200
SALES (est): 330K **Privately Held**
SIC: **2511** 5031 Wood household furniture; kitchen cabinets

(G-7733)
EUROPADISK LLC
2402 Queens Plz S (11101-4602)
PHONE.....................718 407-7300
Fax: 718 361-7961
James P Shelton, *President*
Ron Texley, *Vice Pres*
Jeremy Guttenberg, *Mfg Staff*
Vince Sbarra, *CFO*
Kirk Oetting, *Training Super*
EMP: 50
SQ FT: 75,000
SALES: 6MM **Privately Held**
SIC: **3652** Phonograph record blanks; magnetic tape (audio): prerecorded; compact laser discs, prerecorded

(G-7734)
EXHIBIT CORPORATION AMERICA
Also Called: Exhibit Portables
4623 Crane St Ste 3 (11101-4303)
PHONE.....................718 937-2600
Gregory Abbate, *President*
Ronald A Abbate Jr, *Chairman*
Lorraine Pasieka, *Treasurer*
Giannina Abbate, *Admin Sec*
EMP: 30 EST: 1965
SQ FT: 50,000
SALES: 100K **Privately Held**
SIC: **3993** 7389 2522 2521 Signs & advertising specialties; interior designer; office furniture, except wood; wood office furniture

(G-7735)
EXPERT MACHINE SERVICES INC
3944a 28th St (11101-3729)
PHONE.....................718 786-1200
Stuart Fischer, *President*
EMP: 5
SALES (est): 500.6K **Privately Held**
SIC: **3599** Machine shop, jobbing & repair

(G-7736)
EXPERT METAL SLITTERS CORP
3740 12th St (11101-6009)
PHONE.....................718 361-2735
Fax: 718 361-1808
Kent Derossi, *President*
Henry Rossi, *Vice Pres*
▲ EMP: 6
SQ FT: 22,000
SALES (est): 1.3MM **Privately Held**
SIC: **3549** Cutting & slitting machinery

(G-7737)
FALCON PERSPECTIVES INC
28 Vernon Blvd Ste 45 (11101)
PHONE.....................718 706-9168
Fax: 718 433-0993
Elizabeth Toma, *President*
EMP: 8
SQ FT: 14,000
SALES (est): 1MM **Privately Held**
SIC: **3498** Coils, pipe fabricated from purchased pipe

(G-7738)
FASHION RIBBON CO INC (PA)
Also Called: Pascale Madonna
3401 38th Ave (11101-2223)
PHONE.....................718 482-0100
Fax: 718 482-0177
William Rosenzweig, *Ch of Bd*
Jeffrey Rosenzweig, *President*
Donald Rubin, *President*
▲ EMP: 35 EST: 1949
SQ FT: 28,000

▲ = Import ▼ = Export
◆ = Import/Export

SALES (est): 1.6MM **Privately Held**
WEB: www.fashionribbon.com
SIC: 2241 Ribbons

(G-7739)
FELDMAN MANUFACTURING CORP
3010 41st Ave Ste 3fl (11101-2814)
PHONE.................................718 433-1700
Richard Feldman, *President*
Brenda Johnson, *Vice Pres*
Kent Chong, *Manager*
▲ **EMP:** 93
SALES (est): 5.4MM **Privately Held**
WEB: www.ebathingsuit.com
SIC: 2339 Bathing suits: women's, misses' & juniors'

(G-7740)
FINE ARTS FURNITURE INC
3872 13th St (11101-6120)
PHONE.................................212 744-9139
Fax: 718 754-2186
Robert Longo Sr, *President*
Michelle Longo, *Corp Secy*
Robert Longo Jr, *Vice Pres*
EMP: 7
SQ FT: 12,500
SALES (est): 747.5K **Privately Held**
SIC: 2511 Wood household furniture

(G-7741)
FIREFIGHTERS JOURNAL
2420 Jackson Ave (11101-4323)
PHONE.................................718 391-0283
Tony Coretto, *Officer*
EMP: 25
SALES (est): 499.3K **Privately Held**
SIC: 2711 Newspapers, publishing & printing

(G-7742)
FIRST DISPLAYS INC
2415 43rd Ave Fl 2 (11101-4623)
PHONE.................................347 642-5972
Philip Wong, *Owner*
EMP: 10
SALES (est): 811.1K **Privately Held**
SIC: 2752 Advertising posters, lithographed

(G-7743)
FISONIC CORP
4402 23rd St (11101-5000)
PHONE.................................212 732-3777
Robert Kremer, *CEO*
EMP: 8
SQ FT: 4,000 **Privately Held**
SIC: 3561 3433 Industrial pumps & parts; heating equipment, except electric
PA: Fisonic Corp
  31-00 47th Ave Ste 106
  New York NY 10023

(G-7744)
FOO YUAN FOOD PRODUCTS CO INC
2301 Borden Ave (11101-4517)
PHONE.................................212 925-2840
George Chuang, *President*
▲ **EMP:** 9 **EST:** 1979
SQ FT: 1,200
SALES (est): 605K **Privately Held**
SIC: 2092 Fresh or frozen packaged fish; fish, fresh: prepared; fish, frozen: prepared

(G-7745)
FREEDA VITAMINS INC
4725 34th St Fl 3 (11101-2436)
PHONE.................................718 433-4337
Philip W Zimmerman, *President*
Sylvia Zimmerman, *Vice Pres*
M Kaganoff, *Treasurer*
Eli Zimmerman, *Treasurer*
Samuel Zimmerman, *Treasurer*
EMP: 25
SQ FT: 3,600
SALES (est): 5.9MM **Privately Held**
SIC: 2834 Vitamin, nutrient & hematinic preparations for human use

(G-7746)
FREIRICH JULIAN CO INC (PA)
815 Kerr St (11101)
PHONE.................................718 361-9111
Fax: 718 392-0396
Paul Dardiens, *President*
Jeff Freirich, *President*
Jerry Freirich, *Chairman*
Digna Freirich, *Admin Sec*
EMP: 30 **EST:** 1923
SQ FT: 25,000
SALES (est): 5.2MM **Privately Held**
WEB: www.freirich.com
SIC: 2013 Prepared beef products from purchased beef; corned beef from purchased meat; pastrami from purchased meat; roast beef from purchased meat

(G-7747)
GALAS FRAMING SERVICES
4224 Orchard St Fl 4 (11101-2936)
PHONE.................................718 706-0007
Fax: 718 706-0731
Nilda Brothers, *President*
Elizabeth Madho, *Manager*
EMP: 15
SQ FT: 10,000
SALES (est): 750K **Privately Held**
WEB: www.galaframe.com
SIC: 2499 5023 7699 Picture & mirror frames, wood; frames & framing, picture & mirror; picture framing, custom

(G-7748)
GALMER LTD
Also Called: Galmer Silversmiths
4301 21st St Ste 130b (11101-5082)
PHONE.................................718 392-4609
Fax: 718 472-9390
Michael Izrael, *Ch of Bd*
EMP: 9
SQ FT: 10,000
SALES (est): 770K **Privately Held**
SIC: 3499 3471 Novelties & giftware, including trophies; plating of metals or formed products

(G-7749)
GEM METAL SPINNING & STAMPING
517 47th Rd (11101-5592)
PHONE.................................718 729-7014
Fax: 718 729-7014
Stephen Sloop, *President*
EMP: 5 **EST:** 1944
SQ FT: 12,500
SALES: 175K **Privately Held**
SIC: 3469 Spinning metal for the trade; stamping metal for the trade

(G-7750)
GN PRINTING
4216 34th Ave (11101-1110)
PHONE.................................718 784-1713
Tony Barsamin, *President*
EMP: 20
SALES (est): 1.4MM **Privately Held**
SIC: 2752 Commercial printing, lithographic

(G-7751)
GNOSIS CHOCOLATE INC
4003 27th St (11101-3814)
PHONE.................................646 688-5549
Vanessa Barg, *CEO*
EMP: 8
SALES (est): 540K **Privately Held**
SIC: 2066 Chocolate & cocoa products

(G-7752)
GRAND MERIDIAN PRINTING INC
Also Called: GM Printing
3116 Hunters Point Ave (11101-3131)
PHONE.................................718 937-3888
K Y Chow, *President*
Carol Chiu, *Vice Pres*
Ivy Lung, *Controller*
EMP: 20
SQ FT: 1,500
SALES (est): 3.4MM **Privately Held**
SIC: 2752 2759 Commercial printing, offset; commercial printing

(G-7753)
GRAPHICS 247 CORP
4402 23rd St Ste 113 (11101-5027)
PHONE.................................718 729-2470
Fax: 718 729-2465
George Ibanez, *President*
EMP: 7
SALES (est): 410K **Privately Held**
WEB: www.graphics247.com
SIC: 2759 Publication printing

(G-7754)
GREAT WALL CORP
4727 36th St (11101-1823)
PHONE.................................212 704-4372
Ping Nen Lin, *Ch of Bd*
George Lin, *President*
▲ **EMP:** 120
SQ FT: 86,000
SALES (est): 11.6MM **Privately Held**
SIC: 2339 Athletic clothing: women's, misses' & juniors'

(G-7755)
GUARANTEED PRINTING SVC CO INC
4710 33rd St (11101-2408)
PHONE.................................212 929-2410
Fax: 212 627-0179
Bob Cohen, *President*
Gloria Vargas, *Bookkeeper*
EMP: 20 **EST:** 1931
SQ FT: 3,000
SALES: 3MM **Privately Held**
SIC: 2752 Commercial printing, lithographic

(G-7756)
HANNA ALTINIS CO INC
3601 48th Ave (11101-1815)
PHONE.................................718 706-1134
Fax: 718 706-7824
Kenny Altinis, *President*
John Acello, *Accountant*
EMP: 50
SQ FT: 10,000
SALES (est): 4.9MM **Privately Held**
WEB: www.altunis.com
SIC: 3911 Jewelry, precious metal

(G-7757)
HEALTHY BRAND OIL CORP (PA)
5215 11th St Ste 3 (11101-5830)
PHONE.................................718 937-0806
Bradly Green, *Chairman*
Jason Thomas, *Vice Pres*
Kim Goockner, *Office Mgr*
Kim Glockner, *Administration*
▲ **EMP:** 20
SQ FT: 1,000
SALES (est): 81.4MM **Privately Held**
SIC: 2079 Cooking oils, except corn: vegetable refined

(G-7758)
HERALD PRESS INC
3710 30th St (11101-2614)
PHONE.................................718 784-5255
Anthony Diamataris, *President*
EMP: 6
SQ FT: 4,500
SALES (est): 360K **Privately Held**
SIC: 2711 Newspapers, publishing & printing

(G-7759)
HERBERT JAFFE INC
4011 Skillman Ave (11104-3203)
P.O. Box 4189 (11104-0189)
PHONE.................................718 392-1956
Fax: 718 392-2748
Herbert Jaffe, *President*
Henny Jaffe, *Treasurer*
EMP: 5
SQ FT: 5,000
SALES: 350K **Privately Held**
SIC: 3559 Sewing machines & attachments, industrial

(G-7760)
HERSCO-ORTHOTIC LABS CORP
Also Called: Hersco-Arch Products
3928 Crescent St (11101-3802)
PHONE.................................718 391-0416
Fax: 718 391-0406
James Kennedy, *President*
Cathal Kennedy, *Vice Pres*
EMP: 20
SQ FT: 3,000
SALES (est): 1.5MM **Privately Held**
WEB: www.hersco.com
SIC: 3842 Surgical appliances & supplies; foot appliances, orthopedic

(G-7761)
HOLA PUBLISHING CO
Also Called: Spanish Tele Dirctry Hola 912
2932 Northern Blvd (11101-4013)
PHONE.................................718 424-3129
Hernando Solano, *President*
EMP: 5
SALES (est): 190K **Privately Held**
SIC: 2741 Directories, telephone: publishing only, not printed on site

(G-7762)
I 2 PRINT INC
3819 24th St (11101-3619)
PHONE.................................718 937-8800
Fax: 718 937-8869
Shulan Leong, *President*
EMP: 10
SALES (est): 1.5MM **Privately Held**
WEB: www.i2print.com
SIC: 2752 Commercial printing, lithographic

(G-7763)
ICON ENTERPRISES INTL INC
Also Called: Icon-TV
5025 35th St (11101-2500)
PHONE.................................718 752-9764
Fax: 718 752-9768
Claudio Laraia, *President*
Moe Belin, *Vice Pres*
▲ **EMP:** 23
SQ FT: 7,000
SALES (est): 4.5MM **Privately Held**
WEB: www.icon-tv.org
SIC: 3663 Radio & TV communications equipment; television monitors; radio broadcasting & communications equipment; television broadcasting & communications equipment

(G-7764)
IMPORT-EXPORT CORPORATION
Also Called: Wilda
3814 30th St (11101-2792)
PHONE.................................718 707-0880
Fax: 718 707-9335
William Wu, *President*
Joe Zoo, *Officer*
EMP: 15
SQ FT: 2,500
SALES: 7.5MM **Privately Held**
SIC: 3199 Equestrian related leather articles

(G-7765)
IN TOON AMKOR FASHIONS INC
Also Called: Galaxy Knitting Mills
4809 34th St (11101-2515)
PHONE.................................718 937-4546
Fax: 718 729-5289
Albert Plant, *President*
EMP: 30
SQ FT: 50,000
SALES (est): 1.9MM **Privately Held**
SIC: 2254 Knit underwear mills

(G-7766)
INNOVATIVE INDUSTRIES LLC
4322 22nd St Ste 205 (11101-5004)
P.O. Box 92, Westernville (13486-0092)
PHONE.................................718 784-7300
EMP: 8
SALES (est): 1.2MM **Privately Held**
SIC: 3999 Barber & beauty shop equipment

(G-7767)
INTERIORS-PFT INC
Also Called: Props For Today
3200 Skillman Ave Fl 3 (11101-2308)
PHONE.................................212 244-9600
Fax: 212 244-1053
Dyann Klein, *President*
EMP: 48

Long Island City - Queens County (G-7768)   GEOGRAPHIC SECTION

SALES (est): 4.7MM **Privately Held**
SIC: 2599 Factory furniture & fixtures

(G-7768)
J J CREATIONS INC
4742 37th St (11101-1804)
PHONE....................718 392-2828
John Thor, *President*
EMP: 50
SALES: 22MM **Privately Held**
WEB: www.jjcreations.com
SIC: 3911 3961 Jewelry, precious metal; earrings, precious metal; costume jewelry

(G-7769)
JACKSON DAKOTA INC
3010 41st Ave Ste 3 (11101-2817)
PHONE....................718 786-8600
Fax: 718 706-7718
Ross Conn, *Manager*
EMP: 15
SALES (corp-wide): 6.1MM **Privately Held**
WEB: www.dakotajackson.com
SIC: 2512 Wood upholstered chairs & couches
PA: Jackson Dakota Inc
    979 3rd Ave Ste 503
    New York NY 10022
    212 838-9444

(G-7770)
JADO SEWING MACHINES INC
4008 22nd St (11101-4826)
PHONE....................718 784-2314
Fax: 718 784-2314
Onik Balian, *President*
Alexander Saks, *Vice Pres*
Anneke Stern, *Vice Pres*
EMP: 20
SQ FT: 14,000
SALES: 2.5MM **Privately Held**
WEB: www.jadosewingmachine.com
SIC: 3639 Sewing machines & attachments, domestic

(G-7771)
JLNW INC (PA)
3030 47th Ave (11101-3433)
PHONE....................212 719-4666
Norman Wolf, *CEO*
Jeffrey Leff, *Corp Secy*
Robert Mann, *Sales Mgr*
▲ EMP: 74
SQ FT: 67,000
SALES (est): 25.2MM **Privately Held**
WEB: www.carolewren.com
SIC: 2335 2339 5621 Women's, juniors' & misses' dresses; sportswear, women's; women's clothing stores

(G-7772)
JOHN GAILER INC
3718 Northern Blvd Ste 3 (11101-1631)
PHONE....................212 243-5662
Steven Dourgarian, *President*
Dennis Dourgarian, *Vice Pres*
EMP: 30
SALES (est): 2.2MM **Privately Held**
WEB: www.gailer.com
SIC: 3999 3111 Gold stamping, except books; die-cutting of leather

(G-7773)
JOHN R ROBINSON INC
3805 30th St (11101-2716)
PHONE....................718 786-6088
Fax: 718 786-6090
Frank V Cunningham, *President*
Sharon Racette, *Vice Pres*
EMP: 20
SQ FT: 5,000
SALES (est): 4MM **Privately Held**
SIC: 3443 Heat exchangers, condensers & components

(G-7774)
JURIST COMPANY INC
1105 44th Dr (11101-5107)
PHONE....................212 243-8008
Joseph Jurist, *President*
David Shushansky, *Exec VP*
Jaclyn Belczyk, *Director*
EMP: 7
SQ FT: 13,000
SALES (est): 1.4MM **Privately Held**
WEB: www.juristprinting.com
SIC: 2752 Commercial printing, lithographic

(G-7775)
JUSTA COMPANY
3464 9th St (11106-5102)
PHONE....................718 932-6139
Fax: 718 932-6139
Janechai Sayananon, *Owner*
EMP: 8
SQ FT: 4,000
SALES: 900K **Privately Held**
WEB: www.justacompany.com
SIC: 3873 5199 Watches, clocks, watchcases & parts; gifts & novelties

(G-7776)
JUSTIN ASHLEY DESIGNS INC
4301 21st St Ste 212a (11101-5049)
PHONE....................718 707-0200
Scott Barcvi, *President*
▲ EMP: 6
SALES (est): 540K **Privately Held**
SIC: 3911 Jewelry, precious metal

(G-7777)
KADER LITHOGRAPH COMPANY INC
3002 48th Ave Ste C (11101-3401)
PHONE....................917 664-4380
Fax: 212 265-1663
Roland Katz, *President*
Jack Erlich, *Vice Pres*
EMP: 101
SQ FT: 250,000
SALES (est): 14.5MM **Privately Held**
SIC: 2752 7336 2759 Commercial printing, lithographic; commercial printing, offset; commercial art & graphic design; bookbinding & related work

(G-7778)
KAITERY FURS LTD
2529 49th St (11103-1120)
PHONE....................718 204-1396
Fax: 718 204-0721
Jimmy Kaitery, *President*
◆ EMP: 6
SQ FT: 7,500
SALES (est): 930.4K **Privately Held**
SIC: 2371 Hats, fur; apparel, fur

(G-7779)
KARR GRAPHICS CORP
2219 41st Ave Fl 2a (11101-4807)
PHONE....................718 784-9390
Larry Karr, *President*
Myron Karr, *Vice Pres*
EMP: 20
SQ FT: 25,000
SALES (est): 3.4MM **Privately Held**
SIC: 2754 2752 2759 2796 Commercial printing, gravure; stationery: gravure printing; commercial printing, lithographic; thermography; platemaking services

(G-7780)
KERNS MANUFACTURING CORP (PA)
3714 29th St (11101-2690)
PHONE....................718 784-4044
Fax: 718 786-0534
Simon Srybnik, *Ch of Bd*
Louis Srybnik, *President*
Joe Baronci, *Engineer*
Ben Movaseghi, *CFO*
Rose Amaro, *Controller*
▲ EMP: 125
SQ FT: 60,000
SALES (est): 23.5MM **Privately Held**
WEB: www.kernsmfg.com
SIC: 3469 3724 3812 3714 Electronic enclosures, stamped or pressed metal; aircraft engines & engine parts; search & navigation equipment; motor vehicle parts & accessories

(G-7781)
KEYSTONE IRON & WIRE WORKS INC
217 54th Ave (11101-5922)
PHONE....................718 392-1616
Fax: 718 472-0850
Diana Macchia, *President*
Maria Manzo, *Corp Secy*
Vito Macchia, *Vice Pres*
EMP: 8 EST: 1924
SQ FT: 16,000
SALES (est): 1.2MM **Privately Held**
WEB: www.keystoneironandwireworks.com
SIC: 3534 Elevators & equipment

(G-7782)
KOENIG IRON WORKS INC
814 37th Ave (11101-6011)
PHONE....................718 433-0900
Fax: 718 433-1090
Barry Leistner, *President*
Jane Ross, *President*
Nick Morisset, *Exec VP*
Norman Rosenbaum, *Vice Pres*
Richard Velting, *Vice Pres*
EMP: 50 EST: 1931
SQ FT: 35,000
SALES (est): 13.1MM **Privately Held**
WEB: www.koenigironworks.com
SIC: 3441 3446 Fabricated structural metal; ornamental metalwork

(G-7783)
KONG KEE FOOD CORP
4831 Van Dam St (11101-3101)
PHONE....................718 937-2746
Ip Kong, *President*
Alan Pierroz, *Controller*
EMP: 45
SQ FT: 18,000
SALES (est): 6.1MM **Privately Held**
SIC: 2026 5141 Fermented & cultured milk products; groceries, general line

(G-7784)
KOREA CENTRAL DAILY NEWS INC (HQ)
4327 36th St (11101-1703)
PHONE....................718 361-7700
Fax: 718 361-8891
Byoungsoo Sohn, *CEO*
Wanseob Kong, *Publisher*
Seok J Kim, *General Mgr*
Sangmook Lee, *CFO*
Yondong Kim, *Finance Dir*
▲ EMP: 58
SQ FT: 10,000
SALES (est): 7.6MM
SALES (corp-wide): 299.2MM **Privately Held**
SIC: 2711 Newspapers, publishing & printing
PA: Joongang Ilbo
    100 Seosomun-Ro, Jung-Gu
    Seoul SEO 04513
    275 157-16

(G-7785)
KOREA TIMES NEW YORK INC (HQ)
3710 Skillman Ave (11101-1731)
PHONE....................718 784-4526
Fax: 718 784-9219
Jae Min Chang, *CEO*
Hak Shin, *President*
Chang Yeon, *Editor*
Justin Kim, *Accounts Mgr*
Julianne Lee, *Assoc Editor*
▲ EMP: 80 EST: 1967
SQ FT: 16,000
SALES (est): 12.3MM
SALES (corp-wide): 63.4MM **Privately Held**
SIC: 2711 Newspapers: publishing only, not printed on site
PA: The Korea Times Los Angeles Inc
    4525 Wilshire Blvd
    Los Angeles CA 90010
    323 692-2000

(G-7786)
KOREA TIMES NEW YORK INC
3710 Skillman Ave (11101-1731)
PHONE....................718 729-5555
Jae Min Chang, *Branch Mgr*
EMP: 7
SALES (corp-wide): 63.4MM **Privately Held**
SIC: 2711 Newspapers
HQ: The Korea Times New York Inc
    3710 Skillman Ave
    Long Island City NY 11101
    718 784-4526

(G-7787)
L & L OVERHEAD GARAGE DOORS (PA)
3125 45th St (11103-1620)
PHONE....................718 721-2518
Louis Lauri Jr, *President*
EMP: 9
SQ FT: 5,000
SALES (est): 783.8K **Privately Held**
SIC: 3442 5211 Garage doors, overhead: metal; garage doors, sale & installation

(G-7788)
LARKIN ANYA LTD
4310 23rd St Ste 2b (11101-5020)
PHONE....................718 361-1827
Fax: 212 532-2854
Anya Larkin, *President*
EMP: 9
SQ FT: 4,000
SALES (est): 830K **Privately Held**
WEB: www.anyalarkin.com
SIC: 2679 Wallpaper

(G-7789)
LINCO PRINTING INC
5022 23rd St (11101-4502)
PHONE....................718 937-5141
Yu-Ou Lin, *President*
Sandy Lin, *Vice Pres*
Kelly Shu, *Accounts Mgr*
Tammy Lee, *Manager*
Sherry Mao, *Manager*
EMP: 40 EST: 1975
SQ FT: 34,000
SALES: 4.6MM **Privately Held**
WEB: www.lincoprinting.com
SIC: 2759 Letterpress printing

(G-7790)
LINEAR LIGHTING CORPORATION
3130 Hunters Point Ave (11101-3132)
PHONE....................718 361-7552
Larry Deutsch, *CEO*
Stanley Deutsch, *President*
Fred Jona, *Purch Dir*
Richard Coffin, *Engineer*
Phil Zayes, *Engineer*
EMP: 150
SQ FT: 85,000
SALES (est): 32.2MM **Privately Held**
WEB: www.linearlighting.com
SIC: 3646 5063 Commercial indusl & institutional electric lighting fixtures; electrical apparatus & equipment

(G-7791)
LIQUID KNITS INC
3200 Skillman Ave Fl 2 (11101-2308)
PHONE....................718 706-6600
Jeffrey Schechter, *President*
▲ EMP: 18
SQ FT: 35,000
SALES (est): 3.1MM **Privately Held**
WEB: www.liquidknits.com
SIC: 2339 Women's & misses' athletic clothing & sportswear

(G-7792)
LITELAB CORP
540 54th Ave (11101-5925)
PHONE....................718 361-6829
Rafael Ramirez, *Manager*
EMP: 6
SALES (corp-wide): 27MM **Privately Held**
WEB: www.litelab.com
SIC: 3646 Commercial indusl & institutional electric lighting fixtures
PA: Litelab Corp.
    251 Elm St
    Buffalo NY 14203
    716 856-4300

▲ = Import ▼ = Export
◆ = Import/Export

GEOGRAPHIC SECTION
Long Island City - Queens County (G-7819)

(G-7793)
LOCKWOOD TRADE JOURNAL CO INC
Also Called: Tea & Coffee Trade Journal
3743 Crescent St Fl 2 (11101-3516)
PHONE..................212 391-2060
George E Lockwood Jr, *President*
Frederick Lockwood, *Publisher*
Robert Lockwood Sr, *Vice Pres*
Edward Hoyt III, *Sales Staff*
Fred Lockwood, *Sales Executive*
EMP: 20 **EST:** 1872
SQ FT: 4,000
SALES (est): 1.9MM **Privately Held**
WEB: www.lockwoodpublications.com
SIC: 2721 Trade journals: publishing & printing

(G-7794)
LONG ISLAND BRAND BEVS LLC
3788 Review Ave Ste 15 (11101-2055)
PHONE..................855 542-2832
Philip Thomas, *CEO*
EMP: 100
SQ FT: 25,000
SALES (est): 1.4MM
SALES (corp-wide): 1.9MM **Publicly Held**
SIC: 2086 Iced tea & fruit drinks, bottled & canned
PA: Long Island Iced Tea Corp.
116 Charlotte Ave Ste 1
Hicksville NY 11801
855 542-2832

(G-7795)
LUKAS LIGHTING INC
4020 22nd St Ste 11 (11101-4814)
PHONE..................800 841-4011
Craig Corona, *CEO*
Marilyn Watkins, *Office Mgr*
▲ **EMP:** 30
SALES (est): 6.5MM **Privately Held**
SIC: 3646 Commercial indusl & institutional electric lighting fixtures

(G-7796)
LUXERDAME CO INC
4315 Queens St Ste A (11101-2923)
PHONE..................718 752-9800
Fax: 718 752-9888
Leonard Finkel, *President*
EMP: 20 **EST:** 1933
SALES (est): 1.4MM **Privately Held**
SIC: 2341 2342 Women's & children's underwear; bras, girdles & allied garments

(G-7797)
M A R A METALS LTD
2520 40th Ave (11101-3810)
PHONE..................718 786-7868
Andreas Fiorentino, *President*
Andreas Vassiliou, *Vice Pres*
EMP: 6
SQ FT: 600
SALES (est): 500K **Privately Held**
SIC: 3911 Jewelry, precious metal

(G-7798)
MAC CRETE CORPORATION
Also Called: Mac Donuts of New York
3412 10th St (11106-5108)
PHONE..................718 932-1803
Georga Papadopoulos, *President*
Greg Papadopoulos, *Manager*
EMP: 10
SALES (est): 1.6MM **Privately Held**
SIC: 2051 5149 Cakes, pies & pastries; bakery products

(G-7799)
MANA PRODUCTS INC (PA)
Also Called: Your Name Professional Brand
3202 Queens Blvd Fl 6 (11101-2341)
PHONE..................718 361-2550
Fax: 718 472-1028
Nikos Mouyiaris, *Chairman*
N Masturzo, *Exec VP*
Edward Ewankov, *Vice Pres*
Bruce Meyer, *Vice Pres*
Barbara Novick, *Vice Pres*
▲ **EMP:** 277

SALES (est): 289MM **Privately Held**
WEB: www.manaproducts.com
SIC: 2844 5122 Cosmetic preparations; cosmetics

(G-7800)
MANA PRODUCTS INC
Esthetic Research Group
3202 Queens Blvd Fl 6 (11101-2341)
PHONE..................718 361-5204
Necos Mouyiaris, *Branch Mgr*
EMP: 500
SALES (corp-wide): 289MM **Privately Held**
SIC: 2844 Toilet preparations
PA: Mana Products, Inc.
3202 Queens Blvd Fl 6
Long Island City NY 11101
718 361-2550

(G-7801)
MANE ENTERPRISES INC
3100 47th Ave Unit 5e (11101-3068)
PHONE..................718 472-4955
Bill Mountain, *CEO*
Nicholas Sackett, *President*
John Mountain, *Vice Pres*
Evelyn Kessler, *Manager*
EMP: 55
SQ FT: 12,000
SALES (est): 4.6MM **Privately Held**
SIC: 2323 Men's & boys' neckwear

(G-7802)
MANHATTAN DISPLAY INC
1215 Jackson Ave Ste B (11101-5551)
PHONE..................718 392-1365
Fax: 718 392-1646
John Petursson, *President*
EMP: 6
SQ FT: 1,500
SALES (est): 520K **Privately Held**
WEB: www.manhattandisplay.com
SIC: 2542 5046 Office & store showcases & display fixtures; store fixtures & display equipment

(G-7803)
MARITIME BROADBAND INC
1143 47th Ave (11101-5465)
PHONE..................347 404-6041
Mary Ellen Kramer, *President*
Zebi Kramer, *Admin Sec*
EMP: 30
SALES (est): 6.5MM **Privately Held**
SIC: 3663 Marine radio communications equipment

(G-7804)
MASPETH STEEL FABRICATORS INC
5215 11th St Ste 21 (11101-5832)
PHONE..................718 361-9192
Dominick Lofaso, *Ch of Bd*
EMP: 7
SALES (est): 1.1MM **Privately Held**
SIC: 3441 Fabricated structural metal

(G-7805)
MASTERCRAFT MANUFACTURING CO
3715 11th St (11101-6006)
PHONE..................718 729-5620
Peter Borsits, *President*
EMP: 5
SALES (est): 310K **Privately Held**
SIC: 3993 Advertising novelties

(G-7806)
MATOV INDUSTRIES INC
Also Called: Roxter Lighting
1011 40th Ave (11101-6105)
PHONE..................718 392-5060
Fax: 718 392-9811
Alan Hochster, *President*
Roberta Ackerman, *Human Res Dir*
EMP: 20
SQ FT: 15,000
SALES (est): 3.4MM **Privately Held**
SIC: 3645 3469 3646 5063 Residential lighting fixtures; metal stampings; commercial indusl & institutional electric lighting fixtures; lighting fixtures

(G-7807)
MECHO SYSTEMS
3708 34th St (11101-2213)
PHONE..................718 729-8373
Fax: 718 729-8378
Anthony Gryak, *Manager*
EMP: 15
SALES (corp-wide): 15.8MM **Privately Held**
WEB: www.stretchwall.com
SIC: 3296 Acoustical board & tile, mineral wool
HQ: Mecho Systems
4203 35th St
Long Island City NY 11101
718 729-8376

(G-7808)
MECHOSHADE SYSTEMS INC (DH)
4203 35th St (11101-2301)
PHONE..................718 729-2020
Jan Berman, *President*
Jim Ashmore, *Regional Mgr*
Carlos Herrera, *Business Mgr*
Mel Byars, *Vice Pres*
Brandon Gates, *Materials Mgr*
◆ **EMP:** 200
SQ FT: 45,000
SALES (est): 125.3MM **Privately Held**
WEB: www.soleilshades.com
SIC: 2591 Window shades
HQ: Springs Window Fashions, Llc
7549 Graber Rd
Middleton WI 53562
608 836-1011

(G-7809)
MEDITERREAN DYRO COMPANY
1102 38th Ave (11101-6041)
PHONE..................718 786-4888
Jimmy Austin, *President*
Amalia Malamis, *Principal*
▲ **EMP:** 40 **EST:** 1979
SALES (est): 2.1MM **Privately Held**
SIC: 2099 Food preparations

(G-7810)
METRO DUCT SYSTEMS INC
1219 Astoria Blvd Apt 2 (11102-4478)
PHONE..................718 278-4294
Orson Arroyo, *President*
EMP: 11
SALES (est): 1.2MM **Privately Held**
SIC: 3444 1711 Sheet metalwork; mechanical contractor

(G-7811)
METRO GROUP INC (PA)
Also Called: Metro Grouping
5023 23rd St (11101-4501)
PHONE..................718 392-3616
Bernard Bradpiece, *CEO*
Robert H Seidman, *President*
Richard Blake, *Engineer*
Gary Ho, *Engineer*
M Jackson, *Engineer*
EMP: 74 **EST:** 1925
SQ FT: 15,000
SALES (est): 19.6MM **Privately Held**
WEB: www.metrogroupinc.com
SIC: 3589 1389 Water treatment equipment, industrial; chemically treating wells

(G-7812)
MICHAEL FELDMAN INC
3010 41st Ave Ste 3 (11101-2817)
PHONE..................718 433-1700
Richard Feldman, *President*
Grace Feldman, *Treasurer*
EMP: 95 **EST:** 1964
SQ FT: 20,000
SALES (est): 6.6MM **Privately Held**
WEB: www.permanentfoliage.com
SIC: 2339 Bathing suits: women's, misses' & juniors'

(G-7813)
MING PAO (NEW YORK) INC (HQ)
Also Called: Ming Pay N Y
4331 33rd St (11101-2316)
PHONE..................718 786-2888
Ryan Low, *President*
Francis Tiong, *President*
Ka Lui, *Publisher*
Michael Liu, *Controller*

David Kwan, *Accounting Mgr*
EMP: 70
SQ FT: 21,000
SALES (est): 4.6MM
SALES (corp-wide): 349.1MM **Privately Held**
WEB: www.mingpaousa.com
SIC: 2711 Newspapers, publishing & printing
PA: Media Chinese International Limited
15/F Ming Pao Indl Ctr Blk A
Chai Wan HK
259 531-11

(G-7814)
MISSION CRANE SERVICE INC (PA)
4700 33rd St (11101-2419)
PHONE..................718 937-3333
David Chazen, *President*
EMP: 60
SQ FT: 30,000
SALES (est): 4.5MM **Privately Held**
SIC: 3999 7993 Coin-operated amusement machines; game machines

(G-7815)
MODUTANK INC
4104 35th Ave (11101-1410)
PHONE..................718 392-1112
Fax: 718 786-1008
John Reed Margulis, *President*
Thomas G Carren, *Vice Pres*
Saul Stadtmauer, *Manager*
EMP: 10
SQ FT: 15,000
SALES (est): 3.2MM **Privately Held**
WEB: www.modutank.com
SIC: 3443 Tanks, lined: metal plate

(G-7816)
MONGRU NECKWEAR INC
1010 44th Ave Fl 2 (11101-7032)
PHONE..................718 706-0406
Ramdihal Mongru, *President*
EMP: 40
SQ FT: 10,580
SALES (est): 4.8MM **Privately Held**
SIC: 2253 2323 5136 Neckties, knit; men's & boys' neckwear; neckwear, men's & boys'

(G-7817)
MUTUAL SALES CORP
Also Called: Mutual Harware
545 49th Ave (11101-5610)
PHONE..................718 361-8373
Fax: 718 729-8296
Mary Piotrowski, *President*
Maria Stewart, *Corp Secy*
Vincent Marmallardi, *Vice Pres*
Carol Grassi, *Controller*
Maret Asaro, *Shareholder*
▲ **EMP:** 23
SQ FT: 10,000
SALES (est): 8.4MM **Privately Held**
SIC: 2391 7922 5131 Curtains & draperies; equipment rental, theatrical; textiles, woven

(G-7818)
MZB ACCESSORIES LLC
2976 Northern Blvd Fl 4 (11101-2829)
PHONE..................718 472-7500
Paul Gengler, *Controller*
Galina Dodis, *Accountant*
AMI Alterin, *Mng Member*
▲ **EMP:** 100
SALES (est): 19.4MM
SALES (corp-wide): 76.8MM **Privately Held**
SIC: 2844 Toilet preparations; cosmetic preparations; deodorants, personal; lotions, shaving
PA: M.Z. Berger & Co. Inc.
2976 Northern Blvd Fl 4
Long Island City NY 11101
718 472-7500

(G-7819)
N A ALUMIL CORPORATION
4401 21st St Ste 203 (11101-5009)
PHONE..................718 355-9393
Kyprianos Bazehika, *Ch of Bd*
▲ **EMP:** 8

Long Island City - Queens County (G-7820) — GEOGRAPHIC SECTION

SALES (est): 4.6MM
SALES (corp-wide): 119.9MM **Privately Held**
SIC: 3355 Aluminum rolling & drawing
PA: Alumil Aluminium Industry S.A.
Industrial Area, Stavrochori, P.O. Box 37
Kilkis 61100
234 107-1989

(G-7820)
NATIONAL HERALD INC
Also Called: Greek Nat Hrald Dily Nwsppr In
3710 30th St (11101-2614)
PHONE 718 784-5255
Anthony H Diamataris, *President*
Andy Dabilis, *Editor*
Vasilis Magalios, *Editor*
Aris Papadopoulos, *Editor*
Constantine Sirigos, *Editor*
▲ **EMP:** 35 **EST:** 1915
SQ FT: 4,200
SALES (est): 2.6MM **Privately Held**
WEB: www.nationalherald.com
SIC: 2711 Newspapers: publishing only, not printed on site

(G-7821)
NAZIM IZZAK INC
Also Called: N I Boutique
4402 23rd St Ste 517 (11101-5072)
PHONE 212 920-5546
Nazim I Guity, *President*
EMP: 6
SQ FT: 2,800
SALES (est): 494.4K **Privately Held**
SIC: 2231 5632 Apparel & outerwear broadwoven fabrics; apparel accessories

(G-7822)
NBC UNIVERSAL LLC
210 54th Ave (11101-5923)
PHONE 718 482-8310
Stacy Brady, *General Mgr*
Catherine Konzet, *Business Mgr*
Cameron Blanchard, *Exec VP*
Catherine Balsam-Schwaber, *Senior VP*
Bruce Kallner, *Senior VP*
EMP: 50
SALES (corp-wide): 74.5B **Publicly Held**
WEB: www.nbc.com
SIC: 3663 Radio & TV communications equipment
HQ: Nbc Universal, Llc
1221 Avenue Of The Americ
New York NY 10020
212 664-4444

(G-7823)
NEW CLASSIC INC
4143 37th St (11101-1723)
PHONE 718 609-1100
Fax: 718 609-2509
Simon Yiu, *President*
Rachel Yiu, *Vice Pres*
Alex Quinones, *Sales Mgr*
▲ **EMP:** 14
SQ FT: 20,000
SALES (est): 1.6MM **Privately Held**
WEB: www.newclassic.net
SIC: 2387 5136 5137 Apparel belts; apparel belts, men's & boys'; apparel belts, women's & children's

(G-7824)
NEW SENSOR CORPORATION (PA)
Also Called: Electro-Harmonix
5501 2nd St (11101-5908)
PHONE 718 937-8300
Fax: 212 937-9111
Michael Matthews, *President*
Laura Ho, *Purch Agent*
John Pisani, *Senior Engr*
Minda Lloyd, *Controller*
Matthias Raabe, *Controller*
▲ **EMP:** 52
SQ FT: 89,886
SALES (est): 13.9MM **Privately Held**
WEB: www.newsensor.com
SIC: 3931 3671 5065 Musical instruments, electric & electronic; vacuum tubes; electronic parts & equipment

(G-7825)
NEW YORK BINDING CO INC
2121 41st Ave Ste A (11101-4833)
PHONE 718 729-2454
Fax: 718 392-7070
Roger Levin, *President*
Linda Dine, *Manager*
Linda Van Dine, *Manager*
EMP: 40
SQ FT: 15,000
SALES (est): 4.5MM **Privately Held**
WEB: www.newyorkbindingco.com
SIC: 2241 2396 Bindings, textile; trimmings, textile; automotive & apparel trimmings

(G-7826)
NOVELTY CRYSTAL CORP (PA)
3015 48th Ave (11101-3419)
PHONE 718 458-6700
Rivka Michaeli, *President*
Ed Coslett, *COO*
Asher Michaeli, *Exec VP*
Daniel Weatherly, *Plant Mgr*
▲ **EMP:** 20 **EST:** 1961
SQ FT: 50,000
SALES (est): 9.4MM **Privately Held**
WEB: www.noveltycrystal.com
SIC: 3089 3421 Plastic kitchenware, tableware & houseware; kitchenware, plastic; cutlery

(G-7827)
NY IRON INC
3131 48th Ave Unit C (11101-3021)
PHONE 718 302-9000
Fax: 718 486-8382
Todd Devito, *Ch of Bd*
EMP: 15
SALES (est): 954.8K **Privately Held**
SIC: 7692 Welding repair

(G-7828)
ODEGARD INC
3030 47th Ave Ste 700 (11101-3492)
PHONE 212 545-0069
John Nihoul, *Manager*
EMP: 12
SALES (corp-wide): 5.6MM **Privately Held**
WEB: www.odegardinc.com
SIC: 2273 Carpets & rugs
PA: Odegard, Inc.
200 Lexington Ave Rm 1206
New York NY 10016
212 545-0205

(G-7829)
OLD UE LLC
4511 33rd St (11101-2405)
PHONE 718 707-0700
Steve Franz, *Principal*
Stuart Grover, *Principal*
Willie Hollingswo, *Principal*
Raymond Maragh, *Principal*
John Sorrentino, *Principal*
EMP: 400
SALES (est): 21.8MM **Privately Held**
SIC: 2752 2677 Commercial printing, lithographic; envelopes

(G-7830)
P C RFRS RADIOLOGY
Also Called: Radiology Film Reading Svcs
3630 37th St Frnt (11101-1606)
PHONE 212 586-5700
Fax: 212 586-5726
Joseph Gottesman, *President*
EMP: 8
SQ FT: 1,000
SALES (est): 874.1K **Privately Held**
WEB: www.radiologyreadings.com
SIC: 3577 Film reader devices

(G-7831)
P RYTON CORP
504 50th Ave (11101-5712)
PHONE 718 937-7052
Fax: 718 729-1795
Joseph Palumbo Jr, *President*
Sergio Palumbo, *Vice Pres*
Joseph Palumbo Sr, *Shareholder*
Linda Palumbo, *Admin Sec*
▲ **EMP:** 11
SQ FT: 6,000
SALES (est): 1.7MM **Privately Held**
WEB: www.p-ryton.com
SIC: 3841 5122 Surgical & medical instruments; cosmetics, perfumes & hair products

(G-7832)
PACIFIC POLY PRODUCT CORP
3934 Crescent St (11101-3802)
PHONE 718 786-7129
Fax: 718 706-7855
Henry Ly, *President*
▲ **EMP:** 10
SQ FT: 10,000
SALES: 1MM **Privately Held**
SIC: 2673 Plastic bags: made from purchased materials; garment bags (plastic film): made from purchased materials

(G-7833)
PADDY LEE FASHIONS INC
4709 36th St Fl 2nd (11101-1823)
PHONE 718 786-6020
Fax: 718 786-6876
Ralph Covelli Jr, *CEO*
John Covelli, *Vice Pres*
▲ **EMP:** 15 **EST:** 1955
SQ FT: 46,000
SALES (est): 3MM **Privately Held**
WEB: www.paddylee.com
SIC: 2339 2331 Slacks: women's, misses' & juniors'; blouses, women's & juniors': made from purchased material

(G-7834)
PARSONS-MEARES LTD
2107 41st Ave Ste 1l (11101-4802)
PHONE 212 242-3378
Fax: 212 741-1869
James Mears, *President*
Sally Ann Parsons, *Vice Pres*
EMP: 60
SQ FT: 12,000
SALES (est): 4.8MM **Privately Held**
WEB: www.parsons-meares.com
SIC: 2389 Theatrical costumes

(G-7835)
PASS EM-ENTRIES INC (PA)
3914 Crescent St (11101-3802)
PHONE 718 392-0100
Fax: 718 392-0639
Joseph Stegmayer, *President*
John La Salle, *Vice Pres*
EMP: 18
SALES (est): 1.1MM **Privately Held**
SIC: 2395 Pleating & stitching

(G-7836)
PDM LITHO INC
2219 41st Ave Fl 3 (11101-4807)
PHONE 718 301-1740
Fax: 718 301-1747
Jeffrey M Alpert, *President*
Aaron Craig, *Chairman*
Joel Sachs, *Chairman*
Bob Sussman, *Vice Pres*
Vernice Henderson, *Manager*
EMP: 25
SQ FT: 18,000
SALES (est): 3.7MM **Privately Held**
WEB: www.pdmlitho.com
SIC: 2752 Commercial printing, lithographic

(G-7837)
PEACHTREE ENTERPRISES INC
2219 41st Ave Ste 4a (11101-4807)
PHONE 212 989-3445
Robert Sussman, *President*
Jeffrey Alpert, *Vice Pres*
Bart Sussman, *Treasurer*
Vernice Henderson, *Manager*
EMP: 38
SALES (est): 6MM **Privately Held**
WEB: www.peachtree-printingnyc.com
SIC: 2752 Commercial printing, offset

(G-7838)
PELICAN BAY LTD
Also Called: Ravioli Store, The
3901 22nd St (11101-4809)
PHONE 718 729-9300
Donna Nasoff, *Principal*
Michael Nasoff, *Principal*
EMP: 12

SALES (est): 990K **Privately Held**
SIC: 2099 Food preparations

(G-7839)
PENN & FLETCHER INC
2107 41st Ave Fl 5 (11101-4802)
PHONE 212 239-6868
Fax: 718 239-6914
Ernie Smith, *President*
EMP: 15
SQ FT: 4,500
SALES (est): 1MM **Privately Held**
SIC: 2395 5131 Embroidery products, except schiffli machine; lace fabrics; trimmings, apparel

(G-7840)
PETCAP PRESS CORPORATION
3200 Skillman Ave Ste F (11101-2308)
PHONE 718 609-0910
Joan Caputo, *President*
Peter Caputo, *Vice Pres*
EMP: 10 **EST:** 1968
SALES (est): 1.1MM **Privately Held**
SIC: 2752 Commercial printing, offset

(G-7841)
PETRO MOORE MANUFACTURING CORP
Also Called: Petro Metro Mfg
3641 Vernon Blvd (11106-5123)
P.O. Box 21110, Floral Park (11002-1110)
PHONE 718 784-2516
Fax: 718 784-7099
Robert Murphy, *President*
EMP: 6
SQ FT: 10,000
SALES: 760K **Privately Held**
SIC: 3499 2511 7359 Furniture parts, metal; tables, household: wood; dishes, silverware, tables & banquet accessories rental

(G-7842)
PHEONIX CUSTOM FURNITURE LTD
2107 41st Ave Fl 2 (11101-4802)
PHONE 212 727-2648
Fax: 212 727-2332
John J Clarke, *Principal*
Pauline R De Cosimo, *Business Mgr*
Vito D'Alessandro, *Vice Pres*
Lou Monti, *Controller*
EMP: 20
SQ FT: 10,000
SALES: 2MM **Privately Held**
SIC: 2512 2521 Upholstered household furniture; wood office furniture

(G-7843)
PILOT PRODUCTS INC
2413 46th St (11103-1007)
P.O. Box 3221 (11103-0221)
PHONE 718 728-2141
Fax: 718 728-5190
Carolyn J Hebel, *President*
Herbert Hebel, *President*
Elizabeth Hammell, *Vice Pres*
EMP: 13
SQ FT: 17,000
SALES (est): 1.5MM **Privately Held**
SIC: 3061 Mechanical rubber goods

(G-7844)
PLATINUM SALES PROMOTION INC
Also Called: The Spirited Shipper
3514a Crescent St (11106-3920)
PHONE 718 361-0200
Fax: 718 361-0012
Bruce Cappels, *President*
▲ **EMP:** 7
SQ FT: 12,000
SALES: 1.4MM **Privately Held**
WEB: www.spiritedshipper.com
SIC: 3993 4225 8743 4213 Displays & cutouts, window & lobby; general warehousing; sales promotion; trucking, except local

(G-7845)
PRESTONE PRESS LLC
Also Called: Prestone Printing Company
4750 30th St (11101-3404)
PHONE 347 468-7900

▲ = Import ▼ = Export
◆ = Import/Export

Marci Adler, *Vice Pres*
Jeffrey Horn, *Human Resources*
Ken Sassano, *Sales Executive*
Carlos Ortiz, *Manager*
Dennis Launer, *Director*
EMP: 113
SALES (est): 32.8MM **Privately Held**
SIC: 2752 Commercial printing, lithographic

(G-7846)
PRIME ELECTRIC MOTORS INC
4850 33rd St (11101-2514)
P.O. Box 1374 (11101-0374)
PHONE....................................718 784-1124
Gul Zaman, *President*
EMP: 9
SALES (est): 820K **Privately Held**
SIC: 7694 Electric motor repair

(G-7847)
PRIMO COAT CORP
Also Called: Ciccarelli Custom Taylor
4315 Queens St Fl 3 (11101-2947)
PHONE....................................718 349-2070
Fax: 718 349-7150
Rocco Ciccarelli, *President*
EMP: 35 EST: 1963
SQ FT: 13,500
SALES: 1MM **Privately Held**
SIC: 2311 2337 2339 2325 Suits, men's & boys': made from purchased materials; suits: women's, misses' & juniors'; women's & misses' outerwear; men's & boys' trousers & slacks

(G-7848)
PROMETHEUS INTERNATIONAL INC
4502 11th St (11101-5206)
PHONE....................................718 472-0700
Sayedd Rabb, *President*
EMP: 16
SALES (est): 630K **Privately Held**
SIC: 2711 Commercial printing & newspaper publishing combined

(G-7849)
PULSAR TECHNOLOGY SYSTEMS INC
2720 42nd Rd (11101-4112)
PHONE....................................718 361-9292
Fax: 718 433-4658
Rudolph Robinson, *President*
Joann Pitcher, *Manager*
EMP: 9
SQ FT: 3,750
SALES: 1.3MM **Privately Held**
WEB: www.taxi-meters.com
SIC: 3825 Test equipment for electronic & electrical circuits; meters: electric, pocket, portable, panelboard, etc.

(G-7850)
PURA FRUTA LLC
2323 Borden Ave (11101-4508)
PHONE....................................415 279-5727
Adriana Ayales,
EMP: 12
SALES (est): 1.1MM **Privately Held**
SIC: 2037 Fruit juices

(G-7851)
QUAD/GRAPHICS INC
4402 11th St Fl 1 (11101-5174)
PHONE....................................718 706-7600
James Altadonna, *Branch Mgr*
EMP: 32
SALES (corp-wide): 4.6B **Publicly Held**
SIC: 2752 Commercial printing, lithographic
PA: Quad/Graphics Inc.
  N61w23044 Harrys Way
  Sussex WI 53089
  414 566-6000

(G-7852)
QUADLOGIC CONTROLS CORPORATION
Also Called: Qlc
3300 Northern Blvd Fl 2 (11101-2215)
PHONE....................................212 930-9300
Fax: 212 930-9394
Sayre Swarztrauber, *Ch of Bd*
Doron Shafrir, *President*

Phil Fram, *Vice Pres*
Newman Fruitwala, *Production*
Jordon Herzog, *Technical Mgr*
▲ **EMP**: 75
SQ FT: 36,000
SALES (est): 17MM **Privately Held**
SIC: 3825 7389 Electrical energy measuring equipment; meters: electric, pocket, portable, panelboard, etc.; meter readers, remote

(G-7853)
QUALITY CASTINGS INC
3100 47th Ave Ste 2120b (11101-3023)
PHONE....................................732 409-3203
Carl Morfino, *President*
EMP: 50
SQ FT: 3,200
SALES (est): 7.2MM **Privately Held**
WEB: www.qualitycasting.com
SIC: 3369 3324 Castings, except die-castings, precision; steel investment foundries

(G-7854)
QUALITY OFFSET LLC
4750 30th St (11101-3404)
PHONE....................................347 342-4660
Steve Wong,
EMP: 7
SQ FT: 2,000
SALES (est): 740.2K **Privately Held**
SIC: 2759 Commercial printing

(G-7855)
QUATTRO FRAMEWORKS INC
4310 23rd St Ste 307 (11101-4604)
PHONE....................................718 361-2620
Sebastian Ramundo, *President*
EMP: 11
SALES (est): 468.6K **Privately Held**
SIC: 2499 Picture frame molding, finished

(G-7856)
RAGOZIN DATA
Also Called: Sheets, The
4402 11th St Ste 617 (11101-5184)
PHONE....................................212 674-3123
Len Ragozin, *Owner*
Alex Wolf, *Manager*
EMP: 20
SQ FT: 2,000
SALES (est): 2MM **Privately Held**
WEB: www.thesheets.com
SIC: 2721 Magazines: publishing & printing

(G-7857)
RAPID FAN & BLOWER INC
2314 39th Ave (11101-3612)
PHONE....................................718 786-2060
Fax: 718 706-0951
George J Rogner Jr, *President*
EMP: 10 EST: 1956
SQ FT: 15,000
SALES (est): 1.8MM **Privately Held**
WEB: www.rapidfan.com
SIC: 3564 5084 Blowing fans: industrial or commercial; turbo-blowers, industrial; industrial machinery & equipment

(G-7858)
RAVIOLI STORE INC
4344 21st St (11101-5002)
PHONE....................................718 729-9300
Fax: 212 925-4807
Michael Nasoss, *Manager*
EMP: 5
SALES (est): 500K **Privately Held**
WEB: www.raviolistore.com
SIC: 2098 5411 Macaroni & spaghetti; grocery stores

(G-7859)
RAYANA DESIGNS INC
2520 40th Ave (11101-3810)
PHONE....................................718 786-2040
Andreas Vassiliou, *President*
Andreas Fiorentino, *Corp Secy*
Mihran Panossian, *Vice Pres*
Dennis Fiorentino, *Admin Sec*
EMP: 20 EST: 1979
SQ FT: 5,000
SALES (est): 2.2MM **Privately Held**
WEB: www.rayanadesigns.com
SIC: 3479 Engraving jewelry silverware, or metal

(G-7860)
RELIANCE MACHINING INC
4335 Vernon Blvd (11101-6911)
PHONE....................................718 784-0314
Fax: 718 729-1724
Lloyd Larsen, *President*
EMP: 30
SQ FT: 15,000
SALES: 3MM **Privately Held**
SIC: 3599 Machine shop, jobbing & repair

(G-7861)
RENCO MANUFACTURING INC
1040 45th Ave Fl 2 (11101-7094)
PHONE....................................718 392-8877
AVI Shaul, *President*
EMP: 32
SQ FT: 15,000
SALES: 660K **Privately Held**
SIC: 3915 Jewelers' findings & materials

(G-7862)
ROBERT MILLER ASSOCIATES LLC
4310 23rd St (11101-4604)
PHONE....................................718 392-1640
Fax: 718 392-1601
Robert Miller, *Mng Member*
EMP: 15
SALES: 1MM **Privately Held**
SIC: 2389 Men's miscellaneous accessories

(G-7863)
ROLLHAUS SEATING PRODUCTS INC
2109 Borden Ave Fl 4 (11101-4531)
PHONE....................................718 729-9111
Fax: 718 729-9117
Michael Rollhaus, *President*
Stuart Goldstein, *General Mgr*
Jack Lebewohl, *Counsel*
EMP: 13 EST: 1945
SQ FT: 28,000
SALES (est): 1.9MM **Privately Held**
WEB: www.seatingproducts.com
SIC: 2599 Restaurant furniture, wood or metal; bar furniture

(G-7864)
RONBAR LABORATORIES INC
5202 Van Dam St (11101-3221)
PHONE....................................718 937-6755
Fax: 718 786-1109
Sheldon Borgen, *President*
Barry Borgen, *Vice Pres*
Helen White, *Bookkeeper*
EMP: 11
SQ FT: 12,000
SALES: 2MM **Privately Held**
SIC: 2841 7699 Detergents, synthetic organic or inorganic alkaline; restaurant equipment repair

(G-7865)
RONER INC (PA)
3553 24th St (11106-4416)
P.O. Box 6077 (11106-0077)
PHONE....................................718 392-6020
Ron Meltsner, *President*
Eric Spar, *Vice Pres*
Henry Meltsner, *Treasurer*
Ray Rancourt, *MIS Dir*
Harold Spar, *Admin Sec*
▲ **EMP**: 5 EST: 1959
SQ FT: 20,000
SALES (est): 16.3MM **Privately Held**
SIC: 3842 5047 Hearing aids; medical & hospital equipment

(G-7866)
RONER INC
1433 31st Ave (11106-4536)
PHONE....................................718 392-6020
Fax: 718 267-7191
Marge Weber, *Branch Mgr*
Denise Brantley, *Manager*
Angel Cabrera, *Supervisor*
EMP: 150
SALES (corp-wide): 16.3MM **Privately Held**
SIC: 3842 Hearing aids

PA: Roner, Inc.
  3553 24th St
  Long Island City NY 11106
  718 392-6020

(G-7867)
ROSENWACH TANK CO INC
Also Called: Rose, Herbert
4302 Ditmars Blvd (11105-1337)
PHONE....................................718 274-3250
EMP: 17
SALES (corp-wide): 16.9MM **Privately Held**
SIC: 3993 Signs & advertising specialties
PA: Rosenwach Tank Co. Inc.
  4302 Ditmars Blvd
  Astoria NY 11105
  212 972-4411

(G-7868)
RUBINSTEIN JEWELRY MFG CO
3100 47th Ave (11101-3013)
PHONE....................................718 784-8650
Ernest Rubinstein, *President*
Charles Deutsch, *Corp Secy*
EMP: 12 EST: 1956
SQ FT: 5,000
SALES (est): 74.5K **Privately Held**
SIC: 3911 Jewelry, precious metal

(G-7869)
S & B FASHION INC
4315 Queens St Ste B (11101-2923)
PHONE....................................718 482-1386
Tony Song, *President*
▲ **EMP**: 5 EST: 2000
SALES (est): 279.4K **Privately Held**
SIC: 2389 Apparel & accessories

(G-7870)
S BROOME AND CO INC
Also Called: Samuel Broome Uniform ACC
3300 47th Ave Fl 1 (11101-2428)
PHONE....................................718 663-6800
Michael Broome, *President*
Daniel Broome, *Vice Pres*
David Schaffer, *Treasurer*
ARI Wilker, *MIS Dir*
Kathy Broome, *Info Tech Mgr*
EMP: 80 EST: 1917
SQ FT: 27,000
SALES (est): 8.2MM **Privately Held**
WEB: www.sbroome.com
SIC: 2339 2323 Neckwear & ties: women's, misses' & juniors'; men's & boys' neckwear

(G-7871)
SADOWSKY GUITARS LTD
2107 41st Ave Fl 4 (11101-4802)
PHONE....................................718 433-1990
Fax: 718 422-1125
Roger Sadowsky, *President*
Sam Sadowsky, *Marketing Staff*
Robin Phillips, *Shareholder*
▲ **EMP**: 10
SQ FT: 4,100
SALES: 1.3MM **Privately Held**
WEB: www.sadowsky.com
SIC: 3931 7699 String instruments & parts; musical instrument repair services

(G-7872)
SCOTTI GRAPHICS INC
3200 Skillman Ave Fl 1 (11101-2308)
PHONE....................................212 367-9602
Fax: 212 691-9013
Richard J Scotti, *President*
Carmen Rai, *Bookkeeper*
EMP: 50
SQ FT: 8,000
SALES (est): 7.7MM **Privately Held**
WEB: www.scottigraphics.com
SIC: 2759 2752 2791 Commercial printing; letterpress printing; commercial printing, offset; typesetting

(G-7873)
SCREEN TEAM INC
3402c Review Ave (11101-3242)
PHONE....................................718 786-2424
Fax: 718 786-0399
Richard Grubman, *President*
EMP: 10
SQ FT: 10,000

Long Island City - Queens County (G-7874) — GEOGRAPHIC SECTION

SALES: 1.5MM *Privately Held*
WEB: www.screenteam.com
SIC: 3552 Silk screens for textile industry

(G-7874)
SELECT JEWELRY INC
4728 37th St Fl 3 (11101-1809)
PHONE..................................718 784-3626
Nissim Seliktar, *Ch of Bd*
Ronny Seliktar, *President*
▲ **EMP:** 60
SQ FT: 40,000
SALES (est): 16.2MM *Privately Held*
SIC: 3911 5094 Jewelry, precious metal; jewelry

(G-7875)
SERVICE ADVERTISING GROUP INC
Also Called: Western Queens Gazette
4216 34th Ave (11101-1110)
PHONE..................................718 361-6161
Tony Barsamian, *President*
Tony Barsamiam, *Sales Mgr*
EMP: 15
SQ FT: 2,118
SALES (est): 820K *Privately Held*
WEB: www.qgazette.com
SIC: 2711 2741 7311 7313 Newspapers, publishing & printing; shopping news: publishing only, not printed on site; advertising agencies; newspaper advertising representative

(G-7876)
SIGN DESIGN GROUP NEW YORK INC
3326 Northern Blvd (11101-2224)
PHONE..................................718 392-0779
Mazher Khalfan, *Ch of Bd*
Shokat Khalfan, *Vice Pres*
Mohan Shivram, *Manager*
Sid Walli, *Manager*
Shan Khalfan, *Admin Sec*
▲ **EMP:** 18
SALES (est): 2.6MM *Privately Held*
WEB: www.sdgny.com
SIC: 3993 Signs & advertising specialties

(G-7877)
SIMS GROUP USA HOLDINGS CORP
Sims Metal
3027 Greenpoint Ave (11101-2009)
PHONE..................................718 786-6031
Thomas Ferretti, *Opers-Prdtn-Mfg*
EMP: 66
SALES (corp-wide): 3.4B *Privately Held*
SIC: 3312 3341 Stainless steel; secondary nonferrous metals
HQ: Sims Group Usa Holdings Corp
  16 W 22nd St Fl 10
  New York NY 10010
  212 604-0710

(G-7878)
SIZZAL LLC
Also Called: Influence Graphics
1105 44th Rd (11101-5115)
PHONE..................................212 354-6123
Bill Reeve, *Vice Pres*
Alex Gonzalez, *Prdtn Mgr*
Paul Gonzalez, *Prdtn Mgr*
Al Weiss, *Mng Member*
Ron Sizemore,
EMP: 20
SALES (est): 1.9MM *Privately Held*
SIC: 2752 Commercial printing, lithographic; commercial printing, offset

(G-7879)
SLYDE INC
474 48th Ave Apt 18a (11109-5711)
PHONE..................................917 331-2114
Jason Peltz, *CEO*
Edward Ludvigsen, *Principal*
Kai Blache, *CFO*
EMP: 15
SALES (est): 613.8K *Privately Held*
SIC: 7372 7389 Prepackaged software;

(G-7880)
SM NEW YORK
5216 Barnett Ave (11104-1018)
PHONE..................................718 446-1800

Richard Olicker, *President*
Arvind Dharia, *CFO*
Yingmin Lu, *Accounting Mgr*
▲ **EMP:** 10
SALES (est): 787.9K
SALES (corp-wide): 1.4B *Publicly Held*
WEB: www.mypinecastle.com
SIC: 3144 3149 Women's footwear, except athletic; children's footwear, except athletic
PA: Steven Madden, Ltd.
  5216 Barnett Ave
  Long Island City NY 11104
  718 446-1800

(G-7881)
SPANJER CORP
Also Called: Spanjer Signs
3856 11th St (11101-6114)
PHONE..................................347 448-8033
Fax: 347 448-8032
Steve Silverberg, *President*
Alissa Silverberg, *Vice Pres*
Rose Silverberg, *Admin Sec*
EMP: 6 **EST:** 1908
SQ FT: 5,000
SALES: 446K *Privately Held*
SIC: 3993 Signs & advertising specialties

(G-7882)
STALLION INC (PA)
3620 34th St (11106-1902)
PHONE..................................718 706-0111
Fax: 212 695-4569
John Georgiades, *Ch of Bd*
Ioannis Georgiades, *President*
James Charles, *CFO*
Achilleas Georgiades, *Admin Sec*
▲ **EMP:** 26
SQ FT: 30,000
SALES (est): 45.1MM *Privately Held*
SIC: 2371 5621 Coats, fur; ready-to-wear apparel, women's

(G-7883)
STAMP RITE TOOL & DIE INC
4311 35th St (11101-2303)
PHONE..................................718 752-0334
Jeff Goldberg, *President*
EMP: 5
SQ FT: 1,000
SALES: 200K *Privately Held*
WEB: www.stampritetool.com
SIC: 3544 Special dies & tools

(G-7884)
STANDARD MOTOR PRODUCTS INC (PA)
3718 Northern Blvd # 600 (11101-1637)
PHONE..................................718 392-0200
Fax: 718 472-9334
Lawrence I Sills, *Ch of Bd*
Eric Sills, *President*
Tom Latimer, *General Mgr*
Dale Burks, *Exec VP*
Carmine J Broccole, *Vice Pres*
▲ **EMP:** 500 **EST:** 1919
SQ FT: 74,500
SALES: 971.9MM *Publicly Held*
WEB: www.smpcorp.com
SIC: 3714 3694 3585 3564 Motor vehicle engines & parts; fuel systems & parts, motor vehicle; air conditioner parts, motor vehicle; motor vehicle electrical equipment; ignition systems, high frequency; harness wiring sets, internal combustion engines; battery cable wiring sets for internal combustion engines; compressors for refrigeration & air conditioning equipment; parts for heating, cooling & refrigerating equipment; air conditioning equipment, complete; blowers & fans; rubber & plastics hose & beltings

(G-7885)
STANLEY CREATIONS INC
Also Called: Sgg
3100 47th Ave Ste 4105 (11101-3068)
PHONE..................................718 361-6100
David Lowy, *Branch Mgr*
Harun Ahmed, *Executive*
EMP: 110
SALES (corp-wide): 11.6MM *Privately Held*
SIC: 3911 Jewelry, precious metal

PA: Stanley Creations, Inc.
  1414 Willow Ave
  Elkins Park PA 19027
  215 635-6200

(G-7886)
STANLEY PLEATING STITCHING CO
2219 41st Ave Fl 3 (11101-4807)
PHONE..................................718 392-2417
Fax: 212 868-2939
Stuart Meyer, *President*
EMP: 50
SQ FT: 7,800
SALES (est): 3MM *Privately Held*
SIC: 2395 Permanent pleating & pressing, for the trade; decorative & novelty stitching, for the trade; embroidery products, except schiffli machine

(G-7887)
STARCRAFT PRESS INC
4402 11th St Ste 311 (11101-5150)
PHONE..................................718 383-6700
Robert Glickman, *President*
Jeff Glickman, *Vice Pres*
EMP: 8
SALES (est): 1.3MM *Privately Held*
SIC: 2759 Commercial printing

(G-7888)
STEINWAY INC (DH)
Also Called: Steinway Hall
1 Steinway Pl (11105-1033)
PHONE..................................718 721-2600
Ronald Losby, *CEO*
Kyle R Kirkland, *Exec VP*
▲ **EMP:** 575
SQ FT: 449,000
SALES (est): 115MM
SALES (corp-wide): 229.7MM *Privately Held*
WEB: www.steinway.com
SIC: 3931 5736 Pianos, all types: vertical, grand, spinet, player, etc.; pianos

(G-7889)
STEINWAY AND SONS (DH)
1 Steinway Pl (11105-1033)
PHONE..................................718 721-2600
Michael Sweeney, *Ch of Bd*
Kyle R Kirkland, *President*
Ronald Losby, *President*
Darren Marshall, *Exec VP*
Dana D Messina, *Exec VP*
◆ **EMP:** 112
SQ FT: 450,000
SALES: 96.6MM
SALES (corp-wide): 229.7MM *Privately Held*
WEB: www.steinwaypiano.net
SIC: 3931 5736 Pianos, all types: vertical, grand, spinet, player, etc.; pianos

(G-7890)
STELLAR PRINTING INC
3838 9th St (11101-6110)
PHONE..................................718 361-1600
Fax: 718 786-3200
Dirk Anthonis, *President*
Fred Newton, *President*
Ken Akulin, *General Mgr*
Bill Ednie, *General Mgr*
Jessica Morales, *Human Res Dir*
EMP: 100
SQ FT: 35,000
SALES (est): 15.6MM
SALES (corp-wide): 509.8MM *Privately Held*
WEB: www.americasnewspaper.com
SIC: 2759 Newspapers: printing
HQ: News World Communications, Inc.
  3600 New York Ave Ne
  Washington DC 20002
  202 636-3000

(G-7891)
STEPHEN HANLEY
Also Called: Thomas C Wilson
2111 44th Ave (11101-5007)
PHONE..................................718 729-3360
Charles E Hanley, *CEO*
Jane W Hanley, *Ch of Bd*
Stephen Hanley, *President*
John Heekin, *CFO*
David Hanley, *Sales Staff*

▼ **EMP:** 65 **EST:** 2009
SQ FT: 45,000
SALES (est): 13.4MM *Privately Held*
WEB: www.tcwilson.com
SIC: 3546 3433 Power-driven handtools; heating equipment, except electric

(G-7892)
STEVEN MADDEN LTD (PA)
Also Called: STEVE MADDEN
5216 Barnett Ave (11104-1018)
PHONE..................................718 446-1800
Edward R Rosenfeld, *Ch of Bd*
Amelia Newton Varela, *President*
Awadhesh Sinha, *COO*
Michele Bergerac, *Exec VP*
Jaime Levy, *Vice Pres*
◆ **EMP:** 265
SQ FT: 90,000
SALES: 1.4B *Publicly Held*
WEB: www.mypinecastle.com
SIC: 3143 3144 3149 5632 Men's footwear, except athletic; women's footwear, except athletic; children's footwear, except athletic; handbags; apparel accessories

(G-7893)
STEVEN MADDEN RETAIL INC
5216 Barnett Ave (11104-1018)
PHONE..................................718 446-1800
Edward Rosenfeld, *CEO*
▲ **EMP:** 16
SALES (est): 2.7MM
SALES (corp-wide): 1.4B *Publicly Held*
WEB: www.mypinecastle.com
SIC: 3021 Shoes, plastic soles molded to fabric uppers
PA: Steven Madden, Ltd.
  5216 Barnett Ave
  Long Island City NY 11104
  718 446-1800

(G-7894)
STUART-DEAN CO INC
4350 10th St (11101-6910)
PHONE..................................718 472-1326
Fax: 718 472-1327
Jim Clifford, *Sales Executive*
Kristen Rice, *Branch Mgr*
Maribel Perez, *Admin Asst*
EMP: 13
SALES (corp-wide): 61.3MM *Privately Held*
SIC: 3479 1741 1752 Etching & engraving; stone masonry; wood floor installation & refinishing
PA: Stuart-Dean Co. Inc.
  450 Fashion Ave Ste 3800
  New York NY 10123
  212 273-6900

(G-7895)
SUMMIT AEROSPACE INC
4301 21st St Ste 203 (11101-5039)
PHONE..................................718 433-1326
Fax: 718 433-3964
Moon K Lee, *President*
EMP: 7
SQ FT: 4,000
SALES: 1.2MM *Privately Held*
SIC: 3369 Aerospace castings, nonferrous; except aluminum

(G-7896)
SUPERIOR METALS & PROCESSING
Also Called: Super Stud Building Products
801 26th Ave (11102)
PHONE..................................718 545-7500
Raymond Frobosilo, *President*
Brian Kimmins, *Sales Staff*
John Conneely, *Info Tech Mgr*
▲ **EMP:** 6
SQ FT: 20,500
SALES (est): 340K *Privately Held*
SIC: 3479 Sherardizing of metals or metal products

(G-7897)
SUPREME POULTRY INC
3788 Review Ave (11101-2052)
PHONE..................................718 472-0300
Nasrullah Kamran, *President*
EMP: 5 **EST:** 2015

▲ = Import ▼ = Export
◆ = Import/Export

SALES: 1.5MM **Privately Held**
SIC: 3089 Tableware, plastic

(G-7898)
SUSSMAN-AUTOMATIC CORPORATION (PA)
Also Called: Mr Steam
4320 34th St (11101-2321)
PHONE..................................718 937-4500
Fax: 718 786-4051
Richard Sussman, *Ch of Bd*
Jay Wilsker, *Ch of Bd*
Charles Monteverdi, *President*
Martha Oriena, *General Mgr*
Anthony Diresta, *Vice Pres*
▲ EMP: 73 EST: 1944
SQ FT: 60,000
SALES (est): 16MM **Privately Held**
WEB: www.sussmanelectricboilers.com
SIC: 3569 Generators: steam, liquid oxygen or nitrogen

(G-7899)
TEMPTU INC
522 46th Ave Ste B (11101-5204)
PHONE..................................718 937-9503
Fax: 718 937-9502
Steven Gary, *Manager*
EMP: 5
SALES (corp-wide): 1.9MM **Privately Held**
WEB: www.temptu.com
SIC: 2844 Cosmetic preparations
PA: Temptu Inc.
  26 W 17th St Rm 302
  New York NY 10011
  212 675-4000

(G-7900)
THEODOSIOU INC
Also Called: G T Machine & Tool
3214 49th St (11103-1403)
PHONE..................................718 728-6800
Fax: 718 726-3002
Dean Theodos, *President*
Harry Theodos, *President*
Vj Sukhu, *Manager*
EMP: 8
SQ FT: 7,500
SALES (est): 1.6MM **Privately Held**
WEB: www.gtmachine.com
SIC: 3599 Machine shop, jobbing & repair

(G-7901)
THOMSON PRESS (INDIA) LIMITED
Also Called: Living Media
4 Court Sq Fl 3rm2 (11101-4327)
PHONE..................................646 318-0369
Fax: 718 729-8143
Anup Uniyal, *Branch Mgr*
EMP: 5 **Privately Held**
SIC: 2759 Commercial printing
HQ: Thomson Press (India) Limited
  Thomson Press Building,
  Faridabad HAR 12100
  129 222-3924

(G-7902)
TISH & SNOOKYS NYC INC
Also Called: Manic Panic
2107 Borden Ave Fl 4 (11101-4538)
PHONE..................................718 937-6055
Fax: 718 937-6172
Eileen Bellomo, *Ch of Bd*
Patrice Bellomo, *Corp Secy*
▲ EMP: 15
SQ FT: 15,000
SALES (est): 4MM **Privately Held**
SIC: 2844 Cosmetic preparations

(G-7903)
TOTAL SOLUTION GRAPHICS INC
2511 49th Ave (11101-4429)
PHONE..................................718 706-1540
Ricki Noto, *President*
Jeaneppe Zeh, *Manager*
EMP: 3
SALES: 3MM **Privately Held**
SIC: 2759 Imprinting

(G-7904)
TOWNE HOUSE RESTORATIONS INC
4309 Vernon Blvd (11101-6831)
PHONE..................................718 497-9200
Ivan Cerina, *Principal*
EMP: 5 EST: 2011
SALES (est): 681.9K **Privately Held**
SIC: 3272 Concrete products

(G-7905)
TRANE US INC
4518 Court Sq Ste 100 (11101-4341)
PHONE..................................718 721-8844
Fax: 718 269-3601
Richard Halley, *Branch Mgr*
EMP: 70 **Privately Held**
SIC: 3585 Refrigeration & heating equipment
HQ: Trane U.S. Inc.
  1 Centennial Ave Ste 101
  Piscataway NJ 08854
  732 652-7100

(G-7906)
TRIBORO IRON WORKS INC
3830 31st St (11101-2719)
PHONE..................................718 361-9600
Fax: 718 361-5422
Salvatore Gulino, *President*
EMP: 9
SQ FT: 2,500
SALES (est): 1.4MM **Privately Held**
SIC: 3441 1799 1791 Fabricated structural metal; fire escape installation; iron work, structural

(G-7907)
UNIQUE MBL GRAN ORGNZTION CORP
3831 9th St (11101-6109)
PHONE..................................718 482-0440
John Manassakis, *President*
Hanna Manassakis, *Manager*
EMP: 5
SALES (est): 328K **Privately Held**
SIC: 3281 Marble, building: cut & shaped; granite, cut & shaped

(G-7908)
UNITED PRINT GROUP INC
Also Called: United Business Forms
3636 33rd St Ste 303 (11106-2329)
P.O. Box 1430 (11101-0430)
PHONE..................................718 392-4242
Fax: 718 392-4650
Robert Sanchez, *Ch of Bd*
Bill Linet, *Vice Pres*
Henry Morales, *Vice Pres*
Norma Sanchez, *Treasurer*
EMP: 16
SQ FT: 6,200
SALES (est): 2.1MM **Privately Held**
WEB: www.unitedpg.com
SIC: 2759 3993 Business forms: printing; advertising artwork

(G-7909)
UNITED SHEET METAL CORP
4602 28th St (11101-3402)
PHONE..................................718 482-1197
Fax: 718 482-1197
Joseph Grgas, *President*
Siraj Bora, *Vice Pres*
EMP: 50
SQ FT: 4,000
SALES (est): 4.5MM **Privately Held**
SIC: 3444 Ducts, sheet metal

(G-7910)
UNIVERSAL DESIGNS INC
3517 31st St (11106-2320)
PHONE..................................718 721-1111
Panos Adamopoulos, *President*
Silvia Adamopoulos, *Vice Pres*
EMP: 6
SQ FT: 8,000
SALES: 700K **Privately Held**
SIC: 2511 2521 2541 5712 Wood household furniture; wood office furniture; wood partitions & fixtures; unfinished furniture

(G-7911)
VECTRA INC
3200 Skillman Ave (11101-2309)
PHONE..................................718 361-1000
EMP: 5
SALES (corp-wide): 5.1B **Privately Held**
SIC: 2752 Commercial printing, lithographic
HQ: Vectra, Inc.
  3950 Business Park Dr
  Columbus OH 43204
  614 351-6868

(G-7912)
VENGO INC
4550 30th St Ste 41 (11101-3413)
PHONE..................................866 526-7054
Brian Shimmerlik, *CEO*
Adam Gargenderg, *Vice Pres*
EMP: 6
SALES (est): 390K **Privately Held**
SIC: 3581 Automatic vending machines

(G-7913)
VENUE GRAPHICS SUPPLY INC
1120 46th Rd (11101-5322)
PHONE..................................718 361-1690
EMP: 13
SQ FT: 10,000
SALES: 1.2MM **Privately Held**
SIC: 2899 Mfr Industrial Chemical Solutions

(G-7914)
VERSAILLES DRAPERY UPHOLSTERY
4709 30th St Ste 200 (11101-3400)
PHONE..................................212 533-2059
Fax: 212 995-1681
Jorge Loayza, *President*
Ricardo Loayza, *Treasurer*
EMP: 11
SQ FT: 20,000
SALES: 1MM **Privately Held**
SIC: 2512 5714 2211 Upholstered household furniture; draperies; draperies & drapery fabrics, cotton

(G-7915)
VIAPACK INC
3608 Review Ave (11101-2036)
PHONE..................................718 729-5500
Manash Ortac, *President*
Donald Williams, *Principal*
EMP: 17
SALES (est): 3MM **Privately Held**
SIC: 3089 Injection molded finished plastic products

(G-7916)
VITOBOB FURNITURE INC
3879 13th St (11101-6119)
PHONE..................................516 676-1696
Robert Longo, *President*
Michele Longo, *Admin Sec*
EMP: 5
SQ FT: 5,000
SALES (est): 490K **Privately Held**
SIC: 2426 Frames for upholstered furniture, wood

(G-7917)
WALNUT PRINTING INC
2812 41st Ave (11101-3706)
PHONE..................................718 707-0100
Fax: 718 433-0510
Gerald Paul Pont, *President*
EMP: 5
SQ FT: 3,500
SALES (est): 592.6K **Privately Held**
WEB: www.walnutprinting.com
SIC: 2752 Commercial printing, lithographic

(G-7918)
WARREN PRINTING INC
3718 Northern Blvd # 418 (11101-1636)
PHONE..................................212 627-5000
Fax: 212 691-0857
Warren Pugach, *President*
Priscilla Pugach, *Corp Secy*
Seymour Pugach, *Vice Pres*
Diane Niefin, *Accountant*
EMP: 10
SQ FT: 7,500

SALES (est): 1.8MM **Privately Held**
SIC: 2752 Commercial printing, offset

(G-7919)
WATCHCRAFT INC
2214 40th Ave Ste 4 (11101-4830)
PHONE..................................347 531-0382
Eduardo Milieris, *President*
▲ EMP: 5
SALES (est): 742.5K **Privately Held**
SIC: 3873 5094 Watches, clocks, watchcases & parts; clocks, watches & parts

(G-7920)
WESTMORE LITHO CORP
Also Called: Westmore Litho Printing Co
4017 22nd St (11101-4834)
PHONE..................................718 361-9403
Fax: 718 361-9469
Spike Kalashian, *President*
EMP: 8 EST: 1959
SQ FT: 10,000
SALES (est): 590K **Privately Held**
SIC: 2752 Commercial printing, lithographic

(G-7921)
WILDCAT TERRITORY INC
4401 21st St Ste 202 (11101-5009)
PHONE..................................718 361-6726
Fax: 718 361-6746
Nancy F Reib, *President*
Ibrahim Coban, *Vice Pres*
Vincent Figueroa, *Manager*
Edna Martell, *Manager*
▲ EMP: 15
SQ FT: 10,000
SALES (est): 1.9MM **Privately Held**
WEB: www.wildcatterritory.com
SIC: 2392 2391 Household furnishings; curtains & draperies

(G-7922)
WILLIAM E WILLIAMS VALVE CORP
3850 Review Ave (11101-2019)
P.O. Box 1190 (11101-0190)
PHONE..................................718 392-1660
Fax: 718 729-5106
Richard Sherman, *President*
Nicholas Sherman, *Vice Pres*
▲ EMP: 23 EST: 1918
SQ FT: 60,000
SALES (est): 6.5MM **Privately Held**
SIC: 3494 3491 Valves & pipe fittings; industrial valves

(G-7923)
WILLIAM H JACKSON COMPANY
3629 23rd St (11106-4405)
PHONE..................................718 784-4482
Eric Nelson, *Manager*
EMP: 7
SQ FT: 4,800
SALES (corp-wide): 1.5MM **Privately Held**
WEB: www.bumrails.com
SIC: 3429 Fireplace equipment, hardware: andirons, grates, screens
PA: William H Jackson Company
  18 E 17th St Frnt 1
  New York NY 10003
  212 753-9400

(G-7924)
WINNER PRESS INC
4331 33rd St 1 (11101-2316)
PHONE..................................718 937-7715
Hermi Fu, *President*
Ya Tang Fu, *Principal*
Marissa Santiago, *Admin Sec*
EMP: 25
SQ FT: 20,000
SALES (est): 4MM **Privately Held**
WEB: www.winnerpress.com
SIC: 2752 Commercial printing, lithographic

(G-7925)
WINSON SURNAMER INC
4402 11th St Ste 601 (11101-5149)
PHONE..................................718 729-8787
Gary Levinson, *President*
Lawrence Levinson, *Treasurer*
Robert Levinson, *Admin Sec*
EMP: 5

Long Island City - Queens County (G-7926)   GEOGRAPHIC SECTION

SQ FT: 40,000
SALES (est): 702.1K Privately Held
SIC: 2752 Commercial printing, offset

(G-7926)
WONTON FOOD INC
5210 37th St (11101-2001)
PHONE.............................718 784-8178
Foo Kam Wong, *Manager*
Megan Tong, *Asst Mgr*
EMP: 20
SQ FT: 5,320
SALES (corp-wide): 63MM Privately Held
WEB: www.wontonfood.com
SIC: 2099 2052 Noodles, fried (Chinese); cracker meal & crumbs
PA: Wonton Food Inc.
   220 Moore St 222
   Brooklyn NY 11206
   718 628-6868

(G-7927)
X BRAND EDITIONS
4020 22nd St Ste 1 (11101-4814)
PHONE.............................718 482-7646
Robert Blanton, *President*
EMP: 8 EST: 2010
SALES (est): 916.9K Privately Held
SIC: 3577 Printers & plotters

(G-7928)
XANIA LABS INC
3202 Queens Blvd Fl 6 (11101-2332)
PHONE.............................718 361-2550
Nikos Mouyiaris, *President*
Brenda Gallagher, *Sales Dir*
EMP: 5
SALES (est): 435.3K
SALES (corp-wide): 289MM Privately Held
SIC: 2844 5122 Cosmetic preparations; cosmetics
PA: Mana Products, Inc.
   3202 Queens Blvd Fl 6
   Long Island City NY 11101
   718 361-2550

(G-7929)
YORK INTERNATIONAL CORPORATION
1130 45th Rd (11101-5213)
PHONE.............................718 389-4152
Ben Cohen, *Branch Mgr*
EMP: 94 Privately Held
SIC: 3585 Refrigeration & heating equipment
HQ: York International Corporation
   631 S Richland Ave
   York PA 17403
   717 771-7890

(G-7930)
YORK LADDER INC
3720 12th St (11101-6098)
PHONE.............................718 784-6666
Kenneth J Buettner, *President*
John Ottulich, *Sales Staff*
David Caro, *Manager*
▲ EMP: 8
SALES (est): 829.8K Privately Held
SIC: 2499 Ladders & stepladders, wood

(G-7931)
ZELMAN & FRIEDMAN JWLY MFG CO
4722 37th St (11101-1804)
P.O. Box 547, Woodbury (11797-0547)
PHONE.............................718 349-3400
Fax: 718 349-8159
Irwin Friedman, *President*
Morris Zelman, *Treasurer*
Gary Zelman, *Asst Treas*
Alan Zelman, *Shareholder*
EMP: 25 EST: 1951
SQ FT: 5,000
SALES (est): 2.3MM Privately Held
SIC: 3911 Jewelry, precious metal

(G-7932)
ZENITH COLOR COMM GROUP INC (PA)
4710 33rd St (11101-2408)
PHONE.............................212 989-4400
Peter D Savitt, *President*

Josh Mittleman, *Marketing Staff*
EMP: 20
SALES (est): 4MM Privately Held
SIC: 2711 Commercial printing & newspaper publishing combined

(G-7933)
ZIC SPORTSWEAR INC (PA)
Also Called: Zoe
2107 41st Ave Fl 3 (11101-4802)
PHONE.............................718 361-9022
Fax: 718 392-2813
Susan Mandel, *President*
Alan Gold, *Manager*
EMP: 39
SQ FT: 12,000
SALES (est): 4.9MM Privately Held
WEB: www.zoeltd.com
SIC: 2361 2369 Dresses: girls', children's & infants'; girls' & children's outerwear

---
Lowman
Chemung County

(G-7934)
HORSEHEADS BREWING INC
959 Lattabrook Rd (14861-8926)
PHONE.............................607 734-8055
Edward Samchinsen, *Principal*
EMP: 5
SALES (est): 446.4K Privately Held
SIC: 2082 Malt beverages

Lowville
Lewis County

(G-7935)
CLIMAX PACKAGING INC
7840 State Route 26 (13367-2926)
PHONE.............................315 376-8000
Patrick Purdy, *President*
Mary Wuest, *CFO*
Patty Remick, *Controller*
Peter Dawes, *VP Sales*
EMP: 105
SQ FT: 110,000
SALES (est): 11.7MM Privately Held
WEB: www.stjpkg.com
SIC: 3993 2657 Signs & advertising specialties; folding paperboard boxes

(G-7936)
FARNEY LUMBER CORPORATION
7194 Brewery Rd (13367-2524)
PHONE.............................315 346-6013
Fax: 315 346-1859
Duane Farney, *President*
Terry Farney, *Vice Pres*
Todd Farney, *Vice Pres*
Karen Farney, *Admin Sec*
EMP: 17
SQ FT: 20,000
SALES: 2MM Privately Held
SIC: 2421 Sawmills & planing mills, general

(G-7937)
FIBERMARK NORTH AMERICA INC
5492 Bostwick St (13367)
PHONE.............................315 376-3571
Fax: 315 376-4916
Porter Cathy, *Personnel Exec*
Larry Kieffer, *Branch Mgr*
Roger Perkins, *Info Tech Mgr*
EMP: 179
SALES (corp-wide): 887.7MM Publicly Held
WEB: www.fibermark.com
SIC: 2672 Coated & laminated paper
HQ: Fibermark North America
   70 Front St
   West Springfield MA 01089
   413 533-0699

(G-7938)
KRAFT HEINZ FOODS COMPANY
7388 Utica Blvd (13367-9503)
PHONE.............................315 376-6575

Fax: 315 376-2944
Marc Page, *Plant Mgr*
Tim Reagan, *Plant Mgr*
Marge Kaprin, *Safety Mgr*
Thomas Smith, *Facilities Mgr*
Chris Pomerville, *Opers Spvr*
EMP: 335
SQ FT: 460
SALES (corp-wide): 210.8B Publicly Held
WEB: www.kraftfoods.com
SIC: 2022 Cheese, natural & processed
HQ: Heinz Kraft Foods Company
   1 Ppg Pl Ste 3200
   Pittsburgh PA 15222
   412 456-5700

(G-7939)
LOWVILLE FARMERS COOP INC
5500 Shady Ave (13367-1698)
PHONE.............................315 376-6587
Fax: 315 376-8233
John Williams, *President*
Brian Tabolt, *General Mgr*
Glen Beller, *Corp Secy*
Mark Karelus, *Vice Pres*
Tim Smithling, *CFO*
EMP: 37
SQ FT: 20,000
SALES: 10MM Privately Held
SIC: 2048 5999 2875 5251 Prepared feeds; feed & farm supply; fertilizers, mixing only; hardware; lumber products

(G-7940)
LOWVILLE NEWSPAPER CORPORATION
Also Called: Journal and Republican
7567 S State St (13367-1512)
PHONE.............................315 376-3525
Fax: 315 376-4136
Bonnie Franklin, *Advt Staff*
Jeremiah Papineau, *Manager*
Adam Atkinson, *Manager*
EMP: 7 EST: 1830
SQ FT: 2,000
SALES (est): 442.3K
SALES (corp-wide): 32MM Privately Held
WEB: www.ogd.com
SIC: 2711 Newspapers, publishing & printing
PA: Johnson Newspaper Corporation
   260 Washington St
   Watertown NY
   315 782-1000

(G-7941)
QUBICAAMF WORLDWIDE LLC
Also Called: Pins and Lanes
7412 Utica Blvd (13367-9572)
PHONE.............................315 376-6541
Fax: 315 376-3301
Wayne White, *General Mgr*
Rebecca Purvines, *Human Res Mgr*
William McDonnell, *Manager*
EMP: 150 Privately Held
SIC: 3949 Bowling pins
HQ: Qubicaamf Worldwide, Llc
   8100 Amf Dr
   Mechanicsville VA 23111
   804 569-1000

(G-7942)
ROYAL CUSTOM CABINETS
6149 Patty St (13367-4206)
PHONE.............................315 376-6042
David Lapp, *Owner*
EMP: 8
SALES (est): 815.8K Privately Held
SIC: 2434 Wood kitchen cabinets

Lynbrook
Nassau County

(G-7943)
ADF ACCESSORIES INC
Also Called: Todaysgentleman.com
381 Sunrise Hwy Unit 5r (11563-3040)
PHONE.............................516 450-5755
Jack Fischman, *President*
Chanie Manheimer, *Vice Pres*
▲ EMP: 5

SALES (est): 650.6K Privately Held
WEB: www.todaysgentleman.com
SIC: 2389 Men's miscellaneous accessories

(G-7944)
ADVANCE BIOFACTURES CORP
35 Wilbur St (11563-2358)
PHONE.............................516 593-7000
Edwin Wegman, *President*
Thomas Wegman, *Senior VP*
Larry Dobross, *Admin Sec*
EMP: 20 EST: 1957
SQ FT: 15,000
SALES (est): 1.2MM
SALES (corp-wide): 22.7MM Publicly Held
WEB: www.biospecifics.com
SIC: 2836 8731 Biological products, except diagnostic; biological research
PA: Biospecifics Technologies Corp.
   35 Wilbur St
   Lynbrook NY 11563
   516 593-7000

(G-7945)
ALL METRO EMRGNCY RESPONSE SYS
50 Broadway (11563-2519)
PHONE.............................516 750-9100
Irving Edwards, *President*
EMP: 6
SALES (est): 460K Privately Held
WEB: www.amerslifeline.com
SIC: 3669 Emergency alarms

(G-7946)
ALLOY MACHINE & TOOL CO INC
169 Vincent Ave (11563-2607)
P.O. Box 708 (11563-0708)
PHONE.............................516 593-3445
Fax: 516 593-9031
Paul R Will, *President*
Gary Will, *Vice Pres*
EMP: 8 EST: 1967
SQ FT: 8,000
SALES: 900K Privately Held
SIC: 3679 Electronic circuits

(G-7947)
BIMBO BAKERIES USA INC
669 Sunrise Hwy Spc 4 (11563-3246)
PHONE.............................516 887-1024
George Weston, *Branch Mgr*
EMP: 18
SALES (corp-wide): 13B Privately Held
SIC: 2051 Bread, cake & related products
HQ: Bimbo Bakeries Usa, Inc
   255 Business Center Dr # 200
   Horsham PA 19044
   215 347-5500

(G-7948)
BIOSPECIFICS TECHNOLOGIES CORP (PA)
35 Wilbur St (11563-2358)
PHONE.............................516 593-7000
Thomas L Wegman, *President*
James Goris, *Controller*
Helen Piazza, *Human Res Dir*
▲ EMP: 5
SALES: 22.7MM Publicly Held
WEB: www.biospecifics.com
SIC: 2834 Pharmaceutical preparations

(G-7949)
CASCADE TECHNICAL SERVICES LLC (DH)
Also Called: Zebra Technical Services LLC
30 N Prospect Ave (11563-1313)
PHONE.............................516 596-6300
Tim Smith, *CEO*
Katarzyna Kosarska, *Business Mgr*
Gary Crueger, *Vice Pres*
Tyler Kopet, *CFO*
EMP: 17
SQ FT: 6,400
SALES (est): 6.3MM
SALES (corp-wide): 762.6MM Privately Held
SIC: 3822 Auto controls regulating residntl & coml environmt & applncs

HQ: Cascade Drilling, L.P.
17270 Woodinville Redmond
Woodinville WA 98072
425 527-9700

(G-7950)
ECOLOGICAL LABORATORIES INC (PA)
13 Hendrickson Ave (11563-1201)
P.O. Box 184, Malverne (11565-0184)
PHONE..................................516 823-3441
Barry Richter, *President*
Doug Dent, *Vice Pres*
Mark Krupka, *Vice Pres*
Matthew Richter, *Vice Pres*
Domenic Simone, *Vice Pres*
▲ **EMP:** 15
SQ FT: 5,500
SALES (est): 8.9MM **Privately Held**
WEB: www.propump.com
SIC: 2899 2836 5169 Water treating compounds; biological products, except diagnostic; chemicals & allied products

(G-7951)
IDC PRINTING & STY CO INC (PA)
536 Merrick Rd (11563-2328)
PHONE..................................516 599-0400
Fax: 516 599-8422
Anthony Trani, *President*
Isober Trani, *Admin Sec*
EMP: 4
SQ FT: 2,400
SALES (est): 1.1MM **Privately Held**
SIC: 2759 2761 5943 Commercial printing; letterpress printing; envelopes: printing; computer forms, manifold or continuous; office forms & supplies

(G-7952)
KIMSCO BUSINESS SYSTEMS INC
424 Scranton Ave (11563-3336)
PHONE..................................516 599-5658
Fred Chaplick, *President*
EMP: 5
SALES (est): 390K **Privately Held**
SIC: 2752 Commercial printing, offset

(G-7953)
LABGRAFIX PRINTING INC
43 Rocklyn Ave Unit B (11563-2752)
PHONE..................................516 280-8300
Lev Galkin, *President*
EMP: 6 **EST:** 2010
SALES: 1MM **Privately Held**
SIC: 3861 7384 Photographic equipment & supplies; photographic services

(G-7954)
MASTER CRAFT JEWELRY CO INC
Also Called: L'Etoile Jewelers
150 Vincent Ave (11563-2608)
PHONE..................................516 599-1012
Fax: 516 599-2817
Robert Sharaby, *President*
Marie Coakley, *Bookkeeper*
EMP: 55
SQ FT: 10,000
SALES (est): 5.7MM **Privately Held**
WEB: www.mastercraftjewelry.net
SIC: 3911 Jewelry, precious metal; bracelets, precious metal; earrings, precious metal; rings, finger: precious metal

(G-7955)
ND LABS INC
Also Called: Nutritional Designs
202 Merrick Rd (11563-2622)
PHONE..................................516 612-4900
Beth Beller, *Ch of Bd*
Diane Altos, *President*
Leticia Hanysz-Narvaez, *Facilities Mgr*
Elisa Gross, *Office Mgr*
EMP: 10
SQ FT: 10,000
SALES (est): 1.3MM **Privately Held**
WEB: www.ndlabs.com
SIC: 2834 Vitamin, nutrient & hematinic preparations for human use

(G-7956)
PINQUIST TOOL & DIE CO INC
451 Sunrise Hwy Ste 4 (11563-3037)
PHONE..................................718 389-3900
Fax: 718 349-3168
Richard Pinquist, *President*
Candace Oshinsky, *Vice Pres*
Ann M Troche, *Manager*
EMP: 22 **EST:** 1945
SQ FT: 10,000
SALES (est): 4.2MM **Privately Held**
WEB: www.pinquisttool.com
SIC: 3429 Manufactured hardware (general); door opening & closing devices, except electrical; metal fasteners

(G-7957)
PRO PRINTING
Also Called: PIP Printing
359 Merrick Rd (11563-2517)
PHONE..................................516 561-9700
Raymond Kenney Sr, *Partner*
Raymond Kenney Jr, *Partner*
EMP: 5
SQ FT: 1,000
SALES (est): 370K **Privately Held**
SIC: 2752 2791 2789 Commercial printing, offset; typesetting; bookbinding & related work

(G-7958)
RAYDON PRECISION BEARING CO
75 Merrick Rd (11563-2713)
P.O. Box 679 (11563-0679)
PHONE..................................516 887-2582
Fax: 516 887-2880
Dominick Pinto, *President*
Barbara Pinto, *Treasurer*
EMP: 6 **EST:** 1965
SQ FT: 1,000
SALES (est): 927.7K **Privately Held**
SIC: 3562 5085 Ball & roller bearings; bearings

(G-7959)
REGENCE PICTURE FRAMES INC
12 Cherry Ln (11563-4120)
PHONE..................................718 779-0888
Cecilia Litzak, *President*
Bob O'Donald, *Vice Pres*
Mary Grosse, *Bookkeeper*
EMP: 25 **EST:** 1968
SQ FT: 7,500
SALES: 1MM **Privately Held**
WEB: www.regencepictureframes.com
SIC: 2499 Picture & mirror frames, wood

(G-7960)
RUSSELL INDUSTRIES INC
Also Called: E V G Division
40 Horton Ave (11563-2333)
P.O. Box 807 (11563-0807)
PHONE..................................516 536-5000
Adam Russell, *President*
Stacey Russell, *Manager*
▲ **EMP:** 10 **EST:** 1965
SQ FT: 20,000
SALES (est): 1.5MM **Privately Held**
SIC: 3679 3643 5065 Antennas, receiving; current-carrying wiring devices; video equipment, electronic

(G-7961)
SIGNS OF SUCCESS LTD
247 Merrick Rd Ste 101 (11563-2641)
PHONE..................................516 295-6000
Fax: 516 823-1023
Steven Cohen, *President*
Diane Mastorides, *Manager*
EMP: 21
SQ FT: 4,500
SALES: 700K **Privately Held**
WEB: www.signs-of-success.com
SIC: 3993 Signs & advertising specialties

(G-7962)
SKINZ INC
Also Called: Skinz Mfg
156 Union Ave (11563-3345)
PHONE..................................516 593-3139
Fax: 516 593-0813
Loretta Wax, *President*
Fran Babus, *Admin Sec*
EMP: 20
SQ FT: 2,500
SALES (est): 1.5MM **Privately Held**
SIC: 2335 Women's, juniors' & misses' dresses

(G-7963)
STAND UP MRI OF LYNBROOK PC
229 Broadway (11563-3295)
PHONE..................................516 256-1558
Fax: 516 256-0758
Theresa Gabriel, *Regional Mgr*
Laurie Leimisidi, *Manager*
EMP: 10
SALES (est): 1MM **Privately Held**
SIC: 3845 Electromedical equipment

(G-7964)
SWIFT FULFILLMENT SERVICES
290 Broadway (11563-3293)
PHONE..................................516 593-1198
Barbara Fiegas, *President*
Preston D Theiber, *Vice Pres*
Swist Fulimint, *Manager*
EMP: 7
SQ FT: 5,000
SALES: 999K **Privately Held**
SIC: 2721 5192 Periodicals: publishing only; books

(G-7965)
TOP FORTUNE USA LTD
100 Atlantic Ave Ste 2 (11563-3471)
PHONE..................................516 608-2694
Elan Oved, *CEO*
▲ **EMP:** 6
SALES: 1,000K **Privately Held**
SIC: 2385 Waterproof outerwear

(G-7966)
VALLEY STREAM SPORTING GDS INC
Also Called: Arrowear Athletic Apparel
325 Hendrickson Ave (11563-1055)
PHONE..................................516 593-7800
Robert J Heller, *Ch of Bd*
Joel Napchan, *Manager*
Bob Heller, *Executive*
EMP: 25
SQ FT: 16,000
SALES (est): 3.3MM **Privately Held**
WEB: www.arrowear.com
SIC: 2329 2262 Athletic (warmup, sweat & jogging) suits: men's & boys'; screen printing: manmade fiber & silk broadwoven fabrics

(G-7967)
ZEBRA ENVIRONMENTAL CORP (PA)
30 N Prospect Ave (11563-1398)
PHONE..................................516 596-6300
Fax: 516 596-4422
EMP: 17
SQ FT: 6,400
SALES (est): 5.2MM **Privately Held**
SIC: 3822 Mfg Environmental Controls

Lyndonville
Orleans County

(G-7968)
MIZKAN AMERICA INC
Also Called: Nakano Foods
247 West Ave (14098-9744)
PHONE..................................585 765-9171
Steven Gardepe, *Principal*
Dave Carpenter, *Safety Mgr*
Steve Fortunato, *Purchasing*
EMP: 70
SQ FT: 82,000 **Privately Held**
SIC: 2033 2099 2035 Fruit juices: packaged in cans, jars, etc.; food preparations; pickles, sauces & salad dressings
HQ: Mizkan America, Inc.
1661 Feehanville Dr # 200
Mount Prospect IL 60056
847 590-0059

(G-7969)
SHORELINE FRUIT LLC
Also Called: Atwater Foods
10190 Route 18 (14098-9785)
PHONE..................................585 765-2639
Fax: 585 765-9443
EMP: 70
SALES (corp-wide): 43.3MM **Privately Held**
SIC: 2034 Processor Of Fruit Products
PA: Shoreline Fruit, Llc
10850 E Traverse Hwy # 4001
Traverse City MI 49684
231 941-4336

Lyons
Wayne County

(G-7970)
CASWELL INC
7696 State Route 31 (14489-9116)
PHONE..................................315 946-1213
Fax: 315 946-4456
Lance Caswell, *President*
Carol Caswell, *Vice Pres*
Craige Brooks, *Sales Staff*
Mike Caswell, *Shareholder*
Kelly Campbell, *Administration*
▼ **EMP:** 10
SQ FT: 8,000
SALES (est): 2MM **Privately Held**
WEB: www.caswellplating.net
SIC: 3559 5169 Electroplating machinery & equipment; chemicals & allied products

(G-7971)
CONNEX GRINDING & MACHINING
65 Clyde Rd (14489-9364)
PHONE..................................315 946-4340
Carlton J Collins Jr, *President*
Barbara A Collins, *Treasurer*
EMP: 5
SQ FT: 2,400
SALES (est): 507.8K **Privately Held**
SIC: 3541 Grinding machines, metalworking

(G-7972)
DELOKA LLC
150 Dunn Rd (14489-9772)
PHONE..................................315 946-6910
Scott Lord,
Mike Kunes,
Roger Westerman,
EMP: 5
SQ FT: 21,000
SALES: 800K **Privately Held**
WEB: www.deloka.com
SIC: 3479 Coating of metals & formed products

(G-7973)
LAGASSE WORKS INC
5 Old State Route 31 (14489-9214)
PHONE..................................315 946-9202
Daniel Lagasse, *President*
Kate McCormick, *Controller*
Kate Vosvurgh, *Manager*
EMP: 6
SQ FT: 10,000
SALES (est): 959.8K **Privately Held**
WEB: www.lagasseworks.com
SIC: 7692 3599 Welding repair; machine shop, jobbing & repair

(G-7974)
PENN CAN EQUIPMENT CORPORATION
Also Called: Penn Can Asphalt Materials
300 Cole Rd (14489-9602)
PHONE..................................315 378-0337
EMP: 7
SALES (corp-wide): 1.1MM **Privately Held**
SIC: 3531 Mfg Construction Machinery
PA: Penn Can Equipment Corporation
555 State Fair Blvd
Syracuse NY 13204
315 637-3168

Lyons - Wayne County (G-7975)

(G-7975)
SILGAN CONTAINERS MFG CORP
8673 Lyons Marengo Rd (14489-9726)
PHONE..................................315 946-4826
John Anderson, *Vice Pres*
Tom Kaczynski, *Manager*
Richard Bailey, *Manager*
EMP: 150
SALES (corp-wide): 3.7B **Publicly Held**
WEB: www.silgancontainers.com
SIC: 3411 Metal cans; food containers, metal
HQ: Silgan Containers Manufacturing Corporation
  21800 Oxnard St Ste 600
  Woodland Hills CA 91367

(G-7976)
TIM CRETIN LOGGING & SAWMILL
3607 Wayne Center Rd (14489-9321)
PHONE..................................315 946-4476
Tim Cretin, *President*
EMP: 11
SQ FT: 1,961
SALES: 2MM **Privately Held**
SIC: 2411 Logging

Lyons Falls
Lewis County

(G-7977)
BURROWS PAPER CORPORATION
Lyonsdale Rd (13368)
PHONE..................................315 348-8491
Fax: 315 348-6808
Dennis Gigliotti, *Branch Mgr*
John Dailey, *Maintence Staff*
EMP: 37
SQ FT: 67,484
SALES (corp-wide): 178.2MM **Privately Held**
WEB: www.burrowspaper.com
SIC: 2621 Tissue paper
PA: Burrows Paper Corporation
  501 W Main St Ste 1
  Little Falls NY 13365
  315 823-2300

(G-7978)
OTIS PRODUCTS INC (PA)
Also Called: Otis Technology
6987 Laura St (13368-1802)
P.O. Box 582 (13368-0582)
PHONE..................................315 348-4300
Doreen Garrett, *CEO*
Mike Tuttle, *Opers Mgr*
Nancy Devereaux, *Senior Buyer*
Daniel Szalach, *Buyer*
Steven Buxton, *Engineer*
▲ **EMP:** 122
SQ FT: 12,000
SALES (est): 17.8MM **Privately Held**
WEB: www.otisgun.com
SIC: 3949 Shooting equipment & supplies, general

Macedon
Wayne County

(G-7979)
A&M MODEL MAKERS LLC
1675 Wayneport Rd Ste 1 (14502-8770)
PHONE..................................626 813-9661
Derek Backus,
EMP: 6
SALES: 350K **Privately Held**
SIC: 3999 Manufacturing industries

(G-7980)
ANKOM DEVELOPMENT LLC
2052 Oneil Rd (14502-8953)
PHONE..................................315 986-1937
Andrew Komarek,
EMP: 5 EST: 2006
SALES (est): 680.1K **Privately Held**
SIC: 3534 Elevators & moving stairways

(G-7981)
ANKOM TECHNOLOGY CORP
2052 Oneil Rd (14502-8953)
PHONE..................................315 986-8090
Fax: 315 986-8091
Andrew Komarek, *President*
Christopher Kelley, *Vice Pres*
Ron Komarek, *Vice Pres*
Ronald Komarek, *Vice Pres*
Shawn Ritchie, *Vice Pres*
EMP: 30
SQ FT: 50,000
SALES (est): 7.3MM **Privately Held**
WEB: www.ankom.com
SIC: 3821 5049 Laboratory equipment: fume hoods, distillation racks, etc.; laboratory equipment, except medical or dental

(G-7982)
AUBURN BEARING & MFG INC
4 State Route 350 (14502-9177)
PHONE..................................315 986-7600
Peter Schroth, *CEO*
Barbara McMillan, *Manager*
EMP: 8
SQ FT: 1,280
SALES (est): 888.5K **Privately Held**
SIC: 3714 3599 Motor vehicle transmissions, drive assemblies & parts; custom machinery

(G-7983)
BALDWIN RICHARDSON FOODS CO
3268 Blue Heron Dr (14502-9337)
PHONE..................................315 986-2727
Fax: 315 986-5880
Kelly Holgado, *Sales Mgr*
Matt Mahoney, *Technology*
EMP: 209
SALES (corp-wide): 97.2MM **Privately Held**
SIC: 2087 2035 2099 Flavoring extracts & syrups; extracts, flavoring; syrups, flavoring (except drink); fruit juices: concentrated for fountain use; pickles, sauces & salad dressings; mustard, prepared (wet); food preparations
PA: Baldwin Richardson Foods Company
  1 Tower Ln
  Oakbrook Terrace IL 60181
  815 464-9994

(G-7984)
BERRY PLASTICS CORPORATION
200 Main St (14502-8977)
PHONE..................................315 986-6270
EMP: 400
SALES (corp-wide): 4.8B **Publicly Held**
SIC: 3081 3086 2671 Mfg Unsupported Plastic Film/Sheet Mfg Plastic Foam Products Mfg Packaging Paper/Film
HQ: Berry Plastics Corporation
  101 Oakley St
  Evansville IN 47710
  812 424-2904

(G-7985)
DAU THRMAL SLUTIONS N AMER INC
1657 E Park Dr (14502-8892)
PHONE..................................585 678-9025
Christopher Cutaia, *President*
Shelley Hilfiker, *Controller*
Michael Kulzer, *Sales Dir*
▲ **EMP:** 30
SALES (est): 8.6MM **Privately Held**
SIC: 3823 Thermal conductivity instruments, industrial process type

(G-7986)
EXXONMOBIL CHEMICAL COMPANY
Also Called: Stratford Oriented
729 State Route 31 (14502-9179)
PHONE..................................315 966-1000
Fax: 315 966-5033
Barry Rice, *Facilities Mgr*
Todd Brooks, *Marketing Mgr*
Jean Peterson, *Branch Mgr*
Diane Dobriandobris, *Manager*
Michele Paccagnini, *Research Analys*
EMP: 200
SALES (corp-wide): 268.8B **Publicly Held**
SIC: 2821 Polypropylene resins
HQ: Exxonmobil Chemical Company
  22777 Sprngwoods Vlg Pkwy
  Spring TX 77389
  281 834-5200

(G-7987)
FB SALE LLC
1688 Wayneport Rd (14502-8765)
PHONE..................................315 986-9999
Keith Bleier, *Senior VP*
Aaron Fleischer, *Director*
Marc Fleischer,
EMP: 8 EST: 1974
SQ FT: 42,000
SALES (est): 1MM **Privately Held**
WEB: www.fleischersbagels.com
SIC: 2051 Bagels, fresh or frozen

(G-7988)
LAWSON M WHITING INC
15 State Route 350 (14502-9177)
PHONE..................................315 986-3064
Fax: 315 986-5912
Jay D Whiting, *President*
Barbara Aruck, *Controller*
Van Price, *Controller*
Lawson M Whiting, *Shareholder*
EMP: 8 EST: 1973
SQ FT: 14,000
SALES (est): 1.9MM **Privately Held**
WEB: www.rockcrusher.com
SIC: 3532 Mining machinery; crushing, pulverizing & screening equipment

(G-7989)
PENTA-TECH COATED PRODUCTS LLC
1610 Commons Pkwy (14502-9190)
PHONE..................................315 986-4098
Fax: 315 986-4669
Robert Debruin, *Branch Mgr*
EMP: 12
SALES (corp-wide): 3MM **Privately Held**
WEB: www.ptcp.net
SIC: 2671 Packaging paper & plastics film, coated & laminated
PA: Penta-Tech Coated Products Llc
  58 Main Rd N
  Hampden ME 04444
  207 862-3105

(G-7990)
PLIANT LLC
200 Main St (14502-8977)
PHONE..................................315 986-6286
Kim Kirby, *Manager*
EMP: 400
SALES (est): 61.4MM
SALES (corp-wide): 4.8B **Publicly Held**
SIC: 3081 3086 2671 Unsupported plastics film & sheet; plastics foam products; packaging paper & plastics film, coated & laminated
HQ: Berry Plastics Corporation
  101 Oakley St
  Evansville IN 47710
  812 424-2904

(G-7991)
SHORT JJ ASSOCIATES INC (PA)
1645 Wayneport Rd (14502-9110)
P.O. Box 183, Fairport (14450-0183)
PHONE..................................315 986-3511
Fax: 315 986-2827
John Short Jr, *President*
John J Short Jr, *President*
Peter J Short, *CFO*
EMP: 11 EST: 1977
SQ FT: 12,500
SALES: 750K **Privately Held**
WEB: www.jjshort.com
SIC: 3069 Molded rubber products

(G-7992)
WATER TECHNOLOGIES INC (PA)
Also Called: Columbia
1635 Commons Pkwy (14502-9191)
PHONE..................................315 986-0000
Joe Cupido, *President*
Bruce Dan, *Vice Pres*
▲ **EMP:** 5
SALES (est): 6.5MM **Privately Held**
SIC: 3589 Water filters & softeners, household type

Machias
Cattaraugus County

(G-7993)
MACHIAS FURNITURE FACTORY INC (PA)
3638 Route 242 (14101-9727)
PHONE..................................716 353-8687
Charles I Horning, *President*
Cindy Horning, *Vice Pres*
EMP: 9
SQ FT: 25,000
SALES: 473.1K **Privately Held**
SIC: 2511 Wood desks, bookcases & magazine racks

Madison
Madison County

(G-7994)
SOLID BILT CONSTRUCTION
7561 State Route 20 (13402-9510)
PHONE..................................315 893-1738
Wilmer Zook, *Partner*
Scott Zook, *Partner*
EMP: 5
SALES (est): 440K **Privately Held**
SIC: 2452 Prefabricated wood buildings

Madrid
St. Lawrence County

(G-7995)
MADRID FIRE DISTRICT
26 10 Church St (13660)
PHONE..................................315 322-4346
Theodore Schulz, *Chief*
Marsha Watson, *Admin Sec*
EMP: 6 EST: 1984
SALES (est): 377K **Privately Held**
SIC: 3711 Fire department vehicles (motor vehicles), assembly of

Mahopac
Putnam County

(G-7996)
GATEWAY NEWSPAPERS INC
Also Called: Putnam Press
928 S Lake Blvd Apt 1e (10541-3242)
PHONE..................................845 628-8400
Fax: 914 628-8400
Donald Hall, *President*
EMP: 7
SQ FT: 1,000
SALES (est): 427.4K **Privately Held**
SIC: 2711 Newspapers: publishing only, not printed on site

(G-7997)
MICHAEL BENALT INC
100 Buckshollow Rd (10541-3756)
PHONE..................................845 628-1008
Fax: 845 628-1143
Michael Benalt, *President*
Kevin Briger, *VP Sales*
Kevin Grieger, *Sales Executive*
EMP: 25 EST: 1975
SQ FT: 37,000
SALES (est): 500K **Privately Held**
WEB: www.michaelbenaltinc.com
SIC: 3559 Pharmaceutical machinery

(G-7998)
MORTECH INDUSTRIES INC
961 Route 6 (10541-1796)
P.O. Box 962 (10541-0962)
PHONE..................................845 628-6138
Fax: 845 628-1479
Anthony Morando, *President*

EMP: 8 EST: 1945
SQ FT: 12,000
SALES: 1.5MM Privately Held
SIC: 3541 Grinding, polishing, buffing, lapping & honing machines; buffing & polishing machines

(G-7999)
NORTHEAST DOULAS
23 Hilltop Dr (10541-2815)
PHONE..................................845 621-0654
Debbie Aglietti, *Principal*
EMP: 5
SALES (est): 667K Privately Held
SIC: 2835 Pregnancy test kits

(G-8000)
RICHS STTCHES EMB SCREENPRINT
407 Route 6 (10541-3783)
PHONE..................................845 621-2175
Rich Schnetzinger, *Owner*
EMP: 5
SALES: 210K Privately Held
SIC: 2759 Screen printing

(G-8001)
RMD HOLDING INC
Also Called: X-Press Printing & Office Sup
593 Route 6 (10541-1682)
PHONE..................................845 628-0030
Richard De Cola, *President*
Marie De Cola, *Vice Pres*
EMP: 8
SQ FT: 2,500
SALES (est): 1MM Privately Held
SIC: 2752 5943 2791 2789 Commercial printing, offset; office forms & supplies; typesetting; bookbinding & related work

(G-8002)
T JN ELECTRIC
116 Cortlandt Rd (10541-3620)
PHONE..................................917 560-0981
Tina Giustino, *Owner*
EMP: 12
SALES (est): 1.5MM Privately Held
SIC: 3699 Electrical equipment & supplies

(G-8003)
T JN ELECTRIC INC
901 Route 6 (10541-1717)
PHONE..................................845 628-6970
Tina Giustino, *President*
EMP: 5
SALES (est): 413.8K Privately Held
SIC: 3699 Electrical equipment & supplies

(G-8004)
WALSH & SONS MACHINE INC
15 Secor Rd Ste 5 (10541-2078)
PHONE..................................845 526-0301
Fax: 845 526-8367
Frank Walsh, *President*
EMP: 6
SALES (est): 530K Privately Held
SIC: 3599 Machine shop, jobbing & repair

Malone
Franklin County

(G-8005)
ADIRONDACK ICE & AIR INC
Also Called: Adirondex
26 Railroad St (12953-1014)
PHONE..................................518 483-4340
Fax: 518 481-2468
James McKee, *Ch of Bd*
Tim Boyea, *Vice Pres*
Melanie Andrews, *Project Mgr*
Katie Smith, *Office Mgr*
Molly Mc Kee, *Admin Sec*
EMP: 14 EST: 1968
SQ FT: 4,800
SALES (est): 1.6MM Privately Held
SIC: 2097 4222 5499 7389 Manufactured ice; storage, frozen or refrigerated goods; water: distilled mineral or spring; coffee service

(G-8006)
ADIRONDACK POWER SPORTS
5378 State Route 37 (12953-4114)
P.O. Box 390 (12953-0390)
PHONE..................................518 481-6269
John Waters, *General Mgr*
EMP: 8 EST: 2013
SQ FT: 5,000
SALES (est): 590K Privately Held
SIC: 3799 5012 Recreational vehicles; recreation vehicles, all-terrain

(G-8007)
ASEPT PAK INC
64 West St (12953-1118)
PHONE..................................518 651-2026
Gary L Hanley, *Ch of Bd*
EMP: 22 EST: 2004
SALES (est): 5.2MM Privately Held
SIC: 2833 Organic medicinal chemicals: bulk, uncompounded

(G-8008)
COCA-COLA BOTTLING COMPANY
15 Ida Pkwy (12953)
PHONE..................................518 483-0422
Ron Lavalley, *Branch Mgr*
EMP: 28
SALES (corp-wide): 17.8B Privately Held
SIC: 2086 Bottled & canned soft drinks
HQ: The Coca-Cola Bottling Company Of Northern New England Inc
 1 Executive Park Dr # 330
 Bedford NH 03110
 603 627-7871

(G-8009)
FASPRINT
20 Finney Blvd (12953-1039)
P.O. Box 832 (12953-0832)
PHONE..................................518 483-4631
Fax: 518 483-0504
Tammi M Dupont, *Owner*
Royal Forgues, *Opers-Prdtn-Mfg*
EMP: 6
SQ FT: 2,000
SALES (est): 683.4K Privately Held
SIC: 2752 Commercial printing, lithographic

(G-8010)
GRAYMONT MATERIALS (NY) INC
Also Called: Malone Concrete Products Div
359 Elm St (12953-1500)
P.O. Box 457, North Bangor (12966-0457)
PHONE..................................518 483-2671
Fax: 518 483-7833
Jim Odis, *Manager*
EMP: 6
SALES (corp-wide): 260.9MM Privately Held
WEB: www.graymont-ab.com
SIC: 3272 Concrete products
HQ: Graymont Materials (Ny) Inc.
 111 Quarry Rd
 Plattsburgh NY 12901
 518 561-5321

(G-8011)
JOHNSON NEWSPAPER CORPORATION
Also Called: Malone News
469 E Main St Ste 2 (12953-2128)
PHONE..................................518 483-4700
Chuck Kelly, *Manager*
EMP: 20
SALES (corp-wide): 32MM Privately Held
WEB: www.ogd.com
SIC: 2711 Newspapers: publishing only, not printed on site
PA: Johnson Newspaper Corporation
 260 Washington St
 Watertown NY
 315 782-1000

(G-8012)
LOMIR INC
213 W Main St (12953-9577)
P.O. Box 778 (12953-0778)
PHONE..................................518 483-7697
Fax: 518 483-8195
Teresa Price, *CEO*
Teresa Woodger, *President*
Karen Coles, *General Mgr*
Mr Tom Long, *Chairman*
EMP: 16
SQ FT: 10,000
SALES (est): 1.6MM Privately Held
WEB: www.lomir.com
SIC: 3821 Laboratory equipment: fume hoods, distillation racks, etc.
PA: Lomir Biomedical Inc
 95 Rue Huot
 Notre-Dame-De-L'Ile-Perrot QC J7V 7
 514 425-3604

(G-8013)
MALONE INDUSTRIAL PRESS INC
10 Stevens St (12953-1634)
P.O. Box 267 (12953-0267)
PHONE..................................518 483-5880
Fax: 518 483-4942
Bernard Desnoyers, *President*
EMP: 6 EST: 1939
SQ FT: 3,000
SALES: 725K Privately Held
SIC: 2752 5111 2759 Commercial printing, offset; printing paper; letterpress printing

(G-8014)
MALONE NEWSPAPERS CORP
Also Called: Malone Telegram
469 E Main St Ste 2 (12953-2128)
PHONE..................................518 483-2000
Fax: 518 483-8579
John B Johnson Jr, *CEO*
Connie Jenkins, *Principal*
Russell Webster, *Principal*
Elizabeth Cordes, *Editor*
Betsy McGivney, *Auditor*
EMP: 30
SQ FT: 2,000
SALES (est): 1.9MM
SALES (corp-wide): 32MM Privately Held
WEB: www.malonetelegram.com
SIC: 2711 Newspapers
PA: Johnson Newspaper Corporation
 260 Washington St
 Watertown NY
 315 782-1000

(G-8015)
SCOTTS FEED INC
Also Called: Collins Pet & Garden Center
245 Elm St (12953-1541)
PHONE..................................518 483-3110
Fax: 518 483-3147
Scott Collins, *President*
Tom Schildkamp, *Manager*
EMP: 23
SQ FT: 6,000
SALES (est): 4.9MM Privately Held
SIC: 2048 5191 Prepared feeds; animal feeds

(G-8016)
SEAWAY MATS INC
Also Called: Sea Mats
252 Park St (12953-1234)
P.O. Box 407 (12953-0407)
PHONE..................................518 483-2560
Roy Hamilton, *CEO*
Diane Hamilton, *Vice Pres*
EMP: 7
SALES (est): 945.8K
SALES (corp-wide): 2.2MM Privately Held
SIC: 3069 3949 3089 2391 Mats or matting, rubber; nets: badminton, volleyball, tennis, etc.; composition stone, plastic; doors, folding: plastic or plastic coated fabric; curtains & draperies
PA: Seaway Plastics Ltd
 270 Boul Saint-Joseph
 Lachine QC H8S 2
 514 637-2323

(G-8017)
SIGNS INC
2 Boyer Ave (12953-1628)
P.O. Box 185 (12953-0185)
PHONE..................................518 483-4759
Judy Sousie, *President*
Shannon Niles, *Treasurer*
EMP: 5
SALES (est): 400K Privately Held
SIC: 3993 Signs & advertising specialties

(G-8018)
TITUS MOUNTAIN SAND & GRAV LLC
17 Junction Rd (12953-4217)
P.O. Box 390 (12953-0390)
PHONE..................................518 483-3740
William Hewitt, *Mng Member*
EMP: 8
SALES (est): 761K Privately Held
SIC: 1442 Construction sand & gravel

Malta
Saratoga County

(G-8019)
GLOBALFOUNDRIES US INC
400 Stone Break Rd Ext (12020)
PHONE..................................518 305-9013
Bill Barrett, *Vice Pres*
Deborah Leupold, *Site Mgr*
H Modlin, *Production*
Ram Asra, *Engineer*
Julia Bauwin, *Engineer*
EMP: 144 Privately Held
SIC: 3369 3572 Nonferrous foundries; computer disk & drum drives & components
HQ: Globalfoundries U.S. Inc.
 2600 Great America Way
 Santa Clara CA 95054
 408 462-3900

(G-8020)
GOLUB CORPORATION
Also Called: Price Chopper Pharmacy 184
3 Hemphill Pl Ste 116 (12020-4419)
PHONE..................................518 899-6063
Rob Russell, *Branch Mgr*
EMP: 78
SALES (corp-wide): 3.4B Privately Held
SIC: 3751 Motorcycles & related parts
PA: The Golub Corporation
 461 Nott St
 Schenectady NY 12308
 518 355-5000

(G-8021)
TOKYO ELECTRON AMERICA INC
2 Bayberry Dr (12020-6352)
PHONE..................................518 289-3100
Fax: 518 289-3101
Tetsuo Tsuneishi, *Branch Mgr*
EMP: 5
SALES (corp-wide): 5.6B Privately Held
SIC: 3559 Semiconductor manufacturing machinery
HQ: Tokyo Electron America, Inc.
 2400 Grove Blvd
 Austin TX 78741
 512 424-1000

(G-8022)
WIRED COFFEE AND BAGEL INC
Rr 9 (12020)
PHONE..................................518 506-3194
Matthew J Michele, *President*
EMP: 12
SALES (est): 1.2MM Privately Held
SIC: 3556 5812 Roasting machinery: coffee, peanut, etc.; lunchrooms & cafeterias

Mamaroneck
Westchester County

(G-8023)
AUTOMATED BUILDING CONTROLS
629 N Barry Ave (10543-1608)
PHONE..................................914 381-2860
Barry Novick, *President*
Mary Ellen Keefer, *Office Mgr*
Maryellen Kiefas, *Manager*
EMP: 8
SQ FT: 400

Mamaroneck - Westchester County (G-8024)

SALES: 800K **Privately Held**
SIC: 3822 Auto controls regulating residntl & coml environmt & applncs; temperature controls, automatic

(G-8024)
BASSIN TECHNICAL SALES CO
Also Called: Press Air
1009 W Boston Post Rd # 2 (10543-3329)
PHONE....................914 698-9358
Fax: 914 698-9456
Gilbert Bassin, *Owner*
EMP: 40
SQ FT: 450
SALES (est): 3.6MM **Privately Held**
WEB: www.pressair.com
SIC: 3643 Electric switches

(G-8025)
BRANDS WITHIN REACH LLC
Also Called: AMI Brands
141 Halstead Ave Ste 201 (10543-2652)
PHONE....................847 720-9090
Nicolas Merlen, *District Mgr*
Ryan Sowards, *Regl Sales Mgr*
Oliver Sonnois, *Mng Member*
Olivier Sonnois, *Mng Member*
▲ EMP: 24
SQ FT: 2,500
SALES (est): 5.3MM **Privately Held**
SIC: 2086 Bottled & canned soft drinks

(G-8026)
CARPET FABRICATIONS INTL
628 Waverly Ave Ste 1 (10543-2259)
PHONE....................914 381-6060
Fax: 914 381-6090
Thomas L Budetti, *President*
Edward Soto, *Vice Pres*
▲ EMP: 23
SQ FT: 15,000
SALES (est): 2.3MM **Privately Held**
SIC: 2273 5023 Carpets & rugs; floor coverings

(G-8027)
CATHOLIC NEWS PUBLISHING CO
Also Called: School Guide Publications
606 Halstead Ave (10543-2718)
PHONE....................914 632-7771
Fax: 914 632-3412
Myles A Ridder, *President*
Joseph Ridder, *Treasurer*
EMP: 15
SQ FT: 5,200
SALES: 3MM **Privately Held**
WEB: www.schoolguides.com
SIC: 2741 7372 Directories: publishing only, not printed on site; publishers' computer software

(G-8028)
CHOCOLATIONS LLC
607 E Boston Post Rd (10543-3742)
PHONE....................914 777-3600
Maria Valente,
EMP: 5
SALES: 200K **Privately Held**
SIC: 2064 Candy & other confectionery products

(G-8029)
COLDSTREAM GROUP INC (PA)
Also Called: Nessen Lighting, The
420 Railroad Way (10543-2257)
P.O. Box 187 (10543-0187)
PHONE....................914 698-5959
Fax: 914 698-5577
Bob Henderson, *President*
Ralph Izzi, *Controller*
Jim Hayworth, *Manager*
▲ EMP: 19
SALES (est): 9.6MM **Privately Held**
SIC: 3648 Lighting equipment

(G-8030)
CORIUM CORPORATION (PA)
Also Called: Cromwell Group
147 Palmer Ave (10543-3632)
PHONE....................914 381-0100
Thomas Fleisch, *President*
Margaret Zulkowsky, *Vice Pres*
Richard Gilbert, *Plant Mgr*
Rick Derr, *Treasurer*
Nanci Maida, *Admin Asst*

▲ EMP: 18
SALES (est): 4.3MM **Privately Held**
WEB: www.coriumcorp.com
SIC: 3111 Leather tanning & finishing

(G-8031)
CULIN/COLELLA INC
632 Center Ave (10543-2206)
PHONE....................914 698-7727
Fax: 914 698-6457
Raynsford Culin, *President*
Janice Colella Culin, *Corp Secy*
EMP: 9 EST: 1975
SQ FT: 10,000
SALES: 1.1MM **Privately Held**
WEB: www.culincolella.com
SIC: 2521 2519 Wood office furniture; cabinets, office: wood; household furniture, except wood or metal: upholstered

(G-8032)
DAC LIGHTING INC
420 Railroad Way (10543-2257)
P.O. Box 262 (10543-0262)
PHONE....................914 698-5959
Larry K Powers, *President*
Robert Haidinger Jr, *Vice Pres*
Ralph Izzi, *Treasurer*
▲ EMP: 45
SQ FT: 32,000
SALES (est): 2.8MM
SALES (corp-wide): 9.6MM **Privately Held**
WEB: www.daclighting.com
SIC: 3646 Commercial indusl & institutional electric lighting fixtures
PA: Coldstream Group Inc
   420 Railroad Way
   Mamaroneck NY 10543
   914 698-5959

(G-8033)
DIVISION DEN-BAR ENTERPRISES
Also Called: Arborn Printing & Graphics
745 W Boston Post Rd (10543-3320)
PHONE....................914 381-2220
Fax: 914 381-6404
Barry Arborn, *President*
Denise Arborn, *Vice Pres*
Bruce Sherling, *Vice Pres*
Michael Arborn, *Manager*
Billie Karner, *Manager*
EMP: 5
SQ FT: 1,000
SALES: 650K **Privately Held**
SIC: 2759 2789 Commercial printing; bookbinding & related work

(G-8034)
FAMILY PUBLISHING GROUP INC
Also Called: New York Familypublications
141 Halstead Ave (10543-2607)
PHONE....................914 381-7474
Fax: 914 381-7672
EMP: 20
SQ FT: 1,200
SALES (est): 1.8MM **Privately Held**
SIC: 2721 2731 Periodicals-Publishing/Printing Books-Publishing/Printing

(G-8035)
GANNETT STLLITE INFO NTWRK INC
Also Called: Gannett Suburban Newspapers
700 Waverly Ave (10543-2262)
PHONE....................914 381-3400
Larry James, *Manager*
EMP: 16
SQ FT: 6,000
SALES (corp-wide): 5.7B **Publicly Held**
WEB: www.usatoday.com
SIC: 2711 Newspapers
HQ: Gannett Satellite Information Network, Llc
   7950 Jones Branch Dr
   Mc Lean VA 22102
   703 854-6000

(G-8036)
INFLATION SYSTEMS INC
500 Ogden Ave (10543-2227)
PHONE....................914 381-8070

Sandra Goldman, *President*
Robert Goldman, *Vice Pres*
Sandra Machic, *Vice Pres*
EMP: 20
SQ FT: 7,500
SALES (est): 3.4MM **Privately Held**
SIC: 3069 Valves, hard rubber; hard rubber & molded rubber products

(G-8037)
MARINE & INDUS HYDRAULICS INC
329 Center Ave (10543-2304)
PHONE....................914 698-2036
John J Wright, *President*
Howard Fessel, *Prdtn Mgr*
Brooks Wright, *VP Finance*
Louis Pesapane, *Manager*
▲ EMP: 10
SQ FT: 10,000
SALES (est): 1.9MM **Privately Held**
SIC: 3625 Actuators, industrial

(G-8038)
MARVAL INDUSTRIES INC
Also Called: M I I
315 Hoyt Ave (10543-1899)
PHONE....................914 381-2400
Fax: 914 381-2259
Alan Zimmerman, *CEO*
Thomas Zimmerman, *Ch of Bd*
Emil Kocur, *Vice Pres*
Joyce Zimmerman, *Admin Sec*
▲ EMP: 70
SQ FT: 54,000
SALES (est): 39.6MM **Privately Held**
WEB: www.marvalindustries.com
SIC: 2869 5162 3089 3087 Industrial organic chemicals; plastics materials; thermoformed finished plastic products; custom compound purchased resins

(G-8039)
MDJ SALES ASSOCIATES INC
27 Doris Rd (10543-1009)
PHONE....................914 420-5897
Michael Aaronson, *CEO*
EMP: 5
SALES: 750K **Privately Held**
SIC: 2253 Knit outerwear mills

(G-8040)
ON THE JOB EMBROIDERY & AP
154 E Boston Post Rd # 1 (10543-3755)
PHONE....................914 381-3556
Michael Federici, *President*
Joseph Bilotto, *Vice Pres*
EMP: 5
SALES (est): 320K **Privately Held**
SIC: 2395 Embroidery products, except schiffli machine

(G-8041)
PALETERIA FERNANDEZ INC
350 Mamaroneck Ave (10543-2608)
PHONE....................914 315-1598
Ignacio Fernandez, *CEO*
EMP: 28
SALES (corp-wide): 981.7K **Privately Held**
SIC: 2024 Ice cream, bulk
PA: Paleteria Fernandez Inc.
   33 N Main St
   Port Chester NY 10573
   914 939-3694

(G-8042)
PICONE MEAT SPECIALTIES LTD
Also Called: Picone's Sausage
180 Jefferson Ave (10543-1912)
PHONE....................914 381-3002
Fax: 914 381-1139
Frank Picone, *President*
Anthony Picone, *Vice Pres*
EMP: 8
SQ FT: 6,600
SALES: 3MM **Privately Held**
SIC: 2013 Sausages & other prepared meats

(G-8043)
POLKADOT USA INC
33 Country Rd (10543-1108)
PHONE....................914 835-3697
Debra Schoenau, *President*

Howard Friedman, *Vice Pres*
EMP: 2
SQ FT: 6,000
SALES: 2MM **Privately Held**
WEB: www.polkadotusa.com
SIC: 2396 Apparel & other linings, except millinery

(G-8044)
RICHARD ENGDAL BAKING CORP
Also Called: Hudson Valley Baking Co
421 Waverly Ave (10543-2233)
PHONE....................914 777-9600
Fax: 914 937-9450
Richard Cuozzo, *President*
EMP: 10
SQ FT: 4,000
SALES (est): 1.2MM **Privately Held**
SIC: 2051 Bakery: wholesale or wholesale/retail combined

(G-8045)
ROBERT E DERECKTOR INC
Also Called: Derecktor Shipyards
311 E Boston Post Rd (10543-3738)
PHONE....................914 698-0962
Fax: 914 698-6596
Eric P Derecktor, *Ch of Bd*
E Paul Derecktor, *Ch of Bd*
Mark S Donahue, *Vice Pres*
Mark Donahue, *Vice Pres*
Steve Drago, *Project Mgr*
▲ EMP: 80 EST: 1947
SQ FT: 64,000
SALES (est): 16.3MM **Privately Held**
SIC: 3732 3731 4493 7699 Boat building & repairing; fishing boats: lobster, crab, oyster, etc.: small; yachts, building & repairing; ferryboats, building & repairing; boat yards, storage & incidental repair; boat repair; sheet metalwork; fabricated structural metal

(G-8046)
SECOR MARKETING GROUP INC
Also Called: Nisonger Instrument Sls & Svc
225 Hoyt Ave (10543-1835)
PHONE....................914 381-3600
Fax: 914 381-1786
Peter Bayer, *President*
Robert Castagnetta, *Vice Pres*
Neal Dorf, *Treasurer*
EMP: 6
SQ FT: 3,200
SALES (est): 656.1K **Privately Held**
SIC: 3714 5521 Motor vehicle parts & accessories; fuel systems & parts, motor vehicle; automobiles, used cars only

(G-8047)
SHORE LINE MONOGRAMMING INC
Also Called: Shore Line Momogramming & EMB
115 Hoyt Ave (10543-1891)
PHONE....................914 698-8000
John Moller, *President*
Andrew Moller, *President*
David Griffith, *General Mgr*
Ann Saccomanno, *Bookkeeper*
EMP: 12
SQ FT: 18,000
SALES (est): 1.3MM **Privately Held**
SIC: 2759 5941 Screen printing; sporting goods & bicycle shops

(G-8048)
TOM & JERRY PRINTCRAFT FORMS (PA)
960 Mamaroneck Ave (10543-1631)
P.O. Box 743 (10543-0743)
PHONE....................914 777-7468
Fax: 914 698-1085
Thomas La Guidice, *President*
Phil Caragine, *Treasurer*
Mattie Saporito, *Bookkeeper*
EMP: 22
SQ FT: 5,000
SALES (est): 2.4MM **Privately Held**
WEB: www.printcraftny.com
SIC: 2752 2791 2789 Commercial printing, lithographic; typesetting; bookbinding & related work

(G-8049)
TRIDENT VALVE ACTUATOR CO
329 Center Ave (10543-2304)
PHONE..................................914 698-2650
Fax: 914 698-5629
John Cermanski, *General Mgr*
John Samanski, *General Mgr*
John Wright, *Principal*
Lucille Rende, *Plant Mgr*
Kathleen Wright, *Treasurer*
EMP: 12
SQ FT: 10,000
SALES (est): 1.1MM **Privately Held**
SIC: 3625 5085 Actuators, industrial; valves & fittings

(G-8050)
WHITE PLAINS DRAPERY UPHL INC
Also Called: Commercial Draperies Unlimited
801 E Boston Post Rd (10543-4143)
PHONE..................................914 381-0908
Fax: 914 381-0705
James Lanera, *President*
Sally Lanera, *Vice Pres*
Rose Marie Lanera, *Treasurer*
EMP: 24
SQ FT: 5,000
SALES (est): 3.3MM **Privately Held**
WEB: www.commercialdrape.com
SIC: 2221 5714 5719 5023 Upholstery, tapestry & wall covering fabrics; draperies; curtains; upholstery materials; window furnishings; draperies; window furnishings; reupholstery & furniture repair; curtains & draperies

Manchester
Ontario County

(G-8051)
ELITE MACHINE INC
3 Merrick Cir (14504-9740)
P.O. Box 8 (14504-0008)
PHONE..................................585 289-4733
Steve Hawkins, *President*
EMP: 5
SQ FT: 5,304
SALES (est): 451K **Privately Held**
SIC: 3599 Machine shop, jobbing & repair

(G-8052)
ROCHESTER INSULATED GLASS INC
73 Merrick Cir (14504-9740)
P.O. Box 168 (14504-0168)
PHONE..................................585 289-3611
Fax: 585 289-3610
Richard S Wolk, *President*
Gretchen Wolk, *Corp Secy*
Tyler Wolk, *Vice Pres*
Linda Ralston, *Controller*
Andrew Onofrey, *Accounts Mgr*
◆ **EMP:** 55
SALES (est): 15.1MM **Privately Held**
WEB: www.rochesterinsulatedglass.com
SIC: 3231 Insulating glass: made from purchased glass; safety glass: made from purchased glass

(G-8053)
SIDCO FILTER CORPORATION
58 North Ave (14504-9769)
PHONE..................................585 289-3100
Fax: 585 924-0777
Sidney T Cutt, *Ch of Bd*
Bill Florance, *Sales Dir*
Ebba Donner, *Office Mgr*
EMP: 20
SQ FT: 20,000
SALES (est): 4.8MM **Privately Held**
WEB: www.sidcofilter.com
SIC: 3569 Filters

Manhasset
Nassau County

(G-8054)
ADVANCED PROSTHETICS ORTHOTICS
Also Called: Joyce Center
50 Maple Pl (11030-1927)
PHONE..................................516 365-7225
Fax: 516 365-7112
Michael A Joyce, *President*
Cheryl Caruso, *Manager*
EMP: 10
SALES (est): 1.4MM **Privately Held**
SIC: 3842 Prosthetic appliances; orthopedic appliances

(G-8055)
CABINETRY BY TBR INC
1492 Northern Blvd (11030-3006)
PHONE..................................516 365-8500
Basiliki Ypsilantis, *Principal*
EMP: 8
SALES (est): 430K **Privately Held**
SIC: 2434 Wood kitchen cabinets

(G-8056)
CALIBRATED INSTRUMENTS INC
306 Aerie Ct (11030-4053)
PHONE..................................914 741-5700
John B Shroyer, *President*
Angela Perry, *Bookkeeper*
▲ **EMP:** 10
SALES (est): 1.6MM **Privately Held**
SIC: 3823 On-stream gas/liquid analysis instruments, industrial

(G-8057)
DAVID YURMAN ENTERPRISES LLC
2046 Northern Blvd (11030-3540)
PHONE..................................516 627-1700
Julie Freeman, *Store Mgr*
Caryn Amandola, *Manager*
Evelyn Santiago, *Senior Mgr*
EMP: 6
SALES (corp-wide): 268.2MM **Privately Held**
SIC: 3911 Jewelry, precious metal
PA: David Yurman Enterprises Llc
24 Vestry St
New York NY 10013
212 896-1550

(G-8058)
DEEP DYEING INC
120 Bayview Ave (11030-1849)
PHONE..................................718 418-7187
Fax: 718 418-7188
Edvart Mouradian, *President*
Alis Mouradian, *Vice Pres*
Arsen Mouradian, *Vice Pres*
EMP: 13
SQ FT: 10,000
SALES (est): 1.8MM **Privately Held**
SIC: 2865 Dyes & pigments

(G-8059)
DOHNSCO INC
19 Gracewood Dr (11030-3931)
PHONE..................................516 773-4800
EMP: 5
SQ FT: 2,100
SALES (est): 310K **Privately Held**
SIC: 2741 7379 Misc Publishing Computer Related Services

(G-8060)
FRAME SHOPPE & ART GALLERY
Also Called: Frame Shoppe & Gallery
447 Plandome Rd (11030-1942)
PHONE..................................516 365-6014
Demitri Kazianis, *Partner*
Thomas Walsh, *Partner*
EMP: 6
SALES (est): 429.6K **Privately Held**
SIC: 2499 3499 7699 5999 Picture frame molding, finished; picture frames, metal; picture framing, custom; art dealers; gift shop

(G-8061)
GOLF DIRECTORIES USA INC
39 Orchard St Ste 7 (11030-1969)
PHONE..................................516 365-5351
Ray Cyrgalis, *President*
EMP: 5
SQ FT: 1,000
SALES (est): 296.4K **Privately Held**
SIC: 2741 Telephone & other directory publishing

(G-8062)
MDR PRINTING CORP
Also Called: Minuteman Press
490 Plandome Rd (11030-1944)
PHONE..................................516 627-3221
Fax: 516 365-8271
Les Forrai, *President*
EMP: 5
SQ FT: 1,200
SALES (est): 590K **Privately Held**
WEB: www.manhassetminuteman.com
SIC: 2752 Commercial printing, lithographic

(G-8063)
NATIONAL SECURITY SYSTEMS INC
511 Manhasset Woods Rd (11030-1663)
PHONE..................................516 627-2222
Jay Baron, *President*
John W Walter, *Chairman*
William T Walter, *Vice Pres*
Joan Walter, *Admin Sec*
EMP: 26 **EST:** 1958
SQ FT: 3,200
SALES (est): 34.6MM **Privately Held**
WEB: www.plazaconstruction.com
SIC: 3699 Security control equipment & systems

(G-8064)
PRISCILLA QUART CO FIRTS
160 Plandome Rd Fl 2 (11030-2326)
PHONE..................................516 365-2755
EMP: 6
SALES (est): 278.8K **Privately Held**
SIC: 3131 Quarters

(G-8065)
SUPERIOR FURS INC
1697 Northern Blvd (11030-3026)
PHONE..................................516 365-4123
Tom Djoganopoulos, *President*
EMP: 13
SQ FT: 1,000
SALES (est): 1.1MM **Privately Held**
SIC: 2371 5632 Apparel, fur; furriers

(G-8066)
TECHWEB LLC
600 Community Dr (11030-3802)
PHONE..................................516 562-5000
Charles Babcock, *Editor*
Andrew Conry-Murray, *Editor*
Stacey Peterson, *Editor*
Stephanie Stahl, *Editor*
Rob Koziura, *Sales Staff*
EMP: 16 **EST:** 2010
SALES (est): 1.5MM **Privately Held**
SIC: 2721 Magazines: publishing only, not printed on site

Manlius
Onondaga County

(G-8067)
BASILEUS COMPANY LLC
8104 Cazenovia Rd (13104-6700)
PHONE..................................315 963-3516
Maribeth Homa, *Bookkeeper*
Jacqueline B Wilson, *Sales Mgr*
Gerald E Wilson, *Mng Member*
◆ **EMP:** 10
SQ FT: 2,215
SALES (est): 940K **Privately Held**
SIC: 2211 Apparel & outerwear fabrics, cotton

(G-8068)
CARPENTER MANUFACTURING CO
110 Fairgrounds Dr (13104-2481)
P.O. Box 188 (13104-0188)
PHONE..................................315 682-9176
Fax: 315 682-9160
Thomas Carpenter, *President*
Susan C Sorensen, *Vice Pres*
Andrew Miller, *Engineer*
Kenneth Carpenter, *Shareholder*
EMP: 20 **EST:** 1955
SQ FT: 14,500
SALES (est): 4MM **Privately Held**
WEB: www.carpentermfg.com
SIC: 3549 Wiredrawing & fabricating machinery & equipment, ex. die; cutting & slitting machinery

(G-8069)
CAYUGA ENTERPRISE 21
4384 Pompey Center Rd (13104-9365)
P.O. Box 62 (13104-0062)
PHONE..................................607 441-9166
Mark Ranalli,
EMP: 6
SALES (est): 500K **Privately Held**
SIC: 2075 Soybean oil mills

(G-8070)
CREATIVE YARD DESIGNS INC
8329 Us Route 20 (13104-9536)
PHONE..................................315 706-6143
EMP: 5
SALES (est): 312.1K **Privately Held**
SIC: 3271 Blocks, concrete: landscape or retaining wall

(G-8071)
FILTER TECH INC (PA)
113 Fairgrounds Dr (13104-2497)
P.O. Box 527 (13104-0527)
PHONE..................................315 682-8815
Fax: 315 682-8825
Ahmad E Hindi, *CEO*
Joseph F Scalise, *President*
Elizabeth Elhindi, *Vice Pres*
Tom Horn, *Sales Mgr*
Glenn Davies, *Manager*
▼ **EMP:** 59
SQ FT: 10,000
SALES (est): 11.1MM **Privately Held**
WEB: www.filtertech.com
SIC: 3569 Filters, general line: industrial; lubricating systems, centralized

(G-8072)
GLOBAL INSTRUMENTATION LLC
8104 Cazenovia Rd Ste 2/3 (13104-6700)
PHONE..................................315 682-0272
James Demaso, *Mng Member*
Scott Meyers,
Craig Sellers,
EMP: 10
SALES (est): 1.9MM **Privately Held**
WEB: www.globalinstrumentation.com
SIC: 3845 Ultrasonic scanning devices, medical

(G-8073)
L& JG STICKLEY INCORPORATED (PA)
1 Stickley Dr (13104-2485)
P.O. Box 480 (13104-0480)
PHONE..................................315 682-5500
Fax: 315 682-6306
Aminy I Audi, *Ch of Bd*
Edward Audi, *President*
Jim Christman, *Prdtn Mgr*
Donna Pugh, *Production*
John Brogan, *CFO*
▲ **EMP:** 900 **EST:** 1895
SQ FT: 400,000
SALES (est): 272.4MM **Privately Held**
WEB: www.stickley.com
SIC: 2511 2519 Wood household furniture; household furniture, except wood or metal: upholstered

Manlius - Onondaga County (G-8074) — GEOGRAPHIC SECTION

(G-8074)
MAYBERRY SHOE COMPANY INC
Also Called: Kangaroo Crossing
131 W Seneca St Ste B (13104-2444)
PHONE 315 692-4086
Bruce Mayberry, President
EMP: 5
SQ FT: 500
SALES (est): 530K Privately Held
SIC: 3149 2329 2339 Athletic shoes, except rubber or plastic; men's & boys' athletic uniforms; uniforms, athletic: women's, misses' & juniors'

(G-8075)
MILLER ENTERPRISES CNY INC
Also Called: UPS
131 W Seneca St Ste B (13104-2444)
PHONE 315 682-4999
Christopher Akin, President
EMP: 5
SALES (est): 452.2K Privately Held
SIC: 2752 7334 4783 4513 Commercial printing, lithographic; offset & photolithographic printing; photocopying & duplicating services; packing goods for shipping; package delivery, private air

(G-8076)
VOSS SIGNS LLC
112 Fairgrounds Dr Ste 2 (13104-2437)
P.O. Box 553 (13104-0553)
PHONE 315 682-6418
Fax: 315 682-7335
Debbie Menter, Human Resources
Mary Walser, Sales Mgr
Thomas Tenerovicz, Mktg Dir
Diane Voss, Office Mgr
James Menter, Executive
EMP: 25
SQ FT: 31,000
SALES (est): 4MM Privately Held
WEB: www.vosssigns.com
SIC: 2759 3993 2791 Screen printing; signs & advertising specialties; typesetting

Manorville
Suffolk County

(G-8077)
B&K PRECISION CORPORATION
31 Oakwood Dr (11949-1211)
PHONE 631 369-2665
Ray Kreiger, Branch Mgr
EMP: 5 Privately Held
WEB: www.bkprecision.com
SIC: 3559 Automotive related machinery
PA: B&K Precision Corporation
22820 Savi Ranch Pkwy
Yorba Linda CA 92887

(G-8078)
CPI INDUSTRIES INC
275 Dayton Ave (11949-2029)
PHONE 631 909-3434
Ciro Intini, President
Denise Intini, Opers Mgr
EMP: 55
SALES: 4MM Privately Held
SIC: 3444 Sheet metalwork

(G-8079)
MOTION MESSAGE INC
20 Frontier Trl (11949-2526)
PHONE 631 924-9500
William Sheridan, President
Irene Sheridan, Admin Sec
EMP: 10
SQ FT: 12,000
SALES (est): 820K Privately Held
SIC: 3993 Electric signs

(G-8080)
S A S INDUSTRIES INC
939 Wding River Manor Rd (11949)
P.O. Box 245 (11949-0245)
PHONE 631 727-1441
Fax: 631 727-1387
Steve Steckis, President
A Steckis, Manager
Mitchell Steckis, Info Tech Mgr
▲ EMP: 15 EST: 1973
SQ FT: 10,000
SALES (est): 3.4MM Privately Held
WEB: www.sasindustries.com
SIC: 3053 5085 Gaskets, all materials; industrial supplies

(G-8081)
SPLICE TECHNOLOGIES INC
625 North St (11949-2055)
P.O. Box 644 (11949-0644)
PHONE 631 924-8108
Robert P Auteri, President
Nannette M Auteri, Admin Sec
▼ EMP: 8
SQ FT: 2,000
SALES: 1.2MM Privately Held
WEB: www.splicetechnologies.com
SIC: 3661 Fiber optics communications equipment

(G-8082)
VULCAN IRON WORKS INC
190 Weeks Ave (11949-2034)
PHONE 631 395-6846
Carl Forster, President
Barbara Forster, Office Mgr
EMP: 4 EST: 1926
SQ FT: 1,800
SALES (est): 2MM Privately Held
WEB: www.vulcanironworks.com
SIC: 3441 Fabricated structural metal

Marathon
Cortland County

(G-8083)
GALLERY OF MACHINES LLC
20 Front St (13803-7705)
P.O. Box 460 (13803-0460)
PHONE 607 849-6028
Fax: 607 849-6000
Harry Hartman, President
Brett Hartmam, CFO
Brtittany Donah, Office Mgr
EMP: 9
SQ FT: 46,000
SALES: 12MM Privately Held
WEB: www.galleryofmachines.com
SIC: 3541 Machine tools, metal cutting type

(G-8084)
KURTZ TRUCK EQUIPMENT INC
1085 Mcgraw Marathon Rd (13803-2806)
PHONE 607 849-3468
Mellisa Slack, President
EMP: 18 EST: 1960
SQ FT: 4,000
SALES (est): 3.8MM Privately Held
SIC: 3713 3599 3714 Specialty motor vehicle bodies; machine shop, jobbing & repair; propane conversion equipment, motor vehicle

(G-8085)
MARATHON BOAT GROUP INC
1 Grumman Way (13803-3030)
P.O. Box 549 (13803-0549)
PHONE 607 849-3211
Fax: 607 849-3077
Doug Potter, President
Greg Harvey, Corp Secy
▼ EMP: 15
SQ FT: 24,050
SALES (est): 1MM Privately Held
WEB: www.marathonboat.com
SIC: 3732 5551 Motorized boat, building & repairing; canoes, building & repairing; boat dealers

Marcellus
Onondaga County

(G-8086)
ARMSTRONG TRANSMITTER CORP
4835 N Street Rd (13108-9715)
PHONE 315 673-1269
Fax: 315 673-9972
Sinan Mimaroglu, President
Jim Giatz, General Mgr
Sally Smith, Finance Mgr
Kevin Smith, Marketing Staff
Ahmet Mimaroglu, Manager
EMP: 10
SQ FT: 40,000
SALES (est): 1.2MM Privately Held
WEB: www.armstrongtx.com
SIC: 3663 Transmitting apparatus, radio or television

(G-8087)
CHOCOLATE PIZZA COMPANY INC
3774 Lee Mulroy Rd (13108-9814)
PHONE 315 673-4098
Ryan Novak, Ch of Bd
EMP: 18
SQ FT: 7,000
SALES (est): 3.2MM Privately Held
WEB: www.chocolatepizza.com
SIC: 2066 2064 5149 Chocolate candy, solid; chocolate candy, except solid chocolate; chocolate

(G-8088)
QUIKRETE COMPANIES INC
4993 Limeledge Rd Ste 560 (13108-9798)
PHONE 315 673-2020
Joe Boucher, Sales Staff
Greg Breen, Branch Mgr
EMP: 20 Privately Held
SIC: 3273 Ready-mixed concrete
HQ: Quikrete Companies, Inc.
3490 Piedmont Rd Ne
Atlanta GA 30305
404 634-9100

(G-8089)
SMITH SAND & GRAVEL INC
4782 Shepard Rd (13108-9745)
PHONE 315 673-4124
David J Smith, Ch of Bd
Stacy Feocco, Admin Sec
EMP: 9 EST: 2005
SALES (est): 1.6MM Privately Held
SIC: 1442 Construction sand & gravel

Marcy
Oneida County

(G-8090)
COMMSCOPE TECHNOLOGIES LLC
5662 Mohawk St (13403-2318)
PHONE 315 768-3573
Fax: 315 768-3933
Roger Haines, Manager
EMP: 14
SALES (corp-wide): 5.9B Privately Held
WEB: www.andrew.com
SIC: 3663 Radio & TV communications equipment
HQ: Commscope Technologies Llc
4 Westbrook Corporate Ctr
Westchester IL 60154
708 236-6000

(G-8091)
DEANS PAVING INC
6002 Cavanaugh Rd (13403-2411)
PHONE 315 736-7601
James J Dean, Principal
EMP: 6
SALES: 700K Privately Held
WEB: www.deanspaving.com
SIC: 2951 4959 7521 0782 Asphalt paving mixtures & blocks; sweeping service: road, airport, parking lot, etc.; snowplowing; parking lots; lawn services

(G-8092)
PRAXAIR DISTRIBUTION INC
9432 State Route 49 (13403-2342)
PHONE 315 735-6153
Ron Marson, Manager
EMP: 11
SALES (corp-wide): 10.7B Publicly Held
SIC: 2813 Oxygen, compressed or liquefied; nitrogen; acetylene
HQ: Praxair Distribution, Inc.
39 Old Ridgebury Rd
Danbury CT 06810
203 837-2000

Margaretville
Delaware County

(G-8093)
ROBERT GREENBURG (PA)
Cross Rd (12455)
PHONE 845 586-2226
Robert Greenburg, President
Robert Kane, Vice Pres
Al Bates, Manager
EMP: 5
SQ FT: 2,000
SALES (est): 898.5K Privately Held
SIC: 2851 Epoxy coatings; polyurethane coatings

Marion
Wayne County

(G-8094)
GREEN VALLEY FOODS LLC
3736 S Main St (14505-9751)
PHONE 315 926-4280
Kraig H Kayser,
Timothy Benjamin,
Paul Palmby,
Jeffrey Van Riper,
EMP: 7
SQ FT: 348,000
SALES (est): 283.6K
SALES (corp-wide): 1.2B Publicly Held
SIC: 2033 Vegetables: packaged in cans, jars, etc.; fruits: packaged in cans, jars, etc.
PA: Seneca Foods Corporation
3736 S Main St
Marion NY 14505
315 926-8100

(G-8095)
HADLEYS FAB-WELD INC
4202 Sunset Dr (14505-9538)
PHONE 315 926-5101
Fax: 315 926-0224
Alan Hadley, President
Adriana Hadley, Vice Pres
EMP: 9
SQ FT: 5,800
SALES (est): 1MM Privately Held
WEB: www.hadleyfabweld.com
SIC: 7692 Welding repair

(G-8096)
J & G MACHINE & TOOL CO INC
4510 Smith Rd (14505-9509)
PHONE 315 310-7130
Gary Prutsman, President
EMP: 14
SQ FT: 15,000
SALES: 1.5MM Privately Held
SIC: 3599 Machine shop, jobbing & repair

(G-8097)
PARKER-HANNIFIN CORPORATION
Also Called: Engineered Polymer Systems Div
3967 Buffalo St (14505-9616)
P.O. Box 6 (14505-0006)
PHONE 315 926-4211
Terry Gardner, Mfg Mgr
Sue Remmel, Personnel
Eric Nary, Manager
EMP: 30
SALES (corp-wide): 11.3B Publicly Held
WEB: www.parker.com
SIC: 2821 Plastics materials & resins
PA: Parker-Hannifin Corporation
6035 Parkland Blvd
Cleveland OH 44124
216 896-3000

(G-8098)
PETER C HERMAN INC
5395 Skinner Rd (14505-9406)
PHONE 315 926-4100

Fax: 315 331-0046
Matthew Herman, *President*
Joseph Herman, *Vice Pres*
Diana Harder, *Manager*
EMP: 50
SQ FT: 2,000
SALES (est): 8.1MM **Privately Held**
SIC: 2448 Pallets, wood

(G-8099)
SENECA FOODS CORPORATION (PA)
3736 S Main St (14505-9751)
PHONE 315 926-8100
Fax: 315 926-8300
Arthur S Wolcott, *Ch of Bd*
Kraig H Kayser, *President*
Paul L Palmby, *COO*
Carl A Cichetti, *Senior VP*
Dean E Erstad, *Senior VP*
◆ **EMP:** 50
SQ FT: 348,000
SALES: 1.2B **Publicly Held**
SIC: 2033 2037 Vegetables: packaged in cans, jars, etc.; fruits: packaged in cans, jars, etc.; vegetables, quick frozen & cold pack, excl. potato products; fruits, quick frozen & cold pack (frozen); fruit juices, frozen

(G-8100)
SENECA FOODS CORPORATION
3709 Mill St (14505-9602)
PHONE 315 926-0531
Fax: 315 926-4296
Patricia East, *Accounting Dir*
Mike Hanchette, *Manager*
EMP: 66
SQ FT: 544
SALES (corp-wide): 1.2B **Publicly Held**
SIC: 3411 Metal cans
PA: Seneca Foods Corporation
     3736 S Main St
     Marion NY 14505
     315 926-8100

(G-8101)
SENECA FOODS CORPORATION
Also Called: Vegetable Operations
3732 S Main St (14505-9751)
P.O. Box 996 (14505-0996)
PHONE 315 926-4277
Fax: 315 926-5332
Jim Haukom, *Engineer*
Dan Janke, *Manager*
Jeff Hall, *Manager*
Dennis Magtee, *Manager*
Ben Scherwitz, *Admin Sec*
EMP: 18
SALES (corp-wide): 1.2B **Publicly Held**
SIC: 2033 Vegetables: packaged in cans, jars, etc.
PA: Seneca Foods Corporation
     3736 S Main St
     Marion NY 14505
     315 926-8100

(G-8102)
TEC GLASS & INST LLC
Also Called: Thomas R Schul TEC GL & Inst
4211 Sunset Dr (14505-9556)
PHONE 315 926-7639
Fax: 315 926-5731
Thomas Schul, *Mng Member*
Hope Schul,
EMP: 7
SQ FT: 3,000
SALES: 150K **Privately Held**
WEB: www.tecglass.biz
SIC: 3231 5049 Laboratory glassware; laboratory equipment, except medical or dental

(G-8103)
VERNS MACHINE CO INC
4929 Steel Point Rd (14505-9552)
PHONE 315 926-4223
Fax: 315 926-1005
Al Visingard, *President*
EMP: 28 **EST:** 1975
SQ FT: 8,000
SALES (est): 3.8MM **Privately Held**
SIC: 3541 3599 3451 Machine tools, metal cutting type; machine & other job shop work; screw machine products

(G-8104)
WESSIE MACHINE INC
5229 Steel Point Rd (14505-9534)
PHONE 315 926-4060
Alan Wessie, *President*
EMP: 7
SALES (est): 1MM **Privately Held**
SIC: 3469 Machine parts, stamped or pressed metal

Marlboro
Ulster County

(G-8105)
CIGAR BOX STUDIOS INC
24 Riverview Dr (12542-5310)
PHONE 845 236-9283
Fax: 845 863-1016
Gary Rausenberger, *President*
Michael Girman, *General Mgr*
Nick Rausenberger, *COO*
Lisa Cline, *Project Mgr*
Scott Rausenberger, *Project Mgr*
▲ **EMP:** 14
SQ FT: 20,000
SALES (est): 3.6MM **Privately Held**
WEB: www.cigarboxstudios.com
SIC: 3443 Fabricated plate work (boiler shop)

(G-8106)
ROYAL WINE CORPORATION
Also Called: Royal Kedem Wine
1519 Route 9w (12542-5420)
PHONE 845 236-4000
Solomon Schwartz, *Purchasing*
Michael Herzog, *Branch Mgr*
EMP: 15
SALES (corp-wide): 49.6MM **Privately Held**
SIC: 2084 5182 Wines; wine; liquor
PA: Royal Wine Corporation
     63 Lefante Dr
     Bayonne NJ 07002
     718 384-2400

Masonville
Delaware County

(G-8107)
AXTELL BRADTKE LUMBER CO
113 Beals Pond Rd (13804-2031)
PHONE 607 265-3850
Stuart Axtell, *Partner*
EMP: 6
SALES (est): 554.1K **Privately Held**
SIC: 2421 5211 Sawmills & planing mills, general; lumber products

(G-8108)
MASONVILLE STONE INCORPORATED
12999 State Highway 8 (13804-2119)
PHONE 607 265-3597
David Barnes, *President*
Douglas Barnes, *Vice Pres*
EMP: 8
SQ FT: 7,800
SALES (est): 937.4K **Privately Held**
SIC: 3281 Cut stone & stone products

(G-8109)
WAGNER LOGGING LLC
11188 State Highway 8 (13804-2010)
PHONE 607 467-2347
Dale Wagner, *Partner*
Dana Wagner, *Partner*
Michael Wagner, *Partner*
Richard Wagner, *Partner*
Rodney Wagner, *Partner*
EMP: 5
SALES (est): 310K **Privately Held**
SIC: 2411 Logging

Maspeth
Queens County

(G-8110)
A & A LINE & WIRE CORP
Also Called: Crown Brand Twine
5118 Grand Ave Ste 10 (11378-3031)
PHONE 718 456-2657
Fax: 718 366-8284
Walter Lach, *President*
Fayga Lach, *Treasurer*
Jacob Lach, *Admin Sec*
▲ **EMP:** 15 **EST:** 1963
SQ FT: 16,000
SALES (est): 2.6MM **Privately Held**
SIC: 2298 Twine, cord & cordage; ropes & fiber cables

(G-8111)
AGL INDUSTRIES INC
5912 57th St (11378-3112)
PHONE 718 326-7597
Frank Lofaso, *President*
Farooq Khan, *Controller*
EMP: 50 **EST:** 2012
SQ FT: 4,500
SALES (est): 10MM **Privately Held**
SIC: 3449 Bars, concrete reinforcing: fabricated steel

(G-8112)
AIR LOUVER & DAMPER INC
5670 58th Pl (11378-2348)
PHONE 718 392-3232
Fax: 718 786-5344
James Pascale, *Manager*
EMP: 24
SALES (corp-wide): 3MM **Privately Held**
SIC: 3822 3444 Damper operators: pneumatic, thermostatic, electric; metal ventilating equipment
PA: Air Louver & Damper, Inc
     2121 44th Rd
     Long Island City NY 11101
     718 392-3232

(G-8113)
AIREACTOR INC
5 Railroad Pl (11378-2111)
PHONE 718 326-2433
Fax: 718 326-7179
Ralph Landano, *President*
Paul Pizem, *Manager*
▲ **EMP:** 12 **EST:** 1926
SQ FT: 8,000
SALES (est): 2.2MM **Privately Held**
WEB: www.aireactor.com
SIC: 2842 7699 Specialty cleaning, polishes & sanitation goods; specialty cleaning preparations; deodorants, nonpersonal; miscellaneous building item repair services

(G-8114)
ALL-CITY METAL INC
5435 46th St (11378-1035)
PHONE 718 937-3975
Frank J Buccola, *Ch of Bd*
Roni Lifshitz, *Vice Pres*
Carlene Buccola, *Controller*
EMP: 40
SQ FT: 2,000
SALES (est): 10.1MM **Privately Held**
SIC: 3441 1711 Fabricated structural metal; mechanical contractor

(G-8115)
ALLE PROCESSING CORP
Also Called: Amazing Meals
5620 59th St (11378-2314)
PHONE 718 894-2000
Sam Hollander, *Ch of Bd*
Israel Gross, *President*
Albert Weinstock, *President*
Shlomi Pilo, *General Mgr*
Pinchus Gelbman, *Engineer*
◆ **EMP:** 250 **EST:** 1954
SQ FT: 75,000
SALES (est): 56.9MM **Privately Held**
WEB: www.alleprocessing.com
SIC: 2013 2015 2038 Sausages & other prepared meats; prepared beef products from purchased beef; poultry slaughtering & processing; dinners, frozen & packaged

(G-8116)
AMAX PRINTING INC
6417 Grand Ave (11378-2421)
PHONE 718 384-8600
Fax: 718 384-5628
Anton Chan, *President*
Fanny Fang, *Vice Pres*
EMP: 15
SQ FT: 8,000
SALES (est): 2.1MM **Privately Held**
WEB: www.amaxprinting.com
SIC: 2759 2752 Commercial printing; commercial printing, lithographic

(G-8117)
AMERICA NY RI WANG FD GROUP CO
5885 58th Ave (11378-2721)
PHONE 718 628-8999
Lian You Ye, *President*
Alex Chang, *Administration*
▲ **EMP:** 50 **EST:** 2009
SQ FT: 40,000
SALES: 5MM **Privately Held**
SIC: 2038 Ethnic foods, frozen

(G-8118)
ANDIKE MILLWORK INC (PA)
Also Called: A & M Home Improvement
5818 64th St Fl 2 (11378-2817)
PHONE 718 894-1796
Fax: 718 894-0662
Andrew La Russa, *President*
Mike Machalski, *Vice Pres*
EMP: 1
SQ FT: 6,500
SALES (est): 1MM **Privately Held**
WEB: www.amhomeimprovement.com
SIC: 2434 5211 2499 1521 Wood kitchen cabinets; millwork & lumber; decorative wood & woodwork; single-family home remodeling, additions & repairs

(G-8119)
APEXX OMNI-GRAPHICS INC
5829 64th St (11378-2836)
PHONE 718 326-3330
Fax: 718 326-7317
Larry A Peters, *Ch of Bd*
Luis Arroyo, *Info Tech Mgr*
EMP: 55 **EST:** 1963
SQ FT: 40,000
SALES (est): 10.3MM **Privately Held**
WEB: www.apexxog.com
SIC: 3555 2656 3861 3089 Plates, offset; plates, paper: made from purchased material; plates, photographic (sensitized); plates, plastic; labels, paper: made from purchased material; packaging paper & plastics film, coated & laminated

(G-8120)
ASN INC
Also Called: Tri Star
6020 59th Pl Ste 2 (11378-3349)
PHONE 718 894-0800
Fax: 718 894-4040
Al Nawroth, *President*
Rudy Bove, *Vice Pres*
Rosa Frankly, *Receptionist*
EMP: 40
SALES (est): 1.4MM **Privately Held**
SIC: 2759 2752 Commercial printing; commercial printing, lithographic

(G-8121)
BIMBO BAKERIES USA INC
Also Called: Stroehmann Bakeries 33
5754 Page Pl (11378-2236)
PHONE 718 463-6300
Fax: 718 463-1614
Philip Guglielmetti, *Regl Sales Mgr*
Steven Hartley, *Branch Mgr*
EMP: 117
SALES (corp-wide): 13B **Privately Held**
SIC: 2051 5149 Bread, all types (white, wheat, rye, etc): fresh or frozen; groceries & related products

Maspeth - Queens County (G-8122) — GEOGRAPHIC SECTION

HQ: Bimbo Bakeries Usa, Inc
255 Business Center Dr # 200
Horsham PA 19044
215 347-5500

(G-8122)
COCA-COLA BTLG CO OF NY INC
5902 Borden Ave (11378-1189)
PHONE................................718 326-3334
Fax: 718 326-3491
Anthony Blanchfield, *Opers Mgr*
Mike Linbugh, *Opers Mgr*
Mike Limbaugh, *Mfg Staff*
David Prespitino, *Manager*
Eric Place, *Manager*
EMP: 116
SALES (corp-wide): 44.2B Publicly Held
SIC: 2086 Bottled & canned soft drinks
HQ: The Coca-Cola Bottling Company Of New York Inc
2500 Windy Ridge Pkwy Se
Atlanta GA 30339
770 989-3000

(G-8123)
COCA-COLA BTLG CO OF NY INC
5840 Borden Ave (11378-1106)
PHONE................................718 416-7575
Fax: 718 497-5684
Tom Saliano, *Plant Mgr*
Ricky Ricardo, *Safety Mgr*
Debra Carpianoco, *Finance Mgr*
Sharon Smith, *Manager*
Debra Capobianco, *Executive*
EMP: 20
SALES (corp-wide): 44.2B Publicly Held
SIC: 2086 Bottled & canned soft drinks
HQ: The Coca-Cola Bottling Company Of New York Inc
2500 Windy Ridge Pkwy Se
Atlanta GA 30339
770 989-3000

(G-8124)
CRAFT CUSTOM WOODWORK CO INC
5949 56th Ave (11378-2324)
PHONE................................718 821-2162
Fax: 718 894-6858
Yakov Roitman, *President*
▼ EMP: 10
SQ FT: 3,500
SALES: 600K Privately Held
SIC: 2434 2521 Wood kitchen cabinets; cabinets, office: wood

(G-8125)
CRAFTSMEN WOODWORKERS LTD
5865 Maspeth Ave (11378-2728)
PHONE................................718 326-3350
Fax: 718 326-0269
Joseph Finocchiaro, *Principal*
Maddy Finocchiaro, *Manager*
EMP: 25
SQ FT: 13,000
SALES (est): 3.7MM Privately Held
WEB: www.craftsmenwoodworkers.com
SIC: 2431 Millwork

(G-8126)
CREATIVE IMAGES & APPLIQUE
Also Called: Cyber Swag Merchandise of NY
5208 Grand Ave Ste 2 (11378-3032)
PHONE................................718 821-8700
Bob Andreoli, *President*
Roger Clark, *Vice Pres*
EMP: 63
SQ FT: 14,500
SALES (est): 6.5MM Privately Held
SIC: 2396 Screen printing on fabric articles

(G-8127)
D & G SHEET METAL CO INC
5400 Grand Ave (11378-3006)
PHONE................................718 326-9111
Fax: 718 326-0990
Frank Doka, *President*
EMP: 12
SQ FT: 12,400
SALES (est): 1.3MM Privately Held
SIC: 3444 Sheet metalwork

(G-8128)
DAL-TILE CORPORATION
5840 55th Dr (11378-1152)
PHONE................................718 894-9574
Gary Guarascio, *Manager*
EMP: 6
SALES (corp-wide): 8B Publicly Held
WEB: www.mohawk.com
SIC: 2824 5032 Organic fibers, noncellulosic; ceramic wall & floor tile
HQ: Dal-Tile Corporation
7834 C F Hawn Fwy
Dallas TX 75217
214 398-1411

(G-8129)
DAYLIGHT TECHNOLOGY USA INC
5971 59th St (11378-3229)
PHONE................................973 255-8100
Reawei Lee, *President*
▲ EMP: 5 EST: 2013
SQ FT: 2,000
SALES: 2.3MM Privately Held
SIC: 3229 Bulbs for electric lights

(G-8130)
DIAMOND CORING & CUTTING INC
5919 55th St (11378-3103)
PHONE................................718 381-4545
David Obbink, *President*
EMP: 5
SALES: 80K Privately Held
SIC: 3531 Construction machinery

(G-8131)
DICKARD WIDDER INDUSTRIES INC
5602 Maspeth Ave (11378-2248)
PHONE................................718 326-3700
Fax: 718 894-0326
Steven Slaven, *President*
Charles Hollander, *Exec VP*
James Widder, *Vice Pres*
Steven Weisbrot, *Opers Mgr*
Charles Opolinsky, *Sales Staff*
▲ EMP: 200 EST: 1984
SQ FT: 150,000
SALES (est): 22.9MM Privately Held
WEB: www.dickardwidder.com
SIC: 2782 Sample books

(G-8132)
DSI GROUP INC
Also Called: Ovation Instore
5713 49th St (11378-2020)
PHONE................................800 553-2202
Benjamin S Weshler, *Ch of Bd*
Mindy Kaufman, *COO*
Melissa Oratz, *Exec VP*
Jonathan Palmer, *Senior VP*
Jose Mosquea, *Plant Mgr*
▲ EMP: 200
SQ FT: 130,000
SALES (est): 54.8MM Privately Held
SIC: 3993 Displays & cutouts, window & lobby

(G-8133)
DURA FOAM INC
6302 59th Ave (11378-2808)
PHONE................................718 894-2488
Fax: 718 894-2493
Antony Fontana, *President*
Donna Broselofsky, *Manager*
Gary Hall, *Manager*
EMP: 35 EST: 1977
SQ FT: 50,000
SALES (est): 5.2MM Privately Held
SIC: 3086 Plastics foam products

(G-8134)
DYNASTY STAINLESS STEEL & META
5985 Maurice Ave (11378-1236)
PHONE................................718 205-6623
Peter Liou, *President*
Alicia Lee, *Manager*
Mingkunn Lee, *Manager*
EMP: 30
SQ FT: 120,000
SALES (est): 6.2MM Privately Held
SIC: 3444 1542 Sheet metalwork; nonresidential construction

(G-8135)
EAST CAST ENVLOPE GRAPHICS LLC
5615 55th Dr (11378-1108)
PHONE................................718 326-2424
Fax: 718 894-1570
Leslie Stern, *President*
Alfred Wilkowski, *COO*
Maribel Corchado, *Vice Pres*
Tim Fraraell, *Purch Agent*
Patrick Nunziante, *CFO*
EMP: 41
SQ FT: 78,000
SALES: 8MM Privately Held
WEB: www.interstate-envelope.com
SIC: 2677 Envelopes

(G-8136)
EAST COAST INTL TIRE INC
5746 Flushing Ave Bldg C (11378-3120)
PHONE................................718 386-9088
EMP: 10
SALES (est): 1.3MM Privately Held
SIC: 3011 Tires & inner tubes
PA: Qingdao Taining Industry Co., Ltd.
No.247, 308 National Highway, Hai'er Industrial Zone, Laoshan Di
Qingdao
532 886-0033

(G-8137)
ELDORADO COFFEE ROASTERS LTD
Also Called: Eldorado Coffee Distributors
5675 49th St (11378-2012)
PHONE................................718 418-4100
Segundo Martin, *President*
Amparo Martin, *Vice Pres*
Andres Martin, *Vice Pres*
Juan Martin, *Vice Pres*
Rosendo Cruz, *Financial Exec*
▲ EMP: 80 EST: 1980
SQ FT: 54,000
SALES (est): 19.1MM Privately Held
WEB: www.eldoradocoffee.com
SIC: 2095 Coffee extracts; coffee roasting (except by wholesale grocers)

(G-8138)
FALLON INC
5930 56th Rd (11378-2330)
PHONE................................718 326-7226
Steven Rosenblatt, *President*
EMP: 20
SQ FT: 27,000
SALES (est): 1.6MM Privately Held
WEB: www.structuralprocessing.com
SIC: 3471 Anodizing (plating) of metals or formed products

(G-8139)
FINAL DIMENSION INC
57-401 59th St Fl 1 (11378)
PHONE................................718 786-0100
Labros Magoutas, *President*
EMP: 5
SQ FT: 3,000
SALES: 150K Privately Held
SIC: 2511 Wood household furniture

(G-8140)
FREQUENCY SELECTIVE NETWORKS
5572 61st St (11378-2411)
PHONE................................718 424-7500
Julius Tischkewitsch, *President*
Sid Lande, *Vice Pres*
Mike Izzolo, *Sales Staff*
Christine Wingate, *Office Mgr*
EMP: 15
SQ FT: 10,000
SALES (est): 1.9MM Privately Held
SIC: 3677 Electronic coils, transformers & other inductors; filtration devices, electronic

(G-8141)
GREAT AMERICAN DESSERT CO LLC
5842 Maurice Ave (11378-2333)
PHONE................................718 894-3494
Mike Goodman,
EMP: 55 EST: 1998
SALES (est): 7.6MM Privately Held
SIC: 2051 Cakes, bakery: except frozen

(G-8142)
GYM STORE INC
Also Called: Gym Store.com
5889 57th St (11378-3125)
PHONE................................718 366-7804
Fax: 718 228-9496
Christopher Kelly, *President*
▼ EMP: 5
SQ FT: 10,000
SALES (est): 897K Privately Held
SIC: 3949 Exercise equipment; dumbbells & other weightlifting equipment; treadmills; gymnasium equipment

(G-8143)
HERGO ERGONOMIC SUPPORT (PA)
5601 55th Ave (11378-1104)
PHONE................................718 894-0639
Fax: 718 894-4724
Eli E Hertz, *CEO*
Barry J Goldsammler, *Senior VP*
Albert Hirschson, *Senior VP*
I Marilyn Hertz, *Vice Pres*
Kristen Speranza-Diamond, *Vice Pres*
◆ EMP: 40
SQ FT: 42,000
SALES (est): 5.9MM Privately Held
WEB: www.hergo.com
SIC: 3577 3699 3444 2542 Computer peripheral equipment; electrical equipment & supplies; sheet metalwork; partitions & fixtures, except wood; office furniture, except wood

(G-8144)
HI-TECH METALS INC
5920 56th Ave (11378-2325)
PHONE................................718 894-1212
Fax: 718 894-5021
Manny Tzilzelis, *President*
Menelaos Tzilvelis, *President*
Chris Christodoulou, *Vice Pres*
John Tobin, *Mfg Staff*
Victor Vargas, *Engineer*
EMP: 50
SQ FT: 10,000
SALES (est): 13.8MM Privately Held
WEB: www.hi-techmetals.com
SIC: 3446 Architectural metalwork

(G-8145)
INFINITY DESIGN LLC
5830 Grand Ave (11378-3217)
PHONE................................718 416-3853
Nathan Indig,
EMP: 10
SQ FT: 150,000
SALES (est): 1.1MM
SALES (corp-wide): 25MM Privately Held
SIC: 2434 Wood kitchen cabinets
PA: Cnc Associates N.Y., Inc.
101 Kentile Rd
South Plainfield NJ 07080
718 416-3853

(G-8146)
J & R UNIQUE GIFTWARE
5863 56th St (11378-3105)
PHONE................................718 821-0398
John Daidone, *Owner*
EMP: 20 EST: 2008
SALES (est): 930K Privately Held
SIC: 3999 Manufacturing industries

(G-8147)
JACK LUCKNER STEEL SHELVING CO
Also Called: Kart
5454 43rd St (11378-1028)
PHONE................................718 363-0500
Fax: 718 784-9169
Burton J Gold, *President*
Scott Mair, *Purchasing*
Alan Sheldon, *Controller*
Gardenia McCray, *Credit Mgr*
Lawrence Mass, *Human Res Mgr*
EMP: 75 EST: 1947
SQ FT: 12,000

▲ = Import ▼ = Export ◆ = Import/Export

SALES (est): 7.4MM
SALES (corp-wide): 23MM **Privately Held**
WEB: www.karpinc.com
SIC: 2542 Shelving, office & store: except wood
PA: Karp Associates Inc.
260 Spagnoli Rd
Melville NY 11747
631 768-8300

(G-8148)
KARP OVERSEAS CORPORATION
5454 43rd St (11378-1028)
PHONE.................................718 784-2105
Burton J Gold, *President*
EMP: 40
SQ FT: 30,000
SALES: 500K
SALES (corp-wide): 23MM **Privately Held**
WEB: www.karpinc.com
SIC: 3965 8742 Straight pins: steel or brass; sales (including sales management) consultant
PA: Karp Associates Inc.
260 Spagnoli Rd
Melville NY 11747
631 768-8300

(G-8149)
MASPETH PRESS INC
6620 Grand Ave (11378-2531)
PHONE.................................718 429-2363
Frederick F Strobel, *President*
Frederick J Strobel, *President*
Linda Strobel, *Vice Pres*
EMP: 5
SQ FT: 2,000
SALES (est): 625.4K **Privately Held**
SIC: 2759 Letterpress printing

(G-8150)
MASPETH WELDING INC
5930 54th St (11378-3004)
PHONE.................................718 497-5430
Fax: 718 386-9238
Jeffrey Anschlowar, *Ch of Bd*
Evelyn Agnoli, *VP Finance*
Val Chua, *Manager*
Fred Peterson, *Manager*
Elizabeth Raab, *Manager*
EMP: 40 EST: 1977
SQ FT: 48,000
SALES (est): 10.8MM **Privately Held**
WEB: www.maspethwelding.com
SIC: 3441 7692 Fabricated structural metal; welding repair

(G-8151)
MAXSUN CORPORATION (PA)
Also Called: Maxsun Furnishings
5711 49th St (11378-2020)
PHONE.................................718 418-6800
Johnny Song Lin, *Ch of Bd*
EMP: 14
SALES (est): 716.6K **Privately Held**
SIC: 2599 5719 Restaurant furniture, wood or metal; bar furniture; bar, restaurant & cafeteria furniture; lighting fixtures

(G-8152)
N Y CONTRACT SEATING INC
5560 60th St (11378-2338)
PHONE.................................718 417-9298
John Glantzis, *President*
EMP: 7
SQ FT: 2,100
SALES (est): 710.7K **Privately Held**
SIC: 2211 Upholstery fabrics, cotton

(G-8153)
N Y ELLI DESIGN CORP
5105 Flushing Ave 2 (11378-3019)
PHONE.................................718 228-0014
Fax: 718 418-4629
Dimitra Ligas, *CEO*
Lisa Opera, *Manager*
▲ EMP: 15
SQ FT: 30,000
SALES: 5.1MM **Privately Held**
WEB: www.ellicorp.com
SIC: 2434 2521 2531 Wood kitchen cabinets; cabinets, office: wood; public building & related furniture; library furniture

(G-8154)
NE & WS INC
6050 60th St (11378-3532)
PHONE.................................718 326-4699
Fax: 718 417-7427
Edward Nowakowski, *President*
Margaret Nowakowski, *Admin Sec*
EMP: 9
SQ FT: 4,900
SALES: 950K **Privately Held**
SIC: 2431 Staircases, stairs & railings

(G-8155)
NELSON AIR DEVICE CORPORATION
Also Called: C W Sheet Metal
4628 54th Ave (11378-1012)
PHONE.................................718 729-3801
Fax: 718 729-7181
Nelson Blitz Jr, *President*
Thomas Howard, *COO*
Michael Doff, *Vice Pres*
Peter Unrath, *Vice Pres*
Patrick Boccio, *Project Mgr*
EMP: 200 EST: 1938
SQ FT: 20,000
SALES (est): 81.3MM **Privately Held**
WEB: www.nadcw.com
SIC: 3444 1711 Ducts, sheet metal; heating & air conditioning contractors

(G-8156)
NEW YORK MARBLE AND STONE CORP
4411 55th Ave (11378-1023)
PHONE.................................718 729-7272
Fax: 718 724-7213
Luigi Crecco, *President*
Cathy Crecco, *Vice Pres*
EMP: 10
SALES: 1MM **Privately Held**
SIC: 3281 Stone, quarrying & processing of own stone products

(G-8157)
NEW YORK SAND & STONE LLC
5700 47th St (11378-2105)
PHONE.................................718 596-2897
Tom Dooley,
Randy Waterman,
▲ EMP: 9
SQ FT: 400,000
SALES (est): 834.4K
SALES (corp-wide): 974.7MM **Publicly Held**
SIC: 1442 Construction sand & gravel
HQ: Eastern Concrete Materials, Inc.
250 Pehle Ave Ste 503
Saddle Brook NJ 07663
201 843-5103

(G-8158)
NORAMPAC NEW YORK CITY INC
5515 Grand Ave (11378-3113)
PHONE.................................718 340-2100
Fax: 718 386-7370
Marc Andre Depin, *Ch of Bd*
Nilanjan Sen, *Controller*
Mary Norton, *Human Res Dir*
Richard Etra, *Manager*
Stephen Valjato, *Supervisor*
EMP: 160 EST: 1906
SQ FT: 340,000
SALES (est): 44.6MM
SALES (corp-wide): 2.9B **Privately Held**
SIC: 2653 3993 2675 Boxes, corrugated: made from purchased materials; display items, corrugated: made from purchased materials; signs & advertising specialties; die-cut paper & board
HQ: Norampac Inc
1061 Rue Parent
Saint-Bruno QC J3V 6
450 461-8600

(G-8159)
NORDIC INTERIOR INC
5601 Maspeth Ave Gf (11378-2222)
PHONE.................................718 456-7000
Fax: 718 456-9340
Helge Halvorsen, *President*
Lloyd Jacobsen, *Corp Secy*
Harald Haegeland, *Vice Pres*
Gene Wong, *Manager*
▲ EMP: 150
SQ FT: 55,000
SALES (est): 24.4MM **Privately Held**
WEB: www.nordicinterior.com
SIC: 2431 1742 Woodwork, interior & ornamental; drywall

(G-8160)
NY TEMPERING LLC
6021 Flushing Ave (11378-3220)
PHONE.................................718 326-8989
▲ EMP: 5 EST: 2012
SALES (est): 668.5K **Privately Held**
SIC: 3272 Concrete products

(G-8161)
NYC FIREPLACES & KITCHENS
5830 Maspeth Ave (11378-2214)
PHONE.................................718 326-4328
Frank Alesci, *Principal*
EMP: 5
SALES (est): 340K **Privately Held**
SIC: 3496 Grilles & grillework, woven wire

(G-8162)
OWAYNE ENTERPRISES INC
4901 Maspeth Ave (11378-2219)
PHONE.................................718 326-2200
Owen M Mester, *President*
Wayne Wattenberg, *Vice Pres*
EMP: 38
SQ FT: 30,000
SALES (est): 7.1MM **Privately Held**
SIC: 2051 Cakes, pies & pastries; cakes, bakery: except frozen

(G-8163)
P & F INDUSTRIES OF NY CORP
Also Called: P and F Machine Industries
6006 55th Dr (11378-2351)
PHONE.................................718 894-3501
Fax: 718 894-7820
Frank Passantino, *President*
▲ EMP: 6
SQ FT: 7,000
SALES (est): 440K **Privately Held**
SIC: 3599 Machine shop, jobbing & repair

(G-8164)
PATCO TAPES INC
Also Called: Patco Group
5927 56th St (11378-3395)
PHONE.................................718 497-1527
Fax: 718 366-8845
Michael Rosenberg, *Corp Secy*
Joel Rosenberg, *Vice Pres*
EMP: 8 EST: 1973
SQ FT: 30,000
SALES: 2.5MM **Privately Held**
WEB: www.patcogroup.com
SIC: 2672 2671 5199 Gummed tape, cloth or paper base: from purchased materials; paper coated or laminated for packaging; packaging materials

(G-8165)
PEPSI-COLA BOTTLING CO NY INC
5035 56th Rd (11378-1109)
PHONE.................................718 786-8550
EMP: 5
SALES (corp-wide): 219.3MM **Privately Held**
SIC: 2086 Soft drinks: packaged in cans, bottles, etc.
PA: Pepsi-Cola Bottling Company Of New York, Inc.
11402 15th Ave Ste 5
College Point NY 11356
718 392-1000

(G-8166)
PURVI ENTERPRISES INCORPORATED
Also Called: Sinnara
5556 44th St (11378-2024)
PHONE.................................347 808-9448
Harshi Patel, *President*
▲ EMP: 6
SALES (est): 560.1K **Privately Held**
SIC: 3556 Dehydrating equipment, food processing

(G-8167)
RISA MANAGEMENT CORP
Also Called: Risa's
5501 43rd St Fl 3 (11378-2023)
PHONE.................................718 361-2606
D Savi Prashad, *CEO*
Rishi Prashad, *COO*
Shafqat Tanweer, *CFO*
Karen Henriquez, *Manager*
▲ EMP: 45
SQ FT: 6,500
SALES (est): 8.8MM **Privately Held**
WEB: www.risacorp.com
SIC: 3449 3441 Miscellaneous metalwork; fabricated structural metal

(G-8168)
RM BAKERY LLC
Also Called: Rollo Mio Artisan Bakery
4425 54th Dr (11378-1017)
Rural Route 220 E 42nd St, New York (10017)
PHONE.................................718 472-3036
Christian Mattheus, *Managing Prtnr*
EMP: 24
SALES (est): 4.7MM **Privately Held**
SIC: 2051 Bread, cake & related products

(G-8169)
ROCKMILLS STEEL PRODUCTS CORP
5912 54th St (11378-3004)
P.O. Box 234838, Great Neck (11023-4838)
PHONE.................................718 366-8300
Fax: 718 829-3210
Ann O'Brien, *President*
Daniel Obrien, *Shareholder*
Mary Obrien, *Shareholder*
EMP: 15
SQ FT: 25,200
SALES (est): 4MM **Privately Held**
WEB: www.rockmillsboilers.com
SIC: 3433 Boilers, low-pressure heating: steam or hot water

(G-8170)
S R S INC
5920 56th Ave (11378-2325)
P.O. Box 4277, Metuchen NJ (08840-4277)
PHONE.................................732 548-6630
M Dan Bellware, *President*
Marilyn Russo, *Vice Pres*
EMP: 20
SALES (est): 3.5MM **Privately Held**
WEB: www.srs-metals.com
SIC: 3446 Railings, bannisters, guards, etc.: made from metal pipe

(G-8171)
STAIN RAIL SYSTEMS INC
Also Called: SRS
5920 56th Ave (11378-2325)
P.O. Box 4277, Metuchen NJ (08840-4277)
PHONE.................................732 548-6630
Fax: 732 548-6885
M Daniel Bellware, *President*
Kevin Metz, *Project Mgr*
EMP: 10 EST: 1968
SALES (est): 1.7MM **Privately Held**
SIC: 3446 Railings, bannisters, guards, etc.: made from metal pipe

(G-8172)
T&B BAKERY CORP
5870 56th St (11378-3106)
PHONE.................................646 642-4300
Tomasz Eider, *President*
EMP: 6
SQ FT: 6,000
SALES: 2.8MM **Privately Held**
SIC: 2051 Bakery products, partially cooked (except frozen)

(G-8173)
TRI-STAR OFFSET CORP
6020 59th Pl Ste 3 (11378-3349)
PHONE.................................718 894-5555
Brian Nawroth, *CEO*
Al Nawroth, *President*
Mark Serwetz, *Vice Pres*
Michael Louie, *Sales Staff*
EMP: 25 EST: 1977
SALES (est): 5.3MM **Privately Held**
SIC: 2752 Commercial printing, lithographic

(G-8174)
US ALLEGRO INC
5430 44th St (11378-1034)
PHONE.................................347 408-6601
Yuriy Bogutskiy, *President*
EMP: 30
SQ FT: 10,000
SALES: 4MM **Privately Held**
SIC: 1442 Construction sand & gravel

(G-8175)
VALENTINE PACKAGING CORP
6020 59th Pl Ste 7 (11378-3349)
PHONE.................................718 418-6000
Fax: 718 418-0618
Daniel Suchow, *Vice Pres*
Richard Suchow, *Vice Pres*
Steven Suchow, *Vice Pres*
EMP: 18 EST: 1953
SQ FT: 25,000
SALES (est): 4.9MM **Privately Held**
SIC: 2653 7389 Sheets, corrugated: made from purchased materials; packaging & labeling services

Massapequa
Nassau County

(G-8176)
A & M APPEL DISTRIBUTING INC
500 N Atlanta Ave (11758-2000)
PHONE.................................516 735-1172
Michael Appel, *Principal*
EMP: 5
SALES (est): 320.4K **Privately Held**
SIC: 2051 5149 Bread, cake & related products; bakery products

(G-8177)
ADAMS INTERIOR FABRICATIONS
8 Iroquois Pl (11758-7622)
PHONE.................................631 249-8282
Fax: 516 249-8284
Anthony E Adams, *President*
EMP: 11
SALES (est): 1.4MM **Privately Held**
SIC: 2431 2499 Millwork; decorative wood & woodwork

(G-8178)
AEB SAPPHIRE CORP
152 Ontario Ave (11758-3937)
PHONE.................................516 586-8232
Henry Frankowski, *President*
EMP: 4
SQ FT: 2,000
SALES: 1MM **Privately Held**
SIC: 3699 Chimes, electric

(G-8179)
HUNTINGTON SERVICES INC
Also Called: Vox Systems
727 N Broadway Ste A4 (11758-2348)
PHONE.................................516 795-8500
Richard Vience, *President*
Angel Larocca, *Executive*
EMP: 6
SQ FT: 1,200
SALES (est): 850K **Privately Held**
WEB: www.hsi4service.com
SIC: 7372 Prepackaged software

(G-8180)
LITTLE BIRD CHOCOLATES INC
Also Called: Little Curios Confections
25 Fairchild Ave Ste 200 (11758)
PHONE.................................646 620-6395
Sara Meyer, *President*
EMP: 7 EST: 2013
SALES (est): 575.6K **Privately Held**
SIC: 2064 Candy & other confectionery products

(G-8181)
R KLEIN JEWELRY CO INC
Also Called: Klein & Company
39 Brockmeyer Dr (11758-7804)
PHONE.................................516 482-3260
Richard Klein, *President*
Fred Schrager, *Credit Mgr*
EMP: 55
SQ FT: 30,000
SALES (est): 4.8MM **Privately Held**
WEB: www.kleinjewelry.com
SIC: 3911 Jewelry, precious metal

(G-8182)
S SCHARF INC
278 N Richmond Ave (11758-3231)
PHONE.................................516 541-9552
Irwin Scharf, *President*
Jesse Scharf, *Treasurer*
EMP: 13 EST: 1935
SQ FT: 5,000
SALES (est): 1.2MM **Privately Held**
SIC: 3911 Jewelry, precious metal

(G-8183)
SUNRISE JEWELERS OF NY INC
1220 Sunrise Hwy (11758)
PHONE.................................516 541-1302
EMP: 8
SALES (est): 930K **Privately Held**
SIC: 3911 Mfg Precious Metal Jewelry

(G-8184)
WOODS KNIFE CORPORATION
19 Brooklyn Ave (11758-4855)
PHONE.................................516 798-4972
Fax: 516 798-5864
James S Woods, *President*
Ann Woods, *Vice Pres*
EMP: 24 EST: 1916
SQ FT: 2,600
SALES (est): 2.4MM **Privately Held**
SIC: 3423 3421 Knives, agricultural or industrial; cutlery

Massapequa Park
Nassau County

(G-8185)
CUSTOM MIX INC
31 Clark Blvd (11762-2609)
PHONE.................................516 797-7090
Matthew Lott, *Principal*
EMP: 10
SALES (est): 1MM **Privately Held**
SIC: 3273 Ready-mixed concrete

(G-8186)
IMAGE SALES & MARKETING INC
106 Thornwood Rd (11762-4023)
PHONE.................................516 238-7023
Francine Walk, *President*
Steven Walk, *Vice Pres*
EMP: 2
SQ FT: 3,000
SALES: 4MM **Privately Held**
WEB: www.imagesalesny.com
SIC: 2754 Commercial printing, gravure

(G-8187)
INNOVATIVE SYSTEMS OF NEW YORK
201 Rose St (11762-1022)
PHONE.................................516 541-7410
Joseph Esposito, *President*
EMP: 5
SALES (est): 353.8K **Privately Held**
SIC: 3577 7373 7378 Computer peripheral equipment; computer integrated systems design; computer maintenance & repair

(G-8188)
MASSAPEQUA POST
Also Called: Acj Communications
1045b Park Blvd (11762-2764)
PHONE.................................516 798-5100
Fax: 516 798-5296
Alfred James, *President*
Carolyn James, *Vice Pres*
Karen Pennachio, *Branch Mgr*
Mary A Hayden, *Admin Sec*
Teka McCabe, *Teacher*
EMP: 21
SALES (est): 533.7K **Privately Held**
WEB: www.massapequapost.com
SIC: 2711 Newspapers

(G-8189)
PRINT COTTAGE LLC
1138 Lakeshore Dr (11762-2054)
PHONE.................................516 369-1749
James Altadonna, *Mng Member*
EMP: 10
SQ FT: 1,000
SALES: 4MM **Privately Held**
SIC: 2752 Commercial printing, lithographic

(G-8190)
TVI IMPORTS LLC
178 Abbey St (11762-3430)
PHONE.................................631 793-3077
Anthony Tisi, *Mng Member*
▲ EMP: 6
SQ FT: 2,500
SALES: 19MM **Privately Held**
SIC: 3089 Flower pots, plastic

(G-8191)
WORLD BUSINESS MEDIA LLC
Also Called: Gsn Government Security News
4770 Sunrise Hwy Ste 105 (11762-2911)
PHONE.................................212 344-0759
EMP: 12
SQ FT: 2,000
SALES: 2MM **Privately Held**
SIC: 2721 7313 7382 Periodicals-Publishing/Printing Advertising Representative Security Systems Services

Massena
St. Lawrence County

(G-8192)
COMPOSITE SYSTEMS & TECH LLC
21 Trade Rd (13662-2575)
PHONE.................................716 491-8490
Robert Ziek, *CFO*
Bernadette Sweeney, *Manager*
Steve Rohring,
EMP: 6
SALES (est): 400K **Privately Held**
SIC: 3083 Laminated plastics plate & sheet

(G-8193)
CURRAN RENEWABLE ENERGY LLC
20 Commerce Dr (13662-2576)
PHONE.................................315 769-2000
Ken Ashley, *Controller*
Patrick Curran, *Mng Member*
Tricia Terry, *Manager*
EMP: 30
SALES (est): 19.1MM **Privately Held**
SIC: 2448 Sawmills & planing mills, general

(G-8194)
FARLEY WINDOWS INC
Trade Dr (13662)
PHONE.................................315 764-1111
Fax: 315 764-1194
Steve Mailhot, *Manager*
EMP: 8
SALES (corp-wide): 233.2MM **Privately Held**
SIC: 3211 3231 Window glass, clear & colored; doors, glass: made from purchased glass
HQ: Kp Building Products Ltd
300 Macdonald Blvd
Alexandria ON K0C 1
613 525-3065

(G-8195)
GENERAL MOTORS LLC
56 Chevrolet Rd (13662-1878)
PHONE.................................315 764-2000
Rey Hart, *Prdtn Mgr*
Jim Toth, *Prdtn Mgr*
Daniel J Carroll, *Purchasing*
Larry French, *Engineer*
Ross Johnson, *Engineer*
EMP: 500
SALES (corp-wide): 152.3B **Publicly Held**
SIC: 3369 3714 Castings, except die-castings, precision; motor vehicle parts & accessories
HQ: General Motors Llc
300 Renaissance Ctr L1
Detroit MI 48243
313 556-5000

(G-8196)
HANYAN & HIGGINS COMPANY INC
9772 State Highway 56 (13662-3416)
PHONE.................................315 769-8838
Fax: 315 769-8838
Donald Walters, *CEO*
EMP: 5 EST: 1999
SALES (est): 220K **Privately Held**
SIC: 3297 Castable refractories, nonclay

(G-8197)
KINGSTON PHARMA LLC
Also Called: Kingston Pharmaceuticals
5 County Route 42 (13662-1569)
PHONE.................................315 705-4019
Srikanth Lingen, *Opers Mgr*
Sridhar Thyagarajan,
Venkat Kakani,
EMP: 8
SQ FT: 32,778
SALES (est): 389.9K **Privately Held**
SIC: 2834 Druggists' preparations (pharmaceuticals)

(G-8198)
MASSENA METALS INC
86 S Racquette River Rd (13662-4318)
P.O. Box 5282 (13662-5282)
PHONE.................................315 769-3846
Fax: 315 769-0134
J Goldstein, *President*
Lawrence Leibo, *Corp Secy*
Gary Master, *Vice Pres*
EMP: 15
SQ FT: 10,000
SALES (est): 1.7MM **Privately Held**
SIC: 3365 5093 5051 Aluminum foundries; ferrous metal scrap & waste; steel

(G-8199)
PURINE PHARMA LLC
5 County Route 42 (13662-1569)
PHONE.................................315 705-4030
Venkat Kakani, *Mng Member*
EMP: 25
SQ FT: 32,778
SALES (est): 111.1K
SALES (corp-wide): 1.3MM **Privately Held**
SIC: 2834 Cough medicines; analgesics; vitamin preparations
PA: Geritrex Holdings, Inc.
144 E Kingsbridge Rd
Mount Vernon NY 10550
914 668-4003

(G-8200)
SEAWAY TIMBER HARVESTING INC (PA)
15121 State Highway 37 (13662-6194)
PHONE.................................315 769-5970
Patrick Curran, *President*
Tim Curran, *Vice Pres*
Tricia Terry, *Manager*
Lee Curran, *Admin Sec*
EMP: 60
SQ FT: 15,000
SALES (est): 11.1MM **Privately Held**
SIC: 2411 4789 Logging; log loading & unloading

(G-8201)
STUBBS PRINTING INC
271 E Orvis St Ste B (13662-2352)
P.O. Box 110 (13662-0110)
PHONE.................................315 769-8641
Fax: 315 764-9285
Karen Stubbs, *President*
Robert T Stubbs, *Vice Pres*
EMP: 5
SQ FT: 2,000
SALES (est): 390K **Privately Held**
SIC: 2752 Commercial printing, offset

Mastic
Suffolk County

(G-8202)
EAST END SIGN DESIGN INC
1161 Montauk Hwy (11950-2918)
PHONE..................................631 399-2574
Joseph Colucci, *President*
John Dugan, *Manager*
Mike Powell, *Manager*
EMP: 5
SALES (est): 510K **Privately Held**
SIC: 3993 Signs & advertising specialties

(G-8203)
FUNDA-MANTELS LLC
659 Mastic Rd (11950-5012)
P.O. Box 318, Ridge (11961-0318)
PHONE..................................631 399-3223
Frank Turrigiano, *Mng Member*
Albert Turrigiano,
EMP: 6
SQ FT: 3,000
SALES (est): 1MM **Privately Held**
WEB: www.funda-mantels.com
SIC: 2431 Mantels, wood

Mastic Beach
Suffolk County

(G-8204)
AFFLUENT DESIGN INC
48 Biltmore Dr (11951-1310)
PHONE..................................631 655-2556
Daniel Louis Levine, *Principal*
EMP: 10
SALES (est): 570K **Privately Held**
SIC: 2741 7374 Miscellaneous publishing; computer graphics service

(G-8205)
VINCENT GENOVESE
Also Called: Long Island Radiant Heat
19 Woodmere Dr (11951-2016)
PHONE..................................631 281-8170
Vincent Genovese, *Owner*
EMP: 6
SALES (est): 674.5K **Privately Held**
SIC: 3634 5074 8711 1711 Heating units, electric (radiant heat): baseboard or wall; heating equipment & panels, solar; heating & ventilation engineering; heating & air conditioning contractors; industrial furnaces & ovens; heating equipment, except electric

Mattituck
Suffolk County

(G-8206)
AMEREON LTD
800 Wickham Ave (11952)
P.O. Box 1200 (11952-0921)
PHONE..................................631 298-5100
Joanna Paulsen, *President*
John Clauss, *Vice Pres*
EMP: 5
SQ FT: 30,000
SALES (est): 594.3K **Privately Held**
WEB: www.amereon.com
SIC: 2731 Books: publishing only

(G-8207)
LIEB CELLARS LLC
Also Called: Lieb Cellars Tasting Room
35 Cox Neck Rd (11952-1458)
P.O. Box 907, Cutchogue (11935-0907)
PHONE..................................631 298-1942
Gary Madden, *General Mgr*
EMP: 20
SALES (corp-wide): 7.6MM **Privately Held**
WEB: www.liebcellars.com
SIC: 2084 Wines
PA: Lieb Cellars Llc
 13050 Oregon Rd
 Cutchogue NY 11935
 631 734-1100

(G-8208)
NORTH FORK WOOD WORKS INC
5175 Route 48 (11952-3260)
P.O. Box 1407, Southold (11971-0938)
PHONE..................................631 255-4028
Scott Edgett, *CEO*
EMP: 10
SALES (est): 1.2MM **Privately Held**
SIC: 2431 Millwork

(G-8209)
PREMIUM WINE GROUP LLC
35 Cox Neck Rd (11952-1458)
PHONE..................................631 298-1900
Russell Hearn, *Principal*
John Leo, *Principal*
Andrew Rockwell, *Lab Dir*
▲ **EMP:** 22 **EST:** 2001
SALES (est): 3.5MM **Privately Held**
WEB: www.premiumwinegroup.com
SIC: 2084 Wines

(G-8210)
SHINN WINERY LLC
Also Called: Shinn Vineyard
2000 Oregon Rd (11952-1762)
PHONE..................................631 804-0367
Barbara Shinn,
▲ **EMP:** 7
SALES (est): 600K **Privately Held**
SIC: 2084 Wines, brandy & brandy spirits

(G-8211)
TIMES REVIEW NEWSPAPER CORP
Also Called: News Review, The
7780 Main Rd (11952-1539)
PHONE..................................631 354-8031
Fax: 631 298-3287
Troy Gustavson, *President*
Michael White, *Editor*
Jean Burgond, *VP Mktg*
Karen Cullen, *Manager*
Tim Kelly, *Manager*
EMP: 33
SQ FT: 6,000
SALES (est): 2.7MM **Privately Held**
WEB: www.timesreview.com
SIC: 2711 2791 Newspapers: publishing only, not printed on site; typesetting

Mattydale
Onondaga County

(G-8212)
ERASER COMPANY INC (PA)
123 Oliva Dr (13211-1902)
P.O. Box 4961, Syracuse (13221-4961)
PHONE..................................315 454-3237
Fax: 315 454-3090
Ralph Bevard, *CEO*
Marcus W Bevard, *Ch of Bd*
Renate Bevard, *Vice Pres*
William Jackson, *Engineer*
Anthony R Colella, *Treasurer*
EMP: 115 **EST:** 1911
SQ FT: 7,700
SALES (est): 19.3MM **Privately Held**
WEB: www.eraser.com
SIC: 3069 3291 3549 3991 Erasers: rubber or rubber & abrasive combined; wheels, abrasive; wiredrawing & fabricating machinery & equipment, ex. die; brooms & brushes; engine electrical equipment; miscellaneous fabricated wire products

Mayfield
Fulton County

(G-8213)
KADCO USA INC
17 W Main St (12117-3996)
P.O. Box 584, Amsterdam (12010-0584)
PHONE..................................518 661-6068
Fax: 518 661-5808
Thomas Petherick, *President*
Frank Mc Cleneghen, *Vice Pres*
◆ **EMP:** 7
SQ FT: 5,000
SALES (est): 1.1MM **Privately Held**
WEB: www.kadcousa.com
SIC: 3524 Carts or wagons for lawn & garden; lawn & garden mowers & accessories

(G-8214)
SMITH & SONS FUELS INC
36 2nd Ave (12117-3960)
PHONE..................................518 661-6112
Jeffrey J Smith, *Ch of Bd*
EMP: 7
SALES (est): 877K **Privately Held**
SIC: 2869 Fuels

Mayville
Chautauqua County

(G-8215)
EMPIRE DEVLEOPMENT
5889 Magnolia Stedman Rd (14757-9420)
PHONE..................................716 789-2097
Micah Meredith, *Principal*
EMP: 8 **EST:** 2007
SALES (est): 1MM **Privately Held**
SIC: 3423 Jewelers' hand tools

(G-8216)
KLEINFELDER JOHN
Also Called: Chautauqua Iron Works
5239 W Lake Rd (14757-9507)
PHONE..................................716 753-3163
Fax: 716 753-7018
John Kleinfelder, *Owner*
EMP: 5
SQ FT: 990
SALES (est): 519.8K **Privately Held**
SIC: 3441 3446 5947 4491 Fabricated structural metal; ornamental metalwork; artcraft & carvings; docks, incl. buildings & facilities: operation & maintenance; boat lifts; welding on site

(G-8217)
LYN JO ENTERPRISES LTD
Also Called: Standard Portable
Rr 394 Box 147 (14757)
PHONE..................................716 753-2776
Fax: 716 487-1024
Julie Baraniewicz, *President*
Bernie Newhouse, *Purch Mgr*
Gregory Goerke, *Sales Mgr*
EMP: 7
SQ FT: 288
SALES (est): 750K **Privately Held**
WEB: www.standardportable.com
SIC: 3496 3699 Lamp frames, wire; trouble lights

(G-8218)
RANGE RSURCES - APPALACHIA LLC
Also Called: Lomak Petroleum
100 E Chautauqua St (14757-1040)
P.O. Box 187 (14757-0187)
PHONE..................................716 753-3385
Fax: 716 753-3394
Doug Stebbins, *Manager*
EMP: 30
SALES (corp-wide): 1.6B **Publicly Held**
WEB: www.gl-energy.com
SIC: 1382 Oil & gas exploration services
HQ: Range Resources - Appalachia, Llc.
 3000 Town Center Blvd
 Canonsburg PA 15317
 724 743-6700

(G-8219)
STEDMAN ENERGY INC
4411 Canterbury Dr (14757-9610)
P.O. Box 1006, Chautauqua (14722-1006)
PHONE..................................716 789-3018
Kevin E McChesney, *President*
EMP: 7
SALES (est): 100K **Privately Held**
SIC: 1311 Crude petroleum production; natural gas production

Mc Connellsville
Oneida County

(G-8220)
HARDEN FURNITURE INC (PA)
8550 Mill Pond Way (13401-1844)
PHONE..................................315 675-3600
Fax: 315 245-2884
Gregory Harden, *CEO*
Mike Allen, *Superintendent*
Andy Clark, *COO*
Andrew Clark, *Vice Pres*
Pete Raynford, *Vice Pres*
▼ **EMP:** 216 **EST:** 1844
SQ FT: 400,000
SALES (est): 19.7MM **Privately Held**
WEB: www.cnywinter.com
SIC: 2511 2512 2521 5021 Wood household furniture; dining room furniture: wood; bed frames, except water bed frames: wood; dressers, household: wood; upholstered household furniture; living room furniture: upholstered on wood frames; wood office furniture; desks, office: wood; bookcases, office: wood; furniture

Mc Graw
Cortland County

(G-8221)
COUTURE TIMBER HARVESTING
2760 Phelps Rd (13101-9561)
P.O. Box 66, Cortland (13045-0066)
PHONE..................................607 836-4719
Bruno Couture, *President*
Bruno Coutrue, *Vice Pres*
EMP: 7 **EST:** 1971
SALES (est): 684.9K **Privately Held**
SIC: 2411 Logging camps & contractors

(G-8222)
HIGGINS SUPPLY COMPANY INC
Also Called: Higgins Supl Co
18-23 South St (13101-9475)
PHONE..................................607 836-6474
Fax: 607 836-6913
Terri Maxson, *Ch of Bd*
Cathy Gregg, *President*
Glenn Doran, *Vice Pres*
Terri L Gutchess, *Vice Pres*
EMP: 65 **EST:** 1921
SQ FT: 30,000
SALES (est): 11.3MM **Privately Held**
SIC: 3842 2342 Orthopedic appliances; corset accessories: clasps, stays, etc.

(G-8223)
MCGRAW WOOD PRODUCTS LLC (PA)
1 Charles St (13101-9190)
P.O. Box 652 (13101-0652)
PHONE..................................607 836-6465
Fax: 607 836-6413
Christopher Ousby, *Purchasing*
Jenifer Crisp, *Office Mgr*
Harold J Ousby III, *Mng Member*
EMP: 30 **EST:** 2006
SQ FT: 100,000
SALES (est): 5.7MM **Privately Held**
WEB: www.mcgrawwoodproducts.com
SIC: 2511 2499 2441 2434 Silverware chests: wood; decorative wood & woodwork; nailed wood boxes & shook; wood kitchen cabinets

Mechanicville
Saratoga County

(G-8224)
ALABU INC
Also Called: Alabu Skin Care
30 Graves Rd (12118-3218)
PHONE..................................518 665-0411
Mary Claire, *President*

Mechanicville - Saratoga County (G-8225)

Dean Mayes, *President*
EMP: 7
SALES (est): 1MM Privately Held
WEB: www.alabu.com
SIC: 2841 Soap: granulated, liquid, cake, flaked or chip

(G-8225)
ALONZO FIRE WORKS DISPLAY INC (PA)
12 County Route 75 (12118-3357)
PHONE.................................518 664-9994
Jeff Alonzo, *President*
▲ EMP: 8
SALES (est): 654K Privately Held
WEB: www.alonzofireworks.com
SIC: 2899 7999 Fireworks; fireworks display service

(G-8226)
DECRESCENTE DISTRIBUTING CO
Also Called: D D C
211 N Main St (12118-1242)
P.O. Box 231 (12118-0231)
PHONE.................................518 664-9866
Russ Teplitzky, *General Mgr*
Carmine D Crescente Jr, *Principal*
Andy Laing, *Facilities Mgr*
Ed Keis, *CFO*
Natasha Derby, *HR Admin*
EMP: 67 EST: 2010
SALES (est): 28.4MM Privately Held
SIC: 2082 Beer (alcoholic beverage)

(G-8227)
EMPIRE EXHIBITS & DISPLAYS INC
Also Called: Empire Exhibits and Displays
131 Round Lake Ave (12118-1026)
PHONE.................................518 266-9362
Craig L Koehler, *CEO*
Don Wiesenforth, *President*
Linda Jarvis, *Office Mgr*
EMP: 10
SQ FT: 1,500
SALES: 700K Privately Held
WEB: www.empireexhibits.com
SIC: 2426 Frames for upholstered furniture, wood

(G-8228)
GLAXOSMITHKLINE LLC
108 Woodfield Blvd (12118-3038)
PHONE.................................518 852-9637
EMP: 27
SALES (corp-wide): 36B Privately Held
SIC: 2834 Pharmaceutical preparations
HQ: Glaxosmithkline Llc
  5 Crescent Dr
  Philadelphia PA 19112
  215 751-4000

(G-8229)
POLYSET COMPANY INC
65 Hudson Ave (12118-4517)
P.O. Box 111 (12118-0111)
PHONE.................................518 664-6000
Fax: 518 664-6001
Bart McGonnigal, *President*
Niladri Ghoshal, *Exec VP*
Charlie Simon, *CFO*
Rajat Ghoshal, *Treasurer*
Earl Ramlow, *Manager*
▲ EMP: 36
SQ FT: 40,000
SALES (est): 11.9MM Privately Held
WEB: www.polyset.com
SIC: 2819 3087 2952 2891 Industrial inorganic chemicals; custom compound purchased resins; coating compounds, tar; adhesives & sealants

(G-8230)
RALOID TOOL CO INC
Hc 146 (12118)
P.O. Box 551 (12118-0551)
PHONE.................................518 664-4261
Fax: 518 664-4087
Ronald Brownell, *President*
David Brownell, *Vice Pres*
Stephen Shafts, *Project Mgr*
Molly Montanye, *Info Tech Mgr*
EMP: 19 EST: 1945
SQ FT: 23,200
SALES (est): 3.5MM Privately Held
WEB: www.raloidtool.com
SIC: 3544 3542 Special dies & tools; die casting & extruding machines

(G-8231)
ST SILICONES INC
95 N Central Ave (12118-1543)
PHONE.................................518 664-0745
Fax: 518 664-4179
David A Scagnelli, *President*
EMP: 5
SQ FT: 3,500
SALES: 500K Privately Held
WEB: www.st-silicones.com
SIC: 1446 Silica mining

(G-8232)
VOICES FOR ALL LLC
29 Moreland Dr (12118-3630)
PHONE.................................518 261-1664
Paul Benedetti,
Stan Denis,
EMP: 8
SALES (est): 858.1K Privately Held
SIC: 3679 Voice controls

Medford
Suffolk County

(G-8233)
A & L LIGHTING LTD
15 Commercial Blvd (11763-1522)
PHONE.................................718 821-1188
Glen Altman, *President*
Barbara Ehrhardt, *Manager*
EMP: 10
SQ FT: 11,000
SALES (est): 960K Privately Held
WEB: www.allighting.com
SIC: 3646 Fluorescent lighting fixtures, commercial

(G-8234)
AMERICAN AVIONIC TECH CORP
Also Called: Aatc
25 Industrial Blvd (11763-2243)
PHONE.................................631 924-8200
Amin J Khoury, *Ch of Bd*
Werner Lieberherr, *Ch of Bd*
Salvatore F Scilingo, *President*
Rick Lapp, *Vice Pres*
Ernest Murphy, *Engineer*
EMP: 60
SQ FT: 12,000
SALES (est): 16.8MM
SALES (corp-wide): 2.7B Publicly Held
WEB: www.aatcorp.com
SIC: 3699 8711 Electrical equipment & supplies; engineering services
HQ: Tsi Group, Inc.
  94 Tide Mill Rd
  Hampton NH 03842
  603 964-0296

(G-8235)
B & R INDUSTRIES INC
Also Called: Manifold Center, The
12 Commercial Blvd (11763-1523)
PHONE.................................631 736-2275
Fax: 631 736-2725
Christian P Burian, *President*
EMP: 12
SQ FT: 64,000
SALES (est): 1.3MM Privately Held
WEB: www.bnrindustries.com
SIC: 3599 Machine & other job shop work

(G-8236)
BLAIR INDUSTRIES INC (PA)
3671 Horseblock Rd (11763-2240)
PHONE.................................631 924-6600
William R Lehmann Jr, *Ch of Bd*
Elena Feldman, *Manager*
Gabrielle Piazza, *Manager*
▲ EMP: 30
SQ FT: 8,000
SALES (est): 8MM Privately Held
WEB: www.blair-hsm.com
SIC: 3728 Aircraft parts & equipment; aircraft landing assemblies & brakes

(G-8237)
C & H CSTM BKBINDING EMBOSSING
Also Called: C&H Bookbinding & Embossing
1 Forte Ave (11763-4404)
PHONE.................................800 871-8980
Michael Strauss, *Owner*
Barbara Strauss, *Partner*
EMP: 5
SALES (est): 498.6K Privately Held
WEB: www.chbook.com
SIC: 2789 3111 5199 5948 Binding only: books, pamphlets, magazines, etc.; embossing of leather; leather, leather goods & furs; luggage & leather goods stores; engraving service

(G-8238)
CHEMBIO DIAGNOSTIC SYSTEMS INC
3661 Horseblock Rd Ste A (11763-2244)
PHONE.................................631 924-1135
Fax: 631 924-6033
Javan Esfandiari, *Exec VP*
Tom Ippolito, *Vice Pres*
Paul Lambotte, *Vice Pres*
Michael Steele, *Vice Pres*
Bill Schneider, *Facilities Mgr*
▲ EMP: 105
SQ FT: 14,000
SALES (est): 23.3MM
SALES (corp-wide): 24.2MM Publicly Held
WEB: www.chembio.com
SIC: 2835 In vitro & in vivo diagnostic substances
PA: Chembio Diagnostics, Inc.
  3661 Horseblock Rd Ste C
  Medford NY 11763
  631 924-1135

(G-8239)
CHEMBIO DIAGNOSTICS INC (PA)
3661 Horseblock Rd Ste C (11763-2225)
PHONE.................................631 924-1135
Katherine L Davis, *Ch of Bd*
John J Sperzel III, *President*
Sharon Klugewicz, *COO*
Javan Esfandiari, *Exec VP*
Paul Lambotte, *Vice Pres*
▲ EMP: 40
SQ FT: 39,660
SALES: 24.2MM Publicly Held
WEB: www.chembio.com
SIC: 2835 In vitro & in vivo diagnostic substances

(G-8240)
CHROMA COMMUNICATIONS INC
2030 Route 112 (11763-3644)
P.O. Box 340, Bohemia (11716-0340)
PHONE.................................631 289-8871
Fax: 631 289-8872
Peter Gulyas, *President*
EMP: 5
SALES (est): 310K Privately Held
SIC: 2759 Commercial printing

(G-8241)
CLARKE HESS COMMUNICATION RES
3243 Route 112 Ste 1 (11763-1438)
PHONE.................................631 698-3350
Fax: 631 784-2438
Kenneth Salz, *President*
Doante Alessi, *Vice Pres*
Dan Aless, *Info Tech Mgr*
EMP: 8
SQ FT: 4,500
SALES (est): 1.4MM Privately Held
WEB: www.clarke-hess.com
SIC: 3825 Test equipment for electronic & electrical circuits

(G-8242)
DATA FLOW INC
6 Balsam Dr (11763-4304)
PHONE.................................631 436-9200
Timothy Stead, *President*
Joseph Crook, *Vice Pres*
EMP: 8
SQ FT: 8,500
SALES: 1.7MM Privately Held
WEB: printtomail.com
SIC: 2759 Commercial printing

(G-8243)
ENECON CORPORATION (PA)
Also Called: High Prfmce Plymr Cmposits Div
6 Platinum Ct (11763-2251)
PHONE.................................516 349-0022
Andrew A Janczik, *Ch of Bd*
Andrew A Janczak, *President*
Michael Tedesco, *Exec VP*
Matt Goldberg, *Vice Pres*
Robert L Kneuer, *Vice Pres*
◆ EMP: 56
SQ FT: 30,000
SALES (est): 10.8MM Privately Held
WEB: www.enecon.com
SIC: 2851 Coating, air curing

(G-8244)
ENEFLUX ARMTEK MAGNETICS INC (HQ)
6 Platinum Ct (11763-2251)
PHONE.................................516 576-3434
Tony Mantella, *President*
Dave Gerstacker, *Plant Mgr*
Edward Krensel, *Treasurer*
EMP: 4 EST: 1997
SQ FT: 20,000
SALES (est): 2.8MM
SALES (corp-wide): 10.8MM Privately Held
WEB: www.eamagnetics.com
SIC: 3264 Magnets, permanent: ceramic or ferrite
PA: Enecon Corporation
  6 Platinum Ct
  Medford NY 11763
  516 349-0022

(G-8245)
GLOBAL TISSUE GROUP INC (PA)
870 Expressway Dr S (11763-2027)
PHONE.................................631 924-3019
Meir Elnekaveh, *CEO*
Freydoun Elhekaveh, *Ch of Bd*
David Shaoul, *President*
Philip Shaoul, *COO*
Daniel David, *Exec VP*
◆ EMP: 50
SQ FT: 90,000
SALES (est): 12MM Privately Held
WEB: www.gtgtissue.com
SIC: 2679 Paper products, converted

(G-8246)
H B MILLWORK INC (PA)
500 Long Island Ave (11763-2510)
PHONE.................................631 289-8086
Fax: 631 289-8057
Timothy Hollowell, *President*
Michael Hollowell, *Vice Pres*
EMP: 15
SQ FT: 6,000
SALES (est): 1.9MM Privately Held
WEB: www.hbmillwork.com
SIC: 2431 2436 2426 Millwork; softwood veneer & plywood; hardwood dimension & flooring mills

(G-8247)
HAMPTON ART LLC
19 Scouting Blvd (11763-2220)
PHONE.................................631 924-1335
Robert M Gallagher, *Mktg Dir*
Kevin Gallagher, *Marketing Mgr*
Ronald T Gallagher,
Kevin T Gallagher,
Steven G Gallagher,
▲ EMP: 44
SQ FT: 13,500
SALES: 5.6MM Privately Held
WEB: www.hamptonart.com
SIC: 3069 3953 Stationers' rubber sundries; marking devices

(G-8248)
HAMPTON TECHNOLOGIES LLC
19 Scouting Blvd (11763-2220)
PHONE.................................631 924-1335
Ron Gallagher,
Steven Gallagher,
▲ EMP: 30
SQ FT: 13,500

GEOGRAPHIC SECTION

SALES (est): 5.3MM **Privately Held**
WEB: www.hamptonsecurity.com
SIC: 3699 Security devices

(G-8249)
HEALTHY BASEMENT SYSTEMS LLC
79 Cedarhurst Ave (11763-1503)
PHONE.................................516 650-9046
William Simone,
EMP: 14
SALES (est): 1.5MM **Privately Held**
WEB: www.healthybasementsystems.com
SIC: 3272 Areaways, basement window: concrete

(G-8250)
HSM MACHINE WORKS INC (PA)
Also Called: Blair-Hsm
3671 Horseblock Rd (11763-2295)
PHONE.................................631 924-6600
Fax: 631 924-6409
William R Lehmann Jr, *Ch of Bd*
Bill Lehmann, *President*
Clark Early, *Plant Mgr*
Rex Betita, *QC Mgr*
Frank May, *Manager*
▲ EMP: 40
SQ FT: 30,000
SALES (est): 8MM **Privately Held**
SIC: 3599 3728 Machine shop, jobbing & repair; aircraft parts & equipment

(G-8251)
ISLAND CUSTOM STAIRS INC
23 Scouting Blvd Unit C (11763-2245)
PHONE.................................631 205-5335
Christopher L Brett, *President*
Carol Hodosky, *Treasurer*
Delores Rufrano, *Director*
EMP: 7
SQ FT: 5,800
SALES: 900K **Privately Held**
SIC: 3534 Elevators & moving stairways

(G-8252)
JACOBI TOOL & DIE MFG INC
Also Called: Jacobi Industries
131 Middle Island Rd (11763-1517)
P.O. Box 50 (11763-0050)
PHONE.................................631 736-5394
Fax: 631 732-4643
Roger Jacobi, *Principal*
Dennis Oconnor, *Executive*
EMP: 6
SQ FT: 10,000
SALES (est): 1.1MM **Privately Held**
WEB: www.jacobiindustries.com
SIC: 3599 Machine shop, jobbing & repair

(G-8253)
LIVING DOORS INC
22 Scouting Blvd Ste 3 (11763-2260)
P.O. Box 95, Yaphank (11980-0095)
PHONE.................................631 924-5393
Don Plante, *President*
Elizabeth Plante, *Manager*
EMP: 10
SQ FT: 4,000
SALES: 700K **Privately Held**
WEB: www.livingdoors.com
SIC: 2431 Doors, wood

(G-8254)
M AND M INDUSTRIAL WELDING
2890 Route 112 (11763-1426)
PHONE.................................631 451-6044
Michael Bellasatto, *Owner*
EMP: 5
SALES (est): 232.2K **Privately Held**
SIC: 7692 Welding repair

(G-8255)
MACROLINK INC
25 Scouting Blvd Ste 1 (11763-2243)
PHONE.................................631 924-8265
Fax: 714 777-8807
Mark Cordivari, *CEO*
David Vendor, *President*
Marco Cordibari, *General Mgr*
William Goodale, *Vice Pres*
Don Nelson, *QC Mgr*
EMP: 50 EST: 1975
SQ FT: 30,000

SALES (est): 20MM
SALES (corp-wide): 2.7B **Publicly Held**
WEB: www.macrolink.com
SIC: 3823 3577 Computer interface equipment for industrial process control; computer peripheral equipment
PA: B/E Aerospace, Inc.
1400 Corporate Center Way
Wellington FL 33414
561 791-5000

(G-8256)
MTK ELECTRONICS INC
1 National Blvd (11763-2252)
PHONE.................................631 924-7666
David Radford, *President*
Erik F Meade, *Purch Mgr*
Joseph Alaimo, *Sales Staff*
Tony Digiacomo, *Manager*
▲ EMP: 35
SQ FT: 15,000
SALES (est): 9.1MM **Privately Held**
WEB: www.mtkelec.com
SIC: 3677 3675 Filtration devices, electronic; electronic capacitors

(G-8257)
PHYMETRIX INC
28 Scouting Blvd Ste C (11763-2250)
PHONE.................................631 627-3950
Bedros Bedrossian, *President*
Ani Omer, *Vice Pres*
EMP: 9
SQ FT: 10,000
SALES: 3MM **Privately Held**
SIC: 3826 8734 Moisture analyzers; calibration & certification

(G-8258)
POSIMECH INC
15 Scouting Blvd Unit 3 (11763-2254)
PHONE.................................631 924-5959
Fax: 631 924-3850
Steven R Fazio, *President*
John Fazio, *Managing Dir*
▼ EMP: 22
SQ FT: 12,236
SALES (est): 4MM **Privately Held**
WEB: www.posimech.com
SIC: 3599 3728 Machine shop, jobbing & repair; aircraft assemblies, subassemblies & parts

(G-8259)
SAYEDA MANUFACTURING CORP
20 Scouting Blvd (11763-2221)
PHONE.................................631 345-2525
Fax: 631 345-2342
Ali Khan, *President*
EMP: 10
SQ FT: 5,000
SALES (est): 810K **Privately Held**
WEB: www.sayeda.com
SIC: 3679 Harness assemblies for electronic use: wire or cable

(G-8260)
STAR READY MIX INC
172 Peconic Ave (11763-3244)
P.O. Box 371 (11763-0371)
PHONE.................................631 289-8787
Fax: 631 289-1323
Joseph A Di Silva, *President*
Tom Heff, *Vice Pres*
Frank Otero, *Vice Pres*
Frank Oters, *Project Mgr*
Thomas Hess, *Treasurer*
EMP: 13
SQ FT: 1,000
SALES (est): 1.6MM **Privately Held**
SIC: 3273 Ready-mixed concrete

(G-8261)
TOUGH TRAC INC
22 Industrial Blvd Ste 7 (11763-2260)
P.O. Box 357, Holbrook (11741-0357)
PHONE.................................631 504-6700
Daniel Aiello, *COO*
Andrew Wong, *COO*
Eva Wong, *COO*
▲ EMP: 5 EST: 2009
SQ FT: 3,500
SALES: 250K **Privately Held**
SIC: 3449 Miscellaneous metalwork

(G-8262)
WAVERLY IRON CORP
25 Commercial Blvd (11763-1531)
PHONE.................................631 732-2800
Fax: 631 732-9085
Anthony Pizzichemi, *President*
CAM Jambor, *Bookkeeper*
EMP: 21
SQ FT: 7,000
SALES (est): 6.6MM **Privately Held**
WEB: www.waverlyiron.com
SIC: 3446 Architectural metalwork

(G-8263)
WOOD INNOVATIONS OF SUFFOLK
266 Middle Island Rd # 8 (11763-1525)
PHONE.................................631 698-2345
Fax: 631 698-2396
Gino Genna, *President*
Mary Weiss, *Treasurer*
EMP: 6
SQ FT: 3,000
SALES (est): 856.3K **Privately Held**
WEB: www.woodin.com
SIC: 2431 2499 5712 1799 Interior & ornamental woodwork & trim; exterior & ornamental woodwork & trim; decorative wood & woodwork; outdoor & garden furniture; fence construction

Medina
Orleans County

(G-8264)
AIR PRODUCTS AND CHEMICALS INC
4141 Bates Rd (14103-9706)
P.O. Box 25706, Lehigh Valley PA (18002-5706)
PHONE.................................585 798-2324
Vince Morana, *Office Mgr*
EMP: 6
SALES (corp-wide): 9.8B **Publicly Held**
SIC: 2813 Oxygen, compressed or liquefied
PA: Air Products And Chemicals, Inc.
7201 Hamilton Blvd
Allentown PA 18195
610 481-4911

(G-8265)
BARNES METAL FINISHING INC
3932 Salt Works Rd (14103-9546)
P.O. Box 517 (14103-0517)
PHONE.................................585 798-4817
Fax: 585 798-4359
Wilfred Barnes, *President*
Darrel Barnes, *Vice Pres*
EMP: 17
SQ FT: 6,000
SALES: 800K **Privately Held**
SIC: 3471 Polishing, metals or formed products

(G-8266)
BAXTER HEALTHCARE CORPORATION
711 Park Ave (14103-1078)
PHONE.................................800 356-3454
Mike Smith, *Senior VP*
Dan Wellington, *QC Dir*
Scot Sabo, *Engineer*
Rohan Thadani, *Engineer*
Nelson Tatterson, *Branch Mgr*
EMP: 380
SALES (corp-wide): 9.9B **Publicly Held**
SIC: 3841 Surgical & medical instruments
HQ: Baxter Healthcare Corporation
1 Baxter Pkwy
Deerfield IL 60015
224 948-2000

(G-8267)
BMP AMERICA INC (HQ)
Also Called: B M P
11625 Maple Ridge Rd (14103-9710)
PHONE.................................585 798-0950
Fax: 585 798-4272
Edward D Andrew, *CEO*
Peter Milicia, *President*
Robert Dunning, *Vice Pres*
Jason Gillard, *Vice Pres*

Alan Lebold, *Vice Pres*
▲ EMP: 112
SQ FT: 40,000
SALES (est): 27.3MM
SALES (corp-wide): 102.4MM **Privately Held**
SIC: 3555 Sticks, printers'
PA: Andrew Industries Limited
Walton House
Accrington LANCS BB5 5
128 277-8022

(G-8268)
BRUNNER INTERNATIONAL INC
3959 Bates Rd (14103-9705)
P.O. Box 111 (14103-0111)
PHONE.................................585 798-6000
Fax: 585 798-4963
Peter Brunner, *Ch of Bd*
Paul Fortin, *General Mgr*
Roy Wagner, *Senior Engr*
Jim Carlson, *Controller*
Sandy Bennett, *Human Res Dir*
◆ EMP: 135
SALES (est): 38.3MM **Privately Held**
SIC: 3713 Truck bodies & parts

(G-8269)
COMMUNITY NEWSPPR HOLDINGS INC
Also Called: Medina Journal Register
541-543 Main St (14103)
PHONE.................................585 798-1400
Mark Francis, *Publisher*
Michael Wertman, *Vice Pres*
EMP: 38
SQ FT: 14,301 **Privately Held**
WEB: www.clintonnc.com
SIC: 2711 Newspapers, publishing & printing
PA: Community Newspaper Holdings, Inc.
445 Dexter Ave Ste 7000
Montgomery AL 36104

(G-8270)
D & W ENTERPRISES LLC
10775 W Shelby Rd (14103-9584)
PHONE.................................585 590-6727
Darrel Barnes,
EMP: 17
SALES (est): 960K **Privately Held**
SIC: 3471 Finishing, metals or formed products

(G-8271)
F & H METAL FINISHING CO INC
Also Called: Fearby Enterprises
700 Genesee St (14103-1504)
P.O. Box 486 (14103-0486)
PHONE.................................585 798-2151
Fax: 585 798-2151
Timothy Fearby, *President*
Patricia Caleb, *Corp Secy*
Kim Stevens, *Vice Pres*
EMP: 18
SQ FT: 10,000
SALES: 800K **Privately Held**
SIC: 3479 3471 Enameling, including porcelain, of metal products; lacquering of metal products; varnishing of metal products; painting of metal products; cleaning, polishing & finishing; buffing for the trade; finishing, metals or formed products; polishing, metals or formed products

(G-8272)
GANNETT STLLITE INFO NTWRK INC
Also Called: Greater Niagara Newspaper
413 Main St (14103-1416)
PHONE.................................585 798-1400
Joyce Miles, *Manager*
Dan Caswell, *Director*
EMP: 88
SALES (corp-wide): 5.7B **Publicly Held**
WEB: www.usatoday.com
SIC: 2711 Newspapers, publishing & printing
HQ: Gannett Satellite Information Network, Llc
7950 Jones Branch Dr
Mc Lean VA 22102
703 854-6000

Medina - Orleans County (G-8273)

(G-8273)
GEOPUMP INC
213 State St (14103-1337)
PHONE.................585 798-6666
James Mirand, *President*
Paul Fox, *Vice Pres*
EMP: 5
SQ FT: 1,500
SALES (est): 650.2K **Privately Held**
WEB: www.geopump.com
SIC: 3561 Pumps, domestic: water or sump

(G-8274)
HANSON AGGREGATES EAST LLC
Glenwood Ave (14103)
PHONE.................585 798-0762
EMP: 15
SALES (corp-wide): 18.7B **Privately Held**
SIC: 3273 Mfg Ready-Mixed Concrete
HQ: Hanson Aggregates East Llc
    2300 Gateway Centre Blvd
    Morrisville NC 27560
    919 380-2500

(G-8275)
HINSPERGERS POLY INDUSTRIES
430 W Oak Orchard St (14103-1551)
PHONE.................585 798-6625
Fax: 585 798-6627
Bill Thompson, *Sales Mgr*
Greg Budd, *Manager*
EMP: 27
SALES (corp-wide): 16.9MM **Privately Held**
WEB: www.hinspergers.com
SIC: 3949 Swimming pools, plastic
PA: Hinspergers Poly Industries Ltd
    645 Needham Lane
    Mississauga ON L5A 1
    905 272-0144

(G-8276)
MEDINA MILLWORKS LLC
10694 Ridge Rd (14103-9406)
PHONE.................585 798-2969
Matt Graber,
Jerome Graber,
Philip Graber,
Steven Graber,
EMP: 9
SQ FT: 960
SALES (est): 1.2MM **Privately Held**
WEB: www.medinamillworks.com
SIC: 2431 Millwork

(G-8277)
MILLERS BULK FOOD AND BAKERY
10858 Ridge Rd (14103-9432)
PHONE.................585 798-9700
Steven Miller, *Principal*
EMP: 8
SALES (est): 615K **Privately Held**
SIC: 2051 Bakery: wholesale or wholesale/retail combined

(G-8278)
MIZKAN AMERICAS INC
Also Called: Nakano Foods
711 Park Ave (14103-1078)
PHONE.................585 798-5720
Craig Smith, *President*
EMP: 18 **Privately Held**
SIC: 2099 2035 Vinegar; dressings, salad: raw & cooked (except dry mixes)
HQ: Mizkan America, Inc.
    1661 Feehanville Dr # 200
    Mount Prospect IL 60056
    847 590-0059

(G-8279)
QUORUM GROUP LLC
Also Called: Takeform Archtectural Graphics
11601 Maple Ridge Rd (14103-9710)
PHONE.................585 798-8888
Fax: 585 798-8889
William Hungerford, *President*
Gary Fleckenstein, *Senior Engr*
Dee Ann Courcy, *CFO*
Mary Knapp, *Human Res Mgr*
Megan Vann, *Accounts Mgr*
EMP: 52
SQ FT: 35,000
SALES: 6.3MM **Privately Held**
WEB: www.takeform.net
SIC: 3993 Signs, not made in custom sign painting shops

(G-8280)
S B WHISTLER & SONS INC
11023 W Center Street Ext (14103-9557)
P.O. Box 270 (14103-0270)
PHONE.................585 798-3000
Fax: 585 798-5612
Brendan Whistler, *Owner*
Larry Massey, *CFO*
EMP: 46
SQ FT: 25,000
SALES (est): 14.4MM **Privately Held**
WEB: www.phinneytool.com
SIC: 3544 Special dies & tools

(G-8281)
SHELBY CRUSHED STONE INC
10830 Blair Rd (14103-9590)
PHONE.................585 798-4501
Thomas S Biamonte, *CEO*
EMP: 17
SALES (est): 3.1MM **Privately Held**
SIC: 1429 1442 1422 Sandstone, crushed & broken-quarrying; gravel mining; crushed & broken limestone

(G-8282)
SIGMA INTL GEN MED APPRTUS LLC
711 Park Ave (14103-1078)
PHONE.................585 798-3901
Nelson Tatterson, *President*
Dan Wellington, *President*
Mike Southworth, *Vice Pres*
Jeff Wakefield, *Vice Pres*
Todd Underwood, *Opers Mgr*
▼ EMP: 500
SQ FT: 40,000
SALES (est): 209.2MM
SALES (corp-wide): 9.9B **Publicly Held**
WEB: www.sigmapumps.com
SIC: 3841 IV transfusion apparatus
PA: Baxter International Inc.
    1 Baxter Pkwy
    Deerfield IL 60015
    224 948-2000

(G-8283)
STANDEX AIR DIST PDTS INC
Also Called: Acme Manufacturing Company
214 Commercial St (14103-1206)
PHONE.................585 798-0300
Fax: 585 798-0021
Charles Kreppeneck, *Manager*
Jeffrey Hessel, *Executive*
EMP: 40
SALES (corp-wide): 751.5MM **Publicly Held**
WEB: www.standexadp.com
SIC: 3444 3498 3312 Pipe, sheet metal; fabricated pipe & fittings; blast furnaces & steel mills
HQ: Standex Air Distribution Products, Inc.
    137 Johnson Ferry Rd # 2240
    Marietta GA 30068
    770 999-0841

(G-8284)
WESTERN NEW YORK ENERGY LLC
4141 Bates Rd (14103-9706)
P.O. Box 191 (14103-0191)
PHONE.................585 798-9693
Michael Sawyer, *Vice Pres*
Isahia Schoolcraft, *Opers Staff*
Sara Flansburg, *Accountant*
Michelle Kingdollar, *Accountant*
Andrew L Buck, *Marketing Mgr*
EMP: 40
SALES (est): 19.4MM **Privately Held**
WEB: www.wnyenergy.com
SIC: 2869 Ethanolamines

Medusa
Albany County

(G-8285)
DEGENNARO FUEL SERVICE LLC
242 County Route 357 (12120-2005)
PHONE.................518 239-6350
EMP: 5
SALES (est): 402.2K **Privately Held**
SIC: 2869 Fuels

Melville
Suffolk County

(G-8286)
110 SAND COMPANY (PA)
136 Spagnoli Rd (11747-3502)
PHONE.................631 694-2822
Chester Broman, *Manager*
EMP: 33
SQ FT: 20,000
SALES (est): 8.3MM **Privately Held**
SIC: 1442 Construction sand & gravel

(G-8287)
18 ROCKS LLC
290 Spagnoli Rd (11747-3519)
PHONE.................631 465-9990
Richard Cotler, *Production*
Michael Schatten, *Mng Member*
EMP: 21
SQ FT: 3,000
SALES (est): 1.3MM
SALES (corp-wide): 2.2MM **Privately Held**
SIC: 2331 2335 Women's & misses' blouses & shirts; blouses, women's & juniors': made from purchased material; shirts, women's & juniors': made from purchased materials; women's, juniors' & misses' dresses
PA: Melwood Partners, Inc.
    100 Qentin Roosevelt Blvd
    Garden City NY 11530
    516 307-8030

(G-8288)
ADVANTAGE PLUS DIAGNOSTICS INC
200 Broadhollow Rd (11747-4846)
PHONE.................631 393-5044
Jason Damianio, *President*
Anthony Rollo, *Admin Sec*
EMP: 5
SALES (est): 380K **Privately Held**
SIC: 3841 Diagnostic apparatus, medical

(G-8289)
AERO-VISION TECHNOLOGIES INC (PA)
7 Round Tree Dr (11747-3314)
PHONE.................631 643-8349
Fax: 631 952-3517
Donald P Burkhardt, *President*
EMP: 8
SQ FT: 6,200
SALES (est): 2MM **Privately Held**
WEB: www.aero-vision.com
SIC: 3577 Computer peripheral equipment

(G-8290)
AIP PUBLISHING LLC
1305 Walt Whitman Rd # 300 (11747-4300)
PHONE.................516 576-2200
John Haynes, *CEO*
John Light, *Editor*
Roy Levenson, *CFO*
EMP: 125 EST: 2013
SALES: 48.9MM **Privately Held**
SIC: 2731 Books: publishing only

(G-8291)
AIR TECHNIQUES INC (HQ)
1295 Walt Whitman Rd (11747-3062)
PHONE.................516 433-7676
Christoph Roeer, *CEO*
Robert Nordquist, *Vice Pres*
Kent Searl, *Vice Pres*
Frank Napoli, *VP Opers*
Dominic Giordano, *Plant Mgr*
▲ EMP: 326
SQ FT: 92,000
SALES: 57.5MM
SALES (corp-wide): 269MM **Privately Held**
WEB: www.airtechniques.com
SIC: 3861 3563 3821 3844 Photographic processing equipment & chemicals; air & gas compressors including vacuum pumps; laboratory equipment: fume hoods, distillation racks, etc.; X-ray apparatus & tubes; dental equipment & supplies; pumps & pumping equipment
PA: Durr Dental Ag
    Hopfigheimer Str. 17
    Bietigheim-Bissingen 74321
    714 270-50

(G-8292)
ALL-PRO IMAGING CORP
1295 Walt Whitman Rd (11747-3070)
PHONE.................516 433-7676
Louis E Brooks, *Ch of Bd*
Frank Bader, *President*
Mark S Brooks, *Vice Pres*
Fredrick Fischer, *Vice Pres*
Kenny Keith, *Regl Sales Mgr*
▲ EMP: 20
SQ FT: 10,000
SALES (est): 2.2MM **Privately Held**
WEB: www.allproimaging.com
SIC: 3861 Processing equipment, photographic

(G-8293)
AMERICAN INSTITUTE PHYSICS INC
Hntngton Qad Ste 1n1-2 (11747)
PHONE.................516 576-2410
Catherine Oriordan, *Vice Pres*
Zita Murano, *Opers Staff*
Richard Baccante, *Treasurer*
Doris Lewis, *Branch Mgr*
Debra Dillon, *Manager*
EMP: 250
SALES (corp-wide): 15.6MM **Privately Held**
SIC: 2721 2731 8733 Trade journals: publishing only, not printed on site; books: publishing only; noncommercial research organizations
PA: American Institute Of Physics Incorporated
    1 Physics Ellipse
    College Park MD 20740
    301 209-3100

(G-8294)
AMOROSO WOOD PRODUCTS CO INC
462 Old Country Rd (11747-1825)
PHONE.................631 249-4998
Fax: 631 249-4576
Rocco Amoroso, *President*
EMP: 7
SQ FT: 18,000
SALES (est): 993.9K **Privately Held**
SIC: 2434 Wood kitchen cabinets

(G-8295)
AN GROUP INC
17 Scott Dr (11747-1013)
P.O. Box 895 (11747-0895)
PHONE.................631 549-4090
Steve Hopfenmuller, *President*
Steven Hopfenmuller, *President*
Jill Hopfenmuller, *Vice Pres*
EMP: 5
SALES (est): 287.4K **Privately Held**
WEB: www.smbiz.com
SIC: 2741 Business service newsletters: publishing & printing

(G-8296)
BEC ACQUISITION CO LLC
270 Spagnoli Rd Ste 102 (11747-3515)
PHONE.................516 986-3050
Walden Leverich,
EMP: 6
SALES (est): 310.9K **Privately Held**
SIC: 7372 Prepackaged software

▲ = Import ▼ = Export
◆ = Import/Export

GEOGRAPHIC SECTION

Melville - Suffolk County (G-8321)

(G-8297)
BIG GEYSER INC
150 Broadhollow Rd # 211 (11747-4905)
PHONE.....................................631 549-4940
Fax: 631 549-4948
Jerry Reada, *President*
EMP: 5
SALES (est): 444.3K **Privately Held**
SIC: 2086 Bottled & canned soft drinks

(G-8298)
BLUE RHINO GLOBAL SOURCING INC
Also Called: Mr.-Bar-B-q
10 Hub Dr Ste 101 (11747-3522)
PHONE.....................................516 752-0670
Fax: 516 752-0683
Michael Guadagno, *VP Opers*
Marc Zemel, *Branch Mgr*
EMP: 23
SALES (corp-wide): 2B **Publicly Held**
SIC: 1321 5984 Casing-head butane & propane production; propane gas, bottled
HQ: Blue Rhino Global Sourcing, Inc.
5650 University Pkwy # 400
Winston Salem NC 27105
800 258-7466

(G-8299)
BZ MEDIA LLC
Also Called: SD Times
225 Broadhollow Rd 211e (11747-4807)
PHONE.....................................631 421-4158
Fax: 631 922-5258
Ted Bahr, *President*
H Ted Bahr, *President*
Christina Mulligan, *Editor*
Alan L Zeichick, *Exec VP*
Joe Fernandes, *Vice Pres*
EMP: 18 EST: 1999
SQ FT: 4,000
SALES: 5.5MM **Privately Held**
WEB: www.bzmedia.com
SIC: 2721 Magazines: publishing & printing

(G-8300)
CAPY MACHINE SHOP INC (PA)
114 Spagnoli Rd (11747-3502)
PHONE.....................................631 694-6916
Salvatore Capacchione, *CEO*
Rosemary Capacchione, *Shareholder*
EMP: 40
SQ FT: 7,500
SALES (est): 8.5MM **Privately Held**
SIC: 3599 Machine shop, jobbing & repair

(G-8301)
CELLBOAT DEVELOPMENT CORP
Also Called: Cellboat Company, The
510 Broadhollow Rd (11747-3671)
PHONE.....................................800 973-4659
Andrew Overton, *President*
Keith Brown, *Vice Pres*
David Altman, *Treasurer*
EMP: 7 EST: 2012
SQ FT: 1,800
SALES (est): 413.7K **Privately Held**
SIC: 3732 Sailboats, building & repairing

(G-8302)
CHROMAGRAPHICS PRESS INC
3 Martha Dr (11747-1906)
PHONE.....................................631 367-6160
Frank Cuoco, *President*
Irene Cuoco, *Vice Pres*
Thomas Cuoco, *Vice Pres*
Ed Eng Nancy Lee, *IT/INT Sup*
EMP: 5
SALES (est): 480K **Privately Held**
WEB: www.chromagraphicspress.com
SIC: 2752 8748 Commercial printing, lithographic; business consulting

(G-8303)
CHYRONHEGO CORPORATION (HQ)
5 Hub Dr (11747-3523)
PHONE.....................................631 845-2000
Fax: 516 845-2090
Johan Apel, *President*
Richard Hajdu, *General Mgr*
Neil Foster, *COO*
Rickard Ohrn, *COO*
J M Paul, *Senior VP*
EMP: 100
SQ FT: 47,000
SALES (est): 44.7MM **Privately Held**
WEB: www.chyron.com
SIC: 3663 Radio & TV communications equipment

(G-8304)
COMAX AROMATICS CORPORATION
130 Baylis Rd (11747-3808)
PHONE.....................................631 249-0505
Peter J Calabretta, *President*
Norman Katz, *Vice Pres*
Francis J Keppel, *Admin Sec*
EMP: 50
SQ FT: 40,000
SALES (est): 4.1MM **Privately Held**
SIC: 2869 Flavors or flavoring materials, synthetic

(G-8305)
COMAX MANUFACTURING CORP
Also Called: Comax Flavors
130 Baylis Rd (11747-3808)
PHONE.....................................631 249-0505
Fax: 631 249-9255
Peter J Calabretta Jr, *Ch of Bd*
Agneta Boudreau, *Vice Pres*
Paul Calabretta, *Vice Pres*
Christine Contino, *Purch Agent*
Frank Vollaro, *Manager*
▲ EMP: 55
SQ FT: 40,000
SALES (est): 32MM **Privately Held**
SIC: 2869 Flavors or flavoring materials, synthetic

(G-8306)
COMTECH PST CORP (HQ)
105 Baylis Rd (11747-3833)
PHONE.....................................631 777-8900
Fax: 516 777-8877
Dr Stan Sloane, *CEO*
Michael Hrybenko, *President*
Walter Koprowski, *President*
Donald Podesta, *General Mgr*
Robert McCollum, *Senior VP*
▲ EMP: 120
SQ FT: 46,000
SALES (est): 37.9MM
SALES (corp-wide): 411MM **Publicly Held**
WEB: www.comtechpst.com
SIC: 3663 3825 Microwave communication equipment; amplifiers, RF power & IF; test equipment for electronic & electric measurement
PA: Comtech Telecommunications Corp.
68 S Service Rd Ste 230
Melville NY 11747
631 962-7000

(G-8307)
COMTECH TELECOM CORP (PA)
68 S Service Rd Ste 230 (11747-2350)
PHONE.....................................631 962-7000
Fax: 631 962-7001
Fred Kornberg, *Ch of Bd*
Stanton D Sloane, *President*
Richard L Burt, *Senior VP*
Michael D Porcelain, *CFO*
Jason Dilorenzo, *Manager*
◆ EMP: 136
SQ FT: 9,600
SALES: 411MM **Publicly Held**
WEB: www.comtechtel.com
SIC: 3663 Microwave communication equipment; amplifiers, RF power & IF; mobile communication equipment

(G-8308)
CROWN NOVELTY WORKS INC
42 Elkland Rd (11747-3302)
PHONE.....................................631 253-0949
EMP: 7 EST: 1909
SQ FT: 10,000
SALES: 1.2MM **Privately Held**
SIC: 3364 Mfg Lead Curtain Weights

(G-8309)
DADDARIO & COMPANY INC
99 Marcus Dr (11747-4209)
PHONE.....................................631 439-3300
EMP: 91
SALES (corp-wide): 220.3MM **Privately Held**
SIC: 3931 String instruments & parts
PA: D'addario & Company, Inc.
595 Smith St
Farmingdale NY 11735
631 439-3300

(G-8310)
DESIGNER EPOXY FINISHES INC
445 Broadhollow Rd Ste 25 (11747-3645)
PHONE.....................................646 943-6044
Justin Palladino, *President*
EMP: 6 EST: 2007
SALES (est): 885.2K **Privately Held**
SIC: 2851 1752 Epoxy coatings; floor laying & floor work

(G-8311)
DISTINCTION MAGAZINE INC
Also Called: Island Publications
235 Pinelawn Rd (11747-4226)
PHONE.....................................631 843-3522
Fax: 631 843-4186
Madelyn Roberts, *CEO*
Patrice Golde, *President*
EMP: 25
SALES (est): 2.4MM **Privately Held**
SIC: 2721 Magazines: publishing & printing

(G-8312)
DORIS PANOS DESIGNS LTD
130 Old East Neck Rd (11747-3209)
PHONE.....................................631 245-0580
Doris Panos, *President*
EMP: 6
SQ FT: 250
SALES (est): 710K **Privately Held**
SIC: 3911 Jewelry, precious metal

(G-8313)
E-Z-EM INC (DH)
155 Pinelawn Rd Ste 230n (11747-3249)
PHONE.....................................609 524-2864
Vittorio Puppo, *CEO*
Adrianne Setton, *Manager*
◆ EMP: 39 EST: 1961
SALES (est): 9.1MM
SALES (corp-wide): 97.6MM **Privately Held**
WEB: www.ezem.com
SIC: 2835 3841 In vitro & in vivo diagnostic substances; diagnostic apparatus, medical
HQ: Bracco Diagnostics Inc
259 Prospect Plains Rd
Monroe Township NJ 08831
609 514-2200

(G-8314)
EQUAL OPPRTNITY PBLCATIONS INC
Also Called: Careers and The Disabled
445 Broadhollow Rd # 425 (11747-3669)
PHONE.....................................631 421-9421
John R Miller III, *Ch of Bd*
Debra Kahn, *Business Mgr*
Tamara Flaun, *Exec VP*
Kay Miller, *Exec VP*
Christine Desmond, *Vice Pres*
EMP: 12 EST: 1969
SQ FT: 3,000
SALES (est): 1.6MM **Privately Held**
WEB: www.eop.com
SIC: 2721 7361 Magazines: publishing & printing; employment agencies

(G-8315)
ESTEE LAUDER COMPANIES INC
7 Corporate Center Dr (11747-3115)
PHONE.....................................212 572-4015
John Capotosto, *Exec Dir*
Larry Alonso, *Exec Dir*
EMP: 504
SALES (corp-wide): 11.2B **Publicly Held**
WEB: www.elcompanies.com
SIC: 2844 Toilet preparations
PA: The Estee Lauder Companies Inc
767 5th Ave Fl 37
New York NY 10153
212 572-4200

(G-8316)
ESTEE LAUDER INC
125 Pinelawn Rd (11747-3135)
PHONE.....................................631 531-1000
Fax: 631 531-1604
Ken Marenus, *Senior VP*
Gavin Kaplan, *Vice Pres*
Daniel Kelly, *Vice Pres*
Louis Schapiro, *Vice Pres*
David P Yacko, *Vice Pres*
EMP: 100
SALES (corp-wide): 11.2B **Publicly Held**
WEB: www.esteelauder.com
SIC: 2844 5999 5122 Perfumes & colognes; toiletries, cosmetics & perfumes; cosmetics; perfumes & colognes; drugs, proprietaries & sundries
HQ: Estee Lauder Inc.
767 5th Ave Fl 37
New York NY 10153
212 572-4200

(G-8317)
ESTEE LAUDER INC
350 S Service Rd (11747-3230)
PHONE.....................................631 454-7000
Fax: 631 847-8370
Shahan Nazar, *Senior VP*
Larry Krieb, *Vice Pres*
Frank O'Neil, *Vice Pres*
Jack Deng, *Project Mgr*
Rafael Mercedes, *Mfg Staff*
EMP: 108
SALES (corp-wide): 11.2B **Publicly Held**
WEB: www.esteelauder.com
SIC: 2844 Cosmetic preparations
HQ: Estee Lauder Inc.
767 5th Ave Fl 37
New York NY 10153
212 572-4200

(G-8318)
FALCONSTOR SOFTWARE INC (PA)
2 Huntington Quadrangle 2s (11747-4501)
PHONE.....................................631 777-5188
Fax: 631 501-7633
Eli Oxenhorn, *Ch of Bd*
Gary Quinn, *President*
Philippe Bernard, *General Mgr*
Suresh Nair, *General Mgr*
Herb Siegel, *General Mgr*
EMP: 12
SQ FT: 55,000
SALES: 48.5MM **Publicly Held**
WEB: www.falconstor.com
SIC: 7372 7371 Prepackaged software; application computer software; computer software development; computer software systems analysis & design, custom

(G-8319)
FILMPAK EXTRUSION LLC
125 Spagnoli Rd (11747-3518)
PHONE.....................................631 293-6767
Peter Levy, *President*
EMP: 60
SQ FT: 100,000
SALES: 20MM **Privately Held**
SIC: 2673 Bags: plastic, laminated & coated

(G-8320)
FONAR CORPORATION (PA)
110 Marcus Dr (11747-4292)
PHONE.....................................631 694-2929
Fax: 516 249-3734
Raymond V Damadian, *Ch of Bd*
Lou Bonanni, *CFO*
Sol Ginzburg, *VP Sales*
Claudette J V Chan, *Admin Sec*
EMP: 163
SQ FT: 78,000
SALES: 73.3MM **Publicly Held**
WEB: www.fonar.com
SIC: 3845 8741 Electromedical equipment; management services

(G-8321)
FOUGERA PHARMACEUTICALS INC (DH)
Also Called: Pharmaderm
60 Baylis Rd (11747-3838)
P.O. Box 2006 (11747-0103)
PHONE.....................................631 454-7677

Melville - Suffolk County (G-8322) — GEOGRAPHIC SECTION

Fax: 631 420-1572
Brian A Markison, *CEO*
Donald Degolyer, *Ch of Bd*
Darryl Jackson, *Publisher*
Jeff Bailey, *COO*
Chris Klein, *Senior VP*
▲ **EMP:** 250
SQ FT: 190,000
SALES (est): 266.4MM
SALES (corp-wide): 49.4B **Privately Held**
WEB: www.altanapharma-us.com
SIC: 2834 2851 2821 3479 Pharmaceutical preparations; ointments; paints & paint additives; plasticizer/additive based plastic materials; painting, coating & hot dipping; measuring & controlling devices
HQ: Sandoz Inc.
100 College Rd W
Princeton NJ 08540
609 627-8500

(G-8322)
GPC INTERNATIONAL INC (PA)
510 Broadhollow Rd # 205 (11747-3606)
PHONE 631 752-9600
Steven Roth, *President*
Don Fleisheiar, *CFO*
Joan Middleton, *Manager*
Patrice Masterson, *Asst Director*
EMP: 8
SQ FT: 2,500
SALES (est): 21.9MM **Privately Held**
SIC: 3861 Graphic arts plates, sensitized

(G-8323)
GRAPHIC IMAGE ASSOCIATES LLC
305 Spagnoli Rd (11747-3506)
PHONE 631 249-9600
Thomas Glazer, *Mng Member*
Carol O' Connell,
EMP: 100
SQ FT: 8,500
SALES (est): 8.5MM **Privately Held**
WEB: www.gimageny.com
SIC: 3111 Bookbinders' leather

(G-8324)
GRAPHIC IMAGE INCORPORATED
Also Called: Gigi New York
305 Spagnoli Rd (11747-3506)
PHONE 631 249-9600
Thomas J Glazer, *President*
Carol O' Connell, *Vice Pres*
Rebecca Chin, *Pub Rel Mgr*
Georgette Madura, *Controller*
Edward Mesloh, *Controller*
◆ **EMP:** 150 **EST:** 1969
SQ FT: 50,000
SALES (est): 14.2MM **Privately Held**
WEB: www.graphicimagenewyork.com
SIC: 2782 3111 5137 5632 Blankbooks & looseleaf binders; albums; diaries; handbag leather; handbags; handbags

(G-8325)
GUIDANCE GROUP INC
Also Called: Child's Work-Child's Play
1 Huntington Quad 1n03 (11747-4466)
PHONE 631 756-4618
Jon D Werz, *CEO*
Carmine Russo, *CFO*
Michael Surrey, *Analyst*
EMP: 12
SALES (est): 946.8K **Privately Held**
SIC: 2711 Newspapers, publishing & printing

(G-8326)
HADCO METAL TRADING CO LLC
120 Spagnoli Rd Ste 1 (11747-3513)
PHONE 631 270-9724
Gilad Fishman, *CEO*
Nancy Barcus, *Sales Mgr*
EMP: 6 **EST:** 2011
SALES (est): 799.7K **Privately Held**
SIC: 3353 Aluminum sheet, plate & foil

(G-8327)
HENRY SCHEIN FINCL SVCS LLC (HQ)
Also Called: Henry Schein International Inc
135 Duryea Rd (11747-3834)
PHONE 631 843-5500
Stanley Bergman, *CEO*
Steven Paladino, *CFO*
EMP: 10
SALES (est): 884.9K
SALES (corp-wide): 10.6B **Publicly Held**
SIC: 3843 Dental equipment & supplies
PA: Henry Schein, Inc.
135 Duryea Rd
Melville NY 11747
631 843-5500

(G-8328)
HONEYWELL INTERNATIONAL INC
263 Old Country Rd (11747-2712)
P.O. Box 22324, Brooklyn (11202-2324)
PHONE 212 964-5111
EMP: 657
SALES (corp-wide): 38.5B **Publicly Held**
SIC: 3724 Aircraft Engines And Engine Parts
PA: Honeywell International Inc.
115 Tabor Rd
Morris Plains NJ 07950
973 455-2000

(G-8329)
HONEYWELL INTERNATIONAL INC
2 Corporate Center Dr # 100 (11747-3269)
PHONE 516 577-2000
Ron Rothman, *President*
Manuel Pondillo, *Opers Staff*
Judy Tasch, *Marketing Mgr*
Mike Zimolka, *Sr Project Mgr*
Tom Lange, *Manager*
EMP: 400
SALES (corp-wide): 38.5B **Publicly Held**
WEB: www.honeywell.com
SIC: 3728 Accumulators, aircraft propeller
PA: Honeywell International Inc.
115 Tabor Rd
Morris Plains NJ 07950
973 455-2000

(G-8330)
I W INDUSTRIES INC (PA)
Also Called: Concinnity Division
35 Melville Park Rd (11747-3104)
PHONE 631 293-9494
Fax: 516 293-9499
Jerome Warshawsky, *President*
Murray Cohen, *Vice Pres*
ARI Warshawsky, *Vice Pres*
Glenn M Davis, *Engineer*
Terry Klein, *Credit Mgr*
▲ **EMP:** 230 **EST:** 1931
SQ FT: 110,000
SALES (est): 11.4MM **Privately Held**
WEB: www.iwindustries.com
SIC: 3451 3471 3432 Screw machine products; finishing, metals or formed products; faucets & spigots, metal & plastic

(G-8331)
INTERDGITAL COMMUNICATIONS LLC
2 Huntington Quad Ste 4s (11747-4508)
PHONE 631 622-4000
Fax: 516 622-0100
Daniel Cohen, *Engineer*
Bill Hackett, *Engineer*
Gary Lomp, *Manager*
Richard Cho, *Manager*
Cynthia Hanscom, *Manager*
EMP: 125
SALES (corp-wide): 441.4MM **Publicly Held**
WEB: www.interdigital.com
SIC: 3661 8731 Telephone & telegraph apparatus; commercial physical research
HQ: Interdigital Communications Llc
200 Bellevue Pkwy Ste 300
Wilmington DE 19809
610 878-7800

(G-8332)
KARP ASSOCIATES INC (PA)
Also Called: Adjustable Shelving
260 Spagnoli Rd (11747-3505)
PHONE 631 768-8300
Adam Gold, *Chairman*
Ziggy Midura, *Plant Mgr*
Augustine Lopez, *Safety Mgr*
Ronnie Peterson, *Controller*
Hilda Dejesus, *Human Res Dir*
◆ **EMP:** 95 **EST:** 1956
SALES (est): 23MM **Privately Held**
WEB: www.karpinc.com
SIC: 3442 2541 Metal doors; shelving, office & store, wood

(G-8333)
LEVITION MANUFACTURING CO
201 N Service Rd (11747-3138)
PHONE 631 812-6000
Fax: 718 631-6439
Jennifer Waite, *General Mgr*
Daryoush Larizadeh, *Senior VP*
Patricia O'Hara, *Engineer*
George Hatzigeorgiadis, *Project Engr*
Scot Hale, *Design Engr*
▼ **EMP:** 33
SALES (est): 11.5MM **Privately Held**
SIC: 3699 Electrical equipment & supplies

(G-8334)
LEVITON MANUFACTURING CO INC (PA)
201 N Service Rd (11747-3138)
P.O. Box 10600 (11747-0056)
PHONE 631 812-6000
Stephen Sokolow, *Vice Ch Bd*
Donald J Hendler, *President*
Daryoush Larizadeh, *President*
Brian Groenig, *Principal*
Joseph Helm, *Regional Mgr*
◆ **EMP:** 450 **EST:** 1990
SALES (est): 1.5B **Privately Held**
WEB: www.leviton.com
SIC: 3643 3613 3357 3674 Current-carrying wiring devices; caps & plugs, electric: attachment; connectors, electric cord; sockets, electric; fuses, electric; nonferrous wiredrawing & insulating; building wire & cable, nonferrous; diodes, solid state (germanium, silicon, etc.); transistors; engine electrical equipment; electronic connectors

(G-8335)
LSI COMPUTER SYSTEMS
1235 Walt Whitman Rd (11747-3086)
PHONE 631 271-0400
Fax: 631 271-0405
Alfred Musto, *CEO*
Attila Tetik, *President*
Alvin Kaplan, *Corp Secy*
Burt Cohen, *Vice Pres*
Sherri Smith, *Vice Pres*
EMP: 35
SQ FT: 13,500
SALES (est): 5.8MM **Privately Held**
WEB: www.lsicsi.com
SIC: 3674 Integrated circuits, semiconductor networks, etc.; metal oxide silicon (MOS) devices

(G-8336)
MEYCO PRODUCTS INC (PA)
1225 Walt Whitman Rd (11747-3093)
PHONE 631 421-9800
David W Weissner, *CEO*
John Ciniglio, *President*
Donnie Griffin, *Vice Pres*
John Hughes, *Prdtn Mgr*
Paul Distefano, *Executive*
▼ **EMP:** 30 **EST:** 1898
SQ FT: 70,000
SALES (est): 19.6MM **Privately Held**
WEB: www.meycoproducts.com
SIC: 2394 Liners & covers, fabric: made from purchased materials

(G-8337)
MITSUBISHI ELC PWR PDTS INC
55 Marcus Dr (11747-4209)
PHONE 516 962-2813
EMP: 6
SALES (corp-wide): 37.5B **Privately Held**
SIC: 3699 1731 Electrical equipment & supplies; electrical work
HQ: Mitsubishi Electric Power Products, Inc.
530 Keystone Dr
Warrendale PA 15086
724 772-2555

(G-8338)
NASTEL TECHNOLOGIES INC (PA)
48 S Service Rd Ste 205 (11747-2335)
PHONE 631 761-9100
Fax: 631 761-9101
David Mavashev, *CEO*
Larry Jeshiva, *Vice Pres*
Richard Nikula, *Vice Pres*
Michael Ragusa, *Vice Pres*
Charles Rich, *Vice Pres*
EMP: 78
SQ FT: 7,500
SALES (est): 19.5MM **Privately Held**
WEB: www.nastel.com
SIC: 7372 Prepackaged software

(G-8339)
NATURAL ORGANICS INC (PA)
Also Called: Nature's Plus
548 Broadhollow Rd (11747-3708)
PHONE 631 293-0030
Fax: 631 249-2022
Gerald Kessler, *Ch of Bd*
James Gibbons, *President*
Vic Deventer, *Publisher*
Cheryl Manzione, *Project Mgr*
Scott Devoti, *Opers Mgr*
▲ **EMP:** 250
SQ FT: 100,000
SALES: 0 **Privately Held**
SIC: 2833 Vitamins, natural or synthetic: bulk, uncompounded

(G-8340)
NEW DIMENSIONS RESEARCH CORP
260 Spagnoli Rd (11747-3593)
PHONE 631 694-1356
Fax: 631 694-6097
Timothy L Mason, *Ch of Bd*
Jeffrey Mason, *President*
Kenneth Dasrath, *Vice Pres*
Ranga Kanadam, *Opers Mgr*
Dany Espinal, *Warehouse Mgr*
▲ **EMP:** 125 **EST:** 1957
SQ FT: 155,000
SALES (est): 30.7MM **Privately Held**
WEB: www.ndrc.com
SIC: 3993 7389 Signs & advertising specialties; design, commercial & industrial

(G-8341)
NEWSDAY LLC (DH)
Also Called: Newsday Media Group
235 Pinelawn Rd (11747-4250)
PHONE 631 843-4050
Fax: 516 843-2953
Patrick Dolan, *President*
William H Attwood, *Publisher*
Alicia P Riding, *Publisher*
David Blasband, *Editor*
Percy Foreman, *Editor*
EMP: 400
SALES (est): 45.2MM
SALES (corp-wide): 15.6B **Privately Held**
SIC: 2711 Newspapers, publishing & printing
HQ: Cablevision Systems Corporation
1111 Stewart Ave
Bethpage NY 11714
516 803-2300

(G-8342)
NEWSDAY LLC
25 Deshon Dr (11747-4221)
PHONE 631 843-3135
Raymond Jansen, *Branch Mgr*
EMP: 150
SALES (corp-wide): 15.6B **Privately Held**
SIC: 2711 Newspapers, publishing & printing
HQ: Newsday Llc
235 Pinelawn Rd
Melville NY 11747
631 843-4050

▲ = Import ▼=Export
◆ =Import/Export

(G-8343)
NIKON INSTRUMENTS INC (DH)
1300 Walt Whitman Rd Fl 2 (11747-3064)
PHONE..................................631 547-4200
Yoshinobu Ishikawa, *Ch of Bd*
Toshiaki Nagano, *President*
James Hamlin, *Vice Pres*
Scott Monroe, *Purch Mgr*
Peter Moleski, *Treasurer*
▲ **EMP:** 92
SALES (est): 44.8MM
SALES (corp-wide): 7B **Privately Held**
WEB: www.nikonusa.com
SIC: 3827 Optical instruments & lenses

(G-8344)
OLYMPIC SOFTWARE & CONSULTING
290 Broadhollow Rd 130e (11747-4852)
PHONE..................................631 351-0655
Chris McLean, *Owner*
EMP: 7 **EST:** 2001
SALES (est): 561K **Privately Held**
SIC: 7372 Prepackaged software

(G-8345)
OPUS TECHNOLOGY CORPORATION
10 Gwynne Rd (11747-1414)
PHONE..................................631 271-1883
James Startin, *President*
EMP: 10
SALES (est): 890K **Privately Held**
SIC: 3679 Electronic circuits

(G-8346)
P & F INDUSTRIES INC (PA)
445 Broadhollow Rd # 100 (11747-3615)
PHONE..................................631 694-9800
Fax: 631 694-9804
Richard A Horowitz, *Ch of Bd*
Joseph A Molino Jr, *COO*
◆ **EMP:** 163 **EST:** 1963
SQ FT: 5,000
SALES: 81.7MM **Publicly Held**
WEB: www.pfina.com
SIC: 3546 3429 3714 Power-driven handtools; grinders, portable: electric or pneumatic; manufactured hardware (general); filters: oil, fuel & air, motor vehicle

(G-8347)
PARK ELECTROCHEMICAL CORP (PA)
48 S Service Rd Ste 300 (11747-2335)
PHONE..................................631 465-3600
Fax: 631 465-3100
Brian E Shore, *Ch of Bd*
Ronald Brett, *President*
Howard R Elliott, *President*
Mark A Esquivel, *President*
Manuel Gonzalez, *President*
▲ **EMP:** 145
SQ FT: 8,000
SALES: 145.8MM **Publicly Held**
WEB: www.parkelectro.com
SIC: 3672 3674 Printed circuit boards; microcircuits, integrated (semiconductor)

(G-8348)
POLY-PAK INDUSTRIES INC (PA)
Also Called: Colorpak
125 Spagnoli Rd (11747-3518)
PHONE..................................631 293-6767
Fax: 516 454-6366
Peter Levy, *Ch of Bd*
Leonard Levy, *Chairman*
Rose Matty, *Senior VP*
Mitchell Cohen, *Vice Pres*
Doug Kiesel, *Vice Pres*
◆ **EMP:** 280
SQ FT: 150,000
SALES (est): 91MM **Privately Held**
WEB: www.poly-pak.com
SIC: 2673 2677 Plastic bags: made from purchased materials; envelopes

(G-8349)
PRECISION PHARMA SERVICES INC
155 Duryea Rd (11747-3894)
PHONE..................................631 752-7314
Jim Moose, *President*
Kathleen Beach, *Vice Pres*
Tom Lynch, *Vice Pres*
Allen Williams, *Vice Pres*
Yen Nguyen, *Engineer*
EMP: 125
SQ FT: 100,000
SALES (est): 22.5MM **Privately Held**
WEB: www.precisionpharma.com
SIC: 2834 Pharmaceutical preparations

(G-8350)
PUBLISHERS CLEARING HOUSE LLC
265 Spagnoli Rd Ste 1 (11747-3508)
PHONE..................................516 249-4063
EMP: 21
SALES (corp-wide): 162.6MM **Privately Held**
SIC: 2741 Miscellaneous publishing
PA: Publishers Clearing House Llc
382 Channel Dr
Port Washington NY 11050
516 883-5432

(G-8351)
QUADRANGLE QUICKPRINTS LTD
Also Called: Quadrangle Quick Print
1 Huntington Quad Ll04 (11747-4401)
P.O. Box 2753, North Babylon (11703-0753)
PHONE..................................631 694-4464
Fax: 516 694-4469
Henry Schaja, *Owner*
EMP: 6
SQ FT: 1,000
SALES (est): 780.6K **Privately Held**
WEB: www.cardsandstationery.com
SIC: 2752 Commercial printing, offset

(G-8352)
REDWOOD CLLABORATIVE MEDIA INC
105 Maxess Rd (11747-3851)
PHONE..................................631 393-6051
Andrew Muns, *CEO*
Peggy Libbey, *President*
Kristin Muns, *Marketing Staff*
EMP: 10
SALES (est): 682.3K **Privately Held**
SIC: 3577 Data conversion equipment, media-to-media: computer

(G-8353)
ROSS COMMUNICATIONS ASSOCIATES
200 Broadhollow Rd # 207 (11747-4846)
PHONE..................................631 393-5089
Robert Ross, *President*
Jodie Ross, *Vice Pres*
EMP: 10
SALES (est): 6MM **Privately Held**
SIC: 2721 Magazines: publishing & printing

(G-8354)
RUBIES COSTUME COMPANY INC
1770 Walt Whitman Rd (11747-3068)
PHONE..................................516 326-1500
Howard Biege, *Vice Pres*
Richard Tinari, *Sales Staff*
Lauren Rabinowitz, *Director*
EMP: 40
SALES (corp-wide): 477.7MM **Privately Held**
SIC: 2389 5199 7299 Costumes; fabrics, yarns & knit goods; costume rental
PA: Rubie's Costume Company, Inc.
12008 Jamaica Ave
Richmond Hill NY 11418
718 846-1008

(G-8355)
SIMPLY AMAZING ENTERPRISES INC
68 S Service Rd Ste 1 (11747-2354)
PHONE..................................631 503-6452
EMP: 7 **EST:** 2014
SALES: 390K **Privately Held**
SIC: 2842 Mfg Polish/Sanitation Goods

(G-8356)
STANDARD REGISTER INC
155 Pinelawn Rd Ste 120s (11747-3252)
PHONE..................................937 221-1303
Wendy Matthews, *Finance*
Bob Paradise, *Branch Mgr*
Duard Headley, *Director*
EMP: 10
SALES (corp-wide): 5.1B **Privately Held**
WEB: www.stdreg.com
SIC: 2761 Manifold business forms
HQ: Standard Register, Inc.
600 Albany St
Dayton OH 45417
937 221-1000

(G-8357)
STAR COMMUNITY PUBG GROUP LLC
Also Called: Star Community Pubg Group LLC
235 Pinelawn Rd (11747-4226)
PHONE..................................631 843-4050
Lee Aiello, *Credit Mgr*
Michael Gates, *VP Sales*
Barbara Fisher, *Manager*
EMP: 194
SALES: 45MM
SALES (corp-wide): 15.6B **Privately Held**
WEB: www.tribune.com
SIC: 2711 Newspapers, publishing & printing
HQ: Newsday Llc
235 Pinelawn Rd
Melville NY 11747
631 843-4050

(G-8358)
SUTTON PLACE SOFTWARE INC
13 Tappen Dr (11747-1019)
PHONE..................................631 421-1737
Steve J Sutton, *President*
EMP: 5
SALES (est): 510K **Privately Held**
SIC: 7372 Prepackaged software

(G-8359)
SYSTEMS TRADING INC
48 S Svc Rd Ste Ll90 (11747)
PHONE..................................718 261-8900
Harold Schwartz, *Ch of Bd*
EMP: 7
SQ FT: 1,650
SALES: 8MM **Privately Held**
WEB: www.btn.net
SIC: 7372 7377 Prepackaged software; computer rental & leasing

(G-8360)
TEL TECH INTERNATIONAL
200 Broadhollow Rd # 207 (11747-4846)
PHONE..................................516 393-5174
Donald Wuerfl, *Manager*
EMP: 40
SALES (est): 1MM **Privately Held**
SIC: 7372 Prepackaged software

(G-8361)
TOPTEC PRODUCTS LLC
1225 Walt Whitman Rd (11747-3010)
PHONE..................................631 421-9800
John Ciniglio, *President*
EMP: 13
SALES (est): 1.3MM **Privately Held**
SIC: 2394 Tents: made from purchased materials

(G-8362)
XEROX CORPORATION
155 Pinelawn Rd Ste 200n (11747-3248)
PHONE..................................516 677-1500
Donna Dunlap, *Manager*
EMP: 78
SALES (corp-wide): 18B **Publicly Held**
SIC: 3577 Computer peripheral equipment
PA: Xerox Corporation
45 Glover Ave Ste 700
Norwalk CT 06850
203 968-3000

Menands
Albany County

(G-8363)
A M & J DIGITAL
800 N Pearl St Ste 5 (12204-1893)
PHONE..................................518 434-2579
Lori Squadere,
Beth Cipperly, *Graphic Designe*
EMP: 8
SALES (est): 1MM **Privately Held**
SIC: 2759 Advertising literature: printing

(G-8364)
ACKROYD METAL FABRICATORS INC
966 Broadway Ste 2 (12204-2521)
PHONE..................................518 434-1281
Fax: 518 434-8232
Paul Zabinski, *President*
Bill White, *Controller*
EMP: 12
SQ FT: 40,000
SALES: 1.5MM **Privately Held**
SIC: 3441 Fabricated structural metal

(G-8365)
ALBANY INTERNATIONAL CORP
Appleton Wire Division
1373 Broadway (12204-2697)
PHONE..................................518 445-2230
Fax: 518 445-2265
Michael Moriarty, *Vice Pres*
Tom Rice, *Vice Pres*
Charles J Silva Jr, *Vice Pres*
Chris Spraggins, *Vice Pres*
Norman Fugate, *Opers Mgr*
EMP: 150
SALES (corp-wide): 709.8MM **Publicly Held**
WEB: www.albint.com
SIC: 2621 2296 Paper mills; tire cord & fabrics
PA: Albany International Corp.
216 Airport Dr
Rochester NH 03867
518 445-2200

(G-8366)
ALBANY INTERNATIONAL CORP
Dryer Fabrics Division
1373 Broadway (12204-2697)
P.O. Box 1907, Albany (12201-1907)
PHONE..................................518 447-6400
Al Drinkwater, *Manager*
Alan Perfect, *Administration*
EMP: 100
SALES (corp-wide): 709.8MM **Publicly Held**
WEB: www.albint.com
SIC: 2672 Cloth lined paper: made from purchased paper
PA: Albany International Corp.
216 Airport Dr
Rochester NH 03867
518 445-2200

(G-8367)
ARCADIA MFG GROUP INC
1032 Broadway (12204-2506)
PHONE..................................518 434-6213
William T Sumner, *Ch of Bd*
EMP: 6
SALES (corp-wide): 11.4MM **Privately Held**
SIC: 3498 3446 3444 3999 Fabricated pipe & fittings; ornamental metalwork; sheet metalwork; cigar lighters, except precious metal
PA: Arcadia Manufacturing Group, Inc.
80 Cohoes Ave
Green Island NY 12183
518 434-6213

(G-8368)
ATLANTIC STATES DISTRIBUTING
Also Called: Atlantic States Kitchens Baths
1325 Broadway (12204-2652)
PHONE..................................518 427-6364
Fax: 518 426-8753
Philip Crane, *President*
James Flood, *Vice Pres*
Joey Flood, *VP Finance*
Jamie Flood, *Sales Mgr*
EMP: 8 **EST:** 1959
SALES (est): 1.6MM **Privately Held**
WEB: www.atlanticstateskitchens.com
SIC: 2434 Wood kitchen cabinets

Menands - Albany County

(G-8369)
BLASCH PRECISION CERAMICS INC (PA)
580 Broadway Ste 1 (12204-2896)
PHONE.................518 436-1263
Fax: 518 436-0098
Robert A Baker, *Ch of Bd*
David W Bobrek, *Ch of Bd*
Werner Steinheimer, *Principal*
John Parrish, *Exec VP*
William Johnson, *Vice Pres*
▲ **EMP:** 100
SALES (est): 14.9MM **Privately Held**
WEB: www.powermaterials.com
SIC: 3297 Graphite refractories: carbon bond or ceramic bond

(G-8370)
DYNASTY CHEMICAL CORP
444 N Pearl St (12204-1511)
PHONE.................518 463-1146
Fax: 518 463-3684
Jane Waldman, *President*
Mel R Waldman, *Vice Pres*
Birdus Waldman, *Sales Mgr*
Tabor Waldman, *Mktg Dir*
Chris Babie, *Manager*
▲ **EMP:** 48
SQ FT: 109,000
SALES (est): 17.4MM **Privately Held**
SIC: 2819 5169 Industrial inorganic chemicals; industrial chemicals

(G-8371)
FRAMES PLUS INC
991 Broadway Ste 208 (12204-2539)
PHONE.................518 462-1842
Fax: 518 426-0858
Todd Richless, *President*
Brian Richless, *Vice Pres*
EMP: 18
SQ FT: 15,000
SALES (est): 1.7MM **Privately Held**
WEB: www.framesplusinc.com
SIC: 3952 Frames for artists' canvases

(G-8372)
GEROME TECHNOLOGIES INC
85 Broadway Ste 1 (12204-2791)
PHONE.................518 463-1324
Fax: 518 689-2337
Mark Smisloff, *President*
Justyna Zieba, *Design Engr*
Julie Ferraro, *Manager*
Katie Whalen, *Manager*
▲ **EMP:** 54
SQ FT: 54,000
SALES (est): 18.3MM **Privately Held**
SIC: 3644 3699 7539 Insulators & insulation materials, electrical; electrical equipment & supplies; electrical services

(G-8373)
LEXIS PUBLISHING
Also Called: Lexis Nexis Mathew Bender
1275 Broadway (12204-2638)
PHONE.................518 487-3000
Fax: 518 487-3083
Lou Androzzi, *President*
Kathryn Gruber, *Regional Mgr*
Jenee Moore, *Regional Mgr*
Carlton Dyce, *Vice Pres*
Michelle Guyot, *Vice Pres*
EMP: 113
SALES (est): 8.9MM **Privately Held**
SIC: 2731 Book publishing

(G-8374)
MCALLISTERS PRECISION WLDG INC
Also Called: Precision Co.
1076 Broadway (12204-2507)
PHONE.................518 221-3455
Jason McCallister, *Principal*
April McCallister, *Principal*
EMP: 15
SALES: 1.2MM **Privately Held**
SIC: 3446 3548 Fences or posts, ornamental iron or steel; welding & cutting apparatus & accessories

(G-8375)
MCCARTHY TIRE SVC CO NY INC
Also Called: McCarthy Tire and Auto Ctr
980 Broadway (12204-2504)
PHONE.................518 449-5185
Fax: 518 434-2354
Rick Beckman, *Principal*
EMP: 15
SQ FT: 7,140
SALES (corp-wide): 232MM **Privately Held**
SIC: 3011 Automobile tires, pneumatic
HQ: Mccarthy Tire Service Company Of New York, Inc.
340 Kidder St
Wilkes Barre PA 18702

(G-8376)
MIDLAND FARMS INC (PA)
375 Broadway (12204-2708)
PHONE.................518 436-7038
Demetrios E Haseotes, *CEO*
Bob Walton, *Manager*
EMP: 48
SALES (est): 15.6MM **Privately Held**
WEB: www.midlandfarms.com
SIC: 2026 Milk processing (pasteurization, homogenizing, bottling)

(G-8377)
NEW YORK LEGAL PUBLISHING
120 Broadway Ste 1a (12204-2722)
PHONE.................518 459-1100
Ernest Barvoets, *President*
Edward M Neiles Jr, *Vice Pres*
Suzanne Barvoets, *Sales Staff*
EMP: 7
SALES: 1.2MM **Privately Held**
WEB: www.nylp.com
SIC: 2741 2759 2731 Miscellaneous publishing; commercial printing; book publishing

(G-8378)
SIMMONS MACHINE TOOL CORP
Also Called: Nsh
1700 Broadway (12204-2701)
PHONE.................518 462-5431
Fax: 518 462-0371
John O Naumann, *CEO*
Hans J Naumann, *Ch of Bd*
David William Davis, *President*
Roger Collen, *Vice Pres*
Scott Mitchell, *Project Mgr*
▲ **EMP:** 104
SQ FT: 145,000
SALES (est): 33.2MM **Privately Held**
WEB: www.smtgroup.com
SIC: 3541 5084 Machine tools, metal cutting type; industrial machinery & equipment

(G-8379)
T LEMME MECHANICAL INC
Selby & Smith
1074 Broadway (12204-2507)
PHONE.................518 436-4136
Bill Mattfeld, *Opers Mgr*
EMP: 40
SALES (corp-wide): 21.1MM **Privately Held**
SIC: 3444 Sheet metalwork
PA: T. Lemme Mechanical, Inc.
67 Erie Blvd
Menands NY 12204
518 463-2903

Mendon
Monroe County

(G-8380)
COPIER & PRINTER SUPPLY LLC
27 Locke Dr (14506)
PHONE.................585 329-1077
Rick Johnson, *Sales Staff*
Bill Crocker,
EMP: 2 **EST:** 2009
SALES: 1MM **Privately Held**
SIC: 3555 Printing trades machinery

(G-8381)
N Y B P INC
Also Called: New York Blood Pressure
1355 Pittsford Mendon Rd (14506-9733)
P.O. Box 471 (14506-0471)
PHONE.................585 624-2541
Gregory J Sarkis, *President*
EMP: 3
SALES: 1MM **Privately Held**
SIC: 3841 Blood pressure apparatus

(G-8382)
SAXBY IMPLEMENT CORP (PA)
Also Called: Kubota Authorized Dealer
180 Mendon Victor Rd (14506)
P.O. Box 333 (14506-0333)
PHONE.................585 624-2938
Marvin E Hogan, *President*
Teri H Maxwell, *Vice Pres*
Randall Hogan, *Treasurer*
Joanne Hogan, *Admin Sec*
EMP: 10
SQ FT: 9,400
SALES (est): 1.2MM **Privately Held**
SIC: 3524 5083 Lawn & garden tractors & equipment; farm & garden machinery

Merrick
Nassau County

(G-8383)
D G M GRAPHICS INC
Also Called: Printing Emporium
55 Merrick Ave (11566-3415)
P.O. Box 121 (11566-0121)
PHONE.................516 223-2220
Fax: 516 223-1200
Douglas G Mills, *President*
EMP: 11
SQ FT: 3,300
SALES (est): 1.1MM **Privately Held**
WEB: www.printingemporium.com
SIC: 2752 2791 2789 2759 Photo-offset printing; typesetting; bookbinding & related work; commercial printing

(G-8384)
E J MANUFACTURING INC
2935 Charlotte Dr (11566-5301)
PHONE.................516 313-9380
Elliot S Negrin, *President*
Jeff Negrin, *Vice Pres*
▲ **EMP:** 2
SQ FT: 8,000
SALES: 3MM **Privately Held**
SIC: 2326 Men's & boys' work clothing

(G-8385)
FIORENTINA LLC
1519 Hendrickson Ave (11566-2120)
PHONE.................516 208-5448
Fax: 631 423-3514
Brett Carter, *Mng Member*
Anna Carter,
▲ **EMP:** 6
SQ FT: 800
SALES (est): 674.4K **Privately Held**
SIC: 3199 Equestrian related leather articles

(G-8386)
JON LYN INK INC
Also Called: Minuteman Press
255 Sunrise Hwy Ste 1 (11566-3700)
PHONE.................516 546-2312
Fax: 516 623-0870
John Jutt, *President*
EMP: 6
SQ FT: 1,200
SALES (est): 710.3K **Privately Held**
SIC: 2752 7334 2759 2791 Commercial printing, lithographic; photocopying & duplicating services; invitation & stationery printing & engraving; typesetting; bookbinding & related work

(G-8387)
L I C SCREEN PRINTING INC
2949 Joyce Ln (11566-5209)
PHONE.................516 546-7289
Edward Rosenblum, *President*
EMP: 25
SQ FT: 15,000
SALES (est): 1.7MM **Privately Held**
WEB: www.licscreenprinting.com
SIC: 2759 3089 3993 2396 Letterpress & screen printing; screen printing; plastic processing; signs & advertising specialties; automotive & apparel trimmings

(G-8388)
LEADER PRINTING INC
Also Called: Print-O-Rama Copy Center
2272 Babylon Tpke (11566-3829)
PHONE.................516 546-1544
Steve Leads, *President*
EMP: 10
SALES (est): 907.5K **Privately Held**
SIC: 2752 7334 Photo-offset printing; photocopying & duplicating services

(G-8389)
LEGAL STRATEGIES INC
1795 Harvard Ave (11566-4413)
PHONE.................516 377-3940
Steven Mitchell Sack, *President*
EMP: 7
SALES (est): 519.4K **Privately Held**
SIC: 2731 Book publishing

(G-8390)
NORTHEAST WINDOWS USA INC
1 Kees Pl (11566-3642)
P.O. Box 159 (11566-0159)
PHONE.................516 378-6577
Jill Kaiserman, *President*
Jeffrey Kaiserman, *Vice Pres*
Steven Kaiserman, *Sales Dir*
Phil Reid, *Sales Executive*
Wayne Shoenberger, *Manager*
▲ **EMP:** 48
SQ FT: 35,000
SALES (est): 6MM **Privately Held**
SIC: 3089 Window frames & sash, plastic

(G-8391)
PRESTIGE ENVELOPE & LITHOGRAPH
Also Called: Prestige Litho & Graphics
1745 Merrick Ave Ste 2 (11566-2700)
PHONE.................631 521-7043
Fax: 631 434-3319
Gary Gingo, *CEO*
Angel Irimia, *President*
Gregory Catanese, *Office Mgr*
Joe Nieves, *Admin Sec*
EMP: 12
SQ FT: 30,000
SALES (est): 1.9MM **Privately Held**
WEB: www.prestigelg.com
SIC: 2752 2791 2789 7389 Commercial printing, lithographic; typesetting; bookbinding & related work; printing broker; envelopes

(G-8392)
QUALITY LINEALS USA INC (PA)
Also Called: Quality Fence
1 Kees Pl (11566-3642)
P.O. Box 159 (11566-0159)
PHONE.................516 378-6577
Fax: 516 546-0205
Jill Kaiserman, *President*
Jeffrey Kaiserman, *Vice Pres*
EMP: 2
SALES (est): 7.5MM **Privately Held**
SIC: 3089 Billfold inserts, plastic

(G-8393)
SOURCE ONE PROMOTIONAL PRODUCT
2024 Brian Dr (11566-1731)
PHONE.................516 208-6996
Ken Greenfield, *President*
EMP: 1
SALES: 1.5MM **Privately Held**
SIC: 2752 Promotional printing, lithographic

(G-8394)
WORLDWIDE TICKET CRAFT
1390 Jerusalem Ave (11566-1364)
PHONE.................516 538-6200
Fax: 516 538-4860
Eric Colts, *President*
EMP: 60

SALES (est): 4.7MM **Privately Held**
WEB: www.ticketcraft.com
SIC: 2752 2791 2759 Tickets, lithographed; typesetting; commercial printing

Mexico
Oswego County

(G-8395)
GRANDMA BROWNS BEANS INC
5837 Scenic Ave (13114-3481)
P.O. Box 230 (13114-0230)
PHONE.................................315 963-7221
Fax: 315 963-4072
Sandra L Brown, *President*
EMP: 15 **EST:** 1938
SQ FT: 35,000
SALES (est): 19.7K **Privately Held**
SIC: 2032 Canned specialties

(G-8396)
MEXICO INDEPENDENT INC (PA)
Also Called: Salmon River News
80 N Jefferson St (13114-3001)
P.O. Box 129 (13114-0129)
PHONE.................................315 963-3763
Mark Backus, *President*
R Charles Backus, *Vice Pres*
Horace Backus, *Treasurer*
Shannon Parsons, *Manager*
EMP: 20 **EST:** 1924
SQ FT: 6,139
SALES (est): 1.9MM **Privately Held**
SIC: 2711 2741 Job printing & newspaper publishing combined; catalogs: publishing & printing

(G-8397)
MEXICONE
Also Called: Mexicone Ice Cream
5775 Scenic Ave (13114-3179)
P.O. Box 185, Lycoming (13093-0185)
PHONE.................................315 591-1971
Jan Tripoli, *Owner*
EMP: 5 **EST:** 2013
SQ FT: 300
SALES (est): 190K **Privately Held**
SIC: 2024 Ice cream & frozen desserts

Middle Granville
Washington County

(G-8398)
EVERGREEN SLATE COMPANY INC
2027 County Route 23 (12849-4901)
P.O. Box 248, Granville (12832-0248)
PHONE.................................518 642-2530
Fax: 518 642-9313
Fred Whitridge, *President*
Shannon Humphrey, *General Mgr*
Ray Loomis, *Vice Pres*
Jody Oakman, *Credit Mgr*
Jan Edwards, *Sales Staff*
▲ **EMP:** 70 **EST:** 1916
SQ FT: 1,000
SALES (est): 11MM **Privately Held**
WEB: www.evergreenslate.com
SIC: 3281 Slate products

(G-8399)
HILLTOP SLATE INC
Rr 22 Box A (12849)
PHONE.................................518 642-1453
Fax: 518 642-1220
David Thomas, *President*
Adrian Curtis, *Div Sub Head*
John J Conlon, *Sales Staff*
▲ **EMP:** 30 **EST:** 1948
SQ FT: 50,000
SALES (est): 5.5MM **Privately Held**
WEB: www.hilltopslate.com
SIC: 1411 Slate, dimension-quarrying

(G-8400)
K-D STONE INC
Rr 22 (12849)
PHONE.................................518 642-2082
Nelson Dunster, *President*

Kimberly Dunster, *Vice Pres*
EMP: 12
SALES (est): 1.7MM **Privately Held**
SIC: 2952 Roof cement: asphalt, fibrous or plastic

(G-8401)
SHELDON SLATE PRODUCTS CO INC
Fox Rd (12849)
PHONE.................................518 642-1280
Fax: 518 642-9085
John Tatko Jr, *President*
Beverly Tatko, *Manager*
EMP: 50 **EST:** 1924
SQ FT: 1,200
SALES (est): 5.3MM **Privately Held**
SIC: 3281 2952 2951 Slate products; asphalt felts & coatings; asphalt paving mixtures & blocks

(G-8402)
VERMONT MULTICOLOR SLATE
146 State Route 22a (12849-5431)
P.O. Box 202 (12849-0202)
PHONE.................................518 642-2400
William Enny, *President*
Renold Tang, *CFO*
EMP: 9
SQ FT: 10,000
SALES (est): 406.5K **Privately Held**
SIC: 1411 Slate, dimension-quarrying

(G-8403)
VERMONT NATURAL STONEWORKS
Also Called: Ritchie Brothers Slate Co
146 State Route 22a (12849-5431)
P.O. Box 202 (12849-0202)
PHONE.................................518 642-2460
Fax: 518 642-9327
Bonnie Pratt, *President*
EMP: 30
SALES (est): 2.2MM **Privately Held**
SIC: 3281 Slate products

Middle Grove
Saratoga County

(G-8404)
CUCCIO-ZANETTI INC
Also Called: Zanetti Millwork
455 Middle Grove Rd (12850-1107)
PHONE.................................518 587-1363
John Zanetti, *President*
EMP: 8
SQ FT: 9,000
SALES (est): 1MM **Privately Held**
SIC: 2431 Millwork

Middle Island
Suffolk County

(G-8405)
AFCO PRECAST SALES CORP
Also Called: Old Castle Precast
114 Rocky Point Rd (11953-1216)
PHONE.................................631 924-7114
Fax: 631 924-2243
Richard Affenita, *Ch of Bd*
Peter Kaplin, *President*
Robert Affenita, *Treasurer*
Jackie Densing, *Accountant*
Marion Classi, *Director*
▲ **EMP:** 75
SQ FT: 1,560
SALES (est): 10.7MM **Privately Held**
SIC: 3272 5211 Concrete products, precast; masonry materials & supplies

(G-8406)
ALLEY CAT SIGNS INC
506 Middle Country Rd (11953-2521)
PHONE.................................631 924-7446
Fax: 631 924-9772
Albert Borsella, *President*
EMP: 12

SALES (est): 980K **Privately Held**
SIC: 3993 1799 5999 Signs & advertising specialties; sign installation & maintenance; awnings

(G-8407)
MID ENTERPRISE INC
809 Middle Country Rd (11953-2511)
PHONE.................................631 924-3933
Shahid Ali Khan, *Principal*
EMP: 5
SALES (est): 581.3K **Privately Held**
SIC: 3578 Automatic teller machines (ATM)

(G-8408)
SIMON DEFENSE INC
1533 Rocky Point Rd (11953-1259)
PHONE.................................516 217-6000
CJ Calleson, *Director*
EMP: 7 **EST:** 2014
SQ FT: 2,000
SALES (est): 338.2K **Privately Held**
SIC: 3452 Bolts, metal

Middle Village
Queens County

(G-8409)
ACCURATE SPECIALTY METAL FABRI
6420 Admiral Ave (11379-1614)
PHONE.................................718 418-6895
Fax: 718 418-8325
Ronald Palmerick, *Ch of Bd*
Sebastian Loayas, *Office Mgr*
Gene Griffin, *Manager*
EMP: 35
SQ FT: 30,000
SALES (est): 7.3MM
SALES (corp-wide): 57.2MM **Privately Held**
WEB: www.asm-mech.com
SIC: 3444 Ducts, sheet metal
PA: Aabco Sheet Metal Co., Inc.
47 40 Metropolitan Ave
Ridgewood NY 11385
718 821-1166

(G-8410)
AGLIKA TRADE LLC
5905 74th St (11379-5216)
PHONE.................................727 424-1944
Maya Petkova,
EMP: 10
SALES (est): 495.4K **Privately Held**
SIC: 3552 Textile machinery

(G-8411)
GOLDMONT ENTERPRISES INC
Also Called: Superior Model Form Co
7603 Caldwell Ave (11379-5233)
PHONE.................................212 947-3633
Vito Montalto, *President*
EMP: 15 **EST:** 1940
SQ FT: 7,000
SALES: 1MM **Privately Held**
WEB: www.superiormodel.com
SIC: 3999 Forms: display, dress & show

(G-8412)
J M R PLASTICS CORPORATION
5847 78th St (11379-5305)
PHONE.................................718 898-9825
Fax: 718 898-7967
John Daidone, *President*
Selina Daidone, *Corp Secy*
EMP: 8
SQ FT: 10,000
SALES: 2MM **Privately Held**
SIC: 3089 Plastic kitchenware, tableware & houseware

(G-8413)
JONATHAN DAVID PUBLISHERS INC
6822 Eliot Ave (11379-1131)
PHONE.................................718 456-8611
Fax: 718 894-2818
Alfred J Kolatch, *President*
Thelma Kolatch, *Corp Secy*
Marvin Sekler, *Vice Pres*
Carol Zelezny, *Accounting Mgr*
▲ **EMP:** 10 **EST:** 1949

SQ FT: 2,400
SALES (est): 860K **Privately Held**
WEB: www.jdbooks.com
SIC: 2731 Books: publishing only

(G-8414)
JUNIPER ELBOW CO INC (PA)
Also Called: Juniper Industries
7215 Metropolitan Ave (11379-2198)
P.O. Box 148 (11379-0148)
PHONE.................................718 326-2546
Fax: 718 326-3786
Jesse L Wiener, *CEO*
Marvin Jacobs, *General Mgr*
Celia Wiener, *Vice Pres*
Elliot Wiener, *Vice Pres*
▲ **EMP:** 185 **EST:** 1929
SQ FT: 100,000
SALES (est): 29.3MM **Privately Held**
WEB: www.juniperind.com
SIC: 3444 3498 3433 3312 Elbows, for air ducts, stovepipes, etc.: sheet metal; ventilators, sheet metal; metal ventilating equipment; fabricated pipe & fittings; heating equipment, except electric; blast furnaces & steel mills

(G-8415)
JUNIPER INDUSTRIES FLORIDA INC
7215 Metropolitan Ave (11379-2107)
PHONE.................................718 326-2546
Jesse L Wiener, *President*
Elliot Wiener, *Vice Pres*
Celia Wiener, *Treasurer*
▲ **EMP:** 5
SALES (est): 384.6K **Privately Held**
SIC: 3498 Fabricated pipe & fittings

(G-8416)
PATDAN FUEL CORPORATION
7803 68th Rd (11379-2836)
PHONE.................................718 326-3668
EMP: 6
SALES (est): 743.4K **Privately Held**
SIC: 2869 Fuels

(G-8417)
WETHERALL CONTRACTING NY INC
8312 Penelope Ave Ste 101 (11379-2321)
PHONE.................................718 894-7011
Bryan Wetherall, *President*
EMP: 5
SALES (est): 670.7K **Privately Held**
SIC: 2323 Men's & boys' neckwear

Middleburgh
Schoharie County

(G-8418)
DR REDDYS LABORATORIES NY INC
1974 State Route 145 (12122-5315)
PHONE.................................518 827-7702
Amid Patel, *President*
EMP: 10
SALES (est): 2.3MM **Privately Held**
SIC: 2834 Pharmaceutical preparations

(G-8419)
URREY LUMBER
663 Clauverwie Rd (12122-3411)
PHONE.................................518 827-4851
Fax: 518 827-4859
Allan Urrey, *Partner*
Jeff Urrey, *Partner*
Toni Urrey, *Partner*
EMP: 9
SALES: 2.1MM **Privately Held**
SIC: 2421 Sawmills & planing mills, general

Middleport
Niagara County

(G-8420)
BIRCH MACHINE & TOOL INC
80 Telegraph Rd (14105-9638)
PHONE.................................716 735-9802

Fax: 716 438-0131
Jerry Stadelman, *President*
Mary Stadelman, *Vice Pres*
EMP: 7
SQ FT: 1,500
SALES (est): 500K **Privately Held**
SIC: 3599 Machine & other job shop work; machine shop, jobbing & repair

(G-8421)
FMC CORPORATION
Also Called: F M C Aricultural Chem Group
100 Niagara St (14105-1398)
PHONE.................................716 735-3761
Fax: 585 735-7804
Donna McCloy, *Safety Dir*
Stewart Throop, *Plant Mgr*
A M Hahn, *Finance*
Roger L Krough, *Branch Mgr*
Derek Gammon, *Med Doctor*
EMP: 50
SALES (corp-wide): 3.2B **Publicly Held**
WEB: www.fmc.com
SIC: 2879 2819 Agricultural chemicals; industrial inorganic chemicals
PA: Fmc Corporation
2929 Walnut St
Philadelphia PA 19104
215 299-6000

(G-8422)
PERFORMANCE MFG INC
80 Telegraph Rd (14105-9638)
PHONE.................................716 735-3500
Jody P Herriven, *President*
Tim Worth, *Vice Pres*
Valerie Steltzer, *Office Mgr*
Derek Wagner, *Manager*
EMP: 15
SALES (est): 2.2MM **Privately Held**
WEB: www.pmikartparts.com
SIC: 3599 Machine shop, jobbing & repair

(G-8423)
SIGMAMOTOR INC
3 N Main St (14105-1005)
P.O. Box 298 (14105-0298)
PHONE.................................716 735-3115
Fax: 585 735-3166
Donald Heschke Jr, *President*
Shari Heschke, *Corp Secy*
EMP: 22 **EST:** 1951
SQ FT: 6,500
SALES: 6MM **Privately Held**
SIC: 3599 3494 Machine shop, jobbing & repair; valves & pipe fittings

Middletown
Orange County

(G-8424)
209 DISCOUNT OIL
10 Sands Station Rd (10940-4415)
PHONE.................................845 386-2090
Steve Cortese, *Principal*
EMP: 20
SALES (est): 1.6MM **Privately Held**
SIC: 2911 Oils, fuel

(G-8425)
ADVANCED ENTERPRISES INC
Also Called: Wonder Products
366 Highland Ave Ext (10940-4454)
PHONE.................................845 342-1009
Eugene Polanish, *President*
Christian Al, *Principal*
Colin Dixon, *Vice Pres*
▲ **EMP:** 10
SQ FT: 100
SALES (est): 1.5MM **Privately Held**
SIC: 3842 Cotton & cotton applicators

(G-8426)
ARCHITECTURAL ENHANCEMENTS INC
135 Crotty Rd (10941-4070)
P.O. Box 4680 (10941-8680)
PHONE.................................845 343-9663
Fax: 845 343-0225
Philip Cohen, *President*
Chaim Cohen, *Exec VP*
EMP: 10 **EST:** 1962
SQ FT: 31,000

SALES (est): 1.6MM **Privately Held**
SIC: 2499 Decorative wood & woodwork

(G-8427)
BALL METAL BEVERAGE CONT CORP
Also Called: Ball Metal Beverage Cont Div
95 Ballard Rd (10941-3013)
PHONE.................................845 692-3800
Fax: 845 692-3881
Terree Angerame, *Principal*
Robert Chapin, *Principal*
Noreen Dellay, *Principal*
Rob Lauterbach, *Vice Pres*
Rich Bailey, *Safety Mgr*
EMP: 175
SALES (corp-wide): 8B **Publicly Held**
SIC: 3411 Aluminum cans
HQ: Ball Metal Beverage Container Corp.
9300 W 108th Cir
Westminster CO 80021
303 469-5511

(G-8428)
BRAGA WOODWORKS
19 Montgomery St (10940-5115)
PHONE.................................845 342-4636
Leo Braga, *Owner*
EMP: 5
SALES (est): 410.6K **Privately Held**
SIC: 2431 Millwork

(G-8429)
BRAIDED OAK SPIRITS LLC
12 Roberts St (10940-5007)
P.O. Box 2124 (10940-0949)
PHONE.................................845 381-1525
Peter J Matos,
Peter Matos,
EMP: 17
SALES (est): 5.2MM **Privately Held**
SIC: 2085 Distilled & blended liquors

(G-8430)
CHROMALLOY GAS TURBINE LLC
Also Called: Chromalloy Middletown
105 Tower Dr (10941-2034)
PHONE.................................845 692-8912
Fax: 845 692-8992
Lamarr Taylor, *Safety Mgr*
Mark Levine, *Purch Mgr*
Dean Hoffman, *Engineer*
Scott Irwin, *Engineer*
Judith Quinn, *Engineer*
EMP: 28
SALES (corp-wide): 3B **Publicly Held**
WEB: www.chromalloysatx.com
SIC: 3479 3724 Painting, coating & hot dipping; aircraft engines & engine parts
HQ: Chromalloy Gas Turbine Llc
3999 Rca Blvd
Palm Beach Gardens FL 33410
561 935-3571

(G-8431)
CLASSIC HOSIERY INC
33 Mulberry St Ste 4 (10940-6359)
PHONE.................................845 342-6661
Fax: 845 342-2023
Tuvia Brach, *President*
▲ **EMP:** 35 **EST:** 1980
SQ FT: 18,000
SALES (est): 4.2MM **Privately Held**
SIC: 2251 Women's hosiery, except socks; panty hose; tights, women's

(G-8432)
COMMERCIAL COMMUNICATIONS LLC
Also Called: Msdivisions
14 Montgomery St (10940-5116)
PHONE.................................845 343-9078
Fax: 845 344-2175
Steven Rosenblatt,
EMP: 6
SALES (est): 982.2K **Privately Held**
WEB: www.msdspring.com
SIC: 3495 Wire springs

(G-8433)
COUNTY DRAPERIES INC
64 Genung St (10940-5317)
PHONE.................................845 342-9009
Fax: 845 342-1530

Sara Markowitz, *CEO*
Carl Markowitz, *President*
David C Markowitz, *Vice Pres*
Krystal Bell, *Project Mgr*
Devi Heyer, *Project Mgr*
◆ **EMP:** 45
SQ FT: 50,000
SALES (est): 11MM **Privately Held**
WEB: www.drape.com
SIC: 2391 2392 Draperies, plastic & textile: from purchased materials; curtains, window: made from purchased materials; bedspreads & bed sets: made from purchased materials

(G-8434)
CROWN CORK & SEAL USA INC
21 Industrial Pl (10940-3608)
PHONE.................................845 343-9586
EMP: 118
SALES (corp-wide): 8.7B **Publicly Held**
WEB: www.crowncork.com
SIC: 3411 Metal cans
HQ: Crown Cork & Seal Usa, Inc.
1 Crown Way
Philadelphia PA 19154
215 698-5100

(G-8435)
D & W DESIGN INC (PA)
62 Industrial Pl (10940-3609)
PHONE.................................845 343-3366
Fax: 845 534-7568
Mariam Weiss, *President*
David Weiss, *Vice Pres*
Simon Kraus, *Manager*
Mike Toplamos, *Admin Sec*
EMP: 26
SQ FT: 50,000
SALES: 3MM **Privately Held**
WEB: www.dustinwdesign.com
SIC: 2511 2514 5712 Wood household furniture; metal household furniture; furniture stores

(G-8436)
DELFORD INDUSTRIES INC
82 Washington St 84 (10940-4268)
P.O. Box 863 (10940-0863)
PHONE.................................845 342-3901
Fax: 845 342-3168
Robert L Reach Jr, *President*
Richard Reynolds, *Human Resources*
Allison Reach, *Sales Staff*
EMP: 80 **EST:** 1983
SQ FT: 55,000
SALES: 2MM **Privately Held**
WEB: www.delford-industries.com
SIC: 3061 Mechanical rubber goods

(G-8437)
E TETZ & SONS INC (PA)
130 Crotty Rd (10941-4059)
PHONE.................................845 692-4486
Edward Tetz Jr, *Ch of Bd*
Corinne Tetz, *Bookkeeper*
Liz Raffa, *Manager*
Bob Weber, *Info Tech Mgr*
Denise Tetz, *Admin Sec*
EMP: 55
SQ FT: 3,000
SALES (est): 23.4MM **Privately Held**
WEB: www.etetz-sons.com
SIC: 3273 1442 Ready-mixed concrete; construction sand & gravel

(G-8438)
EAD CASES
43 Smith St (10940-3710)
P.O. Box 957 (10940-0957)
PHONE.................................845 343-2111
Julio Diaz, *President*
EMP: 10
SALES (est): 975.1K **Privately Held**
SIC: 3161 Cases, carrying

(G-8439)
ECO-BAT AMERICA LLC
Also Called: RSR
65 Ballard Rd (10941-3013)
PHONE.................................845 692-4414
Dan Demercurio, *Branch Mgr*
Steve Brooks, *Maintence Staff*
EMP: 45
SQ FT: 20,000

SALES (corp-wide): 2.2B **Privately Held**
SIC: 3356 3339 3341 Nonferrous rolling & drawing; precious metals; lead smelting & refining (secondary)
HQ: Eco-Bat America Llc
2777 N Stemmons Fwy
Dallas TX 75207
214 688-4000

(G-8440)
FAIRBANKS MFG LLC
79 Industrial Pl (10940-3608)
PHONE.................................845 341-0002
Fax: 845 341-1606
Jared Swift, *General Mgr*
Michael Ruppel, *CFO*
Zeke Alenick, *Mng Member*
◆ **EMP:** 145 **EST:** 2011
SQ FT: 100,000
SALES: 34.5MM **Privately Held**
SIC: 2064 Candy & other confectionery products

(G-8441)
FUEL DATA SYSTEMS INC
772 Greenville Tpke (10940-7125)
PHONE.................................800 447-7870
Steve Michalek, *President*
EMP: 6 **EST:** 1989
SALES (est): 457.1K **Privately Held**
WEB: www.fueldatasystems.com
SIC: 7372 7371 Prepackaged software; custom computer programming services

(G-8442)
GENPAK LLC
Republic Plz (10940)
PHONE.................................845 343-7971
Fax: 845 343-0450
Betty Hager, *Opers-Prdtn-Mfg*
Ed Rider, *Engr R&D*
Bill Gentes, *Facilities*
EMP: 200
SQ FT: 150,000
SALES (corp-wide): 14.2B **Privately Held**
WEB: www.genpak.com
SIC: 3089 5046 Plastic processing; commercial cooking & food service equipment
HQ: Genpak Llc
68 Warren St
Glens Falls NY 12801
518 798-9511

(G-8443)
GOLUB CORPORATION
Also Called: Price Chopper Pharmacy
511 Schutt Road Ext (10940-2569)
PHONE.................................845 344-0327
Fax: 845 344-0319
EMP: 104
SALES (corp-wide): 3.4B **Privately Held**
SIC: 3751 Motorcycles & related parts
PA: The Golub Corporation
461 Nott St
Schenectady NY 12308
518 355-5000

(G-8444)
HISTORCAL SOC OF MDDLTOWN WALK
25 East Ave (10940-5818)
P.O. Box 34 (10940-0034)
PHONE.................................845 342-0941
Marvin H Cohen, *President*
Nicholas Cscili, *Vice Pres*
Joanne Norbury, *Treasurer*
Ann Vail, *Director*
Francis Cleary, *Admin Sec*
EMP: 6
SQ FT: 1,974
SALES: 8.8K **Privately Held**
SIC: 2452 8412 Prefabricated wood buildings; museum

(G-8445)
HONEYWELL INTERNATIONAL INC
13 Bedford Ave (10940-6401)
PHONE.................................845 342-4400
EMP: 673
SALES (corp-wide): 38.5B **Publicly Held**
SIC: 3724 Aircraft engines & engine parts
PA: Honeywell International Inc.
115 Tabor Rd
Morris Plains NJ 07950
973 455-2000

Middletown - Orange County (G-8469)

(G-8446)
LOCAL MEDIA GROUP INC (HQ)
40 Mulberry St (10940-6302)
P.O. Box 580 (10940-0580)
PHONE.................................845 341-1100
John Wilcox, *President*
Patrick Purcell, *Chairman*
William T Kennedy, *COO*
Kurt Lozier, *Senior VP*
Patricia Gatto, *Vice Pres*
EMP: 50 **EST:** 1936
SQ FT: 10,000
SALES (est): 13.1MM
SALES (corp-wide): 1.2B **Publicly Held**
WEB: www.ottaway.com
SIC: 2711 7313 Newspapers: publishing only, not printed on site; newspaper advertising representative
PA: New Media Investment Group Inc.
  1345 Avenue Of The Americ
  New York NY 10105
  212 479-3160

(G-8447)
LOCAL MEDIA GROUP INC
Orange County Publications
40 Mulberry St (10940-6302)
P.O. Box 2046 (10940-0558)
PHONE.................................845 341-1100
Fax: 845 343-0163
Jim Moss, *Publisher*
Barry Lewis, *General Mgr*
Dick Bayne, *Editor*
Marc Davis, *Editor*
Gittel Evangelist, *Editor*
EMP: 290
SALES (corp-wide): 1.2B **Publicly Held**
WEB: www.ottaway.com
SIC: 2711 Newspapers, publishing & printing
HQ: Local Media Group, Inc.
  40 Mulberry St
  Middletown NY 10940
  845 341-1100

(G-8448)
LOCAL MEDIA GROUP INC
Also Called: Times Herald-Record
60 Brookline Ave (10940-3404)
PHONE.................................845 341-1100
Andy Mark, *Branch Mgr*
EMP: 68
SALES (corp-wide): 1.2B **Publicly Held**
WEB: www.ottaway.com
SIC: 2711 Commercial printing & newspaper publishing combined
HQ: Local Media Group, Inc.
  40 Mulberry St
  Middletown NY 10940
  845 341-1100

(G-8449)
MANDARIN SOY SAUCE INC
Also Called: Wan Ja Shan
4 Sands Station Rd (10940-4415)
PHONE.................................845 343-1505
Fax: 845 343-0731
Michael Wu, *Ch of Bd*
Mike Shapiro, *Vice Pres*
▲ **EMP:** 25 **EST:** 1974
SQ FT: 85,000
SALES (est): 3.6MM **Privately Held**
WEB: www.wanjashan.com
SIC: 2035 5149 Seasonings & sauces, except tomato & dry; soy sauce; groceries & related products
PA: Wan Ja Shan Brewery Co., Ltd.
  5f-6, 9, De Hui St.,
  Taipei City TAP
  266 180-101

(G-8450)
MEDLINE INDUSTRIES INC
3301 Route 6 (10940-6992)
PHONE.................................845 344-3301
George Vargulish, *Surgery Dir*
EMP: 276
SALES (corp-wide): 5.6B **Privately Held**
SIC: 3842 3841 2326 2392 Surgical appliances & supplies; surgical & medical instruments; men's & boys' work clothing; household furnishings; surgical fabrics, cotton; scrub cloths; surgical equipment & supplies; hospital equipment & supplies; hospital furniture
PA: Medline Industries, Inc.
  1 Medline Pl
  Mundelein IL 60060
  847 949-5500

(G-8451)
MIDDLETOWN PRESS (PA)
20 W Main St 26 (10940-5716)
PHONE.................................845 343-1895
Fax: 845 343-1897
Jo Cover, *Owner*
EMP: 5
SQ FT: 2,800
SALES (est): 401.6K **Privately Held**
WEB: www.mtprintandpromote.com
SIC: 2752 7311 7336 5199 Commercial printing, lithographic; advertising agencies; graphic arts & related design; advertising specialties; commercial printing

(G-8452)
MONROE CABLE COMPANY INC
14 Commercial Ave (10941-1444)
PHONE.................................845 692-2800
Fax: 845 692-8041
Isaac Wieder, *President*
Mendel Wieder, *COO*
Joseph Ungar, *Controller*
Abraham Wieder, *Consultant*
▲ **EMP:** 104 **EST:** 1978
SQ FT: 95,000
SALES (est): 41.5MM **Privately Held**
SIC: 3357 Shipboard cable, nonferrous; coaxial cable, nonferrous

(G-8453)
NEW DYNAMICS CORPORATION
15 Fortune Rd W (10941-1625)
PHONE.................................845 692-0022
Fax: 845 692-2590
James Destefano, *President*
Walter Pawlowski, *Vice Pres*
EMP: 20
SQ FT: 35,000
SALES (est): 5MM **Privately Held**
WEB: www.newdynamics.net
SIC: 3842 5963 7349 Ear plugs; food services, direct sales; janitorial service, contract basis

(G-8454)
NEW YORK CUTTING & GUMMING CO
265 Ballard Rd (10941-3034)
PHONE.................................212 563-4146
Jack Siegel, *President*
Richard Deteresa, *Principal*
Robert Siegel, *Vice Pres*
EMP: 45 **EST:** 1914
SQ FT: 44,000
SALES (est): 4.2MM **Privately Held**
SIC: 3089 2295 2675 2672 Laminating of plastic; laminating of fabrics; die-cut paper & board; coated & laminated paper

(G-8455)
OTTAWAY NEWSPAPERS INC
40 Mulberry St (10940-6302)
PHONE.................................845 343-2181
Joe Vanderhoof, *Principal*
Robin Robinson, *Accounting Dir*
Zeke Fleet, *VP Sales*
Dawn Griffin, *Executive*
EMP: 12
SALES (est): 819.7K **Privately Held**
SIC: 2711 Newspapers

(G-8456)
PILLER USA INC (DH)
Also Called: Piller Power Systems
45 Wes Warren Dr (10941-1772)
PHONE.................................845 695-6600
Fax: 845 692-0295
Dean Richards, *President*
Mike Barron, *President*
Ethel Bargallo, *General Mgr*
Michael Haber, *General Mgr*
Kyle F Burak, *Vice Pres*
▲ **EMP:** 40
SALES (est): 23.9MM
SALES (corp-wide): 939.9MM **Privately Held**
WEB: www.piller.com
SIC: 3699 3612 Electrical equipment & supplies; transformers, except electric
HQ: Piller Group Gmbh
  Abgunst 24
  Osterode Am Harz 37520
  552 231-10

(G-8457)
PRESIDENT CONT GROUP II LLC
Also Called: Manufacturing Facility
290 Ballard Rd (10941-3035)
PHONE.................................845 516-1600
EMP: 69
SALES (corp-wide): 8.8MM **Privately Held**
SIC: 2653 Corrugated boxes, partitions, display items, sheets & pad; sheets, corrugated: made from purchased materials; display items, corrugated: made from purchased materials
PA: President Container Group Ii, Llc
  200 W Commercial Ave
  Moonachie NJ 07074
  201 933-7500

(G-8458)
PRINCETON UPHOLSTERY CO INC (PA)
Also Called: Bright Chair Co
51 Railroad Ave (10940-5117)
P.O. Box 269 (10940-0269)
PHONE.................................845 343-2196
Fax: 845 343-4958
Stan Gottlieb, *Ch of Bd*
Ross Spasato, *Vice Pres*
Shari Morrone, *Controller*
Leigh Spence, *Sales Staff*
Jody Gottlieb, *Admin Sec*
EMP: 100
SQ FT: 100,000
SALES (est): 15.4MM **Privately Held**
WEB: www.brightchair.com
SIC: 2521 2512 Wood office furniture; upholstered household furniture

(G-8459)
RIJ PHARMACEUTICAL CORPORATION
40 Commercial Ave (10941-1444)
PHONE.................................845 692-5799
Fax: 845 692-3023
Hassan Zaidi, *CEO*
Brij Gupta, *President*
EMP: 20
SQ FT: 52,000
SALES (est): 4.4MM **Privately Held**
WEB: www.rijpharm.com
SIC: 2834 Pharmaceutical preparations

(G-8460)
RIMS LIKE NEW INC
507 Union School Rd (10941-5018)
PHONE.................................845 537-0396
Manuel P Heredia Jr, *Owner*
EMP: 10
SALES (est): 630K **Privately Held**
SIC: 3479 Painting of metal products

(G-8461)
S R & R INDUSTRIES INC
45 Enterprise Pl (10941-2043)
PHONE.................................845 692-8329
Fax: 845 692-8330
Paul Rosanelli, *President*
EMP: 6
SQ FT: 10,000
SALES: 450K **Privately Held**
SIC: 3531 3462 3599 Rollers, sheepsfoot & vibratory; gears, forged steel; machine shop, jobbing & repair

(G-8462)
STAFFORD LABS ORTHOTICS/PROSTH
189 Monhagen Ave (10940-6020)
P.O. Box 1004, Goshen (10924-8004)
PHONE.................................845 692-5227
Fax: 845 692-5244
Kimberly Thompson, *President*
Ellen Amodio, *Manager*
EMP: 15
SALES (est): 960K **Privately Held**
WEB: www.staffordlabsoandp.com
SIC: 3842 Prosthetic appliances

(G-8463)
STERLING MOLDED PRODUCTS INC
9-17 Oliver Ave (10940-6095)
PHONE.................................845 344-4546
Fax: 845 344-4548
Stephen Crescimanno, *Ch of Bd*
Janice Fumarola, *Manager*
Caitlin Gulling, *Admin Asst*
▲ **EMP:** 40
SALES (est): 7.5MM **Privately Held**
SIC: 3089 Injection molded finished plastic products; injection molding of plastics

(G-8464)
SURVING STUDIOS
17 Millsburg Rd (10940-8497)
PHONE.................................845 355-1430
Fax: 845 355-1517
Natalie Surving, *Owner*
EMP: 10
SALES (est): 1.2MM **Privately Held**
SIC: 3469 8999 Tile, floor or wall: stamped metal; sculptor's studio

(G-8465)
TPI INDUSTRIES LLC (HQ)
265 Ballard Rd (10941-3034)
PHONE.................................845 692-2820
Fax: 845 692-2946
John Bowe, *President*
Carl Landsman, *Controller*
▲ **EMP:** 42 **EST:** 1978
SQ FT: 50,000
SALES (est): 61.7MM
SALES (corp-wide): 192.8MM **Privately Held**
WEB: www.darlexx.com
SIC: 2295 Laminating of fabrics
PA: Shawmut Corporation
  208 Manley St
  West Bridgewater MA 02379
  508 588-3300

(G-8466)
TRIAD PRINTING INC
Also Called: Chester Printing Service
7 Prospect St (10940-4809)
PHONE.................................845 343-2722
Fax: 845 341-1319
Joseph Stewart, *President*
Ralph Carr, *Corp Secy*
EMP: 5
SALES (est): 791.1K **Privately Held**
SIC: 2752 Commercial printing, lithographic

(G-8467)
TURBINE ARFOIL CATING REPR LLC
Also Called: Tacr
105 Tower Dr (10941-2034)
PHONE.................................845 692-8912
Mathew Wilson, *General Mgr*
Michael Beckert, *CFO*
Gerard Milidantri,
▲ **EMP:** 250
SQ FT: 65,000
SALES (est): 16.8MM **Privately Held**
SIC: 3479 Painting, coating & hot dipping

(G-8468)
UNIQUE QUALITY FABRICS INC
115 Wisner Ave (10940-3635)
PHONE.................................845 343-3070
Henry Klein, *President*
Norman Klein, *Manager*
◆ **EMP:** 7 **EST:** 1980
SQ FT: 13,000
SALES (est): 956.7K **Privately Held**
WEB: www.uniquequalityfabrics.com
SIC: 2221 Draperies & drapery fabrics, manmade fiber & silk

(G-8469)
WANJASHAN INTERNATIONAL LLC
4 Sands Station Rd (10940-4415)
PHONE.................................845 343-1505
Michael Wu, *President*
◆ **EMP:** 15
SALES (est): 2.6MM **Privately Held**
SIC: 2035 Soy sauce

Middletown - Orange County (G-8470)

GEOGRAPHIC SECTION

(G-8470)
WATEC AMERICA CORPORATION
720 Route 17m Ste 4 (10940-4350)
PHONE..................702 434-6111
Chia L Liu, *President*
EMP: 50
SALES (est): 4.3MM **Privately Held**
SIC: 3861 Cameras & related equipment

(G-8471)
ZENITH AUTOPARTS CORP
20 Industrial Pl (10940-3609)
PHONE..................845 344-1382
Fax: 845 344-1462
Moses Goldstein, *President*
Joel Goldstein, *Vice Pres*
▲ EMP: 25
SQ FT: 38,000
SALES: 5MM **Privately Held**
SIC: 3694 Ignition systems, high frequency

Middleville
Herkimer County

(G-8472)
E J WILLIS COMPANY INC
37 N Main St (13406)
PHONE..................315 891-7602
Fax: 315 891-3477
Evelyn Reile, *President*
Rita Huyck, *Bookkeeper*
EMP: 15
SQ FT: 75,000
SALES: 1MM **Privately Held**
SIC: 3599 Machine shop, jobbing & repair

Milford
Otsego County

(G-8473)
COOPERSTOWN BREWING CO LLC
110 River St (13807)
P.O. Box 276 (13807-0276)
PHONE..................607 286-9330
Dennis Haeley, *Partner*
Jewel Hall, *Partner*
Stanley Hall,
EMP: 5
SQ FT: 5,000
SALES (est): 360K **Privately Held**
WEB: www.cooperstownbrewing.com
SIC: 2082 Malt beverages

(G-8474)
PRESSURE WASHING SERVICES INC
26 Maple St (13807)
P.O. Box 417 (13807-0417)
PHONE..................607 286-7458
Mathew Johnson, *President*
EMP: 6
SALES (est): 480K **Privately Held**
SIC: 3582 Washing machines, laundry: commercial, incl. coin-operated

Millbrook
Dutchess County

(G-8475)
GORDON S ANDERSON MFG CO
215 N Mabbettsville Rd (12545-5358)
P.O. Box 1459 (12545-1459)
PHONE..................845 677-3304
Fax: 845 677-5047
Stewart Anderson, *President*
Christine Horihan, *Vice Pres*
EMP: 7 EST: 1946
SQ FT: 7,000
SALES (est): 313.9K **Privately Held**
SIC: 3648 3559 Lighting equipment; pharmaceutical machinery

(G-8476)
MICRO SYSTEMS SPECIALISTS INC
Also Called: Mssi
3280 Franklin Ave Fl 2 (12545-5975)
P.O. Box 347 (12545-0347)
PHONE..................845 677-6150
Fax: 845 677-6620
Catherine Culkin, *President*
Dawn Roeller, *Vice Pres*
Eileen Sunderland, *Treasurer*
Judy Bruning, *Admin Sec*
EMP: 5
SQ FT: 2,000
SALES (est): 431K **Privately Held**
SIC: 7372 Business oriented computer software

(G-8477)
MILLBROOK FAMILY EYECARE
61 Front St (12545-5961)
P.O. Box 570 (12545-0570)
PHONE..................845 677-5012
Linda Krall, *Principal*
EMP: 5 EST: 2011
SALES (est): 563.2K **Privately Held**
SIC: 3851 Contact lenses

(G-8478)
MILLBROOK WINERY INC
Also Called: Millbrook Vineyard
26 Wing Rd (12545-5017)
PHONE..................845 677-8383
Fax: 845 677-6186
John Dyson, *President*
John Graziano, *Vice Pres*
Stacy Hudson, *Marketing Staff*
Lynn Murphy, *Office Mgr*
▲ EMP: 12
SQ FT: 960
SALES (est): 1.2MM **Privately Held**
WEB: www.millbrookwine.com
SIC: 2084 Wines

Millerton
Dutchess County

(G-8479)
ILLINOIS TOOL WORKS INC
5979 N Elm Ave (12546-4525)
PHONE..................860 435-2574
EMP: 89
SALES (corp-wide): 13.4B **Publicly Held**
SIC: 3089 Injection molding of plastics
PA: Illinois Tool Works Inc.
 155 Harlem Ave
 Glenview IL 60025
 847 724-7500

Millport
Chemung County

(G-8480)
BLUE MANUFACTURING CO INC
3852 Watkins Rd (14864-9782)
PHONE..................607 796-2463
Fax: 607 796-4291
Teresa K Liston, *President*
Marlene Liston, *Vice Pres*
EMP: 6
SQ FT: 4,800
SALES (est): 733K **Privately Held**
WEB: www.bluemoonmanufacturing.com
SIC: 3599 Grease cups, metal

(G-8481)
GLASSART INC
2011 Maple St (14864-9630)
PHONE..................607 739-3939
Christian H Thirion, *Ch of Bd*
EMP: 6 EST: 2001
SALES (est): 516.2K **Privately Held**
SIC: 3229 Pressed & blown glass

Milton
Ulster County

(G-8482)
BROOKLYN BTLG MILTON NY INC (PA)
Also Called: Hudson Valley Apple Products
643 South Rd (12547-5119)
P.O. Box 808 (12547-0808)
PHONE..................845 795-2171
Fax: 845 795-2589
Eric Miller, *President*
Neil Richardson, *Prdtn Mgr*
Korese Donaldson, *QC Mgr*
Adam Ela, *QC Mgr*
Theresa Werba, *HR Admin*
◆ EMP: 140
SQ FT: 140,000
SALES (est): 41.2MM **Privately Held**
WEB: www.brooklynbottling.com
SIC: 2086 5149 2033 Bottled & canned soft drinks; iced tea & fruit drinks, bottled & canned; carbonated soft drinks, bottled & canned; juices; soft drinks; canned fruits & specialties

(G-8483)
PRAGMATICS TECHNOLOGY INC
14 Old Indian Trl (12547-5114)
PHONE..................845 795-5071
Chris Mack, *President*
Carissa Dangero, *Office Mgr*
Gaberiela Hughes, *Administration*
EMP: 8 EST: 2000
SQ FT: 700
SALES (est): 1.4MM **Privately Held**
WEB: www.pragmaticstech.com
SIC: 3825 Semiconductor test equipment

(G-8484)
SONO-TEK CORPORATION (PA)
2012 Route 9w Stop 3 (12547-5034)
PHONE..................845 795-2020
Fax: 845 795-2720
Christopher L Coccio, *Ch of Bd*
R Stephen Harshbarger, *President*
Vincent Demaio, *Vice Pres*
Robb W Engle, *Vice Pres*
Joseph Riemer, *Vice Pres*
▲ EMP: 59 EST: 1975
SQ FT: 50,000
SALES: 11.8MM **Publicly Held**
WEB: www.sprayfluxing.com
SIC: 3499 Nozzles, spray: aerosol, paint or insecticide

(G-8485)
SUNDANCE INDUSTRIES INC
36 Greentree Ln (12547-5437)
PHONE..................845 795-5809
Alden Link, *President*
Carol Link, *Treasurer*
EMP: 5
SQ FT: 10,000
SALES: 1.5MM **Privately Held**
WEB: www.sundanceind.com
SIC: 3634 Juice extractors, electric

Mineola
Nassau County

(G-8486)
A & D OFFSET PRINTERS LTD
146 2nd St Apt 3 (11501-4079)
PHONE..................516 746-2476
Fax: 516 746-2859
Mark A Eliassof, *President*
Adam S Eliaof, *Vice Pres*
Adam S Eliassof, *Vice Pres*
Tara A Eliassof, *Vice Pres*
Tara S Eliassof, *Vice Pres*
EMP: 8
SQ FT: 2,000
SALES (est): 590K **Privately Held**
SIC: 2752 7334 7389 5943 Commercial printing, offset; photocopying & duplicating services; laminating service; office forms & supplies

(G-8487)
A & M STEEL STAMPS INC
55 Windsor Ave (11501-1923)
PHONE..................516 741-6223
Fax: 516 248-4202
Paul Argendorf, *President*
EMP: 5
SQ FT: 2,000
SALES: 500K **Privately Held**
SIC: 3953 Embossing seals & hand stamps

(G-8488)
A K ALLEN CO INC
Also Called: Allen Air
255 E 2nd St (11501-3520)
P.O. Box 350 (11501-0350)
PHONE..................516 747-5450
Ronald Buttner, *President*
Tim Byrnes, *General Mgr*
Jim Lyons, *Vice Pres*
Steve Werlinitsch, *Plant Mgr*
Wayne Butner, *Research*
▲ EMP: 120 EST: 1945
SQ FT: 150,000
SALES (est): 17.3MM **Privately Held**
SIC: 3679 3443 3822 3593 Electronic circuits; cylinders, pressure: metal plate; pneumatic relays, air-conditioning type; fluid power cylinders & actuators; valves & pipe fittings; fluid power valves & hose fittings

(G-8489)
AERO TRADES MFG CORP
65 Jericho Tpke (11501-2991)
PHONE..................516 746-3360
Fax: 516 746-3417
Jeffrey E Love, *President*
John Niebuhr, *Vice Pres*
Amy Bernstein, *Manager*
Walter Trimborn, *Manager*
EMP: 33 EST: 1931
SQ FT: 60,000
SALES (est): 6.2MM **Privately Held**
WEB: www.aerotrades.com
SIC: 3728 3444 Aircraft assemblies, sub-assemblies & parts; sheet metalwork

(G-8490)
AERODUCT INC
134 Herricks Rd (11501-2205)
PHONE..................516 248-9550
Alvin Soffler, *President*
Blanche Soffler, *Corp Secy*
Glen Soffler, *Vice Pres*
Marc Soffler, *Vice Pres*
Roberta Yobs, *Controller*
EMP: 20 EST: 1967
SQ FT: 3,500
SALES (est): 2.6MM **Privately Held**
WEB: www.aeroduct.com
SIC: 3444 1711 Sheet metalwork; ventilation & duct work contractor

(G-8491)
AGRECOLOR INC (PA)
400 Sagamore Ave (11501-1987)
PHONE..................516 741-8700
Fax: 516 741-0698
Anthony Greco, *President*
Doreen Greco, *Corp Secy*
Anette Brady, *Bookkeeper*
Frank Ortega, *CPA*
EMP: 18 EST: 1957
SQ FT: 15,000
SALES (est): 2.7MM **Privately Held**
WEB: www.agrecolor.com
SIC: 2752 2791 2789 Commercial printing, offset; typesetting; bookbinding & related work

(G-8492)
ALL STAR AWNINGS & SIGNS
332 Sagamore Ave (11501-1918)
PHONE..................516 742-8469
Tom Shea, *Principal*
EMP: 12
SALES (est): 640K **Privately Held**
SIC: 3993 Signs & advertising specialties

(G-8493)
ALLEN AVIONICS INC
255 E 2nd St (11501-3524)
P.O. Box 350 (11501-0350)
PHONE..................516 248-8080

GEOGRAPHIC SECTION

Mineola - Nassau County (G-8519)

Fax: 516 747-6724
Alton K Allen, *President*
Jim Lyons, *General Mgr*
Richard Mintz, *General Mgr*
Sylvia G Allen, *Vice Pres*
▲ **EMP:** 50
SQ FT: 80,000
SALES (est): 6.7MM **Privately Held**
WEB: www.allenavionics.com
SIC: 3677 3679 Filtration devices, electronic; delay lines

(G-8494)
ALLENAIR CORPORATION
255 E 2nd St (11501-3524)
P.O. Box 350 (11501-0350)
PHONE.................................516 747-5450
Fax: 516 747-5450
Ronald Butner, *President*
Tim Byrnes, *General Mgr*
Daniel Paradino, *QC Dir*
Wayne Butner, *Research*
Sylvia G Allen, *Treasurer*
EMP: 100
SQ FT: 150,000
SALES (est): 13.2MM **Privately Held**
WEB: www.allenair.com
SIC: 3593 Fluid power cylinders, hydraulic or pneumatic

(G-8495)
AQUIFER DRILLING & TESTING INC (PA)
Also Called: A D T
75 E 2nd St (11501-3503)
PHONE.................................516 616-6026
Fax: 516 616-6194
H Leonard Rexrode Jr, *Ch of Bd*
Joseph Miranda, *Vice Pres*
Steffany McIncry, *Manager*
William A Poupis, *Technology*
▲ **EMP:** 60
SQ FT: 22,000
SALES: 24MM **Privately Held**
SIC: 1382 7375 1711 Geological exploration, oil & gas field; information retrieval services; plumbing contractors

(G-8496)
ARISTA INNOVATIONS INC
Also Called: Arista Printing
131 Liberty Ave (11501-3510)
PHONE.................................516 746-2262
Edward Sikorski, *President*
Eleanor Sikorski, *Corp Secy*
Leonard Sikorski, *Vice Pres*
Raymond Sikorski, *Vice Pres*
Greg Turwilliger, *Senior Mgr*
EMP: 30
SQ FT: 25,000
SALES (est): 3.8MM **Privately Held**
WEB: www.aristaprinters.com
SIC: 2752 2791 2789 2759 Commercial printing, offset; typesetting; bookbinding & related work; commercial printing

(G-8497)
BEARDSLEE REALTY
290 E Jericho Tpke (11501-2197)
PHONE.................................516 747-5557
Kan McDowbll, *Manager*
EMP: 6
SALES (corp-wide): 688.4K **Privately Held**
SIC: 2326 6519 Industrial garments, men's & boys'; real property lessors
PA: Beardslee Realty
    27 To 22 Jackson Ave
    Long Island City NY 11101
    718 784-4100

(G-8498)
BIMBO BAKERIES USA INC
12 E Jericho Tpke (11501-3141)
PHONE.................................516 877-2850
EMP: 25
SALES (corp-wide): 13.7B **Privately Held**
SIC: 2051 Mfg Bread/Related Products
HQ: Bimbo Bakeries Usa, Inc
    255 Business Center Dr # 200
    Horsham PA 19044
    215 347-5500

(G-8499)
BLC TEXTILES INC
330 Old Country Rd # 201 (11501-4187)
P.O. Box 5485, New Hyde Park (11042-5485)
PHONE.................................516 791-4500
Mark Lichter, *CEO*
EMP: 26
SALES (est): 2.1MM **Privately Held**
SIC: 2299 Towels & towelings, linen & linen-and-cotton mixtures

(G-8500)
CANVAS PRODUCTS COMPANY INC
234 Herricks Rd (11501-2208)
PHONE.................................516 742-1058
Edwin E Youngstrom, *President*
EMP: 10
SQ FT: 1,500
SALES (est): 1MM **Privately Held**
SIC: 2394 Awnings, fabric: made from purchased materials

(G-8501)
CAROL PERETZ
Also Called: Carol Peretz Workshop
49 Windsor Ave Ste 103 (11501-1933)
PHONE.................................516 248-6300
Carol Peretz, *Owner*
EMP: 18
SQ FT: 4,000
SALES (est): 1.1MM **Privately Held**
WEB: www.carolperetz.com
SIC: 2335 Dresses, paper: cut & sewn

(G-8502)
CAST-ALL CORPORATION (PA)
229 Liberty Ave (11501-3575)
P.O. Box 271 (11501-0271)
PHONE.................................516 741-4025
Jack Mandell, *President*
Rose Mandell, *Corp Secy*
Chaim Mandell, *Vice Pres*
Theodore Mandell, *Vice Pres*
EMP: 35 **EST:** 1962
SALES (est): 2.6MM **Privately Held**
WEB: www.cast-all.com
SIC: 3089 3364 3429 3369 Injection molding of plastics; zinc & zinc-base alloy die-castings; manufactured hardware (general); nonferrous foundries

(G-8503)
CAST-ALL CORPORATION
229 Liberty Ave (11501-3575)
P.O. Box 271 (11501-0271)
PHONE.................................516 741-4025
Jack Mandell, *President*
EMP: 25
SALES (corp-wide): 2.6MM **Privately Held**
WEB: www.cast-all.com
SIC: 3364 3089 Zinc & zinc-base alloy die-castings; injection molding of plastics
PA: Cast-All Corporation
    229 Liberty Ave
    Mineola NY 11501
    516 741-4025

(G-8504)
COMPETICION MOWER REPAIR
75 Windsor Ave (11501-1983)
PHONE.................................516 280-6584
Christopher Sideris, *Owner*
Lisa B Sideris, *Admin Sec*
EMP: 5
SALES (est): 495.7K **Privately Held**
SIC: 7692 Welding repair

(G-8505)
DCL FURNITURE MANUFACTURING
96 Windsor Ave (11501-1922)
PHONE.................................516 248-2683
Fax: 516 248-0417
Domingos Lopes, *President*
Carlos Lopes, *Manager*
EMP: 20
SQ FT: 2,000
SALES (est): 2.2MM **Privately Held**
WEB: www.dclfurniture.com
SIC: 2511 2522 2521 Wood household furniture; office furniture, except wood; wood office furniture

(G-8506)
DISPLAY LOGIC USA INC (PA)
315 Roslyn Rd (11501-1939)
PHONE.................................516 513-1420
Keith Morton, *CEO*
Stanley Schiller, *General Mgr*
EMP: 5 **EST:** 2012
SALES (est): 1MM **Privately Held**
SIC: 3823 Digital displays of process variables

(G-8507)
ELIAS ARTMETAL INC
70 E 2nd St (11501-3505)
P.O. Box 1872 (11501-0909)
PHONE.................................516 873-7501
Fax: 516 873-7505
Constantine Elias, *President*
Ruth Elias, *Vice Pres*
EMP: 19 **EST:** 1976
SQ FT: 9,000
SALES (est): 1MM **Privately Held**
WEB: www.eliasartmetal.com
SIC: 3499 Picture frames, metal; novelties & specialties, metal

(G-8508)
ENVIRONMENTAL TEMP SYSTEMS LLC
Also Called: Ets
111 Roosevelt Ave Ste C (11501-3056)
P.O. Box 701 (11501-0701)
PHONE.................................516 640-5818
Wayman Lee,
Kwon Chan,
Joseph D'Alessio,
EMP: 5
SALES (est): 1.2MM **Privately Held**
SIC: 3585 Refrigeration & heating equipment

(G-8509)
EPS IRON WORKS INC
38 Windsor Ave Ste 101 (11501-1932)
PHONE.................................516 294-5840
Edward Strocchia, *President*
Philip Strocchia, *Vice Pres*
EMP: 8
SQ FT: 2,000
SALES (est): 820K **Privately Held**
SIC: 3441 Fabricated structural metal

(G-8510)
ERICEIRA INC
Also Called: Bakers of All Nations
54 E Jericho Tpke (11501-3141)
PHONE.................................516 294-4034
Fax: 516 877-2472
Paula Rego, *President*
Joao Malheiro, *Treasurer*
EMP: 7
SALES (est): 540K **Privately Held**
WEB: www.ericeira.com
SIC: 2051 Bakery: wholesale or wholesale/retail combined

(G-8511)
F J REMEY CO INC
121 Willis Ave (11501-2612)
P.O. Box 589 (11501-0589)
PHONE.................................516 741-5112
Fax: 516 741-0523
Richard A Haas, *President*
Margaret Haas, *Manager*
Charlie Morano, *Info Tech Mgr*
EMP: 40
SQ FT: 20,000
SALES (est): 6.2MM **Privately Held**
WEB: www.fjremey.com
SIC: 2752 5112 Commercial printing, offset; stationery

(G-8512)
GEOTECHNICAL DRILLING INC
Also Called: Environmental Closures
75 E 2nd St (11501-3503)
PHONE.................................516 616-6055
H L Rexrode Jr, *Ch of Bd*
William Poupis, *Vice Pres*
EMP: 85
SQ FT: 1,250
SALES (est): 3.5MM **Privately Held**
SIC: 1381 Drilling oil & gas wells

(G-8513)
HICKVILLE ILLUSTRATED NEWS
132 E 2nd St (11501-3522)
PHONE.................................516 747-8282
Angela Anton, *Owner*
William Delventhal Jr, *General Mgr*
EMP: 70
SALES (est): 1.6MM **Privately Held**
SIC: 2711 Newspapers

(G-8514)
HYGRADE FUEL INC
260 Columbus Pkwy (11501-3137)
PHONE.................................516 741-0723
R Grieco, *Principal*
EMP: 5
SALES (est): 490.2K **Privately Held**
SIC: 2911 Oils, fuel

(G-8515)
ICONIX INC
315 Roslyn Rd (11501-1939)
PHONE.................................516 307-1324
Fax: 516 513-1421
Jacob Kohn, *Ch of Bd*
Stan Schiller, *General Mgr*
Charlie Forbes, *Buyer*
Steve Molstad, *QC Mgr*
Caralyn Vultaggio, *Marketing Staff*
EMP: 18
SQ FT: 6,200
SALES: 9.1MM **Privately Held**
SIC: 3699 5065 Electrical equipment & supplies; electronic parts & equipment

(G-8516)
INTERCALL SYSTEMS INC
Also Called: Intercall of New York
150 Herricks Rd (11501-2205)
PHONE.................................516 294-4524
Fax: 516 294-4526
Ellis Gurman, *President*
Esther Gurman, *Vice Pres*
Bruno Gray, *Engineer*
Jaco Jacob, *Manager*
▲ **EMP:** 25
SQ FT: 10,000
SALES (est): 4.4MM **Privately Held**
WEB: www.intercallsystems.com
SIC: 3669 Intercommunication systems, electric

(G-8517)
ISLAND MARKETING CORP
95 Searing Ave Ste 2 (11501-3046)
PHONE.................................516 739-0500
Fax: 516 747-4668
Frank Scarangella, *President*
EMP: 5
SALES: 400K **Privately Held**
SIC: 2879 8742 Insecticides, agricultural or household; sales (including sales management) consultant

(G-8518)
ISLAND ORDNANCE SYSTEMS LLC
267 E Jericho Tpke Ste 2 (11501-2100)
PHONE.................................516 746-2100
Fax: 516 746-2405
Amnon Parizat, *President*
Anne Parizat, *Treasurer*
Linda Aguilo, *Controller*
▼ **EMP:** 13
SQ FT: 3,000
SALES (est): 3.4MM **Privately Held**
WEB: www.islandgroup.com
SIC: 3489 5099 5169 Ordnance & accessories; firearms & ammunition, except sporting; explosives

(G-8519)
ISLAND PYROCHEMICAL INDS CORP (PA)
267 E Jericho Tpke Ste 2 (11501-2100)
PHONE.................................516 746-2100
Amnon Parizat, *President*
Robert Massey, *Business Mgr*
Anne Parizat, *Vice Pres*
William Solomon, *VP Sls/Mktg*
Linda Aguilo, *Controller*
◆ **EMP:** 15 **EST:** 1982
SQ FT: 6,000

Mineola - Nassau County (G-8520)

SALES (est): 27.1MM Privately Held
WEB: www.worldvoi.com
SIC: 3081 2899 5169 Film base, cellulose acetate or nitrocellulose plastic; pyrotechnic ammunition: flares, signals, rockets, etc.; chemicals & allied products

(G-8520)
LI COMMUNITY NEWSPAPERS INC
132 E 2nd St (11501-3533)
PHONE..................516 747-8282
Angela Anton, Publisher
Billey Daelventhal, Manager
EMP: 5
SALES (est): 294.2K Privately Held
SIC: 2711 Newspapers, publishing & printing

(G-8521)
LIBERTY PIPE INCORPORATED
128 Liberty Ave (11501-3509)
PHONE..................516 747-2472
John Kritis, President
EMP: 5
SALES (est): 516.5K Privately Held
SIC: 3317 Steel pipe & tubes

(G-8522)
LONG ISLAND CMNTY NWSPPERS INC (PA)
Also Called: Anton Community Newspapers
132 E 2nd St (11501-3522)
PHONE..................516 482-4490
Fax: 516 742-5867
Angela Anton, President
Vicki Caruso, Editor
Denise Nash, Editor
Joe Scotchie, Editor
Rachel Shapiro, Editor
EMP: 85
SALES (est): 10.7MM Privately Held
WEB: www.antonnews.com
SIC: 2711 7313 Newspapers, publishing & printing; newspaper advertising representative

(G-8523)
MAXIM HYGIENE PRODUCTS INC (PA)
Also Called: Organic Peak
121 E Jericho Tpke (11501-2031)
PHONE..................516 621-3323
Kenneth Alvandi, Ch of Bd
▲ EMP: 15
SALES (est): 1.9MM Privately Held
SIC: 2676 Feminine hygiene paper products

(G-8524)
MEDIPOINT INC
Also Called: Medipoint International,
72 E 2nd St (11501-3591)
PHONE..................516 294-8822
Fax: 516 746-6693
Peter Gollobin, President
EMP: 12
SQ FT: 7,200
SALES (est): 1MM Privately Held
SIC: 3841 Surgical & medical instruments; medical instruments & equipment, blood & bone work

(G-8525)
MICHAEL BRITT INC
Also Called: MBI Firearms
89 Mineola Blvd Fl 1 (11501-4063)
PHONE..................516 248-2010
Fax: 516 248-2010
Michael Britt Sr, President
Tatiana Britt, Corp Secy
EMP: 3 EST: 1949
SQ FT: 4,500
SALES: 1MM Privately Held
SIC: 3949 7699 7997 Sporting & athletic goods; baskets (creels); fish & bait; gunsmith shop; gun club, membership

(G-8526)
NASSAU CHROMIUM PLATING CO INC
122 2nd St (11501-3054)
PHONE..................516 746-6666
Fax: 516 747-3791
George Waring, President
Shirley Waring, Corp Secy
EMP: 45 EST: 1929
SQ FT: 10,000
SALES (est): 4.9MM Privately Held
WEB: www.nassaufdrant.com
SIC: 3471 Plating of metals or formed products

(G-8527)
NORTHEAST HARDWARE SPECIALTIES
393 Jericho Tpke Ste 103 (11501-1213)
PHONE..................516 487-6868
Wayne A Reed Jr, Owner
EMP: 10
SALES (est): 174.6K Privately Held
SIC: 3599 Industrial machinery

(G-8528)
NORWOOD SCREW MACHINE PARTS
200 E 2nd St Ste 2 (11501-3519)
PHONE..................516 481-6644
Gary Prchal, President
EMP: 10
SQ FT: 10,000
SALES: 1.5MM Privately Held
WEB: www.norwoodscrewmachine.com
SIC: 3451 Screw machine products

(G-8529)
ORACLE CORPORATION
330 Old Country Rd (11501-4187)
PHONE..................516 247-4500
EMP: 302
SALES (corp-wide): 37B Publicly Held
SIC: 7372 Business oriented computer software
PA: Oracle Corporation
500 Oracle Pkwy
Redwood City CA 94065
650 506-7000

(G-8530)
ORIGIN PRESS INC
131 Liberty Ave (11501-3510)
PHONE..................516 746-2262
Ray Sikorski, President
EMP: 5
SQ FT: 3,000
SALES (est): 378.4K Privately Held
WEB: www.originpress.com
SIC: 2759 Commercial printing

(G-8531)
PRECISION DISC GRINDING CORP
255 E 2nd St (11501-3524)
P.O. Box 350 (11501-0350)
PHONE..................516 747-5450
Ron Buttner, President
Tim Byrnes, President
Richard Mintz, Vice Pres
Sylvia C Allen, Treasurer
Virginia Amato, Personnel
EMP: 15 EST: 1951
SQ FT: 150,000
SALES (est): 1MM Privately Held
WEB: www.precisiondiscgrinding.com
SIC: 3599 8741 Grinding castings for the trade; management services

(G-8532)
RA NEWHOUSE INC (PA)
110 Liberty Ave (11501-3509)
P.O. Box 791 (11501-0791)
PHONE..................516 248-6670
Fax: 516 747-9209
Richard A Newhouse Jr, President
Nancy Appey, Accounts Mgr
EMP: 60 EST: 1955
SQ FT: 20,000
SALES (est): 7.5MM Privately Held
SIC: 2389 Uniforms & vestments; academic vestments (caps & gowns)

(G-8533)
RAYTECH CORP ASBESTOS PERSONAL (PA)
190 Willis Ave (11501-2672)
PHONE..................516 747-0300
Elena Karabatos, Vice Pres
Ron Poepple, Vice Pres
Richard A Lippe, Mng Trustee
EMP: 8
SALES (est): 117.3MM Privately Held
SIC: 3499 Friction material, made from powdered metal

(G-8534)
REIS D FURNITURE MFG
327 Sagamore Ave Ste 2 (11501-1944)
PHONE..................516 248-5676
Fax: 516 746-5223
Domingos Reis, President
Candida C Reis, Corp Secy
▼ EMP: 45
SQ FT: 15,000
SALES (est): 6.3MM Privately Held
WEB: www.mineolachamber.com
SIC: 2511 Wood household furniture

(G-8535)
RUBBER STAMPS INC
174 Herricks Rd (11501-2206)
PHONE..................212 675-1180
Fax: 212 675-3849
Robert A Kowalsky, President
Elsie Cintron, Vice Pres
Abel Kowalsky, Vice Pres
Peter Leinroth, Vice Pres
Patricia Reber, Vice Pres
EMP: 25
SALES (est): 2.7MM Privately Held
WEB: www.rubberstampsinc.com
SIC: 3953 3555 2791 3069 Postmark stamps, hand: rubber or metal; printing plates; typographic composition, for the printing trade; stationers' rubber sundries

(G-8536)
S & V CUSTOM FURNITURE MFG
75 Windsor Ave Unit E (11501-1935)
PHONE..................516 746-8299
Carlos Silva, President
Norman Kurtz, Vice Pres
George Valente, Treasurer
EMP: 10
SQ FT: 2,800
SALES (est): 1.1MM Privately Held
SIC: 2434 Wood kitchen cabinets

(G-8537)
SCHAEFER MACHINE CO INC
100 Hudson St (11501-3581)
PHONE..................516 248-6880
Fax: 516 747-2227
Peter G Walter, President
Paul Rubilotta, Vice Pres
Paul Walter, Vice Pres
EMP: 22
SQ FT: 15,000
SALES (est): 3MM Privately Held
WEB: www.schaeferco.com
SIC: 3542 3452 Machine tools, metal forming type; bolts, nuts, rivets & washers

(G-8538)
VISUAL ID SOURCE INC
65 E 2nd St (11501-3503)
PHONE..................516 307-9759
Fayaz Khalfan, Ch of Bd
EMP: 15
SQ FT: 20,000
SALES: 1.5MM Privately Held
SIC: 3993 Signs & advertising specialties

(G-8539)
WESTBURY TIMES
Also Called: Three Village Times
132 E 2nd St (11501-3522)
PHONE..................516 747-8282
Angela Anton, Owner
William Delventhal Jr, General Mgr
EMP: 75
SALES (est): 5MM Privately Held
WEB: www.westburytimes.com
SIC: 2711 Newspapers

Mineville
Essex County

(G-8540)
ESSEX INDUSTRIES
17 Pilfershire Rd (12956-1092)
P.O. Box 374 (12956-0374)
PHONE..................518 942-6671
Fax: 518 942-3024
John Anello, Manager
EMP: 8
SALES (est): 724.4K Privately Held
SIC: 3999 Manufacturing industries

(G-8541)
PRE-TECH PLASTICS INC
3085 Plank Rd (12956-1050)
P.O. Box 370 (12956-0370)
PHONE..................518 942-5950
Fax: 518 942-5931
Mike Cave, Branch Mgr
EMP: 30
SALES (corp-wide): 11.3MM Privately Held
WEB: www.pretechplastics.com
SIC: 3599 Machine shop, jobbing & repair
PA: Pre-Tech Plastics, Inc.
209 Blair Park Rd
Williston VT 05495
802 879-9441

Mohawk
Herkimer County

(G-8542)
MARY F MORSE
Also Called: Kwik Kut Manufacturing Co
125 Columbia St Ste 1 (13407-1527)
P.O. Box 116 (13407-0116)
PHONE..................315 866-2741
Fax: 315 866-2654
Mary Morse, Owner
EMP: 8
SQ FT: 3,600
SALES (est): 440K Privately Held
WEB: www.kwik-kut.com
SIC: 3556 Choppers, commercial, food

Mohegan Lake
Westchester County

(G-8543)
BARONE OFFSET PRINTING CORP
89 Lake Ridge Cv (10547-1222)
PHONE..................212 989-5500
Sandra Barone, President
Claudio Olnos, Manager
EMP: 5
SALES (est): 541.3K Privately Held
WEB: www.baronepress.com
SIC: 2752 Commercial printing, offset

(G-8544)
SHOPPING CENTER WINE & LIQUOR
Also Called: Kimbri Liquor
3008 E Main St (10547)
PHONE..................914 528-1600
Catheeren Lebleu, Owner
EMP: 5
SALES (est): 175.4K Privately Held
SIC: 2086 Bottled & canned soft drinks

(G-8545)
SOHO EDITIONS INC
2641 Deer St (10547-2019)
PHONE..................914 591-5100
Elliot Burns, CEO
Nicole Mone, Vice Pres
EMP: 25
SALES (est): 2.1MM Privately Held
WEB: www.sohoeditions.com
SIC: 2741 Art copy: publishing & printing

Moira
Franklin County

(G-8546)
MOIRA NEW HOPE FOOD PANTRY
2341 County Route 5 (12957-2118)
PHONE..................518 529-6524
Joanne Deno, Director
EMP: 20

GEOGRAPHIC SECTION

Monsey - Rockland County (G-8576)

SALES (est): 1MM **Privately Held**
SIC: 2099 Food preparations

Monroe
Orange County

(G-8547)
6TH AVE GOURMET INC
51 Forest Rd Unit 116 (10950-2948)
PHONE..................................845 782-9067
Clara Perl, *President*
EMP: 8
SQ FT: 4,000
SALES (est): 617K **Privately Held**
SIC: 2092 Fresh or frozen packaged fish

(G-8548)
ASSOCIATED DRAPERY & EQUIPMENT
Also Called: Novelty Scenic Studios Inc
3 Kosnitz Dr Unit 111 (10950-1163)
PHONE..................................516 671-5245
Fax: 516 674-2213
Feivel Weiss, *Principal*
Howard Kessler, *Corp Secy*
Leslie Kessler, *Vice Pres*
EMP: 10 EST: 1968
SQ FT: 19,000
SALES: 838.6K
SALES (corp-wide): 1.1MM **Privately Held**
SIC: 2391 Curtains & draperies
PA: Novelty Scenic Studios Inc
3 Kosnitz Dr Unit 111
Monroe NY
516 671-5940

(G-8549)
B & H ELECTRONICS CORP
308 Museum Village Rd (10950-1638)
PHONE..................................845 782-5000
Fax: 845 782-0470
Harvey Horowitz, *President*
Bernard Horowitz, *Vice Pres*
EMP: 25
SQ FT: 7,300
SALES (est): 3.3MM **Privately Held**
WEB: www.bhelectronicscorp.com
SIC: 3663 8734 3651 3699 Amplifiers, RF power & IF; testing laboratories; household audio & video equipment; electrical equipment & supplies

(G-8550)
BLOOMING GROVE STAIR CO (PA)
1 Stair Way (10950-1642)
PHONE..................................845 783-4245
Fax: 845 782-2361
Glen Durant, *President*
Serena Aglaff, *Co-Owner*
EMP: 12
SALES (est): 1.4MM **Privately Held**
SIC: 2431 Stair railings, wood

(G-8551)
C T A DIGITAL INC
Also Called: Sol Markowitz
326 State Route 208 (10950-2874)
PHONE..................................845 513-0433
Fax: 718 384-3509
Joseph Markowitz, *Ch of Bd*
Leo Markowitz, *President*
Eli Triteo, *Controller*
Steve Stern, *Sales Mgr*
▲ EMP: 25
SALES: 18.3K **Privately Held**
WEB: www.ctadigital.com
SIC: 3944 Video game machines, except coin-operated

(G-8552)
CHECK-O-MATIC INC
13 D A Weider Blvd # 101 (10950-6124)
P.O. Box 2141 (10949-7141)
PHONE..................................845 781-7675
Chaim Ellenbogen, *President*
Pearl Gruber, *Admin Sec*
EMP: 7
SQ FT: 2,500
SALES (est): 1.3MM **Privately Held**
WEB: www.checkomatic.com
SIC: 2759 Publication printing

(G-8553)
DER BLATT INC
6 Taitch Ct Unit 112 (10950-2195)
PHONE..................................845 783-1148
Aron Muller, *Principal*
EMP: 11
SALES (est): 1.6MM **Privately Held**
SIC: 2711 Newspapers, publishing & printing

(G-8554)
FIVE STAR CREATIONS INC
4 Preshburg Blvd Unit 302 (10950-2968)
PHONE..................................845 783-1187
Baruch Weiss, *President*
Chaya Weiss, *Admin Sec*
EMP: 20
SQ FT: 1,500
SALES (est): 1.7MM **Privately Held**
SIC: 3961 3999 3911 Costume jewelry; bric-a-brac; jewelry, precious metal

(G-8555)
G & M CLEARVIEW INC
Also Called: Clearview Shower Doors
118 Mountain Rd (10950-2128)
PHONE..................................845 781-4877
Chaim Weisberg, *President*
EMP: 6
SALES (est): 370K **Privately Held**
SIC: 3231 Mirrored glass

(G-8556)
HOUSE OF STONE INC
1015 State Route 17m (10950-1626)
PHONE..................................845 782-7271
Raymond Krok Sr, *President*
Eva Crok, *Manager*
EMP: 6
SALES (est): 674.6K **Privately Held**
SIC: 3281 Granite, cut & shaped

(G-8557)
JOEL KIRYAS MEAT MARKET CORP
Also Called: Kirays & Joel Meat Market
51 Forest Rd Ste 345 (10950-2939)
PHONE..................................845 782-9194
Fax: 845 782-2962
Harry Polatchek, *President*
Moses Mewman, *Vice Pres*
Cheskel Landau, *Manager*
EMP: 14
SQ FT: 3,000
SALES (est): 2.1MM **Privately Held**
SIC: 2011 Meat by-products from meat slaughtered on site

(G-8558)
JW CONSULTING INC
Also Called: KJ MEAT DIRECT
20 Chevron Rd Unit 201 (10950-7432)
PHONE..................................845 325-7070
Joel Weiss, *President*
EMP: 2 EST: 1987
SQ FT: 1,000
SALES: 4MM **Privately Held**
SIC: 2015 Poultry slaughtering & processing

(G-8559)
LASER PRINTER CHECKS CORP
7 Vayoel Moshe Ct # 101 (10950-6387)
PHONE..................................845 782-5837
Solomon Klagsbrun, *President*
EMP: 6
SALES (est): 773.9K **Privately Held**
SIC: 2752 Commercial printing, lithographic

(G-8560)
LEGACY FURNITURE INC (PA)
6 Shinev Ct Unit 201 (10950-3829)
P.O. Box 1435 (10949-8435)
PHONE..................................718 527-5331
Herman Sandel, *President*
▲ EMP: 10
SALES (est): 654K **Privately Held**
WEB: www.legacyfurniture.com
SIC: 2434 5021 5712 Wood kitchen cabinets; household furniture; dining room furniture; furniture stores

(G-8561)
MARKOWITZ JEWELRY CO INC
53 Forest Rd Ste 104 (10950-2903)
PHONE..................................845 774-1175
Fax: 212 774-1168
Isaac Markowitz, *President*
Baruch Markowitz, *Vice Pres*
Sam Brisk, *Personnel*
EMP: 30
SQ FT: 10,000
SALES (est): 4.3MM **Privately Held**
WEB: www.markowitzjewelry.com
SIC: 3911 Jewelry, precious metal

(G-8562)
MEDEK LABORATORIES INC
63 First Ave (10950-2063)
PHONE..................................845 943-4988
Isaac Schwartz, *COO*
EMP: 27
SQ FT: 5,000
SALES (est): 1MM **Privately Held**
SIC: 2834 Solutions, pharmaceutical

(G-8563)
MONROE STAIR PRODUCTS INC (PA)
1 Stair Way (10950-1642)
PHONE..................................845 783-4245
Glen T Durant, *President*
Jesse J Kehoe, *Vice Pres*
Paul Graham, *Treasurer*
Serina Durant, *Manager*
EMP: 24
SQ FT: 21,500
SALES (est): 2.8MM **Privately Held**
WEB: www.bloominggrovestair.com
SIC: 2431 Staircases & stairs, wood

(G-8564)
STOP ENTERTAINMENT INC
408 Rye Hill Rd (10950-4509)
PHONE..................................212 242-7867
Ruben Cabrera, *CEO*
EMP: 15
SQ FT: 1,500
SALES (est): 1.1MM **Privately Held**
SIC: 2732 7311 Book printing; advertising agencies

(G-8565)
TRI COUNTY CUSTOM VACUUM
653 State Route 17m (10950-3309)
PHONE..................................845 774-7595
Mike Zahra, *Partner*
EMP: 5
SALES: 200K **Privately Held**
SIC: 3635 Household vacuum cleaners

Monsey
Rockland County

(G-8566)
A&B CONSERVATION LLC
12 Maple Leaf Rd (10952-3030)
PHONE..................................845 282-7272
Baruch Tabak,
Judah Rominek,
EMP: 7
SQ FT: 1,000
SALES (est): 375.3K **Privately Held**
SIC: 3295 Pumice, ground or otherwise treated

(G-8567)
AMERTAC HOLDINGS INC (PA)
25 Robert Pitt Dr (10952-3365)
PHONE..................................610 336-1330
Charles Peifer, *Ch of Bd*
John Cooper, *President*
Peter Hermann, *Vice Pres*
EMP: 6
SALES (est): 29.7MM **Privately Held**
SIC: 3699 3429 5063 5072 Electrical equipment & supplies; manufactured hardware (general); metal fasteners; electrical apparatus & equipment; hardware; tacks

(G-8568)
ARONOWITZ METAL WORKS
5 Edwin Ln (10952-3102)
PHONE..................................845 356-1660
Avigdor Aronowitz, *Owner*
Sal Hurst CPA, *Accountant*
EMP: 5
SQ FT: 2,900
SALES (est): 362.7K **Privately Held**
SIC: 2522 Office furniture, except wood

(G-8569)
ATLANTIC SPECIALTY CO INC
20 Jeffrey Pl (10952-2703)
PHONE..................................845 356-2502
Mark Srulowitz, *President*
Seung Lee, *Treasurer*
EMP: 20 EST: 1908
SQ FT: 5,000
SALES (est): 1.4MM **Privately Held**
SIC: 3172 3161 Personal leather goods; key cases; coin purses; luggage

(G-8570)
CROWN MILL WORK CORP
12 Melnick Dr (10952-3328)
PHONE..................................845 371-2200
Benzion Lebovits, *Ch of Bd*
EMP: 5
SQ FT: 15,500
SALES (est): 1.1MM **Privately Held**
SIC: 2431 Millwork

(G-8571)
DVASH FOODS INC
2 Brewer Rd (10952-4001)
PHONE..................................845 578-1959
Mel Gertner, *President*
▲ EMP: 10 EST: 2008
SALES (est): 3MM **Privately Held**
SIC: 2038 Frozen specialties

(G-8572)
LE CHOCOLAT LLC
41 Main St (10952-3005)
PHONE..................................845 352-8301
Bruce Serkez, *President*
EMP: 5 EST: 1998
SQ FT: 1,500
SALES (est): 460K **Privately Held**
WEB: www.finestchocolate.com
SIC: 2066 Chocolate & cocoa products

(G-8573)
LOLLIPOPS INC
52 Brewer Rd (10952-4007)
PHONE..................................845 352-8642
Fatima Roque, *President*
Vicly Harvey, *Vice Pres*
Jerid Lester, *Treasurer*
EMP: 26
SQ FT: 5,000
SALES: 1.2MM **Privately Held**
SIC: 2361 5641 Dresses: girls', children's & infants'; children's wear

(G-8574)
MAGCREST PACKAGING INC
Also Called: Wally Packaging
5 Highview Rd (10952-2943)
PHONE..................................845 425-0451
Fax: 845 352-8374
Aaron Rubinson, *President*
Gitty Rubinson, *Vice Pres*
Judy Gluck, *Admin Sec*
◆ EMP: 6
SALES (est): 1.1MM **Privately Held**
WEB: www.magcrest.com
SIC: 2673 7389 Bags: plastic, laminated & coated;

(G-8575)
MAVIANO CORP
21 Robert Pitt Dr Ste 207 (10952-5305)
PHONE..................................845 494-2598
Brenda Falk, *President*
EMP: 7
SALES (est): 549.3K **Privately Held**
SIC: 2821 Plastics materials & resins

(G-8576)
NAVY PLUM LLC
47 Plum Rd (10952-1525)
PHONE..................................845 641-7441
Jonathan Joseph,
EMP: 3
SQ FT: 2,500

(PA)=Parent Co (HQ)=Headquarters (DH)=Div Headquarters
✪ = New Business established in last 2 years

2017 Harris
New York Manufacturers Directory

347

Monsey - Rockland County (G-8577)

SALES: 40MM **Privately Held**
SIC: **2299** 5199 Fabrics: linen, jute, hemp, ramie; yarn: flax, jute, hemp & ramie; fabrics, yarns & knit goods

(G-8577)
PLASTICWARE LLC (PA)
13 Wilsher Dr (10952-2328)
PHONE..................845 267-0790
Patricia Belt, *Sales/Mktg Mgr*
David Koegel, *CFO*
Rachel Meltzer, *Office Mgr*
Sam Meth, *Mng Member*
EMP: 16
SQ FT: 10,000
SALES (est): 6.3MM **Privately Held**
SIC: **3089** Plastic containers, except foam

(G-8578)
RESERVE CONFECTIONS INC
Also Called: Reserve Confections Chocolate
9 Butterman Pl (10952-1880)
P.O. Box 186 (10952-0186)
PHONE..................845 371-7744
Juda Fisch, *President*
▲ EMP: 11 EST: 2014
SALES (est): 975.1K **Privately Held**
SIC: **2066** Chocolate

(G-8579)
S B MANUFACTURING LLC
161 Route 59 (10952-7819)
PHONE..................845 352-3700
Michael Bloch, *President*
Ralph Heidings, *CFO*
EMP: 13
SALES (est): 1.8MM **Privately Held**
SIC: **3999** Barber & beauty shop equipment

(G-8580)
SAFE-DENT ENTERPRISES LLC
4 Orchard Hill Dr (10952-1503)
PHONE..................845 362-0141
Hedy Worch, *Mng Member*
EMP: 5
SQ FT: 20,000
SALES (est): 442K **Privately Held**
SIC: **3843** Dental materials

(G-8581)
SB MOLDS LLC
161 Route 59 Ste 203a (10952-7817)
PHONE..................845 352-3700
Michael Bloch, *Mng Member*
EMP: 80
SALES (est): 3MM **Privately Held**
SIC: **3544** Industrial molds

(G-8582)
SENNETH LLC
26 Ronald Dr Ste 500 (10952-2607)
PHONE..................347 232-3170
Aaron Mandel,
EMP: 9 EST: 2015
SALES (est): 700K **Privately Held**
SIC: **2339** Women's & misses' athletic clothing & sportswear

(G-8583)
SZ - DESIGN & PRINT INC
Also Called: S Z Design & Prints
33 Rita Ave (10952-2699)
PHONE..................845 352-0395
Shlomo Zeibe, *President*
EMP: 15
SALES (est): 2.4MM **Privately Held**
SIC: **2752** Commercial printing, lithographic

(G-8584)
TAMI GREAT FOOD CORP
22 Briarcliff Dr (10952-2503)
PHONE..................845 352-7901
David Rosenberg, *President*
Martin Rosenberg, *President*
Renee Rosenberg, *Vice Pres*
EMP: 8
SQ FT: 6,000
SALES (est): 585.6K **Privately Held**
SIC: **2037** 2038 Vegetables, quick frozen & cold pack, excl. potato products; frozen specialties

(G-8585)
TELE-PAK INC
Also Called: Card Printing.us
421 Route 59 (10952-2835)
P.O. Box 430 (10952-0430)
PHONE..................845 426-2300
Jack Steinmetz, *Ch of Bd*
Shoshana Stefansky, *President*
Heath Clemence, *Prdtn Mgr*
Laura Brown, *Production*
Avram Joseph, *Treasurer*
▲ EMP: 43
SQ FT: 7,000
SALES (est): 8.6MM **Privately Held**
WEB: www.tele-pak.com
SIC: **2754** 2759 2752 7929 Commercial printing, gravure; commercial printing; cards, lithographed; entertainers & entertainment groups

(G-8586)
YATED NEEMAN INC
53 Olympia Ln (10952-2829)
PHONE..................845 369-1600
Fax: 845 369-6397
Pinchos Lipschutz, *President*
AVI Yishai, *Editor*
▲ EMP: 12
SALES (est): 600K **Privately Held**
WEB: www.yated.com
SIC: **2711** Newspapers

(G-8587)
ZYLON CORPORATION
Also Called: Zylon Polymers
23 Mountain Ave (10952-2949)
PHONE..................845 425-9469
Fax: 845 352-6508
Alan Zamore, *President*
EMP: 10
SQ FT: 2,500
SALES (est): 580K **Privately Held**
WEB: www.zylon.net
SIC: **3069** Reclaimed rubber & specialty rubber compounds

Montauk
Suffolk County

(G-8588)
JESSE JOECKEL
Also Called: Whalebone Creative
65 Tuthill Rd (11954-5460)
PHONE..................631 668-2772
Jesse Joeckel, *Owner*
Bronson Lamb, *Manager*
EMP: 5 EST: 2010
SQ FT: 600
SALES (est): 357K **Privately Held**
SIC: **2339** Women's & misses' outerwear

(G-8589)
MONTAUK BREWING COMPANY INC
62 S Erie Ave (11954-5370)
P.O. Box 1079 (11954-0802)
PHONE..................631 668-8471
Vaughan Cutillo, *Vice Pres*
EMP: 10
SALES (est): 19.5K **Privately Held**
SIC: **2082** Beer (alcoholic beverage)

(G-8590)
MONTAUK INLET SEAFOOD INC
E Lake Dr Ste 540-541 (11954)
P.O. Box 2148 (11954-0905)
PHONE..................631 668-3419
Charles S Weimar, *President*
David Aripocth, *Owner*
Kevin Maguire, *Owner*
William Grimm, *Vice Pres*
Richard Jones, *Treasurer*
EMP: 3
SQ FT: 5,000
SALES (est): 1.1MM **Privately Held**
SIC: **2092** 5146 5983 Fish, fresh: prepared; fish, fresh; fuel oil dealers

(G-8591)
NYEMAC INC
Also Called: On Montauk
Paradise Ln (11954)
P.O. Box 2087 (11954-0903)
PHONE..................631 668-1303
Joseph Nye, *President*
Carol Macdonald-Nye, *President*
EMP: 8 EST: 1990
SQ FT: 1,200
SALES (est): 690K **Privately Held**
SIC: **2721** 4813 Magazines: publishing only, not printed on site;

Montgomery
Orange County

(G-8592)
CALLANAN INDUSTRIES INC
215 Montgomery Rd (12549-2814)
P.O. Box 505, Maybrook (12543-0505)
PHONE..................845 457-3158
Charlie Tady, *Opers Mgr*
Kevin Schuler, *Manager*
EMP: 25
SALES (corp-wide): 25.3B **Privately Held**
WEB: www.callanan.com
SIC: **2951** 5032 2952 Asphalt & asphaltic paving mixtures (not from refineries); stone, crushed or broken; asphalt felts & coatings
HQ: Callanan Industries, Inc.
1245 Kings Rd Ste 1
Schenectady NY 12303
518 374-2222

(G-8593)
GLAXOSMITHKLINE LLC
3 Tyler St (12549-1609)
PHONE..................845 341-7590
EMP: 26
SALES (corp-wide): 36B **Privately Held**
SIC: **2834** Pharmaceutical preparations
HQ: Glaxosmithkline Llc
5 Crescent Dr
Philadelphia PA 19112
215 751-4000

(G-8594)
GROSSO MATERIALS INC
90 Collabar Rd (12549-1805)
PHONE..................845 361-5211
Fax: 845 361-3576
Allan Grosso, *President*
EMP: 10
SQ FT: 300
SALES (est): 930K **Privately Held**
SIC: **1459** 5261 5032 Shale (common) quarrying; top soil; stone, crushed or broken

(G-8595)
HUNTER PANELS LLC
9 Hudson Crossing Dr (12549-2854)
PHONE..................386 753-0786
Fax: 845 336-4719
Illya Spiecker, *Plant Mgr*
Scott Pearson, *Manager*
Joe Lightfoot, *Manager*
EMP: 65
SALES (corp-wide): 3.5B **Publicly Held**
WEB: www.hpanels.com
SIC: **3086** Insulation or cushioning material, foamed plastic
HQ: Hunter Panels Llc
15 Franklin St Ste B2
Portland ME 04101
888 746-1114

(G-8596)
JOHN WILEY & SONS INC
46 Wavey Willow Ln (12549-1501)
PHONE..................845 457-6250
EMP: 65
SALES (corp-wide): 1.7B **Publicly Held**
SIC: **2731** Textbooks: publishing only, not printed on site
PA: John Wiley & Sons, Inc.
111 River St Ste 2000
Hoboken NJ 07030
201 748-6000

(G-8597)
KAL PAC CORP
10 Factory St (12549-1202)
PHONE..................845 457-7013
Mike Nozawa, *CEO*
▲ EMP: 19
SALES (est): 4.2MM **Privately Held**
SIC: **2671** Plastic film, coated or laminated for packaging

(G-8598)
NORTHEAST CNSTR INDS INC
Also Called: Nci Panel Systems
657 Rte 17 K S St Ste 2 (12549)
PHONE..................845 565-1000
Robert Schroeder, *President*
Harry Gittlitz, *Vice Pres*
EMP: 10 EST: 1999
SQ FT: 12,000
SALES: 630K **Privately Held**
SIC: **3316** Cold finishing of steel shapes

(G-8599)
ON POINT REPS INC
Also Called: Off State Water Group
20a Wellroad Ave (12549)
PHONE..................518 258-2268
Antonio Goncalves, *President*
EMP: 5
SALES: 400K **Privately Held**
SIC: **3088** Plastics plumbing fixtures

(G-8600)
ORANGE COUNTY IRONWORKS LLC
36 Maybrook Rd (12549-2815)
PHONE..................845 769-3000
Todd Cicardo, *Project Mgr*
Daniel Teutul, *Mng Member*
Jenny Stafford, *Manager*
Marie Zeigler, *Manager*
EMP: 44
SQ FT: 65,000
SALES (est): 12.3MM **Privately Held**
SIC: **3449** 3441 1541 Miscellaneous metalwork; fabricated structural metal; industrial buildings, new construction

(G-8601)
QUICK ROLL LEAF MFG CO INC (PA)
118 Bracken Rd (12549-2600)
P.O. Box 53, Middletown (10940-0053)
PHONE..................845 457-1500
Charles E Quick, *Ch of Bd*
Edward Quick Jr, *President*
William Crowley, *Vice Pres*
EMP: 48
SQ FT: 80,000
SALES (est): 45.1MM **Privately Held**
SIC: **3497** Metal foil & leaf

(G-8602)
REUTER PALLET PKG SYS INC
272 Neelytown Rd (12549-2840)
PHONE..................845 457-9937
Joseph A Carfizzi Sr, *President*
George Reuter Jr, *Vice Pres*
EMP: 9
SQ FT: 10,000
SALES (est): 700K **Privately Held**
SIC: **2448** 2441 Wood pallets & skids; nailed wood boxes & shook

(G-8603)
TILCON NEW YORK INC
Also Called: Maybrook Asphalt
215 Montgomery Rd (12549-2814)
PHONE..................845 457-3158
EMP: 63
SALES (corp-wide): 25.3B **Privately Held**
SIC: **1429** Dolomitic marble, crushed & broken-quarrying
HQ: Tilcon New York Inc.
162 Old Mill Rd
West Nyack NY 10994
845 358-4500

Monticello
Sullivan County

(G-8604)
BLOOMING GROVE STAIR CO
309 E Broadway (12701-8839)
PHONE..............................845 791-4016
Glen Durant, *Principal*
EMP: 7
SALES (corp-wide): 1.4MM Privately Held
SIC: 2431 Stair railings, wood
PA: Blooming Grove Stair Co
    1 Stair Way
    Monroe NY 10950
    845 783-4245

(G-8605)
LOCAL MEDIA GROUP INC
Also Called: Times Herald-Record
479 Broadway (12701-1756)
PHONE..............................845 794-3712
EMP: 10
SALES (corp-wide): 610.2MM Publicly Held
SIC: 2711 Newspapers-Publishing/Printing
HQ: Local Media Group, Inc.
    40 Mulberry St
    Middletown NY 10940
    845 294-8181

(G-8606)
MONROE STAIR PRODUCTS INC
309 E Broadway (12701-8839)
PHONE..............................845 791-4016
Glen Durant, *Manager*
EMP: 5
SALES (corp-wide): 2.8MM Privately Held
WEB: www.bloominggrovestair.com
SIC: 2431 Staircases & stairs, wood
PA: Monroe Stair Products Inc.
    1 Stair Way
    Monroe NY 10950
    845 783-4245

(G-8607)
PATRICK ROHAN
Also Called: Wadadda.com
9 Green St (12701-1307)
PHONE..............................718 781-2573
Rohan Patrick, *Owner*
EMP: 5
SALES (est): 170K Privately Held
SIC: 2396 2759 7336 7389 Printing & embossing on plastics fabric articles; woodcuts for use in printing illustrations, posters, etc.; commercial art & graphic design; commercial art & illustration;

(G-8608)
WYDE LUMBER
419 State Route 17b (12701-3525)
PHONE..............................845 513-5571
Fax: 845 794-6420
Wallace Madnick, *Owner*
EMP: 12
SALES (est): 760K Privately Held
SIC: 2421 Lumber: rough, sawed or planed

Montour Falls
Schuyler County

(G-8609)
CHICONE BUILDERS LLC
Chicone Cabinetmakers
302 W South St (14865-9743)
PHONE..............................607 535-6540
Jennifer Chicone, *Office Mgr*
David H Chicone,
EMP: 5 Privately Held
SIC: 2521 2434 Cabinets, office: wood; wood kitchen cabinets
PA: Chicone Builders, Llc
    302 W South St
    Montour Falls NY 14865

(G-8610)
MALINA MANAGEMENT COMPANY INC
Also Called: Castel Grisch Winery
3620 County Road 16 (14865-9708)
PHONE..............................607 535-9614
Fax: 607 535-2994
Thomas Malina, *President*
Barbara A Malina, *Treasurer*
Scott Wachter, *Admin Sec*
EMP: 22
SQ FT: 1,250
SALES (est): 1.5MM Privately Held
SIC: 2084 5812 7011 Wines, brandy & brandy spirits; eating places; bed & breakfast inn

(G-8611)
ROBERT M BROWN
Also Called: Malone Welding
150 Mill St (14865-9734)
PHONE..............................607 426-6250
Robert M Brown, *Owner*
EMP: 11
SALES (est): 368.3K Privately Held
WEB: www.empiregp.com
SIC: 7692 Welding repair

(G-8612)
TAYLOR PRECISION MACHINING
3921 Dug Rd (14865-9722)
PHONE..............................607 535-3101
Mickey Taylor, *Owner*
EMP: 7
SQ FT: 1,056
SALES (est): 922.3K Privately Held
SIC: 3599 Machine shop, jobbing & repair

Montrose
Westchester County

(G-8613)
LEONORE DOSKOW INC
1 Doskow Rd (10548-8801)
P.O. Box 158 (10548-0158)
PHONE..............................914 737-1335
Fax: 914 737-5049
David Doskow, *Ch of Bd*
Lynn Doskow, *President*
Gloria Burchman, *Office Mgr*
EMP: 20 **EST:** 1936
SQ FT: 14,000
SALES (est): 2.3MM Privately Held
WEB: www.leonoredoskow.com
SIC: 3961 5944 Costume jewelry; costume novelties; jewelry stores

(G-8614)
QUALITY CIRCLE PRODUCTS INC
2108 Albany Post Rd (10548-1431)
P.O. Box 36 (10548-0036)
PHONE..............................914 736-6600
Gary Flaum, *President*
Anthony Cenname, *Vice Pres*
◆ **EMP:** 70
SQ FT: 32,500
SALES (est): 14.7MM Privately Held
WEB: www.qualitycircle.com
SIC: 2679 2671 Labels, paper: made from purchased material; tags, paper (un-printed): made from purchased paper; packaging paper & plastics film, coated & laminated

Mooers
Clinton County

(G-8615)
ACME ENGINEERING PRODUCTS INC
2330 State Route 11 (12958-3725)
PHONE..............................518 236-5659
Fax: 518 236-6941
G S Presser, *President*
Robert Presser, *Vice Pres*
David Morginstin, *Project Mgr*
Mohand Amroun, *Engineer*
Martin Costa, *Engineer*
EMP: 25
SALES (est): 4.2MM Privately Held
WEB: www.acmeprod.com
SIC: 3564 8711 Air cleaning systems; engineering services

Moravia
Cayuga County

(G-8616)
BROOKSIDE LUMBER INC
4191 Duryea St (13118-2500)
PHONE..............................315 497-0937
Fax: 315 497-0018
William Millier, *President*
Jennifer Bradshaw, *Manager*
Katherine Millier, *Shareholder*
EMP: 17
SQ FT: 10,000
SALES (est): 2.5MM Privately Held
SIC: 2421 Sawmills & planing mills, general

(G-8617)
REPUBLICAN REGISTRAR INC
Also Called: Community Newspapers
6 Central St (13118-3609)
P.O. Box 591 (13118-0591)
PHONE..............................315 497-1551
Bernard McGuerty III, *President*
Cathy Robinson, *Finance Other*
Janet Mulvaney, *Sales Staff*
EMP: 8
SALES (est): 615.2K Privately Held
SIC: 2759 Newspapers: printing

Morris
Otsego County

(G-8618)
H W NAYLOR CO INC
121 Main St (13808-6920)
P.O. Box 190 (13808-0190)
PHONE..............................607 263-5145
Fax: 607 263-2416
David Lucas, *President*
Jerome Payton, *Human Res Mgr*
▲ **EMP:** 12 **EST:** 1926
SQ FT: 10,000
SALES (est): 1.3MM Privately Held
WEB: www.drnaylor.com
SIC: 2834 Veterinary pharmaceutical preparations

Morrisville
Madison County

(G-8619)
CDC PUBLISHING LLC
19 North St (13408-1721)
PHONE..............................215 579-1695
Ken Borah, *Branch Mgr*
EMP: 30
SALES (corp-wide): 44.4MM Privately Held
WEB: www.cdcpublishing.com
SIC: 2721 2711 Periodicals: publishing only; newspapers
PA: Cdc Publishing, Llc
    2001 9th Ave Fl 2
    Vero Beach FL 32960
    772 770-6003

(G-8620)
COPESETIC INC
62 E Main St (13408)
P.O. Box 1119 (13408-1119)
PHONE..............................315 684-7780
Fax: 315 684-7790
Eric Beyer, *President*
Anthony Lee, *Vice Pres*
David Lee, *VP Opers*
Janice Sebringe, *Office Mgr*
EMP: 15
SQ FT: 10,000
SALES (est): 1.7MM Privately Held
WEB: www.copeseticinc.com
SIC: 3999 Models, except toy

Mount Kisco
Westchester County

(G-8621)
ACCEL PRINTING & GRAPHICS
128 Radio Circle Dr Ste 2 (10549-2640)
PHONE..............................914 241-3369
Bill Harden, *Owner*
Anna Harden, *Vice Pres*
Donna Corti, *Marketing Staff*
EMP: 9
SQ FT: 2,200
SALES: 625K Privately Held
WEB: www.accelprinting.com
SIC: 2759 Commercial printing

(G-8622)
AFP IMAGING CORPORATION (HQ)
Also Called: Dent-X
185 Kisco Ave Ste 202 (10549-1410)
PHONE..............................914 592-6665
Fax: 914 592-6148
R Scott Jones, *CEO*
Pete Steinhausen, *President*
Aida McKinney, *Exec VP*
Kevin Dillon, *Vice Pres*
Elise Nissen, *CFO*
◆ **EMP:** 10
SQ FT: 47,735
SALES (est): 20MM Privately Held
WEB: www.afpimaging.com
SIC: 3844 X-ray apparatus & tubes; radiographic X-ray apparatus & tubes

(G-8623)
BROOKS WOODWORKING INC
15 Kensico Dr (10549-1003)
PHONE..............................914 666-2029
Fax: 914 666-2029
Richard Brooks, *President*
▲ **EMP:** 14
SQ FT: 5,000
SALES: 1.1MM Privately Held
SIC: 2499 Decorative wood & woodwork

(G-8624)
CURTIS INSTRUMENTS INC (PA)
Also Called: Curtis PMC Division
200 Kisco Ave (10549-1400)
PHONE..............................914 666-2971
Fax: 914 666-2188
Stuart Marwell, *Ch of Bd*
Wang Jinghui, *General Mgr*
Randy Miller, *Business Mgr*
Marwell Stuart, *COO*
Mark Ankers, *Vice Pres*
▲ **EMP:** 150 **EST:** 1960
SQ FT: 35,000
SALES (est): 293.6MM Privately Held
SIC: 3825 3824 3629 Elapsed time meters, electronic; speed indicators & recorders, vehicle; electronic generation equipment

(G-8625)
D C I PLASMA CENTER INC (PA)
71 S Bedford Rd (10549-3407)
PHONE..............................914 241-1646
Martin Silver, *President*
Perry Ciarrletta, *Treasurer*
EMP: 3
SQ FT: 700
SALES (est): 2.1MM Privately Held
SIC: 2836 Plasmas

(G-8626)
DATALINK COMPUTER PRODUCTS
165 E Main St 175 (10549-2923)
PHONE..............................914 666-2358
Vickram Bedi, *President*
Chhaya Bedi, *Vice Pres*
Richard Niziak, *Engineer*
EMP: 10
SALES: 2.4MM Privately Held
SIC: 3572 7374 Computer storage devices; service bureau, computer

(G-8627)
ENTERMARKET
280 N Bedford Rd Ste 305 (10549-1148)
PHONE..............................914 437-7268

Mount Kisco - Westchester County (G-8628)

Jeff Tong, *Owner*
Louis Veccaarelli, *Prdtn Mgr*
EMP: 5
SALES (est): 552.9K **Privately Held**
WEB: www.entermarket.com
SIC: 2752 Commercial printing, lithographic

(G-8628)
IAT INTERACTIVE LLC
Also Called: It's About Time
333 N Bedford Rd Ste 110 (10549-1161)
PHONE..................914 273-2233
Thomas Laster, *Co-Owner*
Laurie Kreindler, *Co-Owner*
EMP: 37
SQ FT: 574,600
SALES (est): 2.3MM **Privately Held**
SIC: 2731 Textbooks: publishing & printing

(G-8629)
IMMUDYNE INC
50 Spring Meadow Rd (10549-3846)
PHONE..................914 244-1777
Anthony G Bruzzese, *Ch of Bd*
Mark McLaughlin, *President*
Todd Goldman, *Vice Pres*
Joseph Ditrolio, *Chief Mktg Ofcr*
EMP: 16 EST: 1987
SALES: 1.2MM **Privately Held**
SIC: 2833 Medicinals & botanicals

(G-8630)
INDUSTRY FORECAST
69 S Moger Ave Ste 202 (10549-2222)
PHONE..................914 244-8617
David Levy, *Principal*
EMP: 5
SALES (est): 386.6K **Privately Held**
SIC: 2721 Periodicals

(G-8631)
INTERDYNAMICS
100 S Bedford Rd Ste 300 (10549-3444)
PHONE..................914 241-1423
Ken Motush, *Principal*
Keith Rose, *Info Tech Dir*
▲ **EMP:** 15
SALES (est): 2.6MM **Privately Held**
SIC: 2992 Lubricating oils & greases

(G-8632)
JT ROSELLE LIGHTING & SUP INC
333 N Bedford Rd (10549-1158)
PHONE..................914 666-3700
EMP: 15
SALES (est): 3.5MM **Privately Held**
SIC: 3648 Lighting equipment

(G-8633)
KOHLBERG SPORTS GROUP INC (HQ)
111 Radio Circle Dr (10549-2609)
PHONE..................914 241-7430
Walter W Farley,
EMP: 6
SALES (est): 878.3K
SALES (corp-wide): 9B **Privately Held**
SIC: 3949 Hockey equipment & supplies, general
PA: Kohlberg & Co., L.L.C.
 111 Radio Circle Dr
 Mount Kisco NY 10549
 914 241-7430

(G-8634)
LAURTOM INC
Also Called: It's About Time Publishing
333 N Bedford Rd Ste 100 (10549-1160)
PHONE..................914 273-2233
Laurie Kreindler, *CEO*
Amy Jacaruso, *Editor*
Cheryl Deese, *Vice Pres*
Sal Marottola, *Vice Pres*
Barbara Zahm, *Vice Pres*
EMP: 35
SQ FT: 4,000
SALES (est): 4.6MM
SALES (corp-wide): 1.5B **Privately Held**
WEB: www.its-about-time.com
SIC: 2721 Periodicals
HQ: Herff Jones, Llc
 4501 W 62nd St
 Indianapolis IN 46268
 800 837-4235

(G-8635)
MOUNT KISCO TRANSFER STN INC
10 Lincoln Pl (10549-2614)
PHONE..................914 666-6350
Anthony Orlando, *CEO*
EMP: 6
SALES (est): 623.9K
SALES (corp-wide): 1.6B **Publicly Held**
SIC: 3443 4953 5722 Dumpsters, garbage; garbage: collecting, destroying & processing; garbage disposals
HQ: Covanta Energy, Llc
 445 South St Ste 400
 Morristown NJ 07960
 862 345-5000

(G-8636)
NATIONWIDE COILS INC (PA)
24 Foxwood Cir (10549-1127)
PHONE..................914 277-7396
Ross Stephens, *President*
Andre Ostacoli, *General Mgr*
Stephen Barzelatto, *Vice Pres*
Jay Feldman, *Natl Sales Mgr*
Justin Campanello, *Sales Associate*
EMP: 4
SQ FT: 1,000
SALES (est): 1.3MM **Privately Held**
WEB: www.nationwidecoils.com
SIC: 3585 Refrigeration & heating equipment

(G-8637)
NORCORP INC
Also Called: NORTHERN WESTCHESTER HOSPITAL
400 E Main St (10549-3417)
PHONE..................914 666-1310
Joel Seligman, *President*
John Partenza, *Treasurer*
Micheal Mascia, *Manager*
EMP: 27
SALES: 186.1K
SALES (corp-wide): 250.6MM **Privately Held**
SIC: 2326 8062 Medical & hospital uniforms, men's; general medical & surgical hospitals
PA: Northern Westchester Hospital Association
 400 E Main St
 Mount Kisco NY 10549
 914 666-1200

(G-8638)
ORBIT INDUSTRIES LLC
116 Radio Circle Dr # 302 (10549-2631)
PHONE..................914 244-1500
Marc Shur,
John Katz,
EMP: 14
SALES (est): 1.7MM **Privately Held**
SIC: 2258 Lace & lace products

(G-8639)
PECKER IRON WORKS LLC
137 Ruxton Rd (10549-4025)
PHONE..................914 665-0100
Elliott Pecker, *Mng Member*
EMP: 4
SQ FT: 1,000
SALES (est): 1.5MM **Privately Held**
SIC: 3312 Structural shapes & pilings, steel

(G-8640)
PLASTIC & RECONSTRUCTIVE SVCS
Also Called: Spa Sciara
333 N Bedford Rd (10549-1158)
PHONE..................914 584-5605
Sharon Dechiara, *President*
EMP: 5 EST: 2010
SQ FT: 1,800
SALES (est): 1.2MM **Privately Held**
SIC: 2844 Cosmetic preparations

(G-8641)
R L C ELECTRONICS INC
83 Radio Circle Dr (10549-2622)
PHONE..................914 241-1334
Fax: 914 241-1753
Charles Alan Borck, *CEO*
Doug Borck, *President*
Chris Medina, *Controller*
Jeffrey Borck, *VP Sales*
Peter Jeffery, *Sales Dir*
EMP: 65 EST: 1959
SQ FT: 20,000
SALES (est): 13.5MM **Privately Held**
WEB: www.rlcelectronics.com
SIC: 3679 Electronic circuits; microwave components

(G-8642)
RADIO CIRCLE REALTY INC
136 Radio Circle Dr (10549-2642)
PHONE..................914 241-8742
Arturo Defeo, *President*
Lucia Defeo, *Corp Secy*
Anthony D Feo, *Vice Pres*
Anthony De Feo, *Marketing Staff*
▲ **EMP:** 40
SQ FT: 11,000
SALES (est): 2.4MM **Privately Held**
SIC: 2399 6799 Glove mending on factory basis; real estate investors, except property operators

(G-8643)
RDI INC (PA)
Also Called: RDI ELECTRONICS
333 N Bedford Rd Ste 135 (10549-1160)
PHONE..................914 773-1000
Fax: 914 241-3825
James Diamond, *Ch of Bd*
Barry Miller, *President*
Greg Mozingo, *Regional Mgr*
John Horl, *CFO*
David Del Monte, *Controller*
▲ **EMP:** 18
SQ FT: 10,000
SALES (est): 38.9MM **Privately Held**
WEB: www.rdiusa.com
SIC: 3679 3678 3577 Electronic circuits; electronic connectors; electronic coils, transformers & other inductors; computer peripheral equipment; nonferrous wiredrawing & insulating

(G-8644)
READERS DIGEST ASSN INCTHE
100 S Bedford Rd Ste 340 (10549-3444)
PHONE..................914 238-1000
Fax: 914 238-7653
Robert E Guth, *President*
Susan Cummiskey, *Senior VP*
Albert Perruzza, *Mktg Dir*
George McKeon, *Art Dir*
EMP: 16
SALES (corp-wide): 1.7B **Privately Held**
SIC: 2721 Magazines: publishing only, not printed on site
PA: Trusted Media Brands, Inc.
 750 3rd Ave Fl 3
 New York NY 10017
 914 238-1000

(G-8645)
RPB DISTRIBUTORS LLC
Also Called: Protec Friction Supply
45 Kensico Dr (10549-1025)
PHONE..................914 244-3600
Fax: 914 244-3615
Roy Landesberg, *President*
Parker Silzer, *Vice Pres*
Daniel Martabano, *Manager*
◆ **EMP:** 8
SALES (est): 1.2MM **Privately Held**
WEB: www.protecfriction.com
SIC: 3714 5084 5013 Motor vehicle brake systems & parts; industrial machine parts; clutches

(G-8646)
WESTCHESTER SIGNS INC
Also Called: Sign-A-Rama
145 Kisco Ave (10549-1418)
PHONE..................914 666-7446
Karl Theile, *President*
EMP: 5
SALES (est): 335.2K **Privately Held**
SIC: 3993 Signs & advertising specialties

(G-8647)
XELEUM LIGHTING LLC
333 N Bedford Rd Ste 135 (10549-1160)
PHONE..................954 617-8170
Jon Cooper, *Branch Mgr*
EMP: 11
SALES (corp-wide): 1.9MM **Privately Held**
SIC: 3646 Commercial indusl & institutional electric lighting fixtures
PA: Xeleum Lighting, Llc
 3430 Quantum Blvd
 Boynton Beach FL 33426
 914 773-6250

(G-8648)
ZIERICK MANUFACTURING CORP (PA)
131 Radio Circle Dr (10549-2623)
PHONE..................800 882-8020
Fax: 914 666-0216
Gretchen Zierick, *Ch of Bd*
Russell F Zierick, *Principal*
Joe Comitto, *Purch Agent*
Fred Ackerman, *QC Dir*
Norman Chan, *Engineer*
▲ **EMP:** 80 EST: 1919
SQ FT: 47,500
SALES (est): 13.8MM **Privately Held**
WEB: www.zierick.com
SIC: 3643 3452 3644 3694 Connectors & terminals for electrical devices; solderless connectors (electric wiring devices); nuts, metal; noncurrent-carrying wiring services; terminal boards; ignition apparatus, internal combustion engines; machinery castings, nonferrous: ex. alum., copper, die, etc.

(G-8649)
ZUMBACH ELECTRONICS CORP
Also Called: Elvo
140 Kisco Ave (10549-1412)
PHONE..................914 241-7080
Fax: 914 241-7096
Bruno Zumbach, *Ch of Bd*
Rainer Zumbach, *President*
Jorge Lage, *Area Mgr*
Sven Naegeli, *Vice Pres*
Myrtle Bidwell, *Design Engr*
▲ **EMP:** 55
SQ FT: 15,000
SALES (est): 11.8MM **Privately Held**
SIC: 3825 Instruments to measure electricity

Mount Marion
Ulster County

(G-8650)
LAIRD TELEMEDIA
2000 Sterling Rd (12456)
PHONE..................845 339-9555
Mark Braunstein, *CEO*
Vincent Bruno, *Vice Pres*
EMP: 110
SALES (est): 8.5MM **Privately Held**
WEB: www.lairdtelemedia.com
SIC: 3651 7812 Household audio & video equipment; motion picture & video production

(G-8651)
METHODS TOOLING & MFG INC
635 Glasco Tpke (12456)
P.O. Box 400 (12456-0400)
PHONE..................845 246-7100
Fax: 845 246-0328
Keith Michaels, *President*
Michael Allen, *Vice Pres*
EMP: 31
SQ FT: 30,000
SALES (est): 6.7MM **Privately Held**
WEB: www.methodstooling.com
SIC: 3545 3444 3648 2514 Tools & accessories for machine tools; sheet metalwork; stage lighting equipment; kitchen cabinets: metal; fabricated plate work (boiler shop); wood kitchen cabinets

(G-8652)
NORTHEAST SOLITE CORPORATION
962 Kings Hwy (12456)
P.O. Box 437 (12456-0437)
PHONE..................845 246-2177
Fax: 845 246-2619
Gary Green, *Branch Mgr*

Ian Leaning, *Manager*
EMP: 40
SALES (corp-wide): 17.9MM **Privately Held**
WEB: www.nesolite.com
SIC: 3295 1442 3281 Minerals, ground or treated; construction sand & gravel; slate products
PA: Northeast Solite Corporation
1135 Kings Hwy
Saugerties NY 12477
845 246-2646

Mount Morris
Livingston County

(G-8653)
MT MORRIS SHOPPER INC
85 N Main St (14510-1023)
PHONE.................585 658-3520
Fax: 585 658-2962
Jerry W Rolison, *President*
Evelyn C Rolison, *Corp Secy*
EMP: 6
SQ FT: 1,800
SALES (est): 420K **Privately Held**
WEB: www.mtmorrisshopper.com
SIC: 2741 Guides: publishing only, not printed on site; shopping news: publishing only, not printed on site

Mount Sinai
Suffolk County

(G-8654)
CHEM-PUTER FRIENDLY INC
1 Sevilla Walk (11766-2825)
P.O. Box 650 (11766-0650)
PHONE.................631 331-2259
Linda Ruben, *President*
Bart Ruben, *General Mgr*
EMP: 31
SALES: 3.7MM **Privately Held**
SIC: 2621 2842 3577 5112 Business form paper; specialty cleaning preparations; computer peripheral equipment; business forms; computer peripheral equipment; computer maintenance & repair

(G-8655)
KENDALL CIRCUITS INC
5507-10 Nesconset Hwy 105 (11766)
PHONE.................631 473-3636
Danielle Seaford, *President*
EMP: 37
SALES (est): 4.6MM **Privately Held**
WEB: www.wordcircuits.com
SIC: 3672 Circuit boards, television & radio printed

(G-8656)
OSPREY BOAT
96 Mount Sinai Ave (11766-2311)
P.O. Box 331, Port Jefferson (11777-0331)
PHONE.................631 331-4153
Amanda Cash, *Owner*
EMP: 5 **EST:** 2010
SALES (est): 441.1K **Privately Held**
SIC: 2399 Fishing nets

(G-8657)
TRANSPORTGISTICS INC
28 N Country Rd Ste 103 (11766-1518)
PHONE.................631 567-4100
Fax: 631 563-4698
Alan Miller, *President*
Stewart Miller, *Senior VP*
Kerry Loudenback, *Vice Pres*
Robert Munro, *Vice Pres*
EMP: 12 **EST:** 2001
SQ FT: 3,000
SALES (est): 2.2MM **Privately Held**
WEB: www.transportgistics.com
SIC: 7372 Business oriented computer software

Mount Upton
Chenango County

(G-8658)
LILAC QUARRIES LLC
1702 State Highway 8 (13809-4103)
PHONE.................607 867-4016
Russell Heath,
EMP: 6
SALES (est): 245.9K **Privately Held**
SIC: 1422 Crushed & broken limestone

Mount Vernon
Westchester County

(G-8659)
ABALON PRECISION MFG CORP (PA)
717 S 3rd Ave (10550-4905)
PHONE.................718 589-5682
Fax: 718 589-0300
Norman Orenstein, *President*
Norman Orent, *Manager*
EMP: 15 **EST:** 1945
SQ FT: 42,000
SALES (est): 2.6MM **Privately Held**
SIC: 3441 Fabricated structural metal

(G-8660)
ABALON PRECISION MFG CORP
717 S 3rd Ave (10550-4905)
PHONE.................718 589-5682
Norman Orent, *Manager*
EMP: 15
SALES (corp-wide): 2.6MM **Privately Held**
SIC: 3441 Fabricated structural metal
PA: Abalon Precision Mfg Corp
717 S 3rd Ave
Mount Vernon NY 10550
718 589-5682

(G-8661)
ACCURATE METAL WEATHER STRIP
725 S Fulton Ave (10550-5086)
PHONE.................914 668-6042
Fax: 914 668-6062
Fred O Kammerer, *President*
Ronald R Kammerer, *Corp Secy*
EMP: 7 **EST:** 1898
SQ FT: 15,000
SALES (est): 17.5MM **Privately Held**
SIC: 3442 3449 Weather strip, metal; miscellaneous metalwork

(G-8662)
ACHILLES CONSTRUCTION CO INC
373 Hayward Ave (10552-1028)
PHONE.................718 389-4717
Fax: 718 389-4719
David Braunstein, *CEO*
EMP: 8 **EST:** 1933
SQ FT: 2,200
SALES: 1MM **Privately Held**
SIC: 3441 Fabricated structural metal

(G-8663)
ARIESUN INC
160 W 3rd St (10550-3750)
PHONE.................866 274-3049
Donny McPaggart, *President*
Dennis Everton, *General Mgr*
EMP: 50
SQ FT: 10,000
SALES: 300K **Privately Held**
SIC: 2086 Pasteurized & mineral waters, bottled & canned; mineral water, carbonated: packaged in cans, bottles, etc.

(G-8664)
BALL CHAIN MFG CO INC (PA)
Also Called: BCM
741 S Fulton Ave (10550-5085)
PHONE.................914 664-7500
Fax: 914 664-7460
Valentine Taubner Jr, *President*
Valentine J Taubner III, *Vice Pres*
Steven Kapush, *Safety Mgr*
James Taubner, *Treasurer*
Susan Glaser, *Controller*
▲ **EMP:** 90 **EST:** 1938
SQ FT: 35,000
SALES (est): 13.7MM **Privately Held**
WEB: www.ballchain.com
SIC: 3462 Gear & chain forgings

(G-8665)
BARRETT BRONZE INC
115 Miller Pl (10550-4728)
PHONE.................914 699-6060
Fax: 914 699-6061
Eli Ross, *President*
Jamie Ross, *Principal*
▲ **EMP:** 20
SALES (est): 2.1MM **Privately Held**
WEB: www.barrettbronze.com
SIC: 3299 2821 Statuary: gypsum, clay, papier mache, metal, etc.; plastics materials & resins

(G-8666)
BEACON ADHESIVES INC
Also Called: Beacon Chemical
125 S Macquesten Pkwy (10550-1724)
PHONE.................914 699-3400
Fax: 914 699-2783
Milton Meshirer, *CEO*
David Meshirer, *President*
Barbara Meshirer, *Corp Secy*
Jose Espinosa, *Vice Pres*
Debbie Meshirer-Wojcik, *Vice Pres*
◆ **EMP:** 30
SQ FT: 20,000
SALES (est): 6.4MM **Privately Held**
WEB: www.beacon1.com
SIC: 2891 Adhesives

(G-8667)
BRIDGE METAL INDUSTRIES LLC
717 S 3rd Ave (10550-4905)
PHONE.................914 663-9200
Alan Cowen, *Mng Member*
Frank Giordano, *Manager*
Darryl Veluez, *Manager*
▲ **EMP:** 130
SQ FT: 8,000
SALES (est): 18.2MM **Privately Held**
SIC: 2542 Partitions & fixtures, except wood

(G-8668)
BRONX WSTCHESTER TEMPERING INC
160 S Macquesten Pkwy (10550-1705)
PHONE.................914 663-9400
Miles Kiho, *President*
EMP: 29
SALES (est): 4.1MM **Privately Held**
SIC: 3229 Art, decorative & novelty glassware

(G-8669)
CANAL ASPHALT INC
800 Canal St (10550-4708)
PHONE.................914 667-8500
Fax: 914 667-3879
August M Nigro, *President*
Maria Dioguardi, *Vice Pres*
Sakir Thanawana, *Manager*
EMP: 10
SALES (est): 3.1MM **Privately Held**
SIC: 2951 Asphalt paving mixtures & blocks

(G-8670)
CASTOLEUM CORPORATION
240 E 7th St (10550-4615)
P.O. Box 41, Yonkers (10710-0041)
PHONE.................914 664-5877
Fax: 914 664-9383
S V Goldrich, *President*
Eric Bryan, *General Mgr*
Leslie Schwebel, *Corp Secy*
Steve Neil, *Vice Pres*
Mark House, *Government*
EMP: 15
SQ FT: 25,000
SALES (est): 3.2MM **Privately Held**
WEB: www.sterifab.com
SIC: 2992 2842 5169 Lubricating oils & greases; disinfectants, household or industrial plant; coal tar products, primary & intermediate; gum & wood chemicals

(G-8671)
CHESTER WEST COUNTY PRESS
29 W 4th St (10554-4108)
P.O. Box 152, White Plains (10602-0152)
PHONE.................914 684-0006
Sandra Blackwell, *President*
EMP: 6 **EST:** 1959
SALES (est): 280.2K **Privately Held**
SIC: 2711 Newspapers, publishing & printing

(G-8672)
CLASSIC MEDALLICS INC
520 S Fulton Ave (10550-5010)
PHONE.................718 392-5410
Fax: 914 530-6258
Gerald Singer, *President*
Lucy Walsh, *General Mgr*
Mario Singer, *Vice Pres*
Salma Tasin, *Bookkeeper*
Mobola Sapara, *Comptroller*
▲ **EMP:** 50 **EST:** 1941
SALES (est): 8.8MM **Privately Held**
SIC: 3499 5094 Trophies, metal, except silver; jewelry

(G-8673)
COLD MIX MANUFACTURING CORP
65 Edison Ave (10550-5003)
PHONE.................718 463-1444
Dario Amicucci, *President*
EMP: 17
SQ FT: 2,000
SALES: 5MM **Privately Held**
SIC: 2951 Asphalt paving mixtures & blocks

(G-8674)
COVENTRY MANUFACTURING CO INC (PA)
115 E 3rd St (10550-3606)
PHONE.................914 668-2212
Myron S Gorel, *President*
Edward R Gorel, *Vice Pres*
Phyllis Gorel, *Admin Sec*
EMP: 31 **EST:** 1953
SQ FT: 26,000
SALES (est): 2.8MM **Privately Held**
WEB: www.trulytubular.com
SIC: 3498 3317 3312 Tube fabricating (contract bending & shaping); steel pipe & tubes; blast furnaces & steel mills

(G-8675)
CROWN DIE CASTING CORP
268 W Lincoln Ave (10550-2509)
PHONE.................914 667-5400
Fax: 914 667-4284
Sam Strober, *President*
Bill Gutwein, *Vice Pres*
Lynn Strober, *Office Mgr*
EMP: 28
SQ FT: 17,000
SALES (est): 5.5MM **Privately Held**
WEB: www.crowndiecasting.com
SIC: 3364 3643 3444 3369 Nonferrous die-castings except aluminum; connectors, electric cord; sheet metalwork; nonferrous foundries; aluminum foundries; aluminum die-castings

(G-8676)
DAB-O-MATIC CORP (PA)
896 S Columbus Ave (10550-5074)
P.O. Box 3839 (10553-3839)
PHONE.................914 699-7070
Fax: 914 699-7052
Gerard Magaletti, *Ch of Bd*
James P Bell, *President*
Luke Vaccaro, *Purch Mgr*
Scott Bell, *Purchasing*
Daphne Maurrasse, *Manager*
EMP: 67
SQ FT: 29,000
SALES: 11.9MM **Privately Held**
WEB: www.dabomatic.com
SIC: 3953 Pads, inking & stamping

(G-8677)
DRG NEW YORK HOLDINGS CORP (PA)
700 S Fulton Ave (10550-5014)
PHONE.................914 668-9000

Fax: 914 668-6900
Montague Wolfson, *Ch of Bd*
Stephen Bardfield, *Corp Secy*
Salvatore Ferrera, *Controller*
◆ **EMP:** 100
SQ FT: 40,000
SALES (est): 26MM **Privately Held**
WEB: www.wolfsoncasing.com
SIC: 2011 5149 Meat packing plants; sausage casings

(G-8678)
DUNCAN & SON CARPENTRY INC
1 W Prospect Ave (10550-2008)
PHONE..................914 664-4311
David Duncan, *President*
EMP: 21
SQ FT: 10,000
SALES (est): 2.2MM **Privately Held**
SIC: 2431 Millwork

(G-8679)
DUNLEA WHL GL & MIRROR INC
Also Called: J&T Macquesten Realty
147 S Macquesten Pkwy (10550-1724)
PHONE..................914 664-5277
Fax: 914 664-4427
Timothy Dunlea, *President*
John Arminio, *Vice Pres*
Alex Puranbuda, *Vice Pres*
EMP: 6
SQ FT: 7,000
SALES (est): 837.3K **Privately Held**
SIC: 3231 Insulating glass: made from purchased glass

(G-8680)
E & J OFFSET INC
520 S 4th Ave (10550-4404)
PHONE..................718 663-8850
Howard Moss, *President*
EMP: 5 **EST:** 2000
SQ FT: 4,500
SALES (est): 486.8K **Privately Held**
SIC: 2752 Color lithography

(G-8681)
FINA CABINET CORP
20 N Macquesten Pkwy (10550-1841)
PHONE..................718 409-2900
Fax: 718 409-2956
Annette Alberti, *President*
John Albertti, *Vice Pres*
EMP: 5
SALES (est): 764.8K **Privately Held**
SIC: 2521 2434 2541 Cabinets, office: wood; wood kitchen cabinets; wood partitions & fixtures

(G-8682)
GERITREX LLC
144 E Kingsbridge Rd (10550-4909)
PHONE..................914 668-4003
Fax: 914 668-4047
Mitchell Blashinsky, *CEO*
Anthony Madaio, *President*
Jeff Newton, *Area Mgr*
Melissa Harvey, *QA Dir*
Ricardo Medina, *Marketing Staff*
▲ **EMP:** 40
SQ FT: 47,500 **Privately Held**
WEB: www.geritrex.com
SIC: 2834 Pharmaceutical preparations

(G-8683)
GERITREX HOLDINGS INC (PA)
144 E Kingsbridge Rd (10550-4909)
PHONE..................914 668-4003
Mitch Blashinsky, *CEO*
EMP: 2
SALES (est): 1.3MM **Privately Held**
SIC: 2834 6719 Pharmaceutical preparations; investment holding companies, except banks

(G-8684)
GIAGNI ENTERPRISES LLC
Also Called: Qmi
550 S Columbus Ave (10550-4712)
PHONE..................914 699-6500
Vincent Giagni, *Mng Member*
EMP: 5
SALES (est): 529.9K **Privately Held**
SIC: 3432 Faucets & spigots, metal & plastic

(G-8685)
GIAGNI INTERNATIONAL CORP
548 S Columbus Ave (10550-4712)
PHONE..................914 699-6500
Vincent Giagni, *President*
Dan Gaulin, *Prdtn Mgr*
EMP: 5
SALES (est): 400K **Privately Held**
SIC: 3432 Faucets & spigots, metal & plastic

(G-8686)
GRACE RYAN & MAGNUS MLLWK LLC
17 N Bleeker St (10550-1801)
PHONE..................914 665-0902
Joseph Grace, *Mng Member*
Enrique Lopez, *Manager*
Thor Magnus,
Eamonn Ryan,
EMP: 70
SQ FT: 10,000
SALES (est): 7.4MM **Privately Held**
SIC: 2431 Millwork

(G-8687)
GRANITE TOPS INC
716 S Columbus Ave (10550-4717)
PHONE..................914 699-2909
Fax: 914 699-2425
Christopher Sanzaro, *President*
EMP: 40
SQ FT: 11,000
SALES (est): 4.2MM **Privately Held**
SIC: 3281 Cut stone & stone products

(G-8688)
H & S EDIBLE PRODUCTS CORP
119 Fulton Ln (10550-4607)
PHONE..................914 413-3489
Fax: 914 664-8304
Mari P Sweeney, *President*
Peter J Rowan, *Vice Pres*
Chasity Misserio, *Office Mgr*
EMP: 30
SQ FT: 13,000
SALES (est): 3.2MM **Privately Held**
SIC: 2099 2051 Bread crumbs, not made in bakeries; bread, cake & related products

(G-8689)
HAMLET PRODUCTS INC
221 N Macquesten Pkwy (10550-1005)
PHONE..................914 665-0307
Fax: 914 665-0248
Russ Hamlet, *President*
Marlo Barreto, *Vice Pres*
Randy Hamlet, *Vice Pres*
▲ **EMP:** 12
SQ FT: 12,000
SALES (est): 1.9MM **Privately Held**
WEB: www.hamletproducts.com
SIC: 2542 3089 5046 2541 Fixtures, store: except wood; cases, plastic; commercial equipment; wood partitions & fixtures

(G-8690)
HI SPEED ENVELOPE CO INC
560 S 3rd Ave Ste 1 (10550-4568)
PHONE..................718 617-1600
Charles Romeo, *President*
Mary Romeo-Springman, *Corp Secy*
Anthony Romeo, *Director*
Fortunato C Romeo, *Director*
Jim Romeo, *Director*
EMP: 16 **EST:** 1939
SQ FT: 26,000
SALES (est): 1.9MM **Privately Held**
WEB: www.hispeedprinting.com
SIC: 2752 2759 Commercial printing, offset; letterpress printing

(G-8691)
HI-TECH CNC MACHINING CORP
13 Elm Ave (10550-2305)
PHONE..................914 668-5090
Karl Hormann, *President*
Karl Hormann Jr, *Vice Pres*
EMP: 5 **EST:** 1970
SQ FT: 7,000
SALES (est): 1.2MM **Privately Held**
SIC: 3599 Machine shop, jobbing & repair

(G-8692)
ICE AIR LLC
80 Hartford Ave (10553-1327)
PHONE..................914 668-4700
Alan Shihab, *Vice Pres*
John Accumanno, *CFO*
Kira Kieffer, *Mktg Dir*
Veton Alimi, *Manager*
Anthony Gili, *Manager*
▼ **EMP:** 20
SQ FT: 26,000
SALES (est): 8.4MM **Privately Held**
SIC: 3585 Air conditioning units, complete: domestic or industrial

(G-8693)
INTERNATIONAL MDSE SVCS INC
336 S Fulton Ave Fl 1 (10553-1748)
PHONE..................914 699-4000
Johnny Peralta, *President*
EMP: 5
SALES (est): 639.4K **Privately Held**
SIC: 3578 Automatic teller machines (ATM)

(G-8694)
ISO PLASTICS CORP
160 E 1st St (10553-3435)
PHONE..................914 663-8300
Raul Silva, *President*
Jim Coughlin, *Vice Pres*
Fred Squitire, *Treasurer*
▲ **EMP:** 65
SQ FT: 43,000
SALES (est): 11.2MM **Privately Held**
WEB: www.isoplastics.com
SIC: 3089 3599 Molding primary plastic; machine & other job shop work

(G-8695)
J-K PROSTHETICS & ORTHOTICS
699 N Macquesten Pkwy (10552-2121)
PHONE..................914 699-2077
Fax: 914 699-0676
Jack Caputo, *President*
Kathleen Caputo, *Corp Secy*
Michael J Caputo, *Manager*
EMP: 22
SALES (est): 3.2MM **Privately Held**
WEB: www.trishare.com
SIC: 3842 Prosthetic appliances

(G-8696)
K & B STAMPING CO INC
Also Called: K & B Signs
29 Mount Vernon Ave (10550-2492)
PHONE..................914 664-8555
Fax: 914 664-6667
Albert Aghabekian, *President*
Elaine Dechiara, *Manager*
EMP: 7
SQ FT: 4,500
SALES (est): 530K **Privately Held**
WEB: www.kbsign.com
SIC: 2759 3993 Plateless engraving; screen printing; neon signs; displays & cutouts, window & lobby

(G-8697)
KEY DIGITAL SYSTEMS INC
521 E 3rd St (10553-1606)
PHONE..................914 667-9700
Fax: 914 668-8666
Mikhail Tsingberg, *President*
Edison Yu, *Engineer*
Michael Lakhter, *VP Sales*
Bob Templeman, *Sales Mgr*
Dan O'Donnell, *Regl Sales Mgr*
▲ **EMP:** 20
SQ FT: 24,000
SALES (est): 4.9MM **Privately Held**
WEB: www.keydigital.com
SIC: 3651 Household audio & video equipment

(G-8698)
KING LITHOGRAPHERS INC (PA)
245 S 4th Ave (10550-3804)
PHONE..................914 667-4200
Fax: 914 667-5281
Martin Rego, *President*
Joseph A Rego, *Treasurer*
EMP: 35 **EST:** 1956
SQ FT: 55,000
SALES (est): 4.4MM **Privately Held**
WEB: www.kinglitho.com
SIC: 2752 2789 Commercial printing, lithographic; bookbinding & related work

(G-8699)
LAMPARTS CO INC
160 E 3rd St Ste 2 (10550-3694)
PHONE..................914 723-8986
Fax: 914 668-5941
Anthony Sorbaro Jr, *President*
EMP: 10 **EST:** 1948
SQ FT: 30,000
SALES (est): 1.5MM **Privately Held**
SIC: 3648 3469 Lighting equipment; metal stampings

(G-8700)
LEONARDO PRINTING CORP
Also Called: Leonardo Prntng
529 E 3rd St (10553-1606)
PHONE..................914 664-7890
Fax: 914 664-6767
Frank Leonardo Jr, *President*
Mark Leonardo, *Vice Pres*
Steven Leonardo, *Admin Sec*
EMP: 5 **EST:** 1947
SALES (est): 691K **Privately Held**
SIC: 2754 Job printing, gravure

(G-8701)
LGN MATERIALS & SOLUTIONS
149 Esplanade (10553-1116)
PHONE..................888 414-0005
Maria Nonni, *President*
EMP: 12
SALES (est): 376.5K **Privately Held**
SIC: 2796 Steel line engraving for the printing trade

(G-8702)
LUMINATTA INC
Also Called: Apollo Lighting and Hasco Ltg
717 S 3rd Ave (10550-4905)
PHONE..................914 664-3600
Fax: 914 664-6091
Joseph Sagona, *President*
Paul Verkleij, *Vice Pres*
Paul Verklzij, *Info Tech Mgr*
EMP: 8 **EST:** 1947
SQ FT: 14,000
SALES (est): 1.4MM **Privately Held**
WEB: www.apollolighting.com
SIC: 3646 Commercial indusl & institutional electric lighting fixtures

(G-8703)
M&F STRINGING LLC
2 Cortlandt St (10550-2706)
PHONE..................914 664-1600
Fax: 914 664-1455
Kenneth Jacobs, *Mng Member*
EMP: 20 **EST:** 1953
SQ FT: 8,000
SALES: 2MM **Privately Held**
WEB: www.mfstringing.com
SIC: 2631 Cardboard, tagboard & strawboard

(G-8704)
METAL MAN RESTORATION
254 E 3rd St Fl 1 (10553-5115)
PHONE..................914 662-4218
Fax: 914 665-4219
Anthony Bugliomo, *Principal*
EMP: 10
SALES (est): 700K **Privately Held**
SIC: 3471 Electroplating & plating

(G-8705)
MICHAEL ANTHONY JEWELERS LLC (DH)
115 S Macquesten Pkwy (10550-1724)
P.O. Box 31283, West Palm Beach FL (33420-1283)
PHONE..................914 699-0000
Fax: 914 664-4884
Anthony Paolercio Jr, *Vice Pres*
Linda Levin, *Purch Dir*
Betty Sou, *CFO*
Roseanne Bosco, *Human Res Mgr*
Michael W Paolercio, *Chief Mktg Ofcr*
EMP: 150
SQ FT: 150,000

GEOGRAPHIC SECTION

Mount Vernon - Westchester County (G-8730)

SALES (est): 26.5MM
SALES (corp-wide): 210.8B **Publicly Held**
SIC: **3911** 5944 5094 Jewelry, precious metal; earrings, precious metal; rings, finger: precious metal; bracelets, precious metal; jewelry stores; jewelry & precious stones
HQ: Richline Group, Inc.
   1385 Broadway Fl 12
   New York NY 10018
   212 886-6000

(G-8706)
MICK RADIO NUCLEAR INSTRUMENT
521 Homestead Ave (10550-4619)
PHONE..................................718 597-3999
Fax: 914 665-8834
Felix Mick, *President*
Verena Mick, *Corp Secy*
Maria Saltares, *Admin Asst*
EMP: 19
SQ FT: 25,000
SALES (est): 3.4MM **Privately Held**
SIC: **3841** Surgical & medical instruments

(G-8707)
MITCHELL ELECTRONICS CORP
85 W Grand St (10552-2108)
PHONE..................................914 699-3800
Fax: 914 699-1022
Nancy Lerner, *President*
Jonathan Lerner, *Corp Secy*
EMP: 25 EST: 1956
SQ FT: 5,000
SALES (est): 2.5MM **Privately Held**
WEB: www.mitchellxfmr.com
SIC: **3677** 3612 Electronic coils, transformers & other inductors; specialty transformers

(G-8708)
MOUNT VERNON IRON WORKS INC
130 Miller Pl (10550-4706)
P.O. Box 3009 (10553-3009)
PHONE..................................914 668-7064
Fax: 914 668-7122
Joespeh Lividini, *President*
Peter M Lividini, *Vice Pres*
Grace Lividini, *Treasurer*
EMP: 7
SQ FT: 2,000
SALES (est): 1.4MM **Privately Held**
SIC: **3441** Expansion joints (structural shapes), iron or steel

(G-8709)
NAVAL STORES CO
Also Called: Castoleum Corportation
240 E 7th St (10550-4615)
P.O. Box 41, Yonkers (10710-0041)
PHONE..................................914 664-5877
Steven P Goldrich, *President*
Steve Neil, *Corp Secy*
EMP: 18 EST: 1920
SQ FT: 12,000
SALES (est): 1.7MM **Privately Held**
SIC: **2865** 2861 5169 2911 Cyclic crudes, coal tar; turpentine, pine oil; naval stores, wood & gum; coal tar products, primary & intermediate; gum & wood chemicals; petroleum refining

(G-8710)
NOBLE PINE PRODUCTS CO INC
240 E 7th St (10550-4615)
P.O. Box 41, Yonkers (10710-0041)
PHONE..................................914 664-5877
Sylvia Goldrich, *President*
Leslie Schwebel, *Corp Secy*
Steven Goldrich, *Vice Pres*
Steve Neil, *Vice Pres*
EMP: 12
SQ FT: 12,000
SALES (est): 1.1MM **Privately Held**
SIC: **2842** 2879 Disinfectants, household or industrial plant; insecticides, agricultural or household

(G-8711)
NSI INDUSTRIES LLC
Tork Division
   1 Grove St (10550-2401)
   PHONE..................................800 841-2505
   R Sam Shankar, *Division Pres*
   Leonard Caponigro, *Vice Pres*
   Marie Napoli, *Human Res Dir*
   Jerry Kerensky, *Agent*
   Gil Ledoux, *Agent*
EMP: 200 **Privately Held**
WEB: www.nsipolaris.com
SIC: **3625** 3674 Relays & industrial controls; switches, electric power; light sensitive devices
PA: Nsi Industries, Llc
   9730 Northcross Center Ct
   Huntersville NC 28078

(G-8712)
OWN INSTRUMENT INC
250 E 7th St (10550-4615)
PHONE..................................914 668-6546
Fax: 914 668-8434
Gerald Chapins, *President*
Patricia Chapins, *Treasurer*
EMP: 13 EST: 1957
SQ FT: 5,000
SALES (est): 2.1MM **Privately Held**
WEB: www.owninstrument.com
SIC: **3492** Fluid power valves & hose fittings

(G-8713)
PCI INDUSTRIES CORP
550 Franklin Ave (10550-4516)
PHONE..................................914 662-2700
Richard Persico, *President*
EMP: 24
SALES (est): 3.6MM **Privately Held**
SIC: **3999** Barber & beauty shop equipment

(G-8714)
PEPSI-COLA BOTTLING CO NY INC
601 S Fulton Ave (10550-5094)
PHONE..................................914 699-2600
Fax: 914 699-2638
Mike Freeman, *Sales Executive*
Jim Perry, *Technology*
EMP: 24
SALES (corp-wide): 219.3MM **Privately Held**
SIC: **2086** Soft drinks: packaged in cans, bottles, etc.
PA: Pepsi-Cola Bottling Company Of New York, Inc.
   11402 15th Ave Ste 5
   College Point NY 11356
   718 392-1000

(G-8715)
PERFECT SHOULDER COMPANY INC
2 Cortlandt St (10550-2706)
PHONE..................................914 699-8100
Harold Greenberg, *President*
Julio Figueroa, *Division Mgr*
Ketty Manno, *Sales Staff*
Julius Greenberg, *Administration*
▲ EMP: 25 EST: 1938
SQ FT: 35,000
SALES (est): 2.4MM **Privately Held**
SIC: **2396** Pads, shoulder: for coats, suits, etc.

(G-8716)
PRECISION COSMETICS MFG CO
519 S 5th Ave Ste 6 (10550-4476)
PHONE..................................914 667-1200
Aubrey Fenton Sr, *President*
Aubrey Fenton Jr, *Treasurer*
EMP: 5
SQ FT: 5,000
SALES: 50K **Privately Held**
SIC: **2844** Lipsticks

(G-8717)
PREMIER BRANDS OF AMERICA INC (PA)
31 South St Ste 2s (10550-1748)
PHONE..................................914 667-6200
Steven D Corsun, *Ch of Bd*
Alex Corsun, *Purch Agent*
Vincent Gioffre, *Marketing Staff*
Meisha Bailey, *Manager*
▲ EMP: 120
SQ FT: 75,000
SALES (est): 43MM **Privately Held**
WEB: www.premier-brands.com
SIC: **3842** 3131 2842 Surgical appliances & supplies; orthopedic appliances; footwear cut stock; shoe polish or cleaner

(G-8718)
PREMIER BRANDS OF AMERICA INC
120 Pearl St (10550-1725)
PHONE..................................718 325-3000
Vinnie Gioffre, *VP Sales*
EMP: 25
SALES (corp-wide): 43MM **Privately Held**
SIC: **2842** 2865 Shoe polish or cleaner; polishing preparations & related products; cyclic crudes & intermediates
PA: Premier Brands Of America Inc
   31 South St Ste 2s
   Mount Vernon NY 10550
   914 667-6200

(G-8719)
PRO-LINE SOLUTIONS INC
Also Called: Pry Care Products
18 Sargent Pl (10550-4727)
P.O. Box 651, Bronx (10465-0617)
PHONE..................................914 664-0002
Alex Lodato, *President*
EMP: 7
SQ FT: 10,000
SALES (est): 894.3K **Privately Held**
SIC: **2841** Soap & other detergents

(G-8720)
PROACTIVE MEDICAL PRODUCTS LLC
270 Washington St (10553-1017)
PHONE..................................845 205-6004
Mordecai Light, *President*
Brian Goldstein, *VP Sales*
▲ EMP: 8 EST: 2012
SQ FT: 20,000
SALES: 7MM **Privately Held**
SIC: **3841** Diagnostic apparatus, medical

(G-8721)
PROMPTUS ELECTRONIC HDWR INC
Also Called: Giagni Enterprises
520 Homestead Ave (10550-4620)
PHONE..................................914 699-4700
Vincent Giagni Jr, *President*
Stephen Giagni, *General Mgr*
Steve Giagni, *Sales Executive*
Paul Vamvaketis, *Director*
▲ EMP: 28
SQ FT: 15,000
SALES (est): 5.2MM **Privately Held**
WEB: www.promptusinc.com
SIC: **3699** Electrical equipment & supplies

(G-8722)
R I R COMMUNICATIONS SYSTEMS (PA)
20 Nuvern Ave (10550-4819)
P.O. Box 3660 (10553-3660)
PHONE..................................718 706-9957
Fax: 914 664-0329
Ralph Robinson, *President*
Inez Robinson, *Manager*
EMP: 8
SALES (est): 1.7MM **Privately Held**
SIC: **3661** Telephones & telephone apparatus

(G-8723)
R I R COMMUNICATIONS SYSTEMS
20 Nuvern Ave (10550-4819)
PHONE..................................718 706-9957
Ralph Robinson, *Manager*
EMP: 20
SALES (corp-wide): 1.7MM **Privately Held**
SIC: **3661** Telephones & telephone apparatus
PA: R I R Communications Systems Inc
   20 Nuvern Ave
   Mount Vernon NY 10550
   718 706-9957

(G-8724)
R V H ESTATES INC
138 Mount Vernon Ave (10550-1719)
PHONE..................................914 664-9888
Robert Belluzzi, *President*
Vincent Belluzzi, *Vice Pres*
EMP: 6 EST: 1981
SALES: 390K **Privately Held**
SIC: **2599** Bar, restaurant & cafeteria furniture

(G-8725)
RELIABLE ELEC MT VERNON INC
519 S 5th Ave (10550-4498)
PHONE..................................914 668-4440
Fax: 914 668-4972
Jay Friedman, *President*
Irv Seiger, *Vice Pres*
EMP: 23
SQ FT: 8,000
SALES: 75K **Privately Held**
WEB: www.reliableelectronics.net
SIC: **3577** Computer peripheral equipment

(G-8726)
ROHLFS STINED LEADED GL STUDIO
783 S 3rd Ave (10550-4946)
PHONE..................................914 699-4848
Fax: 914 699-7091
Peter A Rohlf, *CEO*
Gregory Rohlf, *Vice Pres*
EMP: 25
SQ FT: 10,000
SALES (est): 2.9MM **Privately Held**
WEB: www.rohlfstudio.com
SIC: **3231** 3442 Stained glass: made from purchased glass; leaded glass; casements, aluminum

(G-8727)
ROYAL CARIBBEAN JAMAICAN BKY (PA)
Also Called: Royal Caribbean Bakery
620 S Fulton Ave (10550-5012)
PHONE..................................914 668-6868
Jeanette Hosang, *President*
Vincent Hosang, *Vice Pres*
EMP: 50
SQ FT: 20,000
SALES (est): 8.2MM **Privately Held**
SIC: **2051** 5149 Bread, cake & related products; bakery: wholesale or wholesale/retail combined; bakery products

(G-8728)
S & S GRAPHICS INC
521 E 3rd St (10553-1606)
PHONE..................................914 668-4230
Fax: 914 668-3674
Stuart Standard, *President*
Jason Standard, *Vice Pres*
EMP: 11
SQ FT: 21,000
SALES: 2.3MM **Privately Held**
SIC: **2759** Commercial printing

(G-8729)
SAMUEL AARON INC (HQ)
Also Called: Samuel Aaron International
115 S Macquesten Pkwy (10550-1724)
PHONE..................................718 392-5454
Fax: 718 392-5454
Robert Kempler, *President*
Richard Katz, *COO*
Sue MO, *Senior VP*
Elizabeth Bengston, *Vice Pres*
Cindy Chen, *Vice Pres*
▲ EMP: 76
SQ FT: 55,000
SALES (est): 42MM **Privately Held**
WEB: www.samuelaaron.com
SIC: **3911** Jewelry, precious metal; rings, finger: precious metal

(G-8730)
SANDFORD BLVD DONUTS INC
440 E Sandford Blvd (10550-4729)
PHONE..................................914 663-7708
Fax: 914 663-7709
Nick Rassias, *President*
EMP: 6
SALES (est): 350K **Privately Held**
SIC: **2051** Doughnuts, except frozen

Mount Vernon - Westchester County (G-8731)

(G-8731)
SECS INC (PA)
550 S Columbus Ave (10550-4712)
PHONE....................914 667-5600
Fax: 914 699-0377
Vincent Giagni, *Ch of Bd*
Stephen Giagni, *President*
Kevin McBrien, *VP Mktg*
▲ EMP: 20
SQ FT: 15,000
SALES (est): 6MM Privately Held
WEB: www.prosecs.com
SIC: 3462 Gears, forged steel

(G-8732)
SECS INC
550 S Columbus Ave (10550-4712)
PHONE....................914 667-5600
Nichoas Bianculli, *Principal*
EMP: 30
SALES (corp-wide): 6MM Privately Held
WEB: www.prosecs.com
SIC: 3679 3462 Electronic switches; gears, forged steel
PA: Secs, Inc.
    550 S Columbus Ave
    Mount Vernon NY 10550
    914 667-5600

(G-8733)
SENTAGE CORPORATION
Also Called: D P Mount Vernon
161 S Macquesten Pkwy 2 (10550-1724)
PHONE....................914 664-2200
Fax: 914 664-2538
Barry Rothenberg, *Vice Pres*
Michael Petschulat, *Traffic Mgr*
Herman Braverman, *Manager*
Nell Marchetta, *Manager*
Rick West, *Executive*
EMP: 42
SALES (corp-wide): 100MM Privately Held
WEB: www.dentalservices.net
SIC: 3843 Dental laboratory equipment
PA: Sentage Corporation
    801 12th Ave N
    Minneapolis MN 55411
    412 431-3353

(G-8734)
SIGMUND COHN CORP
121 S Columbus Ave (10553-1324)
PHONE....................914 664-5300
Thomas Cohn, *President*
Sue Keneally, *Purchasing*
Michael Myers, *QC Mgr*
George Pilke, *CFO*
Vincent Gataletto, *Manager*
EMP: 55 EST: 1901
SQ FT: 72,000
SALES (est): 13.8MM Privately Held
SIC: 3356 3496 3339 3315 Nonferrous rolling & drawing; precious metals; miscellaneous fabricated wire products; primary nonferrous metals; steel wire & related products

(G-8735)
TALYARPS CORPORATION
716 S Columbus Ave (10550-4717)
PHONE....................914 699-3030
Fax: 914 699-3035
Jack Orentlikher, *Principal*
Tom Klapach, *Controller*
EMP: 30
SALES (corp-wide): 33.6MM Privately Held
WEB: www.spraylat.com
SIC: 2851 Paints & paint additives
PA: Talyarps Corporation
    143 Sparks Ave
    Pelham NY 10803
    914 699-3030

(G-8736)
TAPE SYSTEMS INC
630 S Columbus Ave (10550-4734)
P.O. Box 8612, Pelham (10803-8612)
PHONE....................914 668-3700
Fax: 914 668-3987
Aniello Scotti, *President*
Ana Tongco, *Executive*
▲ EMP: 10
SQ FT: 30,000
SALES (est): 2.2MM Privately Held
SIC: 3842 Adhesive tape & plasters, medicated or non-medicated

(G-8737)
TENNYSON MACHINE CO INC
535 S 5th Ave (10550-4483)
PHONE....................914 668-5468
Fax: 914 668-5002
Lawrence A Castiglia, *President*
EMP: 16 EST: 1961
SQ FT: 10,000
SALES: 1.2MM Privately Held
SIC: 3599 Machine shop, jobbing & repair

(G-8738)
TORK INC (PA)
1 Grove St (10550-2450)
PHONE....................914 664-3542
Fax: 914 664-5052
Victoria White, *Ch of Bd*
R Sam Shankar, *President*
Leonard Caponigro, *Vice Pres*
Nicholas Murlo, *Vice Pres*
Janice Bastin, *Safety Mgr*
▲ EMP: 100 EST: 1934
SQ FT: 40,000
SALES (est): 14.2MM Privately Held
WEB: www.tork.com
SIC: 3625 3674 Relays & industrial controls; switches, electric power; light sensitive devices

(G-8739)
TRAC REGULATORS INC
160 S Terrace Ave (10550-2408)
PHONE....................914 699-9352
Fax: 914 699-9367
Adelmo Costantini, *President*
Cynthia La Sorsa, *Corp Secy*
Tom Notaro, *Vice Pres*
George Witzel, *Shareholder*
EMP: 20
SQ FT: 10,000
SALES (est): 3.4MM Privately Held
SIC: 3613 3491 Regulators, power; industrial valves

(G-8740)
TRI STAR LABEL INC
630 S Columbus Ave (10550-4734)
PHONE....................914 237-4800
Dan Mesisco, *President*
Neil Scotti, *Vice Pres*
Laura Annunziata, *Admin Sec*
▲ EMP: 7
SQ FT: 8,000
SALES: 900K Privately Held
SIC: 2672 Tape, pressure sensitive: made from purchased materials

(G-8741)
TRI-TECHNOLOGIES INC
40 Hartford Ave (10553-5119)
PHONE....................914 699-2001
Fax: 914 699-2002
David Hirsch, *CEO*
Dennis Di Donato, *President*
Lisa Bertuzzi, *Admin Asst*
▲ EMP: 48
SQ FT: 25,000
SALES (est): 11MM Privately Held
SIC: 3484 3451 3444 3469 Small arms; screw machine products; sheet metalwork; metal stampings

(G-8742)
TRULY TUBULAR FITTING CORP
115 E 3rd St (10550-3606)
P.O. Box 1160 (10551-1160)
PHONE....................914 664-8686
Fax: 914 668-2617
Myron S Gorel, *President*
Edward Gorel, *Vice Pres*
Phyllis Gorel, *Admin Sec*
EMP: 19
SQ FT: 26,000
SALES: 800K
SALES (corp-wide): 2.8MM Privately Held
WEB: www.trulytubular.com
SIC: 3498 Fabricated pipe & fittings
PA: Coventry Manufacturing Company, Inc.
    115 E 3rd St
    Mount Vernon NY 10550
    914 668-2212

(G-8743)
TURBOFIL PACKAGING MCHS LLC
30 Beach St (10550-1702)
PHONE....................914 239-3878
Deborah Smook, *VP Mktg*
Eli Uriel, *Branch Mgr*
Elaine Epps, *Director*
▲ EMP: 10
SQ FT: 7,000
SALES (est): 2MM Privately Held
WEB: www.turbofil.com
SIC: 3565 Packing & wrapping machinery

(G-8744)
UFS INDUSTRIES INC
Also Called: Sally Sherman Foods
300 N Macquesten Pkwy (10550-1008)
PHONE....................718 822-1100
Fax: 914 664-2846
Thomas Recine, *President*
Felix Endico, *COO*
Mike Lodolce, *VP Opers*
Ann Colantuono, *Controller*
Debra Gentile, *Accounts Mgr*
EMP: 100 EST: 1930
SQ FT: 50,000
SALES (est): 23.3MM Privately Held
SIC: 2099 Food preparations; cole slaw, in bulk; salads, fresh or refrigerated

(G-8745)
UNITED IRON INC
6 Roslyn Pl (10550-4540)
PHONE....................914 667-5700
Fax: 914 667-5925
Randall Rifelli, *President*
Cecil Bernard, *Safety Mgr*
Luigi Saturnino, *Purch Mgr*
Teodor Valev, *Research*
Pat Zacchi, *Human Res Mgr*
EMP: 30 EST: 1922
SQ FT: 27,000
SALES (est): 7.6MM Privately Held
SIC: 3449 3441 3446 Miscellaneous metalwork; fabricated structural metal; architectural metalwork

(G-8746)
YOUR WAY CUSTOM CABINETS INC
20 N Macquesten Pkwy (10550-1841)
PHONE....................914 371-1870
Annette Alberti, *President*
EMP: 7
SALES (est): 796.6K Privately Held
SIC: 2434 Wood kitchen cabinets

Mountainville - Orange County

(G-8747)
GLUTEN FREE BAKE SHOP INC
Also Called: Katz Gluten Free
19 Industry Dr (10953)
P.O. Box 58, Monroe (10949-0058)
PHONE....................845 782-5307
Rachel Jacobowitz, *President*
Mordche Jacobowitz, *Vice Pres*
▼ EMP: 50
SQ FT: 13,000
SALES (est): 9.3MM Privately Held
SIC: 2051 Bakery: wholesale or wholesale/retail combined

(G-8748)
JP FILLING INC
20 Industry Dr (10953)
P.O. Box 97 (10953-0097)
PHONE....................845 534-4793
Joel Polatsek, *President*
EMP: 65
SQ FT: 3,000
SALES (est): 2.2MM Privately Held
SIC: 2844 Perfumes & colognes

Munnsville - Madison County

(G-8749)
BRIGGS & STRATTON CORPORATION
5375 N Main St (13409-4003)
PHONE....................315 495-0100
Fax: 315 495-0109
Kevin Kiehn, *Plant Mgr*
Asmus Shannon, *Safety Mgr*
John Peters, *Purchasing*
Tim Resig, *Engineer*
Robert Laurin, *Design Engr*
EMP: 175
SALES (corp-wide): 1.8B Publicly Held
WEB: www.briggsandstratton.com
SIC: 3519 3524 Internal combustion engines; lawn & garden equipment
PA: Briggs & Stratton Corporation
    12301 W Wirth St
    Wauwatosa WI 53222
    414 259-5333

(G-8750)
CUSTOM WOODCRAFT LLC
2525 Perry Schumaker Rd (13409-3620)
PHONE....................315 843-4234
Fax: 315 843-7269
Daniel Stoltzfus,
EMP: 12
SQ FT: 11,000
SALES (est): 1.3MM Privately Held
SIC: 2434 5712 2511 Wood kitchen cabinets; cabinet work, custom; wood household furniture

Nanuet - Rockland County

(G-8751)
AZAR INTERNATIONAL INC (PA)
Also Called: Azar Displays
31 W Prospect St (10954-2620)
P.O. Box 250 (10954-0250)
PHONE....................845 624-8808
Fax: 845 624-7156
Elazar Cohen, *CEO*
Loree Cohen, *Controller*
Lisa Barta, *Sales Staff*
▲ EMP: 45
SQ FT: 40,000
SALES (est): 6.9MM Privately Held
WEB: www.azardisplays.com
SIC: 3993 Displays & cutouts, window & lobby

(G-8752)
BRIGADOON SOFTWARE INC (PA)
119 Rockland Ctr 250 (10954-2956)
PHONE....................845 624-0909
Fax: 845 624-0990
Terrance Kawles, *President*
Martin Moran, *Vice Pres*
Tim Albright, *VP Sales*
Cevin Moran, *Manager*
EMP: 2
SALES (est): 1.4MM Privately Held
WEB: www.brigadoonsoftware.com
SIC: 7372 Prepackaged software

(G-8753)
BRUNO & CANIO LTD
130 Blauvelt Rd (10954-3602)
PHONE....................845 624-3060
EMP: 37
SQ FT: 6,500
SALES: 1MM Privately Held
SIC: 2325 2337 Contract Manufacturer Men's Separate Trousers & Women's Skirts

(G-8754)
CITIZEN PUBLISHING CORP
Also Called: Rockland County Times
119 Main St Ste 2 (10954-2883)
PHONE....................845 627-1414
Armand Miele, *Manager*
EMP: 10

SALES (est): 446.5K **Privately Held**
WEB: www.rocklandcountytimes.com
SIC: 2711 Newspapers

(G-8755)
DENMAR ELECTRIC
202 Main St (10954-3324)
PHONE.................................845 624-4430
Dennis Maher, *Owner*
EMP: 17
SALES (est): 3.7MM **Privately Held**
SIC: 3699 Electrical equipment & supplies

(G-8756)
EAGLE INTERNATIONAL LLC
228 E Route 59 Ste 50 (10954-2905)
PHONE.................................917 282-2536
Harry Adler, *Mng Member*
EMP: 5 EST: 2013
SQ FT: 400
SALES: 600K **Privately Held**
SIC: 2835 In vitro & in vivo diagnostic substances

(G-8757)
HNST MOLD INSPECTIONS LLC (PA)
6 Kevin Ct (10954-3828)
PHONE.................................845 215-9258
John Skelly, *Mng Member*
EMP: 4
SALES (est): 1.7MM **Privately Held**
SIC: 3544 Industrial molds

(G-8758)
JAR METALS INC
50 2nd Ave (10954-4405)
PHONE.................................845 425-8901
Andrew Gallina, *President*
John Shepitka, *Vice Pres*
EMP: 15
SQ FT: 10,000
SALES (est): 165.3K **Privately Held**
SIC: 3444 5085 Sheet metalwork; industrial supplies

(G-8759)
MINUTEMAN PRESS INC
121 W Nyack Rd Ste 3 (10954-2962)
PHONE.................................845 623-2277
Brian H Gunn, *President*
EMP: 5
SQ FT: 2,000
SALES (est): 556.3K **Privately Held**
SIC: 2752 Commercial printing, lithographic

(G-8760)
PHILIPP FELDHEIM INC (PA)
Also Called: Feldheim Publishers
208 Airport Executive Par (10954-5262)
PHONE.................................845 356-2282
Yitzchak Feldheim, *President*
Mirian Mendlowitz, *Treasurer*
Moshe Grossman, *Sales Mgr*
Judy Gruenebaum, *Office Mgr*
Chaim Neck, *Comp Spec*
▲ EMP: 9
SALES (est): 607.3K **Privately Held**
WEB: www.feldheim.com
SIC: 2731 Book publishing

(G-8761)
ROCKLAND BAKERY INC (PA)
94 Demarest Mill Rd W (10954-2989)
PHONE.................................845 623-5800
Fax: 845 623-6921
Ignazio Battaglia, *CEO*
Antony Luna, *Exec VP*
Philip Battaglia, *Vice Pres*
Bobbi James, *Purchasing*
Ron Warner, *Plant Engr Mgr*
EMP: 100 EST: 1986
SQ FT: 22,000
SALES (est): 143.5MM **Privately Held**
WEB: www.rocklandbakery.com
SIC: 2051 Bread, cake & related products

(G-8762)
WENDYS AUTO EXPRESS INC
121 Main St (10954-2800)
PHONE.................................845 624-6100
Fax: 845 624-2675
Wendy Winnick, *President*
Cindy Cherny, *Manager*
EMP: 6

SALES (est): 523.1K **Privately Held**
SIC: 3711 Chassis, motor vehicle

(G-8763)
WR SMITH & SONS INC
121 W Nyack Rd (10954-2939)
P.O. Box 225, West Nyack (10994-0225)
PHONE.................................845 620-9400
William Smith, *Principal*
EMP: 7
SQ FT: 1,500
SALES (est): 914.6K **Privately Held**
SIC: 2821 3469 Plastics materials & resins; metal stampings

Naples
Ontario County

(G-8764)
BAKER LOGGING & FIREWOOD
8781 Grlnghuse Atlanta Rd (14512-9247)
PHONE.................................585 374-5733
Richard Baker, *Owner*
EMP: 9
SALES (est): 566.8K **Privately Held**
SIC: 2411 Logging camps & contractors

(G-8765)
L & D ACQUISITION LLC
1 Lake Niagara Ln (14512-9770)
PHONE.................................585 531-9000
Doug Hazlitt, *Principal*
EMP: 16
SALES (est): 950K **Privately Held**
SIC: 2084 Wines, brandy & brandy spirits

(G-8766)
LAKE COUNTRY WOODWORKERS LTD
12 Clark St (14512-9535)
P.O. Box 400 (14512-0400)
PHONE.................................585 374-6353
Fax: 585 374-2505
Donna Fargo, *President*
Karen Wood, *President*
Wayne Haines, *Vice Pres*
Chris Cooney, *Project Mgr*
Ben Heibach, *Engineer*
▲ EMP: 40 EST: 1976
SQ FT: 30,000
SALES (est): 7.8MM **Privately Held**
WEB: www.lcww.com
SIC: 2521 Wood office furniture

(G-8767)
NAPLES VLY MRGERS ACQSTONS LLC
Also Called: Angelic Gourmet
154 N Main St (14512-9156)
P.O. Box 39 (14512-0039)
PHONE.................................585 490-1339
Donna Nichols, *Mng Member*
▼ EMP: 9 EST: 2011
SQ FT: 6,000
SALES: 500K **Privately Held**
SIC: 2064 Cake ornaments, confectionery

Narrowsburg
Sullivan County

(G-8768)
NARROWSBURG FEED & GRAIN CO
Also Called: Honor Brand Feeds
Fifth And Main St (12764)
PHONE.................................845 252-3936
Fax: 845 252-3211
Patrick C Brown, *President*
Raymond Villeneuve, *President*
Roy G Morris, *General Mgr*
EMP: 16 EST: 1970
SQ FT: 20,000
SALES (est): 2.1MM **Privately Held**
WEB: www.narrowsburg.org
SIC: 2048 Prepared feeds; poultry feeds

(G-8769)
STUART COMMUNICATIONS INC
Also Called: The River Reporter
93 Erie Ave (12764-6423)
P.O. Box 150 (12764-0150)
PHONE.................................845 252-7414
Fax: 845 252-3298
Laura Stuart, *President*
EMP: 13
SALES (est): 888.1K **Privately Held**
WEB: www.riverreporter.com
SIC: 2711 Newspapers: publishing only, not printed on site

Nassau
Rensselaer County

(G-8770)
CAPITAL SAWMILL SERVICE
4119 Us Highway 20 (12123-1904)
PHONE.................................518 479-0729
Fax: 518 479-0729
Steven Daniels,
Teresa Eddy,
EMP: 9
SALES (est): 1MM **Privately Held**
WEB: www.capitalsawmill.com
SIC: 2421 Sawmills & planing mills, general

(G-8771)
COPELAND COATING COMPANY INC
3600 Us Highway 20 (12123-1934)
P.O. Box 595 (12123-0595)
PHONE.................................518 766-2932
Fax: 518 766-3603
John R Copeland, *Ch of Bd*
Steven W Hinding, *Vice Pres*
Rick Kment, *Purch Agent*
Matthew Mitchell, *CFO*
Albert Giamei, *Sr Project Mgr*
▲ EMP: 15 EST: 1945
SQ FT: 10,000
SALES (est): 4.7MM **Privately Held**
WEB: www.copelandcoating.com
SIC: 3272 Paving materials, prefabricated concrete

Nedrow
Onondaga County

(G-8772)
BOWEN PRODUCTS CORPORATION
5084 S Onondaga Rd (13120-9702)
PHONE.................................315 498-4481
Charles D Smith, *President*
Louise M Smith, *Vice Pres*
EMP: 9 EST: 1896
SQ FT: 18,000
SALES (est): 1.1MM **Privately Held**
SIC: 3469 3569 Metal stampings; lubricating equipment

(G-8773)
W F SAUNDERS & SONS INC (PA)
5126 S Onondaga Rd (13120-9789)
P.O. Box A (13120-0129)
PHONE.................................315 469-3217
Fax: 315 469-3940
Sherman V Saunders Jr, *President*
Michael Saunders, *Treasurer*
EMP: 15 EST: 1891
SQ FT: 5,000
SALES (est): 7.7MM **Privately Held**
SIC: 3273 3281 Ready-mixed concrete; cut stone & stone products

Nesconset
Suffolk County

(G-8774)
C D A INC
66 Southern Blvd Ste A (11767-1092)
PHONE.................................631 473-1595

Robert Tuniewicz, *President*
Gilbert D Talamo, *Vice Pres*
◆ EMP: 9 EST: 1996
SQ FT: 2,000
SALES (est): 1.2MM **Privately Held**
SIC: 3625 Industrial electrical relays & switches

(G-8775)
KEY HIGH VACUUM PRODUCTS INC
36 Southern Blvd (11767-1097)
PHONE.................................631 584-5959
Fax: 631 360-3973
Anthony Kozyrski, *President*
Elizabeth Kozyrski, *Corp Secy*
Betty Janosick, *Manager*
▲ EMP: 30
SQ FT: 15,000
SALES (est): 5.5MM **Privately Held**
WEB: www.keyhigh.com
SIC: 3589 3494 3492 3429 Vacuum cleaners & sweepers, electric: industrial; valves & pipe fittings; fluid power valves & hose fittings; manufactured hardware (general)

(G-8776)
MOBILE DATA SYSTEMS INC
110 Lake Ave S Ste 35 (11767-1071)
PHONE.................................631 360-3400
Joseph Spiteri, *President*
EMP: 5
SALES (est): 406.3K **Privately Held**
WEB: www.mobiledatasys.com
SIC: 7372 Prepackaged software

(G-8777)
PERFECT POLY INC
1 Gina Ct (11767-2058)
PHONE.................................631 265-0539
Malke Gelbstein, *President*
Elissa Artiles, *Manager*
EMP: 20
SALES (est): 3.5MM **Privately Held**
SIC: 2821 Polyesters

(G-8778)
TRAXEL LABS INC
95 Steuben Blvd (11767-3040)
PHONE.................................631 590-1095
Arthur Lekstutis, *Principal*
EMP: 5
SALES (est): 550K **Privately Held**
WEB: www.traxellabs.com
SIC: 3675 Electronic capacitors

New Berlin
Chenango County

(G-8779)
CHOBANI LLC
669 County Road 25 (13411-4403)
PHONE.................................607 847-6181
Marc Abjean, *Senior VP*
Josh Dean, *Vice Pres*
Ray Magruder, *Safety Dir*
Richard Lake, *Plant Mgr*
Carl Guntle, *Safety Mgr*
EMP: 2351
SALES (corp-wide): 854MM **Privately Held**
SIC: 2026 Yogurt
PA: Chobani, Llc
   147 State Highway 320
   Norwich NY 13815
   607 337-1246

(G-8780)
GOLDEN ARTIST COLORS INC
188 Bell Rd (13411-3616)
PHONE.................................607 847-6154
Fax: 607 847-6767
Mark Golden, *Ch of Bd*
Barbara J Schindler, *President*
Edward Holmquist, *Opers Mgr*
Greg Sheldon, *Opers Mgr*
Ben Gavett, *Safety Mgr*
◆ EMP: 125
SQ FT: 60,000

New City - Rockland County (G-8781)

SALES (est): 31.3MM **Privately Held**
WEB: www.goldenpaint.com
SIC: 3952 Paints, except gold & bronze: artists'; paints, gold or bronze: artists'

New City
Rockland County

(G-8781)
A TRADITION OF EXCELLENCE INC
85b Maple Ave (10956-5020)
PHONE....................845 638-4595
Tom Sullivan, *President*
John Cusick, *Vice Pres*
EMP: 5
SALES (est): 499.1K **Privately Held**
SIC: 2759 Screen printing

(G-8782)
DARK STAR LITHOGRAPH CORP
9 Perth Ln (10956-5808)
P.O. Box 9074, Bardonia (10954-9074)
PHONE....................845 634-3780
Fax: 845 634-2509
Richard Suben, *President*
EMP: 5
SALES (est): 510K **Privately Held**
SIC: 2752 Commercial printing, lithographic

(G-8783)
DOCTOROW COMMUNICATIONS INC
Also Called: Home Lighting & Accessories
180 Phillips Hill Rd 1b (10956-4132)
P.O. Box 293 (10956-0293)
PHONE....................845 708-5166
Jeffrey Doctorow, *President*
Jonathon Doctorow, *Manager*
EMP: 12
SALES (est): 1.2MM **Privately Held**
WEB: www.contractlighting.net
SIC: 2721 Magazines: publishing only, not printed on site

(G-8784)
E L SMITH PRINTING CO INC
3 Lisa Ct (10956-2605)
P.O. Box 6567, Carlstadt NJ (07072-0567)
PHONE....................201 373-0111
Hilton I Kaufman, *President*
Beverly Kaufman, *Admin Sec*
EMP: 20 EST: 1929
SALES (est): 2MM **Privately Held**
SIC: 2752 2789 Commercial printing, lithographic; bookbinding & related work

(G-8785)
EASTERN INDUSTRIAL STEEL CORP (PA)
4 Fringe Ct (10956-6802)
P.O. Box 132, Blauvelt (10913-0132)
PHONE....................845 639-9749
Peter Lacombe, *President*
EMP: 4
SALES: 1MM **Privately Held**
WEB: www.easternindustrialsteel.com
SIC: 3325 3089 Steel foundries; extruded finished plastic products

(G-8786)
JMK ENTERPRISES LLC
301 N Main St Ste 1 (10956-4021)
PHONE....................845 634-8100
John Knutsen, *Partner*
EMP: 7
SALES (est): 484.9K **Privately Held**
SIC: 2389 Apparel & accessories

(G-8787)
LEONARD MARTIN BUS SYSTEMS
120 N Main St Ste 202 (10956-3743)
PHONE....................845 638-9350
Martin Cohen, *President*
Leonard Weiss, *Vice Pres*
EMP: 9

SALES (est): 1.2MM **Privately Held**
SIC: 2752 5199 Commercial printing, lithographic; promotional printing, lithographic; advertising specialties

(G-8788)
MSI INC
329 Strawtown Rd (10956-6634)
PHONE....................845 639-6683
Murray Steinfink, *President*
Carl Roth, *Accountant*
EMP: 10
SALES (est): 880K **Privately Held**
SIC: 3081 Unsupported plastics film & sheet

(G-8789)
PLUS ITS CHEAP LLC (PA)
Also Called: Prestige Xs
873 Route 45 Ste 101 (10956-1123)
PHONE....................845 233-2435
Ralph Newhouse, *CEO*
Joe Sterngold, *CFO*
Yaakov Adams, *Mng Member*
▲ EMP: 32
SQ FT: 30,000
SALES (est): 8.2MM **Privately Held**
SIC: 3634 Electric household cooking appliances

(G-8790)
PRO HITTER CORP
170 S Main St (10956-3323)
P.O. Box 883 (10956-0883)
PHONE....................845 358-8670
Fax: 845 634-1191
Philip Lomedico, *President*
Robert Ingenito, *Treasurer*
EMP: 15
SALES (est): 840K **Privately Held**
WEB: www.prohitter.com
SIC: 3949 Baseball equipment & supplies, general

(G-8791)
REAL GOODS SOLAR INC
22 Third St (10956-4922)
PHONE....................845 708-0800
James Albert, *Branch Mgr*
EMP: 125
SALES (corp-wide): 45.5MM **Publicly Held**
SIC: 3433 Heating equipment, except electric
PA: Real Goods Solar, Inc.
833 W South Boulder Rd B
Louisville CO 80027
303 222-8300

(G-8792)
ROSS MICROSYSTEMS INC
1 Tioga Ct (10956-5710)
PHONE....................845 918-1208
Rick Ross, *President*
EMP: 5
SQ FT: 5,000
SALES: 1.5MM **Privately Held**
WEB: www.rossinspection.com
SIC: 3559 Pharmaceutical machinery

(G-8793)
SHINING CREATIONS INC
Also Called: Strawtown Jewerly
40 S Main St Ste 1 (10956-3533)
PHONE....................845 358-4911
Ellen Arkin, *President*
Glenn Arkin, *Vice Pres*
EMP: 5
SALES (est): 200K **Privately Held**
SIC: 3911 5944 Jewelry mountings & trimmings; jewelry, precious stones & precious metals

(G-8794)
SUPER SOFTWARE
151 S Main St Ste 303 (10956-3544)
PHONE....................845 735-0000
Fax: 845 623-3333
James Flattery, *Owner*
EMP: 6
SALES (est): 310K **Privately Held**
WEB: www.supersoftware.org
SIC: 7372 Prepackaged software

(G-8795)
YELLOW PAGES INC (PA)
222 N Main St (10956-5302)
PHONE....................845 639-6060
Robert Gazzetta, *Ch of Bd*
EMP: 4
SALES (est): 7MM **Privately Held**
WEB: www.ypinc.net
SIC: 2741 Telephone & other directory publishing

(G-8796)
YO FRESH INC
170 S Main St (10956-3323)
PHONE....................845 634-1616
EMP: 30
SALES (corp-wide): 12MM **Privately Held**
SIC: 2026 Yogurt
PA: Yo Fresh Inc.
38 E 29th St Fl 6
New York NY 10016
212 260-4416

New Hampton
Orange County

(G-8797)
BALCHEM CORPORATION (PA)
52 Sunrise Park Rd (10958-4703)
P.O. Box 600 (10958-0600)
PHONE....................845 326-5600
Fax: 845 326-5702
Dino A Rossi, *Ch of Bd*
Theodore L Harris, *President*
Frank J Fitzpatrick, *Vice Pres*
David F Ludwig, *Vice Pres*
Daniel Norton, *Vice Pres*
◆ EMP: 277
SQ FT: 20,000
SALES: 552.4MM **Publicly Held**
WEB: www.balchem.com
SIC: 2869 2899 Industrial organic chemicals; methyl alcohol, synthetic methanol; propylene, butylene; chemical preparations

(G-8798)
BCP INGREDIENTS INC (HQ)
52 Sunrise Park Rd (10958-4703)
PHONE....................845 326-5600
Dino A Rossi, *Ch of Bd*
Richard Bendure, *COO*
John E Kuehner, *Vice Pres*
David F Ludwig, *Vice Pres*
Dana Putnam, *Vice Pres*
▼ EMP: 64
SALES (est): 15MM
SALES (corp-wide): 552.4MM **Publicly Held**
SIC: 2899 Chemical preparations
PA: Balchem Corporation
52 Sunrise Park Rd
New Hampton NY 10958
845 326-5600

(G-8799)
DICKS CONCRETE CO INC (PA)
1053 County Route 37 (10958-4811)
PHONE....................845 374-5966
Fax: 845 374-7262
Richard Penaluna Jr, *President*
Barbara Penaluna, *Vice Pres*
Jan Dodd, *CFO*
Mary Smith, *Manager*
Nettie Smith, *Manager*
EMP: 40
SQ FT: 5,000
SALES (est): 12.7MM **Privately Held**
WEB: www.dicksconcrete.com
SIC: 1442 5032 3273 3271 Sand mining; gravel mining; cement; ready-mixed concrete; concrete block & brick

(G-8800)
EAST COAST SPRING MIX INC
211 Lynch Ave (10958-4504)
PHONE....................845 355-1215
EMP: 7
SALES (est): 1MM **Privately Held**
SIC: 3273 Ready-mixed concrete

New Hartford
Oneida County

(G-8801)
B & D ENTERPRISES OF UTICA (PA)
Also Called: Hemstrought's Bakeries
2 Campion Rd Ste 7 (13413-1647)
PHONE....................315 735-3311
Thomas R Batters, *President*
Michael J Denz, *Vice Pres*
Mary Denz, *Treasurer*
Paul Remizowski, *Shareholder*
EMP: 75
SQ FT: 20,000
SALES (est): 8.6MM **Privately Held**
SIC: 2051 5461 5149 Bread, cake & related products; bakeries; bakery products

(G-8802)
DARTCOM INCORPORATED
Also Called: Dart Communications
2 Oxford Xing Ste 1 (13413-3246)
PHONE....................315 790-5456
Michael Baldwin, *President*
Jamie Jones, *Business Mgr*
Nick Baldwin, *Administration*
EMP: 4
SQ FT: 7,500
SALES (est): 1.3MM **Privately Held**
WEB: www.dart.com
SIC: 7372 Business oriented computer software

(G-8803)
ELM GRAPHICS INC
9694 Mallory Rd (13413-3618)
PHONE....................315 737-5984
Fax: 315 737-0904
Stanley Lebiednik, *President*
Gerald Eischen, *Vice Pres*
EMP: 5
SQ FT: 1,200
SALES (est): 532.6K **Privately Held**
SIC: 2759 Commercial printing

(G-8804)
FASTER-FORM CORP
Also Called: Lifesake Division
1 Faster Form Cir Ste 1 (13413-9564)
P.O. Box 825 (13413-0825)
PHONE....................800 327-3676
Fax: 315 792-9543
J C Waszkiewicz III, *President*
Lawrence P Ulrich, *Vice Pres*
J C Waszkiewicz II, *Treasurer*
Carolyn Kearney, *Accountant*
Jeff Thorpe, *Sales Staff*
▲ EMP: 85 EST: 1959
SQ FT: 200,000
SALES (est): 9.5MM **Privately Held**
WEB: www.vincenzaflowers.com
SIC: 3999 3993 Flowers, artificial & preserved; bric-a-brac; displays, paint process

(G-8805)
GAN KAVOD INC
2050 Tilden Ave (13413-3613)
P.O. Box 1000 (13413-0709)
PHONE....................315 797-3114
Fax: 315 797-6955
Patricia A Hays, *Principal*
EMP: 2
SALES: 5MM **Privately Held**
SIC: 3843 Enamels, dentists'

(G-8806)
HARTFORD HWY DEPT
Also Called: Chadwicks Town Park
48 Genesee St (13413-2337)
PHONE....................315 724-0654
Mike Jeffery, *Director*
EMP: 7 **Privately Held**
SIC: 2531 9111 Picnic tables or benches, park; mayors' offices
PA: Hartford Hwy. Dept
165 Cr 23
Hartford NY 12838
518 632-5255

GEOGRAPHIC SECTION

(G-8807)
LOCKHEED MARTIN CORPORATION
8373 Seneca Tpke (13413-4957)
PHONE..................315 793-5800
Brad McGregor, *Purch Mgr*
Faith Elliott, *Engineer*
Cassaundra Wilkerson, *Business Anlyst*
Richard Kahler, *Manager*
Robert E McAuliffe, *Manager*
EMP: 80
SALES (corp-wide): 46.1B **Publicly Held**
WEB: www.lockheedmartin.com
SIC: 3721 7371 Aircraft; custom computer programming services
PA: Lockheed Martin Corporation
6801 Rockledge Dr
Bethesda MD 20817
301 897-6000

(G-8808)
PAR TECHNOLOGY CORPORATION (PA)
8383 Seneca Tpke Ste 2 (13413-4991)
PHONE..................315 738-0600
Fax: 315 738-0411
Karen E Sammon, *President*
Kevin Jaskolka, *Vice Pres*
Viola A Murdock, *Vice Pres*
Brett Clapham, *Opers Staff*
Larry Billinghurst, *Engineer*
EMP: 99
SQ FT: 216,800
SALES: 229MM **Publicly Held**
WEB: www.partech.com
SIC: 7372 7832 Prepackaged software; motion picture theaters, except drive-in

(G-8809)
RIVERHAWK COMPANY LP
Also Called: Indikon Company
215 Clinton Rd (13413-5306)
PHONE..................315 624-7171
Allen Williams, *Manager*
EMP: 32
SALES (corp-wide): 21.4MM **Privately Held**
WEB: www.indikon.com
SIC: 3823 3829 3674 Industrial process measurement equipment; measuring & controlling devices; semiconductors & related devices
PA: Riverhawk Company L.P.
215 Clinton Rd
New Hartford NY 13413
315 768-4855

(G-8810)
SAES SMART MATERIALS INC
Also Called: Saes Memry
4355 Middle Settlement Rd (13413-5317)
PHONE..................315 266-2026
Richard Lafond, *CEO*
Giorgio Vergani, *Ch of Bd*
John Schosser, *CFO*
Steve Dayton, *Treasurer*
Ronald Rossi, *Controller*
▲ **EMP:** 27
SALES (est): 6.5MM
SALES (corp-wide): 16.6MM **Privately Held**
SIC: 3339 Titanium metal, sponge & granules
PA: Saes Getters Spa
Viale Italia 77
Lainate MI 20020
029 317-81

(G-8811)
SPECIAL METALS CORPORATION
4317 Middle Settlement Rd (13413-5392)
PHONE..................315 798-2900
Fax: 315 798-2001
Joseph I Snowden, *CEO*
Jason Catalino, *General Mgr*
Don Stockton, *General Mgr*
Joe Mack, *Safety Mgr*
Paul Jelinek, *Production*
EMP: 65 EST: 1964
SALES (est): 17.2MM
SALES (corp-wide): 210.8B **Publicly Held**
SIC: 3356 Nickel & nickel alloy: rolling, drawing or extruding

HQ: Precision Castparts Corp.
4650 Sw Mcdam Ave Ste 300
Portland OR 97239
503 946-4800

(G-8812)
TALLMANS EXPRESS LUBE
8421 Seneca Tpke (13413-4959)
PHONE..................315 266-1033
Tim Tallman, *President*
EMP: 5
SALES (est): 488.2K **Privately Held**
SIC: 2992 Lubricating oils

(G-8813)
WESTROCK CP LLC
45 Campion Rd (13413-1601)
PHONE..................770 448-2193
Debbie Millspaugh, *Purch Agent*
Mark Thomson, *Controller*
Nancy Rudnitski, *Human Resources*
William Ross, *Manager*
Dan Fowlkes, *Manager*
EMP: 147
SALES (corp-wide): 11.3B **Publicly Held**
SIC: 2653 Corrugated boxes, partitions, display items, sheets & pad
HQ: Westrock Cp, Llc
504 Thrasher St
Norcross GA 30071

New Hyde Park
Nassau County

(G-8814)
ALNIK SERVICE CORPORATION
20 Tulip Pl (11040-5315)
PHONE..................516 873-7300
Robert Fuchs, *President*
EMP: 8
SALES (est): 1.2MM **Privately Held**
SIC: 3444 Sheet metalwork

(G-8815)
AMERICAN CHALLENGE ENTERPRISES
1804 Plaza Ave Ste 6 (11040-4937)
PHONE..................631 595-7171
Fax: 516 616-0598
Robert Laker Sr, *Ch of Bd*
Robert J Laker Jr, *President*
Bruce Laker, *Vice Pres*
▲ **EMP:** 6
SALES (est): 400K **Privately Held**
SIC: 2329 2339 Men's & boys' athletic uniforms; uniforms, athletic: women's, misses' & juniors'

(G-8816)
APPLE COMMUTER INC
54 Lake Dr (11040-1125)
PHONE..................917 299-0066
Shah Biren, *Principal*
EMP: 5
SALES (est): 626.8K **Privately Held**
SIC: 3571 Personal computers (microcomputers)

(G-8817)
ARNOUSE DIGITAL DEVICES CORP
Also Called: Biodigitalpc
1983 Marcus Ave Ste 104 (11042-2002)
PHONE..................516 673-4444
Fax: 516 626-6001
Michael Arnouse, *President*
Daniel Dellick, *COO*
Dan Gallic, *COO*
Sid M Rezvani, *Project Mgr*
Frank Marano, *CFO*
EMP: 14
SQ FT: 4,963
SALES (est): 3.7MM **Privately Held**
SIC: 3571 Electronic computers

(G-8818)
BARC USA INC
5 Delaware Dr Ste 2 (11042-1100)
PHONE..................516 719-1052
Joseph Jonckheere, *CEO*
Nele Langenaken, *Opers Staff*
Kay Philips, *Accountant*
Dirk Allaert, *Info Tech Dir*

Candice Cheung, *Associate*
EMP: 34
SQ FT: 17,500
SALES (est): 11.7MM
SALES (corp-wide): 121.8MM **Privately Held**
WEB: www.barclab.com
SIC: 2834 Pharmaceutical preparations
HQ: Bio Analytical Research Corporation Nv
Industriepark Zwijnaarde 3b
Gent 9052
932 923-26

(G-8819)
BILLANTI CASTING CO INC
Also Called: Billanti Jewelry Casting
299 S 11th St (11040-5558)
P.O. Box 1117 (11040-7117)
PHONE..................516 775-4800
Rosemarie Billanti, *Exec Officer*
John Billanti, *Vice Pres*
Prudence Billanti, *Treasurer*
Allora Doolittle, *Treasurer*
EMP: 30 EST: 1955
SALES (est): 4.3MM **Privately Held**
WEB: www.billanticasting.com
SIC: 3911 3339 Jewelry, precious metal; primary nonferrous metals

(G-8820)
CAMBRIDGE MANUFACTURING LLC
1700 Jericho Tpke (11040-4742)
PHONE..................516 326-1350
Linda Hofmann, *Controller*
Peter Negri,
EMP: 8
SALES (est): 1.1MM **Privately Held**
SIC: 3826 Laser scientific & engineering instruments

(G-8821)
CHEMICOLLOID LABORATORIES INC
55 Herricks Rd (11040-5340)
P.O. Box 251 (11040-0251)
PHONE..................516 747-2666
Fax: 516 747-4888
Geo Ryder, *President*
▲ **EMP:** 19 EST: 1920
SQ FT: 10,000
SALES (est): 3.2MM **Privately Held**
SIC: 3556 2099 Dairy & milk machinery; emulsifiers, food

(G-8822)
COLORS IN OPTICS LTD
Also Called: Ic Optics
120 Broadway G (11040-5301)
PHONE..................718 845-0300
Gabe Tusk, *Branch Mgr*
EMP: 100
SQ FT: 10,000
SALES (corp-wide): 8.4MM **Privately Held**
SIC: 3851 Eyeglasses, lenses & frames
PA: Colors In Optics, Ltd.
366 5th Ave Rm 804
New York NY
212 465-1200

(G-8823)
COMPUCOLOR ASSOCIATES INC
2200 Marcus Ave Ste C (11042-1043)
PHONE..................516 358-0000
Thomas Weitzmann, *President*
Sharon Nadel, *General Mgr*
Mark Rosner, *Corp Secy*
William Vitale, *Vice Pres*
Cindy Weitzman, *Accounting Mgr*
EMP: 45
SQ FT: 22,000
SALES (est): 6.1MM **Privately Held**
WEB: www.compucolor.com
SIC: 2752 Commercial printing, lithographic

(G-8824)
CORA MATERIALS CORP
Also Called: Cora Matrls
30 Nassau Terminal Rd (11040-4928)
PHONE..................516 488-6300
Robert Raths, *President*

Elissa Raths, *Admin Sec*
EMP: 10
SQ FT: 10,000
SALES (est): 1.5MM **Privately Held**
WEB: www.corarefining.com
SIC: 3341 Secondary nonferrous metals

(G-8825)
DESIGNATRONICS INCORPORATED (PA)
Also Called: Sdp/Si
2101 Jericho Tpke Ste 1 (11040-4702)
P.O. Box 5416 (11042-5416)
PHONE..................516 328-3300
Fax: 516 326-2784
Richard Kufner, *President*
Sue Anderson, *Exec VP*
Hitoshi Tanaka, *Senior VP*
Robert Lindemann, *Vice Pres*
Daniel Raleigh, *Vice Pres*
▲ **EMP:** 2
SQ FT: 40,000
SALES (est): 111.9MM **Privately Held**
WEB: www.designatronics.com
SIC: 3824 3559 3545 3625 Mechanical & electromechanical counters & devices; electronic component making machinery; cams (machine tool accessories); relays & industrial controls; iron & steel forgings

(G-8826)
DESIGNATRONICS INCORPORATED
Also Called: Stock Drive Products Div
55 Denton Ave S (11040-4976)
P.O. Box 5416 (11042-5416)
PHONE..................516 328-3300
Anthony Pagliughi, *Principal*
Robert Lindemann, *Vice Pres*
Billal Hossian, *Engineer*
Herb Arum, *Marketing Mgr*
Shawn Silver, *Data Proc Staff*
EMP: 296
SALES (corp-wide): 111.9MM **Privately Held**
WEB: www.designatronics.com
SIC: 3625 3621 3568 3566 Motor controls & accessories; motors & generators; power transmission equipment; speed changers, drives & gears; manufactured hardware (general); tire cord & fabrics
PA: Designatronics Incorporated
2101 Jericho Tpke Ste 1
New Hyde Park NY 11040
516 328-3300

(G-8827)
DISPLAY TECHNOLOGIES LLC (HQ)
1111 Marcus Ave (11042-1221)
PHONE..................718 321-3100
Fax: 718 939-4034
Marshall Goldberg, *President*
Jon Noce, *President*
Stephen Cress, *Vice Pres*
Bruce Gommermann, *Vice Pres*
Diogo Pereira, *Vice Pres*
▲ **EMP:** 75
SQ FT: 30,000
SALES: 76.1MM
SALES (corp-wide): 2.3B **Privately Held**
WEB: www.display-technologies.com
SIC: 2542 Fixtures: display, office or store: except wood
PA: Imi Plc
4060 Lakeside
Birmingham W MIDLANDS B37 7
121 717-3700

(G-8828)
DOREEN INTERIORS LTD
76 Nottingham Rd (11040-2214)
PHONE..................212 255-9008
Fax: 212 255-8946
Shalom Sharoni, *President*
Boaz Sharoni, *Vice Pres*
Yoav Sharoni, *Vice Pres*
Yona Sharoni, *Treasurer*
EMP: 24
SQ FT: 40,000
SALES (est): 1.9MM **Privately Held**
WEB: www.doreeninteriors.com
SIC: 2512 Upholstered household furniture

New Hyde Park - Nassau County (G-8829)

GEOGRAPHIC SECTION

(G-8829)
DYNASTY BELTS INC
161 Railroad Ave (11040-5016)
PHONE..................516 625-6280
Harbans Lal Chandihok, *President*
Rajinder K Chandihok, *Vice Pres*
EMP: 35
SQ FT: 8,000
SALES (est): 1.4MM **Privately Held**
SIC: 2387 5136 Apparel belts; apparel belts, men's & boys'

(G-8830)
EASTERN FINDING CORP
116 County Courthouse Rd (11040-5342)
PHONE..................516 747-6640
Fax: 516 629-4018
Paul Posner, *President*
Anthony Millaci, *Partner*
Sylvia Posner, *Treasurer*
▲ **EMP:** 10
SQ FT: 5,000
SALES (est): 1.3MM **Privately Held**
WEB: www.easternfindings.com
SIC: 3366 Brass foundry

(G-8831)
ELECTRIC SWTCHBARD SLTIONS LLC
270 Park Ave (11040-5318)
PHONE..................718 643-1105
Fax: 516 855-7017
Timothy Walsh, *Purch Agent*
George Katramados, *Controller*
Steve Levine, *Sales Staff*
Jerry Dicunzolo,
EMP: 8 **EST:** 2006
SQ FT: 25,000
SALES (est): 1.7MM **Privately Held**
SIC: 3613 Switchboards & parts, power

(G-8832)
ELI LILLY AND COMPANY
Also Called: Elanco Animal Health
1979 Marcus Ave (11042-1076)
PHONE..................516 622-2244
James Sweeny, *Manager*
EMP: 14
SALES (corp-wide): 19.9B **Publicly Held**
WEB: www.lilly.com
SIC: 2834 Pharmaceutical preparations
PA: Eli Lilly And Company
  Lilly Corporate Center
  Indianapolis IN 46285
  317 276-2000

(G-8833)
EON LABS INC (DH)
1999 Marcus Ave Ste 300 (11042-1020)
PHONE..................516 478-9700
Thomas Strungmann, *Ch of Bd*
Bernhard Hampl, *President*
Jefferey S Bauer, *Vice Pres*
Pranab Bhattacharyya, *Vice Pres*
Sadie Ciganek, *Vice Pres*
EMP: 19
SQ FT: 25,000
SALES (est): 27.6MM
SALES (corp-wide): 49.4B **Privately Held**
WEB: www.sandoz.com
SIC: 2834 Pharmaceutical preparations
HQ: Sandoz Inc.
  100 College Rd W
  Princeton NJ 08540
  609 627-8500

(G-8834)
FERGUSON ENTERPRISES INC
Also Called: Pollardwater
200 Atlantic Ave (11040-5057)
PHONE..................800 437-1146
Thomas Towler, *General Mgr*
Steven Hancey, *Manager*
EMP: 30
SALES (est): 1.2MM **Privately Held**
SIC: 3589 Sewage & water treatment equipment

(G-8835)
GENERAL FIBRE PRODUCTS CORP
170 Nassau Terminal Rd (11040-4940)
PHONE..................516 358-7500
Fax: 516 358-7503
Stuart Shrode, *CEO*
James Miller, *President*
Michael Petti, *Vice Pres*
Ruth Cartegena, *QC Mgr*
Irene Miller, *CFO*
▲ **EMP:** 70
SQ FT: 52,000
SALES (est): 20.3MM **Privately Held**
WEB: www.generalfibre.com
SIC: 2653 2671 2675 2679 Corrugated boxes, partitions, display items, sheets & pad; packaging paper & plastics film, coated & laminated; die-cut paper & board; corrugated paper: made from purchased material

(G-8836)
HAIN BLUEPRINT INC
1111 Marcus Ave Ste 100 (11042-2033)
PHONE..................212 414-5741
EMP: 29
SALES (est): 6.9MM
SALES (corp-wide): 2.6B **Publicly Held**
SIC: 2037 Fruit juices
PA: The Hain Celestial Group Inc
  1111 Marcus Ave Ste 100
  New Hyde Park NY 11042
  516 587-5000

(G-8837)
HAIN CELESTIAL GROUP INC (PA)
1111 Marcus Ave Ste 100 (11042-2033)
PHONE..................516 587-5000
Fax: 631 730-2550
Irwin D Simon, *Ch of Bd*
Matt Connolly, *Business Mgr*
James R Meiers, *COO*
Michael B McGuinness, *Senior VP*
Tom Arcuri, *Vice Pres*
◆ **EMP:** 130
SQ FT: 86,000
SALES: 2.6B **Publicly Held**
WEB: www.hain-celestial.com
SIC: 2023 2034 2096 2086 Dried & powdered milk & milk products; dried milk preparations; dietary supplements, dairy & non-dairy based; vegetable flour, meal & powder; potato chips & similar snacks; iced tea & fruit drinks, bottled & canned; toilet preparations

(G-8838)
HAL-HEN COMPANY INC
180 Atlantic Ave (11040-5028)
P.O. Box 6077, Astoria (11106-0077)
PHONE..................516 294-3200
Fax: 516 739-5248
Ronald Meltsner, *President*
Eric Spar, *Vice Pres*
Harold Spar, *Treasurer*
Joseph A Vespe, *Director*
Henry Meltsner, *Admin Sec*
▲ **EMP:** 50 **EST:** 1946
SQ FT: 20,000
SALES (est): 7.5MM **Privately Held**
WEB: www.halhen.com
SIC: 3842 Hearing aids

(G-8839)
HARBORS MAINE LOBSTER LLC
969 Lakeville Rd (11040-3008)
PHONE..................516 775-2400
Christian Limbereg,
Peter Cardone,
William Kienke,
EMP: 48 **EST:** 2015
SALES (est): 250K **Privately Held**
SIC: 2091 Seafood products: packaged in cans, jars, etc.

(G-8840)
HASCO COMPONETS
906 Jericho Tpke (11040-4604)
PHONE..................516 328-9292
Tom Marcus, *President*
Wayne Hauser, *Exec VP*
Mike Greenbaum, *Sales Staff*
Warren Pritzker, *Sales Executive*
Larry Ruben, *Sales Executive*
▲ **EMP:** 20
SALES (est): 11MM **Privately Held**
SIC: 3625 Relays, for electronic use

(G-8841)
HOPP COMPANIES INC
815 2nd Ave (11040-4869)
PHONE..................516 358-4170
Fax: 516 358-4178
Robert Hopp, *President*
Rose Fontana, *Manager*
EMP: 12
SQ FT: 5,000
SALES: 2MM **Privately Held**
WEB: www.hoppcompanies.com
SIC: 3578 3086 Point-of-sale devices; plastics foam products

(G-8842)
INTERNTNAL BUS CMMNCATIONS INC (PA)
Also Called: IBC/ Worldwide
1981 Marcus Ave Ste C105 (11042-2028)
PHONE..................516 352-4505
Fax: 516 352-3084
Norman Kay, *President*
Philip Schoonmaker, *Exec VP*
Mike Walker, *Opers Mgr*
▲ **EMP:** 29
SQ FT: 53,000
SALES (est): 27.8MM **Privately Held**
WEB: www.ibcshell.com
SIC: 3086 2679 Packaging & shipping materials, foamed plastic; pressed fiber & molded pulp products except food products

(G-8843)
JOSEPH STRUHL CO INC
Also Called: Super Moderna/Magic Master
195 Atlantic Ave (11040-5027)
PHONE..................516 741-3660
Fax: 516 742-3617
Clifford Struhl, *President*
Harriet Struhl, *Corp Secy*
Joseph Struhl, *Vice Pres*
EMP: 14
SQ FT: 13,000
SALES (est): 960K **Privately Held**
WEB: www.magicmaster.com
SIC: 3993 Displays & cutouts, window & lobby

(G-8844)
JSM VINYL PRODUCTS INC
44 Orchid Ln (11040-1918)
PHONE..................516 775-4520
Fax: 516 239-2879
EMP: 15
SQ FT: 26,000
SALES: 4MM **Privately Held**
SIC: 3089 Mfg Plastic Products

(G-8845)
LAFAYETTE MIRROR & GLASS CO
2300 Marcus Ave (11042-1058)
PHONE..................718 768-0660
Fax: 718 768-3047
Micheal Chuisano, *President*
Barbara Umbria, *Bookkeeper*
EMP: 7 **EST:** 1910
SQ FT: 7,000
SALES (est): 881.2K **Privately Held**
SIC: 3211 3231 1793 Plate glass, polished & rough; mirrored glass; glass & glazing work

(G-8846)
LIQUID MANAGEMENT PARTNERS LLC
1983 Marcus Ave Ste E138 (11042-2000)
PHONE..................516 775-5050
Nick Smith, *Marketing Mgr*
Michael H Lam,
▲ **EMP:** 11
SQ FT: 3,000
SALES (est): 1.1MM **Privately Held**
SIC: 2086 5182 Carbonated beverages, nonalcoholic: bottled & canned; wine & distilled beverages

(G-8847)
MARLOU GARMENTS INC
2115 Jericho Tpke (11040-4703)
P.O. Box 407, West Hempstead (11552-0407)
PHONE..................516 739-7100
Fax: 516 739-1991
Louis De Angelo, *Ch of Bd*
Rose De Angelo, *Admin Sec*
▲ **EMP:** 15 **EST:** 1952
SQ FT: 19,200
SALES (est): 1.4MM **Privately Held**
WEB: www.marlou.com
SIC: 2337 Uniforms, except athletic: women's, misses' & juniors'

(G-8848)
MASON CONTRACT PRODUCTS LLC
85 Denton Ave (11040-4002)
P.O. Box 609, Port Washington (11050-0609)
PHONE..................516 328-6900
Robert Kaye, *Controller*
Janet Vukan, *Manager*
Kevin Connors, *CTO*
Leonard Horowitz,
Lisa Horowitz,
▼ **EMP:** 80
SQ FT: 100,000
SALES (est): 6.6MM **Privately Held**
SIC: 2391 2211 Curtains & draperies; bedspreads, cotton

(G-8849)
NATURAL E CREATIVE LLC
Also Called: Be The Media
1110 Jericho Tpke (11040-4606)
PHONE..................516 488-1143
David Mathison,
Eric Mathison,
Peter Mathison,
EMP: 11
SALES (est): 75K **Privately Held**
WEB: www.bethemedia.com
SIC: 2731 Books: publishing & printing

(G-8850)
NEW YORK PACKAGING CORP
Also Called: Redi-Bag USA
135 Fulton Ave (11040-5305)
P.O. Box 1039 (11040-7039)
PHONE..................516 746-0600
Fax: 516 746-0661
Jeffrey Rabiea, *President*
▲ **EMP:** 90
SQ FT: 50,000
SALES: 25MM **Privately Held**
WEB: www.newyorkpackaging.com
SIC: 2673 Plastic bags: made from purchased materials

(G-8851)
NEW YORK RAVIOLI PASTA CO INC
12 Denton Ave S (11040-4904)
PHONE..................516 270-2852
David Creo, *President*
Paul Moncada, *Corp Secy*
Jeanne Gherity, *Sales Mgr*
Tricia Nacewicz, *Office Mgr*
EMP: 20
SQ FT: 20,000
SALES (est): 3.6MM **Privately Held**
WEB: www.nyravioli.com
SIC: 2099 5499 5149 Packaged combination products: pasta, rice & potato; gourmet food stores; pasta & rice

(G-8852)
NY 1 ART GALLERY INC
32 3rd St (11040-4438)
PHONE..................917 698-0626
Faisal Sheikh, *President*
EMP: 4
SALES (est): 1MM **Privately Held**
SIC: 2389 Men's miscellaneous accessories

(G-8853)
OCALA GROUP LLC
1981 Marcus Ave Ste 227 (11042-1055)
PHONE..................516 233-2750
Rohit Hathiramani, *Controller*
EMP: 15
SALES (est): 2.6MM **Privately Held**
SIC: 3841 3089 Surgical & medical instruments; plastic kitchenware, tableware & houseware

GEOGRAPHIC SECTION

(G-8854)
OVERNIGHT MOUNTINGS INC
1400 Plaza Ave (11040-4921)
PHONE..................516 865-3000
Morris Adwar, CEO
Jeffery Adwar, President
Matthew Roth, Vice Pres
EMP: 55
SQ FT: 550,000
SALES (est): 7.7MM Privately Held
WEB: www.overnightmountings.com
SIC: 3911 Jewelry, precious metal

(G-8855)
P J D PUBLICATIONS LTD
1315 Jericho Tpke (11040-4613)
P.O. Box 966, Westbury (11590-0966)
PHONE..................516 626-0650
Fax: 516 626-5546
Siva Sankar, CEO
Douglas Sankar, Vice Pres
Jason Sankar, Vice Pres
Barbara Kelly, Director
Priscilla Wong,
EMP: 5
SALES (est): 330K Privately Held
WEB: www.pjdonline.com
SIC: 2731 5045 Books: publishing only; computers, peripherals & software

(G-8856)
PERFECT GEAR & INSTRUMENT (HQ)
55 Denton Ave S (11040-4901)
PHONE..................516 328-3330
Morton Hoffman, President
Joseph Rubenfeld, Vice Pres
EMP: 10
SALES (est): 2.5MM
SALES (corp-wide): 111.9MM Privately Held
SIC: 3462 Gears, forged steel
PA: Designatronics Incorporated
2101 Jericho Tpke Ste 1
New Hyde Park NY 11040
516 328-3300

(G-8857)
QUALITY READY MIX INC
1824 Gilford Ave (11040-4031)
PHONE..................516 437-0100
Eugene Messina, President
Mario Messina, Manager
EMP: 15
SALES (est): 2.1MM Privately Held
SIC: 3273 Ready-mixed concrete

(G-8858)
QUANTUM LOGIC CORP
91 5th Ave (11040-5005)
PHONE..................516 746-1380
John Carbone, Ch of Bd
EMP: 9 EST: 2002
SALES (est): 1.1MM Privately Held
SIC: 3572 Computer storage devices

(G-8859)
RASA SERVICES INC
3366 Hillside Ave Ste 10 (11040-2730)
PHONE..................516 294-4292
Maria Nayyar, CEO
EMP: 6
SALES: 752.2K Privately Held
SIC: 3578 Calculating & accounting equipment

(G-8860)
SATCO CASTINGS SERVICE INC
Also Called: Plaza Braceltte Mounting
1400 Plaza Ave (11040-4921)
P.O. Box 1068 (11040-1068)
PHONE..................516 354-1500
Steven Feld, President
EMP: 45
SQ FT: 18,000
SALES (est): 7MM Privately Held
WEB: www.satcocasting.com
SIC: 3915 3911 Jewelers' castings; jewelry, precious metal

(G-8861)
SHELL CONTAINERS INC (NY)
1981 Marcus Ave Ste C105 (11042-2028)
PHONE..................516 352-4505
Norman Kay, President
Philip Schoonmaker, Vice Pres
▲ EMP: 20
SQ FT: 19,000
SALES (est): 3.2MM
SALES (corp-wide): 27.8MM Privately Held
WEB: www.shellcontainers.com
SIC: 3086 2679 Packaging & shipping materials, foamed plastic; building, insulating & packaging paperboard
PA: International Business Communications, Inc.
1981 Marcus Ave Ste C105
New Hyde Park NY 11042
516 352-4505

(G-8862)
SNOW CRAFT CO INC
200 Fulton Ave (11040-5306)
P.O. Box 829 (11040-0829)
PHONE..................516 739-1399
Fax: 516 739-1637
Kirk Guyton, President
Robert Farina, Vice Pres
William Hess, Admin Sec
EMP: 28 EST: 1954
SQ FT: 22,500
SALES (est): 4MM Privately Held
SIC: 3086 Packaging & shipping materials, foamed plastic

(G-8863)
SONOMED INC
Also Called: Sonomed Escalon
1979 Marcus Ave Ste C105 (11042-1002)
PHONE..................516 354-0900
Fax: 516 354-5902
Barry Durante, President
Ronald Hueneke, COO
John Rich, Vice Pres
Frances Shanker, Vice Pres
Judi Herman, Purch Agent
EMP: 30
SQ FT: 11,000
SALES (est): 6.1MM
SALES (corp-wide): 11.5MM Publicly Held
WEB: www.sonomedinc.com
SIC: 3845 3841 Electromedical equipment; ophthalmic instruments & apparatus
PA: Escalon Medical Corp.
435 Devon Park Dr Ste 100
Wayne PA 19087
610 688-6830

(G-8864)
SUNBORN SWISS WATCHES LLC
55 Dail St (11040-2434)
PHONE..................516 967-8836
Raj Patel,
Mamtaben Patel,
▲ EMP: 1
SALES (est): 3MM Privately Held
SIC: 3231 Watch crystals, glass

(G-8865)
TEXAS HOME SECURITY INC (PA)
Also Called: Medallion Security Door & Win
50 Rose Pl (11040-5312)
PHONE..................516 747-2100
Fax: 516 739-9862
Gregory E Falgoust, President
Brian S Falgoust, Vice Pres
Brian Flagoust, Financial Exec
EMP: 50
SALES (est): 6.5MM Privately Held
WEB: www.medalliondoors.com
SIC: 3442 1521 Storm doors or windows, metal; general remodeling, single-family houses

(G-8866)
THREE GEMS INC
Also Called: Sign-A-Rama
2201 Hillside Ave (11040-2714)
PHONE..................516 248-0388
Fax: 516 248-3978
Sal Italiano, President
Jane Italiano, Vice Pres
EMP: 5
SQ FT: 1,200
SALES (est): 692.5K Privately Held
WEB: www.threegems.com
SIC: 3993 Signs & advertising specialties

(G-8867)
U S ENERGY CONTROLS INC
Also Called: US Energy Group
270 Park Ave (11040-5318)
PHONE..................718 380-1004
Fax: 718 380-1432
Gerald Pindus, President
Matthew Rubenstein, President
David Unger, COO
Brian Klansky, Senior VP
Elie Jabbour, Vice Pres
EMP: 12
SQ FT: 10,000
SALES: 300K Privately Held
WEB: www.useci.com
SIC: 3822 Temperature controls, automatic

(G-8868)
ULTRA THIN READY TO BAKE PIZZA
Also Called: Ultra Thin Pzza Shlls Fltbrads
202 Atlantic Ave (11040-5000)
PHONE..................516 679-6655
Douglas Bronsky, Mng Member
Cherise Kramer,
EMP: 30
SQ FT: 15,000
SALES (est): 4.6MM Privately Held
SIC: 2099 Pizza, refrigerated: except frozen

(G-8869)
UNITED METAL INDUSTRIES INC
1008 3rd Ave (11040-5529)
PHONE..................516 354-6800
Fax: 516 354-6715
Richard M Meyers, President
Robert S Meyers, Vice Pres
▲ EMP: 8 EST: 1912
SQ FT: 8,000
SALES (est): 1.1MM Privately Held
WEB: www.unitedmetal.net
SIC: 3429 Clamps & couplings, hose

(G-8870)
UNITED STTES BRNZE SIGN OF FLA
811 2nd Ave (11040-4869)
PHONE..................516 352-5155
Fax: 516 352-1761
George Barbeosch, President
Alan Kasten, Vice Pres
Martha Lamberta, Office Mgr
EMP: 25 EST: 1927
SQ FT: 10,000
SALES (est): 2.7MM Privately Held
WEB: www.usbronze.com
SIC: 3993 3953 Signs & advertising specialties; marking devices

(G-8871)
UNIVERSAL READY MIX INC
197 Atlantic Ave (11040-5048)
PHONE..................516 746-4535
Fax: 516 746-4537
Guilio Viti, President
Anthony Logiudice, Vice Pres
Rocco Viti, Admin Sec
EMP: 5 EST: 1997
SALES (est): 877.9K Privately Held
WEB: www.universalreadymix.com
SIC: 2951 Asphalt paving mixtures & blocks

(G-8872)
WINE MARKET
2337 New Hyde Park Rd (11042-1212)
PHONE..................516 328-8800
Bina Gubda, Owner
EMP: 6
SALES (est): 434.3K Privately Held
SIC: 2084 Wines

New Paltz
Ulster County

(G-8873)
BRUYNSWICK SALES INC
14 Bruynswick Rd (12561-4106)
PHONE..................845 789-2049
Wayne Elliot, President
EMP: 12
SALES (est): 601.8K Privately Held
SIC: 3949 Lures, fishing: artificial

(G-8874)
CATSKILL MTN BREWING CO INC
Also Called: Gilded Otter Brewing
3 Main St (12561-1742)
P.O. Box 57 (12561-0057)
PHONE..................845 256-1700
Fax: 845 256-0955
Rick Rauch, President
EMP: 70
SQ FT: 10,000
SALES (est): 7.6MM Privately Held
WEB: www.gildedotter.com
SIC: 2082 5812 Beer (alcoholic beverage); eating places

(G-8875)
KEVCO INDUSTRIES
Also Called: Engineering Educational Eqp Co
6 Millbrook Rd (12561-1315)
PHONE..................845 255-7407
Peter C Bowers, Owner
Pete Bower, Manager
EMP: 7
SALES (est): 480K Privately Held
WEB: www.eeeco.com
SIC: 3999 Education aids, devices & supplies

(G-8876)
LYOPHILIZATION SYSTEMS INC
14 Hickory Hill Rd (12561-3104)
PHONE..................845 338-0456
Marc Thompson, President
Roger W Grange, Opers Mgr
EMP: 5
SQ FT: 6,000
SALES (est): 540K Privately Held
WEB: www.lyogroup.com
SIC: 3556 Food products machinery

(G-8877)
PDQ SHIPPING SERVICES
Also Called: PDQ Printing
8 New Paltz Plz 299 (12561-1616)
PHONE..................845 255-5500
Fax: 845 255-3202
Craig Shinkles, Owner
EMP: 8
SALES (est): 340K Privately Held
SIC: 2759 7331 Promotional printing; mailing service

(G-8878)
SMALL PACKAGES INC
6 Da Vinci Way (12561-2738)
PHONE..................845 255-7710
Greg Corvell, Principal
Greg Correll, Creative Dir
EMP: 5 EST: 1998
SALES (est): 374K Privately Held
SIC: 2631 Container, packaging & boxboard

(G-8879)
TOTAL WEBCASTING INC
8 Bruce St (12561-2101)
P.O. Box 665 (12561-0665)
PHONE..................845 883-0909
Robert Feldman, President
EMP: 6
SQ FT: 3,000
SALES: 700K Privately Held
SIC: 2741

(G-8880)
ULSTER COUNTY IRON WORKS LLC
64 N Putt Corners Rd (12561-3405)
PHONE..................845 255-0003

New Paltz - Ulster County (G-8881)

Steven Vasalka, *President*
EMP: 8
SQ FT: 5,000
SALES: 750K **Privately Held**
SIC: 3499 Metal household articles

(G-8881)
ULSTER PUBLISHING CO INC
Also Called: New Paltz Times
29 S Chestnut St Ste 101 (12561-1949)
PHONE.................................845 255-7005
Debbie Alexsa, *Principal*
Nan Wilson, *Manager*
EMP: 10
SALES (corp-wide): 3.6MM **Privately Held**
WEB: www.ulsterpublishing.com
SIC: 2711 Newspapers: publishing only, not printed on site
PA: Ulster Publishing Co Inc
    322 Wall St Fl 1
    Kingston NY 12401
    845 334-8205

(G-8882)
VIKING INDUSTRIES INC
89 S Ohioville Rd (12561-4012)
P.O. Box 249 (12561-0249)
PHONE.................................845 883-6325
Fax: 845 883-6228
Richard Croce, *President*
Michael Cozzolino, *Prdtn Mgr*
Mark Nowak, *Controller*
Sharon Wingfield, *Controller*
Cindy Brooks, *Finance*
EMP: 55
SQ FT: 50,000
SALES (est): 13.2MM **Privately Held**
WEB: www.vikingindustries.net
SIC: 2657 Folding paperboard boxes

New Rochelle
Westchester County

(G-8883)
A & T IRON WORKS INC
25 Cliff St (10801-6803)
PHONE.................................914 632-8992
Fax: 914 632-2645
Gessie Tassone, *President*
▲ **EMP:** 28
SQ FT: 20,000
SALES (est): 5MM **Privately Held**
WEB: www.atironworks.com
SIC: 3446 5211 3441 Architectural metalwork; fencing; fabricated structural metal

(G-8884)
ABSOLUTE COATINGS INC
38 Portman Rd (10801-2103)
PHONE.................................914 636-0700
EMP: 35
SQ FT: 40,000
SALES (est): 1.3MM
SALES (corp-wide): 62.6MM **Privately Held**
SIC: 2851 Polyurethane coatings
PA: Valentus Specialty Chemicals, Inc.
    500 Griswold St Ste 2700
    Detroit MI 48226
    313 962-5800

(G-8885)
ALICIAS BAKERY INC
498 Main St Ste A (10801-6326)
PHONE.................................914 235-4689
Alicia Zapien, *President*
EMP: 5
SALES (est): 381.1K **Privately Held**
SIC: 2051 Doughnuts, except frozen

(G-8886)
ALLIED CONVERTERS INC
64 Drake Ave (10805-1598)
P.O. Box 548 (10802-0548)
PHONE.................................914 235-1585
Fax: 914 235-7123
Richard E Ellenbogen, *President*
Wilma J Ellenbogen, *Corp Secy*
♦ **EMP:** 30 **EST:** 1954
SQ FT: 50,000
SALES (est): 6.1MM **Privately Held**
WEB: www.garb-o-liner.com
SIC: 2673 2671 2679 Plastic bags: made from purchased materials; plastic film, coated or laminated for packaging; paperboard products, converted

(G-8887)
BAKERS PRIDE OVEN CO INC
145 Huguenot St Ste Mz1 (10801-6997)
PHONE.................................914 576-0200
Fax: 914 576-0605
Hylton Jones, *CEO*
Howard Kraines, *Vice Pres*
Brian Rosenbloom, *Vice Pres*
Don Wall, *CFO*
Lawrence Rosenbloom, *Admin Sec*
EMP: 150 **EST:** 1995
SQ FT: 120,000
SALES (est): 25.2MM
SALES (corp-wide): 751.5MM **Publicly Held**
WEB: www.associatedamericanindustries.com
SIC: 3589 3631 3556 Commercial cooking & foodwarming equipment; cooking equipment, commercial; household cooking equipment; food products machinery
HQ: Associated American Industries, Inc.
    1307 N Watters Rd
    Allen TX 75013

(G-8888)
BENCHMARK EDUCATION CO LLC (PA)
145 Huguenot St Fl 8 (10801-5233)
PHONE.................................914 637-7200
Fax: 914 738-5063
Carrie Smith, *Vice Pres*
Margie Burton, *Regl Sales Mgr*
Randi Machado, *Mktg Dir*
Daniel Z Liu, *Marketing Staff*
Sha LI, *Marketing Staff*
▲ **EMP:** 75
SALES (est): 21.1MM **Privately Held**
WEB: www.benchmarkeducation.com
SIC: 2731 Book publishing

(G-8889)
BREAD FACTORY LLC
30 Grove Ave (10801-6207)
PHONE.................................914 637-8150
Fax: 914 637-9516
Jean Yves Lebris, *Partner*
Anthony Orza, *Partner*
EMP: 24 **EST:** 2000
SQ FT: 10,000
SALES (est): 1.4MM **Privately Held**
SIC: 2051 Bread, cake & related products

(G-8890)
BRIDGE RECORDS INC
200 Clinton Ave (10801-1525)
PHONE.................................914 654-9270
Fax: 516 773-3397
David Starobin, *President*
Rob Robles, *Editor*
Doron Schachter, *Editor*
Becky Starobin, *Vice Pres*
Charlie Post, *Prdtn Mgr*
EMP: 5
SQ FT: 2,000
SALES (est): 729.4K **Privately Held**
SIC: 3652 Master records or tapes, preparation of

(G-8891)
CASTEK INC (HQ)
20 Jones St (10801-6000)
PHONE.................................914 636-1000
Arthur M Dinitz, *President*
Mike Stento, *Vice Pres*
Robert Welsh, *CFO*
Robert J Welsh, *Treasurer*
▲ **EMP:** 3
SQ FT: 42,000
SALES (est): 2.8MM
SALES (corp-wide): 6.4MM **Privately Held**
WEB: www.castek.net
SIC: 3272 Concrete products, precast
PA: Transpo Industries, Inc.
    20 Jones St Ste 3
    New Rochelle NY 10801
    914 636-1000

(G-8892)
CERAMICA VARM (PA)
Also Called: Ceramica V. A. R. M.
479 5th Ave (10801-2212)
PHONE.................................914 381-6215
Fax: 914 381-3785
EMP: 9
SQ FT: 4,000
SALES: 7.5MM **Privately Held**
SIC: 3263 Mfg Of Ceramic Earthenware-Italy

(G-8893)
CUFFS PLANNING & MODELS LTD
317 Beechmont Dr (10804-4601)
PHONE.................................914 632-1883
David K Combs, *President*
David Combs, *President*
Sandra Kirkendall, *Vice Pres*
EMP: 8
SALES (est): 519.2K **Privately Held**
WEB: www.cuffs88.com
SIC: 7372 Prepackaged software

(G-8894)
DERAFFELE MFG CO INC
2525 Palmer Ave Ste 4 (10801-4476)
PHONE.................................914 636-6850
Fax: 914 636-6596
Philip De Raffele Jr, *President*
Philip Deraffele, *Vice Pres*
Stephen De Raffele, *Treasurer*
Joseph De Raffele, *Admin Sec*
EMP: 25 **EST:** 1933
SQ FT: 30,000
SALES (est): 5.7MM **Privately Held**
SIC: 3448 Prefabricated metal buildings

(G-8895)
DISPLAY PRODUCERS INC
40 Winding Brook Rd (10804-2008)
PHONE.................................718 904-1200
Fax: 718 904-9843
Joseph A Laurite, *President*
Arthur E Landi, *President*
Richard Tevere, *Corp Secy*
Michael Marsigliano, *Administration*
▲ **EMP:** 250
SQ FT: 150,000
SALES (est): 30.9MM **Privately Held**
WEB: www.displayproducersinc.com
SIC: 3993 Signs & advertising specialties

(G-8896)
EMERGENCY BEACON CORP
15 River St (10801-4354)
PHONE.................................914 576-2700
Joan Goodman, *President*
Mary Leonetti, *Vice Pres*
George Ramos, *Vice Pres*
Patricia Wyllie, *Vice Pres*
Judith Weber, *VP Mfg*
EMP: 15
SQ FT: 12,000
SALES: 1MM **Privately Held**
WEB: www.emergencybeaconcorp.com
SIC: 3812 Search & navigation equipment

(G-8897)
ENTERPRISE TECH GROUP INC
15 Irving Pl (10801-1511)
PHONE.................................914 588-0327
Liza Zaneri, *President*
EMP: 12
SALES (est): 950K **Privately Held**
SIC: 7372 Prepackaged software

(G-8898)
ERIC S TURNER & COMPANY INC
Also Called: Turner Plating
3335 Centre Ave (10801)
PHONE.................................914 235-7114
Fax: 914 235-7196
Kenneth Turner, *President*
William Vernon Turner, *Vice Pres*
Angelique Murphy, *Bookkeeper*
EMP: 12 **EST:** 1931
SQ FT: 10,000
SALES: 900K **Privately Held**
WEB: www.turnerplating.com
SIC: 3471 2851 Electroplating of metals or formed products; finishing, metals or formed products; polishing, metals or formed products; paints & allied products

(G-8899)
FLYNN BURNER CORPORATION
425 Fifth Ave (10801-2203)
P.O. Box 431 (10802-0431)
PHONE.................................914 636-1320
Fax: 914 636-3751
Julian Modzeleski, *CEO*
Edward Flynn, *Ch of Bd*
Dom Medina, *President*
♦ **EMP:** 50 **EST:** 1946
SQ FT: 25,000
SALES (est): 8.8MM **Privately Held**
WEB: www.flynnburner.com
SIC: 3433 Gas burners, industrial; oil burners, domestic or industrial

(G-8900)
FORMCRAFT DISPLAY PRODUCTS
42 Beverly Rd (10804-1703)
PHONE.................................914 632-1410
George Bartoli, *President*
Joanne Bartoli, *Vice Pres*
EMP: 5
SQ FT: 5,000
SALES (est): 330K **Privately Held**
SIC: 3229 Christmas tree ornaments, from glass produced on-site

(G-8901)
FORREST ENGRAVING CO INC
Also Called: Forrest Engravg
92 1st St (10801-6121)
P.O. Box 1240, Carmel (10512-8240)
PHONE.................................845 228-0200
Fax: 914 632-7416
Tom Giordano, *President*
EMP: 11
SQ FT: 3,000
SALES (est): 800K **Privately Held**
SIC: 3993 Signs & advertising specialties

(G-8902)
FRADAN MANUFACTURING CORP
499 5th Ave (10801-2212)
PHONE.................................914 632-3653
Frank De Bartolo, *President*
Karen Molia, *Office Mgr*
EMP: 15
SQ FT: 12,000
SALES (est): 2MM **Privately Held**
SIC: 3524 Lawn & garden equipment

(G-8903)
GANNETT CO INC
Also Called: Bronxville Review
92 North Ave (10801-7413)
PHONE.................................914 278-9315
Jerry McKinstry, *Principal*
EMP: 20
SALES (corp-wide): 5.7B **Publicly Held**
WEB: www.gannett.com
SIC: 2711 Newspapers
PA: Gannett Co., Inc.
    7950 Jones Branch Dr
    Mc Lean VA 22102
    703 854-6000

(G-8904)
GARB-O-LINER INC
64 Drake Ave (10805-1598)
P.O. Box 548 (10802-0548)
PHONE.................................914 235-1585
Richard Ellenbogen, *President*
Richard E Ellenbogen, *President*
Wilma Ellenbogen, *Treasurer*
EMP: 7 **EST:** 1986
SALES: 1MM **Privately Held**
SIC: 2673 5113 Trash bags (plastic film): made from purchased materials; bags, paper & disposable plastic

(G-8905)
GEN PUBLISHING INC
Also Called: Genetic Engineering News
140 Huguenot St Fl 3 (10801-5215)
PHONE.................................914 834-3880
Fax: 914 740-2201

Mary Ann Liebert, *President*
Querida Anderson, *Editor*
Harriet Matysko, *Senior VP*
Sharon Spitz, *Sales Mgr*
Luc Selig, *Sales Staff*
EMP: 99
SALES: 950K **Privately Held**
WEB: www.genengnews.com
SIC: 2741 Miscellaneous publishing

(G-8906)
HAGEDORN COMMUNICATIONS INC (PA)
Also Called: Co-Op City News
662 Main St Ste 1 (10801-7145)
P.O. Box 680 (10802-0680)
PHONE.................................914 636-7400
Fax: 914 636-2957
Christopher Hagedorn, *President*
Monique Tolbert, *Accounts Exec*
Al Zezula, *Advt Staff*
▲ **EMP:** 70
SQ FT: 20,000
SALES (est): 10.9MM **Privately Held**
WEB: www.rew-online.com
SIC: 2711 Newspapers

(G-8907)
HAITIAN TIMES INC
80 Lakeside Dr (10801-3130)
PHONE.................................718 230-8700
Garry P Pierre, *President*
Muriel Fenton, *Manager*
Darlie Gervais, *Manager*
EMP: 5 **EST:** 1998
SQ FT: 1,200
SALES (est): 300K **Privately Held**
WEB: www.haitiantimes.com
SIC: 2711 Newspapers

(G-8908)
HALPERN TOOL CORP (PA)
Also Called: Vernon Devices
111 Plain Ave (10801-2206)
PHONE.................................914 633-0038
Fax: 914 633-0059
David Newmark, *President*
Marlene Werner, *Vice Pres*
EMP: 5
SQ FT: 12,500
SALES: 500K **Privately Held**
SIC: 3541 5084 Machine tools, metal cutting type; industrial machinery & equipment

(G-8909)
HARBOR ELC FABRICATION TLS INC
Also Called: Hefti
29 Portman Rd (10801-2104)
PHONE.................................914 636-4400
Jerry Schiff, *President*
Bill Froehlich, *General Mgr*
Anna Campone, *Manager*
EMP: 25
SALES (est): 5.3MM **Privately Held**
SIC: 3444 Metal housings, enclosures, casings & other containers

(G-8910)
HB ATHLETIC INC (PA)
Also Called: Globe-Tex
56 Harrison St Fl 4 (10801-6517)
PHONE.................................914 560-8422
Robert Hurvitz, *Ch of Bd*
Stuart Hurvitz, *President*
▲ **EMP:** 15
SQ FT: 4,500
SALES (est): 1.9MM **Privately Held**
SIC: 2339 2389 Athletic clothing: women's, misses' & juniors'; uniforms, athletic: women's, misses' & juniors'; women's & misses' athletic clothing & sportswear; disposable garments & accessories

(G-8911)
HIGHLANDER REALTY INC
Also Called: Seaboard Electronics
70 Church St (10805-3204)
PHONE.................................914 235-8073
Fax: 914 235-8369
Jerrold Hacker, *President*
Subhas Grandhi, *Vice Pres*
Dorothy Hacker, *Treasurer*
Amy Gibson, *Bookkeeper*
EMP: 35
SQ FT: 15,000
SALES (est): 3.9MM **Privately Held**
WEB: www.highlanderrealty.com
SIC: 3699 Security devices

(G-8912)
HOMEGROWN FOR GOOD LLC
29 Beechwood Ave (10801-6818)
PHONE.................................857 540-6361
Timothy Gibb, *CEO*
Thomas Gibb,
EMP: 10
SALES (est): 1.4MM **Privately Held**
SIC: 3021 Rubber & plastics footwear

(G-8913)
IVY CLASSIC INDUSTRIES INC
40 Plain Ave (10801-2205)
PHONE.................................914 632-8200
Anthony Schwartz, *President*
Greg Schwartz, *Vice Pres*
Justin Schwartz, *Vice Pres*
Stanley Schwartz, *Treasurer*
◆ **EMP:** 30
SQ FT: 30,000
SALES (est): 4.7MM **Privately Held**
SIC: 3423 3546 3547 Hand & edge tools; power-driven handtools; rolling mill machinery

(G-8914)
J P INSTALLATIONS WAREHOUSE
29 Portman Rd (10801-2104)
PHONE.................................914 576-3188
Fax: 914 576-3183
John Pompi, *President*
EMP: 10
SALES (est): 1.1MM **Privately Held**
SIC: 2599 Factory furniture & fixtures

(G-8915)
JOHNS RAVIOLI COMPANY INC
15 Drake Ave (10805-1506)
PHONE.................................914 576-7030
Robert Guarnero, *President*
Lee Key, *Bookkeeper*
▲ **EMP:** 15
SQ FT: 8,800
SALES (est): 2.4MM **Privately Held**
SIC: 2099 5499 Pasta, uncooked: packaged with other ingredients; gourmet food stores

(G-8916)
KORING BROS INC
30 Pine St (10801-6906)
PHONE.................................888 233-1292
EMP: 4
SQ FT: 5,000
SALES: 2MM **Privately Held**
SIC: 2399 Mfg Fabricated Textile Products

(G-8917)
MARY ANN LIEBERT INC
140 Huguenot St Fl 3 (10801-5215)
PHONE.................................914 740-2100
Mary Ann Liebert, *President*
Gerry Williams, *Partner*
Philip Barie, *Editor*
Vicki Cohn, *Editor*
Wendy Cuba, *Editor*
EMP: 70
SQ FT: 4,500
SALES (est): 12.8MM **Privately Held**
WEB: www.mmsionline.com
SIC: 2721 2731 2741 Trade journals: publishing only, not printed on site; books: publishing only; miscellaneous publishing

(G-8918)
ORTHO RITE INC
65 Plain Ave (10801-2206)
PHONE.................................914 235-9100
Fax: 914 235-9697
Gregory Sands, *President*
EMP: 28
SQ FT: 4,000
SALES (est): 3.2MM **Privately Held**
WEB: www.ortho-rite.com
SIC: 3842 Suspensories

(G-8919)
PAINT OVER RUST PRODUCTS INC
Also Called: Last N Last
38 Portman Rd (10801-2103)
PHONE.................................914 636-0700
Fax: 914 636-0822
David Sherman, *CEO*
Jeff Kay, *Controller*
Andres Rivera, *Manager*
◆ **EMP:** 35 **EST:** 1923
SQ FT: 40,000
SALES (est): 14.6MM **Privately Held**
WEB: www.absolutecoatings.com
SIC: 2851 Polyurethane coatings; varnishes

(G-8920)
PLASTIC WORKS
26 Garden St (10801-4204)
P.O. Box 51, Crompond (10517-0051)
PHONE.................................914 576-2050
Fax: 914 576-2628
David J Jeskie, *Owner*
EMP: 8 **EST:** 1978
SALES: 800K **Privately Held**
SIC: 3089 Plastic processing

(G-8921)
PREMCO INC
11 Beechwood Ave (10801-6818)
P.O. Box 266 (10802-0266)
PHONE.................................914 636-7095
Harold Jacobs, *Ch of Bd*
EMP: 18
SQ FT: 22,000
SALES (est): 3.9MM **Privately Held**
SIC: 3621 7694 Motors & generators; motor repair services

(G-8922)
RAM TRANSFORMER TECHNOLOGIES
11 Beechwood Ave (10801-6818)
P.O. Box 266 (10802-0266)
PHONE.................................914 632-3988
Fax: 914 632-3931
Harold Jacobs, *President*
Lisa Ren, *Manager*
EMP: 10
SQ FT: 7,600
SALES (est): 990K **Privately Held**
SIC: 3612 Transformers, except electric

(G-8923)
REINO MANUFACTURING CO INC
34 Circuit Rd (10805-1930)
PHONE.................................914 636-8990
Fax: 914 636-0572
Florence Reino, *President*
Linda Reino, *Corp Secy*
EMP: 10 **EST:** 1945
SALES (est): 615.9K **Privately Held**
SIC: 3961 Costume jewelry

(G-8924)
REPUBLIC CONSTRUCTION CO INC
305 North Ave (10801-4169)
PHONE.................................914 235-3654
Joeseph Pogostin, *President*
EMP: 6 **EST:** 1985
SALES (est): 513.2K **Privately Held**
SIC: 1442 Construction sand & gravel

(G-8925)
TOWSE PUBLISHING CO
Also Called: Furniture World
1333a North Ave (10804-2120)
PHONE.................................914 235-3095
Fax: 914 235-3278
Russell Bienenstock, *President*
Gary Siegel, *Sales Dir*
Gifford Dorival, *Manager*
Barbara Bienenstock, *Director*
EMP: 11
SALES: 1MM **Privately Held**
WEB: www.furnitureworldmagazine.com
SIC: 2721 Magazines: publishing & printing

(G-8926)
TRANSPO INDUSTRIES INC (PA)
20 Jones St Ste 3 (10801-6098)
PHONE.................................914 636-1000
Fax: 914 636-1282
Arthur M Dinitz, *Ch of Bd*
Michael S Stenko, *President*
Janice Fernandez, *General Mgr*
Joan Cornell, *Vice Pres*
Robert Welsh, *Vice Pres*
▲ **EMP:** 38
SQ FT: 33,000
SALES (est): 6.4MM **Privately Held**
WEB: www.transpo.com
SIC: 3089 3272 2821 Plastic hardware & building products; hardware, plastic; concrete products, precast; plastics materials & resins

(G-8927)
VIC-GINA PRINTING COMPANY INC
Also Called: Adrean Printing
1299 North Ave (10804-2642)
PHONE.................................914 636-0200
Victor Diede, *President*
Louise Diede, *Admin Sec*
EMP: 5
SQ FT: 2,500
SALES (est): 619K **Privately Held**
SIC: 2752 Commercial printing, lithographic

New Windsor
Orange County

(G-8928)
24 SEVEN ENTERPRISES INC
1073 State Route 94 Ste 9 (12553-6822)
PHONE.................................845 563-9033
EMP: 9
SALES (est): 1.4MM **Privately Held**
SIC: 3086 Packaging & shipping materials, foamed plastic

(G-8929)
A & R CONCRETE PRODUCTS LLC
7 Ruscitti Rd (12553-6205)
PHONE.................................845 562-0640
Fax: 845 562-1518
Jay Nannini, *President*
Kim Post, *Financial Exec*
Phil Segali, *Sales Staff*
EMP: 25 **EST:** 2013
SALES (est): 1.6MM **Privately Held**
SIC: 3272 Concrete products

(G-8930)
AIGNER LABEL HOLDER CORP
Also Called: Aigner Index,
218 Mac Arthur Ave (12553-7011)
PHONE.................................845 562-4510
Mark Aigner, *President*
Lisa Arestin, *Accounts Mgr*
Lisa Cirig, *Sales Staff*
▲ **EMP:** 11 **EST:** 1930
SALES (est): 2.5MM **Privately Held**
WEB: www.aignerindex.com
SIC: 2679 Paper products, converted

(G-8931)
AMERICAN FELT & FILTER CO INC
Also Called: Affco
361 Walsh Ave (12553-6727)
PHONE.................................845 561-3560
Fax: 845 561-0967
Wilson H Pryne, *Ch of Bd*
Scott H Pryne, *Vice Pres*
▲ **EMP:** 60
SQ FT: 230,000
SALES (est): 25.6MM **Privately Held**
WEB: www.affco.com
SIC: 3569 Filters, general line: industrial

(G-8932)
BELSITO COMMUNICATIONS INC
Also Called: 1st Responder Newspaper
1 Ardmore St (12553-8303)
PHONE.................................845 534-9700
Fax: 845 561-5059
Joseph P Belsito, *President*
Cathy Burak, *General Mgr*
Jim Stankiewicz, *General Mgr*

New Windsor - Orange County (G-8933) — GEOGRAPHIC SECTION

John Rath, *Senior VP*
Anthony Mairo, *Marketing Staff*
EMP: 12 **EST:** 1997
SQ FT: 2,000
SALES (est): 1MM **Privately Held**
SIC: 2711 7374 Newspapers: publishing only, not printed on site; computer graphics service

(G-8933)
BLEND SMOOTHIE BAR
25 Creamery Dr (12553-8011)
PHONE 845 568-7366
EMP: 5
SALES (est): 324.5K **Privately Held**
SIC: 2037 Frozen fruits & vegetables

(G-8934)
CENTER LINE STUDIOS INC (PA)
112 Forge Hill Rd (12553-8061)
PHONE 845 534-7143
Roger Gray, *President*
Anthony Gleason, *Project Mgr*
Prokosch Poni, *Human Resources*
Alexis Gray, *Sales Mgr*
Jennifer Migdal, *Mktg Dir*
▲ **EMP:** 15
SQ FT: 30,000
SALES (est): 1.6MM **Privately Held**
WEB: www.centerlinestudios.com
SIC: 3999 Theatrical scenery

(G-8935)
CLASSIC TOOL DESIGN INC
31 Walnut St (12553-7021)
PHONE 845 562-8700
Fax: 845 562-8596
Ralph Edwards, *President*
Marge Edwards, *Vice Pres*
EMP: 20
SQ FT: 22,000
SALES (est): 1.2MM **Privately Held**
WEB: www.ctd4ac.com
SIC: 3423 Mechanics' hand tools

(G-8936)
COCA-COLA BTLG CO OF NY INC
10 Heampstead Rd (12553-5501)
PHONE 845 562-3037
Fax: 845 568-6335
John Lacey, *Manager*
Lennie Erlanger, *Manager*
James Romano, *Manager*
EMP: 15
SQ FT: 15,000
SALES (corp-wide): 44.2B **Publicly Held**
SIC: 2086 Bottled & canned soft drinks
HQ: The Coca-Cola Bottling Company Of New York Inc
2500 Windy Ridge Pkwy Se
Atlanta GA 30339
770 989-2000

(G-8937)
E W SMITH PUBLISHING CO
Also Called: Sentinel, The
36 Meriline Ave (12553-6520)
P.O. Box 406, Vails Gate (12584-0406)
PHONE 845 562-1218
Everett W Smith, *President*
Michael Smith, *Vice Pres*
Steven Smith, *Vice Pres*
EMP: 11
SALES (est): 804.8K **Privately Held**
WEB: www.ewsmithpublishing.com
SIC: 2711 2752 Commercial printing & newspaper publishing combined; commercial printing, lithographic

(G-8938)
GAMMA PRODUCTS INC
Also Called: A & J Washroom Accessories
509 Temple Hill Rd (12553-5532)
P.O. Box 4569 (12553-0569)
PHONE 845 562-3332
Fax: 845 562-3391
Anthony Granuzzo, *Ch of Bd*
Richard Rebusmen, *President*
Donna G Frenz, *Sr Corp Ofcr*
Jayne F Granuzzo, *Exec VP*
Horacio Sousa, *Plant Mgr*
EMP: 70
SQ FT: 50,000
SALES (est): 12.2MM **Privately Held**
WEB: www.ajwashroom.com
SIC: 3261 Bathroom accessories/fittings, vitreous china or earthenware

(G-8939)
HI-TECH PACKG WORLD-WIDE LLC
110 Corporate Dr (12553-6952)
P.O. Box 4232 (12553-0232)
PHONE 845 947-1912
Robert Trimble, *Owner*
EMP: 2
SQ FT: 10,000
SALES (est): 1.1MM **Privately Held**
SIC: 2759 Commercial printing

(G-8940)
JUST WOOD PALLETS INC
78 Vails Gate Heights Dr (12553-8514)
PHONE 718 644-7013
Carlos Garcia, *Principal*
EMP: 8
SALES (est): 1MM **Privately Held**
SIC: 2448 Pallets, wood & wood with metal

(G-8941)
LARCENT ENTERPRISES INC
Also Called: Angie Washroom
509 Temple Hill Rd (12553-5532)
P.O. Box 4569 (12553-0569)
PHONE 845 562-3332
Anthony J Granuzzo, *Ch of Bd*
▲ **EMP:** 50
SALES (est): 6.4MM **Privately Held**
SIC: 3261 Bathroom accessories/fittings, vitreous china or earthenware

(G-8942)
LSI LIGHTRON INC
500 Hudson Valley Ave (12553-4744)
P.O. Box 4270 (12553-0270)
PHONE 845 562-5500
Fax: 845 562-3082
Gene Littman, *CEO*
Barry White, *President*
▲ **EMP:** 1000
SQ FT: 170,000
SALES (est): 189.3MM
SALES (corp-wide): 322.2MM **Publicly Held**
WEB: www.lsilightron.com
SIC: 3646 5063 Commercial indusl & institutional electric lighting fixtures; electrical apparatus & equipment
PA: Lsi Industries Inc.
10000 Alliance Rd
Blue Ash OH 45242
513 793-3200

(G-8943)
METAL CONTAINER CORPORATION
1000 Breunig Rd (12553-8438)
PHONE 845 567-1500
Fax: 845 567-1522
Russell Lindberg, *Plant Mgr*
Gregg Giaquinto, *QC Dir*
John Voda, *Engineer*
George Ignarra, *Human Res Mgr*
Mark Stafford, *Branch Mgr*
EMP: 200
SALES (corp-wide): 1B **Privately Held**
SIC: 3411 Metal cans
HQ: Metal Container Corporation
3636 S Geyer Rd Ste 400
Saint Louis MO 63127
314 577-2000

(G-8944)
NEW WINDSOR WASTE WATER PLANT
145 Caesars Ln (12553-7742)
P.O. Box 4653 (12553-0653)
PHONE 845 561-2550
Fax: 845 565-0626
John Egitto, *Manager*
EMP: 10
SALES (est): 865.3K **Privately Held**
SIC: 3589 Water treatment equipment, industrial

(G-8945)
NEWBURGH DISTRIBUTION CORP (PA)
463 Temple Hill Rd (12553-5527)
PHONE 845 561-6330
Fax: 845 561-8308
Donald Harkness, *President*
Sharon Harkness, *Vice Pres*
Mary Kratchwil, *Personnel Exec*
▲ **EMP:** 3
SALES (est): 47.6MM **Privately Held**
WEB: www.baricosmetics.com
SIC: 2844 Cosmetic preparations

(G-8946)
NEWLINE PRODUCTS INC (PA)
509 Temple Hill Rd (12553-5532)
PHONE 972 881-3318
Kevin Wang, *CEO*
Chris Bradford, *President*
William Bowers, *CFO*
▲ **EMP:** 20
SQ FT: 30,000
SALES (est): 13MM **Privately Held**
WEB: www.newlineproduct.com
SIC: 3993 Displays & cutouts, window & lobby

(G-8947)
PATTERSON MATERIALS CORP
322 Walsh Ave (12553-6748)
P.O. Box 800, Wingdale (12594-0800)
PHONE 845 832-6000
Fax: 845 832-6724
John Peckham, *Manager*
EMP: 20
SQ FT: 6,171
SALES (corp-wide): 192MM **Privately Held**
SIC: 1422 Crushed & broken limestone
HQ: Patterson Materials Corp
20 Haarlem Ave
White Plains NY 10603
914 949-2000

(G-8948)
PRODUCTION RESOURCE GROUP LLC
539 Temple Hill Rd (12553-5533)
PHONE 845 567-5700
Jerry Harris, *President*
Brian Edwards, *General Mgr*
David James, *General Mgr*
Kevin McKnight, *General Mgr*
Arthur Smith, *General Mgr*
EMP: 50 **Privately Held**
SIC: 3999 7922 Theatrical scenery; equipment rental, theatrical
PA: Production Resource Group Llc
200 Business Park Dr # 109
Armonk NY 10504

(G-8949)
PVH CORP
Also Called: Van Heusen
1073 State Route 94 (12553-6821)
PHONE 845 561-0233
Lenore Dunn, *Branch Mgr*
EMP: 9
SALES (corp-wide): 8B **Publicly Held**
SIC: 2321 Men's & boys' dress shirts
PA: Pvh Corp.
200 Madison Ave Bsmt 1
New York NY 10016
212 381-3500

(G-8950)
REGE INC
110 Corporate Dr (12553-6952)
P.O. Box 4417 (12553-0417)
PHONE 845 565-7772
Fax: 845 565-9452
Cheskel Smilowitz, *CEO*
Ramon Echevarria, *President*
▲ **EMP:** 18
SQ FT: 30,000
SALES (est): 5.3MM **Privately Held**
WEB: www.polyworksinc.com
SIC: 2673 Plastic bags: made from purchased materials

(G-8951)
S M FRANK & COMPANY INC
Also Called: Medico
1073 State Route 94 Ste 7 (12553-6822)
PHONE 914 739-3100
Fax: 914 739-3105
William F Feuerbach Jr, *President*
Lois Kessler, *Manager*
▲ **EMP:** 8 **EST:** 1924
SQ FT: 15,000
SALES (est): 1MM **Privately Held**
WEB: www.smfrankcoinc.com
SIC: 3999 Tobacco pipes, pipestems & bits; cigarette filters; cigar & cigarette holders

(G-8952)
SALKO KITCHENS INC
256 Walsh Ave (12553-5752)
PHONE 845 565-4420
Fax: 845 565-4742
Aron Sandel, *President*
▲ **EMP:** 19
SALES (est): 1.5MM **Privately Held**
WEB: www.salkokitchens.com
SIC: 2434 Wood kitchen cabinets

(G-8953)
SCREEN GEMS INC
41 Windsor Hwy (12553-6225)
PHONE 845 561-0036
Carl Friedwall, *President*
EMP: 5
SQ FT: 3,600
SALES (est): 752.7K **Privately Held**
WEB: www.screengemsny.com
SIC: 2262 2395 Screen printing: man-made fiber & silk broadwoven fabrics; embroidery & art needlework

(G-8954)
SENTINEL PRINTING SERVICES INC
Also Called: Smith, E W Publishing
36 Meriline Ave (12553-6520)
P.O. Box 406, Vails Gate (12584-0406)
PHONE 845 562-1218
Fax: 845 562-0488
Everett Smith, *President*
Michael Smith, *Vice Pres*
Steve Smith, *Vice Pres*
EMP: 55
SQ FT: 4,000
SALES (est): 3.6MM **Privately Held**
SIC: 2741 Catalogs: publishing & printing

(G-8955)
SIMCHA CANDLE CO INC
244 Mac Arthur Ave (12553-7011)
P.O. Box 309, Monroe (10949-0309)
PHONE 845 783-0406
Fax: 845 534-1254
Samuel Marcus, *President*
▲ **EMP:** 6
SQ FT: 15,000
SALES (est): 626.5K **Privately Held**
WEB: www.simchacandle.com
SIC: 3999 Candles

(G-8956)
USA ILLUMINATION INC
Also Called: Usai
1126 River Rd (12553-6728)
PHONE 845 565-8500
Fax: 845 561-1130
Eugene Littman, *President*
Ron Vonwerder, *Design Engr*
Joseph Lynch, *Human Res Mgr*
Janice Rosario, *Director*
▲ **EMP:** 35
SQ FT: 40,000
SALES (est): 18.1MM **Privately Held**
WEB: www.usaillumination.com
SIC: 3648 Public lighting fixtures

(G-8957)
VERLA INTERNATIONAL LTD
463 Temple Hill Rd (12553-5527)
PHONE 845 561-2440
Fax: 845 561-0374
Mario F Maffei, *President*
Robert R Roth, *Vice Pres*
Melissa Gallardo, *Project Mgr*
Matt Haspel, *Manager*
Mike Tiedman, *Maintence Staff*
▲ **EMP:** 400

New York
New York County

(G-8958)
112 JEROME DREYFUSS LLC
475 Broome St (10013-5319)
PHONE.................................212 334-6920
Rachel Chicheportiche, *CEO*
Anne Estrabaut, *Controller*
EMP: 5
SALES (est): 950K **Privately Held**
SIC: 3199 Leather goods

(G-8959)
141 INDUSTRIES LLC
300 E 5th St Apt 11 (10003-8816)
PHONE.................................978 273-8831
Nicolas Lirette,
Erin Young,
EMP: 12
SALES (est): 770K **Privately Held**
SIC: 3999 Manufacturing industries

(G-8960)
1510 ASSOCIATES LLC
1500 Lexington Ave (10029-7349)
PHONE.................................212 828-8720
EMP: 6
SALES (est): 498.4K **Privately Held**
SIC: 2211 Cotton Broadwoven Fabric Mill

(G-8961)
180S LLC (HQ)
1 Liberty Plz (10006-1404)
PHONE.................................410 534-6320
Fax: 410 534-6321
Helen Rockey, *CEO*
Lester C Lee, *CEO*
Brian Le Gette, *President*
Shelley Foland, *Vice Pres*
Flor Andres, *CFO*
▲ **EMP:** 35
SQ FT: 45,000
SALES (est): 6.2MM **Privately Held**
SIC: 2253 Scarves & mufflers, knit
PA: 180s, Inc.
   700 S Caroline St
   New York NY 10006
   410 534-6320

(G-8962)
2 1 2 POSTCARDS INC
121 Varick St Frnt B (10013-1408)
PHONE.................................212 767-8227
Fax: 212 741-1332
Jiff Wed Work, *Manager*
EMP: 25
SALES (est): 2.9MM **Privately Held**
SIC: 2759 2752 Commercial printing; commercial printing, lithographic

(G-8963)
2 X 4 INC
180 Varick St Rm 1518 (10014-5869)
PHONE.................................212 647-1170
Fax: 212 647-0454
Georgie Stout, *President*
Michael Rock, *Partner*
Jane Friesen, *Managing Dir*
Liliana Palau, *Design Engr*
Susan Seller, *Treasurer*
EMP: 22
SQ FT: 2,000
SALES (est): 4.1MM **Privately Held**
WEB: www.2x4.org
SIC: 2752 Commercial printing, lithographic

(G-8964)
212 BIZ LLC (PA)
525 Fashion Ave Rm 2301 (10018-4923)
PHONE.................................212 391-4444
Asheesh Mathur, *VP Sales*
Ira Levinas,
▲ **EMP:** 9 **EST:** 2007
SQ FT: 2,000
SALES (est): 12MM **Privately Held**
SIC: 3161 Clothing & apparel carrying cases

(G-8965)
212 DB CORP
Also Called: Gig-It
30 W 22nd St Fl 6 (10010-5892)
PHONE.................................212 652-5600
John Acunto, *CEO*
EMP: 40 **EST:** 2013
SALES (est): 3MM **Privately Held**
SIC: 3944 Electronic games & toys

(G-8966)
212 MEDIA LLC
460 Park Ave S Fl 4 (10016-7315)
PHONE.................................212 710-3092
Rishi Malhotra, *Managing Prtnr*
Neal Shenoy, *Mng Member*
Clint Balcom, *Creative Dir*
Brian Litvack, *Business Dir*
▲ **EMP:** 40
SALES (est): 2.9MM **Privately Held**
WEB: www.212media.com
SIC: 2741 Miscellaneous publishing

(G-8967)
21ST CENTURY FOX AMERICA INC (HQ)
1211 Ave Of The Americas (10036-8701)
PHONE.................................212 852-7000
Fax: 212 575-5845
Rupert K Murdoch, *Ch of Bd*
Paul V Carlucci, *President*
Michael Regan, *Exec VP*
Rick Lane, *Senior VP*
Gerson Zweifach, *Senior VP*
EMP: 60
SQ FT: 40,000
SALES (est): 1.7B
SALES (corp-wide): 27.3B **Publicly Held**
SIC: 2711 2752 2721 4833 Newspapers: publishing only, not printed on site; promotional printing, lithographic; magazines: publishing only, not printed on site; television broadcasting stations; motion picture production & distribution
PA: Twenty-First Century Fox, Inc.
   1211 Ave Of The Americas
   New York NY 10036
   212 852-7000

(G-8968)
21ST CENTURY FOX AMERICA INC
Mirabella Magazine
200 Madison Ave Fl 8 (10016-3908)
PHONE.................................212 447-4600
Grace Mirabella, *Director*
EMP: 85
SALES (corp-wide): 27.3B **Publicly Held**
SIC: 2721 Periodicals
HQ: 21st Century Fox America, Inc.
   1211 Ave Of The Americas
   New York NY 10036
   212 852-7000

(G-8969)
2K INC
622 Broadway Fl 6 (10012-2600)
PHONE.................................646 536-3007
Strauss Zelnick, *CEO*
Lainie Goldstein, *CFO*
EMP: 5 **EST:** 2013
SALES (est): 248.4K
SALES (corp-wide): 1.4B **Publicly Held**
SIC: 7372 Prepackaged software
PA: Take-Two Interactive Software, Inc.
   622 Broadway Fl 6
   New York NY 10012
   646 536-2842

(G-8970)
30DC INC (PA)
80 Broad St Fl 5 (10004-2257)
PHONE.................................212 962-4400
Henry Pinskier, *Ch of Bd*
Theodore A Greenberg, *CFO*
EMP: 5
SALES: 738.1K **Publicly Held**
SIC: 7372 Prepackaged software

(G-8971)
30DC INC
80 Broad St Fl 5 (10004-2257)
PHONE.................................212 962-4400
Teodore A Greenbird, *CFO*
Greg Laborde, *Director*
EMP: 12
SQ FT: 3,000
SALES: 1MM **Privately Held**
SIC: 7372 Prepackaged software; application computer software

(G-8972)
31 PHILLIP LIM LLC (PA)
304 Hudson St Fl 8 (10013-1015)
PHONE.................................212 354-6540
Wen Zhou, *CEO*
Shirley Cheng, *Bookkeeper*
Hannah Lee, *Marketing Mgr*
Han LI, *Manager*
Bo Zhou, *Manager*
▲ **EMP:** 40
SQ FT: 2,000
SALES (est): 11.4MM **Privately Held**
WEB: www.31philliplim.com
SIC: 2339 Sportswear, women's

(G-8973)
3835 LEBRON REST EQP & SUP INC
Also Called: Lebron Equipment Supply
3835 9th Ave (10034-3740)
PHONE.................................212 942-8258
Catalina Lebron, *Ch of Bd*
Manuel Lebron, *President*
Frepesvinda Perez, *Accountant*
Edward Perez, *Director*
EMP: 20
SQ FT: 400
SALES (est): 3.5MM **Privately Held**
SIC: 3679 Power supplies, all types: static

(G-8974)
3LAB INC
525 Fashion Ave Rm 2300 (10018-5395)
PHONE.................................201 567-9100
Fax: 201 567-2280
David C Chung, *President*
Simon Hong, *Controller*
Brian Chung, *Sales Dir*
Ron De Luca, *Sales Mgr*
Krissy Kim, *Accounts Mgr*
▲ **EMP:** 10
SQ FT: 14,000
SALES (est): 1.4MM **Privately Held**
WEB: www.3lab.com
SIC: 2844 Face creams or lotions

(G-8975)
40 NORTH INDUSTRIES
9 W 57th St Fl 30 (10019-2701)
PHONE.................................212 821-1600
Ronnie Heyman, *President*
Lawrence Palermo, *CFO*
Eric Potoker, *Portfolio Mgr*
Scott Pritchard, *Accountant*
Ethan Leidinger, *Marketing Staff*
EMP: 50
SALES (est): 3.7MM **Privately Held**
SIC: 3999 Manufacturing industries

(G-8976)
4BUMPERS LLC
285 New Wstmnster End Ave (10023)
PHONE.................................212 721-9600
Jeffrey Levine,
Alan Levine,
EMP: 10
SALES (est): 596.8K **Privately Held**
SIC: 3714 Bumpers & bumperettes, motor vehicle

(G-8977)
5 STAR APPAREL LLC
Also Called: Enyce
31 W 34th St Fl 3 (10001-3009)
PHONE.................................212 563-1233
Albert Pardo, *Division Mgr*
EMP: 6
SALES (corp-wide): 86.6MM **Privately Held**
SIC: 2326 Men's & boys' work clothing
HQ: 5 Star Apparel L.L.C.
   31 W 34th St Rm 401
   New York NY 10001
   212 563-1233

(G-8978)
525 AMERICA LLC (PA)
Seventh Ave Rm 701 (10018)
PHONE.................................212 840-1313
Bo Guo,
EMP: 9
SALES (est): 9.2MM **Privately Held**
SIC: 2339 Women's & misses' outerwear

(G-8979)
6TH AVENUE SHOWCASE INC
Also Called: Tempo Paris
241 W 37th St Frnt 2 (10018-6797)
PHONE.................................212 382-0400
Fax: 212 382-0623
Shawn Assil, *President*
▲ **EMP:** 6
SQ FT: 5,300
SALES (est): 998.2K **Privately Held**
SIC: 2339 Women's & misses' outerwear

(G-8980)
79 METRO LTD (PA)
265 W 37th St Rm 205 (10018-5031)
PHONE.................................212 944-4030
Nancy Bossio Hutnick, *President*
Reggy Puma, *Controller*
EMP: 1
SQ FT: 8,500
SALES (est): 1.1MM **Privately Held**
SIC: 2337 2253 2331 Women's & misses' suits & coats; sweaters & sweater coats, knit; blouses, women's & juniors': made from purchased material

(G-8981)
A & M ROSENTHAL ENTPS INC
Also Called: Dessy Group
8 W 38th St Fl 4 (10018-0154)
PHONE.................................646 638-9600
Alan Dessy, *President*
Vivian G Diamond, *Treasurer*
Renee Wyatt, *Manager*
Karla Sanchez, *Director*
▲ **EMP:** 45 **EST:** 1963
SQ FT: 18,400
SALES (est): 7.8MM **Privately Held**
SIC: 2335 Women's, juniors' & misses' dresses; wedding gowns & dresses; gowns, formal; ensemble dresses: women's, misses' & juniors'

(G-8982)
A & V CASTINGS INC
257 W 39th St Fl 16w (10018-3106)
PHONE.................................212 997-0042
Fax: 212 768-3582
Alex Kvitko, *President*
EMP: 8
SALES (est): 1MM **Privately Held**
SIC: 3325 3911 Alloy steel castings, except investment; jewelry, precious metal

(G-8983)
A AND J APPAREL CORP
Also Called: Forwear
209 W 38th St Rm 1207 (10018-4498)
PHONE.................................212 398-8899
Fax: 212 398-1302
Mahin Azizian, *President*
EMP: 9
SALES (est): 1.1MM **Privately Held**
SIC: 2211 Apparel & outerwear fabrics, cotton

(G-8984)
A ESTEBAN & COMPANY INC (PA)
132 W 36th St Rm 1000 (10018-8819)
PHONE.................................212 989-7000
Fax: 212 989-6087
Alphonso C Esteban, *Ch of Bd*
Carl Bednarz, *General Mgr*
Harvey Klipper, *Sales Mgr*
Michelle Mwikoff, *Sales Mgr*
Diane Moralez, *Office Mgr*
▲ **EMP:** 25
SALES (est): 5.9MM **Privately Held**
WEB: www.esteban.com
SIC: 2752 7334 Commercial printing, lithographic; blueprinting service

(G-8985)
A ESTEBAN & COMPANY INC
132 W 36th St Rm 1000 (10018-8819)
PHONE.................................212 714-2227
Esteban Daniel, *Vice Pres*
Tim Gibbaid, *Manager*
EMP: 25

New York - New York County (G-8986) — GEOGRAPHIC SECTION

SALES (corp-wide): 5.9MM **Privately Held**
WEB: www.esteban.com
SIC: 2752 Commercial printing, lithographic
PA: A. Esteban & Company, Inc.
132 W 36th St Rm 1000
New York NY 10018
212 989-7000

(G-8986)
A FLEISIG PAPER BOX CORP
1751 2nd Ave Apt 10a (10128-5377)
PHONE.................................212 226-7490
Fax: 212 941-7840
Robert Fleisig, *President*
EMP: 10 **EST:** 1999
SALES: 1MM **Privately Held**
WEB: www.afleisig.com
SIC: 2652 Setup paperboard boxes

(G-8987)
A GRAPHIC PRINTING INC
49 Market St Frnt 2 (10002-7229)
PHONE.................................212 233-9696
Fax: 212 233-9699
M Siam, *President*
▲ **EMP:** 7
SALES (est): 592.5K **Privately Held**
SIC: 2759 Commercial printing

(G-8988)
A GUIDEPOSTS CHURCH CORP
16 E 34th St Fl 21 (10016-4328)
PHONE.................................212 251-8100
Fax: 212 684-0679
Kevin Eans, *Editor*
Rick Hamlin, *Editor*
Colleen Hughes, *Editor*
Stephanie Samoy, *Editor*
Jim Zappitielli, *Mfg Dir*
EMP: 180
SALES (corp-wide): 21.8MM **Privately Held**
SIC: 2721 Periodicals
PA: A Guideposts Church Corp
39 Old Ridgebury Rd 2ab
Danbury CT 06810
203 749-0203

(G-8989)
A H SCHREIBER CO INC (PA)
460 W 34th St Fl 10 (10001-2320)
PHONE.................................212 594-7234
Fax: 212 594-7234
Joel M Schreiber, *President*
Elliott N Schreiber, *Corp Secy*
Avram Schreiber, *Vice Pres*
David Schreiber, *Vice Pres*
Seth Schreiber, *Vice Pres*
◆ **EMP:** 70 **EST:** 1923
SQ FT: 30,000
SALES (est): 40MM **Privately Held**
SIC: 2339 5621 Bathing suits: women's, misses' & juniors'; athletic clothing: women's, misses' & juniors'; women's sportswear

(G-8990)
A J C JEWELRY CONTRACTING INC
247 W 30th St Fl 3 (10001-2824)
PHONE.................................212 594-3703
Fax: 212 594-3706
Leo Smith, *President*
EMP: 6 **EST:** 1993
SALES (est): 550K **Privately Held**
SIC: 3915 Jewel preparing: instruments, tools, watches & jewelry

(G-8991)
A JAFFE INC
592 5th Ave Fl 3 (10036-4707)
PHONE.................................212 843-7464
Fax: 212 593-1989
Mihir Bhansali, *CEO*
Stanley Sikorski, *President*
Samuel Sandberg, *Chairman*
Ken Karlin, *Prdtn Mgr*
Aj Gandhi, *CFO*
EMP: 175
SQ FT: 30,000
SALES (est): 29.6MM **Privately Held**
WEB: www.ajaffe.com
SIC: 3911 Jewelry, precious metal

(G-8992)
A SCHNELLER SONS INC
129 W 29th St Fl 6 (10001-5105)
PHONE.................................212 695-9440
Fax: 212 563-0944
Jon R Schneller, *President*
Pamela Schenneler, *Corp Secy*
EMP: 15
SQ FT: 7,500
SALES (est): 740K **Privately Held**
SIC: 2512 2521 2391 Upholstered household furniture; wood office furniture; draperies, plastic & textile: from purchased materials

(G-8993)
A THOUSAND CRANES INC
Also Called: Knitty City
208 W 79th St Apt 2 (10024-6269)
PHONE.................................212 724-9596
Pearl Chin, *President*
Arvin Chin, *Vice Pres*
EMP: 10
SALES (est): 1.1MM **Privately Held**
WEB: www.knittycity.com
SIC: 2299 Yarns, specialty & novelty

(G-8994)
A TO Z MEDIA INC (PA)
243 W 30th St Fl 6 (10001-2812)
PHONE.................................212 260-0237
Fax: 212 260-0631
Sarah Robertson, *CEO*
Scott Pollack, *President*
Joe Vent, *General Mgr*
Bret Trach, *Vice Pres*
Stacy Karp, *VP Prdtn*
▲ **EMP:** 12
SALES (est): 12.6MM **Privately Held**
WEB: www.atozmedia.com
SIC: 3652 7389 Compact laser discs, prerecorded; magnetic tape (audio): prerecorded; design services

(G-8995)
A-IMPLANT DENTAL LAB CORP
10 Park Ave (10016-4338)
PHONE.................................212 582-4720
Gina Martin, *Info Tech Mgr*
Bryan Glynson, *Director*
EMP: 7 **EST:** 2012
SALES (est): 676.4K **Privately Held**
SIC: 3843 Teeth, artificial (not made in dental laboratories)

(G-8996)
A2IA CORP
24 W 40th St Fl 3 (10018-1856)
PHONE.................................917 237-0390
Fax: 917 237-0391
Jean-Louis Fages, *President*
Olivier Baret, *Senior VP*
Jorge Tavares, *Sales/Mktg Mgr*
ATI Azemoun, *Sales Mgr*
Bob Degliuomini, *Accounts Mgr*
EMP: 8
SALES (est): 1.3MM
SALES (corp-wide): 9.4MM **Privately Held**
SIC: 7372 Prepackaged software
PA: Analyse Image Intelli Artific
37 Rue De La Bienfaisance
Paris 75008
144 420-080

(G-8997)
A3 APPAREL LLC
1407 Broadway Rm 716a (10018-5293)
PHONE.................................888 403-9669
Peter Regondo, *CEO*
EMP: 7 **EST:** 2014
SQ FT: 1,200
SALES: 8MM **Privately Held**
SIC: 2211 Apparel & outerwear fabrics, cotton

(G-8998)
AAA AMERCN FLAG DCTG CO INC
36 W 37th St Fl 9 (10018-7459)
PHONE.................................212 279-4644
Fax: 212 695-8392
Ian Flamm, *President*
Marian Watson, *Vice Pres*
EMP: 5 **EST:** 1946
SQ FT: 2,500
SALES: 1MM **Privately Held**
SIC: 2399 Flags, fabric; banners, made from fabric

(G-8999)
AAA NOODLE PRODUCTS MFG
102 Bowery (10013-4727)
PHONE.................................212 431-4090
David Ho, *Vice Pres*
K Phan, *Manager*
EMP: 5
SQ FT: 10,800
SALES: 1MM **Privately Held**
SIC: 2098 2052 Noodles (e.g. egg, plain & water), dry; cookies

(G-9000)
ABALENE DECORATING SERVICES
315 W 39th St Rm 611 (10018-4035)
PHONE.................................718 782-2000
Moseha Goldman, *President*
Kalmen Weiss, *President*
Miriam Weiss, *Vice Pres*
EMP: 21
SQ FT: 18,000
SALES (est): 1.8MM **Privately Held**
SIC: 2591 2391 7216 Drapery hardware & blinds & shades; curtains & draperies; curtain cleaning & repair

(G-9001)
ABBEVILLE PRESS INC
Also Called: Abbeville Publishing Group
116 W 23rd St Fl 5 (10011-2599)
PHONE.................................212 366-5585
Fax: 212 366-6966
Robert E Abrams, *Ch of Bd*
Louise Kurtz, *Prdtn Dir*
Ada Rodriguez, *Director*
Misha Beletsky, *Art Dir*
Dorothy Gutterman, *Admin Sec*
▲ **EMP:** 33
SALES (est): 3.6MM **Privately Held**
WEB: www.abbeville.com
SIC: 2731 Books: publishing only

(G-9002)
ABC PEANUT BUTTER LLC
295 Madison Ave Ste 1618 (10017-6304)
PHONE.................................212 661-6886
H J Warden, *Mng Member*
EMP: 355
SALES (est): 23.3MM **Privately Held**
SIC: 2099 Peanut butter

(G-9003)
ABEL NOSER SOLUTIONS LTD
1 Battery Park Plz # 601 (10004-1446)
PHONE.................................646 884-6440
Stanley Abel, *Ch of Bd*
James Noser, *President*
Allison Keane, *Manager*
Eugene Noser, *Director*
EMP: 20
SALES: 4MM **Privately Held**
SIC: 7372 Business oriented computer software

(G-9004)
ABKCO MUSIC & RECORDS INC (PA)
85 5th Ave Fl 11 (10003-3019)
PHONE.................................212 399-0300
Allen Klein, *President*
Alan E Horowitz, *Vice Pres*
Peter J Howard, *Vice Pres*
Iris W Keitel, *Vice Pres*
Jody H Klein, *Vice Pres*
EMP: 20
SQ FT: 11,000
SALES (est): 9.2MM **Privately Held**
SIC: 3652 6794 2741 7922 Phonograph records, prerecorded; magnetic tape (audio): prerecorded; compact laser discs, prerecorded; copyright buying & licensing; music, sheet: publishing only, not printed on site; legitimate live theater producers; motion picture production

(G-9005)
ABRAHAM JWLY DESIGNERS & MFRS
37 W 47th St Ste 202 (10036-2862)
PHONE.................................212 944-1149
Can Akdemir, *Partner*
Ibrahim Akdemir, *Partner*
Iskender Akdemir, *Partner*
EMP: 16
SALES (est): 1.5MM **Privately Held**
SIC: 3911 Jewelry, precious metal

(G-9006)
ABRIMIAN BROS CORP
48 W 48th St Ste 805 (10036-1713)
PHONE.................................212 382-1106
Marty Abrimian, *President*
EMP: 10
SALES (est): 860.2K **Privately Held**
SIC: 3911 Jewelry, precious metal

(G-9007)
ABSOLUTE COLOR CORPORATION
109 W 27th St Frnt 2 (10001-6208)
PHONE.................................212 868-0404
Daniel Shil, *President*
Peter Gordon, *Vice Pres*
EMP: 8
SQ FT: 2,500
SALES (est): 740K **Privately Held**
WEB: www.absolutcolor.com
SIC: 2796 2741 Color separations for printing; miscellaneous publishing

(G-9008)
ACADEMY OF POLITICAL SCIENCE
Also Called: POLITICAL SCIENCE QUARTERLY
475 Riverside Dr Ste 1274 (10115-1298)
PHONE.................................212 870-2500
Fax: 212 870-2202
Demetrios Caraley, *President*
Virgil Conway, *Principal*
Abigail Moses, *Editor*
Diana Murray, *Vice Pres*
Grace Wainer, *Bookkeeper*
EMP: 6
SQ FT: 2,309
SALES: 780.2K **Privately Held**
WEB: www.psqonline.org
SIC: 2721 Periodicals: publishing only

(G-9009)
ACCESS INTELLIGENCE LLC
Also Called: Pbi Media Inc.
249 W 17th St (10011-5390)
PHONE.................................212 204-4269
John French, *President*
Andrea Persily, *COO*
Don Socteart, *Vice Pres*
Allison Witcher, *Controller*
EMP: 950
SALES (est): 33MM
SALES (corp-wide): 95MM **Privately Held**
SIC: 2721 Trade journals: publishing only, not printed on site
PA: Access Intelligence Llc
9211 Corp Blvd Fl 4
Rockville MD 20850
301 354-2000

(G-9010)
ACCESSORY CORPORATION
Also Called: T A C
575 8th Ave Fl 16 (10018-3055)
PHONE.................................212 391-8607
Steven Sutton, *President*
Sherie Dolinoy, *Publisher*
Sharon Sutton, *Principal*
Jesse Sutton, *Vice Pres*
▲ **EMP:** 1200
SQ FT: 4,000
SALES (est): 101.9MM **Privately Held**
WEB: www.tacny.com
SIC: 3089 5199 Clothes hangers, plastic; clothes hangers

(G-9011)
ACCESSORY PLAYS LLC
29 W 36th St (10018-7907)
PHONE.................................212 564-7301
Richard Dauplaise, *President*
EMP: 50
SQ FT: 5,000
SALES (est): 1.4MM **Privately Held**
SIC: 3961 Costume jewelry, ex. precious metal & semiprecious stones

GEOGRAPHIC SECTION

New York - New York County (G-9037)

(G-9012)
ACCESSORY STREET LLC
1370 Broadway (10018-7302)
PHONE.................................212 686-8990
Fax: 212 695-1920
Andrew Pizzo,
Mitchell Grossman,
▲ EMP: 12
SALES (est): 762K Privately Held
SIC: 2339 Women's & misses' outerwear

(G-9013)
ACCUTRAK INC
432 Washington St Ste 113 (10013-1721)
PHONE.................................212 925-5330
Eli Camhi, *President*
Stanford Silverman, *Vice Pres*
EMP: 15
SALES (est): 918.1K Privately Held
SIC: 3812 Electronic detection systems (aeronautical)

(G-9014)
ACE BANNER & FLAG COMPANY
Also Called: Ace Banner Flag & Graphics
107 W 27th St (10001-6213)
PHONE.................................212 620-9111
Fax: 212 463-9128
Carl Calo, *President*
Elizabeth Calo, *Treasurer*
Leah Segarra, *Manager*
EMP: 12 EST: 1916
SQ FT: 10,000
SALES: 1MM Privately Held
WEB: www.acebanner.com
SIC: 2399 Banners, made from fabric; flags, fabric

(G-9015)
ACE DIAMOND CORP
30 W 47th St Ste 808r (10036-8665)
PHONE.................................212 730-8231
Fax: 212 730-8232
Herman Witriol, *President*
Efraim Witriol, *Vice Pres*
Margaret Witriol, *Treasurer*
EMP: 3 EST: 1975
SALES: 1MM Privately Held
SIC: 3915 5094 Diamond cutting & polishing; jewelry & precious stones; diamonds (gems)

(G-9016)
ACF INDUSTRIES HOLDING CORP (DH)
767 5th Ave (10153-0023)
PHONE.................................212 702-4363
Keith Cozza, *CEO*
Carl C Icahn, *President*
Richard T Buonato, *Vice Pres*
EMP: 2
SALES (est): 1.4B
SALES (corp-wide): 1.4B Privately Held
SIC: 3743 4741 4789 6799 Freight cars & equipment; tank freight cars & car equipment; railroad equipment, except locomotives; rental of railroad cars; railroad car repair; security speculators for own account
HQ: Highcrest Investors, Llc
Icahn Associates Corp 767
New York NY 10153
212 702-4323

(G-9017)
ACKER & LI MILLS CORPORATION
44 W 62nd St Apt 3b (10023-7009)
PHONE.................................212 307-7247
Daniel Feder, *President*
▲ EMP: 5
SALES: 2MM Privately Held
SIC: 2231 Broadwoven fabric mills, wool

(G-9018)
ACME PLEATING & FAGOTING CORP
147 W 26th St Fl 2 (10001-6817)
P.O. Box 73, Centerport (11721-0373)
PHONE.................................212 674-3737
Fax: 212 989-7472
Susana Ancona, *President*
Martin Pardee, *Vice Pres*
Stephen Ancona, *Director*

EMP: 14
SQ FT: 3,000
SALES (est): 161.7K Privately Held
SIC: 2395 Pleating & stitching

(G-9019)
ACOLYTE INDUSTRIES INC
251 W 30th St Ste 12e (10001-2822)
PHONE.................................212 629-6830
Guerrieri, *CEO*
Alexander Nicolaides, *Vice Pres*
Johnnie Pechal, *Vice Pres*
Vadryn Pierre, *Design Engr*
Drishti Moktan, *Manager*
EMP: 15
SQ FT: 3,000
SALES (est): 4MM Privately Held
SIC: 3648 6794 Lighting equipment; copyright buying & licensing

(G-9020)
ACOLYTE TECHNOLOGIES CORP
44 E 32nd St Rm 901 (10016-5508)
PHONE.................................212 629-3239
Marvin Figenbaum, *CEO*
Salvatore Guerrieri, *President*
David Hurwitz, *Controller*
▲ EMP: 14
SALES (est): 2.1MM Privately Held
SIC: 3674 Light emitting diodes

(G-9021)
ACTINIUM PHARMACEUTICALS INC
546 5th Ave Fl 14 (10036-5000)
PHONE.................................732 243-9495
Sandesh Seth, *Ch of Bd*
Kaushik J Dave, *President*
Felix Garzon, *Senior VP*
Jeng-Dar Yang, *Vice Pres*
Corey Sohmer, *VP Finance*
EMP: 12 EST: 2013
SALES (est): 2.1MM Privately Held
SIC: 2834 8069 Pharmaceutical preparations; cancer hospital

(G-9022)
ACTV INC (DEL CORP) (DH)
233 Park Ave S Fl 10 (10003-1606)
PHONE.................................212 995-9500
Fax: 212 995-9836
David Reese, *President*
Joel Hassell, *COO*
Bruce Crowley, *Exec VP*
Ben Bennett, *Vice Pres*
Frank Deo, *Vice Pres*
EMP: 100
SQ FT: 12,000
SALES (est): 5.4MM
SALES (corp-wide): 946.1MM Privately Held
WEB: www.actv.com
SIC: 3663 7371 Radio & TV communications equipment; custom computer programming services

(G-9023)
AD VANTAGE PRESS
481 Washington St Fl 7 (10013-1325)
PHONE.................................212 941-8355
Fax: 212 226-6579
Edward J Kachik, *President*
Josephine Rogoff, *Treasurer*
EMP: 5
SQ FT: 2,000
SALES (est): 400K Privately Held
WEB: www.advantagepress.com
SIC: 2752 Commercial printing, offset

(G-9024)
ADAM SCOTT DESIGNS INC
118 E 25th St Fl 11 (10010-2966)
PHONE.................................212 420-8866
Fax: 212 529-0309
Steven Dubler, *President*
Rosanna Rigano, *Mfg Staff*
Anthony Bello, *Controller*
◆ EMP: 20
SQ FT: 8,000

SALES (est): 3.3MM Privately Held
WEB: www.scottadamdesigns.com
SIC: 3111 3161 3069 5199 Accessory products, leather; upholstery leather; luggage; bags, rubber or rubberized fabric; bags, textile; polyvinyl chloride resins (PVC); umbrellas, men's & boys'; hats, men's & boys'; robes, men's & boys'; men's & boys' outerwear

(G-9025)
ADAMOR INC
Also Called: Izi Creations
17 E 48th St Rm 901 (10017-1010)
PHONE.................................212 688-8885
Izidor Kamhi, *President*
EMP: 7
SALES (est): 1.1MM Privately Held
WEB: www.adamor.com
SIC: 3911 Jewelry, precious metal

(G-9026)
ADC DOLLS INC
112 W 34th St Ste 1207 (10120-1207)
PHONE.................................212 244-4500
Fax: 212 283-4901
Herbert E Brown, *Ch of Bd*
Gale Jarvis, *President*
Stu Schwartz, *Vice Pres*
Rob Porell, *CFO*
David Morganstern, *Sales Executive*
◆ EMP: 163
SQ FT: 90,000
SALES (est): 9.5MM Privately Held
WEB: www.alexdoll.com
SIC: 3942 Dolls, except stuffed toy animals

(G-9027)
ADESSO INC (PA)
360 W 31st St Rm 909 (10001-2837)
PHONE.................................212 736-4440
Lee Schaak, *President*
Marvin Traub, *Chairman*
Barney Wenograd, *Vice Pres*
Paul Berk, *VP Sales*
Lia Barbery, *Sales Staff*
◆ EMP: 28
SQ FT: 10,000
SALES (est): 5.3MM Privately Held
SIC: 3645 Floor lamps; table lamps

(G-9028)
ADITIANY INC
37 W 39th St Rm 1100 (10018-0579)
PHONE.................................212 997-8440
Nita K Shah, *President*
EMP: 2
SALES (est): 1.5MM Privately Held
SIC: 2395 Embroidery & art needlework

(G-9029)
ADOBE SYSTEMS INC
1540 Broadway Fl 17 (10036-4039)
PHONE.................................212 471-0904
Fax: 212 471-0990
EMP: 20
SALES (est): 1.9MM Privately Held
SIC: 7372 Prepackaged Software Services

(G-9030)
ADOBE SYSTEMS INCORPORATED
8 W 40th St Fl 8 (10018-2275)
PHONE.................................212 471-0904
Bruce Chizen, *Manager*
Bruno Joncour, *Manager*
Sam Telfer, *Manager*
Jason Knell, *Senior Mgr*
Beatrice Noble, *Senior Mgr*
EMP: 32
SALES (corp-wide): 4.8B Publicly Held
WEB: www.adobe.com
SIC: 7372 Prepackaged software
PA: Adobe Systems Incorporated
345 Park Ave
San Jose CA 95110
408 536-6000

(G-9031)
ADRIENNE LANDAU DESIGNS INC
519 8th Ave Fl 21 (10018-4573)
PHONE.................................212 695-8362
Fax: 212 563-2014
Adrienne Landau, *CEO*
Patti Greco, *Controller*

EMP: 15
SQ FT: 12,000
SALES (est): 1.7MM Privately Held
WEB: www.adriennelandau.com
SIC: 2337 Capes, except fur or rubber: women's, misses' & juniors'

(G-9032)
ADSTREAM AMERICA LLC (DH)
845 3rd Ave Fl 6 (10022-6630)
PHONE.................................845 496-8283
Michael Palmer, *Mng Member*
EMP: 15
SALES (est): 2.7MM Privately Held
SIC: 3993 Advertising artwork
HQ: Adstream (Uk) Limited
7th Floor, Berkshire House
London WC1V
207 539-8400

(G-9033)
ADTECH US INC
770 Broadway Fl 4 (10003-9558)
PHONE.................................212 402-4840
David Jacobs, *Senior VP*
Will Schmahl, *Vice Pres*
Peter Meyer, *Vice Pres*
EMP: 125 EST: 2006
SALES (est): 6.6MM
SALES (corp-wide): 131.6B Publicly Held
SIC: 7372 Prepackaged software
HQ: Adtech Gmbh
Robert-Bosch-Str. 32
Dreieich 63303
610 357-150

(G-9034)
ADVANCE APPAREL INTL INC
265 W 37th St Rm 906 (10018-5728)
PHONE.................................212 944-0984
Charles Hu, *President*
Eugene Hu, *Vice Pres*
▲ EMP: 5
SALES (est): 550K Privately Held
SIC: 2311 Men's & boys' suits & coats

(G-9035)
ADVANCE FINANCE GROUP LLC
101 Park Ave Frnt (10178-0399)
PHONE.................................212 630-5900
Tom Summer, *CFO*
EMP: 100 EST: 2007
SALES (est): 7.6MM Privately Held
SIC: 2759 8721 Publication printing; auditing services

(G-9036)
ADVANCE MAGAZINE PUBLS INC
Also Called: ADVANCE MAGAZINE PUBLISHERS, INC.
1440 Broadway Fl 10 (10018-2304)
PHONE.................................212 286-2860
Daphanie Shaddock, *Principal*
Scott McDonald, *Vice Pres*
Michele Donahue, *Senior VP*
Gina Negron, *Info Tech Mgr*
Tanya Isler, *Business Dir*
EMP: 64
SALES (corp-wide): 322.5MM Privately Held
WEB: www.condenast.com
SIC: 2721 Magazines: publishing & printing
HQ: Advance Magazine Publishers Inc.
1 World Trade Ctr Fl 28
New York NY 10007
212 286-2860

(G-9037)
ADVANCE MAGAZINE PUBLS INC (DH)
Also Called: Conde Nast Publications
1 World Trade Ctr Fl 28 (10007-0090)
PHONE.................................212 286-2860
Fax: 212 286-6763
S I Newhouse Jr, *Ch of Bd*
Richard Beckman, *President*
Jay Felts, *President*
Daniel Lagani, *President*
Robert A Sauerberg Jr, *President*
▲ EMP: 2200

New York - New York County (G-9038)

SALES (est): 1.2B
SALES (corp-wide): 322.5MM **Privately Held**
WEB: www.condenast.com
SIC: 2721 Magazines: publishing & printing

(G-9038)
ADVANCE MAGAZINE PUBLS INC
Also Called: Conde Nast Publications Div
1166 Ave Of The Amrcs 14 (10036-2715)
PHONE..................212 790-4422
Fred Santarpia, *Exec VP*
David Orlin, *Senior VP*
Phyllis Maffai, *Vice Pres*
Kevin Donovan, *Finance*
Karyn Gallant-Zitomer, *Human Res Dir*
EMP: 64
SALES (corp-wide): 322.5MM **Privately Held**
WEB: www.condenast.com
SIC: 2721 Magazines: publishing & printing
HQ: Advance Magazine Publishers Inc.
1 World Trade Ctr Fl 28
New York NY 10007
212 286-2860

(G-9039)
ADVANCE MAGAZINE PUBLS INC
Also Called: ADVANCE MAGAZINE PUBLISHERS, INC.
1166 Ave Of The Amrcs 1 (10036-2708)
PHONE..................212 286-2860
Alexandra Walsh, *Branch Mgr*
EMP: 64
SALES (corp-wide): 322.5MM **Privately Held**
WEB: www.condenast.com
SIC: 2721 Periodicals
HQ: Advance Magazine Publishers Inc.
1 World Trade Ctr Fl 28
New York NY 10007
212 286-2860

(G-9040)
ADVANCE MAGAZINE PUBLS INC
Parade Publications
711 3rd Ave Rm 700 (10017-9210)
PHONE..................212 450-7000
John J Beni, *Vice Chairman*
John Garvey, *Senior VP*
Lee Kravitz, *Senior VP*
Marcel Schloss, *Vice Pres*
Carol Unger, *Vice Pres*
EMP: 195
SALES (corp-wide): 322.5MM **Privately Held**
SIC: 2721 2711 Magazines: publishing only, not printed on site; newspapers
HQ: Advance Magazine Publishers Inc.
1 World Trade Ctr Fl 28
New York NY 10007
212 286-2860

(G-9041)
ADVANCE MAGAZINE PUBLS INC
Also Called: Vogue China
750 3rd Ave Frnt G (10017-2728)
PHONE..................212 697-0126
Jim Gomez, *Editor*
Robert Green, *Senior VP*
Suzanne Reinhardt, *VP Finance*
Alexandra Wolfe, *Branch Mgr*
Brian Cross, *Manager*
EMP: 64
SALES (corp-wide): 322.5MM **Privately Held**
SIC: 2721 Magazines: publishing & printing
HQ: Advance Magazine Publishers Inc.
1 World Trade Ctr Fl 28
New York NY 10007
212 286-2860

(G-9042)
ADVANCED BUSINESS GROUP INC
266 W 37th St Fl 15 (10018-6615)
PHONE..................212 398-1010
Fax: 212 398-1315
Michael J Mulligan, *President*
Kevin Kern, *Vice Pres*
Padmini Liliah, *Accounts Mgr*

Jim Mattiello, *Manager*
Angel Pineiro, *Supervisor*
EMP: 15
SQ FT: 7,000
SALES (est): 3.1MM **Privately Held**
SIC: 2752 Commercial printing, lithographic

(G-9043)
ADVANCED DIGITAL PRINTING LLC
65 W 36th St Fl 11 (10018-7936)
PHONE..................718 649-1500
Aaron Menche, *Mng Member*
Steve Toplan, *Manager*
EMP: 35 EST: 2005
SQ FT: 85,000
SALES (est): 3.7MM **Privately Held**
SIC: 2752 Commercial printing, lithographic

(G-9044)
ADVANCED FASHIONS TECHNOLOGY
110 W 40th St Rm 1100 (10018-8529)
PHONE..................212 221-0606
EMP: 8
SALES (est): 580K **Privately Held**
SIC: 2211 Cotton Broadwoven Fabric Mill

(G-9045)
ADVANCED PRINTING NEW YORK INC
263 W 38th St (10018-4483)
PHONE..................212 840-8108
Carlos Cruz, *President*
EMP: 8
SALES (est): 1MM **Privately Held**
WEB: www.apnyc.com
SIC: 2754 Commercial printing, gravure

(G-9046)
ADVANCED RESPONSE CORPORATION
345 W 58th St Apt 11a (10019-1140)
P.O. Box 2213 (10019)
PHONE..................212 459-0887
Inge Rothenberg, *President*
P G Woog, *Owner*
Lionel Woog, *Director*
▲ EMP: 5
SALES (est): 572.7K **Privately Held**
WEB: www.broxo.com
SIC: 3634 Massage machines, electric, except for beauty/barber shops

(G-9047)
ADVANTAGE QUICK PRINT INC
Also Called: Hampshire Lithographers
30 E 33rd St Frnt B (10016-5337)
PHONE..................212 989-5644
Stuart Menkes, *President*
▲ EMP: 6
SQ FT: 6,000
SALES: 350K **Privately Held**
SIC: 2752 Commercial printing, offset

(G-9048)
ADVD HEART PHYS & SURGS
130 E 77th St Fl 4 (10075-1851)
PHONE..................212 434-3000
Fax: 212 434-2610
Michael Gorman, *Principal*
Konstadinos A Plestis, *Cardiovascular*
EMP: 10
SALES (est): 790K **Privately Held**
SIC: 3845 Surgical support systems: heart-lung machine, exc. iron lung

(G-9049)
ADVENTURE PUBLISHING GROUP
307 7th Ave Rm 1601 (10001-6042)
PHONE..................212 575-4510
Fax: 212 575-4521
Harvey Stern, *Ch of Bd*
Laurie Schacht, *President*
Jonathan Samet, *Publisher*
Bill Reese, *Prdtn Mgr*
Lori Rubin, *Controller*
EMP: 20
SALES (est): 1.7MM **Privately Held**
WEB: www.adventurepub.com
SIC: 2721 Magazines: publishing only, not printed on site

(G-9050)
ADVERTISING LITHOGRAPHERS
121 Varick St Fl 9 (10013-1408)
PHONE..................212 966-7771
Randolph Hafter, *President*
Robert Hafter, *Vice Pres*
EMP: 10 EST: 1950
SQ FT: 11,250
SALES (est): 1.2MM **Privately Held**
SIC: 2752 Commercial printing, lithographic

(G-9051)
AEGIS OIL LIMITED VENTURES LLC
14 Wall St Fl 20 (10005-2123)
PHONE..................646 233-4900
James Freiman, *Manager*
EMP: 11
SALES (corp-wide): 1.6MM **Privately Held**
SIC: 1382 Oil & gas exploration services
PA: Aegis Oil Limited Ventures Llc
100 Crescent Ct Ste 700
Dallas TX 75201
214 431-5201

(G-9052)
AES ELECTRONICS INC
135 E 54th St Apt 10j (10022-4511)
PHONE..................212 371-8120
Fax: 212 688-0891
Abraham E Schenfeld, *President*
Ruth Schenfeld, *Treasurer*
EMP: 7
SQ FT: 1,200
SALES (est): 430K **Privately Held**
SIC: 3633 5065 Household laundry equipment; communication equipment

(G-9053)
AF DESIGN INC
1239 Broadway Ste 701 (10001-4360)
PHONE..................347 548-5273
Ali Ahmad, *CEO*
Behroz Ahmad, *Shareholder*
EMP: 2
SQ FT: 3,000
SALES: 3.5MM **Privately Held**
SIC: 3911 5094 Jewel settings & mountings, precious metal; jewelry

(G-9054)
AFFYMAX INC
630 5th Ave Ste 2260 (10111-2291)
PHONE..................650 812-8700
Fax: 650 424-0832
John A Orwin, *Ch of Bd*
Jonathan M Couchman, *President*
Christine Conroy, *Senior VP*
Mark G Thompson, *CFO*
▲ EMP: 6
SQ FT: 1,500
SALES (est): 1.4MM **Privately Held**
WEB: www.affymax.com
SIC: 2834 Pharmaceutical preparations

(G-9055)
AG NEOVO PROFESSIONAL INC
Also Called: Agn Professional
156 5th Ave Ste 434 (10010-7002)
PHONE..................212 647-9080
Minson Chen, *President*
EMP: 10
SQ FT: 1,900
SALES (est): 1.3MM **Privately Held**
WEB: www.agnpro.com
SIC: 3575 Computer terminals

(G-9056)
AGI BROOKS PRODUCTION CO INC (PA)
7 E 14th St Apt 615 (10003-3130)
PHONE..................212 268-1533
Agi Brooks, *President*
Don Mc Lean, *Vice Pres*
EMP: 11
SQ FT: 5,000
SALES (est): 1.6MM **Privately Held**
WEB: www.agibrooks.com
SIC: 2337 2331 2335 Suits: women's, misses' & juniors'; blouses, women's & juniors'; made from purchased material; women's, juniors' & misses' dresses

(G-9057)
AGILENT TECHNOLOGIES INC
399 Park Ave (10022-4614)
PHONE..................877 424-4536
EMP: 2498
SALES (corp-wide): 4B **Publicly Held**
SIC: 3825 Instruments to measure electricity
PA: Agilent Technologies, Inc.
5301 Stevens Creek Blvd
Santa Clara CA 95051
408 345-8886

(G-9058)
AGNOVOS HEALTHCARE LLC
140 Broadway Fl 46 (10005-1155)
PHONE..................646 502-5860
David Mackey, *CFO*
Dana Krayeski, *Manager*
EMP: 6
SALES (est): 1.1MM
SALES (corp-wide): 7.3MM **Privately Held**
SIC: 3842 Implants, surgical
PA: Agnovos Healthcare Usa, Llc
7301 Calhoun Pl Ste 100
Rockville MD 20855
240 753-6500

(G-9059)
AGRASUN INC
Also Called: Agrasun Renewable Energy
2578 Broadway 117 (10025-5642)
PHONE..................305 377-3337
Stephen Kline, *President*
◆ EMP: 10
SALES (est): 760K **Privately Held**
SIC: 2869 Fuels

(G-9060)
AGUILAR AMPLIFICATION LLC
599 Broadway Fl 7 (10012-3371)
PHONE..................212 431-9109
Dave Avenius, *CEO*
David Boonshoft, *CEO*
Alexander Aguilar, *President*
▲ EMP: 10
SQ FT: 10,000
SALES (est): 1.9MM **Privately Held**
WEB: www.aguilaramp.com
SIC: 3651 Amplifiers: radio, public address or musical instrument

(G-9061)
AHHMIGO LLC
120 Cent Park S Rm 7c (10019)
PHONE..................212 315-1818
Yaacob Dabah, *Manager*
EMP: 12
SALES (est): 820K **Privately Held**
SIC: 2099 Food preparations

(G-9062)
AHQ LLC
Also Called: Accesory Headquarters
10 W 33rd St Rm 306 (10001-3340)
PHONE..................212 328-1560
Isaac Mochon, *Controller*
Abe Chehebar, *Mng Member*
▲ EMP: 40 EST: 2012
SALES: 20MM **Privately Held**
SIC: 3171 Women's handbags & purses

(G-9063)
AI ENTERTAINMENT HOLDINGS LLC (HQ)
730 5th Ave Fl 20 (10019-4105)
PHONE..................212 247-6400
Lincoln Benet, *President*
EMP: 14
SALES (est): 2.9B **Privately Held**
SIC: 2731 Book music: publishing & printing
PA: Access Industries, Inc.
730 5th Ave Fl 20
New York NY 10019
212 247-6400

(G-9064)
AI MEDIA GROUP INC
589 8th Ave Fl 17 (10018-3078)
PHONE..................212 660-2400
Andy Fenster, *CEO*
Sergio Alvarez, *COO*
Krista Dibiccari, *Sales Dir*

▲ = Import ▼ = Export
◆ = Import/Export

GEOGRAPHIC SECTION

New York - New York County (G-9091)

Stella Chen, *Manager*
Ron Trenka, *CIO*
EMP: 16
SQ FT: 2,500
SALES: 9.6MM **Privately Held**
SIC: 2741

(G-9065)
AIP/AEROSPACE HOLDINGS LLC (PA)
Also Called: Aip Aerospace
330 Madison Ave Fl 28 (10017-5018)
PHONE......................212 916-8142
Brian Williams, *CEO*
Steve Littauer, *CFO*
Rajesh Kasaraneni, *CIO*
Dino Cusomano,
▲ **EMP:** 4 **EST:** 2012
SALES: 200MM **Privately Held**
SIC: 3721 6799 Aircraft; investors

(G-9066)
AKH GROUP LLC
Also Called: Marchesa Accesories
601 W 26th St Rm M228 (10001-1122)
PHONE......................646 320-8720
Anneli Hofstrom, *CEO*
Ashley Kennedy, *Founder*
Debra Torres, *CFO*
Lou Wood Kennedy, *Mng Member*
EMP: 6 **EST:** 2015
SQ FT: 1,272
SALES: 800K **Privately Held**
SIC: 3144 3171 Women's footwear, except athletic; women's handbags & purses

(G-9067)
AKOS GROUP LTD
Also Called: Milan Accessories
315 5th Ave Fl 11 (10016-6510)
PHONE......................212 683-4747
Mark Seruya, *Ch of Bd*
Janine Ramsundar, *Director*
EMP: 35
SALES (est): 1.8MM **Privately Held**
SIC: 2326 2339 Men's & boys' work clothing; athletic clothing: women's, misses' & juniors'

(G-9068)
AL ENERGY SOLUTIONS LED LLC
1140 Ave Of The Americas (10036-5803)
PHONE......................646 380-6670
Luis Alvarez, *CEO*
Jose Alvarez, *President*
Juan Alvarez, *Vice Pres*
EMP: 21
SQ FT: 5,000
SALES (est): 2MM **Privately Held**
SIC: 3646 3648 Commercial indusl & institutional electric lighting fixtures; outdoor lighting equipment; street lighting fixtures; spotlights

(G-9069)
ALADDIN MANUFACTURING CORP
295 5th Ave Ste 1412 (10016-7124)
PHONE......................212 561-8715
Dennis Fein, *Manager*
EMP: 187
SALES (corp-wide): 8B **Publicly Held**
SIC: 2273 Carpets & rugs
HQ: Aladdin Manufacturing Corporation
160 S Industrial Blvd
Calhoun GA 30701
706 629-7721

(G-9070)
ALANELLI PSLE
630 5th Ave (10111-0100)
PHONE......................212 828-6600
A Alanelli, *Vice Pres*
EMP: 6
SALES (est): 310K **Privately Held**
SIC: 3861 5043 Photographic equipment & supplies; photographic equipment & supplies

(G-9071)
ALART INC
578 5th Ave Unit 33 (10036-4836)
PHONE......................212 840-1508

Alan Becer, *President*
Arthur Becer, *Vice Pres*
Vivian Becer, *Treasurer*
EMP: 3
SALES: 2MM **Privately Held**
SIC: 3911 3281 Jewelry, precious metal; cut stone & stone products

(G-9072)
ALBALUZ FILMS LLC
954 Lexington Ave (10021-5055)
PHONE......................347 613-2321
Carols Plasencia, *CEO*
EMP: 1
SALES: 1MM **Privately Held**
SIC: 3312 Blast furnaces & steel mills

(G-9073)
ALBEA COSMETICS AMERICA INC (DH)
595 Madison Ave Fl 10 (10022-1955)
PHONE......................212 371-5100
Jean P Imbert, *President*
Tina Sukapdjo, *Controller*
Nancy Gullo, *Manager*
Robert Pelliciari, *Director*
▲ **EMP:** 25
SALES (est): 252.4MM **Privately Held**
SIC: 3089 3911 5162 5051 Plastic containers, except foam; precious metal cases; plastics products; metals service centers & offices
HQ: Albea Services
Zac Des Barbanniers Le Signac
Gennevilliers Cedex 92635
149 686-000

(G-9074)
ALBERT AUGUSTINE LTD
151 W 26th St Fl 4 (10001-6810)
PHONE......................917 661-0220
Fax: 917 661-0223
Stephen Griesgraber, *President*
EMP: 55 **EST:** 1945
SQ FT: 10,500
SALES: 442.7K **Privately Held**
WEB: www.albertaugustine.com
SIC: 3931 5736 Strings, musical instrument; musical instrument stores

(G-9075)
ALBION COSMETICS INC
110 E 42nd St Rm 1506 (10017-8533)
PHONE......................212 869-1052
Yusuke Kobayaski, *President*
Tetsuo Konoishi, *Manager*
▲ **EMP:** 7
SALES (est): 961K
SALES (corp-wide): 2.3B **Privately Held**
SIC: 2844 Cosmetic preparations
HQ: Albion Co., Ltd.
1-7-10, Ginza
Chuo-Ku TKY 104-0
355 241-711

(G-9076)
ALCHEMY SIMYA INC
Also Called: Birthstone Enterprises
161 Avnue Of The Americas (10013-1205)
PHONE......................646 230-1122
Fax: 646 230-1112
Feonia Tilly, *President*
EMP: 30 **EST:** 2004
SALES (est): 2.3MM **Privately Held**
SIC: 3911 Jewelry, precious metal

(G-9077)
ALCOA INC (PA)
390 Park Ave Fl 12 (10022-4608)
PHONE......................212 836-2674
Fax: 212 836-2818
Klaus Kleinfeld, *Ch of Bd*
Roy C Harvey, *President*
Olivier M Jarrault, *President*
Kay H Meggers, *President*
Karl Tragl, *President*
◆ **EMP:** 100 **EST:** 1888
SALES: 22.5B **Publicly Held**
SIC: 3334 3353 1099 Primary aluminum; aluminum sheet & strip; coils, sheet aluminum; plates, aluminum; foil, aluminum; bauxite mining

(G-9078)
ALCOHOLICS ANONYMOUS GRAPEVINE (PA)
475 Riverside Dr Ste 1264 (10115-0052)
PHONE......................212 870-3400
Robin Bromley, *CEO*
Arnold Bros, *Ch of Bd*
John Skillton, *Treasurer*
Eugene O' Brien, *Controller*
Valerie Thomas, *Finance*
▲ **EMP:** 15
SQ FT: 4,000
SALES: 3.1MM **Privately Held**
SIC: 2721 Periodicals: publishing only

(G-9079)
ALDINE INC (NY)
150 Varick St Fl 5 (10013-1218)
PHONE......................212 226-2870
Fax: 212 941-6042
Alan Zuniss, *President*
Greg Zuniss, *Vice Pres*
EMP: 62
SQ FT: 23,000
SALES (est): 12.1MM **Privately Held**
WEB: www.aldine.com
SIC: 2752 2796 2759 Commercial printing, lithographic; embossing plates for printing; engraving

(G-9080)
ALEN SANDS YORK ASSOCIATES LTD
Also Called: Stellar Alliance
236 W 26th St Rm 801 (10001-6882)
PHONE......................212 563-6305
Alen S York, *President*
Joshua Rosen, *Vice Pres*
▲ **EMP:** 10
SALES (est): 790K **Privately Held**
SIC: 2392 Comforters & quilts: made from purchased materials

(G-9081)
ALEX SEPKUS INC
42 W 48th St Ste 501 (10036-1701)
PHONE......................212 391-8466
Alex Sepkus, *President*
Jeffrey D Feero, *Vice Pres*
Blake Mogil, *Representative*
EMP: 11
SALES (est): 1.4MM **Privately Held**
SIC: 3911 Jewelry, precious metal; bracelets, precious metal; necklaces, precious metal

(G-9082)
ALEXANDER PRIMAK JEWELRY INC
Also Called: Platina
529 5th Ave Fl 15 (10017-4674)
PHONE......................212 398-0287
Fax: 212 398-1102
Alexander Primak, *President*
Igor Shersher, *General Mgr*
EMP: 59
SQ FT: 8,000
SALES: 11.3MM **Privately Held**
WEB: www.platinacasting.com
SIC: 3911 Jewelry, precious metal

(G-9083)
ALEXANDER WANG INCORPORATED (PA)
386 Broadway Fl 3 (10013-6021)
PHONE......................212 532-3103
Aimie Wang, *CEO*
Rodrigo Bazan, *President*
Hana Lee, *Opers Staff*
Thiago Pereira, *Opers Staff*
Gerard Amato, *Controller*
▲ **EMP:** 59
SALES (est): 43MM **Privately Held**
SIC: 2331 2329 Blouses, women's & juniors': made from purchased material; shirt & slack suits: men's, youths' & boys'

(G-9084)
ALFRED DUNNER INC (PA)
1411 Broadway Fl 24 (10018-3471)
PHONE......................212 478-4300
Fax: 212 719-9684
Peter Aresty, *President*
Joseph Aresty, *Chairman*
Jerome Aresty, *Vice Pres*

Linda Gold, *Prdtn Mgr*
Ray Barrick, *CFO*
▲ **EMP:** 75 **EST:** 1946
SQ FT: 10,000
SALES: 95.6MM **Privately Held**
WEB: www.alfreddunner.com
SIC: 2337 2331 2339 Skirts, separate: women's, misses' & juniors'; jackets & vests, except fur & leather: women's; T-shirts & tops, women's: made from purchased materials; slacks: women's, misses' & juniors'; shorts (outerwear): women's, misses' & juniors'

(G-9085)
ALL RACKS INDUSTRIES INC
361 W 36th St Frnt A (10018-6408)
PHONE......................212 244-1069
Joseph Desimone, *President*
Charles Desimone, *Vice Pres*
Joseph Mensch, *Director*
EMP: 5
SQ FT: 7,000
SALES: 500K **Privately Held**
SIC: 2542 Garment racks: except wood

(G-9086)
ALLAN JOHN COMPANY
611 5th Ave Fl 7 (10022-6813)
PHONE......................212 940-2210
John Allan Meing, *CEO*
Clare Ludvigsen, *CFO*
Richard Macary, *Treasurer*
▲ **EMP:** 10
SALES (est): 649.8K
SALES (corp-wide): 2MM **Privately Held**
WEB: www.johnallans.com
SIC: 2844 Toilet preparations
PA: The John Allan Company Llc
46 E 46th St
New York NY

(G-9087)
ALLEGHANY CAPITAL CORPORATION (HQ)
7 Times Square Tower (10036)
PHONE......................212 752-1356
David Van Geyzel, *President*
EMP: 10
SALES (est): 102.4MM
SALES (corp-wide): 5B **Publicly Held**
SIC: 3944 Electronic games & toys
PA: Alleghany Corporation
7 Times Sq Tower
New York NY 10036
212 752-1356

(G-9088)
ALLEY MUSIC CORP
126 E 38th St (10016-2602)
PHONE......................212 779-7977
Caroline Bienstock, *President*
EMP: 25
SALES (est): 1.2MM **Privately Held**
SIC: 2741 Music books: publishing & printing

(G-9089)
ALLIED BRONZE CORP (DEL CORP)
32 Avenue Of The Americas (10013-2473)
PHONE......................646 421-6400
Herbert Koenig, *President*
Sandra Browne, *Manager*
Susan Mc Cormick, *Manager*
▲ **EMP:** 40
SQ FT: 55,000
SALES (est): 4.1MM **Privately Held**
WEB: www.alliedbronze.com
SIC: 3446 Architectural metalwork; ornamental metalwork

(G-9090)
ALLIED REPRODUCTIONS INC
121 Varick St Fl 9 (10013-1408)
PHONE......................212 255-2472
Peter Bird, *President*
EMP: 20
SALES (est): 1.9MM **Privately Held**
SIC: 2752 Photo-offset printing

(G-9091)
ALLISON CHE FASHION INC (PA)
1400 Broadway Lbby 5 (10018-5362)
PHONE......................212 391-1433
Fax: 212 391-1508

New York - New York County (G-9092) — GEOGRAPHIC SECTION

Barbara Weiner, *President*
Edith Fisher, *Treasurer*
EMP: 12
SALES (est): 957.8K **Privately Held**
SIC: 2335 Women's, juniors' & misses' dresses

(G-9092)
ALLSTAR CASTING CORPORATION
240 W 37th St Frnt 7 (10018-5091)
PHONE.................................212 563-0909
Robert Winters, *President*
Phyllis Vulcano, *Vice Pres*
Denise Winters, *Vice Pres*
EMP: 40
SQ FT: 2,200
SALES (est): 2.5MM **Privately Held**
SIC: 3915 3369 Jewelers' castings; non-ferrous foundries

(G-9093)
ALLURE JEWELRY AND ACC LLC
15 W 36th St Fl 12 (10018-7113)
P.O. Box 41305, Plymouth MN (55441-0305)
PHONE.................................646 226-8057
Amy Bohaty,
Arlene Tourville,
◆ **EMP:** 36
SQ FT: 5,000
SALES (est): 955.6K **Privately Held**
SIC: 3961 Costume jewelry

(G-9094)
ALLWORTH COMMUNICATIONS INC
Also Called: Allworth Press
10 E 23rd St Ste 510 (10010-4459)
PHONE.................................212 777-8395
Tad Crawford, *President*
Bob Porter, *CFO*
Cindy Peng, *Comptroller*
Cynthia Rivelli, *Mktg Dir*
Gebrina Roberts, *Office Mgr*
▲ **EMP:** 12
SALES (est): 930K **Privately Held**
WEB: www.allworth.com
SIC: 2731 Textbooks: publishing only, not printed on site

(G-9095)
ALM MEDIA LLC (HQ)
Also Called: New York Law Journal
120 Broadway Fl 5 (10271-1100)
PHONE.................................212 457-9400
Fax: 646 417-7705
Bill Carter, *CEO*
Emily Holbrook, *Editor*
Maggie Soladay, *Editor*
Robin Sparkman, *Editor*
Kevin Michielsen, *COO*
EMP: 350 **EST:** 1997
SQ FT: 31,000
SALES (est): 189.2MM
SALES (corp-wide): 190.2MM **Privately Held**
WEB: www.alm.com
SIC: 2721 2711 2741 2731 Magazines: publishing only, not printed on site; newspapers: publishing only, not printed on site; newsletter publishing; book publishing; trade show arrangement
PA: Alm Media Holdings, Inc.
120 Broadway Fl 5
New York NY 10271
212 457-9400

(G-9096)
ALM MEDIA HOLDINGS INC (PA)
120 Broadway Fl 5 (10271-1100)
PHONE.................................212 457-9400
William L Pollak, *President*
Andrew Neblett, *President*
Sherry Costello, *General Mgr*
Jack Berkowitz, *Senior VP*
Jeffrey S Litvack, *Senior VP*
EMP: 400
SQ FT: 31,000
SALES (est): 190.2MM **Privately Held**
SIC: 2721 2711 2741 2731 Magazines: publishing only, not printed on site; newspapers: publishing only, not printed on site; newsletter publishing; book publishing; trade show arrangement

(G-9097)
ALOK INC
7 W 34th St Fl Ste 79105 (10001-8100)
PHONE.................................212 643-4360
Arun Agarwaal, *CEO*
EMP: 5 **EST:** 2007
SALES (est): 401.6K
SALES (corp-wide): 3.5B **Privately Held**
SIC: 2299 5023 Textile goods; sheets, textile
PA: Alok Industries Limited
2nd & 3rd Floor, Tower B Peninsula Business Park
Mumbai MH 40001
226 178-7001

(G-9098)
ALPARGATAS USA INC
Also Called: Havaianas
33 E 33rd St Rm 501 (10016-5335)
PHONE.................................646 277-7171
Marcio Moura, *CEO*
Afonso Fugiyama, *President*
Rona Samaniego, *Accountant*
◆ **EMP:** 30
SQ FT: 7,500
SALES (est): 8.7MM **Privately Held**
SIC: 3144 Women's footwear, except athletic
HQ: Alpargatas S/A.
Av. Doutor Cardoso De Melo 1.336
Sao Paulo SP 04548
310 212-2240

(G-9099)
ALPHA MEDIA GROUP INC (PA)
415 Madison Ave Fl 3 (10017-7927)
PHONE.................................212 302-2626
Kent Brownridge, *CEO*
Felix Dennis, *Ch of Bd*
Stephen Duggan, *COO*
Karen Reed, *Controller*
Cristine Johnston, *Accountant*
▲ **EMP:** 300
SALES (est): 46.6MM **Privately Held**
WEB: www.stuffmagazine.com
SIC: 2721 Magazines: publishing & printing

(G-9100)
ALPINA COLOR GRAPHICS INC
27 Cliff St Rm 502 (10038-2850)
PHONE.................................212 285-2700
Fax: 212 285-2704
Harish Sawhney, *President*
EMP: 7
SALES (est): 800K **Privately Held**
WEB: www.alpinaonline.com
SIC: 2752 Commercial printing, offset

(G-9101)
ALPINA COPYWORLD INC (PA)
Also Called: Alpina Digital
102 Madison Ave Frnt B (10016-7417)
PHONE.................................212 683-3511
Naveen Sawhney, *President*
Roy Shawney, *Accounts Mgr*
Rajeev Sawhney, *Security Mgr*
Harish Sawhney, *Admin Sec*
EMP: 18
SQ FT: 7,000
SALES (est): 1.9MM **Privately Held**
WEB: www.alpina.net
SIC: 2759 7374 2752 Commercial printing; computer graphics service; commercial printing, lithographic

(G-9102)
ALPINE BUSINESS GROUP INC (PA)
Also Called: Alpine Creative Group
30 E 33rd St Frnt B (10016-5337)
PHONE.................................212 989-4198
Fax: 212 989-4182
Steve Paster, *President*
Laura Leigh, *Vice Pres*
Barbara Schaffer, *Sales Staff*
Manali Doshi, *Art Dir*
Rebecca Baker, *Graphic Designe*
EMP: 8
SALES (est): 1.2MM **Privately Held**
WEB: www.alpinecreativegroup.com
SIC: 2759 2752 Invitations: printing; commercial printing, lithographic

(G-9103)
ALPINE CREATIONS LTD
Also Called: TS Manufacturing
17 E 48th St Fl 6 (10017-1010)
PHONE.................................212 308-9353
Fax: 212 308-9736
Samy Sanar, *President*
Zack Sanar, *Vice Pres*
▲ **EMP:** 6
SQ FT: 2,000
SALES (est): 731.9K **Privately Held**
WEB: www.alpineweddingbands.com
SIC: 3911 Jewelry, precious metal

(G-9104)
ALSTOM TRANSPORTATION INC
641 Lexington Ave Fl 28 (10022-4503)
PHONE.................................212 692-5353
Jerome Wallut, *President*
Barbara Schroeder, *Principal*
EMP: 25
SALES (est): 1.4MM **Privately Held**
SIC: 3743 8711 7629 Railroad equipment; engineering services; electrical repair shops

(G-9105)
ALVANON INC
145 W 30th St Fl 10 (10001-4064)
PHONE.................................212 868-4314
Fax: 212 868-4319
Janice Wang Millard, *CEO*
Edward A Gribbin, *President*
Jeff Cheung, *General Mgr*
Jason Wang, *COO*
Hui Lin, *Technical Mgr*
▲ **EMP:** 25
SQ FT: 1,000
SALES (est): 2.8MM **Privately Held**
WEB: www.alvanon.com
SIC: 3999 Mannequins

(G-9106)
ALVIN VALLEY DIRECT LLC
146 W 28th St Apt 5 (10001-6123)
PHONE.................................212 392-4725
Damion Hankejh, *CEO*
Alvin Valley, *President*
Gaepano Rabzieri, *COO*
Caitlin Dieringer, *Manager*
Taetano Razzeri,
EMP: 10 **EST:** 2011
SALES (est): 1MM **Privately Held**
SIC: 2331 Blouses, women's & juniors': made from purchased material

(G-9107)
ALVINA VLENTA COUTURE COLLECTN
525 Fashion Ave Rm 1703 (10018-4935)
PHONE.................................212 921-7058
Joe Murphy, *President*
Jim Hjelm, *Principal*
Joe O'Grady, *Admin Sec*
EMP: 10
SALES (est): 807.8K
SALES (corp-wide): 16MM **Publicly Held**
WEB: www.jimhelmcouture.com
SIC: 2335 Wedding gowns & dresses
PA: Jlm Couture, Inc.
525 Fashion Ave Rm 1703
New York NY 10018
212 921-7058

(G-9108)
ALVINA VLENTA COUTURE COLLECTN
225 W 37th St (10018-5703)
PHONE.................................212 921-7058
Joe Murphy, *President*
Daniel McMillan, *President*
Victoria McMillan, *President*
EMP: 8
SALES: 3MM **Privately Held**
SIC: 2335 5131 Wedding gowns & dresses; bridal supplies

(G-9109)
AMBER BEVER INC
110 W 40th St Rm 204 (10018-8587)
PHONE.................................212 391-4911
Beverly Brown, *CEO*
Mark Brown, *President*
▲ **EMP:** 4
SQ FT: 1,500
SALES: 2MM **Privately Held**
SIC: 2339 Women's & misses' athletic clothing & sportswear

(G-9110)
AMCOM SOFTWARE INC
256 W 38th St Fl 8 (10018-9123)
PHONE.................................212 951-7600
Vincent D Kelly, *Branch Mgr*
Elmer Calonzo, *Software Engr*
EMP: 10
SALES (corp-wide): 189.6MM **Publicly Held**
WEB: www.amcomsoft.com
SIC: 7372 7371 Application computer software; computer software development & applications
HQ: Amcom Software, Inc.
10400 Yellow Circle Dr # 100
Eden Prairie MN 55343
952 230-5200

(G-9111)
AMEREX CORPORATION
512 7th Ave Fl 9 (10018-0861)
PHONE.................................212 221-3151
Fax: 212 391-8702
Dan Raskin, *COO*
Renee McGovern, *Manager*
EMP: 9
SALES (corp-wide): 1.2B **Privately Held**
WEB: www.amerex-fire.com
SIC: 2331 Blouses, women's & juniors': made from purchased material
HQ: Amerex Corporation
7595 Gadsden Hwy
Trussville AL 35173
205 655-3271

(G-9112)
AMERICA CAPITAL ENERGY CORP
Also Called: Acec
405 Lexington Ave Fl 65 (10174-6301)
PHONE.................................212 983-8316
Min Zhaing, *Ch of Bd*
Zhilin Feng, *President*
Kate Reulbach, *Admin Sec*
EMP: 5
SQ FT: 7,299
SALES (est): 430K **Privately Held**
SIC: 1382 Oil & gas exploration services

(G-9113)
AMERICA PRESS INC (PA)
Also Called: National Catholic Wkly Review
106 W 56th St (10019-3893)
PHONE.................................212 581-4640
Fax: 212 399-3596
Thomas Reese, *President*
Drew Christiansen, *Editor*
Joseph Hoover, *Editor*
Maurice Reidy, *Editor*
James Santora, *Controller*
EMP: 35 **EST:** 1909
SQ FT: 36,674
SALES (est): 3.7MM **Privately Held**
SIC: 2721 Magazines: publishing only, not printed on site

(G-9114)
AMERICAN APPAREL TRADING CORP (PA)
Also Called: Vertical Apparel
209 W 38th St Rm 1004 (10018-0391)
PHONE.................................212 764-5990
Peter Marsella, *President*
Ellen Barry, *Vice Pres*
Danny Miser, *Manager*
EMP: 3 **EST:** 2003
SALES (est): 1.2MM **Privately Held**
SIC: 2339 Sportswear, women's

(G-9115)
AMERICAN BPTST CHRCHES MTRO NY
Flemister Housing Services
527 W 22nd St (10011-1179)
PHONE.................................212 870-3195
James D Stallings, *Principal*
EMP: 8
SALES (corp-wide): 692.9K **Privately Held**
WEB: www.abcmny.org
SIC: 2531 Church furniture

▲ = Import ▼ = Export
◆ = Import/Export

PA: American Baptist Churches Of Metropolitan New York
475 Riverside Dr Ste 432
New York NY 10115
212 870-3195

(G-9116)
AMERICAN COMFORT DIRECT LLC
708 3rd Ave Fl 6 (10017-4119)
PHONE..................................201 364-8309
Benzvi Cohen, *CEO*
Timothy Enarson, *Vice Pres*
EMP: 25
SALES (est): 1.3MM **Privately Held**
SIC: 3433 3634 3635 3589 Space heaters, except electric; electric household fans, heaters & humidifiers; household vacuum cleaners; carpet sweepers, except household electric vacuum sweepers; automotive air conditioners;

(G-9117)
AMERICAN DSPLAY DIE CTTERS INC
121 Varick St Rm 301 (10013-1408)
PHONE..................................212 645-1274
Juan Leon, *President*
Christa Leon, *Treasurer*
EMP: 30
SQ FT: 20,000
SALES (est): 202.4K **Privately Held**
SIC: 2675 3544 Die-cut paper & board; dies & die holders for metal cutting, forming, die casting

(G-9118)
AMERICAN GRAPHIC DESIGN AWARDS
Also Called: Graphic Design U S A
89 5th Ave Ste 901 (10003-3046)
PHONE..................................212 696-4380
Gordon Kaye, *CEO*
Milton Kaye, *Publisher*
Eric Bauer, *Director*
Chris Grenier, *Director*
EMP: 5
SALES (est): 430K **Privately Held**
WEB: www.graphicdesignusa.com
SIC: 2721 Magazines: publishing & printing

(G-9119)
AMERICAN HEALTHCARE SUPPLY INC
304 Park Ave S (10010-4301)
PHONE..................................212 674-3636
Fax: 212 202-5173
P H Lee, *President*
Edward Letko, *Managing Dir*
▲ **EMP:** 12
SQ FT: 4,000
SALES (est): 1.2MM **Privately Held**
SIC: 3841 5047 Surgical & medical instruments; medical equipment & supplies

(G-9120)
AMERICAN HOME MFG LLC
302 5th Ave (10001-3604)
PHONE..................................718 855-0617
Nathan Accad, *President*
Isaac Ades, *COO*
Benjamin Akkad, *Vice Pres*
EMP: 65
SQ FT: 125,000
SALES: 9.8MM **Privately Held**
SIC: 2451 Mobile homes

(G-9121)
AMERICAN INST CHEM ENGINEERS (PA)
Also Called: Aiche
120 Wall St Fl 23 (10005-5991)
PHONE..................................646 495-1355
Fax: 212 591-8888
Nasim Hassan, *Research*
Kristine Togneri, *Research*
John Cengel, *Engineer*
Richard Enns, *Engineer*
Noreville Orbe, *Project Engr*
▲ **EMP:** 75
SQ FT: 18,400

SALES: 28.6MM **Privately Held**
WEB: www.naache.net
SIC: 2721 8621 2731 Magazines: publishing only, not printed on site; engineering association; book publishing

(G-9122)
AMERICAN JEWISH COMMITTEE
Also Called: Commentary Magazine
561 Fashion Ave Fl 16 (10018-1816)
PHONE..................................212 891-1400
David Kelsey, *Sales Staff*
Davi Birnstein, *Manager*
EMP: 5
SALES (corp-wide): 55.7MM **Privately Held**
WEB: www.projectinterchange.org
SIC: 2721 Periodicals
PA: American Jewish Committee
165 E 56th St
New York NY 10022
212 751-4000

(G-9123)
AMERICAN JEWISH CONGRESS INC (PA)
Also Called: A J Congress
825 3rd Ave Fl 181800 (10022-7519)
PHONE..................................212 879-4500
Fax: 212 758-1633
David Haberman, *Vice Chairman*
Mark Stern, *Counsel*
Susan Jaffe, *Senior VP*
Simeon Saturn, *Finance Dir*
Rochelle Mancini, *Comms Mgr*
EMP: 20 **EST:** 1918
SQ FT: 9,000
SALES (est): 2.7MM **Privately Held**
SIC: 2721 8661 Magazines: publishing & printing; religious organizations

(G-9124)
AMERICAN MEDIA INC
Also Called: AMI
4 New York Plz Fl 2 (10004-2466)
PHONE..................................212 545-4800
David Pecker, *CEO*
William Frank, *General Mgr*
Dave Leckey, *Exec VP*
Marc Fierman, *Senior VP*
Neil Goldstein, *Vice Pres*
EMP: 62
SALES (corp-wide): 223MM **Privately Held**
SIC: 2711 2741 Newspapers; newspapers: publishing only, not printed on site; miscellaneous publishing
PA: American Media, Inc.
1000 American Media Way
Boca Raton FL 33464
561 997-7733

(G-9125)
AMERICAN MINERALS INC (DH)
Also Called: Prince Minerals
21 W 46th St Fl 14 (10036-4119)
PHONE..................................646 747-4222
Willson Ropp, *President*
Darryl Mayton, *Opers Mgr*
Roderik Alewijnse, *CFO*
Kevin St Germaine, *CFO*
Rob Lannerd, *Controller*
◆ **EMP:** 14 **EST:** 1963
SQ FT: 3,000
SALES (est): 30.3MM
SALES (corp-wide): 2.2B **Privately Held**
WEB: www.princeminerals.com
SIC: 1446 Silica mining; silica sand mining
HQ: Prince Minerals Llc
21 W 46th St Fl 14
New York NY 10036
646 747-4222

(G-9126)
AMERICAN ORIGINALS CORPORATION
Also Called: Gotham Diamonds
1156 Ave Of Ste 710 (10036)
PHONE..................................212 836-4155
Saumil Parikh, *President*
Nagini RAO, *Manager*
EMP: 9
SALES (est): 810K **Privately Held**
SIC: 3911 5094 Jewelry, precious metal; jewelry

(G-9127)
AMERICAN REFRIGERATION INC (HQ)
142 W 57th St Fl 17 (10019-3300)
PHONE..................................212 699-4000
Stephen Presser, *President*
EMP: 4
SALES (est): 44.4MM
SALES (corp-wide): 822.9MM **Privately Held**
SIC: 3585 Refrigeration equipment, complete
PA: Monomoy Capital Partners, L.P.
142 W 57th St Fl 17
New York NY 10019
212 699-4000

(G-9128)
AMERICAN SPRAY-ON CORP
22 W 21st St Fl 2 (10010-6949)
PHONE..................................212 929-2100
Steven Alessio, *President*
Steve Alessio, *President*
Marvin Sweet, *Chairman*
Micheal Boone, *Treasurer*
EMP: 30
SALES (est): 4.3MM **Privately Held**
SIC: 2396 2262 Automotive & apparel trimmings; fire resistance finishing: man-made & silk broadwoven

(G-9129)
AMERICAN T SHIRTS INC
Also Called: Premium Shirts Lerma Mexico
225 W 39th St Fl 6 (10018-3103)
PHONE..................................212 563-7125
Nasser Mokhtar, *President*
American T-Shirt Group, *Shareholder*
EMP: 5
SALES: 5MM **Privately Held**
WEB: www.americantshirts.com
SIC: 2253 T-shirts & tops, knit

(G-9130)
AMERICO GROUP INC
498 7th Ave Fl 8 (10018-6944)
PHONE..................................212 563-2700
EMP: 19
SALES (corp-wide): 13.3MM **Privately Held**
SIC: 2321 Men's & boys' dress shirts
PA: Americo Group Inc.
1411 Broadway Fl 2
New York NY 10018
212 563-2700

(G-9131)
AMERICO GROUP INC (PA)
Also Called: Joseph's Cloak
1411 Broadway Fl 2 (10018-3420)
PHONE..................................212 563-2700
Eli Harari, *Ch of Bd*
Marc Lieber, *Vice Pres*
Joel Weisinger, *CFO*
Kelly Moul, *Controller*
Amer Shabana, *Manager*
▲ **EMP:** 56
SQ FT: 30,000
SALES (est): 13.3MM **Privately Held**
WEB: www.josephscloak.com
SIC: 2321 Men's & boys' dress shirts

(G-9132)
AMERIKOM GROUP INC
247 W 30th St Rm 6w (10001-2808)
PHONE..................................212 675-1329
Yaron Ben-Horin, *COO*
Nitsan Ben-Horin, *Vice Pres*
Derekh Cohen, *Prdtn Mgr*
EMP: 80
SQ FT: 50,000
SALES (est): 10MM **Privately Held**
WEB: www.amerikom.com
SIC: 2759 Commercial printing

(G-9133)
AMERIMADE COAT INC
463 Fashion Ave Rm 802 (10018-8705)
PHONE..................................212 216-0925
Gaspar Ferrara, *President*
Corey Bagget, *Opers Staff*
◆ **EMP:** 9
SQ FT: 20,000

SALES (est): 988.7K **Privately Held**
SIC: 2369 2337 2311 Girls' & children's outerwear; jackets & vests, except fur & leather: women's; men's & boys' suits & coats

(G-9134)
AMG GLOBAL LLC (HQ)
Also Called: AMG Global NY & Enchante ACC
4 E 34th St (10016-4333)
PHONE..................................212 689-6008
Aharon Franco, *Vice Pres*
Duvia Leigh, *Manager*
▼ **EMP:** 5
SQ FT: 5,000
SALES (est): 1.2MM
SALES (corp-wide): 65.5MM **Privately Held**
SIC: 3261 Bathroom accessories/fittings, vitreous china or earthenware
PA: Enchante Accessories Inc.
16 E 34th St Fl 16
New York NY 10016
212 689-6008

(G-9135)
AMG SUPPLY COMPANY LLC
1166 Av Of The Americas (10036-2708)
PHONE..................................212 790-6370
David Chemidlin, *General Mgr*
David Orlin, *Mng Member*
Terry Toloso, *Executive Asst*
EMP: 20
SALES (est): 924.7K
SALES (corp-wide): 322.5MM **Privately Held**
WEB: www.condenast.com
SIC: 2721 Periodicals
HQ: Advance Magazine Publishers Inc.
1 World Trade Ctr Fl 28
New York NY 10007
212 286-2860

(G-9136)
AMINCOR INC
1350 Ave Of Amrcas Fl 24 (10019)
PHONE..................................347 821-3452
John R Rice III, *President*
Joseph F Ingrassia, *CFO*
EMP: 166
SQ FT: 24,806
SALES: 28.6MM **Privately Held**
SIC: 2051 8734 8711 Bread, cake & related products; bakery: wholesale or wholesale/retail combined; pollution testing; petroleum engineering

(G-9137)
AMNEWS CORPORATION
2340 Frdrick Duglass Blvd (10027)
PHONE..................................212 932-7400
Fax: 212 222-3842
Elinor Tatum, *CEO*
Kristin Molroy, *Manager*
EMP: 27 **EST:** 2003
SALES: 25.3K **Privately Held**
WEB: www.amsterdamnews.com
SIC: 2711 Newspapers

(G-9138)
AMOSEASTERN APPAREL INC (PA)
49 W 38th St Fl 7 (10018-1936)
PHONE..................................212 921-1859
Yanling Zhang, *Administration*
EMP: 15
SALES (est): 2MM **Privately Held**
SIC: 2396 Apparel & other linings, except millinery

(G-9139)
AMPEX CASTING CORPORATION
23 W 47th St Unit 3 (10036-2826)
PHONE..................................212 719-1318
Fax: 212 719-3493
Joseph Ipek, *President*
EMP: 19
SQ FT: 3,000
SALES (est): 1.3MM **Privately Held**
SIC: 3915 Jewelers' castings

New York - New York County (G-9140)

(G-9140)
AMSALE ABERRA LLC
318 W 39th St Fl 12 (10018-1484)
PHONE..................212 695-5936
Fax: 212 971-6288
Amsale Aberra, *President*
Clarence O'Neil Brown, *Vice Pres*
Maureen Hirschfield, *Financial Exec*
Allison Alexander, *Mktg Dir*
Emily Lu, *Marketing Mgr*
EMP: 23
SALES (est): 3.3MM **Privately Held**
SIC: 2335 Gowns, formal; wedding gowns & dresses

(G-9141)
AMSCO SCHOOL PUBLICATIONS INC
315 Hudson St Fl 5 (10013-1009)
PHONE..................212 886-6500
Fax: 212 675-7010
Henry Brun, *President*
Irene Rubin, *Vice Pres*
Laurence Beller, *Treasurer*
Inna Kushnir, *Supervisor*
Iris L Beller, *Admin Sec*
▼ EMP: 80 EST: 1935
SQ FT: 20,000
SALES (est): 6.9MM **Privately Held**
WEB: www.amscopub.com
SIC: 2731 Textbooks: publishing only, not printed on site

(G-9142)
AMY SCHERBER INC (PA)
Also Called: Amy's Bread
75 9th Ave (10011-7006)
PHONE..................212 462-4338
Fax: 212 462-4323
Amy Scherber, *President*
Jessica Blank, *Business Mgr*
Ann Burgunder, *Human Res Dir*
Toy Dupree, *Manager*
Robin Keehner, *Manager*
▲ EMP: 18
SQ FT: 7,600
SALES (est): 8.9MM **Privately Held**
WEB: www.amysbread.com
SIC: 2051 Bread, cake & related products

(G-9143)
ANACOR PHARMACEUTICALS INC
235 E 42nd St (10017-5703)
PHONE..................212 733-2323
Fax: 650 543-7660
Douglas E Giordano, *President*
Sanjay Chanda, *Senior VP*
Jacob J Plattner, *Senior VP*
Bob Jacobs, *Vice Pres*
Margaret M Madden, *Vice Pres*
EMP: 110
SALES: 82.3MM
SALES (corp-wide): 48.8B **Publicly Held**
WEB: www.anacor.com
SIC: 2834 Pharmaceutical preparations
PA: Pfizer Inc.
235 E 42nd St
New York NY 10017
212 733-2323

(G-9144)
ANAGE INC
530 Fashion Ave Frnt 5 (10018-4878)
PHONE..................212 944-6533
Fax: 212 904-1787
Kenneth Berkowitz, *President*
Fred Heiser, *Vice Pres*
▲ EMP: 15
SALES (est): 1.1MM **Privately Held**
SIC: 2371 Jackets, fur

(G-9145)
ANALYSTS IN MEDIA (AIM) INC
55 Broad St Fl 9 (10004-2501)
PHONE..................212 488-1777
Alexa Calvarese, *Prdtn Dir*
Garry M Chocky, *Controller*
Jan Iverson, *Manager*
Will Hamilton-Hill, *Director*
EMP: 50
SALES (est): 5.1MM **Privately Held**
SIC: 2721 Magazines: publishing only, not printed on site

(G-9146)
ANALYTICAL TECHNOLOGY INC (PA)
Also Called: ATI
80 Broad St (10004-2209)
PHONE..................646 208-4643
John J Becker, *President*
Raymond B Cromer, *Exec VP*
Patrick J O'Dowd, *Vice Pres*
Steven Oppenheimer, *Director*
EMP: 16
SQ FT: 24,000
SALES (est): 7.9MM **Privately Held**
WEB: www.analyticaltechnology.com
SIC: 3829 3823 Gas detectors; water quality monitoring & control systems

(G-9147)
ANANDAMALI INC
35 N Moore St (10013-5711)
PHONE..................212 343-8964
Cheryl Hazan, *President*
EMP: 10
SQ FT: 2,900
SALES (est): 800K **Privately Held**
SIC: 2519 Garden furniture, except wood, metal, stone or concrete

(G-9148)
ANAREN HOLDING CORP (PA)
590 Madison Ave Fl 41 (10022-2524)
PHONE..................212 415-6700
EMP: 7
SALES (est): 232.2MM **Privately Held**
SIC: 3663 Radio & TV communications equipment

(G-9149)
ANASTASIA FIRST INTERNATIONAL
Also Called: Alexandros
345 7th Ave Fl 19 (10001-5035)
PHONE..................212 868-9241
Tommy Demetriades, *Owner*
Anastasia Demetriades, *Co-Owner*
Tommy Dimitriades, *Vice Pres*
EMP: 10
SALES: 1.2MM **Privately Held**
WEB: www.alexandros.com
SIC: 2371 Coats, fur

(G-9150)
ANASTASIA FURS INTERNATIONAL (PA)
Also Called: Alexandros
345 7th Ave Fl 19 (10001-5035)
PHONE..................212 868-9241
Anastasia Dimitriades, *President*
Tommy Dimitriades, *Vice Pres*
Alex Dimitriades, *Admin Sec*
EMP: 5
SQ FT: 7,000
SALES: 960K **Privately Held**
SIC: 2371 5632 7219 Fur goods; furriers; fur garment cleaning, repairing & storage

(G-9151)
ANCIENT MODERN ART LLC
Also Called: Hill, Lois Accessories
14 E 17th St Ph 1 (10003-1912)
PHONE..................212 302-0080
Elyssa Frank, *Manager*
Lois Hill,
EMP: 10 EST: 1998
SQ FT: 84,000
SALES (est): 1.1MM **Privately Held**
WEB: www.loishill.com
SIC: 3911 Jewelry, precious metal

(G-9152)
ANDES GOLD CORPORATION
405 Lexington Ave (10174-0002)
PHONE..................212 541-2495
Alejandro Diaz, *CEO*
EMP: 95
SALES (est): 2.3MM
SALES (corp-wide): 8.1MM **Privately Held**
SIC: 1041 Gold ores mining
PA: New World Gold Corporation
350 Camino Gardens Blvd
Boca Raton FL 33432
561 962-4139

(G-9153)
ANDIGO NEW MEDIA INC
150 W 25th St Rm 900 (10001-7458)
PHONE..................212 727-8445
Andrew Schulkind, *President*
EMP: 5
SALES (est): 509.4K **Privately Held**
WEB: www.andigo.com
SIC: 7372 Prepackaged software

(G-9154)
ANDREA STRONGWATER
Also Called: A Strongwater Designs
465 W End Ave (10024-4926)
PHONE..................212 873-0905
Andrea Strongwater, *Owner*
EMP: 5
SALES (est): 218K **Privately Held**
SIC: 2253 Knit outerwear mills

(G-9155)
ANDREW M SCHWARTZ LLC
Also Called: Sam NY
71 Gansevoort St Ste 2a (10014-1411)
PHONE..................212 391-7070
Andrew M Schwartz, *Mng Member*
Suzanne Schwartz,
Jessica Avery, *Assistant*
▲ EMP: 9
SALES (est): 1MM **Privately Held**
SIC: 2386 Coats & jackets, leather & sheep-lined

(G-9156)
ANGEL TEXTILES INC
519 8th Ave Fl 21 (10018-6575)
P.O. Box 1169, New Paltz (12561-7169)
PHONE..................212 532-0900
Michael Nist, *CEO*
Helen Prior, *Principal*
EMP: 8
SQ FT: 1,000
SALES (est): 1.2MM **Privately Held**
WEB: www.angelnyc.com
SIC: 3552 2396 Silk screens for textile industry; automotive & apparel trimmings

(G-9157)
ANGEL-MADE IN HEAVEN INC (PA)
525 Fashion Ave Rm 1710 (10018-0440)
PHONE..................212 869-5678
Fax: 212 944-9698
Morris Dahan, *President*
▲ EMP: 3 EST: 1998
SQ FT: 1,000
SALES (est): 1.2MM **Privately Held**
WEB: www.angelmih.com
SIC: 2339 Sportswear, women's

(G-9158)
ANGIOGENEX INC (PA)
Also Called: (A DEVELOPMENT STAGE COMPANY)
425 Madison Ave Ste 902 (10017-1110)
PHONE..................347 468-6799
Fax: 212 874-5027
William A Garland PHD, *CEO*
Richard A Salvador PHD, *President*
Robert Benezra PHD, *Chief*
Michael M Strage, *Vice Pres*
Marty Murray, *Controller*
EMP: 5
SQ FT: 700
SALES (est): 675.7K **Publicly Held**
SIC: 2834 Pharmaceutical preparations

(G-9159)
ANHEUSER-BUSCH LLC
250 Park Ave Fl 2 (10177-0299)
PHONE..................212 573-8800
Carlos Brito, *Branch Mgr*
Maria Barros, *Director*
Fabio Mazza, *Director*
EMP: 162
SALES (corp-wide): 1B **Privately Held**
SIC: 2082 Beer (alcoholic beverage)
HQ: Anheuser-Busch, Llc
1 Busch Pl
Saint Louis MO 63118
314 632-6777

(G-9160)
ANHEUSER-BUSCH INBEV FIN INC
250 Park Ave (10177-0001)
PHONE..................212 573-8800
Carlos Brito, *CEO*
Marianne Amssoms, *Vice Pres*
Ricardo Dias, *Vice Pres*
Washington Dutra, *Vice Pres*
Josh Halpern, *Vice Pres*
EMP: 8
SALES (est): 919.1K **Privately Held**
SIC: 2082 Beer (alcoholic beverage)

(G-9161)
ANIMA GROUP LLC
Also Called: 1884 Collection
435 E 79th St Ph H (10075-1079)
PHONE..................917 913-2053
Alberto Petochi,
▲ EMP: 7
SALES (est): 790K **Privately Held**
SIC: 3911 Jewelry, precious metal

(G-9162)
ANIMAL FAIR MEDIA INC
545 8th Ave Rm 401 (10018-4341)
PHONE..................212 629-0392
Wendy Diamond, *President*
Mike Wang, *Sales Dir*
EMP: 12
SQ FT: 1,200
SALES: 1.2MM **Privately Held**
WEB: www.animalfair.com
SIC: 2721 Magazines: publishing only, not printed on site

(G-9163)
ANN GISH INC (PA)
4 W 20th St (10011-4203)
PHONE..................212 969-9200
Ann P Gish Phillips, *CEO*
David Phillips, *CFO*
Richard Collymore, *Manager*
▲ EMP: 1
SQ FT: 2,000
SALES (est): 2.9MM **Privately Held**
WEB: www.anngish.com
SIC: 2211 2221 2341 2392 Broadwoven fabric mills, cotton; broadwoven fabric mills, manmade; nightgowns & negligees: women's & children's; chemises, camisoles & teddies: women's & children's; household furnishings; blankets, comforters & beddings; finishing plants, manmade fiber & silk fabrics; interior design services

(G-9164)
ANNA SUI CORP (PA)
250 W 39th St Fl 15 (10018-4439)
PHONE..................212 768-1951
Fax: 212 768-8825
Anna Sui, *Ch of Bd*
Bob Sui, *President*
Wen Liao, *Production*
Lauren Grover, *Design Engr*
Gladys Goldsmith, *Controller*
▲ EMP: 39
SQ FT: 3,000
SALES (est): 5.9MM **Privately Held**
WEB: www.annasui.com
SIC: 2331 2339 2335 2337 Blouses, women's & juniors': made from purchased material; women's & misses' athletic clothing & sportswear; slacks: women's, misses' & juniors'; women's, juniors' & misses' dresses; skirts, separate: women's, misses' & juniors'; jackets & vests, except fur & leather: women's

(G-9165)
ANNUALS PUBLISHING CO INC
Also Called: Madison Square Press
10 E 23rd St Ste 510 (10010-4459)
PHONE..................212 505-0950
Fax: 212 979-2207
EMP: 3
SQ FT: 1,000
SALES: 1.5MM **Privately Held**
SIC: 2731 Books-Publishing/Printing

GEOGRAPHIC SECTION

New York - New York County (G-9193)

(G-9166)
ANSWER PRINTING INC
505 8th Ave Rm 1101 (10018-4540)
P.O. Box 3442 (10163-3442)
PHONE.....................212 922-2922
Fax: 212 681-9290
Larry Dunne, *President*
EMP: 17
SQ FT: 3,800
SALES (est): 1.5MM **Privately Held**
WEB: www.answerprinting.com
SIC: 2741 2752 Business service newsletters: publishing & printing; commercial printing, lithographic

(G-9167)
ANTERIOS INC
60 E 42nd St Ste 1160 (10165-6206)
PHONE.....................212 303-1683
Jon Edelson MD, *President*
Fabian Tenenbaum, *CFO*
Klaus Theobald MD, *Osteopathy*
EMP: 6
SALES (est): 987.9K **Privately Held**
SIC: 2834 Pharmaceutical preparations
PA: Allergan Public Limited Company
Euro House
Cork

(G-9168)
ANTHONY L & S LLC (PA)
Also Called: Anthony L&S Footwear Group
500 Fashion Ave Fl 16b (10018-0810)
PHONE.....................212 386-7245
Ashley Ambersinos, *Sales Staff*
Joy Crook, *Manager*
Jenny Rosado, *Manager*
Anthony Loconte,
▲ EMP: 6
SQ FT: 6,000
SALES (est): 3.4MM **Privately Held**
WEB: www.anthonyls.com
SIC: 3021 5139 Rubber & plastics footwear; shoes

(G-9169)
ANTWERP DIAMOND DISTRIBUTORS
6 E 45th St Rm 302 (10017-8451)
PHONE.....................212 319-3300
Fax: 212 207-8168
Phyllis Lisker, *President*
Larry Lisker, *Manager*
EMP: 15 EST: 1955
SQ FT: 4,000
SALES (est): 1.6MM **Privately Held**
WEB: www.antwerpdistributors.com
SIC: 3915 5094 Diamond cutting & polishing; diamonds (gems)

(G-9170)
ANTWERP SALES INTL INC
Also Called: A.S.I. Francies Ltd
576 5th Ave (10036-4807)
PHONE.....................212 354-6515
Fax: 212 768-1209
Norbert May, *President*
Danny Klugman, *Vice Pres*
Yossel Slomovits, *CFO*
Danny Kougman, *Human Res Mgr*
EMP: 18
SQ FT: 3,500
SALES (est): 2.9MM **Privately Held**
SIC: 3915 Diamond cutting & polishing

(G-9171)
AOI PHARMA INC
750 Lexington Ave Fl 20 (10022-9819)
PHONE.....................212 531-5970
Ron Bentsur, *CEO*
James Oliviero, *CFO*
EMP: 17
SALES (est): 1.2MM **Privately Held**
SIC: 2834 Pharmaceutical preparations

(G-9172)
APEC PAPER INDUSTRIES LTD
Also Called: American Printing & Envelope
237 W 37th St Rm 901 (10018-6745)
PHONE.....................212 730-0088
Fax: 212 730-0053
Justin Koplin, *President*
Maureen Best, *Admin Dir*
EMP: 5 EST: 1935
SQ FT: 6,000
SALES: 2.4MM **Privately Held**
SIC: 2677 5112 Envelopes; envelopes

(G-9173)
APEX TEXICON INC (PA)
295 Madison Ave (10017-6304)
P.O. Box 960670, Inwood (11096-0670)
PHONE.....................516 239-4400
Edward Schlussel, *President*
John Kurz, *Vice Pres*
David Kurz, *Treasurer*
EMP: 24 EST: 1943
SQ FT: 9,000
SALES: 1.7MM **Privately Held**
SIC: 2221 2258 2257 Broadwoven fabric mills, manmade; net & netting products; tricot fabrics; weft knit fabric mills

(G-9174)
APICELLA JEWELERS INC
40 W 39th St Fl 4 (10018-2142)
PHONE.....................212 840-2024
Fax: 212 575-4937
John Apicella, *President*
Anthony Apicella, *Vice Pres*
Kevin Khan, *Manager*
EMP: 30 EST: 1946
SQ FT: 2,500
SALES (est): 3.1MM **Privately Held**
SIC: 3911 Jewelry, precious metal

(G-9175)
APOLLO APPAREL GROUP LLC
Also Called: Apollo Jeans
1407 Broadway Rm 2000 (10018-5120)
PHONE.....................212 398-6585
Salim Mann, *Mng Member*
Victor Hasbani, *Manager*
▲ EMP: 10
SALES (est): 1.8MM **Privately Held**
SIC: 2211 2389 Jean fabrics; men's miscellaneous accessories

(G-9176)
APOLLO INVESTMENT FUND VII LP
9 W 57th St Fl 43 (10019-2700)
PHONE.....................212 515-3200
Martin Kelly, *CFO*
Chris Weidler, *Officer*
Leon Black,
Laurence Berg,
EMP: 8
SALES (est): 824.2K **Privately Held**
SIC: 2731 Books: publishing & printing

(G-9177)
APPAREL GROUP LTD
Thyme
469 7th Ave Fl 8 (10018-7605)
PHONE.....................212 328-1200
Thomas Bietrich, *President*
Pam Wyke, *Sales Executive*
EMP: 40 **Privately Held**
SIC: 2331 Women's & misses' blouses & shirts
HQ: The Apparel Group Ltd
883 Trinity Dr
Lewisville TX 75056
214 469-3300

(G-9178)
APPAREL PARTNERSHIP GROUP LLC
250 W 39th St Rm 701 (10018-4719)
PHONE.....................212 302-7722
Matthew Healy, *Mng Member*
EMP: 5
SALES (est): 451.8K **Privately Held**
SIC: 2322 2341 5136 5137 Men's & boys' underwear & nightwear; women's & children's undergarments; underwear, men's & boys'; women's & children's lingerie & undergarments

(G-9179)
APPAREL PRODUCTION INC
270 W 39th St Rm 1701 (10018-0330)
PHONE.....................212 278-8362
Fax: 212 278-8357
Theodore Sadaka, *President*
Teddy Sadaka, *President*
▲ EMP: 5
SALES (est): 471.4K **Privately Held**
SIC: 3949 Sporting & athletic goods

(G-9180)
APPBOY INC
263 W 38th St Fl 16 (10018-0483)
PHONE.....................504 327-7269
Mark Ghermezian, *CEO*
Doug Pepper, *Principal*
Matthew McRoberts, *Vice Pres*
Oliver Bell, *VP Opers*
Paul Szemerenyi, *VP Sales*
EMP: 15 EST: 2013
SALES (est): 1.6MM **Privately Held**
SIC: 7372 Application computer software

(G-9181)
APPFIGURES INC
133 Chrystie St Fl 3 (10002-2810)
PHONE.....................212 343-7900
Eliahu Michaeli, *President*
Jorge Vargas, *Opers Mgr*
Ashley Flores, *Office Admin*
Errol Markland, *Web Dvlpr*
EMP: 14
SALES (est): 1MM **Privately Held**
SIC: 7372 Business oriented computer software

(G-9182)
APPLE BEAUTY INC
214 W 39th St Rm 1006 (10018-5537)
PHONE.....................646 832-3051
Natalia Rusanoba, *Director*
◆ EMP: 5
SQ FT: 1,000
SALES (est): 877K **Privately Held**
SIC: 2844 Toilet preparations

(G-9183)
APPLICATION SECURITY INC (DH)
55 Broad St Rm 10a (10004-2509)
PHONE.....................212 912-4100
Fax: 212 947-8788
Jack Hembrough, *President*
Dave McNamara, *Vice Pres*
Gene Trog, *Research*
Peter Schwartz, *CFO*
Mark Trinidad, *Mktg Dir*
EMP: 75
SALES: 1.6MM **Privately Held**
WEB: www.appsecinc.com
SIC: 7372 Prepackaged software
HQ: Trustwave Holdings, Inc.
70 W Madison St Ste 1050
Chicago IL 60602
312 750-0950

(G-9184)
APPLIED MINERALS INC (PA)
110 Greene St Ste 1101 (10012-3824)
PHONE.....................212 226-4265
John F Levy, *Ch of Bd*
Andre M Zeitoun, *President*
Christopher T Carney, *CFO*
William Gleeson, *General Counsel*
▲ EMP: 29
SALES: 507.4K **Publicly Held**
WEB: www.atlasmining.com
SIC: 1459 2816 Clays, except kaolin & ball; iron oxide pigments (ochers, siennas, umbers)

(G-9185)
APRIL PRINTING CO INC
1201 Broadway Ste 403 (10001-5658)
PHONE.....................212 685-7455
Brad April, *President*
Muriel April, *Vice Pres*
Muriel Horowitz, *Vice Pres*
Ariel April, *Creative Dir*
EMP: 12
SQ FT: 2,500
SALES (est): 1.5MM **Privately Held**
WEB: www.aprilprinting.com
SIC: 2759 Commercial printing

(G-9186)
AR & AR JEWELRY INC
31 W 47th St Fl 15 (10036-2808)
PHONE.....................212 764-7916
Fax: 212 764-7921
Aras Tirtirian, *President*
Aras Tirtir, *Vice Pres*
▲ EMP: 40 EST: 1996
SALES (est): 4.9MM **Privately Held**
SIC: 3911 Jewelry, precious metal

(G-9187)
AR MEDIA INC
601 W 26th St Rm 810 (10001-1153)
PHONE.....................212 352-0731
Fax: 212 352-0738
Raul Martinez, *CEO*
Diane Defroches, *CEO*
Alex Gonzalez, *Founder*
Terry Waters, *COO*
Scott Campbell, *Vice Pres*
EMP: 50
SQ FT: 17,000
SALES (est): 5.6MM **Privately Held**
WEB: www.arnewyork.com
SIC: 2741 7311 Catalogs: publishing only, not printed on site; advertising agencies

(G-9188)
AR PUBLISHING COMPANY INC
55 Broad St Rm 20b (10004-2589)
PHONE.....................212 482-0303
Helen Brusilovsky, *President*
EMP: 10
SALES (est): 479.6K **Privately Held**
WEB: www.vnsnews.com
SIC: 2711 Newspapers, publishing & printing

(G-9189)
ARABELLA TEXTILES LLC
303 5th Ave Rm 1402 (10016-6601)
PHONE.....................212 679-0611
Fax: 212 679-0211
Deborah Connolly, *Mng Member*
▲ EMP: 5
SALES (est): 383.7K **Privately Held**
WEB: www.deborahconnolly.com
SIC: 2299 Batting, wadding, padding & fillings

(G-9190)
ARBEIT BROS INC
345 7th Ave Fl 20 (10001-5034)
PHONE.....................212 736-9761
Sam Arbeit, *President*
EMP: 5 EST: 1948
SQ FT: 2,000
SALES (est): 390K **Privately Held**
SIC: 2371 Apparel, fur

(G-9191)
ARBOR BOOKS INC
244 Madison Ave (10016-2817)
PHONE.....................201 236-9990
Joel Hochman, *President*
Larry Leichman, *Vice Pres*
EMP: 20
SALES: 2.5MM **Privately Held**
WEB: www.arborbooks.com
SIC: 2731 Book publishing

(G-9192)
ARC MUSIC CORPORATION
630 9th Ave Ste 1212 (10036-3742)
PHONE.....................212 492-9414
Fax: 212 262-6299
Eugene Goodman, *President*
Philip Chess, *Vice Pres*
Marshal Chess, *Treasurer*
Jim Leavitt, *Director*
EMP: 13
SALES (est): 1MM **Privately Held**
SIC: 2741 Miscellaneous publishing

(G-9193)
ARCADE INC
1700 Broadway Fl 25 (10019-5925)
PHONE.....................212 541-2600
Richard Kaleta, *Ch of Bd*
Louis Ziafonte, *Senior VP*
Jamie Ross, *Vice Pres*
Briget Tyler, *Purchasing*
Rance Haskew, *Engineer*
EMP: 1838
SALES (est): 208MM
SALES (corp-wide): 5.9B **Publicly Held**
SIC: 2752 Commercial printing, lithographic
HQ: Visant Holding Corp.
3601 Minnesota Dr Ste 400
Minneapolis MN 55435
914 595-8200

(G-9194)
ARCANGEL INC
Also Called: Catherine Deane
209 W 38th St Rm 1001 (10018-4465)
PHONE..................347 771-0789
Catherine Deane, *CEO*
Susan Miller, *Manager*
EMP: 2
SQ FT: 2,000
SALES: 1MM **Privately Held**
SIC: 2335 Wedding gowns & dresses

(G-9195)
ARCHITECTS NEWSPAPER LLC
Also Called: Bd Projects
21 Murray St Fl 5 (10007-2244)
PHONE..................212 966-0630
Becca Blasdel, *Editor*
Molly Sullivan, *Comms Dir*
Susan Kramer, *Director*
Diana Darling,
William Menking,
EMP: 12
SALES (est): 840K **Privately Held**
WEB: www.archpaper.com
SIC: 2711 Newspapers: publishing only, not printed on site

(G-9196)
ARCHITECTURAL TEXTILES USA INC
Also Called: Architex International
36 E 23rd St Ste F (10010-4409)
PHONE..................212 213-6972
Fax: 212 213-8033
Victor Liss, *Manager*
Kim Matanis, *Executive*
EMP: 35
SALES (corp-wide): 59.9MM **Privately Held**
WEB: www.architex-ljh.com
SIC: 2299 5087 Broadwoven fabrics: linen, jute, hemp & ramie; service establishment equipment
PA: Architectural Textiles U.S.A., Inc.
3333 Commercial Ave
Northbrook IL 60062
847 205-1333

(G-9197)
ARCHIVE360 INC
65 Broadway Fl 23 (10006-2503)
PHONE..................212 731-2438
Robert Desteno, *CEO*
Tiberiu Popp, *Founder*
EMP: 22
SALES: 10MM **Privately Held**
SIC: 7372 Prepackaged software

(G-9198)
AREA INC
Also Called: Area Warehouse
58 E 11th St Fl 2 (10003-6019)
PHONE..................212 924-7084
Anki Spets, *President*
Yuko Watatami, *Executive Asst*
▲ EMP: 9
SQ FT: 6,000
SALES (est): 1MM **Privately Held**
WEB: www.lundstrom-id.com
SIC: 2392 Household furnishings

(G-9199)
ARGEE AMERICA INC
Also Called: Argee Sportswear
1400 Broadway Rm 2307 (10018-0390)
PHONE..................212 768-9840
Roshan L Gera, *President*
Shyama Gera, *Vice Pres*
▲ EMP: 8
SQ FT: 3,000
SALES (est): 1.3MM **Privately Held**
SIC: 2339 5137 Sportswear, women's; sportswear, women's & children's

(G-9200)
ARGOSY CERAMIC AROSPC MTLS LLC
225 W 34th St Ste 1106 (10122-1106)
PHONE..................212 268-0003
Richard Rocco, *Mng Member*
Crissy Tecerini, *Administration*
EMP: 12
SALES (est): 767.4K **Privately Held**
SIC: 3299 Ceramic fiber

(G-9201)
ARGUS MEDIA INC
500 5th Ave Ste 2410 (10110-2401)
PHONE..................646 376-6130
Rachel Hosch, *Finance Mgr*
Diego Secaira, *Accounts Mgr*
Kristin Conrey, *Marketing Mgr*
Enrique Arana, *Marketing Staff*
Jennifer Eyring, *Manager*
EMP: 15
SALES (corp-wide): 181.5MM **Privately Held**
SIC: 2741 Miscellaneous publishing
HQ: Argus Media, Inc.
2929 Allen Pkwy
Houston TX 77019
713 968-0000

(G-9202)
ARIELA AND ASSOCIATES INTL LLC (PA)
1359 Broadway Fl 21 (10018-7824)
PHONE..................212 683-4131
Fax: 212 683-4038
Ariela Balk, *President*
Mendel Balk, *COO*
Melissa Dietiker, *Vice Pres*
Barry Graff, *Vice Pres*
Toni Spinelli, *Vice Pres*
▲ EMP: 110
SQ FT: 27,741
SALES (est): 39.3MM **Privately Held**
WEB: www.ariela-alpha.com
SIC: 2341 Women's & children's undergarments

(G-9203)
ARLEE HOME FASHIONS INC (PA)
Also Called: Arlee Group
261 5th Ave Fl Mezz (10016-7600)
PHONE..................212 213-0425
Fax: 212 532-6428
David Frankel, *CEO*
Marsha Cutler, *President*
Marsha Caparelli, *Vice Pres*
Julie Polich, *Vice Pres*
Alan Mandell, *CFO*
▲ EMP: 60 EST: 1976
SQ FT: 20,000
SALES (est): 126.5MM **Privately Held**
SIC: 2392 Pillows, bed: made from purchased materials; chair covers & pads: made from purchased materials

(G-9204)
ARMACEL ARMOR CORPORATION
745 5th Ave Fl 7 (10151-0802)
PHONE..................805 384-1144
Asia Fernandez, *President*
David Fernandez, *Vice Pres*
EMP: 35
SALES (est): 5.6MM **Privately Held**
WEB: www.armacelarmorcorp.com
SIC: 3728 Military aircraft equipment & armament; aircraft assemblies, subassemblies & parts

(G-9205)
ARON STREIT INC
Also Called: Streit Matzoh Co
148-154 Rivington St (10002)
PHONE..................212 475-7000
Fax: 212 505-7650
▲ EMP: 45
SQ FT: 100,000
SALES (est): 8.6MM **Privately Held**
WEB: www.streitsmatzos.com
SIC: 2052 5149 Matzos; bakery products

(G-9206)
ARPA USA
62 Greene St Frnt 1 (10012-4346)
PHONE..................212 965-4099
Thomas Weissbach, *Principal*
Sandro Marini, *Corp Comm Staff*
EMP: 6
SALES (est): 968.7K **Privately Held**
SIC: 3589 High pressure cleaning equipment

(G-9207)
ARPER USA INC
476 Broadway Ste 2f (10013-2641)
P.O. Box 1683 (10013-0870)
PHONE..................212 647-8900
Emanuele Corvo, *President*
Carmela Puleo, *Cust Mgr*
Andrew Floyd, *Manager*
▲ EMP: 6
SALES (est): 941.7K **Privately Held**
SIC: 2599 Factory furniture & fixtures
HQ: Arper Spa
Via Lombardia 16
Monastier Di Treviso TV 31050
042 279-18

(G-9208)
ARRAY MARKETING GROUP INC (PA)
200 Madison Ave Ste 2121 (10016-4000)
PHONE..................212 750-3367
Tom Hendren, *CEO*
Mike Caron, *Vice Pres*
Mark Lattimore, *Design Engr*
Kevin Pattrick, *CFO*
Paul O'Meara, *VP Sales*
▲ EMP: 25
SALES (est): 6.4MM **Privately Held**
WEB: www.arraymarketing.com
SIC: 2541 Store & office display cases & fixtures

(G-9209)
ART ASIAPACIFIC PUBLISHING LLC
410 W 24th St Apt 14a (10011-1356)
PHONE..................212 255-6003
Elaine Ng,
EMP: 8
SALES: 800K **Privately Held**
SIC: 2741 Miscellaneous publishing

(G-9210)
ART FLAG COMPANY INC
8 Jay St Frnt 1 (10013-2891)
PHONE..................212 334-1890
Fax: 212 941-9631
George Weiner, *President*
Carmen Weiner, *Vice Pres*
Daniel Bright, *Manager*
Nancy Maminsky, *Art Dir*
EMP: 18 EST: 1971
SQ FT: 5,000
SALES: 1MM **Privately Held**
SIC: 2399 2396 Flags, fabric; banners, made from fabric; screen printing on fabric articles

(G-9211)
ART INDUSTRIES OF NEW YORK
601 W 26th St Rm 1425 (10001-1160)
PHONE..................212 633-9200
Steve Kaitz, *President*
Neal H Klein, *Vice Pres*
EMP: 50
SQ FT: 80,000
SALES (est): 6.4MM **Privately Held**
WEB: www.salinesolutions.com
SIC: 2675 Die-cut paper & board

(G-9212)
ART PEOPLE INC
594 Broadway Rm 1102 (10012-3289)
PHONE..................212 431-4865
Fax: 212 219-2465
Gary Golkin, *President*
Carrie Golkin, *Treasurer*
EMP: 8
SQ FT: 10,000
SALES (est): 460K **Privately Held**
SIC: 2221 Wall covering fabrics, manmade fiber & silk; upholstery fabrics, manmade fiber & silk

(G-9213)
ART RESOURCES TRANSFER INC
526 W 26th St Rm 614 (10001-5522)
PHONE..................212 255-2919
Yael Meridan Schori, *President*
Bill Bartman, *Exec Dir*
Jennifer Seass, *Director*
▲ EMP: 5
SQ FT: 4,000
SALES: 883.7K **Privately Held**
WEB: www.artretran.com
SIC: 2791 Typesetting

(G-9214)
ART SCROLL PRINTING CORP
230 W 41st St Bsmt 1 (10036-7207)
PHONE..................212 929-2413
Elliot Schwartz, *President*
EMP: 13
SALES (est): 1.8MM **Privately Held**
SIC: 2752 Commercial printing, lithographic

(G-9215)
ART-TEC JEWELRY DESIGNS LTD (PA)
48 W 48th St Ste 401 (10036-1727)
PHONE..................212 719-2941
Fax: 212 719-9456
Edward Zylka, *President*
EMP: 19
SQ FT: 5,000
SALES (est): 4.1MM **Privately Held**
SIC: 3911 Jewelry, precious metal

(G-9216)
ARTEAST LLC
Also Called: Zadig and Voltaire
102 Franklin St Fl 4 (10013-3015)
PHONE..................212 965-8787
Julie Hoepker, *Principal*
Ascher Saddah, *CFO*
Pascaline Audren, *Mng Member*
EMP: 8
SALES (est): 2.1MM **Privately Held**
SIC: 2335 5137 7389 Women's, juniors' & misses' dresses; women's & children's clothing; apparel designers, commercial

(G-9217)
ARTHUR FROMMER MAGAZINES LLC
Also Called: Arthur Frommer Budget Travel
530 7th Ave Uppr 2 (10018-2542)
PHONE..................646 695-6739
Fax: 212 649-6707
Nancy Telliho, *Publisher*
Erik Torkells, *Editor*
Pauline Frommer, *Chief*
Pat O'Donnell, *Adv Mgr*
Donald Welsh, *Mng Member*
EMP: 10
SALES (est): 987.3K
SALES (corp-wide): 2.6MM **Privately Held**
WEB: www.budgettravel.com
SIC: 2721 Magazines: publishing only, not printed on site
PA: Fletcher Asset Management, Inc.
48 Wall St Fl 6
New York NY 10005
212 284-4800

(G-9218)
ARTICULATE GLOBAL INC
244 5th Ave Ste 2960 (10001-7604)
PHONE..................800 861-4880
Adam Schwartz, *CEO*
Frazier Miller, *COO*
Lucy Suros, *Vice Pres*
Patrick Eakin, *QA Dir*
Ronald McGinnis Jr, *QA Dir*
EMP: 130
SQ FT: 20,000
SALES (est): 18.8MM **Privately Held**
WEB: www.articulate.com
SIC: 7372 Prepackaged software

(G-9219)
ARTISTIC FRAME CORP (PA)
979 3rd Ave Ste 1705 (10022-3804)
PHONE..................212 289-2100
Fax: 212 289-2101
David Stevens, *President*
Mark Rosenman, *Purch Agent*
Yossi Dilmani, *Info Tech Mgr*
Morris Sutton, *Executive*
EMP: 110
SQ FT: 400,000
SALES (est): 104.2MM **Privately Held**
SIC: 2426 5021 Frames for upholstered furniture, wood; office furniture

New York - New York County

(G-9220)
ARTISTIC RIBBON NOVELTY CO INC
22 W 21st St Fl 3 (10010-6970)
P.O. Box 126, Hillsdale NJ (07642-0126)
PHONE..................................212 255-4224
Fax: 212 645-6589
Kenneth Hanz, *President*
Kenneth Handz, *President*
Steve Eigner, *Corp Secy*
▲ **EMP:** 20 **EST:** 1928
SQ FT: 15,000
SALES (est): 2.5MM **Privately Held**
WEB: www.artisticribbon.com
SIC: 2396 5131 Ribbons & bows, cut & sewed; sewing supplies & notions; ribbons

(G-9221)
ARTISTIC TYPOGRAPHY CORP (PA)
Also Called: Artistic Group, The
151 W 30th St Fl 8 (10001-4026)
PHONE..................................212 463-8880
Fax: 212 736-6668
Paul J Weinstein, *President*
▲ **EMP:** 6 **EST:** 1959
SQ FT: 7,500
SALES (est): 2MM **Privately Held**
WEB: www.tagimage.com
SIC: 2759 2791 Commercial printing; typographic composition, for the printing trade

(G-9222)
ARTKRAFT STRAUSS LLC
Also Called: Artkraft Sign
1776 Broadway Ste 1810 (10019-2017)
PHONE..................................212 265-5155
Fax: 212 265-5262
Tama Starr, *President*
James Manfredi, *Mfg Spvr*
Neil Vonknoblauch, *CFO*
Kim Ramos, *Office Mgr*
Amy Hu, *Manager*
EMP: 30 **EST:** 1935
SQ FT: 1,500
SALES (est): 3.7MM **Privately Held**
WEB: www.artkraft.com
SIC: 3993 7312 Electric signs; outdoor advertising services

(G-9223)
ARTNEWS LTD (HQ)
Also Called: The Artnewsletter
110 Greene St Ph 2 (10012-3824)
PHONE..................................212 398-1690
Fax: 212 768-4002
Milton Esterow, *Publisher*
Peter M Brant, *Principal*
Joanne Sonntecchio, *Bookkeeper*
Nicole De George, *Assistant*
Julie L Klossner, *Assistant*
▲ **EMP:** 18 **EST:** 1902
SQ FT: 12,000
SALES (est): 3.5MM
SALES (corp-wide): 7.9MM **Privately Held**
WEB: www.artnews.com
SIC: 2721 Magazines: publishing & printing

(G-9224)
ARTSCROLL PRINTING CORP (PA)
53 W 23rd St Fl 4 (10010-4239)
PHONE..................................212 929-2413
Fax: 212 633-1264
Elliot Schwartz, *President*
David Schwartz, *Corp Secy*
Morris Pilicer, *Controller*
Maria Rojas, *Hum Res Coord*
Skip Vesell, *Branch Mgr*
EMP: 24
SALES (est): 4.4MM **Privately Held**
SIC: 2759 2791 2752 7336 Commercial printing; thermography; typesetting; commercial printing, lithographic; commercial art & graphic design; signs & advertising specialties

(G-9225)
ASAHI SHIMBUN AMERICA INC
620 8th Ave (10018-1618)
PHONE..................................212 398-0257
Fax: 212 221-1734
Erika Toh, *Principal*
EMP: 15
SALES (est): 1.1MM **Privately Held**
SIC: 2711 Newspapers, publishing & printing

(G-9226)
ASENCE INC
65 Broadway Fl 7 (10006-2536)
PHONE..................................347 335-2606
Fax: 212 430-6501
EMP: 21
SALES: 3MM **Privately Held**
SIC: 2834 Pharmaceutical Preparations

(G-9227)
ASHBURNS INC
Also Called: Ashburns Engravers
90 John St Rm 409 (10038-3242)
PHONE..................................212 227-5692
Fax: 212 385-1112
Daniel De Prima, *President*
Leonard Zinanti, *Vice Pres*
Jack Natter, *Manager*
EMP: 5
SQ FT: 2,000
SALES (est): 400K **Privately Held**
WEB: www.ashburns.com
SIC: 3479 Engraving jewelry silverware, or metal

(G-9228)
ASHER JEWELRY COMPANY INC
Also Called: Asher Collection
48 W 48th St Ste 303 (10036-1714)
PHONE..................................212 302-6233
Fax: 212 302-6279
Ben Asher, *Ch of Bd*
Fred Asher, *Vice Pres*
Tamara Asher, *Treasurer*
▲ **EMP:** 60
SQ FT: 6,000
SALES (est): 8.2MM **Privately Held**
WEB: www.asherjewelry.com
SIC: 3911 Jewelry apparel

(G-9229)
ASHKO GROUP LLC
10 W 33rd St Rm 1019 (10001-3306)
PHONE..................................212 594-6050
Jack Ashkenazi, *President*
Charles Ashkenazi, *COO*
David Braha, *CFO*
Nympha Phrijdekkar, *VP Sales*
▲ **EMP:** 18
SQ FT: 1,500
SALES (est): 3.8MM **Privately Held**
SIC: 2252 5139 Socks; footwear

(G-9230)
ASI SIGN SYSTEMS INC
192 Lexington Ave Rm 1002 (10016-6823)
PHONE..................................646 742-1320
EMP: 7
SALES (corp-wide): 16.9MM **Privately Held**
SIC: 3993 Signs & advertising specialties
PA: Asi Sign Systems, Inc.
8181 Jetstar Dr Ste 110
Irving TX 75063
214 352-9140

(G-9231)
ASIA CONNECTION LLC
200 E 90th St Apt 4h (10128-3559)
PHONE..................................212 369-4644
Lee Souyun,
▲ **EMP:** 12
SALES (est): 2.2MM **Privately Held**
SIC: 3949 5091 Swimming pools, except plastic; swimming pools, equipment & supplies

(G-9232)
ASITE LLC
375 Park Ave Ste 2607 (10152-2600)
PHONE..................................203 545-3089
Gordon Ashworth, *Principal*
EMP: 60
SALES (est): 1.6MM **Privately Held**
SIC: 7372 Prepackaged software

(G-9233)
ASM USA INC
73 Spring St Rm 309 (10012-5801)
PHONE..................................212 925-2906
EMP: 7
SALES (est): 651.5K
SALES (corp-wide): 188.1K **Privately Held**
SIC: 3444 5051 Sheet metal specialties, not stamped; steel
HQ: Approche Sur Mesure A S M
63 Rue Edouard Vaillant
Levallois Perret 92300
147 481-020

(G-9234)
ASP BLADE INTRMDATE HLDNGS INC (PA)
299 Park Ave Fl 34 (10171-3805)
PHONE..................................212 476-8000
Loren S Easton, *President*
EMP: 2 **EST:** 2015
SALES (est): 866.1MM **Privately Held**
SIC: 3531 3523 6719 Construction machinery; forestry related equipment; farm machinery & equipment; cutters & blowers, ensilage; tractors, farm; investment holding companies, except banks

(G-9235)
ASPEN PUBLISHERS INC (DH)
Also Called: Aspen Law & Business
76 9th Ave Ste 724 (10011-5222)
PHONE..................................212 771-0600
Fax: 212 771-0885
Mark Dorman, *CEO*
Ellen Fischer, *Editor*
Anita Rosepka, *Editor*
Claudia Levine, *Chief*
Susan Yules, *Exec VP*
EMP: 603
SALES (est): 1MM
SALES (corp-wide): 4.5B **Privately Held**
SIC: 2721 2731 2741 Trade journals: publishing only, not printed on site; book publishing; newsletter publishing
HQ: Wolters Kluwer United States Inc.
2700 Lake Cook Rd
Riverwoods IL 60015
847 580-5000

(G-9236)
ASPEN RESEARCH GROUP LTD
17 State St Fl 15 (10004-1532)
PHONE..................................212 425-9588
Fax: 212 425-9349
Tony Rivera, *Sales Staff*
Mike Neff, *Manager*
EMP: 7
SALES (corp-wide): 4.5MM **Privately Held**
SIC: 7372 Business oriented computer software
PA: Aspen Research Group Ltd
802 Grand Ave Ste 120
Glenwood Springs CO 81601
970 945-2921

(G-9237)
ASPEX INCORPORATED
161 Hudson St Apt 1a (10013-2145)
PHONE..................................212 966-0410
Fax: 212 645-8343
Gerald Henrici, *President*
Nicole McLeod, *Bookkeeper*
Johnathan Erbe, *Marketing Staff*
Sonia Ortiz, *Office Admin*
Michael Stoeckel, *Consultant*
EMP: 20
SALES (est): 4MM **Privately Held**
SIC: 3823 3829 Computer interface equipment for industrial process control; measuring & controlling devices

(G-9238)
ASSOCIATED BRANDS INC
111 8th Ave (10011-5201)
P.O. Box 788, Medina (14103-0788)
PHONE..................................585 798-3475
Scott Greenwood, *President*
James Akers, *Vice Pres*
Jurgen Pahl, *VP Opers*
Jim Dimatteo, *Plant Mgr*
Paul Kerr, *Opers Mgr*
◆ **EMP:** 266
SQ FT: 340,000
SALES (est): 63MM
SALES (corp-wide): 3.2B **Publicly Held**
WEB: www.associatedbrands.com
SIC: 2034 2043 2066 2099 Fruits, dried or dehydrated, except freeze-dried; vegetables, dried or dehydrated (except freeze-dried); cereal breakfast foods; chocolate & cocoa products; food preparations
HQ: Associated Brands Inc
1790 Matheson Blvd
Mississauga ON L4W 0
905 643-1211

(G-9239)
ASSOCIATED BUS PUBLICATIONS CO
Also Called: Electronic Tech Briefs
1466 Broadway Ste 910 (10036-7309)
PHONE..................................212 490-3999
Fax: 212 986-7864
Bill Schnirring, *Ch of Bd*
Joseph Pramberger, *President*
Cathleen Lambertson, *Editor*
Domenic Mucchetti, *COO*
William Hague, *Vice Pres*
EMP: 40 **EST:** 1975
SQ FT: 11,000
SALES (est): 5MM **Privately Held**
WEB: www.emhartcontest.com
SIC: 2721 Magazines: publishing only, not printed on site

(G-9240)
ASSOCIATION FOR CMPT MCHY INC (PA)
Also Called: ACM
2 Penn Plz Rm 701 (10121-0799)
P.O. Box 30777 (10087-0777)
PHONE..................................212 869-7440
Fax: 212 869-0481
John R White, *CEO*
Vinton Cerf, *President*
Wendy Hall, *President*
Matthew Smyth, *General Mgr*
John Stanik, *Editor*
EMP: 72
SQ FT: 30,000
SALES (est): 70.2MM **Privately Held**
SIC: 2721 8621 Periodicals: publishing only; scientific membership association

(G-9241)
ASSOULINE PUBLISHING INC (PA)
3 Park Ave Fl 27 (10016-5902)
PHONE..................................212 989-6769
Fax: 212 989-6853
Prosper Assouline, *President*
Rebecca Isenberg, *Editor*
Amy Slingerland, *Editor*
Lindsey Tulloch, *Editor*
Yaffa Assouline, *Vice Pres*
▲ **EMP:** 9
SQ FT: 3,000
SALES (est): 3.2MM **Privately Held**
WEB: www.assouline.com
SIC: 2731 Book publishing

(G-9242)
ASTON LEATHER INC
153 W 27th St Ste 406 (10001-6258)
PHONE..................................212 481-2760
Metin Adam, *Ch of Bd*
▲ **EMP:** 6
SALES (est): 600K **Privately Held**
SIC: 3111 Leather tanning & finishing

(G-9243)
ASTUCCI US LTD (PA)
385 5th Ave Rm 1100 (10016-3340)
PHONE..................................212 725-3171
Fax: 212 725-3236
Dan Benmoshe, *President*
Hanna Levy, *Vice Pres*
Merav Sharon, *Purchasing*
Dan Moshe, *Marketing Mgr*
Channa Levy, *Manager*
▲ **EMP:** 8
SQ FT: 3,000
SALES: 15MM **Privately Held**
SIC: 3172 Cases, jewelry; cases, glasses

New York - New York County (G-9244)

GEOGRAPHIC SECTION

(G-9244)
AT&T CORP
Also Called: Sherwin Commerce
767 5th Ave Fl 12a (10153-0023)
PHONE.....................212 317-7048
Debra Surrette, Manager
EMP: 15
SALES (corp-wide): 146.8B Publicly Held
WEB: www.swbell.com
SIC: 7372 Prepackaged software
HQ: At&T Corp.
1 At&T Way
Bedminster NJ 07921
800 403-3202

(G-9245)
ATC PLASTICS LLC
Also Called: Heller Performance Polymers
555 Madison Ave Fl 5 (10022-3410)
PHONE.....................212 375-2515
Herbert Heller, President
Gordon Smith, Division Mgr
EMP: 39
SALES (corp-wide): 7.8MM Privately Held
SIC: 3087 3643 2851 2821 Custom compound purchased resins; current-carrying wiring devices; paints & allied products; plastics materials & resins
PA: Atc Plastics, Llc
8425 Woodfield Crossing B
Indianapolis IN 46240
317 469-7500

(G-9246)
ATERET LLC
22 W 48th St (10036-1803)
PHONE.....................212 819-0777
Khodahbaksh Levy,
Samuel Levy,
EMP: 5
SALES (est): 410K Privately Held
WEB: www.ateret.com
SIC: 3911 Jewelry, precious metal

(G-9247)
ATERIAN INVESTMENT PARTNERS LP (PA)
11 E 44th St Rm 1803 (10017-3670)
PHONE.....................212 547-2806
Michael Fieldstone, Partner
Eric Dieckman, Partner
Daniel Phan, Vice Pres
Nadine Michel, Office Mgr
Isaac Chalal, Associate
EMP: 19
SALES (est): 117MM Privately Held
SIC: 3398 Metal heat treating

(G-9248)
ATERRA EXPLORATION LLC
230 W 56th St Apt 53d (10019-0077)
PHONE.....................212 315-0030
David G Sepiashvili, President
▲ EMP: 20
SALES (est): 671.8K Privately Held
SIC: 1382 Oil & gas exploration services

(G-9249)
ATHALON SPORTGEAR INC
10 W 33rd St Rm 1012 (10001-3317)
PHONE.....................212 268-8070
Andrew Nitkin, Ch of Bd
Robert Goldener, President
Mike McLoughlin, Vice Pres
Marisol Orellana, Opers Staff
Justin Maged, Marketing Staff
◆ EMP: 7
SALES (est): 600K Privately Held
WEB: www.athalonskyvalet.com
SIC: 3949 Bags, golf

(G-9250)
ATHLON SPT COMMUNICATIONS INC
60 E 42nd St Ste 820 (10165-0820)
PHONE.....................212 478-1910
EMP: 28
SALES (corp-wide): 38.1MM Privately Held
SIC: 2721 Periodicals: publishing only

PA: Athlon Sports Communications, Inc.
2451 Atrium Way Ste 320
Nashville TN 37214
615 327-0747

(G-9251)
ATLANTIC MONTHLY GROUP INC
Also Called: Atlantic, The
60 Madison Ave (10010-1600)
PHONE.....................202 266-7000
Katie Storrs, Principal
Lee Mayer, Facilities Dir
Cindy Reyes, Accountant
Peter Elkins-Williams, Marketing Staff
Laura Trevino, Payroll Mgr
EMP: 25
SALES (corp-wide): 9.1MM Privately Held
WEB: www.theatlantic.com
SIC: 2721 Magazines: publishing only, not printed on site
PA: The Atlantic Monthly Group Inc
600 New Hampshire Ave Nw # 4
Washington DC 20037
202 266-7000

(G-9252)
ATLANTIC RECORDING CORP (DH)
Also Called: Atlantic Records
1633 Broadway Lower 2c1 (10019-6708)
PHONE.....................212 707-2000
Fax: 212 405-5425
Craig Kauman, Ch of Bd
Ahmet M Ertegun, Ch of Bd
Julie Geenwald, President
Greg Kallman, President
Camile Hackney, Partner
EMP: 325
SQ FT: 133,000
SALES (est): 75.5MM
SALES (corp-wide): 2.9B Privately Held
WEB: www.ledzep.com
SIC: 3652 Compact laser discs, prerecorded; master records or tapes, preparation of; phonograph record blanks
HQ: Warner Music Group Corp.
1633 Broadway
New York NY 10019
212 275-2000

(G-9253)
ATLANTIC TROPHY CO INC
866 Avenue Of The America (10001-4168)
PHONE.....................212 684-6020
Fax: 212 689-2665
Arthur Schneider, President
EMP: 6
SQ FT: 1,000
SALES (est): 747.6K Privately Held
SIC: 3914 Trophies, silver; trophies, nickel silver; trophies, pewter; trophies, plated (all metals)

(G-9254)
ATLAS & COMPANY LLC
355 Lexington Ave Fl 6 (10017-6603)
PHONE.....................212 234-3100
Fax: 212 888-3615
James Atlas, Mng Member
David Barker, Manager
Peter Desrochers, Manager
Ulla Schnell, Director
EMP: 6
SALES (est): 500K Privately Held
SIC: 2731 Book publishing

(G-9255)
ATLAS MUSIC PUBLISHING LLC (PA)
6 E 39th St Ste 1104 (10016-0116)
PHONE.....................646 502-5170
Richard Stumpf, CEO
Michael Petersen, COO
Leslie Greene, Vice Pres
Kristen Bushnell, Manager
Jennifer Blakenan, Post Master
EMP: 7
SQ FT: 3,000
SALES (est): 732.5K Privately Held
SIC: 2741 Music books: publishing & printing; music, sheet: publishing only, not printed on site

(G-9256)
ATLAS PRINT SOLUTIONS INC
589 8th Ave Fl 4 (10018-3092)
PHONE.....................212 949-8775
Patrick Fardella, Prdtn Mgr
Kathleen Tan, Finance
Gregg Morgan, Accounts Exec
Allison Philips, CTO
Ken Rosenberg, Creative Dir
EMP: 21
SALES (est): 3.6MM Privately Held
SIC: 2752 Commercial printing, lithographic

(G-9257)
ATLAS RECYCLING LLC
Also Called: Pep Realty
25 Howard St Fl 2 (10013-3164)
PHONE.....................212 925-3280
John Pasquale, CEO
J Pasqual, General Mgr
EMP: 5
SALES (est): 495.9K Privately Held
SIC: 2621 Paper mills

(G-9258)
ATR JEWELRY INC
71 W 47th St Ste 402 (10036-2819)
PHONE.....................212 819-0075
Fax: 212 819-0045
Aron Aranbaev, President
EMP: 10
SALES (est): 1.1MM Privately Held
WEB: www.atrjewelry.com
SIC: 3911 5944 Jewelry, precious metal; jewelry, precious stones & precious metals

(G-9259)
ATTENDS HEALTHCARE INC
200 Park Ave (10166-0005)
PHONE.....................212 338-5100
Michael Fagan, CEO
EMP: 651
SALES (est): 36.6MM
SALES (corp-wide): 5.5B Privately Held
SIC: 2676 Sanitary paper products
PA: Domtar Corporation
395 Boul De Maisonneuve O
Montreal QC H3A 1
514 848-5555

(G-9260)
ATTITUDES FOOTWEAR INC
1040 1st Ave Ste 232 (10022-2991)
PHONE.....................212 754-9113
Paul Mayer, President
Jeff Levy, Vice Pres
EMP: 3
SALES (est): 2MM Privately Held
SIC: 3144 Dress shoes, women's

(G-9261)
ATW RESOURCES LLC
767 3rd Ave Fl 14 (10017-9018)
PHONE.....................212 994-0600
Lawrence G Graev, Mng Member
Alexandra Lorenzen, Administration
EMP: 5
SALES (est): 528.7K Privately Held
SIC: 2842 Specialty cleaning preparations

(G-9262)
AURA INTERNATIONAL MFG INC
512 Fashion Ave Fl 26 (10018-0804)
PHONE.....................212 719-1418
Seth Baum, President
Anthony Wong, Managing Dir
Bob Diamond, Vice Pres
Frances Israel, Admin Sec
EMP: 5
SALES (est): 770K Privately Held
SIC: 2339 Women's & misses' outerwear

(G-9263)
AURATIC INC
41 Madison Ave Ste 1402 (10010-2245)
PHONE.....................914 413-8154
Lewis Wong, President
EMP: 6
SALES (est): 346.1K Privately Held
SIC: 2541 Counter & sink tops

(G-9264)
AURATIC USA INCORPORATED
41 Madison Ave Ste 1904 (10010-2337)
PHONE.....................212 684-8888
Dai Jian-Guo, Principal
▲ EMP: 5
SALES (est): 520.2K
SALES (corp-wide): 25.9MM Privately Held
SIC: 2511 Kitchen & dining room furniture
PA: China Yong Feng Yuan Co., Ltd.
Source Of Yongfeng Ceramic Cultural And Creative Industry Park,S
Shenzhen 51800
755 251-8299

(G-9265)
AURIC TECHNOLOGY LLC
Also Called: Octopus City.com
330 Madison Ave Fl 6 (10017-5041)
PHONE.....................212 573-0911
Fax: 212 573-0943
Jean P Benatar,
Gordon Hartogensis,
EMP: 10
SALES (est): 613.2K Privately Held
WEB: www.aurictechnology.com
SIC: 7372 Business oriented computer software

(G-9266)
AUTODESK INC
38 W 21st St Fl 9 (10010-7183)
PHONE.....................646 613-8680
Joseph M Smith, Sales Mgr
Ana Morillo, Manager
EMP: 12
SALES (corp-wide): 2.5B Publicly Held
WEB: www.autodesk.com
SIC: 7372 Application computer software
PA: Autodesk, Inc.
111 Mcinnis Pkwy
San Rafael CA 94903
415 507-5000

(G-9267)
AUTOMATIC PRESS INC
140 W 30th St Frnt 1 (10001-4005)
PHONE.....................212 924-5573
Isaac Buchinger, President
EMP: 5
SQ FT: 2,500
SALES (est): 450K Privately Held
SIC: 2752 Commercial printing, offset

(G-9268)
AUTOMOTIVE ACCESSORIES GROUP
505 8th Ave Rm 12a05 (10018-6581)
PHONE.....................212 736-8100
Allan J Marrus, President
Stephen Delman, Admin Sec
EMP: 300
SALES (est): 17.9MM Privately Held
SIC: 3714 Motor vehicle parts & accessories; steering mechanisms, motor vehicle

(G-9269)
AUVEN THERAPEUTICS MGT LP
1325 Avenue Of The Americ (10019-6071)
PHONE.....................212 616-4000
Peter B Corr, General Ptnr
Stephen Evans-Freke, General Ptnr
Jim Cooper, CIO
Tara Roulhac, Assistant
EMP: 10
SALES (est): 980K Privately Held
SIC: 2834 Pharmaceutical preparations

(G-9270)
AV DENIM INC
230 W 38th St Fl 8r (10018-9056)
PHONE.....................212 764-6668
David Kubresi, Ch of Bd
▲ EMP: 30
SALES (est): 4.2MM Privately Held
SIC: 2211 Denims

(G-9271)
AV THERAPEUTICS INC
Also Called: A V T
20 E 68th St Ste 204 (10065-5836)
PHONE.....................917 497-5523
Robert Pollock, President

EMP: 25 EST: 2007
SALES (est): 2.7MM Privately Held
SIC: 2836 Vaccines

(G-9272)
AVALANCHE STUDIOS NEW YORK INC
536 Broadway (10012-3915)
PHONE.....................212 993-6447
David Grijns, *Ch of Bd*
EMP: 60 EST: 2011
SALES (est): 4.5MM
SALES (corp-wide): 29MM Privately Held
SIC: 7372 Home entertainment computer software
HQ: Fatalist Holdings Ab

Stockholm 100 6
844 276-70

(G-9273)
AVALIN LLC
221 W 37th St Fl 3 (10018-5782)
PHONE.....................212 842-2286
Fax: 212 997-0022
Zoheir Aghravi, *President*
Matt Cohen, *Vice Pres*
Dawn Smith, *Sales Mgr*
Rose Terriat, *Sales Staff*
▲ EMP: 14
SQ FT: 10,000
SALES (est): 1.6MM Privately Held
WEB: www.avalinknits.com
SIC: 2339 Women's & misses' athletic clothing & sportswear

(G-9274)
AVANTI PRESS INC
6 W 18th St Ste 6l (10011-4630)
PHONE.....................212 414-1025
Frederic Ruffner III, *Branch Mgr*
Jaisi Surowiec, *Manager*
EMP: 27
SALES (corp-wide): 13.2MM Privately Held
SIC: 2771 Greeting cards
PA: Avanti Press, Inc.
155 W Congress St Ste 200
Detroit MI 48226
313 961-0220

(G-9275)
AVAS CORPORATION
225 W 115th St Apt 3a (10026-2476)
PHONE.....................203 470-3587
Sava Kobilarov, *President*
EMP: 5
SQ FT: 1,000
SALES (est): 330K Privately Held
SIC: 2043 Cereal breakfast foods

(G-9276)
AVERY DENNISON CORPORATION
218 W 40th St Fl 8 (10018-1758)
PHONE.....................626 304-2000
Adam Biernat, *Accounts Mgr*
Peter Gunshon, *Manager*
EMP: 115
SALES (corp-wide): 5.9B Publicly Held
SIC: 2672 Adhesive backed films, foams & foils
PA: Avery Dennison Corporation
207 N Goode Ave Fl 6
Glendale CA 91203
626 304-2000

(G-9277)
AVI-SPL EMPLOYEE
8 W 38th St Rm 1101 (10018-6244)
PHONE.....................212 840-4801
EMP: 350
SALES (corp-wide): 596.9MM Privately Held
SIC: 3669 3861 3663 3651 Mfg Communications Equip Mfg Photo Equip/Supplies Mfg Radio/Tv Comm Equip Mfg Home Audio/Video Eqp Whol Photo Equip/Supply
HQ: Avi-Spl Employee Emergency Relief Fund, Inc.
6301 Benjamin Rd Ste 101
Tampa FL 33634
813 884-7168

(G-9278)
AVID TECHNOLOGY INC
90 Park Ave (10016-1301)
PHONE.....................212 983-2424
Fax: 212 983-9770
Kevin Johnston, *Sales Dir*
Adam Taylor, *Branch Mgr*
EMP: 22
SALES (corp-wide): 505.6MM Publicly Held
WEB: www.avid.com
SIC: 3861 Editing equipment, motion picture: viewers, splicers, etc.
PA: Avid Technology, Inc.
75 Network Dr
Burlington MA 01803
978 640-6789

(G-9279)
AVITTO LEATHER GOODS INC
424 W Broadway Frnt A (10012-3796)
PHONE.....................212 219-7501
AVI Sharifi, *President*
EMP: 7
SALES (est): 560K Privately Held
SIC: 2211 Shoe fabrics

(G-9280)
AVOCODE INC
55 E 73rd St Apt Gf (10021-3555)
PHONE.....................646 934-8410
Tomas Hadl, *President*
EMP: 12 EST: 2015
SALES: 500K Privately Held
SIC: 7372 Publishers' computer software

(G-9281)
AVON PRODUCTS INC (PA)
777 3rd Ave (10017-1401)
PHONE.....................212 282-5000
Fax: 212 282-6049
Sherilyn S McCoy, *CEO*
Fernando Acosta, *President*
John P Higson, *President*
David Legher, *President*
Pablo Munoz, *President*
◆ EMP: 250 EST: 1886
SALES: 6.1B Publicly Held
WEB: www.avon.com
SIC: 2844 3961 5961 5023 Toilet preparations; cosmetic preparations; perfumes & colognes; toilet preparations; necklaces, except precious metal; bracelets, except precious metal; earrings, except precious metal; rings, finger: gold plated wire; catalog sales; cosmetics & perfumes, mail order; jewelry, mail order; glassware; stainless steel flatware; decorating supplies; women's & children's clothing; lingerie; blouses; sweaters, women's & children's

(G-9282)
AVS GEM STONE CORP
48 W 48th St Ste 1010 (10036-1713)
PHONE.....................212 944-6380
Antonio Santos, *President*
EMP: 5
SALES (est): 305.5K Privately Held
SIC: 1499 Gemstone & industrial diamond mining

(G-9283)
AWARD PUBLISHING LIMITED
40 W 55th St Apt 9b (10019-5376)
PHONE.....................212 246-0405
Iris Dodge, *Principal*
EMP: 9
SALES (est): 580K Privately Held
SIC: 2741 Miscellaneous publishing

(G-9284)
AXIS NA LLC (PA)
Also Called: Axis Denim
70 W 40th St Fl 11 (10018-2619)
PHONE.....................212 840-4005
Shirley Zheng, *Accountant*
Ling Kwok,
Leigh Martin,
▲ EMP: 10
SALES (est): 1.3MM Privately Held
SIC: 2211 Denims

(G-9285)
AZ YASHIR BAPAZ INC
Also Called: A Yashir Bapa
134 W 37th St (10018-6911)
PHONE.....................212 947-7357
Rasael Yaghoubian, *President*
EMP: 5
SALES (est): 630K Privately Held
SIC: 2339 Sportswear, women's

(G-9286)
AZIBI LTD
Also Called: Luna Luz
270 W 39th St Rm 1501 (10018-4415)
PHONE.....................212 869-6550
Michael Samuels, *President*
Dennis Tilden, *Vice Pres*
Twana Green, *Manager*
EMP: 10
SQ FT: 8,000
SALES (est): 1MM Privately Held
WEB: www.azibi.com
SIC: 3949 Sporting & athletic goods

(G-9287)
B & F ARCHITECTURAL SUPPORT GR
Also Called: Advance Construction Group
450 7th Ave Ste 307 (10123-0307)
PHONE.....................212 279-6488
Stewart Ratzker, *President*
EMP: 30
SALES (est): 2MM Privately Held
SIC: 2851 8712 Paints & allied products; architectural services

(G-9288)
B & R PROMOTIONAL PRODUCTS
Also Called: Beal Blocks
34 W 120th St Apt 1 (10027-6478)
PHONE.....................212 563-0040
Fax: 212 456-1253
Gary Bimblick, *President*
Miriam Del Valle, *Admin Sec*
EMP: 6 EST: 1963
SQ FT: 5,000
SALES (est): 743.4K Privately Held
SIC: 3299 3999 Plaques: clay, plaster or papier mache; plaques, picture, laminated; badges, metal: policemen, firemen, etc.

(G-9289)
B K JEWELRY CONTRACTOR INC
71 W 47th St Fl 11 (10036-2819)
PHONE.....................212 398-9093
Jacob Solomon, *President*
Rachel Solomon, *Admin Sec*
EMP: 20
SQ FT: 5,000
SALES: 1MM Privately Held
SIC: 3911 Jewelry, precious metal

(G-9290)
B LIVE LLC
347 W 36th St Rm 402 (10018-7252)
PHONE.....................212 489-0721
Bill Marpet, *Managing Prtnr*
Todd Galloway, *Partner*
Russell Quy, *Partner*
Matthew Walsh, *Partner*
EMP: 9
SALES: 1.9MM Privately Held
SIC: 3823 Digital displays of process variables

(G-9291)
B S J LIMITED
1400 Broadway Ste 1702 (10018-5300)
PHONE.....................212 764-4600
Fax: 212 764-9340
Shari Levine, *Owner*
EMP: 24
SQ FT: 10,000
SALES (corp-wide): 6.1MM Privately Held
SIC: 2335 Bridal & formal gowns
PA: B S J Limited
1375 Broadway Rm 508
New York NY 10018
212 221-8403

(G-9292)
B S J LIMITED (PA)
1375 Broadway Rm 508 (10018-7179)
PHONE.....................212 221-8403
Fax: 212 354-9454
Shari Levine, *Ch of Bd*
Mike Mann, *President*
Rhea Batterman, *Controller*
▲ EMP: 6
SALES (est): 6.1MM Privately Held
SIC: 2335 Bridal & formal gowns

(G-9293)
B SMITH FURS INC
224 W 30th St Rm 402 (10001-0406)
PHONE.....................212 967-5290
Fax: 212 736-2426
Gary Smith, *President*
Michael Hennessey, *Vice Pres*
Hennessey International, *Shareholder*
EMP: 10
SQ FT: 4,000
SALES (est): 980K Privately Held
SIC: 2371 Fur goods

(G-9294)
B TWEEN LLC
1411 Broadway Rm 2520 (10018-3468)
PHONE.....................212 819-9040
Robert Terzi, *President*
Jack Terzi, *Vice Pres*
Rochelle Terzi, *Vice Pres*
EMP: 12
SQ FT: 3,000
SALES (est): 1.2MM Privately Held
SIC: 2339 Women's & misses' athletic clothing & sportswear

(G-9295)
B-REEL INC
401 Broadway Fl 24 (10013-3007)
PHONE.....................917 388-3836
Anders Wahlquist, *President*
Fredrik Heinig, *Managing Dir*
Charles MA, *Manager*
Courtney Severson, *Manager*
Jonas Hedegard, *Producer*
EMP: 24
SALES (est): 5MM Privately Held
SIC: 3571 Computers, digital, analog or hybrid

(G-9296)
B-SQUARED INC
104 W 29th St Fl 7 (10001-5310)
PHONE.....................212 777-2044
Fax: 212 777-4655
Tim Boucher, *President*
Steve Milillo, *Vice Pres*
Micheal Scully, *Controller*
Karin Boucher, *Human Res Dir*
Lauren Vergara, *Accounts Mgr*
EMP: 29
SQ FT: 10,000
SALES (est): 4.9MM Privately Held
SIC: 2732 Book printing

(G-9297)
B601 V2 INC
315 5th Ave Rm 903 (10016-6510)
PHONE.....................646 391-6431
Steven Cohn, *CEO*
EMP: 5
SALES (est): 117.2K Privately Held
SIC: 7372 Business oriented computer software

(G-9298)
BABY SIGNATURE INC (PA)
Also Called: Dainty Home
251 5th Ave Fl 2l (10016-6515)
PHONE.....................212 686-1700
Hassib Baghdadi, *President*
Merlin Quantam, *Opers Staff*
▲ EMP: 1
SQ FT: 5,000
SALES: 5MM Privately Held
SIC: 2391 2392 5023 Curtains & draperies; placemats, plastic or textile; shower curtains: made from purchased materials; curtains

New York - New York County (G-9299)

(G-9299)
BABYFAIR INC
Also Called: Diversify Apparel
34 W 33rd St Rm 818 (10001-3304)
PHONE.................................212 736-7989
Fax: 212 438-0127
Maurice Shamah, *Ch of Bd*
Ralph Shamah, *Vice Pres*
Jeff Tammam, *Sales Staff*
Edward Riggio, *Manager*
▲ **EMP:** 35 **EST:** 1944
SQ FT: 8,000
SALES (est): 4.7MM **Privately Held**
WEB: www.babyfair.com
SIC: 2369 Play suits; girls', children's & infants'; rompers: infants'

(G-9300)
BACKTECH INC
2 Peter Cooper Rd Apt Mf (10010-6733)
PHONE.................................973 279-0838
Eier Rystedt, *President*
EMP: 2
SALES: 1MM **Privately Held**
SIC: 3842 Surgical appliances & supplies

(G-9301)
BADGLEY MISCHKA LICENSING LLC
Also Called: Jsc Design
550 7th Ave Fl 22 (10018-3223)
PHONE.................................212 921-1585
Fax: 212 921-4171
Taryn Kristal, *Accounts Exec*
Gail Pashka, *Office Mgr*
Neil Cole, *Mng Member*
Christine B Currence, *Manager*
Sonjia Winley, *Manager*
EMP: 29
SQ FT: 3,000
SALES (est): 1.8MM **Privately Held**
WEB: www.badgleymischka.com
SIC: 2326 Men's & boys' work clothing

(G-9302)
BAG ARTS LTD
20 W 36th St Rm 5r (10018-9790)
PHONE.................................212 684-7020
Steve Zagha, *President*
Isaac Cohen, *Vice Pres*
▲ **EMP:** 7
SQ FT: 7,000
SALES (est): 896.6K **Privately Held**
WEB: www.bagarts.com
SIC: 3053 Packing materials

(G-9303)
BAG ARTS THE ART PACKAGING LLC
20 W 36th St Fl 5 (10018-8005)
PHONE.................................212 684-7020
Steve Zagha, *President*
EMP: 7
SQ FT: 7,000
SALES (est): 453.2K
SALES (corp-wide): 1.6MM **Privately Held**
SIC: 2673 2674 Food storage & trash bags (plastic); grocers' bags: made from purchased materials
PA: Mac Swed, Inc.
20 W 36th St Rm 5r
New York NY 10018
917 617-3885

(G-9304)
BAG BAZAAR LTD
Metro Accessories
1 E 33rd St Fl 6 (10016-5099)
PHONE.................................212 689-3508
Joey Shames, *Branch Mgr*
EMP: 25
SALES (corp-wide): 59.2MM **Privately Held**
WEB: www.aeny.com
SIC: 2339 Women's & misses' accessories
PA: Bag Bazaar Ltd.
1 E 33rd St Fl 6
New York NY 10016
212 689-3508

(G-9305)
BAGZNYC CORP
Also Called: Kids
19 W 34th St Rm 318 (10001-0055)
PHONE.................................212 643-8202
Jeff Goldstein, *President*
Larry Zakarin, *Vice Pres*
▲ **EMP:** 18
SQ FT: 5,300
SALES (est): 1.4MM **Privately Held**
SIC: 2339 3171 Women's & misses' outerwear; women's handbags & purses

(G-9306)
BAIKAL INC (PA)
341 W 38th St Fl 3 (10018-9694)
PHONE.................................212 239-4650
Fax: 212 239-4679
Josef Itskovich, *President*
▲ **EMP:** 70
SQ FT: 5,000
SALES (est): 5MM **Privately Held**
WEB: www.baikal.com
SIC: 3171 Handbags, women's

(G-9307)
BAINBRIDGE & KNIGHT LLC
801 2nd Ave Fl 19 (10017-8618)
PHONE.................................212 986-5100
Carl Ruderman, *President*
Mark Horowitz, *VP Sales*
David Bernstein, *Accounts Mgr*
Steven Schwartz, *Mng Member*
Christine Murphy, *Director*
EMP: 50
SQ FT: 12,000
SALES (est): 5.2MM **Privately Held**
SIC: 2099 Food preparations

(G-9308)
BALAJEE ENTERPRISES INC
Also Called: Digitech Printers
150 W 30th St Frnt 2 (10001-4161)
PHONE.................................212 629-6150
Fax: 212 629-6160
Shul Khalfan, *President*
EMP: 8
SQ FT: 2,500
SALES (est): 1MM **Privately Held**
WEB: www.digitechprinters.com
SIC: 2759 Commercial printing

(G-9309)
BALANCED TECH CORP
Also Called: New Balance Underwear
37 W 37th St Fl 10 (10018-6354)
PHONE.................................212 768-8330
Ezra Jack Cattan, *Ch of Bd*
Judah Cattan, *President*
▲ **EMP:** 20
SALES (est): 1.1MM **Privately Held**
WEB: www.newbalanceunderwear.com
SIC: 2254 Underwear, knit

(G-9310)
BALTICARE INC
501 Fashion Ave Rm 414 (10018-8608)
PHONE.................................646 380-9470
Monika Chodkiewicz, *Sales Engr*
Chris Ioannides, *Sales Engr*
Al Rivera, *Sales Engr*
Erica Ross, *Sales Engr*
Edward Villela, *Manager*
EMP: 8
SALES (est): 883.4K **Privately Held**
SIC: 3585 Air conditioning units, complete: domestic or industrial

(G-9311)
BAM SALES LLC (PA)
1407 Broadway Rm 2018 (10018-2863)
PHONE.................................212 781-3000
Marc Moyal,
Alan Cohen,
Scott Danziger,
Nicole Hausman,
Robert Klein,
EMP: 3
SALES (est): 1.2MM **Privately Held**
SIC: 2339 Women's & misses' athletic clothing & sportswear

(G-9312)
BAMBOO GLOBAL INDUSTRIES
339 E 58th St Apt 7e (10022-2268)
PHONE.................................973 943-1878
Matthew Renov, *Principal*
EMP: 5
SALES (est): 396.6K **Privately Held**
SIC: 2869 Industrial organic chemicals

(G-9313)
BANDIER CORP
960 Park Ave Apt 11b (10028-0325)
PHONE.................................212 242-5400
EMP: 10 **EST:** 2013
SALES (est): 1.8MM **Privately Held**
SIC: 2211 5661 Apparel & outerwear fabrics, cotton; shoes, custom

(G-9314)
BANGLA CLOTHING USA INC (PA)
262 W 38th St (10018-5808)
PHONE.................................201 679-2615
Elizabeth Derua, *President*
▲ **EMP:** 6 **EST:** 2009
SQ FT: 5,000
SALES: 16MM **Privately Held**
SIC: 2326 2335 Men's & boys' work clothing; women's, juniors' & misses' dresses

(G-9315)
BARBARA MATERA LTD
890 Broadway Fl 5 (10003-1211)
PHONE.................................212 475-5006
Fax: 212 254-4550
Jared Aswegan, *President*
Larry Feinman, *CFO*
EMP: 100 **EST:** 1967
SQ FT: 8,500
SALES: 5MM **Privately Held**
SIC: 2389 Theatrical costumes

(G-9316)
BARBER BROTHERS JEWELRY MFG
Also Called: B & B Jewelry Mfg Co
580 5th Ave Ste 725 (10036-4724)
PHONE.................................212 819-0666
Fax: 212 768-8735
Abraham Barber, *President*
Simon Barber, *Vice Pres*
Ebba Bai, *Manager*
EMP: 15 **EST:** 1963
SQ FT: 2,200
SALES (est): 1.5MM **Privately Held**
SIC: 3911 Jewelry, precious metal

(G-9317)
BARDWIL INDUSTRIES INC (PA)
Also Called: Bardwil Linens
1071 Ave Of The Americas (10018-3777)
PHONE.................................212 944-1870
Fax: 212 869-3599
George Bardwil, *Ch of Bd*
Robert Paglieri, *Controller*
▲ **EMP:** 3 **EST:** 1906
SQ FT: 12,000
SALES (est): 28.7MM **Privately Held**
WEB: www.beyondmarketing.com
SIC: 2392 2241 Napkins, fabric & nonwoven: made from purchased materials; placemats, plastic or textile; tablecloths: made from purchased materials; chair covers & pads: made from purchased materials; trimmings, textile

(G-9318)
BARE BEAUTY LASER HAIR REMOVAL
5 E 57th St Fl 6 (10022-2553)
PHONE.................................718 278-2273
Debbie Patadopoulas, *Owner*
EMP: 6
SALES (est): 53.7K **Privately Held**
SIC: 3699 Laser systems & equipment

(G-9319)
BARE ESCENTUALS INC
Also Called: Bare Minerals
1140 3rd Ave (10065-6116)
PHONE.................................646 537-0070
Fax: 646 537-0072
Holleigh Motta, *Sales Staff*
Lavette Tursi, *Sales Staff*
Melissa Colom, *Manager*
EMP: 7
SALES (corp-wide): 6.2B **Privately Held**
SIC: 2844 5122 Toilet preparations; toilet preparations
HQ: Bare Escentuals, Inc.
71 Stevenson St Fl 22
San Francisco CA 94105
415 489-5000

(G-9320)
BARI ENGINEERING CORP
240 Bowery (10012-3501)
PHONE.................................212 966-2080
Frank Bari, *President*
EMP: 24
SQ FT: 51,000
SALES (est): 2.9MM **Privately Held**
WEB: www.bariequipment.com
SIC: 3556 5046 Food products machinery; restaurant equipment & supplies

(G-9321)
BARI-JAY FASHIONS INC (PA)
225 W 37th St Fl 7 (10018-5729)
PHONE.................................212 921-1551
Fax: 212 391-0165
Bruce Cohen, *President*
EMP: 20
SQ FT: 20,000
SALES (est): 5.6MM **Privately Held**
WEB: www.barijay.com
SIC: 2335 Gowns, formal; wedding gowns & dresses

(G-9322)
BARNETT PAUL INC
155 Ave Of The Americas 7 (10013-1507)
PHONE.................................212 673-3250
Paul Barnett, *President*
Ryan Darden, *Finance Dir*
EMP: 30
SALES: 9.4MM **Privately Held**
SIC: 2759 Publication printing

(G-9323)
BAROKA CREATIONS INC
36 W 47th St Ste 1402 (10036-8601)
P.O. Box 290744, Brooklyn (11229-0744)
PHONE.................................212 768-0527
Rami Bareket, *President*
Nftali Rockah, *Vice Pres*
Sheri Baroka, *Admin Sec*
EMP: 7
SQ FT: 11,000
SALES: 4MM **Privately Held**
WEB: www.baroka.com
SIC: 3911 3915 Jewelry, precious metal; diamond cutting & polishing

(G-9324)
BARRAGE
401 W 47th St Frnt A (10036-2306)
PHONE.................................212 586-9390
Tom Johnson, *Owner*
EMP: 20
SALES (est): 2MM **Privately Held**
WEB: www.barrage.com
SIC: 3639 Major kitchen appliances, except refrigerators & stoves

(G-9325)
BARRERA JOSE & MARIA CO LTD
29 W 36th St Fl 8 (10018-7668)
PHONE.................................212 239-1994
Fax: 212 302-8480
Jose Barrera, *Owner*
Maria Barrera, *Co-Owner*
EMP: 28
SQ FT: 3,000
SALES (est): 1.8MM **Privately Held**
SIC: 2387 3961 Apparel belts; costume jewelry, ex. precious metal & semi-precious stones

(G-9326)
BARRY INDUSTRIES INC
Also Called: Barry Supply Co Div
36 W 17th St Frnt 1 (10011-5731)
PHONE.................................212 242-5200
Barry Weinberger, *President*
William Wein, *Manager*
EMP: 15
SQ FT: 4,000
SALES (est): 1.1MM **Privately Held**
SIC: 3429 5072 Manufactured hardware (general); hardware

GEOGRAPHIC SECTION

New York - New York County (G-9352)

(G-9327)
BARSKY VENTURES LLC
250 W 57th St Ste 2514 (10107-2500)
PHONE..................212 265-8890
EMP: 5
SALES (est): 389.8K Privately Held
SIC: 2721 Magazines: publishing & printing

(G-9328)
BARTHOLOMEW MAZZA LTD INC
22 W 48th St Ste 805 (10036-1803)
P.O. Box 231444 (10023-0025)
PHONE..................212 935-4530
Fax: 212 355-7801
Hugo Mazza, *President*
Diane Mazza, *Treasurer*
EMP: 50
SQ FT: 4,000
SALES (est): 5.5MM Privately Held
WEB: www.mazzabartholomew.com
SIC: 3911 Jewelry, precious metal

(G-9329)
BASF CORPORATION
545 5th Ave Fl 11 (10017-3609)
PHONE..................212 450-8280
Julianna Wilkins, *Branch Mgr*
EMP: 368
SALES (corp-wide): 75.6B Privately Held
WEB: www.basf.com
SIC: 2819 Industrial inorganic chemicals
HQ: Basf Corporation
   100 Park Ave
   Florham Park NJ 07932
   973 245-6000

(G-9330)
BASIL S KADHIM
Also Called: Eton International
280 Madison Ave Rm 912 (10016-0801)
PHONE..................888 520-5192
Basil S Kadhim, *Owner*
Stephanie Kadhim, *Manager*
Julie A Seward, *Manager*
EMP: 8
SQ FT: 1,000
SALES (est): 1.1MM Privately Held
WEB: www.etoninternational.com
SIC: 3663 5045 7382 5047 Television broadcasting & communications equipment; computers, peripherals & software; protective devices, security; medical equipment & supplies

(G-9331)
BASILOFF LLC
179 Bennett Ave Apt 7f (10040-4059)
PHONE..................646 671-0353
Dmitri Vassiliev, *President*
EMP: 6 EST: 2014
SALES (est): 330K Privately Held
SIC: 2261 Sponging cotton broadwoven cloth for the trade

(G-9332)
BASIN HOLDINGS US LLC (PA)
200 Park Ave Fl 58 (10166-5899)
PHONE..................212 695-7376
John Fitzgibbons, *CEO*
Tyler Hassen, *CFO*
EMP: 39 EST: 2011
SALES (est): 143.3MM Privately Held
SIC: 3533 Oil & gas field machinery

(G-9333)
BAUBLEBAR INC
1115 Broadway Fl 5 (10010-3457)
PHONE..................646 664-4803
Daniella Yacobovsky, *Principal*
Amy Jain, *Principal*
Maritza Mejia, *Opers Mgr*
Kristen Cruz, *Production*
Lauren Yee, *Marketing Staff*
EMP: 55
SALES (est): 12.2MM Privately Held
SIC: 3172 Cases, jewelry

(G-9334)
BAULI USA INC
295 Madison Ave Rm 1705 (10017-6380)
PHONE..................646 380-1891
Michele Bauli, *President*
Samantha Bonanno, *Finance*
▲ EMP: 4

SALES (est): 1.2MM
SALES (corp-wide): 1MM Privately Held
SIC: 2051 Cakes, pies & pastries
HQ: Bauli Spa
   Via Verdi 31
   Castel D'azzano VR 37060

(G-9335)
BAUSCH & LOMB HOLDINGS INC (DH)
450 Lexington Ave (10017-3904)
PHONE..................585 338-6000
Brent L Saunders, *CEO*
Gerald M Ostrov, *Ch of Bd*
EMP: 8
SALES (est): 2.8B
SALES (corp-wide): 10.4B Privately Held
SIC: 3851 2834 Ophthalmic goods; pharmaceutical preparations
HQ: Valeant Pharmaceuticals International Corporation
   400 Somerset Corp Blvd
   Bridgewater NJ 08807
   908 927-1400

(G-9336)
BAZAAR
300 W 57th St Fl 25 (10019-3741)
PHONE..................212 903-5497
Linda Crowley, *Principal*
Lyle Gulley Jr, *Vice Chairman*
John Copeland, *Bd of Directors*
Diana Kaufman, *Bd of Directors*
Ronald J Sulewski, *Admin Sec*
▲ EMP: 5 EST: 2012
SALES (est): 250.6K Privately Held
SIC: 2721 Magazines: publishing & printing

(G-9337)
BDG MEDIA INC
158 W 27th St Fl 11 (10001-6216)
PHONE..................917 951-9768
Bryan Goldberg, *CEO*
Tricia Dellipizzi, *Vice Pres*
EMP: 323
SQ FT: 19,200
SALES (est): 6.1MM Privately Held
SIC: 2741

(G-9338)
BEACHBUTTONS LLC
6 Greene St Apt 4b (10013-5817)
PHONE..................917 306-9369
Stavros Tsibiridis, *Mng Member*
EMP: 1
SALES: 100K Privately Held
SIC: 2253 Beachwear, knit

(G-9339)
BEAR PORT PUBLISHING COMPANY
45 W 21st St 3b (10010-6865)
PHONE..................212 337-8577
Ken Goin, *President*
Katherine Camisa, *Manager*
Adam Siegel, *Director*
Joyce Tavolacci, *Senior Editor*
EMP: 11
SQ FT: 3,000
SALES: 3MM
SALES (corp-wide): 157MM Privately Held
WEB: www.bearportpublishing.com
SIC: 2731 Book publishing
PA: Woongjin Holdings Co., Ltd.
   Jongro Place Bldg.
   Seoul SEO 03130
   220 764-701

(G-9340)
BEAUTY FASHION INC
Also Called: Astor-Honor Division
8 W 38th St Frnt 2 (10018-0133)
PHONE..................212 840-8800
Fax: 212 840-7246
John G Ledes, *Ch of Bd*
George M Ledes, *President*
Hosu Shah, *Controller*
Deborah Davis, *Adv Dir*
Jihad Harkeem, *Director*
EMP: 20
SALES (est): 1.8MM Privately Held
WEB: www.astorhonor.com
SIC: 2731 2721 Book publishing; magazines: publishing only, not printed on site

(G-9341)
BECCA INC
142 W 36th St Fl 15 (10018-8785)
PHONE..................646 568-6250
Robert Debaker, *CEO*
Seymour Zuckerman, *Ch of Bd*
Stephanie Cleghorn, *Accounts Exec*
Taylor Burns, *Asst Mgr*
Kerry Cole, *Director*
▲ EMP: 14 EST: 2011
SALES (est): 2.3MM Privately Held
SIC: 2844 Cosmetic preparations

(G-9342)
BEDFORD FREEMAN & WORTH (DH)
Also Called: Scientific American Library
1 New York Plz Ste 4500 (10004-1562)
PHONE..................212 576-9400
Jessica Fiorillo, *Publisher*
Carlos Marin, *Editor*
Linda Glover, *Business Mgr*
Elizabeth A Widdicombe, *Senior VP*
John Britch, *Sls & Mktg Exec*
EMP: 192
SQ FT: 36,000
SALES (est): 73.9MM
SALES (corp-wide): 2.1B Privately Held
WEB: www.bfwpub.com
SIC: 2731 2759 2732 2721 Book publishing; commercial printing; book printing; periodicals

(G-9343)
BEDFORD FREEMAN & WORTH
Also Called: Saint Martins Press
1 New York Plz Ste 4500 (10004-1562)
PHONE..................212 375-7000
Fax: 212 614-1885
Joan Feinberg, *President*
Tom Kane, *Editor*
Cathy Shin, *Project Mgr*
Raymond Maldonado, *Info Tech Dir*
Spencer Malmad, *Webmaster*
EMP: 70
SALES (corp-wide): 2.1B Privately Held
WEB: www.bfwpub.com
SIC: 2731 Textbooks: publishing only, not printed on site
HQ: Bedford, Freeman & Worth Publishing Group, Llc
   1 New York Plz Ste 4500
   New York NY 10004
   212 576-9400

(G-9344)
BEDFORD COMMUNICATIONS INC
1410 Broadway Frnt 2 (10018-9302)
PHONE..................212 807-8220
Fax: 212 807-1098
Edward D Brown, *President*
Thomas J Fink, *Editor*
Jonathan Pratt, *Editor*
Lisa Brisdane, *Finance*
Kelly Immoor, *Natl Sales Mgr*
EMP: 30
SALES (est): 3.9MM Privately Held
WEB: www.bedfordcommunications.com
SIC: 2721 Magazines: publishing only, not printed on site

(G-9345)
BEDROCK COMMUNICATIONS
Also Called: Facilities
152 Madison Ave Rm 802 (10016-5476)
PHONE..................212 532-4150
Fax: 212 213-6382
Susan Wexner, *President*
Michael Casffin, *Vice Pres*
Sandy Abby, *Assoc Editor*
EMP: 5
SQ FT: 3,500
SALES (est): 479.4K Privately Held
WEB: www.facilitiesonline.com
SIC: 2731 Book publishing

(G-9346)
BEILA GROUP INC
Also Called: City Hats
285 Mott St (10012-3430)
PHONE..................212 260-1948
Alexandra Tiouleneva, *CEO*
EMP: 12

SALES (est): 1MM Privately Held
SIC: 3942 Hats, doll

(G-9347)
BEL AMERICAS INC
122 E 42nd St Rm 2715 (10168-2700)
PHONE..................646 454-8220
Eric Deponcis, *President*
Ingrid Gonzalez, *Manager*
EMP: 5
SALES (est): 202.6K
SALES (corp-wide): 7MM Privately Held
SIC: 2099 Tea blending
HQ: Bel Brands Usa, Inc.
   30 S Wacker Dr Ste 3000
   Chicago IL 60606
   312 462-1500

(G-9348)
BELDEN BRICK SALES & SVC INC (HQ)
Also Called: Belden Tri-State Building Mtls
333 7th Ave Rm 502 (10001-5123)
PHONE..................212 686-3939
Fax: 212 686-4387
William H Belden Jr, *CEO*
Joseph W Ricevito, *President*
David Epstein, *Co-President*
Robert E Belden, *Vice Pres*
Robert Turzilli, *Vice Pres*
▲ EMP: 10
SQ FT: 3,900
SALES (est): 6.7MM
SALES (corp-wide): 79.5MM Privately Held
WEB: www.nynjbrick.com
SIC: 3271 Paving blocks, concrete
PA: The Belden Brick Company Llc
   700 Tuscarawas St W Up
   Canton OH 44702
   330 456-0031

(G-9349)
BELLARNO INTERNATIONAL LTD
1140 Ave Of The Americas (10036-5803)
PHONE..................212 302-4107
Fax: 212 302-5896
Donald Fishoff, *President*
EMP: 8
SALES (est): 494.5K
SALES (corp-wide): 20.2MM Privately Held
SIC: 2844 Toilet preparations
PA: Inter-Ocean Industries Llc
   1208 Avenue M
   Brooklyn NY 11230
   718 375-2532

(G-9350)
BELLATAIRE DIAMONDS INC
19 W 44th St Fl 15 (10036-6101)
PHONE..................212 687-8881
Fax: 212 687-8448
Bill Moryto, *CFO*
Charles A Meyer, *Exec Dir*
EMP: 10
SALES (est): 840K Privately Held
WEB: www.bellatairediamonds.com
SIC: 3911 Jewelry, precious metal

(G-9351)
BELLEROPHON PUBLICATIONS INC
Also Called: Metropolis Magazine
205 Lexington Ave Fl 17 (10016-6022)
PHONE..................212 627-9977
Fax: 212 627-9977
Horace Havemeyer III, *President*
Tamara Stout, *General Mgr*
Mikki Brammer, *Editor*
Samuel Medina, *Editor*
Eugenie Havemeyer, *CFO*
EMP: 35
SQ FT: 4,000
SALES (est): 5.6MM Privately Held
WEB: www.metropolismag.com
SIC: 2721 Magazines: publishing only, not printed on site

(G-9352)
BELSUL AMERICA CORP
125 Park Ave Fl 25 (10017-5550)
PHONE..................212 520-1827
Sergio S Correa, *President*

New York - New York County (G-9353) — GEOGRAPHIC SECTION

Rosemarie Ojeda, *Manager*
Roberto A Santos, *Director*
EMP: 10
SALES: 1MM **Privately Held**
SIC: 2821 Thermoplastic materials

(G-9353)
BELUGA INC (PA)
Also Called: Baby Beluga
463 7th Ave Fl 4 (10018-8725)
PHONE......................212 594-5511
Eric Adjmi, *Ch of Bd*
Mark Adjmi, *Vice Pres*
Steven Bissu, *Vice Pres*
Lori May, *Vice Pres*
Veronica Cabarcas, *Prdtn Mgr*
▲ **EMP:** 40
SQ FT: 15,000
SALES (est): 6.5MM **Privately Held**
WEB: www.beluga.com
SIC: 2329 Men's & boys' sportswear & athletic clothing

(G-9354)
BEN WACHTER ASSOCIATES INC (PA)
Also Called: B W A
36 W 44th St Ste 700 (10036-8105)
PHONE......................212 736-4064
Fax: 212 564-0621
Andrew Lerner, *CEO*
Nuno Lacerda, *Managing Dir*
Carlos Mojich, *Controller*
Charlie Jackson, *Sales Executive*
▲ **EMP:** 5
SALES (est): 1.9MM **Privately Held**
SIC: 2321 2331 5199 Men's & boys' furnishings; women's & misses' blouses & shirts; fabrics, yarns & knit goods; cotton yarns

(G-9355)
BEN-AMUN CO INC (PA)
246 W 38th St Fl 12a (10018-5845)
PHONE......................212 944-6480
Fax: 212 944-9625
Isaac Manevitz, *President*
Regina Manevitz, *Vice Pres*
Lauren Lustica, *Sales Executive*
▼ **EMP:** 20
SQ FT: 10,000
SALES (est): 2.5MM **Privately Held**
WEB: www.ben-amun.com
SIC: 3961 Costume jewelry, ex. precious metal & semiprecious stones

(G-9356)
BEN-SAK TEXTILE INC
Also Called: Bensak
307 W 38th St 9 (10018-2913)
PHONE......................212 279-5122
Benhour Ahdout, *CEO*
David Ahdout, *Vice Pres*
Ned Saki, *CFO*
Alka Cricahi, *Manager*
EMP: 7
SQ FT: 550
SALES (est): 960K **Privately Held**
WEB: www.getinkjet.com
SIC: 2269 Finishing plants

(G-9357)
BENARTEX INC
132 W 36th St Rm 401 (10018-8837)
PHONE......................212 840-3250
Fax: 212 921-8204
David Lochner, *President*
Susan Neill, *VP Mktg*
Janica Cantor, *Manager*
Susan Kemler, *Manager*
Paula Nadelstern, *Manager*
◆ **EMP:** 35
SQ FT: 7,000
SALES (est): 4.4MM **Privately Held**
WEB: www.benartex.com
SIC: 2211 Apparel & outerwear fabrics, cotton

(G-9358)
BENCHMARK GRAPHICS LTD
9 E 37th St Fl 5 (10016-2894)
PHONE......................212 683-1711
Fax: 212 889-1927
EMP: 15
SQ FT: 5,000
SALES (est): 1.8MM **Privately Held**
SIC: 2752 Lithographic Commercial Printing

(G-9359)
BENETTON TRADING USA INC (PA)
601 5th Ave Fl 4 (10017-8258)
P.O. Box 6020, Somerset NJ (08875-6020)
PHONE......................212 593-0290
ARI Hoffman, *Principal*
◆ **EMP:** 6 **EST:** 2014
SALES (est): 1.2MM **Privately Held**
SIC: 2329 Men's & boys' sportswear & athletic clothing

(G-9360)
BENSON INDUSTRIES INC
192 Lexington Ave Rm 502 (10016-6912)
PHONE......................212 779-3230
Robyn Ryan, *Project Mgr*
John Frank, *Manager*
Julissa Maldonado, *Admin Asst*
EMP: 10
SALES (corp-wide): 210.8B **Publicly Held**
SIC: 3231 1793 5031 Products of purchased glass; glass & glazing work; lumber, plywood & millwork
HQ: Benson Industries, Inc.
 1650 Nw Naito Pkwy # 250
 Portland OR 97209
 503 226-7611

(G-9361)
BENTLEY MANUFACTURING INC (PA)
10 W 33rd St Rm 220 (10001-3306)
PHONE......................212 714-1800
Victor Braha, *President*
Ralph Braha, *CFO*
Annett Metir, *Manager*
Eli Braha, *Admin Sec*
◆ **EMP:** 7
SQ FT: 5,200
SALES (est): 2MM **Privately Held**
SIC: 2676 Diapers, paper (disposable): made from purchased paper; napkins, sanitary: made from purchased paper

(G-9362)
BEOWAWE BINARY LLC
1095 Avenue Of The Ave (10036)
PHONE......................646 829-3900
James Pagano,
EMP: 30
SALES: 500K **Privately Held**
SIC: 3511 Turbines & turbine generator sets

(G-9363)
BERGER & WILD LLC
Also Called: Last Magazine, The
401 Broadway Ste 302 (10013-3005)
PHONE......................646 415-8459
Tenzen Wild, *Partner*
Migus Berger, *Partner*
Tenzen Wilt, *Partner*
Sarah Louise, *General Mgr*
Zachary Sniderman, *Assoc Editor*
EMP: 5
SALES (est): 436.2K **Privately Held**
SIC: 2721 Periodicals

(G-9364)
BERNARD CHAUS INC (PA)
530 Fashion Ave Fl 18 (10018-4855)
PHONE......................212 354-1280
Fax: 212 562-4848
Josephine Chaus, *Ch of Bd*
Jaymie Brenner, *General Mgr*
Ken Christmann, *Vice Pres*
Judith Leech, *Vice Pres*
William P Runge, *CFO*
▲ **EMP:** 76
SQ FT: 33,000
SALES (est): 77.9MM **Privately Held**
SIC: 2339 2331 2335 Sportswear, women's; slacks: women's, misses' & juniors'; shorts (outerwear): women's, misses' & juniors'; women's & misses' blouses & shirts; wedding gowns & dresses

(G-9365)
BERNARD CHAUS INC
Also Called: Cynthia Steffe
515 7th Ave Ste 18 (10018-5902)
PHONE......................646 562-4700
Tina Cardell, *Branch Mgr*
EMP: 200
SALES (corp-wide): 77.9MM **Privately Held**
SIC: 2339 2331 Sportswear, women's; slacks: women's, misses' & juniors'; shorts (outerwear): women's, misses' & juniors'; women's & misses' blouses & shirts
PA: Bernard Chaus, Inc.
 530 Fashion Ave Fl 18
 New York NY 10018
 212 354-1280

(G-9366)
BERNETTE APPAREL LLC
42 W 39th St Fl 2 (10018-3895)
PHONE......................212 279-5526
Adam Siskind,
Jeff Siskind,
EMP: 16
SQ FT: 7,000
SALES (est): 1.1MM **Privately Held**
WEB: www.btexusa.com
SIC: 2329 Sweaters & sweater jackets: men's & boys'

(G-9367)
BERNHARD ARNOLD & COMPANY INC (PA)
485 Lexington Ave Fl 9 (10017-2653)
PHONE......................212 907-1500
Howard Brecher, *Vice Pres*
David Henigson, *Vice Pres*
Harold Bernard, *Director*
Stephen Anastasio, *Officer*
EMP: 3 **EST:** 1931
SQ FT: 70,000
SALES: 36MM **Publicly Held**
WEB: www.valueline.com
SIC: 2721 6282 Periodicals: publishing only; investment advice

(G-9368)
BERRYWILD
200 E 30th St Bsmt (10016-8440)
PHONE......................212 686-5848
Samuel Mirelli, *Partner*
Harold Rosen, *Partner*
EMP: 6
SALES (est): 464K **Privately Held**
SIC: 2024 Yogurt desserts, frozen

(G-9369)
BERT WASSERERMAN
370 Lexington Ave (10017-6503)
PHONE......................212 759-5210
Fax: 212 759-5304
Bert Wasserman, *Principal*
EMP: 5
SALES (est): 513.5K **Privately Held**
SIC: 2329 Knickers, dress (separate): men's & boys'

(G-9370)
BERTELSMANN INC (HQ)
1745 Broadway Fl 20 (10019-4640)
PHONE......................212 782-1000
Fax: 212 782-1010
Jaroslaw Gabor, *CEO*
Thomas Rabe, *Ch of Bd*
Joshua Kraus, *President*
Gerd Schulte-Hillen, *Vice Chairman*
Peter Blobel, *COO*
▲ **EMP:** 30
SALES: 1.3B
SALES (corp-wide): 18.4B **Privately Held**
WEB: www.bertelsmann.com
SIC: 2731 2721 7819 3652 Books: publishing & printing; magazines: publishing & printing; trade journals: publishing & printing; video tape or disk reproduction; compact laser discs, prerecorded; commercial & industrial building operation
PA: Bertelsmann Se & Co. Kgaa
 Carl-Bertelsmann-Str. 270
 Gutersloh 33335
 524 180-0

(G-9371)
BERTELSMANN PUBG GROUP INC (DH)
1540 Broadway Fl 24 (10036-4039)
PHONE......................212 782-1000
Thomas Middelhoff, *CEO*
Robert J Sorrentino, *CEO*
Hans-Martin Sorge, *Ch of Bd*
Peter Olson, *President*
Bernhard U Derlath, *Treasurer*
EMP: 1000
SQ FT: 710,000
SALES (est): 80.1MM
SALES (corp-wide): 18.4B **Privately Held**
SIC: 2731 2721 Books: publishing only; magazines: publishing only, not printed on site
HQ: Bertelsmann, Inc.
 1745 Broadway Fl 20
 New York NY 10019
 212 782-1000

(G-9372)
BESPOKE APPAREL INC
214 W 39th St Rm 200b (10018-8321)
PHONE......................212 382-0330
Rong Su, *President*
Chia Hung Yu, *Vice Pres*
▲ **EMP:** 6
SQ FT: 1,500
SALES (est): 390K **Privately Held**
SIC: 2326 Service apparel (baker, barber, lab, etc.), washable: men's

(G-9373)
BEST BRANDS CONSUMER PDTS INC (PA)
20 W 33rd St Fl 5 (10001-3305)
PHONE......................212 684-7456
Peter Felberbaum, *President*
Meyer Kassin, *Vice Pres*
Albert Kassin, *Treasurer*
Isaac Kassin, *Admin Sec*
◆ **EMP:** 8
SQ FT: 26,000
SALES (est): 1.6MM **Privately Held**
SIC: 2369 2371 Headwear: girls', children's & infants'; hats, fur

(G-9374)
BESTYPE DIGITAL IMAGING LLC
285 W Broadway Frnt A (10013-2246)
PHONE......................212 966-6886
Fax: 212 966-6034
John W Lam, *Mng Member*
John Lam, *Manager*
Chick Lam,
EMP: 10
SQ FT: 3,000
SALES: 1MM **Privately Held**
SIC: 2759 Commercial printing

(G-9375)
BET NETWORKS INCORPORATED
1540 Broadway Fl 26 (10036-4039)
PHONE......................212 846-8111
Stephen Hill, *President*
Robert L Johnson, *Principal*
Pete Danielsen, *Exec VP*
MAI K Flournoy, *Senior VP*
Eddie Hill, *Senior VP*
EMP: 20 **EST:** 2008
SALES (est): 3.6MM **Privately Held**
SIC: 3663 Studio equipment, radio & television broadcasting

(G-9376)
BETH KOBLINER COMPANY LLC
1995 Broadway Ste 1800 (10023-5857)
Rural Route 120 W 45th (10036)
PHONE......................212 501-8407
Fax: 212 890-8876
Beth Kobliner,
EMP: 5
SALES (est): 305.1K **Privately Held**
SIC: 2711 Newspapers, publishing & printing

▲ = Import ▼ = Export
◆ = Import/Export

New York - New York County (G-9404)

(G-9377)
BETH WARD STUDIOS LLC
133 W 25th St Rm 8e (10001-7281)
PHONE..................................646 922-7575
Beth Ward, *Mng Member*
EMP: 10
SALES: 3.4MM **Privately Held**
SIC: 3961 Costume jewelry

(G-9378)
BETSY & ADAM LTD (PA)
1400 Broadway Rm 602 (10018-0779)
PHONE..................................212 302-3750
Fax: 212 398-0454
Martin Sklar, *Owner*
Frank Lamourt, *Controller*
Tammy Sklar, *Sales Mgr*
▲ **EMP:** 50
SQ FT: 12,000
SALES (est): 14.6MM **Privately Held**
WEB: www.betsyandadam.com
SIC: 2253 Dresses & skirts

(G-9379)
BETTERTEX INC
Also Called: Bettertex Interioirs
450 Broadway (10013-5822)
PHONE..................................212 431-3373
Raymond Nakash, *President*
EMP: 15 **EST:** 2008
SALES (est): 1.4MM **Privately Held**
SIC: 2391 7641 Curtains & draperies; upholstery work

(G-9380)
BEVERAGE MEDIA GROUP INC (PA)
152 Madison Ave Rm 600 (10016-5471)
PHONE..................................212 571-3232
Mike Roth, *President*
Kristen Wolfe, *Editor*
Jody Slone, *VP Opers*
Lauren Howery, *Marketing Staff*
Lee Stringham, *Director*
▲ **EMP:** 10
SQ FT: 13,300
SALES (est): 1.8MM **Privately Held**
WEB: www.bevmedia.com
SIC: 2721 Magazines: publishing only, not printed on site

(G-9381)
BEVERLY CREATIONS INC
Also Called: Natalie Creations
40 E 34th St Rm 1403 (10016-4501)
PHONE..................................800 439-6855
Jerry Joseph, *President*
Judith Rothman, *Manager*
Dan Strauss, *Manager*
EMP: 12 **EST:** 1968
SALES (est): 770K **Privately Held**
WEB: www.beverlycreations.com
SIC: 2341 Women's & children's undergarments

(G-9382)
BEVILACQUE GROUP LLC
250 Hudson St (10013-1413)
PHONE..................................212 414-8858
Mark Bevilacque,
EMP: 11
SQ FT: 2,750
SALES (est): 800K **Privately Held**
WEB: www.bevilacque.com
SIC: 2752 Commercial printing, lithographic

(G-9383)
BEYOND LOOM INC (PA)
Also Called: Franetta
262 W 38th St Rm 203 (10018-5881)
P.O. Box 105 (10150-0105)
PHONE..................................212 575-3100
Joanne Satin, *President*
Edward Storch, *Vice Pres*
Norden Hahn, *Administration*
▲ **EMP:** 6 **EST:** 1991
SQ FT: 4,000
SALES (est): 607.3K **Privately Held**
WEB: www.beyondtheloom.com
SIC: 2211 2221 2231 Cotton broad woven goods; silk broadwoven fabrics; fabric finishing: wool, mohair or similar fibers

(G-9384)
BEYONDLY INC
Also Called: Everplans
20 W 20th St Ste 1004 (10011-9252)
PHONE..................................646 658-3665
Abby Schneiderman, *President*
Adam Seifer, *President*
Warren Habib, *CTO*
Ammon Brown, *Director*
Gene Newman, *Director*
EMP: 13 **EST:** 2012
SQ FT: 1,700
SALES (est): 1.1MM **Privately Held**
SIC: 7372 Business oriented computer software

(G-9385)
BEYONDSPRING PHRMCEUTICALS INC
28 Liberty St Fl 39 (10005-1451)
PHONE..................................646 305-6387
Lan Huang, *CEO*
G Kenneth Lloyd, *COO*
Steven D Reich, *Vice Pres*
Robert Dickey IV, *CFO*
Gloria Lee, *Chief Mktg Ofcr*
EMP: 11
SALES (est): 912.2K **Privately Held**
SIC: 2834 Pharmaceutical preparations

(G-9386)
BH BRAND INC
Also Called: Bh Brands
10 W 33rd St Rm 218 (10001-3306)
PHONE..................................212 239-1635
Morris Harari, *President*
Kenny Harari, *Vice Pres*
▲ **EMP:** 25
SQ FT: 4,500
SALES: 17MM **Privately Held**
SIC: 2389 2339 Men's miscellaneous accessories; women's & misses' accessories

(G-9387)
BH MULTI COM CORP (PA)
15 W 46th St Fl 6 (10036-4196)
PHONE..................................212 944-0020
Fax: 212 921-7796
Fatolah Hematian, *Ch of Bd*
Effy Hematian, *President*
David Bassalalli, *Corp Secy*
Hertsel Akhavan, *Vice Pres*
Hertsal Athavan, *Controller*
▲ **EMP:** 47 **EST:** 1979
SQ FT: 6,000
SALES (est): 6.5MM **Privately Held*
WEB: www.bhmulti.com
SIC: 3911 Jewelry, precious metal

(G-9388)
BIANCA GROUP LTD
244 W 39th St Fl 4 (10018-4413)
PHONE..................................212 768-3011
Ricardo Garcia, *President*
EMP: 5
SQ FT: 2,200
SALES: 200K **Privately Held**
SIC: 3953 3543 Marking devices; industrial patterns

(G-9389)
BIDPRESS LLC
659 Washington St Apt 5r (10014-2874)
PHONE..................................267 973-8876
Anthony Wavering, *CEO*
EMP: 5 **EST:** 2013
SQ FT: 1,000
SALES (est): 300K **Privately Held**
SIC: 2759 Screen printing

(G-9390)
BIELKA INC
136 E 57th St Ste 907 (10022-2966)
PHONE..................................212 980-6841
Fax: 212 980-6852
Robert Bruce Bielka, *President*
Regina Suzanne Eros, *Vice Pres*
EMP: 5
SQ FT: 1,200
SALES: 600K **Privately Held**
WEB: www.bielkajewelry.com
SIC: 3911 Jewelry, precious metal

(G-9391)
BIG APPLE ELEVTR SRV & CONSULT
247 W 30th St (10001-2824)
PHONE..................................212 279-0700
Jaclyn Hanning, *CEO*
Joseph Hanning, *President*
EMP: 8
SALES (est): 341.4K **Privately Held**
SIC: 3534 Elevators & moving stairways; elevators & equipment; dumbwaiters

(G-9392)
BIG APPLE SIGN CORP (PA)
Also Called: Big Apple Visual Group
247 W 35th St Frnt 1 (10001-1908)
PHONE..................................212 629-3650
Fax: 212 629-4954
Amir Khalfan, *Ch of Bd*
Richi Shah, *CFO*
Habib Shahzad, *Manager*
▲ **EMP:** 35
SQ FT: 40,000
SALES: 12.7MM **Privately Held**
WEB: www.bigapplegroup.com
SIC: 2399 2759 3993 Banners, made from fabric; commercial printing; signs, not made in custom sign painting shops; displays & cutouts, window & lobby

(G-9393)
BIG BANG CLOTHING INC
Also Called: Big Bang Clothing Co
214 W 39th St Rm 1008 (10018-4454)
PHONE..................................212 221-0379
Sam Seungwoo Lee, *Branch Mgr*
EMP: 5 **Privately Held**
SIC: 2339 Women's & misses' outerwear
PA: Big Bang Clothing, Inc
  4507 Staunton Ave
  Vernon CA 90058

(G-9394)
BIG IDEA BRANDS LLC
Also Called: Flow Society
1410 Broadway Frnt 4 (10018-9343)
PHONE..................................212 938-0270
Mark Elenowitz, *CEO*
Anthony Ottimo, *President*
Carlos Vazquez, *COO*
Larry Fihma, *Senior VP*
Brian Frank,
▲ **EMP:** 10
SQ FT: 4,000
SALES (est): 1MM **Privately Held**
SIC: 2329 Athletic (warmup, sweat & jogging) suits: men's & boys'

(G-9395)
BIG WHITE WALL HOLDING INC
41 E 11th St Fl 11 (10003-4602)
PHONE..................................917 281-2649
Tina Trenkler, *CEO*
EMP: 15 **EST:** 2013
SQ FT: 1,200
SALES: 250K **Privately Held**
SIC: 7372 Application computer software

(G-9396)
BILL BLASS GROUP LLC
236 5th Ave Fl 8 (10001-7949)
PHONE..................................212 689-8957
Stuart M Goldblatt, *President*
James Chang, *General Mgr*
Jerry Fallon, *Vice Pres*
Cin Kim, *Mng Member*
Nicolette Cavallo, *Executive Asst*
EMP: 10
SALES (est): 710K **Privately Held**
SIC: 2211 Apparel & outerwear fabrics, cotton

(G-9397)
BILLION TOWER INTL LLC
Also Called: Machine Clothing Company
989 6th Ave Fl 8 (10018-0871)
PHONE..................................212 220-0608
Fax: 212 563-6879
Joeson Ko, *Manager*
Joeson Ko Cho Shun,
▲ **EMP:** 15
SQ FT: 3,000
SALES: 122MM **Privately Held**
SIC: 2326 5136 Men's & boys' work clothing; men's & boys' clothing

(G-9398)
BILLION TOWER USA LLC
989 Avenue Of The America (10018-0871)
PHONE..................................212 220-0608
Joeson Cho Shun Ko,
Ceci Tan, *Executive Asst*
EMP: 5
SALES: 5MM **Privately Held**
SIC: 2329 Men's & boys' sportswear & athletic clothing

(G-9399)
BILLY BEEZ USA LLC (PA)
3 W 35th St Fl 3 (10001-2237)
PHONE..................................646 606-2249
Ron Palerico, *General Mgr*
Elisabetta Varriale, *Regional Mgr*
Mark Bain, *Sales Staff*
EMP: 14
SALES (est): 14.2MM **Privately Held**
SIC: 3949 5137 7999 Playground equipment; women's & children's dresses, suits, skirts & blouses; amusement ride

(G-9400)
BIOCONTINUUM GROUP INC
116 Chambers St (10007-1336)
PHONE..................................212 406-1060
Fax: 212 406-6544
John M Dimor, *President*
EMP: 5
SQ FT: 1,200
SALES (est): 290K **Privately Held**
WEB: www.bioc.net
SIC: 3999 Education aids, devices & supplies

(G-9401)
BIOFEEDBACK INSTRUMENT CORP
Also Called: Allied Products
255 W 98th St Apt 3d (10025-5596)
PHONE..................................212 222-5665
Philip Brotman, *President*
▲ **EMP:** 8
SQ FT: 1,000
SALES: 800K **Privately Held**
WEB: www.biof.com
SIC: 3845 5045 5734 Electromedical apparatus; computers, peripherals & software; computer peripheral equipment; computer & software stores

(G-9402)
BIOLITEC INC
110 E 42nd St Rm 1800 (10017-5648)
PHONE..................................413 525-0600
Wolfgang Neuberger, *CEO*
Arthur Henneberger, *Controller*
Gary Stone, *Manager*
EMP: 50
SQ FT: 16,000
SALES (est): 6.3MM
SALES (corp-wide): 1MM **Privately Held**
WEB: www.biolitec-us.com
SIC: 3229 Fiber optics strands
HQ: Biolitec Biomedical Technology Gmbh
  Otto-Schott-Str. 15
  Jena 07745
  364 151-9530

(G-9403)
BIRNBAUM & BULLOCK LTD
151 W 25th St Rm 2a (10001-7262)
PHONE..................................212 242-2914
Fax: 212 242-0771
Robert Bullock, *CEO*
Steven Birnbaum, *President*
EMP: 8
SQ FT: 1,500
SALES (est): 1.1MM **Privately Held**
SIC: 2335 Wedding gowns & dresses

(G-9404)
BISCUITS & BATH COMPANIES LLC
41 W 13th St (10011-7924)
PHONE..................................212 401-3022
Fax: 212 901-7900
Neshaa Ramoutar, *Human Res Dir*
Laurence Casimir, *Human Res Mgr*
Teague Fleury, *Manager*
Allison Braithwaite, *Manager*
EMP: 25

New York - New York County (G-9405)

SALES (est): 3.9MM **Privately Held**
SIC: 2052 Biscuits, dry

(G-9405)
BISTATE OIL MANAGEMENT CORP
10 E 40th St Rm 2705 (10016-0450)
PHONE..................212 935-4110
Fax: 212 593-1287
Richard D Siegal, *President*
Maria Scibelli, *Principal*
Brian Grossa, *Vice Pres*
Paul H Howard, *Vice Pres*
EMP: 10
SQ FT: 4,500
SALES (est): 2.5MM **Privately Held**
SIC: 1382 Oil & gas exploration services

(G-9406)
BIZBASH MEDIA INC (PA)
Also Called: Bizbash Masterplanner
8 W 38th St Rm 200 (10018-6370)
PHONE..................646 638-3600
Fax: 646 638-3601
David Adler, *CEO*
Richard Aaron, *President*
Ann Keusch, *COO*
Lee Schrager, *Vice Pres*
Jean Jaworek, *Engineer*
EMP: 45
SQ FT: 5,000
SALES (est): 10.5MM **Privately Held**
WEB: www.bizbash.com
SIC: 2759 Advertising literature: printing

(G-9407)
BJ MAGAZINES INC
200 Varick St (10014-4810)
PHONE..................212 367-9705
Renu Hooda, *President*
EMP: 5
SALES (est): 530K **Privately Held**
SIC: 2721 Periodicals

(G-9408)
BJG SERVICES LLC
14 Penn Plz (10122-0049)
PHONE..................516 592-5692
Isaac Newmann, *CEO*
Ben Neuberg, *President*
EMP: 25
SQ FT: 1,600
SALES (est): 7.1MM **Privately Held**
SIC: 3911 Jewelry, precious metal

(G-9409)
BLACK BOOK PHOTOGRAPHY INC
Also Called: Black Book, The
740 Broadway Ste 202 (10003-9518)
PHONE..................212 979-6700
Ted Rubin, *President*
▲ EMP: 19 EST: 1970
SALES (est): 1.5MM
SALES (corp-wide): 3.6MM **Privately Held**
WEB: www.modernholdings.com
SIC: 2741 Directories: publishing only, not printed on site
PA: Modern Holding Company
601 Lexington Ave Rm 5900
New York NY

(G-9410)
BLACKBOOK MEDIA CORP
32 Union Sq E Ste 4l (10003-3209)
PHONE..................212 334-1800
Robert Hoff, *CEO*
Joseph Landry, *President*
David Cohn, *Exec VP*
Haylli Weintraub, *Office Mgr*
Candice Naboicheck, *Manager*
EMP: 21
SQ FT: 1,500
SALES (est): 2.4MM **Privately Held**
SIC: 2721 Magazines: publishing & printing

(G-9411)
BLADES
659 Broadway (10012-2302)
PHONE..................212 477-1059
George Pohntes, *Manager*
▼ EMP: 10
SALES (est): 712.5K **Privately Held**
SIC: 3949 Skateboards

(G-9412)
BLANCHE P FIELD LLC
155 E 56th St Ph (10022-2718)
PHONE..................212 355-6616
Blanche Field, *President*
Lisa Simkin, *Manager*
EMP: 25 EST: 1942
SQ FT: 3,000
SALES (est): 1.5MM **Privately Held**
SIC: 3999 5932 Shades, lamp or candle; antiques

(G-9413)
BLANDI PRODUCTS LLC
Also Called: Oscar Blandi
950 3rd Ave Fl 3 (10022-2793)
PHONE..................908 377-2885
Brian Robinson,
Stuart Litman,
▲ EMP: 15
SALES (est): 1.3MM **Privately Held**
SIC: 3999 Hair & hair-based products

(G-9414)
BLISS FOODS INC
Also Called: Yorganic
275 Greenwich St Frnt 2 (10007-3824)
PHONE..................212 732-8888
Sung Kim, *President*
Shawn Reilly, *Vice Pres*
EMP: 5
SALES (est): 466.3K **Privately Held**
SIC: 2026 Yogurt

(G-9415)
BLISS FOODS INC
Also Called: Yorganic
275 Greenwich St Frnt 2 (10007-3824)
PHONE..................212 732-8888
EMP: 11 **Privately Held**
SIC: 2026 Mfg Fluid Milk

(G-9416)
BLISS-POSTON THE SECOND WIND
928 Broadway Ste 403 (10010-8151)
PHONE..................212 481-1055
Fax: 212 481-7374
Marcia Poston, *Vice Pres*
John Bliss, *Exec Dir*
EMP: 6
SALES (est): 522.9K **Privately Held**
SIC: 2011 Lard from carcasses slaughtered on site

(G-9417)
BLOOMSBURG CARPET INDS INC
Also Called: Silver Creek Carpet
49 W 23rd St Fl 4 (10010-4228)
PHONE..................212 688-7447
Fax: 212 688-9218
Thomas J Habib, *President*
Tracy Hess, *Human Res Mgr*
EMP: 6
SALES (corp-wide): 50MM **Privately Held**
SIC: 2273 Carpets & rugs
PA: Bloomsburg Carpet Industries, Inc.
4999 Columbia Blvd
Bloomsburg PA 17815
570 784-9188

(G-9418)
BLOOMSBURY PUBLISHING INC
Also Called: Bloomsbury USA
1385 Brdwy Fl 5 (10018)
PHONE..................212 419-5300
Fax: 646 727-0984
Nigel Newton, *President*
Doug White, *Principal*
Richard Charkin, *Exec VP*
Colin Adams, *Senior VP*
Wendy Pallot, *Senior VP*
▲ EMP: 100
SALES (est): 28MM
SALES (corp-wide): 173.2MM **Privately Held**
WEB: www.bloomsburyusa.com
SIC: 2731 Book publishing
PA: Bloomsbury Publishing Plc
50 Bedford Square
London WC1B
207 631-5600

(G-9419)
BLU SAND LLC
589 8th Ave Fl 9 (10018-3083)
PHONE..................212 564-1147
Eddie Shomer, *Vice Pres*
Eddie Cheung, *Office Mgr*
Morris Sitt,
EMP: 9
SQ FT: 2,000
SALES (est): 850K **Privately Held**
WEB: www.blusand.com
SIC: 2211 Towels & toweling, cotton

(G-9420)
BLUE AND WHITE PUBLISHING INC
Also Called: Bwog
425 Riverside Dr Apt 3c (10025-7724)
PHONE..................215 431-3339
Jake Hershman, *CEO*
EMP: 10 EST: 2013
SALES (est): 550.6K **Privately Held**
SIC: 2711 Newspapers: publishing only, not printed on site

(G-9421)
BLUE HORIZON MEDIA INC (PA)
11 Park Pl Rm 1508 (10007-2816)
PHONE..................212 661-7878
Geoffrey D Lurie, *COO*
David Bernstein, *CFO*
EMP: 16
SQ FT: 16,000
SALES (est): 3MM **Privately Held**
WEB: www.bluehrzn.com
SIC: 2721 Magazines: publishing only, not printed on site

(G-9422)
BLUE TEE CORP (PA)
Also Called: Brown Strauss Steel Division
387 Park Ave S Fl 5 (10016-8810)
PHONE..................212 598-0880
Fax: 212 598-0896
David P Alldian, *Ch of Bd*
William M Kelly, *President*
Annette Marino D'Arienzo, *Exec Dir*
Brian Hamlin, *Director*
◆ EMP: 7
SQ FT: 2,500
SALES (est): 423MM **Privately Held**
SIC: 3533 3589 5093 3715 Water well drilling equipment; garbage disposers & compactors, commercial; ferrous metal scrap & waste; semitrailers for truck tractors; water quality monitoring & control systems; structural shapes, iron or steel

(G-9423)
BLUE WOLF GROUP LLC (HQ)
11 E 26th St Fl 21 (10010-1413)
PHONE..................866 455-9653
Tim Anderson, *Principal*
Eric Berridge, *Mng Member*
Tom Rahl, *Administration*
Michael Kirven,
EMP: 100
SQ FT: 5,000
SALES (est): 93.6MM
SALES (corp-wide): 81.7B **Publicly Held**
WEB: www.bluewolfgroup.com
SIC: 7372 Prepackaged software; business oriented computer software
PA: International Business Machines Corporation
1 New Orchard Rd Ste 1
Armonk NY 10504
914 499-1900

(G-9424)
BLUEDUCK TRADING LTD
463 7th Ave Rm 806 (10018-8712)
PHONE..................212 268-3122
Barry Novick, *President*
▲ EMP: 8
SQ FT: 4,500
SALES (est): 1.3MM **Privately Held**
WEB: www.blueduckshearling.com
SIC: 2339 2311 Women's & misses' jackets & coats, except sportswear; coats, tailored, men's & boys': from purchased materials

(G-9425)
BLUESOHO (PA)
160 Varick St Fl 2 (10013-1251)
PHONE..................646 805-2583
Jennifer Bergin, *Managing Prtnr*
Janine Crowley, *Opers Mgr*
EMP: 7
SALES (est): 954.4K **Privately Held**
SIC: 2752 Commercial printing, lithographic

(G-9426)
BLUM & FINK INC
158 W 29th St Fl 12 (10001-5300)
PHONE..................212 695-2606
Fax: 212 967-8123
Stanley Blum, *President*
EMP: 12 EST: 1961
SQ FT: 10,000
SALES (est): 1.5MM **Privately Held**
SIC: 2371 5137 Fur coats & other fur apparel; fur clothing, women's & children's

(G-9427)
BM AMERICA LLC (DH)
Also Called: Bruno Magli
4 W 58th St Fl 10 (10019-2515)
PHONE..................201 438-7733
Jay Patel, *Accountant*
Michele Donno,
▲ EMP: 29
SQ FT: 30,000
SALES (est): 2.5MM
SALES (corp-wide): 6.8MM **Privately Held**
WEB: www.brunomagli.com
SIC: 3143 Men's footwear, except athletic
HQ: Bm Usa Incorporated
75 Triangle Blvd
Carlstadt NJ 07072
800 624-5499

(G-9428)
BMC SOFTWARE INC
14 E 47th St Fl 3 (10017-7282)
PHONE..................646 452-4100
Robert Gardos, *Branch Mgr*
EMP: 32
SALES (corp-wide): 2.7B **Privately Held**
SIC: 7372 Prepackaged software
HQ: Bmc Software, Inc.
2103 Citywest Blvd # 2100
Houston TX 77042
713 918-8800

(G-9429)
BMC SOFTWARE INC
1114 Ave Of The Americas (10036-7703)
PHONE..................212 730-1389
Fax: 212 402-1599
Cristina Martinez, *Accounts Mgr*
Jeff Parks, *Branch Mgr*
Mark Settle, *CIO*
Ralph Crosby, *CTO*
EMP: 32
SALES (corp-wide): 2.7B **Privately Held**
WEB: www.bmc.com
SIC: 7372 7371 Utility computer software; custom computer programming services
HQ: Bmc Software, Inc.
2103 Citywest Blvd # 2100
Houston TX 77042
713 918-8800

(G-9430)
BMG RIGHTS MANAGEMENT (US) LLC (HQ)
Also Called: Bmg Chrysalis
1745 Broadway Fl 19 (10019-4640)
PHONE..................212 561-3000
Hartwig Masuch, *CEO*
Jon Cohen, *Exec VP*
Kos Weaver, *Exec VP*
Andy Godfrey, *Vice Pres*
Tim Reid, *Vice Pres*
EMP: 20
SALES (est): 2.7MM
SALES (corp-wide): 18.4B **Privately Held**
SIC: 2731 Book publishing
PA: Bertelsmann Se & Co. Kgaa
Carl-Bertelsmann-Str. 270
Gutersloh 33335
524 180-0

GEOGRAPHIC SECTION

New York - New York County (G-9455)

(G-9431)
BNNS CO INC
71 W 47th St Ste 600-601 (10036-2866)
PHONE.....................................212 302-1844
Fax: 212 302-1844
Nick Barhnakov, *President*
Simon Nikhamin, *Vice Pres*
EMP: 8
SALES (est): 510K **Privately Held**
WEB: www.bnnsco.com
SIC: 3961 Costume jewelry

(G-9432)
BOARDMAN SIMONS PUBLISHING (PA)
Also Called: Davidson Publishing
55 Broad St Fl 26 (10004-2580)
PHONE.....................................212 620-7200
Arthur J McGinnis Jr, *President*
Carol Franklin, *Manager*
EMP: 40
SQ FT: 12,000
SALES (est): 8.8MM **Privately Held**
WEB: www.sbpub.com
SIC: 2721 8249 Periodicals: publishing only; books: publishing only; correspondence school

(G-9433)
BOBBI BROWN PROF COSMT INC
575 Broadway Fl 4 (10012-3237)
PHONE.....................................646 613-6500
Bobbi Brown, *CEO*
Leonard A Lauder, *Ch of Bd*
Donald Robertson, *Senior VP*
Veronika Ullmer, *Vice Pres*
Alicia Valencia, *Vice Pres*
▲ EMP: 36
SALES (est): 394.2K
SALES (corp-wide): 11.2B **Publicly Held**
WEB: www.bobbibrown.com
SIC: 2844 Toilet preparations
PA: The Estee Lauder Companies Inc
   767 5th Ave Fl 37
   New York NY 10153
   212 572-4200

(G-9434)
BOEING COMPANY
304 Park Ave S (10010-4301)
PHONE.....................................201 259-9400
Donald Boeing, *Branch Mgr*
EMP: 897
SALES (corp-wide): 96.1B **Publicly Held**
SIC: 3721 Airplanes, fixed or rotary wing
PA: The Boeing Company
   100 N Riverside Plz
   Chicago IL 60606
   312 544-2000

(G-9435)
BONDI DIGITAL PUBLISHING LLC
88 10th Ave Frnt 6 (10011-4745)
PHONE.....................................212 405-1655
Murat Aktar, *Mng Member*
David Anthony, *Mng Member*
Carey Taylor, *Mng Member*
EMP: 5
SALES (est): 460.4K **Privately Held**
SIC: 2721 Magazines: publishing & printing

(G-9436)
BONELLI FOODS LLC
139 Fulton St Rm 314 (10038-2537)
PHONE.....................................212 346-0942
Tommaso Asaro, *Mng Member*
▲ EMP: 1
SQ FT: 1,000
SALES: 1.4MM **Privately Held**
SIC: 2079 Olive oil

(G-9437)
BONPOINT INC (PA)
396 W Broadway Apt 3 (10012-4681)
PHONE.....................................212 246-3291
Fax: 212 246-3293
Bernard Kolhen, *President*
▲ EMP: 23 EST: 1970
SALES (est): 1.7MM **Privately Held**
WEB: www.bonpoint.com
SIC: 2361 Dresses: girls', children's & infants'

(G-9438)
BOOM LLC
Also Called: Boom Creative Development
800 3rd Ave Fl 2 (10022-7683)
PHONE.....................................646 218-0752
Fax: 212 317-9062
Art Degaetano, *President*
Glenn Marks, *COO*
Karen Higgins, *Manager*
Anthony Mazzarella,
▲ EMP: 35
SQ FT: 12,000
SALES (est): 5.7MM **Privately Held**
WEB: www.boomllc.com
SIC: 3999 5122 Atomizers, toiletry; cosmetics, perfumes & hair products

(G-9439)
BOOSEY & HAWKES INC (DH)
Also Called: Music Library
229 W 28th St Fl 11 (10001-5915)
PHONE.....................................212 358-5300
Fax: 212 358-5301
Jennifer Bilfield, *General Mgr*
Bert Fink, *Senior VP*
Steven Storch, *CFO*
Linda Golding, *Personnel Exec*
Susan Carrigan, *Manager*
▲ EMP: 20
SALES (est): 2.7MM **Privately Held**
WEB: www.christopherrouse.com
SIC: 2741 7389 Music book & sheet music publishing; music copying service; music distribution systems

(G-9440)
BOOTSTRAP SOFTWARE
129 W 29th St Fl 12 (10001-5105)
PHONE.....................................212 871-2020
Richard Levine, *Ch of Bd*
Jay Erickson, *COO*
Kristina V An, *Project Mgr*
Kate Parker, *Project Mgr*
Byron Matto, *Director*
EMP: 6 EST: 1999
SALES (est): 640K **Privately Held**
WEB: www.bootsoft.com
SIC: 7372 Prepackaged software

(G-9441)
BORGHESE INC (PA)
Also Called: Princess Marcella Borghese
3 E 54th St Fl 20 (10022-3130)
PHONE.....................................212 659-5318
Fax: 212 659-5301
Georgette Mosbacher, *President*
Christopher Stephen West, *President*
Neil Petrocelli, *Vice Pres*
Frank Palladino, *CFO*
Michael Tugetman, *Treasurer*
▲ EMP: 25
SQ FT: 10,000
SALES (est): 6.7MM **Privately Held**
WEB: www.chateauxdemeures.com
SIC: 2844 5122 5961 5999 Toilet preparations; cosmetics; cosmetics & perfumes, mail order; cosmetics

(G-9442)
BOUCHERON JOAILLERIE USA INC
Also Called: Parfums Boucheron Jewelry
460 Park Ave Fl 12 (10022-1906)
PHONE.....................................212 715-7330
Thomas Indermuhle, *Ch of Bd*
EMP: 7
SALES (est): 720.1K
SALES (corp-wide): 10.7MM **Privately Held**
SIC: 3915 3423 Jewelers' materials & lapidary work; jewelers' hand tools
HQ: Boucheron Holding
   26 Place Vendome
   Paris 75001
   142 444-244

(G-9443)
BOUNDLESS SPATIAL INC
222 Broadway Fl 19 (10038-2550)
PHONE.....................................646 831-5531
Fax: 212 487-2983
Andy Dearing, *CEO*
Brody Stout, *COO*
Tom Ingold, *Vice Pres*
Zach Rouse, *Vice Pres*
EMP: 35 EST: 2012

SALES (est): 4.3MM **Privately Held**
SIC: 7372 Business oriented computer software

(G-9444)
BOURNE MUSIC PUBLISHERS
Also Called: Bourne Co
5 W 37th St Fl 6 (10018-6275)
PHONE.....................................212 391-4300
Fax: 212 391-4306
Mary Elizabeth Bourne, *Owner*
EMP: 19
SQ FT: 6,500
SALES (est): 920K **Privately Held**
WEB: www.bournemusic.com
SIC: 2741 Music book & sheet music publishing

(G-9445)
BOXBEE INC
134 W 26th St Rm 404 (10001-6865)
PHONE.....................................646 612-7839
Kristoph Matthews, *President*
EMP: 7
SQ FT: 10,000
SALES (est): 733.7K **Privately Held**
SIC: 7372 Business oriented computer software

(G-9446)
BOY SCOUTS OF AMERICA
271 Madison Ave Ste 401 (10016-1001)
PHONE.....................................212 532-0985
Fax: 212 889-4513
Leigh Novog, *Marketing Staff*
Barry Brown, *Manager*
EMP: 7
SALES (corp-wide): 223.4MM **Privately Held**
WEB: www.scouting.org
SIC: 2721 Magazines: publishing & printing
PA: Boy Scouts Of America
   1325 W Walnut Hill Ln
   Irving TX 75038
   972 580-2000

(G-9447)
BOYLAN BOTTLING CO INC
6 E 43rd St Fl 18 (10017-4657)
PHONE.....................................800 289-7978
Ronald C Fiorina, *President*
Steven Hood, *COO*
Mark Fiorina, *Vice Pres*
Nack Modujno, *Office Mgr*
▲ EMP: 30 EST: 1891
SQ FT: 25,000
SALES (est): 6.3MM **Privately Held**
WEB: www.boylanbottling.com
SIC: 2086 2087 Soft drinks: packaged in cans, bottles, etc.; beverage bases, concentrates, syrups, powders & mixes

(G-9448)
BPE STUDIO INC
270 W 38th St Rm 702 (10018-1520)
PHONE.....................................212 868-9896
Fax: 212 302-3270
Dan Ping Zhang, *President*
EMP: 5
SALES (est): 410K **Privately Held**
SIC: 2396 Linings, apparel: made from purchased materials

(G-9449)
BRADLEY MARKETING GROUP INC
1431 Broadway Fl 12 (10018-1912)
PHONE.....................................212 967-6100
James Lemmo, *Principal*
Edward Brucia, *Vice Pres*
Kathy Reccardi, *Vice Pres*
Adam Perry, *VP Sales*
Jackie Sneyers, *Executive Asst*
EMP: 6
SALES (corp-wide): 18.8MM **Privately Held**
WEB: www.bradleymg.com
SIC: 2759 Commercial printing
PA: Bradley Marketing Group, Inc.
   170 Wilbur Pl Ste 700
   Bohemia NY 11716
   631 231-9200

(G-9450)
BRAIFORM ENTERPRISES INC (DH)
Also Called: Plasti-Form
237 W 35th St Ste 504 (10001-1905)
PHONE.....................................800 738-7396
Graeme Andrew S Rutherford, *Ch of Bd*
Peter Wilson, *President*
Josef Farnik, *Chairman*
Stanley Gouldson, *Exec VP*
Chuck Kelly, *Vice Pres*
◆ EMP: 40 EST: 1962
SQ FT: 10,000
SALES (est): 111.8MM
SALES (corp-wide): 2.3B **Privately Held**
SIC: 3089 Clothes hangers, plastic; injection molded finished plastic products
HQ: Spotless Plastics (Usa) Inc.
   100 Motor Pkwy Ste 155
   Hauppauge NY 11788
   631 951-9000

(G-9451)
BRAINPOP LLC
Also Called: Brainpop Group
71 W 23rd St Fl 17 (10010-4183)
PHONE.....................................212 574-6017
Mike Watanabe, *Senior VP*
Daniel Donohue, *Vice Pres*
Avraham Kadar, *Mng Member*
Marcia Flores, *Manager*
Sasha Pettit, *Manager*
EMP: 50
SALES (est): 5.6MM **Privately Held**
SIC: 7372 Educational computer software

(G-9452)
BRAL NADER FINE JEWELRY INC
576 5th Ave (10036-4807)
PHONE.....................................800 493-1222
Nader Bral, *President*
EMP: 5
SALES: 3MM **Privately Held**
SIC: 3911 Jewelry, precious metal

(G-9453)
BRANNKEY INC (PA)
Also Called: Honora
1385 Broadway Fl 14 (10018-6001)
PHONE.....................................212 371-1515
Fax: 212 371-0003
Joel Schechter, *Ch of Bd*
Roberta Schechter, *Vice Pres*
Jeannie Chan, *Human Res Mgr*
Danielle Smith, *VP Sales*
Cynthia Barcia, *Accounts Exec*
▲ EMP: 52 EST: 1969
SQ FT: 6,500
SALES (est): 10.6MM **Privately Held**
WEB: www.honora.com
SIC: 3911 Jewelry, precious metal

(G-9454)
BRANT ART PUBLICATIONS INC
Also Called: Art In America
110 Greene St Ph 2 (10012-3824)
PHONE.....................................212 941-2800
Sandra J Brant, *President*
Lindsay Pollock, *Editor*
Peter Brant, *Vice Pres*
Deborah Blasucci, *CFO*
Jeremy Gaspar, *Manager*
EMP: 27
SQ FT: 20,000
SALES (est): 1.6MM
SALES (corp-wide): 4.8MM **Privately Held**
WEB: www.artinamerica.com
SIC: 2721 Magazines: publishing only, not printed on site
PA: Brant Publications, Inc.
   110 Greene St Ph 2
   New York NY 10012
   212 941-2800

(G-9455)
BRANT PUBLICATIONS INC (PA)
Also Called: Magazine Antiques, The
110 Greene St Ph 2 (10012-3824)
PHONE.....................................212 941-2800
Fax: 212 941-2897
Sandra J Brant, *President*
Jennifer Norton, *Publisher*
Dan Ragone, *Publisher*

New York - New York County (G-9456) GEOGRAPHIC SECTION

Lorrenda Sherrer, *Publisher*
Christopher Bollen, *Editor*
▲ EMP: 28
SQ FT: 20,000
SALES (est): 4.8MM **Privately Held**
WEB: www.themagazineantiques.com
SIC: 2721 Magazines: publishing only, not printed on site

(G-9456)
BRASILANS PRESS PBLCATIONS INC
60 W 46th St Rm 302 (10036)
P.O. Box 985 (10185-0985)
PHONE..........................212 764-6161
Joao De Matos, *President*
Francisco De Matos, *Vice Pres*
EMP: 40
SALES (est): 2.1MM **Privately Held**
SIC: 2711 Newspapers, publishing & printing

(G-9457)
BREAD MARKET CAFE
16 W 45th St Fl 5 (10036-4204)
PHONE..........................212 768-9292
Dan Millman, *President*
EMP: 5 EST: 1997
SALES (est): 270K **Privately Held**
WEB: www.mycafebeyond.com
SIC: 2051 Bread, cake & related products

(G-9458)
BREWER-CANTELMO CO INC
Also Called: Script-Master Div
55 W 39th St Rm 205 (10018-0573)
PHONE..........................212 244-4600
Fax: 212 244-1640
Stephen Kirschenbaum, *President*
David Kirschenbaum, *Vice Pres*
Elissa Christian, *Sales Staff*
EMP: 23 EST: 1928
SQ FT: 9,000
SALES (est): 2.4MM **Privately Held**
WEB: www.brewer-cantelmo.com
SIC: 2782 Looseleaf binders & devices

(G-9459)
BRIGANTINE INC (HQ)
225 W 37th St (10018-5703)
PHONE..........................212 354-8550
Isidore Friedman, *Ch of Bd*
Mark Friedman, *President*
Paul Friedman, *President*
William Fuchs, *Treasurer*
EMP: 5
SQ FT: 10,000
SALES (est): 578.6K
SALES (corp-wide): 8MM **Privately Held**
WEB: www.brigantine.com
SIC: 2329 2339 Men's & boys' leather, wool & down-filled outerwear; women's & misses' jackets & coats, except sportswear
PA: S. Rothschild & Co., Inc.
1407 Broadway Fl 10
New York NY 10018
212 354-8550

(G-9460)
BRIGHT KIDS NYC INC
225 Broadway Ste 1504 (10007-3704)
PHONE..........................917 539-4575
Bige Doruk, *CEO*
Beth Feinkind, *Controller*
Brian Chester, *Office Mgr*
Danielle Kelly, *Manager*
▲ EMP: 40 EST: 2009
SALES (est): 3.6MM **Privately Held**
SIC: 2731 8299 8748 Textbooks: publishing & printing; tutoring school; testing service, educational or personnel

(G-9461)
BRIGHTLINE VENTURES I LLC
1120 Avenue Of The Americ (10036-6700)
PHONE..........................212 626-6829
EMP: 26
SALES (est): 1.5MM **Privately Held**
SIC: 2099 Food preparations

(G-9462)
BRILLIANT JEWELERS/MJJ INC
Also Called: Mjj Brilliant
902 Broadway Fl 18 (10010-6038)
PHONE..........................212 353-2326
Fax: 212 353-0696
Nicolay Yakubovich, *Ch of Bd*
Robert Schwartz, *COO*
Abdul Kampani, *CFO*
Gary Astrow, *Accountant*
Dierdra Walker, *Bookkeeper*
EMP: 120
SALES (est): 24.4MM **Privately Held**
WEB: www.mjjbrilliant.com
SIC: 3911 Jewelry, precious metal

(G-9463)
BRISTOL SEAMLESS RING CORP
209 W 86th St Apt 817 (10024-3337)
PHONE..........................212 874-2645
Irving Skydell, *President*
EMP: 16 EST: 1910
SALES (est): 118.2K **Privately Held**
SIC: 3911 Jewelry, precious metal

(G-9464)
BRISTOL-MYERS SQUIBB COMPANY (PA)
345 Park Ave Bsmt Lc3 (10154-0028)
P.O. Box 4000, Princeton NJ (08543-4000)
PHONE..........................212 546-4000
Fax: 212 546-4390
Giovanni Caforio, *CEO*
Lamberto Andreotti, *Ch of Bd*
Beatrice Cazala, *President*
John Celentano, *President*
Carlo De Notaristefani, *President*
◆ EMP: 1200 EST: 1887
SQ FT: 81,000
SALES: 16.5B **Publicly Held**
WEB: www.bms.com
SIC: 2834 Pharmaceutical preparations; drugs acting on the cardiovascular system, except diagnostic; antibiotics, packaged; drugs acting on the central nervous system & sense organs

(G-9465)
BROADCAST MANAGER INC
Also Called: Promosuite
65 Broadway Ste 602 (10006-2519)
PHONE..........................212 509-1200
Fax: 212 509-6115
Rocco Macri, *CEO*
Christopher Bungo, *President*
Craig Zimmerman, *Vice Pres*
Matthew Jacobson, *Opers Mgr*
Rachel Field, *VP Sales*
EMP: 8
SALES (est): 890K **Privately Held**
WEB: www.broadcastmanager.org
SIC: 3651 Amplifiers: radio, public address or musical instrument

(G-9466)
BROADWAY TECHNOLOGY LLC (PA)
140 Broadway Ste 4320 (10005-1120)
PHONE..........................646 912-6450
Fax: 646 437-3237
Jonathan Fieldman, *COO*
Margaret McManus, *Opers Staff*
Preston Mesick, *Accounts Mgr*
Lindsay Young, *Office Mgr*
Najla Elmachtoub, *Manager*
EMP: 20
SALES: 1MM **Privately Held**
WEB: www.broadwaytechnology.com
SIC: 7372 Business oriented computer software

(G-9467)
BROCADE CMMNCTIONS SYSTEMS INC
1 Penn Plz Ste 1820 (10119-1801)
PHONE..........................212 497-8500
Rosemary Barnett, *Opers Mgr*
Akash Dodwani, *Engineer*
Richard Cortes, *Manager*
John McCormack, *Manager*
Johnny Fonseca, *Technology*
EMP: 9 **Publicly Held**
SIC: 3577 Computer peripheral equipment
PA: Brocade Communications Systems, Inc.
130 Holger Way
San Jose CA 95134

(G-9468)
BROKEN THREADS INC
147 W 35th St Ste 501 (10001-0070)
PHONE..........................212 730-4351
Rohan Shah, *Ch of Bd*
EMP: 2 EST: 2007
SQ FT: 500
SALES (est): 6.3MM **Privately Held**
SIC: 2329 Men's & boys' sportswear & athletic clothing

(G-9469)
BROOKE LEIGH LTD (PA)
Also Called: Ali & Kris
520 8th Ave Fl 20 (10018-6507)
PHONE..........................212 736-9098
Fax: 212 736-9123
Mary Canter, *President*
Francis Fidel, *Bookkeeper*
EMP: 11
SALES (est): 782.3K **Privately Held**
SIC: 2331 2337 2339 Blouses, women's & juniors': made from purchased material; skirts, separate: women's, misses' & juniors'; slacks: women's, misses' & juniors'

(G-9470)
BROOKE MAYA INC
124 W 36th St Fl 7 (10018-8845)
PHONE..........................212 279-2340
Allen Hakimian, *President*
EMP: 35
SQ FT: 11,000
SALES (est): 2.4MM **Privately Held**
SIC: 2361 Dresses: girls', children's & infants'

(G-9471)
BROWN PRINTING COMPANY
1500 Broadway Ste 505 (10036-4055)
PHONE..........................212 782-7800
Fax: 212 782-7878
Volker Peterson, *President*
Del Miller, *Materials Mgr*
Russ Terry, *Accounts Mgr*
Guy Christman, *Department Mgr*
EMP: 25 EST: 2010
SALES (est): 3.2MM **Privately Held**
SIC: 2752 Commercial printing, lithographic

(G-9472)
BROWN PUBLISHING NETWORK INC
122 E 42nd St Rm 2810 (10168-2893)
PHONE..........................212 682-3330
Marie Brown, *Branch Mgr*
Bill Guthrie, *Branch Mgr*
EMP: 5
SALES (corp-wide): 7.2MM **Privately Held**
WEB: www.brownpubnet.com
SIC: 2731 Textbooks: publishing only, not printed on site
PA: Brown Publishing Network, Inc.
10 City Sq Ste 3
Charlestown MA 02129
781 547-7600

(G-9473)
BROWNSTONE CAPITL PARTNERS LLC
251 5th Ave Fl 3 (10016-6515)
PHONE..........................212 889-0069
Lily Calle, *Manager*
Martin Alter,
EMP: 7
SQ FT: 2,500
SALES (est): 713.7K **Privately Held**
SIC: 2752 Commercial printing, offset

(G-9474)
BROWNSTONE PUBLISHERS INC
149 5th Ave Fl 10 (10010-6832)
PHONE..........................212 473-8200
Fax: 212 473-8786
John Striker, *President*
George Chafeffer, *Publisher*
George Schaeffer, *Publisher*
Susan Lipp, *Editor*
Marion Walsh, *Editor*
EMP: 46
SQ FT: 10,000
SALES (est): 3.7MM **Privately Held**
SIC: 2721 2741 Periodicals: publishing only; miscellaneous publishing

(G-9475)
BUCKET LINKS LLC
261 W 35th St Ste 1003 (10001-1902)
PHONE..........................212 290-2900
Steve Ayzen,
EMP: 5 EST: 2014
SALES (est): 134.7K **Privately Held**
SIC: 2741 Miscellaneous publishing;

(G-9476)
BUFFALO INVESTORS CORP (HQ)
1 Wall Street Ct Apt 980 (10005-3404)
PHONE..........................212 702-4363
Richard T Buonato, *Vice Pres*
EMP: 1
SALES (est): 1.4B
SALES (corp-wide): 1.4B **Privately Held**
SIC: 3743 4741 Freight cars & equipment; rental of railroad cars
PA: Starfire Holding Corporation
445 Hamilton Ave Ste 1210
White Plains NY 10601
914 614-7000

(G-9477)
BULKLEY DUNTON (DH)
1 Penn Plz Ste 2814 (10119-2814)
PHONE..........................212 863-1800
Fax: 212 352-0929
Doehner George, *President*
David Backus, *Senior VP*
EMP: 38
SALES (est): 61.3MM
SALES (corp-wide): 8.7B **Publicly Held**
SIC: 2741 Miscellaneous publishing
HQ: Veritiv Operating Company
1000 Abernathy Rd
Atlanta GA 30328
770 391-8200

(G-9478)
BULL STREET LLC
Also Called: Supdates
19 W 69th St Apt 201 (10023-4750)
PHONE..........................212 495-9855
Jared Gettinger,
EMP: 5
SALES (est): 262.1K **Privately Held**
SIC: 7372 Application computer software

(G-9479)
BUREAU OF NATIONAL AFFAIRS INC
25 W 43rd St Ste 1007 (10036-7427)
PHONE..........................212 687-4530
Fax: 212 967-1727
Phyllis Diamond, *Editor*
John Herzfeld, *Manager*
EMP: 23
SALES (corp-wide): 3.6B **Privately Held**
SIC: 2711 Newspapers
HQ: The Bureau Of National Affairs Inc
1801 S Bell St Ste Cn110
Arlington VA 22202
703 341-3000

(G-9480)
BURLEN CORP
6 E 32nd St Fl 10 (10016-5422)
PHONE..........................212 684-0052
Steve Klein, *President*
Linda Arenson, *VP Sales*
Wayne Rooks, *Info Tech Mgr*
EMP: 12
SALES (corp-wide): 1.1B **Privately Held**
SIC: 2342 Girdles & panty girdles
HQ: Burlen Corp.
1904 Mccormick Dr
Tifton GA 31793
229 382-4100

(G-9481)
BURNS ARCHIVE PHOTOGRAPHIC DIS
140 E 38th St Frnt 1 (10016-2686)
PHONE..........................212 889-1938
Stanley Burns MD, *Owner*
Liz Burns, *Director*
▼ EMP: 4
SQ FT: 4,000

SALES: 1MM Privately Held
WEB: www.burnsarchive.com
SIC: 2731 8099 Book publishing; medical photography & art

(G-9482)
BUSINESS INTEGRITY INC (DH)
79 Madison Ave Fl 2 (10016-7805)
PHONE......................................718 238-2008
Tim Allen, *President*
Thomas Mule, *COO*
Geoffrey Goldberg, *Counsel*
Brian Long, *Sales Staff*
EMP: 6
SQ FT: 3,000
SALES (est): 1.1MM
SALES (corp-wide): 521.3K Privately Held
WEB: www.business-integrity.com
SIC: 7372 Business oriented computer software

(G-9483)
BUSINESS JOURNALS
1166 Ave Of The America (10036-2708)
PHONE......................................212 790-5100
Keith Edwards, *Manager*
EMP: 11
SALES (corp-wide): 322.5MM Privately Held
SIC: 2711 Newspapers
HQ: The Business Journals
120 W Morehead St Ste 420
Charlotte NC 28202
704 371-3248

(G-9484)
BUTTONS & TRIMCOM INC
519 8th Ave Rm 26 (10018-5275)
PHONE......................................212 868-1971
Peter Frankel, *President*
Susan Frankel, *Vice Pres*
EMP: 13
SQ FT: 2,200
SALES (est): 1.5MM Privately Held
SIC: 3965 3089 3499 Buttons & parts; buckles & buckle parts; novelties, plastic; novelties & specialties, metal

(G-9485)
BY ROBERT JAMES
74 Orchard St (10002-4515)
PHONE......................................212 253-2121
Robert Loomis, *Principal*
EMP: 5
SALES (est): 658.9K Privately Held
SIC: 2329 5611 Men's & boys' clothing; men's & boys' clothing stores

(G-9486)
BYELOCORP SCIENTIFIC INC (PA)
76 Perry St (10014-3238)
PHONE......................................212 785-2580
Lowell A Mintz, *Ch of Bd*
William Begell, *President*
Kathleen Kent, *Vice Pres*
EMP: 27
SALES (est): 1.6MM Privately Held
SIC: 3491 3443 Industrial valves; industrial vessels, tanks & containers

(G-9487)
BYER CALIFORNIA
1407 Broadway Rm 807 (10018-5149)
PHONE......................................212 944-8989
Fax: 212 719-4290
Amy Madus, *Sales Staff*
Martin Bernstein, *Manager*
EMP: 7
SALES (corp-wide): 361.3MM Privately Held
WEB: www.byer.com
SIC: 3842 Surgical appliances & supplies
PA: Byer California
66 Potrero Ave
San Francisco CA 94103
415 626-7844

(G-9488)
BYLINER INC
27 W 24th St Ste 202 (10010-3299)
PHONE......................................415 680-3608
John Tayman, *CEO*
Deanna Brown, *President*
Theodore Barnett, *COO*
EMP: 20 EST: 2010
SALES (est): 1.4MM Privately Held
SIC: 2731 2741 Book publishing;

(G-9489)
BYTE CONSULTING INC
295 Madison Ave Fl 35 (10017-6414)
PHONE......................................646 500-8606
Rak Chugh, *President*
Lokesh Chugh, *Sales Staff*
Arun Murugavel, *Technology*
Dan Costin, *Director*
Thomas Loop, *Director*
EMP: 8
SALES (est): 857.8K Privately Held
WEB: www.byteconsulting.com
SIC: 7372 Prepackaged software

(G-9490)
C E CHQUIE LTD
Also Called: St Remo
15 W 36th St Ph (10018-7910)
PHONE......................................212 268-0006
Fax: 212 268-1005
Edmond Ebrahimi, *President*
Saeed Shamsian, *Vice Pres*
Masoud Shamsian, *Treasurer*
▲ EMP: 6
SALES (est): 550K Privately Held
SIC: 2325 2329 Men's & boys' trousers & slacks; men's & boys' sportswear & athletic clothing

(G-9491)
CA INC (PA)
520 Madison Ave Fl 22 (10022-4327)
PHONE......................................800 225-5224
Fax: 212 827-2640
Michael P Gregoire, *CEO*
Arthur F Weinbach, *Ch of Bd*
Michael C Bisignano, *Exec VP*
Jacob Lamm, *Exec VP*
Richard J Beckert, *CFO*
▼ EMP: 1500 EST: 1976
SALES: 4B Publicly Held
WEB: www.cai.com
SIC: 7372 8742 Business oriented computer software; application computer software; management consulting services

(G-9492)
CA INC
520 Madison Ave Fl 22 (10022-4327)
PHONE......................................800 225-5224
EMP: 165
SALES (corp-wide): 4B Publicly Held
SIC: 7372 Prepackaged software
PA: Ca, Inc.
520 Madison Ave Fl 22
New York NY 10022
800 225-5224

(G-9493)
CABLES AND CHIPS INC (PA)
121 Fulton St Fl 4 (10038-2795)
PHONE......................................212 619-3132
Fax: 212 619-3982
Howard Feinstein, *CEO*
Susan Feinstein, *President*
Andrew Zadorozny, *Manager*
Rick Scherer, *Shareholder*
EMP: 27
SQ FT: 5,500
SALES (est): 2.8MM Privately Held
WEB: www.cablesandchipsinc.com
SIC: 2298 3644 5734 5063 Cable, fiber; switch boxes, electric; computer peripheral equipment; electronic wire & cable; connectors, electronic; local area network (LAN) systems integrator

(G-9494)
CABRIOLE DESIGNS INC
315 E 91st St Ste 3 (10128-5938)
PHONE......................................212 593-4528
Fax: 212 427-6913
Louis Tonna, *President*
EMP: 6
SALES (est): 476.2K Privately Held
WEB: www.cabrioledesign.com
SIC: 2391 Curtains & draperies

(G-9495)
CACHET INDUSTRIES INC
1400 Broadway Rm 709 (10018-0763)
PHONE......................................212 944-2188

Fax: 212 398-6694
David Darouvar, *President*
Mark Naim, *Admin Sec*
▲ EMP: 30
SQ FT: 12,000
SALES (est): 5MM Privately Held
SIC: 2335 Women's, juniors' & misses' dresses

(G-9496)
CADMUS JOURNAL SERVICES INC
Also Called: William Byrd Press
11 Penn Plz Bsmt 100 (10001-2007)
PHONE......................................212 736-2002
Brenda Donagher, *Corp Comm Staff*
Jim Compton, *Manager*
EMP: 6
SALES (corp-wide): 1.7B Publicly Held
SIC: 2752 Commercial printing, lithographic
HQ: Cadmus Journal Services, Inc.
2901 Byrdhill Rd
Richmond VA 23228
804 287-5680

(G-9497)
CAI INC (PA)
Also Called: Copen International Limited
430 E 56th St (10022-4171)
PHONE......................................212 819-0008
Fax: 212 819-0870
Carin Trundle, *CEO*
Barry Emmanuel, *President*
Tsie Persaud, *Accounts Mgr*
◆ EMP: 4
SQ FT: 2,300
SALES (est): 3.6MM Privately Held
WEB: www.midsouthmfg.com
SIC: 2211 2396 Pocketing twill, cotton; waistbands, trouser

(G-9498)
CAITHNESS EQUITIES CORPORATION (PA)
Also Called: Shepherds Flat
565 5th Ave Fl 29 (10017-2478)
PHONE......................................212 599-2112
James D Bishop Jr, *Ch of Bd*
James C Sullivan, *Senior VP*
Gary Keevill, *Vice Pres*
Christopher T Mc Callion, *Vice Pres*
Gail Conboy, *Admin Sec*
EMP: 23
SALES (est): 34.5MM Privately Held
WEB: www.caithnessenergy.com
SIC: 3491 4911 4961 6162 Compressed gas cylinder valves; generation, electric power; steam supply systems, including geothermal; mortgage bankers

(G-9499)
CALDEIRA USA INC
230 5th Ave Ste 300 (10001-7902)
PHONE......................................212 532-2292
Tony Caldeira, *President*
Lindsey Orrick, *General Mgr*
Jeff Shaffer, *Sales Mgr*
Fahim Khan, *Manager*
▲ EMP: 3 EST: 2006
SQ FT: 2,000
SALES: 2MM
SALES (corp-wide): 16MM Privately Held
SIC: 2399 Emblems, badges & insignia
HQ: Caldeira Limited
Villiers Road
Liverpool L34 9
151 290-9090

(G-9500)
CALIFORNIA PETRO TRNSPT CORP
114 W 47th St (10036-1510)
PHONE......................................212 302-5151
Frank Bilotta, *President*
EMP: 2
SALES: 1.9MM Privately Held
SIC: 2911 Petroleum refining

(G-9501)
CALIFORNIA US HOLDINGS INC
417 5th Ave Lbby 7th (10016-3380)
PHONE......................................212 726-6500
Bruno Bonnell, *President*

Mark Kaiman, *CFO*
Michael Pagnetti, *Controller*
Sherly Roden, *Financial Exec*
Emily Anadu, *Manager*
EMP: 564
SQ FT: 90,000
SALES (est): 28.4MM
SALES (corp-wide): 1.5MM Privately Held
SIC: 7372 5045 Prepackaged software; computers, peripherals & software
PA: Atari
78 Rue Taitbout
Paris 75009
800 814-850

(G-9502)
CALLAWAY ARTS & ENTRMT INC
41 Union Sq W Ste 1101 (10003-3253)
PHONE......................................212 798-3168
John Lee, *CEO*
Nicholas Callaway, *President*
Jennifer Caffrey, *Administration*
EMP: 11
SALES (est): 840K Privately Held
SIC: 2731 Books: publishing & printing

(G-9503)
CALLAWAY DIGITAL ARTS INC
41 Union Sq W Ste 1101 (10003-3253)
PHONE......................................212 675-3050
Rex Ishibashi, *CEO*
John Lee, *President*
Lisa Holton, *Vice Pres*
Nicholas Callaway, *Officer*
EMP: 30
SALES (est): 3.2MM Privately Held
SIC: 7372 Application computer software

(G-9504)
CALLIDUS SOFTWARE INC
152 W 57th St Fl 8 (10019-3386)
PHONE......................................212 554-7300
Fax: 212 554-7252
Leslie Stretch, *CEO*
Robert H Youngjohns, *Ch of Bd*
Bryan Burkhart, *Vice Pres*
Giles House, *Vice Pres*
Swapna Gupta, *Senior Engr*
EMP: 15
SALES (est): 1.2MM Privately Held
SIC: 7372 Prepackaged software

(G-9505)
CALVIN KLEIN INC
654 Madison Ave (10065-8445)
PHONE......................................212 292-9000
Fax: 212 292-9001
Colby Ryan, *Human Res Dir*
Eva Baud, *Manager*
Abe Hernandez, *Clerk*
EMP: 50
SALES (corp-wide): 8B Publicly Held
WEB: www.calvinklein.com
SIC: 3161 Clothing & apparel carrying cases
HQ: Calvin Klein, Inc.
205 W 39th St Lbby 2
New York NY 10018
212 719-2600

(G-9506)
CAMBRIDGE INFO GROUP INC (PA)
Also Called: C I G
888 7th Ave Ste 1701 (10106-1799)
PHONE......................................301 961-6700
Fax: 212 897-6640
Andrew M Snyder, *CEO*
Robert Snyder, *Chairman*
Michael K Chung, *COO*
Barbara Inkellis, *Senior VP*
Larisa Avner Trainor, *Senior VP*
EMP: 12
SQ FT: 24,000
SALES (est): 556.5MM Privately Held
WEB: www.csa.com
SIC: 2741 Technical manual & paper publishing

New York - New York County (G-9507) — GEOGRAPHIC SECTION

(G-9507)
CAMBRIDGE UNIVERSITY PRESS
1 Liberty Plz Fl 20 (10006-1435)
PHONE...................................212 337-5000
Fax: 914 937-4712
Jeffrey Brown, *Editor*
Richard Ziemacki, *Manager*
Barbara Colson, *Manager*
Chris Richter, *Manager*
Aniko Banfi, *Exec Dir*
EMP: 80
SALES (corp-wide): 396.6MM **Privately Held**
SIC: 2731 2721 4226 Books: publishing only; periodicals; special warehousing & storage
PA: Cambridge University Press
University Printing House
Cambridge CAMBS CB2 8
122 335-8331

(G-9508)
CAMINUS CORPORATION (DH)
340 Madison Ave Fl 8 (10173-0899)
PHONE...................................212 515-3600
John A Andrus, *President*
EMP: 65 EST: 1999
SALES (est): 12MM
SALES (corp-wide): 6.6B **Publicly Held**
SIC: 7372 7379 Business oriented computer software; computer related consulting services
HQ: Fis Data Systems Inc.
680 E Swedesford Rd
Wayne PA 19087
484 582-2000

(G-9509)
CAMPBELL ALLIANCE GROUP INC
335 Madison Ave Fl 17 (10017-4677)
PHONE...................................212 377-2740
Patrick Manhard, *CEO*
Alisa Jernigan, *Controller*
Jennifer Krcmery, *Consultant*
Andrew Long, *Consultant*
Mengran Wang, *Consultant*
EMP: 30 EST: 1997
SQ FT: 50
SALES (est): 3.7MM **Privately Held**
SIC: 2834 Pharmaceutical preparations

(G-9510)
CANALI USA INC (DH)
611 Ffth Ave Saks 5th Ave 5 Saks (10014)
PHONE...................................212 767-0205
Fax: 212 586-9775
Paolo Canali, *CEO*
Eugenio Canali, *President*
Georgio Canali, *Assistant VP*
EMP: 7
SALES (est): 1.3MM **Privately Held**
SIC: 2311 Suits, men's & boys': made from purchased materials

(G-9511)
CANCER TARGETING SYSTEMS
100 Wall St (10005-3701)
PHONE...................................212 965-4534
Raymond Tesi, *CEO*
EMP: 5
SALES (est): 300.5K **Privately Held**
SIC: 2834 Pharmaceutical preparations

(G-9512)
CANDEX SOLUTIONS INC
410 Park Ave 1878 (10022-4407)
PHONE...................................215 650-3214
Jeremy Lappin, *CEO*
Mark Steinke, *President*
Marianna Suckova, *Vice Pres*
Shani Vaza, *Vice Pres*
Melissa Deegan, *Office Mgr*
EMP: 6
SALES (est): 1.1MM **Privately Held**
SIC: 7372 Prepackaged software; business oriented computer software

(G-9513)
CANE SUGAR LLC
Also Called: Cane Simple
950 3rd Ave Ste 2200 (10022-2773)
PHONE...................................212 329-2695
Reid Chase, *Mng Member*
EMP: 6
SALES: 230K **Privately Held**
SIC: 2062 Cane syrup from purchased raw sugar

(G-9514)
CANOVA INC
Also Called: Minimal USA
511 W 25th St Ste 809 (10001-5562)
PHONE...................................212 352-3582
Bartolomeo Bellati, *President*
Molly Bates, *Office Mgr*
Stefano Zenier, *Director*
▲ EMP: 10
SQ FT: 1,200
SALES: 1MM **Privately Held**
WEB: www.canova.com
SIC: 2499 Kitchen, bathroom & household ware: wood

(G-9515)
CANTON NOODLE CORPORATION
101 Mott St (10013-5093)
PHONE...................................212 226-3276
Fax: 212 226-8037
James Eng, *Principal*
Michelle Eng, *Manager*
EMP: 8 EST: 1951
SQ FT: 4,000
SALES (est): 600K **Privately Held**
SIC: 2098 Noodles (e.g. egg, plain & water), dry

(G-9516)
CANYON PUBLISHING INC
55 John St Ste 6 (10038-3752)
PHONE...................................212 334-0227
Sandra Vasceannie, *President*
EMP: 10
SALES (est): 880K **Privately Held**
SIC: 2752 Publication printing, lithographic

(G-9517)
CAP USA JERSEYMAN HARLEM INC (PA)
112 W 125th St (10027-4403)
PHONE...................................212 222-7942
Fax: 212 222-7946
Sung R Park, *Ch of Bd*
EMP: 5
SALES (est): 401.6K **Privately Held**
SIC: 2257 Jersey cloth

(G-9518)
CAPCO WAI SHING LLC
132 W 36th St Rm 509 (10018-8643)
PHONE...................................212 268-1976
Jim Capuano, *Mng Member*
EMP: 8
SALES (est): 921.4K **Privately Held**
SIC: 3089 Clothes hangers, plastic

(G-9519)
CAPITAL GOLD CORPORATION (PA)
601 Lexington Ave Fl 36 (10022-4611)
PHONE...................................212 668-0842
Colin Sutherland, *President*
Scott Hazlitt, *COO*
Christopher Chipman, *CFO*
▲ EMP: 8
SALES (est): 13.7MM **Privately Held**
WEB: www.capitalgoldcorp.com
SIC: 1041 1499 Gold ores mining; mineral abrasives mining

(G-9520)
CAPITAL PROGRAMS INC
Also Called: CPI
420 Lexington Ave Lbby 6 (10170-0024)
PHONE...................................212 842-4640
Fax: 212 838-3176
Sabi Kanaan, *CEO*
Aniq Bishop, *Office Mgr*
EMP: 7
SQ FT: 1,000
SALES (est): 590K **Privately Held**
SIC: 7372 Application computer software

(G-9521)
CARANDA EMPORIUM LLC
Also Called: Serengeti Teas and Spices
2292 Frdrick Douglas Blvd (10027)
PHONE...................................212 866-7100
Oseovbie Imoukhuede,
EMP: 15
SALES (est): 528.5K **Privately Held**
SIC: 2095 Roasted coffee

(G-9522)
CARAVAN INTERNATIONAL CORP
641 Lexington Ave Fl 13 (10022-4503)
PHONE...................................212 223-7190
Ursula Cernuschi, *President*
Dennis Friedman, *Vice Pres*
Paulo Sanchez, *Sales Dir*
EMP: 6 EST: 1963
SQ FT: 32,000
SALES: 2.5MM **Privately Held**
WEB: www.caravan-ny.com
SIC: 3728 5065 Aircraft parts & equipment; communication equipment

(G-9523)
CARBERT MUSIC INC
126 E 38th St (10016-2692)
PHONE...................................212 725-9277
Freddy Bienstock, *President*
EMP: 30
SQ FT: 8,000
SALES (est): 1.5MM **Privately Held**
SIC: 2741 Music book & sheet music publishing

(G-9524)
CARELLI COSTUMES INC
109 W 26th St Fl 2 (10001-6821)
PHONE...................................212 765-6166
Fax: 212 765-6168
Carolyn Kostopoulos, *President*
EMP: 20
SALES (est): 1.4MM **Privately Held**
SIC: 2389 Theatrical costumes

(G-9525)
CARIB NEWS INC
Also Called: Caribbean Communication
35 W 35th St Rm 702 (10001-2205)
PHONE...................................212 944-1991
Fax: 212 944-2089
Carl Rodney, *President*
Fay Rodney, *Vice Pres*
EMP: 15
SALES (est): 720K **Privately Held**
WEB: www.nycaribnews.com
SIC: 2711 Newspapers

(G-9526)
CARL FISCHER LLC (PA)
48 Wall St 28 (10005-2903)
PHONE...................................212 777-0900
Fax: 212 477-4129
Hayden Connor, *CEO*
Casey Yu, *Controller*
Michael Kerr, *Finance Other*
Nicole Davenport, *Human Resources*
William Heese, *VP Sales*
EMP: 20 EST: 1872
SALES (est): 2.9MM **Privately Held**
WEB: www.carlfischer.com
SIC: 2741 5736 5099 5199 Music, sheet: publishing & printing; musical instrument stores; sheet music; musical instruments parts & accessories; sheet music

(G-9527)
CARLO MONTE DESIGNS INC
17 E 48th St Fl 8 (10017-1010)
PHONE...................................212 935-5611
Karnik Garipian, *President*
Haci Garipian, *President*
EMP: 6 EST: 1976
SQ FT: 2,400
SALES: 2.5MM **Privately Held**
WEB: www.montecarlodesigns.com
SIC: 3911 Jewelry, precious metal

(G-9528)
CARODA INC
254 W 35th St (10001-2504)
PHONE...................................212 630-9986
Ida Leigh M Law, *CEO*
EMP: 30 EST: 2009
SALES (est): 1.3MM **Privately Held**
SIC: 2329 Athletic (warmup, sweat & jogging) suits: men's & boys'

(G-9529)
CAROL DAUPLAISE LTD (PA)
29 W 36th St Fl 12 (10018-7973)
PHONE...................................212 564-7301
Fax: 212 629-5897
Carol Dauplaise, *Ch of Bd*
Richard Dauplaise, *Vice Pres*
Dan Schuster, *Vice Pres*
Michael Augenblick, *MIS Dir*
▲ EMP: 20 EST: 1978
SQ FT: 18,000
SALES (est): 3MM **Privately Held**
WEB: www.dauplaisejewelry.com
SIC: 3911 5094 Jewelry, precious metal; jewelry & precious stones

(G-9530)
CAROL DAUPLAISE LTD
134 W 37th St Fl 3 (10018-6974)
PHONE...................................212 997-5290
Jeffrey Dauplaise, *Branch Mgr*
EMP: 20
SALES (corp-wide): 3MM **Privately Held**
WEB: www.dauplaisejewelry.com
SIC: 3911 5094 Jewelry, precious metal; jewelry & precious stones
PA: Carol Dauplaise Ltd
29 W 36th St Fl 12
New York NY 10018
212 564-7301

(G-9531)
CAROL FOR EVA GRAHAM INC (PA)
366 5th Ave Rm 815 (10001-2211)
PHONE...................................212 889-8686
Fax: 212 481-3299
Carol Graham, *President*
Eva C Graham, *Vice Pres*
EMP: 8
SQ FT: 10,000
SALES (est): 1.1MM **Privately Held**
SIC: 3961 Costume jewelry, ex. precious metal & semiprecious stones

(G-9532)
CAROL GROUP LTD
Also Called: Habitat Magazine
150 W 30th St Rm 902 (10001-4125)
PHONE...................................212 505-2030
Fax: 212 254-6795
Carol Ott, *President*
Paul Ukena, *Partner*
Frank Lovece, *Editor*
Michael Gentile, *Advt Staff*
Frank Socci Jr, *Director*
EMP: 7 EST: 1980
SQ FT: 1,000
SALES: 891K **Privately Held**
WEB: www.habitatmag.com
SIC: 2721 Magazines: publishing only, not printed on site

(G-9533)
CAROLE HCHMAN DESIGN GROUP INC (HQ)
Also Called: Sara Beth Division
16 E 34th St Fl 10 (10016-4360)
PHONE...................................918 423-3535
Charlie Komar, *CEO*
Peter J Gabbe, *Ch of Bd*
Seth Morris, *President*
Carole Hochman, *Principal*
Paul Shreck, *Principal*
▲ EMP: 150
SQ FT: 26,000
SALES (est): 49.9MM
SALES (corp-wide): 159.3MM **Privately Held**
SIC: 2342 2341 2384 7389 Bras, girdles & allied garments; women's & children's underwear; nightgowns & negligees: women's & children's; women's & children's undergarments; bathrobes, men's & women's: made from purchased materials; interior designer; interior decorating
PA: Charles Komar & Sons, Inc.
16 E 34th St Fl 10
Jersey City NJ 07308
212 725-1500

(G-9534)
CAROLINA AMATO INC
270 W 38th St Rm 902 (10018-1759)
PHONE...................................212 768-9095

▲ = Import ▼ = Export
◆ = Import/Export

GEOGRAPHIC SECTION

Carolina Amato, *President*
Elina Sidler, *Bookkeeper*
▲ **EMP:** 6 **EST:** 1977
SALES: 1.5MM **Privately Held**
WEB: www.carolinaamato.com
SIC: 2339 Women's & misses' accessories

(G-9535)
CAROLINA HERRERA LTD (HQ)
501 Fashion Ave Fl 17 (10018-5911)
PHONE....................212 944-5757
Fax: 212 944-7996
Claudia Thomas, *President*
Julio Viniegra, *Administration*
▼ **EMP:** 45
SALES (est): 15.9MM
SALES (corp-wide): 185.4K **Privately Held**
WEB: www.carolinaherrera.com
SIC: 2337 2339 Skirts, separate: women's, misses' & juniors'; women's & misses' outerwear
PA: Equipamientos Puig Sl
Calle Lardero, 3 - Bj
Logrono
941 202-026

(G-9536)
CARRERA CASTING CORP
64 W 48th St Fl 2 (10036-1708)
PHONE....................212 382-3296
Fax: 212 768-9124
Eric Schwartz, *Ch of Bd*
Owen Schwartz, *President*
Dean Schwartz, *Dean*
Joel Weiss, *Vice Pres*
Joseph Sorrentino, *Draft/Design*
EMP: 160
SQ FT: 8,000
SALES (est): 41.9MM **Privately Held**
WEB: www.carreracasting.net
SIC: 3915 3369 Jewelers' castings; non-ferrous foundries

(G-9537)
CARRY HOT INC
545 W 45th St Rm 501 (10036-3409)
PHONE....................212 279-7535
Fax: 212 279-0734
Sanford Plotkin, *President*
Ron Demaray, *Mktg Dir*
Elizabeth Werner, *Info Tech Dir*
EMP: 10
SALES (est): 550K **Privately Held**
WEB: www.carryhot.com
SIC: 2393 Bags & containers, except sleeping bags: textile

(G-9538)
CARVART GLASS INC (PA)
180 Varick St Rm 1304 (10014-5842)
PHONE....................212 675-0030
Fax: 212 675-8175
Antoly Geyman, *President*
Edward Geyman, *Vice Pres*
Bob Wessel, *Vice Pres*
Amalia Villafranca, *Asst Controller*
▲ **EMP:** 10
SQ FT: 17,000
SALES (est): 4.1MM **Privately Held**
WEB: www.carvart.com
SIC: 3231 Art glass: made from purchased glass

(G-9539)
CARVIN FRENCH JEWELERS INC
515 Madison Ave Rm 1605 (10022-5445)
PHONE....................212 755-6474
Andre Chervin, *President*
Grafinka Chunov, *Controller*
EMP: 20 **EST:** 1954
SQ FT: 4,000
SALES (est): 1.7MM **Privately Held**
SIC: 3911 3961 Jewelry, precious metal; costume jewelry

(G-9540)
CASABLANCA FOODS LLC
135 E 57th St Unit 96 (10022-2168)
PHONE 212 317-1111
Mina Kallamni, *Managing Prtnr*
Fouad Kallamni, *Managing Prtnr*
EMP: 6
SALES: 1MM **Privately Held**
SIC: 2099 Syrups

(G-9541)
CASSINI PARFUMS LTD
3 W 57th St Fl 8 (10019-3407)
PHONE....................212 753-7540
Oleg Cassini, *CEO*
Mary Ann Nestor, *President*
EMP: 8
SQ FT: 8,000
SALES (est): 797.6K **Privately Held**
WEB: www.cassiniparfums.com
SIC: 2844 Perfumes & colognes

(G-9542)
CASTLE BRANDS INC (PA)
122 E 42nd St Rm 5000 (10168-4700)
PHONE....................646 356-0200
Mark E Andrews III, *Ch of Bd*
Richard J Lampen, *President*
John S Glover, *COO*
John Glover, *COO*
Alejandra Pena, *Senior VP*
▲ **EMP:** 51
SQ FT: 5,000
SALES: 72.2MM **Publicly Held**
WEB: www.castlebrandsinc.com
SIC: 2082 2085 Malt beverages; malt liquors; rum (alcoholic beverage); scotch whiskey; vodka (alcoholic beverage)

(G-9543)
CASTLE CONNOLLY MEDICAL LTD
42 W 24th St Fl 2 (10010-3201)
PHONE....................212 367-8400
Fax: 212 367-0964
John K Castle, *Ch of Bd*
Dr John J Connolly, *President*
William Levinson, *COO*
Maria Salvador, *Research*
William Liss-Levinson PHD, *Mktg Dir*
EMP: 25
SQ FT: 500
SALES (est): 3.1MM **Privately Held**
WEB: www.eldercareliving.com
SIC: 2731 2741 Books: publishing only; miscellaneous publishing

(G-9544)
CASUALS ETC INC
Also Called: E T C
16 E 52nd St Fl 4 (10022-5306)
PHONE....................212 838-1319
William Rondina, *President*
David Rosenberg, *Vice Pres*
Steven Steinberg, *CFO*
Mark Schoenfeld, *Controller*
EMP: 100
SALES (est): 5.3MM **Privately Held**
SIC: 2339 5137 Women's & misses' athletic clothing & sportswear; sportswear, women's & children's

(G-9545)
CATALYST GROUP INC
Also Called: Catalyst Group Design
345 7th Ave Rm 1100 (10001-5165)
PHONE....................212 243-7777
Nicholas Gould, *CEO*
Jon Mysel, *President*
Tim Piatek, *Manager*
Janine Coover, *Consultant*
Peter Hughes, *Admin Sec*
EMP: 6
SQ FT: 2,000
SALES (est): 860.7K **Privately Held**
WEB: www.catalystgroupdesign.com
SIC: 7372 Application computer software

(G-9546)
CATAME INC
158 W 29th St (10001-5300)
PHONE....................213 749-2610
EMP: 14
SALES (corp-wide): 4.6MM **Privately Held**
SIC: 3965 Zipper
PA: Catame, Inc.
1930 Long Beach Ave
Los Angeles CA 90058
213 749-2610

(G-9547)
CATCH VENTURES INC
30 W 63rd St Apt 14o (10023-7173)
PHONE....................347 620-4351
Scott Graulich, *President*
EMP: 10
SALES (est): 229.5K **Privately Held**
SIC: 7372 7389 Application computer software;

(G-9548)
CATHAY HOME INC (PA)
261 5th Ave Rm 412 (10016-7601)
PHONE....................212 213-0988
Zhiming Qian, *Ch of Bd*
Liwei Fang, *COO*
▲ **EMP:** 20
SQ FT: 10,000
SALES: 40MM **Privately Held**
SIC: 2392 Blankets, comforters & beddings

(G-9549)
CATHERINE STEIN DESIGNS INC
411 5th Ave Rm 600 (10016-2235)
PHONE....................212 840-1188
Fax: 212 764-4135
Catherine Stein, *President*
Sharon Goldberg, *Vice Pres*
EMP: 30
SQ FT: 10,000
SALES (est): 2MM **Privately Held**
WEB: www.csteindesigns.com
SIC: 3961 Costume jewelry, ex. precious metal & semiprecious stones

(G-9550)
CATHY DANIELS LTD (PA)
Also Called: Ecco Bay Sportswear
1411 Broadway (10018-3496)
PHONE....................212 354-8000
Fax: 212 354-1076
Herb Chestler, *Ch of Bd*
Steven Chestler, *President*
▲ **EMP:** 50
SQ FT: 20,000
SALES (est): 6.8MM **Privately Held**
WEB: www.cathydaniels.com
SIC: 2339 Sportswear, women's

(G-9551)
CAVA SPILIADIS USA
200 W 57th St Ste 908 (10019-3211)
PHONE....................212 247-8214
Martha Tsapanos, *Principal*
▲ **EMP:** 20 **EST:** 2007
SALES (est): 140.2K **Privately Held**
SIC: 2084 Wines

(G-9552)
CCT INC
Also Called: Committee For Color & Trends
60 Madison Ave Ste 1209 (10010-1635)
P.O. Box 1621 (10159-1621)
PHONE....................212 532-3355
Ellen Campuzano, *President*
EMP: 6
SQ FT: 1,500
SALES (est): 440K **Privately Held**
SIC: 2732 Books: printing only

(G-9553)
CEGID CORPORATION
274 Madison Ave Rm 1400 (10016-0701)
PHONE....................212 757-9038
Fax: 212 757-9051
Alan King, *Project Mgr*
Tommy See, *Marketing Mgr*
Arnaud Coste, *Manager*
Hibberd Peter, *Manager*
EMP: 17
SALES (est): 2.1MM
SALES (corp-wide): 5.4MM **Privately Held**
SIC: 7372 Word processing computer software
PA: Cegid Group
52 Quai Paul Sedallian
Lyon 69009
476 443-382

(G-9554)
CEJON INC
390 5th Ave Fl 6 (10018-8152)
PHONE....................201 437-8788
David Seeherman, *President*
Robin Mummert, *Sales Mgr*
Kevin Nolan, *Manager*
▲ **EMP:** 23
SQ FT: 11,000
SALES (est): 2.4MM
SALES (corp-wide): 1.4B **Publicly Held**
WEB: www.cejon.com
SIC: 3111 5137 Accessory products, leather; women's & children's clothing
PA: Steven Madden, Ltd.
5216 Barnett Ave
Long Island City NY 11104
718 446-1800

(G-9555)
CELLUFUN INC
120 Broadway Ste 3330 (10271-3397)
PHONE....................212 385-2255
Lon Otremba, *CEO*
Steve Dacek, *COO*
Andy Bishop, *Vice Pres*
Kevin Cahil, *CFO*
Shannon Kane, *Manager*
EMP: 31
SALES (est): 1.4MM
SALES (corp-wide): 4.4MM **Privately Held**
SIC: 7372 Application computer software
PA: Longworth Venture Partners, L.P
303 Wyman St Ste 300
Waltham MA 02451
781 663-3600

(G-9556)
CELLVATION INC
2 Gansevoort St Fl 9 (10014-1667)
PHONE....................212 554-4520
EMP: 8
SALES (est): 340K **Privately Held**
SIC: 2834 Pharmaceutical preparations

(G-9557)
CELOXICA INC
1133 Broadway (10010-7903)
PHONE....................212 880-2075
Jean-Marc Bouhelier, *Branch Mgr*
EMP: 8
SALES (corp-wide): 3.8MM **Privately Held**
SIC: 3571 Computers, digital, analog or hybrid
HQ: Celoxica, Inc
275 Madison Ave
New York NY 10016
212 880-2075

(G-9558)
CEMENTEX LATEX CORP
121 Varick St Frnt 2 (10013-1408)
PHONE....................212 741-1770
Arthur Gononsky, *President*
Susan Gononsky, *Corp Secy*
Jeffrey Gononsky, *Vice Pres*
Jeff Gonosky, *Vice Pres*
▼ **EMP:** 10 **EST:** 1936
SQ FT: 12,000
SALES (est): 850K **Privately Held**
WEB: www.cementex.com
SIC: 3089 3069 5084 Plastic hardware & building products; reclaimed rubber & specialty rubber compounds; machine tools & accessories

(G-9559)
CEMEX CEMENT INC
590 Madison Ave Fl 41 (10022-2524)
PHONE....................212 317-6000
Javier Garcia, *President*
EMP: 78
SALES (corp-wide): 13.3B **Privately Held**
SIC: 3273 Ready-mixed concrete
HQ: Cemex Cement, Inc.
929 Gessner Rd Ste 1900
Houston TX 77024
713 650-6200

(G-9560)
CEMOI INC (PA)
5 Penn Plz Ste 2325 (10001-1810)
PHONE....................212 583-4920
Thierry Beaujeon, *CEO*
EMP: 2
SALES (est): 4.8MM **Privately Held**
SIC: 2066 Chocolate bars, solid

(G-9561)
CENIBRA INC
335 Madison Ave Fl 23 (10017-4634)
PHONE....................212 818-8242
James Monroe, *Manager*

Yoshida Kazuhiro, *Director*
▲ **EMP:** 6
SALES: 1B **Privately Held**
SIC: 2611 5159 Pulp mills; bristles

(G-9562)
CENTRAL APPAREL GROUP LTD
Also Called: Central Park Active Wear
16 W 36th St Rm 1202 (10018-9751)
PHONE.................................212 868-6505
Shalom Asher, *CEO*
Steve Goldfarb, *President*
◆ **EMP:** 18
SQ FT: 900
SALES: 10MM **Privately Held**
SIC: 2339 5621 Sportswear, women's; women's sportswear

(G-9563)
CENTRAL CNFRNCE OF AMRCN RBBIS
355 Lexington Ave Fl 18 (10017-6603)
PHONE.................................212 972-3636
Fax: 212 692-0819
Jonathan A Stein, *President*
Deborah Smilow, *Editor*
Paul Menitoff, *Exec VP*
Walter Jacob, *Vice Pres*
Richard Block, *Treasurer*
▲ **EMP:** 16
SALES (est): 2.3MM **Privately Held**
WEB: www.ccarnet.org
SIC: 2731 Books: publishing only; pamphlets: publishing only, not printed on site

(G-9564)
CENTRAL GARDEN & PET COMPANY
2475 Broadway (10025-7450)
PHONE.................................212 877-1270
Richard Metzler, *Branch Mgr*
EMP: 9
SALES (corp-wide): 1.6B **Publicly Held**
WEB: www.centralgardenandpet.com
SIC: 2048 Prepared feeds
PA: Central Garden & Pet Company
    1340 Treat Blvd Ste 600
    Walnut Creek CA 94597
    925 948-4000

(G-9565)
CENTRAL MILLS INC
Also Called: Freeze Clothing
1400 Broadway Rm 1605 (10018-5200)
PHONE.................................212 221-0748
Fax: 212 944-1181
Cedric Howe, *Sales Staff*
Maurice Shalam, *Branch Mgr*
Randi Rosenstein, *Info Tech Dir*
EMP: 110
SALES (corp-wide): 93.9MM **Privately Held**
SIC: 2329 2339 2253 Men's & boys' sportswear & athletic clothing; women's & misses' outerwear; T-shirts & tops, knit
PA: Central Mills, Inc.
    473 Ridge Rd
    Dayton NJ 08810
    732 329-0032

(G-9566)
CENTRAL TEXTILES INC
Also Called: Cotswolt Industries
10 E 40th St Rm 3410 (10016-0301)
PHONE.................................212 213-8740
Steve Rosenberg, *Sales Staff*
James McKinnon, *Manager*
EMP: 15
SALES (corp-wide): 60.1MM **Privately Held**
WEB: www.ctextiles.com
SIC: 2261 2262 Finishing plants, cotton; finishing plants, manmade fiber & silk fabrics
PA: Central Textiles, Inc.
    237 Mill Ave
    Central SC 29260
    864 639-2491

(G-9567)
CENTRO INC
841 Broadway Fl 6 (10003-4704)
P.O. Box 13164, Chicago IL (60613-0464)
PHONE.................................212 791-9450

Kelly Wenzel, *Chief Mktg Ofcr*
EMP: 299
SALES (corp-wide): 23.6MM **Privately Held**
SIC: 3089 Plastic processing
PA: Centro, Inc.
    11 E Madison St Ste 300
    Chicago IL 60602
    312 642-7348

(G-9568)
CENTURION DIAMONDS INC
580 5th Ave (10036-4701)
PHONE.................................718 946-6918
Yoel Braun, *Owner*
EMP: 5
SQ FT: 1,000
SALES: 15MM **Privately Held**
SIC: 3915 Diamond cutting & polishing

(G-9569)
CENTURY GRAND INC
Also Called: Century Pharmacy Three
302 Grand St (10002-4465)
PHONE.................................212 925-3838
Steven T Ho, *Principal*
EMP: 12
SALES (est): 1.6MM **Privately Held**
SIC: 2834 Druggists' preparations (pharmaceuticals)

(G-9570)
CEO CAST INC
211 E 43rd St Rm 400 (10017-8620)
PHONE.................................212 732-4300
Kenneth Sgro, *President*
Jim Fallon, *Managing Prtnr*
EMP: 18
SQ FT: 25,000
SALES (est): 1.3MM **Privately Held**
WEB: www.ceocast.com
SIC: 2741 Business service newsletters: publishing & printing

(G-9571)
CEROS INC (PA)
151 W 25th St Rm 200 (10001-7262)
Drawer (10010)
PHONE.................................347 744-9250
Simon Burg, *CEO*
Dominic Duffy, *Managing Dir*
Aaron Wood, *QA Dir*
Kaity Ng, *Controller*
Elina Strizhak, *Human Resources*
EMP: 22
SALES (est): 1.6MM **Privately Held**
SIC: 7372 Publishers' computer software

(G-9572)
CFO PUBLISHING LLC (PA)
45 W 45th St Fl 12 (10036-4602)
PHONE.................................212 459-3004
Fax: 212 258-2185
Alan Glass, *President*
Richard Rivera, *President*
Lissa Short, *Senior VP*
Andreas Droste, *Sales Staff*
Terry Camarillo, *Marketing Staff*
EMP: 42
SQ FT: 7,500
SALES (est): 15.1MM **Privately Held**
SIC: 2721 Magazines: publishing only, not printed on site

(G-9573)
CGI TECHNOLOGIES SOLUTIONS INC
655 3rd Ave Ste 700 (10017-9124)
PHONE.................................212 682-7411
Fax: 212 682-0715
Don O'Brien, *Principal*
Edward Asip, *VP Sales*
Jeremy Douglass, *Manager*
Robert Hicks, *CTO*
Mark Chamberlin, *Info Tech Dir*
EMP: 15
SALES (corp-wide): 7.8B **Privately Held**
SIC: 7372 5045 7379 Prepackaged software; computer software; computer related consulting services
HQ: Cgi Technologies And Solutions Inc.
    11325 Random Hills Rd
    Fairfax VA 22030
    703 267-8000

(G-9574)
CHAIN STORE AGE MAGAZINE
425 Park Ave (10022-3506)
PHONE.................................212 756-5000
EMP: 5
SQ FT: 30,000
SALES (est): 402.6K
SALES (corp-wide): 122.5MM **Privately Held**
SIC: 2731 Book Publisher
PA: Lebhar-Friedman, Inc.
    150 W 30th St Fl 19
    New York NY 10001
    212 756-5000

(G-9575)
CHAINDOM ENTERPRISES INC
48 W 48th St Ste 200 (10036-1779)
PHONE.................................212 719-4778
Fax: 212 398-1318
Fikri Akdemir, *President*
Steve Pinkin, *Treasurer*
EMP: 6
SQ FT: 2,500
SALES (est): 533.5K **Privately Held**
SIC: 3911 Jewelry, precious metal

(G-9576)
CHAMPION ZIPPER CORP
Also Called: Sew True
447 W 36th St Fl 2 (10018-6300)
PHONE.................................212 239-0414
Fax: 212 947-9281
Steven Silberberg, *President*
Chris Roldan, *Principal*
Eugene Silberberg, *Controller*
EMP: 6
SQ FT: 5,000
SALES: 1.3MM **Privately Held**
WEB: www.sewtrue.com
SIC: 3965 2241 Zipper; trimmings, textile

(G-9577)
CHAN LUU LLC
1441 Broadway (10018-1905)
PHONE.................................212 398-3163
Terence Farley, *VP Sales*
Madison Davis, *Accounts Mgr*
Chan Luu, *Branch Mgr*
EMP: 26
SALES (corp-wide): 23.7MM **Privately Held**
SIC: 2752 Fashion plates, lithographed
PA: Chan Luu, Llc
    818 S Broadway Ste 600
    Los Angeles CA 90014
    213 892-0245

(G-9578)
CHANCELLE SUITS INC
Also Called: Chancelle Fashions/Tango
141 W 36th St Rm 900 (10018-9406)
PHONE.................................212 921-5300
Shahram Mobasser, *President*
EMP: 15
SALES (est): 1.4MM **Privately Held**
WEB: www.chancelle.com
SIC: 2337 5137 Suits: women's, misses' & juniors'; suits: women's, children's & infants'

(G-9579)
CHANSE PETROLEUM CORPORATION (PA)
828 5th Ave Apt 1f (10065-7272)
PHONE.................................212 682-3789
Fax: 212 687-5360
Kai Chang, *President*
EMP: 3 **EST:** 1972
SQ FT: 1,000
SALES (est): 1.3MM **Privately Held**
SIC: 1311 Crude petroleum production; natural gas production

(G-9580)
CHARING CROSS MUSIC INC
3 Columbus Cir Ste 1720 (10019-8708)
PHONE.................................212 541-7571
Paul Simon, *President*
EMP: 6
SQ FT: 1,000
SALES (est): 410K **Privately Held**
SIC: 2741 Music, sheet: publishing only, not printed on site

(G-9581)
CHARLES HENRICKS INC
Also Called: Starkey & Henricks
121 Varick St Fl 9 (10013-1408)
PHONE.................................212 243-5800
Fax: 212 966-5913
Peter Bird, *President*
Douglas Bird, *Vice Pres*
EMP: 15
SALES (est): 1.6MM **Privately Held**
SIC: 2796 Gravure printing plates or cylinders, preparation of

(G-9582)
CHARLES P ROGERS BRASS BEDS (PA)
Also Called: Charles P Rogers Brass Ir Bed
26 W 17th St (10011-5710)
PHONE.................................212 675-4400
Fax: 212 675-6495
Linda Klein, *President*
David Klein, *Vice Pres*
Donnie Ray, *Vice Pres*
William Mardorf, *Marketing Staff*
Jeannine Tuttle, *Manager*
▲ **EMP:** 15 **EST:** 1979
SQ FT: 9,000
SALES (est): 3.6MM **Privately Held**
SIC: 2514 5712 5961 Beds, including folding & cabinet, household: metal; beds & accessories; furniture & furnishings, mail order

(G-9583)
CHARLES VAILLANT INC
37 W 57th St Ste 803 (10019-3411)
PHONE.................................212 752-4832
Fax: 212 486-4849
Thomas Renna, *President*
Kenneth Danielsson, *Admin Sec*
▲ **EMP:** 7
SALES (est): 705.3K **Privately Held**
SIC: 3911 Jewelry, precious metal

(G-9584)
CHARMING FASHION INC
247 W 38th St Rm 1400 (10018-0230)
PHONE.................................212 730-2872
Fax: 212 730-2872
Charles Kim, *President*
EMP: 5
SALES (est): 261K **Privately Held**
SIC: 2211 Apparel & outerwear fabrics, cotton

(G-9585)
CHARTER VENTURES LLC
135 W 36th St Rm 1800 (10018-6951)
PHONE.................................212 868-0222
Jennifer Lai,
Howard Cohen,
▲ **EMP:** 10 **EST:** 2000
SQ FT: 4,838
SALES (est): 1.5MM
SALES (corp-wide): 100MM **Privately Held**
SIC: 2253 Sweaters & sweater coats, knit
PA: Charter Ventures Limited
    Rm A 6/F Chiap Luen Indl Bldg
    Kwai Chung NT
    221 106-07

(G-9586)
CHASE CORPORATION
610 Madison Ave (10022-1620)
PHONE.................................212 644-7281
Kamala Harbhajan, *Manager*
EMP: 11
SALES (corp-wide): 238MM **Publicly Held**
SIC: 3644 Noncurrent-carrying wiring services
PA: Chase Corporation
    26 Summer St
    Bridgewater MA 02324
    508 819-4200

(G-9587)
CHECK GROUP LLC
1385 Broadway Fl 16 (10018-6041)
PHONE.................................212 221-4700
Fax: 212 221-1561
Lawrence Jemal,
Richard Tan, *Admin Sec*
▲ **EMP:** 100

GEOGRAPHIC SECTION

New York - New York County (G-9613)

SALES (est): 6.6MM **Privately Held**
WEB: www.checkgroup.com
SIC: 2311 2321 2322 2325 Men's & boys' suits & coats; men's & boys' furnishings; underwear, men's & boys': made from purchased materials; men's & boys' trousers & slacks

(G-9588)
CHECKM8 INC (PA)
307 W 36th St Fl 13 (10018-6434)
PHONE 212 268-0048
Dana Ghavami, *CEO*
David Kedem, *General Mgr*
EMP: 16
SALES (est): 5.3MM **Privately Held**
WEB: www.checkm8.com
SIC: 7372 Business oriented computer software

(G-9589)
CHELSEA PLASTICS INC
200 Lexington Ave Rm 914 (10016-6255)
PHONE 212 924-4530
George Frechter, *President*
EMP: 12
SQ FT: 7,000
SALES (est): 1.5MM **Privately Held**
WEB: www.chelseaplastics.com
SIC: 3082 Unsupported plastics profile shapes

(G-9590)
CHERI PINK INC (PA)
Also Called: Clues Fashion
1430 Broadway Fl 21 (10018-3347)
PHONE 212 869-1948
Fax: 212 869-1953
Mark Naim, *President*
Sam Naim, *Corp Secy*
George Naim, *Vice Pres*
Sammy Rohani, *Manager*
▲ **EMP:** 20
SQ FT: 4,200
SALES (est): 2.2MM **Privately Held**
SIC: 2339 2337 2335 Women's & misses' outerwear; women's & misses' suits & coats; women's, juniors' & misses' dresses

(G-9591)
CHERRY LANE MAGAZINE LLC
1745 Broadway 19 (10019-4640)
PHONE 212 561-3000
Fax: 212 683-2040
Peter Primont, *Mng Member*
EMP: 80
SQ FT: 30,000
SALES (est): 4.9MM **Privately Held**
SIC: 2741 Miscellaneous publishing

(G-9592)
CHESKY RECORDS INC
1650 Broadway Ste 900 (10019-6965)
PHONE 212 586-7799
Norman Chesky, *President*
David Chesky, *Vice Pres*
Lisa Hershfired, *Accounts Mgr*
EMP: 12
SQ FT: 6,000
SALES (est): 1.2MM **Privately Held**
SIC: 3652 Phonograph record blanks; compact laser discs, prerecorded

(G-9593)
CHIA USA LLC
Also Called: Chia Company
315 W 36th St Fl 10 (10018-6527)
PHONE 212 226-7512
John Foss, *CEO*
April Helliwell, *COO*
EMP: 18 **EST:** 2014
SQ FT: 3,000
SALES (est): 20MM **Privately Held**
SIC: 2043 5153 Cereal breakfast foods; grains; barley

(G-9594)
CHILD NUTRITION PROG DEPT ED
1011 1st Ave Fl 6 (10022-4112)
PHONE 212 371-1000
Thomas Smith, *President*
Christine Plantamura, *Admin Asst*
EMP: 99

SALES (est): 3.6MM **Privately Held**
SIC: 2099 Food preparations

(G-9595)
CHILDRENS PROGRESS INC
108 W 39th St Rm 1305 (10018-8258)
PHONE 212 730-0905
Kevin Greaney, *President*
Pat Santo, *Business Mgr*
Sophie Gill, *Sales Associate*
Andrew Morrison, *Info Tech Dir*
EMP: 20
SQ FT: 1,700
SALES (est): 1.7MM **Privately Held**
WEB: www.childrensprogress.com
SIC: 7372 Educational computer software

(G-9596)
CHINA DAILY DISTRIBUTION CORP (HQ)
1500 Broadway Ste 2800 (10036-4097)
PHONE 212 537-8888
Larry Lee, *CEO*
Lili Zhou, *Admin Asst*
EMP: 15
SALES (est): 1.5MM **Privately Held**
SIC: 2711 Newspapers
PA: China Daily
No.15 Huixin Dongjie,Chao Yang District
Beijing
106 499-5388

(G-9597)
CHINA HUAREN ORGANIC PDTS INC
100 Wall St Fl 15 (10005-3701)
PHONE 212 232-0120
Cao Yushu, *CEO*
Pam Cambell, *Opers Dir*
Yushu Cao, *CFO*
▲ **EMP:** 3
SALES (est): 7.4MM **Privately Held**
WEB: www.ultradatasystems.com
SIC: 2099 2844 Food preparations; toilet preparations; cosmetic preparations

(G-9598)
CHINA INDUSTRIAL STEEL INC
110 Wall St Fl 11 (10005-3834)
PHONE 646 328-1502
Shenghong Liu, *Principal*
EMP: 2
SALES (est): 649.3M **Privately Held**
SIC: 3312 Blast furnaces & steel mills

(G-9599)
CHINA LITHIUM TECHNOLOGIES (PA)
15 W 39th St Fl 14 (10018-0626)
PHONE 212 391-2688
Kun Liu, *Ch of Bd*
Jijun Zhang, *Vice Pres*
Chunping Fang, *CFO*
Fang Ai, *CTO*
EMP: 9
SQ FT: 215
SALES (est): 15.7MM **Publicly Held**
SIC: 3691 3629 Storage batteries; batteries, rechargeable; battery chargers, rectifying or nonrotating

(G-9600)
CHINA N E PETRO HOLDINGS LTD
445 Park Ave Ste 900 (10022-8632)
PHONE 212 307-3568
Fax: 718 685-2650
Jingfu LI, *CEO*
Shaohui Chen, *CFO*
EMP: 715
SALES (est): 99.5MM **Privately Held**
WEB: www.cnepetroleum.com
SIC: 1311 Crude petroleum production

(G-9601)
CHINA NEWSWEEK CORPORATION
15 E 40th St Fl 11 (10016-0401)
PHONE 212 481-2510
WEI Xiang Peng, *Ch of Bd*
Fred Teng, *Exec Dir*
EMP: 10
SALES (est): 440K **Privately Held**
SIC: 2711 Newspapers

(G-9602)
CHINA TING FASHION GROUP (USA)
525 7th Ave Rm 1606 (10018-0401)
PHONE 212 716-1600
Fax: 212 716-1605
Ren Shen, *President*
Bruce Bergquist, *Controller*
EMP: 7
SALES: 8.5MM
SALES (corp-wide): 12.4K **Privately Held**
SIC: 2269 2335 2339 Linen fabrics: dyeing, finishing & printing; dresses, paper: cut & sewn; ensemble dresses: women's, misses' & juniors'; women's & misses' outerwear
PA: Zhejiang China Ting Group Co., Ltd.
No.56, Beisha East Road, Yuhang District
Hangzhou
571 862-5908

(G-9603)
CHLOE INTERNATIONAL INC
525 Fashion Ave Rm 1601 (10018-0545)
PHONE 212 730-6661
Leon Hedvat, *CEO*
Faramarz Hedvat, *Ch of Bd*
Behrooz Hedvat, *President*
Alex Uskach, *Controller*
Frankie Hedvat, *Director*
▲ **EMP:** 15
SALES (est): 2.4MM **Privately Held**
SIC: 2339 Service apparel, washable: women's

(G-9604)
CHOCNYC LLC
4996 Broadway (10034-1635)
PHONE 917 804-4848
Brad Jon Doles, *Principal*
Dewayne Jemal Edwards, *Principal*
Jemal Edwards, *Principal*
EMP: 6
SALES (est): 185.1K **Privately Held**
SIC: 2051 Cakes, bakery: except frozen

(G-9605)
CHOCOLAT MODERNE LLC
27 W 20th St Ste 904 (10011-3725)
PHONE 212 229-4797
Joan Coukos, *Mng Member*
▲ **EMP:** 5
SQ FT: 950
SALES (est): 250K **Privately Held**
WEB: www.chocolatmoderne.com
SIC: 2064 5145 5961 Candy & other confectionery products; candy; mail order house

(G-9606)
CHOPT CREATIVE SALAD CO LLC (PA)
853 Broadway (10003-4703)
PHONE 646 374-0386
Fax: 646 336-5513
Drew Alden, *General Mgr*
Michael Caine, *District Mgr*
Anthony Vipond, *Purchasing*
Victor Stevenson, *VP Finance*
Cassie Holtmann, *Marketing Mgr*
EMP: 10
SALES (est): 17.5MM **Privately Held**
SIC: 2099 Ready-to-eat meals, salads & sandwiches

(G-9607)
CHRISTIAN BOOK PUBLISHING
213 Bennett Ave (10040-2675)
PHONE 646 559-2533
Grace Dola Balogun, *Owner*
EMP: 33
SALES (est): 1.4MM **Privately Held**
SIC: 2731 Book clubs: publishing & printing

(G-9608)
CHRISTIAN CASEY LLC (PA)
Also Called: Sean John
1440 Broadway Frnt 3 (10018-2301)
PHONE 212 500-2200
Frank J Dellaquila, *Senior VP*
Vincent Panzanella, *VP Mktg*
Dawn Robertson,
Sean John,

▲ **EMP:** 40
SQ FT: 5,000
SALES (est): 26.3MM **Privately Held**
SIC: 2325 2322 2321 2311 Men's & boys' trousers & slacks; men's & boys' underwear & nightwear; men's & boys' furnishings; men's & boys' suits & coats

(G-9609)
CHRISTIAN CASEY LLC
Also Called: Sean John Clothing
1440 Broadway Frnt 3 (10018-2301)
PHONE 212 500-2200
Juanita Reyes, *Credit Staff*
Kevin Lowney, *Branch Mgr*
EMP: 42
SALES (corp-wide): 26.3MM **Privately Held**
SIC: 2325 2322 2321 2311 Men's & boys' trousers & slacks; men's & boys' underwear & nightwear; men's & boys' furnishings; men's & boys' suits & coats
PA: Christian Casey Llc
1440 Broadway Frnt 3
New York NY 10018
212 500-2200

(G-9610)
CHRISTIAN DIOR PERFUMES LLC (DH)
19 E 57th St (10022-2506)
PHONE 212 931-2200
Fax: 212 751-7473
Pamela Baxter, *CEO*
Scott Johnson, *COO*
Joanna Grillo, *Vice Pres*
Diana Miles, *Vice Pres*
Pertrand Tesra, *Vice Pres*
◆ **EMP:** 35
SALES (est): 34.2MM
SALES (corp-wide): 279MM **Privately Held**
WEB: www.saniflo.com
SIC: 2844 3999 Perfumes, natural or synthetic; cosmetic preparations; atomizers, toiletry
HQ: Parfums Christian Dior
33 Avenue Hoche
Paris Cedex 08 75380
149 538-500

(G-9611)
CHRISTIAN SIRIANO HOLDINGS LLC
260 W 35th St Ste 403 (10001-2525)
PHONE 212 695-5494
Christian Siriano, *Managing Dir*
EMP: 9
SQ FT: 3,000
SALES (est): 1.2MM **Privately Held**
SIC: 2335 Women's, juniors' & misses' dresses

(G-9612)
CHRISTINA SALES INC
1441 Broadway (10018-1905)
PHONE 212 391-0710
Joey Schwebel, *President*
Sharon Fedele, *Credit Mgr*
Rita Mulloy, *Sales Staff*
Brittny Carbel, *Manager*
▲ **EMP:** 10
SQ FT: 5,000
SALES (est): 1.2MM **Privately Held**
SIC: 2339 5137 Bathing suits: women's, misses' & juniors'; swimsuits: women's, children's & infants'

(G-9613)
CHRISTOPHER DESIGNS INC
50 W 47th St Fl 1507 (10036-8687)
PHONE 212 382-1013
Fax: 212 768-8978
Christopher Slowinski, *President*
Ewa Slowinski, *Vice Pres*
Christina Grochowski, *Controller*
Kuba Lipien, *Technology*
Ursula Piekut, *Director*
▲ **EMP:** 27
SQ FT: 3,800
SALES (est): 4MM **Privately Held**
WEB: www.christopherdesigns.com
SIC: 3915 3999 Jewelers' materials & lapidary work; jewelry, precious metal

New York - New York County (G-9614) GEOGRAPHIC SECTION

(G-9614)
CHRISTOS INC
318 W 39th St Fl 12 (10018-1484)
PHONE 212 921-0025
Fax: 212 921-0127
Christos Yiannakou, *President*
Michael Decuollo, *Vice Pres*
Bobbi Wager, *Bookkeeper*
▲ EMP: 37
SQ FT: 7,500
SALES (est): 2.4MM **Privately Held**
WEB: www.christosbridal.com
SIC: 2335 Wedding gowns & dresses

(G-9615)
CHURCH PUBLISHING INCORPORATED (HQ)
Also Called: Morehouse Publishing
445 5th Ave Frnt 1 (10016-0133)
PHONE 212 592-1800
Fax: 212 779-3363
Alan F Blanchard, *President*
Paul Morejon, *Vice Pres*
▼ EMP: 8
SALES (est): 1.2MM
SALES (corp-wide): 443.2MM **Privately Held**
WEB: www.preparingforsunday.com
SIC: 2731 Books: publishing only
PA: Church Pension Group Services Corporation
19 E 34th St Fl 3
New York NY 10016
212 592-1800

(G-9616)
CINDERELLA PRESS LTD
327 Canal St 3 (10013-2513)
PHONE 212 431-3130
Robert Cenedella, *President*
EMP: 6
SALES (est): 420K **Privately Held**
SIC: 2731 Books: publishing only

(G-9617)
CINE DESIGN GROUP LLC
Also Called: Cinedeck
110 Leroy St Fl 8 (10014-3911)
PHONE 646 747-0734
Charles Dautremont,
EMP: 8
SQ FT: 5,000
SALES (est): 658K **Privately Held**
SIC: 3575 Cathode ray tube (CRT), computer terminal

(G-9618)
CINEDIGM SOFTWARE
902 Broadway Fl 9 (10010-6036)
PHONE 212 206-9001
Dan Sherlock, *President*
Jill Calcaterra, *Principal*
Diane Anselmo, *Vice Pres*
Tom Hassell, *Vice Pres*
EMP: 5
SALES (est): 275.8K **Privately Held**
SIC: 7372 Prepackaged software

(G-9619)
CINER MANUFACTURING CO INC
20 W 37th St Fl 10 (10018-7484)
PHONE 212 947-3770
Fax: 212 643-0357
David Hill, *President*
Patricia Ciner Hill, *Vice Pres*
Jackie Rogers, *Sales Staff*
EMP: 28
SQ FT: 6,000
SALES (est): 3.6MM **Privately Held**
SIC: 3961 Costume jewelry, ex. precious metal & semiprecious stones

(G-9620)
CIRCLE PEAK CAPITAL MGT LLC (PA)
1325 Ave Of The Americas (10019-6026)
PHONE 646 230-8812
Fax: 646 349-2743
R Adam Smith, *CEO*
James H Clippard, *Principal*
Holbrook M Forusz, *Principal*
Joseph S Rhodes, *Bd of Directors*
John R Jonge Poerink,
▲ EMP: 30

SALES (est): 816.7MM **Privately Held**
SIC: 2053 6799 Pies, bakery: frozen; venture capital companies

(G-9621)
CIRCLE PRESS INC (PA)
Also Called: Press Room New York Division
121 Varick St Fl 7 (10013-1408)
PHONE 212 924-4277
Fax: 212 675-1163
Richard T Springer, *President*
Lawrence Lembo, *Vice Pres*
Benjamin Caringal, *Treasurer*
Gary Lacinski, *Business Dir*
EMP: 51
SQ FT: 30,000
SALES (est): 5MM **Privately Held**
SIC: 2752 2796 Commercial printing, lithographic; platemaking services

(G-9622)
CISCO SYSTEMS INC
1 Penn Plz Ste 3306 (10119-3306)
PHONE 212 714-4000
Fax: 212 714-4005
Herb Madan, *President*
Adam Pasieka, *Regional Mgr*
Jonathan Carmel, *Business Mgr*
Nick Adomo, *Vice Pres*
Jim Ayers, *Engineer*
EMP: 250
SALES (corp-wide): 49.2B **Publicly Held**
WEB: www.cisco.com
SIC: 3577 7373 Data conversion equipment, media-to-media: computer; computer integrated systems design
PA: Cisco Systems, Inc.
170 W Tasman Dr
San Jose CA 95134
408 526-4000

(G-9623)
CITIFORMS INC
134 W 29th St Rm 704 (10001-5304)
PHONE 212 334-9671
Fax: 212 334-9887
Steven J Slutsky, *President*
EMP: 6
SQ FT: 2,900
SALES (est): 947.1K **Privately Held**
WEB: www.citiformsinc.com
SIC: 2759 Commercial printing

(G-9624)
CITIGROUP INC
388 Greenwich St (10013-2375)
PHONE 212 816-6000
Michael Carpenter, *CEO*
ARI Glazer, *President*
Ron Chakravarti, *Managing Dir*
Peter Charles, *Managing Dir*
Ranjit Chatterji, *Managing Dir*
EMP: 133
SALES (corp-wide): 88.2B **Publicly Held**
SIC: 2621 Parchment, securites & bank note papers
PA: Citigroup Inc.
399 Park Ave
New York NY 10022
212 559-1000

(G-9625)
CITISOURCE INDUSTRIES INC
244 5th Ave Ste 229 (10001-7604)
PHONE 212 683-1033
Dino Sebastiani, *Ch of Bd*
Mario Lacava, *President*
◆ EMP: 30
SALES (est): 4.1MM **Privately Held**
SIC: 2231 5131 Broadwoven fabric mills, wool; woolen & worsted piece goods, woven

(G-9626)
CITIXSYS TECHNOLOGIES INC
1 Rockefeller Plz Fl 11 (10020-2073)
PHONE 212 745-1365
Kamal Karmakar, *CEO*
Pankaj Mathur, *COO*
Paula Da Silva, *Senior VP*
Mick Adamson, *Vice Pres*
Tenny Koshy, *Manager*
EMP: 8
SALES (est): 869.9K **Privately Held**
SIC: 7372 Prepackaged software

(G-9627)
CITY AND STATE NY LLC
Also Called: Think Tank
61 Broadway Rm 1320 (10006-2721)
PHONE 212 268-0442
Fax: 212 401-0810
Tom Allon, *CEO*
Jasmin Freeman, *Business Mgr*
Jim Katocin, *Vice Pres*
Andrew Holt, *Marketing Staff*
Scott Augustine, *Manager*
EMP: 27 EST: 2012
SALES (est): 1.1MM **Privately Held**
SIC: 2721 Magazines: publishing & printing

(G-9628)
CITY BAKERY INC (PA)
Also Called: Maury's Cookie Dough
3 W 18th St Frnt 1 (10011-4610)
PHONE 212 366-1414
Fax: 212 645-0810
Maury Rubin, *President*
Allison Dees, *Sales Staff*
EMP: 30
SQ FT: 2,000
SALES (est): 3.3MM **Privately Held**
SIC: 2051 Bakery: wholesale or wholesale/retail combined

(G-9629)
CITY CASTING CORP
151 W 46th St Fl 5 (10036-8512)
PHONE 212 938-0511
Luis Ontiveros, *CEO*
Lily Londona, *Administration*
EMP: 7
SALES (est): 946.3K **Privately Held**
SIC: 3369 White metal castings (lead, tin, antimony), except die

(G-9630)
CITY SPORTS INC
64 W 48th St Frnt B (10036-1708)
PHONE 212 730-2009
EMP: 6
SALES (corp-wide): 135.8MM **Privately Held**
SIC: 3949 Mfg Sporting/Athletic Goods
PA: City Sports, Inc.
77 N Washington St # 500
Boston MA 02114
617 391-9100

(G-9631)
CITY SPORTS IMAGING INC
20 E 46th St Rm 200 (10017-9287)
PHONE 212 481-3600
Lawrence Silverberg, *President*
EMP: 20
SALES (est): 1MM **Privately Held**
SIC: 3845 Magnetic resonance imaging device, nuclear

(G-9632)
CITYSCAPE OB/GYN PLLC
38 E 32nd St Fl 4 (10016-5507)
PHONE 212 683-3595
Heidi S Rosenberg, *Principal*
Carmit Archibald, *Obstetrician*
EMP: 19
SALES (est): 2.7MM **Privately Held**
SIC: 3842 Gynecological supplies & appliances

(G-9633)
CJ JEWELRY INC
2 W 47th St Ste 1106 (10036-3333)
PHONE 212 719-2464
Chaim Fischman, *President*
▲ EMP: 12
SALES (est): 1.3MM **Privately Held**
WEB: www.cjjewelry.com
SIC: 3911 Jewelry apparel

(G-9634)
CLARITYAD INC ✪
833 Broadway Apt 2 (10003-4700)
PHONE 646 397-4198
Louis-David Mangin, *CEO*
EMP: 6 EST: 2016
SALES (est): 172.7K **Privately Held**
SIC: 7372 Business oriented computer software

(G-9635)
CLARKSON N POTTER INC
1745 Broadway (10019-4640)
PHONE 212 782-9000
Lauren Shakely, *Director*
▲ EMP: 17
SALES (est): 773K
SALES (corp-wide): 18.4B **Privately Held**
WEB: www.anchorbooks.com
SIC: 2731 Books: publishing only
HQ: Penguin Random House Llc
1745 Broadway
New York NY 10019
212 782-9000

(G-9636)
CLASSIC FLAVORS FRAGRANCES INC
878 W End Ave Apt 12b (10025-4957)
PHONE 212 777-0004
Fax: 212 353-0404
George Ivolin, *CEO*
EMP: 6
SQ FT: 750
SALES (est): 560K **Privately Held**
SIC: 2869 2899 5122 5169 Flavors or flavoring materials, synthetic; perfumes, flavorings & food additives; chemical preparations; essential oils; cosmetics, perfumes & hair products; aromatic chemicals; chemical additives; essential oils

(G-9637)
CLASSIC SOFA LTD
130 E 63rd St Ph B (10065-7340)
PHONE 212 620-0485
Fax: 212 924-0953
Jeffrey Stone, *President*
Randal Rogg, *CPA*
Maurice Stone, *Shareholder*
▲ EMP: 55
SQ FT: 15,000
SALES (est): 6.2MM **Privately Held**
SIC: 2512 5712 Couches, sofas & davenports: upholstered on wood frames; furniture stores

(G-9638)
CLASSPASS INC (PA)
275 7th Ave Fl 11 (10001-6708)
PHONE 646 701-2172
EMP: 29
SALES (est): 8.6MM **Privately Held**
SIC: 2741

(G-9639)
CLASSROOM INC
245 5th Ave Fl 20 (10016-8728)
PHONE 212 545-8400
Fax: 212 481-7178
Lisa Holton, *President*
Mindee Barham, *Vice Pres*
Christopher Spivey, *Opers Staff*
Mary Schearer, *Engineer*
Jasmin Greene, *Marketing Staff*
EMP: 25
SALES: 3.4MM **Privately Held**
SIC: 7372 7379 Educational computer software; computer related consulting services

(G-9640)
CLAYTON DUBILIER & RICE FUN (PA)
375 Park Ave Fl 18 (10152-0144)
PHONE 212 407-5200
Joseph L Rice III, *Ch of Bd*
Donald J Gogel, *President*
Joanne Alves, *Vice Pres*
Eileen Smith, *Administration*
▲ EMP: 50 EST: 1985
SALES: 3.1MM **Privately Held**
SIC: 3825 3661 3812 3577 Test equipment for electronic & electric measurement; digital test equipment, electronic & electrical circuits; telephone & telegraph apparatus; switching equipment, telephone; headsets, telephone; search & navigation equipment; computer peripheral equipment; computer terminals; prepackaged software

GEOGRAPHIC SECTION

New York - New York County (G-9666)

(G-9641)
CLEAR CHANNEL OUTDOOR INC
Also Called: Eller
99 Park Ave Fl 2 (10016-1602)
PHONE..................................212 812-0000
Craig Gangi, *Exec VP*
David Sailer, *Exec VP*
Anita Green, *Manager*
Nick Wilkowith, *Manager*
EMP: 16
SALES (corp-wide): 6.2B **Publicly Held**
WEB: www.clearchanneloutdoor.com
SIC: 2759 Posters, including billboards: printing
HQ: Clear Channel Outdoor, Inc
    2325 E Camelback Rd # 400
    Phoenix AZ 85016

(G-9642)
CLEVER GOATS MEDIA LLC
40 Exchange Pl Ste 1602 (10005-2727)
PHONE..................................917 512-0340
Lionel Crear,
EMP: 5
SALES (est): 312.6K **Privately Held**
SIC: 7372 Home entertainment computer software

(G-9643)
CLINIQUE SERVICES INC (DH)
767 5th Ave (10153-0023)
PHONE..................................212 572-4200
Lynne Greene, *Ch of Bd*
William P Lauder, *President*
Natalie Glassman, *Regional Mgr*
Melissa Knapp, *Senior VP*
Joan Poulton, *Senior VP*
EMP: 9
SALES (est): 3.2MM
SALES (corp-wide): 11.2B **Publicly Held**
SIC: 2844 Toilet preparations
HQ: Clinique Laboratories, Inc.
    767 5th Ave Fl 41
    New York NY 10153
    212 572-4200

(G-9644)
CLO-SHURE INTL INC (PA)
224 W 35th St Ste 1000 (10001-2533)
PHONE..................................212 268-5029
Cory Liner, *Principal*
▲ EMP: 7
SALES (est): 1.1MM **Privately Held**
SIC: 3965 Fasteners, buttons, needles & pins

(G-9645)
CLOUDSENSE INC
1325 Avenue Of The Flr 28 (10019)
PHONE..................................917 880-6195
Jonathan Douglas, *Exec VP*
EMP: 6
SALES (est): 498K **Privately Held**
SIC: 7372 Prepackaged software

(G-9646)
CLP PB LLC (PA)
Also Called: Perseus Books Group
250 W 57th St Fl 15 (10107-1307)
PHONE..................................212 340-8100
Fax: 212 340-8105
Meghan Vortherms, *Publisher*
Krista Anderson, *Editor*
Tim Bartlett, *Editor*
Fred Francis, *Editor*
Claire Ivett, *Editor*
◆ EMP: 40
SQ FT: 16,800
SALES (est): 229.8MM **Privately Held**
WEB: www.perseusbooks.com
SIC: 2721 Comic books: publishing only, not printed on site

(G-9647)
CLUB MONACO US INC
601 W 26th St Rm 800 (10001-1127)
PHONE..................................212 886-2660
John Mehas, *President*
Merritt Shwedel, *Director*
EMP: 7
SALES (est): 568.1K
SALES (corp-wide): 7.4B **Publicly Held**
SIC: 2389 Men's miscellaneous accessories

PA: Ralph Lauren Corporation
    650 Madison Ave Fl C1
    New York NY 10022
    212 318-7000

(G-9648)
CLYDE DUNEIER INC (PA)
415 Madison Ave Fl 6 (10017-7929)
PHONE..................................212 398-1122
Dana Duneier, *CEO*
Mark Duneier, *President*
Clyde Duneier, *Corp Secy*
Eddie Garcia, *IT/INT Sup*
▲ EMP: 100
SQ FT: 12,000
SALES (est): 13.8MM **Privately Held**
SIC: 3911 5094 Pearl jewelry, natural or cultured; rings, finger: precious metal; jewelry & precious stones

(G-9649)
CMX MEDIA LLC
Also Called: Complex Magazine
1271 Av Of The Americas (10020-1300)
PHONE..................................917 793-5831
Fax: 917 868-5168
Rich Antoniello, *CEO*
Aleksey Baksheyev, *President*
Moksha Fitzgibbons, *President*
Alvaro Gomez, *President*
Bradley Carbone, *General Mgr*
▲ EMP: 20
SALES (est): 4.7MM **Privately Held**
WEB: www.complex.com
SIC: 2721 Magazines: publishing & printing

(G-9650)
CO2 TEXTILES LLC (PA)
88 Greenwich St Apt 1507 (10006-2238)
PHONE..................................212 269-2222
Melody Levy,
EMP: 3
SALES (est): 1.6MM **Privately Held**
SIC: 2295 Laminating of fabrics

(G-9651)
COACH INC
10 Columbus Cir Ste 101a (10019-1183)
PHONE..................................212 581-4115
Sunshine Sarff, *Manager*
EMP: 15
SALES (corp-wide): 4.4B **Publicly Held**
WEB: www.coach.com
SIC: 3171 Handbags, women's
PA: Coach, Inc.
    10 Hudson Yards
    New York NY 10001
    212 594-1850

(G-9652)
COACH INC
620 5th Ave Frnt 3 (10020-2477)
PHONE..................................212 245-4148
Jack Railing, *Branch Mgr*
EMP: 15
SALES (corp-wide): 4.4B **Publicly Held**
WEB: www.coach.com
SIC: 3171 Handbags, women's
PA: Coach, Inc.
    10 Hudson Yards
    New York NY 10001
    212 594-1850

(G-9653)
COACH INC
143 Prince St Frnt A (10012-3113)
PHONE..................................212 473-6925
Fax: 212 473-6927
Sue Vo, *Vice Pres*
Tim Zawrotney, *Branch Mgr*
Amie Kramer, *Athletic Dir*
EMP: 20
SALES (corp-wide): 4.4B **Publicly Held**
WEB: www.coach.com
SIC: 3171 Handbags, women's
PA: Coach, Inc.
    10 Hudson Yards
    New York NY 10001
    212 594-1850

(G-9654)
COACH INC
595 Madison Ave Frnt 1 (10022-1907)
PHONE..................................212 754-0041
Quinn Barker, *Vice Pres*
Elizabeth Leete, *Vice Pres*

Joe Tate, *Vice Pres*
Courtney Henry, *Branch Mgr*
Michelle Lemay, *Manager*
EMP: 15
SALES (corp-wide): 4.4B **Publicly Held**
WEB: www.coach.com
SIC: 3171 Handbags, women's
PA: Coach, Inc.
    10 Hudson Yards
    New York NY 10001
    212 594-1850

(G-9655)
COACH INC
79 5th Ave Frnt 3 (10003-3034)
PHONE..................................212 675-6403
Jenn Wagner, *Manager*
EMP: 15
SALES (corp-wide): 4.4B **Publicly Held**
WEB: www.coach.com
SIC: 3171 Handbags, women's
PA: Coach, Inc.
    10 Hudson Yards
    New York NY 10001
    212 594-1850

(G-9656)
COACH INC (PA)
10 Hudson Yards (10001-2157)
PHONE..................................212 594-1850
Victor Luis, *CEO*
Jide Zeitlin, *Ch of Bd*
Ian Bickley, *President*
Andre Cohen, *President*
Angus McRae, *Exec VP*
◆ EMP: 277
SALES: 4.4B **Publicly Held**
WEB: www.coach.com
SIC: 3171 3172 2387 3143 Women's handbags & purses; handbags, women's; purses, women's; personal leather goods; apparel belts; men's footwear, except athletic; women's footwear, except athletic

(G-9657)
COACH LEATHERWARE INTL
516 W 34th St Bsmt 5 (10001-1394)
PHONE..................................212 594-1850
Fax: 212 594-1682
EMP: 4
SALES (est): 1.1MM
SALES (corp-wide): 4.4B **Publicly Held**
WEB: www.coach.com
SIC: 3171 Handbags, women's
PA: Coach, Inc.
    10 Hudson Yards
    New York NY 10001
    212 594-1850

(G-9658)
COACH SERVICES INC
516 W 34th St Bsmt 5 (10001-1394)
PHONE..................................212 594-1850
▲ EMP: 7
SALES (est): 861.8K
SALES (corp-wide): 4.4B **Publicly Held**
WEB: www.coach.com
SIC: 3171 Handbags, women's
PA: Coach, Inc.
    10 Hudson Yards
    New York NY 10001
    212 594-1850

(G-9659)
COACH STORES INC
Also Called: Coach Leatherware Company
516 W 34th St Bsmt 5 (10001-1394)
PHONE..................................212 643-9727
Fax: 212 594-8790
Lewis Frankfort, *CEO*
▲ EMP: 3000
SALES (est): 203.3MM **Privately Held**
SIC: 3171 3161 3172 2387 Handbags, women's; briefcases; personal leather goods; apparel belts; handbags, apparel belts, women's & children's; cases, carrying

(G-9660)
COALITION ON POSITIVE HEALTH
1751 Park Ave Fl 4 (10035-2809)
PHONE..................................212 633-2500
Gloria Searson, *Director*
EMP: 14

SALES: 475.6K **Privately Held**
SIC: 7372 Educational computer software

(G-9661)
COCKPIT USA INC
15 W 39th St Fl 12 (10018-0628)
PHONE..................................212 575-1616
Jane Chal, *CFO*
Jacky Clyman, *Branch Mgr*
EMP: 12
SALES (corp-wide): 4.4MM **Privately Held**
WEB: www.avirex.com
SIC: 2386 5136 5611 5961 Coats & jackets, leather & sheep-lined; sportswear, men's & boys'; clothing, sportswear, men's & boys'; clothing, mail order (except women's)
PA: Cockpit Usa, Inc.
    15 W 39th St Fl 12
    New York NY 10018
    212 575-1616

(G-9662)
COCKPIT USA INC (PA)
Also Called: Cockpit, The
15 W 39th St Fl 12 (10018-0628)
PHONE..................................212 575-1616
Jeffrey Clyman, *President*
Jacky Clyman, *President*
Tammy Butler, *Production*
Nestor Sanchez, *Design Engr*
Lydia Yap, *Controller*
▲ EMP: 15
SQ FT: 5,000
SALES (est): 4.4MM **Privately Held**
WEB: www.avirex.com
SIC: 2386 5136 5611 5961 Coats & jackets, leather & sheep-lined; sportswear, men's & boys'; clothing, sportswear, men's & boys'; clothing, mail order (except women's)

(G-9663)
COCKPIT USA INC
15 W 39th St Fl 12 (10018-0628)
PHONE..................................908 558-9704
Andrew Baljeet, *Manager*
EMP: 10
SALES (corp-wide): 4.4MM **Privately Held**
WEB: www.avirex.com
SIC: 2386 Leather & sheep-lined clothing
PA: Cockpit Usa, Inc.
    15 W 39th St Fl 12
    New York NY 10018
    212 575-1616

(G-9664)
CODESTERS INC
900 Broadway Ste 903 (10003-1223)
PHONE..................................646 232-1025
Gordon Smith, *CEO*
Manesh Patel, *Treasurer*
EMP: 7
SQ FT: 4,500
SALES (est): 217K **Privately Held**
SIC: 2731 Textbooks: publishing & printing

(G-9665)
COGNOTION INC
1407 Broadway Fl 24 (10018-5101)
PHONE..................................347 692-0640
Joanna Schneier, *CEO*
Jonathan Dariyanani, *President*
Michael Goldberg, *CFO*
EMP: 4 EST: 2013
SQ FT: 1,000
SALES (est): 8MM **Privately Held**
SIC: 7372 Educational computer software

(G-9666)
COLGAT-PLMOLIVE CENTL AMER INC (HQ)
300 Park Ave (10022-7402)
PHONE..................................212 310-2000
Ian Cook, *Ch of Bd*
EMP: 9
SALES (est): 10.5MM
SALES (corp-wide): 16B **Publicly Held**
SIC: 2844 Toothpastes or powders, dentifrices
PA: Colgate-Palmolive Company
    300 Park Ave Fl 5
    New York NY 10022
    212 310-2000

New York - New York County (G-9667) — **GEOGRAPHIC SECTION**

(G-9667)
COLGATE-PALMOLIVE COMPANY (PA)
300 Park Ave Fl 5 (10022-7499)
PHONE..................212 310-2000
Fax: 212 310-2147
Ian Cook, *Ch of Bd*
Franck Moison, *President*
Gary Palmietto, *President*
Taylor Gordy, *General Mgr*
Issam Bachaalani, *Managing Dir*
▲ EMP: 3000
SALES: 16B Publicly Held
WEB: www.colgate.com
SIC: 2844 3991 2841 2842 Toothpastes or powders, dentifrices; mouthwashes; deodorants, personal; shaving preparations; toothbrushes, except electric; soap & other detergents; detergents, synthetic organic or inorganic alkaline; dishwashing compounds; soap: granulated, liquid, cake, flaked or chip; specialty cleaning, polishes & sanitation goods; fabric softeners; bleaches, household: dry or liquid; dog & cat food

(G-9668)
COLGATE-PALMOLIVE GLOBL TRDG
300 Park Ave Fl 8 (10022-7499)
PHONE..................212 310-2000
Bill Shanahan, *President*
Jacklyn Pierre, *QC Mgr*
EMP: 5
SALES (est): 471.3K
SALES (corp-wide): 16B Publicly Held
WEB: www.colgate.com
SIC: 2844 Toothpastes or powders, dentifrices
PA: Colgate-Palmolive Company
   300 Park Ave Fl 5
   New York NY 10022
   212 310-2000

(G-9669)
COLGATE-PALMOLIVE NJ INC
300 Park Ave Fl 8 (10022-7499)
PHONE..................212 310-2000
Fax: 212 310-3301
Bill Shanahan, *President*
EMP: 20
SALES (est): 2.7MM
SALES (corp-wide): 16B Publicly Held
WEB: www.colgate.com
SIC: 2841 Soap & other detergents
PA: Colgate-Palmolive Company
   300 Park Ave Fl 5
   New York NY 10022
   212 310-2000

(G-9670)
COLLECTION XIIX LTD (PA)
1370 Broadway Fl 17 (10018-7764)
PHONE..................212 686-8990
Fax: 212 683-4789
Andrew Pizzo, *President*
Sean Rimler, *Exec VP*
Ron D'Angelo, *Senior VP*
Ron Dangelo, *Senior VP*
Suzan Kressel, *Vice Pres*
▲ EMP: 10
SQ FT: 14,000
SALES (est): 122MM Privately Held
WEB: www.collection18.com
SIC: 2339 Women's & misses' accessories

(G-9671)
COLONY HOLDINGS INTL LLC
131 W 35th St Fl 6 (10001-2111)
PHONE..................212 868-2800
Douglas Chan, *CEO*
EMP: 10
SALES: 950K Privately Held
SIC: 2321 Men's & boys' furnishings

(G-9672)
COLOR MERCHANTS INC
Also Called: Trac Tech
6 E 45th St Fl 17 (10017-2451)
PHONE..................212 682-4788
Fax: 212 682-1206
Keven Peck, *President*
Helene Packer, *Vice Pres*
Meir Strobel, *Marketing Mgr*
Gina Hartwig, *Director*
EMP: 25
SQ FT: 3,100
SALES (est): 2.1MM Privately Held
WEB: www.colormerchants.com
SIC: 3911 8742 Jewelry, precious metal; materials mgmt. (purchasing, handling, inventory) consultant

(G-9673)
COLOR UNLIMITED INC
244 5th Ave Frnt (10001-7604)
PHONE..................212 802-7547
Henri Boll, *Principal*
EMP: 5
SQ FT: 1,200
SALES: 100K Privately Held
WEB: www.go2museum.com
SIC: 2741 Art copy: publishing & printing

(G-9674)
COLORFAST
121 Varick St Fl 9 (10013-1408)
PHONE..................212 929-2440
John R Arbucci, *President*
Ira Schwidel, *Vice Pres*
Winnie Xil, *Bookkeeper*
EMP: 15
SALES (est): 1MM Privately Held
WEB: www.vividcolorinternational.com
SIC: 2752 Commercial printing, offset

(G-9675)
COLORS FASHION INC
Also Called: Cliquer's
901 Avenue Of The Ste 153 (10001)
PHONE..................212 629-0401
Fax: 212 629-6367
John Kim, *President*
EMP: 10
SQ FT: 10,000
SALES: 2.5MM Privately Held
SIC: 2711 Newspapers, publishing & printing

(G-9676)
COLORTEX INC
1202 Lexington Ave 115 (10028-1439)
P.O. Box 115 (10028-0015)
PHONE..................212 564-2000
Steven Usdan, *President*
▲ EMP: 5
SQ FT: 10,000
SALES (est): 412.8K Privately Held
SIC: 2281 5199 Yarn spinning mills; yarns

(G-9677)
COLUMBIA RECORDS INC
25 Madison Ave Fl 19 (10010-8601)
PHONE..................212 833-8000
Steven E Kober, *CEO*
Bob Semanovich, *VP Mktg*
Audra Kahn, *Marketing Staff*
Garrett Schaefer, *Marketing Staff*
James Grosso, *Manager*
EMP: 17
SALES (est): 2.5MM
SALES (corp-wide): 69.2B Privately Held
SIC: 3652 Pre-recorded records & tapes
HQ: Sony Music Entertainment, Inc.
   25 Madison Ave Fl 19
   New York NY 10010
   212 833-8500

(G-9678)
COLUMBIA UNIVERSITY PRESS INC (HQ)
61 W 62nd St Fl 3 (10023-7015)
PHONE..................212 459-0600
Robert Sedgwick, *Editor*
Dominic Scarpelli, *Sales Mgr*
Todd Lazarus, *Marketing Mgr*
Kevin Kurtz, *Marketing Staff*
Anne McCoy, *Manager*
▲ EMP: 23
SQ FT: 31,500
SALES: 9.4MM
SALES (corp-wide): 3.8B Privately Held
SIC: 2731 Books: publishing only; pamphlets: publishing only, not printed on site
PA: The Trustees Of Columbia University In The City Of New York
   116th And Bdwy Way
   New York NY 10027
   212 854-9970

(G-9679)
COLUMBIA UNIVERSITY PRESS INC
61 W 62nd St Fl 3 (10023-7015)
PHONE..................212 459-0600
EMP: 37
SALES (corp-wide): 3.8B Privately Held
SIC: 2731 Books: publishing only
HQ: Columbia University Press Inc
   61 W 62nd St Fl 3
   New York NY 10023
   212 459-0600

(G-9680)
COLUMBIA UNIVERSITY PRESS INC
61 W 62nd St Fl 3 (10023-7015)
PHONE..................212 459-0600
Angela Ajayi, *Branch Mgr*
EMP: 50
SALES (corp-wide): 3.8B Privately Held
SIC: 2731 5192 Books: publishing only; pamphlets: publishing only, not printed on site; books
HQ: Columbia University Press Inc
   61 W 62nd St Fl 3
   New York NY 10023
   212 459-0600

(G-9681)
COLUMBUS TRADING CORP
Also Called: Columbus Accessories
120 W 31st St Rm 600 (10001-3407)
PHONE..................212 564-1780
Fax: 212 564-1787
Chin C S Kim, *President*
Sue Chung, *Office Mgr*
▲ EMP: 15
SALES (est): 1.4MM Privately Held
SIC: 3961 Costume jewelry

(G-9682)
COMELY INTERNATIONAL TRDG INC
303 5th Ave Rm 1903 (10016-6658)
PHONE..................212 683-1240
Fax: 212 683-4049
Qinghe Liu, *President*
Xu Sue Wang, *Vice Pres*
▲ EMP: 5
SQ FT: 1,800
SALES (est): 2.4MM Privately Held
WEB: www.comelyinternational.com
SIC: 2519 Furniture, household: glass, fiberglass & plastic

(G-9683)
COMINT APPAREL GROUP LLC (PA)
463 7th Ave Fl 4 (10018-8725)
P.O. Box 630, Englewood NJ (07631-0630)
PHONE..................212 947-7474
Graciala Donzin, *Controller*
Carlos Donzis, *Mng Member*
Graciela Donzis,
▲ EMP: 10
SQ FT: 4,000
SALES (est): 3.1MM Privately Held
WEB: www.comintapparel.com
SIC: 2339 Women's & misses' outerwear

(G-9684)
COMMENTARY INC
165 E 56th St Fl 16 (10022-2709)
PHONE..................212 891-1400
Fax: 212 751-1174
Davi Birnstein, *Publisher*
Neal Kozodoy, *Editor*
EMP: 10
SALES: 2.5MM Privately Held
SIC: 2721 Magazines: publishing & printing

(G-9685)
COMMERCIAL GASKETS NEW YORK
247 W 38th St Rm 409 (10018-1047)
PHONE..................212 244-8130
Stewart Shabman, *Principal*
EMP: 11
SALES (est): 1.3MM Privately Held
SIC: 3053 Packing, metallic

(G-9686)
COMMIFY TECHNOLOGY ✪
228 Park Ave S (10003-1502)
PHONE..................917 603-1822
Michael Osborn, *CEO*
EMP: 10 EST: 2016
SALES (est): 237.2K Privately Held
SIC: 7372 Prepackaged software

(G-9687)
COMMONWEAL FOUNDATION INC
Also Called: Commonweal Magazine
475 Riverside Dr Rm 405 (10115-0433)
PHONE..................212 662-4200
Fax: 212 662-4183
Thomas Baker, *President*
James Hannan, *Business Mgr*
Paul Kane, *Business Mgr*
Steven Aubrey, *Manager*
Matthew Boudvay, *Assoc Editor*
EMP: 10 EST: 1924
SALES: 1.5MM Privately Held
WEB: www.catholicsinpublicsquare.org
SIC: 2721 Magazines: publishing only, not printed on site

(G-9688)
COMMONWEALTH TOY NOVELTY INC (PA)
45 W 25th St Fl 7 (10010-2037)
PHONE..................212 242-4070
Fax: 212 645-4279
Steven Greenfield, *Ch of Bd*
Lee Schneider, *President*
Matt Giordano, *Controller*
◆ EMP: 45 EST: 1934
SQ FT: 16,000
SALES (est): 7MM Privately Held
SIC: 3942 Stuffed toys, including animals

(G-9689)
COMMUNITY MEDIA LLC
Also Called: Downtown Express Newspaper
515 Canal St Fl 1 (10013-1330)
PHONE..................212 229-1890
Fax: 212 229-2790
Zera Mussa, *Business Mgr*
Laura Rubin, *Accounts Exec*
John Sutter,
EMP: 20
SALES (est): 1.1MM Privately Held
WEB: www.communitymedialc.com
SIC: 2711 2752 Newspapers; commercial printing, lithographic

(G-9690)
COMPAR MANUFACTURING CORP
308 Dyckman St (10034-5351)
PHONE..................212 304-2777
Alex Neuburger, *President*
Steven Neuburger, *Vice Pres*
EMP: 50 EST: 1965
SALES (est): 3.2MM
SALES (corp-wide): 10MM Privately Held
SIC: 3496 3469 Miscellaneous fabricated wire products; metal stampings
PA: Magic Novelty Co., Inc.
   308 Dyckman St
   New York NY 10034
   212 304-2777

(G-9691)
COMPLETE PUBLISHING SOLUTIONS
Also Called: CPS Creative
350 W 51st St Apt 13b (10019-6445)
PHONE..................212 242-7321
James Hohl, *Mng Member*
EMP: 5
SQ FT: 900
SALES (est): 337.6K Privately Held
WEB: www.cpspress.com
SIC: 2741 Miscellaneous publishing

(G-9692)
COMPLEX MEDIA INC (PA)
1271 Avenue Of Americas (10020)
PHONE..................917 793-5831
Richard Antoniello, *President*
Cheryl Lomaglio, *Opers Mgr*
Richard Sheldon, *CFO*
Brandon Dixon, *Manager*

▲ = Import ▼ = Export ◆ = Import/Export

Jason Killgore, *Manager*
EMP: 9
SALES (est): 10.8MM **Privately Held**
SIC: 2721 Periodicals

(G-9693)
CONCEPTS NYC INC
20 W 33rd St Fl 9 (10001-3305)
PHONE.................................212 244-1033
Joseph Bibi, *President*
Michael Cohen, *Division Mgr*
Reuben J Bibi, *Principal*
Elliott J Bibi, *Vice Pres*
▲ **EMP:** 25
SALES (est): 3.2MM **Privately Held**
SIC: 2221 Apparel & outerwear fabric, manmade fiber or silk

(G-9694)
CONCORD JEWELRY MFG CO LLC
Also Called: Concord Jwlry Mfrs
64 W 48th St Ste 1004 (10036-1708)
PHONE.................................212 719-4030
Ann Seregi, *President*
EMP: 25 **EST:** 1951
SALES (est): 1.8MM **Privately Held**
SIC: 3911 Jewelry, precious metal

(G-9695)
CONCORDE APPAREL COMPANY LLC (PA)
55 W 39th St Fl 11 (10018-3803)
PHONE.................................212 307-7848
Roberta Kromko, *Controller*
Lee Wattenburg,
Paul Wattenburg,
▲ **EMP:** 5
SALES: 20.7MM **Privately Held**
SIC: 2311 Men's & boys' suits & coats

(G-9696)
CONDE NAST (PA)
750 3rd Ave Fl 8 (10017-2703)
PHONE.................................212 630-3642
Charles H Townsend, *CEO*
Robert A Sauerberg Jr, *President*
John Bellando, *COO*
EMP: 30
SALES (est): 7.2MM **Privately Held**
SIC: 2721 2731 Periodicals: publishing only; magazines: publishing & printing; book publishing; books: publishing & printing

(G-9697)
CONDE NAST INTERNATIONAL INC (PA)
Also Called: Cond Nast's
1 World Trade Ctr (10007-0089)
PHONE.................................212 286-2860
Fax: 212 524-6902
Charles H Townsend, *CEO*
Robert A Sauerberg Jr, *CEO*
Edward Menicheschi, *President*
Gina Sanders, *President*
Fred Santarpia, *Exec VP*
EMP: 86
SALES (est): 322.5MM **Privately Held**
SIC: 2721 Magazines: publishing & printing

(G-9698)
CONDECO SOFTWARE INC (DH)
370 Lexington Ave Rm 1409 (10017-6583)
PHONE.................................917 677-7600
Martin Brooker, *COO*
John T Anderson, *Officer*
EMP: 28
SALES (est): 6.2MM
SALES (corp-wide): 293.9K **Privately Held**
SIC: 7372 Prepackaged software
HQ: Condeco Limited
Exchange Tower
London E14 9
207 001-2020

(G-9699)
CONFERENCE BOARD INC (PA)
845 3rd Ave Fl 2 (10022-6600)
PHONE.................................212 759-0900
Fax: 212 339-0238
Jonathan Spector, *President*
Matteo Tonello, *Managing Dir*
Al Vogl, *Editor*
Jason Cross, *Pastor*
Samuel A Dipiazza, *Trustee*
EMP: 180
SQ FT: 49,750
SALES (est): 25.4MM **Privately Held**
WEB: www.conference-board.org
SIC: 2721 8299 Periodicals: publishing only; educational service, nondegree granting: continuing educ.

(G-9700)
CONGRESS FOR JEWISH CULTURE
Also Called: Di Zukunft
1133 Broadway Ste 1019 (10010-7996)
P.O. Box 1590 (10159-1590)
PHONE.................................212 505-8040
Barnett Zumoff, *President*
Shane Baker, *Exec Dir*
EMP: 5
SQ FT: 800
SALES: 94.2K **Privately Held**
SIC: 2731 2721 7922 Book music: publishing only, not printed on site; periodicals: publishing only; theatrical producers & services; theatrical producers

(G-9701)
CONKUR PRINTING CO INC
121 Varick St Rm 400 (10013-1451)
PHONE.................................212 541-5980
Fax: 212 541-5376
Walter Pflumm, *President*
Patricia Pflumm, *Vice Pres*
EMP: 22
SQ FT: 20,000
SALES (est): 2.8MM **Privately Held**
WEB: www.proprintsolutions.com
SIC: 2752 Commercial printing, offset

(G-9702)
CONNECTIVA SYSTEMS INC
19 W 44th St Ste 611 (10036-5900)
PHONE.................................646 722-8741
AVI Basu, *President*
Andrew Doyle, *Vice Pres*
Kaustav Ghosh, *Vice Pres*
Adam Maghrouri, *Vice Pres*
Shankar Mazumder, *Accounts Mgr*
EMP: 350
SALES (est): 33.8MM **Privately Held**
WEB: www.connectivasystems.com
SIC: 3695 Computer software tape & disks: blank, rigid & floppy

(G-9703)
CONSOLIDATED CHILDRENS AP INC (HQ)
Also Called: Bonjour For Kids
100 W 33rd St Ste 1105 (10001-2923)
PHONE.................................212 239-8615
Mark Adjmi, *President*
Jack Adjmi, *Chairman*
Joy Mahana, *Treasurer*
▲ **EMP:** 3
SALES: 8.2MM
SALES (corp-wide): 33.3MM **Privately Held**
SIC: 2361 Girls' & children's dresses, blouses & shirts; dresses: girls', children's & infants'; blouses: girls', children's & infants'; shirts: girls', children's & infants'
PA: Adjmi Apparel Group Llc
463 Fashion Ave Fl 4
New York NY 10018
212 594-5511

(G-9704)
CONSOLIDATED COLOR PRESS INC
307 7th Ave Rm 602 (10001-6171)
PHONE.................................212 929-8197
Fax: 212 627-7530
William D Sommers Jr, *President*
Richard Somers, *Vice Pres*
Richard M Sommers, *Vice Pres*
Paul Cole, *Treasurer*
EMP: 12
SQ FT: 10,000
SALES (est): 840K **Privately Held**
SIC: 2752 2791 Commercial printing, offset; typesetting

(G-9705)
CONSOLIDATED FASHION CORP
225 W 39th St Fl 12 (10018-3129)
PHONE.................................212 719-3000
Steven Sall, *President*
Angela Sall, *Corp Secy*
EMP: 6
SALES (est): 710K **Privately Held**
SIC: 2339 Women's & misses' outerwear

(G-9706)
CONSOLIDATED LOOSE LEAF INC (PA)
989 Avnue Of The Americas (10018-5410)
PHONE.................................212 924-5800
Fax: 212 633-2461
Sol Kleinman, *President*
Martin Schneider, *Corp Secy*
EMP: 3 **EST:** 1943
SQ FT: 32,000
SALES (est): 2.7MM **Privately Held**
SIC: 2782 Looseleaf binders & devices; library binders, looseleaf

(G-9707)
CONSTELLATION BRANDS SMO LLC
111 8th Ave (10011-5201)
PHONE.................................585 396-7161
EMP: 6
SALES (est): 207.5K
SALES (corp-wide): 6.5B **Publicly Held**
SIC: 2084 Wines, brandy & brandy spirits
PA: Constellation Brands, Inc.
207 High Point Dr # 100
Victor NY 14564
585 678-7100

(G-9708)
CONSTELLIUM
830 3rd Ave Rm 901 (10022-6504)
PHONE.................................212 675-5087
Richard B Evans, *Chairman*
Rina Tran, *COO*
Didier Fontaine, *CFO*
Pierre Vareille, *Director*
EMP: 50
SALES (est): 16.6MM
SALES (corp-wide): 5.5B **Privately Held**
SIC: 3354 Aluminum extruded products
HQ: Constellium France Holdco
40 Rue Washington
Paris 75008
158 622-413

(G-9709)
CONTACTIVE INC
137 Varick St Ste 605 (10013-1105)
PHONE.................................646 476-9059
Inaki Berenguer, *CEO*
Julio Viera, *President*
EMP: 50
SALES (est): 3MM
SALES (corp-wide): 77.9MM **Privately Held**
SIC: 7372 Application computer software
PA: Fuze, Inc.
10 Wilson Rd
Cambridge MA 02138
617 453-2052

(G-9710)
CONTINUITY PUBLISHING INC
15 W 39th St Fl 9 (10018-0631)
PHONE.................................212 869-4170
Neil Adams, *President*
Kristine Adams, *Vice Pres*
Marilyn Adams, *Vice Pres*
EMP: 12
SQ FT: 4,000
SALES (est): 750K **Privately Held**
SIC: 2721 Comic books: publishing only, not printed on site

(G-9711)
CONTINUITY SOFTWARE INC
5 Penn Plz Fl 23 (10001-1810)
PHONE.................................646 216-8628
Gil Hecht, *CEO*
Steven B Santos, *Vice Pres*
Liav Even-Chen, *CFO*
Doron Pinhas, *CTO*
Giza Venture Fund, *Shareholder*
EMP: 31
SALES (est): 3.1MM **Privately Held**
SIC: 3695 Computer software tape & disks: blank, rigid & floppy

(G-9712)
CONTINUUM INTL PUBG GROUP INC
15 W 26th St Fl 8 (10010-1065)
PHONE.................................646 649-4215
Fax: 212 953-5944
EMP: 12
SALES (corp-wide): 173.2MM **Privately Held**
SIC: 2731 Book Publishers
HQ: The Continuum International Publishing Group Inc
175 5th Ave Lbby 5
New York NY

(G-9713)
CONVENIENCE STORE NEWS
770 Broadway Fl 5 (10003-9554)
PHONE.................................214 217-7800
Maureen Arzato, *Principal*
Don Longo, *Editor*
EMP: 5
SALES (est): 341.5K **Privately Held**
WEB: www.csnews.com
SIC: 2721 Magazines: publishing & printing

(G-9714)
CONVERSANT LLC
150 E 62nd St (10065-8124)
PHONE.................................212 471-9570
Brian Belhumeur, *Branch Mgr*
EMP: 5
SALES (corp-wide): 6.4B **Publicly Held**
WEB: www.valueclick.com
SIC: 7372 Business oriented computer software
HQ: Conversant, Llc
30699 Russell Ranch Rd # 250
Westlake Village CA 91362
818 575-4500

(G-9715)
COOKIE PNACHE BY BET THE BREAD
250 W 54th St (10019-5515)
PHONE.................................212 757-4145
Ricky I Eisen, *President*
Andrew Dunnavant, *General Mgr*
Stephanie Hanan, *Mktg Dir*
EMP: 6 **EST:** 2004
SALES (est): 389.6K **Privately Held**
SIC: 2052 5149 Cookies; crackers, cookies & bakery products

(G-9716)
COOKIES INC
Also Called: Carnival
1 E 33rd St Fl 6 (10016-5011)
PHONE.................................646 452-5552
Charles Dweck, *President*
Mitch Melamed, *Director*
▲ **EMP:** 575
SALES (est): 31MM **Privately Held**
SIC: 2353 5947 Hats, trimmed: women's, misses' & children's; gift, novelty & souvenir shop

(G-9717)
COOKS INTL LTD LBLTY CO
7 World Trade Ctr Fl 46 (10007-2337)
PHONE.................................212 741-4407
Henry Mandil,
▲ **EMP:** 5
SQ FT: 1,500
SALES (est): 270K **Privately Held**
SIC: 2999 3567 Fuel briquettes or boulets: made with petroleum binder; metal melting furnaces, industrial: electric

(G-9718)
COPEN UNITED LLC
37 W 39th St Rm 603 (10018-0597)
PHONE.................................212 819-0008
EMP: 7
SALES (est): 771.7K **Privately Held**
SIC: 2299 Ramie yarn, thread, roving & textiles
PA: Selecta International Limited
Rm 11-13 16/F One Midtown
Tsuen Wan NT
279 992-80

New York - New York County (G-9719)

(G-9719)
COPIA INTERACTIVE LLC
105 Madison Ave (10016-7418)
PHONE..................212 481-0520
Farimah Schuerman, *Senior VP*
Seth Kaufman, *Vice Pres*
Joann Spyker, *Vice Pres*
EMP: 20
SALES (est): 1.7MM **Privately Held**
SIC: 2711 Newspapers, publishing & printing

(G-9720)
COPY COLOR INC
Also Called: Graphic For Industry
307 W 36th St Fl 10 (10018-6474)
PHONE..................212 889-6202
Fax: 212 545-1276
Mark Palmer, *President*
EMP: 10
SQ FT: 5,000
SALES (est): 1MM **Privately Held**
SIC: 2759 Screen printing

(G-9721)
COPY ROOM INC
885 3rd Ave Lowr 2ll (10022-4804)
PHONE..................212 371-8600
Fax: 212 980-3852
George Dispigno, *President*
Chris Dispigno, *General Mgr*
EMP: 12
SQ FT: 4,000
SALES: 2.5MM **Privately Held**
WEB: www.nydmv.com
SIC: 2759 2789 7389 Commercial printing; magazines, binding; laminating service

(G-9722)
COPY4LES INC
146 W 29th St Rm 9w (10001-8207)
PHONE..................212 487-9778
Davesham Walter Panagoda, *CEO*
Ingrid Singh, *Manager*
EMP: 11
SALES (est): 2MM **Privately Held**
SIC: 3555 Copy holders, printers'

(G-9723)
CORBERTEX LLC
1412 Broadway Rm 1100 (10018-3320)
PHONE..................212 971-0008
Howard Corber, *Prgrmr*
EMP: 5
SALES (est): 310K **Privately Held**
SIC: 3552 Textile machinery

(G-9724)
COREMET TRADING INC
160 Brdwy Ste 1107 (10038)
PHONE..................212 964-3600
Fax: 212 385-8591
Leo Horowitz, *Ch of Bd*
M Elliott Czermak, *Vice Pres*
Warren Katzman, *Treasurer*
Dorothy Leibowitz, *Office Mgr*
◆ EMP: 5
SQ FT: 800
SALES (est): 1MM **Privately Held**
SIC: 1081 Metal mining exploration & development services

(G-9725)
CORINNE MCCORMACK INC
7 W 36th St Fl 9 (10018-7158)
PHONE..................212 868-7919
Corinne McCormack, *President*
Joe Mennella, *Manager*
▲ EMP: 10
SALES (est): 957.3K
SALES (corp-wide): 88.1MM **Privately Held**
WEB: www.corinnemccormack.com
SIC: 3851 Eyeglasses, lenses & frames
HQ: Fgx International Inc.
500 George Washington Hwy
Smithfield RI 02917
401 231-3800

(G-9726)
CORNING INCORPORATED
767 5th Ave Ste 2301 (10153-0012)
PHONE..................646 521-9600
Karen Nelson, *Branch Mgr*
EMP: 6
SALES (corp-wide): 9.1B **Publicly Held**
WEB: www.corning.com
SIC: 3357 Nonferrous wiredrawing & insulating
PA: Corning Incorporated
1 Riverfront Plz
Corning NY 14831
607 974-9000

(G-9727)
CORTICE BIOSCIENCES INC
1345 Avenue Of The Americ (10105-3101)
PHONE..................646 747-9090
Fax: 646 607-9677
George Farmer, *CEO*
EMP: 14
SALES (est): 2MM **Privately Held**
SIC: 2834 Pharmaceutical preparations

(G-9728)
CORTLAND INDUSTRIES INC
1400 Broadway (10018-5300)
PHONE..................212 575-2710
David White, *President*
▲ EMP: 15 EST: 2011
SALES (est): 1.1MM **Privately Held**
SIC: 2389 Disposable garments & accessories

(G-9729)
COTTON EXPRESS INC
1407 Broadway Rm 1807 (10018-2760)
PHONE..................212 921-4588
Manny Sethi, *Owner*
EMP: 20
SALES (est): 763.7K **Privately Held**
SIC: 2329 5137 Men's & boys' sportswear & athletic clothing; women's & children's clothing

(G-9730)
COTY INC (DH)
350 5th Ave Ste 2700 (10118-2700)
PHONE..................212 389-7300
Lambertus J H Becht, *Ch of Bd*
Camillo Pane, *Exec VP*
Mario Reis, *Exec VP*
Sebastien Froidefond, *Senior VP*
Jules P Kaufman, *Senior VP*
◆ EMP: 60
SALES: 4.3B **Publicly Held**
WEB: www.cotyshop.com
SIC: 2844 Toilet preparations; perfumes & colognes; cosmetic preparations
HQ: Jab Holdings B.V.
Oudeweg 147
Haarlem
232 302-866

(G-9731)
COTY US LLC (DH)
Also Called: Private Portfolio
350 5th Ave Fl C1700 (10118-0110)
PHONE..................212 389-7000
Bart Becht, *CEO*
Patrice De Talhout, *Exec VP*
Camillo Pane, *Exec VP*
Mario Reis, *Exec VP*
Jules Kaufman, *Senior VP*
▲ EMP: 130
SALES (est): 428.4MM **Publicly Held**
WEB: www.cotyinc.com
SIC: 2844 Perfumes & colognes; cosmetic preparations

(G-9732)
COUGAR SPORT INC
Also Called: Basic Formula
55 W 39th St Rm 305 (10018-3830)
PHONE..................212 947-3054
Raymond Dayan, *Ch of Bd*
Joseph Soffer, *CFO*
Giselle Dayan, *Treasurer*
Herb Neumann, *Finance Other*
Albert Safdieh, *Admin Sec*
EMP: 14
SALES (est): 1.4MM **Privately Held**
SIC: 2329 Men's & boys' sportswear & athletic clothing

(G-9733)
COUNTER EVOLUTION
37 W 17th St (10011-5503)
PHONE..................212 647-7505
Jim Malone, *Owner*
EMP: 6

SALES (est): 785K **Privately Held**
SIC: 3131 Counters

(G-9734)
COUNTESS CORPORATION
Also Called: Terani Couture
225 W 37th St Fl 12 (10018-5726)
PHONE..................212 869-7070
Fax: 212 869-7044
Daryoush Tehrant, *President*
Victor Hakim, *CPA*
Joyce Hatoum, *Accounts Exec*
▲ EMP: 8
SQ FT: 10,000
SALES (est): 910K **Privately Held**
SIC: 2337 Women's & misses' suits & coats

(G-9735)
COUNTESS MARA INC
120 W 45th St Fl 37 (10036-4041)
PHONE..................212 768-7300
Ross Gershkowitz, *President*
Ronald Griffin, *CTO*
EMP: 6
SQ FT: 3,000
SALES (est): 373.5K
SALES (corp-wide): 448MM **Privately Held**
WEB: www.randacorp.com
SIC: 2323 Neckties, men's & boys': made from purchased materials
HQ: Randa Corporation
417 5th Ave Fl 11
New York NY 10016
212 768-8800

(G-9736)
COURAGE CLOTHING CO INC
1407 Broadway Rm 3604 (10018-2365)
PHONE..................212 354-5690
Noreen Avallon, *CEO*
Ramya Jala, *Administration*
Harssen Mejicanos, *Administration*
▲ EMP: 11
SQ FT: 1,000
SALES (est): 1.1MM **Privately Held**
SIC: 2331 2326 T-shirts & tops, women's: made from purchased materials; men's & boys' work clothing

(G-9737)
COURTAULDS TEXTILES LTD
Also Called: Sara Lee Courtaulds USA
358 5th Ave Fl 6 (10001-2209)
PHONE..................212 946-8000
Jacques Moric, *Senior VP*
Shannon McKeen, *Branch Mgr*
EMP: 14 **Privately Held**
SIC: 2299 Batting, wadding, padding & fillings; felts & felt products; yarns & thread, made from non-fabric materials
PA: Courtaulds Textiles Limited
225 Bath Road
Slough BERKS
115 924-6100

(G-9738)
COUTURE INC
16 W 37th St Frnt 1 (10018-7404)
PHONE..................212 921-1166
Catherine Ansel, *Principal*
▲ EMP: 5 EST: 2007
SALES (est): 470K **Privately Held**
SIC: 2335 Wedding gowns & dresses

(G-9739)
COUTURE PRESS
200 Park Ave (10166-0005)
PHONE..................310 734-4831
Dorita Porter, *President*
Ashley Hammock, *Manager*
Amber Rodriguez, *Exec Dir*
EMP: 15
SALES (est): 593.1K **Privately Held**
SIC: 2741 Miscellaneous publishing

(G-9740)
COVE POINT HOLDINGS LLC (PA)
60 E 42nd St Rm 3210 (10165-0056)
PHONE..................212 599-3388
William C Morris, *Chairman*
EMP: 13

SALES: 27.5K **Privately Held**
SIC: 2671 2672 Paper coated or laminated for packaging; adhesive papers, labels or tapes: from purchased material

(G-9741)
CPT USA LLC (PA)
15 W 39th St Fl 12 (10018-0628)
PHONE..................212 575-1616
Jeffrey Clyman,
EMP: 24
SQ FT: 4,200
SALES (est): 20.7MM **Privately Held**
SIC: 2371 Apparel, fur

(G-9742)
CRABTREE PUBLISHING INC
350 5th Ave Ste 3304 (10118-3304)
PHONE..................212 496-5040
Fax: 800 355-7166
Steve Zito, *Chief Mktg Ofcr*
Laureen Bowman, *Marketing Staff*
Mary J Hull, *Marketing Staff*
Kathy Middleton, *Marketing Staff*
John Siemens, *Branch Mgr*
EMP: 27
SALES (corp-wide): 2.2MM **Privately Held**
WEB: www.crabtreebooks.com
SIC: 2731 Books: publishing & printing
PA: Crabtree Publishing Company Limited
616 Welland Ave
St Catharines ON L2M 5
905 682-5221

(G-9743)
CRAFT CLERICAL CLOTHES INC (PA)
Also Called: Craft Robe Co.
247 W 37th St Rm 1700 (10018-5051)
PHONE..................212 764-6122
Fax: 212 997-7318
Marvin Goldman, *President*
EMP: 8
SQ FT: 3,000
SALES: 1MM **Privately Held**
SIC: 2389 5699 Uniforms & vestments; academic vestments (caps & gowns); clergymen's vestments; uniforms; caps & gowns (academic vestments); clergy vestments

(G-9744)
CRAFTATLANTIC LLC
Also Called: Craft Atlantic
115 Greenwich Ave (10014-1915)
PHONE..................646 726-4205
Pierre Mordacq, *Mng Member*
EMP: 13
SALES (est): 1.2MM **Privately Held**
SIC: 2329 Knickers, dress (separate): men's & boys'

(G-9745)
CRAIN COMMUNICATIONS INC
Business Insurance
685 3rd Ave (10017-4024)
PHONE..................212 210-0100
Fax: 212 210-0237
Martin Ross, *Principal*
Luca Ciferri, *Editor*
Evan Cooper, *Editor*
Katherine Downing, *Editor*
Coleman Glenn, *Editor*
EMP: 200
SALES (corp-wide): 225MM **Privately Held**
WEB: www.crainsnewyork.com
SIC: 2721 7812 Magazines: publishing only, not printed on site; motion picture & video production
PA: Crain Communications, Inc.
1155 Gratiot Ave
Detroit MI 48207
313 446-6000

(G-9746)
CRAIN NEWS SERVICE
440 E 23rd St (10010-5002)
PHONE..................212 254-0890
Rance Crain, *Principal*
Elayne Glick, *Director*
EMP: 7

GEOGRAPHIC SECTION

New York - New York County (G-9773)

SALES (est): 433.6K **Privately Held**
SIC: **2711** 2721 Newspapers, publishing & printing; periodicals: publishing only; magazines: publishing & printing

(G-9747)
CRAINS NEW YORK BUSINESS
711 3rd Ave (10017-4014)
PHONE..................................212 210-0250
Jill Kaplan, *Owner*
Brian Tucker, *Publisher*
EMP: 30 **EST:** 2012
SALES (est): 2.8MM **Privately Held**
SIC: **2721** Periodicals

(G-9748)
CREATIVE COSTUME CO
242 W 36th St Rm 800 (10018-7542)
PHONE..................................212 564-5552
Susan Handler, *Partner*
Linda Carcaci, *Partner*
EMP: 7
SALES (est): 550K **Privately Held**
WEB: www.creativecostume.com
SIC: **2389** Costumes

(G-9749)
CREATIVE FORMS INC
80 Varick St Apt 10a (10013-1945)
P.O. Box 1485 (10013-0878)
PHONE..................................212 431-7540
Donald Macpherson, *President*
EMP: 5
SALES (est): 450K **Privately Held**
SIC: **2752** Commercial printing, offset

(G-9750)
CREATIVE PRINTING CORP
Also Called: Creative Prntng
121 Varick St Fl 9 (10013-1408)
PHONE..................................212 226-3870
Mark Jackson, *President*
Candice Jackson, *Corp Secy*
Dave Bird, *Vice Pres*
Doug Bird, *Vice Pres*
EMP: 7
SQ FT: 6,000
SALES (est): 622.2K **Privately Held**
WEB: www.starkey-henricks.com
SIC: **2752** Commercial printing, offset

(G-9751)
CREATIVE RELATIONS LLC
Also Called: Three Tarts
425 W 23rd St Rm 1f (10011-1436)
PHONE..................................212 462-4392
Marla Durso, *Mng Member*
Marina Brolin, *Mng Member*
EMP: 5
SALES (est): 476K **Privately Held**
WEB: www.creativerelations.net
SIC: **2051** Bakery: wholesale or wholesale/retail combined

(G-9752)
CREATIVE TOOLS & SUPPLY INC
Also Called: All Craft Jewelry Supply
135 W 29th St Rm 205 (10001-5191)
PHONE..................................212 279-7077
Fax: 212 279-6886
Tevel Herbstman, *President*
▲ **EMP:** 9
SQ FT: 2,000
SALES (est): 830K **Privately Held**
SIC: **3915** Jewelers' materials & lapidary work

(G-9753)
CREDIT UNION JOURNAL INC (PA)
Also Called: Source Media
1 State St Fl 26 (10004-1483)
PHONE..................................212 803-8200
Lisa Freeman, *Editor*
Peter Chapman, *Editor*
Allison Colter, *Editor*
Kris Frieswick, *Editor*
Yong Lim, *Editor*
EMP: 5
SALES (est): 401.6K **Privately Held**
WEB: www.cujournal.com
SIC: **2721** Magazines: publishing & printing

(G-9754)
CRESCENT WEDDING RINGS INC
36 W 47th St Ste 306 (10036-8637)
PHONE..................................212 869-8296
Fax: 212 869-2644
Mark Gebhardt, *President*
EMP: 7
SALES (est): 800K **Privately Held**
WEB: www.crescentweddingrings.com
SIC: **3911** Jewelry, precious metal

(G-9755)
CROCS INC
270 Columbus Ave (10023-2905)
PHONE..................................212 362-1655
Robert Brown, *Site Mgr*
Scott Campbell, *Manager*
EMP: 14
SALES (corp-wide): 1.2B **Publicly Held**
SIC: **3021** Shoes, rubber or rubber soled fabric uppers
PA: Crocs, Inc.
  7477 Dry Creek Pkwy
  Niwot CO 80503
  303 848-7000

(G-9756)
CROSS BORDER USA INC
Also Called: Ir Magazine
25 Broadway Fl 9 (10004-1058)
PHONE..................................212 425-9649
Ian Richman, *President*
Charlotte Beugge, *Corp Comm Staff*
Alex Aiken, *Director*
Fiona Stark, *Director*
David Sweet, *Director*
EMP: 6
SALES (corp-wide): 4MM **Privately Held**
WEB: www.irmag.com
SIC: **2731** Books: publishing only
HQ: Cross-Border Publishing (London) Limited
  111-113 Great Titchfield Street
  London

(G-9757)
CROSSWINDS SOURCING LLC
260 W 39th St Fl 10 (10018-4410)
PHONE..................................646 438-6904
Omprakash Batheja, *Mng Member*
EMP: 3
SQ FT: 2,500
SALES (est): 4.3MM
SALES (corp-wide): 5.5MM **Privately Held**
SIC: **2389** Apparel for handicapped
PA: Catalyst Management Holdings Llc
  260 W 39th St Fl 10
  New York NY 10018
  212 398-9300

(G-9758)
CROWLEY TAR PRODUCTS CO INC (PA)
305 Madison Ave Ste 1035 (10165-1036)
PHONE..................................212 682-1200
William A Callaman, *CEO*
Christopher Mortensen, *General Mgr*
William Jennings, *Principal*
John Barry, *Vice Pres*
EMP: 7
SQ FT: 10,000
SALES (est): 3.2MM **Privately Held**
WEB: www.crowleychemical.com
SIC: **2865** Cyclic crudes, coal tar; tar

(G-9759)
CROWN INDUSTRIES INC
220 W 98th St Apt 2b (10025-5669)
PHONE..................................973 672-2277
Hugh Loebner, *President*
Carmen Braime, *Vice Pres*
Mario Camerota, *Plant Mgr*
▲ **EMP:** 10
SQ FT: 25,000
SALES: 1.5MM **Privately Held**
WEB: www.gocrown.com
SIC: **3089** 3499 3993 Floor coverings, plastic; barricades, metal; displays & cutouts, window & lobby

(G-9760)
CROWN JEWELERS INTL INC
168 7th Ave S (10014-2727)
PHONE..................................212 420-7800
Neryo Shimunov, *Ch of Bd*
EMP: 5
SALES (est): 494.9K **Privately Held**
SIC: **3911** 5094 Jewelry, precious metal; jewelry

(G-9761)
CRUZIN MANAGEMENT INC (DH)
401 Park Ave S Fl 7 (10016-8808)
PHONE..................................212 641-8700
Jay S Maltby, *President*
Thomas A Valdes, *Exec VP*
D Chris Mitchell, *Senior VP*
Ousik Yu, *Senior VP*
Ezra Shashoua, *CFO*
▼ **EMP:** 50
SQ FT: 250,000
SALES (est): 34.5MM
SALES (corp-wide): 156.6MM **Privately Held**
WEB: www.cruzanrum.com
SIC: **2085** 2084 5182 Rum (alcoholic beverage); brandy; wines; liquor; wine; brandy & brandy spirits
HQ: The Absolut Spirits Company Inc
  250 Park Ave 17
  New York NY 10177
  914 848-4800

(G-9762)
CSCO LLC (PA)
Also Called: Cherry Stix
525 7th Ave Rm 1006 (10018-0458)
PHONE..................................212 221-5100
David Apperman, *CEO*
Salomon Murciano, *Vice Pres*
Penelope Savinon, *Admin Sec*
EMP: 22 **EST:** 2014
SALES (est): 3.4MM **Privately Held**
SIC: **2335** Women's, juniors' & misses' dresses

(G-9763)
CTS LLC
Also Called: Costello Tagliapietra
211 E 18th St Apt 4d (10003-3624)
PHONE..................................212 278-0058
Aby Saltiel,
Jeffrey Costello,
Regino Nieves,
Robert Tagliapietra,
EMP: 5
SQ FT: 5,000
SALES (est): 472.1K **Privately Held**
SIC: **2335** Women's, juniors' & misses' dresses

(G-9764)
CUBIC TRNSP SYSTEMS INC
245 W 17th St Fl 8 (10011-5373)
PHONE..................................212 255-1810
Michael Ordre, *Division Mgr*
Richard Trenery, *Branch Mgr*
EMP: 15
SALES (corp-wide): 1.4B **Publicly Held**
SIC: **3829** 3714 3581 Fare registers for street cars, buses, etc.; motor vehicle parts & accessories; automatic vending machines
HQ: Cubic Transportation Systems, Inc.
  5650 Kearny Mesa Rd
  San Diego CA 92111
  858 810-1314

(G-9765)
CULT RECORDS LLC
263 Bowery Apt 3 (10002-5656)
PHONE..................................718 395-2077
Julian Casablancas, *Co-Owner*
EMP: 5
SALES (est): 216K **Privately Held**
SIC: **3652** Pre-recorded records & tapes

(G-9766)
CULTUREIQ INC (PA)
7 Penn Plz Ste 1112 (10001-3390)
PHONE..................................212 755-8633
Gregory Besner, *CEO*
Jeremy Hamel, *Marketing Staff*
EMP: 6
SQ FT: 4,500
SALES (est): 3.3MM **Privately Held**
SIC: **7372** Prepackaged software

(G-9767)
CUPID FOUNDATIONS INC (PA)
Also Called: Cupid Intimates
475 Park Ave S Manhattan (10022)
PHONE..................................212 686-6224
Fax: 212 481-9357
David Welsch, *President*
Marilyn Welsch, *Corp Secy*
Ken Langston, *VP Opers*
Tom Richardson, *Sls & Mktg Exec*
Steve Canter, *CFO*
▲ **EMP:** 60 **EST:** 1943
SQ FT: 5,000
SALES (est): 64.3MM **Privately Held**
WEB: www.cshape.com
SIC: **2342** Brassieres; girdles & panty girdles

(G-9768)
CUREATR INC
222 Broadway Fl 19 (10038-2550)
PHONE..................................212 203-3927
Joseph Mayer, *CEO*
Oleksiy Khomenko, *COO*
Vik Shah, *Exec VP*
John Eads, *Executive*
EMP: 10 **EST:** 2011
SQ FT: 300
SALES (est): 710K **Privately Held**
SIC: **7372** Business oriented computer software

(G-9769)
CUREMDCOM INC
Also Called: Cure MD
120 Broadway Fl 35 (10271-3599)
PHONE..................................646 224-2201
Fax: 212 509-6206
Bilal Hashmat, *CEO*
Kamal Hashmat, *Ch of Bd*
John Fletcher, *President*
Adnan Malik, *President*
Mubeen Hayee, *Vice Pres*
EMP: 368
SQ FT: 20,000
SALES (est): 43.6MM **Privately Held**
WEB: www.curemd.com
SIC: **7372** 8621 8082 Prepackaged software; health association; home health care services

(G-9770)
CUSTOM PUBLISHING GROUP LTD
8 W 38th St 204 (10018-6229)
PHONE..................................212 840-8800
John G Ledges, *President*
EMP: 4
SQ FT: 2,000
SALES: 2.5MM **Privately Held**
SIC: **2741** Miscellaneous publishing

(G-9771)
CUSTOM SPORTS LAB INC
Also Called: U S Orthotic Center
515 Madison Ave Rm 1204 (10022-5484)
PHONE..................................212 832-1648
Jeff Rich, *President*
EMP: 5
SALES: 500K **Privately Held**
SIC: **3149** 3842 8734 Athletic shoes, except rubber or plastic; orthopedic appliances; product testing laboratory, safety or performance

(G-9772)
CUSTOMIZE ELITE SOCKS LLC
156 2nd Ave Apt 2c (10003-5759)
PHONE..................................212 533-8551
Roger Cheng, *Principal*
EMP: 5
SALES (est): 481K **Privately Held**
SIC: **2252** Socks

(G-9773)
CUSTOMSHOW INC
216 E 45th St Fl 17 (10017-3304)
PHONE..................................800 255-5303
Paul Shapiro, *CEO*
George Chevalier, *Ch of Bd*
Greg Gordon, *CTO*
EMP: 8
SQ FT: 3,000

New York - New York County (G-9774)

SALES (est): 490K **Privately Held**
SIC: 7372 Application computer software

(G-9774)
CW FASTENERS & ZIPPERS CORP
142 W 36th St Fl 5 (10018-8796)
PHONE.................................212 594-3203
Suk Chun Wong, *Principal*
EMP: 13
SALES (est): 1.5MM **Privately Held**
SIC: 3965 Fasteners; zipper

(G-9775)
CYBERLIMIT INC
257 W 38th St Fl 6 (10018-4457)
PHONE.................................212 840-9597
David MEI, *President*
EMP: 10
SQ FT: 2,000
SALES (est): 210K **Privately Held**
SIC: 2331 2321 Women's & misses' blouses & shirts; men's & boys' furnishings

(G-9776)
CYGNET STUDIO INC
251 W 39th St Fl 17 (10018-3117)
PHONE.................................646 450-4550
Daniel Ehrenard, *Mng Member*
EMP: 12
SALES (est): 943.4K **Privately Held**
SIC: 2389 Costumes

(G-9777)
CYNTHIA ROWLEY INC (PA)
376 Bleecker St (10014-3210)
PHONE.................................212 242-3803
Cynthia Rowley, *Ch of Bd*
Peter Arnold, *President*
Julia Covintree, *Production*
Utem Hynes, *Production*
Robert Shaw, *CFO*
▲ EMP: 12
SQ FT: 7,000
SALES (est): 2.1MM **Privately Held**
SIC: 2331 2335 2339 Women's & misses' blouses & shirts; women's, juniors' & misses' dresses; women's & misses' outerwear; women's & misses' accessories; women's & misses' athletic clothing & sportswear

(G-9778)
CYPRESS BIOSCIENCE INC
110 E 59th St Fl 33 (10022-1315)
PHONE.................................858 452-2323
Jay D Kranzler PHD, *Ch of Bd*
Sabrina Martucci Johnson, *COO*
Sabrina Martucci, *COO*
Larry Kessel, *Marketing Staff*
Manda Hall, *Office Mgr*
EMP: 16
SQ FT: 5,700
SALES (est): 3.3MM **Privately Held**
WEB: www.cypressbio.com
SIC: 2836 Biological products, except diagnostic

(G-9779)
CYTEXONE TECHNOLOGY LLC
50 Hudson St Fl 3 (10013-3389)
PHONE.................................212 792-6700
EMP: 8
SALES (est): 901.4K **Privately Held**
SIC: 3823 Computer interface equipment for industrial process control

(G-9780)
D & A OFFSET SERVICES INC
185 Varick St Ste 3 (10014-4607)
PHONE.................................212 924-0612
Fax: 212 924-0866
Carmine D'Elia, *President*
Al D'Elia, *President*
Henny D'Elia, *Corp Secy*
Vincent D'Elia, *Vice Pres*
EMP: 14
SQ FT: 11,000
SALES (est): 1.4MM **Privately Held**
SIC: 2796 Engraving platemaking services

(G-9781)
D & D CREATIONS CO INC
71 W 47th St Ste 606 (10036-2865)
PHONE.................................212 840-1198
Michael Avrumson, *President*
Dianna Avrumson, *Vice Pres*
EMP: 5
SQ FT: 800
SALES (est): 507.5K **Privately Held**
SIC: 3911 Jewelry, precious metal

(G-9782)
D & D WINDOW TECH INC (PA)
979 3rd Ave Lbby 132 (10022-1298)
PHONE.................................212 308-2822
Amos Regev, *President*
EMP: 5
SQ FT: 250
SALES (est): 401.6K **Privately Held**
SIC: 2591 5023 Window blinds; window shades; venetian blinds; vertical blinds; window shades

(G-9783)
D J NIGHT LTD
225 W 37th St Fl 6 (10018-6741)
PHONE.................................212 302-9050
Roholah Simhaee, *President*
EMP: 30
SALES (est): 2.4MM **Privately Held**
SIC: 2335 Gowns, formal

(G-9784)
D M J CASTING INC
62 W 47th St Ste 508 (10036-3270)
PHONE.................................212 719-1951
Fax: 212 719-1956
David Green, *President*
EMP: 5
SALES (est): 310K **Privately Held**
SIC: 3915 Jewelers' castings

(G-9785)
D R S WATCH MATERIALS
56 W 47th St Fl 2 (10036-8625)
PHONE.................................212 819-0470
Fax: 212 354-2270
Joseph Borella, *Vice Pres*
EMP: 40
SALES (est): 2MM **Privately Held**
SIC: 3915 Jewel preparing: instruments, tools, watches & jewelry

(G-9786)
DABBY-REID LTD
347 W 36th St Rm 701 (10018-7225)
PHONE.................................212 356-0040
Fax: 212 356-0049
Ida Reid, *President*
EMP: 15
SALES (est): 165.6K **Privately Held**
SIC: 3961 5094 Costume jewelry, ex. precious metal & semiprecious stones; jewelry & precious stones

(G-9787)
DAHESHIST PUBLISHING CO LTD
1775 Broadway 501 (10019-1903)
PHONE.................................212 581-8360
Fax: 212 832-7413
Mervat Zahid, *President*
EMP: 10
SQ FT: 2,500
SALES (est): 867.9K **Privately Held**
WEB: www.daheshheritage.org
SIC: 2731 Books: publishing only

(G-9788)
DAILY BEAST COMPANY LLC (HQ)
Also Called: Newsweek/Daily Beast Co LLC
7 Hanover Sq (10004-2616)
PHONE.................................212 445-4600
Goldie Taylor, *Editor*
Baba Shetty, *Mng Member*
Ryan Brown, *Director*
Thomas E Ascheim, *Editor*
Joseph Galarneau,
▲ EMP: 57 EST: 1936
SQ FT: 203,000
SALES (est): 49MM
SALES (corp-wide): 3.2B **Publicly Held**
WEB: www.newsweek.com
SIC: 2721 Magazines: publishing only, not printed on site
PA: Iac/Interactivecorp
  555 W 18th St
  New York NY 10011
  212 314-7300

(G-9789)
DAILY MUSE INC
Also Called: Muse, The
1375 Broadway Fl 20 (10018-7020)
PHONE.................................646 861-0284
Jens Fischer, *Principal*
EMP: 11
SALES (est): 520.3K **Privately Held**
SIC: 2711 Newspapers, publishing & printing

(G-9790)
DAILY NEWS LP (PA)
Also Called: New York Daily News
4 New York Plz Fl 6 (10004-2828)
PHONE.................................212 210-2100
Fax: 212 210-1942
Mort Zuckerman, *Partner*
Linda Lindus, *Publisher*
Omar Aquije, *Editor*
Maria Bailey, *Editor*
Amanda Douville, *Editor*
▲ EMP: 600
SQ FT: 150,000
SALES (est): 351.9MM **Privately Held**
WEB: www.nydailynews.com
SIC: 2711 Commercial printing & newspaper publishing combined

(G-9791)
DAILY RACING FORM
75 Broad St (10004-2415)
PHONE.................................212 514-2180
Fax: 212 366-7773
Lila Kerns, *Marketing Mgr*
EMP: 16
SALES (est): 886.2K **Privately Held**
SIC: 2711 Newspapers, publishing & printing

(G-9792)
DAILY RACING FORM INC (HQ)
708 3rd Ave Fl 12 (10017-4129)
PHONE.................................212 366-7600
Steven Crist, *President*
Irwin Cohen, *Vice Pres*
Charles Hayward, *Vice Pres*
Michael Kravchenko, *Vice Pres*
Richard Rosenbush, *Vice Pres*
▼ EMP: 140 EST: 1894
SQ FT: 34,000
SALES (est): 40MM
SALES (corp-wide): 216.1MM **Privately Held**
WEB: www.drf.com
SIC: 2741 Racing forms & programs: publishing only, not printing
PA: Arlington Capital Partners, L.P.
  5425 Wisconsin Ave # 200
  Chevy Chase MD 20815
  202 337-7500

(G-9793)
DAILY WORLD PRESS INC
Also Called: Daily Sun New York
228 E 45th St Rm 700 (10017-3336)
PHONE.................................212 922-9201
Fax: 212 922-9202
Yoshida Gin, *President*
Yoshiaki Takahashi, *Publisher*
EMP: 10
SALES (est): 460K **Privately Held**
SIC: 2711 Newspapers, publishing & printing

(G-9794)
DAILYCANDY INC
584 Broadway Rm 510 (10012-5244)
PHONE.................................646 230-8719
Fax: 646 230-8729
Danielle Levy, *Ch of Bd*
Leonora Epstein, *Editor*
Jasmine Moir, *Editor*
Catherine Levene, *COO*
Peter A Sheinbaum, *COO*
EMP: 23
SQ FT: 6,100
SALES (est): 3MM **Privately Held**
WEB: www.dailycandy.com
SIC: 2741 Miscellaneous publishing

(G-9795)
DAKOTT LLC
244 Madison Ave Ste 211 (10016-2817)
PHONE.................................888 805-6795
Michael Etedgi, *CEO*

Joshua Martin, *Exec VP*
Vera A Etedgi, *CFO*
▲ EMP: 5
SQ FT: 2,500
SALES (est): 1MM **Privately Held**
SIC: 3944 Scooters, children's

(G-9796)
DAMPITS INTERNATIONAL INC
425 W 57th St (10019-1764)
P.O. Box 493 (10019)
PHONE.................................212 581-3047
David Hollander, *President*
Tair Hollander, *Vice Pres*
EMP: 5 EST: 1966
SALES (est): 480K **Privately Held**
SIC: 3634 Humidifiers, electric: household

(G-9797)
DAN KANE PLATING CO INC
357 W 36th St (10018-6455)
PHONE.................................212 675-4947
Fax: 212 929-4276
Jack Zwas, *Owner*
EMP: 16
SQ FT: 5,000
SALES (est): 1.4MM **Privately Held**
SIC: 3471 Electroplating of metals or formed products

(G-9798)
DANA MICHELE LLC
3 E 84th St (10028-0447)
PHONE.................................917 757-7777
Dana Schiavo, *President*
EMP: 1
SQ FT: 5,000
SALES (est): 2MM **Privately Held**
SIC: 3942 3944 2339 Dolls & stuffed toys; games, toys & children's vehicles; women's & misses' outerwear

(G-9799)
DANAHER CORPORATION
445 E 14th St Apt 3f (10009-2805)
PHONE.................................516 443-9432
Alison Ng, *Engineer*
EMP: 186
SALES (corp-wide): 20.5B **Publicly Held**
SIC: 3823 Water quality monitoring & control systems
PA: Danaher Corporation
  2200 Penn Ave Nw Ste 800w
  Washington DC 20037
  202 828-0850

(G-9800)
DANGELICO GUITARS OF AMERICA
141 W 28th St Fl 4 (10001-6115)
PHONE.................................732 380-0995
John M Ferolito, *CEO*
▲ EMP: 5
SALES (est): 330K **Privately Held**
WEB: www.dangelicodirect.biz
SIC: 3931 Guitars & parts, electric & non-electric

(G-9801)
DANHIER CO LLC
Also Called: Christophe Danhier
380 Rector Pl Apt 3d (10280-1442)
PHONE.................................212 563-7683
Christophe Danhier,
EMP: 14
SQ FT: 1,200
SALES (est): 1.5MM **Privately Held**
WEB: www.danhier.com
SIC: 3915 Jewelers' materials & lapidary work

(G-9802)
DANI II INC (PA)
231 W 39th St Rm 1002 (10018-3167)
PHONE.................................212 869-5999
Kirat Singh, *CEO*
EMP: 14
SALES (est): 1.3MM **Privately Held**
SIC: 2339 Women's & misses' outerwear

(G-9803)
DANICE STORES INC
305 W 125th St (10027-3620)
PHONE.................................212 665-0389
Barry Group, *Manager*
EMP: 15

GEOGRAPHIC SECTION

New York - New York County (G-9831)

SALES (corp-wide): 40.9MM **Privately Held**
SIC: 2339 5137 Sportswear, women's; sportswear, women's & children's
PA: Danice Stores, Inc.
525 Fashion Ave Rm 507
New York NY 10018
212 776-1001

(G-9804)
DANIEL M FRIEDMAN & ASSOC INC
19 W 34th St Fl 4 (10001-3006)
PHONE 212 695-5545
Fax: 212 643-8464
Jamieson A Karson, *Ch of Bd*
Daniel M Friedman, *President*
Steve Lloyd, *CFO*
▲ **EMP:** 30
SQ FT: 5,000
SALES (est): 3.9MM
SALES (corp-wide): 1.4B **Publicly Held**
WEB: www.dmfassociates.com
SIC: 2387 Apparel belts
PA: Steven Madden, Ltd.
5216 Barnett Ave
Long Island City NY 11104
718 446-1800

(G-9805)
DANNY MACAROONS INC
2191 3rd Ave Ste 3 (10035-3520)
PHONE 260 622-8463
Daniel Cohen, *President*
EMP: 6
SALES (est): 524K **Privately Held**
SIC: 2052 Cookies & crackers

(G-9806)
DANNY R COUTURE CORP (PA)
Also Called: Danny Couture
261 W 35th St Ground Fl (10001)
PHONE 212 594-1095
Daniel Rochas, *President*
EMP: 3 **EST:** 2014
SQ FT: 5,000
SALES (est): 1MM **Privately Held**
SIC: 2389 Apparel for handicapped

(G-9807)
DANRAY TEXTILES CORP (PA)
Also Called: Dantex Trimming & Textile Co
270 W 39th St Fl 5 (10018-4409)
PHONE 212 354-5213
Fax: 212 869-9125
Daniel Bergstein, *President*
▲ **EMP:** 13
SQ FT: 2,000
SALES (est): 915.3K **Privately Held**
SIC: 2241 Trimmings, textile

(G-9808)
DANWAK JEWELRY CORP
Also Called: Daniels Jewels Art
55 W 47th St Ste 860 (10036-2849)
PHONE 212 730-4541
Daniel Waknine, *President*
EMP: 5
SALES (est): 590K **Privately Held**
WEB: www.danwak.com
SIC: 3911 5094 Jewelry, precious metal; jewelry & precious stones

(G-9809)
DARCY PRINTING AND LITHOG
121 Varick St Fl 9 (10013-1408)
PHONE 212 924-1554
James Tsiropinas, *President*
EMP: 8
SALES (est): 590K **Privately Held**
SIC: 2759 Commercial printing

(G-9810)
DARMIYAN LLC
450 E 63rd St Apt 5a (10065-7951)
PHONE 917 689-0389
Padideh Kamali-Zare, *CEO*
Thomas Liebmann, *COO*
Kaveh Vejdani, *Development*
EMP: 5
SALES (est): 229.7K **Privately Held**
SIC: 2835 7389 In vivo diagnostics;

(G-9811)
DASAN INC
54 W 39th St Fl 8 (10018-2068)
PHONE 212 244-5410
David Chabbott, *Ch of Bd*
EMP: 36
SALES (est): 4.9MM **Privately Held**
WEB: www.dasan.com
SIC: 3911 5094 Jewelry, precious metal; jewelry

(G-9812)
DASH PRINTING INC
153 W 27th St (10001-6203)
PHONE 212 643-8534
David Ashendorf, *President*
Rachel Feiner, *Exec VP*
EMP: 5
SQ FT: 1,100
SALES (est): 468.1K **Privately Held**
WEB: www.dashprinting.com
SIC: 2759 Commercial printing

(G-9813)
DATA IMPLEMENTATION INC
5 E 22nd St Apt 14t (10010-5325)
PHONE 212 979-2015
Gerald A Goldstein, *President*
William F Hahn, *Vice Pres*
Diana Goldstein, *Treasurer*
Debra Hahn, *Admin Sec*
EMP: 5
SALES (est): 410K **Privately Held**
SIC: 7372 Prepackaged software

(G-9814)
DATADOG INC (PA)
286 5th Ave Fl 12 (10001-4562)
PHONE 866 329-4466
Olivier Promel, *CEO*
Alexis Le-Quoc, *President*
Jay Milkiewicz, *Accounts Exec*
Jake Parsons, *Accounts Exec*
Alex Rosemblat, *Mktg Dir*
EMP: 33
SQ FT: 7,000
SALES (est): 9.6MM **Privately Held**
SIC: 7372 Publishers' computer software

(G-9815)
DATAMAX INTERNATIONAL INC
Also Called: Data Max
132 Nassau St Rm 511 (10038-2433)
PHONE 212 693-0933
Fax: 212 693-1706
Saul Wasser, *CEO*
Max Wasser, *Treasurer*
▲ **EMP:** 45
SQ FT: 15,000
SALES (est): 4.2MM **Privately Held**
WEB: www.datamaxplanners.com
SIC: 2782 3172 Blankbooks & looseleaf binders; diaries; personal leather goods

(G-9816)
DAVE & JOHNNY LTD
225 W 37th St Fl 6 (10018-6741)
PHONE 212 302-9050
Fax: 212 764-3827
Roholah Simhaee, *President*
▲ **EMP:** 25
SQ FT: 9,000
SALES (est): 1.8MM **Privately Held**
WEB: www.daveandjohnny.com
SIC: 2335 Women's, juniors' & misses' dresses

(G-9817)
DAVES ELECTRIC MOTORS & PUMPS
282 E 7th St Apt 1 (10009-6027)
PHONE 212 982-2930
Yefim Vinokur, *President*
EMP: 5
SQ FT: 5,600
SALES (est): 769.9K **Privately Held**
SIC: 7694 7699 Electric motor repair; pumps & pumping equipment repair

(G-9818)
DAVID & YOUNG CO INC
365 5th Ave Rm 707 (10001-2211)
PHONE 212 594-6034
Fax: 212 594-6034
John Yoo, *Owner*
EMP: 6
SALES (est): 556.6K **Privately Held**
SIC: 2389 Apparel & accessories

(G-9819)
DAVID FRIEDMAN CHAIN CO INC
Also Called: David Friedman and Sons
10 E 38th St Fl 6 (10016-0014)
PHONE 212 684-1760
Fax: 212 532-3891
Peter Banyasz, *President*
Matthew Friedman, *Vice Pres*
EMP: 15 **EST:** 1913
SQ FT: 5,000
SALES (est): 1.4MM **Privately Held**
SIC: 3911 Jewelry, precious metal

(G-9820)
DAVID ISSEKS & SONS INC
298 Broome St (10002-3704)
PHONE 212 966-8694
David Hackhauser, *President*
Joyce Hockhauser, *Exec VP*
EMP: 22
SQ FT: 5,000
SALES (est): 1.7MM **Privately Held**
SIC: 3443 7699 2449 Water tanks, metal plate; tank repair; wood containers

(G-9821)
DAVID PEYSER SPORTSWEAR INC
Also Called: 30 Degrees Weatherproof
1071 Ave Americas Fl 12 (10018)
PHONE 212 695-7716
Tony Galvao, *Exec VP*
Ken Brodsky, *CFO*
Jill Quinn, *Accounts Exec*
Eliot Peyser, *Branch Mgr*
Joyce Silverman, *Manager*
EMP: 40
SALES (corp-wide): 94.2MM **Privately Held**
WEB: www.mvsport.com
SIC: 2329 5651 Men's & boys' sportswear & athletic clothing; unisex clothing stores
PA: David Peyser Sportswear, Inc.
88 Spence St
Bay Shore NY 11706
631 231-7788

(G-9822)
DAVID S DIAMONDS INC
546 5th Ave Fl 7 (10036-5000)
PHONE 212 921-8029
David So, *Chairman*
Joan So, *Vice Pres*
EMP: 15
SQ FT: 350
SALES (est): 2.2MM **Privately Held**
WEB: www.davidsdiamonds.com
SIC: 3911 5944 Jewelry, precious metal; jewelry, precious stones & precious metals

(G-9823)
DAVID SUTHERLAND SHOWROOMS - N (PA)
D&D Building 979 3rd (10022)
PHONE 212 871-9717
Thomas William, *Principal*
EMP: 7
SALES (est): 601.7K **Privately Held**
SIC: 2511 Wood household furniture

(G-9824)
DAVID WEEKS STUDIO
38 Walker St Frnt 1 (10013-3589)
PHONE 212 966-3433
David Weeks, *President*
EMP: 18
SALES (est): 2.4MM **Privately Held**
SIC: 3645 5719 Residential lighting fixtures; lighting fixtures

(G-9825)
DAVID WEISZ & SONS INC
20 W 47th St Ste 601 (10036-3768)
PHONE 212 840-4747
Fax: 212 840-4852
David Weisz, *President*
EMP: 8
SALES (est): 890K **Privately Held**
SIC: 3911 5094 Jewelry, precious metal; diamonds (gems)

(G-9826)
DAVID YURMAN ENTERPRISES LLC (PA)
24 Vestry St (10013-1903)
PHONE 212 896-1550
Fax: 212 896-1592
Gabriella Forte, *CEO*
Melissa Anastasia, *General Mgr*
Ruth Sommers, *COO*
Cece Coffin, *Senior VP*
Kate Harrison, *Senior VP*
◆ **EMP:** 300
SQ FT: 75,000
SALES (est): 268.2MM **Privately Held**
SIC: 3911 Jewelry, precious metal

(G-9827)
DAVID YURMAN RETAIL LLC
712 Madison Ave (10065-7207)
PHONE 877 226-1400
EMP: 7
SALES (est): 881.6K
SALES (corp-wide): 275MM **Privately Held**
SIC: 3911 Mfg Precious Metal Jewelry
PA: David Yurman Enterprises Llc
24 Vestry St
New York NY 10013
212 896-1550

(G-9828)
DAVIDOFF GNEVA MADISON AVE INC
Also Called: Davidoff of Geneva Ny., Inc
515 Madison Ave (10022-5403)
PHONE 212 751-9060
Fax: 212 715-0422
James P Young, *President*
Luis Torres, *General Mgr*
Robert Seise, *Store Mgr*
Rich Krutick, *Marketing Mgr*
EMP: 7
SALES (est): 887.5K **Privately Held**
WEB: www.davidoffmadison.com
SIC: 2121 Cigars
HQ: Davidoff Of Geneva Usa Retail, Inc.
3001 Gateway Ctr Pkwy N
Pinellas Park FL 33782
727 828-5400

(G-9829)
DAVIS ZIFF PUBLISHING INC (DH)
Also Called: Ziff-Davis Publishing
28 E 28th St Fl 10 (10016-7939)
PHONE 212 503-3500
Fax: 212 503-5698
James Whitehead, *General Mgr*
Sourabh Kalantri, *Editor*
Tom McGrade, *Exec VP*
Michael J Miller, *Exec VP*
Steve Gladysewski, *Vice Pres*
▲ **EMP:** 100
SQ FT: 310,000
SALES (est): 58.5MM
SALES (corp-wide): 720.8MM **Publicly Held**
WEB: www.zdnet.com
SIC: 2721 2731 7371 Periodicals; book publishing; custom computer programming services

(G-9830)
DAVLER MEDIA GROUP LLC
498 Fashion Ave Fl 10 (10018-6957)
PHONE 212 315-0800
Lisa Ben-Isvy, *President*
David Miller, *Publisher*
Tom Hanlon, *General Mgr*
Ruth Katz, *Editor*
Janet Barbash, *Vice Pres*
EMP: 30
SALES (est): 5MM **Privately Held**
WEB: www.davlermedia.com
SIC: 2721 Magazines: publishing & printing

(G-9831)
DAXOR CORPORATION (PA)
350 5th Ave Ste 4740 (10118-0002)
PHONE 212 244-0555
Fax: 212 244-0806
Michael Feldschuh, *CEO*
Gary Fischman, *Vice Pres*
John Blalock, *Prdtn Mgr*
Sandra Gilbert, *Research*

New York - New York County (G-9832)

Eric P Coleman, *CFO*
EMP: 37
SALES: 1.6MM **Publicly Held**
WEB: www.daxor.com
SIC: 3841 8099 Surgical & medical instruments; sperm bank; blood bank

(G-9832)
DBC INC
Also Called: Photoscribe
35 W 45th St Fl 2 (10036-4918)
PHONE.................................212 819-1177
David Benderly, *President*
Kandy Benderly, *Regional Mgr*
Carroll Dounn, *Vice Pres*
EMP: 60
SQ FT: 20,000
SALES (est) 7.1MM **Privately Held**
WEB: www.photoscribe.com
SIC: 3911 5944 Jewelry, precious metal; jewelry stores

(G-9833)
DEANGELIS LTD
312 E 95th St (10128-5779)
PHONE.................................212 348-8225
Fax: 212 286-3950
Kenneth Deangelis, *President*
Kayel Deangelis, *Vice Pres*
Kristine Deangelis, *MIS Dir*
EMP: 50 **EST:** 1957
SQ FT: 1,500
SALES (est): 4.8MM **Privately Held**
SIC: 2512 2391 Upholstered household furniture; draperies, plastic & textile: from purchased materials

(G-9834)
DEBMAR-MERCURY
75 Rockefeller Plz # 1600 (10019-6908)
PHONE.................................212 669-5025
Ira Bernstein, *President*
Liz Koman, *Exec VP*
Karen Bonck, *Senior VP*
Mike Chinery, *Senior VP*
Alexandra Jewett, *Senior VP*
EMP: 9
SALES (est) 721.7K **Privately Held**
SIC: 2836 Culture media

(G-9835)
DECKERS OUTDOOR CORPORATION
600 Madison Ave (10022-1615)
PHONE.................................212 486-2509
Joseph Bachelder, *Branch Mgr*
EMP: 325
SALES (corp-wide): 1.8B **Publicly Held**
SIC: 3021 Rubber & plastics footwear
PA: Deckers Outdoor Corporation
250 Coromar Dr
Goleta CA 93117
805 967-7611

(G-9836)
DEFINITION PRESS INC
141 Greene St (10012-3201)
PHONE.................................212 777-4490
Arnold Perey, *Info Tech Mgr*
Margot Carpenter, *Exec Dir*
Anne Fielding, *Exec Dir*
Ellen Reiss, *Director*
EMP: 10 **EST:** 1954
SQ FT: 2,210
SALES (est): 780K **Privately Held**
WEB: www.definitionpress.com
SIC: 2731 Books: publishing only

(G-9837)
DEFRAN SYSTEMS INC
1 Penn Plz Ste 1700 (10119-1700)
PHONE.................................212 727-8342
Fax: 212 727-8639
Fran L Turso, *President*
Ron Aceto, *Vice Pres*
Deborah Huyer, *Vice Pres*
Greg Travis, *Vice Pres*
Chris Shaw, *Controller*
EMP: 35
SALES (est): 2.3MM
SALES (corp-wide): 276.7MM **Privately Held**
WEB: www.defran.com
SIC: 7372 7371 Prepackaged software; custom computer programming services

PA: Netsmart Technologies, Inc.
4950 College Blvd
Overland Park KS 66211
913 327-7444

(G-9838)
DELCATH SYSTEMS INC (PA)
1301 Ave Of The Amer 43 (10019-6399)
PHONE.................................212 489-2100
Fax: 212 489-2102
Roger G Stoll, *Ch of Bd*
Jennifer Simpson, *President*
Harold C Mapes, *Exec VP*
John Purpura, *Exec VP*
Barbra C Keck, *CFO*
EMP: 25
SQ FT: 5,818
SALES: 1.7MM **Publicly Held**
WEB: www.delcath.com
SIC: 3841 2834 Surgical & medical instruments; catheters; pharmaceutical preparations

(G-9839)
DELIVERY SYSTEMS INC
19 W 44th St (10036-5902)
PHONE.................................212 221-7007
Sel Silver, *President*
EMP: 15
SALES (est): 1.2MM **Privately Held**
SIC: 7372 Prepackaged software

(G-9840)
DELL COMMUNICATIONS INC
Also Called: Dell Graphics
109 W 27th St Frnt 2 (10001-6208)
PHONE.................................212 989-3434
Steve Dell, *President*
Trg Agiuar, *Manager*
EMP: 5
SQ FT: 5,000
SALES (est): 460K **Privately Held**
WEB: www.dellgraphics.com
SIC: 2752 Commercial printing, offset

(G-9841)
DELTA UPHOLSTERERS INC
619 W 54th St Fl 6 (10019-3545)
PHONE.................................212 489-3308
James Congmea, *President*
EMP: 20 **EST:** 1952
SQ FT: 21,000
SALES (est): 1.4MM **Privately Held**
SIC: 2512 2391 Upholstered household furniture; draperies, plastic & textile: from purchased materials

(G-9842)
DELUXE CORPORATION
979 Lexington Ave (10021-5103)
PHONE.................................212 472-7222
Lee J Schram, *CEO*
EMP: 278
SALES (corp-wide): 1.7B **Publicly Held**
SIC: 2782 Checkbooks
PA: Deluxe Corporation
3680 Victoria St N
Shoreview MN 55126
651 483-7111

(G-9843)
DEMEO BROTHERS INC
Also Called: De Meo Brothers Hair
129 W 29th St Fl 5 (10001-5105)
PHONE.................................212 268-1400
Fax: 212 268-3269
Gabriel Klugmann, *President*
▲ **EMP:** 14
SQ FT: 6,000
SALES (est): 1.1MM **Privately Held**
SIC: 3999 6221 Hair & hair-based products; commodity traders, contracts

(G-9844)
DEMOS MEDICAL PUBLISHING LLC
11 W 42nd St Ste 15c (10036-8002)
PHONE.................................516 889-1791
Fax: 212 683-0118
Phyllis Gold, *President*
David Daddona, *Editor*
Aaron Janoer, *Controller*
Reina Santana, *Manager*
Katherina Gonzalez, *Info Tech Mgr*
EMP: 10
SQ FT: 1,600

SALES (est): 970K **Privately Held**
WEB: www.demosmedpub.com
SIC: 2731 2721 Books: publishing only; trade journals: publishing only, not printed on site

(G-9845)
DENIZ INFORMATION SYSTEMS
Also Called: Dis
208 E 51st St Ste 129 (10022-6557)
P.O. Box 841 (10150-0841)
PHONE.................................212 750-5199
Haluk Deniz, *Ch of Bd*
Nihat Ozkaya, *VP Opers*
Karen Emer, *VP Mktg*
EMP: 9
SQ FT: 600
SALES (est): 528.4K **Privately Held**
SIC: 7372 5045 Prepackaged software; computers, peripherals & software

(G-9846)
DENNIS BASSO COUTURE INC
Also Called: Dennis Basso Furs
825 Madison Ave (10065-5042)
PHONE.................................212 794-4500
Dennis Basso, *President*
Gigi Ferrante, *Production*
Emily Burnett, *Creative Dir*
▲ **EMP:** 12
SALES (est): 1.2MM **Privately Held**
SIC: 2371 Fur goods

(G-9847)
DENNIS PUBLISHING INC
Also Called: Week Publications, The
55 W 39th St Fl 5 (10018-3850)
P.O. Box 111 (10018-0002)
PHONE.................................646 717-9500
Fax: 212 302-9213
Steven Kotok, *CEO*
Scott Cullen, *Publisher*
Eric Effron, *General Mgr*
Collingwood Harris, *Editor*
Chris Mitchell, *Opers Mgr*
EMP: 100
SALES (est): 23.3MM
SALES (corp-wide): 122.1MM **Privately Held**
SIC: 2721 Magazines: publishing only, not printed on site
HQ: Dennis Publishing Limited
30 Cleveland Street
London W1T 4
207 907-6000

(G-9848)
DENTAL TRIBUNE AMERICA LLC
116 W 23rd St Ste 500 (10011-2599)
PHONE.................................212 244-7181
Chadette Maragh, *Publisher*
Sierra Rendon, *Editor*
Rob Selleck, *Editor*
Lorrie Young, *Marketing Staff*
Will Kenyon, *Manager*
EMP: 14
SQ FT: 4,000
SALES (est): 3MM **Privately Held**
SIC: 2759 Publication printing

(G-9849)
DEPARTURES MAGAZINE
Also Called: Travel & Leisure
1120 Ave Of The Amrcs 9 (10036-6700)
PHONE.................................212 382-5600
Fax: 212 768-1568
Richard Story, *Chief*
Mark Brooks, *Info Tech Dir*
Eyal Danon, *Info Tech Dir*
Patty Edwards, *Info Tech Dir*
Cynthia Garippa, *Info Tech Dir*
▲ **EMP:** 20
SALES (est): 1.3MM **Privately Held**
WEB: www.amexpub.com
SIC: 2721 Periodicals

(G-9850)
DESI TALK LLC
Also Called: Parikh Worldwide Media, LLC
115 W 30th St Rm 1206 (10001-4043)
PHONE.................................212 675-7515
Sudhir Parikh,
Shomik Chaudhuri,
EMP: 11

SALES: 300K **Privately Held**
SIC: 2741 Miscellaneous publishing

(G-9851)
DESIGN ARCHIVES INC
1460 Broadway (10036-7306)
PHONE.................................212 768-0617
Veena Advani, *President*
EMP: 5
SQ FT: 2,000
SALES (est): 415.5K **Privately Held**
SIC: 2395 5137 Embroidery & art needlework; women's & children's clothing

(G-9852)
DESIGN FOR ALL LLC
240 W 37th St Rm 601 (10018-5760)
PHONE.................................212 523-0021
Alan Madoff, *President*
Jeffrey Zwiebel, *Vice Pres*
Ann Borton, *Manager*
▲ **EMP:** 22
SALES (est): 3.3MM **Privately Held**
SIC: 2339 Women's & misses' outerwear

(G-9853)
DESIGN LITHOGRAPHERS INC
519 8th Ave Ste 3 (10018-6506)
PHONE.................................212 645-8900
Fax: 212 645-9459
Daniel Green, *President*
EMP: 12
SALES (est): 1.1MM **Privately Held**
WEB: www.designlitho.com
SIC: 2752 Commercial printing, offset

(G-9854)
DESIGN RESEARCH LTD
Also Called: Tom Dixon
243 Centre St (10013-3224)
PHONE.................................212 228-7675
Alex Wisnioski, *Mng Member*
▲ **EMP:** 150
SQ FT: 2,000
SALES (est): 4.1MM **Privately Held**
SIC: 3299 Non-metallic mineral statuary & other decorative products

(G-9855)
DESIGN SOURCE BY LG INC
115 Bowery Frnt 1 (10002-4933)
PHONE.................................212 274-0022
Fax: 212 334-3439
Leo Greisman, *CEO*
Florence Levi, *Manager*
Daniel Olejnik, *Manager*
▲ **EMP:** 23 **EST:** 1968
SQ FT: 1,000
SALES (est): 3.2MM **Privately Held**
SIC: 3423 Plumbers' hand tools

(G-9856)
DESIGNLOGOCOM INC
Also Called: Impressions Prtg & Graphics
200 W 37th St (10018-6603)
PHONE.................................212 564-0200
Arif Jacksi, *Chairman*
Balkrishna Mehta, *Controller*
EMP: 6
SALES (est): 630K **Privately Held**
WEB: www.designlogo.com
SIC: 2752 Commercial printing, lithographic

(G-9857)
DESIGNS ON FIFTH LTD
20 W 47th St Ste 701 (10036-3451)
PHONE.................................212 921-4162
David Ambalo, *Owner*
Min Tun, *Accountant*
EMP: 7
SQ FT: 8,000
SALES (est): 630K **Privately Held**
SIC: 3961 Costume jewelry

(G-9858)
DESIGNWAY LTD
27 E 21st St Fl 7 (10010-6249)
PHONE.................................212 254-2220
Joan Morgan, *President*
EMP: 6
SALES: 1MM **Privately Held**
SIC: 2211 5712 Draperies & drapery fabrics, cotton; custom made furniture, except cabinets

▲ = Import ▼ = Export
◆ = Import/Export

GEOGRAPHIC SECTION
New York - New York County (G-9886)

(G-9859)
DESSIN/FOURNIR INC
Also Called: Rose Cumming
232 E 59th St Fl 2 (10022-1464)
PHONE...................................212 758-0844
Fax: 212 888-2837
Gwendolyn Hitchcock, *Human Resources*
Dennis O'Hara, *Natl Sales Mgr*
Jay Shemwell, *Sales Mgr*
Stephanie Goetz, *Manager*
Ashley Dopita, *General Counsel*
EMP: 18
SALES (corp-wide): 7.7MM Privately Held
WEB: www.dessinfournir.com
SIC: 2511 Wood household furniture
HQ: Dessin/Fournir, Inc.
308 W Mill St
Plainville KS 67663
785 434-2777

(G-9860)
DETNY FOOTWEAR INC
Also Called: Shane & Shawn
1 River Pl Apt 1224 (10036-4369)
PHONE...................................212 423-1040
Shane Ward, *CEO*
Shawn J Ward, *President*
Adam Holmgren, *Opers Mgr*
▲ EMP: 8
SQ FT: 1,800
SALES: 1MM Privately Held
WEB: www.detny.com
SIC: 3143 3144 3021 Men's footwear, except athletic; women's footwear, except athletic; rubber & plastics footwear

(G-9861)
DETOUR APPAREL INC (PA)
Also Called: Chula Girls
530 7th Ave Rm 608 (10018-4888)
PHONE...................................212 221-3265
Lisa Medina, *President*
EMP: 5 EST: 2003
SQ FT: 3,000
SALES (est): 10MM Privately Held
SIC: 2369 Jackets: girls', children's & infants'

(G-9862)
DEUTSCH CORPORATE INC
1633 Broadway Ste 1804 (10019-6708)
PHONE...................................212 710-5870
EMP: 12
SALES (est): 1.1MM
SALES (corp-wide): 10.5MM Privately Held
SIC: 3678 Electronic connectors
PA: Wendel
89 Rue Taitbout
Paris Cedex 09 75312
142 853-000

(G-9863)
DEUX LUX INC
37 W 20th St Ste 1204 (10011-3712)
PHONE...................................212 620-0801
Sarah Jones, *General Mgr*
EMP: 5
SALES (corp-wide): 2.3MM Privately Held
SIC: 3171 Handbags, women's
PA: Deux Lux Inc.
4535 W Valerio St
Burbank CA 91505
213 746-7040

(G-9864)
DEVA CONCEPTS LLC
Also Called: Devacurl
75 Spring St Fl 8 (10012-4071)
PHONE...................................212 343-0344
Mark Pojar, *Sales Staff*
George Sandbrook, *Sales Staff*
EMP: 50
SALES (est): 5.5MM Privately Held
SIC: 3999 Atomizers, toiletry

(G-9865)
DEW GRAPHICS INC
Also Called: Dew Graphics
519 8th Ave Fl 18 (10018-4577)
PHONE...................................212 727-8820
Elaine Weisbrot, *President*
Don Weisbrot, *Vice Pres*
EMP: 35

SQ FT: 17,000
SALES (est): 3.2MM Privately Held
SIC: 2759 Commercial printing

(G-9866)
DFA NEW YORK LLC
240 W 37th St (10018-6604)
PHONE...................................212 523-0021
Alan Madoff, *Mng Member*
Jeff Zwiebel,
▲ EMP: 21
SALES (est): 2MM Privately Held
SIC: 2339 Women's & misses' accessories

(G-9867)
DIA
535 W 22nd St Fl 4 (10011-1119)
PHONE...................................212 675-4097
Nathalie De Gunzburg, *Principal*
EMP: 1
SALES: 13.3MM Privately Held
SIC: 2675 Die-cut paper & board

(G-9868)
DIALASE INC
36 W 47th St Ste 709 (10036-8601)
PHONE...................................212 575-8833
Isace Landerer, *President*
EMP: 5
SQ FT: 1,200
SALES (est): 330K Privately Held
SIC: 3915 Diamond cutting & polishing

(G-9869)
DIAMEX INC
580 5th Ave Ste 625 (10036-4725)
PHONE...................................212 575-8145
Fax: 212 575-8187
David Steinmetz, *President*
Ronald Vanderlinden, *Vice Pres*
Jeffrey Greenwald, *Manager*
EMP: 5
SQ FT: 1,200
SALES (est): 554.9K Privately Held
SIC: 3915 5094 Diamond cutting & polishing; diamonds (gems)

(G-9870)
DIAMOND BRIDAL COLLECTION LTD
260 W 39th St Fl 17 (10018-4410)
PHONE...................................212 302-0210
Fax: 212 302-0203
Paul Diamond, *President*
EMP: 25
SALES (est): 1.2MM Privately Held
SIC: 2335 Wedding gowns & dresses

(G-9871)
DIAMOND CONSTELLATION CORP
37 W 47th St Ste 506 (10036-2809)
P.O. Box 650466, Fresh Meadows (11365-0466)
PHONE...................................212 819-0324
Fax: 212 944-9245
EMP: 6 EST: 1959
SQ FT: 2,500
SALES (est): 470K Privately Held
SIC: 3915 5094 Diamond Cutting & Whol Of Precious Diamonds

(G-9872)
DIAMOND DISTRIBUTORS INC (PA)
608 5th Ave Fl 10 (10020-2303)
PHONE...................................212 921-9188
EMP: 9
SALES (est): 1.8MM Privately Held
SIC: 3911 Jewelry, precious metal

(G-9873)
DIAMOND INSCRIPTION TECH
36 W 47th St Ste 1008 (10036-8601)
PHONE...................................646 366-7944
Jacob Dresdner, *Owner*
EMP: 10
SALES (est): 913.2K Privately Held
WEB: www.dresdiam.com
SIC: 2759 7389 Laser printing; business services

(G-9874)
DIANOS KATHRYN DESIGNS
376 Broadway Apt 13b (10013-3943)
PHONE...................................212 267-1584
Kathryn Dianos, *Owner*
EMP: 5
SALES (est): 520K Privately Held
SIC: 2339 7389 Women's & misses' athletic clothing & sportswear; apparel designers, commercial

(G-9875)
DIGITAL COLOR CONCEPTS INC (PA)
Also Called: D C C
42 W 39th St Fl 6 (10018-2091)
PHONE...................................212 989-4888
Fax: 212 989-5588
Stephen Pandolfi, *CEO*
Christine Grant, *President*
Donald Terwilliger, *Exec VP*
Tom Vetter, *Opers Mgr*
Theresa Bianchi, *Production*
EMP: 24
SQ FT: 15,000
SALES (est): 17.3MM Privately Held
WEB: www.dccnyc.com
SIC: 2752 2791 Commercial printing, lithographic; photocomposition, for the printing trade

(G-9876)
DIGITAL EVOLUTION INC
123 William St Fl 26 (10038-3832)
PHONE...................................212 732-2722
Fax: 212 732-8594
Eric Pulier, *CEO*
Dominic Giordano, *President*
Nicholas Giordano, *Vice Pres*
Kemal Khan, *Controller*
Frankie Giordano, *Manager*
EMP: 23 EST: 2000
SQ FT: 5,000
SALES (est): 4.6MM Privately Held
WEB: www.digitalevolution.com
SIC: 2759 7336 7384 Commercial printing; graphic arts & related design; photograph developing & retouching

(G-9877)
DIGITAL FIRST MEDIA LLC (PA)
20 W 33rd St Fl 7 (10001-3305)
PHONE...................................212 257-7212
John Paton, *CEO*
Kevin Corrado, *President*
Steve Rossi, *President*
Jason Alley, *Editor*
Jim Brady, *Editor*
EMP: 41
SALES (est): 3.9B Privately Held
SIC: 2711 Commercial printing & newspaper publishing combined

(G-9878)
DILIGENT BOARD MEMBER SVCS LLC
310 5th Ave Fl 7 (10001-3605)
PHONE...................................212 741-8181
Tricia Burke, *President*
Bryan Zwahlen, *Vice Pres*
Linsey Manor, *Accountant*
Karen Welby, *Mktg Coord*
Caitlin Derosa, *Marketing Staff*
EMP: 20
SQ FT: 8,000
SALES (est): 1.7MM Privately Held
SIC: 7372 Prepackaged software

(G-9879)
DILIGENT CORPORATION (PA)
1385 Brdwy Fl 19 (10018)
PHONE...................................212 741-8181
Brian Stafford, *President*
Thomas N Tartaro, *Exec VP*
Dennis Comma, *Vice Pres*
Bach Hoang, *Engineer*
Michael Stanton, *CFO*
EMP: 124
SALES (est): 99.3MM Privately Held
SIC: 7372 Prepackaged software

(G-9880)
DIMODA DESIGNS INC
48 W 48th St Ste 403 (10036-1713)
PHONE...................................212 355-8166

Fax: 212 355-3963
Karabet Koroglu, *CEO*
Hayk Ogulluk, *President*
Garo Koroglu, *Vice Pres*
EMP: 25
SALES (est): 2.1MM Privately Held
WEB: www.dimoda.com
SIC: 3911 Jewelry, precious metal

(G-9881)
DIPEXIUM PHARMACEUTICALS INC
14 Wall St Ste 3d (10005-2141)
PHONE...................................212 269-2834
Robert J Deluccia, *Ch of Bd*
David P Luci, *President*
Adam Cutler, *Managing Dir*
David Garrett, *Development*
Robert G Shawah, *Treasurer*
EMP: 8
SALES (est): 1MM Privately Held
SIC: 2834 Pharmaceutical preparations

(G-9882)
DIRECT PRINT INC (PA)
77 E 125th St (10035-1622)
PHONE...................................212 987-6003
Kevin Williams, *President*
EMP: 10
SALES (est): 1.7MM Privately Held
SIC: 2759 Commercial printing

(G-9883)
DISCOVER MEDIA LLC
Also Called: Discover Magazine
90 5th Ave Ste 1100 (10011-2051)
PHONE...................................212 624-4800
Fax: 212 624-4813
Henry Donahue, *CEO*
Bob Guccione, *Ch of Bd*
Jane Bosveld, *Editor*
Jared Diamond, *Editor*
Philip Plait, *Editor*
EMP: 35
SQ FT: 11,500
SALES (est): 3.5MM Privately Held
WEB: www.discovermedia.net
SIC: 2721 Magazines: publishing only, not printed on site

(G-9884)
DISPATCH GRAPHICS INC
Also Called: Dispatch Letter Service
344 W 38th St Fl 4r (10018-8432)
PHONE...................................212 307-5943
Fax: 212 307-6103
Paul A Grech, *President*
Stephen Grech, *Exec VP*
EMP: 10
SQ FT: 8,000
SALES (est): 1.4MM Privately Held
SIC: 2752 7331 2791 2789 Commercial printing, offset; mailing service; typesetting; bookbinding & related work

(G-9885)
DISSENT MAGAZINE
120 Wall St Fl 31 (10005-4007)
PHONE...................................212 316-3120
Michael Walder, *President*
Sarah Leonard, *Editor*
David Marcus, *Editor*
Maxine Phillips, *Editor*
Nick Serpe, *Technology*
EMP: 10
SALES (est): 670K Privately Held
SIC: 2721 Periodicals

(G-9886)
DISTINCTIVE PRINTING INC
225 W 37th St Fl 16 (10018-6637)
PHONE...................................212 727-3000
Fax: 212 727-3004
Meredith Shantz, *President*
Michael Shantz, *Vice Pres*
Steve Cohen, *Manager*
EMP: 6
SQ FT: 5,000
SALES (est): 500K Privately Held
WEB: www.distinctiveprinting.com
SIC: 2752 Offset & photolithographic printing

New York - New York County (G-9887) — GEOGRAPHIC SECTION

(G-9887)
DISTRIBIO USA LLC
Also Called: Biologique Recherche
261 5th Ave Rm 1612 (10016-7706)
PHONE 212 989-6077
Erica Marsh, *Manager*
Philippe Allouche,
EMP: 5
SQ FT: 18,000
SALES (est): 973.9K **Privately Held**
WEB: www.biologiquerecherche.com
SIC: 2844 Face creams or lotions

(G-9888)
DK PUBLISHING
345 Hudson St (10014-4502)
PHONE 212 366-2000
Gary June, *CEO*
Ann Barton, *Editor*
Jennifer Chung, *Editor*
Thomas Leddy, *Prdtn Mgr*
Jessica Lee, *Design Engr*
◆ EMP: 18 EST: 2009
SALES (est): 1.8MM **Privately Held**
SIC: 2741 Miscellaneous publishing

(G-9889)
DM2 MEDIA LLC
Also Called: Digiday
26 Mercer St Apt 4 (10013-4183)
PHONE 646 419-4357
Newton J Friese, *CEO*
Brian Morrissey, *President*
Nancy Picker, *Exec VP*
Elaine Mershon, *Vice Pres*
Andrea Sontz, *Vice Pres*
EMP: 40
SALES (est): 483.9K **Privately Held**
SIC: 3695 Magnetic & optical recording media

(G-9890)
DMD INTERNATIONAL LTD
99 Park Ave Rm 330 (10016-1601)
PHONE 212 944-7300
Fax: 212 302-1561
Jeffrey Zipes, *Ch of Bd*
Steven Klein, *CFO*
Ish Sunder, *Manager*
EMP: 60
SQ FT: 8,000
SALES (est): 4.8MM **Privately Held**
SIC: 2339 Sportswear, women's

(G-9891)
DMX ENTEPRISE
192 Lexington Ave Rm 901 (10016-6823)
PHONE 212 481-1010
Charles Randall, *Principal*
EMP: 10
SALES (est): 730K **Privately Held**
SIC: 3843 Dental equipment & supplies

(G-9892)
DNP ELECTRONICS AMERICA LLC
Also Called: Deal
335 Madison Ave Fl 3 (10017-4616)
PHONE 212 503-1060
Masaru Suzuki, *President*
Kaoru Kando, *CFO*
Kaoru Kondo, *Treasurer*
▲ EMP: 60
SALES (est): 7.3MM
SALES (corp-wide): 12.4B **Privately Held**
SIC: 3861 Screens, projection
HQ: Dnp Corporation Usa
  335 Madison Ave Fl 3
  New York NY 10017
  212 503-1860

(G-9893)
DO IT DIFFERENT INC
59 W 71st St (10023-4111)
PHONE 917 842-0230
EMP: 5
SALES (est): 117.2K **Privately Held**
SIC: 7372 7389 Application computer software;

(G-9894)
DOCUMENT JOURNAL INC
122 W 27th St Fl 8 (10001-6227)
PHONE 917 287-2141
EMP: 7
SALES (est): 330.2K **Privately Held**
SIC: 2711 Newspapers, publishing & printing

(G-9895)
DOG GOOD PRODUCTS LLC
Also Called: Victoria Stilwell Positevely
1407 Broadway Fl 41 (10018-2348)
PHONE 212 789-7000
Steven Hanan, *Manager*
David Cayre,
Sandy Menichelli,
EMP: 6
SQ FT: 20,000
SALES (est): 370K **Privately Held**
SIC: 3199 2047 Dog furnishings: collars, leashes, muzzles, etc.: leather; dog food

(G-9896)
DOLBY LABORATORIES INC
1350 6th Ave Fl 28 (10019-4702)
PHONE 212 767-1700
Fax: 212 767-1705
Richard L Hockenbrock, *Vice Pres*
Bill Allen, *Manager*
EMP: 15
SALES (corp-wide): 970.6MM **Publicly Held**
WEB: www.dolby.com
SIC: 3861 Motion picture film
PA: Dolby Laboratories, Inc.
  1275 Market St
  San Francisco CA 94103
  415 558-0200

(G-9897)
DONALD BRUHNKE
Also Called: Chicago Watermark Company
455 W 37th St Apt 1018 (10018-4785)
PHONE 212 600-1260
Donald Bruhnke, *Owner*
EMP: 10
SQ FT: 1,200
SALES (est): 1.2MM **Privately Held**
SIC: 2621 Commercial printing

(G-9898)
DONNA DISTEFANO LTD (PA)
37 W 20th St Ste 1106 (10011-3713)
PHONE 212 594-3757
Donna Distefano, *President*
EMP: 9
SALES (est): 820.8K **Privately Held**
SIC: 3911 Jewelry, precious metal

(G-9899)
DONNA KARAN COMPANY LLC
Also Called: Dkny Jeans
240 W 40th St Bsmt 2 (10018-1533)
PHONE 212 372-6500
Richard Callari, *VP Prdtn*
Mark Webber, *Branch Mgr*
Serafina Coscia, *Manager*
Cindy Payero, *Manager*
EMP: 16
SALES (corp-wide): 255.7MM **Privately Held**
WEB: www.donnakaran.com
SIC: 2337 Women's & misses' suits & coats
HQ: The Donna Karan Company Llc
  240 W 40th St
  New York NY 10018
  212 789-1500

(G-9900)
DONNA KARAN COMPANY LLC
240 W 40th St Bsmt (10018-1533)
PHONE 212 789-1500
Priscilla Purvis, *District Mgr*
Carol Knouse, *Senior VP*
EMP: 157
SALES (corp-wide): 279MM **Privately Held**
WEB: www.dkny.com
SIC: 2335 2337 2331 2339 Women's, juniors' & misses' dresses; suits: women's, misses' & juniors'; skirts, separate: women's, misses' & juniors'; pantsuits: women's, misses' & juniors'; blouses, women's & juniors': made from purchased material; women's & misses jackets & coats, except sportswear; suits, men's & boys': made from purchased materials; coats, tailored, men's & boys': from purchased materials; slacks, dress: men's, youths' & boys'
HQ: The Donna Karan Company Llc
  550 Fashion Ave Fl 14
  New York NY 10018
  212 789-1500

(G-9901)
DONNA KARAN COMPANY LLC (DH)
Also Called: Dkny
240 W 40th St (10018-1533)
PHONE 212 789-1500
Fax: 212 768-4441
Donna Karan, *CEO*
Carolyn Mariani, *President*
Alexandra Deegan, *General Mgr*
Robert Wolf, *Area Mgr*
Patti Cohen, *Exec VP*
▲ EMP: 300
SQ FT: 67,000
SALES (est): 501.9MM
SALES (corp-wide): 255.7MM **Privately Held**
WEB: www.dkny.com
SIC: 2335 2337 2331 2339 Women's, juniors' & misses' dresses; suits: women's, misses' & juniors'; skirts, separate: women's, misses' & juniors'; pantsuits: women's, misses' & juniors'; blouses, women's & juniors': made from purchased material; women's & misses jackets & coats, except sportswear; suits, men's & boys': made from purchased materials; coats, tailored, men's & boys': from purchased materials; slacks, dress: men's, youths' & boys'
HQ: Donna Karan International Inc.
  550 Fashion Ave Fl 14
  New York NY 10018
  212 789-1500

(G-9902)
DONNA KARAN INTERNATIONAL INC (HQ)
550 Fashion Ave Fl 14 (10018-3250)
PHONE 212 789-1500
Fax: 212 768-6099
Mark Weber, *Ch of Bd*
Donna Karan, *Founder*
Patti Cohen, *Exec VP*
Lee Goldenberg, *Exec VP*
Louis Praino, *Senior VP*
◆ EMP: 1525
SQ FT: 80,000
SALES (est): 509.8MM
SALES (corp-wide): 255.7MM **Privately Held**
WEB: www.donnakaran.com
SIC: 2335 2337 2331 2339 Women's, juniors' & misses' dresses; jackets & vests, except fur & leather: women's; skirts, separate: women's, misses' & juniors'; suits: women's, misses' & juniors'; blouses, women's & juniors': made from purchased material; shirts, women's & juniors': made from purchased materials; women's & misses' outerwear; slacks: women's, misses' & juniors'; jeans: women's, misses' & juniors'; athletic clothing: women's, misses' & juniors'; men's & boys' furnishings; slacks, dress: men's, youths' & boys'; jeans: men's, youths' & boys'
PA: Lvmh Moet Hennessy Louis Vuitton
  22 Avenue Montaigne
  Paris Cedex 08 75382
  144 132-222

(G-9903)
DONNA KARAN INTERNATIONAL INC
240 W 40th St Bsmt (10018-1533)
PHONE 212 768-5800
Fax: 212 768-5868
Fred Wilson, *Manager*
EMP: 8
SALES (corp-wide): 255.7MM **Privately Held**
WEB: www.donnakaran.com
SIC: 2335 2337 2331 2339 Women's, juniors' & misses' dresses; jackets & vests, except fur & leather: women's; blouses, women's & juniors': made from purchased material; women's & misses outerwear; men's & boys' furnishings; slacks, dress: men's, youths' & boys'
HQ: Donna Karan International Inc.
  550 Fashion Ave Fl 14
  New York NY 10018
  212 789-1500

(G-9904)
DONNA MORGAN LLC
Also Called: Ali Ro
132 W 36th St Rm 801 (10018-8824)
PHONE 212 575-2550
Fax: 212 575-4775
Brian Fellner, *Credit Mgr*
Geoffrey Blitz, *Accounts Exec*
Simone Huelser, *Director*
Jaclyn Wagner, *Director*
Kathleen Mc Feeters,
EMP: 25
SALES (est): 4.3MM **Privately Held**
WEB: www.donnamorgan.com
SIC: 3161 Clothing & apparel carrying cases

(G-9905)
DONNE DIEU
315 W 36th St Frnt 3 (10018-6681)
PHONE 212 226-0573
Susan Gosin, *President*
Lisa Switalski, *Prdtn Mgr*
Paul Wong, *Treasurer*
Bridget Donlon, *Program Mgr*
Kathleen Flynn, *Exec Dir*
EMP: 7
SQ FT: 5,000
SALES (est): 796K **Privately Held**
WEB: www.dieudonne.org
SIC: 2621 8999 7999 Art paper; artist's studio; arts & crafts instruction

(G-9906)
DONNELLEY FINANCIAL LLC (HQ)
Also Called: RR Donnelley Financial, Inc.
55 Water St Lowr L1 (10041-0005)
PHONE 212 425-0298
Fax: 212 658-5871
Thomas J Quinlan III, *CEO*
William P Penders, *President*
Sandy McGee, *Senior VP*
Jim Palmiter, *Senior VP*
Scott L Spitzer, *Senior VP*
▲ EMP: 420
SQ FT: 143,000
SALES (est): 914.7MM
SALES (corp-wide): 11.2B **Publicly Held**
WEB: www.bowne.com
SIC: 2752 Commercial printing, lithographic; business forms, lithographed
PA: R.R. Donnelley & Sons Company
  35 W Wacker Dr Ste 3650
  Chicago IL 60601
  312 326-8000

(G-9907)
DONORWALL INC
125 Maiden Ln (10038-4912)
P.O. Box 1005 (10272-1005)
PHONE 212 766-9670
Fax: 212 619-1521
Barry Silverberg, *President*
EMP: 16
SALES (est): 1.3MM **Privately Held**
WEB: www.donorwall.com
SIC: 3999 Plaques, picture, laminated

▲ = Import ▼ = Export
◆ = Import/Export

GEOGRAPHIC SECTION

New York - New York County (G-9931)

(G-9908)
DORAL APPAREL GROUP INC
498 Fashion Ave Fl 10 (10018-6957)
PHONE..................................917 208-5652
Martin Ehrlich, *President*
Andrea Webster, *Manager*
EMP: 9 **EST:** 1999
SQ FT: 5,000
SALES (est): 1.1MM **Privately Held**
SIC: 2339 2326 Women's & misses' athletic clothing & sportswear; men's & boys' work clothing

(G-9909)
DOREMUS FP LLC
228 E 45th St Fl 10 (10017-3331)
PHONE..................................212 366-3800
Fax: 212 366-3640
Dave Wade, *President*
Jed Dorney, *General Mgr*
Greg Cunnion, *Senior VP*
James Bonilla, *VP Opers*
Mickey Hernandez, *Opers Staff*
EMP: 47
SQ FT: 13,800
SALES (est): 7MM **Privately Held**
WEB: www.doremusfp.com
SIC: 2759 Financial note & certificate printing & engraving

(G-9910)
DORLING KINDERSLEY PUBLISHING (DH)
375 Hudson St (10014-3658)
PHONE..................................212 213-4800
Fax: 212 689-4828
Peter Kindersley, *Ch of Bd*
Rosan Tregido, *Finance*
Ebony Lazare, *Sales Staff*
Todd Fries, *Mktg Dir*
Dana Chow, *Analyst*
▲ **EMP:** 60
SQ FT: 5,000
SALES (est): 5.4MM
SALES (corp-wide): 18.4B **Privately Held**
SIC: 2731 3652 Book publishing; pre-recorded records & tapes
HQ: Dorling Kindersley Limited
    Shell Mex House
    London WC2R
    207 010-3000

(G-9911)
DOVER CORPORATION
500 5th Ave Ste 1828 (10110-1807)
PHONE..................................212 922-1640
Fax: 212 922-1656
Bob Livingston, *General Mgr*
Raymond McKay, *Vice Pres*
Robert Tyre, *Vice Pres*
EMP: 5
SALES (corp-wide): 6.9B **Publicly Held**
SIC: 3632 Household refrigerators & freezers
PA: Dover Corporation
    3005 Highland Pkwy # 200
    Downers Grove IL 60515
    630 541-1540

(G-9912)
DOVER GLOBAL HOLDINGS INC
280 Park Ave (10017-1216)
PHONE..................................212 922-1640
Robert A Livingston, *President*
Kenneth Rado, *Managing Dir*
Andy Fincher, *Sr Corp Ofcr*
Lance Fleming, *Sr Corp Ofcr*
Dennis Bester, *Vice Pres*
◆ **EMP:** 24
SALES (est): 4.9MM
SALES (corp-wide): 6.9B **Publicly Held**
SIC: 3531 3542 3565 3534 Construction machinery; machine tools; metal forming type; packaging machinery; elevators & moving stairways
PA: Dover Corporation
    3005 Highland Pkwy # 200
    Downers Grove IL 60515
    630 541-1540

(G-9913)
DOW JONES & COMPANY INC (HQ)
1211 Avenue Of The Americ (10036-8711)
P.O. Box 300, Princeton NJ (08543-0300)
PHONE..................................609 627-2999
Fax: 212 597-5688
William Lewis, *CEO*
Edwin Finn Jr, *President*
Greg Bartalos, *Editor*
Harlan Byrne, *Editor*
Brian Cronk, *Editor*
▲ **EMP:** 500 **EST:** 1882
SALES (est): 2.6B
SALES (corp-wide): 8.2B **Publicly Held**
SIC: 2711 2721 Newspapers; magazines: publishing & printing
PA: News Corporation
    1211 Ave Of The Americas
    New York NY 10036
    212 416-3400

(G-9914)
DOW JONES & COMPANY INC
1211 Avenue Of The (10036)
PHONE..................................212 597-5600
Larry Sukay, *Managing Prtnr*
Thomas Trabucco, *General Mgr*
Brian Callaghan, *Editor*
Thomas Petzinger, *Editor*
Matt Korten, *Business Mgr*
EMP: 200
SALES (corp-wide): 8.2B **Publicly Held**
SIC: 2711 Newspapers, publishing & printing
HQ: Dow Jones & Company, Inc.
    1211 Avenue Of The Americ
    New York NY 10036
    609 627-2999

(G-9915)
DOW JONES & COMPANY INC
1211 Avenue Of The Americ (10036-8711)
PHONE..................................212 597-5983
Edwin Finn, *Branch Mgr*
EMP: 46
SALES (corp-wide): 8.2B **Publicly Held**
SIC: 2711 2721 6289 7383 Newspapers, publishing & printing; magazines: publishing only, not printed on site; statistical reports (periodicals): publishing & printing; financial reporting; stock quotation service; news reporting services for newspapers & periodicals; business oriented computer software
HQ: Dow Jones & Company, Inc.
    1211 Avenue Of The Americ
    New York NY 10036
    609 627-2999

(G-9916)
DOW JONES AER COMPANY INC
1211 Av Of The Am Lwr C3r (10036)
PHONE..................................212 416-2000
Alice Chai, *President*
Claire Ansberry, *General Mgr*
Gail Griffin, *General Mgr*
Donald Marchad, *General Mgr*
Teresa Vozzo, *General Mgr*
EMP: 865
SALES (est): 155.2MM
SALES (corp-wide): 8.2B **Publicly Held**
WEB: www.opinionjournal.com
SIC: 2721 Periodicals
HQ: Dow Jones & Company, Inc.
    1211 Avenue Of The Americ
    New York NY 10036
    609 627-2999

(G-9917)
DOWA INTERNATIONAL CORP
370 Lexington Ave Rm 1002 (10017-6586)
PHONE..................................212 697-3217
Fax: 212 697-3902
Junichi Nagao, *President*
Kimitaka Sato, *Project Mgr*
Akihisa Yamaguchi, *Marketing Mgr*
EMP: 13
SALES (corp-wide): 3.4B **Privately Held**
WEB: www.dicny.com
SIC: 1241 8732 Coal mining services; research services, except laboratory
PA: Dowa Holdings Co.,Ltd.
    4-14-1, Sotokanda
    Chiyoda-Ku TKY 101-0
    368 471-106

(G-9918)
DOWNTOWN INTERIORS INC
250 Hudson St Lbby 1 (10013-1413)
PHONE..................................212 337-0230
Fax: 212 337-0231
Hertzel Abraham, *President*
Helen Conlin, *Bookkeeper*
EMP: 12
SQ FT: 3,600
SALES (est): 1MM **Privately Held**
SIC: 3553 Furniture makers' machinery, woodworking

(G-9919)
DOWNTOWN MEDIA GROUP LLC
Also Called: Tokion Magazine
12 W 27th St Ste 1000 (10001-6903)
PHONE..................................646 723-4510
Maxwell Williams, *Opers Staff*
Kathy Bowden, *Controller*
Larry Rosenblum,
Isam Walji,
EMP: 15 **EST:** 2005
SALES (est): 1.4MM **Privately Held**
SIC: 2721 Periodicals

(G-9920)
DOWNTOWN MUSIC LLC
485 Broadway Fl 3 (10013-3071)
PHONE..................................212 625-2980
Katrancha Jedd, *Vice Pres*
Zach Hancock, *Chief Engr*
Terence Lam,
Sean McGraw, *Administration*
EMP: 9 **EST:** 2008
SALES (est): 1MM **Privately Held**
SIC: 2741 Music book & sheet music publishing

(G-9921)
DOYLE & ROTH MFG CO INC (PA)
39 Broad St Ste 710 (10004-2513)
PHONE..................................212 269-7840
Fax: 212 248-4780
Mary Ann Avella, *President*
Rohit Patel, *Vice Pres*
Kathy Troise, *Buyer*
George Hahn, *Treasurer*
Fred Diestmann, *Director*
EMP: 14 **EST:** 1932
SQ FT: 3,200
SALES (est): 12MM **Privately Held**
WEB: www.doyleroth.com
SIC: 3443 3491 Heat exchangers, condensers & components; pressure valves & regulators, industrial

(G-9922)
DR JAYSCOM
853 Broadway Ste 1900 (10003-4703)
PHONE..................................888 437-5297
▼ **EMP:** 10
SALES (est): 1.2MM **Privately Held**
SIC: 2339 Women's & misses' athletic clothing & sportswear

(G-9923)
DRAGON TRADING INC
Also Called: DRAGON STEEL PRODUCTS
211 E 70th St Apt 20d (10021-5209)
PHONE..................................212 717-1496
James Steindecker, *President*
Chen Tan, *Manager*
◆ **EMP:** 6
SQ FT: 800
SALES (est): 15MM **Privately Held**
SIC: 3462 3321 3731 3315 Iron & steel forgings; chains, forged steel; cast iron pipe & fittings; marine rigging; cable, steel: insulated or armored

(G-9924)
DRAPER ASSOCIATES INCORPORATED
121 Varick St Rm 203 (10013-1455)
PHONE..................................212 255-2727
Joseph Disomma, *President*
Michael Paulmasano, *Vice Pres*
EMP: 15
SQ FT: 1,200
SALES (est): 134.5K **Privately Held**
WEB: www.draperassociates.com
SIC: 2741 2791 Miscellaneous publishing; typesetting

(G-9925)
DREAMWAVE LLC
34 W 33rd St Fl 2 (10001-3304)
PHONE..................................212 594-4250
Morris Dweck, *Ch of Bd*
David Grazi, *President*
Joseph Benun, *Vice Pres*
Fred Goldstein, *Controller*
George Saade, *Controller*
▲ **EMP:** 26
SQ FT: 13,000
SALES (est): 1.4MM **Privately Held**
SIC: 2389 Men's miscellaneous accessories

(G-9926)
DRESDIAM INC
Also Called: Jacob Dresdner Co
36 W 47th St Ste 1008 (10036-8601)
PHONE..................................212 819-2217
Jacob Dresdner, *President*
EMP: 40
SQ FT: 3,000
SALES (est): 3.8MM **Privately Held**
SIC: 3915 Diamond cutting & polishing

(G-9927)
DRESSY TESSY INC (PA)
Also Called: Dt Industry
1410 Broadway Rm 502 (10018-9373)
PHONE..................................212 869-0750
Kitty Koo, *President*
Kathy Ray, *Director*
▲ **EMP:** 9
SQ FT: 5,000
SALES (est): 702.6K **Privately Held**
SIC: 2253 Knit outerwear mills

(G-9928)
DREW PHILIPS CORP (PA)
Also Called: Supply & Demand
231 W 39th St (10018-1070)
PHONE..................................212 354-0095
Andrew Cohen, *President*
Shantee Rickerby, *Editor*
Kasia Franuszkiewicz, *Manager*
▲ **EMP:** 7
SALES (est): 3.9MM **Privately Held**
WEB: www.supplydemand.com
SIC: 2339 Sportswear, women's

(G-9929)
DREYFUS ASHBY INC (DH)
630 3rd Ave Rm 1501 (10017-6745)
PHONE..................................212 818-0770
Fax: 212 953-2366
Chris Ryan, *President*
Micheal Katz, *President*
Daniel Schmalen, *Vice Pres*
Patrick Sere, *Vice Pres*
Gary S Squires, *Vice Pres*
▲ **EMP:** 34
SQ FT: 3,000
SALES (est): 5.3MM
SALES (corp-wide): 981.2K **Privately Held**
WEB: www.dreyfusashby.com
SIC: 3645 3646 2084 Residential lighting fixtures; lamp & light shades; commercial indusl & institutional electric lighting fixtures; wines, brandy & brandy spirits
HQ: Sa Maison Joseph Drouhin
    7 Rue D Enfer
    Beaune 21200
    380 246-888

(G-9930)
DRONE USA INC (PA)
285 Fulton St Fl 85 (10007-0103)
PHONE..................................212 220-8795
EMP: 2 **EST:** 1972
SALES (est): 16.9MM **Privately Held**
SIC: 3721 Motorized aircraft

(G-9931)
DROPCAR INC
511 Ave Of The Amricas (10011-8436)
PHONE..................................212 464-8860
Michael Richardson, *CEO*
EMP: 7
SALES (est): 375.5K **Privately Held**
SIC: 7372 Business oriented computer software

New York - New York County (G-9932)

(G-9932)
DRUMMOND FRAMING INC
38 W 21st St Fl 10 (10010-6969)
PHONE.................................212 647-1701
Fax: 212 254-0242
Donald Delli Paoli, *Owner*
EMP: 14
SQ FT: 2,300
SALES (est): 1.1MM **Privately Held**
WEB: www.drummondframing.com
SIC: 2499 Picture & mirror frames, wood

(G-9933)
DU MONDE TRADING INC
Also Called: Up Country
1407 Brrdwy Rm 1905 (10018)
PHONE.................................212 944-1306
Donald Eatz, *President*
Dale Trienekens, *COO*
▲ EMP: 50
SQ FT: 4,500
SALES: 6.5MM **Privately Held**
SIC: 2339 2326 Women's & misses' jackets & coats, except sportswear; men's & boys' work clothing

(G-9934)
DUANE PARK PATISSERIE INC
179 Duane St Frnt 1 (10013-3397)
PHONE.................................212 274-8447
Madeleine Lanciani, *Owner*
EMP: 12
SALES (est): 1.3MM **Privately Held**
WEB: www.madelines.net
SIC: 2051 Bakery: wholesale or wholesale/retail combined

(G-9935)
DUCDUC LLC
524 Broadway Rm 206 (10012-4408)
PHONE.................................212 226-1868
Bethany Gochie, *Purchasing*
Lelia Byrne, *Mktg Dir*
Philip Eidles, *Mng Member*
Brady Wilcox, *Creative Dir*
EMP: 15
SALES (est): 1.9MM **Privately Held**
SIC: 2511 Children's wood furniture

(G-9936)
DUCK RIVER TEXTILES INC (PA)
295 5th Ave (10016-7103)
PHONE.................................212 679-2980
Eili Alhakim, *President*
Oury Alhakim, *Vice Pres*
Raymond Alhakim, *Controller*
Joel Bren, *VP Mktg*
▲ EMP: 6 EST: 1997
SQ FT: 50,000
SALES (est): 25MM **Privately Held**
WEB: www.duckrivertextile.com
SIC: 2269 Linen fabrics: dyeing, finishing & printing

(G-9937)
DUCON TECHNOLOGIES INC (PA)
5 Penn Plz Ste 2403 (10001-1848)
PHONE.................................631 694-1700
Aron Govil, *Chairman*
William Papa, *Chairman*
Renato Delarama, *Vice Pres*
Bob Gupta, *Vice Pres*
◆ EMP: 15
SQ FT: 35,000
SALES: 479.4MM **Privately Held**
WEB: www.ducon.com
SIC: 3537 3564 Industrial trucks & tractors; blowers & fans

(G-9938)
DUNE INC
200 Lexington Ave Rm 200 (10016-6103)
PHONE.................................212 925-6171
Richard Shemtov, *President*
Aaron Shemtov, *Vice Pres*
Alicia Thibou, *Production*
▲ EMP: 5
SQ FT: 12,000
SALES (est): 722.4K **Privately Held**
WEB: www.dune-ny.com
SIC: 2511 Wood household furniture

(G-9939)
DURAN JEWELRY INC
36 W 47th St Ste 1205 (10036-8637)
PHONE.................................212 431-1959
Erol Civi, *President*
Arlet Tknezi, *Manager*
▲ EMP: 6
SQ FT: 1,000
SALES (est): 460K **Privately Held**
SIC: 3911 Jewelry, precious metal

(G-9940)
DURATA THERAPEUTICS INC
7 Times Sq Ste 3502 (10036-6540)
PHONE.................................646 871-6400
Paul R Edick, *CEO*
Richard U De Schutter, *Ch of Bd*
Corey N Fishman, *COO*
Benjamin Pe, *Opers Staff*
Michael Dunne, *Officer*
EMP: 5
SQ FT: 9,000
SALES (est): 386.3K **Privately Held**
SIC: 2834 8731 Antibiotics, packaged; commercial physical research

(G-9941)
DUXIANA DUX BED
235 E 58th St (10022-1201)
PHONE.................................212 755-2600
Fax: 212 752-4989
Bo Gustafsson, *Principal*
EMP: 6
SALES (est): 529K **Privately Held**
SIC: 2515 5712 5719 Mattresses & bedsprings; beds & accessories; beddings & linens

(G-9942)
DVF STUDIO LLC (PA)
Also Called: Diane Von Furstenberg The Shop
440 W 14th St (10014-1004)
PHONE.................................212 741-6607
Fax: 212 929-4051
Robert McCormick, *COO*
Jeannie Lau, *Exec VP*
Elisa Palomino, *Vice Pres*
Paul Aberasturi, *CFO*
Noelia Navarro, *Human Res Dir*
▲ EMP: 75
SALES (est): 25.6MM **Privately Held**
WEB: www.dvf.com
SIC: 3199 2389 5621 Leather garments; disposable garments & accessories; women's specialty clothing stores

(G-9943)
DWELL LIFE INC
Also Called: Dwell Store The
192 Lexington Ave Fl 16 (10016-6823)
PHONE.................................212 382-2010
Regina Flynn, *Office Mgr*
EMP: 25
SALES (corp-wide): 20MM **Privately Held**
SIC: 2741 Miscellaneous publishing
PA: Dwell Life, Inc.
111 Sutter St Ste 600
San Francisco CA 94104
415 373-5100

(G-9944)
DWNLD INC
13 Laight St Ste 24 (10013-2119)
PHONE.................................484 483-6572
Alexandra Keating, *CEO*
EMP: 28
SALES (est): 498.8K **Privately Held**
SIC: 7372 Application computer software

(G-9945)
DYENAMIX INC
151 Grand St Fl 2 (10013-3176)
PHONE.................................212 941-6642
Fax: 212 941-7407
Raylene Marasco, *President*
EMP: 7
SALES: 250K **Privately Held**
SIC: 2261 2262 Dyeing cotton broadwoven fabrics; screen printing of cotton broadwoven fabrics; dyeing: manmade fiber & silk broadwoven fabrics; screen printing: manmade fiber & silk broadwoven fabrics

(G-9946)
DYLANS CANDY BAR INC
315 E 62nd St Fl 6 (10065-7767)
PHONE.................................212 620-2700
EMP: 18
SALES (est): 2.9MM **Privately Held**
SIC: 2064 Candy & other confectionery products

(G-9947)
DYNAMIC DESIGN GROUP INC
Also Called: Anni Jewels
15 W 47th St Ste 801 (10036-3765)
PHONE.................................212 840-9400
Amit Sanghavi, *President*
Harish Patel, *Accountant*
Steven Das, *Sales Mgr*
Alisha Mudaliar, *Manager*
Vincent Violetta, *Director*
▲ EMP: 10
SQ FT: 500
SALES (est): 1.4MM
SALES (corp-wide): 236MM **Privately Held**
SIC: 3911 Jewelry, precious metal
PA: Sanghavi Exports International Private Limited
No.502, Opera House,
Mumbai MH 40000
222 364-3994

(G-9948)
DYNAMICA INC
930 5th Ave Apt 3f (10021-2680)
PHONE.................................212 818-1900
Daniel Schwartz, *President*
▲ EMP: 9
SALES (est): 1MM **Privately Held**
SIC: 3821 Laboratory apparatus & furniture

(G-9949)
DYNAMO DEVELOPMENT INC
860 Broadway Fl 5 (10003-1228)
PHONE.................................212 385-1552
Dmitry I Grinberg, *President*
Yuri Nakonechny, *Software Dev*
EMP: 6
SALES (est): 2.2MM **Privately Held**
WEB: www.dynamodevelopment.com
SIC: 7372 Prepackaged software

(G-9950)
E M G CREATIONS INC
8 W 37th St (10018-7401)
PHONE.................................212 643-0960
Fax: 212 643-0963
Chasky Samet, *President*
Emil Weiss, *Vice Pres*
◆ EMP: 15
SQ FT: 2,000
SALES (est): 1.3MM **Privately Held**
WEB: www.emgcreations.com
SIC: 3911 Jewelry, precious metal

(G-9951)
E P SEWING PLEATING INC
327 W 36th St Frnt 2 (10018-6405)
PHONE.................................212 967-2575
EMP: 20 EST: 1998
SALES (est): 820K **Privately Held**
SIC: 2342 Mfg Bras/Girdles

(G-9952)
E SCHREIBER INC
580 5th Ave Fl 32a (10036-4716)
PHONE.................................212 382-0280
Norbert Steinmetz, *President*
Ben Moller, *Vice Pres*
▲ EMP: 22
SQ FT: 5,000
SALES (est): 2MM **Privately Held**
WEB: www.eschreiber.com
SIC: 3915 5094 Diamond cutting & polishing; diamonds (gems)

(G-9953)
E W WILLIAMS PUBLICATIONS
Also Called: LDB Interior Textiles
370 Lexington Ave Rm 1409 (10017-6583)
PHONE.................................212 661-1516
Fax: 212 661-1713
Wanda Jankowski, *Editor*
Mark Edgar, *Prdtn Mgr*
Philippa Hochschild, *Manager*
Janys Kuznier, *Director*
EMP: 9

SALES (corp-wide): 41.6MM **Privately Held**
WEB: www.williamspublications.com
SIC: 2721 2731 Magazines: publishing only, not printed on site; textbooks: publishing only, not printed on site
HQ: E W Williams Publications
2125 Center Ave Ste 305
Fort Lee NJ 07024

(G-9954)
E&I PRINTING
545 8th Ave Rm 5e (10018-2441)
PHONE.................................212 206-0506
Fax: 212 268-0226
Eric Eisenberg, *President*
EMP: 15
SALES: 5MM **Privately Held**
WEB: www.eiprints.com
SIC: 2759 Commercial printing

(G-9955)
E-PLAY BRANDS LLC
25 W 39th St Fl 5 (10018-4075)
PHONE.................................212 563-2646
Joseph Esses,
EMP: 6
SQ FT: 1,000
SALES (est): 238.4K **Privately Held**
SIC: 2361 2369 Shirts: girls', children's & infants'; dresses: girls', children's & infants'; coat & legging sets: girls' & children's

(G-9956)
E-WON INDUSTRIAL CO INC
Also Called: New York Trading Co
625 Main St Apt 1532 (10044-0036)
PHONE.................................212 750-9610
Shin Han, *President*
Sun Yu, *Vice Pres*
▲ EMP: 37
SQ FT: 1,000
SALES (est): 4MM **Privately Held**
SIC: 3965 Buttons & parts

(G-9957)
EAGLE ART PUBLISHING INC
475 Park Ave S Rm 2800 (10016-6901)
PHONE.................................212 685-7411
Samuel J Lurie, *President*
EMP: 5
SALES (est): 330K **Privately Held**
SIC: 2731 Book publishing

(G-9958)
EAGLE LACE DYEING CORP
335 W 35th St Fl 2 (10001-1726)
PHONE.................................212 947-2712
Fax: 212 338-0848
Leonard Shally, *President*
EMP: 10
SALES (est): 620K **Privately Held**
SIC: 2258 2396 Dyeing & finishing lace goods & warp knit fabric; automotive & apparel trimmings

(G-9959)
EAGLES NEST HOLDINGS LLC (PA)
Also Called: Sabin Robbins
455 E 86th St (10028-6400)
PHONE.................................513 874-5270
Jack Turcotte, *Purchasing*
Wayne Penrod,
Joseph Hardiman,
EMP: 35
SQ FT: 6,000
SALES (est): 14.8MM **Privately Held**
SIC: 2679 Paper products, converted

(G-9960)
EARL G GRAVES PUBG CO INC (HQ)
Also Called: Black Enterprise
260 Madison Ave Ste 11 (10016-2412)
PHONE.................................212 242-8000
Earl G Graves Sr, *CEO*
Earl Butch Graves Jr, *CEO*
Jacques Jiha, *Principal*
Dirk J Caldwell, *Senior VP*
Angela Mitchell, *Vice Pres*
EMP: 83
SQ FT: 22,000

SALES (est): 9.7MM
SALES (corp-wide): 18.7MM **Privately Held**
SIC: 2721 Magazines: publishing only, not printed on site
PA: Earl G. Graves, Ltd.
260 Madison Ave Ste 11
New York NY 10016
212 242-8000

(G-9961)
EARRING KING JEWELRY MFG INC
62 W 47th St Ste 1202 (10036-3230)
PHONE................................718 544-7947
Fax: 212 471-0011
Kowk Mok, *President*
Jane Mok, *Vice Pres*
EMP: 7
SALES (est): 630K **Privately Held**
SIC: 3911 Jewelry, precious metal

(G-9962)
EAST COAST ORTHOIC & PROS COR
3927 Broadway (10032-1538)
PHONE................................212 923-2161
Lawrence Benenati, *Branch Mgr*
EMP: 5
SALES (corp-wide): 9.8MM **Privately Held**
SIC: 3842 Orthopedic appliances
PA: East Coast Orthotic & Prosthetic Corp.
75 Burt Dr
Deer Park NY 11729
516 248-5566

(G-9963)
EAST MEET EAST INC
347 5th Ave Rm 1402 (10016-5034)
PHONE................................650 450-4446
Mariko Tokioka, *CEO*
Kentaro Ejima, *Admin Sec*
EMP: 7 EST: 2014
SALES (est): 348.1K **Privately Held**
SIC: 2741

(G-9964)
EASTERN HARBOR MEDIA
37 W 17th St Ste 3e (10011-5523)
PHONE................................212 725-9260
Joe Conason, *Editor*
Stephanie Schwartz, *Editor*
Harold Itzkowitz, *Accounts Exec*
Elizabeth Wagley, *Mng Member*
EMP: 8
SALES (est): 557.2K **Privately Held**
SIC: 2741 Miscellaneous publishing

(G-9965)
EASTERN JEWELRY MFG CO INC
48 W 48th St Ste 707 (10036-1714)
PHONE................................212 840-0001
Soloman Witriol, *President*
EMP: 50
SQ FT: 16,000
SALES (est): 3.8MM **Privately Held**
SIC: 3911 Jewelry apparel; bracelets, precious metal; earrings, precious metal; rosaries or other small religious articles, precious metal

(G-9966)
EASTERN SILK MILLS INC
148 W 37th St Fl 3 (10018-6987)
PHONE................................212 730-1300
Fax: 212 302-1665
Andy Ryu, *Controller*
Sheena Suon, *Manager*
EMP: 9
SALES (corp-wide): 4.4MM **Privately Held**
SIC: 2262 2221 Dyeing: manmade fiber & silk broadwoven fabrics; broadwoven fabric mills, manmade
PA: Eastern Silk Mills Inc.
212 Catherine St
Elizabeth NJ

(G-9967)
EASTERN STRATEGIC MATERIALS
45 Rockefeller Plz # 2000 (10111-0100)
PHONE................................212 332-1619

Kai Wong, *President*
Matthew Harris, *Vice Pres*
EMP: 41
SALES (est): 4MM **Privately Held**
SIC: 3365 3812 3822 Aerospace castings, aluminum; defense systems & equipment; space vehicle guidance systems & equipment; energy cutoff controls, residential or commercial types

(G-9968)
EASTNETS AMERICAS CORP
450 Fashion Ave Ste 1509 (10123-1509)
PHONE................................212 631-0666
Hazem Mulhim, *President*
Paul W Chin, *General Mgr*
Mohamed E Bakkali, *CFO*
Kareem Milhem, *Accounts Mgr*
Wanda Rozario, *Manager*
EMP: 10
SALES (est): 1MM **Privately Held**
SIC: 7372 Prepackaged software

(G-9969)
EASTPORT OPERATING PARTNERS LP (PA)
Also Called: Eastport Management
204 E 20th St Fl 3 (10003-1802)
PHONE................................212 387-8791
Fax: 212 674-6821
Edward J Kata, *Partner*
J Andrew McWethy, *General Ptnr*
F Patrick Smith, *Manager*
◆ EMP: 3
SALES (est): 37.4MM **Privately Held**
WEB: www.eastportlp.com
SIC: 3593 3492 Fluid power cylinders, hydraulic or pneumatic; fluid power valves & hose fittings

(G-9970)
EATON CORPORATION
830 3rd Ave Fl 7 (10022-6565)
PHONE................................212 319-2100
Fax: 212 833-0250
Jonathan Knight, *Project Engr*
John Mari, *Sales Engr*
Al Vincenzi, *Manager*
EMP: 218 **Privately Held**
SIC: 3625 Motor controls & accessories
HQ: Eaton Corporation
1000 Eaton Blvd
Cleveland OH 44122
216 523-5000

(G-9971)
EB ACQUISITIONS LLC
444 Madison Ave Ste 501 (10022-6974)
PHONE................................212 355-3310
Nachum Stein,
EMP: 100
SALES (est): 5.7MM **Privately Held**
SIC: 3643 3315 Connectors, electric cord; wire & fabricated wire products

(G-9972)
EBM CARE INC
317 Madison Ave (10017-5201)
PHONE................................212 500-5000
Jack Fitzgibbons, *President*
EMP: 7
SALES (est): 327.8K **Privately Held**
SIC: 7372 Business oriented computer software

(G-9973)
EC PUBLICATIONS INC
1700 Broadway Frnt 5 (10019-5979)
PHONE................................212 728-1844
Paul Levitz, *President*
Dorothy Crouch, *Vice Pres*
EMP: 12 EST: 1942
SALES (est): 1.1MM
SALES (corp-wide): 28.1B **Publicly Held**
SIC: 2721 Magazines: publishing only, not printed on site
HQ: Warner Communications Inc
1 Time Warner Ctr Bsmt B
New York NY 10019
212 484-8000

(G-9974)
ECCLESIASTICAL COMMUNICATIONS
Also Called: Catholic New York
1011 1st Ave Fl 6 (10022-4112)
PHONE................................212 688-2399
Fax: 212 688-2642
Bishop Robert A Brucato, *President*
Arthur L McKenna, *General Mgr*
Mary Gregory, *Accountant*
John Woods, *Manager*
EMP: 13
SALES (est): 750K **Privately Held**
SIC: 2711 Newspapers: publishing only, not printed on site

(G-9975)
ECHO GROUP INC
62 W 39th St Ste 1005 (10018-3818)
PHONE................................917 608-7440
Fax: 212 382-2490
EMP: 15
SALES (est): 980K **Privately Held**
SIC: 3911 Mfg Precious Metal Jewelry

(G-9976)
ECLECTIC CNTRACT FURN INDS INC
450 Fashion Ave Ste 2710 (10123-2710)
PHONE................................212 967-5504
Alex Marc, *President*
▲ EMP: 14
SQ FT: 1,000
SALES (est): 2MM **Privately Held**
WEB: www.eclecticcontract.com
SIC: 2511 Wood household furniture

(G-9977)
ECLIPSE COLLECTION JEWELERS
7 W 45th St Ste 1401 (10036-4905)
PHONE................................212 764-6883
Fax: 212 719-2348
Vatcag Aghjayan, *President*
EMP: 10
SALES (est): 780K **Privately Held**
SIC: 3911 Jewelry, precious metal

(G-9978)
ECONOMIST INTELLIGENCE UNIT NA
750 3rd Ave Fl 5 (10017-2723)
PHONE................................212 554-0600
Fax: 212 245-6413
Chris Stibbs, *Ch of Bd*
David Cox, *Senior VP*
Paul Rossi, *Senior VP*
Fritz Maier, *VP Human Res*
Robin Riddle, *Accounts Mgr*
EMP: 68
SQ FT: 18,000
SALES (est): 13.3MM
SALES (corp-wide): 479.2MM **Privately Held**
WEB: www.eiu.com
SIC: 2721 8732 Periodicals: publishing only; business analysis
HQ: The Economist Newspaper Group Incorporated
750 3rd Ave Fl 5
New York NY 10017
212 541-0500

(G-9979)
ECONOMIST NEWSPAPER GROUP INC (HQ)
Also Called: Economist Group, The
750 3rd Ave Fl 5 (10017-2723)
PHONE................................212 541-0500
Chris Stibbs, *CEO*
James Myers, *Managing Dir*
Mercedes Cardona, *Editor*
Tony Tran, *Vice Pres*
Mary Baksh, *Controller*
▲ EMP: 220

SALES (est): 134.5MM
SALES (corp-wide): 479.2MM **Privately Held**
SIC: 2721 7313 5963 Periodicals: publishing & printing; magazines: publishing & printing; printed media advertising representatives; magazine advertising representative; newspaper advertising representative; encyclopedias & publications, direct sales; magazine subscription sales, excl. mail order, house sales
PA: Economist Newspaper Limited(The)
25 St James's Street
London SW1A
207 830-7000

(G-9980)
ECONOMIST NEWSPAPER NA INC (DH)
Also Called: Economist Magazine, The
750 3rd Ave Fl 5 (10017-2723)
PHONE................................212 554-0676
Chris Stibbs, *CEO*
Paul Rossi, *Exec VP*
David Cox, *CFO*
Richard Hargreaves, *Sales Dir*
Daniel Morris, *Sales Dir*
EMP: 15
SQ FT: 28,900
SALES (est): 18.4MM
SALES (corp-wide): 479.2MM **Privately Held**
SIC: 2711 5192 Newspapers; magazines
HQ: The Economist Newspaper Group Incorporated
750 3rd Ave Fl 5
New York NY 10017
212 541-0500

(G-9981)
EDITH LANCES CORP
247 W 35th St Fl 2 (10001-1927)
PHONE................................212 683-1990
Fax: 212 683-1949
Jay S Gingold, *President*
Marsha Gingold, *Vice Pres*
EMP: 20
SQ FT: 3,000
SALES: 748K **Privately Held**
SIC: 2342 Brassieres

(G-9982)
EDITIONS SCHELLMANN INC
50 Greene St Fl 2 (10013-2663)
PHONE................................212 219-1821
York Schellmann, *President*
EMP: 5
SALES (est): 370K **Privately Held**
SIC: 2731 Book publishing

(G-9983)
EDRINGTON GROUP USA LLC (PA)
150 5th Ave Fl 11 (10011-4347)
PHONE................................212 352-6000
Chris Spalding, *President*
Jessica Tamilio, *Manager*
Mike Zitelli, *General Counsel*
EMP: 24
SALES (est): 9.5MM **Privately Held**
SIC: 2084 Wines, brandy & brandy spirits

(G-9984)
EDSIM LEATHER CO INC (PA)
131 W 35th St Fl 14 (10001-2111)
PHONE................................212 695-8500
Simone Kamali, *President*
Edmond Kamali, *Vice Pres*
Joel Kamali, *Sales Mgr*
Lauren Kamali, *Sales Staff*
Suren Lall, *Information Mgr*
▲ EMP: 11 EST: 1981
SQ FT: 7,000
SALES: 37MM **Privately Held**
WEB: www.hinet.net
SIC: 3111 Leather tanning & finishing

(G-9985)
EDWARD FIELDS INCORPORATED (PA)
Also Called: Paiping Carpets
150 E 58th St Ste 1101 (10155-1101)
PHONE................................212 310-0400
Jim Chaplain, *Ch of Bd*
Ed Goldberg, *Vice Pres*

New York - New York County (G-9986)

Jeffry Brody, *Manager*
Adrian Angelin, *Contract Law*
EMP: 12 **EST:** 1933
SQ FT: 6,500
SALES (est): 13.4MM **Privately Held**
WEB: www.edwardfieldsinc.com
SIC: 2273 Carpets & rugs; rugs, tufted

(G-9986)
EFRONT FINANCIAL SOLUTIONS INC
11 E 44th St Ste 900 (10017-3608)
PHONE 212 220-0660
Eric Bernstein, *COO*
EMP: 25
SALES (corp-wide): 782K **Privately Held**
SIC: 7372 Business oriented computer software
HQ: E Front
    2 Rue Louis David
    Paris 75116
    149 964-060

(G-9987)
EFT ENERGY INC
251 W 30th St Ste 15e (10001-2810)
PHONE 212 290-2300
Craig Ennis, *CEO*
Peter Fagan, *COO*
Jason Kim, *Vice Pres*
EMP: 8
SQ FT: 2,250
SALES (est): 970.8K
SALES (corp-wide): 26.7B **Privately Held**
SIC: 7372 Application computer software
PA: Koch Industries, Inc.
    4111 E 37th St N
    Wichita KS 67220
    316 828-5500

(G-9988)
EIDOSMEDIA INC
14 Wall St Ste 6c (10005-2170)
PHONE 646 795-2100
Steven Ball, *CEO*
EMP: 18
SALES (est): 2.4MM **Privately Held**
SIC: 2721 Periodicals: publishing & printing

(G-9989)
EIGHTEEN LIANA TRADING INC
Also Called: Liana Uniforms
110 W 40th St Rm 606 (10018-8554)
PHONE 718 369-4247
Fax: 718 369-4247
Arie Dervich, *President*
Helen Dervich, *Vice Pres*
▲ **EMP:** 22
SQ FT: 10,000
SALES (est): 2MM **Privately Held**
SIC: 2326 Medical & hospital uniforms, men's

(G-9990)
EILEENS SPECIAL CHEESECAKE
17 Cleveland Pl Frnt A (10012-4052)
PHONE 212 966-5585
Fax: 212 219-9558
Eileen Avezzano, *President*
EMP: 6
SQ FT: 600
SALES (est): 310K **Privately Held**
WEB: www.eileenscheesecake.com
SIC: 2051 Bakery: wholesale or wholesale/retail combined; cakes, bakery: except frozen

(G-9991)
EL AGUILA
137 E 116th St Frnt 1 (10029-1385)
PHONE 212 410-2450
EMP: 7
SALES (est): 393.9K **Privately Held**
SIC: 2711 Newspapers, publishing & printing

(G-9992)
EL-LA DESIGN INC
Also Called: My Apparel
209 W 38th St Rm 901 (10018-4558)
PHONE 212 382-1080
Fax: 212 382-1125
Elaine Lai, *President*
EMP: 5

SALES (est): 590K **Privately Held**
SIC: 2339 Sportswear, women's

(G-9993)
ELANA LADEROS LTD
Also Called: Joanna Mastroianni
230 W 38th St Fl 15 (10018-9026)
PHONE 212 764-0840
Fax: 212 398-6185
Joanna Mastroianni, *President*
EMP: 10
SQ FT: 3,500
SALES (est): 1.3MM **Privately Held**
WEB: www.joannamastroianni.com
SIC: 2335 Women's, juniors' & misses' dresses

(G-9994)
ELDEEN CLOTHING INC
250 W 39th St (10018-4414)
PHONE 212 719-9190
Spenser Alpern, *CEO*
EMP: 10 **EST:** 2014
SALES (est): 573K
SALES (corp-wide): 29.2MM **Privately Held**
SIC: 2231 Apparel & outerwear broadwoven fabrics
PA: H.M.S. Productions Inc.
    250 W 39th St Fl 12
    New York NY 10018
    212 719-9190

(G-9995)
ELEANOR ETTINGER INC
24 W 57th St Ste 609 (10019-3918)
PHONE 212 925-7474
Eleanor Ettinger, *President*
Barbara Stevens, *Vice Pres*
EMP: 20 **EST:** 1975
SALES (est): 1.7MM **Privately Held**
WEB: www.eleanorettinger.com
SIC: 2731 2752 Books: publishing only; commercial printing, offset

(G-9996)
ELECTRIC LIGHTING AGENCIES (PA)
Also Called: Ela
36 W 25th St Fl 6 (10010-2757)
PHONE 212 645-4580
Jaime Levy, *Principal*
Thomas Sica, *Vice Pres*
John Bielen, *Engineer*
Robert J Carr, *Sales Staff*
John Weintraub, *Sales Staff*
EMP: 22
SALES (est): 3.8MM **Privately Held**
SIC: 3646 Commercial indusl & institutional electric lighting fixtures

(G-9997)
ELECTRONIC ARTS INC
1515 Broadway Rm 3601 (10036-8901)
PHONE 212 672-0722
Barbara Gallacher, *Vice Pres*
EMP: 7
SALES (corp-wide): 4.4B **Publicly Held**
WEB: www.ea.com
SIC: 7372 Prepackaged software
PA: Electronic Arts Inc.
    209 Redwood Shores Pkwy
    Redwood City CA 94065
    650 628-1500

(G-9998)
ELEGANT HEADWEAR CO INC
Also Called: ABG Accessories
10 W 33rd St Rm 1122 (10001-3306)
PHONE 212 695-8520
Fax: 212 695-7736
Michael Brett, *Branch Mgr*
EMP: 8
SALES (corp-wide): 41.8MM **Privately Held**
WEB: www.elegantheadwear.com
SIC: 2253 Knit outerwear mills
PA: Elegant Headwear Co. Inc.
    1000 Jefferson Ave
    Elizabeth NJ 07201
    908 558-1200

(G-9999)
ELEGANT JEWELERS MFG CO INC
31 W 47th St Ste 301 (10036-2888)
PHONE 212 869-4951
Sandy Petropoulos, *President*
Nick Seretis, *Vice Pres*
EMP: 12
SQ FT: 1,500
SALES (est): 1.1MM **Privately Held**
WEB: www.elegantsilverjewellery.net
SIC: 3911 Jewelry, precious metal

(G-10000)
ELEPHANT TALK CMMNCATIONS CORP
100 Park Ave (10017-5516)
PHONE 866 901-3309
Tim Payne, *President*
Armin Hessler, *COO*
Mark Nije, *CFO*
Martin Zuurbier, *CTO*
Alex Vermeulen, *General Counsel*
EMP: 252
SALES: 31MM **Privately Held**
SIC: 7372 Prepackaged software

(G-10001)
ELIE TAHARI LTD
501 5th Ave Fl 2 (10017-7825)
PHONE 212 398-2622
Elie Tahari, *Principal*
Birgit Papscoe, *Manager*
EMP: 10
SALES (corp-wide): 241.7MM **Privately Held**
SIC: 2331 2339 2337 5621 Blouses, women's & juniors': made from purchased material; slacks: women's, misses' & juniors'; suits: women's, misses' & juniors'; jackets & vests, except fur & leather: women's; women's clothing stores; men's & boys' clothing stores
PA: Elie Tahari Ltd.
    16 Bleeker St
    Millburn NJ 07041
    973 671-6300

(G-10002)
ELIE TAHARI LTD
510 5th Ave Fl 3 (10036-7507)
PHONE 212 398-2622
Fax: 212 221-6776
Brendan Maher, *Sales Dir*
David Elron, *Branch Mgr*
Rishi Sharma, *Software Dev*
EMP: 75
SALES (corp-wide): 241.7MM **Privately Held**
SIC: 2337 8741 2339 Suits: women's, misses & juniors'; management services; women's & misses' outerwear
PA: Elie Tahari Ltd.
    16 Bleeker St
    Millburn NJ 07041
    973 671-6300

(G-10003)
ELIE TAHARI LTD
1114 Ave Of The Americas (10036-7703)
PHONE 212 763-2000
Fax: 212 763-2298
Robert Goldsmith, *Senior VP*
Julie S Deloca, *Vice Pres*
Jennifer Globus, *Vice Pres*
Jill Safinski, *Mktg Dir*
Arthur S Levine, *Branch Mgr*
EMP: 60
SALES (corp-wide): 241.7MM **Privately Held**
SIC: 2331 2337 Blouses, women's & juniors': made from purchased material; uniforms, except athletic; women's, misses' & juniors'
PA: Elie Tahari Ltd.
    16 Bleeker St
    Millburn NJ 07041
    973 671-6300

(G-10004)
ELIE TAHARI LTD
11 W 42nd St Fl 14 (10036-8002)
PHONE 973 671-6300
Lisanne Kolligs, *President*
Debbie Elmore, *Senior VP*

Scott Currie, *Vice Pres*
Lisa Walsh, *Vice Pres*
Alysha Brock, *Opers Spvr*
EMP: 75
SALES (corp-wide): 241.7MM **Privately Held**
SIC: 2337 Suits: women's, misses' & juniors'
PA: Elie Tahari Ltd.
    16 Bleeker St
    Millburn NJ 07041
    973 671-6300

(G-10005)
ELIS BREAD (ELI ZABAR) INC (PA)
1064 Madison Ave Apt 5 (10028-0252)
PHONE 212 772-2011
Eli Zabar, *President*
Natalie Stettner, *Manager*
Chris Reinhart, *Info Tech Dir*
EMP: 10
SALES (est): 16.7MM **Privately Held**
WEB: www.elisbread.com
SIC: 2045 Bread & bread type roll mixes: from purchased flour

(G-10006)
ELITE GROUP INTERNATIONAL NY
15 W 37th St (10018-6223)
PHONE 917 334-1919
EMP: 11
SALES (est): 1.2MM **Privately Held**
SIC: 3915 Lapidary work, contract or other

(G-10007)
ELITE PARFUMS LTD (HQ)
551 5th Ave Rm 1500 (10176-1599)
PHONE 212 983-2640
Jean Madar, *President*
Philippe Benacin, *President*
Bruce Elbelia, *Exec VP*
Wayne C Hamerling, *Exec VP*
Russell Greenberg, *CFO*
▲ **EMP:** 57
SQ FT: 12,000
SALES (est): 3.6MM
SALES (corp-wide): 468.5MM **Publicly Held**
SIC: 2844 5122 Toilet preparations; perfumes; toiletries
PA: Inter Parfums, Inc.
    551 5th Ave
    New York NY 10176
    212 983-2640

(G-10008)
ELIZABETH EAKINS INC (PA)
654 Madison Ave Rm 1409 (10065-8432)
PHONE 212 628-1950
Elizabeth Eakins, *President*
Scott Lethbridge, *Vice Pres*
Jamie Alencastro, *Manager*
▲ **EMP:** 10
SQ FT: 4,000
SALES (est): 3.1MM **Privately Held**
WEB: www.elizabetheakins.com
SIC: 2273 5713 5023 Carpets, hand & machine made; carpets; carpets

(G-10009)
ELIZABETH FILLMORE LLC
27 W 20th St Ste 705 (10011-3727)
PHONE 212 647-0863
Fax: 212 647-1562
Thomas Allen, *Vice Pres*
Elizabeth Fillmore,
EMP: 7
SQ FT: 1,900
SALES (est): 770.6K **Privately Held**
WEB: www.elizabethfillmorebridal.com
SIC: 2335 Gowns, formal

(G-10010)
ELIZABETH GILLETT LTD
Also Called: Elizabeth Gillett Designs
260 W 36th St Rm 802 (10018-8992)
PHONE 212 629-7993
Fax: 212 629-7993
Elizabeth Gillett, *President*
Tarafawn Marek, *Exec VP*
Stephanie Corren, *Sales Mgr*
EMP: 6
SQ FT: 1,000

▲ = Import ▼ = Export
◆ = Import/Export

SALES (est): 810K **Privately Held**
WEB: www.egillett.com
SIC: 2339 Scarves, hoods, headbands, etc.: women's

(G-10011)
ELLIOTT ASSOCIATES LP (PA)
712 5th Ave Fl 36 (10019-4108)
PHONE..................................212 586-9431
Paul Singer, *Partner*
Brian Kelly, *Engineer*
Brian Corrigan, *Controller*
Steven Kasoff, *Portfolio Mgr*
Anthony Argo, *Accountant*
EMP: 40 EST: 1986
SALES (est): 156.8MM **Privately Held**
WEB: www.elliott-assoc.com
SIC: 1382 6282 Seismograph surveys; investment advisory service

(G-10012)
ELMGANG ENTERPRISES I INC
Also Called: Espostos Fnest Qlty Ssage Pdts
354 W 38th St Frnt (10018-2954)
PHONE..................................212 868-4142
Fax: 212 868-0065
David Samuels, *President*
Kimbal Musk, *General Mgr*
EMP: 10
SQ FT: 5,000
SALES (est): 1.4MM **Privately Held**
WEB: www.espositosausage.com
SIC: 2013 5147 Sausages & related products, from purchased meat; meats & meat products

(G-10013)
ELODINA INC
222 Broadway Fl 19 (10038-2550)
PHONE....................................646 402-5202
Paul Reinitz, *President*
EMP: 5
SALES (est): 117.2K **Privately Held**
SIC: 7372 Business oriented computer software

(G-10014)
ELSEVIER ENGINEERING INFO INC
360 Park Ave S (10010-1710)
PHONE..................................201 356-6800
Martin Tanke, *CEO*
Roland Dietz, *Vice Pres*
Paul Weislogel, *Vice Pres*
Joan Coffey, *Advt Staff*
Tom Matera, *Manager*
EMP: 46
SQ FT: 10,000
SALES (est): 2.9MM
SALES (corp-wide): 9B **Privately Held**
WEB: www.papervillage2.com
SIC: 2741 2731 Miscellaneous publishing; books: publishing only
HQ: Elsevier Inc.
   230 Park Ave Fl 7
   New York NY 10169
   212 633-3773

(G-10015)
ELSEVIER INC (DH)
230 Park Ave Fl 7 (10169-0935)
PHONE..................................212 633-3773
Fax: 212 633-3880
Ron Mobed, *CEO*
Hajo Oltmanns, *President*
Joe Lam, *Managing Dir*
Mj Janse, *Editor*
Jonathan Simpson, *Editor*
◆ EMP: 277 EST: 1962
SQ FT: 65,000
SALES (est): 213.6MM
SALES (corp-wide): 9B **Privately Held**
WEB: www.elsevierfoundation.org
SIC: 2741 Technical manuals: publishing only, not printed on site
HQ: Elsevier Limited
   The Boulevard
   Kidlington OXON OX5 1
   186 584-3000

(G-10016)
ELUMINOCITY US INC
80 Pine St Fl 24 (10005-1732)
PHONE....................................651 528-1165
Sebastian Jagsch, *CEO*
Mike Rockwood, *General Mgr*

EMP: 2 EST: 2015
SQ FT: 200
SALES: 1.8MM **Privately Held**
SIC: 3648 3694 3629 Street lighting fixtures; battery charging generators, automobile & aircraft; battery chargers, rectifying or nonrotating

(G-10017)
ELY BEACH SOLAR LLC
5030 Broadway Ste 819 (10034-1670)
PHONE....................................718 796-9400
Alison Karmel, *Vice Pres*
EMP: 8
SALES (est): 666.4K **Privately Held**
SIC: 3674 Solar cells

(G-10018)
EMA JEWELRY INC
246 W 38th St Fl 6 (10018-5854)
PHONE..................................212 575-8989
Fax: 212 575-9267
Michael Weiss, *CEO*
Edward Weiss, *Vice Pres*
Alex Weiss, *Treasurer*
EMP: 65 EST: 1977
SQ FT: 7,500
SALES (est): 8.9MM **Privately Held**
WEB: www.emajewelry.com
SIC: 3911 3961 Jewelry, precious metal; costume jewelry

(G-10019)
EMBASSY APPAREL INC
37 W 37th St Fl 10 (10018-6354)
PHONE..................................212 768-8330
Ezra Cattan, *President*
Jack Cattan, *Vice Pres*
Judah Cattan, *Vice Pres*
Nadia Ramnauth, *Manager*
EMP: 18
SQ FT: 10,000
SALES (est): 950.8K **Privately Held**
SIC: 2331 5136 5137 Women's & misses' blouses & shirts; men's & boys' furnishings; women's & children's accessories

(G-10020)
EMBLAZE SYSTEMS INC (HQ)
Also Called: Geo Publishing
424 Madison Ave Fl 16 (10017-1137)
PHONE..................................212 371-1100
Bruce Edwards, *President*
Joe Budenholzer, *President*
Brad Grob, *Vice Pres*
Michael Weiss, *Vice Pres*
Lydia Edward, *Treasurer*
EMP: 120
SQ FT: 7,500
SALES (est): 7.6MM
SALES (corp-wide): 59.9MM **Privately Held**
SIC: 7372 Prepackaged software
PA: B.S.D Crown Ltd
   7 Begin Menachem Rd
   Ramat Gan 52681
   976 997-55

(G-10021)
EMC CORPORATION
1180 Ave Of The Americas (10036-8401)
PHONE..................................212 899-5500
Jerry Gross, *Manager*
Walt Kucharski, *Director*
EMP: 46
SALES (corp-wide): 72.7B **Publicly Held**
WEB: www.emc.com
SIC: 7372 Business oriented computer software
HQ: Emc Corporation
   176 South St
   Hopkinton MA 01748
   508 435-1000

(G-10022)
EMCO ELECTRIC SERVICES LLC
526 W 26th St Rm 1012 (10001-5541)
PHONE..................................212 420-9766
Meziar Ghavidel, *Mng Member*
Mehr Mansuri, *Mng Member*
EMP: 5 EST: 2013
SALES: 170K **Privately Held**
SIC: 3699 1731 Electrical equipment & supplies; electronic controls installation

(G-10023)
EMERSON ELECTRIC CO
1250 Broadway Ste 2300 (10018-3726)
PHONE..................................212 244-2490
Jennifer Nichols, *Principal*
Robert Burns, *Director*
EMP: 23
SALES (corp-wide): 22.3B **Publicly Held**
WEB: www.gotoemerson.com
SIC: 3823 Industrial instrmnts msrmnt display/control process variable
PA: Emerson Electric Co.
   8000 W Florissant Ave
   Saint Louis MO 63136
   314 553-2000

(G-10024)
EMPOWRX LLC
249 E 53rd St Apt 2a (10022-4836)
PHONE..................................212 755-3577
Heather Raymond,
EMP: 5
SALES (est): 217.9K **Privately Held**
SIC: 7372 Prepackaged software

(G-10025)
EMSARU USA CORP
Also Called: Hampshire Jewels
608 5th Ave Ste 500 (10020-2303)
PHONE..................................212 459-9355
Fax: 212 459-9354
Harry Molhan, *President*
EMP: 5
SALES (est): 430K **Privately Held**
SIC: 3911 Jewelry, precious metal

(G-10026)
EMSIG MANUFACTURING CORP (PA)
263 W 38th St Fl 5 (10018-0291)
PHONE..................................718 784-7717
Lawrence Jacobs, *President*
John Lerner, *Vice Pres*
Nancy McCaffery, *Manager*
Paula Muster, *Software Dev*
Arthur Klein, *Admin Sec*
◆ EMP: 15 EST: 1965
SQ FT: 19,000
SALES (est): 22.5MM **Privately Held**
SIC: 3965 Buttons & parts

(G-10027)
EMSIG MANUFACTURING CORP
263 W 38th St Fl 5 (10018-0291)
PHONE..................................718 784-7717
Fax: 212 971-0413
Lawrence Jacobs, *President*
EMP: 20
SALES (corp-wide): 22.5MM **Privately Held**
SIC: 3965 Buttons & parts
PA: Emsig Manufacturing Corp.
   263 W 38th St Fl 5
   New York NY 10018
   718 784-7717

(G-10028)
EMUSICCOM INC (PA)
215 Lexington Ave Fl 18 (10016-6023)
PHONE..................................212 201-9240
Peter Chapman, *CEO*
Daniel Stein, *Ch of Bd*
David Packman, *President*
Randy McKelvey, *Vice Pres*
Emusic News, *Vice Pres*
EMP: 54
SALES (est): 10.6MM **Privately Held**
WEB: www.emusic.com
SIC: 3652 Pre-recorded records & tapes

(G-10029)
ENCHANTE ACCESSORIES INC (PA)
16 E 34th St Fl 16 (10016-4359)
PHONE..................................212 689-6008
Fax: 212 684-3622
Ezra Erani, *Chairman*
Gabe Kehzrie, *Vice Pres*
Tanya Kuznetsov, *Controller*
Alan Levy, *VP Sales*
Gabe Kezrie, *Mktg Dir*
◆ EMP: 150

SALES (est): 65.5MM **Privately Held**
WEB: www.emch.com
SIC: 2499 Kitchen, bathroom & household ware: wood

(G-10030)
ENCHANTE LITES LLC (HQ)
15 W 34th St Fl 8 (10001-3015)
PHONE..................................212 602-1818
Ezra Erani, *President*
Abraham Weinberger, *CFO*
▲ EMP: 25
SALES (est): 3.4MM
SALES (corp-wide): 65.5MM **Privately Held**
SIC: 3648 Decorative area lighting fixtures
PA: Enchante Accessories Inc.
   16 E 34th St Fl 16
   New York NY 10016
   212 689-6008

(G-10031)
ENCYSIVE PHARMACEUTICALS INC (HQ)
235 E 42nd St (10017-5703)
PHONE..................................212 733-2323
John M Pietruski, *Ch of Bd*
Bruce D Given, *President*
Ruth Bateshill, *Top Exec*
Richard A F Dixon, *Senior VP*
Paul S Manierre, *Vice Pres*
▲ EMP: 35
SQ FT: 40,730
SALES (est): 12.7MM
SALES (corp-wide): 48.8B **Publicly Held**
SIC: 2834 8733 Pharmaceutical preparations; medical research
PA: Pfizer Inc.
   235 E 42nd St
   New York NY 10017
   212 733-2323

(G-10032)
ENDAVA INC (HQ)
441 Lexington Ave Rm 702 (10017-3922)
PHONE..................................212 920-7240
Dan Sullivan, *President*
EMP: 2
SQ FT: 2,000
SALES (est): 1.3MM
SALES (corp-wide): 129.7MM **Privately Held**
SIC: 7372 7371 7375 Business oriented computer software; custom computer programming services; on-line data base information retrieval
PA: Endava Limited
   125 Old Broad Street
   London EC2N
   207 367-1000

(G-10033)
ENDURANCE LLC
530 7th Ave Rm 902 (10018-4874)
PHONE..................................212 719-2500
Fax: 212 719-2507
Jason Messler, *Vice Pres*
Athanasios Nastos,
Renjie Luo,
Daidai Ni,
Qiwen Zhao,
▲ EMP: 20
SALES (est): 1.5MM **Privately Held**
SIC: 2329 Men's & boys' sportswear & athletic clothing

(G-10034)
ENDURART INC
Also Called: Quality Embedments Mfg Co
132 Nassau St Rm 1100 (10038-2430)
PHONE..................................212 473-7000
Stuart Levine, *President*
Henry Richmond, *Financial Exec*
Raffik Brito, *Art Dir*
EMP: 30
SQ FT: 18,000
SALES (est): 2.4MM **Privately Held**
SIC: 3914 2821 Trophies; plastics materials & resins

(G-10035)
ENER-G COGEN LLC
1261 Broadway (10001-3506)
PHONE..................................718 551-7170
Vishnu Barran, *Sales Staff*
Chis Hayten, *Mng Member*

New York - New York County (G-10036)

EMP: 5 **EST:** 2011
SALES (est): 292.6K **Privately Held**
SIC: 3621 Power generators

(G-10036)
ENER1 INC (HQ)
1540 Broadway Fl 25c (10036-4039)
PHONE................................212 920-3500
Alex Sorokin, *CEO*
Michael Alma, *CEO*
Melissa Debes, *Ch of Bd*
Thomas Snyder, *Ch of Bd*
Tae-Hee Yoon, *Ch of Bd*
EMP: 33
SQ FT: 3,500
SALES (est): 98.9MM
SALES (corp-wide): 103MM **Privately Held**
SIC: 3691 Storage batteries
PA: Ener1 Group, Inc.
550 W Cypress Creek Rd
Fort Lauderdale FL 33309
954 202-4442

(G-10037)
ENERGY BRANDS INC (HQ)
Also Called: Glaceau
260 Madison Ave Fl 10 (10016-2401)
PHONE................................212 545-6000
Fax: 718 747-5900
J Darius Bikoff, *CEO*
Michael Repole, *President*
Carol Dollard, *COO*
William D Hawkins, *Vice Pres*
Glenn Ricks, *Vice Pres*
▼ **EMP:** 61
SQ FT: 15,000
SALES (est): 32.5MM
SALES (corp-wide): 44.2B **Publicly Held**
WEB: www.energybrands.com
SIC: 2086 Soft drinks: packaged in cans, bottles, etc.
PA: The Coca-Cola Company
1 Coca Cola Plz Nw
Atlanta GA 30313
404 676-2121

(G-10038)
ENERGY INTELLIGENCE GROUP INC (PA)
270 Madison Ave Fl 19 (10016-0601)
PHONE................................212 532-1112
Fax: 212 532-4479
Elias Saber, *President*
David Kirsch, *Managing Dir*
David Knapp, *Managing Dir*
Megan Elmore, *Editor*
Jason Fargo, *Editor*
EMP: 30
SQ FT: 7,000
SALES (est): 10.6MM **Privately Held**
SIC: 2741 Newsletter publishing

(G-10039)
ENERTIV INC
555 W 23rd St Ph M (10011-1033)
PHONE................................646 350-3525
Connell McGill, *President*
Sharad Shankar, *Engineer*
Pavel Khodorkovskiy, *Treasurer*
Felix Lipov, *Software Dev*
EMP: 6
SALES (est): 1MM **Privately Held**
SIC: 3825 Instruments to measure electricity

(G-10040)
ENGELACK GEM CORPORATION
36 W 47th St Ste 601 (10036-8636)
PHONE................................212 719-3094
Imre England, *President*
Herman Ackerman, *Vice Pres*
EMP: 2
SALES (est): 1MM **Privately Held**
SIC: 3915 Lapidary work & diamond cutting & polishing

(G-10041)
ENLIGHTEN AIR INC
200 E 71st St (10021-5751)
PHONE................................917 656-1248
William O'Boyle, *CEO*
EMP: 5
SALES: 392MM **Privately Held**
SIC: 3728 Target drones

(G-10042)
ENTERPRISE MANAGEMENT TECH LLC
Also Called: Emt
1 Penn Plz Ste 360025 (10119-0002)
PHONE................................212 835-1557
Ramsey Jallad,
Patrick Stach,
John Terrill,
EMP: 3
SQ FT: 300
SALES (est): 1MM **Privately Held**
WEB: www.em-technology.net
SIC: 7372 Business oriented computer software

(G-10043)
ENTERPRISE PRESS INC
627 Greenwich St (10014-3327)
PHONE................................212 741-2111
Fax: 212 627-7937
Robert Hort, *Ch of Bd*
Benjamin Hort, *President*
Michael Hort, *Principal*
Milton Palenbaum, *Purchasing*
Andrew Hort, *Treasurer*
EMP: 145 **EST:** 1915
SQ FT: 85,000
SALES (est): 12.5MM **Privately Held**
SIC: 2759 2752 Commercial printing; commercial printing, lithographic

(G-10044)
ENTERTAINMENT WEEKLY INC (HQ)
135 W 50th St Fl 3 (10020-1201)
PHONE................................212 522-5600
Fax: 212 522-0074
Andy Sareyan, *President*
Paul Caine, *Publisher*
Mike Bruno, *Editor*
Tim Stack, *Editor*
Steve Edwards, *Vice Pres*
▲ **EMP:** 135
SQ FT: 50,000
SALES (est): 16MM
SALES (corp-wide): 3.1B **Publicly Held**
SIC: 2731 7812 Book publishing; motion picture & video production; television film production; motion picture production
PA: Time Inc.
225 Liberty St
New York NY 10281
212 522-1212

(G-10045)
ENTRAINANT INC
Also Called: Stylesprit
112 W 34th St Fl 18 (10120-0001)
PHONE................................212 946-4724
Ihsan Ugurlu, *President*
EMP: 6 **EST:** 2015
SALES (est): 233.3K **Privately Held**
SIC: 2741

(G-10046)
ENUMERAL BIOMEDICAL CORP (PA)
1370 Broadway Fl 5 (10018-7302)
PHONE................................347 227-4787
Arthur H Tinkelenberg, *CEO*
Kevin Sarney, *Vice Pres*
Derek Brand, *Director*
EMP: 6
SALES (est): 1.1MM **Privately Held**
SIC: 2834 Pharmaceutical preparations

(G-10047)
ENVY PUBLISHING GROUP INC
Also Called: N V Magazine
118 E 25th St Bsmt Ll (10010-2915)
PHONE................................212 253-9874
Fax: 212 253-9874
Kyle Donovan, *CEO*
Maria Gordian, *President*
Kenneth Williams, *Mktg Dir*
Christopher Chaney, *Adv Dir*
EMP: 6
SQ FT: 3,000
SALES: 500K **Privately Held**
WEB: www.nvmagazine.com
SIC: 2721 6282 Periodicals; investment advice

(G-10048)
EON COLLECTIONS
247 W 35th St Rm 401 (10001-1962)
PHONE................................212 695-1263
Alex Andropoulos, *Owner*
EMP: 20
SALES (est): 754.5K **Privately Held**
SIC: 2329 Men's & boys' clothing

(G-10049)
EPIC BEAUTY CO LLC
929 Park Ave 5 (10028-0211)
PHONE................................212 327-3059
Annette McCoy, *Mng Member*
Maggie G Wedemeyer,
EMP: 2
SQ FT: 500
SALES: 1MM **Privately Held**
SIC: 2844 7991 Cosmetic preparations; spas

(G-10050)
EPOCH TIMES INTERNATIONAL INC
229 W 28th St Fl 6 (10001-5905)
PHONE................................212 239-2808
Peter WEI, *Vice Pres*
Amir Talai, *Sales Mgr*
Jim Xie, *Accounts Mgr*
Jan Jekielek, *Mktg Dir*
Dana Cheng, *Manager*
EMP: 4
SALES: 2.3MM **Privately Held**
SIC: 2711 Newspapers, publishing & printing

(G-10051)
EPOST INTERNATIONAL INC
483 10th Ave (10018-1118)
PHONE................................212 352-9390
Justine Brown, *President*
EMP: 5
SALES: 1MM **Privately Held**
SIC: 2741

(G-10052)
EQUILEND HOLDINGS LLC (PA)
225 Liberty St Fl 10 (10281-1049)
PHONE................................212 901-2200
Fax: 212 653-0222
Brian Lamb, *CEO*
Brent Bessire, *COO*
Chris Benedict, *Vice Pres*
Sally Chu, *Vice Pres*
Krista Otis, *Ch Credit Ofcr*
EMP: 30
SQ FT: 5,500
SALES (est): 9.5MM **Privately Held**
WEB: www.equilend.com
SIC: 7372 Business oriented computer software

(G-10053)
EQUIPMENT APPAREL LLC
19 W 34th St Fl 8 (10001-3006)
PHONE................................212 502-1890
Lisa Armstrong, *Credit Mgr*
Gila Dweck,
▲ **EMP:** 100
SALES (est): 7.8MM **Privately Held**
SIC: 2211 Apparel & outerwear fabrics, cotton

(G-10054)
EQUIVITAL INC
19 W 34th St Rm 1018 (10001-3006)
PHONE................................646 513-4169
Anmol Sood, *CEO*
Anand Vasudev, *Vice Pres*
EMP: 22
SALES (est): 1.4MM **Privately Held**
SIC: 3845 Patient monitoring apparatus

(G-10055)
ER BUTLER & CO INC (PA)
55 Prince St (10012-3432)
P.O. Box 272 (10012-0005)
PHONE................................212 925-3565
Fax: 212 925-3305
Edward R Butler, *CEO*
Catherine Anello, *Office Mgr*
▲ **EMP:** 25
SQ FT: 11,000
SALES (est): 4.7MM **Privately Held**
WEB: www.erbutler.com
SIC: 3429 5072 8742 7699 Manufactured hardware (general); builders' hardware; industry specialist consultants; miscellaneous building item repair services; plumbing fixture fittings & trim; residential lighting fixtures

(G-10056)
ERIC WINTERLING INC
Also Called: Winterling, Eric Costumes
20 W 20th St Fl 5 (10011-9257)
PHONE................................212 629-7686
Fax: 212 629-7543
Eric Winterling, *President*
K Larry, *Human Res Mgr*
EMP: 50
SALES (est): 4MM **Privately Held**
SIC: 2389 Costumes

(G-10057)
ERICKSON BEAMON LTD
498 Fashion Ave Rm 2406 (10018-6798)
PHONE................................212 643-4810
Karen Foster Erickson, *President*
Eric Erickson, *Vice Pres*
Jean-Marc Flack, *Manager*
EMP: 15
SQ FT: 7,500
SALES (est): 2MM **Privately Held**
WEB: www.ericksonbeamon.com
SIC: 3961 Costume jewelry, ex. precious metal & semiprecious stones

(G-10058)
ERIKA T SCHWARTZ MD PC
724 5th Ave Fl 10 (10019-4106)
PHONE................................212 873-3420
Erika T Schwartz, *Principal*
EMP: 6
SALES (est): 2MM **Privately Held**
SIC: 2834 8011 Hormone preparations; specialized medical practitioners, except internal

(G-10059)
ESCHEN PROSTHETIC & ORTHOTIC L
510 E 73rd St Ste 201 (10021-4010)
PHONE................................212 606-1262
Fax: 212 249-6103
Andrew Meyers, *President*
Mary Eschen, *Admin Asst*
EMP: 20
SQ FT: 6,000
SALES (est): 3MM **Privately Held**
SIC: 3842 Braces, orthopedic; prosthetic appliances

(G-10060)
ESHEL JEWELRY MFG CO INC
17 E 48th St Fl 9 (10017-1010)
PHONE................................212 588-8800
Fax: 212 588-1308
Manachem Noeh, *President*
Liba Noeh, *Vice Pres*
Sarah Klepner, *Controller*
EMP: 12
SQ FT: 2,000
SALES (est): 1MM **Privately Held**
SIC: 3911 Jewelry, precious metal

(G-10061)
ESI CASES & ACCESSORIES INC
44 E 32nd St Rm 601 (10016-5508)
PHONE................................212 883-8838
Fax: 212 567-3616
Elliot Azoulay, *Ch of Bd*
Karen Kuchta, *Vice Pres*
Scott Heffes, *CFO*
Stephen Bong, *Finance*
▲ **EMP:** 38 **EST:** 1993
SQ FT: 10,000
SALES (est): 12.1MM **Privately Held**
WEB: www.esicellular.com
SIC: 3661 Telephone & telegraph apparatus

(G-10062)
ESSAR AMERICAS
277 Park Ave 47th (10172-0003)
PHONE................................212 292-2600
EMP: 5
SALES (est): 371.9K **Privately Held**
SIC: 1389 Oil & gas field services

GEOGRAPHIC SECTION
New York - New York County (G-10088)

(G-10063)
ESSAR STEEL MINNESOTA LLC (PA)
277 Park Ave Fl 35 (10172-2904)
PHONE....................212 292-2600
Carola Almonte, *Administration*
EMP: 6
SALES (est): 1.7MM **Privately Held**
SIC: 1011 Iron ore mining

(G-10064)
ESSENCE COMMUNICATIONS INC (HQ)
Also Called: Essence Magazine
225 Liberty St (10281-1048)
PHONE....................212 522-1212
Fax: 212 467-5017
Ed Lewis, *CEO*
Christian Juhl, *CEO*
Clarence O Smith, *President*
Donald Fries, *Publisher*
Peter Nakada, *Exec VP*
▲ **EMP:** 119
SQ FT: 30,000
SALES (est): 20.6MM
SALES (corp-wide): 3.1B **Publicly Held**
SIC: 2721 Magazines: publishing only, not printed on site
PA: Time Inc.
225 Liberty St
New York NY 10281
212 522-1212

(G-10065)
ESSENTIAL RIBBONS INC
53 W 36th St Rm 405 (10018-7623)
PHONE....................212 967-4173
Jie Lin, *Ch of Bd*
▲ **EMP:** 7
SALES (est): 620.2K **Privately Held**
SIC: 2241 Ribbons

(G-10066)
ESSEX MANUFACTURING INC
350 5th Ave Ste 2400 (10118-0128)
P.O. Box 190, Washington GA (30673-0190)
PHONE....................212 239-0080
William Baum, *CEO*
Charles J Baum, *Ch of Bd*
Myron Baum, *Ch of Bd*
Peter Baum, *COO*
Thomas Albea, *Plant Mgr*
▲ **EMP:** 75 **EST:** 1961
SQ FT: 85,300
SALES (est): 7.8MM **Privately Held**
SIC: 2385 3171 3999 Waterproof outerwear; raincoats, except vulcanized rubber; purchased materials; women's handbags & purses; umbrellas, canes & parts

(G-10067)
ESSIE COSMETICS LTD
575 5th Ave (10017-2422)
PHONE....................212 818-1500
Fax: 718 726-7680
Esther Weingarten, *President*
Gerry Hill, *VP Opers*
Blanche Weingarten, *Treasurer*
Harvey Perlowitz, *VP Sales*
◆ **EMP:** 75
SQ FT: 25,000
SALES (est): 13.9MM
SALES (corp-wide): 3.1B **Privately Held**
WEB: www.essie.com
SIC: 2844 5122 Manicure preparations; toilet preparations; cosmetics
HQ: L'oreal Usa, Inc.
10 Hudson Yards
New York NY 10001
212 818-1500

(G-10068)
ESTEE LAUDER COMPANIES INC
9 W 22nd St (10010-5101)
PHONE....................917 606-3240
EMP: 504
SALES (corp-wide): 11.2B **Publicly Held**
SIC: 2844 Toilet preparations
PA: The Estee Lauder Companies Inc
767 5th Ave Fl 37
New York NY 10153
212 572-4200

(G-10069)
ESTEE LAUDER COMPANIES INC
767 5th Ave Fl 37 (10153-0003)
PHONE....................212 572-4200
Caroline Geerlings, *Branch Mgr*
EMP: 504
SALES (corp-wide): 11.2B **Publicly Held**
SIC: 2844 5999 Toilet preparations; cosmetic preparations; perfumes & colognes; toiletries, cosmetics & perfumes; cosmetics; perfumes & colognes
PA: The Estee Lauder Companies Inc
767 5th Ave Fl 37
New York NY 10153
212 572-4200

(G-10070)
ESTEE LAUDER COMPANIES INC (PA)
767 5th Ave Fl 37 (10153-0003)
PHONE....................212 572-4200
William P Lauder, *Ch of Bd*
Fabrizio Freda, *President*
John Demsey, *President*
Beth Dinardo, *President*
Jane Hertzmark, *President*
◆ **EMP:** 1000
SQ FT: 739,000
SALES: 11.2B **Publicly Held**
WEB: www.elcompanies.com
SIC: 2844 Toilet preparations; cosmetic preparations; perfumes & colognes

(G-10071)
ESTEE LAUDER COMPANIES INC
65 Bleecker St Frnt 1 (10012-2420)
PHONE....................646 602-7590
EMP: 504
SALES (corp-wide): 11.2B **Publicly Held**
SIC: 2844 Toilet preparations
PA: The Estee Lauder Companies Inc
767 5th Ave Fl 37
New York NY 10153
212 572-4200

(G-10072)
ESTEE LAUDER INC (HQ)
767 5th Ave Fl 37 (10153-0003)
PHONE....................212 572-4200
Fax: 212 572-4292
Freda Fabrizio, *CEO*
Leonard A Lauder, *Ch of Bd*
John Demsey, *President*
Ed Straw, *President*
William P Lauder, *Chairman*
▲ **EMP:** 700
SQ FT: 232,000
SALES: 10.7B
SALES (corp-wide): 11.2B **Publicly Held**
WEB: www.esteelauder.com
SIC: 2844 5999 Toilet preparations; cosmetic preparations; perfumes & colognes; toiletries, cosmetics & perfumes; cosmetics; perfumes & colognes
PA: The Estee Lauder Companies Inc
767 5th Ave Fl 37
New York NY 10153
212 572-4200

(G-10073)
ESTEE LAUDER INC
655 Madison Ave Fl 10 (10065-8043)
PHONE....................212 756-4800
Mercedes H Alvarez, *Principal*
EMP: 55
SALES (corp-wide): 11.2B **Publicly Held**
WEB: www.esteelauder.com
SIC: 2844 Cosmetic preparations
HQ: Estee Lauder Inc.
767 5th Ave Fl 37
New York NY 10153
212 572-4200

(G-10074)
ESTEE LAUDER INTERNATIONAL INC (DH)
767 5th Ave Bsmt 1 (10153-0003)
PHONE....................212 572-4200
Patrick Bousquet-Chavanne, *President*
Joel Bramble, *President*
Larry Berger, *Exec VP*
Nancy Castro, *Exec VP*
Michael Meyer, *Exec VP*
▲ **EMP:** 7
SALES (est): 175.2MM
SALES (corp-wide): 11.2B **Publicly Held**
SIC: 2844 Toilet preparations; face creams or lotions; lipsticks; perfumes & colognes
HQ: Estee Lauder Inc.
767 5th Ave Fl 37
New York NY 10153
212 572-4200

(G-10075)
ET PUBLISHING INTL LLC
Also Called: Editorial America S A
150 E 58th St Ste 2200 (10155-2200)
PHONE....................212 838-7220
Cesar Ruiz, *Manager*
EMP: 14
SALES (corp-wide): 23.6MM **Privately Held**
WEB: www.buyeditorialtelevisa.com
SIC: 2721 Magazines: publishing only, not printed on site
PA: Et Publishing International
6355 Nw 36th St
Virginia Gardens FL 33166
305 871-6400

(G-10076)
ETC HOSIERY & UNDERWEAR LTD
Also Called: Every Toe Covered
350 5th Ave Ste 2525 (10118-0110)
PHONE....................212 947-5151
Richard Fink, *CEO*
Robert Sussaman, *President*
EMP: 8
SALES (est): 842.4K **Privately Held**
SIC: 2252 Hosiery

(G-10077)
ETERNAL FORTUNE FASHION LLC
Also Called: Profile
135 W 36th St Fl 5 (10018-6900)
PHONE....................212 965-5322
Roy Zou, *Mng Member*
Candice Wong,
◆ **EMP:** 12
SQ FT: 5,600
SALES (est): 2MM **Privately Held**
SIC: 2329 Men's & boys' sportswear & athletic clothing

(G-10078)
ETNA PRODUCTS CO INC (PA)
53 W 23rd St Fl 3 (10010-4294)
PHONE....................212 989-7591
Fax: 212 627-4860
Raymond Trinh, *Ch of Bd*
Jeffrey Snyder, *Ch of Bd*
Paula Snyder, *Admin Sec*
▲ **EMP:** 19 **EST:** 1957
SQ FT: 15,000
SALES (est): 3.6MM **Privately Held**
WEB: www.etna.com
SIC: 3089 5021 Plastic kitchenware, tableware & houseware; furniture

(G-10079)
ETNA TOOL & DIE CORPORATION
42 Bond St Frnt A (10012-2476)
PHONE....................212 475-4350
Fax: 212 533-4896
Keranus Galuppo, *President*
Flavia Galuppo, *Manager*
James Galuppo, *Admin Sec*
EMP: 12 **EST:** 1946
SQ FT: 14,000
SALES (est): 1.3MM **Privately Held**
WEB: www.etnatoolanddie.com
SIC: 3599 3544 7692 Machine shop, jobbing & repair; special dies & tools; welding repair

(G-10080)
ETON INSTITUTE
1 Rockefeller Plz Fl 11 (10020-2073)
PHONE....................855 334-3688
EMP: 10
SALES (est): 710K **Privately Held**
SIC: 3999 Mfg Misc Products

(G-10081)
EU DESIGN LLC
73 Spring St Rm 506 (10012-5802)
PHONE....................212 420-7788
Roberto Berardi, *President*
Maryann Russo, *Sales Mgr*
Sergio Terrazzini, *Office Mgr*
▲ **EMP:** 7 **EST:** 1999
SALES (est): 1.2MM **Privately Held**
WEB: www.eu-design.com
SIC: 3965 3961 5131 Buttons & parts; costume jewelry; piece goods & other fabrics; ribbons
HQ: Eu Design, Hk Limited
Rm 301-302 3/F Tins Enterprises Ctr
Cheung Sha Wan KLN
342 115-54

(G-10082)
EUPHORBIA PRODUCTIONS LTD
632 Broadway Fl 9 (10012-2614)
PHONE....................212 533-1700
Philip Glass, *President*
Kurt Munkaisi, *Officer*
EMP: 6
SALES (est): 508.6K **Privately Held**
WEB: www.euphorbia.com
SIC: 2741 7389 Music books: publishing only, not printed on site; music recording producer

(G-10083)
EURO BANDS INC
247 W 37th St Rm 700 (10018-5016)
PHONE....................212 719-9777
Zbignew Jarosh, *President*
EMP: 16
SALES: 500K **Privately Held**
WEB: www.e-bands.net
SIC: 3911 Jewelry, precious metal

(G-10084)
EURO PACIFIC PRECIOUS METALS
152 Madison Ave Rm 1003 (10016-5414)
PHONE....................212 481-0310
Matt Malleo, *Managing Dir*
Peter Schiff, *Principal*
Dickson Buchanan, *Director*
Jonathan Sosnay, *Director*
Michael Freedman, *Assistant*
EMP: 6 **EST:** 2010
SALES (est): 697.5K **Privately Held**
SIC: 3339 Precious metals

(G-10085)
EUROCO COSTUMES INC
254 W 35th St Fl 15 (10001-2504)
PHONE....................212 629-9665
Janet Bloor, *President*
▼ **EMP:** 9
SQ FT: 3,000
SALES (est): 1MM **Privately Held**
SIC: 2389 Theatrical costumes

(G-10086)
EUROPROJECTS INTL INC
Also Called: ADOTTA AMERICA
152 W 25th St Fl 8b (10001-7402)
PHONE....................917 262-0795
Luigi Zannier, *President*
Mona Rubin, *Manager*
EMP: 4
SALES: 8.8MM **Privately Held**
SIC: 3211 1751 3089 Structural glass; window & door (prefabricated) installation; fiberglass doors

(G-10087)
EVADO FILIP
159 Bleecker St (10012-1457)
PHONE....................917 774-8666
Craig Gainsboro, *CFO*
EMP: 12 **EST:** 2013
SQ FT: 2,000
SALES (est): 1MM **Privately Held**
SIC: 3663

(G-10088)
EVANS & PAUL UNLIMITED CORP
Also Called: Corian Design Studio
49 W 23rd St Fl 3 (10010-4229)
PHONE....................212 255-7272
Paul Evans, *President*

New York - New York County (G-10089)   **GEOGRAPHIC SECTION**

EMP: 24
SALES (corp-wide): 6.4MM **Privately Held**
SIC: 2541 Wood partitions & fixtures
PA: Evans & Paul Unlimited Corp.
140 Dupont St
Plainview NY 11803
516 576-0800

(G-10089)
EVERBLOCK SYSTEMS LLC
790 Madison Ave Rm 601 (10065-6124)
PHONE.................................844 422-5625
Arnon Rosan, *President*
EMP: 3 EST: 2015
SALES: 1.5MM **Privately Held**
SIC: 3271 3251 3299 3089 Blocks, concrete: landscape or retaining wall; structural brick & blocks; blocks & brick, sand lime; injection molded finished plastic products

(G-10090)
EVERCORE PARTNERS SVCS E LLC
55 E 52nd St (10055-0002)
PHONE.................................212 857-3100
Stacy Dick, *Vice Pres*
Edward Merrell, *Vice Pres*
Shinji Sugiyama, *Vice Pres*
Marta Guzman, *Manager*
Takajiro Ishikawa, *Manager*
EMP: 2460
SALES (est): 128.3MM **Privately Held**
SIC: 2711 Newspapers, publishing & printing

(G-10091)
EVEREST BBN INC
42 Broadway Ste 1736 (10004-3853)
PHONE.................................212 268-7979
Ruth Shelling, *Principal*
Adrian Carel, *Network Enginr*
EMP: 11 EST: 2011
SALES (est): 1.7MM **Privately Held**
SIC: 3825 Network analyzers

(G-10092)
EVERLAST SPORTS MFG CORP (DH)
42 W 39th St (10018-3809)
PHONE.................................212 239-0990
Neil Morton, *CEO*
Frank Lekram, *Purchasing*
Richard Bonura, *Controller*
Rita C Kriss, *Finance*
Ronni Kornblul, *Manager*
▲ EMP: 41 EST: 1945
SQ FT: 300,000
SALES (est): 13.4MM
SALES (corp-wide): 4.3B **Privately Held**
SIC: 3949 5091 Sporting & athletic goods; sporting & recreation goods
HQ: Everlast Worldwide Inc.
42 W 39th St Fl 3
New York NY 10018
212 239-0990

(G-10093)
EVERLAST WORLDWIDE INC (DH)
42 W 39th St Fl 3 (10018-3832)
Rural Route 40 E 34th St (10016)
PHONE.................................212 239-0990
Neil Morton, *President*
Thomas K Higgerson, *Senior VP*
Jay Senzatimore, *Vice Pres*
Richard Bonura, *Controller*
Michele Walker, *Accounts Exec*
▲ EMP: 41
SQ FT: 12,087
SALES (est): 16.3MM
SALES (corp-wide): 4.3B **Privately Held**
SIC: 3949 8049 3144 3149 Boxing equipment & supplies, general; gloves, sport & athletic: boxing, handball, etc.; nutritionist; women's footwear, except athletic; children's footwear, except athletic
HQ: Brands Holdings Limited
Grenville Court
Slough BERKS
870 838-7200

(G-10094)
EVOLUTION SPIRITS INC
Also Called: Monkey Rum
401 Park Ave S (10016-8808)
PHONE.................................917 543-7880
Ian Crystal, *President*
EMP: 7
SALES (est): 557.7K **Privately Held**
SIC: 2085 Rum (alcoholic beverage)

(G-10095)
EWATCHFACTORY CORP (PA)
Also Called: Pacific Concepts
390 5th Ave Rm 910 (10018-8111)
PHONE.................................212 564-8318
Remi Chabrat, *CEO*
Vanessa Ramirez, *Manager*
Barbara A Rizzo, *Manager*
▲ EMP: 5 EST: 2000
SQ FT: 1,200
SALES (est): 531.9K **Privately Held**
WEB: www.watchfactory.com
SIC: 3873 Watches, clocks, watchcases & parts

(G-10096)
EWT HOLDINGS III CORP (HQ)
666 5th Ave Fl 36 (10103-3102)
PHONE.................................212 644-5900
EMP: 9
SALES (est): 1.2B **Privately Held**
SIC: 3589 3823 3826 4941 Sewage & water treatment equipment; water treatment equipment, industrial; sewage treatment equipment; water purification equipment, household type; water quality monitoring & control systems; water testing apparatus; water supply; iron & steel (ferrous) products; cast iron pipe; piling, iron & steel
PA: Ewt Holdings I Corp.
666 5th Ave Fl 36
New York NY 10103
212 644-5900

(G-10097)
EX EL ENTERPRISES LTD
630 Fort Washington Ave (10040-3900)
PHONE.................................212 489-4500
Henry Lehman, *President*
EMP: 11
SQ FT: 1,900
SALES (est): 960K **Privately Held**
WEB: www.ex-el.com
SIC: 7372 7373 Prepackaged software; systems software development services

(G-10098)
EX-IT MEDICAL DEVICES INC
1330 Ave Of The Americas (10019-5400)
PHONE.................................212 653-0637
Shlomo Shopen, *CEO*
EMP: 3
SALES: 10MM **Privately Held**
SIC: 2844 Cosmetic preparations
PA: Ex-It Medical Devices Limited
3/F Jonsim Place
Wan Chai HK

(G-10099)
EXACT SOLUTIONS INC
139 Fulton St Rm 511 (10038-2535)
PHONE.................................212 707-8627
Fax: 212 707-8632
Hardev Deindsa, *President*
EMP: 11
SALES (est): 1MM **Privately Held**
WEB: www.exact-solutions.com
SIC: 7372 Prepackaged software

(G-10100)
EXACTTARGET INC
155 Av Of The Americas Fl (10013-1507)
PHONE.................................646 560-2275
Scott Dorsey, *CEO*
EMP: 9
SALES (corp-wide): 6.6B **Publicly Held**
SIC: 7372 Prepackaged software
HQ: Exacttarget, Inc.
20 N Meridian St Ste 200
Indianapolis IN 46204
317 423-3928

(G-10101)
EXCEL GRAPHICS SERVICES INC
519 8th Ave Fl 18 (10018-4577)
PHONE.................................212 929-2183
Fax: 212 929-4135
Joseph Risola, *President*
Anthony Fazio III, *Vice Pres*
EMP: 12 EST: 1997
SQ FT: 16,500
SALES (est): 1.3MM **Privately Held**
SIC: 2752 Commercial printing, offset

(G-10102)
EXCEL TECHNOLOGY INC
780 3rd Ave (10017-2024)
PHONE.................................212 355-3400
Fax: 212 355-8125
Donald Hill, *CEO*
EMP: 15
SALES (corp-wide): 373.6MM **Publicly Held**
WEB: www.exceltechinc.com
SIC: 3845 Electromedical equipment
HQ: Excel Technology, Inc.
125 Middlesex Tpke
Bedford MA 01730
781 266-5700

(G-10103)
EXCELLED SHPSKIN LEA COAT CORP (PA)
Also Called: RG Apparel Group
1400 Brdwy Fl 31 (10018)
P.O. Box 659, Carteret NJ (07008-0659)
PHONE.................................212 594-5843
Fax: 212 967-5695
William Goldman, *President*
Myron Goldman, *Chairman*
Michael Holzberg, *Vice Pres*
Jamie Zaino, *Production*
Ken Walton, *CFO*
▲ EMP: 12 EST: 1927
SQ FT: 50,000
SALES (est): 84.9MM **Privately Held**
WEB: www.leathercoatsetc.com
SIC: 2386 3172 2337 2311 Coats & jackets, leather & sheep-lined; personal leather goods; women's & misses' suits & coats; men's & boys' suits & coats

(G-10104)
EXCELSIOR GRAPHICS INC
485 Madison Ave Fl 13 (10022-5803)
PHONE.................................212 730-6200
Harold Siegel, *President*
Patti Cooper, *Marketing Staff*
Jackie Starin, *Director*
EMP: 5
SQ FT: 8,000
SALES (est): 450K **Privately Held**
SIC: 2752 Commercial printing, offset

(G-10105)
EXECUTIVE CREATIONS INC
44 Wall St Fl 12 (10005-2433)
PHONE.................................212 422-2640
Shawn Cahill, *President*
EMP: 2
SQ FT: 1,100
SALES: 1MM **Privately Held**
SIC: 3999 Plaques, picture, laminated

(G-10106)
EXECUTIVE SIGN CORPORATION
347 W 36th St Rm 902 (10018-6491)
PHONE.................................212 397-4050
Fax: 212 239-9684
Isaac Hankins, *President*
Kelle Hankins, *Vice Pres*
EMP: 6
SQ FT: 1,800
SALES: 600K **Privately Held**
SIC: 3993 Signs, not made in custom sign painting shops

(G-10107)
EXOTIC PRINT AND PAPER INC
Also Called: Arthur Invitation
15 E 13th St (10003-4405)
PHONE.................................212 807-0465
Arfa Rejaei, *Ch of Bd*
Arthur Rajaei, *President*
EMP: 11
SQ FT: 1,800
SALES (est): 1.1MM **Privately Held**
SIC: 2759 5947 Commercial printing; gift shop

(G-10108)
EXPERIMENT LLC
260 5th Ave Fl 3 (10001-6408)
PHONE.................................212 889-1659
Matthew Lore, *Principal*
Peter Burri, *Principal*
EMP: 5 EST: 2008
SALES (est): 450K **Privately Held**
SIC: 2732 Book printing

(G-10109)
EXPERIMENT PUBLISHING LLC
220 E 23rd St Ste 301 (10010-4674)
PHONE.................................212 889-1273
Russell Gabay, *Vice Pres*
Matthew Lore, *Mng Member*
▲ EMP: 9
SALES (est): 770K **Privately Held**
SIC: 2741 Miscellaneous publishing

(G-10110)
EXPRESS CHECKOUT LLC
110 E 1st St Apt 20 (10009-7977)
PHONE.................................646 512-2068
William Hogben,
EMP: 6
SQ FT: 300
SALES (est): 320.9K **Privately Held**
SIC: 7372 Application computer software

(G-10111)
EXTREME GROUP HOLDINGS LLC (DH)
550 Madison Ave Fl 6 (10022-3211)
PHONE.................................212 833-8000
▲ EMP: 11
SALES (est): 1.5MM
SALES (corp-wide): 69.2B **Privately Held**
SIC: 3652 Pre-recorded records & tapes
HQ: Sony/Atv Music Publishing Llc
25 Madison Ave Fl 24
New York NY 10010
212 833-7730

(G-10112)
EYELOCK CORPORATION
355 Lexington Ave (10017-6603)
PHONE.................................914 619-5570
Steve Gerber, *Senior VP*
Darlene Crumbaugh, *Vice Pres*
Michael Fiorito, *Vice Pres*
Amy Romeo, *CFO*
Chris Ream, *Security Dir*
EMP: 19
SALES: 3.8MM
SALES (corp-wide): 680.7MM **Publicly Held**
SIC: 3699 Security control equipment & systems
HQ: Eyelock Llc
355 Lexington Ave Fl 12
New York NY 10017
855 393-5625

(G-10113)
EYELOCK LLC (HQ)
355 Lexington Ave Fl 12 (10017-6603)
PHONE.................................855 393-5625
Chris Ream, *Officer*
Jim Demitrieus,
Anthony Antolino,
Samuel Carter,
Marc Levin,
EMP: 5 EST: 2015
SALES (est): 16.2MM
SALES (corp-wide): 680.7MM **Publicly Held**
SIC: 3699 Security control equipment & systems
PA: Voxx International Corporation
2351 J Lawson Blvd
Orlando FL 32824
800 645-7750

(G-10114)
F & J DESIGNS INC
Also Called: Thalian
526 Fashion Ave Fl 8 (10018-4822)
PHONE.................................212 302-8755
Franklin Bergman, *President*
Michael Portnoy, *Accountant*

GEOGRAPHIC SECTION

New York - New York County (G-10141)

Joan Mendlinger, *Admin Sec*
▲ **EMP:** 9
SQ FT: 5,000
SALES (est): 1.3MM **Privately Held**
WEB: www.fjdesigns.com
SIC: 2339 5137 Sportswear, women's; sportswear, women's & children's

(G-10115)
F A PRINTING
690 10th Ave Frnt 1 (10019-7106)
PHONE 212 974-5982
Fax: 212 974-8769
Fazal Ali, *President*
Thomas Black, *Owner*
EMP: 5
SQ FT: 900
SALES (est): 464K **Privately Held**
SIC: 2759 Commercial printing

(G-10116)
F P H COMMUNICATIONS
225 Broadway Ste 2008 (10007-3737)
PHONE 212 528-1728
Steve Young, *President*
EMP: 2
SQ FT: 2,100
SALES: 3.5MM **Privately Held**
SIC: 2731 Book publishing

(G-10117)
F&M ORNAMENTAL DESIGNS LLC
Also Called: Desiron
151 Wooster St Frnt 2 (10012-3185)
PHONE 212 353-2600
Jenna Palin, *Sales Mgr*
Frank J Carfaro, *Manager*
EMP: 6 **Privately Held**
SIC: 2514 Metal household furniture
PA: F&M Ornamental Designs L.L.C.
200 Lexington Ave Rm 702
New York NY 10016

(G-10118)
F&M ORNAMENTAL DESIGNS LLC (PA)
Also Called: Desiron
200 Lexington Ave Rm 702 (10016-6123)
PHONE 908 241-7776
Frank J Carfaro, *Mng Member*
Linda Rox, *Manager*
▲ **EMP:** 17
SQ FT: 20,000
SALES (est): 5.4MM **Privately Held**
SIC: 2514 Metal household furniture

(G-10119)
F+W MEDIA INC
1140 Broadway Fl 14 (10001-7504)
PHONE 212 447-1400
Jessica Canterbury, *Editor*
Kristin Hoerth, *Editor*
Brian Riley, *Editor*
Stephanie White, *Editor*
Scott Roeder, *Human Res Dir*
EMP: 26 **Privately Held**
SIC: 2741 Miscellaneous publishing
HQ: F+W Media, Inc.
10151 Carver Rd Ste 200
Blue Ash OH 45242
513 531-2690

(G-10120)
F-O-R SOFTWARE LLC
Also Called: Two-Four Software
757 3rd Ave Fl 20 (10017-2046)
PHONE 212 231-9506
Steve Davis, *Branch Mgr*
EMP: 15
SALES (corp-wide): 3.9MM **Privately Held**
SIC: 7372 Prepackaged software
PA: F-O-R Software Llc
10 Bank St Ste 830
White Plains NY 10606
914 220-8800

(G-10121)
F-O-R SOFTWARE LLC
100 Park Ave Rm 1600 (10017-5538)
PHONE 212 724-3920
Chris Davis, *Manager*
EMP: 9

SALES (corp-wide): 3.9MM **Privately Held**
SIC: 7372 Prepackaged software
PA: F-O-R Software Llc
10 Bank St Ste 830
White Plains NY 10606
914 220-8800

(G-10122)
F5 NETWORKS INC
424 W 33rd St Rm 530 (10001-2611)
PHONE 888 882-7535
James Reardon, *Principal*
Tamin Sun, *Sales Staff*
Holly Willey, *Manager*
Jon Bartlett, *Technology*
Maxim Zavodchik, *IT/INT Sup*
EMP: 7 **Publicly Held**
SIC: 2752 Commercial printing, lithographic
PA: F5 Networks, Inc.
401 Elliott Ave W Ste 500
Seattle WA 98119

(G-10123)
FABBIAN USA CORP
307 W 38th St Rm 1103 (10018-2946)
PHONE 973 882-3824
Vincenzo Tersigni, *Vice Pres*
Liz Panos, *VP Sales*
Lorie Constantinides, *Manager*
Emanuele Fraccari, *Manager*
▲ **EMP:** 6
SQ FT: 33,000
SALES (est): 866.8K **Privately Held**
SIC: 3648 Lighting equipment

(G-10124)
FABRITEX INC
215 W 40th St Fl 9 (10018-1575)
PHONE 706 376-6584
Larry Golf, *President*
EMP: 5
SALES (est): 387.2K **Privately Held**
SIC: 3499 Aerosol valves, metal

(G-10125)
FACSIMILE CMMNCATIONS INDS INC (PA)
Also Called: Atlantic Business Products
134 W 26th St Fl 3 (10001-6803)
PHONE 212 741-6400
Fax: 212 645-1518
Larry Weiss, *Ch of Bd*
Russell Klin, *CFO*
Karen Flemmig, *HR Admin*
Alan Walker, *Sales Mgr*
Bob Goldman, *Accounts Exec*
EMP: 75
SQ FT: 12,000
SALES (est): 49.9MM **Privately Held**
WEB: www.tomorrowsoffice.com
SIC: 3861 3571 Photocopy machines; computers, digital, analog or hybrid

(G-10126)
FACTS ON FILE INC (HQ)
Also Called: Infobase Learning
132 W 31st St Fl 17 (10001-3406)
PHONE 212 967-8800
Fax: 212 678-3633
Mark D McDonnell, *President*
David Giuffre, *Editor*
Jonathan Leith, *Editor*
Jared McGinley, *Regional Mgr*
Eleanor Jaekel, *Business Mgr*
▲ **EMP:** 70 **EST:** 1940
SALES (est): 11.4MM
SALES (corp-wide): 12.7MM **Privately Held**
WEB: www.factsonfile.com
SIC: 2731 7372 Books: publishing only; prepackaged software
PA: Infobase Publishing Company
132 W 31st St Fl 17
New York NY 10001
212 967-8800

(G-10127)
FAHRENHEIT NY INC
315 W 39th St Rm 700 (10018-4044)
PHONE 212 354-6554
Fax: 212 354-0151
Connie Bates, *President*
Christine Bates, *Admin Sec*
EMP: 7

SQ FT: 2,200
SALES (est): 510K **Privately Held**
SIC: 3199 3172 Leather belting & strapping; personal leather goods

(G-10128)
FAIRCHILD PUBLICATIONS INC (DH)
Also Called: Womens Wear Daily
475 5th Ave (10017-6220)
PHONE 212 630-4000
Fax: 212 630-3563
Charles H Townsend, *President*
Richard Baylef, *President*
Michael Coady, *President*
Marc Berger, *Publisher*
Doug Fierro, *Publisher*
▲ **EMP:** 600
SQ FT: 150,000
SALES (est): 133.8MM
SALES (corp-wide): 322.5MM **Privately Held**
WEB: www.fairchildbooks.com
SIC: 2721 2711 2731 Periodicals; newspapers; book publishing
HQ: Advance Magazine Publishers Inc.
1 World Trade Ctr Fl 28
New York NY 10007
212 286-2860

(G-10129)
FAIRCHILD PUBLISHING LLC
4 Times Sq Fl 17 (10036-6518)
PHONE 212 286-3897
EMP: 7
SALES (est): 730K **Privately Held**
SIC: 2721 Periodicals

(G-10130)
FAIRMOUNT PRESS
121 Varick St Fl 9 (10013-1408)
PHONE 212 255-2300
Fax: 212 215-2035
Peter Bird, *President*
EMP: 6
SALES (est): 518K **Privately Held**
SIC: 2759 7334 Letterpress printing; photocopying & duplicating services

(G-10131)
FAIT USA INC
350 5th Ave Fl 41 (10118-4100)
PHONE 215 674-5310
Massimo Bassi, *President*
Alessandro Bronzini, *Vice Pres*
▲ **EMP:** 4
SQ FT: 8,000
SALES: 1MM
SALES (corp-wide): 24.7MM **Privately Held**
SIC: 3568 Power transmission equipment; shafts, flexible
PA: Fait Group Spa
Via Raffaello Scarpettini 367/369
Montemurlo PO 59013
057 468-121

(G-10132)
FAM CREATIONS
46 W 46th St Fl 4 (10036-4508)
PHONE 212 869-4833
Fax: 212 869-4858
Mario Scimaca, *President*
EMP: 20 **EST:** 1999
SALES (est): 1.9MM **Privately Held**
SIC: 3911 Jewelry apparel

(G-10133)
FAMILY PUBLICATIONS LTD
325 W 38th St Rm 804 (10018-9623)
PHONE 212 947-2177
Gail Granet-Velez, *President*
EMP: 12
SALES (est): 1.2MM **Privately Held**
WEB: www.familypublications.com
SIC: 2741 7999 Guides: publishing only, not printed on site; exposition operation

(G-10134)
FANCY FLAMINGO LLC
450 W 17th St Apt 528 (10011-5846)
PHONE 516 209-7306
Sanchali Sundaram, *CEO*
Senthil Sundaram, *COO*
EMP: 6 **EST:** 2011

SALES (est): 407.5K **Privately Held**
SIC: 2086 Bottled & canned soft drinks

(G-10135)
FANSHAWE FOODS LLC
5 Columbus Cir (10019-1412)
PHONE 212 757-3130
Lee Zalben, *President*
EMP: 10
SALES (est): 564.3K **Privately Held**
SIC: 2099 5149 Food preparations; specialty food items

(G-10136)
FANTASIA JEWELRY INC
42 W 39th St Fl 14 (10018-2082)
PHONE 212 921-9590
Fax: 212 398-6559
Sebastian De Serio, *President*
Joseph De Serio, *Vice Pres*
Edward Deserio, *Treasurer*
Jennifer Deserio, *Marketing Mgr*
Sebastian Deserio, *Manager*
EMP: 42
SQ FT: 7,000
SALES (est): 3.2MM **Privately Held**
WEB: www.fantasiajewelry.com
SIC: 3961 3911 Costume jewelry, ex. precious metal & semiprecious stones; jewelry, precious metal

(G-10137)
FANTASY SPORTS MEDIA GROUP INC
Also Called: Fantasy Sports Network
27 W 20th St Ste 900 (10011-3725)
PHONE 416 917-6002
EMP: 20
SALES: 2.5MM **Privately Held**
SIC: 2741 Miscellaneous publishing

(G-10138)
FARRAR STRAUS AND GIROUX LLC (DH)
Also Called: North Point Press
18 W 18th St Fl 7 (10011-4675)
PHONE 212 741-6900
Fax: 212 633-9384
Melanie Kroupa, *Publisher*
Tom Cansiglio, *Vice Pres*
Frances Foster, *Vice Pres*
Margery Heitbrink, *Vice Pres*
Jeff Seroy, *VP Mktg*
▲ **EMP:** 28 **EST:** 1945
SQ FT: 22,500
SALES (est): 11.6MM
SALES (corp-wide): 2.1B **Privately Held**
WEB: www.petersistibet.com
SIC: 2731 Books: publishing only

(G-10139)
FARROW AND BALL INC (DH)
979 3rd Ave Ste 1519 (10022-3806)
PHONE 212 752-5544
Antonio Moreira, *Principal*
EMP: 9
SALES (est): 930.6K
SALES (corp-wide): 33.6MM **Privately Held**
SIC: 2851 Paints & paint additives
HQ: Farrow & Ball Holdings Limited
33 Uddens Trading Estate
Wimborne BH21
120 287-6141

(G-10140)
FASHION APPAREL INDUSTRIES
Also Called: Judgement Clothing
1412 Broadway Ste 1818 (10018-9228)
PHONE 212 704-0800
Ramin Arasheben, *President*
EMP: 10
SQ FT: 3,000
SALES: 6.5MM **Privately Held**
SIC: 2211 Towels, dishcloths & washcloths: cotton

(G-10141)
FASHION AVE SWEATER KNITS LLC
525 7th Ave Fl 4 (10018-4940)
PHONE 212 302-8282
Melvyn Weiss, *President*
Austin Mallis, *Vice Pres*
Ron Hollandsworth, *Controller*

New York - New York County (G-10142)
GEOGRAPHIC SECTION

EMP: 100
SQ FT: 18,000
SALES (est): 7.9MM Privately Held
SIC: 2339 Service apparel, washable: women's

(G-10142)
FASHION AVENUE KNITS INC
Also Called: Its Our Time
1400 Broadway Rm 2401 (10018-5300)
PHONE..................................718 456-9000
Fax: 212 221-7017
Mel Weiss, *Manager*
EMP: 10
SALES (corp-wide): 125MM Privately Held
WEB: www.fashionavenueknits.com
SIC: 2253 Knit outerwear mills
PA: Fashion Avenue Knits Inc.
525 Fashion Ave Fl 4
New York NY 10018
212 302-8282

(G-10143)
FASHION CALENDAR INTERNATIONAL
153 E 87th St Apt 6a (10128-2705)
PHONE..................................212 289-0420
Fax: 212 289-5917
Ruth Finley, *Owner*
EMP: 7 EST: 1939
SALES (est): 500K Privately Held
WEB: www.fashioncalendar.net
SIC: 2721 Periodicals

(G-10144)
FASHION DELI INC
2353 Fredrck Douglss Blvd Apt 3 (10027)
PHONE..................................818 772-5637
Thulare Monareng, *President*
EMP: 10
SALES (est): 820K Privately Held
SIC: 2335 7389 Housedresses; apparel designers, commercial

(G-10145)
FASHIONDEX INC
153 W 27th St Ste 701 (10001-6255)
PHONE..................................914 271-6121
Fax: 212 691-5873
Andrea Kennedy, *President*
Max Andrews, *Vice Pres*
▲ EMP: 6
SALES: 150K Privately Held
WEB: www.fashiondex.com
SIC: 2741 5192 Telephone & other directory publishing; books, periodicals & newspapers

(G-10146)
FAST-TRAC ENTERTAINMENT LTD
7 E 74th St Apt 5 (10021-2624)
PHONE..................................888 758-8886
Phyllis Keitlen, *Ch of Bd*
EMP: 1
SALES: 1.5MM Privately Held
SIC: 2253 7922 Knit outerwear mills; agent or manager for entertainers

(G-10147)
FAVIANA INTERNATIONAL INC (PA)
320 W 37th St Rm 100 (10018-4229)
PHONE..................................212 594-4422
Parviz Pourmoradi, *President*
Omid Pourmoradi, *Vice Pres*
Shala Pourmoradi, *Treasurer*
Bernard Weiss, *Manager*
▲ EMP: 31
SQ FT: 32,000
SALES: 7.8MM Privately Held
WEB: www.faviana.com
SIC: 2335 Women's, juniors' & misses' dresses

(G-10148)
FEDERAL ENVELOPE INC
22 W 32nd St (10001-3807)
PHONE..................................212 243-8380
Fax: 212 691-8076
EMP: 10 EST: 1953
SQ FT: 10,000
SALES (est): 730K Privately Held
SIC: 2759 2752 Printer Of Printing Envelopes Letterpress & An Offset Printing Service

(G-10149)
FEDERATED MEDIA PUBLISHING LLC
31 W 27th St Fl 8 (10001-6914)
PHONE..................................917 677-7976
Angela Shelby, *Manager*
EMP: 7
SALES (corp-wide): 674.9MM Publicly Held
SIC: 2741 Miscellaneous publishing
HQ: Federated Media Publishing, Llc
350 Sansome St Ste 925
San Francisco CA 94104
415 332-6955

(G-10150)
FELDMAN COMPANY INC
Also Called: Ango Home
7 W 34th St Ste 900 (10001-0054)
PHONE..................................212 966-1303
Alfred Feldman, *President*
Hershel Feldman, *Vice Pres*
Eli Jeidel, *Vice Pres*
▲ EMP: 13
SQ FT: 6,000
SALES (est): 1.4MM Privately Held
WEB: www.feldmanco.com
SIC: 2299 5023 Fabrics: linen, jute, hemp, ramie; home furnishings

(G-10151)
FELLUSS RECORDING
36 E 23rd St Rm 9l (10010-4417)
PHONE..................................212 727-8055
Andrew Fellus, *Owner*
EMP: 6
SALES (est): 320K Privately Held
SIC: 3679 Recording heads, speech & musical equipment

(G-10152)
FEMINIST PRESS INC
365 5th Ave Ste 5406 (10016-4309)
PHONE..................................212 817-7929
Fax: 212 817-1593
Yamberlie Tavarez, *Development*
Sebastian Persico, *CFO*
Jennifer Baumgardner, *Exec Dir*
Sharon Lerner, *Director*
Daniel J Rothenberg, *Director*
EMP: 9
SQ FT: 2,000
SALES: 878.4K Privately Held
SIC: 2731 Book publishing

(G-10153)
FENWAY HOLDINGS LLC
152 W 57th St Fl 59 (10019-3414)
PHONE..................................212 757-0606
Richard C Dresdale,
EMP: 25
SALES (est): 1.8MM Privately Held
SIC: 3949 2431 3842 Archery equipment, general; windows & window parts & trim, wood; doors & door parts & trim, wood; moldings, wood: unfinished & prefinished; surgical appliances & supplies
PA: Fenway Partners Capital Fund Lp
152 W 57th St Fl 59
New York NY 10019

(G-10154)
FERRARA BAKERY & CAFE INC (PA)
195 Grand St (10013-3717)
PHONE..................................212 226-6150
Fax: 212 226-0667
Ernest Lepore, *Ch of Bd*
Peter Lepore, *President*
John Capirchio, *Plant Mgr*
Anthony Sessa, *Opers Staff*
Dennis Canciello, *Treasurer*
▲ EMP: 95 EST: 1892
SALES (est): 10.8MM Privately Held
WEB: www.ferraracafe.com
SIC: 2051 5461 Cakes, bakery: except frozen; pastries, e.g. danish: except frozen; bakeries; cakes; pastries

(G-10155)
FERRIS USA LLC
18 W 108th St (10025-8915)
PHONE..................................617 895-8102
Taylor Conlin, *CEO*
EMP: 8
SALES (est): 275.5K Privately Held
SIC: 2326 2321 2329 Work apparel, except uniforms; men's & boys' dress shirts; men's & boys' sportswear & athletic clothing; field jackets, military

(G-10156)
FETHERSTON DESIGN GROUP LLC
Also Called: Erin Fetherston
225 W Broadway (10013-2909)
PHONE..................................212 643-7537
Raschna Shah, *Finance*
Stefini Zien, *Finance*
Amy Jubb, *Accounts Exec*
Barbara F Fetherston, *Mng Member*
Erin F Fetherston, *Mng Member*
▲ EMP: 20
SALES (est): 2.8MM Privately Held
SIC: 2389 Men's miscellaneous accessories

(G-10157)
FIBER-SEAL OF NEW YORK INC (PA)
979 3rd Ave Ste 903 (10022-3802)
PHONE..................................212 888-5580
Steven Mittman, *President*
Roberta Mittman, *Corp Secy*
▲ EMP: 5 EST: 1954
SALES (est): 7MM Privately Held
WEB: www.lewismittman.com
SIC: 2512 2511 Upholstered household furniture; wood bedroom furniture

(G-10158)
FIBRE CASE & NOVELTY CO INC (PA)
270 Lafayette St Ste 1510 (10012-3377)
PHONE..................................212 254-6060
Fax: 212 460-8794
Elliot Kozer, *President*
Richard Rubin, *Treasurer*
EMP: 4
SALES (est): 2.4MM Privately Held
SIC: 3161 Sample cases; trunks

(G-10159)
FIDELUS TECHNOLOGIES LLC
240 W 35th St Fl 6 (10001-2506)
PHONE..................................212 616-7800
Ron Rosansky, *President*
David Buckenheimer, *Exec VP*
Don Harloff, *Vice Pres*
Nancee Pronsati, *Vice Pres*
Ruben Delgado, *Opers Staff*
EMP: 51
SQ FT: 25,000
SALES (est): 15.6MM Privately Held
WEB: www.fidelus.com
SIC: 7372 Prepackaged software

(G-10160)
FIDESA US CORPORATION
17 State St Unit 122 (10004-1501)
PHONE..................................212 269-9000
Robert Thompson, *Principal*
EMP: 400
SALES (est): 16.9MM
SALES (corp-wide): 445.5MM Privately Held
WEB: www.royalbluefinancial.com
SIC: 7372 7371 Prepackaged software; custom computer programming services
PA: Fidessa Group Plc
Innovation Centre
Belfast BT3 9
289 046-3000

(G-10161)
FIELDSTON CLOTHES INC (HQ)
Also Called: Izzi Clothes
500 Fashion Ave Fl 6a (10018-0820)
PHONE..................................212 354-8550
Isadore Friedman, *Ch of Bd*
Mark Friedman, *President*
Paul Friedman, *Vice Pres*
David Smith, *Credit Mgr*
▲ EMP: 4 EST: 1945

SALES (est): 7.4MM
SALES (corp-wide): 8MM Privately Held
SIC: 2329 2339 Men's & boys' sportswear & athletic clothing; women's & misses' outerwear
PA: S. Rothschild & Co., Inc.
1407 Broadway Fl 10
New York NY 10018
212 354-8550

(G-10162)
FIERCE FUN TOYS LLC
100 Riverside Dr Ste 2 (10024-4822)
P.O. Box 905 (10024-0546)
PHONE..................................646 322-7172
Angela Larson, *Mng Member*
EMP: 7
SALES (est): 447.2K Privately Held
SIC: 3942 5092 Stuffed toys, including animals; toys & hobby goods & supplies

(G-10163)
FINE CUT DIAMONDS CORPORATION
580 5th Ave Ste 901 (10036-0044)
PHONE..................................212 575-8780
Fax: 212 921-2676
Michael Deutsch, *President*
EMP: 5 EST: 1967
SQ FT: 1,100
SALES (est): 410K Privately Held
SIC: 3915 5094 Diamond cutting & polishing; diamonds (gems)

(G-10164)
FINE SHEER INDUSTRIES INC (PA)
350 5th Ave Ste 5001 (10118-5091)
PHONE..................................212 594-4224
Fax: 212 967-9039
Grace Franco, *President*
Isaac Franco, *President*
David Franco, *Info Tech Dir*
▲ EMP: 18
SQ FT: 6,000
SALES (est): 250.1K Privately Held
SIC: 2252 2251 2369 Socks; panty hose; leggings: girls', children's & infants'

(G-10165)
FINE SOUNDS GROUP INC (PA)
Also Called: World of McIntosh
214 Lafayette St (10012-4079)
PHONE..................................212 364-0219
Mauro Grange, *CEO*
Giovanni Palacardo, *CFO*
EMP: 10
SALES (est): 24.3MM Privately Held
SIC: 3679 Recording heads, speech & musical equipment; recording & playback heads, magnetic; recording & playback apparatus, including phonograph

(G-10166)
FIRST GAMES PUBLR NETWRK INC
Also Called: 1gpn
420 Lexington Ave Rm 412 (10170-0499)
PHONE..................................212 983-0501
EMP: 100
SALES: 1,000K Privately Held
SIC: 2741 Developer & Publisher Mmog

(G-10167)
FIRST IMAGE DESIGN CORP
98 Cuttrmill Rd Ste 231 (10036)
PHONE..................................212 221-8282
Fax: 212 221-8484
David Hematian, *Ch of Bd*
Kathy Kamali, *Principal*
EMP: 20
SQ FT: 3,000
SALES (est): 2.4MM Privately Held
WEB: www.firstimage.net
SIC: 3911 Jewelry apparel

(G-10168)
FIRST LOVE FASHIONS LLC
1407 Broadway Rm 2010 (10018-2718)
PHONE..................................212 256-1089
Joseph Hamadani, *President*
EMP: 10 EST: 2014
SALES (est): 1.1MM Privately Held
SIC: 2339 Women's & misses' athletic clothing & sportswear

GEOGRAPHIC SECTION

New York - New York County (G-10194)

(G-10169)
FIRST2PRINT INC
494 8th Ave Fl 12 (10001-2578)
PHONE 212 868-6886
Neil Brasleau, *CEO*
Romalia Mitchell, *Sales Staff*
Lisa Salvato, *Executive Asst*
EMP: 7
SALES (est): 749.6K **Privately Held**
WEB: www.first2print.com
SIC: 2759 Commercial printing

(G-10170)
FISCHER DIAMONDS INC
1212 Avenue Of The Americ (10036-1622)
PHONE 212 869-1990
Fax: 212 354-9775
Jeffrey H Fisher, *President*
Neil Fischer, *Vice Pres*
Marcelle Fischler, *Vice Pres*
EMP: 10
SQ FT: 5,000
SALES (est): 720K **Privately Held**
WEB: www.fischerdiamonds.com
SIC: 3915 Lapidary work & diamond cutting & polishing

(G-10171)
FISCHLER DIAMONDS INC
580 5th Ave Ste 3100 (10036-4701)
PHONE 212 921-8196
Serge Fischler, *Ch of Bd*
Marcella Fischler, *Vice Pres*
▲ **EMP:** 5
SALES (est): 495.7K **Privately Held**
WEB: www.fischlerdiamonds.com
SIC: 3915 5094 Diamond cutting & polishing; diamonds (gems)

(G-10172)
FISCHLER HOCKEY SERVICE
200 W 109th St Apt C5 (10025-2252)
PHONE 212 749-4152
Stan Fischler, *Owner*
EMP: 10
SALES (est): 630K **Privately Held**
SIC: 2741 Newsletter publishing

(G-10173)
FISH & CROWN LTD (PA)
42 W 39th St (10018-3809)
PHONE 212 707-9603
Fax: 212 489-4829
Bergljot Wathne, *President*
Thorunn Wathne, *Corp Secy*
Soffia Wathne, *Vice Pres*
Thomas Faivre, *CFO*
Linda Sanducci, *Accountant*
◆ **EMP:** 100
SQ FT: 14,350
SALES (est): 9.3MM **Privately Held**
WEB: www.wathne.com
SIC: 3161 3999 Luggage; novelties, bric-a-brac & hobby kits

(G-10174)
FISONIC CORP (PA)
Also Called: Fisonic Technology
31-00 47th Ave Ste 106 (10023)
PHONE 716 763-0295
Robert Kremer, *CEO*
Professor Vladimir Fisenko, *Ch of Bd*
Joe Hoose, *President*
▲ **EMP:** 10
SQ FT: 1,000
SALES: 1.8MM **Privately Held**
WEB: www.fisonic.com
SIC: 3561 3433 Pumps & pumping equipment; heating equipment, except electric

(G-10175)
FITCH GRAPHICS LTD
229 W 28th St Fl 9 (10001-5915)
PHONE 212 619-3800
George Pavlides, *CEO*
John K Fitch III, *President*
Micky Padelo, *Manager*
John Fitzsimmons, *Director*
EMP: 32
SQ FT: 25,000
SALES (est): 3.2MM **Privately Held**
WEB: www.fitchdata.com
SIC: 2752 Commercial printing, offset

(G-10176)
FIVE STAR PRTG & MAILING SVCS
225 W 37th St Fl 16 (10018-6637)
PHONE 212 929-0300
Judith Magnus, *President*
Irwin Magnus, *General Mgr*
Steven Magnus, *Vice Pres*
▲ **EMP:** 13
SQ FT: 4,800
SALES: 2MM **Privately Held**
SIC: 2752 7331 Commercial printing, offset; mailing service

(G-10177)
FLASH VENTURES INC
Also Called: Tribeca
853 Broadway Ste 400 (10003-4725)
PHONE 212 255-7070
Albert OH, *CEO*
Katerina Conti, *Manager*
Dan Grabon, *Director*
▲ **EMP:** 12
SQ FT: 2,744
SALES (est): 2.5MM **Privately Held**
SIC: 3571 Electronic computers

(G-10178)
FLAVORS HOLDINGS INC (DH)
35 E 62nd St (10065-8014)
PHONE 212 572-8677
David Kennedy, *CEO*
EMP: 6 **EST:** 2015
SALES (est): 149.9MM
SALES (corp-wide): 5.3B **Privately Held**
SIC: 2869 6712 Sweeteners, synthetic; bank holding companies
HQ: Macandrews & Forbes Inc.
 38 E 63rd St
 New York NY 10065
 212 688-9000

(G-10179)
FLEXSIN
1441 Broadway Fl 5 (10018-1905)
PHONE 212 470-9279
Ankur Bhardwaj, *Principal*
EMP: 10
SALES (est): 500K **Privately Held**
SIC: 7372 Prepackaged software

(G-10180)
FLOORED INC
111 8th Ave Fl 16 (10011-5200)
PHONE 908 347-5845
David Eisenberg, *CEO*
EMP: 10
SQ FT: 2,000
SALES (est): 640K **Privately Held**
SIC: 7372 Business oriented computer software

(G-10181)
FLYCELL INC
80 Pine St Fl 29 (10005-1714)
PHONE 212 400-1212
Cristian Carnevale, *CEO*
Geetha Chandra, *Controller*
Lidiya Voloshko, *Accountant*
Cary Golomb, *Administration*
EMP: 41
SQ FT: 2,000
SALES (est): 3.2MM
SALES (corp-wide): 1.4MM **Privately Held**
WEB: www.flycell.com
SIC: 3663 Mobile communication equipment
PA: Acotel Group Spa
 Via Della Valle Dei Fontanili 29/37
 Roma RM 00168
 066 114-1000

(G-10182)
FLYNNS INC (PA)
Also Called: Flynn's Xerox
115 W 30th St (10001-4010)
PHONE 212 339-8700
Fax: 212 355-3738
Martin Lerner, *Ch of Bd*
Arthur Cantor, *President*
Brian Cantor, *Vice Pres*
Tony Tutura, *Manager*
▲ **EMP:** 27
SQ FT: 4,200

SALES (est): 3.2MM **Privately Held**
WEB: www.lorraineflynn.com
SIC: 2752 5943 Commercial printing, lithographic; stationery stores

(G-10183)
FOG CREEK SOFTWARE INC
1 Exchange Plz Fl 25 (10006-3745)
PHONE 866 364-2733
Joel Spolsky, *CEO*
Damian Brown, *Accounts Mgr*
Anna Lewis, *Manager*
Elizabeth Hall, *Director*
EMP: 5
SALES (est): 920.5K **Privately Held**
WEB: www.fogcreek.com
SIC: 7372 7371 Prepackaged software; custom computer programming services

(G-10184)
FOGEL NECKWEAR CORP
44 W 28th St Fl 15 (10001-4212)
P.O. Box 620820, Little Neck (11362-0820)
PHONE 212 686-7673
Fax: 212 447-9241
Sam Fogel, *President*
Freida Fogel, *Vice Pres*
Howard Fogel, *Treasurer*
EMP: 65 **EST:** 1964
SQ FT: 10,000
SALES (est): 3.4MM **Privately Held**
SIC: 2323 Men's & boys' neckwear

(G-10185)
FOREST LABORATORIES LLC (HQ)
909 3rd Ave Fl 23 (10022-4748)
PHONE 212 421-7850
Fax: 212 350-5665
R Todd Joyce, *President*
Donald Robertson, *President*
Nancy Telliho, *Publisher*
Jessica McNulty, *Division Mgr*
Robert Stewart, *COO*
▲ **EMP:** 227 **EST:** 1956
SQ FT: 169,000
SALES (est): 1.6B **Privately Held**
WEB: www.frx.com
SIC: 2834 5122 Pharmaceutical preparations; pharmaceuticals

(G-10186)
FORMART CORP
Also Called: Bellini Collections
312 5th Ave Fl 6 (10001-3603)
PHONE 212 819-1819
Fax: 212 921-1992
Sheung MEI Liu, *President*
EMP: 12
SQ FT: 2,100
SALES (est): 1.5MM **Privately Held**
WEB: www.cancerpins.com
SIC: 3171 5094 5137 3961 Purses, women's; jewelry; watches & parts; purses; costume jewelry

(G-10187)
FORTRESS BIOTECH INC (PA)
3 Columbus Cir Fl 15 (10019-8716)
PHONE 781 652-4500
Lindsay A Rosenwald, *Ch of Bd*
Eric K Rowinsky, *Ch of Bd*
George Avgerinos, *Senior VP*
Lucy Lu, *CFO*
EMP: 15
SQ FT: 3,200
SALES: 863K **Publicly Held**
SIC: 2834 Pharmaceutical preparations

(G-10188)
FORWARDLANE INC
120 W 21st St Apt 1014 (10011-3228)
PHONE 310 779-8590
Nathan Stevenson, *CEO*
EMP: 12
SQ FT: 1,000
SALES (est): 256K **Privately Held**
SIC: 7372 Business oriented computer software

(G-10189)
FOSCARINI INC
Also Called: Foscarini Showroom
17 Greene St (10013-2534)
PHONE 212 247-2218
Glenn Ludwig, *CEO*

▲ **EMP:** 8
SALES (est): 880.6K
SALES (corp-wide): 45.1MM **Privately Held**
SIC: 3641 5719 Electric lamps; lamps, fluorescent, electric; lamps, incandescent filament, electric; lighting, lamps & accessories; lamps & lamp shades
PA: Foscarini Spa
 Via Delle Industrie 27
 Marcon VE 30020
 041 595-3811

(G-10190)
FOUNDATION CENTER INC (PA)
1 Financial Sq Fl 24 (10005-3076)
PHONE 212 620-4230
Fax: 212 691-1828
Bradford K Smith, *President*
Emily Robbins, *Editor*
Juwon Choi, *Vice Pres*
Loretta Ferrari, *Vice Pres*
Lawrence McGill, *Vice Pres*
▲ **EMP:** 125
SQ FT: 150,000
SALES: 23.5MM **Privately Held**
WEB: www.fdncenter.net
SIC: 2741 8231 Directories: publishing only, not printed on site; libraries

(G-10191)
FOUNDATION FOR CULTURAL REVIEW
Also Called: NEW CRITERION MAGAZINE
900 Broadway Ste 602 (10003-1237)
PHONE 212 247-6980
Fax: 212 247-3127
Roger Kimball, *Principal*
James Panero, *Editor*
Robert Richman, *Corp Secy*
EMP: 7 **EST:** 1982
SALES: 2MM **Privately Held**
WEB: www.newcriterion.com
SIC: 2721 Magazines: publishing only, not printed on site

(G-10192)
FOUR SEASONS FASHION MFG INC
270 W 39th St Fl 12 (10018-0338)
PHONE 212 947-6820
Fax: 212 354-1096
Mohan Singh, *President*
Sandra Gonsalzes, *Administration*
EMP: 45
SALES (est): 3.3MM **Privately Held**
SIC: 2335 2339 2337 Women's, juniors' & misses' dresses; women's & misses' outerwear; women's & misses' suits & coats

(G-10193)
FOURTYS NY INC
231 W 39th St Rm 806 (10018-0734)
PHONE 212 382-0301
Fax: 212 768-7690
Dawn Mayo, *President*
EMP: 10
SQ FT: 4,000
SALES: 900K **Privately Held**
SIC: 2331 Women's & misses' blouses & shirts

(G-10194)
FOWNES BROTHERS & CO INC (PA)
16 E 34th St Fl 5 (10016-4370)
PHONE 212 683-0150
Fax: 212 683-2832
Thomas Gluckman, *Ch of Bd*
Chris Giattino, *Exec VP*
Helmuth Dosch, *Vice Pres*
Bruna Maney, *Vice Pres*
Howard Samuels, *Vice Pres*
◆ **EMP:** 50 **EST:** 1921
SQ FT: 18,000
SALES (est): 59.8MM **Privately Held**
SIC: 3151 2381 5136 5137 Gloves, leather: dress or semidress; gloves, woven or knit: made from purchased materials; gloves, men's & boys'; gloves, women's & children's; gloves, sport & athletic: boxing, handball, etc.

New York - New York County (G-10195)

(G-10195)
FOX UNLIMITED INC
345 7th Ave Rm 2b (10001-5058)
PHONE.....................212 736-3071
Marvin Levenson, *President*
EMP: 5
SQ FT: 4,000
SALES (est): 420K **Privately Held**
WEB: www.foxunlimited.com
SIC: 2371 Apparel, fur

(G-10196)
FOXHILL PRESS INC
37 E 7th St Ste 2 (10003-8027)
PHONE.....................212 995-9620
▲ **EMP:** 20
SQ FT: 1,600
SALES (est): 1.1MM
SALES (corp-wide): 35.2MM **Privately Held**
SIC: 2731 Books-Publishing/Printing
PA: Mcevoy Properties Llc
   85 2nd St Fl 6
   San Francisco CA 94107

(G-10197)
FRAMEDCOM
575 Madison Ave Fl 24 (10022-8538)
PHONE.....................212 400-2200
Ed Dunlap, *CFO*
EMP: 20 **EST:** 2011
SALES (est): 1.8MM **Privately Held**
SIC: 2086 Bottled & canned soft drinks

(G-10198)
FRANCEPRESS LLC (PA)
115 E 57th St Fl 11 (10022-2120)
PHONE.....................646 202-9828
Guenola Pellen, *Editor*
Louis Kyle, *Mng Member*
Lauren Weaver, *Manager*
Matt Viles, *Web Dvlpr*
▲ **EMP:** 4
SQ FT: 1,800
SALES (est): 1.2MM **Privately Held**
SIC: 2711 Newspapers, publishing & printing

(G-10199)
FRANCIS EMORY FITCH INC (PA)
Also Called: Fitch Group
229 W 28th St Fl 9 (10001-5915)
PHONE.....................212 619-3800
Fax: 212 233-1817
George Pavlides, *CEO*
John K Fitch III, *President*
Joseph Barrett, *Exec VP*
Jorge Motta, *Manager*
Frank Riina, *Supervisor*
EMP: 23 **EST:** 1886
SQ FT: 25,000
SALES (est): 6.6MM **Privately Held**
WEB: www.fitchgroup.com
SIC: 2721 2752 Periodicals: publishing only; commercial printing, offset

(G-10200)
FRANCO APPAREL GROUP INC
Also Called: Franco Apparel Group Team
1407 Broadway (10018-5100)
PHONE.....................212 967-7272
Fax: 212 967-7395
Ike Franco, *Ch of Bd*
Albert Shammah, *Vice Pres*
Reuben Eghbali, *Controller*
Allen Franco, *Sales Mgr*
EMP: 100
SQ FT: 15,000
SALES (est): 8.4MM **Privately Held**
WEB: www.francoapparel.com
SIC: 2369 Girls' & children's outerwear

(G-10201)
FRANK BILLANTI CASTING CO INC
42 W 38th St Rm 204 (10018-6220)
PHONE.....................212 221-0440
Frank L Billanti, *President*
Kristin N Billanti, *Principal*
Katherine O Billanti, *Vice Pres*
Frank J Billanti, *Administration*
EMP: 16
SALES: 1MM **Privately Held**
SIC: 3915 Jewelers' castings

(G-10202)
FRANK BLANCATO INC
64 W 48th St Fl 16 (10036-1708)
PHONE.....................212 768-1495
Fax: 212 768-7204
Frank Blancato, *President*
EMP: 10
SALES: 4MM **Privately Held**
WEB: www.fblancato.com
SIC: 3911 Jewelry, precious metal

(G-10203)
FRANK WINES INC
Also Called: HI Wines
345 E 80th St Apt 8b (10075-0688)
PHONE.....................646 765-6637
Olivier Pasquini, *Ch of Bd*
EMP: 5
SALES (est): 330K **Privately Held**
SIC: 2084 Wines

(G-10204)
FRANKLIN REPORT LLC
201 E 69th St Apt 14j (10021-5470)
PHONE.....................212 639-9100
Fax: 212 744-3546
Elizabeth Franklin, *Owner*
Josh Maio, *Editor*
EMP: 8
SALES (est): 600K **Privately Held**
WEB: www.franklinreport.com
SIC: 2731 Book publishing

(G-10205)
FRED WEIDNER & SON PRINTERS
15 Maiden Ln Ste 1505 (10038-5148)
PHONE.....................212 964-8676
Fred Weidner, *President*
EMP: 8
SALES (est): 830K **Privately Held**
SIC: 2759 7336 Commercial printing; commercial art & graphic design

(G-10206)
FREEDOM RAINS INC
Also Called: Northern Goose Polar Project
230 W 39th St Fl 7 (10018-4977)
PHONE.....................646 710-4512
Bobby Reiger, *CEO*
Steven Zellman, *President*
Nick Grazione, *COO*
EMP: 8
SQ FT: 3,500
SALES (est): 12MM **Privately Held**
SIC: 2253 Jackets, knit; sweaters & sweater coats, knit

(G-10207)
FRENCH ACCNT RUGS & TAPESTRIES
36 E 31st St Frnt B (10016-6821)
PHONE.....................212 686-6097
Fax: 212 937-3928
Kevin Rahmanan, *President*
▲ **EMP:** 6
SQ FT: 10,000
SALES (est): 769.9K **Privately Held**
WEB: www.farugs.com
SIC: 2211 Upholstery, tapestry & wall coverings: cotton; casement cloth, cotton; tapestry fabrics, cotton

(G-10208)
FRENCH ATMOSPHERE INC (PA)
Also Called: Urban Rose
421 7th Ave 525 (10001-2002)
P.O. Box 358, Cedarhurst (11516-0358)
PHONE.....................516 371-9100
Lawrence Kessler, *President*
Benjamin Kessler, *Vice Pres*
▲ **EMP:** 9
SQ FT: 1,350
SALES (est): 1.2MM **Privately Held**
SIC: 2339 Sportswear, women's

(G-10209)
FRENCH MORNING LLC
27 W 20th St Ste 800 (10011-3726)
PHONE.....................646 290-7463
Emmanuel Saint-Martin, *President*
EMP: 6
SQ FT: 1,200
SALES (est): 245.8K **Privately Held**
SIC: 2711 Newspapers: publishing only, not printed on site

(G-10210)
FRESH PRINTS LLC
134 E 70th St (10021-5035)
PHONE.....................917 826-2752
Jacob Goodman,
Josh Arbit,
EMP: 40
SALES (est): 1.8MM **Privately Held**
SIC: 2759 7389 Screen printing;

(G-10211)
FRIDGE MAGAZINE INC
108 W 39th St Fl 4 (10018-3614)
PHONE.....................212 997-7673
Jonathon Levine, *President*
EMP: 5
SALES (est): 410K **Privately Held**
WEB: www.fridgemagazine.com
SIC: 2721 Magazines: publishing only, not printed on site

(G-10212)
FROEBE GROUP LLC
154 W 27th St Rm 4 (10001-6215)
PHONE.....................646 649-2150
James Blankenship, *Editor*
Cindy Uh, *Editor*
Paul Sobel, *Production*
Troy Froebe, *Mng Member*
EMP: 8
SALES: 800K **Privately Held**
SIC: 2741 Business service newsletters: publishing & printing

(G-10213)
FROZEN FOOD DIGEST INC
Also Called: Quick Frzen Foods Annual Prcss
271 Madison Ave Ste 805 (10016-1005)
PHONE.....................212 557-8600
Fax: 212 986-9868
Saul Beck, *President*
Audrey Beck, *Publisher*
Anna Beck, *Vice Pres*
▲ **EMP:** 6
SALES (est): 510K **Privately Held**
SIC: 2721 Magazines: publishing only, not printed on site

(G-10214)
FROZEN FOOD PARTNERS LLC (PA)
601 Lexington Ave (10022-4611)
PHONE.....................203 661-7500
David Claroni, *Vice Pres*
EMP: 8
SALES (est): 1.6MM **Privately Held**
SIC: 2099 5141 Ready-to-eat meals, salads & sandwiches; food brokers

(G-10215)
FRP APPAREL GROUP LLC
110 W 40th St Fl 26 (10018-3626)
PHONE.....................212 695-8000
Paul Burghardt, *Business Mgr*
Tsuneaki Yanagida, *Marketing Mgr*
Maggie Felm, *Manager*
Johann Cooke,
Edwin Herman,
▲ **EMP:** 9
SALES (est): 620K **Privately Held**
SIC: 2221 Upholstery, tapestry & wall covering fabrics

(G-10216)
FSI - NEW YORK INC
1407 Broadway Rm 3107 (10018-2319)
PHONE.....................212 730-9545
Kathryn Del Calvo, *President*
Leo Del Calvo, *Vice Pres*
EMP: 6
SQ FT: 2,000
SALES (est): 462.5K **Privately Held**
SIC: 2331 Women's & misses' blouses & shirts

(G-10217)
FSR BEAUTY LTD
411 5th Ave Rm 804 (10016-2234)
PHONE.....................212 447-0036
Jerrold Rauchwerger, *President*
Maxine Rauchwerger, *Vice Pres*
Falen Rauchwerger, *Marketing Staff*
EMP: 6
SQ FT: 1,300
SALES (est): 752.4K **Privately Held**
SIC: 2844 Face creams or lotions; lipsticks

(G-10218)
FT PUBLICATIONS INC (HQ)
Also Called: Financial Times
330 Hudson St (10013-1046)
PHONE.....................212 641-6500
Fax: 212 641-6556
Loredana Beg, *Ch of Bd*
David Bell, *President*
Chris Davies, *Counsel*
Richard Varey, *Vice Pres*
Jo Cunningham, *QC Mgr*
▲ **EMP:** 80
SQ FT: 40,000
SALES (est): 60.5K
SALES (corp-wide): 1.4B **Privately Held**
SIC: 2711 Newspapers: publishing only, not printed on site
PA: Nikkei Inc.
   1-3-7, Otemachi
   Chiyoda-Ku TKY 100-0
   332 700-251

(G-10219)
FT PUBLICATIONS INC
Also Called: Financial Times Newspaper
330 Hudson St (10013-1046)
PHONE.....................212 641-2420
EMP: 46
SALES (corp-wide): 1.4B **Privately Held**
SIC: 2711 Newspapers: publishing only, not printed on site
HQ: F.T. Publications Inc.
   330 Hudson St
   New York NY 10013
   212 641-6500

(G-10220)
FUEL SYSTEMS SOLUTIONS INC (HQ)
780 3rd Ave Fl 25 (10017-2024)
PHONE.....................646 502-7170
Fax: 646 502-7171
Andrea Alghisi, *COO*
Michael Helfand, *Senior VP*
Pietro Bersani, *CFO*
▲ **EMP:** 30
SALES: 263.4MM
SALES (corp-wide): 103.3MM **Privately Held**
SIC: 3714 3592 7363 Fuel systems & parts, motor vehicle; carburetors; engineering help service
PA: Westport Fuel Systems Inc
   1750 75th Ave W Suite 101
   Vancouver BC
   604 718-2000

(G-10221)
FULCRUM PROMOTIONS & PRTG LLC
Also Called: Fulcrum Promos
1460 Broadway New York (10036)
PHONE.....................203 909-6362
Gia-Marie Vacca, *Partner*
Vincent Miceli,
Anthony Monaco,
EMP: 4
SQ FT: 700
SALES: 1MM **Privately Held**
SIC: 2759 7389 Promotional printing; advertising, promotional & trade show services

(G-10222)
FULL CIRCLE HOME LLC
146 W 29th St Rm 9w (10001-8207)
PHONE.....................212 432-0001
Tal Chitayat, *CEO*
David Chitayat, *Managing Dir*
Heather Kauffman, *COO*
Heather Tomasetti, *Manager*
▲ **EMP:** 9
SQ FT: 2,500
SALES: 1.5MM **Privately Held**
SIC: 3991 5199 Brooms & brushes; gifts & novelties

(G-10223)
FUN MEDIA INC
1001 Ave Of The Americas (10018-5460)
PHONE.....................646 472-0135

GEOGRAPHIC SECTION

New York - New York County (G-10248)

Joseph Giarraputo, *President*
A Basodan, *Principal*
P Panerai, *Chairman*
Francesco Librio, *Admin Sec*
EMP: 25
SQ FT: 7,500
SALES (est): 2.4MM **Privately Held**
WEB: www.classeditori.com
SIC: 2721 7319 Magazines: publishing only, not printed on site; transit advertising services
HQ: Class Editori Spa
Via Marco Burigozzo 5
Milano MI 20122
025 821-91

(G-10224)
FUNG WONG BAKERY INC
Also Called: Fung Wong Bakery Shop
30 Mott St Frnt (10013-5037)
PHONE..................................212 267-4037
Sherwin Choy, *President*
Eberline P Choy, *Corp Secy*
EMP: 20
SQ FT: 600
SALES (est): 1.7MM **Privately Held**
SIC: 2051 Bakery: wholesale or wholesale/retail combined

(G-10225)
FUSION BRANDS AMERICA INC
444 Madison Ave Ste 700 (10022-6970)
PHONE..................................212 269-1387
Caroline Piepervogt, *CEO*
Gregory Black, *President*
Michael McNamara, *CFO*
Denise Stein, *Controller*
Shaliza Mithani, *Supervisor*
EMP: 50
SQ FT: 8,500
SALES (est): 12.2MM
SALES (corp-wide): 4.7MM **Privately Held**
WEB: www.fusionbrandscorp.com
SIC: 2844 5122 Cosmetic preparations; cosmetics
PA: Fusion Brands Inc
40 St Clair Ave W Suite 200
Toronto ON M4V 1
800 261-9110

(G-10226)
FUSION PRO PERFORMANCE LTD
Also Called: Ki Pro Performance
16 W 36th St Rm 1202 (10018-9751)
PHONE..................................917 833-0761
Steven Goldfarb, *President*
EMP: 16 EST: 2014
SQ FT: 2,000
SALES (est): 18MM **Privately Held**
SIC: 2339 Athletic clothing: women's, misses' & juniors'

(G-10227)
FUSION TELECOM INTL INC (PA)
420 Lexington Ave Rm 1718 (10170-1707)
PHONE..................................212 201-2400
Fax: 212 972-7884
Matthew D Rosen, *CEO*
Marvin S Rosen, *Ch of Bd*
Gordon Hutchins Jr, *President*
Russell P Markman, *President*
Philip D Turits, *Corp Secy*
EMP: 114
SQ FT: 9,656
SALES: 101.6MM **Publicly Held**
WEB: www.fusiontel.com
SIC: 7372 4813 Business oriented computer software; telephone communication, except radio;

(G-10228)
FUTURE US INC
79 Madison Ave Fl 2 (10016-7805)
PHONE..................................844 779-2822
Fax: 212 944-9279
EMP: 60
SALES (corp-wide): 93.1MM **Privately Held**
WEB: www.futureus-inc.com
SIC: 2731 Book publishing
HQ: Future Us, Inc.
1 Lombard St Ste 200
San Francisco CA 94111
650 238-2400

(G-10229)
G & P PRINTING INC
142 Baxter St (10013-3605)
PHONE..................................212 274-8092
Fax: 212 274-1944
Stanley Chen, *President*
EMP: 5 EST: 1998
SALES (est): 550.1K **Privately Held**
WEB: www.gpprinting.com
SIC: 2752 Offset & photolithographic printing

(G-10230)
G I CERTIFIED INC
623 W 51st St (10019-5008)
PHONE..................................212 397-1945
Michael Borrico, *Ch of Bd*
C Russonello, *Director*
Charlie Rucinelli, *Director*
EMP: 6
SALES: 500K **Privately Held**
WEB: www.certifiedny.com
SIC: 3993 Signs & advertising specialties

(G-10231)
G S W WORLDWIDE LLC
1180 Av Of The Amrcs 10 (10036-8402)
PHONE..................................646 437-4800
Fax: 646 437-4810
Jennifer Oleski, *Senior VP*
Seth Quillin, *Senior VP*
Lori Sayre, *Senior VP*
Mary Krebsbach, *Vice Pres*
Damion Townsend, *Vice Pres*
EMP: 60
SALES (est): 9.9MM **Privately Held**
SIC: 2834 Proprietary drug products

(G-10232)
G SCHIRMER INC (HQ)
Also Called: Music Sales
180 Madison Ave Ste 2400 (10016-5241)
PHONE..................................212 254-2100
Barrie Edwards, *President*
Susan Feder, *Vice Pres*
John Castaldo, *Controller*
Steven Wilson, *Sales Mgr*
Jessica Hobbs, *Manager*
▲ **EMP:** 4
SALES (est): 5.4MM
SALES (corp-wide): 13.6MM **Privately Held**
WEB: www.schirmer.com
SIC: 2741 7929 Music books: publishing only, not printed on site; entertainers & entertainment groups
PA: Music Sales Corporation
180 Madison Ave Ste 2400
New York NY 10016
212 254-2100

(G-10233)
G X ELECTRIC CORPORATION
8 W 38th St (10018-6229)
PHONE..................................212 921-0400
Johnny Hernandez, *President*
EMP: 50 EST: 2013
SALES (est): 2.3MM **Privately Held**
SIC: 3699 Electrical equipment & supplies

(G-10234)
G-III APPAREL GROUP LTD (PA)
512 7th Ave Fl 35 (10018-0832)
PHONE..................................212 403-0500
Morris Goldfarb, *Ch of Bd*
Sammy Aaron, *Vice Ch Bd*
David Winn, *President*
Wayne S Miller, *COO*
Michael Laskau III, *Vice Pres*
▲ **EMP:** 247
SQ FT: 173,000
SALES: 2.3B **Publicly Held**
WEB: www.g-iii.com
SIC: 2337 2339 2311 2329 Women's & misses' suits & coats; women's & misses' outerwear; men's & boys' suits & coats; coats, overcoats & vests; jackets (suede, leatherette, etc.), sport: men's & boys'; garments, leather; coats & jackets, leather & sheep-lined; pants, leather; men's & boys' clothing

(G-10235)
G-III APPAREL GROUP LTD
Jessica Howard
512 Fashion Ave Fl 35 (10018-0832)
PHONE..................................212 403-0500
Karol Gass, *Branch Mgr*
EMP: 50
SALES (corp-wide): 2.1B **Publicly Held**
SIC: 2335 Women's, juniors' & misses' dresses
PA: G-lii Apparel Group, Ltd.
512 7th Ave Fl 35
New York NY 10018
212 403-0500

(G-10236)
G-III LEATHER FASHIONS INC
Also Called: G-III Apparel Group
512 7th Ave Fl 35 (10018-0832)
PHONE..................................212 403-0500
Fax: 212 944-4081
Morris Goldfarb, *Branch Mgr*
Joe Wong, *Info Tech Mgr*
Isaure Renaud, *Director*
EMP: 20
SALES (corp-wide): 2.1B **Publicly Held**
SIC: 2386 2337 2339 Leather & sheep-lined clothing; women's & misses' suits & coats; women's & misses' outerwear
HQ: G-lii Leather Fashions, Inc.
512 Fashion Ave Fl 35
New York NY 10018
212 403-0500

(G-10237)
G18 CORPORATION
215 W 40th St Fl 9 (10018-1575)
PHONE..................................212 869-0010
Laurence Goldfarb, *President*
EMP: 2
SQ FT: 2,500
SALES: 7MM **Privately Held**
SIC: 2337 Women's & misses' suits & coats

(G-10238)
GABRIELLA IMPORTERS INC
305 W 87th St (10024-2602)
PHONE..................................212 579-3945
Jacques Azoulay, *President*
Aymeric Bireau, *Accounts Mgr*
EMP: 11
SALES (corp-wide): 2.3MM **Privately Held**
SIC: 2084 Wines
PA: Gabriella Importers, Inc.
481 Johnson Ave Ste D
Bohemia NY 11716
212 579-3945

(G-10239)
GABRIELLE ANDRA
305 W 21st St (10011-3073)
PHONE..................................212 366-9624
Andra Gabrielle, *Owner*
EMP: 5
SALES (est): 220K **Privately Held**
SIC: 2331 Blouses, women's & juniors': made from purchased material

(G-10240)
GALISON PUBLISHING LLC
Also Called: Galison/Mudpuppy
25 W 43rd St Ste 1411 (10036-7416)
PHONE..................................212 354-8840
Clairissa McLaurin, *Production*
Sam Minnitti, *CFO*
Steven Scott, *Mktg Dir*
Liza Rollins, *Marketing Staff*
Bill Miller, *Mng Member*
▲ **EMP:** 20
SQ FT: 7,500
SALES (est): 3.2MM
SALES (corp-wide): 26MM **Privately Held**
SIC: 2621 Stationery, envelope & tablet papers
PA: The Mcevoy Group Llc
680 2nd St
San Francisco CA 94107
415 537-4200

(G-10241)
GALLERY 57 DENTAL
24 W 57th St Ste 701 (10019-3949)
PHONE..................................212 246-8700
Andrew Koenigsberg DDS, *Principal*
Sandy Chemas, *Pub Rel Dir*
EMP: 20
SALES (est): 2.2MM **Privately Held**
SIC: 3843 Enamels, dentists'

(G-10242)
GALLERY 91
91 Grand St Apt 2 (10013-3075)
PHONE..................................212 966-3722
Fax: 212 219-1684
Daniel T Ebihara, *Partner*
Yoshiko Ebihara, *Partner*
EMP: 4
SQ FT: 1,800
SALES (est): 1MM **Privately Held**
WEB: www.gallery91.com
SIC: 3299 5023 5999 Non-metallic mineral statuary & other decorative products; decorative home furnishings & supplies; art, picture frames & decorations

(G-10243)
GALT INDUSTRIES INC
121 E 71st St (10021-4275)
PHONE..................................212 758-0770
Fax: 212 758-1336
George T Votis, *Ch of Bd*
▲ **EMP:** 9
SQ FT: 2,000
SALES (est): 1.2MM **Privately Held**
SIC: 3089 Injection molding of plastics

(G-10244)
GAME TIME LLC
1407 Broadway Rm 400 (10018-3843)
PHONE..................................914 557-9662
Adam Pennington, *Mng Member*
Belinda Colesanti, *Manager*
Stephanie Raw, *Manager*
Patrick McGeough,
▲ **EMP:** 17 EST: 1999
SQ FT: 30,000
SALES (est): 3.5MM **Privately Held**
SIC: 3873 Watches, clocks, watchcases & parts

(G-10245)
GAMES FOR CHANGE INC
205 E 42nd St Fl 20 (10017-5706)
PHONE..................................212 242-4922
Susanna Pollack, *President*
Emily Treat, *Vice Pres*
Ling Lu, *Controller*
Meghan Ventura, *Mktg Dir*
Deborah Levine, *Director*
EMP: 1 EST: 2004
SALES (est): 1.4MM **Privately Held**
SIC: 7372 Prepackaged software

(G-10246)
GAMETIME MEDIA INC
120 E 87th St Apt R8e (10128-1198)
PHONE..................................212 860-2090
Robert Yan, *CEO*
Liz Yan, *President*
EMP: 6
SALES: 2MM **Privately Held**
WEB: www.gametimemedia.com
SIC: 2741 Guides: publishing & printing

(G-10247)
GAPPA TEXTILES INC
295 5th Ave Ste 1021 (10016-7105)
PHONE..................................212 481-7100
Mahmud Topal, *President*
Boran Batur, *Vice Pres*
Ebru Yildiz, *Analyst*
▲ **EMP:** 11
SALES (est): 1MM
SALES (corp-wide): 2.3B **Privately Held**
WEB: www.gappausa.com
SIC: 2299 Fabrics: linen, jute, hemp, ramie
PA: Calik Holding Anonim Sirketi
No:163 Buyukdere Caddesi
Istanbul (Europe)

(G-10248)
GARAN INCORPORATED (HQ)
200 Madison Ave Fl 4 (10016-3905)
PHONE..................................212 563-1292
Fax: 212 564-7994
Seymour Lichtenstein, *CEO*
Jerald Kamiel, *President*
Wayne C Cooper, *Vice Pres*
Kathie Fiore, *Vice Pres*

New York - New York County (G-10249)

Marvin S Robinson, *Vice Pres*
◆ **EMP:** 120 **EST:** 1941
SQ FT: 38,500
SALES (est): 709.5MM
SALES (corp-wide): 210.8B **Publicly Held**
WEB: www.garanimals.com
SIC: 2361 2369 2331 2339 T-shirts & tops: girls', children's & infants'; slacks: girls' & children's; T-shirts & tops, women's: made from purchased materials; shirts, women's & juniors': made from purchased materials; jeans: women's, misses' & juniors'; men's & boys' furnishings; sport shirts, men's & boys': from purchased materials
PA: Berkshire Hathaway Inc.
  3555 Farnam St Ste 1440
  Omaha NE 68131
  402 346-1400

(G-10249)
GARAN MANUFACTURING CORP (DH)
200 Madison Ave Fl 4 (10016-3905)
PHONE..................212 563-2000
Seymour Lichtenstein, *CEO*
Jerald Kamiel, *President*
David M Fligel, *Vice Pres*
Maria Bothos, *Executive Asst*
▼ **EMP:** 1
SALES (est): 17.5MM
SALES (corp-wide): 210.8B **Publicly Held**
SIC: 2361 2369 2331 2339 T-shirts & tops: girls', children's & infants'; slacks: girls' & children's; T-shirts & tops, women's: made from purchased materials; shirts, women's & juniors': made from purchased materials; jeans: women's, misses' & juniors'; men's & boys' furnishings; sport shirts, men's & boys': from purchased materials
HQ: Garan, Incorporated
  200 Madison Ave Fl 4
  New York NY 10016
  212 563-1292

(G-10250)
GARYS LOFT
28 W 36th St (10018-1284)
PHONE..................212 244-0970
EMP: 6
SALES (est): 764K **Privately Held**
SIC: 3861 Photographic equipment & supplies

(G-10251)
GB GROUP INC
Umpire State Bldg 1808 (10021)
P.O. Box 2293 (10021-0055)
PHONE..................212 594-3748
Howard Zhanz, *President*
EMP: 8
SALES (est): 740K **Privately Held**
WEB: www.crystalisland.com
SIC: 3699 Laser systems & equipment

(G-10252)
GBG NATIONAL BRANDS GROUP LLC
350 5th Ave Lbby 9 (10118-0109)
PHONE..................646 839-7000
Bruce Philip Rockowitz, *CEO*
Dow Peter Famulak, *President*
Ronald Ventricelli, *CFO*
Jason Andrew Rabin, *Chief Mktg Ofcr*
EMP: 5
SALES (est): 374.2K **Privately Held**
SIC: 2321 Men's & boys' furnishings
HQ: Fung Holdings (1937) Limited
  G/F
  Lai Chi Kok KLN
  230 023-00

(G-10253)
GBG SOCKS LLC
350 5th Ave Lbby 9 (10118-0109)
PHONE..................646 839-7000
Dow Famulak, *Mng Member*
EMP: 25
SALES (est): 1.1MM **Privately Held**
SIC: 2252 Socks

(G-10254)
GBG USA INC
350 5th Ave Ste 700 (10118-0701)
PHONE..................646 839-7083
EMP: 93 **Privately Held**
SIC: 2387 Apparel belts
HQ: Gbg Usa Inc.
  350 5th Ave Lbby 9
  New York NY 10118
  646 839-7083

(G-10255)
GBG USA INC
Lf USA Accessories
261 W 35th St Fl 15 (10001-1902)
PHONE..................212 615-3400
Steven Kahn, *Branch Mgr*
EMP: 50 **Privately Held**
SIC: 2387 Apparel belts
HQ: Gbg Usa Inc.
  350 5th Ave Lbby 9
  New York NY 10118
  646 839-7083

(G-10256)
GBG USA INC
Also Called: Max Leather
1333 Broadway Fl 9 (10018-1064)
PHONE..................212 290-8041
Jarrod Kahn, *Manager*
EMP: 20 **Privately Held**
SIC: 2387 Apparel belts
HQ: Gbg Usa Inc.
  350 5th Ave Lbby 9
  New York NY 10118
  646 839-7083

(G-10257)
GBG WEST LLC (DH)
Also Called: Joes Jeans
350 5th Ave Fl 5 (10118-0110)
PHONE..................646 839-7000
Suzy Biszantz, *CEO*
Elena Pickett, *Senior VP*
Joda Han, *Director*
EMP: 110
SQ FT: 150,000
SALES: 88MM **Privately Held**
SIC: 2339 Jeans: women's, misses' & juniors'
HQ: Gbg Usa Inc.
  350 5th Ave Lbby 9
  New York NY 10118
  646 839-7083

(G-10258)
GBT GLOBAL
175-20 Wexford Ter Ste F1 (10001)
PHONE..................718 593-9698
Nick Froner, *Mng Member*
EMP: 30 **EST:** 2012
SQ FT: 5,000
SALES: 200K **Privately Held**
SIC: 3532 Mining machinery

(G-10259)
GCE INTERNATIONAL INC (PA)
Also Called: Great China Empire
1385 Broadway Fl 21 (10018-6022)
PHONE..................212 704-4800
Donald Oberfield, *President*
Peter Markson, *Chairman*
Martin J Kelly, *Treasurer*
Abe Anteby, *Info Tech Mgr*
AVI Sivan, *Info Tech Mgr*
▲ **EMP:** 100 **EST:** 1920
SQ FT: 40,000
SALES (est): 158.4MM **Privately Held**
WEB: www.parisaccessories.com
SIC: 2253 2389 2331 5137 Hats & headwear, knit; scarves & mufflers, knit; handkerchiefs, except paper; T-shirts & tops, women's: made from purchased materials; blouses, women's & juniors': made from purchased material; scarves, women's & children's; gloves, women's & children's; scarves, men's & boys'; gloves, men's & boys'

(G-10260)
GCE INTERNATIONAL INC
Also Called: Baar & Beards
350 5th Ave Ste 616 (10118-0110)
PHONE..................212 868-0500
Fax: 212 564-2915
Martin Kelly, *Manager*
EMP: 12
SALES (corp-wide): 158.4MM **Privately Held**
WEB: www.parisaccessories.com
SIC: 2353 2361 2381 Hats, caps & millinery; girls' & children's dresses, blouses & shirts; fabric dress & work gloves
PA: Gce International, Inc.
  1385 Broadway Fl 21
  New York NY 10018
  212 704-4800

(G-10261)
GCE INTERNATIONAL INC
Also Called: Capital Mercury Shirtmakers Co
1359 Broadway Rm 2000 (10018-7841)
PHONE..................773 263-1210
Peter Markson, *CEO*
Donald Mattson, *General Mgr*
Agnes Kolbig, *Credit Mgr*
EMP: 60
SALES (corp-wide): 158.4MM **Privately Held**
WEB: www.parisaccessories.com
SIC: 2321 Men's & boys' dress shirts
PA: Gce International, Inc.
  1385 Broadway Fl 21
  New York NY 10018
  212 704-4800

(G-10262)
GDS PUBLISHING INC
40 Wall St Ste 500 (10005-1344)
PHONE..................212 796-2000
Dave Cullinane, *Principal*
EMP: 16
SALES (est): 1.6MM
SALES (corp-wide): 35.6MM **Privately Held**
SIC: 2741 Miscellaneous publishing
HQ: Gds Publishing Limited
  18-21 Queen Square
  Bristol BS1 4
  117 921-4000

(G-10263)
GE HEALTHCARE FINCL SVCS INC
299 Park Ave Fl 3 (10171-0022)
PHONE..................212 713-2000
Batcrio Buyo, *Branch Mgr*
EMP: 6
SALES (corp-wide): 25B **Publicly Held**
SIC: 2759 Commercial printing
HQ: Ge Healthcare Financial Services, Inc.
  500 W Monroe St Fl 19
  Chicago IL 60661
  312 697-3999

(G-10264)
GEIGTECH EAST BAY LLC
150 E 58th St Frnt 3 (10155-0007)
PHONE..................844 543-4437
EMP: 13
SALES (corp-wide): 6MM **Privately Held**
SIC: 2591 Window shade rollers & fittings
PA: Geigtech East Bay Llc
  55 Beattie Pl
  Greenville SC 29601
  844 543-4437

(G-10265)
GELIKO LLC
1751 2nd Ave Rm 102 (10128-5363)
PHONE..................212 876-5620
Zach Rubin, *Mng Member*
▲ **EMP:** 20 **EST:** 2009
SALES (est): 2.6MM **Privately Held**
SIC: 2899 Gelatin

(G-10266)
GEM-BAR SETTING INC
15 W 46th St (10036-4117)
PHONE..................212 869-9238
Fred Barilla, *President*
Tina Barilla, *Admin Sec*
EMP: 8
SALES (est): 520K **Privately Held**
SIC: 3911 Jewelry, precious metal

(G-10267)
GEMFIELDS USA INCORPORATED
589 5th Ave Rm 909 (10017-8715)
PHONE..................212 398-5400
Gabriel Jharvy, *President*
EMP: 5
SALES (est): 396.6K **Privately Held**
SIC: 1499 Gem stones (natural) mining

(G-10268)
GEMORO INC
48 W 48th St Ste 1102 (10036-1703)
PHONE..................212 768-8844
Dennis Hakim, *President*
EMP: 5
SALES (est): 530K **Privately Held**
WEB: www.gemoro.com
SIC: 3911 5094 Jewelry, precious metal; jewelry & precious stones

(G-10269)
GEMPRINT CORPORATION
580 5th Ave Bsmt LI05 (10036-4726)
PHONE..................212 997-0007
Angelo Palmieri, *President*
EMP: 20
SQ FT: 5,500
SALES (est): 2.1MM **Privately Held**
SIC: 3826 Laser scientific & engineering instruments

(G-10270)
GEMTEX INC
Also Called: Streetline
1410 Broadway Rm 304 (10018-9376)
PHONE..................212 302-0102
Said Gomaa, *President*
Julia Dodos, *Administration*
▲ **EMP:** 6 **EST:** 2008
SQ FT: 3,500
SALES (est): 765.2K **Privately Held**
SIC: 2329 Men's & boys' sportswear & athletic clothing; men's & boys' athletic uniforms

(G-10271)
GEMVETO JEWELRY COMPANY INC
18 E 48th St Rm 501 (10017-1014)
PHONE..................212 755-2522
Fax: 212 755-2027
Jean Vitau, *President*
Irene Vitau, *Corp Secy*
EMP: 20 **EST:** 1967
SQ FT: 3,500
SALES (est): 2.4MM **Privately Held**
WEB: www.gems-online.org
SIC: 3911 Jewelry, precious metal

(G-10272)
GENERAL ART COMPANY INC
Also Called: General Art Framing
14 E 38th St Fl 6 (10016-0005)
PHONE..................212 255-1298
Jen Chan, *President*
EMP: 10
SQ FT: 4,000
SALES (est): 1MM **Privately Held**
SIC: 2499 5023 Picture frame molding, finished; frames & framing, picture & mirror

(G-10273)
GENERAL MEDIA STRATEGIES INC
Also Called: African American Observer
483 10th Ave Rm 325 (10018-1177)
PHONE..................212 586-4141
Steve Mallory, *President*
EMP: 8 **EST:** 2001
SALES (est): 250K **Privately Held**
SIC: 2711 Newspapers

(G-10274)
GENERAL SPORTWEAR COMPANY INC (PA)
230 W 38th St Fl 4 (10018-9085)
P.O. Box 588, Ellenville (12428-0588)
PHONE..................212 764-5820
Fax: 845 647-4934
Herbert Rosenstock, *Ch of Bd*
David Rosensock, *Corp Secy*
Jeffrey Rosenstock, *Exec VP*
Rich Acunto, *Vice Pres*
Tony Shannahan, *Human Res Mgr*
◆ **EMP:** 5 **EST:** 1927
SQ FT: 20,000

GEOGRAPHIC SECTION

New York - New York County (G-10298)

SALES (est): 31.8MM **Privately Held**
WEB: www.generalsportwear.com
SIC: 2361 2369 2329 T-shirts & tops: girls', children's & infants'; jeans: girls', children's & infants'; men's & boys' sportswear & athletic clothing

(G-10275)
GENESIS MANNEQUINS USA II INC
151 W 25th St Fl 4 (10001-7204)
PHONE 212 505-6600
Joseph Klinow, *President*
EMP: 8
SQ FT: 3,500
SALES: 3.5MM **Privately Held**
SIC: 3999 Mannequins

(G-10276)
GENEVA WATCH COMPANY INC (DH)
1407 Brdway Rm 400 (10018-3843)
PHONE 212 221-1177
Charles Kriete, *President*
Nick Lancellotti, *Vice Pres*
John Cuccurullo, *CFO*
Mary Burns, *Manager*
Mark Meighan, *Manager*
▲ **EMP:** 20
SQ FT: 15,000
SALES (est): 5.7MM
SALES (corp-wide): 98.7K **Privately Held**
WEB: www.advgi.com
SIC: 3873 Watches & parts, except crystals & jewels
HQ: Awc Liquidating Co.
1407 Brdwy Ste 400
New York NY 10018
212 221-1177

(G-10277)
GENIE INSTANT PRINTING CO INC
Also Called: Genie Instant Printing Center
37 W 43rd St (10036-7403)
PHONE 212 575-8258
Fax: 212 382-3408
Sal Cohen, *President*
Ronnie Cohen, *Vice Pres*
EMP: 10
SALES (est): 1MM **Privately Held**
SIC: 2759 2752 Commercial printing; photo-offset printing

(G-10278)
GENOMEWEB LLC
Also Called: Bioinformatics Publishing
40 Fulton St Rm 1002 (10038-5057)
P.O. Box 998 (10272-0998)
PHONE 212 651-5636
Fax: 212 269-3686
Molika Ashford, *Editor*
Adam Bonislawski, *Editor*
Ben Butkus, *Editor*
Madeleine Johnson, *Editor*
Doug Macron, *Editor*
EMP: 17
SQ FT: 3,600
SALES (est): 2.1MM **Privately Held**
SIC: 2721 Periodicals

(G-10279)
GEOFFREY BEENE INC
37 W 57th St Frnt 2 (10019-3410)
PHONE 212 371-5570
Fax: 212 980-6579
Geoffrey Beene, *President*
G Thompson Hutton, *President*
Russell Nardozza, *COO*
Russell Nardoza, *Senior VP*
EMP: 20
SALES: 2.3MM **Privately Held**
WEB: www.geoffreybeene.com
SIC: 2335 2337 2331 2339 Women's, juniors' & misses' dresses; skirts, separate: women's, misses' & juniors'; jackets & vests, except fur & leather: women's; blouses, women's & juniors': made from purchased material; slacks: women's, misses' & juniors'

(G-10280)
GEONEX INTERNATIONAL CORP
200 Park Ave S Ste 920 (10003-1509)
PHONE 212 473-4555
George Nikiforov, *President*
EMP: 6
SQ FT: 1,000
SALES (est): 720K **Privately Held**
SIC: 2435 Hardwood plywood, prefinished

(G-10281)
GEORGE G SHARP INC (PA)
160 Broadway Fl 8 (10038-4230)
PHONE 212 732-2800
Fax: 212 732-2809
I Hilary Rolih, *Ch of Bd*
Allen Chin, *President*
CHI-Cheng Yang, *COO*
Robert Reehl, *QC Mgr*
Al F Seneca, *Treasurer*
EMP: 27
SQ FT: 8,000
SALES (est): 81.6MM **Privately Held**
WEB: www.ggsharp.com
SIC: 3731 4225 8712 Shipbuilding & repairing; commercial cargo ships, building & repairing; military ships, building & repairing; general warehousing; architectural services

(G-10282)
GEORGE KNITTING MILLS CORP
116 W 23rd St Fl 4 (10011-2599)
PHONE 212 242-3300
Fax: 305 885-6747
Lawrence Aibel, *President*
Richard Aibel, *Vice Pres*
George Paez, *Office Mgr*
EMP: 5 **EST:** 1958
SQ FT: 10,000
SALES (est): 787.2K **Privately Held**
SIC: 2258 Pile fabrics, warp or flat knit

(G-10283)
GEORGE LEDERMAN INC
515 Madison Ave Rm 1218 (10022-5452)
PHONE 212 753-4556
Fax: 212 888-3372
Serge Lederman, *President*
Adrienne Lederman, *Vice Pres*
Janine Lederman, *Admin Sec*
EMP: 5 **EST:** 1937
SQ FT: 800
SALES (est): 630.7K **Privately Held**
WEB: www.glederman.com
SIC: 3911 Jewelry, precious metal

(G-10284)
GEORGY CREATIVE FASHIONS INC
Also Called: Georgie Kaye
249 W 29th St (10001-5211)
PHONE 212 279-4885
George Kambouris, *President*
EMP: 6
SQ FT: 3,000
SALES (est): 510.7K **Privately Held**
SIC: 2371 5136 5137 2386 Fur goods; fur clothing, men's & boys'; fur clothing, women's & children's; garments, leather

(G-10285)
GEORLAND CORPORATION
745 5th Ave Fl 5 (10151-0502)
PHONE 212 730-4730
Romain Marteau, *President*
EMP: 2
SQ FT: 3,000
SALES: 1MM **Privately Held**
SIC: 3911 Jewelry, precious metal

(G-10286)
GERLI & CO INC (PA)
Also Called: American Silk Mills
41 Madison Ave Ste 4101 (10010-2203)
PHONE 212 213-1919
Fax: 212 683-2370
Robin L Slough, *President*
Cynthia Douthit, *Vice Pres*
John M Sullivan Jr, *Vice Pres*
Russell Sokolas, *Plant Mgr*
James Harowicz, *CFO*
◆ **EMP:** 35 **EST:** 1883
SQ FT: 7,500
SALES (est): 29.5MM **Privately Held**
SIC: 2211 2221 Cotton broad woven goods; broadwoven fabric mills, manmade; rayon broadwoven fabrics; silk broadwoven fabrics

(G-10287)
GERSON & GERSON INC (PA)
100 W 33rd St Ste 911 (10001-2912)
PHONE 212 244-6775
Fax: 212 244-6794
Matthew Gerson, *Ch of Bd*
Shelley Striar, *Prdtn Mgr*
Phyills Falsone, *Controller*
Beth Smith, *Accounts Exec*
Kevin Gray, *Sales Executive*
▼ **EMP:** 70 **EST:** 1933
SQ FT: 13,000
SALES: 21.7MM **Privately Held**
WEB: www.gersonandgerson.com
SIC: 2369 2361 Girls' & children's outerwear; dresses: girls', children's & infants'

(G-10288)
GFB FASHIONS LTD
Also Called: Jonathan Michael Coats
463 Fashion Ave Rm 1502 (10018-7596)
PHONE 212 239-9230
Paul Cohen, *President*
Steve Schubak, *Controller*
▲ **EMP:** 12
SALES (est): 1.1MM **Privately Held**
SIC: 2339 Women's & misses' jackets & coats, except sportswear

(G-10289)
GG DESIGN AND PRINTING
93 Henry St Frnt 1 (10002-7035)
PHONE 718 321-3220
Allan Yin, *President*
▲ **EMP:** 9
SQ FT: 3,500
SALES: 1MM **Privately Held**
SIC: 2791 7336 Typesetting; graphic arts & related design

(G-10290)
GH BASS & CO (DH)
200 Madison Ave (10016-3903)
PHONE 212 381-3900
Bill Hutchison, *President*
Jannice Gomez, *General Mgr*
Howard Renner, *Senior VP*
Christina Merianos, *Buyer*
Victoria Mann, *Controller*
▲ **EMP:** 300 **EST:** 1987
SALES (est): 84.8MM
SALES (corp-wide): 2.3B **Publicly Held**
WEB: www.ghbass.com
SIC: 3144 3143 3149 5661 Women's footwear, except athletic; men's footwear, except athletic; children's footwear, except athletic; shoe stores
HQ: Am Retail Group, Inc.
7401 Boone Ave N
Brooklyn Park MN 55428
763 391-4000

(G-10291)
GHOSTERY INC (PA)
10 E 39th St Fl 8 (10016-0111)
PHONE 917 262-2530
Scott Meyer, *CEO*
Manny Ataebi, *Vice Pres*
Larry Furr, *Vice Pres*
Todd Ruback, *Vice Pres*
Jim Weber, *CFO*
EMP: 8
SALES (est): 1.8MM **Privately Held**
SIC: 7372 Application computer software

(G-10292)
GIA LINGERIE INC
485 Fashion Ave Rm 1200 (10018-9401)
PHONE 212 448-0918
Lex Hentenaar, *CEO*
Kami Orthmann, *President*
Yolanda Chu, *General Mgr*
Mary Donna, *General Mgr*
Vincent Lee, *Controller*
▲ **EMP:** 20
SALES: 5MM **Privately Held**
SIC: 2341 Nightgowns & negligees: women's & children's

(G-10293)
GIFFORD GROUP INC
Also Called: Just Plastics
250 Dyckman St (10034-5354)
PHONE 212 569-8500
Fax: 212 569-6970
Robert C Vermann, *President*
Tammy Espaillat, *Vice Pres*
Lois Vermann, *Vice Pres*
EMP: 15
SQ FT: 25,000
SALES: 1.5MM **Privately Held**
WEB: www.justplastics.com
SIC: 3089 Plastic processing

(G-10294)
GIFTS SOFTWARE INC
360 Lexington Ave Rm 601 (10017-6562)
PHONE 904 438-6000
Fax: 646 838-9494
Jawaid M Khan, *CEO*
Paul Campanaro, *Vice Pres*
Nasir Farooqui, *Vice Pres*
Sydney Stone, *Vice Pres*
Paul Gdanski, *VP Sales*
EMP: 35
SQ FT: 10,000
SALES (est): 935.2K
SALES (corp-wide): 6.6B **Publicly Held**
WEB: www.giftssoft.com
SIC: 7372 Business oriented computer software
PA: Fidelity National Information Services, Inc.
601 Riverside Ave
Jacksonville FL 32204
904 438-6000

(G-10295)
GILDAN APPAREL USA INC (DH)
Also Called: Anvil Knitwear, Inc.
48 W 38th St Fl 8 (10018-0043)
PHONE 212 476-0341
Fax: 212 265-3159
Anthony Corsano, *Ch of Bd*
Jacob Hollander, *Exec VP*
Heather Stefani, *Exec VP*
Chris Binnicker, *Vice Pres*
J Goldberg, *Vice Pres*
▲ **EMP:** 65
SALES (est): 525.2MM
SALES (corp-wide): 2.1B **Privately Held**
WEB: www.anvilknitwear.com
SIC: 2253 2331 Knit outerwear mills; women's & misses' blouses & shirts

(G-10296)
GILIBERTO DESIGNS INC
142 W 36th St Fl 8 (10018-8792)
PHONE 212 695-0216
Fax: 212 563-0524
Rosario Giliberto Jr, *President*
Anthony Giliberto, *Vice Pres*
Ken Kriegle, *CPA*
EMP: 23
SQ FT: 6,500
SALES (est): 1.5MM **Privately Held**
WEB: www.gilibertodesigns.com
SIC: 2311 5611 Men's & boys' suits & coats; clothing accessories: men's & boys'

(G-10297)
GILMORES SOUND ADVICE INC
599 11th Ave Fl 5 (10036-2110)
PHONE 212 265-4445
Edward Gilmore, *President*
EMP: 12
SALES (est): 1.6MM **Privately Held**
SIC: 3651 Audio electronic systems

(G-10298)
GINA GROUP LLC
Also Called: Gina Hosiery
10 W 33rd St Ph 3 (10001-3317)
PHONE 212 947-2445
Sheryl Becker, *Vice Pres*
Jack Barasch, *Controller*
Allen Gutner, *Controller*
Morris Sakkal, *Asst Controller*
David Gindi, *VP Sales*
◆ **EMP:** 30
SQ FT: 10,500
SALES (est): 7.5MM **Privately Held**
WEB: www.ginagroup.com
SIC: 2252 2251 Hosiery; socks; tights & leg warmers; women's hosiery, except socks

New York - New York County (G-10299)

(G-10299)
GIOVANE LTD
Also Called: Giovane Piranesi
592 5th Ave Ste L (10036-4707)
PHONE................................212 332-7373
Sami Hajibay, *President*
Mishel H H Piranesi, *Vice Pres*
Lavina Punwaney, *Manager*
Mishel H Handreo, *Admin Sec*
EMP: 22
SQ FT: 8,500
SALES (est): 3.2MM **Privately Held**
SIC: 3911 Jewelry, precious metal

(G-10300)
GIOVANNI BAKERY CORP
Also Called: Trio French Bakery
476 9th Ave (10018-5603)
P.O. Box 50057, Staten Island (10305-0057)
PHONE................................212 695-4296
Mario De Giovanni, *President*
Romona De Giovanni, *Corp Secy*
John De Giovanni, *Vice Pres*
EMP: 13 EST: 1953
SALES (est): 30.3K **Privately Held**
SIC: 2051 5461 Bread, all types (white, wheat, rye, etc): fresh or frozen; rolls, bread type: fresh or frozen; bread

(G-10301)
GIULIETTA LLC
25 Peck Slip Apt 4 (10038-1748)
PHONE................................212 334-1859
Sofia Sizzi, *Principal*
EMP: 5
SALES (est): 670K **Privately Held**
SIC: 2339 Women's & misses' accessories

(G-10302)
GIVAUDAN FRAGRANCES CORP
40 W 57th St Fl 11 (10019-4001)
PHONE................................212 649-8800
Fax: 212 649-8898
Jeanine Szweda, *Vice Pres*
Richard Capra, *Production*
Laura Bowser, *QC Mgr*
Gwen Gonzalez, *Research*
Vivian Wasef, *Research*
EMP: 130
SALES (corp-wide): 4.3B **Privately Held**
SIC: 2869 Perfume materials, synthetic; flavors or flavoring materials, synthetic
HQ: Givaudan Fragrances Corporation
1199 Edison Dr Ste 1-2
Cincinnati OH 45216
513 948-3428

(G-10303)
GIVI INC
16 W 56th St Fl 4 (10019-3872)
PHONE................................212 586-5029
Mario Fabris, *President*
EMP: 8
SALES (est): 928.5K
SALES (corp-wide): 136K **Privately Held**
SIC: 3111 5661 3999 Bag leather; shoe stores; atomizers, toiletry
PA: Givi Holding Spa
Via Alessandro Manzoni 38
Milano MI
027 609-31

(G-10304)
GLACEE SKINCARE LLC
611 W 136th St Apt 4 (10031-8137)
PHONE................................212 690-7632
Jose De La Cruz,
EMP: 6 EST: 2015
SALES (est): 276K **Privately Held**
SIC: 2844 Lotions, shaving; cosmetic preparations

(G-10305)
GLAMOUR MAGAZINE
4 Times Sq Fl 16 (10036-6518)
PHONE................................212 286-2860
Fax: 212 286-8336
Denise Gordon, *Editor*
Laura Smith, *COO*
Bill Wackerman, *Vice Pres*
Tom Table, *Asst Controller*
Melissa Halverson, *Mktg Dir*
EMP: 5
SALES (est): 240K **Privately Held**
SIC: 2721 Periodicals

(G-10306)
GLAMOURPUSS NYC LLC
1305 Madison Ave (10128-1327)
PHONE................................212 722-1370
Gigi Mortimer, *Principal*
Courtney Moss, *Principal*
EMP: 8
SALES (est): 794.5K **Privately Held**
SIC: 2331 Women's & misses' blouses & shirts

(G-10307)
GLASS APPS LLC (PA)
25 W 43rd St Ste 902 (10036-7414)
PHONE................................310 987-1536
Thomas Lee,
Sheila Speller, *Executive Asst*
EMP: 10
SQ FT: 1,200
SALES (est): 4.3MM **Privately Held**
SIC: 3211 Laminated glass

(G-10308)
GLASSBOX US INC
234 5th Ave Ste 207 (10001-7607)
PHONE................................917 378-2933
Yaron Morgenstern, *CEO*
Yifat Golan, *Human Res Mgr*
EMP: 48
SALES (est): 762.3K **Privately Held**
SIC: 7372 Prepackaged software

(G-10309)
GLASSES USA LLC
Also Called: Glassesusa.com
954 Lexington Ave Ste 537 (10021-5055)
PHONE................................212 784-6094
Daniel Rothman, *CEO*
Jay Engelmayer, *President*
Eldad Rothman, *COO*
Boaz Ariely, *Vice Pres*
Hili Shani, *Manager*
EMP: 14 EST: 2009
SALES (est): 2.3MM **Privately Held**
SIC: 3851 Ophthalmic goods; glasses, sun or glare; spectacles

(G-10310)
GLOBAL ALLIANCE FOR TB
40 Wall St Fl 24 (10005-1338)
PHONE................................212 227-7540
Fax: 212 227-7541
Melvin K Spigelman, *President*
Maarten Van Cleeff, *President*
Willo Brock, *Senior VP*
Robert C Lorette, *Senior VP*
Carl Mendel, *Senior VP*
EMP: 27
SQ FT: 8,500
SALES (est): 7.3MM **Privately Held**
WEB: www.tballiance.org
SIC: 2834 Druggists' preparations (pharmaceuticals)

(G-10311)
GLOBAL ALUMINA CORPORATION (PA)
277 Park Ave Fl 40 (10172-2902)
PHONE................................212 351-0000
Bruce J Wrobel, *CEO*
Graham Morrey, *President*
Tony McCabe, *Senior VP*
Michael J Cella, *CFO*
EMP: 9
SALES (est): 26MM **Privately Held**
SIC: 3297 Alumina fused refractories

(G-10312)
GLOBAL ALUMINA SERVICES CO
277 Park Ave Fl 40 (10172-2902)
PHONE................................212 309-8060
Bruce Wrobel, *Ch of Bd*
Bernie Cousineau, *President*
Thomas Deleo, *Counsel*
Dirk Straussfeld, *Exec VP*
Jim McGowan, *Senior VP*
EMP: 500
SQ FT: 15,400
SALES (est): 25.8MM
SALES (corp-wide): 26MM **Privately Held**
WEB: www.globalalumina.com
SIC: 3297 Alumina fused refractories

PA: Global Alumina Corporation
277 Park Ave Fl 40
New York NY 10172
212 351-0000

(G-10313)
GLOBAL APPLCTIONS SOLUTION LLC
125 Park Ave Fl 25 (10017-5550)
PHONE................................212 741-9595
Russell Luke, *Managing Dir*
Andy Moors, *Sales Staff*
Vishal Khurana,
EMP: 8
SALES (est): 125.1K **Privately Held**
SIC: 7372 7379 Prepackaged software; computer related maintenance services

(G-10314)
GLOBAL FINANCE MAGAZINE
Also Called: Global Finance Magazine.
411 5th Ave (10016-2203)
PHONE................................212 447-7900
Josepy Giarraputo, *Principal*
Denise Bedell, *Editor*
Andrea Fiano, *Editor*
Peter McManus, *Vice Pres*
Michael Ambrosio, *Mktg Dir*
EMP: 5
SALES (est): 783.4K **Privately Held**
WEB: www.gfmag.com
SIC: 2721 Periodicals

(G-10315)
GLOBAL FINANCE MEDIA INC
Also Called: Global Finance Magazine.
7 E 20th St Fl 2 (10003-1106)
PHONE................................212 447-7900
Andrew Spindler, *CEO*
James Macdonald, *Vice Pres*
Mammen Varkey, *Asst Mgr*
EMP: 12
SALES (est): 1.3MM **Privately Held**
SIC: 2721 5192 Periodicals; magazines

(G-10316)
GLOBAL FIRE CORPORATION
244 5th Ave Ste 2238 (10001-7604)
PHONE................................888 320-1799
Daniel Olszanski, *President*
◆ EMP: 21
SALES (est): 4.8MM **Privately Held**
WEB: www.globalfirecorp.com
SIC: 3711 Fire department vehicles (motor vehicles), assembly of

(G-10317)
GLOBAL GEM CORPORATION
Also Called: Global Creations
425 Madison Ave Rm 400 (10017-1141)
PHONE................................212 350-9936
Moosa Ebrahimian, *President*
Robert Ebrahimian, *Vice Pres*
Steve Ebrahimian, *Manager*
EMP: 5
SQ FT: 1,100
SALES (est): 400K **Privately Held**
WEB: www.globalcreations.com
SIC: 3911 5094 Jewelry, precious metal; diamonds (gems)

(G-10318)
GLOBAL GOLD INC
1410 Broadway Fl 8 (10018-9362)
PHONE................................212 239-4657
Bruce Fisher, *President*
Jeff Fisher, *Vice Pres*
Richard Fleet, *Vice Pres*
Scott Alsberry, *CFO*
▲ EMP: 38
SALES (est): 4.6MM **Privately Held**
SIC: 2337 Women's & misses' suits & coats

(G-10319)
GLOBAL GRIND DIGITAL
512 Fashion Ave Fl 42 (10018-4603)
PHONE................................212 840-9399
Osman Eralt, *CEO*
Tricia Clarke-Stone, *Principal*
Ian Corbin, *Vice Pres*
EMP: 30
SALES (est): 2MM **Privately Held**
SIC: 2741 Miscellaneous publishing

(G-10320)
GLOBAL RESOURCES SG INC
Also Called: Milli Home
267 5th Ave Rm 506 (10016-7512)
PHONE................................212 686-1411
Anil Nayar, *President*
Pavan Uttam, *Exec VP*
Kush Malhotra, *Manager*
Marsha Cutler, *Director*
▲ EMP: 13
SQ FT: 800
SALES (est): 1.7MM **Privately Held**
SIC: 2299 3635 Upholstery filling, textile; household vacuum cleaners

(G-10321)
GLOBAL SECURITY TECH LLC
1407 Broadway Fl 30 (10018-2480)
PHONE................................917 838-4507
Yoram Curiel, *CEO*
Victor Franco, *President*
Samuel Franco, *VP Sales*
Victor Dabah,
EMP: 10
SALES (est): 50K **Privately Held**
SIC: 3089 Identification cards, plastic

(G-10322)
GLORIA APPAREL INC
256 W 38th St Fl 700 (10018-9124)
PHONE................................212 947-0869
Young H Lee, *President*
Sowon Yoon, *Accountant*
Kj Kim, *Director*
▼ EMP: 10
SALES: 59MM **Privately Held**
WEB: www.gloria-texteis.com
SIC: 2386 Coats & jackets, leather & sheep-lined

(G-10323)
GLUCK ORGELBAU INC
170 Park Row Apt 20a (10038-1156)
PHONE................................212 233-2684
Sebastian M Gluck, *President*
Albert Jensenmoulton, *General Mgr*
EMP: 5
SALES (est): 370K **Privately Held**
SIC: 3931 Organs, all types: pipe, reed, hand, electronic, etc.

(G-10324)
GMC MERCANTILE CORP
231 W 39th St Rm 612 (10018-3109)
PHONE................................212 498-9488
Garrick Chan, *President*
Sherman Chan, *Vice Pres*
Agean Chen, *CFO*
▲ EMP: 18
SALES (est): 2MM **Privately Held**
SIC: 2339 Service apparel, washable: women's

(G-10325)
GNCC CAPITAL INC (PA)
244 5th Ave Ste 2525 (10001-7604)
PHONE................................702 951-9793
Peter Voss, *CEO*
Ronald Lowenthal, *Ch of Bd*
EMP: 4
SALES (est): 1.2MM **Privately Held**
SIC: 1041 Gold ores

(G-10326)
GODIVA CHOCOLATIER INC (DH)
333 W 34th St Fl 6 (10001-2566)
PHONE................................212 984-5900
Fax: 212 984-5901
Jim Goldman, *President*
Verna Armstrong, *General Mgr*
Steven Ashworth, *General Mgr*
Stephen Cady, *General Mgr*
Michelle Clark, *General Mgr*
▲ EMP: 35
SQ FT: 15,000
SALES (est): 533.5MM **Privately Held**
WEB: www.godiva.com
SIC: 2066 5149 5441 2064 Chocolate candy, solid; chocolate; candy; candy & other confectionery products

▲ = Import ▼=Export
◆ =Import/Export

GEOGRAPHIC SECTION
New York - New York County (G-10355)

(G-10327)
GODIVA CHOCOLATIER INC
33 Maiden Ln Frnt 1 (10038-4518)
PHONE.................................212 809-8990
Fax: 212 809-8890
Michelle Chin, *Vice Pres*
Erica Perretta, *Manager*
EMP: 6 **Privately Held**
WEB: www.godiva.com
SIC: 2066 Chocolate
HQ: Godiva Chocolatier, Inc.
  333 W 34th St Fl 6
  New York NY 10001
  212 984-5900

(G-10328)
GOLDARAMA COMPANY INC
Also Called: Silvertique Fine Jewelry
56 W 45th St Ste 1504 (10036-4206)
PHONE.................................212 730-7299
Fax: 212 730-0288
Ernie Golan, *President*
Hagay Golan, *Vice Pres*
EMP: 7
SALES (est): 660K **Privately Held**
SIC: 3911 Jewelry, precious metal

(G-10329)
GOLDBERGER COMPANY LLC (PA)
Also Called: Goldberger International
36 W 25th St Fl 14 (10010-2749)
PHONE.................................212 924-1194
Steven Strauss, *Vice Pres*
Jeffrey Holtzman, *Mng Member*
Lawrence Doppelt,
Michael Pietrafesa,
▲ **EMP:** 16 **EST:** 1916
SQ FT: 10,000
SALES: 2MM **Privately Held**
WEB: www.goldbergerdoll.com
SIC: 3942 Dolls & doll clothing; stuffed toys, including animals

(G-10330)
GOLDEN EAGLE MARKETING LLC
244 5th Ave (10001-7604)
PHONE.................................212 726-1242
Monika Sylvester,
EMP: 5 **EST:** 2009
SALES (est): 180K **Privately Held**
SIC: 2741

(G-10331)
GOLDEN HORSE ENTERPRISE NY INC
70 W 36th St Rm 12e (10018-1746)
PHONE.................................212 594-3339
Kenny Fung, *President*
▲ **EMP:** 5
SALES (est): 540K **Privately Held**
SIC: 2331 T-shirts & tops, women's: made from purchased materials

(G-10332)
GOLDEN INTEGRITY INC
Also Called: B K Integrity
37 W 47th St Ste 1601 (10036-3069)
PHONE.................................212 764-6753
Darek Schwartz, *President*
Khris Kornezi, *Vice Pres*
EMP: 20
SALES: 150K **Privately Held**
WEB: www.goldenintegrity.com
SIC: 3911 5944 Jewel settings & mountings, precious metal; jewelry stores

(G-10333)
GOLDEN OWL PUBLISHING COMPANY
Also Called: Jackdaw Publications
29 E 21st St Fl 2 (10010-6256)
PHONE.................................914 962-6911
Roger P Jacques, *President*
EMP: 6
SALES (est): 420K **Privately Held**
WEB: www.jackdaw.com
SIC: 2721 Periodicals

(G-10334)
GOLDEN PACIFIC LXJ INC
156 W 56th St Ste 2002 (10019-3877)
PHONE.................................267 975-6537
Steve Reynolds, *President*

EMP: 2 **EST:** 2011
SALES: 1MM **Privately Held**
SIC: 3131 Footwear cut stock

(G-10335)
GOLDEN SEASON FASHION USA INC
Also Called: Dons Collection
234 W 39th St Fl 7 (10018-4945)
PHONE.................................212 268-6048
Fax: 212 268-6049
Samuel Dong, *President*
Karry Zhang, *Vice Pres*
May Zou, *Manager*
▲ **EMP:** 10
SQ FT: 1,800
SALES (est): 1.1MM **Privately Held**
WEB: www.gsfashion.com
SIC: 2339 Women's & misses' outerwear

(G-10336)
GOLDSTAR LIGHTING LLC
1407 Broadway Fl 30 (10018-2480)
PHONE.................................646 543-6811
EMP: 18
SQ FT: 18,000
SALES (est): 1.3MM **Privately Held**
SIC: 3641 Mfg Electric Lamps

(G-10337)
GOOD HOME CO INC
132 W 24th St (10011-1981)
PHONE.................................212 352-1509
Christine Dimmick, *President*
Arni Halling, *Exec VP*
EMP: 6
SQ FT: 1,800
SALES (est): 1.1MM **Privately Held**
WEB: www.thegoodhomecompany.com
SIC: 2844 Toilet preparations; oral preparations; perfumes & colognes; cosmetic preparations

(G-10338)
GOOD SHOW SPORTWEAR INC
Also Called: Good Show Sportswear
132 Mulberry St 3 (10013-5551)
PHONE.................................212 334-8751
Danny Tsui, *Owner*
EMP: 11
SALES (est): 350K **Privately Held**
SIC: 3949 Sporting & athletic goods

(G-10339)
GORGA FEHREN FINE JEWELRY LLC
Also Called: Eva Fehren
153 E 88th St (10128-2270)
PHONE.................................646 861-3595
Ann Gorga, *CEO*
EMP: 6
SALES: 0 **Privately Held**
SIC: 3911 7389 Jewelry, precious metal;

(G-10340)
GOTHAM ENERGY 360 LLC
48 Wall St Fl 5 (10005-2911)
PHONE.................................917 338-1023
Jennifer Kearney,
EMP: 10 **EST:** 2008
SALES (est): 444.6K **Privately Held**
SIC: 1389 8748 Oil consultants; energy conservation consultant

(G-10341)
GOTHAM VETERINARY CENTER PC
700 Columbus Ave Frnt 5 (10025-6662)
PHONE.................................212 222-1900
Bonnie Brown, *President*
Patricia Dominguez,
Kimberly Kahn,
EMP: 20
SALES (est): 4MM **Privately Held**
SIC: 2835 Veterinary diagnostic substances

(G-10342)
GOTTLIEB & SONS INC
Also Called: Gottlieb Jewelery Mfg
21 W 47th St Fl 4 (10036-2825)
PHONE.................................212 575-1907
Fax: 212 398-9630
Allen Gottlieb, *Owner*
EMP: 25

SALES (corp-wide): 7.9MM **Privately Held**
WEB: www.gottlieb-sons.com
SIC: 3911 Jewelry, precious metal
PA: Gottlieb & Sons, Inc.
  1100 Superior Ave E # 2050
  Cleveland OH 44114
  216 771-4785

(G-10343)
GOYARD INC (HQ)
Also Called: Goyard US
20 E 63rd St (10065-7210)
PHONE.................................212 813-0005
Deborah Ruiz, *Manager*
Patricia Pinheiro, *Manager*
EMP: 4
SALES (est): 1.8MM
SALES (corp-wide): 55.2MM **Privately Held**
SIC: 3161 5137 Wardrobe bags (luggage); handbags
PA: Goyard St Honore
  16 Place Vendome
  Paris 75001
  142 601-881

(G-10344)
GQ MAGAZINE
4 Times Sq Fl 9 (10036-6518)
PHONE.................................212 286-2860
Charles Townsend, *CEO*
Laura Vitale, *Associate*
EMP: 8
SALES (est): 570K **Privately Held**
SIC: 2731 Book publishing

(G-10345)
GRADIAN HEALTH SYSTEMS INC
915 Broadway Ste 1001 (10010-8268)
PHONE.................................212 537-0340
Stephen M Rudy, *CEO*
Stephen Rudy, *CEO*
Erica Frenkel, *Vice Pres*
Lina Sayed, *Director*
Nicole Lund, *Administration*
EMP: 7
SQ FT: 3,400
SALES (est): 715K **Privately Held**
SIC: 3841 Anesthesia apparatus

(G-10346)
GRAMERCY JEWELRY MFG CORP
35 W 45th St Fl 5 (10036-4903)
PHONE.................................212 268-0461
Fax: 212 768-2619
Danny Lai, *President*
Peter Law, *Vice Pres*
▲ **EMP:** 50
SQ FT: 13,000
SALES (est): 6.6MM **Privately Held**
WEB: www.gramercyjewelry.com
SIC: 3911 Jewelry, precious metal

(G-10347)
GRAND CENTRAL PUBLISHING (DH)
1290 Ave Of The Americas (10104-0101)
PHONE.................................212 364-1200
David Young, *Ch of Bd*
Beth Ford, *Principal*
Lawrence Kirshbaum, *Principal*
Mitchell Kinzer, *Business Mgr*
Thomas Maciag, *CFO*
EMP: 240 **EST:** 1960
SQ FT: 140,000
SALES: 38.1MM
SALES (corp-wide): 268.5K **Privately Held**
WEB: www.biggamesmallworld.com
SIC: 2731 Books: publishing only
HQ: Hachette Book Group, Inc.
  1290 Ave Of The Americas
  New York NY 10104
  212 364-1200

(G-10348)
GRAND SLAM HOLDINGS LLC (DH)
Also Called: Blackstone Group
345 Park Ave Bsmt Lb4 (10154-0004)
PHONE.................................212 583-5000
Stephen A Schwarzman, *CEO*

EMP: 20
SALES (est): 1.5B
SALES (corp-wide): 4.6B **Publicly Held**
WEB: www.backstone-gro.com
SIC: 3842 Surgical appliances & supplies

(G-10349)
GRANDEUR CREATIONS INC
146 W 29th St Rm 9e (10001-8207)
PHONE.................................212 643-1277
Jal Billimoria, *President*
Meherukh Billimoria, *Treasurer*
EMP: 6
SQ FT: 2,450
SALES (est): 531.2K **Privately Held**
WEB: www.grandeurcreations.com
SIC: 3911 Rings, finger: precious metal; bracelets, precious metal

(G-10350)
GRANDMA MAES CNTRY NTURALS LLC
340 E 93rd St Apt 30h (10128-5556)
PHONE.................................212 348-8171
Barry Berman, *President*
EMP: 5
SALES (est): 740K **Privately Held**
SIC: 2048 Canned pet food (except dog & cat); dry pet food (except dog & cat); frozen pet food (except dog & cat)

(G-10351)
GRANTOO LLC
60 Broad St Ste 3502 (10004-2356)
PHONE.................................646 356-0460
Tamer Ossama Hassanein, *Vice Pres*
EMP: 5
SALES (est): 223.8K **Privately Held**
SIC: 7372 Application computer software

(G-10352)
GRANTS FINANCIAL PUBLISHING
Also Called: Grant's Interest Rate Observer
2 Wall St Ste 603 (10005-2000)
PHONE.................................212 809-7994
Fax: 212 809-8426
James Grant, *President*
Eric Whitehead, *Controller*
John D'Alberto, *Sales Staff*
Sue Egan, *Manager*
Evan Lorenz, *Analyst*
EMP: 10
SALES (est): 1.6MM **Privately Held**
WEB: www.grantspub.com
SIC: 2721 Periodicals: publishing only

(G-10353)
GRAPHIC LAB INC
228 E 45th St Fl 4 (10017-3303)
PHONE.................................212 682-1815
Fax: 212 682-5067
Richard Campisi, *President*
Carmine Campisi Jr, *Vice Pres*
Robert Campisi, *Treasurer*
Jeannette Duran, *Controller*
Albert Mahoney, *Accounts Exec*
EMP: 34
SQ FT: 7,600
SALES (est): 5.8MM **Privately Held**
WEB: www.gocdp.com
SIC: 2759 Commercial printing

(G-10354)
GRAPHIS INC
389 5th Ave Rm 1105 (10016-3350)
PHONE.................................212 532-9387
Fax: 212 213-3229
B Martin Pedersen, *President*
Arna Pedersen, *Bookkeeper*
Tiffany F Washington, *Sales Mgr*
Mark Laughlin, *Creative Dir*
Stephanie Diani, *Assistant*
▲ **EMP:** 10
SQ FT: 5,000
SALES (est): 1.4MM **Privately Held**
WEB: www.graphis.com
SIC: 2721 2731 Magazines: publishing only, not printed on site; books: publishing only

(G-10355)
GRAVITY EAST VILLAGE INC
515 E 5th St (10009-6703)
PHONE.................................212 388-9788
Michael J Perrine, *Chairman*

New York - New York County (G-10356)

EMP: 6
SALES (est): 679.4K Privately Held
SIC: 3845 Colonoscopes, electromedical

(G-10356)
GREAT IMPRESSIONS INC
Also Called: B C T
135 W 20th St Rm 600 (10011-3614)
PHONE..................................212 989-8555
Fax: 212 989-1115
Lloyd Alpert, *CEO*
Steven Alpert, *Vice Pres*
EMP: 18
SQ FT: 5,500
SALES: 1.5MM Privately Held
SIC: 2752 Commercial printing, lithographic

(G-10357)
GREAT JONES LUMBER CORP
45 Great Jones St (10012-1627)
PHONE..................................212 254-5560
Joseph Lauto, *President*
Anthony Lauto, *Vice Pres*
EMP: 15
SALES (est): 1.3MM Privately Held
SIC: 2421 Lumber: rough, sawed or planed; fuelwood, from mill waste

(G-10358)
GREAT NORTH ROAD MEDIA INC
Also Called: Sparkspread
3115 Broadway Apt 61 (10027-4647)
PHONE..................................646 619-1355
Victor Kremer, *Ch of Bd*
Will Ainger, *Director*
EMP: 10
SALES (est): 537.5K Privately Held
SIC: 2711 Newspapers

(G-10359)
GREAT UNIVERSAL CORP
1441 Broadway Fl 5 (10018-1905)
PHONE..................................917 302-0065
Grace Lu, *President*
◆ EMP: 10
SQ FT: 1,000
SALES: 10MM Privately Held
SIC: 2361 2321 Girls' & children's dresses, blouses & shirts; men's & boys' dress shirts

(G-10360)
GREEN GIRL PRTG & MSGNR INC
44 W 39th St (10018-3802)
PHONE..................................212 575-0357
Alice Harford, *President*
Mark Frelow, *Manager*
EMP: 6
SALES (est): 400K Privately Held
SIC: 2752 Commercial printing, lithographic

(G-10361)
GREENBEADS LLC
Also Called: Emily and Ashley
220 E 72nd St Apt 17d (10021-4531)
PHONE..................................212 327-2765
Emily Green, *Partner*
Ashley Green, *Partner*
EMP: 5
SALES (est): 350K Privately Held
WEB: www.greenbeads.com
SIC: 3961 Costume jewelry

(G-10362)
GRID TYPOGRAPHIC SERVICES INC
Also Called: Grid Typographic Svces
27 W 24th St Ste 9c (10010-3290)
PHONE..................................212 627-1105
Fax: 212 627-0303
Donald Davidson, *President*
John Duffy, *Treasurer*
Robert Kerwick, *Manager*
Sy Schwartz, *Admin Sec*
EMP: 10
SQ FT: 3,300
SALES (est): 1.6MM Privately Held
WEB: www.gridtypography.com
SIC: 2791 Typesetting

(G-10363)
GRIFFON CORPORATION (PA)
712 5th Ave Fl 18 (10019-4108)
PHONE..................................212 957-5000
Fax: 516 938-3779
Ronald J Kramer, *CEO*
Harvey R Blau, *Ch of Bd*
Robert F Mehmel, *President*
Seth L Kaplan, *Senior VP*
Michael Hansen, *Vice Pres*
◆ EMP: 20
SQ FT: 10,000
SALES: 2B Publicly Held
WEB: www.griffoncorp.com
SIC: 3442 2431 1751 1799 Garage doors, overhead: metal; garage doors, overhead: wood; garage door, installation or erection; home/office interiors finishing, furnishing & remodeling; prefabricated fireplace installation; laminated plastics plate & sheet; laminated plastic sheets; radio & TV communications equipment

(G-10364)
GRILLBOT LLC
1562 1st Ave Ste 251 (10028-4004)
PHONE..................................646 258-5639
Ethan Woods, *President*
EMP: 5
SALES (est): 807.2K Privately Held
SIC: 2842 Cleaning or polishing preparations

(G-10365)
GRILLBOT LLC
87 E 116th St Ste 202 (10029-1165)
PHONE..................................646 369-7242
Ethan Woods, *President*
EMP: 5
SALES (est): 61.6K Privately Held
SIC: 3639 Floor waxers & polishers, electric: household

(G-10366)
GRIND
419 Park Ave S Fl 2 (10016-8410)
PHONE..................................646 558-3250
Karina Warshaw, *Opers Staff*
Bettina Warshaw, *Manager*
EMP: 7
SALES (est): 800.2K Privately Held
SIC: 3599 Grinding castings for the trade

(G-10367)
GRINNELL DESIGNS LTD
260 W 39th St Rm 302 (10018-4434)
PHONE..................................212 391-5277
Fax: 212 391-5835
Francis De Ocampo, *President*
Larry Holliday, *Vice Pres*
Patricia Hudson, *Vice Pres*
EMP: 20
SQ FT: 4,000
SALES (est): 2MM Privately Held
WEB: www.grinnelldesigns.com
SIC: 3961 Costume jewelry

(G-10368)
GROLIER INTERNATIONAL INC (HQ)
557 Broadway (10012-3962)
PHONE..................................212 343-6100
Lisa Tarsi, *Principal*
EMP: 3
SALES (est): 1.5MM
SALES (corp-wide): 1.6B Publicly Held
SIC: 2731 Book publishing
PA: Scholastic Corporation
  557 Broadway Lbby 1
  New York NY 10012
  212 343-6100

(G-10369)
GROM COLUMBUS LLC
1796 Broadway (10019-1400)
PHONE..................................212 974-3444
Eran Keren, *Principal*
▲ EMP: 5 EST: 2010
SALES (est): 448.1K Privately Held
SIC: 2024 Ice cream, bulk

(G-10370)
GROUP COMMERCE INC (PA)
902 Broadway Fl 6 (10010-6039)
PHONE..................................646 346-0598
Jonty Kelt, *CEO*
David Lebow, *President*
Vibhav Prasad, *Senior VP*
Jared Augustine, *Vice Pres*
Andrea Gellert, *Vice Pres*
EMP: 13
SALES (est): 2.9MM Privately Held
SIC: 7372 Prepackaged software

(G-10371)
GROUP ENTERAINMENT LLC
115 W 29th St Rm 1102 (10001-5106)
PHONE..................................212 868-5233
Gill Holland,
EMP: 6
SALES (est): 562.1K Privately Held
SIC: 3571 Computers, digital, analog or hybrid

(G-10372)
GROUPE 16SUR20 LLC (PA)
Also Called: Seize Sur Vingt
56 Greene St (10012-4301)
P.O. Box 2280, Lenox MA (01240-5280)
PHONE..................................212 625-1620
James Jurney Jr, *Mng Member*
Eve Geller, *Administration*
EMP: 13
SQ FT: 2,000
SALES (est): 1.6MM Privately Held
SIC: 2329 2321 2325 Men's & boys' sportswear & athletic clothing; men's & boys' furnishings; men's & boys' trousers & slacks

(G-10373)
GROWNBEANS INC
110 Bank St Apt 2j (10014-2164)
PHONE..................................212 989-3486
Fax: 212 633-1181
Karen Groner, *President*
EMP: 5
SQ FT: 2,400
SALES (est): 509K Privately Held
SIC: 3172 Personal leather goods

(G-10374)
GRUNER & JAHR USA
375 Lexington Ave (10017-5644)
PHONE..................................212 782-7870
Fax: 212 499-2199
Gerd Schulte-Hillen, *President*
EMP: 13
SALES (est): 1MM Privately Held
SIC: 2741 Miscellaneous publishing

(G-10375)
GRUNER + JAHR PRTG & PUBG CO
Also Called: New York Times Co Mag Group
110 5th Ave Fl 7 (10011-5632)
PHONE..................................212 463-1000
Holly Netz, *Sales Dir*
Kari Johnston, *Sales Executive*
John Heins, *Manager*
EMP: 160
SALES (corp-wide): 587MM Privately Held
WEB: www.gjusa.com
SIC: 2721 7311 Magazines: publishing only, not printed on site; advertising agencies
PA: Gruner + Jahr Usa Group, Inc.
  1745 Broadway Fl 16
  New York NY 10019
  866 323-9336

(G-10376)
GRUNER + JAHR USA GROUP INC (PA)
Also Called: Gruner Jahr USA Publishing Div
1745 Broadway Fl 16 (10019-4640)
PHONE..................................866 323-9336
Mike Amundson, *President*
Gregg Black, *Exec VP*
Larry Hawkey, *Exec VP*
Dan Nitz, *Exec VP*
Yvette Miller, *Vice Pres*
◆ EMP: 500
SQ FT: 173,000
SALES (est): 587MM Privately Held
WEB: www.gjusa.com
SIC: 2721 2754 Periodicals: publishing & printing; magazines: publishing & printing; commercial printing, gravure

(G-10377)
GS DIRECT LLC
85 Broad St (10004-2434)
PHONE..................................212 902-1000
EMP: 8
SALES (est): 827.6K Privately Held
SIC: 3674 Semiconductors & related devices

(G-10378)
GSCP EMAX ACQUISITION LLC
85 Broad St (10004-2434)
PHONE..................................212 902-1000
Henry M Paulson Jr, *CEO*
Myo Zarny, *Vice Pres*
EMP: 5
SALES (est): 504.9K Privately Held
SIC: 3442 Metal doors, sash & trim

(G-10379)
GUESS INC
575 5th Ave Lbby 1 (10017-2438)
PHONE..................................212 286-9856
EMP: 25
SALES (corp-wide): 2.2B Publicly Held
SIC: 2325 Men's & boys' jeans & dungarees
PA: Guess , Inc.
  1444 S Alameda St
  Los Angeles CA 90021
  213 765-3100

(G-10380)
GUEST INFORMAT LLC
Also Called: Quick Guide
110 E 42nd St Rm 1714 (10017-5649)
PHONE..................................212 557-3010
Fax: 212 557-3822
Lisa Nusynowitz, *Principal*
EMP: 13
SALES (corp-wide): 785.3MM Privately Held
SIC: 2741 Miscellaneous publishing
HQ: Guest Informat, L.L.C.
  21200 Erwin St
  Woodland Hills CA
  818 716-7484

(G-10381)
GUILD DIAMOND PRODUCTS INC (PA)
1212 Avenue Of The Americ (10036-1600)
PHONE..................................212 871-0007
Fax: 212 354-8455
Jacques H Elion, *President*
Douglas Panker, *Corp Secy*
▲ EMP: 13
SQ FT: 7,000
SALES (est): 1.4MM Privately Held
SIC: 3911 3915 Jewelry, precious metal; diamond cutting & polishing

(G-10382)
GUILFORD PUBLICATIONS INC
Also Called: Guilford Press
7 Penn Plz Ste 1200 (10001-1020)
PHONE..................................212 431-9800
Robert Matloff, *President*
Mary Anderson, *Editor*
Martin Coleman, *Editor*
Jane Keislar, *Editor*
Anna Nelson, *Editor*
EMP: 75 EST: 1973
SQ FT: 10,000
SALES (est): 10MM Privately Held
WEB: www.guilford.com
SIC: 2741 2731 2721 7812 Miscellaneous publishing; books: publishing only; trade journals: publishing & printing; audio-visual program production

(G-10383)
GUMUCHIAN FILS LTD
16 E 52nd St Ste 701 (10022-5307)
PHONE..................................212 593-3118
Fax: 212 593-9111
Irma Gumuchdjian, *President*
Patricia Jones, *Vice Pres*
Myriam Schreiber, *Vice Pres*
Andre Gumuchdjian, *Treasurer*
Barbara Palumbo, *CTO*
EMP: 15 EST: 1979
SQ FT: 1,700

SALES (est): 1.5MM **Privately Held**
WEB: www.gumuchianfils.com
SIC: 3911 5094 Jewelry, precious metal; precious stones (gems)

(G-10384)
GUNTHER PARTNERS LLC (HQ)
655 Madison Ave Fl 11 (10065-8043)
PHONE..................................212 521-2930
Barry Bloom, *Principal*
Thomas Tisch, *Mng Member*
Robert Spiegel,
Thomas M Steinberg,
EMP: 3
SALES (est): 14.4MM **Privately Held**
SIC: 3577 Input/output equipment, computer
PA: Four Partners, Llc
666 5th Ave
New York NY
212 841-1547

(G-10385)
H & C CHEMISTS INC
1299 1st Ave (10021-5503)
PHONE..................................212 535-1700
Steven Gelwan, *Principal*
EMP: 12
SALES (est): 1.9MM **Privately Held**
SIC: 2834 Vitamin, nutrient & hematinic preparations for human use

(G-10386)
H & T GOLDMAN CORPORATION
2 W 46th St Ste 607 (10036-4566)
PHONE..................................800 822-0272
Fax: 212 869-0625
Nathan Goldman, *President*
EMP: 5
SQ FT: 1,200
SALES (est): 430K **Privately Held**
SIC: 3911 Jewelry, precious metal

(G-10387)
H BEST LTD
Moret Time
1411 Broadway Fl 8 (10018-3565)
PHONE..................................212 354-2400
Morris Chabott, *Director*
EMP: 10 **Privately Held**
SIC: 3873 Watches, clocks, watchcases & parts
PA: H. Best, Ltd.
1411 Broadway Fl 8
New York NY 10018

(G-10388)
H C KIONKA & CO INC
Also Called: Kimberley Diamond
15 Maiden Ln Ste 908 (10038-5118)
PHONE..................................212 227-3155
Fax: 212 791-7731
Mark Levy, *President*
Mark Baum, *Vice Pres*
EMP: 13 **EST:** 1900
SQ FT: 2,500
SALES: 8MM **Privately Held**
WEB: www.kimberleydiamond.com
SIC: 3911 Jewelry apparel

(G-10389)
H GROUP
462 7th Ave Fl 9 (10018-7436)
PHONE..................................212 719-5500
Joe Dahan, *President*
EMP: 15 **EST:** 2015
SALES (est): 107.9K **Privately Held**
SIC: 2241 Apparel webbing

(G-10390)
H K TECHNOLOGIES INC
303 5th Ave Rm 1707 (10016-6641)
PHONE..................................212 779-0100
Fax: 212 779-4570
Rie Fechita, *Ch of Bd*
Taisuke Hamada, *Sales Staff*
Nobutake Fujimura, *Manager*
EMP: 4
SQ FT: 800
SALES (est): 1MM **Privately Held**
WEB: www.hktechnologies.com
SIC: 3674 Semiconductors & related devices

(G-10391)
HACHETTE BOOK GROUP INC (DH)
1290 Ave Of The Americas (10104-0101)
PHONE..................................212 364-1200
Fax: 212 364-0926
David Young, *Ch of Bd*
Zachary Gordon, *General Mgr*
EMI Battaglia, *Editor*
Tracy Behar, *Editor*
Deb Futter, *Editor*
▲ **EMP:** 350
SALES (est): 312.1MM
SALES (corp-wide): 268.5K **Privately Held**
SIC: 2731 5192 Books: publishing only; books, periodicals & newspapers
HQ: Hachette Livre
58 Rue Jean Bleuzen
Vanves Cedex 92178
141 236-000

(G-10392)
HACHETTE BOOK GROUP USA INC
466 Lexington Ave Ste 13I (10017-3145)
PHONE..................................212 364-1200
Fax: 212 364-0930
David Dyoung, *Chairman*
EMP: 20 **EST:** 2012
SALES (est): 3MM **Privately Held**
SIC: 2732 Book printing

(G-10393)
HADDAD BROS INC (PA)
Also Called: Madonna
28 W 36th St Rm 1026 (10018-1290)
PHONE..................................212 563-2117
Fax: 212 594-7325
Alan Haddad, *President*
Mac Haddad, *Chairman*
◆ **EMP:** 12
SQ FT: 3,500
SALES (est): 7.2MM **Privately Held**
WEB: www.haddadbros.com
SIC: 2321 2361 Men's & boys' furnishings; girls' & children's dresses, blouses & shirts

(G-10394)
HADDAD HOSIERY LLC
34 W 33rd St Rm 401 (10001-3342)
PHONE..................................212 251-0022
Jack Haddad, *President*
▲ **EMP:** 5 **EST:** 2000
SALES (est): 437.6K **Privately Held**
SIC: 2252 Hosiery

(G-10395)
HAIGHTS CROSS CMMNICATIONS INC (PA)
136 Madison Ave Fl 8 (10016-6711)
PHONE..................................212 209-0500
Fax: 212 209-0501
Rick Noble, *CEO*
Kevin R Brueggeman, *President*
Rich Freese, *President*
Julie Latzer, *Senior VP*
Diane Q Curtin, *Vice Pres*
▲ **EMP:** 32
SQ FT: 35,000
SALES (est): 99.1MM **Privately Held**
WEB: www.haightscross.com
SIC: 2731 Book publishing

(G-10396)
HAILO NETWORK USA INC
568 Broadway Fl 11 (10012-3374)
PHONE..................................646 561-8552
EMP: 5 **EST:** 2012
SALES (est): 470K **Privately Held**
SIC: 7372 Prepackaged Software Services

(G-10397)
HALEYS COMET SEAFOOD CORP
605 3rd Ave Fl 34 (10158-3499)
PHONE..................................212 571-1828
Robert Leone, *President*
EMP: 45
SALES: 1.5MM **Privately Held**
SIC: 2211 Long cloth, cotton

(G-10398)
HALMODE APPAREL INC
Also Called: Halmode Petite Div
1400 Brdwy 11th & Fl 16 (10018)
PHONE..................................212 819-9114
Fax: 212 398-6462
Jay Diamond, *CEO*
Bea Myerson, *Exec VP*
Michael M Saunders, *Vice Pres*
John Winston, *CFO*
Meiling Loheng, *Manager*
▲ **EMP:** 600
SQ FT: 240,000
SALES (est): 39.7MM
SALES (corp-wide): 18.3B **Privately Held**
SIC: 2339 2335 5137 Sportswear, women's; uniforms, athletic: women's, misses' & juniors'; maternity clothing; women's, juniors' & misses' dresses; women's & children's clothing
HQ: Kellwood Company, Llc
600 Kellwood Pkwy Ste 200
Chesterfield MO 63017
314 576-3100

(G-10399)
HALO ASSOCIATES
289 Bleecker St Fl 5 (10014-4106)
PHONE..................................212 691-9549
EMP: 6
SQ FT: 7,000
SALES (est): 500K **Privately Held**
SIC: 3299 8999 Art Related Services

(G-10400)
HAMIL AMERICA INC
42 W 39th St Fl 15 (10018-2081)
PHONE..................................212 244-2645
Jerry Miller, *President*
▲ **EMP:** 16
SALES (est): 1.4MM
SALES (corp-wide): 21.7MM **Privately Held**
WEB: www.algo.com
SIC: 2253 Knit outerwear mills
PA: Groupe Algo Inc
5555 Rue Cypihot
Saint-Laurent QC H4S 1
514 388-8888

(G-10401)
HAMMERMAN BROS INC
Also Called: H2 At Hammerman
50 W 57th St Fl 12 (10019-3914)
PHONE..................................212 956-2800
Fax: 212 956-2769
Brett Hammerman, *President*
Philip Begenstein, *General Mgr*
Darcy Hammerman, *Vice Pres*
Rose Dennis, *Controller*
EMP: 9
SQ FT: 10,000
SALES (est): 1.7MM **Privately Held**
WEB: www.hammermanbrothers.com
SIC: 3911 3873 Bracelets, precious metal; earrings, precious metal; necklaces, precious metal; rings, finger: precious metal; watches, clocks, watchcases & parts

(G-10402)
HAMPTON PRESS INCORPORATED
307 7th Ave Rm 506 (10001-6079)
PHONE..................................646 638-3800
Barbara Bernstein, *Owner*
EMP: 9
SALES (est): 730.5K **Privately Held**
SIC: 2741 Miscellaneous publishing

(G-10403)
HAMPTONS MEDIA LLC
915 Broadway Ste 1204 (10010-7124)
PHONE..................................646 835-5211
Jason Binn, *President*
EMP: 40
SALES (est): 4MM **Privately Held**
SIC: 2721 Periodicals: publishing only

(G-10404)
HANDCRAFT MANUFACTURING CORP (PA)
34 W 33rd St Rm 401 (10001-3342)
PHONE..................................212 251-0022
Fax: 212 251-0076
Isaac Mizrahi, *President*
Joseph I Mizrahi, *Corp Secy*
Marshall Mizrahi, *Treasurer*
Asha Shah, *Manager*
Steve Simion, *CTO*
▲ **EMP:** 30
SQ FT: 11,000
SALES (est): 15.2MM **Privately Held**
WEB: www.handcraftmfg.com
SIC: 2341 Women's & children's undergarments

(G-10405)
HANDSOME DANS LLC (PA)
186 1st Ave (10009-4002)
PHONE..................................917 965-2499
EMP: 3 **EST:** 2012
SALES (est): 1.5MM **Privately Held**
SIC: 2064 Candy & other confectionery products

(G-10406)
HANESBRANDS INC
260 Madison Ave Fl 6 (10016-2401)
PHONE..................................212 576-9300
Kimberly Sorrano, *Office Mgr*
Marla Boggs, *Manager*
Bruce Blackwell, *Director*
EMP: 9
SALES (corp-wide): 5.7B **Publicly Held**
WEB: www.hanesbrands.com
SIC: 2211 5699 Apparel & outerwear fabrics, cotton; sports apparel
PA: Hanesbrands Inc.
1000 E Hanes Mill Rd
Winston Salem NC 27105
336 519-8080

(G-10407)
HANGER HEADQUARTERS LLC
32 Broadway Ste 511 (10004-1665)
PHONE..................................212 391-8607
Steven Sutton, *President*
Jesse Sutton,
Sharon Sutton,
▲ **EMP:** 6
SALES: 1.6MM **Privately Held**
SIC: 3089 Clothes hangers, plastic

(G-10408)
HANIA BY ANYA COLE LLC
16 W 56th St Fl 4 (10019-3872)
PHONE..................................212 302-3550
Anya Cole, *Mng Member*
Dhurata Kajtazaj, *Manager*
Sandre Verbeck, *Manager*
EMP: 8
SALES (est): 1MM **Privately Held**
SIC: 2253 Knit outerwear mills

(G-10409)
HANSA USA LLC
18 E 48th St Fl 3 (10017-1014)
PHONE..................................646 412-6407
Abhi Gupta, *Controller*
Beth Wesel, *Accounts Mgr*
Stephanie Teitelbaum, *Manager*
Andrew Fox, *Software Dev*
Eric Hu, *Director*
▲ **EMP:** 20
SALES (est): 3.4MM **Privately Held**
SIC: 3911 Jewelry, precious metal

(G-10410)
HANSAE CO LTD
501 Fashion Ave Rm 208 (10018-8611)
PHONE..................................212 354-6690
Aesun Kim, *Mng Member*
EMP: 8
SALES (est): 855.1K **Privately Held**
SIC: 2331 2329 Women's & misses' blouses & shirts; T-shirts & tops, women's: made from purchased materials; men's & boys' sportswear & athletic clothing
PA: Hansae Co., Ltd.
5je/F Jungu Bldg., Yeouido-Dong
Seoul SEO
377 955-99

(G-10411)
HANSTEEL (USA) INC
230 Grand St Ste 602 (10013-4241)
PHONE..................................212 226-0105
Lin Jie, *President*
EMP: 6

New York - New York County (G-10412)

SALES: 4MM **Privately Held**
SIC: 3531 Construction machinery attachments

(G-10412)
HARD TEN CLOTHING INC
231 W 39th St Rm 606 (10018-0745)
PHONE.................................212 302-1321
Jesse Battino, *Principal*
EMP: 5
SALES: 5MM **Privately Held**
SIC: 2361 5136 Shirts: girls', children's & infants'; shirts, men's & boys'

(G-10413)
HARLEY ROBERT D COMPANY LTD
240 W 35th St Ste 1005 (10001-2514)
PHONE.................................212 947-1872
David Shapiro, *President*
EMP: 6
SALES: 5MM **Privately Held**
SIC: 2211 Apparel & outerwear fabrics, cotton

(G-10414)
HARPERCOLLINS
195 Broadway Fl 2 (10007-3132)
PHONE.................................212 207-7000
Janet Gervasio, *Senior VP*
Amy Halperin, *Vice Pres*
Leah Wasielewski, *Vice Pres*
Jennifer Duckworth, *Human Resources*
Vadim Rozenfeld, *Technology*
EMP: 6 **EST:** 2012
SALES (est): 115.3K **Privately Held**
SIC: 2741 Miscellaneous publishing

(G-10415)
HARPERCOLLINS PUBLISHERS LLC
Harlequin & Silhouette Books
233 Broadway Rm 1001 (10279-1099)
PHONE.................................212 553-4200
Fax: 212 227-8969
David Galloway, *Chairman*
Eisbell Swift, *Branch Mgr*
Margaret Marbury, *Manager*
Leslie Wainger, *Manager*
Joan M Golan, *Senior Editor*
EMP: 43
SALES (corp-wide): 8.2B **Publicly Held**
SIC: 2731 Book publishing
HQ: Harpercollins Publishers L.L.C.
195 Broadway Fl 2
New York NY 10007
212 207-7000

(G-10416)
HARPERCOLLINS PUBLISHERS LLC
Avon Books
10 E 53rd St Fl Cellar2 (10022-5299)
PHONE.................................212 207-7000
Gretchen Rubin, *Publisher*
Heather Schroder, *Publisher*
Michael Greenstein, *Principal*
Margot Schupf, *Senior VP*
Liate Stehlik, *Senior VP*
EMP: 100
SALES (corp-wide): 8.2B **Publicly Held**
WEB: www.harpercollins.com
SIC: 2731 Books: publishing only
HQ: Harpercollins Publishers L.L.C.
195 Broadway Fl 2
New York NY 10007
212 207-7000

(G-10417)
HARPERS MAGAZINE FOUNDATION
666 Broadway Fl 11 (10012-2394)
PHONE.................................212 420-5720
John Macarthur, *President*
John R Mc Arthur, *President*
Giulia Melucci, *President*
James Marcus, *Editor*
Lewis Lapham, *Div Sub Head*
EMP: 28
SQ FT: 7,800
SALES: 7.1MM **Privately Held**
SIC: 2721 Magazines: publishing only, not printed on site

(G-10418)
HARRISON SPORTSWEAR INC
Also Called: Eric Signature
260 W 39th St Fl 7 (10018-4410)
PHONE.................................212 391-1051
Eric Makofsky, *President*
Lemuel Shiuh, *Vice Pres*
Xie Ai Yi, *Vice Pres*
Malou Fernandez, *Accountant*
▲ **EMP:** 12
SQ FT: 3,000
SALES (est): 1.4MM **Privately Held**
WEB: www.randykemper.com
SIC: 2337 Pantsuits: women's, misses' & juniors'; skirts, separate: women's, misses' & juniors'; jackets & vests, except fur & leather: women's

(G-10419)
HARRY N ABRAMS INCORPORATED
Also Called: Stewart Tobori & Chang Div
115 W 18th St Fl 6 (10011-4113)
PHONE.................................212 206-7715
Fax: 212 645-8437
Herve De La Martiniere, *Ch of Bd*
Michael Jacobs, *Ch of Bd*
Shawna Mullen, *Publisher*
Tamar Brazis, *Editor*
Courtney Code, *Editor*
▲ **EMP:** 94 **EST:** 1949
SQ FT: 30,000
SALES (est): 32MM
SALES (corp-wide): 408.6K **Privately Held**
WEB: www.hnabooks.com
SIC: 2731 Books: publishing only
PA: La Martiniere Groupe
25 Boulevard Romain Rolland
Paris 75014
141 488-000

(G-10420)
HARRY WINSTON INC (DH)
718 5th Ave (10019-4195)
PHONE.................................212 399-1000
Nayla Hayek, *CEO*
Robert Scott, *CFO*
Luke Xu, *Sales Executive*
Nina Giambelli, *Director*
Laura Kiernan, *Shareholder*
▲ **EMP:** 110 **EST:** 1932
SQ FT: 18,000
SALES (est): 48.7MM
SALES (corp-wide): 8.4B **Privately Held**
SIC: 3911 5944 Jewelry, precious metal; jewelry, precious stones & precious metals; watches
HQ: Hw Holdings, Inc.
718 5th Ave
New York NY 10019
212 399-1000

(G-10421)
HARRYS INC (PA)
Also Called: Harry's Razor Company
161 Ave Of The (10013)
PHONE.................................888 212-6855
Andy Katz-Mayfield, *CEO*
Jeffrey Raider, *Corp Secy*
Zsolt Bagdi, *Info Tech Dir*
Jon Goldmann, *Director*
Jenni Lee, *Director*
EMP: 49
SALES (est): 14MM **Privately Held**
SIC: 3634 Razors, electric

(G-10422)
HART ENERGY PUBLISHING LLLP
110 William St Fl 18 (10038-3901)
PHONE.................................212 621-4621
Kevin Higgins, *Branch Mgr*
EMP: 5
SALES (corp-wide): 51.3MM **Privately Held**
WEB: www.hartenergynetwork.com
SIC: 2721 2741 Magazines: publishing only, not printed on site; newsletter publishing
PA: Hart Energy Publishing Lllp
1616 S Voss Rd Ste 1000
Houston TX 77057
713 993-9320

(G-10423)
HART REPRODUCTION SERVICES
Also Called: Nyc Thermography
242 W 36th St Rm 801 (10018-8960)
PHONE.................................212 704-0556
Brett Greer, *President*
Patty Franks, *Manager*
EMP: 5
SQ FT: 7,400
SALES: 800K **Privately Held**
WEB: www.hartrepro.com
SIC: 2759 7331 Stationery: printing; mailing service

(G-10424)
HARVARD MAINTENANCE INC
245 Park Ave (10167-0002)
PHONE.................................212 682-2617
Cristina M Johns, *Human Resources*
EMP: 1008
SALES (corp-wide): 239.1MM **Privately Held**
SIC: 3471 Cleaning, polishing & finishing
PA: Harvard Maintenance, Inc.
2 S Biscayne Blvd # 3650
Miami FL 33131
305 351-7300

(G-10425)
HARVARD UNIVERSITY PRESS
150 5th Ave Ste 632 (10011-4311)
PHONE.................................212 337-0280
Fax: 212 337-0259
Elizabeth Gilbert, *Editor*
Dan Wackrow, *CFO*
Brian Distelberg, *Assoc Editor*
Joyce Seltzer, *Director*
Kathleen McDermott, *Executive*
EMP: 100 **EST:** 1995
SALES (est): 6.1MM **Privately Held**
SIC: 2731 Book publishing

(G-10426)
HAUTE BY BLAIR STANLEY LLC
330 E 38th St Apt 23e (10016-2780)
PHONE.................................212 557-7868
Antoine Katbe, *Managing Prtnr*
Roger Blair Stanley, *Managing Prtnr*
EMP: 5
SQ FT: 1,000
SALES: 375K **Privately Held**
SIC: 2335 Women's, juniors' & misses' dresses

(G-10427)
HAX PHEROCEUTICALS INC
228 Park Ave S Ste 35370 (10003-1502)
PHONE.................................212 401-8695
Joseph Herron, *COO*
EMP: 5 **EST:** 2009
SALES (est): 383.2K **Privately Held**
SIC: 2844 Toilet preparations

(G-10428)
HAYMAN-CHAFFEY DESIGNS INC
137 E 25th St (10010-2314)
PHONE.................................212 889-7771
Charles R Hayman Chaffey, *President*
EMP: 10
SQ FT: 10,000
SALES (est): 700K **Privately Held**
SIC: 2511 Wood household furniture

(G-10429)
HAYMARKET GROUP LTD
Also Called: Chocolatier Magazine
12 W 37th St 9 (10018-7480)
PHONE.................................212 239-0855
Fax: 212 967-4184
EMP: 12
SQ FT: 3,000
SALES (est): 950K **Privately Held**
SIC: 2721 Magazine Publishers

(G-10430)
HAYMARKET MEDIA INC (DH)
Also Called: Prweek/Prescribing Reference
275 7th Ave Fl 10 (10001-6756)
PHONE.................................646 638-6000
Fax: 646 638-6119
Kevin Costello, *CEO*
Karmen Maurer, *Publisher*
David Prasher, *Managing Dir*

Andrew Taplin, *Managing Dir*
Steve Barrett, *Editor*
▲ **EMP:** 130
SQ FT: 27,000
SALES (est): 77.1MM
SALES (corp-wide): 106.4MM **Privately Held**
SIC: 2721 Magazines: publishing only, not printed on site

(G-10431)
HAYNES ROBERTS INC
601 W 26th St Rm 1655 (10001-1151)
PHONE.................................212 989-1901
Timothy Haynes, *Owner*
Vanessa Lacson, *Project Mgr*
Melanie Matoba, *Project Mgr*
Esteban Arboleda, *Sr Associate*
Michael Silva, *Associate*
▲ **EMP:** 15
SALES (est): 1.9MM **Privately Held**
SIC: 3679 Electronic components

(G-10432)
HAZAN COHEN GROUP LLC
Also Called: Edgeucational Publishing
1400 Brdwy Rm 700 (10018)
PHONE.................................646 827-0030
Albert Cohen, *CEO*
Albert Hazan, *President*
◆ **EMP:** 14
SQ FT: 2,000
SALES (est): 4.1MM **Privately Held**
SIC: 2731 2741 Book publishing; art copy & poster publishing

(G-10433)
HC CONTRACTING INC
Also Called: Ferrara Manufacturing Company
318 W 39th St Fl 4 (10018-1493)
PHONE.................................212 643-9292
Fax: 212 971-5442
Carolyn Ferrara, *President*
Joseph Ferrara, *Vice Pres*
Alba Lema, *Manager*
◆ **EMP:** 60 **EST:** 1987
SQ FT: 25,000
SALES: 5MM **Privately Held**
WEB: www.ferraramfg.com
SIC: 2339 2326 Service apparel, washable: women's; service apparel (baker, barber, lab, etc.), washable: men's

(G-10434)
HDT GROUP LLC
225 Rector Pl (10280-1116)
PHONE.................................914 490-2107
Michael Costa, *Owner*
EMP: 6
SQ FT: 2,000
SALES: 100K **Privately Held**
SIC: 2731 Book publishing

(G-10435)
HEARST BUS COMMUNICATIONS INC (PA)
300 W 57th St (10019-3741)
PHONE.................................212 649-2000
Richard P Malloch, *President*
Barry J Green, *Vice Pres*
Peter Rowlinson, *Vice Pres*
Robert D Wilbanks, *Treasurer*
David L Kors, *Asst Treas*
EMP: 8 **EST:** 1980
SALES (est): 3.7MM **Privately Held**
SIC: 2721 Magazines: publishing only, not printed on site

(G-10436)
HEARST BUSINESS PUBLISHING INC
Also Called: Diversion Magazine
888 7th Ave Fl 2 (10106-0001)
PHONE.................................212 969-7500
Fax: 212 969-7563
Cathy Cavender, *Principal*
Mike Chan, *MIS Dir*
EMP: 16
SALES (corp-wide): 4.9B **Privately Held**
SIC: 2721 Periodicals
HQ: Hearst Business Publishing, Inc.
214 N Tryon St Fl 33
Charlotte NC 28202
704 348-8614

▲ = Import ▼ = Export
◆ = Import/Export

GEOGRAPHIC SECTION

(G-10437)
HEARST COMMUNICATIONS INC (DH)
Also Called: Hearst Interactive Media
300 W 57th St (10019-3741)
PHONE..................................212 649-2000
Fax: 212 649-2166
Steven R Swartz, *CEO*
Mark E Aldam, *President*
Roberta Kowalishin, *President*
Joanna Coles, *Editor*
Stacy Morrison, *Editor*
EMP: 17
SALES (est): 8MM
SALES (corp-wide): 4.9B Privately Held
SIC: 2741 Miscellaneous publishing
HQ: Hearst Holdings Inc
300 W 57th St
New York NY 10019
212 649-2000

(G-10438)
HEARST CORPORATION (PA)
Also Called: Hearst Magazines
300 W 57th St Fl 42 (10019-3790)
PHONE..................................212 649-2000
Fax: 212 265-0169
Steven R Swartz, *President*
Mark E Aldam, *President*
Nick Brien, *President*
John McKeon, *President*
David A Schirmer, *President*
▲ EMP: 2500
SQ FT: 166,612
SALES (est): 4.9B Privately Held
WEB: www.hearstcorp.com
SIC: 2721 2731 2711 4832 Magazines: publishing only, not printed on site; books: publishing only; newspapers, publishing & printing; newspapers: publishing only, not printed on site; radio broadcasting stations; television broadcasting stations; news feature syndicate

(G-10439)
HEARST CORPORATION
Seventeen Magazine
300 W 57th St Fl 29 (10019-3741)
PHONE..................................212 649-3100
George R Hearst Jr, *Principal*
Joanna Saltz, *Editor*
Ann Shoket, *Editor*
Kelsey Stokes, *Manager*
Carissa Rosenberg, *Director*
EMP: 50
SALES (corp-wide): 4.9B Privately Held
SIC: 2721 Periodicals: publishing only
PA: The Hearst Corporation
300 W 57th St Fl 42
New York NY 10019
212 649-2000

(G-10440)
HEARST CORPORATION
Also Called: Oprah Magazine
224 W 57th St Frnt 1 (10019-3212)
PHONE..................................212 903-5366
Fax: 212 757-6109
Jill Seelig, *Publisher*
Amy Gross, *Principal*
Naomi Barr, *Principal*
Alicia Bridgewater, *Editor*
Maggie Bullock, *Editor*
EMP: 35
SALES (corp-wide): 4.9B Privately Held
WEB: www.hearstcorp.com
SIC: 2721 Magazines: publishing & printing
PA: The Hearst Corporation
300 W 57th St Fl 42
New York NY 10019
212 649-2000

(G-10441)
HEARST CORPORATION
Also Called: Elle Magazine
1633 Broadway Fl 44 (10019-6708)
PHONE..................................212 767-5800
Fax: 212 489-4211
Laurie Abraham, *Principal*
Ingrid Abramovitch, *Editor*
Jade Frampton, *Editor*
Melissa Jewsbury, *Editor*
Roberta Myers, *Editor*
EMP: 300

SALES (corp-wide): 4.9B Privately Held
WEB: www.popphoto.com
SIC: 2759 Magazines: printing
PA: The Hearst Corporation
300 W 57th St Fl 42
New York NY 10019
212 649-2000

(G-10442)
HEARST CORPORATION
Also Called: Popular Mechanics
810 7th Ave (10019-5818)
PHONE..................................516 382-4580
Jay McGill, *Publisher*
Bob Carlquist, *General Mgr*
Greg O'Brien, *General Mgr*
Frank Bennack, *Vice Chairman*
Jeff Cohen, *Exec VP*
EMP: 60
SALES (corp-wide): 4.9B Privately Held
WEB: www.hearstcorp.com
SIC: 2721 Magazines: publishing only, not printed on site
PA: The Hearst Corporation
300 W 57th St Fl 42
New York NY 10019
212 649-2000

(G-10443)
HEARST CORPORATION
Also Called: Marie Claire
1790 Broadway (10019-1412)
PHONE..................................212 830-2980
Fax: 212 541-4295
Lesley Jane Seymour, *Editor*
EMP: 50
SALES (corp-wide): 4.9B Privately Held
WEB: www.hearstcorp.com
SIC: 2741 Miscellaneous publishing
PA: The Hearst Corporation
300 W 57th St Fl 42
New York NY 10019
212 649-2000

(G-10444)
HEARST CORPORATION
Also Called: Esquire Magazine
300 W 57th St Fl 21 (10019-3741)
PHONE..................................212 649-4271
Fax: 212 649-4303
Jack Essig, *Vice Pres*
Natasha Zarinsky, *Manager*
EMP: 70
SALES (corp-wide): 4.9B Privately Held
SIC: 2721 Periodicals
PA: The Hearst Corporation
300 W 57th St Fl 42
New York NY 10019
212 649-2000

(G-10445)
HEARST CORPORATION
Also Called: Seventeen Magazine
1440 Broadway Fl 13 (10018-2301)
PHONE..................................212 204-4300
Sabrina Weill, *Editor*
Abby Kalicka, *Editor*
Kathy Riess, *Finance Mgr*
Howard Grier, *Associate*
EMP: 100
SALES (corp-wide): 4.9B Privately Held
WEB: www.hearstcorp.com
SIC: 2721 Periodicals
PA: The Hearst Corporation
300 W 57th St Fl 42
New York NY 10019
212 649-2000

(G-10446)
HEARST CORPORATION
Also Called: Harper's Bazaar
300 W 57th St Fl 42 (10019-3790)
PHONE..................................212 903-5000
Fax: 212 262-7101
Jennifer Bruno, *Publisher*
Linda Nardi, *General Mgr*
Christopher Tosti, *General Mgr*
Pamela Fiori, *Editor*
Victoria Pedersen, *Editor*
EMP: 65
SALES (corp-wide): 4.9B Privately Held
WEB: www.hearstcorp.com
SIC: 2721 Magazines: publishing & printing

PA: The Hearst Corporation
300 W 57th St Fl 42
New York NY 10019
212 649-2000

(G-10447)
HEARST CORPORATION
Hearst Magazines International
300 W 57th St Fl 42 (10019-3790)
PHONE..................................212 649-2275
Jane Fort, *Editor*
Charles Swift, *Vice Pres*
Ronald Doerfler, *CFO*
John Rohan Jr, *Treasurer*
Vicki Wellington, *Branch Mgr*
EMP: 50
SALES (corp-wide): 4.9B Privately Held
SIC: 2721 2731 2711 Magazines: publishing only, not printed on site; books: publishing only; newspapers, publishing & printing; newspapers: publishing only, not printed on site
PA: The Hearst Corporation
300 W 57th St Fl 42
New York NY 10019
212 649-2000

(G-10448)
HEARST DIGITAL STUDIOS INC
300 W 57th St (10019-3741)
PHONE..................................212 969-7552
Neeraj Khemlani, *Ch of Bd*
Mike Bachmann, *CFO*
EMP: 25
SQ FT: 2,500
SALES (est): 1.1MM Privately Held
SIC: 2741 7371 ; computer software development & applications

(G-10449)
HEARST HOLDINGS INC (HQ)
300 W 57th St (10019-3741)
PHONE..................................212 649-2000
George R Hearst Jr, *Ch of Bd*
Tom Chiarella, *Editor*
Larry Doyle, *Editor*
Ken Kurson, *Editor*
John Richardson, *Editor*
▲ EMP: 10
SALES (est): 580.5MM
SALES (corp-wide): 4.9B Privately Held
SIC: 2721 4841 Magazines: publishing only, not printed on site; cable television services
PA: The Hearst Corporation
300 W 57th St Fl 42
New York NY 10019
212 649-2000

(G-10450)
HEART OF TEA
419 Lafayette St Fl 2f (10003-7033)
PHONE..................................917 725-3164
Gerami Masoud, *CEO*
EMP: 10 EST: 2014
SALES (est): 1.1MM Privately Held
SIC: 2086 Iced tea & fruit drinks, bottled & canned

(G-10451)
HEARTS OF PALM LLC
Also Called: Ruby Road
1411 Broadway Fl 23 (10018-3471)
PHONE..................................212 944-6660
Peter Aresty,
EMP: 45
SALES (corp-wide): 9.2MM Privately Held
SIC: 2339 Women's & misses' athletic clothing & sportswear
PA: Hearts Of Palm, Llc
1411 Broadway Fl 25
New York NY 10018
212 944-6660

(G-10452)
HEARTS OF PALM LLC (PA)
Also Called: Ruby Road
1411 Broadway Fl 25 (10018-3496)
PHONE..................................212 944-6660
Raymond Barrick, *CFO*
Charlene Caminiti, *Credit Mgr*
Peter Aresty,
EMP: 55
SQ FT: 25,000

SALES (est): 9.2MM Privately Held
SIC: 2339 Women's & misses' athletic clothing & sportswear

(G-10453)
HEAT USA II LLC
35 E 21st St (10010-6212)
PHONE..................................212 564-4328
EMP: 28
SALES (corp-wide): 2.4MM Privately Held
SIC: 2911 Oils, fuel
PA: Heat Usa Ii Llc
11902 23rd Ave
College Point NY 11356
212 254-4328

(G-10454)
HELIUM MEDIA INC
Also Called: Heleo.com
165 Duane St Apt 7b (10013-3348)
PHONE..................................917 596-4081
Rufus Griscom, *CEO*
EMP: 5 EST: 2015
SALES (est): 130.5K Privately Held
SIC: 2741 Miscellaneous publishing

(G-10455)
HELLENIC CORPORATION
Also Called: Hellenic Times
823 11th Ave Fl 5 (10019-3557)
PHONE..................................212 986-6881
John Catsimatidis, *Ch of Bd*
Margo Catsimatidis, *President*
EMP: 15
SALES: 144.8K Privately Held
SIC: 2711 Newspapers: publishing only, not printed on site

(G-10456)
HELVETICA PRESS INCORPORATED
Also Called: Vendome Press
244 5th Ave (10001-7604)
PHONE..................................212 737-1857
Fax: 212 737-5340
Mark Magowan, *President*
Alexis Gregory, *Chairman*
Steffanie Rouher, *Controller*
▲ EMP: 5
SQ FT: 3,000
SALES: 31.4K Privately Held
WEB: www.vendomepress.com
SIC: 2731 Books: publishing only

(G-10457)
HENRY B URBAN INC
Also Called: Delta Upholsterers
619 W 54th St Ste 6l (10019-3545)
PHONE..................................212 489-3308
James Congema, *CEO*
EMP: 30
SQ FT: 20,000
SALES: 3MM Privately Held
SIC: 2512 2391 2511 7641 Upholstered household furniture; draperies, plastic & textile: from purchased materials; wood household furniture; reupholstery & furniture repair; household furnishings

(G-10458)
HENRY DUNAY DESIGNS INC
10 W 46th St Ste 1200 (10036-9312)
PHONE..................................212 768-9700
Henry Dunay, *President*
EMP: 30
SQ FT: 6,000
SALES (est): 3.8MM Privately Held
WEB: www.henrydunay.com
SIC: 3911 5944 Jewelry, precious metal; jewelry stores

(G-10459)
HENRY HOLT AND COMPANY LLC
Also Called: Owl Books Div
175 5th Ave Ste 400 (10010-7726)
PHONE..................................646 307-5095
Stephen Rubin, *Publisher*
Maggie Richards, *Vice Pres*
Jason Liebman, *Mktg Dir*
Emily Kobel, *Mktg Coord*
John Sterling, *Mng Member*
▲ EMP: 80
SQ FT: 30,000

New York - New York County (G-10460)

SALES (est): 15.9MM
SALES (corp-wide): 2.1B *Privately Held*
WEB: www.henryholt.com
SIC: 2731 Books: publishing only
HQ: Macmillan Holdings, Llc
175 5th Ave
New York NY 10010

(G-10460)
HERALD PUBLISHING COMPANY LLC
4 Times Sq Fl 23 (10036-6518)
PHONE 315 470-2022
EMP: 5 **EST:** 2013
SALES (est): 226.4K *Privately Held*
SIC: 2711 Newspapers, publishing & printing

(G-10461)
HERBERT WOLF CORP
95 Vandam St Apt C (10013-1019)
PHONE 212 242-0300
Fax: 212 242-1133
Eric Wolf, *President*
EMP: 5 **EST:** 1947
SQ FT: 3,200
SALES: 552K *Privately Held*
SIC: 3534 3599 Elevators & equipment; grinding castings for the trade

(G-10462)
HERMAN KAY COMPANY LTD
Also Called: Herman Kay Div-Mystic
463 7th Ave Fl 12 (10018-7499)
PHONE 212 239-2025
Richard Kringstein, *Ch of Bd*
Barry Kringstein, *President*
▼ **EMP:** 250 **EST:** 2009
SALES (est): 11.5MM
SALES (corp-wide): 80.5MM *Privately Held*
SIC: 2337 2339 2329 Women's & misses' suits & coats; women's & misses' outerwear; men's & boys' leather, wool & down-filled outerwear
PA: Mystic Inc.
463 7th Ave Fl 12
New York NY 10018
212 239-2025

(G-10463)
HERSHEL HOROWITZ CORP
580 5th Ave Ste 901 (10036-0044)
PHONE 212 719-1710
Fax: 212 719-1713
Leibish Horowitz, *President*
Rachel Horowitz, *Treasurer*
Chaya Dachner, *Admin Sec*
EMP: 7
SQ FT: 1,300
SALES (est): 3.1MM *Privately Held*
SIC: 3915 Diamond cutting & polishing

(G-10464)
HESS CORPORATION (PA)
1185 Ave Of The Americas (10036-2601)
PHONE 212 997-8500
Fax: 212 536-8390
John B Hess, *CEO*
James Quigley, *Ch of Bd*
Gerald A Jamin, *President*
Gregory P Hill, *COO*
John Tang, *Counsel*
▲ **EMP:** 254 **EST:** 1920
SALES: 6.5B *Publicly Held*
WEB: www.hess.com
SIC: 1311 2911 5171 5541 Crude petroleum production; natural gas production; petroleum refining; petroleum bulk stations; petroleum terminals; filling stations, gasoline; transmission, electric power

(G-10465)
HESS ENERGY EXPLORATION LTD (HQ)
1185 Ave Of The Americas (10036-2601)
PHONE 732 750-6500
Kevin B Wilcox, *Vice Pres*
Timothy B Goodell, *Vice Pres*
John P Reilly, *Vice Pres*
EMP: 4
SALES (est): 12.7MM
SALES (corp-wide): 6.5B *Publicly Held*
SIC: 1382 1311 Oil & gas exploration services; crude petroleum & natural gas production

PA: Hess Corporation
1185 Ave Of The Americas
New York NY 10036
212 997-8500

(G-10466)
HESS EXPLRTION PROD HLDNGS LTD (DH)
1185 Ave Of The Americas (10036-2601)
PHONE 732 750-6000
John P Rielly, *Vice Pres*
Kevin B Wilcox, *Vice Pres*
EMP: 3
SALES (est): 1MM
SALES (corp-wide): 6.5B *Publicly Held*
SIC: 1382 1311 Oil & gas exploration services; crude petroleum & natural gas production
HQ: Hess Energy Exploration Limited
1185 Ave Of The Americas
New York NY 10036
732 750-6500

(G-10467)
HESS OIL VIRGIN ISLAND CORP
1185 Ave Of The Amer 39 (10036-2603)
PHONE 212 997-8500
John Hess, *Ch of Bd*
Carol Beal, *General Mgr*
Ganesh Bheir, *General Mgr*
Ed Blair, *General Mgr*
Bob Boehm, *General Mgr*
EMP: 3000
SALES (est): 228.8MM
SALES (corp-wide): 6.5B *Publicly Held*
WEB: www.hess.com
SIC: 2911 Petroleum refining
PA: Hess Corporation
1185 Ave Of The Americas
New York NY 10036
212 997-8500

(G-10468)
HESS PIPELINE CORPORATION
1185 Ave Of The Amer 39 (10036-2603)
PHONE 212 997-8500
Fax: 212 536-8245
John Hess, *CEO*
Timothy B Goodell, *Principal*
EMP: 270
SALES (est): 30.8MM
SALES (corp-wide): 6.5B *Publicly Held*
WEB: www.hess.com
SIC: 1311 2911 Crude petroleum production; natural gas production; petroleum refining
PA: Hess Corporation
1185 Ave Of The Americas
New York NY 10036
212 997-8500

(G-10469)
HESS TIOGA GAS PLANT LLC
1185 Ave Of The Americas (10036-2601)
PHONE 212 997-8500
Jonathan C Stein, *Principal*
Theresa Hayden, *Credit Mgr*
John Hess,
EMP: 226 **EST:** 2012
SALES (est): 672.4K
SALES (corp-wide): 7MM *Privately Held*
SIC: 1311 Crude petroleum production; natural gas production
PA: Hess Tgp Holdings Llc
1501 Mckinney St
Houston TX

(G-10470)
HF MFG CORP (PA)
Also Called: Happy Fella
65 W 36th St Fl 11 (10018-7936)
P.O. Box 318, Hewlett (11557-0318)
PHONE 212 594-9142
Fax: 212 967-7148
Bruce Tucker, *President*
Michael Tucker, *Vice Pres*
Irene Weitz, *Controller*
◆ **EMP:** 8 **EST:** 1963
SQ FT: 2,000
SALES (est): 7MM *Privately Held*
WEB: www.hfmfgcorp.com
SIC: 2329 Men's & boys' sportswear & athletic clothing

(G-10471)
HH LIQUIDATING CORP
Also Called: Zinc Corporation America Div
110 E 59th St Fl 34 (10022-1308)
PHONE 646 282-2500
William E Flaherty, *Ch of Bd*
Robert D Scherich, *Vice Pres*
EMP: 843
SALES (est): 86MM *Privately Held*
SIC: 3624 2999 3356 3339 Carbon & graphite products; electrodes, thermal & electrolytic uses: carbon, graphite; carbon specialties for electrical use; coke, calcined petroleum: made from purchased materials; coke (not from refineries), petroleum; lead & zinc; zinc refining (primary), including slabs & dust

(G-10472)
HIGH POINT DESIGN LLC
1411 Broadway Fl 8 (10018-3565)
PHONE 212 354-2400
Mark Lopiparo, *CFO*
Jana Dittmer, *Executive Asst*
▲ **EMP:** 15
SQ FT: 20,000
SALES (est): 1.9MM *Privately Held*
SIC: 2252 Hosiery

(G-10473)
HIGH QUALITY VIDEO INC (PA)
12 W 27th St Fl 7 (10001-6903)
PHONE 212 686-9534
Fax: 212 686-9158
Hirofumy Imoto, *President*
Yuri Fukuda, *Info Tech Dir*
Fukuda Yuri, *Web Proj Mgr*
EMP: 10
SALES (est): 1.1MM *Privately Held*
SIC: 3652 Pre-recorded records & tapes

(G-10474)
HIGHCREST INVESTORS LLC (DH)
Icahn Associates Corp 767 (10153)
PHONE 212 702-4323
Carl C Icahn, *Ch of Bd*
Keef Cozzi, *Manager*
EMP: 80
SQ FT: 25,000
SALES (est): 1.4B
SALES (corp-wide): 1.4B *Privately Held*
SIC: 3743 4741 4789 4813 Freight cars & equipment; rental of railroad cars; railroad car repair; local telephone communications; long distance telephone communications
HQ: Buffalo Investors Corp.
1 Wall Street Ct Apt 980
New York NY 10005
212 702-4363

(G-10475)
HIGHLINE MEDIA LLC
375 Park Ave (10152-0002)
PHONE 859 692-2100
Andrew Goodenough, *President*
Thomas Flynn, *CFO*
EMP: 250
SALES (est): 8.8MM
SALES (corp-wide): 51.2MM *Privately Held*
WEB: www.highlinemedia.com
SIC: 2731 2711 2721 2741 Books: publishing only; pamphlets: publishing only, not printed on site; newspapers: publishing only, not printed on site; periodicals: publishing only; directories: publishing only, not printed on site
PA: Summit Business Media Holding Company
4157 Olympic Blvd Ste 225
Erlanger KY 41018
859 692-2100

(G-10476)
HILLARY MERCHANT INC
2 Wall St Ste 807 (10005-2001)
PHONE 646 575-9242
Zhaoxiong Zhang, *President*
EMP: 8 **EST:** 2012
SQ FT: 500
SALES: 840.6K *Privately Held*
SIC: 2326 5621 Men's & boys' work clothing; ready-to-wear apparel, women's

(G-10477)
HILLS PET PRODUCTS INC (DH)
300 Park Ave (10022-7402)
PHONE 212 310-2000
N Thompson, *Principal*
EMP: 4
SALES (est): 2.7MM
SALES (corp-wide): 16B *Publicly Held*
SIC: 2047 Dog & cat food
HQ: Hill's Pet Nutrition, Inc.
400 Sw 8th Ave Ste 101
Topeka KS 66603
785 354-8523

(G-10478)
HIMATSINGKA AMERICA INC (DH)
261 5th Ave Rm 1400 (10016-7707)
PHONE 212 545-8929
Steve Zaffos, *President*
Dilip J Thakkar, *Chairman*
Ashutosh Halbe, *CFO*
◆ **EMP:** 24 **EST:** 2000
SQ FT: 10,600
SALES (est): 43.6MM
SALES (corp-wide): 146.7MM *Privately Held*
WEB: www.dwholdings.com
SIC: 2392 Bedspreads & bed sets: made from purchased materials
HQ: Himatsingka Holdings Na Inc.
261 5th Ave Rm 1400
New York NY 10016
212 545-8929

(G-10479)
HIMATSINGKA AMERICA INC
Also Called: Global Textile
261 5th Ave Rm 501 (10016-0036)
PHONE 212 252-0802
Diana Cygan, *Director*
EMP: 26
SALES (corp-wide): 146.7MM *Privately Held*
WEB: www.divatex.com
SIC: 2221 Silk broadwoven fabrics
HQ: Himatsingka America Inc.
261 5th Ave Rm 1400
New York NY 10016
212 545-8929

(G-10480)
HIMATSINGKA HOLDINGS NA INC (HQ)
261 5th Ave Rm 1400 (10016-7707)
PHONE 212 545-8929
Amitabh Himatsingka, *Ch of Bd*
Shrikant Himatsingka, *President*
Ajoy Kumar Himatsingka, *Principal*
Dinesh Kumar Himatsingka, *Principal*
Rajiv Khaitan, *Chairman*
EMP: 1
SALES (est): 43.6MM
SALES (corp-wide): 146.7MM *Privately Held*
SIC: 2221 Silk broadwoven fabrics
PA: Himatsingka Seide Limited
10/24, Kumarakrupa Road,
Bengaluru KAR 56000
802 237-8000

(G-10481)
HINGE INC
137 5th Ave Fl 5 (10010-7145)
PHONE 502 445-3111
Justin McLeod, *President*
Jean-Marie McGrath, *Administration*
EMP: 14
SALES (est): 960K *Privately Held*
SIC: 7372 Prepackaged software

(G-10482)
HIPPOCRENE BOOKS INC (PA)
171 Madison Ave Rm 1605 (10016-5113)
PHONE 212 685-4371
Fax: 212 779-9338
George Blagowidow, *President*
Jayne Salomon, *Manager*
▲ **EMP:** 6
SQ FT: 1,200
SALES (est): 825.9K *Privately Held*
WEB: www.hippocrenebooks.com
SIC: 2731 Books: publishing only

GEOGRAPHIC SECTION

New York - New York County (G-10507)

(G-10483)
HIS PRODUCTIONS USA INC
Also Called: Kingstreet Sounds
139 Fulton St Rm 317 (10038-2537)
PHONE 212 594-3737
Fax: 212 594-3636
Hisanao Ishioka, *President*
Robert Wunderman, *Manager*
EMP: 7
SALES (est): 1MM **Privately Held**
WEB: www.kingstreetsounds.com
SIC: 3652 5084 Pre-recorded records & tapes; recording instruments & accessories

(G-10484)
HISTORIC TW INC (HQ)
75 Rockefeller Plz (10019-6908)
PHONE 212 484-8000
RE Turner, *Vice Ch Bd*
Richard D Parsons, *President*
Christopher P Bogart, *Exec VP*
Carl F Dill Jr, *Vice Pres*
Joseph Ripp, *CFO*
▲ **EMP:** 68
SQ FT: 451,000
SALES (est): 2B
SALES (corp-wide): 28.1B **Publicly Held**
SIC: 3652 6794 2741 7812 Compact laser discs, prerecorded; magnetic tape (audio): prerecorded; music licensing to radio stations; performance rights, publishing & licensing; music royalties, sheet & record; music, sheet: publishing only, not printed on site; music books: publishing only, not printed on site; motion picture production & distribution; television film production; motion picture production & distribution, television; video tape production; cable television services; magazines: publishing only, not printed on site
PA: Time Warner Inc.
1 Time Warner Ctr Bsmt B
New York NY 10019
212 484-8000

(G-10485)
HJN INC (PA)
Also Called: Bentones Enterprises
16 W 46th St Ste 900 (10036-4503)
PHONE 212 398-9564
Fax: 212 575-1020
Joel Namdar, *Ch of Bd*
I Raj, *President*
H J Namdar, *Vice Pres*
▲ **EMP:** 15
SALES (est): 2.1MM **Privately Held**
SIC: 3911 Rings, finger: precious metal

(G-10486)
HK METAL TRADING LTD
450 Fashion Ave Ste 2300 (10123-2300)
PHONE 212 868-3333
Kenny Chen, *Partner*
EMP: 6
SQ FT: 350
SALES: 3MM **Privately Held**
SIC: 3399 Metal powders, pastes & flakes

(G-10487)
HKS PRINTING COMPANY INC
Also Called: Official Press, The
115 E 27th St (10016-8945)
PHONE 212 675-2529
Fax: 212 691-6294
Inhyung You, *President*
Sue You, *Corp Secy*
EMP: 10
SALES (est): 940K **Privately Held**
SIC: 2752 2791 Lithographing on metal; typesetting

(G-10488)
HLP KLEARFOLD PACKAGING PDTS
Also Called: Hlp Klearfold Visualize
75 Maiden Ln Rm 808 (10038-4658)
PHONE 718 554-3271
Steve Rothschild, *President*
Ada Lam, *Opers Mgr*
Glenn Levine, *Sales Mgr*
Karen Werther, *Manager*
Derek Brown, *Director*
EMP: 10
SALES (est): 1MM **Privately Held**
SIC: 3089 Closures, plastic

(G-10489)
HMS PRODUCTIONS INC (PA)
Also Called: Spencer Jeremy
250 W 39th St Fl 12 (10018-8215)
PHONE 212 719-9190
Fax: 212 730-3581
Alex Goldberg, *President*
Spenser Alpern, *Chairman*
John Mow, *Exec Officer*
Andrea Nimberger, *Vice Pres*
C K Fung, *Controller*
◆ **EMP:** 69
SQ FT: 14,000
SALES (est): 29.2MM **Privately Held**
WEB: www.nubby.com
SIC: 2399 Hand woven & crocheted products

(G-10490)
HMX LLC (PA)
Also Called: Hmx Operating Co
125 Park Ave Fl 7 (10017-5627)
PHONE 212 682-9073
Loretta Osowski, *Human Res Mgr*
Ajay Khaitan, *Mng Member*
Lisa Branigan, *Manager*
Joseph Abboud,
Doug Williams,
EMP: 68
SALES (est): 206.8MM **Privately Held**
SIC: 2211 Apparel & outerwear fabrics, cotton

(G-10491)
HNI CORPORATION
200 Lexington Ave Rm 1112 (10016-6255)
PHONE 212 683-2232
Tom Talon, *President*
EMP: 226
SALES (corp-wide): 2.3B **Publicly Held**
WEB: www.honi.com
SIC: 2521 Wood office furniture
PA: Hni Corporation
408 E 2nd St
Muscatine IA 52761
563 272-7400

(G-10492)
HNW INC (PA)
666 3rd Ave Frnt A (10017-4081)
PHONE 212 258-9215
Fax: 212 258-9201
Stacey Haefele, *CEO*
Jason Hoffmann, *Exec VP*
Brian Peterson, *Senior VP*
Matthew Warren, *Senior VP*
Rashmi Gupta, *QC Mgr*
▲ **EMP:** 10
SALES (est): 5.3MM **Privately Held**
WEB: www.hnw.com
SIC: 2721 4813 7371 Magazines: publishing & printing; telephone communication, except radio; custom computer programming services

(G-10493)
HOGAN FLAVORS & FRAGRANCES
Also Called: Hogan Fragrances International
130 E 18th St Frnt (10003-2416)
PHONE 212 598-4310
Fax: 212 477-4711
Ray Hogan, *Ch of Bd*
Cory Warner, *Vice Pres*
Sean Hogan, *VP Sales*
EMP: 35
SQ FT: 3,000
SALES (est): 4.3MM **Privately Held**
WEB: www.hoganff.com
SIC: 2844 Perfumes & colognes

(G-10494)
HOLBROOKE INC
Also Called: Holbrooke By Sberry
444 E 20th St Apt 1b (10009-8142)
PHONE 646 397-4674
EMP: 5
SALES (est): 322K **Privately Held**
SIC: 3961 Costume jewelry

(G-10495)
HOLDENS SCREEN SUPPLY CORP
121 Varick St (10013-1408)
PHONE 212 627-2727
Arthur I Gononsky, *President*
EMP: 7
SALES (est): 319.8K **Privately Held**
SIC: 2711 Commercial printing & newspaper publishing combined

(G-10496)
HOLIDAY HOUSE INC
425 Madison Ave Fl 12 (10017-1135)
PHONE 212 688-0085
Fax: 212 421-6134
John H Briggs Jr, *President*
Grace Maccarone, *Editor*
Kate Briggs, *Vice Pres*
Regina Griffin, *Vice Pres*
Lisa Lee, *Opers Staff*
▲ **EMP:** 15 **EST:** 1935
SQ FT: 2,000
SALES (est): 1.9MM **Privately Held**
WEB: www.holidayhouse.com
SIC: 2731 Book publishing

(G-10497)
HOLLAND & SHERRY INC (PA)
Also Called: Holland & Sherry Intr Design
330 E 59th St Ph (10022-1537)
PHONE 212 542-8410
Sergio Casalena, *Ch of Bd*
Bryan Dicker, *President*
Caroline Halsey, *Sales Staff*
Stephanie Sung, *Info Tech Mgr*
▲ **EMP:** 29
SQ FT: 4,700
SALES (est): 17.9MM **Privately Held**
WEB: www.hollandandsherry.com
SIC: 2395 7389 2519 5021 Embroidery & art needlework; design services; garden furniture, except wood, metal, stone or concrete; furniture

(G-10498)
HOLLANDER HM FSHONS HLDNGS LLC
440 Park Ave S Fl 10 (10016-8012)
PHONE 212 575-0400
Jeff Hollander, *President*
EMP: 10
SALES (corp-wide): 196.9MM **Privately Held**
WEB: www.hollander.com
SIC: 2392 Pillows, bed: made from purchased materials
PA: Hollander Home Fashions Holdings, Llc
6501 Congress Ave Ste 300
Boca Raton FL 33487
561 997-6900

(G-10499)
HOLLANDER SLEEP PRODUCTS LLC
440 Park Ave S (10016-8012)
PHONE 212 575-0400
Donald Kelly, *Branch Mgr*
EMP: 79
SALES (corp-wide): 196.9MM **Privately Held**
SIC: 2392 Cushions & pillows
HQ: Hollander Sleep Products, Llc
6501 Congress Ave Ste 300
Boca Raton FL 33487
561 997-6900

(G-10500)
HOLMES GROUP THE INC
Also Called: Saber Awards
271 W 47th St Apt 23a (10036-1447)
PHONE 212 333-2300
Fax: 212 333-2624
Paul Holmes, *President*
Greg Druey, *President*
Ben Edwards, *Vice Pres*
Patrick Drury, *Accounts Exec*
James Colman, *Corp Comm Staff*
EMP: 5
SALES (est): 540K **Privately Held**
WEB: www.holmesreport.com
SIC: 2721 Periodicals

(G-10501)
HOME FASHIONS INTL LLC
Also Called: Hfi
295 5th Ave Ste 1520 (10016-7126)
PHONE 212 684-0091
Tom Goldtsein, *Controller*
EMP: 15

SALES (corp-wide): 19MM **Privately Held**
SIC: 2392 Pillows, bed: made from purchased materials
PA: Home Fashions International, Llc
2255 Glades Rd Ste 324a
Boca Raton FL 33431
212 689-3579

(G-10502)
HONG HOP CO INC
Also Called: Hong Hop Noodle Company
10 Bowery (10013-5101)
PHONE 212 962-1735
Fax: 212 732-0626
Dai Leong Hee, *President*
Sing Leong, *Corp Secy*
Chor Hee, *Manager*
EMP: 30 **EST:** 1931
SQ FT: 5,793
SALES (est): 4MM **Privately Held**
SIC: 2098 2099 2038 Noodles (e.g. egg, plain & water), dry; pasta, uncooked: packaged with other ingredients; snacks, including onion rings, cheese sticks, etc.

(G-10503)
HOOEK PRODUKTION INC
147 W 26th St Fl 6 (10001-6817)
PHONE 212 367-9111
Joseph Primiano, *President*
▲ **EMP:** 7
SQ FT: 2,000
SALES (est): 974.3K **Privately Held**
SIC: 2752 Commercial printing, lithographic

(G-10504)
HOPE INTERNATIONAL PRODUCTIONS
315 W 57th St Apt 6h (10019-3145)
P.O. Box 237078 (10023-0029)
PHONE 212 247-3188
David King, *Ch of Bd*
Hope King, *President*
EMP: 18
SQ FT: 1,800
SALES (est): 1.3MM **Privately Held**
SIC: 3652 3651 5099 1531 Phonograph records, prerecorded; magnetic tape (audio): prerecorded; video cassette recorders/players & accessories; phonograph records; tapes & cassettes, prerecorded; video cassettes, accessories & supplies; operative builders

(G-10505)
HORIZON FLOORS I LLC
11 Broadway Lbby 5 (10004-1330)
PHONE 212 509-9686
Alex Shaoulspour, *President*
EMP: 1
SALES (est): 4MM **Privately Held**
SIC: 2426 Hardwood dimension & flooring mills

(G-10506)
HORIZON IMPORTS INC
Also Called: Horizon Hosiery Mills
10 W 33rd St Rm 606 (10001-3306)
PHONE 212 239-8660
Fax: 212 947-1037
Isaac Cohen, *President*
Howard Gershon, *Purch Agent*
Jack David, *Buyer*
Ssas Wacth, *Human Res Mgr*
Gail Hernandez, *Director*
▲ **EMP:** 60
SQ FT: 6,000
SALES: 16MM **Privately Held**
SIC: 2251 2252 Women's hosiery, except socks; men's, boys' & girls' hosiery

(G-10507)
HORLY NOVELTY CO INC
17 Ludlow St Frnt 2 (10002-6318)
PHONE 212 226-4800
Fax: 212 226-4802
Joe Yip, *President*
Richard Joe, *Vice Pres*
Jack Lee, *Treasurer*
▲ **EMP:** 7
SALES (est): 440K **Privately Held**
SIC: 3961 Costume jewelry, ex. precious metal & semiprecious stones

New York - New York County (G-10508)

(G-10508)
HORO CREATIONS LLC
Also Called: Designs By Hc
71 W 47th St Ste 404 (10036-2865)
PHONE..................212 719-4818
Suresh Krishnani, *President*
Vinay Krishnani,
EMP: 6
SALES (est): 618.8K **Privately Held**
SIC: 3911 Jewelry, precious metal

(G-10509)
HOSEL & ACKERSON INC (PA)
570 Fashion Ave Rm 805 (10018-1647)
PHONE..................212 575-1490
Monte Braverman, *President*
EMP: 5 **EST:** 1944
SALES (est): 559K **Privately Held**
SIC: 2258 2395 2269 Lace, knit; embroidery products, except schiffli machine; finishing plants

(G-10510)
HOSPITALITY GRAPHICS INC
545 8th Ave Rm 401 (10018-4341)
PHONE..................212 643-6700
Fax: 212 643-6784
Louis Melito, *President*
Marshall Silverman, *Treasurer*
Pat McNally, *Office Mgr*
EMP: 9
SQ FT: 3,500
SALES (est): 1.4MM **Privately Held**
WEB: www.hginyc.com
SIC: 2752 Commercial printing, offset

(G-10511)
HOSPITALITY INC
247 W 35th St 4 (10001-1908)
PHONE..................212 268-1930
Howard Pitler, *President*
EMP: 22
SALES (est): 1.1MM **Privately Held**
SIC: 2759 6513 Commercial printing; apartment building operators

(G-10512)
HOT KISS INC
1407 Brdwy Ste 2000 (10018)
PHONE..................212 730-0404
Fax: 212 704-9687
Moshe Tsabag, *President*
EMP: 6
SALES (est): 536.2K **Privately Held**
SIC: 2325 Jeans: men's, youths' & boys'

(G-10513)
HOT SHOT HK LLC
1407 Broadway Rm 2018 (10018-2863)
PHONE..................212 921-1111
Marko Elenron, *Mng Member*
▲ **EMP:** 31
SALES (est): 7.6MM **Privately Held**
SIC: 2339 Women's & misses' athletic clothing & sportswear

(G-10514)
HOT SOX COMPANY INCORPORATED (PA)
Also Called: Polo Ralph Lauren Hosiery Div
95 Madison Ave Fl 15 (10016-7801)
PHONE..................212 957-2000
Fax: 212 957-1050
Gary Wolkowitz, *President*
Mark Gordon, *Senior VP*
Sarah Wolkowitz, *Treasurer*
Josephine Cordero, *Controller*
Eugene Merkushen, *Info Tech Dir*
▼ **EMP:** 40
SQ FT: 18,000
SALES (est): 6.4MM **Privately Held**
SIC: 2252 2251 Men's, boys' & girls' hosiery; women's hosiery, except socks

(G-10515)
HOUGHTON MIFFLIN HARCOURT PUBG
Also Called: Houghton Mifflin Clarion Books
3 Park Ave Fl 18 (10016-5902)
PHONE..................212 420-5800
Dorothy Briley, *Vice Pres*
Dana Baylor, *Sales Mgr*
Ann Healy, *Manager*
Ruth Homberg, *Senior Mgr*
Dinah Stevenson, *Director*
EMP: 40
SALES (corp-wide): 1.4B **Publicly Held**
WEB: www.hmco.com
SIC: 2731 Books: publishing only
HQ: Houghton Mifflin Harcourt Publishing Company
222 Berkeley St
Boston MA 02116
617 351-5000

(G-10516)
HOULES USA INC
979 3rd Ave Ste 1200 (10022-1234)
PHONE..................212 935-3900
Fax: 212 935-3923
Philippe Dasilva, *Manager*
EMP: 5
SALES (corp-wide): 1.3MM **Privately Held**
WEB: www.houlesusa.com
SIC: 3911 Trimmings for canes, umbrellas, etc.: precious metal
HQ: Houles Usa Inc
8687 Melrose Ave Ste B617
West Hollywood CA 90069
310 652-6171

(G-10517)
HOUND & GATOS PET FOODS CORP
14 Wall St Fl 20 (10005-2123)
P.O. Box 11750, Atlanta GA (30355-1750)
PHONE..................212 618-1917
Will Post, *President*
EMP: 8
SQ FT: 25,000
SALES (est): 1.4MM **Privately Held**
WEB: www.houndgatos.com
SIC: 2047 Dog & cat food

(G-10518)
HOUSE OF HEYDENRYK JR INC
Also Called: House of Heydenryk The
601 W 26th St Rm 305 (10001-1159)
PHONE..................212 206-9611
Charles Schreiber, *President*
David Mandel, *Chairman*
Rigmor Heydenryk, *Admin Sec*
EMP: 18 **EST:** 1935
SQ FT: 5,000
SALES (est): 1.4MM **Privately Held**
WEB: www.heydenryk.com
SIC: 2499 Picture & mirror frames, wood

(G-10519)
HOUSE OF PORTFOLIOS CO INC (PA)
133 W 25th St Rm 7w (10001-7282)
PHONE..................212 206-7323
Thomas Lombardo, *President*
Celia Sandiego, *Director*
EMP: 5
SQ FT: 900
SALES (est): 1.5MM **Privately Held**
WEB: www.houseofportfolios.com
SIC: 3172 5948 Personal leather goods; leather goods, except luggage & shoes

(G-10520)
HOUSE OF PORTFOLIOS CO INC
48 W 21st St (10010-6907)
PHONE..................212 206-7323
Thomas Lombardo, *Branch Mgr*
EMP: 17
SALES (corp-wide): 1.5MM **Privately Held**
WEB: www.houseofportfolios.com
SIC: 3172 Personal leather goods
PA: The House Of Portfolios Co Inc
133 W 25th St Rm 7w
New York NY 10001
212 206-7323

(G-10521)
HOUSE PEARL FASHIONS (US) LTD
1410 Broadway Rm 1501 (10018-9834)
PHONE..................212 840-3183
Mehesh Seth, *President*
EMP: 10
SQ FT: 4,000
SALES (corp-wide): 93.1MM **Privately Held**
SIC: 2329 2339 Coats (oiled fabric, leatherette, etc.): men's & boys'; women's & misses' outerwear; women's & misses' accessories
HQ: House Of Pearl Fashions (Us) Ltd.
300-2 D&E Rr 17
Lodi NJ 07644
973 778-7551

(G-10522)
HOVEE INC
722 Saint Nicholas Ave (10031-4002)
PHONE..................646 249-6200
Paul Kogan, *CEO*
EMP: 10
SALES (est): 533.8K **Privately Held**
SIC: 7372 7389 Business oriented computer software;

(G-10523)
HP INC
5 Penn Plz Ste 1912 (10001-1810)
PHONE..................212 835-1640
Alan Stein, *Vice Pres*
Emma Barbian, *Technology*
EMP: 52
SALES (corp-wide): 103.3B **Publicly Held**
WEB: www.3com.com
SIC: 3577 Computer peripheral equipment
PA: Hp Inc.
1501 Page Mill Rd
Palo Alto CA 94304
650 857-1501

(G-10524)
HRG GROUP INC (PA)
450 Park Ave Fl 29 (10022-2640)
PHONE..................212 906-8555
Joseph S Steinberg, *Ch of Bd*
Omar M Asali, *President*
David M Maura, *Exec VP*
Ehsan Zargar, *Vice Pres*
George Nicholson, *CFO*
EMP: 23 **EST:** 1954
SALES (est): 5.8B **Publicly Held**
WEB: www.zapatacorp.com
SIC: 3691 3634 3999 6311 Storage batteries; batteries, rechargeable; electric household cooking appliances; pet supplies; life insurance

(G-10525)
HUDSON ENVELOPE CORPORATION (PA)
Also Called: Jam Paper
135 3rd Ave (10003-2543)
PHONE..................212 473-6666
Fax: 212 473-7300
Michael Jacobs, *President*
Steve Levine, *Marketing Mgr*
Caitlin Hare, *Marketing Staff*
Andrew Jacobs, *Director*
EMP: 25
SQ FT: 7,000
SALES (est): 2.1MM **Privately Held**
SIC: 2752 2759 Commercial printing, offset; envelopes: printing

(G-10526)
HUDSON PARK PRESS INC
232 Madison Ave Rm 1400 (10016-2901)
P.O. Box 774, Pine Plains (12567-0774)
PHONE..................212 929-8898
Gilman Park, *Ch of Bd*
▲ **EMP:** 5
SALES (est): 423.5K **Privately Held**
SIC: 2752 2731 Publication printing, lithographic; books: publishing only

(G-10527)
HUDSON PRINTING CO INC
747 3rd Ave Lbby 3 (10017-2810)
PHONE..................718 937-8600
Fax: 212 937-7710
Robert Bergman, *President*
Jeff Smith, *Mng Member*
Alan Bergman, *Admin Sec*
EMP: 25 **EST:** 1923
SQ FT: 33,000
SALES (est): 3.1MM **Privately Held**
WEB: www.hudsonprints.com
SIC: 2752 2789 Commercial printing, offset; bookbinding & related work

(G-10528)
HUGO BOSS USA INC (HQ)
55 Water St Fl 48 (10041-3204)
PHONE..................212 940-0600
Andre Maeder, *CEO*
Anthony Lucia, *President*
Gretchen Ruoillard, *President*
Camilo Casallas, *General Mgr*
Juan Convers, *General Mgr*
◆ **EMP:** 75
SQ FT: 100,000
SALES (est): 242.9MM
SALES (corp-wide): 3B **Privately Held**
WEB: www.hugobossusa.com
SIC: 2311 2325 2337 5136 Men's & boys' suits & coats; men's & boys' trousers & slacks; women's & misses' suits & coats; suits: women's, misses' & juniors'; skirts, separate: women's, misses' & juniors'; jackets & vests, except fur & leather: women's; men's & boys' suits & trousers; men's & boys' sportswear & work clothing; men's & boys' outerwear; men's & boys' clothing stores; franchises, selling or licensing
PA: Hugo Boss Ag
Dieselstr. 12
Metzingen 72555
712 394-0

(G-10529)
HUMAN LIFE FOUNDATION INC
353 Lexington Ave Rm 802 (10016-0988)
PHONE..................212 685-5210
Fax: 212 725-9793
Maria McFadden, *President*
Faith McFadden, *Vice Pres*
Rose Flynn, *Controller*
Ann Conlon, *Admin Sec*
EMP: 5 **EST:** 1974
SQ FT: 500
SALES: 567K **Privately Held**
WEB: www.humanlifereview.com
SIC: 2721 8399 8733 Periodicals: publishing only; social service information exchange; noncommercial research organizations

(G-10530)
HUMANA PRESS INC
233 Spring St Fl 6 (10013-1522)
PHONE..................212 460-1500
Thomas Lanigan Jr, *President*
Julia Lanigan, *Vice Pres*
Robin Weisberg, *Director*
▲ **EMP:** 40
SQ FT: 8,500
SALES (est): 2.2MM
SALES (corp-wide): 2.1B **Privately Held**
WEB: www.humanapr.com
SIC: 2741 2731 2721 Technical papers: publishing only, not printed on site; book clubs: publishing only, not printed on site; trade journals: publishing only, not printed on site
HQ: Springer Adis Us, Llc
233 Spring St Fl 6
New York NY 10013
212 460-1500

(G-10531)
HUMANSCALE CORPORATION (PA)
11 E 26th St Fl 8 (10010-1425)
PHONE..................212 725-4749
Fax: 212 725-7545
Robert King, *CEO*
Heather Fennimore, *President*
Paul Levy, *President*
Elliot Balis, *District Mgr*
Michele Gerards, *Vice Pres*
◆ **EMP:** 32
SQ FT: 10,000
SALES (est): 171.3MM **Privately Held**
SIC: 3577 2521 Computer peripheral equipment; wood office furniture

(G-10532)
HUMOR RAINBOW INCORPORATED
129 W 29th St Fl 10 (10001-5105)
PHONE..................646 402-9113
Michael Maxim, *President*
EMP: 43
SALES (est): 1.6MM **Privately Held**
SIC: 2741 Miscellaneous publishing

▲ = Import ▼ = Export
◆ = Import/Export

GEOGRAPHIC SECTION

New York - New York County (G-10560)

(G-10533)
HUNTER DOUGLAS INC
979 3rd Ave (10022-1234)
PHONE.....................212 588-0564
David Shmil, *Branch Mgr*
EMP: 191 Privately Held
SIC: 2591 Window blinds
HQ: Hunter Douglas Inc.
   1 Blue Hill Plz Ste 1569
   Pearl River NY 10965
   845 664-7000

(G-10534)
HW HOLDINGS INC (DH)
718 5th Ave (10019-4102)
PHONE.....................212 399-1000
Nayla Hayek, *CEO*
EMP: 3
SALES (est): 48.7MM
SALES (corp-wide): 8.4B Privately Held
SIC: 3911 5944 6719 Jewelry, precious metal; jewelry, precious stones & precious metals; watches; investment holding companies, except banks
HQ: The Swatch Group Far East Distribution Ltd
   Seevorstadt 6
   Biel-Bienne BE 2502
   323 436-811

(G-10535)
HY GOLD JEWELERS INC
Also Called: Jj Marco
1070 Madison Ave Frnt 4 (10028-0229)
PHONE.....................212 744-3202
Mark Cohen, *President*
Julian Jaffe-Cohen, *Treasurer*
EMP: 5
SALES (est): 441.7K Privately Held
SIC: 3911 Jewelry, precious metal

(G-10536)
HYATT TIMES SQUARE NEW YORK
135 W 45th St (10036-4004)
PHONE.....................212 398-2158
EMP: 19
SALES (est): 2MM Privately Held
SIC: 2711 Newspapers

(G-10537)
HYPERLAW INC
17 W 70th St Apt 4 (10023-4544)
PHONE.....................212 873-6982
Fax: 212 496-4138
Alan D Sugarman, *President*
EMP: 10
SALES (est): 830K Privately Held
WEB: www.hyperlaw.com
SIC: 7372 Publishers' computer software

(G-10538)
HYPOXICO INC
50 Lexington Ave Ste 249 (10010-2935)
PHONE.....................212 972-1009
Gary Kotliar, *President*
Yulia Soukhanova, *Vice Pres*
Brian Oe Strike, *Vice Pres*
Matt Eckert, *Manager*
EMP: 6
SQ FT: 3,000
SALES (est): 500K Privately Held
WEB: www.hypoxico.com
SIC: 3949 Exercise equipment

(G-10539)
I LOVE ACCESSORIES INC
10 W 33rd St Rm 210 (10001-3326)
PHONE.....................212 239-1875
Daren Malles, *President*
▲ EMP: 5
SQ FT: 1,200
SALES: 5MM Privately Held
SIC: 3961 Costume jewelry

(G-10540)
I N K T INC
250 W 54th St Fl 9 (10019-5515)
PHONE.....................212 957-2700
Gary Winnick, *CEO*
Scott Jacobson, *COO*
Ed Ickowski, *Senior VP*
Jim Vickers, *Senior VP*
Saurabh Suri, *Vice Pres*
▲ EMP: 10
SALES (est): 1.6MM Privately Held
WEB: www.t-ink.com
SIC: 2759 5085 Commercial printing; ink, printers'

(G-10541)
I S C A CORP (HQ)
Also Called: Elliot Lauren
512 7th Ave Fl 7 (10018-0862)
PHONE.....................212 719-5123
Fax: 212 719-1984
Elliot Grosovsky, *Ch of Bd*
Vijay Malani, *Controller*
▲ EMP: 16
SQ FT: 4,200
SALES (est): 3.4MM
SALES (corp-wide): 15.1MM Privately Held
SIC: 2335 Women's, juniors' & misses' dresses
PA: Lauren Elliott Inc
   512 7th Ave Fl 7
   New York NY 10018
   212 719-5123

(G-10542)
I SPIEWAK & SONS INC
225 W 37th St Fl 15l (10018-6667)
PHONE.....................212 695-1620
Fax: 212 629-4803
Roy J Spiewak, *Ch of Bd*
Jon Van Manen, *General Mgr*
Sol Jacobs, *Vice Pres*
Steve Corsilli, *Opers Staff*
Kevin Nordmann, *Sales Staff*
▲ EMP: 35
SQ FT: 10,000
SALES (est): 5.9MM Privately Held
SIC: 2329 Men's & boys' leather, wool & down-filled outerwear; field jackets, military; down-filled clothing: men's & boys'

(G-10543)
IAC SEARCH LLC (HQ)
555 W 18th St (10011-2822)
PHONE.....................212 314-7300
Barry Diller, *Chairman*
Stacy Simpson, *Senior VP*
Ernest Wurzbach, *Senior VP*
Trish Lounsbury, *Vice Pres*
Dave Smith, *Engineer*
EMP: 47
SALES (est): 4.5MM
SALES (corp-wide): 3.2B Publicly Held
SIC: 7372 7375 Prepackaged software; information retrieval services; on-line data base information retrieval
PA: Iac/Interactivecorp
   555 W 18th St
   New York NY 10011
   212 314-7300

(G-10544)
IAC/INTERACTIVECORP (PA)
555 W 18th St (10011-2822)
PHONE.....................212 314-7300
Joseph Levin, *CEO*
Mandy Ginsberg, *CEO*
Sean Moriarty, *CEO*
Sam Yagan, *CEO*
Barry Diller, *Ch of Bd*
EMP: 200
SQ FT: 202,500
SALES: 3.2B Publicly Held
WEB: www.usanetworks.com
SIC: 7372 7375 5961 Prepackaged software; information retrieval services; on-line data base information retrieval; catalog & mail-order houses

(G-10545)
IBIO INC
600 Madison Ave Ste 1601 (10022-1737)
PHONE.....................302 355-0650
Carlos Picosse, *CEO*
Robert B Kay, *Ch of Bd*
Robert L Erwin, *President*
Andrea Corcoran, *Senior VP*
Renato Lobo, *Chief Mktg Ofcr*
EMP: 9 EST: 2008
SALES: 948K Privately Held
SIC: 2834 Pharmaceutical preparations

(G-10546)
IBIT INC
257 W 38th St Fl 2 (10018-4457)
PHONE.....................212 768-0292
Simon Ting, *President*
EMP: 30
SALES (est): 3.4MM Privately Held
WEB: www.ibit.com
SIC: 3543 7219 Industrial patterns; dressmaking service, material owned by customer

(G-10547)
IBRANDS INTERNATIONAL LLC
230 W 39th St (10018-4411)
PHONE.....................212 354-1330
Marc Garson, *Chairman*
Sylvia Lee, *Manager*
EMP: 16 EST: 2014
SQ FT: 4,200
SALES: 400K Privately Held
SIC: 2321 Polo shirts, men's & boys': made from purchased materials

(G-10548)
IBT MEDIA INC (PA)
Also Called: International Business Times
7 Hanover Sq Fl 5 (10004-2674)
PHONE.....................646 867-7100
Etienne Uzac, *President*
Thomas Hammer, *Senior VP*
Mitchell Caplan, *Chief Mktg Ofcr*
Emily Scheer, *Pub Rel Dir*
Max Willens, *Relations*
EMP: 42
SQ FT: 50,000
SALES (est): 40.6MM Privately Held
SIC: 2741

(G-10549)
IC TECHNOLOGIES LLC
475 Greenwich St (10013-1378)
PHONE.....................212 966-7895
Marcel Bekeyzer, *President*
Norah De Bekker, *Marketing Staff*
▲ EMP: 5
SALES (est): 586.7K Privately Held
SIC: 3674 Light emitting diodes

(G-10550)
ICARUS ENTERPRISES INC
568 Broadway Fl 11 (10012-3374)
PHONE.....................917 969-4461
Nicholas Hubbard, *President*
EMP: 5
SALES: 500K Privately Held
SIC: 2721 Magazines: publishing & printing

(G-10551)
ICER SCRUBS LLC
Also Called: Crocs Medical Apparel
1385 Broadway Fl 16 (10018-6041)
PHONE.....................212 221-4700
Lawrence Jemal, *Mng Member*
Iven Sandler, *Director*
▲ EMP: 10
SQ FT: 2,000
SALES (est): 591.2K Privately Held
SIC: 2335 Women's, juniors' & misses' dresses

(G-10552)
ICER SPORTS LLC
1385 Broadway Fl 16 (10018-6041)
PHONE.....................212 221-4700
Iven Sandler,
▲ EMP: 10
SALES (est): 740K Privately Held
SIC: 2329 2331 Men's & boys' sportswear & athletic clothing; women's & misses' blouses & shirts

(G-10553)
IDALIA SOLAR TECHNOLOGIES LLC
270 Lafayette St Ste 1402 (10012-3364)
PHONE.....................212 792-3913
Marc Dee,
Eric Laufer,
EMP: 9
SQ FT: 2,500
SALES: 500K Privately Held
SIC: 3674 Solar cells

(G-10554)
IDEAL BRILLIANT CO INC
580 5th Ave Ste 600 (10036-4726)
PHONE.....................212 840-2044
Meilech Fastag, *President*
Abe Fastag, *Vice Pres*
Chilly Fastag, *Manager*
EMP: 10
SQ FT: 2,000
SALES (est): 1.1MM Privately Held
WEB: www.idealbrilliant.com
SIC: 3915 Diamond cutting & polishing

(G-10555)
IDEAL CREATIONS INC
10 W 33rd St Rm 708 (10001-3306)
PHONE.....................212 563-5928
Moses Grunbaum, *President*
▲ EMP: 20
SALES (est): 1.1MM Privately Held
WEB: www.idealcreations.net
SIC: 2369 5136 Headwear: girls', children's & infants'; hats, men's & boys'

(G-10556)
IDENTIFYCOM INC
120 W 45th St Ste 2701 (10036-4041)
PHONE.....................212 235-0000
Debra Brown, *General Mgr*
Alexander Valcic, *Manager*
Amanda Lim, *Comp Spec*
EMP: 8
SQ FT: 3,171
SALES (est): 530K Privately Held
SIC: 7372 Application computer software

(G-10557)
IDESCO CORP
37 W 26th St Fl 10 (10010-1097)
PHONE.....................212 889-2530
Andrew Schonzeit, *President*
EMP: 15
SALES (corp-wide): 20.2MM Privately Held
WEB: www.idesco.com
SIC: 2671 Packaging paper & plastics film, coated & laminated
PA: Idesco Corp.
   37 W 26th St Fl 10
   New York NY 10010
   212 889-2530

(G-10558)
IDRA ALTA MODA LLC
200 West St 305 (10282-2102)
PHONE.....................914 644-8202
Jessica Soiser,
Adam Soiser,
EMP: 10 EST: 2009
SQ FT: 1,200
SALES (est): 1.1MM Privately Held
SIC: 2339 Women's & misses' outerwear

(G-10559)
IEH FM HOLDINGS LLC (DH)
Also Called: Icahn
767 5th Ave Ste 4700 (10153-0108)
PHONE.....................212 702-4300
Fax: 212 750-5828
Carl C Icahn,
EMP: 30
SALES (est): 7.4B
SALES (corp-wide): 19.1B Publicly Held
SIC: 3462 3559 3694 3812 Automotive & internal combustion engine forgings; railroad, construction & mining forgings; degreasing machines, automotive & industrial; automotive electrical equipment; acceleration indicators & systems components, aerospace; computer logic modules
HQ: Icahn Enterprises Holdings L.P.
   767 5th Ave Fl 17
   New York NY 10153
   212 702-4300

(G-10560)
IFF INTERNATIONAL INC
521 W 57th St Fl 9 (10019-2960)
PHONE.....................212 765-5500
Richard O'Leary, *Ch of Bd*
Robert Diakon, *VP Accounting*
Alicia Thomas, *Executive Asst*
EMP: 20

New York - New York County (G-10561)

SALES: 668K
SALES (corp-wide): 3B **Publicly Held**
WEB: www.iff.com
SIC: 2844 2087 Toilet preparations; flavoring extracts & syrups
PA: International Flavors & Fragrances Inc.
521 W 57th St
New York NY 10019
212 765-5500

(G-10561)
IFG CORP
1372 Brdwy 12ae 12 Ae (10018)
PHONE 212 629-9600
EMP: 161
SALES (corp-wide): 48.5MM **Privately Held**
SIC: 2329 2339 Athletic (warmup, sweat & jogging) suits: men's & boys'; athletic clothing: women's, misses' & juniors'
PA: Ifg Corp.
1400 Broadway Rm 2202
New York NY 10018
212 239-8615

(G-10562)
IFG CORP
463 7th Ave Fl 4 (10018-8725)
PHONE 212 239-8615
Ronald Adjmi, *President*
EMP: 5
SALES (corp-wide): 48.5MM **Privately Held**
SIC: 2329 Athletic (warmup, sweat & jogging) suits: men's & boys'
PA: Ifg Corp.
1400 Broadway Rm 2202
New York NY 10018
212 239-8615

(G-10563)
IGC NEW YORK INC
580 5th Ave Ste 708 (10036-4725)
PHONE 212 764-0949
Zevi Sterling, *Principal*
EMP: 5
SALES (est): 510K **Privately Held**
WEB: www.igcgroup.com
SIC: 3915 Lapidary work & diamond cutting & polishing

(G-10564)
IHEARTCOMMUNICATIONS INC
Also Called: Lite FM Radio
1133 Ave Of Amricas Fl 34 (10036)
PHONE 212 603-4660
Fax: 212 603-4601
Robert Williams, *President*
EMP: 50
SALES (corp-wide): 6.2B **Publicly Held**
SIC: 3663 Radio receiver networks
HQ: Iheartcommunications, Inc.
200 E Basse Rd
San Antonio TX 78209
210 822-2828

(G-10565)
IKEDDI ENTERPRISES INC (PA)
1407 Brdwy Ste 2900 (10018)
PHONE 212 302-7644
Fax: 212 302-7732
Raymond Salem, *Ch of Bd*
David Salem, *Vice Pres*
Bruce Cotter, *CFO*
▲ **EMP:** 12
SQ FT: 28,000
SALES (est): 4.5MM **Privately Held**
SIC: 2339 Sportswear, women's

(G-10566)
IKEDDI ENTERPRISES INC
1407 Broadway Rm 1805 (10018-2764)
PHONE 212 302-7644
Raymond Salem, *Manager*
EMP: 6
SALES (corp-wide): 4.5MM **Privately Held**
SIC: 2339 Sportswear, women's
PA: Ikeddi Enterprises Inc.
1407 Brdwy Ste 2900
New York NY 10018
212 302-7644

(G-10567)
IMAGINATION PLAYGROUND LLC
5 Union Sq W (10003-3306)
PHONE 212 463-0334
Marc Hacker,
▲ **EMP:** 5
SALES (est): 576.5K **Privately Held**
SIC: 3949 Playground equipment

(G-10568)
IMAGINE COMMUNICATIONS CORP
Also Called: Harris Broadcast
1 Penn Plz Fl 39 (10119-0002)
PHONE 212 303-4200
Charles Vogt, *CEO*
Ron Fehler, *Vice Pres*
Mary Mateo, *Financial Exec*
Frank Gatto, *Sales Engr*
S Rosenfeld, *Branch Mgr*
EMP: 11
SALES (corp-wide): 6.8B **Privately Held**
SIC: 3663 Radio broadcasting & communications equipment; television broadcasting & communications equipment
HQ: Imagine Communications Corp.
3001 Dallas Pkwy Ste 300
Frisco TX 75034
469 803-4900

(G-10569)
IMAGO RECORDING COMPANY (PA)
Also Called: Tigerstar Records
240 E 47th St Apt 20f (10017-2136)
PHONE 212 751-3033
Terry Ellis, *President*
EMP: 5
SALES (est): 626.5K **Privately Held**
SIC: 3652 5099 Pre-recorded records & tapes; compact discs; phonograph records; tapes & cassettes, prerecorded

(G-10570)
IMEK MEDIA LLC
32 Broadway Ste 511 (10004-1665)
PHONE 212 422-9000
Kemi Osukoya,
EMP: 20 **EST:** 2012
SALES (est): 1.5MM **Privately Held**
SIC: 2721 Magazines: publishing only, not printed on site

(G-10571)
IMENA JEWELRY MANUFACTURER INC
2 W 45th St Ste 1000 (10036-4252)
PHONE 212 827-0073
Fax: 212 827-0418
Paul Yan, *President*
Cindy Yan, *Office Mgr*
EMP: 15
SALES (est): 1.7MM **Privately Held**
SIC: 3911 Jewelry, precious metal

(G-10572)
IMG THE DAILY
432 W 45th St Fl 5 (10036-3503)
PHONE 212 541-5640
George Maier, *Principal*
EMP: 7
SALES (est): 473.9K **Privately Held**
SIC: 2711 Newspapers, publishing & printing

(G-10573)
IMMUNE PHARMACEUTICALS INC (PA)
430 E 29th St Ste 940 (10016-8367)
PHONE 646 440-9310
Daniel G Teper, *CEO*
Daniel Kazado, *Ch of Bd*
Miri Ben-AMI, *Exec VP*
Monica E Luchi, *Exec VP*
Karin Hehenberger, *Senior VP*
EMP: 12
SQ FT: 1,674
SALES (est): 2K **Publicly Held**
WEB: www.epicept.com
SIC: 2834 Pharmaceutical preparations; analgesics

(G-10574)
IMPERIAL-HARVARD LABEL CO
Also Called: Harvard Woven Label
225 W 35th St Ste 1102 (10001-1904)
PHONE 212 736-8420
Ira I Altfeder, *President*
Larry Saputo, *Treasurer*
EMP: 10
SQ FT: 3,000
SALES (est): 910K **Privately Held**
SIC: 2241 Labels, woven

(G-10575)
IMPRESSIONS INC
36 W 37th St Rm 400 (10018-7497)
PHONE 212 594-5954
Fax: 212 594-5266
John Baise, *Principal*
EMP: 5
SALES (est): 728.3K **Privately Held**
SIC: 2721 Periodicals: publishing only

(G-10576)
IMTECH GRAPHICS INC
Also Called: Imtech At Avon
1251 Avenue Of The Americ (10020-1104)
PHONE 212 282-7010
Robert Gottlieb, *Principal*
Robert Rose, *Manager*
EMP: 10
SALES (est): 530K **Privately Held**
SIC: 2759 Commercial printing

(G-10577)
IN MOCEAN GROUP LLC (PA)
501 Fashion Ave Fl 12 (10018-5941)
PHONE 732 960-2415
Jerry Harary, *President*
Angelina Jones, *President*
Max Anteby, *Exec VP*
Brian Brinkmann, *Sales Mgr*
Christine Varvaro, *Sales Staff*
▲ **EMP:** 72 **EST:** 2000
SQ FT: 12,000
SALES (est): 15.4MM **Privately Held**
SIC: 2369 Bathing suits & swimwear: girls', children's & infants'

(G-10578)
IN MODA COM INC
241 W 37th St Rm 803 (10018-6810)
PHONE 718 788-4466
Marco Scaba, *President*
Judy Scaba, *Vice Pres*
EMP: 23
SALES (est): 1.6MM **Privately Held**
SIC: 2339 Sportswear, women's

(G-10579)
IN-STEP MARKETING INC (PA)
Also Called: Z Card North America
39 Broadway Fl 32 (10006-3047)
PHONE 212 797-3450
Fax: 212 797-1530
Tim Kunhardt, *President*
Liz Love, *Managing Dir*
Jeremy Shaw, *CFO*
Edgar Millington, *Controller*
Jeffrey Owens, *VP Sales*
EMP: 15
SQ FT: 6,600
SALES (est): 1.5MM **Privately Held**
WEB: www.zcardna.com
SIC: 2752 5199 8742 Promotional printing, lithographic; advertising specialties; marketing consulting services

(G-10580)
INBOXMIND LLC
1 Penn Plz Fl 36th (10119-0002)
PHONE 646 773-7726
Manish Sood,
EMP: 5
SALES (est): 320K **Privately Held**
SIC: 7372 7371 Prepackaged software; business oriented computer software; computer software development & applications

(G-10581)
INCISIVE RWG INC
Also Called: Risk Waters Group
55 Broad St Fl 22 (10004-2511)
PHONE 212 457-9400
Tim Weller, *President*
Ed Bean, *Editor*
Rex Bossert, *Editor*
Pamela Brownstein, *Editor*
Su A Carranza, *Editor*
EMP: 138
SQ FT: 92,000
SALES (est): 12.2MM
SALES (corp-wide): 760.4K **Privately Held**
WEB: www.riskwaters.com
SIC: 2731 Book publishing
HQ: Incisive Media Limited
Haymarket House, 28-29 Haymarket
London
207 316-9000

(G-10582)
INCITEC PIVOT LIMITED
120 Broadway Fl 32 (10271-3299)
PHONE 212 238-3010
EMP: 5
SALES (est): 361.8K **Privately Held**
SIC: 2819 Chemicals, high purity: refined from technical grade

(G-10583)
INCON GEMS INC
Also Called: Jeypore Group
2 W 46th St Ste 603 (10036-4561)
PHONE 212 221-8560
Fax: 212 302-5404
Raju Gupta, *President*
EMP: 15
SQ FT: 2,000
SALES (est): 1.6MM **Privately Held**
SIC: 3911 5094 Jewelry, precious metal; precious stones (gems)

(G-10584)
INCYCLE SOFTWARE CORP (PA)
1120 Ave Of The Americas (10036-6700)
PHONE 212 626-2608
Fredric Persoon, *President*
Claude Ramillard, *Partner*
Leo Vidosola, *Partner*
Martin Rajotte, *COO*
Julie Beaulieu, *CFO*
EMP: 9
SALES (est): 1.4MM **Privately Held**
SIC: 7372 Prepackaged software

(G-10585)
IND REV LLC
1385 Broadway Fl 16 (10018-6041)
PHONE 212 221-4700
Lawrence Jemal, *Mng Member*
▲ **EMP:** 10
SALES (est): 1.2MM **Privately Held**
SIC: 2331 Women's & misses' blouses & shirts

(G-10586)
INDEGY INC
154 Grand St (10013-3141)
PHONE 866 801-5394
EMP: 30
SALES (est): 526.6K **Privately Held**
SIC: 7372 7382 Prepackaged software; security systems services

(G-10587)
INDEX MAGAZINE
526 W 26th St Rm 920 (10001-5540)
PHONE 212 243-1428
Fax: 212 243-1603
Peter Halley, *Owner*
Scott Dixon, *Manager*
EMP: 6
SALES (est): 300K **Privately Held**
WEB: www.indexmagazine.com
SIC: 2721 Magazines: publishing & printing

(G-10588)
INDIA ABROAD PUBLICATIONS INC
102 Madison Ave Frnt B (10016-7417)
PHONE 212 929-1727
Fax: 212 627-9503
Ajit Balakrishnan, *President*
Prem Panicker, *Editor*
Parimal Mehta, *Engineer*
Gopal Raju, *Systems Mgr*
Tony Lobo, *Systems Analyst*
EMP: 59
SQ FT: 6,500

GEOGRAPHIC SECTION

New York - New York County (G-10616)

SALES (est): 4.5MM **Privately Held**
SIC: 2711 Newspapers: publishing only, not printed on site

(G-10589)
INDIGO HOME INC
230 5th Ave Ste 1916 (10001-7730)
PHONE..................................212 684-4146
Taniya Kapoor, *Ch of Bd*
◆ EMP: 6
SALES (est): 806.1K **Privately Held**
WEB: www.indigohome.com
SIC: 2392 Blankets, comforters & beddings

(G-10590)
INDONESIAN IMPORTS INC (PA)
Also Called: Elliot Lucca
339 5th Ave Fl 2 (10016-5016)
PHONE..................................888 800-5899
Fax: 212 545-1207
Mark A Talucchi, *CEO*
Todd Elliott, *President*
Kristin Wilcox, *Vice Pres*
Staci Battino, *Sales Staff*
Lauren Turetsky, *Info Tech Mgr*
▲ EMP: 30
SQ FT: 52,000
SALES (est): 11.6MM **Privately Held**
WEB: www.elliottlucca.com
SIC: 3911 5961 Earrings, precious metal; jewelry, mail order

(G-10591)
INDUSTRIAL COLOR INC (PA)
32 Ave Of The Am (10013)
PHONE..................................212 334-4667
Steve Kalalian, *President*
Giovanni Sblano, *Business Mgr*
Mathieu Champigny, *COO*
Sam Sandoval, *QA Dir*
Andy Goldman, *CFO*
EMP: 3
SQ FT: 30,000
SALES: 5MM **Privately Held**
SIC: 2752 Color lithography

(G-10592)
INEEDMD HOLDINGS INC (PA)
650 1st Ave Fl 3 (10016-3240)
PHONE..................................212 256-9669
Thomas Nicolette, *CEO*
Jonathan Loutzenhiser, *President*
Patrice McMorrow, *Exec VP*
EMP: 3
SALES (est): 1MM **Privately Held**
SIC: 3841 Diagnostic apparatus, medical

(G-10593)
INFINITY AUGMENTED REALITY INC
228 Park Ave S 61130 (10003-1502)
PHONE..................................917 677-2084
Motti Kushnir, *CEO*
Moshe Hogeg, *Ch of Bd*
Enon Landenberg, *President*
Ortal Zanzuri, *CFO*
EMP: 6
SALES (est): 134.9K **Privately Held**
SIC: 7372 7371 Prepackaged software; custom computer programming services; computer software development & applications

(G-10594)
INFINITY SOURCING SERVICES LLC
224 W 35th St Ste 600 (10001-2537)
PHONE..................................212 868-2900
Ray Kim, *Mng Member*
EMP: 8
SALES: 22MM **Privately Held**
SIC: 2335 Women's, juniors' & misses' dresses

(G-10595)
INFOBASE PUBLISHING COMPANY (PA)
Also Called: Films Media Group
132 W 31st St Fl 17 (10001-3406)
PHONE..................................212 967-8800
Mark D McDonnell, *Ch of Bd*
Domenic Durante, *Manager*
Dodd Weisenberger, *Manager*
EMP: 1 EST: 1999

SALES (est): 12.7MM **Privately Held**
SIC: 2731 7372 Books: publishing only; prepackaged software

(G-10596)
INFOR GLOBAL SOLUTIONS INC (DH)
641 Ave Of Americas Fl 4 (10011)
PHONE..................................646 336-1700
James Schaper, *CEO*
Bill Ellis, *President*
Greg Bashar, *Project Mgr*
Allan Nielsen, *Opers Staff*
Harvey Canaan, *QA Dir*
EMP: 94
SALES: 39.5MM
SALES (corp-wide): 2.6B **Privately Held**
SIC: 7372 Prepackaged software
HQ: Infor (Us), Inc.
    13560 Morris Rd Ste 4100
    Alpharetta GA 30004
    678 319-8000

(G-10597)
INFORMA UK LTD
Lloyd's List Intelligence
52 Vanderbilt Ave Fl 7 (10017-3846)
PHONE..................................646 957-8966
Kieran Brown, *Branch Mgr*
EMP: 5 **Privately Held**
SIC: 2711 Newspapers
HQ: Informa Uk Limited
    5 Howick Place
    London W1T 3
    207 017-4555

(G-10598)
INFORMATICA LLC
125 Park Ave Rm 1510 (10017-5694)
PHONE..................................212 845-7650
Fax: 212 845-7651
EMP: 11
SALES (corp-wide): 102.5MM **Privately Held**
SIC: 7372 Prepackaged software
HQ: Informatica Llc
    2100 Seaport Blvd
    Redwood City CA 94063
    650 385-5000

(G-10599)
INFORMERLY INC
35 Essex St (10002-4712)
PHONE..................................646 238-7137
Ranjan Roy, *CEO*
Emily Moss, *President*
EMP: 5
SALES (est): 270K **Privately Held**
SIC: 7372 Prepackaged software

(G-10600)
INKKAS LLC
38 E 29th St Rm 6r (10016-7963)
PHONE..................................646 845-9803
Daniel Ben-Mun, *Mng Member*
EMP: 6
SALES (est): 698K **Privately Held**
SIC: 3021 Canvas shoes, rubber soled

(G-10601)
INNER WORKINGS INC
Also Called: Nycd
1440 Broadway Fl 22 (10018-3041)
PHONE..................................646 352-4394
Eric Belcher, *CEO*
▲ EMP: 27
SALES (est): 7MM **Privately Held**
SIC: 3577 Printers & plotters

(G-10602)
INNOVANT INC
37 W 20th St Ste 209 (10011-3721)
PHONE..................................212 929-4883
Fax: 212 929-5174
Tom Navaretta, *Plant Mgr*
Carl Clark, *Opers Mgr*
Eric Leclaire, *Engineer*
Craig Mulqueen, *Engineer*
Jessica Cuebas, *Sales Mgr*
EMP: 100
SALES (corp-wide): 45.3MM **Privately Held**
WEB: www.innovant.com
SIC: 2521 Wood office furniture

PA: Innovant, Inc.
    21 Locust Ave Ste 2d
    New Canaan CT 06840
    203 966-1305

(G-10603)
INNOVANT INC
37 W 20th St Ste 1101 (10011-3713)
PHONE..................................212 929-4883
Charles Braham, *Branch Mgr*
EMP: 6
SALES (corp-wide): 45.3MM **Privately Held**
WEB: www.innovant.com
SIC: 2511 Kitchen & dining room furniture
PA: Innovant, Inc.
    21 Locust Ave Ste 2d
    New Canaan CT 06840
    203 966-1305

(G-10604)
INNOVATIVE COSMTC CONCEPTS LLC
Also Called: Innovative Design
1430 Broadway Rm 308 (10018-9222)
PHONE..................................212 391-8110
Mark Frankel, *General Mgr*
Don Barresi, *Mng Member*
Norman Greif,
Robert Murello,
▲ EMP: 7 EST: 2001
SALES (est): 1.3MM **Privately Held**
SIC: 2844 Cosmetic preparations

(G-10605)
INNOVATIVE DESIGNS LLC
141 W 36th St Fl 8 (10018-6980)
PHONE..................................212 695-0892
Warren Collin, *Human Res Mgr*
Douglas Haber, *Mng Member*
Jody Rullo, *Manager*
▲ EMP: 34
SQ FT: 8,000
SALES (est): 8.2MM **Privately Held**
SIC: 2678 Stationery products

(G-10606)
INO-TEX LLC
135 W 36th St Fl 6 (10018-9482)
PHONE..................................212 400-2205
Yongjun Yu, *Director*
EMP: 5
SALES (est): 369.1K
SALES (corp-wide): 286.6MM **Privately Held**
SIC: 2299 Batts & batting: cotton mill waste & related material; ramie yarn, thread, roving & textiles
PA: Jiangsu Lianfa Textile Co., Ltd.
    No. 88 Henglian Rd., Chengdong Town, Haian County
    Nantong 22660
    513 888-5915

(G-10607)
INORI JEWELS
580 5th Ave (10036-4701)
PHONE..................................347 703-5078
Guy Israeli, *Owner*
EMP: 10 EST: 2014
SALES (est): 470K **Privately Held**
SIC: 3911 Jewelry, precious metal

(G-10608)
INOVA LLC
685 W End Ave Ste 1b (10025-6819)
PHONE..................................212 932-0366
Loren Sherman, *Purch Mgr*
Guy Bucey, *Manager*
Heheher Curris, *Manager*
Jerry Blackwell,
EMP: 20
SQ FT: 5,000
SALES (est): 1.9MM **Privately Held**
SIC: 2511 Bed frames, except water bed frames: wood

(G-10609)
INPORA TECHNOLOGIES LLC
1501 Broadway (10036-5601)
PHONE..................................646 838-2474
Ron Siddons, *CEO*
EMP: 99
SALES (est): 5.4MM **Privately Held**
SIC: 3577 Computer peripheral equipment

(G-10610)
INPROTOPIA CORPORATION
401 W 110th St Apt 2001 (10025-2445)
PHONE..................................917 338-7501
Souyun Lee, *CEO*
WEl-Yeh Lee, *Exec VP*
EMP: 11 EST: 2011
SALES (est): 654.1K **Privately Held**
SIC: 7372 7373 7371 Business oriented computer software; systems software development services; computer software systems analysis & design, custom

(G-10611)
INSTANT STREAM INC
Also Called: Stream Police
1271 Ave Of The Americas (10020-1300)
PHONE..................................917 438-7182
Michael Daly III, *CEO*
Peggy Wong, *President*
EMP: 32
SALES (est): 3.5MM **Privately Held**
SIC: 2752 Commercial printing, lithographic

(G-10612)
INSTITUTE OF ELECTRICAL AND EL
Ieee Communications Society
3 Park Ave Fl 17 (10016-5902)
PHONE..................................212 705-8900
Davide Dardari, *Vice Chairman*
Sonia Fahmy, *Vice Chairman*
Robert Heath, *Vice Chairman*
Kerrianne Sullivan, *Project Mgr*
Paul Morris, *Manager*
EMP: 25
SALES (corp-wide): 190.1MM **Privately Held**
SIC: 2721 Trade journals: publishing & printing
PA: The Institute Of Electrical And Electronics Engineers Incorporated
    3 Park Ave Fl 17
    New York NY 10016
    212 419-7900

(G-10613)
INSTITUTIONAL INVESTER
225 Park Ave S Fl 7 (10003-1605)
PHONE..................................212 224-3300
Patricia Bertucci, *Publisher*
Steve Brull, *Publisher*
Aaron Finkel, *Publisher*
Elayne Glick, *Publisher*
Kristin Hebert, *Publisher*
EMP: 5 EST: 2008
SALES (est): 352K **Privately Held**
SIC: 2721 Periodicals

(G-10614)
INT TRADING USA LLC
261 W 35th St Ste 1100 (10001-1900)
PHONE..................................212 760-2338
Sung Pak,
▲ EMP: 230 EST: 2004
SALES (est): 37.3MM **Privately Held**
SIC: 2325 2339 Men's & boys' trousers & slacks; women's & misses' outerwear

(G-10615)
INTEGRATED COPYRIGHT GROUP
Also Called: Evergreen
1745 Broadway 19 (10019-4640)
PHONE..................................615 329-3999
Fax: 615 329-4070
John Barker, *President*
EMP: 22
SALES (est): 1.4MM **Privately Held**
SIC: 2741 Music, sheet: publishing only, not printed on site

(G-10616)
INTEGRATED GRAPHICS INC (PA)
Also Called: I C S
7 W 36th St Fl 12 (10018-7154)
PHONE..................................212 592-5600
James Kearns, *President*
Jay Beber, *Vice Pres*
Ronne N Carlton, *Administration*
Ann Todd,
Celeste Oria, *Social Worker*
EMP: 5

New York - New York County (G-10617)

SALES (est): 3.3MM **Privately Held**
WEB: www.integratedgraphics.com
SIC: 2759 8748 Commercial printing; business consulting

(G-10617)
INTELLICELL BIOSCIENCES INC
460 Park Ave Fl 17 (10022-1860)
PHONE..................................646 576-8700
Steven A Victor, *Ch of Bd*
Leonard Mazur, *COO*
Anna Rhodes, *Exec VP*
▼ EMP: 6
SALES (est): 534.9K **Privately Held**
SIC: 2834 Dermatologicals

(G-10618)
INTELLIGIZE INCORPORATED (PA)
261 5th Ave Rm 1414 (10016-7702)
PHONE..................................571 612-8580
Mark Klinker, *Finance Mgr*
Todd Hicks, *VP Sales*
Rodrick Anderson, *Accounts Mgr*
James Batty, *Accounts Mgr*
Sarah Eramo, *Accounts Mgr*
EMP: 2
SALES (est): 3.2MM **Privately Held**
SIC: 7372 Business oriented computer software

(G-10619)
INTELLIGNC THE FTR CMPTNG NWSL
Also Called: Intelligence Newsletter
360 Central Park W (10025-6541)
P.O. Box 20008 (10025-1510)
PHONE..................................212 222-1123
Edward Rosenfeld, *Owner*
EMP: 10
SALES (est): 400K **Privately Held**
WEB: www.eintelligence.com
SIC: 2721 Periodicals

(G-10620)
INTELLITRAVEL MEDIA INC (DH)
530 Fashion Ave Rm 201 (10018-4821)
PHONE..................................646 695-6700
Nancy Telliho, *Ch of Bd*
Harold Shain, *President*
Erik Torkells, *Editor*
Monique Lewis, *Manager*
EMP: 10
SALES (est): 782.3K
SALES (corp-wide): 3.2B **Publicly Held**
SIC: 2721 Magazines: publishing only, not printed on site
HQ: The Daily Beast Company Llc
7 Hanover Sq
New York NY 10004
212 445-4600

(G-10621)
INTER PARFUMS INC (PA)
551 5th Ave (10176-0001)
PHONE..................................212 983-2640
Jean Madar, *Ch of Bd*
Philippe Benacin, *President*
Russell Greenberg, *CFO*
▲ EMP: 98
SQ FT: 16,800
SALES: 468.5MM **Publicly Held**
WEB: www.interparfumsinc.com
SIC: 2844 Toilet preparations; perfumes & colognes; cosmetic preparations

(G-10622)
INTERACTION INSIGHT CORP
750 3rd Ave Fl 9 (10017-2718)
PHONE..................................800 285-2950
Timothy J Feldmann, *President*
Richard Geramia, *Principal*
EMP: 9 EST: 2014
SQ FT: 1,000
SALES: 3MM **Privately Held**
SIC: 3651 Recording machines, except dictation & telephone answering

(G-10623)
INTERAXISSOURCINGCOM INC
41 E 11th St Fl 11 (10003-4602)
PHONE..................................212 905-6001
Donald Taffurelli, *President*
Christopher Jara, *Senior VP*
EMP: 50
SQ FT: 1,000

SALES (est): 4.6MM **Privately Held**
SIC: 2231 Apparel & outerwear broadwoven fabrics

(G-10624)
INTERBRAND LLC
1 W 37th St Fl 9 (10018-5354)
PHONE..................................212 840-9595
Bob McMeekin, *President*
EMP: 9
SALES (corp-wide): 9MM **Privately Held**
WEB: www.interbrandllc.com
SIC: 2321 Men's & boys' furnishings
PA: Interbrand Llc
225 Dupont St Ste 2
Plainview NY 11803
516 349-5884

(G-10625)
INTERCEPT PHARMACEUTICALS INC (PA)
450 W 15th St Ste 505 (10011-7082)
PHONE..................................646 747-1000
Jonathan Silverstein, *Ch of Bd*
Mark Pruzanski, *President*
Juan Carlos Lopez-Talavera, *Senior VP*
Barbara Duncan, *CFO*
Sandip Kapadia, *CFO*
EMP: 72
SQ FT: 20,626
SALES: 2.7MM **Publicly Held**
SIC: 2834 Pharmaceutical preparations

(G-10626)
INTERCOTTON COMPANY INC
888 7th Ave Fl 29 (10106-2899)
PHONE..................................212 265-3809
Herman Landman, *President*
EMP: 3
SALES: 8.9MM **Privately Held**
SIC: 2389 Men's miscellaneous accessories

(G-10627)
INTERFACEFLOR LLC
330 5th Ave Fl 12 (10001-3213)
PHONE..................................212 686-8284
Fax: 212 213-5139
Pete Waldron, *Manager*
EMP: 25
SALES (corp-wide): 1B **Publicly Held**
WEB: www.ca.interfaceinc.com
SIC: 2273 Finishers of tufted carpets & rugs
HQ: Interfaceflor, Llc
1503 Orchard Hill Rd
Lagrange GA 30240
706 882-1891

(G-10628)
INTERHELLENIC PUBLISHING INC
Also Called: Estiator
421 7th Ave Ste 810 (10001-2002)
PHONE..................................212 967-5016
Fax: 212 643-1642
Peter Makrias, *President*
EMP: 7
SQ FT: 1,500
SALES: 1.2MM **Privately Held**
WEB: www.estiator.com
SIC: 2721 Magazines: publishing only, not printed on site

(G-10629)
INTERMEDIA OUTDOORS INC (PA)
1040 Ave Of The Americas (10018-3703)
PHONE..................................212 852-6600
David Koff, *CEO*
Chuck Nelson, *Publisher*
Geoff Mueller, *Editor*
Richard Venola, *Editor*
Peter Kern, *Chairman*
EMP: 66
SALES (est): 42.9MM **Privately Held**
SIC: 2326 5045 Industrial garments, men's & boys'; computer software

(G-10630)
INTERNATIONAL AIDS VACCINE INI (PA)
125 Broad St Fl 9 (10004-2743)
PHONE..................................212 847-1111
Fax: 212 847-1112

Alex Godwin Coutinho, *Ch of Bd*
Margaret McGlynn, *President*
Thomas P Monath, *Partner*
David N Cook, *COO*
Lynn Doren, *Senior VP*
EMP: 143
SQ FT: 32,000
SALES (est): 66.3MM **Privately Held**
WEB: www.iavi.org
SIC: 2836 8731 Vaccines; commercial physical research

(G-10631)
INTERNATIONAL BUS MCHS CORP
Also Called: IBM
55 Broad St Fl 27 (10004-2563)
PHONE..................................212 324-5000
Carol Moore, *Director*
EMP: 40
SALES (corp-wide): 81.7B **Publicly Held**
WEB: www.ibm.com
SIC: 3674 Computer logic modules
PA: International Business Machines Corporation
1 New Orchard Rd Ste 1
Armonk NY 10504
914 499-1900

(G-10632)
INTERNATIONAL DATA GROUP INC
Also Called: Idg Technetwork
117 E 55th St Ste 204 (10022-3502)
PHONE..................................212 331-7883
Lauren Kotara, *Accounts Exec*
Michael Friedenberg, *Branch Mgr*
EMP: 30
SALES (corp-wide): 3.5B **Privately Held**
SIC: 2721 8732 7389 Trade journals: publishing only, not printed on site; market analysis or research; trade show arrangement
PA: International Data Group, Inc.
1 Exeter Plz Fl 15
Boston MA 02116
617 534-1200

(G-10633)
INTERNATIONAL DESIGN ASSOC LTD
Also Called: Life Plus Style
747 3rd Ave Rm 218 (10017-2878)
PHONE..................................212 687-0333
Robin Nedboy, *President*
Steven Kletz, *Vice Pres*
▲ EMP: 8
SQ FT: 3,500
SALES (est): 3.5MM **Privately Held**
SIC: 2678 3999 5999 Stationery products; candles; toiletries, cosmetics & perfumes

(G-10634)
INTERNATIONAL DIRECT GROUP INC
Also Called: Idg
525 7th Ave Rm 208 (10018-5280)
PHONE..................................212 921-9036
Fax: 212 921-9038
Haynes Holding, *CEO*
Wesley Matthews, *CFO*
▲ EMP: 30
SALES (est): 7.6MM **Privately Held**
WEB: www.internationaldg.com
SIC: 2331 7389 Blouses, women's & juniors': made from purchased material; design services

(G-10635)
INTERNATIONAL INSPIRATIONS LTD (PA)
Also Called: Lux Accessories
362 5th Ave Ste 601 (10001-2210)
PHONE..................................212 465-8500
Saul Shaya Reiter, *CEO*
Sherry Burns, *Exec VP*
Maninder Kaur, *Controller*
▲ EMP: 49
SQ FT: 1,000
SALES (est): 14.4MM **Privately Held**
SIC: 3961 Costume jewelry

(G-10636)
INTERNATIONAL INSURANCE SOC
101 Murray St Fl 4 (10007-2132)
PHONE..................................212 815-9291
Fax: 212 815-9297
Douglas Leatherdale, *Ch of Bd*
Patrick W Kenny, *President*
Brian P Greig, *Partner*
Jesper D Jespersen, *Partner*
Andries Terblanche, *Partner*
EMP: 8
SALES: 2.5MM **Privately Held**
WEB: www.iisonline.org
SIC: 3825 Network analyzers

(G-10637)
INTERNATIONAL MGT NETWRK
445 Park Ave Fl 9 (10022-8606)
PHONE..................................646 401-0032
Jeff Krantz, *President*
EMP: 15
SALES: 950K **Privately Held**
SIC: 7372 Prepackaged software

(G-10638)
INTERNATIONL STUDIOS INC
108 W 39th St Rm 1300 (10018-3614)
PHONE..................................212 819-1616
Alan S Ginsberg, *President*
EMP: 5
SALES (est): 360K **Privately Held**
SIC: 2211 Apparel & outerwear fabrics, cotton

(G-10639)
INTERNTNAL FLVORS FRGRNCES INC (PA)
Also Called: Iff
521 W 57th St (10019-2929)
PHONE..................................212 765-5500
Fax: 212 708-7119
Andreas Fibig, *Ch of Bd*
Ahmet Baydar, *Exec VP*
Julian W Boyden, *Exec VP*
Anne Chwat, *Exec VP*
Beth E Ford, *Exec VP*
◆ EMP: 180 EST: 1909
SALES: 3B **Publicly Held**
WEB: www.iff.com
SIC: 2869 2844 2087 Flavors or flavoring materials, synthetic; perfume materials, synthetic; toilet preparations; flavoring extracts & syrups

(G-10640)
INTERNTNL PUBLCATNS MEDIA GRUP
708 3rd Ave Ste 145 (10017-4201)
PHONE..................................917 604-9602
Francois Wilson, *CEO*
EMP: 7
SQ FT: 400
SALES: 269.4K **Privately Held**
SIC: 2731 5112 5085 2721 Books: publishing & printing; laserjet supplies; ink, printers'; comic books: publishing only, not printed on site; computer software; film processing, editing & titling: motion picture

(G-10641)
INTERTEX USA INC
Also Called: B C America
131 W 35th St Fl 10 (10001-2111)
PHONE..................................212 279-3601
Fax: 212 279-3523
Yong Lee, *President*
EMP: 15
SQ FT: 6,500
SALES (est): 1MM **Privately Held**
SIC: 2221 2262 Specialty broadwoven fabrics, including twisted weaves; screen printing: manmade fiber & silk broadwoven fabrics

(G-10642)
INTERVIEW INC
Also Called: Interview Magazine
575 Broadway Fl 5 (10012-3227)
PHONE..................................212 941-2900
Fax: 212 941-2819
Sandra J Brant, *President*
Andrew Wasserstein, *President*
Meghan Dailey, *Editor*

▲ = Import ▼ = Export
◆ = Import/Export

GEOGRAPHIC SECTION

New York - New York County (G-10667)

David Furnish, *Editor*
Pat Hackett, *Editor*
EMP: 29
SQ FT: 20,000
SALES (est): 3.1MM
SALES (corp-wide): 4.8MM **Privately Held**
WEB: www.interviewmagazine.com
SIC: 2721 Magazines: publishing only, not printed on site
PA: Brant Publications, Inc.
  110 Greene St Ph 2
  New York NY 10012
  212 941-2800

(G-10643)
INTEVA PRODUCTS LLC
30 Rockefeller Plz (10112-0015)
PHONE......................248 655-8886
Lon Offenbacher, *Branch Mgr*
EMP: 300
SALES (corp-wide): 4.5B **Privately Held**
SIC: 3089 Injection molding of plastics
HQ: Inteva Products, Llc
  1401 Crooks Rd
  Troy MI 48084
  248 655-8886

(G-10644)
INTIMATECO LLC
Also Called: Inteco Intimates
149 Madison Ave Rm 300 (10016-6713)
PHONE......................212 239-4411
Gaby Sutton,
Eli Levy,
▲ **EMP:** 8 **EST:** 2008
SALES (est): 4.8MM **Privately Held**
SIC: 2341 Women's & children's underwear

(G-10645)
INTRA-CELLULAR THERAPIES INC
430 E 29th St (10016-8367)
PHONE......................212 923-3344
Fax: 212 923-3388
Sharon Mates, *Ch of Bd*
Ashish Dugar, *Vice Pres*
Allen A Fienberg, *Vice Pres*
Michael Halstead, *Vice Pres*
Michael I Halstead, *Vice Pres*
▲ **EMP:** 26
SQ FT: 14,678
SALES: 577.3K **Privately Held**
WEB: www.intracellulartherapies.com
SIC: 2834 8732 Pharmaceutical preparations; research services, except laboratory

(G-10646)
INTRALINKS HOLDINGS INC (PA)
150 E 42nd St Fl 8 (10017-5626)
PHONE......................212 543-7700
Patrick J Wack Jr, *Ch of Bd*
Ronald W Hovsepian, *President*
Jose Almandoz, *Exec VP*
Aditya Joshi, *Exec VP*
Leif O'Leary, *Exec VP*
EMP: 36
SQ FT: 43,304
SALES: 276.1MM **Publicly Held**
SIC: 7372 7382 Prepackaged software; security systems services

(G-10647)
INTRIGUING THREADS APPAREL INC (PA)
552 Fashion Ave Rm 603 (10018-3211)
PHONE......................212 768-8733
Fax: 212 768-4041
Alayne Weinstein, *President*
Frederick Demario, *Corp Secy*
Lori Kamhi, *Vice Pres*
Caryne Marinelli, *Bookkeeper*
Steve Albucher, *Sales Mgr*
▲ **EMP:** 13
SQ FT: 2,500
SALES (est): 3.3MM **Privately Held**
SIC: 2339 Sportswear, women's

(G-10648)
INTUITION PUBLISHING LIMITED
40 E 34th St Rm 1101 (10016-4501)
PHONE......................212 838-7115
Fax: 212 479-2546
David Harrison, *Manager*
EMP: 9
SALES (corp-wide): 30.9MM **Privately Held**
SIC: 2741 Miscellaneous publishing
PA: Intuition Publishing Limited
  I F S C House
  Dublin 1
  160 543-00

(G-10649)
INVENSYS SYSTEMS INC
7 E 8th St (10003-5901)
PHONE......................214 527-3099
EMP: 10
SALES (corp-wide): 224.4K **Privately Held**
SIC: 3823 Industrial instrmnts msrmnt display/control process variable; flow instruments, industrial process type; pressure measurement instruments, industrial; liquid level instruments, industrial process type
HQ: Invensys Systems, Inc.
  10900 Equity Dr
  Houston TX 77041
  713 329-1600

(G-10650)
INVESTMENT NEWS
711 3rd Ave Fl 3 (10017-9214)
PHONE......................212 210-0100
Fax: 212 210-0444
Mary B Franklin, *Editor*
Frederick Gabriel, *Editor*
Suzanne Siracuse, *Vice Pres*
Kate Costanzo, *Prdtn Mgr*
Jim Pavia, *Director*
EMP: 50
SALES (est): 1.9MM **Privately Held**
WEB: www.investmentnews.net
SIC: 2711 Newspapers, publishing & printing

(G-10651)
INVESTMENTWIRES INC
99 Wall St Ste 1700 (10005-4312)
PHONE......................212 331-8995
Sean Hanna, *President*
EMP: 5
SALES (est): 240K **Privately Held**
WEB: www.investmentwires.com
SIC: 2711 6282 Newspapers; investment advice

(G-10652)
INVESTORS BUSINESS DAILY INC
1501 Broadway Fl 12 (10036-5505)
PHONE......................212 626-7676
Fax: 212 626-7699
Janice Janendo, *Branch Mgr*
EMP: 18
SALES (corp-wide): 287.7MM **Privately Held**
WEB: www.investors.com
SIC: 2711 6282 Newspapers, publishing & printing; investment advice
HQ: Investor's Business Daily, Inc.
  12655 Beatrice St
  Los Angeles CA 90066
  310 448-6000

(G-10653)
INVISION INC (HQ)
25 W 43rd St Ste 609 (10036-7422)
PHONE......................212 557-5554
Steve Marshall, *CEO*
Kami Ragsdale, *COO*
Christina Barlowe, *Senior VP*
Travis Howe, *Senior VP*
David Miller, *Vice Pres*
EMP: 2
SALES (est): 1.1MM
SALES (corp-wide): 138.8MM **Privately Held**
SIC: 7372 Prepackaged software
PA: Mediaocean Llc
  45 W 18th St
  New York NY 10011
  212 633-8100

(G-10654)
IPC/RAZOR LLC (PA)
277 Park Ave Fl 39 (10172-2901)
PHONE......................212 551-4500
Douglas Korn, *Mng Member*
EMP: 60 **EST:** 2010
SALES (est): 88.3MM **Privately Held**
SIC: 3541 Machine tools, metal cutting type

(G-10655)
IPM US INC
276 5th Ave Rm 203 (10001-4509)
PHONE......................212 481-7967
Gaelle Pagy, *President*
▲ **EMP:** 6
SALES (est): 479.1K **Privately Held**
SIC: 2258 Lace & warp knit fabric mills

(G-10656)
IRADJ MOINI COUTURE LTD
403 W 46th St (10036-3510)
PHONE......................212 594-9242
Iradj Moini, *President*
Roya Darroudi, *Director*
EMP: 12
SQ FT: 800
SALES: 500K **Privately Held**
SIC: 3911 Jewelry, precious metal

(G-10657)
IRENE GOODMAN LITERARY AGENCY
27 W 24th St Ste 700b (10010-4105)
PHONE......................212 604-0330
Irene Goodman, *President*
Beth Vesel, *Senior VP*
Miriam Kriss, *Vice Pres*
EMP: 5
SALES (est): 454.1K **Privately Held**
SIC: 7372 Publishers' computer software

(G-10658)
IRIDESSE INC
600 Madison Ave Fl 5 (10022-1615)
PHONE......................212 230-6000
Fax: 212 230-6891
Patrick B Dorsey, *President*
Judith A Baldissard, *Principal*
Michael W Connolly, *Principal*
James N Fernandez, *Principal*
Robert L Cepek, *Chairman*
EMP: 15
SALES (est): 1.9MM **Privately Held**
SIC: 3911 Necklaces, precious metal

(G-10659)
IRISH AMERICA INC
Also Called: Irish America Magazine
875 Avnue Of Amricas 2100 (10001)
PHONE......................212 725-2993
Niall O'Dowd, *Publisher*
Kevin Mangan, *Controller*
Brendon Maclua, *Shareholder*
EMP: 20
SQ FT: 3,000
SALES (est): 1.5MM
SALES (corp-wide): 8.7B **Privately Held**
WEB: www.smurfitkappa.com
SIC: 2721 Magazines: publishing only, not printed on site
HQ: Smurfit Kappa Packaging Limited
  Beech Hill
  Dublin

(G-10660)
IRISH ECHO NEWSPAPER CORP
165 Madison Ave Rm 302 (10016-5431)
PHONE......................212 482-4818
Fax: 212 482-6569
Peter Quinn, *Ch of Bd*
Mairtin Muilleoir, *Publisher*
Mairtin Omuilleoir, *Publisher*
Raymond Ohanlon, *Editor*
Mairead Tully, *Sales Staff*
EMP: 19 **EST:** 1928
SQ FT: 3,000
SALES (est): 1.3MM **Privately Held**
WEB: www.irishecho.com
SIC: 2711 Newspapers: publishing only, not printed on site

(G-10661)
IRISH TRIBUNE INC
Also Called: Irish Voice Newspaper
875 Avenue Of The Amerrm2 Rm 2100 (10001)
PHONE......................212 684-3366
Niell O'Dowd, *President*
Robert S Bennett, *Partner*
Sean E Crowley, *Partner*
Ann Marie Zito, *Opers Mgr*
Meghan Sweeney, *Corp Comm Staff*
EMP: 14
SALES (est): 856.2K
SALES (corp-wide): 8.7B **Privately Held**
WEB: www.smurfitkappa.com
SIC: 2711 Newspapers
HQ: Smurfit Kappa Packaging Limited
  Beech Hill
  Dublin

(G-10662)
IRON EAGLE GROUP INC (PA)
Also Called: (A DEVELOPMENT STAGE COMPANY)
160 W 66th St Apt 41g (10023-6565)
PHONE......................888 481-4445
Fax: 917 591-6227
Joseph E Antonini, *Ch of Bd*
Jed M Sabio, *Exec VP*
EMP: 21
SQ FT: 800
SALES (est): 24.8MM **Privately Held**
SIC: 1389 Construction, repair & dismantling services

(G-10663)
IRV INC
Also Called: Warshaw Jacobson Group
540 Broadway Fl 4 (10012-3953)
PHONE......................212 334-4507
Fax: 212 966-4017
Steve Warshaw, *President*
Sal Mercadante, *President*
Jay Warshaw, *Vice Pres*
Jennifer Fernandez, *Office Mgr*
EMP: 23
SALES (est): 2.2MM **Privately Held**
SIC: 7372 7371 Prepackaged software; custom computer programming services

(G-10664)
IRVING FARM COFFEE CO INC (PA)
151 W 19th St Fl 6 (10011-4158)
PHONE......................212 206-0707
David Elwell, *President*
Christien Lauro, *Manager*
Clyde Miller, *Director*
Teresa Von Fuchs, *Director*
Joshua Littlefield, *Advisor*
EMP: 4
SALES (est): 1MM **Privately Held**
WEB: www.irvingfarm.com
SIC: 2095 Roasted coffee

(G-10665)
ISAAC WALDMAN INC
36 W 47th St Ste 1002 (10036-8637)
PHONE......................212 354-8220
Fax: 212 730-9258
Isaac Waldman, *President*
EMP: 7
SALES (est): 750K **Privately Held**
SIC: 3915 Diamond cutting & polishing

(G-10666)
ISABEL TOLEDO ENTERPRISES INC
1181 Broadway Fl 7 (10001-7432)
PHONE......................212 685-0948
Isabel Toledo, *President*
Ruben Toledo, *Vice Pres*
EMP: 6
SALES (est): 720K **Privately Held**
SIC: 2339 Women's & misses' outerwear

(G-10667)
ISFEL CO INC (PA)
Also Called: Top Stuff
110 W 34th St Rm 1101 (10001-2115)
PHONE......................212 736-6216
Fax: 212 465-0645
Joseph Feldman, *President*
Vivian Schwartz, *Production*
Cara Szczygiel, *Production*

New York - New York County (G-10668)

▲ EMP: 8
SQ FT: 2,000
SALES (est): 3.4MM Privately Held
WEB: www.topstuff.com
SIC: 2369 Girls' & children's outerwear

(G-10668)
ISONICS CORPORATION (PA)
535 8th Ave Fl 3 (10018-4305)
PHONE.....................212 356-7400
Christopher Toffales, Ch of Bd
John Sakys, President
Marshall Combs, Vice Pres
Daniel J Grady, Vice Pres
Gregory A Meadows, CFO
EMP: 4
SALES: 22.1MM Publicly Held
WEB: www.isonics.com
SIC: 2819 3674 Isotopes, radioactive; silicon wafers, chemically doped

(G-10669)
ITC MFG GROUP INC
109 W 38th St Rm 701 (10018-3673)
PHONE.....................212 684-3696
Fax: 212 532-2097
Anthony Dadika, President
Irwin Jaeger, Vice Pres
MEI Francese, Manager
EMP: 10
SQ FT: 6,000
SALES (est): 900K Privately Held
SIC: 2241 3965 2759 Labels, woven; fasteners, buttons, needles & pins; tags; printing

(G-10670)
ITEM-EYES INC (HQ)
Also Called: Nouveaux Div
114 W 41st St Fl 5 (10036-7308)
PHONE.....................631 321-0923
Fax: 212 704-0784
Martin Axman, President
Christine Hadjigeorge, Project Mgr
Richard Isaacson, CFO
Robin Jackie, Finance Mgr
Mark Abramson, VP Sales
◆ EMP: 70
SQ FT: 7,000
SALES (est): 17.3MM
SALES (corp-wide): 91.4MM Publicly Held
WEB: www.item-eyes.com
SIC: 2337 2339 5137 Skirts, separate: women's, misses' & juniors'; jackets & vests, except fur & leather: women's; slacks: women's, misses' & juniors'; women's & children's clothing
PA: Hampshire Group, Limited
 1924 Pearman Dairy Rd
 Anderson SC 29625
 212 540-5666

(G-10671)
IZQUIERDO STUDIOS LTD
34 W 28th St 6 (10001-4201)
PHONE.....................212 807-9757
Fax: 212 366-5249
Martin Izquierdo, President
John Inquaqiato, Vice Pres
Jeffrey Scherer, Vice Pres
EMP: 13
SQ FT: 2,000
SALES (est): 1.3MM Privately Held
SIC: 2389 Theatrical costumes

(G-10672)
IZUN PHARMACEUTICALS CORP (PA)
1 Rockefeller Plz Fl 11 (10020-2073)
PHONE.....................212 618-6357
William Levine, CEO
EMP: 6
SALES (est): 1.2MM Privately Held
WEB: www.izunpharma.com
SIC: 2834 Pharmaceutical preparations

(G-10673)
J & H CREATIONS INC
19 W 36th St Fl 3 (10018-7103)
PHONE.....................212 465-0962
Fax: 212 465-0950
Jay Baek, President
▲ EMP: 20
SQ FT: 2,000
SALES (est): 2.6MM Privately Held
WEB: www.jhcreation.com
SIC: 3961 5094 Costume jewelry, ex. precious metal & semiprecious stones; jewelry

(G-10674)
J & M TEXTILE CO INC
505 8th Ave Rm 701 (10018-4552)
PHONE.....................212 268-8000
Fax: 212 268-2152
Maria Wiesiolek, President
▲ EMP: 11
SQ FT: 7,000
SALES (est): 1.1MM Privately Held
SIC: 2241 5131 Glove lining fabrics; piece goods & notions

(G-10675)
J & X PRODUCTION
247 W 37th St Rm 1501 (10018-5056)
PHONE.....................646 366-8288
Guo Jun Lin, Owner
EMP: 10
SALES: 105K Privately Held
SIC: 2311 Men's & boys' suits & coats

(G-10676)
J A G DIAMOND MANUFACTURERS
580 5th Ave Ste 905b (10036-4733)
PHONE.....................212 575-0660
Volf Goldrath, President
Sharon Fink,
EMP: 7
SALES (est): 587.5K Privately Held
SIC: 3915 Diamond cutting & polishing

(G-10677)
J EDLIN INTERIORS LTD
122 W 27th St Fl 2 (10001-6274)
PHONE.....................212 243-2111
Fax: 212 645-0865
Jeffrey Edlin, President
Joyse Edlin, Vice Pres
EMP: 10
SALES (est): 1MM Privately Held
WEB: www.reisner.net
SIC: 2391 Curtains & draperies

(G-10678)
J H JEWELRY CO INC
12 W 32nd St Fl 12 (10001-1293)
PHONE.....................212 239-1330
Fax: 212 564-1087
Jack Leitman, President
Robert Hertz, Vice Pres
EMP: 11
SQ FT: 3,000
SALES (est): 1MM Privately Held
SIC: 3911 Jewelry, precious metal

(G-10679)
J M B APPAREL DESIGNER GROUP
214 W 39th St Rm 508 (10018-4428)
PHONE.....................212 764-8410
Ben Choy, President
Bob Arochas, Vice Pres
Marcella Law, CFO
EMP: 5
SALES: 100K Privately Held
SIC: 2389 Men's miscellaneous accessories

(G-10680)
J PERCY FOR MRVIN RCHARDS LTD (HQ)
512 Fashion Ave (10018-4603)
PHONE.....................212 944-5300
Morris Goldfarb, Ch of Bd
Sammy Aaron, President
Andrew Reid, Vice Pres
Allan Inger, CFO
Lee Lipton, Admin Sec
◆ EMP: 40
SQ FT: 12,000
SALES (est): 4.3MM
SALES (corp-wide): 2.3B Publicly Held
SIC: 2339 2386 2371 2337 Women's & misses' outerwear; women's & misses' jackets & coats, except sportswear; coats & jackets, leather & sheep-lined; fur coats & other fur apparel; women's & misses' suits & coats
PA: G-Iii Apparel Group, Ltd.
 512 7th Ave Fl 35
 New York NY 10018
 212 403-0500

(G-10681)
J R GOLD DESIGNS LTD
555 5th Ave Fl 19 (10017-2416)
PHONE.....................212 922-9292
Fax: 212 922-2992
Rami Uziel, President
Rina Uziel, Principal
EMP: 10
SQ FT: 2,500
SALES (est): 10MM Privately Held
WEB: www.rinalimor.com
SIC: 3911 5094 Jewelry, precious metal; jewelry

(G-10682)
J R NITES (PA)
1400 Broadway 6th Frl (10018)
PHONE.....................212 354-9670
John Klein, Principal
EMP: 8
SALES (est): 1MM Privately Held
SIC: 2335 Women's, juniors' & misses' dresses

(G-10683)
J-TREND SYSTEMS INC
244 5th Ave Ste C294 (10001-7604)
PHONE.....................646 688-3272
Charlotte Chen, President
Sha Wen Chen, COO
▲ EMP: 5
SALES (est): 410K Privately Held
SIC: 3089 Plastic containers, except foam

(G-10684)
J9 TECHNOLOGIES INC
25 Broadway Fl 9 (10004-1058)
PHONE.....................412 586-5038
Allen G Wasserberger, President
Carly Campbell, Controller
Robert C Roach, CTO
EMP: 20
SALES (est): 2MM
SALES (corp-wide): 2.1MM Privately Held
SIC: 7372 Operating systems computer software
PA: Axxiome Usa Llc
 100 Park Ave Fl 16
 New York NY

(G-10685)
JAC USA INC
45 Broadway Fl 18 (10006-3007)
PHONE.....................212 841-7430
Kazunari Okuda, Ch of Bd
Sinji Naka, President
Mary Bailey, Manager
EMP: 5
SQ FT: 1,400
SALES (est): 3.1MM
SALES (corp-wide): 43.4B Privately Held
WEB: www.jacusa.com
SIC: 3728 Aircraft parts & equipment
HQ: Japan Aerospace Corporation
 1-1-1, Minamiaoyama
 Minato-Ku TKY 107-0
 357 855-970

(G-10686)
JACKEL INC
Also Called: Jackel International
1359 Broadway Fl 17 (10018-7117)
PHONE.....................908 359-2039
Pansy Muller, President
Graham Summerfield, CFO
April Wasnick, Manager
▲ EMP: 100
SQ FT: 11,800
SALES (est): 16.1MM Privately Held
WEB: www.jackelus.com
SIC: 2844 Cosmetic preparations

(G-10687)
JACKS AND JOKERS 52 LLC
215 E 68th St Apt 5o (10065-5720)
PHONE.....................917 740-2595
Scot Lerner,
EMP: 5

SALES (est): 602.9K Privately Held
SIC: 2321 Blouses, boys': made from purchased materials

(G-10688)
JACKSON DAKOTA INC (PA)
979 3rd Ave Ste 503 (10022-1393)
PHONE.....................212 838-9444
Fax: 212 758-6413
Dakota Jackson, President
Lucas Leibman, Creative Dir
▲ EMP: 2
SQ FT: 5,500
SALES (est): 6.1MM Privately Held
WEB: www.dakotajackson.com
SIC: 2512 Upholstered household furniture

(G-10689)
JACLYN INC
Also Called: Lindsay Lyn Accessories Div
330 5th Ave Rm 1305 (10001-3101)
PHONE.....................212 736-5657
Howard Rucker, Division Mgr
Bonnie Levy, VP Sales
EMP: 10
SALES (corp-wide): 33.9MM Publicly Held
WEB: www.jaclyninc.com
SIC: 2335 Dresses, paper: cut & sewn
PA: Jaclyn, Inc.
 197 W Spring Valley Ave # 101
 Maywood NJ 07607
 201 909-6000

(G-10690)
JACMEL JEWELRY INC (PA)
1385 Broadway Fl 8 (10018-2102)
PHONE.....................718 349-4300
Fax: 718 349-4466
Jack Rahmey, Ch of Bd
Morris Dweck, Vice Pres
Shelley Tabor, Accounts Mgr
Randy Leder, Accounts Exec
Fred Erani, Manager
▲ EMP: 159 EST: 1977
SQ FT: 60,000
SALES: 100MM Privately Held
WEB: www.jacmel.com
SIC: 3911 Medals, precious or semi-precious metal

(G-10691)
JACOB HIDARY FOUNDATION INC
10 W 33rd St Rm 900 (10001-3317)
PHONE.....................212 736-6540
Abe Hidary, President
Jack A Hidary, Vice Pres
EMP: 10
SALES: 123.4K Privately Held
SIC: 2329 Men's & boys' sportswear & athletic clothing

(G-10692)
JACQUES MORET INC (PA)
Also Called: Moret Group, The
1411 Broadway Fl 8 (10018-3565)
PHONE.....................212 354-2400
Fax: 212 629-8690
Ralph Harary, Ch of Bd
Joey Harary, President
Gary Herwitz, Exec VP
Morris Chehebar, Vice Pres
Allan Sassoon, Vice Pres
▲ EMP: 123
SQ FT: 30,000
SALES: 300MM Privately Held
WEB: www.moret.com
SIC: 2339 5137 Women's & misses' athletic clothing & sportswear; sportswear, women's & children's

(G-10693)
JACQUES TORRES CHOCOLATE LLC
350 Hudson St Frnt 1 (10014-4504)
PHONE.....................212 414-2462
Saida Chabla, Mktg Dir
Andrea Martinez, Office Mgr
Jacques Torres, Mng Member
Christine Brestlin, Executive
▲ EMP: 30
SALES (est): 5.1MM Privately Held
SIC: 2066 Chocolate

▲ = Import ▼ = Export
◆ = Import/Export

GEOGRAPHIC SECTION

(G-10694)
JAGUAR CASTING CO INC
100 United Nations Plz (10017-1713)
PHONE 212 869-0197
Fax: 212 869-1970
Puzant Khatchadourian, *President*
Jean Khatchadourian, *Vice Pres*
EMP: 25 EST: 1966
SQ FT: 5,000
SALES (est): 3MM Privately Held
SIC: 3915 3911 Jewelers' castings; jewelry, precious metal

(G-10695)
JAGUAR JEWELRY CASTING NY INC
48 W 48th St Ste 500 (10036-1713)
PHONE 212 768-4848
Hovig Kajajian, *President*
Kevork Vekerejian, *Owner*
Jack Hallak, *Vice Pres*
Jospeh Nakashian, *Info Tech Mgr*
EMP: 9
SQ FT: 2,500
SALES: 2MM Privately Held
SIC: 3911 Jewelry apparel

(G-10696)
JAKOB SCHLAEPFER INC
307 W 38th St Rm 804 (10018-3539)
PHONE 212 221-2323
Peter Anderegg, *President*
Shkendie Kaziu, *Vice Pres*
David Sommers, *Controller*
EMP: 3
SQ FT: 1,000
SALES: 1.3MM Privately Held
WEB: www.jakobschlaepfer.com
SIC: 2221 2241 Broadwoven fabric mills, manmade; trimmings, textile

(G-10697)
JAMES MORGAN PUBLISHING (PA)
5 Penn Plz Fl 23 (10001-1810)
PHONE 212 655-5470
David L Hancock, *Chairman*
Cindy Sauer, *Vice Pres*
EMP: 1
SALES: 2MM Privately Held
SIC: 2731 Books: publishing & printing

(G-10698)
JAMES THOMPSON & COMPANY INC (PA)
381 Park Ave S Rm 718 (10016-8806)
PHONE 212 686-4242
Fax: 212 686-9528
Robert B Judell, *President*
Gail Boyle, *Senior VP*
Marc Bieler, *Vice Pres*
Steve Luchansky, *Vice Pres*
Sara Loffredo, *MIS Mgr*
▲ EMP: 7 EST: 1860
SQ FT: 1,800
SALES (est): 20.7MM Privately Held
WEB: www.jamesthompson.com
SIC: 2299 Burlap, jute

(G-10699)
JANE BOHAN INC
611 Broadway (10012-2608)
PHONE 212 529-6090
Jane Bohan, *President*
Laura Bothfeld, *Vice Pres*
▲ EMP: 6
SQ FT: 300
SALES: 970K Privately Held
SIC: 3911 Jewelry, precious metal

(G-10700)
JAPAN PRINTING & GRAPHICS INC
160 Broadway Lbby D (10038-4201)
PHONE 212 406-2905
Fax: 212 766-0125
Hiroshi Ono, *President*
EMP: 7
SALES: 500K Privately Held
WEB: www.japanprint.com
SIC: 2759 2752 Commercial printing; commercial printing, lithographic

(G-10701)
JARVIK HEART INC
333 W 52nd St Ste 700 (10019-6238)
PHONE 212 397-3911
Robert Jarvik MD, *President*
Sam McConchie, *Prdtn Mgr*
Pamela Whitehead, *Purch Mgr*
Alani Intintolo, *Engineer*
Latha Kavala, *Engineer*
EMP: 36
SALES (est): 6.6MM Privately Held
WEB: www.jarvikheart.com
SIC: 3845 Surgical support systems: heart-lung machine, exc. iron lung

(G-10702)
JASANI DESIGNS USA INC
25 W 43rd St Ste 704 (10036-7414)
PHONE 212 257-6465
Ameya Joshi, *President*
Sanjay Gokhale, *Accounts Mgr*
Abhay R Jasani, *Director*
Shyam Jasani, *Director*
Satish Joshi, *Director*
EMP: 8
SALES (est): 2.5MM Privately Held
SIC: 3911 Jewelry, precious metal
PA: Jasani
Hw - 6010, 6th Floor,
Mumbai MH

(G-10703)
JAX COCO USA LLC
5 Penn Plz Ste 2300 (10001-1821)
PHONE 347 688-8198
William Craig, *Exec VP*
Joel McMinn, *Sales Mgr*
John Craig,
▲ EMP: 5 EST: 2013
SALES: 300K Privately Held
SIC: 2076 Coconut oil

(G-10704)
JAY IMPORT COMPANY INC (PA)
Also Called: J & H International
41 Madison Ave Fl 12 (10010-2251)
PHONE 212 683-2727
Fax: 212 686-1703
Harry Jay, *President*
Michael Jay, *Vice Pres*
Adrian Haas, *Controller*
Raizy Cousin, *Accountant*
David Jay, *Sales Mgr*
EMP: 20
SQ FT: 8,000
SALES (est): 11MM Privately Held
SIC: 2392 5023 Decorative home furnishings & supplies

(G-10705)
JAYA APPAREL GROUP LLC
1384 Broadway Fl 18 (10018-6122)
PHONE 212 764-4980
Don Lewis, *Branch Mgr*
EMP: 15
SALES (corp-wide): 110MM Privately Held
SIC: 2339 Women's & misses' athletic clothing & sportswear
PA: Jaya Apparel Group Llc
5175 S Soto St
Vernon CA 90058
323 584-3500

(G-10706)
JAYDEN STAR LLC
385 5th Ave Rm 507 (10016-3346)
PHONE 212 686-0400
Maurice Mandelbaum, *Vice Pres*
Winnie Fung, *Accounts Mgr*
Jason Mandelbaum, *Mng Member*
EMP: 0
SQ FT: 5,000
SALES: 5.6MM Privately Held
SIC: 3911 Jewelry apparel

(G-10707)
JAYMAR JEWELRY CO INC
357 W 36th St Rm 203 (10018-6455)
PHONE 212 564-4788
Fax: 212 564-2957
Jayson Levy, *President*
EMP: 5
SQ FT: 3,000
SALES (est): 300K Privately Held
SIC: 3961 Costume jewelry, ex. precious metal & semiprecious stones

(G-10708)
JC CRYSTAL INC
260 W 35th St Fl 10 (10001-2528)
PHONE 212 594-0858
Jimmy Ping Chong Loh, *President*
Lana Hertel, *Sales Dir*
▲ EMP: 50
SQ FT: 5,000
SALES: 5.8MM Privately Held
SIC: 3911 Jewelry apparel

(G-10709)
JCDECAUX MALLSCAPE LLC (DH)
3 Park Ave Fl 33 (10016-5902)
PHONE 646 834-1200
Bernard Pariost, *CEO*
Jean-Luc Decaux, *CEO*
Gabrielle Brussel, *Admin Sec*
EMP: 8
SALES (est): 1.3MM
SALES (corp-wide): 10.8MM Privately Held
SIC: 2531 Benches for public buildings
HQ: Jcdecaux North America, Inc.
3 Park Ave Fl 33
New York NY 10016
646 834-1200

(G-10710)
JD CLASS INC
463 Fashion Ave Rm 600 (10018-8721)
PHONE 212 764-6663
Fax: 212 764-6689
Yeong Seob Shim, *President*
▲ EMP: 6 EST: 2003
SALES (est): 540K Privately Held
SIC: 2329 Athletic (warmup, sweat & jogging) suits: men's & boys'

(G-10711)
JDS GRAPHICS INC
Also Called: Jds Graphics
226 W 37th St Fl 10 (10018-9016)
PHONE 973 330-3300
Debra Yuran, *President*
Sheryl Heller, *Vice Pres*
Jeffery Kirschenbaum, *Vice Pres*
Robert Generale, *Controller*
EMP: 12
SQ FT: 2,500
SALES (est): 1.1MM Privately Held
WEB: www.jdsgraphics.com
SIC: 2752 Commercial printing, offset

(G-10712)
JDT INTERNATIONAL LLC
276 5th Ave Rm 704 (10001-4527)
PHONE 212 400-7570
Tariq Osman, *Branch Mgr*
EMP: 8
SALES (corp-wide): 1.8MM Privately Held
SIC: 2392 5021 Blankets, comforters & beddings; beds & bedding
PA: Jdt International, Llc
3532 Tonkawood Rd
Minnetonka MN 55345
952 933-2558

(G-10713)
JEAN & ALEX JEWELRY MFG & CONS
587 5th Ave Fl 2 (10017-8757)
PHONE 212 935-7621
Fax: 212 935-7645
Zeng Qiang Pu, *President*
Kuofan Chen, *Vice Pres*
Michelle Tsang, *Treasurer*
EMP: 15
SQ FT: 3,000
SALES (est): 1.3MM Privately Held
SIC: 3911 Jewelry apparel

(G-10714)
JEAN PHILIPPE FRAGRANCES LLC
551 5th Ave Rm 1500 (10176-1599)
PHONE 212 983-2640
Fax: 212 983-4197
Terrence Augenbraun, *Exec VP*
Dwyane Williams, *Human Res Mgr*
Gary Roth, *VP Sales*
Jean Madar,
Russell Greenberg,
◆ EMP: 57
SQ FT: 7,000
SALES: 12.4MM
SALES (corp-wide): 468.5MM Publicly Held
WEB: www.interparfumsinc.com
SIC: 2844 Toilet preparations; perfumes & colognes; cosmetic preparations
PA: Inter Parfums, Inc.
551 5th Ave
New York NY 10176
212 983-2640

(G-10715)
JEAN PIERRE INC
Also Called: Jean Pierre Cosmetics
320 5th Ave Fl 3 (10001-3115)
PHONE 718 440-7349
Jeffrey Mamiye, *Vice Pres*
EMP: 10 EST: 2013
SALES (est): 1.2MM Privately Held
SIC: 2844 Cosmetic preparations

(G-10716)
JEANJER LLC
Also Called: Just For Men Div
1400 Broadway Fl 15 (10018-5300)
PHONE 212 944-1330
Joe Nakash, *President*
AVI Naakash, *Vice Pres*
Ralph Nakash, *Treasurer*
Charles Flores, *Sales Mgr*
John Banevicius 6463838123, *Manager*
▲ EMP: 3000
SALES (est): 105.7MM Privately Held
SIC: 2331 2337 2339 2369 Blouses, women's & juniors': made from purchased material; suits: women's, misses' & juniors'; slacks: women's, misses' & juniors'; girls' & children's outerwear

(G-10717)
JEANS INC
1357 Broadway Ste 411 (10018-7101)
PHONE 646 223-1122
Deepak Ramani, *Vice Pres*
Paul Maulucci, *Controller*
EMP: 9 EST: 2015
SALES (est): 283.6K Privately Held
SIC: 2399 5136 Hand woven apparel; men's & boys' clothing

(G-10718)
JEMCAP SERVICING LLC
360 Madison Ave Rm 1902 (10017-7158)
PHONE 212 213-9353
EMP: 5
SALES (est): 278.3K Privately Held
SIC: 1389 Roustabout service

(G-10719)
JENALEX CREATIVE MARKETING INC
116 E 57th St Fl 3 (10022-2613)
PHONE 212 935-2266
Fax: 212 319-6385
Alexandra Grondahl, *President*
Ludwig J Cserhat, *Corp Secy*
Sylvia Lazzari, *Vice Pres*
Saad Bourkadi, *CFO*
▲ EMP: 7
SQ FT: 2,000
SALES (est): 800.2K Privately Held
WEB: www.jenalex.com
SIC: 3999 Boutiquing: decorating gift items with sequins, fruit, etc.

(G-10720)
JENVIE SPORT INC
255 W 36th St 6 (10018-7555)
P.O. Box 856, Bethpage (11714-0017)
PHONE 212 967-2322
Fax: 212 239-8598
Eli Goldstein, *President*
Linda Swobe, *Vice Pres*
Neil Seiden, *Accountant*
Sandy Kanter, *Bookkeeper*
Steven Goldstein, *Admin Sec*
▲ EMP: 7
SQ FT: 9,000

New York - New York County (G-10721) — GEOGRAPHIC SECTION

SALES (est): 1MM **Privately Held**
WEB: www.jenvie.com
SIC: 2339 Sportswear, women's

(G-10721)
JERRY SORBARA FURS INC
39 W 32nd St Rm 1400 (10001-3841)
PHONE.....................................212 594-3897
Fax: 212 643-9098
Jerry Sorbara, *President*
Sal Sorbara, *Vice Pres*
Catherine Wilson, *Treasurer*
EMP: 11
SQ FT: 4,500
SALES: 2MM **Privately Held**
SIC: 2371 Apparel, fur

(G-10722)
JETSON ELECTRIC BIKES LLC
175 Varick St Fl 5 (10014-7411)
PHONE.....................................908 309-8880
Josh Sultan, *CEO*
▲ EMP: 3
SQ FT: 5,000
SALES: 1.3MM **Privately Held**
SIC: 3751 Bicycles & related parts

(G-10723)
JEWELMAK INC
344 E 59th St Fl 1&2 (10022-1593)
PHONE.....................................212 398-2999
Fax: 212 398-0721
Andy Goetz, *President*
Vincent Carotenuto, *Vice Pres*
June Hardy, *Accountant*
Thanh Bui, *Human Res Dir*
Sanya Yeh, *Accounts Exec*
EMP: 25
SQ FT: 7,240
SALES: 35MM **Privately Held**
WEB: www.jewelmak.com
SIC: 3911 Jewelry, precious metal

(G-10724)
JEWELRY ARTS MANUFACTURING
151 W 46th St Fl 12 (10036-8512)
PHONE.....................................212 382-3583
Fax: 212 869-0594
Alberto Tapia, *CEO*
Ligia Tapia, *Vice Pres*
EMP: 40
SALES (est): 2.6MM **Privately Held**
WEB: www.jewelartjewelers.com
SIC: 3915 3961 3911 Jewelers' castings; jewelry polishing for the trade; jewelry soldering for the trade; costume jewelry; jewelry, precious metal

(G-10725)
JEWELS BY STAR LTD
555 5th Ave Fl 7 (10017-9267)
PHONE.....................................212 308-3490
Fax: 212 486-0140
Yehuda Fouzailoff, *President*
Rafael Fouzailoff, *Vice Pres*
EMP: 20
SQ FT: 2,000
SALES: 2.4MM **Privately Held**
WEB: www.jewelsbystar.com
SIC: 3911 Jewelry, precious metal

(G-10726)
JEWELTEX MFG CORP
48 W 48th St Ste 507 (10036-1713)
PHONE.....................................212 921-8188
Fax: 212 921-8706
Barry Rosenfeld, *President*
Joe Itzkowitx, *Admin Sec*
EMP: 13
SQ FT: 1,500
SALES (est): 2.3MM **Privately Held**
SIC: 3911 Jewelry, precious metal

(G-10727)
JEWISH WEEK INC (PA)
1501 Broadway Ste 505 (10036-5504)
PHONE.....................................212 921-7822
Richard Waloff, *Publisher*
Gary Rosenblatt, *Principal*
Robert Goldblum, *Editor*
Jannet Hoffman, *Comptroller*
Stephanie Leone, *Accounts Exec*
♦ EMP: 35 EST: 1970
SQ FT: 6,000

SALES (est): 5.2MM **Privately Held**
WEB: www.thejewishweek.com
SIC: 2711 Newspapers: publishing only, not printed on site

(G-10728)
JFE ENGINEERING CORPORATION
350 Park Ave Fl 27th (10022-6022)
PHONE.....................................212 310-9320
Moriyasu Nagae, *General Mgr*
Hedenori Tawaza, *Branch Mgr*
Shinji Kojima, *Manager*
Youji Ookawa,
EMP: 10
SALES (corp-wide): 29.3B **Privately Held**
SIC: 3312 Sheet or strip, steel, hot-rolled
HQ: Jfe Engineering Corporation
1-8-1, Marunouchi
Chiyoda-Ku TKY 100-0
362 120-800

(G-10729)
JFE STEEL AMERICA INC (PA)
600 3rd Ave Rm 1201 (10016-1921)
PHONE.....................................212 310-9320
Kaoru Okamoto, *President*
Ann Fronimakas, *Admin Sec*
EMP: 7
SALES (est): 1.2MM **Privately Held**
SIC: 3312 Sheet or strip, steel, hot-rolled; sheet or strip, steel, cold-rolled: own hot-rolled; tinplate; iron & steel: galvanized, pipes, plates, sheets, etc.

(G-10730)
JFS INC
Also Called: Joe Fresh
531 W 26th St Unit 531 (10001-5514)
PHONE.....................................646 264-1200
Mario Grauso, *President*
EMP: 14 EST: 2010
SALES (est): 3MM
SALES (corp-wide): 35.2B **Privately Held**
SIC: 2253 T-shirts & tops, knit
HQ: Loblaw Companies Limited
1 Presidents Choice Cir
Brampton ON L6Y 5
905 459-2500

(G-10731)
JGX LLC
1407 Broadway Rm 1416 (10018-2842)
PHONE.....................................212 575-1244
Nouri Jaradeh, *Vice Pres*
Jack Grazi, *Vice Pres*
EMP: 5
SQ FT: 3,000
SALES (est): 59.4K **Privately Held**
SIC: 2369 Leggings: girls', children's & infants'

(G-10732)
JILL FAGIN ENTERPRISES INC (PA)
Also Called: Jillery
107 Avenue B (10009-6264)
PHONE.....................................212 674-9383
Fax: 212 674-9401
Jill Fagin, *President*
EMP: 8
SALES: 670K **Privately Held**
SIC: 3961 3262 Costume jewelry; vitreous china table & kitchenware

(G-10733)
JIM HENSON COMPANY INC
Also Called: Jim Henson Productions
117 E 69th St (10021-5004)
PHONE.....................................212 794-2400
Fax: 212 439-7452
Howard Sharp, *Manager*
EMP: 50
SALES (corp-wide): 11.3MM **Privately Held**
WEB: www.farscape.com
SIC: 3942 3944 2731 Dolls & stuffed toys; games, toys & children's vehicles; book publishing
PA: The Jim Henson Company Inc
1416 N La Brea Ave
Los Angeles CA 90028
323 856-6680

(G-10734)
JIM WACHTLER INC
1212 Avenue Of The Ste 2200 (10036)
PHONE.....................................212 755-4367
James Wachtler, *President*
EMP: 3
SALES: 3MM **Privately Held**
SIC: 3915 5094 5944 Gems, real & imitation: preparation for settings; diamond cutting & polishing; precious stones (gems); jewelry, precious stones & precious metals

(G-10735)
JIMEALE INCORPORATED
130 Church St Ste 163 (10007-2226)
P.O. Box 841, Southport CT (06890-0841)
PHONE.....................................917 686-5383
Jimeale Jorgensen, *Chairman*
▲ EMP: 6
SALES (est): 692.9K **Privately Held**
SIC: 2389 Men's miscellaneous accessories

(G-10736)
JIMMY CRYSTAL NEW YORK CO LTD
47 W 37th St Fl 3 (10018-6294)
PHONE.....................................212 594-0858
Fax: 212 564-0566
Ping Chong Loh, *Ch of Bd*
Alice Chui, *Vice Pres*
▲ EMP: 32
SQ FT: 13,500
SALES (est): 3.5MM **Privately Held**
SIC: 3231 3911 Watch crystals, glass; jewelry, precious metal

(G-10737)
JIRANIMO INDUSTRIES LTD
Also Called: Long Paige
49a W 37th St (10018-6202)
PHONE.....................................212 921-5106
Fax: 212 768-2835
Parviz Shirian, *President*
Aaron Ostad, *President*
Adam Ostad, *Vice Pres*
Shamouiel Ostad, *Treasurer*
Salim Panah, *Accounts Mgr*
▲ EMP: 12
SQ FT: 17,500
SALES (est): 1.3MM **Privately Held**
SIC: 2335 Women's, juniors' & misses' dresses

(G-10738)
JISAN TRADING CORPORATION
519 8th Ave Rm 810 (10018-4586)
PHONE.....................................212 244-1269
SOO Kang, *President*
EMP: 20
SALES (est): 960K **Privately Held**
SIC: 2384 Dressing gowns, men's & women's: from purchased materials

(G-10739)
JJ BASICS LLC (PA)
525 7th Ave Rm 307 (10018-4930)
PHONE.....................................212 768-4779
Steven Bensadigh, *President*
Ivan Sandlers, *COO*
Vivien Zhao, *Vice Pres*
Donna Klein, *Opers Mgr*
Randi Gefen, *VP Sales*
▲ EMP: 21
SQ FT: 5,400
SALES (est): 3MM **Privately Held**
SIC: 2369 Girls' & children's outerwear

(G-10740)
JJ FANTASIA INC
38 W 32nd St (10001-3816)
PHONE.....................................212 868-1198
Fax: 212 868-1195
Cheng Hsuan Wu, *Ch of Bd*
EMP: 7
SALES (est): 628.5K **Privately Held**
SIC: 3961 Jewelry apparel, non-precious metals

(G-10741)
JLM COUTURE INC (PA)
Also Called: J L M
525 Fashion Ave Rm 1703 (10018-4935)
PHONE.....................................212 921-7058

Fax: 212 764-6960
Daniel M Sullivan, *Ch of Bd*
Joseph L Murphy, *President*
Jerry Walkenfeld, *Controller*
Sean Abrams, *Credit Mgr*
Katie Kilbride, *Sales Dir*
▼ EMP: 60
SALES (est): 16MM **Publicly Held**
WEB: www.jlmcouture.com
SIC: 2335 Wedding gowns & dresses

(G-10742)
JM MANUFACTURER INC
241 W 37th St Rm 924 (10018-6970)
PHONE.....................................212 869-0626
Liuchu Jia, *Owner*
EMP: 3
SQ FT: 700
SALES: 4.6MM **Privately Held**
SIC: 2221 Apparel & outerwear fabric, manmade fiber or silk

(G-10743)
JM STUDIO INC
247 W 35th St Fl 3 (10001-1926)
PHONE.....................................646 546-5514
Yim Lan Dong, *CEO*
▲ EMP: 15
SQ FT: 6,000
SALES (est): 1.8MM **Privately Held**
SIC: 2389 5699 Uniforms & vestments; sports apparel

(G-10744)
JOAN BOYCE LTD (PA)
19 W 44th St Ste 417 (10036-5900)
PHONE.....................................212 867-7474
Joan Boyce, *President*
Allen Boyce, *Vice Pres*
EMP: 4
SQ FT: 1,100
SALES: 7MM **Privately Held**
WEB: www.joanboyce.com
SIC: 3911 5944 Jewelry, precious metal; jewelry stores

(G-10745)
JOBSON MEDICAL INFORMATION LLC (PA)
100 Ave Of Amer Fl 9 (10013)
PHONE.....................................212 274-7000
Fax: 212 431-0500
Michael Tansey, *CEO*
Frank Bennicasa, *Publisher*
Marck Ferrera, *Publisher*
Carol Jaxel, *Publisher*
John Orr, *CFO*
▲ EMP: 120
SALES (est): 120MM **Privately Held**
WEB: www.revoptom.com
SIC: 2721 2741 Magazines: publishing & printing; miscellaneous publishing

(G-10746)
JOCKEY INTERNATIONAL INC
Also Called: Jockey Store
1411 Broadway Rm 1010 (10018-3560)
PHONE.....................................212 840-4900
John Brody, *Exec VP*
Janine Forgie, *Branch Mgr*
EMP: 30
SALES (corp-wide): 1.4B **Privately Held**
SIC: 2254 Knit underwear mills
PA: Jockey International, Inc.
2300 60th St
Kenosha WI 53140
262 658-8111

(G-10747)
JOE BENBASSET INC (PA)
213 W 35th St Fl 11 (10001-1903)
PHONE.....................................212 268-4920
Fax: 212 268-4920
Murray Benbasset, *President*
Mila Finkelstein, *Controller*
♦ EMP: 25 EST: 1948
SQ FT: 10,000
SALES (est): 8.1MM **Privately Held**
SIC: 2339 Sportswear, women's

(G-10748)
JOED PRESS
242 W 36th St Fl 8 (10018-7542)
PHONE.....................................212 243-3620
Angela Vann, *General Mgr*
EMP: 5 EST: 2010

GEOGRAPHIC SECTION

New York - New York County (G-10774)

SALES (est): 239.5K **Privately Held**
SIC: 2759 Commercial printing

(G-10749)
JOHN KOCHIS CUSTOM DESIGNS
237 W 35th St Ste 702 (10001-1952)
PHONE..................................212 244-6046
John Kochis, *Owner*
EMP: 7
SALES: 300K **Privately Held**
SIC: 2311 Tailored suits & formal jackets

(G-10750)
JOHN KRISTIANSEN NEW YORK INC
665 Broadway Frnt (10012-2300)
PHONE..................................212 388-1097
John Kristiansen, *President*
Monroe France, *Assistant VP*
EMP: 10
SALES (est): 893.4K **Privately Held**
SIC: 2389 Costumes

(G-10751)
JOHN MARSHALL SOUND INC
630 9th Ave Ste 1108 (10036-3743)
PHONE..................................212 265-6066
Nathan Lincoln, *Editor*
Barbara Vlahides, *Producer*
Beth Laschever, *Office Admin*
Cheary Marshall,
EMP: 8
SALES (est): 1.1MM **Privately Held**
SIC: 3652 Master records or tapes, preparation of

(G-10752)
JOHN N FEHLINGER CO INC (PA)
20 Vesey St Rm 1000 (10007-4225)
PHONE..................................212 233-5656
Fax: 212 233-5717
Kevin Arcuri, *President*
John Capuano, *Treasurer*
Peter Sarkar, *Accountant*
Sheree Pelmen, *Admin Sec*
▲ EMP: 15 EST: 1945
SQ FT: 4,000
SALES (est): 4.9MM **Privately Held**
WEB: www.fehlingerco.com
SIC: 3491 3561 5084 5085 Steam traps; pumps & pumping equipment; industrial pumps & parts; industrial machinery & equipment; water pumps (industrial); valves & fittings

(G-10753)
JOHN SZOKE GRAPHICS INC
Also Called: John Szoke Editions
24 W 57th St Ste 304 (10019-3918)
PHONE..................................212 219-8300
John Szoke, *President*
▲ EMP: 8
SQ FT: 10,000
SALES (est): 520K **Privately Held**
WEB: www.johnszokeeditions.com
SIC: 2741 Miscellaneous publishing

(G-10754)
JOHN VARVATOS COMPANY
26 W 17th St Fl 12 (10011-5710)
PHONE..................................212 812-8000
John Varvatos, *President*
EMP: 30
SALES (est): 1.6MM **Privately Held**
WEB: www.nautica.com
SIC: 2329 5136 5611 6794 Men's & boys' sportswear & athletic clothing; men's & boys' sportswear & work clothing; men's & boys' robes, nightwear & undergarments; clothing, sportswear, men's & boys'; franchises, selling or licensing

(G-10755)
JOHNNY BIENSTOCK MUSIC
126 E 38th St (10016-2602)
PHONE..................................212 779-7977
John Bienstock, *Owner*
EMP: 25
SALES (est): 1.3MM **Privately Held**
SIC: 2741 Music books: publishing & printing

(G-10756)
JON TERI SPORTS INC (PA)
241 W 37th St Frnt 2 (10018-6797)
PHONE..................................212 398-0657
Fax: 212 302-2726
Rickie Freeman, *President*
Leora Platt, *Sales Staff*
Shanta Khairain, *Manager*
▲ EMP: 35 EST: 1981
SQ FT: 6,000
SALES (est): 5.4MM **Privately Held**
SIC: 2335 2337 Women's, juniors' & misses' dresses; suits: women's, misses' & juniors'

(G-10757)
JONATHAN MEIZLER LLC
Also Called: Title of Work
37 W 26th St Ph (10010-1049)
PHONE..................................212 213-2977
Jonathan Meizler, *Mfg Staff*
EMP: 7
SQ FT: 1,500
SALES: 380K **Privately Held**
SIC: 2389 Men's miscellaneous accessories

(G-10758)
JONATHAN MICHAEL COAT CORP
463 Fashion Ave Rm 1502 (10018-7596)
PHONE..................................212 239-9230
Fax: 212 239-9238
Bruce Heart, *President*
Nathan Printz, *Corp Secy*
▲ EMP: 7
SQ FT: 1,500
SALES (est): 810K **Privately Held**
SIC: 2339 Women's & misses' jackets & coats, except sportswear

(G-10759)
JONDEN MANUFACTURING CO INC (PA)
1410 Broadway Rm 1103 (10018-9356)
PHONE..................................516 442-4895
Linda Smilowitz, *CEO*
Jon Smilowitz, *President*
Linda Leal, *Principal*
John Smilowitz, *Chairman*
Denise Smilowitz, *Exec VP*
▲ EMP: 8
SALES (est): 4.8MM **Privately Held**
WEB: www.jonden.com
SIC: 2339 Sportswear, women's

(G-10760)
JORDACHE ENTERPRISES INC
Fubu Jeans By Je Sport Co Div
1400 Broadway Rm 1415 (10018-5336)
PHONE..................................212 944-1330
AVI Nakash, *Exec VP*
Ezri Sirveb, *Branch Mgr*
EMP: 100
SALES (corp-wide): 1.3B **Privately Held**
WEB: www.jordache.com
SIC: 2339 2325 2369 2331 Slacks: women's, misses' & juniors'; men's & boys' trousers & slacks; slacks: girls' & children's; jackets; girls', children's & infants'; shirts, women's & juniors': made from purchased materials; men's & boys' furnishings; shirts: girls', children's & infants'
PA: Jordache Enterprises Inc.
   1400 Broadway Rm 1404b
   New York NY 10018
   212 643-8400

(G-10761)
JORDACHE ENTERPRISES INC (PA)
1400 Broadway Rm 1404b (10018-5336)
PHONE..................................212 643-8400
Fax: 212 768-3096
Joe Nakash, *CEO*
Jonathan Bennett, *Managing Dir*
Ralph Nakash, *Corp Secy*
Eddie Benaderet, *Exec VP*
Bob Ross, *Exec VP*
◆ EMP: 145

SALES (est): 1.3B **Privately Held**
WEB: www.jordache.com
SIC: 2339 2325 2369 2331 Slacks: women's, misses' & juniors'; men's & boys' trousers & slacks; slacks: girls' & children's; jackets; girls', children's & infants'; shirts, women's & juniors': made from purchased materials; men's & boys' furnishings; shirts: girls', children's & infants'

(G-10762)
JORDAN SCOTT DESIGNS LTD
Also Called: Plaza Group Creation
25 W 36th St Fl 12 (10018-7677)
PHONE..................................212 947-4250
Fax: 212 947-4247
Edward Schantz, *CEO*
EMP: 25
SQ FT: 4,500
SALES (est): 2.4MM **Privately Held**
SIC: 3911 Jewelry, precious metal

(G-10763)
JOSEPH (UK) INC
1061 Madison Ave Grnd (10028-0239)
PHONE..................................212 570-0077
Fax: 212 570-0487
Hiroaki Sumi, *Ch of Bd*
Louis Loketch, *Principal*
EMP: 5
SALES (est): 370K **Privately Held**
SIC: 2329 5621 5651 Men's & boys' sportswear & athletic clothing; women's clothing stores; jeans stores

(G-10764)
JOSEPH ABBOUD MANUFACTURING
650 5th Ave Fl 20 (10019-7687)
PHONE..................................212 586-9140
Marty Staff, *Ch of Bd*
Anthony Sapienza, *President*
Eric Spiel, *Vice Pres*
Marisol Fernandez, *Asst Treas*
Brian Hrenenko, *Asst Treas*
EMP: 5
SALES (est): 230K **Privately Held**
SIC: 2326 2339 Men's & boys' work clothing; women's & misses' athletic clothing & sportswear

(G-10765)
JOSEPH INDUSTRIES INC (PA)
Also Called: Color Fx
1410 Broadway Rm 1501 (10018-9834)
PHONE..................................212 764-0010
Prakash Joseph, *President*
▲ EMP: 5
SQ FT: 5,000
SALES (est): 3.8MM **Privately Held**
SIC: 2389 Men's miscellaneous accessories

(G-10766)
JOSEPH TREU SUCCESSORS INC
104 W 27th St Rm 5b (10001-6210)
PHONE..................................212 691-7026
Fax: 212 463-8821
Harvey Schreibman, *President*
Arlene Schreibman, *Corp Secy*
EMP: 5
SQ FT: 3,000
SALES: 700K **Privately Held**
SIC: 3953 Marking devices

(G-10767)
JOSHUA LINER GALLERY LLC
540 W 28th St Frnt (10001-5770)
PHONE..................................212 244-7415
Joshua Liner, *Owner*
EMP: 10
SALES (est): 1.2MM **Privately Held**
SIC: 3443 Liners/lining

(G-10768)
JOSIE ACCESSORIES INC (PA)
Also Called: Elrene Home Fashions
261 5th Ave Fl 10 (10017-7701)
PHONE..................................212 889-6376
Fax: 212 481-1738
◆ EMP: 75 EST: 1945
SQ FT: 20,000

SALES (est): 10.9MM **Privately Held**
SIC: 2392 Tablecloths: made from purchased materials; placemats, plastic or textile

(G-10769)
JOTALY INC
1385 Broadway Fl 12 (10018-6118)
PHONE..................................212 886-6000
Fax: 212 886-6006
Ofer Azrielant, *Ch of Bd*
John C Esposito, *Vice Pres*
Jennifer Bernal, *Facilities Mgr*
Erika Dejesus, *Production*
Cristina Sousa, *Human Res Dir*
▲ EMP: 750
SQ FT: 48,000
SALES: 101.2MM **Privately Held**
SALES (corp-wide): 210.8B **Publicly Held**
WEB: www.andin.com
SIC: 3911 Jewelry, precious metal
HQ: Richline Group, Inc.
   1385 Broadway Fl 12
   New York NY 10018
   212 886-6000

(G-10770)
JOURNAL REGISTER COMPANY
450 W 33rd St Fl 11 (10001-2603)
PHONE..................................212 257-7212
EMP: 66
SALES (corp-wide): 828.3MM **Privately Held**
SIC: 2711 Newspapers, publishing & printing
PA: Journal Register Company
   5 Hanover Sq Fl 25
   New York NY 10004
   212 257-7212

(G-10771)
JOURNAL REGISTER COMPANY (PA)
5 Hanover Sq Fl 25 (10004-4008)
PHONE..................................212 257-7212
John Paton, *CEO*
James W Hall, *Ch of Bd*
Paul Provost, *President*
Matt Derienzo, *Publisher*
Lynette Gannon, *Publisher*
EMP: 40
SQ FT: 36,443
SALES (est): 828.3MM **Privately Held**
WEB: www.journalregister.com
SIC: 2711 Newspapers, publishing & printing

(G-10772)
JOVANI FASHION LTD
1370 Broadway Fl 4 (10018-7786)
PHONE..................................212 279-0222
Fax: 212 279-0133
Saul Maslavi, *President*
Abraham Maslavi, *Vice Pres*
Carol Ramirez, *Cust Mgr*
Jamie Hughes, *Accounts Exec*
Jessica Santiago, *Accounts Exec*
▲ EMP: 30
SQ FT: 8,000
SALES (est): 2.8MM **Privately Held**
WEB: www.jovani.com
SIC: 2335 Women's, juniors' & misses' dresses; gowns, formal

(G-10773)
JOYCE TRIMMING INC
109 W 38th St (10018-3615)
PHONE..................................212 719-3110
Fax: 212 719-2091
Hwe Young Lee, *President*
▲ EMP: 8
SQ FT: 2,000
SALES: 2MM **Privately Held**
WEB: www.ejoyce.com
SIC: 3965 Buttons & parts

(G-10774)
JOYCHARGE INC
510 Madison Ave (10022-5730)
PHONE..................................646 321-1127
Daniel Legziel, *Principal*
EMP: 99
SALES (est): 6.1MM **Privately Held**
SIC: 1381 7389 Drilling oil & gas wells;

New York - New York County (G-10775)

(G-10775)
JRG APPAREL GROUP COMPANY LTD
1407 Broadway Rm 317 (10018-3858)
PHONE.....................212 997-0900
Jay Gorman, *Ch of Bd*
Christina Tierney, *General Mgr*
▲ EMP: 6
SQ FT: 2,100
SALES (est): 450K **Privately Held**
SIC: 2211 Denims

(G-10776)
JS BLANK & CO INC
112 Madison Ave Fl 7 (10016-7484)
PHONE.....................212 689-4835
Fax: 212 696-1659
Joseph S Blank, *CEO*
Barbara Blank, *Vice Pres*
EMP: 25
SQ FT: 7,500
SALES (est): 2.6MM **Privately Held**
SIC: 2323 Men's & boys' neckwear

(G-10777)
JSA JEWELRY INC
2 W 46th St Ste 506 (10036-4555)
PHONE.....................212 764-4504
Norayr Mayisoglu, *President*
EMP: 10
SALES (est): 780K **Privately Held**
SIC: 3911 Jewelry, precious metal

(G-10778)
JSC DESIGNS LTD
550 Fashion Ave Fl 22 (10018-3223)
PHONE.....................212 302-1001
Mitchell Hops, *President*
Alicia Moscovitch, *Accounts Mgr*
▲ EMP: 20
SQ FT: 8,000
SALES (est): 2MM **Privately Held**
SIC: 2339 Service apparel, washable: women's

(G-10779)
JUDYS GROUP INC
1400 Broadway Rm 919 (10018-0698)
PHONE.....................212 921-0515
Fax: 212 302-5259
Howard Schlossberg, *President*
Michele Tepper, *Exec VP*
Michelle Pepper, *CFO*
▲ EMP: 50
SQ FT: 11,000
SALES (est): 9.5MM **Privately Held**
WEB: www.judysgroup.com
SIC: 2337 2339 2335 Suits: women's, misses & juniors'; athletic clothing: women's, misses' & juniors'; women's, juniors' & misses' dresses

(G-10780)
JUICE PRESS LLC (PA)
110 E 59th St Fl 28 (10022-1317)
PHONE.....................212 777-0034
Marcus Antebi, *CEO*
Alex Jay, *Marketing Staff*
EMP: 8
SALES (est): 3.7MM **Privately Held**
SIC: 3556 Juice extractors, fruit & vegetable: commercial type

(G-10781)
JULES SMITH LLC
1369 Broadway Fl 4 (10018-7214)
PHONE.....................718 783-2495
Gina Nigrelli, *Mng Member*
EMP: 5
SQ FT: 400
SALES (est): 520K **Privately Held**
SIC: 3961 Costume jewelry

(G-10782)
JULIA JORDAN CORPORATION
530 Fashion Ave Rm 505 (10018-4890)
PHONE.....................646 214-3090
Mansour Zar, *Owner*
Fernada Navarrete, *Assistant*
EMP: 10
SALES (est): 390.6K **Privately Held**
SIC: 2337 Women's & misses' suits & coats

(G-10783)
JULIUS COHEN JEWELERS INC
699 Madison Ave Fl 4 (10065-8040)
PHONE.....................212 371-3050
Fax: 212 593-2771
Leslie Steinweiss, *President*
Anderson King, *Manager*
EMP: 7 EST: 1956
SALES (est): 590K **Privately Held**
WEB: www.juliuscohen.com
SIC: 3911 5944 Bracelets, precious metal; rings, finger: precious metal; pins (jewelry), precious metal; jewelry stores

(G-10784)
JULIUS KLEIN GROUP
580 5th Ave Ste 500 (10036-4727)
PHONE.....................212 719-1811
Julius Klein, *Owner*
Moshe Klein, *Sales Dir*
Hershy Schwartz, *Sales Executive*
Pearl Rothman, *Admin Sec*
▲ EMP: 50
SALES (est): 4.1MM **Privately Held**
SIC: 3915 Diamond cutting & polishing

(G-10785)
JULIUS LOWY FRAME RESTORING CO
232 E 59th St 4fn (10022-1464)
PHONE.....................212 861-8585
Fax: 212 988-0443
Lawrence A Shar, *President*
John Evans, *Controller*
Patty Tan, *Human Resources*
Lisa Wyer, *VP Sales*
Michael Tramis, *Manager*
EMP: 35
SQ FT: 20,000
SALES (est): 4.4MM **Privately Held**
WEB: www.lowyonline.com
SIC: 2499 8999 Picture frame molding, finished; art restoration

(G-10786)
JUMP DESIGN GROUP INC
Also Called: Jump Apparel Group, The
1400 Broadway Fl 2 (10018-1075)
PHONE.....................212 869-3300
Fax: 212 869-3639
Glenn Schlossberg, *Ch of Bd*
Terry Friedman, *President*
Peter Gabbe, *Principal*
Patrick M Corrigan, *CFO*
Joann Abellar, *Office Mgr*
▲ EMP: 140
SQ FT: 18,000
SALES (est): 38.3MM **Privately Held**
WEB: www.jumpapparel.com
SIC: 2335 Women's, juniors' & misses' dresses

(G-10787)
JUMPROPE INC
121 W 27th St Ste 1204 (10001-6261)
P.O. Box 1616 (10113-1616)
PHONE.....................347 927-5867
Jesse Olsen, *CEO*
Justin Meyer, *COO*
Nathan Patton, *Engineer*
EMP: 9
SQ FT: 500
SALES (est): 580K **Privately Held**
SIC: 7372 Educational computer software

(G-10788)
JUNE JACOBS LABS LLC
460 Park Ave Fl 16 (10022-1829)
PHONE.....................212 471-4830
Tiffany Cavallaro, *Comptroller*
June Jacobs, *Human Resources*
Marvin Sternlicht,
Peter T Roth,
EMP: 65
SALES (corp-wide): 14.7MM **Privately Held**
SIC: 2844 Cosmetic preparations
PA: June Jacobs Labs, Llc
46 Graphic Pl
Moonachie NJ 07074
201 329-9100

(G-10789)
JUNIPER NETWORKS INC
1 Penn Plz Ste 1901 (10119-1901)
PHONE.....................212 520-3300
Carrie Alvarado, *Manager*
Sue Salek, *Senior Mgr*
Pete Fitzgerald, *Account Dir*
EMP: 638 **Publicly Held**
SIC: 3577 Computer peripheral equipment
PA: Juniper Networks, Inc.
1133 Innovation Way
Sunnyvale CA 94089

(G-10790)
JUPITER CREATIONS INC
330 7th Ave Ste 901 (10001-5010)
PHONE.....................917 493-9393
Michael Katina, *President*
Steven Kaplun, *VP Sales*
Kristen Farrell, *Graphic Designe*
▲ EMP: 2
SQ FT: 1,000
SALES: 3MM **Privately Held**
SIC: 3944 3942 Games, toys & children's vehicles; airplanes, toy; automobiles & trucks, toy; dolls & stuffed toys

(G-10791)
JUST BOTTOMS & TOPS INC (PA)
Also Called: Hot Cashews
1412 Broadway Rm 1808 (10018-9228)
PHONE.....................212 564-3202
Fax: 212 564-3205
Mickey Mait, *President*
Sanders Acker, *Vice Pres*
Mitch Levy, *Vice Pres*
Aaron Feder, *Treasurer*
Jerry Hymowitz, *Admin Sec*
EMP: 10
SQ FT: 3,900
SALES (est): 915.3K **Privately Held**
SIC: 2329 2339 Sweaters & sweater jackets: men's & boys'; women's & misses' outerwear

(G-10792)
JUST BRASS INC
215 W 90th St Apt 9a (10024-1224)
PHONE.....................212 724-5447
Fax: 212 875-0124
Ronald Zabinski, *President*
EMP: 5
SALES: 150K **Privately Held**
SIC: 3172 5136 2321 Personal leather goods; shirts, men's & boys'; men's & boys' furnishings

(G-10793)
JUST PERFECT MSP LTD
48 W 48th St Ste 401 (10036-1727)
PHONE.....................877 201-0005
▲ EMP: 45 EST: 1994
SQ FT: 5,000
SALES (est): 1.2MM
SALES (corp-wide): 4.1MM **Privately Held**
SIC: 3911 5094 Jewelry, precious metal; jewelry & precious stones
PA: Art-Tec Jewelry Designs Ltd
48 W 48th St Ste 401
New York NY 10036
212 719-2941

(G-10794)
JUSTYNA KAMINSKA NY INC
1270 Broadway Rm 708 (10001-3224)
PHONE.....................917 423-5527
Justyna Kaminska Cabbad, *President*
▲ EMP: 1
SQ FT: 800
SALES: 1MM **Privately Held**
SIC: 3911 Jewelry, precious metal

(G-10795)
K ROAD MOAPA SOLAR LLC
295 Madison Ave Fl 37 (10017-6343)
PHONE.....................212 351-0535
William V Kriegel,
Gerrit Nicholas,
Daniel Oshea,
Thomas N Tureen,
EMP: 10
SQ FT: 4,000
SALES (est): 723.5K **Privately Held**
SIC: 3621 Power generators

(G-10796)
K ROAD POWER MANAGEMENT LLC (PA)
767 3rd Ave Fl 37 (10017-2077)
PHONE.....................212 351-0535
Fax: 212 351-0530
William Kriegel, *CEO*
Gerrit Nicholas, *Managing Dir*
Mark Friedland, *Exec VP*
Carl Weatherley-White, *CFO*
Buvron Arnelle, *Office Mgr*
EMP: 15
SALES (est): 1.6MM **Privately Held**
SIC: 3612 Transformers, except electric

(G-10797)
K T P DESIGN CO INC
118 E 28th St Rm 707 (10016-8448)
PHONE.....................212 481-6613
Patrick Walsh, *President*
▼ EMP: 15
SALES: 1.6MM **Privately Held**
WEB: www.customtie.com
SIC: 2339 Neckwear & ties: women's, misses' & juniors'

(G-10798)
K2 INTERNATIONAL CORP
22 W 32nd St Fl 9 (10001-3807)
PHONE.....................212 947-1734
John Hyun Kim, *President*
Jennifer Moon, *General Mgr*
Diane Kim, *Accounts Mgr*
▲ EMP: 5
SQ FT: 7,000
SALES (est): 390K **Privately Held**
SIC: 3961 Costume jewelry

(G-10799)
KADMON CORPORATION LLC (PA)
450 E 29th St Fl 5 (10016-8367)
PHONE.....................212 308-6000
Harlan Waksal, *CEO*
Samuel D Waksal, *Chairman*
Harvey Sussman, *Counsel*
Paul Fagan, *Exec VP*
Steve Gordon, *Exec VP*
EMP: 8
SALES (est): 32.3MM **Privately Held**
SIC: 2834 Pharmaceutical preparations

(G-10800)
KADMON HOLDINGS INC
450 E 29th St (10016-8367)
PHONE.....................212 308-6000
Bart M Schwartz, *Ch of Bd*
Harlan W Waksal, *President*
Lawrence K Cohen, *Exec VP*
Eva Heyman, *Exec VP*
Larry Witte, *Exec VP*
EMP: 138
SQ FT: 48,892
SALES (est): 10.5MM **Privately Held**
SIC: 2836 2834 Biological products, except diagnostic; pharmaceutical preparations

(G-10801)
KAHN-LUCAS-LANCASTER INC
112 W 34th St Ste 600 (10120-0700)
PHONE.....................212 239-2407
Justine Berndt, *Vice Pres*
Linda Mulligan, *Design Engr*
Maria Rizzolo, *VP Sales*
Rhonda Shelman, *VP Sales*
Howard Kahn, *Branch Mgr*
EMP: 80
SALES (corp-wide): 41.7MM **Privately Held**
WEB: www.kahnlucas.com
SIC: 2369 Girls' & children's outerwear
PA: Kahn-Lucas-Lancaster, Inc.
306 Primrose Ln
Mountville PA 17554
717 537-4140

(G-10802)
KALEIDOSCOPE IMAGING INC
307 W 38th St Fl 6 (10018-9537)
PHONE.....................212 631-9947
Fax: 212 631-9948
Garo Ksparian, *Partner*
Peter Shaubert, *Manager*
EMP: 30

GEOGRAPHIC SECTION

New York - New York County (G-10828)

SALES (corp-wide): 16.6MM **Privately Held**
SIC: 2752 Commercial printing, lithographic
PA: Kaleidoscope Imaging, Inc.
  700 N Sacramento Blvd # 2
  Chicago IL 60612
  773 722-9300

(G-10803)
KALEKO BROS
580 5th Ave Ste 928 (10036-4726)
PHONE..................212 819-0100
Jerome Kaleko, *Partner*
EMP: 5 EST: 1948
SQ FT: 2,000
SALES (est): 281.6K **Privately Held**
SIC: 3915 Diamond cutting & polishing

(G-10804)
KALIKOW BROTHERS LP
34 W 33rd St Fl 4n (10001-3304)
PHONE..................212 643-0315
Fax: 212 643-0320
Marc Kalikow, *President*
Paul Levine, *Vice Pres*
Jeffrey Rosen, *Controller*
EMP: 30 EST: 1929
SQ FT: 8,000
SALES (est): 2MM **Privately Held**
WEB: www.fishmantobin.com
SIC: 2325 Trousers, dress (separate): men's, youths' & boys'
HQ: F&T Apparel Llc
  4000 Chemical Rd Ste 500
  Plymouth Meeting PA 19462
  610 828-8400

(G-10805)
KALLEN CORP
Also Called: Capstone Printing
99 Hudson St Lbby 2 (10013-2815)
P.O. Box 516 (10014-0516)
PHONE..................212 242-1470
Alan Finkelstein, *President*
EMP: 5
SQ FT: 3,000
SALES (est): 520K **Privately Held**
SIC: 2759 Commercial printing

(G-10806)
KALTEX AMERICA INC
350 5th Ave Ste 7100 (10118-0110)
PHONE..................212 971-0575
Fax: 212 971-0362
Hebe Schecter, *CEO*
Rafael M Kalach, *Ch of Bd*
Jennifer Mason, *CFO*
Fred Walck, *Administration*
EMP: 18 EST: 1987
SQ FT: 1,000
SALES: 161MM **Privately Held**
SIC: 2339 2325 Jeans: women's, misses' & juniors'; jeans: men's, youths' & boys'
HQ: Kaltex North America, Inc.
  350 5th Ave Ste 7100
  New York NY 10118
  212 894-3200

(G-10807)
KALTEX NORTH AMERICA INC (HQ)
350 5th Ave Ste 7100 (10118-0110)
PHONE..................212 894-3200
Rafael Kalach, *Ch of Bd*
Tom McGrath, *Vice Pres*
Nevolia Williams, *Finance*
▲ EMP: 10
SALES (est): 199.4MM **Privately Held**
WEB: www.kaltexhome.com
SIC: 2392 Comforters & quilts: made from purchased materials
PA: Kaltex Textiles, S.A. De C.V.
  Ingenieros Militares No. 2
  Naucalpan EDOMEX. 53380
  773 733-9000

(G-10808)
KAPRIELIAN ENTERPRISES INC
Also Called: Concord Settings
207 W 25th St Fl 8 (10001-7158)
PHONE..................212 645-6623
Fax: 212 255-8128
Hratch Kaprielian, *President*
Maria Chiang, *Accountant*
Timothy Kilburn, *Manager*
▲ EMP: 70
SQ FT: 6,000
SALES (est): 9.4MM **Privately Held**
WEB: www.kaprielian.com
SIC: 3911 3915 Jewel settings & mountings, precious metal; jewelers' materials & lapidary work

(G-10809)
KARBRA COMPANY
151 W 46th St Fl 10 (10036-8512)
PHONE..................212 736-9300
Fax: 212 736-9303
Sing Ming Liu, *Partner*
Carole Roth, *Partner*
Peter Roth, *Partner*
Fiam Ildiko Roth, *Vice Pres*
George Barna, *MIS Dir*
EMP: 140 EST: 1940
SQ FT: 10,000
SALES (est): 13.1MM **Privately Held**
WEB: www.karbra.com
SIC: 3915 3911 3369 3341 Jewelers' castings; jewelry, precious metal; nonferrous foundries; secondary nonferrous metals

(G-10810)
KAREN KANE INC
1441 Broadway Fl 33 (10018-1905)
PHONE..................212 827-0980
Fax: 212 827-0987
Ashly Juskus, *Buyer*
Becky Blair, *Manager*
Tiffany Bowe, *Manager*
EMP: 12
SALES (corp-wide): 53.9MM **Privately Held**
SIC: 2339 Women's & misses' outerwear
PA: Karen Kane, Inc.
  2275 E 37th St
  Vernon CA 90058
  323 588-0000

(G-10811)
KAREN MILLER LTD (PA)
60 W 38th St Rm 200 (10018-0034)
PHONE..................212 819-9550
Fax: 212 819-0016
Mehrdad Sarraf, *President*
Ramin Sarraf, *Vice Pres*
Aghdas Sarraf, *Admin Sec*
▲ EMP: 16
SQ FT: 16,000
SALES: 7MM **Privately Held**
WEB: www.karenmiller.net
SIC: 2335 Ensemble dresses: women's, misses' & juniors'; gowns, formal

(G-10812)
KAS-RAY INDUSTRIES INC
Also Called: Kay-Ray Industries
122 W 26th St (10001-6804)
PHONE..................212 620-3144
Fax: 212 620-4210
Tony Petrizzo, *President*
EMP: 10
SQ FT: 10,000
SALES (est): 1.7MM **Privately Held**
WEB: www.kasray.com
SIC: 2752 5112 5021 Commercial printing, offset; stationery & office supplies; office furniture

(G-10813)
KASEYA US SALES LLC
62 W 22nd St Ste 2r (10010-5147)
PHONE..................415 694-5700
Fred Voccola, *Mng Member*
Isaac Itenberg,
EMP: 99
SALES: 20MM **Privately Held**
SIC: 7372 Prepackaged software

(G-10814)
KASPER GROUP LLC (HQ)
1412 Broadway Fl 5 (10018-3330)
PHONE..................212 354-4311
EMP: 15
SALES (est): 1.7MM
SALES (corp-wide): 244.7MM **Privately Held**
SIC: 2339 Mfg Women's/Misses' Outerwear

PA: Jones Holdings Llc
  1411 Brdwy
  New York NY 10018
  215 785-4000

(G-10815)
KASPER GROUP LLC
1412 Broadway Fl 5 (10018-3330)
PHONE..................212 354-4311
Gregg Marks, *President*
Daniel Fishman, *CFO*
Clark Holm, *Finance*
Adele Askin, *Human Resources*
◆ EMP: 240
SALES: 350MM **Privately Held**
SIC: 2335 Women's, juniors' & misses' dresses

(G-10816)
KATE SPADE & COMPANY (PA)
2 Park Ave Fl 8 (10016-5613)
PHONE..................212 354-4900
Fax: 212 626-1800
Craig A Leavitt, *CEO*
Nancy J Karch, *Ch of Bd*
George M Carrara, *President*
Kirsten Bentley, *District Mgr*
Timothy F Michno, *Senior VP*
▲ EMP: 420
SQ FT: 135,000
SALES: 1.2B **Publicly Held**
WEB: www.lizclaiborne.com
SIC: 2331 5651 5136 5137 Women's & misses' blouses & shirts; family clothing stores; unisex clothing stores; men's & boys' clothing; women's & children's clothing; catalog & mail-order houses

(G-10817)
KATES PAPERIE LTD
188 Lafayette St Frnt A (10013-3200)
PHONE..................212 966-3904
Leonard Flax, *Manager*
Renee Holiday, *Manager*
Asif Iqbal, *Manager*
▲ EMP: 6
SALES (est): 330K **Privately Held**
SIC: 2759 Announcements: engraved

(G-10818)
KATHMANDO VALLEY PRESERVATION
Also Called: H Theophile
36 W 25th St Fl 17 (10010-2706)
PHONE..................212 727-0074
Erich Theophile, *Owner*
Beatriz Faustmann, *Project Mgr*
Axel Paganakis, *Engineer*
EMP: 10
SALES (est): 871.2K **Privately Held**
SIC: 3851 Temples & fronts, ophthalmic

(G-10819)
KATZ MARTELL FASHION TRDG INTL
1385 Broadway Rm 1401 (10018-6057)
PHONE..................212 840-0070
Fax: 212 840-0110
Debbie Martell, *President*
Bonnie Katz, *Vice Pres*
▲ EMP: 7 EST: 1998
SQ FT: 2,500
SALES (est): 820K **Privately Held**
SIC: 2339 Women's & misses' athletic clothing & sportswear

(G-10820)
KAUFMAN BROTHERS PRINTING
327 W 36th St Rm 403 (10018-6971)
PHONE..................212 563-1854
Fax: 212 268-4914
Harvey Kaufman, *Owner*
Bobby Nicol, *Vice Pres*
EMP: 5 EST: 1941
SQ FT: 2,000
SALES (est): 2MM **Privately Held**
SIC: 2752 2759 2789 Commercial printing, offset; letterpress printing; bookbinding & related work

(G-10821)
KAY SEE DENTAL MFG CO
777 Avenue Of The Apt 32 (10001)
PHONE..................816 842-2817
Yachiyo Smith, *President*
Clark Y Smith, *Vice Pres*
EMP: 12
SQ FT: 15,000
SALES (est): 1.4MM **Privately Held**
WEB: www.hydrocast.com
SIC: 3843 Dental equipment; dental materials

(G-10822)
KAYMIL PRINTING COMPANY INC
Also Called: Kaymil Ticket Company
140 W 30th St Frnt (10001-4005)
PHONE..................212 594-3718
Richwar Warner, *President*
EMP: 5 EST: 1961
SQ FT: 6,000
SALES (est): 248.2K **Privately Held**
WEB: www.kaymil.com
SIC: 2759 2752 Letterpress printing; screen printing; offset & photolithographic printing

(G-10823)
KAYO OF CALIFORNIA
525 Fashion Ave Rm 309 (10018-0485)
PHONE..................212 354-6336
Jesse Vasquez, *Office Mgr*
Steven Berman, *Manager*
EMP: 5
SALES (corp-wide): 20.2MM **Privately Held**
WEB: www.kayo.com
SIC: 2337 2339 Skirts, separate: women's, misses' & juniors'; sportswear, women's; shorts (outerwear): women's, misses' & juniors'; slacks: women's, misses' & juniors'
PA: Kayo Of California
  161 W 39th St
  Los Angeles CA 90037
  323 233-6107

(G-10824)
KBL HEALTHCARE LP
757 3rd Ave Fl 20 (10017-2046)
PHONE..................212 319-5555
Fax: 212 319-5591
Dr Marlene Krauss, *Manager*
EMP: 6
SALES (est): 599.2K **Privately Held**
SIC: 2834 Pharmaceutical preparations

(G-10825)
KBS COMMUNICATIONS LLC
Also Called: Mystery Scene Magazine
331 W 57th St Ste 148 (10019-3101)
PHONE..................212 765-7124
Kathleen M Stine, *Mng Member*
Brian Skupin,
EMP: 12
SALES (est): 950.6K **Privately Held**
WEB: www.mysteryscenemag.com
SIC: 2721 Magazines: publishing & printing

(G-10826)
KC COLLECTIONS LLC
1407 Broadway Rm 1710 (10018-2789)
PHONE..................212 302-4412
Fax: 212 840-7581
Bart Yanofsky,
Michael Carbone,
Kirk Oshan,
▲ EMP: 7
SQ FT: 4,000
SALES (est): 701.6K **Privately Held**
SIC: 2253 Cold weather knit outerwear, including ski wear

(G-10827)
KCP HOLDCO INC
603 W 50th St (10019-7029)
PHONE..................212 265-1500
Paul Blum, *CEO*
EMP: 1600
SALES (est): 98.8MM **Privately Held**
SIC: 3143 3171 5661 5632 Mfg Men's Footwear Mfg Womens Handbag/Purse

(G-10828)
KEARNEY-NATIONAL INC (HQ)
Also Called: Coto Technology
565 5th Ave Fl 4 (10017-2424)
PHONE..................212 661-4600
Robert R Dyson, *Ch of Bd*

(PA)=Parent Co (HQ)=Headquarters (DH)=Div Headquarters
✪ = New Business established in last 2 years

2017 Harris
New York Manufacturers Directory

433

New York - New York County (G-10829)

Marc Feldman, *Vice Pres*
Leigh Beck, *Accounts Mgr*
John Fitzsimons, *Admin Sec*
▲ **EMP:** 10 **EST:** 1988
SALES (est): 216.4MM
SALES (corp-wide): 512.4MM **Privately Held**
WEB: www.cotorelay.com
SIC: 3679 3694 3714 3625 Electronic switches; engine electrical equipment; fuel systems & parts, motor vehicle; relays & industrial controls
PA: The Dyson-Kissner-Moran Corporation
2515 South Rd Ste 5
Poughkeepsie NY 12601
212 661-4600

(G-10829)
KEILHAUER
200 Lexington Ave Rm 1101 (10016-6255)
PHONE 646 742-0192
Allen Primason, *Partner*
EMP: 10
SALES (est): 828.9K **Privately Held**
WEB: www.keilhauer.com
SIC: 2522 Chairs, office: padded or plain, except wood

(G-10830)
KELLY GRACE CORP (PA)
Also Called: Danny & Nicole
49 W 37th St Fl 10 (10018-0180)
PHONE 212 704-9603
Fax: 212 704-0462
Jamshid Zar, *Ch of Bd*
Daniel Zar, *President*
Esshagh Zar, *Vice Pres*
Korosh Zar, *Vice Pres*
Kenneth Prizeman, *Controller*
▲ **EMP:** 80
SQ FT: 16,000
SALES (est): 20.5MM **Privately Held**
WEB: www.dannyandnicole.com
SIC: 2335 Women's, juniors' & misses' dresses

(G-10831)
KEMP TECHNOLOGIES INC (PA)
1540 Broadway Fl 23 (10036-4039)
PHONE 917 688-4067
John Becker, *Ch of Bd*
Raymond Downes, *President*
Tim Quinn, *Sales Dir*
Sean Higgins, *Mktg Coord*
Bhargav Shukla, *Director*
▲ **EMP:** 54
SQ FT: 15,000
SALES (est): 6.3MM **Privately Held**
WEB: www.kemptechnologies.com
SIC: 3571 Electronic computers

(G-10832)
KENNETH COLE PRODUCTIONS LP (HQ)
603 W 50th St (10019-7051)
PHONE 212 265-1500
Michele Ferrandino, *Director*
Corinne O'Grady, *Executive Asst*
EMP: 34
SALES (est): 5.3MM
SALES (corp-wide): 731.4MM **Privately Held**
SIC: 3143 Men's footwear, except athletic
PA: Kenneth Cole Productions, Inc.
603 W 50th St
New York NY 10019
212 265-1500

(G-10833)
KENNETH COLE PRODUCTIONS INC (PA)
603 W 50th St (10019-7051)
PHONE 212 265-1500
Fax: 212 713-6670
Marc Schneider, *CEO*
Mia Dellosso-Caputo, *President*
Chris Nakatani, *President*
Joshua Schulman, *President*
Heather Anglin, *General Mgr*
▲ **EMP:** 277
SQ FT: 119,000
SALES (est): 731.4MM **Privately Held**
WEB: www.kennethcole.com
SIC: 3143 3144 3171 5661 Men's footwear, except athletic; women's footwear, except athletic; handbags, women's; purses, women's; shoe stores; women's boots; men's shoes; women's accessory & specialty stores; apparel accessories; costume jewelry; handbags; men's & boys' clothing stores

(G-10834)
KENNETH J LANE INC
20 W 37th St Fl 9 (10018-7367)
PHONE 212 868-1780
Kenneth J Lane, *President*
Susan Fogelman, *Bookkeeper*
EMP: 15
SQ FT: 5,500
SALES (est): 1MM **Privately Held**
SIC: 3961 Jewelry apparel, non-precious metals

(G-10835)
KENSINGTON & SONS LLC
Also Called: Sir Kensington's
270 Lafayette St Ste 200 (10012-3376)
PHONE 646 450-5735
Yan Sim, *Marketing Staff*
Mark Ramadan, *Mng Member*
Laura Villevieille, *Manager*
Scott Norton, *Creative Dir*
EMP: 30
SALES (est): 1.1MM **Privately Held**
SIC: 2035 2033 5149 Mayonnaise; mustard, prepared (wet); catsup: packaged in cans, jars, etc.; condiments

(G-10836)
KENSINGTON PUBLISHING CORP
Also Called: Zebra Books
119 W 40th St Fl 21 (10018-2522)
PHONE 212 407-1500
Fax: 212 935-0699
Steven Zacharius, *CEO*
Vince Kunkemueller, *Editor*
Mike Walters, *Editor*
Laurie Parkin, *Vice Pres*
Michael Rosamilia, *CFO*
EMP: 81
SQ FT: 25,000
SALES (est): 12.1MM **Privately Held**
WEB: www.kensingtonbooks.com
SIC: 2731 5192 Book publishing; books

(G-10837)
KENT ASSOCIATES INC
99 Battery Pl Apt 11p (10280-1324)
PHONE 212 675-0722
Herman Lederfarb, *President*
EMP: 8 **EST:** 1947
SQ FT: 4,000
SALES (est): 870K **Privately Held**
SIC: 2752 Commercial printing, offset

(G-10838)
KENT CHEMICAL CORPORATION
460 Park Ave Fl 7 (10022-1841)
PHONE 212 521-1700
John Farber, *Ch of Bd*
John Oram, *President*
Naveen Chandra, *Vice Pres*
Blaise Sarcone, *Vice Pres*
Susan Aibinder, *Treasurer*
EMP: 25 **EST:** 1983
SQ FT: 15,000
SALES (est): 3.5MM
SALES (corp-wide): 851.2MM **Privately Held**
SIC: 2821 2869 2911 2899 Polyvinyl chloride resins (PVC); flavors or flavoring materials, synthetic; perfume materials, synthetic; paraffin wax; fire retardant chemicals; unsupported plastics film & sheet; solutions, pharmaceutical
PA: Icc Industries Inc.
460 Park Ave Fl 7
New York NY 10022
212 521-1700

(G-10839)
KEY BRAND ENTERTAINMENT INC
104 Franklin St (10013-2923)
PHONE 212 966-5400
EMP: 121
SALES (corp-wide): 473K **Privately Held**
SIC: 2752 Lithographic Commercial Printing
PA: Key Brand Entertainment, Inc.
1619 Broadway Fl 9
New York NY 10019
917 421-5400

(G-10840)
KEY COMPUTER SVCS OF CHELSEA
227 E 56th St (10022-3754)
PHONE 212 206-8060
Fax: 212 206-8398
Paco Valeez, *President*
EMP: 60
SALES (est): 3.5MM **Privately Held**
SIC: 2759 7377 7372 7338 Commercial printing; computer rental & leasing; prepackaged software; resume writing service; facsimile transmission services; telephone communication, except radio

(G-10841)
KIDTELLECT INC
222 Broadway Level19 (10038-2510)
PHONE 617 803-1456
Phylaktis Georgiou, *President*
Charles Bart Clareman, *COO*
Azadeh Jamalian, *Officer*
EMP: 5
SALES (est): 372.3K **Privately Held**
SIC: 3944 Games, toys & children's vehicles

(G-10842)
KIDZ CONCEPTS LLC
Also Called: One Step Up Kids
1412 Brdwy Fl 3 (10018)
PHONE 212 398-1110
Harry Adjmi,
Irwin Gindi,
◆ **EMP:** 52
SQ FT: 15,000
SALES (est): 11.2MM **Privately Held**
WEB: www.kidzconcepts.com
SIC: 2389 5137 Costumes; women's & children's sportswear & swimsuits

(G-10843)
KIDZ WORLD INC
Also Called: High Energy U. S. A.
226 W 37th St Fl 12 (10018-9850)
PHONE 212 563-4949
▲ **EMP:** 15
SQ FT: 2,172
SALES (est): 102.5K **Privately Held**
SIC: 2329 Men's & boys' sportswear & athletic clothing

(G-10844)
KILTRONX ENVIRO SYSTEMS LLC
845 3rd Ave Fl 11 (10022-6601)
PHONE 239 273-8870
Gabriel Kaszovitz, *Ch of Bd*
EMP: 30
SQ FT: 1,500
SALES: 10MM **Privately Held**
SIC: 2295 Chemically coated & treated fabrics

(G-10845)
KIM EUGENIA INC
347 W 36th St Rm 502 (10018-7262)
PHONE 212 674-1345
Fax: 212 674-1769
Eugenia Kim, *President*
Marvin Rodriguez, *Opers Mgr*
Laura Burnosky, *Opers Staff*
Drew Fettner, *Production*
AVI Sanichar, *Controller*
▲ **EMP:** 8
SQ FT: 1,400
SALES (est): 1.5MM **Privately Held**
WEB: www.eugeniakim.com
SIC: 2353 Hats, caps & millinery

(G-10846)
KIM SEYBERT INC (PA)
37 W 37th St Fl 9 (10018-6219)
PHONE 212 564-7850
Fax: 212 695-8803
Kim Seybert, *President*
Shirlene Asmath, *CFO*
Maloney Dyer, *Executive*
▲ **EMP:** 16
SQ FT: 10,000
SALES (est): 2.3MM **Privately Held**
WEB: www.kimseybert.com
SIC: 2392 Household furnishings

(G-10847)
KIMBALL OFFICE INC
215 Park Ave S Fl 3 (10003-1616)
PHONE 212 753-6161
Fax: 212 593-0837
Brian Raynor, *Regional Mgr*
Michael Donahue, *Vice Pres*
Scott Siskind, *Manager*
EMP: 30
SALES (corp-wide): 635.1MM **Publicly Held**
SIC: 2522 Office desks & tables: except wood
HQ: Kimball Office Inc.
1600 Royal St
Jasper IN 47549
812 482-1600

(G-10848)
KIMMERIDGE ENERGY MGT CO LLC (PA)
400 Madison Ave Rm 14c (10017-1937)
PHONE 646 517-7252
Karim Makansi, *Managing Dir*
Alex Inkster, *Vice Pres*
Benjamin Dell, *Mng Member*
Ben Dell,
Andrew Freilich, *Analyst*
EMP: 9 **EST:** 2013
SALES (est): 8.5MM **Privately Held**
SIC: 1311 Sand & shale oil mining

(G-10849)
KIMMIEKAKES LLC
270 W 38th St Rm 1704 (10018-1566)
PHONE 212 946-0311
May Tee, *Prdtn Mgr*
Kim Nguyen,
EMP: 12
SQ FT: 4,000
SALES: 5MM **Privately Held**
SIC: 2326 Work apparel, except uniforms

(G-10850)
KIND GROUP LLC (PA)
19 W 44th St Ste 811 (10036-5901)
PHONE 212 645-0800
Donna Spinillo, *Managing Dir*
Jonathan Teller, *Mng Member*
EMP: 2
SQ FT: 3,000
SALES (est): 16.1MM **Privately Held**
WEB: www.20-10.com
SIC: 2844 Toilet preparations

(G-10851)
KINDLING INC
440 Park Ave S Fl 14 (10016-8012)
PHONE 212 400-6296
Timothy Meaney, *CEO*
Daniel Summa, *President*
Sara Koff, *Business Dir*
Richard Ziade, *Admin Sec*
EMP: 17
SALES (est): 1MM **Privately Held**
SIC: 7372 Business oriented computer software

(G-10852)
KINETIC MARKETING INC
1133 Broadway Ste 221 (10010-8197)
PHONE 212 620-0600
Charles Y Beyda, *Vice Pres*
▲ **EMP:** 7
SQ FT: 2,000
SALES (est): 871.8K **Privately Held**
WEB: www.kineticmarketing.net
SIC: 3699 5065 Household electrical equipment; electronic parts & equipment

▲ = Import ▼ = Export
◆ = Import/Export

GEOGRAPHIC SECTION

(G-10853)
KING DISPLAYS INC
333 W 52nd St (10019-6238)
PHONE 212 629-8455
Fax: 212 629-8457
Wayne Sapper, *President*
Julie Rivkin, *Accountant*
EMP: 14 **EST:** 1938
SQ FT: 7,500
SALES (est): 1.7MM **Privately Held**
WEB: www.kingdisplays.com
SIC: 3999 3993 Theatrical scenery; displays & cutouts, window & lobby

(G-10854)
KINGLIFT ELEVATOR INC
1 Maiden Ln Fl 5 (10038-5154)
PHONE 917 923-3517
Cem Ozalpasan, *President*
EMP: 5
SALES (est): 320.5K **Privately Held**
SIC: 3534 Elevators & moving stairways

(G-10855)
KITON BUILDING CORP
4 E 54th St (10022-4203)
PHONE 212 486-3224
Antonio De Matteis, *Ch of Bd*
Ciro Paone, *President*
Adele Drago, *Accounting Mgr*
EMP: 20
SQ FT: 18,077
SALES (est): 2MM **Privately Held**
SIC: 2389 Costumes

(G-10856)
KKR MILLENNIUM GP LLC
9 W 57th St Ste 4150 (10019-2701)
PHONE 212 750-8300
Lawrence J Rogers, *President*
EMP: 4850
SALES (est): 178.9MM **Privately Held**
SIC: 2515 Mattresses, innerspring or box spring

(G-10857)
KKR NTRAL RSOURCES FUND I-A LP (HQ)
9 W 57th St Ste 4200 (10019-2707)
PHONE 212 750-8300
David J Sorkin, *General Counsel*
EMP: 10
SALES (est): 40.1MM
SALES (corp-wide): 1B **Publicly Held**
SIC: 1382 Oil & gas exploration services
PA: Kkr & Co. L.P.
9 W 57th St Ste 4200
New York NY 10019
212 750-8300

(G-10858)
KLARA TECHNOLOGIES INC
1 State St Fl 25 (10004-1729)
PHONE 844 215-5272
Simon Bolz, *CEO*
EMP: 17
SALES (est): 336.8K
SALES (corp-wide): 538.2K **Privately Held**
SIC: 7372 Business oriented computer software
PA: Klara Holdings, Inc.
1 State St Fl 25
New York NY 10004
844 215-5272

(G-10859)
KLAUBER BROTHERS INC (PA)
980 Ave Of The Ave Frnt 2 (10018)
PHONE 212 686-2531
Fax: 212 481-7194
Roger Klauber, *President*
Mark Klauber, *Vice Pres*
Jay Marcus, *Vice Pres*
Shari Driver, *Production*
Koeun Lee, *Production*
◆ **EMP:** 35 **EST:** 1942
SQ FT: 11,000
SALES (est): 8.9MM **Privately Held**
WEB: www.klauberlace.com
SIC: 2258 5131 Lace, knit; warp & flat knit products; textile converters

(G-10860)
KLUTZ (HQ)
Also Called: Klutz Store
568 Broadway Rm 503 (10012-3264)
PHONE 650 687-2600
Richard Robinson, *CEO*
of Purch, *CEO*
Netta Rabin, *President*
Flora Kim, *Editor*
Dewitt Durham, *Vice Pres*
▲ **EMP:** 31
SALES (est): 9.4MM
SALES (corp-wide): 1.6B **Publicly Held**
WEB: www.klutz.com
SIC: 2731 Books: publishing & printing
PA: Scholastic Corporation
557 Broadway Lbby 1
New York NY 10012
212 343-6100

(G-10861)
KNICKERBOCKER GRAPHICS SVCS
256 W 38th St Rm 504 (10018-5807)
PHONE 212 244-7485
Joseph Schankweiler, *President*
Janet Schankweiler, *Vice Pres*
EMP: 14 **EST:** 1910
SQ FT: 18,000
SALES (est): 1.6MM **Privately Held**
SIC: 2752 Commercial printing, offset

(G-10862)
KNIT ILLUSTRATED INC
247 W 37th St Frnt 3 (10018-5130)
PHONE 212 268-9054
Fax: 212 268-9073
Peter Tam, *President*
Gary Kokin, *Vice Pres*
EMP: 20
SALES: 2MM **Privately Held**
WEB: www.knitillustrated.com
SIC: 2253 Sweaters & sweater coats, knit

(G-10863)
KNIT RESOURCE CENTER LTD
250 W 39th St Rm 207 (10018-4742)
PHONE 212 221-1990
Fax: 212 719-5344
Joseph Katz, *President*
Richard Glanzer, *Manager*
EMP: 7
SQ FT: 2,500
SALES (est): 587.7K
SALES (corp-wide): 269.4MM **Privately Held**
SIC: 2253 Sweaters & sweater coats, knit
HQ: Stoll America Knitting Machinery Inc
250 W 39th St Frnt 1
New York NY 10018
212 398-3869

(G-10864)
KNOLL INC
Also Called: Knoll Textile
1330 Ave Of The A (10019)
PHONE 917 359-8620
Fax: 212 343-4181
Carl Magnusson, *Senior VP*
Benjamin A Pardo, *Senior VP*
Burt Staniar, *Senior VP*
Mindy Rynasko, *Loan Officer*
Karlene McLarty, *Sales Associate*
EMP: 100
SALES (corp-wide): 1.1B **Publicly Held**
WEB: www.knoll.com
SIC: 2521 2522 2511 Wood office furniture; panel systems & partitions, office: except wood; wood household furniture
PA: Knoll, Inc.
1235 Water St
East Greenville PA 18041
215 679-7991

(G-10865)
KOBALT MUSIC PUBG AMER INC (PA)
220 W 42nd St Fl 11 (10036-7200)
PHONE 212 247-6204
Willard Ahdritz, *President*
Nestor Casonu, *Managing Dir*
Kind Matthias, *Managing Dir*
Simon Moor, *Managing Dir*
Michelle Maghise, *Principal*
EMP: 70

SALES (est): 14.6MM **Privately Held**
WEB: www.kobaltmusic.com
SIC: 2731 Book music: publishing & printing

(G-10866)
KOBE STEEL USA HOLDINGS INC (HQ)
535 Madison Ave Fl 5 (10022-4214)
PHONE 212 751-9400
Fax: 212 308-3116
Hiroya Kawasaki, *President*
Carrie Dugan, *Info Tech Dir*
Onuma Hideki, *Info Tech Mgr*
Kazuhiro Ono, *Info Tech Mgr*
Kazunori Yamataki, *Admin Sec*
◆ **EMP:** 8
SQ FT: 5,697
SALES (est): 248.9MM
SALES (corp-wide): 15.5B **Privately Held**
WEB: www.kobelco.com
SIC: 3542 3089 Extruding machines (machine tools), metal; injection molding of plastics
PA: Kobe Steel, Ltd.
2-2-4, Wakinohamakaigandori, Chuo-Ku
Kobe HYO 651-0
782 615-111

(G-10867)
KODANSHA USA INC
451 Park Ave S Fl 7 (10016-7390)
PHONE 917 322-6200
Fax: 212 935-6929
Sawako Noma, *Ch of Bd*
Yoichi Kiyata, *Sr Exec VP*
Tokuo Kanemaru, *Manager*
▲ **EMP:** 9
SQ FT: 7,000
SALES (est): 4MM **Privately Held**
SIC: 2731 5192 Books: publishing only; books

(G-10868)
KOGETO INC (PA)
51 Wooster St Fl 2 (10013-2292)
PHONE 646 490-8169
Jeff Glasse, *Ch of Bd*
Sophie Ziner, *Opers Mgr*
Daniel Nestman, *Opers Staff*
John P Clark, *CFO*
EMP: 7
SQ FT: 1,000
SALES: 579.4K **Publicly Held**
SIC: 3861 Photographic equipment & supplies

(G-10869)
KOHLER CO
37 E (10003)
PHONE 212 529-2800
EMP: 48
SALES (corp-wide): 8.1B **Privately Held**
SIC: 3431 Plumbing fixtures: enameled iron cast iron or pressed metal
PA: Kohler Co.
444 Highland Dr
Kohler WI 53044
920 457-4441

(G-10870)
KOKIN INC
247 W 38th St Rm 701 (10018-4470)
PHONE 212 643-8225
Fax: 212 643-8284
Steven Kokin, *President*
Audrey Kokin, *Corp Secy*
Gary Kokin, *Vice Pres*
▲ **EMP:** 30
SQ FT: 6,800
SALES (est): 3.9MM **Privately Held**
SIC: 2353 2341 Hats, caps & millinery; women's & children's nightwear

(G-10871)
KOLCORP INDUSTRIES LTD (PA)
Also Called: Pro-Print
10 E 36th St (10016-3302)
PHONE 212 354-0400
Fax: 212 768-3550
Charles Kolster, *President*
David Matos, *Bookkeeper*
EMP: 12 **EST:** 1973
SQ FT: 2,500

SALES (est): 1.6MM **Privately Held**
WEB: www.pro-print.com
SIC: 2752 Commercial printing, lithographic

(G-10872)
KOLLAGE WORK TOO LTD
261 W 35th St Ste 302 (10001-1902)
PHONE 212 695-1821
Maria Meunier,
EMP: 7
SALES (est): 329.5K **Privately Held**
SIC: 2326 Men's & boys' work clothing

(G-10873)
KOMAR KIDS LLC (HQ)
16 E 34th St Fl 14 (10016-4360)
PHONE 212 725-1500
Charlie Komar, *CEO*
Jay Harris, *COO*
Harry Gaffney, *CFO*
David Komar, *Admin Sec*
▲ **EMP:** 10
SQ FT: 15,000
SALES (est): 6.4MM
SALES (corp-wide): 159.3MM **Privately Held**
SIC: 2254 Nightwear (nightgowns, negligees, pajamas), knit; underwear, knit
PA: Charles Komar & Sons, Inc.
16 E 34th St Fl 10
Jersey City NJ 07308
212 725-1500

(G-10874)
KOMAR LAYERING LLC (HQ)
Also Called: O'Bryan Bros
16 E 34th St Fl 10 (10016-4360)
PHONE 212 725-1500
Charlie Komar, *President*
David Komar, *Principal*
Allen R Bartine, *CFO*
▲ **EMP:** 40
SQ FT: 13,000
SALES (est): 10.1MM
SALES (corp-wide): 159.3MM **Privately Held**
WEB: www.cuddlduds.com
SIC: 2341 Nightgowns & negligees: women's & children's; pajamas & bed-jackets: women's & children's; slips: women's, misses, children's & infants'; panties: women's, misses', children's & infants'
PA: Charles Komar & Sons, Inc.
16 E 34th St Fl 10
Jersey City NJ 07308
212 725-1500

(G-10875)
KOMAR LUXURY BRANDS
16 E 34th St Fl 10 (10016-4360)
PHONE 646 472-0060
Charles Komar, *President*
Shelly Sosnoff, *Purchasing*
Harry Gaffney, *CFO*
Greg Holland, *Sales Mgr*
Marie Taibbi, *Admin Asst*
▲ **EMP:** 8
SALES (est): 1.1MM
SALES (corp-wide): 159.3MM **Privately Held**
SIC: 2341 2384 5137 2329 Women's & children's nightwear; robes & dressing gowns; nightwear: women's, children's & infants'; sweaters & sweater jackets: men's & boys'
PA: Charles Komar & Sons, Inc.
16 E 34th St Fl 10
Jersey City NJ 07308
212 725-1500

(G-10876)
KORAL INDUSTRIES
1384 Broadway Fl 18 (10018-6122)
PHONE 212 719-0392
Peter Crown, *Owner*
Crystal Slattery, *Sales Executive*
Johan Tavaris, *Office Mgr*
EMP: 10
SALES (est): 450K **Privately Held**
SIC: 2339 Women's & misses' athletic clothing & sportswear

(G-10877)
KORANGY PUBLISHING INC
Also Called: Real Deal, The
158 W 29th St Fl 4 (10001-5300)
PHONE..................................212 260-1332
Amir Korangy, *CEO*
Doug Devine, *Real Est Agnt*
EMP: 60
SALES (est): 1.7MM **Privately Held**
SIC: 2741 Miscellaneous publishing

(G-10878)
KORIN JAPANESE TRADING CORP
57 Warren St Frnt A (10007-1018)
PHONE..................................212 587-7021
Fax: 212 587-7027
Saori Kawano, *President*
John Wong, *CFO*
Sally Cen, *Asst Controller*
Mitsuko Muramatsu, *Sales Associate*
Wendy Yang, *Marketing Staff*
◆ **EMP:** 32
SQ FT: 8,000
SALES (est): 4.8MM **Privately Held**
WEB: www.korin.com
SIC: 3469 3262 3263 3421 Utensils, household; metal, except cast; vitreous china table & kitchenware; commercial tableware or kitchen articles, fine earthenware; cutlery; commercial cooking & food-warming equipment; barbecues, grills & braziers (outdoor cooking)

(G-10879)
KOSSARS BIALYS LLC
367 Grand St (10002-3951)
PHONE..................................212 473-4810
Fax: 212 253-2146
Daniel Cohen, *Owner*
Juda Engelmayer, *Principal*
Debra Engel, *Director*
EMP: 8 **EST:** 1998
SQ FT: 3,000
SALES: 500K **Privately Held**
WEB: www.kossarsbialys.com
SIC: 2051 Bakery: wholesale or wholesale/retail combined

(G-10880)
KOSSARS ON GRAND LLC
367 Grand St (10002-3951)
PHONE..................................212 473-4810
Evan Giniger, *CEO*
EMP: 10
SALES (est): 728.3K **Privately Held**
SIC: 2051 Rolls, bread type: fresh or frozen

(G-10881)
KOTEL IMPORTERS INC
22 W 48th St Ste 607 (10036-1803)
PHONE..................................212 245-6200
Fax: 212 245-5266
Raphel Dagan, *President*
EMP: 12
SQ FT: 1,200
SALES (est): 810K **Privately Held**
SIC: 1499 Gemstone & industrial diamond mining

(G-10882)
KOWA AMERICAN CORPORATION (DH)
55 E 59th St Fl 19 (10022-1112)
PHONE..................................212 303-7800
Fax: 212 310-0101
Reid C Anthony, *Ch of Bd*
Takashi Mamemura, *Ch of Bd*
Masataka Shigenaka, *Credit Mgr*
Noriko Nagamoto, *Accountant*
Tomyouki Mase, *Manager*
▲ **EMP:** 20
SQ FT: 6,400
SALES (est): 4.9MM
SALES (corp-wide): 1.4B **Privately Held**
SIC: 2819 5032 5131 Industrial inorganic chemicals; tile, clay or other ceramic, excluding refractory; textiles, woven
HQ: La Esperanza Delaware Corporation
55 E 59th St Fl 1900a
New York NY 10022
212 303-7800

(G-10883)
KPS CAPITAL PARTNERS LP (PA)
485 Lexington Ave Fl 31 (10017-2641)
PHONE..................................212 338-5100
Michael G Psaros, *Managing Prtnr*
Jay Bernstein, *Partner*
Raquel Palmer, *Partner*
David Shapiro, *Partner*
Daniel Gray, *Managing Dir*
◆ **EMP:** 40
SQ FT: 6,000
SALES (est): 2.1B **Privately Held**
SIC: 3541 6722 3545 5084 Machine tools, metal cutting type; management investment, open-end; machine tool accessories; industrial machinery & equipment

(G-10884)
KRAINZ CREATIONS INC
589 5th Ave (10017-1923)
PHONE..................................212 583-1555
Roland Krainz, *President*
EMP: 35
SALES (est): 3.8MM **Privately Held**
SIC: 3961 Costume jewelry

(G-10885)
KRAMAN IRON WORKS INC
410 E 10th St (10009-4203)
PHONE..................................212 460-8400
Fax: 212 529-2466
Richard Kraman, *President*
EMP: 11 **EST:** 1913
SQ FT: 3,600
SALES: 1.6MM **Privately Held**
SIC: 3449 Miscellaneous metalwork

(G-10886)
KRASNER GROUP INC (PA)
40 W 37th St Ph A (10018-7415)
PHONE..................................212 268-4100
Al Cerbo, *Vice Pres*
Barry Ort, *Vice Pres*
David Pardington, *CFO*
▼ **EMP:** 1
SQ FT: 4,500
SALES (est): 7.9MM **Privately Held**
SIC: 3911 2339 2331 2335 Jewelry, precious metal; women's & misses' accessories; women's & misses' blouses & shirts; women's, juniors' & misses' dresses

(G-10887)
KRAUS & SONS INC
355 S End Ave Apt 10j (10280-1056)
PHONE..................................212 620-0408
Fax: 212 924-4081
Paul Schneider, *President*
Mildred Schneider, *Treasurer*
Saul Brown, *Director*
EMP: 15 **EST:** 1886
SQ FT: 5,000
SALES (est): 1.4MM **Privately Held**
WEB: www.krausbanners.com
SIC: 2399 3993 2394 3965 Banners, made from fabric; signs & advertising specialties; tents: made from purchased materials; buttons & parts

(G-10888)
KRAUS ORGANIZATION LIMITED (PA)
Also Called: Bernan Associates
181 Hudson St Ste 2a (10013-1812)
PHONE..................................212 686-5411
Frank Cermak, *President*
Herbert Gstalder, *Chairman*
Steven Gstalder, *Vice Pres*
Gstalder Steven, *Manager*
Lisa T Provenzano, *Director*
EMP: 5
SALES (est): 8.1MM **Privately Held**
WEB: www.krausorgltd.com
SIC: 2741 7383 7389 Miscellaneous publishing; news pictures, gathering & distributing; photographic library service

(G-10889)
KRAVITZ DESIGN INC (PA)
13 Crosby St Rm 401 (10013-3145)
PHONE..................................212 625-1644
Bill Tannenbaum, *Manager*
Richard Feldstein, *Admin Sec*
◆ **EMP:** 8
SALES (est): 940.6K **Privately Held**
SIC: 2732 Books: printing only

(G-10890)
KRISTEN GRAPHICS INC
44 W 28th St Fl 3 (10001-4212)
PHONE..................................212 929-2183
Joseph Risola, *President*
Anthony Fazio III, *Vice Pres*
Tina Bonaparte, *Manager*
EMP: 14
SQ FT: 20,000
SALES (est): 1.4MM **Privately Held**
SIC: 2796 Platemaking services

(G-10891)
KSK INTERNATIONAL INC (PA)
Also Called: Easel
450 Park Ave Ste 2703 (10022-2646)
PHONE..................................212 354-7770
Neil Weiss, *CEO*
Gus Ayala, *Manager*
EMP: 25
SQ FT: 10,335
SALES (est): 2MM **Privately Held**
SIC: 2331 2339 Women's & misses' blouses & shirts; women's & misses' accessories

(G-10892)
KT GROUP INC
13 W 36th St Fl 3 (10018-7139)
PHONE..................................212 760-2500
Eugene Huh, *President*
Yujin Huh, *Chairman*
Delias Gonzalves, *Prdtn Mgr*
▲ **EMP:** 8
SALES (est): 939.1K **Privately Held**
SIC: 2321 Sport shirts, men's & boys': from purchased materials

(G-10893)
KURARAY AMERICA INC
33 Maiden Ln Fl 6 (10038-5152)
PHONE..................................212 986-2230
Yoshiki Kuroki, *General Mgr*
Scott Landon, *Plant Mgr*
Bob Chvala, *VP Sales*
Deandra Perry, *Sales Staff*
Shuichi Takemoto, *Branch Mgr*
EMP: 26
SALES (corp-wide): 4.2B **Privately Held**
SIC: 2655 Fiber cans, drums & similar products
HQ: Kuraray America, Inc.
2625 Bay Area Blvd # 600
Houston TX 77058

(G-10894)
KUREHA ADVANCED MATERIALS INC
420 Lexington Ave Rm 2510 (10170-1402)
PHONE..................................724 295-3352
Fax: 212 986-8162
Fred Daniell, *President*
Yoshitsugu Nishibayashi, *President*
Lee Pyfitt, *General Mgr*
Leeland Pfeifer, *Corp Secy*
Laura J Uncapher, *Manager*
▲ **EMP:** 10
SQ FT: 23,000
SALES (est): 2MM
SALES (corp-wide): 1.2B **Privately Held**
WEB: www.ttsmatl.com
SIC: 3624 Carbon & graphite products
HQ: Kureha America Inc.
420 Lexington Ave Rm 2510
New York NY 10170
212 867-7040

(G-10895)
KURT GAUM INC
Also Called: Soper Designs
580 5th Ave Ste 303 (10036-4724)
PHONE..................................212 719-2836
Fax: 212 719-2837
Blake Soper, *President*
Peter Boutsas, *Vice Pres*
EMP: 13 **EST:** 1954
SQ FT: 1,250
SALES (est): 1.5MM **Privately Held**
WEB: www.kurtgaum.com
SIC: 3911 Jewel settings & mountings, precious metal

(G-10896)
KWW PRODUCTIONS CORP
Also Called: American Attitude
1410 Broadway Fl 24 (10018-5007)
PHONE..................................212 398-8181
Izzy Pnini, *President*
EMP: 10
SALES (corp-wide): 5.7MM **Privately Held**
WEB: www.knitwork.com
SIC: 2389 Apparel for handicapped
PA: Kww Productions Corp.
1639 Centre St
Ridgewood NY 11385
718 821-2201

(G-10897)
KYBOD GROUP LLC
Also Called: Sriracha2go
222 E 34th St Apt 1005 (10016-4899)
PHONE..................................408 306-1657
Kyle Lewis,
Farbod Deylamian,
EMP: 2
SALES: 1.5MM **Privately Held**
SIC: 3085 Plastics bottles

(G-10898)
KYLE EDITING LLC
15 W 26th St Fl 8 (10010-1065)
PHONE..................................212 675-3464
Eytan Gutman, *General Mgr*
Jackie Sparks, *Info Tech Mgr*
Tina Mintus,
EMP: 9
SALES (est): 977.9K **Privately Held**
WEB: www.kyleedit.com
SIC: 3861 Editing equipment, motion picture: viewers, splicers, etc.

(G-10899)
L & M OPTICAL DISC LLC
Also Called: L & M West
65 W 36th St Fl 11 (10018-7936)
PHONE..................................718 649-3500
Fax: 718 649-9300
Yefit Shahar, *Controller*
Elazar Walder, *CIO*
Aaron Menche,
▲ **EMP:** 100
SALES (est): 12.7MM **Privately Held**
WEB: www.dxbind.com
SIC: 3695 Optical disks & tape, blank

(G-10900)
L ALLMEIER
1201 Broadway Ste 705 (10001-5656)
PHONE..................................212 243-7390
Fax: 212 243-7402
Sandy Perlmutter, *Owner*
▲ **EMP:** 8
SQ FT: 2,500
SALES (est): 740K **Privately Held**
SIC: 2211 5699 2311 Shirting fabrics, cotton; sheets, bedding & table cloths: cotton; shirts, custom made; custom tailor; men's & boys' suits & coats

(G-10901)
L F FASHION ORIENT INTL CO LTD
32 W 40th St Apt 2l (10018-3839)
PHONE..................................917 667-3398
Lisa LI, *President*
Angus Wong, *Controller*
▲ **EMP:** 5
SALES (est): 391.4K **Privately Held**
SIC: 2311 2335 Men's & boys' suits & coats; women's, juniors' & misses' dresses

(G-10902)
L F INTERNATIONAL INC
Also Called: Labhar - Freidman
425 Park Ave Fl 5 (10022-3506)
PHONE..................................212 756-5000
J Roger Friedman, *President*
▼ **EMP:** 90
SALES (est): 4.3MM
SALES (corp-wide): 111.5MM **Privately Held**
WEB: www.lf.com
SIC: 2721 Periodicals

PA: Lebhar-Friedman, Inc.
150 W 30th St Fl 19
New York NY 10001
212 756-5000

(G-10903)
L-3 CMMNCTONS FGN HOLDINGS INC (HQ)
Also Called: L3 Communication
600 3rd Ave Fl 32 (10016-2001)
PHONE...................................212 697-1111
Michael T Strianese, *Principal*
Peter Schleicher, *Asst Treas*
Turchyn Roman, *Human Resources*
Craig Nichols, *Sr Ntwrk Engine*
Danh Dinh, *Administration*
▲ **EMP:** 23
SALES (est): 16.6MM
SALES (corp-wide): 10.4B **Publicly Held**
SIC: 3663 3669 3679 3812 Telemetering equipment, electronic; receiver-transmitter units (transceiver); amplifiers, RF power & IF; signaling apparatus, electric; intercommunication systems, electric; microwave components; search & navigation equipment; guided missile & space vehicle parts & auxiliary equipment
PA: L-3 Communications Holdings, Inc.
600 3rd Ave
New York NY 10016
212 697-1111

(G-10904)
L-3 CMMNCTONS NTRONIX HOLDINGS
600 3rd Ave Fl 34 (10016-2001)
PHONE...................................212 697-1111
Michael T Strianese, *President*
Steven M Post, *Senior VP*
Scott Betchley, *Vice Pres*
Curtis Brunson, *Vice Pres*
Wendall Child, *Vice Pres*
EMP: 65
SALES (est): 17.5MM
SALES (corp-wide): 10.4B **Publicly Held**
SIC: 3625 3699 8711 Marine & navy auxiliary controls; underwater sound equipment; marine engineering
HQ: L-3 Communications Corporation
600 3rd Ave
New York NY 10016
212 697-1111

(G-10905)
L-3 CMMUNICATIONS HOLDINGS INC (PA)
600 3rd Ave (10016-1901)
PHONE...................................212 697-1111
Fax: 212 805-5477
Michael T Strianese, *Ch of Bd*
Steve Kantor, *President*
Christopher E Kubasik, *President*
John S Mega, *President*
Mark Von Schwarz, *President*
◆ **EMP:** 100 **EST:** 1997
SALES: 10.4B **Publicly Held**
SIC: 3663 3669 3679 3812 Telemetering equipment, electronic; receiver-transmitter units (transceiver); signaling apparatus, electric; intercommunication systems, electric; microwave components; search & navigation equipment; guided missile & space vehicle parts & auxiliary equipment

(G-10906)
L-3 COMMUNICATIONS CORPORATION (HQ)
600 3rd Ave (10016-1901)
PHONE...................................212 697-1111
Michael T Strianese, *Ch of Bd*
Christopher E Kubasik, *President*
Steven M Post, *Senior VP*
Dan Azmon, *Vice Pres*
Ralph G D'Ambrosio, *CFO*
EMP: 277 **EST:** 1997

SALES: 3.5B
SALES (corp-wide): 10.4B **Publicly Held**
SIC: 3812 3663 3669 3679 Search & navigation equipment; aircraft control systems, electronic; telemetering equipment, electronic; receiver-transmitter units (transceiver); amplifiers, RF power & IF; signaling apparatus, electric; intercommunication systems, electric; microwave components; guided missile & space vehicle parts & auxiliary equipment
PA: L-3 Communications Holdings, Inc.
600 3rd Ave
New York NY 10016
212 697-1111

(G-10907)
LA COLA 1 INC
529 W 42nd St Apt 5b (10036-6228)
PHONE...................................917 509-6669
Thomas Dugal, *Principal*
EMP: 5
SALES (est): 251.8K **Privately Held**
SIC: 2086 Soft drinks: packaged in cans, bottles, etc.

(G-10908)
LA FINA DESIGN INC
42 W 38th St Rm 1200 (10018-6212)
PHONE...................................212 689-6725
Fax: 212 689-5627
Chol Choi, *President*
Peter Choi, *President*
◆ **EMP:** 7
SALES (est): 890.1K **Privately Held**
SIC: 3911 Jewelry, precious metal

(G-10909)
LA LAME INC
Also Called: La Lame Importers
132 W 36th St Rm 1101 (10018-8818)
PHONE...................................212 921-9770
Fax: 212 302-4359
Benjamin Schneer, *CEO*
Edward Schneer, *Principal*
Glen Schneer, *Principal*
Alan Kerner, *Controller*
▲ **EMP:** 8 **EST:** 1958
SQ FT: 7,500
SALES (est): 1.3MM **Privately Held**
WEB: www.lalame.com
SIC: 2299 2241 2282 2221 Yarns, specialty & novelty; fabrics: linen, jute, hemp, ramie; braids, textile; embroidery yarn: twisting, winding or spooling; spandex broadwoven fabrics; brocade, cotton; textile converters

(G-10910)
LA REGINA DI SAN MARZANO
17 Battery Pl Ste 610 (10004-1133)
PHONE...................................212 269-4202
Felice Romano, *President*
Debra Deoteris, *Vice Pres*
EMP: 8
SQ FT: 7,000
SALES (est): 549.6K **Privately Held**
SIC: 2099 Food preparations

(G-10911)
LABEL SOURCE INC
321 W 35th St (10001-1739)
PHONE...................................212 244-1403
Stuart Rosen, *President*
EMP: 6
SQ FT: 2,000
SALES: 1.2MM **Privately Held**
SIC: 2241 Labels, woven

(G-10912)
LABELS INTER-GLOBAL INC
Also Called: Labels I-G
109 W 38th St Rm 701 (10018-3673)
PHONE...................................212 398-0006
Fax: 212 768-8488
Steve Ziangos, *President*
Effie Ziangos, *Vice Pres*
Andrew Kandial, *Manager*
◆ **EMP:** 13
SQ FT: 3,400
SALES (est): 2.2MM **Privately Held**
WEB: www.labelsig.com
SIC: 2759 5112 2241 Labels & seals: printing; stationery & office supplies; labels, woven

(G-10913)
LABELTEX MILLS INC
1430 Broadway Rm 1510 (10018-3368)
PHONE...................................212 279-6165
Fax: 212 279-6165
Vince McGuire, *Vice Pres*
Ian Kantor, *Manager*
EMP: 7
SALES (corp-wide): 30.6MM **Privately Held**
WEB: www.labeltexmills.com
SIC: 2241 Narrow fabric mills
PA: Labeltex Mills, Inc.
6100 Wilmington Ave
Los Angeles CA 90001
323 582-0228

(G-10914)
LADY ESTER LINGERIE CORP
Also Called: Sliperfection
33 E 33rd St Rm 800 (10016-5335)
PHONE...................................212 689-1729
Robert T Sadock, *CEO*
M William Sadock, *President*
Karen L Sadock, *Exec VP*
Barbara Hoganson, *Purch Mgr*
Fred Adler, *CFO*
EMP: 45 **EST:** 1929
SQ FT: 15,000
SALES (est): 4.6MM **Privately Held**
SIC: 2341 2384 Women's & children's underwear; chemises, camisoles & teddies: women's & children's; slips: women's, misses', children's & infants'; robes & dressing gowns

(G-10915)
LAFAYETTE PUB INC
Also Called: Temple Bar
332 Lafayette St (10012-2739)
PHONE...................................212 925-4242
Fax: 212 219-9763
George Schwartz, *President*
EMP: 25
SALES (est): 1.4MM **Privately Held**
WEB: www.templebarnyc.com
SIC: 2599 5813 Bar, restaurant & cafeteria furniture; drinking places

(G-10916)
LAGARDERE NORTH AMERICA INC (DH)
60 E 42nd St Ste 1940 (10165-6201)
PHONE...................................212 477-7373
Fax: 212 767-5635
David Leckey, *Senior VP*
Richard Rabinowitz, *Vice Pres*
EMP: 20
SALES (est): 551.5MM
SALES (corp-wide): 268.5K **Privately Held**
SIC: 2721 Magazines: publishing only, not printed on site
HQ: Lagardere Media
4 Rue De Presbourg
Paris 75116
140 691-600

(G-10917)
LAGUNATIC MUSIC & FILMWORKS
Also Called: Blackheart Records
636 Broadway Ste 1210 (10012-2624)
PHONE...................................212 353-9600
Fax: 212 353-8300
Kenny Laguna, *President*
Meryl Laguna, *Corp Secy*
Joan Jett, *Vice Pres*
Zander Wolff, *Sls & Mktg Exec*
Alena Amante, *CFO*
EMP: 10
SALES (est): 878.9K **Privately Held**
WEB: www.blackheart.com
SIC: 2741 Music book & sheet music publishing

(G-10918)
LAI APPAREL DESIGN INC
Also Called: Ella Design
209 W 38th St Rm 901 (10018-4558)
PHONE...................................212 382-1075
Elaine Lai, *President*
Jacqueline Wong, *Accounts Mgr*
▲ **EMP:** 21
SQ FT: 7,000

SALES (est): 3.5MM **Privately Held**
SIC: 2339 Women's & misses' athletic clothing & sportswear

(G-10919)
LAKESTAR SEMI INC (PA)
888 7th Ave Ste 3300 (10106-3402)
PHONE...................................212 974-6254
Sailesh Chittipeddi, *President*
Shiva Gowni, *President*
Shu LI, *Chairman*
Julie Hall, *Corp Secy*
Naresh Malipeddi, *COO*
▲ **EMP:** 17
SALES (est): 64.1MM **Privately Held**
WEB: www.conexant.com
SIC: 3674 5065 Semiconductors & related devices; semiconductor devices

(G-10920)
LAKEVIEW INNOVATIONS INC
112 W 34th St Ste 18030 (10120-0101)
PHONE...................................212 502-6702
Scott Colquitt, *President*
Harry Mull, *CFO*
Andrew Mull, *Sales Staff*
EMP: 10
SQ FT: 2,500
SALES (est): 3.4MM **Privately Held**
SIC: 2389 Cummerbunds

(G-10921)
LALI JEWELRY INC
Also Called: Lali Jewels
50 W 47th St Ste 1610 (10036-8734)
PHONE...................................212 944-2277
Arun Bassalali, *President*
Adam Bassalali, *Vice Pres*
EMP: 4 **EST:** 2015
SQ FT: 1,000
SALES: 1MM **Privately Held**
SIC: 3911 Jewelry, precious metal; pearl jewelry, natural or cultured

(G-10922)
LALIQUE NORTH AMERICA INC
Also Called: Lalique Boutique
609 Madison Ave (10022-1901)
PHONE...................................212 355-6550
Fax: 212 752-0203
Maggie WEI, *Marketing Staff*
Marya Samawi, *Branch Mgr*
EMP: 20 **Privately Held**
SIC: 3231 5719 Watch crystals, glass; kitchenware
HQ: Lalique North America, Inc.
133 5th Ave Fl 3
New York NY 10003
212 355-8536

(G-10923)
LAND N SEA INC (PA)
1375 Broadway Fl 2 (10018-7073)
PHONE...................................212 703-2980
Fax: 212 444-6019
Robert Sobel, *Ch of Bd*
Kirk Gellin, *Ch of Bd*
Ed Vanduzer, *Area Mgr*
Scott Aimetti, *Vice Pres*
Fred Mandato, *Vice Pres*
◆ **EMP:** 80 **EST:** 1958
SQ FT: 21,000
SALES (est): 38MM **Privately Held**
SIC: 2369 2361 2331 2339 Girls' & children's outerwear; blouses: girls', children's & infants'; blouses, women's & juniors': made from purchased material; women's & misses' outerwear; family clothing stores

(G-10924)
LANDLORD GUARD INC
1 Maiden Ln Fl 7 (10038-5168)
PHONE...................................212 695-6505
Christine Mathis, *President*
EMP: 10
SALES (est): 780K **Privately Held**
SIC: 2759 Advertising literature: printing

(G-10925)
LANE PARK LITHO PLATE
155 Ave Of The Amer Fl 8 (10013-1507)
PHONE...................................212 255-9100
Linda Salzhauer, *President*
Dan Salzhauer, *Vice Pres*
EMP: 30 **EST:** 1967

New York - New York County (G-10926) — GEOGRAPHIC SECTION

SQ FT: 12,500
SALES (est): 3.4MM Privately Held
WEB: www.parklanelitho.com
SIC: 2796 Color separations for printing

(G-10926)
LANES FLR CVRNGS INTRIORS INC
30 W 26th St Fl 11r (10010-2065)
PHONE.................212 532-5200
Fax: 212 685-7626
Lane Brettschneider, *Ch of Bd*
Gary Ragin, *Sales Staff*
Umberto Aponte, *Manager*
Linda Wolstein, *Info Tech Mgr*
EMP: 25 EST: 1965
SQ FT: 9,000
SALES (est): 5MM Privately Held
WEB: www.lanes-carpets.com
SIC: 2273 Carpets & rugs

(G-10927)
LANGUAGE AND GRAPHICS INC
350 W 57th St Apt 14i (10019-3762)
PHONE.................212 315-5266
Margaret Keppler, *President*
Patricia Encinosa, *Vice Pres*
Michael Keppler, *Treasurer*
EMP: 5
SALES (est): 317.1K Privately Held
SIC: 2741 7389 Miscellaneous publishing; translation services

(G-10928)
LAREGENCE INC
34 W 27th St Fl 2 (10001-6901)
PHONE.................212 736-2548
Fax: 212 736-2547
Jay Perlstein, *President*
Kathy Jones, *Treasurer*
▼ EMP: 20
SALES (est): 2.6MM Privately Held
SIC: 2221 2391 Upholstery, tapestry & wall covering fabrics; curtains & draperies

(G-10929)
LARGO MUSIC INC
425 Park Ave Ste 501 (10022-3519)
PHONE.................212 756-5080
Jay Roger Friedman, *President*
EMP: 7
SQ FT: 10,000
SALES (est): 300.9K
SALES (corp-wide): 111.5MM Privately Held
WEB: www.largomusic.com
SIC: 2741 Music books: publishing only, not printed on site
PA: Lebhar-Friedman, Inc.
150 W 30th St Fl 19
New York NY 10001
212 756-5000

(G-10930)
LARTE DEL GELATO INC
75 9th Ave Frnt 38 (10011-4730)
PHONE.................212 366-0570
Francisco Realmuto, *Owner*
Josephine Pina, *Admin Asst*
▲ EMP: 9
SALES (est): 670.9K Privately Held
SIC: 2052 2099 Cones, ice cream; jelly, corncob (gelatin)

(G-10931)
LATCHABLE INC
450 W 33rd St Fl 12 (10001-2610)
PHONE.................646 833-0604
Luke Schoenfelder, *CEO*
EMP: 25 EST: 2014
SALES (est): 124.6K Privately Held
SIC: 7372 7389 Business oriented computer software;

(G-10932)
LATIN BUSINESS CHRONICLE
72 Madison Ave Fl 11 (10016-8731)
PHONE.................305 441-0002
Ann Cauthen Tworoger, *Principal*
EMP: 5 EST: 2009
SALES (est): 245.7K Privately Held
SIC: 2711 Newspapers, publishing & printing

(G-10933)
LATINA MEDIA VENTURES LLC (PA)
120 Broadway Fl 34 (10271-3499)
PHONE.................212 642-0200
Fax: 212 575-3088
Edward Lewis, *Ch of Bd*
Nicole Solofsky, *Editor*
James Reffler, *Production*
Mattie Reyes, *Sales Staff*
Patty Oppenheimer, *Mktg Dir*
▲ EMP: 40
SQ FT: 11,000
SALES (est): 14MM Privately Held
WEB: www.latinapromotions.com
SIC: 2721 Periodicals

(G-10934)
LATIQUE HANDBAGS AND ACC LLC
10 W 33rd St Rm 405 (10001-3306)
PHONE.................212 564-2914
Donny Greenberger, *Controller*
Lena Jones,
▲ EMP: 12
SALES (est): 870K Privately Held
SIC: 3171 Women's handbags & purses

(G-10935)
LAUFER WIND GROUP LLC
270 Lafayette St Ste 1402 (10012-3364)
PHONE.................212 792-3912
Katherine Corle, *Office Mgr*
Eric Laufer, *Mng Member*
EMP: 15
SALES (est): 2.3MM Privately Held
SIC: 3812 Radar systems & equipment

(G-10936)
LAUMONT LABS INC
Also Called: Laumont Editions
333 W 52nd St Fl 14 (10019-6238)
PHONE.................212 664-0595
Philippe Laumont, *President*
Jake Guenther, *Manager*
EMP: 28
SQ FT: 18,000
SALES (est): 2.7MM Privately Held
WEB: www.laumont.com
SIC: 2752 Commercial printing, lithographic

(G-10937)
LAUNDRESS INC
247 W 30th St Rm 202 (10001-2824)
PHONE.................212 209-0074
Gwen Whiting, *President*
Lindsey Wieber Boyd, *Vice Pres*
Jelina Kallabaku, *Accountant*
Emily Herzig, *Manager*
EMP: 10
SALES (est): 1.1MM Privately Held
SIC: 2842 Laundry cleaning preparations

(G-10938)
LAZARE KAPLAN INTL INC (PA)
19 W 44th St Fl 16 (10036-6101)
PHONE.................212 972-9700
Maurice Tempelsman, *Ch of Bd*
Leon Tempelsman, *President*
Charlie Rosario, *Vice Pres*
William H Moryto, *CFO*
Deborah Hiss, *Director*
EMP: 56 EST: 1903
SQ FT: 17,351
SALES (est): 12.4MM Privately Held
WEB: www.lazarediamonds.com
SIC: 3915 Diamond cutting & polishing

(G-10939)
LBG ACQUISITION LLC
Also Called: Lighting By Gregory
158 Bowery (10012-4601)
PHONE.................212 226-1276
Fax: 212 226-2705
William Skarren, *President*
David Silverstein, *Sales Executive*
Archie Alvarez, *Mktg Dir*
EMP: 35
SALES (est): 14.1MM Privately Held
SIC: 3648 Lighting equipment

(G-10940)
LE BOOK PUBLISHING INC (HQ)
552 Broadway Apt 6s (10012-3956)
PHONE.................212 334-5252
Fax: 212 941-4150
Veronique Kolasa, *President*
Michael Kazam, *Vice Pres*
Mariah Serrano, *Production*
Shirley Leung, *Relations*
▲ EMP: 9
SQ FT: 2,500
SALES (est): 742.6K
SALES (corp-wide): 480.6K Privately Held
WEB: www.lebook.com
SIC: 2731 Books: publishing only
PA: Le Book Editions Sa
4 Rue D Enghien
Paris
147 700-330

(G-10941)
LE CHAMEAU USA INC
60 Broad St Ste 3502 (10004-2356)
PHONE.................646 356-0460
Romain Millet, *Director*
EMP: 5
SALES (est): 372.7K Privately Held
SIC: 3069 Boot or shoe products, rubber

(G-10942)
LE LABO INC (PA)
Also Called: Le Labo Fragrances
584 Broadway Rm 1103 (10012-5238)
PHONE.................212 532-7206
Fabrice Penot, *Ch of Bd*
Edouard Roschi, *Principal*
EMP: 21
SALES (est): 4.8MM Privately Held
SIC: 2844 Perfumes & colognes

(G-10943)
LE PAVEH LTD
23 W 47th St Ste 501 (10036-2826)
PHONE.................212 736-6110
EMP: 10
SALES (est): 850K Privately Held
SIC: 3911 Jewelry, precious metal

(G-10944)
LE VIAN CORP
10 W 46th St (10036-4515)
PHONE.................516 466-7200
Fax: 212 944-7734
EMP: 42
SALES (corp-wide): 21.9MM Privately Held
SIC: 3911 Jewelry, precious metal
PA: Le Vian Corp.
235 Great Neck Rd
Great Neck NY 11021
516 466-7200

(G-10945)
LEA & VIOLA INC
525 Fashion Ave Rm 1401 (10018-4914)
PHONE.................646 918-6866
Minji Kim, *President*
EMP: 6
SQ FT: 4,000
SALES (est): 1MM Privately Held
SIC: 2331 Women's & misses' blouses & shirts

(G-10946)
LEADERSHIP DIRECTORIES INC (PA)
Also Called: Federal Yellow Book
1407 Broadway Rm 318 (10018-3853)
PHONE.................212 627-4140
Fax: 212 645-0538
Gretchen G Teichgraeber, *CEO*
William W Cressey, *Chairman*
Thomas Silver, *Senior VP*
James Gee, *Vice Pres*
Bill Schneider, *Sales Executive*
EMP: 50 EST: 1965
SQ FT: 11,400
SALES (est): 6.4MM Privately Held
SIC: 2741 2721 Miscellaneous publishing; directories: publishing only, not printed on site; periodicals: publishing only

(G-10947)
LEADERTEX INTL INC
Also Called: Leadertex Group
135 W 36th St Fl 12 (10018-6981)
PHONE.................212 563-2242
Fax: 212 563-0220
Joseph Delijani, *President*
▲ EMP: 20
SALES (est): 1.7MM Privately Held
SIC: 2252 Men's, boys' & girls' hosiery

(G-10948)
LEARNINGEXPRESS LLC
80 Broad St Fl 4 (10004-2258)
PHONE.................646 274-6454
Barry Lippman, *CEO*
Kheil McIntyre, *COO*
Steven Nolan, *Senior VP*
Steve Nolan, *Vice Pres*
Kevin Barrett, *VP Sls/Mktg*
EMP: 35
SALES (est): 5.7MM Privately Held
WEB: www.learningexpressllc.com
SIC: 2731 Book publishing

(G-10949)
LEARNVEST INC
113 University Pl Fl 2 (10003-0031)
PHONE.................212 675-6711
Alexa Von Tobel, *CEO*
John Gardner, *COO*
Kelly Leyden, *Vice Pres*
Edwin Quan, *Engineer*
Jeremy Brennan, *Manager*
EMP: 47
SALES (est): 6.5MM
SALES (corp-wide): 26.7B Privately Held
SIC: 2741 6282 ; investment advice
PA: The Northwestern Mutual Life Insurance Company
720 E Wisconsin Ave
Milwaukee WI 53202
414 271-1444

(G-10950)
LEATHER IMPACT INC
240 W 38th St Frnt 1 (10018-5890)
PHONE.................212 382-2788
Demitri P Kermelis, *President*
Margaretha Kermelis, *Treasurer*
◆ EMP: 5
SQ FT: 3,650
SALES (est): 420K Privately Held
WEB: www.leatherfacts.com
SIC: 3172 5199 Personal leather goods; leather, leather goods & furs; chamois leather

(G-10951)
LEBHAR-FRIEDMAN INC (PA)
Also Called: Chain Stores Age
150 W 30th St Fl 19 (10001-4119)
PHONE.................212 756-5000
Fax: 212 207-8167
J Roger Friedman, *President*
Daniel J Mills, *President*
Lebhar Friedman, *Publisher*
Miguel D Haro, *Publisher*
John Kenlon, *Publisher*
▲ EMP: 49 EST: 1925
SQ FT: 30,000
SALES (est): 111.5MM Privately Held
WEB: www.lf.com
SIC: 2721 2711 Magazines: publishing only, not printed on site; newspapers: publishing only, not printed on site

(G-10952)
LEBHAR-FRIEDMAN INC
Also Called: Circulation Dept
425 Park Ave Fl 6 (10022-3520)
PHONE.................212 756-5000
EMP: 125
SALES (corp-wide): 105.2MM Privately Held
SIC: 2721 2711 Periodicals-Publishing/Printing Newspapers-Publishing/Printing
PA: Lebhar-Friedman, Inc.
150 W 30th St Fl 19
New York NY 10001
212 756-5000

▲ = Import ▼ = Export
◆ = Import/Export

GEOGRAPHIC SECTION New York - New York County (G-10978)

(G-10953)
LEBLON HOLDINGS LLC
428 Broadway Fl 4 (10013-2594)
PHONE..................................212 741-2675
Jim Myers, *CFO*
Jaime Keller, *Mktg Dir*
Steven Luttmann,
▲ **EMP**: 35
SQ FT: 3,000
SALES (est): 3.7MM Privately Held
SIC: 2085 Rum (alcoholic beverage)
PA: Bacardi Limited
  65 Pitts Bay Road
  Hamilton
  441 294-1110

(G-10954)
LEBLON LLC
Also Called: Leblon Cachaca
428 Broadway Fl 4 (10013-2594)
PHONE..................................954 649-0148
EMP: 13 **EST**: 2005
SALES (est): 1.5MM Privately Held
SIC: 2085 Distilled & blended liquors

(G-10955)
LEBLON LLC
266 W 26th St Ste 801 (10001-6722)
PHONE..................................786 281-5672
Marcio Silveira, *Dir Ops-Prd-Mfg*
Thomas Bonney, *CFO*
Steve Luttmann, *Mng Member*
Gerrard Schweitzer,
▲ **EMP**: 40
SALES (est): 2.9MM Privately Held
SIC: 2085 Distilled & blended liquors

(G-10956)
LEDES GROUP INC
Also Called: Cosmetic World
85 5th Ave Fl 12 (10003-3019)
PHONE..................................212 840-8800
George M Ledes, *President*
John Ledes, *Publisher*
Joseph Garces, *Vice Pres*
Sally C Ledes, *Vice Pres*
Hasu Shah, *Treasurer*
EMP: 18
SQ FT: 7,000
SALES: 25.4K Privately Held
WEB: www.cosmeticworld.com
SIC: 2741 Miscellaneous publishing; newsletter publishing

(G-10957)
LEE & LOW BOOKS INCORPORATED
Also Called: Bebop Books
95 Madison Ave Rm 1205 (10016-7808)
PHONE..................................212 779-4400
Fax: 212 683-1894
Thomas Low, *President*
Kandace Coston, *Editor*
Jennifer Fox, *Editor*
Emily Hazel, *Editor*
Craig Low, *Vice Pres*
▲ **EMP**: 14
SQ FT: 4,500
SALES (est): 1.4MM Privately Held
WEB: www.leeandlow.com
SIC: 2731 Books: publishing only

(G-10958)
LEE WORLD INDUSTRIES LLC
150 Broadway Ste 1608 (10038-4381)
PHONE..................................212 265-8866
James Lee, *CEO*
Lisa Lee, *Vice Pres*
Lydia Liu, *Project Mgr*
Jeff Lee, *Opers Mgr*
Alex Wang, *Traffic Mgr*
◆ **EMP**: 175
SQ FT: 14,500
SALES: 4MM Privately Held
WEB: www.leeworld.com
SIC: 3714 Motor vehicle parts & accessories

(G-10959)
LEE YUEN FUNG TRADING CO INC (PA)
125 W 29th St Fl 5 (10001-5780)
PHONE..................................212 594-9595
Fax: 212 629-0757
Moon Tong Fok, *President*

EMP: 14
SQ FT: 4,000
SALES: 8MM Privately Held
SIC: 2833 5149 Drugs & herbs: grading, grinding & milling; seasonings, sauces & extracts

(G-10960)
LEFRAK ENTERTAINMENT CO LTD
Also Called: L M R
40 W 57th St Fl 4 (10019-4001)
PHONE..................................212 586-3600
Samuel J Lefrak, *Ch of Bd*
Richard S Lefrak, *Vice Ch Bd*
Herbert Moelis, *President*
EMP: 9
SALES (est): 660K Privately Held
SIC: 2741 3652 Music book & sheet music publishing; pre-recorded records & tapes

(G-10961)
LEG RESOURCE INC (PA)
390 5th Ave Rm 405 (10018-8198)
PHONE..................................212 736-4574
Fax: 212 736-0245
Wayne Lederman, *President*
Nancy Felgueiras, *Accounts Mgr*
Asi Efros, *Creative Dir*
▲ **EMP**: 25
SQ FT: 5,000
SALES: 25MM Privately Held
WEB: www.legresource.com
SIC: 2251 2252 Tights, women's; hosiery; men's, boys' & girls' hosiery; socks

(G-10962)
LEGGIADRO INTERNATIONAL INC (PA)
8 W 36th St Fl 9 (10018-9772)
PHONE..................................212 997-8766
Brooks Ross, *President*
Ann Ross, *Corp Secy*
◆ **EMP**: 50
SQ FT: 6,000
SALES (est): 9.5MM Privately Held
SIC: 2339 Sportswear, women's

(G-10963)
LEHMANN PRINTING COMPANY INC
247 W 37th St Rm 2a (10018-5066)
PHONE..................................212 929-2395
David Lehmann, *President*
EMP: 5
SQ FT: 10,000
SALES (est): 340K Privately Held
WEB: www.lehmannprinting.com
SIC: 2752 Commercial printing, lithographic; commercial printing, offset

(G-10964)
LEMETRIC HAIR CENTERS INC
124 E 40th St Rm 601 (10016-1769)
PHONE..................................212 986-5620
Elline Surianello, *President*
Marvin Blender, *Vice Pres*
EMP: 15
SALES (est): 1.2MM Privately Held
WEB: www.lemetric.com
SIC: 3999 7231 Hairpin mountings; beauty shops

(G-10965)
LENDING TRIMMING CO INC
179 Christopher St (10014-2815)
PHONE..................................212 242-7502
John Benis, *President*
William Jarblum, *Admin Sec*
EMP: 80 **EST**: 1944
SQ FT: 7,000
SALES (est): 4.6MM Privately Held
SIC: 2396 Trimming, fabric

(G-10966)
LENON MODELS INC
236 W 27th St Rm 900 (10001-5906)
PHONE..................................212 229-1581
Elise Hubsher, *President*
EMP: 5
SQ FT: 2,000
SALES (est): 480.2K Privately Held
SIC: 3259 Architectural clay products

(G-10967)
LENORE MARSHALL INC
231 W 29th St Frnt 1 (10001-5209)
PHONE..................................212 947-5945
Fax: 212 629-6056
Leo Marshall, *President*
John Petkanas, *President*
▲ **EMP**: 5 **EST**: 1957
SALES (est): 390K Privately Held
SIC: 2353 Millinery

(G-10968)
LEO D BERNSTEIN & SONS INC (PA)
Also Called: Bernstein Display
151 W 25th St Frnt 1 (10001-7204)
PHONE..................................212 337-9578
Fax: 718 237-5922
Roger Friedman, *Ch of Bd*
Anthony Tripoli, *President*
Edmund Bernstein, *Chairman*
Mitchell Bernstein, *COO*
Geo Pfesser, *Manager*
▲ **EMP**: 20 **EST**: 1965
SQ FT: 192,000
SALES (est): 21.6MM Privately Held
WEB: www.bernsteindisplay.com
SIC: 3999 2541 5046 7389 Forms: display, dress & show; store & office display cases & fixtures; store fixtures; store equipment; design services

(G-10969)
LEO INGWER INC
62 W 47th St Ste 1004 (10036-3286)
PHONE..................................212 719-1342
Fax: 212 869-5462
Kenneth Ingwer, *President*
Danielle I Cohen, *Vice Pres*
Rochelle Ingwer-Levine, *Vice Pres*
Sam Gross, *Sales & Mktg St*
Todd Ingwer, *Sales Executive*
EMP: 42 **EST**: 1941
SQ FT: 3,500
SALES (est): 5.2MM Privately Held
WEB: www.leoingwer.com
SIC: 3911 Mountings, gold or silver: pens, leather goods, etc.

(G-10970)
LEO PAPER INC
27 W 24th St Ste 601 (10010-3275)
PHONE..................................917 305-0708
Fax: 917 305-0709
Bijan Pakzada, *President*
EMP: 7
SALES (est): 469.2K Privately Held
SIC: 2759 Commercial printing

(G-10971)
LEO SCHACHTER & CO INC
529 5th Ave (10017-4608)
PHONE..................................212 688-2000
Michael Metz, *CEO*
Jeremy Crane, *Sales Staff*
EMP: 100
SALES (est): 2.5MM Privately Held
SIC: 3911 5094 Jewelry apparel; diamonds (gems)

(G-10972)
LEO SCHACHTER DIAMONDS LLC
Also Called: Leo Diamond, The
50 W 47th St Fl 2100 (10036-8687)
PHONE..................................212 688-2000
Fax: 212 688-3345
Eric Austein, *Partner*
Rebecca Foerster, *Exec VP*
Jake Weinblatt, *CFO*
Andrew Doenias, *Accountant*
Debbie Goldstein, *Human Res Mgr*
EMP: 100 **EST**: 1981
SQ FT: 11,335
SALES (est): 19.2MM Privately Held
WEB: www.leoschachter.com
SIC: 3915 5094 Jewelers' materials & lapidary work; jewelry & precious stones
PA: Leo Schachter Diamonds Ltd
  Bezalel
  Ramat Gan
  357 662-23

(G-10973)
LESER ENTERPRISES LTD
Also Called: Color Story
18 E 48th St Rm 1104 (10017-1014)
PHONE..................................212 644-8921
Fax: 212 308-7579
Robert Leser, *President*
Hilary Leser, *Manager*
EMP: 11
SALES (est): 1.1MM Privately Held
WEB: www.colorstory.com
SIC: 3911 Jewelry, precious metal

(G-10974)
LESILU PRODUCTIONS INC
Also Called: Hey Doll
60 W 38th St Rm 302 (10018-0281)
PHONE..................................212 947-6419
Steven Sunshine, *CEO*
Lesli Sunshine, *President*
Luanne Trovato, *Corp Secy*
▲ **EMP**: 6 **EST**: 2000
SQ FT: 650
SALES (est): 1.1MM Privately Held
SIC: 3961 Costume jewelry, ex. precious metal & semiprecious stones

(G-10975)
LESLIE STUART CO INC
Also Called: Donna Degan
149 W 36th St Fl 8 (10018-9474)
PHONE..................................212 629-4551
Gene Fobarty, *President*
Donna Degan, *Vice Pres*
Larry Maltzer, *Accountant*
Heshy Feldman, *Sales Mgr*
Eugene Fogarty, *Director*
▲ **EMP**: 17
SQ FT: 4,000
SALES (est): 2MM Privately Held
WEB: www.donnadegnan.com
SIC: 2339 Women's & misses' athletic clothing & sportswear

(G-10976)
LET WATER BE WATER LLC
Also Called: Wataah
40 W 27th St Fl 3 (10001-6908)
P.O. Box 550 (10116-0550)
PHONE..................................212 627-2630
Rose Cameron, *CEO*
Annie Kim, *Accounts Mgr*
Christine Widga, *Mktg Dir*
Carl Nagel, *Marketing Mgr*
David Wills, *Marketing Mgr*
EMP: 8
SALES (est): 3.6MM Privately Held
SIC: 2086 Water, pasteurized: packaged in cans, bottles, etc.

(G-10977)
LEVI STRAUSS & CO
1501 Broadway (10036-5601)
PHONE..................................212 944-8555
Mario David, *Branch Mgr*
EMP: 19
SALES (corp-wide): 4.4B Privately Held
WEB: www.levistrauss.com
SIC: 2325 Jeans: men's, youths' & boys'
PA: Levi Strauss & Co.
  1155 Battery St
  San Francisco CA 94111
  415 501-6000

(G-10978)
LEVINDI (DH)
800 3rd Ave (10022-7649)
PHONE..................................212 572-7000
Gean Fourtou Jr, *President*
Tina Scalise, *General Mgr*
Anita Larson, *Division Pres*
George E Bushnell III, *Vice Pres*
Kevin Conway, *Vice Pres*
▲ **EMP**: 13 **EST**: 1995
SALES (est): 8.8MM
SALES (corp-wide): 45.2MM Privately Held
SIC: 2085 2084 5182 2033 Distilled & blended liquors; neutral spirits, except fruit; bourbon whiskey; cocktails, alcoholic; brandy; wines; wine coolers (beverages); wine & distilled beverages; fruit juices: packaged in cans, jars, etc.; fruit drinks (less than 100% juice): packaged in cans, etc.; fruit juice concentrates, frozen

New York - New York County (G-10979)

HQ: Vivendi Holding I Llc
1755 Broadway Fl 2
New York NY 10019
212 572-7000

(G-10979)
LEVY GROUP INC (PA)
Also Called: Liz Claiborne Coats
1333 Broadway Fl 9 (10018-1064)
PHONE..................212 398-0707
Fax: 212 719-5547
Jack Arthur Levy, *Ch of Bd*
Donald Levy, *Chairman*
Lawrence Levy, *Vice Pres*
Richard Levy, *Vice Pres*
Rich Albom, *QC Mgr*
▲ EMP: 150 EST: 1995
SQ FT: 27,000
SALES (est): 99.8MM **Privately Held**
WEB: www.oasisfarm.com
SIC: 2337 2385 Women's & misses' suits & coats; jackets & vests, except fur & leather; women's; raincoats, except vulcanized rubber; purchased materials

(G-10980)
LEXMARK INTERNATIONAL INC
529 5th Ave (10017-4608)
PHONE..................212 949-1090
Julie Schemerhorn, *Principal*
Heather Auman, *Manager*
Jared Vichengrad, *Manager*
EMP: 20
SALES (corp-wide): 3.5B **Publicly Held**
WEB: www.lexmark.com
SIC: 3577 Printers & plotters
PA: Lexmark International, Inc.
740 W New Circle Rd
Lexington KY 40511
859 232-2000

(G-10981)
LF OUTERWEAR LLC
463 7th Ave Fl 12 (10018-7499)
PHONE..................212 239-2025
Richard Kringstein,
Barry Kringstein,
▲ EMP: 80
SALES (est): 3.1MM **Privately Held**
SIC: 2337 Women's & misses' suits & coats

(G-10982)
LGB INC
Also Called: J Valdi
1410 Broadway Rm 3205 (10018-9633)
PHONE..................212 278-8280
Eduardo Snider, *President*
Peter Reidell, *Corp Secy*
Jason Schwartz, *Manager*
EMP: 20
SALES (est): 836.8K **Privately Held**
SIC: 2339 Women's & misses' outerwear

(G-10983)
LIBERTY APPAREL COMPANY INC
1407 Broadway Rm 214 (10018-3857)
PHONE..................212 221-0101
Hagai Laniado, *Branch Mgr*
EMP: 10 **Privately Held**
WEB: www.libertyapparel.com
SIC: 2339 Women's & misses' outerwear
PA: Liberty Apparel Company Inc.
1407 Broadway Rm 1500
New York NY 10018

(G-10984)
LIBERTY APPAREL COMPANY INC (PA)
1407 Broadway Rm 1500 (10018-2836)
PHONE..................718 625-4000
Fax: 212 768-0660
Hagai Laniado, *President*
Albert Negri, *Principal*
Bryan Lattmen, *Vice Pres*
Jeffrey Wine, *CFO*
▲ EMP: 41
SQ FT: 38,000
SALES (est): 5.2MM **Privately Held**
WEB: www.libertyapparel.com
SIC: 2331 2339 2369 Women's & misses' blouses & shirts; women's & misses' outerwear; girls' & children's outerwear

(G-10985)
LIBRARY TALES PUBLISHING INC
244 5th Ave Ste Q222 (10001-7604)
PHONE..................347 394-2629
Usher Morgan, *CEO*
▼ EMP: 8
SQ FT: 359
SALES (est): 580K **Privately Held**
WEB: www.librarytalespublishing.com
SIC: 2731 Books: publishing & printing

(G-10986)
LICENDERS (PA)
939 8th Ave (10019-4264)
PHONE..................212 759-5200
Fax: 212 759-5250
Adie Horowitz, *Principal*
EMP: 9 EST: 2010
SALES (est): 1.3MM **Privately Held**
SIC: 3647 5087 Headlights (fixtures), vehicular; service establishment equipment

(G-10987)
LIFE STYLE DESIGN GROUP
Also Called: Sag Harbor
1441 Broadway Fl 7 (10018-1905)
PHONE..................212 391-8666
Fax: 212 730-0240
EMP: 35
SQ FT: 12,000
SALES (est): 3MM
SALES (corp-wide): 18.3B **Privately Held**
WEB: www.kellwoodco.com
SIC: 2339 Sportswear, women's
HQ: Kellwood Company, Llc
600 Kellwood Pkwy Ste 200
Chesterfield MO 63017
314 576-3100

(G-10988)
LIFESTYLE DESIGN USA LTD
Also Called: Cyber Knit
315 W 39th St Rm 709 (10018-4043)
PHONE..................212 279-9400
Manachem Katz, *President*
Daniel Honig, *Admin Sec*
Alexis Miller, *Services*
▲ EMP: 5
SALES (est): 540K **Privately Held**
SIC: 2257 Weft knit fabric mills

(G-10989)
LIFTFORWARD INC
261 Madison Ave Fl 9 (10016-2311)
PHONE..................917 693-4993
Jeffrey Rogers, *President*
Barbara Steinberg, *Controller*
Blendi Batusha, *Director*
Christine Reilly, *Officer*
EMP: 13
SQ FT: 1,500
SALES: 15MM **Privately Held**
SIC: 7372 Business oriented computer software

(G-10990)
LIGHT HOUSE HILL MARKETING
Also Called: Signatures
38 W 39th St Fl 4l (10018-2150)
PHONE..................212 354-1338
Donald Schmidt, *President*
▲ EMP: 16
SQ FT: 2,900
SALES (est): 1.5MM **Privately Held**
WEB: www.signaturespromo.com
SIC: 2231 Apparel & outerwear broadwoven fabrics

(G-10991)
LIGHT INC
530 Fashion Ave Rm 1002 (10018-4869)
PHONE..................212 629-1095
Alice Sim, *President*
EMP: 6
SALES (est): 710K **Privately Held**
WEB: www.light.com
SIC: 2339 Women's & misses' outerwear

(G-10992)
LIGHT WAVES CONCEPT INC
1 Bond St Apt 2c (10012-2307)
PHONE..................212 677-6400
Fax: 212 677-6945
Joel Slavis, *President*
▲ EMP: 13
SALES: 2MM **Privately Held**
WEB: www.lightwavesconcept.com
SIC: 3646 3544 Commercial indusl & institutional electric lighting fixtures; special dies, tools, jigs & fixtures

(G-10993)
LIGHTBULB PRESS INC
39 W 28th St (10001-4203)
PHONE..................212 485-8800
Kenneth Morris, *Ch of Bd*
Rickie Kowlessar, *Info Tech Dir*
Mavis Wright, *Director*
Kara Wilson, *Creative Dir*
Rachel Baumgartner, *Admin Asst*
EMP: 30
SQ FT: 7,500
SALES (est): 2.7MM **Privately Held**
WEB: www.lightbulbpress.net
SIC: 2741 Miscellaneous publishing

(G-10994)
LIGHTHOUSE COMPONENTS
14 Wall St (10005-2101)
PHONE..................917 993-6820
Maurice Gaete, *CEO*
EMP: 25
SALES (est): 858.4K **Privately Held**
SIC: 3679 Electronic components

(G-10995)
LIGHTING COLLABORATIVE INC
124 W 24th St (10011-1904)
PHONE..................212 253-7220
Fax: 212 239-7111
Lewis Herman, *Ch of Bd*
Amelia Froom, *Vice Pres*
Nicholas Fisfis, *Manager*
EMP: 6
SQ FT: 1,600
SALES (est): 894.6K **Privately Held**
WEB: www.lightingcollaborative.com
SIC: 3648 Lighting fixtures, except electric: residential

(G-10996)
LIIIIKE SHOPPING INC
37 W 37th St Fl 6 (10018-6283)
PHONE..................914 271-2001
Robert Gardos, *President*
EMP: 10
SALES (est): 800K **Privately Held**
SIC: 7372 7389 Application computer software;

(G-10997)
LILY & TAYLOR INC
Also Called: Lilly Collection
247 W 37th St Frnt 6 (10018-5042)
PHONE..................212 564-5459
Fax: 212 564-2358
Sohail Elyaszadeh, *President*
Morris Elyaszadeh, *Manager*
▲ EMP: 15
SQ FT: 3,500
SALES: 6MM **Privately Held**
WEB: www.lilyandtaylor.com
SIC: 2339 2335 2337 Women's & misses' outerwear; slacks: women's, misses' & juniors'; gowns, formal: suits: women's, misses' & juniors'; skirts, separate: women's, misses' & juniors'

(G-10998)
LINDER NEW YORK LLC
195 Chrystie St Rm 900 (10002-1230)
PHONE..................646 678-5819
Sam Linder, *Mng Member*
EMP: 11 EST: 2007
SALES (est): 1.3MM **Privately Held**
SIC: 2329 2389 Athletic (warmup, sweat & jogging) suits: men's & boys'; men's miscellaneous accessories

(G-10999)
LINDSAY-HOENIG LTD
Also Called: Lindsay & Co
64 W 48th St Ste 1306 (10036-1746)
P.O. Box 196, Rockville Centre (11571-0196)
PHONE..................212 575-9711
Fax: 800 869-0527
David Hoenig, *President*
Henry F Hoenig, *Vice Pres*

Celeste Beckford, *Office Mgr*
EMP: 6
SALES (est): 604.9K **Privately Held**
WEB: www.lindsayco.com
SIC: 3911 Jewelry, precious metal

(G-11000)
LINDT & SPRUNGLI (USA) INC
692 5th Ave (10019-4101)
PHONE..................212 582-3047
Rosita Schumacher, *Manager*
EMP: 5
SALES (corp-wide): 3.6B **Privately Held**
WEB: www.lindtusa.com
SIC: 2066 Chocolate
HQ: Lindt & Sprungli (Usa) Inc.
1 Fine Chocolate Pl
Stratham NH 03885
603 778-8100

(G-11001)
LINEN MICARTA LLC
65 Broadway Ste 1101 (10006-2573)
PHONE..................212 203-5145
Hasan Ozalp, *Mng Member*
EMP: 10 EST: 2014
SQ FT: 2,000
SALES: 1MM **Privately Held**
SIC: 3663 Cellular radio telephone

(G-11002)
LINRICH DESIGNS INC
Also Called: Linda Richards
256 W 38th St Fl 8 (10018-9123)
PHONE..................212 382-2257
Linda Breatti, *Owner*
EMP: 5
SALES (corp-wide): 699.3K **Privately Held**
WEB: www.lindarichards.com
SIC: 2339 2337 Women's & misses' jackets & coats, except sportswear; suits: women's, misses' & juniors'; skirts, separate: women's, misses' & juniors'
PA: Linrich Designs Inc
256 W 38th St Fl 8
New York NY
212 382-2257

(G-11003)
LINTEX LINENS INC
295 5th Ave Ste 1702 (10016-7160)
PHONE..................212 679-8046
Kurt Hamburger, *President*
Rae Ellen Blum, *Vice Pres*
Glorida Matias, *Bookkeeper*
▲ EMP: 450
SQ FT: 6,000
SALES (est): 31.2MM **Privately Held**
SIC: 2299 5023 Fabrics: linen, jute, hemp, ramie; linens, table

(G-11004)
LION BIOTECHNOLOGIES INC (PA)
112 W 34th St Fl 17 (10120-0001)
PHONE..................212 946-4856
Wayne Rothbaum, *Ch of Bd*
Maria Fardis, *President*
Michael T Lotze, *Vice Pres*
James Bender, *VP Mfg*
Molly Henderson, *CFO*
EMP: 14
SALES (est): 6.4MM **Publicly Held**
SIC: 2834 Pharmaceutical preparations

(G-11005)
LIONEL HABAS ASSOCIATES INC
1601 3rd Ave Apt 22d (10128-0028)
PHONE..................212 860-8454
Lionel Habas, *President*
EMP: 10
SQ FT: 200
SALES (est): 840K **Privately Held**
SIC: 2652 Setup paperboard boxes

(G-11006)
LIPPINCOTT MASSIE MCQUILKIN L
27 W 20th St Ste 305 (10011-3731)
PHONE..................212 352-2055
Fax: 212 352-2059
Rob McQuilkin, *Mng Member*
Martin Lemelman, *Professor*

GEOGRAPHIC SECTION

Amanda Panitch, *Associate*
EMP: 10
SALES (est): 845.8K **Privately Held**
SIC: 2731 Book publishing

(G-11007)
LIQUOR BOTTLE PACKG INTL INC
305 Madison Ave Ste 1357 (10165-1319)
PHONE..................................212 922-2813
Andy Fraser, *President*
♦ **EMP:** 5
SQ FT: 2,200
SALES (est): 972.7K **Privately Held**
SIC: 3221 Bottles for packing, bottling & canning: glass

(G-11008)
LITERARY CLASSICS OF US
Also Called: Library of America
14 E 60th St Ste 1101 (10022-7115)
PHONE..................................212 308-3360
Fax: 212 750-8352
Cheryl Hurley, *President*
Daniel Baker, *CFO*
Benjamin Ordover, *Treasurer*
Lily TSE, *Accountant*
Karen Iker, *Marketing Staff*
▲ **EMP:** 16
SQ FT: 4,000
SALES: 4.7MM **Privately Held**
SIC: 2731 2732 Book publishing; book printing

(G-11009)
LITHO PARTNERS INC
Also Called: Happy Printer, The
175 Varick St Fl 8 (10014-7408)
PHONE..................................212 627-9225
Ken Lerman, *President*
Sam Nicholas, *Manager*
EMP: 28
SALES (est): 2.9MM **Privately Held**
SIC: 2752 Commercial printing, lithographic

(G-11010)
LITHOMATIC BUSINESS FORMS INC
233 W 18th St Frnt A (10011-4570)
PHONE..................................212 255-6700
Fax: 212 242-5963
Irwin Ostrega, *President*
Herman Margules, *Accountant*
Carmin Diaz, *Bookkeeper*
EMP: 3
SQ FT: 5,000
SALES: 1.5MM **Privately Held**
SIC: 2752 Commercial printing, offset

(G-11011)
LITTLE BEE BOOKS INC
251 Park Ave S Fl 12 (10010-7302)
PHONE..................................212 321-0237
Shimul Tolia, *President*
Thomas Morgan, *Finance Dir*
EMP: 6
SALES (est): 712.6K
SALES (corp-wide): 3.1B **Privately Held**
SIC: 2731 Books: publishing only
HQ: Bonnier Corporation
    460 N Orlando Ave Ste 200
    Winter Park FL 32789
    407 622-1014

(G-11012)
LITTLE ERIC SHOES ON MADISON
1118 Madison Ave (10028-0406)
PHONE..................................212 717-1513
Robert Pansinkoff, *President*
Robert Pansinkoff, *President*
EMP: 6
SALES (est): 904.7K **Privately Held**
SIC: 3021 Canvas shoes, rubber soled

(G-11013)
LITTLE WOLF CABINET SHOP INC
1583 1st Ave Frnt 1 (10028-4273)
PHONE..................................212 734-1116
Fax: 212 628-1966
Wolfgang Fritsch, *President*
Maureen Fritsch, *Corp Secy*
John Fritsch, *Vice Pres*

John Wolf, *Manager*
EMP: 20
SQ FT: 2,500
SALES (est): 2.7MM **Privately Held**
SIC: 2511 5712 2541 2521 Wood household furniture; furniture stores; wood partitions & fixtures; wood office furniture; wood kitchen cabinets

(G-11014)
LITTLEBITS ELECTRONICS INC
601 W 26th St Ste M274 (10001-1101)
PHONE..................................917 464-4577
Aya Bdeir, *CEO*
EMP: 95
SQ FT: 18,000
SALES (est): 16.6MM **Privately Held**
SIC: 3944 Electronic toys

(G-11015)
LIVERIGHT PUBLISHING CORP
Also Called: Norton, Ww & Company,
500 5th Ave Fl 6 (10110-0699)
PHONE..................................212 354-5500
Drake McSeely, *President*
Victor Schmalzer, *General Mgr*
John G Benedict, *Vice Pres*
James Jordan, *Vice Pres*
Star Lawrence, *Vice Pres*
EMP: 9
SQ FT: 3,000
SALES (est): 902.8K
SALES (corp-wide): 280.3MM **Privately Held**
WEB: www.wwnorton.com
SIC: 2731 Books: publishing only
PA: W. W. Norton & Company, Inc.
    500 5th Ave Fl 6
    New York NY 10110
    212 354-5500

(G-11016)
LIVETILES CORP
60 Madison Ave Fl 8 (10010-1676)
PHONE..................................917 472-7887
Jonathan Green, *Finance Dir*
EMP: 19
SQ FT: 100
SALES (est): 844K **Privately Held**
SIC: 7372 Business oriented computer software

(G-11017)
LM MIGNON LLC
Also Called: Mignon Group, The
499 Fashion Ave Fl 4n (10018-6844)
PHONE..................................212 730-9221
Vincent Mignon, *Mng Member*
♦ **EMP:** 13
SQ FT: 3,500
SALES: 6MM **Privately Held**
SIC: 2335 Women's, juniors' & misses' dresses; bridal & formal gowns

(G-11018)
LOAR GROUP INC (PA)
450 Lexington Ave Fl 31 (10017-3925)
PHONE..................................212 210-9348
Glenn Dalessandro, *CFO*
Jim Mullen, *Sales Staff*
Michael Manella, *General Counsel*
EMP: 144
SALES (est): 22.2MM **Privately Held**
SIC: 3728 Aircraft parts & equipment

(G-11019)
LOCATIONS MAGAZINE
124 E 79th St (10075-0353)
PHONE..................................212 288-4745
Joel Scher, *Owner*
Joel Cher, *Manager*
Sharon Scher, *Admin Sec*
EMP: 5
SALES (est): 290K **Privately Held**
SIC: 2721 Magazines: publishing only, not printed on site

(G-11020)
LOCKHEED MARTIN CORPORATION
420 Lexington Ave Rm 2601 (10170-2702)
PHONE..................................212 953-1510
Ellen Strauss, *Manager*
Kimball Lau, *Administration*
EMP: 8

SALES (corp-wide): 46.1B **Publicly Held**
WEB: www.lockheedmartin.com
SIC: 3721 Aircraft
PA: Lockheed Martin Corporation
    6801 Rockledge Dr
    Bethesda MD 20817
    301 897-6000

(G-11021)
LOCKHEED MARTIN CORPORATION
600 3rd Ave Fl 35 (10016-2001)
PHONE..................................212 697-1105
Lisa McMeekin, *Branch Mgr*
Joe Oparesi, *Info Tech Dir*
EMP: 85
SALES (corp-wide): 46.1B **Publicly Held**
WEB: www.lockheedmartin.com
SIC: 3812 Search & navigation equipment
PA: Lockheed Martin Corporation
    6801 Rockledge Dr
    Bethesda MD 20817
    301 897-6000

(G-11022)
LOGO
1515 Broadway (10036-8901)
PHONE..................................212 846-2568
EMP: 5
SALES (est): 516.8K **Privately Held**
SIC: 2869 Fuels

(G-11023)
LOKAI HOLDINGS LLC
36 E 31st St Rm 602 (10016-6918)
PHONE..................................646 979-3474
Steven Izen, *CEO*
Andrew Actman, *CFO*
EMP: 10
SQ FT: 3,000
SALES (est): 13MM **Privately Held**
SIC: 3911 5199 Bracelets, precious metal; general merchandise, non-durable

(G-11024)
LOLLYTOGS LTD (PA)
Also Called: French Toast
100 W 33rd St Ste 1012 (10001-2914)
PHONE..................................212 502-6000
Fax: 212 594-3030
Richard Sutton, *CEO*
Morris Sutton, *President*
Vishal Chaudhry, *Managing Dir*
Robin Polsley, *Vice Pres*
Alfred Sutton, *Vice Pres*
♦ **EMP:** 80 **EST:** 1958
SQ FT: 40,000
SALES (est): 2.4MM **Privately Held**
SIC: 2369 5137 Girls' & children's outerwear; sportswear, women's & children's

(G-11025)
LONDON THEATER NEWS LTD
12 E 86th St Apt 620 (10028-0511)
PHONE..................................212 517-8608
Fax: 212 249-9371
Roger Harris, *President*
EMP: 19
SALES (est): 130K **Privately Held**
SIC: 2741 7922 Newsletter publishing; ticket agency, theatrical

(G-11026)
LONGO NEW YORK INC
444 W 17th St (10011-5893)
P.O. Box 511, Wharton NJ (07885-0511)
PHONE..................................212 929-7128
Fax: 212 633-9534
Joe M Longo, *President*
EMP: 10
SALES (est): 485.9K **Privately Held**
SIC: 7694 Electric motor repair

(G-11027)
LONGTAIL STUDIOS INC
180 Varick St Rm 820 (10014-5419)
PHONE..................................646 443-8146
Gerard Guillemot, *President*
Claude Guillemot, *Vice Pres*
Michelle Guillemot, *Vice Pres*
Yves Guillemot, *Vice Pres*
Sandeep Bisla, *Manager*
EMP: 26
SQ FT: 4,000

SALES (est): 3.2MM **Privately Held**
WEB: www.longtailstudios.com
SIC: 3695 Computer software tape & disks: blank, rigid & floppy

(G-11028)
LOOK BY M INC
838 Ave Of The Americas (10001-4193)
PHONE..................................212 213-4019
Youjung Kim, *President*
EMP: 5
SALES (est): 329.2K **Privately Held**
SIC: 2252 Tights & leg warmers

(G-11029)
LOOKBOOKS MEDIA INC
208 W 30th St Rm 802 (10001-0883)
PHONE..................................646 737-3360
Adam Helfgott, *CTO*
EMP: 15
SALES (est): 1.1MM **Privately Held**
SIC: 7372 Application computer software

(G-11030)
LOOM CONCEPTS LLC
767 Lexington Ave Rm 405 (10065-8553)
PHONE..................................212 813-9586
John O'Callaghan,
▲ **EMP:** 2
SQ FT: 500
SALES: 1.8MM **Privately Held**
SIC: 2273 Carpets & rugs

(G-11031)
LOOMSTATE LLC
270 Bowery Fl 3 (10012-3674)
PHONE..................................212 219-2300
Berrin Noorata, *Managing Prtnr*
Art Ryan, *Mng Member*
Kevin Ryan,
▲ **EMP:** 25
SALES (est): 4MM **Privately Held**
SIC: 2231 Weaving mill, broadwoven fabrics: wool or similar fabric

(G-11032)
LORAL SPACE & COMMNCTNS HOLDNG
565 5th Ave Fl 19 (10017-2431)
PHONE..................................212 697-1105
EMP: 30
SALES (est): 2MM **Publicly Held**
SIC: 3663 Satellites, communications
HQ: Loral Spacecom Corporation
    565 5th Ave Fl 19
    New York NY 10017
    212 697-1105

(G-11033)
LORAL SPACE COMMUNICATIONS INC (PA)
565 5th Ave (10017-2413)
PHONE..................................212 697-1105
Fax: 212 338-5662
AVI Katz, *President*
Gregory Clark, *COO*
Jeanette Clonan, *Vice Pres*
Barry Sitler, *Vice Pres*
Melody Wang, *Senior Buyer*
EMP: 22
SQ FT: 9,000
SALES (est): 869.9MM **Publicly Held**
WEB: www.ssloral.com
SIC: 3663 4899 Satellites, communications; satellite earth stations; data communication services

(G-11034)
LORAL SPACECOM CORPORATION (HQ)
565 5th Ave Fl 19 (10017-2431)
PHONE..................................212 697-1105
Michael Targoff, *CEO*
Richard Mastoloni, *Treasurer*
John Stack, *Asst Treas*
Carlos Castillo, *Manager*
EMP: 30
SALES: 869.4MM **Publicly Held**
WEB: www.hq.loral.com
SIC: 3663 Satellites, communications

New York - New York County (G-11035)

(G-11035)
LOREAL USA INC
Biotherm
575 5th Ave Bsmt (10017-2446)
PHONE..................212 818-1500
Robert J Cassou, *Senior VP*
Richard Roderick, *Senior VP*
Pierre Rogers, *Senior VP*
Rosemarie Cirminiello, *Assistant VP*
Kurt Bloedel, *Vice Pres*
EMP: 470
SALES (corp-wide): 3.1B **Privately Held**
WEB: www.lorealparisusa.com
SIC: **2844** Hair preparations, including shampoos; cosmetic preparations; perfumes & colognes
HQ: L'oreal Usa, Inc.
   10 Hudson Yards
   New York NY 10001
   212 818-1500

(G-11036)
LOREAL USA INC
435 Hudson St (10014-3941)
PHONE..................917 606-9554
Lindsay Atha, *Manager*
EMP: 373
SALES (corp-wide): 3.1B **Privately Held**
WEB: www.lorealparisusa.com
SIC: **2844 5122** Toilet preparations; cosmetics, perfumes & hair products
HQ: L'oreal Usa, Inc.
   10 Hudson Yards
   New York NY 10001
   212 818-1500

(G-11037)
LOREAL USA INC
575 5th Ave Fl 20 (10017-2422)
PHONE..................212 389-4201
Karen Czajkowski, *Branch Mgr*
EMP: 30
SALES (corp-wide): 3.1B **Privately Held**
WEB: www.lorealparisusa.com
SIC: **2844** Depilatories (cosmetic)
HQ: L'oreal Usa, Inc.
   10 Hudson Yards
   New York NY 10001
   212 818-1500

(G-11038)
LOREAL USA INC
Also Called: L'Oreal Paris
575 5th Ave Fl 23 (10017-2430)
PHONE..................212 984-4704
Joseph Campinell, *Manager*
EMP: 8
SALES (corp-wide): 3.1B **Privately Held**
WEB: www.lorealparisusa.com
SIC: **2844** Hair preparations, including shampoos
HQ: L'oreal Usa, Inc.
   10 Hudson Yards
   New York NY 10001
   212 818-1500

(G-11039)
LOREAL USA INC
575 5th Ave Fl 25 (10017-2422)
PHONE..................646 658-5477
Amanda Leo, *General Mgr*
Elio Travieso, *Engineer*
Katy Holgate, *Director*
EMP: 274
SALES (corp-wide): 3.1B **Privately Held**
SIC: **2844** Hair preparations, including shampoos
HQ: L'oreal Usa, Inc.
   10 Hudson Yards
   New York NY 10001
   212 818-1500

(G-11040)
LOREAL USA PRODUCTS INC (DH)
575 5th Ave Bsmt (10017-2446)
PHONE..................732 873-3520
Frederic Roze, *President*
Rebecca Caruso, *Exec VP*
Paul Sharnsky, *Senior VP*
Arturo Aguayo, *Purch Dir*
Robyn Palang, *Purch Dir*
▲ EMP: 5

SALES (est): 4.9MM
SALES (corp-wide): 3.1B **Privately Held**
SIC: **2844** Hair coloring preparations; shaving preparations; cosmetic preparations; toilet preparations
HQ: L'oreal Usa, Inc.
   10 Hudson Yards
   New York NY 10001
   212 818-1500

(G-11041)
LORELEI ORTHOTICS PROSTHETICS
19 W 21st St Rm 204 (10010-6882)
PHONE..................212 727-2011
Brian Kilcommons, *President*
Alene Chase, *Vice Pres*
EMP: 6
SQ FT: 5,000
SALES (est): 610K **Privately Held**
SIC: **3842** Braces, orthopedic

(G-11042)
LOREMI JEWELRY INC
17 W 45th St Ste 501 (10036-4922)
PHONE..................212 840-3429
Enzo Palmeri, *President*
EMP: 25 EST: 1987
SALES: 1MM **Privately Held**
SIC: **3911 3915** Jewelry, precious metal; jewelers' materials & lapidary work

(G-11043)
LORNAMEAD INC (DH)
1359 Broadway Fl 17 (10018-7117)
PHONE..................914 630-7733
Randy Sloan, *CEO*
B Guth, *Vice Pres*
Colin Lorimer, *Vice Pres*
James Carney, *VP Opers*
Scott Mitchell, *VP Opers*
◆ EMP: 90
SQ FT: 66,000
SALES (est): 17.4MM **Privately Held**
WEB: www.lornameadna.com
SIC: **2844 3843** Toilet preparations; compounds, dental
HQ: Lornamead Group Limited
   Centenary House Centenary Way
   Salford LANCS
   127 641-5740

(G-11044)
LOS ANGELES MAG HOLDG CO INC (DH)
77 W 66th St (10023-6201)
PHONE..................212 456-7777
Joan McCraw, *President*
EMP: 20
SQ FT: 3,500
SALES (est): 6MM **Publicly Held**
SIC: **2721** Magazines: publishing only, not printed on site
HQ: Abc Holding Company Inc.
   77 W 66th St Rm 100
   New York NY 10023
   212 456-7777

(G-11045)
LOST WORLDS INC
920 Riverside Dr Apt 68 (10032-5468)
PHONE..................212 923-3423
Stuart Clurman, *President*
EMP: 9
SALES (est): 670K **Privately Held**
SIC: **2386 5699** Coats & jackets, leather & sheep-lined; leather garments

(G-11046)
LOTTA LUV BEAUTY LLC
1359 Broadway Fl 17 (10018-7117)
PHONE..................646 786-2847
Jeremy Spears, *Manager*
Sabrina Vertucci, *Executive*
Elizabeth Alli,
▲ EMP: 10
SQ FT: 20,000
SALES (est): 1.3MM **Privately Held**
SIC: **2834 5122** Lip balms; cosmetics
PA: Li & Fung Limited
   C/O: Appleby
   Hamilton
   441 295-2244

(G-11047)
LOU SALLY FASHIONS CORP (PA)
Also Called: S L Fashions
1400 Broadway Rm 601 (10018-0728)
PHONE..................212 354-9670
Fax: 212 719-2942
Mitchell Grabow, *CEO*
Bella Postelnik, *Controller*
▲ EMP: 39
SQ FT: 5,500
SALES: 35MM **Privately Held**
SIC: **2335** Women's, juniors' & misses' dresses

(G-11048)
LOU SALLY FASHIONS CORP
1400 Broadway Lbby 3 (10018-5369)
PHONE..................212 354-1283
Tony Porni, *Vice Pres*
EMP: 40
SALES (corp-wide): 35MM **Privately Held**
SIC: **2335** Women's, juniors' & misses' dresses
PA: Lou Sally Fashions Corp
   1400 Broadway Rm 601
   New York NY 10018
   212 354-9670

(G-11049)
LOUIS HORNICK & CO INC
117 E 38th St (10016-2601)
P.O. Box 1584, Quogue (11959-1584)
PHONE..................212 679-2448
Fax: 212 779-7098
Louis Hornick II, *CEO*
Louis Hornick III, *COO*
Sidney Bluming, *Counsel*
◆ EMP: 5 EST: 1918
SALES (est): 913K **Privately Held**
WEB: www.louishornick.com
SIC: **2391 5023** Curtains & draperies; curtains, window: made from purchased materials; curtains; draperies

(G-11050)
LOUIS TAMIS & SONS INC
10 E 38th St Fl 6 (10016-0004)
PHONE..................212 684-1760
Fax: 212 481-3394
William Tamis, *President*
Stephen Tamis, *Corp Secy*
Jeff Tamis, *Vice Pres*
Ariella Cohen, *Admin Asst*
EMP: 25 EST: 1910
SQ FT: 4,500
SALES (est): 3.8MM **Privately Held**
WEB: www.louistamis.com
SIC: **3911** Jewelry, precious metal

(G-11051)
LOUIS VUITTON NORTH AMER INC
1000 3rd Ave (10022-1230)
PHONE..................212 644-2574
Fax: 212 702-0795
Tina Motley, *Manager*
EMP: 7
SALES (corp-wide): 255.7MM **Privately Held**
SIC: **2711** Newspapers, publishing & printing
HQ: Louis Vuitton North America, Inc.
   1 E 57th St
   New York NY 10022
   212 758-8877

(G-11052)
LOUNGEHOUSE LLC
34 W 33rd St Fl 11 (10001-3304)
PHONE..................646 524-2965
Irving Safdieh, *President*
EMP: 20
SQ FT: 10,000
SALES (est): 856.7K **Privately Held**
SIC: **2341** Nightgowns & negligees: women's & children's

(G-11053)
LOVEE DOLL & TOY CO INC
39 W 38th St Rm 4w (10018-5540)
PHONE..................212 242-1545
Fax: 212 242-4596
Sam Horowitz, *President*

▲ EMP: 5 EST: 1962
SQ FT: 40,000
SALES (est): 894.2K **Privately Held**
SIC: **3942** Dolls, except stuffed toy animals

(G-11054)
LOVELY BRIDE LLC
182 Duane St Frnt A (10013-6605)
PHONE..................212 924-2050
Lanie List, *Owner*
EMP: 8
SALES (est): 740.3K **Privately Held**
SIC: **2335** Bridal & formal gowns

(G-11055)
LS POWER EQUITY PARTNERS LP (PA)
1700 Broadway Fl 35 (10019-5905)
PHONE..................212 615-3456
Mike Segal, *Ch of Bd*
Mark Brennan, *Exec VP*
Shimon Edelstein, *Exec VP*
John King, *Exec VP*
David Nanus, *Exec VP*
EMP: 1
SALES (est): 82.1MM **Privately Held**
WEB: www.ziccardi.com
SIC: **3568** 1796 Power transmission equipment; power generating equipment installation

(G-11056)
LT2 LLC
Also Called: Letigre
250 Park Ave S Fl 10 (10003-1402)
PHONE..................212 684-1510
Paul Pagano, *CFO*
Nisha Crooks, *Accountant*
Carol Wang, *Manager*
Ryan O'Sullivan,
EMP: 25
SQ FT: 1,500
SALES: 25MM **Privately Held**
WEB: www.lt2.com
SIC: **2321** 2331 Men's & boys' furnishings; women's & misses' blouses & shirts

(G-11057)
LTB MEDIA (USA) INC
Also Called: Louise Blouin Media
88 Laight St (10013-2070)
PHONE..................212 447-9555
Louise B Macbain, *President*
Kathy Murphy, *Publisher*
Nicolai Hartvig, *Editor*
Derek Page, *Vice Pres*
Andrea Renaud, *Sales Dir*
EMP: 100
SQ FT: 16,000
SALES (est): 16.4MM **Privately Held**
SIC: **2721** Magazines: publishing & printing

(G-11058)
LUCKY MAGAZINE
4 Times Sq Fl 22 (10036-6518)
PHONE..................212 286-6220
EMP: 15
SALES (est): 1.2MM **Privately Held**
SIC: **2721** Periodicals-Publishing/Printing

(G-11059)
LUCKY PEACH LLC
128 Lafayette St (10013-3174)
PHONE..................212 228-0031
Narie Chung, *Finance*
Susan Wright,
EMP: 7
SALES (est): 630.3K **Privately Held**
SIC: **2741** Miscellaneous publishing

(G-11060)
LUDLOW MUSIC INC
266 W 37th St Fl 17 (10018-6655)
PHONE..................212 594-9795
Larry Richmond, *President*
Allen Brackerman, *General Mgr*
Bernard Gartler, *Vice Pres*
EMP: 14 EST: 1949
SALES (est): 645.5K **Privately Held**
SIC: **2741** Music, sheet: publishing only, not printed on site

GEOGRAPHIC SECTION

New York - New York County (G-11088)

(G-11061)
LUKOIL AMERICAS CORPORATION (HQ)
505 5th Ave Fl 9 (10017-4921)
PHONE.................................212 421-4141
Robert Ferluga, *CEO*
Vadim Guzman, *Ch of Bd*
Linda Raynor, *Finance*
Ivan Jackson, *Sales Staff*
EMP: 125 **EST:** 1997
SALES (est): 96.2MM
SALES (corp-wide): 2B **Privately Held**
SIC: 1311 Crude petroleum & natural gas
PA: Lukoil, Pao
    11 Bulvar Sretenski
    Moscow 10100
    495 628-9841

(G-11062)
LUKOIL NORTH AMERICA LLC (DH)
505 5th Ave Fl 9 (10017-4921)
PHONE.................................212 421-4141
Vadim Gulzman, *CEO*
EMP: 25
SALES (est): 23.1MM
SALES (corp-wide): 2B **Privately Held**
SIC: 1381 5541 Drilling oil & gas wells; filling stations, gasoline
HQ: Lukoil-Volgogradenergo, Ooo
    17 Ul. Im Motsarta
    Volgograd 40002
    844 225-2904

(G-11063)
LULU DK LLC
245 E 60th St Apt 1 (10022-1451)
PHONE.................................212 223-4234
Pia Miranda, *Opers Staff*
Alexandra De Kwiatkowski,
Lori Prince,
▲ **EMP:** 4
SALES (est): 1MM **Privately Held**
SIC: 2679 7389 Wallpaper: made from purchased paper; interior design services

(G-11064)
LULUVISE INC
229 W 116th St Apt 5a (10026-2799)
PHONE.................................914 309-7812
Kewhyun Kelly-Yuoh, *CFO*
EMP: 25 **EST:** 2011
SQ FT: 1,000
SALES (est): 1.6MM **Privately Held**
SIC: 7372 Application computer software

(G-11065)
LUTHIER MUSICAL CORP
49 W 24th St Fl 4 (10010-3570)
PHONE.................................212 397-6038
Tony Acosta, *President*
▲ **EMP:** 6
SQ FT: 10,000
SALES (est): 76.7K **Privately Held**
WEB: www.luthiermusic.com
SIC: 3931 Guitars & parts, electric & non-electric

(G-11066)
LUXE IMAGINE CONSULTING LLC
261 W 35th St Ste 404 (10001-1906)
PHONE.................................212 273-9770
EMP: 5
SALES (est): 270K **Privately Held**
SIC: 2329 2339 Mfg Mens Children & Women's Apparel

(G-11067)
M & CO LTD
76 9th Ave Fl 11 (10011-4962)
PHONE.................................212 414-6400
Tibor Kalman, *President*
▲ **EMP:** 6
SQ FT: 3,000
SALES: 450K **Privately Held**
SIC: 3873 Clocks, assembly of

(G-11068)
M & S QUALITY CO LTD
26 W 47th St Ste 502 (10036-8603)
PHONE.................................212 302-8757
Fax: 212 302-2629
Michael Saks, *President*
EMP: 10
SALES (est): 969.5K **Privately Held**
SIC: 3911 Jewelry, precious metal

(G-11069)
M & S SCHMALBERG INC
242 W 36th St Rm 700 (10018-8965)
PHONE.................................212 244-2090
Fax: 212 244-2097
Warren Brand, *President*
Deborah Brand, *Vice Pres*
EMP: 10 **EST:** 1947
SQ FT: 2,500
SALES (est): 700K **Privately Held**
SIC: 3999 5992 Flowers, artificial & preserved; florists

(G-11070)
M G NEW YORK INC
14 E 60th St Ste 400 (10022-7146)
PHONE.................................212 371-5566
Marlyse Gros, *President*
◆ **EMP:** 10
SQ FT: 1,665
SALES: 28.8MM **Privately Held**
SIC: 3172 5122 Cosmetic bags; drugs, proprietaries & sundries

(G-11071)
M H MANUFACTURING INCORPORATED
50 W 47th St (10036-8621)
P.O. Box 1743 (10163-1743)
PHONE.................................212 461-6900
Judah Poupko, *Vice Pres*
EMP: 9 **EST:** 2009
SALES (est): 1MM **Privately Held**
WEB: www.mhdco.com
SIC: 3911 Pins (jewelry), precious metal

(G-11072)
M HESKIA COMPANY INC
98 Cutter Rd Ste 125 (10036)
PHONE.................................212 768-1845
EMP: 5
SALES (est): 450K **Privately Held**
SIC: 3911 Mfg Jewelry

(G-11073)
M HIDARY & CO INC
10 W 33rd St Rm 900 (10001-3317)
PHONE.................................212 736-6540
Fax: 212 268-0304
Margie Valverde, *Managing Dir*
Morris Hidary, *Chairman*
Bert Hidary, *Vice Pres*
Richard Levine, *CFO*
David Hidary, *Treasurer*
▲ **EMP:** 100 **EST:** 1948
SQ FT: 20,000
SALES (est): 17.6MM **Privately Held**
SIC: 2369 2311 2325 2329 Girls' & children's outerwear; men's & boys' suits & coats; men's & boys' trousers & slacks; men's & boys' sportswear & athletic clothing; men's & boys' clothing; women's & children's clothing

(G-11074)
M I T POLY-CART CORP
211 Central Park W (10024-6020)
PHONE.................................212 724-7290
Fax: 212 721-9022
Dan Moss, *President*
Isaac Rinkewich, *Vice Pres*
Tova Moss, *Treasurer*
EMP: 5
SQ FT: 1,000
SALES (est): 300K **Privately Held**
WEB: www.mitpolycart.com
SIC: 3089 Plastic containers, except foam

(G-11075)
M L DESIGN INC (PA)
77 Ludlow St Frnt 1 (10002-3898)
PHONE.................................212 233-0213
Tommy Lam, *President*
▲ **EMP:** 9
SALES (est): 772.8K **Privately Held**
SIC: 2752 Commercial printing, offset

(G-11076)
M S B INTERNATIONAL LTD (PA)
Also Called: Nyc Design Co
1412 Broadway Rm 1210 (10018-9228)
PHONE.................................212 302-5551
Maia Chait, *President*
Robert Guttenberg, *President*
Sunny Leigh, *Vice Pres*
May Woo, *Office Mgr*
Frank Rascati, *Manager*
EMP: 15
SALES (est): 2.7MM **Privately Held**
SIC: 2331 2321 2325 Women's & misses' blouses & shirts; men's & boys' furnishings; men's & boys' trousers & slacks

(G-11077)
M SHANKEN COMMUNICATIONS INC (PA)
825 8th Ave Fl 33 (10019-8872)
PHONE.................................212 684-4224
Marvin R Shanken, *Ch of Bd*
Michael Moaba, *Vice Ch Bd*
Barry Abrams, *Publisher*
Michael Batterberry, *Editor*
Kimberly Carmichael, *Editor*
EMP: 125
SQ FT: 15,000
SALES (est): 36.7MM **Privately Held**
SIC: 2721 Magazines: publishing & printing

(G-11078)
M&S ACCESSORY NETWORK CORP
Also Called: Gabbagoods
10 W 33rd St Rm 718 (10001-3306)
PHONE.................................347 492-7790
Jack Mosseri, *CEO*
Albert Salama, *Vice Pres*
▲ **EMP:** 15 **EST:** 2011
SQ FT: 2,500
SALES (est): 2.2MM **Privately Held**
SIC: 3663 Mobile communication equipment

(G-11079)
M/B MIDTOWN LLC
141 5th Ave Fl 2 (10010-7105)
PHONE.................................212 477-2495
Fax: 212 529-2813
Joe Cayre, *Manager*
EMP: 10
SALES (est): 958K **Privately Held**
SIC: 2731 Book publishing

(G-11080)
M2 FASHION GROUP HOLDINGS INC
Also Called: M2 Apparel
153 E 87th St Apt 10d (10128-2708)
PHONE.................................917 208-2948
Ming Lee Wilcox, *President*
EMP: 6
SQ FT: 1,000
SALES: 2MM **Privately Held**
SIC: 2389 Apparel for handicapped

(G-11081)
MAC FADDEN HOLDINGS INC (PA)
Also Called: Sterling McFadden
333 7th Ave Fl 11 (10001-5824)
PHONE.................................212 614-3980
Peter J Callahan, *Ch of Bd*
Michael J Boylan, *President*
Pete Chapelle, *Publisher*
Anna Blanco, *Vice Pres*
Bobbie Macintosh, *Marketing Mgr*
EMP: 35
SQ FT: 11,000
SALES (est): 10MM **Privately Held**
WEB: www.macfad.com
SIC: 2721 1382 Magazines: publishing only, not printed on site; oil & gas exploration services

(G-11082)
MAC SWED INC (PA)
20 W 36th St Rm 5r (10018-9790)
PHONE.................................917 617-3885
Fax: 212 213-0169
Natham Shams, *Ch of Bd*
Marc Shams, *CFO*
▲ **EMP:** 8
SQ FT: 15,000
SALES (est): 1.6MM **Privately Held**
SIC: 3961 5094 Costume jewelry; jewelry

(G-11083)
MACFADDEN CMMNCTIONS GROUP LLC
Also Called: HSN
333 7th Ave Fl 11 (10001-5824)
PHONE.................................212 979-4800
Fax: 212 979-4825
Peter Callahan, *Managing Prtnr*
Jess Schesser, *Partner*
Lisa Adams, *Publisher*
Barbara Kaplan, *Publisher*
Jeff Cioletti, *Editor*
▲ **EMP:** 105
SQ FT: 33,000
SALES (est): 16.8MM **Privately Held**
SIC: 2721 Magazines: publishing only, not printed on site

(G-11084)
MACGREGOR GOLF NORTH AMER INC (PA)
110 W 57th St Fl 4 (10019-3304)
PHONE.................................646 840-5200
Barry Schneider, *Ch of Bd*
Duff Meyercord, *Principal*
Kenneth Kovasala, *Vice Pres*
Joe Rocco, *Vice Pres*
Davis Jackson, *Purchasing*
▲ **EMP:** 100
SQ FT: 60,000 **Privately Held**
WEB: www.macgregorgolf.com
SIC: 3949 Sporting & athletic goods

(G-11085)
MACMILLAN ACADEMIC PUBG INC (HQ)
75 Varick St Fl 9 (10013-1917)
PHONE.................................212 226-1476
Richard Charkin, *Ch of Bd*
Philip Getz, *Editor*
D M Bagwell, *Vice Pres*
Steve Cohen, *Vice Pres*
Roy Gainsburg, *Vice Pres*
EMP: 19
SALES (est): 3.8MM
SALES (corp-wide): 2.1B **Privately Held**
SIC: 2741 Miscellaneous publishing
PA: Georg Von Holtzbrinck Gmbh & Co.Kg
    Gansheidestr. 26
    Stuttgart 70184
    711 215-00

(G-11086)
MACMILLAN COLLEGE PUBG CO INC
866 3rd Ave Frnt 2 (10022-6221)
PHONE.................................212 702-2000
Walter M Volpi, *CFO*
John Bender, *Manager*
United States, *Agent*
EMP: 10
SALES (corp-wide): 2.1B **Privately Held**
SIC: 2731 Book publishing
HQ: Macmillan Limited
    Macmillan Building
    London
    207 418-5506

(G-11087)
MACMILLAN HOLDINGS LLC
1 New York Plz Ste 4500 (10004-1562)
PHONE.................................212 576-9428
Fritz Foy, *Principal*
Lisa Williams, *Manager*
Andrew Crenshaw, *Director*
EMP: 7
SALES (corp-wide): 2.1B **Privately Held**
SIC: 2721 Magazines: publishing only, not printed on site
HQ: Macmillan Holdings, Llc
    175 5th Ave
    New York NY 10010

(G-11088)
MACMILLAN PUBLISHERS INC
175 5th Ave Ste 400 (10010-7726)
PHONE.................................646 307-5151
John Sargent, *CEO*
Lorraine Keelan, *Publisher*
Whitney Frick, *Editor*
Rose Hilliard, *Editor*
Daniela Rapp, *Editor*
▲ **EMP:** 1200

New York - New York County (G-11089) — GEOGRAPHIC SECTION

SALES (est): 138.5MM
SALES (corp-wide): 2.1B **Privately Held**
SIC: 2731 5192 Books: publishing only; books
HQ: Macmillan Limited
  Macmillan Building
  London
  207 418-5506

(G-11089)
MACMILLAN PUBLISHING GROUP LLC (DH)
Also Called: Palagrave Macmillan
175 5th Ave (10010-7703)
PHONE..................................212 674-5151
Fax: 212 529-0594
Sally Richardson, *President*
Emily Angell, *Editor*
Brenda Copeland, *Editor*
Sylvan Creekmore, *Editor*
Laurie Henderson, *Editor*
◆ EMP: 36
SQ FT: 81,000
SALES (est): 134.3MM
SALES (corp-wide): 2.1B **Privately Held**
WEB: www.stmartins.com
SIC: 2731 5192 Books: publishing only; books

(G-11090)
MACROCHEM CORPORATION (HQ)
80 Broad St Ste 2210 (10004-2209)
PHONE..................................212 514-8094
James M Pachence MD, *CEO*
Robert J Deluccia, *Ch of Bd*
David P Luci, *Officer*
EMP: 6
SALES (est): 196.4K
SALES (corp-wide): 1MM **Publicly Held**
WEB: www.macrochem.com
SIC: 2834 8731 Pharmaceutical preparations; commercial physical research
PA: Abeona Therapeutics Inc.
  3333 Lee Pkwy Ste 600
  Dallas TX 75219
  214 665-9495

(G-11091)
MADAME ALEXANDER DOLL CO LLC
112 W 34th St Ste 1207 (10120-1207)
PHONE..................................212 244-4500
Adolfo Reynoso, *Branch Mgr*
EMP: 100
SALES (corp-wide): 41.7MM **Privately Held**
SIC: 3942 Dolls & stuffed toys
HQ: Madame Alexander Doll Company, Llc
  306 Primrose Ln
  Mountville PA 17554
  717 537-4140

(G-11092)
MADE FRESH DAILY
226 Front St (10038-2009)
PHONE..................................212 285-2253
Jackie Moran, *Manager*
EMP: 6
SALES (est): 398.8K **Privately Held**
SIC: 2711 Newspapers, publishing & printing

(G-11093)
MADHAT INC
108 Charles St Apt 1c (10014-2672)
PHONE..................................518 947-0732
Jude Anasta, *CEO*
EMP: 5
SALES (est): 117.2K **Privately Held**
SIC: 7372 Application computer software

(G-11094)
MADISON INDUSTRIES INC (PA)
295 5th Ave Ste 512 (10016-7103)
PHONE..................................212 679-5110
Michael Schwartz, *Ch of Bd*
Nehemias Nieves, *Controller*
Mike Pandow, *VP Human Res*
Mary McDaniel, *Human Res Dir*
Lisa Billani, *Manager*
◆ EMP: 11
SQ FT: 5,800
SALES (est): 117.4MM **Privately Held**
WEB: www.madisonindustries.com
SIC: 2392 5023 Household furnishings; comforters & quilts: made from purchased materials; pillowcases: made from purchased materials; mattress protectors, except rubber; home furnishings

(G-11095)
MADOFF ENERGY III LLC
319 Lafayette St (10012-2711)
PHONE..................................212 744-1918
Andy Madoff, *Mng Member*
EMP: 8
SQ FT: 3,000
SALES: 29.4K **Privately Held**
SIC: 1382 Oil & gas exploration services

(G-11096)
MAFCO CONSOLIDATED GROUP INC (HQ)
35 E 62nd St (10065-8014)
PHONE..................................212 572-8600
Fax: 212 572-8650
Ronald O Perelman, *Ch of Bd*
EMP: 10
SALES (est): 266.8MM
SALES (corp-wide): 5.3B **Privately Held**
SIC: 2121 2131 2869 Cigars; smoking tobacco; flavors or flavoring materials, synthetic
PA: Macandrews & Forbes Holdings Inc.
  35 E 62nd St
  New York NY 10065
  212 572-8600

(G-11097)
MAG BRANDS LLC
Also Called: Babydoll
463 7th Ave Fl 4 (10018-8725)
PHONE..................................212 629-9600
Raymond A Dayan, *CEO*
Gerard Agoglia, *CFO*
Michael Nagurka, *Controller*
Mark Adjmi,
▲ EMP: 55
SALES (est): 5.9MM **Privately Held**
SIC: 2339 Service apparel, washable: women's

(G-11098)
MAGAZINE I SPECTRUM E
Also Called: I Triple E Spectrum
3 Park Ave Fl 17 (10016-5902)
PHONE..................................212 419-7555
Willie Jones, *General Mgr*
James Vick, *Principal*
EMP: 38
SALES (est): 1.7MM **Privately Held**
SIC: 2721 Periodicals

(G-11099)
MAGEBA USA LLC
575 Lexington Ave Fl 4 (10022-6146)
PHONE..................................212 317-1991
Thomas Spuler, *CEO*
Jim Hatch, *President*
Scott Davis, *Business Mgr*
Gianni Moor, *COO*
Robert Bradley, *Project Mgr*
▲ EMP: 38 EST: 2011
SALES (est): 11.4MM **Privately Held**
SIC: 3441 3562 Expansion joints (structural shapes), iron or steel; ball bearings & parts

(G-11100)
MAGER & GOUGELMAN INC (PA)
345 E 37th St Rm 316 (10016-3256)
PHONE..................................212 661-3939
Fax: 212 661-0576
Henry P Gougelman, *President*
Andrew E Gouglman, *Ophthalmology*
EMP: 7
SALES (est): 855.4K **Privately Held**
WEB: www.artificial-eyes.com
SIC: 3851 Eyes, glass & plastic

(G-11101)
MAGGY BOUTIQUE LTD
Also Called: Maggy London
530 Fashion Ave Fl 6 (10018-4878)
PHONE..................................212 997-5222
Fax: 212 704-9794
Larry Lefkowitz, *President*
Lisa Leavy, *President*
Jerry Sholtz, *CFO*
Julie Monopoli, *Accounting Mgr*
Bob Jagolinzer, *Accounts Exec*
▲ EMP: 50
SQ FT: 5,000
SALES (est): 5.1MM **Privately Held**
SIC: 2339 5137 2337 Women's & misses' outerwear; women's & children's clothing; women's & misses' suits & coats

(G-11102)
MAGGY LONDON INTERNATIONAL LTD (PA)
Also Called: Maggy London Blouse Div
530 Fashion Ave Fl 6 (10018-4896)
PHONE..................................212 944-7199
Fax: 212 840-2483
Larry Lefkowitz, *Ch of Bd*
Milton Cahn, *Chairman*
Sheri Sardella, *Business Mgr*
Devin Fitzpatrick, *Vice Pres*
Lisa West, *Vice Pres*
▲ EMP: 60
SQ FT: 18,000
SALES (est): 37.2MM **Privately Held**
SIC: 2331 Women's & misses' blouses & shirts

(G-11103)
MAGIC BRANDS INTERNATIONAL LLC
31 W 34th St Rm 401 (10001-3036)
PHONE..................................212 563-4999
Sue Embleton, *VP Sales*
Edward J Falack,
Albert Pardo,
▲ EMP: 10
SALES (est): 1.1MM **Privately Held**
SIC: 2211 Apparel & outerwear fabrics, cotton

(G-11104)
MAGIC NOVELTY CO INC (PA)
308 Dyckman St (10034-5397)
PHONE..................................212 304-2777
Fax: 212 567-2597
Alex Neuburger, *President*
David Neuburger, *Vice Pres*
Steven Neuburger, *Vice Pres*
Wendy Torres, *Controller*
Valance Foster, *Director*
▲ EMP: 50 EST: 1940
SQ FT: 40,000
SALES (est): 10MM **Privately Held**
SIC: 3961 5094 3915 3469 Costume jewelry, ex. precious metal & semi-precious stones; jewelry; jewelers' materials & lapidary work; metal stampings; miscellaneous fabricated wire products

(G-11105)
MAGIC NUMBERS INC
Also Called: Glitter
29 Little West 12th St (10014-1393)
PHONE..................................646 839-8578
Christian Rocha, *President*
Joshua Auerbach, *Vice Pres*
Lisa Zhang, *Treasurer*
Saumya Manohar, *Admin Sec*
EMP: 5 EST: 2015
SQ FT: 16,000
SALES (est): 280K **Privately Held**
SIC: 7372 Home entertainment computer software

(G-11106)
MAGIC TANK LLC
80 Maiden Ln Rm 2204 (10038-4815)
PHONE..................................877 646-2442
Steve Distritzky, *President*
EMP: 3
SQ FT: 8,000
SALES: 5MM **Privately Held**
SIC: 2865 Cyclic organic crudes

(G-11107)
MAGIC TOUCH ICEWARES INTL
220 E 72nd St Apt 11g (10021-4527)
PHONE..................................212 794-2852
Susan Gitelson, *President*
◆ EMP: 6
SQ FT: 3,000
SALES (est): 824.7K **Privately Held**
SIC: 3069 5049 Laboratory sundries: cases, covers, funnels, cups, etc.; laboratory equipment, except medical or dental

(G-11108)
MAGNOLIA OPERATING LLC (PA)
Also Called: Magnolia Bakery
1841 Broadway (10023-7603)
PHONE..................................212 265-2777
Steve Abrams, *Principal*
Gary Kraus, *COO*
Sara Schoenborn, *Vice Pres*
Amy Tucker, *Project Mgr*
Ousmane Barry, *Manager*
EMP: 38
SALES (est): 8.6MM **Privately Held**
SIC: 2051 Bakery: wholesale or wholesale/retail combined

(G-11109)
MAGNUM CREATION INC
23 W 47th St Fl 5 (10036-2826)
PHONE..................................212 642-0993
Fax: 212 642-0993
Nathan Cohen, *President*
Mira Cohen, *Vice Pres*
Suri Markowitz, *Bookkeeper*
EMP: 13
SQ FT: 5,500
SALES (est): 1.5MM **Privately Held**
SIC: 3911 Jewelry, precious metal

(G-11110)
MAIDENFORM LLC
260 Madison Ave Fl 6 (10016-2401)
PHONE..................................201 436-9200
Fax: 212 685-1709
Maurice Reznik, *Branch Mgr*
EMP: 10
SALES (corp-wide): 5.7B **Publicly Held**
WEB: www.maidenform.com
SIC: 2259 2254 Girdles & other foundation garments, knit; knit underwear mills
HQ: Maidenform Llc
  1000 E Hanes Mill Rd
  Winston Salem NC 27105
  336 519-8080

(G-11111)
MAILERS-PBLSHER WLFARE TR FUND
1501 Broadway (10036-5601)
PHONE..................................212 869-5986
EMP: 1
SALES: 2.6MM **Privately Held**
SIC: 2741 Miscellaneous publishing

(G-11112)
MAIN STREET FASHIONS INC (PA)
512 Fashion Ave Rm 3700 (10018-0809)
PHONE..................................212 764-2613
Rajesh Bhambri, *President*
Nandini Ali, *Manager*
▲ EMP: 11
SQ FT: 2,000
SALES (est): 846.7K **Privately Held**
SIC: 2339 5137 Sportswear, women's; sportswear, women's & children's

(G-11113)
MAIYET INC
676 Broadway Fl 4 (10012-2319)
PHONE..................................646 602-0000
Paul Van Zyl, *Ch of Bd*
Melanie Copple, *General Mgr*
Minnie Kim, *Prdtn Mgr*
Pearce Thompson, *Production*
Morgan George, *Sales Dir*
EMP: 5
SALES (est): 898.8K **Privately Held**
SIC: 2329 2339 Men's & boys' leather, wool & down-filled outerwear; women's & misses' outerwear

(G-11114)
MAJANI TEA COMPANY
Also Called: Majani Teas
1745 Brdwy Fl 17 (10019)
P.O. Box 87 (10034-0087)
PHONE..................................817 896-5720
Ronald Mutai, *Owner*
EMP: 10

▲ = Import ▼ = Export
◆ = Import/Export

SALES: 250K **Privately Held**
SIC: 2099 Tea blending

(G-11115)
MAJESTIC RAYON CORPORATION
116 W 23rd St Fl 4 (10011-2498)
PHONE..................................212 929-6443
Fax: 212 929-1623
Lawrence Aibel, *President*
Richard Aibel, *Vice Pres*
Sandra Keene, *Vice Pres*
Irina Simon, *Manager*
▲ EMP: 25 EST: 1930
SQ FT: 60,000
SALES: (est): 4.2MM **Privately Held**
SIC: 2282 2269 Twisting yarn; winding yarn; finishing plants

(G-11116)
MAKE HOLDING LLC
850 3rd Ave (10022-6222)
PHONE..................................646 313-1957
Anne Grimes, *Manager*
Daniel Nisssons,
EMP: 30
SALES: (est): 3.1MM **Privately Held**
SIC: 3269 Cookware: stoneware, coarse earthenware & pottery

(G-11117)
MAKE MY CAKE II INC
2380 Adam Clytn Powll Jr (10030-1703)
PHONE..................................212 234-2344
Fax: 212 234-2327
Joann Baylor, *President*
EMP: 7
SALES: 350K **Privately Held**
SIC: 2051 Bread, cake & related products

(G-11118)
MAKERBOT INDUSTRIES LLC
298 Mulberry St (10012-3331)
PHONE..................................347 457-5758
EMP: 7
SALES (est): 470K **Privately Held**
SIC: 2759 Commercial printing

(G-11119)
MAKINS HATS LTD
212 W 35th St Fl 12 (10001-2508)
PHONE..................................212 594-6666
Marsha Akins, *President*
EMP: 7
SQ FT: 5,000
SALES: 500K **Privately Held**
SIC: 2353 Hats, caps & millinery

(G-11120)
MALER TECHNOLOGIES INC
337 E 81st St Bsmt (10028-4068)
PHONE..................................212 391-2070
Stanley Vashovsky, *Ch of Bd*
Ted Weaver, *Vice Pres*
Diane Johnson, *Mktg Dir*
Anatoliy Ryaboy, *CTO*
EMP: 2
SQ FT: 13,617
SALES: 7.2MM **Privately Held**
WEB: www.healthsystemssolutions.com
SIC: 7372 Prepackaged software

(G-11121)
MALIN + GOETZ INC (PA)
210 W 29th St Fl 3 (10001-5205)
PHONE..................................212 244-7771
Matthew Malin, *Ch of Bd*
Andrew Goetz, *President*
Gabriel McVay, *Area Mgr*
Beverly Friedmann, *Accounts Mgr*
Kameren Levingston, *Accounts Mgr*
EMP: 12
SQ FT: 600
SALES: (est): 1.9MM **Privately Held**
WEB: www.malinandgoetz.com
SIC: 2844 5999 Cosmetic preparations; cosmetics

(G-11122)
MALOUF COLETTE INC
594 Broadway Rm 1216 (10012-3289)
PHONE..................................212 941-9588
Fax: 212 431-9561
Colette Malouf, *President*
Lee Tam, *Prdtn Mgr*
EMP: 14
SQ FT: 2,200
SALES: (est): 1.3MM **Privately Held**
WEB: www.colettemalouf.com
SIC: 3999 Hair & hair-based products

(G-11123)
MAMA LUCA PRODUCTION INC
156 W 56th St Ste 1803 (10019-3899)
PHONE..................................212 582-9700
Steven Zandt, *President*
Steven Vandat, *President*
EMP: 2
SALES: 3MM **Privately Held**
SIC: 2399 Aprons, breast (harness)

(G-11124)
MAN OF WORLD
25 W 39th St Fl 5 (10018-4075)
PHONE..................................212 915-0017
EMP: 5
SALES: (est): 839.4K **Privately Held**
SIC: 2836 Culture media

(G-11125)
MANCHU NEW YORK INC
530 Fashion Ave Rm 1906 (10018-4853)
PHONE..................................212 921-5050
Michael Durbin, *President*
▲ EMP: 8
SQ FT: 5,100
SALES: (est): 705.4K **Privately Held**
SIC: 2361 2339 2311 Girls' & children's dresses, blouses & shirts; women's & misses' outerwear; men's & boys' suits & coats

(G-11126)
MANCHU TIMES FASHION INC
530 Sventh Ave Ste 1906 (10018)
PHONE..................................212 921-5050
Michael Durbin, *CEO*
Jay Goldman, *Administration*
EMP: 8 EST: 2014
SQ FT: 2,300
SALES (est): 671.1K
SALES (corp-wide): 63.6MM **Privately Held**
SIC: 2339 Women's & misses' outerwear
HQ: Manchu Times Fashion Limited
Rm 2002 20/F Park-In Coml Ctr
Mongkok KLN
278 161-88

(G-11127)
MANHATTAN CABINETS INC
1349 2nd Ave (10021-4504)
PHONE..................................212 548-2436
Zaheer Akber, *President*
EMP: 3
SQ FT: 1,300
SALES: 1.7MM **Privately Held**
SIC: 2514 1751 Kitchen cabinets: metal; cabinet building & installation

(G-11128)
MANHATTAN COOLING TOWERS INC
540 W 35th St (10001-1317)
PHONE..................................212 279-1045
Richard Silver, *President*
EMP: 15
SQ FT: 80,000
SALES: (est): 1.3MM **Privately Held**
SIC: 3443 Cooling towers, metal plate

(G-11129)
MANHATTAN EASTSIDE DEV CORP
Also Called: Eastside Orthotics Prosthetics
622 W 168th St Ste Vc333 (10032-3720)
PHONE..................................212 305-3275
Matt Flynn, *President*
EMP: 10
SALES: (est): 710K **Privately Held**
SIC: 3841 Medical instruments & equipment, blood & bone work

(G-11130)
MANHATTAN MEDIA LLC (PA)
Also Called: Avenue Magazine
72 Madison Ave Fl 11 (10016-8731)
PHONE..................................212 268-8600
Fax: 212 268-0614
Joanne Harras, *CEO*
Thomas Allon, *President*
Pamela Gross, *Editor*
Harlan Lax, *Info Tech Dir*
Robin Aronow, *Advisor*
EMP: 25
SQ FT: 7,500
SALES: (est): 13.6MM **Privately Held**
SIC: 2711 2721 Newspapers: publishing only, not printed on site; magazines: publishing only, not printed on site

(G-11131)
MANHATTAN NEON SIGN CORP
640 W 28th St Fl 2 (10001-1118)
PHONE..................................212 714-0430
Fax: 212 947-3906
Marylin Tomasso, *President*
Pat Tomasso, *Vice Pres*
EMP: 13
SQ FT: 7,500
SALES: (est): 1.7MM **Privately Held**
SIC: 3993 Neon signs

(G-11132)
MANHATTAN SCIENTIFICS INC (PA)
405 Lexington Ave Fl 26 (10174-2699)
PHONE..................................212 541-2405
Emmanuel Tsoupanarias, *Ch of Bd*
Leonard Friedman, *Admin Sec*
EMP: 8
SQ FT: 300
SALES: 64K **Publicly Held**
SIC: 3699 Electrical equipment & supplies

(G-11133)
MANHATTAN SHADE & GLASS CO INC (PA)
1299 3rd Ave Frnt (10021-3397)
PHONE..................................212 288-5616
Fax: 212 288-7241
Steven Schulman, *President*
Morine Shulman, *Principal*
Douglas Schulman, *Vice Pres*
Mitchell Schulman, *Vice Pres*
Kathleen Maughton, *Controller*
▼ EMP: 56 EST: 1964
SQ FT: 3,500
SALES: (est): 7.8MM **Privately Held**
WEB: www.manhattanshade.com
SIC: 2591 3211 Shade, curtain & drapery hardware; window glass, clear & colored

(G-11134)
MANHATTAN TIMES INC
5030 Broadway Ste 801 (10034-1666)
PHONE..................................212 569-5800
Luis Miranda, *Chairman*
John Guttierez, *Manager*
EMP: 15
SALES: (est): 570K **Privately Held**
SIC: 2711 Newspapers

(G-11135)
MANN PUBLICATIONS INC
450 Fashion Ave Ste 2306 (10123-2306)
PHONE..................................212 840-6266
Jeffrey Mann, *President*
EMP: 20
SQ FT: 4,000
SALES: (est): 2.3MM **Privately Held**
SIC: 2721 Magazines: publishing only, not printed on site

(G-11136)
MANNESMANN CORPORATION
601 Lexington Ave Fl 56 (10022-4611)
PHONE..................................212 258-4000
Peter Prinz Wittgenstein, *President*
Dr Manfred Becker, *Exec VP*
Joseph E Innamorati, *Vice Pres*
Nelson Payne, *Vice Pres*
Olaf Klinger, *Treasurer*
▲ EMP: 100
SALES: 19.7MM
SALES (corp-wide): 83.5B **Privately Held**
SIC: 3536 3544 3511 3547 Hoists; cranes, industrial plant; cranes, overhead traveling; special dies, tools, jigs & fixtures; industrial molds; turbo-generators; hydraulic turbines; rolling mill machinery; steel rolling machinery; pumps & pumping equipment; internal combustion engines
HQ: Siemens Corporation
300 New Jersey Ave Nw A
Washington DC 20001
202 434-4800

(G-11137)
MANNINGTON MILLS INC
200 Lexington Ave Rm 430 (10016-6101)
PHONE..................................212 251-0290
Fax: 212 251-0299
Emily Cring, *District Mgr*
John Maiolo, *Manager*
EMP: 5
SALES (corp-wide): 783.5MM **Privately Held**
WEB: www.mannington.com
SIC: 2273 Floor coverings, textile fiber
PA: Mannington Mills Inc.
75 Mannington Mills Rd
Salem NJ 08079
856 935-3000

(G-11138)
MANNY GRUNBERG INC
62 W 47th St Ste 703 (10036-3185)
PHONE..................................212 302-6173
Fax: 212 382-1569
Manny Grunberg, *President*
EMP: 33
SQ FT: 2,000
SALES: (est): 2.4MM **Privately Held**
SIC: 3911 Jewelry, precious metal

(G-11139)
MANRICO USA INC
Also Called: Manrico Cashmere
922 Madison Ave (10021-3576)
PHONE..................................212 794-4200
Virgile Verellen, *Branch Mgr*
EMP: 5
SALES (corp-wide): 8.9MM **Privately Held**
SIC: 2253 Sweaters & sweater coats, knit
PA: Manrico Usa, Inc.
922 Madison Ave
New York NY 10021
212 794-4200

(G-11140)
MANRICO USA INC (PA)
922 Madison Ave (10021-3576)
PHONE..................................212 794-4200
Manrico Calzoni, *President*
▲ EMP: 5
SQ FT: 750
SALES: (est): 8.9MM **Privately Held**
SIC: 2299 Upholstery filling, textile

(G-11141)
MANSFIELD PRESS INC
599 11th Ave Fl 3 (10036-2110)
PHONE..................................212 265-5411
Fax: 212 262-7279
Stanley J Friedman, *President*
Marc Friedman, *Exec VP*
Frank J Ephraim, *Vice Pres*
Shari Friedman, *Manager*
EMP: 15 EST: 1935
SALES: (est): 1.4MM **Privately Held**
SIC: 2752 Lithographing on metal

(G-11142)
MANSUETO VENTURES LLC
Also Called: Fast Company Magazine
7 World Trade Ctr Fl 29 (10007-2174)
PHONE..................................212 389-5300
Whelan Mahoney, *Publisher*
Jane Hazel, *Principal*
Leigh Buchanan, *Editor*
Tom Foster, *Editor*
Harry McCracken, *Editor*
EMP: 210
SALES: (est): 73.1MM **Privately Held**
SIC: 2721 Magazines: publishing only, not printed on site

(G-11143)
MARBLE DOCTORS LLC
244 5th Ave Ste 2608 (10001-7604)
PHONE..................................203 628-8339
Sergio Gomes Da Silva, *Branch Mgr*
Kelly Dasilca,
EMP: 26
SALES (corp-wide): 1.6MM **Privately Held**
SIC: 3281 1743 Marble, building: cut & shaped; marble installation, interior
PA: Marble Doctors Llc
1198 Mulberry Pl
Wellington FL 33414
203 794-1000

New York - New York County (G-11144)

GEOGRAPHIC SECTION

(G-11144)
MARCASIANO INC
296 Elizabeth St Apt 2f (10012-3590)
PHONE.....................212 614-9412
Mary Jane Marcasiano, *President*
EMP: 5 **EST:** 1977
SQ FT: 3,000
SALES (est): 610K **Privately Held**
SIC: 2339 Sportswear, women's

(G-11145)
MARCO HI-TECH JV LLC (PA)
475 Park Ave S Fl 10 (10016-6901)
PHONE.....................212 798-8114
Michael Barenholtz, *Treasurer*
Nick Larosa, *Controller*
Steven Seltzer, *VP Sales*
Reuben Seltzer,
David Garner,
▲ **EMP:** 8
SQ FT: 4,000
SALES (est): 1.3MM **Privately Held**
WEB: www.marcohi-tech.com
SIC: 2834 Vitamin, nutrient & hematinic preparations for human use

(G-11146)
MARCONI INTL USA CO LTD
214 W 39th St Rm 1100 (10018-5533)
PHONE.....................212 391-2626
Fax: 212 391-1166
Lilian Ching, *President*
Jeremy Setol, *Bookkeeper*
John Matthes, *Director*
▲ **EMP:** 9
SQ FT: 2,500
SALES (est): 1.2MM **Privately Held**
SIC: 2339 Women's & misses' outerwear

(G-11147)
MARCUS GOLDMAN INC
Also Called: Run It Systems
37 W 39th St Rm 1201 (10018-0577)
PHONE.....................212 431-0707
Robert Marcus, *President*
Steven Treiber, *Manager*
Mark Schmidt, *Technical Staff*
Orren Grushkin, *Admin Sec*
EMP: 14
SQ FT: 5,000
SALES (est): 1.7MM **Privately Held**
WEB: www.runit.com
SIC: 7372 Prepackaged software

(G-11148)
MARI STRINGS INC
14 W 71st St (10023-4209)
PHONE.....................212 799-6781
Fax: 212 721-3932
Daniel Mari, *President*
▲ **EMP:** 15
SQ FT: 1,600
SALES: 400K **Privately Held**
SIC: 3931 Strings, musical instrument

(G-11149)
MARIAN GOODMAN GALLERY INC
24 W 57th St Fl 4 (10019-3918)
PHONE.....................212 977-7160
Fax: 212 581-5187
Marian Goodman, *President*
Rebecca Eng, *Accountant*
Alena Marchak, *Librarian*
Steve Griffin, *Manager*
Elaine Budin, *Info Tech Dir*
▲ **EMP:** 23 **EST:** 1974
SQ FT: 5,500
SALES (est): 1.9MM **Privately Held**
WEB: www.mariangoodman.com
SIC: 2741 5999 Catalogs: publishing only, not printed on site; art dealers

(G-11150)
MARIE CLAIRE USA
300 W 57th St Fl 34 (10019-1497)
PHONE.....................212 841-8493
Alix Campbell, *Principal*
Chris Moore, *Editor*
Glenda Bailey, *Chief*
Natalie McCray, *Business Mgr*
Amanda Hearst, *Associate*
▲ **EMP:** 100
SALES (est): 631.1K **Privately Held**
SIC: 2721 Magazines: publishing & printing

(G-11151)
MARILYN MODEL MANAGEMENT INC
32 Union Sq E Ph 1 (10003-3220)
PHONE.....................646 556-7587
Fax: 646 260-0821
Maria Cognata, *President*
Marilyn Gauthier, *President*
Julia Kisla, *CFO*
EMP: 11
SALES (est): 980K **Privately Held**
SIC: 3999 Models, except toy

(G-11152)
MARINA JEWELRY CO INC
Also Called: Jn Marina
42 W 48th St Ste 804 (10036-1712)
PHONE.....................212 354-5027
Fax: 212 575-8086
Joseph Fontana, *President*
Anthony Barona, *Partner*
EMP: 6
SQ FT: 1,200
SALES (est): 540K **Privately Held**
WEB: www.marina-jewellery.com
SIC: 3911 3339 Jewelry, precious metal; primary nonferrous metals

(G-11153)
MARITIME ACTIVITY REPORTS (PA)
118 E 25th St Fl 2 (10010-2994)
PHONE.....................212 477-6700
John C O'Malley, *Vice Pres*
Joel Haka, *Vice Pres*
Esther Rothenberger, *Opers Mgr*
Kristen O'Malley, *Accounting Mgr*
Jocelyn Redfern, *Marketing Mgr*
EMP: 28
SQ FT: 2,500
SALES (est): 2MM **Privately Held**
SIC: 2721 Magazines: publishing only, not printed on site

(G-11154)
MARK KING JEWELRY INC
62 W 47th St Ste 310r (10036-3245)
PHONE.....................212 921-0746
Fax: 212 944-6345
Mark Beznicki, *President*
EMP: 8
SQ FT: 1,000
SALES (est): 570K **Privately Held**
SIC: 3911 5094 Jewelry, precious metal; jewelry & precious stones

(G-11155)
MARK LEVINE
Also Called: Kids Discover
149 5th Ave Fl 10 (10010-6832)
PHONE.....................212 677-4457
Mark Levine, *Owner*
Defi Greene, *Manager*
▲ **EMP:** 11
SQ FT: 2,500
SALES (est): 810K **Privately Held**
SIC: 2721 Magazines: publishing only, not printed on site

(G-11156)
MARK NELSON DESIGNS LLC
404 E 55th St Fl 4 (10022-5136)
PHONE.....................646 422-7020
Debra Harkl, *Office Mgr*
Mark Nelson, *Mng Member*
▲ **EMP:** 10
SALES (est): 1.3MM **Privately Held**
SIC: 2273 Rugs, hand & machine made

(G-11157)
MARK ROBINSON INC
18 E 48th St Rm 1102 (10017-1059)
PHONE.....................212 223-3515
Fax: 212 223-5133
Mark Robinson, *President*
EMP: 9
SQ FT: 200
SALES (est): 1.4MM **Privately Held**
WEB: www.markrobinson.net
SIC: 3911 Jewelry, precious metal

(G-11158)
MARKET FACTORY INC
425 Broadway Fl 3 (10013-2599)
PHONE.....................212 625-9988

James Sinclair, *CEO*
Darren Jer, *COO*
Chris Coletti, *Sales Dir*
Laura Migliozzi, *Office Mgr*
Christian Reiss, *Manager*
EMP: 19
SQ FT: 3,000
SALES (est): 5.2MM **Privately Held**
SIC: 7372 Business oriented computer software

(G-11159)
MARKETING ACTION XCUTIVES INC
50 W 96th St Apt 7b (10025-6529)
P.O. Box 20356 (10025-1519)
PHONE.....................212 971-9155
Karen Korman, *President*
Barry Steinman, *Vice Pres*
Barry Korman, *Marketing Staff*
EMP: 5
SALES (est): 2MM **Privately Held**
WEB: www.mactionx.com
SIC: 2241 Trimmings, textile

(G-11160)
MARKETING EDGE
Also Called: Dmef/Edge
1333 Broadway Rm 301 (10018-1170)
PHONE.....................212 790-1512
Fax: 212 790-1561
Terri L Bartlett, *President*
John Taborosi, *COO*
Linda High, *Exec VP*
Gina Scala, *Vice Pres*
Anissa Lamouchi, *Project Mgr*
EMP: 8
SALES (est): 2.3MM **Privately Held**
WEB: www.the-dmef.com
SIC: 2721 Trade journals: publishing only, not printed on site

(G-11161)
MARKETRESEARCHCOM INC
641 Ave Of The America (10011-2014)
PHONE.....................212 807-2600
Rocco Distefano, *Branch Mgr*
Marzia Marzi, *Manager*
EMP: 15
SALES (corp-wide): 28.3MM **Privately Held**
WEB: www.marketresearch.com
SIC: 2741 Miscellaneous publishing
PA: Marketresearch.Com, Inc.
11200 Rockville Pike # 504
Rockville MD 20852
240 747-3000

(G-11162)
MARKETS MEDIA LLC
110 Wall St Fl 15 (10005-3813)
PHONE.....................646 442-4646
Mohan Virdee, *CEO*
EMP: 5
SALES (est): 451.5K **Privately Held**
SIC: 2711 Newspapers, publishing & printing

(G-11163)
MARLEY SPOON INC
336 W 37th St Rm 1400 (10018-4674)
PHONE.....................646 934-6970
Fabian Siegel, *Principal*
EMP: 8
SALES (est): 697.5K **Privately Held**
SIC: 3411 8742 Food & beverage containers; food & beverage consultant

(G-11164)
MARNIER-LAPOSTOLLE INC
Also Called: Grand Marnier
183 Madison Ave (10016-4501)
PHONE.....................212 207-4350
Fax: 212 207-4351
Elise Seignolle, *Finance Dir*
R Prewitt, *Manager*
Christine Yun, *Manager*
▲ **EMP:** 54
SALES: 538.7K **Privately Held**
WEB: www.grandmarnier.com
SIC: 2082 5182 2085 Malt liquors; liquor; distilled & blended liquors

(G-11165)
MARRETTI USA INC
101 Ave Of The Americas (10013-1941)
PHONE.....................212 255-5565
Marzia Marzi, *President*
EMP: 8 **EST:** 2008
SQ FT: 600
SALES (est): 467.1K **Privately Held**
SIC: 2431 Staircases, stairs & railings

(G-11166)
MARTHA STEWART LIVING (HQ)
601 W 26th St Rm 900 (10001-1143)
PHONE.....................212 827-8000
Fax: 212 827-8204
Daniel W Dienst, *CEO*
Eleni Gage, *Editor*
Angela Law, *Editor*
Ellen Morrissey, *Editor*
Christopher Rudolph, *Editor*
▲ **EMP:** 274
SQ FT: 176,550
SALES: 141.9MM
SALES (corp-wide): 183.7MM **Publicly Held**
WEB: www.marthastewart.com
SIC: 2721 2731 4813 7812 Magazines: publishing only, not printed on site; book publishing; ; motion picture production & distribution, television
PA: Sequential Brands Group, Inc.
5 Bryant Park Fl 30
New York NY 10001
646 564-2577

(G-11167)
MARTHA STEWART LIVING OMNI LLC
20 W 43rd St (10036-7400)
PHONE.....................212 827-8000
Robin Marino, *CEO*
Laura Boberg, *Publisher*
Natalie Ermann, *General Mgr*
Jenn Andrlik, *Editor*
Alanna Fincke, *Editor*
▲ **EMP:** 350
SALES (est): 38.6MM
SALES (corp-wide): 183.7MM **Publicly Held**
WEB: www.msliving.com
SIC: 2721 Magazines: publishing only, not printed on site
HQ: Martha Stewart Living Omnimedia, Inc.
601 W 26th St Rm 900
New York NY 10001
212 827-8000

(G-11168)
MARTIN FLYER INCORPORATED
70 W 36th St Rm 602 (10018-8049)
PHONE.....................212 840-8899
Fax: 212 768-0124
Joshua Kaufman, *COO*
Alan Flyer, *CFO*
Josh Kaufman, *Mng Member*
▲ **EMP:** 27
SQ FT: 8,000
SALES: 11MM **Privately Held**
WEB: www.martinflyer.com
SIC: 3911 Jewelry, precious metal

(G-11169)
MARTINEZ HAND MADE CIGARS
171 W 29th St Frnt A (10001-5100)
PHONE.....................212 239-4049
Antonio Martinez, *Owner*
EMP: 9
SALES (est): 707.3K **Privately Held**
SIC: 2121 Cigars

(G-11170)
MARVEL ENTERTAINMENT LLC (HQ)
135 W 50th St Fl 7 (10020-1201)
P.O. Box 1527, Long Island City (11101-0527)
PHONE.....................212 576-4000
Isaac Perlmutter, *CEO*
Michael Helfant, *President*
Timothy E Rothwell, *President*
Dan Buckley, *Publisher*
Bill Rahn, *Managing Dir*
▲ **EMP:** 217
SQ FT: 65,253

GEOGRAPHIC SECTION

New York - New York County (G-11197)

SALES (est): 97.1MM **Publicly Held**
SIC: 2721 6794 3944 7929 Comic books: publishing only, not printed on site; magazines: publishing only, not printed on site; patent buying, licensing, leasing; electronic games & toys; entertainment service

(G-11171)
MARVELLISSIMA INTL LTD
333 E 46th St Apt 20a (10017-7431)
PHONE.................................212 682-7306
Marvel Perilla, *President*
Shanez Kollnescher, *Vice Pres*
Ellen Stutzer, *Vice Pres*
Abba Kyari, *Shareholder*
Lola Osunsade, *Shareholder*
EMP: 6
SALES (est): 615.2K **Privately Held**
SIC: 2844 5122 Toilet preparations; cosmetics

(G-11172)
MARY BRIGHT INC
269 E 10th St Apt 7 (10009-4849)
PHONE.................................212 677-1970
David Paskin, *President*
Mary Bright, *President*
EMP: 6
SALES: 367K **Privately Held**
WEB: www.marybright.com
SIC: 2258 Curtains & curtain fabrics, lace

(G-11173)
MAS CUTTING INC
257 W 39th St Rm 11e (10018-3228)
PHONE.................................212 869-0826
Kitman MA, *President*
EMP: 6
SALES (est): 350K **Privately Held**
SIC: 2396 Apparel findings & trimmings

(G-11174)
MASTERPIECE COLOR LLC
240 W 35th St Ste 1200 (10001-2514)
PHONE.................................917 279-6056
David Markovits, *Partner*
EMP: 8
SALES: 11MM **Privately Held**
SIC: 3911 Jewelry, precious metal

(G-11175)
MASTERPIECE DIAMONDS LLC
240 W 35th St Ste 1200 (10001-2514)
PHONE.................................212 937-0681
David Markovits,
EMP: 19
SQ FT: 4,500
SALES (est): 1.9MM **Privately Held**
SIC: 3961 Costume jewelry

(G-11176)
MATA FASHIONS LLC
214 W 39th St Ste 608 (10018-4404)
PHONE.................................917 716-7894
Maria Maglaras, *Treasurer*
Dona Elias,
EMP: 2 EST: 2014
SQ FT: 1,200
SALES: 1MM **Privately Held**
SIC: 2384 Dressing gowns, men's & women's: from purchased materials

(G-11177)
MATA IG
Also Called: Ings Mata Stone
332 Bleecker St (10014-2980)
PHONE.................................212 979-7921
Ig Mata, *Owner*
EMP: 5
SALES (est): 207.3K **Privately Held**
WEB: www.igmata.com
SIC: 3229 Art, decorative & novelty glassware

(G-11178)
MATACI INC
Also Called: Lazo Setter Company
247 W 35th St Fl 15 (10001-1915)
PHONE.................................212 502-1899
Adrianna Chico, *President*
▲ EMP: 60
SALES (est): 6.1MM **Privately Held**
SIC: 3961 Costume jewelry

(G-11179)
MATHISEN VENTURES INC
Also Called: Cruise Industry News
441 Lexington Ave Rm 809 (10017-3935)
PHONE.................................212 986-1025
Fax: 212 986-1033
Oivind Mathisen, *President*
Timothy Beebe, *Vice Pres*
Gordon Buck, *Vice Pres*
Camille Olivere, *Vice Pres*
Monty Mathisen, *Sales Staff*
EMP: 6 EST: 1978
SALES (est): 631.8K **Privately Held**
WEB: www.cruiseindustrynews.com
SIC: 2731 2721 2741 Book publishing; periodicals: publishing only; magazines: publishing only, not printed on site; newsletter publishing

(G-11180)
MATT TEXTILE INC
142 W 36th St Fl 3 (10018-8806)
PHONE.................................212 967-6010
Firooz Fred Nili, *President*
Neda Nili, *Principal*
▲ EMP: 7
SQ FT: 8,000
SALES (est): 470K **Privately Held**
SIC: 2231 Fabric finishing: wool, mohair or similar fibers

(G-11181)
MAURICE MAX INC
Also Called: Roxanne Assoulin
49 W 27th St Fl 5 (10001-6936)
PHONE.................................212 334-6573
Fax: 212 334-6152
Roxanne Assoulin, *President*
Meyer Assoulin, *Vice Pres*
Irv Dayan, *Controller*
Jose Torres, *Asst Controller*
EMP: 34
SALES (est): 5.2MM **Privately Held**
WEB: www.leeangel.com
SIC: 3961 Costume jewelry

(G-11182)
MAURYBAKES LLC
18 W 18th St (10011-4607)
PHONE.................................646 722-6570
Maury Rubin, *CEO*
EMP: 20 EST: 2001
SALES (est): 671.8K **Privately Held**
SIC: 2052 Bakery products, dry

(G-11183)
MAVEN MARKETING LLC (PA)
Also Called: Revolution Golf
349 5th Ave Fl 8 (10016-5019)
PHONE.................................615 510-3248
Justin Tapper, *CEO*
Dean Strickler, *Exec Dir*
Wayne Caparas,
Jeff Evans,
EMP: 7 EST: 2008
SALES (est): 3.4MM **Privately Held**
SIC: 7372 7371 8742 Educational computer software; software programming applications; marketing consulting services

(G-11184)
MAVERIK LACROSSE LLC
535 W 24th St Fl 5 (10011-1140)
PHONE.................................516 213-3050
Fax: 516 213-3092
Dilly Pymm, *Manager*
John Gagliardi,
▲ EMP: 5019
SALES (est): 231.9K
SALES (corp-wide): 9B **Privately Held**
SIC: 3949 Lacrosse equipment & supplies, general
HQ: Kohlberg Sports Group, Inc.
  111 Radio Circle Dr
  Mount Kisco NY 10549

(G-11185)
MAVITO FINE JEWELRY LTD INC
37 W 47th St Ste 500 (10036-2861)
PHONE.................................212 398-9384
Fax: 212 398-9384
Victor Scis, *President*
EMP: 11
SQ FT: 4,600
SALES: 1.8MM **Privately Held**
SIC: 3911 7631 3915 Jewel settings & mountings, precious metal; watch, clock & jewelry repair; jewelers' materials & lapidary work

(G-11186)
MAX BRENNER UNION SQUARE LLC
841 Broadway (10003-4704)
PHONE.................................646 467-8803
Ever M Elivo, *Principal*
▲ EMP: 5
SALES (est): 585.6K **Privately Held**
SIC: 2066 Chocolate bars, solid

(G-11187)
MAX KAHAN INC
20 W 47th St Ste 300 (10036-3303)
PHONE.................................212 575-4646
Fax: 212 575-0888
Max Kahan, *President*
David Gluck, *Vice Pres*
Abraham Grossman, *Treasurer*
EMP: 10
SQ FT: 3,000
SALES (est): 980K **Privately Held**
SIC: 3915 Jewelers' materials & lapidary work

(G-11188)
MAXIMILLION COMMUNICATIONS LLC
245 W 17th St Fl 2 (10011-5373)
PHONE.................................212 564-3945
Kathy Hipple,
EMP: 80
SALES (est): 4.6MM **Privately Held**
WEB: www.aypny.com
SIC: 2741 Telephone & other directory publishing

(G-11189)
MAXWORLD INC
Also Called: Promolines
213 W 14th St (10011-7177)
PHONE.................................212 242-7588
Fax: 212 242-7512
Maximino Vazquez, *President*
Richard Garber, *Executive*
▲ EMP: 5
SQ FT: 9,000
SALES: 1.2MM **Privately Held**
WEB: www.maxworldinc.com
SIC: 3993 7336 Signs & advertising specialties; displays & cutouts, window & lobby; displays, paint process; package design

(G-11190)
MAYBELLINE INC
575 5th Ave Bsmt Fl (10017-2446)
PHONE.................................212 885-1310
Robert N Hiatt, *Ch of Bd*
John R Wendt, *President*
Gerald C Beddall, *President*
Jack J Bucher, *President*
Daniel J Coffey Jr, *President*
EMP: 4118 EST: 1915
SALES (est): 40.9K
SALES (corp-wide): 3.1B **Privately Held**
WEB: www.maybelline.com
SIC: 2844 2841 Toilet preparations; cosmetic preparations; toilet preparations; perfumes & colognes; soap: granulated, liquid, cake, flaked or chip
HQ: L'oreal Usa, Inc.
  10 Hudson Yards
  New York NY 10001
  212 818-1500

(G-11191)
MAZ DIGITAL INC (PA)
135 W 26th St Ste 10a (10001-6809)
PHONE.................................646 692-9799
Paul Canetti, *CEO*
Paul Shouvik, *President*
Shikha Arora, *Principal*
Simon Baumer, *Principal*
EMP: 10
SALES (est): 2.7MM **Privately Held**
SIC: 7372 Publishers' computer software

(G-11192)
MBNY LLC (PA)
260 5th Ave Fl 9 (10001-6408)
PHONE.................................646 467-8810
Ever Elivo, *Controller*
Yaniv Shtanger, *Mng Member*
EMP: 10
SALES (est): 1.1MM **Privately Held**
SIC: 2066 Chocolate bars, solid

(G-11193)
MC SQUARED NYC INC
Also Called: Mancum Graphics
121 Varick St Frnt B (10013-1408)
PHONE.................................212 947-2260
Fax: 212 695-7985
Robert Copjec, *President*
EMP: 10
SQ FT: 1,000
SALES (est): 1.3MM **Privately Held**
SIC: 2752 Commercial printing, lithographic

(G-11194)
MCAFEE INC
McAfee Site Advisor
1133 Avenue Of The Americ (10036-6721)
PHONE.................................646 728-1440
Brian Andriolo, *Branch Mgr*
EMP: 6
SALES (corp-wide): 55.3B **Publicly Held**
SIC: 7372 Prepackaged software
HQ: Mcafee, Inc.
  2821 Mission College Blvd
  Santa Clara CA 95054
  408 346-3832

(G-11195)
MCCALL PATTERN COMPANY (HQ)
Also Called: Butterck McCall Vogue Pattern
120 Broadway Fl 34 (10271-3499)
P.O. Box 3755, Manhattan KS (66505-8502)
PHONE.................................212 465-6800
Fax: 212 465-6814
Frank J Rizzo, *Ch of Bd*
Robin Davies, *President*
Kathleen Klausner, *Senior VP*
Nancy Dicocco, *Vice Pres*
Gail Hamilton, *Vice Pres*
▲ EMP: 200
SQ FT: 62,600
SALES (est): 39.3MM
SALES (corp-wide): 48.3MM **Privately Held**
WEB: www.mccallpattern.com
SIC: 2741 2731 2721 Patterns, paper: publishing only, not printed on site; catalogs: publishing only, not printed on site; pamphlets: publishing only, not printed on site; textbooks: publishing only, not printed on site; magazines: publishing only, not printed on site
PA: Mp Holdings Inc
  11 Penn Plz Fl 19
  New York NY 10001
  212 465-6800

(G-11196)
MCCARTHY LLC
Also Called: Blackbook
32 Union Sq E (10003-3209)
PHONE.................................646 862-5354
Jonathan Bond,
EMP: 10 EST: 2013
SALES (est): 875.1K **Privately Held**
SIC: 2721 Periodicals: publishing only

(G-11197)
MCGAW GROUP LLC
Also Called: McGaw Framed Art
233 E 93rd St (10128-3704)
PHONE.................................212 876-8822
Dorris Francies, *Manager*
Bruce McGaw,
Nancy McGaw,
▲ EMP: 10 EST: 2001
SALES (est): 572.7K **Privately Held**
WEB: www.brucemcgaw.com
SIC: 3999 Framed artwork

New York - New York County (G-11198)

(G-11198)
MCGRAW-HILL GLBL EDCTN HLDNGS (PA)
2 Penn Plz Fl 20 (10121-2100)
PHONE...............................646 766-2000
David Levin, President
Sally Shankland, President
Teresa Martin-Retortillo, Senior VP
Heath Morrison, Senior VP
Maryellen Valaitis, Senior VP
EMP: 69
SALES (est): 1.6B Privately Held
SIC: 2731 Textbooks: publishing & printing

(G-11199)
MCGRAW-HILL SCHOOL EDUCATION H (PA)
2 Penn Plz Fl 20 (10121-2100)
PHONE...............................646 766-2000
David Levin, President
Teresa Martin-Retortillo, Senior VP
David B Stafford, Senior VP
Maryellen Valaitis, Senior VP
Patrick Milano, CFO
EMP: 500
SALES: 750MM Privately Held
SIC: 2731 Books: publishing only

(G-11200)
MCGRAW-HILL SCHOOL EDUCATN LLC
2 Penn Plz Fl 20 (10121-2100)
PHONE...............................646 766-2060
David Levin, President
Teresa Martin-Retortillo, Senior VP
Maryellen Valaitis, Senior VP
Patrick Milano, CFO
David Wright, CIO
EMP: 599 EST: 2013
SALES (est): 129.8MM
SALES (corp-wide): 750MM Privately Held
SIC: 2731 Book publishing; books: publishing & printing
PA: Mcgraw-Hill School Education Holdings, Llc
2 Penn Plz Fl 20
New York NY 10121
646 766-2000

(G-11201)
MCM PRODUCTS USA INC
712 5th Ave Ste 702 (10019-4108)
PHONE...............................646 756-4090
Michael R Callahan, CEO
Paolo Fontanelli, CEO
Sung-Joo Kim, Ch of Bd
Patrick Valeo, President
Josephine Redman, Manager
EMP: 36 EST: 2007
SALES (est): 7MM Privately Held
SIC: 3171 3149 3199 Women's handbags & purses; athletic shoes, except rubber or plastic; belt laces, leather

(G-11202)
MCMAHON PUBLISHING COMPANY (PA)
Also Called: Mc Mahon Group
545 W 45th St Fl 8 (10036-3423)
PHONE...............................212 957-5300
Fax: 212 957-7230
Raymond E Mc Mahon, CEO
Van N Velle, President
David Bronstein, Editor
Cynthia Gordon, Editor
Paul Urban, Exec VP
EMP: 64
SALES: 18MM Privately Held
SIC: 2721 Trade journals: publishing only, not printed on site

(G-11203)
MDI HOLDINGS LLC
Also Called: C/O Court Sq Capitl Partners
399 Park Ave Fl 14 (10022-4614)
PHONE...............................212 559-1127
Joseph M Silvestri, President
John Weber, Managing Prtnr
EMP: 2900

SALES (est): 208.8MM Privately Held
SIC: 2899 2842 2874 2992 Chemical preparations; plating compounds; rust resisting compounds; stencil correction compounds; cleaning or polishing preparations; phosphates; lubricating oils; offset & photolithographic printing; printers & plotters

(G-11204)
ME & RO INC (PA)
305 Broadway Ste 1101 (10007-1148)
PHONE...............................212 431-8744
Fax: 212 237-9219
Robin Renzi, CEO
Wu Ena, CFO
EMP: 6
SQ FT: 4,000
SALES (est): 2.1MM Privately Held
WEB: www.meandrojewelry.com
SIC: 3911 3915 Jewelry, precious metal; jewelers' materials & lapidary work

(G-11205)
MEALPLAN CORP
203 E 4th St Apt 6 (10009-7281)
PHONE...............................909 706-8398
Kevin Carter, President
Daniel Mao, Vice Pres
Vinh Thai, Treasurer
Helal Saleh, Sales Mgr
Michelle Chen, Admin Sec
EMP: 5
SALES (est): 128.9K Privately Held
SIC: 7372 Prepackaged software

(G-11206)
MED REVIEWS LLC
247 W 35th St Rm 801 (10001-1921)
PHONE...............................212 239-5860
Fax: 212 201-6850
Steven Black, Exec VP
Charles Benaiah,
John B Simpson, Administration
Miichael Brawer,
Diane Gern,
EMP: 27 EST: 1998
SQ FT: 10,000
SALES (est): 3.6MM Privately Held
WEB: www.medreviews.com
SIC: 2721 Trade journals: publishing & printing

(G-11207)
MEDALLION ASSOCIATES INC
37 W 20th St Fl 4 (10011-3791)
PHONE...............................212 929-9130
Fax: 212 206-7549
Donna Peters, Principal
Michael Decker, Vice Pres
Noelle Pistilli, Project Mgr
Judy Melioli, Personnel Exec
▲ EMP: 50 EST: 1963
SALES (est): 5.9MM Privately Held
WEB: www.medallionltd.com
SIC: 2752 2759 2791 Commercial printing, offset; promotional printing; typesetting

(G-11208)
MEDIA PRESS CORP
55 John St 520 (10038-3752)
PHONE...............................212 791-6347
Givi Topchishvili, President
EMP: 20
SALES (est): 1MM Privately Held
WEB: www.skullman.com
SIC: 2721 Periodicals

(G-11209)
MEDIA TRANSCRIPTS INC
41 W 83rd St Apt 1b (10024-5247)
PHONE...............................212 362-1481
Fax: 212 362-1647
Pat King, President
▲ EMP: 24
SALES (est): 1.5MM Privately Held
WEB: www.mediatranscripts.com
SIC: 2741 Miscellaneous publishing

(G-11210)
MEDIA TRUST LLC (PA)
404 Park Ave S Fl 2 (10016-8412)
PHONE...............................212 802-1162
Peter Bordes, CEO
Keith Cohn, President

Dave Coburn, COO
Mike Stocker, Vice Pres
Trevor Thomas, Officer
EMP: 6
SALES (est): 4.1MM Privately Held
SIC: 2741 7311 ; advertising agencies

(G-11211)
MEDIAPLANET PUBLISHING HSE INC (PA)
3 E 28th St Fl 10 (10016-7408)
PHONE...............................646 922-1409
Luciana Olson, Managing Dir
David Defina, CFO
Richard Hovdsveen, CTO
EMP: 32
SALES (est): 2.9MM Privately Held
SIC: 2731 Book publishing

(G-11212)
MEDIAPOST COMMUNICATIONS LLC
1460 Broadway Fl 12 (10036-7306)
PHONE...............................212 204-2000
Ken Fadner, CEO
Jeff Loechner, President
John Capone, Publisher
Nathan Pollard, Publisher
Phyllis Fine, Editor
EMP: 50
SALES (est): 5.3MM Privately Held
WEB: www.mediapost.com
SIC: 7372 Publishers' computer software

(G-11213)
MEDICAL DAILY INC
7 Hanover Sq Fl 6 (10004-2702)
PHONE...............................646 867-7100
Johnathan Davis, President
Dong-Chan Kim, Principal
Etienne Uzac, Treasurer
EMP: 30
SALES (est): 2.1MM Privately Held
SIC: 2741

(G-11214)
MEDICAL TRANSCRIPTION BILLING
237 W 35th St Ste 1202 (10001-1950)
PHONE...............................631 863-1198
EMP: 504
SALES (corp-wide): 23MM Publicly Held
SIC: 7372 Prepackaged software
PA: Medical Transcription Billing, Corp.
7 Clyde Rd
Somerset NJ 08873
732 873-5133

(G-11215)
MEDIDATA SOLUTIONS INC (PA)
350 Hudson St Fl 9 (10014-4535)
PHONE...............................212 918-1800
Fax: 212 918-1818
Tarek A Sherif, Ch of Bd
Glen M De Vries, President
Michael L Capone, COO
Michael I Otner, Exec VP
Michael C Pinto, Exec VP
EMP: 432
SQ FT: 137,535
SALES: 392.5MM Publicly Held
WEB: www.mdsol.com
SIC: 7372 Prepackaged software; application computer software; business oriented computer software

(G-11216)
MEDIKIDZ USA INC
200 Varick St (10014-4810)
PHONE...............................646 895-9319
Kate Hersov, CEO
Mitzie Garland, CFO
EMP: 7 EST: 2013
SQ FT: 1,000
SALES (est): 4.5MM Privately Held
SIC: 2721 2731 Comic books: publishing & printing; books: publishing only

(G-11217)
MEDIUS SOFTWARE INC
Also Called: Medius North America
14 E 44th St Fl 5 (10017-3632)
PHONE...............................877 295-0058
Fredrik Andre, Mktg Dir
Dmitri Krasik, Director

Mattias Johansson, Director
EMP: 17
SALES (est): 127.5K Privately Held
SIC: 7372 Prepackaged software

(G-11218)
MEE ACCESSORIES LLC (PA)
Also Called: Mark Ecko Enterprises
475 10th Ave Fl 9 (10018-9718)
PHONE...............................917 262-1000
Fax: 917 262-3519
Mark Ecko, CEO
Seth Gerszberg, President
Eli Reinitz, Senior VP
Greg Lucci, Vice Pres
Mark Dilling, Controller
▲ EMP: 189
SQ FT: 30,000
SALES (est): 37.8MM Privately Held
WEB: www.phys-sci.com
SIC: 2329 5136 5621 5611 Men's & boys' sportswear & athletic clothing; sportswear, men's & boys'; women's clothing stores; men's & boys' clothing stores

(G-11219)
MEEGENIUS INC
151 W 25th St Fl 3 (10001-7228)
P.O. Box 287434 (10128-0024)
PHONE...............................212 283-7285
David K Park, CEO
EMP: 5
SALES (est): 60K Privately Held
SIC: 2731 Book publishing

(G-11220)
MEGA POWER SPORTS CORPORATION
1123 Broadway Ph (10010-2084)
PHONE...............................212 627-3380
EMP: 6 EST: 1995
SALES (est): 360K Privately Held
SIC: 2353 5136 5137 Mfg & Whol Hats

(G-11221)
MEKANISM INC
80 Broad St Fl 35 (10004-2216)
PHONE...............................212 226-2772
Laura Peguero, Branch Mgr
EMP: 40
SALES (corp-wide): 8.4MM Privately Held
SIC: 3993 Signs & advertising specialties
PA: Mekanism, Inc.
640 2nd St Fl 3
San Francisco CA 94107
415 908-4000

(G-11222)
MELCHER MEDIA INC
124 W 13th St (10011-7802)
PHONE...............................212 727-2322
Fax: 212 627-1973
Charles Melcher, President
Lauren Nathan, Editor
Bonnie Eldon, COO
Susan Lynch, Prdtn Mgr
Kurt Andrews, Opers Staff
▲ EMP: 11
SQ FT: 1,500
SALES (est): 1.9MM Privately Held
WEB: www.melcher.com
SIC: 2731 2789 Books: publishing only; bookbinding & related work

(G-11223)
MELLANOX TECHNOLOGIES INC
165 Broadway Ste 2301 (10006-1404)
PHONE...............................408 970-3400
EMP: 74
SALES (corp-wide): 461.3MM Privately Held
SIC: 3674 Semiconductors & related devices
HQ: Mellanox Technologies, Inc.
350 Oakmead Pkwy
Sunnyvale CA 94085
408 970-3400

(G-11224)
MEMORY MD INC
205 E 42nd St Fl 14 (10017-5706)
PHONE...............................917 318-0215
Boris Goldstein, Ch of Bd

Yuriy Shirokikh, *CFO*
EMP: 5 **EST:** 2015
SALES (est): 260K **Privately Held**
SIC: 3841 5047 Diagnostic apparatus, medical; diagnostic equipment, medical

(G-11225)
MENS JOURNAL LLC
1290 Ave Of The Americas (10104-0295)
PHONE.................212 484-1616
Fax: 212 767-8204
David Kupiec, *Publisher*
Beth Press, *Publisher*
Tom Foster, *Editor*
Mark Horowitz, *Editor*
Mark Jannot, *Editor*
EMP: 59
SALES (est): 4.5MM **Privately Held**
SIC: 2741 Miscellaneous publishing

(G-11226)
MER GEMS CORP
Also Called: Romir Enterprises
62 W 47th St Ste 614 (10036-3201)
PHONE.................212 714-9129
Fax: 212 221-5743
Roshel Mirzakanzov, *President*
Nelly Mirzakanzov, *Vice Pres*
◆ **EMP:** 5 **EST:** 1998
SQ FT: 800
SALES: 1MM **Privately Held**
SIC: 3911 Jewelry, precious metal

(G-11227)
MERCHANT PUBLISHING INC
34 W 13th St Bsmt (10011-7911)
PHONE.................212 691-6666
Fax: 212 656-1568
Michael Kanbar, *CEO*
EMP: 14
SALES (est): 610K **Privately Held**
SIC: 2741 Miscellaneous publishing

(G-11228)
MEREDITH CORPORATION
125 Park Ave Fl 20 (10017-8545)
PHONE.................212 557-6600
Fax: 212 455-1444
Diane Salvatore, *Chief*
Andrea Gingold, *Branch Mgr*
SOO J Kang, *Director*
EMP: 250
SALES (corp-wide): 1.6B **Publicly Held**
WEB: www.meredith.com
SIC: 2721 Magazines: publishing & printing
PA: Meredith Corporation
1716 Locust St
Des Moines IA 50309
515 284-3000

(G-11229)
MEREDITH CORPORATION
Also Called: Meredith Corporate Solutions
805 3rd Ave Fl 22 (10022-7541)
PHONE.................212 499-2000
Sarah Pappen, *Marketing Mgr*
Noreen Rafferty, *Manager*
Christine Tafuri, *Manager*
Jose Xicohtencatl, *Manager*
Maria Caracci, *Director*
EMP: 17
SALES (corp-wide): 1.6B **Publicly Held**
WEB: www.meredith.com
SIC: 2721 Periodicals
PA: Meredith Corporation
1716 Locust St
Des Moines IA 50309
515 284-3000

(G-11230)
MEREDITH CORPORATION
Also Called: Meredith Hispanic Ventures
805 3rd Ave Fl 29 (10022-7541)
PHONE.................515 284-2157
Mike Lovell, *Branch Mgr*
EMP: 96
SALES (corp-wide): 1.6B **Publicly Held**
SIC: 2721 2731 Magazines: publishing & printing; books: publishing only
PA: Meredith Corporation
1716 Locust St
Des Moines IA 50309
515 284-3000

(G-11231)
MERGENT INC
444 Madison Ave Ste 502 (10022-6976)
PHONE.................212 413-7700
Fax: 212 413-7670
Jonathan Worral, *CEO*
Fred Jenkins, *President*
Mike Winn, *Managing Dir*
Charles E Miller Jr, *CFO*
EMP: 300
SALES (est): 17.2MM **Privately Held**
SIC: 2721 Magazines: publishing only, not printed on site

(G-11232)
MERRILL COMMUNICATIONS LLC
1345 Ave Of The Amrcs 1 (10105-0199)
PHONE.................212 620-5600
Jeannette Rivera, *Research*
Matthew Young, *Accounts Exec*
EMP: 9
SALES (corp-wide): 579.3MM **Privately Held**
SIC: 2759 Commercial printing
HQ: Merrill Communications Llc
1 Merrill Cir
Saint Paul MN 55108
651 646-4501

(G-11233)
MERRILL CORPORATION
25 W 45th St Fl 10 (10036-4916)
PHONE.................917 934-7300
Fax: 212 840-7159
Tom Foley, *Human Res Dir*
Phyliss Salimbene, *VP Sales*
Nancy Skluth, *Sales Staff*
Kathleen Leuba, *VP Mktg*
Peter Jordan, *Branch Mgr*
EMP: 87
SALES (corp-wide): 579.3MM **Privately Held**
WEB: www.merrillcorp.com
SIC: 2759 Commercial printing
PA: Merrill Corporation
1 Merrill Cir
Saint Paul MN 55108
651 646-4501

(G-11234)
MERRILL CORPORATION INC
1345 Ave Of The Ave Fl 17 (10105)
PHONE.................212 620-5600
Fax: 212 229-6630
Lauren Sauter, *General Mgr*
Harold Cooney, *COO*
Grace Triolo, *COO*
Peter Cawley, *Vice Pres*
Robert Chepak, *Vice Pres*
EMP: 100
SALES (corp-wide): 691.4MM **Privately Held**
WEB: www.merrillcorp.com
SIC: 2741 Miscellaneous publishing
PA: Merrill Corporation
1 Merrill Cir
Saint Paul MN 55108
651 646-4501

(G-11235)
MERRILL NEW YORK COMPANY INC
Also Called: Merrill Communications
246 W 54th St (10019-5502)
PHONE.................212 229-6500
Tod Albright, *President*
Robert Talbot, *Controller*
EMP: 200
SALES (est): 13.9MM
SALES (corp-wide): 579.3MM **Privately Held**
WEB: www.merrillcorp.com
SIC: 2759 2752 Financial note & certificate printing & engraving; commercial printing, lithographic
PA: Merrill Corporation
1 Merrill Cir
Saint Paul MN 55108
651 646-4501

(G-11236)
MERYL DIAMOND LTD (PA)
Also Called: M D L
1375 Broadway Fl 9 (10018-7052)
PHONE.................212 730-0333
Fax: 212 730-5933
Meryl Diamond, *President*
▲ **EMP:** 40
SQ FT: 13,000
SALES (est): 95.1MM **Privately Held**
SIC: 2339 Sportswear, women's

(G-11237)
MESH LLC
350 5th Ave Lbby 9 (10118-0109)
PHONE.................646 839-7000
Richard Darling,
▲ **EMP:** 30
SALES (est): 1.8MM **Privately Held**
SIC: 2326 Men's & boys' work clothing
HQ: Gbg Usa Inc.
350 5th Ave Lbby 9
New York NY 10118
646 839-7083

(G-11238)
MESKITA LIFESTYLE BRANDS LLC
336 W 37th St (10018-4212)
PHONE.................212 695-5054
Alexandra Meskita, *Mng Member*
EMP: 40 **EST:** 2013
SALES (est): 2.3MM **Privately Held**
SIC: 2339 Women's & misses' outerwear

(G-11239)
MESOBLAST INC
505 5th Ave Fl 3 (10017-4910)
PHONE.................212 880-2060
Silviu Itescu, *CEO*
Michael Schuster, *Top Exec*
Steve Kornher, *Vice Pres*
Andrea Margiotta, *Vice Pres*
Karen Segal, *Vice Pres*
EMP: 8
SALES (est): 5.1MM
SALES (corp-wide): 18.7MM **Privately Held**
SIC: 2834 Drugs acting on the cardiovascular system, except diagnostic
PA: Mesoblast Limited
L 38 55 Collins St
Melbourne VIC 3000
419 228-128

(G-11240)
MESSEX GROUP INC
244 5th Ave Ste D256 (10001-7604)
PHONE.................646 229-2582
Tom Carmody, *President*
Diana Popescu, *Vice Pres*
EMP: 4 **EST:** 2011
SQ FT: 1,000
SALES (est): 2MM **Privately Held**
SIC: 2325 Men's & boys' jeans & dungarees

(G-11241)
METRO CREATIVE GRAPHICS INC (PA)
519 8th Ave Fl 18 (10018-4577)
PHONE.................212 947-5100
Fax: 917 714-9139
Robert Zimmerman, *CEO*
Andrew Shapiro, *Ch of Bd*
Theodore Vittoria, *Vice Pres*
Millie Tricoles, *Accounting Mgr*
EMP: 38
SQ FT: 22,000
SALES (est): 6.4MM **Privately Held**
WEB: www.metroeditorialservices.com
SIC: 2731 2759 Books: publishing & printing; screen printing

(G-11242)
METROSOURCE PUBLISHING INC
111 W 19th St Fl 6 (10011-4165)
PHONE.................212 691-5127
Fax: 212 741-2978
Rob Davis, *President*
EMP: 12
SALES (est): 1.3MM **Privately Held**
SIC: 2721 Magazines: publishing & printing

(G-11243)
METTLE CONCEPT INC
545 8th Ave Rm 401 (10018-4341)
PHONE.................888 501-0680
Rex Ip, *President*
EMP: 5
SQ FT: 200
SALES: 1MM **Privately Held**
SIC: 3531 Construction machinery

(G-11244)
METZGER SPECIALITY BRANDS
161 W 54th St Apt 802 (10019-5360)
PHONE.................212 957-0055
Fax: 212 957-0918
Tim Metzger, *President*
▲ **EMP:** 2
SQ FT: 300
SALES: 2MM **Privately Held**
SIC: 2037 2035 Frozen fruits & vegetables; pickles, sauces & salad dressings

(G-11245)
MG IMAGING
229 W 28th St Rm 300 (10001-5915)
PHONE.................212 704-4073
Mario Gambuzza, *President*
EMP: 5 **EST:** 2010
SALES (est): 773.3K **Privately Held**
SIC: 3577 Printers & plotters

(G-11246)
MGK GROUP INC
Also Called: Lamontage
979 3rd Ave Ste 1811 (10022-3804)
PHONE.................212 989-2732
Fax: 212 989-8246
Liora Manne, *President*
EMP: 30
SQ FT: 10,000
SALES (est): 4MM **Privately Held**
WEB: www.lamontage.com
SIC: 2273 2211 2221 2392 Rugs, hand & machine made; upholstery fabrics, cotton; tapestry fabrics, cotton; wall covering fabrics, manmade fiber & silk; household furnishings; textile bags; nonwoven fabrics

(G-11247)
MIAMI MEDIA LLC (HQ)
72 Madison Ave Fl 11 (10016-8731)
PHONE.................212 268-8600
Thomas Allon, *Mng Member*
EMP: 14
SALES (est): 1.6MM
SALES (corp-wide): 13.6MM **Privately Held**
SIC: 2711 2721 Newspapers: publishing only, not printed on site; magazines: publishing only, not printed on site
PA: Manhattan Media, Llc
72 Madison Ave Fl 11
New York NY 10016
212 268-8600

(G-11248)
MICHAEL BONDANZA INC
10 E 38th St Fl 6 (10016-0004)
PHONE.................212 869-0043
Fax: 212 921-2565
Michael Bondanza, *President*
Geri Bondanza, *Vice Pres*
EMP: 26
SQ FT: 2,500
SALES (est): 3.3MM **Privately Held**
WEB: www.bondanza.com
SIC: 3911 5094 Jewelry, precious metal; jewelry

(G-11249)
MICHAEL KARP MUSIC INC
Also Called: 39th Street Music-Div
59 W 71st St Apt 7a (10023-4115)
PHONE.................212 840-3285
Fax: 212 840-3923
Michael Karp, *President*
EMP: 6
SQ FT: 5,500
SALES (est): 490K **Privately Held**
WEB: www.michaelkarpmusic.com
SIC: 2741 7389 Music, sheet: publishing only, not printed on site; music & broadcasting services

New York - New York County (G-11250) — GEOGRAPHIC SECTION

(G-11250)
MICHAEL VOLLBRACHT LLC
57 W 57th St Ste 603 (10019-2802)
PHONE..................................212 753-0123
Diane Hanley, *Controller*
Jerry Lynn, *Mng Member*
▲ EMP: 10
SALES (est): 1.2MM **Privately Held**
SIC: 2335 Women's, juniors' & misses' dresses

(G-11251)
MICHAELIAN & KOHLBERG INC
225 E 59th St (10022-1403)
PHONE..................................212 431-9009
EMP: 9
SALES (corp-wide): 4.2MM **Privately Held**
SIC: 2273 Mfg Carpets/Rugs
PA: Michaelian & Kohlberg, Inc.
5216 Brevard Rd
Horse Shoe NC 28742
828 891-8511

(G-11252)
MICKELBERRY COMMUNICATIONS INC (PA)
405 Park Ave (10022-4405)
PHONE..................................212 832-0303
Fax: 212 832-0554
James C Marlas, *Ch of Bd*
Gregory J Garville, *President*
Julian Nemiropsky, *Analyst*
EMP: 8 EST: 1926
SQ FT: 4,000
SALES (est): 50.1MM **Privately Held**
WEB: www.mickelberry.com
SIC: 2752 7311 Commercial printing, lithographic; advertising agencies

(G-11253)
MICRO PUBLISHING INC
Also Called: Micropage
71 W 23rd St Lbby A (10010-3521)
PHONE..................................212 533-9180
Fax: 212 353-1954
Kevin Boyajian, *President*
Steven Carlson, *Systems Admin*
Brian Boyajian, *Admin Sec*
EMP: 5
SQ FT: 9,000
SALES: 3MM **Privately Held**
WEB: www.micropage.com
SIC: 2731 2796 Book publishing; color separations for printing

(G-11254)
MICRO SEMICDTR RESEARCHES LLC (PA)
310 W 52nd St Apt 12b (10019-6292)
PHONE..................................646 863-6070
Seiji Yamashita, *Principal*
▲ EMP: 4
SALES (est): 1.7MM **Privately Held**
SIC: 3674 8748 Semiconductors & related devices; test development & evaluation service

(G-11255)
MICROMEM TECHNOLOGIES
245 Park Ave Fl 24 (10167-2699)
PHONE..................................212 672-1806
Steven Van Fleet, *Principal*
Janet M Garrity, *Treasurer*
Richard F Krakowski, *Director*
Audrey E Prashker, *Director*
Peter D Rutherford, *Director*
EMP: 10
SALES (est): 571.4K **Privately Held**
SIC: 3674 Semiconductors & related devices

(G-11256)
MICROSOFT CORPORATION
11 Times Sq Fl 9 (10036-6619)
PHONE..................................212 245-2100
Fax: 212 225-4479
Bob Buono, *Business Mgr*
Peter Protan, *Engineer*
Amanda Palma, *Accounts Mgr*
Jon Williams, *Regl Sales Mgr*
Michael Jeffers, *Accounts Exec*
EMP: 10
SALES (corp-wide): 85.3B **Publicly Held**
WEB: www.microsoft.com
SIC: 7372 Prepackaged software
PA: Microsoft Corporation
1 Microsoft Way
Redmond WA 98052
425 882-8080

(G-11257)
MICROSTRATEGY INCORPORATED
5 Penn Plz Ste 901 (10001-1837)
PHONE..................................888 537-8135
Fax: 212 896-3965
John Larkin, *CEO*
Stephen Goodson, *Info Tech Mgr*
EMP: 15
SALES (corp-wide): 529.8MM **Publicly Held**
WEB: www.microstrategy.com
SIC: 7372 Application computer software
PA: Microstrategy Incorporated
1850 Towers Crescent Plz # 700
Tysons Corner VA 22182
703 848-8600

(G-11258)
MIDAS MDICI GROUP HOLDINGS INC (PA)
445 Park Ave Frnt 5 (10022-8603)
PHONE..................................212 792-0920
Nana Baffour, *Ch of Bd*
Johnson M Kachidza, *President*
Robert F McCarthy, *Exec VP*
Ricardo Giudice, *Vice Pres*
Mitch Lemons, *Vice Pres*
EMP: 4
SALES: 89.6MM **Publicly Held**
SIC: 7372 Prepackaged software

(G-11259)
MIDURA JEWELS INC
36 W 47th St Ste 809i (10036-8601)
PHONE..................................213 265-8090
EMP: 2 EST: 2013
SALES: 1MM **Privately Held**
SIC: 3911 5094 5944 Mfg Precious Metal Jewelry Whol Jewelry/Precious Stones Ret Jewelry

(G-11260)
MIDWAY NEWS INC
302 E 86th St (10028-3105)
PHONE..................................212 628-3009
Mawani Amjad, *Ch of Bd*
EMP: 5
SALES (est): 234.9K **Privately Held**
SIC: 2711 Newspapers, publishing & printing

(G-11261)
MIGHTY QUINNS BARBEQUE LLC
103 2nd Ave Frnt 1 (10003-8336)
PHONE..................................973 777-8340
Christos Gourmos, *Managing Prtnr*
EMP: 30
SQ FT: 3,000
SALES: 10MM **Privately Held**
SIC: 2099 Food preparations

(G-11262)
MIGUELINA INC
325 W 37th St Fl 2 (10018-4203)
PHONE..................................212 925-0320
Fax: 212 218-4590
Miguelina Ganbiccini, *President*
Miguelina C Ganbiccini, *President*
Riccardo Ganbiccini, *Vice Pres*
Maria Balanta, *Sales Dir*
Patricia Butter, *Administration*
EMP: 10
SQ FT: 6,500
SALES (est): 1.3MM **Privately Held**
WEB: www.miguelina.com
SIC: 2339 Women's & misses' outerwear

(G-11263)
MIKAEL AGHAL LLC
49 W 38th St Fl 4 (10018-1913)
PHONE..................................212 596-4010
Lee Isit, *Accountant*
Michael Hakimi,
Albert Aghalarian,
◆ EMP: 11
SQ FT: 5,000
SALES (est): 1.1MM **Privately Held**
WEB: www.mikaelaghal.com
SIC: 2339 Athletic clothing: women's, misses' & juniors'; women's & misses' athletic clothing & sportswear

(G-11264)
MIKAM GRAPHICS LLC
1440 Broadway Fl 22 (10018-3041)
PHONE..................................212 684-9393
Donald Pesce, *Vice Pres*
Jeff Getelman, *Mng Member*
EMP: 100
SQ FT: 5,000
SALES (est): 13.4MM
SALES (corp-wide): 1B **Publicly Held**
WEB: www.mikam.com
SIC: 2752 Commercial printing, offset
PA: Innerworkings, Inc.
600 W Chicago Ave Ste 850
Chicago IL 60654
312 642-3700

(G-11265)
MILAAYA INC
Also Called: Milaaya Embroideries
566 Fashion Ave Rm 805 (10018-1846)
PHONE..................................212 764-6386
Fax: 212 764-3910
Gayatri Khanna, *President*
EMP: 4
SALES: 1.2MM **Privately Held**
SIC: 2395 Pleating & stitching

(G-11266)
MILLENNIUM MEDICAL PUBLISHING
611 Broadway Rm 310 (10012-2654)
PHONE..................................212 995-2211
Steve Kurlander, *CEO*
Mark Sulkowski, *Bd of Directors*
EMP: 18
SQ FT: 3,000
SALES: 6MM **Privately Held**
SIC: 2741 Miscellaneous publishing

(G-11267)
MILLENNIUM PRODUCTIONS INC
Also Called: Alice & Trixie
265 W 37th St 11 (10018-5707)
PHONE..................................212 944-6203
Andrew Oshrin, *President*
Lynn Harechmak, *Bookkeeper*
▲ EMP: 12
SQ FT: 2,000
SALES (est): 1.3MM **Privately Held**
WEB: www.aliceandtrixie.com
SIC: 2335 2339 Housedresses; sportswear, women's

(G-11268)
MILLER & BERKOWITZ LTD
345 7th Ave Fl 20 (10001-5034)
PHONE..................................212 244-5459
Nathan Berkowitz, *President*
Robert Englander, *Sales Mgr*
EMP: 13 EST: 1949
SQ FT: 13,500
SALES (est): 780K **Privately Held**
SIC: 2371 Fur goods

(G-11269)
MILLER & VEIT INC
22 W 48th St Ste 703 (10036-1820)
PHONE..................................212 247-2275
Fax: 212 245-5908
Edward Ludel, *President*
Edward E Ludel, *Vice Pres*
Barbara Ludel, *Admin Sec*
EMP: 10
SQ FT: 1,566
SALES (est): 880K **Privately Held**
SIC: 3915 5094 Diamond cutting & polishing; diamonds (gems)

(G-11270)
MILLIORE FASHION INC
250 W 39th St Rm 506 (10018-8332)
PHONE..................................212 302-0001
Ws Min, *President*
Kyong Shin, *General Mgr*
▲ EMP: 4
SALES: 7.3MM **Privately Held**
SIC: 2335 Women's, juniors' & misses' dresses

(G-11271)
MILTON MERL & ASSOCIATES INC
647 W 174th St Bsmt B (10033-7716)
PHONE..................................212 634-9292
Fax: 212 634-9262
Milton Merl, *President*
Dan Gray, *Controller*
▲ EMP: 5
SQ FT: 2,000
SALES (est): 725.2K **Privately Held**
WEB: www.miltonmerl.com
SIC: 2542 Partitions & fixtures, except wood

(G-11272)
MILTONS OF NEW YORK INC
110 W 40th St Rm 1001 (10018-8535)
PHONE..................................212 997-3359
Fax: 212 997-3358
Kerman Minbatiwalla, *President*
Shalini Amersey, *Vice Pres*
EMP: 9
SQ FT: 600
SALES (est): 1.1MM **Privately Held**
WEB: www.miltonsny.com
SIC: 2339 2321 2325 2369 Women's & misses' outerwear; men's & boys' furnishings; men's & boys' trousers & slacks; girls' & children's outerwear

(G-11273)
MIMEOCOM INC (PA)
3 Park Ave Fl 22 (10016-5909)
P.O. Box 654018, Dallas TX (75265-4018)
PHONE..................................212 847-3000
Adam Slutsky, *CEO*
Jamie Wardley, *Managing Dir*
John Delbridge, *COO*
Chuck Gehman, *COO*
Nicole P Haughey, *COO*
EMP: 277
SQ FT: 145,000
SALES (est): 247.9MM **Privately Held**
WEB: www.mimeo.com
SIC: 2759 Commercial printing

(G-11274)
MIMI SO INTERNATIONAL LLC
Also Called: Mimi So New York
22 W 48th St Ste 902 (10036-1803)
PHONE..................................212 300-8600
Nick Li, *Production*
Gregory Wong, *Controller*
Mimi So, *Mng Member*
Kamna Gabri, *Manager*
Stephanie Preville, *Director*
EMP: 20
SALES (est): 3.3MM **Privately Held**
SIC: 3911 5944 5094 Jewelry, precious metal; jewelry stores; jewelry

(G-11275)
MIN HO DESIGNS INC
425 Madison Ave Rm 1703 (10017-1150)
PHONE..................................212 838-3667
Fax: 212 838-3689
EMP: 9
SQ FT: 1,600
SALES (est): 740K **Privately Held**
SIC: 3911 Mfg Jewelry

(G-11276)
MINERALS TECHNOLOGIES INC (PA)
Also Called: MTI
622 3rd Ave Fl 38 (10017-6729)
PHONE..................................212 878-1800
Joseph C Muscari, *Ch of Bd*
Gary L Castagna, *Senior VP*
D Randy Harrison, *Senior VP*
Jonathan J Hastings, *Senior VP*
Douglas W Mayger, *Senior VP*
▲ EMP: 50

▲ = Import ▼ = Export
◆ = Import/Export

SALES: 1.8B **Publicly Held**
WEB: www.mineralstech.com
SIC: 3295 2819 3274 1411 Minerals, ground or treated; minerals, ground or otherwise treated; talc, ground or otherwise treated; calcium compounds & salts, inorganic; quicklime; limestone & marble dimension stone; limestone, cut & shaped; limestone

(G-11277)
MING PAO (NEW YORK) INC
265 Canal St Ste 403 (10013-6010)
PHONE..................................212 334-2220
EMP: 10
SALES (corp-wide): 429.1MM **Privately Held**
SIC: 2711 Printing & Circulation Of Newspaper
HQ: Ming Pao (New York), Inc
4331 33rd St
Long Island City NY 11101

(G-11278)
MINK MART INC
345 7th Ave Fl 9 (10001-5049)
PHONE..................................212 868-2785
George J Haralabatos, *President*
EMP: 7 EST: 1960
SQ FT: 7,200
SALES (est): 680K **Privately Held**
SIC: 2371 Apparel, fur

(G-11279)
MINY GROUP INC
148 Lafayette St Fl 2 (10013-3115)
PHONE..................................212 925-6722
Shun Yen Siu, *President*
Harvey Lock, *Vice Pres*
Deirdre Quinn, *Vice Pres*
Anita Wong, *Vice Pres*
EMP: 70
SALES (est): 3.1MM **Privately Held**
SIC: 2337 Women's & misses' suits & coats

(G-11280)
MINYANVILLE MEDIA INC
708 3rd Ave Fl 6 (10017-4119)
PHONE..................................212 991-6200
Todd Harrison, *CEO*
Kevin Wassong, *President*
Allan Millstein, *CFO*
Greg Collins, *Portfolio Mgr*
Guillermo Suarez, *VP Sales*
EMP: 23
SQ FT: 6,000
SALES (est): 1.5MM **Privately Held**
SIC: 2741 Miscellaneous publishing

(G-11281)
MISS GROUP (PA)
1410 Broadway Rm 703 (10018-9365)
PHONE..................................212 391-2535
▲ EMP: 9
SALES (est): 5MM **Privately Held**
SIC: 2329 Mens And Boys Clothing, Nec, Nsk

(G-11282)
MISS JESSIES LLC
Also Called: Miss Jessies Products
441 Broadway Fl 2 (10013-2592)
PHONE..................................718 643-9016
Furner Marquis, *Bookkeeper*
Carissa Ballance, *Marketing Staff*
Miko Branch, *Mng Member*
Piti Branch, *Mng Member*
Reeves Carter, *General Counsel*
EMP: 8
SQ FT: 3,000
SALES (est): 1.3MM **Privately Held**
SIC: 3999 Hair & hair-based products

(G-11283)
MISS SPORTSWEAR INC (PA)
Also Called: Miss Group, The
1410 Broadway Rm 703 (10018-9365)
PHONE..................................212 391-2535
Fax: 212 391-2543
Moses Fallas, *Ch of Bd*
Moey Fallas, *President*
Alan Fallas, *Vice Pres*
Sammy Fallas, *Manager*
Irene Chang, *Admin Asst*
▲ EMP: 3

SQ FT: 8,000
SALES (est): 15.4MM **Privately Held**
SIC: 2339 Women's & misses' athletic clothing & sportswear

(G-11284)
MISTDODA INC (DH)
Also Called: Croscill Home Fashions
261 5th Ave Fl 25 (10016-7601)
PHONE..................................919 735-7111
Fax: 212 481-8656
Douglas Kahn, *CEO*
Marc Navarre, *President*
Bull Armpad, *Business Mgr*
Michelle L Rovere, *Senior VP*
Ken Hedrick, *Vice Pres*
▲ EMP: 50 EST: 1925
SQ FT: 35,000
SALES (est): 70.6MM
SALES (corp-wide): 4.2B **Privately Held**
WEB: www.croscill.com
SIC: 2391 5023 Curtains & draperies; decorative home furnishings & supplies
HQ: Croscill Home Llc
1500 N Carolina St
Goldsboro NC 27530
919 735-7111

(G-11285)
MJM JEWELRY CORP (PA)
Also Called: Berry Jewelry Company
29 W 38th St Rm 1601 (10018-5504)
PHONE..................................212 354-5014
Fax: 212 302-2340
Martha Berry, *President*
Anthony Katsaras, *Engineer*
Jessica Cohen, *Controller*
Joanna Underwood, *Sales Staff*
Morgan Haas, *Manager*
▲ EMP: 35
SQ FT: 10,000
SALES: 14.6MM **Privately Held**
WEB: www.berryjewelry.com
SIC: 3911 Jewelry, precious metal

(G-11286)
MKJ COMMUNICATIONS CORP
174 Hudson St Fl 2 (10013-2161)
PHONE..................................212 206-0072
Jennifer Herman, *President*
EMP: 11
SQ FT: 3,500
SALES: 7.2MM **Privately Held**
SIC: 3699 Security control equipment & systems

(G-11287)
MOBILE HATCH INC
555 W 18th St (10011-2822)
PHONE..................................212 314-7300
Dinesh Moorjani, *CEO*
Adam Huie, *Manager*
Jason Cowlishaw, *Director*
EMP: 6
SQ FT: 2,000
SALES (est): 315.1K
SALES (corp-wide): 3.2B **Publicly Held**
SIC: 7372 Prepackaged software
HQ: Iac Search & Media, Inc.
555 12th St Ste 500
Oakland CA 94607
510 985-7400

(G-11288)
MODERN LANGUAGE ASSN AMER INC
Also Called: M L A
85 Broad St Fl 5 (10004-1789)
PHONE..................................646 576-5000
Fax: 646 576-5160
Margaret W Ferguson, *President*
John Golbach, *Editor*
Kwame Anthony Appiah, *Vice Pres*
Roland Greene, *Vice Pres*
Amilde Hadden, *Finance Dir*
EMP: 110 EST: 1883
SQ FT: 37,500
SALES: 15.4MM **Privately Held**
SIC: 2731 8641 Books: publishing only; educator's association

(G-11289)
MODO RETAIL LLC
Also Called: Modo Eyeware
252 Mott St (10012-3436)
PHONE..................................212 965-4900

Sue Ng, *Controller*
Alex Lenaro,
EMP: 40
SALES (est): 3.1MM **Privately Held**
SIC: 3851 Spectacles

(G-11290)
MODULEX NEW YORK INC
Also Called: Asi Sign Systems
192 Lexington Ave Rm 1002 (10016-6823)
PHONE..................................646 742-1320
Selwyn Josset, *President*
John Jackson, *Sales Associate*
Lauren Corrigan, *Office Mgr*
EMP: 8
SQ FT: 2,200
SALES (est): 2.1MM **Privately Held**
SIC: 3993 Signs & advertising specialties

(G-11291)
MODULIGHTOR INC
246 E 58th St (10022-2011)
PHONE..................................212 371-0336
Fax: 212 371-0335
Ernest Wagner, *President*
Imelda Elpidma, *Bookkeeper*
▲ EMP: 12 EST: 1976
SQ FT: 7,000
SALES (est): 1.2MM **Privately Held**
WEB: www.Modulightor.com
SIC: 3646 3645 Commercial indusl & institutional electric lighting fixtures; residential lighting fixtures

(G-11292)
MOISHE L HOROWITZ
Also Called: Moishe L Horowitz Diamonds
36 W 47th St Ste 303a (10036-8636)
PHONE..................................212 719-4247
Fax: 212 719-4164
Moishe L Horowitz, *Owner*
EMP: 15
SQ FT: 648
SALES (est): 680K **Privately Held**
SIC: 3915 Diamond cutting & polishing

(G-11293)
MOLABS INC
32 Little West 12th St (10014-1303)
PHONE..................................310 721-6828
James Payne, *CEO*
EMP: 6
SALES (est): 135.3K **Privately Held**
SIC: 7372 Application computer software

(G-11294)
MOLESKINE AMERICA INC
210 11th Ave Rm 1004 (10001-1210)
PHONE..................................646 461-3018
Marco Beghin, *Principal*
Anthony Rossi, *Sales Dir*
Shareen Maison, *Info Tech Mgr*
Erik Fabian, *Director*
▲ EMP: 46
SALES (est): 18.9MM
SALES (corp-wide): 98.2MM **Privately Held**
SIC: 2678 Stationery products
PA: Moleskine Spa
Viale Stelvio 66
Milano MI 20159
024 344-981

(G-11295)
MOLLYS CUPCAKES NEW YORK
228 Bleecker St (10014-4420)
PHONE..................................212 255-5441
EMP: 8
SALES (est): 300K **Privately Held**
SIC: 2051 Bakery: wholesale or wholesale/retail combined

(G-11296)
MOM DAD PUBLISHING INC
Also Called: C/O Pdell Ndell Fine Winberger
59 Maiden Ln Fl 27 (10038-4647)
PHONE..................................646 476-9170
Bert Padell, *President*
Bruce Nadell, *CPA*
Annette Paulino, *Manager*
EMP: 30
SALES (est): 2.4MM **Privately Held**
SIC: 2741 Music, sheet: publishing only, not printed on site

(G-11297)
MOMOFUKU 171 FIRST AVENUE LLC
171 1st Ave (10003-2949)
PHONE..................................212 777-7773
David Chang, *Mng Member*
Andrew Salmon,
Susanne Wright,
EMP: 52
SALES (est): 5.8MM **Privately Held**
SIC: 2098 Noodles (e.g. egg, plain & water), dry

(G-11298)
MONACELLI PRESS LLC
236 W 27th St Rm 4a (10001-5906)
PHONE..................................212 229-9925
Gianfranco Monacelli, *President*
Madeleine Compagnon, *Editor*
Victoria Craven, *Editor*
Nancy Green, *Editor*
Michael Vagnetti, *Production*
▲ EMP: 8
SALES (est): 975.3K **Privately Held**
WEB: www.monacellipress.com
SIC: 2731 Books: publishing only

(G-11299)
MONDO PUBLISHING INC (PA)
980 Avenue Of The America (10018-7810)
PHONE..................................212 268-3560
Fax: 212 268-3561
Mark Vineis, *President*
Lucia Chan, *Editor*
Ellen Ungaro, *Editor*
Sallye Drinkard, *Prdtn Mgr*
Yatin Bavishi, *Controller*
▲ EMP: 20
SALES (est): 2.1MM **Privately Held**
WEB: www.mondopub.com
SIC: 2731 Books: publishing only

(G-11300)
MONELLE JEWELRY
608 5th Ave Ste 504 (10020-2303)
PHONE..................................212 977-9535
Avis Swed, *Owner*
EMP: 3
SQ FT: 600
SALES: 1.1MM **Privately Held**
WEB: www.monellejewelry.com
SIC: 3911 Jewelry, precious metal

(G-11301)
MONTE GOLDMAN EMBROIDERY CO
15 W 72nd St Apt 11n (10023-3440)
PHONE..................................212 874-5397
Monte Goldman, *President*
Myrna Goldman, *Corp Secy*
Steven Silverman, *Vice Pres*
EMP: 10
SQ FT: 6,000
SALES: 1MM **Privately Held**
SIC: 2395 Embroidery products, except schiffli machine

(G-11302)
MONTHLY GIFT INC
Also Called: Montly Gift
401 Park Ave S (10016-8808)
PHONE..................................888 444-9661
Lisamarie Scotti, *Vice Pres*
EMP: 6
SQ FT: 350
SALES: 500K **Privately Held**
SIC: 2676 Sanitary paper products

(G-11303)
MONTHLY REVIEW FOUNDATION INC
146 W 29th St Rm 6fw (10001-8202)
PHONE..................................212 691-2555
John Foster, *President*
John Mage, *Vice Pres*
Michael D Yates, *Assoc Editor*
Bill Fletcher Jr, *Director*
Martin Paddio, *Admin Sec*
▲ EMP: 5
SQ FT: 5,000
SALES: 1.1MM **Privately Held**
SIC: 2741 2731 Miscellaneous publishing; books: publishing only

New York - New York County (G-11304) GEOGRAPHIC SECTION

(G-11304)
MORELLE PRODUCTS LTD
Also Called: Philippe Adec Paris
211 E 18th St Apt 4d (10003-3624)
PHONE..................................212 391-8070
Aby Saltiel, *President*
Alexander Fronimos, *Vice Pres*
Bridgets Hutchinsn, *Accountant*
EMP: 17
SQ FT: 13,500
SALES (est): 2.4MM **Privately Held**
WEB: www.philippeadec.com
SIC: 2339 5137 Sportswear, women's; sportswear, women's & children's

(G-11305)
MORGIK METAL DESIGNS
145 Hudson St Frnt 4 (10013-2122)
PHONE..................................212 463-0304
Fax: 212 463-0329
Larry Kaufman, *President*
Joe Kaufman, *Admin Sec*
EMP: 18
SQ FT: 4,000
SALES (est): 1.3MM **Privately Held**
WEB: www.morgik.com
SIC: 3446 1761 3429 Architectural metalwork; architectural sheet metal work; furniture builders' & other household hardware

(G-11306)
MORRIS BROTHERS SIGN SVC INC
37 W 20th St Ste 708 (10011-3717)
PHONE..................................212 675-9130
Fax: 212 675-7708
Peter V Bellantone, *President*
Michael Bellantone, *General Mgr*
EMP: 3
SQ FT: 2,000
SALES: 1MM **Privately Held**
WEB: www.morrisbrotherssigns.com
SIC: 3993 Signs & advertising specialties

(G-11307)
MORRIS COMMUNICATIONS CO LLC
Also Called: Lyons Press
123 W 18th St Fl 6 (10011-4127)
PHONE..................................212 620-9580
Fax: 212 929-1836
Christine Mularoni, *Marketing Staff*
Tony Lyons, *Branch Mgr*
Monica Silva, *Data Proc Exec*
Leigh Rubin, *Exec Dir*
EMP: 23
SALES (corp-wide): 785.3MM **Privately Held**
WEB: www.morris.com
SIC: 2721 Periodicals
HQ: Morris Communications Company Llc
725 Broad St
Augusta GA 30901
706 724-0851

(G-11308)
MOSBY HOLDINGS CORP (DH)
125 Park Ave (10017-5529)
PHONE..................................212 309-8100
Ron Mobed, *President*
EMP: 5
SALES (est): 115.6MM
SALES (corp-wide): 9B **Privately Held**
SIC: 2741 8999 Technical manuals: publishing only, not printed on site; writing for publication
HQ: Relx Inc.
230 Park Ave
New York NY 10169
212 309-8100

(G-11309)
MOSCHOS FURS INC
345 7th Ave Rm 1501 (10001-5042)
PHONE..................................212 244-0255
Fax: 212 465-2039
George Moschos, *President*
Patricia Moschos, *Corp Secy*
Sandy Ross, *Bookkeeper*
EMP: 5
SQ FT: 4,000
SALES (est): 350K **Privately Held**
SIC: 2371 Fur coats & other fur apparel

(G-11310)
MOSCOT WHOLESALE CORP
69 W 14th St Fl 2 (10011-7417)
PHONE..................................212 647-1550
Dr Harvey Moscot, *President*
Kenny Moscot, *Shareholder*
▲ EMP: 6
SQ FT: 2,000
SALES (est): 770.7K **Privately Held**
SIC: 3851 5049 Frames, lenses & parts, eyeglass & spectacle; optical goods

(G-11311)
MOTI GANZ (USA) INC
Also Called: Motiganz Group
1200 Ave Of The Americas (10036-1603)
PHONE..................................212 302-0040
Moti Ganz, *Ch of Bd*
Florence Hon, *Accounting Mgr*
Jack Trister, *Director*
EMP: 6
SALES (est): 550K **Privately Held**
WEB: www.elaradiamonds.com
SIC: 3911 3915 Jewelry, precious metal; jewel cutting, drilling, polishing, recutting or setting

(G-11312)
MOUNT GAY RUM
1290 Ave Of The Americas (10104-0101)
PHONE..................................212 399-4200
Tom Jensen, *CEO*
Alejandra Pena, *Senior VP*
Dennis Floam, *CFO*
Eric Maldonado, *Director*
EMP: 5
SALES (est): 234.3K **Privately Held**
SIC: 2085 2084 5921 Rum (alcoholic beverage); brandy; liquor stores

(G-11313)
MP HOLDINGS INC (PA)
11 Penn Plz Fl 19 (10001-2006)
PHONE..................................212 465-6800
Robin Davy, *President*
▲ EMP: 15
SQ FT: 62,600
SALES (est): 48.3MM **Privately Held**
WEB: www.mccall.com
SIC: 2335 Dresses, paper: cut & sewn

(G-11314)
MP STUDIO INC
147 W 35th St Ste 1603 (10001-2100)
PHONE..................................212 302-5666
EMP: 5 EST: 2013
SALES (est): 300K **Privately Held**
SIC: 2337 Mfg Women's/Misses' Suits/Coats

(G-11315)
MPDRAW LLC
109 Ludlow St (10002-3240)
PHONE..................................212 228-8383
EMP: 25
SALES (est): 1.6MM **Privately Held**
SIC: 3421 Table & food cutlery, including butchers'

(G-11316)
MRINALINI INC
Also Called: M & R Design
469 7th Ave Rm 1254 (10018-7605)
PHONE..................................646 510-2747
Mrinalini Kumari, *President*
Steven Caretsky, *Manager*
EMP: 6
SALES (est): 31.1K **Privately Held**
SIC: 2395 Embroidery & art needlework

(G-11317)
MRS JOHN L STRONG & CO LLC
Also Called: Strong Ventures
699 Madison Ave Fl 5 (10065-8039)
PHONE..................................212 838-3775
Joe Lewis, *President*
Jessica Alfonso, *Accounts Exec*
Ani Acevedo, *Sales Staff*
Nanette Brown,
EMP: 14
SALES (est): 1.5MM **Privately Held**
WEB: www.mrsstrong.com
SIC: 2754 Stationery: gravure printing

(G-11318)
MRT TEXTILE INC
350 5th Ave (10118-0110)
PHONE..................................800 674-1073
Ibrahim Eyidemir, *President*
David Davitoglu, *Vice Pres*
EMP: 3
SQ FT: 7,000
SALES: 4MM **Privately Held**
SIC: 2341 5137 Chemises, camisoles & teddies: women's & children's; women's & children's lingerie & undergarments

(G-11319)
MSKCC RMIPC
Also Called: Memorial Sloan Kttering Cancer
1250 1st Ave Ste S-C24 (10065-6038)
PHONE..................................212 639-6212
Aleksey Khersonskiy, *Business Mgr*
Serge Lyashchenko, *Supervisor*
Jason Lewis, *Director*
EMP: 16
SALES (est): 1.1MM **Privately Held**
SIC: 2834 Solutions, pharmaceutical

(G-11320)
MTM PUBLISHING INC
435 W 23rd St Apt 8c (10011-1437)
PHONE..................................212 242-6930
Valerie Tomaselli, *President*
EMP: 6
SALES (est): 451.3K **Privately Held**
SIC: 2741 Miscellaneous publishing

(G-11321)
MUALEMA LLC
Also Called: Sohha Savory Yogurt
128 W 112th St Apt 1a (10026-3748)
PHONE..................................609 820-6098
Angela Fout, *Mng Member*
John Fout,
EMP: 6
SALES: 600K **Privately Held**
SIC: 2026 Yogurt

(G-11322)
MUD PUDDLE BOOKS INC
36 W 25th St Fl 5 (10010-2718)
PHONE..................................212 647-9168
Gregory Boehm, *President*
▲ EMP: 5
SQ FT: 3,000
SALES (est): 603K **Privately Held**
WEB: www.mudpuddlebooks.com
SIC: 2731 Books: publishing only

(G-11323)
MULITEX USA INC
215 W 40th St Fl 7 (10018-1575)
PHONE..................................212 398-0440
Fax: 212 253-4017
Harry Mohinani, *CEO*
Sivaprakasham Rajakkal, *President*
Arun Mahbubani, *Director*
Vijay Mohinani, *Director*
▲ EMP: 6
SQ FT: 2,000
SALES (est): 7.1MM **Privately Held**
WEB: www.mulitex.com
SIC: 2321 2325 2331 Men's & boys' furnishings; men's & boys' trousers & slacks; women's & misses' blouses & shirts
PA: Mulitex (Exports) Limited
9/F Angel Twr
Lai Chi Kok KLN
225 110-00

(G-11324)
MULTI PACKAGING SOLUTIONS INC (HQ)
150 E 52nd St Ste 2800 (10022-6240)
PHONE..................................646 885-0157
Marc Shore, *CEO*
Dennis Kaltman, *President*
Nancy Smith, *President*
Arthur Kern, *Exec VP*
Rick Smith, *Exec VP*
◆ EMP: 20
SALES (est): 1.1B
SALES (corp-wide): 1.6B **Publicly Held**
WEB: www.ivyhill-wms.com
SIC: 2759 2731 2761 3089 Commercial printing; screen printing; letterpress printing; tags: printing; books: publishing & printing; continuous forms, office & business; identification cards, plastic; arts & crafts equipment & supplies; packaging paper & plastics film, coated & laminated
PA: Multi Packaging Solutions International Limited
150 E 52nd St Fl 28
New York NY 10022
646 885-0005

(G-11325)
MULTI PACKG SOLUTIONS INTL LTD (PA)
150 E 52nd St Fl 28 (10022-6017)
PHONE..................................646 885-0005
Marc Shore, *CEO*
Dennis Kaltman, *President*
Rick Smith, *Exec VP*
William H Hogan, *CFO*
Ross Weiner,
EMP: 8 EST: 2005
SQ FT: 9,772
SALES: 1.6B **Publicly Held**
SIC: 2657 Folding paperboard boxes

(G-11326)
MULTIMEDIA PLUS INC
853 Broadway Ste 1605 (10003-4714)
PHONE..................................212 982-3229
Fax: 212 982-3248
David Harouche, *President*
Robert Guadalupe, *Senior VP*
Anthony Deluca, *CFO*
Bella Etessami, *Director*
Andrew Gaspar, *Director*
EMP: 15
SQ FT: 5,000
SALES (est): 2.3MM **Privately Held**
WEB: www.multimediaplus.com
SIC: 7372 Educational computer software

(G-11327)
MUSIC SALES CORPORATION (PA)
Also Called: Acorn
180 Madison Ave Ste 2400 (10016-5241)
PHONE..................................212 254-2100
Fax: 212 254-2013
Barrie Edwards, *President*
Miles Feinberg, *Exec VP*
Bob Knight, *Vice Pres*
Robert Wise, *Vice Pres*
John Castaldo, *CFO*
▲ EMP: 6
SQ FT: 6,800
SALES (est): 13.6MM **Privately Held**
WEB: www.msc-catalog.com
SIC: 2741 Music books: publishing only, not printed on site; music, sheet: publishing only, not printed on site

(G-11328)
MUST USA INC
1400 Broadway Rm 2204 (10018-5204)
PHONE..................................212 391-8288
Paul Pelssers, *President*
Anil Kamat, *Director*
▲ EMP: 7
SALES (est): 712.3K **Privately Held**
SIC: 2329 5136 Men's & boys' clothing; men's & boys' clothing

(G-11329)
MW SAMARA LLC (PA)
390 5th Ave Fl 2 (10018-8162)
PHONE..................................212 764-3332
Frank Fialkoss, *Mng Member*
Frank Fialkoff, *Mng Member*
Johanna Ortiz, *Manager*
▲ EMP: 50
SALES (est): 3.8MM **Privately Held**
SIC: 3911 Jewelry, precious metal

(G-11330)
MX SOLAR USA LLC
100 Wall St Ste 1000 (10005-3727)
PHONE..................................732 356-7300
◆ EMP: 150

▲ = Import ▼ = Export
◆ = Import/Export

GEOGRAPHIC SECTION

New York - New York County (G-11356)

SALES (est): 10.1MM **Privately Held**
SIC: **3433** Mfg Heating Equipment-Non-electric

(G-11331)
MY MOST FAVORITE FOOD
247 W 72nd St Frnt 1 (10023-2723)
PHONE.................................212 580-5130
Scott A Magram, *Principal*
EMP: 5
SALES (est): 271.8K **Privately Held**
SIC: **2052** 2024 Bakery products, dry; ices, flavored (frozen dessert)

(G-11332)
MY PUBLISHER INC
845 3rd Ave Rm 1410 (10022-6619)
PHONE.................................212 935-5215
Fax: 212 935-3950
Carl Navarre, *CEO*
Dwight Blaha, *COO*
Mark Labbe, *CTO*
EMP: 7
SALES (est): 10MM
SALES (corp-wide): 1B **Publicly Held**
SIC: **2741** Miscellaneous publishing
PA: Shutterfly, Inc.
    2800 Bridge Pkwy Ste 100
    Redwood City CA 94065
    650 610-5200

(G-11333)
MYNT 1792 LLC
300 E 71st St Apt 10g (10021-5253)
PHONE.................................212 249-4562
Ricky Zinn, *Mng Member*
EMP: 3
SALES: 1.5MM **Privately Held**
SIC: **2339** 7389 Women's & misses' athletic clothing & sportswear;

(G-11334)
MYSTIC INC (PA)
Also Called: Herman Kay
463 7th Ave Fl 12 (10018-7499)
PHONE.................................212 239-2025
Fax: 212 643-3465
Richard Kringstein, *President*
Barry Kringstein, *President*
Lawrence Peltz, *CFO*
▲ EMP: 100
SQ FT: 30,000
SALES (est): 80.5MM **Privately Held**
WEB: www.mystic.com
SIC: **2339** Women's & misses' outerwear

(G-11335)
N POLOGEORGIS FURS INC
143 W 29th St Fl 8 (10001-5145)
PHONE.................................212 563-2250
Fax: 212 563-6735
Nick Pologeorgis, *President*
Joan Nathenas, *E-Business*
EMP: 11
SQ FT: 5,000
SALES (est): 1.2MM **Privately Held**
SIC: **2371** Fur coats & other fur apparel

(G-11336)
N Y BIJOUX CORP
1261 Broadway Rm 606 (10001-3539)
PHONE.................................212 244-9585
Hylong Kim, *President*
▲ EMP: 5
SALES (est): 687.6K **Privately Held**
WEB: www.nybijouxcorp.com
SIC: **3911** Jewelry, precious metal

(G-11337)
N Y WINSTONS INC
Also Called: Eko-Blu
5 W 86th St Apt 9e (10024-3664)
PHONE.................................212 665-3166
Lauren Swoszowski, *CEO*
EMP: 5
SALES (est): 224.8K **Privately Held**
SIC: **2086** Bottled & canned soft drinks

(G-11338)
NAME BASE INC
172 Lexington Ave Apt 1 (10016-7481)
PHONE.................................212 545-1400
James Singer, *President*
Margaret Wolfson, *Creative Dir*
EMP: 9

SALES (est): 598.3K **Privately Held**
WEB: www.namebase.com
SIC: **3953** Irons, marking or branding

(G-11339)
NAMM SINGER INC
Also Called: Newco
261 W 35th St Fl 12 (10001-1902)
PHONE.................................212 947-2566
Fax: 212 564-0298
Frank Lee, *President*
Larry Lai, *Vice Pres*
Tim Lee, *Vice Pres*
▲ EMP: 12
SQ FT: 8,000
SALES (est): 1.3MM **Privately Held**
SIC: **3965** Buttons & parts

(G-11340)
NANZ CUSTOM HARDWARE INC (PA)
Also Called: Nanz Company, The
20 Vandam St Fl 5l (10013-1277)
PHONE.................................212 367-7000
Fax: 212 367-7375
Carl Sorenson, *CEO*
Steve Nanz, *President*
Kate Spota, *Project Mgr*
Karl Crowley, *Facilities Mgr*
Ridgely Dodge, *Engineer*
EMP: 76
SQ FT: 7,500
SALES (est): 25.2MM **Privately Held**
WEB: www.nanz.com
SIC: **3429** 5031 Door opening & closing devices, except electrical; building materials, interior

(G-11341)
NAT NAST COMPANY INC (PA)
1370 Broadway Rm 900 (10018-7309)
PHONE.................................212 575-1186
Sonny Haddad, *President*
Lawrence Deparis, *President*
Kerry Ryan, *Vice Pres*
Kristen O'Hara, *Office Mgr*
Sam Haddad, *Manager*
▲ EMP: 5
SALES (est): 1.3MM **Privately Held**
WEB: www.natnast.com
SIC: **2321** Blouses, boys': made from purchased materials

(G-11342)
NATHAN BONING CO LLC
302 W 37th St Fl 4 (10018-2470)
PHONE.................................212 244-4781
Fax: 212 244-4784
Mark Orbach, *Mng Member*
▲ EMP: 7 EST: 1950
SQ FT: 3,000
SALES (est): 750K **Privately Held**
SIC: **3089** Plastic processing

(G-11343)
NATHAN LOVE LLC
407 Broome St Rm 6r (10013-3213)
PHONE.................................212 925-7111
Joe Burrascano,
EMP: 10
SALES: 1.6MM **Privately Held**
SIC: **3931** Musical instruments

(G-11344)
NATION COMPANY LP
Also Called: Nation, The
520 8th Ave Rm 2100 (10018-6507)
PHONE.................................212 209-5400
Scott Klein, *President*
Teresa Stack, *Partner*
Katrina Vanden Heuvel, *Partner*
Maria Margaronis, *Editor*
EMP: 33 EST: 1865
SQ FT: 11,000
SALES (est): 6.6MM **Privately Held**
SIC: **2721** Magazines: publishing only, not printed on site

(G-11345)
NATION MAGAZINE
33 Irving Pl Fl 8 (10003-2307)
PHONE.................................212 209-5400
Victor Navasky, *Publisher*
Ellen Bollinger, *VP Adv*
Miriam Camp, *Manager*
Amanda Hale, *Manager*

EMP: 40 EST: 2008
SALES (est): 390.9K **Privately Held**
SIC: **2721** Periodicals

(G-11346)
NATIONAL ADVERTISING & PRTG
231 W 29th St Frnt (10001-5209)
P.O. Box 1775 (10001)
PHONE.................................212 629-7650
Fax: 212 629-6516
Scott Damashek, *President*
James Ricciardella, *VP Mktg*
EMP: 5
SALES (est): 751.4K **Privately Held**
SIC: **3993** 2679 Advertising novelties; novelties, paper: made from purchased material

(G-11347)
NATIONAL CONTRACT INDUSTRIES
Also Called: Nci
510 E 86th St Apt 16b (10028-7508)
P.O. Box 671 (10028-0044)
PHONE.................................212 249-0045
Maxwell J Moss, *President*
EMP: 5
SQ FT: 1,000
SALES (est): 1.5MM **Privately Held**
WEB: www.ncionline.com
SIC: **2221** Wall covering fabrics, manmade fiber & silk

(G-11348)
NATIONAL FLAG & DISPLAY CO INC (PA)
30 E 21st St Apt 2b (10010-7217)
PHONE.................................212 228-6600
Fax: 212 462-2624
Howard J Siegel, *President*
Alan R Siegel, *Vice Pres*
▲ EMP: 20
SQ FT: 8,500
SALES (est): 8.2MM **Privately Held**
WEB: www.nationalflag.com
SIC: **2399** Flags, fabric

(G-11349)
NATIONAL REPRODUCTIONS INC
229 W 28th St Fl 9 (10001-5915)
PHONE.................................212 619-3800
George Pavoides, *CEO*
John K Fitch III, *President*
EMP: 30 EST: 1946
SQ FT: 5,000
SALES (est): 2.7MM
SALES (corp-wide): 6.6MM **Privately Held**
WEB: www.fitchgroup.com
SIC: **2752** 7334 Photo-offset printing; photocopying & duplicating services
PA: Francis Emory Fitch Inc
    229 W 28th St Fl 9
    New York NY 10001
    212 619-3800

(G-11350)
NATIONAL REVIEW INC (PA)
Also Called: National Review Online
215 Lexington Ave Fl 11 (10016-6019)
PHONE.................................212 679-7330
Fax: 212 696-0309
Thomas L Rhodes, *President*
Rich Lowry, *Editor*
James Kilbridge, *CFO*
Rose Flynn Demaio, *Treasurer*
Ray Lopez, *Manager*
EMP: 30 EST: 1955
SQ FT: 17,000
SALES: 3.2MM **Privately Held**
WEB: www.nationalreview.com
SIC: **2721** Magazines: publishing only, not printed on site; periodicals: publishing only

(G-11351)
NATIONAL SPINNING CO INC
Also Called: Caron Distribution Center
1212 Ave Of The Americ St (10036-1602)
PHONE.................................212 382-6400
Fax: 212 382-6450
Todd Browder, *Principal*
Morgan Miller, *Vice Chairman*

Paula Boyd, *Technical Mgr*
Kevin Whitehurst, *Technical Mgr*
Robert Gordon, *VP Sales*
EMP: 25
SALES (corp-wide): 181.7MM **Privately Held**
WEB: www.natspin.com
SIC: **2281** 2269 5199 Yarn spinning mills; finishing plants; yarns
PA: National Spinning Co., Inc.
    1481 W 2nd St
    Washington NC 27889
    252 975-7111

(G-11352)
NATIONAL TIME RECORDING EQP CO
64 Reade St Fl 2 (10007-1870)
PHONE.................................212 227-3310
Fax: 212 227-5353
Stanley A Akivis, *President*
Richard Akivis, *Vice Pres*
Ethel Akivis, *Treasurer*
Amy Kennedy, *Office Mgr*
EMP: 10 EST: 1932
SQ FT: 10,000
SALES: 1,000K **Privately Held**
WEB: www.national-pinkpages.com
SIC: **3579** 7629 3873 3625 Dating & numbering devices; business machine repair, electric; watches, clocks, watchcases & parts; relays & industrial controls

(G-11353)
NATIONAL TOBACCO COMPANY LP
Also Called: North Atlantic Trading Co
257 Park Ave S Fl 7 (10010-7304)
PHONE.................................212 253-8185
Fax: 212 253-8296
Thomas Holmes, *Chairman*
Camilla Fentress, *VP Finance*
EMP: 10
SALES (corp-wide): 197.2MM **Publicly Held**
SIC: **2131** Chewing tobacco
HQ: National Tobacco Company, L.P.
    5201 Interchange Way
    Louisville KY 40229
    800 579-0975

(G-11354)
NATIVE TEXTILES INC (PA)
411 5th Ave Rm 901 (10016-2203)
PHONE.................................212 951-5100
John Gunyan, *President*
Carl Andersen, *Vice Pres*
EMP: 6 EST: 1975
SQ FT: 7,000
SALES (est): 12.1MM **Privately Held**
SIC: **2253** 2254 Knit outerwear mills; knit underwear mills

(G-11355)
NATORI COMPANY INCORPORATED (PA)
180 Madison Ave Fl 19 (10016-5267)
PHONE.................................212 532-7796
Josie Natori, *Ch of Bd*
David Leung, *Vice Pres*
Cheryl Nowak, *Vice Pres*
Elizabeth Yee, *Vice Pres*
Judith O'Donnell, *Engineer*
▲ EMP: 60
SQ FT: 10,500
SALES (est): 47.9MM **Privately Held**
SIC: **2384** 2341 Bathrobes, men's & women's: made from purchased materials; women's & children's nightwear

(G-11356)
NATORI COMPANY INCORPORATED
Also Called: Natori Company, The
180 Madison Ave Fl 19 (10016-5267)
PHONE.................................212 532-7796
Efren Lota, *Manager*
EMP: 40
SALES (corp-wide): 47.9MM **Privately Held**
SIC: **2341** Women's & children's underwear

New York - New York County (G-11357) — GEOGRAPHIC SECTION

PA: The Natori Company Incorporated
180 Madison Ave Fl 19
New York NY 10016
212 532-7796

(G-11357)
NATURE AMERICA INC (DH)
Also Called: Nature Publishing Group
1 New York Plz Ste 4500 (10004-1562)
P.O. Box 51227, Philadelphia PA (19115-0227)
PHONE..................212 726-9200
Fax: 212 696-9006
Steven Inchcoombe, *President*
Ruth Wilson, *Publisher*
Muctar Ibrahim, *General Mgr*
Christian Dorbrandt, *Managing Dir*
Myles Axton, *Editor*
▼ EMP: 380
SQ FT: 66,000
SALES: 300MM
SALES (corp-wide): 2.1B Privately Held
WEB: www.nature.com
SIC: 2721 Magazines: publishing only, not printed on site
HQ: Macmillan Magazines Limited
Porters South
London
207 833-4000

(G-11358)
NAUTICA INTERNATIONAL INC (DH)
40 W 57th St Fl 3 (10019-4005)
PHONE..................212 541-5757
Fax: 212 245-4717
Karen Murray, *President*
Sarah A Deckey, *President*
Harvey Sanders, *Exec VP*
Christopher Fuentes, *Vice Pres*
Ceasar Fernandez, *Purch Mgr*
▲ EMP: 100
SALES (est): 24.9MM
SALES (corp-wide): 12.3B Publicly Held
SIC: 2329 Men's & boys' sportswear & athletic clothing; men's & boys' leather, wool & down-filled outerwear
HQ: Vf Sportswear, Inc.
545 Wshngton Blvd Fl 8
Jersey City NJ 07310
212 541-5757

(G-11359)
NAVAS DESIGNS INC
200 E 58th St Apt 17b (10022-2035)
PHONE..................818 988-9050
Nava Writz-Shoham, *President*
Moti Shoham, *Controller*
EMP: 25
SQ FT: 4,000
SALES (est): 1.7MM Privately Held
WEB: www.navasdesigns.com
SIC: 2211 Linings & interlinings, cotton

(G-11360)
NAVATAR CONSULTING GROUP INC
90 Brd St (10004)
PHONE..................212 863-9655
Alok Misra, *Branch Mgr*
EMP: 39
SALES (corp-wide): 10.7MM Privately Held
SIC: 7372 Prepackaged software
PA: Navatar Consulting Group Inc
90 Broad St Ste 1703
New York NY 10004
212 863-9655

(G-11361)
NAVATAR CONSULTING GROUP INC (PA)
Also Called: Navatar Group
90 Broad St Ste 1703 (10004-2373)
PHONE..................212 863-9655
Alok Misra, *President*
Christine Millen, *Partner*
Bill Pinzler, *Counsel*
Ketan Khandkar, *Vice Pres*
Amit Chaudhary, *Accounts Exec*
EMP: 41
SALES (est): 10.7MM Privately Held
WEB: www.navatargroup.com
SIC: 7372 Prepackaged software; business oriented computer software

(G-11362)
NBC INTERNET INC
Also Called: Nbci.com
30 Rockefeller Plz Fl 2 (10112-0037)
PHONE..................212 315-9016
William J Lansing, *CEO*
Robert C Wright, *Ch of Bd*
Chris Kitze, *Vice Ch Bd*
Anthony E Altig, *CFO*
Leo Chang, *CTO*
EMP: 500
SALES (est): 596.2K
SALES (corp-wide): 74.5B Publicly Held
WEB: www.nbcinternet.com
SIC: 7372 7375 Business oriented computer software; information retrieval services
HQ: Nbc Universal, Llc
1221 Avenue Of The Americ
New York NY 10020
212 664-4444

(G-11363)
NBM PUBLISHING INC
Also Called: Nantier Ball Minoustchine Pubg
160 Broadway Ste 700e (10038-4201)
PHONE..................212 643-5407
Terry Nantier, *President*
Mart Minoustchine, *Vice Pres*
Martha Samuel, *Controller*
Chris Beall, *Admin Sec*
▲ EMP: 6
SQ FT: 1,200
SALES (est): 510K Privately Held
WEB: www.nbmpub.com
SIC: 2731 2721 Books: publishing only; comic books: publishing only, not printed on site

(G-11364)
NCM PUBLISHERS INC
200 Varick St Rm 608 (10014-7486)
PHONE..................212 691-9100
Fax: 212 645-2571
Michael Zerneck, *President*
Relisa Mitchell, *Office Mgr*
EMP: 8
SQ FT: 10,000
SALES: 1MM Privately Held
SIC: 2721 7812 Trade journals: publishing only, not printed on site; video tape production

(G-11365)
NECESSARY OBJECTS LTD (PA)
530 7th Ave M1 (10018-4878)
PHONE..................212 334-9888
Fax: 212 941-0114
Ady Gluck Frankel, *Ch of Bd*
Bill Kauffman, *CFO*
▼ EMP: 50
SALES (est): 14MM Privately Held
WEB: www.necessaryobjects.com
SIC: 2335 2339 2331 Women's, juniors' & misses' dresses; slacks: women's, misses' & juniors'; blouses, women's & juniors': made from purchased material

(G-11366)
NEMARIS INC
306 E 15th St Apt 1r (10003-4029)
PHONE..................646 794-8648
Frank Schwab, *CEO*
Stephen Schwab, *COO*
Virginie Lafage, *Info Tech Mgr*
EMP: 20
SALES (est): 1.2MM Privately Held
SIC: 7372 Educational computer software

(G-11367)
NEON
1400 Broadway Rm 300 (10018-1078)
PHONE..................212 727-5628
Sabrina Prince, *Senior VP*
Bessie Borja, *Sr Project Mgr*
Kevin McHale, *Creative Dir*
EMP: 14 EST: 2010
SALES (est): 2.4MM Privately Held
SIC: 2813 Neon

(G-11368)
NEPENTHES AMERICA INC
307 W 38th St Rm 201 (10018-3520)
PHONE..................212 343-4262
Fax: 212 343-4261
Keizo Shimizu, *President*
Daiki Suzuki, *Corp Secy*
Akiko Shimizu, *Vice Pres*
Angelo Urritia, *Sales Mgr*
Angelo F Urrutia, *Sales Staff*
▲ EMP: 8 EST: 1996
SQ FT: 1,500
SALES (est): 1.4MM Privately Held
WEB: www.nepenthesny.com
SIC: 2329 Men's & boys' athletic uniforms

(G-11369)
NERVECOM INC
199 Lafayette St Apt 3b (10012-4279)
PHONE..................212 625-9914
Rufus Griscom, *CEO*
Yong Choi, *Web Dvlpr*
EMP: 12
SQ FT: 5,000
SALES (est): 1.5MM Privately Held
WEB: www.nerve.com
SIC: 2721 Periodicals

(G-11370)
NES JEWELRY INC
Also Called: Nes Costume
20 W 33rd St Fl 6 (10001-3305)
PHONE..................212 502-0025
Nemo Gindi, *President*
Jack Yedid, *Vice Pres*
Jay Gassar, *CFO*
Paul Kopyt, *CFO*
Larry Katz, *Controller*
▲ EMP: 115
SQ FT: 14,000
SALES: 42.7MM Privately Held
SIC: 3961 Costume jewelry

(G-11371)
NESHER PRINTING INC
30 E 33rd St Frnt A (10016-5337)
PHONE..................212 760-2521
Sheldon Wrotslavsky, *President*
EMP: 6
SQ FT: 3,500
SALES: 1MM Privately Held
WEB: www.nesherprinting.com
SIC: 2752 Commercial printing, offset

(G-11372)
NETOLOGIC INC
Also Called: Investars
17 State St Fl 38 (10004-1537)
PHONE..................212 269-3796
Kei Kianpoor, *CEO*
John Eagleton, *President*
William Eagleton,
EMP: 45
SQ FT: 1,900
SALES (est): 5.1MM Privately Held
WEB: www.aidworks.com
SIC: 7372 Prepackaged software

(G-11373)
NETSUITE INC
8 W 40th St 5f (10018-3902)
PHONE..................646 652-5700
Zachary Nelson, *CEO*
Lauren Matz, *Business Mgr*
Patricia McMenamin, *Sales Mgr*
EMP: 7
SALES (corp-wide): 741.1MM Privately Held
SIC: 7372 Prepackaged software
PA: Netsuite Inc.
2955 Campus Dr Ste 100
San Mateo CA 94403
650 627-1000

(G-11374)
NETWORK COMPONENTS LLC
52 Vanderbilt Ave Fl 18 (10017-3828)
PHONE..................212 799-5890
Fax: 212 362-3822
Bryan Chin, *Vice Pres*
Taryn Schubert, *Office Mgr*
Ajay Jadhav,
EMP: 15 EST: 2000
SALES (est): 1.2MM Privately Held
WEB: www.networkcomponents.com
SIC: 7372 Prepackaged software

(G-11375)
NETWORK JOURNAL INC
39 Broadway Rm 2120 (10006-3037)
PHONE..................212 962-3791

Fax: 212 962-3537
Aziz Adetimirin, *President*
Robert Wilkins, *Partner*
Joe Milizzo, *Editor*
Pauline Thomas, *Vice Pres*
Edward Woods, *Vice Pres*
EMP: 6
SQ FT: 250
SALES (est): 547K Privately Held
SIC: 2741 Guides: publishing only, not printed on site

(G-11376)
NEUMANN JUTTA NEW YORK INC
355 E 4th St (10009-8513)
PHONE..................212 982-7048
Fax: 212 353-8606
Jutta Neumann, *President*
▲ EMP: 10
SQ FT: 750
SALES: 800K Privately Held
SIC: 3143 3144 3172 Sandals, men's; sandals, women's; personal leather goods

(G-11377)
NEVAEH JEANS COMPANY
450 W 152nd St Apt 31 (10031-1816)
PHONE..................845 641-4255
Corey Reed, *Partner*
▲ EMP: 9
SALES (est): 443.9K Privately Held
SIC: 2329 Men's & boys' clothing

(G-11378)
NEVERWARE INC
112 W 27th St Ste 201 (10001-6242)
PHONE..................516 302-3223
Jonathan Hefter, *CEO*
Andrew Bauer, *COO*
EMP: 12
SQ FT: 2,000
SALES (est): 1MM Privately Held
SIC: 7372 Prepackaged software

(G-11379)
NEW AUDIO LLC
Also Called: Master & Dynamics
132 W 31st St Rm 701 (10001-3478)
PHONE..................212 213-6060
Jonathan Levine, *CEO*
Michael Gonzalez, *CFO*
EMP: 30
SQ FT: 10,000
SALES: 6MM Privately Held
SIC: 3651 Household audio & video equipment; microphones

(G-11380)
NEW AVON LLC
777 3rd Ave Fl 8 (10017-1307)
PHONE..................212 282-8500
Betty Palm, *President*
Steven Bosson, *Mng Member*
Ginny Edwars, *Mng Member*
Helene F Rutledge, *Officer*
EMP: 2500
SQ FT: 100,000
SALES (est): 810MM
SALES (corp-wide): 33.1B Publicly Held
SIC: 2844 5122 5999 Toilet preparations; cosmetics; cosmetics
PA: Cerberus Capital Management, L.P.
875 3rd Ave
New York NY 10022
212 891-2100

(G-11381)
NEW CONCEPTS OF NEW YORK LLC
132 W 36th St Rm 4 (10018-8860)
PHONE..................212 695-4999
Anna Martinez, *Manager*
Robert Schwartz,
▲ EMP: 20
SALES (est): 2.2MM Privately Held
WEB: www.newconceptsllc.com
SIC: 2339 Women's & misses' accessories

(G-11382)
NEW DEAL PRINTING CORP (PA)
Also Called: Altro Business Forms Div
420 E 55th St Apt Grdp (10022-5149)
PHONE..................718 729-5800
David Ruzal, *President*

Jack Tocker, *General Mgr*
Doreen Beynders, *Corp Secy*
▲ **EMP:** 7
SALES: 9MM **Privately Held**
WEB: www.narcainus.com
SIC: 2759 Commercial printing

(G-11383)
NEW DIRECT PRODUCT CORP
150 W 22nd St Fl 12 (10011-6558)
PHONE..................................212 929-0515
Peter Pasteur, *President*
Ed Morris, *CFO*
EMP: 5
SQ FT: 2,500
SALES (est): 2MM **Privately Held**
SIC: 2741 Newsletter publishing

(G-11384)
NEW DIRECTIONS PUBLISHING
80 8th Ave Fl 19 (10011-7146)
PHONE..................................212 255-0230
Fax: 212 255-0231
Peggy Fox, *President*
Jeff Clapper, *Prgrmr*
Declan Spring, *Senior Editor*
EMP: 10 EST: 1936
SQ FT: 2,800
SALES (est): 1.2MM **Privately Held**
WEB: www.ndpublishing.com
SIC: 2731 Books: publishing only

(G-11385)
NEW ENERGY SYSTEMS GROUP
116 W 23rd St Fl 5 (10011-2599)
PHONE..................................917 573-0302
Weihe Yu, *Ch of Bd*
Ken Lin, *Vice Pres*
Jufeng Chen, *CFO*
EMP: 214
SALES (est): 9.9MM **Privately Held**
SIC: 3691 3433 Storage batteries; solar heaters & collectors; space heaters, except electric

(G-11386)
NEW ENGLAND ORTHOTIC & PROST
235 E 38th St (10016-2709)
PHONE..................................212 831-3600
Fax: 212 249-4633
Ryan Murphy, *Manager*
EMP: 5
SALES (corp-wide): 17.9MM **Privately Held**
WEB: www.neops.com
SIC: 3842 Prosthetic appliances
PA: New England Orthotic And Prosthetic Systems, Llc
16 Commercial St
Branford CT 06405
203 483-8488

(G-11387)
NEW GENERATION LIGHTING INC
144 Bowery Frnt 1 (10013-4288)
PHONE..................................212 966-0328
Tony Chu, *Manager*
EMP: 10
SALES (est): 880K **Privately Held**
WEB: www.newgenerationlighting.com
SIC: 3645 Residential lighting fixtures

(G-11388)
NEW GOLDSTAR 1 PRINTING CORP
63 Orchard St (10002-5414)
PHONE..................................212 343-3909
Xue Hua Xie, *President*
EMP: 8
SALES (est): 456.9K **Privately Held**
SIC: 2752 Commercial printing, lithographic

(G-11389)
NEW HAMPTON CREATIONS INC
237 W 35th St Ste 502 (10001-1905)
PHONE..................................212 244-7474
Victor Hoffman, *President*
David P Hoffman, *Corp Secy*
EMP: 5
SQ FT: 1,000
SALES (est): 430K **Privately Held**
WEB: www.nyshose.com
SIC: 2252 Hosiery

(G-11390)
NEW HOPE MEDIA LLC
Also Called: Additude Magazine
108 W 39th St Rm 805 (10018-8277)
PHONE..................................646 366-0830
Eve Gilman, *General Mgr*
Susan Caughman,
EMP: 6
SALES (est): 778.2K **Privately Held**
SIC: 2721 Magazines: publishing & printing

(G-11391)
NEW MEDIA INVESTMENT GROUP INC (PA)
1345 Avenue Of The Americ (10105-0014)
PHONE..................................212 479-3160
Michael E Reed, *CEO*
Wesley R Edens, *Ch of Bd*
Kirk Davis, *COO*
Gregory W Freiberg, *CFO*
Paul Ameden, *CIO*
EMP: 300
SALES: 1.2B **Publicly Held**
SIC: 2711 7373 Newspapers, publishing & printing; systems integration services

(G-11392)
NEW PRESS
120 Wall St Fl 31 (10005-4007)
PHONE..................................212 629-8802
Fax: 212 629-8617
Ellen Adler, *Publisher*
Carline Yup, *Finance*
Rachel Guidera, *Sales Staff*
Maredith Sheridan, *Marketing Staff*
Francienne Forte, *Office Mgr*
EMP: 20
SQ FT: 3,500
SALES: 3.7MM **Privately Held**
WEB: www.thenewpress.com
SIC: 2731 Book publishing

(G-11393)
NEW STYLE SIGNS LIMITED INC
149 Madison Ave Rm 606 (10016-6713)
PHONE..................................212 242-7848
Joseph Fleischer, *President*
EMP: 10
SALES (est): 1.2MM **Privately Held**
SIC: 3993 Displays & cutouts, window & lobby; signs, not made in custom sign painting shops

(G-11394)
NEW TRIAD FOR COLLABORATIVE
205 W 86th St Apt 911 (10024-3344)
PHONE..................................212 873-9610
EMP: 24
SALES (est): 61.5K **Privately Held**
SIC: 7372 Prepackaged software

(G-11395)
NEW YORK ACCESSORY GROUP INC (PA)
Also Called: New York Accessories Group
411 5th Ave Fl 4 (10016-2203)
PHONE..................................212 532-7911
Isaac Shallom, *CEO*
Elizabeth Demaria, *Exec VP*
Joe Tail, *Manager*
Robin Cohen, *Info Tech Dir*
▲ **EMP:** 50
SALES (est): 13.3MM **Privately Held**
SIC: 2389 2339 Men's miscellaneous accessories; women's & misses' accessories

(G-11396)
NEW YORK CARTRIDGE EXCHANGE
225 W 37th St (10018-5703)
PHONE..................................212 840-2227
Jack Rahmur, *President*
Ricky Toweck, *Vice Pres*
▲ **EMP:** 5
SALES (est): 390K **Privately Held**
WEB: www.nycartridgeexchange.com
SIC: 3955 Print cartridges for laser & other computer printers

(G-11397)
NEW YORK CT LOC246 SEIU WEL BF
217 Broadway (10007-2909)
PHONE..................................212 233-0616
Branka Stijovic, *Principal*
EMP: 4
SALES: 2.7MM **Privately Held**
SIC: 3011 Tires & inner tubes

(G-11398)
NEW YORK CVL SRVC EMPLYS PBLSH
Also Called: Chief, The
277 Broadway Ste 1506 (10007-2008)
PHONE..................................212 962-2690
Fax: 212 962-2556
Edward Prial, *President*
EMP: 12
SALES (est): 680K **Privately Held**
SIC: 2711 Newspapers: publishing only, not printed on site

(G-11399)
NEW YORK DAILY NEWS
4 New York Plz Fl 6 (10004-2473)
PHONE..................................212 248-2100
Nikhil Rele, *Principal*
EMP: 5
SALES (est): 371.8K **Privately Held**
SIC: 2711 Newspapers, publishing & printing

(G-11400)
NEW YORK ELEGANCE ENTPS INC
385 5th Ave Rm 709 (10016-3344)
PHONE..................................212 685-7188
Fax: 212 685-3088
Wing CHI Chung, *President*
Andrew Lupo, *VP Sales*
▲ **EMP:** 15
SQ FT: 2,000
SALES (est): 1.3MM **Privately Held**
SIC: 2342 Brassieres

(G-11401)
NEW YORK ENRGY SYNTHETICS INC
375 Park Ave Ste 2607 (10152-2600)
PHONE..................................212 634-4787
EMP: 6
SALES (est): 450K **Privately Held**
SIC: 3825 3229 Mfg Electrical Measuring Instruments Mfg Pressed/Blown Glass

(G-11402)
NEW YORK FINDINGS CORP
70 Bowery Unit 8 (10013-4607)
PHONE..................................212 925-5745
Fax: 212 925-5870
Cheryl Kerber, *President*
Mel Kerber, *Treasurer*
Wanda Holmes, *Manager*
Kim Sam, *Manager*
EMP: 15 EST: 1953
SQ FT: 3,000
SALES (est): 970K **Privately Held**
WEB: www.newyorkfindings.com
SIC: 3915 5094 Jewelers' findings & materials; jewelers' findings

(G-11403)
NEW YORK MEDIA LLC
75 Varick St (10013-1917)
PHONE..................................212 508-0700
Michael Silberman, *General Mgr*
Joe Adalian, *Editor*
David Amsden, *Editor*
Greg Cwik, *Editor*
Mary Duffy, *Editor*
EMP: 250
SQ FT: 73,000
SALES (est): 89.5MM **Privately Held**
SIC: 2721 Periodicals

(G-11404)
NEW YORK NAUTICAL INC
200 Church St Frnt 4 (10013-3831)
PHONE..................................212 962-4522
Fred Walley, *CEO*
Kenneth Maisler, *President*
EMP: 7
SQ FT: 4,000
SALES (est): 989.3K **Privately Held**
WEB: www.newyorknautical.com
SIC: 3812 Nautical instruments

(G-11405)
NEW YORK OBSERVER LLC
321 W 44th St 6th (10036-5404)
PHONE..................................212 887-8460
Kartos Vos, *CFO*
Shweta Mathur, *Controller*
Chrospher Barns, *Mng Member*
Dena Silver, *Senior Editor*
Danielle Balbi, *Relations*
EMP: 90
SQ FT: 10,000
SALES (est): 8.5MM **Privately Held**
SIC: 2711 Newspapers: publishing only, not printed on site

(G-11406)
NEW YORK PRESS INC
72 Madison Ave Fl 11 (10016-8731)
PHONE..................................212 268-8600
Fax: 212 244-9863
Russ Smith, *President*
Ingred Besak, *Human Res Dir*
Alex Schweitzer, *Sales Mgr*
Stephanie Musso, *Adv Dir*
Robynne Carroll, *Marketing Mgr*
EMP: 50
SQ FT: 10,000
SALES (est): 3.8MM **Privately Held**
WEB: www.nypress.com
SIC: 2711 Newspapers, publishing & printing

(G-11407)
NEW YORK SAMPLE CARD CO INC
151 W 26th St Fl 12 (10001-6810)
PHONE..................................212 242-1242
Fax: 212 691-8160
Kenneth Ehrlich, *President*
Roger Ehrlich, *Vice Pres*
Justin Ehrlich, *Treasurer*
EMP: 40
SQ FT: 15,000
SALES (est): 3.1MM **Privately Held**
SIC: 2759 2782 Card printing & engraving, except greeting; sample books

(G-11408)
NEW YORK SPRING WATER INC
517 W 36th St (10018-1100)
PHONE..................................212 777-4649
Richard Zakka, *President*
Luke Zakka, *VP Opers*
Daniel Garcia, *Office Mgr*
▲ **EMP:** 28
SQ FT: 200,000
SALES (est): 28.2MM **Privately Held**
SIC: 2086 Mineral water, carbonated: packaged in cans, bottles, etc.

(G-11409)
NEW YORK SWEATER COMPANY INC
141 W 36th St Rm 17 (10018-9489)
PHONE..................................845 629-9533
Leonard Keff, *President*
EMP: 30
SALES (est): 1.9MM **Privately Held**
SIC: 2253 Sweaters & sweater coats, knit

(G-11410)
NEW YORK TIMES COMPANY (PA)
620 8th Ave (10018-1618)
PHONE..................................212 556-1234
Arthur Sulzberger Jr, *Ch of Bd*
Michael Golden, *Vice Ch Bd*
Mark Thompson, *President*
Scott Heekin-Canedy, *President*
Mary Jacobus, *President*
▲ **EMP:** 277 EST: 1896
SQ FT: 828,000
SALES: 1.5B **Publicly Held**
WEB: www.nytco.com
SIC: 2711 4832 4833 7383 Newspapers, publishing & printing; radio broadcasting stations; television broadcasting stations; news feature syndicate; information retrieval services

New York - New York County (G-11411)

(G-11411)
NEW YORK TIMES COMPANY
Also Called: Times Center, The
620 8th Ave Bsmt 1 (10018-1604)
PHONE.................................212 556-4300
Melanie Masserant, *Branch Mgr*
Mary Walsh, *Relations*
EMP: 12
SALES (corp-wide): 1.5B Publicly Held
SIC: 2711 Newspapers
PA: The New York Times Company
 620 8th Ave
 New York NY 10018
 212 556-1234

(G-11412)
NEW YORK UNIVERSITY
Also Called: Washington Square News
7 E 12th St Ste 800 (10003-4475)
PHONE.................................212 998-4300
Fax: 212 995-4133
David Cosgrove, *General Mgr*
Sue Caporlingua, *Editor*
Jill Filipovic, *Editor*
Elizabeth Tsai, *Editor*
Jasmina Husovic, *Facilities Mgr*
EMP: 25
SQ FT: 7,410
SALES (corp-wide): 8.2B Privately Held
WEB: www.nyu.edu
SIC: 2711 8221 Newspapers, publishing & printing; university
PA: New York University
 70 Washington Sq S
 New York NY 10012
 212 998-1212

(G-11413)
NEW YORK1 NEWS OPERATIONS
75 9th Ave Frnt 6 (10011-7033)
PHONE.................................212 379-3311
Steve Paulus, *CEO*
EMP: 12
SALES (est): 724.1K Privately Held
SIC: 2711 Newspapers, publishing & printing

(G-11414)
NEWPORT GRAPHICS INC
121 Varick St Rm 302 (10013-1408)
PHONE.................................212 924-2600
John Di Somma, *President*
Michael Palmasano, *Vice Pres*
Michael Paulmasano, *Vice Pres*
John Disomma, *Office Mgr*
EMP: 30 EST: 1971
SQ FT: 10,000
SALES (est): 4.1MM Privately Held
WEB: www.newportgraphics.com
SIC: 2752 2789 Commercial printing, offset; bookbinding & related work

(G-11415)
NEWS COMMUNICATIONS INC (PA)
501 Madison Ave Fl 23 (10022-5608)
PHONE.................................212 689-2500
Fax: 212 689-1998
James A Finkelstein, *Ch of Bd*
Jerry A Finkelstein, *Ch of Bd*
E Paul Leishman, *CFO*
Dami Cuadrado, *Director*
Gary Weiss, *Director*
EMP: 11
SQ FT: 2,900
SALES (est): 8.9MM Privately Held
WEB: www.thehill.com
SIC: 2711 Newspapers: publishing only, not printed on site

(G-11416)
NEWS CORPORATION (PA)
1211 Ave Of The Americas (10036-8701)
PHONE.................................212 416-3400
Fax: 212 852-7147
Robert J Thomson, *CEO*
K Rupert Murdoch, *Ch of Bd*
Lachlan K Murdoch, *Ch of Bd*
Bianca Mojica, *Counsel*
Keri Topkins, *Counsel*
EMP: 177
SALES: 8.2B Publicly Held
SIC: 2711 2731 7375 Newspapers; newspapers, publishing & printing; book publishing; on-line data base information retrieval

(G-11417)
NEWS INDIA USA LLC
Also Called: News India Times
37 W 20th St Ste 1109 (10011-3749)
PHONE.................................212 675-7515
Shomik Chaudhuri, *Adv Dir*
Dr Sudhir Parikh,
EMP: 8
SALES: 600K Privately Held
SIC: 2711 Newspapers, publishing & printing

(G-11418)
NEWS INDIA USA INC
Also Called: News India Times
37 W 20th St Ste 1109 (10011-3749)
PHONE.................................212 675-7515
Fax: 212 675-7624
Veena Merchant, *President*
Prakash Parekh, *Mktg Dir*
Vikram Chatwal, *Director*
Dr Bhupendra Patel, *Director*
Ruba Agwani, *Mng Officer*
EMP: 15
SQ FT: 6,000
SALES (est): 720K Privately Held
SIC: 2711 2731 2791 Newspapers, publishing & printing; books: publishing & printing; typesetting

(G-11419)
NEWS/SPRTS MICROWAVE RENTL INC
Also Called: NSM Surveillance
415 Madison Ave Fl 11 (10017-7930)
PHONE.................................619 670-0572
Andrew R Berdy, *President*
Tom Meaney, *General Mgr*
Carlos Arnero, *COO*
John Puetz, *Engineer*
Tony Fede, *Sales Staff*
EMP: 35
SQ FT: 10,000
SALES (est): 6.2MM Privately Held
WEB: www.nsmsurveillance.com
SIC: 3699 Security devices; security control equipment & systems
PA: Solutionpoint International, Inc.
 415 Madison Ave Fl 11
 New York NY 10017

(G-11420)
NEWSPAPER ASSOCIATION AMER INC
20 W 33rd St Fl 7 (10001-3305)
PHONE.................................212 856-6300
Fax: 212 856-6310
Angie Cunningham, *Principal*
Paul C Atkinson, *Senior VP*
Jerry Fragetti, *Senior VP*
Jack Grandcolas, *Senior VP*
Frank Grasso, *Vice Pres*
EMP: 50
SALES (corp-wide): 8.5MM Privately Held
WEB: www.bonafideclassifieds.com
SIC: 2711 Newspapers, publishing & printing
PA: Newspaper Association Of America, Inc.
 4401 Wilson Blvd Ste 900
 Arlington VA 22203
 571 366-1000

(G-11421)
NEXT BIG SOUND INC
125 Park Ave Fl 19 (10017-8545)
PHONE.................................646 657-9837
Alex White, *CEO*
David Hoffman, *Founder*
Samir Rayani, *Founder*
Yu-Ting Lin, *VP Finance*
Kris Schroder, *Sales Engr*
EMP: 6 EST: 2008
SALES (est): 1MM Privately Held
SIC: 3695 Magnetic & optical recording media

(G-11422)
NEXT POTENTIAL LLC
Also Called: Nextpotential
278 E 10th St Apt 5b (10009-4868)
PHONE.................................401 742-5190
Jack Blanchette, *President*
John Blanchette, *Principal*
EMP: 6
SALES (est): 570.2K Privately Held
SIC: 2819 Catalysts, chemical

(G-11423)
NFE MANAGEMENT LLC
1345 Ave Of The Americas (10105-0302)
PHONE.................................212 798-6100
Joseph Adams Jr, *President*
Demetrios Tserpelis, *Principal*
Kenneth Nicholson, *COO*
Cameron Macdougall, *Admin Sec*
Rosario Lualhati, *Administration*
EMP: 15
SQ FT: 2,038,200
SALES (est): 658.4K Privately Held
SIC: 1321 Natural gas liquids

(G-11424)
NICHE MEDIA HOLDINGS LLC (HQ)
711 3rd Ave Rm 501 (10017-9211)
PHONE.................................702 990-2500
Jason Binn, *Ch of Bd*
Katherine Nicholls, *President*
Tim Ocallaghan, *Treasurer*
Karen Whitman, *Accountant*
Stephanie Mitchell, *Human Res Dir*
EMP: 43
SALES (est): 18.3MM
SALES (corp-wide): 60.6MM Privately Held
SIC: 2721 Magazines: publishing & printing
PA: The Greenspun Corporation
 2275 Corp Cir Ste 300
 Henderson NV 89074
 702 259-4023

(G-11425)
NICHOLAS KIRKWOOD LLC (PA)
807 Washington St (10014-1557)
PHONE.................................646 559-5239
EMP: 8
SALES (est): 19.8MM Privately Held
SIC: 3144 3143 Women's footwear, except athletic; men's footwear, except athletic

(G-11426)
NICK LUGO INC
Also Called: La Voz Hispana
159 E 116th St Fl 2 (10029-1399)
PHONE.................................212 348-2100
Nick Lugo, *President*
EMP: 12
SALES (est): 570K Privately Held
SIC: 2711 Newspapers

(G-11427)
NICKELODEON MAGAZINES INC (DH)
1633 Broadway Fl 7 (10019-7637)
PHONE.................................212 541-1949
Herb Scannell, *President*
Jeff Dunn, *COO*
Dan Sullivan, *Senior VP*
Noreen Rafferty, *Vice Pres*
Donna Sabino, *Vice Pres*
EMP: 3
SALES (est): 3.6MM
SALES (corp-wide): 27.1B Publicly Held
SIC: 2721 Magazines: publishing only, not printed on site
HQ: Viacom Inc.
 1515 Broadway
 New York NY 10036
 212 258-6000

(G-11428)
NICOLO RAINERI
Also Called: Nicolo Raineri Jeweler
82 Bowery (10013-4656)
PHONE.................................212 925-6128
Fax: 212 925-1168
Nicolo Raineri, *Owner*
▲ EMP: 6
SQ FT: 3,000
SALES (est): 581.7K Privately Held
WEB: www.rainerijewelers.com
SIC: 3911 5944 Jewelry, precious metal; jewelry, precious stones & precious metals

(G-11429)
NIGHTINGALE FOOD ENTPS INC
2306 1st Ave (10035-4304)
PHONE.................................347 577-1630
Fax: 212 369-2262
Constantinos Kotjias, *Ch of Bd*
Evilyn Kotzias, *Manager*
▼ EMP: 4
SALES: 1.5MM Privately Held
SIC: 2051 Bread, cake & related products

(G-11430)
NIHAO MEDIA LLC
1230 Avenue Of The Flr 7 (10020)
PHONE.................................609 903-4264
Sean Combs, *Co-Owner*
Catherine Lin,
▲ EMP: 9
SALES (est): 493.5K Privately Held
SIC: 2741 2721 Miscellaneous publishing; magazines: publishing only, not printed on site

(G-11431)
NIKE INC
21 Mercer St Frnt A (10013-2771)
PHONE.................................212 226-5433
Wil Whitney, *Branch Mgr*
Chad Easterling, *Manager*
Darah Ross, *Manager*
EMP: 38
SALES (corp-wide): 32.3B Publicly Held
WEB: www.nike.com
SIC: 3021 Rubber & plastics footwear
PA: Nike, Inc.
 1 Sw Bowerman Dr
 Beaverton OR 97005
 503 671-6453

(G-11432)
NIKKEI AMERICA INC (HQ)
1325 Avenue Of The Americ (10019-6055)
PHONE.................................212 261-6200
Hisao Tonedachi, *President*
Hiro Aki Honda, *Exec VP*
Margaret Lim, *Manager*
Yihsuan Wu, *Asst Mgr*
EMP: 40
SQ FT: 33,000
SALES (est): 6MM
SALES (corp-wide): 1.4B Privately Held
WEB: www.nikkeius.com
SIC: 2711 Newspapers, publishing & printing
PA: Nikkei Inc.
 1-3-7, Otemachi
 Chiyoda-Ku TKY 100-0
 332 700-251

(G-11433)
NIKKEI VISUAL IMAGES AMER INC
1325 Ave Of The Americas (10019-6026)
PHONE.................................212 261-6200
Yasayuki Mori, *President*
EMP: 1
SALES (est): 1MM
SALES (corp-wide): 1.4B Privately Held
SIC: 2711 Newspapers
HQ: Nikkei America Holdings, Inc
 1325 Avenue Of The Americ
 New York NY

(G-11434)
NIMBLETV INC
450 Fashion Ave Fl 43 (10123-4399)
PHONE.................................646 502-7010
Anand Subramanian, *CEO*
Peter Von Schlossberg, *President*
Paul George, *CTO*
EMP: 12
SALES (est): 923.4K
SALES (corp-wide): 110.2MM Publicly Held
SIC: 2741
PA: Synacor, Inc.
 40 La Riviere Dr Ste 300
 Buffalo NY 14202
 716 853-1362

GEOGRAPHIC SECTION — New York - New York County (G-11460)

(G-11435)
NINE WEST FOOTWEAR CORPORATION (PA)
1411 Broadway Fl 20 (10018-3471)
PHONE 800 999-1877
Rick Paterno, *President*
Ira Dansky, *Vice Pres*
Stacy Lastina, *Vice Pres*
Dora Thagouras, *Vice Pres*
John T McClain, *CFO*
▲ **EMP**: 400
SQ FT: 366,460
SALES (est): 34.6MM **Privately Held**
WEB: www.ninewest.com
SIC: 3144 3171 5661 5632 Women's footwear, except athletic; boots, canvas or leather; women's; dress shoes, women's; sandals, women's; women's handbags & purses; handbags, women's; purses, women's; shoe stores; women's shoes; women's boots; apparel accessories; handbags; footwear

(G-11436)
NINE WEST HOLDINGS INC
Jones New York
1411 Broadway Fl 38 (10018-3409)
PHONE 212 642-3860
Gail Onorato, *Principal*
Theresa Search, *Director*
EMP: 6
SALES (corp-wide): 2.6B **Privately Held**
WEB: www.jny.com
SIC: 2339 Sportswear, women's
PA: Nine West Holdings, Inc.
 180 Rittenhouse Cir
 Bristol PA 19007
 215 785-4000

(G-11437)
NINE WEST HOLDINGS INC
Jones New York
1411 Broadway Fl 38 (10018-3409)
PHONE 212 221-6376
Lynne Fish, *Manager*
EMP: 7
SALES (corp-wide): 2.6B **Privately Held**
WEB: www.jny.com
SIC: 2339 Women's & misses' athletic clothing & sportswear
PA: Nine West Holdings, Inc.
 180 Rittenhouse Cir
 Bristol PA 19007
 215 785-4000

(G-11438)
NINE WEST HOLDINGS INC
Also Called: Jones New York
1441 Broadway Fl 25 (10018-1905)
PHONE 212 575-2571
Fax: 212 768-7759
Jack Gross, *Branch Mgr*
Frank Bahamonde, *Info Tech Dir*
EMP: 7
SALES (corp-wide): 2.6B **Privately Held**
WEB: www.jny.com
SIC: 2329 2339 Men's & boys' sportswear & athletic clothing; women's & misses' athletic clothing & sportswear
PA: Nine West Holdings, Inc.
 180 Rittenhouse Cir
 Bristol PA 19007
 215 785-4000

(G-11439)
NINE WEST HOLDINGS INC
Also Called: Jones New York
1441 Broadway Fl 10 (10018-1905)
PHONE 215 785-4000
Chris Lorusso, *Exec VP*
Sanjeev Savant, *Project Mgr*
Elisheva Rothstein, *Branch Mgr*
EMP: 22
SALES (corp-wide): 2.6B **Privately Held**
SIC: 2339 Women's & misses' athletic clothing & sportswear
PA: Nine West Holdings, Inc.
 180 Rittenhouse Cir
 Bristol PA 19007
 215 785-4000

(G-11440)
NINE WEST HOLDINGS INC
1411 Broadway Fl 15 (10018-3410)
PHONE 212 642-3860
Wesley Card, *Branch Mgr*
EMP: 120
SALES (corp-wide): 2.6B **Privately Held**
SIC: 2337 Women's & misses' suits & coats
PA: Nine West Holdings, Inc.
 180 Rittenhouse Cir
 Bristol PA 19007
 215 785-4000

(G-11441)
NINE WEST HOLDINGS INC
Also Called: Jones New York
575 Fashion Ave Frnt 1 (10018-1886)
PHONE 212 642-3860
Charles Hostepler, *President*
Lisa Garson, *Branch Mgr*
EMP: 22
SALES (corp-wide): 2.6B **Privately Held**
WEB: www.jny.com
SIC: 2339 Sportswear, women's
PA: Nine West Holdings, Inc.
 180 Rittenhouse Cir
 Bristol PA 19007
 215 785-4000

(G-11442)
NINE WEST HOLDINGS INC
Also Called: Kasper
2 Broadway Frnt 1 (10004-3355)
PHONE 212 968-1521
EMP: 10
SALES (corp-wide): 2.6B **Privately Held**
WEB: www.kasper.net
SIC: 2337 Women's & misses' suits & coats
PA: Nine West Holdings, Inc.
 180 Rittenhouse Cir
 Bristol PA 19007
 215 785-4000

(G-11443)
NINE WEST HOLDINGS INC
Jones New York
1441 Broadway (10018-1905)
PHONE 212 822-1300
Angie Helck, *COO*
EMP: 22
SALES (corp-wide): 2.6B **Privately Held**
SIC: 2339 Jeans: women's, misses' & juniors'
PA: Nine West Holdings, Inc.
 180 Rittenhouse Cir
 Bristol PA 19007
 215 785-4000

(G-11444)
NL SHOES AND BAGS LLC
Also Called: Lepore, Nanette
225 W 35th St Fl 17 (10001-1991)
PHONE 212 594-0012
Ana Restrepo, *General Mgr*
Robert Savage,
Nanette Lepore,
▲ **EMP**: 5
SALES (est): 400K **Privately Held**
SIC: 2392 Shoe bags: made from purchased materials

(G-11445)
NLHE LLC
Also Called: Nanette Lepore
225 W 35th St (10001-1904)
PHONE 212 594-0012
Erica Wolf, *President*
Robert Savage,
EMP: 50 **EST**: 2014
SALES (est): 149.5K **Privately Held**
SIC: 2339 Sportswear, women's

(G-11446)
NLR COUNTER TOPS LLC
902 E 92nd St (10128)
PHONE 347 295-0410
AVI Harel, *Mng Member*
EMP: 5
SALES (est): 447.9K **Privately Held**
SIC: 2541 5211 5084 Counter & sink tops; counter tops; countersinks

(G-11447)
NMNY GROUP LLC ✪
1400 Broadway Fl 16 (10018-5300)
PHONE 212 944-6500
EMP: 25 **EST**: 2016

SALES (est): 612.6K **Privately Held**
SIC: 2389 Men's miscellaneous accessories

(G-11448)
NOAH ENTERPRISES LTD (PA)
520 8th Ave Lbby 2 (10018-6590)
PHONE 212 736-2888
Fax: 212 655-3545
Sam Noah, *President*
▲ **EMP**: 6
SQ FT: 12,000
SALES (est): 1.1MM **Privately Held**
WEB: www.noahenterprises.com
SIC: 2339 5137 Sportswear, women's; sportswear, women's & children's

(G-11449)
NOCHAIRS INC
325 W 38th St Rm 310 (10018-9664)
PHONE 917 748-8731
Anthony Lilore, *President*
Celeste Lilore, *Vice Pres*
EMP: 2
SQ FT: 1,100
SALES: 1MM **Privately Held**
SIC: 2211 2259 5199 Bags & bagging, cotton; bags & bagging, knit; bags, textile

(G-11450)
NOIR JEWELRY LLC
362 5th Ave Fl 6 (10001-2210)
PHONE 212 465-8500
Shaya Reiter, *CEO*
Maninder Kaur, *Controller*
EMP: 6
SQ FT: 10,000
SALES (est): 607.9K
SALES (corp-wide): 14.4MM **Privately Held**
SIC: 3961 Costume jewelry
PA: International Inspirations, Ltd.
 362 5th Ave Ste 601
 New York NY 10001
 212 465-8500

(G-11451)
NOODLE EDUCATION INC
59 Charles St Suite200 (10014-2625)
PHONE 646 289-7800
John Katzman, *CEO*
Darwin Abella, *President*
Aryeh Morris, *Controller*
Dennis Ritell, *Sales Dir*
Jeff Herbst, *Chief Mktg Ofcr*
EMP: 20 **EST**: 2010
SALES (est): 3.2MM **Privately Held**
SIC: 2098 Noodles (e.g. egg, plain & water), dry

(G-11452)
NORDIC PRESS INC
243 E 34th St (10016-4852)
PHONE 212 686-3356
Fax: 212 686-3356
Denis Mets, *President*
Siri Uriko, *Manager*
Anne Karu, *Administration*
EMP: 5
SALES (est): 210K **Privately Held**
WEB: www.metronome.com
SIC: 2711 Newspapers: publishing only, not printed on site

(G-11453)
NORSK TITANIUM US INC
1350 Ave Of The Americas (10019-4702)
PHONE 646 277-7514
Warren Boley, *Ch of Bd*
Gunnar A Skinderhaug, *Senior VP*
Gunnar Aasbo-Skinderhaug,
EMP: 9
SQ FT: 5,000
SALES (est): 399.5K
SALES (corp-wide): 1.4MM **Privately Held**
SIC: 3728 Aircraft assemblies, subassemblies & parts
HQ: Nti Mh As
 Karenslyst Alle 9a
 Oslo

(G-11454)
NORTH AMERICAN BEAR CO INC
1261 Broadway Rm 815 (10001-3532)
PHONE 212 388-0700
Fax: 212 388-0089
Joy Mendez, *Opers Staff*
Barbara Iserberg, *Sales/Mktg Mgr*
Amy Boatman, *Credit Mgr*
Anna Bruno, *Payroll Mgr*
EMP: 10
SALES (corp-wide): 4MM **Privately Held**
WEB: www.nabear.com
SIC: 3942 Stuffed toys, including animals
PA: North American Bear Co., Inc.
 1200 W 35th St
 Chicago IL 60609
 773 376-3457

(G-11455)
NORTH AMERICAN GRAPHICS INC
150 Varick St Rm 303 (10013-1218)
PHONE 212 725-2200
Fax: 212 633-6366
Arthur Ascher, *President*
EMP: 10
SQ FT: 2,500
SALES (est): 1.3MM **Privately Held**
SIC: 2759 7336 Commercial printing; graphic arts & related design

(G-11456)
NORTH AMERICAN MILLS INC
Also Called: Chams
1370 Broadway Rm 1101 (10018-7826)
PHONE 212 695-6146
▲ **EMP**: 15
SQ FT: 6,600
SALES (est): 1MM **Privately Held**
SIC: 2329 Mfg Men's/Boy's Clothing

(G-11457)
NORTH EASTERN FABRICATORS INC
Also Called: Great Gates Etc
910 Park Ave Ph Ph (10075-0277)
PHONE 718 542-0450
Fax: 718 328-6564
Gerald Cohen, *President*
John Fisher, *Vice Pres*
Nereida Segrra, *Manager*
▲ **EMP**: 20 **EST**: 1932
SQ FT: 10,000
SALES (est): 3.4MM **Privately Held**
SIC: 3441 Fabricated structural metal

(G-11458)
NORTH SIX INC
176 Grand St Ste 5f (10013-3786)
PHONE 212 463-7227
Oliver Hicks, *President*
EMP: 12
SALES (est): 13MM **Privately Held**
SIC: 2759 7812 Commercial printing; motion picture & video production

(G-11459)
NORTH-SOUTH BOOKS INC
600 3rd Ave Fl 2 (10016-1919)
PHONE 212 706-4545
Davy Sidjanski, *CEO*
David Reuther, *President*
Marianne Martens, *Vice Pres*
Heather Lennon, *Sales Staff*
Melinda Weigel, *Manager*
▲ **EMP**: 25
SQ FT: 11,000
SALES (est): 1.7MM **Privately Held**
WEB: www.northsouth.com
SIC: 2731 5192 Books: publishing only; books

(G-11460)
NORTHPOINT TRADING INC (PA)
347 5th Ave (10016-5010)
PHONE 212 481-8001
Fax: 212 481-8003
Abe Kassin, *President*
Isaac Kassin, *Vice Pres*
Joshua Kassin, *Sales Mgr*
▲ **EMP**: 10
SQ FT: 4,000

New York - New York County (G-11461) — GEOGRAPHIC SECTION

SALES (est): 39.2MM **Privately Held**
SIC: **2273** 2211 2392 6512 Carpets & rugs; handkerchief fabrics, cotton; blankets, comforters & beddings; shopping center, property operation only

(G-11461)
NORTHWELL HEALTH INC
521 Park Ave (10065-8140)
PHONE.................................888 387-5811
EMP: 502
SALES (corp-wide): 5.3B **Privately Held**
SIC: **3842** Cosmetic restorations
PA: Northwell Health, Inc.
 2000 Marcus Ave
 New Hyde Park NY 11042
 516 321-6000

(G-11462)
NOVARTIS CORPORATION (DH)
608 5th Ave (10020-2303)
PHONE.................................212 307-1122
Christi Shaw, *Ch of Bd*
Susan Damico, *Vice Pres*
Deborah Dunshire, *Vice Pres*
Carole Grabowski, *Vice Pres*
Charles Koen, *Vice Pres*
EMP: 30 EST: 1903
SALES (est): 49.5B
SALES (corp-wide): 49.4B **Privately Held**
WEB: www.novartis.com
SIC: **2834** 2879 0181 2032 Pharmaceutical preparations; drugs acting on the cardiovascular system, except diagnostic; drugs acting on the central nervous system & sense organs; veterinary pharmaceutical preparations; agricultural chemicals; insecticides, agricultural or household; pesticides, agricultural or household; fungicides, herbicides; seeds, vegetable: growing of; baby foods, including meats: packaged in cans, jars, etc.; dyes & pigments
HQ: Novartis International Ag
 Lichtstrasse 35
 Basel BS 4056
 616 971-111

(G-11463)
NOVARTIS PHARMACEUTICALS CORP
230 Park Ave (10169-0005)
PHONE.................................888 669-6682
Jaclyn Feeley, *Branch Mgr*
EMP: 5
SALES (corp-wide): 49.4B **Privately Held**
SIC: **3826** Analytical instruments
HQ: Novartis Pharmaceuticals Corporation
 1 Health Plz
 East Hanover NJ 07936
 862 778-8300

(G-11464)
NOVEN PHARMACEUTICALS INC
350 5th Ave Ste 3700 (10118-3799)
PHONE.................................212 682-4420
Jeffrey F Eisenberg, *CEO*
EMP: 32
SQ FT: 25,000
SALES (corp-wide): 1.3B **Privately Held**
SIC: **2834** Pharmaceutical preparations
HQ: Noven Pharmaceuticals, Inc.
 11960 Sw 144th St
 Miami FL 33186
 305 964-3393

(G-11465)
NP RONIET CREATIONS INC
10 W 46th St Ste 1708 (10036-4515)
PHONE.................................212 302-1847
Fax: 212 768-4172
Naftali Elias, *President*
EMP: 9
SQ FT: 2,200
SALES (est): 1MM **Privately Held**
SIC: **3911** Jewelry, precious metal

(G-11466)
NSGV INC
90 5th Ave (10011-7629)
PHONE.................................212 367-3167
Fax: 212 633-1959
Timothy Forbes, *COO*
Malcolm Forbes, *Branch Mgr*
EMP: 20

SALES (corp-wide): 176.7MM **Privately Held**
WEB: www.forbes.com
SIC: **2721** 6282 6552 Magazines: publishing only, not printed on site; investment advisory service; subdividers & developers
HQ: Nsgv Inc.
 499 Washington Blvd Fl 9
 Jersey City NJ 07310
 212 367-3100

(G-11467)
NSGV INC
Forbes Custom Publishing
90 5th Ave Frnt 2 (10011-7606)
PHONE.................................212 367-4118
Jeff Reilly, *Branch Mgr*
EMP: 20
SALES (corp-wide): 176.7MM **Privately Held**
WEB: www.forbes.com
SIC: **2721** Magazines: publishing only, not printed on site
HQ: Nsgv Inc.
 499 Washington Blvd Fl 9
 Jersey City NJ 07310
 212 367-3100

(G-11468)
NSGV INC
Also Called: American Heritage Magazine
90 5th Ave (10011-7629)
PHONE.................................212 367-3100
Malcolm S Forbes Jr, *Ch of Bd*
Susan Cooney, *Advt Staff*
EMP: 50
SALES (corp-wide): 176.7MM **Privately Held**
WEB: www.forbes.com
SIC: **2721** Periodicals
HQ: Nsgv Inc.
 499 Washington Blvd Fl 9
 Jersey City NJ 07310
 212 367-3100

(G-11469)
NU-TECH LIGHTING CORP (PA)
Also Called: Nutech
608 5th Ave Ste 810 (10020-0036)
PHONE.................................212 541-7397
Phil Thomas, *CEO*
David Wolf, *Admin Sec*
EMP: 5
SQ FT: 10,000
SALES (est): 1MM **Privately Held**
WEB: www.nutechlighting.com
SIC: **3648** Lighting equipment

(G-11470)
NUCARE PHARMACY INC
Also Called: Nucare Pharmacy & Surgical
1789 1st Ave (10128-6901)
PHONE.................................212 426-9300
Fax: 212 426-9305
Harry Wivietsky, *President*
Russell Shvartsshteyn, *Vice Pres*
Kenny Wivietsky, *Administration*
EMP: 14
SQ FT: 2,100
SALES (est): 3MM **Privately Held**
WEB: www.mynucare.com
SIC: **3842** 5912 Surgical appliances & supplies; drug stores & proprietary stores

(G-11471)
NUCARE PHARMACY WEST LLC
Also Called: Nucare Pharmacy & Surgical
250 9th Ave (10001-6602)
PHONE.................................212 462-2525
Fax: 212 462-0040
Robert Marchini, *Mng Member*
Kenny Wivietsky, *Administration*
Russell Shavartsshtyn,
Harry Wivietsky,
EMP: 11
SALES (est): 1.5MM **Privately Held**
WEB: www.mynucare.com
SIC: **3842** 5912 Surgical appliances & supplies; drug stores & proprietary stores

(G-11472)
NUTRACEUTICAL WELLNESS LLC
Also Called: Nutrafol
155 E 37th St Apt 4b (10016-3152)
PHONE.................................888 454-3320
Giorgos Tsetis, *CEO*
Roland Peralta, *President*
EMP: 8
SQ FT: 1,000
SALES: 900K **Privately Held**
SIC: **2834** Vitamin preparations

(G-11473)
NUTRAQUEEN LLC
138 E 34th St Apt 2f (10016-4773)
PHONE.................................347 368-6568
Silvia Demeter, *CEO*
EMP: 12
SALES (est): 911.3K **Privately Held**
WEB: www.nutraqueen.com
SIC: **2833** Vitamins, natural or synthetic: bulk, uncompounded

(G-11474)
NUTRIFAST LLC
244 5th Ave Ste W249 (10001-7604)
PHONE.................................347 671-3181
Andres Ballares,
EMP: 10 EST: 2013
SALES (est): 636.7K **Privately Held**
SIC: **2024** Ice cream & frozen desserts

(G-11475)
NV PRRCONE MD COSMECEUTICALS
1745 Broadway (10019-4640)
PHONE.................................212 734-2537
Fax: 212 734-2567
N V Perricone, *Owner*
Clinical Mirabella, *CFO*
EMP: 7
SALES (est): 839.5K **Privately Held**
SIC: **2834** Pharmaceutical preparations

(G-11476)
NY ACCESSORY GROUP LTD LBLTY (PA)
Also Called: Nyg
130 Madison Ave (10016-7038)
PHONE.................................212 989-6350
Marilyn Cohen, *Principal*
▲ EMP: 7
SALES (est): 952.6K **Privately Held**
SIC: **3143** Dress shoes, men's

(G-11477)
NY DENIM INC
1407 Broadway Rm 1021 (10018-3256)
PHONE.................................212 764-6668
EMP: 10
SALES (est): 720K **Privately Held**
SIC: **2253** Knit Outerwear Mills

(G-11478)
NYC DISTRICT COUNCIL UBCJA
395 Hudson St Lbby 3 (10014-7450)
PHONE.................................212 366-7500
Michael Forde, *Principal*
EMP: 7
SALES: 27.9MM **Privately Held**
SIC: **3423** Carpenters' hand tools, except saws: levels, chisels, etc.

(G-11479)
NYC IDOL APPAREL INC
214 W 39th St Rm 807 (10018-4455)
PHONE.................................212 997-9797
David Shaaya, *President*
EMP: 4 EST: 2008
SQ FT: 700
SALES: 2MM **Privately Held**
SIC: **2329** 2337 Down-filled clothing: men's & boys'; skirts, separate: women's, misses' & juniors'

(G-11480)
NYC KNITWEAR INC
525 Fashion Ave Rm 701 (10018-0473)
PHONE.................................212 840-1313
Fax: 212 398-3157
Jian Guo, *Chairman*
Daniel Romeo, *Supervisor*
▲ EMP: 22
SQ FT: 13,000

SALES (est): 3MM **Privately Held**
SIC: **2331** Women's & misses' blouses & shirts

(G-11481)
NYCJBS LLC
Also Called: Fat Baby
112 Rivington St Frnt (10002-2259)
PHONE.................................212 533-1888
Joseph Blank, *Principal*
EMP: 15
SALES (est): 1.1MM **Privately Held**
SIC: **2064** Candy bars, including chocolate covered bars

(G-11482)
NYLON LLC
Also Called: Nylon Magazine
110 Greene St Ste 607 (10012-3838)
PHONE.................................212 226-6454
Fax: 212 226-7738
Jaclynn Jarrett, *Publisher*
Dana Fields, *Exec VP*
Andrew Haynes, *Manager*
Natalie Toren, *Manager*
Joseph Errico, *Director*
EMP: 20
SALES (est): 3.7MM **Privately Held**
WEB: www.nylonmag.com
SIC: **2721** Magazines: publishing only, not printed on site

(G-11483)
NYLON MEDIA INC
Also Called: Nylonshop
110 Greene St Ste 607 (10012-3838)
PHONE.................................212 226-6454
Paul Greenberg, *CEO*
Marc Luzzatto, *Ch of Bd*
Jamie Elden, *President*
Carrie S Reynolds, *President*
Shruti Ganguly, *Vice Pres*
EMP: 45
SALES (est): 6.1MM **Privately Held**
SIC: **2721** Periodicals: publishing & printing

(G-11484)
NYMAN JEWELRY INC (PA)
66 W 9th St (10011-8972)
PHONE.................................212 944-1976
Fax: 212 944-5716
Corc Aydin, *President*
Gabi Gabriel, *Manager*
EMP: 6
SQ FT: 2,000
SALES (est): 558.2K **Privately Held**
SIC: **3915** 5944 Gems, real & imitation: preparation for settings; jewelry stores

(G-11485)
NYP HOLDINGS INC (DH)
Also Called: New York Post
1211 Avenue Of The Amer (10036-8790)
PHONE.................................212 997-9272
Fax: 212 930-8005
K Rupert Murdoch, *President*
Joe Vincent, *Exec VP*
John Ancona, *Vice Pres*
Michael Carvalhido, *Vice Pres*
Michelle Dalmeida, *Vice Pres*
▲ EMP: 600
SALES (est): 175.5MM
SALES (corp-wide): 8.2B **Publicly Held**
WEB: www.nypost.com
SIC: **2711** Commercial printing & newspaper publishing combined
HQ: News Preferred Holdings Inc.
 20 Westport Rd
 Wilton CT 06897
 203 563-6483

(G-11486)
NYREV INC
Also Called: NEW YORK REVIEW OF BOOKS
435 Hudson St Rm 300 (10014-3949)
P.O. Box 9310, Big Sandy TX (75755-3316)
PHONE.................................212 757-8070
Rae S Hederman, *Ch of Bd*
Michael Grannon, *Corp Secy*
Evan Johnston, *Prdtn Mgr*
Margerie Deblin, *Controller*
Matthew Howard, *Director*
EMP: 35

▲ = Import ▼ = Export
◆ = Import/Export

SQ FT: 12,000
SALES: 93K Privately Held
WEB: www.nybooks.com
SIC: 2721 Magazines: publishing only, not printed on site

(G-11487)
NYS NYU-CNTR INTL COOPERATION
418 Lafayette St (10003-6947)
PHONE 212 998-3680
Chris Jones, *Director*
EMP: 30
SALES (est): 1.6MM Privately Held
SIC: 2759 Publication printing

(G-11488)
NYT CAPITAL LLC (HQ)
620 8th Ave (10018-1618)
PHONE 212 556-1234
Dave Frank, *Vice Pres*
Harrison Sohmer, *Manager*
EMP: 18
SALES: 43.2K
SALES (corp-wide): 1.5B Publicly Held
SIC: 2711 5192 5963 7322 Newspapers, publishing & printing; commercial printing & newspaper publishing combined; newspapers; newspapers, home delivery, not by printers or publishers; collection agency, except real estate; credit reporting services
PA: The New York Times Company
    620 8th Ave
    New York NY 10018
    212 556-1234

(G-11489)
O VAL NICK MUSIC CO INC
254 W 72nd St Apt 1a (10023-2851)
PHONE 212 873-2179
Fax: 212 799-6926
Nicholas Ashford, *President*
EMP: 5
SALES (est): 340K Privately Held
SIC: 2741 Miscellaneous publishing

(G-11490)
OAKHURST PARTNERS LLC
148 Madison Ave Fl 13 (10016-6700)
PHONE 212 502-3220
Gloria Rosenfeld, *Controller*
Boris Shlomm, *Mng Member*
Alexander Shlomm,
Daniel Shlomm,
▲EMP: 5
SQ FT: 5,000
SALES (est): 490K Privately Held
SIC: 2231 Apparel & outerwear broadwoven fabrics

(G-11491)
OAKLEY INC
1515 Broadway Frnt 4 (10036-5701)
PHONE 212 575-0960
Jerome Stewart, *Manager*
EMP: 65 Privately Held
SIC: 3851 Ophthalmic goods
HQ: Oakley, Inc.
    1 Icon
    Foothill Ranch CA 92610
    949 951-0991

(G-11492)
OBVIOUS INC
214 W 39th St Rm 905a (10018-5534)
PHONE 212 278-0007
Sung Choi, *CEO*
Leny Epstien, *Manager*
EMP: 30
SQ FT: 5,000
SALES (est): 2.1MM Privately Held
SIC: 2211 Apparel & outerwear fabrics, cotton

(G-11493)
OCCIDENTAL ENERGY MKTG INC
1230 Av Of The Amrcs 80 (10020-1513)
PHONE 212 632-4950
Kenneth Huffman, *Investment Ofcr*
Francis Sheridan, *Manager*
EMP: 5
SALES (corp-wide): 12.7B Publicly Held
SIC: 1382 Oil & gas exploration services
HQ: Occidental Energy Marketing, Inc.
    5 Greenway Plz Ste 110
    Houston TX 77046
    713 215-7000

(G-11494)
OCEAN WAVES SWIM LLC
231 W 39th St Rm 500 (10018-3151)
PHONE 212 967-4481
Eli Seruya, *CEO*
Lisa Bailey, *President*
EMP: 7
SQ FT: 1,600
SALES (est): 419.4K Privately Held
SIC: 2339 Bathing suits: women's, misses' & juniors'

(G-11495)
OCIP HOLDING LLC (PA)
660 Madison Ave Fl 19 (10065-8415)
PHONE 646 589-6180
Kevin Struve, *Manager*
EMP: 2 EST: 2014
SALES (est): 309.4MM Publicly Held
SIC: 2861 2873 Methanol, natural (wood alcohol); ammonium nitrate, ammonium sulfate

(G-11496)
ODY ACCESSORIES INC
1239 Broadway (10001-4311)
PHONE 212 239-0580
Fax: 212 629-0417
Michael Weiss, *President*
▲EMP: 27
SQ FT: 12,000
SALES (est): 3.5MM Privately Held
SIC: 2339 Women's & misses' accessories

(G-11497)
ODYSSEY MAG PUBG GROUP INC
4 New York Plz (10004-2413)
PHONE 212 545-4800
David J Pecker, *Principal*
EMP: 151
SALES (est): 3.1MM
SALES (corp-wide): 223MM Privately Held
SIC: 2721 Magazines: publishing & printing
PA: American Media, Inc.
    1000 American Media Way
    Boca Raton FL 33464
    561 997-7733

(G-11498)
OHR PHARMACEUTICAL INC (PA)
800 3rd Ave Fl 11 (10022-7651)
PHONE 212 682-8452
Jason S Slakter, *CEO*
Ira Greenstein, *Ch of Bd*
Irach Taraporewala, *President*
Marlene Modi, *Vice Pres*
Sam Backenroth, *CFO*
EMP: 16
SALES (est): 824.5K Publicly Held
SIC: 2834 Pharmaceutical preparations

(G-11499)
OLDCASTLE BUILDING ENVELOPE
1350 Ave Of The Americas (10019-4702)
PHONE 212 957-5400
Melissa Wood, *Assistant*
EMP: 5 EST: 2014
SALES (est): 83.3K
SALES (corp-wide): 25.3B Privately Held
SIC: 3231 Products of purchased glass
PA: Crh Public Limited Company
    Stonemason' S Way
    Dublin 16
    140 410-00

(G-11500)
OLIGOMERIX INC
3960 Broadway Ste 340d (10032-1543)
PHONE 914 997-8877
EMP: 4
SQ FT: 1,000
SALES (est): 1.1MM Privately Held
WEB: www.oligomerix.com
SIC: 2836 2834 Biological products, except diagnostic; pharmaceutical preparations

(G-11501)
OLYMPIC JEWELRY INC
62 W 47th St Ste 509 (10036-3201)
PHONE 212 768-7004
Roberto Ganz, *President*
Mike Genuth, *Vice Pres*
EMP: 4
SALES: 1.2MM Privately Held
SIC: 3873 5094 Watches, clocks, watchcases & parts; clocks, watches & parts

(G-11502)
OLYMPIC PRESS INC
950 3rd Ave Fl 7 (10022-2788)
PHONE 212 242-4934
Fax: 212 242-5727
Howard Bau, *President*
EMP: 15 EST: 1929
SALES: 1.5MM Privately Held
SIC: 2752 Commercial printing, offset

(G-11503)
OMRIX BIOPHARMACEUTICALS INC
1 Rckfller Ctr Ste 2322 (10020)
PHONE 908 218-0707
Robert Taub, *CEO*
Larry Ellberger, *Ch of Bd*
Nissim Mashiach, *President*
V Marc Droppert, *Exec VP*
Nanci Prado, *Vice Pres*
EMP: 212
SQ FT: 8,945
SALES (est): 16.7MM
SALES (corp-wide): 70B Publicly Held
WEB: www.omrix.com
SIC: 2836 Biological products, except diagnostic
HQ: Ethicon Inc.
    Us Route 22
    Somerville NJ 08876
    732 524-0400

(G-11504)
OMX (US) INC
Also Called: Nasdaq Omx
140 Broadway Fl 25 (10005-1142)
PHONE 646 428-2800
Fax: 646 344-0079
Roland Tibell, *President*
Tor Soderquist, *Manager*
Maria Schuck, *Admin Sec*
EMP: 1500
SQ FT: 50,000
SALES (est): 55.9MM Privately Held
SIC: 7372 Application computer software

(G-11505)
ON DEMAND BOOKS LLC
939 Lexington Ave (10065-5771)
PHONE 212 966-2222
Andrew Pate, *Senior VP*
Thor Sigvaldason, *CTO*
Dane Neller,
Herbert Krippner,
Dane J Neller,
EMP: 5
SALES (est): 923.8K Privately Held
WEB: www.ondemandbooks.com
SIC: 7372 Publishers' computer software

(G-11506)
ONE JEANSWEAR GROUP INC (HQ)
Also Called: Jones Jeanswear Group
1441 Broadway (10018-1905)
PHONE 212 835-2500
Jack N Gross, *CEO*
Stuart Bregman, *CEO*
Wesley Card, *Principal*
Ira Margulies, *CFO*
Christopher R Cade, *Admin Sec*
▲EMP: 34
SALES (est): 56.2MM
SALES (corp-wide): 2.6B Privately Held
WEB: www.jny.com
SIC: 2339 2325 Jeans: women's, misses' & juniors'; men's & boys' jeans & dungarees
PA: Nine West Holdings, Inc.
    180 Rittenhouse Cir
    Bristol PA 19007
    215 785-4000

(G-11507)
ONE MOUNTAIN IMPORTS LLC
226 W 37th St Fl 16 (10018-6605)
PHONE 212 643-0805
Antonio Delledonne,
▲EMP: 9
SALES (est): 873.8K Privately Held
SIC: 2339 Women's & misses' accessories

(G-11508)
ONE STEP UP LTD
1412 Broadway Fl 3 (10018-3372)
PHONE 212 398-1110
Fax: 212 302-6596
Harry Adjmi, *President*
Tyrone Davis, *Principal*
Tom Wentley, *Vice Pres*
Sandy Gewercman, *CFO*
▲EMP: 96
SALES (est): 31.7MM Privately Held
SIC: 2339 2329 Women's & misses' athletic clothing & sportswear; men's & boys' sportswear & athletic clothing

(G-11509)
ONE-BLUE LLC
1350 Broadway Rm 1406 (10018-0926)
PHONE 212 223-4380
Roel Kramer, *CEO*
Tom Chen, *CFO*
EMP: 7
SALES (est): 676.5K Privately Held
SIC: 7372 Application computer software

(G-11510)
ONLINE PUBLISHERS ASSOCIATION
1350 Broadway Rm 606 (10018-7205)
PHONE 646 473-1000
Pam Horan, *President*
Caroline Little, *Principal*
Perianne Grignon, *Senior VP*
Rande Price, *Director*
EMP: 27 EST: 2012
SALES: 3.9MM Privately Held
SIC: 2741 Miscellaneous publishing

(G-11511)
ONLY HEARTS LTD (PA)
134 W 37th St Fl 9 (10018-6946)
PHONE 718 783-3218
Fax: 212 268-0922
Jonathan Stewart, *President*
Tina Vito, *Opers Staff*
Esther Neuberg, *Credit Staff*
Keili Leahy, *Accounts Exec*
Nicollette Santos, *Office Mgr*
EMP: 40
SQ FT: 4,000
SALES (est): 7.6MM Privately Held
SIC: 2341 5137 2339 Women's & children's underwear; women's & children's clothing; lingerie; women's & misses' outerwear

(G-11512)
ONTRA PRESENTATIONS LLC
440 Park Ave S Fl 3 (10016-8012)
PHONE 212 213-1315
James Ontra,
Alexandra Ontra,
EMP: 6
SALES: 1MM Privately Held
SIC: 7372 7371 Prepackaged software; business oriented computer software; computer software development

(G-11513)
ONYX SOLAR GROUP LLC
1123 Broadway Ste 908 (10010-2172)
PHONE 917 951-9732
David Mann, *Principal*
▲EMP: 7
SALES (est): 809.6K Privately Held
SIC: 3674 Photovoltaic devices, solid state

(G-11514)
OPENFIN INC
25 Broadway Fl 9 (10004-1058)
PHONE 917 450-8822
Mazy Dar, *CEO*
Fred Doerr, *President*
Jen Collet, *COO*
Chuck Doerr, *COO*
Wenjun Che, *Vice Pres*

New York - New York County (G-11515)

EMP: 9
SQ FT: 1,500
SALES (est): 538K **Privately Held**
SIC: 7372 7371 Prepackaged software; custom computer programming services

(G-11515)
OPENROAD INTEGRATED MEDIA INC
180 Maiden Ln Ste 2803 (10038-4988)
PHONE.................................212 691-0900
Paul Slavin, *CEO*
Jane Friedman, *Ch of Bd*
Jamie Cohen, *Manager*
Samantha Goettlich, *Manager*
EMP: 23
SALES (est): 3.6MM **Privately Held**
SIC: 2741 Miscellaneous publishing

(G-11516)
OPERATIVE MEDIA INC (PA)
6 E 32nd St Fl 3 (10016-5422)
PHONE.................................212 994-8930
Lorne Brown, *CEO*
Venugopal Goteti, *President*
Don Amboyer, *Managing Dir*
Michael Leo, *Principal*
John Briar, *Exec VP*
EMP: 134
SALES (est): 72.6MM **Privately Held**
WEB: www.operative.com
SIC: 7372 Prepackaged software

(G-11517)
OPTHOTECH CORP
1 Penn Plz Ste 1924 (10119-1924)
PHONE.................................212 845-8200
Samir Patel, *President*
Mala Hintzen, *Manager*
EMP: 14
SALES (est): 2.3MM **Privately Held**
SIC: 2834 Pharmaceutical preparations

(G-11518)
OPTIONS PUBLISHING LLC
136 Madison Ave Fl 8 (10016-6711)
PHONE.................................603 429-2698
Barbara Russell,
Sandy Batista, *Admin Sec*
Marty Furlong,
EMP: 14
SQ FT: 2,000
SALES (est): 1MM
SALES (corp-wide): 99.1MM **Privately Held**
WEB: www.optionspublishing.com
SIC: 2741 2731 Miscellaneous publishing; book publishing
PA: Haights Cross Communications, Inc.
136 Madison Ave Fl 8
New York NY 10016
212 209-0500

(G-11519)
ORACLE CORPORATION
520 Madison Ave Fl 30 (10022-4334)
PHONE.................................212 508-7700
Fax: 212 508-7703
Kenneth Berliner, *President*
Drew Goldfarb, *Sales Mgr*
Brian Pennells, *Sales Mgr*
Kevin Gori, *Sales Staff*
Bob Allison, *Branch Mgr*
EMP: 302
SALES (corp-wide): 37B **Publicly Held**
SIC: 7372 Business oriented computer software
PA: Oracle Corporation
500 Oracle Pkwy
Redwood City CA 94065
650 506-7000

(G-11520)
ORACLE CORPORATION
120 Park Ave Fl 26 (10017-5511)
PHONE.................................212 508-7700
David Chow, *Project Mgr*
Tony Cassa, *Engineer*
Jamie Davis, *Sales Mgr*
Art Staple, *Accounts Exec*
EMP: 250
SALES (corp-wide): 37B **Publicly Held**
WEB: www.forcecapital.com
SIC: 7372 Business oriented computer software

PA: Oracle Corporation
500 Oracle Pkwy
Redwood City CA 94065
650 506-7000

(G-11521)
ORANGENIUS INC
115 W 18th St Fl 2 (10011-4113)
PHONE.................................631 742-0648
Grace Cho, *CEO*
Robert Schlackman, *CTO*
EMP: 16 **EST:** 2015
SALES (est): 414.9K **Privately Held**
SIC: 7372 Business oriented computer software

(G-11522)
ORBIS BRYNMORE LITHOGRAPHICS
1735 2nd Ave Frnt 1 (10128-3516)
PHONE.................................212 987-2100
Fax: 212 987-1520
Ceasar Romero, *President*
Anna Romero, *Admin Sec*
EMP: 8 **EST:** 1932
SALES (est): 1MM **Privately Held**
SIC: 2752 Commercial printing, offset

(G-11523)
ORCHARD APPAREL GROUP LTD
212 W 35th St Fl 7 (10001-2508)
PHONE.................................212 268-8701
Robert Fox, *President*
EMP: 5
SALES (est): 342.7K
SALES (corp-wide): 50.9MM **Privately Held**
WEB: www.robertfox.com
SIC: 2331 Blouses, women's & juniors': made from purchased material
PA: Robert Fox Inc.
79 Main St
Mineola NY 11501
516 294-2678

(G-11524)
ORCHID MANUFACTURING CO INC
Also Called: Jessica Michelle
77 W 55th St Apt 4k (10019-4920)
PHONE.................................212 840-5700
Michael Laufer, *Ch of Bd*
Michael H Laufer, *President*
Richard Weiss, *Controller*
EMP: 10 **EST:** 1983
SALES (est): 980K **Privately Held**
SIC: 2331 Women's & misses' blouses & shirts

(G-11525)
OREGE NORTH AMERICA INC (PA)
575 Madison Ave Fl 25 (10022-8509)
PHONE.................................770 862-9388
Kevin Dunlap, *Vice Pres*
Priscilla Brooks, *Office Mgr*
Jonathan Lapin, *Admin Sec*
EMP: 1 **EST:** 2014
SALES: 1MM **Privately Held**
SIC: 3589 Sewage treatment equipment

(G-11526)
ORENS DAILY ROAST INC (PA)
12 E 46th St Fl 6 (10017-2418)
PHONE.................................212 348-5400
Oren Bloostein, *President*
Vijay Rajwani, *Human Resources*
Daniel Earle, *Comms Dir*
Shirley Bethe, *Administration*
▲ **EMP:** 7
SQ FT: 400
SALES (est): 13.7MM **Privately Held**
SIC: 2095 5149 5499 Instant coffee; coffee, green or roasted; coffee

(G-11527)
ORPHEO USA CORP
315 Madison Ave Rm 2601 (10017-5410)
PHONE.................................212 464-8255
Alain Eisenstein, *CEO*
Driss Bellitir, *Manager*
Danelle Downer, *Manager*
Linda Mazeyrie, *Manager*
EMP: 5

SALES (est): 360K **Privately Held**
SIC: 3695 7371 Audio range tape, blank; computer software development & applications

(G-11528)
ORTHO MEDICAL PRODUCTS (PA)
315 E 83rd St (10028-4301)
P.O. Box 847617, Dallas TX (75284-7617)
PHONE.................................212 879-3700
Jane Wilde, *President*
EMP: 13 **EST:** 1944
SQ FT: 7,500
SALES (est): 1.7MM **Privately Held**
SIC: 3841 3842 5999 Surgical & medical instruments; orthopedic appliances; orthopedic & prosthesis applications

(G-11529)
OS33 INC
16 W 22nd St Fl 6 (10010-5969)
PHONE.................................708 336-3466
Jacob Kazakevich, *President*
Aron Derstine, *Vice Pres*
Jennifer Schule, *Executive Asst*
EMP: 6
SALES (est): 5.4MM **Privately Held**
SIC: 7372 7371 Prepackaged software; computer software development; computer software development & applications; computer software systems analysis & design, custom
PA: Os33 Services Corp.
120 Wood Ave S Ste 505
Iselin NJ 08830
866 796-0310

(G-11530)
OSCAR HEYMAN & BROS INC (PA)
501 Madison Ave Fl 15 (10022-5676)
PHONE.................................212 593-0400
Fax: 212 759-8612
Marvin Heyman, *President*
Adam Heyman, *Vice Pres*
Thomas Heyman, *Treasurer*
Whitney Wenk, *Sales Staff*
Lewis Heyman, *Admin Sec*
EMP: 28 **EST:** 1912
SQ FT: 12,000
SALES (est): 4.5MM **Privately Held**
WEB: www.oscarheyman.com
SIC: 3911 Jewelry, precious metal

(G-11531)
OSF FLAVORS INC
259 W 10th St (10014-2510)
P.O. Box 591, Waterbury CT (06720-0591)
PHONE.................................860 298-8350
Oliver Botton, *Branch Mgr*
EMP: 10
SALES (corp-wide): 12.4MM **Privately Held**
WEB: www.osfflavors.com
SIC: 2087 Extracts, flavoring
PA: Osf Flavors, Inc.
40 Baker Hollow Rd
Windsor CT 06095
860 298-8350

(G-11532)
OSNAT GAD INC
Also Called: Ogi Limited
608 5th Ave Ste 609 (10020-2303)
PHONE.................................212 957-0535
Fax: 212 957-0534
Osnat Gad, *President*
Ed Kozin, *CPA*
EMP: 7
SQ FT: 1,450
SALES (est): 780K **Privately Held**
WEB: www.ogi-ltd.com
SIC: 3911 Jewelry, precious metal

(G-11533)
OSPREY PUBLISHING INC
1385 Broadway Fl 5 (10018-6050)
PHONE.................................212 419-5300
Rebecca Smart, *Principal*
▲ **EMP:** 7
SALES (est): 389.2K **Privately Held**
SIC: 2741 Miscellaneous publishing

(G-11534)
OTHER PRESS LLC
267 5th Ave Fl 6 (10016-7508)
PHONE.................................212 414-0054
Judith Gurewich, *CEO*
Corinna Barsan, *Editor*
Amanda Glassman, *Editor*
Katie Henderson, *Editor*
Yvonne Cardenas, *Production*
EMP: 8
SALES (est): 1.2MM **Privately Held**
WEB: www.otherpress.com
SIC: 2731 Book publishing

(G-11535)
OTIS ELEVATOR COMPANY
1 Penn Plz Ste 410 (10119-0499)
PHONE.................................917 339-9600
Fax: 917 339-9677
Ben Petruzella, *Manager*
EMP: 33
SALES (corp-wide): 56.1B **Publicly Held**
SIC: 3534 1796 7699 Elevators & equipment; escalators, passenger & freight; walkways, moving; installing building equipment; elevator installation & conversion; miscellaneous building item repair services; elevators: inspection, service & repair
HQ: Otis Elevator Company
10 Farm Springs Rd
Farmington CT 06032
860 676-6000

(G-11536)
OUTERSTUFF LLC (PA)
1412 Broadway Fl 18 (10018-9258)
PHONE.................................212 594-9700
Fax: 212 239-4268
Sol Werdiger, *President*
Ron Reinisch, *COO*
Randi Blatt, *Vice Pres*
Jonah Blumenfrucht, *CFO*
Maryann Russo, *CFO*
▲ **EMP:** 30
SALES (est): 19.4MM **Privately Held**
SIC: 2369 5137 2339 Girls' & children's outerwear; women's & children's outerwear; women's & misses' outerwear

(G-11537)
OVERTURE MEDIA INC
411 Lafayette St Ste 638 (10003-7032)
PHONE.................................917 446-7455
Jared Weiss, *CEO*
EMP: 7 **EST:** 2014
SQ FT: 153
SALES (est): 285.5K **Privately Held**
SIC: 7372 Prepackaged software

(G-11538)
OXFORD BOOK COMPANY INC
9 Pine St (10005-4701)
PHONE.................................212 227-2120
William Dinger, *President*
Jim Omalley, *Info Tech Mgr*
EMP: 150
SALES (est): 5.8MM
SALES (corp-wide): 65.6MM **Privately Held**
WEB: www.sadlier.com
SIC: 2731 Textbooks: publishing only, not printed on site
PA: William H. Sadlier, Inc.
9 Pine St
New York NY 10005
212 233-3646

(G-11539)
OXFORD CLEANERS
847 Lexington Ave Frnt (10065-6636)
PHONE.................................212 734-0006
Joong Lee, *Owner*
EMP: 5
SALES (est): 280K **Privately Held**
SIC: 3589 7215 Commercial cleaning equipment; coin-operated laundries & cleaning

(G-11540)
OXFORD INDUSTRIES INC
Also Called: Lanier Clothes
600 5th Ave Fl 12 (10020-2325)
PHONE.................................212 247-7712
Alan Rubin, *Branch Mgr*
Tim Brown, *Manager*

GEOGRAPHIC SECTION

New York - New York County (G-11564)

EMP: 25
SALES (corp-wide): 969.2MM **Publicly Held**
SIC: 2329 Athletic (warmup, sweat & jogging) suits: men's & boys'
PA: Oxford Industries, Inc.
999 Peachtree St Ne # 688
Atlanta GA 30309
404 659-2424

(G-11541)
OXFORD INDUSTRIES INC
25 W 39th St (10018-3805)
PHONE 212 840-2288
Fran Hicks, *Manager*
EMP: 14
SALES (corp-wide): 997.8MM **Publicly Held**
WEB: www.oxm.com
SIC: 2321 Men's & boys' furnishings
PA: Oxford Industries, Inc.
999 Peachtree St Ne # 688
Atlanta GA 30309
404 659-2424

(G-11542)
OXFORD UNIVERSITY PRESS LLC (HQ)
Also Called: Oxford University Press, Inc.
198 Madison Ave Fl 8 (10016-4308)
PHONE 212 726-6000
Fax: 212 726-6440
Niko Pfund, *President*
Vineeta Gupta, *Publisher*
Laura Pearson, *General Mgr*
Ameena Saiyid, *Managing Dir*
Joellyn Ausanka, *Editor*
◆ **EMP:** 265 **EST:** 1973
SQ FT: 145,000
SALES (est): 107.9MM
SALES (corp-wide): 1.5B **Privately Held**
SIC: 2731 5961 Book publishing; book & record clubs

(G-11543)
OXFORD UNIVERSITY PRESS LLC
Chancellor Masters & Scholrs
198 Madison Ave Fl 8 (10016-4308)
PHONE 212 726-6000
Giles Kerr, *Finance*
Malcolm Fairbrother, *Manager*
Hilary Henry, *Manager*
Simon Kingston, *Manager*
EMP: 8
SALES (corp-wide): 1.5B **Privately Held**
SIC: 2731 5961 Book publishing; book & record clubs
HQ: Oxford University Press, Llc
198 Madison Ave Fl 8
New York NY 10016
212 726-6000

(G-11544)
OXO INTERNATIONAL INC
601 W 26th St Rm 1050 (10001-1148)
PHONE 212 242-3333
Alex Lee, *President*
Michael Delevante, *Vice Pres*
Todd Cutsuries, *QC Mgr*
Matthew Dolph, *Engineer*
Mark Drayer, *Engineer*
▲ **EMP:** 110
SQ FT: 2,500
SALES (est): 14.1MM **Privately Held**
SIC: 3631 3469 5099 Household cooking equipment; household cooking & kitchen utensils, metal; baby carriages, strollers & related products
PA: Helen Of Troy Limited
C/O Conyers, Dill & Pearman
Hamilton
441 295-1422

(G-11545)
OZMODYL LTD
Also Called: Soho and Tribeca Map
233 Broadway Rm 707 (10279-0705)
PHONE 212 226-0622
EMP: 5
SALES (est): 550K **Privately Held**
SIC: 2731 Publish A Map And Guide Book Of The Soho And Tribeca Area

(G-11546)
P & I SPORTSWEAR INC
384 5th Ave (10018-8103)
PHONE 718 934-4587
Ignacio Bursztyn, *President*
Flora Bursztyn, *Vice Pres*
EMP: 5
SALES: 1.2MM **Privately Held**
SIC: 2339 2329 Women's & misses' athletic clothing & sportswear; men's & boys' sportswear & athletic clothing

(G-11547)
P & W PRESS INC
20 W 22nd St Ste 710 (10010-5877)
PHONE 646 486-3417
Fax: 212 929-2822
Philip Foxman, *President*
Keith Foxman, *Vice Pres*
Anita Foxman, *Sales Mgr*
EMP: 20
SQ FT: 3,000
SALES (est): 1.8MM **Privately Held**
WEB: www.pwpress.com
SIC: 2752 2759 Commercial printing, offset; letterpress printing

(G-11548)
P E GUERIN (PA)
23 Jane St (10014-1999)
PHONE 212 243-5270
Fax: 212 727-2290
Andrew F Ward, *President*
Martin Grubman, *General Mgr*
Candice Cudanes, *Production*
Lila Tublin, *Admin Asst*
◆ **EMP:** 69 **EST:** 1857
SALES (est): 6.5MM **Privately Held**
WEB: www.peguerin.com
SIC: 3429 5072 3432 5074 Door locks, bolts & checks; builders' hardware; plumbing fixture fittings & trim; plumbing fittings & supplies; drapery hardware & blinds & shades; window covering parts & accessories

(G-11549)
PACE EDITIONS INC (PA)
Also Called: Pace Prints
32 E 57th St Fl 3 (10022-8573)
PHONE 212 421-3237
Fax: 212 751-7280
Richard H Solomon, *President*
Jason Schroeder, *VP Opers*
Carlo Bella, *Director*
Kristin Heming, *Director*
EMP: 20
SQ FT: 10,000
SALES (est): 1.7MM **Privately Held**
WEB: www.paceprints.com
SIC: 2741 7999 Art copy & poster publishing; art gallery, commercial

(G-11550)
PACE EDITIONS INC
44 W 18th St Fl 5 (10011-4644)
PHONE 212 675-7431
Richard Soloman, *President*
Kristin Heming, *Director*
Jacob Lewis, *Director*
EMP: 5
SALES (corp-wide): 1.7MM **Privately Held**
WEB: www.paceprints.com
SIC: 2752 2759 2741 Commercial printing, lithographic; commercial printing; miscellaneous publishing
PA: Pace Editions, Inc.
32 E 57th St Fl 3
New York NY 10022
212 421-3237

(G-11551)
PACIFIC ALLIANCE USA INC
350 5th Ave Fl 5 (10118-0110)
PHONE 336 500-8184
Bruce Philip Rockowitz, *Branch Mgr*
EMP: 6 **Privately Held**
SIC: 2339 Women's & misses' outerwear
HQ: Pacific Alliance Usa, Inc.
1359 Broadway Fl 21
New York NY 10018
646 839-7000

(G-11552)
PACIFIC ALLIANCE USA INC (DH)
1359 Broadway Fl 21 (10018-7824)
PHONE 646 839-7000
Bruce Philip Rockowitz, *CEO*
Dow Famulak, *President*
Richard Darling, *Principal*
Ron Ventricelli, *COO*
◆ **EMP:** 26
SALES (est): 11.1MM **Privately Held**
SIC: 2339 Women's & misses' outerwear
HQ: Gbg Usa Inc.
350 5th Ave Lbby 9
New York NY 10118
646 839-7083

(G-11553)
PACIFIC WORLDWIDE INC
20 W 33rd St Fl 11 (10001-3305)
PHONE 212 502-2360
Martin Terzian, *President*
Ronald J Herro, *Vice Pres*
◆ **EMP:** 15
SALES (est): 2MM **Privately Held**
SIC: 3111 Accessory products, leather

(G-11554)
PACK AMERICA CORP (HQ)
108 W 39th St Fl 16 (10018-8255)
PHONE 212 508-6666
Hisao Ueda, *President*
Frank Rizzo, *Exec VP*
Haruyuki Kochi, *Vice Pres*
Steve Walker, *Prdtn Mgr*
◆ **EMP:** 4
SQ FT: 3,100
SALES: 6.3MM
SALES (corp-wide): 714.8MM **Privately Held**
WEB: www.packdash.com
SIC: 2673 2679 Plastic bags: made from purchased materials; paper products, converted
PA: The Pack Corporation
2-9-9, Higashiobase, Higashinari-Ku
Osaka OSK 537-0
669 721-221

(G-11555)
PALETOT LTD
Also Called: Patricia Underwood
499 Fashion Ave Rm 25s (10018-6847)
PHONE 212 268-3774
Judy Hummel, *President*
Patricia Underwood, *Chairman*
EMP: 11
SQ FT: 1,500
SALES (est): 670K **Privately Held**
SIC: 2353 Hats & caps; millinery

(G-11556)
PALGRAVE MACMILLAN LTD
175 5th Ave Frnt 4 (10010-7728)
PHONE 646 307-5028
Fax: 212 307-5035
Ursula Gavin, *Publisher*
Gayatri Patnaik, *General Mgr*
Elisabeth Dyssegaard, *Editor*
Jake Klisivitch, *Editor*
Andy Syson, *Business Mgr*
▲ **EMP:** 9
SALES (est): 1.1MM
SALES (corp-wide): 2.1B **Privately Held**
WEB: www.palgrave-usa.com
SIC: 2731 Book publishing
HQ: Macmillan Publishers Limited
Cromwell Place
Basingstoke HANTS RG24
125 632-9242

(G-11557)
PALLADIA INC
105 W 17th St (10011-5432)
PHONE 212 206-3669
Corinne Workman, *Manager*
EMP: 125
SALES (corp-wide): 43.8MM **Privately Held**
SIC: 3421 Table & food cutlery, including butchers'
PA: Palladia, Inc.
305 7th Ave Fl 10
New York NY 10001

(G-11558)
PAN AMERICAN LEATHERS INC (PA)
347 W 36th St Rm 1204 (10018-6480)
PHONE 978 741-4150
Mark Mendal, *President*
Yania Halman, *Office Mgr*
▲ **EMP:** 3
SQ FT: 3,000
SALES (est): 1.3MM **Privately Held**
WEB: www.panamleathers.com
SIC: 3111 5199 Finishing of leather; leather goods, except footwear, gloves, luggage, belting

(G-11559)
PANGEA BRANDS LLC (PA)
6 W 20th St Fl 3 (10011-9270)
PHONE 617 638-0001
Steve Vuernick, *Senior VP*
Jeremy Bartfield, *VP Sales*
Corey Bradley, *Accounts Mgr*
Joshua Fink, *Mng Member*
Michael London,
▲ **EMP:** 6
SQ FT: 5,000
SALES (est): 1.1MM **Privately Held**
SIC: 2396 Apparel & other linings, except millinery

(G-11560)
PANGEA BRANDS LLC
6 W 20th St Fl 3 (10011-9270)
PHONE 617 638-0001
Joshua Fink, *Branch Mgr*
EMP: 6
SALES (corp-wide): 1.1MM **Privately Held**
SIC: 2396 Apparel & other linings, except millinery
PA: Pangea Brands, Llc
6 W 20th St Fl 3
New York NY 10011
617 638-0001

(G-11561)
PANVIDEA INC
44 W 28th St Fl 14 (10001-4212)
PHONE 212 967-9613
Chiranjeev Bordoloi, *President*
Frank Gatto, *Senior VP*
Chris Cali, *CTO*
EMP: 10
SQ FT: 300
SALES (est): 993.2K **Privately Held**
SIC: 3663 7371 Radio & TV communications equipment; custom computer programming services

(G-11562)
PAPA BUBBLE
380 Broome St Frnt A (10013-3799)
PHONE 212 966-2599
Ryan Grassi, *Owner*
EMP: 7
SALES (est): 552K **Privately Held**
SIC: 2064 Candy & other confectionery products

(G-11563)
PAPER BOX CORP
Also Called: Aaaaaa Creative Designs
1751 2nd Ave Apt 10a (10128-5377)
PHONE 212 226-7490
Robert Fleisig, *President*
EMP: 70 **EST:** 1900
SALES (est): 6.1MM **Privately Held**
SIC: 2631 2657 Folding boxboard; setup boxboard; folding paperboard boxes

(G-11564)
PAPER MAGIC GROUP INC
345 7th Ave Fl 6 (10001-5053)
PHONE 631 521-3682
Fax: 212 868-3648
Nathan Caldwell, *Manager*
Lane Fragomeli, *Exec Dir*
EMP: 450
SALES (corp-wide): 317MM **Publicly Held**
WEB: www.papermagic.com
SIC: 2771 2678 Greeting cards; stationery products

New York - New York County (G-11565) — GEOGRAPHIC SECTION

HQ: Paper Magic Group Inc.
54 Glenmra Ntl Blvd
Moosic PA 18507
570 961-3863

(G-11565)
PAPER PUBLISHING COMPANY INC
Also Called: Paper Magazine
15 E 32nd St (10016-5423)
PHONE....................212 226-4405
Fax: 212 226-0062
David Hershkovits, *President*
Kevin Breen, *Editor*
Tom Guinness, *Editor*
Kim Hastreiter, *Treasurer*
Kim Hasreier, *Personnel Exec*
EMP: 27
SQ FT: 3,000
SALES (est): 3.5MM **Privately Held**
WEB: www.papermag.com
SIC: 2721 Magazines: publishing only, not printed on site

(G-11566)
PAPERCUTZ INC
160 Broadway Rm 700e (10038-4201)
PHONE....................646 559-4681
Terry Nantier, *President*
Jim Salicrup, *Vice Pres*
Beth Scorzato, *Production*
Jeff Whitman, *Production*
Sven P Larsen, *VP Mktg*
▲ EMP: 5
SALES: 4.5MM **Privately Held**
SIC: 2731 Book publishing

(G-11567)
PARACHUTE PUBLISHING LLC
322 8th Ave Ste 702 (10001-6791)
PHONE....................212 337-6743
Arlene West, *Manager*
Joan Waricha,
Jane Stine,
▲ EMP: 30 EST: 1996
SALES (est): 2.9MM **Privately Held**
WEB: www.parachuteproperties.com
SIC: 2731 Books: publishing only

(G-11568)
PARADE PUBLICATIONS INC (DH)
Also Called: Parade Magazine
711 3rd Ave (10017-4014)
PHONE....................212 450-7000
Fax: 212 450-7087
Carlo Vittorini, *CEO*
Brad Dunn, *Editor*
Jo Beddoe, *Vice Pres*
Kevin Craig, *Vice Pres*
Allison White, *Vice Pres*
EMP: 51
SALES (est): 7.2MM
SALES (corp-wide): 322.5MM **Privately Held**
SIC: 2721 Periodicals: publishing only
HQ: The Herald Newspapers Company Inc
220 S Warren St
Syracuse NY 13202
315 470-0011

(G-11569)
PARADIGM SPINE LLC
505 Park Ave Fl 14 (10022-1106)
PHONE....................212 367-7274
Marc Viscigliosi, *CEO*
Gutmar Eisen, *President*
Albert Lee, *Counsel*
Gary Lowery, *Exec VP*
Marci Halevi, *Vice Pres*
EMP: 23
SQ FT: 1,500
SALES (est): 4.7MM **Privately Held**
SIC: 3842 8011 Implants, surgical; offices & clinics of medical doctors

(G-11570)
PARAMOUNT TEXTILES INC
34 Walker St (10013-3514)
PHONE....................212 966-1040
Fax: 212 941-1206
Steven Katz, *CEO*
Estate J Katz, *President*
Ronald Katz, *Vice Pres*
Alan Katz, *Admin Sec*
EMP: 10 EST: 1940
SQ FT: 15,000
SALES (est): 1.2MM **Privately Held**
WEB: www.paramounttextile.com
SIC: 2392 5023 5047 Household furnishings; linens & towels; linens, table; surgical equipment & supplies

(G-11571)
PARENTS GUIDE NETWORK CORP
Also Called: P G Media
419 Park Ave S Rm 505 (10016-8410)
PHONE....................212 213-8840
Fax: 212 447-7734
Steve Elgort, *President*
Donald McDermott, *Editor*
Howard Baum, *Financial Exec*
Samantha Chan, *Assoc Editor*
Rachel Kalina, *Assoc Editor*
EMP: 25
SALES (est): 2.4MM **Privately Held**
WEB: www.parentguidenews.com
SIC: 2721 8351 Magazines: publishing only, not printed on site; child day care services

(G-11572)
PARIJAT JEWELS INC
12 E 46th St Rm 200 (10017-2418)
PHONE....................212 286-2326
Ramesh Vaje, *President*
EMP: 7
SALES (est): 2.5MM **Privately Held**
SIC: 3911 Jewelry, precious metal

(G-11573)
PARIS WEDDING CENTER CORP
45 E Broadway Fl 2 (10002-6804)
PHONE....................212 267-8088
Yuki Lin, *Branch Mgr*
EMP: 22
SALES (corp-wide): 1.5MM **Privately Held**
SIC: 2335 Wedding gowns & dresses
PA: Paris Wedding Center Corp.
42-53 42 55 Main St
Flushing NY 11355
347 368-4085

(G-11574)
PARK WEST JEWELERY INC
565 W End Ave Apt 8b (10024-2734)
PHONE....................646 329-6145
Fax: 212 768-8608
Dale Bearman, *President*
EMP: 6
SQ FT: 900
SALES (est): 490K **Privately Held**
SIC: 3911 Jewelry apparel

(G-11575)
PARKER WARBY RETAIL INC (PA)
Also Called: Warby Parker Eyewear
161 Ave Of The Ave Rm 201 (10013)
PHONE....................646 517-5223
Dave Gilboa, *CEO*
Kirstin Anderson, *Project Mgr*
Janny Wang, *Project Mgr*
Summer Huie, *Opers Spvr*
Shayna Amato, *Sales Mgr*
▲ EMP: 28
SALES (est): 17.3MM **Privately Held**
SIC: 3851 5995 Eyeglasses, lenses & frames; optical goods stores

(G-11576)
PARLOR LABS INC
515 W 19th St (10011-2872)
PHONE....................646 217-0918
Alexander Selkirk, *President*
EMP: 5
SALES (est): 214.5K **Privately Held**
SIC: 7372 Educational computer software

(G-11577)
PASABAHCE USA
41 Madison Ave Fl 7 (10010-2202)
PHONE....................212 683-1600
Neil M Orzeck, *Manager*
Martin Anderson, *Director*
▲ EMP: 4
SALES (est): 25MM **Privately Held**
SIC: 3229 Art, decorative & novelty glassware

(G-11578)
PAT & ROSE DRESS INC
327 W 36th St Rm 3a (10018-7014)
PHONE....................212 279-1357
Fax: 212 279-1413
Rosalia Panebianco, *President*
Maria Milanova, *Bookkeeper*
Pat Capolupo, *Manager*
EMP: 60
SQ FT: 5,000
SALES (est): 3.6MM **Privately Held**
SIC: 2335 2331 2337 2339 Women's, juniors' & misses' dresses; blouses, women's & juniors': made from purchased material; skirts, separate: women's, misses' & juniors'; women's & misses' outerwear; men's & boys' trousers & slacks; men's & boys' suits & coats

(G-11579)
PATMIAN LLC
655 Madison Ave Fl 24 (10065-8043)
PHONE....................212 758-0770
George Botis, *Chairman*
EMP: 350
SALES (est): 22.2MM **Privately Held**
SIC: 3089 3544 Plastic processing; injection molded finished plastic products; special dies, tools, jigs & fixtures

(G-11580)
PATRA LTD
Stenay
318 W 39th St Fl 2 (10018-1496)
PHONE....................212 764-6575
George Beck, *Manager*
Paul Kitos, *Manager*
EMP: 10
SALES (corp-wide): 8.1MM **Privately Held**
SIC: 2335 Gowns, formal
PA: Patra Ltd.
318 W 39th St
New York NY 10018
212 764-6575

(G-11581)
PATRA LTD
Also Called: La Nuit Collection
318 W 39th St (10018-1407)
PHONE....................212 764-6575
Fax: 212 768-7862
Pat Dipietroantonio, *President*
EMP: 10
SALES (corp-wide): 8.1MM **Privately Held**
SIC: 2335 Women's, juniors' & misses' dresses
PA: Patra Ltd.
318 W 39th St
New York NY 10018
212 764-6575

(G-11582)
PATRA LTD (PA)
318 W 39th St (10018-1407)
PHONE....................212 764-6575
Fax: 212 268-6838
Paquale Di Pietrantonio, *CEO*
Pat Di Pietrantonio, *President*
Timothy M Sinatro, *Treasurer*
George C Beck, *Admin Sec*
▲ EMP: 20
SQ FT: 25,000
SALES (est): 8.1MM **Privately Held**
SIC: 2335 Gowns, formal

(G-11583)
PATRON TECHNOLOGY INC
850 7th Ave Ste 704 (10019-5230)
PHONE....................212 271-4328
Eugene Carr, *President*
Lily Traub, *President*
Lorna Dolci, *General Mgr*
Robert Friend, *Vice Pres*
Nathan Anderson, *Opers Staff*
EMP: 7
SQ FT: 800
SALES (est): 1.1MM **Privately Held**
WEB: www.patrontech.com
SIC: 7372 Prepackaged software

(G-11584)
PAUL DAVID ENTERPRISES INC
19 W 34th St Rm 1018 (10001-3006)
PHONE....................646 667-5530
Daniel Korolev, *Vice Pres*
EMP: 9 EST: 2013
SALES (est): 323.8K **Privately Held**
SIC: 2431 Jalousies, glass, wood frame

(G-11585)
PAULA DORF COSMETICS INC
850 7th Ave Ste 801 (10019-5446)
PHONE....................212 582-0073
Sandy Dekovnick, *CEO*
Sandy De Kovnick, *CEO*
Paula Dorf, *President*
Lindsay Santlas, *Manager*
▲ EMP: 30
SALES (est): 4.2MM **Privately Held**
WEB: www.pauladorf.com
SIC: 2844 5122 Toilet preparations; cosmetics, perfumes & hair products

(G-11586)
PAULA VARSALONA LTD
552 Fashion Ave Rm 602 (10018-3239)
PHONE....................212 570-9100
Fax: 212 869-9566
Paula Varsalona, *President*
EMP: 15
SQ FT: 5,000
SALES (est): 1.3MM **Privately Held**
WEB: www.paulavarsalona.com
SIC: 2335 2396 Wedding gowns & dresses; veils & veiling: bridal, funeral, etc.

(G-11587)
PAVANA USA INC
10 W 33rd Rm 408 (10001-3306)
P.O. Box 237191 (10023-0033)
PHONE....................646 833-8811
Avisha Uttamchandani, *President*
Bhavik Patel, *Accountant*
▲ EMP: 5
SALES (est): 905.7K **Privately Held**
SIC: 3873 Watches, clocks, watchcases & parts

(G-11588)
PEAK HOLDINGS LLC
345 Park Ave Fl 30 (10154-0004)
PHONE....................212 583-5000
Brian Jones, *Principal*
EMP: 5262
SALES (est): 228.8MM **Privately Held**
SIC: 2038 2092 2099 2045 Frozen specialties; breakfasts, frozen & packaged; pizza, frozen; waffles, frozen; prepared fish or other seafood cakes & sticks; pancake syrup, blended & mixed; cake flour: from purchased flour; bread & bread type roll mixes: from purchased flour; pancake mixes, prepared: from purchased flour

(G-11589)
PEARL ERWIN INC (PA)
389 5th Ave Fl 9 (10016-3352)
PHONE....................212 889-7410
Fax: 212 889-3076
Erwin Pearl, *President*
Peter Indiveri, *Senior VP*
Michael Elswit, *Vice Pres*
Joel Weinstein, *CFO*
Anita Rosenberg, *Manager*
EMP: 30 EST: 1954
SALES (est): 41.5MM **Privately Held**
SIC: 3961 3911 Costume jewelry; jewelry, precious metal

(G-11590)
PEARL ERWIN INC
300 Madison Ave Frnt 1 (10017-6250)
PHONE....................212 883-0650
Erwin Pearl, *President*
EMP: 27
SALES (corp-wide): 41.5MM **Privately Held**
SIC: 3961 Costume jewelry
PA: Pearl Erwin Inc
389 5th Ave Fl 9
New York NY 10016
212 889-7410

(G-11591)
PEARSON EDUCATION INC
1185 Avenue Of The Americ (10036-2601)
PHONE....................212 782-3337
EMP: 16

▲ = Import ▼ = Export
◆ = Import/Export

GEOGRAPHIC SECTION
New York - New York County (G-11613)

SALES (corp-wide): 6.7B Privately Held
WEB: www.phgenit.com
SIC: 2731 Book publishing
HQ: Pearson Education, Inc.
  1 Lake St
  Upper Saddle River NJ 07458
  201 236-7000

(G-11592)
PEARSON EDUCATION INC
375 Hudson St (10014-3658)
PHONE.................................212 366-2000
Dennis Swaim, *Adv Dir*
Tom Altier, *Branch Mgr*
Sean Stowers, *Director*
EMP: 27
SALES (corp-wide): 7.7B Privately Held
WEB: www.phgenit.com
SIC: 2731 Book publishing
HQ: Pearson Education, Inc.
  1 Lake St
  Upper Saddle River NJ 07458
  201 236-7000

(G-11593)
PEARSON EDUCATION HOLDINGS INC (HQ)
330 Hudson St Fl 9 (10013-1048)
PHONE.................................201 236-6716
Will Ethridge, *President*
Helena Hung, *General Mgr*
Jim Tognolini, *Managing Dir*
Wendy Craven, *Editor*
Paul Crockett, *Editor*
◆ EMP: 2000 EST: 1998
SQ FT: 475,000
SALES (est): 2.1B
SALES (corp-wide): 6.7B Privately Held
WEB: www.pearsoned.com
SIC: 2731 Textbooks: publishing & printing
PA: Pearson Plc
  Shell Mex House
  London WC2R
  207 010-2000

(G-11594)
PEARSON INC (HQ)
330 Hudson St Fl 9 (10013-1048)
PHONE.................................212 641-2400
John Fallon, *CEO*
Fred Becker, *General Mgr*
Boone Novy, *Principal*
Glen Moreno, *Chairman*
Christopher Howard, *Business Mgr*
▼ EMP: 58
SALES (est): 2.6B
SALES (corp-wide): 6.7B Privately Held
SIC: 2711 2731 Newspapers; books: publishing & printing; textbooks: publishing & printing
PA: Pearson Plc
  Shell Mex House
  London WC2R
  207 010-2000

(G-11595)
PEARSON LONGMAN LLC
51 Madison Ave Fl 27 (10010-1609)
PHONE.................................917 981-2200
Bruce Styron, *Facilities Mgr*
Roth Wilkofsky, *Manager*
EMP: 120
SALES (corp-wide): 7.7B Privately Held
SIC: 2731 Books: publishing & printing
HQ: Pearson Longman Llc
  10 Bank St Ste 1030
  White Plains NY 10606
  212 641-2400

(G-11596)
PEER INTERNATIONAL CORP (HQ)
Also Called: 3239603400 La Head Quarters
250 W 57th St Ste 820 (10107-0814)
PHONE.................................212 265-3910
Ralph Peer II, *President*
Elizabeth W Peer, *Vice Pres*
Cecile Russo, *Vice Pres*
Kathryn Spanberger, *Vice Pres*
Todd Vunderink, *Vice Pres*
▲ EMP: 30
SQ FT: 11,448

SALES (est): 2.9MM
SALES (corp-wide): 10MM Privately Held
SIC: 2741 Music books: publishing only, not printed on site
PA: Southern Music Publishing Co., Inc.
  810 7th Ave Fl 36
  New York NY 10019
  212 265-3910

(G-11597)
PEER-SOUTHERN PRODUCTIONS INC (HQ)
250 W 57th St (10107-0001)
PHONE.................................212 265-3910
Ralph Peer II, *President*
Mariano Hegi, *Marketing Staff*
Marilyn La Vine, *Admin Sec*
EMP: 30 EST: 1961
SALES (est): 1.7MM
SALES (corp-wide): 10MM Privately Held
SIC: 3652 Master records or tapes, preparation of
PA: Southern Music Publishing Co., Inc.
  810 7th Ave Fl 36
  New York NY 10019
  212 265-3910

(G-11598)
PEERMUSIC III LTD (PA)
250 W 57th St Ste 820 (10107-0814)
PHONE.................................212 265-3910
EMP: 6 EST: 2013
SALES (est): 1.8MM Privately Held
SIC: 2741 Music books: publishing only, not printed on site

(G-11599)
PEERMUSIC LTD (HQ)
250 W 57th St Ste 820 (10107-0814)
PHONE.................................212 265-3910
Ralph Peer II, *President*
Elizabeth W Peer, *Vice Pres*
Cecile Russo, *Vice Pres*
Katheryn Spanberger, *Vice Pres*
EMP: 12
SQ FT: 1,000
SALES (est): 5MM
SALES (corp-wide): 10MM Privately Held
WEB: www.digitalpressure.com
SIC: 2741 7922 Music books: publishing only, not printed on site; theatrical producers & services
PA: Southern Music Publishing Co., Inc.
  810 7th Ave Fl 36
  New York NY 10019
  212 265-3910

(G-11600)
PEFIN TECHNOLOGIES LLC
39 W 32nd St Rm 1500 (10001-3841)
PHONE.................................917 715-3720
Ramya Joseph, *CEO*
EMP: 10
SALES (est): 590K Privately Held
SIC: 7372 Application computer software

(G-11601)
PEGASYSTEMS INC
1120 Ave Of The Americas (10036-6700)
PHONE.................................212 626-6550
Fax: 212 626-6966
Beth Saperstein, *Branch Mgr*
EMP: 25
SALES (corp-wide): 682.7MM Publicly Held
WEB: www.pega.com
SIC: 7372 7379 Business oriented computer software; computer related consulting services
PA: Pegasystems Inc.
  1 Rogers St
  Cambridge MA 02142
  617 374-9600

(G-11602)
PELOTON INTERACTIVE INC
158 W 27th St Fl 4 (10001-6216)
PHONE.................................818 571-7236
John Foley, *CEO*
Graham Stanton, *President*
Thomas Cortese, *COO*
Ben Holstein, *Vice Pres*
Johnny Jiang, *Vice Pres*

▲ EMP: 50
SQ FT: 9,000
SALES (est): 8.8MM Privately Held
SIC: 3949 Gymnasium equipment
PA: Peloton Land Solutions, Inc.
  5751 Kroger Dr Ste 185
  Fort Worth TX 76244
  817 562-3350

(G-11603)
PENGUIN RANDOM HOUSE LLC
1540 Broadway (10036-4039)
PHONE.................................212 782-1000
Markus Dohle, *CEO*
Pankaj Makkar, *Managing Dir*
Mallory Loehr, *Editor*
Krista Marino, *Editor*
Jurand Honisch, *Senior VP*
EMP: 25
SALES (corp-wide): 18.4B Privately Held
SIC: 2731 Book publishing
HQ: Penguin Random House Llc
  1745 Broadway
  New York NY 10019
  212 782-9000

(G-11604)
PENGUIN RANDOM HOUSE LLC (HQ)
1745 Broadway (10019-4640)
PHONE.................................212 782-9000
Markus Dohle, *CEO*
Madeline McIntosh, *President*
Shasta Clinch, *Editor*
Julia Maguire, *Editor*
Lauren Shakely, *Senior VP*
EMP: 277
SALES (est): 1.5B
SALES (corp-wide): 18.4B Privately Held
SIC: 2731 Books: publishing only
PA: Bertelsmann Se & Co. Kgaa
  Carl-Bertelsmann-Str. 270
  Gutersloh 33335
  524 180-0

(G-11605)
PENGUIN RANDOM HOUSE LLC
1745 Broadway Frnt 3 (10019-4641)
PHONE.................................212 572-6162
Markus Dohle, *CEO*
EMP: 513
SALES (corp-wide): 18.4B Privately Held
SIC: 2731 5942 Books: publishing only; book stores
HQ: Penguin Random House Llc
  1745 Broadway
  New York NY 10019
  212 782-9000

(G-11606)
PENGUIN RANDOM HOUSE LLC
1745 Broadway Frnt 3 (10019-4641)
PHONE.................................212 782-9000
Markus Dohle, *CEO*
EMP: 1000
SALES (corp-wide): 18.4B Privately Held
SIC: 2731 Books: publishing only
HQ: Penguin Random House Llc
  1745 Broadway
  New York NY 10019
  212 782-9000

(G-11607)
PENHOUSE MEDIA GROUP INC (PA)
11 Penn Plz Fl 12 (10001-2027)
PHONE.................................212 702-6000
Fax: 212 702-6262
John Prebich, *President*
Eric Danville, *Editor*
Claude Bertin, *Exec VP*
Nina Guccione, *Exec VP*
Hal Halpner, *Exec VP*
▲ EMP: 150
SALES (est): 11.5MM Privately Held
SIC: 2721 5999 6512 6794 Magazines: publishing only, not printed on site; art dealers; commercial & industrial building operation; copyright buying & licensing

(G-11608)
PENTON MEDIA INC (DH)
Also Called: Penton Media - Aviation Week
1166 Avenue Of The Americ (10036-2743)
PHONE.................................212 204-4200
Fax: 212 206-3622

David Kieselstein, *Ch of Bd*
Paul Miller, *President*
Francine Brasseur, *Publisher*
Bill Rodman, *Publisher*
Ellen Romanow, *Managing Dir*
▲ EMP: 500 EST: 1976
SQ FT: 189,000
SALES (est): 234.8MM
SALES (corp-wide): 348.9MM Privately Held
WEB: www.penton.com
SIC: 2721 7389 7313 7375 Periodicals; periodicals: publishing & printing; magazines: publishing & printing; advertising, promotional & trade show services; printed media advertising representatives; on-line data base information retrieval
HQ: Penton Business Media, Inc.
  9800 Metcalf Ave
  Shawnee Mission KS 66212
  913 341-1300

(G-11609)
PENTON MEDIA INC
Also Called: Used Equipment Directory
1166 Avenue Of The Americ (10036-2743)
PHONE.................................212 204-4200
James Mack, *Principal*
Angela Daunis, *Editor*
Olivia Labarre, *Editor*
Andrew Zvonek, *Personnel Exec*
Dan Elm, *Accounts Exec*
EMP: 9
SALES (corp-wide): 348.9MM Privately Held
WEB: www.penton.com
SIC: 2721 Magazines: publishing & printing
HQ: Penton Media, Inc.
  1166 Avenue Of The Americ
  New York NY 10036
  212 204-4200

(G-11610)
PEPE CREATIONS INC
2 W 45th St Ste 1003 (10036-4253)
PHONE.................................212 391-1514
Frank Gomez, *President*
EMP: 12
SALES: 1.5MM Privately Held
WEB: www.pepecreations.com
SIC: 3961 Costume jewelry

(G-11611)
PEPSI-COLA BOTTLING CO NY INC
1 Pepsi Way (10016)
P.O. Box 14035 (10249-4035)
PHONE.................................718 392-1000
David Burnette, *Director*
EMP: 12
SALES (corp-wide): 219.3MM Privately Held
SIC: 2087 Flavoring extracts & syrups
PA: Pepsi-Cola Bottling Company Of New York, Inc.
  11402 15th Ave Ste 5
  College Point NY 11356
  718 392-1000

(G-11612)
PER ANNUM INC
555 8th Ave Rm 202 (10018-4386)
PHONE.................................212 647-8700
Fax: 212 647-8716
Alicia Settle, *President*
Tom Settle, *Corp Secy*
Lauren Romero, *Sls & Mktg Exec*
EMP: 25
SQ FT: 14,000
SALES (est): 1.8MM Privately Held
WEB: www.perannum.com
SIC: 2741 Miscellaneous publishing

(G-11613)
PERCEPTIVE PIXEL INC (HQ)
641 Avenue Of The Ste 7 (10011)
PHONE.................................701 367-5845
Jefferson Y Han, *CEO*
Fred Allman, *Vice Pres*
Diane Carlson, *Vice Pres*
Bob Pette, *Vice Pres*
Natalie Vien, *Project Mgr*
EMP: 32

New York - New York County (G-11614) — GEOGRAPHIC SECTION

SALES (est): 10.7MM
SALES (corp-wide): 85.3B **Publicly Held**
WEB: www.perceptivepixel.com
SIC: 3577 Computer peripheral equipment
PA: Microsoft Corporation
   1 Microsoft Way
   Redmond WA 98052
   425 882-8080

(G-11614)
PEREGRINE INDUSTRIES INC
40 Wall St (10005-1304)
PHONE.....................631 838-2870
Richard Rubin, *CEO*
EMP: 5
SALES (est): 513K
SALES (corp-wide): 572.3K **Privately Held**
SIC: 3569 Filters
PA: Dolomite Holdings Ltd
   7 Jabotinsky
   Ramat Gan 52520
   488 100-21

(G-11615)
PERFUME AMERICANA INC (PA)
Also Called: Perfume Americana Wholesale
1216 Broadway (10001-4301)
PHONE.....................212 683-8029
Fax: 212 779-2383
Mukstar Cheema, *Principal*
▲ EMP: 8
SALES (est): 5.2MM **Privately Held**
SIC: 2844 Perfumes & colognes

(G-11616)
PERFUME AMRCANA WHLESALERS INC
11 W 30th St Betwe Broad Between (10001)
PHONE.....................212 683-8029
Mukhtar S Cheema, *President*
Bharati Cheema, *President*
Oscar Singh, *Sales Mgr*
▼ EMP: 10
SALES (est): 1.5MM **Privately Held**
SIC: 2844 Perfumes & colognes

(G-11617)
PERFUMERS WORKSHOP INTL LTD (PA)
350 7th Ave Rm 802 (10001-1941)
PHONE.....................212 644-8950
Donald G Bauchner, *President*
Steven Levenson, *Exec VP*
▲ EMP: 8
SQ FT: 1,800
SALES (est): 1MM **Privately Held**
SIC: 2844 Perfumes & colognes

(G-11618)
PERIMONDO LLC
331 W 84th St Apt 2 (10024-4215)
P.O. Box 200 (10024-0200)
PHONE.....................212 749-0721
Matthias Rebmann, *Mng Member*
EMP: 6
SALES (est): 814.8K **Privately Held**
SIC: 2074 Lecithin, cottonseed

(G-11619)
PERMA GLOW LTD INC
48 W 48th St Ste 301 (10036-1713)
PHONE.....................212 575-9677
Fax: 212 575-9733
Richard Scandaglia, *President*
Joseph Scandaglia, *President*
▲ EMP: 15 EST: 1972
SQ FT: 2,000
SALES (est): 1.6MM **Privately Held**
SIC: 3915 Jewel cutting, drilling, polishing, recutting or setting

(G-11620)
PERMIT FASHION GROUP INC
135 W 36th St Fl 16 (10018-7172)
PHONE.....................212 912-0988
Zhouping Zheng, *CEO*
▲ EMP: 8 EST: 2012
SALES (est): 870K **Privately Held**
SIC: 2331 2337 2339 Blouses, women's & juniors': made from purchased material; skirts, separate: women's, misses' & juniors'; jackets & vests, except fur & leather: women's; slacks: women's, misses' & juniors'

(G-11621)
PERNOD RICARD USA LLC (DH)
250 Park Ave Ste 17a (10177-1702)
PHONE.....................914 848-4800
Fax: 914 848-4777
Bryan Fry, *President*
Lauren Simkin, *General Mgr*
Philippe Coutin, *Managing Dir*
Filip Slowinski, *Area Mgr*
Gopi Nambiar, *Exec VP*
◆ EMP: 100
SALES (est): 472.9MM
SALES (corp-wide): 156.6MM **Privately Held**
WEB: www.pernod-ricard-usa.com
SIC: 2085 Distilled & blended liquors
HQ: Pernod Ricard North America
   12 Place Des Etats Unis
   Paris 75116
   141 004-100

(G-11622)
PERRY ELLIS INTERNATIONAL INC
1126 Avenue Of The Americ (10036-6708)
PHONE.....................212 536-5400
Fax: 212 354-3614
Jennifer Bollinger, *Vice Pres*
John Griffin, *Branch Mgr*
Amanda Apple, *Director*
EMP: 12
SALES (corp-wide): 899.5MM **Publicly Held**
SIC: 2321 2325 6794 Men's & boys' furnishings; sport shirts, men's & boys': from purchased materials; polo shirts, men's & boys': made from purchased materials; men's & boys' dress shirts; men's & boys' trousers & slacks; trousers, dress (separate): men's, youths' & boys'; shorts (outerwear): men's, youths' & boys'; franchises, selling or licensing
PA: Perry Ellis International Inc
   3000 Nw 107th Ave
   Doral FL 33172
   305 592-2830

(G-11623)
PERRY ELLIS INTERNATIONAL INC
42 W 39th St Fl 4 (10018-3841)
PHONE.....................212 536-5499
Saundra James, *Vice Pres*
Hope Wright, *VP Finance*
Kevin Kiley, *Branch Mgr*
Angela Hyndman, *Manager*
EMP: 11
SALES (corp-wide): 889.9MM **Publicly Held**
WEB: www.cubabera.com
SIC: 2339 Women's & misses' outerwear
PA: Perry Ellis International Inc
   3000 Nw 107th Ave
   Doral FL 33172
   305 592-2830

(G-11624)
PERRY ELLIS MENSWEAR LLC (HQ)
Also Called: Perry Ellis America
1120 Ave Of The Americas (10036-6700)
PHONE.....................212 221-7500
Doug Jakubowski, *Ch of Bd*
Awadhesh K Sinha, *COO*
Elliot M Lavigne, *Exec VP*
Brian Root, *Senior VP*
Felice Schulaner, *Senior VP*
◆ EMP: 150 EST: 1893
SQ FT: 27,000
SALES (est): 75.2MM
SALES (corp-wide): 899.5MM **Publicly Held**
WEB: www.perryellis.com
SIC: 2325 5611 2321 2387 Slacks, dress: men's, youths' & boys'; jeans: men's, youths' & boys'; men's & boys' clothing stores; men's & boys' furnishings; apparel belts; suspenders; neckties, men's & boys': made from purchased materials
PA: Perry Ellis International Inc
   3000 Nw 107th Ave
   Doral FL 33172
   305 592-2830

(G-11625)
PERRY STREET SOFTWARE INC
489 5th Ave Rm 2900 (10017-6115)
PHONE.....................415 935-1429
John Skandros, *President*
Eric Silverberg, *Admin Sec*
EMP: 5 EST: 2011
SALES (est): 430K **Privately Held**
SIC: 7372 Prepackaged software

(G-11626)
PERSISTENT SYSTEMS LLC
303 5th Ave Rm 306 (10016-6635)
PHONE.....................212 561-5895
Herbert B Rubens, *CEO*
Adrien Robenhymer, *Vice Pres*
Will Haggerty, *Opers Staff*
Ruben Neira, *Production*
Michael Landry, *Engineer*
EMP: 50
SQ FT: 5,000
SALES (est): 16.8MM **Privately Held**
SIC: 3663 Radio broadcasting & communications equipment

(G-11627)
PERSONAL ALARM SEC SYSTEMS
379 5th Ave Fl 3 (10016-3324)
PHONE.....................212 448-1944
Leonard Meyerson, *President*
Sam Minzer, *Vice Pres*
Richard Burton, *Sales Mgr*
Jay Black, *Office Mgr*
EMP: 12
SQ FT: 3,000
SALES (est): 1.2MM **Privately Held**
SIC: 3669 5999 Emergency alarms; alarm signal systems

(G-11628)
PESSELNIK & COHEN INC
82 Bowery Unit 10 (10013-4656)
PHONE.....................212 925-0287
Salvatore Diadema, *President*
Stephen De Angelo, *Admin Sec*
EMP: 7
SALES (est): 550K **Privately Held**
SIC: 3911 5094 Jewelry, precious metal; jewelry; watches & parts

(G-11629)
PET PROTEINS LLC
347 W 36th St Rm 1204 (10018-6480)
PHONE.....................888 293-1029
Steven Mendal,
Jayme Mendal,
Mark Mendal,
◆ EMP: 7
SQ FT: 500
SALES: 1MM **Privately Held**
SIC: 2047 Dog & cat food

(G-11630)
PETER ATMAN INC
6 E 45th St Rm 1100 (10017-2475)
PHONE.....................212 644-3888
Fax: 212 644-8882
Peter Philipakos, *Ch of Bd*
Peter Phillips, *President*
EMP: 10
SALES (est): 1.3MM **Privately Held**
WEB: www.peteratman.com
SIC: 3911 5944 Jewelry, precious metal; jewelry, precious stones & precious metals

(G-11631)
PETER LANG PUBLISHING INC (DH)
29 Broadway Rm 1800 (10006-3221)
PHONE.....................212 647-7700
Fax: 212 647-7707
Michelle Salyga, *Editor*
Sophie Appel, *Opers Staff*
Shergill Kelly, *Sales Staff*
Patricia Mulrane, *Marketing Staff*
Christopher Myers, *Director*
EMP: 12
SQ FT: 8,000
SALES (est): 1.1MM
SALES (corp-wide): 274.9K **Privately Held**
WEB: www.peterlangusa.com
SIC: 2731 Textbooks: publishing only, not printed on site
HQ: Peter Lang Ag Internationaler Verlag Der Wissenschaften
   Wabernstrasse 40
   Bern BE 3007
   313 061-717

(G-11632)
PETER MAYER PUBLISHERS INC
Also Called: Overlook Press, The
141 Wooster St Fl 4 (10012-3163)
PHONE.....................212 673-2210
Peter Mayer, *President*
George Davidson, *Production*
Maura Diamond, *Manager*
▲ EMP: 13
SQ FT: 5,000
SALES: 1MM **Privately Held**
WEB: www.overlookpress.com
SIC: 2731 Books: publishing only

(G-11633)
PETER THOMAS ROTH LABS LLC (PA)
460 Park Ave Fl 16 (10022-1829)
PHONE.....................212 581-5800
Peter Thomasroth, *Vice Pres*
June Jacobs,
June Jacbos,
Peter Roth,
▲ EMP: 40
SQ FT: 5,500
SALES (est): 27.1MM **Privately Held**
SIC: 2844 Cosmetic preparations

(G-11634)
PEXIP INC (HQ)
240 W 35th St Ste 1002 (10001-2506)
PHONE.....................703 338-3544
Adam Marlin, *Vice Pres*
Richard Coder, *Vice Pres*
Matt Hansen, *VP Opers*
EMP: 32 EST: 2012
SQ FT: 3,000
SALES (est): 3MM
SALES (corp-wide): 4.7MM **Privately Held**
SIC: 7372 Application computer software

(G-11635)
PFIZER HCP CORPORATION (HQ)
235 E 42nd St (10017-5703)
PHONE.....................212 733-2323
Fax: 212 573-7851
Ian C Read, *CEO*
Geno Germano, *President*
Frank D'Amelio, *Exec VP*
Rady Johnson, *Exec VP*
Freda C Lewis-Hall, *Exec VP*
▲ EMP: 12
SALES (est): 4.5MM
SALES (corp-wide): 48.8B **Publicly Held**
WEB: www.pfizer.com
SIC: 2834 Pharmaceutical preparations
PA: Pfizer Inc.
   235 E 42nd St
   New York NY 10017
   212 733-2323

(G-11636)
PFIZER INC (PA)
235 E 42nd St (10017-5703)
PHONE.....................212 733-2323
Fax: 212 309-0896
Ian C Read, *Ch of Bd*
Shaileen English, *Exec VP*
Karine Gravel, *Exec VP*
Charles H Hill III, *Exec VP*
Douglas M Lankler, *Exec VP*
◆ EMP: 2500 EST: 1942
SALES: 48.8B **Publicly Held**
WEB: www.pfizer.com
SIC: 2834 2833 Pharmaceutical preparations; drugs acting on the cardiovascular system, except diagnostic; drugs affecting parasitic & infective diseases; veterinary pharmaceutical preparations; antibiotics

▲ = Import ▼ = Export
◆ = Import/Export

(G-11637)
PFIZER INC
150 E 42nd St Bsmt 2 (10017-5642)
PHONE.................................937 746-3603
Daniel Reardon, *Principal*
Dianbo Cao, *Project Mgr*
Maritza Rosener, *Hum Res Coord*
Netu Verma, *Hum Res Coord*
Brendan Sheehan, *Corp Counsel*
EMP: 214
SALES (corp-wide): 48.8B **Publicly Held**
SIC: 2834 Pharmaceutical preparations
PA: Pfizer Inc.
   235 E 42nd St
   New York NY 10017
   212 733-2323

(G-11638)
PFIZER INC
150 E 42nd St Bsmt 2 (10017-5642)
PHONE.................................212 733-6276
Hugh Oconnor, *Vice Pres*
Macdara Lynch, *Plant Mgr*
Anthony P Carcich, *Engineer*
Delano F Randolph, *Controller*
William Waldin, *Persnl Mgr*
EMP: 70
SALES (corp-wide): 48.8B **Publicly Held**
WEB: www.pfizer.com
SIC: 2834 Pharmaceutical preparations
PA: Pfizer Inc.
   235 E 42nd St
   New York NY 10017
   212 733-2323

(G-11639)
PFIZER INC
235 E 42nd St (10017-5703)
PHONE.................................804 257-2000
Lucile Callahan, *President*
Michael Mead, *Vice Pres*
Robert Hunter, *VP Opers*
EMP: 146
SALES (corp-wide): 48.8B **Publicly Held**
WEB: www.wyeth.com
SIC: 2834 Pharmaceutical preparations
PA: Pfizer Inc.
   235 E 42nd St
   New York NY 10017
   212 733-2323

(G-11640)
PFIZER INC
235 E 42nd St (10017-5703)
PHONE.................................212 733-2323
EMP: 146
SALES (corp-wide): 48.8B **Publicly Held**
SIC: 2834 Pharmaceutical preparations
PA: Pfizer Inc.
   235 E 42nd St
   New York NY 10017
   212 733-2323

(G-11641)
PFIZER OVERSEAS LLC
235 E 42nd St (10017-5703)
PHONE.................................212 733-2323
Ian C Read, *Ch of Bd*
Mikael Dolsten, *President*
Frank D'Amelio, *Exec VP*
Chuck Hill, *Exec VP*
Rady Johnson, *Exec VP*
EMP: 5
SALES (est): 364K
SALES (corp-wide): 48.8B **Publicly Held**
SIC: 2834 2833 Pharmaceutical preparations; antibiotics
PA: Pfizer Inc.
   235 E 42nd St
   New York NY 10017
   212 733-2323

(G-11642)
PGS MILLWORK INC (PA)
535 8th Ave Rm 20n (10018-4493)
PHONE.................................212 244-6610
Fax: 212 244-0587
Thomas Spurge, *CEO*
Scott Manchester, *VP Opers*
David Zale, *Engineer*
Nick Ference, *Marketing Staff*
Peggy Moon, *Manager*
▲ **EMP:** 65
SQ FT: 44,000
SALES (est): 12.2MM **Privately Held**
WEB: www.pgsmillwork.com
SIC: 2431 2434 2499 5211 Millwork; wood kitchen cabinets; decorative wood & woodwork; millwork & lumber

(G-11643)
PHAIDON PRESS INC
65 Bleecker St Fl 8 (10012-2420)
PHONE.................................212 652-5400
Fax: 212 652-5410
Keith Fox, *CEO*
Andrew Price, *Vice Pres*
James Clibborn, *Sales Staff*
Chris Conti, *Sales Staff*
James Whittaker, *Sales Executive*
▲ **EMP:** 20
SALES (est): 2.6MM
SALES (corp-wide): 399.9K **Privately Held**
SIC: 2731 Book publishing
HQ: Phaidon Press Limited
   Regent's Wharf
   London

(G-11644)
PHC RESTORATION HOLDINGS LLC
Also Called: Philip Crangi
147 W 29th St Fl 4 (10001-5107)
PHONE.................................212 643-0517
Courtney Crangi, *Mng Member*
Jeffry Aronsson,
Philip Crangi,
EMP: 10
SQ FT: 2,000
SALES: 1.5MM **Privately Held**
SIC: 3911 Jewelry, precious metal
PA: Phc Restoration, Inc.
   147 W 29th St Ste 4e
   New York NY 10001
   212 643-0517

(G-11645)
PHILIP MORRIS INTL INC (PA)
120 Park Ave Fl 6 (10017-5592)
PHONE.................................917 663-2000
Fax: 212 907-5355
Andre Calantzopoulos, *CEO*
Louis C Camilleri, *Ch of Bd*
Drago Azinovic, *President*
Frederic De Wilde, *President*
Martin King, *President*
◆ **EMP:** 102
SALES: 73.9B **Publicly Held**
SIC: 2111 Cigarettes

(G-11646)
PHILIPP PLEIN MADISON AVE LLC
Also Called: Philipp Plein North America
625 Madison Ave (10022-1801)
PHONE.................................212 644-3304
Grazziano De Boni, *CEO*
Palma Settini, *Asst Treas*
▲ **EMP:** 14
SALES (est): 715.2K **Privately Held**
SIC: 2311 2337 Coats, overcoats & vests; formal jackets, men's & youths': from purchased materials; suits: women's, misses' & juniors'
PA: Philipp Plein International Ag
   Via Pietro Capelli 18
   Lugano TI
   919 703-933

(G-11647)
PHILIPS LIGHTING N AMER CORP
267 5th Ave (10016-7503)
PHONE.................................646 265-7170
Jeffrey Cassis, *CEO*
Leverda Wallace, *Surgery Dir*
EMP: 190 **Privately Held**
SIC: 3646 Commercial indusl & institutional electric lighting fixtures
HQ: Philips Lighting North America Corporation
   3 Burlington Woods Dr # 4
   Burlington MA 01803
   617 423-9999

(G-11648)
PHILLIFOX MUSIC
239 W 145th St Apt 2g (10039-4002)
PHONE.................................646 260-9300
Mitzi Jones, *Owner*
EMP: 10
SALES (est): 370K **Privately Held**
SIC: 2741 Miscellaneous publishing

(G-11649)
PHILLIPS-VAN HEUSEN EUROPE
Also Called: Pvh Europe
200 Madison Ave Bsmt 1 (10016-3913)
PHONE.................................212 381-3500
Ellen Constantinides, *President*
Dominic Catalfamo, *Vice Pres*
Marcela Manubens, *Vice Pres*
Carlos Heredia, *Project Mgr*
Richard Alfonso, *Technical Mgr*
EMP: 12
SALES: 20MM
SALES (corp-wide): 8B **Publicly Held**
SIC: 2321 2331 2253 3143 Men's & boys' dress shirts; blouses, women's & juniors': made from purchased material; sweaters & sweater coats, knit; men's footwear, except athletic; ready-to-wear apparel, women's; men's & boys' clothing stores
PA: Pvh Corp.
   200 Madison Ave Bsmt 1
   New York NY 10016
   212 381-3500

(G-11650)
PHOEBE COMPANY LLC
Also Called: Kay Unger
230 W 38th St Fl 11 (10018-9053)
PHONE.................................212 302-5556
Fax: 212 302-5965
Rob Fineberg, *Mng Member*
Richard Honig,
▲ **EMP:** 55
SQ FT: 8,000
SALES (est): 4.6MM **Privately Held**
SIC: 2335 Women's, juniors' & misses' dresses

(G-11651)
PHOENIX RIBBON CO INC
20 W 36th St Fl 7 (10018-8086)
PHONE.................................212 239-0155
Fax: 212 268-1897
Irving Besterman, *President*
Anne Besterman, *Treasurer*
Astill Matt, *Manager*
▲ **EMP:** 8
SQ FT: 6,500
SALES (est): 660.9K **Privately Held**
SIC: 2396 Ribbons & bows, cut & sewed

(G-11652)
PHOENIX USA LLC
315 W 33rd St Apt 30h (10001-2795)
PHONE.................................646 351-6598
Roger Garcia,
▲ **EMP:** 2
SALES (est): 5MM **Privately Held**
SIC: 2211 7389 Apparel & outerwear fabrics, cotton;

(G-11653)
PHOENIX VENTURE FUND LLC
70 E 55th St Fl 10 (10022-3334)
PHONE.................................212 759-1909
Philip S Sassower, *Ch of Bd*
EMP: 21
SALES (est): 1.8MM **Privately Held**
SIC: 3577 Computer peripheral equipment

(G-11654)
PHREESIA NEW YORK
432 Park Ave S Fl 12 (10016-8013)
PHONE.................................888 654-7473
Chaim Indig, *CEO*
Michael Davidoff, *Vice Pres*
Evan Roberts, *Vice Pres*
Thomas Altier, *CFO*
EMP: 275
SQ FT: 18,000
SALES: 60MM **Privately Held**
SIC: 3695 Computer software tape & disks: blank, rigid & floppy

(G-11655)
PHYSICALMIND INSTITUTE
84 Wooster St Ste 605 (10012-4363)
PHONE.................................212 343-2150
Joan Breibart, *General Mgr*
▲ **EMP:** 10
SALES (est): 600K **Privately Held**
SIC: 3949 7812 8621 Exercise equipment; video tape production; professional membership organizations

(G-11656)
PIAGET
663 5th Ave Fl 7 (10022-5353)
PHONE.................................212 355-6444
Fax: 212 355-6996
Adriana Gravier, *Area Mgr*
Kyle Wilcher, *Sales Staff*
Federico Iossa, *Manager*
Jaime Jara, *Manager*
Pablo Lafforgue, *Manager*
EMP: 15 EST: 2010
SALES (est): 1.5MM **Privately Held**
SIC: 2329 Men's & boys' clothing

(G-11657)
PIAGGIO GROUP AMERICAS INC
257 Park Ave S Fl 4 (10010-7304)
PHONE.................................212 380-4400
Miguel Martinez, *President*
Roberto M Zerbi, *Exec VP*
Mauro Prignoli, *Vice Pres*
Michael Fiduk, *Regl Sales Mgr*
Antonio Verga, *Manager*
◆ **EMP:** 22
SALES (est): 5.4MM
SALES (corp-wide): 4.7MM **Privately Held**
WEB: www.piaggiousa.com
SIC: 3751 Motor scooters & parts
PA: Immsi Spa
   Piazza Vilfredo Pareto 3
   Mantova MN
   064 229-51

(G-11658)
PICADOR USA
175 5th Ave (10010-7703)
PHONE.................................646 307-5629
Frances Coady, *Vice Pres*
Kelsey Smith, *Manager*
EMP: 12
SALES (est): 954.2K
SALES (corp-wide): 2.1B **Privately Held**
SIC: 2731 Book publishing
HQ: Macmillan Holdings, Llc
   175 5th Ave
   New York NY 10010

(G-11659)
PIDYON CONTROLS INC (PA)
141 W 24th St Apt 4 (10011-1958)
PHONE.................................212 683-9523
Yochi Cohen, *CEO*
EMP: 1
SQ FT: 10,000
SALES: 10MM **Privately Held**
SIC: 3944 3751 Child restraint seats, automotive; gears, motorcycle & bicycle

(G-11660)
PIEMONTE HOME MADE RAVIOLI CO
190 Grand St (10013-3712)
PHONE.................................212 226-0475
Fax: 212 226-0476
Mario Bertorelli, *President*
EMP: 6
SALES (corp-wide): 1.6MM **Privately Held**
WEB: www.piemonteravioli.com
SIC: 2098 Macaroni & spaghetti
PA: Piemonte Home Made Ravioli Co, Inc
   3436 65th St
   Woodside NY 11377
   718 429-1972

(G-11661)
PIN PHARMA INC
3960 Broadway Fl 2 (10032-1543)
PHONE.................................212 543-2583
Hestaline Reynolds, *Principal*
EMP: 8

New York - New York County (G-11662)

SALES (est): 894.3K **Privately Held**
SIC: 3452 Pins

(G-11662)
PINGMD INC
136 Madison Ave Fl 6 (10016-6711)
PHONE..................................212 632-2665
Susan Driscoll, *CEO*
Lawrence Sosnow, *Ch of Bd*
Ancil Lea III, *Sales Dir*
EMP: 6 EST: 2009
SALES (est): 492.9K **Privately Held**
SIC: 7372 Application computer software

(G-11663)
PINK INC
23 E 10th St Apt 1b (10003-6114)
PHONE..................................212 352-8282
Debra Roth, *President*
EMP: 22
SQ FT: 2,000
SALES: 1.6MM **Privately Held**
WEB: www.pinkinc.org
SIC: 2395 Quilted fabrics or cloth

(G-11664)
PINK CRUSH LLC
1410 Broadway Rm 1002 (10018-9359)
PHONE..................................718 788-6978
Rori Nadrich, *President*
Raymond Kassin, *Vice Pres*
EMP: 4
SQ FT: 1,800
SALES: 2MM **Privately Held**
SIC: 2369 Girls' & children's outerwear

(G-11665)
PINNACLE WINE VAULT LLC (PA)
810 7th Ave Fl 28 (10019-9000)
PHONE..................................212 736-0040
Ted Wilson,
▲ EMP: 9
SALES (est): 4.4MM **Privately Held**
SIC: 2084 Wines

(G-11666)
PINS N NEEDLES
1045 Lexington Ave (10021-3252)
PHONE..................................212 535-6222
Rachel Low, *CEO*
EMP: 9
SALES (est): 1.1MM **Privately Held**
SIC: 3452 Pins

(G-11667)
PITNEY BOWES INC
637 W 27th St Fl 8 (10001-1019)
PHONE..................................212 564-7548
Fax: 917 351-2965
Giberti Alberti, *Exec VP*
James Euchner, *Vice Pres*
Gregory Forbes, *Project Mgr*
Benjamin Dock, *Engineer*
Joseph Guiles, *Engineer*
EMP: 35
SALES (corp-wide): 3.5B **Publicly Held**
SIC: 3579 7359 Postage meters; business machine & electronic equipment rental services
PA: Pitney Bowes Inc.
3001 Summer St
Stamford CT 06926
203 356-5000

(G-11668)
PITNEY BOWES INC
90 Park Ave Rm 1110 (10016-1301)
PHONE..................................203 356-5000
Michael Levitan, *Principal*
Tom Focone, *VP Human Res*
EMP: 35
SALES (corp-wide): 3.5B **Publicly Held**
SIC: 3579 7359 Postage meters; business machine & electronic equipment rental services
PA: Pitney Bowes Inc.
3001 Summer St
Stamford CT 06926
203 356-5000

(G-11669)
PITUITARY SOCIETY
423 E 23rd St Rm 16048 (10010-5011)
PHONE..................................212 263-6772
David L Kleinberg, *Principal*

EMP: 12 EST: 2008
SALES: 291.3K **Privately Held**
SIC: 2834 Pituitary gland pharmaceutical preparations

(G-11670)
PIWIK PRO LLC
222 Broadway Fl 19 (10038-2550)
PHONE..................................888 444-0049
Maiciej Zawadski, *CEO*
EMP: 30 EST: 2015
SALES (est): 815.9K **Privately Held**
SIC: 7372 Application computer software

(G-11671)
PJ DESIGNS INC
Also Called: Peggy Jennings Designs
100 E 50th St Ste 38a (10022-6844)
PHONE..................................212 355-3100
Herbert Kosterlitz, *Manager*
EMP: 40
SALES (corp-wide): 4.3MM **Privately Held**
SIC: 2335 Dresses, paper; cut & sewn
PA: P.J. Designs, Inc.
2830 46th Ave N
Saint Petersburg FL 33714
727 525-0599

(G-11672)
PKG GROUP
560 Broadway Rm 406 (10012-3946)
PHONE..................................212 965-0112
Edward Csaszar, *Manager*
EMP: 7
SALES (est): 702.1K **Privately Held**
SIC: 2631 Container, packaging & boxboard

(G-11673)
PLASCOLINE INC
275 Madison Ave Fl 14 (10016-1100)
PHONE..................................917 410-5754
Rafael Faramand, *CEO*
EMP: 18
SQ FT: 2,000
SALES: 4MM **Privately Held**
SIC: 3089 Organizers for closets, drawers, etc.: plastic; plastic kitchenware, tableware & houseware

(G-11674)
PLAYBILL INCORPORATED (PA)
729 7th Ave Fl 4 (10019-6827)
PHONE..................................212 557-5757
Fax: 212 661-5866
Philip S Birsh, *President*
Clifford Tinder, *Editor*
Arthur T Birsh, *Chairman*
Joan Alleman-Birsh, *Exec VP*
Susan Ludlow, *Accounts Mgr*
EMP: 20 EST: 1882
SQ FT: 4,500
SALES (est): 21.6MM **Privately Held**
SIC: 2721 Periodicals: publishing & printing

(G-11675)
PLAYLIFE LLC
297 Church St Fl 5 (10013-5716)
PHONE..................................646 207-9082
Mattias Stanghed,
EMP: 5
SALES (est): 250K **Privately Held**
SIC: 2741 7389 ;

(G-11676)
PLC APPAREL LLC
137 Grand St Fl 3 (10013-3169)
PHONE..................................212 239-3434
Kate Gordon, *President*
EMP: 6
SALES (corp-wide): 2.3MM **Privately Held**
SIC: 2339 Service apparel, washable: women's
PA: Plc Apparel, Llc
2360 Corp Cir Ste 400
Henderson NV

(G-11677)
PLEXI CRAFT QUALITY PRODUCTS
200 Lexington Ave Rm 914 (10016-6255)
PHONE..................................212 924-3244
George Frechter, *President*

EMP: 15
SQ FT: 10,000
SALES (est): 2.3MM **Privately Held**
WEB: www.plexi-craft.com
SIC: 2821 Thermoplastic materials

(G-11678)
PLUGG LLC
Also Called: Coliseum
1410 Broadway Frnt 2 (10018-9302)
PHONE..................................212 840-6655
Fax: 212 840-3078
Laureen Emilius, *Sales Staff*
John Kiplani, *Branch Mgr*
EMP: 10
SALES (corp-wide): 12.4MM **Privately Held**
WEB: www.coliseum.com
SIC: 2331 2335 2339 Women's & misses' blouses & shirts; women's, juniors' & misses' dresses; slacks: women's, misses' & juniors'
PA: Plugg Llc
250 Moonachie Rd Ste 501
Moonachie NJ 07074
201 662-8200

(G-11679)
PMI GLOBAL SERVICES INC
120 Park Ave Fl 7 (10017-5577)
PHONE..................................917 663-2000
James R Mortensen, *President*
Matthieu Banks, *Hum Res Coord*
EMP: 23
SALES (est): 3.6MM
SALES (corp-wide): 73.9B **Publicly Held**
SIC: 2111 Cigarettes
PA: Philip Morris International Inc.
120 Park Ave Fl 6
New York NY 10017
917 663-2000

(G-11680)
POETS HOUSE INC
10 River Ter (10282-1240)
PHONE..................................212 431-7920
Margo Viscusi, *President*
Frank Platt, *Vice Pres*
Martin Gomez, *Treasurer*
Carlin Wragg, *Manager*
Jane Preston, *Exec Dir*
EMP: 14 EST: 1985
SALES: 1.7MM **Privately Held**
SIC: 2731 8231 Book publishing; libraries

(G-11681)
POLLACK GRAPHICS INC
601 W 26th St Ste M204 (10001-1101)
PHONE..................................212 727-8400
Fax: 212 727-1056
Glenn Pollack, *President*
Peter Mirenda, *Sales Mgr*
EMP: 5
SQ FT: 1,600
SALES (est): 450K **Privately Held**
SIC: 2752 Commercial printing, offset

(G-11682)
POLYMER SLUTIONS GROUP FIN LLC (PA)
100 Park Ave Fl 31 (10017-5584)
PHONE..................................212 771-1717
Mike Ivany, *CEO*
EMP: 4 EST: 2015
SALES (est): 38.5MM **Privately Held**
SIC: 2869 Industrial organic chemicals

(G-11683)
POP BAR LLC
5 Carmine St Frnt 6 (10014-4440)
PHONE..................................212 255-4874
Daniel Yaghoubi,
◆ EMP: 6
SALES (est): 348.6K **Privately Held**
SIC: 2024 Ice cream & frozen desserts

(G-11684)
POPNYC 1 LLC
Also Called: Pop Nyc
75 Saint Nicholas Pl 2e (10032-8030)
PHONE..................................646 684-4600
Gina Panella, *Mng Member*
Joseph Peraino,
▲ EMP: 5
SQ FT: 1,000

SALES: 2MM **Privately Held**
SIC: 2339 Women's & misses' accessories

(G-11685)
POPPIN INC
Also Called: Www.poppin.com
1115 Broadway Fl 3 (10010-3457)
PHONE..................................212 391-7200
Randy Nicolau, *CEO*
Chris Robison, *General Mgr*
Michael Chauliac, *Principal*
Andrew Benoit, *COO*
Jimmy Abbott, *Vice Pres*
▲ EMP: 52 EST: 2009
SALES (est): 12.2MM **Privately Held**
SIC: 2521 2522 Cabinets, office: wood; tables, office: wood; chairs, office: padded or plain, except wood

(G-11686)
PORTFOLIO DECISIONWARE INC
250 W 57th St Ste 1032 (10107-1024)
PHONE..................................212 947-1326
Jeff Hewitt, *President*
Phil Wolf, *Senior VP*
Judy Neustadter, *Accounts Exec*
Brenda Faucher, *Sales Associate*
EMP: 30
SALES (est): 2.9MM **Privately Held**
SIC: 7372 Prepackaged software

(G-11687)
PORTFOLIO MEDIA INC
Also Called: Law360
111 W 19th St Ste 507 (10011-4115)
PHONE..................................646 783-7100
Fax: 646 783-7161
Scott Roberts, *CEO*
Jackie Bell, *Editor*
Christian Lewis, *Editor*
Alyssa Anzur, *Accounts Exec*
Sam Howard, *Corp Comm Staff*
EMP: 200
SQ FT: 46,000
SALES (est): 9.1MM
SALES (corp-wide): 9B **Privately Held**
WEB: www.portfoliomedia.com
SIC: 2741 Business service newsletters: publishing & printing
HQ: Relx Inc.
230 Park Ave
New York NY 10169
212 309-8100

(G-11688)
PORTWARE LLC (HQ)
233 Broadway Fl 24 (10279-2502)
PHONE..................................212 425-5233
Fax: 212 571-4634
Alfred Eskandar, *CEO*
Scott Depetris, *President*
Eric Goldberg, *Founder*
Ary Khatchikian, *Founder*
Jackson Ling, *Asst Controller*
EMP: 75
SALES (est): 21.5MM
SALES (corp-wide): 1B **Publicly Held**
SIC: 7372 Prepackaged software
PA: Factset Research Systems Inc.
601 Merritt 7
Norwalk CT 06851
203 810-1000

(G-11689)
POSITIVE PRINT LITHO OFFSET
121 Varick St Rm 204 (10013-1461)
PHONE..................................212 431-4850
Fax: 212 431-0414
Garry Koppel, *President*
EMP: 8
SQ FT: 2,000
SALES (est): 1MM **Privately Held**
SIC: 2752 Commercial printing, offset

(G-11690)
POST ROAD
101 E 16th St Apt 4b (10003-2150)
PHONE..................................203 545-2122
David Ryan, *President*
John Todd, *Managing Prtnr*
EMP: 14 EST: 2001
SALES (est): 925.9K **Privately Held**
SIC: 2752 7371 Publication printing, lithographic; computer software development & applications

GEOGRAPHIC SECTION

New York - New York County (G-11716)

(G-11691)
POWA TECHNOLOGIES INC
1 Bryant Park Ste 39 (10036-6747)
PHONE...................................347 344-7848
Jeff Dumbrell, *CEO*
Jeff Max, *President*
Ilan Levine, *COO*
Paul Rasori, *Exec VP*
EMP: 40
SQ FT: 10,000
SALES (est): 5.3MM
SALES (corp-wide): 3.6MM **Privately Held**
SIC: 7372 3578 Business oriented computer software; point-of-sale devices
HQ: Powa Technologies Limited
35th Floor Heron Tower
London

(G-11692)
POWERCOMPLETE LLC
636 Broadway Rm 1000 (10012-2609)
PHONE...................................212 228-4129
Fax: 212 591-2831
Jason Feingold,
Ben Boyd,
EMP: 6
SALES (est): 690K **Privately Held**
WEB: www.powercomplete.com
SIC: 3621 Motors & generators

(G-11693)
PRAGER METIS CPAS LLC
675 3rd Ave (10017-5704)
PHONE...................................212 972-7555
Dawn Minogue, *Manager*
Kamal Shah, *Manager*
Ryan Shaw, *Manager*
Bozena Targonski, *Manager*
Walter Lacoste, *Senior Mgr*
EMP: 10
SALES (corp-wide): 35MM **Privately Held**
SIC: 3661 Communication headgear, telephone
HQ: Prager Metis Cpas, Llc
14 Penn Plz Ste 1800
New York NY 10122
212 643-0099

(G-11694)
PRC LIQUIDATING COMPANY
Also Called: New York Running Co
10 Columbus Cir (10019-1158)
PHONE...................................212 823-9626
Eugene Mitchell, *Bd of Directors*
EMP: 30
SALES (corp-wide): 1.8B **Publicly Held**
SIC: 3949 Sporting & athletic goods
HQ: Prc Liquidating Company
632 Overhill Rd
Ardmore PA 19003
610 649-1876

(G-11695)
PRECISION CSTM COATINGS I LLC
234 W 39th St (10018-4412)
PHONE...................................212 868-5770
Peter Longo, *Branch Mgr*
EMP: 210
SALES (corp-wide): 152MM **Privately Held**
SIC: 2295 Coated fabrics, not rubberized
PA: Precision Custom Coatings Llc
200 Maltese Dr
Totowa NJ 07512
973 785-4390

(G-11696)
PRECISION DIAMOND CUTTERS INC
2 W 46th St Ste 1007 (10036-4502)
PHONE...................................212 719-4438
Fax: 212 719-4582
David Lew, *President*
Kathy Paykany, *Vice Pres*
EMP: 6
SALES (est): 500K **Privately Held**
WEB: www.bellnor.com
SIC: 3915 Diamond cutting & polishing

(G-11697)
PRECISION INTERNATIONAL CO INC
Also Called: Cenere
201 E 28th St 9n (10016-8538)
PHONE...................................212 268-9090
Fax: 212 268-9094
Michelle Kim, *President*
James Cioffi, *Sales Staff*
▲ **EMP:** 6
SQ FT: 4,200
SALES (est): 410K **Privately Held**
SIC: 3873 5094 Watches, clocks, watchcases & parts; jewelry & precious stones

(G-11698)
PREMIER GROUP NY
18 W 23rd St Fl 3 (10010-5233)
PHONE...................................212 229-1200
EMP: 10
SALES (est): 651.4K **Privately Held**
SIC: 3281 1741 Marble, building: cut & shaped; masonry & other stonework

(G-11699)
PRESCRIBING REFERENCE INC
275 7th Ave Fl 10 (10001-6756)
PHONE...................................646 638-6000
William Pecover, *Ch of Bd*
Lee Maniscalco, *President*
Alex Benady, *Editor*
Ian Griggs, *Editor*
Danny Rogers, *Editor*
EMP: 85
SQ FT: 18,000
SALES (est): 4MM
SALES (corp-wide): 106.4MM **Privately Held**
SIC: 2721 Magazines: publishing only, not printed on site
HQ: Haymarket Media, Inc.
275 7th Ave Fl 10
New York NY 10001
646 638-6000

(G-11700)
PRESS OF FREMONT PAYNE INC
55 Broad St Frnt 3 (10004-2569)
PHONE...................................212 966-6570
Charles J Esposito, *President*
John Esposito, *Vice Pres*
Logan Ripley, *Systems Analyst*
Thomas D Esposito, *Admin Sec*
EMP: 8 **EST:** 1890
SQ FT: 3,500
SALES (est): 610K **Privately Held**
SIC: 2752 Commercial printing, offset

(G-11701)
PRESTEL PUBLISHING INC
900 Broadway Ste 603 (10003-1237)
PHONE...................................212 995-2720
Fax: 212 995-2733
Juergen Krieger, *Principal*
Judy Hardin, *Executive*
Nola Tully, *Executive*
▲ **EMP:** 6
SQ FT: 1,620
SALES (est): 642.6K
SALES (corp-wide): 18.4B **Privately Held**
SIC: 2731 Book publishing
HQ: Verlagsgruppe Random House Gmbh
Neumarkter Str. 28
Munchen 81673
894 136-0

(G-11702)
PRETLIST
545 W 110th St Apt 2b (10025-2016)
PHONE...................................646 368-1849
Rashid Altayer, *President*
EMP: 5 **EST:** 2013
SALES (est): 351.7K **Privately Held**
SIC: 7372 Prepackaged software

(G-11703)
PRICING ENGINE INC
175 Varick St Fl 4 (10014-7412)
PHONE...................................917 549-3289
Jeremy Kagan, *CEO*
Peter Kingswell, *Senior Engr*
Shobu Filho, *Accounts Mgr*
Marissa Fung, *Accounts Mgr*
EMP: 10

SALES (est): 221.8K **Privately Held**
SIC: 7372 Business oriented computer software

(G-11704)
PRIDE & JOYS INC
Also Called: Olivea Mathews
1400 Broadway Rm 503 (10018-1044)
PHONE...................................212 594-9820
Fax: 212 594-8369
Eli Rousso, *Ch of Bd*
Rochelle Reis, *Corp Secy*
Neil Rousso, *Vice Pres*
EMP: 15
SQ FT: 4,000
SALES: 8.6MM **Privately Held**
SIC: 2339 2329 Sportswear, women's; knickers, dress (separate): men's & boys'

(G-11705)
PRIMARY WAVE PUBLISHING LLC
116 E 16th St Fl 9 (10003-2123)
PHONE...................................212 661-6990
Winston Simone, *Principal*
Joe Ades, *Project Mgr*
Ranon Villa, *CFO*
Erica Emerson, *Controller*
Robert Dippold, *VP Sales*
EMP: 9
SALES (est): 660K **Privately Held**
SIC: 2741 Miscellaneous publishing

(G-11706)
PRIME GARMENTS INC
1407 Broadway Rm 1200 (10018-2850)
PHONE...................................212 354-7294
Joseph Hamdar, *President*
Beth Matran, *Bookkeeper*
▲ **EMP:** 15
SALES (est): 2.6MM **Privately Held**
SIC: 2342 Bras, girdles & allied garments

(G-11707)
PRIME MARKETING AND SALES LLC
111 W Hmpstead Tpke Fl 3 (10001)
PHONE...................................888 802-3836
▲ **EMP:** 4
SQ FT: 7,000
SALES: 1MM **Privately Held**
SIC: 2066 3089 Chocolate; plastic kitchenware, tableware & houseware

(G-11708)
PRIME PACK LLC
Also Called: Prime Pharmaceutical
303 5th Ave Rm 1007 (10016-6681)
PHONE...................................732 253-7734
Sreedara Nagarajan, *Mng Member*
Amrita Gupta,
Lakshmi Nagarajan,
▲ **EMP:** 10
SQ FT: 13,598
SALES (est): 870K **Privately Held**
SIC: 2834 Pharmaceutical preparations

(G-11709)
PRIMEDIA SPECIAL INTEREST PUBL (DH)
260 Madison Ave Fl 8 (10016-2401)
PHONE...................................212 726-4300
Fax: 212 545-1238
Dean Nelson, *President*
David Branch, *Publisher*
Carol Campbell, *Publisher*
Mike Irish, *Publisher*
Mark Terry, *Division Mgr*
EMP: 100
SALES (est): 15.5MM **Privately Held**
WEB: www.films.com
SIC: 2731 2721 Books: publishing only; trade journals: publishing & printing; magazines: publishing & printing
HQ: Rentpath, Inc.
950 E Paces Ferry Rd Ne # 2600
Atlanta GA 30326
678 421-3000

(G-11710)
PRINCE MINERAL HOLDING CORP (PA)
21 W 46th St Fl 14th (10036-4119)
PHONE...................................646 747-4222
Willson Ropp, *CEO*

Peter Joseph, *Director*
David Perez, *Director*
EMP: 9
SALES (est): 84.7MM **Privately Held**
SIC: 2819 Industrial inorganic chemicals

(G-11711)
PRINCE MINERALS LLC (HQ)
Also Called: Prince Foundry
21 W 46th St Fl 14 (10036-4119)
Po Box 251 IL
PHONE...................................646 747-4222
John Ropp, *President*
Axel Strack, *Business Mgr*
Alan Petefish, *Vice Pres*
J F Alewijnse, *CFO*
Roderik J F Alewijnse, *CFO*
▼ **EMP:** 53
SQ FT: 8,000
SALES (est): 291.6MM
SALES (corp-wide): 2.2B **Privately Held**
SIC: 3295 3356 Minerals, ground or treated; silicon, ultra high purity: treated; zirconium
PA: Palladium Equity Partners Iii, L.P.
1270 Ave Of The
New York NY 10020
212 218-5150

(G-11712)
PRINCESS MUSIC PUBLISHING CO
1650 Broadway Ste 701 (10019-6966)
PHONE...................................212 586-0240
Fax: 212 586-4306
Hal Webman, *Owner*
EMP: 20
SALES (est): 1MM **Privately Held**
SIC: 2741 Music books: publishing & printing

(G-11713)
PRINCIPIA PARTNERS LLC
140 Broadway Fl 46 (10005-1155)
PHONE...................................212 480-2270
Dan Smith, *CFO*
Suzanne Brower, *Sr Software Eng*
Theresa Adams,
Mark Kovach, *Administration*
Brian Donnally,
EMP: 55
SALES (est): 4.8MM **Privately Held**
WEB: www.ppllc.com
SIC: 7372 8742 Business oriented computer software; financial consultant

(G-11714)
PRINCTON ARCHTCTURAL PRESS LLC
37 E 7th St Ste 2 (10003-8027)
PHONE...................................212 995-9620
Fax: 212 995-9454
Joe Watson, *Manager*
Kevin Lippert,
▲ **EMP:** 24
SALES: 5MM
SALES (corp-wide): 26MM **Privately Held**
SIC: 2731 Book publishing
PA: The Mcevoy Group Llc
680 2nd St
San Francisco CA 94107
415 537-4200

(G-11715)
PRINT BEAR LLC (PA)
411 Lafayette St Fl 6 (10003-7035)
PHONE...................................518 703-6098
Timothy Song,
EMP: 7
SALES (est): 2.9MM **Privately Held**
SIC: 2752 Color lithography

(G-11716)
PRINT BY PREMIER LLC
Also Called: Premier Supplies
212 W 35th St Fl 2 (10001-2508)
PHONE...................................212 947-1365
Sheldon Lehman, *Mng Member*
EMP: 6
SALES (est): 1.7MM **Privately Held**
SIC: 2752 Publication printing, lithographic

New York - New York County (G-11717) GEOGRAPHIC SECTION

(G-11717)
PRINT CITY CORP
165 W 29th St (10001-5101)
PHONE.....................212 487-9778
Anna Wadolowska-Panagoda, *Ch of Bd*
Walter Panagoda, *President*
EMP: 16
SALES (est): 495.5K **Privately Held**
SIC: 2759 Commercial printing

(G-11718)
PRINT MANAGEMENT GROUP CORP
33 E 33rd St Fl 3 (10016-5335)
PHONE.....................212 213-1555
John Scalli, *President*
Tony Santaniello, *Prdtn Mgr*
EMP: 7
SALES (est): 1.5MM **Privately Held**
SIC: 2752 Commercial printing, lithographic

(G-11719)
PRINT MEDIA INC
350 7th Ave Rm 401 (10001-1960)
PHONE.....................212 563-4040
Fax: 212 563-4041
Jordan H Wachtell, *Ch of Bd*
Lisa Iddings, *President*
Kady Myers, *Accountant*
▲ EMP: 100
SQ FT: 2,000
SALES (est): 12.5MM **Privately Held**
SIC: 2752 Commercial printing, lithographic

(G-11720)
PRINTECH BUSINESS SYSTEMS INC
519 8th Ave Fl 3 (10018-4594)
PHONE.....................212 290-2542
Fax: 212 290-2541
Frank Passantino, *President*
Marc Zaransky, *Vice Pres*
Ralph Pantuso, *Senior Engr*
Sue Teraghty, *Office Mgr*
Jose Gomez, *Info Tech Dir*
EMP: 18
SQ FT: 15,000
SALES (est): 3.2MM **Privately Held**
WEB: www.printechny.com
SIC: 2789 2752 7374 2759 Binding only: books, pamphlets, magazines, etc.; commercial printing, lithographic; commercial printing, offset; optical scanning data service; promotional printing

(G-11721)
PRINTFACILITY INC
225 Broadway Fl 3 (10007-3001)
PHONE.....................212 349-4009
Fax: 212 406-5575
Farah Khan, *CEO*
Sarah Shabbir, *Manager*
EMP: 8
SQ FT: 2,000
SALES (est): 670K **Privately Held**
WEB: www.printfacility.com
SIC: 2759 Commercial printing

(G-11722)
PRINTINGHOUSE PRESS LTD
10 E 39th St Rm 700 (10016-0111)
PHONE.....................212 719-0990
Fax: 212 398-9253
Myron Schonfeld, *Principal*
Sean Leary, *Production*
Maria Ali, *Mktg Dir*
Antonia Thornton, *Mktg Coord*
Beth Bersson, *Marketing Staff*
EMP: 6
SALES (est): 1MM **Privately Held**
WEB: www.phpny.com
SIC: 2752 Commercial printing, lithographic

(G-11723)
PRIORITY PRINTING ENTPS INC
Also Called: Priority Enterprise
315 W 36th St (10018-6404)
PHONE.....................646 285-0684
Ronald Bright, *President*
EMP: 12

SALES (est): 3.9MM **Privately Held**
WEB: www.priorityenterpriseinc.com
SIC: 2759 Commercial printing

(G-11724)
PRO DRONES USA LLC
115 E 57th St Fl 11 (10022-2120)
PHONE.....................718 530-3558
Vivien Heriard Dubreuil, *President*
EMP: 12
SALES (est): 670K **Privately Held**
SIC: 3721 Aircraft

(G-11725)
PRO PUBLICA INC
155 Ave Of The Americas (10013-1507)
PHONE.....................212 514-5250
Richard Tofel, *President*
Stephen Engelberg, *Editor*
Robin Fields, *Editor*
Terry Parris, *Editor*
Paul Steiger, *Editor*
EMP: 52
SALES: 17MM **Privately Held**
SIC: 2731 Book publishing

(G-11726)
PROCTER & GAMBLE COMPANY
120 W 45th St Fl 3 (10036-4041)
PHONE.....................646 885-4201
Nancy Medici, *Branch Mgr*
EMP: 150
SALES (corp-wide): 65.3B **Publicly Held**
SIC: 2676 2844 Towels, napkins & tissue paper products; diapers, paper (disposable): made from purchased paper; feminine hygiene paper products; toilet preparations; hair preparations, including shampoos; oral preparations; deodorants, personal
PA: The Procter & Gamble Company
1 Procter And Gamble Plz
Cincinnati OH 45202
513 983-1100

(G-11727)
PRODUCT DEVELOPMENT INTL LLC
215 W 40th St Fl 8 (10018-1575)
PHONE.....................212 279-6170
Sue Sun, *Accountant*
Donald L Foss, *Mng Member*
Eric Chu,
▲ EMP: 9
SQ FT: 5,000
SALES (est): 1MM **Privately Held**
SIC: 2335 Women's, juniors' & misses' dresses

(G-11728)
PROFESSNAL SPT PBLICATIONS INC (PA)
Also Called: Touchdown
519 8th Ave (10018-6506)
PHONE.....................212 697-1460
Fax: 212 286-8154
Mitchell Zeifman, *President*
Ryan Mattos, *Editor*
Steven Fox, *Exec VP*
Martin Lewis, *Exec VP*
Robert Fulton, *Senior VP*
EMP: 70 EST: 1990
SALES (est): 31.3MM **Privately Held**
WEB: www.pspsports.com
SIC: 2721 7941 Magazines: publishing only, not printed on site; sports promotion

(G-11729)
PROGENICS PHARMACEUTICALS INC (PA)
1 World Trade Ctr Fl 47 (10007-0089)
PHONE.....................646 975-2500
Fax: 914 789-2817
Mark R Baker, *CEO*
Peter J Crowley, *Ch of Bd*
Paul J Maddon, *Vice Ch Bd*
Sheldon H Hirt, *Exec VP*
Vivien Wong, *Exec VP*
EMP: 66
SALES: 8.6MM **Publicly Held**
WEB: www.progenics.com
SIC: 2834 Pharmaceutical preparations

(G-11730)
PROGRESSIVE FIBRE PRODUCTS CO
160 Broadway Rm 1105 (10038-4212)
PHONE.....................212 566-2720
Fax: 212 566-2726
Elliot Kozer, *President*
EMP: 40
SALES (est): 3.8MM **Privately Held**
WEB: www.fibrecase.com
SIC: 3161 Sample cases

(G-11731)
PROMOTIONAL SALES BOOKS LLC
30 W 26th St Frnt (10010-2011)
PHONE.....................212 675-0364
EMP: 5
SQ FT: 2,500
SALES (est): 410K **Privately Held**
SIC: 2732 Publisher

(G-11732)
PROMPT BINDERY CO INC
350 W 38th St (10018-5206)
PHONE.....................212 675-5181
Fax: 212 255-5925
Louis Levine, *President*
EMP: 12
SQ FT: 5,800
SALES (est): 759.3K **Privately Held**
SIC: 2789 Bookbinding & related work

(G-11733)
PRONOVIAS USA INC
14 E 52nd St (10022-5308)
PHONE.....................212 897-6393
Alberto Palatchi, *Ch of Bd*
Joseluis Perez Herrero, *President*
Jordi Morral, *Exec VP*
Llouis Sole, *Opers Mgr*
Nuria Salazar, *Credit Mgr*
▲ EMP: 30
SQ FT: 20,000
SALES (est): 5.4MM **Privately Held**
WEB: www.pronoviasusa.com
SIC: 2335 Gowns, formal
PA: Pronovias SI
Poligono Industrial Mas Mateu, S/N
El Prat De Llobregat
934 799-700

(G-11734)
PRONTO JEWELRY INC
23 W 47th St (10036-2826)
PHONE.....................212 719-9455
Fax: 212 302-5413
Misak Terjinian, *President*
EMP: 23
SALES (est): 1.8MM **Privately Held**
SIC: 3911 Jewelry, precious metal

(G-11735)
PROOF 7 LTD
121 Varick St Rm 301 (10013-1408)
PHONE.....................212 680-1843
Joshua Cooper, *President*
Laurence Chandler, *Vice Pres*
Max Cantatore, *Sales Staff*
EMP: 10
SQ FT: 3,000
SALES (est): 1MM **Privately Held**
SIC: 2759 7336 7299 Card printing & engraving, except greeting; advertising literature: printing; catalogs: printing; announcements: engraved; graphic arts & related design; party planning service

(G-11736)
PROPER CLOTH LLC
450 Broadway Ste 2 (10013-5822)
PHONE.....................646 964-4221
Joseph Skerritt, *Mng Member*
EMP: 8
SQ FT: 3,000
SALES (est): 779K **Privately Held**
SIC: 2311 Men's & boys' suits & coats

(G-11737)
PROPS DISPLAYS & INTERIORS
Also Called: Pdi
132 W 18th St (10011-5403)
PHONE.....................212 620-3840
Fax: 212 620-5472
Stephen Sebbane, *President*

Wendy Isaacson, *President*
EMP: 15
SALES (est): 950K **Privately Held**
SIC: 3993 3999 2431 Displays, paint process; stage hardware & equipment, except lighting; interior & ornamental woodwork & trim

(G-11738)
PROSPECT NEWS
6 Maiden Ln Fl 9 (10038-5134)
PHONE.....................212 374-2800
Bernard Dankowski, *Principal*
Janene Geiss, *Editor*
Lisa Mayntz, *Marketing Staff*
Zhaniece Springer, *Admin Asst*
EMP: 14 EST: 2007
SALES (est): 654K **Privately Held**
SIC: 2711 Newspapers, publishing & printing

(G-11739)
PROSPECTOR NETWORK
350 5th Ave Fl 59 (10118-5999)
PHONE.....................212 601-2781
Claude Duhamel, *President*
EMP: 50
SALES (est): 1.5MM **Privately Held**
SIC: 7372 Application computer software

(G-11740)
PROSTHODONTIC & IMPLANT DEN
693 5th Ave (10022-3110)
PHONE.....................212 319-6363
Fax: 212 319-4995
Dean Vafiadis, *President*
EMP: 8
SALES (est): 996.3K **Privately Held**
SIC: 3842 Implants, surgical

(G-11741)
PROVISIONAIRE & CO LLC
Also Called: Field Trip Jerky
155 W 68th St Apt 611 (10023-5812)
PHONE.....................315 491-8240
Thomas Donigan,
M Scott Fiesinger,
Matthew Levey,
EMP: 20
SALES (est): 1.5MM **Privately Held**
SIC: 2013 Snack sticks, including jerky: from purchased meat

(G-11742)
PS38 LLC
Also Called: Public School
545 8th Ave Rm 350 (10018-4647)
PHONE.....................212 819-1123
Alan Mak,
EMP: 12 EST: 2012
SALES (est): 692.5K **Privately Held**
SIC: 2329 Men's & boys' sportswear & athletic clothing

(G-11743)
PSYCHONOMIC SOCIETY INC
233 Spring St Fl 7 (10013-1522)
PHONE.....................512 381-1494
EMP: 26
SQ FT: 6,000
SALES: 954.7K **Privately Held**
SIC: 2721 2789 2752 Periodical-Publish/Print Bookbinding/Related Work Lithographic Coml Print

(G-11744)
PTI-PACIFIC INC
166 5th Ave Fl 4t (10010-5909)
PHONE.....................212 414-8495
Simon Chong, *President*
EMP: 5 EST: 2009
SQ FT: 2,000
SALES: 10MM **Privately Held**
SIC: 2329 2339 2369 Men's & boys' athletic uniforms; women's & misses' outerwear; girls' & children's outerwear

(G-11745)
PTS FINANCIAL TECHNOLOGY LLC
1001 Ave Of The Americas (10018-5460)
PHONE.....................844 825-7634
Farid Naib, *CEO*
EMP: 40 EST: 1999

▲ = Import ▼=Export
◆ =Import/Export

GEOGRAPHIC SECTION

New York - New York County (G-11771)

SALES (est): 881.6K **Privately Held**
SIC: 7372 Application computer software

(G-11746)
PUBLIC RELATIONS SOC AMER INC (PA)
Also Called: Prsa
33 Maiden Ln Fl 11 (10038-5149)
PHONE..................212 460-1400
Joseph P Truncale, *CEO*
William Murray, *President*
Mary L Vannatta, *President*
Jeffrey P Julin, *Principal*
Jennifer Clark, *Vice Pres*
EMP: 50
SQ FT: 22,000
SALES: 11.6MM **Privately Held**
WEB: www.newyorkcity.com
SIC: 2721 8621 Trade journals: publishing only, not printed on site; professional membership organizations

(G-11747)
PUBLISHING GROUP AMERICA INC
Also Called: American Profile Magazine
60 E 42nd St Ste 1146 (10165-1146)
PHONE..................646 658-0550
Fax: 646 865-1921
Peggy Bosco, *Branch Mgr*
EMP: 18
SALES (corp-wide): 6.5MM **Privately Held**
WEB: www.pubgroupofamerica.com
SIC: 2711 Newspapers: publishing only, not printed on site
PA: Publishing Group Of America, Inc.
1200 Clinton St Ste 219
Nashville TN 37203
615 468-6000

(G-11748)
PUBLISHING SYNTHESIS LTD
39 Crosby St Apt 2n (10013-3254)
PHONE..................212 219-0135
Fax: 212 219-0136
Otto H Barz, *Partner*
Ellen Small, *Vice Pres*
George Ernsberger, *Manager*
Bryan Meek, *Senior Editor*
EMP: 6
SQ FT: 1,000
SALES (est): 420K **Privately Held**
WEB: www.pubsyn.com
SIC: 2791 Typesetting

(G-11749)
PUGLISI & CO
800 3rd Ave Ste 902 (10022-7768)
PHONE..................212 300-2285
Jeff Puglisi, *Principal*
Craig Klein, *CFO*
EMP: 5
SALES (est): 223.2K **Privately Held**
SIC: 1231 Anthracite mining

(G-11750)
PUIG USA INC (PA)
40 E 34th St Fl 19 (10016-4501)
PHONE..................212 271-5940
Marc Puig, *President*
Gary Ragusa, *CFO*
Pascal Jodra, *Sales Staff*
▲ EMP: 15 EST: 1981
SALES (est): 1.9MM **Privately Held**
SIC: 2844 Toilet preparations

(G-11751)
PURE TRADE US INC
347 5th Ave Rm 604 (10016-5031)
PHONE..................212 256-1600
Stefane Ladous, *CEO*
EMP: 40
SALES (est): 3.4MM **Privately Held**
SIC: 2652 3171 Setup paperboard boxes; women's handbags & purses

(G-11752)
PUREBASE NETWORKS INC
37 Wall St Apt 9a (10005-2019)
PHONE..................646 670-8964
Steven Ridder, *CEO*
EMP: 8
SALES (est): 186.1K **Privately Held**
SIC: 7372 Business oriented computer software

(G-11753)
PURELY MAPLE LLC
902 Broadway Fl 6 (10010-6039)
PHONE..................203 997-9309
ARI Tolwin, *CEO*
EMP: 15 EST: 2013
SALES (est): 639.5K **Privately Held**
SIC: 2086 Fruit drinks (less than 100% juice): packaged in cans, etc.

(G-11754)
PUREOLOGY RESEARCH LLC
565 5th Ave (10017-2413)
PHONE..................212 984-4360
Pat Parenty, *General Mgr*
EMP: 18
SALES (est): 1.6MM
SALES (corp-wide): 3.1B **Privately Held**
WEB: www.pureology.com
SIC: 2844 Hair preparations, including shampoos
HQ: L'oreal Usa, Inc.
10 Hudson Yards
New York NY 10001
212 818-1500

(G-11755)
PUTNAM ROLLING LADDER CO INC (PA)
32 Howard St (10013-3112)
PHONE..................212 226-5147
Fax: 212 941-1836
Warren R Monsees, *President*
Lloyd Javois, *Sales Staff*
K Laura Monsees, *Director*
Gregg Monsees, *Admin Sec*
▲ EMP: 15 EST: 1897
SQ FT: 45,000
SALES (est): 3.6MM **Privately Held**
WEB: www.putnamrollingladder.com
SIC: 2499 5084 Ladders, wood; woodworking machinery

(G-11756)
PVH CORP (PA)
200 Madison Ave Bsmt 1 (10016-3913)
P.O. Box 64945, Saint Paul MN (55164-0945)
PHONE..................212 381-3500
Fax: 212 381-3950
Francis K Duane, *CEO*
Daniel Grieder, *CEO*
Steven B Shiffman, *CEO*
Emanuel Chirico, *Ch of Bd*
Michael A Shaffer, *COO*
◆ EMP: 100 EST: 1881
SQ FT: 209,000
SALES: 8B **Publicly Held**
WEB: www.pvh.com
SIC: 2321 2331 2253 3143 Men's & boys' dress shirts; sport shirts, men's & boys': from purchased materials; blouses, women's & juniors': made from purchased material; shirts, women's & juniors': made from purchased materials; sweaters & sweater coats, knit; shirts (outerwear), knit; men's footwear, except athletic; ready-to-wear apparel, women's; men's & boys' clothing stores

(G-11757)
PVH CORP
Van Heusen
200 Madison Ave Bsmt 1 (10016-3913)
PHONE..................212 381-3800
Ken Duane, *Branch Mgr*
John Hayes, *Executive*
EMP: 7
SALES (corp-wide): 8B **Publicly Held**
WEB: www.pvh.com
SIC: 2329 2339 Men's & boys' sportswear & athletic clothing; sportswear, women's
PA: Pvh Corp.
200 Madison Ave Bsmt 1
New York NY 10016
212 381-3500

(G-11758)
PVH CORP
Also Called: Van Heusen
404 5th Ave Fl 4 (10018-7566)
PHONE..................212 502-6300
Allain Russo, *President*
EMP: 60

SALES (corp-wide): 8B **Publicly Held**
WEB: www.pvh.com
SIC: 2339 Women's & misses' outerwear
PA: Pvh Corp.
200 Madison Ave Bsmt 1
New York NY 10016
212 381-3500

(G-11759)
PVH CORP
Also Called: Van Heusen
205 W 39th St Fl 4 (10018-3102)
PHONE..................212 719-2600
Barb Nykolichuk, *District Mgr*
Sherrie Seymour, *District Mgr*
Jeffrey Hui, *COO*
Pamela Bradford, *Senior VP*
Natalie M Turpan, *Senior VP*
EMP: 9
SALES (corp-wide): 8B **Publicly Held**
SIC: 2321 2331 Men's & boys' dress shirts; sport shirts, men's & boys': from purchased materials; blouses, women's & juniors': made from purchased material; shirts, women's & juniors': made from purchased materials
PA: Pvh Corp.
200 Madison Ave Bsmt 1
New York NY 10016
212 381-3500

(G-11760)
PVI SOLAR INC
599 11th Ave Bby (10036-2110)
PHONE..................212 280-2100
Paul Mladineo, *Managing Dir*
Ted Hasenstaub, *Exec VP*
Ed Shenker, *Exec VP*
Ryan McKeever, *Vice Pres*
EMP: 8
SALES (est): 570K **Privately Held**
SIC: 3674 3679 Integrated circuits, semiconductor networks, etc.; electronic loads & power supplies

(G-11761)
PWXYZ LLC
Also Called: Publishers Weekly
71 W 23rd St Ste 1608 (10010-4186)
PHONE..................212 377-5500
George W Slowik Jr, *President*
Cevin Bryerman, *Publisher*
Matia Burnett, *Editor*
Michael Coffey, *Editor*
Jim Milliot, *Editor*
EMP: 5
SALES (est): 480K **Privately Held**
SIC: 2721 2731 Trade journals: publishing only, not printed on site; books: publishing only

(G-11762)
Q COMMUNICATIONS INC
Also Called: Passport Magazine
247 W 35th St Rm 1200 (10001-1917)
PHONE..................212 594-6520
Don Tuthill, *President*
Andrew Mersmann, *Editor*
Robert Adams, *Treasurer*
Brett Caldwell, *Mktg Dir*
David Molano, *Mktg Coord*
EMP: 7
SALES (est): 890K **Privately Held**
WEB: www.passportmagazine.net
SIC: 2721 Magazines: publishing only, not printed on site

(G-11763)
Q SQUARED DESIGN LLC
41 Madison Ave Ste 1905 (10010-2343)
P.O. Box 1550, Sanibel FL (33957-1550)
PHONE..................212 686-8860
Shannon McAlpine, *Sales Dir*
Nancy Mosny, *Mng Member*
Rudolf Mosny,
▲ EMP: 25
SALES (est): 2.4MM **Privately Held**
SIC: 3089 2392 Tableware, plastic; household furnishings

(G-11764)
QUAD/GRAPHICS INC
140 E 42nd St Bsmt 2 (10017-5616)
PHONE..................212 672-1300
EMP: 447

SALES (corp-wide): 4.6B **Publicly Held**
SIC: 2752 Commercial printing, lithographic
PA: Quad/Graphics Inc.
N61w23044 Harrys Way
Sussex WI 53089
414 566-6000

(G-11765)
QUAD/GRAPHICS INC
60 5th Ave Lowr Level (10011-8868)
PHONE..................212 206-5535
EMP: 509
SALES (corp-wide): 4.6B **Publicly Held**
SIC: 2752 Commercial printing, lithographic
PA: Quad/Graphics Inc.
N61w23044 Harrys Way
Sussex WI 53089
414 566-6000

(G-11766)
QUAD/GRAPHICS INC
375 Hudson St (10014-3658)
PHONE..................212 741-1001
Fax: 212 741-1077
Mike Horton, *Branch Mgr*
EMP: 509
SALES (corp-wide): 4.6B **Publicly Held**
SIC: 2752 Commercial printing, lithographic
PA: Quad/Graphics Inc.
N61w23044 Harrys Way
Sussex WI 53089
414 566-6000

(G-11767)
QUALITY IMPRESSIONS INC
163 Varick St Fl 6 (10013-1108)
PHONE..................646 613-0002
Fax: 646 613-0002
Brennan Ganga, *President*
EMP: 6
SALES: 600K **Privately Held**
SIC: 2759 Commercial printing

(G-11768)
QUALITY PATTERN CORP
246 W 38th St Fl 9 (10018-9076)
PHONE..................212 704-0355
Fax: 212 921-0568
Mario Lipari, *President*
Joe Lipari, *Vice Pres*
EMP: 70
SQ FT: 14,000
SALES (est): 5.3MM **Privately Held**
WEB: www.qualitypatterns.com
SIC: 2335 2741 Women's, juniors' & misses' dresses; miscellaneous publishing

(G-11769)
QUARTET FINANCIAL SYSTEMS INC (PA)
1412 Broadway Rm 2300 (10018-9240)
PHONE..................845 358-6071
Kathleen Perrotte, *President*
Georges Bory, *Managing Dir*
Zevier Dellouard, *Managing Dir*
Allen Whipple, *Managing Dir*
Dennis Kachintsev, *Software Engr*
EMP: 17
SALES (est): 6.7MM **Privately Held**
SIC: 7372 Prepackaged software

(G-11770)
QUARTO GROUP INC (DH)
276 5th Ave Rm 205 (10001-8308)
PHONE..................212 779-0700
Lawrence Orbach, *Chairman*
▲ EMP: 30
SALES (est): 61.4MM
SALES (corp-wide): 5MM **Privately Held**
WEB: www.quarto.com
SIC: 2731 Books: publishing only
HQ: Quarto Group Inc(The)
The Old Brewery
London N7 9B
207 700-9000

(G-11771)
QUEST BEAD & CAST INC
Also Called: Quest Beads
49 W 37th St Fl 16 (10018-6226)
PHONE..................212 354-1737
Fax: 212 354-0978

New York - New York County (G-11772) — GEOGRAPHIC SECTION

Marcelle Rosenstrauch, *President*
Josephine Polizzi, *Manager*
▼ **EMP:** 8
SQ FT: 2,000
SALES (est): 510K **Privately Held**
WEB: www.questbeads.com
SIC: 3914 Pewter ware

(G-11772)
QUEST MEDIA LLC
Also Called: Quest Magazine
920 3rd Ave Fl 6 (10022-3627)
PHONE 646 840-3404
Fax: 212 840-3408
Alex Travers, *Assoc Editor*
Christopher Meigher,
EMP: 19
SQ FT: 9,000
SALES (est): 2.6MM **Privately Held**
SIC: 2721 Magazines: publishing only, not printed on site

(G-11773)
QUILTED KOALA LTD
1384 Broadway Rm 1501 (10018-0502)
PHONE 800 223-5678
EMP: 11 **EST:** 2007
SALES (est): 92K **Privately Held**
SIC: 3171 5137 5632 Mfg Women's Handbags/Purses Ret Women's Accessories/Specialties

(G-11774)
QUINN AND CO OF NY LTD
520 8th Ave Rm 2101 (10018-4110)
PHONE 212 868-1900
Florence Quinn, *President*
Gregory McGunagle, *Vice Pres*
Suzanne Rosnowski, *Real Estate*
EMP: 32
SALES (est): 3.9MM **Privately Held**
SIC: 2084 5141 7011 4724 Wines, brandy & brandy spirits; food brokers; resort hotel; travel agencies

(G-11775)
QUOGUE CAPITAL LLC
1285 Ave Of The Ave Fl 35 (10019)
PHONE 212 554-4475
Wayne Rothbaum, *Mng Member*
EMP: 5 **EST:** 2001
SALES (est): 446.6K **Privately Held**
SIC: 2834 Pharmaceutical preparations

(G-11776)
QUOTABLE CARDS INC
611 Broadway Rm 810 (10012-2648)
PHONE 212 420-7552
Gillian Simon, *CEO*
Leslye Reaves, *Editor*
Carol Monte, *Opers Staff*
Kris Ohlsen, *Director*
▲ **EMP:** 6
SALES: 500K **Privately Held**
WEB: www.quotablecards.com
SIC: 2771 2782 Greeting cards; memorandum books, printed

(G-11777)
QUOVO INC
251 W 30th St Ste 16e (10001-2810)
PHONE 646 216-9437
Lowell Putnam, *CEO*
EMP: 20
SALES (est): 1.1MM **Privately Held**
SIC: 7372 Application computer software

(G-11778)
QWORLDSTAR INC
200 Park Ave S Fl 8 (10003-1526)
PHONE 212 768-4500
Lee Odenat, *President*
EMP: 8 **EST:** 2013
SALES (est): 427.9K **Privately Held**
SIC: 2741

(G-11779)
R & M GRAPHICS OF NEW YORK
121 Varick St Fl 9 (10013-1408)
PHONE 212 929-0294
Mario Balzano, *President*
Ron Balzano, *Vice Pres*
EMP: 15 **EST:** 1991
SQ FT: 10,000
SALES: 1.5MM **Privately Held**
SIC: 2759 Commercial printing

(G-11780)
R & M INDUSTRIES INC
111 Broadway Rm 1112 (10006-1933)
PHONE 212 366-6414
Erik Van Kreuninger, *CEO*
Metje Saffir, *Principal*
Robert Van Kreuninger, *Vice Pres*
Sherry Moore, *Controller*
▲ **EMP:** 14
SQ FT: 198,000
SALES (est): 1.1MM **Privately Held**
SIC: 2392 Pillows, bed: made from purchased materials; tablecloths: made from purchased materials

(G-11781)
R & M RICHARDS INC (PA)
1400 Broadway Fl 9 (10018-5300)
PHONE 212 921-8820
Fax: 212 398-1813
Mario Dellanno, *CEO*
Richard Dellanno, *President*
Robert Dellanno, *Vice Pres*
Robert Dellano, *Vice Pres*
Stephanie Louis, *Production*
▲ **EMP:** 65
SQ FT: 19,000
SALES (est): 30.1MM **Privately Held**
WEB: www.rmrich.com
SIC: 2337 2335 Women's & misses' suits & skirts; women's, juniors' & misses' dresses

(G-11782)
R & R GROSBARD INC
1156 Avenue Of The Americ (10036-2702)
PHONE 212 575-0077
Robert Grosbard, *Ch of Bd*
Amish Shah, *COO*
Grendy Raymonds, *Controller*
Fran Laucella, *Relations*
EMP: 30
SALES (est): 3.2MM **Privately Held**
SIC: 3911 Jewelry apparel

(G-11783)
R-PAC INTERNATIONAL CORP (PA)
132 W 36th St Fl 7 (10018-8825)
PHONE 212 465-1818
Michael Teitelbaum, *President*
Daniel Teitelbaum, *Chairman*
Peter D'Amico, *CFO*
▲ **EMP:** 40
SQ FT: 15,000
SALES (est): 10.1MM **Privately Held**
SIC: 2241 Labels, woven

(G-11784)
R-S RESTAURANT EQP MFG CORP (PA)
Also Called: Preferred Wholesale
272 Bowery (10012-3674)
PHONE 212 925-0335
Chekee Ho, *President*
Fu Ho, *Vice Pres*
▲ **EMP:** 10
SQ FT: 2,500
SALES (est): 2MM **Privately Held**
SIC: 3589 5046 Commercial cooking & foodwarming equipment; restaurant equipment & supplies

(G-11785)
RAFFETTOS CORP
144 W Houston St (10012-2546)
PHONE 212 777-1261
Fax: 212 727-0047
Richard Raffetto, *President*
Andrew Raffetto, *Vice Pres*
EMP: 20
SQ FT: 7,000
SALES (est): 2.4MM **Privately Held**
SIC: 2098 5499 Macaroni & spaghetti; noodles (e.g. egg, plain & water), dry; gourmet food stores

(G-11786)
RAG & BONE INDUSTRIES LLC
416 W 13th St (10014-1117)
PHONE 212 249-3331
Shannon Overman, *Area Mgr*
Chris Vieth, *CFO*
Fernando Victoria, *Credit Mgr*
Farrell Crowley, *Marketing Mgr*

Litisha Daring, *Branch Mgr*
EMP: 56
SALES (corp-wide): 43.7MM **Privately Held**
SIC: 2326 Men's & boys' work clothing
PA: Rag & Bone Industries Llc
425 W 13th St Ofc 2
New York NY 10014
212 278-8214

(G-11787)
RAG & BONE INDUSTRIES LLC (PA)
425 W 13th St Ofc 2 (10014-1123)
PHONE 212 278-8214
Mike Tucci, *Managing Prtnr*
Ray Guerra, *General Mgr*
Kay Wright, *General Mgr*
Jennie McCormick, *Managing Dir*
Shelly Parker, *Area Mgr*
▲ **EMP:** 70
SALES (est): 43.7MM **Privately Held**
SIC: 2326 Men's & boys' work clothing

(G-11788)
RAILWORKS TRANSIT SYSTEMS INC (HQ)
5 Penn Plz (10001-1810)
PHONE 212 502-7900
Jeffrey M Levy, *President*
Daniel Brown, *Principal*
Gene Cellini, *Senior VP*
John August, *Vice Pres*
Geane Jospeh Celoini, *Vice Pres*
EMP: 28
SALES (est): 84.4MM
SALES (corp-wide): 905.2MM **Privately Held**
SIC: 3531 Railway track equipment
PA: Railworks Corporation
5 Penn Plz
New York NY 10001
212 502-7900

(G-11789)
RAINFOREST APPAREL LLC
1385 Broadway Fl 24 (10018-6009)
PHONE 212 840-0880
Jack Wo, *President*
EMP: 8
SALES (est): 452.3K **Privately Held**
SIC: 2389 Disposable garments & accessories

(G-11790)
RAINFOREST INC
Also Called: Rft
420 5th Ave Fl 27 (10018-0271)
PHONE 212 575-7620
Fax: 212 575-7630
Jack Wu, *Ch of Bd*
Daisy Wu, *CFO*
Ike Tippettes, *Financial Exec*
▲ **EMP:** 10
SQ FT: 11,850
SALES: 3MM **Privately Held**
SIC: 2329 8742 6794 Men's & boys' leather, wool & down-filled outerwear; down-filled clothing: men's & boys'; jackets (suede, leatherette, etc.), sport: men's & boys'; marketing consulting services; patent owners & lessors

(G-11791)
RALEIGH AND DRAKE PBC
110 E 25th St Fl 3 (10010-2913)
PHONE 212 625-8212
Patrick Sarkissian, *CEO*
Gilad Goren,
EMP: 15 **EST:** 2013
SALES (est): 860K **Privately Held**
SIC: 7372 Application computer software

(G-11792)
RALPH LAUREN CORPORATION (PA)
650 Madison Ave Fl C1 (10022-1070)
PHONE 212 318-7000
Ralph Lauren, *Ch of Bd*
Stefan Larsson, *President*
Valerie Hermann, *President*
Sara Olinger, *Editor*
David Lauren, *Exec VP*
◆ **EMP:** 500 **EST:** 1967
SQ FT: 270,000

SALES: 7.4B **Publicly Held**
WEB: www.polo.com
SIC: 2325 2321 2253 2323 Men's & boys' trousers & slacks; men's & boys' dress shirts; men's & boys' sports & polo shirts; shirts (outerwear), knit; sweaters & sweater coats, knit; ties, handsewn: made from purchased materials; topcoats, men's & boys': made from purchased materials; men's & boys' sportswear & athletic clothing; sweaters & sweater jackets: men's & boys'

(G-11793)
RALPH LAUREN CORPORATION
979 3rd Ave Ste 404 (10022-1270)
PHONE 212 421-1570
Brittany Adler, *Vice Pres*
Misty McGee, *Vice Pres*
Jeffrey Wheeler, *Vice Pres*
Genemarie Crowe, *Human Resources*
Stephanie Ring, *Manager*
EMP: 12
SALES (corp-wide): 7.4B **Publicly Held**
SIC: 2321 Men's & boys' furnishings
PA: Ralph Lauren Corporation
650 Madison Ave Fl C1
New York NY 10022
212 318-7000

(G-11794)
RALPH LAUREN CORPORATION
205 W 39th St Fl 13 (10018-3532)
PHONE 917 934-4200
EMP: 8
SALES (corp-wide): 7.4B **Publicly Held**
SIC: 2339 Women's & misses' outerwear
PA: Ralph Lauren Corporation
650 Madison Ave Fl C1
New York NY 10022
212 318-7000

(G-11795)
RALPH LAUREN CORPORATION
25 W 39th St Fl 8 (10018-4073)
PHONE 212 221-7751
Lori Kahn, *Finance*
Michael Arahill, *Branch Mgr*
Patrick McCombb, *Technician*
EMP: 10
SALES (corp-wide): 7.4B **Publicly Held**
SIC: 2335 Women's, juniors' & misses' dresses
PA: Ralph Lauren Corporation
650 Madison Ave Fl C1
New York NY 10022
212 318-7000

(G-11796)
RAMSBURY PROPERTY US INC (DH)
Also Called: Benetton Services
601 5th Ave Fl 4 (10017-8258)
P.O. Box 6020, Somerset NJ (08875-6020)
PHONE 212 223-6250
Fax: 212 371-1438
Carlo Tunioli, *Vice Pres*
Diane Mravcak, *Vice Pres*
Kurt Andersen, *Manager*
Robyn Forest, *Manager*
Angie Maximo, *Manager*
▲ **EMP:** 13
SQ FT: 10,000
SALES (est): 3.9MM
SALES (corp-wide): 9.4MM **Privately Held**
SIC: 2329 2339 5651 8742 Men's & boys' sportswear & athletic clothing; sportswear, women's; family clothing stores; marketing consulting services
HQ: Benetton Group Srl
Via Villa Minelli 1
Ponzano Veneto TV 31050
042 251-9111

(G-11797)
RAMY BROOK LLC
231 W 39th St Rm 720 (10018-1089)
PHONE 212 744-2789
Ramy Sharp, *President*
Nellie Roch, *Opers Mgr*
Aryeh Melaris, *CFO*
▲ **EMP:** 30
SQ FT: 5,000

▲ = Import ▼ = Export
◆ = Import/Export

GEOGRAPHIC SECTION

New York - New York County (G-11826)

SALES (est): 4.2MM **Privately Held**
SIC: 2331 Women's & misses' blouses & shirts

(G-11798)
RAND LUXURY INC
276 5th Ave Rm 906 (10001-4509)
PHONE..................................212 655-4505
Bradford Rand, *Principal*
Michelle Weiser, *Marketing Mgr*
Alex Reiff, *Director*
EMP: 6 EST: 2011
SALES (est): 242.1K **Privately Held**
SIC: 3131 Rands

(G-11799)
RANDA ACCESSORIES LEA GDS LLC
417 5th Ave Fl 11 (10016-2238)
PHONE..................................212 354-5100
John Hastings, *Branch Mgr*
EMP: 100
SALES (corp-wide): 448MM **Privately Held**
SIC: 2387 3161 3172 2389 Apparel belts; attache cases; briefcases; suitcases; wallets; suspenders; neckties, men's & boys': made from purchased materials
PA: Randa Accessories Leather Goods Llc
5600 N River Rd Ste 500
Rosemont IL 60018
847 292-8300

(G-11800)
RANDALL LOEFFLER INC
588 Broadway Rm 1203 (10012-5237)
PHONE..................................212 226-8787
Jessica L Randall, *CEO*
Amanda Thomas, *COO*
Brian Murphy, *CFO*
▲ EMP: 15
SQ FT: 2,500
SALES (est): 3.8MM **Privately Held**
SIC: 3131 Boot & shoe accessories

(G-11801)
RANDGOLD RESOURCES LTD
101 Barclay St (10007-2550)
PHONE..................................212 815-2129
Graham Shuttleworth, *CFO*
Martin Welsh, *General Counsel*
EMP: 5
SALES (est): 235.7K **Privately Held**
SIC: 1241 Coal mining services

(G-11802)
RASCO GRAPHICS INC
519 8th Ave Fl 18 (10018-4577)
PHONE..................................212 206-0447
Fax: 212 242-2818
Howard Frank, *President*
Jackie Romano, *Bookkeeper*
EMP: 6
SQ FT: 2,000
SALES (est): 570K **Privately Held**
SIC: 2752 Commercial printing, offset

(G-11803)
RAVEN NEW YORK LLC
450 W 15th St (10011-7097)
PHONE..................................212 584-9690
Molly Young, *Accounting Mgr*
Mazdack Rassi,
Moishe Mama,
Erez Shternlicht,
▲ EMP: 6
SQ FT: 2,500
SALES (est): 710K **Privately Held**
SIC: 2331 2335 Women's & misses' blouses & shirts; women's, juniors' & misses' dresses

(G-11804)
RAXON FABRICS CORP (HQ)
261 5th Ave (10016-7701)
PHONE..................................212 532-6816
Fax: 212 481-9219
Joe Berasi, *President*
Ruud Averson, *President*
Harry Ellis, *Vice Pres*
Eve Singer, *Design Engr*
Claus Maenzsiebje, *Treasurer*
▲ EMP: 13 EST: 1947
SQ FT: 7,400

SALES (est): 4.4MM **Privately Held**
WEB: www.raxon.com
SIC: 2262 Silk broadwoven fabric finishing
PA: Vescom B.V.
V Diepenheim Scheltusln 32
Leusden
334 944-010

(G-11805)
RAY GRIFFITHS INC
303 5th Ave Rm 1901 (10016-6658)
PHONE..................................212 689-7209
Ray Griffiths, *Principal*
EMP: 7
SALES (est): 453K **Privately Held**
SIC: 1499 Gem stones (natural) mining

(G-11806)
RAY MEDICA INC
505 Park Ave Ste 1400 (10022-9315)
PHONE..................................952 885-0500
Todd Johnson, *Vice Pres*
Mary Fuller, *CFO*
Monique Priest, *Supervisor*
EMP: 45
SALES (est): 1.9MM **Privately Held**
SIC: 3845 Electromedical equipment

(G-11807)
RAYDOOR INC
134 W 29th St Rm 909 (10001-5304)
PHONE..................................212 421-0641
Fax: 212 349-1856
Luke Sigel, *President*
Lana Abraham, *Vice Pres*
Ted Fotopoulos, *Opers Mgr*
Matt Cashman, *Prdtn Mgr*
Dhruv Patel, *Prdtn Mgr*
EMP: 6
SALES (est): 1MM **Privately Held**
WEB: www.raydoor.com
SIC: 3442 Metal doors, sash & trim

(G-11808)
RAZORFISH LLC
1440 Broadway Fl 18 (10018-2312)
PHONE..................................212 798-6600
Lorna Colgan, *Publisher*
Maggie Boyer, *General Mgr*
Paul Brownlow, *Project Mgr*
Melanie Bean, *Buyer*
Nate Carlson, *Buyer*
EMP: 8
SALES (corp-wide): 65.7MM **Privately Held**
WEB: www.avenuea.com
SIC: 7372 Prepackaged software
HQ: Razorfish, Llc
424 2nd Ave W
Seattle WA 98119
206 816-8800

(G-11809)
RB DIAMOND INC
22 W 48th St Ste 904 (10036-1803)
PHONE..................................212 398-4560
Fax: 212 366-0078
Rafael Inoyatov, *Principal*
EMP: 5
SALES (est): 396.3K **Privately Held**
SIC: 3356 Gold & gold alloy bars, sheets, strip, etc.

(G-11810)
RD INTRNTNL STYLE
275 W 39th St Fl 7 (10018-0748)
PHONE..................................212 382-2360
Kenneth Hollinger, *Ch of Bd*
▲ EMP: 8
SALES (est): 750K **Privately Held**
SIC: 2339 Women's & misses' outerwear

(G-11811)
READERS DIGEST ASSN INCTHE
16 E 34th St Fl 14 (10016-4360)
PHONE..................................414 423-0100
Diane Jones, *Branch Mgr*
EMP: 16
SALES (corp-wide): 1.7B **Privately Held**
WEB: www.rd.com
SIC: 2721 Magazines: publishing only, not printed on site

PA: Trusted Media Brands, Inc.
750 3rd Ave Fl 3
New York NY 10017
914 238-1000

(G-11812)
READING ROOM INC (PA)
48 Wall St Fl 5 (10005-2911)
PHONE..................................212 463-1029
EMP: 6
SALES (est): 2.2MM **Privately Held**
SIC: 2731 Book publishing

(G-11813)
REAL ESTATE MEDIA INC
120 Broadway Fl 5 (10271-1100)
PHONE..................................212 929-6976
Jonathan Schein, *President*
Jessica Dume, *Human Resources*
EMP: 45
SALES (est): 3.9MM **Privately Held**
SIC: 2721 Magazines: publishing only, not printed on site

(G-11814)
RECORD PRESS INC
157 Chambers St (10007-1015)
PHONE..................................212 619-4949
Fax: 212 608-3141
Hugh Wilmot Jr, *President*
EMP: 8
SALES (est): 605K **Privately Held**
SIC: 2741 Miscellaneous publishing

(G-11815)
REDBOOK MAGAZINE
224 W 57th St Lbby Fl22 (10019-3212)
PHONE..................................212 649-3331
Fax: 212 581-8114
Daniel Zucchi, *Principal*
Ellen Kumes, *Chief*
EMP: 12
SALES (est): 1.4MM **Privately Held**
SIC: 2721 7313 Magazines: publishing & printing; radio, television, publisher representatives

(G-11816)
REDKEN 5TH AVENUE NYC LLC
565 5th Ave (10017-2413)
PHONE..................................212 984-5113
Sheri Doss, *Vice Pres*
Claire Buxton, *Director*
EMP: 8
SALES (est): 1.3MM **Privately Held**
SIC: 2844 Cosmetic preparations

(G-11817)
REENTRY GAMES INC
215 E 5th St (10003-8563)
PHONE..................................646 421-0080
Andrew Kutruff, *President*
EMP: 5
SALES (est): 258.4K **Privately Held**
SIC: 7372 Home entertainment computer software

(G-11818)
REFUEL INC (PA)
1384 Broadway Rm 407 (10018-6140)
PHONE..................................917 645-2974
Srinivas RAO, *President*
Greg Anthony, *Natl Sales Mgr*
▲ EMP: 2
SQ FT: 1,800
SALES (est): 4MM **Privately Held**
SIC: 2211 5091 5699 Apparel & outerwear fabrics, cotton; sporting & recreation goods; sports apparel

(G-11819)
REGAL EMBLEM CO INC
250 W Broadway Fl 2 (10013-2431)
PHONE..................................212 925-8833
Fax: 212 925-3413
Judith Nadelson, *President*
Michael Bottino, *Vice Pres*
EMP: 15 EST: 1931
SQ FT: 5,000
SALES (est): 1.8MM **Privately Held**
SIC: 2399 Emblems, badges & insignia: from purchased materials

(G-11820)
REGAN ARTS LLC
65 Bleecker St Fl 4 (10012-2420)
PHONE..................................646 488-6613
Judith Regan, *CEO*
EMP: 10
SALES (est): 1.2MM
SALES (corp-wide): 399.9K **Privately Held**
SIC: 2741 Miscellaneous publishing
HQ: Phaidon Press Limited
Regent's Wharf
London

(G-11821)
REINHOLD BROTHERS INC
799 Park Ave (10021-3275)
PHONE..................................212 867-8310
John Reinhold, *President*
EMP: 20
SALES (est): 1.5MM **Privately Held**
SIC: 3911 5944 Jewel settings & mountings, precious metal; pearl jewelry, natural or cultured; jewelry, precious stones & precious metals

(G-11822)
REISS LTD (PA)
309 Bleecker St 313 (10014-3427)
PHONE..................................212 488-2411
David Reiss, *Principal*
EMP: 7
SALES (est): 1.6MM **Privately Held**
SIC: 2389 Apparel & accessories

(G-11823)
RELAVIS CORPORATION
40 Wall St Ste 3300 (10005-1304)
PHONE..................................212 995-2900
Robert De Maio, *President*
Michael Baum, *President*
Jean-Pierre Ducondi, *Vice Pres*
EMP: 45
SQ FT: 2,500
SALES (est): 3MM **Privately Held**
SIC: 7372 Business oriented computer software

(G-11824)
RELIANT SECURITY
450 Fashion Ave Ste 503 (10123-0591)
PHONE..................................917 338-2200
Richard Newman, *CEO*
Mark Weiner, *Principal*
Traci Weiner, *Finance Dir*
Tom Juliani, *Info Tech Dir*
EMP: 23
SALES (est): 2.8MM **Privately Held**
SIC: 7372 Prepackaged software

(G-11825)
RELMADA THERAPEUTICS INC
275 Madison Ave Ste 702 (10016-1101)
PHONE..................................646 677-3853
Sergio Traversa, *CEO*
Danny KAO, *Senior VP*
Michael D Becker, *CFO*
Richard M Mangano, *Security Dir*
EMP: 22 EST: 2007
SALES (est): 4.4MM **Privately Held**
SIC: 2834 Pharmaceutical preparations

(G-11826)
RELX INC (DH)
Also Called: Reed Business Information
230 Park Ave (10169-0005)
PHONE..................................212 309-8100
Fax: 212 309-5480
Mark Kelsey, *CEO*
Dominic Feltham, *President*
Nicholas Luff, *President*
Koos Admiraal, *Publisher*
Joe Lam, *Managing Dir*
◆ EMP: 40
SQ FT: 30,000
SALES (est): 7.1B
SALES (corp-wide): 9B **Privately Held**
WEB: www.lexis-nexis.com
SIC: 2721 2731 7389 7374 Trade journals: publishing only, not printed on site; books: publishing only; trade show arrangement; data processing & preparation; systems analysis or design

New York - New York County (G-11827)

HQ: Reed Elsevier Us Holdings, Inc.
1105 N Market St Ste 501
Wilmington DE 19801
302 427-2672

(G-11827)
RELX INC
249 W 17th St (10011-5390)
PHONE..................212 463-6644
Cheryl Miller, *Manager*
EMP: 35
SALES (corp-wide): 9B **Privately Held**
WEB: www.lexis-nexis.com
SIC: 2721 Magazines: publishing only, not printed on site
HQ: Relx Inc.
230 Park Ave
New York NY 10169
212 309-8100

(G-11828)
RELX INC
655 6th Ave (10010-5107)
PHONE..................212 633-3900
Russell White, *President*
Assaf Rozenberg, *Sales Staff*
Lisa Layton, *Manager*
Marc Palmer, *Sr Software Eng*
EMP: 260
SALES (corp-wide): 9B **Privately Held**
WEB: www.lexis-nexis.com
SIC: 2721 Periodicals
HQ: Relx Inc.
230 Park Ave
New York NY 10169
212 309-8100

(G-11829)
REMAINS LIGHTING
130 W 28th St Frnt 1 (10001-6151)
PHONE..................212 675-8051
Fax: 212 675-8052
David Calligeros, *Owner*
Katie Brennan, *Sales Dir*
Hayley Mace, *Sales Staff*
Alice Kriz, *Mktg Dir*
Lauren Reed, *Marketing Staff*
EMP: 20
SQ FT: 1,500
SALES (est): 2.8MM **Privately Held**
SIC: 3646 3645 Commercial indusl & institutional electric lighting fixtures; residential lighting fixtures

(G-11830)
RENAISSANCE BIJOU LTD
20 W 47th St Ste 18 (10036-3303)
PHONE..................212 869-1969
Fax: 212 869-1371
Elias Theodoropoulos, *President*
EMP: 8
SQ FT: 3,000
SALES (est): 680K **Privately Held**
SIC: 3911 Jewelry, precious metal

(G-11831)
RENAISSNCE CRPT TAPESTRIES INC
200 Lexington Ave Rm 912 (10016-6255)
PHONE..................212 696-0080
Fax: 212 696-4248
Jan Soleimani, *President*
Jeffrey Soleimani, *Vice Pres*
John Lally, *Office Mgr*
Bergi Andonian, *Admin Sec*
▲ EMP: 12
SQ FT: 7,000
SALES (est): 1.3MM **Privately Held**
SIC: 2273 2211 Rugs, hand & machine made; tapestry fabrics, cotton

(G-11832)
RENCO GROUP INC (PA)
1 Rockefeller Plz Fl 29 (10020-2021)
PHONE..................212 541-6000
Fax: 212 541-6197
Ira Leon Rennert, *President*
ARI Rennert, *Chairman*
Marvin Koenig, *Exec VP*
Roger L Fay, *Vice Pres*
John Siegel, *Vice Pres*
◆ EMP: 4
SQ FT: 10,000
SALES (est): 4.5B **Privately Held**
WEB: www.rencogroup.net
SIC: 3312 3316 2514 2511 Sheet or strip, steel, cold-rolled: own hot-rolled; corrugating iron & steel, cold-rolled; metal kitchen & dining room furniture; wood household furniture; kitchen & dining room furniture; handbags, women's; cages, wire

(G-11833)
RENEGADE NATION LTD
434 Av Of The Amercs Fl 6 (10011-8411)
PHONE..................212 868-9000
Jerry Eisner, *Principal*
Geoff Sanoff, *Chief Engr*
Gloria Winter, *Office Mgr*
Louis Arzonico, *Art Dir*
Dennis Mortensen, *Executive*
EMP: 15 EST: 1993
SQ FT: 4,400
SALES (est): 1.4MM **Privately Held**
WEB: www.renegadenation.com
SIC: 2782 Record albums

(G-11834)
RENEGADE NATION ONLINE LLC
434 Av Of The Americas Fl Flr 6 (10011)
PHONE..................212 868-9000
Jerome Eisner, *Accountant*
EMP: 8
SQ FT: 2,400
SALES (est): 269K **Privately Held**
SIC: 2741

(G-11835)
REPERTOIRE INTERNATIONAL DE LI
Also Called: RILM
365 5th Ave Fl 3 (10016-4309)
PHONE..................212 817-1990
Jason Oakes, *Editor*
Lori Rothstein, *Editor*
Rachael Brungard, *Assoc Editor*
Michael Lupo, *Assoc Editor*
Insia Malik, *Assoc Editor*
EMP: 25
SALES (est): 2.6MM **Privately Held**
SIC: 2731 2741 Book publishing; miscellaneous publishing

(G-11836)
REPUBLIC CLOTHING CORPORATION
Also Called: Republic Clothing Group
1411 Broadway Fl 37 (10018-3413)
PHONE..................212 719-3000
Fax: 212 719-3057
Steven M Sall, *Ch of Bd*
Michael Warner, *President*
Jerry Kau, *Office Mgr*
▲ EMP: 30
SQ FT: 7,500
SALES (est): 8.1MM **Privately Held**
SIC: 2339 Women's & misses' outerwear

(G-11837)
REPUBLIC CLOTHING GROUP INC
1411 Broadway Fl 37 (10018-3413)
PHONE..................212 719-3000
Michael Warner, *President*
Steven M Sall, *Chairman*
Alison Cho, *Controller*
EMP: 150
SQ FT: 7,500
SALES (est): 1.2MM **Privately Held**
SIC: 2339 Aprons, except rubber or plastic: women's, misses', juniors'

(G-11838)
RES MEDIA GROUP INC
Also Called: RES Magazine
601 W 26th St Fl 11 (10001-1101)
PHONE..................212 320-3750
Fax: 212 937-7134
David Beal, *CEO*
Les Garland, *President*
Jonathan Wells, *Vice Pres*
EMP: 12
SALES (est): 813.7K **Privately Held**
WEB: www.res.com
SIC: 2721 8742 Periodicals; management consulting services
PA: Sputnik7.Com Llc
601 W 26th St Fl 11
New York NY

(G-11839)
RESERVOIR MEDIA MANAGEMENT INC (PA)
225 Varick St Fl 6 (10014-4388)
PHONE..................212 675-0541
Golnar Khosrowshahi, *CEO*
Rell Lafargue, *COO*
Faith Newman, *Senior VP*
Steven Storch, *CFO*
Catherine Addo, *Director*
EMP: 12
SQ FT: 8,000
SALES (est): 1.5MM **Privately Held**
SIC: 2741 Music book & sheet music publishing

(G-11840)
RESONANT LEGAL MEDIA LLC
1040 Av Of The Amrcs 18 (10018-3703)
PHONE..................212 687-7100
Fax: 212 687-0411
Patrick Swart, *Branch Mgr*
EMP: 20
SALES (corp-wide): 34.9MM **Privately Held**
SIC: 2752 7336 8748 Commercial printing, lithographic; commercial art & graphic design; business consulting
PA: Resonant Legal Media, Llc
1 Penn Plz Ste 1514
New York NY 10119
800 781-3591

(G-11841)
RESONANT LEGAL MEDIA LLC (PA)
Also Called: Trialgraphix
1 Penn Plz Ste 1514 (10119-1514)
PHONE..................800 781-3591
Richard S Pennell, *CEO*
Steven Stolberg, *President*
Luis E Otero, *Vice Pres*
Patrick Paulin, *Vice Pres*
Elizabeth Noble, *Prdtn Mgr*
EMP: 90
SQ FT: 35,000
SALES (est): 34.9MM **Privately Held**
SIC: 2752 7336 3993 2761 Commercial printing, offset; graphic arts & related design; signs & advertising specialties; manifold business forms

(G-11842)
RESOURCE PTRLM&PTROCHMCL INTL
3 Columbus Cir Fl 15 (10019-8716)
PHONE..................212 537-3856
Damon Lee, *Ch of Bd*
Daunette Lee, *Vice Pres*
Akpan Ekpo, *Director*
EMP: 20
SALES (est): 289.2K **Privately Held**
SIC: 1311 Crude petroleum production

(G-11843)
RESPONCER INC
1781 Riverside Dr Apt 3g (10034-5346)
PHONE..................917 572-0895
Miguel Cabrera, *CEO*
Tony Aviles, *Bd of Directors*
Josh Gosier, *Bd of Directors*
Jordan Gosin, *Bd of Directors*
Adam Levinson, *Bd of Directors*
EMP: 5
SALES (est): 300K **Privately Held**
SIC: 7372 Application computer software

(G-11844)
RESTAURANT 570 8TH AVENUE LLC
Also Called: Wok To Walk
213 W 40th St Fl 3 (10018-1627)
PHONE..................646 722-8191
Aviv Schwietzer,
EMP: 15 EST: 2013
SALES (est): 1.5MM **Privately Held**
SIC: 2599 Food wagons, restaurant

(G-11845)
RETAIL MANAGEMENT PUBG INC
Also Called: Instore Magazine
12 W 37th St Rm 502 (10018-7544)
PHONE..................212 981-0217
Fred Mouawad, *Ch of Bd*
Chris Burslem, *Editor*
Krista Collins, *Sales Staff*
Fran Zimnuich, *Sales Staff*
Candace Carlisle, *Art Dir*
EMP: 13
SALES (est): 1.7MM **Privately Held**
SIC: 2721 7313 8741 Magazines: publishing only, not printed on site; electronic media advertising representatives; management services

(G-11846)
RETROPHIN LLC
330 Madison Ave Fl 6 (10017-5041)
PHONE..................212 983-1310
Martin Shkreli, *CEO*
Alvin Shih, *Exec VP*
Bill Benvenuto, *Vice Pres*
Nils Olsson, *Vice Pres*
Kristyn Bogli, *Opers Staff*
EMP: 8
SALES (est): 764.1K **Privately Held**
SIC: 2834 Pharmaceutical preparations

(G-11847)
RETURN TEXTILES LLC
187 Lafayette St Fl 5 (10013-3221)
PHONE..................646 408-0108
Pinothy Coombs, *Mng Member*
Tyson Toussant, *Mng Member*
Pharrell Williams,
Angela Stuart, *Coordinator*
EMP: 6
SALES (est): 440K **Privately Held**
SIC: 2299 Apparel filling: cotton waste, kapok & related material; upholstery filling, textile

(G-11848)
REV HOLDINGS INC
466 Lexington Ave Fl 21 (10017-3153)
PHONE..................212 527-4000
Ronald O Perelman, *Ch of Bd*
Mary Massimo, *Exec VP*
Barry F Schwartz, *Exec VP*
Martine Williamson, *Senior VP*
Barretto Carlos, *Vice Pres*
EMP: 8000
SALES (est): 228.8MM
SALES (corp-wide): 5.3B **Privately Held**
SIC: 2844 3421 5122 5199 Toilet preparations; cosmetic preparations; perfumes & colognes; hair preparations, including shampoos; clippers, fingernail & toenail; scissors, hand; cosmetics, perfumes & hair products; toilet preparations; wigs; toiletries, cosmetics & perfumes
HQ: Revlon Holdings Inc.
237 Park Ave
New York NY 10017
212 527-4000

(G-11849)
REVANA INC
Also Called: Revana Digital
350 5th Ave Ste 5912 (10118-0110)
PHONE..................212 244-6137
EMP: 50 **Publicly Held**
WEB: www.webmetro.com
SIC: 7372 Prepackaged software
HQ: Revana, Inc.
8123 S Hardy Dr
Tempe AZ 85284
480 902-5900

(G-11850)
REVLON INC
Also Called: Revlon Co
237 Park Ave (10017-3140)
PHONE..................212 527-6330
EMP: 50
SALES (corp-wide): 1.9B **Publicly Held**
SIC: 2844 Toilet preparations
PA: Revlon, Inc.
1 New York Plz
New York NY 10004
212 527-4000

GEOGRAPHIC SECTION
New York - New York County (G-11873)

(G-11851)
REVLON INC (PA)
1 New York Plz (10004-1901)
PHONE.....................212 527-4000
Fax: 212 527-4130
Ronald O Perelman, *Ch of Bd*
Fabian T Garcia, *President*
Nancy Bonhomme, *General Mgr*
Giovanni Pieraccioni, *COO*
Nelson Griggs, *Exec VP*
▲ **EMP:** 251
SQ FT: 91,000
SALES: 1.9B **Publicly Held**
WEB: www.revlon.com
SIC: 2844 Toilet preparations; perfumes & colognes; deodorants, personal; hair coloring preparations

(G-11852)
REVLON CONSUMER PRODUCTS CORP (HQ)
1 New York Plz (10004-1901)
PHONE.....................212 527-4000
Ronald O Perelman, *Ch of Bd*
Jessica T Graziano, *Senior VP*
Deena Fishman, *Vice Pres*
Larry Winoker, *Treasurer*
Lawrence B Alletto, *Officer*
▲ **EMP:** 277
SQ FT: 91,000
SALES: 1.9B **Publicly Held**
SIC: 2844 3421 Toilet preparations; cosmetic preparations; perfumes & colognes; hair preparations, including shampoos; clippers, fingernail & toenail; scissors, hand
PA: Revlon, Inc.
1 New York Plz
New York NY 10004
212 527-4000

(G-11853)
REVLON HOLDINGS INC (DH)
237 Park Ave (10017-3140)
PHONE.....................212 527-4000
Ronald O Perelman, *Ch of Bd*
David Kennedy, *President*
Donald G Drapkin, *Principal*
Howard Gittis, *Principal*
Ronald Blitstein, *Senior VP*
▲ **EMP:** 60 **EST:** 1985
SQ FT: 345,000
SALES (est): 622.9MM
SALES (corp-wide): 5.3B **Privately Held**
SIC: 2844 3421 5122 5199 Toilet preparations; cosmetic preparations; perfumes & colognes; hair preparations, including shampoos; clippers, fingernail & toenail; scissors, hand; cosmetics, perfumes & hair products; toilet preparations; wigs; toiletries, cosmetics & perfumes
HQ: Rgi Group Incorporated
625 Madison Ave Frnt 4
New York NY 10022
212 527-4000

(G-11854)
REVMAN INTERNATIONAL INC (DH)
350 5th Ave Fl 70 (10118-7000)
PHONE.....................212 894-3100
Rafael Kalach, *Ch of Bd*
Richard Roman, *President*
Normand Savaria, *Senior VP*
Tom Derosa, *Vice Pres*
Diane Piemonte, *Vice Pres*
▲ **EMP:** 40
SQ FT: 20,000
SALES (est): 38.4MM **Privately Held**
WEB: www.revman.com
SIC: 2391 2392 Draperies, plastic & textile: from purchased materials; comforters & quilts: made from purchased materials
HQ: Kaltex North America, Inc.
350 5th Ave Ste 7100
New York NY 10118
212 894-3200

(G-11855)
RFP LLC
Also Called: Bridal Guide
228 E 45th St Fl 11 (10017-3345)
PHONE.....................212 838-7733
Fax: 212 308-7165
Barry Rosenbloom, *Partner*
Jeremy Bucovetsky, *Partner*
Yelena Malinovskaya, *Partner*
Mike Rosenbloom, *Partner*
Jeff Hendlin, *Publisher*
EMP: 35
SQ FT: 11,000
SALES (est): 5.3MM **Privately Held**
WEB: www.bridalguide.com
SIC: 2721 4724 Magazines: publishing only, not printed on site; travel agencies

(G-11856)
RG BARRY CORPORATION
Also Called: Dearfoams Div
9 E 37th St Fl 11 (10016-2822)
PHONE.....................212 244-3145
Howard Eisenberg, *Manager*
EMP: 10
SALES (corp-wide): 25.3MM **Privately Held**
WEB: www.rgbarry.com
SIC: 3142 House slippers
HQ: R.G. Barry Corporation
13405 Yarmouth Rd Nw
Pickerington OH 43147
614 864-6400

(G-11857)
RG GLASS CREATIONS INC
Also Called: R G Glass
180 Varick St Rm 1304 (10014-5842)
PHONE.....................212 675-0030
Edward Geyman, *President*
EMP: 38
SALES (est): 9MM **Privately Held**
SIC: 3211 Construction glass

(G-11858)
RGI GROUP INCORPORATED (DH)
625 Madison Ave Frnt 4 (10022-1801)
PHONE.....................212 527-4000
Ronald O Perelman, *Ch of Bd*
Howard Gittis, *Vice Chairman*
Carol Moral, *Office Mgr*
EMP: 40
SQ FT: 286,000
SALES (est): 628.7MM
SALES (corp-wide): 5.3B **Privately Held**
WEB: www.mafgrp.com
SIC: 2844 3421 5122 5199 Toilet preparations; cosmetic preparations; perfumes & colognes; hair preparations, including shampoos; clippers, fingernail & toenail; scissors, hand; cosmetics, perfumes & hair products; toilet preparations; wigs; toiletries, cosmetics & perfumes
HQ: Macandrews & Forbes Inc.
38 E 63rd St
New York NY 10065
212 688-9000

(G-11859)
RHODA LEE INC
77 W 55th St Apt 4k (10019-4920)
PHONE.....................212 840-5700
Fax: 212 819-1269
Michael Laufer, *President*
Henry Alcalay, *Vice Pres*
Audrey Laufer, *Vice Pres*
▲ **EMP:** 75 **EST:** 1947
SQ FT: 11,000
SALES (est): 6.2MM **Privately Held**
SIC: 2331 2337 2339 Blouses, women's & juniors': made from purchased material; skirts, separate: women's, misses' & juniors'; slacks: women's, misses' & juniors'

(G-11860)
RIAZUL IMPORTS LLC
310 W 120th St Apt 5d (10027-6194)
PHONE.....................713 894-9177
Inaki Orozco,
EMP: 10
SALES (est): 615.7K **Privately Held**
SIC: 2085 Distilled & blended liquors

(G-11861)
RIBZ LLC
1407 Broadway Rm 1402 (10018-2838)
PHONE.....................212 764-9595
EMP: 5
SALES (est): 330K **Privately Held**
SIC: 2389 Mfg Apparel/Accessories

(G-11862)
RICHARD LEEDS INTL INC (PA)
Also Called: True Colors
135 Madison Ave Fl 10 (10016-6712)
PHONE.....................212 532-4546
Fax: 212 683-8571
Marcia L Leeds, *President*
Richard M Leeds, *Chairman*
Bruce Migliaccio, *CFO*
Beth Shindelman, *CFO*
Sudesh Chonkar, *Controller*
▲ **EMP:** 54
SQ FT: 12,500
SALES (est): 15.1MM **Privately Held**
WEB: www.richardleeds.com
SIC: 2339 2384 2341 Women's & misses' athletic clothing & sportswear; bathrobes, men's & women's: made from purchased materials; women's & children's nightwear

(G-11863)
RICHEMONT NORTH AMERICA INC
Also Called: A. Lange & Sohne Corporate
645 5th Ave Fl 6 (10022-5923)
PHONE.....................212 891-2440
EMP: 5
SALES (corp-wide): 12.3B **Privately Held**
SIC: 3873 Watches, clocks, watchcases & parts
HQ: Richemont North America, Inc.
645 5th Ave Fl 5
New York NY 10022
212 891-2440

(G-11864)
RICHEMONT NORTH AMERICA INC
Also Called: Vacheron New York Btq
729 Madison Ave (10065-8003)
PHONE.....................212 644-9500
EMP: 5
SALES (corp-wide): 12.3B **Privately Held**
SIC: 3873 Watches, clocks, watchcases & parts
HQ: Richemont North America, Inc.
645 5th Ave Fl 5
New York NY 10022
212 891-2440

(G-11865)
RICHLINE GROUP INC
Eclipse Design Div
245 W 29th St Rm 900 (10001-5396)
PHONE.....................212 643-2908
Eric Frid, *Branch Mgr*
EMP: 45
SALES (corp-wide): 210.8B **Publicly Held**
WEB: www.aurafin.net
SIC: 3911 Earrings, precious metal
HQ: Richline Group, Inc.
1385 Broadway Fl 12
New York NY 10018
212 886-6000

(G-11866)
RICHLINE GROUP INC
1385 Broadway Fl 12 (10018-6118)
PHONE.....................212 764-8454
EMP: 194
SALES (corp-wide): 194.6B **Publicly Held**
SIC: 3911 5094 Mfg Precious Metal Jewelry Whol Jewelry/Precious Stones
HQ: Richline Group, Inc.
1385 Broadway Fl 12
New York NY 10018
212 886-6000

(G-11867)
RICHLINE GROUP INC
Also Called: Aurafin Oroamerica
1385 Broadway Fl 12 (10018-6118)
PHONE.....................914 699-0000
EMP: 177
SALES (corp-wide): 194.6B **Publicly Held**
SIC: 3911 Mfg Precious Metal Jewelry
HQ: Richline Group, Inc.
1385 Broadway Fl 12
New York NY 10018
212 886-6000

(G-11868)
RICHLOOM CORP
Also Called: Richloom Home Fashion
261 5th Ave Fl 12 (10016-7794)
PHONE.....................212 685-5400
James Richman, *President*
Richard Wold, *Finance Dir*
▲ **EMP:** 10 **EST:** 1995
SALES (est): 6MM **Privately Held**
SIC: 2392 Bedspreads & bed sets: made from purchased materials

(G-11869)
RICHLOOM FABRICS CORP (PA)
261 5th Ave Fl 12 (10016-7794)
PHONE.....................212 685-5400
Fax: 212 696-4407
James Richman, *Ch of Bd*
Fred M Richman, *President*
Ralph Geller, *Vice Pres*
Marvin Karp, *CFO*
Sidney J Silverman, *Admin Sec*
▲ **EMP:** 10
SQ FT: 12,000
SALES (est): 66.1MM **Privately Held**
SIC: 2391 5131 2392 Curtains & draperies; drapery material, woven; household furnishings

(G-11870)
RICHLOOM FABRICS GROUP INC
Also Called: Berkshire Weaving
261 5th Ave Fl 12 (10016-7794)
PHONE.....................212 685-5400
Fax: 212 689-0230
Great Neck Richman, *CEO*
James Richman, *Ch of Bd*
Louise C Robinson, *Vice Pres*
Marci Cohen, *Sls & Mktg Exec*
Richard Schaefer, *Controller*
▲ **EMP:** 5
SQ FT: 1,500
SALES (est): 64.8MM
SALES (corp-wide): 66.1MM **Privately Held**
SIC: 2392 2391 Blankets, comforters & beddings; curtains & draperies
PA: Richloom Fabrics Corp.
261 5th Ave Fl 12
New York NY 10016
212 685-5400

(G-11871)
RICHLOOM HOME FASHIONS CORP
Also Called: Coham/Rvrdale Dcrative Fabrics
261 5th Ave Fl 12 (10016-7794)
PHONE.....................212 685-5400
Fax: 212 646-4907
Ralph Geller, *President*
Fred Richman, *Treasurer*
Michel Spaniel, *Manager*
▲ **EMP:** 10 **EST:** 1966
SQ FT: 1,500
SALES (est): 913.1K
SALES (corp-wide): 66.1MM **Privately Held**
WEB: www.richloom.com
SIC: 2391 2211 2221 Curtains & draperies; draperies & drapery fabrics, cotton; draperies & drapery fabrics, man-made fiber & silk
PA: Richloom Fabrics Corp.
261 5th Ave Fl 12
New York NY 10016
212 685-5400

(G-11872)
RIGHT FIT SHOES LLC
1385 Broadway (10018-6001)
PHONE.....................212 575-9445
Edward Alfax, *President*
Faraj Salameh, *Vice Pres*
▼ **EMP:** 4
SALES: 4MM **Privately Held**
SIC: 3144 Women's footwear, except athletic

(G-11873)
RIMMEL INC
2 Park Ave Rm 1800 (10016-9307)
PHONE.....................212 479-4300
EMP: 5

New York - New York County (G-11874)

GEOGRAPHIC SECTION

SALES (est): 1MM **Publicly Held**
SIC: 2844 Toilet preparations
HQ: Coty Us Llc
350 5th Ave Fl C1700
New York NY 10118
212 389-7000

(G-11874)
RINGS WIRE INC
Also Called: Rome Fastener
24 W 25th St Fl 7 (10010-2727)
PHONE..................................212 741-9779
Fax: 212 741-9774
Dr Stanley Reiter, *President*
Stanley Rieter, *Manager*
EMP: 5
SALES (corp-wide): 2.4MM **Privately Held**
SIC: 3965 Fasteners, snap; buckles & buckle parts
PA: Rings Wire Inc
257 Depot Rd
Milford CT 06460
203 874-6719

(G-11875)
RIO APPAREL USA INC
237 W 37th St Rm 13l (10018-6768)
PHONE..................................212 869-9150
Tong Kyoon Lee, *President*
▲ **EMP:** 5
SALES (est): 640K **Privately Held**
SIC: 2331 Women's & misses' blouses & shirts

(G-11876)
RIO GARMENT SA
114 W 41st St Fl 4 (10036-7308)
PHONE..................................212 822-3182
David Gren, *President*
EMP: 831
SALES (est): 120MM
SALES (corp-wide): 91.4MM **Publicly Held**
SIC: 2331 Women's & misses' blouses & shirts
PA: Hampshire Group, Limited
1924 Pearman Dairy Rd
Anderson SC 29625
212 540-5666

(G-11877)
RIRI USA INC (DH)
350 5th Ave Ste 6700 (10118-6704)
PHONE..................................212 268-3866
L Benjamin Howell II, *Ch of Bd*
Mark Teel, *Vice Pres*
▲ **EMP:** 6
SQ FT: 5,000
SALES (est): 521K **Privately Held**
SIC: 3965 Zipper
HQ: Riri Sa
Viale Della Regione Veneto 3
Padova PD
049 899-6611

(G-11878)
RISION INC
306 E 78th St Apt 1b (10075-2243)
PHONE..................................212 987-2628
Kate Cornick, *CEO*
Earle Harper, *COO*
Ryan O'Donnell, *Vice Pres*
Steven Salsberg, *General Counsel*
EMP: 7 **EST:** 2015
SALES (est): 390K **Privately Held**
SIC: 7372 7389 Business oriented computer software;

(G-11879)
RISK SOCIETY MANAGEMENT PUBG
Also Called: Risk Management Magazine
655 3rd Ave Fl 2 (10017-5621)
PHONE..................................212 286-9364
Fax: 212 655-2693
Jack Hampton, *Exec Dir*
Colin Ferenbach, *Administration*
EMP: 43
SALES: 1.5MM
SALES (corp-wide): 15.3MM **Privately Held**
SIC: 2721 Magazines: publishing only, not printed on site

PA: Risk And Insurance Management Society, Inc.
1065 Ave Of The Amrcs 1
New York NY 10018
212 286-9292

(G-11880)
RITCHIE CORP
263 W 38th St Fl 13 (10018-0280)
PHONE..................................212 768-0083
Fax: 212 768-7773
Lynn Ritchie, *President*
▲ **EMP:** 16 **EST:** 1990
SQ FT: 3,000
SALES (est): 1.4MM **Privately Held**
WEB: www.lynn-ritchie.com
SIC: 2339 Sportswear, women's

(G-11881)
RIZZOLI INTL PUBLICATIONS INC (DH)
300 Park Ave S Fl 4 (10010-5399)
PHONE..................................212 387-3400
Fax: 212 387-3535
Antonio Polito, *President*
Margaret Chace, *Publisher*
Joe Davidson, *Editor*
Loren Olson, *Editor*
Anthony Petrillose, *Editor*
▲ **EMP:** 40
SALES (est): 35MM
SALES (corp-wide): 113.8MM **Privately Held**
WEB: www.rizzoliusa.com
SIC: 2731 5192 5942 5961 Books: publishing only; books; book stores; books, mail order (except book clubs)
HQ: Rcs International Books B.V.
Herengracht 124
Amsterdam
207 944-700

(G-11882)
RIZZOLI INTL PUBLICATIONS INC
Also Called: Universe Publishing
300 Park Ave S Fl 3 (10010-5399)
PHONE..................................212 387-3572
Fax: 212 387-3644
Antonio Polito, *President*
EMP: 15
SALES (corp-wide): 113.8MM **Privately Held**
SIC: 2731 Book publishing
HQ: Rizzoli International Publications, Inc.
300 Park Ave S Fl 4
New York NY 10010
212 387-3400

(G-11883)
RIZZOLI INTL PUBLICATIONS INC
Also Called: Amica Magazine
300 Park Ave Frnt 4 (10022-7404)
PHONE..................................212 308-2000
Fax: 212 308-3718
Imma Vaccaro, *Manager*
Pietro Banas, *Correspondent*
EMP: 12
SALES (corp-wide): 113.8MM **Privately Held**
SIC: 2711 Newspapers
HQ: Rizzoli International Publications, Inc.
300 Park Ave S Fl 4
New York NY 10010
212 387-3400

(G-11884)
RJM2 LTD
241 W 37th St Rm 926 (10018-6963)
PHONE..................................212 944-1660
Richard Weinsieder, *President*
Meryl Weinsieder, *Vice Pres*
▲ **EMP:** 5
SALES (est): 442.9K **Privately Held**
WEB: www.rjm2ltd.com
SIC: 2389 Men's miscellaneous accessories

(G-11885)
RMLL CORP
Also Called: CAROLE WREN
1385 Broadway Rm 1100 (10018-6011)
PHONE..................................212 719-4666
Fax: 212 869-0119

Hoon Lee, *CEO*
Robert Mann, *President*
Lucas MO, *Controller*
Sinead Carroll, *Assistant*
EMP: 20
SQ FT: 4,500
SALES: 22.8MM **Privately Held**
SIC: 2339 Sportswear, women's & children's

(G-11886)
RND ENTERPRISES INC
Also Called: Next Magazine
121 Varick St (10013-1408)
PHONE..................................212 627-0165
David Moyal, *President*
EMP: 19
SALES (est): 1.4MM
SALES (corp-wide): 2.3MM **Privately Held**
SIC: 2721 Magazines: publishing & printing
PA: Multimedia Platforms, Inc.
2929 E Coml Blvd Ph D
Fort Lauderdale FL 33308
954 440-4678

(G-11887)
ROADRUNNER RECORDS INC (DH)
1290 Av Of The Amrcs Fl (10104)
PHONE..................................212 274-7500
Fax: 212 219-0301
Jones Nachsin, *President*
Rodney King, *Vice Pres*
David Rath, *Vice Pres*
Jeffery Teldman, *Personnel Exec*
Ross Anderson, *Manager*
EMP: 35
SQ FT: 8,000
SALES (est): 2.7MM
SALES (corp-wide): 3B **Privately Held**
WEB: www.roadrunnerrecords.com
SIC: 3652 Pre-recorded records & tapes; magnetic tape (audio): prerecorded; phonograph records, prerecorded
HQ: Warner Chappell Music Group (Netherlands) B.V.
Middenweg 1
Hilversum
356 465-600

(G-11888)
ROBELL RESEARCH INC
Also Called: Supersmile
635 Madison Ave Fl 13 (10022-1009)
PHONE..................................212 755-6577
Irwin Smigel, *CEO*
Lucia Smigel, *President*
Joel Levy, *COO*
Phil Mussman, *Sales Dir*
Meredith Johnson, *Sales Executive*
▲ **EMP:** 8
SQ FT: 1,500
SALES (est): 1.8MM **Privately Held**
SIC: 2844 5122 Oral preparations; mouthwashes; toiletries

(G-11889)
ROBERT DANES DANES INC (PA)
481 Greenwich St Apt 5b (10013-1398)
PHONE..................................212 226-1351
Rachel Danes, *President*
Robert Danes, *Treasurer*
EMP: 4
SQ FT: 1,500
SALES: 1.6MM **Privately Held**
WEB: www.robertdanes.com
SIC: 2331 Women's & misses' blouses & shirts

(G-11890)
ROBERT EHRLICH
Also Called: Blackswirl
75 Saint Marks Pl (10003-7944)
PHONE..................................516 353-4617
Robert Ehrlich, *Owner*
EMP: 5
SALES (est): 194.6K **Privately Held**
SIC: 7372 Application computer software

(G-11891)
ROBERTO COIN INC (PA)
579 5th Ave Fl 17 (10017-8760)
PHONE..................................212 486-4545
Fax: 212 486-0111

Anthony Peter Webster, *Ch of Bd*
Victoria Simons, *Accounts Exec*
▼ **EMP:** 13
SQ FT: 3,500
SALES (est): 3MM **Privately Held**
WEB: www.robertocoin.com
SIC: 3911 Jewelry, precious metal

(G-11892)
ROBESPIERRE INC
Also Called: Nanette Lepore Showroom
214 W 39th St Ph Ste 602 (10018-4404)
PHONE..................................212 764-8810
Fax: 212 764-8796
Megan Darling, *Manager*
EMP: 8
SALES (corp-wide): 19.6MM **Privately Held**
WEB: www.nanettelepore.com
SIC: 2339 Women's & misses' athletic clothing & sportswear
PA: Robespierre, Inc.
225 W 35th St Ste 600
New York NY 10001
212 594-0012

(G-11893)
ROBESPIERRE INC (PA)
Also Called: Nanette Lepore
225 W 35th St Ste 600 (10001-1980)
PHONE..................................212 594-0012
Fax: 212 594-0038
Robert Savage, *President*
Nanette Lepore, *Vice Pres*
Ana Restrepo, *CFO*
Jenny Rodriguez, *Accountant*
▲ **EMP:** 115
SQ FT: 39,000
SALES (est): 19.6MM **Privately Held**
WEB: www.nanettelepore.com
SIC: 2339 Sportswear, women's

(G-11894)
ROBIN STANLEY INC
Also Called: Pearltek
1212 Avenue Of The Americ (10036-1600)
PHONE..................................212 871-0007
Stanley Robin, *President*
EMP: 6 **EST:** 1975
SALES (est): 510K **Privately Held**
SIC: 3911 Pearl jewelry, natural or cultured

(G-11895)
ROBLY DIGITAL MARKETING LLC
93 Leonard St Apt 6 (10013-3459)
PHONE..................................917 238-0730
Adam Robinson, *Mng Member*
EMP: 40
SALES (est): 660.4K **Privately Held**
SIC: 7372 Prepackaged software

(G-11896)
ROCCO BORMIOLI GLASS CO INC (PA)
41 Madison Ave Ste 1603 (10010-2236)
PHONE..................................212 719-0606
Fax: 212 719-3606
Davide Sereni, *Ch of Bd*
Rocco Bormioli, *Owner*
Maurizio Amari, *Treasurer*
▲ **EMP:** 20
SALES (est): 3.3MM **Privately Held**
SIC: 3221 Glass containers

(G-11897)
ROCKEFELLER UNIVERSITY
Press Office
950 3rd Ave Fl 2 (10022-2705)
PHONE..................................212 327-8568
Fax: 212 327-8587
Michael Rossner, *General Mgr*
Lorna Petersen, *Advt Staff*
Michael Held, *Branch Mgr*
David W Greene, *Manager*
Torsten N D, *Director*
EMP: 6
SQ FT: 3,000
SALES (corp-wide): 537MM **Privately Held**
SIC: 2741 Miscellaneous publishing
PA: The Rockefeller University
1230 York Ave
New York NY 10065
212 327-8078

GEOGRAPHIC SECTION

New York - New York County (G-11924)

(G-11898)
ROCKET FUEL INC
195 Broadway 10 (10007-3100)
PHONE...................212 594-8888
Fax: 212 594-8889
Yasmine Decosterd, *Vice Pres*
Scott Spaulding, *VP Sales*
Doug Herko, *Sales Dir*
Jennifer Stein, *Sales Staff*
Peter Sulick, *Manager*
EMP: 266
SALES (corp-wide): 461.6MM **Publicly Held**
SIC: 3993 Advertising artwork
PA: Rocket Fuel Inc.
 1900 Seaport Blvd
 Redwood City CA 94063
 650 595-1300

(G-11899)
ROCKPORT PA LLC
477 Madison Ave Fl 18 (10022-5831)
PHONE...................212 482-8580
William Trepp, *Principal*
Kimberly Carter, *Counsel*
EMP: 10
SALES (est): 849.5K **Privately Held**
SIC: 7372 Prepackaged software

(G-11900)
RODALE INC
Also Called: Men's Health Magazine
733 3rd Ave Fl 15 (10017-3293)
PHONE...................212 697-2040
Fax: 212 949-9455
Kristina McMahon, *Publisher*
Thomas Bair, *Principal*
Leah Flickinger, *Editor*
Debbie McHugh, *Editor*
Tom Reifinger, *COO*
EMP: 300
SALES (corp-wide): 458.7MM **Privately Held**
WEB: www.rodale.com
SIC: 2721 Magazines: publishing & printing
PA: Rodale Inc.
 400 S 10th St
 Emmaus PA 18049
 800 848-4735

(G-11901)
RODEM INCORPORATED
Also Called: Galian Handbags
120 W 29th St Frnt A (10001-5596)
PHONE...................212 779-7122
John Woo, *General Mgr*
▲ EMP: 10
SALES (est): 667.4K **Privately Held**
SIC: 3171 Women's handbags & purses

(G-11902)
RODEO OF NY INC
62 W 47th St Ste 14a2 (10036-3231)
PHONE...................212 730-0744
Joseph Janfar, *President*
Christine Chang, *Bookkeeper*
▲ EMP: 20
SQ FT: 1,200
SALES (est): 20MM **Privately Held**
SIC: 3366 Castings (except die)

(G-11903)
ROFFE ACCESSORIES INC (PA)
833 Broadway Apt 4 (10003-4700)
PHONE...................212 213-1440
Murray Roffe, *Ch of Bd*
Mark Ptak, *Vice Pres*
▲ EMP: 15
SQ FT: 50,000
SALES (est): 2.6MM **Privately Held**
SIC: 2321 2323 5136 Men's & boys' furnishings; men's & boys' neckwear; neckwear, men's & boys'

(G-11904)
ROGAN LLC
330 Bowery (10012-2414)
PHONE...................212 680-1407
Kevin Ryan, *Branch Mgr*
EMP: 5
SALES (corp-wide): 2.1MM **Privately Held**
WEB: www.roganandcompany.com
SIC: 2335 Women's, juniors' & misses' dresses

PA: Rogan, Llc
 270 Bowery 3
 New York NY 10012
 646 496-9339

(G-11905)
ROGAN LLC (PA)
270 Bowery 3 (10012-3674)
PHONE...................646 496-9339
Dulce Camacho, *Credit Mgr*
Kevin Ryan,
Roger Gregory,
▲ EMP: 20
SALES (est): 2.1MM **Privately Held**
WEB: www.roganandcompany.com
SIC: 2335 Women's, juniors' & misses' dresses

(G-11906)
ROGER & SONS INC (PA)
268 Bowery Frnt 6 (10012-3992)
PHONE...................212 226-4734
Carl Saitta, *Ch of Bd*
Anthony Saitta, *Ch of Bd*
Maria Saitta, *President*
Joe Cirone, *Vice Pres*
EMP: 8
SQ FT: 15,000
SALES (est): 1.9MM **Privately Held**
SIC: 3589 5046 5719 Commercial cooking & foodwarming equipment; restaurant equipment & supplies; kitchenware

(G-11907)
ROGERS GROUP INC
Also Called: Ferrara Manufacturing
318 W 39th St Fl 4 (10018-1493)
PHONE...................212 643-9292
Joe Ferrara, *Ch of Bd*
Carolyn Ferrara, *President*
Joseph Ferrara, *Vice Pres*
Alva Lama, *Manager*
EMP: 50
SQ FT: 25,000
SALES (est): 4MM **Privately Held**
SIC: 2369 2339 Girls' & children's outerwear; women's & misses' outerwear

(G-11908)
ROLI USA INC
100 5th Ave (10011-6903)
PHONE...................412 600-4840
Danny Siger, *Manager*
EMP: 15 EST: 2015 **Privately Held**
SIC: 3931 Musical instruments

(G-11909)
ROLLING STONE MAGAZINE
1290 Ave Of The Amer Fl 2 (10104-0295)
PHONE...................212 484-1616
Fax: 212 767-8205
Steven Deluca, *Publisher*
Jill Thiry, *Publisher*
R Brownridge, *Principal*
John Gruber, *Controller*
Ed Needham, *Manager*
EMP: 9
SALES (est): 920K **Privately Held**
WEB: www.rollingstone.com
SIC: 2741 2721 Miscellaneous publishing; periodicals

(G-11910)
ROMA INDUSTRIES LLC
12 W 37th St Fl 10 (10018-7379)
PHONE...................212 268-0723
Kristin Franz, *Manager*
EMP: 8
SALES (corp-wide): 51.3MM **Privately Held**
WEB: www.watchstraps.com
SIC: 3172 Watch straps, except metal
PA: Roma Industries Llc
 12821 Starkey Rd Ste 4500
 Largo FL 33773
 727 545-9009

(G-11911)
ROMAN MALAKOV DIAMONDS LTD
1 W 47th St Frnt 5 (10036-4785)
PHONE...................212 944-8500
Roman Malakov, *President*
Rajendra Takel, *Office Mgr*
EMP: 5

SALES (est): 553.4K **Privately Held**
SIC: 3544 3911 Diamond dies, metalworking; jewelry, precious metal

(G-11912)
ROMANCE & CO INC
2 W 47th St Ste 1111 (10036-3329)
PHONE...................212 382-0337
Uriel Kaykov, *CEO*
EMP: 5
SALES (est): 260.1K **Privately Held**
SIC: 1499 5094 Diamond mining, industrial; diamonds (gems)

(G-11913)
RONNI NICOLE GROUP LLC
1400 Broadway Rm 2102 (10018-0649)
PHONE...................212 764-1000
Ronnie Russell, *President*
Andy Hilowitz, *Controller*
Cindy Garcia, *Manager*
◆ EMP: 35
SQ FT: 2,500
SALES (est): 3.9MM **Privately Held**
SIC: 2335 Women's, juniors' & misses' dresses

(G-11914)
ROOMACTUALLY LLC
175 Varick St (10014-4604)
PHONE...................646 388-1922
William Keck,
EMP: 5
SALES (est): 307.8K **Privately Held**
SIC: 7372 7373 7371 Prepackaged software; business oriented computer software; systems software development services; computer software development

(G-11915)
ROSEMONT PRESS INCORPORATED (PA)
253 Church St Apt 2 (10013-3438)
PHONE...................212 239-4770
Fax: 212 268-8619
James J Reardon, *Ch of Bd*
Patricia Reardon, *Manager*
EMP: 43 EST: 1963
SQ FT: 12,800
SALES (est): 9.6MM **Privately Held**
WEB: www.rosemontpress.com
SIC: 2752 2789 Commercial printing, offset; bookbinding & related work

(G-11916)
ROSEN MANDELL & IMMERMAN INC
Also Called: Rmi Printing
121 Varick St Rm 301 (10013-1408)
PHONE...................212 691-2277
Fax: 212 675-4243
Steve Visoky, *President*
Joel Kubie, *VP Finance*
Bobbi Peters, *Manager*
EMP: 24
SQ FT: 3,500
SALES (est): 3.3MM **Privately Held**
WEB: www.rmiprinting.com
SIC: 2789 2752 Bookbinding & related work; commercial printing, lithographic

(G-11917)
ROSEN PUBLISHING GROUP INC
29 E 21st St Fl 2 (10010-6256)
P.O. Box 29278 (10087-9278)
PHONE...................212 777-3017
Fax: 212 777-0277
Roger C Rosen, *President*
Holly Cefrey, *Editor*
Tricia Bauer, *Vice Pres*
Gina Hayn, *Vice Pres*
Nancy Nelson, *Human Resources*
▲ EMP: 150
SQ FT: 12,000
SALES (est): 31.3MM **Privately Held**
WEB: www.rosenpublishing.com
SIC: 2731 Book publishing

(G-11918)
ROSENAU BECK INC
135 W 36th St Rm 10l (10018-9473)
PHONE...................212 279-6202
Fax: 212 563-4786
Thomas Rosenau, *President*

EMP: 12
SALES (corp-wide): 1.5MM **Privately Held**
SIC: 2361 Dresses: girls', children's & infants'
PA: Beck Rosenau Inc
 1310 Industrial Blvd # 201
 Southampton PA 18966
 215 364-1714

(G-11919)
ROSETTI HANDBAGS AND ACC (DH)
1333 Broadway Fl 9 (10018-1064)
PHONE...................212 273-3765
Jane Thompson, *President*
Nanette Acost, *Office Mgr*
▲ EMP: 45
SQ FT: 4,000
SALES (est): 4.6MM **Privately Held**
SIC: 2389 Men's miscellaneous accessories
HQ: Gbg Usa Inc.
 350 5th Ave Lbby 9
 New York NY 10118
 646 839-7083

(G-11920)
ROUGH DRAFT PUBLISHING LLC
Also Called: Proof Magazine
1916 Old Chelsea Sta (10113)
PHONE...................212 741-4773
Stephen Davis,
EMP: 15
SALES (est): 1.2MM **Privately Held**
SIC: 2721 Periodicals

(G-11921)
ROUGH GUIDES US LTD
345 Hudson St Fl 4 (10014-4536)
PHONE...................212 414-3635
Martin Dunford, *Exec Dir*
▲ EMP: 75 EST: 1982
SALES (est): 3.9MM **Privately Held**
WEB: www.roughguides.com
SIC: 2741 Miscellaneous publishing

(G-11922)
ROVI CORPORATION
Also Called: Information Commerce Group
18 W 18th St Fl 11 (10011-4650)
PHONE...................212 524-7000
Jonathan Lewin, *Branch Mgr*
EMP: 110
SALES (corp-wide): 526.2MM **Privately Held**
WEB: www.macrovision.com
SIC: 7372 Prepackaged software
PA: Rovi Corporation
 2 Circle Star Way
 San Carlos CA 94070
 408 562-8400

(G-11923)
ROVI CORPORATION
1345 Avenue Of The Americ (10105-0014)
PHONE...................212 824-0355
Dan Tyack, *Sr Project Mgr*
Trev Huxley, *Manager*
EMP: 110
SALES (corp-wide): 526.2MM **Privately Held**
SIC: 7372 Prepackaged software
PA: Rovi Corporation
 2 Circle Star Way
 San Carlos CA 94070
 408 562-8400

(G-11924)
ROYAL HOME FASHIONS INC (DH)
261 5th Ave Fl 25 (10016-7601)
PHONE...................212 689-7222
Myron Kahn, *CEO*
Douglas Kahn, *President*
Stanley Kahn, *Corp Secy*
David Kahn, *Exec VP*
Anthony Cassella, *CFO*
▲ EMP: 2
SALES (est): 57MM
SALES (corp-wide): 4.2B **Privately Held**
SIC: 2391 2392 Curtains & draperies; comforters & quilts: made from purchased materials

New York - New York County (G-11925) — GEOGRAPHIC SECTION

HQ: Mistdoda, Inc.
261 5th Ave Fl 25
New York NY 10016
919 735-7111

(G-11925)
ROYAL MIRACLE CORP
2 W 46th St Rm 9209 (10036-4811)
PHONE 212 921-5797
Edmond Elyassian, *President*
EMP: 30
SQ FT: 5,000
SALES (est): 25MM **Privately Held**
WEB: www.royalmiracle.com
SIC: 3911 Jewelry, precious metal

(G-11926)
ROYAL NEWS CORP
Also Called: Royal Media Group
80 Broad St Ste 1701 (10004-2245)
PHONE 212 564-8972
Fax: 212 564-8973
Jonathan Hornblass, *President*
EMP: 12
SQ FT: 2,000
SALES (est): 1.1MM **Privately Held**
WEB: www.momentic.com
SIC: 2711 Newspapers

(G-11927)
ROYAL PROMOTION GROUP INC
Also Called: Rpg
119 W 57th St Ste 906 (10019-2401)
PHONE 212 246-3780
Fax: 212 399-9135
Bruce E Teitelbaum, *CEO*
Ellen L Friedman, *Exec VP*
Andrea Millner, *Exec VP*
Eric Williams, *Exec VP*
Adam Lurie, *Purchasing*
▲ EMP: 60
SQ FT: 20,000
SALES (est): 10.7MM **Privately Held**
WEB: www.royalpromo.com
SIC: 3993 Signs & advertising specialties; displays & cutouts, window & lobby; displays, paint process

(G-11928)
ROYALTY NETWORK INC (PA)
224 W 30th St Rm 1007 (10001-1077)
PHONE 212 967-4300
Fax: 212 967-3447
Frank Liwall, *President*
Renato Olivari, *Vice Pres*
Lawson Higgins, *Admin Asst*
Ben Gray, *Administration*
Elinor Wilcox, *Administration*
EMP: 7
SQ FT: 2,500
SALES (est): 754.9K **Privately Held**
WEB: www.roynet.com
SIC: 2741 Patterns, paper: publishing & printing

(G-11929)
RP55 INC
230 W 39th St Fl 7 (10018-4977)
PHONE 212 840-4035
Fax: 212 840-7684
Lisa Blumenthal, *Vice Pres*
Sabai Burnett, *VP Mktg*
Ron Poisson, *Manager*
EMP: 6
SALES (corp-wide): 12.9MM **Privately Held**
SIC: 2329 Men's & boys' sportswear & athletic clothing
PA: Rp55, Inc.
520 Viking Dr
Virginia Beach VA 23452
757 428-0300

(G-11930)
RR DONNELLEY & SONS COMPANY
Also Called: Studio 26
250 W 26th St Rm 402 (10001-6737)
PHONE 646 755-8125
Fax: 212 336-5165
Mike James, *Manager*
EMP: 8
SALES (corp-wide): 11.2B **Publicly Held**
WEB: www.rrdonnelley.com
SIC: 2759 Commercial printing
PA: R.R. Donnelley & Sons Company
35 W Wacker Dr Ste 3650
Chicago IL 60601
312 326-8000

(G-11931)
RSL MEDIA LLC
Also Called: New York Enterprise Report
1001 Ave Of The Ave Fl 11 (10018)
PHONE 212 307-6760
Robert Lebin,
EMP: 9
SALES (est): 934K **Privately Held**
SIC: 2721 2741 Magazines: publishing only, not printed on site; miscellaneous publishing

(G-11932)
RTR BAG & CO LTD
27 W 20th St (10011-3707)
PHONE 212 620-0011
Ron Raznick, *President*
EMP: 6
SALES (est): 457.6K **Privately Held**
SIC: 2673 2674 Plastic bags: made from purchased materials; shopping bags: made from purchased materials

(G-11933)
RUBY NEWCO LLC
1211 Ave Of The Americas (10036-8701)
PHONE 212 852-7000
Keith Rupert Murdoch, *CEO*
EMP: 6
SALES (est): 281.7K
SALES (corp-wide): 8.2B **Publicly Held**
SIC: 2711 2721 6289 Newspapers, publishing & printing; magazines: publishing only, not printed on site; statistical reports (periodicals): publishing & printing; financial reporting; stock quotation service
HQ: News Preferred Holdings Inc.
20 Westport Rd
Wilton CT 06897
203 563-6483

(G-11934)
RUDOLF FRIEDMAN INC
42 W 48th St Ste 1102 (10036-1701)
PHONE 212 869-5070
Fax: 212 944-7114
Alexander Nadaner, *President*
Glenn Nadaner, *Vice Pres*
Fay Nadaner, *Treasurer*
Celena Hecht, *Admin Sec*
EMP: 12 EST: 1946
SQ FT: 1,200
SALES (est): 940K **Privately Held**
WEB: www.rudolffriedmann.com
SIC: 3911 Jewelry, precious metal

(G-11935)
RULEVILLE MANUFACTURING CO INC (PA)
469 Fashion Ave Fl 10 (10018-7640)
PHONE 212 695-1620
Gerald Spiewak, *Ch of Bd*
Roy Spiewak, *President*
Pat Cunningham, *Controller*
▲ EMP: 2
SQ FT: 10,000
SALES (est): 16.1MM **Privately Held**
WEB: www.spiewak.com
SIC: 2326 2329 Men's & boys' work clothing; men's & boys' sportswear & athletic clothing

(G-11936)
RUMSON ACQUISITION LLC
Also Called: Stephen Dweck
1385 Broadway Fl 9 (10018-6001)
PHONE 718 349-4300
Jack Rahmey, *President*
EMP: 18
SQ FT: 4,500
SALES (est): 3MM **Privately Held**
SIC: 3911 Jewelry, precious metal

(G-11937)
RUSSIAN STANDARD VODKA USA INC
Also Called: Roust USA
232 Madison Ave Fl 16 (10016-2909)
PHONE 212 679-1894
Leonid Yangarber, *CEO*
Michael Stoner, *President*
Nelia Nuriakhmetova, *Principal*
Igor Galburt, *Exec VP*
Dan Liguori, *Vice Pres*
▲ EMP: 5
SALES (est): 812.8K **Privately Held**
SIC: 2085 Vodka (alcoholic beverage)

(G-11938)
RUTHYS CHEESECAKE RUGELACH BKY
Also Called: Ruthy's Bakery & Cafe
300 E 54th St Apt 31b (10022-5037)
PHONE 212 463-8800
Patrizia Alessi, *President*
Patricia Alessi, *President*
EMP: 18
SQ FT: 7,000
SALES (est): 2MM **Privately Held**
WEB: www.ruthys.com
SIC: 2051 5461 Bread, cake & related products; bakery: wholesale or wholesale/retail combined; bakeries

(G-11939)
RVC ENTERPRISES LLC (PA)
Also Called: Dereon/24 K Style
1384 Broadway Fl 17 (10018-0508)
P.O. Box 607 (10150-0607)
PHONE 212 391-4600
Michael Alestra, *Credit Staff*
Victor Azrak, *Mng Member*
Ryan Steele, *Info Tech Dir*
Charles Azrak,
Reuben Azrak,
▲ EMP: 29
SALES (est): 8.3MM **Privately Held**
SIC: 2339 Women's & misses' outerwear

(G-11940)
RYAN GEMS INC
20 E 46th St Rm 200 (10017-9287)
PHONE 212 697-0149
Edison Akhavan, *President*
Jeffrey Eischen, *Vice Pres*
▲ EMP: 38
SQ FT: 4,500
SALES (est): 9MM **Privately Held**
WEB: www.ryangems.com
SIC: 3911 Jewelry, precious metal

(G-11941)
RYLAND PETERS & SMALL INC
341 E 116th St (10029-1502)
PHONE 646 791-5410
David Peters, *President*
Jeremy Scholl, *CFO*
▲ EMP: 6
SALES (est): 586.9K **Privately Held**
WEB: www.rylandpeters.com
SIC: 2731 Books: publishing only

(G-11942)
S & C BRIDALS LLC (PA)
Also Called: US Angels
1407 Broadway Fl 41 (10018-2348)
PHONE 212 789-7000
Diane O'Brien, *Controller*
Stanley Cayre, *Mng Member*
Amin Cayre,
Hank Shalom,
▲ EMP: 9
SQ FT: 10,000
SALES: 6.5MM **Privately Held**
WEB: www.usangels.com
SIC: 2361 5641 Girls' & children's dresses, blouses & shirts; children's wear

(G-11943)
S & S MANUFACTURING CO INC (PA)
1375 Broadway Fl 2 (10018-7073)
PHONE 212 444-6000
Kirk Gellin, *Co-President*
Robert Sobel, *Co-President*
Robert Frederick, *Vice Pres*
Fred Mandato, *CFO*
▲ EMP: 75
SQ FT: 21,000
SALES (est): 6MM **Privately Held**
SIC: 2331 2339 Blouses, women's & juniors': made from purchased material; sportswear, women's

(G-11944)
S & W METAL TRADING CORP
36 W 47th St Ste 1606 (10036-8601)
PHONE 212 719-5070
Fax: 212 719-5753
Abraham Slomovics, *President*
Abraham Weisz, *Vice Pres*
EMP: 8
SQ FT: 1,000
SALES (est): 650K **Privately Held**
SIC: 3339 3341 Primary nonferrous metals; secondary nonferrous metals

(G-11945)
S G I
40 E 52nd St Frnt A (10022-5911)
PHONE 917 386-0385
Richard L Miller, *Principal*
EMP: 5 EST: 2010
SALES (est): 260K **Privately Held**
SIC: 3577 Computer peripheral equipment

(G-11946)
S P BOOKS INC
99 Spring St Fl 3 (10012-3929)
PHONE 212 431-5011
Pearson Allen, *President*
EMP: 6
SALES: 1.5MM **Privately Held**
WEB: www.spibooks.com
SIC: 2731 5192 Book publishing; books

(G-11947)
S ROTHSCHILD & CO INC (PA)
Also Called: Rothschild Mens Div
1407 Broadway Fl 10 (10018-3271)
PHONE 212 354-8550
Fax: 212 921-5564
Isidore Friedman, *CEO*
Mark Friedman, *President*
Zac Greene, *Mfg Staff*
William Mitchell, *CFO*
Nancy Tassoni, *Sales Mgr*
▼ EMP: 110 EST: 1881
SQ FT: 50,000
SALES (est): 8MM **Privately Held**
SIC: 2369 Girls' & children's outerwear

(G-11948)
S1 BIOPHARMA INC
7 World Trade Ctr 250g (10007-2140)
PHONE 201 839-0941
John Kaufmann, *CFO*
EMP: 5 EST: 2013
SALES (est): 576K **Privately Held**
SIC: 2834 Pharmaceutical preparations

(G-11949)
SAAD COLLECTION INC (PA)
1165 Broadway Ste 305 (10001-7450)
PHONE 212 937-0341
Mohammad Younus, *President*
EMP: 10
SALES (est): 1MM **Privately Held**
SIC: 2321 2331 Men's & boys' furnishings; women's & misses' blouses & shirts

(G-11950)
SABIN ROBBINS PAPER COMPANY
455 E 86th St Apt 5e (10028-6486)
PHONE 513 874-5270
Fax: 513 874-5785
Thomas Roberts, *President*
EMP: 33
SALES (est): 11.5MM **Privately Held**
SIC: 2621 Building paper, sheathing

(G-11951)
SABON MANAGEMENT LLC
123 Prince St Frnt A (10012-5312)
PHONE 212 982-0968
Irina Stepanova, *Branch Mgr*
EMP: 16
SALES (corp-wide): 16.8MM **Privately Held**
SIC: 2841 Soap & other detergents
PA: Sabon Management, Llc
38 Greene St Fl 5
New York NY 10013
212 473-1009

▲ = Import ▼ = Export ◆ = Import/Export

GEOGRAPHIC SECTION

New York - New York County (G-11978)

(G-11952)
SACKS AND COMPANY NEW YORK (PA)
423 W 14th St Ste 429-3f (10014-1028)
PHONE..................212 741-1000
Fax: 212 741-9007
Carla Sacks, *President*
Mary Moyer, *Vice Pres*
Krista Williams, *Sales Staff*
Chris Schimpf, *Agent*
Samantha Tillman, *Director*
EMP: 9
SALES (est): 691.8K **Privately Held**
SIC: 2741 Miscellaneous publishing

(G-11953)
SAFE SKIES LLC (PA)
Also Called: TSA Luggage Locks
954 3rd Ave Ste 504 (10022-2013)
PHONE..................888 632-5027
David Tropp, *Mng Member*
▲ EMP: 9
SQ FT: 70,000
SALES (est): 106.4MM **Privately Held**
SIC: 3429 Locks or lock sets

(G-11954)
SAINT LAURIE LTD
22 W 32nd St Fl 5 (10001-0590)
PHONE..................212 643-1916
Fax: 212 695-4709
Andrew Kozinn, *CEO*
Allan Stricoff, *Controller*
Fernanda Maffra-Narvaez, *Sales Mgr*
▲ EMP: 26
SQ FT: 7,500
SALES (est): 3.5MM **Privately Held**
WEB: www.saintlaurie.com
SIC: 2311 2337 5611 5621 Suits, men's & boys': made from purchased materials; suits: women's, misses' & juniors'; suits, men's; women's clothing stores

(G-11955)
SAKONNET TECHNOLOGY LLC
11 E 44th St Fl 1000 (10017-0058)
PHONE..................212 849-9267
Fax: 212 343-3103
Alarik Myrin, *Partner*
Eric Min, *COO*
Melanie Penachio, *Vice Pres*
Angela Santos, *Finance*
Melanie Tenachio, *Finance*
EMP: 30
SALES (est): 2.9MM **Privately Held**
WEB: www.sknt.com
SIC: 7372 Prepackaged software

(G-11956)
SALE 121 CORP
1324 Lexington Ave # 111 (10128-1145)
PHONE..................240 855-8988
Mohammad Naz, *Branch Mgr*
EMP: 99
SALES (corp-wide): 5.2MM **Privately Held**
SIC: 3572 8748 7371 7373 Disk drives, computer; systems engineering consultant, ex. computer or professional; computer software development; systems software development services; office computer automation systems integration
PA: Sale 121 Corp
 1467 68th Ave
 Sacramento CA 95822
 888 233-7667

(G-11957)
SALENTICA SYSTEMS INC
245 Park Ave Fl 39 (10167-4000)
PHONE..................212 672-1777
Bil Rourke, *Principal*
Dave Ireland, *Vice Pres*
Jonathan Lucas, *Manager*
EMP: 20
SALES (est): 1.5MM **Privately Held**
SIC: 7372 Prepackaged software

(G-11958)
SALMCO JEWELRY CORP (PA)
Also Called: Bay Sales Company
22 W 32nd St Fl 16 (10001-1698)
PHONE..................212 695-8792
Fax: 212 564-5609
Errol Salm, *President*
Morton Salm, *Principal*
Jarred Salm, *Manager*
Lance Salm, *Manager*
▲ EMP: 17
SQ FT: 6,000
SALES (est): 7MM **Privately Held**
WEB: www.baysalesinc.com
SIC: 3961 Costume jewelry, ex. precious metal & semiprecious stones

(G-11959)
SALONCLICK LLC
Also Called: Min New York
117 Crosby St (10012-3301)
PHONE..................718 643-6793
Chad Muranczyk,
EMP: 12
SQ FT: 2,000
SALES (est): 2.1MM **Privately Held**
SIC: 2844 Hair coloring preparations; hair preparations, including shampoos

(G-11960)
SALUTEM GROUP LLC
44 Wall St Fl 12 (10005-2433)
PHONE..................347 620-2640
Mikhail Abarshalin, *Principal*
EMP: 6
SALES (est): 557.4K **Privately Held**
SIC: 2834 Pharmaceutical preparations

(G-11961)
SAM HEE INTERNATIONAL INC
213 W 35th St Ste 503 (10001-1903)
PHONE..................212 594-7815
Fax: 212 594-7844
Hoon Lee, *CEO*
Caroline Lee, *Accountant*
Eric Chong, *Manager*
▲ EMP: 7
SQ FT: 3,000
SALES (est): 1.9MM **Privately Held**
SIC: 2339 Athletic clothing: women's, misses' & juniors'

(G-11962)
SAMUEL FRENCH INC (PA)
235 Park Ave S Fl 5 (10003-1405)
PHONE..................212 206-8990
Fax: 212 206-1429
Nathan Collins, *Ch of Bd*
Charles Nostrand, *President*
Merle Cosgrove, *Vice Pres*
John Graham, *Vice Pres*
Casey McLain, *Opers Spvr*
EMP: 45 EST: 1830
SQ FT: 17,000
SALES (est): 7.1MM **Privately Held**
WEB: www.samuelfrench.com
SIC: 2731 5942 5192 Books: publishing & printing; book stores; books

(G-11963)
SAMUEL SCHULMAN FURS INC
Also Called: Alexandre Furs
150 W 30th St Fl 13 (10001-4185)
PHONE..................212 736-5550
Fax: 212 564-8079
Edwin L Schulman, *President*
Larry Schulman, *Vice Pres*
Stanley R Schulman, *Treasurer*
EMP: 25 EST: 1940
SQ FT: 12,000
SALES (est): 1.4MM **Privately Held**
SIC: 2371 Fur coats & other fur apparel; jackets, fur

(G-11964)
SANCTUARY BRANDS LLC (PA)
Also Called: Tailorbyrd
70 W 40th St Fl 5 (10018-2626)
PHONE..................212 704-4014
Lisa Crider, *Director*
Larry Stemerman,
EMP: 6
SALES (est): 699.8K **Privately Held**
SIC: 2329 5136 5611 Riding clothes:, men's, youths' & boys'; men's & boys' clothing; men's & boys' clothing stores

(G-11965)
SANDBOX BRANDS INC
26 W 17th St Lbby (10011-5710)
PHONE..................212 647-8877
David Barber, *President*
Tom Hubben, *Vice Pres*
EMP: 7
SALES: 490K **Privately Held**
WEB: www.sandboxbrands.com
SIC: 3944 Games, toys & children's vehicles

(G-11966)
SANDOW MEDIA LLC
1271 Ave Of The Ave Fl 17 (10020)
PHONE..................646 805-0200
Arlyn Hernandez, *Editor*
Pamela McNally, *Vice Pres*
Yolanda Yoh, *Vice Pres*
Barbara Mabie, *Controller*
Karlee Linman, *Marketing Staff*
EMP: 10
SALES (corp-wide): 90.7MM **Privately Held**
SIC: 2721 Magazines: publishing only, not printed on site
PA: Sandow Media, Llc
 3651 Nw 8th Ave Ste 200
 Boca Raton FL 33431
 561 961-7700

(G-11967)
SANDY DALAL LTD
220 Central Park S 10f (10019-1417)
PHONE..................212 532-5822
Michael Agashiwala, *President*
Loma Agashiwala, *Admin Sec*
EMP: 5
SQ FT: 1,200
SALES (est): 330K **Privately Held**
WEB: www.sandydalal.com
SIC: 2329 Men's & boys' sportswear & athletic clothing

(G-11968)
SANOY INC
Also Called: Bonnie J
19 W 36th St Fl 11 (10018-7699)
PHONE..................212 695-6384
Larry Jonas, *President*
Bonnie Jonas, *Vice Pres*
EMP: 28
SQ FT: 5,000
SALES (est): 4.1MM **Privately Held**
SIC: 3911 3961 Jewelry, precious metal; costume jewelry

(G-11969)
SANTEE PRINT WORKS (PA)
58 W 40th St Fl 11 (10018-2638)
PHONE..................212 997-1570
Fax: 212 869-7230
Martin Barocas, *Chairman*
Joe Turbeville, *Human Res Mgr*
Mary Grooms, *Manager*
Furman Dominick, *MIS Mgr*
Leon Barocas, *Admin Sec*
▲ EMP: 15 EST: 1949
SQ FT: 1,500,000
SALES (est): 56.3MM **Privately Held**
WEB: www.classiccottons.com
SIC: 2261 Finishing plants, cotton; printing of cotton broadwoven fabrics

(G-11970)
SAPPHIRE SYSTEMS INC (PA)
405 Lexington Ave Fl 49 (10174-0002)
PHONE..................212 905-0100
Uys Moller, *Vice Pres*
Lorenzo Zecca, *Vice Pres*
Derek Dieringer, *Finance*
George Powers, *Accounts Mgr*
Lakesha Stuldivant, *Office Mgr*
EMP: 10
SALES (est): 2MM **Privately Held**
SIC: 7372 Business oriented computer software

(G-11971)
SARATOGA LIGHTING HOLDINGS LLC (PA)
535 Madison Ave Fl 4 (10022-4291)
PHONE..................212 906-7800
Christian L Oberbeck,
Damon H Ball,
Richard A Petrocelli,
▲ EMP: 3
SALES (est): 218.1MM **Privately Held**
SIC: 3641 3645 3646 3648 Electric lamps & parts for generalized applications; residential lighting fixtures; commercial indusl & institutional electric lighting fixtures; lighting equipment

(G-11972)
SARGENT MANUFACTURING INC
120 E 124th St (10035-1933)
P.O. Box 740607, Bronx (10474-9425)
PHONE..................212 722-7000
Richard Oswald, *President*
Robert Oswald, *Vice Pres*
Andrew Geraci, *Engineer*
Roland McNary, *Engineer*
Susan Gnida, *Manager*
EMP: 2 EST: 1973
SQ FT: 5,000
SALES: 1.4MM
SALES (corp-wide): 3.4MM **Privately Held**
SIC: 3443 Chutes & troughs
PA: H. C. Oswald Supply Co., Inc.
 725 Whittier St
 Bronx NY 10474
 718 620-1400

(G-11973)
SARINA ACCESSORIES LLC
Also Called: Dp Accessories
445 5th Ave (10016-0133)
PHONE..................212 239-8106
Dana Heisler, *VP Opers*
Marc Faham, *Mng Member*
▲ EMP: 20
SQ FT: 4,000
SALES (est): 4.1MM **Privately Held**
SIC: 3961 2339 3873 Costume jewelry; scarves, hoods, headbands, etc.: women's; watches, clocks, watchcases & parts

(G-11974)
SARKISIANS JEWELRY CO
17 W 45th St Ste 201 (10036-4922)
PHONE..................212 869-1060
Fax: 212 398-4045
Vazgen Sarkisian, *President*
EMP: 5
SALES (est): 360K **Privately Held**
WEB: www.sarkisiansjewelry.com
SIC: 3911 Medals, precious or semi-precious metal

(G-11975)
SAS INSTITUTE INC
787 Seventh Ave Fl 47 (10019-6018)
PHONE..................212 757-3826
Fax: 212 308-0127
Michael Rosenthal, *Partner*
Kristie Collins, *Principal*
Fiona McNeill, *Principal*
Wes Strom, *Principal*
Tim Fairchlld, *Business Mgr*
EMP: 15
SALES (corp-wide): 2.9B **Privately Held**
WEB: www.sas.com
SIC: 7372 Prepackaged software
PA: Sas Institute Inc.
 100 Sas Campus Dr
 Cary NC 27513
 919 677-8000

(G-11976)
SATELLITE INCORPORATED
43 W 46th St Ste 503 (10036-4121)
PHONE..................212 221-6687
Paula STA Cruz, *General Mgr*
EMP: 5
SALES (est): 319.7K **Privately Held**
SIC: 3911 Jewelry, precious metal

(G-11977)
SAVEUR MAGAZINE
304 Park Ave S Fl 8 (10010-4310)
PHONE..................212 219-7400
Fax: 212 219-1260
Russ Cherami, *Publisher*
Max Falkowitz, *Editor*
Coleman Andrews, *Manager*
Farideh Sadeghin, *Director*
Stefanie McNamara, *Associate Dir*
EMP: 32
SALES (est): 2.2MM **Privately Held**
SIC: 2721 Periodicals

(G-11978)
SAVWATT USA INC (PA)
475 Park Ave S Fl 30 (10016-6901)
PHONE..................646 478-2676
Michael Haug, *CEO*

New York - New York County (G-11979)

GEOGRAPHIC SECTION

Isaac H Sutton, *Ch of Bd*
EMP: 13
SQ FT: 2,000
SALES (est): 3.1MM **Publicly Held**
SIC: 3646 3645 Commercial indusl & institutional electric lighting fixtures; residential lighting fixtures

(G-11979)
SB CORPORATION
114 W 41st St Fl 4 (10036-7308)
PHONE..........................212 822-3166
Rob Cohen, *Principal*
Eric Olmsted, *Info Tech Dir*
▼ **EMP:** 5
SALES (est): 360K **Privately Held**
SIC: 2329 Men's & boys' sportswear & athletic clothing

(G-11980)
SB NEW YORK INC (HQ)
Also Called: Metro New York
120 Broadway (10271-0002)
PHONE..........................212 457-7790
Fax: 212 952-1246
Oskar Bjorner, *CFO*
Al Romei, *Credit Mgr*
Juliano Michael, *Sales Executive*
Lisa Dell, *Senior Mgr*
Bessie Bazile, *Assistant*
EMP: 57
SALES (est): 12.1MM
SALES (corp-wide): 15.4MM **Privately Held**
WEB: www.metronewyork.com
SIC: 2711 Newspapers
PA: Seabay Media Holdings Llc
    120 Broadway Fl 6
    New York NY 10271
    212 457-7790

(G-11981)
SC SUPPLY CHAIN MANAGEMENT LLC
Also Called: SCM
90 Broad St Ste 1504 (10004-2276)
PHONE..........................212 344-3322
Anan Bishara, *Mng Member*
Denise Barrel, *Manager*
▲ **EMP:** 6
SQ FT: 2,600
SALES: 3MM **Privately Held**
SIC: 3569 Filters

(G-11982)
SCALAMANDRE SILKS INC (PA)
979 3rd Ave Ste 202 (10022-1294)
PHONE..........................212 980-3888
Edwin W Bitter, *CEO*
Adriana Bitter, *Ch of Bd*
Robert F Bitter, *President*
Mark Bitter, *Chairman*
Mark J Bitter, *CFO*
▲ **EMP:** 65
SALES (est): 62.1MM **Privately Held**
WEB: www.scalamandre.com
SIC: 2221 2241 5131 2273 Upholstery fabrics, manmade fiber & silk; wall covering fabrics, manmade fiber & silk; trimmings, textile; drapery material, woven; upholstery fabrics, woven; carpets, textile fiber

(G-11983)
SCALAMANDRE SILKS INC
942 3rd Ave (10022-2701)
PHONE..........................212 376-2900
Doris Farno, *Branch Mgr*
EMP: 70
SALES (corp-wide): 62.1MM **Privately Held**
SIC: 2221 Upholstery fabrics, manmade fiber & silk
PA: Scalamandre Silks, Inc.
    979 3rd Ave Ste 202
    New York NY 10022
    212 980-3888

(G-11984)
SCEPTER PUBLISHERS
10 E 39th St Ste 908 (10016-0111)
P.O. Box 1391, New Rochelle (10802-1391)
PHONE..........................212 354-0670
Fax: 212 354-0736
John Powers, *President*

Angel Camardese, *Manager*
Violet Sukdeo, *Manager*
◆ **EMP:** 5
SALES (est): 933.5K **Privately Held**
SIC: 2741 Miscellaneous publishing

(G-11985)
SCH DPX CORPORATION
22 W 21st St Ste 700 (10010-6982)
PHONE..........................917 405-5377
Joe Schoenfelder, *President*
Ricardo Hurtado, *Sales Mgr*
EMP: 7
SALES (est): 510K **Privately Held**
WEB: www.schoenfelder.com
SIC: 2369 Girls' & children's outerwear

(G-11986)
SCHALLER MANUFACTURING CORP (PA)
Also Called: Schaller & Weber
1654 2nd Ave Apt 2n (10028-3109)
PHONE..........................718 721-5480
Fax: 718 956-9157
Ralph Schaller, *Ch of Bd*
Marianne Schaller, *Vice Pres*
Harold Nagel, *Plant Mgr*
George Nici, *Engineer*
Maryanne Karis, *Controller*
EMP: 70 **EST:** 1937
SQ FT: 16,000
SALES (est): 9.7MM **Privately Held**
WEB: www.schallerweber.com
SIC: 2013 5421 Prepared pork products from purchased pork; meat & fish markets

(G-11987)
SCHINDLER ELEVATOR CORPORATION
620 12th Ave Fl 4 (10036-1016)
PHONE..........................212 708-1000
Fax: 212 582-4092
Michael Joseph, *Project Mgr*
Jack Walsh, *Manager*
Claude Brun, *Manager*
URS Singer, *Manager*
Albert Coleman, *Supervisor*
EMP: 250
SALES (corp-wide): 9.3B **Privately Held**
WEB: www.us.schindler.com
SIC: 3534 1796 Elevators & moving stairways; installing building equipment
HQ: Schindler Elevator Corporation
    20 Whippany Rd
    Morristown NJ 07960
    973 397-6500

(G-11988)
SCHINDLER ELEVATOR CORPORATION
1211 6th Ave Ste 2950 (10036-8705)
PHONE..........................800 225-3123
Fax: 212 398-8222
James Iannaccone, *Manager*
EMP: 30
SALES (corp-wide): 9.3B **Privately Held**
WEB: www.us.schindler.com
SIC: 3534 1796 Elevators & equipment; elevator installation & conversion
HQ: Schindler Elevator Corporation
    20 Whippany Rd
    Morristown NJ 07960
    973 397-6500

(G-11989)
SCHLESINGER SIEMANS ELEC LLC
527 Madison Ave Fl 8 (10022-4376)
PHONE..........................718 386-6230
Ralph Scotti, *Manager*
Lana Petrocelli, *Manager*
EMP: 13
SALES (est): 2.2MM
SALES (corp-wide): 83.5B **Privately Held**
SIC: 3634 Electric housewares & fans
PA: Siemens Ag
    Wittelsbacherplatz 2
    Munchen 80333
    896 360-0

(G-11990)
SCHNEEMAN STUDIO LIMITED
330 W 38th St Rm 505 (10018-8639)
PHONE..........................212 244-3330
John Schneeman, *President*

EMP: 5
SQ FT: 2,000
SALES: 500K **Privately Held**
SIC: 2389 Theatrical costumes

(G-11991)
SCHNEIDER AMALCO INC
600 3rd Ave Fl 2 (10016-1919)
PHONE..........................917 470-9674
Thomas Schneider, *CEO*
EMP: 10
SQ FT: 3,500
SALES (est): 547.2K **Privately Held**
SIC: 1381 1389 6792 Drilling oil & gas wells; oil field services; oil royalty traders; oil leases, buying & selling on own account

(G-11992)
SCHNEIDER ELECTRIC IT CORP
Also Called: APC-Mge
520 8th Ave Rm 2103 (10018-4164)
PHONE..........................646 335-0216
George Chappas, *Manager*
Tanya Tomlin, *Manager*
EMP: 10
SALES (corp-wide): 224.4K **Privately Held**
WEB: www.apcc.com
SIC: 3612 Power & distribution transformers
HQ: Schneider Electric It Corporation
    132 Fairgrounds Rd
    West Kingston RI 02892
    401 789-5735

(G-11993)
SCHNEIDER ELECTRIC USA INC
112 W 34th St Ste 908 (10120-0999)
PHONE..........................646 335-0220
James Montemarano, *Principal*
EMP: 136
SALES (corp-wide): 224.4K **Privately Held**
SIC: 3613 Switchgear & switchboard apparatus
HQ: Schneider Electric Usa, Inc.
    800 Federal St
    Andover MA 01810
    978 975-9600

(G-11994)
SCHNEIDER MILLS INC (PA)
1430 Broadway Rm 1202 (10018-3390)
PHONE..........................212 768-7500
Fax: 212 768-0909
Peter M Campanelli, *President*
Mark A Labbe, *Vice Pres*
Mark Mincieli, *Engineer*
Bruce Bodinger, *Controller*
Eva Pang, *Office Mgr*
EMP: 12 **EST:** 1921
SQ FT: 4,500
SALES (est): 110.1MM **Privately Held**
SIC: 2221 Manmade & synthetic broadwoven fabrics; acetate broadwoven fabrics; nylon broadwoven fabrics; polyester broadwoven fabrics

(G-11995)
SCHNELL PUBLISHING COMPANY INC (DH)
360 Park Ave S Fl 10 (10010-1710)
PHONE..........................212 791-4200
Feliza Mirasol, *General Mgr*
Helga Tilton, *Editor*
Marlen Guayara, *Finance Mgr*
EMP: 11 **EST:** 1941
SQ FT: 9,600
SALES: 13MM
SALES (corp-wide): 9B **Privately Held**
SIC: 2721 Trade journals: publishing only, not printed on site
HQ: Relx (Uk) Limited
    Grand Buildings, 1-3 Strand
    London WC2N
    207 930-7077

(G-11996)
SCHOEN TRIMMING & CORD CO INC
151 W 25th St Fl 10 (10001-7250)
PHONE..........................212 255-3949
Fax: 212 924-4945
Martin Silver, *President*
▲ **EMP:** 17 **EST:** 1939

SQ FT: 6,000
SALES: 2.6MM **Privately Held**
SIC: 2241 2298 Narrow fabric mills; braids, textile; cords, fabric; cordage & twine

(G-11997)
SCHOLASTIC CORPORATION (PA)
557 Broadway Lbby 1 (10012-3999)
PHONE..........................212 343-6100
Fax: 212 343-6737
Richard Robinson, *Ch of Bd*
Alan Boyko, *President*
Andrew S Hedden, *Exec VP*
Judith A Newman, *Exec VP*
Richard Dye, *Sr Software Eng*
▲ **EMP:** 9
SQ FT: 500,000
SALES: 1.6B **Publicly Held**
WEB: www.scholastic.com
SIC: 2731 2721 7372 7812 Book publishing; books: publishing only; textbooks: publishing only, not printed on site; magazines: publishing only, not printed on site; educational computer software; non-theatrical motion picture production, television; video production; motion picture production; copyright buying & licensing; advertising agencies

(G-11998)
SCHOLASTIC INC (HQ)
557 Broadway Lbby 1 (10012-3999)
PHONE..........................800 724-6527
Fax: 212 343-4638
Richard Robinson, *Ch of Bd*
Neal Goff, *President*
John Cassidy, *Publisher*
Rosamund Else-Mitchell, *Publisher*
Wayne Friedman, *Publisher*
▲ **EMP:** 2000 **EST:** 1920
SQ FT: 300,000
SALES (est): 1.5B
SALES (corp-wide): 1.6B **Publicly Held**
WEB: www.scholasticdealer.com
SIC: 2731 2721 7372 7812 Books: publishing only; textbooks: publishing only, not printed on site; magazines: publishing only, not printed on site; statistical reports (periodicals): publishing only; educational computer software; video production; television film production; motion picture production & distribution
PA: Scholastic Corporation
    557 Broadway Lbby 1
    New York NY 10012
    212 343-6100

(G-11999)
SCHOLASTIC INC
Also Called: Scholastic Copy Center
557 Broadway Lbby 1 (10012-3999)
PHONE..........................212 343-6100
Richard Robinson, *CEO*
EMP: 25
SALES (corp-wide): 1.6B **Publicly Held**
WEB: www.scholasticdealer.com
SIC: 2731 Book publishing
HQ: Scholastic Inc.
    557 Broadway Lbby 1
    New York NY 10012
    800 724-6527

(G-12000)
SCHOLASTIC INC
568 Broadway Rm 809 (10012-3253)
PHONE..........................212 343-7100
Fax: 212 343-4951
Chris Lick, *Vice Pres*
Natnaree Junboonta, *Production*
Seth Radwell, *Branch Mgr*
John Paul, *Manager*
Tara Currie, *Producer*
EMP: 100
SALES (corp-wide): 1.6B **Publicly Held**
WEB: www.scholasticdealer.com
SIC: 2741 Business service newsletters: publishing & printing
HQ: Scholastic Inc.
    557 Broadway Lbby 1
    New York NY 10012
    800 724-6527

▲ = Import ▼ = Export
◆ = Import/Export

GEOGRAPHIC SECTION

New York - New York County (G-12030)

(G-12001)
SCHOOLNET INC (DH)
525 Fashion Ave Fl 4 (10018-4940)
PHONE..........................646 496-9000
Fax: 212 675-0815
Jonathan D Harber, *CEO*
Mark Chernis, *President*
Jane Lockett, *Senior VP*
Diane Malanowski, *Senior VP*
Susan Aspey, *Vice Pres*
EMP: 116
SQ FT: 11,500
SALES (est): 14.3MM
SALES (corp-wide): 6.7B **Privately Held**
WEB: www.schoolnet.com
SIC: 7372 7373 Educational computer software; systems software development services
HQ: Pearson Education, Inc.
 1 Lake St
 Upper Saddle River NJ 07458
 201 236-7000

(G-12002)
SCHURMAN RETAIL GROUP
275 7th Ave Frnt 6 (10001-5821)
PHONE..........................212 206-0067
Nhan Truong, *Branch Mgr*
EMP: 158
SALES (corp-wide): 1.2B **Privately Held**
SIC: 2771 Greeting cards
PA: Schurman Fine Papers
 500 Chadbourne Rd
 Fairfield CA 94534
 707 425-8006

(G-12003)
SCI BORE INC
70 Irving Pl Apt 5c (10003-2218)
PHONE..........................212 674-7128
Robert Olsen, *Partner*
Nadiya D Jinnah, *Partner*
EMP: 7
SALES (est): 550K **Privately Held**
SIC: 3496 Miscellaneous fabricated wire products

(G-12004)
SCIENTIFIC PLASTICS INC
243 W 30th St Fl 8 (10001-2812)
PHONE..........................212 967-1199
Fax: 212 967-9609
Steven Stegman, *President*
Jeffrey Stegman, *Vice Pres*
EMP: 12 EST: 1940
SALES (est): 1.1MM **Privately Held**
WEB: www.scientificplastics.com
SIC: 3842 Surgical appliances & supplies

(G-12005)
SCOOPS R US INCORPORATED
1514 Broadway (10036-4002)
PHONE..........................212 730-7959
EMP: 8
SALES (est): 652.9K **Privately Held**
SIC: 2024 Mfg Ice Cream/Frozen Desert

(G-12006)
SCOTT KAY INC
154 W 14th St Fl 6 (10011-7334)
PHONE..........................201 287-0100
David Minster, *CEO*
Scott Kay, *Principal*
Jeffrey Simon, *CFO*
EMP: 120
SQ FT: 12,000
SALES (est): 20.6MM **Privately Held**
WEB: www.scottkay.com
SIC: 3911 5944 Jewelry, precious metal; jewelry stores

(G-12007)
SCREEN GEMS-EMI MUSIC INC (DH)
Also Called: EMI Music Publishing
150 5th Ave Fl 7 (10011-4372)
PHONE..........................212 786-8000
Martin Bandier, *CEO*
Santiago Men Ndez-Pidal, *Managing Dir*
Joanne Boris, *Exec VP*
EMP: 60
SQ FT: 45,200

SALES (est): 36.9MM
SALES (corp-wide): 45.2MM **Privately Held**
SIC: 2741 Music, sheet: publishing only, not printed on site

(G-12008)
SCROLL MEDIA INC
235 W 102nd St Apt 14i (10025-8432)
PHONE..........................617 395-8904
Samir Patil, *President*
EMP: 5 EST: 2013
SALES: 660K **Privately Held**
SIC: 3577 Data conversion equipment, media-to-media: computer

(G-12009)
SEABAY MEDIA HOLDINGS LLC (PA)
Also Called: Metro Nespaper
120 Broadway Fl 6 (10271-0002)
PHONE..........................212 457-7790
Pelle Tornberg, *CEO*
EMP: 1
SALES (est): 15.4MM **Privately Held**
SIC: 2711 2741 Newspapers; miscellaneous publishing

(G-12010)
SEAN JOHN CLOTHING INC
1710 Broadway Frnt 1 (10019-5254)
PHONE..........................212 500-2200
Sean John, *Manager*
EMP: 28
SALES (corp-wide): 6.3MM **Privately Held**
SIC: 2325 Men's & boys' trousers & slacks
PA: Sean John Clothing, Inc.
 1440 Broadway Frnt 3
 New York NY 10018
 212 500-2200

(G-12011)
SEAN JOHN CLOTHING INC (PA)
1440 Broadway Frnt 3 (10018-2301)
PHONE..........................212 500-2200
Jeff Tweedy, *President*
Derek Ferguson, *CFO*
EMP: 25
SALES (est): 6.3MM **Privately Held**
SIC: 2325 Men's & boys' trousers & slacks

(G-12012)
SECRET CELEBRITY LICENSING LLC
1431 Broadway Fl 10 (10018-1910)
PHONE..........................212 812-9277
Kathryn Sio, *Mng Member*
EMP: 5
SALES (est): 912.7K **Privately Held**
SIC: 3648 5023 Decorative area lighting fixtures; decorative home furnishings & supplies

(G-12013)
SECURED SERVICES INC (PA)
110 William St Fl 14 (10038-3901)
PHONE..........................866 419-3900
King T Moore, *President*
EMP: 4
SALES (est): 3.2MM **Privately Held**
WEB: www.secured-services.com
SIC: 7372 Prepackaged software

(G-12014)
SECURITIES DATA PUBLISHING INC (PA)
Also Called: Venture Economics
11 Penn Plz Fl 17 (10001-2006)
PHONE..........................212 631-1411
Bruce Morris, *President*
Wendi Winshall, *Vice Pres*
William Johnston, *CFO*
▲ EMP: 4
SALES (est): 17.1MM **Privately Held**
SIC: 2721 Magazines: publishing & printing

(G-12015)
SECURITY LETTER
166 E 96th St Apt 3b (10128-2512)
PHONE..........................212 348-1553
Fax: 212 534-2957
Robert McCrie, *Owner*
EMP: 5 EST: 1970

SALES (est): 270K **Privately Held**
SIC: 2721 8742 Trade journals: publishing only, not printed on site; business consultant

(G-12016)
SEED MEDIA GROUP LLC
405 Greenwich St Apt 2 (10013-2047)
P.O. Box 2092 (10013-0875)
PHONE..........................646 502-7050
Vera Savcic, *CFO*
Adam Bly, *Mng Member*
Franchesca Arkus, *Manager*
Gita Linkeviciute, *Info Tech Mgr*
EMP: 40
SALES (est): 3.8MM **Privately Held**
SIC: 7372 8748 Application computer software; business consulting

(G-12017)
SEEDLNGS LF SCNCE VENTURES LLC
230 E 15th St Apt 1a (10003-3941)
PHONE..........................917 913-8511
Keith Rubin, *CEO*
Ken Solovay,
EMP: 7
SALES (est): 546.8K **Privately Held**
SIC: 3841 Surgical & medical instruments

(G-12018)
SEFAIRA INC
115 E 23rd St Fl 11 (10010-4597)
PHONE..........................855 733-2472
Mads Jensen, *CEO*
Sandeep Menon, *Vice Pres*
Stephen Grist, *CFO*
Ryan Farrell, *Sales Mgr*
Glen Halperin, *Accounts Mgr*
EMP: 35
SALES (est): 3.6MM **Privately Held**
SIC: 7372 Business oriented computer software
HQ: Sefaira Limited
 22 Soho Square, 4th Floor
 London

(G-12019)
SEGOVIA TECHNOLOGY CO
115 W 18th St Fl 2 (10011-4113)
PHONE..........................212 868-4412
Michael Faye, *CEO*
EMP: 10
SQ FT: 1,500
SALES (est): 530.1K **Privately Held**
SIC: 7372 Prepackaged software

(G-12020)
SEIDLIN CONSULTING
580 W End Ave (10024-1723)
PHONE..........................212 496-2043
Mindell Seidlin, *Owner*
EMP: 1
SALES: 1MM **Privately Held**
SIC: 2834 Pharmaceutical preparations

(G-12021)
SEKAS INTERNATIONAL LTD
345 7th Ave Fl 9 (10001-5049)
PHONE..........................212 629-6095
Fax: 212 629-6097
Nicholas Sekas, *President*
Gus Sekas, *Director*
Athina Orthodoxou, *Admin Sec*
EMP: 10
SQ FT: 2,500
SALES (est): 3.1MM **Privately Held**
SIC: 2371 Fur goods

(G-12022)
SELECT INDUSTRIES NEW YORK INC
450 Fashion Ave Ste 3002 (10123-3002)
PHONE..........................800 723-5333
Jerry Friedman, *Principal*
▲ EMP: 17 EST: 2011
SALES (est): 3.3MM **Privately Held**
SIC: 3999 Manufacturing industries

(G-12023)
SELECT INFORMATION EXCHANGE
175 W 79th St 3a (10024-6450)
PHONE..........................212 496-6435
Fax: 212 787-4269

George H Wein, *Owner*
Alex Wein, *Manager*
Dan Lam, *Prgrmr*
Terri Chiodo, *Director*
EMP: 18
SQ FT: 2,200
SALES (est): 700K **Privately Held**
WEB: www.siecom.com
SIC: 2741 7331 Catalogs: publishing only, not printed on site; mailing list compilers

(G-12024)
SELECTIVE BEAUTY CORPORATION
315 Bleecker St 109 (10014-3427)
PHONE..........................585 336-7600
Sylvie Ganter, *President*
EMP: 10
SALES (est): 980K **Privately Held**
WEB: www.selective-beauty.com
SIC: 2844 Perfumes & colognes

(G-12025)
SELIA YANG INC
Also Called: Selia Yang Bridal
15 Broad St Apt 714 (10005-1963)
PHONE..........................212 480-4252
Sam Yang, *President*
EMP: 6 EST: 1997
SALES (est): 836.3K **Privately Held**
SIC: 2335 Bridal & formal gowns

(G-12026)
SELINI NECKWEAR INC
248 W 37th St (10018-6603)
PHONE..........................212 268-5488
Fax: 212 725-6595
Paul Park, *President*
▲ EMP: 8
SQ FT: 3,500
SALES (est): 990K **Privately Held**
SIC: 2323 Men's & boys' neckwear

(G-12027)
SEMI-LINEAR INC
1123 Broadway Ste 718 (10010-2097)
PHONE..........................212 243-2108
Linda Holliday, *CEO*
Michael Kostadinovich, *CTO*
EMP: 6
SALES (est): 585.1K **Privately Held**
SIC: 3599 Industrial machinery

(G-12028)
SENDYNE CORP
250 W Broadway Fl 6 (10013-2431)
PHONE..........................212 966-0663
John Milios, *CEO*
Aakar Patel, *Vice Pres*
Victor Marten, *Engineer*
Ellen Gooch, *Marketing Staff*
EMP: 6
SALES (est): 550K **Privately Held**
SIC: 3674 Semiconductors & related devices

(G-12029)
SENSATIONAL COLLECTION INC (PA)
1410 Broadway Rm 505 (10018-9372)
PHONE..........................212 840-7388
Azar Kada, *Owner*
▲ EMP: 2
SQ FT: 5,600
SALES (est): 4.3MM **Privately Held**
SIC: 2339 5137 Women's & misses' athletic clothing & sportswear; women's & children's sportswear & swimsuits

(G-12030)
SENSUAL INC
Also Called: Icy Hot Lingerie
183 Madison Ave Rm 401 (10016-4402)
PHONE..........................212 869-1450
Sami Souid, *CEO*
EMP: 20
SQ FT: 4,000
SALES (est): 1.9MM **Privately Held**
SIC: 2342 Bras, girdles & allied garments
PA: Usa Apparel Group Inc
 183 Madison Ave Rm 401
 New York NY 10016
 212 869-1450

New York - New York County (G-12031) — GEOGRAPHIC SECTION

(G-12031)
SERVICENOW INC
60 E 42nd St Ste 1230 (10165-1203)
PHONE.................................914 318-1168
Tom Moore, *Branch Mgr*
Britta Koch, *Manager*
EMP: 10
SALES (corp-wide): 1B Publicly Held
SIC: 7372 Prepackaged software
PA: Servicenow, Inc.
   2225 Lawson Ln
   Santa Clara CA 95054
   408 501-8550

(G-12032)
SEVEN STORIES PRESS INC
140 Watts St (10013-1738)
PHONE.................................212 226-8760
Daniel Simon, *President*
Phoebe Hwang, *Publisher*
Lauren Hooker, *Editor*
Crystal Yakacki, *Editor*
Howard Zinn, *Editor*
▲ EMP: 7
SQ FT: 2,500
SALES (est): 720K Privately Held
WEB: www.sevenstories.com
SIC: 2731 Book publishing

(G-12033)
SG BLOCKS INC (PA)
115 W 18th St Fl 3 (10011-4113)
PHONE.................................212 520-6218
Paul M Galvin, *CEO*
Stevan Armstrong, *President*
Brian Wasserman, *CFO*
Jennifer Strumingher, *Officer*
▼ EMP: 7
SALES: 2.4MM Publicly Held
WEB: www.newvalley.com
SIC: 2448 5032 8711 8741 Cargo containers, wood & metal combination; building blocks; engineering services; construction management

(G-12034)
SG NYC LLC
385 5th Ave Rm 809 (10016-3343)
PHONE.................................310 210-1837
Daniel Chiu, *Managing Prtnr*
Stephanie Garcia, *Managing Prtnr*
EMP: 20
SQ FT: 4,000
SALES: 4.2MM Privately Held
SIC: 2335 Women's, juniors' & misses' dresses

(G-12035)
SGD NORTH AMERICA
900 3rd Ave Fl 4 (10022-4998)
PHONE.................................212 753-4200
Fax: 212 355-6073
Peter Acerra, *President*
Eleonor Sylio, *Administration*
▲ EMP: 33 EST: 2007
SALES (est): 4.1MM Privately Held
SIC: 3221 Glass containers

(G-12036)
SGL SERVICES CORP
1221 Ave Of Americas 42 (10020)
PHONE.................................718 630-0392
Rudolph Jones, *Managing Dir*
Erwin Lontok, *Principal*
Lauren Jones, *Opers Staff*
▲ EMP: 10 EST: 2007
SALES (est): 1.9MM Privately Held
SIC: 3534 Elevators & moving stairways

(G-12037)
SHADOWTV INC
630 9th Ave Ste 1000 (10036-3744)
PHONE.................................212 445-2540
Joachim Kim, *President*
Carl Rischar, *President*
Tracy Fred, *Bookkeeper*
Kevin Riley, *Sales Mgr*
Phil Gove, *Director*
EMP: 6
SALES (est): 720K Privately Held
WEB: www.shadowtv.com
SIC: 3575 Computer terminals, monitors & components

(G-12038)
SHAH DIAMONDS INC
Also Called: Venus
22 W 48th St Ste 600 (10036-1820)
PHONE.................................212 888-9393
Natwar Shah, *President*
Danny Gagasia, *Business Mgr*
Gita Shah, *Admin Sec*
▲ EMP: 19
SQ FT: 4,000
SALES (est): 3.2MM Privately Held
WEB: www.hoc.com
SIC: 3911 3915 5094 Jewelry, precious metal; diamond cutting & polishing; jewelry; diamonds (gems)

(G-12039)
SHAHIN DESIGNS LTD
766 Madison Ave Fl 3 (10065-6563)
PHONE.................................212 737-7225
Samouhi Shahin, *President*
EMP: 5
SALES (est): 390K Privately Held
SIC: 2211 Apparel & outerwear fabrics, cotton

(G-12040)
SHAKE INC
175 Varick St Fl 4 (10014-7412)
PHONE.................................650 544-5479
Abraham Geiger, *CEO*
EMP: 13 EST: 2012
SQ FT: 1,000
SALES (est): 922.9K Privately Held
SIC: 7372 Business oriented computer software

(G-12041)
SHAMRON MILLS LTD
242 W 38th St Fl 14 (10018-9062)
PHONE.................................212 354-0430
Fax: 212 302-7776
Ronnye Shamron, *President*
◆ EMP: 3
SQ FT: 3,000
SALES: 3MM Privately Held
WEB: www.shamron.com
SIC: 2389 Hospital gowns

(G-12042)
SHANU GEMS INC
1212 Ave Of The Americas (10036-1602)
P.O. Box 680, New City (10956-0680)
PHONE.................................212 921-4470
Fax: 212 921-4522
Pramod Agrawal, *President*
Manensha Agrawal, *Vice Pres*
EMP: 10
SALES (est): 840K Privately Held
WEB: www.shanugems.com
SIC: 3911 5094 Jewelry, precious metal; jewelry

(G-12043)
SHAPEWAYS INC (PA)
419 Park Ave S Fl 9 (10016-8409)
PHONE.................................914 356-5816
Peter Weijmarshausen, *CEO*
Charlie Maddock, *President*
Martin Meyer, *CFO*
Jay Kiecolt-Wahl, *Accountant*
Justine Trubey, *Accounts Mgr*
EMP: 94
SALES (est): 20.8MM Privately Held
SIC: 2759 Commercial printing

(G-12044)
SHAPIRO BERNSTEIN & CO INC
488 Madison Ave Fl 1201 (10022-5708)
PHONE.................................212 588-0878
Micheal Brettler, *President*
Debbie Rose, *Vice Pres*
Alexa Cabellon, *Manager*
Fay Pickens, *Admin Asst*
▲ EMP: 12
SALES (est): 850K Privately Held
WEB: www.shapirobernstein.com
SIC: 2741 Music, sheet: publishing only, not printed on site

(G-12045)
SHAREDBOOK INC
110 William St Fl 30 (10038-3901)
PHONE.................................646 442-8840
Caroline Vanderlip, *CEO*
Josef Hollander, *President*
Liza Murphy, *Senior VP*
Caroline Weng, *Accountant*
Jim Agostine, *Director*
EMP: 30
SQ FT: 8,000
SALES (est): 271.5K Privately Held
WEB: www.sharedbook.com
SIC: 2741 5942 Miscellaneous publishing; book stores

(G-12046)
SHARMEEN TEXTILE INC
469 Fashion Ave Fl 4 (10018-8738)
PHONE.................................646 298-5757
Mujtaba Karim, *President*
▲ EMP: 5
SALES: 12MM Privately Held
SIC: 3552 Beaming machines, textile

(G-12047)
SHAW CONTRACT FLRG SVCS INC
521 5th Ave Fl 37 (10175-0094)
PHONE.................................212 953-7429
Fax: 212 953-2589
Bruce Birnberg, *Marketing Staff*
Joe Sulima, *Manager*
Richard Butrym, *Manager*
Leon Martin, *Manager*
Laura Mahadeo, *Commercial*
EMP: 8
SALES (corp-wide): 210.8B Publicly Held
SIC: 2273 Carpets & rugs
HQ: Shaw Contract Flooring Services, Inc.
   616 E Walnut Ave
   Dalton GA 30721
   706 278-3812

(G-12048)
SHAWMUT WOODWORKING & SUP INC
Also Called: Shawmutdesign and Construction
3 E 54th St Fl 8 (10022-3141)
PHONE.................................212 920-8900
Jack Fickes, *Superintendent*
Leszek Piotrowski, *Superintendent*
Larry Campana, *Marketing Staff*
Michael Simon, *Branch Mgr*
Hes Abdollahi, *Manager*
EMP: 7
SALES (corp-wide): 957.6MM Privately Held
WEB: www.shawmut.com
SIC: 2431 Millwork
PA: Shawmut Woodworking & Supply, Inc.
   560 Harrison Ave Ste 200
   Boston MA 02118
   617 338-6200

(G-12049)
SHELLEY PROMOTIONS INC
87 5th Ave (10003-3002)
PHONE.................................212 924-4987
James Scott Shelley, *President*
EMP: 5
SALES (est): 370K Privately Held
SIC: 3861 Photographic film, plate & paper holders

(G-12050)
SHIELD PRESS INC
9 Lispenard St Fl 1 (10013-2290)
PHONE.................................212 431-7489
Bryan Shield, *President*
Stephen Shield, *Treasurer*
Ellen Shield, *Admin Sec*
EMP: 6 EST: 1940
SQ FT: 1,500
SALES: 750K Privately Held
SIC: 2752 7389 Commercial printing, offset; printers' services: folding, collating

(G-12051)
SHINDO USA INC
162 W 36th St (10018-6901)
PHONE.................................212 868-9311
Tadashi Shindo, *CEO*
Shingo Nagai, *Principal*
Junichiro Tanaka, *Regl Sales Mgr*
Viviana Velasquez, *Marketing Staff*
EMP: 6
SALES (est): 390.2K Privately Held
SIC: 2211 Stretch fabrics, cotton

(G-12052)
SHIRA ACCESSORIES LTD
30 W 36th St Rm 504 (10018-9791)
PHONE.................................212 594-4455
Fax: 212 594-4466
Barry Shapiro, *President*
EMP: 15
SQ FT: 2,000
SALES (est): 1.7MM Privately Held
SIC: 3961 Costume jewelry

(G-12053)
SHIRO LIMITED
928 Broadway Ste 806 (10010-8128)
PHONE.................................212 780-0007
Fax: 212 614-8526
Gary Mandel, *President*
▲ EMP: 5
SQ FT: 2,000
SALES (est): 390K Privately Held
SIC: 3911 Jewelry, precious metal

(G-12054)
SHISEIDO AMERICAS CORPORATION (HQ)
Also Called: Shiseido Cosmetics
900 3rd Ave Fl 15 (10022-4792)
PHONE.................................212 805-2300
Nobuo Takahashi, *President*
Edward W Klause, *Vice Pres*
Tatsuya Toda, *Vice Pres*
Ronald Gee, *CFO*
George Grossi Jr, *CFO*
◆ EMP: 7
SQ FT: 108,000
SALES (est): 449.9MM
SALES (corp-wide): 6.2B Privately Held
SIC: 2844 5122 Cosmetic preparations; toilet preparations; cosmetics; toilet preparations
PA: Shiseido Company, Limited
   7-5-5, Ginza
   Chuo-Ku TKY 104-0
   335 725-111

(G-12055)
SHRINEETA PHARMACY
1749 Amsterdam Ave Frnt (10031-4618)
PHONE.................................212 234-7959
Robby Annamaneni, *Principal*
EMP: 5
SALES (est): 812.6K Privately Held
SIC: 2834 Pharmaceutical preparations

(G-12056)
SHRINEETA PHARMACY INC
Also Called: Amsterdam Pharmacy
1743 Amsterdam Ave (10031-4614)
PHONE.................................212 234-7959
Sreenivasa R Gade, *Ch of Bd*
Ravinder Annamaneni, *Director*
EMP: 21
SQ FT: 1,600
SALES (est): 9MM Privately Held
SIC: 2834 Pharmaceutical preparations

(G-12057)
SHYAM AHUJA LIMITED
201 E 56th St Frnt A (10022-3724)
PHONE.................................212 644-5910
Fax: 212 644-5787
Azmina Merali, *Branch Mgr*
EMP: 7
SALES (corp-wide): 1.4MM Privately Held
WEB: www.shyamahujahome.com
SIC: 2391 2273 3999 Curtains & draperies; carpets & rugs; atomizers, toiletry
PA: Shyam Ahuja Private Limited
   A - 6 Poonam Apartment
   Mumbai MH 40001
   226 524-6967

(G-12058)
SHYK INTERNATIONAL CORP
258 Riverside Dr Apt 7b (10025-6160)
PHONE.................................212 663-3302
Steven Kline, *President*
EMP: 2
SQ FT: 2,500
SALES: 75MM Privately Held
SIC: 3651 Home entertainment equipment, electronic

▲ = Import ▼ = Export ◆ = Import/Export

GEOGRAPHIC SECTION

New York - New York County (G-12083)

(G-12059)
SIBEAU HANDBAGS INC
Also Called: Finesse La Model Handbags
33 E 33rd St Rm 1001 (10016-5335)
PHONE..................................212 686-0210
Fax: 212 684-6089
David Weber, *President*
Larry Weber, *Vice Pres*
EMP: 20
SQ FT: 6,000
SALES (est): 1.2MM **Privately Held**
SIC: 3171 2387 3172 Women's handbags & purses; apparel belts; leather cases

(G-12060)
SIDE HUSTLE MUSIC GROUP LLC
600 3rd Ave Fl 2 (10016-1919)
PHONE..................................800 219-4003
Fabian Cummings, *Prgrmr*
EMP: 10
SQ FT: 574,000
SALES (est): 851.4K **Privately Held**
WEB: www.sidehustlemusicgroup.com
SIC: 3652 Pre-recorded records & tapes

(G-12061)
SIEGFRIEDS BASEMENT INC
Also Called: House of Tarling
320 W 37th St Ground Fl (10018)
PHONE..................................212 629-3523
Gordon Link, *President*
Francis Parkman, *President*
EMP: 11
SALES (est): 1MM **Privately Held**
SIC: 2431 Woodwork, interior & ornamental

(G-12062)
SIEMENS CORPORATION
527 Madison Ave Fl 8 (10022-4376)
PHONE..................................202 434-7800
Terry Heath, *Senior VP*
Alison Taylor, *Vice Pres*
Klaus P Stegemann, *CFO*
Michael Panigel, *Director*
Paul McDonald, *Director*
EMP: 10
SALES (corp-wide): 83.5B **Privately Held**
SIC: 3661 3641 3844 3612 Telephones & telephone apparatus; electric lamps; radiographic X-ray apparatus & tubes; distribution transformers, electric; voltage regulators, transmission & distribution; nonferrous wiredrawing & insulating
HQ: Siemens Corporation
300 New Jersey Ave Nw A
Washington DC 20001
202 434-4800

(G-12063)
SIEMENS ELECTRO INDUSTRIAL SA
527 Madison Ave Fl 8 (10022-4376)
PHONE..................................212 258-4000
Kees Smaling, *Managing Dir*
Steffen Meyer, *Principal*
Pete Tubolino, *Business Mgr*
Thomas Leubner, *Senior VP*
Scott Bennett, *Vice Pres*
EMP: 854
SALES (est): 78.4MM
SALES (corp-wide): 83.5B **Privately Held**
SIC: 3648 Lighting equipment
PA: Siemens Ag
Wittelsbacherplatz 2
Munchen 80333
896 360-0

(G-12064)
SIEMENS USA HOLDINGS INC
601 Lexington Ave Fl 56 (10022-4611)
PHONE..................................212 258-4000
Fax: 212 258-4370
George C Nolan, *President*
James Harris, *General Mgr*
Joseph N Gunn, *Counsel*
Timothy M McVey, *Counsel*
Michael J Palumbo, *Counsel*
EMP: 300

SALES (est): 53.2MM
SALES (corp-wide): 83.5B **Privately Held**
SIC: 3612 3844 3641 3357 Distribution transformers, electric; voltage regulators, transmission & distribution; radiographic X-ray apparatus & tubes; electric lamps; nonferrous wiredrawing & insulating; telephones & telephone apparatus
PA: Siemens Ag
Wittelsbacherplatz 2
Munchen 80333
896 360-0

(G-12065)
SIFONYA INC
Also Called: Cego Custom Shirts
303 Park Ave S Frnt 2 (10010-3677)
PHONE..................................212 620-4512
Carl Goldberg, *President*
EMP: 6
SQ FT: 300
SALES: 600K **Privately Held**
WEB: www.cego.com
SIC: 2321 5131 Men's & boys' furnishings; piece goods & other fabrics

(G-12066)
SIGA TECHNOLOGIES INC (PA)
660 Madison Ave Ste 1700 (10065-8446)
PHONE..................................212 672-9100
Eric A Rose, *Ch of Bd*
William J Haynes II, *Exec VP*
Dennis E Hruby, *Vice Pres*
Daniel J Luckshire, *CFO*
Dana Tettamanti, *Accounting Mgr*
EMP: 34
SALES: 8.1MM **Privately Held**
WEB: www.siga.com
SIC: 2834 2836 Pharmaceutical preparations; vaccines & other immunizing products

(G-12067)
SIGMA WORLDWIDE LLC
65 W 83rd St Apt 5 (10024-5237)
PHONE..................................646 217-0629
Jeffrey Muti, *CEO*
Peter Devries, *Opers Staff*
EMP: 40
SALES: 15MM **Privately Held**
SIC: 3161 5099 3089 Cases, carrying; cases, carrying; cases, plastic

(G-12068)
SIGN CENTER INC
Also Called: Sign Company, The
54 W 21st St Rm 201 (10010-7374)
PHONE..................................212 967-2113
Fax: 212 967-4119
Mark Dressman, *President*
James Kelly, *Vice Pres*
EMP: 10
SQ FT: 2,000
SALES (est): 897.7K **Privately Held**
SIC: 3993 Signs, not made in custom sign painting shops; displays & cutouts, window & lobby

(G-12069)
SIGN COMPANY
Also Called: Sjm Interface
54 W 21st St Rm 201 (10010-7374)
PHONE..................................212 967-2113
James Kelly, *Owner*
EMP: 9
SALES (est): 440K **Privately Held**
SIC: 3993 5812 Signs & advertising specialties; eating places

(G-12070)
SIGN EXPO ENTERPRISES (PA)
127 W 26th St Rm 401 (10001-6870)
PHONE..................................212 925-8585
Offer Sharady, *Partner*
Steve Cohen, *Partner*
Michelle Shapiro, *General Mgr*
EMP: 10
SALES (est): 806.3K **Privately Held**
SIC: 3993 Signs & advertising specialties

(G-12071)
SIGNA CHEMISTRY INC (PA)
400 Madison Ave Fl 21 (10017-8901)
PHONE..................................212 933-4101
Michael Lefenfeld, *President*
Paul F Vogt, *Vice Pres*

David Field, *Manager*
EMP: 14
SQ FT: 7,000
SALES (est): 8.6MM **Privately Held**
WEB: www.signachem.com
SIC: 2819 3511 Catalysts, chemical; hydraulic turbine generator set units, complete

(G-12072)
SIGNATURE DIAMOND ENTPS LLC
15 W 47th St Ste 203 (10036-5708)
PHONE..................................212 869-5115
Jeremy S Hill,
EMP: 40
SQ FT: 3,000
SALES (est): 3.2MM **Privately Held**
SIC: 1499 Diamond mining, industrial

(G-12073)
SIGNATURE SYSTEMS GROUP LLC
38 E 29th St Fl 3l (10016-7911)
PHONE..................................800 569-2751
Timothy Kirk, *Sales Staff*
Daniel Ryan, *Sales Staff*
EMP: 6
SALES (corp-wide): 90MM **Privately Held**
SIC: 3996 Hard surface floor coverings
HQ: Signature Systems Group, Llc
1201 Lkeside Pkwy Ste 150
Flower Mound TX 75028
972 684-5736

(G-12074)
SIGNPOST INC
127 W 26th St Fl 2 (10001-6881)
PHONE..................................646 503-4231
Seth Purcell, *President*
Christopher Depatria, *Vice Pres*
Reid Erardy, *Accountant*
Henry Edelson, *Persnl Dir*
Christopher Penn, *Sales Mgr*
EMP: 15
SALES (est): 2MM **Privately Held**
SIC: 7372 Application computer software

(G-12075)
SILVATRIM CORP
Also Called: Silvatrim Corporation America
324 W 22nd St (10011-2602)
PHONE..................................212 675-0933
William Shanok, *President*
Daniel Shanock, *Vice Pres*
Frederick Shanok, *Vice Pres*
Victor Shanok, *Treasurer*
EMP: 120 EST: 1931
SQ FT: 120,000
SALES (est): 8MM **Privately Held**
SIC: 3089 Plastic processing; molding primary plastic

(G-12076)
SIMCO MANUFACTURING JEWELERS
62 W 47th St Ste 903 (10036-3271)
PHONE..................................212 575-8390
Fax: 212 768-0376
David Unger, *President*
EMP: 10 EST: 1953
SALES: 1.5MM **Privately Held**
SIC: 3911 Jewelry, precious metal

(G-12077)
SIMKA DIAMOND CORP
580 5th Ave Ste 709 (10036-4728)
PHONE..................................212 921-4420
Philip Katz, *President*
Isaac Friedman, *Vice Pres*
Surie Friedman, *Admin Sec*
Raizel Katz, *Admin Sec*
EMP: 15
SQ FT: 3,000
SALES (est): 1.4MM **Privately Held**
WEB: www.simkadiamond.com
SIC: 3911 Jewelry, precious metal

(G-12078)
SIMMONS-BOARDMAN PUBG CORP (HQ)
55 Broad St Fl 26 (10004-2580)
PHONE..................................212 620-7200
Arthur J Mc Ginnis Jr, *President*

Carol Franklin, *Manager*
Morene Cooney, *Director*
EMP: 3 EST: 1928
SQ FT: 10,000
SALES (est): 8.8MM **Privately Held**
WEB: www.marinelog.com
SIC: 2721 2731 8249 Periodicals: publishing only; book music: publishing only, not printed on site; correspondence school
PA: Simons Boardman Publishing Inc
55 Broad St Fl 26
New York NY 10004
212 620-7200

(G-12079)
SIMON & SCHUSTER INC
Pocket Books
1230 Ave Of The Americas (10020-1586)
PHONE..................................212 698-7000
Carolyn Kroll Reidy, *Branch Mgr*
EMP: 51
SALES (corp-wide): 27.1B **Publicly Held**
SIC: 2731 Book publishing
HQ: Simon & Schuster, Inc.
1230 Ave Of The Americas
New York NY 10020
212 698-7000

(G-12080)
SIMON & SIMON LLC
Also Called: Magic Maestro Music
1745 Broadway Fl 17 (10019-4642)
PHONE..................................202 419-0490
Bonnie Simon, *Mng Member*
Stephen Simon,
EMP: 5
SALES: 10K **Privately Held**
SIC: 2782 Record albums

(G-12081)
SIMON SCHUSTER DIGITAL SLS INC
51 W 52d St (10019)
PHONE..................................212 698-4391
Carolyn Reidy, *Chairman*
Robert Riger, *Vice Pres*
EMP: 53
SALES (est): 3.4MM
SALES (corp-wide): 27.1B **Publicly Held**
SIC: 2731 Book publishing
HQ: Simon & Schuster, Inc.
1230 Ave Of The Americas
New York NY 10020
212 698-7000

(G-12082)
SIMPLICITY CREATIVE GROUP INC (DH)
261 Madison Ave Fl 4 (10016-3906)
PHONE..................................212 686-7676
J Cary Findlay, *Ch of Bd*
Konstance J K Findlay, *Senior VP*
William M Stewart, *VP Mfg*
David Sears, *VP Sales*
Jennifer Pegram, *Marketing Mgr*
◆ EMP: 725
SQ FT: 220,000
SALES (est): 125.3MM
SALES (corp-wide): 683.9MM **Privately Held**
WEB: www.conso.com
SIC: 2241 2221 2396 2298 Narrow fabric mills; fringes, woven; trimmings, textile; fabric tapes; jacquard woven fabrics, manmade fiber & silk; automotive & apparel trimmings; cordage & twine
HQ: Wilton Brands Llc
2240 75th St
Woodridge IL 60517
630 963-7100

(G-12083)
SIMPLY GUM INC
270 Lafayette St Ste 1301 (10012-3327)
PHONE..................................917 721-8032
Caron Proschan, *CEO*
EMP: 12
SALES (est): 652.2K **Privately Held**
SIC: 2067 Chewing gum

New York - New York County (G-12084)

(G-12084)
SING TAO NEWSPAPERS NY LTD (PA)
Also Called: Sing Tao Daily
188 Lafayette St (10013-3200)
PHONE..................................212 699-3800
Fax: 212 431-1816
Robin Mui, *CEO*
Alice Lee, *Corp Secy*
Jerry Du, *Accounts Exec*
Charles Fu, *Manager*
James Duan, *Info Tech Mgr*
▲ EMP: 20
SALES: 22.5MM **Privately Held**
WEB: www.nysingtao.com
SIC: 2711 2741 Newspapers: publishing only, not printed on site; miscellaneous publishing

(G-12085)
SING TRIX
118 W 22nd St Fl 3 (10011-2416)
PHONE..................................212 352-1500
Al Roque, *Principal*
John Devecka, *Vice Pres*
Eric Berkowitz, *Mng Member*
EMP: 10
SALES (est): 869.4K **Privately Held**
SIC: 3651 Home entertainment equipment, electronic

(G-12086)
SINO PRINTING INC
30 Allen St Frnt A (10002-5363)
PHONE..................................212 334-6896
Craig Marsden, *Principal*
◆ EMP: 15
SALES (est): 1.1MM **Privately Held**
SIC: 2759 Commercial printing

(G-12087)
SISTER SISTER INC (PA)
463 7th Ave Fl 4 (10018-8725)
PHONE..................................212 629-9600
Fax: 212 629-6699
Jack Adjmi, *Ch of Bd*
Joseph Dwek, *President*
Joseph Dweck, *President*
Mark Adjmi, *Vice Pres*
Terry Dwek, *Vice Pres*
◆ EMP: 6
SQ FT: 15,000
SALES (est): 4.9MM **Privately Held**
SIC: 2369 2329 Headwear: girls', children's & infants'; men's & boys' sportswear & athletic clothing

(G-12088)
SITECOMPLI LLC
45 W 25th St Fl 3 (10010-2080)
PHONE..................................800 564-1152
Jonathan Fertel, *Vice Pres*
Brian Sakevich, *Vice Pres*
Taylor Rhodes, *Sales Staff*
Grace Yuan, *Business Anlyst*
Jeannie Cambria, *Marketing Staff*
EMP: 19
SALES (est): 2.1MM **Privately Held**
SIC: 7372 Application computer software

(G-12089)
SIX BORO PUBLISHING
221 E 122nd St Apt 1703 (10035-2015)
P.O. Box 1811 (10035-0816)
PHONE..................................347 589-6756
Danielle Sullivan, *Principal*
EMP: 5
SALES: 26K **Privately Held**
SIC: 2731 Book publishing

(G-12090)
SKETCH STUDIO TRADING INC
221 W 37th St (10018-5782)
PHONE..................................212 244-2875
ARI Merabi, *President*
Isaac Merabi, *Manager*
Arry Miraly, *Manager*
Priscilla Chan, *Administration*
EMP: 3
SQ FT: 2,500
SALES (est): 10MM **Privately Held**
SIC: 2384 Dressing gowns, men's & women's: from purchased materials

(G-12091)
SKILLS ALLIANCE INC
135 W 29th St 201 (10001-5188)
PHONE..................................646 492-5300
Joseph Wolf CPA, *Principal*
EMP: 8
SALES (est): 896.2K **Privately Held**
SIC: 2834 Pharmaceutical preparations

(G-12092)
SKIN NUTRITION INTL INC
410 Park Ave Fl 15 (10022-4407)
PHONE..................................212 231-8355
Richard Purvis, *CEO*
EMP: 21
SQ FT: 400
SALES (est): 2.2MM **Privately Held**
SIC: 2844 Cosmetic preparations

(G-12093)
SKINCARE PRODUCTS INC
118 E 57th St (10022-2663)
PHONE..................................917 837-5255
Allan Vanhoven, *CEO*
EMP: 9
SALES: 900K **Privately Held**
SIC: 2834 7991 7389 Dermatologicals; spas; design services

(G-12094)
SKY ART MEDIA INC
Also Called: Whitewall Magazine
175 Varick St Fl 8 (10014-7408)
PHONE..................................917 355-9022
Michael Klug, *President*
Margaux Cerruti, *Marketing Mgr*
EMP: 7
SALES (est): 1.3MM **Privately Held**
SIC: 2721 Periodicals: publishing & printing

(G-12095)
SKY FRAME & ART INC (PA)
Also Called: Pop A2z
141 W 28th St Fl 12 (10001-6115)
PHONE..................................212 925-7856
Fax: 212 695-8577
Robert Benrimon, *President*
Sheila Benrimon, *Vice Pres*
Jonny Benrimon, *Sales Dir*
EMP: 23
SQ FT: 7,000
SALES (est): 4.5MM **Privately Held**
SIC: 2499 Picture frame molding, finished

(G-12096)
SKYHORSE PUBLISHING INC
307 W 36th St Fl 11 (10018-6592)
PHONE..................................212 643-6816
Tony Lyons, *President*
Bill Wolfsthal, *Publisher*
Joseph Sverchek, *Editor*
Lora Sturat, *Manager*
Kathryn Mennone, *Director*
▲ EMP: 40
SALES (est): 8MM **Privately Held**
WEB: www.skyhorsepublishing.com
SIC: 2731 Book publishing

(G-12097)
SKYLER BRAND VENTURES LLC
590 Madison Ave Fl 19 (10022-2544)
PHONE..................................646 979-5904
Betsy Schmalz Ferguson, *President*
Konstantinos M Lahanas, *Vice Pres*
EMP: 5 EST: 2013
SALES: 1MM **Privately Held**
SIC: 3841 Skin grafting equipment

(G-12098)
SKYSTEM LLC
100 W 92nd St Apt 20d (10025-7504)
PHONE..................................877 778-3320
Shagun Malhotra, *CEO*
EMP: 5
SALES (est): 207.8K **Privately Held**
SIC: 7372 Prepackaged software

(G-12099)
SLOANE DESIGN INC
336 W 37th St Rm 204 (10018-4242)
PHONE..................................212 539-0184
Sloane Madureira, *President*
Tim Chapman, *Vice Pres*
EMP: 5 EST: 2005
SALES (est): 227.6K **Privately Held**
SIC: 2752 Commercial printing, lithographic

(G-12100)
SMART & STRONG LLC
Also Called: Poz Publishing
212 W 35th St Fl 8 (10001-2508)
PHONE..................................212 938-2051
Brad Peebles, *Partner*
Sean O'Brien Strub, *Founder*
Tom Doyle, *COO*
Megan Strub, *Sales Executive*
Michelle Lopez, *Admin Sec*
EMP: 25
SALES (est): 2.4MM **Privately Held**
WEB: www.poz.com
SIC: 2721 Magazines: publishing only, not printed on site

(G-12101)
SMART SPACE PRODUCTS LLC (PA)
244 5th Ave Ste 2487 (10001-7604)
PHONE..................................877 777-2441
Adam Rozen, *Mng Member*
EMP: 5
SQ FT: 1,200
SALES: 1MM **Privately Held**
SIC: 2599 5712 Hotel furniture; furniture stores

(G-12102)
SMILE SPECIALISTS
236 E 36th St (10016-3777)
PHONE..................................877 337-6135
Marvin Lagstein, *Principal*
EMP: 11
SALES (est): 1.5MM **Privately Held**
SIC: 3843 Cutting instruments, dental

(G-12103)
SMITH & JOHNSON DRY GOODS (PA)
295 5th Ave Ste 114 (10016-7103)
PHONE..................................212 951-7067
Park B Smith Sr, *President*
Linda Johnson, *Vice Pres*
EMP: 9
SQ FT: 5,000
SALES (est): 702.6K **Privately Held**
SIC: 2392 Household furnishings

(G-12104)
SMITH & WATSON
200 Lexington Ave Rm 805 (10016-6111)
PHONE..................................212 686-6444
Fax: 212 686-6606
Robert Ryan, *President*
John P Ryan, *Chairman*
Barbara R Pilcher, *Vice Pres*
Jeffrey Soleimani, *Vice Pres*
Teresa Hoang, *Finance Mgr*
▲ EMP: 20 EST: 1907
SQ FT: 8,000
SALES: 2MM **Privately Held**
WEB: www.smith-watson.com
SIC: 2512 Upholstered household furniture

(G-12105)
SMITH INTERNATIONAL INC
601 Lexington Ave Fl 57 (10022-4627)
PHONE..................................212 350-9400
Kenneth Liang, *Vice Pres*
Susan Herron, *Project Mgr*
Ann Marie Copo, *Office Mgr*
Udit Guru, *Director*
William T McCormick Jr, *Director*
EMP: 89 **Privately Held**
SIC: 1382 1389 Geophysical exploration, oil & gas field; well logging
HQ: Smith International, Inc.
1310 Rankin Rd
Houston TX 77073
281 443-3370

(G-12106)
SMK WINES & LIQUORS LLC
23 E 28th St (10016-7921)
PHONE..................................212 685-7651
Steve Kaiden, *Mng Member*
EMP: 5
SALES (est): 323.8K **Privately Held**
SIC: 2084 Wines, brandy & brandy spirits

(G-12107)
SML USA INC (PA)
5 Penn Plz Ste 1500 (10001-1810)
PHONE..................................212 736-8800
Paul Gnieser, *CEO*
Thomas Blaze, *Manager*
EMP: 50
SQ FT: 16,000
SALES (est): 11.6MM **Privately Held**
SIC: 2679 2241 2269 5131 Tags & labels, paper; building, insulating & packaging paper; labels, woven; labels, cotton: printed; labels; textile machinery & equipment

(G-12108)
SMM - NORTH AMERICA TRADE CORP
Also Called: Sims Metal Management
16 W 22nd St Fl 10 (10010-5967)
PHONE..................................212 604-0710
Robert A Kelman, *President*
Michael S Collins, *Vice Pres*
Marian Arnold, *Manager*
Chrystelle Ball, *Manager*
Nina Goryntseva, *Manager*
EMP: 5
SALES (est): 1.2MM **Privately Held**
SIC: 3291 Grit, steel

(G-12109)
SMOOTH INDUSTRIES INCORPORATED
1411 Broadway Rm 3000 (10018-3437)
PHONE..................................212 869-1080
Fax: 212 302-5699
Celeste Chan, *President*
Alice Kalenial, *Accountant*
▲ EMP: 25
SQ FT: 7,000
SALES (est): 1.6MM **Privately Held**
WEB: www.smoothny.com
SIC: 2339 Women's & misses' outerwear

(G-12110)
SMOOTH MAGAZINE
55 John St Ste 800 (10038-3752)
PHONE..................................212 925-1150
Sandra Vasceannie, *President*
EMP: 10
SALES (est): 730K **Privately Held**
SIC: 2721 Periodicals

(G-12111)
SNEAKER NEWS INC
41 Elizabeth St Ste 301 (10013-4637)
PHONE..................................347 687-1588
Yu-Ming Wu, *President*
EMP: 9
SALES: 1.8MM **Privately Held**
SIC: 2741 Shopping news: publishing only, not printed on site

(G-12112)
SNEAKERS SOFTWARE INC
Also Called: Dvmax
519 8th Ave Rm 812 (10018-4588)
PHONE..................................800 877-9221
Paul R Greenman, *CEO*
Larry White, *Engineer*
Kathie Stecher, *Office Mgr*
EMP: 18
SQ FT: 800
SALES: 3MM **Privately Held**
WEB: www.DVMAX.com
SIC: 7372 Prepackaged software

(G-12113)
SNOWMAN
1181 Broadway Fl 6 (10001-7433)
PHONE..................................212 239-8818
Baekkyu Suh, *Mng Member*
EMP: 5
SALES (est): 557.2K **Privately Held**
SIC: 2339 Sportswear, women's

(G-12114)
SOCIETY FOR THE STUDY
Also Called: PARABOLA
20 W 20th St Fl 2 (10011-9260)
PHONE..................................212 822-8806
Steven Schiff, *President*
Joseph Kulin, *Publisher*
Bob Doto, *Manager*
Erynn Sosinski, *Assistant*

GEOGRAPHIC SECTION

New York - New York County (G-12137)

EMP: 7
SQ FT: 1,500
SALES: 429.3K Privately Held
SIC: 2721 5735 5942 Magazines: publishing only, not printed on site; video tapes, prerecorded; audio tapes, prerecorded; book stores

(G-12115)
SOFT SERVE APPLE LLC
Also Called: Chloe's Soft Serve Fruit Co
37 W 17th St Ste 4w (10011-5522)
PHONE..................646 442-8002
Michael Sloan, *CEO*
Chloe Epstein, *President*
Jason Epstein, *Owner*
Todd Hoffman, *CFO*
▲ EMP: 50
SQ FT: 3,000
SALES (est): 6.1MM
SALES (corp-wide): 8.7MM Privately Held
SIC: 2024 5143 Yogurt desserts, frozen; frozen dairy desserts
PA: Soft Serve Fruit Co Llc
    37 W 17th St Ste 4w
    New York NY 10011
    646 442-8002

(G-12116)
SOFT SERVE FRUIT CO LLC (PA)
Also Called: Chloe's Soft Serve Fruit Co
37 W 17th St Ste 4w (10011-5522)
PHONE..................646 442-8002
Michael Sloan, *CEO*
Chloe Epstein, *President*
Jason Epstein, *Owner*
Todd Hoffman, *CFO*
EMP: 34
SQ FT: 2,000
SALES (est): 8.7MM Privately Held
SIC: 2024 5143 Fruit pops, frozen; frozen dairy desserts

(G-12117)
SOFT SHEEN PRODUCTS INC (DH)
575 5th Ave (10017-2422)
PHONE..................212 818-1500
Patricia Cumberland, *President*
Candace Matthews, *Principal*
Gut Peyrelongue, *Div Sub Head*
Diane Wade, *Assistant VP*
Adu Darkwa, *Vice Pres*
▼ EMP: 21
SALES (est): 4.7MM
SALES (corp-wide): 3.1B Privately Held
WEB: www.softsheen-carson.com
SIC: 2844 Shampoos, rinses, conditioners: hair
HQ: L'oreal Usa, Inc.
    10 Hudson Yards
    New York NY 10001
    212 818-1500

(G-12118)
SOHO APPAREL LTD
Also Called: Flirtatious
525 Fashion Ave Fl 6 (10018-4960)
PHONE..................212 840-1109
Nikou Achouri, *President*
Jeffrey Stein, *Exec VP*
EMP: 5
SQ FT: 3,140
SALES (est): 550.2K Privately Held
SIC: 2331 5137 Women's & misses' blouses & shirts; women's & children's clothing

(G-12119)
SOHO PRESS INC
853 Broadway Ste 1402 (10003-4716)
PHONE..................212 260-1900
Fax: 212 260-1902
Juris Jurjevics, *President*
Bronwen Hruska, *Publisher*
Mark Doten, *Editor*
Amara Hoshijo, *Editor*
Laura Hruska, *Vice Pres*
EMP: 5
SQ FT: 1,250
SALES (est): 510K Privately Held
WEB: www.sohopress.com
SIC: 2731 5942 Books: publishing only; book stores

(G-12120)
SOLABIA USA INC
60 Broad St Lbby A (10004-2351)
PHONE..................212 847-2397
Michael J Conti, *President*
▲ EMP: 80
SALES (est): 7.4MM Privately Held
SIC: 2844 Cosmetic preparations

(G-12121)
SOLARPATH INC
Also Called: Solarpath Sun Solutions
415 Madison Ave Fl 14 (10017-7935)
PHONE..................201 490-4499
Ori Aldubi, *CEO*
Amir Warshazsky, *President*
Scott Marquartt, *Manager*
EMP: 6
SQ FT: 5,000
SALES (est): 760K Privately Held
SIC: 3646 Commercial indusl & institutional electric lighting fixtures

(G-12122)
SOLENIS
240 E 82nd St (10028-2703)
PHONE..................212 772-0560
EMP: 9
SALES (corp-wide): 5.3B Publicly Held
SIC: 2891 Adhesives
HQ: Hercules Incorporated
    500 Hercules Rd
    Wilmington DE 19808
    302 594-5000

(G-12123)
SOLENIS
108 E 38th St (10016-2648)
PHONE..................212 204-6679
EMP: 9
SALES (corp-wide): 5.3B Publicly Held
SIC: 2891 Adhesives
HQ: Hercules Incorporated
    500 Hercules Rd
    Wilmington DE 19808
    302 594-5000

(G-12124)
SOLENIS
310 W 85th St (10024-3819)
PHONE..................212 362-1759
EMP: 9
SALES (corp-wide): 5.3B Publicly Held
SIC: 2891 Adhesives
HQ: Hercules Incorporated
    500 Hercules Rd
    Wilmington DE 19808
    302 594-5000

(G-12125)
SOLO LICENSING CORP
358 5th Ave Rm 1205 (10001-2209)
PHONE..................212 244-5505
Fax: 212 244-5535
David Freed, *President*
Fern Pochtar, *Vice Pres*
Barbara Freed, *Admin Sec*
▲ EMP: 8
SQ FT: 2,200
SALES (est): 1MM Privately Held
SIC: 2341 2322 Women's & children's underwear; men's & boys' underwear & nightwear

(G-12126)
SOLSTARS INC
Also Called: Solstarny
575 Madison Ave Ste 1006 (10022-8511)
PHONE..................212 605-0430
Haim Hassin, *President*
▲ EMP: 7
SALES (est): 690K Privately Held
SIC: 2084 Wine cellars, bonded: engaged in blending wines

(G-12127)
SOLSTISS INC
561 Fashion Ave Fl 16 (10018-1816)
PHONE..................212 719-9194
Fax: 212 302-8109
Francois Damide, *President*
Sandrine Bernard, *Exec VP*
Ahsan Masood, *Controller*
Sara Campos, *Sales Staff*
EMP: 6
SQ FT: 3,500
SALES (est): 624.7K Privately Held
SIC: 2241 2258 Silk narrow fabrics; lace & lace products

(G-12128)
SOLUTIA BUSINESS ENTPS INC
111 8th Ave (10011-5201)
PHONE..................314 674-1000
Timothy J Spihlman, *Ch of Bd*
Charles Petracra, *Credit Mgr*
EMP: 15
SALES (est): 1.2MM
SALES (corp-wide): 9.6B Publicly Held
SIC: 2824 Organic fibers, noncellulosic
HQ: Solutia Inc.
    575 Maryville Centre Dr
    Saint Louis MO 63141
    618 271-5835

(G-12129)
SONIC BOOM INC
259 W 30th St Rm 801 (10001-2864)
PHONE..................212 242-2852
Fax: 212 242-2852
David Danon, *CEO*
Josh Grant, *COO*
William F Deslauriers, *Exec VP*
Bruno Moirn, *Vice Pres*
Christopher Small, *Manager*
EMP: 11
SALES (est): 981.2K
SALES (corp-wide): 2.9MM Privately Held
SIC: 2451 Mobile homes
PA: Sonic Branding Solutions, Inc.
    259 W 30th St Rm 803
    New York NY 10001
    212 242-4200

(G-12130)
SONTEK INDUSTRIES INC (PA)
36 E 12th St Fl 6 (10003-4604)
PHONE..................781 749-3055
Garry A Prime, *President*
Gary Prime, *President*
James Gerson, *Chairman*
Donald I McCarthy, *Treasurer*
David H Drohan, *Clerk*
EMP: 6
SQ FT: 3,000
SALES (est): 8.1MM Privately Held
SIC: 3842 5047 Respiratory protection equipment, personal; medical equipment & supplies

(G-12131)
SONY BROADBAND ENTERTAINMENT (DH)
550 Madison Ave Fl 6 (10022-3811)
PHONE..................212 833-6800
Howard Stringer, *Ch of Bd*
Peter Jensen, *Senior VP*
Janel Clausen, *Vice Pres*
Jonathan Pearl, *Vice Pres*
Carolyn Rice, *Vice Pres*
▲ EMP: 12
SQ FT: 20,000
SALES (est): 1.4B
SALES (corp-wide): 69.2B Privately Held
SIC: 3652 7812 5734 7832 Pre-recorded records & tapes; motion picture production & distribution; motion picture production & distribution, television; software, computer games; motion picture theaters, except drive-in; video discs & tapes, pre-recorded
HQ: Sony Corporation Of America
    25 Madison Ave Fl 27
    New York NY 10010
    212 833-8000

(G-12132)
SONY CORPORATION OF AMERICA (HQ)
Also Called: Sony Music Entertainment
25 Madison Ave Fl 27 (10010-8601)
PHONE..................212 833-8000
Fax: 212 833-6924
Kazuo Hirai, *Ch of Bd*
Howard Stringer, *President*
Peter Viot, *General Mgr*
Hironori Wada, *General Mgr*
Michelle McManus, *Principal*
◆ EMP: 250
SQ FT: 20,000
SALES (est): 11.4B
SALES (corp-wide): 69.2B Privately Held
WEB: www.sony.com
SIC: 3695 3652 3651 3577 Optical disks & tape, blank; compact laser discs, prerecorded; household audio & video equipment; computer peripheral equipment; computer storage devices
PA: Sony Corporation
    1-7-1, Konan
    Minato-Ku TKY 108-0
    367 482-111

(G-12133)
SONY DADC US INC
Also Called: Sony Style
550 Madison Ave (10022-3211)
PHONE..................212 833-8800
David Rubenstein, *Branch Mgr*
Catherine Wozney, *Manager*
EMP: 386
SALES (corp-wide): 69.2B Privately Held
SIC: 3695 Optical disks & tape, blank
HQ: Sony Dadc Us Inc.
    1800 N Fruitridge Ave
    Terre Haute IN 47804
    812 462-8100

(G-12134)
SONY MUSIC ENTERTAINMENT INC
Also Called: Sony Music Holdings
25 Madison Ave Fl 19 (10010-8601)
PHONE..................212 833-8000
Fax: 212 833-8338
Thomas Mottola, *CEO*
Catherine Wozney, *Manager*
Kevin Kiernan, *Director*
EMP: 2000
SALES (corp-wide): 69.2B Privately Held
WEB: www.sonymusic.com
SIC: 3652 Pre-recorded records & tapes
HQ: Sony Music Entertainment, Inc.
    25 Madison Ave Fl 19
    New York NY 10010
    212 833-8500

(G-12135)
SONY MUSIC ENTERTAINMENT INC (DH)
Also Called: Sony Wonder
25 Madison Ave Fl 19 (10010-8601)
PHONE..................212 833-8500
Fax: 212 833-4007
Hartwig Masuch, *CEO*
Antonio Reid, *CEO*
Robert Sorrentino, *Ch of Bd*
Michael Block, *President*
Colin Currie, *Managing Dir*
▲ EMP: 2000
SQ FT: 500,000
SALES (est): 1.4B
SALES (corp-wide): 69.2B Privately Held
WEB: www.sonymusic.com
SIC: 3652 5064 Pre-recorded records & tapes; electrical appliances, television & radio
HQ: Sony Broadband Entertainment Corp
    550 Madison Ave Fl 6
    New York NY 10022
    212 833-6800

(G-12136)
SONY MUSIC ENTERTAINMENT INC
Tristar Music
79 5th Ave Fl 16 (10003-3034)
PHONE..................212 833-5057
Rich Isaacson, *President*
Jeff Swierk, *Manager*
Catherine Wozney, *Manager*
EMP: 45
SALES (corp-wide): 69.2B Privately Held
WEB: www.sonymusic.com
SIC: 3652 Pre-recorded records & tapes
HQ: Sony Music Entertainment, Inc.
    25 Madison Ave Fl 19
    New York NY 10010
    212 833-8500

(G-12137)
SONY MUSIC HOLDINGS INC (DH)
550 Madison Ave Fl 6 (10022-3211)
PHONE..................212 833-8000

New York - New York County (G-12138)

Douglas P Morris, *CEO*
Steven E Kober, *President*
Charles Goldstuck, *President*
Richard Griffiths, *President*
Robert Jamieson, *President*
◆ **EMP:** 800
SQ FT: 300,000
SALES (est): 322.4MM
SALES (corp-wide): 69.2B **Privately Held**
WEB: www.bmgentertainment.com
SIC: 3652 5099 2741 Pre-recorded records & tapes; phonograph records; tapes & cassettes, prerecorded; compact discs; miscellaneous publishing
HQ: Sony Corporation Of America
25 Madison Ave Fl 27
New York NY 10010
212 833-8000

(G-12138)
SONY/ATV MUSIC PUBLISHING LLC (DH)
25 Madison Ave Fl 24 (10010-8601)
PHONE..................212 833-7730
Martin N Bandier, *Ch of Bd*
Robert S Wiesenthal, *President*
Aki Shimazu, *Comms Mgr*
Ginny Peirats,
▲ **EMP:** 20 **EST:** 1995
SALES (est): 20.6MM
SALES (corp-wide): 69.2B **Privately Held**
SIC: 2741 Music book & sheet music publishing
HQ: Sony Corporation Of America
25 Madison Ave Fl 27
New York NY 10010
212 833-8000

(G-12139)
SOS CHEFS OF NEW YORK INC
104 Avenue B Apt 1 (10009-6286)
P.O. Box 517 (10021-0011)
PHONE..................212 505-5813
Fax: 212 505-5815
Atef Boulaabi, *President*
▲ **EMP:** 5
SALES (est): 503.6K **Privately Held**
WEB: www.sos-chefs.com
SIC: 2099 Seasonings & spices

(G-12140)
SOS INTERNATIONAL LLC (HQ)
Also Called: Sosi
40 Fulton St Fl 26 (10038-5007)
PHONE..................212 742-2410
Sosi Setian, *President*
Jim Edwards, *Vice Pres*
Frank Helmick, *Vice Pres*
Julian Setian, *Vice Pres*
Bruce Crowell, *CFO*
EMP: 22 **EST:** 2011
SALES: 95MM
SALES (corp-wide): 100MM **Privately Held**
SIC: 3724 8711 7389 8732 Aircraft engines & engine parts; engineering services; translation services; opinion research
PA: Sos International Ltd.
40 Fulton St Fl 26
New York NY 10038
212 742-2410

(G-12141)
SOTERIX MEDICAL INC
Also Called: Soterix Medical Technologies
237 W 35th St Ste 1401 (10001-1950)
PHONE..................888 990-8327
Lucas Parra, *President*
Pragya Bista, *Engineer*
Rakshya Bista, *Engineer*
Nitish Shrestha, *Design Engr*
Rabinson Shakya, *Electrical Engi*
EMP: 12
SALES (est): 407K **Privately Held**
SIC: 3845 Electromedical equipment

(G-12142)
SOUL JOURN LLC
Also Called: Guide Group
251 W 136th St Apt 2b (10030-2617)
PHONE..................646 823-9882
Patrick Riley, *President*
Adrian Ingram, *Vice Pres*
EMP: 12

SALES (est): 840K **Privately Held**
SIC: 2731 Book publishing

(G-12143)
SOURCE MEDIA INC (HQ)
1 State St Fl 26 (10004-1561)
PHONE..................212 803-8200
Douglas J Manoni, *CEO*
Tim Whiting, *Publisher*
Benjamin Felix, *General Mgr*
Robert Barba, *Editor*
Allison Bisbey, *Editor*
▲ **EMP:** 269
SQ FT: 60,000
SALES (est): 193MM **Privately Held**
WEB: www.sourcemedia.com/
SIC: 2721 Magazines: publishing & printing

(G-12144)
SOUTH BRIDGE PRESS INC
122 W 26th St Fl 3 (10001-6804)
PHONE..................212 233-4047
Mitch Nochlin, *President*
EMP: 8
SALES (est): 946.9K **Privately Held**
SIC: 2752 Commercial printing, lithographic

(G-12145)
SOUTINE INC
104 W 70th St Frnt 1 (10023-4454)
PHONE..................212 496-1450
Fax: 212 496-1791
Madge Rosenberg, *President*
Barry Rosenberg, *Vice Pres*
EMP: 6
SQ FT: 600
SALES (est): 497.2K **Privately Held**
WEB: www.soutine.com
SIC: 2051 5812 Bakery: wholesale or wholesale/retail combined; caterers

(G-12146)
SOVEREIGN BRANDS LLC
81 Greene St Apt 2 (10012-5349)
PHONE..................212 343-8366
Brett R Berish, *CEO*
Finn Briggs, *Regional Mgr*
Allison Kolos, *Area Mgr*
Scott Cohen, *VP Opers*
Shannon Bullinger, *Opers Staff*
▲ **EMP:** 6
SQ FT: 1,800
SALES (est): 1.1MM **Privately Held**
WEB: www.sovereignbrands.com
SIC: 2085 Distilled & blended liquors

(G-12147)
SPARK CREATIONS INC
10 W 46th St Fl 9 (10036-4515)
PHONE..................212 575-8385
Fax: 212 764-5455
Eli Aviram, *President*
Benjamin Aviram, *Vice Pres*
▲ **EMP:** 17
SQ FT: 4,000
SALES (est): 1.8MM **Privately Held**
WEB: www.sparkcreations.com
SIC: 3911 Jewelry, precious metal

(G-12148)
SPARTACIST PUBLISHING CO
48 Warren St (10007-1017)
P.O. Box 1377 (10116-1377)
PHONE..................212 732-7860
Fax: 212 406-2210
Elizabeth R Gordis, *CEO*
James M Robertson, *President*
A Robinson Hunt, *Treasurer*
Robinson A Hunt, *Treasurer*
EMP: 20
SALES (est): 1.8MM **Privately Held**
SIC: 2731 2711 Pamphlets: publishing only, not printed on site; newspapers: publishing only, not printed on site

(G-12149)
SPARTAN BRANDS INC (PA)
451 Park Ave S Fl 5 (10016-7390)
PHONE..................212 340-0320
Fax: 212 684-0625
Gary Grey, *President*
Eli Motovich, *CFO*
Cynthia Murphy, *Manager*
Sean Murphy, *MIS Dir*
◆ **EMP:** 12 **EST:** 1946

SQ FT: 2,500
SALES (est): 12.5MM **Privately Held**
WEB: www.spartanbrands.com
SIC: 3999 Hair & hair-based products

(G-12150)
SPARTAN BRANDS INC
451 Park Ave S Fl 5 (10016-7390)
PHONE..................212 340-0320
Bill Moser, *Manager*
EMP: 11
SALES (corp-wide): 12.5MM **Privately Held**
WEB: www.spartanbrands.com
SIC: 2252 2254 Hosiery; knit underwear mills
PA: Spartan Brands, Inc.
451 Park Ave S Fl 5
New York NY 10016
212 340-0320

(G-12151)
SPATULA LLC
2165 Broadway (10024-6603)
PHONE..................917 582-8684
Nicolo Derienzo, *Mng Member*
Stesano Ciravegna,
▲ **EMP:** 17
SALES (est): 780K **Privately Held**
SIC: 2024 Ice cream & frozen desserts

(G-12152)
SPECIALTY MINERALS INC (HQ)
Also Called: S M I
622 3rd Ave Fl 38 (10017-6729)
PHONE..................212 878-1800
Paul R Saueracker, *Ch of Bd*
Timothy South, *Managing Prtnr*
Dj Monagle, *Principal*
Kenneth Mueller, *Business Mgr*
Andy Payne, *Purch Mgr*
◆ **EMP:** 50
SQ FT: 42,000
SALES (est): 314.5MM
SALES (corp-wide): 1.8B **Publicly Held**
WEB: www.specialtyminerals.com
SIC: 2819 5032 1422 5169 Industrial inorganic chemicals; calcium carbide; lime building products; crushed & broken limestone; chemical additives; chemical preparations
PA: Minerals Technologies Inc.
622 3rd Ave Fl 38
New York NY 10017
212 878-1800

(G-12153)
SPECIALTY SIGNS CO INC
54 W 21st St Rm 201 (10010-7374)
PHONE..................212 243-8521
Fax: 212 243-6457
Marc Frankel, *President*
Kelly Bedwell, *General Mgr*
Edna Batounis, *Project Mgr*
EMP: 13 **EST:** 1971
SQ FT: 6,000
SALES (est): 850K **Privately Held**
SIC: 3993 Signs & advertising specialties

(G-12154)
SPECILTY BUS MCHS HOLDINGS LLC
260 W 35th St Fl 11 (10001-2528)
PHONE..................212 587-9600
Steven Schaps, *Mng Member*
EMP: 26
SALES (est): 3.6MM **Privately Held**
SIC: 3555 Printing trades machinery

(G-12155)
SPECTATOR PUBLISHING CO INC
Also Called: Columbia Daily Spectator
2875 Broadway Ste 3 (10025-7847)
PHONE..................212 854-9550
Fax: 212 854-9553
Maggie Alden, *Editor*
Catie Edmondson, *Editor*
Tiffany Fang, *Editor*
Maxwell Hu, *Editor*
Noah Jackson, *Editor*
EMP: 20
SALES (est): 343.2K **Privately Held**
WEB: www.columbiaspectator.com
SIC: 2711 Newspapers

(G-12156)
SPECTRALINK CORPORATION
1 Penn Plz Ste 4800 (10119-0002)
PHONE..................212 372-6997
EMP: 64
SALES (corp-wide): 97.1MM **Privately Held**
SIC: 3663 Radio & TV communications equipment
PA: Spectralink Corporation
2560 55th St
Boulder CO 80301
303 441-7500

(G-12157)
SPECTRUM APPAREL INC
463 Fashion Ave Fl 12 (10018-7499)
PHONE..................212 239-2025
Richard Kringstein, *President*
EMP: 85
SALES (est): 5.7MM **Privately Held**
SIC: 2339 Women's & misses' jackets & coats, except sportswear

(G-12158)
SPECTRUM PRTG LITHOGRAPHY INC
Also Called: Earth Spectrum
505 8th Ave Rm 1802 (10018-4707)
PHONE..................212 255-3131
Peter Mandelkern, *President*
Karen Targrove, *Vice Pres*
Lauren Moore, *Manager*
EMP: 10
SQ FT: 5,000
SALES (est): 1.9MM **Privately Held**
SIC: 2752 2789 2759 2675 Color lithography; bookbinding & related work; commercial printing; die-cut paper & board

(G-12159)
SPEKTRIX INC
115 W 30th St Rm 501 (10001-4071)
PHONE..................646 741-5110
Rebecca Kahn, *Mng Member*
EMP: 6
SQ FT: 1,200
SALES (est): 135.3K **Privately Held**
SIC: 7372 Publishers' computer software

(G-12160)
SPENCER AB INC
265 W 37th St Rm 2388 (10018-5757)
PHONE..................646 831-3728
Tommy Tsui, *President*
Joel Glentz, *VP Sales*
Lisa Tsui, *Admin Asst*
EMP: 7
SALES: 1.5MM **Privately Held**
SIC: 2335 2331 Women's, juniors' & misses' dresses; women's & misses' blouses & shirts

(G-12161)
SPF HOLDINGS II LLC (HQ)
9 W 57th St Ste 4200 (10019-2707)
PHONE..................212 750-8300
Dave West, *President*
EMP: 12
SALES (est): 2.1B
SALES (corp-wide): 5.6B **Publicly Held**
SIC: 2033 5149 6719 2099 Fruits & fruit products in cans, jars, etc.; vegetables & vegetable products in cans, jars, etc.; tomato products: packaged in cans, jars, etc.; canned goods: fruit, vegetables, seafood, meats, etc.; pet foods; personal holding companies, except banks; syrups; frosting, ready-to-use; sandwiches, assembled & packaged: for wholesale market; peanut butter
PA: The J M Smucker Company
1 Strawberry Ln
Orrville OH 44667
330 682-3000

(G-12162)
SPH GROUP HOLDINGS LLC (PA)
590 Madison Ave Fl 32 (10022-2524)
PHONE..................212 520-2300
Jack L Howard, *CEO*
EMP: 9 **EST:** 2013

GEOGRAPHIC SECTION

New York - New York County (G-12186)

SALES (est): 782MM **Publicly Held**
SIC: **3339** 3011 3312 Precious metals; tire & inner tube materials & related products; wire products, steel or iron

(G-12163)
SPIN MAGAZINE MEDIA
276 5th Ave Rm 800 (10001-4509)
PHONE..................................212 231-7400
Fax: 212 231-7312
Nion McEvoy, *CEO*
Jack Jensen, *President*
Malcom Kimball, *Publisher*
Mary Howard, *General Mgr*
Mike Redmond, *Editor*
EMP: 9
SALES (est): 198.3K
SALES (corp-wide): 6.1MM **Privately Held**
WEB: www.spinmag.com
SIC: **2721** Periodicals
PA: Buzz Media Inc.
    6464 W Sunset Blvd # 650
    Los Angeles CA 90028
    213 252-8999

(G-12164)
SPINMEDIA GROUP INC
276 5th Ave Fl 7 (10001-4509)
PHONE..................................646 274-9110
Stephen Blackwell, *Branch Mgr*
Matt Russoniello, *Manager*
Kate O'Malley, *Producer*
EMP: 65
SALES (corp-wide): 10.8MM **Privately Held**
SIC: **2741** Miscellaneous publishing
PA: Spinmedia Group, Inc.
    6464 W Sunset Blvd # 520
    Los Angeles CA 90028
    323 203-1333

(G-12165)
SPIRIT MUSIC GROUP INC (HQ)
235 W 23rd St Ste 4 (10011-2302)
PHONE..................................212 533-7672
Fax: 212 979-8566
Mark Fried, *President*
David Renzer, *Chairman*
Jennifer Scher, *CFO*
David Fedon, *Manager*
EMP: 20
SALES (est): 1.4MM
SALES (corp-wide): 17.2MM **Privately Held**
WEB: www.spiritmusicgroup.com
SIC: **2741** Music books: publishing & printing
PA: Pegasus Capital Advisors, L.P.
    99 River Rd
    Cos Cob CT 06807
    203 869-4400

(G-12166)
SPORTS ILLUSTRATED FOR KIDS
1271 Ave Of The Americas (10020-1300)
PHONE..................................212 522-1212
Fax: 212 522-0120
Don Logan, *CEO*
Paul Caine, *Publisher*
Sherrill Clarke, *Publisher*
Charles Kammer, *Publisher*
Diane Oshin, *Publisher*
▲ **EMP:** 50
SALES (est): 5.2MM
SALES (corp-wide): 3.1B **Publicly Held**
WEB: www.siphoto.com
SIC: **2721** Magazines: publishing only, not printed on site
PA: Time Inc.
    225 Liberty St
    New York NY 10281
    212 522-1212

(G-12167)
SPORTS PBLICATIONS PROD NY LLC
708 3rd Ave Fl 12 (10017-4129)
PHONE..................................212 366-7700
Brent Diamond,
EMP: 80
SALES (est): 5.6MM **Privately Held**
SIC: **2711** Newspapers, publishing & printing

(G-12168)
SPORTS PRODUCTS AMERICA LLC
Popsicle Playwear
34 W 33rd St Fl 2 (10001-3304)
PHONE..................................212 594-5511
Fax: 212 564-0174
EMP: 50
SALES (corp-wide): 33.3MM **Privately Held**
SIC: **2361** Girls' & children's dresses, blouses & shirts; girls' & children's blouses & shirts
HQ: Sports Products Of America Llc
    463 7th Ave
    New York NY 10018
    212 629-9600

(G-12169)
SPORTS REPORTER INC
527 3rd Ave Ste 327 (10016-4168)
PHONE..................................212 737-2750
Lindsay Hamilton, *President*
EMP: 6
SALES (est): 280K **Privately Held**
WEB: www.sportsreporter.com
SIC: **2711** Newspapers, publishing & printing

(G-12170)
SPRING INC
41 E 11th St Fl 11 (10003-4602)
PHONE..................................646 732-0323
Ofer Leidner, *President*
EMP: 6
SALES (est): 416.7K **Privately Held**
SIC: **7372** Application computer software

(G-12171)
SPRINGER ADIS US LLC (DH)
233 Spring St Fl 6 (10013-1578)
PHONE..................................212 460-1500
Derk Haank, *CEO*
Tom Lee, *Finance*
EMP: 24
SALES (est): 2.2MM
SALES (corp-wide): 2.1B **Privately Held**
SIC: **2721** 2731 Trade journals: publishing only, not printed on site; magazines: publishing only, not printed on site; books: publishing only
HQ: Springer Science + Business Media, Llc
    233 Spring St Fl 6
    New York NY 10013
    781 871-6600

(G-12172)
SPRINGER CUSTOMER SVC CTR LLC
233 Spring St Fl 6 (10013-1578)
PHONE..................................212 460-1500
Edward Woods, *CFO*
EMP: 400
SQ FT: 80,000
SALES (est): 16.6MM **Privately Held**
SIC: **2731** Book publishing

(G-12173)
SPRINGER HEALTHCARE LLC
233 Spring St Fl 6 (10013-1578)
PHONE..................................212 460-1500
Fax: 212 460-1575
Rick Werdann, *Principal*
Martin Mos, *COO*
Jan De Boer, *Exec VP*
Myrtle Bannis, *Facilities Mgr*
Ulrich Vest, *CFO*
EMP: 25
SALES (est): 950K **Privately Held**
SIC: **2721** Periodicals

(G-12174)
SPRINGER PUBLISHING CO LLC
11 W 42nd St Fl 15 (10036-8002)
PHONE..................................212 431-4370
Fax: 212 941-7842
Ursula Springer, *President*
Jeffrey Meltzer, *Vice Pres*
Jason Roth, *Vice Pres*
Pascal Schwarzer, *Vice Pres*
Diana Osborne, *Prdtn Mgr*
EMP: 38 **EST:** 1950
SQ FT: 9,000
SALES (est): 7.3MM **Privately Held**
WEB: www.springerpub.com
SIC: **2721** 2721 Books: publishing only; trade journals: publishing only, not printed on site

(G-12175)
SPRINGER SCNCE + BUS MEDIA LLC (DH)
Also Called: Springer Business Media
233 Spring St Fl 6 (10013-1578)
PHONE..................................781 871-6600
Carolyn Honour, *Managing Dir*
Charlotte Cusumano, *Editor*
Herma Drees, *Editor*
Elizabeth Dziubela, *Editor*
Melissa Fearon, *Editor*
◆ **EMP:** 119 **EST:** 1964
SQ FT: 40,000
SALES (est): 74.5MM
SALES (corp-wide): 2.1B **Privately Held**
WEB: www.telospub.com
SIC: **2721** 2731 Trade journals: publishing only, not printed on site; books: publishing only
HQ: Springer Science+Business Media Gmbh
    Heidelberger Platz 3
    Berlin 14197
    308 278-70

(G-12176)
SRP APPAREL GROUP INC
530 Fashion Ave Rm 809 (10018-4802)
PHONE..................................212 764-4810
Scott Pianin, *President*
▲ **EMP:** 5
SALES (est): 896.3K **Privately Held**
SIC: **2339** Women's & misses' athletic clothing & sportswear

(G-12177)
SS&C TECHNOLOGIES INC
Also Called: Security Software & Consulting
675 3rd Ave (10017-5704)
PHONE..................................212 503-6400
Fax: 212 503-6450
Bob Moitoso, *Senior VP*
Dan Colucci, *Vice Pres*
Stuart Weinberg, *Project Mgr*
Richard Shalowitz, *Branch Mgr*
Dennis Ross, *Info Tech Dir*
EMP: 50
SALES (corp-wide): 1B **Publicly Held**
WEB: www.ssctech.com
SIC: **7372** Prepackaged software
HQ: Ss&C Technologies, Inc.
    80 Lamberton Rd
    Windsor CT 06095
    860 298-4500

(G-12178)
SSA TRADING LTD
226 W 37th St Fl 6 (10018-9020)
PHONE..................................646 465-9500
Gary Cohen, *President*
Robert Klein, *CFO*
Bernard Stern, *CFO*
Marc Klein, *Treasurer*
EMP: 12
SQ FT: 5,000
SALES (est): 1.4MM **Privately Held**
SIC: **2339** Sportswear, women's

(G-12179)
SSG FASHIONS LTD
27 E 37th St Frnt 1 (10016-3004)
PHONE..................................212 221-0933
William Seng, *President*
Tim Burman, *Controller*
▲ **EMP:** 6
SQ FT: 3,000
SALES (est): 1MM **Privately Held**
WEB: www.ssgfashions.com
SIC: **2339** 2335 Sportswear, women's; women's, juniors' & misses' dresses

(G-12180)
ST TROPEZ INC
530 Broadway Fl 10 (10012-3920)
PHONE..................................800 366-6383
Isaac Naim, *President*
EMP: 6
SQ FT: 4,300
SALES (est): 300K
SALES (corp-wide): 1.2B **Privately Held**
SIC: **2844** Suntan lotions & oils
PA: Pz Cussons Plc
    3500 Aviator Way Manchester Business Park
    Manchester M22 5
    161 435-1000

(G-12181)
STANDARD ANALYTICS IO INC
7 World Trade Ctr 46th (10007-2140)
PHONE..................................917 882-5422
Tiffany Bogich, *COO*
EMP: 6
SALES (est): 370K **Privately Held**
SIC: **2721** 2741 7371 7374 Periodicals; ; computer software development; data processing & preparation; distribution channels consultant

(G-12182)
STANDARD SCREEN SUPPLY CORP (PA)
Also Called: Active Process Supply
121 Varick St Rm 200 (10013-1408)
PHONE..................................212 627-2727
Fax: 212 627-2770
Arthur Gononsky, *President*
Sue Gonosky, *Vice Pres*
Susan Gononsky, *Treasurer*
▼ **EMP:** 11 **EST:** 1951
SALES (est): 1.2MM **Privately Held**
WEB: www.standardscreen.com
SIC: **2893** Screen process ink

(G-12183)
STANMARK JEWELRY INC
64 W 48th St Ste 1303 (10036-1708)
PHONE..................................212 730-2557
Stanley Krukowski, *President*
EMP: 6
SQ FT: 10,000
SALES (est): 510K **Privately Held**
WEB: www.stanmark.com
SIC: **3911** 5944 Jewelry, precious metal; jewelry stores

(G-12184)
STAR CHILDRENS DRESS CO INC (PA)
Also Called: Rare Editions
1250 Broadway Rm 1800 (10001-3734)
PHONE..................................212 244-1390
Fax: 212 594-7532
Edward Rosen, *Ch of Bd*
Andy Brown, *General Mgr*
Sue Cella, *Manager*
Ken Dippold, *Info Tech Mgr*
Marilyn Collazo, *Executive*
▲ **EMP:** 60 **EST:** 1953
SQ FT: 12,000
SALES: 53MM **Privately Held**
WEB: www.rareeditions.com
SIC: **2361** Dresses: girls', children's & infants'

(G-12185)
STAR WIRE MESH FABRICATORS
518 E 119th St (10035-4432)
P.O. Box 678 (10035-0678)
PHONE..................................212 831-4133
Fax: 212 876-0634
Alex Pavur, *President*
Anistasia Pavur, *Treasurer*
EMP: 5
SQ FT: 2,500
SALES (est): 510K **Privately Held**
WEB: www.starwiremesh.com
SIC: **3496** Screening, woven wire: made from purchased wire; mesh, made from purchased wire

(G-12186)
STARLITE MEDIA LLC (PA)
151 W 19th St Fl 4 (10011-4116)
PHONE..................................212 909-7700
Fax: 212 838-4533
Harold Lueken, *CEO*
Ronald Mendez, *Managing Dir*
Lisa Gaglia, *Director*
Tim Daly,
Karen Jolicoeur,
EMP: 4

New York - New York County (G-12187)

GEOGRAPHIC SECTION

SQ FT: 1,000
SALES (est): 4.1MM **Privately Held**
WEB: www.starlitemedia.com
SIC: 3993 Signs & advertising specialties

(G-12187)
STARMARK APPAREL INC
255 W 36th St Lbby (10018-7555)
PHONE...................................212 967-6347
Fax: 212 239-1486
Michael Fox, *Co-President*
Martin Fox, *Manager*
EMP: 20
SALES (est): 1.5MM **Privately Held**
SIC: 2326 Industrial garments, men's & boys'

(G-12188)
STATE BAGS LLC
495 Broadway Rm 3f (10012-4457)
PHONE...................................617 895-8532
Scott Tatelman, *CEO*
Jacqueline Tatelman, *Director*
EMP: 14 EST: 2013
SALES: 2MM **Privately Held**
SIC: 2392 Bridge sets, cloth & napkin: from purchased materials

(G-12189)
STEEL PARTNERS HOLDINGS LP (PA)
Also Called: Splp
590 Madison Ave Rm 3202 (10022-8536)
PHONE...................................212 520-2300
Warren G Lichtenstein, *Ch of Bd*
Jack L Howard, *President*
Amanda Lamson, *Counsel*
Leonard J McGill, *Senior VP*
Pete Marciniak, *Vice Pres*
EMP: 24
SALES: 998MM **Publicly Held**
SIC: 3479 3497 1381 6141 Etching & engraving; copper foil; gold foil or leaf; nickel foil; silver foil or leaf; drilling oil & gas wells; consumer finance companies

(G-12190)
STEEZYS LLC
80 8th Ave 202 (10011-5126)
PHONE...................................646 276-5333
Robert Lebowitz, *Mng Member*
Edina Sultanik,
EMP: 7
SALES (est): 592.2K **Privately Held**
SIC: 3961 Costume jewelry, ex. precious metal & semiprecious stones

(G-12191)
STEFAN FURS INC
150 W 30th St Fl 15 (10001-4138)
PHONE...................................212 594-2788
Alex Amanatides, *President*
EMP: 5 EST: 1978
SQ FT: 800
SALES (est): 350K **Privately Held**
SIC: 2371 Fur goods

(G-12192)
STEINWAY MUSICAL INSTRS INC (HQ)
1133 Ave Of The Am Fl 33 (10036)
PHONE...................................781 894-9770
Michael T Sweeney, *President*
Ron Losby, *President*
John Stoner Jr, *President*
Dennis Hanson, *Sr Exec VP*
Donna M Lucente, *Vice Pres*
◆ EMP: 40
SALES (est): 269.6MM
SALES (corp-wide): 229.7MM **Privately Held**
WEB: www.steinwaymusical.com
SIC: 3931 Musical instruments; pianos, all types: vertical, grand, spinet, player, etc.; string instruments & parts; woodwind instruments & parts

(G-12193)
STEMLINE THERAPEUTICS INC
750 Lexington Ave Fl 11 (10022-9817)
PHONE...................................646 502-2311
Ivan Bergstein, *Ch of Bd*
Kenneth Hoberman, *COO*
Eric K Rowinsky, *Chief Mktg Ofcr*
Jonathan Schwartz, *Med Doctor*
Stephen P Hall,
EMP: 22
SALES: 654.1K **Privately Held**
WEB: www.stemline.com
SIC: 2834 Pharmaceutical preparations

(G-12194)
STEPHAN & COMPANY ACC LTD (PA)
10 E 38th St Fl 9 (10016-0004)
PHONE...................................212 481-3888
Fax: 212 481-4244
Stephan Rubin, *President*
Shellie Rubin, *VP Sales*
Lella Anceschi, *MIS Dir*
▲ EMP: 20
SQ FT: 2,400
SALES: 28.6K **Privately Held**
WEB: www.stephanco.com
SIC: 3961 Costume jewelry, ex. precious metal & semiprecious stones

(G-12195)
STEPHEN GOULD CORPORATION
450 7th Ave Fl 32 (10123-3299)
PHONE...................................212 497-8180
Rachel Golden, *Office Mgr*
Justin Golben, *Branch Mgr*
EMP: 5
SALES (corp-wide): 594.7MM **Privately Held**
WEB: www.stephengould.com
SIC: 3086 Packaging & shipping materials, foamed plastic
PA: Stephen Gould Corporation
35 S Jefferson Rd
Whippany NJ 07981
973 428-1500

(G-12196)
STEPHEN SINGER PATTERN CO INC
Also Called: Popular Pattern
340 W 39th St Fl 4 (10018-1345)
PHONE...................................212 947-2902
Fax: 212 643-0025
Stephen Singer, *President*
EMP: 12
SQ FT: 7,000
SALES (est): 1.9MM **Privately Held**
SIC: 2621 2741 Pattern tissue; miscellaneous publishing

(G-12197)
STERLING POSSESSIONS LTD
251 W 39th St (10018-3105)
PHONE...................................212 594-0418
Fax: 212 594-2529
William Callaghan, *Ch of Bd*
Richard Castagna, *President*
▲ EMP: 8
SQ FT: 3,000
SALES (est): 740K **Privately Held**
WEB: www.sterlingposs.com
SIC: 3911 5094 2329 2339 Jewelry apparel; jewelry; men's & boys' sportswear & athletic clothing; sportswear, women's; sportswear, men's & boys'; sportswear, women's & children's

(G-12198)
STERLING SOUND INC
88 10th Ave Frnt 6 (10011-4745)
PHONE...................................212 604-9433
Fax: 212 604-9964
Murat Aktar, *President*
Justin Guip, *Facilities Mgr*
EMP: 30
SALES (est): 4.7MM **Privately Held**
SIC: 3652 Master records or tapes, preparation of

(G-12199)
STEVE & ANDYS ORGANICS INC
102 E 7th St Apt 6 (10009-6141)
PHONE...................................718 499-7933
Michelle Schwartz, *President*
Arjan Khiani, *Vice Pres*
Steve Marino, *Treasurer*
Quinn Rhone, *Director*
EMP: 5
SALES (est): 255.4K **Privately Held**
SIC: 2064 Candy & other confectionery products

(G-12200)
STEVEN MADDEN LTD
41 W 34th St (10001-3081)
PHONE...................................212 736-3283
Kelly Paytner, *Branch Mgr*
EMP: 25
SALES (corp-wide): 1.4B **Publicly Held**
SIC: 3143 Men's footwear, except athletic
PA: Steven Madden, Ltd.
5216 Barnett Ave
Long Island City NY 11104
718 446-1800

(G-12201)
STEVEN MADDEN LTD
Also Called: Madden Zone
19 W 34th St Fl 4 (10001-3006)
PHONE...................................718 446-1800
Jeff Goldstein, *Branch Mgr*
EMP: 75
SALES (corp-wide): 1.4B **Publicly Held**
SIC: 3144 Women's footwear, except athletic; boots, canvas or leather: women's
PA: Steven Madden, Ltd.
5216 Barnett Ave
Long Island City NY 11104
718 446-1800

(G-12202)
STEVENS BANDES GRAPHICS CORP
333 Hudson St Fl 3 (10013-1006)
PHONE...................................212 675-1128
Fax: 212 924-6362
Stephen Kilduff, *President*
Kevin Roach, *Admin Sec*
EMP: 10
SQ FT: 2,500
SALES: 1.5MM **Privately Held**
WEB: www.stevensbandes.com
SIC: 2752 Commercial printing, lithographic

(G-12203)
STEVES ORIGINAL FURS INC
150 W 30th St Rm 700 (10001-4155)
PHONE...................................212 967-8007
Steve Panaretos, *President*
Aspasia Panaretos, *Admin Sec*
EMP: 20
SALES (est): 1.1MM **Privately Held**
WEB: www.stevesoriginalfurs.com
SIC: 2371 Fur finishers & liners for the fur goods trade

(G-12204)
STICKY ADS TV INC
747 3rd Ave Fl 2 (10017-2803)
PHONE...................................646 668-1346
Hervet Brunet, *President*
Pascal Eang, *Treasurer*
EMP: 5
SALES (est): 117.2K **Privately Held**
SIC: 7372 Prepackaged software

(G-12205)
STICKY SOCKS LLC
200 W 60th St Apt 7g (10023-8504)
PHONE...................................212 541-5927
Eva Di Nardo, *President*
EMP: 5
SALES (est): 280.9K **Privately Held**
SIC: 2252 Socks

(G-12206)
STITCH & COUTURE INC (PA)
Also Called: Lela Rose
224 W 30th St Fl 14 (10001-1493)
PHONE...................................212 947-9204
Lela Rose, *Ch of Bd*
Nandini Amrit, *Finance*
Betsy Kilough, *VP Sales*
Caroline Faulkner, *Accounts Exec*
Tricia Starr, *Marketing Mgr*
EMP: 25
SQ FT: 3,000
SALES: 11MM **Privately Held**
WEB: www.lelarose.com
SIC: 2331 2335 Blouses, women's & juniors': made from purchased material; shirts, women's & juniors': made from purchased materials; bridal & formal gowns

(G-12207)
STONE HOUSE ASSOCIATES INC
37 W 47th St Ste 910 (10036-2809)
PHONE...................................212 221-7447
Elaine Wong, *President*
EMP: 5
SALES: 450K **Privately Held**
WEB: www.theidea-network.com
SIC: 3911 Jewelry, precious metal

(G-12208)
STONESONG PRESS LLC
270 W 39th St Rm 201 (10018-0137)
PHONE...................................212 929-4600
Emmanuelle Morgen, *Principal*
Jessica Rosen, *Editor*
Judy Linden, *Exec VP*
Alison Fargis, *Mng Member*
Ellen Scordato,
EMP: 6 EST: 1978
SALES (est): 450K **Privately Held**
SIC: 2731 Book publishing

(G-12209)
STONY APPAREL CORP
Also Called: Eye Shadow
1407 Broadway Rm 3300 (10018-2395)
PHONE...................................212 391-0022
Fax: 212 819-9456
Shaun Jackson, *Manager*
Charity Fox, *Manager*
EMP: 5 **Privately Held**
SIC: 2339 Women's & misses' athletic clothing & sportswear
PA: Stony Apparel Corp.
1500 S Evergreen Ave
Los Angeles CA 90023

(G-12210)
STRAIGHT ARROW PUBLISHING CO
Also Called: Mens Journal
1290 Ave Of The Amer Fl 2 (10104-0298)
PHONE...................................212 484-1616
Fax: 212 767-8209
John Gruber, *CFO*
Hugh T Scogin Jr, *General Counsel*
John F Walsh Jr, *Officer*
Frank Janoscak, *Administration*
EMP: 200
SALES (est): 12.4MM
SALES (corp-wide): 118.1MM **Privately Held**
WEB: www.mensjournal.com
SIC: 2741 Miscellaneous publishing
PA: Wenner Media Llc
1290 Ave Of The Amer Fl 2
New York NY 10104
212 484-1616

(G-12211)
STRATCONGLOBAL INC
685 3rd Ave Fl 4 (10017-8408)
PHONE...................................212 989-2355
Joanna Peters, *Principal*
Tatum Pursell, *Opers Staff*
EMP: 5 EST: 2008
SALES (est): 215.4K **Privately Held**
SIC: 2711 Newspapers

(G-12212)
STREET KING LLC
Also Called: Sk Energy Shots
575 Madison Ave Fl 24 (10022-8538)
PHONE...................................212 400-2200
Sabrina Peterson, *President*
Rosie Jonker, *Manager*
EMP: 8
SALES: 1MM **Privately Held**
SIC: 2086 Bottled & canned soft drinks

(G-12213)
STREET SMART DESIGNS INC
29 W 35th St Fl 6 (10001-2299)
PHONE...................................646 865-0056
Fax: 646 865-0052
Richard H Bienen, *Ch of Bd*
Dera Jairam, *Manager*
▲ EMP: 6
SALES (est): 888.8K **Privately Held**
WEB: www.streetsmartdesigns.com
SIC: 3111 5137 Handbag leather; handbags

▲ = Import ▼ = Export
◆ = Import/Export

GEOGRAPHIC SECTION

New York - New York County (G-12240)

(G-12214)
STRIATA INC
48 Wall St Ste 1100 (10005-2903)
PHONE..................................212 918-4677
Michael Wright, *President*
Garin Toren, *COO*
Jacqui Michelson, *CFO*
Chad Somodi, *Natl Sales Mgr*
Sue Ellner, *Sales Mgr*
EMP: 85
SQ FT: 6,000
SALES (est): 7MM **Privately Held**
WEB: www.striata.com
SIC: 7372 Application computer software

(G-12215)
STRIDER GLOBAL LLC
261 W 28th St Apt 6a (10001-5936)
PHONE..................................212 726-1302
Leon Rawlings,
EMP: 5
SALES: 100K **Privately Held**
SIC: 3648 Lighting equipment

(G-12216)
STRUCTURED RETAIL PRODUCTS
Also Called: SRP
225 Park Ave S Fl 8 (10003-1604)
PHONE..................................212 224-3692
Sunny Singh, *Principal*
Joe Burris, *Principal*
EMP: 5
SQ FT: 60,000
SALES (est): 291.7K
SALES (corp-wide): 628.1MM **Privately Held**
SIC: 7372 Prepackaged software
HQ: Euromoney Global Limited
6-8 Bouverie Street
London EC4Y
207 779-8888

(G-12217)
STRUCTUREDWEB INC
20 W 20th St Ste 402 (10011-9258)
PHONE..................................201 325-3110
Daniel Nissan, *President*
Michael Coscetta, *VP Sales*
Sam Oliff, *Sales Associate*
Matthew Thompson, *Marketing Mgr*
Angela Silva, *Marketing Staff*
EMP: 40
SQ FT: 7,500
SALES (est): 4.6MM **Privately Held**
WEB: www.structuredweb.com
SIC: 7372 7371 Business oriented computer software; computer software development; software programming applications

(G-12218)
STUART WEITZMAN LLC
625 Madison Ave Frnt 3 (10022-1801)
PHONE..................................212 823-9560
Fax: 212 355-2639
Randi Berman, *Principal*
Annie Frylinck, *Vice Pres*
Barbara Kreger, *Vice Pres*
Rhashaied Clarke, *Store Mgr*
Lane Schilling, *Store Mgr*
▲ **EMP:** 40
SALES (est): 5.4MM **Privately Held**
SIC: 2392 3171 Shoe bags: made from purchased materials; handbags, women's

(G-12219)
STUDIO ASSOCIATES OF NEW YORK
242 W 30th St Rm 902 (10001-4903)
PHONE..................................212 268-1163
Fax: 212 268-2646
Edward Jenner, *President*
Joseph Perilla, *Corp Secy*
EMP: 6
SALES (est): 450K **Privately Held**
WEB: www.sanylaser.com
SIC: 3299 Architectural sculptures: gypsum, clay, papier mache, etc.

(G-12220)
STUDIO KRP LLC
210 11th Ave Rm 500 (10001-1210)
PHONE..................................310 589-5777
Carol Rosenstein, *CEO*

EMP: 13
SQ FT: 1,500
SALES: 3MM **Privately Held**
SIC: 2335 Women's, juniors' & misses' dresses

(G-12221)
STUDIO ONE LEATHER DESIGN INC
270 W 39th St Rm 505 (10018-0334)
PHONE..................................212 760-1701
Fax: 212 760-1702
Arthur Coines, *President*
EMP: 12
SQ FT: 2,500
SALES (est): 977.5K **Privately Held**
SIC: 2386 3543 Garments, leather; industrial patterns

(G-12222)
STUFF MAGAZINE
1040 Ave Of The Amrcas (10018-3703)
PHONE..................................212 302-2626
Steven Collvin, *President*
EMP: 5
SALES (est): 500K **Privately Held**
SIC: 2721 Magazines: publishing & printing

(G-12223)
STYLE PARTNERS INC
Also Called: Jana Kos Collection, The
318 W 39th St Fl 7 (10018-1465)
PHONE..................................212 904-1499
Jana Kos, *President*
Victor Ruiz, *Controller*
▲ **EMP:** 15
SALES (est): 965K **Privately Held**
WEB: www.janakos.com
SIC: 2335 2331 2337 Women's, juniors' & misses' dresses; women's & misses' blouses & shirts; women's & misses' suits & coats

(G-12224)
STYLECLICK INC (HQ)
810 7th Ave Fl 18 (10019-5879)
PHONE..................................212 329-0300
Lisa Brown, *CEO*
Robert Halper, *President*
Bruce Goldstein, *Exec VP*
Barry W Hall, *CFO*
EMP: 52
SALES (est): 3.7MM
SALES (corp-wide): 3.2B **Publicly Held**
WEB: www.styleclick.com
SIC: 7372 Business oriented computer software
PA: Iac/Interactivecorp
555 W 18th St
New York NY 10011
212 314-7300

(G-12225)
STYLISTIC PRESS INC
99 Battery Pl Apt 11p (10280-1324)
PHONE..................................212 675-0797
Jeff Lederfarb, *President*
EMP: 15
SQ FT: 2,500
SALES (est): 1.5MM **Privately Held**
SIC: 2752 Commercial printing, offset

(G-12226)
SUGAR & PLUMM UPPER WEST LLC
377 Amsterdam Ave (10024-6207)
PHONE..................................201 334-1600
Desiree Wedlaw, *Controller*
Lamia Jacobs, *Mng Member*
EMP: 60
SALES: 3.9MM **Privately Held**
SIC: 2053 Cakes, bakery: frozen

(G-12227)
SUGAR FOODS CORPORATION (PA)
950 3rd Ave Fl 21 (10022-2786)
PHONE..................................212 753-6900
Fax: 212 753-6988
Donald G Tober, *Ch of Bd*
Marty Wilson, *President*
Stephen Odell, *President*
Myron Stein, *Vice Pres*
Brian Thomson, *Opers Mgr*
▼ **EMP:** 34

SQ FT: 10,000
SALES (est): 323.9MM **Privately Held**
WEB: www.sugarfoods.com
SIC: 2869 2023 2099 2068 Sweeteners, synthetic; cream substitutes; sugar; seasonings & spices; packaged combination products: pasta, rice & potato; bread crumbs, not made in bakeries; salted & roasted nuts & seeds; packaging & labeling services

(G-12228)
SULLIVAN ST BKY - HLLS KIT INC
533 W 47th St (10036-7903)
PHONE..................................212 265-5580
James Lahey, *Principal*
Daniel Solbany, *Manager*
▲ **EMP:** 29
SALES (est): 4.4MM **Privately Held**
SIC: 2051 Bread, cake & related products

(G-12229)
SULPHUR CREATIONS INC
71 W 47th St Ste 402 (10036-2819)
PHONE..................................212 719-2223
Elliott Delshad, *President*
EMP: 5
SQ FT: 1,240
SALES (est): 374.5K **Privately Held**
SIC: 3911 Jewelry, precious metal

(G-12230)
SUMA INDUSTRIES INC
345 E 52nd St Apt 9d (10022-6344)
PHONE..................................646 436-5202
Arthur Forst, *President*
Robert Katz, *Exec VP*
Christopher Patterson, *Vice Pres*
Myra Hyman, *Executive*
EMP: 5
SALES (est): 420K **Privately Held**
WEB: www.sumaindustries.com
SIC: 3993 Signs, not made in custom sign painting shops

(G-12231)
SUMER GOLD LTD
33 W 46th St Fl 4 (10036-4103)
PHONE..................................212 354-8677
Fax: 212 354-8697
Juan Merchan, *President*
Suzanna Merchan, *Treasurer*
EMP: 6
SQ FT: 700
SALES (est): 590K **Privately Held**
SIC: 3911 Jewelry, precious metal

(G-12232)
SUMITOMO ELC USA HOLDINGS INC (HQ)
600 5th Ave Fl 18 (10020-2320)
PHONE..................................212 490-6610
Yoshitomo Kasui, *President*
David Saleeby, *Editor*
Jim Pierce, *Plant Mgr*
Kim Dawkins, *Materials Mgr*
Joe Beck, *Maint Spvr*
▲ **EMP:** 8
SALES: 46MM
SALES (corp-wide): 25B **Privately Held**
WEB: www.engsin.com
SIC: 3674 Semiconductors & related devices
PA: Sumitomo Electric Industries, Ltd.
4-5-33, Kitahama, Chuo-Ku
Osaka OSK 541-0
662 204-141

(G-12233)
SUMMIT FINANCIAL PRINTING LLC
216 E 45th St Fl 15 (10017-3304)
PHONE..................................212 913-0510
James W Palmiter, *Owner*
Kenneth M McClure, *Owner*
Scott Damico, *COO*
EMP: 40
SQ FT: 15,000
SALES (est): 7.7MM **Privately Held**
SIC: 2621 Printing paper

(G-12234)
SUMMIT PROFESSIONAL NETWORKS
469 Fashion Ave Fl 10 (10018-7640)
PHONE..................................212 557-7480
Joyce Coots, *Manager*
EMP: 60
SALES (corp-wide): 190.2MM **Privately Held**
SIC: 2721 Magazines: publishing & printing
HQ: Summit Professional Networks
4157 Olympic Blvd Ste 225
Erlanger KY 41018
859 692-2100

(G-12235)
SUNA BROS INC
10 W 46th St Fl 5 (10036-4515)
PHONE..................................212 869-5670
Aron Suna, *President*
Jonathan Suna, *Admin Sec*
EMP: 30 **EST:** 1934
SQ FT: 5,000
SALES (est): 4.2MM **Privately Held**
WEB: www.sunabros.com
SIC: 3911 5944 Jewelry, precious metal; jewelry stores

(G-12236)
SUNHAM HOME FASHIONS LLC (PA)
136 Madison Ave Fl 16 (10016-6711)
PHONE..................................212 695-1218
Howard Yung, *CEO*
Jane Bognacki, *President*
Arthur Coubanou, *COO*
Gregory Chletsos, *Vice Pres*
Simpi Singh, *Opers Mgr*
◆ **EMP:** 58
SQ FT: 15,000
SALES: 200MM **Privately Held**
WEB: www.sunham.com
SIC: 2392 Blankets, comforters & beddings

(G-12237)
SUNSHINE DIAMOND CUTTER INC
38 W 48th St Ste 905 (10036-1805)
PHONE..................................212 221-1028
Manglaben Dhanani, *President*
EMP: 7
SALES: 400K **Privately Held**
SIC: 3915 Lapidary work & diamond cutting & polishing

(G-12238)
SUNSHINE DISTRIBUTION CORP
555 Madison Ave Ste 1800 (10022-3301)
PHONE..................................888 506-7051
EMP: 6 **EST:** 2015
SALES (est): 220.7K **Privately Held**
SIC: 2051 3651 Bakery: wholesale or wholesale/retail combined; music distribution apparatus

(G-12239)
SUNWIN GLOBAL INDUSTRY INC
295 5th Ave Ste 515 (10016-7103)
PHONE..................................646 370-6196
Sophie Cheng, *President*
Lily Zhang, *General Mgr*
Susan Rybnick, *Director*
EMP: 5
SQ FT: 850
SALES: 423.6K
SALES (corp-wide): 125.1MM **Privately Held**
SIC: 2258 5137 Lace & warp knit fabric mills; baby goods; apparel belts, women's & children's
PA: Shanghai Sunwin Investment Holding Group Co.,Ltd.
No.17,Lane 688, Hengnan Road, Minhang District
Shanghai 20111
216 036-0288

(G-12240)
SUNYNAMS FASHIONS LTD
Also Called: Sunny Names
270 W 38th St Fl 2 (10018-1563)
PHONE..................................212 268-5200
Fax: 212 268-4842
Sunny Neman, *President*

New York - New York County (G-12241)   **GEOGRAPHIC SECTION**

▲ **EMP:** 7
SQ FT: 5,000
SALES (est): 1.3MM **Privately Held**
SIC: 2339 Women's & misses' outerwear

(G-12241)
SUPER-TRIM INC
30 W 24th St Fl 4 (10010-3558)
PHONE.....................................212 255-2370
Fax: 212 243-8414
Daniel Noy, *President*
Rafael Noy, *Vice Pres*
EMP: 20
SQ FT: 5,000
SALES (est): 1.1MM **Privately Held**
WEB: www.supertrim.com
SIC: 2258 5131 Lace & lace products; lace fabrics

(G-12242)
SUPERCHAT LLC
310 E 70th St Apt 6lm (10021-8609)
PHONE.....................................212 352-8581
Kevin Koplin, *Principal*
EMP: 6
SQ FT: 500
SALES (est): 112.6K **Privately Held**
SIC: 7372 Application computer software

(G-12243)
SUPERMEDIA LLC
Also Called: Verizon
2 Penn Plz Fl 22 (10121-2299)
PHONE.....................................212 513-9700
Jeanne Ryans, *Manager*
EMP: 100
SALES (corp-wide): 1.8B **Privately Held**
WEB: www.verizon.superpages.com
SIC: 2741 8741 Directories: publishing only, not printed on site; administrative management
HQ: Supermedia Llc
2200 W Airfield Dr
Dfw Airport TX 75261
972 453-7000

(G-12244)
SURE FIT INC
58 W 40th St Rm 2a (10018-2647)
PHONE.....................................212 395-9340
Fax: 212 869-6644
Dean Smith, *Opers Staff*
EMP: 25
SALES (corp-wide): 199MM **Privately Held**
SIC: 2392 Household furnishings
HQ: Sure Fit Inc.
8000 Quarry Rd Ste C
Alburtis PA 18011
610 264-7300

(G-12245)
SUREPURE INC
405 Lexington Ave Fl 25 (10174-0002)
PHONE.....................................917 368-8480
Guy Kebble, *President*
Stephen Robinson, *CFO*
EMP: 11
SALES: 2.4MM **Privately Held**
SIC: 3559 Chemical machinery & equipment; refinery, chemical processing & similar machinery

(G-12246)
SURFACE MAGAZINE
Also Called: Surface Publishing
134 W 26th St Frnt 1 (10001-6803)
PHONE.....................................646 805-0200
Richard Klein, *Owner*
Lance Crapo, *Principal*
Adriana Gelves, *Adv Dir*
Courtney Kenefick, *Associate*
EMP: 25
SALES (est): 1.9MM **Privately Held**
SIC: 2721 Periodicals

(G-12247)
SUSSEX PUBLISHERS INC (PA)
Also Called: Psychology Today
115 E 23rd St Fl 9 (10010-4559)
PHONE.....................................212 260-7210
Fax: 212 260-7445
John P Colman, *President*
Lybi MA, *Editor*
Jennifer Redmond, *Med Doctor*
EMP: 20

SQ FT: 7,400
SALES (est): 3.7MM **Privately Held**
WEB: www.blues-buster.com
SIC: 2721 Magazines: publishing only, not printed on site

(G-12248)
SWANK INC
90 Park Ave Rm 1302 (10016-1395)
PHONE.....................................212 867-2600
Fax: 212 370-1039
John A Tulin, *Ch of Bd*
Eric P Luft, *President*
Paul Duckett, *Senior VP*
Melvin Goldfeder, *Senior VP*
James E Tulin, *Senior VP*
▲ **EMP:** 256 **EST:** 1936
SQ FT: 242,000
SALES (est): 352.9K
SALES (corp-wide): 448MM **Privately Held**
WEB: www.swankaccessories.com
SIC: 2389 5611 Men's miscellaneous accessories; clothing accessories: men's & boys'
PA: Randa Accessories Leather Goods Llc
5600 N River Rd Ste 500
Rosemont IL 60018
847 292-8300

(G-12249)
SWAPS MONITOR PUBLICATIONS INC
29 Broadway Rm 1315 (10006-3252)
PHONE.....................................212 742-8550
Paul Spraos, *President*
EMP: 10
SALES (est): 1.1MM **Privately Held**
WEB: www.financialcalendar.com
SIC: 2721 6282 Periodicals; investment advice

(G-12250)
SWAROVSKI NORTH AMERICA LTD
1 Penn Plz Frnt 4 (10119-0202)
PHONE.....................................212 695-1502
EMP: 7
SALES (corp-wide): 4.2B **Privately Held**
SIC: 3961 Costume jewelry
HQ: Swarovski North America Limited
1 Kenney Dr
Cranston RI 02920
401 463-6400

(G-12251)
SWATFAME INC
530 Fashion Ave Rm 1204 (10018-4862)
PHONE.....................................212 944-8022
Marcy Olin, *Branch Mgr*
EMP: 6
SALES (corp-wide): 81.2MM **Privately Held**
WEB: www.swatfame.com
SIC: 2339 2369 Women's & misses' athletic clothing & sportswear; girls' & children's outerwear
PA: Swat.Fame, Inc.
16425 Gale Ave
City Of Industry CA 91745
626 961-7928

(G-12252)
SWED MASTERS WORKSHOP LLC
214 E 82nd St Frnt 1 (10028-2723)
PHONE.....................................212 644-8822
Eyal Fogelnest, *Store Mgr*
Lee Fogelnest, *Manager*
Yossi Swed, *Executive*
EMP: 11
SALES (est): 1.3MM **Privately Held**
WEB: www.swedllc.com
SIC: 3914 Silversmithing

(G-12253)
SWEET MOUTH INC
244 5th Ave Ste L243 (10001-7604)
PHONE.....................................800 433-7758
Lucas Dawson, *President*
EMP: 20
SQ FT: 2,000
SALES (est): 655K **Privately Held**
SIC: 2731 Book publishing

(G-12254)
SWEETRIOT INC
131 Varick St Ste 936 (10013-1443)
P.O. Box 140441, Brooklyn (11214-0441)
PHONE.....................................212 431-7468
Sarah Endline, *President*
Andy Neiterman, *Controller*
▲ **EMP:** 5
SALES (est): 726K **Privately Held**
SIC: 2066 Chocolate & cocoa products

(G-12255)
SYBASE INC
1114 Avenue Of The Americ (10036-7703)
PHONE.....................................212 596-1100
Fax: 212 596-1900
Sandy Toscano, *Office Mgr*
Claudia Pernath, *Manager*
Bill Prapani, *Manager*
Nancy Groskopf, *Network Mgr*
Ricardo Murcia, *Sr Consultant*
EMP: 60
SALES (corp-wide): 22.3B **Privately Held**
WEB: www.sybase.com
SIC: 7372 Prepackaged software
HQ: Sybase, Inc.
1 Sybase Dr
Dublin CA 94568
925 236-5000

(G-12256)
SYMANTEC CORPORATION
1 Penn Plz Ste 5420 (10119-5420)
PHONE.....................................646 487-6000
Chris Klein, *Natl Sales Mgr*
Robert Zampolin, *Sales Executive*
Ken Lowe, *Manager*
EMP: 65
SALES (corp-wide): 3.6B **Publicly Held**
WEB: www.symantec.com
SIC: 7372 Prepackaged software
PA: Symantec Corporation
350 Ellis St
Mountain View CA 94043
650 527-8000

(G-12257)
SYMPHONY TALENT LLC (PA)
45 Rockefeller Plz # 659 (10111-0502)
PHONE.....................................212 999-9000
Richard Campione, *CEO*
Romesh Wadhwani, *Chairman*
Paul Slakey, *Exec VP*
Sal Apuzzio, *Senior VP*
Samantha Loveland, *Senior VP*
EMP: 75 **EST:** 2007
SALES (est): 134.6MM **Privately Held**
SIC: 7372 7361 Business oriented computer software; employment agencies

(G-12258)
SYMRISE INC
505 Park Ave Fl 15 (10022-9333)
PHONE.....................................646 459-5000
Fax: 646 459-5020
Magali Leogrande, *Sales Staff*
Achim Daub, *Branch Mgr*
John Teffenhart, *Consultant*
EMP: 25
SALES (corp-wide): 2.7B **Privately Held**
WEB: www.symriseinc.com
SIC: 2869 Perfume materials, synthetic; flavors or flavoring materials, synthetic
HQ: Symrise Inc.
300 North St
Teterboro NJ 07608
201 462-5559

(G-12259)
SYNCED INC
120 Walker St Ste 4 (10013-4117)
PHONE.....................................917 565-5591
Andrew Ferenci, *CEO*
Scott Paladini, *COO*
Michael Paladini, *Risk Mgmt Dir*
EMP: 5 **EST:** 2013
SALES: 5MM **Privately Held**
SIC: 7372 Application computer software

(G-12260)
SYNCO TECHNOLOGIES INC
54 W 21st St Rm 602 (10010-7347)
P.O. Box 976 (10113-0976)
PHONE.....................................212 255-2031
Fax: 212 255-1464
John Rau, *President*

Terry Cook, *Vice Pres*
Steve Schimmele, *Controller*
Carly Cadet, *Manager*
EMP: 6
SQ FT: 1,250
SALES: 1MM **Privately Held**
WEB: www.syncotec.com
SIC: 7372 Prepackaged software

(G-12261)
SYNERGY PHARMACEUTICALS INC (HQ)
420 Lexington Ave Rm 2500 (10170-0020)
PHONE.....................................212 227-8611
Donald Picker, *CEO*
Marino Garcia, *Senior VP*
Gary Sender, *CFO*
Craig Talluto, *Exec Dir*
Bernadette Hickey, *Director*
EMP: 6
SQ FT: 1,750
SALES (est): 902.1K
SALES (corp-wide): 7.6MM **Publicly Held**
SIC: 2836 8731 Biological products, except diagnostic; biological research
PA: Synergy Pharmaceuticals Inc.
420 Lexington Ave Rm 2012
New York NY 10170
212 297-0020

(G-12262)
SYNERGY PHARMACEUTICALS INC (PA)
420 Lexington Ave Rm 2012 (10170-2099)
PHONE.....................................212 297-0020
Fax: 212 297-0019
Gary S Jacob, *Ch of Bd*
Marino Garcia, *Exec VP*
Patrick H Griffin, *Exec VP*
Kunwar Shailubhai, *Exec VP*
Stephen Comiskey, *Vice Pres*
EMP: 42
SQ FT: 8,500
SALES (est): 7.6MM **Publicly Held**
SIC: 2834 Pharmaceutical preparations

(G-12263)
SYNTEL INC
1 Exchange Plz Ste 2001 (10006-3736)
PHONE.....................................212 785-9810
Fax: 212 785-9811
Bhares Bissa, *President*
EMP: 14
SALES (corp-wide): 968.6MM **Publicly Held**
SIC: 7372 8748 Prepackaged software; systems analysis & engineering consulting services
PA: Syntel, Inc.
525 E Big Beaver Rd # 300
Troy MI 48083
248 619-2800

(G-12264)
T & M PLATING INC
357 W 36th St Fl 7 (10018-6455)
PHONE.....................................212 967-1110
Joseph AMI, *President*
Steve Amiriam, *Director*
EMP: 30
SQ FT: 24,000
SALES (est): 3.2MM **Privately Held**
SIC: 3471 Electroplating of metals or formed products; polishing, metals or formed products

(G-12265)
T & R KNITTING MILLS INC
Also Called: Direct Alliance
214 W 39th St (10018-4404)
PHONE.....................................212 840-8665
Rocco Marini, *Branch Mgr*
EMP: 16
SALES (corp-wide): 20MM **Privately Held**
SIC: 2253 Knit outerwear mills
PA: T & R Knitting Mills Inc.
8000 Cooper Ave Ste 6
Glendale NY 11385
718 497-4017

(G-12266)
T M W DIAMONDS MFG CO (PA)
15 W 47th St Ste 302 (10036-3442)
PHONE.....................................212 869-8444
Leibis Morgenstern, *President*

GEOGRAPHIC SECTION

New York - New York County (G-12293)

Jonah Morgenstern, *Vice Pres*
EMP: 9
SALES: 1.5MM **Privately Held**
SIC: 3915 5094 Diamond cutting & polishing; diamonds (gems)

(G-12267)
T O DEY SERVICE CORP
Also Called: To Dey
151 W 46th St Fl 3 (10036-8512)
PHONE..................................212 683-6300
Fax: 212 683-3445
Rose Bifulco, *President*
Thomas Bifulco, *Vice Pres*
Gino Fulco, *Vice Pres*
Ciro Bifulco, *Treasurer*
EMP: 16
SQ FT: 6,700
SALES (est): 1.7MM **Privately Held**
SIC: 3144 3143 Orthopedic shoes, women's; men's footwear, except athletic

(G-12268)
T O GRONLUND COMPANY INC
200 Lexington Ave Rm 1515 (10016-6112)
PHONE..................................212 679-3535
Fax: 212 725-3847
Robert L Gronlund, *President*
Brooks Grounlund, *Corp Secy*
EMP: 18
SQ FT: 3,600
SALES (est): 2.3MM **Privately Held**
SIC: 2599 Cabinets, factory

(G-12269)
T V TRADE MEDIA INC
Also Called: TV Executive
216 E 75th St Apt 1w (10021-2921)
PHONE..................................212 288-3933
Fax: 212 734-3424
Dom Serafini, *President*
EMP: 12
SQ FT: 2,000
SALES (est): 890K **Privately Held**
SIC: 2721 Magazines: publishing & printing

(G-12270)
TABRISSE COLLECTIONS INC
Also Called: Oberon
1412 Broadway (10018-9228)
PHONE..................................212 921-1014
Fax: 212 869-8608
Mark Naim, *President*
Ebi Shaer, *Vice Pres*
Sam Naim, *Treasurer*
Jeannine Simpson, *Sales Staff*
EMP: 10
SQ FT: 5,500
SALES (est): 790K **Privately Held**
SIC: 2335 Women's, juniors' & misses' dresses

(G-12271)
TACTICA INTERNATIONAL INC (PA)
11 W 42nd St (10036-8002)
PHONE..................................212 575-0500
Fax: 212 354-5323
Prem Ramchandani, *President*
Kurt Streams, *CFO*
AVI Sivan, *Director*
Paul Greenfield, *Admin Sec*
▲ **EMP:** 12
SQ FT: 11,500
SALES (est): 1.6MM **Privately Held**
SIC: 3999 3634 Electric housewares & fans; hair & hair-based products

(G-12272)
TAHARI ASL LLC
Also Called: Tahari Arthur S Levine
1114 Ave Of The Americas (10036-7703)
PHONE..................................212 763-2800
Linda Vinceslio, *Prdtn Mgr*
Lester Schreiber, *Manager*
EMP: 305
SALES (corp-wide): 63.2MM **Privately Held**
SIC: 2331 2335 2339 Blouses, women's & juniors': made from purchased material; women's, juniors' & misses' dresses; slacks: women's, misses' & juniors'
PA: Tahari A.S.L. Llc
16 Bleeker St
Millburn NJ 07041
888 734-7459

(G-12273)
TAIKOH USA INC
369 Lexington Ave Fl 2 (10017-6516)
PHONE..................................646 556-6652
Masaki Nomura, *President*
Gen Sato, *Vice Pres*
▲ **EMP:** 13
SALES (est): 1.6MM
SALES (corp-wide): 429.7K **Privately Held**
SIC: 2211 Canvas
HQ: Futamura Chemical Co.,Ltd.
2-29-16, Meieki, Nakamura-Ku
Nagoya AIC 450-0
525 651-212

(G-12274)
TAILORED SPORTSMAN LLC
Also Called: Ogulnick Uniforms
230 W 38th St Fl 6 (10018-9058)
PHONE..................................646 366-8733
Fax: 646 366-0590
Peter Loferfo, *General Mgr*
Van Isaacs,
▲ **EMP:** 12
SALES (est): 1.8MM **Privately Held**
WEB: www.thetailoredsportsman.com
SIC: 2339 Neckwear & ties: women's, misses & juniors'; riding habits: women's, misses' & juniors'

(G-12275)
TAMBER KNITS INC
Also Called: Gilber Braid
231 W 39th St Fl 8 (10018-1070)
PHONE..................................212 730-1121
Fax: 212 730-8484
Richard Lansey, *President*
EMP: 20
SQ FT: 6,000
SALES (est): 1.6MM **Privately Held**
SIC: 2241 3965 Trimmings, textile; braids, textile; fasteners, buttons, needles & pins

(G-12276)
TAMBETTI INC
48 W 48th St Ste 501 (10036-1713)
PHONE..................................212 751-9584
Fax: 212 751-9698
Dvora Horvitz, *President*
Joseph Segal, *Corp Secy*
EMP: 5
SQ FT: 1,612
SALES (est): 340K **Privately Held**
SIC: 3911 Jewelry, precious metal

(G-12277)
TAMSEN Z LLC
350 Park Ave Fl 4 (10022-6067)
PHONE..................................212 292-6412
Tamsen Ziff, *Mng Member*
Victoria Wallace, *Manager*
EMP: 5
SALES (est): 348.3K **Privately Held**
SIC: 3911 Jewelry, precious metal

(G-12278)
TANAGRO JEWELRY CORP
36 W 44th St Ste 1101 (10036-8104)
PHONE..................................212 753-2817
Fax: 212 753-1328
Pietro Dibenedetto, *President*
Antonio Dibenedetto, *Vice Pres*
EMP: 20
SQ FT: 2,200
SALES: 4.3MM **Privately Held**
WEB: www.tanagro.com
SIC: 3911 Jewelry, precious metal

(G-12279)
TANDUS CENTIVA INC
71 5th Ave Fl 2 (10003-3004)
PHONE..................................212 206-7170
EMP: 171
SALES (corp-wide): 35.9MM **Privately Held**
SIC: 2273 Carpets & rugs
HQ: Tandus Centiva Inc.
311 Smith Industrial Blvd
Dalton GA 30721
706 259-9711

(G-12280)
TARSIER LTD
488 Madison Ave Fl 23 (10022-5703)
PHONE..................................212 401-6181

Isaac H Sutton, *Ch of Bd*
EMP: 106
SALES (est): 11MM **Privately Held**
SIC: 3648 3645 3674 Lighting equipment; public lighting fixtures; residential lighting fixtures; light emitting diodes

(G-12281)
TAYLOR & FRANCIS GROUP LLC
711 3rd Ave Fl 8 (10017-9209)
PHONE..................................212 216-7800
Naomi Silverman, *Publisher*
Len Cornacchia, *Principal*
Liz Levine, *Editor*
Kristine Mednansky, *Editor*
Rachael Panthier, *Editor*
EMP: 133 **Privately Held**
SIC: 2741 Miscellaneous publishing
HQ: Taylor & Francis Group, Llc
6000 Broken Sound Pkwy Nw # 300
Boca Raton FL 33487
561 994-0555

(G-12282)
TBHL INTERNATIONAL LLC
Also Called: Globe-Tex Apparel
252 W 38th St Fl 11 (10018-5806)
PHONE..................................212 799-2007
Stuart Hurvitz, *Principal*
Jodi Gallagher, *Production*
Robert Hurvitz,
Joel Limenes,
EMP: 10 **EST:** 1995
SQ FT: 1,400
SALES (est): 1MM **Privately Held**
SIC: 2329 2339 Men's & boys' sportswear & athletic clothing; women's & misses' outerwear

(G-12283)
TBT GROUP INC
267 5th Ave Bsmt B-103 (10016-7503)
PHONE..................................212 685-1836
Daniel Declemnet, *CEO*
Eric M Weiss, *President*
Sabine Ohler, *Vice Pres*
EMP: 11
SQ FT: 1,700
SALES (est): 1.5MM **Privately Held**
SIC: 3675 8711 Electronic capacitors; engineering services

(G-12284)
TDG OPERATIONS LLC
200 Lexington Ave Rm 1314 (10016-6201)
PHONE..................................212 779-4300
Mark Nestler, *Owner*
EMP: 7
SALES (corp-wide): 422.4MM **Publicly Held**
SIC: 2273 Carpets & rugs
HQ: Tdg Operations, Llc
716 Bill Myles Dr
Saraland AL 36571
251 675-9080

(G-12285)
TE NEUES PUBLISHING COMPANY (PA)
7 W 18th St Fl 9 (10011-4663)
PHONE..................................212 627-9090
Hendrik Teneues, *Managing Prtnr*
Hendrik Te Neues, *Partner*
Sebastian Te Neues, *Partner*
Harold Thieck, *Managing Dir*
Allison Stern, *Vice Pres*
▲ **EMP:** 11
SQ FT: 5,000
SALES (est): 1.3MM **Privately Held**
WEB: www.teneues-usa.com
SIC: 2741 5192 Miscellaneous publishing; books

(G-12286)
TEACHERGAMING LLC
809 W 181st St 231 (10033-4516)
PHONE..................................866 644-9323
Joel Levin, *Principal*
Santeri Koivisto, *Principal*
Carl Syren, *Principal*
EMP: 12 **EST:** 2012
SQ FT: 200
SALES (est): 281.6K **Privately Held**
SIC: 7372 Educational computer software

(G-12287)
TEACHERS COLLEGE COLUMBIA UNIV
Also Called: Teachers College Press
1234 Amsterdam Ave (10027-6602)
PHONE..................................212 678-3929
Fax: 212 678-4149
Sarah Biondello, *Editor*
Noelle De La Paz, *Editor*
Christina Brianik, *Manager*
Carole Saltz, *Director*
Emily Spangler, *Teacher*
EMP: 25
SALES (corp-wide): 228.3MM **Privately Held**
WEB: www.teacherscollege.edu
SIC: 2731 Book publishing
PA: Teachers College, Columbia University
525 W 120th St
New York NY 10027
212 678-3000

(G-12288)
TECHGRASS
77 Water St (10005-4401)
PHONE..................................646 719-2000
Susan Aexander, *Mng Member*
EMP: 10
SALES (est): 479.9K **Privately Held**
SIC: 3999 Grasses, artificial & preserved

(G-12289)
TECHNOLOGY CROSSOVER MGT VII
280 Park Ave Fl 26e (10017-1265)
PHONE..................................212 808-0200
Eric Goldberg, *Branch Mgr*
EMP: 205
SALES (corp-wide): 8.5MM **Privately Held**
SIC: 7372 Business oriented computer software
PA: Technology Crossover Management Vii, Ltd
528 Ramona St
Palo Alto CA 94301
650 614-8200

(G-12290)
TECHNOLOGY DESKING INC
39 Broadway Rm 1640 (10006-3057)
PHONE..................................212 257-6998
Lee Markwick, *President*
Phil Clay, *Senior VP*
Kallita Phipps, *Administration*
▲ **EMP:** 26
SQ FT: 6,100
SALES: 4.1MM **Privately Held**
SIC: 2521 Wood office furniture

(G-12291)
TECHTRADE LLC
274 Madison Ave Rm 1001 (10016-0715)
PHONE..................................212 481-2515
Andrea Song, *Prdtn Mgr*
Rose Mezzina-Smith, *Accounting Mgr*
Andy Shapiro, *Manager*
EMP: 5
SALES (est): 524.6K **Privately Held**
SIC: 3821 Clinical laboratory instruments, except medical & dental

(G-12292)
TECTONIC FLOORING USA LLC
1140 1st Ave Frnt 1 (10065-7961)
PHONE..................................212 686-2700
Mondo Pallon,
Rupert Dowd,
EMP: 4
SQ FT: 2,100
SALES: 7MM **Privately Held**
SIC: 2426 Flooring, hardwood

(G-12293)
TED-STEEL INDUSTRIES LTD
Also Called: Ted-Steel Indstries
361 W 36th St Frnt A (10018-6408)
PHONE..................................212 279-3878
Fax: 212 279-3878
Charles Desimone, *President*
Joseph Desimone, *Vice Pres*
Saml T Grayburn,
EMP: 6 **EST:** 1959
SQ FT: 10,000

New York - New York County (G-12294) GEOGRAPHIC SECTION

SALES (est): 530K **Privately Held**
SIC: 2542 Garment racks: except wood

(G-12294)
TEEN FIRE MAGAZINE
280 1st Ave (10009-1834)
PHONE.................................646 415-3703
Ngozi Maduakolam, *Owner*
EMP: 7
SALES (est): 330K **Privately Held**
SIC: 2721 Periodicals

(G-12295)
TELEPHONE SALES & SERVICE CO (PA)
132 W Broadway (10013-3396)
PHONE.................................212 233-8505
Fax: 212 233-8507
William Bradley, *President*
Neil Bradley, *Vice Pres*
James Woods, *Engineer*
Lynette Serrano, *Human Resources*
EMP: 23
SQ FT: 4,000
SALES (est): 3MM **Privately Held**
SIC: 3612 1731 Transmission & distribution voltage regulators; sound equipment specialization

(G-12296)
TELESCA-HEYMAN INC
304 E 94th St 6 (10128-5688)
PHONE.................................212 534-3442
Mario Dire, *President*
Remo Dire, *Vice Pres*
EMP: 15
SQ FT: 14,500
SALES (est): 605K **Privately Held**
SIC: 2541 7641 Cabinets, except refrigerated: show, display, etc..: wood; furniture refinishing; antique furniture repair & restoration

(G-12297)
TELMAR INFORMATION SERVICES (PA)
711 3rd Ave (10017-4014)
PHONE.................................212 725-3000
Stanley Federman, *Ch of Bd*
Corey V Panno, *President*
Corey Panno, *President*
Jennfer Potter, *Sr Corp Ofcr*
Susan Lanzetta, *Exec VP*
EMP: 30 EST: 1968
SQ FT: 4,400
SALES (est): 19MM **Privately Held**
WEB: www.telmar.com
SIC: 7372 Business oriented computer software

(G-12298)
TEMPLE ST CLAIR LLC
594 Broadway Rm 306 (10012-3234)
PHONE.................................212 219-8664
Fax: 212 219-8740
Frank Trent, *CFO*
Temple St Clair Carr, *VP Human Res*
Jamie McGrath, *Natl Sales Mgr*
Melanie Oswald, *Marketing Staff*
Temple St Clair, *Mng Member*
EMP: 27
SALES: 13MM **Privately Held**
SIC: 3911 Jewelry, precious metal

(G-12299)
TEMPTU INC (PA)
Also Called: Tempt Body Art
26 W 17th St Rm 302 (10011-5730)
PHONE.................................212 675-4000
Fax: 212 675-4075
Michael Benjamin, *Ch of Bd*
Roy Zuckerman, *President*
Greg Mandor, *CFO*
Alberto Mayoral, *Senior Mgr*
Amy Madonia, *Director*
▲ EMP: 6
SQ FT: 2,200
SALES (est): 1.9MM **Privately Held**
WEB: www.temptu.com
SIC: 2844 5999 Toilet preparations; cosmetics

(G-12300)
TENBY LLC ✪
344 W 38th St Fl 3 (10018-8414)
PHONE.................................646 863-5890

Toni Palmarini, *Manager*
EMP: 101 EST: 2016
SALES (est): 1.9MM
SALES (corp-wide): 191MM **Privately Held**
SIC: 2337 Skirts, separate: women's, misses' & juniors'
PA: The Kittrich Corporation
1585 W Mission Blvd
Pomona CA 91766
714 736-1000

(G-12301)
TEP EVENTS INTERNATIONAL INC
Also Called: Event Pad
379 W Broadway Lbby 1 (10012-5121)
PHONE.................................646 393-4723
Paul Beck, *CEO*
Charles Levitan, *Vice Pres*
EMP: 15 EST: 2013
SALES (est): 1.6MM **Privately Held**
SIC: 7372 Application computer software

(G-12302)
TERRA ENRGY RESOURCE TECH INC (PA)
99 Park Ave Ph A (10016-1601)
PHONE.................................212 286-9197
Fax: 917 591-5988
Dmitry Vilbaum, *CEO*
Alexandre Agaian PHD, *Ch of Bd*
EMP: 10
SALES (est): 3MM **Publicly Held**
WEB: www.terrainsight.com
SIC: 1389 Testing, measuring, surveying & analysis services

(G-12303)
TERRANUA US CORP
535 5th Ave Fl 4 (10017-8020)
PHONE.................................212 852-9028
Brian Fahey, *CEO*
Frank Hourihane, *CFO*
EMP: 16
SALES (est): 1.7MM **Privately Held**
SIC: 7372 Prepackaged software
HQ: Terranua Limited
Unit 2c
Dublin

(G-12304)
TESLA MOTORS INC
10 Columbus Cir Ste 102d (10019-1215)
PHONE.................................212 206-1204
EMP: 663
SALES (corp-wide): 4B **Publicly Held**
SIC: 3711 3714 Mfg Motor Vehicle/Car Bodies & Components
PA: Tesla Motors, Inc.
3500 Deer Creek Rd
Palo Alto CA 94304
650 681-5000

(G-12305)
TEXPORT FABRICS CORP
Also Called: Rose-Ann Division
495 Broadway Fl 7 (10012-4457)
PHONE.................................212 226-6066
Fax: 212 966-6785
Sonia Essebag, *President*
EMP: 10
SQ FT: 48,000
SALES (est): 1.1MM **Privately Held**
SIC: 2335 Women's, juniors' & misses' dresses

(G-12306)
TEXWOOD INC (U S A)
850 7th Ave Ste 1000 (10019-5438)
PHONE.................................212 262-8383
Fax: 212 262-9787
Herbert Tam, *President*
Herbert Tam Shiu, *President*
Jeanette Shi, *Exec VP*
EMP: 5
SQ FT: 3,000
SALES (est): 361.2K **Privately Held**
SIC: 2339 5136 Jeans: women's, misses' & juniors'; trousers, men's & boys'
HQ: Texwood Limited
3/F Texwood Plz
Kwun Tong KLN
279 773-33

(G-12307)
TG THERAPEUTICS INC
3 Columbus Cir Fl 15 (10019-8716)
PHONE.................................212 554-4484
Fax: 212 582-3957
Michael S Weiss, *Ch of Bd*
Peter Sportelli, *COO*
Christian Mayorga, *Vice Pres*
Sean A Power, *CFO*
▲ EMP: 24
SALES: 152.3K **Privately Held**
WEB: www.manhattanpharma.com
SIC: 2834 Pharmaceutical preparations

(G-12308)
TGP FLYING CLOUD HOLDINGS LLC
565 5th Ave Fl 27 (10017-2478)
PHONE.................................646 829-3900
James Pagano, *Principal*
Ashlynn Smith, *Principal*
EMP: 25
SALES (est): 500K **Privately Held**
SIC: 3511 Turbines & turbine generator sets

(G-12309)
THE DESIGN GROUP INC
Also Called: J.hoaglund
240 Madison Ave Fl 8 (10016-2820)
PHONE.................................212 681-1548
Robert Rosen, *President*
Daniel Cohen, *Chairman*
▲ EMP: 10
SALES: 3MM **Privately Held**
SIC: 2339 Women's & misses' outerwear

(G-12310)
THE SWATCH GROUP U S INC
56 Grand Central Terminal (10017-5622)
PHONE.................................212 297-9192
Kyle Hoffman, *Manager*
EMP: 5
SALES (corp-wide): 8.4B **Privately Held**
WEB: www.mcrystal.com
SIC: 3423 Jewelers' hand tools
HQ: The Swatch Group U S Inc
1200 Harbor Blvd Fl 7
Weehawken NJ 07086
201 271-1400

(G-12311)
THEHUFFINGTONPOSTCOM INC (DH)
Also Called: Huffington Post, The
770 Broadway Fl 4 (10003-9558)
PHONE.................................212 245-7844
Eric Hippeau, *CEO*
Gregory Beyer, *Editor*
Ethan Fedida, *Editor*
David Freeman, *Editor*
Ethan Klapper, *Editor*
EMP: 46
SALES (est): 3.8MM
SALES (corp-wide): 131.6B **Publicly Held**
SIC: 2741
HQ: Aol Inc.
770 Broadway Fl 4
New York NY 10003
212 652-6400

(G-12312)
THEIRAPP LLC
Also Called: Apprise Mobile
880 3rd Ave (10022-4730)
PHONE.................................212 896-1255
Ben Gholian, *Partner*
Jeff Corbin, *Mng Member*
Jeffrey Corbin, *Mng Member*
EMP: 35
SALES (est): 2.2MM
SALES (corp-wide): 4.5MM **Privately Held**
SIC: 7372 Application computer software
PA: Kanan, Corbin, Schupak & Aronow, Inc.
880 3rd Ave Fl 6
New York NY 10022
212 682-6300

(G-12313)
THEORY LLC
1114 Avenue Of The Americ (10036-7703)
PHONE.................................212 762-2300
Fax: 212 997-7409

Shaye Vercollone, *Managing Dir*
Andrew Rosen, *Manager*
Rudolph Gopie, *Supervisor*
Alexander Rakovsky, *Info Tech Dir*
Leanne Fremar, *Director*
EMP: 100
SALES (corp-wide): 13.7B **Privately Held**
SIC: 2337 Suits: women's, misses' & juniors'
HQ: Theory Llc
38 Gansevoort St
New York NY 10014
212 300-0800

(G-12314)
THEORY LLC
1157 Madison Ave (10028-0409)
PHONE.................................212 879-0265
Sylke Cunha, *Branch Mgr*
EMP: 7
SALES (corp-wide): 13.7B **Privately Held**
SIC: 2337 Suits: women's, misses' & juniors'
HQ: Theory Llc
38 Gansevoort St
New York NY 10014
212 300-0800

(G-12315)
THESKIMM INC
49 W 23rd St Fl 10 (10010-4224)
PHONE.................................212 228-4628
Carly Zakin, *CEO*
Dheerja Kaur, *Prdtn Mgr*
Kaylin Marcotte, *Manager*
EMP: 15
SQ FT: 1,500
SALES (est): 1MM **Privately Held**
SIC: 2741 Miscellaneous publishing

(G-12316)
THESTREET INC (PA)
14 Wall St Fl 15 (10005-2139)
PHONE.................................212 321-5000
Fax: 212 321-5016
Lawrence S Kramer, *CEO*
Eric F Lundberg, *CFO*
Richard Broitman,
Vanessa J Soman, *Admin Sec*
EMP: 93
SQ FT: 35,000
SALES: 67.6MM **Publicly Held**
WEB: www.thestreet.com
SIC: 2711 2721 Newspapers: publishing only, not printed on site; periodicals: publishing only

(G-12317)
THING DAEMON INC
Also Called: Fancy
96 Spring St Fl 5 (10012-3923)
PHONE.................................917 696-5794
Joseph Einhorn, *CEO*
Jack Einhorn, *President*
Michael Silverman, *COO*
Andrew Tuch, *Vice Pres*
Paige Williams, *Manager*
EMP: 25 EST: 2010
SALES (est): 5.2MM **Privately Held**
SIC: 7372 Application computer software

(G-12318)
THINKTREK INC
Also Called: Complystream
420 Lexington Ave Rm 300 (10170-0399)
PHONE.................................212 884-8399
Jyoti Prasanna, *Principal*
Tridib Majumder, *Director*
Prasanna Kumar, *Director*
EMP: 10
SQ FT: 1,000
SALES (est): 520K **Privately Held**
SIC: 7372 Business oriented computer software

(G-12319)
THOMAS GROUP INC
Also Called: Thomas Group, The
131 Varick St Rm 1016 (10013-1417)
PHONE.................................212 947-6400
Fax: 212 947-6462
Jamie H Tomashoff, *President*
Charlene Schoen, *Controller*
Vera Caras, *Manager*
EMP: 10
SQ FT: 18,000

GEOGRAPHIC SECTION — New York - New York County (G-12342)

SALES (est): 1.1MM **Privately Held**
WEB: www.thethomasgroup.com
SIC: 2752 2791 2789 Commercial printing, offset; typesetting; bookbinding & related work

(G-12320)
THOMAS INTERNATIONAL PUBG CO (HQ)
5 Penn Plz Fl 15 (10001-1810)
PHONE.............................212 613-3441
Fax: 212 629-1542
John L Lindsey, *President*
Bonnie Kantor, *Manager*
EMP: 9
SALES (est): 699.1K
SALES (corp-wide): 248.9MM **Privately Held**
SIC: 2721 Trade journals: publishing only, not printed on site
PA: Thomas Publishing Company Llc
5 Penn Plz Fl 10
New York NY 10001
212 695-0500

(G-12321)
THOMAS PUBLISHING COMPANY LLC (PA)
5 Penn Plz Fl 10 (10001-1860)
PHONE.............................212 695-0500
Fax: 212 290-7288
Jos E Andrade, *Ch of Bd*
Tom Holst Knudsen, *President*
Robert Ferguson, *Publisher*
Heather Holst-Knudsen, *Publisher*
Matt Campbell, *Editor*
EMP: 300 **EST:** 1898
SQ FT: 100,000
SALES (est): 248.9MM **Privately Held**
WEB: www.inboundlogistics.com
SIC: 2741 2721 7374 7331 Directories: publishing only, not printed on site; catalogs: publishing only, not printed on site; trade journals: publishing only, not printed on site; data processing service; direct mail advertising services

(G-12322)
THOMAS PUBLISHING COMPANY LLC
5 Penn Plz Fl 10 (10001-1860)
PHONE.............................212 629-2127
Fax: 212 290-7307
Ilene Markowitz, *President*
Sandra Batzel, *Engineer*
Ed Edwards, *Sales Staff*
Tom Marren, *Marketing Staff*
Delimar Melendez, *Manager*
EMP: 70
SALES (corp-wide): 248.9MM **Privately Held**
WEB: www.inboundlogistics.com
SIC: 2741 Catalogs: publishing & printing
PA: Thomas Publishing Company Llc
5 Penn Plz Fl 10
New York NY 10001
212 695-0500

(G-12323)
THOMAS PUBLISHING COMPANY LLC
Also Called: Magazine Group
5 Penn Plz Fl 8 (10001-1810)
PHONE.............................212 695-0500
Ralph Richardson, *Manager*
EMP: 9
SALES (corp-wide): 248.9MM **Privately Held**
WEB: www.inboundlogistics.com
SIC: 2721 Magazines: publishing only, not printed on site
PA: Thomas Publishing Company Llc
5 Penn Plz Fl 10
New York NY 10001
212 695-0500

(G-12324)
THOMAS PUBLISHING COMPANY LLC
Managing Automation Magazine
5 Penn Plz Fl 10 (10001-1860)
PHONE.............................212 290-7297
Fax: 212 629-1170
Karen Molitz, *Marketing Staff*
Margret Bresto, *Manager*

EMP: 9
SALES (corp-wide): 248.9MM **Privately Held**
WEB: www.inboundlogistics.com
SIC: 2721 Magazines: publishing & printing
PA: Thomas Publishing Company Llc
5 Penn Plz Fl 10
New York NY 10001
212 695-0500

(G-12325)
THOMAS SASSON CO INC
555 5th Ave Rm 1900 (10017-9250)
PHONE.............................212 697-4998
Jeffery Thomas, *President*
Lois Dianne Sasson, *Vice Pres*
EMP: 2
SQ FT: 1,000
SALES: 1MM **Privately Held**
SIC: 3911 Jewelry apparel

(G-12326)
THOMPSON FERRIER LLC
230 5th Ave Ste 1004 (10001-7834)
PHONE.............................212 244-2212
Essie Gonzales, *Bookkeeper*
Raffi Arslanian,
Pauline Dana,
▲ **EMP:** 9
SQ FT: 2,000
SALES (est): 1.1MM **Privately Held**
SIC: 3999 2844 Candles; concentrates, perfume

(G-12327)
THOMPSON PACKAGING NOVLT INC (HQ)
381 Park Ave S Rm 718 (10016-8806)
PHONE.............................212 686-4242
Robert B Judell, *President*
Fred Betzag, *Vice Pres*
Barry Garr, *Controller*
Robert Lang, *Admin Sec*
▲ **EMP:** 4 **EST:** 1960
SALES (est): 3.1MM
SALES (corp-wide): 20.7MM **Privately Held**
SIC: 2258 2673 2392 Lace & warp knit fabric mills; bags: plastic, laminated & coated; household furnishings
PA: James Thompson & Company, Inc.
381 Park Ave S Rm 718
New York NY 10016
212 686-4242

(G-12328)
THOMSON REUTERS CORPORATION
500 Pearl St (10007-1316)
PHONE.............................212 393-9461
Gail Appleson, *Principal*
Bill Dickinson, *Manager*
EMP: 15
SALES (corp-wide): 3.8B **Publicly Held**
SIC: 2741 Miscellaneous publishing
HQ: Thomson Reuters Corporation
3 Times Sq Lbby Mailroom
New York NY 10036
646 223-4000

(G-12329)
THOMSON REUTERS CORPORATION (DH)
3 Times Sq Lbby Mailroom (10036-6564)
PHONE.............................646 223-4000
David Thomson, *Ch of Bd*
James C Smith, *President*
Vin Caraher, *President*
David W Craig, *President*
Gonzalo Lissarrague, *President*
▲ **EMP:** 16600
SQ FT: 558,500
SALES: 12.2B
SALES (corp-wide): 3.8B **Publicly Held**
WEB: www.thomsonreuters.com
SIC: 2741 8111 7372 7383 Miscellaneous publishing; legal services; prepackaged software; news syndicates
HQ: Woodbridge Company Limited, The
65 Queen St W Suite 2400
Toronto ON M5H 2
416 364-8700

(G-12330)
THOMSON RTERS TAX ACCNTING INC
195 Broadway Fl 2 (10007-3132)
PHONE.............................212 367-6300
Gregg Wirth, *General Mgr*
Lori Sheehy, *Manager*
EMP: 68
SALES (corp-wide): 3.8B **Publicly Held**
SIC: 2721 7371 Periodicals: publishing only; computer software development
HQ: Thomson Reuters (Tax & Accounting) Inc.
2395 Midway Rd
Carrollton TX 75006
800 431-9025

(G-12331)
THORNWILLOW PRESS LTD
57 W 58th St Ste 11e (10019-1630)
P.O. Box 1202 (10028-0048)
PHONE.............................212 980-0738
Luke Pontifell, *President*
EMP: 3
SALES: 1MM **Privately Held**
WEB: www.thornwillow.com
SIC: 2731 5942 Book publishing; book stores

(G-12332)
THREAD LLC (PA)
26 W 17th St Rm 301 (10011-5730)
PHONE.............................212 414-8844
Fax: 212 414-9169
Beth Blake,
Melissa Akey,
▲ **EMP:** 5 **EST:** 1999
SALES (est): 517.6K **Privately Held**
WEB: www.threaddesign.com
SIC: 2335 Bridal & formal gowns

(G-12333)
THREE FIVE III-V MATERIALS INC
1261 Broadway Rm 401 (10001-3548)
PHONE.............................212 213-8043
Thomas Guan, *President*
Peter Wong, *Manager*
EMP: 10
SALES (est): 931K **Privately Held**
SIC: 3679 Electronic loads & power supplies

(G-12334)
THYSSENKRUPP ELEVATOR CORP
519 8th Ave Fl 6 (10018-4591)
PHONE.............................212 268-2020
Fax: 212 344-2090
Ben Siano, *Branch Mgr*
EMP: 58
SALES (corp-wide): 47.2B **Privately Held**
WEB: www.tyssenkrupp.com
SIC: 3534 Elevators & moving stairways
HQ: Thyssenkrupp Elevator Corporation
11605 Haynes Bridge Rd # 650
Alpharetta GA 30009
678 319-3240

(G-12335)
THYSSENKRUPP MATERIALS NA INC
Thyssnkrupp Mtllrgcal Pdts USA
489 5th Ave Fl 20 (10017-6125)
PHONE.............................212 972-8800
Herr Thorsten Sorje, *Branch Mgr*
EMP: 8
SALES (corp-wide): 47.2B **Privately Held**
SIC: 3499 3313 Fire- or burglary-resistive products; ferroalloys
HQ: Thyssenkrupp Materials Na, Inc.
22355 W 11 Mile Rd
Southfield MI 48033
248 233-5600

(G-12336)
TIE KING INC
Jimmy's Sales
42 W 38th St Rm 1200 (10018-6212)
PHONE.............................212 714-9611
Jimmy Azizo, *President*
EMP: 5

SALES (corp-wide): 4.6MM **Privately Held**
WEB: www.thetieking.com
SIC: 2323 Ties, handsewn: made from purchased materials
PA: The Tie King Inc
243 44th St
Brooklyn NY 11232
718 768-8484

(G-12337)
TIGER 21 LLC
6 E 87th St (10128-0505)
PHONE.............................212 360-1700
Michael Sonnenfeldt, *Principal*
Ron Brown, *Broker*
Amanda Passarella, *Marketing Staff*
Kristyn Comei, *Manager*
Courtney Simpkins, *Manager*
EMP: 7
SALES (est): 1.5MM **Privately Held**
SIC: 2273 Carpets & rugs

(G-12338)
TIGER FASHION INC
20 W 36th St Frnt (10018-9781)
PHONE.............................212 244-1175
John Joo, *President*
▲ **EMP:** 20
SALES (est): 1.3MM **Privately Held**
SIC: 2337 5137 Women's & misses' suits & skirts; suits: women's, children's & infants'

(G-12339)
TIGER J LLC (PA)
1430 Broadway Fl 19 (10018-3349)
PHONE.............................212 764-5624
Fax: 212 435-7412
Jeffrey Steinberg, *Ch of Bd*
Mark Locks, *President*
Aycan Baransel, *Production*
Arnold Brodsky, *CFO*
Andrew Steinberg, *Info Tech Dir*
▲ **EMP:** 44
SQ FT: 15,600
SALES: 33.6MM **Privately Held**
WEB: www.terrytiger.com
SIC: 2339 2337 Women's & misses' outerwear; sportswear, women's; jackets & vests, except fur & leather: women's; women's & misses' suits & skirts; skirts, separate: women's, misses' & juniors'

(G-12340)
TIKA MOBILE INC
112 W 34th St Fl 18 (10120-0001)
PHONE.............................516 635-1696
Anthony Bowden, *Principal*
Manish Sharma, *Principal*
EMP: 12
SQ FT: 500
SALES (est): 612.2K **Privately Held**
SIC: 7372 Business oriented computer software

(G-12341)
TILLSONBURG COMPANY USA INC
37 W 39th St Rm 1101 (10018-3894)
PHONE.............................267 994-8096
Tony Cooper, *CEO*
Ramaswamy Arakoni, *Ch of Bd*
Indira Sukdeo, *Office Mgr*
Sandy Jabaly, *Director*
Alex Lam, *Director*
▲ **EMP:** 50
SQ FT: 3,000
SALES (est): 5MM **Privately Held**
SIC: 2339 2329 Women's & misses' athletic clothing & sportswear; men's & boys' sportswear & athletic clothing
PA: Tillsonburg Company Limited
18/F Corporation Sq
Kowloon Bay KLN
233 138-84

(G-12342)
TIME HOME ENTERTAINMENT INC
1271 Ave Of The Americas (10020-1300)
PHONE.............................212 522-1212
Jim Childs, *Publisher*
Barbara Kaczynski, *Officer*
EMP: 32

New York - New York County (G-12343) — GEOGRAPHIC SECTION

SALES (est): 3.5MM
SALES (corp-wide): 3.1B **Publicly Held**
SIC: **2731** Book publishing
PA: Time Inc.
  225 Liberty St
  New York NY 10281
  212 522-1212

(G-12343)
TIME INC
Sports Illustrated Magazine
1271 Avenue Of The Americ (10020-1300)
PHONE..................................212 522-1212
Fax: 212 522-0318
David Morris, *Publisher*
Bradford Wallick, *Principal*
EMP: 25
SALES (corp-wide): 3.1B **Publicly Held**
SIC: **2721 2731** Magazines: publishing & printing; book publishing
PA: Time Inc.
  225 Liberty St
  New York NY 10281
  212 522-1212

(G-12344)
TIME INC
Also Called: Fortune Magazine
135 W 50th St (10020-1201)
P.O. Box 5979 (10087-5979)
PHONE..................................212 522-1633
Christine DiLauro, *Sr Project Mgr*
Abigail Baker, *Executive Asst*
EMP: 23
SALES (corp-wide): 3.1B **Publicly Held**
SIC: **2721** Magazines: publishing only, not printed on site
PA: Time Inc.
  225 Liberty St
  New York NY 10281
  212 522-1212

(G-12345)
TIME INC (PA)
225 Liberty St (10281-1048)
PHONE..................................212 522-1212
Fax: 212 522-0096
Rich Battista, *President*
Richard Battista, *President*
Jennifer Wong, *President*
Lori Dente, *General Mgr*
Evan Kypreos, *Editor*
◆ EMP: 2800
SQ FT: 670,000
SALES: 3.1B **Publicly Held**
WEB: www.timeinc.com
SIC: **2721** Magazines: publishing only, not printed on site

(G-12346)
TIME INC
Time/Fortune Money Group
1271 Ave Of The Amer Sb7 (10020-1393)
PHONE..................................212 522-0361
Ann Moore, *CEO*
EMP: 28
SALES (corp-wide): 3.1B **Publicly Held**
SIC: **2721** Magazines: publishing only, not printed on site
PA: Time Inc.
  225 Liberty St
  New York NY 10281
  212 522-1212

(G-12347)
TIME INC AFFLUENT MEDIA GROUP (HQ)
Also Called: American Express Publishing
1120 Ave Of The Americas (10036-6700)
PHONE..................................212 382-5600
Fax: 212 382-5878
Edward F Kelly Jr, *President*
Corinne Ng, *Partner*
Dana Cowin, *Senior VP*
Michael Crotty, *Senior VP*
Nikki Upshaw, *Senior VP*
▲ EMP: 300 EST: 1938
SALES (est): 37.6MM
SALES (corp-wide): 3.1B **Publicly Held**
WEB: www.fwmediakit.com
SIC: **2721** Magazines: publishing only, not printed on site
PA: Time Inc.
  225 Liberty St
  New York NY 10281
  212 522-1212

(G-12348)
TIME OUT NEW YORK PARTNERS LP
475 10th Ave Fl 12 (10018-1175)
PHONE..................................646 432-3000
Fax: 646 432-3010
Alison Tocci, *President*
Tony Elliott, *Partner*
Marisa Fari A, *Publisher*
Michael Freidson, *Principal*
Raven Snook, *Editor*
▲ EMP: 91
SALES (est): 19.8MM
SALES (corp-wide): 42.9MM **Privately Held**
SIC: **2721** Periodicals
HQ: Time Out Digital Limited
  4th Floor
  London
  207 813-3000

(G-12349)
TIME TO KNOW INC
655 3rd Ave Fl 21 (10017-9103)
PHONE..................................212 230-1210
Yonit Tzadok, *CFO*
Bryan Fryer, *Controller*
Jamie Iesner, *Director*
Lawrence Malkin, *Director*
EMP: 10
SALES (est): 875K **Privately Held**
SIC: **7372** Educational computer software

(G-12350)
TIME WARNER COMPANIES INC (DH)
1 Time Warner Ctr Bsmt B (10019-6010)
PHONE..................................212 484-8000
Jeff Bewkes, *Ch of Bd*
Howard M Averill, *Exec VP*
Paul T Cappuccio, *Exec VP*
Gary L Ginsberg, *Exec VP*
Karen Magee, *Exec VP*
EMP: 62 EST: 1922
SQ FT: 451,000
SALES (est): 28.9MM
SALES (corp-wide): 28.1B **Publicly Held**
SIC: **3652 6794 2741 7812** Compact laser discs, prerecorded; music licensing to radio stations; music, sheet: publishing only, not printed on site; motion picture production & distribution; cable television services; magazines: publishing only, not printed on site

(G-12351)
TIMELESS FASHIONS LLC
530 Fashion Ave Rm 707 (10018-5163)
PHONE..................................212 730-9328
Syed Sajid, *CFO*
Navin Mahtani, *Mng Member*
Ravi Datwani,
▲ EMP: 7
SQ FT: 2,900
SALES: 10MM **Privately Held**
SIC: **2389** Apparel for handicapped

(G-12352)
TIMES SQUARE STUDIOS LTD
Also Called: ABC Television Network
1500 Broadway Fl 2 (10036-4055)
PHONE..................................212 930-7720
Fax: 212 930-7790
Ruth Anne Alsop, *Senior VP*
Jeff Braet, *Vice Pres*
Jeff Hartnett, *Manager*
EMP: 200
SALES (est): 30.5MM **Publicly Held**
WEB: www.go.com
SIC: **3663** Studio equipment, radio & television broadcasting
PA: The Walt Disney Company
  500 S Buena Vista St
  Burbank CA 91521

(G-12353)
TIMING GROUP LLC
237 W 37th St Ste 1100 (10018-6770)
P.O. Box 275, Tallman (10982-0275)
PHONE..................................646 878-2600
AVI Schwebel, *Mng Member*
Michelle Jacobs, *Manager*
Alan Friedman,
▲ EMP: 15

SALES (est): 1.7MM **Privately Held**
SIC: **3021** Rubber & plastics footwear

(G-12354)
TITAN CONTROLS INC
122 W 27th St Fl 5 (10001-6227)
PHONE..................................516 358-2407
Paul Deronde, *President*
Gary Sefcheck, *Vice Pres*
EMP: 11 EST: 1998
SQ FT: 2,000
SALES (est): 820K **Privately Held**
WEB: www.titancontrols.com
SIC: **3829** Temperature sensors, except industrial process & aircraft

(G-12355)
TLC-LC INC (PA)
115 E 57th St Bsmt (10022-2090)
PHONE..................................212 756-8900
Loida Nicolas Lewis, *Ch of Bd*
Reynaldo P Glover, *President*
▲ EMP: 30
SQ FT: 2,500
SALES (est): 69MM **Privately Held**
SIC: **2024 2096 5149 5411** Ice cream & ice milk; dairy based frozen desserts; potato chips & similar snacks; potato chips & other potato-based snacks; beverages, except coffee & tea; grocery stores

(G-12356)
TM MUSIC INC
Also Called: Casablanca Records
9 E 63rd St Apt 2-3 (10065-7236)
PHONE..................................212 471-4000
Fax: 212 471-4010
Thomas Mottola, *President*
Susan Steinsapir, *Business Mgr*
Kamal Darraz, *Business Anlyst*
EMP: 10
SQ FT: 12,000
SALES: 5MM **Privately Held**
SIC: **2782** Record albums

(G-12357)
TOHO SHOJI (NEW YORK) INC
990 Avenue Of The America (10018-5419)
PHONE..................................212 868-7466
Fax: 212 868-7464
T Mishide, *President*
▲ EMP: 15
SALES (est): 1.1MM
SALES (corp-wide): 19.6MM **Privately Held**
SIC: **3961** Costume jewelry
PA: Toho Shoji Co.,Ltd.
  5-29-8, Asakusabashi
  Taito-Ku TKY 111-0
  338 613-274

(G-12358)
TOLTEC FABRICS INC
437 5th Ave Fl 10 (10016-2205)
PHONE..................................212 706-9310
Fax: 212 684-2522
Barbara Nymark, *President*
Judy Lester, *Vice Pres*
Claudia Rycz, *Vice Pres*
EMP: 155
SQ FT: 6,000
SALES (est): 10.1MM
SALES (corp-wide): 86.6K **Privately Held**
WEB: www.interfacefabricsgroup.com
SIC: **2262 2221** Finishing plants, manmade fiber & silk fabrics; decorative finishing of manmade broadwoven fabrics; broadwoven fabric mills, manmade
HQ: True Textiles, Inc.
  5300 Corprte Grv Dr Se
  Grand Rapids MI 49512
  616 301-7540

(G-12359)
TOM & LINDA PLATT INC
29 W 38th St Rm 6l (10018-2174)
PHONE..................................212 221-7208
Fax: 212 727-1912
Linda Platt, *President*
Tom Platt, *Treasurer*
EMP: 13
SALES (est): 1.4MM **Privately Held**
WEB: www.tomandlindaplatt.com
SIC: **2335** Women's, juniors' & misses' dresses

(G-12360)
TOM DOHERTY ASSOCIATES INC
Also Called: Tor Books
175 5th Ave Frnt 1 (10010-7704)
PHONE..................................212 388-0100
Fax: 212 388-0191
Tom Doherty, *President*
Roy Gainsburg, *Exec VP*
Philip Schwartz, *Exec VP*
Mark Goldfarb, *CFO*
Chitra Bopardikar, *Sales Mgr*
EMP: 44
SQ FT: 7,000
SALES (est): 7MM
SALES (corp-wide): 2.1B **Privately Held**
WEB: www.stmartins.com
SIC: **2731** Books: publishing only
HQ: Macmillan Holdings, Llc
  175 5th Ave
  New York NY 10010

(G-12361)
TOM JAMES COMPANY
641 Lexington Ave Fl 19 (10022-4503)
PHONE..................................212 581-6968
John Minhain, *Branch Mgr*
EMP: 10
SALES (corp-wide): 317.5MM **Privately Held**
WEB: www.englishamericanco.com
SIC: **2311** Suits, men's & boys': made from purchased materials
PA: Tom James Company
  263 Seaboard Ln
  Franklin TN 37067
  615 771-6633

(G-12362)
TOM JAMES COMPANY
717 5th Ave (10022-8101)
PHONE..................................212 593-0204
George Mattos, *Branch Mgr*
EMP: 10
SALES (corp-wide): 317.5MM **Privately Held**
WEB: www.englishamericanco.com
SIC: **2311** Suits, men's & boys': made from purchased materials
PA: Tom James Company
  263 Seaboard Ln
  Franklin TN 37067
  615 771-6633

(G-12363)
TOM MORIBER FURS INC
345 7th Ave Fl 19 (10001-5035)
PHONE..................................212 244-2180
Tom Moriber, *President*
EMP: 10
SQ FT: 15,000
SALES (est): 760K **Privately Held**
SIC: **2371** Fur goods

(G-12364)
TOMAS MAIER
956 Madison Ave Frnt 1 (10021-2635)
PHONE..................................212 988-8686
Tomas Maier, *Owner*
EMP: 7 EST: 2014
SALES (est): 422.3K
SALES (corp-wide): 19MM **Privately Held**
SIC: **2253** Bathing suits & swimwear, knit; jerseys, knit
HQ: B.V. Servizi Srl
  Viale Della Scienza 9/11
  Vicenza VI 36100

(G-12365)
TOMMY BOY ENTERTAINMENT LLC
220 E 23rd St Ste 400 (10010-4669)
PHONE..................................212 388-8300
Thomas Silverman,
EMP: 12
SQ FT: 5,500
SALES (est): 1.3MM **Privately Held**
WEB: www.tommyboy.com
SIC: **2782** Record albums

(G-12366)
TOMMY JOHN INC
100 Broadway Ste 1101 (10005-4504)
PHONE..................................800 708-3490

GEOGRAPHIC SECTION

New York - New York County (G-12389)

Thomas J Patterson, *President*
John Wu, *COO*
Matt Kritzer, *Vice Pres*
Al Valdes, *Vice Pres*
Al Valdez, *Controller*
▲ **EMP:** 50
SQ FT: 17,500
SALES: 31MM **Privately Held**
SIC: 2322 Men's & boys' underwear & nightwear

(G-12367)
TONIX PHRMCEUTICALS HOLDG CORP (PA)
509 Madison Ave Rm 306 (10022-5583)
PHONE..................212 980-9155
Fax: 212 923-5700
Seth Lederman, *Ch of Bd*
Jessica Morris, *Exec VP*
Jessica Edgar Morris, *CFO*
Bradley Saenger, *CFO*
Bruce Daugherty, *Officer*
EMP: 13
SQ FT: 4,800
SALES (est): 2.5MM **Publicly Held**
SIC: 2834 Pharmaceutical preparations

(G-12368)
TOP COPI REPRODUCTIONS INC
Also Called: Hard Copy Printing
160 Broadway Fl 3 (10038-4237)
PHONE..................212 571-4141
Fax: 212 571-4154
Abraham Faerberg, *President*
Gene R Ruscigno, *Vice Pres*
Thihira S Mangal, *VP Mktg*
EMP: 10 **EST:** 1967
SQ FT: 4,000
SALES: 2.4MM **Privately Held**
WEB: www.hardcopyprinting.com
SIC: 2752 2759 Commercial printing, offset; commercial printing

(G-12369)
TOP QUALITY PRODUCTS INC
1173 Broadway (10001-7505)
PHONE..................212 213-1988
Phu Thanh Nguyen, *Principal*
▲ **EMP:** 6
SALES (est): 735.4K **Privately Held**
SIC: 3081 Unsupported plastics film & sheet

(G-12370)
TOPPAN PRINTING CO AMER INC (HQ)
747 3rd Ave Rm 1700 (10017-2855)
PHONE..................212 975-9060
Fax: 212 246-3067
Toru Moriyama, *Ch of Bd*
David Hathaway, *General Mgr*
Zach Watts, *General Mgr*
James Violette, *Corp Secy*
Minoru Kamigahira, *Senior VP*
▲ **EMP:** 20
SQ FT: 12,000
SALES: 35.1MM
SALES (corp-wide): 12.6B **Privately Held**
WEB: www.toppan.com
SIC: 2752 7384 Commercial printing, offset; film processing & finishing laboratory
PA: Toppan Printing Co., Ltd.
1, Kandaizumicho
Chiyoda-Ku TKY 101-0
338 355-111

(G-12371)
TOPPAN VITE (NEW YORK) INC (PA)
747 3rd Ave Fl 7 (10017-2821)
PHONE..................212 596-7747
Jeff Riback, *President*
Lee Asher, *Senior VP*
Glen Buchbaum, *Senior VP*
Bill Lee, *Senior VP*
Edward Vaccaro, *Vice Pres*
EMP: 70
SALES (est): 17.6MM **Privately Held**
SIC: 2759 8732 Commercial printing; merger, acquisition & reorganization research

(G-12372)
TORAY HOLDING (USA) INC (HQ)
461 5th Ave Fl 9 (10017-7730)
PHONE..................212 697-8150
Akihiro Nikkaku, *President*
Yasuke Orito, *Principal*
K Nakajima, *Admin Sec*
◆ **EMP:** 50
SALES (est): 593.1MM
SALES (corp-wide): 17.9B **Privately Held**
SIC: 2821 Plastics materials & resins
PA: Toray Industries,Inc.
2-1-1, Nihombashimuromachi
Chuo-Ku TKY 103-0
332 455-111

(G-12373)
TORAY INDUSTRIES INC
600 3rd Ave Fl 5 (10016-1919)
PHONE..................212 697-8150
Fax: 212 972-4279
Patrick Dewitt, *CFO*
Yvette Kosar, *Branch Mgr*
EMP: 7
SALES (corp-wide): 17.9B **Privately Held**
WEB: www.toray.co.jp
SIC: 2221 2821 3089 3081 Broadwoven fabric mills, manmade; plastics materials & resins; plastic processing; unsupported plastics film & sheet
PA: Toray Industries,Inc.
2-1-1, Nihombashimuromachi
Chuo-Ku TKY 103-0
332 455-111

(G-12374)
TORCH GRAPHICS INC
1001 Ave Of The Americas (10018-5460)
PHONE..................212 679-4334
Gary Handis, *President*
Rosemary Johnson, *Info Tech Dir*
EMP: 20
SALES (est): 2.4MM **Privately Held**
SIC: 2796 Color separations for printing

(G-12375)
TORRE PRODUCTS CO INC
479 Washington St (10013-1381)
PHONE..................212 925-8989
Liberty F Raho, *President*
Peter N Raho, *Treasurer*
Philip Raho, *Admin Sec*
EMP: 9 **EST:** 1917
SALES (est): 1MM **Privately Held**
SIC: 2899 2087 Essential oils; flavoring extracts & syrups

(G-12376)
TOSHIBA AMER INFO SYSTEMS INC (DH)
1251 Ave Of The Ste 4110 (10020)
P.O. Box 19724, Irvine CA (92623-9724)
PHONE..................949 583-3000
Fax: 949 583-3205
Mark Simons, *CEO*
Ted Flati, *Vice Pres*
Scott Moore, *Purch Mgr*
Michael Bone, *Engineer*
Erik Monisera, *Engineer*
▲ **EMP:** 277
SQ FT: 446,000
SALES (est): 279.7MM
SALES (corp-wide): 48.4B **Privately Held**
WEB: www.toshiba-components.com
SIC: 3571 3577 3572 3661 Electronic computers; computer peripheral equipment; disk drives, computer; telephones & telephone apparatus; facsimile equipment; computers, peripherals & software
HQ: Toshiba America Inc
1251 Ave Of Ameri Ste 4100
New York NY 10020
212 596-0600

(G-12377)
TOSHIBA AMERICA INC (HQ)
1251 Ave Of Ameri Ste 4100 (10020)
PHONE..................212 596-0600
Fax: 212 593-3875
Hideo Ito, *CEO*
Takeshi Okatomi, *Ch of Bd*
Hiromitsu Igarashi, *President*
Hisashi Izumi, *President*
Toru Uchiike, *President*
◆ **EMP:** 28
SALES (est): 2B
SALES (corp-wide): 48.4B **Privately Held**
SIC: 3651 3631 5064 5075 Television receiving sets; video cassette recorders/players & accessories; microwave ovens, including portable: household; video cassette recorders & accessories; high fidelity equipment; compressors, air conditioning; personal computers (microcomputers); multiplex equipment, telephone & telegraph
PA: Toshiba Corporation
1-1-1, Shibaura
Minato-Ku TKY 105-0
334 574-511

(G-12378)
TOTAL CONCEPT GRAPHIC INC
519 8th Ave Rm 805a (10018-5182)
PHONE..................212 229-2626
Fax: 212 229-2677
Joe Ferrara, *President*
John Chessa, *Vice Pres*
EMP: 4
SQ FT: 500
SALES (est): 2MM **Privately Held**
SIC: 2752 Commercial printing, offset

(G-12379)
TOTAL OFFSET INC
Also Called: Total Offset Graphic
200 Hudson St Fl 11 (10013-1807)
PHONE..................212 966-4482
Fax: 212 219-3009
Phil Deluca, *President*
George Stern, *Treasurer*
EMP: 11
SQ FT: 3,600
SALES (est): 1.1MM **Privately Held**
SIC: 3555 Plates, offset

(G-12380)
TOTO USA INC
20 W 22nd St Ste 1505 (10010-5944)
PHONE..................917 237-0665
Kazuo Sako, *Principal*
EMP: 5
SALES (corp-wide): 4.8B **Privately Held**
SIC: 3432 Plumbing fixture fittings & trim
HQ: Toto U.S.A., Inc.
1800 Murphy Ave Sw
Atlanta GA 30310
404 752-8998

(G-12381)
TOTO USA INC
20 W 22nd St Ste 1505 (10010-5944)
PHONE..................770 282-8686
Fax: 917 237-0654
Kazuo Sako, *Principal*
Lori Peterson, *Human Res Mgr*
Masataka Okubo, *Sales Mgr*
EMP: 5
SALES (est): 520K **Privately Held**
SIC: 3432 Plumbing fixture fittings & trim

(G-12382)
TOUCHTUNES MUSIC CORPORATION (PA)
Also Called: Touch Tunes
850 3rd Ave Ste 15c (10022-7263)
PHONE..................847 419-3300
Fax: 646 365-0011
Charles Goldstuck, *CEO*
Charles Branchaud, *Principal*
Jim Wilson, *COO*
Phil Cohn, *Senior VP*
Eric Saint-Jacques, *Senior VP*
EMP: 3
SALES (est): 6.5MM **Privately Held**
SIC: 3651 Household audio & video equipment; audio electronic systems

(G-12383)
TOWNLEY INC
Also Called: Townley Cosmetics
10 W 33rd St Rm 418 (10001-3324)
PHONE..................212 779-0544
Abraham Safdieh, *President*
Ron Sassoon, *Senior VP*
Wandy Abreau, *Controller*
Felena Jagarnauth, *VP Finance*
▲ **EMP:** 30
SQ FT: 9,000
SALES (est): 7.2MM **Privately Held**
SIC: 3915 Jewelers' materials & lapidary work

(G-12384)
TOYMAX INC (DH)
Also Called: Candy Planet Division
200 5th Ave (10010-3302)
PHONE..................212 633-6611
David Ki Kwan Chu, *Ch of Bd*
Steven Lebensfeld, *President*
Carmine Russo, *COO*
Harvey Goldberg, *Exec VP*
Kenneth Price, *Senior VP*
EMP: 6
SQ FT: 30,000
SALES (est): 4.4MM **Publicly Held**
WEB: www.toymax.com
SIC: 3944 5092 Games, toys & children's vehicles; toys

(G-12385)
TR APPAREL LLC
609 Greenwich St Fl 3 (10014-3610)
PHONE..................310 595-4337
Andrew Wong, *Branch Mgr*
EMP: 40
SALES (corp-wide): 11.4MM **Privately Held**
SIC: 2389 Academic vestments (caps & gowns)
HQ: Tr Apparel, Llc
609 Greenwich St Fl 3
New York NY 10014
646 358-3888

(G-12386)
TR APPAREL LLC (HQ)
Also Called: Row, The
609 Greenwich St Fl 3 (10014-3610)
PHONE..................646 358-3888
Francois Kress, *President*
Ashley Olsen, *Owner*
Mary Kate Olsen, *Owner*
Greg Eyink, *CFO*
Amy Ocampo, *Accountant*
EMP: 9
SALES (est): 10.9MM **Privately Held**
WEB: www.therow.com
SIC: 2389 Academic vestments (caps & gowns)
PA: Dualstar Entertainment Group Llc
3525 Hayden Ave
Culver City CA 90232
310 945-3705

(G-12387)
TR DESIGNS INC
Also Called: Tracy Reese
260 W 39th St Fl 19 (10018-0360)
PHONE..................212 398-9300
Karen Castelano, *CEO*
Tracy Reese, *President*
Om Batheja, *VP Finance*
Alyssa Jones, *Comms Dir*
▼ **EMP:** 32
SQ FT: 11,000
SALES (est): 4.6MM **Privately Held**
SIC: 2339 Sportswear, women's

(G-12388)
TRADER JOES COMPANY
Also Called: Trader Joe's 541
138 E 14th St (10003-4170)
PHONE..................212 529-6326
John Martinelli, *Manager*
EMP: 40 **Privately Held**
SIC: 2084 Wines
HQ: Trader Joe's Company
800 S Shamrock Ave
Monrovia CA 91016
626 599-3700

(G-12389)
TRADING SERVICES INTERNATIONAL
Also Called: Tsi Technologies
133 W 72nd St Rm 601 (10023-3236)
PHONE..................212 501-0142
Joel Darr, *President*
Judy Darr, *Vice Pres*
▲ **EMP:** 14
SQ FT: 2,000

New York - New York County (G-12390)

SALES (est): 24MM **Privately Held**
WEB: www.tsitec.com
SIC: 3679 5013 Electronic circuits; motor vehicle supplies & new parts

(G-12390)
TRAFALGAR COMPANY LLC (HQ)
417 5th Ave Fl 11 (10016-2238)
PHONE.................................212 768-8800
Jeffrey Spiegel, *Mng Member*
John Hastings,
▲ EMP: 5 EST: 2003
SQ FT: 6,500
SALES (est): 626.9K
SALES (corp-wide): 448MM **Privately Held**
WEB: www.ghurka.com
SIC: 2387 3172 3161 2389 Apparel belts; wallets; attache cases; briefcases; suitcases; suspenders
PA: Randa Accessories Leather Goods Llc
5600 N River Rd Ste 500
Rosemont IL 60018
847 292-8300

(G-12391)
TRANS-HIGH CORPORATION
250 W 57th St Ste 920 (10107-0003)
PHONE.................................212 387-0500
Mary McCvoy, *Principal*
EMP: 22 EST: 2013
SALES (est): 2.4MM **Privately Held**
SIC: 2721 Magazines: publishing & printing

(G-12392)
TRANS-LUX CORPORATION (PA)
445 Park Ave Ste 2001 (10022-8613)
PHONE.................................800 243-5544
George W Schiele, *Ch of Bd*
Jean-Marc Allain, *President*
Brian Laroche, *President*
Alberto Shaio, *COO*
Alex Gomez, *Senior VP*
▲ EMP: 84
SALES: 23.5MM **Publicly Held**
WEB: www.trans-lux.com
SIC: 3993 Electric signs

(G-12393)
TRANSPARENCY LIFE SCIENCES LLC
225 W 60th St Apt 15d (10023-7430)
PHONE.................................862 252-1216
Alex Greenberg, *Marketing Mgr*
Tomasz Sablinski,
Marc Foster,
EMP: 10
SALES (est): 778.8K **Privately Held**
SIC: 2834 Pharmaceutical preparations

(G-12394)
TRAVIS AYERS INC
Also Called: Isabel and Nina
1412 Broadway Fl 8 (10018-3528)
PHONE.................................212 921-5165
Fax: 212 921-5068
Maia Chiat, *President*
Fred Chill, *Vice Pres*
Cheryl Feld, *Vice Pres*
Karen Wilson, *Accounting Dir*
Frank Rascati, *Manager*
EMP: 21
SQ FT: 4,000
SALES (est): 1.5MM **Privately Held**
SIC: 2337 5137 Suits: women's, misses' & juniors'; suits: women's, children's & infants'

(G-12395)
TREAUU INC
60 E 120th St Fl 2 (10035-3571)
PHONE.................................703 731-0196
Tahira White, *Principal*
Marcus Scott, *Principal*
EMP: 6
SALES (est): 340K **Privately Held**
SIC: 7372 7389 Application computer software;

(G-12396)
TREBBIANNO LLC (PA)
Also Called: Lucky Brand
19 W 34th St Fl 7 (10001-0055)
PHONE.................................212 868-2770
Terry McCormick, *President*

Victoria Maresco, *CFO*
Richard Schaefer, *CFO*
▲ EMP: 53
SQ FT: 25,000
SALES (est): 27.2MM **Privately Held**
SIC: 3111 Handbag leather

(G-12397)
TREND POT INC
411 Lafayette St Ste 301 (10003-7032)
PHONE.................................212 431-9970
Tetsuji Shintani, *President*
▲ EMP: 25
SALES (est): 2.6MM **Privately Held**
WEB: www.trendpot.com
SIC: 2721 Periodicals

(G-12398)
TRENDLYTICS INNVATION LABS INC
79 Madison Ave Fl 2 (10016-7805)
PHONE.................................415 971-4123
Karen Moon, *CEO*
Jian He, *Chief Engr*
EMP: 7 EST: 2010
SALES (est): 325.7K **Privately Held**
SIC: 7372 Application computer software; business oriented computer software

(G-12399)
TRI-FORCE SALES LLC
767 3rd Ave Rm 35b (10017-2082)
PHONE.................................732 261-5507
Robert Bracebic, *President*
Scp Crusader LLC, *Principal*
Matthew Marone, *Vice Pres*
Hemang Mehta, *Vice Pres*
▼ EMP: 24 EST: 2008
SQ FT: 5,500
SALES: 12MM **Privately Held**
SIC: 3999 8742 Models, except toy; marketing consulting services

(G-12400)
TRI-LON CLOR LITHOGRAPHERS LTD
Also Called: Trilon Color Lithographers
233 Spring St Frnt 9th (10013-1522)
PHONE.................................212 255-6140
Fax: 212 929-1690
Marc Strickler, *President*
David Strickler, *Chairman*
Esther Strickler, *Corp Secy*
Dave Strickler, *Vice Pres*
EMP: 26 EST: 1964
SQ FT: 10,000
SALES (est): 3.4MM **Privately Held**
SIC: 2752 2791 2789 2759 Commercial printing, lithographic; typesetting; bookbinding & related work; commercial printing

(G-12401)
TRI-PLEX PACKAGING CORPORATION
307 5th Ave Fl 7 (10016-6517)
PHONE.................................212 481-6070
Fax: 212 481-1550
Ken Golden, *President*
Barry Walsh, *Opers Staff*
Ron Verblaauw, *CFO*
Adam Caraher, *Director*
▲ EMP: 26
SALES: 10MM **Privately Held**
WEB: www.lieberman-nyc.com
SIC: 3999 2671 Advertising display products; paper coated or laminated for packaging

(G-12402)
TRI-STATE BRICK & STONE NY INC (PA)
333 7th Ave Fl 5 (10001-5829)
PHONE.................................212 366-0300
Fax: 212 366-0339
Robert Turzilli, *President*
Michael Falcone, *Vice Pres*
Vincent Falcone, *Vice Pres*
Louis J Formica, *Vice Pres*
▲ EMP: 60
SQ FT: 6,500
SALES (est): 24.4MM **Privately Held**
SIC: 2421 5031 Building & structural materials, wood; building materials, exterior

(G-12403)
TRIANON COLLECTION INC
16 W 46th St Fl 10 (10036-4503)
PHONE.................................212 921-9450
Fax: 212 921-9454
Anthony Hopenka JM, *CEO*
Joseph Bauer, *President*
Anthony Hopenhajm, *Vice Pres*
Manwant Walia, *Manager*
▲ EMP: 24
SQ FT: 3,390
SALES (est): 3.3MM **Privately Held**
WEB: www.trianonnet.com
SIC: 3911 Jewelry, precious metal
PA: Banisa Corporation
20981 Island Sound Cir # 103
Estero FL 33928
239 949-2309

(G-12404)
TRIBUNE ENTERTAINMENT CO DEL
220 E 42nd St Fl 26 (10017-5806)
PHONE.................................203 866-2204
Milan Chilla, *Sales Mgr*
Michael Fischer, *Manager*
EMP: 40
SALES (corp-wide): 2B **Publicly Held**
SIC: 2711 2741 4833 Newspapers, publishing & printing; miscellaneous publishing; television broadcasting stations
HQ: Tribune Entertainment Company (Del)
435 N Michigan Ave Fl 19
Chicago IL 60611
312 222-4441

(G-12405)
TRICYCLE FOUNDATION INC
89 5th Ave Ste 301 (10003-3020)
PHONE.................................800 873-9871
Fax: 212 645-1493
Elizabeth Lees, *President*
Alyssa Snow, *Controller*
Joellen Sommer, *Controller*
James Shaheen, *Exec Dir*
EMP: 9
SQ FT: 2,500
SALES: 1.6MM **Privately Held**
SIC: 2711 Newspapers: publishing only, not printed on site

(G-12406)
TRITON INFOSYS INC
1230 Avenue Of The Americ (10020-1513)
PHONE.................................877 308-2388
Mike Patel, *President*
Babubhai Patel, *Shareholder*
EMP: 30
SALES (est): 3.2MM **Privately Held**
SIC: 3699 Security devices; security control equipment & systems

(G-12407)
TRIUMPH APPAREL CORPORATION (PA)
530 Fashion Ave Ste M1 (10018-4878)
PHONE.................................212 302-2606
Carol Hockman, *President*
Donald Schupak, *Principal*
Philip Davis, *Vice Pres*
John A Sarto, *CFO*
Henry T Mortmer Jr, *Director*
▲ EMP: 42
SALES (est): 87.7MM **Privately Held**
WEB: www.danskin.com
SIC: 2331 Women's & misses' blouses & shirts

(G-12408)
TRIUMPH LEARNING LLC (DH)
Also Called: Options Publishing
136 Madison Ave Fl 7 (10016-6711)
PHONE.................................212 652-0200
Fax: 212 652-0277
Rick Noble, *President*
Raj Chary, *President*
Thomas Emrick, *President*
Wendy Fischer, *President*
Heather Watson, *President*
▲ EMP: 50 EST: 1963
SALES (est): 17.1MM
SALES (corp-wide): 99.1MM **Privately Held**
SIC: 2741 Miscellaneous publishing

HQ: Haights Cross Operating Company
10 New King St Ste 102
White Plains NY 10604
914 289-9400

(G-12409)
TROPP PRINTING CORP
Also Called: Tropp Prntng
181 Broadway Fl 3 (10007-3129)
PHONE.................................212 233-4519
Fax: 212 791-2953
Lee Tropp, *President*
William Tropp, *Vice Pres*
EMP: 6
SQ FT: 4,000
SALES (est): 752.9K **Privately Held**
SIC: 2752 Commercial printing, offset; lithographing on metal

(G-12410)
TRUEEX LLC
162 5th Ave (10010-5902)
PHONE.................................646 786-8526
Sunil Hirani, *CEO*
Karen O'Connor, *COO*
Harry Katz, *CFO*
Danielle Hamann, *Sales Dir*
Lauren McFall, *Chief Mktg Ofcr*
EMP: 48
SALES (est): 260.8K **Privately Held**
SIC: 7372 Business oriented computer software

(G-12411)
TRUNK & TROLLEY LLC
15 W 34th St (10001-3015)
PHONE.................................212 947-9001
Jade Corff, *Manager*
Sammy Sitt,
Steven Russo,
▲ EMP: 5
SQ FT: 25,000
SALES (est): 290K **Privately Held**
SIC: 3161 Luggage

(G-12412)
TRUST OF COLUM UNIVE IN THE CI
Also Called: Columbia Univ Publications
2929 Broadway Fl 3 (10025-7819)
PHONE.................................212 854-2793
Fax: 212 854-9509
Sandy Kaufman, *Director*
EMP: 19
SALES (corp-wide): 3.8B **Privately Held**
WEB: www.columbia.edu
SIC: 2754 8221 Labels: gravure printing; letter, circular & form: gravure printing; university
PA: The Trustees Of Columbia University In The City Of New York
116th And Bdwy Way
New York NY 10027
212 854-9970

(G-12413)
TRUSTED MEDIA BRANDS INC (PA)
Also Called: Reader's Digest
750 3rd Ave Fl 3 (10017-2723)
P.O. Box 2182 (10116-2182)
PHONE.................................914 238-1000
Randall Curran, *Ch of Bd*
Bonnie Kintzer, *President*
Lee Dashiell, *Editor*
Spencer Mary, *Editor*
Howard Halligan, *COO*
◆ EMP: 1100 EST: 1922
SQ FT: 445,193
SALES (est): 1.7B **Privately Held**
WEB: www.rd.com
SIC: 2721 2731 5961 2741 Magazines: publishing only, not printed on site; books: publishing only; books, mail order (except book clubs); record &/or tape (music or video) club, mail order; miscellaneous publishing

(G-12414)
TRUSTED MEDIA BRANDS INC
Reader's Digest
750 3rd Ave Fl 4 (10017-2723)
PHONE.................................646 293-6025
Fax: 212 366-8999
Linda Vaughan, *Publisher*
Randee Cohen, *Editor*

▲ = Import ▼ = Export
◆ = Import/Export

GEOGRAPHIC SECTION

New York - New York County (G-12439)

Richard Hessney, *Editor*
Jennifer Lenhart, *Editor*
Margaret Hoh, *Production*
EMP: 16
SQ FT: 30,000
SALES (corp-wide): 1.7B **Privately Held**
WEB: www.rd.com
SIC: 2721 2731 Magazines: publishing only, not printed on site; books: publishing only
PA: Trusted Media Brands, Inc.
750 3rd Ave Fl 3
New York NY 10017
914 238-1000

(G-12415)
TSAR USA LLC
99 Madison Ave Fl 5 (10016-7419)
PHONE....................646 415-7968
Lucy Tupu, *General Mgr*
David Sharpley, *Mng Member*
EMP: 10 **EST:** 2011
SALES (est): 1.2MM
SALES (corp-wide): 1.7MM **Privately Held**
SIC: 2273 Carpets, hand & machine made
PA: Dakee Australia Pty. Ltd.
3 Wellington Street
St Kilda VIC 3182
395 250-488

(G-12416)
TSC LLC
Also Called: Spaceship Company, The
65 Bleecker St (10012-2420)
PHONE....................661 824-6609
Julia Tizard, *Opers Staff*
Chris Madden, *Asst Controller*
AC Charania, *Director*
Jonathan Peachey,
EMP: 5
SQ FT: 7,500
SALES (est): 1.2MM **Privately Held**
SIC: 3721 Aircraft

(G-12417)
TSS-TRANSPORT SNLTN SSTMS
20 W 22nd St Ste 612 (10010-6067)
PHONE....................917 267-8534
Alex Gerodimos, *President*
Alejandro Molina, *Managing Dir*
Grant Mackinnon, *Consultant*
EMP: 5
SALES (est): 593.1K
SALES (corp-wide): 3.1MM **Privately Held**
SIC: 7372 Prepackaged software
PA: Tss Transport Simulation Systems Sl
Ronda Universitat, 22 - At
Barcelona 08007
933 171-693

(G-12418)
TTG LLC
Also Called: Titan Technology Group
115 W 30th St Rm 209 (10001-4218)
PHONE....................917 777-0959
Mark Liebmam, *Mng Member*
Paula Deverse, *Manager*
Danny Keren,
EMP: 9
SQ FT: 1,600
SALES (est): 992.8K **Privately Held**
WEB: www.titantechgroup.com
SIC: 7372 Prepackaged software

(G-12419)
TUCANO USA INC
377 5th Ave Fl 4 (10016-3300)
PHONE....................212 966-9211
Franco Luini, *President*
Sergio Musati, *Exec VP*
Mattia Cesco, *Manager*
▲ **EMP:** 6
SQ FT: 1,200
SALES (est): 4.8MM **Privately Held**
SIC: 3199 Leather garments

(G-12420)
TUDOR ELECTRICAL SUPPLY CO INC
137 W 24th St (10011-1901)
PHONE....................212 867-7550
Jay Wittner, *President*
Steve Kramer, *Vice Pres*
EMP: 8

SQ FT: 8,500
SALES (est): 1.4MM **Privately Held**
SIC: 3645 5063 Residential lighting fixtures; electrical supplies

(G-12421)
TULA LIFE LLC
660 Madison Ave Ste 1600 (10065-8418)
PHONE....................201 895-3309
Julia Steraus, *Mng Member*
Andi Christian,
Julia Straus,
EMP: 6 **EST:** 2013
SALES (est): 349.9K **Privately Held**
SIC: 2844 Toilet preparations

(G-12422)
TUMERIC HEALING ENTPS INC
Also Called: Tumericalive
39 Broadway Fl 1110 (10006-3092)
PHONE....................508 364-7597
Daniel Sullivan, *CEO*
Jesal Sheth, *CFO*
EMP: 10
SQ FT: 6,000
SALES (est): 1MM **Privately Held**
SIC: 2086 Bottled & canned soft drinks

(G-12423)
TUMI INC
261 5th Ave Rm 2010 (10016-7704)
PHONE....................212 447-8747
Jamie Webb, *Vice Pres*
EMP: 160 **Privately Held**
SIC: 3161 Hat boxes
HQ: Tumi, Inc.
1001 Durham Ave Ste 1b
South Plainfield NJ 07080
908 756-4400

(G-12424)
TUMI INC
Also Called: Tumi Stores
67 Wall St Frnt 3 (10005-3101)
PHONE....................212 742-8020
Larry Holmes, *Branch Mgr*
EMP: 160 **Privately Held**
SIC: 3161 Traveling bags; attache cases; cases, carrying; briefcases
HQ: Tumi, Inc.
1001 Durham Ave Ste 1b
South Plainfield NJ 07080
908 756-4400

(G-12425)
TURING PHARMACEUTICALS LLC
1177 Ave Of The (10036)
PHONE....................646 356-5577
Ron Tilles, *Ch of Bd*
Eliseo Salinas, *President*
Howard L Dorfman, *Senior VP*
Nicholas Pelliccione, *Vice Pres*
Michael Harrison, *CFO*
EMP: 25
SALES (est): 6.3MM
SALES (corp-wide): 1.1MM **Privately Held**
SIC: 2836 5122 Biological products, except diagnostic; pharmaceuticals
PA: Turing Pharmaceuticals Ag
Haldenstrasse 5
Baar ZG 6340
760 242-4

(G-12426)
TURN ON PRODUCTS INC (PA)
Also Called: Almost Famous Clothing
270 W 38th St Rm 1200 (10018-1573)
PHONE....................212 764-2121
Peter Kossoy, *President*
Robert Regina, *Vice Pres*
Marc Wasserman, *CFO*
Desiree Reghubeer, *Controller*
▲ **EMP:** 80
SQ FT: 20,000
SALES (est): 170MM **Privately Held**
WEB: www.youniqueclothing.com
SIC: 2339 2331 Sportswear, women's; women's & misses' blouses & shirts

(G-12427)
TURN ON PRODUCTS INC
Also Called: Younique Clothing
525 7th Ave Rm 1403 (10018-4967)
PHONE....................212 764-4545

Fax: 212 768-1289
Peter Kossoy, *President*
EMP: 12
SALES (corp-wide): 170MM **Privately Held**
WEB: www.youniqueclothing.com
SIC: 2331 2339 2337 2335 Blouses, women's & juniors': made from purchased material; slacks: women's, misses' & juniors'; skirts, separate: women's, misses' & juniors'; women's, juniors' & misses' dresses
PA: Turn On Products Inc.
270 W 38th St Rm 1200
New York NY 10018
212 764-2121

(G-12428)
TURTLE POND PUBLICATIONS LLC
1 W 72nd St Apt 84 (10023-3425)
PHONE....................212 579-4393
Craig Hatkoff,
Craig M Hatkoff,
EMP: 5
SALES (est): 420K **Privately Held**
SIC: 2731 5942 Book publishing; children's books

(G-12429)
TUTOR PERINI CORPORATION
360 W 31st St Rm 1102 (10001-2862)
PHONE....................646 473-2924
EMP: 431
SALES (corp-wide): 4.9B **Publicly Held**
SIC: 1389 Construction, repair & dismantling services
PA: Tutor Perini Corporation
15901 Olden St
Sylmar CA 91342
818 362-8391

(G-12430)
TV GUIDE MAGAZINE LLC (HQ)
50 Rockefeller Plz Fl 14 (10020-1617)
PHONE....................212 852-7500
Fax: 212 852-7323
David J Fishman, *CEO*
Michell Lindquist, *CFO*
Vincent Ohanyan, *CFO*
Mark Gudewitz, *Manager*
Rose Fiorentino, *Creative Dir*
EMP: 5
SALES (est): 121.9MM
SALES (corp-wide): 124.2MM **Privately Held**
SIC: 2721 Magazines: publishing & printing
PA: Ntvb Media, Inc.
209 Park Dr
Troy MI 48083
248 583-4190

(G-12431)
TV GUIDE MAGAZINE GROUP INC (DH)
1211 Ave Of The Americas (10036-8701)
PHONE....................212 852-7500
John Loughlin, *CEO*
Stacy Jolna, *Senior VP*
Danila Koverman, *Senior VP*
Kayne Lanahan, *Senior VP*
Stacy Lifton, *Senior VP*
▲ **EMP:** 100 **EST:** 2008
SQ FT: 40,000
SALES (est): 11.8MM
SALES (corp-wide): 124.2MM **Privately Held**
SIC: 2721 Magazines: publishing only, not printed on site; television schedules: publishing only, not printed on site
HQ: Tv Guide Magazine, Llc
50 Rockefeller Plz Fl 14
New York NY 10020
212 852-7500

(G-12432)
TWCC PRODUCT AND SALES
122 5th Ave (10011-5605)
PHONE....................212 614-9364
Katrina Hanritty, *Vice Pres*
EMP: 50
SALES (est): 2.7MM **Privately Held**
SIC: 2389 7389 Apparel & accessories; design services

(G-12433)
TWIST INTIMATE GROUP LLC (PA)
Also Called: Twist Intimate Apparel
35 W 35th St Rm 903 (10001-2238)
PHONE....................212 695-5990
Jack Saldar, *Mng Member*
David Sutone,
◆ **EMP:** 7
SQ FT: 5,000
SALES (est): 1.1MM **Privately Held**
SIC: 2322 Underwear, men's & boys': made from purchased materials

(G-12434)
TWO PALMS PRESS INC
476 Broadway Ste 3f (10013-2641)
PHONE....................212 965-8598
David Lasry, *President*
Abelan Lasry, *Co-Owner*
EMP: 10
SALES (est): 950K **Privately Held**
WEB: www.twopalmspress.com
SIC: 2741 Miscellaneous publishing

(G-12435)
TWP AMERICA INC (DH)
Also Called: Tien Wah Press
299 Broadway Ste 720 (10007-1987)
PHONE....................212 274-8090
Fax: 212 274-0771
Christina Hockin, *Vice Pres*
Bella Lukovsky, *Sales Dir*
Gary Watson, *Manager*
Deah Gerard, *Officer*
◆ **EMP:** 7
SQ FT: 4,500
SALES (est): 589.7K
SALES (corp-wide): 12.4B **Privately Held**
WEB: www.twpny.com
SIC: 2732 Books: printing only
HQ: Tien Wah Press (Pte.) Limited
4 Pandan Crescent
Singapore 12847
646 662-22

(G-12436)
TYCOON INTERNATIONAL INC
3436 W 32nd St Fl 4 (10001)
PHONE....................212 563-7107
Young Eun Kin, *President*
▲ **EMP:** 6
SALES (est): 490K **Privately Held**
SIC: 3961 Costume jewelry

(G-12437)
TYME GLOBAL TECHNOLOGIES LLC
Also Called: Hotelexpert
60 W 66th St Apt 15a (10023-6288)
PHONE....................212 796-1950
David Cristescu, *CFO*
Ryan Levin,
EMP: 21
SALES (est): 397.7K **Privately Held**
SIC: 7372 Business oriented computer software

(G-12438)
U S JAPAN PUBLICATION NY INC
147 W 35th St Ste 1705 (10001-2100)
PHONE....................212 252-8833
Nobuo Ijichi, *Ch of Bd*
Kazuyo Nakagawa, *Manager*
Naoki Hishida, *Art Dir*
▲ **EMP:** 7
SQ FT: 2,500
SALES (est): 760K **Privately Held**
SIC: 2721 Magazines: publishing only, not printed on site

(G-12439)
U SERVE BRANDS INC
Also Called: Insomnia Cookies On The Hill
440 Park Ave S Fl 14 (10016-8012)
PHONE....................212 286-2403
Seth Berkowitz, *Chairman*
EMP: 9
SALES (est): 974.1K **Privately Held**
SIC: 2052 Cookies & crackers

New York - New York County (G-12440)

(G-12440)
UBM INC
2 Penn Plz (10121-0101)
PHONE...................................212 600-3000
David Levin, *CEO*
Michelle Tan, *General Mgr*
Marilyn Cohodas, *Editor*
Douglas Henschen, *Editor*
Tim Wilson, *Editor*
EMP: 3500
SALES (est): 228.8MM
SALES (corp-wide): 1.1B **Privately Held**
WEB: www.unm.com
SIC: 2721 2711 8732 2741 Periodicals; newspapers; commercial nonphysical research; business research service; business service newsletters: publishing & printing
PA: Ubm Plc
240 Blackfriars Road
London SE1 8
207 921-5000

(G-12441)
UBM LLC (HQ)
Also Called: Ubm Tech
2 Penn Plz Fl 15 (10121-1700)
PHONE...................................516 562-5085
Robert Faletra, *CEO*
Steve Johnston, *President*
Amy Birnbach, *Publisher*
Christie Dang, *Publisher*
Will Wise, *Publisher*
EMP: 700
SQ FT: 230,000
SALES (est): 583.6MM
SALES (corp-wide): 1.1B **Privately Held**
WEB: www.cmp.com
SIC: 2721 2711 7319 7389 Periodicals; publishing only; newspapers; media buying service; decoration service for special events
PA: Ubm Plc
240 Blackfriars Road
London SE1 8
207 921-5000

(G-12442)
UBM LLC
Also Called: Cmp Media
2 Penn Plz Fl 15 (10121-1700)
PHONE...................................516 562-5000
Fax: 516 562-5131
Dan Dignam, *Senior VP*
Pamala McGlinchey, *Vice Pres*
Maureen Passaro, *Accounting Mgr*
Edwin Lothrock, *Director*
Mike Tan, *Director*
EMP: 10
SALES (corp-wide): 1.1B **Privately Held**
WEB: www.cmp.com
SIC: 2711 2721 Commercial printing & newspaper publishing combined; magazines: publishing & printing
HQ: Ubm Llc
2 Penn Plz Fl 15
New York NY 10121
516 562-5085

(G-12443)
UDISENSE INC
Also Called: Nannit
620 8th Ave Fl 38 (10018-1442)
PHONE...................................858 442-9875
Assaf Glazer, *CEO*
Andrew Berman, *COO*
Tor Ivry, *Officer*
EMP: 8
SQ FT: 10,000
SALES (est): 609.9K **Privately Held**
SIC: 7372 Home entertainment computer software

(G-12444)
UFO CONTEMPORARY INC
42 W 38th St Rm 1204 (10018-0054)
P.O. Box 20505 (10017-0005)
PHONE...................................212 226-5400
Fax: 212 219-8928
Lorna Brody, *President*
▲ EMP: 10
SALES (est): 1.1MM **Privately Held**
WEB: www.ufojeans.com
SIC: 2389 Men's miscellaneous accessories

(G-12445)
UFX HOLDING I CORPORATION (HQ)
55 E 52nd St Fl 35 (10055-0110)
PHONE...................................212 644-5900
Vincent MAI, *Principal*
▲ EMP: 1
SALES (est): 50.9MM
SALES (corp-wide): 2.7B **Privately Held**
SIC: 3299 Ceramic fiber
PA: Aea Investors Lp
666 5th Ave Fl 36
New York NY 10103
212 644-5900

(G-12446)
UFX HOLDING II CORPORATION (DH)
55 E 52nd St Fl 35 (10055-0110)
PHONE...................................212 644-5900
Vincent MAI, *Principal*
EMP: 1
SALES (est): 50.9MM
SALES (corp-wide): 2.7B **Privately Held**
SIC: 3299 Ceramic fiber

(G-12447)
UNCHARTED PLAY INC
246 Lenox Ave (10027-5543)
PHONE...................................646 675-7783
Jessica O Matthews, *Ch of Bd*
Christopher Strunk, *Finance*
Nicholas Navarro, *Director*
EMP: 25
SALES (est): 4.3MM **Privately Held**
SIC: 3699 Generators, ultrasonic

(G-12448)
UNCO UNITED OIL HOLDINGS LLC
100 Park Ave Fl 16 (10017-5538)
PHONE...................................212 481-1003
Paulette Long, *President*
John C Long, *Treasurer*
EMP: 10 EST: 2006
SQ FT: 2,400
SALES: 1.4MM **Privately Held**
SIC: 1382 Oil & gas exploration services

(G-12449)
UNDERLINE COMMUNICATIONS LLC
12 W 27th St Fl 14 (10001-6903)
PHONE...................................212 994-4340
Fax: 212 686-8224
Monika Gmochowska, *President*
Lauren Ciarleglio, *Project Mgr*
Liyo Hsieh, *Project Mgr*
Ariella Raviv, *Production*
Michelle Duda, *Director*
EMP: 10
SALES (est): 1.2MM **Privately Held**
WEB: www.underlinecom.com
SIC: 2741 Miscellaneous publishing

(G-12450)
UNI JEWELRY INC
48 W 48th St Ste 1401 (10036-1718)
PHONE...................................212 398-1818
Frank Lee, *President*
▲ EMP: 7
SQ FT: 1,000
SALES (est): 540K **Privately Held**
SIC: 3911 5094 Jewelry, precious metal; jewelry

(G-12451)
UNIBRANDS CORPORATION
745 5th Ave Ste 500 (10151-0099)
PHONE...................................212 897-2278
Michael H Rahbari, *President*
EMP: 12
SQ FT: 5,000
SALES: 5MM **Privately Held**
SIC: 3631 3669 3648 Barbecues, grills & braziers (outdoor cooking); emergency alarms; lanterns: electric, gas, carbide, kerosene or gasoline; flashlights; lighting fixtures, except electric: residential

(G-12452)
UNICOM GRAPHIC COMMUNICATIONS
230 Park Ave Rm 1000 (10169-1001)
PHONE...................................212 221-2456
Khaled Sawaf, *President*
Karim Sawaf, *Vice Pres*
EMP: 7
SQ FT: 1,500
SALES: 3MM
SALES (corp-wide): 528.4K **Privately Held**
SIC: 2752 Commercial printing, offset
PA: Unicom Communications Graphiques Inc
5000 Rue Jean-Talon O Bureau 100
Montreal QC H4P 1
514 731-3677

(G-12453)
UNIFIED INC IED
35 W 36th St (10018-7906)
PHONE...................................646 370-4650
EMP: 10
SALES (est): 500K **Privately Held**
SIC: 2389 Mfg Apparel/Accessories

(G-12454)
UNIFIED MEDIA INC
180 Madison Ave Lbby L (10016-5267)
PHONE...................................917 595-2710
Sheldon Owen, *CEO*
EMP: 19
SALES (est): 1.2MM **Privately Held**
SIC: 2711 Newspapers, publishing & printing

(G-12455)
UNIFOR INC
149 5th Ave Ste 3r (10010-6899)
PHONE...................................212 673-3434
Fax: 212 673-7317
Gianfranco Marinelli, *President*
Mersiha Makota, *Project Mgr*
Shannon Devine, *Comms Dir*
Stefano Rubino, *Sr Project Mgr*
Matthew Pych, *Manager*
▲ EMP: 19
SALES (est): 3MM **Privately Held**
SIC: 2531 Public building & related furniture

(G-12456)
UNIFRAX HOLDING CO (DH)
55 E 52nd St Fl 35 (10055-0110)
PHONE...................................212 644-5900
Joseph D Carrabino, *Managing Dir*
Martin C Eltrich, *Managing Dir*
Daniel H Klebes, *Managing Dir*
Vincent MAI, *Principal*
EMP: 1
SALES (est): 50.9MM
SALES (corp-wide): 2.7B **Privately Held**
SIC: 3299 Ceramic fiber
HQ: Ufx Holding Ii Corporation
55 E 52nd St Fl 35
New York NY 10055
212 644-5900

(G-12457)
UNIMAX SUPPLY CO INC (PA)
269 Canal St (10013-3568)
PHONE...................................212 925-1051
Fax: 646 925-7424
Westley Wood, *President*
◆ EMP: 27
SQ FT: 10,000
SALES (est): 2.8MM **Privately Held**
WEB: www.unimaxsupply.com
SIC: 3911 Earrings, precious metal

(G-12458)
UNIMEX CORPORATION (PA)
Also Called: Lee Spring Company Div
54 E 64th St (10065-7306)
PHONE...................................212 755-8800
Fax: 212 486-5737
Arthur L Carter, *Ch of Bd*
Tom Scheinman, *President*
Vincent A Bohn Jr, *Vice Pres*
Brian G Kempner, *Vice Pres*
Ezra Berger, *Treasurer*
EMP: 100
SQ FT: 10,000
SALES (est): 33.4MM **Privately Held**
SIC: 3495 Wire springs

(G-12459)
UNIPHARM INC (PA)
350 5th Ave Ste 6701 (10118-0110)
PHONE...................................212 564-3634
Victor Sapritsky, *President*
Robert D Sires, *President*
Chris Adamo, *General Mgr*
Mike Carollo, *VP Opers*
Bernie Hubert, *Buyer*
▼ EMP: 31
SALES (est): 13.7MM **Privately Held**
WEB: www.unipharmus.com
SIC: 2834 5122 Vitamin preparations; vitamins & minerals

(G-12460)
UNIQLO USA LLC
546 Broadway (10012-3912)
PHONE...................................877 486-4756
Andrew Rosen, *Mng Member*
EMP: 14
SALES (est): 1.4MM
SALES (corp-wide): 13.7B **Privately Held**
SIC: 2329 2337 5621 Sweaters & sweater jackets: men's & boys' & misses' capes & jackets; women's clothing stores
PA: Fast Retailing Co., Ltd.
9-7-1, Akasaka
Minato-Ku TKY 107-0
368 650-050

(G-12461)
UNIQUE DESIGNS INC
521 5th Ave Rm 820 (10175-0800)
PHONE...................................212 575-7701
Tejas Shah, *CEO*
Ben Yep, *President*
Chai Lin, *Vice Pres*
Karen Lin, *Controller*
Dolly Ng, *Office Mgr*
EMP: 19
SQ FT: 1,000
SALES: 65MM
SALES (corp-wide): 1.1B **Privately Held**
WEB: www.uniquedesigns.com
SIC: 3911 Jewelry, precious metal
PA: Kiran Gems Private Limited
Fe-5011, G Block, Bandra Kurla Complex,
Mumbai MH 40005
224 050-4444

(G-12462)
UNIQUE PETZ LLC
10 W 33rd St Rm 220 (10001-3306)
PHONE...................................212 714-1800
Adam Ash, *President*
EMP: 25
SALES: 20MM **Privately Held**
SIC: 3999 Pet supplies

(G-12463)
UNISYSTEMS INC (PA)
Also Called: Modern Publishing
155 E 55th St Apt 203 (10022-4051)
PHONE...................................212 826-0850
Fax: 212 759-9069
Larry Steinberg, *Ch of Bd*
Andrew Steinberg, *President*
Warren Cohen, *Exec VP*
Fill Lapinig, *Controller*
Shini Parker, *Administration*
▲ EMP: 36
SQ FT: 8,200
SALES (est): 3.6MM **Privately Held**
WEB: www.modernpublishing.com
SIC: 2731 Books: publishing only

(G-12464)
UNITED BROTHERS JEWELRY INC
Also Called: U B J
48 W 48th St Ste 700 (10036-1703)
PHONE...................................212 921-2558
Fax: 212 398-9482
Gabriel Nisanov, *CEO*
Roman Nisanov, *Vice Pres*
Israel Nisanov, *Treasurer*
Nadya Nisanov, *Manager*
Katanov Rafi, *Manager*
EMP: 50
SQ FT: 6,000
SALES (est): 4.4MM **Privately Held**
SIC: 3911 Jewelry, precious metal

▲ = Import ▼ = Export
◆ = Import/Export

GEOGRAPHIC SECTION

New York - New York County (G-12492)

(G-12465)
UNITED KNITWEAR INTERNATIONAL (PA)
1384 Broadway Rm 1210 (10018-0509)
PHONE 212 354-2920
Fax: 212 354-2921
Carlos Hausner, *President*
Winter Evans, *Sales Staff*
Shy Efter, *Manager*
▲ EMP: 3
SQ FT: 860
SALES (est): 4.4MM **Privately Held**
WEB: www.unitedknitwear.com
SIC: 2253 5136 5137 Sweaters & sweater coats, knit; men's & boys' clothing; women's & children's clothing

(G-12466)
UNITED STRUCTURE SOLUTION INC
240 W 65th St Apt 26c (10023-6412)
PHONE 347 227-7526
Ying Lu, *President*
Tc Yuan, *Project Mgr*
EMP: 15 EST: 2010
SALES: 2MM **Privately Held**
SIC: 3441 Fabricated structural metal

(G-12467)
UNITED SYNGGUE CNSRVTIVE JDISM (PA)
120 Broadway Ste 1540 (10271-0032)
PHONE 212 533-7800
Rabbi Steven Wernick, *CEO*
Rabbi Jerome Epstein, *Exec VP*
Breanne Bornstein, *Vice Pres*
Brian Boczko, *CFO*
Mark Gapski, *CFO*
▲ EMP: 50
SQ FT: 50,000
SALES (est): 19.1MM **Privately Held**
WEB: www.uscj.org
SIC: 2731 8661 Books: publishing only; religious organizations

(G-12468)
UNITONE COMMUNICATION SYSTEMS
220 E 23rd St (10010-4606)
PHONE 212 777-9090
Fax: 212 777-9094
Lucien Bohbot, *President*
Preya Khusial, *Vice Pres*
Andrew Doilodov, *Manager*
EMP: 6
SALES (est): 983.4K **Privately Held**
WEB: www.unitonecom.com
SIC: 3669 7622 Burglar alarm apparatus, electric; fire alarm apparatus, electric; intercommunication systems, electric; communication equipment repair

(G-12469)
UNIVERSAL CMMNCATIONS OF MIAMI
Also Called: Elite Traveler Magazine
801 2nd Ave Lbby (10017-4706)
PHONE 212 986-5100
Geoffrey Lurie, *CEO*
Carl Reuderman, *Ch of Bd*
Douglas Gollan, *President*
Mikki Dorsey, *Exec VP*
Mikki Dosey, *Exec VP*
EMP: 125
SALES (est): 10.5MM **Privately Held**
SIC: 2721 Magazines: publishing & printing

(G-12470)
UNIVERSAL EDITION INC
Also Called: Ue Music
331 W 57th St Ste 380 (10019-3101)
PHONE 917 213-2177
Robert Thompson, *President*
Wolfgang Schaufler, *Manager*
▲ EMP: 65
SQ FT: 5,000
SALES: 8MM **Privately Held**
WEB: www.roxannapanufnik.com
SIC: 2741 Music books: publishing & printing

(G-12471)
UNIVERSAL ELLIOT CORP
327 W 36th St Rm 700 (10018-6929)
PHONE 212 736-8877
Fax: 212 736-8611
Mike Gadh, *President*
Ush Gadh, *Vice Pres*
Gurpal Gadh, *Admin Sec*
EMP: 9
SALES (est): 550K **Privately Held**
SIC: 2387 Apparel belts

(G-12472)
UNLIMITED JEANS CO INC
401 Broadway Frnt A (10013-3005)
PHONE 212 661-6355
EMP: 5
SALES (corp-wide): 1.8MM **Privately Held**
SIC: 2253 Pants, slacks or trousers, knit
PA: Unlimited Jeans Co., Inc.
  850 2nd Ave
  New York NY 10017
  212 661-6355

(G-12473)
UPPER EAST VERERINARY CENTER
1435 Lexington Ave Frnt 6 (10128-1660)
PHONE 212 369-8387
Talia G Goldberg, *Principal*
EMP: 6
SALES (est): 738.8K **Privately Held**
SIC: 3131 Uppers

(G-12474)
UPPER NINTY LLC
Also Called: Upper Ninty Soccer and Sport
697 Amsterdam Ave (10025-6933)
PHONE 646 863-3105
Shaquille Robinson, *Sales Associate*
Jack Rubin,
Douglas Gatanis,
EMP: 9
SALES (est): 2.5MM **Privately Held**
SIC: 3131 Uppers

(G-12475)
UPTOWN LOCAL
1606 1st Ave (10028-4311)
PHONE 212 988-1704
Scott Stringer, *Admin Sec*
EMP: 11
SQ FT: 2,000
SALES (est): 487.2K **Privately Held**
SIC: 2082 5149 Beer (alcoholic beverage); sandwiches

(G-12476)
UPTOWN MEDIA GROUP LLC
113 E 125th St Frnt 1 (10035-1661)
PHONE 212 360-5073
Brett Wright,
Leonard Burnett,
EMP: 36
SALES (est): 4MM **Privately Held**
SIC: 2721 Magazines: publishing & printing

(G-12477)
UPTOWN NAILS LLC
500 5th Ave (10110-0002)
P.O. Box 20456 (10021-0067)
PHONE 800 748-1881
Larry G Kapfer, *Principal*
EMP: 106
SALES (est): 315.4K **Privately Held**
SIC: 3999 Fingernails, artificial

(G-12478)
URBAN APPAREL GROUP INC
226 W 37th St Fl 17 (10018-9011)
PHONE 212 947-7009
Fax: 212 947-7218
Karen Camporeale, *President*
Noreen Camporeale, *Vice Pres*
David A Dulinski, *CFO*
Glenn Ald, *VP Sales*
Anna Imperati, *Manager*
▲ EMP: 37
SQ FT: 9,000
SALES (est): 4.5MM **Privately Held**
WEB: www.urbanapparel.com
SIC: 2339 Sportswear, women's

(G-12479)
URBAN GREEN ENERGY INC
Also Called: Uge
330 W 38th St Rm 1103 (10018-8446)
PHONE 917 720-5681
Nick Blitterswyk, *CEO*
Joshua Rogol, *President*
Henry Hatch, *Business Mgr*
Mateo Chaskel, *Vice Pres*
Anthony Ditietro, *Vice Pres*
◆ EMP: 31
SQ FT: 35,000
SALES: 5MM **Privately Held**
SIC: 3825 Energy measuring equipment, electrical

(G-12480)
URBAN MAPPING INC
Also Called: Umi
295 Madison Ave Rm 1010 (10017-6340)
PHONE 415 946-8170
Ian White, *President*
John Marshall, *CTO*
Timothy Caro-Bruce, *Prgrmr*
Amy Ocasio, *Admin Sec*
EMP: 11
SALES (est): 1.1MM **Privately Held**
WEB: www.urbanmapping.com
SIC: 2741 Atlas, map & guide publishing

(G-12481)
URBAN TEXTILES INC
Also Called: Forest Uniforms
49 Elizabeth St Fl 6 (10013-4636)
PHONE 212 777-1900
Fax: 212 777-1980
Michael Schackett, *President*
Mary Cuevas, *Manager*
▲ EMP: 10
SQ FT: 5,000
SALES (est): 1.4MM **Privately Held**
SIC: 2311 Men's & boys' uniforms

(G-12482)
URBANDADDY INC
900 Broadway Ste 1003 (10003-1215)
PHONE 212 929-7905
Lance Broumand, *CEO*
Jerry Wang, *President*
Jim Bridges, *Editor*
Dionne Buxton, *Editor*
Sam Eichner, *Editor*
EMP: 14
SALES (est): 3.7MM **Privately Held**
SIC: 2721 Magazines: publishing & printing

(G-12483)
URTHWORX INC
320 W 106th St Apt 2f (10025-3470)
PHONE 646 373-7535
Michael Fox, *CEO*
EMP: 5 EST: 2014
SALES (est): 276.6K **Privately Held**
SIC: 7372 7389 Home entertainment computer software;

(G-12484)
US CHINA MAGAZINE
200 W 95th St Apt 21 (10025-6315)
PHONE 212 663-4333
Zhong Vhan, *President*
Angila Chan, *Vice Pres*
Andrew Heermans, *Exec Dir*
Andrew Jee, *Director*
EMP: 25 EST: 1994
SALES: 500K **Privately Held**
SIC: 2721 Periodicals

(G-12485)
US DESIGN GROUP LTD
Also Called: Request Jeans
1385 Broadway Rm 1905 (10018-6001)
PHONE 212 354-4070
Fax: 212 354-4418
Frank Jbara, *President*
Frank Jebara, *President*
Assad Charles Jebara, *Vice Pres*
Imad Jebara, *Admin Sec*
▲ EMP: 18
SQ FT: 10,000
SALES (est): 1.2MM **Privately Held**
SIC: 2211 Apparel & outerwear fabrics, cotton

(G-12486)
US FRONTLINE NEWS INC
228 E 45th St Rm 700 (10017-3336)
PHONE 212 922-9090
Fax: 212 922-9119
Ryu Fujiwara, *President*
Yuri Yamane, *Vice Pres*
EMP: 30
SQ FT: 5,000
SALES (est): 3.5MM **Privately Held**
WEB: www.usfl.com
SIC: 2721 Magazines: publishing only, not printed on site

(G-12487)
US HOME TEXTILES GROUP LLC
1400 Broadway Fl 18 (10018-5300)
PHONE 212 768-3030
▲ EMP: 6
SALES (est): 570K **Privately Held**
SIC: 2221 Manmade Broadwoven Fabric Mill

(G-12488)
US NEWS & WORLD REPORT INC (PA)
4 New York Plz Fl 6 (10004-2473)
PHONE 212 716-6800
Fax: 212 916-7400
Mortimer B Zuckerman, *CEO*
Brian Duffy, *Editor*
Fred Drasner, *Co-COB*
Bill Frischling, *Vice Pres*
Niel Maheshwari, *Vice Pres*
▲ EMP: 150 EST: 1933
SQ FT: 100,000
SALES (est): 107.3MM **Privately Held**
WEB: www.usnews.com
SIC: 2721 Magazines: publishing & printing

(G-12489)
US WEEKLY LLC
1290 Ave Of The Am Fl 2 (10104)
PHONE 212 484-1616
Will Schenck, *Publisher*
Kent Brownridge, *General Mgr*
Will Brownrigeg, *General Mgr*
Elizabeth Crow, *Chief*
Anso Wintour, *Chief*
EMP: 75
SQ FT: 15,000
SALES (est): 10.5MM **Privately Held**
WEB: www.usweekly.com
SIC: 2721 Magazines: publishing only, not printed on site

(G-12490)
USA FURS BY GEORGE INC
212 W 30th St (10001-4901)
PHONE 212 643-1415
George Chrisomalides, *President*
Johanna Chrisomalides, *Vice Pres*
EMP: 4
SQ FT: 2,500
SALES: 1MM **Privately Held**
SIC: 2371 Fur coats & other fur apparel

(G-12491)
USA TODAY INTERNATIONAL CORP
535 Madison Ave Fl 27 (10022-4216)
PHONE 703 854-3400
Fax: 212 371-0241
David Mazzarella, *Manager*
EMP: 7
SALES (corp-wide): 5.7B **Publicly Held**
SIC: 2711 Newspapers
HQ: Usa Today International Corp
  7950 Jones Branch Dr
  Mc Lean VA 22102
  703 854-3400

(G-12492)
USPA ACCESSORIES LLC
Also Called: Concept One Accessories
119 W 40th St Fl 3 (10018-2526)
PHONE 212 868-2590
Fax: 212 868-2595
Margaret Close, *Vice Pres*
Jack Gindi, *Vice Pres*
Harvey Mallis, *Vice Pres*
David Shaoul, *Vice Pres*
Kim White, *Vice Pres*
▲ EMP: 150

New York - New York County (G-12493)

GEOGRAPHIC SECTION

SQ FT: 38,000
SALES (est): 24.5MM Privately Held
SIC: 2339 Women's & misses' accessories

(G-12493)
USQ GROUP LLC
222 Broadway Fl 19 (10038-2550)
PHONE..................212 777-7351
Shanto Goswami, *CEO*
Spencer Hawes, *Mktg Dir*
EMP: 5
SALES (est): 300K Privately Held
SIC: 7372 Application computer software; home entertainment computer software

(G-12494)
VALENTIN & KALICH JWLY MFG LTD
Also Called: Valentin Magro
42 W 48th St Ste 903 (10036-1712)
PHONE..................212 575-9044
Valente Magro, *President*
Terry Magro, *Vice Pres*
EMP: 24
SALES (est): 3.1MM Privately Held
SIC: 3911 Jewelry, precious metal

(G-12495)
VALENTINE JEWELRY MFG CO INC
31 W 47th St Ste 602 (10036-2833)
PHONE..................212 382-0606
Fax: 212 382-0608
Emil Feiger, *President*
EMP: 20 EST: 1969
SQ FT: 2,000
SALES (est): 1.9MM Privately Held
SIC: 3911 Jewelry, precious metal

(G-12496)
VALMONT INC (PA)
1 W 34th St Rm 303 (10001-3011)
PHONE..................212 685-1653
Fax: 212 689-6325
Nicholas Vales, *President*
Nicholas Vale, *President*
Errol Lewis, *Mfg Mgr*
John Graboski, *VP Human Res*
Sarah Peterman, *Marketing Mgr*
▲ EMP: 15 EST: 1944
SQ FT: 1,000
SALES (est): 3.1MM Privately Held
SIC: 2342 5961 Brassieres; catalog & mail-order houses

(G-12497)
VALUE LINE INC (HQ)
485 Lexington Ave Fl 9 (10017-2653)
PHONE..................212 907-1500
Fax: 212 661-2807
Howard A Brecher, *Ch of Bd*
Steve Grant, *Vice Pres*
Stephen R Anastasio, *Treasurer*
Mary Bernstein, *Accountant*
EMP: 75
SQ FT: 44,493
SALES: 34.5MM
SALES (corp-wide): 36MM Publicly Held
SIC: 2721 6282 2741 Periodicals: publishing only; investment advisory service; miscellaneous publishing
PA: Bernhard Arnold & Company Inc
   485 Lexington Ave Fl 9
   New York NY 10017
   212 907-1500

(G-12498)
VALUE LINE PUBLISHING LLC
485 Lexington Ave Fl 9 (10017-2653)
PHONE..................212 907-1500
Howard Brether, *CEO*
George Moy, *Manager*
Christine Gould, *CTO*
Ted Krismann, *Director*
EMP: 175
SQ FT: 80,000
SALES (est): 31MM
SALES (corp-wide): 36MM Publicly Held
SIC: 2721 Periodicals: publishing only
HQ: Value Line, Inc.
   485 Lexington Ave Fl 9
   New York NY 10017
   212 907-1500

(G-12499)
VANDAM INC
121 W 27th St Ste 1102 (10001-6261)
PHONE..................212 929-0416
Fax: 212 929-0426
Stephan Muth Vandam, *President*
Jacob Benjamin, *Editor*
Jessy Cerda, *Opers Staff*
Eamonn Fitzmaurice, *Production*
Bob Troast, *VP Sales*
▲ EMP: 12
SQ FT: 2,500
SALES: 1.5MM Privately Held
SIC: 2741 2731 6794 Maps: publishing only, not printed on site; books: publishing only; patent buying, licensing, leasing

(G-12500)
VANDER HEYDEN WOODWORKING
Also Called: Tapestries Etc
151 W 25th St Fl 8 (10001-7204)
PHONE..................212 242-0525
Fax: 212 242-0988
Marcia Vander Heyden, *President*
EMP: 6
SQ FT: 3,000
SALES (est): 480K Privately Held
WEB: www.metookids.com
SIC: 2431 0742 Interior & ornamental woodwork & trim; veterinary services, specialties

(G-12501)
VANITY FAIR
4 Times Sq Bsmt C1b (10036-6518)
PHONE..................212 286-6052
Fax: 212 286-6916
Graydon Carter, *Chief*
Edward Menicheschi, *Vice Pres*
Susan White, *Director*
◆ EMP: 15
SALES (est): 2MM Privately Held
WEB: www.vf.com
SIC: 2721 Magazines: publishing & printing

(G-12502)
VANITY FAIR BRANDS LP
25 W 39th St (10018-3805)
PHONE..................212 548-1548
Pat Lager, *Manager*
EMP: 250
SALES (corp-wide): 210.8B Publicly Held
SIC: 2341 Nightgowns & negligees: women's & children's
HQ: Vanity Fair Brands, Lp
   1 Fruit Of The Loom Dr
   Bowling Green KY 42103
   270 781-6400

(G-12503)
VANITY ROOM INC
Also Called: Four Star
230 W 39th St Fl 9 (10018-4411)
PHONE..................212 921-7154
Fax: 212 391-5520
Geneva Goldsmith, *President*
Teresa Boanco, *Assistant*
EMP: 10
SALES (est): 2.8MM Privately Held
SIC: 2331 2335 Women's & misses' blouses & shirts; women's, juniors' & misses' dresses

(G-12504)
VANTAGE PRESS INC
419 Park Ave S Fl 18 (10016-8410)
PHONE..................212 736-1767
Fax: 212 736-2273
Martin Kleinwald, *President*
Martin Littlefield, *Controller*
Donna Kempe, *Bd of Directors*
Susanne Camilleri, *Admin Sec*
▲ EMP: 26 EST: 1949
SQ FT: 8,000
SALES (est): 3.2MM Privately Held
WEB: www.vantagepress.com
SIC: 2731 Books: publishing only

(G-12505)
VARIABLE GRAPHICS LLC
15 W 36th St Rm 601 (10018-7122)
PHONE..................212 691-2323
Keneth Ratskin,
Arthur Raskin,
Kenneth Ratskin,
▲ EMP: 6
SALES (est): 540K Privately Held
WEB: www.variablegraphics.com
SIC: 2752 Commercial printing, lithographic

(G-12506)
VARICK STREET LITHO INC
121 Varick St (10013-1408)
PHONE..................646 843-0800
EMP: 6
SALES (est): 480K Privately Held
SIC: 2759 Commercial printing

(G-12507)
VARNISH SOFTWARE INC
85 Broad St Fl 18 (10004-2783)
PHONE..................201 857-2832
Lars Larsson, *President*
Daniel Jacobs, *Sales Mgr*
EMP: 5
SALES (est): 121K Privately Held
SIC: 7372 Prepackaged software

(G-12508)
VARONIS SYSTEMS INC (PA)
1250 Broadway Fl 29 (10001-3720)
PHONE..................877 292-8767
Yakov Faitelson, *Ch of Bd*
Eric Mann, *COO*
James O'Boyle, *Senior VP*
Gili Iron, *CFO*
Ohad Korkus, *CTO*
EMP: 113
SQ FT: 31,000
SALES (est): 127.2MM Publicly Held
SIC: 7372 Prepackaged software

(G-12509)
VARSITY MONITOR LLC
50 5th Ave Fl 3 (10011)
PHONE..................212 691-6292
Sam Carnahan, *Managing Prtnr*
Farrah Carnahan, *Managing Dir*
EMP: 9
SALES (est): 470K Privately Held
SIC: 7372 Business oriented computer software

(G-12510)
VASQUEZ TITO
Also Called: Tito Moldmaker Co
36 W 47th St Ste 206 (10036-8636)
PHONE..................212 944-0441
Tito Vasquez, *Owner*
EMP: 10
SALES (est): 718.1K Privately Held
SIC: 2822 Silicone rubbers

(G-12511)
VAULTCOM INC (PA)
Also Called: Vault.com, Vault Media
132 W 31st St Rm 1501 (10001-3406)
PHONE..................212 366-4212
Fax: 212 366-6712
Eric Ober, *President*
Samer Hamadeh, *Chairman*
Hussam Hamadeh, *Vice Pres*
Mark Oldman, *Vice Pres*
Vera Djordjevich, *Engineer*
EMP: 40 EST: 1992
SALES (est): 6.1MM Privately Held
WEB: www.vaultmatch.com
SIC: 2731 7361 Books: publishing only; employment agencies

(G-12512)
VECTOR GROUP LTD
712 5th Ave (10019-4108)
PHONE..................212 409-2800
Ellen Jorgenson, *Manager*
EMP: 387
SALES (corp-wide): 1.6B Publicly Held
SIC: 2111 Cigarettes
PA: Vector Group Ltd.
   4400 Biscayne Blvd Fl 10
   Miami FL 33137
   305 579-8000

(G-12513)
VEERHOUSE VODA HAITI LLC
Also Called: Veerhouse Voda Haiti SA
42 Broadway Fl 12 (10004-3892)
PHONE..................917 353-5944
Farooq Hassan,
Brendon Brewster,
EMP: 25
SALES (est): 1.4MM Privately Held
SIC: 3448 Buildings, portable: prefabricated metal

(G-12514)
VEGA COFFEE INC
300 E 46th St Apt 9h (10017-3010)
PHONE..................415 881-7969
William Deluca, *Co-Owner*
Noushin Ketabi, *Co-Owner*
Robert Terenzi, *Co-Owner*
EMP: 5
SALES (est): 139.9K Privately Held
SIC: 2095 Roasted coffee

(G-12515)
VELOCITY OUTSOURCING LLC
750 3rd Ave (10017-2703)
PHONE..................212 891-4043
Charles Weinstein, *Manager*
EMP: 24
SALES (est): 2.2MM Privately Held
SIC: 7372 Business oriented computer software

(G-12516)
VENDOME GROUP LLC
216 E 45th St Fl 6 (10017-3304)
PHONE..................646 795-3899
Fax: 212 228-1308
Jane Butler, *CEO*
Mark Fried, *President*
Daniel Gross, *Exec VP*
Ann Hendrich, *Vice Pres*
Ron Lowy, *Vice Pres*
EMP: 89
SQ FT: 10,000
SALES (est): 18.7MM Privately Held
SIC: 2741 Miscellaneous publishing

(G-12517)
VENTURA ENTERPRISE CO INC
512 Fashion Ave Fl 38 (10018-0827)
PHONE..................212 391-0170
Saul Tawil, *Ch of Bd*
Shelley Rindner, *Exec VP*
Henry Dweck, *Vice Pres*
Kim Spencer, *Controller*
Anne King, *Director*
▲ EMP: 40
SQ FT: 8,000
SALES (est): 4.7MM Privately Held
SIC: 2326 2331 Men's & boys' work clothing; women's & misses' blouses & shirts

(G-12518)
VERA WANG GROUP LLC (PA)
Also Called: V E W
15 E 26th St Fl 4 (10010-1536)
PHONE..................212 575-6400
Vera W Becker, *Ch of Bd*
Pamela Anthony, *Accountant*
Cary Jackson, *Sales Dir*
Ivan Valle, *Accounts Mgr*
Marc Kotsines, *Info Tech Dir*
▲ EMP: 190 EST: 2004
SQ FT: 14,000
SALES (est): 52.5MM Privately Held
WEB: www.verawang.com
SIC: 2335 5621 Bridal & formal gowns; wedding gowns & dresses; gowns, formal; bridal shops; dress shops

(G-12519)
VERANDA PUBLICATIONS INC
Also Called: Veranda Magazine
300 W 57th St Fl 28 (10019-5288)
PHONE..................212 903-5206
Lisa Newsom, *President*
EMP: 8
SALES (est): 655.2K
SALES (corp-wide): 4.9B Privately Held
WEB: www.hearstcorp.com
SIC: 2721 Magazines: publishing only, not printed on site
PA: The Hearst Corporation
   300 W 57th St Fl 42
   New York NY 10019
   212 649-2000

▲ = Import ▼ = Export
◆ = Import/Export

GEOGRAPHIC SECTION

New York - New York County (G-12548)

(G-12520)
VERATEX INC (PA)
254 5th Ave Fl 3 (10001-6406)
P.O. Box 682 (10108-0682)
PHONE.................................212 683-9300
Fax: 212 889-5573
Claude Simon, *President*
John Simon, *Vice Pres*
▲ EMP: 10
SQ FT: 2,500
SALES (est): 2.2MM **Privately Held**
SIC: 2258 Tricot fabrics

(G-12521)
VERDONETTE INC
270 W 39th St Fl 5 (10018-4409)
PHONE.................................212 719-2003
EMP: 5
SALES (est): 310K **Privately Held**
SIC: 2395 Pleating/Stitching Services

(G-12522)
VERIFYME INC (PA)
12 W 21st St Fl 8 (10010-6912)
PHONE.................................212 994-7002
Thomas A Nicolette, *CEO*
Ben Burrell, *COO*
Scott McPherson, *CFO*
Sandy Fliderman, *CTO*
EMP: 8
SALES: 217.2K **Publicly Held**
WEB: www.laserlocktech.com
SIC: 3699 Security devices

(G-12523)
VERRAGIO LTD (PA)
132 W 36th St Bsmt (10018-6903)
PHONE.................................212 868-8181
Barry Nisguretsky, *President*
Jeff Sullivan, *Natl Sales Mgr*
Tab Judd, *Regl Sales Mgr*
Neha Shah, *Accounts Exec*
Lindsay Conrath, *Mktg Dir*
▲ EMP: 27
SQ FT: 8,000
SALES (est): 4.3MM **Privately Held**
WEB: www.verragio.com
SIC: 3911 Jewelry apparel

(G-12524)
VERSAILLES INDUSTRIES LLC
485 Fashion Ave Rm 500 (10018-9438)
PHONE.................................212 792-9615
Freddy Hamra, *Mng Member*
▲ EMP: 6
SALES (est): 579.6K **Privately Held**
SIC: 2329 Riding clothes:, men's, youths' & boys'

(G-12525)
VERSE MUSIC GROUP LLC
330 W 38th St Rm 405 (10018-2942)
PHONE.................................212 564-0977
Curt Frasca, *CEO*
Sabelle Breer, *Exec VP*
Faith Newman Orbach, *Exec VP*
Lizzie Moncrief, *Director*
EMP: 6
SALES (est): 312.8K **Privately Held**
SIC: 2741 Music book & sheet music publishing
PA: Verse Music Group Holdings Llc
    400 Park Ave Ste 702
    New York NY 10022

(G-12526)
VERSO CORPORATION
370 Lexington Ave Rm 802 (10017-6510)
PHONE.................................212 599-2700
Gerhard Nussbaumer, *Principal*
EMP: 400
SALES (corp-wide): 3.1B **Publicly Held**
SIC: 2621 3554 Paper mills; paper industries machinery
PA: Verso Corporation
    6775 Lenox Center Ct # 400
    Memphis TN 38115
    901 369-4100

(G-12527)
VERSO PAPER MANAGEMENT LP
370 Lexington Ave Rm 802 (10017-6510)
PHONE.................................781 320-8660
Alvin Smart, *Branch Mgr*
EMP: 1449
SALES (corp-wide): 1B **Privately Held**
SIC: 2621 Paper mills
PA: Verso Paper Management Lp
    60 W 42nd Ste 1942
    New York NY 10165
    212 599-2700

(G-12528)
VERSO PAPER MANAGEMENT LP (PA)
60 W 42nd Ste 1942 (10165)
PHONE.................................212 599-2700
Michael A Jackson, *President*
Susan Frye, *Manager*
Jesse Rothfork, *Network Mgr*
Patricia Oetken, *Analyst*
EMP: 3
SALES (est): 1B **Privately Held**
SIC: 2621 Paper mills

(G-12529)
VERTANA GROUP LLC (PA)
35 W 20th St Ste 804 (10011-3709)
PHONE.................................646 706-7210
Emmanuel Tesone, *President*
EMP: 18 EST: 2013
SALES (est): 4.3MM **Privately Held**
SIC: 7372 Prepackaged software

(G-12530)
VERTICAL RESEARCH PARTNERS LLC
52 Vanderbilt Ave Rm 200 (10017-3860)
PHONE.................................212 257-6499
EMP: 18
SALES (corp-wide): 4.4MM **Privately Held**
SIC: 2591 Drapery Hardware And Blinds And Shades
PA: Vertical Research Partners Llc
    1 Landmark Sq Fl 4
    Stamford CT 06901
    203 276-5680

(G-12531)
VETTA JEWELRY INC (PA)
Also Called: Spring Street Design Group
70 W 36th St Fl 9 (10018-1798)
PHONE.................................212 564-8250
Edwin Peissis, *Ch of Bd*
Mary Walsh, *President*
◆ EMP: 20
SALES (est): 5.7MM **Privately Held**
WEB: www.cosmotronics.com
SIC: 3961 Costume jewelry

(G-12532)
VF SPORTSWEAR INC
Nautica Womens Sportswear
40 W 57th St Fl 3 (10019-4001)
PHONE.................................212 541-5757
James Williams, *Counsel*
Kathy Hines, *Vice Pres*
Sarah Wallace, *Vice Pres*
Lisa Whitney, *Vice Pres*
Christopher Young, *Vice Pres*
EMP: 23
SALES (corp-wide): 12.3B **Publicly Held**
SIC: 2339 Athletic clothing: women's, misses' & juniors'
HQ: Vf Sportswear, Inc.
    545 Wshngton Blvd Fl 8
    Jersey City NJ 07310
    212 541-5757

(G-12533)
VGG HOLDING LLC
590 Madison Ave Fl 41 (10022-2524)
PHONE.................................212 415-6700
EMP: 6
SALES (est): 653.1K **Privately Held**
SIC: 3674 Semiconductors & related devices

(G-12534)
VHX CORPORATION
555 W 18th St (10011-2822)
PHONE.................................347 689-1446
Jamie Wilkinson, *CEO*
Katleen Barrett, *Finance*
Kevin Sheurs, *CTO*
EMP: 13 EST: 2013
SALES (est): 1.4MM
SALES (corp-wide): 3.2B **Publicly Held**
SIC: 7372 Prepackaged software
PA: Iac/Interactivecorp
    555 W 18th St
    New York NY 10011
    212 314-7300

(G-12535)
VIA AMERICA FINE JEWELRY INC
578 5th Ave Unit 26 (10036-4836)
PHONE.................................212 302-1218
Fax: 212 768-2731
Mary Yogurtcu, *President*
Sadik Yogurtco, *Vice Pres*
Harutyn Temurco, *Admin Sec*
EMP: 5
SQ FT: 3,000
SALES (est): 420K **Privately Held**
SIC: 3915 Jewelers' materials & lapidary work

(G-12536)
VIBE MEDIA GROUP LLC
Also Called: Vibe Magazine
120 Wall St Fl 21 (10005-4024)
P.O. Box 618180, Chicago IL (60661-8180)
PHONE.................................212 448-7300
Fax: 212 448-7400
Danyel Smith, *Vice Pres*
Nicky Booth, *Manager*
Gary R Lewis, *Officer*
Steve Aaron,
EMP: 65
SALES (est): 4.7MM **Privately Held**
SIC: 2721 Periodicals

(G-12537)
VICKERS STOCK RESEARCH CORP (HQ)
61 Broadway Rm 1910 (10006-2761)
PHONE.................................212 425-7500
Fax: 212 344-1755
Fern Dorsey, *President*
Kathy Kareseboom, *Human Resources*
EMP: 40
SQ FT: 5,000
SALES (est): 2.6MM
SALES (corp-wide): 12.8MM **Privately Held**
WEB: www.vickers-stock.com
SIC: 2721 Periodicals
PA: Argus Research Group Inc Del
    61 Broadway Rm 1702
    New York NY 10006
    212 425-7500

(G-12538)
VICTOIRE LATAM ASSET MGT LLC
Also Called: Voctoire Finance Capital
598 Madison Ave Fl 9 (10022-1668)
PHONE.................................212 319-6550
Nadim Razzouck, *Chairman*
EMP: 10
SALES (est): 1.3MM **Privately Held**
SIC: 3524 6799 Hedge trimmers, electric; venture capital companies
PA: Sindicatum Holdings Limited
    25 Eccleston Place
    London

(G-12539)
VICTORIA ALBI INTL INC
Also Called: Makari
1178 Broadway Fl 5 (10001-5404)
PHONE.................................212 689-2600
Raquel Aini, *CEO*
Adja Fall, *Marketing Staff*
▲ EMP: 10
SALES (est): 2.4MM **Privately Held**
SIC: 2844 Cosmetic preparations

(G-12540)
VICTORY GARDEN
31 Carmine St Frnt A (10014-4427)
PHONE.................................212 206-7273
Sophia Brittain, *Owner*
EMP: 5
SALES (est): 318.4K **Privately Held**
SIC: 2024 Ice cream, bulk

(G-12541)
VIDAL CANDIES USA INC
845 3rd Ave Fl 6 (10022-6630)
PHONE.................................609 781-8169
Mitchell Bernstein, *Director*
▲ EMP: 10
SALES (est): 1.1MM
SALES (corp-wide): 96.4MM **Privately Held**
SIC: 2064 Candy & other confectionery products
PA: Vidal Golosinas Sa
    Avenida Gutierrez Mellado, S/N
    Molina De Segura 30500
    968 647-100

(G-12542)
VIEW COLLECTIONS INC
265 W 37th St Rm 5w (10018-5750)
PHONE.................................212 944-4030
David Shavolian, *President*
Nathan Shavolian, *Chairman*
EMP: 12
SQ FT: 6,000
SALES (est): 910K **Privately Held**
SIC: 2337 Suits: women's, misses' & juniors'

(G-12543)
VIEWFINDER INC
Also Called: First View
101 W 23rd St Ste 2303 (10011-2490)
PHONE.................................212 831-0939
Donald Asbey, *President*
Marcio Moraes, *Vice Pres*
EMP: 5
SALES (est): 475.1K **Privately Held**
WEB: www.firstview.com
SIC: 2741 Miscellaneous publishing

(G-12544)
VIKTOR GOLD ENTERPRISE CORP
58 W 47th St Unit 36 (10036-8610)
PHONE.................................212 768-8885
Boris Yakutilov, *Principal*
EMP: 3 EST: 1996
SALES: 1MM **Privately Held**
SIC: 3911 Jewelry, precious metal

(G-12545)
VILLEROY & BOCH USA INC
41 Madison Ave Ste 1801 (10010-2226)
PHONE.................................212 213-8149
Macha McQueen, *Accounting Mgr*
Awilda Munno, *Manager*
EMP: 5
SALES (corp-wide): 863.3MM **Privately Held**
SIC: 3089 Plastic kitchenware, tableware & houseware
HQ: Villeroy & Boch Usa, Inc.
    3a S Middlesex Ave
    Monroe Township NJ 08831
    800 536-2284

(G-12546)
VIP PAPER TRADING INC
1140 Ave Of The (10036)
PHONE.................................212 382-4642
Rebecca Silver, *President*
▼ EMP: 20
SALES (est): 2.8MM **Privately Held**
SIC: 2679 Paper products, converted

(G-12547)
VIRGIL MOUNTAIN INC (PA)
1 E 28th St Fl 4 (10016-7432)
PHONE.................................212 378-0007
Fax: 212 779-4066
Stephen Dignam, *President*
Edmund Mandrala, *Corp Secy*
Gerard Glenn, *Vice Pres*
▲ EMP: 8
SQ FT: 5,000
SALES (est): 1MM **Privately Held**
SIC: 2752 Commercial printing, lithographic

(G-12548)
VIROPRO INC
49 W 38th St Fl 11 (10018-1933)
PHONE.................................650 300-5190
Bruce A Cohen, *Ch of Bd*
Joseph J Vallner, *President*
Scott M Brown, *Security Dir*
EMP: 34
SALES (est): 2MM **Privately Held**
SIC: 2834 Pharmaceutical preparations

New York - New York County (G-12549)

GEOGRAPHIC SECTION

(G-12549)
VIRTUAL FRAMEWORKS INC
841 Broadway Ste 504 (10003-4704)
PHONE.....................................646 690-8207
EMP: 16
SALES (est): 321.1K **Privately Held**
SIC: 7372 Application computer software

(G-12550)
VIRTUAL SUPER LLC
116 E 27th St Fl 3 (10016-8942)
PHONE.....................................212 685-6400
Joshua Smith,
EMP: 5
SALES: 50K **Privately Held**
SIC: 3822 Building services monitoring controls, automatic

(G-12551)
VIRTUVENT INC
1221 Av Of The Amrcas4200 (10020-1009)
PHONE.....................................646 845-0387
Saul Sutcher, *COO*
EMP: 7 **EST:** 2012
SALES (est): 384.3K **Privately Held**
SIC: 7372 7389 Business oriented computer software;

(G-12552)
VISAGE SWISS WATCH LLC
Also Called: Visage Watches
29 W 30th St Rm 701 (10001-4463)
PHONE.....................................212 594-7991
Fax: 212 356-0016
Richa Patel, *Mng Member*
EMP: 6 **EST:** 2014
SALES (est): 295.2K **Privately Held**
SIC: 3873 Watches & parts, except crystals & jewels

(G-12553)
VISIONAIRE PUBLISHING LLC
Also Called: V Magazine
30 W 24th St (10010-3207)
PHONE.....................................646 434-6091
Fax: 212 343-2595
Jorge Garcia, *Publisher*
Donald Hearn, *Prdtn Dir*
Sooraya Pariag, *Controller*
Stephen Gan,
Farzana Khan, *Admin Sec*
▲ **EMP:** 20
SALES (est): 3.1MM **Privately Held**
WEB: www.visionaireworld.com
SIC: 2721 Magazines: publishing only, not printed on site

(G-12554)
VITAFEDE (PA)
25 W 26th St Fl 5 (10010-1039)
PHONE.....................................213 488-0136
Mitch Naidrich, *Principal*
Alice Kim, *Vice Pres*
Bryant Bene, *Sales Staff*
EMP: 11
SALES (est): 5.4MM **Privately Held**
SIC: 3961 Bracelets, except precious metal

(G-12555)
VITALIS LLC
902 Broadway Fl 6 (10010-6039)
PHONE.....................................646 831-7338
Joseph Habboushe,
EMP: 5 **EST:** 2012
SALES (est): 40.1K **Privately Held**
SIC: 2834 Pharmaceutical preparations

(G-12556)
VITALIZE LABS LLC
Also Called: Eboost
560 Broadway Rm 604 (10012-3946)
PHONE.....................................212 966-6130
Christine Cummings, *Opers Staff*
Malijian Sjam, *CFO*
John McDonald,
Josh Taekman,
EMP: 5
SQ FT: 1,000
SALES: 3MM **Privately Held**
SIC: 2833 Vitamins, natural or synthetic: bulk, uncompounded

(G-12557)
VITEX PACKAGING GROUP INC (HQ)
45 Rockefeller Plz (10111-0100)
PHONE.....................................212 265-6575
Bela Szigethy, *President*
Jerome F Anderson, *Vice Pres*
John Phifer, *CFO*
Robert Fitzsimmons, *Treasurer*
Kara Pajarillo, *Admin Sec*
◆ **EMP:** 10
SALES (est): 28.3MM
SALES (corp-wide): 41.2MM **Privately Held**
SIC: 2759 3497 2671 2754 Flexographic printing; metal foil & leaf; packaging paper & plastics film, coated & laminated; commercial printing, gravure; bags: plastic, laminated & coated; adhesives & sealants
PA: Kirtland Capital Partners Iii L.P.
2550 Som Center Rd # 105
Willoughby Hills OH
440 585-9010

(G-12558)
VITRA INC (DH)
29 9th Ave (10014-1205)
PHONE.....................................212 463-5700
Fax: 212 929-6424
Stefan Golinski, *President*
Rolf Gisler, *General Mgr*
Patrick Guntzburger, *Managing Dir*
Josef Kaiser, *Managing Dir*
Rolf Fehlbaum, *Chairman*
▲ **EMP:** 16
SALES (est): 9.5MM **Privately Held**
SIC: 2522 Chairs, office: padded or plain, except wood
HQ: Vitra Collections Ag
Klunenfeldstrasse 22
Muttenz BL
811 132-7

(G-12559)
VIVREAU ADVANCED WATER SYSTEMS
545 8th Ave Rm 401 (10018-4341)
PHONE.....................................212 502-3749
Andrew Hamilton, *Principal*
EMP: 10
SALES (est): 1MM **Privately Held**
SIC: 3221 3589 5963 Bottles for packing, bottling & canning: glass; water purification equipment, household type; bottled water delivery

(G-12560)
VIZBEE INC
120 E 23rd St Fl 5 (10010-4519)
PHONE.....................................650 787-1424
Darren Feher, *CEO*
Prashanth Pappu, *Principal*
EMP: 8
SALES (est): 136.6K **Privately Held**
SIC: 7372 7371 Home entertainment computer software; computer software systems analysis & design, custom

(G-12561)
VIZIO MEDICAL DEVICES LLC
200 Chambers St Apt 28a (10007-1350)
PHONE.....................................646 845-7382
EMP: 10
SALES (est): 600K **Privately Held**
SIC: 3841 Mfg Surgical/Medical Instruments

(G-12562)
VNOVOM SVETE
55 Broad St Fl 20 (10004-2501)
PHONE.....................................212 302-9480
Helen Brusilovski, *Principal*
EMP: 9 **EST:** 2012
SALES (est): 280K **Privately Held**
SIC: 2711 Newspapers, publishing & printing

(G-12563)
VOGEL APPLIED TECHNOLOGIES
Also Called: Brainwave Toys-New York
36 E 12th St Fl 7 (10003-4604)
PHONE.....................................212 677-3136
Fax: 212 677-4346
David Vogel, *President*
EMP: 1
SQ FT: 500
SALES: 1MM **Privately Held**
WEB: www.brainwavetoys.com
SIC: 3944 Games, toys & children's vehicles

(G-12564)
VOGUE MAGAZINE
4 Times Sq Bsmt C1b (10036-6595)
PHONE.....................................212 286-2860
Fax: 212 286-4341
Taylor Antrim, *General Mgr*
Charles Townsend, *Principal*
Jillian Demling, *Editor*
Rebecca Johnson, *Editor*
Douglas Keeve, *Director*
EMP: 61
SALES (est): 5.9MM **Privately Held**
SIC: 2721 Periodicals

(G-12565)
VOGUE TOO PLTING STITCHING EMB
265 W 37th St Fl 14 (10018-5707)
PHONE.....................................212 354-1022
Fax: 212 704-0038
Larry Geffner, *President*
EMP: 13 **EST:** 2001
SALES (est): 1.1MM **Privately Held**
SIC: 2395 Pleating & tucking, for the trade

(G-12566)
VOICE ANALYSIS CLINIC
326 W 55th St Apt 4d (10019-5112)
PHONE.....................................212 245-3803
James Lynn, *Owner*
EMP: 6
SALES (est): 310K **Privately Held**
SIC: 3829 Vibration meters, analyzers & calibrators

(G-12567)
VON MUSULIN PATRICIA
148 W 24th St Fl 10 (10011-1951)
PHONE.....................................212 206-8345
Fax: 212 627-7216
Patricia Von Musulin, *President*
EMP: 8
SALES (est): 610K **Privately Held**
SIC: 3911 3961 Jewelry, precious metal; jewelry apparel, non-precious metals

(G-12568)
VON POK & CHANG NEW YORK INC
4 E 43rd St Fl 7 (10017-4607)
PHONE.....................................212 599-0556
Omega Chang, *Ch of Bd*
Bernd Guhl, *Finance Mgr*
▲ **EMP:** 6
SQ FT: 1,000
SALES: 4.8MM **Privately Held**
WEB: www.vonpok.com
SIC: 3993 Advertising novelties

(G-12569)
VONDOM LLC
979 3rd Ave Ste 1532 (10022-3806)
PHONE.....................................212 207-3252
Olga Tomas, *CFO*
Antonio Esteve,
▲ **EMP:** 4
SALES: 1.6MM **Privately Held**
SIC: 2519 Furniture, household: glass, fiberglass & plastic

(G-12570)
VOSS USA INC
236 W 30th St Rm 900 (10001-0900)
PHONE.....................................212 995-2255
Fax: 212 995-2425
Jack Baelsito, *CEO*
Joe Bayern, *COO*
Jan Saboe, *CFO*
Jan Eystein Saeboe, *CFO*
Patrick Larkin, *VP Sales*
▲ **EMP:** 150
SQ FT: 1,000
SALES (est): 49.5MM
SALES (corp-wide): 60MM **Privately Held**
SIC: 3561 Pumps & pumping equipment
PA: Voss Of Norway As
Vatnestrom Industriomrade 5
Vatnestrom 4730
231 316-16

(G-12571)
VSM INVESTORS LLC (PA)
245 Park Ave Fl 41 (10167-0002)
PHONE.....................................212 351-1600
John Magliana, *Managing Dir*
Anna McGoldrick, *Accountant*
▲ **EMP:** 1
SALES (est): 578MM **Privately Held**
SIC: 3842 2599 2515 Wheelchairs; personal safety equipment; respirators; hospital beds; hospital furniture, except beds; mattresses & foundations

(G-12572)
W B BOW TIE CORP
Also Called: Bentley Cravats
521 W 26th St Fl 6 (10001-5531)
PHONE.....................................212 683-6130
Fax: 212 779-2108
Walter Schick, *President*
Robert Schick, *Vice Pres*
Marion Schick, *Admin Sec*
EMP: 10 **EST:** 1948
SQ FT: 10,000
SALES (est): 990K **Privately Held**
SIC: 2323 Men's & boys' neckwear; neckties, men's & boys': made from purchased materials

(G-12573)
W W NORTON & COMPANY INC (PA)
500 5th Ave Fl 6 (10110-0054)
PHONE.....................................212 354-5500
Fax: 212 869-0856
W Drake McFeely, *President*
Krista Azer, *Publisher*
Amber Watkins, *Publisher*
Katie Callahan, *Editor*
Remy Cawley, *Editor*
▲ **EMP:** 130 **EST:** 1923
SQ FT: 30,000
SALES (est): 253.9MM **Privately Held**
WEB: www.wwnorton.com
SIC: 2731 5192 Textbooks: publishing only, not printed on site; books: publishing only; books

(G-12574)
W W NORTON & COMPANY INC
Countryman Press
500 5th Ave Lbby 1 (10110-0105)
PHONE.....................................212 354-5500
Lisa Sacks, *Editor*
Doug Yeager, *COO*
Kermit Hummel, *Branch Mgr*
Chuck Forsman, *Executive*
EMP: 6
SALES (corp-wide): 253.9MM **Privately Held**
SIC: 2731 Book publishing
PA: W. W. Norton & Company, Inc.
500 5th Ave Fl 6
New York NY 10110
212 354-5500

(G-12575)
WACOAL AMERICA INC
Also Called: Dkny Underwear
136 Madison Ave Fl 15 (10016-6711)
PHONE.....................................212 743-9600
Fax: 212 696-5608
Susan Malinowski, *Vice Pres*
Rich Murray, *Branch Mgr*
Maria Reyes, *Supervisor*
Stan Briggs, *CTO*
Ernie Charles, *CTO*
EMP: 30
SALES (corp-wide): 1.7B **Privately Held**
WEB: www.wacoal-america.com
SIC: 2342 Bras, girdles & allied garments
HQ: Wacoal America, Inc.
1 Wacoal Plz
Lyndhurst NJ 07071
201 933-8400

(G-12576)
WACOAL INTERNATIONAL CORP
136 Madison Ave Fl 15 (10016-6711)
PHONE.....................................212 532-6100

▲ = Import ▼=Export
◆ =Import/Export

Richard C Murray, *President*
EMP: 100
SALES (corp-wide): 1.7B **Privately Held**
SIC: 2341 Women's & children's undergarments
HQ: Wacoal International Corp
1 Wacoal Plz
Lyndhurst NJ 07071
201 933-8400

(G-12577)
WALCO LEATHER CO INC
22 W 32nd St Fl 8 (10001-0890)
PHONE.................................212 243-2244
Fax: 212 989-2766
Monroe Jay Chaikin, *President*
Rosalie Tenzer, *Director*
EMP: 50
SQ FT: 15,000
SALES (est): 6.4MM **Privately Held**
SIC: 3111 3199 3172 2512 Specialty leathers; leather belting & strapping; personal leather goods; upholstered household furniture; apparel belts

(G-12578)
WALDMAN ALEXANDER M DIAMOND CO
Also Called: Waldman Diamond Company
30 W 47th St Ste 805 (10036-8644)
PHONE.................................212 921-8098
Fax: 212 869-8238
Alexander M Waldman, *President*
Leon Waldman, *Admin Sec*
Rose Lafurge, *Technician*
EMP: 35
SQ FT: 3,500
SALES (est): 4.6MM **Privately Held**
WEB: www.wdcgroup.com
SIC: 3915 5094 Diamond cutting & polishing; diamonds (gems)

(G-12579)
WALDMAN PUBLISHING CORPORATION (PA)
570 Fashion Ave Rm 800 (10018-1608)
P.O. Box 1587 (10028-0013)
PHONE.................................212 730-9590
Rachel Waldman, *Ch of Bd*
Michael Gober, *Managing Dir*
▲ **EMP:** 10 **EST:** 1961
SQ FT: 3,200
SALES (est): 2.4MM **Privately Held**
SIC: 2731 Books: publishing only

(G-12580)
WALL STREET BUSINESS PDTS INC
151 W 30th St Fl 8 (10001-4026)
PHONE.................................212 563-4014
Steven Altman, *President*
Ed Walker, *Vice Pres*
Glinda Adams, *Administration*
EMP: 31
SQ FT: 7,500
SALES (est): 3.1MM **Privately Held**
WEB: www.wallmail.com
SIC: 2752 Commercial printing, offset

(G-12581)
WALL STREET REPORTER MAGAZINE
419 Lafayette St Fl 2 (10003-7033)
PHONE.................................212 363-2600
Jack Marks, *President*
Nadejda Bojinova, *Research*
Alan Wolski, *Treasurer*
EMP: 62 **EST:** 1993
SQ FT: 9,000
SALES: 4MM **Privately Held**
WEB: www.wallstreetreporter.com
SIC: 2721 Magazines: publishing & printing

(G-12582)
WALLACE REFINERS INC
15 W 47th St Ste 808 (10036-5703)
PHONE.................................212 391-2649
EMP: 5
SQ FT: 1,500
SALES (est): 510K **Privately Held**
SIC: 3339 5094 Refine Buys And Wholesales Precious Metals

(G-12583)
WALLICO SHOES CORP
417 Park Ave (10022-4401)
PHONE.................................212 826-7171
Fax: 212 826-7720
Walter Steiger, *Owner*
Antonia Trimarchi, *Manager*
EMP: 5
SALES (est): 512.7K **Privately Held**
SIC: 3021 5139 5661 Rubber & plastics footwear; footwear; shoe stores

(G-12584)
WALTER EDBRIL INC
10 E 38th St Fl 6 (10016-0014)
PHONE.................................212 532-3253
Clifford Tamis, *President*
Jeffrey Tamis, *Vice Pres*
EMP: 30
SQ FT: 4,500
SALES (est): 3MM **Privately Held**
SIC: 3911 Jewelry, precious metal

(G-12585)
WARM
181 Mott St Frnt 1 (10012-4581)
PHONE.................................212 925-1200
EMP: 5 **EST:** 2014
SALES (est): 265.1K **Privately Held**
SIC: 2253 Warm weather knit outerwear, including beachwear

(G-12586)
WARNACO GROUP INC (HQ)
501 Fashion Ave (10018-5903)
PHONE.................................212 287-8000
Fax: 212 287-8297
Helen McCluskey, *CEO*
James B Gerson, *President*
Joanne Kaye, *President*
Martha Olson, *President*
Michael Prendergast, *President*
◆ **EMP:** 51
SALES (est): 825.5MM
SALES (corp-wide): 8B **Publicly Held**
SIC: 2322 2329 2339 2369 Underwear, men's & boys': made from purchased materials; men's & boys' sportswear & athletic clothing; women's & misses' outerwear; bathing suits: women's, misses' & juniors'; beachwear: women's, misses' & juniors'; children's bathing suits & beachwear; bras, girdles & allied garments; brassieres; girdles & panty girdles; panties: women's, misses', children's & infants'; women's & children's nightwear
PA: Pvh Corp.
200 Madison Ave Bsmt 1
New York NY 10016
212 381-3500

(G-12587)
WARNACO INC (DH)
Also Called: Warner S
501 Fashion Ave Fl 14 (10018-5942)
PHONE.................................212 287-8000
Joseph R Gromek, *Ch of Bd*
Charles R Perrin, *Ch of Bd*
Helen McCluskey, *President*
Les Hall, *President*
Larry Rutkowski, *Exec VP*
◆ **EMP:** 300 **EST:** 1874
SQ FT: 25,000
SALES (est): 688.6MM
SALES (corp-wide): 8B **Publicly Held**
WEB: www.warnaco.com
SIC: 2342 2341 2321 2329 Bras, girdles & allied garments; brassieres; girdles & panty girdles; panties: women's, children's & infants'; women's & children's nightwear; men's & boys' dress shirts; men's & boys' sportswear & athletic clothing; underwear, men's & boys': made from purchased materials; men's & boys' neckwear
HQ: The Warnaco Group Inc
501 Fashion Ave
New York NY 10018
212 287-8000

(G-12588)
WARNER MUSIC GROUP CORP (DH)
1633 Broadway (10019-6708)
PHONE.................................212 275-2000
Fax: 212 757-3985
Stephen Cooper, *CEO*
Stu Bergen, *CEO*
Cameron Strang, *CEO*
Len Blavatnik, *Vice Ch Bd*
Michael Fleisher, *Vice Chairman*
EMP: 277
SALES: 2.9B **Privately Held**
SIC: 3652 6794 Pre-recorded records & tapes; music licensing & royalties

(G-12589)
WARNER MUSIC INC (DH)
75 Rockefeller Plz Bsmt 1 (10019-0011)
PHONE.................................212 275-2000
Fax: 212 275-4760
Paul Rene' Albertini, *President*
David H Johnson, *Exec VP*
Olafur Olafsson, *Exec VP*
Jim Noonan, *Senior VP*
Liz Rosenberg, *Vice Pres*
▼ **EMP:** 100
SQ FT: 333,500
SALES (est): 774MM
SALES (corp-wide): 2.9B **Privately Held**
SIC: 3652 2741 Pre-recorded records & tapes; phonograph records, prerecorded; magnetic tape (audio): prerecorded; compact laser discs, prerecorded; music, sheet: publishing & printing
HQ: Wmg Acquisition Corp.
75 Rockefeller Plz
New York NY 10019
212 275-2000

(G-12590)
WARREN CORPORATION (DH)
711 5th Ave Fl 11 (10022-3113)
PHONE.................................860 684-2766
Pier Guerci, *President*
Guy Birkhead, *Senior VP*
Lisa Cornish, *Vice Pres*
Richard Anderman, *Admin Sec*
Giuseppe Monteoeone, *Maintence Staff*
▲ **EMP:** 180 **EST:** 1853
SQ FT: 330,000
SALES (est): 33.2MM
SALES (corp-wide): 255.7MM **Privately Held**
WEB: www.warrencorp.com
SIC: 2231 Overcoatings: wool, mohair or similar fibers; suitings: wool, mohair or similar fibers
HQ: Loro Piana Spa
Corso Pietro Rolandi 10
Quarona VC 13017
016 320-1911

(G-12591)
WARREN ENERGY SERVICES LLC
1114 Ave Of The Americas (10036-7703)
PHONE.................................212 697-9660
Robert Wimbush, *Accountant*
James A Watt,
EMP: 10
SQ FT: 4,200
SALES (corp-wide): 372.4K
SALES (corp-wide): 88.3MM **Publicly Held**
SIC: 1382 Oil & gas exploration services
PA: Warren Resources, Inc.
1331 17th St Ste 720
Denver CO 80202
720 403-8125

(G-12592)
WASTECORP PUMPS LLC (PA)
345 W 85th St Apt 23 (10024-3834)
P.O. Box 70, Grand Island (14072-0070)
PHONE.................................888 829-2783
Maggie Domingos, *General Mgr*
Daniel Soja, *General Mgr*
Marc Johnson, *Manager*
Dan Starr,
◆ **EMP:** 10
SQ FT: 2,000,000
SALES (est): 1.1MM **Privately Held**
SIC: 3561 Pumps & pumping equipment

(G-12593)
WATCH JOURNAL LLC
110 E 25th St Fl 4 (10010-2913)
PHONE.................................212 229-1500
Marc Lotenberg,
EMP: 6
SALES: 1.7MM **Privately Held**
SIC: 2721 Magazines: publishing & printing

(G-12594)
WATCHANISH LLC
1 Rockefeller Plz Fl 11 (10020-2073)
PHONE.................................917 558-0404
EMP: 10
SALES (est): 298.1K **Privately Held**
SIC: 2741 Miscellaneous publishing

(G-12595)
WATCHITOO INC
24 W 40th St Fl 14 (10018-1093)
PHONE.................................212 354-5888
Eyal Hillman, *General Mgr*
Eric Lipkind, *Principal*
Tom Clark, *Exec VP*
Mike Marsico, *Research*
Yael Carmel, *Office Mgr*
EMP: 5
SALES (est): 591.9K **Privately Held**
SIC: 7372 Prepackaged software

(G-12596)
WATER ENERGY SYSTEMS LLC
1 Maiden Ln (10038-4015)
PHONE.................................844 822-7665
EMP: 8 **EST:** 2015
SALES (est): 431K **Privately Held**
SIC: 3589 Mfg Service Industry Machinery

(G-12597)
WATERBURY GARMENT LLC
Also Called: Jackie's Girls
16 E 34th St Fl 10 (10016-4360)
PHONE.................................212 725-1500
Daniel Livingston, *President*
Harry Gaffney, *CFO*
▲ **EMP:** 30 **EST:** 1921
SQ FT: 19,000
SALES: 1.7MM
SALES (corp-wide): 159.3MM **Privately Held**
WEB: www.waterburygarment.com
SIC: 2341 2369 2322 Women's & children's nightwear; children's robes & housecoats; men's & boys' underwear & nightwear
HQ: Komar Kids, L.L.C.
16 E 34th St Fl 14
New York NY 10016
212 725-1500

(G-12598)
WATSON ADVENTURES LLC
330 W 38th St Rm 407 (10018-8307)
PHONE.................................212 564-8293
Daniel Maranon, *Principal*
EMP: 6
SALES (est): 611.3K **Privately Held**
SIC: 3949 Sporting & athletic goods

(G-12599)
WAY OUT TOYS INC
230 5th Ave Ste 800 (10001-7851)
PHONE.................................212 689-9094
Eddie Mishan, *President*
Al Mishan, *Vice Pres*
Jeffrey Mishan, *Vice Pres*
Morris Mishan, *Vice Pres*
Steven Mishan, *Vice Pres*
EMP: 6
SALES (est): 660K **Privately Held**
SIC: 3944 5092 Games, toys & children's vehicles; toys & games

(G-12600)
WE WORK
1 Little West 12th St (10014-1302)
PHONE.................................877 673-6628
Adam Wacenske, *Associate*
EMP: 6
SALES (est): 493.2K **Privately Held**
SIC: 2011 Meat packing plants

(G-12601)
WEA INTERNATIONAL INC (DH)
75 Rockefeller Plz (10019-6908)
PHONE.................................212 275-1300
Keith Bruce, *Senior VP*
Ramon Lopez, *Vice Pres*
EMP: 100
SQ FT: 3,500

New York - New York County (G-12602)

SALES (est): 100.1MM
SALES (corp-wide): 2.9B **Privately Held**
SIC: 3652 Master records or tapes, preparation of
HQ: Warner Music Inc.
  75 Rockefeller Plz Bsmt 1
  New York NY 10019
  212 275-2000

(G-12602)
WEAR ABOUTS APPAREL INC
260 W 36th St Rm 602 (10018-7603)
PHONE..................212 827-0888
Kim Yu, *President*
Geri Nelson, *Executive*
▲ EMP: 12
SQ FT: 4,500
SALES (est): 4.6MM **Privately Held**
SIC: 2335 Women's, juniors' & misses' dresses

(G-12603)
WEEKLY BUSINESS NEWS CORP
274 Madison Ave Rm 1101 (10016-0700)
PHONE..................212 689-5888
Yoshiaki Takahashi, *President*
Akiko Kudo, *Editor*
Akiko Kido, *Office Mgr*
EMP: 6
SALES: 202.2K **Privately Held**
SIC: 2711 Newspapers

(G-12604)
WEIDER PUBLICATIONS LLC
Also Called: A M I
1 Park Ave Fl 10 (10016-5802)
PHONE..................212 545-4800
Sean Hyson, *Editor*
Mike Kahane, *Senior VP*
Stuart Zakim, *Senior VP*
David Obey, *Vice Pres*
Beverly Levy, *Branch Mgr*
EMP: 200
SALES (corp-wide): 245.1MM **Privately Held**
WEB: www.fitnessonline.com
SIC: 2721 Magazines: publishing only, not printed on site
HQ: Weider Publications, Llc
  6420 Wilshire Blvd # 720
  Los Angeles CA 90048
  818 884-6400

(G-12605)
WEISCO INC
246 W 38th St Fl 6 (10018-5854)
PHONE..................212 575-8989
Alex Weiss, *President*
Edward Weiss, *Vice Pres*
Peter Weiss, *Treasurer*
EMP: 15
SQ FT: 7,000
SALES (est): 1.3MM **Privately Held**
WEB: www.weisco.com
SIC: 3911 Jewelry, precious metal

(G-12606)
WELCOME RAIN PUBLISHERS LLC
Also Called: South Brooklyn Book Company
230 5th Ave Ste 1806 (10001-7719)
PHONE..................212 686-1909
John Weber,
EMP: 2
SALES: 1.5MM **Privately Held**
SIC: 2741 Miscellaneous publishing

(G-12607)
WELDING CHAPTER OF NEW YORK
44 W 28th St Fl 12 (10001-4291)
PHONE..................212 481-1496
Ray Hopkins, *President*
EMP: 5
SALES (est): 307.6K **Privately Held**
SIC: 7692 Welding repair

(G-12608)
WELLQUEST INTERNATIONAL INC (PA)
230 5th Ave Ste 800 (10001-7851)
PHONE..................212 689-9094
Eddie Mishan, *President*
Al Mishan, *Vice Pres*
Isaac Mishan, *Vice Pres*
Morris Mishan, *Vice Pres*
▲ EMP: 6
SQ FT: 2,000
SALES (est): 847.4K **Privately Held**
WEB: www.wellquestinternational.com
SIC: 2833 5122 Vitamins, natural or synthetic: bulk, uncompounded; vitamins & minerals

(G-12609)
WELLSPRING CORP (PA)
54a Ludlow St (10002-5410)
PHONE..................212 529-5454
Fax: 212 979-6779
Yon K Lai, *Ch of Bd*
Danny Lai, *President*
EMP: 5
SQ FT: 1,000
SALES (est): 741.4K **Privately Held**
WEB: www.wellspringcorp.com
SIC: 2064 5149 Candy & other confectionery products; groceries & related products; chocolate; mineral or spring water bottling; crackers, cookies & bakery products

(G-12610)
WELLSPRING OMNI HOLDINGS CORP
390 Park Ave Fl 6 (10022-4623)
PHONE..................212 318-9800
William F Dawson Jr, *President*
Joshua C Cascade, *Corp Secy*
EMP: 950
SALES (est): 13.2MM **Privately Held**
SIC: 1382 1389 7349 Seismograph surveys; lease tanks, oil field: erecting, cleaning & repairing; cleaning service, industrial or commercial

(G-12611)
WENNER MEDIA LLC (PA)
Also Called: Rolling Stone
1290 Ave Of The Amer Fl 2 (10104-0295)
P.O. Box 30895 (10087-0895)
PHONE..................212 484-1616
Fax: 212 484-1713
Hugh Scogin, *CEO*
Dana L Fields, *Publisher*
Elizabeth Abts, *Editor*
Jenna Lemoncelli, *Editor*
Steven Schwartz, *Chairman*
▲ EMP: 250 EST: 1967
SQ FT: 75,000
SALES (est): 118.1MM **Privately Held**
SIC: 2721 Magazines: publishing & printing

(G-12612)
WEST INTERNET TRADING COMPANY
Also Called: Idonethis
47 Great Jones St Fl 5 (10012-1196)
PHONE..................415 484-5848
EMP: 6
SALES (est): 320K **Privately Held**
SIC: 7372 Prepackaged Software Services

(G-12613)
WEST PACIFIC ENTERPRISES CORP
260 W 39th St Rm 5w (10018-4432)
PHONE..................212 564-6800
Daniel Kwok Sui Chuen, *Vice Pres*
Jackie Lee, *Manager*
Ray Denyer, *Legal Staff*
▲ EMP: 5
SQ FT: 700
SALES: 17MM
SALES (corp-wide): 134.4MM **Privately Held**
SIC: 2339 Sportswear, women's
PA: Tungtex (Holdings) Company Limited
  12/F Tungtex Bldg
  Kwun Tong KLN
  279 770-00

(G-12614)
WEST PUBLISHING CORPORATION
Also Called: West Information Center
530 5th Ave Fl 7 (10036-5101)
PHONE..................212 922-1920
Fax: 212 548-7401
Dan Zawislak, *General Mgr*
Allen Hobbs, *Pub Rel Mgr*
Maria Tedesco, *Human Res Dir*
EMP: 40
SALES (corp-wide): 3.8B **Publicly Held**
WEB: www.ruttergroup.com
SIC: 2711 Newspapers, publishing & printing
HQ: West Publishing Corporation
  610 620 Opperman Dr
  Eagan MN 55123
  651 687-7000

(G-12615)
WESTPOINT HOME LLC (DH)
28 E 28th St Rm 8 (10016-7962)
PHONE..................212 930-2074
Fax: 212 930-2525
Christopher N Baker, *Senior VP*
Tyler Bolden, *Vice Pres*
Meredith Mele, *Vice Pres*
Stephen Peters, *Vice Pres*
Cindy Norman, *Senior Buyer*
◆ EMP: 800
SALES (est): 629.5MM
SALES (corp-wide): 19.1B **Publicly Held**
SIC: 2211 2221 Broadwoven fabric mills, cotton; sheets, bedding & table cloths: cotton; towels, dishcloths & washcloths: cotton; bedding, manmade or silk fabric
HQ: Westpoint International, Inc.
  28 E 28th St Bsmt 2
  New York NY 10016
  212 930-2044

(G-12616)
WESTPOINT INTERNATIONAL INC (HQ)
28 E 28th St Bsmt 2 (10016-7914)
PHONE..................212 930-2044
Joseph Pennacchio, *CEO*
EMP: 14
SALES (est): 629.5MM
SALES (corp-wide): 19.1B **Publicly Held**
SIC: 2211 Broadwoven fabric mills, cotton
PA: Icahn Enterprises L.P.
  767 5th Ave Ste 4700
  New York NY 10153
  212 702-4300

(G-12617)
WESTPRINT INC
873 Washington St (10014-1108)
PHONE..................212 989-3805
Tim Bissell, *President*
EMP: 5
SQ FT: 5,000
SALES (est): 350K **Privately Held**
SIC: 2759 2752 Commercial printing; commercial printing, lithographic

(G-12618)
WESTROCK MWV LLC
299 Park Ave Fl 13 (10171-3800)
PHONE..................212 688-5000
Luke John, *Trustee*
Jeff Jensen, *Vice Pres*
Tony Milikin, *Vice Pres*
John Cherry, *Sales Staff*
John A Luke, *Branch Mgr*
EMP: 227
SALES (corp-wide): 11.3B **Publicly Held**
WEB: www.meadwestvaco.com
SIC: 2631 2671 2678 2677 Linerboard; packaging paper & plastics film, coated & laminated; stationery products; envelopes; gum & wood chemicals
HQ: Westrock Mwv, Llc
  501 S 5th St
  Richmond VA 23219
  804 444-1000

(G-12619)
WESTSIDE CLOTHING CO INC
240 W 35th St Ste 1000 (10001-2514)
PHONE..................212 273-9898
Jeff Borer, *President*
EMP: 4
SALES (est): 1.7MM **Privately Held**
WEB: www.westsideclothingco.co
SIC: 2331 Women's & misses' blouses & shirts

(G-12620)
WETPAINTCOM INC
Also Called: Wet Paint
902 Broadway Fl 11 (10010-6034)
PHONE..................206 859-6300
Ben Elowitz, *CEO*
Bert Hogue, *CFO*
Ji Mun, *Software Dev*
EMP: 38
SALES (est): 3.4MM
SALES (corp-wide): 4.5MM **Publicly Held**
WEB: www.wetpaint.com
SIC: 7372 7371 Prepackaged software; custom computer programming services
PA: X Function Inc
  902 Broadway Fl 11
  New York NY 10010
  212 231-0092

(G-12621)
WEY INC
21 W 39th St Fl 6 (10018-0614)
PHONE..................212 532-3299
Matt Zierdniewski, *President*
Matt Cierzniewski, *Managing Dir*
Armin Klingler, *Managing Dir*
Giuseppe Zaccaria, *Managing Dir*
EMP: 8
SALES (est): 586.8K **Privately Held**
SIC: 3575 Keyboards, computer, office machine

(G-12622)
WHEELER/RINSTAR LTD
242 W 30th St (10001-4903)
PHONE..................212 244-1130
Fax: 212 594-4697
Noel Shavzin, *President*
Anatol Shavzin, *Vice Pres*
EMP: 10
SQ FT: 2,400
SALES (est): 1MM **Privately Held**
SIC: 2759 Commercial printing

(G-12623)
WHENTECH LLC (DH)
55 E 52nd St Fl 40 (10055-0005)
PHONE..................212 571-0042
David Wender,
EMP: 10
SALES (est): 2.3MM
SALES (corp-wide): 4.6B **Publicly Held**
WEB: www.whentech.com
SIC: 7372 Business oriented computer software
HQ: Intercontinental Exchange Inc.
  1415 Moonstone
  Brea CA 92821
  770 857-4700

(G-12624)
WHITE COAT INC
Also Called: Dynamic Diamond
580 5th Ave Ste 501 (10036-4724)
PHONE..................212 575-8880
Fax: 212 575-2049
Moshe Lax, *Ch of Bd*
Debbi Rudich, *Manager*
EMP: 50
SALES (est): 7.7MM **Privately Held**
WEB: www.dynamicdiamond.com
SIC: 3915 Diamond cutting & polishing

(G-12625)
WHITE GATE HOLDINGS INC (PA)
22 W 38th St Fl 6 (10018-0107)
PHONE..................212 564-3266
Michael Nolan, *President*
Kevin Joss, *Vice Pres*
Stephi Ruben, *Vice Pres*
Chloe Nolan, *Opers Mgr*
Kimberly Patterson, *Prdtn Mgr*
▲ EMP: 20
SALES (est): 4.1MM **Privately Held**
WEB: www.nolanglove.com
SIC: 2339 Women's & misses' accessories

(G-12626)
WHITE LABEL PARTNERS LLC
250 Mercer St Apt B1205 (10012-6125)
PHONE..................917 445-6650
Benedict Aitkenhead, *Business Mgr*
Mark Kaplan,
EMP: 5

▲ = Import ▼ = Export
◆ = Import/Export

GEOGRAPHIC SECTION

SALES (est): 259.5K **Privately Held**
SIC: 7372 Application computer software

(G-12627)
WHITE WORKROOM INC
40 W 27th St Fl 11 (10001-6944)
PHONE.................................212 941-5910
Vivian White, *Partner*
Gary Weisner, *Partner*
EMP: 6
SQ FT: 1,000
SALES (est): 280K **Privately Held**
SIC: 2391 Curtains & draperies

(G-12628)
WHITEBOARD VENTURES INC
Also Called: Xpand
31 W 34th St Ste 7020 (10001-3009)
PHONE.................................855 972-6346
Deb Bardhan, *CEO*
Kalyan Anumula, *President*
EMP: 16
SALES (est): 35.2K **Privately Held**
SIC: 7372 Application computer software

(G-12629)
WHITTALL & SHON (PA)
1201 Broadway Ste 904a (10001-5656)
PHONE.................................212 594-2626
Fax: 212 268-2862
Elliot Whittall, *President*
Richard Shon, *Vice Pres*
Charlaine Bivens, *Sales Mgr*
EMP: 3
SALES (est): 14.2MM **Privately Held**
SIC: 2353 2321 Hats: cloth, straw & felt; millinery; men's & boys' furnishings

(G-12630)
WICKED SPOON INC
127 W 24th St Fl 6 (10011-1943)
PHONE.................................646 335-2890
Alex Rozhitsky, *President*
EMP: 11
SALES: 750K **Privately Held**
SIC: 2024 Ice cream & frozen desserts

(G-12631)
WIDMER TIME RECORDER COMPANY
27 Park Pl Rm 219 (10007-2526)
PHONE.................................212 227-0405
Fax: 212 227-0526
Robert Widmer, *President*
Robert Reese, *Vice Pres*
EMP: 10
SALES (corp-wide): 8.9MM **Privately Held**
WEB: www.widmertime.com
SIC: 3579 Time clocks & time recording devices
PA: Widmer Time Recorder Company Inc
228 Park St
Hackensack NJ 07601
201 489-3810

(G-12632)
WILLCO FINE ART LTD
145 Nassau St Apt 9c (10038-1514)
PHONE.................................718 935-9567
William Wolod, *President*
EMP: 10
SALES: 700K **Privately Held**
SIC: 2759 Commercial printing

(G-12633)
WILLIAM GOLDBERG DIAMOND CORP
589 5th Ave Fl 14 (10017-7293)
PHONE.................................212 980-4343
Fax: 212 980-6120
Saul Goldberg, *CEO*
Benjamin Goldberg, *Principal*
Eve Goldberg, *Vice Pres*
Lili Goldberg, *CFO*
EMP: 20 EST: 1954
SQ FT: 6,000
SALES (est): 4.5MM **Privately Held**
SIC: 3915 3911 5094 Diamond cutting & polishing; jewelry, precious metal; jewelry & precious stones

(G-12634)
WILLIAM H SADLIER INC (PA)
9 Pine St (10005-4701)
P.O. Box 5685, Hicksville (11802-5685)
PHONE.................................212 233-3646
Fax: 212 312-6080
Frank S Dinger, *Ch of Bd*
William S Dinger Jr, *President*
Suzan Larroquette, *Division Mgr*
Rosemary Calicchio, *Exec VP*
John Bonenberger, *Vice Pres*
◆ EMP: 111 EST: 1928
SQ FT: 56,000
SALES (est): 65.6MM **Privately Held**
WEB: www.sadlier.com
SIC: 2731 Book publishing

(G-12635)
WILLIAM H SHAPIRO
Also Called: Shapiro Wlliam NY Univ Med Ctr
530 1st Ave Ste 3e (10016-6402)
PHONE.................................212 263-7037
William H Shapiro, *Owner*
EMP: 5 EST: 1999
SALES (est): 438.9K **Privately Held**
SIC: 3842 Hearing aids

(G-12636)
WILLIAM SOMERVILLE MAINTENANCE
166 E 124th St (10035-1712)
PHONE.................................212 534-4600
Merna Miller, *President*
EMP: 68
SQ FT: 40,000
SALES (est): 5.3MM **Privately Held**
SIC: 2511 Wood household furniture

(G-12637)
WILLIAMS-SONOMA STORES INC
Also Called: Williams-Sonoma Store 154
110 7th Ave (10011-1801)
PHONE.................................212 633-2203
Donnie Cassell, *Manager*
EMP: 13
SALES (corp-wide): 4.9B **Publicly Held**
SIC: 3263 Cookware, fine earthenware
HQ: Williams-Sonoma Stores, Inc.
3250 Van Ness Ave
San Francisco CA 94109
415 421-7900

(G-12638)
WILLIS MC DONALD CO INC
44 W 62nd St Ph A (10023-7039)
PHONE.................................212 366-1526
Jerry Dennehy, *President*
EMP: 15 EST: 1874
SQ FT: 10,000
SALES: 1.3MM **Privately Held**
SIC: 2759 2732 Periodicals: printing; pamphlets: printing only, not published on site

(G-12639)
WILMAX USA LLC
315 5th Ave Rm 505 (10016-6583)
PHONE.................................917 388-2790
Maksym Kyrylov,
EMP: 15
SQ FT: 1,500
SALES (est): 1MM **Privately Held**
SIC: 3469 Cooking ware, porcelain enameled

(G-12640)
WINDOW TECHNOLOGIES LLC
555 5th Ave Fl 14 (10017-9257)
PHONE.................................402 464-0202
Craig Anderson,
EMP: 10
SQ FT: 135,000
SALES (est): 1.6MM **Privately Held**
SIC: 2431 Windows, wood

(G-12641)
WINE & SPIRITS MAGAZINE INC (PA)
2 W 32nd St Ste 601 (10001-3834)
PHONE.................................212 695-4660
Joshua Greene, *President*
Tara Thomas, *Editor*
Marcy Crimmins, *Vice Pres*
Vivian Ho, *Prdtn Mgr*
Roy Schneider, *Finance Dir*
EMP: 6
SQ FT: 2,300
SALES (est): 1MM **Privately Held**
WEB: www.wineandspiritsmagazine.com
SIC: 2721 Magazines: publishing only, not printed on site

(G-12642)
WINE ON LINE INTERNATIONAL
Also Called: Walman, Jerome
400 E 59th St Apt 9f (10022-2344)
PHONE.................................212 755-4363
Jerome Walman, *Principal*
Jerry Preiser, *Editor*
Beth Wilson, *Editor*
Mary Price, *Info Tech Dir*
▲ EMP: 8
SQ FT: 1,000
SALES (est): 374.1K **Privately Held**
SIC: 2721 Magazines: publishing only, not printed on site

(G-12643)
WING HEUNG NOODLE INC
144 Baxter St (10013-3605)
PHONE.................................212 966-7496
Fax: 212 966-7496
Ng Shoong Kwong, *Ch of Bd*
Tippy T Yuan Gong, *Vice Pres*
EMP: 13
SQ FT: 2,000
SALES (est): 910K **Privately Held**
WEB: www.chicago-chinatown.com
SIC: 2098 Noodles (e.g. egg, plain & water), dry

(G-12644)
WING KEI NOODLE INC
102 Canal St (10002-6004)
PHONE.................................212 226-1644
Yik Pui Kong, *Ch of Bd*
EMP: 17
SQ FT: 1,200
SALES (est): 1.6MM **Privately Held**
SIC: 2098 Macaroni products (e.g. alphabets, rings & shells), dry

(G-12645)
WING TEL INC ○
79 Madison Ave Fl 3 (10016-7802)
PHONE.................................347 508-5802
David Arabov, *CEO*
Yury Yakubchyk, *CTO*
EMP: 5 EST: 2016
SALES: 500K **Privately Held**
SIC: 7372 Prepackaged software

(G-12646)
WINK INC
606 W 28th St Fl 6 (10001-1108)
PHONE.................................212 389-1382
EMP: 45 EST: 2013
SALES (est): 2.2MM
SALES (corp-wide): 19.5MM **Privately Held**
SIC: 7372 5961 Prepackaged Software Services Ret Mail-Order House
PA: Quirky, Inc.
606 W 28th St Fl 7
New York NY 10001
212 389-4759

(G-12647)
WINK LABS INC (DH)
Also Called: Wink Acquisition Corp.
606 W 28th St Fl 7 (10001-1108)
PHONE.................................916 717-0437
Nathan Smith, *President*
EMP: 30
SQ FT: 6,000
SALES (est): 10.7MM
SALES (corp-wide): 24.4B **Privately Held**
SIC: 7372 Application computer software

(G-12648)
WINSIGHT LLC
90 Broad St Ste 402 (10004-3312)
PHONE.................................646 708-7309
Heather Cleveland, *Social Dir*
EMP: 5
SALES (corp-wide): 14.4MM **Privately Held**
SIC: 2721 Periodicals
HQ: Winsight, Llc
1 Tower Ln Ste 2000
Oakbrook Terrace IL 60181
630 574-5075

(G-12649)
WIZQ INC
307 5th Ave Fl 8 (10016-6517)
PHONE.................................586 381-9048
Marcus Kay, *CEO*
Wing Tung LI, *Controller*
EMP: 10 EST: 2011
SQ FT: 3,000
SALES (est): 358.3K **Privately Held**
SIC: 7372 Prepackaged software

(G-12650)
WMG ACQUISITION CORP (DH)
75 Rockefeller Plz (10019-6908)
PHONE.................................212 275-2000
Stephen F Cooper, *President*
Mark Ansorge, *Exec VP*
Paul M Robinson, *Exec VP*
Will Tanous, *Exec VP*
Steven Macri, *CFO*
EMP: 12
SALES (est): 774MM
SALES (corp-wide): 2.9B **Privately Held**
SIC: 2782 2741 7929 Record albums; music books: publishing & printing; music, sheet: publishing & printing; musical entertainers
HQ: Warner Music Group Corp.
1633 Broadway
New York NY 10019
212 275-2000

(G-12651)
WOBBLEWORKS INC (PA)
Also Called: 3doodler
316 E 11th St Apt 3c (10003-7433)
P.O. Box 153 (10009-0153)
PHONE.................................415 987-1534
Maxwell Bogue, *CEO*
Daniel Cowen, *CEO*
Peter Cilworth, *CTO*
EMP: 7
SALES (est): 1.9MM **Privately Held**
SIC: 3944 Electronic toys

(G-12652)
WOLTERS KLUWER US INC
111 8th Ave Fl 13 (10011-5213)
PHONE.................................212 894-8920
Susan Chazin, *Publisher*
Chris Puype, *Managing Dir*
Lora West, *Business Mgr*
Edward Kramer, *Exec VP*
Doug Lavin, *Vice Pres*
EMP: 12
SALES (corp-wide): 4.5B **Privately Held**
SIC: 2731 Book publishing
HQ: Wolters Kluwer United States Inc.
2700 Lake Cook Rd
Riverwoods IL 60015
847 580-5000

(G-12653)
WOMENS E NEWS INC
6 Barclay St Fl 6 (10007-2721)
PHONE.................................212 244-1720
Fax: 212 244-2320
Rita Henley Jensen, *President*
Katina Paron, *Editor*
Cassandra Leveille, *Marketing Staff*
Kristen Elechko, *Exec Dir*
EMP: 7
SALES: 1MM **Privately Held**
WEB: www.womensenews.org
SIC: 2721 Periodicals

(G-12654)
WONTON FOOD INC
183 E Broadway (10002-5503)
PHONE.................................212 677-8865
Fax: 212 777-6308
Chan Wai, *Principal*
Derrick Wong, *VP Sales*
John Lee, *Sales Mgr*
EMP: 15
SALES (corp-wide): 63MM **Privately Held**
WEB: www.wontonfood.com
SIC: 2099 2098 Noodles, fried (Chinese); noodles (e.g. egg, plain & water), dry

New York - New York County (G-12655)

PA: Wonton Food Inc.
220 Moore St 222
Brooklyn NY 11206
718 628-6868

(G-12655)
WOOD FLOOR EXPO INC
Also Called: Scerri Quality Wood Floors
426 E 73rd St Frnt 1 (10021-3866)
PHONE 212 472-0671
Fax: 212 737-4280
Joseph Scerri, *President*
Edward Laboy, *Vice Pres*
Peter Palagian, *Controller*
EMP: 5
SALES (est): 510K **Privately Held**
WEB: www.woodfloorexpo.com
SIC: 2426 Flooring, hardwood

(G-12656)
WOODMERE FABRICS INC
35 W 35th St (10001-2205)
PHONE 212 695-0144
Ira Schantz, *President*
EMP: 5
SQ FT: 2,000
SALES: 5MM **Privately Held**
SIC: 2311 Men's & boys' suits & coats

(G-12657)
WOOLMARK AMERICAS INC
Also Called: WOOLMARK COMPANY, THE
110 E 25th St Fl 3 (10010-2913)
PHONE 347 767-3160
Velma George, *Principal*
EMP: 1
SALES: 2.2MM **Privately Held**
SIC: 2231 Cloth, wool; mending

(G-12658)
WORKERS VANGUARD
299 Broadway Ste 318 (10007-4104)
P.O. Box 1377 (10116-1377)
PHONE 212 732-7862
Robin Hunt, *Treasurer*
EMP: 23
SALES (est): 801.1K **Privately Held**
SIC: 2711 Newspapers

(G-12659)
WORKING MOTHER MEDIA INC
Also Called: Diversity Best Practices
2 Park Ave Fl 10 (10016-5604)
PHONE 212 351-6400
Carol Evans, *President*
Joan Labarge, *Publisher*
Barbara Turvett, *Editor*
Nancy Colter, *CFO*
Laquanda Murray, *Sales Dir*
EMP: 51 **EST:** 2001
SQ FT: 15,000
SALES (est): 5.9MM
SALES (corp-wide): 3.1B **Privately Held**
WEB: www.workingmother.com
SIC: 2721 4813 Magazines: publishing only, not printed on site;
HQ: Bonnier Corporation
460 N Orlando Ave Ste 200
Winter Park FL 32789
407 622-1014

(G-12660)
WORKMAN PUBLISHING CO INC (PA)
Also Called: Algonquin Books Chapel Hl Div
225 Varick St Fl 9 (10014-4381)
PHONE 212 254-5900
Fax: 212 614-7783
Dan Reynolds, *CEO*
Chuck Adams, *Editor*
Sarah Brady, *Editor*
Kate Karol, *Editor*
Krestyna Lypen, *Editor*
▲ **EMP:** 200
SQ FT: 57,000
SALES (est): 98.9MM **Privately Held**
WEB: www.pageaday.com
SIC: 2731 Books: publishing only

(G-12661)
WORKMAN PUBLISHING CO INC
Artisan House Div
708 Broadway Fl 6 (10003-9508)
PHONE 212 254-5900
Fax: 212 254-8198
Richard Petry, *Controller*

Trent Duffy, *Manager*
Mairead Duffy, *Technical Staff*
Elizabeth Hermann, *Director*
Peter Workman, *Director*
EMP: 150
SALES (corp-wide): 98.9MM **Privately Held**
WEB: www.pageaday.com
SIC: 2731 Books: publishing only
PA: Workman Publishing Co. Inc.
225 Varick St Fl 9
New York NY 10014
212 254-5900

(G-12662)
WORLD GUIDE PUBLISHING
1271 Ave Of The Americas (10020-1300)
PHONE 800 331-7840
Tina Threston, *CEO*
EMP: 40
SQ FT: 600
SALES (est): 1.5MM **Privately Held**
SIC: 2721 Periodicals: publishing only

(G-12663)
WORLD WATERS LLC
Also Called: Wtrmln Wtr
191 7th Ave Apt 2r (10011-1818)
PHONE 212 905-2393
Rob Paladino, *CEO*
Jeffrey Rubenstein, *Principal*
EMP: 20
SQ FT: 5,000
SALES: 323K **Privately Held**
SIC: 2037 Fruit juices

(G-12664)
WORLDSCALE ASSOCIATION NYC
132 Nassau St Rm 619 (10038-2432)
PHONE 212 422-2786
Sara Bierman, *President*
EMP: 6
SQ FT: 2,000
SALES: 1.3MM **Privately Held**
WEB: www.scanalysis.com
SIC: 2741 Guides: publishing only, not printed on site

(G-12665)
WORTH COLLECTION LTD (PA)
520 8th Ave Rm 2301 (10018-4108)
PHONE 212 268-0312
David Defeo, *CEO*
Caroline Davis, *Ch of Bd*
Jay Rosenberg, *Ch of Bd*
David F Defeo, *President*
Seth Grossman, *COO*
▲ **EMP:** 50
SQ FT: 8,000
SALES (est): 45.8MM **Privately Held**
WEB: www.worthny.com
SIC: 2335 Women's, juniors' & misses' dresses

(G-12666)
WORTH PUBLISHERS INC
1 New York Plz Ste 4500 (10004-1562)
PHONE 212 475-6000
Fax: 212 505-9570
Elizabeth Widdicombe, *President*
Valerie Raymond, *Editor*
Michelle Schmidt, *Vice Pres*
Michael Ross, *Treasurer*
Jeff Harris, *VP Finance*
EMP: 110
SQ FT: 14,000
SALES (est): 28.7MM
SALES (corp-wide): 2.1B **Privately Held**
WEB: www.hbpubny.com
SIC: 2731 Textbooks: publishing only, not printed on site
HQ: Macmillan Holdings, Llc
175 5th Ave
New York NY 10010

(G-12667)
WORZALLA PUBLISHING COMPANY
222 W 37th St Fl 10 (10018-9001)
PHONE 212 967-7909
Lynn Carroll, *Branch Mgr*
EMP: 189
SALES (corp-wide): 90MM **Privately Held**
SIC: 2732 Book printing

PA: Worzalla Publishing Company
3535 Jefferson St
Stevens Point WI 54481
715 344-9600

(G-12668)
WP LAVORI USA INC (DH)
597 Broadway Fl 2 (10012-3211)
PHONE 212 244-6074
Cristina Calori, *President*
Ethem Gungor, *Vice Pres*
Arianna Marcollo, *Manager*
◆ **EMP:** 5
SALES (est): 1.5MM **Privately Held**
SIC: 2311 5136 Men's & boys' suits & coats; men's & boys' clothing
HQ: W.P. Lavori In Corso Srl
Via Dell' Arcoveggio 59/5
Bologna BO 40129
051 416-1411

(G-12669)
WR DESIGN CORP
Also Called: Wr9000
1407 Broadway Rm 448 (10018-3820)
PHONE 212 354-9000
Sunny Lam, *President*
EMP: 20
SALES: 8.4MM **Privately Held**
SIC: 2253 Sweaters & sweater coats, knit

(G-12670)
WSN INC
Also Called: World Screen News
1123 Broadway Ste 1207 (10010-2007)
PHONE 212 924-7620
Fax: 212 924-6940
Ricardo Guise, *President*
Jeff Bewkes, *Vice Pres*
Nathalie Jaspar, *Vice Pres*
Jamie LI, *Vice Pres*
Matt Rippetoe, *Production*
EMP: 6
SQ FT: 500
SALES (est): 540K **Privately Held**
WEB: www.worldscreen.com
SIC: 2721 Magazines: publishing only, not printed on site

(G-12671)
WYETH LLC (HQ)
235 E 42nd St (10017-5703)
PHONE 973 660-5000
Ian Reid, *CEO*
Etienne N Attar, *President*
Richard R Deluca, *President*
Michael Kamarck, *President*
Joseph Mahady, *President*
◆ **EMP:** 850 **EST:** 1926
SALES (est): 4.1B
SALES (corp-wide): 48.8B **Publicly Held**
WEB: www.wyeth.com
SIC: 2834 2836 Analgesics; cough medicines; veterinary pharmaceutical preparations; biological products, except diagnostic; allergens, allergenic extracts; vaccines; veterinary biological products
PA: Pfizer Inc.
235 E 42nd St
New York NY 10017
212 733-2323

(G-12672)
X FUNCTION INC (PA)
902 Broadway Fl 11 (10010-6034)
PHONE 212 231-0092
Robert F X Sillerman, *Ch of Bd*
Robert Haag, *Managing Prtnr*
Mitchell J Nelson, *Exec VP*
Julie Gerola, *Vice Pres*
Olga Bashkatova,
EMP: 21
SQ FT: 16,500
SALES: 4.5MM **Publicly Held**
SIC: 7372 7371 Prepackaged software; custom computer programming services

(G-12673)
X MYLES MAR INC
Also Called: Marx Myles Graphic Services
875 Av Of The Americas (10001-3507)
PHONE 212 683-2015
Fax: 212 213-0015
Arthur Marx, *President*
Sheldon Marx, *Vice Pres*
Nancy Lupton, *Controller*

Barry Heaney, *Sales Dir*
EMP: 40
SQ FT: 7,000
SALES (est): 6.1MM **Privately Held**
WEB: www.marxmyles.com
SIC: 2759 2791 2789 2752 Commercial printing; typesetting; bookbinding & related work; commercial printing, lithographic

(G-12674)
XANADU
150 W 30th St Rm 702 (10001-4155)
PHONE 212 465-0580
Gus Xanthoudakis, *Owner*
EMP: 5
SQ FT: 5,000
SALES: 750K **Privately Held**
SIC: 2371 Apparel, fur

(G-12675)
XEROX CORPORATION
245 Park Ave Fl 21 (10167-2900)
PHONE 212 716-4000
Fax: 212 916-1577
Alfonso Lopez, *Principal*
David Lezinsky, *Vice Pres*
Ann Smith, *Vice Pres*
Jeff Fowler, *Engineer*
Glenn Keenan, *Engineer*
EMP: 260
SALES (corp-wide): 18B **Publicly Held**
WEB: www.xerox.com
SIC: 3861 Photographic equipment & supplies
PA: Xerox Corporation
45 Glover Ave Ste 700
Norwalk CT 06850
203 968-3000

(G-12676)
XEROX CORPORATION
115 Barrow St (10014-2826)
PHONE 212 633-8190
EMP: 80
SALES (corp-wide): 18B **Publicly Held**
SIC: 3861 Photocopy machines
PA: Xerox Corporation
45 Glover Ave Ste 700
Norwalk CT 06850
203 968-3000

(G-12677)
XEROX CORPORATION
485 Lexington Ave Fl 10 (10017-2652)
PHONE 212 330-1386
EMP: 80
SALES (corp-wide): 18B **Publicly Held**
SIC: 3861 Photocopy machines
PA: Xerox Corporation
45 Glover Ave Ste 700
Norwalk CT 06850
203 968-3000

(G-12678)
XING LIN USA INTL CORP
1410 Broadway Fl 34 (10018-5007)
PHONE 212 947-4846
Wen Y Wu, *President*
Richard Jacobs, *General Mgr*
Maggie Yeoh, *Opers Mgr*
Glenn Barnett, *VP Sales*
▲ **EMP:** 5
SQ FT: 900
SALES: 6.5MM **Privately Held**
SIC: 2211 Denims

(G-12679)
XINYA INTERNATIONAL TRADING CO
Also Called: Polly Treating
115 W 30th St Rm 1109 (10001-4056)
PHONE 212 216-9681
Fax: 212 216-9681
Peng Sen Liu, *President*
EMP: 6
SALES: 700K **Privately Held**
SIC: 2387 3851 Apparel belts; glasses, sun or glare

(G-12680)
XL GRAPHICS INC
121 Varick St Rm 300 (10013-1408)
PHONE 212 929-8700
Jeff Baltimore, *Ch of Bd*
Michelle Darpa, *Office Mgr*

GEOGRAPHIC SECTION

New York - New York County (G-12709)

Hank Briody, *Manager*
EMP: 5
SQ FT: 4,000
SALES (est): 610.9K **Privately Held**
SIC: 2759 Commercial printing

(G-12681)
XOMOX JEWELRY INC
151 W 46th St Fl 15 (10036-8512)
PHONE 212 944-8428
Mark Bugnacki, *President*
EMP: 7
SQ FT: 1,200
SALES (est): 850K **Privately Held**
WEB: www.xomoxjewelry.com
SIC: 3911 Jewelry, precious metal

(G-12682)
XPOGO LLC
440 9th Ave Fl 17 (10001-1612)
PHONE 717 650-5232
Nicholas Ryan, *Mng Member*
EMP: 5
SQ FT: 300
SALES: 533.8K **Privately Held**
SIC: 3949 Sporting & athletic goods

(G-12683)
XPRESSPA HOLDINGS LLC (PA)
3 E 54th St Fl 9 (10022-3108)
PHONE 212 750-9595
Richard Bachman, *Principal*
EMP: 13
SALES (est): 4.2MM **Privately Held**
SIC: 2392 Cushions & pillows

(G-12684)
XSTELOS HOLDINGS INC
630 5th Ave Ste 2600 (10111-2697)
PHONE 212 729-4962
Jonathan M Couchman, *President*
EMP: 3
SALES: 28.7MM **Privately Held**
SIC: 2834 Pharmaceutical preparations

(G-12685)
Y LIFT NEW YORK LLC
61 E 66th St (10065-6114)
PHONE 212 861-7787
Yan Trokel, *Principal*
EMP: 10
SALES (est): 414.8K **Privately Held**
SIC: 3842 Cosmetic restorations

(G-12686)
YACOUBIAN JEWELERS INC
2 W 45th St Ste 1104 (10036-4248)
PHONE 212 302-6729
Fax: 212 302-3439
Mike Yacoubian, *President*
EMP: 30
SALES (est): 2.7MM **Privately Held**
SIC: 3961 Costume jewelry

(G-12687)
YALE ROBBINS INC
Also Called: Manhattan Map Co
205 Lexington Ave Fl 12 (10016-6022)
PHONE 212 683-5700
Fax: 212 545-0764
Yale Robbins, *President*
Jim Douglass, *Editor*
Debra Estock, *Editor*
Henry Robbins, *Vice Pres*
Sofia Sapeg, *Research*
EMP: 60
SQ FT: 4,000
SALES (est): 8.8MM **Privately Held**
WEB: www.yalerobbins.com
SIC: 2721 8742 6531 Periodicals: publishing & printing; business consultant; real estate brokers & agents

(G-12688)
YAM TV LLC
144 W 23rd St Apt 8e (10011-9403)
PHONE 917 932-5418
Matan Koren,
EMP: 2
SALES: 5MM **Privately Held**
SIC: 2741 7819 Miscellaneous publishing; services allied to motion pictures

(G-12689)
YARNZ INTERNATIONAL INC
260 W 36th St Rm 201 (10018-7524)
PHONE 212 868-5883
Mujadid Shah, *Chairman*
▲ **EMP:** 6
SALES (est): 709.6K **Privately Held**
WEB: www.yarnz.com
SIC: 2231 Apparel & outerwear broadwoven fabrics

(G-12690)
YEOHLEE INC
12 W 29th St (10001-4516)
PHONE 212 631-8099
Fax: 212 631-0918
Yeohlee Teng, *President*
Arthur Laurel, *Manager*
EMP: 13 **EST:** 1975
SQ FT: 6,000
SALES (est): 1.4MM **Privately Held**
WEB: www.yeohlee.com
SIC: 2331 2335 2337 Women's & misses' blouses & shirts; women's, juniors' & misses' dresses; women's & misses' suits & coats

(G-12691)
YIGAL-AZROUEL INC
225 W 39th St Fl 5 (10018-3498)
PHONE 212 302-1194
Fax: 212 221-3870
Yigal Azrouel, *President*
Flora Cervantes, *Principal*
Andre Edwards, *Accounts Exec*
Susan Wetts, *Office Mgr*
Kristen Caruso, *Director*
EMP: 30
SALES (est): 4.7MM **Privately Held**
WEB: www.yigal-azrouel.com
SIC: 2339 2369 Women's & misses' outerwear; girls' & children's outerwear

(G-12692)
YINGLI GREEN ENRGY AMRICAS INC (DH)
Also Called: Yingli Solar
33 Irving Pl Fl 3 (10003-2332)
PHONE 888 686-8820
Robert Petrina, *Ch of Bd*
Liansheng Miao, *Chairman*
Tori Clifford, *Marketing Staff*
Brian Grenko, *Director*
Matthew Sachs, *Director*
◆ **EMP:** 20
SALES (est): 4.2MM **Privately Held**
SIC: 3674 Solar cells
HQ: Baoding Tianwei Yingli New Energy Resources Co., Ltd.
No.3399, Chaoyang(N) St.
Baoding
312 892-9899

(G-12693)
YIWEN USA INC
60 E 42nd St Ste 2107 (10165-6233)
PHONE 212 370-0828
You Chang, *President*
EMP: 10
SALES (est): 1.3MM **Privately Held**
SIC: 2899 Chemical preparations

(G-12694)
YMOBIZ INC
40 Wall St Ste 1700 (10005-1375)
PHONE 917 470-9280
Jose Carlos Garcia, *President*
Thomas Szabo, *Vice Pres*
EMP: 10 **EST:** 2013
SALES: 45MM **Privately Held**
SIC: 7372 Prepackaged software

(G-12695)
YOMIURI INTERNATIONAL INC
747 3rd Ave Fl 28 (10017-2803)
PHONE 212 752-2196
Fax: 212 752-2575
Michiro Okamoto, *Principal*
Masashi Kobari, *Asst Treas*
EMP: 7
SALES (est): 806.4K
SALES (corp-wide): 18.9MM **Privately Held**
SIC: 3714 Motor vehicle parts & accessories
HQ: Yomiuri Shimbun,The
1-7-1, Otemachi
Chiyoda-Ku TKY 100-0
332 421-111

(G-12696)
YONG XIN KITCHEN SUPPLIES INC
50 Delancey St Frnt A (10002-2967)
PHONE 212 995-8908
Chang Wang, *President*
Yvette Lang, *Accountant*
▲ **EMP:** 18
SALES (est): 122.8K **Privately Held**
SIC: 3993 Signs & advertising specialties

(G-12697)
YOOCONNECT1 LLC
244 5th Ave Ste G-269 (10001-7604)
PHONE 212 726-2062
Gerard Lynn Kimble, *CEO*
EMP: 5
SALES (est): 270K **Privately Held**
SIC: 7372 Application computer software

(G-12698)
YOU AND ME LEGWEAR LLC
10 W 33rd St Rm 300 (10001-3306)
PHONE 212 279-9292
Fax: 212 268-0543
Sam Hemaoui, *Controller*
Albert Cohen,
▲ **EMP:** 18
SQ FT: 5,000
SALES: 6.7MM **Privately Held**
SIC: 2252 Hosiery

(G-12699)
YS PUBLISHING CO INC
228 E 45th St Rm 700 (10017-3336)
PHONE 212 682-9360
Fax: 212 682-3916
Hitoshi Yoshida, *President*
Miyuki Hanakoshi, *Accountant*
▲ **EMP:** 9
SALES (est): 1.2MM **Privately Held**
WEB: www.us-benricho.com
SIC: 2731 Book publishing

(G-12700)
YURMAN RETAIL INC
Also Called: David Yurman
712 Madison Ave (10065-7207)
PHONE 888 398-7626
David Yurman, *President*
Scott Vogel, *Vice Pres*
EMP: 8
SQ FT: 1,000
SALES (est): 1.2MM
SALES (corp-wide): 268.2MM **Privately Held**
WEB: www.davidyurman.com
SIC: 3911 Jewelry, precious metal
PA: David Yurman Enterprises Llc
24 Vestry St
New York NY 10013
212 896-1550

(G-12701)
Z-PLY CORP
Also Called: Texray
213 W 35th St Ste 5w (10001-1903)
PHONE 212 398-7011
Fax: 212 398-7647
Timothy Chung, *Ch of Bd*
J J Hou, *Exec VP*
Sharon Grosso, *Prdtn Mgr*
Sam Chang, *CFO*
Elizabeth Searle, *Mktg Dir*
▲ **EMP:** 40
SQ FT: 5,000
SALES (est): 5.1MM **Privately Held**
WEB: www.z-ply.com
SIC: 2339 2369 Women's & misses' athletic clothing & sportswear; girls' & children's outerwear

(G-12702)
ZAK JEWELRY TOOLS INC
55 W 47th St Fl 2 (10036-2812)
PHONE 212 768-8122
Roman Zak, *President*
Robert Zak, *Vice Pres*
◆ **EMP:** 14
SQ FT: 7,500
SALES (est): 1.5MM **Privately Held**
SIC: 3915 5251 Jewel preparing: instruments, tools, watches & jewelry; tools

(G-12703)
ZAR GROUP LLC
Also Called: Zar Apparel Group
1375 Broadway Fl 12 (10018-7044)
PHONE 212 944-2510
Bobby Zar, *CEO*
Bruce Bond, *President*
Mansour Zar, *Chairman*
▼ **EMP:** 150 **EST:** 2014
SQ FT: 20,000
SALES: 100MM **Privately Held**
SIC: 2339 Women's & misses' outerwear

(G-12704)
ZARALO LLC
Also Called: Shugaray Division of Zaralo
500 7th Ave Fl 18 (10018-4502)
PHONE 212 764-4590
David Lomita, *Principal*
EMP: 2
SALES (corp-wide): 138MM **Privately Held**
SIC: 2337 Women's & misses' suits & skirts
HQ: Zaralo, Llc
1 Cape May St Ste 3
Harrison NJ 07029

(G-12705)
ZARO BAKE SHOP INC
Also Called: Zaro's Bread Basket
370 Lexington Ave (10017-6503)
PHONE 212 292-0175
Fax: 212 292-0188
Joseph Zaro, *Manager*
EMP: 59
SALES (corp-wide): 80.3MM **Privately Held**
WEB: www.zaro.com
SIC: 3556 Ovens, bakery
PA: Zaro Bake Shop, Inc.
138 Bruckner Blvd
Bronx NY 10454
718 993-7327

(G-12706)
ZAZOOM LLC (PA)
Also Called: Zazoom Media Group
1 Exchange Plz Ste 801 (10006-3754)
PHONE 212 321-2100
Tim Minton, *CEO*
Megan Mullins, *Editor*
Greg Morey, *Exec VP*
Steve Charlier, *Vice Pres*
Amanda Kabbabe, *Production*
EMP: 17
SALES (est): 2.6MM **Privately Held**
SIC: 2741

(G-12707)
ZDNY & CO INC (PA)
Also Called: Universal Jewelry Designs
31 W 47th St Ste 403 (10036-0013)
PHONE 212 354-1233
Fax: 212 719-4970
Zak Dulgeroglu, *President*
▲ **EMP:** 10
SQ FT: 1,500
SALES (est): 733K **Privately Held**
WEB: www.zdnyco.com
SIC: 3911 5944 Jewelry, precious metal; jewelry stores

(G-12708)
ZEDGE INC
22 Cortlandt St Fl 14 (10007-3152)
PHONE 330 577-3424
Tom Arnoy, *CEO*
Eduardo Mestre, *Business Mgr*
Jonathan Reich, *COO*
EMP: 53
SQ FT: 500
SALES: 9MM **Privately Held**
SIC: 7372 Prepackaged software

(G-12709)
ZEEBA JEWELRY MFG INC
Also Called: Zeeba Jewelry Manufacturing
36 W 47th St Ste 902 (10036-8601)
PHONE 212 997-1009
Fred Navi, *President*
Ray Lavi, *Vice Pres*

New York - New York County (G-12710)

EMP: 3
SQ FT: 2,000
SALES: 1MM Privately Held
SIC: 3911 Jewelry, precious metal

(G-12710)
ZETEK CORPORATION
Also Called: Zeteck
13 E 37th St Ste 701 (10016-2841)
PHONE....................212 668-1485
Fax: 212 668-1487
Bertrand Dorfman, President
Raymond McKee, Director
EMP: 10
SQ FT: 1,500
SALES (est): 1.1MM Privately Held
WEB: www.zetek.com
SIC: 3663 3669 7622 7629 Radio & TV communications equipment; fire detection systems, electric; communication equipment repair; electrical equipment repair services

(G-12711)
ZG APPAREL GROUP LLC
1450 Broadway Fl 7 (10018-2201)
PHONE....................646 930-1113
Maurice Salama, Finance
Babak Zar, Mng Member
Mansur Zar,
◆ EMP: 40 EST: 2014
SQ FT: 5,000
SALES: 30MM Privately Held
SIC: 2339 Women's & misses' athletic clothing & sportswear; athletic clothing: women's, misses' & juniors'

(G-12712)
ZIA POWER INC
116 E 27th St (10016-8942)
PHONE....................845 661-8388
Nathaniel Thompkins, President
EMP: 36
SQ FT: 2,000
SALES (est): 1.4MM Privately Held
SIC: 2339 Women's & misses' outerwear

(G-12713)
ZINEPAK LLC
349 5th Ave (10016-5019)
PHONE....................212 706-8621
Brittney Hodak, Mng Member
Brittany Hodak, Mng Member
Abby Downing, Creative Dir
EMP: 9
SALES: 2.9MM Privately Held
SIC: 2731 Book publishing

(G-12714)
ZIRCONIA CREATIONS INTL
134 W 29th St Rm 801 (10001-0107)
PHONE....................212 239-3730
Fax: 212 239-3733
Michael Halpert, President
Yisha Weber, Vice Pres
EMP: 8
SQ FT: 3,000
SALES: 1.1MM Privately Held
SIC: 3915 Jewelers' materials & lapidary work

(G-12715)
ZITOMER LLC
969 Madison Ave Fl 1 (10021-2763)
PHONE....................212 737-5560
Thanh Tran, Principal
Sharmin Rai, Marketing Mgr
▲ EMP: 9 EST: 1997
SALES (est): 1.5MM Privately Held
SIC: 2834 Solutions, pharmaceutical

(G-12716)
ZIVA GEM LLC (PA)
200 Madison Ave Ste 2225 (10016-4000)
PHONE....................646 416-5828
Marc Klein, President
Ronnie Dushey, Vice Pres
EMP: 10 EST: 2015
SALES: 1MM Privately Held
SIC: 3961 Costume jewelry

(G-12717)
ZOE SAKOUTIS LLC
Also Called: Blueprint Cleanse
135 W 29th St Rm 704 (10001-5172)
PHONE....................212 414-5741

Zoe Sakoutis, Principal
Erica Huss, Principal
Patrick Burlingham, Manager
EMP: 19
SALES (est): 2.9MM
SALES (corp-wide): 2.6B Publicly Held
SIC: 2037 Fruit juices
PA: The Hain Celestial Group Inc
1111 Marcus Ave Ste 100
New Hyde Park NY 11042
516 587-5000

(G-12718)
ZOLA BOOKS INC
242 W 38th St Fl 2 (10018-5820)
PHONE....................917 822-4950
Michael Strong, CEO
Maryann Regal, Cust Mgr
Tad Floridis, Director
Phil Hanrahan, Director
EMP: 23
SALES (est): 2.2MM Privately Held
SIC: 2731 Book publishing

(G-12719)
ZORLU USA INC (PA)
295 5th Ave Ste 503 (10016-7103)
PHONE....................212 689-4622
Fax: 212 689-4380
Vedat Aydin, President
Sevket Celikkanat, Vice Pres
Filiz Ozpicak, Vice Pres
Alihan Altunbas, Controller
Elena Ivena, Office Mgr
▲ EMP: 10
SALES (est): 7.2MM Privately Held
WEB: www.zorluusa.com
SIC: 2221 5131 Textile mills, broadwoven: silk & manmade, also glass; textiles, woven

New York Mills
Oneida County

(G-12720)
DELFT BLUE LLC
36 Garden St A (13417-1301)
PHONE....................315 768-7100
Fax: 315 768-7992
John Gorea, Plant Mgr
Kimberly Milller, Accountant
Jerry Bartelsi,
EMP: 108
SQ FT: 3,000
SALES (est): 15.9MM Privately Held
SIC: 2011 Veal from meat slaughtered on site

(G-12721)
DI HIGHWAY SIGN STRUCTURE CORP
40 Greenman Ave (13417-1004)
P.O. Box 123 (13417-0123)
PHONE....................315 736-8312
Fax: 315 736-7172
Jane Mulvihill, Ch of Bd
Steven Mulvihill, General Mgr
Kevin Fee, Prdtn Mgr
Jeff Welch, Production
Alex Baisley, QC Mgr
EMP: 40
SQ FT: 35,000
SALES (est): 14.3MM Privately Held
SIC: 3499 Metal household articles; trophies, metal, except silver

(G-12722)
FOUNTAINHEAD GROUP INC (PA)
Also Called: Burgess Products Division
23 Garden St (13417-1318)
PHONE....................315 736-0037
John F Romano, CEO
John O'Toole, President
George Mitchell, Vice Pres
Linda E Romano, Vice Pres
James Siepiola, Vice Pres
◆ EMP: 150 EST: 1973
SQ FT: 40,000

SALES (est): 36.7MM Privately Held
WEB: www.thefountainheadgroup.com
SIC: 3563 3523 3569 Spraying outfits: metals, paints & chemicals (compressor); sprayers & spraying machines, agricultural; fertilizing, spraying, dusting & irrigation machinery; firefighting apparatus

(G-12723)
FOUNTAINHEAD GROUP INC
Smith, D B & Company
23 Garden St (13417-1318)
PHONE....................315 736-0037
Fax: 315 736-0335
F Eugene Romano, Ch of Bd
John F Romano, President
EMP: 40
SALES (corp-wide): 36.7MM Privately Held
WEB: www.thefountainheadgroup.com
SIC: 3563 Spraying outfits: metals, paints & chemicals (compressor)
PA: The Fountainhead Group Inc
23 Garden St
New York Mills NY 13417
315 736-0037

(G-12724)
FOUNTAINHEAD GROUP INC
Bridgeview Aerosol
3 Graden St (13417)
PHONE....................708 598-7100
Jack Young, COO
Richard Bannon, Controller
Carol Nelson, Human Res Mgr
EMP: 170
SALES (corp-wide): 36.7MM Privately Held
SIC: 3563 2813 Spraying outfits: metals, paints & chemicals (compressor); aerosols
PA: The Fountainhead Group Inc
23 Garden St
New York Mills NY 13417
315 736-0037

(G-12725)
HERMOSA CORP
102 Main St (13417-1103)
P.O. Box 274 (13417-0274)
PHONE....................315 768-4320
Fax: 315 768-3818
Steven Mulvihill, President
Michael Sheridan Pe, Vice Pres
Alan Morgan, Opers Mgr
Patrick Sullivan, QC Mgr
Joann Western, Office Mgr
EMP: 20
SQ FT: 40,000
SALES (est): 3.7MM Privately Held
WEB: www.hermosacorp.com
SIC: 3993 Signs, not made in custom sign painting shops

(G-12726)
MOHAWK VALLEY KNT MCHY CO INC
561 Main St (13417-1431)
P.O. Box 120 (13417-0120)
PHONE....................315 736-3038
Thomas P Firsching, President
EMP: 19
SQ FT: 40,000
SALES (est): 3.6MM Privately Held
SIC: 3552 Textile machinery

(G-12727)
QUALITY MACHINING SERVICE INC
70 Sauquoit St (13417-1018)
PHONE....................315 736-5774
Tom Ostrander, President
EMP: 5
SQ FT: 3,000
SALES: 150K Privately Held
SIC: 3599 Machine shop, jobbing & repair

Newark
Wayne County

(G-12728)
ADDEX INC
251 Murray St (14513-1216)
PHONE....................315 331-7700
Barb Cree, Owner
Robert Cree, Exec VP
Dan Carey, Manager
EMP: 9
SALES (corp-wide): 1.7MM Privately Held
WEB: www.addexinc.com
SIC: 3625 Control equipment, electric
PA: Addex, Inc.
251 Murray St
Newark NY 14513
781 344-5800

(G-12729)
ADDEX INC (PA)
251 Murray St (14513-1216)
PHONE....................781 344-5800
Fax: 781 344-5766
Rudiger Von Kraus, President
Robert E Cree, Exec VP
Bill Randolph, Engineer
Kathy McCluskey, Manager
▲ EMP: 5
SQ FT: 10,000
SALES (est): 1.7MM Privately Held
WEB: www.addexinc.com
SIC: 3559 Plastics working machinery

(G-12730)
C&C AUTOMATICS INC
127 W Shore Blvd (14513-1259)
PHONE....................315 331-1436
Craig T Parsons, President
Craig Halstead, Vice Pres
EMP: 20
SQ FT: 9,000
SALES (est): 2.3MM Privately Held
WEB: www.ccautomatics.com
SIC: 3451 Screw machine products

(G-12731)
HALLAGAN MANUFACTURING CO INC
500 Hoffman St (14513-1858)
P.O. Box 268 (14513-0268)
PHONE....................315 331-4640
Charles W Hallagan, Ch of Bd
Stephen Hallagan, President
Walter Hallagan, Vice Pres
EMP: 80
SQ FT: 97,000
SALES (est): 10.3MM Privately Held
SIC: 2512 Living room furniture: upholstered on wood frames

(G-12732)
IEC ELECTRONICS CORP (PA)
105 Norton St (14513-1298)
P.O. Box 271 (14513-0271)
PHONE....................315 331-7742
Fax: 315 331-3547
Jeffery T Schlarbaum, Ch of Bd
Jens Hauvn, Senior VP
Justin Whitlow, Opers Mgr
Tom Giuliani, Opers Staff
Denise Marone, Production
EMP: 277 EST: 1966
SQ FT: 235,000
SALES: 127MM Publicly Held
WEB: www.iec-electronics.com
SIC: 3672 3679 Printed circuit boards; electronic circuits

(G-12733)
IEC ELECTRONICS WIRE CABLE INC
105 Norton St (14513-1218)
P.O. Box 271 (14513-0271)
PHONE....................585 924-9010
Jeffrey T Schlarbaum, President
Donald S Doody, Vice Pres
Debbie Bridger, Prdtn Mgr
Vincent Leo, CFO
Christi Rollo, Credit Mgr
EMP: 100
SQ FT: 19,000

▲ = Import ▼ = Export
◆ = Import/Export

GEOGRAPHIC SECTION

Newburgh - Orange County (G-12757)

SALES (est): 12.9MM
SALES (corp-wide): 127MM **Publicly Held**
WEB: www.val-u-tech.com
SIC: 3672 Printed circuit boards
PA: Iec Electronics Corp.
    105 Norton St
    Newark NY 14513
    315 331-7742

(G-12734)
LEGENDARY AUTO INTERIORS LTD
121 W Shore Blvd (14513-1259)
PHONE..................315 331-2244
Fax: 315 331-2244
Martin J Beckenbach, *Ch of Bd*
▲ EMP: 40
SQ FT: 12,000
SALES (est): 5.8MM **Privately Held**
WEB: www.legendaryautointeriors.com
SIC: 2396 5013 5531 3429 Automotive trimmings, fabric; automotive trim; automotive accessories; manufactured hardware (general); leather tanning & finishing; nonwoven fabrics

(G-12735)
MACO BAG CORPORATION
412 Van Buren St (14513-9205)
PHONE..................315 226-1000
Fax: 315 226-1050
J Scott Miller, *Ch of Bd*
Craig Miller, *President*
Susan Miller, *Corp Secy*
Bob Finley, *Safety Dir*
Robert Finley, *Safety Dir*
▲ EMP: 140 EST: 1929
SQ FT: 60,000
SALES (est): 35.1MM **Privately Held**
WEB: www.macobag.com
SIC: 3081 2673 Plastic film & sheet; plastic & pliofilm bags

(G-12736)
MCDOWELL RESEARCH CO INC (HQ)
2000 Technology Pkwy (14513-2175)
PHONE..................315 332-7100
John D Kavazanjian, *President*
Julius Cirin, *Vice Pres*
Dede Emery, *Senior Buyer*
Molly Hedges, *Controller*
Dan Espinosa, *Manager*
▲ EMP: 100
SQ FT: 54,000
SALES (est): 88.2MM
SALES (corp-wide): 76.4MM **Publicly Held**
WEB: www.mrc-power.com
SIC: 3669 Intercommunication systems, electric
PA: Ultralife Corporation
    2000 Technology Pkwy
    Newark NY 14513
    315 332-7100

(G-12737)
MICRO-TECH MACHINE INC
301 W Shore Blvd (14513-1261)
PHONE..................315 331-6671
Fax: 315 331-0142
Michael R Davis, *President*
Lance Mebb, *General Mgr*
Lori Ramsey, *Purchasing*
Bill Guinup, *Engineer*
Amy Davis, *CFO*
EMP: 44
SQ FT: 13,000
SALES (est): 7.4MM **Privately Held**
WEB: www.microtechmachine.com
SIC: 3599 Machine shop, jobbing & repair

(G-12738)
NEWCHEM INC
Also Called: Newcut
434 E Union St (14513-1610)
PHONE..................315 331-7680
Sean Whittaker, *President*
Richard Boerman, *Human Res Dir*
Kirk Cranston, *Manager*
EMP: 22
SALES (est): 3.2MM **Privately Held**
SIC: 3479 Etching, photochemical

(G-12739)
NORTH AMERICAN FILTER CORP (PA)
Also Called: Nafco
200 W Shore Blvd (14513-1258)
PHONE..................800 265-8943
Fax: 315 331-4750
Steve Taylor, *President*
Jerry Dusharm, *Opers Staff*
Dave Shuler, *Opers Staff*
Shawnna Wirth, *Purch Agent*
Tim Hall, *Engineer*
♦ EMP: 74
SQ FT: 75,000
SALES (est): 14.3MM **Privately Held**
WEB: www.nafcoinc.com
SIC: 3569 3564 Filters, general line: industrial; blowers & fans

(G-12740)
P V C MOLDING TECHNOLOGIES
122 W Shore Blvd (14513-1258)
PHONE..................315 331-1212
Martin Beckenbach, *President*
EMP: 12
SQ FT: 14,198
SALES (est): 670K **Privately Held**
SIC: 3089 Plastic processing

(G-12741)
PROGRESSIVE GRAPHICS & PRTG
1171 E Union St (14513-9201)
P.O. Box 492 (14513-0492)
PHONE..................315 331-3635
Robert Kelly, *President*
Dennis Chasse, *Vice Pres*
EMP: 6
SQ FT: 10,000
SALES (est): 380K **Privately Held**
SIC: 2752 2791 2789 Commercial printing, offset; typesetting; bookbinding & related work

(G-12742)
SMITH METAL WORKS NEWARK INC
1000 E Union St (14513-1643)
PHONE..................315 331-1651
Fax: 315 331-0910
Wayne F Smith, *President*
Janice Smith, *Treasurer*
Barbara Jones, *Manager*
Joe Cosentino, *IT/INT Sup*
EMP: 27 EST: 1942
SQ FT: 5,000
SALES (est): 7.5MM **Privately Held**
WEB: www.smithspreaders.com
SIC: 3714 3599 Sanders, motor vehicle safety; machine shop, jobbing & repair; custom machinery

(G-12743)
SPINCO METAL PRODUCTS INC
1 Country Club Dr (14513-1250)
PHONE..................315 331-6285
Fax: 315 331-9535
C Robert Straubing Jr, *Ch of Bd*
David Gardner, *Engineer*
Thurlow Hammond, *Controller*
Ryan Fanning, *Sales Staff*
John Bulger, *Admin Sec*
▲ EMP: 80
SQ FT: 48,000
SALES (est): 24MM **Privately Held**
WEB: www.spincometal.com
SIC: 3498 Tube fabricating (contract bending & shaping)

(G-12744)
SUPERGEN PRODUCTS LLC
320 Hoffman St (14513-1830)
PHONE..................315 573-7887
Paul Cole, *Mng Member*
EMP: 9
SALES: 140K **Privately Held**
SIC: 3621 Motors & generators

(G-12745)
ULTRALIFE CORPORATION (PA)
2000 Technology Pkwy (14513-2175)
PHONE..................315 332-7100
Bradford T Whitmore, *Ch of Bd*
Michael D Popielec, *President*
Andrew Naukam, *Exec VP*
Steve Szamocki, *Exec VP*
Bob Green, *Vice Pres*
▲ EMP: 272
SQ FT: 250,000
SALES: 76.4MM **Publicly Held**
WEB: www.ulbi.com
SIC: 3691 3679 Storage batteries; alkaline cell storage batteries; batteries, rechargeable; electronic loads & power supplies; harness assemblies for electronic use: wire or cable; parametric amplifiers

(G-12746)
UPSTATE REFRACTORY SVCS INC
100 Erie Blvd (14513-1163)
PHONE..................315 331-2955
Fax: 315 364-4594
David Wetmore, *President*
Diane Wetmore, *Vice Pres*
Bill Wilck, *Senior Engr*
Diana Harder, *Manager*
EMP: 29
SQ FT: 18,000
SALES (est): 5.8MM **Privately Held**
WEB: www.upstaterefractoryservices.com
SIC: 3255 5085 Clay refractories; refractory material

(G-12747)
VAN LAEKEN RICHARD
Also Called: Harris Machine
2680 Parker Rd (14513-9750)
PHONE..................315 331-0289
Richard Van Laeken, *Owner*
EMP: 5 EST: 1995
SQ FT: 2,600
SALES: 450K **Privately Held**
SIC: 3599 Machine shop, jobbing & repair

Newburgh
Orange County

(G-12748)
ALUMIL FABRICATION INC
1900 Corporate Blvd (12550-6412)
PHONE..................845 469-2874
Kyt Bazenikas, *President*
▲ EMP: 12
SALES (est): 2.4MM **Privately Held**
SIC: 3442 Screens, window, metal

(G-12749)
AMERICAN ICON INDUSTRIES INC
392 N Montgomery St Ste 2 (12550-6802)
PHONE..................845 561-1299
Fax: 845 913-9067
Robert Kucharek, *CEO*
Gary Rausenberger, *Principal*
Drew Abate, *COO*
Roger Conant, *COO*
Jimmy Phaneuf, *COO*
EMP: 6
SALES (est): 991.4K **Privately Held**
SIC: 2752 Commercial printing, lithographic

(G-12750)
ARCTIC GLACIER NEWBURGH INC (HQ)
225 Lake St (12550-5242)
PHONE..................845 561-0549
Robert Nagy, *President*
Al Feller, *General Mgr*
Keith McMahon, *Vice Pres*
Scott Hinson, *Manager*
Hugh Adams, *Admin Sec*
EMP: 15
SQ FT: 40,000
SALES (est): 2.6MM
SALES (corp-wide): 310.9MM **Privately Held**
SIC: 2097 Manufactured ice
PA: Arctic Glacier Inc
    625 Henry Ave
    Winnipeg MB R3A 0
    204 772-2473

(G-12751)
BIMBO BAKERIES USA INC
98 Scobie Dr (12550-3257)
PHONE..................845 568-0943
Michael D'Adamo, *Director*
EMP: 53
SALES (corp-wide): 13B **Privately Held**
SIC: 2051 Bread, cake & related products
HQ: Bimbo Bakeries Usa, Inc
    255 Business Center Dr # 200
    Horsham PA 19044
    215 347-5500

(G-12752)
CLEVER DEVICES LTD
546 Fostertown Rd (12550-8853)
PHONE..................845 566-0051
Fax: 845 566-0120
Maryellen Collins, *Vice Pres*
EMP: 7
SALES (corp-wide): 18.7MM **Privately Held**
WEB: www.cleverdevices.net
SIC: 3679 Recording & playback apparatus, including phonograph
PA: Clever Devices Ltd.
    300 Crossways Park Dr
    Woodbury NY 11797
    516 433-6100

(G-12753)
COMMODORE CHOCOLATIER USA INC
482 Broadway (12550-5333)
PHONE..................845 561-3960
John Courtsunis, *President*
EMP: 10 EST: 1935
SQ FT: 5,000
SALES: 1MM **Privately Held**
SIC: 2066 5149 5441 Chocolate; chocolate; candy

(G-12754)
E & O MARI INC
Also Called: La Bella Strings
256 Broadway (12550-5487)
P.O. Box 869 (12551-0869)
PHONE..................845 562-4400
Fax: 845 562-4491
Richard Cocco Jr, *President*
Robert Archigian, *Sales/Mktg Dir*
▲ EMP: 89 EST: 1915
SQ FT: 29,000
SALES (est): 12.8MM **Privately Held**
SIC: 3931 Strings, musical instrument

(G-12755)
FRAGRANCE ACQUISITIONS LLC
1900 Corporate Blvd (12550-6412)
PHONE..................845 534-9172
Glenn Palmer, *Partner*
▲ EMP: 70 EST: 2011
SALES (est): 9.6MM **Privately Held**
SIC: 2844 Perfumes & colognes

(G-12756)
GASOFT EQUIPMENT INC
231 Dubois St (12550-3410)
PHONE..................845 863-1010
Tony M Colandrea, *President*
Nick Gurlakis, *Vice Pres*
♦ EMP: 14
SQ FT: 5,000
SALES: 5.6MM **Privately Held**
SIC: 3577 5045 Computer peripheral equipment; computers, peripherals & software

(G-12757)
GENERAL ELECTRIC COMPANY
169 New York 17k 17 K (12550)
PHONE..................845 567-7410
EMP: 21
SALES (corp-wide): 117.3B **Publicly Held**
WEB: www.gecapital.com
SIC: 3743 Train cars & equipment, freight or passenger
PA: General Electric Company
    41 Farnsworth St
    Boston MA 02210
    617 443-3000

Newburgh - Orange County (G-12758)

(G-12758)
GENERAL TRAFFIC EQUIPMENT CORP
259 Broadway (12550-5452)
PHONE 845 569-9000
Fax: 845 569-1800
Raymond Staffon, *President*
Jackie Deleon, *Office Mgr*
▲ EMP: 15
SQ FT: 15,000
SALES (est): 2.4MM Privately Held
WEB: www.generaltrafficequip.com
SIC: 3669 Traffic signals, electric

(G-12759)
GLASBAU HAHN AMERICA LLC
15 Little Brook Ln Ste 2 (12550-1687)
PHONE 845 566-3331
Jamie Ponton, *Principal*
Cathy Lima, *Accounting Mgr*
Hideki Shiozawa, *Representative*
▲ EMP: 5
SALES (est): 390K Privately Held
SIC: 2542 Counters or counter display cases: except wood

(G-12760)
GTI GRAPHIC TECHNOLOGY INC (PA)
211 Dupont Ave (12550-4019)
P.O. Box 3138 (12550-0651)
PHONE 845 562-7066
Fax: 845 562-2543
Robert Mc Curdy, *President*
Louis Chappo, *Vice Pres*
Robert McCurdy, *Vice Pres*
Elizabeth Mc Curdy, *Treasurer*
Nancy Marjollet, *Sales Staff*
EMP: 32
SQ FT: 40,000
SALES: 4.9MM Privately Held
WEB: www.graphiclite.com
SIC: 3648 Lighting equipment

(G-12761)
HOME DEPOT USA INC
Also Called: Home Depot, The
1220 Route 300 (12550-5006)
PHONE 845 561-6540
Fax: 845 563-9016
Steve Fee, *Human Res Dir*
Michael J Pleskach, *Manager*
Scott Procia, *Manager*
EMP: 240
SALES (corp-wide): 88.5B Publicly Held
WEB: www.homerentalsdepot.com
SIC: 3699 Electrical equipment & supplies
HQ: Home Depot U.S.A., Inc.
2455 Paces Ferry Rd Se
Atlanta GA 30339
770 433-8211

(G-12762)
HUDSON VALLEY BLACK PRESS
343 Broadway (12550-5301)
P.O. Box 2160 (12550-0332)
PHONE 845 562-1313
Charles Stewart, *President*
John Callahan, *Accounts Exec*
EMP: 7
SQ FT: 4,000
SALES (est): 378.6K Privately Held
SIC: 2711 Newspapers: publishing only, not printed on site

(G-12763)
HUDSON VALLEY OFFICE FURN INC
7 Wisner Ave (12550-5133)
PHONE 845 565-6673
Fax: 845 565-7269
Tom Chickery, *Owner*
EMP: 8
SALES (corp-wide): 4MM Privately Held
WEB: www.thewowguys.com
SIC: 2522 Office furniture, except wood
PA: Hudson Valley Office Furniture, Inc.
375 Main St
Poughkeepsie NY 12601
845 471-7910

(G-12764)
HUDSON VALLEY PAPER WORKS INC
8 Lander St 15 (12550-4938)
PHONE 845 569-8883
Luke Pontifell, *President*
▲ EMP: 15
SALES (est): 1.2MM Privately Held
SIC: 2732 Book printing

(G-12765)
LA ESCONDIDA INC
129 Lake St (12550-5242)
PHONE 845 562-1387
Andres Garcia, *President*
Emigdio Carrera, *Vice Pres*
EMP: 8
SQ FT: 2,000
SALES (est): 670K Privately Held
WEB: www.laescondida.com
SIC: 2099 Tortillas, fresh or refrigerated

(G-12766)
MAGNETIC AIDS INC
201 Ann St (12550-5417)
P.O. Box 2502 (12550-0610)
PHONE 845 863-1400
Joe Formoso, *President*
George Klapiscak, *Sales Staff*
Eve Formoso, *Manager*
Stacy Pecka, *Manager*
Daniel Formoso, *Master*
▲ EMP: 8 EST: 1958
SQ FT: 12,000
SALES: 750K Privately Held
WEB: www.magneticaids.com
SIC: 3499 3429 Magnets, permanent: metallic; manufactured hardware (general); hangers, wall hardware

(G-12767)
MIXTURE SCREEN PRINTING
1607 Route 300 100 (12550-1738)
PHONE 845 561-2857
Christopher D Fahrbach, *Owner*
EMP: 7
SALES (est): 468.8K Privately Held
SIC: 2759 3993 5099 Screen printing; signs & advertising specialties; signs, except electric

(G-12768)
MOKAI MANUFACTURING INC
13 Jeanne Dr (12550-1788)
PHONE 845 566-8287
Rick Murray, *President*
Justin Bruyn, *Design Engr*
Misses Jones, *Manager*
EMP: 6
SALES (est): 1.2MM Privately Held
WEB: www.mokai.com
SIC: 3732 Boat building & repairing

(G-12769)
NEWBURGH BREWING COMPANY LLC
88 S Colden St (12550-5640)
Rural Route 72, Salisbury Mills (12577)
PHONE 845 569-2337
Paul Halayko,
EMP: 14 EST: 2012
SALES (est): 1.9MM Privately Held
SIC: 2082 Beer (alcoholic beverage)

(G-12770)
NEWBURGH ENVELOPE CORP
1720 Route 300 (12550-8930)
PHONE 845 566-4211
Fax: 845 566-4212
Carl Stillwaggon, *President*
Stuart Stillwaggon, *Vice Pres*
EMP: 7
SQ FT: 1,800
SALES (est): 640K Privately Held
SIC: 2752 Commercial printing, offset

(G-12771)
ORANGE COUNTY CHOPPERS INC
Also Called: O C Choppers
14 Crossroads Ct (12550-5064)
PHONE 845 522-5200
Paul Teutul Sr, *President*
Jim Quinn, *Engineer*
Jessica Miller, *Executive*
EMP: 4
SALES: 1MM Privately Held
SIC: 3751 Motorcycles & related parts

(G-12772)
ORANGE DIE CUTTING CORP
Also Called: Orange Packaging
1 Favoriti Ave (12550-4015)
P.O. Box 2295 (12550-0441)
PHONE 845 562-0900
Fax: 845 562-1020
Anthony Esposito Sr, *Ch of Bd*
Anthony Esposito Jr, *President*
Hector Torres, *General Mgr*
Brenda Benevides, *Sales Staff*
Tom Pederson, *Mktg Dir*
▲ EMP: 120 EST: 1950
SQ FT: 40,000
SALES (est): 30.6MM Privately Held
SIC: 2675 Die-cut paper & board

(G-12773)
ORNAMETAL INC
216 S William St (12550-5845)
PHONE 845 562-5151
Richard Cohen, *Owner*
EMP: 5
SALES (est): 355K Privately Held
SIC: 3446 Stairs, staircases, stair treads: prefabricated metal

(G-12774)
PEPSI-COLA NEWBURGH BTLG INC
Also Called: Pepsico
1 Pepsi Way (12550-3921)
PHONE 845 562-5400
Fax: 845 562-7480
Charles T Tenney Jr, *President*
Jim Brannigan, *Division Mgr*
Richard Ryan, *Division Mgr*
Mike Travis, *Division Mgr*
Laureen Fee, *General Mgr*
EMP: 150 EST: 1939
SALES (est): 31.2MM Privately Held
SIC: 2086 Carbonated soft drinks, bottled & canned

(G-12775)
PRISMATIC DYEING & FINSHG INC
40 Wisner Ave (12550-5132)
P.O. Box 2456 (12550-0732)
PHONE 845 561-1800
Gary Innocenti, *President*
Deborah Emerick, *Manager*
EMP: 60
SQ FT: 110,000
SALES (est): 11.7MM Privately Held
WEB: www.prismaticdyeing.com
SIC: 2861 2269 2262 2261 Dyeing materials, natural; finishing plants; finishing plants, manmade fiber & silk fabrics; finishing plants, cotton

(G-12776)
PROKOSCH AND SONN SHEET METAL
772 South St (12550-4149)
PHONE 845 562-4211
Fax: 845 562-8782
Alfred Prokosch Jr, *Ch of Bd*
Annunciata Prokosch, *President*
EMP: 21
SQ FT: 2,400
SALES (est): 4.2MM Privately Held
SIC: 3444 1711 Sheet metalwork; heating & air conditioning contractors

(G-12777)
PROSTHETIC REHABILITATION CTR (PA)
2 Winding Ln (12550-2223)
PHONE 845 565-8255
Fax: 845 565-4409
Andrew Carubia, *President*
Carol Hatcher, *Admin Sec*
EMP: 6
SALES (est): 750.9K Privately Held
SIC: 3842 5999 Limbs, artificial; artificial limbs

(G-12778)
RUSSIN LUMBER CORP
Also Called: Staining Plant
75 Pierces Rd (12550-3263)
PHONE 845 457-4000
Barry Russin, *President*
EMP: 10
SALES (corp-wide): 47.6MM Privately Held
WEB: www.russinlumber.com
SIC: 2431 Millwork
PA: Russin Lumber Corp.
21 Leonards Dr
Montgomery NY 12549
800 724-0010

(G-12779)
SANDY LITTMAN INC
Also Called: American Glass Light
420 N Montgomery St (12550-3680)
P.O. Box 11089, Greenwich CT (06831-1089)
PHONE 845 562-1112
Fax: 212 371-4874
Sandy Littman, *President*
Kim Gabriel, *Manager*
Irene Higgins, *Manager*
EMP: 6
SQ FT: 800
SALES (est): 1.2MM Privately Held
WEB: www.americanglasslight.com
SIC: 3646 3645 Commercial indusl & institutional electric lighting fixtures; residential lighting fixtures

(G-12780)
STEELWAYS INC
Also Called: Steelways Shipyard
401 S Water St (12553-6038)
PHONE 845 562-0860
David Plotkins, *Ch of Bd*
Brian Plotkin, *Exec VP*
Brian Plotkins, *Exec VP*
Steve Laker, *CFO*
EMP: 29
SQ FT: 15,000
SALES (est): 8.4MM Privately Held
WEB: www.steelwaysinc.com
SIC: 3731 3443 Commercial cargo ships, building & repairing; tanks, standard or custom fabricated: metal plate
PA: Steelways Holdings Group, Inc.
401 S Water St
Newburgh NY 12553
845 562-0860

(G-12781)
TELECHEMISCHE INC
222 Dupont Ave (12550-4060)
PHONE 845 561-3237
Mary Mallavarapu, *Ch of Bd*
Leo Mallavarapu PHD, *President*
Anita Soares, *Admin Sec*
EMP: 6
SALES: 100K Privately Held
WEB: www.telechemische.en.ecplaza.net
SIC: 2821 2869 Plastics materials & resins; industrial organic chemicals

(G-12782)
UNICO INC
25 Renwick St (12550-6029)
PHONE 845 562-9255
Fax: 845 562-7759
Michael Guarneri, *President*
Joseph Guarneri Jr, *Vice Pres*
Regina Guarneri, *Vice Pres*
Edward Guarneri, *Treasurer*
EMP: 15 EST: 1948
SQ FT: 12,000
SALES (est): 2.3MM Privately Held
SIC: 3431 3231 2821 2541 Metal sanitary ware; doors, glass: made from purchased glass; plastics materials & resins; wood partitions & fixtures

(G-12783)
UNICO SPECIAL PRODUCTS INC
25 Renwick St (12550-6029)
PHONE 845 562-9255
Joseph Guarneri Jr, *President*
Edward Guarneri, *Corp Secy*
Michael Guarneri, *Vice Pres*
▲ EMP: 50
SQ FT: 44,000

GEOGRAPHIC SECTION

SALES: 250K **Privately Held**
SIC: 3083 Plastic finished products, laminated

(G-12784)
UNIVERSAL THIN FILM LAB CORP
232 N Plank Rd (12550-1775)
PHONE..................845 562-0601
Carmelo Comito, *President*
Jordan Comito, *Prdtn Mgr*
Christopher Infante, *Engineer*
Mike Middleton, *Engineer*
Alison Comito, *Treasurer*
EMP: 7 EST: 1997
SQ FT: 3,000
SALES: 1MM **Privately Held**
SIC: 3559 Optical lens machinery

(G-12785)
WAGNER TECHNICAL SERVICES INC
1658 Route 300 (12550-1757)
PHONE..................845 566-4018
Gerald L Wagner, *President*
Gerald Wagner, *President*
EMP: 17
SALES: 2MM **Privately Held**
WEB: www.wagnertech.com
SIC: 7372 Utility computer software

(G-12786)
WALLKILL VALLEY PUBLICATIONS
Also Called: Wallkill Valley Times
300 Stony Brook Ct Ste B (12550-6535)
PHONE..................845 561-0170
Carl Aiello, *President*
EMP: 20
SQ FT: 1,500
SALES (est): 1.1MM **Privately Held**
WEB: www.tcnewspapers.com
SIC: 2711 2791 2752 2721 Newspapers: publishing only, not printed on site; typesetting; commercial printing, lithographic; periodicals

Newfane
Niagara County

(G-12787)
KSM GROUP LTD
2905 Beebe Rd (14108-9655)
PHONE..................716 751-6006
Fax: 716 751-6335
Daniel King, *President*
Judith M King, *Vice Pres*
EMP: 5
SQ FT: 18,000
SALES (est): 430K **Privately Held**
WEB: www.ksmgroup.org
SIC: 3444 Sheet metalwork

(G-12788)
SAVACO INC
2905 Beebe Rd (14108-9655)
PHONE..................716 751-9455
Judith King, *President*
Brad Few, *Info Tech Mgr*
EMP: 7
SQ FT: 18,000
SALES: 500K **Privately Held**
WEB: www.savacoinc.com
SIC: 3444 Sheet metalwork

(G-12789)
VANTE INC
Also Called: Plasticweld Systems
3600 Coomer Rd (14108-9651)
PHONE..................716 778-7691
Fax: 716 778-5671
Brian Strini, *CEO*
Norman Strobel, *President*
Scott Dewitt, *General Mgr*
Ziggy Franusiak, *Electrical Engi*
Pete Strobel, *Manager*
▲ EMP: 10
SQ FT: 4,800

SALES (est): 1.9MM
SALES (corp-wide): 19MM **Privately Held**
WEB: www.plasticweldsystems.com
SIC: 3841 3548 Catheters; welding apparatus
PA: Machine Solutions, Inc.
2951 W Shamrell Blvd # 107
Flagstaff AZ 86005
928 556-3109

Newport
Herkimer County

(G-12790)
FULLER TOOL INCORPORATED
225 Platform Rd (13416-2217)
PHONE..................315 891-3183
Rodney Fuller, *CEO*
EMP: 10
SQ FT: 2,800
SALES: 500K **Privately Held**
WEB: www.fullertool.com
SIC: 3312 3544 Tool & die steel & alloys; special dies, tools, jigs & fixtures

(G-12791)
NEWPORT MAGNETICS INC
396 Old State Rd (13416)
P.O. Box 533 (13416-0533)
PHONE..................315 845-8878
Fax: 315 845-8876
Ronald Fusco, *President*
▲ EMP: 9
SQ FT: 5,000
SALES: 500K **Privately Held**
WEB: www.newportmagnetics.com
SIC: 3493 Coiled flat springs

(G-12792)
REYNOLDS DRAPERY SERVICE INC
Also Called: Country Coin-Op
7440 Main St (13416-7707)
PHONE..................315 845-8632
Fax: 315 845-8645
Richard Reynolds, *President*
Michael Moody, *Vice Pres*
EMP: 10 EST: 1964
SQ FT: 6,500
SALES (est): 877.1K **Privately Held**
SIC: 2391 5023 5714 7216 Draperies, plastic & textile: from purchased materials; draperies; draperies; curtain cleaning & repair; fire resistance finishing of cotton broadwoven fabrics; laundry, coin-operated

Niagara Falls
Niagara County

(G-12793)
A - MIC CORPORATION
4600 Witmer Indus Est (14305-1364)
PHONE..................909 598-1814
Feng Chuanhuang, *President*
▲ EMP: 10
SQ FT: 10,000
SALES (est): 740K **Privately Held**
SIC: 3499 Novelties & giftware, including trophies

(G-12794)
AAVID NIAGARA LLC (DH)
3315 Haseley Dr (14304-1460)
PHONE..................716 297-0652
Barry Heckman, *CEO*
Alan Wong, *President*
Chris Soule, *President*
Scott Mowry, *Vice Pres*
Dennis Baer, *Plant Mgr*
▲ EMP: 19
SQ FT: 45,000
SALES (est): 27.3MM **Privately Held**
WEB: www.niagarathermal.com
SIC: 3443 5084 Heat exchangers, condensers & components; heat exchange equipment, industrial

HQ: Aavid Thermalloy, Llc
1 Aavid Cir
Laconia NH 03246
603 528-3400

(G-12795)
ADVANTAGE MACHINING INC
6421 Wendt Dr (14304-1100)
PHONE..................716 731-6418
Scott Ranney, *President*
EMP: 10
SALES (est): 940.1K **Privately Held**
SIC: 3441 Fabricated structural metal

(G-12796)
ANGUS CHEMICAL COMPANY
Also Called: Angus Buffers & Biochemicals
2236 Liberty Dr (14304-3756)
PHONE..................716 283-1434
John Gabrielson, *Safety Mgr*
Fred Dlugos, *CFO*
Mark Deuble, *Manager*
Bill Brewer, *Manager*
EMP: 23
SALES (corp-wide): 7.7B **Privately Held**
SIC: 2836 Culture media
HQ: Angus Chemical Company
1500 E Lake Cook Rd
Buffalo Grove IL 60089
847 215-8600

(G-12797)
APOLLO STEEL CORPORATION
4800 Tomson Ave (14304-2150)
PHONE..................716 283-8758
Fax: 716 283-1136
George J Merkling III, *President*
Bill Crissy, *Business Mgr*
EMP: 16
SQ FT: 15,000
SALES (est): 6.4MM **Privately Held**
SIC: 3441 Bridge sections, prefabricated highway; bridge sections, prefabricated railway; expansion joints (structural shapes), iron or steel; floor jacks, metal

(G-12798)
BRAUN HORTICULTURE INC
3302 Highland Ave (14305-2013)
P.O. Box 260 (14305-0260)
PHONE..................716 282-6101
Peter Braun, *President*
Ken Young, *Controller*
▲ EMP: 7
SQ FT: 31,500
SALES (est): 1.2MM
SALES (corp-wide): 202.9K **Privately Held**
WEB: www.braungroup.com
SIC: 3315 Baskets, steel wire
HQ: Braun Nursery Limited
2004 Glancaster Rd
Mount Hope ON L0R 1
905 648-1911

(G-12799)
BRODA MACHINE CO INC
8745 Packard Rd (14304-1497)
PHONE..................716 297-3221
Fax: 716 297-0270
Matthew Broda, *President*
Thomas J Broda, *President*
Lillian Broda, *Corp Secy*
Mark Broda, *Vice Pres*
Jeff Kilroy, *Plant Mgr*
EMP: 13
SQ FT: 10,000
SALES (est): 3.3MM **Privately Held**
WEB: www.brodamachine.com
SIC: 3451 Screw machine products

(G-12800)
CALSPAN CORPORATION
Also Called: Calspan Flight Research Center
2041 Niagara Falls Blvd (14304-1617)
PHONE..................716 236-1040
Paul Nafziger, *Branch Mgr*
EMP: 40
SALES (corp-wide): 41.1MM **Privately Held**
WEB: www.windtunnel.com
SIC: 3721 Research & development on aircraft by the manufacturer

PA: Calspan Corporation
4455 Genesee St
Buffalo NY 14225
716 631-6955

(G-12801)
CASCADES CNTNERBOARD PACKG INC
4001 Packard Rd (14303-2202)
PHONE..................716 285-3681
Clark Willett, *Maint Spvr*
Mary Malone, *Manager*
EMP: 140
SALES (corp-wide): 2.9B **Privately Held**
SIC: 2631 Linerboard
HQ: Cascades Containerboard Packaging Inc.
4001 Packard Rd
Niagara Falls NY 14303
450 923-3031

(G-12802)
CASCADES CNTNERBOARD PACKG INC (DH)
Also Called: Norampac Industries Inc.
4001 Packard Rd (14303-2202)
PHONE..................450 923-3031
Jean Goulet, *General Mgr*
Mario Lacharit, *General Mgr*
Luc Langevin, *General Mgr*
Charles Malo, *Vice Pres*
Robert Lanthier, *Vice Pres*
▲ EMP: 191
SALES (est): 958.6MM
SALES (corp-wide): 2.9B **Privately Held**
SIC: 2631 2653 Container board; corrugated & solid fiber boxes
HQ: Cascades Canada Ulc
404 Boul Marie-Victorin
Kingsey Falls QC J0A 1
819 363-5100

(G-12803)
CCT (US) INC
2221 Niagara Falls Blvd # 5 (14304-5709)
PHONE..................716 297-7509
Fax: 716 297-3262
Yves Therrien, *President*
Jacques Chevrette, *Admin Sec*
▲ EMP: 15
SQ FT: 20,000
SALES (est): 541.2K
SALES (corp-wide): 5.7MM **Privately Held**
SIC: 2679 Building, insulating & packaging paper; building, insulating & packaging paperboard
PA: Papiers C.C.T. Inc
830 Rue Saint-Viateur
Berthierville QC J0K 1
450 836-3846

(G-12804)
CHEMOURS COMPANY FC LLC
3181 Buffalo Ave (14303-2158)
P.O. Box 787 (14302-0787)
PHONE..................716 278-5100
Fax: 716 278-5195
Kelly Kober, *Human Res Dir*
Tim Reece, *Manager*
Jeffrey Manning, *Manager*
Marie Kandt, *Supervisor*
Esther Lorence, *Director*
EMP: 50
SALES (corp-wide): 5.7B **Publicly Held**
WEB: www.dupont.com
SIC: 2819 2865 2812 Industrial inorganic chemicals; cyclic crudes & intermediates; alkalies & chlorine
HQ: The Chemours Company Fc Llc
1007 Market St
Wilmington DE 19898
302 774-1000

(G-12805)
COMMUNITY NEWSPPR HOLDINGS INC
Also Called: Tonanwanda News
473 3rd St Ste 201 (14301-1500)
PHONE..................716 693-1000
Wayne Lowman, *Branch Mgr*
EMP: 100
SQ FT: 21,892 **Privately Held**
WEB: www.clintonnc.com
SIC: 2711 Newspapers: publishing only, not printed on site

Niagara Falls - Niagara County (G-12806)

PA: Community Newspaper Holdings, Inc.
445 Dexter Ave Ste 7000
Montgomery AL 36104

(G-12806)
COMMUNITY NEWSPPR HOLDINGS INC
Also Called: Niagara Gazette
473 3rd St Ste 201 (14301-1500)
PHONE..................716 282-2311
Fax: 716 285-5610
Steve Braver, *Principal*
Samantha Dreverman, *Manager*
Cheryl Phillips, *Director*
EMP: 55
SQ FT: 21,534 **Privately Held**
WEB: www.clintonnc.com
SIC: 2711 2741 Newspapers; miscellaneous publishing
PA: Community Newspaper Holdings, Inc.
445 Dexter Ave Ste 7000
Montgomery AL 36104

(G-12807)
COSTANZOS WELDING INC (PA)
Also Called: Cataract Steel Industries
22nd Allen St (14302)
P.O. Box 862 (14302-0862)
PHONE..................716 282-0845
Scott Costanzo, *President*
Thomas Costanzo, *Vice Pres*
Rich Winchel, *Maintence Staff*
▼ **EMP:** 37
SQ FT: 100,000
SALES (est): 8.5MM **Privately Held**
WEB: www.cataractsteel.com
SIC: 3443 Heat exchangers, plate type

(G-12808)
CRYSTAL CERES INDUSTRIES INC
2250 Liberty Dr (14304-3756)
PHONE..................716 283-0445
Michael Lynch, *Vice Pres*
Nancy Lynch, *Plant Mgr*
Douglas Scouten, *Project Mgr*
Robin Selino, *Technology*
▲ **EMP:** 58
SALES (est): 8.2MM **Privately Held**
WEB: www.cerescrystal.com
SIC: 1481 7631 Nonmetallic mineral services; diamond setter

(G-12809)
CSI INTERNATIONAL INC
1001 Main St (14301-1111)
PHONE..................716 282-5408
Fax: 716 285-6332
Steven Brown, *President*
Erika Lorange, *Opers Mgr*
Maria Vapri, *Controller*
Jim Drakakis, *VP Sales*
Theresa Ventry, *Sales Staff*
▲ **EMP:** 40
SQ FT: 37,000
SALES (est): 7.2MM **Privately Held**
SIC: 3911 3914 Jewelry, precious metal; trophies, plated (all metals)

(G-12810)
DELFINGEN US-NEW YORK INC
Also Called: Sofanou
2221 Niagara Falls Blvd # 12 (14304-5709)
PHONE..................716 215-0300
Fax: 716 215-0304
Bernard Streit, *President*
Olivier Mathieu, *General Mgr*
David Streit, *Vice Pres*
Mark Blanke, *Treasurer*
Larry Weatherston, *Exec Dir*
▲ **EMP:** 25
SALES (est): 5MM
SALES (corp-wide): 6.6MM **Privately Held**
SIC: 3643 Caps & plugs, electric: attachment
HQ: Delfingen Us, Inc.
3985 W Hamlin Rd
Rochester Hills MI 48309
716 215-0300

(G-12811)
DONNA KARAN COMPANY LLC
1900 Military Rd (14304-1737)
PHONE..................716 297-0752
Fax: 716 298-5724
Elizabeth Carroll, *Branch Mgr*
EMP: 157
SALES (corp-wide): 279MM **Privately Held**
SIC: 2335 Women's, juniors' & misses' dresses
HQ: The Donna Karan Company Llc
550 Fashion Ave Fl 14
New York NY 10018
212 789-1500

(G-12812)
DUREZ CORPORATION
5000 Packard Rd (14304-1510)
PHONE..................716 286-0100
John W Fisher, *CEO*
EMP: 13
SALES (corp-wide): 1.7B **Privately Held**
SIC: 2865 2821 Cyclic crudes & intermediates; plastics materials & resins
HQ: Durez Corporation
46820 Magellan Dr Ste C
Novi MI 48377
248 313-7000

(G-12813)
EASTERN MACHINE AND ELECTRIC
1041 Niagara Ave (14305-2639)
PHONE..................716 284-8271
Fax: 716 284-0277
Louis Destino, *President*
Daniel Destino, *Corp Secy*
EMP: 6 **EST:** 1957
SQ FT: 7,200
SALES (est): 514.2K **Privately Held**
SIC: 3599 Machine shop, jobbing & repair

(G-12814)
ENSIL TECHNICAL SERVICES INC
1901 Maryland Ave (14305-1722)
PHONE..................716 282-1020
Farsad Kiani, *President*
Lewi Koykas, *General Mgr*
Louis Koikas, *Principal*
EMP: 50
SALES (est): 7.3MM **Privately Held**
SIC: 3728 Aircraft parts & equipment

(G-12815)
ERIC S HAPEMAN
Also Called: Hapeman's Seal Coating
6611 Hunt St (14304-2006)
PHONE..................716 731-5416
Eric S Hapeman, *Owner*
EMP: 8
SALES (est): 970.4K **Privately Held**
SIC: 3531 0781 Snow plow attachments; landscape services

(G-12816)
EUROTEX INC
Also Called: Eurotex North America
4600 Witmer Rd (14305-1217)
PHONE..................716 205-8861
Sasha Mitic, *President*
Stacee Sokoloff, *Marketing Mgr*
▲ **EMP:** 12
SALES (est): 1.3MM **Privately Held**
SIC: 2295 Coated fabrics, not rubberized

(G-12817)
EYE DEAL EYEWEAR INC
4611 Military Rd (14305-1337)
PHONE..................716 297-1500
Mike Trombley, *President*
EMP: 5
SALES (est): 516.4K **Privately Held**
WEB: www.eyedealeyewear.com
SIC: 3851 3229 Frames, lenses & parts, eyeglass & spectacle; pressed & blown glass

(G-12818)
FCC ACQUISITION LLC
Also Called: Flame Control Coatings
4120 Hyde Park Blvd (14305-1712)
PHONE..................716 282-1399
Fax: 716 285-6303
Tim Walker, *Prdtn Mgr*
Tim Lockhart, *Marketing Mgr*
Amy Jeary, *Manager*
Jeff Fallon,
Jonathan Hatch,
▼ **EMP:** 26 **EST:** 1976
SQ FT: 26,000
SALES (est): 7.2MM **Privately Held**
WEB: www.flamecontrol.com
SIC: 2899 Fire retardant chemicals

(G-12819)
FELICETTI CONCRETE PRODUCTS
4129 Hyde Park Blvd (14305-1711)
PHONE..................716 284-5740
Fax: 716 284-5751
Gene Felicetti, *Corp Secy*
Henry Felicetti, *Vice Pres*
Frank M Felicetti, *Shareholder*
Phillip Felicetti, *Shareholder*
Richard B Felicetti, *Shareholder*
EMP: 7
SQ FT: 1,750
SALES (est): 1.1MM **Privately Held**
SIC: 3271 Blocks, concrete or cinder: standard; brick, concrete

(G-12820)
FELTON MACHINE CO INC
2221 Niagara Falls Blvd (14304-5709)
P.O. Box 239 (14304-0239)
PHONE..................716 215-9001
Fax: 716 731-9048
Robert J Schroeder, *President*
Jeff Gorney, *Mfg Staff*
Bridget M Schroeder, *Treasurer*
Mike Schroder, *Info Tech Mgr*
EMP: 38
SQ FT: 42,000
SALES (est): 5.8MM **Privately Held**
WEB: www.feltonmachine.com
SIC: 3599 Machine shop, jobbing & repair

(G-12821)
FERRO ELECTRONICS MATERIALS
4511 Hyde Park Blvd (14305-1215)
PHONE..................716 278-9400
Lyndon La Brake, *Branch Mgr*
Pat Jones, *Branch Mgr*
EMP: 200
SALES (corp-wide): 1B **Publicly Held**
SIC: 3264 2819 Porcelain electrical supplies; industrial inorganic chemicals
HQ: Ferro Electronics Materials Inc
1789 Transelco Dr
Penn Yan NY 14527
315 536-3357

(G-12822)
FINGER FOOD PRODUCTS INC
2045 Niagara Falls Blvd # 1 (14304-1675)
P.O. Box 560 (14304-0560)
PHONE..................716 297-4888
Fax: 716 297-4944
Robert Cordova, *President*
Ronald A Canestro, *Vice Pres*
Jason Cordova, *Vice Pres*
Ann Henderson, *Office Mgr*
Ann Anderson, *Manager*
EMP: 48
SALES (est): 6.9MM **Privately Held**
WEB: www.fingerfoodproducts.com
SIC: 2038 Frozen specialties

(G-12823)
FROSS INDUSTRIES INC
Also Called: Niagara Development & Mfg Div
3315 Haseley Dr (14304-1460)
PHONE..................716 297-0652
Fax: 716 297-2550
Silvio Derubeis, *President*
Robert Schultz, *Vice Pres*
Donald H Smith, *Treasurer*
Mark Parisi, *Business Dir*
Gordon Smith, *Admin Sec*
EMP: 50 **EST:** 1981
SQ FT: 16,000
SALES (est): 6.2MM **Privately Held**
SIC: 3443 3599 Heat exchangers, plate type; machine shop, jobbing & repair

(G-12824)
GENERAL WELDING & FABG INC
360 Rainbow Blvd (14303-1122)
PHONE..................716 304-3622
EMP: 7
SALES (corp-wide): 5.3MM **Privately Held**
SIC: 7692 Welding repair
PA: General Welding & Fabricating, Inc.
991 Maple Rd
Elma NY 14059
716 652-0033

(G-12825)
GLOBE METALLURGICAL INC
Also Called: Globe Specialty Metals
3807 Highland Ave (14305-1723)
PHONE..................716 804-0862
Fax: 716 278-6199
David Nau, *Plant Mgr*
David Shaw, *Prdtn Mgr*
Tammy Mack, *Controller*
Paul Kwapiszeski, *Branch Mgr*
Richard Schmidt, *Security Mgr*
EMP: 90
SALES (corp-wide): 651.6K **Privately Held**
WEB: www.globemetallurgical.com
SIC: 3339 3313 Silicon refining (primary, over 99% pure); ferromanganese, not made in blast furnaces
HQ: Globe Metallurgical Inc.
County Road 32
Waterford OH 45786
740 984-2361

(G-12826)
GRAPHICOMM INC
Also Called: Insty-Prints
7703 Niagara Falls Blvd (14304-1739)
PHONE..................716 283-0830
Fax: 716 283-2217
John Jones, *President*
Jill Welsby, *Graphic Designe*
EMP: 5
SQ FT: 2,200
SALES (est): 520K **Privately Held**
SIC: 2752 7334 2791 2789 Commercial printing, lithographic; photocopying & duplicating services; typesetting; bookbinding & related work

(G-12827)
GREATER NIAGARA BLDG CTR INC
9540 Niagara Falls Blvd (14304-4909)
PHONE..................716 299-0543
EMP: 10
SALES (est): 1.8MM **Privately Held**
SIC: 2421 Building & structural materials, wood

(G-12828)
GREEN GLOBAL ENERGY INC
2526 Niagara Falls Blvd (14304-4519)
PHONE..................716 501-9770
Dan Schriber, *President*
EMP: 6
SALES (est): 850K **Privately Held**
SIC: 2911 Fuel additives

(G-12829)
GREENPAC MILL LLC (DH)
4400 Royal Ave (14303-2128)
PHONE..................716 299-0560
Veronique Dion, *Manager*
Rhonda Perry, *Manager*
Luc Nadeau,
▲ **EMP:** 93
SALES (est): 42.9MM
SALES (corp-wide): 2.9B **Privately Held**
SIC: 2631 Linerboard
HQ: Cascades Containerboard Packaging Inc.
4001 Packard Rd
Niagara Falls NY 14303
450 923-3031

(G-12830)
GUESS INC
1826 Military Rd Spc 113 (14304-1772)
PHONE..................716 298-3561
Danielle Guetta, *Manager*
EMP: 25
SALES (corp-wide): 2.2B **Publicly Held**
WEB: www.guess.com
SIC: 2325 Men's & boys' jeans & dungarees

GEOGRAPHIC SECTION

Niagara Falls - Niagara County (G-12855)

PA: Guess, Inc.
1444 S Alameda St
Los Angeles CA 90021
213 765-3100

(G-12831)
HEAVEN FRESH USA INC
4600 Witmer Industrial Es (14305-1364)
PHONE..................................800 642-0367
Mohammad Kamal Anwar, *President*
Imran Bashir, *Vice Pres*
Taoufik Lahrache, *Treasurer*
Abrar Shaikh, *Supervisor*
▲ **EMP:** 5
SALES (est): 521.4K **Privately Held**
SIC: 3634 3585 5722 Air purifiers, portable; humidifiers & dehumidifiers; electric household appliances, small

(G-12832)
HELMEL ENGINEERING PDTS INC
6520 Lockport Rd (14305-3512)
PHONE..................................716 297-8644
Fax: 716 297-9405
Erwin Helmel, *President*
Arthur Whistler, *Marketing Staff*
Robert Cliffe, *Asst Mgr*
Dora Helmel, *Admin Sec*
▲ **EMP:** 22
SQ FT: 23,000
SALES: 2.9MM **Privately Held**
WEB: www.helmel.com
SIC: 3829 Measuring & controlling devices

(G-12833)
IMERYS FSED MNRL NGARA FLS INC
3455 Hyde Park Blvd (14305-2201)
PHONE..................................716 286-1234
Laura Nowak, *Purchasing*
EMP: 5
SALES (corp-wide): 1.2MM **Privately Held**
SIC: 3291 Abrasive products
HQ: Imerys Fused Minerals Niagara Falls, Inc.
2000 College Ave
Niagara Falls NY 14305
716 286-1250

(G-12834)
IMERYS FSED MNRL NGARA FLS INC (DH)
2000 College Ave (14305-1734)
P.O. Box 1438 (14302-1438)
PHONE..................................716 286-1250
Fax: 716 286-1224
Christian Pfeifer, *CEO*
Laura Nowak, *Purchasing*
▲ **EMP:** 35
SQ FT: 4,950
SALES (est): 7.9MM
SALES (corp-wide): 1.2MM **Privately Held**
SIC: 3291 Abrasive products
HQ: Imerys Usa, Inc.
100 Mansell Ct E Ste 300
Roswell GA 30076
770 645-3300

(G-12835)
IMERYS STEELCASTING USA INC (DH)
4111 Witmer Rd (14305-1720)
P.O. Box 368 (14302-0368)
PHONE..................................716 278-1634
Fax: 716 284-8753
Gilles Michel, *CEO*
Jurgen Sardemann, *Ch of Bd*
Manfred Beck, *President*
Tim Wilson, *Corp Secy*
Michael Monberg, *Vice Pres*
▲ **EMP:** 81
SALES (est): 17.4MM **Privately Held**
WEB: www.stollberg.com
SIC: 3399 Powder, metal
HQ: Imerys Metalcasting Germany Gmbh
Duisburger Str. 69-73
Oberhausen 46049
208 850-0500

(G-12836)
INDUSTRIAL SERVICES OF WNY
7221 Niagara Falls Blvd (14304-1715)
Rural Route 7221 Niaga (14304)
PHONE..................................716 799-7788
Georgena Dinieri, *Owner*
EMP: 5
SALES (est): 210K **Privately Held**
SIC: 3599 Machine & other job shop work

(G-12837)
J D CALATO MANUFACTURING CO (PA)
Also Called: Regal Tip
4501 Hyde Park Blvd (14305-1215)
PHONE..................................716 285-3546
Fax: 716 285-2710
Carol Calato, *CEO*
Joseph D Calato, *CEO*
Catherine Calato, *Vice Pres*
EMP: 35 **EST:** 1961
SQ FT: 17,000
SALES (est): 4.1MM **Privately Held**
WEB: www.calato.com
SIC: 3931 Musical instruments; drums, parts & accessories (musical instruments)

(G-12838)
JOHNNIE RYAN CO INC
3084 Niagara St (14303-2030)
PHONE..................................716 282-1606
Fax: 716 282-6737
Paul Janik, *Vice Pres*
Kathy Tedesco, *Office Mgr*
EMP: 15
SQ FT: 10,000
SALES (est): 1.5MM **Privately Held**
WEB: www.johnnieryan.com
SIC: 2086 Soft drinks: packaged in cans, bottles, etc.

(G-12839)
KINTEX INC
Also Called: Niagara Thermo Products
3315 Haseley Dr (14304-1460)
PHONE..................................716 297-0652
Barry Heckman, *Owner*
Frank Yang, *Manager*
EMP: 90
SALES (est): 6.3MM **Privately Held**
SIC: 3443 Heat exchangers, condensers & components

(G-12840)
L A R ELECTRONICS CORP
2733 Niagara St (14303-2027)
PHONE..................................716 285-0555
Lawrence Kutner, *President*
EMP: 7
SQ FT: 3,500
SALES: 150K **Privately Held**
WEB: www.laraudio.com
SIC: 3651 5065 1731 Speaker systems; sound equipment, electronic; sound equipment specialization

(G-12841)
LAFARGE NORTH AMERICA INC
8875 Quarry Rd (14304-1041)
PHONE..................................716 297-3031
Courtland Hess, *Branch Mgr*
EMP: 27
SALES (corp-wide): 23.4B **Privately Held**
SIC: 3241 Cement, hydraulic
HQ: Lafarge North America Inc.
8700 W Bryn Mawr Ave Ll
Chicago IL 60631
703 480-3600

(G-12842)
LIDDELL CORPORATION
4600 Witmer Ind Est 5 (14305-1364)
PHONE..................................716 297-8557
Lon Flick, *President*
EMP: 14
SALES: 1.3MM **Privately Held**
WEB: www.nicel.com
SIC: 2844 Cosmetic preparations

(G-12843)
LIQUID INDUSTRIES INC
7219 New Jersey Ave (14305)
P.O. Box 1862 (14302-1862)
PHONE..................................716 628-2999
Hamish Shaw, *President*
EMP: 6
SALES (est): 724.3K **Privately Held**
SIC: 3589 Car washing machinery

(G-12844)
LOCKHEED MARTIN CORPORATION
2221 Niagara Falls Blvd (14304-5709)
PHONE..................................716 297-1000
Mike Davis, *Safety Mgr*
Donald Kellner, *QC Dir*
Clive A Affleck, *Engineer*
H M Neeson, *Sales/Mktg Dir*
Vincent Chiarenza, *Finance*
EMP: 40
SALES (corp-wide): 46.1B **Publicly Held**
WEB: www.lockheedmartin.com
SIC: 3721 3812 3769 Motorized aircraft; search & navigation equipment; guided missile & space vehicle parts & auxiliary equipment
PA: Lockheed Martin Corporation
6801 Rockledge Dr
Bethesda MD 20817
301 897-6000

(G-12845)
MARIPHARM LABORATORIES
2045 Niagara Falls Blvd (14304-1675)
PHONE..................................716 984-6520
Christopher Dean, *Owner*
EMP: 10
SALES (est): 564.9K **Privately Held**
SIC: 3821 Laboratory apparatus & furniture

(G-12846)
METAL PRODUCTS INTL LLC
7510 Porter Rd Ste 4 (14304-1692)
PHONE..................................716 215-1930
Laurine Stamborski, *Controller*
Thomas Fleckestien,
Kenneth Koedinger,
▲ **EMP:** 5
SALES: 12MM **Privately Held**
WEB: www.metalproducts.com
SIC: 3449 Miscellaneous metalwork

(G-12847)
METRO MATTRESS CORP
2212 Military Rd (14304-1760)
PHONE..................................716 205-2300
Randy Pegan, *Branch Mgr*
EMP: 28
SALES (corp-wide): 38.1MM **Privately Held**
SIC: 2515 5712 5719 Mattresses & bedsprings; beds & accessories; beddings & linens
PA: Metro Mattress Corp.
3545 John Glenn Blvd
Syracuse NY 13209
315 218-1200

(G-12848)
MOOG INC
Also Called: Moog - Isp
6686 Walmore Rd (14304-1638)
PHONE..................................716 731-6300
Fax: 716 731-6329
James Zappa, *Engineer*
Donna Lough, *Accountant*
Jerry Fritz, *Branch Mgr*
Cheryl Gray, *Manager*
Christopher Cummings, *Assistant*
EMP: 100
SALES (corp-wide): 2.5B **Publicly Held**
SIC: 2819 Industrial inorganic chemicals
PA: Moog Inc.
400 Jamison Rd Plant26
Elma NY 14059
716 652-2000

(G-12849)
NATIONAL MAINT CONTG CORP
Also Called: Nmcc
5600 Niagara Falls Blvd (14304-1532)
P.O. Box 258 (14304-0258)
PHONE..................................716 285-1583
Samuel D Lehr, *President*
Linda Lehr, *Office Mgr*
EMP: 54
SALES: 5MM **Privately Held**
SIC: 3499 Welding tips, heat resistant: metal

(G-12850)
NIAGARA SAMPLE BOOK CO INC
1717 Mackenna Ave (14303-1715)
PHONE..................................716 284-6151
Fax: 716 284-7117
Joseph P Pinzotti, *President*
Marsha A Pinzotti, *Vice Pres*
Mary B Pinzotti, *Treasurer*
Marcella Pinzotti, *Admin Sec*
EMP: 15 **EST:** 1945
SQ FT: 20,000
SALES (est): 1.3MM **Privately Held**
WEB: www.niagarasample.com
SIC: 2782 2759 Sample books; commercial printing

(G-12851)
NORTH AMERICAN HOGANAS INC
5950 Packard Rd (14304-1584)
P.O. Box 310 (14304-0310)
PHONE..................................716 285-3451
Avinash Gore, *President*
Terry Heinrich, *Corp Secy*
Nagarjuna Nandivada, *Vice Pres*
Patricia Burkstone, *Purchasing*
Eric Reynolds, *Accountant*
◆ **EMP:** 41
SALES (est): 15.6MM
SALES (corp-wide): 869.5MM **Privately Held**
SIC: 2819 Iron (ferric/ferrous) compounds or salts
HQ: North American Hoganas Holdings, Inc.
111 Hoganas Way
Hollsopple PA 15935
814 479-2551

(G-12852)
NORTHEAST WIRE AND CABLE CO
8635 Packard Rd (14304-5612)
P.O. Box 503, Grand Island (14072-0503)
PHONE..................................716 297-8483
Fax: 716 297-1412
Gregory Barker, *President*
EMP: 5
SQ FT: 15,000
SALES (est): 750.4K **Privately Held**
WEB: www.northeastwire.com
SIC: 3315 Cable, steel: insulated or armored

(G-12853)
NORTHKNIGHT LOGISTICS INC
7724 Buffalo Ave (14304-4134)
PHONE..................................716 283-3090
John Rendle, *CEO*
◆ **EMP:** 15 **EST:** 2007
SQ FT: 14,000
SALES (est): 2MM **Privately Held**
SIC: 3429 Builders' hardware

(G-12854)
NUTTALL GEAR L L C (HQ)
Also Called: Delroyd Worm Gear
2221 Niagara Falls Blvd # 17 (14304-5710)
PHONE..................................716 298-4100
Fax: 716 298-4101
Michael Hurt, *CEO*
Scott Jimbroni, *General Mgr*
Greg Klein, *Project Mgr*
Jeannine Jackson, *Purch Mgr*
Denis Hadden, *QC Mgr*
▲ **EMP:** 62
SQ FT: 107,000
SALES (est): 15.3MM
SALES (corp-wide): 746.6MM **Publicly Held**
WEB: www.nuttallgear.com
SIC: 3566 Speed changers, drives & gears
PA: Altra Industrial Motion Corp.
300 Granite St Ste 201
Braintree MA 02184
781 917-0600

(G-12855)
OCCIDENTAL CHEMICAL CORP
4700 Buffalo Ave (14304-3821)
P.O. Box 344 (14302-0344)
PHONE..................................716 278-7795
Fax: 716 278-7880
Joseph G Dewey, *Human Res Mgr*

Niagara Falls - Niagara County (G-12856) GEOGRAPHIC SECTION

Tom Feeney, *Branch Mgr*
James Czapla, *Technology*
EMP: 35
SALES (corp-wide): 12.7B **Publicly Held**
WEB: www.oxychem.com
SIC: 2812 Alkalies & chlorine
HQ: Occidental Chemical Corporation
  5005 Lyndon B Johnson Fwy # 2200
  Dallas TX 75244
  972 404-3800

(G-12856)
OCCIDENTAL CHEMICAL CORP
56 Street & Energy Blvd (14302)
P.O. Box 344 (14302-0344)
PHONE..................................716 278-7794
Herb Jones, *General Mgr*
EMP: 200
SALES (corp-wide): 12.7B **Publicly Held**
SIC: 2812 2874 Alkalies & chlorine; phosphatic fertilizers
HQ: Occidental Chemical Corporation
  5005 Lyndon B Johnson Fwy # 2200
  Dallas TX 75244
  972 404-3800

(G-12857)
OLIN CHLOR ALKALI LOGISTICS
Also Called: Chlor Alkali Products & Vinyls
2400 Buffalo Ave (14303-1959)
P.O. Box 748 (14302-0748)
PHONE..................................716 278-6411
Fax: 716 278-6495
Brian Vain, *COO*
Pamela Harvey, *Purchasing*
J Murphy, *Purchasing*
Mike Bentley, *Human Res Dir*
Tanner Deaton, *Human Res Mgr*
EMP: 150
SALES (corp-wide): 2.8B **Publicly Held**
WEB: www.olin.com
SIC: 2812 2842 Alkalies & chlorine; specialty cleaning, polishes & sanitation goods
HQ: Olin Chlor Alkali Logistics Inc
  490 Stuart Rd Ne
  Cleveland TN 37312
  423 336-4850

(G-12858)
OXAIR LTD
8320 Quarry Rd (14304-1068)
P.O. Box 4039 (14304-8039)
PHONE..................................716 298-8288
Fax: 716 298-8889
Flavio Zeni, *President*
▼ **EMP:** 5
SQ FT: 10,000
SALES (est): 550K **Privately Held**
WEB: www.oxair.com
SIC: 2813 Oxygen, compressed or liquefied

(G-12859)
PENETRADAR CORPORATION
2509 Niagara Falls Blvd (14304-4518)
PHONE..................................716 731-2629
Fax: 716 731-5040
Anthony J Alongi, *President*
Rick Geltz, *Purch Agent*
Carol Eames, *CIO*
EMP: 15
SQ FT: 15,000
SALES (est): 1.4MM **Privately Held**
WEB: www.penetradar.com
SIC: 3812 Radar systems & equipment

(G-12860)
PLIOTRON COMPANY AMERICA LLC
4650 Witmer Indus Est (14305-1360)
PHONE..................................716 298-4457
Fax: 716 298-4459
Robert Leiathton, *Plant Mgr*
Richard Rohm, *Manager*
Albert E Matthews,
Linda Matthews,
EMP: 5 **EST:** 1962
SQ FT: 8,125
SALES (est): 330K **Privately Held**
WEB: www.pliotron.com
SIC: 3564 Filters, air: furnaces, air conditioning equipment, etc.

(G-12861)
PRAXAIR INC
4501 Royal Ave (14303-2121)
PHONE..................................716 286-4600
Fax: 716 286-4619
Elizabeth Casciani, *Safety Mgr*
Brian McKie, *Branch Mgr*
EMP: 50
SALES (corp-wide): 10.7B **Publicly Held**
SIC: 2813 Industrial gases
PA: Praxair, Inc.
  39 Old Ridgebury Rd
  Danbury CT 06810
  203 837-2000

(G-12862)
PRECIOUS PLATE INC
2124 Liberty Dr (14303-3799)
PHONE..................................716 283-0690
Fax: 716 283-9185
David R Hurst, *President*
William Copping, *Vice Pres*
Scott Law, *Vice Pres*
David Miller, *Vice Pres*
Ken Russell, *Safety Mgr*
▲ **EMP:** 75
SQ FT: 65,000
SALES (est): 13.9MM **Privately Held**
SIC: 3471 Plating & polishing

(G-12863)
PRECISION ELCTRO MNRL PMCO INC
150 Portage Rd (14303-1535)
P.O. Box 8 (14302-0008)
PHONE..................................716 284-2484
Fax: 716 284-2483
Abdul Labi, *President*
Manny Trinidad, *Office Mgr*
EMP: 25
SQ FT: 40,000
SALES (est): 2MM **Privately Held**
WEB: www.pemco-niagara.com
SIC: 2819 3291 1446 Silica compounds; abrasive products; industrial sand

(G-12864)
PRECISION PROCESS INC (PA)
2111 Liberty Dr (14304-3744)
PHONE..................................,716 731-1587
Fax: 716 236-7802
David Hurst, *CEO*
Bill Copping, *Vice Pres*
Jeannine Jackson, *Purchasing*
Joe Hoyt, *VP Finance*
John Bondi, *Sales Mgr*
▲ **EMP:** 83
SQ FT: 65,000
SALES (est): 15.8MM **Privately Held**
WEB: www.precisionprocess.com
SIC: 3559 Electroplating machinery & equipment

(G-12865)
QUANTUM COLOR INC
Also Called: Niagara Printing
8742 Buffalo Ave (14304-4342)
PHONE..................................716 283-8700
Fax: 716 283-3527
Darry Finn, *President*
David Finn, *Vice Pres*
Jack Birkman, *Accounts Exec*
Bob Edwards, *Accounts Exec*
Jonathan Sanford, *Sales Staff*
EMP: 40
SQ FT: 41,000
SALES (est): 4.7MM **Privately Held**
SIC: 2752 Periodicals, lithographed

(G-12866)
RANNEY PRECISION
Also Called: Ranney Precision Machining
6421 Wendt Dr (14304-1100)
PHONE..................................716 731-6418
Fax: 716 731-6521
David Ranney, *Owner*
Joanne Ranney, *Co-Owner*
EMP: 17
SQ FT: 10,000
SALES (est): 1.3MM **Privately Held**
WEB: www.ranneyprecision.com
SIC: 3451 Screw machine products

(G-12867)
RELIANCE FLUID TECH LLC
3943 Buffalo Ave (14303-2136)
PHONE..................................716 332-0988
John Garguiolo,
Ryan Sanders, *Clerk*
EMP: 40
SALES (est): 875.3K **Privately Held**
SIC: 2899 Corrosion preventive lubricant

(G-12868)
RT MACHINED SPECIALTIES
2221 Niagara Falls Blvd (14304-5709)
P.O. Box 281, Sanborn (14132-0281)
PHONE..................................716 731-2055
Fax: 716 731-2055
Rebecca Christie, *President*
Jon Christie, *Manager*
EMP: 5
SALES: 300K **Privately Held**
SIC: 3599 Machine shop, jobbing & repair

(G-12869)
RUS INDUSTRIES INC
3255 Lockport Rd (14305-2398)
PHONE..................................716 284-7828
Fax: 716 284-0514
Alice G Carlson, *Ch of Bd*
James A Ryding, *Vice Pres*
Greg Robinson, *VP Sales*
Erik Davis, *Marketing Mgr*
Eric Carlson, *Manager*
▲ **EMP:** 32
SQ FT: 29,000
SALES (est): 4.8MM **Privately Held**
WEB: www.rusindustries.com
SIC: 3441 3661 Fabricated structural metal; communication headgear, telephone

(G-12870)
SAINT GOBAIN GRAINS & POWDERS
6600 Walmore Rd (14304-1638)
PHONE..................................716 731-8200
Tom Vincent, *Principal*
Annie Marcantonio, *Administration*
▲ **EMP:** 1526
SALES (est): 102.5MM
SALES (corp-wide): 189MM **Privately Held**
SIC: 3221 3269 2891 Glass containers; food containers, glass; bottles for packing, bottling & canning: glass; vials, glass; laboratory & industrial pottery; chemical porcelain; adhesives; adhesives, plastic; cement, except linoleum & tile; epoxy adhesives
HQ: Saint-Gobain Corporation
  20 Moores Rd
  Malvern PA 19355
  610 893-6000

(G-12871)
SAINT-GBAIN ADVNCED CRMICS LLC (HQ)
Also Called: Structural Ceramics Division
23 Acheson Dr (14305-1555)
PHONE..................................716 278-6066
Ron Lambright, *CEO*
Jean Louis Beffa, *Ch of Bd*
Curtis Schmit, *General Mgr*
Michael J Fricano, *Controller*
Donald Cafarella, *Sales Dir*
▲ **EMP:** 150
SQ FT: 1,064
SALES (est): 29.9MM
SALES (corp-wide): 207.6MM **Privately Held**
WEB: www.hexoloy.com
SIC: 3269 Laboratory & industrial pottery
PA: Compagnie De Saint Gobain
  18 Avenue D Alsace
  Paris La Defense Cedex 92096
  147 623-000

(G-12872)
SAINT-GOBAIN DYNAMICS INC
Also Called: Structural Ceramics Group
23 Acheson Dr (14303-1555)
PHONE..................................716 278-6007
Curtis M Schmit, *President*
EMP: 10
SALES (est): 1.1MM **Privately Held**
SIC: 3297 Nonclay refractories

(G-12873)
SAINT-GOBAIN STRL CERAMICS
23 Acheson Dr (14301-1555)
PHONE..................................716 278-6233
John Crowe, *President*
Lawrence Banach, *President*
John Bevilacqua, *Manager*
◆ **EMP:** 2518
SALES (est): 187.2MM
SALES (corp-wide): 189MM **Privately Held**
SIC: 3255 Brick, clay refractory
HQ: Saint-Gobain Corporation
  20 Moores Rd
  Malvern PA 19355
  610 893-6000

(G-12874)
SATURN SALES INC
4500 Witmer Indstrl 202 (14305-1386)
PHONE..................................519 658-5125
Zafar Syed, *President*
EMP: 20
SALES (est): 1.4MM
SALES (corp-wide): 6.3MM **Privately Held**
SIC: 2522 Office furniture, except wood
PA: Saturn Sales Inc
  130 Guelph Ave
  Cambridge ON N3C 1
  519 658-6263

(G-12875)
SENTRY METAL BLAST INC
Also Called: Sentry Metal Services
401 47th St (14304-2101)
P.O. Box 160, Grand Island (14072-0160)
PHONE..................................716 285-5241
Fax: 716 692-6245
Gary D Verost, *President*
James Verost, *Vice Pres*
Mark Verost, *Vice Pres*
Karen Schiro, *Manager*
EMP: 30
SQ FT: 47,000
SALES (est): 7.3MM **Privately Held**
WEB: www.sentrymetal.com
SIC: 3441 3479 Fabricated structural metal; coating of metals & formed products

(G-12876)
SHIPMAN PRINTING INDS INC
Also Called: Shipman Print Solutions
2424 Niagara Falls Blvd (14304-4562)
P.O. Box 357 (14304-0357)
PHONE..................................716 504-7700
Fax: 716 504-7710
Gary Blum, *Ch of Bd*
Richard Faiola, *Exec VP*
Randy Duncan, *Vice Pres*
Michael Fiore, *Vice Pres*
Diane Donner, *Accounts Mgr*
EMP: 34 **EST:** 1905
SQ FT: 20,000
SALES (est): 6.8MM **Privately Held**
WEB: www.shipmanprint.com
SIC: 2752 2789 2759 Commercial printing, offset; bookbinding & related work; envelopes: printing

(G-12877)
SILIPOS HOLDING LLC
7049 Williams Rd (14304-3731)
PHONE..................................716 283-0700
Richard Margolis, *President*
Ian Shaw, *Director*
◆ **EMP:** 40
SQ FT: 35,000
SALES (est): 2.5MM **Privately Held**
SIC: 3842 Surgical appliances & supplies

(G-12878)
STEPHENSON CUSTOM CASE COMPANY
Also Called: Portequip Work Stations
1623 Military Rd (14304-1745)
PHONE..................................905 542-8762
John Stephenson, *Owner*
EMP: 30
SALES: 950K **Privately Held**
SIC: 3949 Sporting & athletic goods

▲ = Import ▼=Export
◆ =Import/Export

GEOGRAPHIC SECTION

(G-12879)
SWISSMAR INC
6391 Walmore Rd (14304-1613)
PHONE...................905 764-1121
Daniel Oehy, *President*
George Hobson, *VP Finance*
Erik Reid, *Director*
EMP: 8 **EST:** 1990
SQ FT: 15,000
SALES (est): 689.3K **Privately Held**
SIC: 3262 5719 China cookware; housewares

(G-12880)
TAM CERAMICS GROUP OF NY LLC
4511 Hyde Park Blvd (14305-1298)
PHONE...................716 278-9400
George Bilkey, *President*
Mike Chu, *
EMP: 62
SQ FT: 3,750
SALES: 30MM **Privately Held**
SIC: 3399 Powder, metal

(G-12881)
TAM CERAMICS LLC
4511 Hyde Park Blvd (14305-1298)
PHONE...................716 278-9480
Fax: 716 278-9571
Chris Merry, *Controller*
George H Bilkey IV, *Mng Member*
George Bilkey, *Technology*
Shamus Crean, *Technology*
John Hess, *Technology*
▲ **EMP:** 52
SQ FT: 373,593
SALES (est): 21.8MM **Privately Held**
SIC: 2899 Chemical preparations
PA: All American Holdings, Llc
3714 W End Ave
Nashville TN 37205
615 969-3411

(G-12882)
TECMOTIV (USA) INC
1500 James Ave (14305-1222)
PHONE...................905 669-5911
Arthur Hayden, *President*
Lorna Earrett, *Vice Pres*
Gary Sheedy, *Vice Pres*
Sally L Yan, *CFO*
◆ **EMP:** 31
SQ FT: 27,000
SALES: 9MM
SALES (corp-wide): 2.6MM **Privately Held**
WEB: www.tecmotiv.com
SIC: 3795 Tanks & tank components
PA: Tecmotiv Corporation
131 Saramia Cres 2nd Fl
Concord ON L4K 4
905 669-5911

(G-12883)
TORONTO METAL SPINNING AND LTG
4500 Witmer Indus Ests (14305-1386)
PHONE...................905 793-1174
EMP: 32
SALES (est): 80.8K **Privately Held**
SIC: 3469 Spinning metal for the trade

(G-12884)
TRANSCEDAR INDUSTRIES LTD
Also Called: Motorad of America
6292 Walmore Rd (14304-5703)
PHONE...................716 731-6442
Fax: 716 731-6436
Kelly Runkle, *Branch Mgr*
Aaron Musgrave, *Technician*
EMP: 7
SALES (corp-wide): 3.1MM **Privately Held**
SIC: 3714 Air conditioner parts, motor vehicle
PA: Transcedar Industries Ltd
120 Silver Star Blvd Unit A
Scarborough ON M1V 3

(G-12885)
TULIP MOLDED PLASTICS CORP
Also Called: Niagara Falls Plant
3125 Highland Ave (14305-2051)
PHONE...................716 282-1261
Fax: 716 285-6075
S Shoecraft, *Research*
David Delange, *Personnel*
G Moran, *Personnel*
John Signore, *Manager*
EMP: 80
SALES (corp-wide): 35.2MM **Privately Held**
WEB: www.tulipcorp.com
SIC: 3089 Plastic processing
HQ: Tulip Molded Plastics Corporation
714 E Keefe Ave
Milwaukee WI 53212
414 963-3120

(G-12886)
UNIFRAX CORPORATION
2351 Whirlpool St (14305-2413)
PHONE...................716 278-3800
Fax: 716 278-3900
Mark Travers, *COO*
Matt W Colbert, *Senior VP*
Paul Boymel, *Vice Pres*
Bruce Zoitos, *Facilities Mgr*
Brian Mellett, *Engineer*
EMP: 41
SALES (est): 5.8MM **Privately Held**
SIC: 3296 Mineral wool insulation products

(G-12887)
US DRIVES INC
2221 Niagara Falls Blvd # 41 (14304-5711)
P.O. Box 281 (14304-0281)
PHONE...................716 731-1606
Fax: 716 731-1524
Kader Laroussi, *President*
Dick Torbenson, *President*
James S Grisante, *Vice Pres*
Paul Wizner, *VP Prdtn*
Theodore G Nuding, *VP Finance*
EMP: 60
SQ FT: 70,000
SALES (est): 10.5MM **Privately Held**
WEB: www.usdrivesinc.com
SIC: 3625 Motor controls, electric

(G-12888)
VIOLA CABINET CORPORATION
Also Called: Viola Construction
4205 Hyde Park Blvd (14305-1709)
PHONE...................716 284-6327
Fax: 716 284-6336
Pat Viola, *President*
EMP: 6
SQ FT: 3,500
SALES: 1MM **Privately Held**
SIC: 2434 Wood kitchen cabinets

(G-12889)
VISHAY THIN FILM LLC
2160 Liberty Dr (14304-3727)
PHONE...................716 283-4025
Fax: 716 283-3205
Dr Felix Zandman, *President*
Justin Gefell, *Production*
Rachel Corulli, *Purch Mgr*
Rachel Bricca, *Purchasing*
Robert A Freece, *Treasurer*
▲ **EMP:** 154
SQ FT: 33,000
SALES (est): 24.7MM
SALES (corp-wide): 2.3B **Publicly Held**
SIC: 3676 3861 3577 Electronic resistors; photographic equipment & supplies; computer peripheral equipment
HQ: Dale Vishay Electronics Llc
1122 23rd St
Columbus NE 68601
605 665-9301

(G-12890)
WASHINGTOM MILLS ELEC MNRLS (HQ)
1801 Buffalo Ave (14303-1528)
P.O. Box 423 (14302-0423)
PHONE...................716 278-6600
Fax: 716 278-6650
Don McLeod, *President*
Donald McLeod, *Vice Pres*
Kirk Hartog, *Safety Mgr*
Larry Brown, *Maint Spvr*
Gary Asbach, *Purch Mgr*
◆ **EMP:** 100
SALES (est): 36.5MM
SALES (corp-wide): 170.9MM **Privately Held**
WEB: www.washingtonmills.com
SIC: 3291 2819 Abrasive grains; industrial inorganic chemicals
PA: Washington Mills Group, Inc.
20 N Main St
North Grafton MA 01536
508 839-6511

(G-12891)
YORKVILLE SOUND INC
4625 Witmer Indus Est (14305-1390)
PHONE...................716 297-2920
Fax: 716 297-3689
Steven Long, *Owner*
Jack Long, *Founder*
Jay Hohmann, *Opers Staff*
Terry Sherwood, *Controller*
Joe Colantonio, *Sales Mgr*
▲ **EMP:** 7
SALES (est): 1.3MM **Privately Held**
SIC: 3651 Audio electronic systems

Nichols
Tioga County

(G-12892)
WOODS MACHINE AND TOOL LLC
150 Howell St (13812-2146)
PHONE...................607 699-3253
Fax: 607 699-3725
Ricky E Woods,
Michael Woods,
Richard Woods,
EMP: 16
SQ FT: 2,400
SALES (est): 1.4MM **Privately Held**
SIC: 3599 Machine shop, jobbing & repair

Niskayuna
Schenectady County

(G-12893)
ADC ACQUISITION COMPANY
Also Called: Automated Dynamics
2 Commerce Park Rd (12309-3545)
PHONE...................518 377-6471
Fax: 518 377-5628
Robert Langone, *President*
Hauber David, *Vice Pres*
Ralph Marcario, *Vice Pres*
Becker Robert, *Vice Pres*
Raymond R Johnston, *Treasurer*
▼ **EMP:** 35
SQ FT: 30,000
SALES: 5.7MM **Privately Held**
WEB: www.automateddynamics.com
SIC: 3083 Thermoplastic laminates: rods, tubes, plates & sheet

(G-12894)
GE GLOBAL RESEARCH ✪
1 Research Cir (12309-1027)
PHONE...................518 387-5000
George Dalakos, *Managing Dir*
Victor R Abate, *Senior VP*
Beth Dorn, *Project Mgr*
Chris Allen, *Facilities Mgr*
Xianglei Chen, *Research*
EMP: 5 **EST:** 2016
SALES (est): 204.6K
SALES (corp-wide): 117.3B **Publicly Held**
SIC: 3511 8742 Turbines & turbine generator sets; industrial consultant
PA: General Electric Company
41 Farnsworth St
Boston MA 02210
617 443-3000

(G-12895)
GENERAL ELECTRIC COMPANY
2690 Balltown Rd Bldg 600 (12309-1004)
PHONE...................518 385-7620
Doug Wood, *Branch Mgr*
Phil Tolbert, *Manager*
Steve Fo, *CIO*
EMP: 50
SALES (corp-wide): 117.3B **Publicly Held**
SIC: 3724 3511 3612 Aircraft engines & engine parts; research & development of aircraft engines & parts; steam turbines; gas turbines, mechanical drive; autotransformers, electric (power transformers)
PA: General Electric Company
41 Farnsworth St
Boston MA 02210
617 443-3000

(G-12896)
SILICON IMAGING INC
25 Covington Ct (12309-1323)
PHONE...................518 374-3367
ARI Presler, *President*
Tom Gielow, *Vice Pres*
Mark Kolvites, *Vice Pres*
Steve Nordhauser, *Vice Pres*
Allison Russell, *Manager*
EMP: 8
SQ FT: 5,000
SALES (est): 982.6K **Privately Held**
WEB: www.siliconimaging.com
SIC: 3663 Cameras, television

Norfolk
St. Lawrence County

(G-12897)
APC PAPER COMPANY INC
100 Remington Ave (13667-4136)
P.O. Box 756 (13667-0756)
PHONE...................315 384-4225
Kyle Dansereau, *Safety Dir*
Al Ames, *Manager*
EMP: 55
SALES (corp-wide): 13.1MM **Privately Held**
WEB: www.apcpaper.com
SIC: 2621 4953 2674 2611 Kraft paper; refuse systems; bags: uncoated paper & multiwall; pulp mills
PA: Apc Paper Company, Inc.
130 Sullivan St
Claremont NH 03743
603 542-0411

(G-12898)
CRANESVILLE BLOCK CO INC
Also Called: Cranesville Concrete
8405 State Highway 56 (13667-4221)
PHONE...................315 384-4000
Fax: 315 384-3419
Randy Braul, *Manager*
EMP: 6
SALES (corp-wide): 41.2MM **Privately Held**
SIC: 3273 5211 Ready-mixed concrete; masonry materials & supplies
PA: Cranesville Block Co., Inc.
1250 Riverfront Ctr
Amsterdam NY 12010
518 684-6000

(G-12899)
LENCORE ACOUSTICS CORP
1 S Main St (13667-3111)
P.O. Box 616 (13667-0616)
PHONE...................315 384-9114
Fax: 315 384-4974
Brian Leonard, *Branch Mgr*
EMP: 10
SALES (corp-wide): 5.9MM **Privately Held**
WEB: www.lencore.com
SIC: 3296 Acoustical board & tile, mineral wool
PA: Lencore Acoustics Corp.
1 Crossways Park Dr W
Woodbury NY 11797
516 682-9292

(G-12900)
NORTHERN MACHINING INC
2a N Main St (13667-4154)
PHONE...................315 384-3189
Fax: 315 384-4164
Ted Ashley, *President*

North Babylon - Suffolk County (G-12901)

Kathie Ashley, *Vice Pres*
Marie Delosh, *Admin Sec*
EMP: 10
SQ FT: 7,000
SALES: 1.2MM **Privately Held**
WEB: www.northernmachininginc.com
SIC: 3599 Machine shop, jobbing & repair

North Babylon
Suffolk County

(G-12901)
GO BLUE TECHNOLOGIES LTD
325 August Rd (11703-1014)
PHONE..................................631 404-6285
Carlo Drago, *CEO*
EMP: 1
SALES: 1MM **Privately Held**
SIC: 3624 3842 Carbon & graphite products; gas masks

(G-12902)
PMB PRECISION PRODUCTS INC
Also Called: Spartan Instruments
725 Mount Ave (11703)
PHONE..................................631 491-6753
Michael Belesis, *President*
Jan Craw, *Principal*
Richard Jackson, *Sales Mgr*
EMP: 16
SALES (est): 2.8MM **Privately Held**
SIC: 3399 Metal fasteners

(G-12903)
QUALITY FUEL 1 CORPORATION
1235 Deer Park Ave (11703-3112)
PHONE..................................631 392-4090
EMP: 6
SALES (est): 664.8K **Privately Held**
SIC: 2869 Fuels

North Baldwin
Nassau County

(G-12904)
DURA SPEC INC
Also Called: Jamaica Electroplating
1239 Village Ct (11510-1138)
PHONE..................................718 526-3053
Fax: 718 657-8867
C Samuel Williams, *President*
Violet Williams, *Vice Pres*
EMP: 18
SQ FT: 5,000
SALES (est): 1.5MM **Privately Held**
SIC: 3471 Electroplating of metals or formed products

(G-12905)
GENESIS MACHINING CORP
725 Brooklyn Ave (11510-2708)
PHONE..................................516 377-1197
Michael A Chin, *President*
EMP: 12
SQ FT: 4,000
SALES (est): 1.7MM **Privately Held**
SIC: 3599 Machine & other job shop work

(G-12906)
GUOSA LIFE SCIENCES INC
846 Center Dr (11510-1104)
PHONE..................................516 481-1540
Charles Oviawe, *Principal*
EMP: 12 **EST:** 2012
SALES (est): 920K **Privately Held**
SIC: 2834 8999 Solutions, pharmaceutical; tablets, pharmaceutical; scientific consulting

(G-12907)
HUBRAY INC
Also Called: Stu-Art Supplies
2045 Grand Ave (11510-2915)
PHONE..................................800 645-2855
Fax: 516 377-3512
Lisa Hubley, *President*
Andrew Ray, *Vice Pres*
EMP: 12
SQ FT: 10,000
SALES: 1MM **Privately Held**
WEB: www.stu-artsupplies.com
SIC: 2675 2499 5961 Panels, cardboard, die-cut: made from purchased materials; picture & mirror frames, wood; mail order house

(G-12908)
SANDY DUFTLER DESIGNS LTD
775 Brooklyn Ave Ste 105 (11510-2948)
PHONE..................................516 379-3084
Fax: 516 379-4156
Irwin Duftler, *CEO*
Sandra Duftler, *Ch of Bd*
Gregg Duftler, *President*
EMP: 12
SALES (est): 1.1MM **Privately Held**
SIC: 2387 Apparel belts

(G-12909)
SPLIT SYSTEMS CORP (PA)
Also Called: Johnson Contrls Authorized Dlr
1593 Grand Ave (11510-1849)
PHONE..................................516 223-5511
Charles Solon, *President*
Mike Solon, *Vice Pres*
EMP: 1
SALES (est): 1.8MM **Privately Held**
SIC: 3585 5075 Air conditioning equipment, complete; refrigeration equipment, complete; warm air heating & air conditioning

(G-12910)
SWIRL BLISS LLC
1777 Grand Ave (11510-2429)
PHONE..................................516 867-9475
Jeanette Reed,
EMP: 5
SALES (est): 311.5K **Privately Held**
SIC: 2024 Yogurt desserts, frozen

(G-12911)
V C N GROUP LTD INC
1 Clifton St (11510-2114)
PHONE..................................516 223-4812
Florence Abate, *President*
Vincent Abate, *Vice Pres*
Anthony Abate, *Admin Sec*
EMP: 5
SQ FT: 500
SALES (est): 502.9K **Privately Held**
SIC: 2752 Advertising posters, lithographed

(G-12912)
VORTEX VENTURES INC
857 Newton Ave (11510-2826)
PHONE..................................516 946-8345
Kevin Walters, *President*
EMP: 5
SALES (est): 193.4K **Privately Held**
SIC: 7372 7389 Publishers' computer software;

(G-12913)
W & B MAZZA & SONS INC
Also Called: Mazza Co, The
2145 Marion Pl (11510-2921)
PHONE..................................516 379-4130
Fax: 516 379-4152
William Mazza, *President*
William Mazza Jr, *Treasurer*
Steven Mazza, *VP Mktg*
Jeffrey Mazza, *Admin Sec*
EMP: 28
SQ FT: 8,000
SALES (est): 3MM **Privately Held**
WEB: www.mazzajewelry.com
SIC: 3911 Jewelry, precious metal; rings, finger: precious metal; pins (jewelry), precious metal; earrings, precious metal

North Bellmore
Nassau County

(G-12914)
21ST CENTURY FINISHES INC
1895 Newbridge Rd (11710-2218)
P.O. Box 471, Bellmore (11710-0471)
PHONE..................................516 221-7000
Al Doerbecker, *President*
EMP: 15

SALES (est): 1.5MM **Privately Held**
SIC: 3471 Finishing, metals or formed products

(G-12915)
CAPITOL RESTORATION CORP
2473 Belmond Ave (11710-1205)
PHONE..................................516 783-1425
Seeme Rizvi, *President*
EMP: 6
SALES (est): 627.6K **Privately Held**
SIC: 3297 1771 1521 Brick refractories; concrete repair; new construction, single-family houses

(G-12916)
CHERRY HOLDING LTD
Also Called: Cherry Metal Works
1536 Broad St (11710-2146)
PHONE..................................516 679-3748
Michale Kersch, *President*
EMP: 5
SALES (est): 574.2K **Privately Held**
SIC: 3444 Sheet metalwork

(G-12917)
COMPUMATIC TIME RECORDERS INC
1518 Bellmore Ave (11710-5506)
PHONE..................................718 531-5749
Harvey Kipnes, *Vice Pres*
◆ **EMP:** 6
SALES (est): 540K **Privately Held**
WEB: www.compumatictime.com
SIC: 3873 5087 Clocks, except time-clocks; service establishment equipment

(G-12918)
COSTANZA READY MIX INC
1345 Newbridge Rd (11710-1629)
PHONE..................................516 334-7788
Frank Costanza, *Principal*
EMP: 6
SALES (est): 545.7K **Privately Held**
SIC: 3273 Ready-mixed concrete

(G-12919)
CUPCAKE CONTESSAS CORPORATION
1242 Julia Ln (11710-1925)
PHONE..................................516 307-1222
Laura Andreacchi, *Chairman*
EMP: 7
SALES (est): 457.8K **Privately Held**
SIC: 2051 Cakes, bakery: except frozen

(G-12920)
CUSTOM DISPLAY MANUFACTURE
1686 Logan St (11710-2528)
PHONE..................................516 783-6491
Paul Kassbaum, *President*
EMP: 5
SQ FT: 8,000
SALES (est): 440K **Privately Held**
SIC: 2511 3993 Chairs, household, except upholstered: wood; signs & advertising specialties

(G-12921)
GEORGE BASCH CO INC
1554 Peapond Rd (11710-2925)
P.O. Box 188, Freeport (11520-0188)
PHONE..................................516 378-8100
Fax: 516 378-8140
Laurie Basch-Levy, *President*
Mildred Basch, *Treasurer*
Rhonda Ax, *Admin Sec*
EMP: 10 **EST:** 1929
SQ FT: 6,800
SALES (est): 1MM **Privately Held**
WEB: www.nevrdull.com
SIC: 2842 Cleaning or polishing preparations

(G-12922)
KP INDUSTRIES INC
Also Called: K P Signs
2481 Charles Ct Ste 1 (11710-2761)
P.O. Box 1000, Bethpage (11714-0019)
PHONE..................................516 679-3161
Fax: 516 679-3668
Karen A Puchacz, *President*
Dee Smith, *Admin Sec*
EMP: 11

SQ FT: 3,600
SALES (est): 1.9MM **Privately Held**
SIC: 3993 Signs & advertising specialties

(G-12923)
TOWER INSULATING GLASS LLC
2485 Charles Ct (11710-2733)
PHONE..................................516 887-3300
Fax: 516 887-3323
Barry Litt, *President*
EMP: 22
SQ FT: 12,000
SALES (est): 3.7MM **Privately Held**
SIC: 3211 Insulating glass, sealed units

North Chili
Monroe County

(G-12924)
ALBERT GATES INC
3434 Union St (14514-9731)
PHONE..................................585 594-9401
Fax: 585 594-4305
Andrew J Laniak, *Ch of Bd*
Robert J Brinkman, *President*
Dan Ferries, *General Mgr*
James Adams, *Vice Pres*
Denise Sarkis, *QC Mgr*
EMP: 75
SQ FT: 26,000
SALES (est): 24.1MM **Privately Held**
WEB: www.gatesalbert.com
SIC: 3451 Screw machine products

(G-12925)
P TOOL & DIE CO INC
3535 Union St (14514-9709)
P.O. Box 369 (14514-0369)
PHONE..................................585 889-1340
Fax: 585 889-4636
Michael J Sucese, *President*
Pam McCormick, *Office Mgr*
James Allen, *Manager*
Paul Bradler, *Manager*
EMP: 22
SQ FT: 18,000
SALES (est): 3.6MM **Privately Held**
SIC: 3544 Special dies, tools, jigs & fixtures

North Collins
Erie County

(G-12926)
AMERICAN WIRE TIE INC (PA)
2073 Franklin St (14111-9636)
P.O. Box 696 (14111-0696)
PHONE..................................716 337-2412
Fax: 716 337-3728
James W Smith, *President*
Ronald Lehnortt, *Sales Staff*
Amelia Jarzynski, *Sales Associate*
Gregory C Mumbach, *Admin Sec*
◆ **EMP:** 30
SQ FT: 54,000
SALES (est): 15.3MM **Privately Held**
WEB: www.americanwiretie.com
SIC: 3599 3496 3315 2631 Ties, form: metal; miscellaneous fabricated wire products; steel wire & related products; paperboard mills

(G-12927)
CRESCENT MARKETING INC (PA)
Also Called: Crescent Manufacturing
10285 Eagle Dr (14111)
P.O. Box 1500 (14111-1500)
PHONE..................................716 337-0145
Fax: 716 337-0146
Richard Frazer Jr, *President*
Tom Laski, *COO*
Paul Mosher, *Safety Dir*
Rick Taber, *Plant Mgr*
Charlene Mehnert, *Production*
▲ **EMP:** 123
SQ FT: 110,000

GEOGRAPHIC SECTION

North Syracuse - Onondaga County (G-12949)

SALES (est): 16.7MM **Privately Held**
SIC: **2842** Specialty cleaning, polishes & sanitation goods; specialty cleaning preparations; polishing preparations & related products

(G-12928)
E & D SPECIALTY STANDS INC
2081 Franklin St (14111-9636)
P.O. Box 700 (14111-0700)
PHONE..................................716 337-0161
Fax: 716 337-2903
David A Metzger, *President*
Dean Metzger, *Treasurer*
Charlene Heppel, *Accountant*
Dee Pelz, *Human Res Dir*
Mark Caroll, *Technology*
EMP: 50 EST: 1956
SQ FT: 85,000
SALES (est): 9.8MM **Privately Held**
WEB: www.edstands.com
SIC: **2531** Bleacher seating, portable

(G-12929)
NITRO MANUFACTURING LLC
440 Shirley Rd (14111)
PHONE..................................716 646-9900
Christine Frascella, *Mng Member*
Tim Frascella,
William Frascella,
Dave Kota,
EMP: 5
SALES (est): 576.8K **Privately Held**
SIC: **3599** Machine & other job shop work

(G-12930)
NITRO WHEELS INC
4440 Shirley Rd (14111-9783)
PHONE..................................716 337-0709
Louis Frascella, *Principal*
EMP: 10 EST: 2012
SALES (est): 1MM **Privately Held**
SIC: **3312** Wheels, locomotive & car: iron & steel

(G-12931)
RENALDOS SALES AND SERVICE CTR
1770 Milestrip Rd (14111-9753)
P.O. Box 820 (14111-0820)
PHONE..................................716 337-3760
James V Renaldo, *President*
Joan E Renaldo, *Vice Pres*
EMP: 8
SQ FT: 3,800
SALES: 1.9MM **Privately Held**
SIC: **3523** **3713** Trailers & wagons, farm; planting machines, agricultural; truck bodies (motor vehicles)

(G-12932)
WINTERS RAILROAD SERVICE INC
11309 Sisson Hwy (14111-9729)
PHONE..................................716 337-2668
Fax: 716 337-2503
David Winter, *President*
Michael Winter, *Corp Secy*
EMP: 6
SQ FT: 15,000
SALES: 530K **Privately Held**
SIC: **3423** **3441** Hand & edge tools; fabricated structural metal

North Creek
Warren County

(G-12933)
CREATIVE STAGE LIGHTING CO INC
Also Called: C S L
149 State Route 28n (12853-2707)
P.O. Box 567 (12853-0567)
PHONE..................................518 251-3302
Fax: 518 251-2908
George B Studnicky III, *President*
Darrell Barnes, *Business Mgr*
Steve Smith, *Safety Mgr*
Jason Lemery, *Financial Exec*
Lily Studnicky, *Admin Sec*
◆ **EMP: 43**
SQ FT: 32,000
SALES: 8MM **Privately Held**
WEB: www.creativestagelighting.com
SIC: **3648** **5063** **7922** Lighting equipment; lighting fixtures, commercial & industrial; lighting, theatrical

North Java
Wyoming County

(G-12934)
SELECT INTERIOR DOOR LTD
Also Called: Select Door
2074 Perry Rd (14113-9722)
P.O. Box 178 (14113-0178)
PHONE..................................585 535-9900
Fax: 585 535-9923
John Angelbeck, *President*
Maureen Ronan, *CFO*
EMP: 40
SQ FT: 25,000
SALES (est): 6.1MM **Privately Held**
WEB: www.sidl.com
SIC: **2431** **3231** Doors, wood; products of purchased glass

North Lawrence
St. Lawrence County

(G-12935)
UPSTATE NIAGARA COOP INC
Also Called: North Country Dairy
22 County Route 52 (12967-9539)
PHONE..................................315 389-5111
Tim Gominiack, *Branch Mgr*
EMP: 59
SALES (corp-wide): 775.5MM **Privately Held**
SIC: **2026** Fluid milk; milk & cream, except fermented, cultured & flavored; fermented & cultured milk products
PA: Upstate Niagara Cooperative, Inc.
25 Anderson Rd
Buffalo NY 14225
716 892-3156

North Rose
Wayne County

(G-12936)
FLEISCHMANNS VINEGAR CO INC
Also Called: Fleischman Vinegar
4754 State Route 414 (14516-9704)
PHONE..................................315 587-4414
John Wilson, *Manager*
EMP: 20
SALES (corp-wide): 71.6MM **Privately Held**
WEB: www.breadworld.com
SIC: **2099** Vinegar
HQ: Fleischmann's Vinegar Company, Inc.
12604 Hiddencreek Way A
Cerritos CA 90703
562 483-4619

(G-12937)
GARGRAVES TRACKAGE CORPORATION (PA)
Also Called: Gardner The Train Doctor
8967 Ridge Rd (14516-9753)
PHONE..................................315 483-6577
Fax: 315 483-2425
Michael Roder, *President*
Thomas Roder, *Vice Pres*
EMP: 5
SQ FT: 5,000
SALES: 516.5K **Privately Held**
WEB: www.gargraves.com
SIC: **3944** **5945** Trains & equipment, toy: electric & mechanical; hobby, toy & game shops

(G-12938)
OLMSTEAD MACHINE INC
10399 Warehouse Ave (14516-9537)
P.O. Box 331 (14516-0331)
PHONE..................................315 587-9864
Fax: 315 587-9110
Dale Liechti, *President*
EMP: 10
SQ FT: 10,000
SALES (est): 1.4MM **Privately Held**
SIC: **3599** Machine shop, jobbing & repair

North Salem
Westchester County

(G-12939)
METROPOLITAN FINE MLLWK CORP
Also Called: Metro Millwork
230 Hardscrabble Rd (10560-1019)
PHONE..................................914 669-4900
Fax: 914 669-4904
Robert Sposato, *President*
Michael Duignan, *Vice Pres*
Linda Dengler, *Office Mgr*
EMP: 18
SQ FT: 5,000
SALES: 250K **Privately Held**
SIC: **2431** Millwork; doors, wood

(G-12940)
TOTAL ENERGY FABRICATION CORP
2 Hardscrabble Rd (10560-1014)
PHONE..................................580 363-1500
Robert Armentano, *CEO*
Gary Harvey, *Principal*
Frank Kovacs, *Principal*
▲ **EMP: 6**
SALES (est): 1.3MM **Privately Held**
SIC: **3491** Pressure valves & regulators, industrial

North Syracuse
Onondaga County

(G-12941)
DISPLAYS BY RIOUX INC
6090 E Taft Rd (13212-3303)
P.O. Box 3008, Syracuse (13220-3008)
PHONE..................................315 458-3639
Fax: 315 458-3722
Robert A Rioux Jr, *President*
EMP: 7
SQ FT: 12,200
SALES (est): 972.5K **Privately Held**
WEB: www.displaysbyrioux.com
SIC: **3083** **3089** Laminated plastics plate & sheet; cases, plastic

(G-12942)
DL MANUFACTURING INC
340 Gateway Park Dr (13212-3758)
PHONE..................................315 432-8977
Donald L Metz, *Ch of Bd*
Rick Woytan, *Controller*
Lee Eslicker, *Human Res Mgr*
Joseph Markert, *Natl Sales Mgr*
Patricia Dawson, *Marketing Staff*
EMP: 30
SQ FT: 22,000
SALES: 12MM **Privately Held**
WEB: www.dlmanufacturing.com
SIC: **3537** **5084** **5031** Loading docks: portable, adjustable & hydraulic; industrial machinery & equipment; doors

(G-12943)
G A BRAUN INC (PA)
79 General Irwin Blvd (13212-5279)
P.O. Box 3029, Syracuse (13220-3029)
PHONE..................................315 475-3123
JB Werner, *Ch of Bd*
Joe Gudenburr, *President*
David Clark, *Vice Pres*
Daniel Hertig, *Vice Pres*
Todd Pfeiffer, *Vice Pres*
▲ **EMP: 90**
SQ FT: 75,000
SALES (est): 26.4MM **Privately Held**
WEB: www.gabraun.com
SIC: **3582** **5087** Washing machines, laundry: commercial, incl. coin-operated; laundry equipment & supplies

(G-12944)
GAYLORD BROS INC
Also Called: Gaylord Archival
7282 William Barry Blvd (13212-3347)
P.O. Box 4901, Syracuse (13221-4901)
PHONE..................................315 457-5070
Fax: 315 451-4760
R Keith George, *CEO*
Gony Green, *Credit Staff*
Mark Anderson, *Manager*
Danny McCartin, *Manager*
Courtney McEvoy, *Manager*
▼ **EMP: 60**
SQ FT: 80,000
SALES (est): 18.6MM
SALES (corp-wide): 118MM **Privately Held**
WEB: www.gaylord.com
SIC: **2679** **2657** **2542** Adding machine rolls, paper: made from purchased material; folding paperboard boxes; fixtures: display, office or store: except wood
PA: Demco, Inc.
4810 Forest Run Rd
Madison WI 53704
800 356-1200

(G-12945)
GEDDES BAKERY CO INC
421 S Main St (13212-2800)
PHONE..................................315 437-8084
Fax: 315 410-1971
Vasilios Pappas, *President*
Bill Pappas, *Office Mgr*
EMP: 24 EST: 1957
SQ FT: 5,600
SALES (est): 3.3MM **Privately Held**
WEB: www.geddesbakery.com
SIC: **2051** **5461** Bakery: wholesale or wholesale/retail combined; bakeries

(G-12946)
GRYPHON SENSORS LLC
7351 Round Pond Rd (13212-2552)
PHONE..................................315 452-8810
Anthony Albanese, *President*
EMP: 15 EST: 2014
SQ FT: 1,000
SALES (est): 1.9MM **Privately Held**
SIC: **3812** Antennas, radar or communications

(G-12947)
ICM CONTROLS CORP
7313 William Barry Blvd (13212-3384)
PHONE..................................315 233-5266
Hassan B Kadah, *Ch of Bd*
Andrew Kadah, *President*
Laurie Kadah, *Treasurer*
▲ **EMP: 56**
SALES (est): 2.6MM
SALES (corp-wide): 50MM **Privately Held**
SIC: **3625** Electric controls & control accessories, industrial
PA: International Controls & Measurements Corp.
7313 William Barry Blvd
North Syracuse NY 13212
315 233-5266

(G-12948)
INTERNTNAL CNTRLS MSRMNTS CORP (PA)
Also Called: ICM
7313 William Barry Blvd (13212-3384)
PHONE..................................315 233-5266
Hassan B Kadah, *Ch of Bd*
Andrew Kadah, *President*
Christina Staniec, *Purch Dir*
Laurie Kadah, *Treasurer*
Joe Nappi, *Accounting Mgr*
▲ **EMP: 194**
SQ FT: 85,000
SALES: 50MM **Privately Held**
WEB: www.icmcontrols.com
SIC: **3625** Electric controls & control accessories, industrial

(G-12949)
JADAK LLC (HQ)
7279 William Barry Blvd (13212-3349)
PHONE..................................315 701-0678
Jeffrey Pine, *President*
Ronald Blair, *Engineer*
MO Chen, *Engineer*

North Syracuse - Onondaga County (G-12950)

Andrew Litteer, *Engineer*
John Pettinelli, *Engineer*
EMP: 15
SALES (est): 8.2MM
SALES (corp-wide): 373.6MM **Publicly Held**
SIC: 3577 3845 Optical scanning devices; ultrasonic scanning devices, medical
PA: Novanta Inc.
125 Middlesex Tpke
Bedford MA 01730
781 266-5700

(G-12950)
JADAK TECHNOLOGIES INC (DH)
7279 William Barry Blvd (13212-3349)
PHONE 315 701-0678
Fax: 315 701-0679
David Miller, *President*
Jan Douma, *Managing Dir*
Frank Borghese, *Vice Pres*
Mark Raymond, *Mfg Mgr*
Jennifer Cruse, *Purch Mgr*
EMP: 100
SALES (est): 17.4MM
SALES (corp-wide): 373.6MM **Publicly Held**
WEB: www.jadaktech.com
SIC: 3577 Bar code (magnetic ink) printers
HQ: Novanta Corporation
125 Middlesex Tpke
Bedford MA 01730
781 266-5700

(G-12951)
KELLOGG COMPANY
7350 Round Pond Rd (13212-2553)
PHONE 315 452-0310
Nick Carlucci, *Manager*
EMP: 30
SALES (corp-wide): 13.5B **Publicly Held**
WEB: www.kelloggs.com
SIC: 2043 Cereal breakfast foods
PA: Kellogg Company
1 Kellogg Sq
Battle Creek MI 49017
269 961-2000

(G-12952)
TERRYS TRANSMISSION
6217 E Taft Rd (13212-2527)
PHONE 315 458-4333
Terry Bish, *President*
Charlene Bish, *Vice Pres*
EMP: 6
SQ FT: 5,500
SALES (est): 610K **Privately Held**
WEB: www.terrystransmission.com
SIC: 3714 Motor vehicle transmissions, drive assemblies & parts

North Tonawanda
Niagara County

(G-12953)
369 RIVER ROAD INC
369 River Rd (14120-7108)
PHONE 716 694-5001
Michael Deakin, *President*
EMP: 25 **EST:** 2007
SQ FT: 25,000
SALES (est): 942.6K **Privately Held**
SIC: 3496 Miscellaneous fabricated wire products

(G-12954)
AN-COR INDUSTRIAL PLASTICS INC
900 Niagara Falls Blvd (14120-2096)
PHONE 716 695-3141
Fax: 716 695-0465
Merrill W Arthur, *President*
Joseph Gates, *Vice Pres*
Norman Hirschey, *Engineer*
Paul Biondi, *CFO*
Ronald Hughes, *Manager*
EMP: 83
SQ FT: 96,000
SALES (est): 24.1MM **Privately Held**
WEB: www.an-cor.com
SIC: 3089 3088 Plastic & fiberglass tanks; plastics plumbing fixtures

(G-12955)
ARMSTRONG PUMPS INC
93 East Ave (14120-6594)
PHONE 716 693-8813
Fax: 716 693-8970
J A C Armstrong, *CEO*
Bruce Van Nus, *Managing Dir*
Karl Ziolek, *Safety Mgr*
Steven Yung, *Controller*
Catherine Holesko, *Human Res Mgr*
▲ **EMP:** 100
SQ FT: 150,000
SALES (est): 43.7MM
SALES (corp-wide): 143.9MM **Privately Held**
WEB: www.armstrongpumps.com
SIC: 3561 Pumps & pumping equipment
PA: S. A. Armstrong Limited
23 Bertrand Ave
Toronto ON M1L 2
416 755-2291

(G-12956)
ASCENSION INDUSTRIES INC (PA)
1254 Erie Ave (14120-3036)
PHONE 716 693-9381
Fax: 716 693-9381
Jack Kopczynski Jr, *Ch of Bd*
Donald Naab, *President*
Gary Vincent, *Regional Mgr*
Christian Nobel, *Plant Supt*
Michael Conti, *Project Mgr*
▲ **EMP:** 85 **EST:** 1975
SQ FT: 140,000
SALES (est): 23.5MM **Privately Held**
WEB: www.asmfab.com
SIC: 3544 3541 3444 Special dies, tools, jigs & fixtures; machine tools, metal cutting type; sheet metalwork

(G-12957)
AUDUBON MACHINERY CORPORATION (PA)
Also Called: Oxygen Generating Systems Intl
814 Wurlitzer Dr (14120-3042)
PHONE 716 564-5165
Joseph M McMahon, *President*
Robert Schlehr, *Vice Pres*
Dave White, *Prdtn Mgr*
Timothy Blach, *CFO*
Bob Schlehr, *VP Sales*
◆ **EMP:** 60
SQ FT: 40,000
SALES (est): 13.1MM **Privately Held**
WEB: www.ogsi.com
SIC: 3569 Gas producers, generators & other gas related equipment

(G-12958)
BAKER TOOL & DIE
48 Industrial Dr (14120-3244)
PHONE 716 694-2025
Jon C Olstad, *President*
EMP: 8
SALES (est): 690K **Privately Held**
SIC: 3312 Blast furnaces & steel mills

(G-12959)
BAKER TOOL & DIE & DIE
48 Industrial Dr (14120-3244)
PHONE 716 694-2025
Fax: 716 694-2026
Jon C Olstad, *President*
Dottie Harvey, *Bookkeeper*
EMP: 6
SQ FT: 6,000
SALES (est): 480K **Privately Held**
SIC: 3312 Tool & die steel

(G-12960)
BATTENFELD GREASE OIL CORP NY
1174 Erie Ave (14120-3036)
P.O. Box 728 (14120-0728)
PHONE 716 695-2100
Fax: 716 695-0367
Barbara A Bellanti, *Ch of Bd*
John A Bellanti, *President*
Paul Carpenter, *Plant Mgr*
Don Bowen, *Sales Executive*
Mark Swanson, *CTO*
▲ **EMP:** 38
SALES (est): 11.4MM **Privately Held**
SIC: 2992 Lubricating oils & greases

(G-12961)
BROADWAY KNITTING MILLS INC
1333 Strad Ave Ste 216 (14120-3061)
PHONE 716 692-4421
Craig Boyce, *President*
Russell Boyce, *Vice Pres*
Susan Boyce, *Treasurer*
Molly Boyce, *Admin Sec*
EMP: 5 **EST:** 1932
SQ FT: 8,400
SALES (est): 210K **Privately Held**
WEB: www.broadwayknitting.com
SIC: 2329 5611 2326 Jackets (suede, leatherette, etc.), sport: men's & boys'; clothing accessories: men's & boys'; men's & boys' work clothing

(G-12962)
BUFFALO ABRASIVES INC (PA)
960 Erie Ave (14120-3503)
PHONE 716 693-3856
Fax: 716 693-4092
Arthur A Russ Jr, *President*
Jeffrey J Binkley, *Chairman*
Tim Wagner, *Vice Pres*
Fred Williams, *Vice Pres*
Frank Pawlik, *Safety Mgr*
▲ **EMP:** 45
SQ FT: 65,000
SALES (est): 15.7MM **Privately Held**
WEB: www.buffaloabrasives.com
SIC: 3291 Abrasive products

(G-12963)
BUFFALO PUMPS INC (HQ)
Also Called: A Division A & Liquid Systems
874 Oliver St (14120-3298)
PHONE 716 693-1850
Fax: 716 693-6303
Robert Paul, *Ch of Bd*
Charles Kistner, *President*
Robert Schultz, *Vice Pres*
Kathy Kalczynski, *Plant Mgr*
Marty Kraft, *QC Dir*
▲ **EMP:** 153
SQ FT: 140,000
SALES (est): 24.1MM
SALES (corp-wide): 238.4MM **Publicly Held**
WEB: www.buffalopumps.com
SIC: 3561 Pumps & pumping equipment
PA: Ampco-Pittsburgh Corporation
726 Bell Ave Ste 301
Carnegie PA 15106
412 456-4400

(G-12964)
CALGON CARBON CORPORATION
830 River Rd (14120-6557)
PHONE 716 531-9113
EMP: 9
SALES (est): 1.2MM **Privately Held**
SIC: 2819 Charcoal (carbon), activated

(G-12965)
CANALSIDE CREAMERY INC
985 Ruie Rd (14120-1727)
PHONE 716 695-2876
Barbara Labruna, *Owner*
EMP: 8
SALES (est): 671.1K **Privately Held**
SIC: 2021 Creamery butter

(G-12966)
COMMERCIAL FABRICS INC
908 Niagara Falls Blvd (14120-2019)
PHONE 716 694-0641
Fax: 716 694-3803
Michel Senecal, *President*
James Senecal, *Corp Secy*
EMP: 15
SQ FT: 30,000
SALES (est): 1.7MM **Privately Held**
WEB: www.commercialfabrics.com
SIC: 3999 Hot tub & spa covers

(G-12967)
CONFER PLASTICS INC
97 Witmer Rd (14120-2421)
PHONE 800 635-3213
Fax: 716 694-3102
Douglas C Confer, *President*
Bob Confer, *Vice Pres*
Peter Miller, *Plant Mgr*
Cliff Hoover, *QC Mgr*
Dave Lipnianski, *Engineer*
▼ **EMP:** 130
SQ FT: 100,000
SALES (est): 38.4MM **Privately Held**
WEB: www.conferladders.com
SIC: 3089 Blow molded finished plastic products

(G-12968)
DELAWARE MFG INDS CORP (PA)
3776 Commerce Ct (14120-2024)
PHONE 716 743-4360
Fax: 716 743-4370
Renzo Mestieri, *Ch of Bd*
Michelle Lattuca, *Vice Pres*
Mike Cotterell, *Purch Mgr*
▼ **EMP:** 58
SQ FT: 55,000
SALES (est): 12.3MM **Privately Held**
WEB: www.dmic.com
SIC: 3494 Valves & pipe fittings

(G-12969)
DMIC INC
Also Called: Delaware Manufacturing Inds
3776 Commerce Ct (14120-2024)
PHONE 716 743-4360
Chuck Wolski, *Principal*
Eric Stanczyk, *Engineer*
EMP: 10
SALES (est): 1.5MM **Privately Held**
SIC: 3492 3714 Fluid power valves for aircraft; motor vehicle parts & accessories

(G-12970)
EXPEDIENT HEAT TREATING CORP
61 Dale Dr (14120-4201)
PHONE 716 433-1177
Paul Waild, *President*
EMP: 5 **EST:** 1979
SQ FT: 2,000
SALES (est): 400K **Privately Held**
SIC: 3398 Metal heat treating

(G-12971)
FAIRVIEW FITTING & MFG INC
3777 Commerce Ct (14120-2024)
PHONE 716 614-0320
Fax: 716 614-0327
Leslie Woodward, *Ch of Bd*
Joseph B Kozak, *General Mgr*
Dale Slisz, *Materials Mgr*
Ron Hageman, *Manager*
Gordon Shanor, *Manager*
▲ **EMP:** 53
SQ FT: 50,000
SALES (est): 8.9MM **Privately Held**
SIC: 3599 Flexible metal hose, tubing & bellows

(G-12972)
FEI PRODUCTS LLC (PA)
825 Wurlitzer Dr (14120-3041)
PHONE 716 693-6230
Fax: 716 693-6368
Charles S Craig, *President*
Lance Bronnenkant, *Research*
Jennifer Gates, *CFO*
Paul G Baldetti, *Manager*
Patrick Kilcullen, *Network Mgr*
EMP: 35
SQ FT: 23,500
SALES (est): 5.2MM **Privately Held**
SIC: 3089 Plastic processing

(G-12973)
GARDEI INDUSTRIES LLC (PA)
Also Called: F K Williams Division
1087 Erie Ave (14120-3532)
PHONE 716 693-7100
Lori Ferraraccio, *Mng Member*
Jordon Lizy,
▲ **EMP:** 17 **EST:** 1936
SQ FT: 25,000
SALES (est): 1.6MM **Privately Held**
WEB: www.gardei.net
SIC: 2679 3545 Paper products, converted; machine tool accessories

GEOGRAPHIC SECTION
North Tonawanda - Niagara County (G-12998)

(G-12974)
GERALD FRD PACKG DISPLAY LLC
550 Gilmore Ave (14120-4311)
PHONE.................716 692-2705
Gerald Fried, *President*
EMP: 16
SALES (corp-wide): 2.3MM **Privately Held**
SIC: 2789 Display mounting
PA: Gerald Fried Packaging & Display Co., Llc
  550 Fillmore Ave
  Tonawanda NY 14150
  716 692-2705

(G-12975)
GLI-DEX SALES CORP
Also Called: Glidden Machine & Tool
855 Wurlitzer Dr (14120-3041)
PHONE.................716 692-6501
Fax: 716 692-6551
James Gerace, *President*
Marcia Gerace, *Corp Secy*
Robert Gerace, *Vice Pres*
EMP: 35 **EST:** 1946
SQ FT: 12,000
SALES (est): 2.3MM **Privately Held**
WEB: www.glidex.biz
SIC: 3599 Machine shop, jobbing & repair

(G-12976)
GRIFFIN CHEMICAL COMPANY LLC
Also Called: W.O.w Brand Products
889 Erie Ave Ste 1 (14120-3533)
PHONE.................716 693-2465
Gregory Robinson, *Mng Member*
Bernard Zysman,
EMP: 9
SQ FT: 15,000
SALES: 500K **Privately Held**
SIC: 2842 Specialty cleaning preparations

(G-12977)
IMPRESSIVE IMPRINTS
601 Division St (14120-4461)
PHONE.................716 692-0905
Fax: 716 693-8997
Robert Albert, *Owner*
Kyle Crotty, *Vice Pres*
Judy Albert, *Manager*
EMP: 12
SQ FT: 3,000
SALES (est): 1MM **Privately Held**
SIC: 2759 Commercial printing

(G-12978)
ISLAND STREET LUMBER CO INC
11 Felton St (14120-6503)
PHONE.................716 692-4127
James Le Blanc, *President*
Joan Le Blanc, *Vice Pres*
EMP: 5 **EST:** 1949
SQ FT: 11,500
SALES (est): 600.8K **Privately Held**
SIC: 2431 5211 Millwork; millwork & lumber

(G-12979)
ISOLATION SYSTEMS INC
889 Erie Ave Ste 1 (14120-3533)
PHONE.................716 694-6390
Ted Arts, *President*
Susan Arts, *Comptroller*
EMP: 10
SQ FT: 98,000
SALES (est): 2MM **Privately Held**
WEB: www.isolation-systems.com
SIC: 3564 Filters, air: furnaces, air conditioning equipment, etc.

(G-12980)
L & S METALS INC
111 Witmer Rd (14120-2443)
PHONE.................716 692-6865
Gary Schade, *President*
Steven Oslen, *Purchasing*
Tiffany Shaffer, *Controller*
Dave Orth, *Sales Staff*
Becky Beutel, *Manager*
EMP: 23
SQ FT: 17,000
SALES (est): 4.5MM **Privately Held**
WEB: www.ls-metals.com
SIC: 3599 7692 Machine shop, jobbing & repair; welding repair

(G-12981)
LISTON MANUFACTURING INC
421 Payne Ave (14120-6987)
P.O. Box 178 (14120-0178)
PHONE.................716 695-2111
Fax: 716 695-0443
Theodore Pyrak, *Ch of Bd*
Joseph Laduca, *Vice Pres*
Russell Laduca, *Vice Pres*
Charles E Pyrak, *Treasurer*
Edward Pyrak, *Treasurer*
EMP: 50 **EST:** 1954
SQ FT: 60,000
SALES (est): 9.7MM **Privately Held**
WEB: www.listonmfg.com
SIC: 3568 Bearings, bushings & blocks

(G-12982)
MODU-CRAFT INC
337 Payne Ave (14120-7236)
PHONE.................716 694-0709
Kenneth Babka, *President*
EMP: 7
SALES (corp-wide): 1MM **Privately Held**
SIC: 2599 3821 Factory furniture & fixtures; laboratory furniture
PA: Modu-Craft Inc
  276 Creekside Dr
  Tonawanda NY 14150
  716 694-0709

(G-12983)
NIAGARA SHEETS LLC
7393 Shawnee Rd (14120-1325)
PHONE.................716 692-1129
Fax: 716 799-8320
John Bolender, *President*
Skip Polowy, *Vice Pres*
Kurt Schuler, *Controller*
▲ **EMP:** 75 **EST:** 2007
SALES (est): 29.4MM
SALES (corp-wide): 116MM **Privately Held**
SIC: 2653 Corrugated boxes, partitions, display items, sheets & pad
PA: Jamestown Container Corp
  14 Deming Dr
  Falconer NY 14733
  716 665-4623

(G-12984)
OCCIDENTAL CHEMICAL CORP
3780 Commerce Ct Ste 600 (14120-2025)
PHONE.................716 694-3827
Rose Zenturin, *General Mgr*
EMP: 5
SALES (corp-wide): 12.7B **Publicly Held**
WEB: www.oxychem.com
SIC: 2874 Phosphatic fertilizers
HQ: Occidental Chemical Corporation
  5005 Lyndon B Johnson Fwy # 2200
  Dallas TX 75244
  972 404-3800

(G-12985)
PELLETS LLC
63 Industrial Dr Ste 3 (14120-3248)
PHONE.................716 693-1750
Fax: 716 693-1880
Mike Deakin, *President*
Kevin Deakin, *General Mgr*
◆ **EMP:** 6
SQ FT: 7,500
SALES (est): 1MM
SALES (corp-wide): 2.7MM **Privately Held**
WEB: www.pelletsllc.com
SIC: 3291 Abrasive metal & steel products
PA: Val-Kro, Inc.
  369 River Rd
  North Tonawanda NY
  716 694-5001

(G-12986)
PIONEER PRINTERS INC
Also Called: Gardei Manufacturing
1087 Erie Ave (14120-3532)
PHONE.................716 693-7100
Fax: 716 692-8671
Carl Hoover, *CEO*
Courtney Frank, *Manager*
Jim Hoffman, *Administration*
EMP: 16
SQ FT: 7,000
SALES (est): 2.8MM **Privately Held**
WEB: www.pioneerprinters.com
SIC: 2752 Commercial printing, offset

(G-12987)
PROTOTYPE MANUFACTURING CORP
836 Wurlitzer Dr (14120-3042)
PHONE.................716 695-1700
Fax: 716 695-2735
Richard A Christie, *President*
Timothy G Christie, *Vice Pres*
EMP: 10
SQ FT: 8,000
SALES (est): 1.5MM **Privately Held**
SIC: 3544 Special dies & tools

(G-12988)
RECORD ADVERTISER
435 River Rd (14120-6809)
P.O. Box 668 (14120-0668)
PHONE.................716 693-1000
Fax: 716 693-8573
Wayne Lowman, *President*
Robert Kazeangin, *Manager*
EMP: 40
SALES (est): 2MM **Privately Held**
SIC: 2711 Newspapers

(G-12989)
RILEY GEAR CORPORATION
61 Felton St (14120-6598)
PHONE.................716 694-0900
Fax: 716 694-9094
David Sambuchi, *Vice Pres*
Donn Neffke, *Manager*
Douglas Caswell, *Manager*
EMP: 20
SALES (corp-wide): 16.1MM **Privately Held**
WEB: www.rileygear.com
SIC: 3462 Gears, forged steel
PA: Riley Gear Corporation
  1 Precision Dr
  Saint Augustine FL 32092
  904 829-5652

(G-12990)
RIVERFRONT COSTUME DESIGN
Also Called: A D M
200 River Rd (14120-5708)
PHONE.................716 693-2501
Fax: 716 693-2502
Paul Tucker, *President*
Barbara Tucker, *Vice Pres*
EMP: 9
SQ FT: 12,500
SALES (est): 1MM **Privately Held**
SIC: 2521 2522 Cabinets, office: wood; cabinets, office: except wood

(G-12991)
ROEMAC INDUSTRIAL SALES INC
Also Called: Buffalo Snowmelter
27 Fredericka St (14120-6590)
PHONE.................716 692-7332
Fax: 716 692-7366
Mitchell Roemer, *President*
Greg Roemer, *Corp Secy*
Nicholas B Roemer, *Vice Pres*
EMP: 9 **EST:** 1947
SQ FT: 7,000
SALES: 900K **Privately Held**
WEB: www.roemac.com
SIC: 3443 3585 Fabricated plate work (boiler shop); evaporative condensers, heat transfer equipment

(G-12992)
ROGER L URBAN INC (PA)
Also Called: Platter's Chocolates
954 Oliver St (14120-3230)
PHONE.................716 693-5391
Fax: 716 692-2055
Joseph Urban, *President*
Sherry Di Guiseppe, *Vice Pres*
Sherry Diguiseppe, *Vice Pres*
Michael Urban, *Shareholder*
EMP: 21
SQ FT: 11,000
SALES (est): 2.4MM **Privately Held**
WEB: www.platterschocolate.com
SIC: 2066 5141 5145 2064 Chocolate candy, solid; candy; confectionery; candy & other confectionery products

(G-12993)
SHANNON ENTPS WSTN NY INC
Also Called: Insultech
75 Main St (14120-5903)
P.O. Box 199 (14120-0199)
PHONE.................716 693-7954
Fax: 716 693-1647
Frank Kovacs, *President*
Dennis Dombrowski, *Controller*
Robert Weir, *Admin Sec*
▼ **EMP:** 58
SQ FT: 20,000
SALES (est): 6.1MM **Privately Held**
WEB: www.corian-countertop.com
SIC: 2299 Insulating felts

(G-12994)
SOLID SURFACE ACRYLICS INC
800 Walck Rd Ste 14 (14120-3500)
PHONE.................716 743-1870
John Linde,
Bob Barenthaler,
EMP: 10
SQ FT: 60,000
SALES (est): 1.3MM **Privately Held**
SIC: 3083 Plastic finished products, laminated

(G-12995)
SOLID SURFACE ACRYLICS LLC
800 Walck Rd Ste 14 (14120-3500)
PHONE.................716 743-1870
Fax: 716 743-0475
Paul Biondi, *Controller*
Jack Tillotsom,
Merrill Arthur,
EMP: 16
SQ FT: 76,000
SALES (est): 3.8MM **Privately Held**
WEB: www.ssacrylics.com
SIC: 2824 Acrylic fibers

(G-12996)
SOLIVAIRA SPECIALTIES INC
4 Detroit St (14120-6843)
PHONE.................716 693-4009
Jerry Bianchi, *Manager*
EMP: 58
SALES (corp-wide): 129.4MM **Privately Held**
WEB: www.ifcfiber.com
SIC: 2023 2299 2823 Dry, condensed, evaporated dairy products; flock (recovered textile fibers); cellulosic manmade fibers
PA: Solvaira Specialties Inc.
  50 Bridge St
  North Tonawanda NY 14120
  716 693-4040

(G-12997)
SOLVAIRA SPECIALTIES INC (PA)
50 Bridge St (14120-6842)
PHONE.................716 693-4040
L J Baillargeon, *CEO*
Dean Newby, *Exec VP*
Ron Evans, *Senior VP*
Jit Ang, *Vice Pres*
Lawrence A McKee, *Vice Pres*
◆ **EMP:** 110 **EST:** 1917
SQ FT: 270,000
SALES (est): 129.4MM **Privately Held**
WEB: www.ifcfiber.com
SIC: 2823 2299 Cellulosic manmade fibers; flock (recovered textile fibers)

(G-12998)
SUPERIOR TOOL CO INC
1020 Oliver St (14120-2796)
PHONE.................716 692-3900
Fax: 716 692-3937
James Durkee, *President*
Richard Rog, *Vice Pres*
EMP: 12
SQ FT: 10,000
SALES (est): 2.1MM **Privately Held**
WEB: www.superiortoolllc.com
SIC: 3545 Cutting tools for machine tools

North Tonawanda - Niagara County (G-12999)

GEOGRAPHIC SECTION

(G-12999)
T-S-K ELECTRONICS INC
908 Niagara Falls Blvd # 122 (14120-2016)
PHONE..................................716 693-3916
Fax: 716 692-6433
Kevin Kedzierski, *President*
Michael Kedzierski, *Vice Pres*
EMP: 5 EST: 1958
SQ FT: 15,000
SALES (est): 727.7K **Privately Held**
SIC: 3679 Electronic circuits

(G-13000)
TABER ACQUISITION CORP
Also Called: Taber Industries
455 Bryant St (14120-7043)
PHONE..................................716 694-4000
Fax: 716 694-1450
Daniel Slawson, *Ch of Bd*
Rocer Foore, *Vice Pres*
James Stawitzky, *Vice Pres*
Lori Anderson, *VP Opers*
Danny Thaler, *Opers Staff*
EMP: 60
SQ FT: 72,000
SALES (est): 19.1MM **Privately Held**
WEB: www.taberindustries.com
SIC: 3823 Pressure measurement instruments, industrial

(G-13001)
TAYLOR DEVICES INC (PA)
90 Taylor Dr (14120-6894)
P.O. Box 748 (14120-0748)
PHONE..................................716 694-0800
Fax: 716 695-6015
Douglas P Taylor, *Ch of Bd*
Richard G Hill, *Vice Pres*
Ben Kujawinski, *Opers Mgr*
John Metzger, *Engineer*
Eric Roth, *Engineer*
▲ EMP: 114 EST: 1955
SALES: 35.6MM **Publicly Held**
WEB: www.taylordevices.com
SIC: 3569 Industrial shock absorbers

(G-13002)
TEVA WOMENS HEALTH INC
825 Wurlitzer Dr (14120-3041)
PHONE..................................716 693-6230
Paul Wasielewski, *Opers Staff*
Paul McCarthy, *Engineer*
Jennifer Gates, *Branch Mgr*
EMP: 17
SALES (corp-wide): 20.3B **Privately Held**
WEB: www.barrlabs.com
SIC: 3089 Plastic processing
HQ: Teva Women's Health, Inc.
    5040 Duramed Rd
    Cincinnati OH 45213
    513 731-9900

(G-13003)
TRINITY TOOLS INC
261 Main St (14120-7106)
PHONE..................................716 694-1111
Fax: 716 692-0959
Mitchell Banas, *President*
Chris Wein, *Vice Pres*
Michael Ostrowski, *Admin Sec*
EMP: 20 EST: 1956
SQ FT: 18,000
SALES (est): 2.2MM **Privately Held**
WEB: www.trinitytoolrentals.com
SIC: 3544 3545 Special dies & tools; jigs & fixtures; gauges (machine tool accessories)

(G-13004)
UNITED MATERIALS LLC (PA)
3949 Frest Pk Way Ste 400 (14120)
PHONE..................................716 683-1432
Ross Eckert, *Ch of Bd*
Peter Romano, *President*
Roger Ball, *CFO*
EMP: 57 EST: 1997
SQ FT: 15,000
SALES (est): 19.3MM **Privately Held**
SIC: 3273 Ready-mixed concrete

(G-13005)
VIATRAN CORPORATION (DH)
3829 Frest Pk Way Ste 500 (14120)
PHONE..................................716 629-3800
George A Fraas, *CEO*
Kenneth H Brown, *Ch of Bd*
Tony Sauer, *Business Mgr*
Frank Sorce, *Vice Pres*
Carol Starck, *Opers Mgr*
EMP: 50 EST: 1965
SQ FT: 18,000
SALES (est): 5.7MM
SALES (corp-wide): 3.5B **Publicly Held**
WEB: www.viatran.com
SIC: 3823 3825 5084 Pressure measurement instruments, industrial; instruments to measure electricity; industrial machinery & equipment
HQ: Dynisco Llc
    38 Forge Pkwy
    Franklin MA 02038
    508 541-3195

(G-13006)
WESTROCK CP LLC
51 Robinson St (14120-6805)
PHONE..................................716 694-1000
Dave Hromowyk, *Safety Mgr*
Don Laurie, *Branch Mgr*
Mark Savre, *Manager*
EMP: 165
SALES (corp-wide): 11.3B **Publicly Held**
WEB: www.sto.com
SIC: 2653 3412 Boxes, corrugated: made from purchased materials; metal barrels, drums & pails
HQ: Westrock Cp, Llc
    504 Thrasher St
    Norcross GA 30071

(G-13007)
WESTROCK CP LLC
51 Robinson St (14120-6805)
PHONE..................................716 692-6510
Fax: 716 694-9262
Mike McGugan, *Branch Mgr*
EMP: 101
SALES (corp-wide): 11.3B **Publicly Held**
WEB: www.smurfit-stone.com
SIC: 2653 Corrugated boxes, partitions, display items, sheets & pad
HQ: Westrock Cp, Llc
    504 Thrasher St
    Norcross GA 30071

Northport
Suffolk County

(G-13008)
BIO-CHEM BARRIER SYSTEMS LLC
11 W Scudder Pl (11768-3040)
PHONE..................................631 261-2682
Patricia J Maloney,
Raymond Maloney,
EMP: 8
SQ FT: 1,200
SALES: 1.6MM **Privately Held**
WEB: www.bio-chembarriersystemllc.com
SIC: 3842 Personal safety equipment

(G-13009)
CHASE CORPORATION
Also Called: Chase Partners
7 Harbour Point Dr (11768-1556)
PHONE..................................631 827-0476
EMP: 11
SALES (corp-wide): 238MM **Publicly Held**
SIC: 3644 Noncurrent-carrying wiring services
PA: Chase Corporation
    26 Summer St
    Bridgewater MA 02324
    508 819-4200

(G-13010)
CYPRESS SEMICONDUCTOR CORP
Also Called: Sales Office
34 Rowley Dr (11768-3246)
PHONE..................................631 261-1358
Carl Finke, *Branch Mgr*
EMP: 14
SALES (corp-wide): 1.6B **Publicly Held**
WEB: www.cypress.com
SIC: 3674 5065 Semiconductors & related devices; electronic parts & equipment
PA: Cypress Semiconductor Corporation
    5883 Rue Ferrari Ste 100
    San Jose CA 95138
    408 943-2600

(G-13011)
FRANKLIN PACKAGING INC (PA)
96 Sea Cove Rd (11768-1847)
PHONE..................................631 582-8900
Steven Lincon, *CEO*
Joan Lincoln, *Treasurer*
EMP: 6
SQ FT: 1,500
SALES: 800K **Privately Held**
SIC: 2759 Commercial printing

(G-13012)
HAMMER COMMUNICATIONS INC
Also Called: Hammer Magazine
28 Sunken Meadow Rd (11768-2719)
PHONE..................................631 261-5806
John Rigrod, *President*
Michaelina Rigrod, *Vice Pres*
Michalina Rigrod, *Vice Pres*
EMP: 10
SALES: 1.5MM **Privately Held**
SIC: 2721 Periodicals

(G-13013)
KEEP HEALTHY INC
1019 Fort Salonga Rd (11768-2270)
PHONE..................................631 651-9090
Ronald Sowa, *President*
EMP: 12
SALES: 500K **Privately Held**
SIC: 2064 Breakfast bars

(G-13014)
LEDAN INC
Also Called: Ledan Design Group
6 Annetta Ave (11768-1802)
PHONE..................................631 239-1226
Fax: 516 747-5933
Daniel Leo Sr, *CEO*
Steven Leo, *President*
Dan Leo Jr, *Vice Pres*
Carla Polizzi, *Sales Staff*
EMP: 25
SQ FT: 20,000
SALES (est): 3.1MM **Privately Held**
WEB: www.ledan.com
SIC: 2542 Office & store showcases & display fixtures

(G-13015)
LIK LLC
6 Bluff Point Rd (11768-1516)
PHONE..................................516 848-5135
Laura Kampa, *President*
EMP: 10
SALES (est): 761.8K **Privately Held**
SIC: 3669 Communications equipment

(G-13016)
MARKETING GROUP INTERNATIONAL
Also Called: Mgi
225 Main St Ste 301 (11768-1787)
P.O. Box 539 (11768-0539)
PHONE..................................631 754-8095
Bruce Chautin, *Partner*
Linda Kupcewicz, *Partner*
▲ EMP: 7
SALES (est): 840K **Privately Held**
SIC: 2679 Paper products, converted

(G-13017)
MILLHOUSE 1889 LLC
24 Woodbine Ave Ste 8 (11768-2878)
PHONE..................................631 259-4777
Tad Schrantz, *Principal*
EMP: 5
SALES (est): 380.2K **Privately Held**
SIC: 3069 Roofing, membrane rubber

(G-13018)
WACF ENTERPRISE INC
275 Asharoken Ave (11768-1120)
PHONE..................................631 745-5841
Richard Orofino, *Owner*
Jim Peterson, *General Mgr*
EMP: 50
SQ FT: 4,000
SALES (est): 6.4MM **Privately Held**
SIC: 2833 Botanical products, medicinal: ground, graded or milled

Northville
Fulton County

(G-13019)
BEST TINSMITH SUPPLY INC
4 Zetta Dr (12134-5322)
PHONE..................................518 863-2541
John Crawford Jr, *President*
Claudia Hutchins, *Treasurer*
EMP: 5
SQ FT: 6,000
SALES: 507.1K **Privately Held**
SIC: 3444 Sheet metalwork

Norwich
Chenango County

(G-13020)
BYTHEWAY PUBLISHING SERVICES
365 Follett Hill Rd (13815-3378)
PHONE..................................607 334-8365
Betty Bytheway, *Owner*
Jean Blackburn, *Vice Pres*
Lori Holland, *Office Mgr*
EMP: 17
SALES (est): 810K **Privately Held**
WEB: www.bytheway.com
SIC: 2791 Typesetting

(G-13021)
CHENANGO ASPHALT PRODUCTS
23 State St (13815-1400)
P.O. Box 270 (13815-0270)
PHONE..................................607 334-3117
Fax: 607 334-4843
Barry Christophgrsen, *Manager*
EMP: 10 EST: 2002
SALES (est): 431.2K **Privately Held**
SIC: 1442 Construction sand & gravel

(G-13022)
CHENANGO UNION PRINTING INC
15 American Ave (13815-1834)
P.O. Box 149 (13815-0149)
PHONE..................................607 334-2112
Fax: 607 334-9205
Andrew Phelps, *President*
David Phelps, *Shareholder*
EMP: 8
SALES (est): 1.2MM **Privately Held**
WEB: www.chenangounion.com
SIC: 2759 2752 Letterpress printing; commercial printing, offset

(G-13023)
CHENTRONICS CORPORATION
115 County Rd 45 (13815)
P.O. Box 2256
PHONE..................................607 334-5531
Fax: 607 336-7447
John Killean, *President*
Stephen Biviano, *Vice Pres*
Karen Graham, *QC Mgr*
Andrew Strong, *Engineer*
Allen Pardon, *Admin Sec*
▲ EMP: 22
SALES (est): 6.1MM
SALES (corp-wide): 26.7B **Privately Held**
WEB: www.chentronics.com
SIC: 3433 Heating equipment, except electric
PA: Koch Industries, Inc.
    4111 E 37th St N
    Wichita KS 67220
    316 828-5500

(G-13024)
CHOBANI LLC (PA)
147 State Highway 320 (13815-3561)
PHONE..................................607 337-1246
Hamdi Ulukaya, *CEO*
Michael Gonda, *President*
Kurt Atkinson, *Division Mgr*

GEOGRAPHIC SECTION

Nyack - Rockland County (G-13044)

Brynn Cox, *Editor*
Nick Hansen, *Area Mgr*
▲ **EMP:** 176
SQ FT: 60,000
SALES (est): 854MM **Privately Held**
SIC: 2026 Yogurt

(G-13025)
COMMERCIAL DISPLAY DESIGN LLC
120 Kemper Ln (13815-3579)
PHONE..................607 336-7353
Fax: 607 336-7357
Michael H Beggs, *Manager*
W Russell Hurd,
Thomas G Naughton,
Gregory C Yungbluth,
EMP: 15
SALES (est): 100K
SALES (corp-wide): 17.9MM **Privately Held**
SIC: 2521 Cabinets, office: wood
PA: Burt Rigid Box, Inc.
  58 Browne St
  Oneonta NY 13820
  607 433-2510

(G-13026)
DAN WESSON CORP
Also Called: Cz USA Dwf Dan Wesson Firearm
65 Borden Ave (13815-1105)
PHONE..................607 336-1174
Robert W Serva, *President*
EMP: 18
SQ FT: 24,000
SALES (est): 1.4MM **Privately Held**
WEB: www.danwessonfirearms.com
SIC: 3484 Small arms

(G-13027)
ELECTRON COIL INC
Also Called: Eci
141 Barr Rd (13815)
P.O. Box 71 (13815-0071)
PHONE..................607 336-7414
Douglas Marchant, *CEO*
John Barnett, *General Mgr*
Richard Marchant, *Vice Pres*
Paula McCall, *Purch Agent*
Jeff Cola, *QC Mgr*
EMP: 55
SQ FT: 10,000
SALES (est): 9.9MM **Privately Held**
WEB: www.electroncoil.com
SIC: 3621 3612 3675 3677 Coils, for electric motors or generators; power & distribution transformers; electronic capacitors; electronic coils, transformers & other inductors

(G-13028)
GOLUB CORPORATION
Also Called: Price Chopper Pharmacy
5631 State Highway 12 (13815-3205)
PHONE..................607 336-2588
Vincent Mainella, *Branch Mgr*
EMP: 78
SALES (corp-wide): 3.4B **Privately Held**
SIC: 3751 Motorcycles & related parts
PA: The Golub Corporation
  461 Nott St
  Schenectady NY 12308
  518 355-5000

(G-13029)
KERRY INC (DH)
Also Called: Kerry Bio-Science
158 State Highway 320 (13815-3561)
PHONE..................607 334-1700
Stan McCarthy, *CEO*
Gerry Behan, *Chairman*
Kelly Anderson, *Controller*
Crystal Dunninger, *Manager*
Michael Woods, *Manager*
▼ **EMP:** 97
SQ FT: 127,353
SALES (est): 17.2MM **Privately Held**
SIC: 2099 2079 2023 Food preparations; seasonings: dry mixes; edible fats & oils; dry, condensed, evaporated dairy products
HQ: Kerry Inc.
  3330 Millington Rd
  Beloit WI 53511
  608 363-1200

(G-13030)
LABEL GALLERY INC
1 Lee Ave 11 (13815-1108)
PHONE..................607 334-3244
Fax: 607 334-4815
Christopher Ulatowski, *President*
Anna Ulatowski, *Vice Pres*
Gail Lawrence, *Human Res Dir*
Dennis Rifanburg, *Sales Mgr*
EMP: 30
SQ FT: 15,000
SALES (est): 6.5MM **Privately Held**
WEB: www.labelgallery.net
SIC: 2672 2752 Labels (unprinted), gummed: made from purchased materials; commercial printing, lithographic

(G-13031)
NEW BERLIN GAZETTE
29 Lackawanna Ave (13815-1404)
P.O. Box 151 (13815-0151)
PHONE..................607 847-6131
Dick Snyder, *Owner*
EMP: 20
SQ FT: 2,400
SALES (est): 920K **Privately Held**
SIC: 2711 Commercial printing & newspaper publishing combined

(G-13032)
NORWICH AERO PRODUCTS INC (HQ)
50 Ohara Dr (13815-2029)
P.O. Box 109 (13815-0109)
PHONE..................607 336-7636
Fax: 607 336-2610
Richard Brad Lawrence, *Ch of Bd*
Tj Grady, *Vice Pres*
Tim Doyle, *QC Mgr*
Ronald Charles, *Project Engr*
Terry Keister, *CFO*
EMP: 79
SQ FT: 56,000
SALES (est): 17.5MM
SALES (corp-wide): 3.8B **Publicly Held**
WEB: www.norwichaero.com
SIC: 3812 3829 3823 Search & navigation equipment; measuring & controlling devices; temperature instruments: industrial process type
PA: Esterline Technologies Corp
  500 108th Ave Ne Ste 1500
  Bellevue WA 98004
  425 453-9400

(G-13033)
NORWICH PHARMACEUTICALS INC
Also Called: Norwich Pharma Services
6826 State Highway 12 (13815-3335)
PHONE..................607 335-3000
Chris Calhoun, *President*
Darren Alkins, *President*
Richard Bachelder, *Business Mgr*
Lisa Graver, *Exec VP*
Carolyn Gerardi, *Vice Pres*
▲ **EMP:** 375
SQ FT: 375,000
SALES (est): 50MM **Privately Held**
SIC: 2834 Pharmaceutical preparations
PA: Alvogen Group, Inc.
  10 Bloomfield Ave
  Pine Brook NJ 07058

(G-13034)
PPG ARCHITECTURAL FINISHES INC
Glidden Professional Paint Ctr
158 State Highway 320 (13815-3561)
P.O. Box 630 (13815-0630)
PHONE..................607 334-9951
Walter Schermerhorn, *Controller*
Jack Rush, *Marketing Mgr*
Tim O'Reilly, *Branch Mgr*
Vijai K Pasupuleti, *Manager*
Wayne Tilley, *Manager*
EMP: 125
SALES (corp-wide): 15.3B **Publicly Held**
WEB: www.gliddenpaint.com
SIC: 2821 Acrylic resins
HQ: Ppg Architectural Finishes, Inc.
  1 Ppg Pl
  Pittsburgh PA 15272
  412 434-3131

(G-13035)
PRECISION BUILT TOPS LLC
89 Borden Ave (13815-1105)
PHONE..................607 336-5417
Fax: 607 336-7585
Steven Serafan,
EMP: 6
SALES (est): 440K **Privately Held**
WEB: www.precisionbuilttops.com
SIC: 2541 Counter & sink tops

(G-13036)
PRIME TOOL & DIE LLC
6277 County Road 32 (13815-3560)
P.O. Box 83 (13815-0083)
PHONE..................607 334-5435
Steve Prime, *Manager*
George H Prime,
EMP: 6
SALES: 400K **Privately Held**
SIC: 3544 Jigs & fixtures

(G-13037)
SUN PRINTING INCORPORATED
57 Borden Ave 65 (13815-1105)
P.O. Box 151 (13815-0151)
PHONE..................607 337-3034
Fax: 607 334-5136
Bradford R Dick, *Principal*
EMP: 29 EST: 2001
SALES (est): 2.5MM **Privately Held**
SIC: 2752 Commercial printing, lithographic

(G-13038)
SURESEAL CORPORATION
Also Called: Norwich Aero
50 Ohara Dr (13815-2029)
P.O. Box 109 (13815-0109)
PHONE..................607 336-6676
Randy Mohr, *President*
Mike Crandell, *Engineer*
Terry Keister, *CFO*
Edward Campbell, *Executive*
EMP: 7
SQ FT: 56,000
SALES (est): 876.6K
SALES (corp-wide): 3.8B **Publicly Held**
WEB: www.norwichaero.com
SIC: 3678 Electronic connectors
HQ: Norwich Aero Products, Inc.
  50 Ohara Dr
  Norwich NY 13815
  607 336-7636

(G-13039)
UNISON INDUSTRIES LLC
5345 State Highway 12 (13815-1246)
P.O. Box 310 (13815-0310)
PHONE..................607 335-5000
Steve Logan, *Purch Agent*
Debbie Morgan, *Buyer*
Timothy Carr, *Project Engr*
Gary Cummings, *Manager*
Jerry Irwin, *Manager*
EMP: 350
SALES (corp-wide): 117.3B **Publicly Held**
WEB: www.unisonindustries.com
SIC: 3679 3769 Electronic circuits; guided missile & space vehicle parts & auxiliary equipment
HQ: Unison Industries, Llc
  7575 Baymeadows Way
  Jacksonville FL 32256
  904 739-4000

Norwood
St. Lawrence County

(G-13040)
BARRETT PAVING MATERIALS INC
Also Called: Norwood Quar Btmnous Con Plnts
Rr 56 (13668)
P.O. Box 203 (13668-0203)
PHONE..................315 353-6611
Fax: 315 353-2768
David R Wright, *Superintendent*
EMP: 25

SALES (corp-wide): 84.5MM **Privately Held**
WEB: www.barrettpaving.com
SIC: 2951 5032 1611 2952 Concrete, bituminous; paving materials; surfacing & paving; asphalt felts & coatings
HQ: Barrett Paving Materials Inc.
  3 Becker Farm Rd Ste 307
  Roseland NJ 07068
  973 533-1001

Nunda
Livingston County

(G-13041)
ONCE AGAIN NUT BUTTER COLLECTV (PA)
12 S State St (14517)
P.O. Box 429 (14517-0429)
PHONE..................585 468-2535
Fax: 585 468-5995
Robert Gelser, *President*
Jake Rawleigh, *QC Mgr*
Peter Millen, *Engineer*
Lawrence Filipski, *CFO*
Gael Orr, *Comms Mgr*
▲ **EMP:** 64
SQ FT: 20,000
SALES (est): 12.9MM **Privately Held**
WEB: www.onceagainnutbutter.com
SIC: 2099 Peanut butter; almond pastes; honey, strained & bottled

(G-13042)
SEATING INC
60 N State St (14517)
P.O. Box 898 (14517-0898)
PHONE..................800 468-2475
Fax: 585 468-2804
Judy Hart, *President*
Doug Hart, *Vice Pres*
Tammy Everts, *Manager*
Tammy McCallum, *Info Tech Mgr*
EMP: 31
SQ FT: 65,000
SALES (est): 3.7MM **Privately Held**
WEB: www.seatinginc.com
SIC: 2522 2531 Office chairs, benches & stools, except wood; public building & related furniture

Nyack
Rockland County

(G-13043)
AIR CHEX EQUIPMENT CORP
50 Lydecker St (10960-2104)
PHONE..................845 358-8179
Mark Wallach, *President*
Richard Fussell, *Vice Pres*
Elizabeth Wallach, *Vice Pres*
EMP: 5
SQ FT: 4,300
SALES (est): 150K **Privately Held**
WEB: www.airchexcorp.com
SIC: 2499 Decorative wood & woodwork

(G-13044)
BECTON DICKINSON AND COMPANY
Also Called: Bd Initiative-Hlthcare Wrkr SA
1 Main St Apt 3307 (10960-3236)
PHONE..................845 353-3371
Johannes Gustafsson, *Engineer*
Amit Limaye, *Engineer*
John Manocchio, *Senior Engr*
Jill Garnette, *Manager*
Lourdes P Lopez Amora,
EMP: 379
SALES (corp-wide): 10.2B **Publicly Held**
SIC: 3841 Surgical & medical instruments
PA: Becton, Dickinson And Company
  1 Becton Dr
  Franklin Lakes NJ 07417
  201 847-6800

Nyack - Rockland County (G-13045) — GEOGRAPHIC SECTION

(G-13045)
BERRY INDUSTRIAL GROUP INC (PA)
30 Main St (10960-3202)
PHONE.................................845 353-8338
Debra Berry, *CEO*
Peter Berry, *President*
Lori Lichtig, *General Mgr*
Jessica Kane, *Bookkeeper*
Lenny Kochuba, *Natl Sales Mgr*
EMP: 5
SQ FT: 1,800
SALES (est): 915.7K **Privately Held**
WEB: www.berryindustrial.com
SIC: 2448 5031 Wood pallets & skids; lumber: rough, dressed & finished

(G-13046)
CHARLES PERRELLA INC
78 S Broadway (10960-6802)
PHONE.................................845 348-4777
Marie Somos, *President*
Richard Townsend, *Corp Secy*
Phyllis Townsend, *Vice Pres*
EMP: 20
SQ FT: 7,500
SALES (est): 1.5MM **Privately Held**
WEB: www.perrellainc.com
SIC: 3911 5944 Jewelry, precious metal; jewelry stores

(G-13047)
CONCEPT PRINTING INC
Also Called: Concept Printing and Promotion
40 Lydecker St (10960-2104)
PHONE.................................845 353-4040
Fax: 201 387-6363
Kerry Gaughan Monahan, *President*
▲ EMP: 4
SALES: 1.3MM **Privately Held**
WEB: www.conceptprintinginc.com
SIC: 2752 5199 Commercial printing, offset; advertising specialties

(G-13048)
DESIGNPLEX LLC
107 Cedar Hill Ave (10960-3705)
PHONE.................................845 358-6647
Loren Bloom, *President*
EMP: 5
SQ FT: 1,500
SALES (est): 200K **Privately Held**
WEB: www.designplex.org
SIC: 3993 Signs & advertising specialties

(G-13049)
DIRECTORY MAJOR MALLS INC
20 N Broadway Ste 2 (10960-2644)
P.O. Box 837 (10960-0837)
PHONE.................................845 348-7000
Tama J Shor, *President*
EMP: 8
SALES (est): 800.4K **Privately Held**
WEB: www.directoryofmajormalls.com
SIC: 2741 6531 Atlases: publishing only, not printed on site; real estate agents & managers

(G-13050)
EASTERN PRECISION MFG
76 S Franklin St 78 (10960-3734)
PHONE.................................845 358-1951
Harold Hill, *President*
EMP: 6 EST: 1973
SQ FT: 600
SALES (est): 500K **Privately Held**
SIC: 3569 Firefighting apparatus

(G-13051)
EDROY PRODUCTS CO INC
245 N Midland Ave (10960-1949)
P.O. Box 998 (10960-0998)
PHONE.................................845 358-6600
Fax: 845 358-4098
Steven Stoltze, *President*
EMP: 7 EST: 1937
SQ FT: 4,700
SALES: 606.2K **Privately Held**
WEB: www.edroyproducts.com
SIC: 3851 Magnifiers (readers & simple magnifiers)

(G-13052)
GLOBAL BRANDS INC
1031 Route 9w S (10960-4907)
PHONE.................................845 358-1212
Ralph Ferrante, *CEO*
Herbert M Paul, *President*
Lawernce Ackemern, *Office Mgr*
EMP: 8
SQ FT: 1,250
SALES (est): 600K **Privately Held**
SIC: 2086 Mineral water, carbonated: packaged in cans, bottles, etc.

(G-13053)
SARAVAL INDUSTRIES
348 N Midland Ave (10960-1531)
PHONE.................................516 768-9033
Dave Schwartz, *Owner*
Maria Vestal, *Managing Dir*
EMP: 9
SALES (est): 480K **Privately Held**
SIC: 2521 Wood office furniture

(G-13054)
TANDY LEATHER FACTORY INC
298 Main St (10960-2418)
PHONE.................................845 480-3588
Kelly Perini, *Manager*
EMP: 5
SALES (corp-wide): 84.1MM **Publicly Held**
SIC: 3111 5199 5948 Accessory products, leather; lace leather; leather, leather goods & furs; leather goods, except luggage & shoes
PA: Tandy Leather Factory, Inc.
1900 Se Loop 820
Fort Worth TX 76140
817 872-3200

(G-13055)
TEKA PRECISION INC
251 Mountainview Ave (10960-1700)
PHONE.................................845 753-1900
Fax: 845 727-4040
Helen Roderick, *President*
EMP: 7
SQ FT: 1,500
SALES (est): 660K **Privately Held**
SIC: 3496 3541 3495 3452 Miscellaneous fabricated wire products; machine tools, metal cutting type; wire springs; bolts, nuts, rivets & washers

(G-13056)
WIRELESS COMMUNICATIONS INC
4 Chemong Ct (10960-2307)
PHONE.................................845 353-5921
Robert H Colten, *Owner*
EMP: 5
SALES (est): 317.7K **Privately Held**
SIC: 3663 Radio broadcasting & communications equipment

Oakdale
Suffolk County

(G-13057)
CJ COMPONENT PRODUCTS LLC
624 Tower Mews (11769-2449)
PHONE.................................631 567-3733
David Howe, *CEO*
▼ EMP: 5
SQ FT: 880
SALES (est): 798.9K **Privately Held**
WEB: www.cjcomponents.com
SIC: 3663 Radio & TV communications equipment

(G-13058)
GALAXY SOFTWARE LLC
154 Middlesex Ave (11769-1975)
P.O. Box 229 (11769-0229)
PHONE.................................631 244-8405
Andrew Cohen,
Cathline Cohen,
EMP: 8
SALES (est): 664.9K **Privately Held**
WEB: www.galaxy-software.com
SIC: 7372 7371 Application computer software; software programming applications

(G-13059)
MODERN ITLN BKY OF W BABYLON
301 Locust Ave (11769-1652)
PHONE.................................631 589-7300
Fax: 631 589-7383
James Turco, *CEO*
Kevin Connors, *Controller*
Bridgette Johnston, *Controller*
Frank Dibenedetto, *Natl Sales Mgr*
Michael Dunn, *Corp Comm Staff*
EMP: 170
SQ FT: 54,000
SALES (est): 43.9MM **Privately Held**
WEB: www.modernbakedprod.com
SIC: 2051 5142 5149 Bread, all types (white, wheat, rye, etc); fresh or frozen; bakery products, frozen; bakery products

(G-13060)
MORELAND HOSE & BELTING CORP
4118 Sunrise Hwy (11769-1013)
PHONE.................................631 563-7071
Fax: 631 563-3457
William Delmore, *Manager*
EMP: 8
SALES (corp-wide): 6.4MM **Privately Held**
WEB: www.morelandhose.com
SIC: 3052 Hose, pneumatic: rubber or rubberized fabric
PA: Moreland Hose & Belting Corp
135 Adams Ave
Hempstead NY 11550
516 485-9898

(G-13061)
PUPELLOS ORGANIC CHIPS INC
509 Ockers Dr (11769-1410)
P.O. Box 542, Bohemia (11716-0542)
PHONE.................................718 710-9154
John Adam Pupello, *CEO*
EMP: 15
SALES: 950K **Privately Held**
SIC: 2096 Potato sticks

(G-13062)
SPECIALTY FABRICATORS
4120 Sunrise Hwy (11769-1079)
PHONE.................................631 256-6982
Charlie Aguilera, *Principal*
EMP: 10
SALES (est): 1.2MM **Privately Held**
SIC: 3399 Primary metal products

(G-13063)
STEEL-BRITE LTD
Also Called: September Associates
2 Dawn Dr (11769-1624)
PHONE.................................631 589-4044
Marilyn Cohen, *President*
Susan McCarthy, *Managing Dir*
EMP: 10
SQ FT: 2,500
SALES (est): 770K **Privately Held**
SIC: 3993 5072 Displays & cutouts, window & lobby; hardware

Oakfield
Genesee County

(G-13064)
BONDUELLE USA INC
40 Stevens St (14125-1227)
PHONE.................................585 948-5252
Daniel Vielfaure, *CEO*
EMP: 33
SALES (est): 8.8MM **Privately Held**
SIC: 3556 Smokers, food processing equipment

(G-13065)
KEEBLER COMPANY
2999 Judge Rd (14125-9771)
PHONE.................................585 948-8010
Fax: 585 948-8023
Ed Watson, *Manager*
EMP: 17
SALES (corp-wide): 13.5B **Publicly Held**
WEB: www.keebler.com
SIC: 2052 Cookies
HQ: Keebler Company
1 Kellogg Sq
Battle Creek MI 49017
269 961-2000

(G-13066)
UNITED STATES GYPSUM COMPANY
2750 Maple Ave (14125-9722)
PHONE.................................585 948-5221
Fax: 585 948-5018
Jim Perry, *Plant Mgr*
Jim Roz, *Opers Staff*
Debbie Rich, *Purchasing*
Ray Dunlevy, *Personnel*
Gregg Diefenbacher, *Branch Mgr*
EMP: 123
SALES (corp-wide): 3.7B **Publicly Held**
WEB: www.usg.com
SIC: 3275 Gypsum products
HQ: United States Gypsum Company Inc
550 W Adams St Ste 1300
Chicago IL 60661
312 606-4000

Oakland Gardens
Queens County

(G-13067)
SLIMS BAGELS UNLIMITED INC (PA)
22118 Horace Harding Expy (11364-2390)
P.O. Box 640206 (11364-0206)
PHONE.................................718 229-1140
Fax: 718 225-0514
Joseph Dvir, *President*
David Katz, *Vice Pres*
EMP: 27 EST: 1999
SQ FT: 5,000
SALES (est): 1.5MM **Privately Held**
SIC: 2051 5641 Bakery: wholesale or wholesale/retail combined; children's & infants' wear stores

(G-13068)
SRTECH INDUSTRY CORP
5022 201st St (11364-1014)
PHONE.................................718 496-7001
S Chung, *President*
EMP: 25
SQ FT: 5,000
SALES: 3MM **Privately Held**
SIC: 3663 Amplifiers, RF power & IF

Oaks Corners
Ontario County

(G-13069)
ELDERLEE INCORPORATED (HQ)
729 Cross Rd (14518)
P.O. Box 10 (14518-0010)
PHONE.................................315 789-6670
Fax: 315 789-4262
Basil A Shorb III, *Ch of Bd*
William J Shorb, *President*
David Dejohn, *Vice Pres*
Robert Rook, *Vice Pres*
Paul R Strain, *Vice Pres*
EMP: 120
SQ FT: 240,000
SALES (est): 44.3MM
SALES (corp-wide): 74.9MM **Privately Held**
WEB: www.elderlee.com
SIC: 3312 1611 3444 3993 Iron & steel: galvanized, pipes, plates, sheets, etc.; guardrail construction, highways; guard rails, highway: sheet metal; signs & advertising specialties; concrete products
PA: Reh Holdings, Inc
150 S Sumner St
York PA 17404
717 843-0021

(G-13070)
HANSON AGGREGATES PA LLC
2026 County Rd Ste 6 (14518)
P.O. Box 9 (14518-0009)
PHONE.................................315 789-6202

▲ = Import ▼ = Export
◆ = Import/Export

GEOGRAPHIC SECTION

Oceanside - Nassau County (G-13098)

Fax: 315 789-1030
Kenny Thurston, *Opers-Prdtn-Mfg*
Mike Cool, *Personnel Exec*
EMP: 25
SALES (corp-wide): 14.4B **Privately Held**
SIC: 1442 3281 1422 Gravel mining; stone, quarrying & processing of own stone products; crushed & broken limestone
HQ: Hanson Aggregates Pennsylvania, Llc
7660 Imperial Way
Allentown PA 18195
610 366-4626

Oceanside
Nassau County

(G-13071)
3KRF LLC
3516 Hargale Rd (11572-5820)
PHONE..................516 208-6824
Mark Gruenspecht, *Mng Member*
Timothy Hopper,
EMP: 5
SALES (est): 410K **Privately Held**
SIC: 3699 Electrical welding equipment

(G-13072)
AHW PRINTING CORP
Also Called: PIP Printing
2920 Long Beach Rd (11572-3114)
PHONE..................516 536-3600
Fax: 516 536-9290
Alan Waldman, *President*
Harriet Waldman, *Treasurer*
EMP: 11
SQ FT: 1,900
SALES (est): 1.5MM **Privately Held**
SIC: 2752 Commercial printing, offset

(G-13073)
ASTRODYNE INC
18 Neil Ct (11572-5816)
P.O. Box 354, Rockville Centre (11571-0354)
PHONE..................516 536-5755
Fax: 516 536-5063
David J Salwen, *CEO*
Ira M Salwen, *President*
Barbara Salwen, *Admin Sec*
EMP: 6
SQ FT: 5,000
SALES (est): 931.1K **Privately Held**
SIC: 3861 5045 5734 Photographic equipment & supplies; computers, peripherals & software; computer software; computer & software stores; computer software & accessories

(G-13074)
CHUDNOW MANUFACTURING CO INC
3055 New St (11572-2743)
PHONE..................516 593-4222
Fax: 516 593-4156
Richard B Cohen, *President*
Ralph Pierro, *General Mgr*
EMP: 45 **EST:** 1934
SQ FT: 28,000
SALES: 5MM **Privately Held**
SIC: 3585 Soda fountain & beverage dispensing equipment & parts; soda fountains, parts & accessories

(G-13075)
D & M CUSTOM CABINETS INC
2994 Long Beach Rd (11572-3205)
PHONE..................516 678-2818
Fax: 516 678-0042
Michael J Lastella, *President*
Doris Lastella, *Admin Sec*
EMP: 12
SQ FT: 7,500
SALES (est): 1.3MM **Privately Held**
WEB: www.d-mcc.com
SIC: 2434 Wood kitchen cabinets

(G-13076)
DDC TECHNOLOGIES INC
311 Woods Ave (11572-2128)
PHONE..................516 594-1533
Dimitri Donskoy, *President*
Alex Chernovets, *Marketing Mgr*
EMP: 5
SALES (est): 847.9K **Privately Held**
WEB: www.ddctech.com
SIC: 3845 Laser systems & equipment, medical

(G-13077)
DRILL AMERICA INC
3574 Lawson Blvd (11572-4909)
PHONE..................516 764-5700
▲ **EMP:** 6
SALES (est): 420K **Privately Held**
SIC: 3545 Mfg Machine Tool Accessories

(G-13078)
EAST COAST MOLDERS INC
3001 New St Ste F (11572-2747)
PHONE..................516 240-6000
Richard Mandell, *President*
EMP: 225
SQ FT: 7,000
SALES (est): 10MM **Privately Held**
SIC: 2342 Brassieres

(G-13079)
EXPRESS BUILDING SUPPLY INC
Also Called: Wholesale Window Warehouse
3550 Lawson Blvd (11572-4908)
PHONE..................516 608-0379
Robert Freedman, *President*
EMP: 25 **EST:** 1996
SQ FT: 9,000
SALES: 2.5MM **Privately Held**
SIC: 3211 5031 5211 Window glass, clear & colored; windows; windows, storm: wood or metal

(G-13080)
HENNIG CUSTOM WOODWORK CORP
Also Called: Hennig Custom Woodworking
2497 Long Beach Rd (11572-1321)
PHONE..................516 536-3460
James Hennig, *President*
EMP: 5
SALES: 500K **Privately Held**
SIC: 2421 7389 5031 2499 Furniture dimension stock, softwood; laminating service; kitchen cabinets; decorative wood & woodwork; cabinet & finish carpentry

(G-13081)
INDUSTRIAL MACHINE & GEAR WORK
Also Called: Industrial Machs & Gear Wks
9 Neil Ct (11572-5800)
PHONE..................516 569-4820
Richard Lehrman, *Principal*
EMP: 5
SALES (est): 250K **Privately Held**
SIC: 3599 7389 Machine shop, jobbing & repair; grinding, precision: commercial or industrial

(G-13082)
IP MED INC
3571 Hargale Rd (11572-5821)
PHONE..................516 766-3800
Judah Isaacs, *President*
EMP: 7
SALES (est): 304.1K **Privately Held**
SIC: 2836 3841 2834 5122 Bacterial vaccines; inhalators, surgical & medical; proprietary drug products; drugs & drug proprietaries

(G-13083)
JONDEN MANUFACTURING CO INC
3069 Lawson Blvd (11572-2939)
PHONE..................718 369-4925
Fax: 718 369-4927
Jon Smilowitze, *Owner*
Jennifer Matera, *Sales Staff*
Jean Mondesir Jr, *Manager*
EMP: 10
SALES (corp-wide): 4.8MM **Privately Held**
WEB: www.jonden.com
SIC: 2339 Athletic clothing: women's, misses' & juniors'
PA: Jonden Manufacturing Co., Inc.
1410 Broadway Rm 1103
New York NY 10018
516 442-4895

(G-13084)
KANTEK INC
Also Called: Spectrum
3460a Hampton Rd (11572-4803)
PHONE..................516 594-4600
Fax: 516 594-1555
Herman Kappel, *President*
AVI Kappel, *General Mgr*
▲ **EMP:** 30
SQ FT: 25,000
SALES (est): 15MM **Privately Held**
WEB: www.kantek.com
SIC: 3577 5045 Computer peripheral equipment; computers, peripherals & software

(G-13085)
L N D INCORPORATED
Also Called: Lnd
3230 Lawson Blvd (11572-3796)
PHONE..................516 678-6141
Fax: 516 678-6704
Peter T Neyland, *President*
Spencer B Neyland, *Vice Pres*
Robert Sears, *Purchasing*
Bill Chatfield, *Controller*
William J Lehnert, *VP Sales*
EMP: 45 **EST:** 1964
SQ FT: 14,000
SALES (est): 11.5MM **Privately Held**
WEB: www.lndinc.com
SIC: 3829 Nuclear radiation & testing apparatus

(G-13086)
LOVE BRIGHT JEWELRY INC
Also Called: Lovebrightjewelry.com
3446 Frederick St (11572-4713)
PHONE..................516 620-2509
Bhupen Kapadia, *President*
EMP: 25
SQ FT: 2,000
SALES (est): 1.4MM **Privately Held**
SIC: 3911 5094 5944 Jewelry apparel; jewelry; jewelry stores

(G-13087)
MARK PERI INTERNATIONAL
3516 Hargale Rd (11572-5820)
PHONE..................516 208-6824
Mark Gruenspecht, *Director*
EMP: 10
SALES (est): 725.2K **Privately Held**
SIC: 3663 Radio & TV communications equipment

(G-13088)
MARKPERICOM
3516 Hargale Rd (11572-5820)
PHONE..................516 208-6824
Mark Gruenstpecht, *President*
EMP: 9
SALES (est): 641.9K **Privately Held**
SIC: 3569 General industrial machinery

(G-13089)
PIER-TECH INC
7 Hampton Rd (11572-4808)
PHONE..................516 442-5420
Robert Sackaris, *Ch of Bd*
Jennifer Sackaris, *Manager*
Irene Sackaris, *Admin Sec*
EMP: 42
SALES (est): 8.8MM **Privately Held**
SIC: 3531 Construction machinery

(G-13090)
POETRY MAILING LIST MARSH HAWK
2823 Rockaway Ave (11572-1018)
P.O. Box 206, East Rockaway (11518-0206)
PHONE..................516 766-1891
Jane Augustine, *President*
EMP: 5
SALES (est): 45.4K **Privately Held**
SIC: 2731 Book publishing

(G-13091)
RADAR SPORTS LLC
Also Called: Radarsport.com
2660 Washington Ave (11572-1540)
PHONE..................516 678-1919
Barbara Schure,
Allen Web,
EMP: 4 **EST:** 1990
SQ FT: 1,500
SALES: 1.2MM **Privately Held**
SIC: 3949 Sporting & athletic goods

(G-13092)
RADIANT PRO LTD
245 Merrick Rd (11572-1428)
PHONE..................516 763-5678
John Cioento, *Owner*
EMP: 7 **EST:** 2000
SALES (est): 643K **Privately Held**
SIC: 3567 Radiant heating systems, industrial process

(G-13093)
ROSE TRUNK MFG CO INC
3935 Sally Ln (11572-5934)
PHONE..................516 766-6686
Melvin Lapidus, *President*
Mark Lapidus, *Vice Pres*
▼ **EMP:** 15 **EST:** 1945
SQ FT: 15,000
SALES (est): 1.4MM **Privately Held**
WEB: www.rosetrunk.com
SIC: 3161 Luggage; trunks

(G-13094)
ROYAL MARBLE & GRANITE INC
3295 Royal Ave (11572-3625)
PHONE..................516 536-5900
Richard Tafuri, *President*
Anthony Tafuri, *Vice Pres*
▲ **EMP:** 8
SQ FT: 8,000
SALES (est): 738.4K **Privately Held**
SIC: 3281 3272 Granite, cut & shaped; art marble, concrete

(G-13095)
RUSSCO METAL SPINNING CO INC
3064 Lawson Blvd (11572-2711)
PHONE..................516 872-6055
Fax: 516 872-8199
William Russ, *President*
Mary Russ, *Corp Secy*
Michael Byrne, *Plant Mgr*
EMP: 10
SQ FT: 5,300
SALES (est): 1.2MM **Privately Held**
SIC: 3469 Spinning metal for the trade

(G-13096)
SEA WAVES INC (PA)
2425 Long Beach Rd (11572-1320)
PHONE..................516 766-4201
Brian Corhan, *President*
Harold Corhan, *Vice Pres*
▲ **EMP:** 5
SQ FT: 2,000
SALES (est): 660.1K **Privately Held**
SIC: 2339 Bathing suits: women's, misses' & juniors'; beachwear: women's, misses' & juniors'

(G-13097)
STRONG GROUP INC
222 Atlantic Ave Unit B (11572-2045)
PHONE..................516 766-6300
Fax: 516 766-6307
Walter Bistrong, *President*
Ann Sigel, *Corp Secy*
EMP: 8
SALES (est): 550K **Privately Held**
SIC: 2311 Policemen's uniforms: made from purchased materials

(G-13098)
STYLES MANUFACTURING CORP
3571 Hargale Rd (11572-5821)
PHONE..................516 763-5303
Louis Fuchs, *President*
Ron Keyes, *Vice Pres*
Irene Sassaman, *Manager*
▲ **EMP:** 5

Oceanside - Nassau County (G-13099)

SALES (est): 5MM **Privately Held**
SIC: 3315 Hangers (garment), wire

(G-13099)
SUM SUM LLC
3595 Lawson Blvd Whse D Warehouse D (11572)
PHONE..................516 812-3959
Jaymie Dahan, *CEO*
David Dahan, *Vice Pres*
EMP: 5
SQ FT: 1,000
SALES: 250K **Privately Held**
SIC: 2035 Dressings, salad: raw & cooked (except dry mixes)

(G-13100)
TAG FLANGE & MACHINING INC
3375 Royal Ave (11572-4812)
PHONE..................516 536-1300
Theodore A Gallucci III, *President*
Sean F Gallucci, *Vice Pres*
EMP: 6
SQ FT: 10,000
SALES (est): 500K **Privately Held**
SIC: 3498 Fabricated pipe & fittings

(G-13101)
THE NUGENT ORGANIZATION INC
Also Called: Nugent Printing Company
3433 Ocean Harbor Dr (11572-3516)
PHONE..................212 645-6600
Fax: 212 645-6605
Antonino Longo, *President*
Vincent Longo, *Vice Pres*
EMP: 18
SQ FT: 10,000
SALES (est): 2.3MM **Privately Held**
WEB: www.nugentprint.com
SIC: 2752 7331 2732 Commercial printing, offset; mailing service; book printing

(G-13102)
UNITED THREAD MILLS CORP (PA)
3530 Lawson Blvd Gf (11572-4908)
P.O. Box 766, Rockville Centre (11571-0766)
PHONE..................516 536-3900
Fax: 516 536-3547
Ira Henkus, *President*
▼ **EMP:** 6 **EST:** 1948
SQ FT: 66,000
SALES (est): 60.2MM **Privately Held**
SIC: 2284 2281 Thread mills; yarn spinning mills

(G-13103)
VENEER ONE INC
3415 Hampton Rd (11572-4835)
PHONE..................516 536-6480
Victor Giaime, *Ch of Bd*
Arnold Lanzillotta, *President*
Steve Horan, *Admin Sec*
▲ **EMP:** 28 **EST:** 2000
SQ FT: 19,000
SALES (est): 4.1MM **Privately Held**
WEB: www.veneer1.com
SIC: 2435 Hardwood veneer & plywood

(G-13104)
VIANA SIGNS CORP
3520 Lawson Blvd (11572-4908)
PHONE..................516 887-2000
Leo Viana, *President*
EMP: 10
SALES (est): 750K **Privately Held**
SIC: 3993 Signs & advertising specialties

(G-13105)
WESTRON CORPORATION
Also Called: Westron Lighting
18 Neil Ct (11572-5816)
PHONE..................516 678-2300
Irving Allerhand, *Ch of Bd*
Hershel Allerhand, *President*
Les Deutsch, *Sales/Mktg Dir*
Rosary Holmes, *Manager*
▲ **EMP:** 50
SQ FT: 25,000
SALES (est): 5.9MM **Privately Held**
WEB: www.westronlighting.com
SIC: 3641 Electric lamps

(G-13106)
WHITTIER PUBLICATIONS INC
3115 Long Beach Rd # 301 (11572-3253)
PHONE..................516 432-8120
Judith Etra, *President*
Marcia Binns, *Prdtn Mgr*
Gerald Etra, *Admin Asst*
EMP: 5
SALES: 500K **Privately Held**
WEB: www.whitbooks.com
SIC: 2731 Books: publishing & printing

(G-13107)
YALE TROUSER CORPORATION
Also Called: Smokey Joes
3670 Oceanside Rd W Ste 6 (11572-5961)
PHONE..................516 255-0700
Arnold Bloom, *President*
Gary Bloom, *Vice Pres*
EMP: 10 **EST:** 1950
SALES (est): 1.1MM **Privately Held**
WEB: www.yaletrouser.com
SIC: 2325 2321 Slacks, dress: men's, youths' & boys'; trousers, dress (separate): men's, youths' & boys'; men's & boys' furnishings

Odessa
Schuyler County

(G-13108)
FINGER LAKES CHEESE TRAIL
4970 County Road 14 (14869-9730)
PHONE..................607 857-5726
Carmella Hoffman, *Treasurer*
EMP: 13
SALES (est): 718.6K **Privately Held**
SIC: 2026 Fluid milk

Ogdensburg
St. Lawrence County

(G-13109)
ACCO BRANDS USA LLC
Also Called: Acco North America
941 Acco Way (13669-4438)
PHONE..................847 541-9500
Fax: 315 393-7887
Chad Kiah, *Controller*
Sandra Fazio, *Manager*
Kyle Foster, *Manager*
Balaji Padmanabhan, *Technology*
Jeffery Almasian, *Director*
EMP: 120
SALES (corp-wide): 1.5B **Publicly Held**
WEB: www.accobrands.com
SIC: 2782 Looseleaf binders & devices
HQ: Acco Brands Usa Llc
 4 Corporate Dr
 Lake Zurich IL 60047
 800 222-6462

(G-13110)
ALGONQUIN POWER
19 Mill St (13669-1304)
PHONE..................315 393-5595
Walter Bracy, *Manager*
EMP: 7
SALES (est): 886.8K **Privately Held**
SIC: 3634 Electric housewares & fans

(G-13111)
ANSEN CORPORATION (PA)
100 Chimney Point Dr (13669-2206)
PHONE..................315 393-3573
James Kingman, *CEO*
Jerry W Slusser, *President*
Kenneth Emter, *Corp Secy*
Nadia Cutler, *Senior Buyer*
Jason W Slusser, *Director*
▲ **EMP:** 7
SQ FT: 72,000
SALES (est): 87.8MM **Privately Held**
WEB: www.ansencorp.com
SIC: 3672 Printed circuit boards

(G-13112)
ANSEN CORPORATION
100 Chimney Point Dr (13669-2206)
PHONE..................315 393-3573
Craig D Kelley, *Vice Pres*
Don McCormick, *Vice Pres*
Jeff Hilk, *Sales Staff*
Rodney Bush, *Branch Mgr*
EMP: 110
SQ FT: 71,000
SALES (corp-wide): 87.8MM **Privately Held**
WEB: www.ansencorp.com
SIC: 3672 Printed circuit boards
PA: Ansen Corporation
 100 Chimney Point Dr
 Ogdensburg NY 13669
 315 393-3573

(G-13113)
CANARM LTD (HQ)
808 Commerce Park Dr (13669-2208)
PHONE..................800 267-4427
David Beatty, *CEO*
James Cooper, *President*
▲ **EMP:** 2
SQ FT: 1,500
SALES: 75MM
SALES (corp-wide): 80.1MM **Privately Held**
SIC: 3564 3645 3646 5064 Blowing fans: industrial or commercial; exhaust fans: industrial or commercial; ventilating fans: industrial or commercial; residential lighting fixtures; commercial indusl & institutional electric lighting fixtures; fans, household: electric; fans, industrial; lighting fixtures, commercial & industrial; lighting fixtures, residential
PA: Canarm Ltd
 2157 Parkedale Ave
 Brockville ON K6V 0
 613 342-5424

(G-13114)
DEFELSKO CORPORATION
800 Proctor Ave (13669-2205)
PHONE..................315 393-4450
Fax: 315 393-8471
Frank Koch, *President*
Terry Larue, *General Mgr*
David Beamish, *Chairman*
Linda K Beamish, *Vice Pres*
Steven Nowell, *QC Mgr*
◆ **EMP:** 60 **EST:** 1965
SQ FT: 15,000
SALES (est): 17.9MM **Privately Held**
WEB: www.defelsko.com
SIC: 3823 3829 Industrial instrmnts msrmnt display/control process variable; measuring & controlling devices

(G-13115)
HANSON AGGREGATES PA LLC
701 Cedar St (13669-3000)
P.O. Box 250 (13669-0250)
PHONE..................315 393-3743
Daniel O'Connor, *Manager*
Robert Bismarck, *Manager*
Mark Macklen, *Manager*
EMP: 14
SQ FT: 2,196
SALES (corp-wide): 14.4B **Privately Held**
SIC: 1429 1422 Grits mining (crushed stone); limestones, ground
HQ: Hanson Aggregates Pennsylvania, Llc
 7660 Imperial Way
 Allentown PA 18195
 610 366-4626

(G-13116)
HOOSIER MAGNETICS INC
110 Denny St (13669-1797)
PHONE..................315 393-1813
Fax: 315 393-0017
B Thomas Shirk, *President*
Joe Vierno, *Manager*
Mary Alice Shirk, *Admin Sec*
◆ **EMP:** 55
SQ FT: 30,000
SALES (est): 9.7MM **Privately Held**
WEB: www.hoosiermagnetics.com
SIC: 3264 Ferrite & ferrite parts

(G-13117)
LAWTONS ELECTRIC MOTOR SERVICE
Also Called: Lawton Electric Co
148 Cemetery Rd (13669-4179)
PHONE..................315 393-2728
Bernard Lawton, *Partner*
Timothy Lawton, *Partner*
EMP: 7
SALES: 500K **Privately Held**
SIC: 7694 Electric motor repair

(G-13118)
MAXAM NORTH AMERICA INC
3 Cemetary Dr (13669-4528)
PHONE..................313 322-8651
EMP: 7
SALES (corp-wide): 37.8MM **Privately Held**
SIC: 2892 5169 Explosives; explosives
HQ: Maxam North America, Inc.
 6975 S Union Park Ctr # 525
 Midvale UT 84047
 801 233-6000

(G-13119)
MED-ENG LLC
103 Tulloch Dr (13669-2215)
PHONE..................315 713-0103
Scott Obrien, *CEO*
Dennis Morris, *President*
Cindy Levi, *Manager*
Aris Makris, *CTO*
Maureen Mackie, *Info Tech Mgr*
EMP: 40
SALES (est): 3.7MM
SALES (corp-wide): 791.5MM **Privately Held**
WEB: www.allen-vanguard.com
SIC: 2311 Military uniforms, men's & youths': purchased materials
HQ: Safariland, Llc
 13386 International Pkwy
 Jacksonville FL 32218
 904 741-5400

(G-13120)
QUEENAIRE TECHNOLOGIES INC
9483 State Highway 37 (13669-4467)
PHONE..................315 393-5454
Susan Duffy, *President*
Paul McGrath, *Opers Dir*
Nicole Plumley, *Finance*
Tom Coplen, *Sales Staff*
▼ **EMP:** 6
SQ FT: 6,600
SALES (est): 1.2MM **Privately Held**
SIC: 3559 Ozone machines

(G-13121)
RIVER RAT DESIGN
Also Called: Roethel
1801 Ford St Ste A (13669-1845)
PHONE..................315 393-4770
Laurel Roethel, *Owner*
EMP: 15
SQ FT: 6,600
SALES (est): 712.7K **Privately Held**
SIC: 2395 Embroidery & art needlework

(G-13122)
ST LAWRENCE COUNTY NEWSPAPERS (HQ)
Also Called: Courier Observer
230 Caroline St Ste 1 (13669-1629)
PHONE..................315 393-1003
Fax: 315 393-5108
Charles Kelly, *Publisher*
Chuck Kelley, *General Mgr*
Brenda La Brake, *VP Finance*
Cindy Ford, *Accounts Exec*
Sean Cameron, *Manager*
▲ **EMP:** 60
SQ FT: 15,000
SALES (est): 6.3MM
SALES (corp-wide): 32MM **Privately Held**
WEB: www.courierobserver.com
SIC: 2711 2752 Newspapers, publishing & printing; commercial printing, lithographic
PA: Johnson Newspaper Corporation
 260 Washington St
 Watertown NY
 315 782-1000

(G-13123)
T-BASE COMMUNICATIONS USA INC
806 Commerce Park Dr (13669-2208)
PHONE..................315 713-0013
Sharylyn Ayotte, *President*

▲ = Import ▼ = Export
◆ = Import/Export

GEOGRAPHIC SECTION

Bruce Moszcelt, *Managing Dir*
Christine Roy, *Human Res Dir*
Paula Woods, *Manager*
EMP: 40
SALES (est): 3.2MM **Privately Held**
SIC: 2759 Commercial printing

Old Bethpage
Nassau County

(G-13124)
ALJO PRECISION PRODUCTS INC
205 Bethpge Sweet Holw (11804-1309)
PHONE..................516 420-4419
Fax: 516 756-1995
John Adelmann, *President*
Albert Adelmann, *Vice Pres*
Michael Mattern, *Vice Pres*
Gary Setteeucto, *Sales Mgr*
Marilyn Platz, *Office Mgr*
EMP: 35 **EST:** 1953
SQ FT: 24,000
SALES (est): 4.8MM **Privately Held**
WEB: www.aljogefa.com
SIC: 3599 Machine shop, jobbing & repair

(G-13125)
ALJO-GEFA PRECISION MFG LLC
205 Bethpage Sweet Holw (11804-1309)
PHONE..................516 420-4419
John Addleman, *Partner*
Michael Mattern, *General Mgr*
Suanne Hippner, *Office Mgr*
EMP: 33 **EST:** 1999
SQ FT: 26,000
SALES (est): 6.4MM **Privately Held**
SIC: 3674 Integrated circuits, semiconductor networks, etc.

(G-13126)
BARSON COMPOSITES CORPORATION (PA)
Also Called: Hitemco
160 Bethpage Sweet (11804)
PHONE..................516 752-7882
Fax: 516 752-7951
Terrell Barnard, *CEO*
Edwin Garofalo, *Vice Pres*
Doug Kowaczek, *Opers Mgr*
Dana Barnard, *CFO*
Noel G Gibilaro, *Marketing Staff*
EMP: 50
SQ FT: 32,500
SALES (est): 18MM **Privately Held**
WEB: www.hitemco.com
SIC: 3479 2899 2851 Painting, coating & hot dipping; chemical preparations; paints & allied products

(G-13127)
GEFA INSTRUMENT CORP
205 Bethpage Sweet (11804)
PHONE..................516 420-4419
Gunther Faas, *President*
Tyrone Faas, *Treasurer*
Susan Hippner, *Office Mgr*
Collette Faas, *Shareholder*
EMP: 12 **EST:** 1966
SQ FT: 10,000
SALES (est): 740K **Privately Held**
SIC: 3599 Machine shop, jobbing & repair

(G-13128)
HITEMCO MEDICAL APPLICATIONS
Also Called: Hi-Med
160 Bethpage Sweet Holw (11804-1315)
PHONE..................516 752-7882
Terrill E Barnard, *Ch of Bd*
Edwin Garofalo, *President*
John Lagaros, *Vice Pres*
Dana Barnard, *CFO*
EMP: 134
SQ FT: 5,000
SALES (est): 14.9MM
SALES (corp-wide): 18MM **Privately Held**
WEB: www.hitemco.com
SIC: 3479 Painting, coating & hot dipping

PA: Barson Composites Corporation
160 Bethpage Sweet
Old Bethpage NY 11804
516 752-7882

(G-13129)
INTELLIGEN POWER SYSTEMS LLC
301 Winding Rd (11804-1322)
PHONE..................212 750-0373
David H Lesser,
Stephen Bellone,
EMP: 8
SALES (est): 990K **Privately Held**
SIC: 3621 Power generators

(G-13130)
SEVILLE CENTRAL MIX CORP
495 Wining Rd (11804)
PHONE..................516 293-6190
Peter Scalamandre, *Vice Pres*
Peter Buck, *Branch Mgr*
EMP: 60
SALES (corp-wide): 13.6MM **Privately Held**
WEB: www.sevillecentralmix.com
SIC: 3273 3531 Ready-mixed concrete; concrete plants
PA: Seville Central Mix Corp.
157 Albany Ave
Freeport NY 11520
516 868-3000

(G-13131)
TRULITE LOUVRE CORP
148 Bethpage Sweet Holw (11804-1315)
PHONE..................516 756-1850
Robert Marchart, *President*
EMP: 27
SQ FT: 25,000
SALES (est): 1.5MM **Privately Held**
SIC: 3646 3443 3442 5031 Commercial indusl & institutional electric lighting fixtures; fabricated plate work (boiler shop); metal doors, sash & trim; doors & windows

Old Forge
Herkimer County

(G-13132)
ADIRONDACK OUTDOOR CENTER
2839 State Route 28 (13420)
P.O. Box 1146 (13420-1146)
PHONE..................315 369-2300
John Nemjo, *Principal*
EMP: 6
SALES (est): 490K **Privately Held**
SIC: 3949 5091 Camping equipment & supplies; camping equipment & supplies

Old Westbury
Nassau County

(G-13133)
NU LIFE RESTORATIONS OF L I
Also Called: Nu-Life Long Island
51 Valley Rd (11568-1015)
PHONE..................516 489-5200
Fax: 516 481-9791
Mark Marinbach, *President*
EMP: 84
SQ FT: 8,500
SALES (est): 10.2MM **Privately Held**
WEB: www.nulifeli.com
SIC: 3843 Dental laboratory equipment

Olean
Cattaraugus County

(G-13134)
AVX CORPORATION
Also Called: Olean Advanced Products
1695 Seneca Ave (14760-9532)
PHONE..................716 372-6611
Fax: 585 372-6635
Philip Ghent, *General Mgr*

Wayne Floyd, *Vice Pres*
Richard Gerringer, *Purch Agent*
Stan Cygan, *Engineer*
Norman J Malick, *Senior Engr*
EMP: 95
SALES (corp-wide): 12.6B **Publicly Held**
WEB: www.avxcorp.com
SIC: 3675 5065 Electronic capacitors; capacitors, electronic
HQ: Avx Corporation
1 Avx Blvd
Fountain Inn SC 29644
864 967-2150

(G-13135)
BIMBO BAKERIES
111 N 2nd St (14760-2501)
PHONE..................800 289-7876
EMP: 8
SALES (est): 748K **Privately Held**
SIC: 2051 Bread, cake & related products

(G-13136)
BIMBO BAKERIES USA INC
Also Called: Stroehmann Bakeries 56
111 N 2nd St (14760-2501)
PHONE..................716 372-8444
Fax: 585 372-7808
Nancy Fox, *Human Res Dir*
Frank Catarisano, *Sales Staff*
Ted Lipeowski, *Branch Mgr*
EMP: 140
SALES (corp-wide): 13B **Privately Held**
SIC: 2051 Bakery: wholesale or wholesale/retail combined
HQ: Bimbo Bakeries Usa, Inc
255 Business Center Dr # 200
Horsham PA 19044
215 347-5500

(G-13137)
BRADFORD PUBLICATIONS INC
Also Called: Times Herald, The
639 W Norton Dr (14760-1402)
PHONE..................716 373-2500
Fax: 585 372-0740
Rick Miller, *Editor*
Jeff Cole, *Accountant*
Jim Bonn, *Mktg Dir*
Lori Coffman, *Manager*
Bill Fitzpatrick, *Manager*
EMP: 130
SQ FT: 22,300
SALES (corp-wide): 10.7MM **Privately Held**
WEB: www.oleantimesherald.com
SIC: 2711 7313 Newspapers, publishing & printing; newspaper advertising representative
PA: Bradford Publications Inc
43 Main St
Bradford PA 16701
814 368-3173

(G-13138)
CITY OF OLEAN
Also Called: Olean Waste Water Treatment
174 S 19th St (14760-3326)
PHONE..................716 376-5694
Fax: 585 376-5629
William Quinlan, *Mayor*
Jeremy Meerdink, *Manager*
John Anastasia, *Hlthcr Dir*
Mary George, *Associate*
EMP: 9
SQ FT: 1,080 **Privately Held**
SIC: 3589 9111 Water treatment equipment, industrial; mayors' offices
PA: City Of Olean
101 E State St Ste 1
Olean NY 14760
716 376-5683

(G-13139)
CONCRETE MIXER SUPPLYCOM INC (PA)
1721 Cornell Dr (14760-9753)
PHONE..................716 375-5565
Fax: 716 701-6747
Audrey D Pavia, *President*
Rick Pavia, *Manager*
▲ **EMP:** 9
SQ FT: 3,000
SALES (est): 1.6MM **Privately Held**
SIC: 3713 Truck bodies & parts

(G-13140)
COOPER POWER SYSTEMS LLC
1648 Dugan Rd (14760-9527)
PHONE..................716 375-7100
Fax: 585 375-7202
Cindy Peterson, *Buyer*
Wayne E Traugh, *Purchasing*
Herce Alcocer, *Engineer*
Dave Custard, *Engineer*
Jim Lee, *Engineer*
EMP: 300 **Privately Held**
WEB: www.cooperpower.com
SIC: 3612 3699 3674 3643 Transformers, except electric; electrical equipment & supplies; semiconductors & related devices; current-carrying wiring devices; switchgear & switchboard apparatus
HQ: Cooper Power Systems, Llc
2300 Badger Dr
Waukesha WI 53188
262 524-4227

(G-13141)
CUTCO CUTLERY CORPORATION (HQ)
1116 E State St (14760-3814)
P.O. Box 810 (14760-0810)
PHONE..................716 372-3111
Fax: 585 373-6145
James E Stitt, *Ch of Bd*
James M Stitt, *President*
Carey F Litteer, *Exec VP*
Dan Wenke, *Opers Staff*
Brent A Driscoll, *Treasurer*
▲ **EMP:** 300
SQ FT: 226,370
SALES (est): 78.2MM
SALES (corp-wide): 155.4MM **Privately Held**
WEB: www.campusrelations.com
SIC: 3421 Cutlery
PA: Cutco Corporation
1116 E State St
Olean NY 14760
716 372-3111

(G-13142)
CYTEC INDUSTRIES INC
1405 Buffalo St (14760-1197)
PHONE..................716 372-9650
Fax: 716 372-1594
Jeff Maley, *Site Mgr*
Tara Tepp, *Corp Comm Staff*
David Lilley, *Branch Mgr*
John Clarke, *Manager*
Travis Martin, *Manager*
EMP: 66
SALES (corp-wide): 135.3MM **Privately Held**
SIC: 2899 2821 2672 2851 Water treating compounds; plastics materials & resins; adhesive backed films, foams & foils; paints & allied products; cellulosic manmade fibers
HQ: Cytec Industries Inc.
5 Garret Mountain Plz
Woodland Park NJ 07424
973 357-3100

(G-13143)
CYTEC OLEAN INC
1405 Buffalo St (14760-1197)
PHONE..................716 372-9650
William Work, *Purch Mgr*
Leonard Riker, *Manager*
Maureen Dearmitt, *Info Tech Mgr*
Marsha Topor, *Administration*
▼ **EMP:** 75
SQ FT: 105,000
SALES (est): 11.7MM
SALES (corp-wide): 135.3MM **Privately Held**
WEB: www.conap.com
SIC: 2821 5169 Plastics materials & resins; thermoplastic materials; chemicals & allied products
HQ: Cytec Industries Inc.
5 Garret Mountain Plz
Woodland Park NJ 07424
973 357-3100

(G-13144)
DRESSER-RAND GROUP INC
500 Paul Clark Dr (14760-9560)
PHONE..................716 375-3000

Olean - Cattaraugus County (G-13145)   GEOGRAPHIC SECTION

Fax: 585 375-3178
Jean Chevrier, *Vice Pres*
Dwight D Everetts, *Vice Pres*
Edmund Reybitz, *Project Dir*
Glenn Grosso, *Technical Mgr*
Job Barboza, *Engineer*
EMP: 66
SALES (corp-wide): 83.5B **Privately Held**
SIC: 3563 3511 Air & gas compressors; turbines & turbine generator sets
HQ: Dresser-Rand Group Inc
10205 Westheimer Rd # 1000
Houston TX 77042
713 354-6100

(G-13145)
DSTI INC
Also Called: Scott Rotary Seals
301 W Franklin St (14760-1211)
PHONE 716 557-2362
Fax: 716 557-8613
Jeffrey Meister, *President*
Scott Ilstrup, *Vice Pres*
John Knoll, *Vice Pres*
Dave Schenfield, *Project Mgr*
Bob Kwiatkowski, *Engineer*
EMP: 7
SQ FT: 13,000
SALES (est): 1.6MM
SALES (corp-wide): 16.1MM **Privately Held**
WEB: www.scottrotaryseals.com
SIC: 3492 Control valves, fluid power: hydraulic & pneumatic
PA: Dynamic Sealing Technologies, Inc.
13829 Jay St Nw
Anoka MN 55304
763 786-3758

(G-13146)
DYNAMIC SEALING TECH INC
Also Called: Scott Rotary Seals
301 W Franklin St (14760-1211)
PHONE 716 376-0708
Jeffrey Meister, *Branch Mgr*
EMP: 8
SQ FT: 15,000
SALES (corp-wide): 16.1MM **Privately Held**
SIC: 3492 Control valves, fluid power: hydraulic & pneumatic
PA: Dynamic Sealing Technologies, Inc.
13829 Jay St Nw
Anoka MN 55304
763 786-3758

(G-13147)
EATON HYDRAULICS LLC
1648 Dugan Rd (14760-9527)
PHONE 716 375-7132
Dennis Edwards, *Maint Spvr*
William Sorokes, *Manager*
EMP: 7 **Privately Held**
SIC: 3625 Motor controls & accessories
HQ: Eaton Hydraulics Llc
14615 Lone Oak Rd
Eden Prairie MN 55344
952 937-9800

(G-13148)
G & H WOOD PRODUCTS LLC
Also Called: Pallets Plus
2427 N Union Street Ext (14760-1529)
PHONE 716 372-5510
Terrance Grant,
EMP: 10
SQ FT: 4,343
SALES (est): 1.1MM **Privately Held**
SIC: 2448 Pallets, wood

(G-13149)
KAMERYS WHOLESALE MEATS INC
322 E Riverside Dr (14760-3964)
PHONE 716 372-6756
David A Kamery, *President*
EMP: 6
SALES (est): 573.4K **Privately Held**
SIC: 2011 5147 Meat packing plants; meats, fresh

(G-13150)
L AMERICAN LTD
Also Called: Swatt Baking Co
222 Homer St (14760-1132)
PHONE 716 372-9480

Fax: 716 373-6019
Leonard Anzivine, *President*
Lee Anzivine, *Vice Pres*
EMP: 16
SQ FT: 9,400
SALES (est): 2MM **Privately Held**
WEB: www.lamerican.com
SIC: 2051 5461 Bread, all types (white, wheat, rye, etc): fresh or frozen; rolls, bread type: fresh or frozen; bakeries

(G-13151)
NES BEARING COMPANY INC
1601 Johnson St (14760-1127)
PHONE 716 372-6532
Fax: 585 372-1448
Christopher Napoleon, *President*
Jim Hardy, *QC Mgr*
Hatther Piatte, *Administration*
▲ **EMP:** 48
SALES (est): 13.8MM **Privately Held**
WEB: www.nesbearings.com
SIC: 3562 8711 Ball bearings & parts; sanitary engineers

(G-13152)
PIERCE STEEL FABRICATORS
430 N 7th St (14760-2330)
P.O. Box 504 (14760-0504)
PHONE 716 372-7652
Fax: 585 372-3102
Michael Derose, *President*
Daniel Derose, *Vice Pres*
Janice Bronson, *Manager*
EMP: 11
SQ FT: 20,000
SALES (est): 2.1MM **Privately Held**
WEB: www.piercesteel.com
SIC: 3449 Curtain wall, metal

(G-13153)
SOLEPOXY INC
211 W Franklin St (14760-1211)
PHONE 716 372-6300
Jeff Belt, *Ch of Bd*
Robert Groele, *President*
◆ **EMP:** 55 **EST:** 2010
SQ FT: 250,000
SALES (est): 13.6MM **Privately Held**
SIC: 3087 Custom compound purchased resins

(G-13154)
TOTAL PIPING SOLUTIONS INC
1760 Haskell Rd (14760-9756)
P.O. Box 525 (14760-0525)
PHONE 716 372-0160
Daryl Piontek, *President*
Mark Langenhan, *President*
▲ **EMP:** 10
SQ FT: 35,000
SALES (est): 1.9MM **Privately Held**
WEB: www.tps.us
SIC: 3494 Pipe fittings

Oneida
Madison County

(G-13155)
GOLUB CORPORATION
Also Called: Price Chopper Pharmacy
142 Genesee St (13421-2704)
PHONE 315 363-0679
Nena Crowne, *Branch Mgr*
EMP: 78
SALES (corp-wide): 3.4B **Privately Held**
SIC: 3751 Motorcycles & related parts
PA: The Golub Corporation
461 Nott St
Schenectady NY 12308
518 355-5000

(G-13156)
HARTMAN ENTERPRISES INC
455 Elizabeth St (13421-2438)
P.O. Box 360 (13421-0360)
PHONE 315 363-7300
Fax: 315 363-0314
Robert E Sweet Jr, *CEO*
Bob Sweep, *President*
Jim Rager, *General Mgr*
Merry Dailey, *Manager*
Tim Shetler, *Director*
EMP: 55

SQ FT: 18,000
SALES (est): 9.3MM **Privately Held**
WEB: www.hartmanenterprisesinc.com
SIC: 3599 7692 Machine shop, jobbing & repair; welding repair

(G-13157)
HP HOOD LLC
252 Genesee St (13421-2709)
P.O. Box 491 (13421-0491)
PHONE 315 363-3870
Fax: 315 363-9534
Gary Musial, *Vice Pres*
Jim Sylvester, *Opers Mgr*
Ross Hasty, *Prdtn Mgr*
Ray Johnson, *Safety Mgr*
Brandon Cook, *Warehouse Mgr*
EMP: 200
SALES (corp-wide): 1.9B **Privately Held**
WEB: www.hphood.com
SIC: 2026 5143 Fluid milk; dairy products, except dried or canned
PA: Hp Hood Llc
6 Kimball Ln Ste 400
Lynnfield MA 01940
617 887-8441

(G-13158)
M M WELDING
558 Lenox Ave (13421-1522)
PHONE 315 363-3980
Michael Marley, *Owner*
Denice Marley, *Partner*
EMP: 20
SALES (est): 451.2K **Privately Held**
SIC: 7692 Welding repair

(G-13159)
ONEIDA FOUNDRIES INC
559 Fitch St (13421-1515)
PHONE 315 363-4570
Fax: 315 363-4692
John Albanse, *President*
Harry Hood, *Vice Pres*
Shelly Albanese, *Office Mgr*
EMP: 20 **EST:** 1900
SQ FT: 30,000
SALES (est): 5.4MM **Privately Held**
SIC: 3321 Gray iron castings; ductile iron castings

(G-13160)
ONEIDA INTERNATIONAL INC
163-181 Kenwood Ave (13421)
PHONE 315 361-3000
Fax: 315 361-3745
Terry G Westbrook, *President*
EMP: 5
SALES (est): 323K
SALES (corp-wide): 571.3MM **Privately Held**
WEB: www.oneida.net
SIC: 3262 3231 3914 3421 Vitreous china table & kitchenware; ornamental glass: cut, engraved or otherwise decorated; silverware & plated ware; cutlery
HQ: Oneida Ltd.
163 Kenwood Ave
Oneida NY 13421
315 361-3000

(G-13161)
ONEIDA MOLDED PLASTICS LLC (PA)
104 S Warner St (13421-1510)
PHONE 315 363-7990
Barry Uber, *Ch of Bd*
Steve Thalmann, *President*
Raymond E Randall Jr, *Business Mgr*
James Seipola, *Vice Pres*
Richard Harrington, *Plant Mgr*
▲ **EMP:** 130 **EST:** 2006
SQ FT: 82,000
SALES (est): 40.8MM **Privately Held**
WEB: oneidamoldedplastics.com
SIC: 3089 Injection molding of plastics

(G-13162)
ONEIDA MOLDED PLASTICS LLC
104 S Warner St (13421-1510)
PHONE 315 363-7990
Joe Kiah, *CEO*
David Harrington, *President*
Tim Mc Cullough, *Vice Pres*
Kenneth Morey, *Vice Pres*

Robert Wiehl, *VP Finance*
EMP: 72
SQ FT: 41,000
SALES (est): 4.7MM
SALES (corp-wide): 40.8MM **Privately Held**
SIC: 3089 Plastic containers, except foam
PA: Oneida Molded Plastics, Llc
104 S Warner St
Oneida NY 13421
315 363-7990

(G-13163)
ONEIDA PUBLICATIONS INC
Also Called: Oneida Dispatch
130 Broad St (13421-1684)
PHONE 315 363-5100
Fax: 315 363-9832
Phil Austin, *CEO*
Kyle Mennig, *Editor*
Perry L Novak, *Editor*
Maryann Hawthorne, *Accounting Dir*
Janice Collins, *Sales Associate*
EMP: 40 **EST:** 1851
SQ FT: 10,000
SALES (est): 2.4MM **Privately Held**
SIC: 2711 Newspapers

(G-13164)
ONEIDA SILVERSMITHS INC
163 Kenwood Ave 181 (13421-2829)
PHONE 315 361-3000
Fax: 315 361-3290
Terry G Westbrook, *President*
EMP: 8
SALES (est): 967.3K
SALES (corp-wide): 571.3MM **Privately Held**
WEB: www.oneida.net
SIC: 3262 3231 3914 3421 Vitreous china table & kitchenware; ornamental glass: cut, engraved or otherwise decorated; silverware & plated ware; cutlery
HQ: Oneida Ltd.
163 Kenwood Ave
Oneida NY 13421
315 361-3000

(G-13165)
PATHFINDER 103 INC
229 Park Ave (13421-2021)
PHONE 315 363-4260
Larry Manser, *President*
EMP: 8
SALES (est): 961.4K **Privately Held**
SIC: 3589 Sewer cleaning equipment, power

(G-13166)
S K CIRCUITS INC (PA)
483 Foxwood Ter (13421-2609)
PHONE 703 376-8718
Vijay K Kodali, *President*
EMP: 14
SALES (est): 1.8MM **Privately Held**
SIC: 3672 Printed circuit boards

(G-13167)
SHIRL-LYNN OF NEW YORK (PA)
266 Wilson St (13421-1722)
PHONE 315 363-5898
Fax: 315 363-5936
Shirley Thurston, *Partner*
Mary Blau, *Partner*
EMP: 12
SQ FT: 4,300
SALES: 1MM **Privately Held**
SIC: 2339 5699 5632 Women's & misses' athletic clothing & sportswear; bathing suits: women's, misses' & juniors'; bathing suits; sports apparel; costumes, masquerade or theatrical; dancewear

(G-13168)
THOMAS FOUNDRY LLC
559 Fitch St (13421-1515)
P.O. Box 175 (13421-0175)
PHONE 315 361-9048
John D Albanese III,
Shelly M Albanese,
John Albanese III,
EMP: 8
SQ FT: 7,400

GEOGRAPHIC SECTION

Oneonta - Otsego County (G-13191)

SALES: 600K *Privately Held*
WEB: www.thomasfoundry.com
SIC: 3471 3364 Sand blasting of metal parts; nonferrous die-castings except aluminum

(G-13169)
V & J GRAPHICS INC
153 Phelps St (13421-1708)
PHONE......................315 363-1933
Vernon Waters, *President*
Janice Waters, *Treasurer*
Sandy Harrison,
EMP: 8
SQ FT: 4,960
SALES (est): 989.5K *Privately Held*
SIC: 2752 Commercial printing, offset

(G-13170)
VISIBLE SYSTEMS CORPORATION (PA)
248 Main St Ste 2 (13421-2100)
PHONE......................508 628-1510
Fax: 315 363-7488
George Cagliuso, *President*
Michael Paul, *Vice Pres*
Ellen Shoner, *CFO*
Mike Cesino, *Manager*
EMP: 20
SQ FT: 6,000
SALES (est): 4MM *Privately Held*
SIC: 7372 5045 8748 Prepackaged software; computer software; systems analysis or design

Oneonta
Otsego County

(G-13171)
ARNAN DEVELOPMENT CORP (PA)
Also Called: Pickett Building Materials
6459 State Highway 23 (13820-6542)
PHONE......................607 432-6641
Fax: 607 433-6284
Robert A Harlem Jr, *Ch of Bd*
Rebecca Lloyd, *Vice Pres*
Kevin Curnalia, *Store Mgr*
Larry Covell, *Purchasing*
Tom Ballard, *Sales Staff*
EMP: 52
SQ FT: 40,000
SALES: 10.9MM *Privately Held*
WEB: www.oneontablock.com
SIC: 3271 3272 5082 5211 Architectural concrete: block, split, fluted, screen, etc.; concrete products; septic tanks, concrete; masonry equipment & supplies; lumber & other building materials; management services

(G-13172)
ASTROCOM ELECTRONICS INC
115 Dk Lifgren Dr (13820-3682)
PHONE......................607 432-1930
Fax: 607 432-1286
Terry D Lifgren, *President*
Kim Roseboom, *General Mgr*
Doug Lifgren, *COO*
Dan Berard, *Vice Pres*
Kenny Morrell, *Safety Mgr*
▲ EMP: 93 EST: 1961
SQ FT: 65,000
SALES (est): 16.3MM *Privately Held*
WEB: www.astrocom-electronics.com
SIC: 3661 Communication headgear, telephone

(G-13173)
BK ASSOCIATES INTL INC
127 Commerce Rd (13820-3539)
P.O. Box 1238 (13820-5238)
PHONE......................607 432-1499
Fax: 607 432-1592
Paul Karabinis, *President*
Eugene Bettiol Sr, *Treasurer*
Steve Palmer, *Office Mgr*
EMP: 15
SQ FT: 20,000
SALES (est): 2.1MM *Privately Held*
SIC: 2095 Coffee roasting (except by wholesale grocers)

(G-13174)
BROOKS BOTTLING CO LLC
5560 State Highway 7 (13820-3699)
PHONE......................607 432-1782
Wendy Hunter, *Accountant*
Ryan Brooks, *Mng Member*
Angelina Shultis, *Admin Asst*
EMP: 10
SALES (est): 1.2MM *Privately Held*
SIC: 3565 Bottling machinery: filling, capping, labeling

(G-13175)
BURT RIGID BOX INC
58 Browne St (13820-1092)
PHONE......................607 433-2510
Ron Bolaird, *Managing Dir*
William Howard, *Vice Pres*
Ralph Underwood, *Plant Mgr*
Penny Timer, *Production*
Dave Van Pelt, *Purch Agent*
EMP: 52
SQ FT: 77,280
SALES (corp-wide): 17.9MM *Privately Held*
WEB: www.burtbox.com
SIC: 2653 2657 2652 Boxes, solid fiber: made from purchased materials; folding paperboard boxes; setup paperboard boxes
PA: Burt Rigid Box, Inc.
  58 Browne St
  Oneonta NY 13820
  607 433-2510

(G-13176)
BURT RIGID BOX INC (PA)
58 Browne St (13820-1092)
P.O. Box 1883, Buffalo (14225-8883)
PHONE......................607 433-2510
Fax: 607 433-2512
W Russell Hurd, *President*
William Howard, *Vice Pres*
Bill Howard, *Safety Mgr*
Laura Hurd, *Treasurer*
Julie Gillentine, *Controller*
▲ EMP: 10
SQ FT: 500,000
SALES (est): 17.9MM *Privately Held*
WEB: www.burtbox.com
SIC: 2631 Folding boxboard; setup boxboard

(G-13177)
CHARLES LAY (PA)
Also Called: G C Casting
138 Roundhouse Rd (13820-1200)
PHONE......................607 432-4518
Charles Lay, *Owner*
EMP: 10 EST: 1946
SQ FT: 1,500
SALES (est): 1MM *Privately Held*
WEB: www.charleslay.com
SIC: 3366 3365 Bronze foundry; aluminum foundries

(G-13178)
CITY OF ONEONTA
Also Called: Oneonta City Wtr Trtmnt Plant
110 East St (13820-1304)
PHONE......................607 433-3470
Fax: 607 433-3486
Stanley Shaffer, *Manager*
EMP: 5 *Privately Held*
SIC: 3589 9111 Water treatment equipment, industrial; mayors' offices
PA: City Of Oneonta
  258 Main St Ste 1
  Oneonta NY 13820
  607 432-6450

(G-13179)
CO-OPTICS AMERICA LAB INC
Also Called: Co-Optics Groups, The
297 River Street Svc Rd Service (13820)
PHONE......................607 432-0557
Fax: 607 432-1668
Paul Strenn, *President*
Israel Soto, *Vice Pres*
EMP: 20
SQ FT: 3,300
SALES (est): 3MM *Privately Held*
WEB: www.co-optics.com
SIC: 3851 3229 Lenses, ophthalmic; pressed & blown glass

(G-13180)
COBLESKILL STONE PRODUCTS INC
Also Called: Oneonta Asphalt
57 Ceperley Ave (13820-2182)
PHONE......................607 432-8321
Fax: 607 432-7960
Lennie Goodspeed, *Branch Mgr*
Cliff Cooper, *Manager*
EMP: 10
SQ FT: 1,353
SALES (corp-wide): 114.3MM *Privately Held*
WEB: www.cobleskillstone.com
SIC: 2951 Asphalt & asphaltic paving mixtures (not from refineries)
PA: Cobleskill Stone Products, Inc.
  112 Rock Rd
  Cobleskill NY 12043
  518 234-0221

(G-13181)
COMMUNITY NEWSPAPER GROUP LLC
Daily Star, The
102 Chestnut St (13820-2584)
P.O. Box 250 (13820-0250)
PHONE......................607 432-1000
Fax: 607 432-5847
David Kiehm, *Editor*
Daniel Swift, *Editor*
Peter Hill, *Counsel*
Kay Helms, *Finance Mgr*
Rocky Jackson, *Finance Mgr*
EMP: 17 *Privately Held*
WEB: www.clintonnc.com
SIC: 2711 2752 Newspapers: publishing only, not printed on site; commercial printing, lithographic
HQ: Community Newspaper Group, Llc
  3500 Colonnade Pkwy # 600
  Birmingham AL 35243

(G-13182)
CORNING INCORPORATED
275 River St (13820-2299)
PHONE......................607 433-3100
Fax: 607 433-3161
Marla Kelly, *Engineer*
Mark Maroz, *Engineer*
Teri Mauk, *Enginr/R&D Mgr*
Marcial Vasco, *Manager*
Don Capelluto, *Senior Mgr*
EMP: 25
SQ FT: 20,106
SALES (corp-wide): 9.1B *Publicly Held*
WEB: www.corning.com
SIC: 3229 Pressed & blown glass
PA: Corning Incorporated
  1 Riverfront Plz
  Corning NY 14831
  607 974-9000

(G-13183)
CREATIVE ORTHOTICS PROSTHETICS
Also Called: Hanger Clinic
37 Associate Dr (13820-2266)
PHONE......................607 431-2526
Chris German, *Manager*
Sheryl Price, *Director*
EMP: 7
SALES (corp-wide): 51.9MM *Privately Held*
WEB: www.creativeoandp.com
SIC: 3842 Surgical appliances & supplies
PA: Creative Orthotics & Prosthetics Inc
  1300 College Ave Ste 1
  Elmira NY 14901
  607 734-7215

(G-13184)
CUSTOM ELECTRONICS INC
87 Browne St (13820-1096)
PHONE......................607 432-3880
Fax: 607 432-3913
Peter Dokuchitz, *Ch of Bd*
Michael Pentaris, *President*
Jonathan Dokuchitz, *VP Opers*
Cathy Smith, *Opers Mgr*
Carol Brower, *Purchasing*
▲ EMP: 62 EST: 1964
SQ FT: 27,500
SALES (est): 14.1MM *Privately Held*
WEB: www.customelec.com
SIC: 3675 Electronic capacitors

(G-13185)
EQUISSENTIALS LLC
3200 Chestnut St Ste 5 (13820-1072)
PHONE......................607 432-2856
Fax: 607 432-2951
Joseph Creighton,
Tracie Jones,
EMP: 12 EST: 1999
SQ FT: 5,000
SALES (est): 900K *Privately Held*
WEB: www.equissentials.net
SIC: 2231 Apparel & outerwear broadwoven fabrics

(G-13186)
FOTIS ONEONTA ITALIAN BAKERY
42 River St (13820-4320)
PHONE......................607 432-3871
James Tomaino, *Owner*
EMP: 6
SALES (est): 508.7K *Privately Held*
SIC: 2051 Bakery: wholesale or wholesale/retail combined

(G-13187)
G C CASTINGS INC
138 Roundhouse Rd (13820-1200)
PHONE......................607 432-4518
Charles R Lay, *President*
EMP: 10
SQ FT: 14,000
SALES (est): 700K *Privately Held*
SIC: 3531 Snow plow attachments

(G-13188)
MEDICAL COACHES INCORPORATED (PA)
399 County Highway 58 (13820-3422)
P.O. Box 129 (13820-0129)
PHONE......................607 432-1333
Fax: 607 432-8190
Geoffrey A Smith, *President*
Ian Smith, *Founder*
Leonard W Marsh, *COO*
Joseph Fazio, *Opers Staff*
Kathy Caffery, *Purch Agent*
◆ EMP: 50 EST: 1952
SQ FT: 100,000
SALES: 10MM *Privately Held*
WEB: www.medcoach.com
SIC: 3711 Automobile assembly, including specialty automobiles

(G-13189)
MOLD-A-MATIC CORPORATION
Also Called: Mamco
147 River St (13820-2276)
PHONE......................607 433-2121
Fax: 607 432-7861
Siro Vergari, *Ch of Bd*
Mark Vergari, *Vice Pres*
Joel Stanley, *Purch Mgr*
William Giese, *Finance Mgr*
Francis Colone, *Director*
▲ EMP: 45 EST: 1964
SQ FT: 31,000
SALES: 4MM *Privately Held*
WEB: www.mamcomolding.com
SIC: 3549 3089 Assembly machines, including robotic; plastic processing

(G-13190)
ONEONTA FENCE
2 Washburn St (13820-2721)
PHONE......................607 433-6707
EMP: 5
SALES (est): 474.9K *Privately Held*
SIC: 3089 3315 Fences, gates & accessories: plastic; fence gates posts & fittings: steel

(G-13191)
OTSEGO READY MIX INC
2 Wells Ave (13820-2723)
PHONE......................607 432-3400
Fax: 607 433-6287
Robert Harlem Jr, *President*
EMP: 16
SQ FT: 8,000
SALES: 3.4MM *Privately Held*
SIC: 3273 Ready-mixed concrete

Oneonta - Otsego County (G-13192)

(G-13192)
PONY FARM PRESS & GRAPHICS
Also Called: Village Print Room
330 Pony Farm Rd (13820-3591)
PHONE 607 432-9020
Edward May, *President*
Chris Chase, *IT/INT Sup*
EMP: 7
SQ FT: 12,000
SALES (est): 594.5K **Privately Held**
WEB: www.ponyfarmpress.com
SIC: 2759 Commercial printing

(G-13193)
RJ MILLWORKERS INC
12 Lewis St (13820-2652)
PHONE 607 433-0525
Fax: 607 433-0478
Randy J Morley, *President*
Ellen Morley, *Vice Pres*
EMP: 20
SALES (est): 3.6MM **Privately Held**
WEB: www.rjmillworkers.com
SIC: 2431 Millwork

(G-13194)
T S PINK CORP
Also Called: TS Pink
139 Pony Farm Rd (13820-3537)
PHONE 607 432-1100
Fax: 607 433-0500
Todd Pink, *President*
Diana Colone, *Vice Pres*
▲ EMP: 16
SQ FT: 15,000
SALES (est): 2MM **Privately Held**
WEB: www.tspink.com
SIC: 2841 Textile soap

Ontario
Wayne County

(G-13195)
ARIEL OPTICS INC
261 David Pkwy (14519-8955)
PHONE 585 265-4820
Frederick Koch, *President*
EMP: 8
SALES: 525K **Privately Held**
WEB: www.arieloptics.com
SIC: 3827 Prisms, optical

(G-13196)
AVALANCHE FABRICATION INC
6314 Dean Pkwy (14519-9011)
PHONE 585 545-4000
Paul Duerr, *President*
Thad Spaulding, *Vice Pres*
EMP: 14 EST: 1998
SQ FT: 5,500
SALES: 1.1MM **Privately Held**
WEB: www.afinc.biz
SIC: 3444 Sheet metalwork

(G-13197)
CLAUDE TRIBASTONE INC
6367 Dean Pkwy (14519-8939)
PHONE 585 265-3776
Claude Tribastone, *President*
Tom Kelly, *Controller*
EMP: 6
SALES (est): 611.8K
SALES (corp-wide): 31.5MM **Privately Held**
WEB: www.photonicsolutionsusa.com
SIC: 3827 Lenses, optical: all types except ophthalmic
PA: Optimax Systems, Inc.
6367 Dean Pkwy
Ontario NY 14519
585 265-1020

(G-13198)
CS AUTOMATION INC
Also Called: C S Welding
518 Berg Rd (14519-9376)
PHONE 315 524-5123
Craig Schieven, *Principal*
EMP: 10
SALES (est): 480K **Privately Held**
SIC: 7692 7389 8742 Welding repair; inspection & testing services; automation & robotics consultant

(G-13199)
DATA CONTROL INC
277 David Pkwy (14519-8955)
PHONE 585 265-2980
Lori Ferguson, *President*
EMP: 4
SQ FT: 12,712
SALES: 1MM **Privately Held**
WEB: www.datacontrolinc.com
SIC: 2542 Fixtures: display, office or store: except wood

(G-13200)
DJ ACQUISITION MANAGEMENT CORP
Also Called: Weco Metal Products
6364 Dean Pkwy (14519-8970)
PHONE 585 265-3000
Fax: 585 265-3447
Donald Cornwell, *President*
John R Gillan, *Vice Pres*
Bill Connor, *Purch Agent*
Christopher Sherland, *Human Resources*
▲ EMP: 75
SQ FT: 55,000
SALES (est): 16.6MM **Privately Held**
WEB: www.wecometal.com
SIC: 3444 Sheet metalwork

(G-13201)
FRED A NUDD CORPORATION (PA)
1743 State Route 104 (14519-8935)
P.O. Box 577 (14519-0577)
PHONE 315 524-2531
Fax: 315 524-4249
Thomas Nudd, *President*
Bonnie Judware, *Accountant*
Tim Wilson, *Sales Mgr*
Lyle Nudd, *Manager*
EMP: 32
SQ FT: 40,000
SALES (est): 7.3MM **Privately Held**
WEB: www.nuddtowers.com
SIC: 3444 3441 1799 1622 Sheet metalwork; tower sections, radio & television transmission; antenna installation; bridge, tunnel & elevated highway

(G-13202)
G&G SEALCOATING AND PAVING INC
1449 Ontario (14519)
PHONE 585 787-1500
Fax: 585 265-9016
Manny Giudice, *President*
EMP: 23
SALES (est): 3.1MM **Privately Held**
SIC: 2951 Asphalt paving mixtures & blocks

(G-13203)
HARBEC INC
369 State Route 104 (14519-8958)
PHONE 585 265-0010
Fax: 585 265-1306
Robert Bechtold, *President*
Gerald Wahl, *Counsel*
John Hoefen, *Production*
Kate Chamberlain, *Engineer*
Jeffrey Eisenhauer, *Engineer*
EMP: 100
SQ FT: 15,000
SALES (est): 30.2MM **Privately Held**
WEB: www.harbec.com
SIC: 3089 Injection molded finished plastic products

(G-13204)
INTEGRITY TOOL INCORPORATED
6485 Furnace Rd (14519-8920)
PHONE 315 524-4409
Mike Freidler, *President*
Les Saiers, *Plant Mgr*
Terri Nichols, *Manager*
EMP: 13 EST: 1996
SQ FT: 6,000
SALES (est): 1.5MM **Privately Held**
SIC: 3449 Miscellaneous metalwork

(G-13205)
LAKE IMMUNOGENICS INC
348 Berg Rd (14519-9374)
PHONE 585 265-1973
Fax: 585 265-2306
James Bowman, *President*
Barbara Bowman, *Vice Pres*
Anne Rowlands, *Cust Mgr*
Ginger Sullivan, *Manager*
EMP: 15
SQ FT: 8,000
SALES (est): 3.1MM **Privately Held**
WEB: www.lakeimmunogenics.com
SIC: 2836 Plasmas; veterinary biological products

(G-13206)
NORTHERN BIODIESEL INC
317 State Route 104 (14519-8958)
PHONE 585 545-4534
Jason Masters, *Ch of Bd*
Robert Bethold, *Vice Pres*
Jeff Frank, *Technician*
EMP: 5
SALES (est): 690K **Privately Held**
WEB: www.northernbiodiesel.com
SIC: 2911 Diesel fuels

(G-13207)
OPTIMAX SYSTEMS INC (PA)
6367 Dean Pkwy (14519-8939)
PHONE 585 265-1020
Fax: 585 265-1033
Rick Plympton, *CEO*
Michael P Mandina, *Ch of Bd*
Robert Sawyer, *Managing Dir*
Mark Palvino, *Vice Pres*
Richard Plympton, *Vice Pres*
EMP: 178
SQ FT: 40,000
SALES (est): 31.5MM **Privately Held**
WEB: www.optimaxsi.com
SIC: 3827 Lenses, optical: all types except ophthalmic; prisms, optical

(G-13208)
OPTIPRO SYSTEMS LLC
6368 Dean Pkwy (14519-8970)
PHONE 585 265-0160
Fax: 585 265-9416
Tim Ansalvi, *Controller*
Mike Bechtold, *Mng Member*
▲ EMP: 54
SQ FT: 20,000
SALES (est): 12.8MM
SALES (corp-wide): 9.1MM **Privately Held**
WEB: www.optipro.com
SIC: 3559 3827 Optical lens machinery; optical instruments & lenses
PA: Brightside 09 Inc.
6368 Dean Pkwy
Ontario NY 14519
585 265-0160

(G-13209)
PHOTON GEAR INC
245 David Pkwy (14519-8955)
PHONE 585 265-3360
Fax: 315 524-2681
Gary Blough, *President*
EMP: 11
SQ FT: 5,400
SALES (est): 2.4MM **Privately Held**
WEB: www.photongear.com
SIC: 3827 8711 Optical elements & assemblies, except ophthalmic; engineering services

(G-13210)
R C KOLSTAD WATER CORP
73 Lake Rd (14519-9311)
PHONE 585 216-2230
William Kolstad, *President*
EMP: 5
SALES: 2MM **Privately Held**
SIC: 3589 Water treatment equipment, industrial

(G-13211)
RANGER DESIGN US INC
6377 Dean Pkwy (14519-8939)
PHONE 800 565-5321
Derek Cowie, *President*
Randal Cowie, *Chairman*
Paul Rogers, *Manager*
▲ EMP: 20
SQ FT: 80,000
SALES (est): 2.4MM **Privately Held**
SIC: 3711 Motor vehicles & car bodies

(G-13212)
ROCHESTER INDUSTRIAL CTRL INC (PA)
6400 Furnace Rd (14519-9744)
PHONE 315 524-4555
Fax: 315 524-5733
John Little, *Ch of Bd*
Mike Clancy, *Plant Mgr*
Heather Glanzel, *Purch Mgr*
Donna Perry, *Purch Mgr*
Kathy Ferguson, *QC Mgr*
▲ EMP: 99
SQ FT: 23,600
SALES (est): 22MM **Privately Held**
SIC: 3625 3679 3672 Relays & industrial controls; electronic circuits; printed circuit boards

(G-13213)
ROCHESTER INDUSTRIAL CTRL INC
Also Called: R I C
6345 Furnace Rd (14519-9744)
PHONE 315 524-4555
Eric Albert, *President*
EMP: 100
SQ FT: 8,050
SALES (corp-wide): 22MM **Privately Held**
SIC: 3679 Electronic circuits
PA: Rochester Industrial Control, Inc.
6400 Furnace Rd
Ontario NY 14519
315 524-4555

(G-13214)
SCIENTIFIC POLYMER PRODUCTS
6265 Dean Pkwy (14519-8997)
PHONE 585 265-0413
Fax: 585 265-1390
Bret Vanzo, *Ch of Bd*
Leslie Twist, *Manager*
EMP: 5
SQ FT: 10,000
SALES (est): 570K **Privately Held**
WEB: www.scientificpolymer.com
SIC: 2819 Industrial inorganic chemicals

(G-13215)
SMITH INTERNATIONAL INC
Also Called: Smith Service Corps
1915 Lake Rd (14519-9792)
PHONE 585 265-2330
Fax: 315 524-6369
Drew Smith, *Principal*
EMP: 12 **Privately Held**
WEB: www.smith-intl.com
SIC: 3533 Oil & gas field machinery
HQ: Smith International, Inc.
1310 Rankin Rd
Houston TX 77073
281 443-3370

(G-13216)
VETTE CORP NEW YORK
Also Called: Erm Thermal Technologies Inc
6377 Dean Pkwy (14519-8939)
PHONE 585 265-0330
Fax: 585 265-1941
Christopher Cutaia, *President*
David C Arena, *Vice Pres*
Alesha Garrett, *Sales Associate*
EMP: 100 EST: 1958
SQ FT: 40,000
SALES: 14.2MM
SALES (corp-wide): 1.8B **Privately Held**
WEB: www.heatsink.com
SIC: 3443 Heat exchangers, plate type
HQ: Vette Thermal Solutions, Llc
33 Bridge St
Pelham NH 03076
603 635-2800

▲ = Import ▼ = Export
◆ = Import/Export

GEOGRAPHIC SECTION

Orangeburg
Rockland County

(G-13217)
AALBORG INSTRS & CONTRLS INC
20 Corporate Dr (10962-2616)
PHONE.................................845 398-3160
Fax: 845 398-3165
T J Baan, *CEO*
Christine Pomponio, *Human Res Mgr*
Karen Baan, *Admin Sec*
EMP: 54
SQ FT: 33,000
SALES (est): 12.1MM **Privately Held**
WEB: www.aalborg.com
SIC: 3823 3824 3577 3494 Primary elements for process flow measurement; fluid meters & counting devices; computer peripheral equipment; valves & pipe fittings; fluid power valves & hose fittings

(G-13218)
API INDUSTRIES INC (PA)
Also Called: Aluf Plastics Division
2 Glenshaw St (10962-1207)
PHONE.................................845 365-2200
Fax: 845 365-2294
Susan Rosenberg, *CEO*
Reuven Rosenberg, *President*
Gabriel Kahana, *General Mgr*
Isaac Rosenberg, *Assistant VP*
David Anderson, *VP Opers*
◆ **EMP:** 280
SQ FT: 300,000
SALES (est): 122.8MM **Privately Held**
SIC: 2673 3081 Plastic bags: made from purchased materials; unsupported plastics film & sheet

(G-13219)
API INDUSTRIES INC
Base Plastics
2 Glenshaw St (10962-1207)
PHONE.................................845 365-2200
Fax: 845 680-0421
Susan Rosenberg, *CEO*
David Nezri, *Accounts Exec*
Sam Schiller, *Accounts Exec*
David Sabo, *Marketing Mgr*
Jennifer Gill, *Info Tech Mgr*
EMP: 125
SALES (corp-wide): 122.8MM **Privately Held**
SIC: 2673 3081 Plastic bags: made from purchased materials; unsupported plastics film & sheet
PA: Api Industries, Inc.
2 Glenshaw St
Orangeburg NY 10962
845 365-2200

(G-13220)
AVERY DENNISON CORPORATION
524 Route 303 (10962-1309)
PHONE.................................845 680-3873
Tesh Patel, *Research*
Mike Wright, *Sales Executive*
EMP: 116
SALES (corp-wide): 5.9B **Publicly Held**
SIC: 2672 Adhesive papers, labels or tapes: from purchased material
PA: Avery Dennison Corporation
207 N Goode Ave Fl 6
Glendale CA 91203
626 304-2000

(G-13221)
CEROVENE INC
10 Corporate Dr (10962-2614)
PHONE.................................845 359-1101
Manish Shah, *President*
EMP: 10
SALES (corp-wide): 8MM **Privately Held**
SIC: 2834 Pharmaceutical preparations
PA: Cerovene Inc.
612 Corporate Way Ste 10
Valley Cottage NY 10989
845 267-2055

(G-13222)
CHROMALLOY AMERICAN LLC (DH)
330 Blaisdell Rd (10962-2510)
PHONE.................................845 230-7355
Armand F Lauzon Jr, *CEO*
EMP: 27 **EST:** 1986
SALES (est): 21.4MM
SALES (corp-wide): 3B **Publicly Held**
SIC: 3724 7699 Aircraft engines & engine parts; engine repair & replacement, non-automotive
HQ: Chromalloy Gas Turbine Llc
3999 Rca Blvd
Palm Beach Gardens FL 33410
561 935-3571

(G-13223)
CHROMALLOY GAS TURBINE LLC
Also Called: Chromalloy New York
330 Blaisdell Rd (10962-2510)
PHONE.................................845 359-2462
Fax: 845 359-4409
Vince Martling, *General Mgr*
Zenon Piatnyczka, *General Mgr*
Tim Ulles, *General Mgr*
Dan Albert, *Vice Pres*
Keith Chessum, *Vice Pres*
EMP: 200
SALES (corp-wide): 3B **Publicly Held**
WEB: www.chromalloysatx.com
SIC: 3724 Aircraft engines & engine parts
HQ: Chromalloy Gas Turbine Llc
3999 Rca Blvd
Palm Beach Gardens FL 33410
561 935-3571

(G-13224)
DHS SYSTEMS LLC (HQ)
560 Route 303 Ste 206 (10962-1329)
PHONE.................................845 359-6066
Samuel R Marrone, *CEO*
A Jon Prusmack, *President*
Samuel Marrone, *COO*
Brian Mindich, *Mfg Dir*
Mike Hall, *Prdtn Mgr*
▲ **EMP:** 15
SQ FT: 75,000
SALES: 80MM
SALES (corp-wide): 369.3MM **Privately Held**
WEB: www.drash.com
SIC: 2394 Tents: made from purchased materials
PA: Hdt Global, Inc.
30500 Aurora Rd Ste 100
Solon OH 44139
216 438-6111

(G-13225)
EMMI USA INC
100 Dutch Hill Rd Ste 220 (10962-2198)
PHONE.................................845 268-9990
Fax: 845 268-9991
Steven Millard, *President*
Paul Schilt, *President*
Jim Delaurentis, *General Mgr*
Mattaias Kinz, *Chairman*
Brett Mize, *Business Mgr*
▲ **EMP:** 19
SQ FT: 12,000
SALES (est): 4.8MM
SALES (corp-wide): 227.9MM **Privately Held**
WEB: www.emmiusa.com
SIC: 2096 Cheese curls & puffs
HQ: Emmi International Ag
Landenbergstrasse 1
Luzern LU 6005
227 272-7

(G-13226)
ESSILOR LABORATORIES AMER INC
Also Called: Nova Optical
165 Route 303 (10962-2209)
PHONE.................................845 365-6700
EMP: 50
SALES (corp-wide): 100.9MM **Privately Held**
SIC: 3851 Mfg Ophthalmic Goods

HQ: Essilor Laboratories Of America, Inc.
13515 N Stemmons Fwy
Dallas TX 75234
972 241-4141

(G-13227)
EUROMED INC
25 Corporate Dr (10962-2615)
PHONE.................................845 359-4039
Richard Wildnauer, *Ch of Bd*
Thomas E Gardner, *President*
Stephen Powell, *COO*
Brian Coughlin, *Vice Pres*
Ravi Ramjit, *Vice Pres*
▲ **EMP:** 95
SQ FT: 42,000
SALES (est): 29.3MM **Privately Held**
WEB: www.euromedinc.com
SIC: 3842 Bandages & dressings

(G-13228)
FERRO MACHINE CO INC
70 S Greenbush Rd (10962-1323)
PHONE.................................845 398-3641
John Ferrogari, *President*
Susan Ferrogari, *Vice Pres*
EMP: 5
SQ FT: 4,500
SALES (est): 490K **Privately Held**
SIC: 3599 Machine shop, jobbing & repair

(G-13229)
INERTIA SWITCH INC
70 S Greenbush Rd (10962-1323)
PHONE.................................845 359-8300
Fax: 845 359-6227
Ruth Fischer, *President*
Brian Digirolamo, *Vice Pres*
Nadine Nodhturft, *Controller*
EMP: 25 **EST:** 1959
SQ FT: 9,500
SALES (est): 5.4MM **Privately Held**
WEB: www.inertiaswitch.com
SIC: 3625 3812 3643 3613 Control circuit devices, magnet & solid state; acceleration indicators & systems components, aerospace; current-carrying wiring devices; switchgear & switchboard apparatus

(G-13230)
INNOVATIVE PLASTICS CORP (PA)
400 Route 303 (10962-1340)
PHONE.................................845 359-7500
Fax: 845 359-0237
Judith Hershaft, *Ch of Bd*
Jim Parrish, *President*
Stephen Hershaft, *Vice Pres*
Rick Colton, *VP Opers*
Mac Freeman, *Plant Mgr*
▼ **EMP:** 150 **EST:** 1982
SQ FT: 100,000
SALES: 40.4MM **Privately Held**
WEB: www.innovative-plastics.com
SIC: 3089 Plastic processing; thermoformed finished plastic products; molding primary plastic

(G-13231)
INSTRUMENTATION LABORATORY CO
526 Route 303 (10962-1309)
PHONE.................................845 680-0028
Fax: 845 365-8031
Doug Ward, *General Mgr*
Randy Vlasak, *Facilities Mgr*
Maryann Kocubinski, *Senior Buyer*
Lori Bailey, *Buyer*
Kathy Ottinger, *QC Dir*
EMP: 180
SQ FT: 54,883
SALES (est): 49.2MM **Privately Held**
WEB: www.ilww.com
SIC: 2836 3842 3821 2899 Blood derivatives; surgical appliances & supplies; laboratory apparatus & furniture; chemical preparations
HQ: Instrumentation Laboratory Company
180 Hartwell Rd
Bedford MA 01730
800 955-9525

(G-13232)
KEEBLER COMPANY
29 Corporate Dr (10962-2615)
PHONE.................................845 365-5200
Fax: 845 365-5286
Kirk Cunningham, *Mktg Dir*
Joseph Aidio, *Manager*
EMP: 40
SALES (corp-wide): 13.5B **Publicly Held**
WEB: www.keebler.com
SIC: 2052 Cookies
HQ: Keebler Company
1 Kellogg Sq
Battle Creek MI 49017
269 961-2000

(G-13233)
KELLOGG COMPANY
29 Corporate Dr (10962-2615)
PHONE.................................845 365-5284
Joseph Aidio, *Branch Mgr*
EMP: 699
SALES (corp-wide): 13.5B **Publicly Held**
WEB: www.kelloggs.com
SIC: 2043 Cereal breakfast foods
PA: Kellogg Company
1 Kellogg Sq
Battle Creek MI 49017
269 961-2000

(G-13234)
LTS (CHEMICAL) INC
37 Ramland Rd 2 (10962-2606)
PHONE.................................845 494-2940
Hirak Aarmaker, *President*
Slava Kogan, *Treasurer*
▲ **EMP:** 12
SQ FT: 1,400
SALES (est): 1.7MM **Privately Held**
WEB: www.ltschem.com
SIC: 2865 Chemical indicators

(G-13235)
MACHIDA INCORPORATED
Also Called: Vision-Sciences
40 Ramland Rd S Ste 1 (10962-2698)
PHONE.................................845 365-0600
Fax: 845 365-0620
Ron Hadani, *CEO*
Jitu Patel, *Vice Pres*
Patricia Ippolito, *Purch Agent*
Liad Vitman, *Buyer*
Don McPhail, *Purchasing*
EMP: 7
SQ FT: 10,000
SALES (est): 2.1MM
SALES (corp-wide): 26.5MM **Publicly Held**
WEB: www.visionsciences.com
SIC: 3827 Boroscopes
PA: Cogentix Medical, Inc.
5420 Feltl Rd
Minnetonka MN 55343
952 426-6140

(G-13236)
NICE-PAK PRODUCTS INC (PA)
2 Nice Pak Park (10962-1376)
PHONE.................................845 365-2772
Fax: 845 365-1717
Robert Julius, *President*
John Culligan, *President*
Jon Kupperman, *President*
Zachary Julius, *Exec VP*
William E Dwan, *Senior VP*
◆ **EMP:** 400 **EST:** 1955
SQ FT: 168,000
SALES (est): 440.6MM **Privately Held**
WEB: www.nicepak.com
SIC: 2621 7389 2676 Towels, tissues & napkins: paper & stock; sanitary tissue paper; packaging & labeling services; sanitary paper products

(G-13237)
OCTAGON PROCESS LLC (DH)
30 Ramland Rd S Ste 103 (10962-2626)
PHONE.................................845 680-8800
Joe McGrail, *President*
Jeff B Crevoiserat, *President*
Michael Beraota, *Controller*
EMP: 5 **EST:** 1940
SALES (est): 1.2MM
SALES (corp-wide): 5.7B **Privately Held**
SIC: 2899 Chemical preparations; deicing or defrosting fluid

Orangeburg - Rockland County (G-13238)

HQ: Clariant Corporation
4000 Monroe Rd
Charlotte NC 28205
704 331-7000

(G-13238)
PAXAR CORPORATION (HQ)
Also Called: Avery Dennison
524 Route 303 (10962-1397)
PHONE....................845 398-3229
Fax: 845 359-0380
Susan C Miller, *Ch of Bd*
Robert Van Der Merwe, *President*
Joseph Fetzner, *Vice Pres*
Paul S Huyffer, *Vice Pres*
John Jordan, *Vice Pres*
◆ EMP: 50
SQ FT: 30,000
SALES (est): 15.7MM
SALES (corp-wide): 5.9B **Publicly Held**
WEB: www.paxar.com
SIC: 2269 2752 3555 3577 Labels, cotton: printed; tags, lithographed; printing trades machinery; bar code (magnetic ink) printers
PA: Avery Dennison Corporation
207 N Goode Ave Fl 6
Glendale CA 91203
626 304-2000

(G-13239)
PICCINI INDUSTRIES LTD
37 Ramland Rd (10962-2606)
PHONE....................845 365-0614
John Piccininni, *Ch of Bd*
Senolisa Santos, *Admin Asst*
EMP: 30
SQ FT: 23,000
SALES (est): 3.2MM **Privately Held**
WEB: www.piccini.net
SIC: 2421 2522 2521 2511 Sawmills & planing mills, general; office furniture, except wood; wood office furniture; wood household furniture; wood kitchen cabinets; millwork

(G-13240)
PLEATING PLUS LTD
34 Route 340 (10962-2222)
PHONE....................201 863-2991
Ernest Vega, *President*
EMP: 10
SQ FT: 2,800
SALES (est): 536.1K **Privately Held**
WEB: www.deltafiltration.com
SIC: 2395 2339 2337 7219 Permanent pleating & pressing, for the trade; lace, burnt-out, for the trade; women's & misses' outerwear; women's & misses' suits & coats; garment making, alteration & repair

(G-13241)
PRAXAIR INC
542 Route 303 (10962-1309)
PHONE....................845 359-4200
Mark Murphy, *President*
Nicole Mitchell, *Human Res Dir*
Paul Gilman, *Info Tech Dir*
Richard Mallard, *Director*
David Strauss, *Director*
EMP: 150
SALES (corp-wide): 10.7B **Publicly Held**
SIC: 2813 Industrial gases
PA: Praxair, Inc.
39 Old Ridgebury Rd
Danbury CT 06810
203 837-2000

(G-13242)
PRAXAIR SURFACE TECH INC
560 Route 303 (10962-1329)
PHONE....................845 398-8322
Nicole Mitchell, *Human Res Dir*
David Strauff, *Manager*
Mark Nestle, *Director*
EMP: 160
SALES (corp-wide): 10.7B **Publicly Held**
SIC: 3471 Plating & polishing
HQ: Praxair Surface Technologies, Inc.
1500 Polco St
Indianapolis IN 46222
317 240-2500

(G-13243)
PRODUCTO ELECTRIC CORP
Also Called: Peco Conduit Fittings
11 Kings Hwy (10962-1897)
PHONE....................845 359-4900
Fax: 845 359-4978
Arthur Lemay, *President*
John Fischer, *Vice Pres*
Nancy Jaccoi, *Administration*
◆ EMP: 30 EST: 1935
SQ FT: 54,000
SALES (est): 5.2MM **Privately Held**
WEB: www.pecoelect.com
SIC: 3644 Electric conduits & fittings

(G-13244)
PROFESSIONAL DISPOSABLES INC
2 Nice Pak Park (10962-1317)
PHONE....................845 365-1700
Robert P Julius, *President*
William E Dwan, *Senior VP*
Ed Ostendorf, *Project Mgr*
Frank Gagliano, *Maint Spvr*
Rich Eberle, *Purch Agent*
◆ EMP: 810
SALES (est): 181MM **Privately Held**
SIC: 2676 7389 2621 Sanitary paper products; packaging & labeling services; towels, tissues & napkins: paper & stock; sanitary tissue paper

(G-13245)
SENSORMATIC ELECTRONICS LLC
10 Corporate Dr (10962-2614)
PHONE....................845 365-3125
EMP: 15 **Privately Held**
WEB: www.sensormatic.com
SIC: 3812 Detection apparatus: electronic/magnetic field, light/heat
HQ: Sensormatic Electronics, Llc
6600 Congress Ave
Boca Raton FL 33487
561 912-6000

(G-13246)
SEQUA CORPORATION
300 Blaisdell Rd (10962-2506)
PHONE....................813 434-4522
Armand Lauzon, *Branch Mgr*
Gary Palomba, *Director*
EMP: 29
SALES (corp-wide): 3B **Publicly Held**
SIC: 3724 Aircraft engines & engine parts
HQ: Sequa Corporation
3999 Rca Blvd
Palm Beach Gardens FL 33410
201 343-1122

(G-13247)
SEQUA CORPORATION
300 Blaisdell Rd (10962-2506)
PHONE....................201 343-1122
John Lansdale, *President*
Mitchell Bittman, *Counsel*
Peter Howard, *Vice Pres*
William Johnson, *Purch Mgr*
Roberto Santilli, *Design Engr*
EMP: 50
SQ FT: 367,000
SALES (corp-wide): 3B **Publicly Held**
WEB: www.sequa.com
SIC: 3479 Coating of metals & formed products
HQ: Sequa Corporation
3999 Rca Blvd
Palm Beach Gardens FL 33410
201 343-1122

(G-13248)
ZACKS ENTERPRISES INC
Also Called: Zagwear
33 Corporate Dr (10962-2615)
PHONE....................800 366-4924
Fax: 845 398-0303
Toby Zacks, *CEO*
Judd Karofsky, *President*
John Marshall, *President*
Lenny Polakoff, *Exec VP*
Nate Jacobs, *Senior VP*
▲ EMP: 50
SQ FT: 48,000
SALES (est): 17.4MM **Privately Held**
SIC: 2759 8742 Screen printing; marketing consulting services

Orchard Park
Erie County

(G-13249)
303 CONTRACTING INC (HQ)
5486 Powers Rd (14127-3111)
P.O. Box 831, Buffalo (14240-0831)
PHONE....................716 896-2122
Edward Janowski, *Ch of Bd*
Henry Van Mollenberg, *President*
Joseph Kilijanski, *Exec VP*
James P Camarre, *CFO*
EMP: 27
SQ FT: 10,000
SALES (est): 4.1MM
SALES (corp-wide): 56.6MM **Privately Held**
SIC: 3444 1799 7692 3699 Sheet metalwork; ducts, sheet metal; welding on site; welding repair; electrical equipment & supplies
PA: Mollenberg-Betz Holdings Llc
300 Scott St
Buffalo NY 14204
716 614-7473

(G-13250)
A LUNT DESIGN INC
5755 Big Tree Rd (14127-4115)
P.O. Box 247 (14127-0247)
PHONE....................716 662-0781
Fax: 716 662-0784
Audrey Lunt, *President*
Thomas Lunt, *Vice Pres*
Nicholas Buccieri CPA, *Accountant*
Robert Kresse, *Shareholder*
▲ EMP: 16
SQ FT: 15,000
SALES (est): 1.4MM **Privately Held**
WEB: www.alunt.com
SIC: 2389 Disposable garments & accessories

(G-13251)
ADVAN-TECH MANUFACTURING INC
3645 California Rd (14127-1715)
PHONE....................716 667-1500
Fax: 716 667-2860
Peter Munschauer, *President*
Denise Dietz, *Manager*
Tim Smith, *Consultant*
EMP: 23
SQ FT: 7,750
SALES (est): 3.7MM **Privately Held**
SIC: 3599 Machine shop, jobbing & repair

(G-13252)
AURORA INDUS MACHINING INC
3380 N Benzing Rd (14127-1538)
PHONE....................716 826-7911
Fax: 716 827-1041
Robert T Hesse, *President*
Mary C Hesse, *Vice Pres*
John Breen, *Treasurer*
EMP: 25
SQ FT: 20,000
SALES (est): 4.8MM
SALES (corp-wide): 32.8MM **Privately Held**
WEB: www.auroraheatexchangers.com
SIC: 3443 Heat exchangers, condensers & components; vessels, process or storage (from boiler shops); metal plate
PA: Hesse Industrial Sales, Inc.
3370 N Benzing Rd
Orchard Park NY 14127
716 827-4951

(G-13253)
BOS-HATTEN INC
Also Called: Ipe
50 Cobham Dr (14127-4121)
PHONE....................716 662-7030
Fax: 716 662-6548
Warner G Martin, *Ch of Bd*
Anthony Paliwoda, *Vice Pres*
Shirley Martin, *Admin Sec*
EMP: 10
SQ FT: 5,500
SALES (est): 832.2K
SALES (corp-wide): 68.2MM **Privately Held**
WEB: www.bos-hatten.com
SIC: 3443 Heat exchangers, condensers & components
PA: Peerless Mfg. Co.
14651 Dallas Pkwy Ste 500
Dallas TX 75254
214 357-6181

(G-13254)
BOSTON VALLEY POTTERY INC (PA)
Also Called: Boston Valley Terra Cotta
6860 S Abbott Rd (14127-4707)
PHONE....................716 649-7490
Fax: 716 649-7688
John B Krouse, *President*
Gretchen E Krouse, *Vice Pres*
Richard O Krouse, *Vice Pres*
William D Krouse, *Vice Pres*
Gary Jamoni, *Safety Mgr*
▲ EMP: 95
SQ FT: 95,300
SALES (est): 51.1MM **Privately Held**
SIC: 3259 Architectural terra cotta; roofing tile, clay

(G-13255)
BUCKLEY QC FASTENERS INC
3874 California Rd (14127-2262)
PHONE....................716 662-1490
Fax: 716 662-0669
Ruth M Kohl, *General Mgr*
Kris Furjanic, *Sales Staff*
EMP: 32
SQ FT: 11,000
SALES (est): 4.5MM **Privately Held**
SIC: 3452 Nuts, metal; bolts, metal; screws, metal

(G-13256)
BUFFALO CIRCUITS INC
105 Mid County Dr (14127-1773)
PHONE....................716 662-2113
Fax: 716 662-2696
Peter Messina Jr, *President*
Liz Bever, *Manager*
EMP: 7
SQ FT: 4,920
SALES (est): 760K **Privately Held**
SIC: 3672 7336 Printed circuit boards; silk screen design

(G-13257)
BURGESS-MANNING INC (HQ)
Also Called: Skimovex USA
50 Cobham Dr (14127-4121)
PHONE....................716 662-6540
Warner G Martin, *Ch of Bd*
Robert Sherman, *President*
Philip Otto, *Plant Mgr*
Edward Rucker, *Controller*
Anthony Paliwoda, *VP Finance*
▲ EMP: 60
SQ FT: 5,500
SALES (est): 16.4MM
SALES (corp-wide): 68.2MM **Privately Held**
WEB: www.burgessmanning.com
SIC: 3625 Noise control equipment
PA: Peerless Mfg. Co.
14651 Dallas Pkwy Ste 500
Dallas TX 75254
214 357-6181

(G-13258)
CARBON ACTIVATED CORPORATION
336 Stonehenge Dr (14127-2841)
PHONE....................716 662-2005
Chris Allen, *Branch Mgr*
EMP: 8
SALES (corp-wide): 35.4MM **Privately Held**
WEB: www.carbonactivatedcorp.com
SIC: 2819 Charcoal (carbon), activated
PA: Carbon Activated Corporation
2250 S Central Ave
Compton CA 90220
310 885-4555

(G-13259)
CARLETON TECHNOLOGIES INC (DH)
10 Cobham Dr (14127-4195)
PHONE...................................716 662-0006
Fax: 716 662-0747
Kenneth Kota, *Ch of Bd*
Kelly Coffield, *President*
Nicholas Dziama, *General Mgr*
Kenneth A Kota, *General Mgr*
Chuck Connelly, *Safety Dir*
EMP: 277
SQ FT: 93,000
SALES (est): 235.8MM
SALES (corp-wide): 3.1B Privately Held
SIC: 3728 Aircraft parts & equipment
HQ: Cobham Holdings Inc.
    10 Orchard Park Dr
    Orchard Park NY 14127
    716 662-0006

(G-13260)
CENVEO INC
Mail-Well
100 Centre Dr (14127-4122)
PHONE...................................716 662-2800
Mike A Zaietar, *Manager*
EMP: 67
SALES (corp-wide): 1.7B Publicly Held
SIC: 2677 Envelopes
PA: Cenveo, Inc.
    200 First Stamford Pl # 200
    Stamford CT 06902
    203 595-3000

(G-13261)
CHET KRUSZKAS SERVICE INC
Also Called: Chet Kruszka's Svce
3536 Southwestern Blvd (14127-1707)
PHONE...................................716 662-7450
Fax: 716 662-9593
Michael Kruszka, *President*
Rose Kruszka, *Office Mgr*
Jan Hoelscher, *Manager*
EMP: 12
SQ FT: 18,000
SALES: 1MM Privately Held
SIC: 3493 5013 5531 7538 Steel springs, except wire; automobile springs; truck parts & accessories; truck equipment & parts; general truck repair; body shop, automotive; body shop, trucks; collision shops, automotive

(G-13262)
COBHAM HOLDINGS (US) INC
10 Cobham Dr (14127-4121)
PHONE...................................716 662-0006
Betty Bible, *President*
Robert Atkins, *Business Mgr*
Michael Odonnell, *Business Mgr*
Rob Schaeffer, *Business Mgr*
Marilyn Kail, *Assistant VP*
EMP: 3700
SALES (est): 228.8MM
SALES (corp-wide): 3.1B Privately Held
SIC: 3679 3812 Microwave components; acceleration indicators & systems components, aerospace
HQ: Lockman Investments Limited
    Brook Road
    Wimborne

(G-13263)
COBHAM HOLDINGS INC (DH)
10 Orchard Park Dr (14127)
PHONE...................................716 662-0006
Bob Murphy, *CEO*
Terry Lang, *Info Tech Mgr*
EMP: 15
SALES (est): 2.1B
SALES (corp-wide): 3.1B Privately Held
SIC: 3679 3812 Microwave components; acceleration indicators & systems components, aerospace

(G-13264)
COBHAM MANAGEMENT SERVICES INC
Also Called: Cobham Mission Systems Div
10 Cobham Dr (14127-4121)
PHONE...................................716 662-0006
Warren Tucker, *President*
Adreanne Lippa, *Opers Mgr*
Tim Thommen, *Opers Mgr*
Mike Rapp, *Production*
Barbara Walters, *Buyer*
◆ EMP: 2650
SQ FT: 37,024
SALES (est): 228.8MM
SALES (corp-wide): 3.1B Privately Held
SIC: 3568 Couplings, shaft: rigid, flexible, universal joint, etc.
HQ: Cobham Holdings Inc.
    10 Orchard Park Dr
    Orchard Park NY 14127
    716 662-0006

(G-13265)
CONTECH ENGNERED SOLUTIONS LLC
34 Birdsong Pkwy (14127-3067)
PHONE...................................716 870-9091
Gene Majchrzack, *Branch Mgr*
EMP: 12
SALES (corp-wide): 695.2MM Privately Held
SIC: 3443 Fabricated plate work (boiler shop)
HQ: Contech Engineered Solutions Llc
    9025 Ctr Pinte Dr Ste 400
    West Chester OH 45069
    513 645-7000

(G-13266)
CURBELL MEDICAL PRODUCTS INC
20 Centre Dr (14127-4102)
PHONE...................................716 667-2520
Craig Fenske, *Senior Buyer*
Chris Camacho, *Design Engr*
Dave Zavah, *Branch Mgr*
EMP: 11
SALES (corp-wide): 190.5MM Privately Held
SIC: 3669 Intercommunication systems, electric
HQ: Curbell Medical Products, Inc.
    7 Cobham Dr
    Orchard Park NY 14127
    716 667-2520

(G-13267)
CURBELL MEDICAL PRODUCTS INC (HQ)
7 Cobham Dr (14127-4180)
PHONE...................................716 667-2520
Thomas E Leone, *Ch of Bd*
Christine L Sabuda, *Vice Ch Bd*
Abdulkadir Sarac, *President*
Art Gosh, *COO*
Shawn Heeter, *Mfg Dir*
▲ EMP: 159
SALES: 50.4MM
SALES (corp-wide): 190.5MM Privately Held
WEB: www.curbell.com
SIC: 3669 Intercommunication systems, electric
PA: Curbell, Inc.
    7 Cobham Dr
    Orchard Park NY 14127
    716 667-3377

(G-13268)
CUSTOM COUNTERTOPS INC
5260 Armor Duells Rd (14127-4409)
PHONE...................................716 646-1579
Gloria Marino, *President*
EMP: 5
SQ FT: 7,588
SALES (corp-wide): 750K Privately Held
WEB: www.customcountertops.com
SIC: 3131 Counters
PA: Custom Countertops Inc
    3192 Walden Ave
    Depew NY 14043
    716 685-2871

(G-13269)
DESMI-AFTI INC
227 Thorn Ave Bldg C (14127-2600)
P.O. Box 575 (14127-0575)
PHONE...................................716 662-0632
Fax: 716 662-0636
Peter Lane, *President*
Carole Lane, *Production*
David Kuczma, *Engineer*
Charlene Cousineau, *Accountant*
Roy R Uebelhoer, *Sales Mgr*
▲ EMP: 20
SQ FT: 26,131
SALES (est): 5MM Privately Held
WEB: www.afti.com
SIC: 3533 3535 Oil field machinery & equipment; belt conveyor systems, general industrial use

(G-13270)
FLOW-SAFE INC
3865 Taylor Rd (14127-2297)
PHONE...................................716 662-2585
Warner Martin, *Ch of Bd*
Kevin Martin, *President*
Edward Rucker, *Controller*
Dawn Hawell, *Accounts Mgr*
Dennis Maines, *Sales Engr*
EMP: 40
SQ FT: 25,000
SALES (est): 9.1MM Privately Held
SIC: 3491 5074 Industrial valves; plumbing & heating valves

(G-13271)
GAYMAR INDUSTRIES INC
10 Centre Dr (14127-2280)
PHONE...................................800 828-7341
Fax: 716 662-6120
Bradford L Saar, *CEO*
Kent J Davies, *Principal*
Pradeep Gupta, *QA Dir*
Timothy Bialek, *Engineer*
David McKay, *Director*
▲ EMP: 350 EST: 1956
SQ FT: 110,000
SALES (est): 44.9MM
SALES (corp-wide): 9.9B Publicly Held
WEB: www.gaymar.com
SIC: 3841 Surgical & medical instruments
PA: Stryker Corporation
    2825 Airview Blvd
    Portage MI 49002
    269 385-2600

(G-13272)
GENIUS TOOLS AMERICAS CORP
Also Called: Genius Tool Americas
15 Cobham Dr (14127-4101)
PHONE...................................716 662-6872
Winni Chang, *Branch Mgr*
EMP: 10
SALES (corp-wide): 2.4MM Privately Held
WEB: www.geniustoolsusa.com
SIC: 3545 Tools & accessories for machine tools
PA: Genius Tools Americas Corp
    1440 E Cedar St
    Ontario CA 91761
    909 230-9588

(G-13273)
GOODNATURE PRODUCTS INC (PA)
3860 California Rd (14127-2262)
PHONE...................................716 855-3325
Fax: 716 667-3328
Dale Wettlaufer, *President*
Larry Colucci, *Engineer*
Eric Wettlaufer, *Engineer*
Diane Massett, *Finance*
Lori Sonnenfeld, *Human Res Mgr*
EMP: 12
SQ FT: 18,000
SALES: 5MM Privately Held
WEB: www.goodnature.com
SIC: 3634 3556 Juice extractors, electric; pasteurizing equipment, dairy machinery

(G-13274)
GRASERS DENTAL CERAMICS
5020 Armor Duells Rd # 2 (14127-4441)
PHONE...................................716 649-5100
Thomas John Graser Jr, *Owner*
EMP: 6
SQ FT: 600
SALES: 60K Privately Held
SIC: 3843 Dental materials

(G-13275)
ITT ENIDINE INC (DH)
Also Called: Enivate - Aerospace Division
7 Centre Dr (14127-2281)
PHONE...................................716 662-1900
Fax: 716 662-1909
Dennise Ramos, *CEO*
Munish Nanda, *Ch of Bd*
Dennis Schully, *President*
Christophe Lee, *Vice Pres*
Mike Semo, *Vice Pres*
▲ EMP: 275
SQ FT: 85,000
SALES (est): 126.1MM
SALES (corp-wide): 2.4B Publicly Held
WEB: www.enidine.com
SIC: 3724 3714 3593 Aircraft engines & engine parts; motor vehicle parts & accessories; fluid power cylinders & actuators
HQ: Itt, Llc
    1133 Westchester Ave N-100
    White Plains NY 10604
    914 641-2000

(G-13276)
J H BUSCHER INC
227 Thorn Ave Ste 30 (14127-2671)
PHONE...................................716 667-2003
John H Buscher, *President*
Margaret G Buscher, *Vice Pres*
EMP: 5
SQ FT: 3,000
SALES: 700K Privately Held
WEB: www.jhbi.com
SIC: 3491 Industrial valves

(G-13277)
KELSON PRODUCTS INC
3300 N Benzing Rd (14127-1538)
PHONE...................................716 825-2585
Joseph P Merz, *President*
EMP: 7
SQ FT: 10,864
SALES: 700K Privately Held
WEB: www.kelsonproducts.com
SIC: 3069 Rubberized fabrics

(G-13278)
KINEDYNE INC
Also Called: Engineered Lifting Tech
3566 S Benzing Rd (14127-1703)
PHONE...................................716 667-6833
William Hanes, *President*
Matthew Filion, *Project Engr*
Jeremy Inda, *Design Engr*
Sue Sherry, *Office Mgr*
EMP: 18
SQ FT: 17,000
SALES (est): 4.6MM Privately Held
SIC: 3531 Cranes

(G-13279)
LAKE REGION MEDICAL INC
3902 California Rd (14127-2275)
P.O. Box 637 (14127-0637)
PHONE...................................716 662-5025
Fax: 716 662-5772
Lisa Kull, *Vice Pres*
Michael Ekstrum, *Opers Staff*
Alexander Nastevski, *Engineer*
Michael Clayback, *Director*
EMP: 110
SALES (corp-wide): 800.4MM Publicly Held
SIC: 3841 Surgical instruments & apparatus; medical instruments & equipment, blood & bone work
HQ: Lake Region Medical, Inc.
    100 Fordham Rd
    Wilmington MA 01887
    978 570-6900

(G-13280)
LD MCCAULEY LLC
3875 California Rd (14127-2239)
PHONE...................................716 662-6744
Durham S McCauley, *CEO*
Peter L McCauley, *President*
David Powers, *Vice Pres*
Darryl Rieger, *Manager*
EMP: 120
SALES (est): 15.5MM Privately Held
SIC: 3452 Bolts, nuts, rivets & washers

(G-13281)
MANZELLA KNITTING
3345 N Benzing Rd (14127-1539)
PHONE...................................716 825-0808
Ed Masanovic, *Owner*
▲ EMP: 7

Orchard Park - Erie County (G-13282)

SALES (est): 608.3K *Privately Held*
SIC: 2381 Gloves, work: woven or knit, made from purchased materials

(G-13282)
MARATHON ROOFING PRODUCTS INC
3310 N Benzing Rd (14127-1538)
PHONE.................................716 685-3340
Tod Cislo, *President*
Tim Krawczyk, *Sales Dir*
Tony Venturoli, *Sales Associate*
Cindy Fiordaliso, *Manager*
◆ **EMP:** 10
SQ FT: 30,000
SALES (est): 3MM *Privately Held*
WEB: www.marathondrains.com
SIC: 2952 5033 Roofing materials; roofing & siding materials

(G-13283)
MEDSOURCE TECHNOLOGIES LLC
3902 California Rd (14127-2275)
PHONE.................................716 662-5025
Jim Hillman, *General Mgr*
Mark Lee, *Plant Mgr*
Jim Clark, *Manager*
EMP: 100
SALES (corp-wide): 800.4MM *Publicly Held*
WEB: www.medsourcetech.com
SIC: 3841 Surgical & medical instruments
HQ: Medsource Technologies, Llc
100 Fordham Rd Ste 1
Wilmington MA 01887
978 570-6900

(G-13284)
MENTHOLATUM COMPANY (DH)
707 Sterling Dr (14127-1587)
PHONE.................................716 677-2500
Fax: 716 677-9528
Akiyoshi Yoshida PHD, *CEO*
Kunio Yamada, *President*
Barbara Regan, *Regional Mgr*
Randal Beard, *Business Mgr*
David Moore, *Sr Corp Ofcr*
◆ **EMP:** 34 **EST:** 1889
SQ FT: 102,000
SALES (est): 53.3MM
SALES (corp-wide): 1.4B *Privately Held*
WEB: www.mentholatum.com
SIC: 2834 2844 Pharmaceutical preparations; analgesics; lip balms; toilet preparations
HQ: Rohto Usa Inc
707 Sterling Dr
Orchard Park NY 14127
716 677-2500

(G-13285)
NITRAM ENERGY INC
Also Called: Alco Products Div
50 Cobham Dr (14127-4121)
PHONE.................................716 662-6540
Peter J Burlage, *CEO*
Robert Sherman, *President*
Bob Wicher, *Engineer*
Joe Hasler, *Controller*
John Buczynskyj, *Sales Staff*
EMP: 50
SQ FT: 5,500
SALES (est): 4.6MM
SALES (corp-wide): 68.2MM *Privately Held*
SIC: 3625 3443 Control equipment, electric; heat exchangers: coolers (after, inter), condensers, etc.
PA: Peerless Mfg. Co.
14651 Dallas Pkwy Ste 500
Dallas TX 75254
214 357-6181

(G-13286)
P M PLASTICS INC
1 Bank St Ste 1 (14127-2997)
PHONE.................................716 662-1255
Paul Sparks, *President*
Mark Zybert, *Corp Secy*
EMP: 25
SQ FT: 46,000
SALES: 3.5MM *Privately Held*
SIC: 3089 Injection molding of plastics

(G-13287)
PANAGRAPHICS INC
Also Called: Polish American Journal
30 Quail Run (14127-4611)
P.O. Box 198, Bowmansville (14026-0198)
PHONE.................................716 312-8088
Mark A Cohan, *President*
Christopher Misztal, *Vice Pres*
Caroline Szczepanski, *Treasurer*
Scott Oziemek, *Manager*
Barbara Pinkowski, *Director*
EMP: 5
SQ FT: 1,200
SALES (est): 462K *Privately Held*
SIC: 2791 2711 Typesetting; newspapers

(G-13288)
PARATUS INDUSTRIES INC
6659 E Quaker St (14127-2503)
PHONE.................................716 826-2000
Stephen Idziur, *President*
Thomas Zimmermann, *Vice Pres*
Trish Kernitz, *Controller*
EMP: 30
SQ FT: 20,000
SALES (est): 5.3MM *Privately Held*
WEB: www.paratusindustries.com
SIC: 3553 Woodworking machinery

(G-13289)
PEERLESS MFG CO
Also Called: Alco Products USA
50 Cobham Dr (14127-4121)
PHONE.................................716 539-7400
Steve Lefavour, *Mfg Dir*
Peter J Burlage, *Branch Mgr*
EMP: 40
SALES (corp-wide): 68.2MM *Privately Held*
WEB: www.peerlessmfg.com
SIC: 3569 Separators for steam, gas, vapor or air (machinery)
PA: Peerless Mfg. Co.
14651 Dallas Pkwy Ste 500
Dallas TX 75254
214 357-6181

(G-13290)
POLYMER CONVERSIONS INC
5732 Big Tree Rd (14127-4196)
PHONE.................................716 662-8550
Jack E Bertsch, *CEO*
Joan Bertsch, *Corp Secy*
Benjamin Harp, *COO*
Ken Cook, *Maint Spvr*
Tom Rybicki, *Opers Staff*
EMP: 70
SQ FT: 35,000
SALES (est): 21.9MM *Privately Held*
WEB: www.polymerconversions.com
SIC: 3089 Molding primary plastic

(G-13291)
PRECISION ABRASIVES CORP
3176 Abbott Rd (14127-1069)
PHONE.................................716 826-5833
Kevin Wyckoff, *President*
Pam Vogel, *VP Opers*
Jeff Kraatz, *Plant Mgr*
Stacey Coyne, *Purch Mgr*
David Menzer, *Treasurer*
▲ **EMP:** 50
SQ FT: 25,000
SALES (est): 6.7MM
SALES (corp-wide): 32.3MM *Privately Held*
WEB: www.wesand.com
SIC: 3291 Coated abrasive products
PA: Sopark Corp.
3300 S Park Ave
Buffalo NY 14218
716 822-0534

(G-13292)
QUAKER BOY INC (PA)
Also Called: Quaker Boy Turkey Calls
5455 Webster Rd (14127-1742)
PHONE.................................716 662-3979
Fax: 716 662-9426
Richard C Kirby, *President*
Laurie Rizzo, *Manager*
▲ **EMP:** 50
SQ FT: 13,000

SALES (est): 5.3MM *Privately Held*
WEB: www.quakerboy.com
SIC: 3949 5961 Game calls; hunting equipment; mail order house

(G-13293)
QUAKER MILLWORK & LUMBER INC
77 S Davis St (14127-2684)
PHONE.................................716 662-3388
Robert J Raber, *President*
Lyn Raber, *Office Mgr*
Joan Siarek, *Manager*
EMP: 40
SQ FT: 36,000
SALES (est): 6.9MM *Privately Held*
WEB: www.quakermills.com
SIC: 2431 Millwork; doors & door parts & trim, wood; staircases, stairs & railings

(G-13294)
QUALITY INDUSTRIAL SERVICES
Also Called: Bws Specialty Fabrication
75 Bank St (14127-2908)
PHONE.................................716 667-7703
John E Sisson, *CEO*
Cindee Fahey, *Accounting Mgr*
EMP: 14
SQ FT: 52,800
SALES (est): 2.9MM *Privately Held*
SIC: 3496 7692 Miscellaneous fabricated wire products; welding repair

(G-13295)
ROHTO USA INC (HQ)
707 Sterling Dr (14127-1557)
PHONE.................................716 677-2500
Peter Arena, *Supervisor*
James W Ingham, *Admin Sec*
◆ **EMP:** 1
SALES (est): 53.3MM
SALES (corp-wide): 1.4B *Privately Held*
SIC: 2834 8731 Pharmaceutical preparations; analgesics; lip balms; medical research, commercial
PA: Rohto Pharmaceutical Co., Ltd.
1-8-1, Tatsuminishi, Ikuno-Ku
Osaka OSK 544-0
667 581-231

(G-13296)
S & K COUNTER TOPS INC
4708 Duerr Rd (14127-3141)
PHONE.................................716 662-7986
Fax: 716 648-4776
Bob Hayes, *President*
Tim Huwes, *Vice Pres*
EMP: 7
SQ FT: 2,400
SALES: 500K *Privately Held*
SIC: 2542 5211 Cabinets: show, display or storage: except wood; counters or counter display cases: except wood; cabinets, kitchen; counter tops

(G-13297)
STI-CO INDUSTRIES INC
11 Cobham Dr Ste A (14127-4187)
PHONE.................................716 662-2680
Fax: 716 662-5150
Antoinette Kaiser, *CEO*
Antoinette P Kaiser, *CEO*
Kyle Sawiat, *President*
Kyle Swiat, *Business Mgr*
Joseph M Collura, *Prdtn Mgr*
EMP: 48
SQ FT: 10,000
SALES (est): 16MM *Privately Held*
WEB: www.sti-co.com
SIC: 3663 Radio & TV communications equipment

(G-13298)
TAYLOR METALWORKS INC
3925 California Rd (14127-2276)
PHONE.................................716 662-3113
Peter G Taylor, *President*
Gary Lumley, *Managing Dir*
Jason Taylor, *Vice Pres*
Paul Johnson, *Engineer*
Kathy Mecca, *Human Res Mgr*
EMP: 110 **EST:** 1948
SQ FT: 37,000

SALES (est): 21.9MM *Privately Held*
WEB: www.taylorcnc.com
SIC: 3451 3365 Screw machine products; aluminum & aluminum-based alloy castings

(G-13299)
TRANSPORT NATIONAL DEV INC (PA)
Also Called: North American Carbide
5720 Ellis Rd (14127-2223)
PHONE.................................716 662-0270
Robert E Gralke, *CEO*
Carl Dischner, *Plant Mgr*
Elizabeth Liebich, *Treasurer*
Tim Gelder, *Controller*
Debby Oconnor, *VP Finance*
EMP: 50
SQ FT: 30,000
SALES (est): 13MM *Privately Held*
SIC: 3541 Machine tools, metal cutting type

(G-13300)
TRANSPORT NATIONAL DEV INC
Also Called: North American Carbide of NY
5720 Ellis Rd (14127-2223)
PHONE.................................716 662-0270
Marsha Gralke, *Opers Mgr*
Robert Gralke, *Enginr/R&D Mgr*
Cindy Donnelly, *Office Mgr*
EMP: 50
SALES (corp-wide): 13MM *Privately Held*
SIC: 2819 3545 Carbides; machine tool accessories
PA: Transport National Development, Inc.
5720 Ellis Rd
Orchard Park NY 14127
716 662-0270

(G-13301)
UNITED MATERIALS LLC
Also Called: Frey Concrete Incoporated
75 Bank St (14127-2908)
PHONE.................................716 662-0564
Richard Holmes, *Owner*
Leslie Stewart, *Human Res Dir*
Peter J Romano, *Director*
EMP: 6
SALES (corp-wide): 19.3MM *Privately Held*
SIC: 3273 1442 Ready-mixed concrete; construction sand & gravel
PA: United Materials, L.L.C.
3949 Frest Pk Way Ste 400
North Tonawanda NY 14120
716 683-1432

(G-13302)
VIBRATION & NOISE ENGRG CORP
Also Called: Vanec
3374 N Benzing Rd (14127-1538)
PHONE.................................716 827-4959
Art Cagney, *President*
Thomas Love, *President*
Jim McGrath, *Cust Mgr*
Charlie Dias, *Manager*
EMP: 3
SQ FT: 2,000
SALES (est): 2MM *Privately Held*
WEB: www.vanec.com
SIC: 3625 5084 Noise control equipment; industrial machinery & equipment

---

Oriskany
Oneida County

(G-13303)
ALFRED PUBLISHING CO INC
Also Called: Alfred Music
123 Dry Rd (13424-4312)
PHONE.................................315 736-1572
Daniel Mayack, *Branch Mgr*
Brian Simpson, *Info Tech Mgr*
EMP: 70
SALES (corp-wide): 74.4MM *Privately Held*
WEB: www.alfred.com
SIC: 2731 5192 Book music: publishing & printing; books, periodicals & newspapers

GEOGRAPHIC SECTION

Ossining - Westchester County (G-13326)

PA: The Full Void 2 Inc
16320 Roscoe Blvd Ste 100
Van Nuys CA 91406
818 891-5999

(G-13304)
BONIDE PRODUCTS INC
6301 Sutliff Rd (13424-4326)
PHONE....................315 736-8231
James J Wurz, *CEO*
Edward T Wurz, *Vice Pres*
Tom Wurz, *Vice Pres*
Nancy Long, *Technical Mgr*
Michael Klein, *Human Res Mgr*
▲ EMP: 200
SQ FT: 27,000
SALES (est): 67.9MM **Privately Held**
WEB: www.bonideproducts.com
SIC: 2899 Chemical preparations

(G-13305)
CALDWELL BENNETT INC
Also Called: C B I
6152 County Seat Rd (13424-4308)
P.O. Box 610, Rome (13442-0610)
PHONE....................315 337-8540
Fax: 315 337-0215
Douglas Brazinski, *President*
Brian Branzinski, *Vice Pres*
Brian Brazinski, *Vice Pres*
Joan Brazinski, *Vice Pres*
Paul Brazinski, *Vice Pres*
EMP: 45
SQ FT: 40,000
SALES (est): 8.9MM **Privately Held**
WEB: www.cbicables.com
SIC: 3357 Communication wire

(G-13306)
COVENTYA INC
132 Ceral Ln (13424-4702)
PHONE....................315 768-6635
Amanda Liberatore, *Purch Agent*
Debra Torchia, *Human Res Dir*
Karen B Mathis, *Director*
EMP: 6
SALES (corp-wide): 22.8MM **Privately Held**
WEB: www.sirius-tech.com
SIC: 2899 Plating compounds
HQ: Coventya, Inc.
4639 Van Epps Rd
Brooklyn Heights OH 44131
216 351-1500

(G-13307)
CPP - STEEL TREATERS
100 Furnace St (13424-4816)
PHONE....................315 736-3081
Fax: 315 736-8849
Joseph Weber, *President*
Pat Fonner, *Vice Pres*
Kevin Thomas, *Vice Pres*
Rob Thompson, *QC Dir*
Ronald Russell, *Treasurer*
EMP: 29 EST: 1957
SQ FT: 4,000
SALES (est): 6.5MM
SALES (corp-wide): 6.7B **Privately Held**
SIC: 3398 Metal heat treating
HQ: Cpp-Syracuse, Inc.
901 E Genesee St
Chittenango NY 13037
315 687-0014

(G-13308)
DAIMLER BUSES NORTH AMER INC
165 Base Rd (13424)
P.O. Box 748 (13424-0748)
PHONE....................315 768-8101
Fax: 315 768-3513
Bernd Voigt, *Ch of Bd*
Andreas Strecker, *President*
Harry Rendel, *CFO*
▲ EMP: 560
SQ FT: 40,000
SALES: 79.2MM
SALES (corp-wide): 160.5B **Privately Held**
WEB: www.orionbus.com
SIC: 3713 3711 Truck & bus bodies; motor buses, except trackless trollies, assembly of

HQ: Daimler Trucks North America Llc
4747 N Channel Ave
Portland OR 97217
503 745-8011

(G-13309)
FIBER INSTRUMENT SALES INC (PA)
Also Called: F I S
161 Clear Rd (13424-4339)
PHONE....................315 736-2206
Fax: 315 736-2285
Frank Giotto, *President*
Susan Grabinsky, *President*
Kirk Donley, *Senior VP*
Valerie Sitler, *Senior VP*
John Bruno, *Vice Pres*
◆ EMP: 150
SQ FT: 90,000
SALES (est): 56.1MM **Privately Held**
WEB: www.fisfiber.com
SIC: 3661 3643 2298 3699 Fiber optics communications equipment; connectors & terminals for electrical devices; cable, fiber; security devices

(G-13310)
GOLD MEDAL PACKING INC
8301 Old River Rd (13424)
P.O. Box 652 (13424-0652)
PHONE....................315 337-1911
Fax: 315 339-5854
Joseph Rocco III, *President*
Nancy Stilwell, *Controller*
Liz Shapano, *Admin Sec*
EMP: 60
SQ FT: 10,000
SALES (est): 8.8MM **Privately Held**
WEB: www.goldmedalpacking.com
SIC: 2011 Meat packing plants

(G-13311)
INDUSTRIAL OIL TANK SERVICE
120 Dry Rd (13424-4311)
PHONE....................315 736-6080
John E Hitchings Jr, *President*
John E Hitchings Sr, *Admin Sec*
EMP: 10
SQ FT: 11,580
SALES (est): 1.1MM **Privately Held**
SIC: 2992 Re-refining lubricating oils & greases

(G-13312)
ORISKANY ARMS INC
175 Clear Rd (13424-4301)
PHONE....................315 737-2196
Frank Giotto, *CEO*
Jim Rabbia, *President*
EMP: 2
SQ FT: 10,000
SALES: 5MM **Privately Held**
SIC: 3484 Guns (firearms) or gun parts, 30 mm. & below

(G-13313)
SEIFERT GRAPHICS INC
Also Called: Seifert Transit Graphics
6133 Judd Rd (13424-4220)
PHONE....................315 736-2744
Fax: 315 736-6602
Karen M Seifert, *President*
Robert J Dunn, *COO*
Emmett Seifert, *Accounts Exec*
Todd Stern, *Manager*
EMP: 15
SQ FT: 20,000
SALES (est): 2.8MM **Privately Held**
WEB: www.seifertgraphics.com
SIC: 2752 Commercial printing, lithographic

(G-13314)
SUIT-KOTE CORPORATION
Also Called: Central Asphalt
191 Dry Rd (13424-4312)
PHONE....................315 735-8501
Fax: 315 735-4604
Lee Wall, *Branch Mgr*
EMP: 13
SALES (corp-wide): 278.7MM **Privately Held**
WEB: www.suit-kote.com
SIC: 2951 Asphalt paving mixtures & blocks

PA: Suit-Kote Corporation
1911 Lorings Crossing Rd
Cortland NY 13045
607 753-1100

(G-13315)
SUMAX CYCLE PRODUCTS INC
122 Clear Rd (13424-4300)
PHONE....................315 768-1058
Fax: 315 768-1046
Linda Van Scoten, *President*
Kirk Van Scotten, *Vice Pres*
EMP: 16
SQ FT: 11,000
SALES: 611.4K **Privately Held**
WEB: www.sumax.com
SIC: 3751 Motorcycles & related parts; motorcycle accessories

(G-13316)
TERAHERTZ TECHNOLOGIES INC
Also Called: T T I
169 Clear Rd (13424-4301)
PHONE....................315 736-3642
John Gentile, *President*
Donald Biron, *Director*
Donna Gentile, *Admin Sec*
EMP: 6
SQ FT: 28,000
SALES (est): 1.8MM **Privately Held**
WEB: www.terahertztechnologies.com
SIC: 3661 8742 8731 Fiber optics communications equipment; industrial & labor consulting services; electronic research

(G-13317)
TLC-THE LIGHT CONNECTION INC
132 Base Rd (13424-4204)
PHONE....................315 736-7384
Fax: 315 736-1927
Brian Mohar, *President*
Brain Mohar, *President*
Fritz Barns, *Principal*
Doug Rouse, *Principal*
Keith Vanderzell, *Principal*
EMP: 70
SQ FT: 19,500
SALES (est): 19.5MM
SALES (corp-wide): 56.1MM **Privately Held**
WEB: www.thelightconnection.com
SIC: 3357 Fiber optic cable (insulated)
PA: Fiber Instrument Sales, Inc.
161 Clear Rd
Oriskany NY 13424
315 736-2206

Oriskany Falls
Oneida County

(G-13318)
HANSON AGGREGATES PA LLC
1780 State Route 12b (13425)
P.O. Box 368 (13425-0368)
PHONE....................315 821-7222
Donald Hennings, *Plant Mgr*
Donald Henings, *Manager*
EMP: 15
SALES (corp-wide): 14.4B **Privately Held**
SIC: 1442 1429 1422 Common sand mining; grits mining (crushed stone); crushed & broken limestone
HQ: Hanson Aggregates Pennsylvania, Llc
7660 Imperial Way
Allentown PA 18195
610 366-4626

(G-13319)
ZIELINSKIS ASPHALT INC
4989 State Route 12b (13425-4541)
PHONE....................315 306-4057
Kevin J Zielinski, *Principal*
EMP: 5
SALES (est): 2MM **Privately Held**
SIC: 2951 Asphalt paving mixtures & blocks

Ossining
Westchester County

(G-13320)
ALLIANCE MAGNETIC LLC
100 Executive Blvd # 202 (10562-2557)
PHONE....................914 944-1690
Martin Kuo,
▲ EMP: 5
SALES (est): 527.2K **Privately Held**
WEB: www.alliancemagnetics.net
SIC: 3571 Electronic computers

(G-13321)
CATARACT HOSE CO
Also Called: Cataract Hose Co No 2
6 Waller Ave (10562-4711)
PHONE....................914 941-9019
Louie Diloreto, *President*
EMP: 40
SALES (est): 2.7MM **Privately Held**
SIC: 3052 Fire hose, rubber

(G-13322)
CLEAR CAST TECHNOLOGIES INC (PA)
99 N Water St (10562-3255)
PHONE....................914 945-0848
Fax: 914 945-0436
Peter Goldstein, *President*
Jerry Brown, *General Mgr*
Chris Beigle, *VP Sales*
Janice McAlevy, *Accounts Mgr*
Gary Schambs, *Regl Sales Mgr*
▲ EMP: 30
SQ FT: 28,000
SALES (est): 5.2MM **Privately Held**
WEB: www.clearcasttech.com
SIC: 3083 Laminated plastics plate & sheet

(G-13323)
METALLIZED CARBON CORPORATION (PA)
Also Called: Metcar Products
19 S Water St (10562-4633)
PHONE....................914 941-3738
Fax: 914 941-4050
Matt Brennan, *Ch of Bd*
Bruce Hard, *General Mgr*
Manuel Debarros, *Prdtn Mgr*
Frank Puentes, *Opers Staff*
Donald Destefano, *Purchasing*
EMP: 140
SQ FT: 50,000
SALES (est): 20.3MM **Privately Held**
WEB: www.carbongraphite.net
SIC: 3624 3568 Electric carbons; carbon specialties for electrical use; fibers, carbon & graphite; power transmission equipment

(G-13324)
OSSINING BAKERY LMP INC
50 N Highland Ave (10562-3432)
PHONE....................914 941-2654
Tony Martins, *President*
EMP: 7 EST: 1973
SQ FT: 3,000
SALES: 490K **Privately Held**
SIC: 2051 Bread, cake & related products

(G-13325)
OSSINING VILLAGE OF INC
Also Called: Indian Water Treatment Plant
25 Fowler Ave (10562-1919)
P.O. Box 1166 (10562-0996)
PHONE....................914 202-9668
Fax: 914 923-6239
George Gibson, *Chief*
EMP: 5 **Privately Held**
SIC: 3589 Water treatment equipment, industrial
PA: Ossining, Village Of Inc
16 Croton Ave Ste 2
Ossining NY 10562
914 941-3554

(G-13326)
PAN AMERICAN ROLLER INC
5 Broad Ave (10562-4601)
P.O. Box 1225 (10562-0057)
PHONE....................914 762-8700
Fax: 914 762-8700

Ossining - Westchester County (G-13327)

Gertrude Wolf, *Corp Secy*
Michael Wolf, *Vice Pres*
Jean Black, *Office Mgr*
EMP: 10
SQ FT: 15,000
SALES: 1MM **Privately Held**
SIC: 3991 Paint rollers

(G-13327)
REMUS INDUSTRIES
11 Oakbrook Rd (10562-2650)
PHONE.................914 906-1544
Robert Leggio, *Principal*
Deborah Ardino, *Office Mgr*
EMP: 8
SALES (est): 839.4K **Privately Held**
SIC: 3999 Manufacturing industries

(G-13328)
SABRA DENTAL PRODUCTS
24 Quail Hollow Rd (10562-2545)
PHONE.................914 945-0836
Adrian Avram, *Owner*
EMP: 2
SALES (est): 1.5MM **Privately Held**
SIC: 3843 Dental equipment & supplies

Oswego
Oswego County

(G-13329)
DESIGNER HARDWOOD FLRG CNY INC
193 E Seneca St (13126-1644)
PHONE.................315 207-0044
Joseph Marmon, *Vice Pres*
EMP: 10 **EST:** 2014
SALES (est): 553.5K **Privately Held**
SIC: 2426 Flooring, hardwood

(G-13330)
DOTTO WAGNER
Also Called: Local News
185 E Seneca St (13126-1600)
P.O. Box 276 (13126-0276)
PHONE.................315 342-8020
Wagner Dotto, *Owner*
EMP: 6
SALES (est): 681K **Privately Held**
WEB: www.cnyfall.com
SIC: 2721 Magazines: publishing only, not printed on site

(G-13331)
ENERGY NUCLEAR OPERATIONS
Also Called: Chemistry Department
268 Lake Rd (13126-6325)
P.O. Box 110, Lycoming (13093-0110)
PHONE.................315 342-0055
Ted Sullivan, *Vice Pres*
EMP: 30
SALES (est): 6.5MM **Privately Held**
SIC: 3443 Nuclear reactors, military or industrial

(G-13332)
HEALTHWAY PRODUCTS COMPANY
249a Mitchell St (13126-1279)
PHONE.................315 207-1410
William O'Hara, *President*
Michael Daly, *Vice Pres*
EMP: 25
SQ FT: 33,000
SALES (est): 3.8MM **Privately Held**
SIC: 3564 3585 Blowers & fans; refrigeration & heating equipment

(G-13333)
INDUSTRIAL PRECISION PDTS INC
350 Mitchell St (13126-1270)
PHONE.................315 343-4421
Fax: 315 342-5662
William J Gallagher, *Chairman*
George Savas, *Controller*
Steve Standish, *Sales Staff*
Chris Fregale, *Office Mgr*
Kevin Doovan, *Manager*
EMP: 20 **EST:** 1951
SQ FT: 26,000
SALES: 1.7MM **Privately Held**
WEB: www.indprecision.com
SIC: 3599 Machine & other job shop work; custom machinery

(G-13334)
LAZAREK INC
209 Erie St (13126-2459)
PHONE.................315 343-1242
Fax: 315 343-2916
Walter Lazarek Jr, *President*
Jean Lararek, *Office Mgr*
Stanley Lazarek, *Admin Sec*
EMP: 5 **EST:** 1936
SQ FT: 950
SALES (est): 705.8K **Privately Held**
SIC: 3273 5032 1442 Ready-mixed concrete; concrete & cinder block; construction sand mining; gravel mining

(G-13335)
MITCHELL PRTG & MAILING INC (PA)
125 E 1st St 129 (13126-2104)
P.O. Box 815 (13126-0815)
PHONE.................315 343-3531
Fax: 315 343-3577
John Henry, *President*
Kathleen Henry, *Vice Pres*
Helen Henry, *Office Mgr*
EMP: 15 **EST:** 1930
SQ FT: 2,112
SALES: 400K **Privately Held**
WEB: www.mpcny.com
SIC: 2752 Commercial printing, offset

(G-13336)
NORTHLAND FILTER INTL LLC
249a Mitchell St (13126-1279)
PHONE.................315 207-1410
Dawn Moreau, *Office Mgr*
Gilles Morin,
◆ **EMP:** 20
SALES (est): 4.5MM **Privately Held**
WEB: www.northlandfilter.com
SIC: 3564 Filters, air: furnaces, air conditioning equipment, etc.

(G-13337)
NOVELIS CORPORATION
448 County Route 1a (13126-5962)
P.O. Box 28 (13126-0028)
PHONE.................315 342-1036
Thomas Walpole, *Engineer*
Larry Hudson, *Engineer*
Gordon Barkley, *Controller*
Mark Dawson, *Personnel*
Bernard Sanders, *Systems Mgr*
EMP: 300
SALES (corp-wide): 5B **Privately Held**
SIC: 3353 Aluminum sheet, plate & foil
HQ: Novelis Corporation
3560 Lenox Rd Ne Ste 2000
Atlanta GA 30326
404 760-4000

(G-13338)
NOVELIS CORPORATION
72 Alcan W Entrance Rd (13126)
P.O. Box 28 (13126-0028)
PHONE.................315 349-0121
Jack Morrison, *Principal*
EMP: 300
SALES (corp-wide): 5B **Privately Held**
SIC: 3353 Aluminum sheet, plate & foil
HQ: Novelis Corporation
3560 Lenox Rd Ne Ste 2000
Atlanta GA 30326
404 760-4000

(G-13339)
NOVELIS INC
448 County Route 1a (13126-5963)
P.O. Box 28 (13126-0028)
PHONE.................315 349-0121
Steve Fisher, *CEO*
Philip Robert Martens, *Ch of Bd*
Michael Herron, *Purch Mgr*
Lorena Bastian, *Engineer*
Dan Harrington, *Engineer*
EMP: 19
SALES (est): 2.6MM **Privately Held**
SIC: 3355 Aluminum rolling & drawing; aluminum ingot

(G-13340)
SAMPLE NEWS GROUP LLC
Also Called: Palladium Times
140 W 1st St (13126-1514)
PHONE.................315 343-3800
Fax: 315 343-0273
John Spalding, *Manager*
Ron Waer, *Manager*
Sarah McCrobie, *Relations*
EMP: 55
SQ FT: 9,620
SALES (corp-wide): 13.5MM **Privately Held**
WEB: www.gatehousemedia.com
SIC: 2711 2752 Newspapers; commercial printing, lithographic
PA: Sample News Group, L.L.C.
28 W South St
Corry PA 16407
814 665-8291

(G-13341)
SPEEDWAY PRESS INC
Also Called: Mitchell's Speedway Press
1 Burkle St (13126-3271)
P.O. Box 2006 (13126-0606)
PHONE.................315 343-3531
Fax: 315 342-0217
George Caruso Jr, *President*
Romeo Caruso, *Corp Secy*
Douglas Caruso, *Vice Pres*
Kathy Henry, *VP Sales*
EMP: 9
SQ FT: 9,000
SALES (est): 240K
SALES (corp-wide): 400K **Privately Held**
WEB: www.speedwaypress.com
SIC: 2752 Commercial printing, offset
PA: Mitchell Printing & Mailing, Inc.
125 E 1st St 129
Oswego NY 13126
315 343-3531

(G-13342)
STONES HOMEMADE CANDIES INC
145 W Bridge St (13126-1440)
PHONE.................315 343-8401
Margaret Stanchowicz, *President*
Margaret Stachowicz, *President*
EMP: 7 **EST:** 1946
SQ FT: 3,000
SALES (est): 591.2K **Privately Held**
SIC: 2064 Candy & other confectionery products

(G-13343)
SURE-LOCK INDUSTRIES LLC
193 E Seneca St (13126-1644)
PHONE.................315 207-0044
Fax: 315 207-0400
Art Brown,
Barbara Brown,
Irving Brown,
EMP: 13
SALES (est): 1.6MM **Privately Held**
SIC: 2435 Hardwood veneer & plywood

Otisville
Orange County

(G-13344)
FEDERAL PRISON INDUSTRIES
Also Called: Unicor
2 Mile Dr (10963)
PHONE.................845 386-6819
William Bondy, *Superintendent*
EMP: 150 **Publicly Held**
WEB: www.unicor.gov
SIC: 3795 Tanks, military, including factory rebuilding
HQ: Federal Prison Industries, Inc
320 1st St Nw
Washington DC 20534
202 305-3500

Ovid
Seneca County

(G-13345)
CROSSWINDS FARM & CREAMERY
6762 Log City Rd (14521-9789)
PHONE.................607 327-0363
EMP: 5
SALES (est): 262.3K **Privately Held**
SIC: 2022 5451 Natural cheese; dairy products stores

(G-13346)
HOSMER INC
Also Called: Hosmer's Winery
6999 State Route 89 (14521-9569)
PHONE.................888 467-9463
Cameron Hosmer, *President*
Maren Hosmer, *Vice Pres*
Virginia Graber, *Manager*
EMP: 15
SALES: 500K **Privately Held**
WEB: www.hosmerwinery.com
SIC: 2084 Wines

(G-13347)
SENECA COUNTY AREA SHOPPER
1885 State Route 96a (14521-9712)
PHONE.................607 532-4333
Joan E Hendrix, *Principal*
EMP: 5
SALES (est): 261.9K **Privately Held**
SIC: 2711 Newspapers, publishing & printing

(G-13348)
SHELDRAKE POINT VINEYARD LLC
Also Called: Sheldrake Point Winery
7448 County Road 153 (14521-9564)
PHONE.................607 532-8967
Fax: 607 532-8967
Chuck Tauck, *Managing Prtnr*
Robert Madill, *General Mgr*
EMP: 10
SQ FT: 4,063
SALES: 800K **Privately Held**
SIC: 2084 Wines

(G-13349)
THIRSTY OWL WINE COMPANY
6861 State Route 89 (14521-9599)
PHONE.................607 869-5805
Fax: 607 869-5851
Jonathan C Cupp, *President*
John Cupp, *President*
EMP: 7
SALES (est): 697.7K **Privately Held**
WEB: www.thirstyowl.com
SIC: 2084 Wines

Owego
Tioga County

(G-13350)
APPLIED TECHNOLOGY MFG CORP
71 Temple St (13827-1338)
P.O. Box 189 (13827-0189)
PHONE.................607 687-2200
Fax: 607 687-8145
Stephen M Lounsberry III, *President*
Peter C Lounsberry, *Vice Pres*
Steve Bean, *Manager*
EMP: 30 **EST:** 1927
SQ FT: 25,000
SALES: 7.9MM **Privately Held**
WEB: www.appliedtechmfg.com
SIC: 3531 3599 Railway track equipment; railroad related equipment; machine & other job shop work

GEOGRAPHIC SECTION

(G-13351)
C & C READY-MIX CORPORATION
3818 Rt 17 C (13827)
P.O. Box 174 (13827-0174)
PHONE.................................607 687-1690
Andy Cerretani, *Enginr/R&D Mgr*
EMP: 10
SALES (corp-wide): 5.3MM **Privately Held**
WEB: www.ccreadymix.com
SIC: 3273 2951 Ready-mixed concrete; asphalt paving mixtures & blocks
PA: C & C Ready-Mix Corporation
  3112 Vestal Rd
  Vestal NY 13850
  607 797-5108

(G-13352)
INDUSTRIAL PAINT SERVICES CORP
60 W Main St 62 (13827-1537)
PHONE.................................607 687-0107
Fax: 607 687-0208
Jean Chapman, *President*
John Spencer, *General Mgr*
Margo Padgett, *Supervisor*
EMP: 17
SQ FT: 20,000
SALES (est): 1.2MM **Privately Held**
WEB: www.ipsowego.com
SIC: 3479 Painting of metal products

(G-13353)
KYOCERA PRECISION TOOLS INC
Also Called: New York Division
1436 Taylor Rd (13827-1833)
PHONE.................................607 687-0012
Stephen Hansen, *Branch Mgr*
EMP: 14
SALES (corp-wide): 12.6B **Publicly Held**
WEB: www.tycom.com
SIC: 3541 Machine tools, metal cutting type
HQ: Kyocera Precision Tools, Inc
  102 Industrial Park Rd
  Hendersonville NC 28792
  828 698-4181

(G-13354)
LOCKHEED MARTIN CORPORATION
1801 State Route 17 (13827)
PHONE.................................607 751-2000
Deborah Grant, *Engineer*
Bryan Ruskavich, *Mktg Dir*
Joseph Trench, *Manager*
Martin Patchett, *Manager*
Mike McNeil, *Senior Mgr*
EMP: 1261
SALES (corp-wide): 46.1B **Publicly Held**
WEB: www.lockheedmartin.com
SIC: 3812 3761 Search & navigation equipment; guided missiles & space vehicles
PA: Lockheed Martin Corporation
  6801 Rockledge Dr
  Bethesda MD 20817
  301 897-6000

(G-13355)
LOCKHEED MARTIN CORPORATION
Also Called: Mission Systems & Training
1801 State Rd 17c 17 C (13827)
PHONE.................................607 751-7434
Wayne Wilson, *Senior Engr*
Deborah Zacharias, *Manager*
EMP: 100
SALES (corp-wide): 46.1B **Publicly Held**
WEB: www.lockheedmartin.com
SIC: 3812 3761 Search & navigation equipment; guided missiles & space vehicles
PA: Lockheed Martin Corporation
  6801 Rockledge Dr
  Bethesda MD 20817
  301 897-6000

(G-13356)
NATIONAL PAPER CONVERTING INC
207 Corporate Dr (13827-3249)
PHONE.................................607 687-6049
Eric Kretzmer, *President*
EMP: 5
SQ FT: 8,000
SALES (est): 837.5K **Privately Held**
WEB: www.nationaladh.com
SIC: 2621 Absorbent paper

(G-13357)
NORWESCO INC
263 Corporate Dr (13827-3249)
PHONE.................................607 687-8081
Fax: 607 687-7585
Rich Barto, *Manager*
EMP: 11
SALES (corp-wide): 54.5MM **Privately Held**
WEB: www.ncmmolding.com
SIC: 3089 Plastic & fiberglass tanks
PA: Norwesco, Inc.
  4365 Steiner St
  Saint Bonifacius MN 55375
  952 446-1945

(G-13358)
OWEGO PENNYSAVER PRESS INC
181 Front St (13827-1520)
PHONE.................................607 687-2434
Fax: 607 687-6858
George V Lynett, *President*
Wendy Post, *Publisher*
EMP: 10
SALES (est): 534.5K
SALES (corp-wide): 32.1MM **Privately Held**
WEB: www.sundayreview.com
SIC: 2711 Newspapers, publishing & printing
PA: Towanda Printing Co Inc
  116 N Main St
  Towanda PA 18848
  570 265-2151

(G-13359)
SANMINA CORPORATION
1200 Taylor Rd (13827-1292)
PHONE.................................607 689-5000
James Griffin, *Vice Pres*
Richard Day, *Mfg Staff*
Ed Fisher, *Purch Agent*
Brian Barber, *Purchasing*
Chuck Pigos, *Senior Engr*
EMP: 500
SALES (corp-wide): 6.3B **Publicly Held**
WEB: www.sanmina.com
SIC: 3672 Printed circuit boards
PA: Sanmina Corporation
  2700 N 1st St
  San Jose CA 95134
  408 964-3500

(G-13360)
TIOGA COUNTY COURIER
59 Church St (13827-1439)
PHONE.................................607 687-0108
Mary Jones, *Owner*
EMP: 5
SALES (est): 224.6K **Privately Held**
SIC: 2711 Newspapers: publishing only, not printed on site

(G-13361)
WAGNER MILLWORK INC
Also Called: Wagner Lumber
4060 Gaskill Rd (13827-4741)
PHONE.................................607 687-5362
Fax: 607 687-2633
Jeffrey S Meyer, *CEO*
Leslie Wagner, *President*
Steven Schaeffer, *Vice Pres*
Terry Bouck, *Buyer*
Ernie Creeden, *Buyer*
EMP: 70 **EST:** 1976
SQ FT: 60,000
SALES (est): 22MM **Privately Held**
WEB: www.wagnerlumber.com
SIC: 2421 2431 2426 Sawmills & planing mills, general; millwork; hardwood dimension & flooring mills

(G-13362)
WHOLESALE MULCH & SAWDUST INC
Also Called: Tioga County Waste Wood Recycl
3711 Waverly Rd (13827-2860)
PHONE.................................607 687-2637
Fax: 607 687-1907
Philip Nestor, *President*
Cynthia Nestor, *Vice Pres*
EMP: 5
SQ FT: 1,624
SALES (est): 460K **Privately Held**
SIC: 2499 Mulch or sawdust products, wood

Oxford
Chenango County

(G-13363)
AUTOMECHA INTERNATIONAL LTD (PA)
48 S Canal St (13830)
P.O. Box 660 (13830-0660)
PHONE.................................607 843-2235
Fax: 607 843-7075
Kenneth E St John, *President*
Mike Sawyer, *Manager*
Norell Bates, *Admin Sec*
Sonjia Strobach, *Admin Sec*
EMP: 28
SQ FT: 23,000
SALES (est): 5.2MM **Privately Held**
WEB: www.asmarc.com
SIC: 3579 5044 3565 3554 Addressing machines, plates & plate embossers; address labeling machines; mailing, letter handling & addressing machines; office equipment; packaging machinery; paper industries machinery

(G-13364)
RAPID REPRODUCTIONS LLC
4511 State Hwy 12 (13830)
P.O. Box 598 (13830-0598)
PHONE.................................607 843-2221
Fax: 607 843-6487
Barbara Blackman, *General Mgr*
Bryant Latourette,
EMP: 8
SQ FT: 11,000
SALES (est): 680K **Privately Held**
SIC: 2752 Commercial printing, lithographic

Oyster Bay
Nassau County

(G-13365)
AMERICAN TRANS-COIL CORP
Also Called: A T C
69 Hamilton Ave Ste 3 (11771-1573)
P.O. Box 629 (11771-0629)
PHONE.................................516 922-9640
Fax: 516 922-3361
Mark Masin, *President*
William Rogers, *Principal*
Robert Booker, *Purch Agent*
Ken Winheim, *Design Engr*
Stewart Goldberg, *Analyst*
EMP: 15 **EST:** 1960
SQ FT: 5,000
SALES (est): 2.3MM **Privately Held**
WEB: www.atc-us.com
SIC: 3677 Electronic coils, transformers & other inductors

(G-13366)
APOTHECUS PHARMACEUTICAL CORP (PA)
220 Townsend Sq (11771-2339)
PHONE.................................516 624-8200
Thomas Leon, *Ch of Bd*
Daniel Leon, *President*
Jonathan Leon, *Vice Pres*
Paul Gabel, *VP Opers*
Michael Lesser, *CFO*
EMP: 14
SQ FT: 7,000
SALES (est): 4.6MM **Privately Held**
WEB: www.apothecus.com
SIC: 2834 5122 Pharmaceutical preparations; proprietary (patent) medicines

(G-13367)
CIRCO FILE CORP
Also Called: Circo-O-File
69 Hamilton Ave Ste 1 (11771-1573)
PHONE.................................516 922-1848
Thomas Carrella, *President*
Ralph Carrella, *Shareholder*
EMP: 7 **EST:** 1955
SQ FT: 2,000
SALES (est): 1MM **Privately Held**
WEB: www.circofile.com
SIC: 3423 3545 Hand & edge tools; machine tool accessories

(G-13368)
COMANDER TERMINALS LLC
1 Commander Sq (11771-1536)
PHONE.................................516 922-7600
Abrham Prznaski, *President*
EMP: 14
SALES (est): 1.4MM **Privately Held**
SIC: 2843 Oils & greases

(G-13369)
ENGINEERING MAINT PDTS INC
Also Called: Hippo Industries
250 Berry Hill Rd (11771-3121)
P.O. Box 548 (11771-0548)
PHONE.................................516 624-9774
Fax: 516 624-9860
Ansuya Dave, *President*
Peter Dave, *Vice Pres*
Shashidhar H Dave, *Vice Pres*
EMP: 14
SQ FT: 4,000
SALES (est): 4MM **Privately Held**
SIC: 2899 5169 Corrosion preventive lubricant; anti-corrosion products

(G-13370)
IMREX LLC (PA)
55 Sandy Hill Rd (11771-3110)
P.O. Box 154 (11771-0154)
PHONE.................................516 479-3675
Jacob Armon, *Mng Member*
Harry Armon,
Alan J Weiss,
EMP: 350
SQ FT: 32,000
SALES (est): 53.1MM **Privately Held**
WEB: www.imrex.com
SIC: 3679 Electronic circuits

(G-13371)
MILL-MAX MFG CORP
190 Pine Hollow Rd (11771-4711)
P.O. Box 300 (11771-0300)
PHONE.................................516 922-6000
Fax: 516 922-9253
Roger L Bahnik, *Ch of Bd*
James W Litke, *President*
Claude A Bahnik, *Vice Pres*
Bradley E Kuczinski, *Vice Pres*
Marge Ruzicka, *Purchasing*
▲ **EMP:** 190
SQ FT: 135,000
SALES (est): 50.7MM **Privately Held**
WEB: www.mil-max.com
SIC: 3678 5065 Electronic connectors; electronic parts & equipment

(G-13372)
MIRODDI IMAGING INC (PA)
Also Called: M Squared Graphics
27 Centre View Dr (11771-2815)
PHONE.................................516 624-6898
Cherrise Miroddi, *Ch of Bd*
EMP: 2
SQ FT: 8,000
SALES (est): 1MM **Privately Held**
WEB: www.msquaredgraphics.com
SIC: 2796 Gravure printing plates or cylinders, preparation of

(G-13373)
PRINTERY
Also Called: Printing House of W S Miller
43 W Main St (11771-2215)
PHONE.................................516 922-3250
Fax: 516 922-2823
William Miller, *President*

Oyster Bay - Nassau County (G-13374)

Mary Abbene, *Vice Pres*
EMP: 5 **EST:** 1973
SALES (est): 522.7K **Privately Held**
SIC: 2759 2791 Card printing & engraving, except greeting; typesetting

(G-13374)
R F GIARDINA CO
200 Lexington Ave Apt 3a (11771-2114)
P.O. Box 562 (11771-0562)
PHONE..................516 922-1364
Robert Giardina, *President*
EMP: 10
SALES (est): 430K **Privately Held**
WEB: www.rfgco.com
SIC: 3944 Craft & hobby kits & sets

Ozone Park
Queens County

(G-13375)
ABIGAL PRESS INC
9735 133rd Ave (11417-2119)
P.O. Box 170704 (11417-0704)
PHONE..................718 641-5350
Salvatore Stratis, *CEO*
Jeff Gaines, *President*
Jeffrey Gaines, *President*
Lois Berl, *Vice Pres*
Angela Zuniga, *Purchasing*
◆ **EMP:** 98 **EST:** 1956
SQ FT: 30,000
SALES (est): 13.5MM **Privately Held**
WEB: www.abigal.com
SIC: 2759 Card printing & engraving, except greeting

(G-13376)
CENTRE INTERIORS WDWKG CO INC
10001 103rd Ave (11417-1712)
PHONE..................718 323-1343
Fax: 718 323-1856
Alex Lee, *President*
EMP: 20
SALES (est): 3.5MM **Privately Held**
SIC: 2521 Wood office desks & tables

(G-13377)
ELEVATOR VENTURES CORPORATION
Also Called: Ver-Tech Elevator
9720 99th St (11416-2602)
PHONE..................212 375-1900
Fax: 718 850-9533
Don Gelestino, *Owner*
Don Celestino, *General Mgr*
Jonathan Gatmaitan, *Manager*
EMP: 99
SALES (est): 10.2MM **Privately Held**
SIC: 3534 Elevators & moving stairways

(G-13378)
FASTENER DIMENSIONS INC
9403 104th St (11416-1723)
PHONE..................718 847-6321
Fax: 718 847-8414
Darryl A Hinkle, *President*
Debbie Blizzard, *Manager*
EMP: 35
SQ FT: 24,000
SALES: 3.2MM **Privately Held**
WEB: www.fastdim.com
SIC: 3429 5085 5088 3452 Aircraft hardware; fasteners, industrial; nuts, bolts, screws, etc.; aircraft equipment & supplies; bolts, nuts, rivets & washers

(G-13379)
FOOD GEMS LTD
8423 Rockaway Blvd (11416-1249)
PHONE..................718 296-7788
Fax: 718 296-7788
Bradley Stroll, *President*
Frank Kurt, *Vice Pres*
Jean Walker, *Manager*
EMP: 24
SQ FT: 10,000
SALES (est): 1.2MM **Privately Held**
WEB: www.foodgems.com
SIC: 2051 5812 Bread, cake & related products; eating places

(G-13380)
JOLDESON ONE AEROSPACE INDS
Also Called: Joldeson One Aerospace Inds
10002 103rd Ave (11417-1713)
PHONE..................718 848-7396
Fax: 718 848-7396
Ecatarina Joldeson, *President*
George Joldeson, *Vice Pres*
Richard Joldeson, *Admin Sec*
EMP: 93
SALES: 8.5MM **Privately Held**
SIC: 3728 3496 3812 3643 Aircraft parts & equipment; woven wire products; search & navigation equipment; current-carrying wiring devices; conveyors & conveying equipment; partitions & fixtures, except wood

(G-13381)
JULIA KNIT INC
8050 Pitkin Ave (11417-1211)
PHONE..................718 848-1900
Avraham Lip, *President*
EMP: 6
SALES (est): 820K **Privately Held**
SIC: 2253 Sweaters & sweater coats, knit

(G-13382)
KW DISTRIBUTORS GROUP INC
9018 Liberty Ave (11417-1350)
PHONE..................718 843-3500
Vito Altesi, *President*
Riccardo Altesi, *Vice Pres*
Daniel Altesi, *Treasurer*
▲ **EMP:** 10
SQ FT: 3,600
SALES (est): 820K **Privately Held**
SIC: 2434 Wood kitchen cabinets

(G-13383)
MAMITAS ICES LTD
10411 100th St (11417-2206)
PHONE..................718 738-3238
Fax: 718 738-0784
Javier Morel, *Partner*
EMP: 10
SALES: 780K **Privately Held**
SIC: 2097 Manufactured ice

(G-13384)
PREMIER KNITS LTD
9735 133rd Ave (11417-2119)
PHONE..................718 323-8264
Fax: 718 323-8274
Panta Ardeljan, *President*
Petar Ardeljan Jr, *Vice Pres*
EMP: 10
SQ FT: 35,000
SALES (est): 610K **Privately Held**
WEB: www.premierknits.com
SIC: 2253 5199 Sweaters & sweater coats, knit; knit goods

(G-13385)
ROBERT COHEN
Also Called: Allied Orthopedics
10540 Rockaway Blvd Ste A (11417-2304)
PHONE..................718 789-0996
Fax: 718 789-3716
Robert F Cohen, *Owner*
EMP: 6
SQ FT: 4,000
SALES (est): 516.3K **Privately Held**
SIC: 3842 Limbs, artificial; braces, orthopedic

(G-13386)
WALL TOOL & TAPE CORP
Also Called: Wall Tool Manufacturing
8111 101st Ave (11416-2008)
P.O. Box 20637, Floral Park (11002-0637)
PHONE..................718 641-6813
Fax: 718 641-6758
Dorothy Kaliades, *President*
Steven Kaliades, *Sales Mgr*
EMP: 20
SQ FT: 12,000
SALES (est): 3.2MM **Privately Held**
SIC: 3423 Edge tools for woodworking: augers, bits, gimlets, etc.

(G-13387)
WORKSMAN TRADING CORP
Also Called: Worksman Cycles
9415 100th St (11416-1707)
PHONE..................718 322-2000
Jeffrey A Mishkin, *President*
Donnalee Quintana, *General Mgr*
Al Venditti, *General Mgr*
Brian Mishkin, *General Mgr*
Wayne Sosin, *Vice Pres*
◆ **EMP:** 50 **EST:** 1898
SQ FT: 100,000
SALES (est): 12.6MM **Privately Held**
SIC: 3751 3444 Bicycles & related parts; sheet metalwork

(G-13388)
ZONE FABRICATORS INC
10780 101st St (11417-2609)
PHONE..................718 272-0200
Peter Scaminaci, *President*
Frances Hultin, *Vice Pres*
James Matera, *Opers Mgr*
Matt Vowell, *Manager*
EMP: 16
SQ FT: 8,000
SALES (est): 1.7MM **Privately Held**
WEB: www.zonefabinc.com
SIC: 3089 3443 Plastic processing; metal parts

Painted Post
Steuben County

(G-13389)
AUTOMATED CELLS & EQP INC
9699 Enterprise Dr (14870-9166)
PHONE..................607 936-1341
James Morris, *President*
Charlie Claes, *Engineer*
Mike Joyce, *Design Engr*
Mindi McCann, *Controller*
Jerry North, *Sales Engr*
EMP: 38
SQ FT: 27,000
SALES (est): 11MM **Privately Held**
WEB: www.autocells.com
SIC: 3569 5084 Robots, assembly line: industrial & commercial; robots, industrial

(G-13390)
CORNING INCORPORATED
905 Addison Rd (14870-9726)
PHONE..................607 974-1274
Samuel Owusu, *Engineer*
John Rector, *Project Engr*
Richard Jack, *Branch Mgr*
EMP: 50
SALES (corp-wide): 9.1B **Publicly Held**
WEB: www.corning.com
SIC: 3229 3264 Pressed & blown glass; porcelain electrical supplies
PA: Corning Incorporated
1 Riverfront Plz
Corning NY 14831
607 974-9000

(G-13391)
CORNING INCORPORATED
9261 Addison Rd (14870-9650)
PHONE..................607 974-6729
Jim Blade, *Principal*
Thomas Moag, *Engineer*
EMP: 5
SALES (corp-wide): 9.1B **Publicly Held**
WEB: www.corning.com
SIC: 3357 3661 3211 3229 Fiber optic cable (insulated); telephone & telegraph apparatus; flat glass; pressed & blown glass; semiconductors & related devices; analytical instruments
PA: Corning Incorporated
1 Riverfront Plz
Corning NY 14831
607 974-9000

(G-13392)
PACE MANUFACTURING COMPANY
894 Addison Rd (14870-9726)
PHONE..................607 936-0431
Dennis Friends, *Branch Mgr*
EMP: 5

SALES (corp-wide): 7.4MM **Privately Held**
SIC: 2048 5191 Prepared feeds; animal feeds
HQ: Pace Manufacturing Company Inc
30 N Harrison St Ste 2
Easton MD 21601

(G-13393)
SCHULER-HAAS ELECTRIC CORP
598 Ritas Way (14870-8546)
PHONE..................607 936-3514
EMP: 37
SALES (corp-wide): 21MM **Privately Held**
SIC: 3699 1731 Electrical equipment & supplies; electrical work
PA: Schuler-Haas Electric Corp.
240 Commerce Dr
Rochester NY 14623
585 325-1060

(G-13394)
SIRIANNI HARDWOODS INC
912 Addison Rd (14870-9729)
PHONE..................607 962-4688
Fax: 607 936-6237
James Sirianni, *CEO*
Mary Sirianni, *Corp Secy*
Tom Armentano, *Purch Agent*
Ann Short, *Manager*
EMP: 24
SQ FT: 69,024
SALES (est): 3.5MM **Privately Held**
WEB: www.siriannihardwoods.com
SIC: 2426 Lumber, hardwood dimension

Palatine Bridge
Montgomery County

(G-13395)
LEE NEWSPAPERS INC
6113 State Highway 5 (13428-2809)
PHONE..................518 673-3237
Fred Lee, *Principal*
EMP: 9
SALES (est): 606.6K **Privately Held**
SIC: 2711 Newspapers

(G-13396)
LEE PUBLICATIONS INC (PA)
Also Called: Waste Management
6113 State Highway 5 (13428-2809)
P.O. Box 121 (13428-0121)
PHONE..................518 673-3237
Fax: 518 673-2322
Fred Lee, *President*
Bruce Button, *Division Mgr*
John Casey, *Editor*
Joan Kark-Wren, *Editor*
Janet Lee Button, *Treasurer*
EMP: 99
SQ FT: 25,000
SALES (est): 9.8MM **Privately Held**
WEB: www.leepub.com
SIC: 2711 Newspapers, publishing & printing

Palenville
Greene County

(G-13397)
NATIONAL MILITARY INDUSTRIES
78 White Rd Ext (12463)
P.O. Box 245 (12463-0245)
PHONE..................908 782-1646
Larry Krueger, *President*
Jeanette Krueger, *Sales Staff*
EMP: 6
SQ FT: 4,500
SALES: 1.1MM **Privately Held**
WEB: www.nationalparachute.com
SIC: 2399 Parachutes

GEOGRAPHIC SECTION

(G-13398)
NATIONAL PARACHUTE INDUSTRIES
Also Called: National Parachute Industry
78 White Rd Extensio (12463)
P.O. Box 245 (12463-0245)
PHONE.................................908 782-1646
Larry Krueger, *President*
Jeanette Krueger, *Admin Sec*
EMP: 20 **EST:** 1976
SQ FT: 6,000
SALES (est): 1.2MM **Privately Held**
SIC: 2399 Parachutes

(G-13399)
PRECISION TOOL AND MFG
314 Pennsylvania Ave (12463-2615)
P.O. Box 160 (12463-0160)
PHONE.................................518 678-3130
Fax: 518 678-3570
Alan Schneck, *President*
EMP: 27
SALES (est): 3.2MM **Privately Held**
SIC: 3599 Machine shop, jobbing & repair

Palisades
Rockland County

(G-13400)
ADVANCED DISTRIBUTION SYSTEM
275 Oak Tree Rd (10964-1003)
PHONE.................................845 848-2357
Jean Higgins, *Manager*
Ron Gittens, *Manager*
Chris Sheldon, *Manager*
Tomaj Vadasz, *Info Tech Dir*
▲ **EMP:** 80
SALES (est): 5.4MM **Privately Held**
SIC: 3084 Plastics pipe

(G-13401)
HISTORY PUBLISHING COMPANY LLC
173 Route 9w (10964-1616)
P.O. Box 700 (10964-0700)
PHONE.................................845 398-8161
Don Bracken, *Mng Member*
EMP: 6
SALES (est): 459.1K **Privately Held**
WEB: www.historypublishingco.com
SIC: 2741 Posters: publishing only, not printed on site

(G-13402)
SKAE POWER SOLUTIONS LLC (PA)
348 Route 9w (10964-1200)
P.O. Box 615 (10964-0615)
PHONE.................................845 365-9103
Jason Ketcham, *Electrical Engi*
Hitesh Gandhi, *Controller*
Russ Mykytyn, *Accounts Exec*
John McPartland, *Marketing Mgr*
Cathy Skae, *Manager*
EMP: 30
SQ FT: 6,000
SALES (est): 7.5MM **Privately Held**
WEB: www.skaepower.com
SIC: 3699 8711 Electrical equipment & supplies; consulting engineer

(G-13403)
TRI VALLEY IRON INC
700 Oak Tree Rd (10964-1533)
P.O. Box 234 (10964-0234)
PHONE.................................845 365-1013
Nancy Bucciarelli, *President*
James McCarthy, *Vice Pres*
EMP: 15
SALES: 1.5MM **Privately Held**
SIC: 3312 Bars, iron: made in steel mills

(G-13404)
VELL COMPANY INC
700 Oak Tree Rd (10964-1533)
P.O. Box 622 (10964-0622)
PHONE.................................845 365-1013
Larry Bucciarelli, *Principal*
EMP: 8

SALES (est): 1MM **Privately Held**
SIC: 3312 Bars & bar shapes, steel, hot-rolled

Palmyra
Wayne County

(G-13405)
FARADYNE MOTORS LLC
Also Called: Juan Motors
2077 Division St (14522-9211)
PHONE.................................315 331-5985
Chris Osgood, *Engineer*
Grace Dewey, *Accountant*
Juan Lugo, *Accountant*
Mellisa Kidd, *Mng Member*
Kathy Cox, *Manager*
▲ **EMP:** 14
SQ FT: 28,000
SALES (est): 4.6MM **Privately Held**
WEB: www.faradynemotors.com
SIC: 3621 Motors & generators

(G-13406)
FINZER HOLDING LLC
Also Called: Finzer Roller New York
2085 Division St (14522-9211)
PHONE.................................315 597-1147
David Finzer, *President*
Kevin Byer, *Plant Mgr*
Grace Devito, *Accountant*
Brian La Due, *Financial Exec*
EMP: 27
SALES (corp-wide): 13.2MM **Privately Held**
SIC: 3069 3061 Roll coverings, rubber; mechanical rubber goods
PA: Finzer Holding Llc
    129 Rawls Rd
    Des Plaines IL 60018
    847 390-6200

(G-13407)
GARLOCK SEALING TECH LLC
1666 Division St (14522-9350)
PHONE.................................315 597-4811
Paul Baldetti, *President*
Ray Davis, *Vice Pres*
James Erven, *Vice Pres*
Al Lariviere, *Vice Pres*
K B Schoenfelder, *Vice Pres*
EMP: 950
SALES (corp-wide): 1.2B **Publicly Held**
SIC: 3053 Gaskets, packing & sealing devices
HQ: Garlock Sealing Technologies Llc
    1666 Division St
    Palmyra NY 14522
    315 597-4811

(G-13408)
GENTNER PRECISION COMPONENTS
406 Stafford Rd (14522-9426)
PHONE.................................315 597-5734
Richard Genter, *President*
John E Gentner Jr, *Principal*
EMP: 5
SALES (est): 383K **Privately Held**
SIC: 3599 Machine & other job shop work

(G-13409)
JRLON INC
4344 Fox Rd (14522-9423)
P.O. Box 244 (14522-0244)
PHONE.................................315 597-4067
Fax: 315 597-9781
James F Redmond, *President*
Lindsey Redmond, *Corp Secy*
Brandon Redmond, *Marketing Mgr*
Chad Redmond, *Manager*
▲ **EMP:** 80 **EST:** 1981
SQ FT: 60,000
SALES (est): 19.5MM **Privately Held**
WEB: www.jrlon.com
SIC: 2821 3566 3479 3462 Molding compounds, plastics; gears, power transmission, except automotive; painting, coating & hot dipping; iron & steel forgings; paints & allied products

(G-13410)
LABCO OF PALMYRA INC
904 Canandaigua Rd (14522-9701)
P.O. Box 216 (14522-0216)
PHONE.................................315 597-5202
Fax: 315 597-2112
Gary Laberge, *President*
Lynette McTigue, *Vice Pres*
Sharyl Digiovanni, *Treasurer*
Marybeth Laberge, *Admin Sec*
EMP: 12 **EST:** 1956
SQ FT: 7,800
SALES (est): 1.7MM **Privately Held**
WEB: www.labco-ny.com
SIC: 3599 Machine shop, jobbing & repair

(G-13411)
MODERN COATING AND RESEARCH
400 E Main St (14522-1132)
PHONE.................................315 597-3517
Fax: 315 597-6045
James Deagman, *President*
Ed Meyer, *Director*
James Hollingsworth, *Shareholder*
Kevin Marvin, *Administration*
EMP: 11
SQ FT: 26,000
SALES (est): 700K **Privately Held**
WEB: www.moderncoatings.com
SIC: 3479 Coating of metals & formed products

(G-13412)
PARRY MACHINE CO INC
2081a Division St (14522-9211)
P.O. Box 421 (14522-0421)
PHONE.................................315 597-5014
Fax: 315 546-6499
Mike Coughlin, *President*
EMP: 7 **EST:** 2007
SALES (est): 582.1K **Privately Held**
SIC: 3599 Industrial machinery

(G-13413)
PAUL T FREUND CORPORATION (PA)
216 Park Dr (14522-1114)
P.O. Box 475 (14522-0475)
PHONE.................................315 597-4873
Fax: 315 597-4188
Dennis Baron, *President*
Paul T Freund Jr, *Corp Secy*
Thomas Farnham, *Vice Pres*
▲ **EMP:** 85
SQ FT: 126,000
SALES (est): 7.2MM **Privately Held**
WEB: www.freundcarton.com
SIC: 2652 Filing boxes, paperboard: made from purchased materials

Parish
Oswego County

(G-13414)
BIOSPHERIX LTD
Also Called: Biospherix Medical
25 Union St (13131)
PHONE.................................315 387-3414
Randy Yerden, *Ch of Bd*
George Down, *General Mgr*
Mark Simpson, *Human Res Dir*
Ray Gould, *Sales Mgr*
Kayla Nolan, *Sales Associate*
EMP: 50
SQ FT: 30,000
SALES (est): 10.6MM **Privately Held**
WEB: www.biospherix.com
SIC: 3821 Laboratory equipment: fume hoods, distillation racks, etc.

Patchogue
Suffolk County

(G-13415)
BAKERY INNOVATIVE TECH CORP
139 N Ocean Ave (11772-2018)
PHONE.................................631 758-3081
Fax: 631 758-3779

Robert White, *President*
Maryann Rose, *Manager*
EMP: 15
SQ FT: 8,000
SALES (est): 1.5MM **Privately Held**
WEB: www.bit-corp.com
SIC: 3625 Motor control accessories, including overload relays

(G-13416)
BAYSHORE ELECTRIC MOTORS
Also Called: Bayshore Motors
33 Suffolk Ave (11772-1651)
PHONE.................................631 475-1397
Paul Phillips, *Owner*
EMP: 5
SALES (est): 244.5K **Privately Held**
SIC: 7694 Electric motor repair

(G-13417)
CLASSIC LABELS INC
217 River Ave (11772-3312)
PHONE.................................631 467-2300
Fax: 718 358-3262
John Orta, *President*
EMP: 21 **EST:** 1978
SQ FT: 29,000
SALES (est): 2.4MM **Privately Held**
WEB: www.classiclabels.com
SIC: 2759 2891 2672 2671 Labels & seals; printing; adhesives & sealants; coated & laminated paper; packaging paper & plastics film, coated & laminated

(G-13418)
DEPOT LABEL COMPANY INC
Also Called: Colonial Label
217 River Ave (11772-3312)
PHONE.................................631 467-2952
Mike Juliano, *President*
Russell England, *Branch Mgr*
EMP: 8
SALES (est): 1.8MM **Privately Held**
SIC: 2679 5013 2671 2241 Tags & labels, paper; automotive supplies & parts; packaging paper & plastics film, coated & laminated; narrow fabric mills

(G-13419)
EQUICHECK LLC
20 Medford Ave Ste 7 (11772-1220)
PHONE.................................631 987-6356
Fax: 631 447-0084
Warren Rothstein, *Owner*
EMP: 5
SALES (est): 300K **Privately Held**
WEB: www.equicheck.com
SIC: 3851 Lens coating, ophthalmic

(G-13420)
GEM WEST INC
Also Called: Cya Action Funwell
433 E Main St Unit 1 (11772-3177)
PHONE.................................631 567-4228
Sylvia Stephanie, *President*
EMP: 6
SALES (est): 285.7K **Privately Held**
SIC: 2759 Commercial printing

(G-13421)
GROVER ALUMINUM PRODUCTS INC
Also Called: Grover Home Headquarters
577 Medford Ave (11772-1307)
PHONE.................................631 475-3500
Fax: 631 475-3569
Arthur R Spencer, *President*
Irving Fine, *Corp Secy*
Lorrine Heuthe, *Bookkeeper*
EMP: 20 **EST:** 1956
SQ FT: 20,000
SALES (est): 3.3MM **Privately Held**
WEB: www.groverhome.com
SIC: 3442 Louver windows, metal; metal doors

(G-13422)
HOPTRON BREWTIQUE
22 W Main St Ste 11 (11772-3007)
PHONE.................................631 438-0296
Amanda Danielsen, *Owner*
EMP: 8
SALES (est): 587.1K **Privately Held**
SIC: 2082 5182 Beer (alcoholic beverage); wine coolers, alcoholic

Patchogue - Suffolk County (G-13423)

(G-13423)
INNER-PAK CONTAINER INC
116 West Ave (11772-3525)
PHONE..........................631 289-9700
Fax: 631 289-9797
Judith M Nadler, *Ch of Bd*
EMP: 15
SALES (est): 2.9MM **Privately Held**
SIC: 2653 5113 Boxes, corrugated: made from purchased materials; corrugated & solid fiber boxes

(G-13424)
JABO AGRICULTURAL INC
9 Northwood Ln (11772-2228)
PHONE..........................631 475-1800
Robert Muchnick, *CEO*
Jacob Gurewich, *President*
EMP: 5
SQ FT: 1,000
SALES (est): 430K **Privately Held**
SIC: 2452 Farm & agricultural buildings, prefabricated wood

(G-13425)
JOHN LOR PUBLISHING LTD
Also Called: Islip Bulletin
20 Medford Ave Ste 1 (11772-1220)
P.O. Box 780 (11772-0780)
PHONE..........................631 475-1000
Fax: 631 589-2460
John Tuthill III, *President*
Lorerir Mary Lou Cohalon, *Vice Pres*
EMP: 20 EST: 1950
SALES (est): 930.7K **Privately Held**
WEB: www.islipbulletin.net
SIC: 2711 Newspapers: publishing only, not printed on site

(G-13426)
KEVIN FREEMAN
Also Called: Rf Inter Science Co
414 S Service Rd Ste 119 (11772-2254)
PHONE..........................631 447-5321
Kevin Freeman, *President*
EMP: 5
SALES (est): 398.6K **Privately Held**
SIC: 3827 Optical instruments & apparatus

(G-13427)
L-3 COMMUNICATIONS CORPORATION
L3 Communications Narda - Atm
49 Rider Ave (11772-3915)
PHONE..........................631 289-0363
EMP: 50
SALES (corp-wide): 10.4B **Publicly Held**
SIC: 3679 Microwave components
HQ: L-3 Communications Corporation
600 3rd Ave
New York NY 10016
212 697-1111

(G-13428)
NEW LIVING INC
99 Waverly Ave Apt 6d (11772-1922)
PHONE..........................631 751-8819
Christine Harvey, *Principal*
EMP: 6
SALES (est): 289.8K **Privately Held**
SIC: 2711 Newspapers, publishing & printing

(G-13429)
PARIS ART LABEL CO INC
217 River Ave (11772-3312)
PHONE..........................631 467-2300
Fax: 631 467-1729
Ronald P Tarantino, *Ch of Bd*
John Raguso, *Sales Mgr*
EMP: 100 EST: 1925
SQ FT: 20,000
SALES (est): 28.6MM **Privately Held**
WEB: www.parisartlabel.com
SIC: 2672 Labels (unprinted), gummed: made from purchased materials

(G-13430)
PATCHOGUE ADVANCE INC
Also Called: Long Island Advance
20 Medford Ave Ste 1 (11772-1220)
PHONE..........................631 475-1000
Fax: 631 475-1565
John T Tuthill III, *President*
Mark Nolan, *Chief*
Lorelei T Tuthill, *Admin Sec*
EMP: 35 EST: 1821
SQ FT: 7,000
SALES (est): 2MM **Privately Held**
WEB: www.longislandadvance.net
SIC: 2711 Newspapers: publishing only, not printed on site

(G-13431)
PATCHOGUE ELECTRIC MOTORS INC
71 Sycamore St (11772-2886)
P.O. Box 537 (11772-0537)
PHONE..........................631 475-0117
Paul Tabone, *President*
Mary Tabone, *Corp Secy*
EMP: 6
SQ FT: 8,000
SALES (est): 801.4K **Privately Held**
WEB: www.patchelect.com
SIC: 7694 5063 Electric motor repair; motors, electric

(G-13432)
PEPSI BOTTLING VENTURES LLC
Also Called: Pepsi-Cola
4141 Parklane Ave Ste 600 (11772)
PHONE..........................631 772-6144
Theresa Dunton, *Manager*
Wes Krupp, *Administration*
EMP: 53
SALES (corp-wide): 64.4MM **Privately Held**
SIC: 2086 Bottled & canned soft drinks
HQ: Pepsi Bottling Ventures Llc
4141 Parklake Ave Ste 600
Raleigh NC 27612
919 865-2300

(G-13433)
PRINCETON LABEL & PACKAGING
217 River Ave (11772-3312)
PHONE..........................609 490-0800
Fax: 609 490-0272
Donald J Guli, *President*
John Muccino, *Sales Staff*
EMP: 35
SQ FT: 7,800
SALES (est): 6.3MM **Privately Held**
WEB: www.princetonlabel.com
SIC: 2672 7389 Coated & laminated paper; packaging & labeling services

(G-13434)
RELIABLE WELDING & FABRICATION
214 W Main St (11772-3004)
PHONE..........................631 758-2637
EMP: 7
SALES (est): 490K **Privately Held**
SIC: 7692 5051 5021 1799 Welding Repair Metals Service Center Whol Furniture Special Trade Contractor

(G-13435)
SUFFOLK MCHY & PWR TL CORP (PA)
Also Called: Gschwind Group
12 Waverly Ave (11772-1902)
PHONE..........................631 289-7153
Fax: 631 289-7156
Arthur F Gschwind Sr, *President*
Debbie Freyre, *General Mgr*
Tom Davies, *Director*
▼ EMP: 3
SQ FT: 4,000
SALES (est): 1.2MM **Privately Held**
WEB: www.timberwolf1.com
SIC: 3425 Saw blades & handsaws

(G-13436)
T & SMOOTHIE INC
499 N Service Rd Ste 83 (11772-2290)
PHONE..........................631 804-6653
Tiffany Wirth, *Principal*
EMP: 5
SALES (est): 287.8K **Privately Held**
SIC: 2037 Frozen fruits & vegetables

Patterson
Putnam County

(G-13437)
DICAMILLO MARBLE AND GRANITE
20 Jon Barrett Rd (12563-2164)
PHONE..........................845 878-0078
Fax: 845 878-2250
EMP: 20 EST: 1991
SALES (est): 1.6MM **Privately Held**
SIC: 3281 Mfg Cut Stone/Products

(G-13438)
EAST HUDSON WATERSHED CORP
2 Route 164 (12563-2813)
PHONE..........................845 319-6349
Peter Parsons, *President*
Kevin Fitzpatrick, *Project Mgr*
EMP: 5
SQ FT: 1,000
SALES (est): 3.1MM **Privately Held**
SIC: 3822 Auto controls regulating residntl & coml environmt & applncs

(G-13439)
EURO FUEL CO
2499 Route 22 (12563-6207)
PHONE..........................914 424-5052
Vebi Mushkolaj, *Principal*
EMP: 5 EST: 2012
SALES (est): 616.8K **Privately Held**
SIC: 2869 Fuels

(G-13440)
GOLDEN GROUP INTERNATIONAL LTD
305 Quaker Rd (12563-2191)
P.O. Box 407, Brewster (10509-0407)
PHONE..........................845 440-1025
Jacqueline Transue, *President*
Kevin Hanna, *Info Tech Mgr*
EMP: 6
SALES (est): 530K **Privately Held**
SIC: 2673 5113 3444 5199 Trash bags (plastic film): made from purchased materials; food storage & trash bags (plastic); bags, paper & disposable plastic; bins, prefabricated sheet metal; art goods & supplies

(G-13441)
JRS PHARMA LP (DH)
2981 Route 22 Ste 1 (12563-2359)
PHONE..........................845 878-8300
Josef Rettenmaier, *Partner*
J Rettenmaier America, *Partner*
Josef Otto Rettenmaier, *Partner*
J Rettenmaier Holding USA, *Partner*
Jennifer Good, *Vice Pres*
▲ EMP: 48
SQ FT: 46,000
SALES (est): 17.6MM **Privately Held**
SIC: 2834 Pharmaceutical preparations
HQ: Jrs Pharma Gmbh & Co. Kg
Holzmuhle 1
Rosenberg 73494
796 715-2312

(G-13442)
LANE PARK GRAPHICS INC
93 Mcmanus Rd S (12563-2900)
PHONE..........................914 273-5898
Susan Scholer, *President*
Rich Harmon, *Manager*
Kris Smith, *Manager*
EMP: 7
SQ FT: 1,000
SALES (est): 866.5K **Privately Held**
SIC: 2754 7336 Commercial printing, gravure; commercial art & graphic design

(G-13443)
REELEX PACKAGING SOLUTIONS INC
39 Jon Barrett Rd (12563-2165)
PHONE..........................845 878-7878
Thomas R Copp, *President*
Frank Kotzur, *Vice Pres*
Ronald Zajac, *Vice Pres*
Gregory Kotzur, *Engineer*
Mike Muller, *Electrical Engi*
▲ EMP: 40
SQ FT: 50,000
SALES (est): 9.2MM
SALES (corp-wide): 5MM **Privately Held**
SIC: 3549 6794 Metalworking machinery; patent buying, licensing, leasing
PA: Da Capo Al Fine Ltd
81 Stone Crop Ln
Cold Spring NY 10516
845 265-2011

(G-13444)
SPANISH ARTISAN WINE GROUP LLC
Also Called: Spanish Artisan Wine Group Ltd
370 Cushman Rd (12563-2638)
PHONE..........................914 414-6982
Gerry Dawes, *Principal*
Gerald Dawes, *Mng Member*
EMP: 5
SALES (est): 1MM **Privately Held**
SIC: 2084 5182 7389 Wines; neutral spirits; brokers, business: buying & selling business enterprises

(G-13445)
TAUMEL METALFORMING CORP
Also Called: Taumel Assembly Systems
25 Jon Barrett Rd (12563-2165)
PHONE..........................845 878-3100
Ernest Bodmer, *President*
Tony A Huber, *Vice Pres*
Werner Stutz, *Vice Pres*
Peter Bodmer, *Treasurer*
Phil Huber, *Manager*
EMP: 8
SQ FT: 10,000
SALES (est): 520K **Privately Held**
WEB: www.taumel.com
SIC: 3542 Machine tools, metal forming type

(G-13446)
WERLATONE INC
17 Jon Barrett Rd (12563-2165)
P.O. Box 47, Brewster (10509-0047)
PHONE..........................845 278-2220
Fax: 845 279-7404
Glen C Werlau, *Ch of Bd*
Diane Wolpert, *General Mgr*
Austin Kile, *Corp Secy*
Eric Kowalik, *Opers Staff*
Patrick Youlio, *QC Mgr*
EMP: 38 EST: 1965
SQ FT: 7,000
SALES (est): 7.6MM **Privately Held**
WEB: www.werlatone.com
SIC: 3679 Electronic circuits

Pattersonville
Schenectady County

(G-13447)
DJ PIRRONE INDUSTRIES INC
8865 Mariaville Rd (12137-3007)
PHONE..........................518 864-5496
David Pirrone, *Principal*
EMP: 5
SALES (est): 234.2K **Privately Held**
SIC: 3999 Manufacturing industries

Paul Smiths
Franklin County

(G-13448)
MOUNTAIN GIFT AND POWDER CO
1353 Blue Mountain Rd (12970-2417)
PHONE..........................518 327-3516
Gay Relyea, *President*
EMP: 5
SALES: 150K **Privately Held**
WEB: www.mountaingift.com
SIC: 2844 Powder: baby, face, talcum or toilet

Pavilion
Genesee County

(G-13449)
HANSON AGGREGATES NEW YORK LLC
6895 Ellicott Street Rd (14525-9614)
PHONE..................585 638-5841
Daniel M Meehan, *Principal*
Scott Wheaton, *Plant Mgr*
Craig Green, *Opers Staff*
Dennis Dolan, *Controller*
Doug Fuess, *Sales Dir*
EMP: 15
SALES (corp-wide): 14.4B **Privately Held**
SIC: 3273 Ready-mixed concrete
HQ: Hanson Aggregates New York Llc
8505 Freport Pkwy Ste 500
Irving TX 75063

Pawling
Dutchess County

(G-13450)
JOE PIETRYKA INCORPORATED (PA)
85 Charles Colman Blvd (12564-1160)
PHONE..................845 855-1201
Joseph W Pietryka, *Ch of Bd*
John Drake, *Sales Staff*
EMP: 53
SQ FT: 65,000
SALES (est): 12.4MM **Privately Held**
WEB: www.dwconcepts.net
SIC: 3089 Injection molded finished plastic products

(G-13451)
PAWLING CORPORATION (PA)
Also Called: Pawling Engineered Products
157 Charles Colman Blvd (12564-1188)
PHONE..................845 855-1000
Fax: 845 855-1937
Craig Busby, *President*
Roger W Smith, *Chairman*
Gregory S Holen, *Vice Pres*
John C Rickert, *Vice Pres*
Jason W Smith, *Vice Pres*
EMP: 180
SQ FT: 250,000
SALES (est): 42MM **Privately Held**
WEB: www.pawling.com
SIC: 3061 3069 3089 2821 Mechanical rubber goods; custom compounding of rubber materials; rubber floor coverings, mats & wallcoverings; mats or matting, rubber; molding primary plastic; extruded finished plastic products; silicone resins

(G-13452)
PAWLING ENGINEERED PDTS INC
157 Charles Colman Blvd (12564-1121)
PHONE..................845 855-1000
Craig Busby, *President*
John Rickert, *Vice Pres*
EMP: 120
SQ FT: 250,000
SALES (est): 13.7MM **Privately Held**
SIC: 3061 3089 Mechanical rubber goods; extruded finished plastic products

(G-13453)
WIRED UP ELECTRIC INC
90 Harmony Rd (12564-3101)
PHONE..................845 878-3122
Michael C Murphy, *President*
EMP: 7
SALES (est): 1MM **Privately Held**
SIC: 3699 Electrical equipment & supplies

Pearl River
Rockland County

(G-13454)
21ST CENTURY FOX AMERICA INC
Also Called: Corporate News
1 Blue Hill Plz Ste 1525 (10965-3129)
PHONE..................845 735-1116
EMP: 8
SALES (corp-wide): 27.3B **Publicly Held**
SIC: 2711 Newspapers: publishing only, not printed on site
HQ: 21st Century Fox America, Inc.
1211 Ave Of The Americas
New York NY 10036
212 852-7000

(G-13455)
C B MANAGEMENT SERVICES INC
Also Called: Beitals Aquarium Sales & Svc
73 S Pearl St (10965-2235)
PHONE..................845 735-2300
Craig Beital, *President*
Creig Beital, *President*
EMP: 13
SQ FT: 5,000
SALES (est): 970K **Privately Held**
WEB: www.cbmanagementservices.com
SIC: 3231 5999 7389 Aquariums & reflectors, glass; aquarium supplies; aquarium design & maintenance

(G-13456)
FIVE STAR MILLWORK LLC
6 E Dexter Plz (10965-2360)
PHONE..................845 920-0247
Marco Santos,
Dario Fonseca,
Tiago Fonseca,
EMP: 12
SQ FT: 15,000
SALES (est): 4MM **Privately Held**
SIC: 2431 Millwork

(G-13457)
FUJITSU NTWRK CMMNICATIONS INC
2 Blue Hill Plz Ste 1609 (10965-3115)
PHONE..................845 731-2000
Henry Chang, *Engineer*
Bob Demarco, *Manager*
EMP: 18
SALES (corp-wide): 39.9B **Privately Held**
WEB: www.fnc.fujitsu.com
SIC: 3661 8731 3663 Fiber optics communications equipment; commercial physical research; radio & TV communications equipment
HQ: Fujitsu Network Communications, Inc.
2801 Telecom Pkwy
Richardson TX 75082
972 479-6000

(G-13458)
HEARTLAND COMMERCE INC
Also Called: Pcamerica
1 Blue Hill Plz Ste 16 (10965-3100)
PHONE..................845 920-0800
Steve Messemer, *Sales Mgr*
Steve Rimpici, *Sales Mgr*
Tony Scarpa, *Sales Mgr*
Ted Raymundo, *Technology*
Ronny Polo, *Software Engr*
EMP: 21
SALES (corp-wide): 2.9B **Publicly Held**
SIC: 7372 Business oriented computer software
HQ: Heartland Commerce, Inc.
90 Nassau St Fl 2
Princeton NJ 08542
609 683-3831

(G-13459)
HUDSON TECHNOLOGIES COMPANY (PA)
1 Blue Hill Plz Ste 1541 (10965-3110)
P.O. Box 1541 (10965)
PHONE..................845 735-6000
Kevin Zugibe, *Ch of Bd*
Briann Coleman, *President*
Stephen Mandracchia, *Vice Pres*
Marylyn Hu, *Accountant*
EMP: 38
SQ FT: 4,500
SALES: 48.6MM **Privately Held**
SIC: 2869 Fluorinated hydrocarbon gases

(G-13460)
HUNTER DOUGLAS INC (DH)
1 Blue Hill Plz Ste 1569 (10965-6101)
PHONE..................845 664-7000
Ralph Sonnenberg, *Ch of Bd*
Marvin B Hopkins, *President*
David H Sonnenberg, *President*
Marko H Sonnenberg, *President*
Bryan Clabeaux, *General Mgr*
◆ **EMP:** 100
SQ FT: 32,000
SALES (est): 1.9B **Privately Held**
WEB: www.hunterdouglas.com
SIC: 2591 3444 5084 Window blinds; window shades; venetian blinds; sheet metalwork; industrial machinery & equipment
HQ: Hunter Douglas N.V.
Piekstraat 2
Rotterdam 3071
104 869-911

(G-13461)
KRAFT HAT MANUFACTURERS INC
7 Veterans Pkwy (10965-1328)
PHONE..................845 735-6200
Israel Rosenzweig, *President*
Steven Rosenzweig, *Corp Secy*
Lawrence Rosenzweig, *Vice Pres*
Stacey Fromowitz, *Systems Mgr*
▲ **EMP:** 100
SQ FT: 34,000
SALES (est): 9.3MM **Privately Held**
WEB: www.krafthat.com
SIC: 2353 Hats, caps & millinery; millinery

(G-13462)
LEVOLOR WINDOW FURNISHINGS INC (DH)
1 Blue Hill Plz (10965-3104)
PHONE..................845 664-7000
Marvin B Hopkins, *President*
Mark Carroll, *Vice Pres*
Jim Morando, *Vice Pres*
Craig York, *Vice Pres*
Jerome Danson, *Finance Mgr*
▲ **EMP:** 300
SALES (est): 47.8MM **Privately Held**
SIC: 2591 Window blinds; blinds vertical
HQ: Hunter Douglas Inc.
1 Blue Hill Plz Ste 1569
Pearl River NY 10965
845 664-7000

(G-13463)
PIEZO ELECTRONICS RESEARCH
Also Called: Peri
30 Walter St (10965-1722)
PHONE..................845 735-9349
David Marsh, *President*
EMP: 12 **EST:** 1946
SQ FT: 3,000
SALES: 1MM **Privately Held**
SIC: 3674 7389 Solid state electronic devices; packaging & labeling services

(G-13464)
POLY SOFTWARE INTERNATIONAL
7 Kerry Ct (10965-3034)
P.O. Box 60 (10965-0060)
PHONE..................845 735-9301
Xiaowu Wang, *CEO*
Linda Hu, *Office Mgr*
EMP: 6
SALES (est): 448.8K **Privately Held**
WEB: www.polysoftware.com
SIC: 7372 Prepackaged software

(G-13465)
QUALITY GRAPHICS TRI STATE
171 Center St (10965-1630)
PHONE..................845 735-2523
Fax: 845 735-0182
Phyllis Schweizer, *President*
Bruce Schweizer, *Vice Pres*
EMP: 5
SALES (est): 779.2K **Privately Held**
SIC: 2752 Commercial printing, lithographic

(G-13466)
SKIN PRINTS INC
63 Walter St (10965-1723)
PHONE..................845 920-8756
Diane Kaufman, *President*
EMP: 3
SQ FT: 10,000
SALES (est): 1.2MM **Privately Held**
SIC: 2269 Finishing plants

(G-13467)
STRATEGIC MKTG PROMOTIONS INC (PA)
Also Called: S M P
10 N Main St (10965-2317)
PHONE..................845 623-7777
Jennifer Pagels-Caglione, *Ch of Bd*
Robert Russo, *President*
Greg Caglione, *Vice Pres*
Jennifer Caglione, *Director*
▼ **EMP:** 15
SQ FT: 3,000
SALES (est): 1.8MM **Privately Held**
SIC: 3999 Advertising display products

(G-13468)
UTILITY ENGINEERING CO
40 Walter St (10965-1795)
PHONE..................845 735-8900
Fax: 845 735-0363
George Huston, *President*
Mike Taylor, *Engineer*
EMP: 10 **EST:** 1952
SQ FT: 7,400
SALES (est): 620K **Privately Held**
WEB: www.utilitydisplays.com
SIC: 3496 Miscellaneous fabricated wire products

(G-13469)
WYETH HOLDINGS LLC
Also Called: Wyeth Pharmaceutical
401 N Middletown Rd (10965-1298)
PHONE..................845 602-5000
Fax: 845 602-5599
David Zisa, *Principal*
Andy Schaschl, *Engineer*
James S Morrissey, *Project Leader*
Clive Pepper, *IT/INT Sup*
Debbie Bertero, *Director*
EMP: 100
SALES (corp-wide): 48.8B **Publicly Held**
SIC: 2834 2836 3842 3841 Pharmaceutical preparations; biological products, except diagnostic; surgical appliances & supplies; surgical & medical instruments; ophthalmic goods; chemical preparations
HQ: Wyeth Holdings Llc
5 Giralda Farms
Madison NJ 07940
973 660-5000

Peconic
Suffolk County

(G-13470)
DORSET FARMS INC
Also Called: Lenz
38355 Main Rd (11958-1515)
P.O. Box 28 (11958-0028)
PHONE..................631 734-6010
Fax: 631 734-6069
Peter Carroll, *President*
Deborah Carroll, *Vice Pres*
▲ **EMP:** 10
SALES (est): 1MM **Privately Held**
SIC: 2084 Wines

(G-13471)
J PETROCELLI WINE CELLARS LLC
Also Called: Raphael
39390 Route 25 (11958-1501)
P.O. Box 17 (11958-0017)
PHONE..................631 765-1100
Joseph Vergari, *General Mgr*
Chip Cheek, *Sales Mgr*
Jennifer Elten, *Marketing Staff*
Jack Petrocelli, *Mng Member*

Diane Ferruzzi, *Manager*
▲ **EMP:** 25
SALES: 450K **Privately Held**
SIC: 2084 5921 Wines; wine

(G-13472)
PINDAR VINEYARDS LLC
37645 Route 25 (11958-1514)
P.O. Box 332 (11958-0332)
PHONE..................................631 734-6200
Fax: 631 734-6205
Kathy Krejci, *Business Mgr*
Steve Ciuffo, *Sales Mgr*
Elizabeth Rolison, *Marketing Staff*
Herdotes Damianos, *Mng Member*
Jason Damianos, *Director*
EMP: 20
SQ FT: 5,000
SALES (est): 2.4MM **Privately Held**
WEB: www.pindar.net
SIC: 2084 Wines

Peekskill
Westchester County

(G-13473)
BASF CORPORATION
1057 Lower South St (10566-5302)
PHONE..................................914 737-2554
Michael Kimble, *Engineer*
Bart Reith, *Project Engr*
Daniel S Gulley, *Branch Mgr*
Rick King, *Info Tech Mgr*
Patrick Therrien, *Systs Prg Mgr*
EMP: 344
SALES (corp-wide): 75.6B **Privately Held**
WEB: www.basf.com
SIC: 2816 Inorganic pigments
HQ: Basf Corporation
  100 Park Ave
  Florham Park NJ 07932
  973 245-6000

(G-13474)
BASF CORPORATION
1057 Lower South St (10566-5302)
PHONE..................................914 788-1627
EMP: 368
SALES (corp-wide): 75.6B **Privately Held**
WEB: www.basf.com
SIC: 2819 Industrial inorganic chemicals
HQ: Basf Corporation
  100 Park Ave
  Florham Park NJ 07932
  973 245-6000

(G-13475)
CANDLES BY FOSTER
810 South St (10566-3431)
P.O. Box 89 (10566-0089)
PHONE..................................914 739-9226
Donald Foster, *Owner*
EMP: 6
SQ FT: 6,500
SALES (est): 260K **Privately Held**
SIC: 3999 5999 Candles; candle shops

(G-13476)
ECONOMY ENERGY LLC
500 Highland Ave (10566-2320)
PHONE..................................845 222-3384
Henry E Seger,
Patricia V McGrath,
EMP: 5
SALES (est): 652.4K **Privately Held**
SIC: 2869 Fuels

(G-13477)
ELEVATOR ACCESSORIES MFG
Also Called: Paxton Metal Craft Division
1035 Howard St 37 (10566-2819)
P.O. Box 430 (10566-0430)
PHONE..................................914 739-7004
Fax: 914 736-3366
Alan Messing, *President*
John Johnson, *Vice Pres*
Vicki Messing, *Admin Sec*
EMP: 12
SALES (est): 2.4MM **Privately Held**
SIC: 3534 3441 3446 3444 Elevators & equipment; fabricated structural metal; architectural metalwork; sheet metalwork

(G-13478)
GIULIANTE MACHINE TOOL INC
12 John Walsh Blvd (10566-5323)
PHONE..................................914 835-0008
Martha Giuliante, *President*
Armando Giuliante, *Vice Pres*
Marcelo Giuliante, *Vice Pres*
EMP: 25
SQ FT: 27,000
SALES: 4.5MM **Privately Held**
WEB: www.gmtgear.com
SIC: 3599 Machine shop, jobbing & repair

(G-13479)
HUDSON MIRROR LLC
Also Called: Mirrorlite Superscript
710 Washington St (10566-5418)
PHONE..................................914 930-8906
Dwayne Reith, *Vice Pres*
Gary Reith,
EMP: 25
SQ FT: 2,000
SALES (est): 4MM **Privately Held**
SIC: 3827 Mirrors, optical

(G-13480)
RESCUESTUFF INC
962 Washington St (10566-5816)
PHONE..................................718 318-7570
Greg Grimaldi, *President*
Seth Porter, *CFO*
EMP: 5
SQ FT: 2,000
SALES: 250K **Privately Held**
WEB: www.rescuestuff.net
SIC: 2395 2262 Embroidery products, except schiffli machine; screen printing: manmade fiber & silk broadwoven fabrics

(G-13481)
RMS PACKAGING INC
Also Called: Aurora Sef
1050 Lower South St (10566-5313)
PHONE..................................914 205-2070
Sheldon Rosenberg, *President*
Ernest Peiffer, *VP Opers*
Stacy Christensen, *Manager*
▲ **EMP:** 16
SALES (est): 5.2MM **Privately Held**
SIC: 2671 Plastic film, coated or laminated for packaging

(G-13482)
SD CHRISTIE ASSOCIATES INC
424 Central Ave Ste 5 (10566-2056)
P.O. Box 5158, Cary NC (27512-5158)
PHONE..................................914 734-1800
Thomas Christie, *President*
EMP: 5
SALES (est): 548.7K **Privately Held**
SIC: 3069 5085 Molded rubber products; mattress protectors, rubber; fasteners, industrial: nuts, bolts, screws, etc.; rubber goods, mechanical

(G-13483)
VIVID RGB LIGHTING LLC
824 Main St Ste 1 (10566-2052)
PHONE..................................718 635-0817
Brian Fassett, *Managing Dir*
EMP: 7
SQ FT: 3,000
SALES (est): 721.8K **Privately Held**
SIC: 3648 Lighting equipment

(G-13484)
W DESIGNE INC
Also Called: Wood Design
5 John Walsh Blvd (10566-5307)
PHONE..................................914 736-1058
Fax: 914 736-7376
Alex Bernabo, *President*
Gladys Pagan, *Manager*
▲ **EMP:** 20
SQ FT: 25,000
SALES (est): 3.1MM **Privately Held**
SIC: 2434 2517 Wood kitchen cabinets; wood television & radio cabinets

(G-13485)
WALTER G LEGGE COMPANY INC
Also Called: Legge System
444 Central Ave (10566-2003)
PHONE..................................914 737-5040
Fax: 800 332-2636
Elizabeth Bauer, *President*
Jane Fejes, *General Mgr*
▲ **EMP:** 9 **EST:** 1936
SQ FT: 10,000
SALES (est): 1.6MM **Privately Held**
WEB: www.leggesystems.com
SIC: 2842 3272 3679 Sanitation preparations, disinfectants & deodorants; tile, precast terrazzo or concrete; power supplies, all types: static

(G-13486)
WESTCHESTER TECHNOLOGIES INC
8 John Walsh Blvd Ste 311 (10566-5347)
PHONE..................................914 736-1034
Fax: 914 736-1217
Roger Prahl, *CEO*
Carol Townley, *Office Mgr*
Thomas Ross, *Manager*
EMP: 23
SQ FT: 4,000
SALES: 4.1MM **Privately Held**
WEB: www.microoptics.com
SIC: 3827 Optical instruments & apparatus

(G-13487)
WESTYPO PRINTERS INC
540 Harrison Ave (10566-2318)
PHONE..................................914 737-7394
Fax: 914 739-7717
Mike Mc Guggart, *President*
Teri Mc Guggart, *Treasurer*
EMP: 6 **EST:** 1964
SQ FT: 8,000
SALES: 470K **Privately Held**
SIC: 2752 2759 Commercial printing, offset; commercial printing

Pelham
Westchester County

(G-13488)
ARCHIE COMIC PUBLICATIONS INC
Also Called: Archie Comics Publishers
629 Fifth Ave (10803-1251)
PHONE..................................914 381-5155
Fax: 914 381-2335
Michael Silberkleit, *Chairman*
Victor Gorelick, *Vice Pres*
Ed Spallone, *Controller*
Harold Buchholz, *Exec Dir*
Rik Offenberger, *Relations*
EMP: 75 **EST:** 1939
SQ FT: 10,000
SALES: 13.5MM **Privately Held**
WEB: www.archiecomics.com
SIC: 2721 Comic books: publishing only, not printed on site

(G-13489)
BANK-MILLER CO INC
333 Fifth Ave (10803-1203)
PHONE..................................914 227-9357
Steven Bank, *President*
Anna Paljuski, *Manager*
▲ **EMP:** 20
SQ FT: 5,500
SALES (est): 2.7MM **Privately Held**
WEB: www.bankmiller.com
SIC: 2259 2339 5131 Convertors, knit goods; women's & misses' outerwear; textile converters

(G-13490)
EASTCO MANUFACTURING CORP
Also Called: K & S & East
323 Fifth Ave (10803-1203)
PHONE..................................914 738-5667
Fax: 914 738-1859
Jack Koff, *President*
Philip Schwartzman, *Vice Pres*
Adam Sanchez, *Engineer*
Stanley Rothman, *Sales Mgr*
EMP: 12
SQ FT: 5,000
SALES (est): 1.8MM **Privately Held**
SIC: 3699 Electrical equipment & supplies

(G-13491)
ENVENT SYSTEMS INC
62 Harmon Ave (10803-1708)
PHONE..................................646 294-6980
Michael Curtin, *President*
EMP: 6
SALES: 2MM **Privately Held**
SIC: 3571 7389 Electronic computers;

(G-13492)
IMPERIA MASONRY SUPPLY CORP (PA)
57 Canal Rd (10803-2706)
PHONE..................................914 738-0900
Fax: 914 738-0243
Joseph Imperia, *President*
Janice Piszczatowski, *CFO*
Lisa Carabello, *Admin Sec*
▲ **EMP:** 30 **EST:** 1927
SQ FT: 8,400
SALES (est): 2.6MM **Privately Held**
WEB: www.imperiabros.com
SIC: 3271 5031 5032 5211 Concrete block & brick; lumber, plywood & millwork; brick, stone & related material; brick, except refractory; stone, crushed or broken; lumber & other building materials; lumber products; brick; masonry materials & supplies

(G-13493)
MANACRAFT PRECISION INC
945 Spring Rd (10803-2714)
PHONE..................................914 654-0967
Fax: 914 654-9006
Richard Osterer, *President*
EMP: 10 **EST:** 1946
SQ FT: 3,000
SALES (est): 1.1MM **Privately Held**
SIC: 3451 Screw machine products

(G-13494)
SHORELINE PUBLISHING INC
629 Fifth Ave Ste B01 (10803-3708)
PHONE..................................914 738-7869
Fax: 914 738-7876
Edward Shapiro, *President*
EMP: 7
SQ FT: 1,000
SALES (est): 911K **Privately Held**
WEB: www.shorelinepub.com
SIC: 2721 2752 Periodicals; commercial printing, offset

(G-13495)
STANDARDWARE INC
424 Pelham Manor Rd (10803-2524)
PHONE..................................914 738-6382
David Evans, *President*
EMP: 8
SALES: 1.7MM **Privately Held**
WEB: www.standardware.com
SIC: 7372 7371 Educational computer software; custom computer programming services

(G-13496)
TALYARPS CORPORATION (PA)
143 Sparks Ave (10803-1810)
PHONE..................................914 699-3030
Michael E Borner, *CEO*
Raymond Chlodney, *President*
James E Borner, *Chairman*
William J Borner, *Vice Pres*
Al Sarnotsky, *Vice Pres*
◆ **EMP:** 85
SQ FT: 9,000
SALES (est): 33.6MM **Privately Held**
WEB: www.spraylat.com
SIC: 2851 Paints & paint additives

Penfield
Monroe County

(G-13497)
ALUMI-TECH LLC
1640 Harris Rd (14526-1816)
PHONE..................................585 663-7010
Elizabeth Pantalo, *Manager*
James Putnam,
EMP: 8
SQ FT: 2,500

GEOGRAPHIC SECTION

Penn Yan - Yates County (G-13523)

SALES (est): 77.8K **Privately Held**
WEB: www.saddlestackers.com
SIC: 3354 Aluminum extruded products

(G-13498)
DOLOMITE PRODUCTS COMPANY INC
746 Whalen Rd (14526-1022)
PHONE............................585 586-2568
Fax: 585 389-1577
Don Hosensele, *Manager*
EMP: 20
SQ FT: 2,280
SALES (corp-wide): 25.3B **Privately Held**
WEB: www.dolomitegroup.com
SIC: 2951 1429 Paving mixtures; trap rock, crushed & broken-quarrying
HQ: Dolomite Products Company Inc.
  1150 Penfield Rd
  Rochester NY 14625
  315 524-1998

(G-13499)
IRPENSCOM
4 Katsura Ct (14526-2612)
PHONE............................585 507-7997
Sabatino Agnitti Jr, *Owner*
EMP: 5
SALES (est): 381.3K **Privately Held**
SIC: 3571 Electronic computers

(G-13500)
JORDAN PRODUCTS INC
Also Called: Dell Tool
430 Whitney Rd (14526-2326)
PHONE............................585 385-7777
Janis E Jordan, *President*
William E Jordan, *Vice Pres*
Paul Jordan, *VP Opers*
EMP: 20
SQ FT: 20,000
SALES (est): 1.6MM **Privately Held**
WEB: www.delltool.com
SIC: 3451 Screw machine products

(G-13501)
NIFTY BAR GRINDING & CUTTING
450 Whitney Rd (14526-2326)
PHONE............................585 381-0450
Fax: 585 381-4712
John Raimondi, *President*
EMP: 23 EST: 1967
SQ FT: 24,000
SALES (est): 5.4MM **Privately Held**
WEB: www.niftybar.com
SIC: 3541 Machine tools, metal cutting type

(G-13502)
RANGE REPAIR WAREHOUSE
421 Penbrooke Dr Ste 2 (14526-2045)
PHONE............................585 235-0980
Paul V Ciminelli, *Owner*
EMP: 5
SALES (est): 274.5K **Privately Held**
SIC: 3499 Fabricated metal products

(G-13503)
ROBINSON TOOLS LLC
Also Called: Garco
477 Whitney Rd (14526-2328)
PHONE............................585 586-5432
James D Keppel, *President*
Judy Jahn, *Plant Mgr*
EMP: 7 EST: 1836
SQ FT: 5,000
SALES (est): 650K **Privately Held**
WEB: www.robinsontools.com
SIC: 3423 Hand & edge tools

(G-13504)
SCHNEIDER ELECTRIC USA INC
441 Penbrooke Dr Ste 9 (14526-2046)
PHONE............................585 377-1313
Brian Hoffman, *Manager*
EMP: 11
SALES (corp-wide): 224.4K **Privately Held**
WEB: www.squared.com
SIC: 3612 Transformers, except electric
HQ: Schneider Electric Usa, Inc.
  800 Federal St
  Andover MA 01810
  978 975-9600

(G-13505)
VIEWSPORT INC
11 Feathery Cir (14526-2816)
PHONE............................585 738-6803
Benjamin Wood, *CEO*
EMP: 5
SALES (est): 573.2K **Privately Held**
SIC: 2329 3552 Men's & boys' sportswear & athletic clothing; silk screens for textile industry

Penn Yan
Yates County

(G-13506)
BIRKETT MILLS (PA)
163 Main St Ste 2 (14527-1284)
PHONE............................315 536-3311
Fax: 315 536-6740
Wayne W Wagner, *President*
Jeffrey S Gifford, *Exec VP*
Andrew Schuck, *Plant Mgr*
Cliff Orr, *Sls & Mktg Exec*
Wayne Agner, *Manager*
◆ EMP: 5 EST: 1797
SQ FT: 12,018
SALES (est): 8.5MM **Privately Held**
WEB: www.thebirkettmills.com
SIC: 2041 5999 5261 Flour & other grain mill products; farm equipment & supplies; nurseries & garden centers; lawn & garden supplies

(G-13507)
BIRKETT MILLS
163 Main St Ste 3 (14527-1284)
PHONE............................315 536-4112
Jeff Gifford, *Manager*
EMP: 32
SQ FT: 60,455
SALES (corp-wide): 8.1MM **Privately Held**
WEB: www.thebirkettmills.com
SIC: 2041 Flour & other grain mill products
PA: The Birkett Mills
  163 Main St Ste 2
  Penn Yan NY 14527
  315 536-3311

(G-13508)
CHRONICLE EXPRESS
138 Main St (14527-1299)
PHONE............................315 536-4422
Fax: 315 536-0682
George Barnes, *President*
Irene Vanderlinder, *Sales/Mktg Mgr*
Robert Corey, *Manager*
Michael Hansen, *Graphic Designe*
EMP: 15
SALES (est): 640K **Privately Held**
WEB: www.chronicleexpress.com
SIC: 2711 5994 Newspapers; news dealers & newsstands

(G-13509)
FERRO CORPORATION
1789 Transelco Dr (14527-9752)
PHONE............................315 536-3357
Fax: 315 536-8091
Gary Braun, *General Mgr*
John Prendergast, *Business Mgr*
Terry Fennelly, *Opers Mgr*
Michael O'Loughlin, *Facilities Mgr*
Lisa Button, *Purch Mgr*
EMP: 200
SALES (corp-wide): 1B **Publicly Held**
WEB: www.ferro.com
SIC: 2819 Industrial inorganic chemicals
PA: Ferro Corporation
  6060 Parkland Blvd # 250
  Mayfield Heights OH 44124
  216 875-5600

(G-13510)
FERRO ELECTRONICS MATERIALS (HQ)
Also Called: Ferro Electronic Mtl Systems
1789 Transelco Dr (14527-9752)
PHONE............................315 536-3357
Arleen Jensen, *HR Admin*
Lyn Labrake, *Manager*
Bob Gage, *Manager*
Mary Champln, *Admin Asst*
◆ EMP: 2
SALES (est): 21MM
SALES (corp-wide): 1B **Publicly Held**
SIC: 3264 Porcelain electrical supplies
PA: Ferro Corporation
  6060 Parkland Blvd # 250
  Mayfield Heights OH 44124
  216 875-5600

(G-13511)
FERRO ELECTRONICS MATERIALS
Also Called: Ferro Electronic Mtl Systems
1789 Transelco Dr (14527-9752)
PHONE............................315 536-3357
EMP: 101
SALES (corp-wide): 1B **Publicly Held**
SIC: 3264 Porcelain electrical supplies
HQ: Ferro Electronics Materials Inc
  1789 Transelco Dr
  Penn Yan NY 14527
  315 536-3357

(G-13512)
FOX RUN VINEYARDS INC
670 State Route 14 (14527-9622)
PHONE............................315 536-4616
Fax: 315 536-1383
Scott Osbourne, *President*
Ruth Osborn, *Vice Pres*
Jarrod Crytzer, *Executive*
EMP: 12
SQ FT: 8,000
SALES (est): 3.7MM **Privately Held**
WEB: www.foxrunvineyards.com
SIC: 2084 Wines

(G-13513)
HANSON AGGREGATES EAST LLC
131 Garfield Ave (14527-1655)
P.O. Box 168 (14527-0168)
PHONE............................315 536-9391
Kenny Thurston, *Manager*
EMP: 6
SALES (corp-wide): 14.4B **Privately Held**
WEB: www.hansonaggeast.com
SIC: 1442 Common sand mining
HQ: Hanson Aggregates East Llc
  3131 Rdu Center Dr
  Morrisville NC 27560
  919 380-2500

(G-13514)
HOFFMAN & HOFFMAN
Also Called: Rooster Hill Vineyards
489 State Route 54 (14527-9595)
P.O. Box 11 (14527-0011)
PHONE............................315 536-4773
David W Hoffman, *Partner*
Amy E Hoffman, *Partner*
Ron Reals, *Director*
EMP: 7
SALES (est): 620.3K **Privately Held**
WEB: www.roosterhill.com
SIC: 2084 Wines, brandy & brandy spirits

(G-13515)
JASPER TRANSPORT LLC
1680 Flat St (14527-9024)
P.O. Box 441 (14527-0441)
PHONE............................315 729-5760
Ross Newcomb,
EMP: 6
SALES (est): 570K **Privately Held**
SIC: 3537 Trucks, tractors, loaders, carriers & similar equipment

(G-13516)
PREJEAN WINERY INC
2634 State Route 14 (14527-9735)
PHONE............................315 536-7524
Fax: 315 536-7635
Elizabeth Prejean, *President*
Thomas Prejean, *Vice Pres*
EMP: 11
SQ FT: 6,000
SALES (est): 1.2MM **Privately Held**
WEB: www.prejeanwinery.com
SIC: 2084 Wines

(G-13517)
RED TAIL RIDGE INC
Also Called: Red Tail Ridge Winery
846 State Route 14 (14527-9622)
PHONE............................315 536-4580
Nancy Irelan, *Ch of Bd*
Mike Schnelle, *President*
EMP: 5
SALES (est): 441.1K **Privately Held**
SIC: 2084 Wines

(G-13518)
RIBBLE LUMBER INC
249 1/2 Lake St (14527-1812)
PHONE............................315 536-6221
Roger C Ribble, *President*
Roger A Ribble Sr, *Corp Secy*
EMP: 5
SALES (est): 360K **Privately Held**
SIC: 2434 1794 4212 Wood kitchen cabinets; excavation work; dump truck haulage

(G-13519)
ROTO SALT COMPANY INC
118 Monell St (14527-1404)
PHONE............................315 536-3742
Fax: 315 536-7273
Brett M Oakes, *President*
Susan Ettinger, *Vice Pres*
Ann Olney, *Controller*
EMP: 32
SQ FT: 20,000
SALES (est): 7.8MM **Privately Held**
SIC: 2899 3281 Salt; building stone products

(G-13520)
SENCER INC
1 Keuka Business Park (14527-8995)
PHONE............................315 536-3474
David Burt, *President*
Donald Burt, *Chairman*
EMP: 5
SQ FT: 16,000
SALES: 1MM **Privately Held**
WEB: www.sencer.com
SIC: 3674 Semiconductors & related devices

(G-13521)
SILGAN PLASTICS LLC
40 Powell Ln (14527-1072)
PHONE............................315 536-5690
Rodney Olevnik, *Senior Engr*
Donald Oakleas, *Controller*
Diana Brown, *HR Admin*
Joseph Pollhein, *Manager*
Stacy Fisher, *Manager*
EMP: 250
SQ FT: 100,000
SALES (corp-wide): 3.7B **Publicly Held**
WEB: www.silganplastics.com
SIC: 3089 Plastic containers, except foam
HQ: Silgan Plastics Llc
  14515 North Outer 40 Rd # 210
  Chesterfield MO 63017
  800 274-5426

(G-13522)
VR FOOD EQUIPMENT INC
7 Bush Park Ln (14527-1727)
P.O. Box 216 (14527-0216)
PHONE............................315 531-8133
Fax: 315 531-8134
Steven A Von Rhedey, *Ch of Bd*
Isaac Von Rhedey, *Vice Pres*
Steven P Von Rhedey, *Vice Pres*
Peter Von Rhedey, *CFO*
Steven Rhedey, *Sales Staff*
▲ EMP: 10
SQ FT: 15,000
SALES (est): 3.2MM **Privately Held**
WEB: www.vrfoodequipment.com
SIC: 3556 5084 Food products machinery; food industry machinery

(G-13523)
WARRIOR SPORTS INC
Also Called: In The Crease
26 Powell Ln (14527-1072)
PHONE............................315 536-0937
Fax: 315 536-3128
Steve Trombley, *Branch Mgr*
EMP: 5

SALES (corp-wide): 1.8B **Privately Held**
SIC: 3949 2329 2339 Team sports equipment; lacrosse equipment & supplies, general; soccer equipment & supplies; men's & boys' athletic uniforms; sportswear, women's
HQ: Warrior Sports, Inc.
32125 Hollingsworth Ave
Warren MI 48092
586 978-2595

Perry
Wyoming County

(G-13524)
J N WHITE ASSOCIATES INC
Also Called: J.N. White Designs
129 N Center St (14530-9701)
P.O. Box 219 (14530-0219)
PHONE.................................585 237-5191
Fax: 585 237-2115
Randy White, *President*
Ken Boss, *Vice Pres*
John Steff, *Vice Pres*
Susan C White, *Vice Pres*
Donald Fryling, *Purch Mgr*
EMP: 95
SQ FT: 25,000
SALES (est): 16.8MM **Privately Held**
WEB: www.jnwhitedesigns.com
SIC: 2759 7389 Screen printing; printed circuitry graphic layout

(G-13525)
R J LIEBE ATHLETIC COMPANY
Also Called: Liebe NY
200 Main St N (14530-1211)
PHONE.................................585 237-6111
Jim Liebe, *Mng Member*
Rob Knoll,
EMP: 95
SQ FT: 200,000
SALES (est): 7.5MM **Privately Held**
WEB: www.americanclassicoutfitters.com
SIC: 2329 Men's & boys' athletic uniforms

(G-13526)
SIGN LANGUAGE INC
Also Called: Sign Language Custom WD Signs
6491 State Route 20a (14530-9758)
PHONE.................................585 237-2620
Fax: 585 237-5868
Dave Caito, *President*
Jeff Fitch, *Corp Secy*
EMP: 8
SQ FT: 3,000
SALES (est): 570K **Privately Held**
WEB: www.signlanguageinc.com
SIC: 3993 Signs, not made in custom sign painting shops

Peru
Clinton County

(G-13527)
ROBERT W BUTTS LOGGING CO
420 Mannix Rd (12972-4529)
PHONE.................................518 643-2897
Robert Butts, *Owner*
EMP: 6
SALES (est): 625.6K **Privately Held**
SIC: 2411 Logging camps & contractors

Petersburg
Rensselaer County

(G-13528)
TONOGA INC (PA)
Also Called: Taconic
136 Coon Brook Rd (12138-4303)
P.O. Box 69 (12138-0069)
PHONE.................................518 658-3202
Fax: 518 658-3988
Andrew G Russell, *Chairman*
Lawrence Carroll, *Exec VP*
Sharon Goodermote, *Vice Pres*
Manfred Huschka, *Vice Pres*

Scott Schulz, *Vice Pres*
▲ EMP: 180 EST: 1961
SQ FT: 150,000
SALES (est): 155.1MM **Privately Held**
WEB: www.taconic-afd.com
SIC: 2295 3629 Resin or plastic coated fabrics; electronic generation equipment

Phelps
Ontario County

(G-13529)
AMERICAN CRMIC PROCESS RES LLC
835 Mcivor Rd (14532-9535)
P.O. Box 213 (14532-0213)
PHONE.................................315 828-6268
Jesse Sheckler,
EMP: 6
SQ FT: 18,670
SALES (est): 279.8K **Privately Held**
SIC: 3299 Nonmetallic mineral products

(G-13530)
BENEMY WELDING & FABRICATION
8 Pleasant Ave (14532-1100)
PHONE.................................315 548-8500
Fax: 315 548-8550
Dave Suhr, *President*
Christine Suhr, *Vice Pres*
EMP: 6
SQ FT: 1,852
SALES (est): 675.2K **Privately Held**
SIC: 7692 Welding repair

(G-13531)
DORGAN WELDING SERVICE
1378 White Rd (14532-9502)
PHONE.................................315 462-9030
Bob Dorgan, *Owner*
EMP: 5
SQ FT: 7,000
SALES: 450K **Privately Held**
SIC: 7692 1799 Welding repair; welding on site

(G-13532)
GW LISK COMPANY INC
Also Called: Lisk Coils
1369 Phelps Junction Rd (14532-9747)
PHONE.................................315 548-2165
EMP: 40
SALES (corp-wide): 113.1MM **Privately Held**
SIC: 3629 Mfg Electrical Industrial Apparatus
PA: G.W. Lisk Company, Inc.
2 South St
Clifton Springs NY 14432
315 462-2611

(G-13533)
HANSON AGGREGATES EAST LLC
392 State Route 96 (14532-9531)
PHONE.................................315 548-2911
Mike Cool, *Manager*
Bob Clapp, *Manager*
EMP: 26
SQ FT: 6,756
SALES (corp-wide): 14.4B **Privately Held**
SIC: 3273 1442 Ready-mixed concrete; construction sand & gravel
HQ: Hanson Aggregates East Llc
3131 Rdu Center Dr
Morrisville NC 27560
919 380-2500

(G-13534)
MAGNUS PRECISION MFG INC
1912 State Route 96 (14532-9705)
PHONE.................................315 548-8032
Fax: 315 548-8041
Thomas Shepard, *Principal*
Alfred Mustardo, *Vice Pres*
John Hallett, *Engineer*
Alan Raymond, *Engineer*
Dunfey Gretchen, *Human Res Dir*
EMP: 68
SQ FT: 55,000

SALES (est): 14.8MM
SALES (corp-wide): 93MM **Privately Held**
WEB: www.magnuscnc.com
SIC: 3625 3544 Relays & industrial controls; special dies & tools
PA: Floturn, Inc.
4236 Thunderbird Ln
West Chester OH 45014
513 860-8040

(G-13535)
PHELPS CEMENT PRODUCTS INC
5 S Newark St (14532-9708)
P.O. Box 40 (14532-0040)
PHONE.................................315 548-9415
Fax: 315 548-2235
Gerald Haers, *Ch of Bd*
Michael Haers, *President*
Philip Haers, *Manager*
Chris Wheelers, *Manager*
Gerry Haers, *Admin Sec*
EMP: 23
SQ FT: 4,000
SALES (est): 4.7MM **Privately Held**
WEB: www.phelpscement.com
SIC: 3271 5211 5032 Concrete block & brick; lumber & other building materials; brick, stone & related material

(G-13536)
SENECA CERAMICS CORP
835 Mcivor Rd (14532-9535)
P.O. Box 213 (14532-0213)
PHONE.................................315 781-0100
Chad Scheckler, *President*
Howard Hersey, *Treasurer*
Larisa Scheckler, *Admin Sec*
EMP: 6
SALES: 300K **Privately Held**
SIC: 3469 Utensils, household: porcelain enameled

(G-13537)
TRIPLETT MACHINE INC
1374 Phelps Junction Rd (14532-9747)
PHONE.................................315 548-3198
Fax: 315 548-4143
Douglas A Triplett Jr, *CEO*
Jeffrey Triplett, *Vice Pres*
Grant Abrams, *Engineer*
James Cheney, *Manager*
Douglas Triplett Sr, *Shareholder*
EMP: 65
SQ FT: 30,000
SALES (est): 18.6MM **Privately Held**
WEB: www.triplettmachine.com
SIC: 3599 Machine & other job shop work

(G-13538)
VALVETECH INC
1391 Phelps Junction Rd (14532-9747)
P.O. Box 118 (14532-0118)
PHONE.................................315 548-4551
Fax: 315 548-4200
Michael Mullally, *President*
Russell Williams Jr, *Vice Pres*
Mary Edwards, *Treasurer*
Timothy Mullally, *Sales Mgr*
Paul Welker, *Manager*
EMP: 35
SQ FT: 1,000
SALES (est): 7.6MM
SALES (corp-wide): 136.9MM **Privately Held**
WEB: www.valvetech.net
SIC: 3592 Valves, aircraft
PA: G.W. Lisk Company, Inc.
2 South St
Clifton Springs NY 14432
315 462-2611

(G-13539)
Z-AXIS INC
Also Called: Boundless Technologies
1916 State Route 96 (14532-9705)
PHONE.................................315 548-5000
Fax: 315 548-5100
Michael Allen, *President*
Chris Friel, *Purch Mgr*
Donna Smith, *Purch Mgr*
Bob Sparlin, *Purch Mgr*
Will Eygnor, *Engineer*
▲ EMP: 55
SQ FT: 30,000

SALES (est): 15.4MM **Privately Held**
WEB: www.zaxis.net
SIC: 3699 3845 3577 Electrical equipment & supplies; electromedical equipment; computer peripheral equipment

Philmont
Columbia County

(G-13540)
FALLS MANUFACTURING INC (PA)
95 Main St (12565)
P.O. Box 798 (12565-0798)
PHONE.................................518 672-7189
Fax: 518 672-7195
Frederick A Meyer, *President*
EMP: 8
SQ FT: 4,800
SALES (est): 2.3MM **Privately Held**
SIC: 2381 2339 Fabric dress & work gloves; women's & misses' outerwear

(G-13541)
PVC CONTAINER CORPORATION
Also Called: Nova Pack
370 Stevers Crossing Rd (12565)
P.O. Box 784 (12565-0784)
PHONE.................................518 672-7721
Fax: 518 672-7351
Gary Gendron, *Plant Mgr*
Edna Hover, *Manager*
Sharad Prasad, *Technology*
EMP: 160
SALES (corp-wide): 827.1MM **Privately Held**
WEB: www.airopak.com
SIC: 3085 3089 Plastics bottles; molding primary plastic
HQ: Pvc Container Corporation
15450 South Outer 40 Rd # 120
Chesterfield MO 63017
732 542-0060

Phoenix
Oswego County

(G-13542)
MAJESTIC MOLD & TOOL INC
177 Volney St (13135-3116)
PHONE.................................315 695-2079
Fax: 315 695-3493
Timothy King, *President*
Dennis Lyons, *Vice Pres*
Stephen Corsette, *Treasurer*
Pam Najdul, *Manager*
EMP: 16
SQ FT: 8,000
SALES (est): 4MM **Privately Held**
WEB: www.majesticmold.com
SIC: 2821 Molding compounds, plastics

(G-13543)
PHOENIX WELDING & FABG INC
Also Called: Phoenix Material Handling
10 County Route 6 (13135-2118)
PHONE.................................315 695-2223
Fax: 315 695-3437
Brian D Dates, *Ch of Bd*
Michelle Wagner, *Office Mgr*
EMP: 5
SQ FT: 2,500
SALES (est): 882.1K **Privately Held**
SIC: 7692 Welding repair

(G-13544)
SOUTHERN GRAPHIC SYSTEMS LLC
67 County Route 59 (13135-2116)
PHONE.................................315 695-7079
Fax: 315 695-3160
Vic Baranowski, *Manager*
Frank Palmieri, *Manager*
Ginny Paparo, *Manager*
Jennifer Shutts, *Technology*
EMP: 27
SALES (corp-wide): 281.2MM **Privately Held**
SIC: 3555 Printing trades machinery

HQ: Southern Graphic Systems, Llc
626 W Main St Ste 500
Louisville KY 40202
502 637-5443

Piermont
Rockland County

(G-13545)
ROCKLAND COLLOID CORP (PA)
Also Called: Rockaloid
44 Franklin St (10968-1010)
P.O. Box 3120, Oregon City OR (97045-0306)
PHONE.....................845 359-5559
Robert Cone, *President*
Francis Cooper, *Corp Secy*
Robert Cone Jr, *Vice Pres*
EMP: 5
SQ FT: 3,000
SALES (est): 739.8K **Privately Held**
WEB: www.rockloid.com
SIC: 3861 5043 Photographic equipment & supplies; photographic equipment & supplies

Piffard
Livingston County

(G-13546)
ARKEMA INC
Also Called: Genesee Plant
3289 Genesee St (14533-9745)
P.O. Box 188, Geneseo (14454-0188)
PHONE.....................585 243-6359
Richard Gahagan, *Safety Mgr*
Joe Marcin, *Safety Mgr*
Daryl Roberts, *Mfg Staff*
Jake Zimmerman, *Engineer*
Martin Foess, *Branch Mgr*
EMP: 170
SALES (corp-wide): 19.3MM **Privately Held**
SIC: 2869 2819 Industrial organic chemicals; industrial inorganic chemicals
HQ: Arkema Inc.
900 First Ave
King Of Prussia PA 19406
610 205-7000

(G-13547)
EXXELIA-RAF TABTRONICS LLC
2854 Genesee St (14533-9749)
P.O. Box 128, Geneseo (14454-0128)
PHONE.....................585 243-4331
James Charles Tabbi, *Manager*
EMP: 43
SALES (corp-wide): 26.4MM **Privately Held**
SIC: 3677 3643 3612 Electronic transformers; coil windings, electronic; current-carrying wiring devices; transformers, except electric
PA: Exxelia-Raf Tabtronics, Llc
1221 N Us Highway 17 92
Longwood FL 32750
386 736-1698

Pine Bush
Orange County

(G-13548)
MOBILE MEDIA INC (PA)
24 Center St (12566-6004)
P.O. Box 177 (12566-0177)
PHONE.....................845 744-8080
Fax: 845 744-8090
Lance Pennington, *President*
Nancy Pennington, *Vice Pres*
Angela Ruggiero, *Accounts Mgr*
Renee Turcott, *Accounts Mgr*
Robin Vitacco, *Accounts Mgr*
▲ **EMP:** 23
SQ FT: 31,000
SALES: 10.9MM **Privately Held**
WEB: www.rolleasy.com
SIC: 2542 Partitions & fixtures, except wood

(G-13549)
P & B WOODWORKING INC
2415 State Route 52 (12566-7041)
P.O. Box 225 (12566-0225)
PHONE.....................845 744-2508
Fax: 845 744-5548
Jake Donnell, *President*
Steven Reinhardt, *Vice Pres*
EMP: 10
SQ FT: 11,000
SALES: 1.1MM **Privately Held**
SIC: 2541 Cabinets, lockers & shelving

Pine City
Chemung County

(G-13550)
DALRYMPLE GRAV & CONTG CO INC (HQ)
2105 S Broadway (14871-9700)
PHONE.....................607 739-0391
Fax: 607 737-1056
David J Dalrymple, *Ch of Bd*
Robert H Dalrymple, *President*
Edward C Dalrymple Jr, *Vice Pres*
Roger Burris, *Plant Mgr*
Al Murphy, *Controller*
EMP: 18 EST: 1890
SQ FT: 10,000
SALES (est): 37.2MM
SALES (corp-wide): 98.5MM **Privately Held**
SIC: 1442 3273 Construction sand & gravel; ready-mixed concrete
PA: Dalrymple Holding Corp
2105 S Broadway
Pine City NY 14871
607 737-6200

(G-13551)
DALRYMPLE HOLDING CORP (PA)
2105 S Broadway (14871-9700)
PHONE.....................607 737-6200
David J Dalrymple, *President*
Edward C Dalrymple Jr, *Vice Pres*
Robert H Dalrymple, *Admin Sec*
EMP: 20
SQ FT: 5,000
SALES (est): 98.5MM **Privately Held**
SIC: 3273 1611 1442 1622 Ready-mixed concrete; highway & street construction; construction sand & gravel; bridge construction; stone, quarrying & processing of own stone products

(G-13552)
SENECA STONE CORPORATION (HQ)
2105 S Broadway (14871-9700)
PHONE.....................607 737-6200
David J Dalrymple, *President*
Edward C Dalrymple Jr, *Vice Pres*
Robert H Dalrymple, *Vice Pres*
Edward C Dalrymple Sr, *Treasurer*
Sandy Strong, *Manager*
EMP: 4 EST: 1979
SQ FT: 800
SALES (est): 1.6MM
SALES (corp-wide): 98.5MM **Privately Held**
SIC: 3281 1771 1442 Cut stone & stone products; concrete work; construction sand & gravel
PA: Dalrymple Holding Corp
2105 S Broadway
Pine City NY 14871
607 737-6200

Pine Island
Orange County

(G-13553)
REELCOLOGY INC
39 Transport Ln (10969-1223)
P.O. Box 305 (10969-0305)
PHONE.....................845 258-1880
Kenneth H Smith, *President*
EMP: 15
SQ FT: 7,000
SALES (est): 1.7MM **Privately Held**
SIC: 3496 3499 Cable, uninsulated wire: made from purchased wire; reels, cable: metal

Pine Plains
Dutchess County

(G-13554)
ABRA MEDIA INC
Also Called: Live Oak Media
2773 W Church St (12567-5421)
P.O. Box 652 (12567-0652)
PHONE.....................518 398-1010
Arnold Cardillo, *President*
Debra Cardillo, *Admin Sec*
EMP: 6
SALES (est): 480K **Privately Held**
WEB: www.liveoakmedia.com
SIC: 2741 7812 Miscellaneous publishing; audio-visual program production

(G-13555)
DUTCH SPIRITS LLC
Also Called: Dutch's Spirits
98 Ryan Rd (12567-5022)
PHONE.....................518 398-1022
Ariel Schlein, *Mng Member*
John Adams,
Ronit Schlein,
EMP: 17
SQ FT: 7,424,000
SALES: 250K **Privately Held**
SIC: 2084 5999 2085 Neutral spirits, fruit; alcoholic beverage making equipment & supplies; cocktails, alcoholic

Pine Valley
Chemung County

(G-13556)
AMES COMPANIES INC
114 Smith Rd (14872)
P.O. Box 126 (14872-0126)
PHONE.....................607 739-4544
Fax: 607 739-0030
John Stoner, *Owner*
Mark Schrage, *Manager*
EMP: 20
SQ FT: 13,235
SALES (corp-wide): 2B **Publicly Held**
WEB: www.ames.com
SIC: 3423 Hand & edge tools
HQ: The Ames Companies Inc
465 Railroad Ave
Camp Hill PA 17011
717 737-1500

Pittsford
Monroe County

(G-13557)
COMET INFORMATICS LLC
642 Kreag Rd Ste 300 (14534-3736)
PHONE.....................585 385-2310
Thomas Guhl, *Sales Mgr*
Dirk Hightower,
Daniel Draper,
Leonard Gingello,
Serge Lossa,
EMP: 5 EST: 2011
SALES (est): 266.6K **Privately Held**
SIC: 7372 Educational computer software; publishers' computer software

(G-13558)
EASTMAN KODAK COMPANY
1818 W Jefferson Rd (14534-1033)
PHONE.....................585 722-9695
Dawn Schweitze, *Principal*
EMP: 67
SALES (corp-wide): 1.8B **Publicly Held**
SIC: 3861 Film, sensitized motion picture, X-ray, still camera, etc.
PA: Eastman Kodak Company
343 State St
Rochester NY 14650
585 724-4000

(G-13559)
FLUOROLOGIC INC
33 Bishops Ct (14534-2882)
PHONE.....................585 248-2796
Laura Weller-Brophy, *CEO*
EMP: 7
SALES (est): 410K **Privately Held**
SIC: 3841 Surgical & medical instruments

(G-13560)
FREESCALE SEMICONDUCTOR INC
135 Sullys Trl Ste 9 (14534-4564)
PHONE.....................585 425-4000
Mike Farciglia, *Sales Executive*
Gordy Carlson, *Branch Mgr*
Larry Simpson, *Manager*
EMP: 7
SALES (corp-wide): 6.1B **Privately Held**
WEB: www.freescale.com
SIC: 3674 Semiconductors & related devices
HQ: Freescale Semiconductor, Inc.
6501 W William Cannon Dr
Austin TX 78735
512 895-2000

(G-13561)
GATEHOUSE MEDIA LLC (HQ)
175 Sullys Trl Ste 300 (14534-4560)
PHONE.....................585 598-0030
Fax: 585 248-2631
Adam Reinebach, *CEO*
Rick Daniels, *President*
Peter Newton, *President*
Paul Ameden, *Principal*
Walter Belback, *Editor*
▲ **EMP:** 70
SQ FT: 15,000
SALES: 1.2B
SALES (corp-wide): 1.2B **Publicly Held**
WEB: www.gatehousemedia.com
SIC: 2711 7311 2759 Newspapers, publishing & printing; advertising agencies; commercial printing
PA: New Media Investment Group Inc.
1345 Avenue Of The Americ
New York NY 10105
212 479-3160

(G-13562)
GATEHOUSE MEDIA MO HOLDINGS
Also Called: Rolla Daily News Plus
175 Sullys Trl Ste 300 (14534-4560)
PHONE.....................530 846-3661
Michael E Reed, *CEO*
EMP: 7 EST: 2013
SALES (est): 374K **Privately Held**
SIC: 2711 Newspapers, publishing & printing

(G-13563)
GATEHUSE MEDIA PA HOLDINGS INC (HQ)
175 Sullys Trl Fl 3 (14534-4560)
PHONE.....................585 598-0030
Kirk Davis, *CEO*
EMP: 68
SALES (est): 4.1MM
SALES (corp-wide): 1.2B **Publicly Held**
SIC: 2711 Commercial printing & newspaper publishing combined
PA: New Media Investment Group Inc.
1345 Avenue Of The Americ
New York NY 10105
212 479-3160

Pittsford - Monroe County

(G-13564)
IMAGINANT INC
Also Called: Jsr Ultrasonics Division
3800 Monroe Ave Ste 29 (14534-1330)
PHONE.................................585 264-0480
Fax: 585 264-9642
Todd Jackson, *CEO*
Samuel Rosenberg, *President*
Robert Hibbard, *Corp Secy*
Valerie Sill, *Engineer*
Steve Smith, *Engineer*
EMP: 32
SQ FT: 10,000
SALES (est): 5.9MM **Privately Held**
WEB: www.jsrultrasonics.com
SIC: **3829** Measuring & controlling devices

(G-13565)
INFIMED INC
15 Fishers Rd (14534-9544)
PHONE.................................585 383-1710
Pat Rox, *Branch Mgr*
Jack Mooney, *Manager*
Tim Seeler, *Manager*
EMP: 7
SALES (corp-wide): 8.3MM **Privately Held**
SIC: **3845** Electromedical equipment
PA: Infimed, Inc.
    121 Metropolitan Park Dr
    Liverpool NY 13088
    315 453-4545

(G-13566)
KERNOW NORTH AMERICA
5 Park Forest Dr (14534-3557)
PHONE.................................585 586-3590
Bosy Colak, *Owner*
EMP: 11 EST: 2010
SALES (est): 830K **Privately Held**
SIC: **3089** Plastic containers, except foam

(G-13567)
LIFE JUICE BRANDS LLC
115 Brook Rd (14534-1144)
PHONE.................................585 944-7982
Peter Schulick, *CEO*
EMP: 4
SQ FT: 1,400
SALES: 1.7MM **Privately Held**
SIC: **2033** Vegetable juices: packaged in cans, jars, etc.

(G-13568)
MAGNUM SHIELDING CORPORATION
3800 Monroe Ave Ste 14f (14534-1330)
P.O. Box 827 (14534-0827)
PHONE.................................585 381-9957
Fax: 585 381-9956
Scott Hurwitz, *President*
Tom Vierthaler, *General Mgr*
Chad Conklin, *Manager*
Sue Myer, *Manager*
Jeremy Austin, *Senior Mgr*
▲ EMP: 50
SQ FT: 15,000
SALES (est): 9.1MM **Privately Held**
WEB: www.magnumshielding.com
SIC: **3694** Ignition apparatus & distributors

(G-13569)
MARDEK LLC
73 N Wilmarth Rd (14534-9775)
P.O. Box 134, North Hero VT (05474-0134)
PHONE.................................585 735-9333
Charles Dekar, *President*
Nick Dekar, *President*
▲ EMP: 5
SALES: 2MM **Privately Held**
SIC: **3312** Rods, iron & steel: made in steel mills

(G-13570)
MILLERCOORS LLC
1000 Pittsford Victor Rd (14534-3822)
PHONE.................................585 385-0670
Dennis Perreault, *Branch Mgr*
EMP: 25
SALES (corp-wide): 19.8B **Privately Held**
SIC: **2082** Malt beverages
HQ: Millercoors Llc
    250 S Wacker Dr Ste 800
    Chicago IL 60606
    312 496-2700

(G-13571)
OPTICS TECHNOLOGY INC
3800 Monroe Ave Ste 3 (14534-1330)
PHONE.................................585 586-0950
Fax: 585 248-2371
John Warda, *President*
EMP: 6
SQ FT: 6,000
SALES (est): 1.3MM **Privately Held**
WEB: www.opticstechnology.com
SIC: **3827** 3599 8711 Lenses, optical: all types except ophthalmic; lens mounts; optical elements & assemblies, except ophthalmic; machine & other job shop work; machine shop, jobbing & repair; engineering services

(G-13572)
PA PELLETS LLC (HQ)
1 Fischers Rd Ste 160 (14534)
PHONE.................................814 848-9970
Dan Wetzel, *Principal*
▼ EMP: 16 EST: 2010
SALES (est): 2.6MM
SALES (corp-wide): 26.6MM **Privately Held**
SIC: **2421** Fuelwood, from mill waste
PA: Biomaxx, Inc.
    1 Fishers Rd Ste 160
    Pittsford NY 14534
    585 314-7304

(G-13573)
PACTIV LLC
1169 Pittsford Victor Rd (14534-3809)
P.O. Box 5032, Lake Forest IL (60045-5032)
PHONE.................................585 248-1213
EMP: 50 **Privately Held**
WEB: www.pactiv.com
SIC: **2631** 2653 Paperboard mills; container board; folding boxboard; corrugated & solid fiber boxes
HQ: Pactiv Llc
    1900 W Field Ct
    Lake Forest IL 60045
    847 482-2000

(G-13574)
UNITED TECHNOLOGIES CORP
Lenel
1212 Pittsford Victor Rd (14534-3820)
PHONE.................................866 788-5095
Tom Parks, *Regl Sales Mgr*
Mark Kozik, *Sales Engr*
Diego Ponti, *Sales Engr*
John Merlino, *Director*
Brian Beideman, *Director*
EMP: 500
SALES (corp-wide): 56.1B **Publicly Held**
SIC: **3699** Electrical equipment & supplies
PA: United Technologies Corporation
    10 Farm Springs Rd
    Farmington CT 06032
    860 728-7000

(G-13575)
XELIC INCORPORATED
1250 Pittsford Victor Rd # 370 (14534-9541)
PHONE.................................585 415-2764
Mark Gibson, *President*
Doug Bush, *Vice Pres*
Kenny Chung, *Design Engr*
Jamie Howard, *Design Engr*
Mark Grabosky, *Treasurer*
EMP: 18
SQ FT: 2,400
SALES: 3MM **Privately Held**
WEB: www.xelic.com
SIC: **3825** Integrated circuit testers

Plainview
Nassau County

(G-13576)
ADART POLYETHYLENE BAG MFG
Also Called: Adart Poly Bag Mfg
1 W Ames Ct Ste 201 (11803-2328)
P.O. Box 615 (11803-0019)
PHONE.................................516 932-1001
Robert Wolk, *President*
Gabriella Grama, *Manager*
EMP: 6 EST: 1968
SQ FT: 13,500
SALES (est): 1.1MM **Privately Held**
SIC: **2673** Bags: plastic, laminated & coated

(G-13577)
AEROFLEX HOLDING CORP (DH)
35 S Service Rd (11803-4117)
P.O. Box 6022 (11803-0622)
PHONE.................................516 694-6700
Hugh Evans, *Ch of Bd*
Leonard Borow, *President*
John Buyko, *Exec VP*
Andrew F Kaminsky, *Senior VP*
Edward Wactlar, *Senior VP*
▼ EMP: 25
SQ FT: 90,000
SALES (est): 528.5MM
SALES (corp-wide): 3.1B **Privately Held**
SIC: **3674** Semiconductors & related devices
HQ: Cobham Holdings Inc.
    10 Orchard Park Dr
    Orchard Park NY 14127
    716 662-0006

(G-13578)
AEROFLEX INCORPORATED (DH)
35 S Service Rd (11803-4117)
P.O. Box 6022 (11803-0622)
PHONE.................................516 694-6700
Fax: 516 694-0658
Robert B McKeon, *Ch of Bd*
Leonard J Borow, *President*
Michael G Gorin, *Vice Chairman*
Matt Gordon, *Area Mgr*
Leslie Collins, *COO*
▲ EMP: 450
SQ FT: 69,000
SALES (est): 528.5MM
SALES (corp-wide): 3.1B **Privately Held**
WEB: www.aeroflex.com
SIC: **3812** 3621 3677 3674 Acceleration indicators & systems components, aerospace; torque motors, electric; electronic coils, transformers & other inductors; microcircuits, integrated (semiconductor); mesh, made from purchased wire; optical instruments & apparatus
HQ: Aeroflex Holding Corp.
    35 S Service Rd
    Plainview NY 11803
    516 694-6700

(G-13579)
AEROFLEX PLAINVIEW INC (DH)
35 S Service Rd (11803-4117)
P.O. Box 6022 (11803-0622)
PHONE.................................516 694-6700
Fax: 516 694-6715
Leonard Borow, *Ch of Bd*
Carl Caruso, *Senior VP*
William Brown, *Vice Pres*
Kevin J Finnegan, *Vice Pres*
Rob Sichenzia, *Vice Pres*
EMP: 422
SQ FT: 69,000
SALES (est): 192.8MM
SALES (corp-wide): 3.1B **Privately Held**
SIC: **3679** 3621 3674 3827 Electronic circuits; motors, electric; microcircuits, integrated (semiconductor); microprocessors; optical instruments & lenses
HQ: Cobham Aes Holdings Inc.
    2121 Crystal Dr Ste 625
    Arlington VA 22202
    703 414-5300

(G-13580)
ALCATEL-LUCENT USA INC
1 Fairchild Ct Ste 340 (11803-1720)
PHONE.................................516 349-4900
EMP: 58
SALES (corp-wide): 597.5MM **Privately Held**
SIC: **3661** Telephone & telegraph apparatus
HQ: Alcatel-Lucent Usa Inc.
    600 Mountain Ave Ste 700
    New Providence NJ 07974

(G-13581)
AMERICAN CASTING AND MFG CORP (PA)
51 Commercial St (11803-2490)
PHONE.................................800 342-0333
Fax: 516 349-8389
Norman Wenk, *President*
H L Christian Wenk IV, *Corp Secy*
Joseph Wenk, *Vice Pres*
Al Micucci, *Plant Mgr*
Carlos Cuadros, *Manager*
◆ EMP: 70 EST: 1916
SQ FT: 40,000
SALES: 16.5MM **Privately Held**
WEB: www.americancasting.com
SIC: **3089** 3364 2759 5085 Injection molding of plastics; lead die-castings; labels & seals: printing; seals, industrial

(G-13582)
AMERICAN CASTING AND MFG CORP
65 S Terminal Dr (11803-2310)
PHONE.................................516 349-7010
Jim Wenk, *Mktg Dir*
Norman Wenk, *Branch Mgr*
EMP: 5
SALES (corp-wide): 16.5MM **Privately Held**
WEB: www.americancasting.com
SIC: **3089** 3364 3429 Injection molding of plastics; lead die-castings; manufactured hardware (general)
PA: American Casting And Manufacturing Corporation
    51 Commercial St
    Plainview NY 11803
    800 342-0333

(G-13583)
AUDIO VIDEO INVASION INC
Also Called: AVI
53 Werman Ct (11803-4507)
PHONE.................................516 345-2636
Panos Anassis, *Principal*
Christina Anassis, *Manager*
EMP: 15
SALES (est): 1.9MM **Privately Held**
SIC: **3651** 5999 Household audio & video equipment; audio-visual equipment & supplies

(G-13584)
AUFHAUSER CORPORATION (PA)
Also Called: I R M
39 West Mall (11803-4209)
PHONE.................................516 694-8696
Fax: 516 694-8690
R K Aufhauser, *CEO*
Pl Tsang Wu, *Vice Pres*
Fred Wu, *Marketing Staff*
Chris Ll, *Info Tech Mgr*
▲ EMP: 18
SQ FT: 28,000
SALES: 30MM **Privately Held**
WEB: www.aufhauser.net
SIC: **3356** 2899 5051 Welding rods; solder: wire, bar, acid core, & rosin core; fluxes: brazing, soldering, galvanizing & welding; metals service centers & offices

(G-13585)
AUFHAUSER MANUFACTURING CORP
Also Called: Aufhauser Corp Canada
39 West Mall (11803-4209)
PHONE.................................516 694-8696
R Keith Aufhauser, *President*
Wu Pl Tsang, *Vice Pres*
Fred Wu, *Treasurer*
EMP: 20
SQ FT: 25,000
SALES: 25MM **Privately Held**
WEB: www.brazing.com
SIC: **3356** Welding rods

(G-13586)
CENTROID INC
111 E Ames Ct Unit 1 (11803-2311)
PHONE.................................516 349-0070
Fax: 516 349-9141
Gerald I Starr, *Ch of Bd*
Marc A Starr, *President*
Nancy Budd, *Purch Agent*

GEOGRAPHIC SECTION

Plainview - Nassau County (G-13610)

Steve Apelman, *Engineer*
Peggy Carey, *Controller*
EMP: 23 **EST:** 1965
SQ FT: 8,000
SALES (est): 3.8MM **Privately Held**
WEB: www.centroidinc.com
SIC: 3679 Oscillators

(G-13587)
CHERRY LANE LITHOGRAPHING CORP
15 E Bethpage Rd Unit A (11803-4217)
PHONE.................516 293-9294
William Citterbart Jr, *President*
Joann Citterbart, *Corp Secy*
William Citterbart III, *Vice Pres*
Bill Fuchf, *Safety Mgr*
Tony Federicic, *CFO*
EMP: 48 **EST:** 1962
SQ FT: 54,000
SALES (est): 10.7MM **Privately Held**
WEB: www.cherrylanelitho.com
SIC: 2752 Lithographing on metal

(G-13588)
COINMACH SERVICE CORP
303 Sunnyside Blvd # 70 (11803-1598)
PHONE.................516 349-8555
Robert M Doyle, *Ch of Bd*
Carol A Siebuhr, *President*
Adrian Verquer, *President*
VA Richmond, *Regional Mgr*
NC Charlotte, *Vice Pres*
EMP: 805
SQ FT: 11,600
SALES (est): 129.5MM
SALES (corp-wide): 333.8MM **Privately Held**
SIC: 3633 5087 Household laundry equipment; laundry equipment & supplies
HQ: Spin Holdco Inc.
303 Sunnyside Blvd # 70
Plainview NY 11803
516 349-8555

(G-13589)
COLONIAL GROUP LLC
150 Express St Ste 2 (11803-2421)
PHONE.................516 349-8010
Pierre Lavi,
EMP: 25
SALES (est): 1.8MM **Privately Held**
SIC: 3724 Aircraft engines & engine parts

(G-13590)
CONRAD BLASIUS EQUIPMENT CO
Also Called: Cbe/New York
199 Newtown Rd (11803-4308)
PHONE.................516 753-1200
Fax: 516 756-1209
Richard Fiordelisi Sr, *President*
Richard C Fiordelisi Jr, *President*
EMP: 6
SQ FT: 10,000
SALES (est): 630K **Privately Held**
SIC: 3599 3291 2842 5084 Tubing, flexible metallic; coated abrasive products; metal polish; industrial machinery & equipment

(G-13591)
CONTROLLED CASTINGS CORP
31 Commercial Ct (11803-2403)
PHONE.................516 349-1718
Fax: 516 349-1126
Carmella Fratello, *Ch of Bd*
Peter Fratello Jr, *President*
Clifford Fratello, *Vice Pres*
EMP: 30 **EST:** 1961
SQ FT: 32,500
SALES (est): 4.3MM **Privately Held**
SIC: 3369 Castings, except die-castings, precision

(G-13592)
CORAL CAST LLC
31 Commercial Ct (11803-2403)
PHONE.................516 349-1300
Joseph Marden,
EMP: 21
SALES (est): 3.5MM **Privately Held**
SIC: 3272 Precast terrazo or concrete products

(G-13593)
COX & COMPANY INC
1664 Old Country Rd (11803-5013)
PHONE.................212 366-0200
Fax: 212 366-0222
John Smith, *Ch of Bd*
Thomas Ferguson, *Senior VP*
Kevin Pierce, *Buyer*
Christian Asitimbay, *QC Mgr*
Kamel Al-Khalil, *Engineer*
▲ **EMP:** 185 **EST:** 1944
SQ FT: 90,000
SALES (est): 61.8MM **Privately Held**
SIC: 3625 3743 3822 3812 Relays & industrial controls; railroad equipment; auto controls regulating residntl & coml environmt & applncs; search & navigation equipment; current-carrying wiring devices; aircraft parts & equipment; deicing equipment, aircraft

(G-13594)
CSC SERVICEWORKS INC (HQ)
303 Sunnyside Blvd # 70 (11803-1597)
PHONE.................516 349-8555
Mark Hjelle, *CEO*
Lydia Neal, *Area Mgr*
EMP: 43
SALES (est): 168.1MM
SALES (corp-wide): 333.8MM **Privately Held**
SIC: 3633 5087 Household laundry equipment; laundry equipment & supplies
PA: Csc Serviceworks Holdings, Inc
303 Sunnyside Blvd # 70
Plainview NY 11803
516 349-8555

(G-13595)
CSC SERVICEWORKS HOLDINGS (PA)
303 Sunnyside Blvd # 70 (11803-1597)
PHONE.................516 349-8555
EMP: 31 **EST:** 2013
SALES (est): 333.8MM **Privately Held**
SIC: 3633 5087 Household laundry equipment; laundry equipment & supplies

(G-13596)
DERM/BURO INC (PA)
229 Newtown Rd (11803-4309)
PHONE.................516 694-8300
Frank Guthart, *President*
Kathy Daponce, *Manager*
EMP: 2
SQ FT: 1,100
SALES (est): 3.4MM **Privately Held**
WEB: www.gforces.com
SIC: 3841 5122 5047 3842 Surgical & medical instruments; pharmaceuticals; instruments, surgical & medical; surgical appliances & supplies

(G-13597)
DIE-MATIC PRODUCTS LLC
130 Express St (11803-2477)
PHONE.................516 433-7900
Fax: 516 433-7966
Arnold Klein, *President*
Bill Oehrlein, *Opers Mgr*
Evelyn Martinez, *Controller*
Dan Farber, *Info Tech Mgr*
Sheldon Fox,
EMP: 30 **EST:** 1944
SQ FT: 30,000
SALES (est): 5.3MM **Privately Held**
WEB: www.diematicproducts.com
SIC: 3469 Stamping metal for the trade

(G-13598)
EBY ELECTRO INC
210 Express St (11803-2423)
PHONE.................516 576-7777
Fax: 516 576-1414
Mitchell Solomon, *President*
Rick Mitukiewicz, *President*
Charles Louie, *Opers Mgr*
Jim Fennell, *Opers Staff*
John Mancini, *Opers Staff*
▲ **EMP:** 28
SQ FT: 20,000
SALES (est): 5.7MM **Privately Held**
WEB: www.ebyelectro.com
SIC: 3678 Electronic connectors

(G-13599)
EMERSON NETWORK POWER
79 Express St Fl 14 (11803-2419)
PHONE.................516 349-8500
Tammy Burns, *Branch Mgr*
Jay Mohr, *Network Mgr*
EMP: 8
SALES (corp-wide): 22.3B **Publicly Held**
SIC: 3823 Industrial instrmnts msrmnt display/control process variable
HQ: Emerson Network Power, Liebert Services, Inc.
610 Executive Campus Dr
Westerville OH 43082
614 841-6400

(G-13600)
EVANS & PAUL LLC
140 Dupont St (11803-1603)
PHONE.................516 576-0800
Janis White, *CFO*
Jeffrey Evans, *Mng Member*
Suzanne Ray,
EMP: 50
SQ FT: 30,000
SALES: 5.1MM **Privately Held**
SIC: 2599 2542 1799 Hospital furniture, except beds; fixtures, office: except wood; office furniture installation

(G-13601)
FACTORY WHEEL WAREHOUSE INC
30 W Ames Ct (11803-2319)
PHONE.................516 605-2131
EMP: 9 **EST:** 2012
SALES (est): 1MM **Privately Held**
SIC: 3714 5013 5015 5085 Motor vehicle wheels & parts; wheel rims, motor vehicle; wheels, motor vehicle; wheels, motor vehicle; wheels, used: motor vehicle; bearings, bushings, wheels & gears

(G-13602)
FIBRE MATERIALS CORP
40 Dupont St (11803-1679)
PHONE.................516 349-1660
Fax: 516 349-1671
Glenn Fellows, *CEO*
Brian Grossberg, *President*
Elvira Minerva, *Controller*
▲ **EMP:** 27 **EST:** 1963
SQ FT: 34,000
SALES (est): 4.7MM **Privately Held**
WEB: www.fibrematerials.com
SIC: 3089 5162 Washers, plastic; plastics materials & basic shapes

(G-13603)
FULL MOTION BEVERAGE INC (PA)
998 Old Country Rd (11803-4928)
PHONE.................631 585-1100
Peter Frazzetto, *CEO*
Vincent Butta, *President*
Chris Mollica, *President*
Paul Dua, *Vice Pres*
Tim Mayette, *CFO*
EMP: 6
SALES: 396.4K **Publicly Held**
WEB: www.web2corp.com
SIC: 2869 Alcohols, non-beverage

(G-13604)
HOSHIZAKI NRTHEASTERN DIST CTR
150 Dupont St Ste 100 (11803-1603)
PHONE.................516 605-1411
Toshio Mase, *President*
Mitsuhiro Nomura, *CFO*
Ron Podolsky, *Accounts Mgr*
Artic Rade, *Admin Sec*
▲ **EMP:** 6
SALES (est): 1MM
SALES (corp-wide): 2.1B **Privately Held**
WEB: www.hoshizaki.com
SIC: 3585 Ice making machinery
HQ: Hoshizaki America, Inc.
618 Highway 74 S
Peachtree City GA 30269
770 487-2331

(G-13605)
HOT LINE INDUSTRIES INC (PA)
Also Called: Casttle Harbor
28 South Mall (11803-4208)
PHONE.................516 764-0400
Fax: 516 764-6009
Howard Negrin, *President*
Jeff Negrin, *Corp Secy*
Elliot Negrin, *Vice Pres*
▲ **EMP:** 14
SQ FT: 9,000
SALES (est): 915.3K **Privately Held**
WEB: www.hotlineindustries.com
SIC: 2339 Women's & misses' outerwear

(G-13606)
HOWARD J MOORE COMPANY INC
Also Called: Morco
210 Terminal Dr Ste B (11803-2322)
PHONE.................631 351-8467
Eric Moore, *President*
Margaret Bram, *Director*
EMP: 28 **EST:** 1945
SQ FT: 17,000
SALES (est): 5.5MM **Privately Held**
WEB: www.morcofab.com
SIC: 3082 2679 Unsupported plastics profile shapes; building, insulating & packaging paper

(G-13607)
INDUSTRIAL RAW MATERIALS LLC
Also Called: Industrial Wax
39 West Mall (11803-4209)
PHONE.................212 688-8080
Fax: 212 759-3656
Keith Aufhauser, *Mng Member*
◆ **EMP:** 19 **EST:** 1946
SQ FT: 6,000
SALES (est): 4.6MM
SALES (corp-wide): 30MM **Privately Held**
WEB: www.industrialwax.com
SIC: 2911 5172 Paraffin wax; petroleum products
PA: Aufhauser Corporation
39 West Mall
Plainview NY 11803
516 694-8696

(G-13608)
INTELLIDYNE LLC
303 Sunnyside Blvd # 75 (11803-1508)
PHONE.................516 676-0777
Michelle David, *Manager*
Jack Hammer,
EMP: 17
SQ FT: 4,500
SALES (est): 3.5MM **Privately Held**
WEB: www.intellidynellc.com
SIC: 3822 Temperature controls, automatic

(G-13609)
INTERNATIONAL PATTERNS INC
8 Arthur Ct (11803-3708)
PHONE.................631 952-2000
Fax: 631 952-7602
Paul Kaplan, *Ch of Bd*
Shelley Beckwith, *President*
Keith Huntington, *Vice Pres*
Leona Weiner, *Treasurer*
▲ **EMP:** 100
SQ FT: 37,000
SALES (est): 13.7MM **Privately Held**
WEB: www.internationalpatterns.com
SIC: 3993 Signs & advertising specialties

(G-13610)
INTERPARTS INTERNATIONAL INC (PA)
190 Express St (11803-2405)
PHONE.................516 576-2000
Hung Da Yang, *President*
Frank Buquicchio, *Controller*
Andrew Feng, *Asst Controller*
Dauphine Yang, *Director*
▲ **EMP:** 20
SQ FT: 40,000
SALES (est): 3.2MM **Privately Held**
SIC: 3714 5013 3566 Motor vehicle brake systems & parts; automotive brakes; speed changers, drives & gears

Plainview - Nassau County (G-13611)

(G-13611)
JAYEN CHEMICAL SUPPLIES INC
1120 Old Country Rd # 311 (11803-5021)
PHONE..................516 933-3311
Jeff Nemeth, *President*
EMP: 1
SALES: 1MM **Privately Held**
WEB: www.jayenchemical.com
SIC: 2841 Soap & other detergents

(G-13612)
JEM CONTAINER CORP
151 Fairchild Ave Ste 1 (11803-1716)
P.O. Box 456, Farmingdale (11735-0456)
PHONE..................516 349-7770
John Mc Laughlin, *President*
EMP: 10 **EST:** 1982
SALES (est): 1.2MM **Privately Held**
SIC: 3086 Packaging & shipping materials, foamed plastic

(G-13613)
KAREY KASSL CORP
Also Called: Karey Products
180 Terminal Dr (11803-2324)
PHONE..................516 349-8484
Fax: 516 349-9329
Gary J Kassl, *CEO*
Ronald Kassl, *President*
Carlos Gomez, *Info Tech Mgr*
▲ **EMP:** 30
SQ FT: 40,000
SALES: 2.5MM **Privately Held**
SIC: 3442 Storm doors or windows, metal

(G-13614)
KENSTAN LOCK & HARDWARE CO INC
Also Called: Kenstan Lock Co.
101 Commercial St Ste 100 (11803-2408)
PHONE..................631 423-1977
Fax: 516 576-0100
Hans E R Bosch, *President*
Anne Judd-Raye, *Human Res Mgr*
Craig Lynn, *VP Sales*
Matty Youngs, *Sales Staff*
Bob Harrison, *Executive*
▲ **EMP:** 38 **EST:** 1964
SQ FT: 10,000
SALES (est): 8.2MM **Privately Held**
WEB: www.kenstan.com
SIC: 3429 Cabinet hardware

(G-13615)
LAWRENCE PACKAGING INC
43 Sheer Plz (11803-4205)
PHONE..................516 420-1930
Harry Schein, *President*
EMP: 9
SQ FT: 5,000
SALES (est): 795.6K **Privately Held**
SIC: 3083 Laminated plastics plate & sheet

(G-13616)
LIFETIME CHIMNEY SUPPLY LLC
171 E Ames Ct (11803-2332)
PHONE..................516 576-8144
Fax: 516 576-8145
Abraham J Finkler, *President*
Deborah Grandison, *General Mgr*
Dennis Martinez, *Vice Pres*
Susan Esswein, *Controller*
Joshua Lang, *Director*
▲ **EMP:** 5
SQ FT: 6,000
SALES (est): 1.2MM **Privately Held**
WEB: www.lifetimechimneysupply.com
SIC: 3443 5023 Liners, industrial: metal plate; kitchenware

(G-13617)
MACHINE COMPONENTS CORP
70 Newtown Rd (11803-4382)
PHONE..................516 694-7222
Fax: 516 694-7252
Joseph Kaplan, *President*
Miriam Kaplan, *President*
Jay Kaplan, *Corp Secy*
Gregory Ahmad, *Engineer*
Rana Klein, *Administration*
EMP: 25 **EST:** 1959
SQ FT: 10,000
SALES (est): 5MM **Privately Held**
WEB: www.machinecomp.com
SIC: 3568 3625 Clutches, except vehicular; switches, electronic applications

(G-13618)
MARCEL FINISHING CORP
4 David Ct (11803-6009)
PHONE..................718 381-2889
Marcel Brenka, *President*
Floarea Brenka, *Admin Sec*
EMP: 30
SQ FT: 7,000
SALES (est): 1.9MM **Privately Held**
SIC: 2269 2261 2262 Finishing plants; finishing plants, cotton; finishing plants, manmade fiber & silk fabrics

(G-13619)
METROFAB PIPE INCORPORATED
15 Fairchild Ct (11803-1701)
PHONE..................516 349-7373
Elizabeth Ficken, *President*
Joe Magliato, *Vice Pres*
Cathy Karp, *Manager*
EMP: 10
SALES (est): 2.6MM **Privately Held**
SIC: 3462 3443 Flange, valve & pipe fitting forgings, ferrous; pipe, standpipe & culverts

(G-13620)
MGD BRANDS INC
Also Called: Finesse Accessories
30 Commercial Ct (11803-2415)
PHONE..................516 545-0150
Arthur Damast, *CEO*
Scott Damast, *Vice Pres*
▲ **EMP:** 51
SALES (est): 8.8MM **Privately Held**
WEB: www.finessenovelty.com
SIC: 3911 3999 5094 5131 Jewelry, precious metal; hair & hair-based products; jewelry; hair accessories; ribbons; novelties

(G-13621)
MICRO CENTRIC CORPORATION (PA)
25 S Terminal Dr (11803-2314)
PHONE..................800 573-1139
Fax: 516 349-9354
Nicholas Fink, *Ch of Bd*
Dan Olsen, *VP Opers*
Eva Fink, *Treasurer*
Maria Koski, *Controller*
Terry Korndoerfer, *Manager*
◆ **EMP:** 28
SQ FT: 14,000
SALES (est): 4.3MM **Privately Held**
WEB: www.microcentric.com
SIC: 3545 5084 Machine tool accessories; collets (machine tool accessories); industrial machinery & equipment

(G-13622)
N & G OF AMERICA INC
28 W Lane Dr (11803-5436)
PHONE..................516 428-3414
Najmi Hussain, *President*
EMP: 12
SALES: 500K **Privately Held**
SIC: 3571 Electronic computers

(G-13623)
NASH PRINTING INC
Also Called: Sir Speedy
101 Dupont St Ste 2 (11803-1612)
PHONE..................516 935-4567
Fax: 516 935-4736
Noor Baqueri, *President*
Ali Baqueri, *Manager*
Marc Saltzman, *Manager*
EMP: 10
SQ FT: 4,500
SALES (est): 890K **Privately Held**
SIC: 2752 Commercial printing, lithographic

(G-13624)
NUCLEAR DIAGNOSTIC PDTS NY INC
130 Commercial St (11803-2414)
PHONE..................516 575-4201
Wayne Wong, *Ch of Bd*
Tom Poland, *Manager*
EMP: 7
SALES (est): 986.7K **Privately Held**
SIC: 3829 Medical diagnostic systems, nuclear

(G-13625)
OMEGA INDUSTRIES & DEVELOPMENT
Also Called: Turbo Dynamics
150 Express St Ste 2 (11803-2421)
PHONE..................516 349-8010
Fax: 516 349-0677
Pierre Lavi, *President*
Edward Lavi, *Treasurer*
EMP: 26
SQ FT: 25,000
SALES (est): 2.9MM **Privately Held**
SIC: 3519 3511 3728 6512 Jet propulsion engines; gas turbines, mechanical drive; aircraft parts & equipment; nonresidential building operators; aircraft engines & engine parts; motor vehicle parts & accessories

(G-13626)
P D R INC
Also Called: Sir Speedy
101 Dupont St (11803-1608)
PHONE..................516 829-5300
Fax: 516 829-5650
Pat Riccardi, *President*
EMP: 8
SQ FT: 4,500
SALES (est): 1.1MM **Privately Held**
SIC: 2752 2791 Commercial printing, lithographic; typesetting

(G-13627)
PB LEINER-USA
143 Orchard St (11803-4718)
PHONE..................516 822-4040
Cheryl Michaels, *Principal*
EMP: 5
SALES (est): 549.3K **Privately Held**
SIC: 3565 Bottling & canning machinery

(G-13628)
PETER DIGIOIA
Also Called: Medsurg Direct
7 Sherwood Dr (11803-3218)
PHONE..................516 644-5517
Peter Digioia, *Owner*
EMP: 5
SALES (est): 424.1K **Privately Held**
SIC: 3841 5047 Surgical & medical instruments; medical equipment & supplies

(G-13629)
PETRO INC
3 Fairchild Ct (11803-1701)
PHONE..................516 686-1717
Brian Boschert, *Branch Mgr*
EMP: 8 **Publicly Held**
SIC: 1389 Gas field services
HQ: Petro, Inc.
9 W Broad St Ste 3
Stamford CT 06902
203 325-5400

(G-13630)
PORT EVERGLADES MACHINE WORKS
Also Called: P E Machine Works
57 Colgate Dr (11803-1803)
PHONE..................516 367-2280
Steven Bellask, *President*
John Schaefer, *Vice Pres*
EMP: 10
SQ FT: 10,000
SALES (est): 1MM **Privately Held**
SIC: 3599 3731 Machine shop, jobbing & repair; shipbuilding & repairing

(G-13631)
PURITY PRODUCTS INC
200 Terminal Dr (11803-2312)
PHONE..................516 767-1967
Jahn Levin, *President*
Michael Iwanciw, *Controller*
Matt Soreco, *Marketing Staff*
Harry Badwal, *Manager*
Joseph Tirino, *Web Dvlpr*
▲ **EMP:** 57
SALES (est): 14.1MM **Privately Held**
SIC: 2834 Vitamin, nutrient & hematinic preparations for human use

(G-13632)
ROMAC ELECTRONICS INC
155 E Ames Ct Unit 1 (11803-2383)
PHONE..................516 349-7900
Fax: 516 349-7573
Jerome Bloomberg, *President*
Al Debello, *General Mgr*
Lee Bloomberg, *Vice Pres*
Michael Bloomberg, *Vice Pres*
Ronald Bloomberg, *Vice Pres*
EMP: 49 **EST:** 1952
SQ FT: 42,000
SALES (est): 10.1MM **Privately Held**
WEB: www.romacelectronics.com
SIC: 3499 Shims, metal

(G-13633)
S E A SUPPLIES LTD
Also Called: S E A Supls
1670 Old Country Rd # 104 (11803-5000)
PHONE..................516 694-6677
Martin Reynolds, *Vice Pres*
Paul Hastings, *Manager*
EMP: 15
SQ FT: 1,400
SALES (est): 1.5MM **Privately Held**
WEB: www.seasupplies.com
SIC: 2819 3646 Industrial inorganic chemicals; commercial indusl & institutional electric lighting fixtures

(G-13634)
SCORE INTERNATIONAL
137 Commercial St Ste 300 (11803-2410)
PHONE..................407 322-3230
Henry Hardy, *President*
John Millonig IV, *Vice Pres*
Rosemary Starnes, *Purchasing*
Joanne Crespo, *Treasurer*
◆ **EMP:** 20
SQ FT: 9,000
SALES (est): 4.3MM **Privately Held**
WEB: www.scoredental.com
SIC: 3843 7699 Dental tools; dental instrument repair

(G-13635)
SPIN HOLDCO INC (DH)
303 Sunnyside Blvd # 70 (11803-1597)
PHONE..................516 349-8555
Bob Doyl, *Principal*
EMP: 1
SALES (est): 168.1MM
SALES (corp-wide): 333.8MM **Privately Held**
SIC: 3633 5087 Household laundry equipment; laundry equipment & supplies
HQ: Csc Serviceworks, Inc
303 Sunnyside Blvd # 70
Plainview NY 11803
516 349-8555

(G-13636)
STEVAL GRAPHICS CONCEPTS INC
Also Called: Graphic Concepts
7 Fairchild Ct Ste 200 (11803-1734)
PHONE..................516 576-0220
Fax: 516 576-2002
Stephen Trigg, *CEO*
EMP: 12
SQ FT: 5,000
SALES (est): 760K **Privately Held**
SIC: 2752 Commercial printing, offset

(G-13637)
SUPREME SCREW PRODUCTS INC
10 Skyline Dr Unit B (11803-2517)
PHONE..................718 293-6600
Fax: 718 293-6602
Misha Migdal, *Ch of Bd*
Gerald Lopez, *President*
Reinaldo Lopez, *Vice Pres*
EMP: 17 **EST:** 1963
SQ FT: 11,000
SALES (est): 4.5MM **Privately Held**
SIC: 3451 Screw machine products

GEOGRAPHIC SECTION

Plattsburgh - Clinton County (G-13661)

(G-13638)
TECHNIC INC
Also Called: Advanced Technology Division
111 E Ames Ct Unit 2 (11803-2311)
PHONE..................................516 349-0700
Rob Sheddy, *Branch Mgr*
EMP: 15
SALES (corp-wide): 125.9MM **Privately Held**
WEB: www.technic.com
SIC: 2899 3559 Metal treating compounds; electroplating machinery & equipment
PA: Technic, Inc.
47 Molter St
Cranston RI 02910
401 781-6100

(G-13639)
TRANE US INC
245 Newtown Rd Ste 500 (11803-4300)
PHONE..................................631 952-9477
Fax: 631 269-3601
Steve Wey, *District Mgr*
Eric Barkowitz, *Branch Mgr*
Richard Hailey, *Manager*
Deborah Hole, *Manager*
EMP: 20 **Privately Held**
SIC: 3585 Refrigeration & heating equipment
HQ: Trane U.S. Inc.
1 Centennial Ave Ste 101
Piscataway NJ 08854
732 652-7100

(G-13640)
ULTRA FINE JEWELRY MFG
180 Dupont St Unit C (11803-1616)
PHONE..................................516 349-2848
Benjamin Matalon, *President*
Sandra Matalon, *Vice Pres*
▲ **EMP:** 20 **EST:** 1978
SALES (est): 1.3MM **Privately Held**
SIC: 3911 Jewelry, precious metal

(G-13641)
VASOMEDICAL INC (PA)
137 Commercial St Ste 200 (11803-2410)
PHONE..................................516 997-4600
Fax: 516 997-2299
Joshua Markowitz, *Ch of Bd*
David Lieberman, *Vice Ch Bd*
Jun MA, *President*
Peter C Castle, *COO*
Randy Hill, *Senior VP*
▲ **EMP:** 23
SQ FT: 8,700
SALES: 57MM **Publicly Held**
WEB: www.vasomedical.com
SIC: 3845 3841 Electromedical equipment; surgical & medical instruments

(G-13642)
VASOMEDICAL SOLUTIONS INC
137 Commercial St Ste 200 (11803-2410)
PHONE..................................516 997-4600
Jai Daodat, *Accountant*
EMP: 99 **EST:** 2013
SALES (est): 9.5MM
SALES (corp-wide): 57MM **Publicly Held**
SIC: 3841 Diagnostic apparatus, medical
PA: Vasomedical, Inc.
137 Commercial St Ste 200
Plainview NY 11803
516 997-4600

(G-13643)
VEECO INSTRUMENTS INC
Also Called: Veeco Process Equipment
1 Terminal Dr (11803-2313)
PHONE..................................516 349-8300
Susan Troncale, *Engineer*
Emmanuel Lakios, *Branch Mgr*
Jim Hopkins, *Network Enginr*
EMP: 150
SALES (corp-wide): 477MM **Publicly Held**
WEB: www.veeco.com
SIC: 3612 5932 Transformers, except electric; building materials, secondhand
PA: Veeco Instruments Inc.
1 Terminal Dr
Plainview NY 11803
516 677-0200

(G-13644)
VEECO INSTRUMENTS INC (PA)
1 Terminal Dr (11803-2313)
PHONE..................................516 677-0200
Fax: 516 349-6232
John R Peeler, *Ch of Bd*
William J Miller, *President*
John P Kiernan, *Senior VP*
John Kiernan, *Senior VP*
Ajit Paranjpe, *Senior VP*
▲ **EMP:** 277
SQ FT: 80,000
SALES: 477MM **Publicly Held**
WEB: www.veeco.com
SIC: 3559 Semiconductor manufacturing machinery

(G-13645)
VEECO PROCESS EQUIPMENT INC (HQ)
1 Terminal Dr (11803-2313)
PHONE..................................516 677-0200
John R Peeler, *CEO*
Russell Low, *President*
David Glass, *Exec VP*
Bill Miller, *Exec VP*
John Kiernan, *Senior VP*
EMP: 178
SQ FT: 18,000
SALES (est): 183.5MM
SALES (corp-wide): 477MM **Publicly Held**
SIC: 3569 Assembly machines, non-metalworking
PA: Veeco Instruments Inc.
1 Terminal Dr
Plainview NY 11803
516 677-0200

(G-13646)
WILLIAM CHARLES PRTG CO INC
7 Fairchild Ct Ste 100 (11803-1701)
PHONE..................................516 349-0900
Fax: 516 349-0935
Chris Pellegrini, *President*
Joseph Pelligrini, *President*
Charles Pelligrini, *Principal*
Ed Simon, *Cust Mgr*
Jeanne Marin, *Marketing Mgr*
EMP: 35 **EST:** 1935
SQ FT: 17,000
SALES (est): 5.8MM **Privately Held**
WEB: www.williamcharlesprinting.com
SIC: 2752 2759 2789 Commercial printing, offset; letterpress printing; bookbinding & related work

(G-13647)
XPRESS PRINTING INC
Also Called: T L X
7 Fairchild Ct Ste 100 (11803-1701)
PHONE..................................516 605-1000
Chris Moscatl, *President*
EMP: 8
SQ FT: 60,000
SALES (est): 816K **Privately Held**
SIC: 2759 Promotional printing

(G-13648)
Y & Z PRECISION INC
Also Called: Y & Z Precision Machine Shop
155 E Ames Ct Unit 4 (11803-2300)
PHONE..................................516 349-8243
Fax: 516 349-7615
Zoltan Vays, *President*
Ryszard Dobrogowski, *Admin Sec*
EMP: 15
SQ FT: 7,400
SALES (est): 2.5MM **Privately Held**
SIC: 3671 Electron tubes

Plattsburgh
Clinton County

(G-13649)
A D K DENTAL LAB
87 Hammond Ln (12901-2000)
PHONE..................................518 563-6093
Robert Squire, *Owner*
EMP: 5
SQ FT: 7,000
SALES (est): 250K **Privately Held**
SIC: 3843 Dental laboratory equipment

(G-13650)
ADIRONDACK PENNYSAVER INC
177 Margaret St (12901-1837)
PHONE..................................518 563-0100
Fax: 518 562-0303
Corinne Rigby, *President*
Mark Rigby, *Corp Secy*
EMP: 25
SQ FT: 5,000
SALES (est): 2.2MM **Privately Held**
WEB: www.adkpennysaver.com
SIC: 2741 2759 Shopping news: publishing & printing; commercial printing

(G-13651)
APGN INC
Also Called: Apg Neuros
160 Banker Rd (12901-7309)
PHONE..................................518 324-4150
Omar Hammoud, *Branch Mgr*
EMP: 19
SALES (corp-wide): 27.4MM **Privately Held**
SIC: 3564 Blowing fans: industrial or commercial
HQ: Apgn Inc
1270 Boul Michele-Bohec
Blainville QC J7C 5
450 939-0799

(G-13652)
AWR ENERGY INC
35 Melody Ln (12901-6414)
P.O. Box 3027 (12901-0298)
PHONE..................................585 469-7750
Steve Baiocchi, *President*
George Klemann, *Treasurer*
EMP: 10
SALES (est): 911.9K **Privately Held**
SIC: 3511 Turbines & turbine generator sets

(G-13653)
B3CG INTERCONNECT USA INC
1523 Military Tpke # 200 (12901-7457)
PHONE..................................450 491-4040
Stefan Baumans, *President*
Marc Brosseau, *Vice Pres*
EMP: 17 **EST:** 2008
SALES (est): 2.8MM
SALES (corp-wide): 37.2MM **Privately Held**
SIC: 3679 Harness assemblies for electronic use: wire or cable
HQ: B3cg Interconnect Inc
310 Boul Industriel
Saint-Eustache QC J7R 5
450 491-4040

(G-13654)
BIOTECH ENERGY INC
Also Called: Biotech Energy Systems
35a Smithfield Blvd (12901-2111)
PHONE..................................800 340-1387
Bradley Noviski, *Vice Pres*
EMP: 6 **EST:** 2015
SALES (est): 237.7K **Privately Held**
SIC: 3433 Burners, furnaces, boilers & stokers

(G-13655)
BOMBARDIER MASS TRANSIT CORP
71 Wall St (12901-3755)
PHONE..................................518 566-0150
Fax: 518 566-0052
William Spurr, *President*
Serge Planchet, *General Mgr*
Rene Lalande, *Vice Pres*
James Tooley, *Vice Pres*
Mike Mitchell, *Opers Staff*
▲ **EMP:** 380
SALES (est): 82.7MM
SALES (corp-wide): 2.7B **Privately Held**
SIC: 3743 Railroad equipment
HQ: Brp Us Inc.
10101 Science Dr
Sturtevant WI 53177
715 842-8886

(G-13656)
BRUSHTECH (DISC) INC
4 Matt Ave (12901-3736)
P.O. Box 1130 (12901-0068)
PHONE..................................518 563-8420
Fax: 518 563-0581
Nora Gunjian, *President*
Zaven Gunjian, *Vice Pres*
Ralph Downey, *Plant Mgr*
▲ **EMP:** 18
SQ FT: 34,000
SALES (est): 3.3MM **Privately Held**
WEB: www.brushtech.com
SIC: 3991 Brushes, household or industrial

(G-13657)
CAMSO MANUFACTURING USA LTD (HQ)
1 Martina Cir (12901-7421)
PHONE..................................518 561-7528
Fax: 518 561-7651
Ivan Warmuth, *Ch of Bd*
Mario Bouchard, *Treasurer*
Wanda Haby, *Human Res Mgr*
Pierre Milot, *Director*
▲ **EMP:** 70
SALES (est): 14.8MM
SALES (corp-wide): 999.2MM **Privately Held**
SIC: 3061 Oil & gas field machinery rubber goods (mechanical)
PA: Camso Inc
2633 Rue Macpherson
Magog QC J1X 0
819 823-1777

(G-13658)
CEIT CORP
625 State Route 3 Unit 2 (12901-6530)
PHONE..................................518 825-0649
Fax: 518 825-0651
▲ **EMP:** 10
SQ FT: 15,000
SALES (est): 950K **Privately Held**
SIC: 3648 Mfg Lighting Equipment

(G-13659)
CINTUBE LTD
139 Distribution Way (12901-3734)
PHONE..................................518 324-3333
EMP: 10
SALES (est): 1.2MM **Privately Held**
SIC: 3399 Primary metal products

(G-13660)
COMMUNITY NEWSPAPER GROUP LLC
Also Called: Plattsburgh Press-Republican
170 Margaret St (12901-1838)
P.O. Box 459 (12901-0459)
PHONE..................................518 565-4114
Fax: 518 561-3362
Kevin Richard, *President*
Bob Parks, *Branch Mgr*
Jim Dynko, *Manager*
EMP: 28 **Privately Held**
WEB: www.clintonnc.com
SIC: 2711 Newspapers: publishing only, not printed on site
HQ: Community Newspaper Group, Llc
3500 Colonnade Pkwy # 600
Birmingham AL 35243

(G-13661)
DENTON PUBLICATIONS INC
Also Called: Free Trader
21 Mckinley Ave Ste 3 (12901-3800)
PHONE..................................518 561-9680
Cindy Tucker, *General Mgr*
James Fields, *Manager*
EMP: 20
SALES (corp-wide): 10.1MM **Privately Held**
WEB: www.denpubs.com
SIC: 2711 2721 Commercial printing & newspaper publishing combined; periodicals
PA: Denton Publications, Inc.
14 Hand Ave
Elizabethtown NY 12932
518 873-6368

Plattsburgh - Clinton County (G-13662) — GEOGRAPHIC SECTION

(G-13662)
EURO GEAR (USA) INC
1 Cumberland Ave (12901-1833)
PHONE...............................518 578-1775
Eloise Beauche, *Branch Mgr*
EMP: 8
SALES (corp-wide): 5.3MM **Privately Held**
SIC: 3241 3599 Natural cement; machine & other job shop work
PA: Euro Gear (Usa), Inc.
  1395 Brickell Ave Ste 800
  Miami FL 33131
  518 578-1775

(G-13663)
GBG DENIM USA LLC
Also Called: Buffalo
14 Area Dev Dr Ste 200 (12901)
PHONE...............................646 839-7000
EMP: 5
SALES (est): 230.7K **Privately Held**
SIC: 2325 2339 5651 Jeans: men's, youths' & boys'; jeans: women's, misses' & juniors'; jeans stores

(G-13664)
GEORGIA-PACIFIC LLC
327 Margaret St (12901-1719)
PHONE...............................518 561-3500
Fax: 518 562-6598
Kirk Stallsmith, *Vice Pres*
Mike Bell, *Maint Spvr*
Ray Desso, *QC Dir*
Gary Frenia, *Manager*
Judy Tallada, *Manager*
EMP: 540
SQ FT: 14,464
SALES (corp-wide): 26.7B **Privately Held**
WEB: www.gp.com
SIC: 2621 2676 Paper mills; sanitary paper products
HQ: Georgia-Pacific Llc
  133 Peachtree St Ne # 4810
  Atlanta GA 30303
  404 652-4000

(G-13665)
GRAYMONT MATERIALS (NY) INC (HQ)
111 Quarry Rd (12901-6215)
PHONE...............................518 561-5321
Stephane Godin, *CEO*
Todd Kempainen, *President*
Jim Wossar, *Site Mgr*
Debora L Richards, *Treasurer*
Scott Bombard, *Sales Staff*
EMP: 68 EST: 1943
SQ FT: 5,000
SALES (est): 25.8MM
SALES (corp-wide): 260.9MM **Privately Held**
WEB: www.graymont-ab.com
SIC: 1429 3273 2951 Grits mining (crushed stone); ready-mixed concrete; asphalt & asphaltic paving mixtures (not from refineries)
PA: Graymont Inc
  301 S 700 E 3950
  Salt Lake City UT 84102
  801 262-3942

(G-13666)
GRAYMONT MATERIALS (NY) INC
Also Called: Potsdam Stone Concrete
111 Quarry Rd (12901-6215)
PHONE...............................315 265-8036
Fax: 315 265-3402
Judy Fuhr, *Superintendent*
Dave Gordon, *Plant Mgr*
Donny Smith, *Manager*
EMP: 17
SQ FT: 3,769
SALES (corp-wide): 260.9MM **Privately Held**
WEB: www.graymont-ab.com
SIC: 3273 5083 Ready-mixed concrete; landscaping equipment
HQ: Graymont Materials (Ny) Inc.
  111 Quarry Rd
  Plattsburgh NY 12901
  518 561-5321

(G-13667)
GRAYMONT MATERIALS INC
Also Called: Plattsburgh Quarry
111 Quarry Rd (12901-6215)
PHONE...............................518 561-5200
Todd Kempainen, *President*
EMP: 28
SALES (est): 692.7K **Privately Held**
SIC: 3281 2951 Stone, quarrying & processing of own stone products; asphalt paving mixtures & blocks

(G-13668)
HANET PLASTICS USA INC
139 Distribution Way (12901-3734)
PHONE...............................518 324-5850
EMP: 5
SALES (est): 370K **Privately Held**
SIC: 2821 Mfg Plastic Materials/Resins

(G-13669)
HERITAGE PRINTING CENTER
94 Margaret St (12901-2925)
PHONE...............................518 563-8240
Fax: 518 563-9377
Roger A Conant, *Partner*
Roger W Conant, *Partner*
EMP: 7 EST: 1976
SQ FT: 2,200
SALES (est): 590K **Privately Held**
WEB: www.heritageprint.com
SIC: 2752 Commercial printing, offset

(G-13670)
IEC HOLDEN CORPORATION
51 Distribution Way (12901-3731)
PHONE...............................518 213-3991
Robert Briscoe, *Ch of Bd*
EMP: 19
SALES (est): 3.6MM **Privately Held**
SIC: 3621 Inverters, rotating: electrical

(G-13671)
INTRAPAC INTERNATIONAL CORP
4 Plant St (12901-3771)
PHONE...............................518 561-2030
Steve Braido, *Plant Mgr*
Marlon Moreno, *Plant Mgr*
Tony Searing, *Plant Mgr*
Robert Thiessen, *Plant Mgr*
Rick Gahagen, *Accounts Exec*
EMP: 150
SALES (corp-wide): 120MM **Privately Held**
SIC: 3085 3221 Plastics bottles; glass containers
PA: Intrapac International Corporation
  136 Fairview Rd Ste 320
  Mooresville NC 28117
  704 360-8910

(G-13672)
ISLAND MACHINE INC
86 Boynton Ave (12901-1236)
PHONE...............................518 562-1232
Fax: 518 561-0307
Marvin C Benton, *President*
Marvin Benton, *President*
Bonnie Benton, *Vice Pres*
EMP: 9
SQ FT: 2,100
SALES: 600K **Privately Held**
SIC: 3599 Machine & other job shop work

(G-13673)
JOHNS MANVILLE CORPORATION
1 Kaycee Loop Rd (12901-2010)
PHONE...............................518 565-3000
Fax: 518 565-3010
Tim Barnewall, *Safety Dir*
David Hardway, *Production*
Steve Kuhn, *Manager*
EMP: 28
SALES (corp-wide): 210.8B **Publicly Held**
WEB: www.jm.com
SIC: 2952 Roofing materials
HQ: Johns Manville Corporation
  717 17th St Ste 800
  Denver CO 80202
  303 978-2000

(G-13674)
KNORR BRAKE COMPANY LLC
613 State Route 3 Unit 1 (12901-6530)
PHONE...............................518 561-1387
Fax: 518 561-1344
Phil Rockwell, *Site Mgr*
EMP: 6 **Privately Held**
WEB: www.knorrbrakecorp.com
SIC: 3743 Brakes, air & vacuum: railway; rapid transit cars & equipment
HQ: Knorr Brake Company Llc
  1 Arthur Peck Dr
  Westminster MD 21157
  410 875-0900

(G-13675)
LAKESIDE CONTAINER CORP (PA)
299 Arizona Ave (12903-4429)
P.O. Box 845 (12901-0845)
PHONE...............................518 561-6150
George Bouyea, *President*
Paige Raville, *Vice Pres*
Miki Worden, *Program Mgr*
Dennis Carrier, *Manager*
EMP: 19 EST: 1958
SQ FT: 65,000
SALES (est): 2.1MM **Privately Held**
WEB: www.lakesidecontainer.com
SIC: 2653 Boxes, corrugated: made from purchased materials

(G-13676)
LEROUX FUELS
994 Military Tpke (12901-5926)
PHONE...............................518 563-3653
Nicholas Leroux, *Principal*
EMP: 9
SALES (est): 1.6MM **Privately Held**
SIC: 2869 Fuels

(G-13677)
MATROX GRAPHICS INC
625 State Route 3 1/2 (12901-6530)
PHONE...............................518 561-4417
Robert Lasalle Jr, *Manager*
EMP: 8
SALES (corp-wide): 14.8MM **Privately Held**
SIC: 3572 Computer tape drives & components
PA: Graphiques Matrox Inc
  1055 Boul Saint-Regis
  Dorval QC H9P 2
  514 822-6000

(G-13678)
MOLD-RITE PLASTICS LLC (HQ)
1 Plant St (12901-3788)
P.O. Box 160 (12901-0160)
PHONE...............................518 561-0017
Fax: 518 561-0017
Brian Bauerbach, *President*
Dennis Houpt, *Senior VP*
Barry Daggett, *Vice Pres*
Keith Kelble, *Opers Mgr*
Rick Gardner, *Facilities Mgr*
◆ EMP: 208
SQ FT: 335,000
SALES (est): 119.6MM
SALES (corp-wide): 1.5B **Privately Held**
WEB: www.mrpcap.com
SIC: 3089 Closures, plastic
PA: Irving Place Capital, Llc
  745 5th Ave Fl 7
  New York NY 10151
  212 551-4500

(G-13679)
MONAGHAN MEDICAL CORPORATION (PA)
5 Latour Ave Ste 1600 (12901-7271)
PHONE...............................518 561-7330
Fax: 518 561-5660
Gerald Slemko, *President*
Dominic Coppolo, *Vice Pres*
William Seitz, *Vice Pres*
Dick Thayer, *Purchasing*
Ronald Grahm, *Controller*
▲ EMP: 52
SALES (est): 11.9MM **Privately Held**
WEB: www.monaghanmed.com
SIC: 3841 Surgical & medical instruments

(G-13680)
NORTH AMERICAN DOOR CORP
Also Called: Nadcor
1471 Military Tpke (12901-7453)
PHONE...............................518 566-0161
Fax: 518 566-6172
Antonio Gervasi, *President*
Anna Montesano, *Corp Secy*
Bruno Gervasi, *Vice Pres*
Connie Carrozza, *Office Mgr*
▼ EMP: 12
SQ FT: 20,000
SALES (est): 4MM **Privately Held**
WEB: www.nadcor.com
SIC: 3442 Metal doors, sash & trim

(G-13681)
NORTHEAST CONCRETE PDTS INC
1024 Military Tpke (12901-5959)
PHONE...............................518 563-0700
Arthur Spiegel, *President*
James L Neverett, *Senior VP*
Darren C Babbie, *Vice Pres*
Suzanne Arlt, *Finance Dir*
Jill Friedrich, *Administration*
EMP: 15 EST: 1938
SQ FT: 31,500
SALES (est): 1.4MM **Privately Held**
WEB: www.concretebuildingsupply.com
SIC: 3272 Precast terrazo or concrete products

(G-13682)
NORTHEAST GROUP
Also Called: Strictly Business
12 Nepco Way (12903-3961)
PHONE...............................518 563-8214
Herb Carpenter, *Partner*
Mary Carpenter, *Partner*
Mike Carpenter, *Partner*
Travis Carter, *Manager*
▲ EMP: 55
SALES (est): 7.3MM **Privately Held**
WEB: www.sbmonthly.com
SIC: 2721 Periodicals

(G-13683)
NORTHEAST PRTG & DIST CO INC (PA)
12 Nepco Way (12903-3961)
PHONE...............................518 563-8214
Fax: 518 563-3320
Herb Carpenter, *President*
Mary E Carpenter, *Vice Pres*
Michael Carpenter, *Vice Pres*
Marcia Vicencio, *Purch Mgr*
Donna Martin, *CFO*
▲ EMP: 44
SQ FT: 115,000
SALES (est): 7.5MM **Privately Held**
WEB: www.thenortheastgroup.com
SIC: 2752 Commercial printing, offset

(G-13684)
PACTIV LLC
74 Weed St (12901-1260)
PHONE...............................518 562-6101
Michael Petit, *Plant Mgr*
Tony Scaring, *Plant Mgr*
Matt Labombard, *QC Mgr*
Mark Lowther, *Engineer*
Damijan Vujanovic, *Engineer*
EMP: 200
SQ FT: 64,904 **Privately Held**
WEB: www.pactiv.com
SIC: 2656 2657 2671 Plates, paper: made from purchased material; food containers, folding: made from purchased material; packaging paper & plastics film, coated & laminated
HQ: Pactiv Llc
  1900 W Field Ct
  Lake Forest IL 60045
  847 482-2000

(G-13685)
PACTIV LLC
74 Weed St (12901-1260)
PHONE...............................518 562-6120
Anthony Searing, *Manager*
EMP: 120 **Privately Held**
WEB: www.pactiv.com
SIC: 3089 Plastic containers, except foam

GEOGRAPHIC SECTION

HQ: Pactiv Llc
1900 W Field Ct
Lake Forest IL 60045
847 482-2000

(G-13686)
PERFORMANCE DIESEL SERVICE LLC
24 Latour Ave (12901-7206)
PHONE..................................315 854-5269
Scott Roketenetz,
EMP: 11
SALES (est): 1.8MM **Privately Held**
SIC: 2911 Diesel fuels

(G-13687)
PLATTCO CORPORATION (PA)
7 White St (12901-3471)
PHONE..................................518 563-4640
Fax: 518 563-4892
Douglas J Crozierm, *Ch of Bd*
Dean Surprenant, *Production*
Stacie Chapman, *Purch Mgr*
Logan Miller, *Design Engr*
Dianne Lynch, *Sales Staff*
▲ **EMP:** 50 **EST:** 1897
SQ FT: 60,000
SALES (est): 7.3MM **Privately Held**
WEB: www.plattco.com
SIC: 3369 3491 3322 Machinery castings, nonferrous: ex. alum., copper, die, etc.; industrial valves; malleable iron foundries

(G-13688)
PLATTSBURGH SHEET METAL INC
95 Sailly Ave (12901-1726)
PHONE..................................518 561-4930
Sandra Carlo, *President*
EMP: 5
SALES: 1MM **Privately Held**
SIC: 3444 Sheet metalwork

(G-13689)
PREVOST CAR US INC
Also Called: Nova Bus Lfs, A Division of PR
260 Banker Rd (12901-7310)
PHONE..................................518 957-2052
Corrine Govinden, *Controller*
Mathew Nadal, *Sales Mgr*
EMP: 202
SQ FT: 140,000
SALES (est): 104.2MM **Privately Held**
SIC: 3711 Buses, all types, assembly of

(G-13690)
PRICE CHOPPER OPERATING CO
19 Centre Dr (12901-6553)
PHONE..................................518 562-3565
Tom Tsounis, *Manager*
Lori L Duprey, *Manager*
Sharon Wood, *Manager*
EMP: 11
SALES (corp-wide): 3.4B **Privately Held**
SIC: 3751 Motorcycles & related parts
HQ: Price Chopper Operating Co., Inc
501 Duanesburg Rd
Schenectady NY 12306
518 379-1600

(G-13691)
PRIM HALL ENTERPRISES INC
11 Spellman Rd (12901-5326)
PHONE..................................518 561-7408
Fax: 518 563-1472
John Prim, *President*
David Hall, *Vice Pres*
Thomas Venne, *Engineer*
Bill Kelting, *Accounts Mgr*
Mat Demers, *Manager*
EMP: 12
SQ FT: 43,000
SALES (est): 1.4MM **Privately Held**
WEB: www.primhall.com
SIC: 3555 7699 3542 7389 Printing trades machinery; industrial machinery & equipment repair; machine tools, metal forming type; design, commercial & industrial

(G-13692)
RAILTECH COMPOSITES INC
80 Montana Dr (12903-4933)
PHONE..................................518 324-6190
John Natale, *President*
Nestor Lewyckyj, *Vice Pres*
Lisa Hufnagel, *Regl Sales Mgr*
Mark Beaudoin, *Manager*
EMP: 14
SQ FT: 10,000
SALES (est): 1.9MM
SALES (corp-wide): 20MM **Privately Held**
WEB: www.railtechcomposites.com
SIC: 2439 Structural wood members
HQ: Skyfold Inc
325 Av Lee
Baie-D'urfe QC H9X 3
514 457-4767

(G-13693)
RAMBACHS INTERNATIONAL BAKERY
65 S Peru St (12901-3834)
PHONE..................................518 563-1721
Gerard Rambach, *President*
Joan Rambach, *Treasurer*
EMP: 18
SQ FT: 3,500
SALES (est): 830K **Privately Held**
SIC: 2051 Bakery: wholesale or wholesale/retail combined

(G-13694)
RAPA INDEPENDENT NORTH AMERICA
Also Called: Rina
124 Connecticut Rd (12903-4955)
PHONE..................................518 561-0513
Manil Whig, *President*
▲ **EMP:** 6
SQ FT: 5,000
SALES (est): 200K **Privately Held**
SIC: 2013 Sausage casings, natural

(G-13695)
SALERNO PLASTIC FILM (HQ)
14 Gus Lapham Ln (12901-6534)
PHONE..................................518 563-3636
Fax: 518 563-3839
Kurt Strater, *President*
Roger Sullivan, *Senior VP*
Mac Elgin, *Vice Pres*
Matt Ramsey, *Marketing Staff*
Greg Crites, *Manager*
EMP: 6
SALES (est): 33.3MM
SALES (corp-wide): 3.2MM **Privately Held**
SIC: 2673 Plastic bags: made from purchased materials
PA: Inteplast Group Corporation
9 Peach Tree Hill Rd
Livingston NJ 07039
973 994-8000

(G-13696)
SEMEC CORP
20 Gateway Dr (12901-5371)
PHONE..................................518 825-0160
Deborah Wells, *Admin Mgr*
EMP: 15
SALES (est): 1.2MM **Privately Held**
SIC: 3743 Railroad equipment

(G-13697)
SSF PRODUCTION LLC
194 Pleasant Ridge Rd (12901-5841)
PHONE..................................518 324-3407
Frank Filbir, *Mng Member*
Tilo Hilderbrand,
▲ **EMP:** 10
SQ FT: 17,000
SALES (est): 1.8MM **Privately Held**
SIC: 3296 Acoustical board & tile, mineral wool

(G-13698)
STEELE TRUSS COMPANY INC
118 Trade Rd (12901-6259)
PHONE..................................518 562-4663
Robert Steele, *CEO*
Joel C Steele, *President*
Thomas E Steele Sr, *President*
Loretta Steele, *Corp Secy*
Marvin Hooper, *VP Engrg*
EMP: 25
SQ FT: 80,000
SALES: 2MM **Privately Held**
WEB: www.steeltrusses.net
SIC: 2439 Trusses, wooden roof

(G-13699)
STERRX LLC (PA)
141 Idaho Ave (12903-3987)
PHONE..................................518 324-7879
Terry Wiley, *VP Mfg*
Gary Hanley,
EMP: 22
SALES (est): 5.9MM **Privately Held**
SIC: 2834 Solutions, pharmaceutical

(G-13700)
STERRX LLC
Also Called: Sterrx Cmo
141 Idaho Ave Ste 1 (12903-3987)
PHONE..................................518 324-7879
Terry Wiley, *VP Mfg*
EMP: 10
SALES (corp-wide): 5.9MM **Privately Held**
SIC: 2834 Water, sterile: for injections
PA: Sterrx, Llc
141 Idaho Ave
Plattsburgh NY 12903
518 324-7879

(G-13701)
STUDLEY PRINTING & PUBLISHING
Also Called: Lake Champlain Weekly
4701 State Route 9 (12901-6036)
PHONE..................................518 563-1414
Fax: 518 563-7060
William Studley, *President*
Caroline Kehne, *Editor*
Lynn Roberts-Devins, *Accounts Exec*
Kim Mousseau, *Director*
EMP: 18
SALES (est): 2.9MM **Privately Held**
WEB: www.studleyprinting.com
SIC: 2752 8743 Commercial printing, lithographic; public relations & publicity

(G-13702)
SWAROVSKI LIGHTING LTD (PA)
Also Called: Schonbek
61 Industrial Blvd (12901-1908)
PHONE..................................518 563-7500
Fax: 518 563-4228
John Simms, *CEO*
Andrew Schonbek, *President*
Scott Anderson, *COO*
Mike Stratte, *Project Mgr*
Joe Walsh, *Purch Dir*
◆ **EMP:** 267
SQ FT: 200,000
SALES (est): 59.4MM **Privately Held**
SIC: 3645 Residential lighting fixtures

(G-13703)
SWAROVSKI LIGHTING LTD
Also Called: Schonbek Shipping Bldg
1483 Military Tpke Ste B (12901-7453)
PHONE..................................518 324-6378
PR Llier, *Principal*
EMP: 400
SALES (corp-wide): 59.4MM **Privately Held**
SIC: 3645 Chandeliers, residential
PA: Swarovski Lighting, Ltd.
61 Industrial Blvd
Plattsburgh NY 12901
518 563-7500

(G-13704)
TITHERINGTON DESIGN & MFG
102 Sharron Ave Unit 1 (12903-3828)
PHONE..................................518 324-2205
Philip D Titherington, *CEO*
EMP: 11
SALES (est): 1.6MM **Privately Held**
SIC: 3089 7336 Injection molding of plastics; package design

(G-13705)
UMS MANUFACTURING LLC
194 Pleasant Ridge Rd (12901-5841)
PHONE..................................518 562-2410
Ed Martin, *Controller*
Mark Schulter,
Udo Schulter,
EMP: 10
SQ FT: 57,000
SALES: 1.2MM **Privately Held**
SIC: 2675 Waterproof cardboard: made from purchased materials

(G-13706)
VIDEOTEC SECURITY INCORPORATED
35 Gateway Dr Ste 100 (12901-5382)
PHONE..................................518 825-0020
Enrico Campana, *Research*
Edvina TSE, *Accounting Dir*
Salvatore Menna, *Sales Dir*
Marta Stocchero, *Sales Staff*
Maureen Carlo, *Marketing Staff*
▲ **EMP:** 5
SALES (est): 792.6K
SALES (corp-wide): 203.6K **Privately Held**
SIC: 3699 Security devices
HQ: Videotec Spa
Via Friuli 6
Schio VI 36015
044 569-7411

(G-13707)
WEBER INTL PACKG CO LLC
318 Cornelia St (12901-2300)
PHONE..................................518 561-8282
K Heinz Weber, *CEO*
Michael Hanley, *Engineer*
Alice Barcomb, *Finance*
Tihamer Monostori,
EMP: 54
SQ FT: 44,000
SALES (est): 13.1MM **Privately Held**
WEB: www.weberintl.com
SIC: 3085 Plastics bottles

(G-13708)
WESTINGHOUSE A BRAKE TECH CORP
72 Arizona Ave (12903-4427)
PHONE..................................518 561-0044
Bob Brassee, *Manager*
Alisa Langille, *Administration*
EMP: 70
SALES (corp-wide): 3.3B **Publicly Held**
WEB: www.wabtecglobalservices.com
SIC: 3743 Brakes, air & vacuum: railway; locomotives & parts; freight cars & equipment; rapid transit cars & equipment
PA: Westinghouse Air Brake Technologies Corporation
1001 Airbrake Ave
Wilmerding PA 15148
412 825-1000

(G-13709)
WOODFALLS INDUSTRIES
434 Burke Rd (12901-5214)
PHONE..................................518 236-7201
Tammy Deyo, *Owner*
EMP: 10 **EST:** 2010
SALES (est): 450K **Privately Held**
SIC: 3999 Manufacturing industries

(G-13710)
XBORDER ENTERTAINMENT LLC
568 State Route 3 (12901-6526)
PHONE..................................518 726-7036
Casey Spiegel, *Mng Member*
EMP: 7
SQ FT: 35,000
SALES (est): 175.8K **Privately Held**
SIC: 7372 Application computer software

Pleasant Valley
Dutchess County

(G-13711)
DETECTOR PRO
Also Called: Hudson River Met Detector Sls
1447 Route 44 (12569-7832)
PHONE..................................845 635-3488
Gary Storm, *Owner*
EMP: 5
SALES (est): 300K **Privately Held**
WEB: www.detectorpro.com
SIC: 3669 Metal detectors

Pleasantville - Westchester County (G-13712) GEOGRAPHIC SECTION

Pleasantville
Westchester County

(G-13712)
CARLARA GROUP LTD
Also Called: Sir Speedy
467 Bedford Rd (10570-2928)
PHONE..................................914 769-2020
Fax: 914 769-4680
Carlos Bernard, *President*
Susana Lara, *Vice Pres*
EMP: 5
SQ FT: 3,000
SALES (est): 580K **Privately Held**
SIC: 2752 2791 2789 Commercial printing, lithographic; typesetting; bookbinding & related work

(G-13713)
COUNTY FABRICATORS
175 Marble Ave (10570-3421)
PHONE..................................914 741-0219
Kristina Benza, *Mng Member*
Phillip R Benza,
EMP: 18
SQ FT: 13,200
SALES: 1.5MM **Privately Held**
WEB: www.countyfabricators.com
SIC: 3441 Fabricated structural metal

(G-13714)
HOME SERVICE PUBLICATIONS (DH)
1 Readers Digest Rd (10570-7000)
PHONE..................................914 238-1000
Bonnie Dachar, *President*
Clifford Dupree, *Admin Sec*
Peggy Cassin,
EMP: 5
SALES (est): 1.2MM
SALES (corp-wide): 1.7B **Privately Held**
SIC: 2741 Miscellaneous publishing
HQ: Rd Publications, Inc.
    1 Readers Digest Rd
    Pleasantville NY 10570
    914 238-1000

(G-13715)
OPTIMIZED DEVICES INC
220 Marble Ave (10570-3465)
PHONE..................................914 769-6100
Fax: 914 769-6102
Arthur Zuch, *President*
Robert Zuch, *Vice Pres*
EMP: 13
SQ FT: 6,000
SALES (est): 1.1MM **Privately Held**
WEB: www.optdev.com
SIC: 3825 Instruments to measure electricity

(G-13716)
R D MANUFACTURING CORP
Readers Digest Rd (10570)
PHONE..................................914 238-1000
Albert Perruzza, *President*
Melvin Williams, *Div Sub Head*
Bonnie Monahan, *Treasurer*
Clifford Dupree, *Admin Sec*
▲ EMP: 7
SQ FT: 500,000
SALES (est): 1.2MM
SALES (corp-wide): 1.7B **Privately Held**
WEB: www.rd.com
SIC: 2732 2759 Book printing; magazines: printing
PA: Trusted Media Brands, Inc.
    750 3rd Ave Fl 3
    New York NY 10017
    914 238-1000

(G-13717)
RD PUBLICATIONS INC (HQ)
1 Readers Digest Rd (10570-7000)
PHONE..................................914 238-1000
Thomas O Ryder, *President*
Robert J Krefting, *Senior VP*
Michael Geltzeiler, *Vice Pres*
Eric Gruseke, *Vice Pres*
George Scimone, *CFO*
EMP: 120
SQ FT: 50,000
SALES (est): 19.8MM
SALES (corp-wide): 1.7B **Privately Held**
WEB: www.rdpublications.com
SIC: 2721 Magazines: publishing only, not printed on site
PA: Trusted Media Brands, Inc.
    750 3rd Ave Fl 3
    New York NY 10017
    914 238-1000

(G-13718)
READERS DGEST LATINOAMERICA SA
Readers Digest Rd (10570)
PHONE..................................914 238-1000
Thomas O Ryder, *CEO*
Clifford H Dupree, *Corp Secy*
Mike Geltzeiler, *CFO*
William Magill, *Treasurer*
William Adler, *Director*
EMP: 500
SQ FT: 7,700
SALES: 750.2K
SALES (corp-wide): 1.7B **Privately Held**
WEB: www.rd.com
SIC: 2721 Magazines: publishing only, not printed on site
PA: Trusted Media Brands, Inc.
    750 3rd Ave Fl 3
    New York NY 10017
    914 238-1000

(G-13719)
READERS DGEST YUNG FMILIES INC
Readers Digest Rd (10570)
PHONE..................................914 238-1000
Thomas O Ryder, *Ch of Bd*
EMP: 25
SALES: 717.7K
SALES (corp-wide): 1.7B **Privately Held**
WEB: www.rd.com
SIC: 2731 Book publishing
PA: Trusted Media Brands, Inc.
    750 3rd Ave Fl 3
    New York NY 10017
    914 238-1000

(G-13720)
SAW MILL PEDIATRICS PLLC
95 Locust Rd (10570-3333)
PHONE..................................914 449-6064
Maryann Hammel, *Principal*
Maryann Hamel, *Office Mgr*
Jeanne M Wilson, *Pediatrics*
Jeannie Leclere, *Nurse Practr*
EMP: 9
SALES (est): 996.9K **Privately Held**
SIC: 2421 Sawmills & planing mills, general

(G-13721)
STAUB USA INC
270 Marble Ave (10570-3464)
PHONE..................................914 747-0300
Francis Staub, *President*
Alain Stammur, *Vice Pres*
▲ EMP: 5
SALES (est): 466.3K
SALES (corp-wide): 3.4B **Privately Held**
WEB: www.staubusa.com
SIC: 3321 Cooking utensils, cast iron
HQ: Zwilling J.A. Henckels, Llc
    270 Marble Ave
    Pleasantville NY 10570
    914 749-3440

Poestenkill
Rensselaer County

(G-13722)
CANTON BIO-MEDICAL INC (PA)
Also Called: Saint-Gobain Performance Plas
11 Sicho Rd (12140-3102)
PHONE..................................518 283-5963
Fax: 518 283-1418
John Bedell, *Principal*
Bob Pellerin, *Controller*
EMP: 36
SQ FT: 36,000
SALES (est): 2.4MM **Privately Held**
SIC: 2822 Silicone rubbers

(G-13723)
DYNAMIC SYSTEMS INC
Also Called: D S I
323 Rte 355 (12140)
P.O. Box 1234 (12140-1234)
PHONE..................................518 283-5350
Fax: 518 283-3160
David Ferguson, *President*
Peggy Jacobsen, *General Mgr*
Jean Jacon, *Vice Pres*
Todd Bonesteel, *Production*
Mark Budesheim, *Purchasing*
▲ EMP: 38
SQ FT: 29,000
SALES (est): 12.3MM **Privately Held**
WEB: www.gleeble.com
SIC: 3829 Measuring & controlling devices

(G-13724)
INTER STATE LAMINATES INC
44 Main St (12140-3201)
P.O. Box 270 (12140-0270)
PHONE..................................518 283-8355
Fax: 518 283-8358
Harold Crandall, *President*
Cheryl Littlefield, *Sales Staff*
Debbie Crandall, *Admin Sec*
EMP: 46
SALES (est): 6.1MM **Privately Held**
WEB: www.isltops.com
SIC: 3083 2541 Plastic finished products, laminated; wood partitions & fixtures

(G-13725)
SAINT-GOBAIN PRFMCE PLAS CORP
11 Sicho Rd (12140-3102)
PHONE..................................518 283-5963
Lynn Monrow, *General Mgr*
Tammy L Teal, *Manager*
EMP: 41
SALES (corp-wide): 207.6MM **Privately Held**
SIC: 3089 Spouting, plastic & glass fiber reinforced
HQ: Saint-Gobain Performance Plastics Corporation
    31500 Solon Rd
    Solon OH 44139
    440 836-6900

(G-13726)
VAN SLYKE BELTING LLC
606 Snyders Corners Rd (12140-2914)
PHONE..................................518 283-5479
H Van, *Principal*
EMP: 6
SALES (est): 652.2K **Privately Held**
SIC: 3052 Rubber belting

Poland
Herkimer County

(G-13727)
PERFEX CORPORATION
32 Case St (13431)
PHONE..................................315 826-3600
Fax: 315 826-7471
Michael E Kubick, *President*
Mike Dougherty, *Sales Staff*
Cynthia Chmielewski, *Manager*
▲ EMP: 13 EST: 1924
SQ FT: 24,000
SALES (est): 2.3MM **Privately Held**
WEB: www.perfexonline.com
SIC: 3991 2392 Brooms & brushes; mops, floor & dust

Pomona
Rockland County

(G-13728)
BARR LABORATORIES INC
2 Quaker Rd (10970-2931)
PHONE..................................845 362-1100
Fax: 845 353-3843
Connie Losito, *Senior Buyer*
Tim Breuninger, *Research*
Bruce L Downey, *Branch Mgr*
Joseph Kevra, *Manager*
Lianli LI, *Manager*
EMP: 173
SALES (corp-wide): 20.3B **Privately Held**
WEB: www.barrlabs.com
SIC: 2834 Pharmaceutical preparations
HQ: Barr Laboratories, Inc.
    1090 Horsham Rd
    North Wales PA 19454
    215 591-3000

(G-13729)
CAMBRIDGE SECURITY SEALS LLC
1 Cambridge Plz (10970-2676)
PHONE..................................845 520-4111
Brian Lyle, *VP Sales*
Elisha Tropper, *Mng Member*
▲ EMP: 20
SQ FT: 25,000
SALES (est): 6MM **Privately Held**
SIC: 3089 Injection molding of plastics

(G-13730)
ELITE SIGNS INC
238 Quaker Rd (10970-2913)
PHONE..................................718 993-7342
David Cabillis, *Ch of Bd*
Mark Cabillis, *President*
Jodie Iagnocco, *Admin Sec*
EMP: 8 EST: 1934
SQ FT: 10,000
SALES: 100K **Privately Held**
SIC: 3993 Signs & advertising specialties

(G-13731)
NUTRA-SCIENTIFICS LLC
108 Overlook Rd (10970-2115)
PHONE..................................917 238-8510
Patrice Mouehla,
EMP: 9 EST: 2012
SALES (est): 543.6K **Privately Held**
SIC: 2834 5122 Pharmaceutical preparations; pharmaceuticals

(G-13732)
PARKWAY BREAD DISTRIBUTORS INC
15 Conklin Rd (10970-3601)
PHONE..................................845 362-1221
Debra L Smith, *Principal*
EMP: 8
SALES (est): 475.9K **Privately Held**
SIC: 2051 Bread, cake & related products

(G-13733)
SAN JAE EDUCATIONAL RESOU
9 Chamberlain Ct (10970-2837)
PHONE..................................845 364-5458
James Butler, *CEO*
Sandy Butler, *President*
EMP: 4
SALES (est): 1MM **Privately Held**
WEB: www.sanjaeco.com
SIC: 7372 Educational computer software

Port Byron
Cayuga County

(G-13734)
MARTENS COUNTRY KIT PDTS LLC
1323 Towpath Rd (13140)
P.O. Box 428 (13140-0428)
PHONE..................................315 776-8821
Jill Skrupa, *Sales Staff*
Timothy Martens,
▲ EMP: 10
SALES (est): 859.8K **Privately Held**
SIC: 2099 Potatoes, dried: packaged with other ingredients

(G-13735)
MAX 200 PERFORMANCE DOG EQP
2113 State Route 31 (13140-9423)
PHONE..................................315 776-9588
Fax: 315 776-9603
Irene Lamphere, *President*
Alfred Lamphere, *Vice Pres*
Joyce Scott, *Director*
EMP: 22
SQ FT: 18,000

▲ = Import ▼ = Export
◆ = Import/Export

Port Chester
Westchester County

SALES: 1.5MM Privately Held
WEB: www.max200.com
SIC: 3199 Dog furnishings: collars, leashes, muzzles, etc.: leather

(G-13736)
PRECISION DIECUTTING INC
1381 Spring Lake Rd (13140-3375)
PHONE 315 776-8465
Norma Compson, *President*
Jamie Compson, *Vice Pres*
EMP: 6
SALES: 300K Privately Held
SIC: 2675 Die-cut paper & board; stencil board, die-cut: made from purchased materials; stencil cards, die-cut: made from purchased materials

(G-13737)
AIR STRUCTURES AMERCN TECH INC
211 S Ridge St Ste 3 (10573-3445)
PHONE 914 937-4500
Fax: 914 937-6331
Donato A Fraioli, *CEO*
Jan Ligas Jr, *Vice Pres*
Robert Tornquist, *CFO*
Julia Ross, *Sales Mgr*
Erika Britton, *Manager*
▼ **EMP:** 50
SQ FT: 2,500
SALES (est): 10MM Privately Held
WEB: www.asati.com
SIC: 2394 Tents: made from purchased materials

(G-13738)
ALBUMX CORP
Also Called: Renanssance The Book
21 Grace Church St (10573-4911)
PHONE 914 939-6878
Fax: 212 274-0128
Terry Huang, *President*
Albert Huang, *Prdtn Mgr*
Yung Kwong, *Treasurer*
Victor Huang, *Human Resources*
Tasha Homyak, *Manager*
▲ **EMP:** 80
SQ FT: 27,000
SALES (est): 7.9MM Privately Held
WEB: www.renaissancealbums.com
SIC: 2782 Albums

(G-13739)
ALWAYS PRINTING
149 Highland St (10573-3301)
PHONE 914 481-5209
Jodi McCredo, *Owner*
EMP: 5
SALES (est): 483.6K Privately Held
SIC: 2759 Commercial printing

(G-13740)
COMPOSITE FORMS INC
7 Merritt St (10573-3502)
PHONE 914 937-1808
Fax: 914 937-1952
Frank J Madonia, *CEO*
Frank Madonia Jr, *President*
Frank Madonia Sr, *Director*
EMP: 10
SQ FT: 6,500
SALES (est): 930K Privately Held
WEB: www.sidingsolutions.com
SIC: 2752 5112 Commercial printing, offset; business forms

(G-13741)
D & M ENTERPRISES INCORPORATED
Also Called: A W S
1 Mill St Ste 2 (10573-6301)
PHONE 914 937-6430
Dino Alampi, *President*
Mary Alampi, *Vice Pres*
Angie Glosser, *Consultant*
Alison Bayer, *Supervisor*
Barbara J Grote, *Admin Asst*
EMP: 8
SQ FT: 5,000

SALES: 327K Privately Held
SIC: 3088 3999 Hot tubs, plastic or fiberglass; hot tubs

(G-13742)
DESIGNS BY NOVELLO INC
505 N Main St (10573-3360)
PHONE 914 934-7711
George Bulger, *Owner*
EMP: 5
SALES (est): 440K Privately Held
SIC: 3449 Miscellaneous metalwork

(G-13743)
EAGLE INSTRUMENTS INC
35 Grove St (10573-4501)
PHONE 914 939-6843
Robert Schneider, *President*
EMP: 7
SQ FT: 4,000
SALES (est): 580K Privately Held
SIC: 3599 Machine shop, jobbing & repair

(G-13744)
EHS GROUP LLC
69 Townsend St (10573-4311)
PHONE 914 937-6162
Fax: 914 937-6365
Steven Kennedy, *President*
Lisa Cartolano, *Corp Secy*
EMP: 8
SQ FT: 6,000
SALES (est): 1.6MM Privately Held
SIC: 2759 Envelopes: printing

(G-13745)
EMPIRE COFFEE COMPANY INC
106 Purdy Ave (10573-4624)
PHONE 914 934-1100
Fax: 914 934-1190
Steven Dunefsky, *President*
Todd Good, *Manager*
Laura Thoden, *Manager*
Robert Richter, *Admin Sec*
Tasha Alicea, *Admin Asst*
EMP: 35
SQ FT: 30,000
SALES (est): 6.5MM Privately Held
WEB: www.empire-coffee.com
SIC: 2095 Coffee roasting (except by wholesale grocers)

(G-13746)
FMC INTERNATIONAL LTD
Also Called: Biologic Solutions
8 Slater St Ste 2 (10573-4984)
PHONE 914 935-0918
Harvey Fishman, *President*
Peter Blumenthal, *CFO*
EMP: 2
SALES: 2MM Privately Held
WEB: www.biologicsolutions.com
SIC: 2844 Toilet preparations

(G-13747)
GMP LLC
Also Called: Graphic Management Partners
47 Purdy Ave Ste 2 (10573-5043)
PHONE 914 939-0571
Fax: 914 939-1670
Stuart Levinson, *Vice Pres*
Ellen Moman, *Controller*
Leah Karosos, *Credit Mgr*
Rosanna Burgio, *Human Res Mgr*
Felix A Lugo, *Accounts Mgr*
EMP: 86
SQ FT: 20,000
SALES: 12.6MM Privately Held
SIC: 2752 Promotional printing, lithographic

(G-13748)
GOOD BREAD BAKERY
Also Called: Best Bread
33 New Broad St Ste 1 (10573-4651)
PHONE 914 939-3900
Fax: 914 939-2513
Michael Beldotti, *Owner*
Chris Beldotti, *Owner*
EMP: 15
SALES (est): 1.4MM Privately Held
SIC: 2051 Bakery: wholesale or wholesale/retail combined

(G-13749)
INTEGRATED SOLAR TECH LLC
181 Westchester Ave (10573-4534)
PHONE 914 249-9364
Oliver Koehler, *CEO*
EMP: 5
SQ FT: 500
SALES (est): 289.6K Privately Held
SIC: 3433 Solar heaters & collectors

(G-13750)
JJ CASSONE BAKERY INC
202 S Regent St (10573-4791)
PHONE 914 939-1568
Fax: 914 939-3811
Mary Lou Cassone, *President*
Linda Fitzpatrick, *COO*
Dominic Ambrose, *Vice Pres*
Tony Crusco, *Vice Pres*
Jack Guarcello, *Vice Pres*
▲ **EMP:** 280
SQ FT: 180,000
SALES (est): 54.9MM Privately Held
WEB: www.jjcassone.com
SIC: 2051 5461 Bread, cake & related products; bread, all types (white, wheat, rye, etc): fresh or frozen; bakeries

(G-13751)
LANZA CORP
Also Called: Sign Design
404 Willett Ave (10573-3132)
PHONE 914 937-6360
Fax: 914 939-0105
Joseph Lanza, *President*
Ray Carpenter, *General Mgr*
Nicholas Pagnozzi, *Technical Mgr*
EMP: 9
SQ FT: 4,000
SALES (est): 1.3MM Privately Held
WEB: www.clicksignage.com
SIC: 3993 2394 7389 5999 Signs & advertising specialties; electric signs; neon signs; canvas awnings & canopies; sign painting & lettering shop; awnings, carved & turned wood; sign installation & maintenance

(G-13752)
LONGFORDS ICE CREAM LTD
Also Called: Longford's Own
151 Wilkins Ave (10573-3324)
PHONE 914 935-9469
Nolan West, *President*
Patricia Sudbay West, *Vice Pres*
Ralph Pietrasesa, *CTO*
EMP: 12
SQ FT: 3,000
SALES: 1.2MM Privately Held
WEB: www.longfordsicecream.com
SIC: 2024 5143 Ice cream & frozen desserts; dairy products, except dried or canned

(G-13753)
MAGJAK PRINTING CORPORATION
Also Called: Magjak Graphic Communications
114 Pearl St (10573-4663)
PHONE 914 939-8800
Fax: 914 933-0392
Bruce Browning, *President*
Tom Marron, *Vice Pres*
Margaret Goldberg, *Treasurer*
EMP: 9
SQ FT: 7,500
SALES: 3MM Privately Held
SIC: 2752 Commercial printing, lithographic

(G-13754)
MATTHEW SHIVELY LLC
28 Bulkley Ave (10573-3902)
PHONE 914 937-3531
Matthew Shively,
EMP: 7
SQ FT: 5,000
SALES (est): 300.4K Privately Held
SIC: 2519 Household furniture

(G-13755)
NATIONAL PROF RESOURCES
Also Called: Dude Publishing
25 S Regent St Ste 2 (10573-3512)
PHONE 914 937-8879
Fax: 914 937-9327

Robert Hanson, *President*
Andrea Cerone, *Graphic Designe*
EMP: 20
SALES (est): 1.9MM Privately Held
WEB: www.nprinc.com
SIC: 2721 5192 5099 8748 Periodicals: publishing only; books, periodicals & newspapers; video & audio equipment; educational consultant

(G-13756)
PARSONS & WHITTEMORE INC (HQ)
4 International Dr # 300 (10573-1064)
PHONE 914 937-9009
Arthur L Schwartz, *President*
George F Landegger, *Chairman*
Robert H Masson, *Vice Pres*
Steve Sweeney, *Vice Pres*
Jose Alvelo, *Treasurer*
EMP: 40 **EST:** 1853
SQ FT: 16,650
SALES (est): 59.3MM
SALES (corp-wide): 85.6MM Privately Held
SIC: 2611 Pulp mills
PA: Parsons & Whittemore Enterprises Corp.
  4 International Dr # 300
  Port Chester NY 10573
  914 937-9009

(G-13757)
PARSONS WHITTEMORE ENTPS CORP (PA)
4 International Dr # 300 (10573-1064)
PHONE 914 937-9009
George F Landegger, *Ch of Bd*
Carl C Landegger, *Vice Ch Bd*
Steven Sweeney, *CFO*
Frank Grasso, *Treasurer*
EMP: 25
SQ FT: 16,650
SALES (est): 85.6MM Privately Held
SIC: 2611 Pulp mills

(G-13758)
QUEMERE INTERNATIONAL
330 N Main St (10573-3307)
PHONE 914 934-8366
Fax: 914 934-8401
Celine Quemere, *Owner*
EMP: 8
SALES (est): 619.7K Privately Held
SIC: 3253 Ceramic wall & floor tile

(G-13759)
STEILMANN EUROPEAN SELECTIONS
354 N Main St (10573-3307)
PHONE 914 997-0015
Bruni Butschek, *President*
Paul Knerr, *VP Sales*
EMP: 60
SALES: 2.2MM
SALES (corp-wide): 1.4B Privately Held
SIC: 2339 Sportswear, women's
HQ: Klaus Steilmann Gmbh & Co. Kg
  Industriestr. 24
  Bergkamen 59192
  238 990-070

(G-13760)
SWISSBIT NA INC
18 Willett Ave 202 (10573-4326)
PHONE 914 935-1400
Anthony Cerreta, *President*
Grady Lambert, *Business Mgr*
Roland Ochoa, *Engineer*
David Gray, *Sales Associate*
Rae Lingblom, *Office Mgr*
EMP: 3
SQ FT: 2,050
SALES: 20MM Privately Held
WEB: www.swissbitna.com
SIC: 3674 Semiconductors & related devices
HQ: Swissbit Ag
  Industriestrasse 4-8
  Bronschhofen SG
  719 130-303

Port Chester - Westchester County

(G-13761)
WESTMORE NEWS INC
Also Called: America Latina
38 Broad St Ste 1 (10573-4197)
PHONE..............................914 939-6864
Fax: 914 939-6877
Richard Abel, *President*
Jananne Abel, *Corp Secy*
Angie Storino, *Assistant*
EMP: 9
SQ FT: 3,000
SALES (est): 500K Privately Held
WEB: www.westmorenews.com
SIC: 2711 Newspapers: publishing only, not printed on site

(G-13762)
ZYLOWARE CORPORATION (PA)
Also Called: Zyloware Eyewear
8 Slater St Ste 1 (10573-4984)
PHONE..............................914 708-1200
Christopher Shyer, *President*
Robert Shyer, *Principal*
Jennifer Derryberry, *Vice Pres*
James Shyer, *Vice Pres*
Carol Ambler, *Sales Mgr*
▲ EMP: 66
SQ FT: 21,000
SALES (est): 13.5MM Privately Held
WEB: www.zyloware.com
SIC: 3851 Frames & parts, eyeglass & spectacle

Port Jeff STA
Suffolk County

(G-13763)
BILTRON AUTOMOTIVE PRODUCTS
509 Bicycle Path Unit Q (11776-3491)
PHONE..............................631 928-8613
Fax: 631 928-5028
Ron Stoll, *President*
David Gayle, *Controller*
▲ EMP: 30
SQ FT: 21,000
SALES (est): 4.4MM Privately Held
WEB: www.biltronauto.com
SIC: 3714 3566 3462 Steering mechanisms, motor vehicle; speed changers, drives & gears; iron & steel forgings

(G-13764)
CABLE YOUR WORLD INC
1075 Route 112 Ste 4 (11776-8050)
P.O. Box 1214, Miller Place (11764-1154)
PHONE..............................631 509-1180
Eric Levy, *President*
EMP: 4
SQ FT: 3,000
SALES (est): 1.2MM Privately Held
SIC: 3357 Fiber optic cable (insulated)

(G-13765)
COLUMBIA METAL FABRICATORS
801 Hallock Ave (11776-1226)
PHONE..............................631 476-7527
Dean T Hough, *Ch of Bd*
Don Hoeffner, *General Mgr*
EMP: 6 EST: 1997
SALES (est): 500K Privately Held
SIC: 3441 Fabricated structural metal

(G-13766)
DESIGN/OL INC
200 Wilson St Unit D2 (11776-1150)
PHONE..............................631 474-5536
Fax: 631 474-9310
William Delongis, *President*
August Oetting, *Vice Pres*
Chris Siemes, *Finance Mgr*
EMP: 16
SQ FT: 12,500
SALES: 2.5MM Privately Held
WEB: www.design-ol.com
SIC: 3728 Aircraft assemblies, subassemblies & parts

(G-13767)
NORTH SHORE HOME IMPROVER
200 Wilson St (11776-1100)
PHONE..............................631 474-2824
David Kielhurn, *CEO*
EMP: 16
SALES (est): 910K Privately Held
WEB: www.lihomeshows.com
SIC: 2731 Books: publishing only

(G-13768)
NORTH SHORE ORTHTICS PRSTHTICS
591 Bicycle Path Ste D (11776-3421)
PHONE..............................631 928-3040
Fax: 631 474-8020
Robert Biaggi, *President*
EMP: 7
SQ FT: 1,000
SALES (est): 994.5K Privately Held
WEB: www.nsop.com
SIC: 3842 5999 Limbs, artificial; artificial limbs

(G-13769)
OCCUNOMIX INTERNATIONAL LLC
585 Bicycle Path Ste 52 (11776-3431)
PHONE..............................631 741-1940
Richard Hauser, *President*
Joel Cooper, *Business Mgr*
Jon Smith, *Vice Pres*
Christine Hadjigeorge, *CFO*
Jim Preston, *Controller*
▲ EMP: 45
SQ FT: 48,500
SALES (est): 9.8MM Privately Held
WEB: www.occunomix.com
SIC: 3842 2311 2326 5047 Personal safety equipment; men's & boys' uniforms; men's & boys' work clothing; medical & hospital equipment

(G-13770)
ST GERARD ENTERPRISES INC
Also Called: St Gerard Printing
507 Bicycle Path (11776-3446)
P.O. Box 834, East Setauket (11733-0644)
PHONE..............................631 473-2003
Fax: 631 473-2025
Eugene Gerrard, *CEO*
Paul Gerrard, *Vice Pres*
EMP: 11 EST: 1965
SQ FT: 7,100
SALES (est): 1.2MM Privately Held
WEB: www.stgerardprinting.com
SIC: 2752 Commercial printing, offset

(G-13771)
STARGATE COMPUTER CORP
24 Harmony Dr (11776-3168)
P.O. Box 11161, Hauppauge (11788-0702)
PHONE..............................516 474-4799
EMP: 5
SALES (est): 400K Privately Held
SIC: 3571 Mfg Electronic Computers

(G-13772)
T EASON LAND SURVEYOR
27 Poplar St (11776-1415)
PHONE..............................631 474-2200
Treimane Eason, *Owner*
Pam Easton, *Controller*
EMP: 6
SALES (est): 411.9K Privately Held
WEB: www.teasonlandsurveyor.com
SIC: 2499 Surveyors' stakes, wood

(G-13773)
TKM TECHNOLOGIES INC
623 Bicycle Path Ste 5 (11776-3444)
P.O. Box 665, Mount Sinai (11766-0665)
PHONE..............................631 474-4700
Fax: 631 736-7991
Mike Moroff, *President*
Monika Moroff, *Vice Pres*
EMP: 6
SQ FT: 1,200
SALES: 950K Privately Held
WEB: www.tkmtechnologies.com
SIC: 3651 8711 Household audio & video equipment; electrical or electronic engineering

Port Jefferson
Suffolk County

(G-13774)
CHIP IT ALL LTD
366 Sheep Pasture Rd (11777-2059)
P.O. Box 959, Port Jeff STA (11776-0812)
PHONE..............................631 473-2040
Richard Edgar, *President*
Linda Edgar, *Admin Sec*
EMP: 7
SQ FT: 720
SALES (est): 885.9K Privately Held
SIC: 2411 Wood chips, produced in the field

(G-13775)
ELEGANCE LIGHTING LTD
326 Mn St (11777)
PHONE..............................631 509-0640
EMP: 11
SALES (est): 2.7MM Privately Held
SIC: 3646 Commercial indusl & institutional electric lighting fixtures

(G-13776)
LONG ISLAND GEOTECH
6 Berkshire Ct (11777-1906)
PHONE..............................631 473-1044
Micheal Verruto, *President*
EMP: 5
SALES (est): 308.6K Privately Held
SIC: 3272 Concrete products

(G-13777)
M H MANDELBAUM ORTHOTIC
116 Oakland Ave (11777-2172)
PHONE..............................631 473-8668
Fax: 631 473-8691
Martin H Mandelbaum, *President*
Marc Werner, *Vice Pres*
Terri Conigliaro, *Office Mgr*
EMP: 10
SQ FT: 5,300
SALES (est): 890K Privately Held
WEB: www.mhmoandp.com
SIC: 3842 5999 8011 Orthopedic appliances; prosthetic appliances; artificial limbs; offices & clinics of medical doctors

(G-13778)
PACE WALKERS OF AMERICA INC
Also Called: Thomas Jefferson Press
105 Washington Ave (11777-2003)
P.O. Box 843, East Setauket (11733-0653)
PHONE..............................631 444-2147
Steven Jonas, *President*
EMP: 12
SALES (est): 1.1MM Privately Held
SIC: 2731 Book publishing

(G-13779)
SARTEK INDUSTRIES INC (PA)
Also Called: Snr Cctv Systems Division
34 Jamaica Ave Ste 1 (11777-2270)
PHONE..............................631 473-3555
Carl Saieva, *President*
EMP: 6
SQ FT: 5,200
SALES (est): 950.3K Privately Held
WEB: www.sarind.com
SIC: 3663 1731 Television closed circuit equipment; closed circuit television installation

(G-13780)
WHITFORD DEVELOPMENT INC
646 Main St Ste 301 (11777-2230)
PHONE..............................631 471-7711
Fax: 631 471-0332
Victor Irizarry, *President*
EMP: 11
SALES (est): 1.1MM Privately Held
WEB: www.whitfordhomes.com
SIC: 2789 Trade binding services

Port Jervis
Orange County

(G-13781)
CERAMATERIALS LLC
226 Route 209 (12771-5124)
PHONE..............................518 701-6722
Jerry Weinstein,
▲ EMP: 5
SQ FT: 3,000
SALES (est): 519.3K Privately Held
SIC: 3624 8748 5945 3297 Carbon & graphite products; business consulting; ceramics supplies; nonclay refractories

(G-13782)
CONIC SYSTEMS INC
11 Rebel Ln (12771-3547)
PHONE..............................845 856-4053
Fax: 845 858-2824
Vincent Genovese, *President*
◆ EMP: 10
SQ FT: 12,000
SALES (est): 1.4MM Privately Held
WEB: www.conicsystems.com
SIC: 3625 Control equipment, electric

(G-13783)
DATATRAN LABS INC
Also Called: Nireco America
11 Rebel Ln (12771-3547)
PHONE..............................845 856-4313
Fax: 845 858-2384
Vincent Genovesse, *President*
EMP: 7
SQ FT: 11,000
SALES (est): 640K Privately Held
WEB: www.datatranlabs.com
SIC: 3625 3577 Industrial controls: push button, selector switches, pilot; computer peripheral equipment

(G-13784)
FLANAGANS CREATIVE DISP INC
55 Jersey Ave (12771-2514)
P.O. Box 98 (12771-0098)
PHONE..............................845 858-2542
Fax: 845 856-5931
Michael Flanagan, *President*
Kelly Flanagan, *Office Mgr*
EMP: 35 EST: 1998
SQ FT: 30,000
SALES (est): 6.9MM Privately Held
SIC: 3496 Miscellaneous fabricated wire products

(G-13785)
GILLINDER BROTHERS INC
Also Called: Gillinder Glass
39 Erie St 55 (12771-2809)
P.O. Box 1007 (12771-0187)
PHONE..............................845 856-5375
Fax: 845 858-5931
Charles E Gillinder, *Ch of Bd*
Dave Fox, *General Mgr*
Susan Gillinder, *Corp Secy*
Ken Moore, *Plant Mgr*
Walter Kozlowski, *Controller*
▲ EMP: 70 EST: 1912
SQ FT: 120,000
SALES: 7MM Privately Held
WEB: www.gillinderglass.com
SIC: 3229 Pressed & blown glass

(G-13786)
KALTEC FOOD PACKAGING INC
36 Center St 40 (12771-2808)
PHONE..............................845 856-9888
Nick Mascarra, *CEO*
Ed Mascara, *President*
Harriet L Mascara, *Shareholder*
▲ EMP: 30
SQ FT: 20,000
SALES (est): 5.7MM Privately Held
SIC: 2052 Cookies & crackers

(G-13787)
KALTECH FOOD PACKAGING INC
3640 Center St (12771)
PHONE..............................845 856-1210
Harriet L Mascara, *CEO*

GEOGRAPHIC SECTION
Port Washington - Nassau County (G-13812)

Frank Mascara, *Exec VP*
Edward Mascara, *Vice Pres*
Debra Salazar, *Office Mgr*
EMP: 26
SQ FT: 70,000
SALES: 2.2MM **Privately Held**
SIC: 2033 Spaghetti & other pasta sauce: packaged in cans, jars, etc.

(G-13788)
KLG USA LLC
20 W King St (12771-3061)
P.O. Box 1111 (12771-0154)
PHONE.................................845 856-5311
Joseph Healey, *Ch of Bd*
Rob Edmonds, *President*
James Skelton, *COO*
Jack Fallon, *Vice Pres*
Robert Jaegly, *Vice Pres*
▲ **EMP:** 1000
SQ FT: 4,210
SALES (est): 183.3MM **Privately Held**
WEB: www.kolmar.com
SIC: 2844 7389 2834 Toilet preparations; packaging & labeling services; pharmaceutical preparations

(G-13789)
MORGAN FUEL & HEATING CO INC
6 Sleepy Hollow Rd (12771-5308)
PHONE.................................845 856-7831
Dave Wood, *Branch Mgr*
EMP: 38
SALES (corp-wide): 53.3MM **Privately Held**
SIC: 2869 Fuels
PA: Morgan Fuel & Heating Co., Inc.
2785 W Main St
Wappingers Falls NY 12590
845 297-5580

(G-13790)
PORT JERVIS MACHINE CORP
176 1/2 Jersey Ave (12771-2612)
PHONE.................................845 856-6210
Sal Spiezio, *Manager*
EMP: 8
SALES (corp-wide): 737K **Privately Held**
SIC: 3599 Machine shop, jobbing & repair
PA: Port Jervis Machine Corporation
180 Jersey Ave
Port Jervis NY
845 856-3333

(G-13791)
SAMAKI INC
62 Jersey Ave (12771-2513)
P.O. Box 554, Westbrookville (12785-0554)
PHONE.................................845 858-1012
Simon Marrian, *President*
Laura Marrian, *Treasurer*
EMP: 7
SQ FT: 2,800
SALES (est): 880.8K **Privately Held**
WEB: www.samaki.com
SIC: 2091 Fish, smoked; fish, cured

(G-13792)
SKY DIVE
Also Called: Hgi Skydyne
100 River Rd (12771-2931)
PHONE.................................845 858-6400
Jay Benson, *CEO*
Donald J Paris, *President*
Steve Quick, *Exec VP*
David Coker, *Vice Pres*
Robert Fitch, *Vice Pres*
EMP: 70
SQ FT: 68,000
SALES: 8MM **Privately Held**
WEB: www.hornetgroup.com
SIC: 3089 3449 7336 3412 Boxes, plastic; miscellaneous metalwork; package design; metal barrels, drums & pails; metal cans; luggage

(G-13793)
SKYDYNE COMPANY
100 River Rd (12771-2997)
PHONE.................................845 858-6400
Peter M Keay, *President*
Peter A Siebert, *Corp Secy*
Nicole Flood, *Purch Mgr*
Michael Stewart, *VP Sales*
▲ **EMP:** 70

SALES (est): 21.3MM **Privately Held**
WEB: www.skydyne.com
SIC: 2655 Containers, laminated phenolic & vulcanized fiber

(G-13794)
SWIMWEAR ANYWHERE INC
Also Called: Finals, The
21 Minisink Ave (12771-2320)
PHONE.................................845 858-4141
Fax: 845 858-4193
Art Conway, *Exec VP*
Nancy Piccolo, *Manager*
Rosemarie Dilorenzo, *Creative Dir*
EMP: 40
SALES (corp-wide): 45.5MM **Privately Held**
SIC: 2329 2339 Bathing suits & swimwear: men's & boys'; athletic (warmup, sweat & jogging) suits: men's & boys'; bathing suits: women's, misses' & juniors'; athletic clothing: women's, misses' & juniors'
PA: Swimwear Anywhere, Inc.
85 Sherwood Ave
Farmingdale NY 11735
631 420-1400

Port Washington
Nassau County

(G-13795)
ACTIONCRAFT PRODUCTS INC
2 Manhasset Ave (11050-2008)
PHONE.................................516 883-6423
Nina Straus, *President*
EMP: 8 **EST:** 1951
SQ FT: 4,000
SALES (est): 381.6K **Privately Held**
WEB: www.industrialtest.com
SIC: 2759 Tags: printing

(G-13796)
ADVANCED POLYMER SOLUTIONS LLC
99 Seaview Blvd Ste 1a (11050-4632)
PHONE.................................516 621-5800
Rita Ryan, *Senior VP*
Purushoth Kesavan, *Prdtn Mgr*
John M Ryan,
John Ryan,
Rita M Ryan,
EMP: 9
SQ FT: 10,000
SALES (est): 1.6MM **Privately Held**
WEB: www.advancedpolymersolutions.com
SIC: 2891 8731 Adhesives & sealants; chemical laboratory, except testing

(G-13797)
ALAN F BOURGUET
63 Essex Ct (11050-4222)
PHONE.................................516 883-4315
Alan F Bourguet, *President*
EMP: 15 **EST:** 2001
SALES (est): 862.8K **Privately Held**
SIC: 2844 Perfumes & colognes

(G-13798)
ALERE INC
14 Vanderventer Ave (11050-3759)
PHONE.................................516 767-1112
EMP: 375
SALES (corp-wide): 2.4B **Publicly Held**
SIC: 2835 In vitro & in vivo diagnostic substances
PA: Alere Inc.
51 Sawyer Rd Ste 200
Waltham MA 02453
781 647-3900

(G-13799)
ALMOND JEWELERS INC
Also Called: Almond Group
16 S Maryland Ave (11050-2913)
P.O. Box 471 (11050-0135)
PHONE.................................516 933-6000
Jonathan Mandelbaum, *President*
Maurice Mandelbaum, *Vice Pres*
Jason Mandelbaum, *Mfg Staff*
Henry Bubrow, *CFO*
Barbara Schmidt, *Persnl Mgr*
▲ **EMP:** 15

SQ FT: 3,500
SALES: 100MM **Privately Held**
SIC: 3911 Jewelry, precious metal

(G-13800)
APPLE & EVE LLC (DH)
2 Seaview Blvd Ste 100 (11050-4634)
PHONE.................................516 621-1122
Gordon Crane, *President*
John Emerson, *President*
Sol Jacobs, *General Mgr*
Chris McFadden, *Regional Mgr*
Robert Mortati, *Senior VP*
▲ **EMP:** 65
SQ FT: 14,000
SALES (est): 53MM
SALES (corp-wide): 274.7MM **Privately Held**
WEB: www.appleandeve.com
SIC: 2033 Fruit juices: packaged in cans, jars, etc.
HQ: Us Juice Partners, Llc
2 Seaview Blvd
Port Washington NY 11050
516 621-1122

(G-13801)
ARENA GRAPHICS INC
Also Called: Arena Sports Center
52 Main St Frnt (11050-2952)
PHONE.................................516 767-5108
Fax: 516 944-5626
Christopher J Avazis, *President*
Steven Avazis, *Vice Pres*
EMP: 9
SQ FT: 4,700
SALES (est): 1.2MM **Privately Held**
WEB: www.arenagraphics.com
SIC: 2759 5941 2395 Screen printing; sporting goods & bicycle shops; embroidery products, except schiffli machine

(G-13802)
BOMBAY KITCHEN FOODS INC
76 S Bayles Ave (11050-3729)
PHONE.................................516 767-7401
Fax: 516 767-7402
Sanjiv Mody, *President*
Ajit Mody, *Treasurer*
Sachin Mody, *Admin Sec*
▲ **EMP:** 15
SQ FT: 18,000
SALES: 2.5MM **Privately Held**
SIC: 2099 Food preparations

(G-13803)
CARNELS PRINTING INC
Also Called: Carnel Printing and Copying
22 Main St Frnt A (11050-2933)
PHONE.................................516 883-3355
Fax: 516 883-0085
Kay W Ray, *President*
EMP: 6
SQ FT: 2,500
SALES (est): 758.9K **Privately Held**
SIC: 2752 2791 2789 Commercial printing, offset; typesetting; bookbinding & related work

(G-13804)
CHANNEL MANUFACTURING INC (PA)
55 Channel Dr (11050-2216)
PHONE.................................516 944-6271
Jordan Klein, *President*
Carol Caplen, *Controller*
Carole Kaplan, *Controller*
Mia Kelly, *Sales Associate*
Bill Koines, *Manager*
▲ **EMP:** 25 **EST:** 2000
SALES (est): 2.9MM **Privately Held**
WEB: www.channelmfg.com
SIC: 2499 3537 Food handling & processing products, wood; industrial trucks & tractors

(G-13805)
CHOICE MAGAZINE LISTENING INC
85 Channel Dr Ste 3 (11050-2278)
PHONE.................................516 883-8280
Fax: 516 944-5849
William O'Conner, *Chairman*
Lois Miller, *Manager*
Sondra Mochson, *Director*
EMP: 7

SALES (est): 520K **Privately Held**
WEB: www.choicemagazinelistening.org
SIC: 2721 8322 Periodicals; social services for the handicapped

(G-13806)
COMPOZ A PUZZLE INC
2 Secatoag Ave (11050-2107)
PHONE.................................516 883-2311
Robert F Krisch, *Chairman*
Richard Hinchey, *Vice Pres*
Livon Bailey, *Manager*
EMP: 5
SQ FT: 4,000
SALES: 500K **Privately Held**
WEB: www.compozapuzzle.com
SIC: 3944 5945 Puzzles; hobby, toy & game shops

(G-13807)
DATA PALETTE INFO SVCS LLC
35 Marino Ave (11050-4207)
PHONE.................................718 433-1060
Fax: 718 433-1074
Walter Reinhardt, *Manager*
Fred Disalvatore, *Consultant*
Stephen Lee, *Software Engr*
Ramil Cargullo, *Software Dev*
Joel Ronis,
▲ **EMP:** 75
SQ FT: 35,000
SALES (est): 11.2MM **Privately Held**
SIC: 2759 7331 7374 7389 Laser printing; mailing service; data processing & preparation;

(G-13808)
DIAMOND BOUTIQUE
77 Main St (11050-2929)
PHONE.................................516 444-3373
Joseph Daniel, *Owner*
EMP: 6
SALES: 2.5MM **Privately Held**
SIC: 3915 5944 Jewel cutting, drilling, polishing, recutting or setting; jewelry stores

(G-13809)
DIAMOND SEAFOODS LLC
150 Main St (11050-2859)
PHONE.................................503 351-3240
Wendy Schwartz, *Mng Member*
Wendi Schwartz, *Mng Member*
Jonathan Schwartz,
▲ **EMP:** 5
SALES (est): 550K **Privately Held**
SIC: 2091 Seafood products: packaged in cans, jars, etc.

(G-13810)
DJ PUBLISHING INC
25 Willowdale Ave (11050-3716)
PHONE.................................516 767-2500
Vincent P Testa, *President*
Tom McCarty, *Sales Mgr*
EMP: 50
SALES (est): 2.8MM **Privately Held**
WEB: www.testabags.com
SIC: 2721 Magazines: publishing only, not printed on site

(G-13811)
DOMA MARKETING INC
28 Haven Ave Ste 226 (11050-3646)
PHONE.................................516 684-1111
Doron Katz, *Owner*
EMP: 5 **EST:** 2012
SQ FT: 2,000
SALES: 100K **Privately Held**
SIC: 2066 Chocolate

(G-13812)
E GLOBAL SOLUTIONS INC
Also Called: E G S
8 Haven Ave Ste 221 (11050-3636)
P.O. Box 771 (11050-0771)
PHONE.................................516 767-5138
Anthony Straggi, *Ch of Bd*
EMP: 6
SQ FT: 9,000
SALES (est): 690K **Privately Held**
SIC: 3822 Auto controls regulating residntl & coml environmt & applncs

Port Washington - Nassau County (G-13813)

(G-13813)
ELCO MANUFACTURING CO INC (PA)
26 Ivy Way (11050-3802)
P.O. Box 1759 (11050-7759)
PHONE..................516 767-3577
Eric Weintraub, *President*
Stanley Weintraub, *Vice Pres*
E Nash, *Admin Sec*
EMP: 19 EST: 1904
SQ FT: 10,000
SALES (est): 1.5MM **Privately Held**
WEB: www.elcomfg.com
SIC: 3172 5199 Personal leather goods; advertising specialties

(G-13814)
EVOLVE GUEST CONTROLS LLC (PA)
16 S Maryland Ave (11050-2913)
PHONE..................855 750-9090
Staffan Encrantz, *Ch of Bd*
Len Horowitz, *President*
David Korcz, *CFO*
Robert Kaye, *Controller*
EMP: 15
SQ FT: 10,000
SALES (est): 5MM **Privately Held**
SIC: 3822 7371 2591 1731 Auto controls regulating residntl & coml environmt & applncs; building services monitoring controls, automatic; computer software development; shade, curtain & drapery hardware; electronic controls installation; energy management controls

(G-13815)
FINER TOUCH PRINTING CORP
4 Yennicock Ave (11050-2131)
PHONE..................516 944-8000
Fax: 516 944-9439
Kenny Cummings, *President*
Sharon Verity, *Office Mgr*
EMP: 10
SQ FT: 2,500
SALES: 1.1MM **Privately Held**
WEB: www.comiccastle.com
SIC: 2752 Commercial printing, offset

(G-13816)
FRANKLIN-DOUGLAS INC
Also Called: Omnimusic
52 Main St Side (11050-2965)
PHONE..................516 883-0121
Fax: 516 883-0271
Douglas Wood, *President*
Patricia Wood, *Vice Pres*
EMP: 12 EST: 1975
SQ FT: 4,000
SALES (est): 1MM **Privately Held**
WEB: www.omnimusic.com
SIC: 2741 Music book & sheet music publishing

(G-13817)
G & C WELDING CO INC
39 Annette Dr (11050-2803)
PHONE..................516 883-3228
Carmine Meluzio, *President*
EMP: 5
SALES (est): 179.5K **Privately Held**
SIC: 7692 1799 Welding repair; welding on site

(G-13818)
GANNETT CO INC
Also Called: U S A Today
99 Seaview Blvd Ste 200 (11050-4632)
PHONE..................516 484-7510
Fax: 516 621-5307
Peter Donohue, *Branch Mgr*
EMP: 40
SALES (corp-wide): 5.7B **Publicly Held**
WEB: www.gannett.com
SIC: 2711 Newspapers, publishing & printing
PA: Gannett Co., Inc.
  7950 Jones Branch Dr
  Mc Lean VA 22102
  703 854-6000

(G-13819)
GE HEALTHCARE INC
Also Called: Medi-Physics
80 Seaview Blvd Ste E (11050-4618)
PHONE..................516 626-2799
Fax: 516 621-5807
Franklyn Robinson, *Manager*
EMP: 14
SALES (corp-wide): 117.3B **Publicly Held**
SIC: 2833 5912 Medicinals & botanicals; drug stores
HQ: Ge Healthcare Inc.
  100 Results Way
  Marlborough MA 01752
  800 292-8514

(G-13820)
HENLEY BRANDS LLC
1 Channel Dr (11050-2216)
PHONE..................516 883-8220
Anne Marco, *Director*
David Long,
Corey Lieblein,
EMP: 12 EST: 2012
SALES (est): 920K **Privately Held**
SIC: 3651 Home entertainment equipment, electronic

(G-13821)
HERCULES GROUP INC
27 Seaview Blvd (11050-4610)
PHONE..................212 813-8000
Fax: 212 899-5559
Sara Amani, *President*
Jennifer Ryder, *Controller*
Rosan Jesdine, *Manager*
▲ EMP: 20
SQ FT: 2,000
SALES (est): 3.8MM **Privately Held**
WEB: www.herculesgroup.com
SIC: 2385 Diaper covers, waterproof: made from purchased materials

(G-13822)
HURRYWORKS LLC
990 Seaview Blvd (11050)
PHONE..................516 998-4600
Richard Kolodny, *CEO*
EMP: 99
SQ FT: 10,000
SALES (est): 2.5MM **Privately Held**
SIC: 3841 Surgical & medical instruments

(G-13823)
IDENTFICATION DATA IMAGING LLC
Also Called: IDI
26 Harbor Park Dr (11050-4602)
PHONE..................516 484-6500
Fax: 516 484-4486
Mohammed Abu-Khraybeh, *Vice Pres*
Pat Schrenzel, *Accounts Exec*
Pat Screnzel,
Jeffrey Brodsky,
EMP: 6
SQ FT: 1,300
SALES (est): 590.7K **Privately Held**
WEB: www.idius.com
SIC: 3999 Identification badges & insignia

(G-13824)
INDUSTRIAL TEST EQP CO INC
2 Manhasset Ave (11050-2008)
PHONE..................516 883-6423
Fax: 516 886-7155
Jay Monroe, *President*
Hugo Harnella, *Purch Dir*
Barbara Assa, *Persnl Dir*
Sam Lou, *Marketing Staff*
Barbara Monroe, *Admin Sec*
EMP: 20
SQ FT: 8,000
SALES: 1MM **Privately Held**
WEB: www.rf-pwr-amps.com
SIC: 3621 3829 2759 Generating apparatus & parts, electrical; gas detectors; tags: printing

(G-13825)
INTECH 21 INC
21 Harbor Park Dr (11050-4658)
PHONE..................516 626-7221
Fax: 516 626-7021
George Y Bilenko, *President*
Joe Adinolfi, *General Mgr*
Victor Zelmanovich, *Exec VP*
Aleksandr Baranov, *Software Engr*
Jules Leibman, *Shareholder*
▲ EMP: 12
SQ FT: 8,000
SALES (est): 1.2MM **Privately Held**
WEB: www.intech21.com
SIC: 3674 Computer logic modules

(G-13826)
IVY ENTERPRISES INC (HQ)
3 Seaview Blvd (11050-4610)
PHONE..................516 621-9779
Fax: 516 621-9779
Hee J Chang, *President*
Belle Park, *Manager*
Tom Brancato, *Director*
▲ EMP: 120
SALES (est): 11.4MM
SALES (corp-wide): 26.2MM **Privately Held**
SIC: 3999 5087 Fingernails, artificial; beauty parlor equipment & supplies
PA: Kiss Nail Products, Inc.
  57 Seaview Blvd
  Port Washington NY 11050
  516 625-9292

(G-13827)
JAIDAN INDUSTRIES INC
Also Called: Absolute Business Products
16 Capi Ln (11050-3410)
PHONE..................516 944-3650
Richard Sussman, *President*
Louise Feliciano, *Manager*
▲ EMP: 16
SALES (est): 3.6MM **Privately Held**
WEB: www.jaidan.com
SIC: 3442 Window & door frames; moldings & trim, except automobile: metal

(G-13828)
JESCO LIGHTING INC (PA)
15 Harbor Park Dr (11050-4604)
PHONE..................718 366-3211
Richard Kurtz, *Chairman*
Edward MA, *Chairman*
Joan Miller, *Accounts Exec*
Mike Wright, *Sales Associate*
Paulin Tham, *VP Mktg*
◆ EMP: 50
SQ FT: 70,000
SALES (est): 21MM **Privately Held**
SIC: 3646 Commercial indusl & institutional electric lighting fixtures

(G-13829)
JESCO LIGHTING GROUP LLC (PA)
15 Harbor Park Dr (11050-4604)
PHONE..................718 366-3211
Richard Kurtz, *President*
▲ EMP: 50 EST: 2008
SQ FT: 70,000
SALES (est): 7MM **Privately Held**
SIC: 3646 Commercial indusl & institutional electric lighting fixtures

(G-13830)
JP BUS & TRUCK REPAIR LTD (PA)
Also Called: Bird Bus Sales
135 Haven Ave (11050-3925)
PHONE..................516 767-2700
Robert Reichenbach, *President*
Stephanie Chavez, *Principal*
James Filomena, *Principal*
Ivan Soto, *Vice Pres*
EMP: 18 EST: 2004
SALES (est): 7.6MM **Privately Held**
SIC: 3711 Buses, all types, assembly of

(G-13831)
JWIN ELECTRONICS CORP (PA)
Also Called: Iluv
2 Harbor Park Dr (11050-4602)
PHONE..................516 626-7188
Fax: 516 533-8766
Justin Kim, *Ch of Bd*
Dena Kim, *Exec VP*
Kevin Vinlim, *Controller*
Deon Lookmauth, *Credit Mgr*
Joe Im, *Human Resources*
◆ EMP: 100
SQ FT: 132,000
SALES (est): 18.2MM **Privately Held**
WEB: www.jwin.com
SIC: 3651 Television receiving sets; radio receiving sets; home entertainment equipment, electronic

(G-13832)
KELLER INTERNATIONAL PUBG LLC (PA)
150 Main St Ste 10 (11050-2849)
PHONE..................516 829-9210
Fax: 516 829-5414
Terry Beirne, *Publisher*
Felicia M Morales, *Editor*
Carel Letschert, *Vice Pres*
Kelly Keller, *Sales Dir*
Brad Berger, *Sales Mgr*
EMP: 40 EST: 1882
SQ FT: 7,000
SALES (est): 2.8MM **Privately Held**
WEB: www.glscs.com
SIC: 2721 Magazines: publishing only, not printed on site

(G-13833)
KITTYWALK SYSTEMS INC
10 Farmview Rd (11050-4511)
PHONE..................516 627-8418
Jeff King, *CEO*
Lise King, *President*
▲ EMP: 2
SALES: 1MM **Privately Held**
SIC: 3999 Pet supplies

(G-13834)
KLEARBAR INC
8 Graywood Rd (11050-1516)
PHONE..................516 684-9892
Mark Klein, *President*
Scott Bercu, *Admin Sec*
▲ EMP: 5
SALES (est): 410K **Privately Held**
SIC: 3585 Soda fountain & beverage dispensing equipment & parts

(G-13835)
KRAUS USA INC
12 Harbor Park Dr (11050-4649)
PHONE..................516 621-1300
Russel Levi, *President*
Russell Levi, *President*
Michael Rukhlin, *Principal*
Dmitry Rukhlin, *COO*
Jeff Rukhlin, *Assistant VP*
▲ EMP: 10
SQ FT: 15,000
SALES (est): 2.4MM **Privately Held**
SIC: 3431 Bathroom fixtures, including sinks

(G-13836)
KRUG PRECISION INC
7 Carey Pl (11050-2421)
PHONE..................516 944-9350
Fax: 516 944-5841
Michael Krug, *President*
Rosemarie Krug, *Corp Secy*
EMP: 9
SQ FT: 6,500
SALES: 1.3MM **Privately Held**
SIC: 3599 Machine shop, jobbing & repair

(G-13837)
LIF INDUSTRIES INC (PA)
Also Called: Long Island Fireproof Door
5 Harbor Park Dr Ste 1 (11050-4698)
PHONE..................516 390-6800
Vincent Gallo, *Ch of Bd*
Joseph Gallo Jr, *President*
Anthony Gallo, *Vice Pres*
David Kanner, *Sales Mgr*
John Ciampi, *Manager*
EMP: 63
SQ FT: 85,000
SALES (est): 18.9MM **Privately Held**
WEB: www.lifi.net
SIC: 3442 5031 Metal doors; window & door frames; door frames, all materials

(G-13838)
LIFC CORP
101 Haven Ave (11050-3936)
PHONE..................516 426-5737
Brian Kenny, *President*
EMP: 5

SALES: (est): 410K **Privately Held**
SIC: 3569 5812 Firefighting apparatus & related equipment; caterers

(G-13839)
M R C INDUSTRIES INC
Also Called: Mason Medical Products
99 Seaview Blvd Ste 210 (11050-4632)
P.O. Box 609 (11050-0609)
PHONE.................516 328-6900
Fax: 516 328-6622
Leonard Horowitz, *CEO*
Brian Goldstein, *Vice Pres*
Bernice Wien, *Treasurer*
◆ EMP: 200
SQ FT: 60,000
SALES: (est): 20.7MM **Privately Held**
WEB: www.masonmedical.com
SIC: 2515 Mattresses & foundations

(G-13840)
MEDER TEXTILE CO INC
20 Lynn Rd (11050-4437)
PHONE.................516 883-0409
Bruce T Lindemann, *President*
EMP: 4 EST: 1936
SQ FT: 500
SALES: 1MM **Privately Held**
SIC: 2211 Broadwoven fabric mills, cotton; upholstery fabrics, cotton

(G-13841)
MEDICAL DEPOT INC (PA)
99 Seaview Blvd Ste 210 (11050-4632)
P.O. Box 842450, Boston MA (02284-2450)
PHONE.................516 998-4600
Fax: 631 420-4468
Harvey P Diamond, *CEO*
Nick Gargano, *President*
Richard S Kolodny, *President*
Ryan Mahoney, *President*
David Pugh, *President*
◆ EMP: 300
SQ FT: 83,000
SALES: (est): 540.9MM **Privately Held**
WEB: www.drivemedical.com
SIC: 3841 Surgical & medical instruments

(G-13842)
MEDICAL INFORMATION SYSTEMS
2 Seaview Blvd Ste 104 (11050-4634)
PHONE.................516 621-7200
Fax: 516 423-0161
Irving Silverberg, *President*
Roy Silverberg, *Vice Pres*
Hazel Silverberg, *Admin Sec*
EMP: 5
SQ FT: 5,000
SALES: 2.3MM **Privately Held**
WEB: www.medinfosystems.com
SIC: 2741 Miscellaneous publishing

(G-13843)
MEDSAFE SYSTEMS INC
46 Orchard Farm Rd (11050-3338)
PHONE.................516 883-8222
Bernard Shore, *President*
EMP: 6
SQ FT: 1,000
SALES: 1.2MM **Privately Held**
SIC: 3823 Telemetering instruments, industrial process type

(G-13844)
MEKATRONICS INCORPORATED
85 Channel Dr Ste 2 (11050-2248)
PHONE.................516 883-6805
Jack Bendror, *President*
Kenneth Lines, *Engineer*
EMP: 24
SQ FT: 30,000
SALES: (est): 4MM **Privately Held**
SIC: 3679 3555 3861 Electronic circuits; printing trades machinery; microfilm equipment: cameras, projectors, readers, etc.

(G-13845)
MIN RUN (USA) INC
14 West Dr (11050-1433)
PHONE.................646 331-1018
Micheal Zheng, *President*
▲ EMP: 3
SQ FT: 2,700

SALES: 5MM **Privately Held**
SIC: 2211 Apparel & outerwear fabrics, cotton

(G-13846)
MINERALBIOUS CORP
Also Called: Dr Mineral
46 Graywood Rd (11050-1538)
PHONE.................516 498-9715
Dong Young Kim, *CEO*
▲ EMP: 12
SALES: (est): 1.2MM **Privately Held**
SIC: 3295 Minerals, ground or treated

(G-13847)
MUSIC & SOUND RETAILER INC
Also Called: Retailer, The
25 Willowdale Ave (11050-3716)
PHONE.................516 767-2500
Vincent Testa, *President*
EMP: 28
SQ FT: 1,500
SALES: (est): 1.7MM **Privately Held**
SIC: 2721 Magazines: publishing only, not printed on site

(G-13848)
NEWBAY MEDIA LLC
Mp & A Editorial
6 Manhasset Ave (11050-2008)
PHONE.................516 944-5940
Martin Porter, *Branch Mgr*
EMP: 17
SALES: (corp-wide): 138.1MM **Privately Held**
SIC: 2741 8999 2721 Miscellaneous publishing; commercial & literary writings; periodicals
HQ: Newbay Media Llc
28 E 28th St Fl 12
New York NY 10016
212 378-0400

(G-13849)
OSWALD MANUFACTURING CO INC
65 Channel Dr (11050-2216)
PHONE.................516 883-8850
Fax: 516 883-7857
Fred Oswald, *President*
Angella Oswald, *Vice Pres*
▲ EMP: 30
SQ FT: 22,000
SALES: (est): 3.9MM **Privately Held**
SIC: 3531 Construction machinery

(G-13850)
OZTECK INDUSTRIES INC
65 Channel Dr (11050-2216)
PHONE.................516 883-8857
Fred Oswald, *President*
Angella Oswald, *Vice Pres*
Tiffany Shackatano, *Vice Pres*
Joanna Stupar, *Bookkeeper*
◆ EMP: 40
SQ FT: 22,000
SALES: (est): 10.8MM **Privately Held**
WEB: www.oztec.com
SIC: 3531 Vibrators for concrete construction; surfacers, concrete grinding

(G-13851)
PALL BIOMEDICAL INC
Also Called: Pall Medical
25 Harbor Park Dr (11050-4605)
PHONE.................516 484-3600
Fax: 516 484-3637
Eric Kransnoff, *Principal*
Stella Rivera, *Human Res Mgr*
Ricardo Alfonso, *VP Mktg*
Jacques Hestres, *Manager*
Tim Lynch, *Manager*
▲ EMP: 200
SALES: (est): 27.3MM
SALES: (corp-wide): 20.5B **Publicly Held**
WEB: www.pall.com
SIC: 3842 Surgical appliances & supplies
HQ: Pall Corporation
25 Harbor Park Dr
Port Washington NY 11050
516 484-5400

(G-13852)
PALL CORPORATION (HQ)
25 Harbor Park Dr (11050-4664)
PHONE.................516 484-5400

Fax: 516 484-3633
Rainer Blair, *President*
Yves Baratelli, *President*
Michael Egholm, *President*
Naresh Narasimhan, *President*
Brian Burnett, *Senior VP*
▲ EMP: 1200 EST: 2015
SQ FT: 25,000
SALES: 2.7B
SALES: (corp-wide): 20.5B **Publicly Held**
WEB: www.pall.com
SIC: 3569 3599 3714 2834 Filters; filters, general line: industrial; filter elements, fluid, hydraulic line; separators for steam, gas, vapor or air (machinery); air intake filters, internal combustion engine, except auto; gasoline filters, internal combustion engine, except auto; oil filters, internal combustion engine, except automotive; filters: oil, fuel & air, motor vehicle; solutions, pharmaceutical; surgical & medical instruments; IV transfusion apparatus
PA: Danaher Corporation
2200 Penn Ave Nw Ste 800w
Washington DC 20037
202 828-0850

(G-13853)
PALL CORPORATION
Also Called: Pall Life Sciences
25 Harbor Park Dr (11050-4664)
PHONE.................516 484-2818
Cathy Klock, *Opers Mgr*
Man Ng, *QC Mgr*
Joanna Fielding, *Research*
Rhonda Kingery, *Research*
Huy Thach, *Engineer*
EMP: 750
SALES: (corp-wide): 20.5B **Publicly Held**
WEB: www.pall.com
SIC: 3842 Surgical appliances & supplies
HQ: Pall Corporation
25 Harbor Park Dr
Port Washington NY 11050
516 484-5400

(G-13854)
PALL INTERNATIONAL CORPORATION
25 Harbor Park Dr (11050-4605)
PHONE.................516 484-5400
Jeremy Haywood Serey, *President*
Donald Nicholls, *Exec VP*
Sakae Isohata, *Senior VP*
Denise M Dick, *Vice Pres*
Chris Donegan, *Vice Pres*
EMP: 350
SALES: (est): 34.8MM
SALES: (corp-wide): 20.5B **Publicly Held**
WEB: www.pall.com
SIC: 3677 Filtration devices, electronic
HQ: Pall Corporation
25 Harbor Park Dr
Port Washington NY 11050
516 484-5400

(G-13855)
PARAGON CORPORATION
21 Forest Dr (11050-1910)
PHONE.................516 484-6090
Serena Jen, *President*
▲ EMP: 12
SQ FT: 4,466
SALES: (est): 1MM **Privately Held**
WEB: www.paradigmsw.com
SIC: 2399 3911 5199 Emblems, badges & insignia; jewelry, precious metal; badges

(G-13856)
PLAY-IT PRODUCTIONS INC
735 Port Washington Blvd (11050-3735)
PHONE.................212 695-6530
Fax: 212 695-4304
Terri Tyler, *Vice Pres*
EMP: 10
SQ FT: 3,000
SALES: (est): 1.2MM **Privately Held**
WEB: www.play-itproductions.net
SIC: 2752 7336 7812 7819 Commercial printing, lithographic; graphic arts & related design; audio-visual program production; video tape or disk reproduction

(G-13857)
PROFICIENT SURGICAL EQP INC
99 Seaview Blvd Ste 1c (11050-4632)
PHONE.................516 487-1175
Steven Baum, *President*
Harold Mondschein, *Sales Mgr*
Michael Albano, *Sales Executive*
Alicia Mamarella, *Office Mgr*
▲ EMP: 6 EST: 1996
SALES: (est): 710K **Privately Held**
WEB: www.proficientsurgical.com
SIC: 3842 Surgical appliances & supplies

(G-13858)
RADNOR-WALLACE (PA)
921 Port Washington Blvd # 1 (11050-2976)
PHONE.................516 767-2131
Michael O'Beirne, *Director*
EMP: 5
SQ FT: 600
SALES: 500K **Privately Held**
WEB: www.radnorwallace.com
SIC: 7372 Prepackaged software

(G-13859)
ROBERT BARTHOLOMEW LTD
Also Called: Magnus Sands Point Shop
15 Main St (11050-2916)
PHONE.................516 767-2970
Fax: 516 767-7774
Robert C Mazza, *President*
Robert S Mazza, *President*
Donal Keogh, *Vice Pres*
Bob Mazza, *Manager*
Laura Mazza, *Admin Sec*
EMP: 32
SQ FT: 12,000
SALES: (est): 5.3MM **Privately Held**
WEB: www.robertbartholomew.com
SIC: 3911 Jewelry, precious metal

(G-13860)
SAFAVIEH INC
40 Harbor Park Dr (11050-4602)
PHONE.................516 945-1900
Mohsen Yaraghi, *Ch of Bd*
EMP: 500
SALES: 300MM **Privately Held**
SIC: 2273 5712 Rugs, hand & machine made; furniture stores

(G-13861)
SAINT HONORE PASTRY SHOP INC
993 Port Washington Blvd (11050-2910)
PHONE.................516 767-2555
Jacques Leguelaf, *President*
EMP: 5
SQ FT: 1,500
SALES: (est): 270K **Privately Held**
SIC: 2051 5461 Bread, cake & related products; bakeries

(G-13862)
SAMMBA PRINTING INC
Also Called: Minuteman Press
437 Port Washington Blvd (11050-4225)
PHONE.................516 944-4449
Fax: 516 944-4428
Mark Gutner, *President*
Susan Spira, *Vice Pres*
EMP: 6
SQ FT: 1,700
SALES: 900K **Privately Held**
SIC: 2752 2759 Commercial printing, lithographic; invitation & stationery printing & engraving

(G-13863)
SCHOLIUM INTERNATIONAL INC
151 Cow Neck Rd (11050-1143)
PHONE.................516 883-8032
Fax: 516 944-9824
Arthur A Candido, *President*
Elena M Candido, *Vice Pres*
EMP: 5 EST: 1970
SQ FT: 1,800
SALES: (est): 303.2K **Privately Held**
WEB: www.scholium.com
SIC: 2731 5192 Book publishing; books

Port Washington - Nassau County (G-13864) — GEOGRAPHIC SECTION

(G-13864)
SHAKE-N-GO FASHION INC (PA)
85 Harbor Rd (11050-2535)
PHONE..................................516 944-7777
James K Kim, *Ch of Bd*
Mike Kim, *Vice Pres*
Betty Kim, *Treasurer*
Jessica Cho, *Controller*
◆ EMP: 62
SQ FT: 75,000
SALES (est): 25.3MM **Privately Held**
WEB: www.shake-n-gofashions.com
SIC: 3999 Hairpin mountings; wigs, including doll wigs, toupees or wiglets

(G-13865)
SHARODINE INC
18 Haven Ave Frnt 2 (11050-3642)
PHONE..................................516 767-3548
Ron Sharoni, *President*
EMP: 9
SALES (est): 1.3MM **Privately Held**
SIC: 3911 Jewelry, precious metal

(G-13866)
SOUND COMMUNICATIONS INC
25 Willowdale Ave (11050-3716)
PHONE..................................516 767-2500
Vincent Testa, *President*
John Carr, *Publisher*
John Beresford, *Editor*
Dan Ferrisi, *Editor*
Shonan Noronha, *Editor*
EMP: 40
SALES (est): 2.2MM **Privately Held**
SIC: 2721 Magazines: publishing only, not printed on site

(G-13867)
SWITCH BEVERAGE COMPANY LLC
2 Seaview Blvd Fl 3 (11050-4634)
PHONE..................................203 202-7383
Brian Boyd, *CEO*
Maura Mottolese, *President*
Richard Beswick, *Sales Staff*
EMP: 11
SQ FT: 1,200
SALES (est): 947.3K
SALES (corp-wide): 274.7MM **Privately Held**
WEB: www.switchbev.com
SIC: 2096 2086 Potato chips & similar snacks; carbonated beverages, nonalcoholic: bottled & canned
HQ: Apple & Eve, Llc
  2 Seaview Blvd Ste 100
  Port Washington NY 11050
  516 621-1122

(G-13868)
TESTA COMMUNICATIONS INC
Also Called: Sound & Communication
25 Willowdale Ave (11050-3716)
PHONE..................................516 767-2500
Vincent Testa, *President*
Steve Thorakos, *Prdtn Mgr*
Shane Jacobs, *Manager*
EMP: 40
SQ FT: 1,500
SALES (est): 4.6MM **Privately Held**
WEB: www.testa.com
SIC: 2721 Magazines: publishing only, not printed on site

(G-13869)
THETA INDUSTRIES INC
26 Valley Rd Ste 1 (11050-2498)
PHONE..................................516 883-4088
Fax: 516 883-4599
Gerhard Clusener, *President*
Brigette Clusener, *Admin Sec*
EMP: 10
SQ FT: 10,000
SALES (est): 890K **Privately Held**
WEB: www.theta-us.com
SIC: 3821 7699 Laboratory apparatus & furniture; laboratory equipment: fume hoods, distillation racks, etc.; laboratory instrument repair

(G-13870)
US JUICE PARTNERS LLC (DH)
2 Seaview Blvd (11050-4614)
PHONE..................................516 621-1122
Pierre-Paul Lassonde, *Ch of Bd*

EMP: 4
SALES (est): 53MM
SALES (corp-wide): 274.7MM **Privately Held**
SIC: 2033 Fruit juices: packaged in cans, jars, etc.
HQ: Industries Lassonde Inc
  755 Rue Principale
  Rougemont QC J0L 1
  450 469-4926

(G-13871)
WELL-MADE TOY MFG CORPORATION
146 Soundview Dr (11050-1751)
PHONE..................................718 381-4225
Fax: 718 381-5532
Fred F Catapano, *President*
Susan Cook, *Vice Pres*
Gilbert Edovas, *Controller*
Susan Small, *Sales Staff*
▲ EMP: 20
SALES (est): 2.8MM **Privately Held**
WEB: www.wellmadetoy.com
SIC: 3942 Stuffed toys, including animals

Portageville
Wyoming County

(G-13872)
FILLMORE GREENHOUSES INC
11589 State Route 19a (14536-9611)
PHONE..................................585 567-2678
Fax: 585 567-2247
Mario Van Logten, *Chairman*
▲ EMP: 45
SALES (est): 6.6MM **Privately Held**
SIC: 3448 Greenhouses: prefabricated metal

Portland
Chautauqua County

(G-13873)
OLDE CHTQUA VNEYARDS LTD LBLTY
Also Called: Twentyone Brix Winery
6654 W Main St (14769-9621)
PHONE..................................716 792-2749
Marion Jordan, *General Mgr*
Kris Kane,
Bryan Jordan,
Michael Jordan,
EMP: 12
SQ FT: 10,000
SALES (est): 910K **Privately Held**
SIC: 2084 5921 Wines; wine

Portville
Cattaraugus County

(G-13874)
FIBERCEL PACKAGING LLC (HQ)
46 Brooklyn St (14770-9529)
P.O. Box 610 (14770-0610)
PHONE..................................716 933-8703
Fax: 585 933-6948
Mitch Gray, *General Mgr*
Bruce E Olson,
Richard Flanagan,
Gale Hastings,
Robert T Hinett,
EMP: 28
SQ FT: 7,200
SALES (est): 8.6MM
SALES (corp-wide): 21.8MM **Privately Held**
SIC: 2621 Molded pulp products
PA: Orcon Industries Corp.
  8715 Lake Rd
  Le Roy NY 14482
  585 768-7000

(G-13875)
I A CONSTRUCTION CORPORATION
Also Called: Portville Sand & Gravel Div
Rr 305 Box S (14770)
P.O. Box 367 (14770-0367)
PHONE..................................716 933-8787
Fax: 585 933-8787
John Taylor, *Sales/Mktg Mgr*
EMP: 5
SQ FT: 1,800
SALES (corp-wide): 84.5MM **Privately Held**
WEB: www.iaconstruction.com
SIC: 1442 Gravel mining
HQ: Ia Construction Corporation
  24 Gibb Rd
  Franklin PA 16323
  814 432-3184

Potsdam
St. Lawrence County

(G-13876)
3 BEARS GLUTEN FREE BAKERY
51 Market St (13676-1744)
PHONE..................................315 323-0277
Christopher Durand, *President*
Faye Ori, *Vice Pres*
EMP: 11 EST: 2014
SALES (est): 921.9K **Privately Held**
SIC: 2051 Bakery: wholesale or wholesale/retail combined

(G-13877)
ATLANTIS SOLAR INC
Also Called: Atlantis Solar and Wind
2302 River Rd (13676-3491)
PHONE..................................916 226-9183
Lance Thomas, *President*
Michael Becker, *Manager*
EMP: 12
SQ FT: 47,000
SALES (est): 926.7K
SALES (corp-wide): 3.6MM **Publicly Held**
SIC: 3433 Solar heaters & collectors
PA: Solar Thin Films Inc
  1136 Rxr Plz
  Uniondale NY 11556
  516 341-7787

(G-13878)
DONALD SNYDER JR
Also Called: Donald Snyder Jr Logging
528 Allen Falls Rd (13676-4032)
PHONE..................................315 265-4485
Donald Snyder Jr, *Owner*
EMP: 15
SALES (est): 1.1MM **Privately Held**
SIC: 2411 Logging

(G-13879)
LCDRIVES CORP
65 Main St Pytn Hl 3204 Rm 3204 Peyton Hall (13676)
PHONE..................................860 712-8926
Russel Marvin, *CEO*
EMP: 13 EST: 2012
SALES (est): 2.1MM **Privately Held**
SIC: 3621 Motors & generators

(G-13880)
NORTH COUNTRY THIS WEEK
19 Depot St Ste 1 (13676-1143)
P.O. Box 975 (13676-0975)
PHONE..................................315 265-1000
Fax: 315 268-8701
William C Shumway, *President*
Craig Freilich, *Assoc Editor*
Julie Spadaccini, *Relations*
EMP: 9
SQ FT: 2,000
SALES: 850K **Privately Held**
WEB: www.northcountrynow.com
SIC: 2711 Newspapers

(G-13881)
POTSDAM SPECIALTY PAPER INC (HQ)
Also Called: Potsdam Specialty Paper, Inc.
547a Sissonville Rd (13676-3549)
PHONE..................................315 265-4000
Fax: 315 265-4005
Mike Huth, *CEO*
WEI Qun Zhang, *President*
Ronald Charette, *General Mgr*
Doug Drumm, *Opers Mgr*
Roxanne Kilgore, *Senior Buyer*
▼ EMP: 70
SQ FT: 18,400
SALES (est): 32.4MM
SALES (corp-wide): 13.8MM **Privately Held**
SIC: 2621 Specialty papers

(G-13882)
POTTERS INDUSTRIES LLC
72 Reynolds Rd (13676-3588)
P.O. Box 697 (13676-0697)
PHONE..................................315 265-4920
Fax: 315 265-2474
Andy Gray, *Manager*
Andrew Gray, *Manager*
EMP: 40
SALES (corp-wide): 1.1B **Privately Held**
WEB: www.flexolite.com
SIC: 3231 Reflector glass beads, for highway signs or reflectors
HQ: Potters Industries, Llc
  300 Lindenwood Dr
  Malvern PA 19355
  610 651-4700

(G-13883)
RANDY SIXBERRY
Also Called: Great Northern Printing Co
6 Main St Ste 101 (13676-2066)
P.O. Box 270 (13676-0270)
PHONE..................................315 265-6211
Randy Sixberry, *Owner*
Ranah Matott, *Corp Secy*
EMP: 7
SQ FT: 3,800
SALES: 700K **Privately Held**
SIC: 2396 5699 Screen printing on fabric articles; T-shirts, custom printed

(G-13884)
SNYDER LOGGING
528 Allen Falls Rd (13676-4032)
PHONE..................................315 265-1462
Donald Snyder, *Owner*
EMP: 12
SALES (est): 605.6K **Privately Held**
SIC: 2411 Logging camps & contractors

(G-13885)
SUNFEATHER NATURAL SOAP CO INC
Also Called: Sunfeather Herbal Soap
1551 State Highway 72 (13676-4031)
PHONE..................................315 265-1776
Fax: 315 265-2902
Sandra Maine, *CEO*
Kelly Deshaw, *Vice Pres*
Winona Crump, *Production*
EMP: 8
SQ FT: 6,000
SALES (est): 930K **Privately Held**
WEB: www.sunsoap.com
SIC: 2841 Soap & other detergents

Poughkeepsie
Dutchess County

(G-13886)
AMERICAN HORMONES INC
69 W Cedar St Ste 2 (12601-1351)
PHONE..................................845 471-7272
Sal Rubino, *President*
Govind Gill, *Principal*
Ashok Kadambi, *Principal*
Debbie Carey, *Office Mgr*
EMP: 12
SALES (est): 2.3MM **Privately Held**
WEB: www.americanhormones.com
SIC: 2834 Hormone preparations

▲ = Import ▼ = Export
◆ = Import/Export

GEOGRAPHIC SECTION
Poughkeepsie - Dutchess County (G-13911)

(G-13887)
APPARATUS MFG INC
13 Commerce St (12603-2608)
PHONE...................................845 471-5116
Norman Murley, *President*
Chris Murley, *Manager*
EMP: 6
SQ FT: 7,500
SALES: 600K Privately Held
WEB: www.apparatusmfg.com
SIC: 3444 Sheet metalwork

(G-13888)
ARCHITECTURAL DCTG CO LLC
Also Called: Hyde Park
130 Salt Point Tpke (12603-1016)
PHONE...................................845 483-1340
Fax: 845 483-1343
Eli Nassim, *President*
EMP: 20
SALES (est): 1.6MM Privately Held
SIC: 2499 Carved & turned wood

(G-13889)
ATLANTIS ENERGY SYSTEMS INC (PA)
7 Industry St (12603-2617)
PHONE...................................845 486-4052
Frank Pao, *Principal*
Joe Morrissey, *Vice Pres*
Jack Kennedy, *Plant Mgr*
Keith Mack, *Manager*
▲ **EMP:** 13
SALES (est): 2.3MM Privately Held
SIC: 3674 Solar cells

(G-13890)
ATLANTIS ENERGY SYSTEMS INC (PA)
7 Industry St (12603-2617)
PHONE...................................916 438-2930
Frank Pao, *President*
Joe Morrissey, *Vice Pres*
Carolyn Courtney, *Accounts Mgr*
Terri Lucas, *Admin Mgr*
Eleanor Pao, *Director*
EMP: 3
SQ FT: 10,000
SALES (est): 1.4MM Privately Held
SIC: 3674 3433 Semiconductors & related devices; solar heaters & collectors

(G-13891)
AW MACK MANUFACTURING CO INC
1098 Dutchess Tpke (12603-1150)
PHONE...................................845 452-4050
Fax: 845 452-4057
Albert Mack, *CEO*
John Mack, *Vice Pres*
Diane Conners, *Office Mgr*
EMP: 16
SQ FT: 19,000
SALES (est): 1.6MM Privately Held
SIC: 3599 Machine shop, jobbing & repair

(G-13892)
CETEK INC (PA)
19 Commerce St (12603-2608)
PHONE...................................845 452-3510
Fayiz Hilal, *President*
John Hilal, *Vice Pres*
▲ **EMP:** 25
SQ FT: 20,000
SALES (est): 3.2MM Privately Held
SIC: 3299 3599 3444 3825 Ceramic fiber; machine shop, jobbing & repair; forming machine work, sheet metal; instruments to measure electricity; porcelain electrical supplies

(G-13893)
CHOCOVISION CORPORATION
14 Catharine St (12601-3104)
PHONE...................................845 473-4970
Babu Mandava, *CEO*
Ian Lazarus, *Manager*
▲ **EMP:** 10
SALES (est): 1.9MM Privately Held
WEB: www.chocovision.com
SIC: 3599 Custom machinery

(G-13894)
CREATIVE COUNTER TOPS INC
17 Van Kleeck Dr (12601-2163)
PHONE...................................845 471-6480
Andrew Schor, *President*
EMP: 12
SALES: 600K Privately Held
SIC: 2541 Counters or counter display cases, wood; cabinets, except refrigerated: show, display, etc.: wood

(G-13895)
DORSEY METROLOGY INTL INC
53 Oakley St (12601-2004)
PHONE...................................845 229-2929
Fax: 845 454-3888
Devon Luty, *President*
Peter Klepp, *President*
Mark Swenson, *Vice Pres*
Courtney Britton, *Engineer*
John Giannetti, *Engineer*
EMP: 40
SQ FT: 18,000
SALES: 6MM Privately Held
WEB: www.dorseymetrology.com
SIC: 3545 5084 3827 3699 Gauges (machine tool accessories); precision tools, machinists'; industrial machinery & equipment; optical instruments & lenses; optical comparators; electrical equipment & supplies

(G-13896)
DYSON-KISSNER-MORAN CORP (PA)
2515 South Rd Ste 5 (12601-5474)
PHONE...................................212 661-4600
Fax: 212 986-2268
Robert R Dyson, *Ch of Bd*
Michael J Harris, *President*
Henry Beinstein, *Director*
John H Fitzsimons, *General Counsel*
John Fitzsimons, *Admin Sec*
▲ **EMP:** 30
SALES (est): 512.4MM Privately Held
SIC: 3433 3625 3699 Gas burners, industrial; motor controls, electric; security devices

(G-13897)
EAW ELECTRONIC SYSTEMS INC
16 Victory Ln Ste 3 (12603-1563)
PHONE...................................845 471-5290
Victoria Winiarski, *President*
Edward Winiarski, *Vice Pres*
Anna Tastro, *Sales Mgr*
Ana Castro, *Admin Asst*
EMP: 7
SALES (est): 820K Privately Held
WEB: www.eawelectro.com
SIC: 3568 Power transmission equipment

(G-13898)
FACES MAGAZINE INC (PA)
46 Violet Ave (12601-1521)
PHONE...................................201 843-4004
Scott Figman, *President*
Adrianne Moore, *Editor*
▲ **EMP:** 18
SALES (est): 3.3MM Privately Held
SIC: 2721 Magazines: publishing only, not printed on site

(G-13899)
FACES MAGAZINE INC
40 Violet Ave (12601-1521)
PHONE...................................845 454-7420
Timothy Perretta, *Manager*
EMP: 100
SALES (corp-wide): 3.3MM Privately Held
SIC: 2731 Book music: publishing & printing
PA: Faces Magazine Inc
46 Violet Ave
Poughkeepsie NY 12601
201 843-4004

(G-13900)
GANNETT STLLITE INFO NTWRK LLC
Also Called: Poughkeepsie Journal
85 Civic Center Plz (12601-2498)
P.O. Box 1231 (12602-1231)
PHONE...................................845 454-2000
Fax: 845 437-4903
James Konrad, *Editor*
Nora Pietrafesa, *Human Res Mgr*
Ellen Smith, *Adv Dir*
Barry Rothfeld, *Branch Mgr*
Richard L Kleban, *Manager*
EMP: 250
SALES (corp-wide): 5.7B Publicly Held
WEB: www.usatoday.com
SIC: 2711 Newspapers, publishing & printing
HQ: Gannett Satellite Information Network, Llc
7950 Jones Branch Dr
Mc Lean VA 22102
703 854-6000

(G-13901)
GET REAL SURFACES INC (PA)
121 Washington St (12601-1806)
PHONE...................................845 337-4483
Fax: 845 483-9580
George Bishop, *President*
Avis Bishop, *Vice Pres*
▼ **EMP:** 15
SQ FT: 19,800
SALES (est): 3.9MM Privately Held
WEB: www.getrealsurfaces.com
SIC: 3271 3272 Architectural concrete: block, split, fluted, screen, etc.; concrete products

(G-13902)
GLOEDE NEON SIGNS LTD INC
97 N Clinton St (12601-2032)
PHONE...................................845 471-4366
Fax: 845 471-0987
Barbara Fitzgerald, *President*
Todd Lanthier, *Opers Mgr*
Lori Giustino, *Office Mgr*
EMP: 12 **EST:** 1922
SQ FT: 9,500
SALES (est): 1.7MM Privately Held
WEB: www.gloedesigns.com
SIC: 3993 1799 Electric signs; neon signs; sign installation & maintenance

(G-13903)
GREAT EASTERN COLOR LITH (PA)
46 Violet Ave (12601-1599)
PHONE...................................845 454-7420
Lawrence Perretta, *President*
Louis Perretta Jr, *Vice Pres*
EMP: 100
SQ FT: 115,000
SALES (est): 15.5MM Privately Held
WEB: www.magnapublishing.com
SIC: 2752 Commercial printing, lithographic

(G-13904)
GREY HOUSE PUBLISHING INC
Also Called: Greyhouse Publshng
84 Patrick Ln Stop 3 (12603-2950)
PHONE...................................845 483-3535
Fax: 845 483-3542
Jennifer Patrick, *Manager*
EMP: 25
SALES (corp-wide): 6.9MM Privately Held
WEB: www.greyhouse.com
SIC: 2731 2741 Book publishing; miscellaneous publishing
PA: Grey House Publishing, Inc.
4919 Route 22
Amenia NY 12501
518 789-8700

(G-13905)
HARMON AND CASTELLA PRINTING
164 Garden St (12601-1934)
PHONE...................................845 471-9163
Fax: 845 471-2590
Frank Castella, *President*
Karen Castella, *Vice Pres*
EMP: 13 **EST:** 1974
SQ FT: 4,500
SALES (est): 2.1MM Privately Held
WEB: www.hcprinting.com
SIC: 2752 2759 Commercial printing, offset; letterpress printing

(G-13906)
HATFIELD METAL FAB INC
16 Hatfield Ln (12603-6250)
PHONE...................................845 454-9078
Fax: 845 454-9036
Ann Hatfield, *Ch of Bd*
Christopher Hatfield, *Vice Pres*
Henry Hatfield, *Vice Pres*
Ann Schwarzbarg, *Bookkeeper*
EMP: 45
SQ FT: 60,000
SALES (est): 11MM Privately Held
WEB: www.hatfieldmetal.com
SIC: 3444 5051 3479 3499 Sheet metalwork; sheets, metal; painting, coating & hot dipping; metal household articles

(G-13907)
INTERNATIONAL BUS MCHS CORP
Also Called: IBM
2455 South Rd (12603-5463)
PHONE...................................845 433-1234
Dave Turek, *President*
Kevin Cleary, *General Mgr*
Dino Quintero, *General Mgr*
Michael Laffin, *Business Mgr*
Nancy Pearson, *Vice Pres*
EMP: 4500
SALES (corp-wide): 81.7B Publicly Held
WEB: www.ibm.com
SIC: 3575 Computer terminals
PA: International Business Machines Corporation
1 New Orchard Rd Ste 1
Armonk NY 10504
914 499-1900

(G-13908)
JABIL CIRCUIT INC
2455 South Rd (12603-5463)
PHONE...................................845 471-9237
Daniel Whalen, *Manager*
EMP: 421
SALES (corp-wide): 18.3B Publicly Held
SIC: 3672 Printed circuit boards
PA: Jabil Circuit, Inc.
10560 Dr Martin Luther
Saint Petersburg FL 33716
727 577-9749

(G-13909)
JAMES L TAYLOR MFG CO (PA)
Also Called: James L. Taylor Mfg.
130 Salt Point Tpke (12603-1016)
PHONE...................................845 452-3780
Fax: 845 452-0764
Michael Burdis, *CEO*
Joseph Burdis, *Editor*
Bradley Quick, *Vice Pres*
Gordon Burdis, *Engineer*
Judi Paolillow, *Office Mgr*
▼ **EMP:** 21 **EST:** 1911
SALES (est): 4.1MM Privately Held
WEB: www.jltclamps.com
SIC: 3553 Woodworking machinery

(G-13910)
JAMES L TAYLOR MFG CO
Jlt Lancaster Clamps Div
130 Salt Point Tpke (12603-1016)
PHONE...................................845 452-3780
Michael Burdis, *President*
EMP: 9
SALES (corp-wide): 4.1MM Privately Held
WEB: www.jltclamps.com
SIC: 3553 Woodworking machinery
PA: James L. Taylor Manufacturing Co.
130 Salt Point Tpke
Poughkeepsie NY 12603
845 452-3780

(G-13911)
KOSHII MAXELUM AMERICA INC
12 Van Kleeck Dr (12601-2164)
P.O. Box 352 (12602-0352)
PHONE...................................845 471-0500
Mick Morita, *Ch of Bd*

Poughkeepsie - Dutchess County (G-13912)

Stan Posluszny, *Business Mgr*
Michele Niles, *Financial Exec*
Michelle Niles, *Human Resources*
Stanley Poluesny, *Sales Executive*
▲ **EMP:** 34
SQ FT: 60,000
SALES: 7.5MM
SALES (corp-wide): 81.8MM **Privately Held**
WEB: www.kmamax.com
SIC: 3743 Railway maintenance cars
PA: Koshii & Co., Ltd.
1-2-158, Hirabayashikita, Suminoe-Ku
Osaka OSK 559-0
666 852-061

(G-13912)
LJMM INC
Also Called: Nilda Desserts
188 Washington St (12601-1357)
PHONE...............................845 454-5876
Linda Tritto, *President*
Jason Tritto, *Vice Pres*
EMP: 20
SQ FT: 4,000
SALES: 1.2MM **Privately Held**
SIC: 2051 Bakery: wholesale or wholesale/retail combined

(G-13913)
MACHINE TECHNOLOGY INC
104 Bushwick Rd (12603-3813)
PHONE...............................845 454-4030
Fax: 845 454-4031
Klaus Greinacher, *President*
EMP: 5
SQ FT: 3,500
SALES (est): 430K **Privately Held**
SIC: 3829 Measuring & controlling devices

(G-13914)
MARCO MANUFACTURING INC
55 Page Park Dr (12603-2583)
P.O. Box 3733 (12603-0733)
PHONE...............................845 485-1571
Fax: 845 485-1649
Michael Ratliff, *President*
Brian Lowe, *Opers Mgr*
Jim Burger, *Materials Mgr*
Jolanta Skrok, *Buyer*
Patty Jessup, *QC Mgr*
EMP: 40
SQ FT: 10,000
SALES (est): 12MM **Privately Held**
WEB: www.marcomanf.com
SIC: 3577 Computer peripheral equipment

(G-13915)
MID HDSON WKSHP FOR THE DSBLED
188 Washington St (12601-1357)
PHONE...............................845 471-3820
Fax: 845 452-3407
Robert Nellis, *President*
Richard Stark, *Vice Pres*
▲ **EMP:** 25
SQ FT: 52,000
SALES: 709.7K **Privately Held**
WEB: www.midhudsonworkshop.com
SIC: 3679 Electronic circuits

(G-13916)
MID HUDSON PLATING INC
132 Smith St (12601-2109)
PHONE...............................845 849-1277
Wayne Newlin, *President*
Barbara Newlin, *Corp Secy*
Phillip Newlin, *Vice Pres*
EMP: 5 **EST:** 1964
SQ FT: 4,000
SALES (est): 536.9K **Privately Held**
WEB: www.midhudsonplaters.com
SIC: 3471 Electroplating of metals or formed products

(G-13917)
MODERN CABINET COMPANY INC
Also Called: Kitchen Cabinet Co
17 Van Kleeck Dr (12601-2163)
PHONE...............................845 473-4900
Andrew Schor, *President*
Lisa Turner, *Vice Pres*
Maxine Schor, *Treasurer*
EMP: 45
SQ FT: 21,000
SALES (est): 6.4MM **Privately Held**
SIC: 2434 Wood kitchen cabinets

(G-13918)
MPI INCORPORATED
165 Smith St Stop 5 (12601-2108)
PHONE...............................845 471-7630
Fax: 845 471-2485
Bruce S Phipps, *Ch of Bd*
Chris Dyson, *Vice Pres*
Bill Nicholas, *Plant Mgr*
Dan Phillips, *Opers Staff*
Chris Freeman, *Engineer*
▼ **EMP:** 65 **EST:** 1951
SQ FT: 30,000
SALES (est): 16.7MM **Privately Held**
WEB: www.mpi-systems.com
SIC: 3542 Pressing machines

(G-13919)
MR SMOOTHIE
207 South Ave Ste F102 (12601-4815)
PHONE...............................845 296-1686
Aaron S Goldberg, *Vice Pres*
Robert Botllieri, *Branch Mgr*
EMP: 5
SALES (corp-wide): 696.9K **Privately Held**
SIC: 2087 Concentrates, drink
PA: Mr Smoothie
1000 Ross Park Mall Dr Vc13
Pittsburgh PA 15237
412 630-9065

(G-13920)
NEW BGNNNGS WIN DOOR DSTRS LLC
28 Willowbrook Hts (12603-5708)
PHONE...............................845 214-0698
Domenica Haines, *Mng Member*
EMP: 10 **EST:** 2009
SALES (est): 1.2MM **Privately Held**
SIC: 3442 5031 Window & door frames; windows

(G-13921)
NEW ENGLAND ORTHOTIC & PROST
2656 South Rd Ste B (12601-5279)
PHONE...............................845 471-7777
EMP: 5
SALES (corp-wide): 17.9MM **Privately Held**
SIC: 3842 Surgical appliances & supplies
PA: New England Orthotic And Prosthetic Systems, Llc
16 Commercial St
Branford CT 06405
203 483-8488

(G-13922)
NILDAS DESSERTS LIMITED
188 Washington St (12601-1357)
PHONE...............................845 454-5876
Fax: 845 471-9479
James Milano, *President*
EMP: 10 **EST:** 1989
SQ FT: 5,000
SALES: 500K **Privately Held**
SIC: 2051 Bakery: wholesale or wholesale/retail combined

(G-13923)
NUTRA-VET RESEARCH CORP
201 Smith St (12601-2198)
PHONE...............................845 473-1900
Robert Abady, *President*
EMP: 10 **EST:** 1971
SQ FT: 14,000
SALES (est): 1MM **Privately Held**
SIC: 2048 Mineral feed supplements

(G-13924)
OPTIMUM APPLIED SYSTEMS INC
16 Victory Ln Ste 5 (12603-1563)
P.O. Box 3572 (12603-0572)
PHONE...............................845 471-3333
Edward Awiniarski, *President*
EMP: 19
SALES: 950K **Privately Held**
SIC: 3699 Electrical equipment & supplies

(G-13925)
PERRETTA GRAPHICS CORP
46 Violet Ave (12601-1521)
PHONE...............................845 473-0550
Fax: 845 473-2919
Lawrence Perretta, *President*
Louis Perretta Jr, *Vice Pres*
Bruce Quilliam Sr, *Vice Pres*
Todd Doughty, *Mfg Mgr*
Richard Piccoli, *Purch Agent*
EMP: 40
SQ FT: 115,000
SALES (est): 8.8MM **Privately Held**
SIC: 3555 Printing trades machinery

(G-13926)
PROTECTIVE POWER SYSTMS & CNTR
Also Called: AC DC Power Systems & Contrls
259 N Grand Ave (12603-1007)
P.O. Box 119, Staatsburg (12580-0119)
PHONE...............................845 773-9016
Andrea Patierno, *CEO*
John Patierno, *Vice Pres*
Joe Szabo, *Sales Mgr*
EMP: 11
SALES (est): 3MM **Privately Held**
WEB: www.protectivepowersystems.com
SIC: 3621 Motors & generators

(G-13927)
QUENCH IT INC
Also Called: Half Time
2290 South Rd (12601-5586)
PHONE...............................845 462-5400
Fax: 845 462-5401
Allan Daniels, *Ch of Bd*
▲ **EMP:** 20
SALES (est): 2.5MM **Privately Held**
WEB: www.halftimebeverage.com
SIC: 2086 Bottled & canned soft drinks

(G-13928)
ROBERT ABADY DOG FOOD CO LTD
201 Smith St (12601-2198)
PHONE...............................845 473-1900
Robert Abady, *President*
EMP: 12
SALES (est): 1.5MM **Privately Held**
SIC: 2047 Dog food; cat food

(G-13929)
ROYAL COPENHAGEN INC (PA)
63 Page Park Dr (12603-2583)
P.O. Box 610, Belmar NJ (07719-0610)
PHONE...............................845 454-4442
Nicolai Lindhardt, *President*
Lisa Roberson, *Controller*
▲ **EMP:** 10
SQ FT: 6,000
SALES (est): 722.9K **Privately Held**
SIC: 2392 Tablecloths & table settings

(G-13930)
SCHATZ BEARING CORPORATION
10 Fairview Ave (12601-1312)
PHONE...............................845 452-6000
Dr Stephen D E Pomeroy, *CEO*
Bob Lanser, *Plant Mgr*
Dorothy Pomeroy, *Shareholder*
Walter S Pomeroy, *Shareholder*
EMP: 75
SQ FT: 50,000
SALES (est): 21.2MM **Privately Held**
WEB: www.schatzbearing.com
SIC: 3562 Ball bearings & parts

(G-13931)
SOLARTECH RENEWABLES LLC
75 Vassar Rd (12603-5450)
PHONE...............................646 675-1853
Todd Roberts, *CEO*
Chris Alsante, *Director*
▲ **EMP:** 12
SALES: 5MM **Privately Held**
SIC: 3674 Semiconductors & related devices

(G-13932)
SPECTRA VISTA CORPORATION
29 Firemens Way (12603-6522)
PHONE...............................845 471-7007
Fax: 845 471-7020
William G Goffe, *Ch of Bd*
Tom Corl, *President*
Larry Slomer, *Senior Engr*
Ward Duffield, *Manager*
EMP: 6
SQ FT: 2,000
SALES (est): 1.2MM **Privately Held**
SIC: 3826 Spectrometers

(G-13933)
SPECTRUM GRAPHICS & PRINT
306 Main St (12601-3110)
PHONE...............................845 473-4400
Scott Mallen, *Owner*
Jodie Mallen, *Co-Owner*
Jody Mallen, *Office Mgr*
EMP: 17
SQ FT: 2,500
SALES (est): 2.3MM **Privately Held**
WEB: www.spectrum-graphics.com
SIC: 2752 7336 7334 Commercial printing, offset; commercial art & graphic design; photocopying & duplicating services

(G-13934)
STANFORDVILLE MCH & MFG CO INC (PA)
Also Called: Kent Gage & Tool Company
29 Victory Ln (12603-1562)
P.O. Box B, Stanfordville (12581-0152)
PHONE...............................845 868-2266
Fax: 845 868-7259
Neal Johnsen, *Ch of Bd*
Ann Marie Johnsen, *Corp Secy*
Peter Johnsen, *Vice Pres*
Joe La Falce, *CFO*
Bob Jones, *Manager*
EMP: 57 **EST:** 1975
SALES (est): 10.7MM **Privately Held**
WEB: www.stanfordville.com
SIC: 3599 Machine shop, jobbing & repair

(G-13935)
STEBE SHCJHJFF
18 Lynbrook Rd (12603-4608)
PHONE...............................839 383-9833
EMP: 10
SALES (est): 480K **Privately Held**
SIC: 2051 Mfg Bread/Related Products

(G-13936)
SUBURBAN PUBLISHING INC (PA)
Also Called: Hudson Valley Magazine
2678 South Rd Ste 202 (12601-5254)
PHONE...............................845 463-0542
Fax: 845 463-1544
Nancy Walbridge, *Publisher*
Angelo Martinello, *Chairman*
Robert Martinella, *Vice Pres*
Robert Martinelli, *Vice Pres*
Michael Martinelli, *Marketing Staff*
EMP: 12
SQ FT: 3,000
SALES (est): 942.4K **Privately Held**
WEB: www.hudsonvalleymagazine.com
SIC: 2721 Magazines: publishing only, not printed on site

(G-13937)
SUPERIOR WLLS OF HDSON VLY INC
Also Called: Superior Walls of Hudson Vly
68 Violet Ave (12601-1521)
PHONE...............................845 485-4033
Fax: 845 485-2501
Karen Ackert, *President*
Arthur Ackert Sr, *General Mgr*
Tammi Ackert, *Treasurer*
Louis Foscaldi, *Controller*
EMP: 50
SALES (est): 5.9MM **Privately Held**
WEB: www.superiorwallshv.com
SIC: 3272 Precast terrazo or concrete products; concrete products, precast

(G-13938)
VANTAGE MFG & ASSEMBLY LLC
Also Called: Vma
900 Dutchess Tpke (12601-1554)
P.O. Box 3623 (12603-0623)
PHONE...............................845 471-5290
Edward Winiarski, *President*
Micheal Sterbenz, *Finance*

Scott Syska, *Sales Dir*
Ana Castro, *Manager*
Greg Devine, *Manager*
EMP: 48
SALES (est): 19.6MM Privately Held
SIC: 3824 Electromechanical counters

(G-13939)
VETERINARY BIOCHEMICAL LTD
201 Smith St (12601-2110)
PHONE.................................845 473-1900
Robert Abady, *President*
EMP: 5
SQ FT: 14,000
SALES (est): 650K Privately Held
SIC: 2048 Feed supplements

(G-13940)
VIKING IRON WORKS INC
37 Hatfield Ln (12603-6249)
PHONE.................................845 471-5010
Fax: 845 471-7925
Richard J Kunkel, *Ch of Bd*
Richard J Kunke, *President*
Paul Kunkel, *Vice Pres*
Jennifer George, *Accounts Mgr*
Laurie Lunden, *Manager*
EMP: 14
SQ FT: 6,000
SALES (est): 3.3MM Privately Held
WEB: www.vikingironworks.com
SIC: 3462 Iron & steel forgings

Poughquag
Dutchess County

(G-13941)
FRED SCHULZ INC
Also Called: Schulz Interiors
4 Jordan Ct (12570-5039)
PHONE.................................845 724-3409
Fax: 845 724-3681
Fred Schulz, *President*
Mary Schulz, *Corp Secy*
EMP: 6
SALES (est): 549.6K Privately Held
WEB: www.fredschulz.com
SIC: 2511 Wood household furniture

Pound Ridge
Westchester County

(G-13942)
BIORESEARCH INC (PA)
4 Sunset Ln (10576-2318)
PHONE.................................212 734-5315
Fax: 631 249-8027
Leonard Kirth, *President*
EMP: 9
SQ FT: 7,000
SALES (est): 928.8K Privately Held
WEB: www.bioresearch.com
SIC: 3841 Surgical & medical instruments

(G-13943)
DYNAX CORPORATION
79 Westchester Ave (10576-1702)
P.O. Box 285 (10576-0285)
PHONE.................................914 764-0202
Fax: 914 764-0553
Eduard K Kleiner PHD, *President*
▲ **EMP:** 6
SQ FT: 3,600
SALES (est): 1.3MM Privately Held
WEB: www.dynaxcorp.com
SIC: 2822 2824 Fluoro rubbers; fluorocarbon fibers

(G-13944)
LLOYD PRICE ICON FOOD BRANDS
Also Called: Lawdy Miss Clawdy
95 Horseshoe Hill Rd (10576-1636)
PHONE.................................914 764-8624
Lloyd Price, *Ch of Bd*
Bill Waller, *COO*
Jacqueline Battle, *Admin Sec*
EMP: 15
SQ FT: 2,500
SALES (est): 950K Privately Held
WEB: www.lawdymissclawdy.com
SIC: 2052 Cookies

Prattsville
Greene County

(G-13945)
COBLESKILL STONE PRODUCTS INC
Also Called: Falke's Quarry
395 Falke Rd (12468-5811)
P.O. Box 268 (12468-0268)
PHONE.................................518 299-3066
Fax: 518 299-3067
Richard Mahar, *Branch Mgr*
EMP: 10
SALES (corp-wide): 103.9MM Privately Held
WEB: www.cobleskillstone.com
SIC: 1422 Crushed & broken limestone
PA: Cobleskill Stone Products, Inc.
  112 Rock Rd
  Cobleskill NY 12043
  518 234-0221

Pulaski
Oswego County

(G-13946)
FELIX SCHOELLER NORTH AMER INC
Also Called: Felix Schoeller Technical Pprs
179 County Route 2a (13142-2546)
P.O. Box 250 (13142-0250)
PHONE.................................315 298-5133
Fax: 315 298-4337
Michael Szidat, *President*
Gunter Raabe, *General Mgr*
Jim Belser, *Opers Mgr*
Steve Evans, *Controller*
Arthur Steinbrecher, *Administration*
▲ **EMP:** 110
SQ FT: 500,000
SALES: 168MM
SALES (corp-wide): 482.3MM Privately Held
WEB: www.felix-schoeller.com
SIC: 2679 Paper products, converted
HQ: Schoeller Beteiligungen Gmbh
  Burg Gretesch 1
  Osnabruck
  541 380-00

(G-13947)
FULTON BOILER WORKS INC (PA)
3981 Port St (13142-4604)
P.O. Box 257 (13142-0257)
PHONE.................................315 298-5121
Fax: 315 298-6390
Ronald B Palm, *Ch of Bd*
Nelson Lewis, *Engineer*
Scott Redden, *Info Tech Dir*
Fred Farnarier, *Info Tech Mgr*
Jyri Palm, *Info Tech Mgr*
▲ **EMP:** 60 EST: 1949
SQ FT: 120,000
SALES (est): 98.2MM Privately Held
WEB: www.fulton.com
SIC: 3443 Boilers: industrial, power, or marine

(G-13948)
FULTON BOILER WORKS INC
972 Centerville Rd (13142-2595)
PHONE.................................315 298-5121
Amy Dust, *Purch Mgr*
Jeanne Wall, *Buyer*
Ronald Palm, *Manager*
EMP: 250
SALES (corp-wide): 98.2MM Privately Held
SIC: 3443 Fabricated plate work (boiler shop)
PA: Fulton Boiler Works, Inc.
  3981 Port St
  Pulaski NY 13142
  315 298-5121

(G-13949)
FULTON HEATING SOLUTIONS INC
972 Centerville Rd (13142-2595)
P.O. Box 257 (13142-0257)
PHONE.................................315 298-5121
Ronald B Palm Jr, *Ch of Bd*
Karen Currier, *Credit Mgr*
▲ **EMP:** 55
SQ FT: 200,000
SALES (est): 5.7MM Privately Held
SIC: 3433 Burners, furnaces, boilers & stokers
PA: Hangzhou Fulton Thermal Equipment Co., Ltd.
  No.9, No.18th Street, Xiasha Economic & Technologic Development
  Hangzhou 31001
  571 867-2589

(G-13950)
FULTON VOLCANIC INC (PA)
Also Called: Fulton Companies
3981 Port St (13142-4604)
P.O. Box 257 (13142-0257)
PHONE.................................315 298-5121
Ronald B Palm, *President*
Kathy Sega, *Exec VP*
Mark Hilton, *VP Mfg*
Josh Brown, *Project Mgr*
Tony Carusone, *Mfg Staff*
▼ **EMP:** 70
SQ FT: 20,000
SALES (est): 35.9MM Privately Held
WEB: www.volcanic-heater.com
SIC: 3433 3567 3634 Heating equipment, except electric; heating units & devices, industrial: electric; electric housewares & fans

(G-13951)
HEALTHWAY HOME PRODUCTS INC
3420 Maple Ave (13142-4502)
P.O. Box 485 (13142-0485)
PHONE.................................315 298-2904
Vincent G Lobdell Sr, *Ch of Bd*
Jeffrey Herberger, *Vice Pres*
Vince Lobdell Jr, *Vice Pres*
Terri Moot, *Hum Res Coord*
Jennifer Casler, *Mktg Coord*
▲ **EMP:** 30
SQ FT: 20,000
SALES (est): 7.7MM Privately Held
WEB: www.healthway.com
SIC: 3564 Filters, air: furnaces, air conditioning equipment, etc.

(G-13952)
SOLITEC INCORPORATED
3981 Port St (13142-4614)
P.O. Box 257 (13142-0257)
PHONE.................................315 298-4213
R Bramley Palm Jr, *President*
Ronald B Palm, *Vice Pres*
EMP: 19
SQ FT: 14,400
SALES (est): 1.5MM Privately Held
SIC: 3585 Refrigeration & heating equipment

Purchase
Westchester County

(G-13953)
BOVIE MEDICAL CORPORATION
4 Manhattanville Rd (10577-2139)
PHONE.................................727 384-2323
Shailesh Chokshi, *QA Dir*
Tom Feldhaus, *QC Mgr*
Scott McArdle, *Engineer*
Janis Dezso, *VP Sls/Mktg*
Marsha Oswald, *Sales Staff*
EMP: 7
SALES (corp-wide): 29.5MM Publicly Held
SIC: 3841 Surgical & medical instruments
PA: Bovie Medical Corporation
  4 Manhattanville Rd # 106
  Purchase NY 10577
  914 468-4009

(G-13954)
BOVIE MEDICAL CORPORATION (PA)
4 Manhattanville Rd # 106 (10577-2139)
PHONE.................................914 468-4009
Robert Gershon, *CEO*
Robert L Gershon, *CEO*
Andrew Makrides, *Ch of Bd*
Moshe Citronowicz, *Senior VP*
Janis Dezso, *Vice Pres*
▲ **EMP:** 108
SALES (est): 29.5MM Publicly Held
WEB: www.boviemedical.com
SIC: 3841 Surgical & medical instruments

(G-13955)
CENTRAL NAT PULP & PPR SLS INC
3 Manhattanville Rd (10577-2116)
PHONE.................................914 696-9000
Kenneth L Wallach, *Chairman*
EMP: 2500
SALES (est): 69.9MM
SALES (corp-wide): 2B Privately Held
SIC: 2611 Pulp mills; pulp mills, mechanical & recycling processing
PA: Central National Gottesman Inc.
  3 Manhattanville Rd # 301
  Purchase NY 10577
  914 696-9000

(G-13956)
DR MIRACLES INC
2900 Westchester Ave (10577-2552)
PHONE.................................212 481-3584
Randy R Zeno, *President*
Richard Lombardi, *COO*
Ollie Johnson, *Ch Credit Ofcr*
Tanya Martinez, *Manager*
▼ **EMP:** 17
SQ FT: 1,000
SALES (est): 5.1MM Privately Held
WEB: www.drmiracles.com
SIC: 2844 Hair preparations, including shampoos

(G-13957)
HITACHI CABLE AMERICA INC (DH)
2 Manhattanville Rd # 301 (10577-2118)
PHONE.................................914 694-9200
Fax: 914 993-0997
Toro Aoki, *CEO*
Tatsuo Kinoshita, *Corp Secy*
John Gibson, *Senior VP*
Katsura Ishikawa, *Vice Pres*
Miwa Burns, *Buyer*
▲ **EMP:** 13
SQ FT: 6,000
SALES (est): 165.1MM
SALES (corp-wide): 85.7B Privately Held
WEB: www.hitachi-cable.com
SIC: 3052 Rubber & plastics hose & beltings
HQ: Hitachi Metals America, Ltd.
  2 Manhattanville Rd # 301
  Purchase NY 10577
  914 694-9200

(G-13958)
HITACHI METALS AMERICA LTD
HI Specialties America Div
2 Manhattanville Rd # 301 (10577-2103)
PHONE.................................914 694-9200
Ernie Stricsck, *President*
Christine Mandracchia, *Human Res Mgr*
David Whigham, *Manager*
Stewart Barton, *Programmer Anys*
EMP: 24
SALES (corp-wide): 85.7B Privately Held
SIC: 3312 3496 3316 3315 Rods, iron & steel: made in steel mills; miscellaneous fabricated wire products; cold finishing of steel shapes; steel wire & related products
HQ: Hitachi Metals America, Ltd.
  2 Manhattanville Rd # 301
  Purchase NY 10577
  914 694-9200

(G-13959)
HITACHI METALS AMERICA LTD (DH)
2 Manhattanville Rd # 301 (10577-2103)
PHONE.................................914 694-9200

Purchase - Westchester County (G-13960)

Fax: 914 694-9279
Hideaki Takahashi, CEO
Tomoyasu Kubota, Ch of Bd
Tomoyuki Hatano, President
Hiroaki Nakanishi, President
Akira Kitahara, Purchasing
◆ EMP: 45 EST: 1965
SQ FT: 25,000
SALES (est): 901.7MM
SALES (corp-wide): 85.7B Privately Held
SIC: 3264 3577 3365 5051 Magnets, permanent: ceramic or ferrite; computer peripheral equipment; aluminum & aluminum-based alloy castings; steel; castings, rough: iron or steel; ductile iron castings; gray iron castings; automotive related machinery
HQ: Hitachi Metals, Ltd.
1-2-70, Konan
Minato-Ku TKY 108-0
367 743-001

(G-13960)
LIGHTING HOLDINGS INTL LLC (PA)
4 Manhattanville Rd (10577-2139)
P.O. Box 25, Mahopac Falls (10542-0025)
PHONE..........................845 306-1850
Dionne Gadsden, CEO
Steve Imgham, CEO
Jan Germis, Exec VP
Tom Mullally, Exec VP
Marcos Paganini, Exec VP
◆ EMP: 10
SQ FT: 1,700
SALES (est): 69.3MM Privately Held
WEB: www.sli-lighting.com
SIC: 3641 5719 5063 4225 Electric lamps & parts for generalized applications; lamps & lamp shades; lighting fixtures; general warehousing; current-carrying wiring devices; lamp sockets & receptacles (electric wiring devices); pressed & blown glass

(G-13961)
MAM USA CORPORATION
2700 Westchester Ave # 315 (10577-2554)
PHONE..........................914 269-2500
Michael Tedesco, CEO
Fritz Hirsch, CEO
Niklaus Schertenlieb, President
Bernd Deussen, Vice Pres
Stefan Roehrig, Vice Pres
▲ EMP: 10
SALES (est): 2.2MM Privately Held
SIC: 3069 5999 Baby pacifiers, rubber; infant furnishings & equipment
HQ: Mam Babyartikel Gesellschaft M.B.H.
Lorenz Mandl-Gasse 50
Wien 1160
149 141-0

(G-13962)
NXXI INC
4 Manhattanville Rd # 205 (10577-2139)
PHONE..........................914 701-4500
Michael A Zeher, President
Alan J Kirschbaum, CFO
Alpha Jallow, Accountant
Robert E Pollack, Director
Robert Pollack,
EMP: 11
SQ FT: 5,383
SALES: 6.6MM Privately Held
WEB: www.nutrition21.com
SIC: 2836 8733 Biological products, except diagnostic; noncommercial biological research organization

(G-13963)
PEPSI BOTTLING HOLDINGS INC (PA)
700 Anderson Hill Rd (10577-1401)
PHONE..........................800 433-2652
EMP: 16
SALES (est): 13.4MM Privately Held
SIC: 2086 Bottled And Canned Soft Drinks

(G-13964)
PEPSI LIPTON TEA PARTNERSHIP
700 Anderson Hill Rd Fl 3 (10577-1401)
PHONE..........................914 253-2000
Roger Gormley, Principal
Cecelia McKenney, Human Res Dir

Marianne Pugni, Human Res Dir
Melanie Wambach, Human Res Dir
Nathan Cady, CIO
EMP: 20
SALES (est): 2.1MM Privately Held
SIC: 2086 Carbonated soft drinks, bottled & canned

(G-13965)
PEPSI-COLA METRO BTLG CO INC
700 Anderson Hill Rd (10577-1444)
PHONE..........................914 253-2000
Deborah Hoskins, Accounts Mgr
Edgar Basilio, Sales Staff
Charmika Bros, Manager
Jerry Brown, Manager
Aaron Copa, Manager
EMP: 23 EST: 2012
SALES (est): 2.3MM Privately Held
SIC: 2086 Carbonated soft drinks, bottled & canned

(G-13966)
PEPSICO INC (PA)
700 Anderson Hill Rd (10577-1444)
PHONE..........................914 253-2000
Fax: 914 253-2070
Sanjeev Chadha, CEO
Ramon Laguarta, CEO
Laxman Narasimhan, CEO
Vivek Sankaran, CEO
Indra K Nooyi, Ch of Bd
◆ EMP: 1500 EST: 1919
SALES: 63B Publicly Held
WEB: www.pepsico.com
SIC: 2096 2087 2086 2037 Potato chips & similar snacks; corn chips & other corn-based snacks; potato chips & other potato-based snacks; cheese curls & puffs; flavoring extracts & syrups; syrups, drink; fruit juices: concentrated for fountain use; concentrates, drink; bottled & canned soft drinks; iced tea & fruit drinks, bottled & canned; soft drinks: packaged in cans, bottles, etc.; carbonated beverages, non-alcoholic: bottled & canned; fruit juices; cookies & crackers; cereal breakfast foods; oatmeal: prepared as cereal breakfast food

(G-13967)
PEPSICO INC
Anderson Hill Rd (10577)
PHONE..........................914 253-2000
D Wayne Calloway, Ch of Bd
Joseph Sim, Vice Pres
EMP: 700
SALES (corp-wide): 63B Publicly Held
SIC: 2086 Carbonated soft drinks, bottled & canned
PA: Pepsico, Inc.
700 Anderson Hill Rd
Purchase NY 10577
914 253-2000

(G-13968)
PEPSICO INC
700 Anderson Hill Rd (10577-1444)
PHONE..........................914 253-2713
Denise Passarella, Branch Mgr
EMP: 10
SALES (corp-wide): 63B Publicly Held
SIC: 2086 Carbonated soft drinks, bottled & canned
PA: Pepsico, Inc.
700 Anderson Hill Rd
Purchase NY 10577
914 253-2000

(G-13969)
PEPSICO CAPITAL RESOURCES INC
700 Anderson Hill Rd (10577-1444)
PHONE..........................914 253-2000
Judy Germano, Principal
EMP: 6
SALES (est): 395.2K Privately Held
SIC: 2086 Bottled & canned soft drinks

(G-13970)
REGAL TRADING INC
Also Called: Regal Commodities
2975 Westchester Ave # 210 (10577-2500)
PHONE..........................914 694-6100
Joseph Apuzzo Jr, CEO

Sid Abramowitz, Vice Pres
Arlene Zimmer, Accounts Mgr
▲ EMP: 35
SALES (est): 6.4MM Privately Held
SIC: 2095 Coffee roasting (except by wholesale grocers)

(G-13971)
RIGHT WORLD VIEW
2900 Purchase St 528 (10577-2131)
PHONE..........................914 406-2994
Daniel Parzow, Owner
Andrew Berman, Chief
Logan Osberg, Manager
EMP: 30
SALES (est): 1.3MM Privately Held
SIC: 2711 Newspapers, publishing & printing

Purdys
Westchester County

(G-13972)
DATA INTERCHANGE SYSTEMS INC
Also Called: Peltrix
9 Ridge Way (10578-1405)
PHONE..........................914 277-7775
Amit Peleg, President
EMP: 8
SQ FT: 8,000
SALES: 3MM Privately Held
SIC: 3651 Audio electronic systems

Putnam Valley
Putnam County

(G-13973)
ARGOS INC
58 Seifert Ln (10579-1707)
PHONE..........................845 528-0576
Fax: 845 278-6769
Steven A Roy, President
Roger Eriksen, Vice Pres
Dennis Klubnick, Admin Sec
EMP: 24
SQ FT: 10,000
SALES (est): 3.7MM Privately Held
WEB: www.argos.net
SIC: 3366 3369 Bronze foundry; nonferrous foundries

Queens Village
Queens County

(G-13974)
ALL TIME PRODUCTS INC
21167 Jamaica Ave (11428-1621)
PHONE..........................718 464-1400
Fax: 718 464-4967
Junior Lindo, President
Vinton Lindo, Admin Sec
EMP: 6
SALES (est): 600K Privately Held
SIC: 2752 Commercial printing, lithographic

(G-13975)
COLGATE-PALMOLIVE COMPANY
21818 100th Ave (11429-1209)
PHONE..........................718 506-3961
Ian M Cook, President
EMP: 279
SALES (corp-wide): 16B Publicly Held
SIC: 2844 Toothpastes or powders, dentifrices
PA: Colgate-Palmolive Company
300 Park Ave Fl 5
New York NY 10022
212 310-2000

(G-13976)
EAST END VINEYARDS LLC
Also Called: Clovis Point
21548 Jamaica Ave (11428-1716)
P.O. Box 669, Jamesport (11947-0669)
PHONE..........................718 468-0500

Hal R Ginsburg, Mng Member
▲ EMP: 7
SQ FT: 5,000
SALES: 300K Privately Held
SIC: 2084 Wines

(G-13977)
GM ICE CREAM INC
8911 207th St (11427-2238)
P.O. Box 5064, Astoria (11105-5064)
PHONE..........................646 236-7383
George Mylonas, President
EMP: 6
SALES (est): 429K Privately Held
SIC: 2024 Ice cream & frozen desserts

(G-13978)
GRAY GLASS INC
21744 98th Ave Ste C (11429-1252)
PHONE..........................718 217-2943
Fax: 718 217-0280
Christopher A Viggiano, Ch of Bd
William O Bryan, Vice Pres
Dave Costa, Plant Mgr
Kenneth Rutowicz, Site Mgr
Val Krejci, Financial Exec
▲ EMP: 49 EST: 1946
SQ FT: 50,000
SALES: 7.8MM Privately Held
WEB: www.grayglass.net
SIC: 3229 3231 Glass tubes & tubing; products of purchased glass

(G-13979)
IGNELZI INTERIORS INC
9805 217th St (11429-1234)
PHONE..........................718 464-0279
Fax: 718 464-1986
Paul Ignelzi, President
Hugo Pomies, Vice Pres
EMP: 20
SQ FT: 16,000
SALES (est): 3.3MM Privately Held
WEB: www.ignelziinteriors.com
SIC: 2431 2434 Woodwork, interior & ornamental; wood kitchen cabinets

(G-13980)
JAMAICA LAMP CORP
21220 Jamaica Ave (11428-1618)
PHONE..........................718 776-5039
Irving Shernock, President
Norman Weiselberg, Manager
▲ EMP: 30 EST: 1955
SQ FT: 20,000
SALES (est): 2.8MM Privately Held
SIC: 3999 3645 Shades, lamp or candle; residential lighting fixtures

(G-13981)
LAMS FOODS INC
9723 218th St (11429-1251)
PHONE..........................718 217-0476
Fax: 718 217-0655
Sherlock Lam, President
Shervin Lam, Vice Pres
Cesar Cercado, Accountant
▲ EMP: 17
SQ FT: 20,000
SALES (est): 3.3MM Privately Held
WEB: www.lamsnacks.com
SIC: 2099 Noodles, fried (Chinese)

(G-13982)
MSQ CORPORATION
21504 Hempstead Ave (11429-1222)
PHONE..........................718 465-0900
Craig Zoly, President
EMP: 7
SALES (est): 268.7K Privately Held
SIC: 2024 Ice cream & frozen desserts; ice cream & ice milk

(G-13983)
SCENT-SATION INC
9312 Vanderveer St (11428-1729)
PHONE..........................718 672-4300
Fax: 718 672-4337
Robert Pirzata, Manager
EMP: 65
SQ FT: 20,000
SALES (corp-wide): 8.8MM Privately Held
WEB: www.scent-sation.com
SIC: 2221 2392 Satins; household furnishings

▲ = Import ▼=Export
◆ =Import/Export

PA: Scent-Sation, Inc.
350 5th Ave Ste 4202
New York NY 10118
212 244-4125

(G-13984)
VOLKERT PRECISION TECH INC
22240 96th Ave Ste 3 (11429-1330)
PHONE..................................718 464-9500
Fax: 718 464-8536
Kenneth J Heim, *Ch of Bd*
Jerome Bloomberg, *Vice Pres*
EMP: 47
SQ FT: 50,000
SALES (est): 9.8MM **Privately Held**
WEB: www.volkertprecision.com
SIC: 3469 Stamping metal for the trade; machine parts, stamped or pressed metal

(G-13985)
XEDIT CORP
Also Called: Servo Reeler System
21831 97th Ave (11429-1232)
PHONE..................................718 380-1592
Fax: 718 464-9435
Claude Karczmer, *President*
Eileen Karczmer, *Sales Staff*
EMP: 7
SQ FT: 1,800
SALES (est): 660K **Privately Held**
WEB: www.servoreelers.com
SIC: 3679 Electronic circuits

Queensbury
Warren County

(G-13986)
ADIRONDACK PRECISION CUT STONE (PA)
536 Queensbury Ave (12804-7612)
PHONE..................................518 681-3060
Kris Johnston, *Owner*
EMP: 10
SALES (est): 948.1K **Privately Held**
SIC: 3281 Cut stone & stone products

(G-13987)
AMSTERDAM PRINTING & LITHO INC
Resource One
428 Corinth Rd (12804-7816)
P.O. Box 267, Hagaman (12086-0267)
PHONE..................................518 792-6501
Bill Matte, *Purch Agent*
Kevin Kirbey, *Manager*
EMP: 9
SQ FT: 24,000
SALES (corp-wide): 5.1B **Privately Held**
WEB: www.amsterdamprinting.com
SIC: 2752 Commercial printing, offset
HQ: Amsterdam Printing & Litho, Inc.
166 Wallins Corners Rd
Amsterdam NY 12010
518 842-6000

(G-13988)
AMSTERDAM PRINTING & LITHO INC
Also Called: Web Graphics
428 Corinth Rd (12804-7816)
PHONE..................................518 792-6501
Bill Matte, *Purch Agent*
Bob Mongin, *Natl Sales Mgr*
Connie Marcotte, *Cust Mgr*
Jane Costello, *Sales Associate*
Tim Taylor, *Branch Mgr*
EMP: 11
SALES (corp-wide): 5.1B **Privately Held**
WEB: www.amsterdamprinting.com
SIC: 2759 Laser printing
HQ: Amsterdam Printing & Litho, Inc.
166 Wallins Corners Rd
Amsterdam NY 12010
518 842-6000

(G-13989)
ANGIODYNAMICS INC
543 Queensbury Ave (12804-7629)
PHONE..................................518 742-4430
EMP: 275
SALES (corp-wide): 353.8MM **Publicly Held**
SIC: 3841 Surgical & medical instruments

PA: Angiodynamics, Inc.
14 Plaza Dr
Latham NY 12110
518 795-1400

(G-13990)
ANGIODYNAMICS INC
603 Queensbury Ave (12804-7619)
PHONE..................................518 975-1400
Lynn Wadleigh, *Controller*
EMP: 400
SALES (corp-wide): 353.8MM **Publicly Held**
SIC: 3841 Surgical & medical instruments
PA: Angiodynamics, Inc.
14 Plaza Dr
Latham NY 12110
518 795-1400

(G-13991)
ARCA INK
4 Highland Ave (12804-3834)
PHONE..................................518 798-0100
Wendy Chadwick, *Owner*
EMP: 6
SALES (est): 290K **Privately Held**
SIC: 2759 Screen printing

(G-13992)
ARLINGTON EQUIPMENT CORP
588 Queensbury Ave (12804-7612)
P.O. Box 4557 (12804-0557)
PHONE..................................518 798-5867
Pauline Burnett, *President*
Debbie Burnett, *Vice Pres*
EMP: 8
SALES (est): 700K **Privately Held**
SIC: 3537 Industrial trucks & tractors

(G-13993)
C R BARD INC
289 Bay Rd (12804-2015)
PHONE..................................518 793-2531
Fax: 518 793-1012
David Freeman, *President*
Ronald Greene, *Vice Pres*
Brian Battease, *Warehouse Mgr*
David Walls, *Buyer*
Debbie Welch, *Purchasing*
EMP: 485
SALES (corp-wide): 3.4B **Publicly Held**
SIC: 3841 Surgical & medical instruments
PA: C. R. Bard, Inc.
730 Central Ave
New Providence NJ 07974
908 277-8000

(G-13994)
CAR ESSENTIALS INC
Also Called: Coomer McLoud
299 Dix Ave (12804-3933)
PHONE..................................518 745-1300
Bill Hayner, *Manager*
EMP: 5
SALES (corp-wide): 4MM **Privately Held**
WEB: www.boomer-mcloud.com
SIC: 3699 Electronic training devices
PA: Car Essentials, Inc.
1021 Central Ave
Albany NY
518 438-3000

(G-13995)
DUKE CONCRETE PRODUCTS INC
50 Duke Dr (12804-2048)
PHONE..................................518 793-7743
Fax: 518 793-0179
O E S Hedbring, *Ch of Bd*
John Hedbring, *President*
Gary Hukey, *Vice Pres*
Joanne Major, *Info Tech Dir*
Richard Schumaker, *Admin Sec*
EMP: 25
SQ FT: 9,000
SALES (est): 5.5MM
SALES (corp-wide): 144.9MM **Privately Held**
WEB: www.dukeconcrete.com
SIC: 3271 5211 5082 Blocks, concrete or cinder: standard; concrete & cinder block; masonry materials & supplies; masonry equipment & supplies

PA: The Fort Miller Service Corp
688 Wilbur Ave
Greenwich NY 12834
518 695-5000

(G-13996)
GLENS FALLS BUSINESS FORMS INC
Also Called: G F Labels
10 Ferguson Ln (12804-7641)
PHONE..................................518 798-6643
Fax: 518 798-0741
Robert Gray, *CEO*
Steve Badera, *General Mgr*
Jacob Vanness, *Vice Pres*
Betsy Carney, *Admin Sec*
EMP: 14
SQ FT: 12,000
SALES (est): 3.3MM **Privately Held**
WEB: www.gflabels.com
SIC: 2675 Die-cut paper & board

(G-13997)
GLENS FALLS READY MIX INC
Also Called: Crainville Block Co
112 Big Boom Rd (12804-7861)
PHONE..................................518 793-1695
Fax: 518 684-6141
John Tesiero, *President*
EMP: 12
SQ FT: 195
SALES (est): 770K **Privately Held**
SIC: 3272 3273 Concrete products, pre-cast; ready-mixed concrete

(G-13998)
HARRIS LOGGING INC
39 Mud Pond Rd (12804-7313)
PHONE..................................518 792-1083
Fax: 518 639-8351
Keith L Harris, *President*
Pamela Harris, *Corp Secy*
EMP: 30
SALES (est): 2.2MM **Privately Held**
SIC: 2411 Logging

(G-13999)
HJE COMPANY INC
820 Quaker Rd (12804-3811)
PHONE..................................518 792-8733
Joseph Tunick Strauss, *President*
EMP: 5
SQ FT: 4,500
SALES (est): 605K **Privately Held**
SIC: 3549 3399 Metalworking machinery; powder, metal

(G-14000)
JAMES KING WOODWORKING INC
656 County Line Rd (12804-7621)
PHONE..................................518 761-6091
Scott Kingsley, *President*
James Morris, *Vice Pres*
Wandi Abbote, *Office Mgr*
EMP: 6
SQ FT: 76,230
SALES (est): 410K **Privately Held**
SIC: 2499 Decorative wood & woodwork

(G-14001)
JE MONAHAN FABRICATIONS LLC
559 Queensbury Ave 1/2 (12804-7613)
PHONE..................................518 761-0414
Lois Bennett, *Office Mgr*
Harold A Smith,
Joe E Monahan,
Walter R Smith,
EMP: 11
SQ FT: 25,000
SALES: 1.2MM **Privately Held**
SIC: 3499 Welding tips, heat resistant: metal

(G-14002)
KINGSBURY PRINTING CO INC
813 Bay Rd (12804-5906)
PHONE..................................518 747-6606
Robert Bombard, *President*
Robert L Bombard, *Vice Pres*
Victoria Bombard-Bushey, *Director*
EMP: 6

SALES: 600K **Privately Held**
WEB: www.kingsburyprinting.com
SIC: 2752 Commercial printing, offset

(G-14003)
KOKE INC
582 Queensbury Ave (12804-7612)
PHONE..................................800 535-5303
Richard Koke, *President*
Michael Nelson, *CFO*
Tom Miksch, *Mktg Dir*
◆ EMP: 20
SQ FT: 36,000
SALES (est): 5.2MM **Privately Held**
SIC: 3537 5084 Trucks, tractors, loaders, carriers & similar equipment; materials handling machinery

(G-14004)
M & S PRECISION MACHINE CO LLC
27 Casey Rd (12804-7627)
PHONE..................................518 747-1193
Dave Mc Donald, *Mng Member*
Joyllen Sporiwski, *Manager*
Michael Spirowski,
▲ EMP: 10
SALES: 1.2MM **Privately Held**
SIC: 3545 3599 Machine tool accessories; machine & other job shop work

(G-14005)
MORRIS PRODUCTS INC
53 Carey Rd (12804-7880)
PHONE..................................518 743-0523
Jeff Schwartz, *President*
Yani Cruz, *General Mgr*
▲ EMP: 10
SQ FT: 20,000
SALES (est): 1.9MM **Privately Held**
WEB: www.morrisproducts.com
SIC: 3625 5063 Electric controls & control accessories, industrial; electrical construction materials

(G-14006)
NORTHERN DESIGN & BLDG ASSOC
Also Called: Hamilton Design Kit Homes
100 Park Rd (12804-7616)
P.O. Box 47, Hudson Falls (12839-0047)
PHONE..................................518 747-2200
Fax: 518 747-8032
Richard Kent McNairy, *CEO*
Douglas Thayer, *Exec VP*
Bob Niedermeyer, *Vice Pres*
Kent McNairy, *Treasurer*
Brian Thayer, *Sales Staff*
EMP: 21
SQ FT: 20,000
SALES (est): 3.4MM **Privately Held**
SIC: 2452 7389 Prefabricated wood buildings; design services

(G-14007)
PRAXIS POWDER TECHNOLOGY INC
604 Queensbury Ave (12804-7618)
PHONE..................................518 812-0112
Joseph A Grohowski, *President*
Tracy Macneal, *Vice Pres*
Susan Purinton, *Office Mgr*
Kathryn Lecours, *Info Tech Mgr*
EMP: 24
SQ FT: 8,400
SALES (est): 5.4MM **Privately Held**
SIC: 3841 Surgical & medical instruments

(G-14008)
PRIME WOOD PRODUCTS
1288 Vaughn Rd (12804-7356)
PHONE..................................518 792-1407
Fax: 518 792-4357
Richard Caravaggio, *Owner*
EMP: 6
SALES (est): 364.6K **Privately Held**
SIC: 2499 Decorative wood & woodwork

(G-14009)
RWS MANUFACTURING INC
22 Ferguson Ln (12804-7641)
PHONE..................................518 361-1657
Eric Fortin, *President*
Yvin Fortin, *Vice Pres*
EMP: 5

Queensbury - Warren County (G-14010)

GEOGRAPHIC SECTION

SALES (est): 808.4K
SALES (corp-wide): 5MM **Privately Held**
SIC: **2429** Shavings & packaging, excelsior
PA: Litiere Royal Inc
  2327 Boul Du Versant-Nord Bureau
  250
  Quebec QC G1N 4
  418 780-3373

(G-14010)
S & H ENTERPRISES INC
Also Called: Nationwide Lifts
10b Holden Ave (12804-3316)
PHONE 888 323-8755
Andrew Darnley, *President*
EMP: 5
SALES (est): 465.9K **Privately Held**
SIC: **3534** **3999** Stair elevators, motor powered; wheelchair lifts

(G-14011)
SEELEY MACHINE INC
Also Called: Seeley Machine & Fabrication
75 Big Boom Rd (12804-7858)
PHONE 518 798-9510
Fax: 518 798-0687
Daryl W Pechtel, *Ch of Bd*
Craig Seeley, *President*
Barbara Seeley, *Corp Secy*
Charles Seeley, *Vice Pres*
EMP: 25
SQ FT: 14,000
SALES (est): 5.6MM **Privately Held**
WEB: www.seeleymachine.com
SIC: **3599** Machine shop, jobbing & repair

(G-14012)
SINCLAIR INTERNATIONAL COMPANY (PA)
85 Boulevard (12804-3903)
PHONE 518 798-2361
Fax: 518 798-3028
David H Sinclair Jr, *President*
Brian Phelps, *Chief Engr*
Mark Havens, *Engineer*
Jason Viele, *Manager*
Donald Weaver, *Manager*
EMP: 48
SQ FT: 28,000
SALES (est): 5.9MM **Privately Held**
SIC: **3496** **3554** **3569** Wire cloth & woven wire products; paper industries machinery; filters

(G-14013)
TRIBUNE MEDIA SERVICES INC (HQ)
Also Called: TV Data
40 Media Dr (12804-4086)
PHONE 518 792-9914
Fax: 518 792-4671
Daniel Kazan, *CEO*
John B Kelleher, *President*
Richard Cusick, *General Mngr*
John Kelleher, *General Mngr*
Kathleen Tolstrup, *General Mngr*
EMP: 300
SQ FT: 38,000
SALES (est): 45MM
SALES (corp-wide): 2B **Publicly Held**
WEB: www.tvdata.com
SIC: **2741** Miscellaneous publishing
PA: Tribune Media Company
  435 N Michigan Ave Fl 2
  Chicago IL 60611
  212 210-2786

(G-14014)
WF LAKE CORP
65 Park Rd (12804-7615)
P.O. Box 4214 (12804-0214)
PHONE 518 798-9934
Fax: 518 798-9936
Jim Meyer, *President*
John L Hodgkins III, *Corp Secy*
EMP: 25
SQ FT: 33,000
SALES (est): 5.4MM **Privately Held**
WEB: www.wflake.com
SIC: **3052** Rubber & plastics hose & beltings

Quogue
Suffolk County

(G-14015)
PECONIC PLASTICS INC
6062 Old Country Rd (11959)
P.O. Box 1425 (11959-1425)
PHONE 631 653-3676
Fax: 631 653-3649
Ralph Ponto, *President*
Gerhart Ponto, *Vice Pres*
Elizabeth Ponto, *Manager*
EMP: 10
SALES (est): 786.7K **Privately Held**
WEB: www.peconicplastics.com
SIC: **3089** Molding primary plastic

Randolph
Cattaraugus County

(G-14016)
METALLIC LADDER MFG CORP
Also Called: Alumidock
41 S Washington St (14772-1326)
PHONE 716 358-6201
Fax: 716 358-4736
William Wadsworth, *President*
Christian Monroe, *Sales Staff*
Charles Jarosz, *Executive*
Daryl Wadsworth, *Admin Sec*
Elizabeth Lerow, *Administration*
▼ EMP: 15 EST: 1949
SQ FT: 12,000
SALES (est): 3.2MM **Privately Held**
WEB: www.alumidock.com
SIC: **3448** **3499** Docks: prefabricated metal; ladders, portable: metal

(G-14017)
RANDOLPH DIMENSION CORPORATION
216 Main St Ste 216 (14772)
PHONE 716 358-6901
EMP: 10 EST: 1965
SQ FT: 72,000
SALES (est): 130.2K **Privately Held**
SIC: **2426** **2431** Hardwood Dimension/Floor Mill Mfg Millwork

(G-14018)
REGISTER GRAPHICS INC
220 Main St (14772-1213)
P.O. Box 98 (14772-0098)
PHONE 716 358-2921
Fax: 716 358-5695
Robert G Beach, *President*
Tim Beach, *President*
Mark Hinman, *Corp Secy*
Jean D Beach, *Vice Pres*
Sandra Simmons, *Manager*
EMP: 23 EST: 1865
SQ FT: 13,000
SALES (est): 3.7MM **Privately Held**
WEB: www.registergraphics.com
SIC: **2752** Commercial printing, offset

Ransomville
Niagara County

(G-14019)
J F MACHINING COMPANY INC
2382 Balmer Rd (14131-9787)
P.O. Box 249 (14131-0249)
PHONE 716 791-3910
Fax: 716 791-3913
Joseph Fleckenstein, *President*
Kelly Fleckenstein, *Vice Pres*
EMP: 10
SQ FT: 2,000
SALES (est): 800K **Privately Held**
SIC: **3599** Machine shop, jobbing & repair

Ravena
Albany County

(G-14020)
BLEEZARDE PUBLISHING INC
Also Called: Greenville Local
164 Main St (12143-1112)
PHONE 518 756-2030
Fax: 518 756-8555
Richard G Bleezarde, *President*
Keith Shoemaker, *Advt Staff*
EMP: 8 EST: 1880
SQ FT: 5,400
SALES (est): 305K **Privately Held**
SIC: **2711** Commercial printing & newspaper publishing combined

(G-14021)
HOOTZ FAMILY BOWLING INC
100 Main St (12143-1709)
PHONE 518 756-4668
Brian Hotaoing, *President*
EMP: 10
SALES (est): 738.8K **Privately Held**
SIC: **3949** Bowling alleys & accessories

(G-14022)
LAFARGE BUILDING MATERIALS INC
Rr (12143)
P.O. Box 3 (12143-0003)
PHONE 518 756-5000
Martin Turecky, *Manager*
EMP: 14
SALES (corp-wide): 23.4B **Privately Held**
SIC: **3241** Masonry cement
HQ: Lafarge Building Materials Inc.
  8700 W Bryn Mawr Ave 300n
  Chicago IL 60631
  678 746-2000

(G-14023)
LAFARGE NORTH AMERICA INC
1916 Route 9 W (12143)
P.O. Box 3 (12143-0003)
PHONE 518 756-5000
Bernie Dushane, *Maint Spvr*
Martin Turecky, *Branch Mgr*
Sarah Sweeney, *Manager*
Morgan Huffman, *Supervisor*
EMP: 27
SALES (corp-wide): 23.4B **Privately Held**
WEB: www.lafargenorthamerica.com
SIC: **3241** **3273** **3272** **3271** Cement, hydraulic; portland cement; ready-mixed concrete; concrete products; precast terrazo or concrete products; prestressed concrete products; cylinder pipe, prestressed or pretensioned concrete; blocks, concrete or cinder: standard; construction sand & gravel; construction sand mining; gravel mining; asphalt paving mixtures & blocks; paving mixtures; asphalt & asphaltic paving mixtures (not from refineries)
HQ: Lafarge North America Inc.
  8700 W Bryn Mawr Ave Ll
  Chicago IL 60631
  703 480-3600

Ray Brook
Essex County

(G-14024)
FEDERAL PRISON INDUSTRIES
Also Called: Unicor
Old Ray Brook Rd (12977)
PHONE 518 897-4000
Steve Priddell, *Principal*
Jon Hensley, *Principal*
Diane Klusman, *Principal*
EMP: 99 **Publicly Held**
WEB: www.unicor.gov
SIC: **2299** Textile mill waste & remnant processing
HQ: Federal Prison Industries, Inc
  320 1st St Nw
  Washington DC 20534
  202 305-3500

Red Creek
Wayne County

(G-14025)
RED CREEK COLD STORAGE LLC (PA)
14127 Keeley St (13143-9513)
P.O. Box 622 (13143-0622)
PHONE 315 576-2069
Joel Daugherty, *President*
Joseph Dougherty, *CFO*
EMP: 5
SALES: 500K **Privately Held**
SIC: **2022** Natural cheese

(G-14026)
SMOOTHBORE INTERNATIONAL INC
13881 Westbury Cutoff Rd (13143)
PHONE 315 754-8124
Jason Smith, *President*
EMP: 7
SALES (est): 708.9K **Privately Held**
SIC: **2411** Logging camps & contractors

(G-14027)
WAYUGA COMMUNITY NEWSPAPERS (PA)
Also Called: Wayuga News
6784 Main St (13143)
PHONE 315 754-6229
Fax: 315 594-6331
Angelo Palermo, *President*
Carol Palermo, *Vice Pres*
EMP: 20 EST: 1894
SQ FT: 9,520
SALES (est): 2.5MM **Privately Held**
WEB: www.wayuga.com
SIC: **2711** **2741** Newspapers, publishing & printing; miscellaneous publishing

Red Hook
Dutchess County

(G-14028)
CORT CONTRACTING
188 W Market St (12571-2710)
PHONE 845 758-1190
Ralph Cort, *Owner*
EMP: 10
SALES (est): 680K **Privately Held**
WEB: www.cortcontracting.com
SIC: **2452** Prefabricated wood buildings

(G-14029)
HOTROCK OVENS LLC
886 Gusky Rd (12571)
PHONE 917 224-4342
Nobile Attie, *Mng Member*
EMP: 14
SALES: 360K **Privately Held**
SIC: **3556** Ovens, bakery

(G-14030)
UNIVERSAL BUILDERS SUPPLY INC
45 Ocallaghan Ln (12571-1776)
PHONE 845 758-8801
Fax: 845 758-5510
Paul Grenon, *Purch Agent*
Dave Rice, *CFO*
EMP: 16
SALES (corp-wide): 20MM **Privately Held**
WEB: www.ubs1.com
SIC: **3357** Nonferrous wiredrawing & insulating
PA: Universal Builders Supply Inc
  27 Horton Ave Ste 5
  New Rochelle NY 10801
  914 699-2400

▲ = Import ▼ = Export
◆ = Import/Export

GEOGRAPHIC SECTION

Rego Park
Queens County

(G-14031)
CARMONA NYC LLC
9830 67th Ave Apt 1d (11374-4942)
PHONE...................................718 227-6662
Tammy Carmona,
Steve Bistritzky, *Administration*
EMP: 5
SALES (est): 410K **Privately Held**
SIC: 3262 Tableware, vitreous china

(G-14032)
DIDCO INC
8570 67th Ave (11374-5225)
PHONE...................................212 997-5022
Malcolm Doyle, *President*
EMP: 12 **EST:** 2012
SALES (est): 831.8K **Privately Held**
SIC: 1499 Gemstone & industrial diamond mining

(G-14033)
J I INTRNTNAL CONTACT LENS LAB
6352 Saunders St Ste A (11374-2000)
PHONE...................................718 997-1212
Joseph Itzkowitz, *President*
EMP: 7 **EST:** 1964
SQ FT: 2,000
SALES: 750K **Privately Held**
SIC: 3851 Contact lenses

(G-14034)
KEFA INDUSTRIES GROUP INC
9219 63rd Dr (11374-2926)
PHONE...................................718 568-9297
Keyan Xing, *Principal*
Huicong Cong, *Manager*
▲ **EMP:** 7
SALES (est): 469.3K **Privately Held**
SIC: 3499 Machine bases, metal

(G-14035)
MARK I PUBLICATIONS INC
Also Called: Queens Chronicle
6233 Woodhaven Blvd (11374-3731)
P.O. Box 747769 (11374-7769)
PHONE...................................718 205-8000
Fax: 718 205-0150
Mark Wilder, *President*
Estelle Torino, *President*
Raymond G Sito, *General Mgr*
Betty M Cooney, *Editor*
Rebecca Cooney, *Counsel*
EMP: 50
SQ FT: 1,800
SALES (est): 3MM **Privately Held**
WEB: www.qchron.com
SIC: 2711 Newspapers

(G-14036)
METRO LUBE (PA)
9110 Metropolitan Ave (11374-5328)
PHONE...................................718 947-1167
Fernando Magalhaes, *Principal*
EMP: 5
SALES (est): 1.4MM **Privately Held**
SIC: 3589 Car washing machinery

(G-14037)
MILESTONE CONSTRUCTION CORP
9229 Queens Blvd Ste C2 (11374-1099)
PHONE...................................718 459-8500
Mike S Lee, *Ch of Bd*
EMP: 6
SALES (est): 570K **Privately Held**
SIC: 1442 Construction sand & gravel

(G-14038)
PCB COACH BUILDERS CORP
Also Called: Picasso Coach Builders
6334 Austin St (11374-2923)
PHONE...................................718 897-7606
Gualberto Diaz, *President*
Laura Diaz, *Treasurer*
EMP: 6
SQ FT: 20,000
SALES (est): 1.6MM **Privately Held**
WEB: www.picassocoachbuilders.com
SIC: 3711 Automobile assembly, including specialty automobiles

(G-14039)
PROFESSIONAL PAVERS CORP
6605 Woodhaven Blvd Bsmt (11374-5235)
P.O. Box 790186, Middle Village (11379-0186)
PHONE...................................718 784-7853
Duarte N Lopes, *Ch of Bd*
Nunu Lopes, *President*
Joseph Foley, *Vice Pres*
Veronica Garcia, *Manager*
Melissa Rodriguez, *Manager*
▲ **EMP:** 30
SALES (est): 6MM **Privately Held**
SIC: 3531 Road construction & maintenance machinery

Remsen
Oneida County

(G-14040)
GRAPHICS OF UTICA
10436 Dustin Rd (13438-4241)
PHONE...................................315 797-4868
Elaine B Kovach, *CEO*
EMP: 5
SQ FT: 3,319
SALES (est): 460K **Privately Held**
SIC: 2752 7334 Commercial printing, offset; photocopying & duplicating services

(G-14041)
METAL PARTS MANUFACTURING INC
9498 State Route 12 (13438-3713)
PHONE...................................315 831-2530
Fax: 315 831-2397
William Noeth, *President*
Paul Lopus, *Admin Sec*
EMP: 5
SQ FT: 3,000
SALES: 375K **Privately Held**
WEB: www.mpminc.net
SIC: 3599 Machine shop, jobbing & repair

Rensselaer
Rensselaer County

(G-14042)
ALBANY INTERNATIONAL CORP
Press Fabrics Division
253 Troy Rd (12144-9473)
P.O. Box 1907, Albany (12201-1907)
PHONE...................................518 445-2200
Fax: 518 285-4253
Steve Sassaman, *General Mgr*
Andy Dolan, *Vice Pres*
Jack Taffe, *Marketing Staff*
Gard Emond, *MIS Dir*
Thomas Curry, *Director*
EMP: 180
SALES (corp-wide): 709.8MM **Publicly Held**
WEB: www.albint.com
SIC: 2221 2297 2241 Paper broadwoven fabrics; nonwoven fabrics; narrow fabric mills
PA: Albany International Corp.
216 Airport Dr
Rochester NH 03867
518 445-2200

(G-14043)
ALBANY MOLECULAR RESEARCH INC
Also Called: Amri Rensselaer
81 Columbia Tpke (12144-3411)
PHONE...................................518 433-7700
Thomas E D'Ambra, *Ch of Bd*
Gerry Wilcox, *Purch Mgr*
Mark Klompas, *CIO*
EMP: 10
SALES (corp-wide): 402.3MM **Publicly Held**
SIC: 2833 Medicinals & botanicals
PA: Albany Molecular Research, Inc.
26 Corporate Cir
Albany NY 12203
518 512-2000

(G-14044)
ALBANY MOLECULAR RESEARCH INC
Also Called: Amri
33 Riverside Ave (12144-2951)
PHONE...................................518 512-2000
Norberto Cintron, *Facilities Mgr*
Michael Reynolds, *Engineer*
Kyle Peters, *Controller*
Steven R Hagen, *Branch Mgr*
Karen Veltman, *Senior Mgr*
EMP: 10
SALES (corp-wide): 276.5MM **Publicly Held**
SIC: 2833 Medicinals & botanicals
PA: Albany Molecular Research, Inc.
26 Corporate Cir
Albany NY 12203
518 512-2000

(G-14045)
BASF CORPORATION
Chemicals Division
70 Riverside Ave (12144-2938)
PHONE...................................518 465-6534
Fax: 518 472-8370
Michael Murphy, *Safety Mgr*
Dave Wos, *Production*
Vishal Vora, *Engineer*
Wayne Sinclair, *Manager*
Mike Pietrko, *Manager*
EMP: 280
SALES (corp-wide): 75.6B **Privately Held**
WEB: www.basf.com
SIC: 2869 Industrial organic chemicals
HQ: Basf Corporation
100 Park Ave
Florham Park NJ 07932
973 245-6000

(G-14046)
GRAPES & GRAINS
279 Troy Rd Ste 4 (12144-9752)
PHONE...................................518 283-9463
Andrew Stasky, *Owner*
EMP: 9
SQ FT: 3,000
SALES (est): 2.1MM **Privately Held**
SIC: 2084 Wines

(G-14047)
GREAT 4 IMAGE
Also Called: G4i
5 Forest Hills Blvd (12144-5831)
PHONE...................................518 424-2058
Daren Arakelian, *President*
▲ **EMP:** 35
SALES (est): 1MM **Privately Held**
WEB: www.g4i.com
SIC: 2311 Men's & boys' suits & coats

(G-14048)
INTEGRATED LINER TECH INC (PA)
45 Discovery Dr (12144-3466)
PHONE...................................518 621-7422
Fax: 518 432-9146
Paul Petrosino, *Ch of Bd*
Ken Greene, *Project Engr*
▲ **EMP:** 48
SQ FT: 30,000
SALES (est): 10.5MM **Privately Held**
WEB: www.integratedliner.com
SIC: 3821 2822 Chemical laboratory apparatus; synthetic rubber

(G-14049)
POCONO POOL PRODUCTS-NORTH
15 Krey Blvd (12144-9746)
PHONE...................................518 283-1023
Fax: 518 283-1059
Mark Vultaggio, *President*
Charles Boomhower, *Vice Pres*
EMP: 25
SQ FT: 10,000
SALES: 1MM **Privately Held**
WEB: www.completepoolsource.com
SIC: 3081 3949 Vinyl film & sheet; sporting & athletic goods

(G-14050)
REGENERON PHARMACEUTICALS INC
33 Riverside Ave (12144-2951)
PHONE...................................518 488-6000
Randy Rupp, *Branch Mgr*
EMP: 40
SALES (corp-wide): 4.1B **Publicly Held**
WEB: www.regeneron.com
SIC: 2833 Medicinals & botanicals
PA: Regeneron Pharmaceuticals Inc
777 Old Saw Mill River Rd # 10
Tarrytown NY 10591
914 847-7000

(G-14051)
REGENERON PHARMACEUTICALS INC
81 Columbia Tpke (12144-3423)
PHONE...................................518 488-6000
Fax: 518 488-6030
Dr Randall Rupp, *General Mgr*
Deborah Teggan, *Purch Mgr*
Carol Jones, *Engineer*
Diane Yocum, *Supervisor*
EMP: 40
SALES (corp-wide): 4.1B **Publicly Held**
WEB: www.regeneron.com
SIC: 2833 Medicinals & botanicals
PA: Regeneron Pharmaceuticals Inc
777 Old Saw Mill River Rd # 10
Tarrytown NY 10591
914 847-7000

(G-14052)
STEMCULTURES LLC
1 Discovery Dr (12144-3448)
PHONE...................................518 621-0848
Jeffrey Stern, *CEO*
William Price, *COO*
Christopher Fasano, *Bd of Directors*
EMP: 7
SALES (est): 304.1K **Privately Held**
SIC: 2836 Biological products, except diagnostic; culture media

(G-14053)
ULTRADIAN DIAGNOSTICS LLC
5 University Pl A324 (12144-3461)
PHONE...................................518 618-0046
Douglas Pickard, *CFO*
John P Willis,
EMP: 5
SQ FT: 2,000
SALES (est): 600.5K **Privately Held**
SIC: 3845 Electromedical equipment

Retsof
Livingston County

(G-14054)
AMERICAN ROCK SALT COMPANY LLC (PA)
3846 Retsof Rd (14539)
P.O. Box 190, Mount Morris (14510-0190)
PHONE...................................585 991-6878
Fax: 585 243-7676
Gunther Buerman, *Ch of Bd*
Justin Curley, *General Mgr*
Joseph G Bucci, *Principal*
John Goho, *Facilities Mgr*
Ann Blake, *CFO*
EMP: 20
SALES (est): 1B **Privately Held**
WEB: www.americanrocksalt.com
SIC: 1479 5169 Rock salt mining; salts, industrial

Rexford
Saratoga County

(G-14055)
WERNER BROTHERS ELECTRIC INC
677 Riverview Rd (12148-1427)
PHONE...................................518 377-3056
Craig Werner, *Owner*
EMP: 8
SALES (est): 530K **Privately Held**
SIC: 3699 Electrical equipment & supplies

Rhinebeck
Dutchess County

(G-14056)
DUTCHESS WINES LLC
Also Called: Alison Wine & Vineyard
39 Lorraine Dr (12572-1203)
P.O. Box 619 (12572-0619)
PHONE...............................845 876-1319
Richard Lewit, *President*
EMP: 5
SALES: 280K **Privately Held**
WEB: www.alisonwine.com
SIC: 2084 Wines, brandy & brandy spirits

(G-14057)
PDQ MANUFACTURING CO INC
29 Hilee Rd (12572-2349)
PHONE...............................845 889-3123
Fax: 845 889-8241
Scott Hutchins, *Ch of Bd*
Kristin Hutchins, *President*
Kerri Tiano, *Opers Mgr*
Brian Hutchins, *Facilities Mgr*
EMP: 45 EST: 1975
SQ FT: 40,000
SALES (est): 8.1MM **Privately Held**
WEB: www.pdqmfg.com
SIC: 3444 Sheet metalwork

(G-14058)
SMITHERS TOOLS & MCH PDTS INC
Also Called: Stamp
3718 Route 9g (12572-1139)
P.O. Box 391 (12572-0391)
PHONE...............................845 876-3063
Roland Jennings, *Ch of Bd*
Gary L Hosey, *President*
Robert Nevins, *Vice Pres*
Joann Russell, *Vice Pres*
EMP: 63 EST: 1947
SQ FT: 35,000
SALES (est): 11.1MM **Privately Held**
WEB: www.stampinc.com
SIC: 3699 3469 7692 3599 Electrical equipment & supplies; stamping metal for the trade; welding repair; machine shop, jobbing & repair

(G-14059)
UMBRO MACHINE & TOOL CO INC
3811 Route 9g (12572-1042)
PHONE...............................845 876-4669
Fax: 845 876-0720
Gerald Umbro, *President*
Claire Umbro, *Vice Pres*
Rosemary Kavanaugh, *Admin Sec*
EMP: 12 EST: 1959
SQ FT: 1,800
SALES: 1MM **Privately Held**
SIC: 3451 Screw machine products

(G-14060)
WARREN CUTLERY CORP
3584 Route 9g (12572-3309)
P.O. Box 289 (12572-0289)
PHONE...............................845 876-3444
Fax: 845 876-5664
James Zitz, *President*
Richard Von Husen, *Vice Pres*
EMP: 10
SQ FT: 3,500
SALES (est): 1.5MM **Privately Held**
WEB: www.warrencutlery.com
SIC: 3421 3291 5072 5085 Cutlery; abrasive products; cutlery; abrasives

Richfield Springs
Otsego County

(G-14061)
ANDELA TOOL & MACHINE INC
Also Called: Andela Products
493 State Route 28 (13439-3739)
PHONE...............................315 858-0055
Fax: 315 858-2669
Cynthia Andela, *President*
Michelle Proctor, *General Mgr*
James Andela, *Vice Pres*
Janice Arkema, *Admin Sec*
▼ EMP: 8
SQ FT: 10,000
SALES (est): 1.9MM **Privately Held**
WEB: www.andelaproducts.com
SIC: 3559 Recycling machinery

(G-14062)
WELDING AND BRAZING SVCS INC
2761 County Highway 26 (13439-3049)
PHONE...............................607 397-1009
David R Parker, *President*
Kay Parker, *Vice Pres*
Carter Cook, *Manager*
EMP: 5
SALES (est): 412K **Privately Held**
SIC: 7692 Welding repair; brazing

Richford
Tioga County

(G-14063)
MARATHON HEATER CO INC
13 Town Barn Rd (13835)
P.O. Box 58 (13835-0058)
PHONE...............................607 657-8113
Fax: 607 657-8114
Thomas J Parker, *President*
EMP: 6
SQ FT: 16,000
SALES: 500K **Privately Held**
WEB: www.marathonheaterco.com
SIC: 3585 3433 Furnaces, warm air: electric; burners, furnaces, boilers & stokers

Richmond Hill
Queens County

(G-14064)
131-11 ATLANTIC RE INC
Also Called: Premier
13111 Atlantic Ave Ste 1 (11418-3305)
PHONE...............................718 441-7700
Kevin Leichter, *CEO*
Harry Leichter, *President*
Sari Nathan, *COO*
Guillermo Soto, *Supervisor*
◆ EMP: 75
SQ FT: 250,000
SALES (est): 15.1MM **Privately Held**
WEB: www.premierpaintroller.com
SIC: 3991 Paint rollers

(G-14065)
ALL AMERICAN STAIRS & RAILING
13023 91st Ave (11418-3320)
PHONE...............................718 441-8400
Fax: 718 850-3080
Marie Bottari, *President*
EMP: 12
SALES (est): 2.4MM **Privately Held**
SIC: 3446 Stairs, fire escapes, balconies, railings & ladders

(G-14066)
ATLANTIC FARM & FOOD INC
11415 Atlantic Ave (11418-3139)
PHONE...............................718 441-3152
Gurcharn Singh, *Principal*
EMP: 13
SALES (est): 1.7MM **Privately Held**
SIC: 2037 8611 Frozen fruits & vegetables; growers' marketing advisory service

(G-14067)
BARALAN USA INC (DH)
Also Called: Arrowpak
12019 89th Ave (11418-3235)
PHONE...............................718 849-5768
Fax: 718 849-1343
Roland Baranes, *President*
Ellis Rudman, *Corp Secy*
Chris Llamas, *Opers Mgr*
Steve Consection, *Manager*
Carol Carbone, *Executive Asst*
▲ EMP: 35 EST: 1980
SQ FT: 70,000
SALES (est): 5.4MM
SALES (corp-wide): 861.5K **Privately Held**
WEB: www.arrowpak.com
SIC: 3221 3089 Cosmetic jars, glass; plastic containers, except foam
HQ: Baralan International Spa
Via Nicolo' Copernico 34
Trezzano Sul Naviglio MI 20090
024 844-961

(G-14068)
BELLE MAISON USA LTD
Also Called: Stylemaster
8950 127th St (11418-3323)
PHONE...............................718 805-0200
Elizabeth Romano, *Ch of Bd*
Ethel Romano, *Vice Pres*
◆ EMP: 30
SALES (est): 3.5MM **Privately Held**
WEB: www.stylemasterusa.com
SIC: 2392 2391 Bedspreads & bed sets: made from purchased materials; curtains, window: made from purchased materials

(G-14069)
BEST TIME PROCESSOR LLC
8746 Van Wyck Expy (11418-1958)
PHONE...............................917 455-4126
Charlie Bachu,
Somdat Bachu,
EMP: 5
SALES (est): 384.5K **Privately Held**
SIC: 2679 Paper products, converted

(G-14070)
CARLOS & ALEX ATELIER INC
Also Called: C & A Atelier
10010 91st Ave Fl 2 (11418-2118)
PHONE...............................718 441-8911
Carlos Queiroz, *CEO*
Claudio Goncalves, *COO*
EMP: 24
SQ FT: 22,000
SALES (est): 2MM **Privately Held**
SIC: 2434 2511 Wood kitchen cabinets; wood household furniture

(G-14071)
DIAMOND COLLECTION LLC
1 Rubie Plz (11418)
PHONE...............................718 846-1008
Richard Roche, *Administration*
EMP: 50
SALES (est): 1MM
SALES (corp-wide): 6.2MM **Privately Held**
SIC: 2389 Costumes
PA: Rubietoy Company, Inc
540 Broadhollow Rd
Melville NY 11747
516 326-1500

(G-14072)
ELECTRON TOP MFG CO INC
12615 89th Ave (11418-3337)
PHONE...............................718 846-7400
Fax: 718 846-8426
Craig Strauss, *President*
Frederick W Strauss III, *Vice Pres*
Kimberly S Hess, *Treasurer*
EMP: 41 EST: 1947
SQ FT: 20,000
SALES (est): 6.4MM **Privately Held**
WEB: www.electrontop.com
SIC: 3714 Tops, motor vehicle

(G-14073)
EMPIRE STATE METAL PDTS INC
10110 Jamaica Ave (11418-2007)
PHONE...............................718 847-1617
Fax: 718 805-1189
David Millshauser, *President*
▲ EMP: 20 EST: 1946
SQ FT: 20,475
SALES: 2MM **Privately Held**
SIC: 3965 Buttons & parts; buckles & buckle parts

(G-14074)
GAUGHAN CONSTRUCTION CORP
13034 90th Ave (11418-3309)
PHONE...............................718 850-9577
Anthony Gaughan, *President*
Margaret Gaughan, *Admin Sec*
EMP: 5
SQ FT: 6,000
SALES (est): 731.1K **Privately Held**
SIC: 2541 Wood partitions & fixtures

(G-14075)
HILL KNITTING MILLS INC
10005 92nd Ave Ste Mgmt (11418-2910)
PHONE...............................718 846-5000
Jeff Rosen, *President*
Peter Cruciata, *Corp Secy*
EMP: 23
SQ FT: 30,000
SALES (est): 2.1MM **Privately Held**
SIC: 2257 Pile fabrics, circular knit

(G-14076)
J & E TALIT INC
13011 Atlantic Ave Fl 2 (11418-3304)
PHONE...............................718 850-1333
Fax: 718 850-1666
Eitan Talit, *President*
EMP: 8
SQ FT: 6,000
SALES (est): 1MM **Privately Held**
WEB: www.jandetalit.com
SIC: 2253 2339 T-shirts & tops, knit; sportswear, women's

(G-14077)
OLYMPIC ICE CREAM CO INC (PA)
Also Called: Marinos Italian Ices
12910 91st Ave (11418-3317)
PHONE...............................718 849-6200
Fax: 718 805-0455
Michael Barone Sr, *President*
Frank Barone, *Vice Pres*
Frank Stracucca, *Sales Staff*
▲ EMP: 35
SQ FT: 50,000
SALES (est): 12.4MM **Privately Held**
WEB: www.marinositalianices.com
SIC: 2024 Ice cream & frozen desserts; ices, flavored (frozen dessert)

(G-14078)
PREMIER PAINT ROLLER CO LLC
13111 Atlantic Ave (11418-3397)
PHONE...............................718 441-7700
Kevin Leichter, *CEO*
EMP: 11 EST: 2004
SALES (est): 399.9K **Privately Held**
SIC: 3991 5198 Paint rollers; paint brushes, rollers, sprayers

(G-14079)
RESEARCH CENTRE OF KABBALAH
Also Called: Kabbalah Centre
8384 115th St (11418-1303)
PHONE...............................718 805-0380
Philip Berg, *President*
Beatrice Cohen, *Treasurer*
Karen Berg, *Admin Sec*
EMP: 6
SQ FT: 40,000
SALES (est): 536.6K **Privately Held**
WEB: www.kabbalah.com
SIC: 2731 Books: publishing only; pamphlets: publishing only, not printed on site

(G-14080)
RN FURNITURE CORP
11409 Atlantic Ave (11418-3139)
PHONE...............................347 960-9622
Tamesh Nankumar, *President*
EMP: 5 EST: 2009
SALES (est): 460K **Privately Held**
SIC: 3231 Furniture tops, glass: cut, beveled or polished

(G-14081)
RUBIES COSTUME COMPANY INC (PA)
12008 Jamaica Ave (11418-2521)
PHONE...............................718 846-1008
Marc P Beige, *Ch of Bd*
Joanne Rudis, *Division Mgr*
Howard Beige, *Vice Pres*
Michael Esposito, *Sales Staff*
Sandy Fernandez, *Marketing Mgr*
◆ EMP: 400

▲ = Import ▼ = Export
◆ = Import/Export

SQ FT: 55,000
SALES (est): 477.7MM **Privately Held**
SIC: 2389 7299 Costumes; costume rental

(G-14082)
RUBIES COSTUME COMPANY INC
12017 Jamaica Ave (11418-2522)
PHONE.....................................718 441-0834
Rosalie Rubies, *Vice Pres*
Francesca Labita, *Accountant*
Charlie Flohr, *Credit Staff*
Jenn Deseve, *Sales Staff*
Arthur Savarese, *Branch Mgr*
EMP: 148
SALES (corp-wide): 477.7MM **Privately Held**
SIC: 2389 Costumes
PA: Rubie's Costume Company, Inc.
  12008 Jamaica Ave
  Richmond Hill NY 11418
  718 846-1008

(G-14083)
RUBIES COSTUME COMPANY INC
1 Rubie Plz (11418)
PHONE.....................................718 846-1008
Michael Shtadtlender, *Project Mgr*
Catherine Zubrovich, *Prdtn Mgr*
Michael Andreoli, *Production*
Debra Contegni, *Production*
Maryann Depaola, *Purchasing*
EMP: 148
SALES (corp-wide): 477.7MM **Privately Held**
SIC: 2389 7299 Costumes; costume rental
PA: Rubie's Costume Company, Inc.
  12008 Jamaica Ave
  Richmond Hill NY 11418
  718 846-1008

(G-14084)
RUBIES MASQUERADE COMPANY LLC (PA)
1 Rubie Plz (11418)
PHONE.....................................718 846-1008
Dick Roche,
EMP: 4
SALES (est): 11.9MM **Privately Held**
SIC: 2389 Masquerade costumes

(G-14085)
STAIRWORLD INC
10114 Jamaica Ave (11418-2007)
PHONE.....................................718 441-9722
John Franklin, *President*
Kenneth Franklin, *President*
EMP: 5
SQ FT: 3,000
SALES (est): 390K **Privately Held**
WEB: www.stairworld.com
SIC: 2431 Stair railings, wood; staircases & stairs, wood

(G-14086)
SUPER EXPRESS USA PUBG CORP
8410 101st St Apt 4l (11418-1150)
PHONE.....................................212 227-5800
Fax: 212 227-5910
Ana Gierzphall, *President*
EMP: 12
SALES (est): 801.2K **Privately Held**
SIC: 2741 Miscellaneous publishing

(G-14087)
TERBO LTD
Also Called: Interiors By Robert
8905 130th St (11418-3328)
PHONE.....................................718 847-2860
Fax: 718 847-2826
Robert Boccard, *President*
EMP: 9
SQ FT: 3,400
SALES (est): 893.1K **Privately Held**
SIC: 2391 2392 7641 Curtains & draperies; household furnishings; upholstery work

(G-14088)
WOMENS HEALTH CARE PC (PA)
Also Called: Park Avenue Nutrition
11311 Jamaica Ave Ste C (11418-2476)
PHONE.....................................718 850-0009
Rehana Sajjad, *CEO*
EMP: 4
SALES (est): 1.3MM **Privately Held**
SIC: 3842 7991 7299 Gynecological supplies & appliances; physical fitness facilities; personal appearance services

---
Richmondville
Schoharie County

(G-14089)
CHENANGO CONCRETE CORP (PA)
145 Podpadic Rd (12149-2205)
PHONE.....................................518 294-9964
Martin Galasso, *President*
Timothy Gaffney Sr, *CFO*
Emil Galasso, *Treasurer*
Cathy Manchester, *Manager*
EMP: 12
SALES (est): 6.5MM **Privately Held**
SIC: 3273 Ready-mixed concrete

(G-14090)
TRI-CITY HIGHWAY PRODUCTS INC
145 Podpadic Rd (12149-2205)
PHONE.....................................518 294-9964
Martin Galasso, *CEO*
David Black, *Chairman*
Martin A Galasso Jr, *Chairman*
Warner Hodddon, *Manager*
EMP: 23
SALES (est): 5.3MM **Privately Held**
SIC: 2951 1442 Asphalt paving mixtures & blocks; construction sand & gravel

---
Ridge
Suffolk County

(G-14091)
AIRWELD INC
1740 Middle Country Rd (11961-2407)
PHONE.....................................631 924-6366
John Zak, *Branch Mgr*
EMP: 5
SALES (corp-wide): 30MM **Privately Held**
SIC: 7692 Welding repair
PA: Airweld, Inc.
  94 Marine St
  Farmingdale NY 11735
  631 694-4343

(G-14092)
OCEANS CUISINE LTD
367 Sheffield Ct (11961-2028)
PHONE.....................................631 209-9200
Fax: 631 209-9630
Philip Melfi, *President*
Linda Melfi, *Admin Sec*
EMP: 15
SQ FT: 1,000
SALES (est): 1.9MM **Privately Held**
WEB: www.oceanscuisine.com
SIC: 2092 Seafoods, frozen: prepared

(G-14093)
QUALITY AND ASRN TECH CORP
Also Called: Qna Tech
18 Marginwood Dr (11961-2902)
PHONE.....................................646 450-6762
Marcos Merced, *CEO*
Antonio Cefalo, *Engineer*
Daniel Corozza, *Engineer*
Jean Machado, *Engineer*
EMP: 7
SALES: 500K **Privately Held**
SIC: 7372 7379 Business oriented computer software; computer hardware requirements analysis

(G-14094)
RESIDENTIAL FENCES CORP
1760 Middle Country Rd (11961-2415)
PHONE.....................................631 205-9758
John Gulino, *Branch Mgr*
EMP: 29
SALES (corp-wide): 14.9MM **Privately Held**
SIC: 3273 Ready-mixed concrete
PA: Residential Fences Corp.
  1775 Middle Country Rd
  Ridge NY 11961
  631 924-3011

(G-14095)
WEATHER TIGHT EXTERIORS
8 Woodbrook Dr (11961-2132)
PHONE.....................................631 375-5108
Rick Dandria, *Owner*
EMP: 8
SALES (est): 550K **Privately Held**
SIC: 2421 Siding (dressed lumber)

Ridgewood
Queens County

(G-14096)
333 J & M FOOD CORP
Also Called: Allsupermarkets
333 Seneca Ave (11385-1338)
PHONE.....................................718 381-1493
Jose Espinal, *Ch of Bd*
EMP: 12 EST: 2011
SALES (est): 2.4MM **Privately Held**
SIC: 2674 Grocers' bags: made from purchased materials

(G-14097)
AABCO SHEET METAL CO INC (PA)
Also Called: Asm Mechanical Systems
47 40 Metropolitan Ave (11385)
PHONE.....................................718 821-1166
Ronald J Palmerick, *President*
Richard Minieri, *President*
Edmund MEI, *President*
Tom Brady, *Purchasing*
George Quattlander, *Information Mgr*
EMP: 75
SQ FT: 85,000
SALES (est): 57.2MM **Privately Held**
SIC: 3444 1711 1761 Ducts, sheet metal; metal housings, enclosures, casings & other containers; ventilation & duct work contractor; sheet metalwork

(G-14098)
ABR MOLDING ANDY LLC
1624 Centre St (11385-5336)
PHONE.....................................212 576-1821
Andy Skoczek, *Owner*
▲ EMP: 15
SALES (est): 2.5MM **Privately Held**
SIC: 3089 Molding primary plastic

(G-14099)
ARAMSCO INC
1819 Flushing Ave Ste 2 (11385-1002)
PHONE.....................................718 361-7540
Toll Free:......................................888 -
Mike Dambrosio, *Manager*
EMP: 10
SALES (corp-wide): 231.3MM **Privately Held**
SIC: 3842 Personal safety equipment
HQ: Aramsco, Inc.
  1480 Grandview Ave
  Paulsboro NJ 08066
  856 686-7700

(G-14100)
ARCADE BOOKBINDING CORP
801 Wyckoff Ave (11385-4742)
PHONE.....................................718 366-8484
Fax: 718 366-8682
Eugene Weiss, *President*
Jacob Hollender, *Vice Pres*
EMP: 50
SQ FT: 30,000
SALES (est): 6.1MM **Privately Held**
SIC: 2789 Binding only: books, pamphlets, magazines, etc.

(G-14101)
BARKER BROTHERS INCORPORATED
1666 Summerfield St Ste 1 (11385-5748)
PHONE.....................................718 456-6400
Kenneth A Doyle, *Ch of Bd*
Edwin Doyle, *Ch of Bd*
Walter Doyle, *Vice Pres*
David Thomas, *Vice Pres*
Thomas Vissichelli, *Vice Pres*
▲ EMP: 100 EST: 1911
SQ FT: 50,000
SALES (est): 17.2MM **Privately Held**
WEB: www.bardoabrasives.com
SIC: 3291 Buffing or polishing wheels, abrasive or nonabrasive

(G-14102)
BEST ADHESIVES COMPANY INC
4702 Metropolitan Ave (11385-1047)
PHONE.....................................718 417-3800
Sholm Singer, *President*
EMP: 6
SQ FT: 10,000
SALES (est): 670K **Privately Held**
SIC: 2891 Adhesives

(G-14103)
BRICK & BALLERSTEIN INC
1085 Irving Ave (11385-5745)
P.O. Box 1158, Yorktown Heights (10598-8158)
PHONE.....................................718 497-1400
Fax: 718 366-0149
Robert Levinson, *Ch of Bd*
Gary Levinson, *President*
Bruce Levinson, *Vice Pres*
Gladys Kaplan, *Purchasing*
▲ EMP: 82
SQ FT: 54,000
SALES (est): 15.1MM **Privately Held**
WEB: www.brickandballerstein.com
SIC: 2652 Setup paperboard boxes

(G-14104)
COSCO ENTERPRISES INC
Also Called: Cosco Soap & Detergent
1930 Troutman St (11385-1020)
PHONE.....................................718 383-4488
Andrew Cook, *President*
Lawrence McGreevy, *Vice Pres*
Pat Loy, *Office Mgr*
EMP: 7 EST: 1966
SQ FT: 10,000
SALES (est): 1.4MM **Privately Held**
SIC: 2841 Soap & other detergents

(G-14105)
ELECTRO-OPTICAL PRODUCTS CORP
6240 Forest Ave Fl 2 (11385-1929)
P.O. Box 650441, Fresh Meadows (11365-0441)
PHONE.....................................718 456-6000
Fax: 718 456-6050
Ziva Tuchman, *President*
Israel Tuchman, *CIO*
EMP: 6
SQ FT: 1,600
SALES: 1MM **Privately Held**
WEB: www.eopc.com
SIC: 3829 Measuring & controlling devices

(G-14106)
FANTASY FURNITURE INC
Also Called: G W Manufacturing
24a Woodward Ave (11385-1175)
PHONE.....................................718 386-8078
Fax: 718 386-7950
George Stavilla, *President*
▲ EMP: 32
SALES (est): 5.8MM **Privately Held**
SIC: 2431 Millwork

(G-14107)
FIVE STAR AWNINGS INC
5923 Decatur St (11385-5942)
PHONE.....................................718 860-6070
Christopher Rice, *Principal*
EMP: 12
SALES (est): 1.4MM **Privately Held**
SIC: 3444 Awnings & canopies

Ridgewood - Queens County (G-14108)

(G-14108)
GENERAL COATINGS TECH INC (PA)
24 Woodward Ave (11385-1022)
PHONE.................................718 821-1232
Fax: 718 381-6935
Michael Ghitelman, *President*
Robert Ghitelman, *Vice Pres*
EMP: 25
SQ FT: 160,000
SALES (est): 8.3MM **Privately Held**
SIC: 2851 Paints & paint additives; varnishes

(G-14109)
GRIMALDIS HOME BREAD INC
Also Called: Grimaldi Bakery
2101 Menahan St (11385-2046)
PHONE.................................718 497-1425
Fax: 718 366-0590
Vito J Grimaldi, *President*
Joseph Anobile, *COO*
Joseph Grimaldi, *Vice Pres*
Joseph Anovile, *Purch Agent*
John Lamonaca, *Sales Executive*
EMP: 85
SQ FT: 30,000
SALES (est): 11.7MM **Privately Held**
WEB: www.grimaldibakery.com
SIC: 2051 Bread, cake & related products

(G-14110)
J & C FINISHING
1067 Wyckoff Ave (11385-5751)
PHONE.................................718 456-1087
Jose Hernandez, *President*
EMP: 20
SALES (est): 1.2MM **Privately Held**
SIC: 2389 Apparel & accessories

(G-14111)
JULIAN A MCDERMOTT CORPORATION
Also Called: McDermott Light & Signal
1639 Stephen St (11385-5345)
PHONE.................................718 456-3606
Fax: 718 381-0229
Vernon McDermott, *Ch of Bd*
Andrea McDermott, *Vice Pres*
Resa Thomsan, *Manager*
▲ EMP: 45 EST: 1943
SQ FT: 25,000
SALES: 6MM **Privately Held**
WEB: www.mcdermottlight.com
SIC: 3648 Lighting equipment

(G-14112)
LONG ISLAND STAMP & SEAL CO
Also Called: L I Stamp
5431 Myrtle Ave Ste 2 (11385-3403)
P.O. Box 863990 (11386-3990)
PHONE.................................718 628-8550
Fax: 718 628-8560
Harriet Pollak, *President*
Harry Pollak, *Vice Pres*
EMP: 15
SQ FT: 4,000
SALES (est): 980K **Privately Held**
SIC: 3953 Date stamps, hand: rubber or metal

(G-14113)
LYRIC LIGHTING LTD INC
4825 Metro Ave Ste 3 (11385-1008)
PHONE.................................718 497-0109
Fax: 718 497-2351
Chester Mudick, *President*
EMP: 6 EST: 1962
SQ FT: 25,000
SALES (est): 570K **Privately Held**
SIC: 3645 Residential lighting fixtures

(G-14114)
MIB INDUSTRIES INC
Also Called: Rite Price Printing
4805 Metro Ave Ste 1 (11385-1007)
PHONE.................................718 497-2200
Isaac Mutzen, *President*
Ben Mutzen, *Vice Pres*
Nathan Hersch, *Admin Sec*
EMP: 50
SQ FT: 55,000
SALES (est): 9.4MM **Privately Held**
SIC: 2752 Commercial printing, offset

(G-14115)
NEW YORK KNITTING PROCESSOR
5900 Decatur St Ste 3 (11385-5900)
PHONE.................................718 366-3469
Fax: 718 366-2355
Farhat Pervaiz, *President*
EMP: 5
SQ FT: 5,000
SALES (est): 537.3K **Privately Held**
SIC: 2253 7389 2339 Sweaters & sweater coats, knit; textile & apparel services; women's & misses' outerwear

(G-14116)
NULUX INC
1717 Troutman St (11385-1034)
PHONE.................................718 383-1112
Fax: 718 383-1118
Delia Price, *President*
Frank Conti, *Vice Pres*
Karen Jackson, *Manager*
EMP: 33
SQ FT: 4,500
SALES (est): 6.5MM **Privately Held**
WEB: www.nulux.com
SIC: 3645 3646 Residential lighting fixtures; commercial indusl & institutional electric lighting fixtures

(G-14117)
ON THE SPOT BINDING INC
4805 Metropolitan Ave (11385-1007)
P.O. Box 863104 (11386-3104)
PHONE.................................718 497-2200
Isaac Mutzen, *President*
Nathan Hirsch, *Corp Secy*
Jerry Josefson, *Vice Pres*
EMP: 26
SQ FT: 10,000
SALES (est): 2MM **Privately Held**
SIC: 2789 Binding & repair of books, magazines & pamphlets

(G-14118)
PLANET EMBROIDERY
6695 Forest Ave (11385-3839)
PHONE.................................718 381-4827
Edwin Sotto, *Owner*
EMP: 12
SALES (est): 69.2K **Privately Held**
SIC: 2395 Embroidery & art needlework

(G-14119)
PRINT BETTER INC
5939 Myrtle Ave (11385-5657)
PHONE.................................347 348-1841
Ayman Naguib, *Ch of Bd*
▲ EMP: 6
SALES (est): 534.4K **Privately Held**
SIC: 2752 Commercial printing, lithographic

(G-14120)
PRISMA GLASS & MIRROR INC
1815 Decatur St (11385-6017)
PHONE.................................718 366-7191
Fax: 718 628-5444
Candice Tonkowich, *President*
Teresa Oneil, *Principal*
EMP: 5 EST: 1947
SQ FT: 5,000
SALES (est): 330K **Privately Held**
SIC: 3231 Mirrors, truck & automobile: made from purchased glass

(G-14121)
PUBLIMAX PRINTING CORP
6615 Traffic Ave (11385-3307)
PHONE.................................718 366-7133
Patricia Flores, *President*
Taniya Flores, *Office Mgr*
▲ EMP: 6
SALES (est): 881.9K **Privately Held**
WEB: www.publimaxprinting.com
SIC: 2759 Commercial printing

(G-14122)
RIDGEWOOD TIMES PRTG & PUBG
Also Called: Times News Weekly
6071 Woodbine St Fl 1 (11385-3242)
PHONE.................................718 821-7500
Fax: 718 456-0125
Maureen E Walthers, *President*
William Mitchell, *Manager*
EMP: 30
SQ FT: 3,500
SALES (est): 1.6MM **Privately Held**
WEB: www.timesnewsweekly.com
SIC: 2711 Newspapers, publishing & printing

(G-14123)
SARUG INC
Also Called: Sarug Knitwear
1616 Summerfield St (11385-5748)
PHONE.................................718 381-7300
Steve Virbasthe, *President*
EMP: 6
SALES (est): 549K **Privately Held**
SIC: 2253 Sweaters & sweater coats, knit

(G-14124)
SCHNEIDER M SOAP & CHEMICAL CO
1930 Troutman St (11385-1020)
PHONE.................................718 389-1000
Andrew Cook, *President*
EMP: 8 EST: 1969
SQ FT: 10,000
SALES (est): 740K **Privately Held**
SIC: 2841 Soap: granulated, liquid, cake, flaked or chip

(G-14125)
STUDIO SILVERSMITHS INC
6315 Traffic Ave (11385-2629)
PHONE.................................718 418-6785
Fax: 718 418-6863
Arnold Godinger, *Ch of Bd*
Issac Godinger, *President*
Larry Lack, *Vice Pres*
Max Harris, *Manager*
▲ EMP: 40
SQ FT: 300,000
SALES (est): 3.8MM **Privately Held**
SIC: 3914 5199 Silverware; gifts & novelties

(G-14126)
TEC - CRETE TRANSIT MIX CORP
4673 Metropolitan Ave (11385-1044)
PHONE.................................718 657-6880
Linda Gisond, *Ch of Bd*
Dale Lahman, *Bookkeeper*
EMP: 25
SQ FT: 20,000
SALES (est): 4.2MM **Privately Held**
SIC: 3273 Ready-mixed concrete

(G-14127)
TIBANA FINISHING INC
1630 Cody Ave (11385-5734)
PHONE.................................718 417-5375
Fax: 718 417-0372
Tiberija Miksa, *President*
▼ EMP: 20
SQ FT: 21,000
SALES (est): 2.5MM **Privately Held**
WEB: www.tibana.com
SIC: 2329 2331 Men's & boys' sportswear & athletic clothing; women's & misses' blouses & shirts

(G-14128)
TRADING EDGE LTD
1923 Bleecker St Apt 1r (11385-9200)
PHONE.................................347 699-7079
Michael Oniszczuk, *Purch Mgr*
EMP: 5
SALES (est): 130.5K **Privately Held**
SIC: 2741

(G-14129)
TRI-BORO SHLVING PRTITION CORP
1940 Flushing Ave (11385-1043)
PHONE.................................434 315-5600
Antoinette P Demaio, *Ch of Bd*
EMP: 12
SALES (corp-wide): 9.1MM **Privately Held**
SIC: 2542 Shelving, office & store: except wood
PA: Tri-Boro Shelving & Partition Corp.
300 Dominion Dr
Farmville VA 23901
434 315-5600

(G-14130)
TRI-BORO SHLVING PRTITION CORP
1940 Flushing Ave (11385-1043)
PHONE.................................718 782-8527
Fax: 718 963-0457
Fred Demaio, *President*
A P Demaio, *Vice Pres*
Cathy Mitchell, *Traffic Mgr*
John De Maio, *Sales/Mktg Mgr*
Nelson Cantillo, *Mktg Dir*
EMP: 15
SQ FT: 11,950
SALES (corp-wide): 9.1MM **Privately Held**
WEB: www.triboroshelving.com
SIC: 2542 5046 5084 Shelving, office & store: except wood; shelving, commercial & industrial; materials handling machinery
PA: Tri-Boro Shelving & Partition Corp.
300 Dominion Dr
Farmville VA 23901
434 315-5600

(G-14131)
VIP FOODS INC
1080 Wyckoff Ave (11385-5757)
PHONE.................................718 821-5330
Edward Fruend, *President*
Mendel Fruend, *Vice Pres*
Esther Fruend, *Purchasing*
Tobias Fruend, *Treasurer*
▲ EMP: 25
SQ FT: 13,000
SALES (est): 3.4MM **Privately Held**
WEB: www.vipfoodsinc.com
SIC: 2099 Dessert mixes & fillings; gelatin dessert preparations

Rifton
Ulster County

(G-14132)
COMMUNITY PRODUCTS LLC (PA)
Also Called: COMMUNITY PLAYTHINGS AND RIFTO
2032 Route 213 St (12471-7700)
P.O. Box 260 (12471-0260)
PHONE.................................845 658-8799
John Rhodes, *CEO*
Carol Kleinsasser, *Manager*
Eric Nelson, *Manager*
Nancy Voll, *Manager*
William Wiser, *Manager*
▲ EMP: 120
SQ FT: 5,000
SALES: 88.5MM **Privately Held**
WEB: www.communityplaythings.com
SIC: 3842 2511 3844 Orthopedic appliances; children's wood furniture; therapeutic X-ray apparatus & tubes

(G-14133)
COMMUNITY PRODUCTS LLC
2032 Route 213 St (12471-7700)
P.O. Box 903 (12471-0903)
PHONE.................................845 658-8351
Christoph Meier,
EMP: 30
SALES (corp-wide): 88.5MM **Privately Held**
SIC: 3993 Signs & advertising specialties
PA: Community Products, Llc
2032 Route 213 St
Rifton NY 12471
845 658-8799

(G-14134)
KEITH LEWIS STUDIO INC
35 Rifton Ter (12471)
P.O. Box 357 (12471-0357)
PHONE.................................845 339-5629
EMP: 9
SQ FT: 2,000
SALES: 375K **Privately Held**
SIC: 3911 5094 Jewelry, precious metal; jewelry

Ripley
Chautauqua County

(G-14135)
CHROMA LOGIC
6651 Wiley Rd (14775-9527)
PHONE...............................716 736-2458
Jason W Peterson, *President*
Jhon Mara, *Vice Pres*
EMP: 2
SQ FT: 5,000
SALES: 1.5MM **Privately Held**
SIC: 3552 Dyeing, drying & finishing machinery & equipment

(G-14136)
RIPLEY MACHINE & TOOL CO INC
9825 E Main Rd (14775-9504)
PHONE...............................716 736-3205
Fax: 716 736-3215
Andrew Reinwald, *President*
Quentin Bensink, *Vice Pres*
EMP: 17 **EST:** 1944
SQ FT: 15,000
SALES (est): 2.6MM **Privately Held**
SIC: 3599 Machine shop, jobbing & repair

Riverhead
Suffolk County

(G-14137)
ADCHEM CORP (PA)
Also Called: Adchem Industries
1852 Old Country Rd (11901-3116)
PHONE...............................631 727-6000
Fax: 631 727-6010
Joseph Pufahl, *President*
Pamela S Fardelos, *General Mgr*
Dave Hagen, *Business Mgr*
Walter Polifka, *Business Mgr*
Roopram Anderson, *Vice Pres*
▲ **EMP:** 135
SQ FT: 180,000
SALES (est): 31.8MM **Privately Held**
WEB: www.adchem.com
SIC: 2672 Tape, pressure sensitive: made from purchased materials; coated paper, except photographic, carbon or abrasive

(G-14138)
ANDREW MARC OUTLET
Also Called: Marc New York
408 Tanger Mall Dr (11901-6404)
PHONE...............................631 727-2520
K Anne Messinas, *General Mgr*
Kellie Anne Messinas, *General Mgr*
EMP: 7
SALES (est): 464.1K **Privately Held**
SIC: 3643 Outlets, electric: convenience

(G-14139)
AUTO-MATE TECHNOLOGIES LLC
34 Hinda Blvd (11901-4804)
PHONE...............................631 727-8886
Fax: 631 369-3903
Kenneth Herzog,
▼ **EMP:** 12
SALES (est): 1.9MM **Privately Held**
WEB: www.automatetech.com
SIC: 3365 Machinery castings, aluminum

(G-14140)
CUSTOM WOODWORK LTD
Also Called: Heritage Wide Plank Flooring
205 Marcy Ave (11901-3029)
PHONE...............................631 727-5260
Cathaleen Lanieri, *President*
Genie Rindfuss, *Manager*
EMP: 16
SQ FT: 3,500
SALES (est): 3.2MM **Privately Held**
WEB: www.heritagewideplankflooring.com
SIC: 2426 Flooring, hardwood

(G-14141)
DYNASTY METAL WORKS INC
787 Raynor Ave (11901-2949)
PHONE...............................631 284-3719
John Harold Jr, *President*
John Harold Sr, *Treasurer*
EMP: 7
SALES (est): 1MM **Privately Held**
SIC: 3272 3441 Concrete products, pre-cast; fabricated structural metal

(G-14142)
EASTERN WELDING INC
274 Mill Rd (11901-3145)
PHONE...............................631 727-0306
Fax: 631 727-4682
William Stubelek, *President*
Brian Stubelek, *Vice Pres*
EMP: 6
SQ FT: 10,000
SALES: 228.4K **Privately Held**
SIC: 3713 3523 3732 4226 Truck bodies (motor vehicles); farm machinery & equipment; boat building & repairing; special warehousing & storage; fabricated structural metal

(G-14143)
FREDERICK COWAN & COMPANY INC
48 Kroemer Ave (11901-3108)
PHONE...............................631 369-0360
Fax: 631 369-0637
Thomas L Cowan, *President*
Mildred Cowan, *Corp Secy*
EMP: 14
SQ FT: 20,000
SALES (est): 2.4MM **Privately Held**
WEB: www.fcowan.com
SIC: 3612 3433 Ignition transformers, for use on domestic fuel burners; gas burners, industrial

(G-14144)
HALLOCK FABRICATING CORP
324 Doctors Path (11901-1509)
PHONE...............................631 727-2441
Corey Hallock, *President*
Doreen Hallock, *Admin Sec*
EMP: 6
SQ FT: 10,000
SALES (est): 1MM **Privately Held**
SIC: 3312 3599 3441 1799 Stainless steel; machine shop, jobbing & repair; fabricated structural metal; welding on site

(G-14145)
KAPS-ALL PACKAGING SYSTEMS
200 Mill Rd (11901-3125)
PHONE...............................631 574-8778
Fax: 631 369-5939
Kenneth Herzog, *Ch of Bd*
▼ **EMP:** 57
SQ FT: 60,000
SALES (est): 14.8MM **Privately Held**
WEB: www.kapsall.com
SIC: 3565 Bottling machinery: filling, capping, labeling

(G-14146)
LEHNEIS ORTHOTICS PROSTHETIC
518 E Main St (11901-2529)
PHONE...............................631 369-3115
EMP: 7
SALES (corp-wide): 5MM **Privately Held**
SIC: 3842 5047 5999 Mfg Surgical Appliances/Supplies Whol Medical/Hospital Equipment Ret Misc Merchandise
PA: Lehneis Orthotics & Prosthetic Associates Ltd
13 Bedells Landing Rd
Roslyn NY
516 621-7277

(G-14147)
LONG IRELAND BREWING LLC
723 Pulaski St (11901-3039)
PHONE...............................631 403-4303
Gregory Martin, *President*
EMP: 5
SALES: 668K **Privately Held**
SIC: 2082 Malt beverages

(G-14148)
LONG ISLAND GREEN GUYS
26 Silverbrook Dr (11901-4269)
PHONE...............................631 664-4306
Martin Hand, *Principal*
EMP: 5
SALES (est): 473.9K **Privately Held**
SIC: 3272 Grease traps, concrete

(G-14149)
LUXFER MAGTECH INC
680 Elton St (11901-2555)
PHONE...............................631 727-8600
Brian Purves, *CEO*
Marc Lamensdorf, *President*
Deepak Madan, *Vice Pres*
Tim Zimmerman, *Vice Pres*
Deborah Simsen, *Treasurer*
EMP: 80
SALES (est): 12.3MM
SALES (corp-wide): 460.3MM **Privately Held**
SIC: 2899 5149 Desalter kits, sea water; oxidizers, inorganic; groceries & related products
PA: Luxfer Holdings Plc
Ancorage Gateway
Salford LANCS M50 3
161 300-0611

(G-14150)
NORTH COAST OUTFITTERS LTD
1015 E Main St Ste 1 (11901-2678)
PHONE...............................631 727-5580
Charles Darling III, *President*
Horst Ehinger, *Vice Pres*
Maria Lafrance, *Administration*
▼ **EMP:** 20 **EST:** 1996
SQ FT: 30,000
SALES (est): 2.2MM **Privately Held**
WEB: www.charlieshorse.com
SIC: 3949 3444 3354 Sporting & athletic goods; sheet metalwork; aluminum extruded products

(G-14151)
PHOENIX WOOD WRIGHTS LTD
132 Kroemer Ave 3 (11901-3117)
PHONE...............................631 727-9691
James Gleason, *President*
EMP: 14 **EST:** 2007
SALES (est): 2.3MM **Privately Held**
SIC: 3553 Bandsaws, woodworking

(G-14152)
PRECISION CONSULTING
Also Called: Planet Going
760 Osborn Ave (11901-2931)
PHONE...............................631 727-0847
Ted Diachun, *Owner*
EMP: 6
SALES (est): 390.3K **Privately Held**
SIC: 3556 Smokers, food processing equipment

(G-14153)
QUANTUM KNOWLEDGE LLC
356 Reeves Ave (11901-1109)
PHONE...............................631 727-6111
Alexander Pozamantir,
EMP: 6
SALES (est): 848.5K **Privately Held**
SIC: 3572 Computer storage devices

(G-14154)
ROBERT & WILLIAM INC (PA)
224 Griffing Ave (11901-3214)
PHONE...............................631 727-5780
Wil S Field, *CEO*
William Schofield Sr, *CEO*
Robert Frankel, *President*
Julie Brooke, *Manager*
Kim Curry, *Administration*
▼ **EMP:** 5 **EST:** 1997
SQ FT: 3,200
SALES: 30.1MM **Privately Held**
WEB: www.randw.com
SIC: 2011 Meat by-products from meat slaughtered on site

(G-14155)
SCHILLER STORES INC (PA)
Also Called: Le Creuset
509 Tanger Mall Dr (11901-6405)
PHONE...............................631 208-9400
Michael Kryivski, *Manager*
EMP: 5
SALES (est): 491K **Privately Held**
SIC: 3469 Cooking ware, porcelain enameled

(G-14156)
SENTRY AUTOMATIC SPRINKLER
735 Flanders Rd (11901-3828)
PHONE...............................631 723-3095
Thomas Andracchi, *President*
EMP: 10
SALES (est): 980K **Privately Held**
SIC: 3569 Sprinkler systems, fire: automatic

(G-14157)
SPIRENT INC (HQ)
303 Griffing Ave (11901-3010)
PHONE...............................631 208-0680
L John Knox, *President*
Frank V Pizzi, *Treasurer*
▲ **EMP:** 7
SQ FT: 51,000
SALES (est): 105.9MM
SALES (corp-wide): 477.1MM **Privately Held**
SIC: 3699 High-energy particle physics equipment
PA: Spirent Communications Plc
Northwood Park
Crawley W SUSSEX RH10
129 376-7676

(G-14158)
TUTHILL CORPORATION
75 Kings Dr (11901-6202)
PHONE...............................631 727-1097
EMP: 467
SALES (corp-wide): 469.3MM **Privately Held**
SIC: 3511 Mfg Steel Turbines
PA: Tuthill Corporation
8500 S Madison St
Burr Ridge IL 60527
630 382-4900

(G-14159)
WEDEL SIGN COMPANY INC
705 W Main St (11901-2843)
PHONE...............................631 727-4577
Fax: 631 727-4578
Barry Wedel, *President*
EMP: 5
SQ FT: 2,000
SALES: 276.8K **Privately Held**
SIC: 3993 Signs & advertising specialties

(G-14160)
WINE SERVICES INC
1129 Cross River Dr Ste A (11901-1703)
PHONE...............................631 722-3800
John White, *President*
John Flock, *Director*
EMP: 5
SQ FT: 21,000
SALES (est): 420.1K **Privately Held**
WEB: www.wineservices.com
SIC: 2084 Wine cellars, bonded: engaged in blending wines

Rochester
Monroe County

(G-14161)
A Q P INC
Also Called: Advanced Quickprinting
2975 Brighton Henrietta T (14623-2787)
PHONE...............................585 256-1690
Fax: 585 256-1694
James L Roach, *President*
Kim Dodson, *Office Mgr*
EMP: 7
SQ FT: 3,700
SALES (est): 1.1MM **Privately Held**
SIC: 2752 7334 Commercial printing, offset; photocopying & duplicating services

Rochester - Monroe County (G-14162) — GEOGRAPHIC SECTION

(G-14162)
A R ARENA PRODUCTS INC
2101 Mount Read Blvd (14615-3708)
PHONE.................................585 277-1680
Fax: 585 254-1046
Anthony R Arena, *CEO*
Charles Arena, *Vice Pres*
Mike Brunhuber, *Vice Pres*
Jeff Reeves, *Mfg Mgr*
Stephen Kruger, *Engineer*
▲ **EMP:** 20
SQ FT: 30,000
SALES (est): 8.6MM **Privately Held**
WEB: www.arenaproducts.com
SIC: 3089 7359 Plastic containers, except foam; shipping container leasing

(G-14163)
AAA WELDING AND FABRICATION OF
1085 Lyell Ave (14606-1935)
PHONE.................................585 254-2830
Fax: 585 254-7951
Sam Dinch, *President*
Steven Stadtmiller, *Corp Secy*
EMP: 9
SQ FT: 16,000
SALES (est): 1.9MM **Privately Held**
WEB: www.aaawelding.com
SIC: 3441 1623 7692 Fabricated structural metal; pipe laying construction; welding repair

(G-14164)
AARON TOOL & MOLD INC
620 Trolley Blvd (14606-4215)
PHONE.................................585 426-5100
Daniel Morgan, *President*
Ellen Morgan, *Vice Pres*
EMP: 8
SQ FT: 6,000
SALES (est): 1MM **Privately Held**
WEB: www.aaronmold.com
SIC: 3544 Industrial molds

(G-14165)
ACCEDE MOLD & TOOL CO INC
1125 Lexington Ave (14606-2995)
PHONE.................................585 254-6490
Fax: 585 254-0954
Roger Fox, *CEO*
Alton L Fox, *President*
Nancy Fox, *Vice Pres*
Brett Lindenmuth, *VP Opers*
Camille Sackett, *Engineer*
▲ **EMP:** 58
SQ FT: 38,000
SALES (est): 12.7MM **Privately Held**
WEB: www.accedemold.com
SIC: 3544 3599 Forms (molds), for foundry & plastics working machinery; custom machinery

(G-14166)
ACCU COAT INC
111 Humboldt St Ste 8 (14609-7415)
PHONE.................................585 288-2330
Paul Meier-Wang, *President*
Patrick Iuliamello, *Vice Pres*
Janeen Tsymbal, *Office Mgr*
EMP: 7
SQ FT: 4,500
SALES (est): 1MM **Privately Held**
WEB: www.accucoatinc.com
SIC: 3851 Ophthalmic goods

(G-14167)
ACCURATE PNT POWDR COATING INC
606 Hague St (14606-1214)
PHONE.................................585 235-1650
Fax: 585 235-3884
Christopher Ralph, *President*
Jeremy Seaver, *General Mgr*
Gina Sorokti, *Opers Mgr*
EMP: 17
SQ FT: 40,000
SALES: 1.2MM **Privately Held**
SIC: 3479 3999 Etching & engraving; coating of metals & formed products; barber & beauty shop equipment

(G-14168)
ACCURATE TOOL & DIE LLC
1085 Lyell Ave (14606-1935)
PHONE.................................585 254-2830
Sam Dinch,
Mark Drewiega,
Steve Drewiega,
Gene Lippa,
EMP: 15
SQ FT: 15,000
SALES: 1.1MM **Privately Held**
SIC: 3544 Special dies, tools, jigs & fixtures

(G-14169)
ACES OVER EIGHTS INC
Also Called: Woodcraft
1100 Jefferson Rd Ste 22 (14623-3135)
PHONE.................................585 292-9690
Sean Clayton, *President*
Andrea Clayton, *Admin Sec*
EMP: 8 **EST:** 2001
SQ FT: 7,500
SALES (est): 1.2MM **Privately Held**
SIC: 2499 Decorative wood & woodwork

(G-14170)
ACME PRECISION SCREW PDTS INC
623 Glide St (14606-1345)
P.O. Box 60649 (14606-0649)
PHONE.................................585 328-2028
Fax: 585 235-0601
Rodney Czudak, *President*
Barbara Czudak, *Manager*
EMP: 18
SQ FT: 10,000
SALES (est): 3.5MM **Privately Held**
SIC: 3451 Screw machine products

(G-14171)
ACRO INDUSTRIES INC
554 Colfax St (14606-3112)
PHONE.................................585 254-3661
Fax: 585 254-0415
Joseph A Noto, *President*
Robert Coyne, *COO*
John H Gefell, *Vice Pres*
Al Caruso, *Safety Dir*
James Francisco, *Opers Mgr*
▲ **EMP:** 148
SQ FT: 150,000
SALES (est): 65.2MM **Privately Held**
WEB: www.acroind.com
SIC: 3444 3599 3443 3469 Sheet metalwork; custom machinery; fabricated plate work (boiler shop); metal stampings

(G-14172)
ADDISON PRECISION MFG CORP
500 Avis St (14615-3308)
P.O. Box 15393 (14615-0393)
PHONE.................................585 254-1386
Fax: 585 254-5342
Robert E Champagne, *CEO*
Rodney C Champagne, *President*
Eric Caudill, *COO*
Roger C Champagne, *Vice Pres*
Rick Pursel, *Safety Mgr*
EMP: 72 **EST:** 1950
SQ FT: 40,000
SALES (est): 13.9MM **Privately Held**
WEB: www.addisonprec.com
SIC: 3599 Machine & other job shop work

(G-14173)
ADFLEX CORPORATION
300 Ormond St (14605-3090)
PHONE.................................585 454-2950
Fax: 585 454-5583
Joseph Andolora, *Ch of Bd*
Jeffery Andolora, *President*
Christopher Andolora, *Vice Pres*
Daniel Valentine, *Controller*
EMP: 36
SQ FT: 25,000
SALES (est): 7.7MM **Privately Held**
WEB: www.adflexcorp.com
SIC: 2796 7336 2754 2672 Platemaking services; engraving platemaking services; art design services; labels: gravure printing; coated & laminated paper; commercial printing

(G-14174)
ADRIAN JULES LTD
Also Called: Adrian-Jules Custom Tailor
1392 E Ridge Rd (14621-2005)
PHONE.................................585 342-5886
Fax: 585 342-0345
Adriano P Roberti, *Ch of Bd*
Arnald J Roberti, *President*
Peter E Roberti, *President*
Angela Lolas, *Human Res Dir*
Scotti Gaylor, *Manager*
▲ **EMP:** 80 **EST:** 1964
SQ FT: 14,000
SALES (est): 7MM **Privately Held**
WEB: www.adrianjules.com
SIC: 2311 5699 2325 Men's & boys' suits & coats; custom tailor; men's & boys' trousers & slacks

(G-14175)
ADVANCE CIRCUIT TECHNOLOGY INC
19 Jetview Dr (14624-4903)
PHONE.................................585 328-2000
Fax: 585 328-2019
James Morrison, *Ch of Bd*
Robert Kajfasz, *Vice Pres*
Kalman Zsamboky, *Vice Pres*
Adrianne Maxwell, *Production*
▲ **EMP:** 42 **EST:** 1998
SQ FT: 35,000
SALES (est): 11.3MM **Privately Held**
WEB: www.advcircuit.com
SIC: 3679 3672 Electronic circuits; printed circuit boards

(G-14176)
ADVANCED COATING SERVICE LLC
15 Hytec Cir (14606-4255)
P.O. Box 60387 (14606-0387)
PHONE.................................585 247-3970
Mark Romach, *Engineer*
Donald Titus, *Mng Member*
Donald E Titus Jr, *Mng Member*
EMP: 7
SALES (est): 920.8K **Privately Held**
WEB: www.acscoating.com
SIC: 3479 Etching & engraving

(G-14177)
ADVANCED GLASS INDUSTRIES INC
Also Called: A G I
1335 Emerson St (14606-3006)
P.O. Box 60467 (14606-0467)
PHONE.................................585 458-8040
Anthony Marino, *President*
H John Fischer, *Vice Pres*
Bill Neylor, *Engrg Mgr*
Alicia Gionta, *Marketing Mgr*
Henry Louis, *Marketing Staff*
▲ **EMP:** 51
SQ FT: 42,000
SALES (est): 20.7MM **Privately Held**
WEB: www.agi.com
SIC: 3827 Lenses, optical: all types except ophthalmic

(G-14178)
ADVANCED MACHINE INC
439 Central Ave Ste 108 (14605-3016)
PHONE.................................585 423-8255
Fax: 585 423-9804
John Bauman, *President*
Jacqueline De Mario, *Treasurer*
Dana Byron, *Admin Sec*
EMP: 10 **EST:** 1999
SQ FT: 5,600
SALES (est): 1.4MM **Privately Held**
SIC: 3599 Machine shop, jobbing & repair

(G-14179)
ADVANCED MOLD & TOOLING INC
769 Trabold Rd (14624-2588)
PHONE.................................585 426-2110
Fax: 585 426-8041
Peter Grassl, *President*
Julius Bartl Jr, *Vice Pres*
Julius Bartl, *Vice Pres*
Hannelore Grassl, *Treasurer*
Elfriede Bartl, *Admin Sec*
▲ **EMP:** 30 **EST:** 1978
SQ FT: 27,000
SALES (est): 5.8MM **Privately Held**
WEB: www.advancedmold.us
SIC: 3544 Industrial molds

(G-14180)
ADVANTAGE METALWORK FINSHG LLC
1000 University Ave # 700 (14607-1286)
PHONE.................................585 454-0160
Fax: 585 454-0173
Chet Wester, *CEO*
Arthur Carroll, *Exec VP*
Dale Campbell, *Vice Pres*
Greg Miller, *Opers Mgr*
Thomas Coburn, *Engineer*
EMP: 86
SALES (est): 21.5MM **Privately Held**
SIC: 3542 Machine tools, metal forming type

(G-14181)
ADVANTECH INDUSTRIES INC
3850 Buffalo Rd (14624-1104)
PHONE.................................585 247-0701
Fax: 585 247-0745
James Gizzi, *Ch of Bd*
EMP: 115
SALES (est): 26.4MM **Privately Held**
WEB: www.advantechindustries.com
SIC: 3399 3444 Laminating steel; sheet metalwork

(G-14182)
AIRGAS INC
77 Deep Rock Rd (14624-3519)
PHONE.................................585 436-7780
Fax: 585 436-8907
Bob Hewitt, *CEO*
EMP: 23
SALES (corp-wide): 189.3MM **Privately Held**
SIC: 2813 Industrial gases
HQ: Airgas, Inc.
  259 N Radnor Chester Rd
  Radnor PA 19087
  610 687-5253

(G-14183)
AIRGAS USA LLC
77 Deep Rock Rd (14624-3519)
PHONE.................................585 436-7781
Robert Gross, *Opers Mgr*
Bob Hewitt, *Branch Mgr*
EMP: 15
SQ FT: 12,330
SALES (corp-wide): 189.3MM **Privately Held**
WEB: www.airgas.com
SIC: 2813 Industrial gases
HQ: Airgas Usa Llc
  259 N Radnor Chester Rd # 100
  Radnor PA 19087
  610 687-5253

(G-14184)
AJL MANUFACTURING INC
100 Holleder Pkwy (14615-3800)
PHONE.................................585 254-1128
David Zink, *General Mgr*
Albert F Porter, *Chairman*
Mark Burch, *Facilities Dir*
Joe Frillici, *Plant Mgr*
Patrick Palermo, *Opers Mgr*
▲ **EMP:** 112
SQ FT: 165,000
SALES (est): 30.8MM **Privately Held**
WEB: www.ajlmfg.com
SIC: 3469 Stamping metal for the trade

(G-14185)
ALCOA FASTENING SYSTEMS
181 Mckee Rd (14611-2011)
PHONE.................................585 368-5049
Vitaliy Rusakov, *CEO*
EMP: 7 **EST:** 2015
SALES (est): 611K **Privately Held**
SIC: 3353 Aluminum sheet & strip

(G-14186)
ALKEMY MACHINE LLC
Also Called: Aurora Machine
1600 Lexington Ave 103c (14606-3000)
PHONE.................................585 436-8730
Jonathan Amoia, *General Mgr*
Jordan Kowalczyk, *General Mgr*
EMP: 8

▲ = Import ▼ = Export
◆ = Import/Export

GEOGRAPHIC SECTION

Rochester - Monroe County (G-14255)

SALES (est): 150.1MM
SALES (corp-wide): 2B **Privately Held**
SIC: 2033 2013 2035 2096 Fruits & fruit products in cans, jars, etc.; fruit pie mixes & fillings; packaged in cans, jars, etc.; canned meats (except baby food) from purchased meat; beef stew from purchased meat; pickles, vinegar; dressings, salad: raw & cooked (except dry mixes); potato chips & other potato-based snacks; cheese curls & puffs
HQ: Vestar/Agrilink Holdings Llc
  90 Linden Park
  Rochester NY

(G-14233)
BITTNER COMPANY LLC
Also Called: AlphaGraphics
75 Goodway Dr Ste 3 (14623-3000)
PHONE 585 214-1790
EMP: 13
SALES (est): 1.5MM **Privately Held**
SIC: 2752 Comm Prtg Litho

(G-14234)
BLACKBOX BIOMETRICS INC
125 Tech Park Dr Ste 1131 (14623-2438)
PHONE 585 329-3399
Joseph V Bridgeford, *Ch of Bd*
Michael Ostertag, *Electrical Engi*
Scott Featherman, *Sales Staff*
David Borkholder, *CTO*
EMP: 22
SALES (est): 2.2MM **Privately Held**
SIC: 3999 Barber & beauty shop equipment

(G-14235)
BLOCH INDUSTRIES LLC
140 Commerce Dr (14623-3504)
P.O. Box 25806 (14625-0806)
PHONE 585 334-9600
Fax: 585 334-9636
Diane Miller, *Office Mgr*
Brian Geary, *Mng Member*
EMP: 60
SQ FT: 54,000
SALES (est): 8.4MM **Privately Held**
WEB: www.blochindustries.com
SIC: 2434 2541 2431 2521 Wood kitchen cabinets; counters or counter display cases, wood; millwork; wood office furniture

(G-14236)
BLUE CHIP MOLD INC
95 Lagrange Ave (14613-1509)
PHONE 585 647-1790
Fax: 585 647-2138
Paul A Engert, *President*
Daniellle Champeney, *Manager*
EMP: 13
SQ FT: 10,250
SALES: 1.3MM **Privately Held**
SIC: 3544 Industrial molds

(G-14237)
BLUE TOAD HARD CIDER
120 Mushroom Blvd (14623-3263)
PHONE 585 424-5508
Todd Rath, *Co-Owner*
EMP: 20
SALES (est): 1.9MM **Privately Held**
SIC: 3556 Presses, food: cheese, beet, cider & sugarcane

(G-14238)
BMA MEDIA SERVICES INC
Also Called: Spinergy
1655 Lyell Ave (14606-2311)
PHONE 585 385-2060
EMP: 29 **EST:** 2013
SQ FT: 79,000
SALES (est): 1.7MM **Privately Held**
SIC: 3695 Mfg Magnetic/Optical Recording Media

(G-14239)
BOB PERANI SPORT SHOPS INC
1225 Jefferson Rd (14623-3163)
PHONE 585 427-2930
Raymund House, *Branch Mgr*
EMP: 8

SALES (corp-wide): 11.6MM **Privately Held**
SIC: 3949 Sporting & athletic goods
PA: Bob Perani Sport Shops, Inc.
  3600 S Dort Hwy Ste 19
  Flint MI 48507
  810 744-3338

(G-14240)
BODYCOTE THERMAL PROC INC
620 Buffalo Rd (14611-2006)
PHONE 585 436-7876
Keith Stewart, *Div Sub Head*
Milton Cage, *Opers Mgr*
Al Rogers, *Sales Staff*
Tony Schaut, *Branch Mgr*
EMP: 24
SQ FT: 10,000
SALES (corp-wide): 968.6MM **Privately Held**
SIC: 3398 Metal heat treating
HQ: Bodycote Thermal Processing, Inc.
  12700 Park Central Dr # 700
  Dallas TX 75251
  214 904-2420

(G-14241)
BOEHM SURGICAL INSTRUMENT
966 Chili Ave Ste 3 (14611-2896)
PHONE 585 436-6584
Fax: 585 436-6428
Paul Boehm, *President*
Mary L Cooper, *Corp Secy*
Jean Sullivan, *Treasurer*
EMP: 11 **EST:** 1915
SQ FT: 13,000
SALES: 1MM **Privately Held**
SIC: 3841 3843 3429 3641 Surgical & medical instruments; dental equipment; keys, locks & related hardware; electric lamps & parts for specialized applications

(G-14242)
BOOK1ONE LLC
655 Driving Park Ave (14613-1566)
PHONE 585 458-2101
Peter Pape, *CEO*
Jim Gleason, *Credit Mgr*
Corey Upright, *Marketing Mgr*
Marc Bardeen,
EMP: 7
SALES (est): 1MM **Privately Held**
WEB: www.book1one.com
SIC: 2732 Books: printing & binding

(G-14243)
BOYDELL & BREWER INC
Also Called: Camden House
668 Mount Hope Ave (14620-2731)
PHONE 585 275-0419
Fax: 585 271-8778
Sue Smit, *President*
Sue Miller, *Marketing Staff*
Sue Smith, *Exec Dir*
Eloise Puls, *Director*
Richard Barber, *Intl Dir*
EMP: 12
SQ FT: 1,500
SALES (est): 1.3MM
SALES (corp-wide): 1.9MM **Privately Held**
SIC: 2731 Book music: publishing only, not printed on site
PA: Boydell & Brewer Group Limited
  Bridge Farm Business Park
  Woodbridge IP12
  139 461-0600

(G-14244)
BRAYLEY TOOL & MACHINE INC
1685 Lyell Ave (14606-2311)
PHONE 585 342-7190
Fax: 585 342-0972
Stephen Roeger, *President*
Rena Roeger, *Vice Pres*
EMP: 8
SQ FT: 6,500
SALES: 700K **Privately Held**
WEB: www.brayleytool.com
SIC: 3544 Special dies, tools, jigs & fixtures

(G-14245)
BRINKMAN INTL GROUP INC (PA)
167 Ames St (14611-1701)
PHONE 585 429-5000
Andrew J Laniak, *CEO*
Robert Brinkman, *Ch of Bd*
Daniel Bavineau, *Mfg Dir*
Dan Robinson, *Engineer*
Ella Gardner, *Controller*
EMP: 1
SQ FT: 12,000
SALES (est): 81.2MM **Privately Held**
WEB: www.brinkmanig.com
SIC: 3545 3451 3325 3542 Thread cutting dies; screw machine products; steel foundries; machine tools, metal forming type

(G-14246)
BRINKMAN PRODUCTS INC (HQ)
Also Called: Davenport
167 Ames St (14611-1701)
PHONE 585 235-4545
Andrew Laniak, *Ch of Bd*
Andrew J Laniak, *President*
Robert J Brinkman, *Principal*
David Long, *Opers Mgr*
Alle Gardner, *Controller*
▲ **EMP:** 290
SQ FT: 118,000
SALES (est): 61.2MM
SALES (corp-wide): 81.2MM **Privately Held**
WEB: www.davenportmachine.com
SIC: 3541 5084 Machine tools, metal cutting type; industrial machinery & equipment
PA: Brinkman International Group, Inc.
  167 Ames St
  Rochester NY 14611
  585 429-5000

(G-14247)
BRISTOL BOARDING INC
1336 Culver Rd (14609-5336)
PHONE 585 271-7860
Fax: 585 271-3679
Bille McDonald, *President*
Mary McDonald, *Vice Pres*
EMP: 6 **EST:** 1974
SALES (est): 865.8K **Privately Held**
WEB: www.bristolcase.com
SIC: 2441 5099 Shipping cases, wood: nailed or lock corner; cases, carrying

(G-14248)
BRUCE WOEHR
Also Called: Plastikoil Binding Systems
146 Halstead St (14610-1946)
PHONE 585 654-6746
Bruce Woehr, *Owner*
EMP: 10
SQ FT: 2,500
SALES: 800K **Privately Held**
SIC: 2789 Bookbinding & related work

(G-14249)
BUFFALO SPREE PUBLISHING INC
100 Allens Creek Rd Ste 8 (14618-3303)
PHONE 585 413-0040
Laurence Levite, *Branch Mgr*
EMP: 5
SALES (corp-wide): 2.3MM **Privately Held**
SIC: 2721 Periodicals: publishing only
PA: Buffalo Spree Publishing, Inc.
  1738 Elmwood Ave Ste 103
  Buffalo NY 14207
  716 783-9119

(G-14250)
BURKE & BANNAYAN
2465 W Ridge Rd Ste 2 (14626-3046)
PHONE 585 723-1010
Fax: 585 723-1070
Vic Bannayan, *President*
EMP: 5
SQ FT: 2,480
SALES (est): 370K **Privately Held**
SIC: 3911 7631 5944 Jewelry, precious metal; jewelry repair services; jewelry stores

(G-14251)
BURKE FRGING HEAT TREATING INC
30 Sherer St (14611-1618)
PHONE 585 235-6060
Fax: 585 235-6068
Ronald Thompson, *Ch of Bd*
James Granville, *Vice Pres*
Martha Vanderhoof, *Treasurer*
Suzanne Adam, *Credit Mgr*
James Warner, *Sales Mgr*
EMP: 24
SQ FT: 58,000
SALES (est): 5.3MM **Privately Held**
SIC: 3462 3398 Iron & steel forgings; metal heat treating

(G-14252)
BURNETT PROCESS INC (HQ)
545 Colfax St (14606-3111)
PHONE 585 254-8080
Jack Cannon, *Ch of Bd*
Tim McCauley, *General Mgr*
Melissa Shea-Brooks, *Info Tech Mgr*
Peat Howlard, *Assistant*
▲ **EMP:** 1
SQ FT: 60,000
SALES (est): 5.4MM
SALES (corp-wide): 43.9MM **Privately Held**
WEB: www.burnettprocessinc.com
SIC: 3296 3086 7699 Fiberglass insulation; plastics foam products; industrial equipment services
PA: Cannon Industries, Inc.
  525 Lee Rd
  Rochester NY 14606
  585 254-8080

(G-14253)
BURNETT PROCESS INC
545 Colfax St (14606-3111)
PHONE 585 277-1623
Paul Campbell, *Purchasing*
Ronald Salayda, *Manager*
Gerhard Drechsler, *Manager*
EMP: 30
SALES (corp-wide): 43.9MM **Privately Held**
WEB: www.burnettprocessinc.com
SIC: 3569 Filters
HQ: Burnett Process, Inc.
  545 Colfax St
  Rochester NY 14606
  585 254-8080

(G-14254)
C J WINTER MACHINE TECH (HQ)
167 Ames St (14611-1701)
PHONE 585 429-5000
Robert Brinkman, *President*
Dave Ostrander, *Plant Mgr*
Liberato Pietrantoni, *Research*
Philip Daggar, *Treasurer*
Connie Tribotte, *Personnel*
EMP: 18 **EST:** 1933
SQ FT: 118,000
SALES (est): 4MM
SALES (corp-wide): 81.2MM **Privately Held**
WEB: www.cjwinter.com
SIC: 3545 3542 3325 Thread cutting dies; machine tools, metal forming type; steel foundries
PA: Brinkman International Group, Inc.
  167 Ames St
  Rochester NY 14611
  585 429-5000

(G-14255)
C R C MANUFACTURING INC
37 Curlew St (14606-2535)
PHONE 585 254-8820
Fax: 585 254-8859
Todd Chapman, *CEO*
Brian Van Ocker, *Admin Sec*
EMP: 10
SQ FT: 7,000
SALES (est): 1MM **Privately Held**
SIC: 3599 3451 Machine shop, jobbing & repair; screw machine products

Rochester - Monroe County (G-14256)

(G-14256)
CAMPUS CRAFTS INC
160 Murray St (14606-1151)
P.O. Box 60650 (14606-0650)
PHONE.....................585 328-6780
Fax: 585 328-0898
Greg Weinrieb, *President*
Kathleen Weinrieb, *Corp Secy*
▲ EMP: 6
SQ FT: 7,000
SALES (est): 864.1K **Privately Held**
WEB: www.campuscrafts.com
SIC: 3231 Strengthened or reinforced glass; mirrored glass

(G-14257)
CANFIELD & TACK INC
Also Called: Dellas Graphics
925 Exchange St (14608-2802)
PHONE.....................585 235-7710
Fax: 585 235-4166
Michael Guche, *CEO*
Ray Brown, *President*
Gary Cvejic, *COO*
EMP: 85 EST: 1926
SQ FT: 45,000
SALES (est): 29.2MM **Privately Held**
WEB: www.canfieldtack.com
SIC: 2752 4225 Commercial printing, offset; general warehousing & storage

(G-14258)
CANNON INDUSTRIES INC (PA)
525 Lee Rd (14606-4236)
PHONE.....................585 254-8080
Jack Cannon, *CEO*
Reggie Cannon, *President*
Bruce Canon, *Prdtn Mgr*
Soledad Centeno, *QC Dir*
Rudy Dean, *CFO*
▲ EMP: 97
SQ FT: 100,000
SALES (est): 43.9MM **Privately Held**
WEB: www.cannonind.com
SIC: 3444 3469 5051 3861 Sheet metalwork; metal stampings; metals service centers & offices; photocopy machines

(G-14259)
CARESTREAM HEALTH INC
1669 Lake Ave (14652-0001)
PHONE.....................585 627-1800
EMP: 300
SALES (corp-wide): 4.1B **Privately Held**
SIC: 3861 Photographic equipment & supplies
HQ: Carestream Health, Inc.
  150 Verona St
  Rochester NY 14608
  585 627-1800

(G-14260)
CARTA USA LLC
1600 Lexington Ave # 116 (14606-3061)
PHONE.....................585 436-3012
Fax: 585 436-3018
Mike Welch, *General Mgr*
Jake Carey, *Vice Pres*
Paul Dalle, *Prdtn Mgr*
Wayne Clarke, *CFO*
Josh Cummings, *Sales Mgr*
▲ EMP: 20
SALES (est): 422.8K
SALES (corp-wide): 86MM **Privately Held**
SIC: 2621 Paper mills
PA: Flower City Printing, Inc.
  1725 Mount Read Blvd
  Rochester NY 14606
  585 663-9000

(G-14261)
CARTER STREET BAKERY INC
580 Child St (14606-1158)
PHONE.....................585 749-7104
Takele Delnesa, *President*
EMP: 8 EST: 2015
SALES (est): 306.7K **Privately Held**
SIC: 2051 Bakery: wholesale or wholesale/retail combined

(G-14262)
CASUAL FRIDAY INC
1561 Lyell Ave (14606-2123)
PHONE.....................585 544-9470
Anthony Germano, *President*
John Lansdown, *Manager*
Renee Yell, *Art Dir*
EMP: 12
SQ FT: 6,000
SALES (est): 1.6MM **Privately Held**
SIC: 2396 Fabric printing & stamping

(G-14263)
CDJ STAMPING INC
146 Halstead St Ste 123 (14610-1954)
PHONE.....................585 224-8120
Fax: 585 224-8201
Timothy Merklinger, *President*
Jason Schulmerich, *Vice Pres*
EMP: 5
SQ FT: 4,000
SALES (est): 275K **Privately Held**
WEB: www.cdjstamping.com
SIC: 3089 Plastic processing

(G-14264)
CEIPAL LLC
722 Weiland Rd (14626-3957)
PHONE.....................585 351-2934
EMP: 5 EST: 2014
SQ FT: 3,000
SALES (est): 300K **Privately Held**
SIC: 7372 Prepackaged Software Services

(G-14265)
CEIPAL LLC
722 Weiland Rd (14626-3957)
PHONE.....................585 351-2934
Sameer Penakalapati,
Mitch Meller,
EMP: 5
SALES (est): 300K **Privately Held**
SIC: 7372 Prepackaged software; application computer software; business oriented computer software

(G-14266)
CENTURY MOLD COMPANY INC (PA)
25 Vantage Point Dr (14624-1142)
PHONE.....................585 352-8600
Fax: 585 352-5799
Ron Ricotta, *CEO*
Jacob Vinocour, *President*
David F Dick, *Exec VP*
Terry Hodge, *Exec VP*
Meg Collins, *Vice Pres*
▲ EMP: 100 EST: 1978
SQ FT: 80,000
SALES (est): 227MM **Privately Held**
WEB: www.centurymold.com
SIC: 3089 3544 Injection molding of plastics; industrial molds

(G-14267)
CENTURY MOLD MEXICO LLC (HQ)
25 Vantage Point Dr (14624-1142)
PHONE.....................585 352-8600
Melissa Hayes, *Controller*
Ronald Ricotta,
▲ EMP: 3
SALES (est): 35.2MM
SALES (corp-wide): 227MM **Privately Held**
SIC: 3089 Injection molding of plastics
PA: Century Mold Company, Inc.
  25 Vantage Point Dr
  Rochester NY 14624
  585 352-8600

(G-14268)
CERION ENERGY INC
1 Blossom Rd (14610-1009)
PHONE.....................585 271-5630
George M Stadler, *CEO*
Landon Mertz, *Ch of Bd*
Douglas Singer, *Exec VP*
Matt Winslow, *Exec VP*
Bruce Brown, *VP Sales*
▼ EMP: 25
SALES (est): 5MM **Privately Held**
SIC: 2819 Industrial inorganic chemicals

(G-14269)
CERION LLC
1 Blossom Rd (14610-1009)
PHONE.....................585 271-5630
Douglas Singer, *Exec VP*
Carl Testa, *Exec VP*
Bob Curtis, *Senior VP*
Brad Stadler, *Vice Pres*
Matt Winslow, *Vice Pres*
EMP: 15
SALES (est): 1.7MM **Privately Held**
SIC: 2819 Industrial inorganic chemicals

(G-14270)
CHAMBERLIN RUBBER COMPANY INC
3333 Brighton Henrietta (14623-2842)
P.O. Box 22700 (14692-2700)
PHONE.....................585 427-7780
Fax: 585 427-2429
Philip Collins, *President*
Stephen Anderson, *Vice Pres*
Jerome Stomper, *Vice Pres*
John Giancursio, *Opers Mgr*
Scott Bready, *Opers Staff*
▲ EMP: 31
SQ FT: 30,000
SALES (est): 8.8MM **Privately Held**
WEB: www.crubber.com
SIC: 3069 Rubber automotive products

(G-14271)
CHAMPION PHOTOCHEMISTRY INC
1669 Lake Ave (14615)
PHONE.....................585 760-6444
R Fraser Mason, *Ch of Bd*
Peter Newton, *President*
Brian Bingaman, *Finance Mgr*
◆ EMP: 65
SQ FT: 375,000
SALES (est): 11.7MM
SALES (corp-wide): 216.7K **Privately Held**
WEB: www.championphotochemistry.com
SIC: 3861 Photographic processing chemicals
HQ: Champion Photochemistry Limited
  1760 Meyerside Dr
  Mississauga ON L5T 1
  905 670-7900

(G-14272)
CHAMTEK MFG INC
123 Louise St (14606-1321)
PHONE.....................585 328-4900
Fax: 585 328-2938
Donald Zenkel, *President*
Franklin Chamberlain, *Corp Secy*
Thomas Williams, *Vice Pres*
Derick Samson, *Sales Staff*
Kathy Johnson, *Office Mgr*
EMP: 27
SQ FT: 18,000
SALES (est): 2.3MM **Privately Held**
WEB: www.chamtek.com
SIC: 3544 3444 Special dies, tools, jigs & fixtures; sheet metalwork

(G-14273)
CHECKLIST BOARDS CORPORATION
763 Linden Ave Ste 2 (14625-2725)
PHONE.....................585 586-0152
Rick Taylor, *President*
Jim Wemett, *Vice Pres*
EMP: 5
SALES (est): 500K **Privately Held**
SIC: 3993 Signs, not made in custom sign painting shops

(G-14274)
CHINA IMPRINT LLC
750 Saint Paul St (14605-1737)
PHONE.....................585 563-3391
Christopher Adams, *CFO*
William A Dolan II,
▲ EMP: 5
SQ FT: 20,000
SALES (est): 2MM **Privately Held**
SIC: 2752 Promotional printing, lithographic

(G-14275)
CHRISTI PLASTICS INC
215 Tremont St (14608-2393)
PHONE.....................585 436-8510
Fax: 585 436-8519
Earl Martin, *President*
Deborah Scally, *Corp Secy*
EMP: 4
SQ FT: 10,500
SALES: 1.1MM **Privately Held**
SIC: 3089 Extruded finished plastic products

(G-14276)
CITY NEWSPAPER
250 N Goodman St Ste 1 (14607-1199)
PHONE.....................585 244-3329
Fax: 585 244-1126
Mary Towler, *Publisher*
Bill Towler, *Publisher*
Chris Fien, *Editor*
Eric Rezsnyak, *Editor*
Betsy Matthews, *Sales Mgr*
EMP: 7
SALES (est): 467.6K **Privately Held**
SIC: 2711 Newspapers, publishing & printing

(G-14277)
CJK MANUFACTURING LLC
100 Boxart St (14612-5656)
PHONE.....................585 663-6370
Keith Woodward,
Charles Tutty,
EMP: 14
SQ FT: 20,000
SALES (est): 2.6MM **Privately Held**
WEB: www.cjkmanufacturing.com
SIC: 3089 Thermoformed finished plastic products

(G-14278)
CLARSONS CORP
Also Called: Express Press
215 Tremont St Ste 8 (14608-2366)
PHONE.....................585 235-8775
Fax: 585 235-7847
David Clar, *President*
Robert M Clar, *President*
Michael Cwikinski, *VP Prdtn*
Joan Clar, *Admin Sec*
EMP: 11 EST: 1978
SQ FT: 4,000
SALES (est): 1MM **Privately Held**
WEB: www.expresspress.com
SIC: 2752 2791 7334 Commercial printing, offset; typesetting; photocopying & duplicating services

(G-14279)
CLERIO VISION INC
312 Susquehanna Rd (14618-2940)
PHONE.....................617 216-7881
Mikael Totterman, *President*
EMP: 12
SQ FT: 2,000
SALES (est): 710.7K **Privately Held**
SIC: 3841 Surgical lasers

(G-14280)
CLUB 1100
1100 Jay St (14611-1131)
PHONE.....................585 235-3478
Louis Vertiz, *Owner*
EMP: 5
SQ FT: 4,112
SALES (est): 230K **Privately Held**
WEB: www.1100club.com
SIC: 2033 5813 Fruit juices: fresh; tavern (drinking places)

(G-14281)
COAST TO COAST CIRCUITS INC
Metro Circuits
205 Lagrange Ave (14613-1562)
PHONE.....................585 254-2980
Fax: 585 254-4614
Walter Stender, *CEO*
Water Stender, *CEO*
Cheryl Covert, *Principal*
Burhen Capar, *Opers-Prdtn-Mfg*
Lance Miller, *Controller*
EMP: 45
SALES (corp-wide): 21.2MM **Privately Held**
WEB: www.speedycircuits.com
SIC: 3672 Wiring boards
PA: Coast To Coast Circuits, Inc.
  5331 Mcfadden Ave
  Huntington Beach CA 92647
  585 254-2980

GEOGRAPHIC SECTION

Rochester - Monroe County (G-14306)

(G-14282)
COATING TECHNOLOGY INC
800 Saint Paul St (14605-1032)
PHONE..................................585 546-7170
Fax: 585 546-7202
Stanley Dahle, *Ch of Bd*
Ronald L Feeley, *President*
Bryant Dunham, *QC Mgr*
EMP: 30
SQ FT: 40,000
SALES (est): 3.6MM
SALES (corp-wide): 17.1MM **Privately Held**
WEB: www.coatingtechnologyinc.com
SIC: 3471 Plating of metals or formed products
PA: The Metal Arts Company Inc
 800 Saint Paul St
 Rochester NY

(G-14283)
COLOR ME MINE
3349 Monroe Ave Ste 32 (14618-5513)
PHONE..................................585 383-8420
Fax: 585 383-8425
Joe Maxon, *Owner*
Lynn Maxon, *Co-Owner*
EMP: 15
SALES (est): 660.7K **Privately Held**
SIC: 3479 Painting, coating & hot dipping

(G-14284)
CONDOR ELECTRONICS CORP
295 Mount Read Blvd (14611-1931)
P.O. Box 60590 (14606-0590)
PHONE..................................585 235-1500
Fax: 585 235-0552
Wayne S Corso, *President*
Lisa Corso, *Corp Secy*
Margaret Fox, *Purchasing*
▲ EMP: 30
SQ FT: 18,000
SALES (est): 4.9MM **Privately Held**
WEB: www.condorelectronics.com
SIC: 3679 Harness assemblies for electronic use: wire or cable

(G-14285)
CONE BUDDY SYSTEM INC
3495 Winton Pl Ste E290 (14623-2819)
PHONE..................................585 427-9940
Fax: 585 427-2403
Robert Sotile, *President*
EMP: 15 EST: 1994
SALES (est): 1.5MM **Privately Held**
WEB: www.buddysystemusa.com
SIC: 2052 Cones, ice cream

(G-14286)
CONNECTION MOLD INC
585 Ling Rd (14612-1936)
PHONE..................................585 458-6463
Fax: 585 254-7825
Thomas Strecker, *President*
Reiner Strecker, *Vice Pres*
Tom Hockborn, *Design Engr*
David Lee, *Design Engr*
David Schwenger, *Design Engr*
EMP: 7
SQ FT: 6,800
SALES (est): 1MM **Privately Held**
WEB: www.connectionmold.com
SIC: 3965 Button blanks & molds

(G-14287)
CONOPCO INC
28 Mansfield St (14606-2327)
PHONE..................................585 647-8322
John Frank, *Branch Mgr*
EMP: 35 **Privately Held**
SIC: 2844 Toilet preparations
HQ: Conopco, Inc.
 700 Sylvan Ave
 Englewood Cliffs NJ 07632
 201 894-2727

(G-14288)
CONSOLIDATED CONTAINER CO LLC
Also Called: Liquitane
18 Champeney Ter (14605-2711)
PHONE..................................585 262-6470
Fax: 585 262-3521
Jerry Zaklick, *Plant Mgr*
Peter Schulick, *Mfg Staff*
Brian Avery, *Executive*
EMP: 150
SALES (corp-wide): 22B **Privately Held**
WEB: www.ccllc.com
SIC: 2655 2656 Fiber cans, drums & containers; sanitary food containers
HQ: Consolidated Container Company, Llc
 3101 Towercreek Pkwy Se
 Atlanta GA 30339
 678 742-4600

(G-14289)
CORBETT STVES PTTERN WORKS INC
80 Lowell St (14605-1831)
PHONE..................................585 546-7109
Fax: 585 546-6157
John K Steeves Jr, *President*
Kevin Steeves, *Vice Pres*
George Williams, *Controller*
Jorge Williams, *Controller*
Sandy Erickson, *Manager*
EMP: 20 EST: 1914
SQ FT: 20,000
SALES (est): 3.8MM **Privately Held**
WEB: www.corbett-steeves.com
SIC: 3365 3599 3553 3469 Machinery castings, aluminum; machine shop, jobbing & repair; pattern makers' machinery, woodworking; patterns on metal

(G-14290)
COUNTY WD APPLNC & TV SRVC OF
95 Mount Read Blvd Ste 14 (14611-1936)
PHONE..................................585 328-7417
Fax: 585 328-0983
Stephen Greczyn, *President*
Judy Greczyn, *Vice Pres*
EMP: 10 EST: 1996
SQ FT: 2,600
SALES (est): 1.6MM **Privately Held**
SIC: 3357 Appliance fixture wire, nonferrous

(G-14291)
CRAFTSMAN MANUFACTURING CO IN
1279 Mount Read Blvd (14606-2817)
PHONE..................................585 426-5780
Fax: 585 426-2617
Kevin Contestabile, *President*
EMP: 5
SQ FT: 3,000
SALES: 320K **Privately Held**
SIC: 3599 Machine shop, jobbing & repair

(G-14292)
CRYSTAL LINTON TECHNOLOGIES
2180 Brigh Henri Town Lin (14623)
PHONE..................................585 444-8784
Rick Webb, *COO*
EMP: 11 EST: 2013
SQ FT: 15,713
SALES (est): 2.4MM **Privately Held**
SIC: 3821 Furnaces, laboratory

(G-14293)
CSW INC
Also Called: Diegraphics Group
70 Pixley Industrial Pkwy (14624-2377)
PHONE..................................585 247-4010
Ann Lukasik, *General Mgr*
Ed Begy, *Prdtn Mgr*
Mark Buchanan, *Prdtn Mgr*
Tom Harris, *Prdtn Mgr*
James Mootz, *Production*
EMP: 15
SALES (corp-wide): 15.3MM **Privately Held**
WEB: www.citystamp.com
SIC: 3555 2796 2791 Printing plates; platemaking services; typesetting
PA: Csw, Inc.
 45 Tyburski Rd
 Ludlow MA 01056
 413 589-1311

(G-14294)
CURAEGIS TECHNOLOGIES INC (PA)
1999 Mount Read Blvd # 3 (14615-3700)
PHONE..................................585 254-1100
Richard A Kaplan, *CEO*
Gary A Siconolfi, *Ch of Bd*
Keith E Gleasman, *President*
Douglas Hemink, *Senior Engr*
Bill Jackson, *Design Engr*
EMP: 13
SQ FT: 13,650
SALES (est): 4.1MM **Publicly Held**
WEB: www.torvec.com
SIC: 7372 3561 Business oriented computer software; pumps & pumping equipment

(G-14295)
CURBELL PLASTICS INC (PA)
100 Aviation Ave (14624-4776)
PHONE..................................585 426-1690
Fax: 585 426-1125
Art Ghose, *President*
Patrick Castrechini, *Sales Staff*
Mike Steblein, *Sales Associate*
Robert Dutcher, *Marketing Staff*
Tim McPherson, *Branch Mgr*
EMP: 19
SALES (est): 5MM **Privately Held**
SIC: 3086 Plastics foam products

(G-14296)
CUSTOM SOUND AND VIDEO
Also Called: Casco Security
40 Rutter St (14606-1806)
PHONE..................................585 424-5000
Casimer S Plonczynski, *President*
Rosa F Ladelfa, *Business Mgr*
Richard Pool, *Project Mgr*
Bee Ong, *Accountant*
Cecelia Percle, *Finance*
EMP: 20
SQ FT: 6,500
SALES (est): 2.2MM **Privately Held**
SIC: 3699 5731 7629 Security devices; radio, television & electronic stores; electronic equipment repair

(G-14297)
CVI LASER LLC
Also Called: Melles Griot
55 Science Pkwy (14620-4258)
PHONE..................................585 244-7220
David Durfee, *Engineer*
Carrie Royer, *Engineer*
David Stephenson, *Engineer*
William Polito, *Controller*
Chuck Synborski, *Branch Mgr*
EMP: 100
SALES (corp-wide): 2B **Publicly Held**
SIC: 3827 3699 Optical instruments & lenses; laser systems & equipment
HQ: Cvi Laser, Llc
 200 Dorado Pl Se
 Albuquerque NM 87123
 505 296-9541

(G-14298)
DAGOSTINO IRON WORKS INC
10 Deep Rock Rd (14624-3520)
PHONE..................................585 235-8850
Fax: 585 328-5710
Kenneth J D'Agostino Jr, *President*
Kenneth Dagostino, *Project Mgr*
Amy King, *Manager*
EMP: 9
SQ FT: 4,000
SALES (est): 750K **Privately Held**
SIC: 3312 Blast furnaces & steel mills

(G-14299)
DAILY RECORD (PA)
Also Called: Daily Media
16 W Main St Ste G9 (14614-1604)
PHONE..................................585 232-2035
Fax: 585 232-2740
Jim Dolan, *President*
Tracy Bartlett, *Advt Staff*
EMP: 10
SQ FT: 36,000
SALES (est): 654K **Privately Held**
WEB: www.dailyrecord.com
SIC: 2752 2711 Commercial printing, lithographic; newspapers, publishing & printing

(G-14300)
DANISCO US INC
Also Called: Genencor Division Danisco US
3490 Winton Pl (14623-2829)
PHONE..................................585 256-5200
Robert Metheny, *General Mgr*
Randy Fisher, *Production*
Kelly Altman, *QC Mgr*
Janet Remus, *Technical Mgr*
Scott Kinsella, *Engineer*
EMP: 75
SALES (corp-wide): 25.1B **Publicly Held**
SIC: 2835 8731 2899 2869 In vitro & in vivo diagnostic substances; commercial physical research; chemical preparations; industrial organic chemicals
HQ: Danisco Us Inc.
 925 Page Mill Rd
 Palo Alto CA 94304
 650 846-7500

(G-14301)
DANISCO US INC
Also Called: Genencor International
1700 Lexington Ave (14606-3140)
PHONE..................................585 277-4300
Nancy Ritz, *Human Resources*
Cindy Boston, *Marketing Staff*
Thomas Mitchell, *Branch Mgr*
Peggy Kriger, *Manager*
Robert Villas, *Manager*
EMP: 100
SALES (corp-wide): 25.1B **Publicly Held**
SIC: 2819 2087 Industrial inorganic chemicals; flavoring extracts & syrups
HQ: Danisco Us Inc.
 925 Page Mill Rd
 Palo Alto CA 94304
 650 846-7500

(G-14302)
DAYTON ROGERS NEW YORK LLC
150 Fedex Way (14624-1174)
PHONE..................................585 349-4040
Fax: 585 349-4049
Ron Lowry, *CEO*
Rich Vanaernum, *General Mgr*
Thomas A Pilon, *Vice Pres*
Jesse Wolsanger, *Safety Mgr*
Mark D Spiczka, *Treasurer*
EMP: 60
SQ FT: 38,000
SALES (est): 10.7MM
SALES (corp-wide): 65.1MM **Privately Held**
SIC: 3469 Metal stampings
PA: Dayton Rogers Manufacturing Co.
 8401 W 35w Service Dr Ne
 Minneapolis MN 55449
 763 717-6450

(G-14303)
DEAD RINGER LLC
2100 Brghton Hnrtta St375 Ste 375 (14623)
PHONE..................................585 355-4685
Kristian Meyer, *Vice Pres*
Greg Hopf, *Director*
Jesse Erdle,
▲ EMP: 2 EST: 2011
SALES: 2.6MM **Privately Held**
SIC: 3423 5091 Hand & edge tools; sharpeners, sporting goods

(G-14304)
DEAL INTERNATIONAL INC
110 Halstead St Ste 1 (14610-1952)
P.O. Box 10088 (14610-0088)
PHONE..................................585 288-4444
Menish Damani, *President*
▲ EMP: 24
SQ FT: 6,000
SALES (est): 4.6MM **Privately Held**
WEB: www.diihq.com
SIC: 2891 Sealants

(G-14305)
DEES AUDIO & VISION
347 Seneca Pkwy (14613-1416)
PHONE..................................585 719-9256
EMP: 5
SALES (est): 150K **Privately Held**
SIC: 3571 Electronics/Audio/Sales

(G-14306)
DIAMOND PACKAGING HOLDINGS LLC
111 Commerce Dr (14623-3503)
PHONE..................................585 334-8030
Dave Rydell, *Vice Pres*
Keith Robinson,

Rochester - Monroe County (G-14307)

EMP: 8
SALES (est): 1.1MM **Privately Held**
SIC: 2657 3089 Food containers, folding; made from purchased material; air mattresses, plastic

(G-14307)
DIEMAX OF ROCHESTER INC
1555 Lyell Ave Ste 141 (14606-2148)
PHONE 585 288-3912
Richard J Oliver, *President*
Wayne Rotella, *Vice Pres*
Ryan Prue, *Treasurer*
▲ **EMP:** 7
SQ FT: 900
SALES (est): 1MM **Privately Held**
WEB: www.diemax.com
SIC: 3544 Special dies & tools

(G-14308)
DIGITRONIK DEV LABS INC
Also Called: Digitronik Labs
181 Saint Paul St Apt 6d (14604-1127)
PHONE 585 360-0043
Shawn Mott, *Ch of Bd*
Christopher Coon, *Vice Pres*
Stephan Mokey, *Treasurer*
Darren Dewispelaere, *Marketing Staff*
David Coon, *Admin Sec*
EMP: 8
SQ FT: 1,000
SALES: 350K **Privately Held**
SIC: 3823 8731 8711 7371 Controllers for process variables, all types; computer (hardware) development; engineering services; custom computer programming services

(G-14309)
DIMENSION TECHNOLOGIES INC
Also Called: D T I
315 Mount Read Blvd Ste 5 (14611-1900)
PHONE 585 436-3530
Fax: 585 436-3280
Arnold Lagergren, *CEO*
Arnold D Lagergren, *President*
Michael Casciano, *President*
Jesse B Eichenlaub, *Vice Pres*
Michael Farrell, *Purch Mgr*
EMP: 5
SQ FT: 3,400
SALES (est): 1MM **Privately Held**
WEB: www.dti3d.com
SIC: 3679 Liquid crystal displays (LCD)

(G-14310)
DIPAOLO BAKING CO INC
598 Plymouth Ave N (14608-1691)
PHONE 585 303-5013
Fax: 585 423-5975
Dominick P Massa, *President*
Stephen Woerner, *Vice Pres*
EMP: 80 **EST:** 1910
SQ FT: 30,000
SALES (est): 12.7MM **Privately Held**
WEB: www.dipaolobread.com
SIC: 2051 5461 Bread, all types (white, wheat, rye, etc): fresh or frozen; rolls, bread type: fresh or frozen; bakeries; bread

(G-14311)
DISTECH SYSTEMS INC (HQ)
1000 University Ave # 400 (14607-1286)
PHONE 585 254-7020
Fax: 585 254-1905
John J Perrotti, *CEO*
Dan Schwab, *President*
Thomas Fitzsimmons, *VP Opers*
Loreen Deperna, *Buyer*
Christine Martin, *Buyer*
▲ **EMP:** 2
SQ FT: 12,900
SALES (est): 6.9MM
SALES (corp-wide): 999.5MM **Privately Held**
WEB: www.distechsystems.com
SIC: 3569 Assembly machines, non-metalworking
PA: Gleason Corporation
1000 University Ave
Rochester NY 14607
585 473-1000

(G-14312)
DIVERSIFIED ENVELOPE LTD
95 Mount Read Blvd # 103 (14611-1973)
PHONE 585 615-4697
Fax: 585 527-8106
Robert Eckert, *President*
EMP: 10
SQ FT: 13,000
SALES: 1MM **Privately Held**
WEB: www.diversifiedenvelope.com
SIC: 2759 2752 5112 Envelopes: printing; commercial printing, lithographic; envelopes

(G-14313)
DIXON TOOL AND MANUFACTURING
240 Burrows St (14606-2637)
PHONE 585 235-1352
Fax: 585 235-8465
Rober Hyder, *President*
Gary Putnam, *Buyer*
EMP: 10
SQ FT: 5,224
SALES (est): 1.2MM **Privately Held**
SIC: 3544 Special dies & tools

(G-14314)
DOCK HARDWARE INCORPORATED
Also Called: Rogers Enterprises
24 Seneca Ave Ste 4 (14621-2387)
P.O. Box 17266 (14617-0266)
PHONE 585 266-7920
Garry Rogers, *President*
Mike Chiumento, *Director*
EMP: 10
SALES (est): 960K **Privately Held**
WEB: www.dockhardware.com
SIC: 3545 Machine tool accessories

(G-14315)
DOCUMENT STRATEGIES LLC
185 Gibbs St (14605-2907)
PHONE 585 506-9000
James Bowen, *Principal*
EMP: 12
SALES (est): 561.5K **Privately Held**
SIC: 7372 Application computer software

(G-14316)
DOLOMITE PRODUCTS COMPANY INC (DH)
Also Called: Shadow Lake Golf & Racquet CLB
1150 Penfield Rd (14625-2202)
PHONE 315 524-1998
John M Odenbach Jr, *President*
John Siel, *Chairman*
Russ Larocca, *Senior VP*
Gardner Odenbach, *Treasurer*
Mike Bagne, *Manager*
EMP: 25 **EST:** 1920
SQ FT: 5,000
SALES (est): 22.9MM
SALES (corp-wide): 25.3B **Privately Held**
WEB: www.dolomitegroup.com
SIC: 2951 1422 5031 8741 Paving mixtures; dolomite, crushed & broken-quarrying; building materials, exterior; building materials, interior; circuit management for motion picture theaters; golf club, membership; golf, tennis & ski shops
HQ: Oldcastle Materials, Inc.
900 Ashwood Pkwy Ste 700
Atlanta GA 30338
770 522-5600

(G-14317)
DPI OF ROCHESTER LLC
1560 Emerson St (14606-3118)
PHONE 585 325-3610
Sandra Dano, *Principal*
Brian Steblen, *Director*
EMP: 8
SALES (est): 1MM **Privately Held**
SIC: 3089 Plastics products

(G-14318)
DRAPERY INDUSTRIES INC
175 Humboldt St Ste 222 (14610-1060)
PHONE 585 232-2992
Fax: 585 325-6290
Mark Kosinski, *President*
David Geen, *Vice Pres*
Diane Russell, *Manager*
EMP: 14
SQ FT: 8,000
SALES (est): 1.6MM **Privately Held**
WEB: www.draperyindustries.com
SIC: 2391 2591 1799 Curtains, window: made from purchased materials; draperies, plastic & textile: from purchased materials; window blinds; home/office interiors finishing, furnishing & remodeling; drapery track installation

(G-14319)
DRT POWER SYSTEMS LLC - LANE
500 Mile Crossing Blvd (14624-6205)
PHONE 585 247-5940
Gary Van Gundy, *President*
EMP: 55
SQ FT: 25,000
SALES (est): 3.4MM **Privately Held**
SIC: 3545 3761 3728 Precision tools, machinists'; guided missiles & space vehicles; aircraft parts & equipment
PA: Drt Holdings, Inc.
618 Greenmount Blvd
Dayton OH 45419

(G-14320)
DYNA-TECH QUALITY INC
1570 Emerson St (14606-3118)
PHONE 585 458-9970
Andy Masters, *President*
EMP: 5 **EST:** 1998
SALES (est): 371.1K **Privately Held**
SIC: 3599 Machine shop, jobbing & repair

(G-14321)
DYNAMASTERS INC
1570 Emerson St (14606-3118)
PHONE 585 458-9970
Andy Mastrodonato Sr, *President*
EMP: 5 **EST:** 2008
SALES (est): 400K **Privately Held**
SIC: 3569 Assembly machines, non-metalworking

(G-14322)
DYNAMIC DIES INC
70 Pixley Industrial Pkwy (14624-2377)
PHONE 585 247-4010
Fax: 585 247-7203
EMP: 14
SALES (corp-wide): 22.2MM **Privately Held**
SIC: 3544 Mfg Dies/Tools/Jigs/Fixtures
PA: Dynamic Dies, Inc.
1705 Commerce Rd
Holland OH 43528
419 865-0249

(G-14323)
E I DU PONT DE NEMOURS & CO
Also Called: Dupont
69 Seneca Ave (14621-2316)
PHONE 585 339-4200
Donna Newhart, *Human Res Mgr*
Shona Fullerton, *Marketing Staff*
Frank Pinkosky, *Planning Mgr*
EMP: 50
SQ FT: 24,546
SALES (corp-wide): 25.1B **Publicly Held**
WEB: www.dupont.com
SIC: 2819 2899 Industrial inorganic chemicals; chemical preparations
PA: E. I. Du Pont De Nemours And Company
974 Centre Rd
Wilmington DE 19805
302 774-1000

(G-14324)
EAGLE GRAPHICS INC
149 Anderson Ave (14607-1106)
PHONE 585 244-5006
Fax: 585 244-5884
Nancy Powell, *President*
Michael W Powell, *Vice Pres*
EMP: 9 **EST:** 1977
SQ FT: 10,000
SALES: 1.5MM **Privately Held**
WEB: www.eaglegraphicsinc.com
SIC: 2752 Commercial printing, lithographic

(G-14325)
EAST RIDGE QUICK PRINT
1249 Ridgeway Ave Ste Y (14615-3761)
PHONE 585 266-4911
Fax: 585 266-2721
Richard San Angelo, *President*
Janice San Angelo, *Vice Pres*
EMP: 15
SQ FT: 6,000
SALES (est): 1.5MM **Privately Held**
WEB: www.eastridgequickprint.com
SIC: 2752 Commercial printing, offset

(G-14326)
EASTMAN CHEMICAL COMPANY
2255 Mount Read Blvd (14615-2712)
PHONE 585 722-2905
Brian Bennett, *Research*
Anthony Debboli, *Manager*
EMP: 60
SALES (corp-wide): 9.6B **Publicly Held**
WEB: www.eastman.com
SIC: 2869 Industrial organic chemicals
PA: Eastman Chemical Company
200 S Wilcox Dr
Kingsport TN 37660
423 229-2000

(G-14327)
EASTMAN KODAK COMPANY
233 Olde Harbour Trl (14612-2936)
PHONE 585 722-2187
Fax: 585 726-2700
Gus Gleichauf, *Principal*
Dale Lipscomb, *Human Res Mgr*
EMP: 65
SALES (corp-wide): 1.8B **Publicly Held**
SIC: 3861 Film, sensitized motion picture, X-ray, still camera, etc.
PA: Eastman Kodak Company
343 State St
Rochester NY 14650
585 724-4000

(G-14328)
EASTMAN KODAK COMPANY (PA)
343 State St (14650-0001)
PHONE 585 724-4000
Fax: 585 724-0447
Jeffrey J Clarke, *CEO*
James V Continenza, *Ch of Bd*
Philip Cullimore, *Senior VP*
Brad W Kruchten, *Senior VP*
Eric-Yves Mahe, *Senior VP*
EMP: 277 **EST:** 1880
SALES: 1.8B **Publicly Held**
SIC: 3861 3577 7384 Film, sensitized motion picture, X-ray, still camera, etc.; cameras, still & motion picture (all types); photographic paper & cloth, all types; computer peripheral equipment; graphic displays, except graphic terminals; optical scanning devices; photofinish laboratories

(G-14329)
EASTMAN KODAK COMPANY
1669 Lake Ave Bldg 31-4 (14652-0001)
PHONE 585 724-5600
Fax: 585 477-5361
Jerome Johnson, *Exec VP*
Patricia Parisi, *Buyer*
Thomas McKeehan, *Senior Engr*
Tim Kiehle, *Branch Mgr*
John Chiazza, *MIS Dir*
EMP: 60
SALES (corp-wide): 1.8B **Publicly Held**
SIC: 3861 Film, sensitized motion picture, X-ray, still camera, etc.
PA: Eastman Kodak Company
343 State St
Rochester NY 14650
585 724-4000

(G-14330)
EASTMAN KODAK COMPANY
39 Kaywood Dr (14626-3753)
PHONE 585 726-6261
Ed Schranz, *Design Engr*
Raul Santiago, *Branch Mgr*
Larry Wolfe, *Manager*
EMP: 65
SALES (corp-wide): 1.8B **Publicly Held**
SIC: 3861 Film, sensitized motion picture, X-ray, still camera, etc.

GEOGRAPHIC SECTION — Rochester - Monroe County

PA: Eastman Kodak Company
343 State St
Rochester NY 14650
585 724-4000

(G-14331)
EASTMAN KODAK COMPANY
2600 Manitou Rd (14650-0001)
PHONE..................585 724-4000
EMP: 74
SALES (corp-wide): 1.8B Publicly Held
SIC: 3861 Film, sensitized motion picture, X-ray, still camera, etc.
PA: Eastman Kodak Company
343 State St
Rochester NY 14650
585 724-4000

(G-14332)
EASTMAN KODAK COMPANY
343 State St (14650-0001)
PHONE..................800 698-3324
Lori Perez, *Branch Mgr*
EMP: 15
SALES (corp-wide): 1.8B Publicly Held
SIC: 3861 Film, sensitized motion picture, X-ray, still camera, etc.
PA: Eastman Kodak Company
343 State St
Rochester NY 14650
585 724-4000

(G-14333)
EASTMAN KODAK COMPANY
1999 Lake Ave 6/83/RI (14650-0001)
PHONE..................585 722-4385
Rudy Hicks, *Division Mgr*
Dennis Butterfield, *Research*
Frances Schantz, *Research*
Duane Courtney, *Electrical Engi*
Mary J Hellyar, *Branch Mgr*
EMP: 99
SALES (corp-wide): 1.8B Publicly Held
SIC: 3861 Film, sensitized motion picture, X-ray, still camera, etc.
PA: Eastman Kodak Company
343 State St
Rochester NY 14650
585 724-4000

(G-14334)
EASTMAN KODAK COMPANY
300 Weiland Road (14650-0001)
PHONE..................585 588-5598
EMP: 78
SALES (corp-wide): 1.8B Publicly Held
SIC: 3861 Film, sensitized motion picture, X-ray, still camera, etc.
PA: Eastman Kodak Company
343 State St
Rochester NY 14650
585 724-4000

(G-14335)
EASTMAN KODAK COMPANY
343 State St (14650-0001)
PHONE..................585 726-7000
Baerbel Post, *CFO*
Robert Yelencsics, *Sales Mgr*
Donna Gozia, *Technology*
Alan Priebe, *Technology*
Bonnie Saravullo, *Administration*
EMP: 130
SALES (corp-wide): 1.8B Publicly Held
SIC: 3861 Film, sensitized motion picture, X-ray, still camera, etc.
PA: Eastman Kodak Company
343 State St
Rochester NY 14650
585 724-4000

(G-14336)
EASTMAN KODAK COMPANY
2400 Mount Read Blvd (14615-2744)
PHONE..................585 722-4007
Tomas McHugh, *Plant Mgr*
Dennis Boldt, *Project Mgr*
Susan Shattuck, *Purch Agent*
David Bishop, *Engineer*
John Milazzo, *CIO*
EMP: 5
SQ FT: 14,909
SALES (corp-wide): 1.8B Publicly Held
SIC: 3861 Film, sensitized motion picture, X-ray, still camera, etc.

PA: Eastman Kodak Company
343 State St
Rochester NY 14650
585 724-4000

(G-14337)
EASTMAN KODAK COMPANY
100 Latona Rd Gate 340 (14652-0001)
PHONE..................585 588-3896
Jack Kosoff, *Branch Mgr*
EMP: 78
SALES (corp-wide): 1.8B Publicly Held
SIC: 3861 Film, sensitized motion picture, X-ray, still camera, etc.
PA: Eastman Kodak Company
343 State St
Rochester NY 14650
585 724-4000

(G-14338)
EASTMAN KODAK COMPANY
343 State St (14650-0001)
P.O. Box 15399 (14615-0399)
PHONE..................585 724-4000
EMP: 45
SALES (corp-wide): 1.8B Publicly Held
SIC: 3861 Photographic equipment & supplies
PA: Eastman Kodak Company
343 State St
Rochester NY 14650
585 724-4000

(G-14339)
EASTMAN PARK MICROGRAPHICS INC
100 Latona Rd Bldg 318 (14652-0001)
PHONE..................866 934-4376
William D Oates, *President*
Robert Breslawski, *Manager*
Richard McDaniel, *Manager*
Kim Young, *Consultant*
Susanna Records, *Info Tech Mgr*
EMP: 38 Privately Held
SIC: 3861 Film, sensitized motion picture, X-ray, still camera, etc.
PA: Park Eastman Micrographics Inc
6300 Cedar Springs Rd
Dallas TX 75235

(G-14340)
EBERHARDT ENTERPRISES INC
1325 Mount Read Blvd (14606-2819)
PHONE..................585 458-7681
Fax: 585 458-6018
Peter Eberhardt, *President*
Carla Madau, *Office Mgr*
▲ EMP: 10
SQ FT: 18,000
SALES (est): 1.5MM Privately Held
SIC: 3544 Special dies, tools, jigs & fixtures

(G-14341)
EIS INC
Also Called: Light Fabrications
40 Hytec Cir (14606-4255)
PHONE..................585 426-5330
Jim Cucinelli, *Principal*
Mary Lochner, *CTO*
Jim Theodorakakos, *Exec Dir*
EMP: 62
SALES (corp-wide): 15.2B Publicly Held
SIC: 2672 3842 7699 Adhesive backed films, foams & foils; adhesive papers, labels or tapes: from purchased material; adhesive tape & plasters, medicated or non-medicated; industrial equipment services
HQ: Eis, Inc.
2018 Powers Ferry Rd Se # 500
Atlanta GA 30339
678 255-3600

(G-14342)
EKOSTINGER INC
33 Saginaw Dr (14623-3131)
PHONE..................585 739-0450
Parr Wiegel, *CEO*
Steven Chatwin, *COO*
EMP: 11 EST: 2012
SQ FT: 13,500
SALES (est): 760.6K Privately Held
SIC: 3713 Truck bodies & parts

(G-14343)
ELAB SMOKERS BOUTIQUE
4373 Lake Ave (14612-4864)
PHONE..................585 865-4513
Steve J Glover, *Partner*
Steve Glover, *Partner*
Mark Landon, *Partner*
EMP: 5
SALES (est): 621.1K Privately Held
SIC: 2131 5621 Chewing & smoking tobacco; boutiques

(G-14344)
ELECTRONICS & INNOVATION LTD
150 Research Blvd (14623-3436)
PHONE..................585 214-0598
Fax: 585 214-0580
Tony Harris, *President*
John Andrews, *Vice Pres*
John Stratakos, *Exec Dir*
▼ EMP: 10
SALES (est): 1.8MM Privately Held
WEB: www.electronicsandinnovation.com
SIC: 3679 Parametric amplifiers

(G-14345)
ELO TOUCH SOLUTIONS INC
2245 Brdgtn Hnrtta Twn Ln (14623)
PHONE..................585 427-2802
Craig Witsoe, *CEO*
Jim Melton, *Vice Pres*
Sean Miller, *Vice Pres*
Dave Renner, *Vice Pres*
Bruno Thuillier, *Vice Pres*
▲ EMP: 22 EST: 2012
SALES (est): 5.1MM Privately Held
SIC: 3571 Computers, digital, analog or hybrid

(G-14346)
EMPIRE FABRICATORS INC
Also Called: Cusimano, Michael
95 Saginaw Dr (14623-3131)
PHONE..................585 235-3050
Fax: 585 235-3055
Michael Cusimano, *President*
EMP: 7
SQ FT: 10,000
SALES (est): 1.1MM Privately Held
WEB: www.empirefabricators.com
SIC: 2541 5084 Counter & sink tops; countersinks

(G-14347)
EMPIRE METAL FABRICATORS INC
1385 Empire Blvd Ste 3 (14609-5915)
PHONE..................585 288-2140
Fax: 585 288-2145
John Singer, *President*
EMP: 7
SQ FT: 4,000
SALES: 520K Privately Held
SIC: 3441 Fabricated structural metal

(G-14348)
EMPIRE OPTICAL INC
1249 Ridgeway Ave Ste P (14615-3761)
P.O. Box 40320 (14604-0820)
PHONE..................585 454-4470
Fax: 585 454-3128
James Willoth, *President*
Barbara Willoth, *Treasurer*
Elaine Kleehammer, *Manager*
EMP: 12
SQ FT: 2,400
SALES (est): 1.1MM Privately Held
SIC: 3851 Lens grinding, except prescription: ophthalmic

(G-14349)
ENBI INDIANA INC
1661 Lyell Ave (14606-2311)
PHONE..................585 647-1627
Jim Maulucci, *Plant Mgr*
Tom Brod, *Sales Mgr*
Mike McMindes, *Branch Mgr*
EMP: 25
SALES (corp-wide): 44.9MM Privately Held
SIC: 3069 Printers' rolls & blankets: rubber or rubberized fabric

PA: Indiana Enbi Inc
1703 Mccall Dr
Shelbyville IN 46176
317 398-3267

(G-14350)
ENCORE CHOCOLATES INC
147 Pattonwood Dr (14617-1409)
PHONE..................585 266-2970
Nancy Stiebitz, *President*
EMP: 5
SALES (est): 410K Privately Held
WEB: www.encorechocolates.com
SIC: 2066 Chocolate candy, solid

(G-14351)
ENGRAV-O-TYPE PRESS INC
Also Called: Epi Printing & Finishing
30 Bermar Park Ste 2 (14624-1541)
PHONE..................585 262-7590
Fax: 585 262-7594
Rick Speciale, *President*
Emile L Speciale Jr, *Treasurer*
Tracey Kohl, *VP Sales*
EMP: 17
SQ FT: 12,000
SALES (est): 3.5MM Privately Held
WEB: www.epiprinting.com
SIC: 2752 Commercial printing, offset

(G-14352)
ENI MKS PRODUCTS GROUP
100 Highpower Rd (14623-3498)
PHONE..................585 427-8300
Paul Eyerman, *General Mgr*
▲ EMP: 12
SALES (est): 1.6MM
SALES (corp-wide): 813.5MM Publicly Held
SIC: 3663 Airborne radio communications equipment
PA: Mks Instruments, Inc.
2 Tech Dr Ste 201
Andover MA 01810
978 645-5500

(G-14353)
ENI TECHNOLOGY INC (HQ)
100 Highpower Rd (14623-3498)
PHONE..................585 427-8300
John R Bertucci, *CEO*
Edward Maier, *General Mgr*
Cristiano Salino, *General Mgr*
Alessandro Puliti, *Managing Dir*
Baltazar Belo, *Research*
▲ EMP: 500
SQ FT: 160,000
SALES (est): 24.6MM
SALES (corp-wide): 813.5MM Publicly Held
WEB: www.enipower.com
SIC: 3679 3677 3663 3621 Electronic loads & power supplies; electronic coils, transformers & other inductors; radio & TV communications equipment; motors & generators
PA: Mks Instruments, Inc.
2 Tech Dr Ste 201
Andover MA 01810
978 645-5500

(G-14354)
EPP TEAM INC
Also Called: Empire Precision Plastics
500 Lee Rd Ste 400 (14606-4260)
PHONE..................585 454-4995
Neal P Elli, *Ch of Bd*
Bob Zygulski, *COO*
Rick Wilson, *Vice Pres*
Mark Ward, *Project Mgr*
Steve Steinmetz, *Prdtn Mgr*
▲ EMP: 60
SQ FT: 45,000
SALES (est): 15.8MM Privately Held
WEB: www.empireprecision.com
SIC: 3089 Injection molded finished plastic products; injection molding of plastics

(G-14355)
ERDLE PERFORATING HOLDINGS INC (PA)
100 Pixley Indus Pkwy (14624-2325)
PHONE..................585 247-4700
Fax: 585 247-4716
Frank Pfau, *President*
Thomas J Pariso, *Exec VP*

Rochester - Monroe County (G-14356)

Clint Stevens, *Safety Mgr*
Jim Garand, *Opers Staff*
Chuck Gartley, *Engineer*
EMP: 100 **EST:** 1870
SQ FT: 92,000
SALES (est): 23.8MM **Privately Held**
SIC: 3469 Perforated metal, stamped

(G-14356)
ERNIE GREEN INDUSTRIES INC
85 Pixley Industrial Pkwy (14624-2322)
PHONE................................585 295-8951
Lubomira Rochet, *Manager*
EMP: 100
SALES (corp-wide): 639MM **Privately Held**
SIC: 3089 Injection molding of plastics
PA: Ernie Green Industries, Inc.
2030 Dividend Dr
Columbus OH 43228
614 219-1423

(G-14357)
ERNIE GREEN INDUSTRIES INC
Also Called: Eg Industries
1667 Emerson St (14606-3119)
PHONE................................585 647-2300
Bob Lannon, *Purch Agent*
Aaron Leighton, *Controller*
Nartign Vanmanen, *Manager*
EMP: 240
SALES (corp-wide): 639MM **Privately Held**
SIC: 3089 Injection molding of plastics; blow molded finished plastic products
PA: Ernie Green Industries, Inc.
2030 Dividend Dr
Columbus OH 43228
614 219-1423

(G-14358)
ERNIE GREEN INDUSTRIES INC
Also Called: Eg Indsturies
460 Buffalo Rd Ste 220 (14611-2022)
PHONE................................585 647-2300
Diane Crispino, *VP Opers*
Chris Payne, *Opers Mgr*
Scott McDermott, *Purch Mgr*
Dave King, *QC Mgr*
Mike Lee, *Engineer*
EMP: 100
SALES (corp-wide): 639MM **Privately Held**
SIC: 3089 Injection molding of plastics; blow molded finished plastic products
PA: Ernie Green Industries, Inc.
2030 Dividend Dr
Columbus OH 43228
614 219-1423

(G-14359)
ESTEBANIA ENTERPRISES INC
Also Called: Aries Precision Products
15 Mcardle St Ste A (14611-1513)
PHONE................................585 529-9330
Jose L Suro, *President*
EMP: 7
SQ FT: 9,600
SALES (est): 1.1MM **Privately Held**
WEB: www.connectorindustry.com
SIC: 3599 Machine shop, jobbing & repair

(G-14360)
ET PRECISION OPTICS INC
33 Curlew St (14606-2535)
PHONE................................585 254-2560
Fax: 585 254-2966
Thomas R Eckler, *President*
Vanessa Distrul, *Manager*
EMP: 71
SQ FT: 3,000
SALES (est): 12.5MM **Privately Held**
WEB: www.etprecision.com
SIC: 3599 Machine shop, jobbing & repair

(G-14361)
EVOLUTION IMPRESSIONS INC
160 Commerce Dr (14623-3504)
P.O. Box 12788 (14612-0788)
PHONE................................585 473-6600
Thomas A Gruber, *President*
Craig Miller, *Principal*
Mike Buell, *Vice Pres*
Thomas Kelly, *Vice Pres*
EMP: 60 **EST:** 1971
SQ FT: 28,000
SALES (est): 7.4MM **Privately Held**
WEB: www.evolutionimpressions.com
SIC: 2752 7334 Commercial printing, lithographic; photocopying & duplicating services

(G-14362)
EXACT MACHINING & MFG
305 Commerce Dr Ste 7 (14623-3538)
PHONE................................585 334-7090
Dan Bleier, *President*
Tim Bleier, *Corp Secy*
Jay Pryor, *Vice Pres*
EMP: 5
SQ FT: 3,600
SALES: 600K **Privately Held**
SIC: 3599 Machine shop, jobbing & repair

(G-14363)
EXCELSUS SOLUTIONS LLC
300b Commerce Dr (14623-3508)
PHONE................................585 533-0003
Mark Laniak, *CEO*
Chris Laniak, *Production*
John Bennett, *CFO*
Chris Batdorf, *Marketing Staff*
Sheryl Wilcox, *Marketing Staff*
EMP: 24
SQ FT: 18,000
SALES (est): 4.5MM **Privately Held**
WEB: www.excelsussolutions.com
SIC: 2759 Commercial printing

(G-14364)
EXIGO PRECISION INC
190 Murray St (14606-1126)
P.O. Box 60917 (14606-0917)
PHONE................................585 254-5818
EMP: 7
SALES (est): 499.5K **Privately Held**
SIC: 3599 Mfg Industrial Machinery

(G-14365)
EXPOSITOR NEWSPAPERS INC
Also Called: Rochester Golf Week
2535 Brighton Henrietta (14623-2711)
PHONE................................585 427-2468
Fax: 585 427-8521
Barbara Morgenstern, *President*
George Morgenstern, *Editor*
EMP: 6 **EST:** 1924
SALES (est): 270K **Privately Held**
SIC: 2711 Newspapers: publishing only, not printed on site

(G-14366)
EYEWORKS INC
1249 Ridgeway Ave Ste M (14615-3761)
PHONE................................585 454-4470
Mark Keehammer, *President*
Elaine Kleehammer, *Vice Pres*
▲ **EMP:** 7
SALES: 950K **Privately Held**
SIC: 3851 Ophthalmic goods

(G-14367)
F OLIVERS LLC
747 Park Ave (14607-3020)
PHONE................................585 244-2585
Leah Wolanski, *Branch Mgr*
EMP: 5
SALES (corp-wide): 377.3K **Privately Held**
SIC: 2079 Olive oil
PA: F. Oliver's Llc
129 S Main St
Canandaigua NY 14424
585 396-2585

(G-14368)
FARO INDUSTRIES INC
340 Lyell Ave (14606-1697)
PHONE................................585 647-6000
Fax: 585 647-2886
Matthew Mc Conville, *President*
William Bashford, *General Mgr*
Ray Fitcher, *Engineer*
Matt McConville, *Info Tech Mgr*
Chuck Zimmerman, *Director*
EMP: 17
SQ FT: 26,000
SALES (est): 3.3MM **Privately Held**
WEB: www.faroindustries.com
SIC: 3089 Injection molding of plastics; plastic processing

(G-14369)
FIELDTEX PRODUCTS INC
3055 Brighton Henrietta (14623-2749)
PHONE................................585 427-2940
Fax: 585 427-8666
Sanford R Abbey, *President*
Jonathan Abbey, *General Mgr*
Patricia Draper, *General Mgr*
Mike Ferris, *Plant Mgr*
Cynthia Helander, *Plant Mgr*
▲ **EMP:** 130
SQ FT: 40,000
SALES (est): 27.3MM **Privately Held**
WEB: www.e-firstaidsupplies.com
SIC: 3151 3161 Leather gloves & mittens; cases, carrying

(G-14370)
FINGER LAKES CHEMICALS INC (PA)
Also Called: Finger Lakes/Castle
420 Saint Paul St (14605-1734)
PHONE................................585 454-4760
Ewald Blatter, *President*
Hans Blatter, *Vice Pres*
Andy Santerre, *Director*
Ron Wells, *Executive*
EMP: 50
SQ FT: 100,000
SALES: 10MM **Privately Held**
WEB: www.castlepackspower.com
SIC: 2842 5169 Specialty cleaning preparations; chemicals & allied products

(G-14371)
FIRTH RIXSON INC (DH)
Also Called: Firth Rixson Monroe
181 Mckee Rd (14611-2011)
PHONE................................585 328-1383
Fax: 585 328-2885
David C Mortimer, *CEO*
David Hebert, *President*
Michael Belmont, *General Mgr*
Shawn Gould, *General Mgr*
Chris Gratton, *General Mgr*
▲ **EMP:** 80
SQ FT: 23,821
SALES (est): 113.6MM
SALES (corp-wide): 22.5B **Publicly Held**
WEB: www.firthrixson.com
SIC: 3462 Iron & steel forgings; aircraft forgings, ferrous
HQ: Firth Rixson Limited
Centre Court Building
Sheffield S4 7Q
114 219-3000

(G-14372)
FIVE STAR TOOL CO INC
125 Elmgrove Park (14624-1359)
PHONE................................585 328-9580
Fax: 585 328-0106
Kenneth Klalonde, *President*
Julio Ahumada, *President*
Mark Schaefer, *Design Engr*
Alicia Hunt, *Accounting Mgr*
Kenneth Lalonde, *VP Sales*
EMP: 23 **EST:** 1965
SQ FT: 9,200
SALES (est): 4.7MM **Privately Held**
SIC: 3451 3541 Screw machine products; milling machines

(G-14373)
FLINT GROUP INCORPORATED
Also Called: Flint Ink North America Div
1128 Lexington Ave Bldg 3 (14606-2909)
PHONE................................585 458-1223
Fax: 585 458-7569
Kathy Marx, *Vice Pres*
Robert Heath, *Purchasing*
Harry Reeves, *Manager*
Tim Angel, *Manager*
EMP: 26 **Privately Held**
WEB: www.flintink.com
SIC: 2893 Printing ink
HQ: Flint Group Us Llc
14909 N Beck Rd
Plymouth MI 48170
734 781-4600

(G-14374)
FLOWER CITY PRINTING INC (PA)
1725 Mount Read Blvd (14606-2827)
P.O. Box 60680 (14606-0680)
PHONE................................585 663-9000
Fax: 585 663-4908
Audrey Hardenburg, *Editor*
Timothy Welch, *Chairman*
William Oliveri, *Exec VP*
Tim Welch, *Exec VP*
Carin Laniak, *Vice Pres*
EMP: 197
SQ FT: 135,000
SALES (est): 86MM **Privately Held**
WEB: www.flowercityprinting.com
SIC: 2657 2752 Folding paperboard boxes; commercial printing, offset

(G-14375)
FLOWER CITY PRINTING INC
1001 Lee Rd (14606-4243)
PHONE................................585 512-1235
Matt Bryant, *Principal*
EMP: 5
SALES (corp-wide): 86MM **Privately Held**
SIC: 2752 Commercial printing, lithographic
PA: Flower City Printing, Inc.
1725 Mount Read Blvd
Rochester NY 14606
585 663-9000

(G-14376)
FLOWER CY TISSUE MILLS CO INC (PA)
700 Driving Park Ave (14613-1506)
P.O. Box 13497 (14613-0497)
PHONE................................585 458-9200
Fax: 585 458-3812
William F Shafer III, *Ch of Bd*
William F Shafer IV, *Vice Pres*
Thomas Myers, *Treasurer*
Don Macdonald, *Sales Dir*
Luke Schafer, *Accounts Mgr*
▲ **EMP:** 50
SQ FT: 46,000
SALES (est): 8.7MM **Privately Held**
WEB: www.flowercitytissue.com
SIC: 2621 Wrapping paper

(G-14377)
FLUXDATA INCORPORATED
176 Anderson Ave Ste F304 (14607-1169)
PHONE................................800 425-0176
Pano Spiliotis, *CEO*
Tracie Spiliotis, *CFO*
Lawrence Taplin, *CTO*
EMP: 6
SQ FT: 4,665
SALES (est): 650K **Privately Held**
SIC: 3861 Aerial cameras

(G-14378)
FORBES PRECISION INC
100 Boxart St Ste 105 (14612-5658)
PHONE................................585 865-7069
Michael Forbes, *Ch of Bd*
EMP: 11
SQ FT: 3,000
SALES (est): 1.5MM **Privately Held**
SIC: 3599 Machine shop, jobbing & repair

(G-14379)
FORWARD ENTERPRISES INC
Also Called: Brewer & Newell Printing
215 Tremont St Ste 8 (14608-2366)
PHONE................................585 235-7670
Fax: 585 235-7789
Gerald Ward, *President*
Dick Shellman, *Vice Pres*
Melinda Ward, *Vice Pres*
Lisa Fairchild, *Sales Staff*
Stan Phillips, *Representative*
EMP: 10
SQ FT: 4,000
SALES: 1.1MM **Privately Held**
SIC: 2759 2752 Letterpress printing; commercial printing, offset

(G-14380)
FRAMING TECHNOLOGY INC
137 Syke St (14611-1738)
PHONE................................585 464-8470

GEOGRAPHIC SECTION

Rochester - Monroe County (G-14404)

Fax: 585 464-8471
Chris Hill, *President*
Jim Hartke, *Vice Pres*
John Bryce, *Engineer*
Kyle Blemel, *Sales Staff*
Daniel Johnstone, *Manager*
▲ **EMP:** 20
SALES: 2.2MM **Privately Held**
WEB: www.framingtech.com
SIC: 3448 Prefabricated metal buildings

(G-14381)
FRANK J MARTELLO
Also Called: Countertop Creations
1227 Maple St (14611-1545)
PHONE 585 235-2780
Fax: 585 235-2788
Frank J Martello, *Owner*
Cynthia Martello, *Manager*
EMP: 6
SQ FT: 6,000
SALES (est): 430K **Privately Held**
WEB: www.countertop-creations.com
SIC: 2541 Counter & sink tops

(G-14382)
FREETIME MAGAZINE INC
1255 University Ave # 270 (14607-1643)
PHONE 585 473-2266
Fax: 585 473-5214
Thomas Cannon, *President*
EMP: 8
SQ FT: 1,000
SALES (est): 430K **Privately Held**
WEB: www.freetime.com
SIC: 2711 Newspapers: publishing only, not printed on site

(G-14383)
FRESHOP INC
125 Tech Park Dr (14623-2446)
PHONE 585 738-6035
Brian Moyer, *CEO*
Karthik Balasubramanian, *President*
EMP: 15
SQ FT: 20,000
SALES (est): 305.2K **Privately Held**
SIC: 7372 Application computer software

(G-14384)
FTT MEDICAL INC (PA)
Also Called: Esi
37 Centennial St (14611-1732)
PHONE 585 235-1430
Fax: 585 235-1438
John Longuil, *CEO*
EMP: 8
SQ FT: 9,000
SALES (est): 625.5K **Privately Held**
WEB: www.electrosurgicalinstrument.com
SIC: 3841 Surgical & medical instruments

(G-14385)
FX SILK SCREEN PRINTING I
1555 Lyell Ave (14606-2145)
PHONE 585 266-6773
Tom Dunne, *President*
EMP: 27
SALES (est): 2MM **Privately Held**
SIC: 2752 Commercial printing, lithographic

(G-14386)
GADABOUT USA WHEELCHAIRS INC
892 E Ridge Rd (14621-1718)
P.O. Box 17890 (14617-0890)
PHONE 585 338-2110
Fax: 585 338-2696
Michael Fonte, *President*
EMP: 15
SALES (est): 853.6K **Privately Held**
SIC: 3842 Wheelchairs

(G-14387)
GANNETT CO INC
Also Called: Democrat & Chronicle
245 E Main St (14604-2103)
PHONE 585 232-7100
Brian Ambor, *Branch Mgr*
EMP: 76
SALES (corp-wide): 5.7B **Publicly Held**
SIC: 2711 Newspapers, publishing & printing

PA: Gannett Co., Inc.
7950 Jones Branch Dr
Mc Lean VA 22102
703 854-6000

(G-14388)
GATTI TOOL & MOLD INC
997 Beahan Rd (14624-3548)
PHONE 585 328-1350
Fax: 585 328-1679
Gino Gatti, *President*
EMP: 12
SALES (est): 1.2MM **Privately Held**
WEB: www.gattitool.com
SIC: 3544 Industrial molds

(G-14389)
GE MDS LLC (HQ)
Also Called: Aferge Mds
175 Science Pkwy (14620-4260)
PHONE 585 242-9600
Henry Garcia, *Opers Mgr*
Stephen Cyran, *Engineer*
Bradford Laundry, *Engineer*
Ken Robson, *Engineer*
Thomas Hodge, *Senior Engr*
▲ **EMP:** 200
SALES (est): 31.6MM
SALES (corp-wide): 117.3B **Publicly Held**
WEB: www.microwavedata.com
SIC: 3663 Radio & TV communications equipment
PA: General Electric Company
41 Farnsworth St
Boston MA 02210
617 443-3000

(G-14390)
GEM MANUFACTURING INC
853 West Ave Bldg 17a (14611-2413)
PHONE 585 235-1670
Fax: 585 235-3666
Scott Keller, *President*
Thad Spaulding, *Vice Pres*
Stuart Kristensen, *Engineer*
Daniel Frankenberger, *Manager*
EMP: 5
SQ FT: 7,000
SALES (est): 679.6K **Privately Held**
WEB: www.gemmachine.com
SIC: 3599 Machine shop, jobbing & repair

(G-14391)
GENERAL PLATING LLC
850 Saint Paul St Ste 10 (14605-1065)
PHONE 585 423-0830
Fax: 585 423-2257
Tom Schenkel, *Partner*
Don Schenkel, *Partner*
John Schenkel, *Partner*
Richard Schenkel, *Partner*
Roger Schenkel, *Partner*
EMP: 20 **EST:** 1890
SQ FT: 35,000
SALES (est): 450K **Privately Held**
SIC: 3471 Finishing, metals or formed products

(G-14392)
GENERAL WELDING & FABG INC
60 Saginaw Dr Ste 4 (14623-3159)
PHONE 585 697-7660
Fax: 585 697-7660
EMP: 8
SALES (corp-wide): 5.3MM **Privately Held**
WEB: www.gwfab.com
SIC: 3713 5531 7539 Truck bodies & parts; trailer hitches, automotive; trailer repair
PA: General Welding & Fabricating, Inc.
991 Maple Rd
Elma NY 14059
716 652-0033

(G-14393)
GENESCO INC
Also Called: Hat World & Lids
271 Greece Rdg 69a (14626-2818)
PHONE 585 227-3080
Matthew Toor, *Manager*
EMP: 5

SALES (corp-wide): 3B **Publicly Held**
WEB: www.genesco.com
SIC: 2353 Hats & caps
PA: Genesco Inc.
1415 Murfreesboro Pike
Nashville TN 37217
615 367-7000

(G-14394)
GENESEE MANUFACTURING CO INC
566 Hollenbeck St (14621-2288)
PHONE 585 266-3201
Kevin Hite, *President*
Donald A Kohler Jr, *Vice Pres*
EMP: 9 **EST:** 1905
SQ FT: 8,000
SALES (est): 558.3K **Privately Held**
WEB: www.geneseemfg.com
SIC: 3545 5084 Cutting tools for machine tools; industrial machinery & equipment

(G-14395)
GENESEE VLY MET FINSHG CO INC
244 Verona St (14608-1708)
PHONE 585 232-4412
Fax: 585 232-2106
Peter N Dresser, *President*
Salvatore Vittozzi, *Corp Secy*
Cathy Heuft, *Manager*
EMP: 6 **EST:** 1948
SQ FT: 11,400
SALES (est): 568.3K **Privately Held**
SIC: 3471 Electroplating of metals or formed products; finishing, metals or formed products

(G-14396)
GENESIS DIGITAL IMAGING INC
150 Verona St (14608-1733)
PHONE 310 305-7358
Joseph Eliafan, *President*
EMP: 10
SALES (est): 1MM
SALES (corp-wide): 4.1B **Privately Held**
WEB: www.genesisdigitalimaging.com
SIC: 3844 Radiographic X-ray apparatus & tubes
HQ: Carestream Health, Inc.
150 Verona St
Rochester NY 14608
585 627-1800

(G-14397)
GENESIS VISION INC
Also Called: Rochester Optical
1260 Lyell Ave (14606-2040)
PHONE 585 254-0193
Jeremy Ho, *CEO*
Patrick Ho, *Ch of Bd*
Steve Asch, *Controller*
▲ **EMP:** 25
SQ FT: 22,500
SALES (est): 6.1MM **Privately Held**
SIC: 3827 Optical instruments & lenses

(G-14398)
GERMAN MACHINE & ASSEMBLY INC
226 Jay St (14608-1623)
PHONE 585 546-4200
Fax: 585 546-4400
Kim Beasley, *Ch of Bd*
Scott Boheen, *President*
Margaret Blair, *Bookkeeper*
EMP: 25
SALES (est): 3.5MM **Privately Held**
WEB: www.germanmach.com
SIC: 3469 Machine parts, stamped or pressed metal

(G-14399)
GERMANOW-SIMON CORPORATION
Also Called: G-S Plastic Optics
408 Saint Paul St (14605-1788)
PHONE 585 232-1440
Fax: 585 232-3857
Andrew Germanow, *Ch of Bd*
Kathye Simon, *General Mgr*
Lori Steffenilla, *Mfg Dir*
Chris Smock, *Plant Mgr*
Pat Sisca, *Mfg Mgr*
◆ **EMP:** 40 **EST:** 1916

SQ FT: 125,000
SALES (est): 9.9MM **Privately Held**
WEB: www.gsoptics.com
SIC: 3089 3559 3829 3545 Plastic processing; plastics working machinery; thermometers, liquid-in-glass & bimetal type; machine tool accessories; pressed & blown glass

(G-14400)
GETINGE SOURCING LLC
1777 E Henrietta Rd (14623-3133)
PHONE 585 475-1400
Fax: 585 272-5291
John Aymong, *President*
Darren Soudan, *CFO*
▲ **EMP:** 174
SALES: 28.5MM
SALES (corp-wide): 3.4B **Privately Held**
SIC: 3842 Sterilizers, hospital & surgical
PA: Getinge Ab
Theres Svenssons Gata 7
Goteborg 417 5
103 350-000

(G-14401)
GETINGE USA INC (HQ)
1777 E Henrietta Rd (14623-3133)
PHONE 585 475-1400
Andrew Ray, *Ch of Bd*
Charles Carrier, *President*
Mike Kotsch, *President*
Charles Dacey, *Area Mgr*
Terry D Cooke, *Vice Pres*
▲ **EMP:** 150
SQ FT: 250,000
SALES (est): 105.2MM
SALES (corp-wide): 3.4B **Privately Held**
SIC: 3842 3841 Sterilizers, hospital & surgical; surgical & medical instruments
PA: Getinge Ab
Theres Svenssons Gata 7
Goteborg 417 5
103 350-000

(G-14402)
GH INDUCTION ATMOSPHERES LLC
35 Industrial Park Cir (14624-2403)
PHONE 585 368-2120
Fax: 585 368-2123
Becky Sheldon, *Manager*
Steve Skewes, *Manager*
Rebecca Sheldon, *Info Tech Mgr*
Steven Skewes,
Dale Wilcox,
▲ **EMP:** 35
SQ FT: 19,000
SALES (est): 8.5MM
SALES (corp-wide): 39.6K **Privately Held**
WEB: www.inductionatmospheres.com
SIC: 3542 Machine tools, metal forming type
HQ: Gh Electrotermia Sa
Calle Vereda Real, S/N
San Antonio De Benageber 46184
961 352-020

(G-14403)
GIZMO PRODUCTS INC
205 Seneca Pkwy (14613-1414)
PHONE 585 301-0970
EMP: 5
SALES (est): 828.5K **Privately Held**
SIC: 3823 Mfg Process Control Instruments

(G-14404)
GLASSFAB INC
257 Ormond St (14605-3024)
P.O. Box 31880 (14603-1880)
PHONE 585 262-4000
Fax: 585 454-4305
Robert Saltzman, *Ch of Bd*
Daniel Saltzman, *President*
Timothy Guenther, *QC Mgr*
Mary Leach, *Controller*
George Dean, *Sales Staff*
▲ **EMP:** 30
SQ FT: 30,000
SALES (est): 5.9MM **Privately Held*
WEB: www.glassfab.com
SIC: 3231 Products of purchased glass

Rochester - Monroe County (G-14405)

(G-14405)
GLASTEEL PARTS & SERVICES INC (DH)
1000 West Ave (14611-2442)
P.O. Box 23600 (14692-3600)
PHONE..................585 235-1010
Gary Brewer, *President*
EMP: 50
SQ FT: 18,000
SALES (est): 9.8MM
SALES (corp-wide): 14.7B Publicly Held
SIC: 3229 Pressed & blown glass
HQ: Pfaudler, Inc.
  1000 West Ave
  Rochester NY 14611
  585 464-5663

(G-14406)
GLAXOSMITHKLINE LLC
1177 Winton Rd S (14618-2240)
PHONE..................585 738-9025
EMP: 26
SALES (corp-wide): 36B Privately Held
SIC: 2834 Pharmaceutical preparations
HQ: Glaxosmithkline Llc
  5 Crescent Dr
  Philadelphia PA 19112
  215 751-4000

(G-14407)
GLEASON CORPORATION (PA)
1000 University Ave (14607-1286)
P.O. Box 22970 (14692-2970)
PHONE..................585 473-1000
Fax: 585 461-4092
John J Perrotti, *President*
Johannes Becker, *General Mgr*
He Bo, *General Mgr*
Klaus Kremmin, *General Mgr*
Rudolf Moser, *General Mgr*
◆ EMP: 800
SQ FT: 721,400
SALES (est): 999.5MM Privately Held
SIC: 3541 3829 Machine tools, metal cutting type; gear cutting & finishing machines; numerically controlled metal cutting machine tools; machine tool replacement & repair parts, metal cutting types; physical property testing equipment

(G-14408)
GLEASON WORKS (HQ)
1000 University Ave (14607-1286)
PHONE..................585 473-1000
Fax: 585 461-4348
James S Gleason, *Ch of Bd*
John J Perrotti, *President*
Nanci Malin Peck, *Vice Pres*
Edward J Pelta, *Vice Pres*
John W Pysnack, *Vice Pres*
◆ EMP: 925 EST: 1865
SQ FT: 721,000
SALES (est): 257.2MM
SALES (corp-wide): 999.5MM Privately Held
WEB: www.gleason.com
SIC: 3714 3728 3566 3541 Gears, motor vehicle; gears, aircraft power transmission; gears, power transmission, except automotive; gear cutting & finishing machines; numerically controlled metal cutting machine tools; machine tool replacement & repair parts, metal cutting types; physical property testing equipment; metal stampings
PA: Gleason Corporation
  1000 University Ave
  Rochester NY 14607
  585 473-1000

(G-14409)
GLOBAL PRECISION INDS INC
955 Millstead Way (14624-5107)
PHONE..................585 254-0010
Mark Wheeler, *CEO*
Bob Nuccitelli, *President*
Ryan Moyer, *Opers Mgr*
EMP: 15
SALES (est): 2.1MM Privately Held
WEB: www.global-precision.com
SIC: 3999 Barber & beauty shop equipment

(G-14410)
GM COMPONENTS HOLDINGS LLC
Also Called: Gmch Rochester
1000 Lexington Ave (14606-2810)
P.O. Box 92700 (14692-8800)
PHONE..................585 647-7000
Chuck Gifford, *Principal*
Jane Shewman, *Senior Buyer*
Eugene Bovenzi, *Engineer*
John Butler, *Engineer*
John Johnson, *Manager*
EMP: 350
SQ FT: 2,250
SALES (corp-wide): 152.3B Publicly Held
SIC: 3714 Motor vehicle parts & accessories
HQ: Gm Components Holdings, Llc
  300 Renaissance Ctr
  Detroit MI 48243
  313 556-5000

(G-14411)
GOLD PRIDE PRESS INC
12 Pixley Industrial Pkwy (14624-2364)
PHONE..................585 224-8800
Fax: 585 224-9633
Ted Rhodes, *Vice Pres*
Gloria Cambisi, *Office Mgr*
Tom Steele, *Supervisor*
EMP: 20
SQ FT: 30,000
SALES (est): 4.4MM Privately Held
WEB: www.goldpride.com
SIC: 2789 Trade binding services

(G-14412)
GRADIENT LENS CORPORATION
207 Tremont St Ste 1 (14608-2398)
PHONE..................585 235-2620
Fax: 585 235-6645
Douglas Kindred, *President*
Linda Plate, *Business Mgr*
Leland Atkinson, *Vice Pres*
Imelda Griffith, *Sales Staff*
Kenneth Harrington, *Marketing Staff*
EMP: 35
SQ FT: 9,500
SALES (est): 4.4MM Privately Held
WEB: www.gradientlens.com
SIC: 3827 Optical instruments & lenses; interferometers

(G-14413)
GRAYWOOD COMPANIES INC (PA)
Also Called: Jasco Cutting Tools
1390 Mount Read Blvd (14606-2820)
P.O. Box 60497 (14606-0497)
PHONE..................585 254-7000
Fax: 585 254-2655
John M Summers, *Ch of Bd*
Eugene Baldino, *President*
Dave Krigeer, *Vice Pres*
Sam Eberhard, *Purch Mgr*
Mary Schiltz, *Purchasing*
EMP: 40 EST: 2005
SQ FT: 36,000
SALES (est): 107.2MM Privately Held
SIC: 3541 3545 3544 3398 Machine tools, metal cutting type; boring mills; countersinking machines; deburring machines; machine tool accessories; drill bits, metalworking; taps, machine tool; reamers, machine tool; special dies, tools, jigs & fixtures; metal heat treating

(G-14414)
GSP COMPONENTS INC
1190 Brooks Ave (14624-3112)
PHONE..................585 436-3377
Fax: 585 436-5123
Ronald J Motsay, *CEO*
Tim Lynn, *Opers Mgr*
EMP: 62 EST: 1951
SQ FT: 34,000
SALES (est): 18.9MM Privately Held
WEB: www.gspcomponents.com
SIC: 3451 Screw machine products

(G-14415)
H RISCH INC
44 Saginaw Dr (14623-3132)
PHONE..................585 442-0110
Fax: 585 442-0189
Sara Tartaglia, *CEO*
Michael Pauly, *President*
Matt Meddaugh, *Sales Mgr*
Tammy Omay, *Sales Staff*
Laurie Mannhardt, *Manager*
EMP: 60 EST: 1935
SQ FT: 15,000
SALES (est): 9.5MM Privately Held
WEB: www.hrisch.com
SIC: 3089 Floor coverings, plastic

(G-14416)
H S ASSEMBLY INC
570 Hollandback (14605)
PHONE..................585 266-4287
David Marcellus, *President*
EMP: 5
SALES (est): 550K Privately Held
WEB: www.hsassembly.com
SIC: 3541 8711 Machine tools, metal cutting type; engineering services

(G-14417)
H T SPECIALTY INC
70 Bermar Park (14624-1541)
PHONE..................585 458-4060
Fax: 585 458-7592
Russel W Thiel, *President*
Donna Thiel, *Vice Pres*
Susan Thomas, *Office Mgr*
Judy Thiel, *Manager*
EMP: 18
SQ FT: 8,400
SALES: 2.2MM Privately Held
SIC: 3599 Machine shop, jobbing & repair

(G-14418)
HAARSTICK SAILMAKERS INC
1461 Hudson Ave (14621-1716)
PHONE..................585 342-5200
Fax: 585 342-8360
Steven Haarstick, *President*
EMP: 10 EST: 1970
SQ FT: 8,760
SALES (est): 926K Privately Held
WEB: www.haarsticksailmakers.com
SIC: 2394 Sails: made from purchased materials

(G-14419)
HAMTRONICS INC
39 Willnick Cir (14626-4748)
PHONE..................585 392-9430
Fax: 585 392-9420
G Francis Vogt, *President*
Joan Vogt, *Sales Executive*
EMP: 7
SALES: 500K Privately Held
SIC: 3663 5961 Radio broadcasting & communications equipment; mail order house

(G-14420)
HANGER PRSTHETCS & ORTHO INC
333 Metro Park Ste F200 (14623-2632)
PHONE..................585 292-9510
Zoltan Pallagi, *Branch Mgr*
Sheryl Price, *Director*
Zulfiqar Ahmed, *Executive*
EMP: 7
SALES (corp-wide): 500.5MM Privately Held
SIC: 3842 Surgical appliances & supplies
HQ: Hanger Prosthetics & Orthotics, Inc.
  10910 Main Dr
  Austin TX 78758
  512 777-3800

(G-14421)
HANSON AGGREGATES PA LLC
1535 Scottsville Rd (14623-1934)
PHONE..................585 436-3250
Jeff Kramarz, *Branch Mgr*
EMP: 15
SALES (corp-wide): 14.4B Privately Held
SIC: 2899 1442 Concrete curing & hardening compounds; gravel mining
HQ: Hanson Aggregates Pennsylvania, Llc
  7660 Imperial Way
  Allentown PA 18195
  610 366-4626

(G-14422)
HARRIS CORPORATION
Harris Long Range Radio
1680 University Ave (14610-1887)
PHONE..................585 244-5830
Fax: 585 242-4755
Madjid Abdi, *Principal*
Bob Griffith, *Opers Staff*
Jim Rogers, *Engineer*
Steven Trumpiniski, *Engineer*
Mark Turner, *Engineer*
EMP: 2600
SALES (corp-wide): 7.4B Publicly Held
SIC: 3663 Radio & TV communications equipment
PA: Harris Corporation
  1025 W Nasa Blvd
  Melbourne FL 32919
  321 727-9100

(G-14423)
HARRIS CORPORATION
Also Called: Exelis Geospatial Systems
400 Initiative Dr (14624-6219)
P.O. Box 60488 (14606-0488)
PHONE..................585 269-6600
Christopher Young, *CEO*
William Brown, *President*
William Gattle, *President*
David Melcher, *President*
Conrad Cierniak, *Vice Pres*
EMP: 800
SALES (corp-wide): 7.4B Publicly Held
SIC: 3812 Space vehicle guidance systems & equipment
PA: Harris Corporation
  1025 W Nasa Blvd
  Melbourne FL 32919
  321 727-9100

(G-14424)
HARRIS CORPORATION
Also Called: Exelis Geospatial Systems
800 Lee Rd Bldg 601 (14606)
P.O. Box 60488 (14606-0488)
PHONE..................585 269-5001
William Brown, *CEO*
William Gattle, *President*
David Melcher, *President*
Richard W Wambach, *Branch Mgr*
Kathryn Lloyd, *MIS Mgr*
EMP: 400
SALES (corp-wide): 7.4B Publicly Held
SIC: 3812 Space vehicle guidance systems & equipment
PA: Harris Corporation
  1025 W Nasa Blvd
  Melbourne FL 32919
  321 727-9100

(G-14425)
HARRIS CORPORATION
Also Called: Exelis
800 Lee Rd (14606)
P.O. Box 60488 (14606-0488)
PHONE..................413 263-6200
Christopher Young, *CEO*
William Gattle, *President*
David McCaffrey, *Branch Mgr*
Kathryn Lloyd, *MIS Mgr*
EMP: 509
SALES (corp-wide): 7.4B Publicly Held
SIC: 3669 Burglar alarm apparatus, electric
PA: Harris Corporation
  1025 W Nasa Blvd
  Melbourne FL 32919
  321 727-9100

(G-14426)
HARRIS CORPORATION
2696 Manitou Rd Bldg 101 (14624-1173)
PHONE..................585 269-5000
Robert Golightly, *Business Mgr*
Tommy Brazie, *Vice Pres*
Michael Ognenovski, *Vice Pres*
Joe Westbay, *Vice Pres*
Joan Gardner, *Project Mgr*
EMP: 163

SALES (corp-wide): 7.4B **Publicly Held**
SIC: 3812 Space vehicle guidance systems & equipment
PA: Harris Corporation
 1025 W Nasa Blvd
 Melbourne FL 32919
 321 727-9100

(G-14427)
HARRIS CORPORATION
Also Called: Rf Communications
570 Culver Rd (14609-7442)
PHONE.................................585 244-5830
Dana Mehnert, *Manager*
Melissa Revilla, *Manager*
Bill Fisher, *MIS Dir*
EMP: 20
SALES (corp-wide): 7.4B **Publicly Held**
SIC: 3661 3671 Telephone & telegraph apparatus; electron tubes
PA: Harris Corporation
 1025 W Nasa Blvd
 Melbourne FL 32919
 321 727-9100

(G-14428)
HARRIS CORPORATION
50 Carlson Rd (14610-1021)
PHONE.................................585 244-5830
EMP: 441
SALES (corp-wide): 7.4B **Publicly Held**
SIC: 3663 Radio & TV communications equipment
PA: Harris Corporation
 1025 W Nasa Blvd
 Melbourne FL 32919
 321 727-9100

(G-14429)
HARRIS CORPORATION
Also Called: Harris Rf Communications
1350 Jefferson Rd (14623-3106)
PHONE.................................585 244-5830
Frank Connolly, *Exec VP*
EMP: 441
SALES (corp-wide): 7.4B **Publicly Held**
SIC: 3663 Radio & TV communications equipment
PA: Harris Corporation
 1025 W Nasa Blvd
 Melbourne FL 32919
 321 727-9100

(G-14430)
HAWVER DISPLAY INC (PA)
140 Carter St (14621-5136)
PHONE.................................585 544-2290
Fax: 585 544-2292
Timothy Culver, *President*
EMP: 29
SQ FT: 44,000
SALES (est): 3.6MM **Privately Held**
WEB: www.hawver.com
SIC: 2542 Fixtures: display, office or store: except wood

(G-14431)
HAZLOW ELECTRONICS INC
49 Saint Bridgets Dr (14605-1899)
PHONE.................................585 325-5323
Fax: 585 325-4308
Alma Publow, *President*
David Publow, *Admin Sec*
EMP: 25
SQ FT: 40,000
SALES (est): 5.7MM **Privately Held**
WEB: www.hazlow.com
SIC: 3679 3672 Harness assemblies for electronic use: wire or cable; printed circuit boards

(G-14432)
HEDONIST ARTISAN CHOCOLATES
674 South Ave Ste B (14620-1378)
PHONE.................................585 461-2815
Jennifer Posey, *Partner*
Zahra Langford, *Partner*
EMP: 11
SALES (est): 1.3MM **Privately Held**
SIC: 2064 Candy & other confectionery products

(G-14433)
HICKEY FREEMAN TAILORED CL INC
1155 N Clinton Ave (14621-4454)
PHONE.................................585 467-7240
Stephen Granovsky, *CEO*
Paulette Garafalo, *President*
Eric Jennings, *Director*
EMP: 50
SALES (est): 8.9MM
SALES (corp-wide): 1.7MM **Privately Held**
SIC: 2311 Men's & boys' suits & coats; jackets, tailored suit-type: men's & boys'; suits, men's & boys': made from purchased materials; tuxedos: made from purchased materials
HQ: Samuelsohn Limitee
 6930 Av Du Parc
 Montreal QC H3N 1
 514 273-7741

(G-14434)
HIGH FALLS BREWING COMPANY LLC (DH)
Also Called: North Americas Breweries
445 Saint Paul St (14605-1726)
P.O. Box 30762 (14603-0762)
PHONE.................................585 546-1030
Michael Gaesser, *Vice Pres*
Andrew Yeager, *Treasurer*
William A Neilson, *VP Human Res*
Jessica Chatterton, *Info Tech Mgr*
Samuel T Hubbard Jr,
▲ **EMP:** 142
SQ FT: 900,000
SALES (est): 70.8MM **Privately Held**
WEB: www.highfalls.com
SIC: 2082 Beer (alcoholic beverage); ale (alcoholic beverage)
HQ: North American Breweries, Inc.
 445 Saint Paul St
 Rochester NY 14605
 585 546-1030

(G-14435)
HIGH FALLS OPERATING CO LLC
445 Saint Paul St (14605-1726)
PHONE.................................585 546-1030
Katie Blahowicz, *Controller*
Kenneth Yartz, *Mng Member*
EMP: 800
SALES (est): 109MM **Privately Held**
SIC: 2082 Malt beverage products
HQ: North American Breweries, Inc.
 445 Saint Paul St
 Rochester NY 14605
 585 546-1030

(G-14436)
HIGH SPEED HAMMER COMPANY INC
Also Called: Assembly Equipment Division
313 Norton St (14621-3331)
PHONE.................................585 266-4287
Fax: 585 544-8921
David Marcellus, *President*
Richard Marcellus, *Corp Secy*
EMP: 15 EST: 1917
SQ FT: 12,000
SALES: 1MM **Privately Held**
SIC: 3542 3541 Riveting machines; machine tools, metal cutting: exotic (explosive, etc.); machine tool replacement & repair parts, metal cutting types

(G-14437)
HIS VISION INC
1260 Lyell Ave (14606-2040)
PHONE.................................585 254-0022
Patrick Ho, *President*
Wayne Ohl, *Admin Sec*
EMP: 48 EST: 1941
SQ FT: 21,000
SALES: 3.5MM **Privately Held**
WEB: www.rochesteroptical.com
SIC: 3851 Frames & parts, eyeglass & spectacle

(G-14438)
HOBART CORPORATION
3495 Winton Pl (14623-2824)
PHONE.................................585 427-9000
Fax: 585 427-8818
Pat Allen, *Manager*
EMP: 50
SALES (corp-wide): 13.4B **Publicly Held**
SIC: 3589 Dishwashing machines, commercial
HQ: Hobart Corporation
 701 S Ridge Ave
 Troy OH 45374
 937 332-3000

(G-14439)
HOVER-DAVIS INC (DH)
100 Paragon Dr (14624-1129)
PHONE.................................585 352-9590
John Hover, *President*
Peter Davis, *Vice Pres*
Chris Bennette, *Controller*
Kraig Cotter, *Director*
▲ **EMP:** 125
SQ FT: 66,000
SALES (est): 15.6MM
SALES (corp-wide): 145.4MM **Privately Held**
WEB: www.hoverdavis.com
SIC: 3549 Assembly machines, including robotic
HQ: Ui Holding Company
 33 Broome Corporate Pkwy
 Conklin NY 13748
 607 779-7522

(G-14440)
HUDSON STEEL FABRICATORS
444 Hudson Ave (14605-1359)
P.O. Box 31547 (14603-1547)
PHONE.................................585 454-3923
Fax: 585 454-6141
Rosario La Delfa, *President*
Russ La Delfa, *Purch Agent*
Don Brown, *Controller*
EMP: 40
SQ FT: 18,000
SALES (est): 7.2MM **Privately Held**
SIC: 3441 Fabricated structural metal

(G-14441)
HY-TECH MOLD INC
60 Elmgrove Park (14624-1363)
PHONE.................................585 247-2450
Fax: 585 247-2461
Donald Philipp, *President*
Patricia Philipp, *Vice Pres*
Stuart Norris, *Treasurer*
EMP: 10
SQ FT: 10,000
SALES: 800K **Privately Held**
WEB: www.hy-techmold.com
SIC: 3544 Industrial molds

(G-14442)
ID SIGNSYSTEMS INC
410 Atlantic Ave Ste 401 (14609-7352)
PHONE.................................585 266-5750
Fax: 585 266-5798
Katrina Beatty, *CEO*
Paul Dudley, *President*
Jeff Ureles, *COO*
Stephanie Marquez, *Controller*
Phillip Dotson, *Marketing Staff*
◆ **EMP:** 48
SQ FT: 15,000
SALES (est): 4.3MM **Privately Held**
WEB: www.idsignsystems.com
SIC: 3993 Signs & advertising specialties

(G-14443)
IDEX CORPORATION
2883 Brghtn Hnretta Tl Rd (14623-2790)
PHONE.................................585 292-8121
Michael Bonomo, *Manager*
Jeff Sill, *Director*
EMP: 5
SALES (corp-wide): 2B **Publicly Held**
SIC: 3563 Air & gas compressors
PA: Idex Corporation
 1925 W Field Ct Ste 200
 Lake Forest IL 60045
 847 498-7070

(G-14444)
IEC ELECTRONICS CORP
Celmet
1365 Emerson St (14606-3006)
PHONE.................................585 647-1760
Fax: 585 647-2308
Rich Ramell, *Marketing Staff*
Tom Guiliani, *Director*
EMP: 319
SALES (corp-wide): 127MM **Publicly Held**
SIC: 3444 Sheet metalwork
PA: Iec Electronics Corp.
 105 Norton St
 Newark NY 14513
 315 331-7742

(G-14445)
IHEARTCOMMUNICATIONS INC
Also Called: Wham 1180 AM
100 Chestnut St Ste 1700 (14604-2418)
PHONE.................................585 454-4884
Fax: 585 262-9426
Karen Carey, *President*
Nick Francesco, *Social Dir*
EMP: 120
SALES (corp-wide): 6.2B **Publicly Held**
SIC: 3663 4832 Radio receiver networks; radio broadcasting stations
HQ: Iheartcommunications, Inc.
 200 E Basse Rd
 San Antonio TX 78209
 210 822-2828

(G-14446)
IMAGE360
Also Called: Signs Now
275 Marketplace Dr (14623-6001)
PHONE.................................585 272-1234
Fax: 585 272-1252
Julie St Germaine, *President*
Jackie Ciresi, *Treasurer*
EMP: 5
SALES (est): 712.9K **Privately Held**
WEB: www.signsnow405.com
SIC: 3993 Signs & advertising specialties

(G-14447)
IMPRESSIONS INTERNATIONAL INC
1255 University Ave # 150 (14607-1643)
PHONE.................................585 442-5240
Terry Gersey, *President*
Harry Gersey, *Vice Pres*
▲ **EMP:** 7
SQ FT: 2,500
SALES (est): 969.7K **Privately Held**
WEB: www.checkfraud.com
SIC: 3555 Printing plates

(G-14448)
INNEX INDUSTRIES INC
6 Marway Dr (14624-2349)
PHONE.................................585 247-3575
Fax: 585 247-1903
Luka Gakovic, *President*
Helen J Gakovic, *Vice Pres*
▼ **EMP:** 28
SQ FT: 20,000
SALES (est): 7MM **Privately Held**
WEB: www.innexind.com
SIC: 3545 Milling machine attachments (machine tool accessories)

(G-14449)
INSTANT AGAIN LLC
1277 Mount Read Blvd # 2 (14606-2850)
PHONE.................................585 436-8003
Fax: 585 436-8012
James Webster, *Sales Staff*
Andrew Gross III,
EMP: 20
SALES (est): 3.1MM **Privately Held**
WEB: www.instantagain.com
SIC: 2752 Commercial printing, lithographic

(G-14450)
INSTANT MONOGRAMMING INC
1150 University Ave Ste 5 (14607-1647)
PHONE.................................585 654-5550
Fax: 585 654-5554
Daniel Bloom, *President*
Deborah Bloom, *Corp Secy*
EMP: 7
SALES (est): 683.1K **Privately Held**
SIC: 2395 Embroidery & art needlework; emblems, embroidered

(G-14451)
INTELLIMETAL INC
2025 Brighton Henrietta (14623-2509)
PHONE.................................585 424-3260

Rochester - Monroe County (G-14452) — GEOGRAPHIC SECTION

Kim Lazzara Zapiach, *President*
Scott Lazzara, *General Mgr*
Shannon Pryce, *Accountant*
EMP: 57
SALES (est): 11.9MM **Privately Held**
SIC: 3444 Sheet metalwork

(G-14452)
INTERNATIONAL PAPER COMPANY
200 Boxart St (14612-5646)
PHONE..................585 663-1000
Mike Rougeux, *Mfg Mgr*
Les Senft, *Manager*
Rex Roy, *Maintence Staff*
EMP: 150
SALES (corp-wide): 22.3B **Publicly Held**
WEB: www.internationalpaper.com
SIC: 2653 2671 Boxes, corrugated: made from purchased materials; packaging paper & plastics film, coated & laminated
PA: International Paper Company
6400 Poplar Ave
Memphis TN 38197
901 419-9000

(G-14453)
INTERNATIONAL TOOL & MCH INC
121 Lincoln Ave (14611-2444)
P.O. Box 24334 (14624-0334)
PHONE..................585 654-6955
Fax: 585 654-8919
Eric Moore, *President*
▲ **EMP:** 10
SQ FT: 8,000
SALES: 800K **Privately Held**
SIC: 3599 Machine shop, jobbing & repair

(G-14454)
INTRINSIQ MATERIALS INC
1200 Ridgeway Ave Ste 110 (14615-3758)
PHONE..................585 301-4432
Robert Cournoyer, *President*
Sujatha Ramanujan, *Vice Pres*
Scott Walton, *Engineer*
EMP: 7 **EST:** 2011
SALES (est): 1.2MM **Privately Held**
WEB: www.intrinsiqmaterials.com
SIC: 2893 8731 Printing ink; electronic research

(G-14455)
ISOFLUX INCORPORATED
Also Called: Isoflux Hollow Cathodes
10 Vantage Point Dr Ste 4 (14624-1151)
P.O. Box 190, Pittsford (14534-0190)
PHONE..................585 349-0640
David A Glocker, *President*
Joseph E Miller Jr, *Vice Pres*
Mark Romach, *Manager*
EMP: 5
SQ FT: 2,800
SALES (est): 795.4K **Privately Held**
WEB: www.isofluxinc.com
SIC: 3479 Coating of metals & formed products

(G-14456)
J MACKENZIE LTD
234 Wallace Way (14624-6216)
P.O. Box 22678 (14692-2678)
PHONE..................585 321-1770
Fax: 585 321-3277
James E Hammer, *President*
John Fischer, *Manager*
Christopher F Wieser, *Admin Sec*
▲ **EMP:** 39
SQ FT: 56,000
SALES (est): 3.5MM
SALES (corp-wide): 119.2MM **Privately Held**
WEB: www.jmackenzie.com
SIC: 2789 Paper cutting
PA: Hammer Packaging Corp.
200 Lucius Gordon Dr
West Henrietta NY 14586
585 424-3880

(G-14457)
J VOGLER ENTERPRISE LLC
15 Evelyn St (14606-5533)
P.O. Box 24361 (14624-0361)
PHONE..................585 247-1625
Fax: 585 247-1637
James Vogler,
EMP: 10
SQ FT: 6,000
SALES (est): 1.7MM **Privately Held**
WEB: www.jvogler.com
SIC: 3541 Machine tools, metal cutting type

(G-14458)
JAM INDUSTRIES INC
Also Called: Ace Manufacturing
1580 Emerson St (14606-3118)
PHONE..................585 458-9830
Fax: 585 458-7696
Eric L Johnson, *Ch of Bd*
Martha Moriarty, *Vice Pres*
Bill Farrell, *Purchasing*
Scott Brownstein, *Branch Mgr*
▲ **EMP:** 45
SQ FT: 25,000
SALES (est): 7.9MM **Privately Held**
WEB: www.jamindustries.com
SIC: 3599 Machine & other job shop work

(G-14459)
JAMES CONOLLY PRINTING CO
72 Marway Cir (14624-2380)
PHONE..................585 426-4150
Fax: 585 426-4198
Robert Conolly, *President*
Luke Burnahy, *Manager*
Beth Calkins, *Manager*
EMP: 21 **EST:** 1968
SQ FT: 13,000
SALES (est): 3.3MM **Privately Held**
SIC: 2752 2789 2791 Commercial printing, offset; bookbinding & related work; typesetting

(G-14460)
JAMESTOWN CONT OF ROCHESTER
82 Edwards Deming Dr (14606-2842)
PHONE..................585 254-9190
Bruce Janowsky, *Ch of Bd*
Lou Petitti, *General Mgr*
Dick P Weimer, *Corp Secy*
Joseph R Palmeri, *Vice Pres*
EMP: 70
SALES (est): 18.8MM
SALES (corp-wide): 107.4MM **Privately Held**
WEB: www.jamestowncontainer.com
SIC: 2653 Corrugated & solid fiber boxes
PA: Jamestown Container Corp
14 Deming Dr
Falconer NY 14733
716 665-4623

(G-14461)
JK JEWELRY INC
Also Called: ELEKTRA DESIGNS
1500 Brighton Henrietta (14623-2340)
PHONE..................585 346-3464
John S Kaupp, *President*
Joni Lucas, *COO*
John Berg, *Sales Staff*
Ron Koenigs, *Sales Staff*
Melvin Koh, *Info Tech Dir*
▲ **EMP:** 70
SQ FT: 18,000
SALES: 17.1MM **Privately Held**
WEB: www.jkfindings.com
SIC: 3911 Jewelry, precious metal

(G-14462)
JML OPTICAL INDUSTRIES LLC
Also Called: Gregg Sadwick
820 Linden Ave (14625-2710)
PHONE..................585 248-8900
Bob Bicksler, *CEO*
Joseph Lobozzo II, *President*
Trett Sadwick, *COO*
Graldine Lynch, *Vice Pres*
Michael McCusker, *Vice Pres*
▲ **EMP:** 86
SQ FT: 72,000
SALES: 14.1MM **Privately Held**
SIC: 3827 Lenses, optical: all types except ophthalmic; mirrors, optical; prisms, optical

(G-14463)
JMT PROGRAM LEADERSHIP GROUP
1305 Emerson St (14606-3006)
PHONE..................585 217-1134
Mike Hockenberger, *President*
EMP: 6
SALES (est): 391.8K
SALES (corp-wide): 19.3MM **Privately Held**
SIC: 3544 Special dies & tools
PA: Precision Grinding And Manufacturing Corporation
1305 Emerson St
Rochester NY 14606
585 458-4300

(G-14464)
JOHNSON CONTROLS INC
1669 Lake Ave Bldg 333 (14652-0001)
PHONE..................585 724-2232
Lee Arbagast, *Branch Mgr*
EMP: 120 **Privately Held**
SIC: 2531 3714 3691 3822 Seats, automobile; motor vehicle body components & frame; instrument board assemblies, motor vehicle; lead acid batteries (storage batteries); building services monitoring controls, automatic; facilities support services
HQ: Johnson Controls, Inc.
5757 N Green Bay Ave
Milwaukee WI 53209
414 524-1200

(G-14465)
JTEKT TORSEN NORTH AMERICA
2 Jetview Dr (14624-4904)
PHONE..................585 464-5000
Fax: 585 328-5477
Hiroyuki Kaijima, *President*
Y Kataoka, *President*
Thomas Sipples, *Engineer*
Gary Lynch, *Controller*
Joseph Parisi, *Admin Sec*
▲ **EMP:** 10
SQ FT: 30,000
SALES (est): 2MM
SALES (corp-wide): 11.9B **Privately Held**
SIC: 3714 3711 Motor vehicle parts & accessories; motor vehicles & car bodies
HQ: Jtekt North America, Inc.
47771 Halyard Dr
Plymouth MI 48170
734 454-1500

(G-14466)
K BARTHELMES MFG CO INC
61 Brooklea Dr (14624-2701)
PHONE..................585 328-8140
Fax: 585 328-5932
John Wischmeyer, *President*
Janet Wischmeyer, *Admin Sec*
EMP: 15 **EST:** 1917
SQ FT: 55,000
SALES (est): 1.9MM **Privately Held**
WEB: www.barthelmes.com
SIC: 3444 Sheet metalwork

(G-14467)
KAMAN AUTOMATION INC
1000 University Ave (14607-1286)
PHONE..................585 254-8840
EMP: 7
SALES (corp-wide): 1.7B **Publicly Held**
SIC: 3625 Relays & industrial controls; motor controls & accessories
HQ: Kaman Automation, Inc.
1 Vision Way
Bloomfield CT 06002
860 687-5000

(G-14468)
KATHLEEN B MEAD
Also Called: Automatic Bar Machining Co
1675 Buffalo Rd (14624-1637)
PHONE..................585 247-0146
Fax: 585 247-2141
Kathleen B Mead, *Owner*
EMP: 5 **EST:** 1957
SQ FT: 16,800
SALES (est): 273.9K **Privately Held**
SIC: 3451 Screw machine products

(G-14469)
KEVIN J KASSMAN
Also Called: Uniform Express
1408 Buffalo Rd (14624-1827)
PHONE..................585 529-4245
Fax: 585 529-4247
Kevin J Kassman, *Owner*
EMP: 6
SQ FT: 4,500
SALES: 600K **Privately Held**
SIC: 2395 2396 Embroidery & art needlework; screen printing on fabric articles

(G-14470)
KLEE CORP
Also Called: Klees Car Wash and Detailing
340 Jefferson Rd (14623-2644)
PHONE..................585 272-0320
Daniel Edelman, *Manager*
EMP: 7
SQ FT: 5,625
SALES (corp-wide): 14.8MM **Privately Held**
SIC: 3589 Car washing machinery
PA: Klee Corp
3044 E Henrietta Rd
Henrietta NY 14467
585 321-1510

(G-14471)
KODAK ALARIS INC (HQ)
2400 Mount Read Blvd # 1175 (14615-2744)
PHONE..................585 290-2891
Jeff Goodman, *CEO*
Rick Costanzo, *President*
Rick Costanzom, *President*
Dennis Olbrich, *President*
Nicki Zongrone, *President*
◆ **EMP:** 277
SQ FT: 340,000
SALES (est): 319.7MM
SALES (corp-wide): 1B **Privately Held**
SIC: 3861 Photographic equipment & supplies
PA: Kodak Alaris Holdings Limited
Hemel One Boundary Way
Hemel Hempstead HERTS HP2 7
845 293-7855

(G-14472)
KURZ AND ZOBEL INC
688 Colfax St (14606-3193)
PHONE..................585 254-9060
Fax: 585 254-0123
Michael Zobel Jr, *President*
Sandy Rosengrant, *Office Mgr*
EMP: 8
SQ FT: 15,000
SALES (est): 867.9K **Privately Held**
SIC: 3599 3462 Machine shop, jobbing & repair; gear & chain forgings

(G-14473)
LAGOE-OSWEGO CORP
429 Antlers Dr (14618-2103)
PHONE..................315 343-3160
Fax: 315 343-5882
David A Falk, *President*
Bertram Falk, *Vice Pres*
Ben Bailey, *Manager*
Glenn Sharkey, *Manager*
EMP: 30
SQ FT: 19,000
SALES (est): 4.5MM **Privately Held**
SIC: 3599 7692 Machine shop, jobbing & repair; welding repair

(G-14474)
LASERMAX INC
3495 Winton Pl Ste A37 (14623-2898)
PHONE..................585 272-5420
Fax: 585 272-5427
Susan H Walter, *President*
Will H Walter, *Exec VP*
Brian Olmsted, *Vice Pres*
Joanne Morrow, *Purch Mgr*
Jeff Tuller, *Design Engr*
EMP: 54
SQ FT: 10,250
SALES (est): 12.7MM **Privately Held**
WEB: www.lasermax.com
SIC: 3699 3674 Laser systems & equipment; semiconductors & related devices

(G-14475)
LASSER PRODUCTS INCORPORATED
63 Winfield Rd (14622-2212)
PHONE..................585 249-5180
Mark Zazubec, *President*
Angela Zazubec, *Office Mgr*

GEOGRAPHIC SECTION
Rochester - Monroe County (G-14500)

EMP: 5
SALES: 450K **Privately Held**
SIC: 2431 Storm windows, wood

(G-14476)
LAZER INCORPORATED (PA)
Also Called: Lazer Photo Engraving
1465 Jefferson Rd Ste 110 (14623-3149)
PHONE..................................336 744-8047
Fax: 585 247-9647
Gary Staford, *President*
Ken McCurdy, *CFO*
Lesia Telega, *Director*
EMP: 50
SQ FT: 10,000
SALES (est): 3.6MM **Privately Held**
WEB: www.lazerinc.com
SIC: 2796 Color separations for printing

(G-14477)
LENS TRIPTAR CO INC
439 Monroe Ave Ste 1 (14607-3787)
PHONE..................................585 473-4470
Fax: 585 473-3945
Allen Krisiloff, *President*
EMP: 5
SQ FT: 3,300
SALES (est): 912.7K **Privately Held**
WEB: www.triptar.com
SIC: 3827 Lenses, optical: all types except ophthalmic

(G-14478)
LEXINGTON MACHINING LLC
677 Buffalo Rd (14611-2014)
PHONE..................................585 235-0880
Ken Vivlamore, *Vice Pres*
Rick Donofrio, *Controller*
Kathi Horch, *Systems Staff*
EMP: 100
SALES (corp-wide): 25.9MM **Privately Held**
SIC: 3451 Screw machine products
PA: Lexington Machining Llc
  677 Buffalo Rd
  Rochester NY 14611
  585 235-0880

(G-14479)
LEXINGTON MACHINING LLC (PA)
677 Buffalo Rd (14611-2014)
PHONE..................................585 235-0880
Michael Lubin, *Ch of Bd*
Warren Delano, *President*
Robert S Ducharme, *Engineer*
Tim Duemmel, *Manager*
Dave Giannavola, *Manager*
EMP: 185
SALES: 25.9MM **Privately Held**
WEB: www.lexingtonmachining.com
SIC: 3451 Screw machine products

(G-14480)
LIDESTRI FOODS INC
1000 Lee Rd (14606)
PHONE..................................585 458-8335
EMP: 22
SALES (corp-wide): 271.6MM **Privately Held**
SIC: 2033 Apple sauce: packaged in cans, jars, etc.
PA: Lidestri Foods, Inc.
  815 Whitney Rd W
  Fairport NY 14450
  585 377-7700

(G-14481)
LOAD/N/GO BEVERAGE CORP (PA)
Also Called: Fiz Beverages
355 Portland Ave (14605-1565)
PHONE..................................585 218-4019
Fax: 585 467-7114
Paul Johnson, *President*
Linda Povlock, *Office Mgr*
EMP: 10 **EST:** 1964
SQ FT: 11,000
SALES (est): 1.6MM **Privately Held**
SIC: 2086 5181 5149 5921 Soft drinks: packaged in cans, bottles, etc.; beer & other fermented malt liquors; soft drinks; beer (packaged)

(G-14482)
LOGICAL OPERATIONS INC
3535 Winton Pl (14623-2803)
PHONE..................................585 350-7000
Fax: 585 288-7411
Bill Rosenthal, *President*
Jeff Felice, *Managing Dir*
Michelle Mattick, *CFO*
▲ **EMP:** 110
SALES (est): 15.9MM **Privately Held**
SIC: 2732 Books: printing & binding

(G-14483)
LOUIS HEINDL & SON INC
Also Called: Heindl Printers
306 Central Ave (14605-3007)
P.O. Box 31121 (14603-1121)
PHONE..................................585 454-5080
Fax: 585 454-5350
P J Heindl, *President*
Debra Heindl, *Vice Pres*
Craig Schinsing, *Manager*
EMP: 6 **EST:** 1873
SQ FT: 3,500
SALES: 540K **Privately Held**
SIC: 2752 2759 2791 2789 Commercial printing, offset; letterpress printing; typesetting; bookbinding & related work

(G-14484)
LUMETRICS INC
1565 Jefferson Rd Ste 420 (14623-3190)
PHONE..................................585 214-2455
John Hart, *President*
Filipp Ignatovich, *General Mgr*
Todd Blalock, *Vice Pres*
Steve Heveron-Smith, *Vice Pres*
Steve Kelly, *Vice Pres*
▼ **EMP:** 17
SQ FT: 4,416
SALES (est): 4.4MM **Privately Held**
WEB: www.lumetrics.com
SIC: 3827 Optical instruments & apparatus

(G-14485)
MACAUTO USA INC
80 Excel Dr (14621-3470)
PHONE..................................585 342-2060
Fax: 585 342-2085
J J Liao, *President*
Jerry Hsu, *QC Mgr*
Douglas Chang, *Treasurer*
▲ **EMP:** 30
SQ FT: 15,000
SALES (est): 4.8MM
SALES (corp-wide): 114.6MM **Privately Held**
SIC: 3089 Automotive parts, plastic
PA: Macauto Industrial Co., Ltd.
  No. 6, Yongke 5th Rd.,
  Tainan City 71041
  623 310-88

(G-14486)
MACHINECRAFT INC
1645 Lyell Ave Ste 125 (14606-2331)
PHONE..................................585 436-1070
Alan D Lintz, *Ch of Bd*
EMP: 25
SQ FT: 8,750
SALES (est): 2.4MM **Privately Held**
SIC: 3544 Special dies & tools

(G-14487)
MACINNES TOOL CORPORATION
1700 Hudson Ave Ste 3 (14617-5155)
PHONE..................................585 467-1920
Fax: 585 467-7807
Gary Haines, *President*
Sherry Haines, *Treasurer*
Emily Haines, *Accountant*
Janet Lawson, *Office Mgr*
EMP: 20 **EST:** 1953
SQ FT: 6,000
SALES (est): 2.8MM **Privately Held**
WEB: www.macto.com
SIC: 3545 5085 Cutting tools for machine tools; industrial supplies

(G-14488)
MADISON & DUNN
850 Saint Paul St Ste 29 (14605-1065)
PHONE..................................585 563-7760
Christine Baliva, *Owner*
EMP: 6
SALES (est): 779.5K **Privately Held**
SIC: 2426 Flooring, hardwood

(G-14489)
MAGNA PRODUCTS CORP
777 Mount Read Blvd (14606-2129)
PHONE..................................585 647-2280
Fax: 585 647-2155
Kenneth Morrow, *President*
Pat Morrow, *Vice Pres*
Brian Reeves, *Accounting Mgr*
Andrew Bolton, *Manager*
EMP: 20
SALES (est): 4.2MM **Privately Held**
WEB: www.magnaproducts.com
SIC: 3621 3566 Servomotors, electric; drives, high speed industrial, except hydrostatic

(G-14490)
MAGNETIC TECHNOLOGIES CORP (DH)
770 Linden Ave (14625-2764)
PHONE..................................585 385-9010
Gordon H McNeil, *Ch of Bd*
Steve Gleckler, *Facilities Mgr*
Kathleen Palia, *Controller*
Kevin Maier, *Finance*
Debbie Deitloff, *Sales Associate*
▲ **EMP:** 60
SQ FT: 70,000
SALES (est): 12MM
SALES (corp-wide): 805.3MM **Publicly Held**
WEB: www.arnoldmagnetics.com
SIC: 3579 Typing & word processing machines
HQ: Arnold Magnetic Technologies Corporation
  770 Linden Ave
  Rochester NY 14625
  585 385-9010

(G-14491)
MAIDSTONE COFFEE CO
60 Mushroom Blvd (14623-3202)
PHONE..................................585 272-1040
Fax: 585 272-8495
Garrett Dobesh, *CEO*
Ken Mottshaw, *Maintence Staff*
EMP: 38
SALES (est): 4MM
SALES (corp-wide): 34.8MM **Privately Held**
SIC: 2095 Roasted coffee
HQ: Restaurant Brands International Inc
  226 Wyecroft Rd
  Oakville ON L6K 3
  905 845-6511

(G-14492)
MANITOU CONCRETE
1260 Jefferson Rd (14623-3104)
PHONE..................................585 424-6040
Fax: 585 424-1846
John Pelrier, *Manager*
J McCarthy, *Manager*
Jim Wagner, *Director*
EMP: 65
SQ FT: 2,536
SALES (est): 6.6MM **Privately Held**
SIC: 3273 Ready-mixed concrete

(G-14493)
MANUFACTURING RESOURCES INC
2392 Innovation Way # 4 (14624-6225)
PHONE..................................631 481-0041
James Wildman, *Ch of Bd*
James Widman, *Ch of Bd*
EMP: 40 **EST:** 2002
SQ FT: 30,000
SALES (est): 605.3K **Privately Held**
WEB: www.mfgresource.com
SIC: 3444 3549 Sheet metalwork; assembly machines, including robotic

(G-14494)
MANUFACTURING SOLUTIONS INC
850 Saint Paul St Ste 11 (14605-1065)
PHONE..................................585 235-3320
Fax: 585 235-3324
Oscar Wilson, *President*
Jane Murray, *Manager*
EMP: 25
SQ FT: 5,000
SALES (est): 3.8MM **Privately Held**
WEB: www.mfgsolonline.com
SIC: 3699 Electrical equipment & supplies

(G-14495)
MARACLE INDUSTRIAL FINSHG CO
93 Kilbourn Rd (14618-3607)
PHONE..................................585 387-9077
Fax: 585 872-0285
Thomas Maracle, *President*
Nelson Maracle, *Vice Pres*
Valerie Eaton, *Office Mgr*
EMP: 30 **EST:** 1960
SQ FT: 30,000
SALES (est): 3MM **Privately Held**
SIC: 3471 Finishing, metals or formed products

(G-14496)
MARDON TOOL & DIE CO INC
19 Lois St (14606-1801)
PHONE..................................585 254-4545
Fax: 585 254-8258
Donald Fox, *President*
EMP: 13 **EST:** 1981
SQ FT: 4,000
SALES (est): 1.7MM **Privately Held**
SIC: 3599 Machine shop, jobbing & repair

(G-14497)
MAREX AQUISITION CORP
1385 Emerson St (14606-3027)
PHONE..................................585 458-3940
Gary Baxter, *Ch of Bd*
John Olivieri Sr, *Ch of Bd*
Leonard Olivieri, *Vice Pres*
▲ **EMP:** 115
SQ FT: 55,000
SALES (est): 10.7MM
SALES (corp-wide): 42.2MM **Privately Held**
WEB: www.martecindustries.com
SIC: 3469 3444 3443 3441 Metal stampings; sheet metalwork; fabricated plate work (boiler shop); fabricated structural metal
PA: Peko Precision Products, Inc.
  1400 Emerson St
  Rochester NY 14606
  585 647-3010

(G-14498)
MARTEC INDUSTRIES
1385 Emerson St (14606-3027)
PHONE..................................585 458-3940
Fax: 585 458-5412
John Olivieri, *Principal*
EMP: 16
SALES (est): 2.2MM **Privately Held**
SIC: 3999 Manufacturing industries

(G-14499)
MASTRO GRAPHIC ARTS INC
67 Deep Rock Rd (14624-3519)
PHONE..................................585 436-7570
Fax: 585 436-4245
Rae Mastrofilippo, *Ch of Bd*
Ms Rae Mastrofilippo, *Ch of Bd*
William Betteridge, *President*
Thomas Tortora, *CFO*
Nick Mastro, *Treasurer*
EMP: 34
SQ FT: 23,000
SALES (est): 8.4MM **Privately Held**
WEB: www.mastrographics.com
SIC: 2759 2754 Screen printing; rotary photogravure printing

(G-14500)
MCALPIN INDUSTRIES INC (PA)
255 Hollenbeck St (14621-3294)
PHONE..................................585 266-3060
Kenneth McAlpin, *CEO*
Mike McAlpin, *Exec VP*
Dave Krieger, *Plant Mgr*
Lisa Kendrick, *Opers Mgr*
Patti Closson, *Mfg Mgr*
▲ **EMP:** 150 **EST:** 1964
SQ FT: 140,000
SALES (est): 28MM **Privately Held**
WEB: www.mcalpin-ind.com
SIC: 3444 Sheet metalwork

Rochester - Monroe County (G-14501)   GEOGRAPHIC SECTION

(G-14501)
MCALPIN INDUSTRIES INC
Also Called: Monroe Plating Div
265 Hollenbeck St (14621-3294)
PHONE 585 544-5335
Fax: 585 266-8091
Gus Douglas, *QC Dir*
Gus Norwalk, *QC Dir*
Mike Mumm, *Branch Mgr*
EMP: 45
SQ FT: 8,000
SALES (corp-wide): 28MM **Privately Held**
WEB: www.mcalpin-ind.com
SIC: 3471 Plating & polishing
PA: Mcalpin Industries, Inc.
255 Hollenbeck St
Rochester NY 14621
585 266-3060

(G-14502)
MCM NATURAL STONE INC
860 Linden Ave Ste 1 (14625-2718)
PHONE 585 586-6510
EMP: 12 EST: 1998
SALES (est): 1.1MM **Privately Held**
SIC: 3281 5032 Natural Stone Granite Limestone Fabrication & Sales

(G-14503)
MELIORUM TECHNOLOGIES INC
620 Park Ave 145 (14607-2943)
PHONE 585 313-0616
Jason Rama, *President*
John Gibson, *Bd of Directors*
▼ EMP: 5
SALES (est): 487.3K **Privately Held**
SIC: 2821 2819 Silicone resins; aluminum oxide

(G-14504)
MERCURY PRINT PRODUCTIONS INC (PA)
2332 Innovation Way 4 (14624-6225)
PHONE 585 458-7900
Fax: 585 458-2896
Valerie D Mannix, *CEO*
John Place, *President*
Scott Fox, *Vice Pres*
Christian Schaumburger, *Vice Pres*
Paul Sawyer, *Warehouse Mgr*
▲ EMP: 200
SQ FT: 80,000
SALES (est): 65.1MM **Privately Held**
WEB: www.mercuryprint.com
SIC: 2752 7334 2791 2789 Commercial printing, offset; photocopying & duplicating services; typesetting; bookbinding & related work

(G-14505)
METROPOLITAN GRANITE & MBL INC
860 Maple St Ste 100 (14611-1612)
PHONE 585 342-7020
Fax: 585 342-7032
Helmettin Cakir, *President*
Melissa Zeaso, *Manager*
EMP: 5
SALES: 450K **Privately Held**
SIC: 2541 Counter & sink tops

(G-14506)
MICHAEL TODD STEVENS
Also Called: Rochester Screen Printing
95 Mount Read Blvd # 125 (14611-1923)
PHONE 585 436-9957
Michael Stevens, *Owner*
EMP: 5
SALES (est): 319.4K **Privately Held**
SIC: 3953 Screens, textile printing

(G-14507)
MICRO INSTRUMENT CORP
Also Called: Automated Systems Group
1199 Emerson St (14606-3038)
P.O. Box 60619 (14606-0619)
PHONE 585 458-3150
John Pfeffer, *Ch of Bd*
Anthony De Salvo, *President*
William Gunther, *President*
Steve Hakes, *Materials Mgr*
Michelle Blando, *Purchasing*
EMP: 100 EST: 1944
SQ FT: 56,000
SALES (est): 23.6MM **Privately Held**
WEB: www.microinst.com
SIC: 3599 3613 7389 6552 Machine & other job shop work; control panels, electric; grinding, precision: commercial or industrial; land subdividers & developers, commercial; special dies, tools, jigs & fixtures; aluminum foundries

(G-14508)
MICRO THREADED PRODUCTS INC
325 Mount Read Blvd Ste 4 (14611-1928)
PHONE 585 288-0080
Robert Osipovitch, *President*
EMP: 5
SALES (est): 500K **Privately Held**
SIC: 3451 Screw machine products

(G-14509)
MICROERA PRINTERS INC
304 Whitney St (14606-1110)
PHONE 585 783-1300
Bruno Coccia, *Ch of Bd*
Raphael Coccia, *Vice Pres*
EMP: 22
SQ FT: 20,000
SALES (est): 4.4MM **Privately Held**
WEB: www.microera.com
SIC: 2752 Commercial printing, lithographic

(G-14510)
MICROMOD AUTOMATION INC
3 Townline Cir Ste 4 (14623-2537)
PHONE 585 321-9200
Fax: 585 321-9291
Richard Keane, *President*
Carol McNelly, *Vice Pres*
Nancy Gilbride, *Treasurer*
Donna Marsocci, *Manager*
EMP: 20
SALES (est): 4.2MM **Privately Held**
WEB: www.micmod.com
SIC: 3625 Industrial controls: push button, selector switches, pilot

(G-14511)
MICROMOD AUTOMTN & CONTRLS INC
3 Townline Cir Ste 4 (14623-2537)
PHONE 585 321-9209
Wayne France, *General Mgr*
Nancy Gilbride, *CFO*
EMP: 13
SALES (est): 2.2MM **Privately Held**
SIC: 3823 Industrial process control instruments

(G-14512)
MICRON INDS ROCHESTER INC
31 Industrial Park Cir (14624-2403)
PHONE 585 247-6130
Fax: 585 247-0783
Stephen K Schmidt, *President*
Kirk Schmidt, *Vice Pres*
Eric Schmidt, *Admin Sec*
EMP: 9
SQ FT: 20,000
SALES (est): 1.3MM **Privately Held**
WEB: www.micronindustries.com
SIC: 3544 Special dies & tools; industrial molds

(G-14513)
MICROSOFT CORPORATION
100 Corporate Woods # 240 (14623-1423)
PHONE 585 240-6037
Michelle Datey, *Accounts Mgr*
Amjad Khan, *Sales Staff*
Keith Partington, *Branch Mgr*
Sandy Burke, *Manager*
Peter Harrington, *Manager*
EMP: 100
SALES (corp-wide): 85.3B **Publicly Held**
WEB: www.microsoft.com
SIC: 7372 Prepackaged software
PA: Microsoft Corporation
1 Microsoft Way
Redmond WA 98052
425 882-8080

(G-14514)
MILLER METAL FABRICATING INC
315 Commerce Dr (14623-3507)
PHONE 585 359-3400
Steven Mertz, *President*
EMP: 9
SQ FT: 10,500
SALES (est): 960K **Privately Held**
SIC: 3443 3441 3545 7692 Weldments; fabricated structural metal for bridges; precision tools, machinists'; welding repair; sandblasting of building exteriors

(G-14515)
MINORITY REPORTER INC (PA)
19 Borrowdale Dr (14626-1751)
P.O. Box 26352 (14626-0352)
PHONE 585 225-3628
Dave McCleary, *Principal*
EMP: 6
SALES (est): 469.6K **Privately Held**
SIC: 2711 Newspapers, publishing & printing

(G-14516)
MITCHELL MACHINE TOOL LLC
190 Murray St (14606-1126)
PHONE 585 254-7520
Michael Mitchell,
Maryland Mitchell,
EMP: 5
SALES (est): 330K **Privately Held**
WEB: www.mitchellmachinetool.com
SIC: 3599 Machine & other job shop work

(G-14517)
MKS INSTRUMENTS INC
100 Highpower Rd (14623-3498)
PHONE 585 292-7472
Paul Eyerman, *General Mgr*
Bill Schumacher, *Opers Mgr*
Teri Mueller, *Prdtn Mgr*
Mary Hoopes, *Senior Buyer*
Karen Savastano, *Senior Buyer*
EMP: 20
SALES (corp-wide): 813.5MM **Publicly Held**
WEB: www.mksinst.com
SIC: 3823 Industrial instrmnts msrmnt display/control process variable
PA: Mks Instruments, Inc.
2 Tech Dr Ste 201
Andover MA 01810
978 645-5500

(G-14518)
MKS MEDICAL ELECTRONICS
Also Called: M K S
100 Highpower Rd (14623-3498)
PHONE 585 292-7400
Paul M Eyerman, *General Mgr*
Yogendra Chawla, *Engng Exec*
Kemble Morrison, *Controller*
Jonna Gearry, *Office Mgr*
Don Fowler, *Director*
EMP: 112 EST: 1970
SQ FT: 20,000
SALES (est): 8.5MM
SALES (corp-wide): 813.5MM **Publicly Held**
WEB: www.mksinst.com
SIC: 3621 3663 Generating apparatus & parts, electrical; amplifiers, RF power & IF
PA: Mks Instruments, Inc.
2 Tech Dr Ste 201
Andover MA 01810
978 645-5500

(G-14519)
MOLECULAR GLASSES INC
1667 Lake Ave Ste 278b (14615-3047)
PHONE 585 210-2861
Michel Molaire, *CEO*
Mark Juba, *COO*
EMP: 5 EST: 2015
SQ FT: 1,000
SALES (est): 210.1K **Privately Held**
SIC: 2869 High purity grade chemicals, organic

(G-14520)
MONROE COUNTY AUTO SVCS INC (PA)
Also Called: Ziebart
1505 Lyell Ave (14606-2109)
PHONE 585 764-3741
Fax: 585 458-0614
Anthony Mattiacio, *President*
EMP: 30
SALES: 7MM **Privately Held**
SIC: 3479 5012 Coating, rust preventive; automotive brokers

(G-14521)
MOONEY-KEEHLEY INC
38 Saginaw Dr (14623-3132)
PHONE 585 271-1573
Fax: 585 271-1579
David Hedges, *President*
Kenneth Hempson, *Owner*
Elihu Hedges Jr, *Vice Pres*
Judith Gessner, *Treasurer*
Elizabeth Hedges, *Admin Sec*
EMP: 6 EST: 1944
SQ FT: 12,000
SALES (est): 910.3K **Privately Held**
WEB: www.mooneykeehley.com
SIC: 2752 7389 Cards, lithographed; engraving service
PA: 22 Winston, Inc.
22 Winston Pl
Rochester NY 14607
585 271-1573

(G-14522)
MORGOOD TOOLS INC
940 Millstead Way (14624-5108)
P.O. Box 24997 (14624-0997)
PHONE 585 436-8828
Fax: 585 436-2426
Virginia L Marshall, *CEO*
Doug Meier, *President*
James Faas, *Engineer*
Diane Soper, *CFO*
Janet Garrison, *Bookkeeper*
EMP: 60 EST: 1945
SQ FT: 30,000
SALES (est): 9MM **Privately Held**
WEB: www.morgood.com
SIC: 3545 Cutting tools for machine tools; cams (machine tool accessories)

(G-14523)
MORRIS MACHINING SERVICE INC
95 Mount Read Blvd (14611-1923)
PHONE 585 527-8100
James Morris, *President*
EMP: 5
SQ FT: 4,000
SALES (est): 220K **Privately Held**
SIC: 3599 Machine shop, jobbing & repair

(G-14524)
MUESLI FUSION INC
Also Called: Evoke Healthy Foods
875 Atlantic Ave Ste C (14609-7583)
P.O. Box 93344 (14692-8344)
PHONE 716 984-0855
Ian Szalinski, *President*
EMP: 11
SALES (est): 1.6MM **Privately Held**
SIC: 2043 Granola & muesli, except bars & clusters

(G-14525)
MULTIPLE IMPRSSONS OF RCHESTER (PA)
Also Called: Minuteman Press
41 Chestnut St (14604-2303)
PHONE 585 546-1160
William Malone Sr, *President*
Jay Malone, *Corp Secy*
Brad Amedeo, *Prdtn Mgr*
EMP: 8
SQ FT: 3,600
SALES (est): 799.8K **Privately Held**
WEB: www.dtmmp.com
SIC: 2752 7334 2791 2789 Commercial printing, lithographic; photocopying & duplicating services; typesetting; bookbinding & related work

▲ = Import ▼ = Export
◆ = Import/Export

GEOGRAPHIC SECTION

(G-14526)
MWI INC (PA)
1269 Brighton Henrietta T (14623-2485)
PHONE..................................585 424-4200
David Mc Mahon, *Ch of Bd*
Kevin Mc Mahon, *President*
Brian Mc Mahon, *COO*
Ryan Mc Mahon, *Vice Pres*
Ryan McMahon, *Vice Pres*
▲ EMP: 100
SQ FT: 28,000
SALES (est): 23.2MM Privately Held
WEB: www.mwiedm.com
SIC: 3624 Carbon & graphite products

(G-14527)
NALGE NUNC INTERNATIONAL CORP (DH)
75 Panorama Creek Dr (14625-2303)
PHONE..................................585 586-8800
Fax: 585 264-3709
Michaeline Reed, *Principal*
Ken Bunn, *VP Opers*
Gregory Pankratz, *Engineer*
Robert Relyea, *Engineer*
David Sauter, *Engineer*
◆ EMP: 903
SQ FT: 275,000
SALES (est): 265.3MM
SALES (corp-wide): 16.9B Publicly Held
WEB: www.nuncbrand.com
SIC: 3089 3949 3821 3085 Plastic processing; plastic & fiberglass tanks; sporting & athletic goods; laboratory apparatus & furniture; plastics bottles; laminated plastics plate & sheet
HQ: Fisher Scientific International Llc
    81 Wyman St
    Waltham MA 02451
    781 622-1000

(G-14528)
NATIONWIDE CIRCUITS INC
1444 Emerson St (14606-3009)
PHONE..................................585 328-0791
Fax: 585 328-9152
Alan Austin, *President*
Judith Austin, *Vice Pres*
Tim Sauer, *Engineer*
Elaine Weber, *Financial Exec*
Brett Austin, *Human Res Mgr*
EMP: 28 EST: 1971
SQ FT: 20,000
SALES (est): 3.6MM Privately Held
WEB: www.nciproto.com
SIC: 3672 Wiring boards

(G-14529)
NATIONWIDE PRECISION PDTS CORP
Also Called: Hn Precision-Ny
200 Tech Park Dr (14623-2445)
PHONE..................................585 272-7100
Fax: 585 272-0171
Dan Nash, *CEO*
Dan Brooks, *Vice Pres*
Rick Menaldino, *Vice Pres*
Sharon Pierce, *Vice Pres*
James Rice, *Production*
▲ EMP: 425 EST: 1999
SQ FT: 160,000
SALES (est): 136.2MM Privately Held
WEB: www.nationwideprecision.com
SIC: 3356 Nonferrous rolling & drawing

(G-14530)
NAVITAR INC (PA)
200 Commerce Dr (14623-3589)
PHONE..................................585 359-4000
Julian Goldstein, *Ch of Bd*
Robert Prato, *General Mgr*
Donna Backus, *COO*
Thomas McCune, *COO*
Jeremy Goldstein, *Vice Pres*
EMP: 58
SQ FT: 19,000
SALES (est): 9.5MM Privately Held
WEB: www.navitar.com
SIC: 3699 3651 3827 3674 Laser systems & equipment; household audio & video equipment; optical instruments & lenses; semiconductors & related devices; radio & TV communications equipment; pressed & blown glass

(G-14531)
NBN TECHNOLOGIES LLC
136 Wilshire Rd (14618-1221)
PHONE..................................585 355-5556
Shimon Miamon PHD,
Joseph Wodenscheck,
EMP: 6
SALES (est): 698.4K Privately Held
SIC: 3699 Electrical equipment & supplies

(G-14532)
NEW YORK MANUFACTURED PRODUCTS
6 Cairn St (14611-2416)
PHONE..................................585 254-9353
Salvatore Anselmo, *Partner*
Boubane Aselmo, *Partner*
EMP: 10
SALES (est): 2MM Privately Held
SIC: 3441 3499 3089 Fabricated structural metal; metal household articles; injection molding of plastics

(G-14533)
NEW YORK MANUFACTURING CORP
6 Cairn St (14611-2416)
PHONE..................................585 254-9353
Salvatore Anselmo,
Bouabane Anselmo,
EMP: 6
SQ FT: 20,000
SALES (est): 1.1MM Privately Held
WEB: www.newyorkmanufacturing.com
SIC: 7692 Welding repair

(G-14534)
NEW YORK MARKING DEVICES CORP
C H Morse Stamp Co
700 Clinton Ave S Ste 2 (14620-1383)
PHONE..................................585 454-5188
Fax: 585 454-5446
Peter J Stummer, *Branch Mgr*
EMP: 6
SALES (corp-wide): 2.5MM Privately Held
WEB: www.nymarking.com
SIC: 3953 Marking devices
PA: New York Marking Devices Corp
    2207 Teall Ave
    Syracuse NY 13206
    315 463-8641

(G-14535)
NEWPORT CORPORATION
705 Saint Paul St (14605-1730)
PHONE..................................585 248-4246
Kim Messerschmidt, *Project Mgr*
Linda Nittolo, *Purchasing*
Jeff Olson, *Engineer*
Ann M Brennan, *Human Resources*
Christophe Palmer, *Manager*
EMP: 15
SALES (corp-wide): 813.5MM Publicly Held
WEB: www.newport.com
SIC: 3821 Laboratory apparatus & furniture
HQ: Newport Corporation
    1791 Deere Ave
    Irvine CA 92606
    949 863-3144

(G-14536)
NEWPORT ROCHESTER INC
705 Saint Paul St (14605-1730)
PHONE..................................585 262-1325
Chris Palmer, *General Mgr*
Paula Gullo, *Manager*
▲ EMP: 60
SALES: 19.3MM
SALES (corp-wide): 813.5MM Publicly Held
WEB: www.newport.com
SIC: 3827 Gratings, diffraction
HQ: Newport Corporation
    1791 Deere Ave
    Irvine CA 92606
    949 863-3144

(G-14537)
NICOFORM INC
72 Cascade Dr (14614-1143)
PHONE..................................585 454-5530
Fax: 585 454-5167
Berl Stein, *President*
Richard Kraynik, *Vice Pres*
John Contino, *Engineer*
Joe Jachlewski, *Engineer*
Diane Cotton, *Sales Executive*
▼ EMP: 17
SQ FT: 12,000
SALES (est): 2.2MM Privately Held
WEB: www.nicoform.com
SIC: 3544 3599 Industrial molds; bellows, industrial: metal

(G-14538)
NORDON INC (PA)
691 Exchange St (14608-2714)
PHONE..................................585 546-6200
Fax: 585 546-7748
Terry J Donovan, *CEO*
Gary Ebert, *Engineer*
Richard Sullivan, *Sales Engr*
Sara Bruzda, *Manager*
Theresa Dickerson, *CIO*
◆ EMP: 100
SQ FT: 64,000
SALES (est): 29MM Privately Held
WEB: www.nordon.org
SIC: 3089 3544 Injection molding of plastics; industrial molds

(G-14539)
NORTH AMERICAN BREWERIES INC (DH)
Also Called: Northamerican Breweries
445 Saint Paul St (14605-1726)
PHONE..................................585 546-1030
Kris Sirchio, *CEO*
Richard Lozyniak, *Ch of Bd*
Raquel Vargas, *President*
Larry Cornish, *District Mgr*
Brock Elmore, *District Mgr*
▼ EMP: 10
SALES (est): 310.6MM Privately Held
SIC: 2082 Beer (alcoholic beverage)
HQ: Florida Bebidas Sa
    Rio Segundo De Alajuela
    Alajuela
    243 767-00

(G-14540)
NORTH AMERICAN MINT INC
1600 Lexington Ave 240a (14606-3062)
PHONE..................................585 654-8500
William La Mere Jr, *President*
Brad La Mere, *Principal*
Michael La Mere, *Principal*
EMP: 6
SQ FT: 1,200
SALES (est): 727.6K Privately Held
SIC: 3911 Medals, precious or semi-precious metal

(G-14541)
NORTH AMERICAN STONE INC
1358 E Ridge Rd (14621-2005)
PHONE..................................585 266-4020
Fax: 585 266-4042
Dave Julian, *President*
EMP: 7
SALES (est): 945.8K Privately Held
SIC: 3281 Cut stone & stone products

(G-14542)
NORTH AMRCN BRWRIES HLDNGS LLC (PA)
445 Saint Paul St (14605-1726)
PHONE..................................585 546-1030
Rich Lozyniak, *CEO*
Katie Blahowicz, *Controller*
EMP: 29
SALES (est): 73.1MM Privately Held
SIC: 2082 Beer (alcoholic beverage)

(G-14543)
NORTHERN AIR SYSTEMS INC (PA)
3605 Buffalo Rd (14624-1120)
PHONE..................................585 594-5050
Fax: 585 594-8888
Timothy Confer, *President*
Garland Beasley, *Vice Pres*
Joseph Denninger, *Vice Pres*
Gerald Christie, *Project Mgr*
Kirk Hoak, *Mfg Staff*
EMP: 46
SQ FT: 45,000
SALES (est): 12.6MM Privately Held
SIC: 3585 Heating & air conditioning combination units

(G-14544)
NORTHERN AIR TECHNOLOGY INC (PA)
3605 Buffalo Rd (14624-1120)
PHONE..................................585 594-5050
Timothy J Confer, *President*
Joseph Denninger, *Vice Pres*
EMP: 1 EST: 2000
SQ FT: 1,000
SALES (est): 1.1MM Privately Held
SIC: 3648 Outdoor lighting equipment

(G-14545)
NORTHERN KING LURES INC (PA)
167 Armstrong Rd (14616-2703)
P.O. Box 12482 (14612-0482)
PHONE..................................585 865-3373
Fax: 585 865-7176
Patsy Distaffen, *President*
Etta Distaffen, *Treasurer*
Beverly Cahill, *Bookkeeper*
EMP: 5
SALES (est): 733K Privately Held
WEB: www.northernkinglures.com
SIC: 3949 Lures, fishing: artificial

(G-14546)
NU WAYS INC
655 Pullman Ave (14615-3334)
PHONE..................................585 254-7510
Edward A Coleman, *President*
Richard Albert, *Treasurer*
Michael Bater, *Finance*
EMP: 6 EST: 1996
SALES: 1.2MM Privately Held
SIC: 2591 Window blinds

(G-14547)
OLEDWORKS LLC (PA)
1645 Lyell Ave Ste 140 (14606-2331)
PHONE..................................585 287-6802
David Dejoy, *CEO*
Joh Hamer, *COO*
Michael Boroson, *CTO*
Giana Phelan,
EMP: 28
SALES (est): 5.4MM Privately Held
SIC: 3641 3646 3999 3674 Electric lamps; commercial indusl & institutional electric lighting fixtures; barber & beauty shop equipment; light emitting diodes

(G-14548)
OMG DESSERTS INC
1227 Ridgeway Ave Ste J (14615-3759)
PHONE..................................585 698-1561
Mary Graham, *President*
EMP: 10
SALES (est): 900K Privately Held
SIC: 2099 Desserts, ready-to-mix

(G-14549)
OMNI-ID USA INC
1200 Ridgeway Ave Ste 106 (14615-3758)
PHONE..................................585 697-9913
George E Daddis Jr, *President*
Tony Kington, *COO*
Ed Nabrotzky, *Exec VP*
Andre Cote, *Senior VP*
Tracy Gay, *Vice Pres*
EMP: 37
SALES (est): 5.6MM Privately Held
WEB: www.omni-id.com
SIC: 3825 Radio frequency measuring equipment

(G-14550)
ONTARIO PLASTICS INC (PA)
Also Called: O P I
2503 Dewey Ave (14616-4728)
PHONE..................................585 663-2644
Fax: 585 865-7774
Gerard Reynolds, *President*
Jim Beifus, *Principal*
Ralph E Barnes, *Vice Pres*
Kevin P Hayes, *Vice Pres*
Dorraine Coughlin, *Asst Controller*
▲ EMP: 34 EST: 1945
SQ FT: 40,000

Rochester - Monroe County (G-14551) — GEOGRAPHIC SECTION

SALES (est): 5.8MM **Privately Held**
WEB: www.ontario-plastics.com
SIC: 3082 3089 Unsupported plastics profile shapes; plastic containers, except foam; boxes, plastic

(G-14551)
ORACLE CORPORATION
400 Linden Oaks Ste 310 (14625-2818)
PHONE 585 383-1998
Scott Strong, *Sales Executive*
Diane Maccowan, *Admin Asst*
Barbara Higgins, *Assistant*
EMP: 302
SALES (corp-wide): 37B **Publicly Held**
SIC: 7372 Business oriented computer software
PA: Oracle Corporation
500 Oracle Pkwy
Redwood City CA 94065
650 506-7000

(G-14552)
ORMEC SYSTEMS CORP (PA)
19 Linden Park (14625-2776)
PHONE 585 385-3520
Fax: 585 385-6833
Edward J Krasnicki, *CEO*
David Goodwin, *Research*
Jesse Barr, *Engineer*
Robert McMillen, *Engineer*
John Greve, *Controller*
EMP: 35
SQ FT: 15,600
SALES (est): 6MM **Privately Held**
WEB: www.ormec.com
SIC: 3823 3672 Controllers for process variables, all types; printed circuit boards

(G-14553)
OROLIA USA INC
Also Called: Spectracom
1565 Jefferson Rd Ste 460 (14623-3190)
PHONE 585 321-5800
Elizabeth Withers, *President*
John Fischer, *Vice Pres*
Josh Harris, *Sls & Mktg Exec*
Philip Teece, *Sls & Mktg Exec*
Keith Wing, *Manager*
EMP: 55 EST: 1972
SQ FT: 26,000
SALES (est): 20.7MM
SALES (corp-wide): 2MM **Privately Held**
WEB: www.spectracomcorp.com
SIC: 3829 Measuring & controlling devices
PA: Orolia
Batiment Drakkar 2
Valbonne 06560
492 907-040

(G-14554)
ORTHO-CLINICAL DIAGNOSTICS INC
Also Called: Ortho/Rochester Tech
2402 Innovation Way # 3 (14624-6226)
PHONE 585 453-5200
EMP: 14
SALES (corp-wide): 1B **Privately Held**
SIC: 3841 Diagnostic apparatus, medical
PA: Ortho-Clinical Diagnostics, Inc.
1001 Us Highway 202
Raritan NJ 08869
908 218-8000

(G-14555)
ORTHO-CLINICAL DIAGNOSTICS INC
100 Latona Rd Bldg 313 (14626)
PHONE 585 453-4771
EMP: 400
SALES (corp-wide): 1B **Privately Held**
SIC: 3841 Diagnostic apparatus, medical
PA: Ortho-Clinical Diagnostics, Inc.
1001 Us Highway 202
Raritan NJ 08869
908 218-8000

(G-14556)
ORTHO-CLINICAL DIAGNOSTICS INC
1000 Lee Rd (14626)
PHONE 585 453-3000
EMP: 33

SALES (corp-wide): 1B **Privately Held**
WEB: www.orthoclinical.com
SIC: 2835 Blood derivative diagnostic agents
PA: Ortho-Clinical Diagnostics, Inc.
1001 Us Highway 202
Raritan NJ 08869
908 218-8000

(G-14557)
ORTHOGONAL
1999 Lake Ave (14650-0001)
PHONE 585 254-2775
John Defranco, *CEO*
Fox Holt, *Principal*
Victor Hsia, *Vice Pres*
EMP: 5
SALES (est): 390K **Privately Held**
SIC: 3679 Liquid crystal displays (LCD)

(G-14558)
ORTHOTICS & PROSTHETICS DEPT
Also Called: Strong Hospital
4901 Lac De Ville Blvd (14618-5647)
PHONE 585 341-9299
Rob Brown, *Manager*
EMP: 15
SALES (est): 1MM **Privately Held**
SIC: 3842 Orthopedic appliances

(G-14559)
OTEX PROTECTIVE INC
2180 Brighton Henrietta (14623-2704)
PHONE 585 232-7160
Jacob Weidert, *CEO*
EMP: 6
SALES (est): 610.6K **Privately Held**
SIC: 2311 Men's & boys' uniforms

(G-14560)
OZIPKO ENTERPRISES INC
Also Called: Printing Plus
125 White Spruce Blvd # 5 (14623-1607)
PHONE 585 424-6740
Rita Ozipko, *President*
Carl Ozipko, *Vice Pres*
Jim Ozipko, *Admin Sec*
EMP: 8
SQ FT: 3,000
SALES: 890K **Privately Held**
SIC: 2752 2791 2789 Commercial printing, offset; typesetting; bookbinding & related work

(G-14561)
P & H MACHINE SHOP INC
40 Industrial Park Cir (14624-2404)
PHONE 585 247-5500
Fax: 585 247-5572
EMP: 5
SQ FT: 3,000
SALES (est): 360K **Privately Held**
SIC: 3544 Mfg Dies/Tools/Jigs/Fixtures

(G-14562)
P & R INDUSTRIES INC (PA)
1524 N Clinton Ave (14621-2206)
PHONE 585 266-6725
Fax: 585 266-0075
Lawrence F Coyle, *President*
Charles Sheelar, *Vice Pres*
Donna Stein, *Purch Agent*
Bob Brawn, *Engineer*
Brian Stein, *Sls & Mktg Exec*
EMP: 32
SQ FT: 22,000
SALES: 16.7MM **Privately Held**
SIC: 3544 3541 Special dies, tools, jigs & fixtures; machine tools, metal cutting type

(G-14563)
P & R INDUSTRIES INC
1524 N Clinton Ave (14621-2206)
PHONE 585 544-1811
Nick Natali, *Branch Mgr*
EMP: 10
SALES (corp-wide): 16.7MM **Privately Held**
SIC: 3544 Special dies & tools
PA: P & R Industries, Inc.
1524 N Clinton Ave
Rochester NY 14621
585 266-6725

(G-14564)
P K G EQUIPMENT INCORPORATED
367 Paul Rd (14624-4925)
PHONE 585 436-4650
Fax: 585 436-3751
Stephen Pontarelli, *CEO*
Stephen T Pontarelli, *Ch of Bd*
Tambe Hartman, *Project Mgr*
Timothy Brunke, *Engineer*
Maria Parker, *Treasurer*
EMP: 30
SQ FT: 35,000
SALES (est): 9.1MM **Privately Held**
WEB: www.pkgequipment.com
SIC: 3559 3441 Metal finishing equipment for plating, etc.; fabricated structural metal

(G-14565)
P3 TECHNOLOGIES
383 Buell Rd (14624-3123)
PHONE 585 730-7340
Mark Shaw, *President*
EMP: 6 EST: 2012
SQ FT: 10,000
SALES (est): 622.1K **Privately Held**
SIC: 3471 Anodizing (plating) of metals or formed products

(G-14566)
PACTECH PACKAGING LLC
2605 Manitou Rd (14624-1109)
PHONE 585 458-8008
Fax: 585 647-9116
John Ferber, *Vice Pres*
Chad Buchta, *Mng Member*
Pat Morris, *Administration*
▲ **EMP:** 65
SALES (est): 24.3MM **Privately Held**
WEB: www.pactechpackaging.com
SIC: 2671 Packaging paper & plastics film, coated & laminated
PA: Barrier Packaging, Inc.
2605 Manitou Rd 200
Rochester NY

(G-14567)
PALEY STUDIOS LTD
1677 Lyell Ave A (14606-2311)
PHONE 585 232-5260
Fax: 585 232-5507
Albert Paley, *President*
Frances Welley-Paley, *Treasurer*
▲ **EMP:** 16 EST: 1967
SQ FT: 18,000
SALES: 1.4MM **Privately Held**
WEB: www.albertpaley.com
SIC: 3446 8412 Architectural metalwork; ornamental metalwork; museums & art galleries

(G-14568)
PALLET DIVISION INC
40 Silver St (14611-2208)
PHONE 585 328-3780
Fax: 585 227-2766
Bernie Mangold, *President*
EMP: 7
SALES (est): 922.9K **Privately Held**
SIC: 2448 Pallets, wood & metal combination

(G-14569)
PALLET SERVICES INC
1681 Lyell Ave (14606-2311)
PHONE 585 647-4020
Fax: 585 647-1756
Donald Matre, *Branch Mgr*
EMP: 40
SALES (corp-wide): 9.2MM **Privately Held**
SIC: 2448 Wood pallets & skids
PA: Pallet Services, Inc.
4055 Casillio Pkwy
Clarence NY 14031
716 873-7700

(G-14570)
PANE VITA LLC
Also Called: Panevita Foods
10 White St (14608-1444)
P.O. Box 585, Victor (14564-0585)
PHONE 888 509-3310
John Scanlon, *CFO*
EMP: 15

SALES (est): 2.8MM **Privately Held**
SIC: 2099 Food preparations

(G-14571)
PANTHER GRAPHICS INC (PA)
465 Central Ave (14605-3012)
PHONE 585 546-7163
Fax: 585 325-3943
Daryll A Jackson Sr, *President*
Josh Cummings, *General Mgr*
Carolyn Stewart, *Accountant*
Henry Ehindero, *Sales Staff*
Rachael Hudson-Rodvik, *Office Mgr*
▲ **EMP:** 46
SQ FT: 12,000
SALES (est): 48.7MM **Privately Held**
WEB: www.panthergraphics.net
SIC: 2752 Commercial printing, offset

(G-14572)
PARAGON STEEL RULE DIES INC
979 Mount Read Blvd (14606-2829)
PHONE 585 254-3395
Fax: 585 254-8839
Michael McDeid, *President*
Teresa McDeid, *Manager*
EMP: 13
SQ FT: 13,000
SALES (est): 1.9MM **Privately Held**
WEB: www.paragonsrd.com
SIC: 3544 Dies, steel rule

(G-14573)
PARK ENTERPRISES ROCHESTER INC
226 Jay St (14608-1623)
PHONE 585 546-4200
Fax: 585 546-7088
Sook Cha Park, *President*
Rob Brunskill, *Principal*
Hyo Sang Park, *Principal*
Tom Sydeski, *Principal*
▲ **EMP:** 200
SQ FT: 60,000
SALES (est): 40.3MM **Privately Held**
WEB: www.parkent.com
SIC: 3545 Precision tools, machinists'

(G-14574)
PEKO PRECISION PRODUCTS INC
70 Holworthy St (14606-1313)
PHONE 585 301-1386
Scott H Baube, *Project Mgr*
Donald Delaney, *Project Mgr*
Timothy Knox, *Project Mgr*
Sonny Sok, *Manager*
Louis E Emerson, *Manager*
EMP: 12
SALES (corp-wide): 42.2MM **Privately Held**
WEB: www.pekoprecision.com
SIC: 3599 Crankshafts & camshafts, machining
PA: Peko Precision Products, Inc.
1400 Emerson St
Rochester NY 14606
585 647-3010

(G-14575)
PENNANT INGREDIENTS INC
64 Chester St (14611-2110)
PHONE 585 235-8160
Simon Teel, *President*
Karel Zimmermann, *President*
EMP: 90 EST: 2015
SALES (est): 2.8MM **Privately Held**
SIC: 2099 Food preparations
HQ: Puratos Corporation
1941 Old Cuthbert Rd
Cherry Hill NJ 08034

(G-14576)
PERFORMANCE TECHNOLOGIES INC (HQ)
3500 Winton Pl Ste 4 (14623-2860)
PHONE 585 256-0200
Fax: 585 256-0791
John M Slusser, *Ch of Bd*
John J Peters, *Senior VP*
J Patrick Rice, *Senior VP*
Dorrance W Lamb, *CFO*
Bob Appolito, *Sales Staff*
EMP: 53

SQ FT: 32,000
SALES (est): 23.3MM
SALES (corp-wide): 249MM **Publicly Held**
WEB: www.pt.com
SIC: 3672 3661 3577 7373 Printed circuit boards; telephone & telegraph apparatus; computer peripheral equipment; computer integrated systems design
PA: Sonus Networks, Inc.
4 Technology Park Dr
Westford MA 01886
978 614-8100

(G-14577)
PERI-FACTS ACADEMY
601 Elmwood Ave (14642-0001)
PHONE.................................585 275-6037
Dr James Woods, *Senior Editor*
EMP: 5
SALES (est): 257.5K **Privately Held**
SIC: 2731 Textbooks: publishing & printing

(G-14578)
PFAUDLER INC (HQ)
Also Called: Glassteel Parts and Services
1000 West Ave (14611-2442)
P.O. Box 23600 (14692-3600)
PHONE.................................585 464-5663
Fax: 585 423-9644
Micheal F Powers, *Principal*
Philip McGrath, *Engineer*
Lewis Fabricius, *Manager*
Bud Gruver, *Manager*
Keith Quintana, *Manager*
◆ EMP: 300
SQ FT: 500,000
SALES (est): 117MM
SALES (corp-wide): 14.7B **Publicly Held**
SIC: 3559 Refinery, chemical processing & similar machinery; pharmaceutical machinery
PA: National Oilwell Varco, Inc.
7909 Parkwood Circle Dr
Houston TX 77036
713 346-7500

(G-14579)
PFAUDLER US INC
1000 West Ave (14611-2442)
PHONE.................................585 235-1000
Bob Waddell, *Vice Pres*
Pat Coleman, *Vice Pres*
Donald Cornwell, *Vice Pres*
Russ Bennett, *Plant Mgr*
▲ EMP: 200 EST: 1883
SALES (est): 18.5K **Privately Held**
SIC: 3443 Fabricated plate work (boiler shop)

(G-14580)
PGM OF NEW ENGLAND LLC
1305 Emerson St (14606-3006)
PHONE.................................585 458-4300
Mike Hockenberger, *Mng Member*
Douglas Cauwels,
William Hockenberger,
EMP: 58
SQ FT: 62,500
SALES (est): 6MM
SALES (corp-wide): 19.3MM **Privately Held**
WEB: www.pgmcorp.com
SIC: 3599 Machine & other job shop work
PA: Precision Grinding And Manufacturing Corporation
1305 Emerson St
Rochester NY 14606
585 458-4300

(G-14581)
PHARMA-SMART INTERNATIONAL INC
Also Called: Pharmasmart
773 Elmgrove Rd Bldg 2 (14624-6200)
PHONE.................................585 427-0730
Fax: 585 427-8165
Frederick W Sarkis II, *CEO*
Drew Knopfel, *President*
Ashton S Maaraba, *COO*
Lisa M Goodwin, *Exec VP*
Ashton Maaraba, *Senior VP*
▼ EMP: 39 EST: 2004
SQ FT: 52,000

SALES (est): 7MM **Privately Held**
SIC: 3841 5047 8099 Diagnostic apparatus, medical; diagnostic equipment, medical; health screening service

(G-14582)
PHOENIX GRAPHICS INC
464 State St 470 (14608-1739)
PHONE.................................585 232-4040
Fax: 585 232-5642
Sal De Biase III, *President*
Mark Stavalone, *Vice Pres*
Kim Randall, *Human Resources*
Keith Boas, *Manager*
Roxanne Grace, *Manager*
EMP: 20
SALES (est): 5.9MM **Privately Held**
WEB: www.phoenix-graphics.com
SIC: 2752 Commercial printing, lithographic

(G-14583)
PHOTONAMICS INC
Also Called: Elmgrove Technologies Div
558 Elmgrove Rd (14606-3348)
PHONE.................................585 426-3774
Fax: 585 426-3754
Hank Carbucci, *CEO*
Henry Carducci, *CEO*
Terry B Cooley, *President*
Kay Carducci, *Manager*
EMP: 10 EST: 1971
SQ FT: 4,000
SALES (est): 1.9MM **Privately Held**
WEB: www.elmgrovetechnologies.com
SIC: 3679 Electronic circuits

(G-14584)
PIERCE INDUSTRIES LLC
465 Paul Rd (14624-4779)
PHONE.................................585 458-0888
Dick Webb, *CEO*
Rick Schopinsky, *President*
Pat Sennett, *Opers Staff*
Elaine Deacon, *Engineer*
Craig Neubauer, *Engineer*
▲ EMP: 40
SQ FT: 60,000
SALES (est): 15.6MM **Privately Held**
WEB: www.pierceindustries.com
SIC: 3441 Fabricated structural metal

(G-14585)
PIERREPONT VISUAL GRAPHICS
15 Elser Ter (14611-1607)
PHONE.................................585 305-9672
Fax: 585 328-8376
Scott Zappia, *President*
Terence Zappia, *Vice Pres*
EMP: 2 EST: 1958
SQ FT: 15,000
SALES (est): 1MM **Privately Held**
WEB: www.pierrepont.com
SIC: 2759 Screen printing

(G-14586)
PMI INDUSTRIES LLC
350 Buell Rd (14624-3124)
PHONE.................................585 464-8050
Fax: 585 328-6509
V Sheldon Alfiero, *President*
Roger Reiner, *General Mgr*
◆ EMP: 30
SQ FT: 48,500
SALES (est): 9.1MM
SALES (corp-wide): 43.6MM **Privately Held**
WEB: www.pro-moldinc.com
SIC: 3544 3089 Industrial molds; injection molded finished plastic products
PA: Bam Enterprises, Inc.
2243 Corning Rd
Grand Island NY 14072
716 773-7634

(G-14587)
POLYMAG TEK INC
215 Tremont St Ste 2 (14608-2371)
PHONE.................................585 235-8390
Gary Larsen, *President*
Brian Giardino, *Engineer*
Ronald W Sweet, *Treasurer*
Jennifer Sweet, *Manager*
Pete Byam, *Executive*
EMP: 12

SALES (est): 2.4MM **Privately Held**
WEB: www.polymagtek.com
SIC: 3547 7389 Rolling mill machinery; design services

(G-14588)
POLYMER ENGINEERED PDTS INC
23 Moonlanding Rd (14624-2505)
PHONE.................................585 426-1811
Fax: 585 426-1444
George Peroutka, *President*
Sharon Niederschmiet, *Accounting Mgr*
Dan Dicicco, *Manager*
Mark Bestram, *Supervisor*
Mike Bruno, *Analyst*
EMP: 100
SQ FT: 55,000
SALES (corp-wide): 13.9MM **Privately Held**
SIC: 3089 Injection molding of plastics
PA: Polymer Engineered Products, Inc.
595 Summer St Ste 2
Stamford CT 06901
203 324-3737

(G-14589)
POSEIDON SYSTEMS LLC
200 Canal View Blvd # 300 (14623-2851)
PHONE.................................585 239-6025
Ryan Brewer, *President*
Nikhil Beke, *Engineer*
Robert Livolsi, *Engineer*
Theodore Meyer, *Project Engr*
Lemen Robert, *CFO*
EMP: 11
SQ FT: 6,000
SALES (est): 2.2MM **Privately Held**
SIC: 3829 3823 Measuring & controlling devices; industrial instrmnts msrmnt display/control process variable; flow instruments, industrial process type; data loggers, industrial process type

(G-14590)
PPG ARCHITECTURAL FINISHES INC
Also Called: Glidden Professional Paint Ctr
566 Clinton Ave S (14620-1135)
PHONE.................................585 271-1363
Fax: 716 271-2449
Rochard Puzzolo, *Branch Mgr*
EMP: 5
SALES (corp-wide): 15.3B **Publicly Held**
WEB: www.gliddenpaint.com
SIC: 2891 Adhesives
HQ: Ppg Architectural Finishes, Inc.
1 Ppg Pl
Pittsburgh PA 15272
412 434-3131

(G-14591)
PRECISE TOOL & MFG INC
9 Coldwater Cres (14624-2512)
PHONE.................................585 247-0700
Fax: 585 247-0746
John S Gizzi, *President*
John P Gizzi, *President*
Rose A Poirier, *Corp Secy*
Gary Mastro, *Vice Pres*
Dale Sloan, *Controller*
▲ EMP: 100
SQ FT: 150,000
SALES (est): 23MM **Privately Held**
WEB: www.precisetool.com
SIC: 3541 Numerically controlled metal cutting machine tools; milling machines; boring mills

(G-14592)
PRECISION DESIGN SYSTEMS INC
1645 Lyell Ave Ste 136 (14606-2386)
PHONE.................................585 426-4500
William J West, *President*
Jeff Sutton, *Vice Pres*
EMP: 20
SQ FT: 18,000
SALES (est): 3.5MM **Privately Held**
SIC: 3829 3479 Measuring & controlling devices; name plates: engraved, etched, etc.

(G-14593)
PRECISION GRINDING & MFG CORP (PA)
Also Called: P G M
1305 Emerson St (14606-3098)
PHONE.................................585 458-4300
Fax: 585 458-6465
Michael Hockenberger, *CEO*
William C Hockenberger, *Ch of Bd*
Nick Baldassaia, *General Mgr*
Nick Baldassara, *General Mgr*
Todd Hockenberger, *Vice Pres*
▲ EMP: 119
SQ FT: 62,000
SALES (est): 19.3MM **Privately Held**
WEB: www.pgmcorp.com
SIC: 3545 3544 Precision tools, machinists'; special dies & tools

(G-14594)
PRECISION LASER TECHNOLOGY LLC
1001 Lexington Ave Ste 4 (14606-2847)
PHONE.................................585 458-6208
Ron Natale Jr,
James Garcia,
EMP: 10
SQ FT: 7,000
SALES (est): 766.5K **Privately Held**
SIC: 3479 Etching & engraving

(G-14595)
PRECISION MACHINE TECH LLC
Also Called: Spex
85 Excel Dr (14621-3471)
PHONE.................................585 467-1840
Michael Nolan, *President*
William Martinez, *VP Sales*
Lisa Fess, *Manager*
EMP: 60
SQ FT: 16,000
SALES (est): 15.9MM **Privately Held**
WEB: www.spex1.com
SIC: 3451 Screw machine products

(G-14596)
PRECISION MAGNETICS LLC
770 Linden Ave (14625-2716)
PHONE.................................585 385-9010
Yhuang Wang, *Controller*
Andrew Albers,
Terence R Loughrey,
▲ EMP: 50
SQ FT: 12,000
SALES (est): 5.9MM **Privately Held**
WEB: www.precisionmagnetics.com
SIC: 3499 Magnets, permanent: metallic

(G-14597)
PREMIER METALS GROUP
11 Cairn St (14611-2415)
PHONE.................................585 436-4020
Fax: 585 436-4021
Marc Olgin, *CEO*
Mike Diamond, *Principal*
Steve Olgin, *Exec VP*
Ed Czemeryck, *CFO*
Sharna Larson, *Controller*
EMP: 32
SALES (est): 5.1MM
SALES (corp-wide): 2.4B **Privately Held**
SIC: 3469 Metal stampings
PA: Scholz Holding Gmbh
Berndt-Ulrich-Scholz-Str. 1
Essingen 73457
736 584-0

(G-14598)
PREMIER SIGN SYSTEMS LLC
10 Excel Dr (14621-3470)
PHONE.................................585 235-0390
Fax: 585 235-0392
Jeff Sherwood, *Owner*
James Peacock, *Principal*
Jamie Rawleigh, *Project Mgr*
Lori Herold, *Controller*
EMP: 27
SALES (est): 4.6MM **Privately Held**
SIC: 3993 Signs & advertising specialties

Rochester - Monroe County (G-14599)

(G-14599)
PRESSTEK PRINTING LLC
Also Called: Washburn Litho Envirgo Prtg
20 Balfour Dr (14621-3202)
P.O. Box 67211 (14617-7211)
PHONE 585 266-2770
Fax: 585 266-6065
Antony Disalvo, *President*
Dennis Collins, *Vice Pres*
Stephanie Weber, *Office Mgr*
EMP: 14
SQ FT: 6,600
SALES (est): 1.6MM **Privately Held**
SIC: 2759 2752 Commercial printing; commercial printing, lithographic

(G-14600)
PRINT ON DEMAND INITIATIVE INC
1240 Jefferson Rd (14623-3104)
PHONE 585 239-6044
Gaurav Govil, *President*
Tracy Burkovich, *Manager*
EMP: 19
SQ FT: 900
SALES: 239.1K **Privately Held**
SIC: 2752 Commercial printing, lithographic

(G-14601)
PRINTROC INC
620 South Ave (14620-1316)
PHONE 585 461-2556
Fax: 585 461-3673
Ronald Schutt, *President*
Daniel McCarthy, *Vice Pres*
Jesse McCarthy, *Director*
EMP: 12
SQ FT: 6,000
SALES (est): 1.2MM **Privately Held**
WEB: www.pinnacleprinters.com
SIC: 2752 Commercial printing, offset

(G-14602)
PRIVATE LBEL FODS RCHESTER INC
1686 Lyell Ave (14606-2312)
P.O. Box 60805 (14606-0805)
PHONE 585 254-9205
Fax: 585 254-0186
Bonnie Lavorato, *Ch of Bd*
Frank Lavorato III, *Vice Pres*
Russ Eliason, *CFO*
EMP: 30
SQ FT: 125,000
SALES (est): 11.4MM **Privately Held**
WEB: www.privatelabelfoods.com
SIC: 2033 Tomato products: packaged in cans, jars, etc.

(G-14603)
PRO-TECH WLDG FABRICATION INC
Also Called: Pro-Tech Sno Pusher
711 West Ave (14611-2412)
PHONE 585 436-9855
Fax: 585 436-5645
Michael P Weagley, *President*
EMP: 35
SQ FT: 30,000
SALES (est): 9.3MM **Privately Held**
SIC: 3531 7692 Snow plow attachments; welding repair

(G-14604)
PRO-VALUE DISTRIBUTION INC
1547 Lyell Ave Ste 3 (14606-2123)
PHONE 585 783-1461
Thomas W Mayberry, *President*
EMP: 6
SQ FT: 4,000
SALES (est): 839.3K **Privately Held**
SIC: 3714 Motor vehicle parts & accessories

(G-14605)
PRODUCT INTEGRATION & MFG INC
55 Fessenden St (14611-2815)
PHONE 585 436-6260
Tyrone Reaves, *Ch of Bd*
Tom Bare, *General Mgr*
Brenda Wilson, *Human Res Mgr*
Long Nguyen, *Manager*
Lorriane Reeve, *Manager*
EMP: 22
SQ FT: 25,000
SALES (est): 5MM **Privately Held**
SIC: 3444 Sheet metalwork; forming machine work, sheet metal

(G-14606)
PRODUCTION METAL CUTTING INC
1 Curlew St (14606-2535)
P.O. Box 60535 (14606-0535)
PHONE 585 458-7136
Fax: 585 458-1215
Leo T Glogowski, *President*
▲ EMP: 12
SQ FT: 34,000
SALES (est): 2.1MM
SALES (corp-wide): 2.5MM **Privately Held**
WEB: www.zedcomachinery.com
SIC: 3545 Machine tool accessories
PA: Zedco Machinery Inc
 1 Curlew St
 Rochester NY 14606
 585 458-6920

(G-14607)
PSB LTD
543 Atlantic Ave Ste 2 (14609-7396)
PHONE 585 654-7078
Robert Armitage, *President*
EMP: 13
SQ FT: 30,000
SALES: 2.5MM **Privately Held**
WEB: www.psb.net
SIC: 3471 Electroplating & plating

(G-14608)
PULLMAN MFG CORPORATION
77 Commerce Dr (14623-3501)
PHONE 585 334-1350
Fax: 585 359-4460
Chris Biegel, *CEO*
William A Palmer, *Shareholder*
▼ EMP: 6 EST: 1886
SQ FT: 36,000
SALES (est): 1.2MM **Privately Held**
WEB: www.pullmanmfg.com
SIC: 3495 Sash balances, spring

(G-14609)
PULSAFEEDER INC (HQ)
Also Called: Engineered Products Oper Epo
2883 Brighton Henrietta T (14623-2794)
PHONE 585 292-8000
Fax: 585 424-6268
Richard C Morgan, *Ch of Bd*
John Carter, *Ch of Bd*
Dieter Sauer, *President*
Joe Patarino, *Prdtn Mgr*
Cathy Haywood, *Controller*
▲ EMP: 122
SQ FT: 45,000
SALES (est): 23.3MM
SALES (corp-wide): 2B **Publicly Held**
WEB: www.pulsa.com
SIC: 3561 3825 3823 3822 Pumps & pumping equipment; measuring instruments & meters, electric; industrial instrmnts msrmnt display/control process variable; auto controls regulating residntl & coml environmt & applncs; relays & industrial controls; measuring & dispensing pumps
PA: Idex Corporation
 1925 W Field Ct Ste 200
 Lake Forest IL 60045
 847 498-7070

(G-14610)
QED TECHNOLOGIES INTL INC
Also Called: Q.E.d
1040 University Ave (14607-1282)
PHONE 585 256-6540
Fax: 585 256-3211
Andrew Kulawiec, *CEO*
Gary Devries, *General Mgr*
Ralph Scialo, *Facilities Mgr*
Chris Hoyng, *QC Mgr*
Mugdha Patwardhan, *Research*
◆ EMP: 45
SALES (est): 12.6MM
SALES (corp-wide): 414.1MM **Publicly Held**
WEB: www.qedmrf.com
SIC: 3577 Computer peripheral equipment
PA: Cabot Microelectronics Corporation
 870 N Commons Dr
 Aurora IL 60504
 630 375-6631

(G-14611)
QES SOLUTIONS INC (PA)
1547 Lyell Ave (14606-2123)
PHONE 585 254-8693
Thomas W Mayberry, *CEO*
Jerry Parker, *Materials Mgr*
Karen Knapp, *Accounts Mgr*
▲ EMP: 98
SQ FT: 15,000
SALES (est): 15.6MM **Privately Held**
SIC: 3559 Metal finishing equipment for plating, etc.

(G-14612)
QUALITY CONTRACT ASSEMBLIES
Also Called: Qca
100 Boxart St Ste 251 (14612-5656)
P.O. Box 12868 (14612-0868)
PHONE 585 663-9030
Fax: 585 663-1432
Richard Frank, *President*
Dawn Moore, *Purch Mgr*
Lynn Gongwer, *Bookkeeper*
John Newton, *Lab Dir*
▲ EMP: 12
SQ FT: 5,500
SALES (est): 1.9MM **Privately Held**
WEB: www.qcacorp.com
SIC: 3679 Electronic circuits; harness assemblies for electronic use: wire or cable

(G-14613)
QUALITY VISION INTL INC (PA)
Also Called: Optical Gaging Products Div
850 Hudson Ave (14621-4839)
PHONE 585 544-0400
Fax: 585 544-4998
Edward T Polidor, *CEO*
Andrea Walker, *General Mgr*
David Hansen, *Vice Pres*
Tim Tieppo, *Traffic Mgr*
Ronald Verschage, *Senior Buyer*
▲ EMP: 3
SALES (est): 93.5MM **Privately Held**
SIC: 3827 Optical test & inspection equipment

(G-14614)
QUALITY VISION SERVICES INC
Also Called: Quality Vision International
1175 North St (14621-4942)
PHONE 585 544-0450
Fax: 585 506-4307
Timothy Moriarty, *President*
Raymond Go, *Regional Mgr*
Tim Sladden, *Regional Mgr*
Joe Soistman, *Regional Mgr*
Frank Opett, *Opers Staff*
▲ EMP: 56
SALES (est): 11.4MM
SALES (corp-wide): 93.5MM **Privately Held**
SIC: 3827 8734 Optical comparators; optical test & inspection equipment; calibration & certification
PA: Quality Vision International Inc.
 850 Hudson Ave
 Rochester NY 14621
 585 544-0400

(G-14615)
QUANTUM SAILS ROCHESTER LLC
1461 Hudson Ave (14621-1716)
PHONE 585 342-5200
Kristofer Werner, *President*
EMP: 5 EST: 2015
SALES (est): 268.6K **Privately Held**
SIC: 2394 Convertible tops, canvas or boat: from purchased materials

(G-14616)
QUB9 INC
181 Saint Paul St Apt 3a (14604-1192)
PHONE 585 484-1808
Amy Jerman, *Principal*
EMP: 6 EST: 2015
SALES (est): 245.2K **Privately Held**
SIC: 3448 7389 Buildings, portable: prefabricated metal;

(G-14617)
QUINTEL USA INC
1200 Ridgeway Ave Ste 132 (14615-3758)
PHONE 585 420-8364
Alastair Westgarth, *CEO*
Bob Fishback, *CFO*
▲ EMP: 50
SALES (est): 8MM **Privately Held**
SIC: 3663 Radio & TV communications equipment

(G-14618)
R P FEDDER CORP (PA)
740 Driving Park Ave B (14613-1596)
PHONE 585 288-1600
Fax: 585 288-2481
Stephen Quinn, *Ch of Bd*
Joseph Vancura, *President*
Joseph Pennise, *Vice Pres*
Gordon Leonard, *Engineer*
Tammy Gioseffi, *Controller*
▲ EMP: 28 EST: 1958
SQ FT: 65,000
SALES: 15MM **Privately Held**
WEB: www.rpfedder.com
SIC: 3564 5075 2674 Filters, air: furnaces, air conditioning equipment, etc.; air filters; bags: uncoated paper & multi-wall

(G-14619)
R V DOW ENTERPRISES INC
Also Called: B J Long Co
466 Central Ave (14605-3011)
PHONE 585 454-5862
Fax: 585 454-2836
Richard V Dow, *President*
▲ EMP: 17
SQ FT: 9,000
SALES (est): 700K **Privately Held**
WEB: www.bjlong.com
SIC: 3999 Pipe cleaners

(G-14620)
RAPID PRECISION MACHINING INC
Also Called: Quality Plus
50 Lafayette Rd (14609-3119)
PHONE 585 467-0780
John Nolan, *President*
EMP: 70
SQ FT: 51,000
SALES (est): 6.6MM **Privately Held**
SIC: 3541 Mfg Machine Tools-Cutting

(G-14621)
RECHARGE NET INC
439 Central Ave Ste 108 (14605-3016)
PHONE 585 546-1060
Fax: 585 546-1061
Hugh Chambers, *President*
MAI Leaty, *Vice Pres*
EMP: 6
SQ FT: 7,500
SALES (est): 741.6K **Privately Held**
WEB: www.rechargenetworks.com
SIC: 3955 5999 5065 Print cartridges for laser & other computer printers; photocopy machines; diskettes, computer

(G-14622)
RED OAK SOFTWARE INC
3349 Monroe Ave Ste 175 (14618-5513)
PHONE 585 454-3170
Greg Waffen, *Branch Mgr*
EMP: 5
SALES (corp-wide): 2.1MM **Privately Held**
WEB: www.redoaksw.com
SIC: 7372 Prepackaged software
PA: Red Oak Software Inc
 115 Us Highway 46 F1000
 Mountain Lakes NJ 07046
 973 316-6064

(G-14623)
RESPONSE CARE INC
1450 E Ridge Rd (14621-2007)
PHONE 585 671-4144
Myron Kowal, *President*
Richard Moore, *Co-Owner*
EMP: 7
SQ FT: 6,500
SALES (est): 690K **Privately Held**
SIC: 3669 Intercommunication systems, electric

▲ = Import ▼ = Export
◆ = Import/Export

GEOGRAPHIC SECTION

Rochester - Monroe County (G-14647)

(G-14624)
RHINO TRUNK & CASE INC
Also Called: Trunk Outlet
565 Blossom Rd Ste J (14610-1859)
PHONE 585 244-4553
Gregory Hurwitz, *President*
Bob Eastwood, *Manager*
EMP: 15
SALES: 5MM **Privately Held**
WEB: www.trunkoutlet.com
SIC: 3161 Luggage

(G-14625)
RID LOM PRECISION MFG
50 Regency Oaks Blvd (14624-5901)
PHONE 585 594-8600
Fax: 585 594-5550
John D Rider, *President*
Kari Trimer, *Office Mgr*
Jack Trimer, *Manager*
EMP: 20
SQ FT: 7,100
SALES (est): 3.2MM **Privately Held**
WEB: www.ridlom.com
SIC: 3544 Special dies & tools

(G-14626)
RIDGE CABINET & SHOWCASE INC
1545 Mount Read Blvd # 2 (14606-2848)
PHONE 585 663-0560
Fax: 585 663-1445
Steve Lader, *Ch of Bd*
EMP: 20
SQ FT: 6,200
SALES (est): 3.6MM **Privately Held**
SIC: 2541 Counter & sink tops

(G-14627)
RIVERSIDE MFG ACQUISITION LLC
655 Driving Park Ave (14613-1566)
PHONE 585 458-2090
Fax: 585 458-2123
Mike Hill, *President*
Dannie Simons, *General Mgr*
Gerard Shafer, *Vice Pres*
EMP: 110
SQ FT: 120,000
SALES (est): 16.5MM **Privately Held**
SIC: 2789 Bookbinding & related work; bookbinding & repairing: trade, edition, library, etc.; paper cutting; display mounting

(G-14628)
RIVERVIEW ASSOCIATES INC
Also Called: Riverside Automation
1040 Jay St (14611-1110)
PHONE 585 235-5980
Fax: 585 235-8626
John A Christopher, *Ch of Bd*
Debbie Smardz, *Engineer*
Jeremey Duell, *Controller*
EMP: 13
SQ FT: 20,000
SALES: 2.5MM **Privately Held**
WEB: www.riversideautomation.com
SIC: 3559 Automotive related machinery

(G-14629)
RMB EMBROIDERY SERVICE
176 Anderson Ave Ste F110 (14607-1169)
PHONE 585 271-5560
Ruta Szabo, *Partner*
Birute Collier, *Partner*
Maria Stankus, *Partner*
EMP: 7 **EST:** 1995
SQ FT: 850
SALES: 140K **Privately Held**
SIC: 2397 Schiffli machine embroideries

(G-14630)
ROBERT J FARAONE
Also Called: O Tex
1600 N Clinton Ave (14621-2200)
PHONE 585 232-7160
Robert J Faraone, *Owner*
EMP: 7
SALES: 500K **Privately Held**
WEB: www.otex.com
SIC: 3545 Tool holders

(G-14631)
ROBOTIC DIRECTIONS
8 Black Spruce Ct (14616-5007)
PHONE 585 453-9417
Ronald Metzinger, *Owner*
EMP: 5
SALES: 100K **Privately Held**
SIC: 3699 Electrical equipment & supplies

(G-14632)
ROCCERA LLC
771 Elmgrove Rd Bldg No2 (14624-6200)
PHONE 585 426-0887
Syamal Ghosh, *President*
Frank Kaduc, *Vice Pres*
EMP: 18
SQ FT: 10,000
SALES (est): 2.2MM **Privately Held**
SIC: 3297 3432 3599 Heat resistant mixtures; alumina fused refractories; plumbing fixture fittings & trim; machine & other job shop work; custom machinery

(G-14633)
ROCHESTER 100 INC
40 Jefferson Rd (14623-2132)
P.O. Box 92801 (14692-8901)
PHONE 585 475-0200
Fax: 585 475-0340
Nicholas Sfikas, *President*
Catherine Sfikas, *Principal*
Geraldine E Warner, *Corp Secy*
William Fish, *Vice Pres*
Carleen Fien, *Admin Sec*
▲ **EMP:** 129 **EST:** 1962
SQ FT: 100,000
SALES: 19.6MM **Privately Held**
WEB: www.rochester100.com
SIC: 2677 2672 Envelopes; adhesive papers, labels or tapes: from purchased material

(G-14634)
ROCHESTER ASPHALT MATERIALS (DH)
1150 Penfield Rd (14625-2202)
PHONE 585 381-7010
John M Odenbach Jr, *President*
Gardner Odenbach, *Treasurer*
Mary Swierkos, *Admin Sec*
EMP: 8
SQ FT: 5,000
SALES (est): 9.7MM
SALES (corp-wide): 25.3B **Privately Held**
SIC: 2951 3273 Road materials, bituminous (not from refineries); ready-mixed concrete
HQ: Oldcastle Materials, Inc.
900 Ashwood Pkwy Ste 700
Atlanta GA 30338
770 522-5600

(G-14635)
ROCHESTER ATOMATED SYSTEMS INC
40 Regency Oaks Blvd (14624-5901)
PHONE 585 594-3222
Fax: 585 594-5810
Jerrold Potter, *President*
Frank Denaro, *Vice Pres*
George Gamer, *Vice Pres*
Bob Conklin, *Engineer*
Giovanni Dallicardillo, *Design Engr*
EMP: 20
SQ FT: 12,000
SALES (est): 3.8MM **Privately Held**
WEB: www.rochauto.com
SIC: 3599 Machine & other job shop work; custom machinery

(G-14636)
ROCHESTER BUSINESS JOURNAL
45 East Ave Ste 500 (14604-2292)
PHONE 585 546-8303
Fax: 585 546-3398
Susan Holliday, *President*
Lisa Granite, *Editor*
John Bouchard, *Vice Pres*
Karen Martin, *Vice Pres*
Daniel Peck, *Sls & Mktg Exec*
EMP: 35
SALES (est): 2.4MM **Privately Held**
WEB: www.rbj.net
SIC: 2711 Newspapers: publishing only, not printed on site

(G-14637)
ROCHESTER CATHOLIC PRESS (PA)
Also Called: Catholic Courier
1150 Buffalo Rd (14624-1823)
P.O. Box 24379 (14624-0379)
PHONE 585 529-9530
Fax: 585 529-9532
Bishop Salvatore R Matano, *President*
Karen M Franz, *General Mgr*
William H Kedley, *Treasurer*
Arlene Gall, *Manager*
Rev Daniel Condon, *Admin Sec*
EMP: 15
SQ FT: 3,188
SALES: 1.3MM **Privately Held**
WEB: www.catholiccourier.com
SIC: 2711 Newspapers: publishing only, not printed on site

(G-14638)
ROCHESTER COCA COLA BOTTLING
Also Called: Coca-Cola
123 Upper Falls Blvd (14605-2156)
PHONE 585 546-3900
Fax: 585 325-1816
George Keim, *Manager*
Jeff Alchowiak, *IT/INT Sup*
EMP: 65
SALES (corp-wide): 44.2B **Publicly Held**
SIC: 2086 5149 Bottled & canned soft drinks; groceries & related products
HQ: Rochester Coca Cola Bottling Corp
300 Oak St
Pittston PA 18640
570 655-2874

(G-14639)
ROCHESTER COLONIAL MFG CORP (PA)
1794 Lyell Ave (14606-2316)
PHONE 585 254-8191
Fax: 585 254-1768
Mark S Gionta, *CEO*
Norm Dix, *President*
Paul Gionta, *Plant Mgr*
Ed Johnson, *Opers Staff*
Caroline Wail, *Controller*
EMP: 100
SQ FT: 100,000
SALES (est): 11.6MM **Privately Held**
WEB: www.rochestercolonial.com
SIC: 2431 3442 3231 3444 Windows & window parts & trim, wood; metal doors, sash & trim; strengthened or reinforced glass; sheet metalwork

(G-14640)
ROCHESTER COUNTERTOP INC (PA)
Also Called: Premier Cabinet Wholesalers
3300 Monroe Ave Ste 212 (14618-4621)
PHONE 585 338-2260
Fax: 585 338-2265
Dean Pelletier, *President*
Dean Pelleiter, *Controller*
EMP: 10
SQ FT: 9,000
SALES (est): 1MM **Privately Held**
WEB: www.premiercabinetwholesalers.com
SIC: 2541 1799 Counter & sink tops; counter top installation; kitchen cabinets

(G-14641)
ROCHESTER DEMOCRAT & CHRONICLE
55 Exchange Blvd (14614-2001)
PHONE 585 232-7100
Fax: 585 258-2734
EMP: 26
SALES (est): 2.1MM **Privately Held**
SIC: 2711 Newspapers-Publishing/Printing

(G-14642)
ROCHESTER GEAR INC
213 Norman St (14613-1875)
PHONE 585 254-5442
Fax: 585 254-0427
Anthony J Fedor, *President*
Scott Caccamise, *Exec VP*
Robert Eckelberger, *Mfg Mgr*
Jim Horan, *Manager*
EMP: 37
SQ FT: 25,000
SALES (est): 5.4MM **Privately Held**
WEB: www.rochestergear.com
SIC: 3566 Speed changers, drives & gears

(G-14643)
ROCHESTER MIDLAND CORPORATION (PA)
155 Paragon Dr (14624-1167)
P.O. Box 64462 (14624-6862)
PHONE 585 336-2200
Fax: 585 266-1606
H Bradley Calkins, *CEO*
Harlan D Calkins, *Ch of Bd*
Glenn A Paynter, *President*
Vince Marcucci, *Regional Mgr*
Michael Coyner, *COO*
▲ **EMP:** 170 **EST:** 1888
SQ FT: 190,000
SALES (est): 135MM **Privately Held**
WEB: www.rochestermidland.com
SIC: 2842 2676 2899 Specialty cleaning, polishes & sanitation goods; floor waxes; cleaning or polishing preparations; disinfectants, household or industrial plant; feminine hygiene paper products; chemical preparations

(G-14644)
ROCHESTER ORTHOPEDIC LABS (PA)
460 White Spruce Blvd (14623-1648)
PHONE 585 272-1060
Fax: 585 272-0871
David Forbes, *President*
Ronald McKay, *Vice Pres*
Jennifer Moncrief, *Vice Pres*
Gerald Tendall, *Vice Pres*
Eric Ober, *Admin Sec*
EMP: 8 **EST:** 1962
SQ FT: 12,000
SALES (est): 1.8MM **Privately Held**
WEB: www.rochesterorthopediclabs.com
SIC: 3842 Limbs, artificial; braces, elastic; braces, orthopedic

(G-14645)
ROCHESTER OVERNIGHT PLTG LLC
2 Cairn St (14611-2416)
PHONE 585 328-4590
Fax: 585 328-1984
Catherine Hurd, *President*
Shirley Tallman, *Office Mgr*
Tom Rohack, *Executive*
EMP: 60
SQ FT: 40,000
SALES (est): 5.9MM **Privately Held**
WEB: www.rochesterplatingworks.com
SIC: 3471 Plating of metals or formed products

(G-14646)
ROCHESTER PHOTONICS CORP
115 Canal Landing Blvd (14626-5105)
PHONE 585 387-0674
Michael Morris, *CEO*
Paul Marx, *President*
EMP: 60
SQ FT: 52,000
SALES (est): 4.4MM
SALES (corp-wide): 9.1B **Publicly Held**
WEB: www.corning.com
SIC: 3827 Optical instruments & lenses
PA: Corning Incorporated
1 Riverfront Plz
Corning NY 14831
607 974-9000

(G-14647)
ROCHESTER SILVER WORKS LLC
100 Latona Rd Bldg 110 (14652-0001)
P.O. Box 15397 (14615-0397)
PHONE 585 477-9501
EMP: 50
SALES (est): 12MM **Privately Held**
SIC: 1044 Silver ores processing

Rochester - Monroe County (G-14648)

(G-14648)
ROCHESTER SILVER WORKS LLC
240 Aster St (14615)
P.O. Box 15397 (14615-0397)
PHONE..................585 743-1610
David Dix, *Opers Mgr*
Ralph Holmes, *Purch Mgr*
Bob Surash, *Technical Mgr*
EMP: 7
SALES (est): 755.6K **Privately Held**
SIC: 3339 Silver refining (primary)

(G-14649)
ROCHESTER STAMPINGS INC
400 Trade Ct (14624-4773)
PHONE..................585 467-5241
Fax: 585 467-2518
L Charles Hicks, *President*
EMP: 16 **EST:** 1958
SQ FT: 15,000
SALES (est): 3MM **Privately Held**
WEB: www.rochstamp.com
SIC: 3544 3469 3452 Special dies & tools; metal stampings; bolts, nuts, rivets & washers

(G-14650)
ROCHESTER STEEL TREATING WORKS
962 E Main St (14605-2780)
PHONE..................585 546-3348
Fax: 585 546-1684
Eugene Miller, *President*
Bryan Miller, *Production*
EMP: 18 **EST:** 1932
SQ FT: 13,000
SALES: 2MM **Privately Held**
WEB: www.rstwinc.com
SIC: 3398 Metal heat treating

(G-14651)
ROCHESTER STRUCTURAL LLC
961 Lyell Ave Bldg 5 (14606-1956)
PHONE..................585 436-1250
David Yelle, *President*
Brian Carmer,
EMP: 25
SQ FT: 15,000
SALES (est): 7.2MM **Privately Held**
SIC: 3312 1791 Structural shapes & pilings, steel; structural steel erection

(G-14652)
ROCHESTER TOOL AND MOLD INC
515 Lee Rd (14606-4236)
PHONE..................585 464-9336
Fax: 585 464-8043
Al Kapoor, *President*
Paul Tolley, *Vice Pres*
Elise Engelberger, *Office Mgr*
Franky Arndt, *Manager*
EMP: 11
SQ FT: 5,600
SALES (est): 1.8MM **Privately Held**
WEB: www.rochestertoolandmold.com
SIC: 3544 3599 Industrial molds; machine shop, jobbing & repair

(G-14653)
ROCHESTER TUBE FABRICATORS
1128 Lexington Ave 5d (14606-2909)
PHONE..................585 254-0290
James R Bunting, *Principal*
EMP: 9
SALES (est): 1.2MM **Privately Held**
SIC: 3498 Fabricated pipe & fittings

(G-14654)
ROCHLING ADVENT TOOL & MOLD LP
999 Ridgeway Ave (14615-3819)
PHONE..................585 254-2000
Ken Desrosiers, *General Ptnr*
EMP: 39
SALES (est): 13.2MM
SALES (corp-wide): 1.6B **Privately Held**
SIC: 3089 3544 3545 Injection molding of plastics; industrial molds; tools & accessories for machine tools
HQ: Rochling Engineering Plastics Se & Co. Kg
Rochlingstr. 1
Haren (Ems) 49733
593 470-10

(G-14655)
ROCK IROQUOIS PRODUCTS INC (DH)
1150 Penfield Rd (14625-2202)
PHONE..................585 381-7010
John Odenbach Jr, *President*
Richard E Williams, *President*
David Fingar, *Vice Pres*
Frederick J Odenbach, *Vice Pres*
Gerard Odenbach, *Vice Pres*
EMP: 10
SQ FT: 5,000
SALES (est): 3.6MM
SALES (corp-wide): 25.3B **Privately Held**
SIC: 3281 2951 3273 Stone, quarrying & processing of own stone products; paving mixtures; asphalt & asphaltic paving mixtures (not from refineries); road materials, bituminous (not from refineries); ready-mixed concrete
HQ: Oldcastle Materials, Inc.
900 Ashwood Pkwy Ste 700
Atlanta GA 30338
770 522-5600

(G-14656)
ROCKWELL AUTOMATION INC
300 Red Creek Dr Ste 100 (14623-4283)
PHONE..................585 487-2700
Brian Blaisdell, *Area Mgr*
Kevin Phelps, *Vice Pres*
Scott Turling, *Manager*
Dave Cicero, *Technical Staff*
Carol Caranddo, *Clerk*
EMP: 27 **Publicly Held**
SIC: 3625 Relays & industrial controls
PA: Rockwell Automation, Inc.
1201 S 2nd St
Milwaukee WI 53204

(G-14657)
ROESSEL & CO INC
199 Lagrange Ave (14613-1593)
PHONE..................585 458-5560
Fax: 585 458-6074
William R Laitenberger, *President*
Kathy Laitenberger, *President*
Alfred P Laitenberger, *Treasurer*
Patrick Mulrooney, *Manager*
EMP: 8 **EST:** 1952
SQ FT: 6,000
SALES: 2MM **Privately Held**
WEB: www.roessel.com
SIC: 3823 Water quality monitoring & control systems

(G-14658)
ROMOLD INC
5 Moonlanding Rd (14624-2505)
PHONE..................585 529-4440
Louis Romano, *President*
Diane Romano, *Corp Secy*
Thomas Fumia, *Plant Mgr*
EMP: 16
SQ FT: 11,500
SALES (est): 1.3MM **Privately Held**
WEB: www.romold.net
SIC: 3544 Industrial molds

(G-14659)
ROTORK CONTROLS INC
Also Called: Jordon Controls
675 Mile Crossing Blvd (14624-6212)
PHONE..................585 328-1550
EMP: 12
SALES (corp-wide): 823.9MM **Privately Held**
SIC: 3625 Actuators, industrial
HQ: Rotork Controls Inc.
675 Mile Crossing Blvd
Rochester NY 14624
585 328-1550

(G-14660)
ROTORK CONTROLS INC (DH)
675 Mile Crossing Blvd (14624-6212)
PHONE..................585 328-1550
Fax: 585 247-2308
Robert H Arnold, *Ch of Bd*
William H Whiteley, *President*
Karl Klopfenstein, *Area Mgr*
Fred Dowdeswell, *Vice Pres*
Michael Knapp, *VP Opers*
▲ **EMP:** 160 **EST:** 1967
SALES (est): 58.3MM
SALES (corp-wide): 823.9MM **Privately Held**
SIC: 3625 Actuators, industrial
HQ: Rotork Overseas Limited
Rotork House
Bath
122 573-3200

(G-14661)
RPC PHOTONICS INC
330 Clay Rd (14623-3227)
PHONE..................585 272-2840
Fax: 585 272-5845
Dr G Michael Morris, *CEO*
Mark A Hirschler, *Facilities Mgr*
Jeffrey Shaw, *Design Engr*
Laura Weller-Brophy, *Info Tech Mgr*
Lorna Maier, *Administration*
EMP: 19
SALES (est): 3.3MM **Privately Held**
SIC: 3827 Optical instruments & lenses

(G-14662)
RT SOLUTIONS LLC
Also Called: Worm Power
80 Linden Oaks Ste 210 (14625-2809)
PHONE..................585 245-3456
Thomas Herlihy, *President*
Shawn Ferro, *Manager*
EMP: 8
SQ FT: 80,000
SALES (est): 1.3MM **Privately Held**
SIC: 2873 8711 Nitrogenous fertilizers; engineering services

(G-14663)
RY-GAN PRINTING INC
111 Humboldt St (14609-7463)
PHONE..................585 482-7770
Fax: 585 482-7039
Craig Schinsing, *President*
EMP: 9
SQ FT: 8,000
SALES (est): 1.4MM **Privately Held**
WEB: www.rygan.com
SIC: 2752 Commercial printing, lithographic

(G-14664)
S C T
3000 E Ridge Rd (14622-3028)
PHONE..................585 467-7740
Fax: 585 339-2550
Nancy Keucher, *Principal*
EMP: 14
SALES (est): 1.3MM **Privately Held**
SIC: 7372 Prepackaged software

(G-14665)
SAFE PASSAGE INTERNATIONAL INC
333 Metro Park Ste F204 (14623-2632)
PHONE..................585 292-4910
Andrew Figiel, *Owner*
Michael Rooksby, *COO*
Lew Pulvino, *Sales Executive*
Vicki Tran, *Mktg Coord*
Barb Gibson, *Manager*
EMP: 14
SQ FT: 3,500
SALES (est): 1.2MM **Privately Held**
WEB: www.safe-passage.com
SIC: 7372 7371 Prepackaged software; custom computer programming services

(G-14666)
SAMCO SCIENTIFIC CORPORATION
75 Panorama Creek Dr (14625-2303)
PHONE..................800 522-3359
Tuyen Nguyen, *Manager*
Sandy McKinsey, *Manager*
EMP: 167
SQ FT: 80,000
SALES (est): 14.5MM
SALES (corp-wide): 16.9B **Publicly Held**
WEB: www.samcosci.com
SIC: 3085 Plastics bottles
HQ: Fisher Scientific International Llc
81 Wyman St
Waltham MA 02451
781 622-1000

(G-14667)
SANDSTONE TECHNOLOGIES CORP (PA)
2117 Buffalo Rd 245 (14624-1507)
PHONE..................585 785-5537
Timothy Williams, *President*
Matthew Brodie, *Manager*
◆ **EMP:** 1 **EST:** 2012
SALES: 1MM **Privately Held**
SIC: 3661 Fiber optics communications equipment

(G-14668)
SANDSTONE TECHNOLOGIES CORP
2117 Buffalo Rd Unit 245 (14624-1507)
PHONE..................585 785-5537
Matthew Brodie, *Branch Mgr*
EMP: 7
SALES (corp-wide): 1MM **Privately Held**
SIC: 3661 Fiber optics communications equipment
PA: Sandstone Technologies Corp.
2117 Buffalo Rd 245
Rochester NY 14624
585 785-5537

(G-14669)
SASSY SAUCE INC
740 Driving Park Ave F (14613-1534)
PHONE..................585 621-1050
Fax: 585 621-1099
Salvatore Nalbone, *President*
Sal Nalbone, *President*
Terry O'Brien, *Vice Pres*
EMP: 7
SALES (est): 572.2K **Privately Held**
SIC: 2035 Seasonings & sauces, except tomato & dry

(G-14670)
SATISPIE LLC
155 Balta Dr (14623-3142)
PHONE..................716 982-4600
Keith Woodward, *Senior VP*
Dan Mulvaney, *CFO*
Vernon Miller, *Controller*
Ann Pasqual, *Controller*
Mike Pinkowski,
▲ **EMP:** 20
SALES (est): 5MM **Privately Held**
WEB: www.satispie.com
SIC: 2051 Cakes, pies & pastries

(G-14671)
SAVAGE & SON INSTALLATIONS LLC
676 Pullman Ave (14615-3335)
P.O. Box 12647 (14612-0647)
PHONE..................585 342-7533
Gerald Champman,
EMP: 30 **EST:** 2008
SALES (est): 3.7MM **Privately Held**
SIC: 2952 Mastic roofing composition

(G-14672)
SCAIFE ENTERPRISES INC
Also Called: PETRILLO'S BAKERY
67 Lyell Ave (14608-1414)
PHONE..................585 454-5231
Richard Scaife, *President*
EMP: 18
SALES (est): 920K **Privately Held**
SIC: 2051 Cakes, bakery; except frozen

(G-14673)
SCHLEGEL ELECTRONIC MTLS INC (PA)
1600 Lexington Ave 236a (14606-3062)
PHONE..................585 295-2030
Johnny C C Lo, *President*
Haydee Dibble, *Manager*
Christina Pachett, *Manager*
Lorrie Fairey, *Admin Asst*
EMP: 15
SQ FT: 25,000
SALES (est): 2.3MM **Privately Held**
SIC: 3053 Gaskets & sealing devices

GEOGRAPHIC SECTION
Rochester - Monroe County (G-14698)

(G-14674)
SCHLEGEL SYSTEMS INC (DH)
1555 Jefferson Rd (14623-3109)
PHONE..................................585 427-7200
Fax: 585 427-7216
Jeff Grady, *CEO*
Jonathan Petromelis, *Ch of Bd*
Lenny Witmeyer, *Design Engr*
Paula Toland, *Accounts Mgr*
Santiago Garcia, *Sales Staff*
◆ EMP: 200 EST: 1885
SQ FT: 150,000
SALES (est): 326.4MM
SALES (corp-wide): 532.9MM **Privately Held**
WEB: www.schlegel.com
SIC: 3053   3089 3069 Gaskets, packing & sealing devices; plastic hardware & building products; pillows, sponge rubber

(G-14675)
SCHWAB CORP (DH)
900 Linden Ave (14625-2700)
PHONE..................................585 381-4900
James Brush, *President*
Denise Booream, *Partner*
Mechelle Corwin, *COO*
Ellen Boesner, *Counsel*
Linn Ferguson, *Senior VP*
EMP: 30 EST: 1872
SQ FT: 10,000
SALES (est): 14.3MM
SALES (corp-wide): 4.5B **Publicly Held**
WEB: www.schwabcorp.com
SIC: 3499   3442 2522 Safes & vaults, metal; fire doors, metal; file drawer frames: except wood
HQ: Sentry Safe, Inc.
   137 W Forest Hill Ave
   Oak Creek WI 53154
   585 381-4900

(G-14676)
SCHWAB CORP
900 Linden Ave (14625-2700)
PHONE..................................812 547-2956
Fax: 812 547-4487
Bill Nave, *Safety Mgr*
Charles Jasper, *QC Dir*
Pamela Krieg, *Persnl Mgr*
Harold May, *Manager*
David Miller, *Manager*
EMP: 130
SALES (corp-wide): 4.5B **Publicly Held**
WEB: www.schwabcorp.com
SIC: 3499   2522 Safes & vaults, metal; office furniture, except wood
HQ: Schwab Corp.
   900 Linden Ave
   Rochester NY 14625
   585 381-4900

(G-14677)
SCJ ASSOCIATES INC
60 Commerce Dr (14623-3502)
PHONE..................................585 359-0600
Fax: 585 359-0856
Scott Sutherland, *Ch of Bd*
Jone Holdforth, *Purch Mgr*
Gary Brusdal, *Engineer*
Richard Figueras, *Engineer*
David Sutherland, *Controller*
EMP: 40
SQ FT: 15,000
SALES (est): 13.4MM **Privately Held**
WEB: www.scjassociates.com
SIC: 3825 Test equipment for electronic & electric measurement

(G-14678)
SDJ MACHINE SHOP INC
1215 Mount Read Blvd # 1 (14606-2895)
PHONE..................................585 458-1236
Fax: 585 254-0912
Don Celestino, *President*
Aggie Polny, *Office Mgr*
EMP: 11
SQ FT: 20,000
SALES (est): 2MM **Privately Held**
WEB: www.sdjmachine.com
SIC: 3599 Machine shop, jobbing & repair

(G-14679)
SEABREEZE PAVEMENT OF NY LLC
14 Maryknoll Park (14622-1542)
PHONE..................................585 338-2333
Keruin Negron, *CEO*
Kelly Mahoney,
EMP: 8 EST: 2015
SALES (est): 452.7K **Privately Held**
SIC: 2951 Concrete, asphaltic (not from refineries)

(G-14680)
SECUPRINT INC
1560 Emerson St (14606-3118)
PHONE..................................585 341-3100
Patrick White, *Ch of Bd*
Tiffany Carthen, *Office Mgr*
EMP: 10
SALES (est): 1.6MM
SALES (corp-wide): 17.5MM **Publicly Held**
SIC: 3577 Printers & plotters
PA: Document Security Systems Inc
   200 Canal View Blvd # 300
   Rochester NY 14623
   585 325-3610

(G-14681)
SEMROK INC (HQ)
Also Called: Semrock
3625 Buffalo Rd Ste 6 (14624-1179)
PHONE..................................585 594-7050
Fax: 585 594-3898
Victor Mizrahi, *President*
Craig Hodgson, *Research*
Brian O'Flaherty, *Engineer*
Neil Brown, *Finance*
Amy Pitoniak, *Sales Associate*
▲ EMP: 99
SQ FT: 22,000
SALES (est): 12.8MM
SALES (corp-wide): 2B **Publicly Held**
WEB: www.semrock.com
SIC: 3229 Optical glass
PA: Idex Corporation
   1925 W Field Ct Ste 200
   Lake Forest IL 60045
   847 498-7070

(G-14682)
SERI SYSTEMS INC
172 Metro Park (14623-2610)
PHONE..................................585 272-5515
Ron Lablanc, *Vice Pres*
Martin Sondervan, *Vice Pres*
Dan Wagner, *Vice Pres*
Robert McJury, *VP Sales*
EMP: 20
SQ FT: 6,000
SALES: 2MM **Privately Held**
SIC: 2759 Decals: printing; labels & seals: printing; screen printing

(G-14683)
SHAMROCK PLASTICS & TOOL INC
95 Mount Read Blvd # 149 (14611-1973)
PHONE..................................585 328-6040
Timothy Kelly, *President*
EMP: 6
SALES (est): 812K **Privately Held**
SIC: 3089 Plastic processing

(G-14684)
SHORETEL INC
300 State St Ste 100 (14614-1047)
PHONE..................................877 654-3573
Don Joos, *Branch Mgr*
EMP: 7 **Publicly Held**
SIC: 3661 3663 7372 Telephone & telegraph apparatus; radio & TV communications equipment; prepackaged software
PA: Shoretel, Inc.
   960 Stewart Dr
   Sunnyvale CA 94085

(G-14685)
SIGN IMPRESSIONS INC
2590 W Ridge Rd Ste 6 (14626-3041)
PHONE..................................585 723-0420
Fax: 585 723-0535
Gerald Mallaber, *President*
EMP: 8
SQ FT: 3,000
SALES (est): 1.1MM **Privately Held**
WEB: www.signimpressions.com
SIC: 3993 Signs, not made in custom sign painting shops

(G-14686)
SIGNATURE NAME PLATE CO INC
292 Commerce Dr (14623-3506)
PHONE..................................585 321-9960
William Monell, *President*
Harry T Bain Jr, *Vice Pres*
EMP: 7
SQ FT: 9,000
SALES (est): 784.9K **Privately Held**
WEB: www.signaturenp.com
SIC: 3993 Name plates: except engraved, etched, etc.: metal

(G-14687)
SIKORSKY AIRCRAFT CORPORATION
Also Called: Impact Tech A Skrsky Innvtions
300 Canal View Blvd (14623-2811)
PHONE..................................585 424-1977
Fax: 585 424-1177
James Cycon, *General Mgr*
EMP: 68
SALES (corp-wide): 46.1B **Publicly Held**
SIC: 3721 Aircraft
HQ: Sikorsky Aircraft Corporation
   6900 Main St
   Stratford CT 06614
   203 386-4000

(G-14688)
SIMPLEXGRINNELL LP
90 Goodway Dr (14623-3039)
PHONE..................................585 288-6200
Fax: 585 475-1126
Tom Deveronica, *Opers Mgr*
Kerry Maier, *Human Res Dir*
Mark Goergen, *Sales Staff*
Gary Gokey, *Branch Mgr*
Ruth Sardone, *Traffic Dir*
EMP: 74 **Privately Held**
WEB: www.simplexgrinnell.com
SIC: 3669 Emergency alarms
HQ: Simplexgrinnell Lp
   4700 Exchange Ct
   Boca Raton FL 33431
   561 988-7200

(G-14689)
SLIM LINE CASE CO INC
64 Spencer St (14608-1423)
PHONE..................................585 546-3639
Bette Thomas, *CEO*
Andrea Coulter, *President*
EMP: 15
SQ FT: 14,000
SALES (est): 560K **Privately Held**
WEB: www.slimlinecase.com
SIC: 3172 Leather cases

(G-14690)
SOCIAL SCIENCE ELECTRONIC PUBG
2171 Monroe Ave Ste 203 (14618-2432)
PHONE..................................585 442-8170
Fax: 585 442-8171
Greg Gordon, *President*
Robert McCormick, *Research*
EMP: 16
SALES (est): 1.2MM **Privately Held**
WEB: www.ssrn.com
SIC: 2741 8299 Miscellaneous publishing; educational services

(G-14691)
SOLID CELL INC
771 Elmgrove Rd (14624-6200)
PHONE..................................585 426-5000
Arkady Malakhov, *CEO*
EMP: 9 EST: 2010
SALES (est): 993K **Privately Held**
SIC: 3674 Fuel cells, solid state

(G-14692)
SOLID SURFACES INC
1 Townline Cir (14623-2513)
PHONE..................................585 292-5340
Mitchell A Makowski, *President*
Mark E Makowski, *Vice Pres*
EMP: 20
SQ FT: 7,800
SALES (est): 3.7MM **Privately Held**
WEB: www.solidsurfacesinc.net
SIC: 2541 2821 Counter & sink tops; table or counter tops, plastic laminated; plastics materials & resins

(G-14693)
SOUND SOURCE INC
161 Norris Dr (14610-2422)
PHONE..................................585 271-5370
Fax: 585 271-5373
John Castronova, *President*
Robert Storms, *Vice Pres*
EMP: 7
SQ FT: 7,500
SALES (est): 570K **Privately Held**
SIC: 3931 5731 Musical instruments; consumer electronic equipment

(G-14694)
SPECTRUM CABLE CORPORATION
295 Mount Read Blvd Ste 2 (14611-1967)
PHONE..................................585 235-7714
Fax: 585 235-7739
Mark Philip, *President*
Simon Braitman, *Corp Secy*
EMP: 9
SQ FT: 17,000
SALES (est): 1MM **Privately Held**
WEB: www.spectrumcablecorp.com
SIC: 3315 1731 Wire & fabricated wire products; electrical work

(G-14695)
SPIN-RITE CORPORATION
30 Dubelbeiss Ln (14622-2402)
P.O. Box 67184 (14617-7184)
PHONE..................................585 266-5200
Gary Bohrer, *President*
EMP: 16
SQ FT: 1,400
SALES (est): 1.8MM **Privately Held**
SIC: 3312 Tool & die steel & alloys

(G-14696)
SPX CORPORATION
Kaytex
1000 Millstead Way (14624-5110)
PHONE..................................585 279-1216
Tom Fitzimmons, *Manager*
EMP: 50
SALES (corp-wide): 1.7B **Publicly Held**
SIC: 3559 Semiconductor manufacturing machinery
PA: Spx Corporation
   13320a Balntyn Corp Pl
   Charlotte NC 28277
   980 474-3700

(G-14697)
SPX CORPORATION
SPX Flow Technology
135 Mount Read Blvd (14611-1921)
P.O. Box 31370 (14603-1370)
PHONE..................................585 436-5550
Fax: 585 436-5589
Andrwe Creathorn, *General Mgr*
Hock Teoh, *General Mgr*
Tom Kaufman, *Business Mgr*
Laura Dwyer, *Vice Pres*
James Stanton, *Vice Pres*
EMP: 480
SALES (corp-wide): 1.7B **Publicly Held**
WEB: www.spx.com
SIC: 3443 Cooling towers, metal plate
PA: Spx Corporation
   13320a Balntyn Corp Pl
   Charlotte NC 28277
   980 474-3700

(G-14698)
SPX FLOW US LLC
Also Called: SPX Flow Technology
135 Mount Read Blvd (14611-1921)
PHONE..................................585 436-5550
Andrew Creathorn, *General Mgr*
Jim Myers, *General Mgr*
Christopher J Kearney, *Chairman*
Rick Bourbonnais, *Sales Associate*
Kathleen Spath, *Info Tech Mgr*
EMP: 5

Rochester - Monroe County (G-14699) GEOGRAPHIC SECTION

SALES (est): 216K
SALES (corp-wide): 2.3B **Publicly Held**
SIC: 3824 7699 Impeller & counter driven flow meters; cash register repair
PA: Spx Flow, Inc.
 13320 Balntyn Corp Pl
 Charlotte NC 28277
 704 752-4400

(G-14699)
ST VINCENT PRESS INC
250 Cumberland St Ste 260 (14605-2811)
PHONE...................................585 325-5320
Fax: 585 325-2571
Barbara Anzalone, *President*
Ken Holeperl, *Vice Pres*
Vincent Anzalone, *CFO*
EMP: 15
SQ FT: 18,000
SALES (est): 2.3MM **Privately Held**
WEB: www.stvincentpress.com
SIC: 2752 Commercial printing, offset

(G-14700)
STAMPER TECHNOLOGY INC
232 Wallace Way (14624-6216)
PHONE...................................585 247-8370
Bruce Ha, *President*
▲ EMP: 7
SQ FT: 5,000
SALES (est): 1.1MM **Privately Held**
SIC: 3695 Magnetic & optical recording media

(G-14701)
STEEL WORK INC
340 Oak St (14608-1727)
PHONE...................................585 232-1555
Tim Grove, *President*
EMP: 9
SQ FT: 7,000
SALES (est): 1.4MM **Privately Held**
WEB: www.steelwork.com
SIC: 3446 3444 Architectural metalwork; sheet metalwork

(G-14702)
STEFAN SYDOR OPTICS INC
31 Jetview Dr (14624-4903)
P.O. Box 20001 (14602-0001)
PHONE...................................585 271-7300
Fax: 585 271-7309
James Sydor, *President*
Michael Naselaris, *General Mgr*
John Escolas, *Opers Mgr*
Sam Ezzezew, *Prdtn Mgr*
Nicole Cafolla, *QA Dir*
▼ EMP: 43
SQ FT: 40,000
SALES (est): 10.1MM **Privately Held**
WEB: www.sydor.com
SIC: 3827 3229 3211 Optical instruments & lenses; pressed & blown glass; flat glass

(G-14703)
STERILIZ LLC
95 Allens Creek Rd (14618-3250)
PHONE...................................585 415-5411
James T Townsend,
Samuel R Trapani,
EMP: 5
SALES (est): 390K **Privately Held**
SIC: 3821 3842 Sterilizers; sterilizers, hospital & surgical

(G-14704)
STEVEN COFFEY PALLET S INC
3376 Edgemere Dr (14612-1128)
PHONE...................................585 261-6783
Steven Coffey, *Principal*
EMP: 8
SALES (est): 942.6K **Privately Held**
SIC: 2448 Pallets, wood & wood with metal

(G-14705)
STRAUSS EYE PROSTHETICS INC
360 White Spruce Blvd (14623-1604)
PHONE...................................585 424-1350
James V Strauss, *President*
Josie Strauss, *Admin Sec*
EMP: 5
SQ FT: 2,024
SALES (est): 310K **Privately Held**
WEB: www.strausseye.com
SIC: 3851 Eyes, glass & plastic

(G-14706)
SUIT-KOTE CORPORATION
Also Called: Western Bituminous
2 Rockwood St Frnt (14610-2611)
PHONE...................................585 473-6321
Fax: 585 473-1774
Tom Hackwelder, *Vice Pres*
Frank Suits, *Vice Pres*
Steve Rebman, *Sales & Mktg St*
EMP: 25
SALES (corp-wide): 278.7MM **Privately Held**
WEB: www.suit-kote.com
SIC: 2951 5032 Asphalt & asphaltic paving mixtures (not from refineries); asphalt mixture
PA: Suit-Kote Corporation
 1911 Lorings Crossing Rd
 Cortland NY 13045
 607 753-1100

(G-14707)
SUPERIOR TECHNOLOGY INC
200 Paragon Dr (14624-1159)
PHONE...................................585 352-6556
Fax: 585 352-6559
John P Shortino, *President*
Anthony J Shortino, *Vice Pres*
Joseph Shortino, *Vice Pres*
Aaron Mandarano, *Manager*
Robin Grandusky, *Admin Asst*
▲ EMP: 50 EST: 1987
SQ FT: 36,500
SALES (est): 12.7MM **Privately Held**
WEB: www.superiortech.org
SIC: 3599 Machine shop, jobbing & repair

(G-14708)
SWEETWATER ENERGY INC
500 Lee Rd Ste 200 (14606-4261)
PHONE...................................585 647-5760
Jack Baron, *CEO*
Ron Boillat, *Exec VP*
James Hvisdas, *Vice Pres*
Nina Pearlmutter, *Vice Pres*
Jonathan Sherwood, *Vice Pres*
▲ EMP: 7
SALES (est): 750K **Privately Held**
SIC: 2046 Corn sugar

(G-14709)
SWIFT MULTIGRAPHICS LLC
55 Southwood Ln (14618-4019)
PHONE...................................585 442-8000
Kenneth Stahl, *Principal*
EMP: 2
SQ FT: 200
SALES (est): 1MM **Privately Held**
SIC: 2759 3999 Promotional printing; advertising display products

(G-14710)
SYNAPTICS INCORPORATED
90 Linden Oaks Ste 100 (14625-2830)
PHONE...................................585 899-4300
Rick Bergman, *President*
Joe Muczynski, *Manager*
EMP: 15
SALES (corp-wide): 1.6B **Publicly Held**
SIC: 3577 Computer peripheral equipment
PA: Synaptics Incorporated
 1251 Mckay Dr
 San Jose CA 95131
 408 904-1100

(G-14711)
SYNERGY FLAVORS NY COMPANY LLC
Also Called: Vanlab
86 White St (14608-1435)
PHONE...................................585 232-6648
Richard Hatch, *Plant Mgr*
Bob Strassner, *Branch Mgr*
Jim Abraham, *Manager*
Paulete Lanzoff, *Manager*
EMP: 6 **Privately Held**
SIC: 2087 Flavoring extracts & syrups
HQ: Synergy Flavors (Ny) Company Llc
 1500 Synergy Dr
 Wauconda IL 60084
 585 232-6648

(G-14712)
SYNTEC TECHNOLOGIES INC (PA)
Also Called: Syntec Optics
515 Lee Rd (14606-4236)
PHONE...................................585 768-2513
Alok Kapoor, *President*
Richard Arndt, *Vice Pres*
Steve Polvinen, *Vice Pres*
Ryan Kromm, *Foreman/Supr*
Phil Marra, *Engineer*
EMP: 50 EST: 1981
SQ FT: 25,000
SALES (est): 15.1MM **Privately Held**
WEB: www.syntecoptics.com
SIC: 3089 Injection molding of plastics

(G-14713)
SYNTEC TECHNOLOGIES INC
Also Called: Syntec Optics
515 Lee Rd (14606-4236)
PHONE...................................585 464-9336
Phil Race, *Branch Mgr*
EMP: 11
SALES (corp-wide): 14.9MM **Privately Held**
WEB: www.syntecoptics.com
SIC: 3544 3599 Industrial molds; machine shop, jobbing & repair
PA: Syntec Technologies, Inc.
 7100 Junction Rd
 Pavilion NY 14606
 585 768-2513

(G-14714)
T & C POWER CONVERSION INC
132 Humboldt St (14610-1046)
PHONE...................................585 482-5551
Fax: 585 482-8487
Tomasz Mokrzan, *President*
Noam Sarfati, *Opers Staff*
Golan Jacob, *Engineer*
Andrzej Marcinkowski, *Project Engr*
Jolanta Mokrzan, *CFO*
EMP: 13
SQ FT: 3,000
SALES (est): 2.5MM **Privately Held**
WEB: www.tcpowerconversion.com
SIC: 3825 Radio frequency measuring equipment

(G-14715)
T & L AUTOMATICS INC
770 Emerson St (14613-1895)
PHONE...................................585 647-3717
Fax: 585 647-1126
Thomas W Hassett, *President*
Vincent Buzzelli, *Senior VP*
David Murphy, *Vice Pres*
Vince Vuzzelli, *VP Opers*
William Green, *Marketing Staff*
EMP: 120 EST: 1975
SQ FT: 120,000
SALES (est): 25.4MM **Privately Held**
WEB: www.tandlautomatics.com
SIC: 3451 Screw machine products

(G-14716)
T L F GRAPHICS INC
Also Called: Tlf Graphics
235 Metro Park (14623-2618)
PHONE...................................585 272-5500
Fax: 585 272-5525
Ronald Leblanc, *Ch of Bd*
Mike Goupil, *General Mgr*
Dan Wagner, *Vice Pres*
Rich Cromwell, *Materials Mgr*
Ray McHargue, *Safety Mgr*
EMP: 59
SQ FT: 12,000
SALES (est): 29.4MM **Privately Held**
SIC: 2672 2759 Tape, pressure sensitive: made from purchased materials; labels (unprinted), gummed: made from purchased materials; screen printing

(G-14717)
TAC SCREW PRODUCTS INC
170 Bennington Dr (14616-4754)
PHONE...................................585 663-5840
Fax: 585 663-8221
Julius Papp, *President*
Mark Laisure, *Vice Pres*
EMP: 10
SQ FT: 4,000
SALES (est): 1.4MM **Privately Held**
SIC: 3451 Screw machine products

(G-14718)
TCS INDUSTRIES INC
400 Trabold Rd (14624-2529)
PHONE...................................585 426-1160
Fax: 585 426-1162
Manoj Shekar, *President*
Mark Wright, *Engineer*
Bill Rankin, *Manager*
▲ EMP: 80
SQ FT: 110,000
SALES: 17MM **Privately Held**
WEB: www.tcsindustries.com
SIC: 3444 Sheet metalwork

(G-14719)
TEALE MACHINE COMPANY INC
1425 University Ave (14607-1617)
P.O. Box 10340 (14610-0340)
PHONE...................................585 244-6700
Fax: 585 473-1271
Ronald E Larock, *Ch of Bd*
Aimee Ciulla, *Vice Pres*
Michael E Larock, *Vice Pres*
Gary Bergen, *Opers Staff*
Aimee R Larock, *Treasurer*
EMP: 70
SQ FT: 22,000
SALES (est): 20.1MM **Privately Held**
WEB: www.tealemachine.com
SIC: 3451 3625 Screw machine products; numerical controls

(G-14720)
TEL-TRU INC (PA)
Also Called: Tel-Tru Manufacturing Company
408 Saint Paul St (14605-1734)
PHONE...................................585 295-0225
Andrew Germanow, *President*
Felisha Bostick, *Purchasing*
Steve Deweese, *Manager*
Brian Watson, *Manager*
Suzanne Mayer, *Consultant*
EMP: 56
SALES (est): 7.3MM **Privately Held**
SIC: 3823 Temperature measurement instruments, industrial; resistance thermometers & bulbs, industrial process type

(G-14721)
THE CALDWELL MANUFACTURING CO (PA)
2605 Manitou Rd Ste 100 (14624-1199)
P.O. Box 92891 (14692-8991)
PHONE...................................585 352-3790
Fax: 585 352-3729
Edward A Boucher, *CEO*
Eric W Mertz, *Ch of Bd*
James Boucher, *Ch of Bd*
Carmen Berretta, *District Mgr*
Peter M Egberts, *Vice Pres*
◆ EMP: 100 EST: 1888
SQ FT: 126,000
SALES: 50MM **Privately Held**
WEB: www.caldwellmfgco.com
SIC: 3495 Wire springs

(G-14722)
THERMO FISHER SCIENTIFIC INC
1999 Mnt Rd Blvd 1-3 Bldg 13 (14615)
PHONE...................................585 458-8008
Chad Buchta, *Technical Mgr*
Helene Diederich, *Branch Mgr*
EMP: 307
SALES (corp-wide): 16.9B **Publicly Held**
WEB: www.thermo.com
SIC: 3826 Analytical instruments
PA: Thermo Fisher Scientific Inc.
 168 3rd Ave
 Waltham MA 02451
 781 622-1000

(G-14723)
THERMO FISHER SCIENTIFIC INC
75 Panorama Creek Dr (14625-2385)
PHONE...................................585 899-7610
Katrina Kusovski, *General Mgr*
Dan Biggs, *Vice Pres*
Barbara Dorsey, *Opers Mgr*
David Eddy, *Opers Staff*
Peter Baird, *Engineer*

▲ = Import ▼ = Export
◆ = Import/Export

GEOGRAPHIC SECTION

EMP: 900
SALES (corp-wide): 16.9B **Publicly Held**
SIC: 3826 Analytical instruments
PA: Thermo Fisher Scientific Inc.
168 3rd Ave
Waltham MA 02451
781 622-1000

(G-14724)
THREE POINT VENTURES LLC
Also Called: Skooba Design
3495 Winton Pl Ste E120 (14623-2838)
PHONE...................................585 697-3444
Fax: 585 697-3447
Nancy Laniak, *Manager*
Michael J Hess,
▲ **EMP:** 10
SQ FT: 20,000
SALES (est): 640K **Privately Held**
WEB: www.roadwired.com
SIC: 3161 Cases, carrying

(G-14725)
THREE R ENTERPRISES INC
Also Called: Jason Manufacturing Company
447 Adirondack St (14606-2213)
PHONE...................................585 254-5050
Richard Wallenhorst II, *President*
Patty Wallenhorst, *Admin Sec*
EMP: 30
SQ FT: 10,000
SALES (est): 4MM **Privately Held**
SIC: 2431 2541 2521 Millwork; store fixtures, wood; office fixtures, wood; cabinets, office: wood

(G-14726)
TILE SHOP INC
420 Jefferson Rd Ste 3 (14623-2447)
PHONE...................................585 424-2180
Tara Yost, *Manager*
EMP: 5
SALES (est): 352.3K **Privately Held**
SIC: 3253 Floor tile, ceramic

(G-14727)
TODD WALBRIDGE
Also Called: T M Design Screen Printing
1916 Lyell Ave (14606-2306)
PHONE...................................585 254-3018
Fax: 585 254-8657
Todd Walbridge, *Owner*
EMP: 7
SQ FT: 3,500
SALES (est): 605.6K **Privately Held**
WEB: www.tmdesigncorp.com
SIC: 2759 3993 2396 2395 Screen printing; signs & advertising specialties; automotive & apparel trimmings; pleating & stitching

(G-14728)
TOUCHSTONE TECHNOLOGY INC
350 Mile Crossing Blvd (14624-6207)
PHONE...................................585 458-2690
Fax: 585 458-2733
Eric B Snavely, *Ch of Bd*
David J Meisenzahl, *CFO*
Kelly Fairchild, *Controller*
Courtney Armstrong, *Cust Mgr*
Alan Robertson, *Manager*
▲ **EMP:** 16
SQ FT: 13,000
SALES (est): 5.5MM **Privately Held**
WEB: www.touchstn.com
SIC: 3575 Computer terminals, monitors & components; keyboards, computer, office machine

(G-14729)
TRANE US INC
75 Town Centre Dr Ste I (14623-4259)
PHONE...................................585 256-2500
Fax: 585 256-0067
Vincent Ferrer, *Engineer*
Dan Wendo, *Systems Staff*
EMP: 47 **Privately Held**
SIC: 3585 Refrigeration & heating equipment
HQ: Trane U.S. Inc.
1 Centennial Ave Ste 101
Piscataway NJ 08854
732 652-7100

(G-14730)
TREAD QUARTERS (PA)
200 Holleder Pkwy (14615-3808)
PHONE...................................800 876-6676
EMP: 8
SALES (est): 1.8MM **Privately Held**
SIC: 3131 Quarters

(G-14731)
TRIPLEX INDUSTRIES INC
100 Boxart St Ste 27 (14612-5659)
PHONE...................................585 621-6920
Fax: 585 621-7068
Christa Roesner, *President*
Patrick Moran, *Opers Staff*
Scott Patrick, *QC Mgr*
EMP: 10 **EST:** 1981
SQ FT: 8,500
SALES (est): 960K **Privately Held**
SIC: 3599 Machine shop, jobbing & repair

(G-14732)
TROYER INC
4555 Lyell Rd (14606-4316)
PHONE...................................585 352-5590
Fax: 585 352-5593
William Colton, *President*
Kris Kettlewell, *Manager*
EMP: 15
SQ FT: 18,000
SALES (est): 1.7MM **Privately Held**
SIC: 3711 3714 5531 Motor vehicles & car bodies; motor vehicle parts & accessories; speed shops, including race car supplies

(G-14733)
TRUESENSE IMAGING INC
1964 Lake Ave (14615-2316)
PHONE...................................585 784-5500
Fax: 585 784-5602
Chris McNiffe, *CEO*
Michael Miller, *Opers Dir*
David Nichols, *Research*
Rachel Kielon, *CFO*
Wes Micket, *Director*
EMP: 207 **EST:** 2011
SQ FT: 260,000
SALES: 36MM
SALES (corp-wide): 3.5B **Publicly Held**
SIC: 3861 Film, sensitized motion picture, X-ray, still camera, etc.
HQ: Semiconductor Components Industries, Llc
5005 E Mcdowell Rd
Phoenix AZ 85008
602 244-6600

(G-14734)
TRUFORM MANUFACTURING CORP
1500 N Clinton Ave (14621-2206)
PHONE...................................585 458-1090
Fax: 585 458-1155
Tyrone Reaves, *Ch of Bd*
Bryan Putt, *General Mgr*
Cathy Seaver, *Buyer*
Pat Small, *Engineer*
Sharon McCullough, *Manager*
EMP: 70
SQ FT: 45,000
SALES (est): 13.4MM **Privately Held**
WEB: www.truformmfg.com
SIC: 3444 Sheet metalwork

(G-14735)
TURNER BELLOWS INC
Also Called: Tb
526 Child St Ste 1 (14606-1187)
PHONE...................................585 235-4456
Fax: 585 235-4593
Marilyn Yeager, *CEO*
Amanda Pontaella, *Ch of Bd*
Phyllis Rosenhack, *General Mgr*
▲ **EMP:** 45
SQ FT: 85,000
SALES (est): 8.5MM **Privately Held**
WEB: www.turnerbellows.com
SIC: 3081 3069 3861 Unsupported plastics film & sheet; foam rubber; photographic sensitized goods

(G-14736)
TURNING POINT TOOL LLC
1197 Mount Read Blvd (14606-2831)
PHONE...................................585 288-7380

Rob Kirby, *Opers Mgr*
Connie Pezzulo, *Office Mgr*
Frank Pezzulo,
Robert Kirby,
EMP: 6
SALES (est): 590K **Privately Held**
WEB: www.turningpointtool.com
SIC: 3544 Special dies, tools, jigs & fixtures

(G-14737)
TYCO ELECTRONICS CORPORATION
2245 Brighton Henrta Twn (14623-2705)
PHONE...................................585 785-2500
John Rowe, *Manager*
EMP: 50
SALES (corp-wide): 12.2B **Privately Held**
WEB: www.raychem.com
SIC: 3679 Electronic circuits
HQ: Tyco Electronics Corporation
1050 Westlakes Dr
Berwyn PA 19312
717 986-7275

(G-14738)
U-LACE LLC
465 Central Ave (14605-3012)
PHONE...................................716 848-0939
Timothy Talley, *CEO*
Royce Russell, *Vice Pres*
EMP: 3
SQ FT: 5,000
SALES: 1MM **Privately Held**
SIC: 3131 Laces, shoe & boot: leather

(G-14739)
UCB PHARMA INC (PA)
755 Jefferson Rd (14623-3233)
PHONE...................................919 767-2555
Roch Doliveux, *CEO*
Fabrice Enderlin, *Exec VP*
Ismail Kola, *Exec VP*
Iris Lw-Friedrich, *Exec VP*
Mark McDade, *Exec VP*
▲ **EMP:** 400
SQ FT: 556,000
SALES (est): 63.1MM **Privately Held**
SIC: 2833 2834 5122 Anesthetics, in bulk form; drugs & herbs: grading, grinding & milling; pharmaceutical preparations; pharmaceuticals

(G-14740)
ULTRA TOOL AND MANUFACTURING
129 Seneca Ave (14621-2318)
P.O. Box 17860 (14617-0860)
PHONE...................................585 467-3700
Daniel E Herzog, *President*
James M Schmeer, *Vice Pres*
Carol Herzog, *Office Mgr*
EMP: 13
SQ FT: 4,000
SALES: 1.3MM **Privately Held**
SIC: 3599 Machine & other job shop work; machine shop, jobbing & repair

(G-14741)
UNICELL BODY COMPANY INC
1319 Brighton Henrietta (14623-2408)
PHONE...................................585 424-2660
Fax: 585 424-2782
Dale Wunsch, *Purch Mgr*
Steven Bones, *Manager*
EMP: 14
SQ FT: 7,200
SALES (corp-wide): 20MM **Privately Held**
WEB: www.unicell.com
SIC: 3713 Truck & bus bodies
PA: Unicell Body Company, Inc
571 Howard St
Buffalo NY 14206
716 853-8628

(G-14742)
UNIFAB INC
215 Tremont St Ste 31 (14608-2370)
PHONE...................................585 235-1760
Fax: 585 235-1762
Brian Malark, *President*
William S Martin, *Vice Pres*
EMP: 7
SQ FT: 2,500

SALES: 1MM **Privately Held**
SIC: 3089 Plastic processing

(G-14743)
UNITHER MANUFACTURING LLC
755 Jefferson Rd (14623-3233)
PHONE...................................585 475-9000
Kevin Haehl, *General Mgr*
Kathleen Mruk, *Senior Buyer*
Amy Gould, *Human Resources*
EMP: 250
SALES (est): 66.8MM
SALES (corp-wide): 1.9MM **Privately Held**
SIC: 2834 Pharmaceutical preparations
HQ: Unither Pharmaceuticals
Espace Industriel Nord Cs 2802
Amiens 80080
322 547-300

(G-14744)
UNIVERSAL PRECISION CORP
40 Commerce Dr (14623-3502)
PHONE...................................585 321-9760
Fax: 585 321-9828
Michael J Schmitt, *President*
Michael Domenico, *Vice Pres*
Dana Goodman, *Opers Mgr*
Sonya Dotson, *QA Dir*
Jeff Hooper, *Treasurer*
EMP: 24
SQ FT: 12,000
SALES (est): 4.5MM **Privately Held**
WEB: www.universalprecision.com
SIC: 3444 Sheet metalwork

(G-14745)
UNIVERSITY OF ROCHESTER
Also Called: Labortory For Laser Energetics
250 E River Rd (14623-1212)
PHONE...................................585 275-3483
Fax: 585 275-5960
Jody Mayer, *Purch Agent*
Michael Bock, *Engineer*
Brian Charles, *Engineer*
Alex Maltsev, *Engineer*
Sam Morse, *Engineer*
EMP: 400
SALES (corp-wide): 2.1B **Privately Held**
WEB: www.rochester.edu
SIC: 3845 8221 Laser systems & equipment, medical; university
PA: University Of Rochester
601 Elmwood Ave
Rochester NY 14642
585 275-5000

(G-14746)
UPSTATE CABINET CO INC
32 Marway Cir (14624-2321)
PHONE...................................585 429-5090
Fax: 585 429-5096
Todd Whelehan, *President*
Vincenzo Delucia, *Vice Pres*
Jon Ingrick, *Sales Executive*
Annette Whelehan, *Manager*
Donna Demanchick, *Admin Asst*
EMP: 14
SQ FT: 30,000
SALES (est): 1.9MM **Privately Held**
WEB: www.upstatecabinet.com
SIC: 2434 Wood kitchen cabinets

(G-14747)
UPSTATE INCRETE INCORPORATED
49 Adelaide St (14606-2205)
PHONE...................................585 254-2010
Jeff Barlette, *Principal*
EMP: 9
SALES (est): 1.1MM **Privately Held**
SIC: 2421 Building & structural materials, wood

(G-14748)
UPSTATE NIAGARA COOP INC
Also Called: Sealtest Dairy Products
45 Fulton Ave (14608-1032)
PHONE...................................585 458-1880
Fax: 585 458-2887
John Gould, *Vice Pres*
Christine Krawczyk, *Safety Dir*
Stephan Hranjec, *Plant Mgr*
Roger Grove, *Opers Mgr*
Terry Wihlen, *Maint Spvr*
EMP: 150

Rochester - Monroe County (G-14749) — GEOGRAPHIC SECTION

SQ FT: 40,000
SALES (corp-wide): 775.5MM **Privately Held**
SIC: **2026** Milk processing (pasteurizing, homogenizing, bottling)
PA: Upstate Niagara Cooperative, Inc.
25 Anderson Rd
Buffalo NY 14225
716 892-3156

(G-14749)
USAIRPORTS SERVICES INC
Also Called: US Airports Flight Support Svc
1295 Scottsville Rd (14624-5125)
PHONE..............................585 527-6835
Fax: 585 529-5581
Anthony Castillo, *President*
Patrick Smelt, *Controller*
Barbara Marianetti, *Human Res Dir*
EMP: 22
SQ FT: 29,800 **Privately Held**
WEB: www.usairportsflight.com
SIC: **3728** Refueling equipment for use in flight, airplane
PA: Usairports Services, Inc
1 Airport Way Ste 300
Rochester NY 14624

(G-14750)
VA INC
Also Called: Vincent Associates
803 Linden Ave Ste 1 (14625-2723)
PHONE..............................585 385-5930
Kevin Farrell, *Ch of Bd*
Stephen Pasquarella, *Vice Pres*
Dave Krieger, *Engineer*
Helen Yan, *Engineer*
EMP: 25
SQ FT: 6,500
SALES (est): 4.9MM **Privately Held**
WEB: www.uniblitz.com
SIC: **3861** 3827 Shutters, camera; optical instruments & lenses

(G-14751)
VAN THOMAS INC
Also Called: Ruggeri Manufacturing
740 Driving Park Ave G1 (14613-1594)
PHONE..............................585 426-1414
Fax: 585 247-0661
Charles E Thomas, *President*
Gary Vander Mallie, *Vice Pres*
Lisa Rutenberg, *Bookkeeper*
Dale Palmer, *Sales Mgr*
▲ EMP: 35
SQ FT: 37,000
SALES: 850K **Privately Held**
SIC: **3599** 3544 Machine & other job shop work; special dies, tools, jigs & fixtures

(G-14752)
VETERANS OFFSET PRINTING INC
Also Called: Veteran Offset Printing
500 N Goodman St (14609-6136)
PHONE..............................585 288-2900
Fax: 585 288-2908
Louie Difilippo, *President*
John Dukay, *Vice Pres*
John Duque, *Vice Pres*
EMP: 3 EST: 1940
SALES: 2MM **Privately Held**
SIC: **2752** 2759 Commercial printing, offset; commercial printing

(G-14753)
VIGNERI CHOCOLATE INC
810 Emerson St (14613-1804)
PHONE..............................585 254-6160
Alex Vigneri, *CEO*
◆ EMP: 7 EST: 2012
SQ FT: 10,000
SALES: 500K **Privately Held**
SIC: **2064** Candy bars, including chocolate covered bars; chocolate candy, except solid chocolate

(G-14754)
VILLAGE METALS INC
87 Belmont St (14620-1620)
PHONE..............................585 271-1250
Rodney Schlesing, *Principal*
EMP: 5
SALES (est): 409.4K **Privately Held**
SIC: **3469** Metal stampings

(G-14755)
W M T PUBLICATIONS INC
250 N Goodman St Ste 1 (14607-1150)
PHONE..............................585 244-3329
Mary Anna Towler, *President*
Michael Alo, *Vice Pres*
William J Towler, *Treasurer*
EMP: 16
SALES (est): 939.1K **Privately Held**
SIC: **2711** Newspapers, publishing & printing

(G-14756)
WATER WISE OF AMERICA INC
90 Canal St (14608-1958)
PHONE..............................585 232-1210
Bob Beach, *Branch Mgr*
EMP: 7 **Privately Held**
WEB: www.waterwiseofamerica.com
SIC: **2899** Water treating compounds
PA: Water Wise Of America, Inc
75 Bermar Park Ste 5
Rochester NY 14624

(G-14757)
WATER WISE OF AMERICA INC (PA)
75 Bermar Park Ste 5 (14624-1500)
PHONE..............................585 232-1210
Michael Bromley, *President*
Anne Jefferson, *Corp Secy*
EMP: 7
SQ FT: 2,500
SALES (est): 952.9K **Privately Held**
WEB: www.waterwiseofamerica.com
SIC: **2899** 5169 Water treating compounds; chemicals & allied products

(G-14758)
WEB SEAL INC (PA)
15 Oregon St (14605-3094)
PHONE..............................585 546-1320
Fax: 585 546-5746
John F Hurley, *President*
Betty A Hurley, *Treasurer*
Marie Martin, *Finance*
Nick Riola, *Regl Sales Mgr*
Julia Magone, *Manager*
EMP: 20 EST: 1960
SQ FT: 13,000
SALES (est): 4.7MM **Privately Held**
WEB: www.websealinc.com
SIC: **3053** 5085 Gaskets & sealing devices; seals, industrial

(G-14759)
WELCH MACHINE INC
961 Lyell Ave Bldg 1-6 (14606-1956)
PHONE..............................585 647-3578
Martin Welch, *President*
EMP: 5
SQ FT: 5,000
SALES (est): 633.4K **Privately Held**
SIC: **3541** Machine tool replacement & repair parts, metal cutting types

(G-14760)
WELDRITE CLOSURES INC
2292 Innovation Way (14624-6224)
PHONE..............................585 429-8790
Jason Nelson, *President*
Richard Knapp, *General Mgr*
Greg Scace, *Vice Pres*
Mary J Maier, *Manager*
EMP: 40 EST: 2008
SALES (est): 9.6MM **Privately Held**
SIC: **3731** Offshore supply boats, building & repairing

(G-14761)
WERE FORMS INC
500 Helendale Rd Ste 190 (14609-3125)
PHONE..............................585 482-4400
Fax: 585 482-5243
Kim Hostutler, *President*
Chris Accorso, *Accounts Mgr*
John Duggan, *Accounts Mgr*
EMP: 6
SQ FT: 2,000
SALES (est): 480K **Privately Held**
WEB: www.wereforms.com
SIC: **2759** Commercial printing

(G-14762)
WHIRLWIND MUSIC DISTRS INC
99 Ling Rd (14612-1965)
PHONE..............................585 663-8820
Fax: 585 865-8930
Michael Laiacona, *Ch of Bd*
Al Keltz, *General Mgr*
Scott Harvey, *Prdtn Mgr*
Debbie Noble, *Prdtn Mgr*
Holly Bryan, *Purch Agent*
▲ EMP: 100
SQ FT: 28,000
SALES (est): 22.3MM **Privately Held**
WEB: www.whirlwindusa.com
SIC: **3651** 3678 3663 3643 Audio electronic systems; amplifiers: radio, public address or musical instrument; public address systems; electronic connectors; radio & TV communications equipment; current-carrying wiring devices; nonferrous wiredrawing & insulating

(G-14763)
WIKOFF COLOR CORPORATION
686 Pullman Ave (14615-3335)
PHONE..............................585 458-0653
EMP: 16
SALES (corp-wide): 152.7MM **Privately Held**
SIC: **2893** Printing ink
PA: Wikoff Color Corporation
1886 Merritt Rd
Fort Mill SC 29715
803 548-2210

(G-14764)
WINDSOR TECHNOLOGY LLC
1527 Lyell Ave (14606-2121)
PHONE..............................585 461-2500
Grant Randall, *President*
Douglas Green, *Vice Pres*
Ann Shattuck, *QA Dir*
Chad Notebaert, *Engineer*
Mary Carlson, *Design Engr*
EMP: 10
SQ FT: 40,000
SALES: 10MM **Privately Held**
WEB: www.windsortec.com
SIC: **3672** Printed circuit boards

(G-14765)
WOERNER INDUSTRIES INC
Also Called: Wizer Equipment
485 Hague St (14606-1296)
PHONE..............................585 436-1934
Philip Collins, *President*
EMP: 40
SALES (corp-wide): 4.4MM **Privately Held**
WEB: www.lasscowizer.com
SIC: **3555** Printing trades machinery
PA: Woerner Industries, Inc.
485 Hague St
Rochester NY
585 235-1991

(G-14766)
WORDINGHAM MACHINE CO INC
Also Called: Wordingham Technologies
515 Lee Rd (14606-4236)
PHONE..............................585 924-2294
Fax: 585 924-7660
Alok Kapoor, *CEO*
Todd Close, *QC Mgr*
Bob Orcutt, *VP Sales*
Tony Phillips, *Sales Staff*
Mike Jackson, *Manager*
EMP: 45
SQ FT: 26,000
SALES (est): 9MM **Privately Held**
SIC: **3599** Machine & other job shop work

(G-14767)
XACTRA TECHNOLOGIES INC
9 Marway Cir (14624-2320)
PHONE..............................585 426-2030
David W Binn, *President*
Kevin Yackel, *Sales Mgr*
Michael Binn, *Manager*
John Bartlett, *Supervisor*
EMP: 55
SQ FT: 33,000
SALES (est): 8MM **Privately Held**
WEB: www.prestigeprecision.com
SIC: **3545** Precision tools, machinists'

(G-14768)
XEROX CORPORATION
100 S Clinton Ave Fl 4 (14604-1877)
PHONE..............................585 423-4711
Fax: 585 423-5620
Carl Langsenkamp, *Principal*
Greg Jones, *Top Exec*
John M Kelly, *Exec VP*
Munish Agrawal, *Vice Pres*
Michael Frey, *Vice Pres*
EMP: 10
SALES (corp-wide): 18B **Publicly Held**
WEB: www.xerox.com
SIC: **3861** Photographic equipment & supplies
PA: Xerox Corporation
45 Glover Ave Ste 700
Norwalk CT 06850
203 968-3000

(G-14769)
XEROX CORPORATION
100 S Clinton Ave (14604-1877)
PHONE..............................585 423-3538
James Danylyshyn, *Manager*
Stella Naugle, *Officer*
EMP: 25
SALES (corp-wide): 18B **Publicly Held**
WEB: www.xerox.com
SIC: **3577** Computer peripheral equipment
PA: Xerox Corporation
45 Glover Ave Ste 700
Norwalk CT 06850
203 968-3000

(G-14770)
XEROX CORPORATION
80 Linden Oaks (14625-2809)
PHONE..............................585 264-5584
EMP: 200
SALES (corp-wide): 21.4B **Publicly Held**
SIC: **3861** Mfg Photographic Equipment/Supplies
PA: Xerox Corporation
45 Glover Ave Ste 700
Norwalk CT 06850
203 968-3000

(G-14771)
XLI CORPORATION
55 Vanguard Pkwy (14606-3101)
PHONE..............................585 436-2250
Peter Schott, *Ch of Bd*
Camille Declerck, *Project Mgr*
Curt Hampton, *Safety Mgr*
Vlade Kordovich, *Engineer*
Jim Ours, *Engineer*
EMP: 60 EST: 1967
SQ FT: 35,000
SALES (est): 12MM **Privately Held**
WEB: www.xlionline.com
SIC: **3544** Special dies, tools, jigs & fixtures

(G-14772)
XMH-HFI INC (HQ)
Also Called: Bobby Jones Sportswear
1155 N Clinton Ave (14621-4454)
PHONE..............................585 467-7240
Fax: 585 467-1236
Walter Hickey, *Ch of Bd*
Mike Cohen, *President*
Steve Dell'olio, *President*
Paulette Garafalo, *President*
Fruno Castagna, *Exec VP*
▲ EMP: 700
SQ FT: 200,000
SALES (est): 206.8MM **Privately Held**
WEB: www.hickeyfreeman.com
SIC: **2311** 2325 Suits, men's & boys': made from purchased materials; tailored dress & sport coats: men's & boys'; slacks, dress: men's, youths' & boys'
PA: Hmx Llc
125 Park Ave Fl 7
New York NY 10017
212 682-9073

(G-14773)
YELLOWPAGECITYCOM
280 Kenneth Dr Ste 300 (14623-5263)
PHONE..............................585 410-6688
Rachel Dubey, *Production*
Michelle Quilitzsch, *Accounts Exec*
Matthew Smeltzer, *Consultant*
Richard Smith, *Consultant*

▲ = Import ▼ = Export
◆ = Import/Export

EMP: 15
SALES (est): 2MM Privately Held
SIC: 3993 Signs & advertising specialties

(G-14774)
ZEROVALENT NANOMETALS INC
693 East Ave Ste 103 (14607-2160)
PHONE................585 298-8592
Joseph Fargnoli, *Principal*
EMP: 7
SALES (est): 286.2K Privately Held
SIC: 3339 Antimony refining (primary); cobalt refining (primary); babbitt metal (primary); beryllium metal

(G-14775)
ZIP PRODUCTS INC
565 Blossom Rd Ste E (14610-1873)
PHONE................585 482-0044
Fax: 585 482-0040
Nikolay Petukhov, *President*
Joseph Zinger, *Vice Pres*
EMP: 14
SQ FT: 8,000
SALES: 800K Privately Held
SIC: 3599 Machine & other job shop work

(G-14776)
ZWEIGLES INC
651 Plymouth Ave N (14608-1689)
PHONE................585 546-1740
Fax: 585 546-8721
Roberta Camardo, *President*
Tina Steinmetz, *Purch Mgr*
Dominic Lippa, *CFO*
Michael Keller, *Treasurer*
Julie Camardo-Steron, *Sales Mgr*
EMP: 55 EST: 1880
SQ FT: 37,000
SALES (est): 10.4MM Privately Held
WEB: www.zweigles.com
SIC: 2013 Sausages & other prepared meats; sausages from purchased meat

Rock City Falls
Saratoga County

(G-14777)
COTTRELL PAPER COMPANY INC
1135 Rock City Rd (12863-1208)
P.O. Box 35 (12863-0035)
PHONE................518 885-1702
Fax: 518 885-0741
Jack L Cottrell, *Ch of Bd*
Ben Cottrell, *Vice Pres*
Darren Costanzo, *Purchasing*
Tom Harrington, *Sales Mgr*
Kathy Vandyk, *Manager*
▲ EMP: 36 EST: 1926
SQ FT: 40,000
SALES (est): 9.2MM Privately Held
WEB: www.cottreilpaper.com
SIC: 2621 Specialty papers; insulation siding, paper

(G-14778)
ELECTRIC BOAT CORPORATION
Atomic Project Rd (12863)
PHONE................518 884-1596
Allen Spadafora, *Manager*
Martha Ward, *Manager*
EMP: 200
SALES (corp-wide): 31.4B Publicly Held
SIC: 3731 8711 Submarines, building & repairing; engineering services
HQ: Electric Boat Corporation
75 Eastern Point Rd
Groton CT 06340

Rock Stream
Schuyler County

(G-14779)
ROCK STREAM VINEYARDS
162 Fir Tree Point Rd (14878-9700)
PHONE................607 243-8322
Mark Karasz, *Owner*
EMP: 7

SALES (est): 682.6K Privately Held
SIC: 2084 Wines

Rock Tavern
Orange County

(G-14780)
CREATIVE DESIGN AND MCH INC
197 Stone Castle Rd (12575-5000)
PHONE................845 778-9001
Fax: 845 778-9086
Clifford Broderick, *CEO*
Mark Pugh, *Project Engr*
Brian Robertson, *Sales Mgr*
Alan Gelb, *Technical Staff*
▲ EMP: 25
SQ FT: 24,000
SALES (est): 5.5MM Privately Held
SIC: 3469 Machine parts, stamped or pressed metal

Rockaway Beach
Queens County

(G-14781)
DESIGNS BY LANIE INC
Also Called: Hillary Hats & Accessories
211 Beach 90th St (11693-1501)
PHONE................718 945-4221
Fax: 718 945-7580
Helene Cohen, *President*
Brad Cohen, *Vice Pres*
EMP: 7
SQ FT: 2,300
SALES: 500K Privately Held
SIC: 2339 Sportswear, women's

(G-14782)
MADELAINE CHOCOLATE NOVLT INC (PA)
Also Called: Madelaine Chocolate Company
9603 Beach Channel Dr (11693-1398)
PHONE................718 945-1500
Fax: 718 318-4607
Jorge Farber, *CEO*
Scott Wright, *COO*
Vivian Farber, *Exec VP*
Norman Gold, *Vice Pres*
Jeremy Kaye, *Plant Mgr*
▲ EMP: 100 EST: 1949
SQ FT: 200,000
SALES (est): 22MM Privately Held
WEB: www.madelainechocolate.com
SIC: 2066 Chocolate candy, solid

(G-14783)
WAVE PUBLISHING CO INC
Also Called: Wave of Long Island, The
8808 Rockaway Beach Blvd (11693-1608)
PHONE................718 634-4000
Fax: 718 945-0913
Susan Locke, *President*
Howie Schwach, *Editor*
Sanford Bernstein, *Treasurer*
Felisha Edwards, *Adv Mgr*
EMP: 15
SQ FT: 4,500
SALES: 850K Privately Held
SIC: 2711 8111 Newspapers: publishing only, not printed on site; legal services

Rockaway Park
Queens County

(G-14784)
A-1 STAMPING & SPINNING CORP
225 Beach 143rd St (11694-1106)
PHONE................718 388-2626
Fax: 718 486-8317
Ira Zapolsky, *President*
▲ EMP: 15 EST: 1947
SQ FT: 14,000

SALES (est): 2MM Privately Held
SIC: 3469 3646 3645 Stamping metal for the trade; spinning metal for the trade; commercial indusl & institutional electric lighting fixtures; residential lighting fixtures

(G-14785)
EVELO INC
327 Beach 101st St (11694-2831)
PHONE................917 251-8743
Yevgeniy Morekovic, *President*
Boris Morekovic, *Vice Pres*
▲ EMP: 2
SALES: 1MM Privately Held
SIC: 3751 Bicycles & related parts

(G-14786)
NICKEL GROUP LLC
212 Beach 141st St (11694-1230)
PHONE................212 706-7906
EMP: 5
SALES (est): 554.3K Privately Held
SIC: 3356 Nickel

(G-14787)
RELIANCE MICA CO INC
336 Beach 149th St (11694-1027)
PHONE................718 788-0282
Fax: 718 768-2593
Peter Yanello Jr, *President*
Michael Parrella, *Div Sub Head*
Frank Callahan, *Vice Pres*
▲ EMP: 6 EST: 1924
SQ FT: 10,000
SALES (est): 480K Privately Held
SIC: 3299 Mica products

Rockville Centre
Nassau County

(G-14788)
BIANCA BURGERS LLC
Also Called: Janowski Hamburger
15 S Long Beach Rd (11570-5621)
PHONE................516 764-9591
Fax: 516 764-1908
William Vogelsberg, *President*
EMP: 12
SALES (est): 1.8MM Privately Held
SIC: 2013 Prepared beef products from purchased beef

(G-14789)
CHAMPION CUTTING TOOL CORP
11-15 Saint Marks Ave (11570-4244)
P.O. Box 368 (11571-0368)
PHONE................516 536-8200
Lowell Frey, *President*
Diane Ruggiero, *Controller*
Andy Lebrecque, *Regl Sales Mgr*
Bob Farrar, *Sales Staff*
Frank Suarez, *Sales Staff*
▲ EMP: 50
SQ FT: 15,000
SALES (est): 8.4MM
SALES (corp-wide): 17.9MM Privately Held
WEB: www.championcuttingtool.com
SIC: 3545 Cutting tools for machine tools
PA: The Frey Company Inc
190 Madison Ave
Rockville Centre NY 11572
516 536-8200

(G-14790)
CREATION BAUMANN USA INC
114 N Centre Ave (11570-3948)
PHONE................516 764-7431
George Baumann, *President*
Gloria Mastranni, *Human Res Mgr*
Harry Persaus, *Executive*
EMP: 30
SALES (est): 1.9MM Privately Held
SIC: 2211 2221 5949 5131 Apparel & outerwear fabrics, cotton; broadwoven fabric mills, manmade; fabric stores piece goods; piece goods & other fabrics

(G-14791)
GRAPHIC FABRICATIONS INC
Also Called: Minuteman Press
488a Sunrise Hwy (11570-5037)
PHONE................516 763-3222
Fax: 516 764-9334
George Dormani, *President*
EMP: 6
SQ FT: 4,000
SALES (est): 843.4K Privately Held
SIC: 2752 7334 2791 Commercial printing, lithographic; photocopying & duplicating services; typesetting

(G-14792)
HANGER INC
556 Merrick Rd Ste 101 (11570-5545)
PHONE................516 678-3650
Fax: 516 678-3654
EMP: 19
SALES (corp-wide): 500.5MM Privately Held
SIC: 3841 Surgical & medical instruments
PA: Hanger, Inc.
10910 Domain Dr Ste 300
Austin TX 78758
512 777-3800

(G-14793)
J SOEHNER CORPORATION
200 Brower Ave (11570-2603)
PHONE................516 599-2534
Fax: 516 599-2718
James Soehner, *President*
William F Soehner, *Vice Pres*
▲ EMP: 17 EST: 1948
SQ FT: 18,000
SALES (est): 1.9MM Privately Held
SIC: 3599 Custom machinery

(G-14794)
MEGAMATT INC
Also Called: Whistle Stop Bakery
35 Vassar Pl (11570-2830)
PHONE................516 536-3541
Jeff Tierney, *President*
Mary Tierney, *Treasurer*
EMP: 10
SQ FT: 4,600
SALES (est): 530K Privately Held
WEB: www.megamatt.com
SIC: 2051 5461 Bread, cake & related products; cakes, bakery: except frozen; bakeries; cakes

(G-14795)
MERCURY ENVELOPE CO INC
Also Called: Mercury Envelope Printing
100 Merrick Rd Ste 204e (11570-4801)
P.O. Box 200 (11571-0200)
PHONE................516 678-6744
Fax: 516 678-6764
Maurice Deutsch, *Ch of Bd*
Scott Deutsch, *President*
Maury Deutsch, *Vice Pres*
Vicky Vital, *Comptroller*
EMP: 75
SQ FT: 2,500
SALES (est): 19.4MM Privately Held
SIC: 2677 Envelopes

(G-14796)
PROGRESSUS COMPANY INC
100 Merrick Rd Ste 510w (11570-4825)
PHONE................516 255-0245
Fax: 516 255-0243
Lawrence Hutzler, *President*
Lillian Ehrenhaus, *Vice Pres*
Glenn Ehrenhaus, *VP Sales*
▲ EMP: 10
SQ FT: 60,000
SALES (est): 880K Privately Held
WEB: www.progressus.com
SIC: 3469 Household cooking & kitchen utensils, metal

(G-14797)
QUALITY METAL STAMPING LLC (PA)
100 Merrick Rd Ste 310w (11570-4884)
PHONE................516 255-9000
Robert Serling, *Owner*
Steven White, *Engineer*
Joe Downing, *Senior Engr*
Stephen Serling, *Sales & Mktg St*
Jerry Flecker, *Controller*

Rockville Centre - Nassau County (G-14798)

(G-14798)
SLEEP IMPROVEMENT CENTER INC
178 Sunrise Hwy Fl 2 (11570-4704)
PHONE...............................516 536-5799
Reza Naghavi, *President*
EMP: 12
SALES (est): 1MM Privately Held
SIC: 2515 Sleep furniture

(G-14799)
SOLVE ADVISORS INC
265 Sunrise Hwy Ste 22 (11570-4912)
PHONE...............................646 699-5041
Yevgeniy Grinberg, *President*
Gerard Nealon, *President*
Sanjeev Handa, *Advisor*
EMP: 8 EST: 2011
SQ FT: 2,000
SALES (est): 687.2K Privately Held
SIC: 7372 Business oriented computer software

(G-14800)
SOUTHBAY FUEL INJECTORS
566 Merrick Rd Ste 3 (11570-5547)
PHONE...............................516 442-4707
EMP: 5
SALES (est): 604.9K Privately Held
SIC: 2869 Fuels

(G-14801)
TRUEFORGE GLOBAL MCHY CORP
100 Merrick Rd Ste 208e (11570-4817)
PHONE...............................516 825-7040
Ronald E Jaggie, *President*
▲ EMP: 3
SQ FT: 2,500
SALES: 9MM Privately Held
WEB: www.trueforge.com
SIC: 3542 Forging machinery & hammers

(G-14802)
VENDING TIMES INC
55 Maple Ave Ste 304 (11570-4267)
PHONE...............................516 442-1850
Alicia Lavay, *President*
Nicolas Montano, *Vice Pres*
Frances Lavay, *Treasurer*
EMP: 11 EST: 1961
SQ FT: 4,000
SALES (est): 1.1MM Privately Held
SIC: 2721 2741 Magazines: publishing only, not printed on site; miscellaneous publishing

Rome
Oneida County

(G-14803)
ALLIANCE PAVING MATERIALS INC
846 Lawrence St (13440-8102)
PHONE...............................315 337-0795
Kimberly Ocuto, *President*
Roger Krol, *Manager*
Mark Tibbetts, *Manager*
Daniel Armstrong, *Director*
James Fahey, *Director*
EMP: 6
SQ FT: 4,000
SALES (est): 820K Privately Held
SIC: 2951 1771 Road materials, bituminous (not from refineries); driveway, parking lot & blacktop contractors

(G-14804)
BARTELL MACHINERY SYSTEMS LLC (DH)
6321 Elmer Hill Rd (13440-9325)
PHONE...............................315 336-7600
Pat Morocco, *President*
Robert Bono, *Vice Pres*
Frank Elias, *Materials Mgr*
Sue Young, *Buyer*
Rick Foland, *Engineer*
EMP: 3
SQ FT: 2,000
SALES (est): 10.2MM Privately Held
SIC: 3469 Metal stampings

▲ EMP: 140
SQ FT: 115,000
SALES (est): 31.1MM
SALES (corp-wide): 1.3B Privately Held
WEB: www.bartellmachinery.com
SIC: 3549 Metalworking machinery
HQ: Pettibone L.L.C.
   27501 Bella Vista Pkwy
   Warrenville IL 60555
   630 353-5000

(G-14805)
BAUMS CASTORINE COMPANY INC
200 Matthew St (13440-6533)
PHONE...............................315 336-8154
Fax: 315 336-3854
Charles F Mowry, *President*
Paul H Berger Jr, *Chairman*
Theodore Mowry, *Vice Pres*
Kathy Cardinal, *Manager*
▼ EMP: 7 EST: 1879
SQ FT: 22,000
SALES (est): 1.4MM Privately Held
WEB: www.baumscastorine.com
SIC: 2992 2841 Lubricating oils & greases; soap & other detergents

(G-14806)
BECK VAULT COMPANY
6648 Shank Ave (13440-9357)
PHONE...............................315 337-7590
Paul Beck, *Partner*
Peter Beck, *Partner*
EMP: 5 EST: 1946
SQ FT: 4,500
SALES: 500K Privately Held
SIC: 3272 7359 Burial vaults, concrete or precast terrazzo; equipment rental & leasing

(G-14807)
CAPTECH INDUSTRIES LLC
6 Revere Park (13440-5567)
PHONE...............................347 374-1182
Asher Wagh,
EMP: 9
SALES (est): 950K Privately Held
SIC: 3398 Brazing (hardening) of metal

(G-14808)
CATHEDRAL CORPORATION (PA)
632 Ellsworth Rd (13441-4808)
PHONE...............................315 338-0021
Fax: 315 338-5874
Marianne W Gaige, *President*
Lucie Shoen, *President*
Tom Wetjen, *Senior VP*
Donna Eychner, *Vice Pres*
Aart Knyff, *Vice Pres*
EMP: 138
SQ FT: 58,000
SALES: 33.4MM Privately Held
WEB: www.cathedralcorporation.com
SIC: 2752 Commercial printing, lithographic

(G-14809)
COLD POINT CORPORATION
Also Called: Adirondack-Aire
7500 Cold Point Dr (13440-1852)
PHONE...............................315 339-2331
Gary F Brockett, *President*
Terry L Crawford, *Vice Pres*
▲ EMP: 30
SQ FT: 18,000
SALES (est): 6.6MM Privately Held
WEB: www.coldpointcorp.com
SIC: 3585 Air conditioning condensers & condensing units

(G-14810)
ENVIROMASTER INTERNATIONAL LLC
Also Called: E M I
5780 Success Dr (13440-1769)
P.O. Box 4729, Utica (13504-4729)
PHONE...............................315 336-3716
Fax: 315 336-3981
Joe Hughes, *Engineer*
Gary Martin, *Manager*
Thomas Stull, *Info Tech Dir*
Earl C Reed,
Timothy Reed,

▲ EMP: 100
SQ FT: 52,000
SALES (est): 14MM
SALES (corp-wide): 119MM Privately Held
WEB: www.ecrinternational.com
SIC: 3585 Heating & air conditioning combination units
PA: Ecr International, Inc.
   2201 Dwyer Ave
   Utica NY 13501
   315 797-1310

(G-14811)
GOODRICH CORPORATION
104 Otis St (13441-4714)
PHONE...............................315 838-1200
Jeff Meredith, *Managing Prtnr*
Ed Marron, *Business Mgr*
Steve Croke, *Vice Pres*
Judith Knox, *Opers Mgr*
Joshua Clark, *Engineer*
EMP: 200
SALES (corp-wide): 56.1B Publicly Held
WEB: www.bfgoodrich.com
SIC: 3728 Aircraft parts & equipment
HQ: Goodrich Corporation
   4 Coliseum Ctr 2730 W
   Charlotte NC 28217
   704 423-7000

(G-14812)
HARRIS CORPORATION
474 Phoenix Dr (13441-4911)
PHONE...............................703 668-6239
Dave Melcher, *Principal*
EMP: 143
SALES (corp-wide): 7.4B Publicly Held
SIC: 3823 3812 Industrial instrmnts msrmnt display/control process variable; search & navigation equipment
PA: Harris Corporation
   1025 W Nasa Blvd
   Melbourne FL 32919
   321 727-9100

(G-14813)
HARRIS CORPORATION
Also Called: Exelis
474 Phoenix Dr (13441-4911)
PHONE...............................315 838-7000
Fax: 315 334-4964
Daniel Snell, *Branch Mgr*
Scot Tucker, *Info Tech Dir*
Liz Palumbo, *Executive*
Phil King, *Administration*
EMP: 40
SALES (corp-wide): 7.4B Publicly Held
WEB: www.ittind.com
SIC: 3625 Control equipment, electric
PA: Harris Corporation
   1025 W Nasa Blvd
   Melbourne FL 32919
   321 727-9100

(G-14814)
HCI ENGINEERING
5880 Bartlett Rd (13440-1111)
PHONE...............................315 336-3450
Jim Carrol, *General Mgr*
James Carroll, *Engineer*
Staurt Hatzinder, *Manager*
EMP: 3
SALES: 1MM Privately Held
SIC: 3829 Measuring & controlling devices

(G-14815)
HUBBARD TOOL AND DIE CORP
Rome Indus Ctr Bldg 5 (13440)
PHONE...............................315 337-7840
Fax: 315 337-7865
Eric Hubbard, *President*
Randall Hubbard, *Treasurer*
Robin Yaworski, *Manager*
EMP: 22 EST: 1957
SQ FT: 12,000
SALES: 3MM Privately Held
SIC: 3599 3545 Machine shop, jobbing & repair; precision tools, machinists'

(G-14816)
J DAVIS MANUFACTURING CO INC
Also Called: R-Tronics
222 Erie Blvd E (13440-6814)
PHONE...............................315 337-7574

Fax: 315 337-0804
Lucille Kroeger, *CEO*
Rocco Garro, *Principal*
William Abrams, *Webmaster*
EMP: 20
SQ FT: 8,000
SALES (est): 4.6MM Privately Held
WEB: www.r-tronics.com
SIC: 3496 Cable, uninsulated wire: made from purchased wire

(G-14817)
KRIS-TECH WIRE COMPANY INC (PA)
80 Otis St (13441-4712)
P.O. Box 4377 (13442-4377)
PHONE...............................315 339-5268
Fax: 315 339-5277
Jon C Brodock, *CEO*
Cheryl Ingersoll, *COO*
Chuck Dillman, *Plant Mgr*
Steven Benjamin, *Mfg Spvr*
EMP: 32
SQ FT: 50,000
SALES (est): 6.6MM Privately Held
WEB: www.kristechwire.com
SIC: 3357 Nonferrous wiredrawing & insulating

(G-14818)
L & L TRUCKING INC
1 Revere Park (13440-5568)
PHONE...............................315 339-2550
Joe Mammone, *President*
Mike Barrilo, *Sales Staff*
Bob Galbraith, *Sales Staff*
Andrew Hovest, *Sales Staff*
Dan Karley, *Sales Staff*
EMP: 20
SALES (est): 807.9K Privately Held
SIC: 2741 Miscellaneous publishing

(G-14819)
LEONARD BUS SALES INC
730 Ellsworth Rd (13441-4309)
PHONE...............................607 467-3100
Mike Leonard, *President*
EMP: 6
SALES (corp-wide): 36.8MM Privately Held
SIC: 3711 5012 Buses, all types, assembly of; buses
PA: Leonard Bus Sales, Inc.
   4 Leonard Way
   Deposit NY 13754
   607 467-3100

(G-14820)
MCINTOSH BOX & PALLET CO INC
200 6th St (13440-6069)
PHONE...............................315 446-9350
Fax: 315 337-4196
Dan Balitz, *Manager*
Vayeli Rivera, *Manager*
EMP: 26
SALES (corp-wide): 24.8MM Privately Held
WEB: www.mcintoshbox.com
SIC: 2499 2448 2441 5085 Spools, wood; wood pallets & skids; nailed wood boxes & shook; bins & containers, storage
PA: Mcintosh Box & Pallet Co., Inc.
   5864 Pyle Dr
   East Syracuse NY 13057
   315 446-9350

(G-14821)
MGS MANUFACTURING INC (PA)
Also Called: Mgs Group, The
122 Otis St (13441-4714)
P.O. Box 4259 (13442-4259)
PHONE...............................315 337-3350
Fax: 315 337-4502
Robert Johnson, *Ch of Bd*
Scott Stephan, *COO*
Tom Comiskey, *Vice Pres*
William Gurecki, *Vice Pres*
Joe Davis, *Plant Mgr*
▲ EMP: 50 EST: 1957
SQ FT: 20,000
SALES (est): 18.3MM Privately Held
SIC: 3549 Wiredrawing & fabricating machinery & equipment, ex. die

GEOGRAPHIC SECTION

(G-14822)
MSI-MOLDING SOLUTIONS INC
6247 State Route 233 (13440-1037)
PHONE..................315 736-2412
Frank Giotto, *Ch of Bd*
Thomas Bashant, *President*
Cindy Waterman, *Manager*
▲ **EMP:** 20
SALES: 2.8MM
SALES (corp-wide): 56.1MM **Privately Held**
SIC: 3089 Molding primary plastic
PA: Fiber Instrument Sales, Inc.
  161 Clear Rd
  Oriskany NY 13424
  315 736-2206

(G-14823)
NASH METALWARE CO INC
Also Called: American Metal
200 Railroad St (13440-6951)
PHONE..................315 339-5794
Fax: 315 339-0933
Donald Beebe, *Manager*
EMP: 11
SALES (corp-wide): 10.3MM **Privately Held**
SIC: 3469 5719 Household cooking & kitchen utensils, metal; kitchenware
PA: Nash Metalware Co Inc
  1 Nassau Ave
  Brooklyn NY 11222
  718 384-1500

(G-14824)
NCI GROUP INC
Metal Building Components Mbci
6168 State Route 233 (13440-1033)
P.O. Box 4141 (13442-4141)
PHONE..................315 339-1245
Fax: 315 339-6284
Chuck Glady, *Branch Mgr*
EMP: 100
SALES (corp-wide): 1.5B **Publicly Held**
SIC: 3448 3444 3441 Prefabricated metal buildings; prefabricated metal components; sheet metalwork; fabricated structural metal
HQ: Nci Group, Inc.
  10943 N Sam Huston Pkwy W
  Houston TX 77064
  281 897-7500

(G-14825)
NORAS CANDY SHOP
Also Called: Candy Land
321 N Doxtator St (13440-3121)
PHONE..................315 337-4530
Spiro Haritatos, *Owner*
EMP: 14
SALES (est): 1.2MM **Privately Held**
SIC: 2064 5441 2066 Candy & other confectionery products; candy; chocolate & cocoa products

(G-14826)
NORTEK POWDER COATING LLC
5900 Success Dr (13440-1743)
PHONE..................315 337-2339
Bunrith Lach, *Vice Pres*
Tom Serwatka, *Sales Mgr*
Borin Chea, *Mng Member*
Borin Keith,
EMP: 16
SALES (est): 3.2MM **Privately Held**
SIC: 2851 Paints & allied products

(G-14827)
NORTHROP GRUMMAN SYSTEMS CORP
Rr 26 Box N (13440)
PHONE..................315 336-0500
Steve Maiser, *Manager*
EMP: 25 **Publicly Held**
WEB: www.logicon.com
SIC: 7372 Operating systems computer software
HQ: Northrop Grumman Systems Corporation
  2980 Fairview Park Dr
  Falls Church VA 22042
  703 280-2900

(G-14828)
OLIVEPLASTE LLC
1 Olive Grove St (13441-4815)
PHONE..................315 356-2670
Tim Morrison, *Manager*
Rui Abelho,
EMP: 24
SQ FT: 5,600
SALES (est): 1.5MM **Privately Held**
SIC: 3221 Bottles for packing, bottling & canning: glass

(G-14829)
OMEGA WIRE INC
900 Railroad St (13440-6900)
PHONE..................315 337-4300
James A Spargo IV, *Manager*
EMP: 50
SQ FT: 50,980
SALES (corp-wide): 442.1MM **Privately Held**
WEB: www.omegawire.com
SIC: 3366 Copper foundries
HQ: Omega Wire, Inc.
  12 Masonic Ave
  Camden NY 13316
  315 245-3800

(G-14830)
PROFESSIONAL TECHNOLOGY INC
Also Called: Professional Technologies
5433 Lowell Rd (13440-7815)
PHONE..................315 337-4156
John Puleo, *President*
EMP: 5
SALES (est): 540K **Privately Held**
SIC: 3651 1731 Speaker systems; communications specialization

(G-14831)
R&S STEEL LLC
412 Canal St (13440-6835)
PHONE..................315 281-0123
Fax: 315 281-0124
Paul Raulli, *Mng Member*
Patty Huey, *Manager*
Richie T Raulli,
Thomas Raulli,
EMP: 21
SQ FT: 5,600
SALES (est): 3.9MM **Privately Held**
SIC: 3441 Fabricated structural metal

(G-14832)
RAULLI IRON WORKS INC
133 Mill St (13440-6945)
PHONE..................315 337-8070
Fax: 315 337-3960
Agostino Raulli, *President*
Mark Raulli, *Vice Pres*
EMP: 10 **EST:** 1938
SQ FT: 3,600
SALES: 900K **Privately Held**
WEB: www.raulliandsonsincornamental.com
SIC: 3446 Architectural metalwork

(G-14833)
ROME SIGN & DISPLAY CO
510 Erie Blvd W (13440-4806)
PHONE..................315 336-0550
Randall Denton, *President*
Terrance Denton, *Vice Pres*
EMP: 7
SQ FT: 1,000
SALES (est): 906.7K **Privately Held**
SIC: 3993 Signs, not made in custom sign painting shops

(G-14834)
ROME SPECIALTY COMPANY INC
Also Called: Rosco Div
501 W Embargo St (13440-4061)
P.O. Box 109 (13442-0109)
PHONE..................315 337-8200
Fax: 315 339-2523
Judith Kiernan, *President*
Michael Bleem, *Finance Dir*
John Butts, *Supervisor*
▲ **EMP:** 20 **EST:** 1926
SQ FT: 35,000
SALES (est): 2MM **Privately Held**
WEB: www.roscoinc.com
SIC: 3949 Fishing equipment; fishing tackle, general

(G-14835)
RTD MANUFACTURING INC
6273 State Route 233 (13440-1037)
PHONE..................315 337-3151
Brian P Getbehead, *President*
Robert Getbehead, *Vice Pres*
Sandra Vanslyke, *Office Mgr*
Mike Waterman, *Executive*
Iva S Getbehead, *Admin Sec*
EMP: 7
SQ FT: 3,500
SALES (est): 600K **Privately Held**
WEB: www.rtdmfg.com
SIC: 3599 Machine shop, jobbing & repair

(G-14836)
SERWAY BROS INC (PA)
Also Called: Serway Cabinet Trends
Plant 2 Rome Indus Ctr (13440)
PHONE..................315 337-0601
Fax: 315 336-0169
Christine N Serway, *Ch of Bd*
Dorothy Alexander, *Manager*
James Pacific, *Director*
Sophia Pelose, *Admin Sec*
EMP: 22
SQ FT: 20,800
SALES (est): 2.3MM **Privately Held**
WEB: www.serway.com
SIC: 2541 5211 3648 5719 Counters or counter display cases, wood; cabinets, kitchen; lighting fixtures, except electric: residential; lighting fixtures; wood kitchen cabinets

(G-14837)
TIPS & DIES INC
505 Rome Industrial Park (13440-6948)
PHONE..................315 337-4161
Randall Hubbard, *President*
Gary Johnson, *Sales Staff*
Peter Scribner, *Sales Staff*
EMP: 12
SALES: 2.3MM **Privately Held**
WEB: www.tipsanddies.com
SIC: 3544 Special dies & tools

(G-14838)
TONYS ORNAMENTAL IR WORKS INC
6757 Martin St (13440-7106)
P.O. Box 4425 (13442-4425)
PHONE..................315 337-3730
Fax: 315 337-0213
Anthony J Pettinelli Jr, *President*
Toni Olejarczyk, *Corp Secy*
EMP: 20
SQ FT: 13,800
SALES (est): 3.4MM **Privately Held**
SIC: 3449 3446 Miscellaneous metalwork; architectural metalwork

(G-14839)
VARFLEX CORPORATION
512 W Court St (13440-4000)
P.O. Box 551 (13442-0551)
PHONE..................315 336-4400
Fax: 315 336-0005
Daniel J Burgdorf, *President*
William L Griffin, *Vice Pres*
Christine Ruben, *Safety Mgr*
Charles J Schoff, *Treasurer*
Lisa Dombrowski, *Sales Associate*
EMP: 150 **EST:** 1924
SQ FT: 144,000
SALES (est): 10MM **Privately Held**
WEB: www.varflex.com
SIC: 3644 Insulators & insulation materials, electrical

(G-14840)
WORTHINGTON INDUSTRIES INC
530 Henry St (13440-5639)
PHONE..................315 336-5500
EMP: 72
SALES (corp-wide): 2.8B **Publicly Held**
SIC: 3316 Strip steel, cold-rolled: from purchased hot-rolled
PA: Worthington Industries, Inc.
  200 W Wilson Bridge Rd
  Worthington OH 43085
  614 438-3210

Romulus
Seneca County

(G-14841)
COBBLESTONE FRM WINERY VINYRD
5102 State Route 89 (14541-9779)
PHONE..................315 549-1004
Jennifer Clark, *Principal*
EMP: 10
SALES (est): 840.1K **Privately Held**
SIC: 2084 Wines, brandy & brandy spirits

(G-14842)
SCHRADER MEAT MARKET
1937 Summerville Rd (14541-9800)
PHONE..................607 869-6328
Keith Schrader, *Owner*
EMP: 19
SALES: 600K **Privately Held**
SIC: 3421 2013 Table & food cutlery, including butchers'; sausages & other prepared meats

(G-14843)
SOUTH SENECA VINYL LLC
1585 Yale Farm Rd (14541-9761)
PHONE..................315 585-6050
Nelson Sensenig,
EMP: 9
SQ FT: 5,000
SALES (est): 1.1MM **Privately Held**
SIC: 3211 Window glass, clear & colored

(G-14844)
SWEDISH HILL VINEYARD INC
Also Called: Swedish Hill Winery
4565 State Route 414 (14541-9769)
PHONE..................607 403-0029
Fax: 315 549-8477
David Peterson, *CEO*
Richard Peterson, *President*
Cynthia Peterson, *Vice Pres*
Jarred Ingram, *Manager*
Marissa Taylor, *Manager*
EMP: 70
SALES: 6MM **Privately Held**
SIC: 2084 0721 Wines; vines, cultivation of

Ronkonkoma
Suffolk County

(G-14845)
A A TECHNOLOGY INC
101 Trade Zone Dr (11779-7363)
PHONE..................631 913-0400
Fax: 631 563-3994
Henry Tang, *CEO*
Frank Rosselli, *Vice Pres*
James Stapleton, *Manager*
James Unser, *QC Mgr*
Roberta Besso, *Office Mgr*
◆ **EMP:** 30
SQ FT: 15,700
SALES (est): 8.3MM **Privately Held**
SIC: 3672 Printed circuit boards

(G-14846)
ACCELA INC
100 Comac St Ste 2 (11779-6928)
PHONE..................631 563-5005
Daryl Blowes, *General Mgr*
EMP: 10
SALES (corp-wide): 80MM **Privately Held**
SIC: 7372 Prepackaged software
PA: Accela, Inc.
  2633 Camino Ramon Ste 500
  San Ramon CA 94583
  925 659-3200

Ronkonkoma - Suffolk County (G-14847)

(G-14847)
ACCENT LABEL & TAG CO INC (PA)
348 Woodlawn Ave (11779-5055)
PHONE.................................631 244-7066
Fax: 631 244-7108
Larry Gutman, *President*
EMP: 6
SALES (est): 592.2K **Privately Held**
WEB: www.accentlabelandtag.com
SIC: 2679 7336 Labels, paper: made from purchased material; graphic arts & related design

(G-14848)
ACE CANVAS & TENT CORP
155 Raynor Ave (11779-6666)
PHONE.................................631 648-0614
Fax: 631 981-4430
Vincent Cardillo, *Vice Pres*
▲ EMP: 10 EST: 1954
SQ FT: 5,500
SALES (est): 1.5MM **Privately Held**
SIC: 3081 2394 7359 Vinyl film & sheet; canvas & related products; tent & tarpaulin rental

(G-14849)
ACME INDUSTRIES OF W BABYLON
125 Gary Way Ste 2 (11779-6576)
PHONE.................................631 737-5231
John Landrio, *President*
EMP: 10
SQ FT: 3,000
SALES (est): 1.7MM **Privately Held**
SIC: 3599 7389 Machine shop, jobbing & repair; grinding, precision: commercial or industrial

(G-14850)
ADAPTIVE MFG TECH INC
181 Remington Blvd (11779-6911)
PHONE.................................631 580-5400
Terence Larocca, *Ch of Bd*
EMP: 32
SQ FT: 18,000
SALES (est): 7.6MM **Privately Held**
WEB: www.amtautomation.com
SIC: 3542 3599 Machine tools, metal forming type; custom machinery

(G-14851)
ADDMM LLC
4155 Veterans Memorial Hw (11779-6063)
PHONE.................................631 913-4400
John Masterson, *CFO*
Chung Lam, *Mng Member*
Randy Bonella,
EMP: 10
SQ FT: 1,700
SALES (est): 650K **Privately Held**
SIC: 3674 Memories, solid state

(G-14852)
ADVANCE MICRO POWER CORP
2190 Smithtown Ave (11779-7355)
PHONE.................................631 471-6157
Jasbir Mahajan, *President*
▲ EMP: 15
SQ FT: 14,000
SALES (est): 1.6MM **Privately Held**
SIC: 3672 Printed circuit boards

(G-14853)
ADVANCED LAMP COATINGS CORP
2165 5th Ave (11779-6908)
PHONE.................................631 585-5505
Michael Johnson, *President*
Luisa Flores, *Production*
James Silvestri, *CFO*
Gabrielle Russell, *Manager*
EMP: 27
SQ FT: 8,000
SALES (est): 4.2MM **Privately Held**
WEB: advancedlampcoatings.com
SIC: 3479 Coating or wrapping steel pipe

(G-14854)
ADVANCED MANUFACTURING SVC INC
100 13th Ave Ste 2 (11779-6820)
PHONE.................................631 676-5210
John Nucatola, *President*
Laura Patanella, *Buyer*
Alan Kaufman, *Purchasing*
EMP: 28
SALES (est): 6.5MM **Privately Held**
SIC: 3672 Printed circuit boards

(G-14855)
ADVANCED PHOTONICS INC
151 Trade Zone Dr (11779-7384)
PHONE.................................631 471-3693
Fax: 631 471-3750
Robert Turner, *President*
Richard Turner, *Vice Pres*
Jack Raybin, *CFO*
EMP: 14
SQ FT: 5,000
SALES: 1.4MM **Privately Held**
WEB: www.advancedphotonicsusa.com
SIC: 3699 5084 Laser systems & equipment; industrial machinery & equipment

(G-14856)
AERO-DATA METAL CRAFTERS INC
2085 5th Ave (11779-6903)
PHONE.................................631 471-7733
Fax: 631 471-9161
Robert De Luca, *President*
David Rubinstein, *Project Mgr*
Andrea Savino, *Human Res Mgr*
Ed Fiance, *Sales Executive*
Sarah Marshall, *Manager*
EMP: 110
SQ FT: 100,000
SALES (est): 23.3MM **Privately Held**
WEB: www.metal-crafters.com
SIC: 3444 3446 3443 3441 Sheet metal specialties, not stamped; architectural metalwork; fabricated plate work (boiler shop); fabricated structural metal; cold finishing of steel shapes

(G-14857)
AIR CRAFTERS INC
2085 5th Ave (11779-6903)
PHONE.................................631 471-7788
Fax: 631 471-9161
Robert Deluca, *President*
Ed Fiance, *General Mgr*
Michael Hennessey, *Vice Pres*
Chris Behr, *Manager*
William Mabanta, *Admin Sec*
EMP: 105
SQ FT: 40,000
SALES: 12MM **Privately Held**
WEB: www.air-crafters.com
SIC: 2542 5085 3625 3564 Fixtures, office: except wood; clean room supplies; relays & industrial controls; blowers & fans

(G-14858)
AKSHAR EXTRACTS INC
59 Remington Blvd (11779-6954)
PHONE.................................631 588-9727
Jay Patel, *President*
Nat Patel, *Vice Pres*
Dee Patel, *Treasurer*
▲ EMP: 5
SQ FT: 3,000
SALES: 500K **Privately Held**
WEB: www.pureextracts.com
SIC: 2836 Extracts

(G-14859)
ALKEN INDUSTRIES INC
2175 5th Ave (11779-6217)
PHONE.................................631 467-2000
Fax: 631 467-2877
Kimberly Senior, *President*
Tricia Voigt, *General Mgr*
Tami Senior-Humanitizki, *Vice Pres*
Amanda Cartwright, *Purch Mgr*
Cynthia Lang, *Purch Agent*
EMP: 70
SQ FT: 52,000
SALES (est): 24.7MM **Privately Held**
WEB: www.alkenind.com
SIC: 3728 Aircraft parts & equipment

(G-14860)
ALL AROUND SPIRAL INC
10 Fleetwood Ct (11779-6907)
PHONE.................................631 588-0220
Richard Kern, *Ch of Bd*
EMP: 9
SALES (est): 1.2MM **Privately Held**
SIC: 3444 Sheet metalwork

(G-14861)
ALL PACKAGING MCHY & SUPS CORP
90 13th Ave Unit 11 (11779-6818)
PHONE.................................631 588-7310
Fax: 631 467-4690
Albert Bolla, *President*
Joel Busel, *Vice Pres*
Samul Posner, *Controller*
Eric Wassing, *Controller*
Lynn Miranda, *Comms Mgr*
EMP: 10
SQ FT: 10,000
SALES: 2.7MM
SALES (corp-wide): 20.6MM **Privately Held**
WEB: www.triopackaging.com
SIC: 3565 Packaging machinery
PA: Trio Packaging Corp.
    90 13th Ave Unit 11
    Ronkonkoma NY 11779
    631 588-0800

(G-14862)
ALL PHASES ASP & LDSCPG DSGN
60 18th Ave (11779-6204)
PHONE.................................631 588-1372
Vincent Schlosser, *Principal*
EMP: 10
SALES (est): 886.8K **Privately Held**
SIC: 2951 Asphalt paving mixtures & blocks

(G-14863)
ALLIANT TCHSYSTEMS OPRTONS LLC
77 Raynor Ave (11779-6649)
PHONE.................................631 737-6100
Robert Bakos, *Vice Pres*
John Tilleli, *Finance*
EMP: 20
SALES (corp-wide): 6.8B **Publicly Held**
WEB: www.mrcwdc.com
SIC: 3721 Research & development on aircraft by the manufacturer
HQ: Alliant Techsystems Operations Llc
    4700 Nathan Ln N
    Plymouth MN 55442

(G-14864)
ALLURE METAL WORKS INC
71 Hoffman Ln (11749-5007)
PHONE.................................631 588-0220
Jillian Guido, *Principal*
EMP: 10
SALES (est): 1.5MM **Privately Held**
SIC: 3444 1711 Sheet metalwork; plumbing, heating, air-conditioning contractors

(G-14865)
ALPHABET HOLDING COMPANY INC (HQ)
2100 Smithtown Ave (11779-7347)
PHONE.................................631 200-2000
Jeffrey A Nagel, *CEO*
Sandra Horbach, *President*
Anita Balaji, *Vice Pres*
Dipak Golechha, *CFO*
Harvey Kamil, *CFO*
EMP: 23
SALES: 3.2B
SALES (corp-wide): 3B **Publicly Held**
SIC: 2833 5122 5499 5961 Vitamins, natural or synthetic: bulk, uncompounded; vitamins & minerals; health & dietetic food stores; vitamin food stores; health foods; dietetic foods; pharmaceuticals, mail order
PA: The Carlyle Group L P
    1001 Pennsylvania Ave Nw 220s
    Washington DC 20004
    202 729-5626

(G-14866)
ALROD ASSOCIATES INC
710 Union Pkwy Ste 9 (11779-7428)
PHONE.................................631 981-2193
Fax: 631 981-2197
Evan Alrod, *President*
Peggy Axelrod, *Vice Pres*
Evan Axelrod, *Treasurer*
EMP: 10
SQ FT: 6,000
SALES (est): 1.3MM **Privately Held**
SIC: 2541 2542 5046 Store fixtures, wood; fixtures, store: except wood; store fixtures

(G-14867)
ALTAQUIP LLC
200 13th Ave Unit 6 (11779-6815)
PHONE.................................631 580-4740
EMP: 8
SALES (corp-wide): 194.6B **Publicly Held**
SIC: 3699 Mfg Electrical Equipment/Supplies
HQ: Altaquip Llc
    100 Production Dr
    Harrison OH 45030
    513 674-6464

(G-14868)
AMERICAN BOTTLING COMPANY
Also Called: Snapple Distributors
2004 Orville Dr N (11779-7645)
PHONE.................................516 714-0002
Ray Russo, *Manager*
EMP: 19
SALES (corp-wide): 6.2B **Publicly Held**
SIC: 2086 Bottled & canned soft drinks
HQ: The American Bottling Company
    5301 Legacy Dr
    Plano TX 75024

(G-14869)
AMERICAN QUALITY EMBROIDERY (PA)
740 Koehler Ave (11779-7406)
PHONE.................................631 467-3200
Fax: 631 467-0273
Robert Kalinowski, *President*
EMP: 1
SQ FT: 1,600
SALES (est): 17.8MM **Privately Held**
SIC: 2284 2395 Embroidery thread; embroidery products, except schiffli machine

(G-14870)
AMRON ELECTRONICS INC
160 Gary Way (11779-6509)
PHONE.................................631 737-1234
Rick Foora, *CEO*
James Flora, *Vice Pres*
EMP: 50
SALES (est): 2.9MM **Privately Held**
SIC: 3679 Commutators, electronic

(G-14871)
APOLLO DISPLAY TECH CORP (PA)
87 Raynor Ave Ste 1 (11779-6667)
PHONE.................................631 580-4360
Fax: 631 580-4370
Bernhard Staller, *President*
Werner Schubert, *Managing Dir*
Joanne Sottile, *Senior VP*
Jim Rossi, *Opers Staff*
Adam Larkinith, *Engineer*
▲ EMP: 35
SQ FT: 15,000
SALES (est): 5.9MM **Privately Held**
WEB: www.apollodisplays.com
SIC: 3679 5065 Liquid crystal displays (LCD); electronic parts & equipment

(G-14872)
ARTISAN MACHINING INC
49 Remington Blvd (11779-6909)
PHONE.................................631 589-1416
John Caccavale, *President*
EMP: 7
SALES (est): 800K **Privately Held**
WEB: www.artisanmachining.com
SIC: 3599 Machine shop, jobbing & repair

(G-14873)
ASSOCIATED MATERIALS LLC
Also Called: Alside Supply Center
1830 Lakeland Ave (11779-7404)
PHONE.................................631 467-4535
Debbie Gittleman, *Site Mgr*
William Prush, *Manager*
EMP: 10 **Privately Held**
WEB: www.associatedmaterials.com

GEOGRAPHIC SECTION

Ronkonkoma - Suffolk County (G-14899)

SIC: 3089 Plastic hardware & building products
HQ: Associated Materials, Llc
3773 State Rd
Cuyahoga Falls OH 44223
330 929-1811

(G-14874)
ATK GASL INC
77 Raynor Ave (11779-6649)
PHONE.................................631 737-6100
John Tilleli, *Principal*
Vladimir Balepin, *Research*
Ralph Woelfel, *Engineer*
Richard Stone, *Manager*
Tara Calomino, *Info Tech Mgr*
EMP: 19
SALES (est): 3.1MM **Privately Held**
SIC: 3721 Research & development on aircraft by the manufacturer

(G-14875)
AZTEC INDUSTRIES INC
200 13th Ave Unit 5 (11779-6815)
PHONE.................................631 585-1331
Phil Del Giudice, *President*
EMP: 6
SQ FT: 2,500
SALES: 500K **Privately Held**
SIC: 2522 Panel systems & partitions, office: except wood

(G-14876)
B & B PRECISION COMPONENTS INC
301 Christopher St # 303 (11779-6922)
PHONE.................................631 273-3321
Fax: 631 273-3936
Lucille Bricker, *President*
August Bricker, *COO*
Kathryn Richichi, *Manager*
EMP: 9
SQ FT: 12,000
SALES (est): 1.4MM **Privately Held**
WEB: www.bbprecisioncomponents.com
SIC: 3728 Aircraft parts & equipment

(G-14877)
B H AIRCRAFT COMPANY INC (PA)
2230 Smithtown Ave (11779-7329)
PHONE.................................631 580-9747
Vincent E Kearns, *Ch of Bd*
Daniel Kearns, *President*
Sebastian F Digiacomo, *Principal*
Dan Fugua, *Principal*
Paul Goggi, *Principal*
EMP: 90 **EST:** 1933
SQ FT: 100,000
SALES (est): 16.1MM **Privately Held**
WEB: www.bhaircraft.com
SIC: 3724 Aircraft engines & engine parts

(G-14878)
BANNER METALCRAFT INC
300 Trade Zone Dr (11779-7345)
PHONE.................................631 563-7303
Fax: 631 563-7655
Kenneth R Bednar, *President*
Nancy E Bednar, *Corp Secy*
Richard Martin, *Foreman/Supr*
Linda Herzing, *Office Mgr*
EMP: 70
SQ FT: 32,000
SALES: 12.1MM **Privately Held**
WEB: www.bannermetalcraft.com
SIC: 3444 Sheet metalwork

(G-14879)
BECKER ELECTRONICS INC
50 Alexander Ct Ste 2 (11779-6568)
PHONE.................................631 619-9100
Fax: 631 699-0138
David M Sosnow, *CEO*
Sharon Becker, *Vice Pres*
Kathleen Fauteux, *Purch Mgr*
Patrick Spagnuolo, *Treasurer*
Glenn Clifford, *Manager*
EMP: 80
SQ FT: 14,000
SALES: 12MM **Privately Held**
WEB: www.beckerelectronicsinc.com
SIC: 3679 5065 Harness assemblies for electronic use; wire or cable; electronic parts & equipment

(G-14880)
BOBLEY-HARMANN CORPORATION
Also Called: Gift Valleys.com
200 Trade Zone Dr Unit 2 (11779-7359)
PHONE.................................516 433-3800
Mark Bobley, *President*
Barbara Monks, *Opers Mgr*
Bob Hagenburger, *Executive*
▲ **EMP:** 8
SQ FT: 500
SALES (est): 860K **Privately Held**
WEB: www.bobley.com
SIC: 2731 2759 Book publishing; promotional printing

(G-14881)
BROADWAY NEON SIGN CORP
Also Called: Broadway National
1900 Ocean Ave (11779-6520)
PHONE.................................908 241-4177
William Paparella, *President*
Joy Sparano, *Manager*
Phil Varca, *Manager*
EMP: 18
SQ FT: 50,000
SALES (est): 3MM **Privately Held**
WEB: www.broadwaynational.com
SIC: 3993 3444 2431 2394 Neon signs; sheet metalwork; millwork; canvas & related products

(G-14882)
C TO C DESIGN & PRINT INC
1850 Pond Rd Unit B (11779-7210)
PHONE.................................631 885-4020
Anthony Aceto, *Ch of Bd*
EMP: 10
SALES (est): 1.3MM **Privately Held**
SIC: 2752 Commercial printing, lithographic

(G-14883)
CALCHEM CORPORATION (PA)
2001 Ocean Ave (11779-6500)
P.O. Box 4258, Huntington (11743-0777)
PHONE.................................631 423-5696
John H Chen, *President*
Molly Chen, *Exec VP*
▲ **EMP:** 7
SQ FT: 12,000
SALES (est): 1.9MM **Privately Held**
WEB: www.calchemcorp.com
SIC: 2893 Printing ink

(G-14884)
CANFIELD AEROSPACE & MAR INC
90 Remington Blvd (11779-6910)
PHONE.................................631 648-1050
Lynn Zaun, *President*
Raymond Zaun, *General Mgr*
Laura Holm, *Executive*
Michael Zaun, *Administration*
EMP: 20 **EST:** 2000
SALES (est): 2.6MM **Privately Held**
WEB: www.canfieldam.com
SIC: 3728 Aircraft parts & equipment

(G-14885)
CAROLINA PRECISION PLAS LLC
Also Called: Cpp Global
115 Comac St (11779-6931)
PHONE.................................631 981-0743
Fax: 631 585-1405
EMP: 94
SALES (corp-wide): 70.3MM **Privately Held**
SIC: 3089 Injection molding of plastics
PA: Carolina Precision Plastics Llc
405 Commerce Pl
Asheboro NC 27203
336 498-2654

(G-14886)
CEDAR WEST INC (PA)
1700 Ocean Ave Ste 1 (11779-6570)
PHONE.................................631 467-1444
Joanne D Herman, *President*
Michael Clark, *Vice Pres*
Robert Herman, *Vice Pres*
Gloria J Smalley, *CFO*
EMP: 2

SALES (est): 3.6MM **Privately Held**
WEB: www.cedarwest.com
SIC: 2752 Commercial printing, offset

(G-14887)
CHOCOLATE BY DESIGN INC
700 Union Pkwy Ste 4 (11779-7427)
PHONE.................................631 737-0082
Fax: 631 737-0188
Richard Motlin, *President*
Ellen Motlin, *Corp Secy*
EMP: 5 **EST:** 1979
SQ FT: 5,000
SALES (est): 380K **Privately Held**
WEB: www.chocolatebydesigninc.com
SIC: 2066 Chocolate & cocoa products

(G-14888)
COPY X/PRESS LTD
Also Called: Ocean Printing
700 Union Pkwy Ste 5 (11779-7427)
PHONE.................................631 585-2200
Fax: 631 585-0071
John Harkins, *President*
Jeanette Johnston, *Prdtn Mgr*
Terri Bligh, *Human Resources*
EMP: 63
SQ FT: 30,000
SALES (est): 9.3MM **Privately Held**
WEB: www.oceanprinting.com
SIC: 2759 Commercial printing

(G-14889)
CORNING RUBBER COMPANY INC
Also Called: Corning Wax
1744 Julia Goldbach Ave (11779-6413)
PHONE.................................631 738-0041
Fax: 631 738-0045
Robert Schiemel, *President*
Claudio Acquafredda, *Vice Pres*
▲ **EMP:** 14 **EST:** 1946
SQ FT: 10,000
SALES (est): 1.2MM **Privately Held**
WEB: www.corningwax.com
SIC: 3843 Wax, dental

(G-14890)
COSMOPOLITAN CABINET COMPANY
40 Fleetwood Ct Ste 1 (11779-6944)
P.O. Box 2797, North Babylon (11703-0797)
PHONE.................................631 467-4960
Fax: 631 467-0869
James M Harvell, *CEO*
EMP: 8 **EST:** 2000
SALES (est): 670K **Privately Held**
SIC: 2434 Wood kitchen cabinets

(G-14891)
CRYSTALONICS INC
2805 Veterans Mem Hwy 14 (11779-7680)
PHONE.................................631 981-6140
Paul Weinstein, *President*
Brian Gomes, *Treasurer*
Joseph Plescia, *Treasurer*
Fred Boening, *Controller*
EMP: 12
SQ FT: 14,000
SALES (est): 1.5MM **Privately Held**
WEB: www.crystalonics.com
SIC: 3674 Semiconductors & related devices; hybrid integrated circuits; transistors

(G-14892)
DAK MICA AND WOOD PRODUCTS
Also Called: Coronet Kitchen & Bath
2147 5th Ave (11779-6908)
PHONE.................................631 467-0749
Fax: 631 467-6137
David Kaplan, *President*
Micheline Auchenbaugh, *Office Mgr*
EMP: 5
SQ FT: 5,800
SALES: 1MM **Privately Held**
SIC: 2434 5031 1751 Wood kitchen cabinets; kitchen cabinets; cabinet & finish carpentry

(G-14893)
DELLA SYSTEMS INC
951 S 2nd St (11779-7203)
PHONE.................................631 580-0010
Fax: 631 567-0040
John Della Croce, *President*
John Odella, *Purch Agent*
Melissa Gordon, *Purchasing*
EMP: 14
SQ FT: 3,000
SALES (est): 2.2MM **Privately Held**
WEB: www.dellasystems.com
SIC: 3672 8711 Printed circuit boards; engineering services

(G-14894)
DESIGNS FOR VISION INC
760 Koehler Ave (11779-7405)
PHONE.................................631 585-3300
Fax: 631 585-3404
Richard Feinbloom, *Chairman*
John Walsh, *COO*
Judy Bowers, *Purchasing*
Tracy Mayer, *Design Engr Mgr*
Tom Mackiewicz, *Engineer*
▲ **EMP:** 130 **EST:** 1961
SQ FT: 30,000
SALES (est): 27.3MM **Privately Held**
WEB: www.designsforvision.com
SIC: 3841 3851 Surgical & medical instruments; ophthalmic goods

(G-14895)
DYNAMIC LABORATORIES INC
Also Called: Dynamic Labs
30 Haynes Ct (11779-7220)
PHONE.................................631 231-7474
David Beauchamp, *President*
Steven Zwerman, *Vice Pres*
Rick Beauchamp, *Production*
Chris Cabal, *Engineer*
▲ **EMP:** 38
SQ FT: 18,000
SALES: 8.7MM **Privately Held**
SIC: 3827 5049 Optical instruments & lenses; optical goods

(G-14896)
EAST/WEST INDUSTRIES INC
80 13th Ave (11779-6812)
PHONE.................................631 981-5900
Fax: 631 981-5990
Teresa Ferraro, *President*
Mary Spinosa, *Corp Secy*
Joseph Spinosa, *Vice Pres*
Frank Schieferstein, *VP Finance*
Patricia Romano, *Admin Asst*
EMP: 45
SQ FT: 38,000
SALES (est): 10MM **Privately Held**
WEB: www.eastwestindustries.com
SIC: 3728 2531 Seat ejector devices, aircraft; oxygen systems, aircraft; seats, aircraft

(G-14897)
EASTERN STOREFRONTS & MTLS INC
1739 Julia Goldbach Ave (11779-6412)
P.O. Box 431, Bohemia (11716-0431)
PHONE.................................631 471-7065
Timothy Dittmeier, *Ch of Bd*
EMP: 14
SALES (est): 2.3MM **Privately Held**
SIC: 3442 Store fronts, prefabricated, metal

(G-14898)
EASTLAND ELECTRONICS CO INC
700 Union Pkwy Ste 9 (11779-7427)
PHONE.................................631 580-3800
William Mercurio, *President*
Prem Dally, *Admin Asst*
▲ **EMP:** 7
SQ FT: 2,000
SALES (est): 1.1MM **Privately Held**
WEB: www.eastlandny.com
SIC: 3679 Electronic circuits

(G-14899)
EXECUTIVE MIRROR DOORS INC
1 Comac Loop Unit 7 (11779-6816)
PHONE.................................631 234-1090

Ronkonkoma - Suffolk County (G-14900)

Fax: 631 234-6939
Robert Cozzie, *President*
Carol Cozzie, *Vice Pres*
EMP: 7
SQ FT: 5,400
SALES (est): 720K Privately Held
WEB: www.executivemirror.com
SIC: 3231 5211 5085 Doors, glass: made from purchased glass; door & window products; industrial supplies

(G-14900)
FIRST IMPRESSIONS FINISHING
132 Remington Blvd (11779-6912)
PHONE......................................631 467-2244
Fax: 631 467-0368
Scott Shapiro, *President*
Laura Shapiro, *Vice Pres*
EMP: 6
SQ FT: 4,000
SALES: 351.9K Privately Held
SIC: 3471 Finishing, metals or formed products

(G-14901)
FORMATIX CORP
9 Colt Ct (11779-6949)
PHONE......................................631 467-3399
Radjesh Guptar, *CEO*
Carmine Russo, *Accountant*
Aviska Dabiveen, *Bookkeeper*
EMP: 20
SALES (est): 3.7MM Privately Held
SIC: 3089 Blister or bubble formed packaging, plastic

(G-14902)
FOUR PAWS PRODUCTS LTD
3125 Vtrans Mem Hwy Ste 1 (11779-7644)
PHONE......................................631 436-7421
Allen Simon, *President*
Barry Askin, *Vice Pres*
Hector Melgar, *Purchasing*
Ray Gallagher, *CFO*
Haley Birke, *Human Res Mgr*
▲ EMP: 85 EST: 1970
SQ FT: 50,000
SALES (est): 8.5MM
SALES (corp-wide): 1.6B Publicly Held
WEB: www.fourpaws.com
SIC: 3999 2844 Pet supplies; toilet preparations
PA: Central Garden & Pet Company
    1340 Treat Blvd Ste 600
    Walnut Creek CA 94597
    925 948-4000

(G-14903)
GENERAL CUTTING INC
2111 9th Ave (11779-6280)
PHONE......................................631 580-5011
Fax: 631 585-3712
Ralph Viteritti, *President*
EMP: 12
SQ FT: 8,000
SALES (est): 860K Privately Held
SIC: 3599 Machine shop, jobbing & repair

(G-14904)
GLIPTONE MANUFACTURING INC
Also Called: Camco
1740 Julia Goldbach Ave (11779-6409)
PHONE......................................631 285-7250
Rocco Caporaso Jr, *President*
▲ EMP: 10
SQ FT: 6,500
SALES (est): 1.7MM Privately Held
WEB: www.gliptone.com
SIC: 2842 Specialty cleaning preparations; automobile polish

(G-14905)
GLOBAL ENTITY MEDIA INC
2090 5th Ave Ste 2 (11779-6958)
PHONE......................................631 580-7772
Michael J Cutino, *Principal*
EMP: 5
SALES (est): 600.5K Privately Held
SIC: 2721 Periodicals: publishing only

(G-14906)
GOT POWER INC
5 Campus Ln (11779-1924)
PHONE......................................631 767-9493
Luis Duarte, *Owner*

EMP: 5
SALES: 100K Privately Held
SIC: 3621 Motors & generators

(G-14907)
H & H TECHNOLOGIES INC
10 Colt Ct (11779-6948)
PHONE......................................631 567-3526
Henry J Kleitsch, *President*
Georgette Adora, *Controller*
David Puckett, *Manager*
Frank Dimato, *Supervisor*
EMP: 40
SQ FT: 14,000
SALES (est): 9MM Privately Held
WEB: www.hhtech.com
SIC: 3599 Machine shop, jobbing & repair

(G-14908)
H A GUDEN COMPANY INC
99 Raynor Ave (11779-6634)
PHONE......................................631 737-2900
Fax: 631 737-2933
Paul A Guden, *President*
Kirby D Moyers, *Vice Pres*
Mary L Schwarz, *Admin Sec*
▲ EMP: 25
SQ FT: 20,000
SALES: 8.5MM Privately Held
SIC: 3429 5072 Manufactured hardware (general); hardware

(G-14909)
HADFIELD INC
840 S 2nd St (11779-7202)
PHONE......................................631 981-4314
Charles Hadfield, *President*
EMP: 10
SALES (est): 980K Privately Held
SIC: 7692 1799 Welding repair; welding on site

(G-14910)
HASTINGS TILE & BATH INC (PA)
711 Koehler Ave Ste 8 (11779-7410)
PHONE......................................516 379-3500
Lee Kohrman, *President*
Michael Homola, *President*
Richard Kucera, *Corp Secy*
Janet Allison, *Purch Mgr*
Charlene Hymes, *Accounting Mgr*
▲ EMP: 18
SQ FT: 36,000
SALES: 5.4MM Privately Held
WEB: www.hastingstilebath.com
SIC: 3253 Ceramic wall & floor tile

(G-14911)
IMPALA PRESS LTD
931 S 2nd St (11779-7203)
PHONE......................................631 588-4262
Fax: 631 588-4029
Peter Wolf, *President*
EMP: 8
SQ FT: 6,000
SALES (est): 850K Privately Held
WEB: www.impalapress.com
SIC: 2752 Commercial printing, lithographic

(G-14912)
INGENIOUS DESIGNS LLC
Also Called: Idl
2060 9th Ave (11779-6253)
PHONE......................................631 254-3376
Joy Mangano, *Ch of Bd*
Ronni Fauci, *Vice Pres*
Alan Mandell, *Finance*
◆ EMP: 110
SQ FT: 63,000
SALES (est): 36.7MM
SALES (corp-wide): 3.6B Publicly Held
WEB: www.ingeniousdesigns.com
SIC: 2392 5199 3089 5099 Mops, floor & dust; broom, mop & paint handles; plastic containers, except foam; containers: glass, metal or plastic
PA: Hsn, Inc.
    1 Hsn Dr
    Saint Petersburg FL 33729
    727 872-1000

(G-14913)
INSTRUMENTS FOR INDUSTRY INC
Also Called: I F I
903 S 2nd St (11779-7201)
PHONE......................................631 467-8400
Mark Swanson, *President*
Leon Benatar, *Vice Pres*
Richard Janiec, *Sales Dir*
Bernie Papocchia, *Manager*
Dennis Tucker, *Manager*
EMP: 25 EST: 1953
SQ FT: 10,600
SALES (est): 8.2MM
SALES (corp-wide): 3.9B Publicly Held
WEB: www.ifi.com
SIC: 3663 Amplifiers, RF power & IF
HQ: Teseq Holding Ag
    Sternenhofstrasse 15
    Reinach
    728 737-3

(G-14914)
ISINE INC (PA)
4155 Veterans Memorial Hw (11779-6063)
PHONE......................................631 913-4400
Louis J Morales, *President*
Louis A Morales, *Vice Pres*
Gary Stevens, *Vice Pres*
Robert Gross, *Senior Engr*
John Masterson, *Finance*
▲ EMP: 7
SQ FT: 1,800
SALES (est): 1.4MM Privately Held
WEB: www.isine.com
SIC: 3672 3674 Printed circuit boards; semiconductors & related devices

(G-14915)
ISLAND RESEARCH AND DEV CORP
Also Called: Island Technology
200 13th Ave Unit 12 (11779-6815)
PHONE......................................631 471-7100
Robert Guy Ward, *President*
EMP: 75
SQ FT: 10,000
SALES (est): 10.6MM Privately Held
WEB: www.islandresearch.net
SIC: 3679 Electronic circuits

(G-14916)
J F M SHEET METAL INC
2090 Pond Rd (11779-7216)
PHONE......................................631 737-8494
Joseph Magri, *President*
Jeff Stern, *Manager*
EMP: 5
SALES: 450K Privately Held
SIC: 3441 Fabricated structural metal

(G-14917)
J R S PRECISION MACHINING
40 Raynor Ave Ste 2 (11779-6623)
PHONE......................................631 737-1330
Fax: 631 737-3065
Scott Sopko, *President*
EMP: 8 EST: 1970
SQ FT: 2,000
SALES (est): 737K Privately Held
SIC: 3599 Machine shop, jobbing & repair

(G-14918)
JAAB PRECISION INC
180 Gary Way (11779-6509)
PHONE......................................631 218-3725
Joseph W Aloi, *President*
Josephine Blasso, *Office Mgr*
EMP: 9
SALES (est): 2.6MM Privately Held
SIC: 3441 Fabricated structural metal

(G-14919)
JET REDI MIX CONCRETE INC
Also Called: J E T
2101 Pond Rd Ste 1 (11779-7213)
PHONE......................................631 580-3640
Fax: 631 580-3641
Steve Jensen, *President*
Harold Jensen, *President*
Linda Lavzaro, *Office Mgr*
EMP: 14
SQ FT: 15,000

SALES (est): 2MM Privately Held
WEB: www.jetredimixconcrete.com
SIC: 3273 Ready-mixed concrete

(G-14920)
JMG FUEL INC
3 Fowler Ave (11779-4105)
PHONE......................................631 579-4319
Brian Gauci, *Principal*
EMP: 6 EST: 2010
SALES (est): 689.4K Privately Held
SIC: 2869 Fuels

(G-14921)
KELTRON ELECTRONICS (DE CORP)
Also Called: Keltron Connector Co.
3385 Vtrans Mem Hwy Ste E (11779-7660)
PHONE......................................631 567-6300
Fax: 631 567-6363
David Levison, *President*
Joanne Perks, *Mfg Staff*
Elaine Carucci, *Controller*
Robert Pellicane, *Sales Dir*
Diane Kearns, *Sales Staff*
▲ EMP: 15
SALES (est): 2.6MM Privately Held
WEB: www.keltronconnectors.com
SIC: 3679 Electronic circuits

(G-14922)
KETCHAM MEDICINE CABINETS
3505 Vtrans Mem Hwy Ste L (11779-7613)
PHONE......................................631 615-6151
Tracey Bonham, *General Mgr*
Gina Lacarrubba, *Vice Pres*
EMP: 25
SALES: 10MM Privately Held
SIC: 3431 Bathroom fixtures, including sinks

(G-14923)
KNF CLEAN ROOM PRODUCTS CORP
1800 Ocean Ave (11779-6532)
PHONE......................................631 588-7000
Philip J Carcara, *Ch of Bd*
Chuck McAteer, *Sls & Mktg Exec*
John Stuerzel, *Human Res Dir*
Patricia Floro, *Mktg Dir*
Randy Ferdinand, *Director*
EMP: 50
SQ FT: 22,000
SALES (est): 9.5MM Privately Held
SIC: 3699 1541 3081 5085 Electrical equipment & supplies; pharmaceutical manufacturing plant construction; unsupported plastics film & sheet; clean room supplies

(G-14924)
KONDOR TECHNOLOGIES INC
206 Christopher St (11779-6921)
PHONE......................................631 471-8832
Fax: 631 471-8834
Nils Youngwall, *President*
Carie Lanarca, *Manager*
EMP: 10
SQ FT: 3,500
SALES (est): 990K Privately Held
SIC: 3599 Machine shop, jobbing & repair

(G-14925)
L W S INC
125 Gary Way Ste 1 (11779-6576)
PHONE......................................631 580-0472
Leon Shapiro, *President*
EMP: 15
SQ FT: 3,000
SALES (est): 1.4MM Privately Held
SIC: 3471 Finishing, metals or formed products; polishing, metals or formed products

(G-14926)
LAB CRAFTERS INC
2085 5th Ave (11779-6903)
PHONE......................................631 471-7755
Bob Deluca Sr, *President*
Robert Deluca, *Principal*
Edward Fiance, *Principal*
Coryn Skolnick, *Project Mgr*
Brittany Savino, *Human Resources*
EMP: 25
SQ FT: 90,000

GEOGRAPHIC SECTION

Ronkonkoma - Suffolk County (G-14951)

SALES (est): 7.1MM **Privately Held**
SIC: **3821** 5049 Laboratory apparatus & furniture; laboratory equipment, except medical or dental

(G-14927)
LAB-AIDS INC
17 Colt Ct (11779-6949)
PHONE.................................631 737-1133
Fax: 631 737-1286
Morton Frank, *President*
David M Frank, *President*
John Garrett, *Regional Mgr*
Dilani Rosa, *Regional Mgr*
Zach Smith, *Regional Mgr*
▲ EMP: 49 EST: 1963
SQ FT: 41,000
SALES (est): 9.5MM **Privately Held**
WEB: www.lab-aid.com
SIC: **3999** Education aids, devices & supplies

(G-14928)
LAKELAND INDUSTRIES INC (PA)
3555 Vtrans Mem Hwy Ste C (11779-7636)
PHONE.................................631 981-9700
Fax: 631 981-9751
Christopher J Ryan, *President*
Charles D Roberson, *Senior VP*
Teri W Hunt, *CFO*
▼ EMP: 226
SALES: 99.6MM **Publicly Held**
WEB: www.lakeland-ind.com
SIC: **3842** 2389 Personal safety equipment; clothing, fire resistant & protective; gloves, safety; disposable garments & accessories

(G-14929)
LANCO CORPORATION
Also Called: Brijon
2905 Vtrans Mem Hwy Ste 3 (11779-7655)
PHONE.................................631 231-2300
Fax: 631 231-2731
Brian Landow, *President*
Tom Kronberger, *Regional Mgr*
Irwin Landow, *Vice Pres*
John Whitaker, *Vice Pres*
Bernardo Romero, *Prdtn Mgr*
◆ EMP: 250
SQ FT: 40,000
SALES (est): 48.5MM **Privately Held**
WEB: www.lancopromo.com
SIC: **3993** 2066 5149 2064 Signs & advertising specialties; chocolate & cocoa products; chocolate; candy & other confectionery products

(G-14930)
LANGER BIOMECHANICS INC
2905 Vtrans Mem Hwy Ste 2 (11779-7655)
PHONE.................................800 645-5520
Bruce Marrison, *CEO*
Jason Kraus, *President*
Terence Fitzmaurice, *Controller*
EMP: 71
SALES (est): 11.1MM
SALES (corp-wide): 13.4MM **Privately Held**
SIC: **3842** Orthopedic appliances
PA: Orthotic Holdings, Inc.
   2905 Veterans Mem Hwy
   Ronkonkoma NY 11779
   416 479-8609

(G-14931)
LEE PHILIPS PACKAGING INC
750 Union Pkwy (11779-7413)
PHONE.................................631 580-3306
Fax: 631 580-3298
Lee Schnitzer, *President*
EMP: 14
SQ FT: 26,000
SALES (est): 3.3MM **Privately Held**
WEB: www.leephilipspackaging.com
SIC: **2653** Corrugated & solid fiber boxes

(G-14932)
LINK CONTROL SYSTEMS INC
16 Colt Ct (11779-6948)
PHONE.................................631 471-3950
Fax: 631 471-2390
William F Bowden, *President*
David Cotte, *Engineer*
Francine Abramowitz, *Manager*

Clive Dillon, *Info Tech Mgr*
EMP: 15
SQ FT: 12,000
SALES (est): 3.3MM **Privately Held**
WEB: www.linkconsys.com
SIC: **3613** Control panels, electric

(G-14933)
LONG ISLAND BUSINESS NEWS
2150 Smithtown Ave Ste 7 (11779-7348)
PHONE.................................631 737-1700
Fax: 631 737-1890
James Dolan, *President*
Jordan Zeigler, *Partner*
John Kominicki, *Principal*
Michael H Samuels, *Regional Mgr*
Mike Gates, *Adv Dir*
EMP: 22 EST: 1953
SQ FT: 6,000
SALES (est): 1.4MM
SALES (corp-wide): 147.2MM **Privately Held**
WEB: www.libn.com
SIC: **2711** Newspapers
HQ: Dolan Llc
   222 S 9th St Ste 2300
   Minneapolis MN 55402
   612 317-9420

(G-14934)
LUX MUNDI CORP
10 Colt Ct (11779-6948)
PHONE.................................631 244-4596
Henry Kleitsch, *President*
EMP: 8
SALES (est): 803.8K **Privately Held**
SIC: **3999** Candles

(G-14935)
LWS PRECISION DEBURRING INC
125 Gary Way Ste 1 (11779-6576)
PHONE.................................631 580-0472
Fax: 631 580-0496
Leon Shaperio, *President*
EMP: 10 EST: 1994
SALES (est): 977K **Privately Held**
SIC: **3761** 3471 Rockets, space & military, complete; cleaning, polishing & finishing

(G-14936)
MAHARLIKA HOLDINGS LLC
Also Called: Atis Colojet
111 Trade Zone Ct Unit A (11779-7367)
PHONE.................................631 319-6203
Erez Shoshoni, *General Mgr*
▲ EMP: 14
SALES: 3MM **Privately Held**
SIC: **3559** Chemical machinery & equipment

(G-14937)
MANTEL & MANTEL STAMPING CORP
802 S 4th St (11779-7200)
PHONE.................................631 467-1916
Fax: 631 467-1916
Edward Mantel, *President*
EMP: 8 EST: 1977
SQ FT: 7,500
SALES: 1MM **Privately Held**
SIC: **3544** 3469 Special dies & tools; metal stampings

(G-14938)
MARCOVICCI-WENZ ENGINEERING
33 Comac Loop Unit 10 (11779-6856)
PHONE.................................631 467-9040
Ted Wenz, *President*
Peter Marcovicci, *Vice Pres*
EMP: 6
SQ FT: 4,000
SALES (est): 490K **Privately Held**
SIC: **3714** 5531 3711 Motor vehicle engines & parts; speed shops, including race car supplies; automobile assembly, including specialty automobiles

(G-14939)
MASTER-HALCO INC
25 Mill Rd Unit 1 (11779-4597)
PHONE.................................631 585-8150
Bob Locurto, *Manager*
Bob Locurrto, *Manager*

EMP: 14
SALES (corp-wide): 43.4B **Privately Held**
WEB: www.fenceonline.com
SIC: **3315** 5039 5031 1799 Chain link fencing; wire fence, gates & accessories; fencing, wood; fence construction
HQ: Master-Halco, Inc.
   3010 Lbj Fwy Ste 800
   Dallas TX 75234
   972 714-7300

(G-14940)
MAYFAIR MACHINE COMPANY INC
128 Remington Blvd (11779-6912)
PHONE.................................631 981-6644
EMP: 6
SQ FT: 1,500
SALES (est): 610K **Privately Held**
SIC: **3599** Machine Shop

(G-14941)
MICRO CONTRACT MANUFACTURING
119 Comac St (11779-6931)
PHONE.................................631 738-7874
Fax: 631 738-7879
Michael L Matula, *President*
Thomas Degasperi, *President*
Josephine Matula, *Corp Secy*
EMP: 60
SQ FT: 12,000 **Privately Held**
WEB: www.microcontractmfg.com
SIC: **3674** Semiconductors & related devices

(G-14942)
MICRO PHOTO ACOUSTICS INC
105 Comac St (11779-6931)
PHONE.................................631 750-6035
Xiaojie Zhao, *President*
EMP: 5
SALES (est): 754.7K
SALES (corp-wide): 3.9MM **Privately Held**
SIC: **3826** Laser scientific & engineering instruments
PA: Advanced Optowave Corporation
   105 Comac St
   Ronkonkoma NY 11779
   631 750-6035

(G-14943)
MIN-MAX MACHINE LTD
1971 Pond Rd (11779-7244)
PHONE.................................631 585-4378
Fax: 631 585-4610
Randy Neubauer, *Ch of Bd*
Rodney Neubauer, *Corp Secy*
Ralph Neubauer, *Vice Pres*
EMP: 37
SQ FT: 18,000
SALES: 4MM **Privately Held**
SIC: **3728** Aircraft parts & equipment; aircraft assemblies, subassemblies & parts

(G-14944)
MINUTEMEN PRECSN MCHNING TOOL
135 Raynor Ave (11779-6666)
PHONE.................................631 467-4900
Fax: 631 467-6850
Michael Castoro, *President*
Michael Lane, *Vice Pres*
Carlo J Castoro, *Treasurer*
EMP: 37
SQ FT: 14,900
SALES: 8.1MM **Privately Held**
SIC: **3728** 3599 Aircraft parts & equipment; machine shop, jobbing & repair

(G-14945)
MNS FUEL CORP
2154 Pond Rd (11779-7216)
P.O. Box 344, East Islip (11730-0344)
PHONE.................................516 735-3835
Irene F Walsh, *Principal*
EMP: 12
SALES (est): 2.5MM **Privately Held**
SIC: **2869** Fuels

(G-14946)
MULTILINE TECHNOLOGY INC
75 Roebling Ct (11779-9202)
P.O. Box 548, Centerport (11721-0548)
PHONE.................................631 249-8300
Michael Angelo, *President*
David Angelo, *Vice Pres*
John Pereira, *Purchasing*
John A Karcher, *CFO*
Mary Endres, *Sales Mgr*
▲ EMP: 160
SQ FT: 37,000
SALES (est): 26.6MM **Privately Held**
WEB: www.multiline.com
SIC: **3559** Electronic component making machinery

(G-14947)
MULTIMATIC PRODUCTS INC
900 Marconi Ave (11779-7212)
PHONE.................................800 767-7633
Hyman Jack Kipnes, *President*
Rohit C Chodha, *Managing Dir*
Irving Kipnes, *Corp Secy*
EMP: 74 EST: 1962
SQ FT: 20,000
SALES: 3MM **Privately Held**
WEB: www.multimaticproducts.com
SIC: **3451** 3541 Screw machine products; machine tools, metal cutting type

(G-14948)
N & L INSTRUMENTS INC
90 13th Ave Unit 1 (11779-6818)
PHONE.................................631 471-4000
Fax: 631 471-0339
John Walz, *President*
Anthony Kearney, *Treasurer*
Teresa Smith, *Manager*
EMP: 17
SQ FT: 20,000
SALES (est): 2MM **Privately Held**
WEB: www.namf.com
SIC: **3571** 3444 Electronic computers; sheet metalwork

(G-14949)
NATECH PLASTICS INC
85 Remington Blvd (11779-6923)
PHONE.................................631 580-3506
Fax: 631 580-5448
Gerd Nagler, *Ch of Bd*
Thomas Nagler, *President*
Carol Nagler, *Vice Pres*
Ray Schneider, *Engineer*
Jennifer Nagler, *Manager*
EMP: 45 EST: 1998
SQ FT: 10,000
SALES (est): 11.2MM **Privately Held**
WEB: www.natechplastics.com
SIC: **3089** Injection molding of plastics

(G-14950)
NATURES BOUNTY INC (DH)
2100 Smithtown Ave (11779-7347)
PHONE.................................631 580-6137
Scott Rudolph, *Ch of Bd*
Michael Collins, *Ch of Bd*
Harvey Kamil, *President*
Jim Flaherty, *Senior VP*
Kristine Urea, *Vice Pres*
▲ EMP: 4000
SQ FT: 15,000
SALES (est): 614.7MM
SALES (corp-wide): 3B **Publicly Held**
WEB: www.nbty.com
SIC: **2834** Vitamin preparations
HQ: Nbty, Inc.
   2100 Smithtown Ave
   Ronkonkoma NY 11779
   631 200-2000

(G-14951)
NBTY INC
Also Called: Accounts Payable Department
2100 Smithtown Ave (11779-7347)
P.O. Box 9011 (11779-9011)
PHONE.................................631 244-2065
Jeff Nagel, *Branch Mgr*
EMP: 12
SALES (corp-wide): 3B **Publicly Held**
SIC: **2833** Vitamins, natural or synthetic; bulk, uncompounded

Ronkonkoma - Suffolk County (G-14952)

HQ: Nbty, Inc.
2100 Smithtown Ave
Ronkonkoma NY 11779
631 200-2000

(G-14952)
NBTY INC
2100 Smithtown Ave (11779-7347)
PHONE................631 244-2021
Fax: 631 244-1777
Dorie Greenblatt, *Principal*
EMP: 90
SALES (corp-wide): 3B **Publicly Held**
SIC: 2833 5122 5499 5961 Vitamins, natural or synthetic: bulk, uncompounded; vitamins & minerals; health & dietetic food stores; vitamin food stores; health foods; pharmaceuticals, mail order
HQ: Nbty, Inc.
2100 Smithtown Ave
Ronkonkoma NY 11779
631 200-2000

(G-14953)
NBTY INC (DH)
Also Called: Arco Pharmaceutical
2100 Smithtown Ave (11779-7347)
P.O. Box 9014 (11779-9014)
PHONE................631 200-2000
Jeffrey A Nagel, *CEO*
Harvey Kamil, *Vice Ch Bd*
Andre Branch, *President*
Glenn Schneider, *President*
Kevin Warren, *President*
◆ EMP: 800 EST: 1971
SQ FT: 110,000
SALES: 3.2B
SALES (corp-wide): 3B **Publicly Held**
WEB: www.nbty.com
SIC: 2833 5122 5499 5961 Vitamins, natural or synthetic: bulk, uncompounded; vitamins & minerals; health & dietetic food stores; vitamin food stores; health foods; dietetic foods; pharmaceuticals, mail order

(G-14954)
NBTY INC
2145 9th Ave (11779-6280)
PHONE................631 200-7338
Laura Bode, *Sales Staff*
EMP: 90
SALES (corp-wide): 3B **Publicly Held**
SIC: 2833 Vitamins, natural or synthetic: bulk, uncompounded
HQ: Nbty, Inc.
2100 Smithtown Ave
Ronkonkoma NY 11779
631 200-2000

(G-14955)
NBTY MANUFACTURING LLC (DH)
2100 Smithtown Ave (11779-7347)
PHONE................631 567-9500
Joe Looney, *Vice Pres*
Harvey Kamil, *Mng Member*
▲ EMP: 29
SQ FT: 6,000,000
SALES (est): 69.4MM
SALES (corp-wide): 3B **Publicly Held**
SIC: 2833 5122 Vitamins, natural or synthetic: bulk, uncompounded; vitamins & minerals
HQ: Nbty, Inc.
2100 Smithtown Ave
Ronkonkoma NY 11779
631 200-2000

(G-14956)
NEW AGE PRECISION TECH INC
151 Remington Blvd (11779-6911)
PHONE................631 588-1692
Mario Costa, *President*
Robert Flower, *Sales Mgr*
EMP: 20
SALES: 1MM **Privately Held**
SIC: 3599 Machine & other job shop work

(G-14957)
OAKDALE INDUSTRIAL ELEC CORP
1995 Pond Rd (11779-7259)
PHONE................631 737-4090
Fax: 631 737-4349
Abraham Mamoor, *President*

Allen Mamoor, *Vice Pres*
▼ EMP: 15
SQ FT: 5,000
SALES (est): 4.2MM **Privately Held**
SIC: 3679 3672 5065 Electronic circuits; printed circuit boards; electronic parts

(G-14958)
OAKLEE INTERNATIONAL INC
Also Called: Pro-Tek Packaging Group
125 Raynor Ave (11779-6666)
PHONE................631 436-7900
Leo Lee, *President*
Alice Zebrowski, *Exec VP*
Donna Neumann, *Exec Dir*
EMP: 75
SALES (est): 9.4MM **Privately Held**
WEB: www.oaklee.com
SIC: 2672 3081 Adhesive papers, labels or tapes: from purchased material; unsupported plastics film & sheet

(G-14959)
OMEGA HEATER COMPANY INC
2059 9th Ave (11779-6233)
PHONE................631 588-8820
Fax: 631 588-8953
Alfred Gaudio, *President*
Gina Gaudio, *Manager*
▲ EMP: 60 EST: 1970
SQ FT: 30,000
SALES: 3MM **Privately Held**
WEB: www.omegaheater.com
SIC: 3433 Heating equipment, except electric

(G-14960)
OMNTEC MFG INC
1993 Pond Rd (11779-7259)
P.O. Box 30 (11779-0030)
PHONE................631 981-2001
Fax: 631 981-2007
Lee J Nicholson, *President*
Gregg Nicholson, *General Mgr*
Tom Dalessandro, *Exec VP*
Tom D'Alessandro, *Vice Pres*
▲ EMP: 34
SQ FT: 13,600
SALES (est): 8.4MM **Privately Held**
WEB: www.omntec.com
SIC: 3625 5065 Relays & industrial controls; electronic parts & equipment

(G-14961)
P R B METAL PRODUCTS INC
200 Christopher St (11779-6921)
PHONE................631 467-1800
Fax: 631 467-1894
Ronald Breunig, *President*
Peter Breunig, *Vice Pres*
EMP: 10
SQ FT: 10,000
SALES: 1MM **Privately Held**
SIC: 3444 3465 3469 Sheet metal specialties, not stamped; automotive stampings; metal stampings

(G-14962)
PAAL TECHNOLOGIES INC
152 Remington Blvd Ste 1 (11779-6964)
PHONE................631 319-6262
Latha Chandran, *Ch of Bd*
Prem Chandran, *Vice Pres*
EMP: 5
SALES: 300K **Privately Held**
WEB: www.paaltech.com
SIC: 3679 Harness assemblies for electronic use: wire or cable

(G-14963)
PACE TECHNOLOGY INC
Also Called: API Technologies
2200 Smithtown Ave (11779-7329)
PHONE................631 981-2400
Benidict Pace, *President*
Fran Albert, *Sales Mgr*
Duli Yariv, *VP Mktg*
EMP: 45 EST: 1995
SALES (est): 4.4MM
SALES (corp-wide): 232.2MM **Privately Held**
WEB: www.nationalhybrid.com
SIC: 3549 3571 Assembly machines, including robotic; electronic computers

HQ: National Hybrid, Inc.
345 Pomroys Dr
Windber PA 15963
814 467-9060

(G-14964)
PARAMOUNT EQUIPMENT INC
Also Called: O P I Industries
201 Christopher St (11779-6956)
PHONE................631 981-4422
Jerome Bernzweig, *President*
Matt Barbaro, *Vice Pres*
Steve Bearman, *Vice Pres*
Ken Muller, *Vice Pres*
▲ EMP: 20
SQ FT: 10,000
SALES (est): 4.7MM **Privately Held**
SIC: 2673 5113 Plastic bags: made from purchased materials; bags, paper & disposable plastic

(G-14965)
PARSLEY APPAREL CORP
2153 Pond Rd (11779-7214)
PHONE................631 981-7181
Ronald Colnick, *President*
EMP: 50
SQ FT: 5,000
SALES (est): 3MM **Privately Held**
SIC: 2335 Wedding gowns & dresses

(G-14966)
PAUL MICHAEL GROUP INC
Also Called: PMG
460 Hawkins Ave (11779-4248)
PHONE................631 585-5700
Vincent Gennaro, *President*
▲ EMP: 7
SQ FT: 1,500
SALES (est): 930.9K **Privately Held**
SIC: 2752 7389 Commercial printing, offset; packaging & labeling services

(G-14967)
PCX AEROSTRUCTURES LLC
70 Raynor Ave (11779-6650)
PHONE................631 249-7901
Paul Iannotta, *Branch Mgr*
EMP: 50
SALES (corp-wide): 100MM **Privately Held**
SIC: 3441 Fabricated structural metal
PA: Pcx Aerostructures, Llc
300 Fenn Rd
Newington CT 06111
860 666-2471

(G-14968)
PHOTONICS INDUSTRIES INTL INC (PA)
1800 Ocean Ave Unit A (11779-6532)
PHONE................631 218-2240
Fax: 631 218-2275
Yusong Yin, *Ch of Bd*
Joe Wysk, *Buyer*
Matt Corrello, *Mktg Dir*
Joe Echolitc, *Manager*
Laura Bjorke, *Assistant*
▲ EMP: 60
SQ FT: 184,000
SALES (est): 12.6MM **Privately Held**
WEB: www.photonix.com
SIC: 3845 Laser systems & equipment, medical

(G-14969)
PHYSIOLOGICS LLC
2100 Smithtown Ave (11779-7347)
PHONE................800 765-6775
Chris De Petris, *Manager*
EMP: 14
SALES (est): 1.4MM **Privately Held**
WEB: www.physiologics.com
SIC: 2023 Dietary supplements, dairy & non-dairy based

(G-14970)
PIC A POC ENTERPRISES INC
53 Union Ave (11779-5814)
P.O. Box 338, Holbrook (11741-0338)
PHONE................631 981-2094
Fax: 631 981-2105
Nicholas J Ullrich II, *President*
Marilyn Ullrich, *Principal*
EMP: 5
SQ FT: 2,000

SALES: 500K **Privately Held**
SIC: 2752 7336 Commercial printing, lithographic; graphic arts & related design

(G-14971)
PRINTCORP INC
2050 Ocean Ave (11779-6536)
PHONE................631 696-0641
Joseph C Fazzingo Jr, *CEO*
Arthur Foti, *Marketing Staff*
EMP: 20 EST: 1994
SALES (est): 3.1MM **Privately Held**
SIC: 2752 Commercial printing, lithographic

(G-14972)
PRONTO TOOL & DIE CO INC
50 Remington Blvd (11779-6910)
PHONE................631 981-8920
Fax: 631 981-8344
Michael Silvestri, *President*
Donna Schecker, *Corp Secy*
Marion Silvestri, *Vice Pres*
Linda Young, *Manager*
EMP: 30 EST: 1980
SQ FT: 10,000
SALES (est): 4.7MM **Privately Held**
SIC: 3544 3599 3469 Special dies & tools; machine & other job shop work; metal stampings

(G-14973)
QUALITY KING DISTRIBUTORS INC
201 Comac St (11779-6950)
PHONE................631 439-2027
Glenn H Nussdorf, *CEO*
EMP: 133
SALES (corp-wide): 869.7MM **Privately Held**
SIC: 2844 5122 Toilet preparations; toilet preparations
PA: Quality King Distributors, Inc.
35 Sawgrass Dr Ste 3
Bellport NY 11713
631 439-2000

(G-14974)
QUALITY ONE WIRELESS LLC
2127 Lakeland Ave Unit 2 (11779-7431)
PHONE................631 233-3337
John Chiorando, *CEO*
EMP: 250
SALES (corp-wide): 440.3MM **Privately Held**
SIC: 3661 Headsets, telephone
PA: Quality One Wireless, Llc
1500 Tradeport Dr Ste B
Orlando FL 32824
407 857-3737

(G-14975)
QUANTUM MEDICAL IMAGING LLC
2002 Orville Dr N (11779-7661)
PHONE................631 567-5800
Fax: 631 567-5074
Scott Matovich, *President*
Shalom Cohen, *President*
Keith Matovich, *Vice Pres*
Gil Ruiz, *QA Dir*
Dennis Iuliucci, *VP Finance*
▲ EMP: 100
SQ FT: 55,000
SALES (est): 25MM
SALES (corp-wide): 4.1B **Privately Held**
WEB: www.qmiteam.com
SIC: 3844 5047 Radiographic X-ray apparatus & tubes; medical equipment & supplies
HQ: Carestream Health, Inc.
150 Verona St
Rochester NY 14608
585 627-1800

(G-14976)
R S T CABLE AND TAPE INC
2130 Pond Rd Ste B (11779-7239)
PHONE................631 981-0096
Fax: 631 981-0130
David M Rothert, *President*
William Hilder, *Vice Pres*
Stephen Thomas, *Director*
EMP: 8
SQ FT: 6,500

SALES (est): 2MM **Privately Held**
SIC: 3479 Painting, coating & hot dipping; coating of metals with plastic or resins

(G-14977)
RATAN RONKONKOMA
3055 Veterans Mem Hwy (11779-7612)
PHONE.................................631 588-6800
Mahesh Ratanji, *Administration*
EMP: 8 EST: 2011
SALES (est): 1MM **Privately Held**
SIC: 3421 Table & food cutlery, including butchers'

(G-14978)
RESONANCE TECHNOLOGIES INC
109 Comac St (11779-6931)
PHONE.................................631 237-4901
George Szenczy, *President*
Mark Anatov, *Director*
EMP: 35
SALES (est): 5MM **Privately Held**
WEB: www.res-tek.info
SIC: 3678 Electronic connectors

(G-14979)
RICK-MIC INDUSTRIES INC
1951 Ocean Ave Ste 6 (11779-6564)
PHONE.................................631 563-8389
Rod Dimiano, *President*
EMP: 6
SALES (est): 420K **Privately Held**
SIC: 3599 Machine shop, jobbing & repair

(G-14980)
ROGER LATARI
Also Called: Island Precision
30 Raynor Ave Ste 1 (11779-6628)
PHONE.................................631 580-2422
Roger Licari, *Owner*
EMP: 5
SALES (est): 300K **Privately Held**
WEB: www.rogerblench.info
SIC: 3599 Machine shop, jobbing & repair

(G-14981)
RONA PRECISION INC
Also Called: Rona Precision Mfg
142 Remington Blvd Ste 2 (11779-6960)
PHONE.................................631 737-4034
Fax: 631 737-4064
Ronald Alber, *President*
Marie Alber, *Treasurer*
EMP: 6
SQ FT: 3,500
SALES (est): 752.4K **Privately Held**
SIC: 3599 Machine shop, jobbing & repair

(G-14982)
SENTRY TECHNOLOGY CORPORATION
Also Called: Knogo
1881 Lakeland Ave (11779-7416)
PHONE.................................631 739-2000
Peter Murdoch, *CEO*
Elizabeth Heyder, *Corp Secy*
Joane Miller, *CFO*
Maryanne Owens, *Credit Mgr*
▲ EMP: 30
SQ FT: 20,000
SALES (est): 3MM **Privately Held**
SIC: 3812 7359 Detection apparatus: electronic/magnetic field, light/heat; electronic equipment rental, except computers
PA: Sentry Technology Corporation
    1881 Lakeland Ave
    Ronkonkoma NY 11779

(G-14983)
SENTRY TECHNOLOGY CORPORATION (PA)
Also Called: Sentry Funding Partnership
1881 Lakeland Ave (11779-7416)
PHONE.................................800 645-4224
Fax: 631 232-2812
Peter L Murdoch, *Ch of Bd*
Joseph Ryan, *Vice Pres*
Nelson Hocker, *Project Dir*
Matt Eckert, *Senior Engr*
Joseph J Ryan, *VP Sls/Mktg*
▲ EMP: 13
SQ FT: 20,000

SALES (est): 7.9MM **Privately Held**
SIC: 3812 3663 Detection apparatus: electronic/magnetic field, light/heat; television closed circuit equipment

(G-14984)
SETAUKET MANUFACTURING CO
202 Christopher St (11779-6921)
PHONE.................................631 231-7272
Michael Horrigan, *President*
Linda Horrigan, *Vice Pres*
EMP: 5
SQ FT: 4,000
SALES: 500K **Privately Held**
SIC: 2833 5499 Medicinals & botanicals; health & dietetic food stores

(G-14985)
SHERRY-MICA PRODUCTS INC
45 Remington Blvd Ste D (11779-9500)
PHONE.................................631 471-7513
Fax: 631 471-2675
Anthony Villano, *President*
EMP: 5
SQ FT: 2,000
SALES (est): 380K **Privately Held**
SIC: 2434 5031 Wood kitchen cabinets; vanities, bathroom: wood; kitchen cabinets

(G-14986)
SOC AMERICA INC
3505 Veterans Memorial Hw (11779-7613)
PHONE.................................631 472-6666
Neil Sato, *President*
Karl Lindquist, *Vice Pres*
Yuichi Sato, *Vice Pres*
Sharon Terry, *Electrical Engi*
Dawn Minichello, *Executive Asst*
EMP: 15
SQ FT: 3,200
SALES (est): 2.6MM **Privately Held**
WEB: www.san-o.com
SIC: 3613 Fuses, electric
PA: Soc Corporation
    3-16-17, Takanawa
    Minato-Ku TKY
    354 201-011

(G-14987)
SPECIALTY MICROWAVE CORP
120 Raynor Ave (11779-6655)
PHONE.................................631 737-2175
Fax: 631 737-2175
Stephen Faber, *President*
EMP: 18
SQ FT: 7,500
SALES (est): 3.4MM **Privately Held**
WEB: www.specialtymicrowave.com
SIC: 3663 Microwave communication equipment

(G-14988)
SPX CORPORATION
Also Called: SPX Precision Components
70 Raynor Ave (11779-6650)
PHONE.................................631 249-7900
Steve Souffronc, *Branch Mgr*
Mike Yannetti, *Info Tech Mgr*
EMP: 50
SALES (corp-wide): 1.7B **Publicly Held**
WEB: www.spx.com
SIC: 3443 Cooling towers, metal plate
PA: Spx Corporation
    13320a Balntyn Corp Pl
    Charlotte NC 28277
    980 474-3700

(G-14989)
ST JAMES PRINTING INC
656 Rosevale Ave (11779-3098)
PHONE.................................631 981-2095
Fax: 631 981-4646
Gert Kuehnel, *President*
EMP: 5
SQ FT: 5,000
SALES (est): 300K **Privately Held**
SIC: 2759 2752 Commercial printing; commercial printing, lithographic

(G-14990)
SWITCHING POWER INC
3601 Veterans Mem Hwy (11779-7691)
PHONE.................................631 981-7231
Fax: 631 981-7266

Melvin Kravitz, *President*
John Bellone, *Vice Pres*
Mike Costanzo, *Safety Mgr*
Carmen Midiri, *Purch Mgr*
Peter Herringer, *Engineer*
EMP: 65 EST: 1976
SQ FT: 30,000
SALES (est): 13MM **Privately Held**
WEB: www.switchpwr.com
SIC: 3613 5065 3643 3612 Power switching equipment; electronic parts & equipment; current-carrying wiring devices; transformers, except electric

(G-14991)
SYNERGY INTRNTNAL OPTRNICS LLC
101 Comac St (11779-6931)
PHONE.................................631 277-0500
Richard Heathcote, *President*
Robert Tartaglia, *Vice Pres*
Lydia Bozymowski, *Manager*
Lori Pflug, *Teacher*
EMP: 36
SQ FT: 12,500
SALES (est): 6.1MM **Privately Held**
WEB: www.siollc.com
SIC: 3827 Optical instruments & lenses

(G-14992)
TRANSISTOR DEVICES INC
125 Comac St (11779-6931)
PHONE.................................631 471-7492
Fax: 631 471-7497
Ron Deluca, *Manager*
EMP: 27
SALES (corp-wide): 341.4MM **Privately Held**
WEB: www.transdev.com
SIC: 3625 3612 3672 3812 Switches, electric power; power transformers, electric; printed circuit boards; search & navigation equipment
PA: Transistor Devices, Inc.
    36 Newburgh Rd
    Hackettstown NJ 07840
    908 850-1595

(G-14993)
TRUEMADE PRODUCTS INC
910 Marconi Ave (11779-7212)
PHONE.................................631 981-4755
Carmen Yvonne Mender, *President*
EMP: 5
SQ FT: 4,000
SALES: 400K **Privately Held**
SIC: 3541 Machine tools, metal cutting type

(G-14994)
U S AIR TOOL CO INC (PA)
Also Called: U S Air Tool International
60 Fleetwood Ct (11779-6907)
PHONE.................................631 471-3300
Fax: 631 471-3308
Geoffrey J Percz, *Ch of Bd*
Laurence Percz, *Vice Pres*
David Lombardo, *Controller*
▲ EMP: 14 EST: 1951
SQ FT: 14,000
SALES (est): 5MM **Privately Held**
SIC: 3423 5084 3542 Hand & edge tools; pneumatic tools & equipment; sheet metalworking machines; riveting machines

(G-14995)
ULTRAFLEX POWER TECHNOLOGIES
158 Remington Blvd Ste 2 (11779-6966)
PHONE.................................631 467-6814
Mario Metodiev, *President*
Nedelina Metodieva, *Treasurer*
EMP: 5
SQ FT: 3,000
SALES (est): 523K **Privately Held**
SIC: 3567 Induction heating equipment

(G-14996)
ULTRAVOLT INC
1800 Ocean Ave Unit A (11779-6532)
PHONE.................................631 471-4444
Fax: 631 471-4696
James Morrison, *CEO*
Craig Hembach, *Facilities Mgr*
April Gelo, *Purchasing*
Carlos Alicea, *Engineer*

Dianne Burkard, *Engineer*
EMP: 100
SQ FT: 20,000
SALES (est): 23.2MM
SALES (corp-wide): 414.8MM **Publicly Held**
WEB: www.ultravolt.com
SIC: 3679 5065 5084 Power supplies, all types: static; electronic parts & equipment; power plant machinery
PA: Advanced Energy Industries, Inc.
    1625 Sharp Point Dr
    Fort Collins CO 80525
    970 221-4670

(G-14997)
VACUUM INSTRUMENT CORPORATION (PA)
Also Called: Vic Leak Detection
2099 9th Ave (11779-6276)
PHONE.................................631 737-0900
Fax: 631 737-0949
Frederick Ewing II, *CEO*
John Schreiner, *Vice Pres*
Art Hoffmann, *Engineer*
John Xu, *Sales Engr*
EMP: 100
SQ FT: 48,000
SALES (est): 19.1MM **Privately Held**
WEB: www.vacuuminst.com
SIC: 3823 3829 3812 Industrial instrmnts msrmnt display/control process variable; measuring & controlling devices; search & navigation equipment

(G-14998)
VISION QUEST LIGHTING INC
90 13th Ave Unit 1 (11779-6818)
PHONE.................................631 737-4800
Larry Lieberman, *Ch of Bd*
Torrey Bievenour, *Vice Pres*
Janelle Norton, *Vice Pres*
▲ EMP: 33
SQ FT: 2,500
SALES (est): 8.9MM **Privately Held**
WEB: www.vql.com
SIC: 3646 3645 Commercial indusl & institutional electric lighting fixtures; fluorescent lighting fixtures, commercial; ornamental lighting fixtures, commercial; residential lighting fixtures; fluorescent lighting fixtures, residential; garden, patio, walkway & yard lighting fixtures: electric

(G-14999)
VORMITTAG ASSOCIATES INC (PA)
Also Called: V A I
120 Comac St Ste 1 (11779-6941)
PHONE.................................800 824-7776
Fax: 631 588-9770
Robert Vormittag, *President*
Russ Cereola, *Vice Pres*
Ira Dannenberg, *Vice Pres*
Larry Murphy, *Vice Pres*
Michael Gallagher, *Project Dir*
EMP: 130
SQ FT: 15,000
SALES (est): 43.8MM **Privately Held**
WEB: www.vaihome.com
SIC: 7372 7371 5045 Prepackaged software; computer software systems analysis & design, custom; computers, peripherals & software

(G-15000)
VOSKY PRECISION MACHINING CORP
70 Air Park Dr (11779-7360)
PHONE.................................631 737-3200
Mourad Voskinarian, *President*
Eddy Voskinarian, *Manager*
Anthony Voskinarian, *Info Tech Mgr*
Keven Boris, *Administration*
EMP: 18
SQ FT: 11,000
SALES (est): 4.3MM **Privately Held**
WEB: www.voskyprecision.com
SIC: 3728 3469 3599 Aircraft parts & equipment; machine parts, stamped or pressed metal; machine shop, jobbing & repair

Ronkonkoma - Suffolk County (G-15001)   GEOGRAPHIC SECTION

(G-15001)
WILCO INDUSTRIES INC
788 Marconi Ave (11779-7230)
P.O. Box 277 (11779-0277)
PHONE..............................631 676-2593
Fax: 631 588-5578
Otto Wildmann, *President*
Robert Fischer, *QC Mgr*
EMP: 9
SQ FT: 8,000
SALES (est): 970K **Privately Held**
WEB: www.wilcoindustries.com
SIC: 3728 Aircraft assemblies, subassemblies & parts

(G-15002)
ZETA MACHINE CORP
206 Christopher St (11779-6921)
PHONE..............................631 471-8832
Frank Castelli, *President*
Carol Castelli, *Vice Pres*
EMP: 8 **EST:** 1975
SQ FT: 8,000
SALES (est): 660K **Privately Held**
SIC: 3469 Machine parts, stamped or pressed metal

Roosevelt
Nassau County

(G-15003)
AUTOSTAT CORPORATION
209 Nassau Rd 11 (11575-1756)
P.O. Box 170 (11575-0170)
PHONE..............................516 379-9447
Fax: 516 868-5568
Arthur Baer, *President*
▲ **EMP:** 10 **EST:** 1955
SQ FT: 9,000
SALES (est): 1.2MM **Privately Held**
SIC: 3549 Marking machines, metalworking

(G-15004)
GENERAL DIE AND DIE CUTNG INC
151 Babylon Tpke (11575-2122)
PHONE..............................516 665-3584
Fax: 516 623-5142
Peter Vallone Sr, *CEO*
Peter Vallone Jr, *President*
Louann Vallone Pepi, *Vice Pres*
Richard Vallone, *Treasurer*
▲ **EMP:** 55 **EST:** 1961
SQ FT: 30,000
SALES (est): 35.8K **Privately Held**
WEB: www.gendiecut.com
SIC: 2653 2675 3544 Display items, corrugated: made from purchased materials; boxes, corrugated: made from purchased materials; corrugated boxes, partitions, display items, sheets & pad; die-cut paper & board; special dies, tools, jigs & fixtures

(G-15005)
INTRIGUE CONCEPTS INC
8 Gilbert Pl Ste 8 (11575-1718)
PHONE..............................800 424-8170
Dennis Barclift, *President*
EMP: 6
SALES (est): 430K **Privately Held**
SIC: 2326 Work shirts: men's, youths' & boys'

(G-15006)
K F I INC
33 Debevoise Ave (11575-1711)
PHONE..............................516 546-2904
Sion Elalouf, *President*
▲ **EMP:** 8
SALES (est): 491.7K **Privately Held**
WEB: www.euroyarns.com
SIC: 2299 Yarns, specialty & novelty

(G-15007)
LONG ISLAND CATHOLIC NEWSPAPER
200 W Centennial Ave # 201 (11575-1937)
PHONE..............................516 594-1212
Liz O'Conner, *Principal*
EMP: 30
SALES (est): 2.9MM **Privately Held**
SIC: 2721 2711 Periodicals; newspapers

(G-15008)
PARABIT SYSTEMS INC
35 Debevoise Ave (11575-1711)
P.O. Box 481 (11575-0481)
PHONE..............................516 378-4800
Fax: 516 378-4843
Robert Leiponis, *President*
Pat Zajicek, *General Mgr*
Andrew Sherman, *Foreman/Supr*
Olesya Maggio, *Accountant*
Bob Hricisak, *VP Sales*
▲ **EMP:** 50
SQ FT: 25,000
SALES (est): 12.4MM **Privately Held**
SIC: 3699 3661 3578 2542 Security devices; telephone & telegraph apparatus; telephone station equipment & parts, wire; automatic teller machines (ATM); telephone booths: except wood

(G-15009)
SOUTH SHORE ICE CO INC
89 E Fulton Ave (11575-2212)
PHONE..............................516 379-2056
Al Farina, *President*
EMP: 10
SQ FT: 4,500
SALES (est): 1MM **Privately Held**
SIC: 2097 5999 5169 Manufactured ice; ice; dry ice

(G-15010)
TROPICAL DRIFTWOOD ORIGINALS
Also Called: Tdo Sandblasting
499 Nassau Rd (11575-1019)
PHONE..............................516 623-0980
John O'Brien Sr, *President*
EMP: 5
SQ FT: 4,000
SALES (est): 270K **Privately Held**
SIC: 3441 3446 3471 Fabricated structural metal; architectural metalwork; sand blasting of metal parts

Roscoe
Sullivan County

(G-15011)
PROHIBITION DISTILLERY LLC
10 Union St (12776-5210)
PHONE..............................917 685-8989
Brian Facquet, *Mng Member*
EMP: 8
SALES (est): 384.5K **Privately Held**
SIC: 2085 Distilled & blended liquors

(G-15012)
ROSCOE LITTLE STORE INC
Also Called: Little Store, The
59 Stewart Ave (12776-5105)
PHONE..............................607 498-5553
Elwin Wood, *President*
Deborah Gabry, *Corp Secy*
EMP: 9
SQ FT: 3,200
SALES (est): 980.4K **Privately Held**
SIC: 3949 Sporting & athletic goods

Rosedale
Queens County

(G-15013)
LARRY KINGS CORPORATION
13708 250th St (11422-2110)
PHONE..............................718 481-8741
Fax: 718 481-9859
Larry Yoen, *President*
Clara Wong, *Treasurer*
Ken Klein, *Systems Mgr*
Johnny Yoen, *Shareholder*
Penny Yoen, *Admin Sec*
EMP: 6
SALES (est): 663.4K **Privately Held**
SIC: 3825 Instruments to measure electricity

(G-15014)
MASTRO CONCRETE INC
15433 Brookville Blvd (11422-3163)
PHONE..............................718 528-6788
Tony Mastronardi, *President*
Mario Mastronardi, *Vice Pres*
EMP: 8
SQ FT: 10,000
SALES (est): 1.4MM **Privately Held**
SIC: 3273 Ready-mixed concrete

(G-15015)
WATER COOLING CORP
Also Called: Robert Miller Associate
24520 Merrick Blvd (11422-1464)
P.O. Box 220056 (11422-0056)
PHONE..............................718 723-6500
Elliott Miller, *President*
Robert Miller, *Consultant*
EMP: 7 **EST:** 1939
SQ FT: 5,500
SALES (est): 860K **Privately Held**
WEB: www.watcopumps.com
SIC: 3443 3561 Water tanks, metal plate; tanks, standard or custom fabricated: metal plate; pumps, domestic: water or sump; industrial pumps & parts

Roslyn
Nassau County

(G-15016)
BEACON SPCH LNGE PTHLGY PHYS
Also Called: Beacon Therapy Services
1441 Old Northern Blvd (11576-2146)
PHONE..............................516 626-1635
Barbar Lehrer, *Partner*
Barbara Lehrer, *Partner*
EMP: 16
SQ FT: 5,500
SALES (est): 7MM **Privately Held**
SIC: 3841 Inhalation therapy equipment

(G-15017)
CLOUD ROCK GROUP LLC
525 Bryant Ave (11576-1146)
PHONE..............................516 967-6023
Leon Hedvat, *Manager*
EMP: 5
SALES (est): 350K **Privately Held**
SIC: 7372 7389 Application computer software;

(G-15018)
CUSTOM ECO FRIENDLY LLC (PA)
Also Called: Custom Eco Friendly Bags
50 Spruce Dr (11576-2330)
PHONE..............................347 227-0229
Matthew Kesten, *CEO*
Jonathon Wollman, *President*
▲ **EMP:** 9
SQ FT: 250
SALES (est): 2.4MM **Privately Held**
SIC: 2674 Shopping bags: made from purchased materials

(G-15019)
DYNAMIC PHOTOGRAPHY INC
Also Called: Daisy Memory Products
48 Flamingo Rd N (11576-2606)
PHONE..............................516 381-2951
Robert M Deangelo Jr, *President*
Richard J Deangelo, *Vice Pres*
EMP: 5
SALES (est): 7MM **Privately Held**
SIC: 3674 7336 7221 Magnetic bubble memory device; commercial art & graphic design; photographer, still or video

(G-15020)
HAND CARE INC
42 Sugar Maple Dr (11576-3207)
P.O. Box 331, Albertson (11507-0331)
PHONE..............................516 747-5649
Harrison Fuller, *President*
Patricia Fuller, *Admin Sec*
▲ **EMP:** 2
SQ FT: 15,000
SALES: 2MM **Privately Held**
WEB: www.handcare.net
SIC: 3842 Gloves, safety; adhesive tape & plasters, medicated or non-medicated

(G-15021)
NEW YORK LASER & AESTHETICKS
1025 Nthrn Blvd Ste 206 (11576)
PHONE..............................516 627-7777
Ofra Grinbaum, *Owner*
EMP: 5
SALES (est): 445.8K **Privately Held**
SIC: 3845 Laser systems & equipment, medical

(G-15022)
NORTHWEST COMPANY LLC (PA)
Also Called: Wilmington Products USA
49 Bryant Ave (11576-1123)
P.O. Box 263 (11576-0263)
PHONE..............................516 484-6996
Ross Auerbach, *President*
Marc Friedman, *COO*
Glenn Auerbach, *Exec VP*
Kim Rizzardi, *Vice Pres*
Robert Jolson, *CFO*
▲ **EMP:** 80
SQ FT: 15,000
SALES (est): 158MM **Privately Held**
WEB: www.thenorthwest.com
SIC: 2211 Blankets & blanketings, cotton

(G-15023)
ROVEL MANUFACTURING CO INC
52 Wimbledon Dr (11576-3082)
PHONE..............................516 365-2752
William Levor, *President*
Andrew A Levor, *Vice Pres*
EMP: 5
SQ FT: 10,000
SALES: 400K **Privately Held**
SIC: 2299 Batts & batting: cotton mill waste & related material; batting, wadding, padding & fillings

(G-15024)
WM E MARTIN AND SONS CO INC
55 Bryant Ave Ste 300 (11576-1158)
PHONE..............................516 605-2444
Fax: 718 291-0331
William Martin Jr, *President*
William S Martin, *Vice Pres*
Abby Zeifman, *Director*
Spencer Martin, *Administration*
▲ **EMP:** 22 **EST:** 1954
SQ FT: 60,000
SALES (est): 7.8MM **Privately Held**
SIC: 2099 2034 Spices, including grinding; vegetables, dried or dehydrated (except freeze-dried)

Roslyn Heights
Nassau County

(G-15025)
ERGUN INC
10 Mineola Ave Unit B (11577-1067)
PHONE..............................631 721-0049
Omer Eguner, *President*
EMP: 2
SQ FT: 200
SALES: 15.9MM **Privately Held**
SIC: 2911 Oils, fuel

(G-15026)
HIGHWAY TOLL ADM LLC
66 Powerhouse Rd Ste 402 (11577-1372)
PHONE..............................516 684-9584
David Centner, *CEO*
Keith Baylor, *CTO*
Jonathan Schweiger,
▲ **EMP:** 15
SALES (est): 4.7MM **Privately Held**
SIC: 3829 Toll booths, automatic

GEOGRAPHIC SECTION

(G-15027)
IET LABS INC (PA)
1 Expressway Plz Ste 120 (11577-2031)
PHONE..................................516 334-5959
Fax: 516 334-5988
Sam Sheena, *President*
David Sheena, *Vice Pres*
▲ EMP: 12
SQ FT: 11,000
SALES (est): 5.2MM **Privately Held**
SIC: 3825 Test equipment for electronic & electrical circuits

(G-15028)
KIM JAE PRINTING CO INC
249 Parkside Dr (11577-2211)
PHONE..................................212 691-6289
Jae Kye Kim, *President*
Yun Kim, *Vice Pres*
EMP: 5
SQ FT: 6,000
SALES (est): 500K **Privately Held**
SIC: 2759 2752 Newspapers: printing; commercial printing, lithographic

(G-15029)
MASON SCOTT INDUSTRIES LLC
159 Westwood Cir (11577-1844)
PHONE..................................516 349-1800
Scott Fishkind, *Mng Member*
EMP: 13
SQ FT: 20,000
SALES: 12MM **Privately Held**
SIC: 3444 Sheet metalwork

(G-15030)
NATIONAL MARKETING SERVICES
Also Called: Cars Magazine
200 S Service Rd Ste 100 (11577-2133)
PHONE..................................516 942-9595
Bryan Flyn, *President*
EMP: 12
SALES (est): 1.1MM **Privately Held**
SIC: 2721 Periodicals

(G-15031)
ROSLYN BREAD COMPANY INC
190 Mineola Ave (11577-2093)
PHONE..................................516 625-1470
EMP: 35
SQ FT: 3,500
SALES: 1.1MM **Privately Held**
SIC: 2051 5149 5461 5812 Mfg Whol Ret Bread & Restaurant

(G-15032)
SIMPLY LOGIC LABS LLC
200 S Service Rd Ste 211 (11577-2118)
P.O. Box 386, Roslyn (11576-0386)
PHONE..................................516 626-6228
Roseanne Ruttner, *Manager*
Gabriel Ruttner,
EMP: 7 EST: 2009
SALES (est): 530K **Privately Held**
WEB: www.simplylogiclabs.com
SIC: 7372 Utility computer software

(G-15033)
SOMERSET MANUFACTURERS INC
36 Glen Cove Rd (11577-1703)
PHONE..................................516 626-3832
Jacob Ambalu, *President*
Esther Ambalu, *Vice Pres*
EMP: 20
SALES (est): 1.6MM **Privately Held**
SIC: 3911 Jewelry, precious metal

(G-15034)
US CONCRETE INC
Also Called: Kings Ready Mix
10 Powerhouse Rd (11577-1311)
PHONE..................................718 853-4644
EMP: 50
SALES (corp-wide): 974.7MM **Publicly Held**
SIC: 3273 Ready-mixed concrete
PA: U.S. Concrete, Inc.
331 N Main St
Euless TX 76039
817 835-4105

Rotterdam Junction
Schenectady County

(G-15035)
SI GROUP INC
Rr 5 Box South (12150)
P.O. Box 1046, Schenectady (12301-1046)
PHONE..................................518 347-4200
Andy Barrett, *General Mgr*
EMP: 150
SALES (corp-wide): 1.1B **Privately Held**
WEB: www.schenectadyinternational.com
SIC: 2851 Varnishes
PA: Si Group, Inc.
2750 Balltown Rd
Schenectady NY 12309
518 347-4200

Round Lake
Saratoga County

(G-15036)
ALCO INDUSTRIES INC
Also Called: Catalyst Systms Div of US Chmc
2103 Route 9 (12151-1711)
PHONE..................................740 254-4311
Amber Wood, *Safety Dir*
John Nelson, *Plant Mgr*
Jack B Wyrie, *Sales & Mktg St*
EMP: 25
SQ FT: 27,200
SALES (corp-wide): 225.9MM **Privately Held**
WEB: www.alcoind.com
SIC: 2879 2899 2821 Pesticides, agricultural or household; chemical preparations; plastics materials & resins
PA: Alco Industries, Inc.
1275 Glenlivet Dr Ste 100
Allentown PA 18106
610 666-0930

(G-15037)
DEATH WISH COFFEE COMPANY LLC
19 Wood Rd Ste 500 (12151-1718)
PHONE..................................518 400-1050
Michael Brown, *CEO*
EMP: 10 EST: 2015
SALES (est): 1.5MM **Privately Held**
SIC: 2095 5499 Coffee extracts; coffee roasting (except by wholesale grocers); coffee

(G-15038)
USHERS MACHINE AND TOOL CO INC
180 Ushers Rd (12151-1806)
PHONE..................................518 877-5501
Fax: 518 877-8575
Donald Lincoln, *Ch of Bd*
Joseph Hopeck, *President*
Patte Prevost, *Manager*
EMP: 20
SQ FT: 5,000
SALES (est): 4.6MM **Privately Held**
WEB: www.ushersm.com
SIC: 3599 Machine shop, jobbing & repair

(G-15039)
WYRESTORM TECHNOLOGIES LLC
23 Wood Rd (12151-1708)
PHONE..................................518 289-1293
Derek Hulbert, *President*
Todd Akins, *Marketing Staff*
▲ EMP: 15
SQ FT: 2,500
SALES: 4MM
SALES (corp-wide): 1.5MM **Privately Held**
SIC: 3651 Household audio & video equipment
PA: Wyrestorm Technologies Europe Limited
Unit 22 Kelvin Road
Swindon WILTS SN3 3
179 323-0343

Round Top
Greene County

(G-15040)
ROUND TOP KNIT & SCREENING
Rr 31 (12473)
P.O. Box 188 (12473-0188)
PHONE..................................518 622-3600
Fax: 518 622-9041
Manny Voss, *Owner*
Dolly Cavicchioni, *Office Mgr*
EMP: 8
SQ FT: 6,000
SALES: 750K **Privately Held**
SIC: 2759 5651 2395 2396 Screen printing; family clothing stores; embroidery & art needlework; automotive & apparel trimmings

Rouses Point
Clinton County

(G-15041)
CHAMPLAIN PLASTICS INC
Also Called: Champlain Hanger
87 Pillsbury Rd (12979-1701)
P.O. Box 2947, Plattsburgh (12901-0269)
PHONE..................................518 297-3700
Fax: 518 297-3777
Alan L Taveroff, *Ch of Bd*
Joe Zalter, *President*
Joanne Palliotti, *Accounting Mgr*
Monique Perez, *Accountant*
Beverly McKernan, *Accounts Mgr*
▲ EMP: 60 EST: 1998
SALES (est): 16.3MM
SALES (corp-wide): 3.2MM **Privately Held**
WEB: www.olympicpoolaccessories.com
SIC: 3089 Injection molding of plastics
PA: Canadian Buttons Limited
7020 Boul Newman
Lasalle QC H8N 3
514 363-0210

(G-15042)
PFIZER INC
Also Called: Wyeth
64 Maple St (12979-1424)
P.O. Box 697 (12979-0697)
PHONE..................................518 297-6611
Fax: 518 297-8122
John Nichols, *Opers Mgr*
Tony Pilcher, *Engineer*
Thomas Trombley, *Engineer*
Lynn Jock, *Corp Comm Staff*
William Brooks, *Branch Mgr*
EMP: 440
SALES (corp-wide): 48.8B **Publicly Held**
WEB: www.wyeth.com
SIC: 2834 Pharmaceutical preparations
PA: Pfizer Inc.
235 E 42nd St
New York NY 10017
212 733-2323

(G-15043)
POWERTEX INC (PA)
1 Lincoln Blvd Ste 101 (12979-1087)
PHONE..................................518 297-4000
Fax: 518 297-2634
Stephen Podd, *President*
Victor I Podd, *Vice Pres*
Karen M Lamberton, *Treasurer*
Heather Cayea, *Accounts Mgr*
Heather Laforest, *Accounts Mgr*
▲ EMP: 34 EST: 1977
SQ FT: 65,900
SALES (est): 3.7MM **Privately Held**
WEB: www.powertex.com
SIC: 3089 Plastic containers, except foam

(G-15044)
SANDYS DELI INC ✪
Also Called: Last Resort, The
90 Montgomery St (12979-1018)
PHONE..................................518 297-6951
Carolyn Reid, *President*
EMP: 6 EST: 2016
SQ FT: 1,000
SALES: 145K
SALES (corp-wide): 450K **Privately Held**
SIC: 2599 Bar, restaurant & cafeteria furniture
PA: Sandy's Deli Inc
133 Lake St
Rouses Point NY 12979
518 297-6951

(G-15045)
VWR CHEMICALS LLC (DH)
3 Lincoln Blvd (12979-1037)
PHONE..................................518 297-4444
Fax: 518 297-2960
Theodore Pulkownick, *President*
Tom Caramia, *Production*
Meredith Earnest, *Accounts Mgr*
Christopher Karambelas, *Manager*
▲ EMP: 30
SQ FT: 30,000
SALES (est): 20.8MM
SALES (corp-wide): 4.3B **Publicly Held**
WEB: www.anachemiachemicals.com
SIC: 2819 Industrial inorganic chemicals
HQ: Vwr Funding, Inc.
100 Matsonford Rd
Radnor PA 19087
610 386-1700

Rush
Monroe County

(G-15046)
CONVERGENT AUDIO TECH INC
85 High Tech Dr (14543-9746)
PHONE..................................585 359-2700
Ken Stevens, *President*
Truddy Stevens, *Vice Pres*
Cheri Milliman, *Office Mgr*
EMP: 5
SQ FT: 3,300
SALES (est): 842.4K **Privately Held**
SIC: 3651 Household audio equipment

(G-15047)
EXTEK INC
7500 W Henrietta Rd (14543-9790)
PHONE..................................585 533-1672
John Demanaco, *Engineer*
Caroline Eastman, *Branch Mgr*
Glen Crast, *Branch Mgr*
Tom Bienias, *Manager*
Anne Rowlinds, *Manager*
EMP: 50
SALES (corp-wide): 5.5MM **Privately Held**
WEB: www.sts.ethoxint.com
SIC: 3841 Surgical & medical instruments
PA: Extek, Inc.
370 Summit Point Dr
Henrietta NY
585 321-5000

(G-15048)
G & G WINDOW REPAIR INC
6710 W Henrietta Rd Ste 4 (14543-9770)
PHONE..................................585 334-3370
Gary Donald Larzelere, *President*
EMP: 12
SALES (est): 1.6MM **Privately Held**
SIC: 2431 Windows & window parts & trim, wood

(G-15049)
GLOBAL PRECISION PRODUCTS INC
90 High Tech Dr (14543-9746)
PHONE..................................585 334-4640
Fax: 585 334-2815
Mark Labell, *CEO*
Doug Labell, *Vice Pres*
Charles Cornelius, *Engineer*
EMP: 22
SQ FT: 250,000
SALES (est): 4.6MM **Privately Held**
WEB: www.globalppi.com
SIC: 3599 Machine & other job shop work

(G-15050)
GPM ASSOCIATES LLC
Graphik Promotional Products
45 High Tech Dr Ste 100 (14543-9746)
PHONE..................................585 359-1770

Rush - Monroe County (G-15051)

Sean Fraser, *Sales Dir*
Kevin Webster, *Marketing Mgr*
Lauren A Wrobel, *Marketing Staff*
Mark Hughes, *Manager*
Jim McDermott,
EMP: 6
SALES (corp-wide): 15.8MM **Privately Held**
SIC: 2393 Textile bags
PA: Gpm Associates Llc
  45 High Tech Dr
  Rush NY 14543
  585 334-4800

(G-15051)
KEUKA STUDIOS INC
1011 Rush Henrietta Townl (14543-9763)
PHONE.................................585 624-5960
Dan White, *President*
Jeanne White, *Corp Secy*
▼ **EMP:** 8
SALES (est): 740K **Privately Held**
WEB: www.keuka-studios.com
SIC: 3446 Architectural metalwork

(G-15052)
SPS MEDICAL SUPPLY CORP (DH)
6789 W Henrietta Rd (14543-9797)
PHONE.................................585 359-0130
Gary Steinberg, *President*
Charles A Hughes, *General Mgr*
John Hughes, *General Mgr*
Jennifer Griffin, *QA Dir*
Mary Reed, *Finance Mgr*
▲ **EMP:** 73
SQ FT: 40,000
SALES (est): 18.3MM
SALES (corp-wide): 664.7MM **Publicly Held**
WEB: www.spsmedical.com
SIC: 3842 Surgical appliances & supplies
HQ: Crosstex International, Inc.
  10 Ranick Rd
  Hauppauge NY 11788
  631 582-6777

Rushville
Yates County

(G-15053)
RUSH MACHINERY INC
4761 State Route 364 (14544-9721)
PHONE.................................585 554-3070
Fax: 585 554-4077
William P Freese, *President*
David Burdett, *General Mgr*
Rob Robbins, *Sales Mgr*
Maggie Atkins, *Admin Mgr*
▲ **EMP:** 9
SQ FT: 7,000
SALES (est): 2.1MM **Privately Held**
SIC: 3541 Centering machines

Rye
Westchester County

(G-15054)
AUXILIUM PHARMACEUTICALS INC
70 High St (10580-1506)
PHONE.................................484 321-2022
Brian Wogram, *Director*
EMP: 10
SALES (est): 870K **Privately Held**
SIC: 2834 Pharmaceutical preparations

(G-15055)
CONSOLIDATED EDISON CO NY INC
511 Theodore Fremd Ave (10580-1432)
PHONE.................................914 933-2936
William McGrath, *Principal*
EMP: 130
SALES (corp-wide): 12.5B **Publicly Held**
SIC: 2869 Fuels

HQ: Consolidated Edison Company Of New York, Inc.
  4 Irving Pl
  New York NY 10003
  212 460-4600

(G-15056)
GAZETTE PRESS INC
2 Clinton Ave (10580-1629)
PHONE.................................914 963-8300
Richard Martinelli, *CEO*
Angelo R Martinelli, *President*
Angelo Martinelli, *Chairman*
Carol Martinelli, *Treasurer*
EMP: 20 **EST:** 1864
SQ FT: 10,000
SALES (est): 2.8MM **Privately Held**
SIC: 2759 2796 2791 2789 Letterpress printing; platemaking services; typesetting; bookbinding & related work; commercial printing, lithographic

(G-15057)
GB AERO ENGINE LLC
555 Theodore Fremd Ave (10580-1451)
PHONE.................................914 925-9600
Raynard D Benvenuti,
Noah Roy,
Rob Wolf,
EMP: 390
SALES (est): 25.2MM **Privately Held**
SIC: 3724 3541 3769 Aircraft engines & engine parts; machine tools, metal cutting type; guided missile & space vehicle parts & auxiliary equipment

(G-15058)
GLOBAL GOLD CORPORATION (PA)
555 Theodore Fremd Ave C208 (10580-1437)
PHONE.................................914 925-0020
Fax: 203 422-2330
Van Z Krikorian, *Ch of Bd*
W E S Urquhart, *Vice Pres*
Jan Dulman, *CFO*
Drury J Gallagher, *Treasurer*
EMP: 12
SALES (est): 3.2MM **Privately Held**
WEB: www.globalgoldcorp.com
SIC: 1021 1041 1094 1044 Copper ores; gold ores; uranium ore mining; silver ores

(G-15059)
HIBERT PUBLISHING LLC
222 Purchase St (10580-2101)
PHONE.................................914 381-7474
Jean Sheff, *Editor*
Nina Spiegelman, *Accounts Mgr*
Gary Hibert, *Branch Mgr*
EMP: 13
SALES (corp-wide): 1MM **Privately Held**
SIC: 2741 Miscellaneous publishing
PA: Hibert Publishing Llc
  7555 E Hampden Ave # 405
  Denver CO 80231
  303 312-1000

(G-15060)
HYDRIVE ENERGY
350 Theodore Fremd Ave (10580-1573)
PHONE.................................914 925-9100
Michael F Weinstein, *Chairman*
EMP: 6
SALES (est): 451.8K **Privately Held**
SIC: 2086 Carbonated beverages, nonalcoholic: bottled & canned

(G-15061)
JUDITH N GRAHAM INC
Also Called: Pink and Palmer
64 Halls Ln (10580-3124)
PHONE.................................914 921-5446
James Graham, *Principal*
EMP: 7
SALES (est): 539.9K **Privately Held**
SIC: 2844 Toilet preparations

(G-15062)
MARTINELLI HOLDINGS LLC
Also Called: Today Media
2 Clinton Ave (10580-1629)
PHONE.................................302 504-1361
Dianne Green, *Controller*
EMP: 50

SALES (corp-wide): 15K **Privately Held**
SIC: 2721 Magazines: publishing only, not printed on site
PA: Martinelli Holdings Llc
  3301 Lancaster Pike 5c
  Wilmington DE 19805
  302 656-1809

(G-15063)
MASON & GORE INC
Also Called: Gazette & Press
2 Clinton Ave (10580-1629)
PHONE.................................914 921-1025
Fax: 914 476-1052
Angelo R Martinelli, *President*
EMP: 20 **EST:** 1956
SQ FT: 4,500
SALES (est): 2MM **Privately Held**
WEB: www.gazettepress.com
SIC: 2752 7331 7311 Commercial printing, offset; mailing service; advertising consultant

(G-15064)
MONEYPAPER INC
411 Theodore Fremd Ave # 132 (10580-1482)
P.O. Box 451 (10580-0451)
PHONE.................................914 925-0022
Fax: 914 921-9318
Vita Nelson, *President*
EMP: 12
SALES (est): 875.8K **Privately Held**
WEB: www.giftsofstock.com
SIC: 2711 6282 Newspapers, publishing & printing; investment advice

(G-15065)
O C TANNER COMPANY
27 Park Dr S (10580-1826)
PHONE.................................914 921-2025
Thomas Rosato, *Manager*
EMP: 5
SALES (corp-wide): 344.1MM **Privately Held**
WEB: www.octanner.com
SIC: 3911 5944 Pins (jewelry), precious metal; jewelry, precious stones & precious metals
PA: O. C. Tanner Company
  1930 S State St
  Salt Lake City UT 84115
  801 486-2430

(G-15066)
QUOIN LLC
555 Theodore Fremd Ave B302 (10580-1451)
PHONE.................................914 967-9400
Martin Franklin, *CEO*
EMP: 1402
SALES (est): 365.4MM
SALES (corp-wide): 5.9B **Publicly Held**
WEB: www.jarden.com
SIC: 3089 Plastic containers, except foam
HQ: Jarden Corporation
  1800 N Military Trl # 210
  Boca Raton FL 33431
  561 447-2520

(G-15067)
RYE RECORD
14 Elm Pl Ste 200 (10580-2951)
PHONE.................................914 713-3213
Dolores Eyler, *Partner*
Allen Clarck, *Partner*
Robin Jovanovich, *Partner*
Susan Bontempo, *Marketing Staff*
EMP: 8
SALES (est): 500K **Privately Held**
SIC: 2721 Periodicals

(G-15068)
SMN MEDICAL PC
Also Called: Docchat
2 Allendale Dr (10580-2402)
PHONE.................................844 362-2428
Michael Okhravi, *CEO*
Steve Okhravi, *President*
EMP: 10
SALES (est): 821.7K **Privately Held**
SIC: 7372 8011 7389 Application computer software; offices & clinics of medical doctors;

(G-15069)
WESTERN OIL AND GAS JV INC
Also Called: Michael Neuman
7 Mccullough Pl (10580-2934)
PHONE.................................914 967-4758
Michael Neuman, *Principal*
EMP: 3 **EST:** 2008
SALES: 2.1MM **Privately Held**
SIC: 1321 8748 1381 Natural gas liquids; energy conservation consultant; drilling oil & gas wells

Rye Brook
Westchester County

(G-15070)
ELIAS FRAGRANCES INC (PA)
3 Hunter Dr (10573-1406)
PHONE.................................718 693-6400
Robert Elias, *President*
Barbara Elias, *Corp Secy*
Lewis Elias, *Exec VP*
Jackie James, *Bookkeeper*
EMP: 17 **EST:** 1972
SQ FT: 8,000
SALES (est): 1.3MM **Privately Held**
SIC: 2844 5122 Perfumes, natural or synthetic; perfumes

(G-15071)
IDEAS INTERNATIONAL INC
800 Westchester Ave # 337 (10573-1354)
PHONE.................................914 937-4302
Ian Birks, *President*
Liam Carthy, *Vice Pres*
Chris Ober, *Vice Pres*
Paul Sowerby, *CFO*
Nancy Wolfberg, *Admin Sec*
EMP: 50
SQ FT: 5,484
SALES: 5.6MM
SALES (corp-wide): 2.1B **Publicly Held**
WEB: www.ideasintl.com
SIC: 2741 8742 Technical papers: publishing only, not printed on site; training & development consultant
HQ: Ideas International Pty Limited
  Level 3 20 George Street
  Hornsby NSW 2077
  294 727-777

(G-15072)
MITSUI CHEMICALS AMERICA INC (HQ)
800 Westchester Ave N607 (10573-1328)
PHONE.................................914 253-0777
Naoto Tani, *President*
Keiichi Sano, *Managing Dir*
Toshikazu Tanaka, *Exec VP*
Furukawa Manabu, *Vice Pres*
Kenji Doi, *Prdtn Mgr*
◆ **EMP:** 40
SQ FT: 13,000
SALES (est): 284.3MM
SALES (corp-wide): 11.4B **Privately Held**
SIC: 2821 2865 3082 8731 Plastics materials & resins; plasticizer/additive based plastic materials; cyclic crudes & intermediates; unsupported plastics profile shapes; computer (hardware) development; chemical additives; loan institutions, general & industrial
PA: Mitsui Chemicals, Inc.
  1-5-2, Higashishimbashi
  Minato-Ku TKY 105-0
  362 532-100

(G-15073)
PARACO GAS CORPORATION (PA)
800 Westchester Ave S604 (10573-1397)
PHONE.................................800 647-4427
Joseph Armentano, *CEO*
Michael Gioffre, *President*
Patrick Brennan, *Regional Mgr*
Bob Pearce, *Regional Mgr*
Peter Teresi, *Regional Mgr*
EMP: 13
SALES (est): 326.7MM **Privately Held**
SIC: 1321 Propane (natural) production

▲ = Import ▼ = Export
◆ = Import/Export

GEOGRAPHIC SECTION   Saint Johnsville - Montgomery County (G-15098)

(G-15074)
PROGRESSIVE PRODUCTS LLC
Also Called: Wipesplus
4 International Dr # 224 (10573-1065)
PHONE..................................914 417-6022
Jason Englander, *CEO*
Gabby Hunter, *Bookkeeper*
Mary Delsranco, *Manager*
Carol Lugo, *Administration*
Mark Zeitler,
▲ **EMP:** 8
SQ FT: 2,000
SALES: 12MM **Privately Held**
SIC: 2842 Cleaning or polishing preparations

(G-15075)
XYLEM INC (PA)
1 International Dr (10573-1058)
PHONE..................................914 323-5700
Fax: 914 323-5800
Markos I Tambakeras, *Ch of Bd*
Patrick K Decker, *President*
Tomas Brannemo, *President*
David Flinton, *President*
Pak Steven Leung, *President*
EMP: 277
SQ FT: 67,000
SALES: 3.6B **Publicly Held**
SIC: 3561 Pumps & pumping equipment

Sag Harbor
Suffolk County

(G-15076)
COASTAL PUBLICATIONS INC
22 Division St (11963)
P.O. Box 1620 (11963-0058)
PHONE..................................631 725-1700
Gavin Menu, *Principal*
EMP: 10
SALES (est): 702.1K **Privately Held**
SIC: 2741 Miscellaneous publishing

(G-15077)
DORTRONICS SYSTEMS INC
1668 Bhmpton Sag Hbr Tpke (11963-3706)
PHONE..................................631 725-0505
Fax: 631 725-8148
Paul R Scheerer, *CEO*
John Fitzpaprick, *President*
John Fitzpatrick, *President*
John Fitzgerald, *Vice Pres*
Mary Scheerer, *Vice Pres*
EMP: 21
SQ FT: 10,000
SALES (est): 3.9MM
SALES (corp-wide): 14.2MM **Privately Held**
WEB: www.dortronics.com
SIC: 3429 3679 3625 3089 Locks or lock sets; electronic switches; switches, electronic applications; timing devices, electronic; plastic hardware & building products
PA: Sag Harbor Industries, Inc.
    1668 Bhmpton Sag Hbr Tpke
    Sag Harbor NY 11963
    631 725-0440

(G-15078)
DWJ BOOKS LLC
21 Division St (11963-3155)
P.O. Box 996 (11963-0029)
PHONE..................................631 899-4500
Darrell Kozlowski, *Director*
Lauren Fedorko,
EMP: 5
SALES (est): 390K **Privately Held**
SIC: 2731 Book publishing

(G-15079)
SAG HARBOR EXPRESS
35 Main St (11963-3012)
P.O. Box 1620 (11963-0058)
PHONE..................................631 725-1700
Fax: 631 725-1584
Bryan Boyhan, *Manager*
EMP: 7
SALES (est): 507.4K **Privately Held**
WEB: www.sagharboronline.com
SIC: 2741 2711 Miscellaneous publishing; newspapers

(G-15080)
SAG HARBOR INDUSTRIES INC (PA)
1668 Bhmpton Sag Hbr Tpke (11963-3714)
PHONE..................................631 725-0440
Fax: 631 725-4234
Paul R Scheerer Jr, *Ch of Bd*
Mary Scheerer, *President*
John Fitzpatrick, *Vice Pres*
Dave Leeney, *Vice Pres*
Christopher Murphy, *Purchasing*
EMP: 50 **EST:** 1946
SQ FT: 50,000
SALES (est): 15.1MM **Privately Held**
WEB: www.sagharborind.com
SIC: 3621 3672 3677 5065 Coils, for electric motors or generators; printed circuit boards; electronic coils, transformers & other inductors; electronic parts & equipment; transformers, except electric

(G-15081)
SECOND CHANCE PRESS INC
Also Called: Permanent Press
4170 Noyac Rd (11963-2809)
PHONE..................................631 725-1101
Martin Shepard, *President*
Cathy Suter, *Editor*
Judith Shepard, *Vice Pres*
EMP: 6
SALES: 420K **Privately Held**
WEB: www.thepermanentpress.com
SIC: 2731 5942 Books: publishing only; book stores

Sagaponack
Suffolk County

(G-15082)
WOLFFER ESTATE VINEYARD INC
Also Called: Wolffer Estate Winery
139 Sagg Rd (11962-2006)
P.O. Box 9002 (11962-9002)
PHONE..................................631 537-5106
Christian Wolffer, *President*
Lara Brown, *CFO*
Judy Malone, *Comms Dir*
Mindy Crawford, *Marketing Staff*
Roman Roth, *Technical Staff*
▲ **EMP:** 50
SALES (est): 8.2MM **Privately Held**
WEB: www.wolffer.com
SIC: 2084 5813 Wines, brandy & brandy spirits; wine bar

Saint Albans
Queens County

(G-15083)
HOUSE OF THE FOAMING CASE INC
110 08 Dunkirk St (11412)
PHONE..................................718 454-0101
Mark Levy, *Principal*
EMP: 5
SALES (est): 873.3K **Privately Held**
SIC: 3523 Farm machinery & equipment

(G-15084)
INTEGRATED TECH SUPPORT SVCS
Also Called: Itss
18616 Jordan Ave (11412-2308)
PHONE..................................718 454-2497
Gerald Cortez, *President*
Damon Kinebrew, *Sales/Mktg Dir*
Michael Greaves, *Admin Mgr*
EMP: 7 **EST:** 2001
SQ FT: 1,000
SALES: 150K **Privately Held**
SIC: 2522 Office furniture, except wood

(G-15085)
ZZZ MATTRESS MANUFACTURING
Also Called: Purest of America
11080 Dunkirk St (11412-1950)
PHONE..................................718 454-1468
Charlie Jad, *Ch of Bd*
EMP: 30 **EST:** 2012
SQ FT: 40,000
SALES: 3MM **Privately Held**
SIC: 2515 5719 Mattresses & bedsprings; beddings & linens

Saint James
Suffolk County

(G-15086)
2600 ENTERPRISES INC
Also Called: The Hacker Quarterly
2 Flowerfield Ste 30 (11780-1507)
P.O. Box 848, Middle Island (11953-0848)
PHONE..................................631 474-2677
Emmanuelle Goldstein, *Principal*
Eric Corley, *Editor*
▲ **EMP:** 10
SALES (est): 1MM **Privately Held**
WEB: www.2600.net
SIC: 2721 Magazines: publishing only, not printed on site

(G-15087)
CREATE-A-CARD INC
16 Brasswood Rd (11780-3410)
PHONE..................................631 584-2273
Arthur Messina, *President*
Kathleen Messina, *Vice Pres*
Drew Messina, *Sales Staff*
Marian Abrilz, *Marketing Staff*
EMP: 5
SALES: 375K **Privately Held**
WEB: www.createacardinc.com
SIC: 2752 2759 Color lithography; post cards, picture: lithographed; visiting cards (including business): printing

(G-15088)
DESIGN SOLUTIONS LI INC
711 Middle Country Rd (11780-3209)
PHONE..................................631 656-8700
Mario Adragna, *Owner*
EMP: 1
SQ FT: 6,000
SALES: 4MM **Privately Held**
SIC: 3639 Major kitchen appliances, except refrigerators & stoves

(G-15089)
FOREVER YOURS INTL CORP
50 James Nck (11780-4102)
PHONE..................................516 443-2743
Fax: 631 951-4700
David Lesser, *President*
EMP: 28
SQ FT: 10,000
SALES (est): 2.3MM **Privately Held**
SIC: 2335 Bridal & formal gowns

(G-15090)
IMAGE SPECIALISTS INC
80 Elderwood Dr (11780-3445)
PHONE..................................631 475-0867
Fax: 631 475-2244
Doris Costello, *Ch of Bd*
Joseph P Costello, *Vice Pres*
Stephen J Costello Sr, *Vice Pres*
Tom Domino, *Plant Mgr*
Bryan Ford, *Warehouse Mgr*
▲ **EMP:** 18
SQ FT: 30,000
SALES (est): 3.4MM **Privately Held**
WEB: www.imagespecialists.com
SIC: 2893 Printing ink

(G-15091)
SMITHTOWN CONCRETE PRODUCTS
441 Middle Country Rd (11780-3201)
P.O. Box 612, Smithtown (11787-0612)
PHONE..................................631 265-1815
Neil Spevak, *President*
Barbara Spevak, *Treasurer*
Rob Barttlett, *Adv Mgr*
EMP: 16 **EST:** 1940
SALES: 950K **Privately Held**
WEB: www.smithtownconcrete.com
SIC: 3271 Concrete block & brick

Saint Johnsville
Montgomery County

(G-15092)
CELLECT LLC
10 New St (13452-1313)
PHONE..................................508 744-6906
Richard Bambara, *Manager*
Michael Tuza, *Manager*
Carl Ursi, *Manager*
Scott Smith,
▲ **EMP:** 140
SQ FT: 200,000
SALES (est): 14.7MM **Privately Held**
WEB: www.cellectfoam.com
SIC: 3086 Packaging & shipping materials, foamed plastic

(G-15093)
CELLECT PLASTICS LLC
12 New St (13452-1313)
PHONE..................................518 568-7036
Scott Smith, *CEO*
▲ **EMP:** 100
SQ FT: 197,952
SALES (est): 5.3MM **Privately Held**
SIC: 3086 Plastics foam products

(G-15094)
HANSON AGGREGATES PA INC
7904 St Hwy 5 (13452-3514)
PHONE..................................518 568-2444
Don Sheldon, *Superintendent*
EMP: 10
SALES (corp-wide): 14.4B **Privately Held**
SIC: 1442 1422 Common sand mining; limestones, ground
HQ: Hanson Aggregates Pennsylvania, Llc
    7660 Imperial Way
    Allentown PA 18195
    610 366-4626

(G-15095)
HELMONT MILLS INC (HQ)
15 Lion Ave (13452-1398)
PHONE..................................518 568-7913
Fax: 518 568-7866
George G Gehring Jr, *CEO*
John Davidson, *Controller*
EMP: 1 **EST:** 1992
SALES: 8.9MM
SALES (corp-wide): 60.2MM **Privately Held**
SIC: 2258 Lace & warp knit fabric mills
PA: Gehring Tricot Corporation
    1225 Franklin Ave Ste 300
    Garden City NY 11530
    315 429-8551

(G-15096)
HIGHWAY GARAGE
110 State Highway 331 (13452-2818)
PHONE..................................518 568-2837
Rich Crum, *Manager*
EMP: 7 **EST:** 2011
SALES (est): 405.9K **Privately Held**
SIC: 3531 Drags, road (construction & road maintenance equipment)

(G-15097)
RC ENTPS BUS & TRCK INC
5895 State Highway 29 (13452-2413)
P.O. Box 193 (13452-0193)
PHONE..................................518 568-5753
Robert Crum, *Ch of Bd*
EMP: 6
SALES (est): 460K **Privately Held**
SIC: 7694 Motor repair services

(G-15098)
SENTINEL PRODUCTS CORP
12 New St (13452-1396)
PHONE..................................518 568-7036
Fax: 518 568-2614
Michael Tuza, *Manager*
Michael Bambara, *Manager*
EMP: 14
SALES (corp-wide): 1MM **Privately Held**
WEB: www.sentinelproducts.net
SIC: 3081 Polyethylene film

Salamanca
Cattaraugus County

(G-15099)
ALICE PERKINS
Also Called: A & F Trucking & Excavating
148 Washington St (14779-1045)
PHONE..................716 378-5100
Alice Perkins, *Co-Owner*
Fred Perkins, *Co-Owner*
EMP: 6
SQ FT: 3,212
SALES: 1.5MM **Privately Held**
SIC: 1389 4212 1411 Excavating slush pits & cellars; dump truck haulage; granite dimension stone

(G-15100)
CAPSTREAM TECHNOLOGIES LLC
16 Main St (14779-1528)
PHONE..................716 945-7100
Dale M Wymer, *Project Mgr*
Michael Krysick,
EMP: 6
SALES (est): 818.8K **Privately Held**
SIC: 3669 Intercommunication systems, electric

(G-15101)
MCHONE INDUSTRIES INC
110 Elm St (14779-1500)
P.O. Box 69 (14779-0069)
PHONE..................716 945-3380
Fax: 716 945-3780
Arnold McHone, *President*
Eva Hone, *Vice Pres*
Eva McHone, *Vice Pres*
Marlin Robbins, *Vice Pres*
Mike Redden, *Purch Mgr*
EMP: 75 **EST:** 1952
SQ FT: 75,000
SALES (est): 18.9MM **Privately Held**
WEB: www.mchoneind.com
SIC: 3469 3317 3569 3444 Metal stampings; steel pipe & tubes; robots, assembly line: industrial & commercial; sheet metalwork

(G-15102)
MONROE TABLE COMPANY INC
255 Rochester St Ste 15 (14779-1563)
PHONE..................716 945-7700
Douglas Kirchner, *CEO*
Orville Johnston, *President*
EMP: 10
SALES (est): 1MM **Privately Held**
SIC: 2599 Bar, restaurant & cafeteria furniture

(G-15103)
NORTON-SMITH HARDWOODS INC (PA)
Also Called: Arbor Valley Flooring
25 Morningside Ave (14779-1210)
PHONE..................716 945-0346
Art Smith, *Co-President*
Dan Smith, *Co-President*
Dorothy Jacoby, *Office Mgr*
▼ **EMP:** 7
SQ FT: 18,000
SALES (est): 2MM **Privately Held**
SIC: 2426 Dimension, hardwood

(G-15104)
SALAMANCA LUMBER COMPANY INC
59 Rochester St (14779-1508)
P.O. Box 416 (14779-0416)
PHONE..................716 945-4810
Fax: 716 945-1531
Reinier Taapken, *CEO*
Rinus Vollenberg, *Vice Pres*
Mike Gilbert, *Safety Mgr*
Susan Rockwell, *Financial Exec*
▼ **EMP:** 45
SQ FT: 3,000
SALES (est): 6.9MM
SALES (corp-wide): 33.2MM **Privately Held**
WEB: www.salamancalumber.com
SIC: 2421 Kiln drying of lumber
PA: Leyenaar Taapken Lamaker Holding B.V.
Kamerlingh Onnesweg 7
Vianen Ut 4131
347 374-844

(G-15105)
SALAMANCA PRESS PENNY SAVER
Also Called: Salamanca Penny Saver
36 River St (14779-1495)
PHONE..................716 945-1500
Fax: 716 945-4285
F David Radler, *President*
Kevin Burleson, *Principal*
Ernie Sage, *Sales/Mktg Mgr*
John H Satterwhite, *Treasurer*
Ellen Dougherty, *Office Mgr*
EMP: 30
SALES (est): 1.7MM **Privately Held**
SIC: 2741 2759 2711 Shopping news: publishing & printing; commercial printing; newspapers

(G-15106)
SENECA MANUFACTURING COMPANY
175 Rochester St (14779-1508)
P.O. Box 496 (14779-0496)
PHONE..................716 945-4400
Gary Sanden, *Partner*
Travis Heron, *Partner*
Dave Sanden, *Office Mgr*
▲ **EMP:** 8
SQ FT: 40,000
SALES (est): 780K **Privately Held**
SIC: 2111 Cigarettes

(G-15107)
SNYDER MANUFACTURING INC
Also Called: SMI
255 Rochester St Unit 1 (14779-1563)
PHONE..................716 945-0354
James F Snyder, *President*
Cynthia Snyder, *Corp Secy*
John Doyle, *VP Mktg*
▲ **EMP:** 25 **EST:** 2000
SQ FT: 40,000
SALES (est): 5.3MM **Privately Held**
WEB: www.snyder-mfg.com
SIC: 3423 Hand & edge tools

(G-15108)
STRATEGIES NORTH AMERICA INC
Also Called: Ellicottville Kitchen Eqp
150 Elm St (14779-2002)
P.O. Box 1549, Ellicottville (14731-1549)
PHONE..................716 945-6053
John Karassik, *President*
EMP: 5
SQ FT: 4,000
SALES (est): 814.1K **Privately Held**
SIC: 3589 Dishwashing machines, commercial

(G-15109)
SUBCON INDUSTRIES
65 South Ave (14779-1771)
PHONE..................716 945-4430
Nancy Jiardini, *Principal*
Charles Townsend, *Manager*
Lisa Sagana, *Director*
EMP: 1
SALES (est): 2.4MM
SALES (corp-wide): 1.3B **Privately Held**
WEB: www.subconindustries.com
SIC: 3999 Manufacturing industries
HQ: Nysarc, Inc., Cattaraugus County Chapter
1439 Buffalo St
Olean NY 14760
716 375-4747

(G-15110)
SUN-TIMES MEDIA GROUP INC
Also Called: Salamanca Daily Reporter
36 River St (14779-1474)
P.O. Box 111 (14779-0111)
PHONE..................716 945-1644
Kevin Burleson, *Manager*
EMP: 32
SALES (corp-wide): 304.8MM **Privately Held**
SIC: 2711 Newspapers
HQ: Sun-Times Media Group, Inc.
350 N Orleans St Fl 10
Chicago IL 60654
312 321-2299

Salem
Washington County

(G-15111)
CAROLINA EASTERN-VAIL INC
Also Called: Carol Vail
4134 State Route 22 (12865-3420)
PHONE..................518 854-9785
Charles Tucker, *Branch Mgr*
EMP: 25
SALES (corp-wide): 74.9MM **Privately Held**
SIC: 2875 Fertilizers, mixing only
PA: Carolina Eastern-Vail, Inc.
831 County Rte 28
Niverville NY 12130
518 784-9166

Salisbury Mills
Orange County

(G-15112)
CALLAHAN & NANNINI QUARRY INC
276 Clove Rd (12577-5224)
P.O. Box 164 (12577-0164)
PHONE..................845 496-4323
Fax: 845 496-8910
Robert Nannini, *President*
Bob Nannini, *Vice Pres*
Jay Nannini, *Vice Pres*
Leslie Nannini, *Admin Sec*
EMP: 5
SQ FT: 3,600
SALES (est): 5.3MM **Privately Held**
SIC: 1459 5032 Shale (common) quarrying; stone, crushed or broken

Sanborn
Niagara County

(G-15113)
BRIDGE COMPONENTS INC
2122 Cory Dr (14132-9338)
PHONE..................716 731-1184
Silvio G Derubeis, *Principal*
EMP: 6
SALES (est): 628.8K **Privately Held**
SIC: 3399 Primary metal products

(G-15114)
BRIDGESTONE APM COMPANY
6350 Inducon Dr E (14132-9015)
PHONE..................419 423-9552
Duke Kawai, *Manager*
EMP: 60
SALES (corp-wide): 30.7B **Privately Held**
SIC: 3061 Automotive rubber goods (mechanical)
HQ: Bridgestone Apm Company
2030 Production Dr
Findlay OH 45840
419 423-9552

(G-15115)
BRUCE PIERCE
Also Called: Core Welding
2386 Lockport Rd (14132-9011)
P.O. Box 209 (14132-0209)
PHONE..................716 731-9310
Fax: 716 731-9310
Bruce Pierce, *Owner*
Coreen Froman, *Admin Sec*
EMP: 5
SQ FT: 4,080
SALES (est): 500K **Privately Held**
WEB: www.brucepierce.com
SIC: 3443 3599 7692 1799 Fabricated plate work (boiler shop); machine shop, jobbing & repair; welding repair; sandblasting of building exteriors

(G-15116)
BUFFALO GEAR INC
3635 Lockport Rd (14132-9704)
PHONE..................716 731-2100
Fax: 716 731-2100
Daniel Szczygiel, *President*
Gail Nichols, *Vice Pres*
John Jerge, *Manager*
Allan Monich, *Manager*
▲ **EMP:** 20 **EST:** 1962
SQ FT: 22,000
SALES (est): 4MM **Privately Held**
WEB: www.buffalogear.com
SIC: 3566 Speed changers, drives & gears

(G-15117)
CERTIFIED FABRICATIONS INC
2127 Cory Dr (14132-9338)
PHONE..................716 731-8123
Fax: 716 731-8123
Christopher Karnavas, *President*
EMP: 15
SQ FT: 12,000
SALES (est): 1.3MM **Privately Held**
SIC: 7692 3599 Welding repair; machine shop, jobbing & repair

(G-15118)
COMMERCIAL SOLUTIONS INC
6359 Ward Rd (14132-9266)
PHONE..................716 731-5825
James C Kaiser, *Ch of Bd*
EMP: 12
SALES (est): 1.2MM **Privately Held**
SIC: 3589 Commercial cleaning equipment

(G-15119)
EDWARDS VACUUM LLC (DH)
6416 Inducon Dr W (14132-9019)
PHONE..................800 848-9800
Matthew Taylor, *CEO*
John O'Sullivan, *Ch of Bd*
Butch Paddock, *President*
Michael Allison, *Vice Pres*
Nigel Wenden, *Vice Pres*
▲ **EMP:** 100
SALES (est): 178.4MM
SALES (corp-wide): 11.7B **Privately Held**
SIC: 3563 Vacuum (air extraction) systems, industrial
HQ: Edwards Limited
Crawley Business Quarter
Crawley W SUSSEX RH10
129 352-8844

(G-15120)
GAMBLE & GAMBLE INC (PA)
Also Called: Unit Step Company
5890 West St (14132-9245)
PHONE..................716 731-3239
Fax: 716 731-3239
Ronald H Gamble, *President*
EMP: 4
SQ FT: 2,500
SALES (est): 1.4MM **Privately Held**
SIC: 3272 Concrete products, precast

(G-15121)
INNOVATIVE CLEANING SOLUTIONS
2990 Carney Dr (14132-9305)
PHONE..................716 731-4408
EMP: 5
SQ FT: 1,600
SALES (est): 727.2K **Privately Held**
SIC: 3559 Mfg Misc Industry Machinery

(G-15122)
KATZ GROUP AMERICAS INC
Also Called: Katz Americas
3685 Lockport Rd (14132-9404)
PHONE..................716 995-3071
Frank Muraca, *CEO*
Michael Elbers, *COO*
Michael Dimartino, *CFO*
Craig Erisman, *Controller*
Kelly Barry, *Accountant*
▲ **EMP:** 50
SQ FT: 70,000

SALES (est): 12.6MM **Privately Held**
WEB: www.american-coaster.com
SIC: 2679 Paper products, converted

(G-15123)
KINSHOFER USA INC
6420 Inducon Dr W Ste G (14132-9025)
PHONE.................................716 731-4333
Martin Francois, *General Mgr*
Francois Martin, *General Mgr*
▲ **EMP:** 19
SALES (est): 4.7MM
SALES (corp-wide): 4.8B **Privately Held**
SIC: 3531 Excavators: cable, clamshell, crane, derrick, dragline, etc.; cranes
HQ: Kinshofer Gmbh
 Hauptstr. 76
 Waakirchen 83666
 802 188-990

(G-15124)
MYLES TOOL COMPANY INC
6300 Inducon Corporate Dr (14132-9346)
PHONE.................................716 731-1300
Fax: 716 731-9140
Myles Barraclough, *President*
Sandra Barraclough, *Vice Pres*
Tim Barraclough, *Vice Pres*
James Thiel, *Vice Pres*
Paul Reding, *Prdtn Mgr*
EMP: 42 EST: 1977
SQ FT: 4,500
SALES (est): 9.5MM **Privately Held**
WEB: www.mylestool.com
SIC: 3545 3541 Machine tool accessories; machine tools, metal cutting type

(G-15125)
PRECISION PLUS VACUUM PARTS
6416 Inducon Dr W (14132-9019)
PHONE.................................716 297-2039
Joe Miller, *President*
Joseph Miller, *Superintendent*
Sarah De, *Accounts Mgr*
Micheal Willis, *Marketing Mgr*
Ron Aloisio, *Manager*
▲ **EMP:** 62
SQ FT: 20,000
SALES (est): 11.9MM
SALES (corp-wide): 11.7B **Privately Held**
WEB: www.precisionplus.com
SIC: 3563 Vacuum pumps, except laboratory
HQ: Edwards Vacuum Llc
 6416 Inducon Dr W
 Sanborn NY 14132
 800 848-9800

(G-15126)
PYROTEK INCORPORATED
Metaullics Systems Division
2040 Cory Dr (14132-9388)
PHONE.................................716 731-3221
Fax: 716 731-4943
George Bitler, *Principal*
Kevin Scott, *Manager*
Dave Burkholder, *Manager*
Claudia Lisman, *Executive*
EMP: 50
SALES (corp-wide): 632.7MM **Privately Held**
SIC: 3624 3569 3999 Carbon & graphite products; filters; chairs, hydraulic, barber & beauty shop
PA: Pyrotek Incorporated
 705 W 1st Ave
 Spokane WA 99201
 509 926-6212

(G-15127)
SHARP PRINTING INC
3477 Lockport Rd (14132-9491)
PHONE.................................716 731-3994
Slade Sharpsteen, *President*
EMP: 7
SQ FT: 1,200
SALES (est): 715K **Privately Held**
WEB: www.sharpprinting.com
SIC: 2759 Commercial printing

(G-15128)
UNITED BIOCHEMICALS LLC
6351 Inducon Dr E (14132-9016)
PHONE.................................716 731-5161
Fax: 716 731-5163

Dr Duane Mazur, *Vice Pres*
Paul Parwulski, *VP Opers*
Manuel Brocke-Benz, *Mng Member*
▲ **EMP:** 56
SALES (est): 17.2MM
SALES (corp-wide): 4.3B **Publicly Held**
SIC: 2869 Industrial organic chemicals
HQ: Vwr International, Llc
 100 Matsonford Rd Bldg 1
 Radnor PA 19087
 610 386-1700

(G-15129)
UNITED MATERIALS LLC
2186 Cory Dr (14132-9338)
PHONE.................................716 731-2332
Jim Pierce, *Mfg Staff*
Lean Guilinan, *Manager*
Leon Juiliani, *Manager*
Jeff Whalen, *Manager*
EMP: 22
SALES (corp-wide): 19.3MM **Privately Held**
SIC: 3273 Ready-mixed concrete
PA: United Materials, L.L.C.
 3949 Frest Pk Way Ste 400
 North Tonawanda NY 14120
 716 683-1432

(G-15130)
VOSS MANUFACTURING INC
2345 Lockport Rd (14132-9636)
PHONE.................................716 731-5062
Fax: 716 731-5868
Rita Voss Kammerer, *President*
Thomas Kammerer, *Vice Pres*
Dave Siegmann, *Foreman/Supr*
Pete Lute, *Engineer*
Mark Targus, *Engineer*
▲ **EMP:** 73
SQ FT: 55,000
SALES (est): 24.6MM **Privately Held**
WEB: www.vossmfg.com
SIC: 3444 3599 7389 3549 Sheet metalwork; custom machinery; design, commercial & industrial; metalworking machinery

Sandy Creek
Oswego County

(G-15131)
CASTERS CUSTOM SAWING
6323 Us Route 11 (13145-2191)
PHONE.................................315 387-5104
Fax: 315 387-5104
Edith Caster, *Principal*
EMP: 19
SALES (est): 1.6MM **Privately Held**
SIC: 2421 Sawmills & planing mills, general

Sangerfield
Oneida County

(G-15132)
CHAMPION HOME BUILDERS INC
951 Rte 12 S (13455)
P.O. Box 177 (13455-0177)
PHONE.................................315 841-4122
Fax: 315 841-3538
John Copeletti, *General Mgr*
Lloyd Black, *Div Sub Head*
Ed Ostrander, *Purchasing*
James Sigsbee, *Engineer*
Jack Susanburger, *Personnel*
EMP: 150
SQ FT: 115,000 **Privately Held**
WEB: www.championaz.com
SIC: 2451 Mobile homes
HQ: Champion Home Builders, Inc.
 755 W Big Beaver Rd # 1000
 Troy MI 48084
 248 614-8200

Saranac
Clinton County

(G-15133)
OPTIC SOLUTION LLC
133 Standish Rd (12981-2630)
PHONE.................................518 293-4321
Darrell McGee,
Gregory Gibbons, *Administration*
EMP: 13
SALES: 675K **Privately Held**
SIC: 3652 Compact laser discs, prerecorded; aircraft flight instruments

Saranac Lake
Franklin County

(G-15134)
ADIRONDACK PUBLISHING CO INC (HQ)
Also Called: Adirondack Daily Enterprise
54 Broadway (12983-1704)
P.O. Box 318 (12983-0318)
PHONE.................................518 891-2600
Fax: 518 891-2756
George Ogden Nutting, *President*
Cathy Moore, *Publisher*
Peter Crowley, *Editor*
Alec Bieber, *Manager*
EMP: 32 EST: 1904
SQ FT: 5,000
SALES (est): 2.5MM
SALES (corp-wide): 553.9MM **Privately Held**
SIC: 2711 2752 Job printing & newspaper publishing combined; commercial printing, lithographic
PA: The Ogden Newspapers Inc
 1500 Main St
 Wheeling WV 26003
 304 233-0100

(G-15135)
COMPASS PRINTING PLUS
42 Main St (12983-1708)
PHONE.................................518 891-7050
John Gagnon, *Branch Mgr*
EMP: 11
SALES (corp-wide): 986K **Privately Held**
SIC: 2752 Commercial printing, lithographic
PA: Compass Printing Plus
 42 Main St
 Saranac Lake NY 12983
 518 523-3308

(G-15136)
COMPASS PRINTING PLUS (PA)
42 Main St (12983-1708)
PHONE.................................518 523-3308
Tom Connors, *Owner*
John Gagnon, *Branch Mgr*
EMP: 7
SALES (est): 986K **Privately Held**
SIC: 2752 Commercial printing, lithographic

(G-15137)
GETTING THE WORD OUT INC
Also Called: ADIRONDACK EXPLORER
36 Church St Apt 106 (12983-1850)
PHONE.................................518 891-9352
Dick Beamish, *President*
Debra Stover, *Office Mgr*
Andreas Mowka, *Director*
Keith McKeever, *Spokesman*
EMP: 5
SALES: 881.3K **Privately Held**
SIC: 2721 Magazines: publishing only, not printed on site

(G-15138)
GRAYMONT MATERIALS (NY) INC
909 State Route 3 (12983-5109)
PHONE.................................518 891-0236
Stephane Godin, *Vice Pres*
Phil Marquis, *Plant Mgr*
Nathan Dutil, *Project Mgr*
Shawn Stedman, *Human Res Dir*

Sunil Joshi, *Sales Mgr*
EMP: 22
SALES (corp-wide): 260.9MM **Privately Held**
WEB: www.graymont-ab.com
SIC: 1422 Crushed & broken limestone
HQ: Graymont Materials (Ny) Inc.
 111 Quarry Rd
 Plattsburgh NY 12901
 518 561-5321

(G-15139)
NORTHERN NEW YORK RURAL
Also Called: North Country Behavioral
126 Kiwassa Rd (12983-2357)
P.O. Box 891 (12983-0891)
PHONE.................................518 891-9460
Fax: 518 891-9461
Samantha Dashnaw, *Manager*
Samantha Denshaw, *Manager*
Barry Brogan, *Director*
EMP: 5
SALES: 390.3K **Privately Held**
SIC: 3999 Education aids, devices & supplies

Saratoga Springs
Saratoga County

(G-15140)
09 FLSHY BLL/DSERT SUNRISE LLC
2 Smith Bridge Rd (12866-5617)
PHONE.................................518 583-6638
Lindsey Heumann CPA, *Principal*
EMP: 5
SALES (est): 320.1K **Privately Held**
SIC: 3291 Hones

(G-15141)
ADIRONDACK SIGN PERFECT INC
72 Ballston Ave (12866-4427)
PHONE.................................518 409-7446
John Natale, *Principal*
Adam Wakalenko, *Principal*
EMP: 8
SQ FT: 3,500
SALES: 740K **Privately Held**
SIC: 3993 Signs & advertising specialties

(G-15142)
ADVANTAGE PRESS INC
74 Warren St (12866-2534)
PHONE.................................518 584-3405
Fax: 518 583-2763
Mark Sutton, *President*
Kimberly Sutton, *Corp Secy*
EMP: 12
SQ FT: 4,800
SALES (est): 900K **Privately Held**
WEB: www.myadvantagepress.com
SIC: 2752 Commercial printing, offset

(G-15143)
AGROCHEM INC
3 Duplainville Rd (12866-9073)
PHONE.................................518 226-4850
Robert J Demarco, *President*
John Demarco, *Vice Pres*
Amiee Trader, *Manager*
EMP: 20
SQ FT: 30,000
SALES (est): 7MM **Privately Held**
WEB: www.agrocheminc.com
SIC: 2879 Agricultural chemicals

(G-15144)
BALL METAL BEVERAGE CONT CORP
Also Called: Ball Metal Beverage Cont Div
11 Adams Rd (12866-9061)
PHONE.................................518 587-6030
Fax: 518 587-5272
Steve Di Loreto, *Plant Mgr*
Steven Di Lorto, *Plant Mgr*
Harry Monroe, *Maint Spvr*
Robert Nelson, *Engineer*
Tracy Ellis, *CPA*
EMP: 225
SALES (corp-wide): 8B **Publicly Held**
SIC: 3411 Metal cans

Saratoga Springs - Saratoga County (G-15145)

HQ: Ball Metal Beverage Container Corp.
9300 W 108th Cir
Westminster CO 80021
303 469-5511

(G-15145)
BIG JOHNS ADIRONDACK INC
Also Called: Big John's Beef Jerky
45 N Milton Rd (12866-6137)
PHONE.................................518 587-3680
John Ponessa, *President*
EMP: 5
SALES: 60K **Privately Held**
SIC: 2013 Snack sticks, including jerky: from purchased meat

(G-15146)
C C INDUSTRIES INC
344 Burgoyne Rd (12866-5493)
PHONE.................................518 581-7633
Charles Carlstrom, *President*
EMP: 13
SQ FT: 9,500
SALES: 450K **Privately Held**
SIC: 2754 Imprinting, gravure

(G-15147)
CAPITAL STONE SARATOGA LLC
4295 Route 50 (12866-2962)
PHONE.................................518 226-8677
Paul Sicluna,
EMP: 6
SALES (est): 599.9K **Privately Held**
SIC: 3281 Granite, cut & shaped

(G-15148)
CAPITOL EQ 2 LLC
376 Broadway Ste 27 (12866-3115)
PHONE.................................518 886-8341
Daniel Grignon,
EMP: 3
SALES: 5MM **Privately Held**
SIC: 3531 Construction machinery

(G-15149)
CHEQUEDCOM INC
513 Broadway Ste 1 (12866-6730)
PHONE.................................888 412-0699
Greg Moran, *CEO*
Michael Gladden, *President*
John Tobison, *COO*
George Ehinger, *Vice Pres*
Gary Ito, *CFO*
EMP: 30
SALES (est): 3MM
SALES (corp-wide): 693.6K **Privately Held**
SIC: 7372 8742 Business oriented computer software; human resource consulting services
PA: Chequed Holdings, Llc
513 Broadway Ste 1
Saratoga Springs NY 12866
888 412-0699

(G-15150)
ENCORE ELECTRONICS INC
4400 Route 50 (12866-2924)
PHONE.................................518 584-5354
Fax: 518 584-5963
Thomas J Barrett, *General Mgr*
Nancy Zucchino, *Vice Pres*
Rosemary Lafreniere, *Mfg Staff*
Rick Leonard, *Manager*
Tom Moeller, *Info Tech Mgr*
EMP: 25
SQ FT: 15,000
SALES (est): 5.8MM **Privately Held**
WEB: www.encore-elec.com
SIC: 3824 Mechanical & electromechanical counters & devices; electromechanical counters

(G-15151)
ESPEY MFG & ELECTRONICS CORP (PA)
233 Ballston Ave (12866-4767)
PHONE.................................518 245-4400
Fax: 518 245-4421
Howard Pinsley, *Ch of Bd*
Patrick T Enright Jr, *President*
David A O'Neil, *CFO*
Katrina L Sparano,
Peggy A Murphy, *Admin Sec*
EMP: 150 **EST:** 1928

SQ FT: 151,000
SALES: 27.4MM **Publicly Held**
WEB: www.espey.com
SIC: 3679 Power supplies, all types: static

(G-15152)
FREEDOM MFG LLC
3 Duplainville Rd Bldg 4 (12866-9073)
PHONE.................................518 584-0441
Scott Mummert, *Principal*
Joe Patton, *Info Tech Mgr*
EMP: 13
SALES (est): 1.4MM **Privately Held**
SIC: 3999 Manufacturing industries

(G-15153)
FRIENDLY FUEL INCORPORATED
54 Church St (12866-2007)
PHONE.................................518 581-7036
Manjinder Grewal, *Principal*
EMP: 5
SALES (est): 406.5K **Privately Held**
SIC: 2869 Fuels

(G-15154)
GOLUB CORPORATION
3045 Route 50 (12866-2919)
PHONE.................................518 583-3697
Fax: 518 583-3110
Paul Flatley, *Site Mgr*
Paul R Flately, *Manager*
EMP: 104
SALES (corp-wide): 3.4B **Privately Held**
SIC: 3751 Motorcycles & related parts
PA: The Golub Corporation
461 Nott St
Schenectady NY 12308
518 355-5000

(G-15155)
GREAT AMERICAN BICYCLE LLC
41 Geyser Rd (12866-9038)
PHONE.................................518 584-8100
Jason Bierlotta, *Engineer*
Ben Serotta, *Mng Member*
Stephen Fairchild, *Manager*
Rick Laspesa, *IT/INT Sup*
Brendan Quirk, *IT/INT Sup*
EMP: 50
SQ FT: 15,000
SALES (est): 6.9MM **Privately Held**
WEB: www.serotta.com
SIC: 3751 5941 Bicycles & related parts; frames, motorcycle & bicycle; sporting goods & bicycle shops

(G-15156)
GREENFIELD MANUFACTURING INC
25 Freedom Way (12866-9076)
PHONE.................................518 581-2368
Duane R Palmateer, *President*
Mary McChesney, *Bookkeeper*
▲ **EMP:** 11
SQ FT: 40,000
SALES (est): 2.2MM **Privately Held**
WEB: www.greenfieldmfg.com
SIC: 2899 Acid resist for etching

(G-15157)
GUYSON CORPORATION OF USA (PA)
13 Grande Blvd (12866-9090)
PHONE.................................518 587-7894
Steve Byrnes, *President*
Mark Butler, *Engineer*
Stephen M Donohue, *VP Sales*
◆ **EMP:** 46
SQ FT: 78,000
SALES (est): 10.4MM **Privately Held**
WEB: www.guyson.com
SIC: 3569 Blast cleaning equipment, dustless

(G-15158)
HAPPY SOFTWARE INC
11 Federal St (12866-4111)
PHONE.................................518 584-4668
Fax: 518 584-5388
Joseph Mastrianni, *President*
Jennifer Terito, *Opers Mgr*
Kirsten Cleveland, *Sales Mgr*
Jessica Yerdon, *Mktg Coord*

Sean McGuckin, *Marketing Staff*
EMP: 7 **EST:** 1994
SQ FT: 1,500
SALES (est): 881.8K **Privately Held**
WEB: www.happysoftware.com
SIC: 7372 Prepackaged software

(G-15159)
HUNTINGTON INGALLS INC
33 Cady Hill Blvd (12866-9047)
PHONE.................................518 884-3834
Peter Wedesky, *Branch Mgr*
Benjamin England, *Associate*
EMP: 50 **Publicly Held**
SIC: 3731 Shipbuilding & repairing
HQ: Huntington Ingalls Incorporated
4101 Washington Ave
Newport News VA 23607
757 380-2000

(G-15160)
INCENTIVATE HEALTH LLC
60 Railroad Pl Ste 101 (12866-3045)
PHONE.................................518 469-8491
J Lawrence Toole, *President*
Patricia Hasbrouck, *Co-Owner*
Robert Legrande II, *Co-Owner*
EMP: 5
SALES (est): 117.2K **Privately Held**
SIC: 7372 Application computer software

(G-15161)
JOURNAL REGISTER COMPANY
Also Called: Saratogian USA Today
20 Lake Ave (12866-2314)
PHONE.................................518 584-4242
Fax: 518 583-8014
Charles Kraebel, *Editor*
Paul Tackett, *Editor*
Stephany Quevillon, *Cust Mgr*
Sean Fagan, *Accounts Exec*
Jaclyn Grady, *Accounts Exec*
EMP: 80
SALES (corp-wide): 828.3MM **Privately Held**
SIC: 2711 Newspapers: publishing only, not printed on site
PA: Journal Register Company
5 Hanover Sq Fl 25
New York NY 10004
212 257-7212

(G-15162)
LYONS & SULLIVAN INC
376 Caroline St (12866-3739)
PHONE.................................518 584-1523
Charles Sullivan, *President*
EMP: 5
SALES (est): 300K **Privately Held**
SIC: 2421 Sawmills & planing mills, general

(G-15163)
NALCO COMPANY LLC
6 Butler Pl 2 (12866-2155)
PHONE.................................518 796-1985
Joseph Fitzhenry, *Manager*
EMP: 20
SALES (corp-wide): 13.5B **Publicly Held**
WEB: www.nalco.com
SIC: 2899 5169 Chemical preparations; chemicals & allied products
HQ: Nalco Company Llc
1601 W Diehl Rd
Naperville IL 60563
630 305-1000

(G-15164)
NANOBIONOVUM LLC
117 Grand Ave (12866-4118)
P.O. Box 4434 (12866-8026)
PHONE.................................518 581-1171
Lance Bell, *CEO*
EMP: 10
SQ FT: 5,000
SALES (est): 710.4K **Privately Held**
SIC: 3841 Diagnostic apparatus, medical

(G-15165)
OLDE SARATOGA BREWING
131 Excelsior Ave (12866-8545)
PHONE.................................518 581-0492
Colleen Clark, *Owner*
Meg Thompson, *Manager*
EMP: 12

SALES (est): 1.5MM **Privately Held**
SIC: 2082 5181 Malt beverages; beer & ale

(G-15166)
PHYTOFILTER TECHNOLOGIES INC
9 Kirby Rd Apt 19 (12866-9287)
PHONE.................................518 507-6399
Martin Mittelmark, *CEO*
EMP: 5 **EST:** 2010
SALES (est): 400K **Privately Held**
SIC: 3564 Air purification equipment

(G-15167)
POST COMMUNITY MEDIA LLC
376 Broadway (12866-3127)
P.O. Box 1090 (12866-0890)
PHONE.................................518 374-4141
Dennis Donoghue, *Manager*
Tom Woodman, *Manager*
EMP: 139
SALES (corp-wide): 1.7B **Privately Held**
WEB: www.postnewsweektech.com
SIC: 2711 2752 Newspapers, publishing & printing; commercial printing, lithographic
HQ: Post Community Media Llc
1301 K St Nw
Washington DC 20071
301 670-2565

(G-15168)
QUAD/GRAPHICS INC
56 Duplainville Rd (12866-9050)
PHONE.................................518 581-4000
Fax: 518 581-4874
Dave Calmes, *General Mgr*
Davida Scripter, *Buyer*
Tom Kazda, *Engineer*
John Atkinson, *Human Res Mgr*
Janette Spieldenner, *Accounts Mgr*
EMP: 900
SALES (corp-wide): 4.6B **Publicly Held**
WEB: www.qg.com
SIC: 2752 2791 2789 Commercial printing, offset; typesetting; bookbinding & related work
PA: Quad/Graphics Inc.
N61w23044 Harrys Way
Sussex WI 53089
414 566-6000

(G-15169)
RECORD
Also Called: Sunday Record, The
20 Lake Ave (12866-2314)
PHONE.................................518 270-1200
Fax: 518 270-1202
Chad Beatty, *President*
Fred Degesco, *President*
Linda Gunther, *Human Res Dir*
EMP: 1
SQ FT: 35,000
SALES (est): 1.6MM
SALES (corp-wide): 828.3MM **Privately Held**
WEB: www.troyrecord.com
SIC: 2711 Newspapers, publishing & printing
PA: Journal Register Company
5 Hanover Sq Fl 25
New York NY 10004
212 257-7212

(G-15170)
REDSPRING COMMUNICATIONS INC
125 High Rock Ave (12866-2307)
PHONE.................................518 587-0547
James Hill, *President*
EMP: 44
SQ FT: 10,500
SALES (est): 3MM **Privately Held**
WEB: www.redspring.com
SIC: 2741 Newsletter publishing; posters: publishing only, not printed on site

(G-15171)
SARATOGA SPRING WATER COMPANY
11 Geyser Rd (12866-9038)
PHONE.................................518 584-6363
Fax: 518 584-0380
Adam Madkour, *CEO*
Steve Gilbank, *Principal*

▲ = Import ▼ = Export
◆ = Import/Export

Michael Lawson, *Plant Mgr*
Mark Horwitz, *Controller*
Shanon Green, *Human Res Mgr*
EMP: 22
SQ FT: 40,000
SALES (est): 5.9MM **Privately Held**
WEB: www.saratogaspringwater.com
SIC: 2086 Mineral water, carbonated: packaged in cans, bottles, etc.

(G-15172)
SCA TISSUE NORTH AMERICA LLC
49 Geyser Rd (12866-9038)
PHONE 518 583-2785
Tim Cutler, *Manager*
EMP: 219
SALES (corp-wide): 14B **Privately Held**
SIC: 2621 Paper mills
HQ: Sca Tissue North America, Llc
1451 Mcmahon Rd
Neenah WI 54956
920 725-7031

(G-15173)
SENSIO AMERICA
18 Division St Ste 207a (12866-2197)
PHONE 877 501-5337
Paul Bardwell, *General Mgr*
Terry V Delong, *Principal*
EMP: 15
SALES (est): 2.9MM **Privately Held**
SIC: 3648 Lighting equipment

(G-15174)
STRATEGIC SIGNAGE SOURCING LLC
2 Gilbert Rd (12866-9701)
PHONE 518 450-1093
Robert L Keyser, *President*
Kenneth W Wasson, *Vice Pres*
Amber-Lee Ranalli, *Project Mgr*
Carole Van Buren, *Project Mgr*
Suzanne K Nelson, *Marketing Staff*
EMP: 10
SALES (est): 1.2MM **Privately Held**
SIC: 3993 Signs & advertising specialties

(G-15175)
TMC USA LLC (PA)
60 Railroad Pl Ste 501 (12866-3048)
PHONE 518 587-8920
John Halnan,
EMP: 7
SALES (est): 4.5MM **Privately Held**
WEB: www.tmcusallc.com
SIC: 2721 Periodicals

(G-15176)
WARD LAFRANCE TRUCK CORP
26 Congress St Ste 259f (12866-4168)
PHONE 518 893-1865
Daniel Olszansky, *President*
EMP: 15 **EST:** 1978
SALES (est): 12.8MM **Privately Held**
SIC: 3537 Trucks: freight, baggage, etc.: industrial, except mining

(G-15177)
WILLIAM J BLUME WORLDWIDE SVCS
Also Called: Blume Worldwide Services
732 Route 9p (12866-7291)
PHONE 914 723-6185
Fax: 914 723-6085
William J Blume, *President*
Betty Blume, *Vice Pres*
EMP: 6
SALES (est): 900K **Privately Held**
WEB: www.blumeworldwideservices.com
SIC: 3648 5088 Lighting equipment; marine propulsion machinery & equipment; marine supplies

---

Saugerties
Ulster County

(G-15178)
ADIRONDACK STAIRS INC
990 Kings Hwy (12477-4373)
P.O. Box 419 (12477-0419)
PHONE 845 246-2525
Fax: 845 246-3131

Karl H Neumann, *President*
Mattie Anttila, *Vice Pres*
EMP: 12 **EST:** 1966
SALES (est): 1.3MM **Privately Held**
SIC: 2431 Staircases & stairs, wood

(G-15179)
AMETEK TCHNICAL INDUS PDTS INC
Also Called: Ametek Rtron Technical Mtr Div
75 North St (12477-1039)
PHONE 845 246-3401
Mark Dwyer, *Plant Mgr*
Edward Hopp, *Plant Mgr*
David Cade, *Engineer*
Lee Denman, *Engineer*
Jeremy Roberts, *Engineer*
EMP: 26
SALES (corp-wide): 3.9B **Publicly Held**
WEB: www.rotronmilaero.com
SIC: 3564 Blowers & fans
HQ: Ametek Technical & Industrial Products, Inc
100 E Erie St Ste 130
Kent OH 44240
330 677-3754

(G-15180)
ARISTA FLAG CORPORATION
157 W Saugerties Rd (12477-3532)
P.O. Box 319 (12477-0319)
PHONE 845 246-7700
Fax: 845 246-7786
Stephen Suma, *President*
Susan Suma, *Corp Secy*
Rita Mary Suma, *Vice Pres*
EMP: 12
SQ FT: 5,500
SALES (est): 1.1MM **Privately Held**
WEB: www.aristaflag.com
SIC: 2399 Banners, made from fabric; flags, fabric; pennants

(G-15181)
CERES TECHNOLOGIES INC
5 Tower Dr (12477-4386)
P.O. Box 209 (12477-0209)
PHONE 845 247-4701
Kevin Brady, *President*
Partha Buragohain, *President*
Sharon Burton, *General Mgr*
Petra Klein, *Vice Pres*
Kira Cozzolino, *Project Mgr*
EMP: 70
SQ FT: 50,000
SALES (est): 21.1MM **Privately Held**
SIC: 3674 3823 3826 Semiconductors & related devices; industrial instrmnts msrmnt display/control process variable; analytical instruments

(G-15182)
CVD EQUIPMENT CORPORATION
1117 Kings Hwy (12477-4343)
PHONE 845 246-3631
Kevin Collions, *Manager*
EMP: 20
SALES (corp-wide): 38.9MM **Publicly Held**
WEB: www.cvdequipment.com
SIC: 3559 Sewing machines & hat & zipper making machinery
PA: Cvd Equipment Corporation
355 S Technology Dr
Central Islip NY 11722
631 981-7081

(G-15183)
DE LUXE PACKAGING CORP
63 North St (12477-1039)
PHONE 416 754-4633
Richard Goulet, *President*
Paul Fischer, *Plant Supt*
EMP: 50 **EST:** 2003
SALES (est): 6.6MM
SALES (corp-wide): 3.2B **Privately Held**
SIC: 2671 3497 Packaging paper & plastics film, coated & laminated; paper coated or laminated for packaging; plastic film, coated or laminated for packaging; waxed paper: made from purchased material; foil containers for bakery goods & frozen foods

HQ: Packaging Dynamics Corporation
3900 W 43rd St
Chicago IL 60632
773 254-8000

(G-15184)
DELUXE PACKAGING CORP
63 North St (12477-1039)
P.O. Box 269 (12477-0269)
PHONE 845 246-6090
Fax: 845 246-0511
Jim Tarrant, *Sales Staff*
Richard Goulet, *Branch Mgr*
Lisa Gardner, *Relations*
EMP: 19
SQ FT: 32,740
SALES (corp-wide): 10.5MM **Privately Held**
WEB: www.deluxepack.com
SIC: 2676 Toilet paper: made from purchased paper
PA: De Luxe Paper Products Inc
120 Nugget Ave
Scarborough ON M1S 3
416 291-0598

(G-15185)
INQUIRING MINDS INC (PA)
65 S Partition St (12477-1413)
PHONE 845 246-5775
Bryan Donahue, *President*
EMP: 9 **EST:** 2012
SALES (est): 1MM **Privately Held**
SIC: 3421 Table & food cutlery, including butchers'

(G-15186)
KENBENCO INC
Also Called: Benson Steel Fabricators
437 Route 212 (12477-4620)
P.O. Box 480 (12477-0480)
PHONE 845 246-3066
Myron E Benson, *Owner*
Jeniffer Benson, *Manager*
EMP: 15
SQ FT: 12,000
SALES (est): 3.2MM **Privately Held**
WEB: www.bensonsteelfabricators.com
SIC: 3312 3431 Blast furnaces & steel mills; metal sanitary ware

(G-15187)
LODOLCE MACHINE CO INC
196 Malden Tpke (12477-5015)
PHONE 845 246-7017
James Lodolce, *Ch of Bd*
Michael Lodolce, *President*
Dennis Barringer, *Engineer*
Robin Charlton, *Office Mgr*
Joseph Fisco, *Manager*
▲ **EMP:** 38 **EST:** 1963
SQ FT: 65,000
SALES (est): 8.3MM **Privately Held**
WEB: www.lodolce.com
SIC: 3599 1761 3479 Machine shop, jobbing & repair; sheet metalwork; painting, coating & hot dipping

(G-15188)
MORGAN FUEL & HEATING CO INC
240 Ulster Ave (12477-1221)
PHONE 845 246-4931
EMP: 28
SALES (corp-wide): 53.3MM **Privately Held**
SIC: 2869 Fuels
PA: Morgan Fuel & Heating Co., Inc.
2785 W Main St
Wappingers Falls NY 12590
845 297-5580

(G-15189)
NORTHEAST SOLITE CORPORATION (PA)
1135 Kings Hwy (12477-4343)
P.O. Box 437, Mount Marion (12456-0437)
PHONE 845 246-2646
Fax: 845 246-3356
John W Roberts, *Ch of Bd*
Philip M Nesmith, *President*
Jessica Eng, *Senior VP*
James Gregory, *Vice Pres*
Max Kalafat, *Vice Pres*
EMP: 40

SALES (est): 17.9MM **Privately Held**
WEB: www.nesolite.com
SIC: 3295 Minerals, ground or treated

(G-15190)
PAPER HOUSE PRODUCTIONS INC
160 Malden Tpke Bldg 2 (12477-5015)
P.O. Box 259 (12477-0259)
PHONE 845 246-7261
Donald A Guidi, *CEO*
Pam Gardeski, *Vice Pres*
Linda Vansteenburg, *CFO*
Sarah Ardila, *VP Sales*
Gretchen Vonderlieth, *Marketing Mgr*
◆ **EMP:** 25
SQ FT: 16,000
SALES (est): 3.7MM **Privately Held**
WEB: www.paperhouseproductions.com
SIC: 2771 2752 5112 5945 Greeting cards; decals, lithographed; greeting cards; hobby & craft supplies

(G-15191)
PESCES BAKERY INC
Also Called: Pesce Bakery
20 Pesce Ct (12477-5054)
PHONE 845 246-4730
Richard Pesce, *President*
Rich Pesce, *President*
EMP: 6 **EST:** 1946
SQ FT: 3,000
SALES (est): 410K **Privately Held**
SIC: 2051 5461 Bakery: wholesale or wholesale/retail combined; bakeries

(G-15192)
PETE LEVIN MUSIC INC
598 Schoolhouse Rd (12477-3325)
PHONE 845 247-9211
Peter Levin, *President*
Theresa Levin, *Vice Pres*
EMP: 5
SALES (est): 340K **Privately Held**
WEB: www.petelevin.com
SIC: 3652 Pre-recorded records & tapes

(G-15193)
ROTHE WELDING INC
1455 Route 212 (12477-3040)
PHONE 845 246-3051
Fax: 845 246-6351
Dorothy L Fauci, *Chairman*
Raymond Scally, *Corp Secy*
EMP: 8
SQ FT: 11,500
SALES (est): 1.8MM **Privately Held**
WEB: www.hvaccess.com
SIC: 3441 7692 Fabricated structural metal; welding repair

(G-15194)
SIMULAIDS INC
16 Simulaids Dr (12477-5067)
P.O. Box 1289 (12477-8289)
PHONE 845 679-2475
Dean T Johnson, *CEO*
J Boyce, *Vice Pres*
Jack McNeff, *Vice Pres*
Gus Hof, *Plant Mgr*
Warren Johnson, *Marketing Staff*
EMP: 93 **EST:** 1963
SQ FT: 50,000
SALES (est): 22.3MM
SALES (corp-wide): 802.3MM **Publicly Held**
WEB: www.simulaids.com
SIC: 3841 7841 3699 Surgical & medical instruments; video tape rental; electrical equipment & supplies
HQ: Nasco Healthcare Inc.
901 Janesville Ave
Fort Atkinson WI 53538
920 568-5600

(G-15195)
STAINLESS DESIGN CONCEPTS LTD
Also Called: SDC
1117 Kings Hwy (12477-4343)
P.O. Box 514, Smithtown (11787-0514)
PHONE 845 246-3631
Fax: 845 246-1595
Len Rosenbaum, *Ch of Bd*
Kevin Collins, *General Mgr*
Bill Iacobellis, *Purch Mgr*

Saugerties - Ulster County (G-15196) — GEOGRAPHIC SECTION

Glen Charles, *CFO*
Mary Sauer, *Human Res Mgr*
EMP: 35
SQ FT: 25,000
SALES (est): 8.1MM
SALES (corp-wide): 38.9MM **Publicly Held**
WEB: www.stainlessdesign.com
SIC: 3559 Chemical machinery & equipment
PA: Cvd Equipment Corporation
355 S Technology Dr
Central Islip NY 11722
631 981-7081

(G-15196)
STUART SPECTOR DESIGNS LTD
1450 Route 212 (12477-3028)
PHONE..................845 246-6124
Fax: 845 246-0833
Stuart Spector, *President*
Mike Kropp, *Marketing Staff*
▲ **EMP:** 9
SQ FT: 4,500
SALES: 850K **Privately Held**
WEB: www.ssdbass.com
SIC: 3931 Guitars & parts, electric & non-electric

(G-15197)
THE SMOKE HOUSE OF CATSKILLS
724 Route 212 (12477-4617)
PHONE..................845 246-8767
Charles Rothe, *President*
EMP: 7 **EST:** 1952
SQ FT: 2,400
SALES (est): 220K **Privately Held**
SIC: 2011 5421 Meat packing plants; meat markets, including freezer provisioners

(G-15198)
WORKING FAMILY SOLUTIONS INC
359 Washington Avenue Ext (12477-5221)
P.O. Box 88, Malden On Hudson (12453-0088)
PHONE..................845 802-6182
Danielle N Heller, *CEO*
EMP: 5
SALES (est): 360.9K **Privately Held**
SIC: 2835 Pregnancy test kits

Sauquoit
Oneida County

(G-15199)
CUSTOM STAIR & MILLWORK CO
Also Called: Kitchen Design Center
6 Gridley Pl (13456-3416)
PHONE..................315 839-5793
John Dweyer, *President*
EMP: 9
SQ FT: 10,000
SALES (est): 750K **Privately Held**
SIC: 2431 Millwork; staircases & stairs, wood

(G-15200)
LEATHERSTOCKING MOBILE HOME PA
2089 Doolittle Rd (13456-2409)
PHONE..................315 839-5691
Jane W Brennan, *Ch of Bd*
EMP: 5
SALES (est): 613.7K **Privately Held**
SIC: 2451 Mobile homes

(G-15201)
PARKS PAVING & SEALING INC
Also Called: Parks TRUcking&paving
3220 Valley Pl (13456-2808)
P.O. Box 508 (13456-0508)
PHONE..................315 737-5761
Tadd Aparks, *President*
Marietha Parks, *Office Mgr*
EMP: 11
SALES: 900K **Privately Held**
SIC: 2951 Asphalt & asphaltic paving mixtures (not from refineries)

Savannah
Wayne County

(G-15202)
PEARL TECHNOLOGIES INC
13297 Seneca St (13146-9663)
P.O. Box 196 (13146-0196)
PHONE..................315 365-2632
Fax: 315 365-3433
Robert Tewksbury, *President*
Linda Gillette, *VP Opers*
Bill Gillette, *Mfg Mgr*
Gary Stover, *Purch Agent*
Andrew Prudhomme, *Engineer*
EMP: 35
SQ FT: 35,000
SALES (est): 8.7MM
SALES (corp-wide): 278.3MM **Privately Held**
SIC: 3559 Plastics working machinery
HQ: Gloucester Engineering Co., Inc.
11 Dory Rd
Gloucester MA 01930
978 281-1800

Sayville
Suffolk County

(G-15203)
AQUARIUM PUMP & PIPING SYSTEMS
528 Chester Rd (11782-1808)
PHONE..................631 567-5555
Fax: 631 589-0154
Charles Eckstein, *Owner*
Virginia Eckstein, *Finance Other*
EMP: 11
SQ FT: 2,500
SALES (est): 604.5K **Privately Held**
SIC: 3499 3089 Aquarium accessories, metal; aquarium accessories, plastic

(G-15204)
BRAINWORKS SOFTWARE DEV CORP (PA)
100 S Main St Ste 102 (11782-3148)
PHONE..................631 563-5000
John Barry, *President*
Richard Kitzmiller, *General Mgr*
Elly Barry, *Office Mgr*
EMP: 9
SQ FT: 4,000
SALES (est): 9.7MM **Privately Held**
SIC: 7372 Publishers' computer software

(G-15205)
BUNGERS SURF SHOP
Also Called: Bunger Sayville
247 W Main St (11782-2522)
PHONE..................631 244-3646
Sammy Hito, *Principal*
EMP: 8 **EST:** 2012
SALES (est): 481.4K **Privately Held**
SIC: 3949 Surfboards; water sports equipment

(G-15206)
CNA SPECIALTIES INC
226 Mcneil St (11782-2249)
PHONE..................631 567-7929
Carolyn Ward, *CEO*
EMP: 5
SALES (est): 632.7K **Privately Held**
SIC: 2541 3431 5046 Cabinets, lockers & shelving; shower stalls, metal; partitions

(G-15207)
ESC CONTROL ELECTRONICS LLC
98 Lincoln Ave (11782-2711)
PHONE..................631 467-5328
Daniel Barnett Jr, *IT/INT Sup*
Paul Alessandrini,
EMP: 2
SQ FT: 10,000
SALES: 3MM **Privately Held**
SIC: 3559 Electronic component making machinery

(G-15208)
ESC CONTROL ELECTRONICS LLC
Also Called: Control Elec Div Fil-Coil
98 Lincoln Ave (11782-2711)
PHONE..................631 467-5328
Syed Zaidi, *Accountant*
Paul Alessandrini,
▲ **EMP:** 35
SQ FT: 2,000
SALES (est): 5.2MM **Privately Held**
SIC: 3677 3679 3841 3851 Electronic transformers; filtration devices, electronic; delay lines; surgical & medical instruments; ophthalmic goods
PA: Fil-Coil (Fc) Corp.
98 Lincoln Ave
Sayville NY 11782
631 467-5328

(G-15209)
FIL-COIL (FC) CORP (PA)
Also Called: Custom Power System
98 Lincoln Ave (11782-2711)
PHONE..................631 467-5328
Carrol Trust, *CEO*
Paul Alessandrini Sr, *Ch of Bd*
Batt Trust, *Vice Pres*
Dan Barnett Jr, *Director*
▲ **EMP:** 25
SQ FT: 6,000
SALES (est): 5.2MM **Privately Held**
SIC: 3677 Filtration devices, electronic

(G-15210)
FIRE ISLAND TIDE PUBLICATION
Also Called: Fire Island Tide The
40 Main St (11782-2552)
P.O. Box 70 (11782-0070)
PHONE..................631 567-7470
Fax: 631 567-1271
Patricia E King, *President*
Warren McDowell, *Publisher*
John Lee, *Editor*
EMP: 12
SALES: 500K **Privately Held**
SIC: 2711 7313 Newspapers; newspaper advertising representative

(G-15211)
KKW CORP
Also Called: Koster Keunen Waxes
90 Bourne Blvd (11782-3307)
PHONE..................631 589-5454
Richard B Koster, *Ch of Bd*
Jay Ehring, *QC Mgr*
▲ **EMP:** 40
SQ FT: 5,000
SALES (est): 6.8MM **Privately Held**
WEB: www.paramold.com
SIC: 3999 Candles

(G-15212)
KOSTER KEUNEN WAXES LTD
90 Bourne Blvd (11782-3307)
PHONE..................631 589-0400
Fax: 631 589-1232
Richard Koster, *President*
Kathryn Koster, *QC Dir*
Randolph Bruckner, *CFO*
Joanne Whitney, *Bookkeeper*
Randy Bruckner, *Finance*
▲ **EMP:** 15
SQ FT: 45,000
SALES (est): 2MM **Privately Held**
SIC: 2911 Mineral waxes, natural

(G-15213)
OPTIKA EYES LTD
153 Main St Unit 1 (11782-2566)
PHONE..................631 567-8852
Nancy Pacella, *President*
EMP: 8
SQ FT: 1,000
SALES (est): 610K **Privately Held**
SIC: 3851 5995 Frames, lenses & parts, eyeglass & spectacle; contact lenses; optical goods stores

(G-15214)
REDDI CAR CORP
174 Greeley Ave (11782-2396)
PHONE..................631 589-3141
Kenneth Johnson, *President*
EMP: 7 **EST:** 1957
SQ FT: 5,000
SALES (est): 648.1K **Privately Held**
SIC: 2851 2899 5085 Paints & paint additives; chemical preparations; fasteners, industrial: nuts, bolts, screws, etc.

(G-15215)
WEEKS & REICHEL PRINTING INC
131 Railroad Ave (11782-2799)
PHONE..................631 589-1443
Fax: 631 589-2723
John A Weeks, *President*
Robert Reichel, *Corp Secy*
EMP: 5
SQ FT: 2,400
SALES (est): 537.1K **Privately Held**
SIC: 2759 2752 Letterpress printing; commercial printing, offset

Scarsdale
Westchester County

(G-15216)
AMERICAN EPOXY AND METAL INC
83 Cushman Rd (10583-3403)
PHONE..................718 828-7828
Samer Daniel, *President*
Ralph Maccarino, *Vice Pres*
EMP: 8
SALES (est): 996.7K **Privately Held**
WEB: www.americanepoxy.com
SIC: 2821 2511 Epoxy resins; whatnot shelves: wood; tables, household: wood

(G-15217)
GOTHAM CITY INDUSTRIES INC
372 Fort Hill Rd (10583-2411)
PHONE..................985 851-5474
Barbara Chalton, *Ch of Bd*
Jay Chalson, *Vice Pres*
Todd Petre, *Vice Pres*
Lucia Silva, *Office Mgr*
Roger Nafziger, *Director*
▲ **EMP:** 20
SQ FT: 17,000
SALES (est): 3.4MM **Privately Held**
WEB: www.gothamind.com
SIC: 2541 Wood partitions & fixtures

(G-15218)
JAPAN AMERICA LEARNING CTR INC (PA)
Also Called: Enjoy
81 Montgomery Ave (10583-5104)
P.O. Box 606, Hartsdale (10530-0606)
PHONE..................914 723-7600
Fax: 914 723-1515
Kazuko Maeda, *President*
EMP: 10
SQ FT: 2,000
SALES: 300K **Privately Held**
SIC: 2721 8299 Trade journals: publishing only, not printed on site; language school

(G-15219)
KONTROLSCAN INC
22 Murray Hill Rd (10583-2828)
PHONE..................917 743-0481
Sanjeev Dheer, *CEO*
EMP: 8
SALES (est): 204.7K **Privately Held**
SIC: 7372 Application computer software; business oriented computer software

(G-15220)
LAND PACKAGING CORP
7 Black Birch Ln (10583-7456)
PHONE..................914 472-5976
Lawrence Rosefeld, *President*
Lawrence Rosenfeld, *President*
EMP: 10
SQ FT: 3,000
SALES: 5MM **Privately Held**
SIC: 2653 Corrugated boxes, partitions, display items, sheets & pad

▲ = Import ▼=Export
◆ =Import/Export

GEOGRAPHIC SECTION
Schenectady - Schenectady County (G-15245)

(G-15221)
NATHAN PRINTING EXPRESS INC
740 Central Park Ave (10583-2504)
PHONE.....................914 472-0914
Fax: 914 472-5398
Nathan Wong, *President*
Neil Moreton, *Vice Pres*
Alex Wong, *Vice Pres*
EMP: 7
SQ FT: 1,600
SALES (est): 871.5K **Privately Held**
SIC: 2759 Commercial printing

(G-15222)
S I COMMUNICATIONS INC
Also Called: Scarsdale Inquirer
8 Harwood Ct (10583-4104)
P.O. Box 418 (10583-0418)
PHONE.....................914 725-2500
Fax: 914 725-1552
Deborah White, *Owner*
Todd Sliss, *Editor*
EMP: 18
SALES (est): 1MM **Privately Held**
WEB: www.scarsdaleinquirer.com
SIC: 2711 Newspapers: publishing only, not printed on site

(G-15223)
SHERIDAN HOUSE INC
230 Nelson Rd (10583-5908)
PHONE.....................914 725-5431
Fax: 914 693-0776
Lothar Simon, *President*
Jeannine Simon, *Vice Pres*
▲ **EMP:** 5
SQ FT: 4,000
SALES (est): 709.7K **Privately Held**
WEB: www.sheridanhouse.com
SIC: 2731 Book publishing

(G-15224)
SPAGHETTI BRIDGE LLC
Also Called: Coolit
27 Dorchester Rd (10583-6037)
PHONE.....................646 369-7505
Matthew Kahn, *Mng Member*
Mathew Ammiradi,
Carrie Kahn,
Heath Mathias,
Scott Underwood,
EMP: 5
SALES: 5K **Privately Held**
SIC: 3569 Generators: steam, liquid oxygen or nitrogen

(G-15225)
ZANZANO WOODWORKING INC
91 Locust Ave (10583-6230)
PHONE.....................914 725-6025
Michael Zanzano, *Principal*
EMP: 13
SALES (est): 1.6MM **Privately Held**
SIC: 2431 Millwork

Schenectady
Schenectady County

(G-15226)
A W HAMEL STAIR MFG INC
3111 Amsterdam Rd (12302-6328)
PHONE.....................518 346-3031
Fax: 518 346-3523
Joseph Lucarelli, *President*
Donald Lucarelli, *Vice Pres*
Scott Ressel, *Manager*
EMP: 16
SQ FT: 30,000
SALES (est): 1.3MM **Privately Held**
SIC: 2431 Staircases & stairs, wood; stair railings, wood

(G-15227)
ADIRONDACK BEVERAGE CO INC
701 Corporation Park (12302-1060)
PHONE.....................518 370-3621
Ralph Crowley Jr, *President*
Angelo Mastrangelo, *Chairman*
Michael Mulrain, *Corp Secy*
Christopher Crowley, *Vice Pres*
Douglas Martin, *Vice Pres*
▲ **EMP:** 1000
SQ FT: 240,000
SALES (est): 228.8MM
SALES (corp-wide): 374.2MM **Privately Held**
WEB: www.adirondackbeverages.com
SIC: 2086 Soft drinks: packaged in cans, bottles, etc.; pasteurized & mineral waters, bottled & canned
PA: Polar Corp.
   1001 Southbridge St
   Worcester MA 01610
   508 753-6383

(G-15228)
ALSTOM SIGNALING INC (DH)
Also Called: Alstrom Trnspt Info Solutions
1 River Rd (12345-6000)
PHONE.....................585 783-2000
Fax: 585 783-2009
Ulisses Camillo, *CEO*
Jamie Van Scoter, *General Mgr*
Thierry Best, *Managing Dir*
William Wilson, *Managing Dir*
Franck Lecoq, *Senior VP*
▲ **EMP:** 270
SALES (est): 57.5MM
SALES (corp-wide): 110.3MM **Privately Held**
WEB: www.alstomsignalingsolutions.com
SIC: 3669 Railroad signaling devices, electric; signaling apparatus, electric

(G-15229)
ALSTOM SIGNALING INC
1 River Rd (12345-6000)
PHONE.....................585 274-8700
John Desmond, *Opers Mgr*
Ken Witt, *Electrical Engi*
Lisa Critchly, *Human Res Mgr*
Ian Desousa, *Manager*
EMP: 50
SALES (corp-wide): 110.3MM **Privately Held**
WEB: www.alstomsignalingsolutions.com
SIC: 3669 3743 3643 Railroad signaling devices, electric; signaling apparatus, electric; railroad equipment; current-carrying wiring devices
HQ: Alstom Signaling Inc.
   1 River Rd
   Schenectady NY 12345
   585 783-2000

(G-15230)
AMERICAN HSPTALS PATIENT GUIDE
1890 Maxon Rd Ext (12308-1140)
P.O. Box 1031 (12301-1031)
PHONE.....................518 346-1099
Fax: 518 346-1461
Robert J Kosineski Sr, *President*
Tim Chace, *VP Opers*
Donna Gauman, *Accounts Mgr*
EMP: 10
SALES (est): 630K **Privately Held**
SIC: 2741 Miscellaneous publishing

(G-15231)
ASTRIA SOLUTIONS GROUP LLC
Docstar
2165 Technology Dr (12308-1143)
PHONE.....................518 346-7799
Greg D Cooke, *VP Sales*
Eric McCracken, *Sales Dir*
Nancy Hauss, *Sales Mgr*
Jim Greco, *Sales Engr*
Suren Pai, *Branch Mgr*
EMP: 45
SALES (corp-wide): 30.4MM **Privately Held**
SIC: 7372 Application computer software
PA: Astria Solutions Group, Llc
   2165 Technology Dr
   Schenectady NY 12308
   518 346-7799

(G-15232)
AUTERRA INC
2135 Technology Dr (12308-1143)
PHONE.....................518 382-9600
Eric Burnett, *Ch of Bd*
Steven T Jackson, *Vice Pres*
EMP: 9 **EST:** 2006
SALES (est): 2.2MM **Privately Held**
SIC: 2819 Industrial inorganic chemicals

(G-15233)
AXLE EXPRESS
729 Broadway (12305-2703)
PHONE.....................518 347-2220
Samuel Caldarazzo, *President*
EMP: 25
SALES (est): 2.2MM **Privately Held**
SIC: 3714 Motor vehicle parts & accessories

(G-15234)
BENCHEMARK PRINTING INC
1890 Maxon Rd Ext (12308-1149)
P.O. Box 1031 (12301-1031)
PHONE.....................518 393-1361
Fax: 518 372-1336
Robert Kosineski, *President*
Denise Hecker, *Human Resources*
Joe Coli, *Accounts Exec*
Carl Roser, *Accounts Exec*
Betsy Saltsman, *Accounts Exec*
▲ **EMP:** 55
SQ FT: 75,000
SALES (est): 12.4MM **Privately Held**
SIC: 2752 2791 2789 2759 Commercial printing, lithographic; typesetting; bookbinding & related work; commercial printing

(G-15235)
BESTLINE INTERNATIONAL RES INC
224 State St (12305-1806)
PHONE.....................518 631-2177
John Polster, *Principal*
EMP: 8
SALES (est): 1.1MM **Privately Held**
SIC: 2992 Lubricating oils & greases

(G-15236)
CALLANAN INDUSTRIES INC (DH)
1245 Kings Rd Ste 1 (12303-2824)
P.O. Box 15097, Albany (12212-5097)
PHONE.....................518 374-2222
Fax: 518 374-2222
Jonas Havens, *President*
Kevin D Browne, *Safety Dir*
Peter Skelly, *Credit Mgr*
Don Fane, *Mktg Dir*
Darlene Brunner, *Marketing Mgr*
▲ **EMP:** 205
SQ FT: 24,000
SALES (est): 131.4MM
SALES (corp-wide): 25.3B **Privately Held**
WEB: www.callanan.com
SIC: 3272 2951 Concrete products, precast; asphalt paving mixtures & blocks
HQ: Oldcastle Materials, Inc.
   900 Ashwood Pkwy Ste 700
   Atlanta GA 30338
   770 522-5600

(G-15237)
CALLANAN INDUSTRIES INC
145 Cordell Rd (12303-2701)
P.O. Box 40, Selkirk (12158-0040)
PHONE.....................518 382-5354
Joe Decelle, *Branch Mgr*
EMP: 7
SALES (corp-wide): 23.5B **Privately Held**
SIC: 3999 Barber & beauty shop equipment
HQ: Callanan Industries, Inc.
   1245 Kings Rd Ste 1
   Schenectady NY 12303
   518 374-2222

(G-15238)
CAPITAL DST PRINT & IMAGING
Also Called: Allegra Print & Imaging
2075 Central Ave (12304-4426)
PHONE.....................518 456-6773
Jim Cazavilan, *President*
Janet Calise, *Vice Pres*
Janet C Cazavilan, *Vice Pres*
EMP: 7
SQ FT: 2,500
SALES (est): 933.7K **Privately Held**
WEB: www.allegraalbany.com
SIC: 2752 7334 Commercial printing, offset; photocopying & duplicating services

(G-15239)
CAPITAL STONE LLC
2241 Central Ave (12304-4379)
PHONE.....................518 382-7588
James Nass, *President*
Caron Beggan, *General Mgr*
Paul Sicluna, *Manager*
EMP: 9
SQ FT: 5,000
SALES: 1MM **Privately Held**
SIC: 3281 Granite, cut & shaped

(G-15240)
CASCADE TECHNICAL SERVICES LLC
2846 Curry Rd Ste B (12303-3463)
PHONE.....................518 355-2201
Matthew Ednie, *Manager*
EMP: 5
SALES (corp-wide): 762.6MM **Privately Held**
WEB: www.teamzebra.com
SIC: 3822 Auto controls regulating residntl & coml environmt & applncs
HQ: Cascade Technical Services Llc
   30 N Prospect Ave
   Lynbrook NY 11563
   516 596-6300

(G-15241)
CDS PRODUCTIONS INC
108 Erie Blvd Ste 400 (12305-2223)
PHONE.....................518 385-8255
Fax: 518 385-8290
Anthony Casapullo, *President*
James Fuller, *Vice Pres*
EMP: 16
SQ FT: 15,000
SALES: 937.7K **Privately Held**
SIC: 2752 2791 7334 Commercial printing, lithographic; typesetting, computer controlled; photocopying & duplicating services

(G-15242)
CHURCH & DWIGHT CO INC
Also Called: Arm & Hammer
706 Ennis Rd (12306-7420)
PHONE.....................518 887-5109
Douglas Waddell, *Branch Mgr*
EMP: 12
SALES (corp-wide): 3.3B **Publicly Held**
WEB: www.churchdwight.com
SIC: 2812 Sodium bicarbonate
PA: Church & Dwight Co., Inc.
   500 Charles Ewing Blvd
   Ewing NJ 08628
   609 806-1200

(G-15243)
CLEMENTE LATHAM CONCRETE CORP
Also Called: Clemente Latham North Div
1245 Kings Rd (12303-2831)
P.O. Box 15097, Albany (12212-5097)
PHONE.....................518 374-2222
Frank A Clemente, *Ch of Bd*
EMP: 100 **EST:** 1993
SALES (est): 11.8MM
SALES (corp-wide): 25.3B **Privately Held**
SIC: 3273 5032 Ready-mixed concrete; brick, stone & related material
HQ: Oldcastle Materials, Inc.
   900 Ashwood Pkwy Ste 700
   Atlanta GA 30338
   770 522-5600

(G-15244)
CODINOS LIMITED INC
704 Corporation Park # 5 (12302-1091)
PHONE.....................518 372-3308
Scott Devantier, *President*
Glen Brown, *Plant Mgr*
Rita Vose, *Shareholder*
EMP: 33
SQ FT: 33,000
SALES: 6.1MM **Privately Held**
SIC: 2038 Frozen specialties

(G-15245)
CON REL AUTO ELECTRIC INC
3637 Carman Rd (12303-5401)
PHONE.....................518 356-1646
Fax: 518 356-9080
Kevin Relyea, *President*

Schenectady - Schenectady County (G-15246) — GEOGRAPHIC SECTION

Michael Relyea, *Corp Secy*
David O'Connell, *Vice Pres*
Gloria Mc Cue, *Financial Exec*
Gloria McCue, *Office Mgr*
EMP: 35
SQ FT: 9,000
SALES: 3.9MM **Privately Held**
SIC: 3621 3694 3625 Starters, for motors; alternators, automotive; relays & industrial controls

(G-15246)
DAILY GAZETTE COMPANY (PA)
2345 Maxon Rd Ext (12308-1150)
P.O. Box 1090 (12301-1090)
PHONE 518 374-4141
Fax: 518 395-3072
John Hume, *President*
James P Murphy, *President*
Tom Boggie, *Editor*
Mark Mahoney, *Editor*
Steven Yansak, *District Mgr*
EMP: 325 **EST:** 1894
SQ FT: 111,000
SALES (est): 79.9MM **Privately Held**
WEB: www.dailygazette.com
SIC: 2711 Newspapers, publishing & printing

(G-15247)
DAILY GAZETTE COMPANY
2345 Maxon Rd Ext (12308-1150)
P.O. Box 1090 (12301-1090)
PHONE 518 395-3060
Lance Geda, *VP Finance*
Luis Borreli, *Financial Exec*
Richard Dwyer, *Branch Mgr*
Steve Amedio, *Manager*
Lee Brill, *Manager*
EMP: 110
SALES (corp-wide): 79.9MM **Privately Held**
SIC: 2711 Newspapers, publishing & printing
PA: Daily Gazette Company
2345 Maxon Rd Ext
Schenectady NY 12308
518 374-4141

(G-15248)
DIMENSION FABRICATORS INC
2000 7th St (12302-1051)
PHONE 518 374-1936
Fax: 518 374-4830
Scott Stevens, *President*
Joel C Patrie, *Principal*
Coleen Stevens, *Corp Secy*
Scott A Mushaw, *Vice Pres*
Valerie M Borst, *Manager*
▲ **EMP:** 50
SQ FT: 46,000
SALES (est): 19.6MM **Privately Held**
WEB: www.dimensionfab.com
SIC: 3449 Bars, concrete reinforcing: fabricated steel

(G-15249)
DSM NUTRITIONAL PRODUCTS LLC (DH)
Also Called: D S M
2105 Technology Dr (12308-1143)
P.O. Box 910, Nutley NJ (07110)
PHONE 518 372-5155
Richard Polacek, *President*
Dorothy Y Towns, *General Mgr*
Michael Effing, *Managing Dir*
Nitin Kothari, *Managing Dir*
Luis Pereira, *Area Mgr*
◆ **EMP:** 277
SQ FT: 106,000
SALES (est): 468.3MM **Privately Held**
WEB: www.nutraaccess.com
SIC: 2834 2836 Pharmaceutical preparations; vitamin, nutrient & hematinic preparations for human use; biological products, except diagnostic; veterinary biological products
HQ: Dsm Holding Company Usa, Inc.
45 Waterview Blvd
Parsippany NJ 07054
973 257-1031

(G-15250)
ENER-G-ROTORS INC
17 Fern Ave (12306-2708)
PHONE 518 372-2608
Michael Newell, *Ch of Bd*
Edward Zampella III, *President*
EMP: 5
SALES (est): 946K **Privately Held**
SIC: 3621 7694 5084 5063 Motors & generators; armature rewinding shops; hydraulic systems equipment & supplies; electrical apparatus & equipment

(G-15251)
ENERGY PANEL STRUCTURES INC
Also Called: Fingerlakes Construction
864 Burdeck St (12306-1218)
PHONE 518 355-6708
Kirt Burghdorf, *Vice Pres*
EMP: 6
SALES (corp-wide): 700K **Privately Held**
SIC: 3448 2452 Prefabricated metal buildings; prefabricated wood buildings
HQ: Energy Panel Structures, Inc.
603 N Van Gordon Ave
Graettinger IA 51342
712 859-3219

(G-15252)
ENVIRONMENT-ONE CORPORATION
Also Called: E/One Utility Systems
2773 Balltown Rd (12309-1090)
PHONE 518 346-6161
Fax: 518 346-6188
Mark Donegan, *Ch of Bd*
George A Earle III, *President*
Eric Lacoppola, *President*
Philip Welsh, *President*
Irwin Hyman, *Exec VP*
◆ **EMP:** 135
SQ FT: 78,000
SALES (est): 45.7MM
SALES (corp-wide): 210.8B **Publicly Held**
WEB: www.eone.com
SIC: 3589 3824 Sewage treatment equipment; mechanical & electromechanical counters & devices
HQ: Precision Castparts Corp.
4650 Sw Mcdam Ave Ste 300
Portland OR 97239
503 946-4800

(G-15253)
EVERI GAMES INC
1 Broadway Ctr Fl 7 (12305-2554)
PHONE 518 881-1122
Donna Weckesser, *Supervisor*
EMP: 6
SALES (corp-wide): 827MM **Publicly Held**
SIC: 3944 Electronic games & toys
HQ: Everi Games Inc.
206 Wild Basin Rd Bldg B
West Lake Hills TX 78746
512 334-7500

(G-15254)
F CAPPIELLO DAIRY PDTS INC
115 Van Guysling Ave (12305-2708)
PHONE 518 374-5064
Fax: 518 374-4015
Peter Cappiello, *President*
Julio Cappiello, *Accounts Mgr*
EMP: 40
SALES (est): 5.3MM **Privately Held**
WEB: www.cappiello.com
SIC: 2022 Cheese, natural & processed

(G-15255)
FORTITECH INC (HQ)
2105 Technology Dr (12308-1151)
PHONE 518 372-5155
Walter S Borisenok, *Ch of Bd*
Dr Ram Chaudhari Sr, *Exec VP*
Ed Webster, *Prdtn Mgr*
Rich Sthleis, *Marketing Mgr*
Joseph Vozna, *MIS Staff*
◆ **EMP:** 137
SQ FT: 68,000
SALES (est): 34.2MM **Privately Held**
SIC: 2834 3295 2087 Vitamin, nutrient & hematinic preparations for human use; vitamin preparations; minerals, ground or treated; flavoring extracts & syrups

PA: Koninklijke Dsm N.V.
Het Overloon 1
Heerlen 6411
455 788-111

(G-15256)
GE TRANSPORTATION ENG SYSTEMS
Also Called: GE Transportation Energy
1 River Rd Bldg 2-333d (12345-6000)
PHONE 518 258-9276
EMP: 12
SALES (corp-wide): 117.3B **Publicly Held**
SIC: 3511 Turbines & turbine generator sets
HQ: Ge Transportation Engine Systems Company
6 Northway Ln
Latham NY
518 786-2352

(G-15257)
GENERAL ELECTRIC COMPANY
1 River Rd Bldg 55 (12305-2551)
PHONE 518 385-4022
Teddy Schiopu, *Buyer*
Andrew Crapo, *Engineer*
Cynthia O'Connor, *Marketing Staff*
Teal Reeves, *Program Mgr*
Jeff Shaffer, *Manager*
EMP: 603
SQ FT: 23,808
SALES (corp-wide): 117.3B **Publicly Held**
SIC: 3724 3511 3612 3641 Aircraft engines & engine parts; research & development on aircraft engines & parts; steam turbines; gas turbines, mechanical drive; autotransformers, electric (power transformers); electric lamps & parts for generalized applications; electric light bulbs, complete; lamps, incandescent filament, electric; lamps, fluorescent, electric; refrigerators, mechanical & absorption: household; freezers, home & farm; television broadcasting stations
PA: General Electric Company
41 Farnsworth St
Boston MA 02210
617 443-3000

(G-15258)
GENERAL ELECTRIC COMPANY
1 River Rd Bldg 33 (12305-2551)
PHONE 518 385-2211
John G Rice, *Branch Mgr*
EMP: 500
SALES (corp-wide): 117.3B **Publicly Held**
SIC: 3511 Turbines & turbine generator sets
PA: General Electric Company
41 Farnsworth St
Boston MA 02210
617 443-3000

(G-15259)
GENERAL ELECTRIC COMPANY
1 River Rd (12345-6000)
PHONE 518 385-3716
Damian D Foti, *Principal*
EMP: 491
SALES (corp-wide): 117.3B **Publicly Held**
SIC: 3511 Gas turbine generator set units, complete
PA: General Electric Company
41 Farnsworth St
Boston MA 02210
617 443-3000

(G-15260)
GENERAL ELECTRIC COMPANY
1 River Rd Bldg 43 (12345-6000)
PHONE 203 373-2756
Steve Bolze, *President*
EMP: 458
SALES (corp-wide): 117.3B **Publicly Held**
SIC: 3511 Turbines & turbine generator sets
PA: General Electric Company
41 Farnsworth St
Boston MA 02210
617 443-3000

(G-15261)
GENERAL ELECTRIC COMPANY
1 River Rd Bldg 37 (12345-6000)
PHONE 518 385-2211
John G Rice, *President*
Tom Saddlemeyer, *Finance*
John C Loomis, *Human Resources*
Jim Suciu, *Sales Staff*
Dell Williamson, *Marketing Staff*
EMP: 500
SALES (corp-wide): 117.3B **Publicly Held**
SIC: 3511 3621 Gas turbine generator set units, complete; steam turbine generator set units, complete; motors & generators
PA: General Electric Company
41 Farnsworth St
Boston MA 02210
617 443-3000

(G-15262)
GENERAL ELECTRIC COMPANY
1 Research Cir (12309-1027)
P.O. Box 8 (12301-0008)
PHONE 518 387-5000
Tom Shaginaw, *Business Mgr*
Mark M Little, *Vice Pres*
Mike Hartman, *Project Mgr*
Ralph Cox, *QC Mgr*
Jonathan Janssen, *Research*
EMP: 500
SALES (corp-wide): 117.3B **Publicly Held**
SIC: 3511 Turbines & turbine generator sets
PA: General Electric Company
41 Farnsworth St
Boston MA 02210
617 443-3000

(G-15263)
GENERAL ELECTRIC COMPANY
705 Corporation Park (12302-1092)
PHONE 518 385-3439
EMP: 8
SALES (corp-wide): 117.3B **Publicly Held**
SIC: 3511 Turbines & turbine generator sets
PA: General Electric Company
41 Farnsworth St
Boston MA 02210
617 443-3000

(G-15264)
GEORGIA-PACIFIC LLC
801 Corporation Park (12302-1097)
PHONE 518 346-6151
Fax: 518 346-8504
Sheri Nolan, *Human Res Mgr*
P J Hand, *Manager*
EMP: 180
SALES (corp-wide): 26.7B **Privately Held**
WEB: www.gp.com
SIC: 2653 Boxes, corrugated: made from purchased materials
HQ: Georgia-Pacific Llc
133 Peachtree St Ne # 4810
Atlanta GA 30303
404 652-4000

(G-15265)
GRANDVIEW BLOCK & SUPPLY CO
1705 Hamburg St (12304-4699)
PHONE 518 346-7981
Fax: 518 374-3908
Salvatore Salamone, *President*
Samuel Salamone, *Vice Pres*
James Salamone, *Admin Sec*
EMP: 20 **EST:** 1946
SQ FT: 22,500
SALES (est): 3.3MM **Privately Held**
SIC: 3271 5032 Blocks, concrete or cinder: standard; masons' materials

(G-15266)
GRANDVIEW CONCRETE CORP
1705 Hamburg St (12304-4673)
PHONE 518 346-7981
George Salamone, *President*
Attilio A Salamone, *Shareholder*
Frank J Salamone, *Shareholder*
EMP: 24
SQ FT: 22,500

2017 Harris New York Manufacturers Directory

▲ = Import ▼ = Export
◆ = Import/Export

SALES (est): 3.1MM **Privately Held**
SIC: 3273 Ready-mixed concrete

(G-15267)
GUARDIAN CONCRETE INC
Also Called: Guardian Concrete Steps
2140 Maxon Rd Ext (12308-1102)
PHONE................................518 372-0080
Fax: 518 372-6729
W K Stanton, *President*
EMP: 12
SQ FT: 13,000
SALES (est): 1.2MM **Privately Held**
SIC: 3272 5211 5039 Concrete products, precast; masonry materials & supplies; septic tanks

(G-15268)
HOHMANN & BARNARD INC
Sandell Moisture
310 Wayto Rd (12303-4538)
PHONE................................518 357-9757
Fax: 518 357-9636
Paul Napora, *Plant Mgr*
Vickie Daniel, *Sales Staff*
EMP: 21
SALES (corp-wide): 210.8B **Publicly Held**
SIC: 3496 3462 Clips & fasteners, made from purchased wire; iron & steel forgings
HQ: Hohmann & Barnard, Inc.
30 Rasons Ct
Hauppauge NY 11788
631 234-0600

(G-15269)
IGT GLOBAL SOLUTIONS CORP
1 Broadway Ctr Fl 2 (12305-2554)
PHONE................................518 382-2900
Ed Bourghan, *Branch Mgr*
Paul Stelmaszyk, *Manager*
EMP: 70
SALES (corp-wide): 4.7B **Privately Held**
WEB: www.gtech.com
SIC: 3575 Computer terminals
HQ: Igt Global Solutions Corporation
10 Memorial Blvd
Providence RI 02903
401 392-1000

(G-15270)
JIM QUINN
Also Called: Jim Quinn and Associates
12 Morningside Dr (12303-5610)
PHONE................................518 356-0398
Jim Quinn, *Owner*
EMP: 10
SALES (est): 783.6K **Privately Held**
SIC: 2426 7641 Carvings, furniture: wood; office furniture repair & maintenance

(G-15271)
JOHN C DOLPH COMPANY INC
200 Von Roll Dr (12306-2443)
PHONE................................732 329-2333
Fax: 732 329-1143
Jack Hasson, *President*
▲ **EMP:** 26 **EST:** 1910
SQ FT: 50,000
SALES (est): 9.3MM
SALES (corp-wide): 353MM **Privately Held**
WEB: www.johncdolph.com
SIC: 2851 2821 Varnishes; epoxy resins
PA: Von Roll Holding Ag
Passwangstrasse 20
Breitenbach SO
442 043-000

(G-15272)
KERYAKOS INC
1080 Catalyn St Fl 2 (12303-1835)
PHONE................................518 344-7092
Fax: 518 344-7096
Charles Contompasis, *President*
Marika Contompasis, *Principal*
Laurie Ives, *Vice Pres*
EMP: 15
SALES (est): 1.7MM **Privately Held**
SIC: 2253 5137 Sweaters & sweater coats, knit; sweaters, women's & children's

(G-15273)
KING ROAD MATERIALS INC (DH)
Also Called: King Paving
1245 Kings Rd (12303-2831)
P.O. Box 15097, Albany (12212-5097)
PHONE................................518 381-9995
Fax: 518 374-1721
Donald E Fane, *President*
EMP: 35 **EST:** 1959
SQ FT: 2,552
SALES (est): 22.5MM
SALES (corp-wide): 25.3B **Privately Held**
SIC: 2951 Asphalt & asphaltic paving mixtures (not from refineries)
HQ: Oldcastle Materials, Inc.
900 Ashwood Pkwy Ste 700
Atlanta GA 30338
770 522-5600

(G-15274)
KING ROAD MATERIALS INC
145 Cordell Rd (12303-2701)
PHONE................................518 382-5354
Fax: 518 382-5442
Chris Hensler, *Manager*
EMP: 11
SQ FT: 500
SALES (corp-wide): 25.3B **Privately Held**
SIC: 2951 Asphalt & asphaltic paving mixtures (not from refineries)
HQ: King Road Materials, Inc
1245 Kings Rd
Schenectady NY 12303
518 381-9995

(G-15275)
L BUILDERS SUPPLY INC
Also Called: Bellevue Builders Supply
500 Duanesburg Rd (12306-1015)
PHONE................................518 355-7190
Fax: 518 355-3178
Greg Gaskell, *President*
Billy Deorazio, *General Mgr*
Mark Auspelmyer, *Safety Mgr*
Robert Hansen, *Purch Agent*
Chad Ahr, *Engineer*
EMP: 380
SQ FT: 500,000
SALES (est): 77.9MM
SALES (corp-wide): 2B **Privately Held**
SIC: 2431 2439 2541 5211 Millwork; trusses, wooden roof; trusses, except roof: laminated lumber; wood partitions & fixtures; millwork & lumber; cabinets, kitchen; home centers
HQ: Us Lbm Holdings, Llc
1000 Corporate Grove Dr
Buffalo Grove IL 60089
877 787-5267

(G-15276)
LATHAM INTERNATIONAL INC
Also Called: Latham Manufacturing
706 Corporation Park 1 (12302-1047)
PHONE................................518 346-5292
Tony Pagano, *Branch Mgr*
EMP: 11
SALES (corp-wide): 218.9MM **Privately Held**
WEB: www.pacificpools.com
SIC: 3081 Vinyl film & sheet
PA: Latham International, Inc.
787 Watervliet Shaker Rd
Latham NY 12110
518 783-7776

(G-15277)
MASTROIANNI BROS INC
Also Called: Mastroianni Bros Bakery
51 Opus Blvd (12306-1219)
PHONE................................518 355-5310
Tracy Mastroianni, *President*
Bill Busacker, *General Mgr*
Will Doherty, *Sales Mgr*
▲ **EMP:** 35
SQ FT: 25,000
SALES (est): 7.5MM **Privately Held**
SIC: 2045 2051 Pizza doughs, prepared: from purchased flour; doughs, frozen or refrigerated: from purchased flour; bread, all types (white, wheat, rye, etc): fresh or frozen

(G-15278)
METAL COATED FIBERS INC
679 Mariaville Rd (12306-6806)
PHONE................................518 280-8514
Robert Duval, *President*
EMP: 22 **EST:** 2012
SALES (est): 1.5MM **Privately Held**
SIC: 3624 Fibers, carbon & graphite

(G-15279)
MILLIVAC INSTRUMENTS INC
2818 Curry Rd (12303-3463)
PHONE................................518 355-8300
Imek Metzger, *President*
Pola Metzger, *Corp Secy*
Jan Metzger, *Vice Pres*
EMP: 7
SQ FT: 12,000
SALES (est): 600K **Privately Held**
WEB: www.millivacinstruments.com
SIC: 3825 Test equipment for electronic & electric measurement

(G-15280)
MISCELLNOUS IR FABRICATORS INC
1404 Dunnsville Rd (12306-5509)
PHONE................................518 355-1822
Fax: 518 355-2337
Helmut Giesselmann, *Ch of Bd*
Gunther Giesselmann, *President*
Daniel Eaton, *Financial Exec*
Tom Giesselmann, *Sales Staff*
Reinhart Giesselmann, *Admin Sec*
EMP: 22 **EST:** 1966
SQ FT: 22,000
SALES (est): 5.6MM **Privately Held**
SIC: 3441 1791 7699 Fabricated structural metal; iron work, structural; metal reshaping & replating services

(G-15281)
NEW MOUNT PLEASANT BAKERY
941 Crane St (12303-1140)
PHONE................................518 374-7577
Fax: 518 374-5548
Joe Riitano, *President*
Debra Riitano, *Vice Pres*
Ann Moore, *Manager*
EMP: 50 **EST:** 1932
SQ FT: 15,000
SALES (est): 4.8MM **Privately Held**
SIC: 2051 5461 2052 Bread, cake & related products; bakeries; cookies & crackers

(G-15282)
NORAMPAC NEW ENGLAND INC
Also Called: Norampac Thompson Inc.
801 Corporation Park (12302-1061)
PHONE................................860 923-9563
Bryan Fagan, *General Mgr*
Joe Distesano, *Plant Mgr*
Lee Kozlowski, *Controller*
Firas Mando, *Controller*
Jim Rafetry, *Sales Dir*
EMP: 120 **EST:** 1958
SQ FT: 150,000
SALES (est): 1.6MM
SALES (corp-wide): 2.9B **Privately Held**
SIC: 2653 Boxes, corrugated: made from purchased materials; pads, corrugated: made from purchased materials; sheets, corrugated: made from purchased materials
HQ: Cascades Canada Ulc
404 Boul Marie-Victorin
Kingsey Falls QC J0A 1
819 363-5100

(G-15283)
NORAMPAC SCHENECTADY INC
801 Corporation Park (12302-1097)
PHONE................................518 346-6151
Marc Andre Depin, *President*
Charles Smith, *President*
Craig Griffith, *General Mgr*
Scott Russell, *General Mgr*
Jay Toland, *Plant Mgr*
EMP: 150
SALES: 55MM
SALES (corp-wide): 2.9B **Privately Held**
SIC: 2653 Corrugated & solid fiber boxes
HQ: Norampac Inc
1061 Rue Parent
Saint-Bruno QC J3V 6
450 461-8600

(G-15284)
OLSON SIGN COMPANY INC
Also Called: Olson Signs & Graphics
1750 Valley Rd Ext (12302)
PHONE................................518 370-2118
Fax: 518 370-3873
Richard Olson, *President*
Kelly Lee Olson, *Vice Pres*
EMP: 8
SQ FT: 6,200
SALES: 580K **Privately Held**
SIC: 3993 Electric signs; displays & cutouts, window & lobby

(G-15285)
PACKAGE ONE INC (PA)
414 Union St (12305-1107)
P.O. Box 414 (12301-0414)
PHONE................................518 344-5425
David W Dussault, *President*
Lawrence Pigliavento, *CFO*
▲ **EMP:** 59
SQ FT: 30,000
SALES (est): 21MM **Privately Held**
SIC: 3568 Power transmission equipment

(G-15286)
PRINTZ AND PATTERNZ LLC
Also Called: Printz Pttrnz Scrn-Prnting EMB
1550 Altamont Ave Ste 1 (12303-2140)
PHONE................................518 944-6020
Mike Crowley, *Vice Pres*
Daniel Crowley, *Mng Member*
Kristie Crowley, *Administration*
EMP: 6 **EST:** 2009
SALES (est): 697K **Privately Held**
SIC: 2752 2281 2396 Commercial printing, lithographic; embroidery yarn, spun; screen printing on fabric articles

(G-15287)
RAILEX CORP
105 Rotterdam Indus Park (12306-1920)
PHONE................................518 347-6040
Chris Franz, *Transptn Dir*
Dan Murtagh, *Opers Mgr*
Margie Hart, *Office Admin*
EMP: 80
SALES (est): 37.2MM **Privately Held**
SIC: 3537 Platforms, stands, tables, pallets & similar equipment

(G-15288)
RAND PRODUCTS MANUFACTURING CO
Also Called: Rand Mfg
1602 Van Vranken Ave (12308-2239)
PHONE................................518 374-9871
Henry W Frick, *President*
Karen Frick Connlly, *Manager*
Karen Lewis, *Manager*
EMP: 5 **EST:** 1977
SQ FT: 7,000
SALES (est): 470K **Privately Held**
WEB: www.randmfg.com
SIC: 3444 Radiator shields or enclosures, sheet metal

(G-15289)
RAY SIGN INC
Also Called: Color Pro Sign
28 Colonial Ave (12304-4122)
PHONE................................518 377-1371
Fax: 518 377-2704
Russell Hazen, *President*
EMP: 13 **EST:** 1980
SQ FT: 5,000
SALES (est): 1.6MM **Privately Held**
SIC: 3993 1799 7389 Electric signs; sign installation & maintenance; sign painting & lettering shop

(G-15290)
REN TOOL & MANUFACTURING CO
1801 Chrisler Ave (12303-1517)
PHONE................................518 377-2123
Fax: 518 393-8986
Renato Belletti, *President*
Ellen Belletti, *Corp Secy*
EMP: 10 **EST:** 1949

Schenectady - Schenectady County (G-15291)

SQ FT: 7,000
SALES (est): 1.5MM **Privately Held**
SIC: 3599 Machine shop, jobbing & repair

(G-15291)
SAMPSONS PRSTHTIC ORTHOTIC LAB
Also Called: Sampsons Prsthtic Orthotic Lab
1737 State St (12304-1832)
PHONE..................................518 374-6011
Fax: 518 393-3292
William Sampson, *President*
Pat Johnson, *Manager*
EMP: 24
SQ FT: 3,500
SALES (est): 2.4MM **Privately Held**
WEB: www.sampsons.com
SIC: 3842 5999 Prosthetic appliances; orthopedic & prosthesis applications

(G-15292)
SANZDRANZ LLC
388 Broadway (12305-2520)
PHONE..................................518 894-8625
Sandro Gerbini, *Branch Mgr*
EMP: 6
SALES (corp-wide): 210K **Privately Held**
SIC: 2043 Cereal breakfast foods
PA: Sanzdranz Llc
  83 Dumbarton Dr
  Delmar NY 12054
  518 894-8625

(G-15293)
SCHENECTADY STEEL CO INC
18 Mariaville Rd (12306-1398)
PHONE..................................518 355-3220
Fax: 518 355-3284
Anthony J Tebano, *President*
David M Derott, *Vice Pres*
David Mc Dermott, *Vice Pres*
Charles Chamulak, *Treasurer*
John Sportman, *Controller*
EMP: 51
SQ FT: 77,700
SALES: 20.6MM **Privately Held**
SIC: 3441 Fabricated structural metal

(G-15294)
SEALED AIR CORPORATION
201 A St (12302)
PHONE..................................518 370-1693
Fax: 518 370-3530
Dave Brown, *CEO*
Imad Safady, *Maint Spvr*
Joe Callahan, *Director*
Steven Nicholson, *Director*
EMP: 150
SALES (corp-wide): 7B **Publicly Held**
SIC: 3086 Plastics foam products
PA: Sealed Air Corporation
  8215 Forest Point Blvd # 100
  Charlotte NC 28273
  980 221-3235

(G-15295)
SEALED AIR CORPORATION
Also Called: Polyethylene Foam Div
Scotia Glenvl Ind Pk A St (12302)
PHONE..................................518 370-1693
Earle Booths, *Branch Mgr*
EMP: 130
SALES (corp-wide): 7B **Publicly Held**
WEB: www.sealedair.com
SIC: 3086 2671 Packaging & shipping materials, foamed plastic; packaging paper & plastics film, coated & laminated
PA: Sealed Air Corporation
  8215 Forest Point Blvd # 100
  Charlotte NC 28273
  201 791-7600

(G-15296)
SI GROUP INC (PA)
2750 Balltown Rd (12309-1006)
P.O. Box 1046 (12301-1046)
PHONE..................................518 347-4200
Fax: 518 346-6908
Wallace A Graham, *CEO*
Paul Tilley, *Senior VP*
Emmanuel Hess, *Vice Pres*
Traci Hockstra, *Vice Pres*
Christopher T Roberts, *Vice Pres*
◆ EMP: 150 EST: 1906

SALES (est): 1.1B **Privately Held**
WEB: www.schenectadyinternational.com
SIC: 2865 3087 2851 Phenol, alkylated & cumene; custom compound purchased resins; enamels

(G-15297)
SIERRA PROCESSING LLC
2 Moyer Ave (12306-1308)
PHONE..................................518 433-0020
Fax: 518 356-1720
William Wilczak,
Dave Fusco,
EMP: 15
SALES (est): 1.7MM **Privately Held**
SIC: 2611 Pulp manufactured from waste or recycled paper

(G-15298)
SKYTRAVEL (USA) LLC
20 Talon Dr (12309-1839)
PHONE..................................518 888-2610
Hongwei Jin, *Owner*
EMP: 10 EST: 2015
SALES (est): 502.5K **Privately Held**
SIC: 3593 Fluid power cylinders, hydraulic or pneumatic

(G-15299)
SQP INC
Also Called: Speciality Quality Packaging
602 Potential Pkwy (12302-1041)
PHONE..................................518 831-6800
Fax: 518 374-8542
Barbara Slaming, *President*
Dominick Fontana, *Opers Mgr*
▲ EMP: 140
SALES (est): 25MM
SALES (corp-wide): 23.1B **Publicly Held**
WEB: www.usfoodservice.com
SIC: 2676 2656 Sanitary paper products; straws, drinking: made from purchased material
HQ: Us Foods, Inc.
  9399 W Higgins Rd Ste 500
  Rosemont IL 60018
  847 720-8000

(G-15300)
STARFIRE SYSTEMS INC
8 Sarnowski Dr (12302-3504)
PHONE..................................518 899-9336
Andrew Skinner, *CEO*
Richard M Saburro, *Ch of Bd*
Caron Buresh, *Controller*
Karen Buresh, *Technology*
▲ EMP: 12
SALES (est): 1.8MM **Privately Held**
WEB: www.starfiresystems.com
SIC: 3299 8731 Ceramic fiber; commercial physical research

(G-15301)
STS STEEL INC
301 Nott St Ste 2 (12305-1053)
PHONE..................................518 370-2693
Fax: 518 370-2696
James A Stori, *Ch of Bd*
Jim Stori, *President*
Glenn Tabolt, *Vice Pres*
David McDermott, *Project Mgr*
Debbie Clements, *Finance Mgr*
EMP: 65
SQ FT: 85,000
SALES (est): 16.6MM **Privately Held**
WEB: www.stssteel.com
SIC: 3441 Fabricated structural metal; fabricated structural metal for bridges

(G-15302)
SUPERPOWER INC
450 Duane Ave Ste 1 (12304-2631)
PHONE..................................518 346-1414
Fax: 518 346-6080
Yusei Shirasaka, *President*
Drew Hazelton, *Principal*
Arthur P Kazanjian, *Vice Pres*
Hisaki Sakamoto, *Vice Pres*
Ross B McClure, *Opers Mgr*
▲ EMP: 56
SALES (est): 12.7MM
SALES (corp-wide): 7.4B **Privately Held**
SIC: 3643 Current-carrying wiring devices

PA: Furukawa Electric Co.,Ltd.
  2-2-3, Marunouchi
  Chiyoda-Ku TKY 100-0
  332 863-001

(G-15303)
TABLECLOTHS FOR GRANTED LTD
510 Union St (12305-1117)
PHONE..................................518 370-5481
Fax: 518 723-2009
Rudolph R Grant, *President*
Gary Lombardi, *Vice Pres*
David Siders, *Vice Pres*
Richard Walsh, *Admin Sec*
EMP: 11
SALES (est): 890K **Privately Held**
SIC: 2392 Tablecloths; made from purchased materials; towels, dishcloths & dust cloths

(G-15304)
TATTERSALL INDUSTRIES LLC
Also Called: Frank Murken Products
2125 Technology Dr (12308-1143)
PHONE..................................518 381-4270
Fax: 518 381-4351
James Dominelli, *Sales Mgr*
Donna Compton, *Accounts Mgr*
John Tattersall, *Mng Member*
▼ EMP: 20 EST: 1963
SQ FT: 35,000
SALES (est): 7.7MM **Privately Held**
WEB: www.fmproducts.com
SIC: 3429 5085 5169 Manufactured hardware (general); rubber goods, mechanical; chemicals & allied products

(G-15305)
THERESE THE CHILDRENS COLLECTN
301 Nott St (12305-1039)
PHONE..................................518 346-2315
Fax: 518 346-7351
Marie Guidarelli, *President*
Sally Racicot, *Bookkeeper*
EMP: 1
SQ FT: 4,000
SALES: 1.2MM **Privately Held**
SIC: 2369 5137 2353 2335 Girls' & children's outerwear; women's & children's clothing; hats, caps & millinery; women's, juniors' & misses' dresses; men's & boys' suits & coats

(G-15306)
TRAC MEDICAL SOLUTIONS INC
2165 Technology Dr (12308-1143)
PHONE..................................518 346-7799
John Botti, *Ch of Bd*
Jeff Frankel, *President*
Brad Pivar, *Vice Pres*
EMP: 7
SALES: 500K
SALES (corp-wide): 3.6MM **Publicly Held**
WEB: www.tracmed.com
SIC: 7372 Application computer software
PA: Authentidate Holding Corp.
  300 Connell Dr Ste 1000
  Berkeley Heights NJ 07922
  908 787-1700

(G-15307)
UNICELL BODY COMPANY INC
170 Cordell Rd (12303-2702)
PHONE..................................716 853-8628
Dale Wunsch, *Purch Mgr*
Carmin Sperduti, *Branch Mgr*
EMP: 14
SALES (corp-wide): 20MM **Privately Held**
WEB: www.unicell.com
SIC: 3713 5084 Truck bodies & parts; industrial machinery & equipment
PA: Unicell Body Company, Inc
  571 Howard St
  Buffalo NY 14206
  716 853-8628

(G-15308)
UNILUX ADVANCED MFG LLC
30 Commerce Park Rd (12309-3545)
PHONE..................................518 344-7490
Fax: 518 344-7495
Dean Wadland, *Sales Executive*
Lawrence Farrelly,

EMP: 50
SQ FT: 70,000
SALES: 11MM **Privately Held**
SIC: 3433 Heating equipment, except electric; boilers, low-pressure heating: steam or hot water

(G-15309)
VINCYS PRINTING LTD
1832 Curry Rd (12306-4237)
PHONE..................................518 355-4363
Fax: 518 355-2416
Evelyn L Vincinguerra, *President*
EMP: 10 EST: 1967
SQ FT: 3,000
SALES (est): 990K **Privately Held**
WEB: www.vincysprinting.com
SIC: 2752 2741 Commercial printing, offset; miscellaneous publishing

(G-15310)
VON ROLL USA INC (HQ)
200 Von Roll Dr (12302-2443)
PHONE..................................518 344-7100
Fax: 518 344-7286
Jon Roberts, *CEO*
Eran Rosenzweig, *Ch of Bd*
Andrew T Harrin, *President*
Jurg Brunner, *Vice Pres*
Lawrence Ostwald, *Controller*
▲ EMP: 130
SQ FT: 200,000
SALES (est): 49.5MM
SALES (corp-wide): 353MM **Privately Held**
SIC: 3644 Insulators & insulation materials, electrical
PA: Von Roll Holding Ag
  Passwangstrasse 20
  Breitenbach SO
  442 043-000

(G-15311)
WA PACKAGING LLC
604 Corporation Park (12302-1074)
PHONE..................................518 724-6466
Doug McGill, *Accounts Mgr*
Dominic Scialdone, *Accounts Mgr*
Todd Kletter, *Mng Member*
Heather Martin, *Manager*
EMP: 40
SALES (est): 5.8MM **Privately Held**
SIC: 2653 Boxes, corrugated: made from purchased materials

(G-15312)
WESTERN BLENDING INC
1411 Rottrdm Indstl Park (12306)
PHONE..................................518 356-6650
Bob Morris, *Manager*
Butch Mitchell, *Executive*
EMP: 7
SALES (corp-wide): 4.5MM **Privately Held**
SIC: 2045 2041 Prepared flour mixes & doughs; pizza dough, prepared
PA: Western Blending Inc
  5357 N Marine Dr
  Portland OR

(G-15313)
WHITE EAGLE PACKING CO INC
922 Congress St (12303-1728)
PHONE..................................518 374-4366
Gary Markiewicz, *President*
George Markiewicz, *Vice Pres*
EMP: 12 EST: 1951
SQ FT: 15,000
SALES (est): 1.4MM **Privately Held**
SIC: 2013 Sausages & other prepared meats; frankfurters from purchased meat; sausages from purchased meat; bologna from purchased meat

---

Schenevus
Otsego County

(G-15314)
A AND L HOME FUEL LLC
601 Smokey Ave (12155-4012)
PHONE..................................607 638-1994
Frank Competiello, *Principal*
EMP: 10

▲ = Import ▼ = Export
◆ = Import/Export

SALES (est): 1.4MM **Privately Held**
SIC: 2869 Fuels

(G-15315)
SCEHENVUS FIRE DIST
Also Called: Scehenvus Gram Hose Co
40 Main St (12155-2020)
PHONE.................................607 638-9017
Chief Pete Comion, *CEO*
EMP: 65 **EST:** 1900
SALES (est): 3.8MM **Privately Held**
SIC: 3711 Fire department vehicles (motor vehicles), assembly of

Schoharie
Schoharie County

(G-15316)
COBLESKILL STONE PRODUCTS INC
Also Called: Schoharie Quarry/Asphalt
163 Eastern Ave (12157-3209)
P.O. Box 220, Cobleskill (12043-0220)
PHONE.................................518 295-7121
Shae Adams, *Vice Pres*
Tim Adams, *Vice Pres*
Mike Moore, *Vice Pres*
Pete Gray, *Manager*
EMP: 12
SQ FT: 1,104
SALES (corp-wide): 114.3MM **Privately Held**
WEB: www.cobleskillstone.com
SIC: 1422 Crushed & broken limestone
PA: Cobleskill Stone Products, Inc.
112 Rock Rd
Cobleskill NY 12043
518 234-0221

(G-15317)
MASICK SOIL CONSERVATION CO
Also Called: Carver Sand & Gravel
4860 State Route 30 (12157-2906)
PHONE.................................518 827-5354
Fax: 518 827-5307
Carver Laraway, *Owner*
EMP: 11
SQ FT: 800
SALES (est): 500K **Privately Held**
SIC: 3274 0711 Agricultural lime; lime spreading services

Schroon Lake
Essex County

(G-15318)
PARADOX BREWERY LLC
154 Us 9 (12870)
PHONE.................................518 351-5036
Joan Mrocka, *CFO*
EMP: 7
SALES (est): 210.5K **Privately Held**
SIC: 2082 Malt beverages

Schuylerville
Saratoga County

(G-15319)
EMPIRE BUILDING PRODUCTS INC
12 Spring St (12871-1049)
PHONE.................................518 695-6094
Thomas R Harrison, *President*
Derek Harrison, *General Mgr*
Cindy Giantomasi, *Exec VP*
Paul J Martin, *Vice Pres*
EMP: 5
SQ FT: 1,500
SALES (est): 572K
SALES (corp-wide): 3.7MM **Privately Held**
WEB: www.vtf.com
SIC: 2439 2431 Timbers, structural: laminated lumber; panel work, wood

PA: Vermont Timber Frames, Inc
458 Morse Rd
Bennington VT 05201
802 445-3007

(G-15320)
GASSHO BODY & MIND INC
76 Broad St (12871-1301)
P.O. Box 910, Saratoga Springs (12866-0836)
PHONE.................................518 695-9991
Louis Hotchkiss, *President*
Junko Kobori, *Vice Pres*
▼ **EMP:** 5
SALES (est): 815.8K **Privately Held**
SIC: 2844 2044 5122 Face creams or lotions; bran, rice; toiletries

Scio
Allegany County

(G-15321)
HYDRAMEC INC
4393 River St (14880-9702)
P.O. Box 69 (14880-0069)
PHONE.................................585 593-5190
Fax: 585 593-5194
Gregg D Shear, *President*
James Vossler, *Vice Pres*
Erik Potter, *Buyer*
Karen Torrence, *Info Tech Dir*
Karen Jandrew, *Director*
▲ **EMP:** 23 **EST:** 1924
SQ FT: 23,000
SALES (est): 4.6MM **Privately Held**
WEB: www.hydrameconline.com
SIC: 3423 3542 Hand & edge tools; machine tools, metal forming type

Scipio Center
Cayuga County

(G-15322)
CUSTOM CONTROLS
2804 Skillett Rd (13147-3127)
PHONE.................................315 253-4785
Fax: 315 253-7970
Jay Horst, *Owner*
EMP: 6
SALES (est): 689.5K **Privately Held**
SIC: 3613 Control panels, electric

Scotia
Schenectady County

(G-15323)
ARCHITCTRAL SHETMETAL PDTS INC
1329 Amsterdam Rd (12302-6306)
P.O. Box 2150 (12302-0150)
PHONE.................................518 381-6144
Toll Free:..................................888 -
Gary Curcio, *President*
William Donnan, *Vice Pres*
EMP: 6
SQ FT: 8,000
SALES (est): 640K **Privately Held**
SIC: 3444 Sheet metalwork; metal roofing & roof drainage equipment

(G-15324)
BEECHE SYSTEMS CORP
Scotia Glenville Indl Par (12302)
PHONE.................................518 381-6000
Fax: 518 381-4613
John T Hedbring, *President*
Richard Schumaker, *Corp Secy*
EMP: 60
SQ FT: 52,000
SALES (est): 7MM
SALES (corp-wide): 144.9MM **Privately Held**
WEB: www.beeche.com
SIC: 3446 Scaffolds, mobile or stationary: metal

PA: The Fort Miller Service Corp
688 Wilbur Ave
Greenwich NY 12834
518 695-5000

(G-15325)
GRENO INDUSTRIES INC (PA)
2820 Amsterdam Rd (12302-6323)
P.O. Box 542, Schenectady (12301-0542)
PHONE.................................518 393-4195
Fax: 518 393-4182
Robert W Golden, *CEO*
Eileen Guarino, *President*
Joe Vainauskas, *VP Opers*
Bill Slocum, *QC Mgr*
Vincent Guarino, *Treasurer*
▲ **EMP:** 6
SQ FT: 70,000
SALES: 15.4MM **Privately Held**
WEB: www.greno.com
SIC: 3599 Machine shop, jobbing & repair

(G-15326)
INTERACTIVE INSTRUMENTS INC
704 Corporation Park # 1 (12302-1078)
PHONE.................................518 347-0955
Robert Skala, *President*
James Hutchison, *Vice Pres*
EMP: 6
SQ FT: 9,000
SALES (est): 929.6K **Privately Held**
WEB: www.interactiveinstruments.com
SIC: 3599 Custom machinery; machine shop, jobbing & repair

(G-15327)
JBS LLC
Also Called: J B S
6 Maple Ave (12302-4612)
PHONE.................................518 346-0001
Tommy Bouck, *Engineer*
John Busino, *Mng Member*
EMP: 20
SQ FT: 18,000
SALES (est): 3.7MM **Privately Held**
SIC: 3441 Fabricated structural metal

(G-15328)
NEFAB PACKAGING NORTH EAST LLC
203 Glenville Indus Park (12302-1072)
PHONE.................................518 346-9105
Paul Frisch, *General Mgr*
Jerry Dolly, *Sales Staff*
Brad Lawyer, *Manager*
EMP: 37
SALES (corp-wide): 23.7MM **Privately Held**
SIC: 2448 Wood pallets & skids
HQ: Nefab Packaging North East, Llc
204 Airline Dr Ste 100
Coppell TX 75019
469 444-5264

(G-15329)
OAK-BARK CORPORATION
Also Called: Silar Laboratories Division
37 Maple Ave (12302-4613)
PHONE.................................518 372-5691
Fax: 518 372-5720
Bob Ruskino, *Manager*
Mike Hewitt, *Manager*
EMP: 8
SQ FT: 256
SALES (corp-wide): 13MM **Privately Held**
WEB: www.wrightcorp.com
SIC: 2869 Industrial organic chemicals; formaldehyde (formalin)
PA: Oak-Bark Corporation
1224 Old Nc Highway 87
Riegelwood NC 28456
910 655-9225

(G-15330)
SHIPMTES/PRINTMATES HOLDG CORP (PA)
Also Called: Velocity Print Solutions
705 Corporation Park # 2 (12302-1092)
PHONE.................................518 370-1158
James Stiles, *CEO*
David Benny, *General Mgr*
Michael Mello, *CFO*
Gail Jefts, *Human Res Mgr*

Paul Dellaripa, *Accounts Exec*
EMP: 85
SQ FT: 60,000
SALES (est): 32.6MM **Privately Held**
WEB: www.sm-pm.com
SIC: 2752 5111 7334 7319 Commercial printing, lithographic; printing & writing paper; photocopying & duplicating services; distribution of advertising material or sample services; direct mail advertising services

(G-15331)
SPECIALTY QUALITY PACKG LLC
Also Called: Sqp
602 Potential Pkwy (12302-1041)
PHONE.................................914 580-3200
Maria Gutierrez, *Controller*
Peter Stull, *Credit Mgr*
Paul Epstein, *Mng Member*
▲ **EMP:** 81
SQ FT: 267,000
SALES: 30.2MM **Privately Held**
SIC: 2679 Papier mache articles, except statuary & art goods

Scottsville
Monroe County

(G-15332)
ADRIA MACHINE & TOOL INC
966 North Rd (14546-9770)
P.O. Box 208 (14546-0208)
PHONE.................................585 889-3360
Fax: 585 889-3365
Janos Poloznik, *President*
EMP: 4
SQ FT: 7,000
SALES: 1MM **Privately Held**
WEB: www.adriamachine.com
SIC: 3541 Machine tool replacement & repair parts, metal cutting types

(G-15333)
AMBRELL INC
39 Main St Ste 1 (14546-1356)
PHONE.................................585 889-9000
Richard Rosenbloom, *President*
EMP: 6 **EST:** 2012
SALES (est): 568.9K
SALES (corp-wide): 52.9MM **Privately Held**
SIC: 3567 Induction heating equipment
HQ: Ameritherm, Inc.
39 Main St Ste 1
Scottsville NY 14546
585 889-0236

(G-15334)
AMERITHERM INC (HQ)
Also Called: Ambrell
39 Main St Ste 1 (14546-1356)
PHONE.................................585 889-0236
Fax: 585 889-2066
Richard Rosenbloom, *President*
Bruce Stewart, *President*
Girish Dahake, *Vice Pres*
Skip Thompson, *Vice Pres*
Lee Stratford, *Prdtn Mgr*
▲ **EMP:** 13
SQ FT: 25,000
SALES: 21.4MM
SALES (corp-wide): 52.9MM **Privately Held**
WEB: www.ameritherm.com
SIC: 3567 Induction heating equipment
PA: Graycliff Partners, Lp
500 5th Ave Fl 47
New York NY 10110
212 300-2900

(G-15335)
COOPERVISION INC
711 North Rd (14546-1238)
PHONE.................................585 889-3301
Fax: 585 385-6145
Michael Schaenen, *Vice Chairman*
Mona Swanson, *COO*
Robert Steen, *Prdtn Mgr*
Dennis Snyder, *Mfg Staff*
Jim Galloway, *Purch Dir*
EMP: 660

SCOTTSVILLE - Monroe County (G-15336)

SALES (corp-wide): 1.8B **Publicly Held**
SIC: 3851 Contact lenses
HQ: Coopervision, Inc.
209 High Point Dr
Victor NY 14564
585 385-6810

(G-15336)
HEANY INDUSTRIES INC
249 Briarwood Ln (14546-1244)
P.O. Box 38 (14546-0038)
PHONE 585 889-2700
Fax: 585 889-2708
S Scott Zolnier, *Ch of Bd*
Charles Aldridge, *Vice Pres*
Brian Roberts, *Safety Mgr*
Joan Smith, *Accounts Mgr*
Jim Collins, *Manager*
▲ **EMP:** 58 **EST:** 1937
SQ FT: 18,000
SALES (est): 10MM **Privately Held**
WEB: www.heany.com
SIC: 3299 3479 2851 2816 Ceramic fiber; coating of metals with plastic or resins; paints & allied products; inorganic pigments

(G-15337)
JACK W MILLER
Also Called: Miller Truck Rental
2339 North Rd (14546-9737)
PHONE 585 538-2399
Fax: 585 538-2107
Jack W Miller, *Owner*
EMP: 9
SQ FT: 13,000
SALES (est): 1.3MM **Privately Held**
SIC: 3519 7538 Diesel engine rebuilding; diesel engine repair: automotive

(G-15338)
POWER AND CNSTR GROUP INC
Also Called: Livingston Lighting and Power
86 River Rd (14546-9503)
PHONE 585 889-6020
Fax: 585 889-1194
John Cleveland, *Vice Pres*
Philip Brooks, *Branch Mgr*
EMP: 26
SALES (corp-wide): 37.3MM **Privately Held**
WEB: www.valleysandandgravel.com
SIC: 3648 3647 Street lighting fixtures; streetcar lighting fixtures
PA: Power And Construction Group, Inc.
119 River Rd
Scottsville NY 14546
585 889-8500

(G-15339)
SABIN METAL CORPORATION
1647 Wheatland Center Rd (14546-9709)
P.O. Box 905 (14546-0905)
PHONE 585 538-2194
Fax: 585 538-2593
John Waldon, *Maint Spvr*
Mike Nichols, *Research*
Vicki Strong, *Accounting Dir*
Sherrye Cook, *Human Res Dir*
Rick Dolby, *Human Resources*
EMP: 125
SALES (corp-wide): 56.6MM **Privately Held**
WEB: www.sabinmetal.com
SIC: 3341 3339 Secondary precious metals; primary nonferrous metals
PA: Sabin Metal Corporation
300 Pantigo Pl Ste 102
East Hampton NY 11937
631 329-1695

(G-15340)
SWAIN TECHNOLOGY INC
963 North Rd (14546-1228)
PHONE 585 889-2786
Fax: 585 889-5218
Daniel Swain, *President*
Richard Tucker, *General Mgr*
Linda Swain, *Vice Pres*
EMP: 15
SQ FT: 11,000
SALES (est): 1.6MM **Privately Held**
WEB: www.swaintech.com
SIC: 3479 Coating of metals & formed products

Sea Cliff
Nassau County

(G-15341)
GOTHAM T-SHIRT CORP
211 Glen Cove Ave Unit 5 (11579-1432)
PHONE 516 676-0900
Howard Zwang, *Ch of Bd*
EMP: 5
SALES (est): 440K **Privately Held**
SIC: 2211 Shirting fabrics, cotton

(G-15342)
ROBS REALLY GOOD LLC
100 Roslyn Ave (11579-1274)
P.O. Box 355 (11579-0355)
PHONE 516 671-4411
Drew Giardino, *Sales Dir*
Robert Ehrlich, *Mng Member*
Carey Johnston, *Manager*
EMP: 11
SALES (est): 1.8MM **Privately Held**
SIC: 2096 Potato chips & similar snacks

Seaford
Nassau County

(G-15343)
A & A GRAPHICS INC II
615 Arlington Dr (11783-1135)
PHONE 516 735-0078
Eli P Pandolfi, *President*
EMP: 3
SQ FT: 5,000
SALES (est): 1.7MM **Privately Held**
SIC: 2759 Commercial printing

(G-15344)
KYRA COMMUNICATIONS CORP
3864 Bayberry Ln (11783-1503)
PHONE 516 783-6244
Fax: 516 679-8167
Richard Doherty, *President*
Carol Doherty, *Vice Pres*
William Taczak, *Vice Pres*
Richard Dougherty, *Manager*
Elise Tanaka, *Director*
EMP: 14
SALES (est): 750K **Privately Held**
SIC: 2741 8734 Miscellaneous publishing; testing laboratories

(G-15345)
LUCAS ELECTRIC
3524 Merrick Rd (11783-2824)
PHONE 516 809-8619
EMP: 7
SALES (est): 100.3K **Privately Held**
SIC: 3699 Electrical equipment & supplies

(G-15346)
MEETHAPPY INC
2122 Bit Path (11783-2402)
PHONE 917 903-0591
Joana Gutierrez, *CEO*
EMP: 18
SALES (est): 352.3K **Privately Held**
SIC: 7372 7389 7375 Application computer software; ; information retrieval services

(G-15347)
TRIMTEC INC
4057 Judge Ct (11783-2262)
PHONE 516 783-5428
Linda Luckman, *Ch of Bd*
EMP: 5
SALES (est): 464.3K **Privately Held**
SIC: 3496 Fabrics, woven wire

Selden
Suffolk County

(G-15348)
BLUE TORTILLA LLC
1070 Middle Country Rd # 4 (11784-2529)
PHONE 631 451-0100
Eric Gorber, *Owner*
EMP: 6
SALES (est): 492.4K **Privately Held**
SIC: 2099 Tortillas, fresh or refrigerated

(G-15349)
CENTRAL GARDEN & PET COMPANY
1100 Middle Country Rd (11784-2513)
PHONE 631 451-8021
Stacey Rossi, *Manager*
EMP: 9
SALES (corp-wide): 1.6B **Publicly Held**
WEB: www.centralgardenandpet.com
SIC: 2048 Prepared feeds
PA: Central Garden & Pet Company
1340 Treat Blvd Ste 600
Walnut Creek CA 94597
925 948-4000

(G-15350)
CREATIVE STONE & CABINETS
448 Middle Country Rd # 1 (11784-2657)
PHONE 631 772-6548
Juan Cuzco, *President*
EMP: 6 **EST:** 2010
SALES (est): 871.7K **Privately Held**
SIC: 2599 Cabinets, factory

(G-15351)
DATORIB INC
Also Called: Minuteman Press
974 Middle Country Rd (11784-2535)
PHONE 631 698-6222
Fax: 631 698-6153
William J Passeggio, *President*
Rita Passeggio, *Sales Mgr*
EMP: 5
SQ FT: 1,850
SALES (est): 657.4K **Privately Held**
SIC: 2752 Commercial printing, lithographic

(G-15352)
ILAB AMERICA INC
45 Hemlock St (11784-1327)
PHONE 631 615-5053
Wayne Boyle, *President*
EMP: 6
SALES: 800K **Privately Held**
WEB: www.ilabamerica.com
SIC: 3651 Amplifiers: radio, public address or musical instrument

(G-15353)
PROGRESSIVE ORTHOTICS LTD (PA)
280 Middle Country Rd G (11784-2532)
PHONE 631 732-5556
Fax: 631 732-0218
Bruce Goodman, *President*
EMP: 9
SQ FT: 2,400
SALES (est): 905.9K **Privately Held**
WEB: www.progressiveorthotics.com
SIC: 3842 3841 5999 5047 Limbs, artificial; orthopedic appliances; surgical & medical instruments; orthopedic & prosthesis applications; medical & hospital equipment

Selkirk
Albany County

(G-15354)
CQ TRAFFIC CONTROL DEVICES LLC
Also Called: Cq Traffic Control Products
1521 Us Rte 9w (12158)
P.O. Box 192 (12158-0192)
PHONE 518 767-0057
Fax: 518 767-0058
William Quattrochi,
Frank Conrad,
Carol Quattrochi,
Douglas Robbins,
EMP: 5
SALES (est): 843.4K **Privately Held**
SIC: 3669 Pedestrian traffic control equipment

(G-15355)
GE PLASTICS
1 Noryl Ave (12158-9784)
PHONE 518 475-5011
Fax: 518 475-5650
Jeffery Immelt, *Principal*
Massimo Spiezia, *Safety Mgr*
Everett Teller, *Maint Spvr*
Dave Ehlinger, *IT/INT Sup*
◆ **EMP:** 5
SALES (est): 782K **Privately Held**
SIC: 2821 Plastics materials & resins

(G-15356)
OLDCASTLE PRECAST INC
Also Called: Oldcastle Precast Bldg Systems
123 County Route 101 (12158-2606)
PHONE 518 767-2112
Bob Jones, *Safety Dir*
Edward Soler, *Manager*
Sheila Conners, *Manager*
EMP: 40
SALES (corp-wide): 25.3B **Privately Held**
WEB: www.oldcastle-precast.com
SIC: 3272 Concrete products, precast
HQ: Oldcastle Precast, Inc.
1002 15th St Sw Ste 110
Auburn WA 98001
253 833-2777

(G-15357)
PALPROSS INCORPORATED
Also Called: L P Transportation
Maple Ave Rr 396 (12158)
P.O. Box 95 (12158-0095)
PHONE 845 469-2188
Andrew Palmer, *Manager*
EMP: 10
SQ FT: 2,400
SALES (corp-wide): 17MM **Privately Held**
SIC: 3537 Trucks, tractors, loaders, carriers & similar equipment
PA: Palpross Incorporated
Rr Box 17m
Chester NY 10918
845 469-2188

(G-15358)
SABIC INNOVATIVE PLAS US LLC
1 Noryl Ave (12158-9765)
PHONE 518 475-5011
Charlie Crew, *Manager*
EMP: 258 **Privately Held**
WEB: www.sabic-ip.com
SIC: 2821 Plastics materials & resins
HQ: Sabic Innovative Plastics Us Llc
1 Plastics Ave
Pittsfield MA 01201
413 448-7110

Seneca Castle
Ontario County

(G-15359)
CASTLE HARVESTER CO INC
Also Called: Castle Harvstr Met Fabricators
3165 Seneca Castle Rd (14547)
P.O. Box 167 (14547-0167)
PHONE 585 526-5884
Michael Kunes, *President*
Linda Gulvin, *Office Mgr*
EMP: 9
SQ FT: 10,000
SALES (est): 1MM **Privately Held**
SIC: 3441 Fabricated structural metal

Seneca Falls
Seneca County

(G-15360)
GOULDS PUMPS INCORPORATED (DH)
240 Fall St (13148-1573)
PHONE 315 568-2811
Fax: 315 568-5737
Robert Pagano, *Ch of Bd*
Aris Chicles, *President*
Ken Napolitano, *President*

▲ = Import ▼ = Export
◆ = Import/Export

Paul Sember, *Superintendent*
Stan Knecht, *Opers Mgr*
▲ **EMP:** 1100 **EST:** 1984
SALES (est): 1B
SALES (corp-wide): 2.4B **Publicly Held**
WEB: www.gouldspumps.com
SIC: 3561 5084 Pumps & pumping equipment; industrial pumps & parts; pumps, oil well & field; pumps, domestic: water or sump; industrial machinery & equipment
HQ: Itt Fluid Technology Corp
1133 Westcstr Ave N100 Ste N
White Plains NY 10604
914 641-2000

(G-15361)
ITT CORPORATION
2881 E Bayard Street Ext (13148-8745)
PHONE 914 641-2000
Peter Verdehem, *Engineer*
EMP: 58
SALES (corp-wide): 2.4B **Publicly Held**
WEB: www.ittind.com
SIC: 3625 3823 3363 3812 Control equipment, electric; fluidic devices, circuits & systems for process control; aluminum die-castings; radar systems & equipment; infrared object detection equipment
HQ: Itt, Llc
1133 Westchester Ave N-100
White Plains NY 10604
914 641-2000

(G-15362)
ITT CORPORATION
A-C Pump Division
240 Fall St (13148-1590)
PHONE 315 568-2811
Aaron Hagen, *Purch Agent*
Gene Sabini, *Engineer*
Robert Matusek, *Senior Engr*
Tolis Pitsalidis, *Cust Mgr*
Doug Brown, *Manager*
EMP: 58
SALES (corp-wide): 2.4B **Publicly Held**
SIC: 3625 3823 3363 3812 Control equipment, electric; fluidic devices, circuits & systems for process control; aluminum die-castings; radar systems & equipment; infrared object detection equipment; fluid power pumps & motors; pumps & pumping equipment
HQ: Itt, Llc
1133 Westchester Ave N-100
White Plains NY 10604
914 641-2000

(G-15363)
ITT ENGINEERED VALVES LLC (DH)
240 Fall St (13148-1590)
Rural Route 750 (13148)
PHONE 662 257-6982
Randy Garman, *General Mgr*
Fred Bose, *General Mgr*
Roland Howell, *Human Res Mgr*
David Nicholas, *Manager*
EMP: 30
SALES (est): 7.6MM
SALES (corp-wide): 2.4B **Publicly Held**
SIC: 2611 Pulp mills
HQ: Itt, Llc
1133 Westchester Ave N-100
White Plains NY 10604
914 641-2000

(G-15364)
ITT GOULDS PUMPS INC (HQ)
240 Fall St (13148-1573)
PHONE 914 641-2129
EMP: 4500
SALES (est): 1.1B
SALES (corp-wide): 2.4B **Publicly Held**
SIC: 3561 5084 Pumps & pumping equipment; industrial machinery & equipment
PA: Itt Inc.
1133 Westchester Ave N-100
White Plains NY 10604
914 641-2000

(G-15365)
ITT WATER TECHNOLOGY INC
Also Called: Goulds Pumps
2881 E Bayard Street Ext (13148-8745)
PHONE 315 568-2811

Fax: 315 568-2046
Douglas Bingler, *President*
Robert T Butera, *Vice Pres*
Douglas M Lawrence, *Vice Pres*
Maria Tzortzatos, *Treasurer*
Robert Kilmer, *VP Mktg*
▲ **EMP:** 350
SALES (est): 68.5MM
SALES (corp-wide): 2.4B **Publicly Held**
SIC: 3561 Pumps & pumping equipment
HQ: Itt, Llc
1133 Westchester Ave N-100
White Plains NY 10604
914 641-2000

(G-15366)
MONTEZUMA WINERY LLC
2981 Us Route 20 (13148-9423)
PHONE 315 568-8190
Bill Martin,
EMP: 9
SALES (est): 826.5K **Privately Held**
WEB: www.montezumawinery.com
SIC: 2084 Wines

(G-15367)
SCEPTER INC
Also Called: Scepter New York
11 Lamb Rd (13148-8432)
PHONE 315 568-4225
Fax: 315 568-4240
Garney Scott III, *Manager*
EMP: 30
SALES (corp-wide): 71.2MM **Privately Held**
WEB: www.scepterinc.com
SIC: 3341 Secondary nonferrous metals
PA: Scepter, Inc.
1485 Scepter Ln
Waverly TN 37185
931 535-3565

(G-15368)
SENECA FALLS CAPITAL INC (PA)
Also Called: Seneca Falls Machine
314 Fall St (13148-1543)
PHONE 315 568-5804
Fax: 315 568-5800
Attila Libertiny, *President*
EMP: 2
SQ FT: 115,000
SALES (est): 4.7MM **Privately Held**
SIC: 3541 Machine tools, metal cutting type

(G-15369)
SENECA FALLS MACHINE TOOL CO
Also Called: Seneca Falls Technology Group
314 Fall St (13148-1543)
PHONE 315 568-5804
Attila Libertiny, *President*
Dave Matteson, *Senior VP*
EMP: 60
SQ FT: 115,000
SALES: 3MM
SALES (corp-wide): 4.7MM **Privately Held**
WEB: www.sftg.com
SIC: 3541 3545 Machine tools, metal cutting type; machine tool accessories
PA: Seneca Falls Capital, Inc.
314 Fall St
Seneca Falls NY 13148
315 568-5804

(G-15370)
SENECA FLS SPC & LOGISTICS CO (PA)
50 Johnston St (13148-1235)
PHONE 315 568-4139
Fax: 585 388-0184
Stephen M Bregande, *President*
Bruce Hilton, *Vice Pres*
Christopher Woods, *Vice Pres*
Matthew Dukat, *Opers Mgr*
David Krager, *Traffic Mgr*
▲ **EMP:** 80 **EST:** 1880
SALES (est): 37.8MM **Privately Held**
SIC: 2653 2652 Boxes, corrugated: made from purchased materials; setup paperboard boxes

(G-15371)
TI GROUP AUTO SYSTEMS LLC
240 Fall St (13148-1590)
PHONE 315 568-7042
Danielle Roetting, *Manager*
EMP: 5
SALES (corp-wide): 1.7B **Privately Held**
WEB: www.tiautomotive.com
SIC: 3317 3312 3599 3052 Tubes, seamless steel; tubes, steel & iron; hose, flexible metallic; plastic hose; fuel systems & parts, motor vehicle
HQ: Ti Group Automotive Systems, Llc
2020 Taylor Rd
Auburn Hills MI 48326
248 296-8000

(G-15372)
WILSON PRESS LLC
56 Miller St (13148-1585)
PHONE 315 568-9693
Fax: 315 568-9693
Don Johnson, *Sales Staff*
Richard Ricci, *Manager*
Sharon Tyler, *Manager*
Nora Ricci,
EMP: 20
SQ FT: 5,500
SALES: 2MM **Privately Held**
SIC: 2752 2791 2789 2759 Commercial printing, lithographic; typesetting; bookbinding & related work; commercial printing

(G-15373)
XYLEM INC
2881 E Bayard Street Ext (13148-8745)
P.O. Box 750 (13148-0750)
PHONE 716 862-4123
Douglas Bingler, *Branch Mgr*
William Ritchie, *Manager*
Marlene Fingar, *Info Tech Dir*
Linda Lynch, *Director*
Liz Coakley, *Executive Asst*
EMP: 15 **Publicly Held**
SIC: 3561 Pumps & pumping equipment
PA: Xylem Inc.
1 International Dr
Rye Brook NY 10573

Setauket
Suffolk County

(G-15374)
BC SYSTEMS INC
200 N Belle Mead Ave # 2 (11733-3463)
PHONE 631 751-9370
Fax: 631 751-9378
Gus Blazek, *President*
Gustav Blazek, *President*
Dennis Carrigan, *Vice Pres*
Art Charych, *Vice Pres*
Carl Balk, *Mfg Staff*
EMP: 50
SQ FT: 16,000
SALES (est): 13.1MM **Privately Held**
WEB: www.bcpowersys.com
SIC: 3679 Power supplies, all types: static

(G-15375)
CAREFREE DAILY MONEY MANAGEMEN
5 Cedarwood Ct (11733-1844)
PHONE 631 751-1281
Jim Lindiakos, *Principal*
EMP: 5
SALES (est): 251.1K **Privately Held**
SIC: 2711 Newspapers, publishing & printing

(G-15376)
EATINGEVOLVED LLC
10 Technology Dr (11733-4063)
PHONE 631 675-2440
EMP: 16
SALES (est): 557.8K **Privately Held**
SIC: 2064 Candy bars, including chocolate covered bars

(G-15377)
MAUSNER EQUIPMENT CO INC
8 Heritage Ln (11733-3018)
PHONE 631 689-7358

Seymour Mausner, *President*
Dorothy Mausner, *Corp Secy*
Leonard Mausner, *Vice Pres*
EMP: 137
SQ FT: 17,000
SALES: 27.5MM **Privately Held**
SIC: 3545 5084 3823 Precision measuring tools; measuring & testing equipment, electrical; industrial instrmnts msrmnt display/control process variable

(G-15378)
RETIREMENT INSIDERS
15 Triangle Dr (11733-1431)
PHONE 631 751-1329
David Rogers, *President*
EMP: 6
SALES: 225K **Privately Held**
SIC: 2741 7389 Business service newsletters: publishing & printing; financial services

(G-15379)
RICHARD H WILLIAMS ASSOCIATES
Also Called: Bakery Associates
7 White Pine Ln (11733-3953)
PHONE 631 751-4156
Fax: 631 751-4156
John Granger, *President*
Jane Granger, *Corp Secy*
EMP: 5
SALES: 1MM **Privately Held**
WEB: www.bakeryassociates.net
SIC: 3556 Ovens, bakery

(G-15380)
SUCH INTL INCORPORATION
10 Mill River Rd (11733-2204)
PHONE 212 686-9888
Shumin Chou, *President*
Sergey Bagbasarov, *Bookkeeper*
▲ **EMP:** 5
SALES (est): 310K **Privately Held**
WEB: www.suchinternational.com
SIC: 2392 Household furnishings

(G-15381)
SUN CIRCUITS INTERNATIONAL INC
7 S Jersey Ave Ste 3 (11733-2065)
PHONE 631 240-9251
Nick Vitarelly, *CEO*
Anthony Petrelli, *Vice Pres*
EMP: 350
SALES (est): 19MM **Privately Held**
SIC: 3679 3824 Electronic circuits; mechanical & electromechanical counters & devices

Sharon Springs
Schoharie County

(G-15382)
ADELPHI PAPER HANGINGS
102 Main St (13459-3136)
P.O. Box 135 (13459-0135)
PHONE 518 284-9066
Fax: 518 284-3011
Chris Ohrstrom, *President*
Steve Larson, *Manager*
EMP: 5
SALES: 380K **Privately Held**
WEB: www.adelphipaperhangings.com
SIC: 2679 Wallpaper

(G-15383)
AMT INCORPORATED
883 Chestnut St (13459-2131)
P.O. Box 338 (13459-0338)
PHONE 518 284-2910
Fax: 518 284-2911
Lanning Brandel, *President*
Al Smrstik, *General Mgr*
Beth Brandel, *Corp Secy*
Dorinda Hamilton, *QA Dir*
Ryan Pillsbury, *Sales Mgr*
EMP: 33
SQ FT: 22,000

Sharon Springs - Schoharie County (G-15384)

GEOGRAPHIC SECTION

SALES (est): 7.6MM **Privately Held**
WEB: www.amtcastings.com
SIC: **3366** 3365 3354 3341 Bushings & bearings, copper (nonmachined); aluminum foundries; aerospace castings, aluminum; machinery castings, aluminum; aluminum extruded products; secondary nonferrous metals; steel foundries; miscellaneous nonferrous products; ferrous metals

(G-15384)
MONOLITHIC COATINGS INC
916 Highway Route 20 (13459-3108)
PHONE..................................914 621-2765
EMP: 5
SALES (est): 566.1K **Privately Held**
SIC: **3674** Read-only memory (ROM)

(G-15385)
TIMOTHY L SIMPSON
5819 State Route 145 (13459-3205)
PHONE..................................518 234-1401
Timothy L Simpson, *Principal*
EMP: 6
SALES (est): 492.5K **Privately Held**
SIC: **2411** Logging

Shelter Island
Suffolk County

(G-15386)
COECLES HBR MARINA & BOAT YARD
68 Cartwright Rd (11964)
PHONE..................................631 749-0856
John Needham, *President*
EMP: 15
SALES (corp-wide): 1.2MM **Privately Held**
SIC: **3732** Boat building & repairing
PA: Coecles Harbor Marina & Boat Yard Inc
18 Hudson Ave
Shelter Island NY 11964
631 749-0700

(G-15387)
GOODING & ASSOCIATES INC
15 Dinah Rock Rd (11964)
P.O. Box 1690 (11964-1690)
PHONE..................................631 749-3313
A Gordon Gooding Jr, *President*
Joy Strasser, *Office Mgr*
EMP: 14
SALES (est): 1.3MM **Privately Held**
SIC: **2741** Catalogs; publishing & printing

(G-15388)
SHELTER ISLAND REPORTER INC
Also Called: Shelter Island Cmnty Nwspapers
50 N Ferry Rd (11964)
P.O. Box 756 (11964-0756)
PHONE..................................631 749-1000
Troy Gustavson, *President*
Andrew Olsen, *Vice Pres*
◆ EMP: 8
SALES (est): 490K **Privately Held**
SIC: **2711** Newspapers, publishing & printing

Sherburne
Chenango County

(G-15389)
CHENANGO VALLEY TECH INC
328 Route 12b (13460)
P.O. Box 1038 (13460-1038)
PHONE..................................607 674-4115
Lloyd Baker, *CEO*
Lucille Baker, *President*
John Davis, *President*
John Clark, *Plant Mgr*
Norman Wynn, *Production*
EMP: 35 EST: 1997
SQ FT: 30,000
SALES (est): 6.6MM **Privately Held**
WEB: www.chenangovalleytech.com
SIC: **3544** 3089 Industrial molds; injection molding of plastics

(G-15390)
COLUMBUS WOODWORKING INC
164 Casey Cheese Fctry Rd (13460-5006)
PHONE..................................607 674-4546
Michael Tomaselli, *President*
Stacy Tomaselli, *Corp Secy*
EMP: 5
SQ FT: 15,000
SALES (est): 653.2K **Privately Held**
SIC: **2431** Millwork

(G-15391)
EGG LOW FARMS INC
35 W State St (13460-9424)
PHONE..................................607 674-4653
Fax: 607 674-9216
Helen Dunckel, *President*
David Dunckel, *Vice Pres*
Thena Russell, *Manager*
EMP: 10
SQ FT: 38,000
SALES: 850K **Privately Held**
SIC: **2015** Egg substitutes made from eggs

(G-15392)
KENYON PRESS INC
1 Kenyon Press Dr (13460-5670)
P.O. Box 710 (13460-0710)
PHONE..................................607 674-9066
Fax: 607 674-4952
Ray Kenyon, *President*
Debra Ford, *General Mgr*
Donald Washburn, *Prdtn Mgr*
Carrie Guyer, *Opers Staff*
Heather Norton, *Production*
EMP: 50
SQ FT: 75,000
SALES (est): 10MM **Privately Held**
SIC: **2752** Commercial printing, offset

(G-15393)
MID-YORK PRESS INC
2808 State Highway 80 (13460-4549)
P.O. Box 733 (13460-0733)
PHONE..................................607 674-4491
Fax: 607 674-4088
Robert W Tenney, *Ch of Bd*
Jane Eaton, *Principal*
Mary Mahoney, *Principal*
Cynthia Tenney, *Principal*
Pat Dowdall, *COO*
EMP: 70 EST: 1946
SQ FT: 56,000
SALES (est): 29.3MM **Privately Held**
WEB: www.midyorkpress.com
SIC: **2679** 2752 2711 Paperboard products, converted; commercial printing, offset; newspapers, publishing & printing
PA: Media Tenney Group
28 Robinson Rd
Clinton NY 13323
315 853-5569

(G-15394)
READY EGG FARMS INC
35 W State St (13460-9424)
P.O. Box 843, Silverton OR (97381-0843)
PHONE..................................607 674-4653
Patrick Green, *President*
EMP: 9
SQ FT: 40,000
SALES: 1.5MM **Privately Held**
WEB: www.readyeggfarms.com
SIC: **2015** Egg processing

(G-15395)
SHERBURNE METAL SALES INC (PA)
40 S Main St (13460-9804)
PHONE..................................607 674-4441
Fax: 607 674-9576
David Harvey, *President*
Gregory Panagiotakis, *Vice Pres*
EMP: 19
SQ FT: 60,000
SALES (est): 36.6MM **Privately Held**
WEB: www.sherburnemetals.com
SIC: **3331** 3351 Primary copper; rolled or drawn shapes: copper & copper alloy

(G-15396)
SMITH TOOL & DIE INC
714 Pleasant Valley Rd (13460-3101)
P.O. Box 205 (13460-0205)
PHONE..................................607 674-4165
Fax: 607 674-4335
Kenneth Smith, *President*
EMP: 6
SQ FT: 2,000
SALES (est): 340K **Privately Held**
WEB: www.cncsurfacegrinding.com
SIC: **3599** Machine shop, jobbing & repair

(G-15397)
STEEL SALES INC
8085 New York St Hwy 12 (13460)
P.O. Box 539 (13460-0539)
PHONE..................................607 674-6363
Fax: 607 674-9706
Brenda Westcott, *Ch of Bd*
Barbie Joe, *Sales Mgr*
EMP: 20
SQ FT: 20,000
SALES (est): 6.7MM **Privately Held**
WEB: www.steelsalesinc.com
SIC: **3446** 3444 3449 5051 Architectural metalwork; sheet metalwork; bars, concrete reinforcing: fabricated steel; metals service centers & offices; steel

(G-15398)
TECNOFIL CHENANGO SAC
40 S Main St (13460-9804)
PHONE..................................607 674-4441
Jose Babadia, *Principal*
Belinda Fairess, *Human Resources*
◆ EMP: 30
SALES (est): 9.5MM **Privately Held**
SIC: **3331** Primary copper

(G-15399)
WHITE HOUSE CABINET SHOP LLC
11 Knapp St (13460-9791)
P.O. Box 877 (13460-0877)
PHONE..................................607 674-9358
Jeff Webster, *COO*
Bruce Webster,
Mike Webster,
EMP: 8
SQ FT: 5,112
SALES (est): 786.5K **Privately Held**
SIC: **2434** Wood kitchen cabinets

Sheridan
Chautauqua County

(G-15400)
COTTON WELL DRILLING CO INC
Center Rd (14135)
P.O. Box 203 (14135-0203)
PHONE..................................716 672-2788
Fax: 716 672-6183
Donald D Cotton, *President*
Mollie Cotton, *Office Mgr*
EMP: 8
SQ FT: 2,400
SALES (est): 916K **Privately Held**
SIC: **1389** Oil & gas wells: building, repairing & dismantling

Sherman
Chautauqua County

(G-15401)
BISSEL-BABCOCK MILLWORK INC
3866 Kendrick Rd (14781-9628)
PHONE..................................716 761-6976
James Babcock, *President*
Paula Babcock, *Admin Sec*
EMP: 11
SQ FT: 5,000
SALES: 1.1MM **Privately Held**
SIC: **2421** Sawmills & planing mills, general

(G-15402)
FIRE APPARATUS SERVICE TECH
7895 Lyons Rd (14781-9609)
PHONE..................................716 753-3538
Danny Karges, *Executive*
EMP: 7
SALES (est): 931K **Privately Held**
SIC: **3669** Fire alarm apparatus, electric

(G-15403)
TRIPLE E MANUFACTURING
117 Osborn St (14781-9790)
P.O. Box 438 (14781-0438)
PHONE..................................716 761-6996
Fax: 716 761-6688
Richard Watrous, *Partner*
Pamela Watrous, *Partner*
▲ EMP: 18
SQ FT: 12,000
SALES (est): 1.8MM **Privately Held**
SIC: **2399** Horse & pet accessories, textile

Sherrill
Oneida County

(G-15404)
BRIGGS & STRATTON CORPORATION
4245 Highbridge Rd (13461)
PHONE..................................315 495-0100
Philip Wenzel, *Manager*
EMP: 15
SALES (corp-wide): 1.8B **Publicly Held**
SIC: **3519** Internal combustion engines
PA: Briggs & Stratton Corporation
12301 W Wirth St
Wauwatosa WI 53222
414 259-5333

(G-15405)
DUTCHLAND PLASTICS CORP
102 E Seneca St (13461-1008)
PHONE..................................315 280-0247
Daven Claerbout, *Branch Mgr*
EMP: 223
SALES (corp-wide): 107.2MM **Privately Held**
SIC: **3089** Molding primary plastic
PA: Dutchland Plastics Llc
54 Enterprise Ct
Oostburg WI 53070
920 564-3633

(G-15406)
JDLR ENTERPRISES LLC
Also Called: Noble Wood Shavings
104 E Seneca St (13461-1008)
PHONE..................................315 813-2911
EMP: 5
SALES (est): 751K **Privately Held**
SIC: **2421** Sawmill/Planing Mill

(G-15407)
SHERRILL MANUFACTURING INC
102 E Seneca St (13461-1008)
PHONE..................................315 280-0727
Gregory L Owens, *CEO*
Matthew A Roberts, *President*
EMP: 140
SQ FT: 1,000,000
SALES (est): 32.6MM **Privately Held**
WEB: www.sherrillmfg.com
SIC: **3421** 3914 3471 Cutlery; silverware, silver plated; gold plating

(G-15408)
SILVER CITY GROUP INC
Also Called: Silver City Metals
27577 W Seneca St (13461)
PHONE..................................315 363-0344
Fax: 315 361-1125
Dennis Tormey, *President*
Cliff Wittman, *Vice Pres*
EMP: 5
SQ FT: 2,500
SALES (est): 400K **Privately Held**
SIC: **3914** Pewter ware

▲ = Import ▼ = Export
◆ = Import/Export

GEOGRAPHIC SECTION

(G-15409)
TIBRO WATER TECHNOLOGIES LTD
106 E Seneca St Unit 25 (13461-1008)
PHONE..................................647 426-3415
Dhiren Chandaria, *President*
Dharmendra Variya, *Controller*
EMP: 15
SQ FT: 7,000
SALES: 1.2MM
SALES (corp-wide): 1.3MM **Privately Held**
SIC: 2819 Sodium & potassium compounds, exc. bleaches, alkalies, alum.
PA: Tibro International Ltd
    1 Scarsdale Rd Unit 300
    North York ON M3B 2
    647 426-3415

(G-15410)
WESTMOOR LTD
Also Called: Conde Pumps Div
906 W Hamilton Ave (13461-1366)
P.O. Box 99 (13461-0099)
PHONE..................................315 363-1500
Fax: 315 363-0193
James R Hendry, *Ch of Bd*
EMP: 10 EST: 1939
SQ FT: 18,000
SALES (est): 2.5MM **Privately Held**
WEB: www.westmoorltd.com
SIC: 3561 3523 Pumps & pumping equipment; milking machines

Shirley
Suffolk County

(G-15411)
AMERICAN REGENT INC
Also Called: American Regent Laboratories
5 Ramsey Rd (11967-4701)
P.O. Box 9001 (11967-9001)
PHONE..................................631 924-4000
Fax: 631 924-1731
Ralf Lange, *President*
Jean Poulos, *Vice Pres*
Anna Kirk, *Purch Agent*
Brian Goodman, *Buyer*
Christine Lydon-Rakov, *Research*
EMP: 425
SQ FT: 95,000
SALES (est): 52.3MM
SALES (corp-wide): 8.4B **Privately Held**
WEB: www.osteohealth.com
SIC: 2834 Pharmaceutical preparations
HQ: Luitpold Pharmaceuticals, Inc.
    5 Ramsey Rd
    Shirley NY 11967
    631 924-4000

(G-15412)
ANTHONY GIGI INC
Also Called: Russo's Gluten Free Gourmet
45 Ramsey Rd Unit 28 (11967-4712)
PHONE..................................860 984-1943
Neil Russo, *President*
EMP: 5
SQ FT: 2,000
SALES: 300K **Privately Held**
SIC: 2046 Gluten meal

(G-15413)
ATLANTIC COLOR CORP
14 Ramsey Rd (11967-4704)
PHONE..................................631 345-3800
Richard Reina, *Ch of Bd*
Joe Calandra, *Vice Pres*
EMP: 20
SALES (est): 3.1MM **Privately Held**
WEB: www.atlanticcolor.com
SIC: 2752 Commercial printing, offset

(G-15414)
ATLANTIC INDUSTRIAL TECH INC
90 Precision Dr (11967-4702)
PHONE..................................631 234-3131
Robert Ferrara, *Ch of Bd*
Thomas Ferrara, *Vice Pres*
EMP: 35
SQ FT: 20,000
SALES (est): 15MM **Privately Held**
WEB: www.aitzone.com
SIC: 3443 8711 7699 3594 Fabricated plate work (boiler shop); engineering services; industrial machinery & equipment repair; fluid power pumps & motors

(G-15415)
B V M ASSOCIATES
999-32 Montrell 414 (11967)
PHONE..................................631 254-6220
Mike Lucyk, *Owner*
EMP: 8
SQ FT: 5,000
SALES (est): 510K **Privately Held**
SIC: 3577 Computer peripheral equipment

(G-15416)
BIODEX MEDICAL SYSTEMS INC (PA)
20 Ramsey Rd (11967-4704)
PHONE..................................631 924-9000
Fax: 631 924-9338
James Reiss, *Ch of Bd*
Allyson Scerri, *President*
Kate Dimeglio, *Vice Pres*
Bill Johnson, *Vice Pres*
Bob Ranieri, *Vice Pres*
▲ EMP: 170
SQ FT: 83,000
SALES (est): 29.3MM **Privately Held**
WEB: www.biodex.com
SIC: 3842 3841 3844 Radiation shielding aprons, gloves, sheeting, etc.; muscle exercise apparatus, ophthalmic; X-ray apparatus & tubes

(G-15417)
BIODEX MEDICAL SYSTEMS INC
49 Natcon Dr (11967-4700)
PHONE..................................631 924-3146
John Ryan, *Manager*
EMP: 30
SALES (corp-wide): 29.3MM **Privately Held**
WEB: www.biodex.com
SIC: 3842 3841 Radiation shielding aprons, gloves, sheeting, etc.; muscle exercise apparatus, ophthalmic
PA: Biodex Medical Systems, Inc.
    20 Ramsey Rd
    Shirley NY 11967
    631 924-9000

(G-15418)
FIRE ISLAND FUEL
106 Parkwood Dr (11967-3918)
PHONE..................................631 772-1482
Joseph Intravaia, *Principal*
EMP: 6
SALES (est): 616.7K **Privately Held**
SIC: 2869 Fuels

(G-15419)
FRANK LOWE RBR & GASKET CO INC
44 Ramsey Rd (11967-4704)
PHONE..................................631 777-2707
Ira M Warren, *Ch of Bd*
Judy Rosalez, *Vice Pres*
Azhar Chishti, *Manager*
Ruth Kowalski, *Manager*
EMP: 35
SQ FT: 60,000
SALES (est): 8.3MM **Privately Held**
WEB: www.franklowe.com
SIC: 3053 Gaskets, all materials

(G-15420)
INNOVATION MGT GROUP INC
999 Montauk Hwy (11967-2130)
PHONE..................................800 889-0987
Jerry Hussong, *Vice Pres*
EMP: 10
SALES (corp-wide): 950K **Privately Held**
WEB: www.imgpresents.com
SIC: 7372 Prepackaged software
PA: Innovation Management Group, Inc.
    5348 Vegas Dr Ste 285
    Las Vegas NV 89108
    800 889-0987

(G-15421)
J & M FEED CORPORATION
675 Montauk Hwy (11967-2105)
PHONE..................................631 281-2152
John Colondona, *President*
EMP: 6
SQ FT: 7,500
SALES (est): 843.2K **Privately Held**
SIC: 2048 5999 Prepared feeds; feed supplements; pet food

(G-15422)
L I F PUBLISHING CORP (PA)
Also Called: The Fisherman
14 Ramsey Rd (11967-4704)
PHONE..................................631 345-5200
Richard Reina Sr, *President*
Fred Galofaro, *Publisher*
Toby Lapinski, *Editor*
Richard S Reina, *Vice Pres*
Madalyn Lechner, *Finance Other*
EMP: 20
SQ FT: 14,000
SALES (est): 5.1MM **Privately Held**
SIC: 2721 2752 Periodicals; commercial printing, offset

(G-15423)
LUITPOLD PHARMACEUTICALS INC (HQ)
5 Ramsey Rd (11967-4701)
P.O. Box 9001 (11967-9001)
PHONE..................................631 924-4000
William Berger, *General Mgr*
Liz Tilton, *Safety Mgr*
Kathleen Washington, *Opers Staff*
Bob Culkin, *Production*
Robert Locorriere, *Production*
▲ EMP: 500 EST: 1946
SALES (est): 209.4MM
SALES (corp-wide): 8.4B **Privately Held**
WEB: www.osteohealth.com
SIC: 2834 Pharmaceutical preparations
PA: Daiichi Sankyo Company, Limited
    3-5-1, Nihonbashihoncho
    Chuo-Ku TKY 103-0
    362 251-111

(G-15424)
LUITPOLD PHARMACEUTICALS INC
Also Called: Osteohealth Company
5 Ramsey Rd (11967-4701)
PHONE..................................631 924-4000
Mary Jane Helenek, *President*
Anna Kirk, *Purch Agent*
John Maiero, *QA Dir*
Gary Coughlen, *CFO*
Elizabeth Allen, *Finance Mgr*
EMP: 20
SALES (corp-wide): 8.4B **Privately Held**
WEB: www.osteohealth.com
SIC: 3843 Dental equipment & supplies
HQ: Luitpold Pharmaceuticals, Inc.
    5 Ramsey Rd
    Shirley NY 11967
    631 924-4000

(G-15425)
MID ATLANTIC GRAPHICS CORP
14 Ramsey Rd (11967-4704)
PHONE..................................631 345-3800
Fax: 631 345-5304
Madaline Lechner, *CEO*
Richard Reina Sr, *President*
Richard S Reina, *Vice Pres*
EMP: 20
SQ FT: 14,000
SALES (est): 2.4MM
SALES (corp-wide): 5.1MM **Privately Held**
SIC: 2752 Commercial printing, offset
PA: L I F Publishing Corp
    14 Ramsey Rd
    Shirley NY 11967
    631 345-5200

(G-15426)
MODULAR DEVICES INC
Also Called: M D I
1 Roned Rd (11967-4706)
PHONE..................................631 345-3100
Fax: 631 345-3106
Steven E Summer, *President*
Henry Striegl, *Regional Mgr*
Greg Mink, *COO*
Henry Striegel, *Vice Pres*
Henry F Striegl Jr, *Vice Pres*
▲ EMP: 55
SQ FT: 20,000
SALES (est): 12.1MM **Privately Held**
WEB: www.modev.com
SIC: 3621 Motors & generators

(G-15427)
NJF PUBLISHING CORP
Also Called: The Fisherman
14 Ramsey Rd (11967-4704)
PHONE..................................631 345-5200
Richard Reina, *President*
Peter Barrett, *Vice Pres*
Adrienne Kucharewshi, *Office Mgr*
Linda Barrett, *Manager*
EMP: 6
SQ FT: 1,800
SALES (est): 680K **Privately Held**
SIC: 2721 8412 Periodicals; museums & art galleries

(G-15428)
POWR-UPS CORP
1 Roned Rd (11967-4707)
PHONE..................................631 345-5700
Fax: 631 345-0060
Steven Summer, *President*
Debbie Wheeler, *Mktg Dir*
EMP: 25 EST: 1981
SQ FT: 20,000
SALES: 2.7MM **Privately Held**
WEB: www.powrupscorp.com
SIC: 3625 5063 Motor controls & accessories; electrical apparatus & equipment

(G-15429)
PRMS INC
Also Called: Prms Electronic Components
45 Ramsey Rd Unit 26 (11967-4712)
PHONE..................................631 851-7945
Ron Roybal, *Owner*
Linda Roybal, *Vice Pres*
EMP: 6
SQ FT: 5,000
SALES: 1.7MM **Privately Held**
WEB: www.prmsinc.com
SIC: 3677 Filtration devices, electronic

(G-15430)
UNCLE WALLYS LLC
41 Natcon Dr (11967-4700)
PHONE..................................631 205-0455
Wallace Amos, *Chairman*
Jerry Ceccio, *Vice Pres*
Michael Petrucelli, *CFO*
Denise Weber, *Controller*
Kathy Lennon, *Sales Mgr*
EMP: 35
SQ FT: 60,000
SALES (est): 1MM **Privately Held**
WEB: www.unclewallys.com
SIC: 2051 Bread, cake & related products

(G-15431)
UNITED BAKING CO INC (PA)
Also Called: Uncle Wally's
41 Natcon Dr (11967-4700)
PHONE..................................631 205-0455
Fax: 631 205-9691
Louis Avignone, *Ch of Bd*
John Avignone, *Plant Mgr*
Frank Sivilli, *Opers Staff*
Susan Vizzi, *Controller*
Kim Massa, *Accountant*
EMP: 3
SQ FT: 60,000
SALES (est): 33.4MM **Privately Held**
SIC: 2052 Cookies & crackers

Shokan
Ulster County

(G-15432)
MACK WOOD WORKING
Also Called: General Specialties
2792 State Route 28 (12481-5002)
PHONE..................................845 657-6625
Fax: 845 657-6630
Ben Mack, *Owner*
EMP: 8
SQ FT: 8,000

Shortsville - Ontario County (G-15433) — GEOGRAPHIC SECTION

SALES (est): 500K *Privately Held*
SIC: 2431 Millwork

Shortsville
Ontario County

(G-15433)
GLK FOODS LLC
Curtice Burns Foods
11 Clark St (14548-9755)
P.O. Box 450 (14548-0450)
PHONE 585 289-4414
Dave Flanagan, *Opers-Prdtn-Mfg*
Tom Palmer, *CFO*
David Pico, *Controller*
Chris Klahn, *Maintence Staff*
EMP: 40
SALES (corp-wide): 33.8MM *Privately Held*
SIC: 2035 2033 Sauerkraut, bulk; sauerkraut; packaged in cans, jars, etc.
PA: Glk Foods, Llc
    158 E Northland Ave
    Appleton WI 54911
    715 752-4105

Sidney
Delaware County

(G-15434)
ACCO BRANDS
101 Oneil Rd (13838-1055)
PHONE 607 561-5515
Jeffery Burnett, *Project Engr*
Craig Biondi, *Human Res Mgr*
Heidi Williams, *Sales Staff*
Ryan Tesiero, *Senior Mgr*
EMP: 32
SALES (est): 4.4MM
SALES (corp-wide): 1.5B *Publicly Held*
SIC: 2782 Blankbooks & looseleaf binders
PA: Acco Brands Corporation
    4 Corporate Dr
    Lake Zurich IL 60047
    847 541-9500

(G-15435)
AMERICAN BLUESTONE LLC
760 Quarry Rd (13838)
P.O. Box 117 (13838-0117)
PHONE 607 369-2235
Robert McDuffey, *Mng Member*
Deborah McDuffey,
EMP: 12
SALES (est): 1.5MM *Privately Held*
SIC: 3281 Cut stone & stone products

(G-15436)
AMPHENOL CORPORATION
Also Called: Amphenol Aerospace Industrial
40-60 Delaware Ave (13838-1395)
PHONE 607 563-5364
Rick Aiken, *General Mgr*
Mark Tompkins, *Superintendent*
Robert Stewart, *Business Mgr*
Carolyn Tian, *Business Mgr*
Dan Williams, *QC Mgr*
EMP: 345
SQ FT: 675,000
SALES (corp-wide): 5.5B *Publicly Held*
SIC: 3678 Electronic connectors
PA: Amphenol Corporation
    358 Hall Ave
    Wallingford CT 06492
    203 265-8900

(G-15437)
AMPHENOL CORPORATION
Amphenol Aerospace Operations
40-60 Delaware Ave (13838-1395)
PHONE 607 563-5011
Fax: 607 563-5118
Stan Backus, *District Mgr*
Brendan Harder, *Opers Mgr*
Mark Philpott, *Opers Mgr*
Richard Barnes, *Engineer*
Bob Boecke, *Engineer*
EMP: 1500
SALES (corp-wide): 5.5B *Publicly Held*
SIC: 3678 Electronic connectors

PA: Amphenol Corporation
    358 Hall Ave
    Wallingford CT 06492
    203 265-8900

(G-15438)
DECKER FOREST PRODUCTS INC
New York State Rte 8 (13838)
P.O. Box 205 (13838-0205)
PHONE 607 563-2345
Floyd Decker, *President*
Mark Decker, *Vice Pres*
Carol Decker, *Admin Sec*
EMP: 5
SQ FT: 15,000
SALES (est): 330K *Privately Held*
SIC: 2411 Logging camps & contractors

(G-15439)
EGLI MACHINE COMPANY INC
240 State Highway 7 (13838-2716)
PHONE 607 563-3663
Fax: 607 563-1160
Denis Egli, *President*
Charles Howand, *Engineer*
Ellen Egli, *Treasurer*
Dorthea Christensen, *Admin Sec*
EMP: 28
SQ FT: 18,000
SALES: 3.5MM *Privately Held*
WEB: www.eglimachine.com
SIC: 3545 3544 3089 Precision tools, machinists'; special dies, tools, jigs & fixtures; molding primary plastic

(G-15440)
JP OIL GROUP INC
49 Union St (13838-1442)
PHONE 607 563-1360
John Tal, *President*
EMP: 5
SALES (est): 306.7K *Privately Held*
SIC: 1382 Oil & gas exploration services

(G-15441)
REFILL SERVICES LLC
16 Winkler Rd (13838-1056)
PHONE 607 369-5864
Austin Wilson, *Mng Member*
EMP: 5
SALES (est): 320K *Privately Held*
SIC: 2621 Stationery, envelope & tablet papers

(G-15442)
TRI-TOWN NEWS INC (PA)
Also Called: Sidney Favorite Printing Div
74 Main St (13838-1134)
PHONE 607 561-3515
Fax: 607 563-7116
Paul Hamilton Sr, *President*
Wiley Vincent, *Vice Pres*
EMP: 25 EST: 1925
SQ FT: 10,080
SALES (est): 1.7MM *Privately Held*
WEB: www.powerofprint.com
SIC: 2752 2711 Commercial printing, offset; newspapers, publishing & printing

(G-15443)
UFP NEW YORK LLC (PA)
Also Called: Universal Forest Products
13 Winkler Rd (13838-1057)
PHONE 607 563-1556
Ralph Gschwind, *Principal*
EMP: 20
SALES (est): 10.1MM *Privately Held*
WEB: www.ufpinc.com
SIC: 2439 Trusses, wooden roof

(G-15444)
UNADILLA SILO COMPANY INC
Also Called: Unadilla Laminated Products
100 West Rd (13838)
PHONE 607 369-9341
Barb Deblasio, *Human Res Mgr*
Phillip Holowacz, *VP Sales*
Floyd Spencer, *Manager*
EMP: 62
SALES (corp-wide): 6.4MM *Privately Held*
SIC: 2431 3444 2439 Silo staves, wood; sheet metalwork; structural wood members

PA: Unadilla Silo Company, Inc.
    18 Clifton St
    Unadilla NY 13849
    607 369-9341

(G-15445)
USA CUSTOM PAD CORP (PA)
16 Winkler Rd (13838-1056)
PHONE 607 563-9550
Fax: 607 563-9553
Eric T Wilson, *Chairman*
Marcia Wilson, *Admin Sec*
▲ EMP: 29
SQ FT: 20,000
SALES (est): 6.5MM *Privately Held*
WEB: www.memopads.com
SIC: 2678 2759 2741 Tablets & pads, book & writing: from purchased materials; commercial printing; miscellaneous publishing

Silver Bay
Warren County

(G-15446)
HACKER BOAT COMPANY INC (PA)
8 Delaware Ave (12874-1815)
PHONE 518 543-6731
Fax: 518 543-6732
Ernest George Badcock III, *Ch of Bd*
Lynn R Wagemann, *President*
Dolores Kunker, *Sales Mgr*
▲ EMP: 20
SALES (est): 6.1MM *Privately Held*
WEB: www.hackerboatco.com
SIC: 3732 Boat building & repairing

Silver Creek
Chautauqua County

(G-15447)
CHAUTAUQUA WINE COMPANY INC
Also Called: Willow Creek Winery
2627 Chapin Rd (14136-9760)
PHONE 716 934-9463
Fax: 716 934-9463
Holly Metzger, *President*
Holly Metzter, *President*
EMP: 5 EST: 2000
SALES (est): 418.6K *Privately Held*
WEB: www.willowcreekwinery.com
SIC: 2084 Wines

(G-15448)
EXCELCO DEVELOPMENTS INC
65 Main St (14136-1467)
P.O. Box 230 (14136-0230)
PHONE 716 934-2651
Christopher J Lanski, *President*
Douglas A Newman, *Exec VP*
Jeff Wagner, *Project Mgr*
Keith Pelz, *Opers Mgr*
Philip J Azzarella, *CFO*
EMP: 37
SQ FT: 40,000
SALES (est): 7MM *Privately Held*
SIC: 3728 3731 3429 Aircraft assemblies, subassemblies & parts; shipbuilding & repairing; manufactured hardware (general)

(G-15449)
EXCELCO/NEWBROOK INC
16 Mechanic St (14136-1202)
P.O. Box 231 (14136-0231)
PHONE 716 934-2644
Fax: 716 854-9285
Christopher J Lanski, *CEO*
Geoff Rondeau, *General Mgr*
Paul Narraway, *Engineer*
P J Azzarella, *CFO*
Georgia Rengert, *Office Mgr*
EMP: 85 EST: 1952
SQ FT: 93,000
SALES (est): 12.2MM *Privately Held*
WEB: www.excelco.net
SIC: 3728 3731 7692 Aircraft assemblies, subassemblies & parts; shipbuilding & repairing; welding repair

(G-15450)
SILVER CREEK ENTERPRISES INC
25 Howard St (14136-1007)
PHONE 716 934-2611
Fax: 716 934-2081
Frederick Mertz, *Ch of Bd*
Wayne Mertz, *President*
Paul Allen, *Mfg Mgr*
Ben Davis, *Research*
Michael Reedy, *Senior Engr*
EMP: 2 EST: 1856
SQ FT: 60,000
SALES (est): 4.8MM *Privately Held*
WEB: www.showes.com
SIC: 3559 3565 Chemical machinery & equipment; pharmaceutical machinery; packaging machinery

Silver Springs
Wyoming County

(G-15451)
MORTON SALT INC
45 Ribaud Ave (14550-9805)
P.O. Box 342 (14550-0342)
PHONE 585 493-2511
Fax: 585 493-2067
Matt Ashley, *Project Engr*
Tim Declerck, *Electrical Engi*
Norbert Fuest, *Human Res Dir*
Steve Hull, *Human Res Mgr*
Daniel Border, *Branch Mgr*
EMP: 12
SALES (corp-wide): 4.4B *Privately Held*
SIC: 1479 Salt & sulfur mining
HQ: Morton Salt, Inc.
    123 N Wacker Dr Fl 24
    Chicago IL 60606

Sinclairville
Chautauqua County

(G-15452)
CARLSON WOOD PRODUCTS INC (PA)
1705 Bates Rd (14782-9726)
PHONE 716 287-2923
Fax: 716 287-2657
William Carlson, *President*
Ivetta Carlson, *Vice Pres*
EMP: 6
SQ FT: 4,000
SALES: 1.3MM *Privately Held*
SIC: 2426 2421 Lumber, hardwood dimension; kiln drying of lumber

(G-15453)
CONTAINER TSTG SOLUTIONS LLC (PA)
17 Lester St (14782-9724)
PHONE 716 487-3300
Brian Johnson, *Ch of Bd*
EMP: 10
SALES (est): 1.7MM *Privately Held*
SIC: 2834 Solutions, pharmaceutical

(G-15454)
RAND MACHINE PRODUCTS INC
Spartan Tool Division
5035 Route 60 (14782-9731)
PHONE 716 985-4681
Fax: 716 985-4683
Herman C Ruhlman, *Sales/Mktg Mgr*
Chad Ruhlman, *Manager*
EMP: 9
SALES (corp-wide): 29.6MM *Privately Held*
WEB: www.randmachine.com
SIC: 3544 2865 Special dies, tools, jigs & fixtures; dyes & pigments
PA: Rand Machine Products, Inc.
    2072 Allen Street Ext
    Falconer NY 14733
    716 665-5217

Skaneateles
Onondaga County

(G-15455)
ANYELAS VINEYARDS LLC
2433 W Lake Rd (13152-9471)
PHONE.................................315 685-3797
James Nocek,
EMP: 13
SQ FT: 5,000
SALES: 200K **Privately Held**
SIC: 2084 Wines

(G-15456)
BURDICK PUBLICATIONS INC
Also Called: EB&I Marketing
2352 E Lake Rd (13152-8924)
P.O. Box 977 (13152-0977)
PHONE.................................315 685-9500
Elaina K Burdick, *CEO*
EMP: 6
SQ FT: 1,200
SALES (est): 900K **Privately Held**
WEB: www.burdickpubs.com
SIC: 2741 Miscellaneous publishing

(G-15457)
CHOHEHCO LLC
78 State St (13152-1218)
PHONE.................................315 420-4624
Vedran Psenicnik,
EMP: 7 **EST:** 2014
SALES (est): 330.7K **Privately Held**
SIC: 2086 Carbonated beverages, nonalcoholic: bottled & canned

(G-15458)
DIGITAL ANALYSIS CORPORATION
716 Visions Dr (13152-6475)
P.O. Box 95 (13152-0095)
PHONE.................................315 685-0760
Fax: 315 685-0766
Richard Pinkowski, *President*
Marge Pinkowski, *Manager*
Sherri Stringer, *Manager*
EMP: 17
SQ FT: 12,000
SALES: 4.4MM **Privately Held**
WEB: www.digital-analysis.com
SIC: 3823 Industrial instrmnts msrmnt display/control process variable

(G-15459)
DIVINE PHOENIX LLC
Also Called: Divine Phoenix Books
2985 Benson Rd (13152-9638)
P.O. Box 1001 (13152-5001)
PHONE.................................585 737-1482
Laura Ponticello, *Principal*
EMP: 585
SQ FT: 850
SALES: 30K **Privately Held**
SIC: 2731 Book publishing

(G-15460)
G E INSPECTION TECHNOLOGIES LP
721 Visions Dr (13152-6475)
PHONE.................................315 554-2000
Todd Brugger, *Branch Mgr*
Maureen Omeara, *Associate*
EMP: 175
SALES (corp-wide): 117.3B **Publicly Held**
SIC: 3829 8734 7359 3651 Physical property testing equipment; testing laboratories; equipment rental & leasing; household audio & video equipment
HQ: G E Inspection Technologies, Lp
721 Visions Dr
Skaneateles NY 13152
315 554-2000

(G-15461)
GENERAL ELC CAPITL SVCS INC
721 Visions Dr (13152-6475)
PHONE.................................315 554-2000
Melissa Lainhart, *General Mgr*
William Kelly, *Design Engr*
Dennis McEnery, *Engng Exec*
Jeff Anderson, *Branch Mgr*
Jeff Register, *Manager*
EMP: 7
SALES (corp-wide): 117.3B **Publicly Held**
WEB: www.gecommercialfinance.com
SIC: 3699 3651 3634 Electrical equipment & supplies; household audio & video equipment; electric housewares & fans
HQ: General Electric Capital Services, Inc.
3135 Easton Tpke
Fairfield CT 06828
203 373-2211

(G-15462)
HABERMAASS CORPORATION
Also Called: T C Timber
4407 Jordan Rd (13152-8300)
P.O. Box 42 (13152-0042)
PHONE.................................315 685-8919
Fax: 315 685-3792
Klaus Habermaass, *President*
Hugh Reed, *Vice Pres*
Rolf Sievers, *Vice Pres*
Janet Walker, *Accounts Mgr*
▲ **EMP:** 12
SQ FT: 150,000
SALES (est): 2.3MM
SALES (corp-wide): 121.9MM **Privately Held**
SIC: 3944 5092 Games, toys & children's vehicles; toys & hobby goods & supplies
PA: HabermaaB Gmbh
August-Grosch-Str. 28-38
Bad Rodach 96476
956 492-90

(G-15463)
HANSON AGGREGATES PA LLC
Rr 321 (13152)
P.O. Box 7 (13152-0007)
PHONE.................................315 685-3321
Dirk Field, *Vice Pres*
Phil Wheeler, *Manager*
EMP: 25
SQ FT: 2,160
SALES (corp-wide): 14.4B **Privately Held**
SIC: 1442 1422 Common sand mining; crushed & broken limestone
HQ: Hanson Aggregates Pennsylvania, Llc
7660 Imperial Way
Allentown PA 18195
610 366-4626

(G-15464)
PATIENCE BREWSTER INC
3872 Jordan Rd (13152-9317)
P.O. Box 689 (13152-0689)
PHONE.................................315 685-8336
Patience Brewster Gregg, *CEO*
Holland Gregg, *President*
Hubbard Stout, *President*
▲ **EMP:** 10
SALES: 5MM **Privately Held**
SIC: 3999 Christmas tree ornaments, except electrical & glass

(G-15465)
SCALE-TRONIX INC (PA)
4341 State Street Rd (13152-9338)
PHONE.................................914 948-8117
Fax: 914 948-0581
Carolyn Lepler, *President*
David C Hale, *Principal*
EMP: 15
SQ FT: 5,000
SALES (est): 4.1MM **Privately Held**
SIC: 3596 Baby scales; bathroom scales; weighing machines & apparatus

(G-15466)
TESSY PLASTICS CORP (PA)
700 Visions Dr (13152-6475)
PHONE.................................315 689-3924
Fax: 315 689-6595
Henry Beck, *Ch of Bd*
Roland Beck, *President*
Joseph Raffa, *General Mgr*
Greg Levengood, *COO*
Matthew Biernacki, *Vice Pres*
◆ **EMP:** 500
SQ FT: 240,000
SALES (est): 177.8MM **Privately Held**
WEB: www.tessy.com
SIC: 3089 3549 Injection molding of plastics; assembly machines, including robotic

Skaneateles Falls
Onondaga County

(G-15467)
CLEAR EDGE CROSIBLE INC
Also Called: Clear Edge Filtration
4653 Jordan Rd (13153-7704)
PHONE.................................315 685-3466
Michael Kriever, *Branch Mgr*
Mike Reichert, *Supervisor*
EMP: 100
SALES (corp-wide): 26.8MM **Privately Held**
WEB: www.crosible.com
SIC: 2393 Textile bags
PA: Clear Edge Crosible Inc
11607 E 43rd St N
Tulsa OK 74116
918 984-6000

(G-15468)
HAND HELD PRODUCTS INC (HQ)
Also Called: Honeywell Imaging and Mobility
700 Visions Dr (13153-5312)
P.O. Box 208 (13153-0208)
PHONE.................................315 554-6000
Kevin Jost, *CEO*
John F Waldron, *Ch of Bd*
Darius Adamczyk, *Chairman*
Michael A Ehrhart, *Vice Pres*
David Guido, *Vice Pres*
▲ **EMP:** 500
SQ FT: 120,000
SALES (est): 192.5MM
SALES (corp-wide): 38.5B **Publicly Held**
WEB: www.handheld.com
SIC: 3577 3571 3663 3578 Magnetic ink & optical scanning devices; electronic computers; radio & TV communications equipment; calculating & accounting equipment
PA: Honeywell International Inc.
115 Tabor Rd
Morris Plains NJ 07950
973 455-2000

(G-15469)
HAND HELD PRODUCTS INC
Also Called: Honeywell Scanning & Mobility
700 Visions Dr (13153-5312)
PHONE.................................315 554-6000
Ej Riley, *Regional Mgr*
Bill Coleman, *Purch Mgr*
Rick Witkowski, *Engineer*
Dave Guido, *CFO*
Joe Henningan, *CFO*
EMP: 13
SALES (corp-wide): 38.5B **Publicly Held**
SIC: 3577 Magnetic ink & optical scanning devices
HQ: Hand Held Products, Inc.
700 Visions Dr
Skaneateles Falls NY 13153
315 554-6000

(G-15470)
HONEYWELL INTERNATIONAL INC
700 Visions Dr (13153-5311)
PHONE.................................315 554-6643
Kevin Jost, *President*
Joanne Plis, *Sales Associate*
Eileen Clancy, *Technical Staff*
Donald Thompson, *Director*
EMP: 657
SALES (corp-wide): 38.5B **Publicly Held**
SIC: 3724 Aircraft engines & engine parts
PA: Honeywell International Inc.
115 Tabor Rd
Morris Plains NJ 07950
973 455-2000

(G-15471)
WELCH ALLYN INC
Data Collection Division
4341 State Street Rd (13153-5301)
P.O. Box 220 (13153-0220)
PHONE.................................315 685-4100
Tim McGilloway, *Sales Mgr*
Mary Adams, *Marketing Staff*
Dewey Shimer, *Branch Mgr*
EMP: 1000
SALES (corp-wide): 1.9B **Publicly Held**
SIC: 3841 3577 Diagnostic apparatus, medical; computer peripheral equipment
HQ: Welch Allyn Inc
4341 State Street Rd
Skaneateles Falls NY 13153
315 685-4100

(G-15472)
WELCH ALLYN INC (HQ)
4341 State Street Rd (13153-5301)
P.O. Box 220 (13153-0220)
PHONE.................................315 685-4100
Fax: 315 685-1769
Stephen Meyer, *President*
Naveen Velagapudi, *General Mgr*
Chris Bragg, *Business Mgr*
Tom Pelchy, *Business Mgr*
Mike Ehrhart, *Exec VP*
▲ **EMP:** 1400
SALES (est): 517.3MM
SALES (corp-wide): 1.9B **Publicly Held**
SIC: 3841 2835 3827 Diagnostic apparatus, medical; otoscopes, except electromedical; ophthalmic instruments & apparatus; blood pressure apparatus; in vitro & in vivo diagnostic substances; optical instruments & lenses
PA: Hill-Rom Holdings, Inc.
2 Prudential Plz Ste 4100
Chicago IL 60601
312 819-7200

(G-15473)
WELCH ALLYN INC
Also Called: Lighting Products Division
4619 Jordan Rd (13153-5313)
P.O. Box 187 (13153-0187)
PHONE.................................315 685-4347
Fax: 315 685-2854
Michael Slaton, *Regional Mgr*
William Allyn, *Research*
John Lane, *Engineer*
Scott Martin, *Engineer*
Jason Mirisoloff, *Engineer*
EMP: 1000
SALES (corp-wide): 1.9B **Publicly Held**
SIC: 3841 3641 Diagnostic apparatus, medical; electric lamps
HQ: Welch Allyn Inc
4341 State Street Rd
Skaneateles Falls NY 13153
315 685-4100

Slate Hill
Orange County

(G-15474)
RICHARD ROTHBARD INC
1866 Route 284 (10973-4208)
P.O. Box 480 (10973-0480)
PHONE.................................845 355-2300
Richard Rothbard, *President*
Joanna Rothbard, *Admin Sec*
EMP: 9
SQ FT: 1,500
SALES (est): 675.2K **Privately Held**
SIC: 2499 Decorative wood & woodwork

Sleepy Hollow
Westchester County

(G-15475)
TRADER INTERNTNAL PUBLICATIONS
50 Fremont Rd (10591-1118)
P.O. Box 687, Tarrytown (10591-0687)
PHONE.................................914 631-6856
Jean Sudol, *President*
Edward R Sudol, *Corp Secy*
EMP: 6
SALES: 500K **Privately Held**
SIC: 2741 2721 Miscellaneous publishing; periodicals: publishing only; trade journals: publishing only, not printed on site

(G-15476)
VALERIE BOHIGIAN
Also Called: Valian Associates
225 Hunter Ave (10591-1316)
PHONE.................................914 631-8866

Valerie Bohigian, *Owner*
EMP: 6
SALES (est): 230K **Privately Held**
WEB: www.valianassociates.com
SIC: 3914 Trophies, pewter

Slingerlands
Albany County

(G-15477)
LONG LUMBER AND SUPPLY CORP
2100 New Scotland Rd (12159-3419)
PHONE..................................518 439-1661
Fax: 518 439-8832
Richard L Long Jr, *President*
Robert P Long, *Vice Pres*
EMP: 10 EST: 1945
SQ FT: 10,000
SALES (est): 790K **Privately Held**
SIC: 2511 2499 5712 5211 Wood lawn & garden furniture; fencing, wood; furniture stores; fencing

(G-15478)
SABRE ENERGY SERVICES LLC
1891 New Scotland Rd (12159-3628)
PHONE..................................518 514-1572
Steven D Oesterle, *CEO*
John Y Mason, *Ch of Bd*
Gillian Webster, *Administration*
EMP: 15
SALES (est): 3.9MM **Privately Held**
SIC: 2819 1389 Sulfur chloride; cementing oil & gas well casings

Sloansville
Schoharie County

(G-15479)
FLORIDA NORTH INC
134 Vanderwerken Rd (12160-2211)
PHONE..................................518 868-2888
Fax: 518 868-4888
Daniel Nelson, *President*
EMP: 15
SQ FT: 85,000
SALES (est): 650K **Privately Held**
WEB: www.makarioscondos.com
SIC: 3949 Swimming pools, plastic

Sloatsburg
Rockland County

(G-15480)
CUSTOM EUROPEAN IMPORTS INC
100 Sterling Mine Rd (10974-2502)
PHONE..................................845 357-5718
Martin Lichtman, *President*
▲ EMP: 20
SALES (est): 1.5MM **Privately Held**
SIC: 2394 Canvas & related products

Smithtown
Suffolk County

(G-15481)
A & G HEAT SEALING
1 Albatross Ln (11787-3301)
PHONE..................................631 724-7764
George Ciunga, *President*
EMP: 8
SQ FT: 12,000
SALES (est): 790.6K **Privately Held**
WEB: www.agheatsealing.com
SIC: 3089 3565 Plastic processing; packaging machinery

(G-15482)
ALL PRODUCTS DESIGNS
227a Route 111 (11787-4754)
PHONE..................................631 748-6901
Xiurong Liu, *Owner*
EMP: 7

SALES (est): 346.7K **Privately Held**
SIC: 3669 Communications equipment

(G-15483)
ANCHOR CANVAS LLC
556 W Jericho Tpke (11787-2601)
PHONE..................................631 265-5602
Fax: 631 265-5632
Jo A Hnsen, *Finance Mgr*
Jon Hansen,
Rita Zelig, *Administration*
EMP: 6
SQ FT: 8,000
SALES (est): 540K **Privately Held**
SIC: 2394 Canvas & related products

(G-15484)
CERTIFIED FLAMEPROOFING CORP
17 N Ingelore Ct (11787-1544)
PHONE..................................631 265-4824
Edwards Fallom, *President*
EMP: 6
SALES (est): 436.1K **Privately Held**
SIC: 3251 Fireproofing tile, clay

(G-15485)
DIGITAL ASSOCIATES LLC
50 Karl Ave Ste 303 (11787-2744)
PHONE..................................631 983-6075
Vincent RE,
EMP: 8 EST: 2015
SALES (est): 186.1K **Privately Held**
SIC: 7372 Publishers' computer software

(G-15486)
DUKE OF IRON INC
1039 W Jericho Tpke (11787-3205)
PHONE..................................631 543-3600
Fax: 631 543-3629
Paul Montelbano, *President*
EMP: 6
SQ FT: 8,000
SALES: 1MM **Privately Held**
WEB: www.dukeofiron.com
SIC: 3446 Ornamental metalwork

(G-15487)
G N R PLASTICS INC
Also Called: G N R Co
11 Wandering Way (11787-1147)
PHONE..................................631 724-8758
EMP: 9
SQ FT: 10,000
SALES (est): 760K **Privately Held**
SIC: 3544 3089 Mfg Dies/Tools/Jigs/Fixtures Mfg Plastic Products

(G-15488)
HOTELINTERACTIVE INC
155 E Main St Ste 140 (11787-2853)
PHONE..................................631 424-7755
Richard Viola, *President*
Andrew Noce, *President*
Glenn Haussman, *Editor*
Joseph Viola, *COO*
Michael Chalfin, *Vice Pres*
EMP: 15
SQ FT: 3,000
SALES (est): 2.3MM **Privately Held**
WEB: www.hotelinteractive.com
SIC: 2721 7389 Trade journals: publishing & printing; decoration service for special events

(G-15489)
IRON WORKER
1039 W Jericho Tpke (11787-3205)
PHONE..................................516 338-2756
Fax: 516 543-3629
Paul Montelbano, *President*
EMP: 14
SALES (est): 1.1MM **Privately Held**
SIC: 3446 Stairs, staircases, stair treads: prefabricated metal

(G-15490)
JERIC KNIT WEAR
61 Hofstra Dr (11787-2053)
PHONE..................................631 979-8827
Jerry Lobel, *Owner*
EMP: 5
SALES (est): 452.3K **Privately Held**
SIC: 2253 Sweaters & sweater coats, knit

(G-15491)
KANTIAN SKINCARE LLC
496 Smithtown Byp (11787-5005)
PHONE..................................631 780-4711
Jonathan Klein,
Richard Klein,
EMP: 5 EST: 2012
SALES (est): 475.3K **Privately Held**
SIC: 2844 Cosmetic preparations

(G-15492)
NATURALLY FREE FOOD INC
35 Roundabout Rd (11787-1822)
P.O. Box 1365 (11787-0896)
PHONE..................................631 361-9710
Christine Mitchell, *Principal*
EMP: 6
SALES (est): 425.6K **Privately Held**
SIC: 2099 Food preparations

(G-15493)
PBL INDUSTRIES CORP
49 Dillmont Dr (11787-1635)
PHONE..................................631 979-4266
William Loffman, *President*
EMP: 10
SALES: 950K **Privately Held**
SIC: 3499 Fabricated metal products

(G-15494)
PERFECT FORMS AND SYSTEMS INC
35 Riverview Ter (11787-1155)
PHONE..................................631 462-1100
Fax: 631 382-4976
Joseph Messana, *President*
Jacquelyn Cully, *Business Dir*
EMP: 15
SALES (est): 1.6MM **Privately Held**
SIC: 2752 Business form & card printing, lithographic

(G-15495)
PRECISION DENTAL CABINETS INC (PA)
900 W Jericho Tpke (11787-3206)
PHONE..................................631 543-3870
Fax: 631 543-1609
Peter Loscialpo, *President*
Joseph Pisk, *Vice Pres*
Antoinette Frumusa, *Bookkeeper*
EMP: 13
SQ FT: 12,000
SALES (est): 2.5MM **Privately Held**
SIC: 3843 2434 1751 Cabinets, dental; wood kitchen cabinets; cabinet building & installation

(G-15496)
PSI TRANSIT MIX CORP
34 E Main St (11787-2804)
P.O. Box 178 (11787-0178)
PHONE..................................631 382-7930
Albino Almeida, *President*
EMP: 5
SALES (est): 478K **Privately Held**
SIC: 2951 Concrete, asphaltic (not from refineries); concrete, bituminous

(G-15497)
QUALTRONIC DEVICES INC
130 Oakside Dr (11787-1132)
PHONE..................................631 360-0859
Peter A Ferentinos, *CEO*
Steven Ferentinos, *President*
Antoine Dominic, *Project Mgr*
EMP: 18
SQ FT: 3,000
SALES (est): 2.2MM **Privately Held**
SIC: 3571 Electronic computers

(G-15498)
SMITHTOWN NEWS INC
Also Called: North Shore News Group
1 Brooksite Dr (11787-3493)
P.O. Box 805 (11787-0805)
PHONE..................................631 265-2100
Fax: 631 265-6237
Bernard Paley, *President*
Mary Lavecchia, *Office Mgr*
EMP: 32
SQ FT: 7,000
SALES (est): 1.8MM **Privately Held**
WEB: www.thesmithtownnews.com
SIC: 2711 Newspapers

(G-15499)
SYMANTEC CORPORATION
98 Sunrise Ln (11787-4436)
PHONE..................................631 656-0185
EMP: 70
SALES (corp-wide): 3.6B **Publicly Held**
SIC: 7372 Prepackaged software
PA: Symantec Corporation
   350 Ellis St
   Mountain View CA 94043
   650 527-8000

(G-15500)
T-COMPANY LLC
16 Monitor Rd (11787-1867)
PHONE..................................646 290-6365
Mark Grottano, *Mng Member*
Lisa Frizol,
Agatha Grottano,
EMP: 5
SQ FT: 2,100
SALES (est): 400K **Privately Held**
SIC: 2599 Factory furniture & fixtures

(G-15501)
TRADEWINS PUBLISHING CORP
19 Bellemeade Ave Ste B (11787-1877)
PHONE..................................631 361-6916
Steve Schmidt, *President*
Jane Schmidt, *Admin Sec*
EMP: 5
SQ FT: 1,000
SALES (est): 440K **Privately Held**
WEB: www.tradewinspublishing.com
SIC: 7372 Publishers' computer software

(G-15502)
VITAKEM NUTRACEUTICAL INC
811 W Jericho Tpke (11787-3232)
PHONE..................................631 956-8343
EMP: 250
SQ FT: 35,000
SALES: 15MM **Privately Held**
SIC: 2023 Mfg Dietary Supplements Products

Sodus
Wayne County

(G-15503)
MIZKAN AMERICAS INC
7673 Sodus Center Rd (14551-9539)
PHONE..................................315 483-6944
Carlos Mansinho, *Plant Mgr*
Kevin Perry, *Opers Staff*
Ted Pouley, *Manager*
EMP: 10 **Privately Held**
SIC: 2099 Vinegar
HQ: Mizkan America, Inc.
   1661 Feehanville Dr # 200
   Mount Prospect IL 60056
   847 590-0059

(G-15504)
NYKON INC
Also Called: Ramco Arts
8175 Stell Rd (14551-9530)
PHONE..................................315 483-0504
Alice Cuvelier, *Principal*
Craig Cuvelier, *Controller*
EMP: 9
SQ FT: 5,000
SALES (est): 817.8K **Privately Held**
WEB: www.nykon.net
SIC: 3651 Music distribution apparatus

(G-15505)
TERMATEC MOLDING INC
28 Foley Dr (14551-1044)
P.O. Box 96 (14551-0096)
PHONE..................................315 483-4150
Fax: 315 483-6365
Brad Cuvelier, *President*
James Peerson, *Plant Mgr*
James Peterson, *Plant Mgr*
EMP: 15
SQ FT: 6,500
SALES (est): 1.2MM **Privately Held**
SIC: 3089 Molding primary plastic

Solvay
Onondaga County

(G-15506)
BERRY PLASTICS CORPORATION
1500 Milton Ave (13209-1622)
PHONE..................................315 484-0397
David Heigel, *Manager*
Tom Taylor, *Info Tech Mgr*
EMP: 178
SALES (corp-wide): 4.8B **Publicly Held**
SIC: 3089 Plastic containers, except foam
HQ: Berry Plastics Corporation
   101 Oakley St
   Evansville IN 47710
   812 424-2904

(G-15507)
EASTERN COMPANY
Also Called: Frazer & Jones Division
3000 Milton Ave (13209)
P.O. Box 4955, Syracuse (13221-4955)
PHONE..................................315 468-6251
Stan Newsome, *Plant Supt*
Sadmir Brkanovic, *QC Mgr*
Michael Reilley, *Technical Mgr*
Thomas Giannone, *Controller*
A T Giannone, *Comptroller*
EMP: 100
SALES (corp-wide): 144.5MM **Publicly Held**
WEB: www.easterncompany.com
SIC: 3322 Malleable iron foundries
PA: The Eastern Company
   112 Bridge St
   Naugatuck CT 06770
   203 729-2255

(G-15508)
EVENT SERVICES CORPORATION
6171 Airport Rd (13209-9754)
P.O. Box 587 (13209-0587)
PHONE..................................315 488-9357
Kevin Jankiewicz, *President*
EMP: 6
SALES (est): 440K **Privately Held**
SIC: 2099 Food preparations

Somers
Westchester County

(G-15509)
GENERAL CINEMA BEVS OF OHIO
Also Called: Pepsi Bottle and Group
1 Pepsi Way Ste 1 (10589-2212)
PHONE..................................914 767-6000
Craig Weatherup, *President*
Christian Luther, *Info Tech Mgr*
Chris Knox, *Director*
EMP: 1200
SALES (est): 75.2MM
SALES (corp-wide): 63B **Publicly Held**
WEB: www.joy-of-cola.com
SIC: 2086 Soft drinks: packaged in cans, bottles, etc.
HQ: Pepsi-Cola Metropolitan Bottling Company, Inc.
   1111 Westchester Ave
   White Plains NY 10604
   914 767-6000

(G-15510)
GRAYHAWK LEASING LLC (HQ)
1 Pepsi Way (10589-2212)
PHONE..................................914 767-6000
Saad Abdul-Latif, *CEO*
EMP: 8
SALES (est): 2.3MM
SALES (corp-wide): 63B **Publicly Held**
SIC: 2086 7359 Bottled & canned soft drinks; rental store, general
PA: Pepsico, Inc.
   700 Anderson Hill Rd
   Purchase NY 10577
   914 253-2000

(G-15511)
PEPSI BTLG GROUP GLOBL FIN LLC (DH)
1 Pepsi Way Ste 1 (10589-2212)
PHONE..................................914 767-6000
Eric J Ross, *President*
EMP: 4
SALES (est): 2.1MM
SALES (corp-wide): 63B **Publicly Held**
SIC: 2086 Carbonated soft drinks, bottled & canned
HQ: Pepsi-Cola Metropolitan Bottling Company, Inc.
   1111 Westchester Ave
   White Plains NY 10604
   914 767-6000

(G-15512)
RICHARD C OWEN PUBLISHERS INC
243 Route 100 (10589-3203)
P.O. Box 585, Katonah (10536-0585)
PHONE..................................914 232-3903
Fax: 914 232-3977
Richard C Owen, *President*
Phyllis Morrison, *Office Mgr*
▲ EMP: 11
SQ FT: 5,000
SALES (est): 1.5MM **Privately Held**
WEB: www.rcowen.com
SIC: 2731 Books: publishing only

Sound Beach
Suffolk County

(G-15513)
PREFAB CONSTRUCTION INC
16 Jackson Ave (11789-2623)
PHONE..................................631 821-9613
Charles Kapp, *Ch of Bd*
EMP: 12 EST: 2001
SALES (est): 800K **Privately Held**
WEB: www.prefabconstruction.com
SIC: 1389 Construction, repair & dismantling services

South Bethlehem
Albany County

(G-15514)
OLDCASTLE PRECAST INC
100 S County Rte 101 (12161)
PHONE..................................518 767-2116
Fax: 518 767-2183
Emilie Herrald, *Sales Mgr*
Sheila Connor, *Manager*
EMP: 10
SALES (corp-wide): 25.3B **Privately Held**
WEB: www.oldcastle-precast.com
SIC: 3272 3446 3273 Concrete products, precast; pipe, concrete or lined with concrete; open flooring & grating for construction; ready-mixed concrete
HQ: Oldcastle Precast, Inc.
   1002 15th St Sw Ste 110
   Auburn WA 98001
   253 833-2777

South Colton
St. Lawrence County

(G-15515)
J & S LOGGING INC
3860 State Highway 56 (13687-3403)
P.O. Box 458 (13687-0458)
PHONE..................................315 262-2112
Stephen Poste, *President*
Patricia Poste, *Vice Pres*
Teresa Fisher, *Director*
Jerry Poste, *Director*
EMP: 20
SALES (est): 2.4MM **Privately Held**
SIC: 2411 4212 Logging camps & contractors; local trucking, without storage

(G-15516)
NORTHEASTERN SIGN CORP
102 Cold Brook Dr (13687)
P.O. Box 340 (13687-0340)
PHONE..................................315 265-6657
Anne Clarkson, *President*
EMP: 8
SQ FT: 1,600
SALES (est): 740K **Privately Held**
SIC: 3993 Signs & advertising specialties

South Dayton
Cattaraugus County

(G-15517)
BIRDS EYE FOODS INC
Also Called: Comstock Foods Division
Mechanic St (14138)
PHONE..................................716 988-3218
Sam Chiavetta, *Branch Mgr*
EMP: 6
SALES (corp-wide): 2.5B **Publicly Held**
SIC: 2037 Vegetables, quick frozen & cold pack, excl. potato products
HQ: Birds Eye Foods, Inc.
   121 Woodcrest Rd
   Cherry Hill NJ 08003
   585 383-1850

(G-15518)
CHERRY CREEK WOODCRAFT INC (PA)
Also Called: Great Impressions
1 Cherry St (14138-9736)
P.O. Box 267 (14138-0267)
PHONE..................................716 988-3211
Fax: 716 988-3109
Michael Lord, *Ch of Bd*
Martin Goldman, *President*
Jennifer Brown, *Finance Dir*
Jennifer Morey, *Finance*
Charlene Sterlace, *Executive*
EMP: 34
SQ FT: 60,000
SALES (est): 4MM **Privately Held**
SIC: 2499 Trophy bases, wood

(G-15519)
COUNTRY SIDE SAND & GRAVEL
8458 Route 62 (14138-9756)
PHONE..................................716 988-3271
Fax: 716 988-3272
Mark Smith, *Vice Pres*
Jason Rosier, *Manager*
EMP: 10
SALES (corp-wide): 33.7MM **Privately Held**
SIC: 1442 Construction sand mining; gravel mining
HQ: Country Side Sand & Gravel Inc
   Taylor Hollow Rd
   Collins NY 14034
   716 988-3271

South Fallsburg
Sullivan County

(G-15520)
MB FOOD PROCESSING INC
5190 S Fallsburg Main St (12779)
P.O. Box 13 (12779-0013)
PHONE..................................845 436-5001
Dean Koplik, *President*
EMP: 350
SALES (est): 1.5MM **Privately Held**
WEB: www.murrayschicken.com
SIC: 2015 Poultry slaughtering & processing
PA: M.B. Consulting Group, Ltd.
   5190 S Fallsburg Main
   South Fallsburg NY 12779
   845 434-5050

(G-15521)
MURRAY BRESKY CONSULTANTS LTD (PA)
Also Called: Murray's Chicken
5190 Main St (12779)
P.O. Box P (12779-2015)
PHONE..................................845 436-5001
Murray Bresky, *President*
Ellen Gold, *Corp Secy*
Dean Koplik, *Vice Pres*
Allen Schwartz, *Opers Mgr*
Maureen J Pinto, *Human Res Dir*
EMP: 299
SQ FT: 40,000
SALES (est): 47MM **Privately Held**
SIC: 2015 Poultry slaughtering & processing

South Glens Falls
Saratoga County

(G-15522)
AMES ADVANCED MATERIALS CORP (HQ)
50 Harrison Ave (12803-4912)
PHONE..................................518 792-5808
Frank Barber, *President*
EMP: 87
SALES (est): 38MM
SALES (corp-wide): 44.9MM **Privately Held**
SIC: 3399 Silver powder; flakes, metal
PA: Ames Goldsmith Corp.
   50 Harrison Ave
   South Glens Falls NY 12803
   518 792-5808

(G-15523)
CASTLE POWER SOLUTIONS LLC
22 Hudson Falls Rd Ste 55 (12803-5072)
PHONE..................................518 743-1000
Maureen Losito, *President*
▲ EMP: 9
SQ FT: 3,200
SALES (est): 2.7MM **Privately Held**
SIC: 3699 Electrical equipment & supplies

(G-15524)
ERBESSD RELIABILITY LLC
Also Called: Erbessd Reliability Instrs
22 Hudson Falls Rd (12803-5050)
PHONE..................................518 874-2700
Michael Howard, *President*
EMP: 27
SALES (est): 1.1MM **Privately Held**
SIC: 3829 Measuring & controlling devices

(G-15525)
HEXION INC
64 Fernan Rd (12803-5047)
P.O. Box B (12803)
PHONE..................................518 792-8040
Mike Karpinski, *Purchasing*
Kathleen Ervine, *Manager*
EMP: 20 **Publicly Held**
SIC: 2821 2869 2891 Melamine resins, melamine-formaldehyde; formaldehyde (formalin); adhesives & sealants
HQ: Hexion Inc.
   180 E Broad St Fl 26
   Columbus OH 43215
   614 225-4000

(G-15526)
MDI EAST INC
Also Called: Bates Industries
22 Hudson Falls Rd Ste 6 (12803-5069)
PHONE..................................518 747-8730
Randy Bodkin, *Plant Mgr*
Tom Pendergrass, *Plant Mgr*
Rhonda Sharp, *Materials Mgr*
Rose Bates, *Financial Exec*
Chuck Bates, *Manager*
EMP: 50
SALES (corp-wide): 13.2MM **Privately Held**
SIC: 3841 Surgical & medical instruments
HQ: Mdi East, Inc.
   6918 Ed Perkic St
   Riverside CA 92504
   951 509-6918

South Glens Falls - Saratoga County (G-15527)

GEOGRAPHIC SECTION

(G-15527)
NORTHEAST PROMOTIONAL GROUP IN
75 Main St (12803-4706)
PHONE..................518 793-1024
Deana Endieveri, *President*
Jim Chamberlin, *Vice Pres*
Mike Endieveri, *Vice Pres*
Kindra Chamberlin, *Treasurer*
Kate Cochran, *Representative*
EMP: 5
SALES (est): 666.9K **Privately Held**
WEB: www.nepromo.com
SIC: 3993 7389 Advertising novelties; embroidering of advertising on shirts, etc.

(G-15528)
NORTHEAST STITCHES & INK INC
Also Called: Sperry Advertising
95 Main St (12803-4706)
PHONE..................518 798-5549
Deana Endieveri, *President*
Kindra Chamberlin, *Corp Secy*
James Chamberlin, *Vice Pres*
Michael Endieveri, *Vice Pres*
Jeremy Terry, *Manager*
EMP: 34
SQ FT: 20,000
SALES (est): 2.8MM **Privately Held**
WEB: www.nestitchesink.com
SIC: 2395 2396 Embroidery & art needlework; automotive & apparel trimmings

South Hempstead
Nassau County

(G-15529)
ACCESSORIES FOR ELECTRONICS
Also Called: Afe
620 Mead Ter (11550-8011)
PHONE..................631 847-0158
William J Epstein, *President*
Peter Wright, *Treasurer*
EMP: 26
SQ FT: 3,000
SALES (est): 5.4MM **Privately Held**
WEB: www.afeaccess.com
SIC: 3678 3679 Electronic connectors; electronic circuits

(G-15530)
MIRANDY PRODUCTS LTD
1078 Grand Ave (11550-7902)
PHONE..................516 489-6800
Ira Breiter, *President*
Mike Glassman, *Treasurer*
EMP: 28
SQ FT: 5,000
SALES (est): 3.5MM **Privately Held**
WEB: www.mirandy.com
SIC: 2842 5087 Industrial plant disinfectants or deodorizers; service establishment equipment

South Otselic
Chenango County

(G-15531)
GLADDING BRAIDED PRODUCTS LLC
1 Gladding St (13155)
P.O. Box 164 (13155-0164)
PHONE..................315 653-7211
Fax: 315 653-4492
Sparky Christakos, *President*
Mike Radziwon, *Vice Pres*
Rick Burt, *Manager*
▲ EMP: 45
SQ FT: 85,000
SALES (est): 8.4MM **Privately Held**
WEB: www.gladdingbraid.com
SIC: 2298 Rope, except asbestos & wire; cordage: abaca, sisal, henequen, hemp, jute or other fiber; cord, braided

South Ozone Park
Queens County

(G-15532)
CONTINENTAL LIFT TRUCK INC
12718 Foch Blvd (11420-2824)
PHONE..................718 738-4738
Giuseppe Donofrio, *CEO*
Julia Adeleke, *Analyst*
▲ EMP: 16
SALES (est): 3.9MM **Privately Held**
SIC: 3537 Forklift trucks

(G-15533)
EXTREME AUTO ACCESSORIES CORP (PA)
Also Called: Rennen International
12019 Rockaway Blvd (11420-2423)
PHONE..................718 978-6722
Fax: 718 504-9637
Takang Lee, *Ch of Bd*
Weizrung Lee, *COO*
Rich Sha, *Vice Pres*
Linda Liu, *Administration*
▲ EMP: 15
SQ FT: 15,000
SALES (est): 3.6MM **Privately Held**
WEB: www.renneninternational.com
SIC: 3714 5013 Wheel rims, motor vehicle; automotive supplies

South Richmond Hill
Queens County

(G-15534)
MAIZTECA FOODS INC
13005 Liberty Ave (11419-3121)
PHONE..................718 641-3933
Sixto Reyes, *Ch of Bd*
EMP: 40
SQ FT: 10,000
SALES (est): 4.8MM **Privately Held**
SIC: 2099 Tortillas, fresh or refrigerated

South Salem
Westchester County

(G-15535)
GUITAR SPECIALIST INC
219 Oakridge Cmn (10590)
PHONE..................914 533-5589
EMP: 5
SQ FT: 2,400
SALES (est): 310K **Privately Held**
SIC: 3931 7699 Mfg Musical Instruments Repair Services

(G-15536)
SERENDIPITY CONSULTING CORP
48 Twin Lakes Rd (10590-1009)
PHONE..................914 763-8251
Senia E Feiner, *President*
Mark Feiner, *Info Tech Mgr*
EMP: 10
SQ FT: 3,200
SALES (est): 638.7K **Privately Held**
WEB: www.sccny.com
SIC: 7372 8742 Application computer software; training & development consultant

(G-15537)
THE CENTRO COMPANY INC
215 Silver Spring Rd (10590-2525)
PHONE..................914 533-2200
Alan Greene, *Ch of Bd*
Susan Green, *President*
EMP: 5
SALES (est): 508.6K **Privately Held**
SIC: 3061 Mechanical rubber goods

Southampton
Suffolk County

(G-15538)
AMERICAN COUNTRY QUILTS & LIN
Also Called: Judi Boisson American Country
134 Mariner Dr Unit C (11968-3482)
PHONE..................631 283-5466
Judi Boisson, *President*
Erin Boisson, *Vice Pres*
EMP: 8
SQ FT: 4,000
SALES (est): 490K **Privately Held**
SIC: 2395 2269 3269 5023 Quilted fabrics or cloth; linen fabrics: dyeing, finishing & printing; art & ornamental ware, pottery; linens & towels; linens, table; decorative home furnishings & supplies; mail order house; antiques

(G-15539)
ATLANTIC COAST EMBROIDERY INC
172 Mariner Dr (11968-3479)
P.O. Box 702 (11969-0702)
PHONE..................631 283-2175
Fax: 631 283-2249
Emoke Boldvay, *President*
EMP: 7
SQ FT: 4,000
SALES: 785K **Privately Held**
SIC: 2395 2759 Embroidery & art needlework; screen printing

(G-15540)
BEST MDLR HMS AFRBE P Q& S IN
495 County Road 39 (11968-5236)
PHONE..................631 204-0049
Fax: 631 204-1534
John Distefano, *Ch of Bd*
Laureiann Distefano, *Vice Pres*
Susan Ehrlich, *Manager*
EMP: 14
SALES (est): 1.6MM **Privately Held**
SIC: 2452 Modular homes, prefabricated, wood

(G-15541)
CENTRAL KITCHEN CORP
871 County Road 39 (11968-5227)
PHONE..................631 283-1029
Fax: 631 283-1138
Robert Grigo, *President*
Doreen Grigo, *Corp Secy*
Kurt Grigo, *Sales Mgr*
William Grigo, *Real Est Agnt*
EMP: 10
SQ FT: 4,000
SALES (est): 1MM **Privately Held**
WEB: www.centralkitchenscorp.com
SIC: 2434 5712 1751 5031 Wood kitchen cabinets; cabinet work, custom; cabinets, except custom made: kitchen; cabinet & finish carpentry; cabinet building & installation; kitchen cabinets

(G-15542)
DANS PAPER INC
Also Called: South of The Highway
158 County Road 39 (11968-5252)
PHONE..................631 537-0500
Fax: 631 537-3330
Margo C Abrams, *General Mgr*
Lee Meyer, *Editor*
Roy E Brown, *Chairman*
Allison Bourquin, *Sales Staff*
Leslie Ernst, *Sales Staff*
EMP: 68
SQ FT: 2,500
SALES (est): 5.3MM
SALES (corp-wide): 8.9MM **Privately Held**
WEB: www.danspapers.com
SIC: 2711 Newspapers: publishing only, not printed on site
PA: News Communications Inc
501 Madison Ave Fl 23
New York NY 10022
212 689-2500

(G-15543)
FRONTIERS UNLIMITED INC
Also Called: Homes Land Eastrn Long Island
52 Jagger Ln (11968-4822)
PHONE..................631 283-4663
Fax: 631 283-4018
James Miller, *President*
EMP: 8
SQ FT: 1,300
SALES: 1.5MM **Privately Held**
WEB: www.hamptonshomes.com
SIC: 2721 Periodicals

(G-15544)
GABANI INC
81 Lee Ave (11968-4518)
PHONE..................631 283-4930
Gabrielle Sampietro, *President*
Miguel Sampietro, *Treasurer*
EMP: 6
SQ FT: 900
SALES (est): 32K **Privately Held**
SIC: 2253 Knit outerwear mills

(G-15545)
HAMPTONS MAGAZINE
67 Hampton Rd Unit 5 (11968-4962)
PHONE..................631 283-7125
Randy Schindler, *President*
Jason Binn, *Publisher*
Debra Halpert, *Publisher*
Samantha Yanks, *Publisher*
Avery Andon, *Editor*
EMP: 50
SQ FT: 2,400
SALES: 3.5MM **Privately Held**
SIC: 2721 2791 2752 Periodicals-Publishing/Printing Typesetting Services Lithographic Commercial Printing

(G-15546)
HAMPTONS MEDIA LLC
Also Called: Hamptons Magazine
67 Hampton Rd Unit 5 (11968-4962)
PHONE..................631 283-6900
Fax: 631 283-7854
Jason Binn,
EMP: 5
SALES: 149.3K
SALES (corp-wide): 60.6MM **Privately Held**
SIC: 2721 Periodicals
HQ: Niche Media Holdings, L.L.C
711 3rd Ave Rm 501
New York NY 10017
702 990-2500

(G-15547)
MORRIS GOLF VENTURES
Sebonac Inlet Rd (11968)
PHONE..................631 283-0559
James Morris, *Owner*
EMP: 25
SALES (est): 1.7MM **Privately Held**
SIC: 3949 Golf equipment

(G-15548)
PAULPAC LLC
104 Foster Xing (11968-4955)
PHONE..................631 283-7610
Michela Keszlies,
EMP: 6
SALES: 500K **Privately Held**
WEB: www.paulpac.com
SIC: 2393 Textile bags

(G-15549)
PECONIC IRONWORKS LTD
33 Flying Point Rd # 108 (11968-5280)
PHONE..................631 204-0323
Patrick Grace, *President*
Thomas Berglin, *Vice Pres*
Don Gauthir, *Manager*
EMP: 13 EST: 1997
SALES (est): 2.4MM **Privately Held**
SIC: 3446 Architectural metalwork

(G-15550)
ROCKWELL VIDEO SOLUTIONS LLC
10 Koral Dr (11968-4307)
PHONE..................631 745-0582
Adam Cusack,
EMP: 15

GEOGRAPHIC SECTION

SALES: 950K **Privately Held**
SIC: 3999 Manufacturing industries

(G-15551)
SHADE & SHUTTER SYSTEMS OF NY
260 Hampton Rd (11968-5028)
PHONE 631 208-0275
EMP: 6
SALES (est): 630K **Privately Held**
SIC: 3442 Louvers, shutters, jalousies & similar items

(G-15552)
SOUTHAMPTON TOWN NEWSPAPERS (PA)
Also Called: Press of Manorville & Moriches
135 Windmill Ln (11968-4840)
PHONE 631 283-4100
Fax: 631 283-4927
Joseph Louchheim, *President*
Nick Thomas, *Business Mgr*
Scott Enstine, *Prdtn Mgr*
Paul Conroy, *Sales Mgr*
David Macmillan, *Sales Executive*
EMP: 30
SQ FT: 1,500
SALES (est): 3.9MM **Privately Held**
WEB: www.southamptonpress.com
SIC: 2711 2741 Newspapers: publishing only, not printed on site; miscellaneous publishing

(G-15553)
THEORY LLC
98 Main St (11968-4834)
PHONE 631 204-0231
EMP: 5
SALES (corp-wide): 13.7B **Privately Held**
SIC: 2337 Suits: women's, misses' & juniors'
HQ: Theory Llc
 38 Gansevoort St
 New York NY 10014
 212 300-0800

(G-15554)
THOMAS MATTHEWS WDWKG LTD
15 Powell Ave (11968-3425)
PHONE 631 287-3657
Thomas Matthews, *Branch Mgr*
EMP: 14
SALES (corp-wide): 1.1MM **Privately Held**
SIC: 2499 Woodenware, kitchen & household
PA: Thomas Matthews Woodworking Ltd.
 225 Ocean View Pkwy
 Southampton NY 11968
 631 287-2023

(G-15555)
THOMAS MATTHEWS WDWKG LTD (PA)
225 Ocean View Pkwy (11968-5523)
P.O. Box 520, Bridgehampton (11932-0520)
PHONE 631 287-2023
Thomas Matthew, *President*
EMP: 6
SALES (est): 1.1MM **Privately Held**
SIC: 2499 Woodenware, kitchen & household

Southfields
Orange County

(G-15556)
KARLYN INDUSTRIES INC
16 Spring St (10975-2614)
P.O. Box 310 (10975-0310)
PHONE 845 351-2249
Fax: 845 351-2256
Hans Bierdumpfel, *President*
Margaret Bierdumpfel, *Vice Pres*
Joyce Lasalle, *Treasurer*
▲ EMP: 15
SQ FT: 10,000

SALES (est): 1.3MM **Privately Held**
WEB: www.karlynsti.com
SIC: 3714 3694 Motor vehicle parts & accessories; spark plugs for internal combustion engines

Southold
Suffolk County

(G-15557)
ACADEMY PRINTING SERVICES INC
Also Called: Peconic B Shopper
42 Hortons Ln (11971-1686)
P.O. Box 848 (11971-0848)
PHONE 631 765-3346
Fax: 631 765-3369
Michael Hagerman, *President*
Rita Hagerman, *Vice Pres*
EMP: 6
SQ FT: 4,000
SALES (est): 866.4K **Privately Held**
SIC: 2752 2759 Photo-offset printing; commercial printing

(G-15558)
FUTURE SCREW MACHINE PDTS INC
41155 County Road 48 (11971-5041)
PHONE 631 765-1610
Fax: 631 765-2683
Ellen Hufe, *President*
Glen Grathwhol, *Manager*
EMP: 10
SQ FT: 2,700
SALES (est): 1.1MM **Privately Held**
SIC: 3599 Machine shop, jobbing & repair

(G-15559)
INTERNODAL INTERNATIONAL INC
54800 Route 25 (11971-4648)
P.O. Box 1173 (11971-0934)
PHONE 631 765-0037
Fax: 631 765-2337
Rosemary Verrecchio, *President*
Joe Stadler, *Vice Pres*
EMP: 25
SALES (est): 2.5MM **Privately Held**
WEB: www.internodalinternational.com
SIC: 7372 7389 Prepackaged software; design services

(G-15560)
NEW ENGLAND BARNS INC
45805 Route 25 (11971-4670)
P.O. Box 1447, Mattituck (11952-0925)
PHONE 631 445-1461
William Gorman, *Owner*
EMP: 22
SALES (est): 1.7MM **Privately Held**
SIC: 2439 Timbers, structural: laminated lumber

(G-15561)
WALLACE HOME DESIGN CTR
44500 County Road 48 (11971-5034)
P.O. Box 181, Peconic (11958-0181)
PHONE 631 765-3890
George Wallace, *President*
Rene Lisowy, *Owner*
EMP: 6
SQ FT: 2,400
SALES (est): 800.6K **Privately Held**
SIC: 2211 2511 2512 5713 Draperies & drapery fabrics, cotton; wood household furniture; upholstered household furniture; carpets; window furnishings

Sparrow Bush
Orange County

(G-15562)
ETERNAL LINE
1237 State Route 42 (12780-5042)
PHONE 845 856-1999
Marius Winograd, *Owner*
Agnes Winograd, *Co-Owner*
EMP: 2

SALES: 1.2MM **Privately Held**
SIC: 3911 Jewelry, precious metal

Speculator
Hamilton County

(G-15563)
STEPHENSON LUMBER COMPANY INC
Rr 8 (12164)
PHONE 518 548-7521
Fax: 518 548-4136
John Shaw, *Manager*
EMP: 5
SALES (corp-wide): 5.6MM **Privately Held**
WEB: www.riversidetruss.com
SIC: 2439 5211 Arches, laminated lumber; millwork & lumber
PA: Stephenson Lumber Company, Inc.
 Riverside Station Rd
 Riparius NY 12862
 518 494-4733

Spencer
Tioga County

(G-15564)
STARFIRE SWORDS LTD INC
74 Railroad Ave (14883-9543)
PHONE 607 589-7244
Fax: 607 589-6630
Maciej Zakrzewski, *President*
Sandy Russell, *Vice Pres*
Alexandra White, *Vice Pres*
EMP: 20
SALES (est): 2.5MM **Privately Held**
WEB: www.starfireswords.com
SIC: 3421 Swords

Spencerport
Monroe County

(G-15565)
AZTEC MFG OF ROCHESTER
19 Hickory Ln (14559-2511)
PHONE 585 352-8152
James Monsees, *Ch of Bd*
Mary Monsees, *Manager*
EMP: 7
SQ FT: 5,382
SALES (est): 903.8K **Privately Held**
SIC: 3541 Machine tools, metal cutting type

(G-15566)
BOSS PRECISION LTD
2440 S Union St (14559-2230)
PHONE 585 352-7070
Fax: 585 352-7059
Gerd Herrman, *Ch of Bd*
Paul Dugan, *Vice Pres*
Alec Ollies, *Treasurer*
EMP: 60
SQ FT: 45,000
SALES (est): 13MM **Privately Held**
SIC: 3444 Sheet metalwork

(G-15567)
BSV METAL FINISHERS INC
Also Called: Bsv Enterprises
11 Aristocrat Cir (14559-1042)
PHONE 585 349-7072
Benjamin S Vasquez, *President*
EMP: 26
SQ FT: 13,000
SALES (est): 5.4MM **Privately Held**
SIC: 3398 Metal heat treating

(G-15568)
BULLET INDUSTRIES INC
Also Called: Coyote Motorsports
7 Turner Dr (14559-1930)
PHONE 585 352-0836
Mark Lipari, *CEO*
EMP: 5 EST: 2007

SALES (est): 410.7K **Privately Held**
SIC: 3799 7539 Recreational vehicles; machine shop, automotive

(G-15569)
DOLOMITE PRODUCTS COMPANY INC
2540 S Union St (14559-2232)
PHONE 585 352-0460
EMP: 16
SALES (corp-wide): 25.3B **Privately Held**
SIC: 2951 Asphalt paving mixtures & blocks
HQ: Dolomite Products Company Inc.
 1150 Penfield Rd
 Rochester NY 14625
 315 524-1998

(G-15570)
IMCO INC
15 Turner Dr (14559-1930)
PHONE 585 352-7810
Fax: 585 352-7809
David Demallie, *Principal*
Susan Rinere, *Manager*
Audrey Mair, *Director*
EMP: 47
SQ FT: 25,000
SALES (est): 10.1MM **Privately Held**
SIC: 3089 Injection molding of plastics

(G-15571)
KLEIN REINFORCING SERVICES INC
11 Turner Dr (14559-1930)
PHONE 585 352-9433
Fax: 585 352-4474
Mark Kulzer, *President*
EMP: 15
SQ FT: 15,000
SALES (est): 4MM **Privately Held**
SIC: 3449 Bars, concrete reinforcing: fabricated steel

(G-15572)
MANUFACTURERS TOOL & DIE CO
3 Turner Dr (14559-1930)
P.O. Box 139 (14559-0139)
PHONE 585 352-1080
Fax: 585 352-1086
Douglas Sullivan, *President*
Dan Sullivan, *Vice Pres*
Gail Sullivan, *Office Mgr*
EMP: 5 EST: 1918
SQ FT: 10,000
SALES: 300K **Privately Held**
SIC: 3544 Special dies, tools, jigs & fixtures

(G-15573)
ROTATION DYNAMICS CORPORATION
Rotadyne
3581 Big Ridge Rd (14559-1709)
PHONE 585 352-9023
Dave Baldwin, *Plant Mgr*
Scott Bleier, *Opers Staff*
EMP: 36
SALES (corp-wide): 128.8MM **Privately Held**
SIC: 3069 2796 Rolls, solid or covered rubber; platemaking services
PA: Rotation Dynamics Corporation
 8140 Cass Ave
 Darien IL 60561
 630 769-9255

(G-15574)
WESTSIDE NEWS INC
Also Called: Suburban News
1835 N Union St (14559-1153)
P.O. Box 106 (14559-0106)
PHONE 585 352-3411
Fax: 585 352-4811
Keith Ryan, *Ch of Bd*
Debbie Day, *Sales Associate*
Evelyn Dow, *Advt Staff*
Barbara Burke, *Manager*
EMP: 18
SQ FT: 1,000
SALES (est): 1.4MM **Privately Held**
SIC: 2711 Newspapers: publishing only, not printed on site

Speonk
Suffolk County

(G-15575)
HENPECKED HUSBAND FARMS CORP
1212 Speonk Riverhead Rd (11972)
P.O. Box 752 (11972-0752)
PHONE.................................631 728-2800
Raayah Churgin, *Principal*
Jennifer Roberts, *Administration*
EMP: 6
SQ FT: 12,000
SALES (est): 440K **Privately Held**
SIC: 2869 Industrial organic chemicals

(G-15576)
JOHN T MONTECALVO INC
1233 Speonk River Head Rd (11972)
PHONE.................................631 325-1492
Margaret Fig, *Branch Mgr*
EMP: 5
SALES (corp-wide): 4.2MM **Privately Held**
SIC: 2951 1611 Asphalt paving mixtures & blocks; surfacing & paving
PA: John T. Montecalvo, Inc.
48 Railroad Ave
Center Moriches NY
631 325-1492

Sprakers
Montgomery County

(G-15577)
BILL LAKE HOMES CONSTRUCTION
188 Flanders Rd (12166-4519)
P.O. Box 105 (12166-0105)
PHONE.................................518 673-2424
Fax: 518 673-5039
William Lake, *President*
John Connolly, *Purchasing*
Rick Leto, *Marketing Mgr*
Cindy Jackland, *Manager*
EMP: 56
SALES (est): 8MM **Privately Held**
WEB: www.billlakehomes.com
SIC: 2452 Modular homes, prefabricated, wood

Spring Valley
Rockland County

(G-15578)
AMERICAN MEDICAL & DENTAL SUPS
100 Red Schoolhouse Rd A6 (10977-7057)
PHONE.................................845 517-5876
Dinesh Sakhrani, *CEO*
EMP: 13 EST: 2008
SALES (est): 1.9MM **Privately Held**
SIC: 3843 Dental equipment & supplies

(G-15579)
CITATION MANUFACTURING CO INC
42 Harmony Rd (10977-2328)
P.O. Box 418 (10977-0418)
PHONE.................................845 425-6868
Margo Nelson, *CEO*
Phil Nelson, *President*
EMP: 5
SQ FT: 900
SALES (est): 625K **Privately Held**
SIC: 3651 Sound reproducing equipment

(G-15580)
DELUXE CORPORATION
9 Lincoln Ave (10977-8938)
PHONE.................................845 362-4054
Yakov Breuer, *Branch Mgr*
EMP: 267
SALES (corp-wide): 1.7B **Publicly Held**
SIC: 2782 Checkbooks
PA: Deluxe Corporation
3680 Victoria St N
Shoreview MN 55126
651 483-7111

(G-15581)
DJS NYC INC
Also Called: Deejays
34 Union Rd (10977-3936)
PHONE.................................845 445-8618
Chaim Einhorn, *President*
Sarah Koenig, *Treasurer*
EMP: 6
SALES (est): 669.5K **Privately Held**
SIC: 3674 Solid state electronic devices

(G-15582)
EAGLE REGALIA CO INC
Also Called: Abbot Flag Co Div
747 Chestnut Ridge Rd # 101 (10977-6225)
PHONE.................................845 425-2245
Fax: 845 425-2637
Michael Kartzmer, *President*
J Cohen, *Mfg Staff*
▲ EMP: 10 EST: 1910
SQ FT: 4,000
SALES (est): 730K **Privately Held**
SIC: 2399 3999 2395 3911 Flags, fabric; banners, made from fabric; badges, metal: policemen, firemen, etc.; plaques, picture, laminated; emblems, embroidered; medals, precious or semiprecious metal

(G-15583)
ECKERSON DRUGS INC
275 N Main St Ste 12 (10977-2917)
PHONE.................................845 352-1800
Ashish Amin, *Principal*
EMP: 14
SALES (est): 2.2MM **Privately Held**
SIC: 2834 Tablets, pharmaceutical

(G-15584)
EZ LIFT OPERATOR CORP
Also Called: EZ Lift Garage Door Service
111 S Main St (10977-5617)
PHONE.................................845 356-1676
EMP: 10
SALES: 870K **Privately Held**
SIC: 3699 5084 5211 1751 Mfg Elec Mach/Equip/Supp Whol Industrial Equip Ret Lumber/Building Mtrl Carpentry Contractor

(G-15585)
FINAL TOUCH PRINTING INC
29 Decatur Ave Unit 1 (10977-4782)
PHONE.................................845 352-2677
Shmiel Elger, *Chairman*
EMP: 12
SALES (est): 1.3MM **Privately Held**
SIC: 2752 Commercial printing, lithographic

(G-15586)
FROZEN PASTRY PRODUCTS CORP
41 Lincoln Ave (10977-1918)
PHONE.................................845 364-9833
Fax: 845 364-9833
Dov Sandburg, *President*
Michael Schwartz, *Manager*
EMP: 33
SQ FT: 8,000
SALES (est): 3.2MM **Privately Held**
SIC: 2041 Doughs, frozen or refrigerated

(G-15587)
GOLDEN TASTE INC
318 Roosevelt Ave (10977-5824)
PHONE.................................845 356-4133
Fax: 845 356-4231
Rachel Perlmutter, *President*
Rafiel Perlmutter, *Vice Pres*
Jacob Taub, *Manager*
EMP: 32
SQ FT: 10,000
SALES: 6MM **Privately Held**
SIC: 2099 Salads, fresh or refrigerated

(G-15588)
GUARDIAN BOOTH LLC
29 Roosevelt Ave Ste 301 (10977-7844)
PHONE.................................844 992-6684
Abraham Taub, *Owner*
EMP: 10
SALES (est): 672.1K **Privately Held**
SIC: 3448 Docks: prefabricated metal

(G-15589)
HOLY COW KOSHER LLC
750 Chestnut Ridge Rd (10977-6438)
PHONE.................................347 788-8620
Gilead Mooseek,
Gabi Harkham,
EMP: 5 EST: 2010
SALES: 400K **Privately Held**
SIC: 2013 Snack sticks, including jerky: from purchased meat

(G-15590)
JAY BAGS INC
55 Union Rd Ste 107 (10977-3900)
PHONE.................................845 459-6500
Gitty Rubin, *Principal*
Joseph Pultman, *Manager*
▲ EMP: 3 EST: 2010
SQ FT: 20,000
SALES: 2MM **Privately Held**
SIC: 2673 Bags: plastic, laminated & coated

(G-15591)
LECHLER LABORATORIES INC
Also Called: Lechler Labs
100 Red Schoolhse Rd C2 (10977-7049)
PHONE.................................845 426-6800
Fax: 845 426-1515
Martin Melik, *President*
Jimmy Varghese, *Research*
Thomas Miller, *Accountant*
Denise Viola, *Office Mgr*
EMP: 25 EST: 1957
SALES (est): 4.1MM **Privately Held**
WEB: www.lechlerlabs.com
SIC: 2844 5961 Cosmetic preparations; colognes; catalog & mail-order houses

(G-15592)
LIPTIS PHARMACEUTICALS USA INC
110 Red Schoolhouse Rd (10977-7032)
PHONE.................................845 627-0260
Sherin Awad, *CEO*
Dick Klaus, *President*
Jenny Avalos, *Vice Pres*
▲ EMP: 1022
SALES (est): 125.2MM **Privately Held**
WEB: www.liptis.com
SIC: 2834 Pharmaceutical preparations

(G-15593)
LOUIS SCHWARTZ
Also Called: Supreme Leather Products
28 Lawrence St (10977-5038)
PHONE.................................845 356-6624
Louis Schwartz, *Owner*
EMP: 6 EST: 1949
SQ FT: 7,500
SALES (est): 220K **Privately Held**
SIC: 2386 Garments, leather

(G-15594)
MASTER ART CORP
131 Clinton Ln Ste E (10977-8918)
PHONE.................................845 362-6430
Tzipprah Austerlitz, *Principal*
▲ EMP: 8
SALES (est): 1.1MM **Privately Held**
SIC: 3944 Craft & hobby kits & sets

(G-15595)
MBH FURNITURE INNOVATIONS INC
28 Lincoln Ave (10977-1915)
P.O. Box 28 (10977-0028)
PHONE.................................845 354-8202
Simcha Greenberg, *Ch of Bd*
EMP: 6
SALES (est): 578.4K **Privately Held**
SIC: 2519 Household furniture, except wood or metal: upholstered

(G-15596)
MEASUPRO INC (PA)
Also Called: Smart Weigh
1 Alpine Ct (10977-5647)
PHONE.................................845 425-8777
EMP: 12
SALES (est): 3.5MM **Privately Held**
SIC: 3596 Weighing machines & apparatus

(G-15597)
PALISADES PAPER INC
13 Jackson Ave (10977-1910)
PHONE.................................845 354-0333
Jochanan Schwaite, *President*
EMP: 6
SALES: 2MM **Privately Held**
SIC: 2621 Parchment paper

(G-15598)
PAR PHARMACEUTICAL INC (DH)
1 Ram Ridge Rd (10977-6714)
PHONE.................................845 425-7100
Fax: 845 425-7167
Paul V Campanelli, *CEO*
Thomas J Haughey, *President*
Kenneth I Sawyer, *Principal*
Michael A Tropiano, *Exec VP*
Joseph Barbarite, *Senior VP*
▲ EMP: 277 EST: 1978
SQ FT: 92,000
SALES (est): 207MM **Privately Held**
SIC: 2834 Pharmaceutical preparations; druggists' preparations (pharmaceuticals); tablets, pharmaceutical; medicines, capsuled or ampuled
HQ: Par Pharmaceutical Companies, Inc.
1 Ram Ridge Rd
Chestnut Ridge NY 10977
845 573-5500

(G-15599)
PIN PEOPLE LLC
35 West St (10977-4778)
PHONE.................................888 309-7467
Andrew Dale,
EMP: 10
SQ FT: 12,000
SALES: 9.5MM **Privately Held**
WEB: www.thepinpeople.com
SIC: 3911 Pins (jewelry), precious metal

(G-15600)
RAMI SHEET METAL INC
25 E Hickory St (10977-3709)
PHONE.................................845 426-2948
Nathan Gdanski, *President*
EMP: 6
SALES (est): 489.8K **Privately Held**
SIC: 3444 Sheet metalwork

(G-15601)
REGAL SCREEN PRINTING INTL
Also Called: Shirt Shack
42 Grove St (10977-4852)
PHONE.................................845 356-8181
Fax: 845 352-8575
Stan Mesnick, *President*
Barbara Mesnick, *Vice Pres*
EMP: 6
SQ FT: 2,200
SALES (est): 717.8K **Privately Held**
SIC: 2759 Letterpress & screen printing

(G-15602)
STRATIVA PHARMACEUTICALS
1 Ram Ridge Rd (10977-6714)
PHONE.................................201 802-4000
Paul V Campanelli, *CEO*
Terrance J Coughlin, *COO*
Michael A Tropiano, *Exec VP*
EMP: 13
SALES (est): 1MM **Privately Held**
SIC: 2834 Pharmaceutical preparations

(G-15603)
TRAFFIC LOGIX CORPORATION
3 Harriet Ln (10977-1302)
PHONE.................................866 915-6449
Louis Newman, *CEO*
Mindy N Cohen, *General Mgr*
Ben Cohen, *Treasurer*
▼ EMP: 7
SQ FT: 100
SALES (est): 1.1MM **Privately Held**
SIC: 3812 3069 5084 Radar systems & equipment; molded rubber products; safety equipment

(G-15604)
ULTRA CLARITY CORP
3101 Parkview Dr (10977-4979)
PHONE..................................719 470-1010
Goldie Halpert, *CEO*
Samuel Halpert, *Principal*
EMP: 5 **EST:** 2014
SALES (est): 289.2K **Privately Held**
SIC: 3496 5051 Cable, uninsulated wire: made from purchased wire; cable, wire

(G-15605)
UNEEDA ENTERPRIZES INC
640 Chestnut Ridge Rd (10977-5653)
P.O. Box 209 (10977-0209)
PHONE..................................877 863-3321
Fax: 845 426-2810
Bruce Fuchs, *President*
Herman Fuchs, *President*
Richard Caporusso, *Vice Pres*
Kenneth Chilson, *Plant Mgr*
Bruce Fuge, *Safety Mgr*
◆ **EMP:** 110 **EST:** 1967
SQ FT: 58,000
SALES (est): 20.5MM **Privately Held**
WEB: www.uneeda.com
SIC: 3291 5084 5085 Abrasive products; industrial machinery & equipment; abrasives

(G-15606)
UNIVERSITY TABLE CLOTH COMPANY
10 Centre St (10977-5025)
P.O. Box 82 (10977-0082)
PHONE..................................845 371-3876
Debra Timco, *President*
Lu Temco, *Manager*
▲ **EMP:** 11 **EST:** 1998
SQ FT: 5,000
SALES (est): 918.9K **Privately Held**
SIC: 2392 Tablecloths: made from purchased materials

(G-15607)
US POLYCHEMICAL HOLDING CORP
584 Chestnut Ridge Rd (10977-5648)
PHONE..................................845 356-5530
David Cherry, *CEO*
Bruce Gebhardt, *Vice Pres*
Mark Paul, *Director*
EMP: 21 **EST:** 2012
SALES (est): 4.1MM **Privately Held**
SIC: 2842 Cleaning or polishing preparations

Springfield Gardens
Queens County

(G-15608)
DUNDY GLASS & MIRROR CORP
12252 Montauk St (11413-1034)
PHONE..................................718 723-5800
Eric Latin, *President*
Florence Latin, *Treasurer*
Angelique Beamon, *Manager*
Ellen Latin, *Admin Sec*
▲ **EMP:** 25 **EST:** 1900
SQ FT: 17,000
SALES (est): 4.2MM **Privately Held**
WEB: www.dundyglass.com
SIC: 3231 Mirrored glass; furniture tops, glass: cut, beveled or polished

Springville
Erie County

(G-15609)
DELOCON WHOLESALE INC
270 W Main St (14141-1070)
P.O. Box 4 (14141-0004)
PHONE..................................716 592-2711
Sherwin Lape, *President*
Laurel Swartz, *Sales Mgr*
Ryan Beebe, *Sales Staff*
Theresa Chase, *Consultant*
EMP: 15

SALES (est): 2.2MM **Privately Held**
WEB: www.delocon.com
SIC: 2541 5211 Counter & sink tops; lumber & other building materials

(G-15610)
GERNATT ASPHALT PRODUCTS INC
Benz Dr (14141)
PHONE..................................716 496-5111
Fax: 716 592-7352
Mark Smith, *Vice Pres*
EMP: 7
SALES (corp-wide): 33.7MM **Privately Held**
WEB: www.gernatt.com
SIC: 2951 Asphalt paving mixtures & blocks
PA: Gernatt Asphalt Products, Inc.
 13870 Taylor Hollow Rd
 Collins NY 14034
 716 532-3371

(G-15611)
GRAMCO INC (PA)
299 Waverly St (14141-1055)
P.O. Box 68 (14141-0068)
PHONE..................................716 592-2845
Fax: 716 592-2091
Robert D Mattison, *President*
Nancy J Human, *Vice Pres*
Torrance H Brooks, *Admin Sec*
EMP: 3
SQ FT: 800
SALES (est): 5.2MM **Privately Held**
WEB: www.gramcoonline.com
SIC: 2048 5999 Feed concentrates; feed & farm supply

(G-15612)
HEARY BROS LGHTNING PROTECTION
11291 Moore Rd (14141-9614)
PHONE..................................716 941-6141
Fax: 716 941-3828
Kenneth Heary, *President*
Edwin Heary, *Vice Pres*
EMP: 40
SQ FT: 22,800
SALES (est): 3MM **Privately Held**
WEB: www.hearybros.com
SIC: 3643 Lightning protection equipment

(G-15613)
J KRAFT MICROSCOPY SVCS INC
243 W Main St Ste 2 (14141-1089)
PHONE..................................716 592-4402
EMP: 8
SALES (est): 928.7K **Privately Held**
SIC: 2022 Processed cheese

(G-15614)
PEERLESS-WINSMITH INC
172 Eaton St (14141-1197)
PHONE..................................716 592-9311
Fax: 716 592-9311
Karen Omphalius, *General Mgr*
Tom Idcik, *Plant Mgr*
Boyd Thomas, *Opers Staff*
Janice Carder, *Senior Buyer*
H Koelbel, *Purchasing*
EMP: 225
SALES (corp-wide): 230.1MM **Privately Held**
WEB: www.peerlesswinsmith.com
SIC: 3566 5063 Speed changers, drives & gears; power transmission equipment, electric
HQ: Peerless-Winsmith, Inc.
 5200 Upper Metro Pl # 110
 Dublin OH 43017
 614 526-7000

(G-15615)
PERFECTION GEAR INC
172 Eaton St (14141-1165)
PHONE..................................716 592-9310
Kim Neyrett, *Manager*
EMP: 150
SALES (corp-wide): 255MM **Privately Held**
SIC: 3566 Reduction gears & gear units for turbines, except automotive

HQ: Perfection Gear, Inc.
 9 N Bear Creek Rd
 Asheville NC 28806
 828 253-0000

(G-15616)
SPRINGVILLE MFG CO INC
8798 North St (14141-9648)
P.O. Box 367 (14141-0367)
PHONE..................................716 592-4957
Fax: 716 592-9834
Daniel J Schmauss, *President*
William Kneeland, *Counsel*
Carol Chowaniec, *Accountant*
Mary Boberg, *Director*
Joseph Schmauss, *Shareholder*
EMP: 31 **EST:** 1958
SQ FT: 28,000
SALES (est): 7MM **Privately Held**
WEB: www.springvillemfg.com
SIC: 3593 3599 Fluid power cylinders, hydraulic or pneumatic; machine shop, jobbing & repair

Staatsburg
Dutchess County

(G-15617)
CURRANT COMPANY LLC
Also Called: Currantc
59 Walnut Ln (12580-6346)
PHONE..................................845 266-8999
Greg Quinn,
▲ **EMP:** 5
SALES (est): 540.1K **Privately Held**
WEB: www.currantc.com
SIC: 2026 Yogurt

(G-15618)
DUTCHESS PLUMBING & HEATING
28 Reservoir Rd (12580-5317)
PHONE..................................845 889-8255
Fax: 845 876-2986
Steven Eckelman, *President*
Maryanne Eckelman, *Vice Pres*
EMP: 5
SALES (est): 420K **Privately Held**
SIC: 2759 Commercial printing

(G-15619)
UNIFUSE LLC
2092 Route 9g (12580-5426)
PHONE..................................845 889-4000
Jeff Bookstein, *Managing Dir*
Dan Aiello, *Principal*
Andrew Flynn, *Manager*
EMP: 15
SQ FT: 50,000
SALES (est): 3.1MM **Privately Held**
WEB: www.unifuse.com
SIC: 3089 Plastic processing

Stafford
Genesee County

(G-15620)
GENESEE BUILDING PRODUCTS LLC
7982 Byron Stafford Rd (14143)
PHONE..................................585 548-2726
Ronald Wheeler, *President*
EMP: 7
SQ FT: 20,000
SALES (est): 820.4K **Privately Held**
SIC: 3444 Gutters, sheet metal

(G-15621)
HANSON AGGREGATES EAST LLC
5870 Main Rd (14143-9519)
PHONE..................................585 343-1787
Scott Wheaton, *Plant Mgr*
Kelly Kinney, *Office Mgr*
Jeff Curry, *Manager*
EMP: 22
SALES (corp-wide): 14.4B **Privately Held**
SIC: 2951 Asphalt paving mixtures & blocks

HQ: Hanson Aggregates East Llc
 3131 Rdu Center Dr
 Morrisville NC 27560
 919 380-2500

(G-15622)
RJ PRECISION LLC
6662 Main Rd (14143-9554)
PHONE..................................585 768-8030
Kathleen Johns, *Partner*
Robert Johns,
EMP: 5
SQ FT: 5,300
SALES (est): 820K **Privately Held**
SIC: 3441 Fabricated structural metal

Stamford
Delaware County

(G-15623)
AUDIO-SEARS CORP
2 South St (12167-1211)
PHONE..................................607 652-7305
Fax: 607 652-3653
David Hartwell, *President*
Shawn Hartwell, *Vice Pres*
Nicholas Knoll, *Purch Mgr*
Glenn Bertrand, *QC Dir*
Karen Chichester, *Controller*
▲ **EMP:** 81 **EST:** 1956
SQ FT: 25,000
SALES (est): 13.7MM **Privately Held**
WEB: www.audiosears.com
SIC: 3661 Telephones & telephone apparatus

(G-15624)
CATSKILL CRAFTSMEN INC
15 W End Ave (12167-1296)
PHONE..................................607 652-7321
Fax: 607 652-7293
Duncan Axtell, *Ch of Bd*
Ken Smith, *CFO*
Hank Cioccari, *Manager*
▲ **EMP:** 55
SQ FT: 94,000
SALES (est): 7.7MM **Privately Held**
WEB: www.catskillcraftsmen.com
SIC: 2434 2499 2511 Wood kitchen cabinets; woodenware, kitchen & household; kitchen & dining room furniture

(G-15625)
MACADOODLES
26 River St (12167-1014)
PHONE..................................607 652-9019
Michelle Caiazza, *Owner*
EMP: 6
SALES (est): 190K **Privately Held**
WEB: www.macadoodles.com
SIC: 2024 Ice cream & frozen desserts

(G-15626)
STONE CREST INDUSTRIES INC
Also Called: Generic Compositors
152 Starheim Rd (12167-1757)
PHONE..................................607 652-2665
Fax: 607 652-2416
Gerald Stoner, *President*
Ellen Thorn, *CFO*
EMP: 5
SALES (est): 275K **Privately Held**
WEB: www.genericcomp.com
SIC: 2791 Typesetting

Stanfordville
Dutchess County

(G-15627)
GALLANT GRAPHICES LTD INC
242 Attlebury Hill Rd (12581-5635)
PHONE..................................845 868-1166
Melvin Eiger, *President*
Ralph Brunks, *Vice Pres*
Julian Thorn, *Vice Pres*
▲ **EMP:** 26
SALES (est): 4.8MM **Privately Held**
WEB: www.gallantgraphics.com
SIC: 2752 2796 2791 2759 Commercial printing, offset; platemaking services; typesetting; commercial printing

Star Lake
St. Lawrence County

(G-15628)
CLEARLAKE LAND CO INC
Hanks Rd (13690)
P.O. Box 280 (13690-0280)
PHONE.................................315 848-2427
Gordon Gardner, *President*
Lynn Gardner, *Treasurer*
EMP: 10
SALES: 900K **Privately Held**
SIC: 2411 Logging

Staten Island
Richmond County

(G-15629)
828 EXPRESS INC
619 Elbe Ave (10304-3412)
PHONE.................................917 577-9019
Nelson Liu, *President*
EMP: 9
SALES (est): 1.1MM **Privately Held**
SIC: 3443 Containers, shipping (bombs, etc.): metal plate

(G-15630)
A K A COMPUTER CONSULTING INC
881 Richmond Rd (10304-2421)
PHONE.................................718 351-5200
Alex Kleyff, *Founder*
Eva Kleyff, *Vice Pres*
Leonardo Vasquez, *Prgrmr*
EMP: 5
SQ FT: 1,200
SALES (est): 755.7K **Privately Held**
WEB: www.akaconsulting.com
SIC: 7372 Prepackaged software

(G-15631)
A&B MCKEON GLASS INC
69 Roff St (10304-1856)
PHONE.................................718 525-2152
Charles Bell, *President*
Terri Barbato, *Manager*
EMP: 5 EST: 1976
SQ FT: 750
SALES (est): 560K **Privately Held**
SIC: 3449 1542 1793 1761 Curtain wall, metal; store front construction; glass & glazing work; architectural sheet metal work

(G-15632)
A/C DESIGN & FABRICATION CORP
638 Sharrotts Rd (10309-1992)
PHONE.................................718 227-8100
Fax: 718 227-8100
Jeff Arcello, *President*
EMP: 5
SALES (est): 828.6K **Privately Held**
SIC: 3441 Fabricated structural metal

(G-15633)
ALBA HOUSE PUBLISHERS
2187 Victory Blvd (10314-6603)
PHONE.................................718 698-2759
Ignatius Staniszewski, *CEO*
▲ EMP: 25
SALES (est): 1.2MM **Privately Held**
SIC: 2731 Book publishing

(G-15634)
ALL SHORE INDUSTRIES INC
1 Edgewater St Ste 215 (10305-4900)
PHONE.................................718 720-0018
Fax: 718 720-0225
Sandor Goldner, *CEO*
Norman Goldner, *President*
Hannah Goldner, *Corp Secy*
Elizabeth Torres, *Accountant*
Jean Steinmetz, *Info Tech Mgr*
▲ EMP: 10
SQ FT: 5,000
SALES (est): 890K **Privately Held**
SIC: 3679 3677 3699 Electronic circuits; electronic coils, transformers & other inductors; appliance cords for household electrical equipment

(G-15635)
ALL SIGNS
Also Called: Woodside Decorator
63 Bridgetown St (10314-6211)
PHONE.................................973 736-2113
Vincent Iannuzzelli, *Owner*
EMP: 7
SALES (est): 600K **Privately Held**
SIC: 3993 Signs & advertising specialties

(G-15636)
ALPHA MARINE REPAIR
88 Coursen Pl (10304-2506)
PHONE.................................718 816-7150
Eutrice Robinson, *Principal*
Heather Robinson, *Principal*
EMP: 45
SALES (est): 950K **Privately Held**
SIC: 3731 Shipbuilding & repairing

(G-15637)
AMERICAN ROLLING DOOR LTD
40 Dolson Pl (10303-1402)
PHONE.................................718 273-0485
Ed Simone, *President*
Peter Paloscio, *Vice Pres*
EMP: 8
SQ FT: 7,600
SALES (est): 992.1K **Privately Held**
SIC: 3442 Garage doors, overhead: metal

(G-15638)
ANGIE MANGINO
366 Craig Ave (10307-1211)
PHONE.................................347 489-4009
Angela Mangino, *Principal*
EMP: 5
SALES (est): 254.7K **Privately Held**
SIC: 2711 Newspapers, publishing & printing

(G-15639)
ARC TEC WLDG & FABRICATION INC
15 Harrison Ave (10302-1328)
PHONE.................................718 982-9274
Kim R Genduso, *President*
EMP: 5
SALES (est): 556.5K **Privately Held**
SIC: 7692 Welding repair

(G-15640)
ARIMED ORTHOTICS PROSTHETICS P
235 Dongan Hills Ave 2d (10305-1224)
PHONE.................................718 979-6155
Fax: 718 668-9431
Steven Mirones, *Branch Mgr*
EMP: 13
SALES (corp-wide): 3.7MM **Privately Held**
SIC: 3842 Braces, orthopedic
PA: Arimed Orthotics Prosthetics Pedorthics
302 Livingston St
Brooklyn NY 11217
718 875-8754

(G-15641)
ATHLETIC CAP CO INC
123 Fields Ave (10314-5066)
PHONE.................................718 398-1300
Fax: 718 399-0999
Arthur Farkas, *President*
Ira Farkas, *Vice Pres*
EMP: 40
SQ FT: 9,000
SALES (est): 1.2MM **Privately Held**
SIC: 2353 2396 2395 Hats & caps; automotive & apparel trimmings; pleating & stitching

(G-15642)
B & R TOOL INC
955 Rensselaer Ave (10309-2227)
PHONE.................................718 948-2729
William Nobile, *President*
EMP: 6
SALES (est): 567K **Privately Held**
SIC: 3469 Metal stampings

(G-15643)
BANDS N BOWS
34 Fieldway Ave (10308-2930)
PHONE.................................718 984-4316
Ted Mazola, *Principal*
EMP: 5
SALES (est): 235.6K **Privately Held**
SIC: 2339 Scarves, hoods, headbands, etc.: women's

(G-15644)
BARBERA TRANSDUSER SYSTEMS
21 Louis St (10304-2111)
PHONE.................................718 816-3025
Richard Barbera, *Partner*
Katherine Sanfilippo, *Partner*
EMP: 10
SALES (est): 520K **Privately Held**
SIC: 3931 5736 String instruments & parts; musical instrument stores

(G-15645)
BEETINS WHOLESALE INC
125 Ravenhurst Ave (10310-2633)
PHONE.................................718 524-0899
Gamade Perera, *CEO*
EMP: 13
SALES (est): 1.5MM **Privately Held**
SIC: 2679 Paper products, converted

(G-15646)
BEST LINE INC
101 Manila Ave Fl 2 (10306-5605)
PHONE.................................917 670-6210
Andrey Kanevsky, *President*
▼ EMP: 6
SALES (est): 189.4K **Privately Held**
WEB: www.mozga.net
SIC: 2711 5192 Newspapers; newspapers

(G-15647)
BILLING BLOCKS INC
147 North Ave (10314-2653)
PHONE.................................718 442-5006
Fax: 718 504-6015
Dan Kuper, *President*
EMP: 10
SALES (est): 860K **Privately Held**
WEB: www.billingblocks.com
SIC: 7372 7371 Prepackaged software; custom computer programming services

(G-15648)
BLINDS TO GO (US) INC
2845 Richmond Ave (10314-5883)
PHONE.................................718 477-9523
Fax: 718 477-9525
Bill Forte, *Manager*
Shawna Bodemer, *Manager*
EMP: 30
SALES (corp-wide): 98.9MM **Privately Held**
SIC: 2591 5719 Drapery hardware & blinds & shades; window furnishings
HQ: Blinds To Go (U.S.) Inc.
101 E State Rt 4
Paramus NJ 07652
201 441-9260

(G-15649)
BLOOD MOON PRODUCTIONS LTD
75 Saint Marks Pl (10301-1606)
PHONE.................................718 556-9410
Danforth Prince, *CEO*
EMP: 7
SALES (est): 494.9K **Privately Held**
WEB: www.bloodmoonproductions.com
SIC: 2741 Miscellaneous publishing

(G-15650)
BORO PARK CUTTING TOOL CORP
106b Wakefield Ave (10314-3624)
PHONE.................................718 720-0610
Fax: 718 720-1084
Vito Rubino, *President*
Steven Bruzese, *General Mgr*
Vincent Bruzese, *Treasurer*
EMP: 21
SQ FT: 10,000
SALES (est): 1MM **Privately Held**
SIC: 3545 5251 Cutting tools for machine tools; tools

(G-15651)
BRAZE ALLOY INC
3075 Richmond Ter (10303-1303)
PHONE.................................718 815-5757
Princie Sevaratnam, *President*
EMP: 5
SALES (est): 534.6K **Privately Held**
SIC: 3356 Solder: wire, bar, acid core, & rosin core

(G-15652)
BRITISH SCIENCE CORPORATION (PA)
100 Wheeler Ave (10314-4018)
PHONE.................................212 980-8700
David H Kingsley, *President*
Yvonne Kingsley, *Corp Secy*
EMP: 8
SALES (est): 676.3K **Privately Held**
SIC: 2844 7299 Shampoos, rinses, conditioners: hair; scalp treatment service

(G-15653)
C & R DE SANTIS INC
Also Called: Royal Press
2645 Forest Ave Ste 2 (10303-1503)
PHONE.................................718 447-5076
Fax: 718 448-7573
Robert De Santis, *President*
Janet Sher, *Office Mgr*
Beth Cotroneo, *Art Dir*
EMP: 22 EST: 1926
SQ FT: 5,000
SALES: 83.9K **Privately Held**
WEB: www.royalpress.com
SIC: 2752 2672 Commercial printing, lithographic; commercial printing, offset; coated & laminated paper

(G-15654)
CADDELL DRY DOCK & REPR CO INC
Also Called: Caddell Ship Yards
Foot Of Broadway 1 W (10310)
PHONE.................................718 442-2112
Fax: 718 981-7493
John B Caddell II, *Ch of Bd*
Steven Kalil, *President*
Cynthia Patelli, *Corp Secy*
Brian Donato, *Safety Mgr*
Maritza Castillo, *Human Res Mgr*
EMP: 180 EST: 1903
SQ FT: 100,000
SALES (est): 35MM **Privately Held**
WEB: www.caddelldrydock.com
SIC: 3731 Shipbuilding & repairing

(G-15655)
CALIA TECHNICAL INC
Also Called: Calia Consultants
420 Jefferson Blvd (10312-2334)
PHONE.................................718 447-3928
Fax: 718 815-2887
Anthony Calia, *President*
Robert Santagata, *Vice Pres*
EMP: 6
SALES: 650K **Privately Held**
SIC: 3625 8742 Control equipment, electric; training & development consultant

(G-15656)
CARMINE STREET BAGELS INC
Also Called: Bagels On The Square
107 Park Dr N (10314-5702)
PHONE.................................212 691-3041
Joseph Turchiano, *Ch of Bd*
Neil Guy, *President*
EMP: 10
SQ FT: 2,000
SALES (est): 870.7K **Privately Held**
SIC: 2051 Bakery: wholesale or wholesale/retail combined

(G-15657)
CARTERS INC
430 New Dorp Ln (10306-4946)
PHONE.................................718 980-1759
EMP: 9
SALES (corp-wide): 3B **Publicly Held**
SIC: 2361 Dresses: girls', children's & infants'

GEOGRAPHIC SECTION

Staten Island - Richmond County (G-15686)

PA: Carter's, Inc.
3438 Peachtree Rd Ne # 1800
Atlanta GA 30326
678 791-1000

(G-15658)
CHEESE EXPERTS USA LTD LBLTY
14 Notus Ave (10312-3123)
PHONE...................908 275-3889
Richard Falcone, *President*
Joseph Pastorello, *Principal*
EMP: 9
SALES (est): 760K **Privately Held**
SIC: 2022 Cheese spreads, dips, pastes & other cheese products

(G-15659)
CLASSIC NEWS
2655 Richmond Ave (10314-5821)
PHONE...................718 698-5256
Tony Nazir, *Chairman*
EMP: 5
SALES (est): 219.5K **Privately Held**
SIC: 2711 Newspapers, publishing & printing

(G-15660)
COCA-COLA BTLG CO OF NY INC
400 Western Ave (10303-1199)
PHONE...................718 420-6800
Fax: 718 420-6801
Susan Stavan, *Branch Mgr*
Sam Campanello, *Manager*
EMP: 12
SALES (corp-wide): 44.2B **Publicly Held**
SIC: 2086 Bottled & canned soft drinks
HQ: The Coca-Cola Bottling Company Of New York Inc
2500 Windy Ridge Pkwy Se
Atlanta GA 30339
770 989-3000

(G-15661)
COFFEE HOLDING CO INC (PA)
3475 Victory Blvd Ste 4 (10314-6785)
PHONE...................718 832-0800
Andrew Gordon, *President*
David Gordon, *Exec VP*
◆ **EMP:** 69
SALES: 118.1MM **Publicly Held**
WEB: www.coffeeholding.com
SIC: 2095 5149 5499 Roasted coffee; coffee, green or roasted; coffee

(G-15662)
CONTEMPRA DESIGN INC
20 Grille Ct (10309-1400)
PHONE...................718 984-8586
Fax: 718 356-9813
James Pelligrino, *President*
Dominique Bifiory, *Corp Secy*
EMP: 6
SQ FT: 4,000
SALES: 800K **Privately Held**
SIC: 2541 1799 Table or counter tops, plastic laminated; showcases, except refrigerated; wood; counter top installation

(G-15663)
CRAFT PAK INC
67 Gateway Dr (10304-4440)
PHONE...................718 257-2700
Anthony Deviasi, *Owner*
EMP: 6 **EST:** 2015
SALES (est): 341.1K **Privately Held**
SIC: 2673 Bags: plastic, laminated & coated

(G-15664)
CYCLONE AIR POWER INC
Also Called: Four Wheel Drive
12 Van St (10310-1311)
PHONE...................718 447-3038
Robert J Meeker, *President*
Veronica Larney, *Manager*
Demaira Vontana, *Administration*
▲ **EMP:** 9
SALES (est): 1MM **Privately Held**
WEB: www.cycloneair.com
SIC: 3599 3563 7539 Machine shop, jobbing & repair; air & gas compressors; automotive repair shops

(G-15665)
DI DOMENICO PACKAGING CO INC
304 Bertram Ave (10312-5200)
PHONE...................718 727-5454
Fax: 718 727-5577
Vincent A Di Domenico, *President*
Michael A Di Domenico, *President*
Steven M Di Domenico, *Vice Pres*
Lisa Marchase, *Manager*
EMP: 6
SQ FT: 21,000
SALES (est): 1.1MM **Privately Held**
SIC: 2631 3089 Folding boxboard; setup boxboard; blister or bubble formed packaging, plastic

(G-15666)
DIMARZIO INC
1388 Richmond Ter (10310-1115)
P.O. Box 100387 (10310-0387)
PHONE...................718 442-6655
Fax: 718 720-5296
Lawrence Dimarzio, *President*
Steven Blucher II, *Vice Pres*
Glenn Simmons, *Director*
▲ **EMP:** 30
SQ FT: 2,000
SALES (est): 4.9MM **Privately Held**
WEB: www.dimarzio.com
SIC: 3931 Guitars & parts, electric & non-electric

(G-15667)
E & Y GENERAL CNSTR CO INC
16 Bradley Ave 2 (10314-4403)
PHONE...................718 567-7011
Fax: 718 567-7012
Yasar Tahmaz, *President*
Jennifer Brown, *Manager*
EMP: 10
SQ FT: 2,500
SALES (est): 1.1MM **Privately Held**
SIC: 3441 Fabricated structural metal

(G-15668)
E I DU PONT DE NEMOURS & CO
10 Teleport Dr (10311-1001)
PHONE...................718 761-0043
Jennifer Dupont, *Branch Mgr*
EMP: 182
SALES (corp-wide): 25.1B **Publicly Held**
SIC: 2879 Agricultural chemicals
PA: E. I. Du Pont De Nemours And Company
974 Centre Rd
Wilmington DE 19805
302 774-1000

(G-15669)
EAG ELECTRIC INC
496 Mosel Ave (10304-1621)
PHONE...................201 376-5103
Christopher Todd, *Vice Pres*
EMP: 6
SALES (est): 500K **Privately Held**
SIC: 3534 Elevators & moving stairways

(G-15670)
EASTERN ENTERPRISE CORP
Also Called: Vinyl Tech Window
465 Bay St Ste 2 (10304-3842)
PHONE...................718 727-8600
Fax: 718 727-8684
Al Gargiulo Jr, *President*
Mary Waller, *Manager*
EMP: 15
SALES (est): 1.2MM **Privately Held**
SIC: 3089 Windows, plastic

(G-15671)
ENVIRO SERVICE & SUPPLY CORP
45b Marble Loop (10309-1326)
PHONE...................347 838-6500
Dom Guercio, *President*
Christopher Lorippo, *Vice Pres*
EMP: 10
SALES (est): 1.1MM **Privately Held**
SIC: 2842 2869 2841 Specialty cleaning preparations; sanitation preparations, disinfectants & deodorants; disinfectants, household or industrial plant; industrial organic chemicals; soap & other detergents

(G-15672)
F & D SERVICES INC
Also Called: F & D Printing
34 E Augusta Ave (10308-1323)
PHONE...................718 984-1635
Fax: 718 987-8075
Frank Sisino, *President*
Donald Marcus, *Vice Pres*
EMP: 14
SQ FT: 2,400
SALES (est): 1.2MM **Privately Held**
SIC: 2752 Letters, circular or form: lithographed; commercial printing, offset

(G-15673)
FEDEX OFFICE & PRINT SVCS INC
2456 Richmond Ave Ste C (10314-5804)
PHONE...................718 982-5223
Fax: 718 982-8310
Sandy Sneiderman, *Manager*
Julee Cruz, *Manager*
EMP: 5
SALES (corp-wide): 50.3B **Publicly Held**
WEB: www.kinkos.com
SIC: 2759 5099 7334 Commercial printing; signs, except electric; photocopying & duplicating services
HQ: Fedex Office And Print Services, Inc.
7900 Legacy Dr
Plano TX 75024
214 550-7000

(G-15674)
FRANK TORRONE & SONS INC
Also Called: Torrone Outdoor Displays
400 Broadway (10310-2036)
PHONE...................718 273-7600
Fax: 718 447-5103
Arthur Torrone Jr, *President*
EMP: 15 **EST:** 1944
SQ FT: 9,000
SALES (est): 1.2MM **Privately Held**
SIC: 3993 Neon signs

(G-15675)
G & M ROASTER
680 Sharrotts Rd Ste 4 (10309-1912)
PHONE...................718 984-5235
Will Lahara, *Manager*
EMP: 5
SALES (est): 402.3K **Privately Held**
SIC: 2095 Roasted coffee

(G-15676)
GANGI DISTRIBUTORS INC
Also Called: Snapple Distributors
135 Mcclean Ave (10305-4655)
PHONE...................718 442-5745
Santo Spallina, *President*
EMP: 12
SQ FT: 5,000
SALES (est): 890K **Privately Held**
SIC: 2086 Bottled & canned soft drinks

(G-15677)
GENERAL TRADE MARK LA
31 Hylan Blvd Apt 14c (10305-2079)
PHONE...................718 979-7261
Fax: 718 448-9808
Richard Capuozzo, *President*
Virginia Kruse, *Corp Secy*
EMP: 30 **EST:** 1924
SQ FT: 20,000
SALES (est): 3.4MM **Privately Held**
WEB: www.incrediblelabels.com
SIC: 2759 2671 Labels & seals: printing; tags: printing; packaging paper & plastics film, coated & laminated

(G-15678)
GLENDA INC
Also Called: Victory Sports
1732 Victory Blvd (10314-3510)
PHONE...................718 442-8981
Fax: 718 442-2730
George Siller, *President*
Glenda Siller, *Corp Secy*
EMP: 5
SQ FT: 2,500
SALES (est): 500K **Privately Held**
SIC: 2395 5941 Emblems, embroidered; sporting goods & bicycle shops

(G-15679)
GOTTLIEB SCHWARTZ FAMILY
724 Collfield Ave (10314-4253)
PHONE...................718 761-2010
Michael Gottlieb, *Owner*
EMP: 50 **EST:** 1973
SALES (est): 4.5MM **Privately Held**
SIC: 3444 Skylights, sheet metal

(G-15680)
GRADO GROUP INC
66 Willow Ave (10305-1829)
PHONE...................718 556-4200
Richard Grado, *President*
Nadiane Cintia, *Admin Asst*
EMP: 7 **EST:** 2000
SQ FT: 2,900
SALES (est): 610K **Privately Held**
SIC: 2759 Advertising literature: printing

(G-15681)
GRAPHIC SIGNS & AWNINGS LTD
165 Industrial Loop Ste 1 (10309-1109)
PHONE...................718 227-6000
Fax: 718 227-2057
Mike Demarco, *Vice Pres*
EMP: 5
SALES: 355K **Privately Held**
SIC: 3993 5999 Signs & advertising specialties; awnings

(G-15682)
GREAT ATL PR-CAST CON STATUARY
225 Ellis St (10307-1128)
PHONE...................718 948-5677
Frank Fresca, *President*
EMP: 4
SQ FT: 5,000
SALES: 4MM **Privately Held**
SIC: 3272 Concrete products

(G-15683)
HENRY MORGAN
Also Called: Pensrus
433 Tennyson Dr (10312-6545)
P.O. Box 90219 (10309-0219)
PHONE...................718 317-5013
Henry Morgan, *Owner*
Sandy Aubry, *Sales Staff*
Amanda Carbone, *Technology*
Christine Votaggio, *Executive Asst*
Laurie Necco, *Graphic Designe*
EMP: 11
SALES: 5MM **Privately Held**
WEB: www.pensrus.com
SIC: 3951 Pens & mechanical pencils

(G-15684)
HOMESELL INC
4010 Hylan Blvd (10308-3331)
PHONE...................718 514-0346
Frank Lopa, *CEO*
Paul Lopa, *General Mgr*
Tracy Hardyal, *Admin Sec*
EMP: 10
SQ FT: 1,200
SALES (est): 620K **Privately Held**
WEB: www.homesell.com
SIC: 2721 Magazines: publishing & printing

(G-15685)
I D TEL CORP
Also Called: Metro Tel Communications
55 Canal St (10304-3809)
PHONE...................718 876-6000
Fax: 718 876-6003
Anthony Giammanco, *President*
Edward Pavia, *Vice Pres*
Barbara Syracuse, *Sales Staff*
▲ **EMP:** 12
SQ FT: 4,000
SALES: 1MM **Privately Held**
SIC: 3661 Telephones & telephone apparatus

(G-15686)
IADC INC
845 Father Capodanno Blvd (10305-4039)
PHONE...................718 238-0623
EMP: 10
SALES (est): 690K **Privately Held**
SIC: 3089 Mfg Plastic Products

Staten Island - Richmond County (G-15687)

(G-15687)
INFINITE SOFTWARE SOLUTIONS
Also Called: Md-Reports
1110 South Ave Ste 303 (10314-3403)
PHONE.................................718 982-1315
Fax: 718 477-3692
Srikanth Gosike, *President*
Hari Gandham, *Vice Pres*
Naina Gosike, *Vice Pres*
EMP: 12
SALES (est): 1.3MM **Privately Held**
WEB: www.infinitesoftsol.com
SIC: 3695 5045 Computer software tape & disks: blank, rigid & floppy; computer software

(G-15688)
INTERNTIONAL GOURMET SOUPS INC
Also Called: Famous Manhattan Soup Chef
1110 South Ave Ste 300 (10314-3414)
PHONE.................................212 768-7687
Jamieson Karson, *CEO*
Robert Bertrand, *President*
Jessy Parez, *Admin Sec*
EMP: 20
SALES (est): 1.8MM **Privately Held**
WEB: www.manhattansoupchef.com
SIC: 2034 5499 Dried & dehydrated soup mixes; soups, dehydrated; gourmet food stores

(G-15689)
ISLAND STAIRS CORP
178 Industrial Loop (10309-1145)
PHONE.................................347 645-0560
Fax: 347 967-1708
Vassili Lijnev, *President*
EMP: 6
SQ FT: 5,000
SALES (est): 488.8K **Privately Held**
WEB: www.islandstairs.com
SIC: 2431 Staircases & stairs, wood

(G-15690)
ITTS INDUSTRIAL INC
165 Industrial Loop Ste C (10309-1109)
PHONE.................................718 605-6934
Harvey Itts, *CEO*
Felix Tricoche, *Vice Pres*
▲ EMP: 8
SQ FT: 8,000
SALES (est): 1.3MM **Privately Held**
SIC: 3354 Aluminum extruded products

(G-15691)
J V HARING & SON
Also Called: Haring, J V & Son
1277 Clove Rd Ste 2 (10301-4339)
PHONE.................................718 720-1947
Fax: 718 448-0608
Connie Mauro, *President*
EMP: 10
SQ FT: 1,000
SALES (est): 760K **Privately Held**
SIC: 2752 Commercial printing, lithographic

(G-15692)
JMS ICES INC
Also Called: Ralph's Ices
501 Port Richmond Ave (10302-1720)
PHONE.................................718 448-0853
Michael Scolaro, *President*
Larry Silvestro, *Corp Secy*
John Scolaro, *Vice Pres*
EMP: 15
SQ FT: 5,000
SALES (est): 4.5MM **Privately Held**
SIC: 2024 Ices, flavored (frozen dessert)

(G-15693)
JOSEPH A FILIPPAZZO SOFTWARE
106 Lovell Ave (10314-4905)
PHONE.................................718 987-1626
EMP: 5 EST: 2010
SALES (est): 230K **Privately Held**
SIC: 7372 Prepackaged Software Services

(G-15694)
JOSEPH FEDELE
Also Called: Rainbow Custom Counter Tops
1950b Richmond Ter (10302-1206)
PHONE.................................718 448-3658
Fax: 718 273-4368
Joseph Fedele, *Owner*
Rachael Fedele, *Bookkeeper*
EMP: 6
SQ FT: 5,000
SALES (est): 580K **Privately Held**
SIC: 2541 5211 5031 1799 Counter & sink tops; cabinets, lockers & shelving; cabinets, kitchen; kitchen cabinets; counter top installation

(G-15695)
JPMORGAN CHASE BANK NAT ASSN
1690 Hylan Blvd (10305-1930)
PHONE.................................718 668-0346
EMP: 6
SALES (corp-wide): 101B **Publicly Held**
SIC: 3578 Automatic teller machines (ATM)
HQ: Jpmorgan Chase Bank, National Association
    1111 Polaris Pkwy
    Columbus OH 43240
    614 436-3055

(G-15696)
KLEEN STIK INDUSTRIES INC
44 Lenzie St (10312-6118)
PHONE.................................718 984-5031
Edwin Wallace, *President*
Rosalie Wallace, *Admin Sec*
▲ EMP: 17
SQ FT: 20,000
SALES (est): 1.8MM **Privately Held**
WEB: www.kleenstik.net
SIC: 2672 Tape, pressure sensitive: made from purchased materials

(G-15697)
LAROSA CUPCAKES
314 Lake Ave (10303-2610)
PHONE.................................347 866-3920
EMP: 8
SALES (est): 386.1K **Privately Held**
SIC: 2051 Bread, cake & related products

(G-15698)
LASER AND VARICOSE VEIN TRTMNT
500 Seaview Ave Ste 240 (10305-3403)
PHONE.................................718 667-1777
Inam Haq, *Principal*
EMP: 8
SALES (est): 963.8K **Privately Held**
SIC: 3845 Laser systems & equipment, medical

(G-15699)
LOFFRENO CSTM INTERIORS CONTG
33 Ada Pl (10301-3801)
PHONE.................................718 981-0319
Frank Loffreno, *President*
EMP: 25
SALES: 2.9MM **Privately Held**
SIC: 2521 2517 Cabinets, office: wood; wood television & radio cabinets

(G-15700)
LOOBRICA INTERNATIONAL CORP
41 Darnell Ln (10309-1933)
PHONE.................................347 997-0296
Marshall Weinberg, *Principal*
Jason Weinberg, *Administration*
▲ EMP: 8 EST: 2012
SALES (est): 960K **Privately Held**
SIC: 2992 8733 Lubricating oils & greases; scientific research agency

(G-15701)
M & L STEEL & ORNAMENTAL IRON
27 Housman Ave (10303-2701)
PHONE.................................718 816-8660
Fax: 718 815-6104
Lubomir P Svoboda, *President*
Pete Svoboda, *Executive*
▲ EMP: 14
SALES (est): 3.4MM **Privately Held**
SIC: 3441 1791 Fabricated structural metal; iron work, structural

(G-15702)
MADISONS DELIGHT LLC
711 Forest Ave (10310-2506)
PHONE.................................718 720-8900
David Saraf, *Mng Member*
Danny Saraf, *Manager*
EMP: 10
SQ FT: 2,200
SALES (est): 496.7K **Privately Held**
SIC: 2066 Chocolate

(G-15703)
MAIDENFORM LLC
2655 Richmond Ave (10314-5821)
PHONE.................................718 494-0268
EMP: 178
SALES (corp-wide): 5.7B **Publicly Held**
SIC: 2341 Women's & children's underwear
HQ: Maidenform Llc
    1000 E Hanes Mill Rd
    Winston Salem NC 27105
    336 519-8080

(G-15704)
MAXINE DENKER INC (PA)
Also Called: Tokens
212 Manhattan St (10307-1805)
PHONE.................................212 689-1440
Fax: 212 689-1517
Maxine Denker, *President*
Carla Elson, *Vice Pres*
EMP: 1
SALES (est): 1.2MM **Privately Held**
SIC: 3911 3965 Jewelry, precious metal; buckles & buckle parts; hair curlers

(G-15705)
MAY SHIP REPAIR CONTG CORP
3075 Richmond Ter Ste 3 (10303-1300)
PHONE.................................718 442-9700
Fax: 718 494-4499
Mohamed M Adam, *President*
Yvonne Heredia, *Office Mgr*
Angel Heredia, *Supervisor*
EMP: 45
SQ FT: 1,800
SALES (est): 10.4MM **Privately Held**
WEB: www.mayship.com
SIC: 3731 3732 Shipbuilding & repairing; boat building & repairing

(G-15706)
MILANO GRANITE AND MARBLE CORP
3521 Victory Blvd (10314-6763)
PHONE.................................718 477-7200
Fax: 718 477-3910
Joseph Moreale, *President*
EMP: 12
SALES (est): 1.7MM **Privately Held**
SIC: 3272 Art marble, concrete

(G-15707)
MORAN SHIPYARD CORPORATION (DH)
2015 Richmond Ter (10302-1298)
PHONE.................................718 981-5600
Fax: 718 448-4147
Malcolm W McLeod, *President*
Peter Keyes, *Vice Pres*
Brian Burtner, *Purchasing*
Lee Christensen, *Treasurer*
Joseph De'angelo, *Treasurer*
▲ EMP: 187
SQ FT: 26,400
SALES (est): 11.8MM
SALES (corp-wide): 67.5MM **Privately Held**
SIC: 3731 Shipbuilding & repairing
HQ: Moran Towing Corporation
    50 Locust Ave Ste 10
    New Canaan CT 06840
    203 442-2800

(G-15708)
MORAN TOWING CORPORATION
Also Called: Moran Ship Yard
2015 Richmond Ter (10302-1298)
PHONE.................................718 981-5600
Fax: 718 447-4076
Patty Boncoraglio, *Branch Mgr*
EMP: 9
SALES (corp-wide): 67.5MM **Privately Held**
WEB: www.morantug.com
SIC: 3731 Shipbuilding & repairing
HQ: Moran Towing Corporation
    50 Locust Ave Ste 10
    New Canaan CT 06840
    203 442-2800

(G-15709)
MOTHER MOUSSE LTD (PA)
3767 Victory Blvd Ste D (10314-6706)
PHONE.................................718 983-8366
Fax: 718 698-5282
Theresa Rutigilano, *President*
Joan Ingrisani, *Vice Pres*
EMP: 9
SQ FT: 3,500
SALES (est): 1.5MM **Privately Held**
WEB: www.mamamousse.com
SIC: 2051 Bakery: wholesale or wholesale/retail combined

(G-15710)
NEWSPAPER DELIVERY SOLUTIONS
309 Bradley Ave (10314-5154)
PHONE.................................718 370-1111
Peter Priolo, *CEO*
EMP: 5 EST: 2011
SALES (est): 216.2K **Privately Held**
SIC: 2711 Newspapers

(G-15711)
NORTH AMERICAN DF INC (PA)
280 Watchogue Rd (10314-3100)
PHONE.................................718 698-2500
Chrissy Mazzola, *President*
EMP: 8
SQ FT: 5,000
SALES (est): 2MM **Privately Held**
SIC: 2759 Advertising literature: printing

(G-15712)
NORTH AMERICAN MFG ENTPS INC (PA)
Also Called: Mht Lighting
1961 Richmond Ter (10302-1201)
PHONE.................................718 524-4370
Thomas Spinelli, *Ch of Bd*
Mark Shotton, *Vice Pres*
Angela Santana, *Office Mgr*
Rob Reiner, *Manager*
▲ EMP: 28
SQ FT: 56,000
SALES (est): 3.2MM **Privately Held**
SIC: 3646 Commercial indusl & institutional electric lighting fixtures

(G-15713)
NORTH AMERICAN MFG ENTPS INC
1961 Richmond Ter (10302-1201)
PHONE.................................718 524-4370
Joe Scalice, *Director*
EMP: 15
SALES (corp-wide): 3.2MM **Privately Held**
SIC: 3646 Commercial indusl & institutional electric lighting fixtures
PA: North American Manufacturing Enterprises, Inc.
    1961 Richmond Ter
    Staten Island NY 10302
    718 524-4370

(G-15714)
NORTH EAST FUEL GROUP INC
51 Stuyvesant Ave (10312-3721)
PHONE.................................718 984-6774
Richard D Auria, *Principal*
EMP: 7
SALES (est): 724.9K **Privately Held**
SIC: 2869 Fuels

(G-15715)
NORTHEASTERN FUEL CORP
51 Stuyvesant Ave (10312-3721)
PHONE.................................917 560-6241
Richard Dauria, *Principal*
EMP: 6
SALES (est): 832.9K **Privately Held**
SIC: 2869 Fuels

GEOGRAPHIC SECTION

Staten Island - Richmond County (G-15746)

(G-15716)
NORTHEASTERN FUEL NY INC
414 Spencer St (10303-3627)
PHONE..................................718 761-5360
Richard D'Auria, *Principal*
EMP: 7
SALES (est): 772.7K **Privately Held**
SIC: 2869 Fuels

(G-15717)
NOVA METAL INC
351 Walker St Ste 4 (10303-2719)
PHONE..................................718 981-4000
God Israilov, *Ch of Bd*
▲ EMP: 9
SALES (est): 1MM **Privately Held**
SIC: 2522 Office furniture, except wood

(G-15718)
OCCHIOEROSSO JOHN
Also Called: All Gone Restoration
75 Santa Monica Ln (10309-2833)
PHONE..................................718 541-7025
John Occhiogrosso, *Owner*
EMP: 10
SALES (est): 258.6K **Privately Held**
SIC: 1389 Construction, repair & dismantling services

(G-15719)
OH HOW CUTE INC
38 Androvette St (10309-1302)
PHONE..................................347 838-6031
Margaret Delia, *President*
EMP: 6
SQ FT: 800
SALES: 80K **Privately Held**
SIC: 2064 5199 5092 5145 Cake ornaments, confectionery; gifts & novelties; balloons, novelty; candy

(G-15720)
PHILLIP JUAN
9 Union Ave (10303-2424)
PHONE..................................800 834-4543
Philip Juan, *Owner*
Fu-Chang Juan, *Maintence Staff*
EMP: 7
SQ FT: 2,500
SALES (est): 340K **Privately Held**
WEB: www.juanscorp.com
SIC: 2032 Chinese foods: packaged in cans, jars, etc.

(G-15721)
PIAZZAS ICE CREAM ICE HSE INC
41 Housman Ave (10303-2701)
PHONE..................................718 818-8811
Salvatore J Piazz, *Ch of Bd*
Sam Conte, *Manager*
EMP: 16 EST: 2010
SALES (est): 2.4MM **Privately Held**
SIC: 2024 Ice cream & frozen desserts

(G-15722)
PLAYFITNESS CORP
27 Palisade St (10305-4711)
PHONE..................................917 497-5443
Pavel Asanov, *CEO*
EMP: 5
SALES (est): 351.8K **Privately Held**
SIC: 7372 7999 7389 Educational computer software; physical fitness instruction;

(G-15723)
PORT AUTHORITY OF NY & NJ
2777 Goethals Rd N Fl 2 (10303-1107)
PHONE..................................718 390-2534
Jerry Deltufo, *Manager*
Kelly Murphy, *Admin Asst*
EMP: 90
SALES (corp-wide): 981.3MM **Privately Held**
WEB: www.portnynj.com
SIC: 3441 Bridge sections, prefabricated highway
PA: The Port Authority Of New York & New Jersey
4 World Trade Ctr 150
New York NY 10007
212 435-7000

(G-15724)
PREPARATORY MAGAZINE GROUP
1200 South Ave Ste 202 (10314-3424)
PHONE..................................718 761-4800
Luciano Rammairone, *President*
Gina Biancardi, *President*
EMP: 55
SQ FT: 9,000
SALES: 2.5MM **Privately Held**
SIC: 2721 Magazines: publishing only, not printed on site

(G-15725)
QPS DIE CUTTERS FINISHERS CORP
140 Alverson Ave (10309-1776)
PHONE..................................718 966-1811
Eva Choina, *President*
Semion Goldsman, *Vice Pres*
EMP: 42
SQ FT: 35,000
SALES (est): 3.2MM **Privately Held**
SIC: 3999 Advertising display products

(G-15726)
R & L PRESS INC
896 Forest Ave (10310-2413)
PHONE..................................718 447-8557
Fax: 718 448-4261
Ron Patterson, *President*
EMP: 5
SQ FT: 4,000
SALES (est): 695.9K **Privately Held**
SIC: 2752 Promotional printing, lithographic; commercial printing, offset

(G-15727)
RAMHOLTZ PUBLISHING INC
Also Called: Collegebound Teen Magazine
1200 South Ave Ste 202 (10314-3424)
PHONE..................................718 761-4800
Luciano Rammairone, *CEO*
Gina Biancardi, *Vice Pres*
Aleks Danilov, *Accounts Mgr*
Joseph Cardinale, *Accounts Exec*
Kristy Fallon, *Accounts Exec*
EMP: 60
SQ FT: 10,000
SALES (est): 6.1MM **Privately Held**
SIC: 2721 Magazines: publishing only, not printed on site

(G-15728)
RD2 CONSTRUCTION & DEM LLC
63 Trossach Rd (10304-2131)
PHONE..................................718 980-1650
Kathleen Cloppse, *Controller*
Peter Dagostino,
EMP: 15
SALES (est): 2.2MM **Privately Held**
SIC: 1442 Construction sand & gravel

(G-15729)
REEBOK INTERNATIONAL LTD
2655 Richmond Ave (10314-5821)
PHONE..................................718 370-0471
EMP: 205
SALES (corp-wide): 18.1B **Privately Held**
SIC: 3149 Athletic shoes, except rubber or plastic
HQ: Reebok International Ltd.
1895 J W Foster Blvd
Canton MA 02021
781 401-5000

(G-15730)
REMSEN FUEL INC
4668 Amboy Rd (10312-4150)
PHONE..................................718 984-9551
Natha Singh, *President*
EMP: 6 EST: 2012
SALES (est): 595.4K **Privately Held**
SIC: 2869 Fuels

(G-15731)
REYNOLDS SHIPYARD CORPORATION
200 Edgewater St (10305-4996)
P.O. Box 50010 (10305-0010)
PHONE..................................718 981-2800
Fax: 718 447-2710
Michael Reynolds, *President*
▲ EMP: 10
SQ FT: 30,000
SALES (est): 1.3MM **Privately Held**
SIC: 3731 Cargo vessels, building & repairing; tugboats, building & repairing; barges, building & repairing; scows, building & repairing

(G-15732)
RGM SIGNS INC
Also Called: Blue Boy
1234 Castleton Ave (10310-1717)
PHONE..................................718 442-0598
Fax: 718 442-2343
Ron Malanga, *President*
EMP: 6
SQ FT: 684
SALES (est): 593.9K **Privately Held**
WEB: www.rgmsigns.com
SIC: 3993 2752 5999 1799 Signs & advertising specialties; offset & photolithographic printing; awnings; sign installation & maintenance

(G-15733)
RICHMOND READY MIX CORP
328 Park St (10306-1859)
PHONE..................................917 731-8400
EMP: 7 EST: 2015
SALES (est): 740.6K **Privately Held**
SIC: 3273 Ready-mixed concrete

(G-15734)
SCARA-MIX INC
2537 Richmond Ter (10303-2390)
P.O. Box 30313 (10303-0313)
PHONE..................................718 442-7357
Fax: 718 948-7198
Philip Castellano, *President*
Peter Mauro, *Manager*
EMP: 45 EST: 1981
SQ FT: 17,000
SALES (est): 5.2MM **Privately Held**
SIC: 3273 Ready-mixed concrete

(G-15735)
SPECIAL TEES
250 Buel Ave (10305-1204)
PHONE..................................718 980-0987
Fax: 718 980-1048
Joanne Homsey, *Prgrmr*
Vincent Bonomi, *Director*
Vicent Bonomi, *Program Dir*
EMP: 24
SALES (est): 1.4MM **Privately Held**
WEB: www.specialtees-si.com
SIC: 2396 Screen printing on fabric articles

(G-15736)
SPEEDWAY LLC
951 Bay St (10305-4938)
PHONE..................................718 815-6897
Antonio Balle, *Manager*
EMP: 10 **Publicly Held**
WEB: www.hess.com
SIC: 1389 Gas field services
HQ: Speedway Llc
500 Speedway Dr
Enon OH 45323
937 864-3000

(G-15737)
ST JOHN
229 Morrison Ave (10310-2836)
PHONE..................................718 720-8367
Barbara A Logan, *Principal*
EMP: 5 EST: 2011
SALES (est): 219.5K **Privately Held**
SIC: 2339 Sportswear, women's

(G-15738)
STATED ISLAND STAIR INC
439 Sharrotts Rd (10309-1414)
PHONE..................................718 317-9276
Fran Imber, *President*
EMP: 5
SQ FT: 4,500
SALES: 450K **Privately Held**
SIC: 2431 Staircases & stairs, wood; stair railings, wood

(G-15739)
STATEN ISLAND PARENT MAGAZINE
16 Shenandoah Ave Ste 2 (10314-3652)
PHONE..................................718 761-4800
Orlando Frank, *Owner*

Giulio Rammairone, *Vice Pres*
Nicole Puglia, *Manager*
Patrick Mok, *Info Tech Mgr*
EMP: 5
SALES (est): 373.2K **Privately Held**
SIC: 2721 Periodicals

(G-15740)
STATEN ISLAND STAIR INC
439 Sharrotts Rd (10309-1414)
PHONE..................................718 317-9276
Fax: 718 966-8176
Fran Imber, *President*
Benjamin Imber, *Manager*
Fran Imder, *Executive*
EMP: 5
SALES: 500K **Privately Held**
SIC: 2431 Staircases & stairs, wood

(G-15741)
STONEY CROFT CONVERTERS INC
Also Called: Alltek Labeling Systems
364 Sharrotts Rd (10309-1990)
PHONE..................................718 608-9800
Fax: 718 608-9200
John Conti, *President*
Ann Conti, *Vice Pres*
Ann Holbert, *Vice Pres*
Alan Sherman, *Accounts Mgr*
EMP: 16
SQ FT: 7,000
SALES (est): 3.9MM **Privately Held**
WEB: www.allteklabeling.com
SIC: 2672 2679 Adhesive papers, labels or tapes: from purchased material; labels, paper: made from purchased material

(G-15742)
STRADA SOFT INC
20 Clifton Ave (10305-4912)
PHONE..................................718 556-6940
Lou Esposito, *Principal*
EMP: 8
SALES: 300K **Privately Held**
WEB: www.stradasoft.com
SIC: 7372 Prepackaged software

(G-15743)
SUPERIOR CONFECTIONS INC
1150 South Ave (10314-3404)
PHONE..................................718 698-3300
Fax: 718 494-4576
George Kaye, *President*
Michael K Katsoris, *Exec VP*
Peter Kaye, *Vice Pres*
▲ EMP: 100 EST: 1951
SQ FT: 40,000
SALES (est): 10.1MM **Privately Held**
SIC: 2066 Chocolate candy, solid

(G-15744)
SUPREME CHOCOLATIER LLC
1150 South Ave Fl 1 (10314-3404)
PHONE..................................718 761-9600
Fax: 718 761-5279
George Kaye, *Info Tech Dir*
Kraichen Tracey, *Administration*
▲ EMP: 50 EST: 1999
SALES (est): 11.8MM **Privately Held**
WEB: www.supremechocolatier.com
SIC: 2061 Raw cane sugar

(G-15745)
TDS WOODWORKING INC
Also Called: TDS Woodcraft
104 Port Richmond Ave (10302-1334)
PHONE..................................718 442-5298
Fax: 718 816-8403
Salvatore Piscicelli, *President*
Diane Steoppiell, *Admin Sec*
EMP: 10
SALES (est): 1.2MM **Privately Held**
SIC: 2431 Millwork

(G-15746)
TEACHLEY LLC
56 Marx St (10301-4125)
PHONE..................................347 552-1272
Rachael Labrecque, *Partner*
Kara Carpenter, *Partner*
Dana Pagar, *Partner*
Herbert Ginsburg, *Research*
EMP: 5
SALES (est): 458.2K **Privately Held**
SIC: 7372 Educational computer software

Staten Island - Richmond County (G-15747)

(G-15747)
TEAM BUILDERS INC
Also Called: Team Builders Management
88 New Dorp Plz S Ste 303 (10306-2902)
P.O. Box 778 (10302-0778)
PHONE..................................718 979-1005
Christine B Fasier, *President*
Daniel Harris, *Manager*
EMP: 11
SQ FT: 1,100
SALES: 2MM Privately Held
SIC: 7372 Business oriented computer software

(G-15748)
TECH PRODUCTS INC
105 Willow Ave (10305-1896)
PHONE..................................718 442-4900
Fax: 718 442-2124
Kenneth Nelson Sr, *President*
Carey Nelson, *Corp Secy*
Robert Rosenbaum, *CFO*
Daniel Oconnor, *VP Sales*
Dan O'Connor, *Business Dir*
▼ EMP: 49 EST: 1948
SQ FT: 1,600
SALES (est): 8.4MM Privately Held
WEB: www.techproducts.com
SIC: 3953 3993 Marking devices; signs & advertising specialties

(G-15749)
TODT HILL AUDIOLOGICAL SVCS
78 Todt Hill Rd Ste 202 (10314-4528)
PHONE..................................718 816-1952
Theresa Cannon, *President*
EMP: 5
SALES (est): 660.1K Privately Held
SIC: 3842 8049 Hearing aids; audiologist

(G-15750)
ULTIMATE PAVERS CORP
659 Quincy Ave (10305-4100)
PHONE..................................917 417-2652
EMP: 27
SALES (est): 5MM Privately Held
SIC: 2951 Asphalt paving mixtures & blocks

(G-15751)
VCP MOBILITY INC
4131 Richmond Ave (10312-5633)
PHONE..................................718 356-7827
EMP: 400
SALES (corp-wide): 578MM Privately Held
SIC: 3842 Wheelchairs
HQ: Vcp Mobility, Inc.
   6899 Winchester Cir # 200
   Boulder CO 80301
   303 218-4500

(G-15752)
VEZ INC
Also Called: Fastsigns
1209 Forest Ave (10310-2416)
PHONE..................................718 273-7002
Fax: 718 273-7006
Rich Vezzuto, *President*
Kurt Kracsun, *Vice Pres*
EMP: 6
SQ FT: 1,400
SALES: 600K Privately Held
WEB: www.veztek.com
SIC: 3993 Signs & advertising specialties

(G-15753)
VF OUTDOOR INC
2655 Richmond Ave # 1570 (10314-5821)
PHONE..................................718 698-6215
EMP: 46
SALES (corp-wide): 12.3B Publicly Held
SIC: 2329 Men's & boys' leather, wool & down-filled outerwear
HQ: Vf Outdoor, Llc
   2701 Harbor Bay Pkwy
   Alameda CA 94502
   510 618-3500

(G-15754)
WELSH GOLD STAMPERS INC
44 Lenzie St (10312-6118)
PHONE..................................718 984-5031
Fax: 212 505-9206

Edwin Wallace, *President*
▲ EMP: 27
SALES (est): 1.6MM Privately Held
SIC: 3999 2759 2675 2796 Gold stamping, except books; embossing on paper; die-cut paper & board; platemaking services; bookbinding & related work

(G-15755)
YPIS OF STATEN ISLAND INC
130 Stuyvesant Pl Ste 5 (10301-1900)
PHONE..................................718 815-4557
Dominick Brancato, *Exec Dir*
EMP: 2
SALES: 4.1MM Privately Held
SIC: 7372 Business oriented computer software

Stephentown
Rensselaer County

(G-15756)
ATLANTIS EQUIPMENT CORPORATION (PA)
16941 Ny 22 (12168)
PHONE..................................518 733-5910
Fax: 518 733-6834
Louis Schroeter, *President*
Richard W Keeler Jr, *Vice Pres*
Kate Beach, *Manager*
Catherine Beach, *Technology*
EMP: 18
SQ FT: 40,000
SALES: 5MM Privately Held
SIC: 3599 3441 7692 3444 Machine shop, jobbing & repair; fabricated structural metal; welding repair; sheet metalwork

(G-15757)
FOUR FAT FOWL INC
324 State Route 43 Stop B (12168-2933)
PHONE..................................518 733-5230
Willard Bridgham IV, *President*
Josie Madison, *Opers Mgr*
Shaleena Bridgham, *Sales Mgr*
EMP: 5
SALES: 325K Privately Held
SIC: 2022 Natural cheese

(G-15758)
ZWACK INCORPORATED
15875 Ny 22 (12168)
P.O. Box 100 (12168-0100)
PHONE..................................518 733-5135
Fax: 518 733-6135
Frank J Zwack, *President*
Maria Zwack, *Admin Sec*
EMP: 50 EST: 1971
SQ FT: 30,000
SALES (est): 9.6MM Privately Held
WEB: www.zwackinc.com
SIC: 3541 3714 5082 Machine tools, metal cutting type; sanders, motor vehicle safety; general construction machinery & equipment

Stillwater
Saratoga County

(G-15759)
FANTASY FIREWORKS DISPLAY
28 Flike Rd (12170-1231)
PHONE..................................518 664-1809
Scott Demarco, *Owner*
EMP: 5
SALES: 400K Privately Held
SIC: 2899 Fireworks

(G-15760)
H2O SOLUTIONS INC
61 Major Dickinson Ave (12170-7729)
P.O. Box 721 (12170-0721)
PHONE..................................518 527-0915
Daniel Reilly, *Principal*
EMP: 15
SALES (est): 900K Privately Held
SIC: 3589 Water filters & softeners, household type

(G-15761)
STILLWATER WOOD & IRON
114 Hudson Ave (12170-1146)
P.O. Box 736 (12170-0736)
PHONE..................................518 664-4501
Charles Robert Hallum, *Owner*
C Robert Hallum, *Owner*
Bob Hallum, *Partner*
EMP: 5
SQ FT: 13,000
SALES: 650K Privately Held
WEB: www.stillwaterfdny.com
SIC: 2511 Wood household furniture; unassembled or unfinished furniture, household: wood

Stittville
Oneida County

(G-15762)
DYNA-VAC EQUIPMENT INC
8963 State Route 365 (13469-1021)
PHONE..................................315 865-8084
Hal Reigi, *President*
Laurie Reigi, *Vice Pres*
Mike Simpson, *Sales Mgr*
EMP: 11
SQ FT: 6,000
SALES: 1.8MM Privately Held
WEB: www.dynavacequipment.com
SIC: 3589 Sewer cleaning equipment, power

Stone Ridge
Ulster County

(G-15763)
FTS SYSTEMS INC (DH)
3538 Main St (12484-5601)
PHONE..................................845 687-5300
Fax: 845 687-7481
Claus Kinder, *Principal*
Peter Nissen, *Engineer*
Thomas Verdey, *Technology*
EMP: 85
SQ FT: 34,000
SALES (est): 7.6MM
SALES (corp-wide): 1.6B Privately Held
WEB: www.ftssystems.com
SIC: 3821 3823 3585 Laboratory equipment: fume hoods, distillation racks, etc.; industrial instrmnts msrmnt display/control process variable; refrigeration & heating equipment
HQ: S P Industries, Inc.
   935 Mearns Rd
   Warminster PA 18974
   215 672-7800

(G-15764)
PK30 SYSTEM LLC
3607 Atwood Rd (12484-5446)
P.O. Box 656 (12484-0656)
PHONE..................................212 473-8050
Philip Kerzner, *Owner*
EMP: 13
SALES (est): 2MM Privately Held
SIC: 3442 3446 3429 Store fronts, prefabricated, metal; architectural metalwork; builders' hardware

(G-15765)
REID K DALLAND
5 Silver Fox Rd (12484-5231)
PHONE..................................845 687-8728
Reid K Dalland, *Owner*
EMP: 6
SQ FT: 3,000
SALES: 250K Privately Held
SIC: 2394 Liners & covers, fabric: made from purchased materials

Stony Brook
Suffolk County

(G-15766)
BASF BEAUTY CARE SOLUTIONS LLC
50 Health Sciences Dr (11790-3349)
PHONE..................................631 689-0200
John Marchese, *Safety Mgr*
Steve Palmberg, *Purchasing*
Kevin Regan, *QC Mgr*
James Haywood, *Manager*
EMP: 10
SALES (est): 1.3MM
SALES (corp-wide): 75.6B Privately Held
SIC: 2816 Inorganic pigments
HQ: Basf Catalysts Llc
   25 Middlesex Tpke
   Iselin NJ 08830
   732 205-5000

(G-15767)
BASF CORPORATION
25 Health Sciences Dr # 220 (11790-3384)
PHONE..................................631 380-2490
B Gorbov, *President*
Robert Carver, *Research*
EMP: 104
SALES (corp-wide): 75.6B Privately Held
SIC: 2869 Industrial organic chemicals
HQ: Basf Corporation
   100 Park Ave
   Florham Park NJ 07932
   973 245-6000

(G-15768)
COGNITIVEFLOW SENSOR TECH
9 Melville Ct (11790-1851)
PHONE..................................631 513-9369
Mitchell Fourman, *CEO*
EMP: 9 EST: 2011
SALES (est): 780K Privately Held
SIC: 3841 Surgical & medical instruments

(G-15769)
CREATIVE CABINET CORP AMERICA
3 Onyx Dr (11790-3013)
PHONE..................................631 751-5768
Arthur A Daniels, *President*
Barbara Giordano, *Bookkeeper*
Mark Daniels, *Sales Mgr*
Tony Peterford, *Info Tech Dir*
EMP: 25 EST: 1975
SQ FT: 40,000
SALES: 3.2MM Privately Held
SIC: 2434 5031 5211 Wood kitchen cabinets; kitchen cabinets; cabinets, kitchen

(G-15770)
SAFINA CENTER
118 Administration (11794-0001)
PHONE..................................808 888-9440
Mayra Marino, *Manager*
EMP: 9 EST: 2015
SQ FT: 564
SALES (est): 550K Privately Held
SIC: 3545 Mandrels

(G-15771)
SLEEP CARE ENTERPRISES INC
1212 N Country Rd Ste 3b (11790-1919)
PHONE..................................631 246-9000
Stephen L Frederico, *Principal*
EMP: 8
SALES (est): 671.3K Privately Held
SIC: 2511 5046 5047 5712 Bed frames, except water bed frames: wood; commercial equipment; medical & hospital equipment; mattresses

(G-15772)
STONY BROOK UNIVERSITY
Also Called: University Advertising Agency
310 Administration Bldg (11794-0001)
PHONE..................................631 632-6434
Richard Fine, *Dean*
Suzanne Shane, *Counsel*
Bruce Schroffel, *Exec VP*
Michael Teta, *Facilities Mgr*
Samantha Thomas, *Transportation*

▲ = Import ▼ = Export
◆ = Import/Export

EMP: 40 Privately Held
WEB: www.sunysb.edu
SIC: 2752 8221 9411 Commercial printing, lithographic; colleges universities & professional schools; administration of educational programs;
HQ: Stony Brook University
100 Nicolls Rd
Stony Brook NY 11794
631 632-6000

Stony Point
Rockland County

(G-15773)
FANTASY GLASS COMPAN
61 Beach Rd (10980-2035)
PHONE..................845 786-5818
Greggory Barbutl, *Owner*
EMP: 5
SALES (est): 338.7K Privately Held
SIC: 3732 Boats, fiberglass: building & repairing

(G-15774)
GOTHAM INK & COLOR CO INC
19 Holt Dr (10980-1919)
PHONE..................845 947-4000
Fax: 845 947-3270
William Olson, *General Mgr*
Joseph Simons, *Vice Pres*
Bill Olsen, *Manager*
EMP: 20
SQ FT: 25,000
SALES (est): 3.4MM Privately Held
SIC: 2893 Printing ink

(G-15775)
KEON OPTICS INC
30 John F Kennedy Dr (10980-3207)
PHONE..................845 429-7103
Kevin McKeon, *President*
EMP: 10
SQ FT: 1,300
SALES (est): 815.2K Privately Held
SIC: 3827 Optical instruments & lenses

(G-15776)
LIGHTING SERVICES (PA)
2 Holt Dr (10980-1920)
PHONE..................845 942-2800
Fax: 914 942-2392
Daniel Gelman, *President*
Ken Kane, *Exec VP*
Rose Miller, *Purch Agent*
Jame Brown, *Controller*
Alexander Gonzales, *Accountant*
▲ EMP: 100 EST: 1958
SQ FT: 50,000
SALES (est): 16.2MM Privately Held
WEB: www.lightingservicesinc.com
SIC: 3646 Commercial indusl & institutional electric lighting fixtures

(G-15777)
STONY POINT GRAPHICS LTD
Also Called: Shell Ann Printing
1 S Liberty Dr (10980-1811)
PHONE..................845 786-3322
Fax: 845 786-2122
Phillip Laquidara, *President*
Felix Laquidara, *Vice Pres*
Loraine Laquidara, *Admin Sec*
EMP: 5
SQ FT: 4,000
SALES: 300K Privately Held
SIC: 2752 2759 Commercial printing, offset; letterpress printing

(G-15778)
TIMES SQUARE STAGE LTG CO INC
Also Called: Time Square Lighting
5 Holt Dr (10980-1919)
PHONE..................845 947-3034
Fax: 845 947-3047
Robert Riccadelli, *President*
Bruce Turk, *General Mgr*
Thomas Tyler, *Engineer*
Eric Leskin, *Accounting Dir*
Bruce M Farlane, *Finance Mgr*
▲ EMP: 50 EST: 1938
SQ FT: 32,000

SALES (est): 11.7MM Privately Held
WEB: www.tslight.com
SIC: 3648 Lighting equipment

Stormville
Dutchess County

(G-15779)
GALLI SHIRTS AND SPORTS AP
246 Judith Dr (12582-5262)
PHONE..................845 226-7305
Fax: 845 227-6984
Vincent Gallipani, *President*
Erika Gallipani, *Vice Pres*
EMP: 5
SALES: 300K Privately Held
WEB: www.gallishirts.com
SIC: 2396 7311 Screen printing on fabric articles; advertising consultant

(G-15780)
PACKAGE PAVEMENT COMPANY INC
3530 Route 52 (12582-5651)
P.O. Box 408 (12582-0408)
PHONE..................845 221-2224
Fax: 845 221-0433
Darren Doherty, *Ch of Bd*
Frank J Doherty, *President*
Paul Doherty, *General Mgr*
Gary Lancour, *General Mgr*
Eileen Doherty, *Vice Pres*
▲ EMP: 95 EST: 1951
SQ FT: 5,000
SALES (est): 26.9MM Privately Held
SIC: 2951 Asphalt paving mixtures & blocks; asphalt & asphaltic paving mixtures (not from refineries); concrete, asphaltic (not from refineries); concrete, bituminous

Stottville
Columbia County

(G-15781)
IRV SCHRODER & SONS INC
2906 Atlantic Ave (12172-7700)
P.O. Box 300 (12172-0300)
PHONE..................518 828-0194
Fax: 518 828-2402
Jim Schroder, *President*
EMP: 20
SQ FT: 6,000
SALES (est): 3.8MM Privately Held
SIC: 3441 1791 Fabricated structural metal; structural steel erection

Stuyvesant
Columbia County

(G-15782)
MAPLE HILL CREAMERY LLC
285 Allendale Rd W (12173-2611)
PHONE..................518 758-7777
Tim Joseph, *President*
Peter Meck, *Vice Pres*
Charles Zentay, *CFO*
Peter T Joseph,
EMP: 20
SQ FT: 6,000
SALES: 8MM Privately Held
SIC: 2026 Yogurt

Stuyvesant Falls
Columbia County

(G-15783)
BETHS FARM KITCHEN
504 Rte 46 (12174)
P.O. Box 113 (12174-0113)
PHONE..................518 799-3414
Fax: 518 799-2042
Beth Linskey, *Owner*
EMP: 8

SALES (est): 400K Privately Held
WEB: www.bethsfarmkitchen.com
SIC: 2033 Jams, jellies & preserves: packaged in cans, jars, etc.

Suffern
Rockland County

(G-15784)
ADVANCED MEDICAL MFG CORP
Also Called: Crown Medical Products
7-11 Suffern Pl Ste 2 (10901-5501)
PHONE..................845 369-7535
Ron Resnick, *Owner*
Carol Wynee, *Controller*
Linda Montemarano, *Cust Svc Dir*
EMP: 20
SALES (est): 1.4MM Privately Held
SIC: 2393 Cushions, except spring & carpet: purchased materials

(G-15785)
AMERICAN BEST CABINETS INC
Also Called: Malibu Cabinets
397 Spook Rock Rd (10901-5319)
PHONE..................845 369-6666
Fax: 845 369-7777
Sam Blum, *President*
Aron Feldman, *Vice Pres*
Gitty Samet, *Sales Mgr*
▲ EMP: 39
SQ FT: 26,000
SALES (est): 3.9MM Privately Held
WEB: www.malibucabinets.com
SIC: 2514 Kitchen cabinets: metal

(G-15786)
BEER MARKETERS INSIGHTS INC
49 E Maple Ave (10901-5507)
PHONE..................845 507-0040
Benj Steinman, *President*
Irene Steinman, *Treasurer*
Christopher Shepard, *Assoc Editor*
EMP: 8
SALES (est): 620K Privately Held
WEB: www.beerinsights.com
SIC: 2721 8742 Trade journals: publishing & printing; management consulting services

(G-15787)
CLASSIC CABINETS
375 Spook Rock Rd (10901-5314)
PHONE..................845 357-4331
John Cheman, *Owner*
EMP: 10
SALES (est): 767.5K Privately Held
WEB: www.classcabs.com
SIC: 2434 Wood kitchen cabinets

(G-15788)
DYNAMIC INTL MFRS & DISTRS INC
78 Lafayette Ave Ste 201 (10901-5551)
PHONE..................347 993-1914
Avery Engel, *President*
▲ EMP: 10
SALES (est): 730.2K Privately Held
SIC: 2678 Stationery products

(G-15789)
EMPIRE COACHWORKS INTL LLC
475 Haverstraw Rd (10901-3135)
PHONE..................732 257-7981
Ron Dubiel, *Controller*
Edward Vergopia, *Mng Member*
Micheal Misseri,
EMP: 70
SQ FT: 88,000
SALES (est): 5.3MM Privately Held
SIC: 3711 Automobile bodies, passenger car, not including engine, etc.

(G-15790)
GRAPHIC ARTISAN LTD
3 Cross St (10901-4622)
PHONE..................845 368-1700
Peter Aron, *President*

Sandra Aron, *Treasurer*
EMP: 8
SQ FT: 4,000
SALES (est): 695.6K Privately Held
SIC: 2752 Lithographing on metal

(G-15791)
HUDSON ENERGY SERVICES LLC (PA)
4 Executive Blvd Ste 301 (10901-4190)
PHONE..................630 300-0013
Fax: 845 228-3422
Holly Hopper, *Business Mgr*
Joanna Magnani, *Business Mgr*
Susan Persson, *Business Mgr*
Robert Vera, *Business Mgr*
Kelly Zuniga, *Accountant*
EMP: 6
SQ FT: 1,500
SALES (est): 990.3K Privately Held
WEB: www.hudsonenergyservices.com
SIC: 2911 Gases & liquefied petroleum gases

(G-15792)
I TRADE TECHNOLOGY LTD
400 Rella Blvd Ste 165 (10901-8114)
PHONE..................615 348-7233
Andy Gordon, *Branch Mgr*
EMP: 6
SALES (corp-wide): 1.5MM Privately Held
SIC: 3678 5999 5065 Electronic connectors; electronic parts & equipment; connectors, electronic
PA: I Trade Technology, Ltd.
115 Franklin Tpke Ste 144
Mahwah NJ 07430
615 348-7233

(G-15793)
LA VITA HEALTH FOODS LTD
257 Route 59 (10901-5303)
PHONE..................845 368-4101
Zina Minz, *President*
Eli Minz, *Vice Pres*
▼ EMP: 6
SQ FT: 6,000
SALES: 500K Privately Held
SIC: 2052 Cookies

(G-15794)
LE CHOCOLATE OF ROCKLAND LLC
1 Ramapo Ave (10901-5805)
PHONE..................845 533-4125
Simon Rottenburg,
▲ EMP: 6
SALES (est): 4.3MM Privately Held
SIC: 2066 Chocolate

(G-15795)
NOVARTIS CORPORATION
25 Old Mill Rd (10901-4106)
PHONE..................845 368-6000
Fax: 845 368-6380
EMP: 200
SALES (corp-wide): 49.4B Privately Held
SIC: 2834 Mfg Pharmaceutical Preparations
HQ: Novartis Corporation
608 5th Ave
New York NY 10020
212 307-1122

(G-15796)
OUTLOOK NEWSPAPER
145 College Rd (10901-3620)
PHONE..................845 356-6261
Fax: 845 574-4476
Ian Newman, *Director*
EMP: 25
SALES (est): 752.1K Privately Held
SIC: 2711 2741 Newspapers, publishing & printing; miscellaneous publishing

(G-15797)
PRECISION LATHE WORK CO INC
395 Spook Rock Rd (10901-5319)
PHONE..................845 357-3110
Fax: 845 357-6682
Jeno Szvetecz, *President*
Steve Pados, *Vice Pres*
EMP: 6

Suffern - Rockland County (G-15798)

SQ FT: 3,000
SALES (est): 470K **Privately Held**
SIC: 3599 Machine shop, jobbing & repair

(G-15798)
PRIME FEATHER INDUSTRIES LTD
7-11 Suffern Pl (10901-5501)
PHONE..............................718 326-8701
Fax: 718 326-8436
Justin J Shipper, *President*
EMP: 10
SQ FT: 5,500
SALES (est): 760K **Privately Held**
SIC: 2392 Cushions & pillows

(G-15799)
RADIATION SHIELDING SYSTEMS
415 Spook Rock Rd (10901-5308)
PHONE..............................888 631-2278
Ed Delia, *CEO*
Seth Warnock, *Vice Pres*
Brenda Velez, *Manager*
EMP: 11
SALES (est): 2.1MM
SALES (corp-wide): 40.7MM **Privately Held**
WEB: www.radiationshieldingsystems.com
SIC: 3444 3271 Radiator shields or enclosures, sheet metal; blocks, concrete: radiation-proof
PA: New England Lead Burning Company, Inc.
2 Burlington Woods Dr # 300
Burlington MA 01803
781 933-1940

(G-15800)
ROYAL TEES INC
29 Lafayette Ave (10901-5405)
PHONE..............................845 357-9448
Fax: 845 357-9490
Al Rosenblatt, *President*
EMP: 5
SQ FT: 8,000
SALES: 750K **Privately Held**
WEB: www.royaltees.com
SIC: 2759 2395 2752 5611 Screen printing; embroidery & art needlework; transfers, decalcomania or dry: lithographed; clothing, sportswear, men's & boys'; women's sportswear

(G-15801)
SUPER CONDUCTOR MATERIALS INC
Also Called: SCM
391 Spook Rock Rd (10901-5319)
P.O. Box 701, Tallman (10982-0701)
PHONE..............................845 368-0240
Fax: 845 368-0250
Aftab Dar, *President*
Neelam Dar, *Corp Secy*
▼ EMP: 14
SQ FT: 10,000
SALES (est): 2.3MM **Privately Held**
WEB: www.scm-inc.com
SIC: 3674 Semiconductors & related devices

(G-15802)
UNITED ROCKLAND HOLDING CO INC
9 N Airmont Rd (10901-5101)
P.O. Box 68, Tallman (10982-0068)
PHONE..............................845 357-1900
Paul Wishnoff, *President*
Stanley Wishnoff, *Chairman*
Mitchell Kolata, *Treasurer*
Linda Olivo, *Manager*
EMP: 20 EST: 1961
SQ FT: 20,000
SALES (est): 1.6MM **Privately Held**
WEB: www.unitedrocklandstairs.com
SIC: 2431 Staircases & stairs, wood; stair railings, wood

(G-15803)
XEROX CORPORATION
30 Dunnigan Dr Ste 3 (10901-4185)
PHONE..............................845 918-3147
Norb Stampfel, *Manager*
EMP: 50

SALES (corp-wide): 18B **Publicly Held**
WEB: www.xerox.com
SIC: 3861 Photographic equipment & supplies
PA: Xerox Corporation
45 Glover Ave Ste 700
Norwalk CT 06850
203 968-3000

Sugar Loaf
Orange County

(G-15804)
IRINIRI DESIGNS LTD
1358 Kings Hwy (10981)
P.O. Box 378 (10981-0378)
PHONE..............................845 469-7934
Rit Goldman, *Ch of Bd*
Nirit Rechtman, *President*
EMP: 12
SQ FT: 1,653
SALES (est): 1MM **Privately Held**
SIC: 3911 5944 Jewelry, precious metal; jewelry stores

Sunnyside
Queens County

(G-15805)
DEANCO DIGITAL PRINTING LLC
Also Called: NY Print Partners
4545 39th St (11104-4401)
PHONE..............................212 371-2025
Joe Aziz, *Mng Member*
Pete Lamba,
EMP: 10
SQ FT: 2,500
SALES: 1.2MM **Privately Held**
SIC: 2752 Commercial printing, lithographic

(G-15806)
DEELKA VISION CORP
Also Called: New York Style Eats
4502 Queens Blvd (11104-2304)
PHONE..............................718 937-4121
Fax: 718 937-1338
Mark Stroubosm, *Ch of Bd*
Mark Stroubos, *Principal*
EMP: 20
SALES (est): 2.3MM **Privately Held**
SIC: 2091 Canned & cured fish & seafoods

(G-15807)
EASTERN CONCEPTS LTD
Also Called: Green Mountain Graphics
4125 39th St (11104-4201)
P.O. Box 1417, Long Island City (11101-0417)
PHONE..............................718 472-3377
Fax: 718 472-4040
Eric Greenberg, *President*
Yugnik Singh, *General Mgr*
Elsie Gerena, *Purch Mgr*
Rhonda Greenberg, *Admin Sec*
EMP: 11
SQ FT: 6,000
SALES (est): 980K **Privately Held**
WEB: www.gm-graphics.com
SIC: 3993 Signs & advertising specialties

(G-15808)
NODUS NOODLE CORPORATION
4504 Queens Blvd (11104-2304)
PHONE..............................718 309-3725
Thomas SAE Tang, *CEO*
EMP: 8
SALES (est): 329K **Privately Held**
SIC: 2098 Noodles (e.g. egg, plain & water), dry

(G-15809)
S DONADIC WOODWORKING INC
4525 39th St (11104-4401)
PHONE..............................718 361-9888
Steven Donadic, *President*
Gene Abbazio, *Project Mgr*
Cavan Dunne, *Project Mgr*

Maya Lexa, *Project Mgr*
Nicholas Naimo, *Project Mgr*
EMP: 60
SQ FT: 7,000
SALES: 2MM **Privately Held**
SIC: 2434 2431 2426 2421 Wood kitchen cabinets; millwork; hardwood dimension & flooring mills; sawmills & planing mills, general

(G-15810)
T S B A GROUP INC (PA)
3830 Woodside Ave (11104-1004)
PHONE..............................718 565-6000
Samuel Brown, *Chairman*
Duane Fuller, *Purchasing*
Mark Grossman, *Controller*
Anthony Difiglia, *Marketing Mgr*
EMP: 30
SQ FT: 70,000
SALES (est): 21.3MM **Privately Held**
SIC: 3822 1731 Temperature controls, automatic; energy management controls

Surprise
Greene County

(G-15811)
ROYAL METAL PRODUCTS INC
463 West Rd (12176-1709)
PHONE..............................518 966-4442
Fax: 518 966-5148
David M Johannesen, *President*
Steven Johannesen, *Vice Pres*
Robert Johannesen, *Treasurer*
EMP: 40 EST: 1956
SQ FT: 49,600
SALES (est): 4.2MM **Privately Held**
WEB: www.royalmetalproducts.com
SIC: 2514 3446 2522 3444 Metal household furniture; architectural metalwork; office furniture, except wood; sheet metalwork; products of purchased glass

Syosset
Nassau County

(G-15812)
ANDOR DESIGN CORP
20 Pond View Dr (11791-4409)
PHONE..............................516 364-1619
Fax: 516 364-5428
Ralph Silvera, *President*
EMP: 7
SALES: 800K **Privately Held**
WEB: www.andordesign.com
SIC: 3829 Tensile strength testing equipment; testing equipment: abrasion, shearing strength, etc.

(G-15813)
BEKTROM FOODS INC
Also Called: Lots O' Luv
155 Foxhunt Cres (11791-1707)
PHONE..............................516 802-3800
Thomas Barbella, *President*
Marguerite Barbella, *Office Mgr*
▲ EMP: 50
SALES (est): 13MM **Privately Held**
SIC: 2045 2099 Prepared flour mixes & doughs; packaged combination products: pasta, rice & potato

(G-15814)
BEKTROM FOODS INC (PA)
155 Foxhunt Cres (11791-1707)
PHONE..............................516 802-3800
Thomas Barbella, *President*
Shannon Erickson, *General Mgr*
Steve Barbella, *Exec VP*
Aldon Reed, *Exec VP*
John Adams, *QC Dir*
EMP: 20
SALES (est): 23.4MM **Privately Held**
SIC: 2099 Spices, including grinding

(G-15815)
BUFFALO DENTAL MFG CO INC
Also Called: Bdm
159 Lafayette Dr (11791-3933)
P.O. Box 678 (11791-0678)
PHONE..............................516 496-7200
Fax: 516 496-7751
Donald Nevin, *President*
Marshall Nevin, *Chairman*
Doris Nevin, *Admin Sec*
▲ EMP: 50 EST: 1869
SQ FT: 25,000
SALES (est): 8.7MM **Privately Held**
SIC: 3843 Dental equipment & supplies

(G-15816)
CONTI AUTO BODY CORP
44 Jericho Tpke (11791-4530)
PHONE..............................516 921-6435
Liam Martin, *Principal*
EMP: 7
SALES (est): 775.7K **Privately Held**
SIC: 3711 3713 7532 Automobile bodies, passenger car, not including engine, etc.; truck & bus bodies; top & body repair & paint shops

(G-15817)
COSENSE INC
125 Coachman Pl W (11791-3059)
PHONE..............................516 364-9161
Fax: 631 231-0838
Naim Dam, *President*
Sal Stiperi, *Vice Pres*
Melt Boyatan, *Purchasing*
Christine Legrande, *Purchasing*
Shamine Dam, *Controller*
EMP: 35
SQ FT: 10,000
SALES (est): 5.7MM
SALES (corp-wide): 12.2B **Privately Held**
WEB: www.cosense.com
SIC: 3829 Measuring & controlling devices
HQ: Measurement Specialties, Inc.
1000 Lucas Way
Hampton VA 23666
757 766-1500

(G-15818)
DANDREA INC
115 Eileen Way Ste 106 (11791-5314)
P.O. Box 391, Port Washington (11050-0392)
PHONE..............................516 496-2200
Fax: 516 496-2425
Anthony J D'Andrea, *President*
Rosemary D'Andrea, *Corp Secy*
Terry Day, *Manager*
Giovanni Maggioni, *Manager*
▲ EMP: 40 EST: 1922
SQ FT: 12,000
SALES (est): 5MM **Privately Held**
SIC: 3931 5736 Musical instruments; musical instrument stores

(G-15819)
DELANEY BOOKS INC
212 Michael Dr (11791-5379)
PHONE..............................516 921-8888
Michael Rudman, *President*
Frances Rudman, *Vice Pres*
EMP: 15
SQ FT: 5,000
SALES (est): 1.5MM **Privately Held**
WEB: www.passbooks.com
SIC: 2731 Books: publishing only
PA: National Learning Corp
212 Michael Dr
Syosset NY 11791
516 921-8888

(G-15820)
ELEGANT ENTRIES INC (PA)
235 Robbins Ln Unit F (11791-6014)
PHONE..............................631 595-1000
Fax: 631 595-2481
Gary Arcieri, *President*
Gary Ragucin, *Vice Pres*
Cheryl Borman, *Admin Sec*
EMP: 18
SQ FT: 24,000
SALES (est): 3.1MM **Privately Held**
SIC: 3442 Metal doors

GEOGRAPHIC SECTION

Syracuse - Onondaga County (G-15846)

(G-15821)
ETERNAL LOVE PARFUMS CORP
Also Called: Eternal Love Perfumes
485 Underhill Blvd # 207 (11791-3434)
PHONE..................................516 921-6100
Fax: 516 921-6142
Mahender Sabhnani, *President*
◆ EMP: 4
SALES: 4.2MM **Privately Held**
WEB: www.eternalloveparfums.com
SIC: 2844 5122 Toilet preparations; perfumes

(G-15822)
FLUID METERING INC (HQ)
5 Aerial Way Ste 500 (11791-5593)
PHONE..................................516 922-6050
Harry E Pinkerton III, *President*
Robert A Warren Jr, *Vice Pres*
Anthony Mennella, *Purch Mgr*
Daniel Lee, *Design Engr*
EMP: 50 EST: 1959
SALES (est): 11.8MM
SALES (corp-wide): 3.5B **Publicly Held**
WEB: www.fmipump.com
SIC: 3825 Meters: electric, pocket, portable, panelboard, etc.
PA: Roper Technologies, Inc.
    6901 Prof Pkwy E Ste 200
    Sarasota FL 34240
    941 556-2601

(G-15823)
FRANK MERRIWELL INC
212 Michael Dr (11791-5305)
PHONE..................................516 921-8888
Jack Rudman, *President*
Frances Rudman, *Vice Pres*
EMP: 15
SQ FT: 5,000
SALES (est): 1.5MM **Privately Held**
WEB: www.frankmerriwell.com
SIC: 2731 Books: publishing only
PA: National Learning Corp
    212 Michael Dr
    Syosset NY 11791
    516 921-8888

(G-15824)
GENERAL MICROWAVE CORPORATION (DH)
Also Called: Kratos General Microwave
227a Michael Dr (11791-5306)
PHONE..................................516 802-0900
Deanna Lund, *CEO*
Eric Demarco, *President*
Michael Fink, *Vice Pres*
Michael W Fink, *Vice Pres*
Laura Siegal, *Treasurer*
EMP: 11 EST: 1960
SQ FT: 3,000
SALES: 4.3MM
SALES (corp-wide): 1.1B **Privately Held**
SIC: 3674 5065 3825 6794 Hybrid integrated circuits; electronic parts & equipment; electronic parts; test equipment for electronic & electrical circuits; patent owners & lessors; microwave components; analytical instruments
HQ: Herley Industries, Inc.
    3061 Industry Dr
    Lancaster PA 17603
    717 397-2777

(G-15825)
GOTHAM INK CORP
19 Teibrook Ave (11791-3831)
PHONE..................................516 677-1969
Edward Feldstein, *President*
Paul Weinstein, *Vice Pres*
EMP: 7
SQ FT: 5,000
SALES: 925K **Privately Held**
SIC: 2752 7331 Commercial printing, lithographic; direct mail advertising services

(G-15826)
KNOLL PRINTING & PACKAGING INC
Also Called: Knoll Worldwide
149 Eileen Way (11791-5302)
PHONE..................................516 621-0100
Jeremy Cohen, *Ch of Bd*
Linda Drew, *Vice Pres*
Coleen Corporal, *Prdtn Mgr*
▲ EMP: 24
SALES: 5MM **Privately Held**
WEB: www.knollpack.com
SIC: 2657 3081 3086 Folding paperboard boxes; packing materials, plastic sheet; packaging & shipping materials, foamed plastic

(G-15827)
KUSH OASIS ENTERPRISES LLC
228 Martin Dr (11791-5406)
PHONE..................................516 513-1316
Jyoti Jaiswal,
▲ EMP: 5
SALES (est): 210K **Privately Held**
SIC: 2393 Textile bags

(G-15828)
MESTEL BROTHERS STAIRS & RAILS
11 Gary Rd Ste 102 (11791-6211)
PHONE..................................516 496-4127
Fax: 516 496-4127
Barry Mestel, *President*
EMP: 236
SALES (est): 16.1MM **Privately Held**
WEB: www.mestelbrothersstairs.com
SIC: 2431 3446 1751 Staircases & stairs, wood; architectural metalwork; carpentry work

(G-15829)
NASCO ENTERPRISES INC
95 Woodcrest Dr (11791-3037)
PHONE..................................516 921-9696
Naimish P Shah, *President*
▲ EMP: 1
SALES: 1MM **Privately Held**
SIC: 3841 Catheters

(G-15830)
NATIONAL LEARNING CORP (PA)
212 Michael Dr (11791-5379)
PHONE..................................516 921-8888
Fax: 516 921-8743
Michael Rudman, *President*
Frances Rudman, *Vice Pres*
EMP: 15
SQ FT: 15,000
SALES: 1.5MM **Privately Held**
WEB: www.delaneybooks.com
SIC: 2731 Book clubs: publishing & printing

(G-15831)
NATIONAL RDING STYLES INST INC
Also Called: N R S I
179 Lafayette Dr (11791-3933)
P.O. Box 737 (11791-0737)
PHONE..................................516 921-5500
Fax: 516 921-5591
Marie Carbo, *President*
Juliet Ditroia, *Corp Secy*
Gail Banks, *Bookkeeper*
EMP: 12
SQ FT: 6,400
SALES: 1.5MM **Privately Held**
WEB: www.nrsi.com
SIC: 2741 8748 Miscellaneous publishing; educational consultant

(G-15832)
NEW JERSEY PULVERIZING CO INC (PA)
4 Rita St (11791-5918)
PHONE..................................516 921-9595
Fax: 516 921-9575
Martin Tanzer, *President*
Barbara Tanzer, *Vice Pres*
Barbara Deegan, *Treasurer*
EMP: 3 EST: 1915
SQ FT: 2,500
SALES (est): 2.4MM **Privately Held**
SIC: 1446 Industrial sand

(G-15833)
NORTH HILLS SIGNAL PROC CORP (HQ)
6851 Jericho Tpke Ste 170 (11791-4454)
PHONE..................................516 682-7700
Fax: 516 682-7704
Estro Vitantonio, *CEO*
Warren Esanu, *Ch of Bd*
Richard Schwartz, *General Mgr*
Richard Schwarz, *General Mgr*
Leslie Brand, *CFO*
▲ EMP: 1
SQ FT: 12,000
SALES (est): 5.3MM
SALES (corp-wide): 495K **Privately Held**
WEB: www.northhills-sp.com
SIC: 3679 Harness assemblies for electronic use: wire or cable
PA: North Hills Holding Company Llc
    6851 Jericho Tpke Ste 170
    Syosset NY 11791
    516 682-7705

(G-15834)
NORTH HILLS SIGNAL PROC CORP
North Hill Signal Prossesing
6851 Jericho Tpke Ste 170 (11791-4454)
PHONE..................................516 682-7740
Richard Schwartz, *General Mgr*
Renee Taylor, *Administration*
EMP: 10
SALES (corp-wide): 495K **Privately Held**
SIC: 3669 Signaling apparatus, electric
HQ: North Hills Signal Processing Corp.
    6851 Jericho Tpke Ste 170
    Syosset NY 11791
    516 682-7700

(G-15835)
PARADIGM MKTG CONSORTIUM INC
Also Called: United Supply Systems
350 Michael Dr (11791-5307)
PHONE..................................516 677-6012
Fax: 516 677-6013
Ralph Bianculli Jr, *CEO*
Pamela Bianculli, *President*
Thomas Bathe, *VP Sales*
Marsha Pearl, *Administration*
▲ EMP: 50
SQ FT: 100,000
SALES (est): 15.7MM **Privately Held**
SIC: 2679 5087 Paper products, converted; cleaning & maintenance equipment & supplies

(G-15836)
RAMLER INTERNATIONAL LTD
485 Underhill Blvd # 100 (11791-3434)
PHONE..................................516 353-3106
Garry Ramler, *President*
▲ EMP: 24
SALES: 12MM **Privately Held**
SIC: 2599 Hotel furniture

(G-15837)
REAL EST BOOK OF LONG ISLAND
575 Underhill Blvd # 110 (11791-3426)
PHONE..................................516 364-5000
Bryan Flynn, *President*
Julie Lindh, *Office Mgr*
EMP: 10
SQ FT: 1,600
SALES: 2MM **Privately Held**
SIC: 2721 7319 Periodicals: publishing only; magazines: publishing only, not printed on site; distribution of advertising material or sample services

(G-15838)
ROTA FILE CORPORATION
Also Called: Rota Tool
159 Lafayette Dr (11791-3933)
P.O. Box 678 (11791-0678)
PHONE..................................516 496-7200
Don Nevin, *President*
Richard Byalick, *General Mgr*
EMP: 20
SALES (est): 2.2MM **Privately Held**
WEB: www.rotafile.com
SIC: 3545 Cutting tools for machine tools

(G-15839)
SDS BUSINESS CARDS INC
Also Called: B C T
170 The Vale (11791-4312)
PHONE..................................516 747-3131
Fax: 516 746-3425

Todd Peters, *President*
Sharon Peters, *Vice Pres*
EMP: 10
SQ FT: 3,000
SALES: 1.2MM **Privately Held**
SIC: 2752 2759 Commercial printing, lithographic; commercial printing

(G-15840)
SUNQUEST PHARMACEUTICALS INC
150 Eileen Way Unit 1 (11791-5313)
PHONE..................................855 478-6779
Atul Sharma, *President*
EMP: 16
SALES (est): 3.5MM **Privately Held**
SIC: 2834 Pharmaceutical preparations

(G-15841)
VIDEO TECHNOLOGY SERVICES INC
5 Aerial Way Ste 300 (11791-5594)
PHONE..................................516 937-9700
Andres Sierra, *President*
Philip Lapierre, *Engineer*
Phillip Pierre, *Engineer*
Richard Rouse, *Engineer*
Lisa Morreale, *Manager*
EMP: 12
SQ FT: 7,200
SALES (est): 1.9MM **Privately Held**
WEB: www.videotechnologyservices.com
SIC: 3651 7622 5099 Household video equipment; video repair; video & audio equipment

(G-15842)
VIVONA BUSINESS PRINTERS INC
Also Called: PIP Printing
343 Jackson Ave (11791-4123)
PHONE..................................516 496-3453
Fax: 516 496-8949
Joseph Vivonia, *CEO*
Joe Vivona, *President*
Anne Marie Bono, *Vice Pres*
Fran Galligan, *Office Mgr*
EMP: 8
SALES (est): 1.3MM **Privately Held**
SIC: 2752 Commercial printing, offset

(G-15843)
ZASTECH INC
15 Ryan St (11791-2129)
PHONE..................................516 496-4777
Raymond Zhou, *CEO*
▲ EMP: 20
SALES (est): 1.3MM **Privately Held**
SIC: 3674 Semiconductors & related devices

Syracuse
Onondaga County

(G-15844)
219 SOUTH WEST
219 S West St (13202-1874)
PHONE..................................315 474-2065
EMP: 8
SALES (est): 560K **Privately Held**
SIC: 2448 Mfg Wood Pallets/Skids

(G-15845)
A ZIMMER LTD
Also Called: Syracuse New Times
W Tenesee St (13204)
PHONE..................................315 422-7011
Arthur Zimmer, *President*
Gregg Gambell, *General Mgr*
Christine Scheuerman, *General Mgr*
Shirley Zimmer, *CFO*
Jill Hutchinson, *Finance*
EMP: 84
SQ FT: 24,000
SALES (est): 5.2MM **Privately Held**
WEB: www.syracusenewtimes.com
SIC: 2711 5521 Newspapers; used car dealers

(G-15846)
AIRGAS USA LLC
121 Boxwood Ln (13206-1802)
PHONE..................................315 433-1295

Syracuse - Onondaga County (G-15847)

Fax: 315 463-7346
Bill Hartsock, *Branch Mgr*
EMP: 20
SALES (corp-wide): 189.3MM **Privately Held**
SIC: 2813 Industrial gases
HQ: Airgas Usa Llc
  259 N Radnor Chester Rd # 100
  Radnor PA 19087
  610 687-5253

(G-15847)
ALL TIMES PUBLISHING LLC
Also Called: Syracuse New Times
1415 W Genesee St (13204-2119)
PHONE..................................315 422-7011
Fax: 315 422-1721
William Brod, *CEO*
Bill Brod, *Publisher*
Art Zimmer, *Publisher*
Larry Dietrich, *Editor*
James Coleman, *Vice Pres*
EMP: 24
SALES (est): 2MM **Privately Held**
SIC: 2741 Miscellaneous publishing

(G-15848)
ALL-STATE DIVERSIFIED PDTS INC
8 Dwight Park Dr (13209-1034)
PHONE..................................315 472-4728
EMP: 50
SALES (est): 5.3MM **Privately Held**
SIC: 3443 Mfg Fabricated Plate Work

(G-15849)
ALLIED DECORATIONS CO INC
Also Called: Allied Sign Co
720 Erie Blvd W (13204-2226)
PHONE..................................315 637-0273
Fax: 315 476-3756
Michael E Pfohl, *President*
Ken Colton, *Natl Sales Mgr*
Kim Charette, *Office Mgr*
EMP: 15
SQ FT: 45,000
SALES (est): 1.2MM **Privately Held**
WEB: www.alliedsigncompany.com
SIC: 3993 7389 Signs & advertising specialties; decoration service for special events; trade show arrangement

(G-15850)
ALPHA DC MOTORS INC
5949 E Molloy Rd (13211-2125)
P.O. Box 3166 (13220-3166)
PHONE..................................315 432-9039
Fax: 315 432-9085
Elton Mantle, *CEO*
Josh Rauscher, *Manager*
EMP: 10
SALES (est): 890K **Privately Held**
WEB: www.alphadcmotors.com
SIC: 7694 Electric motor repair

(G-15851)
ALPHA PRINTING CORP
131 Falso Dr (13211-2106)
P.O. Box 26 (13211-0026)
PHONE..................................315 454-5507
Stephen Larose, *President*
Chris Graney, *Sales Staff*
Castro Dyane, *Manager*
Sally Godkin, *Manager*
EMP: 12
SQ FT: 5,000
SALES (est): 1.5MM **Privately Held**
SIC: 2752 Commercial printing, offset

(G-15852)
ALTIUS AVIATION LLC
113 Tuskegee Rd Ste 2 (13211-1332)
PHONE..................................315 455-7555
Vaughn J Crawford, *Mng Member*
EMP: 6
SALES (est): 860.2K **Privately Held**
SIC: 3721 6722 8742 Aircraft; management investment, open-end; management consulting services

(G-15853)
AMERICAN FOUNDRYMENS SOCIETY
Also Called: Frasier and Jones
3000 Milton Ave (13209)
P.O. Box 4955 (13221-4955)
PHONE..................................315 468-6251
Fax: 315 468-3676
Mark Novakowski, *Principal*
Stew Paice, *Foreman/Supr*
Noel Ebner, *Director*
EMP: 90
SQ FT: 182,784
SALES (est): 10.8MM **Privately Held**
WEB: www.frazerandjones.com
SIC: 3325 Steel foundries

(G-15854)
ANSUN GRAPHICS INC
6392 Deere Rd Ste 4 (13206-1317)
PHONE..................................315 437-6869
Fax: 315 437-6979
Jeff Schoenfeld, *President*
Patricia Craine, *Manager*
Joe Marrinan, *Shareholder*
Todd Thomas, *Admin Sec*
EMP: 12
SALES (est): 1.7MM **Privately Held**
WEB: www.ansun.biz
SIC: 2759 Commercial printing

(G-15855)
ANTHONY RIVER INC
116 Granger St (13202-2388)
PHONE..................................315 475-1315
Fax: 315 475-6341
Ken Abramson, *President*
EMP: 15
SQ FT: 21,500
SALES (est): 2MM **Privately Held**
SIC: 3471 3083 2851 Finishing, metals or formed products; plastic finished products, laminated; paints & allied products

(G-15856)
ARCOM AUTOMATICS LLC
185 Ainsley Dr (13210-4202)
P.O. Box 6729 (13217-6729)
PHONE..................................315 422-1230
Fax: 315 422-2963
Gregory A Tresness, *President*
Mary Tresness, *Vice Pres*
William Warwick, *Engineer*
Barb Beckner, *VP Sales*
Nick Chunka, *VP Sales*
EMP: 8
SALES (est): 1.4MM **Privately Held**
WEB: www.arcomlabs.com
SIC: 3663 Cable television equipment

(G-15857)
ARO-GRAPH CORPORATION
Also Called: Aro-Graph Displays
847 North Ave (13206-1630)
PHONE..................................315 463-8693
Fax: 315 463-0026
Neal Burrei, *President*
Carol Burrei, *Vice Pres*
EMP: 5 **EST:** 1946
SQ FT: 7,000
SALES (est): 785.3K **Privately Held**
WEB: www.arograph.com
SIC: 2752 2396 Decals, lithographed; screen printing on fabric articles

(G-15858)
ARPAC LLC
6581 Townline Rd (13206-1175)
PHONE..................................315 471-5103
EMP: 10
SALES (corp-wide): 68.5MM **Privately Held**
SIC: 3537 Palletizers & depalletizers
PA: Arpac, Llc
  9555 Irving Park Rd
  Schiller Park IL 60176
  847 678-9034

(G-15859)
ARROW-COMMUNICATION LABS INC
Also Called: Arcom Labs
185 Ainsley Dr (13210-4202)
P.O. Box 6729 (13217-6729)
PHONE..................................315 422-1230

Andrew Tresness, *President*
Dave Kozlowski, *Regional Mgr*
David Dixon, *Vice Pres*
Michael Thayer, *Safety Dir*
David Dickson, *Controller*
▲ **EMP:** 300
SQ FT: 30,000
SALES (est): 52.6MM
SALES (corp-wide): 53.8MM **Privately Held**
SIC: 3663 Cable television equipment
PA: Northern Catv Sales Inc
  185 Ainsley Dr
  Syracuse NY
  315 422-1230

(G-15860)
ATLAS BITUMINOUS CO INC
173 Farrell Rd (13209-1823)
PHONE..................................315 457-2394
Charmaine Jones, *President*
Robert Shattel, *Treasurer*
Robert Shattell Sr, *Treasurer*
James Shattel, *Admin Sec*
EMP: 11 **EST:** 1963
SQ FT: 2,500
SALES (est): 1.9MM **Privately Held**
SIC: 2951 6513 Asphalt & asphaltic paving mixtures (not from refineries); apartment hotel operation

(G-15861)
AUTOMATION CORRECT LLC
Also Called: Automationcorrect.com
405 Parrish Ln (13205-3323)
PHONE..................................315 299-3589
Neil Waelder, *Manager*
EMP: 5
SALES (est): 530K **Privately Held**
WEB: www.automationcorrect.com
SIC: 3825 Test equipment for electronic & electrical circuits

(G-15862)
AUTOMATION PAPERS INC
Also Called: National Pad & Paper
6361 Thompson Rd Stop 1 (13206-1412)
P.O. Box 572, Fayetteville (13066-0572)
PHONE..................................315 432-0565
David T Carroll, *President*
Donald T Carroll, *Vice Pres*
Jean Carroll, *Admin Sec*
▼ **EMP:** 7
SQ FT: 17,000
SALES (est): 1.1MM **Privately Held**
SIC: 2621 Writing paper

(G-15863)
AVALON COPY CENTERS AMER INC (PA)
Also Called: Avalon Document Services
901 N State St (13208-2515)
PHONE..................................315 471-3333
Fax: 315 471-3334
John P Midgley, *CEO*
Shawn Thrall, *President*
Jon Willette, *COO*
David Paulick, *Opers Staff*
Melissa Pidanick, *Opers Staff*
EMP: 65
SQ FT: 13,000
SALES (est): 23.5MM **Privately Held**
SIC: 2741 7375 7336 7334 Art copy: publishing & printing; information retrieval services; commercial art & graphic design; photocopying & duplicating services

(G-15864)
BABBITT BEARINGS INC (PA)
Also Called: Babbit Bearings
734 Burnet Ave (13203-2999)
PHONE..................................315 479-6603
Fax: 315 479-5103
Tracy S Stevenson, *CEO*
H Thomas Wart, *Vice Pres*
Charles R Wat, *Plant Mgr*
John Cerrone, *Treasurer*
Marian Wart, *Admin Sec*
EMP: 90
SQ FT: 34,000
SALES (est): 15.6MM **Privately Held**
SIC: 3599 Machine shop, jobbing & repair

(G-15865)
BABBITT BEARINGS INCORPORATED
734 Burnet Ave (13203-2999)
PHONE..................................315 479-6603
Charles R Wart Jr, *President*
Jeffrey Rossman, *Purchasing*
John Cerrone, *Treasurer*
Marian Wart, *Admin Sec*
EMP: 75 **EST:** 1970
SQ FT: 60,000
SALES (est): 7.1MM
SALES (corp-wide): 15.6MM **Privately Held**
WEB: www.babbitt-inc.com
SIC: 3599 3568 Machine shop, jobbing & repair; power transmission equipment
PA: Babbitt Bearings, Inc.
  734 Burnet Ave
  Syracuse NY 13203
  315 479-6603

(G-15866)
BADOUD COMMUNICATIONS INC
Also Called: Scotsman Press
750 W Genesee St (13204-2306)
P.O. Box 130, Camillus (13031-0130)
PHONE..................................315 472-7821
John Badoud, *President*
Nancy Badoud, *Admin Sec*
EMP: 225
SQ FT: 51,682
SALES (est): 13.2MM **Privately Held**
SIC: 2752 2741 Commercial printing, lithographic; shopping news: publishing & printing

(G-15867)
BARNES GROUP INC
Associated Spring
1225 State Fair Blvd (13209-1011)
PHONE..................................315 457-9200
Fax: 315 457-9228
Kenneth Martin, *Division Mgr*
Malinda Peterman, *Sales Executive*
Larry Johnson, *Branch Mgr*
Sean Foran, *Manager*
Eric Condreay, *Executive*
EMP: 8
SQ FT: 22,448
SALES (corp-wide): 1.1B **Publicly Held**
WEB: www.barnesgroupinc.com
SIC: 3495 3469 Wire springs; metal stampings
PA: Barnes Group Inc.
  123 Main St
  Bristol CT 06010
  860 583-7070

(G-15868)
BENCHMARK MEDIA SYSTEMS INC
203 E Hampton Pl Ste 2 (13206-1676)
PHONE..................................315 437-6300
Fax: 315 437-8119
Ruth S Burdick, *CEO*
Allen H Burdick, *President*
Peter Depuy, *Prdtn Mgr*
Richard Kalinowski, *Purch Mgr*
Rory Rall, *Sales Mgr*
EMP: 14
SQ FT: 5,500
SALES (est): 2.4MM **Privately Held**
WEB: www.benchmarkmedia.com
SIC: 3663 Radio & TV communications equipment

(G-15869)
BILLY BEEZ USA LLC
9090 Destiy Usa Dr L301 Unit L 301 (13204)
PHONE..................................315 741-5099
EMP: 19
SALES (corp-wide): 14.2MM **Privately Held**
SIC: 3949 5137 7999 Playground equipment; women's & children's dresses, suits, skirts & blouses; amusement ride
PA: Billy Beez Usa, Llc
  3 W 35th St Fl 3
  New York NY 10001
  646 606-2249

▲ = Import ▼ = Export
◆ = Import/Export

GEOGRAPHIC SECTION
Syracuse - Onondaga County (G-15896)

(G-15870)
BITZER SCROLL INC
6055 Court Street Rd (13206-1749)
PHONE....................................315 463-2101
Peter P Narreau, *CEO*
Richard Kobor, *President*
Peter Schaufler, *Principal*
Joseph Beckley, *Production*
Gary Vittorio, *QC Mgr*
▲ **EMP:** 92
SALES (est): 44.7MM
SALES (corp-wide): 195.3K **Privately Held**
SIC: 3822 Air conditioning & refrigeration controls
HQ: Bitzer Se
Eschenbrunnlestr. 15
Sindelfingen 71065
703 193-20

(G-15871)
BIZEVENTZ INC
269 W Jefferson St (13202-2334)
PHONE....................................315 579-3901
Norman Poltenson, *President*
Joyl Clance, *Manager*
EMP: 5
SALES (est): 273.8K **Privately Held**
SIC: 2711 Newspapers

(G-15872)
BOMAC INC
6477 Ridings Rd (13206-1110)
PHONE....................................315 433-9181
Fax: 315 433-1910
Kevin T Knecht, *President*
Mark Pauls, *Vice Pres*
William Decoursey, *Foreman/Supr*
Thomas Pauls, *Purchasing*
Jeff Allen, *Engineer*
EMP: 18 **EST:** 1959
SQ FT: 22,000
SALES (est): 4.7MM **Privately Held**
WEB: www.bomacinc.com
SIC: 3625 Electric controls & control accessories, industrial

(G-15873)
BOXCAR PRESS INCORPORATED
509 W Fayette St Ste 135 (13204-2987)
PHONE....................................315 473-0930
Harold Kyle, *Ch of Bd*
Debbi Urbanski, *Vice Pres*
Adriana Sosnowski, *Opers Mgr*
Erich Dixon, *Prdtn Mgr*
Cathy Smith, *Accounts Mgr*
EMP: 30
SALES (est): 5.4MM **Privately Held**
WEB: www.boxcarpress.com
SIC: 2752 5084 Commercial printing, lithographic; printing trades machinery, equipment & supplies

(G-15874)
BRIGHTON BAKERY
335 E Brighton Ave (13210-4141)
PHONE....................................315 475-2948
Mark Stefanski, *Owner*
EMP: 7
SQ FT: 3,000
SALES (est): 240K **Privately Held**
SIC: 2051 5461 Bread, all types (white, wheat, rye, etc): fresh or frozen; pastries, e.g. danish: except frozen; rolls, bread type: fresh or frozen; bakeries

(G-15875)
BROADNET TECHNOLOGIES INC
2-212 Center For Science (13244-0001)
PHONE....................................315 443-3694
Michael Sun, *CEO*
Humenn Polar, *Web Proj Mgr*
EMP: 15 **EST:** 2000
SQ FT: 2,000
SALES (est): 1.2MM **Privately Held**
SIC: 3577 Optical scanning devices

(G-15876)
BUCKEYE CORRUGATED INC
151 Midler Park Dr (13206-1817)
PHONE....................................315 437-1181
EMP: 8

SALES (corp-wide): 196.7MM **Privately Held**
SIC: 2653 Boxes, corrugated: made from purchased materials
PA: Buckeye Corrugated, Inc
822 Kumho Dr Ste 400
Fairlawn OH 44333
330 576-0590

(G-15877)
BURR & SON INC
Also Called: Dover Enterprises
119 Seeley Rd (13224-1113)
PHONE....................................315 446-1550
Fax: 315 446-9976
J Peter Burr, *President*
EMP: 5
SQ FT: 3,000
SALES (est): 360K **Privately Held**
WEB: www.doverent.com
SIC: 2759 Imprinting; engraving

(G-15878)
BUSCH PRODUCTS INC
110 Baker St (13206-1701)
PHONE....................................315 474-8422
Robert Brown Sr, *President*
Darlene Brown, *Vice Pres*
Paul Conley, *Engineer*
EMP: 50
SALES (est): 6.8MM **Privately Held**
WEB: www.buschproducts.com
SIC: 3281 Cut stone & stone products

(G-15879)
BYRNE DAIRY INC
Also Called: Byrne Distribution Center
275 Cortland Ave (13202)
PHONE....................................315 475-2111
Mike Haldane, *Manager*
EMP: 20
SQ FT: 54,928
SALES (corp-wide): 287.4MM **Privately Held**
WEB: www.byrnedairy.com
SIC: 2024 Ice cream, bulk
PA: Byrne Dairy Inc.
2394 Us Route 11
La Fayette NY 13084
315 475-2121

(G-15880)
C & M PRODUCTS INC
1209 N Salina St Ste 1 (13208-1581)
PHONE....................................315 471-3303
Fax: 315 471-4406
Charles Mott, *President*
EMP: 6 **EST:** 1965
SQ FT: 5,600
SALES (est): 579.5K **Privately Held**
SIC: 3479 3499 3089 Name plates: engraved, etched, etc.; trophies, metal, except silver; laminating of plastic

(G-15881)
C M E CORP
Also Called: Central Marking Equipment
1005 W Fayette St Ste 3c (13204-2840)
PHONE....................................315 451-7101
Leedom Kettell, *President*
Andrew Kettell, *General Mgr*
Elena Brusa, *Office Mgr*
Heather Finn, *Office Mgr*
EMP: 11
SQ FT: 12,000
SALES: 1MM **Privately Held**
SIC: 3555 3953 Printing plates; marking devices

(G-15882)
CAFE KUBAL
202 Lockwood Rd (13214-2035)
PHONE....................................315 278-2812
Matthew Godard, *Branch Mgr*
EMP: 12
SALES (corp-wide): 1MM **Privately Held**
SIC: 2095 Roasted coffee
PA: Cafe Kubal
3501 James St Ste 2
Syracuse NY 13206
315 278-2812

(G-15883)
CALTEX INTERNATIONAL LTD
60 Presidential Plz # 1405 (13202-2444)
PHONE....................................315 425-1040

Kapil Kevin Sodhi, *President*
Jennifer Hetherington, *Vice Pres*
EMP: 39
SQ FT: 26,000
SALES: 6.4MM **Privately Held**
WEB: www.iscbiostrat.com
SIC: 2869 2842 3826 Industrial organic chemicals; specialty cleaning preparations; environmental testing equipment

(G-15884)
CAMFIL USA INC
6600 Deere Rd (13206-1311)
PHONE....................................518 456-6085
EMP: 8
SALES (est): 1.3MM **Privately Held**
SIC: 3564 Blowers & fans

(G-15885)
CAROLS POLAR PARLOR
3800 W Genesee St (13219-1928)
PHONE....................................315 468-3404
Carol Franceschetti, *Owner*
EMP: 5
SALES (est): 358.5K **Privately Held**
SIC: 2024 Ice cream & frozen desserts

(G-15886)
CARPENTER INDUSTRIES INC
1 General Motors Dr # 10 (13206-1129)
P.O. Box 888 (13206-0888)
PHONE....................................315 463-4284
Fax: 315 463-4051
Edward Tibbits, *President*
Ed Downs, *Manager*
EMP: 11
SQ FT: 25,000
SALES (est): 890K **Privately Held**
WEB: www.carpenterindustries.com
SIC: 3471 3441 Sand blasting of metal parts; fabricated structural metal

(G-15887)
CARRIER CORPORATION
Also Called: Carrier Globl Engrg Conference
Carrier Pkwy Trl 20 (13221)
P.O. Box 4808 (13221-4808)
PHONE....................................315 432-6000
EMP: 34
SALES (corp-wide): 56.1B **Publicly Held**
WEB: www.carrier.com
SIC: 3585 Air conditioning equipment, complete
HQ: Carrier Corporation
17900 Bee Line Hwy
Jupiter FL 33478
561 796-2000

(G-15888)
CARRIER CORPORATION
Carrier Pkwy Tr 20 (13221)
P.O. Box 4808 (13221-4808)
PHONE....................................315 432-6000
Randall J Hogan, *President*
Nassem Shaikh, *Vice Pres*
Bruce Poplawski, *Engineer*
Dick Ferguson, *Accounting Mgr*
Patrick Preux, *VP Human Res*
EMP: 400
SALES (corp-wide): 56.1B **Publicly Held**
WEB: www.carrier.com
SIC: 3822 3585 3433 Refrigeration/air-conditioning defrost controls; refrigeration & heating equipment; heating equipment, except electric
HQ: Carrier Corporation
17900 Bee Line Hwy
Jupiter FL 33478
561 796-2000

(G-15889)
CARRIER CORPORATION
Carrier Global Account (13221)
P.O. Box 4808 (13221-4808)
PHONE....................................315 432-6000
Geraud Darnis, *Branch Mgr*
EMP: 1200
SALES (corp-wide): 56.1B **Publicly Held**
WEB: www.carrier.com
SIC: 3585 Refrigeration & heating equipment
HQ: Carrier Corporation
17900 Bee Line Hwy
Jupiter FL 33478
561 796-2000

(G-15890)
CATHEDRAL CANDLE CO
510 Kirkpatrick St (13208-2100)
PHONE....................................315 422-9119
Fax: 315 478-1610
Louis J Steigerwald III, *Ch of Bd*
Mark Steigerwald, *Vice Pres*
John Hogan, *Treasurer*
Linda D Rohde, *Admin Sec*
▲ **EMP:** 52 **EST:** 1897
SQ FT: 17,000
SALES (est): 7.2MM **Privately Held**
WEB: www.cathedralcandle.com
SIC: 3999 5049 Candles; religious supplies

(G-15891)
CAVALRY SOLUTIONS
449 E Wshngtn St Ste 100 (13202-1967)
PHONE....................................315 422-1699
John Devendorf, *Owner*
EMP: 5
SALES (est): 248.9K **Privately Held**
SIC: 7372 Prepackaged software

(G-15892)
CHAMPION MILLWORK INC
140 Hiawatha Pl (13208-1268)
PHONE....................................315 463-0711
Fax: 315 463-0655
Micheal Duffy, *President*
Mark J Zapisek, *Co-Owner*
EMP: 25
SALES (est): 4.4MM **Privately Held**
SIC: 2541 Wood partitions & fixtures

(G-15893)
CHEMTRADE CHEMICALS US LLC
Also Called: General Chemical
1421 Willis Ave (13204-1051)
P.O. Box 16 (13209-0016)
PHONE....................................315 430-7650
Fax: 315 478-6247
Biagio Vavala, *Plant Mgr*
Biagio Bavala, *Opers-Prdtn-Mfg*
EMP: 40
SALES (corp-wide): 128MM **Privately Held**
SIC: 2819 Industrial inorganic chemicals
HQ: Chemtrade Chemicals Us Llc
90 E Halsey Rd
Parsippany NJ 07054
973 515-0900

(G-15894)
CHEMTRADE CHEMICALS US LLC
Also Called: Syracuse Technical Center
344 W Genesee St Ste 100 (13202-1010)
PHONE....................................315 478-2323
Joseph Hurd, *Manager*
Kathy Baker, *Manager*
Ben Shultes, *Manager*
EMP: 5
SALES (corp-wide): 128MM **Privately Held**
SIC: 2819 Sodium compounds or salts, inorg., ex. refined sod. chloride
HQ: Chemtrade Chemicals Us Llc
90 E Halsey Rd
Parsippany NJ 07054
973 515-0900

(G-15895)
CITY PATTERN SHOP INC
4052 New Court Ave (13206-1639)
P.O. Box 6 (13206-0006)
PHONE....................................315 463-5239
Fax: 315 463-1138
Paul M Clisson, *President*
Robert Leonard, *Vice Pres*
Mike Davranv, *Manager*
EMP: 10 **EST:** 1961
SQ FT: 7,500
SALES (est): 1.2MM **Privately Held**
WEB: www.citypatternshop.com
SIC: 3543 Industrial patterns

(G-15896)
CLARK CONCRETE CO INC (PA)
Also Called: Clark Trucking Co Div
434 E Brighton Ave (13210-4144)
PHONE....................................315 478-4101
Fax: 315 452-3150

Syracuse - Onondaga County (G-15897) — GEOGRAPHIC SECTION

Donald W Clark, *President*
Lyndon S Clark, *Vice Pres*
Stephen Clark, *Vice Pres*
John Wehrle, *Sales Staff*
EMP: 6 **EST:** 1920
SQ FT: 8,000
SALES (est): 1.8MM **Privately Held**
SIC: 3273 4212 Ready-mixed concrete; local trucking, without storage

(G-15897)
CLEAN ALL OF SYRACUSE LLC
838 Erie Blvd W (13204-2228)
PHONE 315 472-9189
Fax: 315 472-3904
Severino Gonnella, *President*
Angela Gonnella, *Vice Pres*
EMP: 9
SQ FT: 40,000
SALES (est): 980K **Privately Held**
SIC: 2842 5999 Cleaning or polishing preparations; swimming pool chemicals, equipment & supplies

(G-15898)
CNY BUSINESS REVIEW INC
Also Called: Business Journal
269 W Jefferson St (13202-2334)
PHONE 315 472-3104
Fax: 315 472-3644
Norman Poltenson, *President*
Marny Nesher, *COO*
Vance Marriner, *Engineer*
Mary Lamacchia, *Accounts Mgr*
Kurt Bramer, *Manager*
EMP: 14
SQ FT: 3,000
SALES (est): 1MM **Privately Held**
WEB: www.cnybj.com
SIC: 2711 2721 Newspapers; periodicals

(G-15899)
COASTEL CABLE TOOLS INC
Also Called: Coastel Cable Tools Intl
344 E Brighton Ave (13210-4142)
PHONE 315 471-5361
Edward Dale, *President*
Mary Shaver, *Vice Pres*
John Lumia, *Manager*
EMP: 21
SQ FT: 42,000
SALES (est): 2MM **Privately Held**
WEB: www.coasteltools.com
SIC: 3541 3423 Machine tools, metal cutting type; hand & edge tools

(G-15900)
COCA-COLA BTLG CO OF NY INC
298 Farrell Rd (13209-1876)
PHONE 315 457-9221
Lucky Wyrick, *Sales/Mktg Mgr*
Heaven Donner, *Manager*
EMP: 10
SQ FT: 117,740
SALES (corp-wide): 44.2B **Publicly Held**
SIC: 2086 Bottled & canned soft drinks
HQ: The Coca-Cola Bottling Company Of New York Inc
2500 Windy Ridge Pkwy Se
Atlanta GA 30339
770 989-3000

(G-15901)
COLD SPRINGS R & D INC
1207 Van Vleck Rd Ste A (13209-1017)
PHONE 315 413-1237
Fax: 315 413-0456
Scott Grimshaw, *President*
Valerie Grimshaw, *Vice Pres*
EMP: 10
SQ FT: 10,000
SALES (est): 1.3MM **Privately Held**
WEB: www.csrdinc.com
SIC: 3674 Semiconductors & related devices

(G-15902)
COMMERCIAL MILLWORKS INC
221 W Division St (13204-1411)
PHONE 315 475-7479
John Tortorello, *Ch of Bd*
Theodore Kinder, *Vice Pres*
EMP: 9
SQ FT: 10,000
SALES (est): 850.7K **Privately Held**
SIC: 2434 Wood kitchen cabinets

(G-15903)
COMMUNICATIONS & ENERGY CORP
204 Ambergate Rd (13214-2204)
PHONE 315 446-5723
Emily Bostick, *Ch of Bd*
Christopher Bostick, *President*
EMP: 10
SQ FT: 5,500
SALES (est): 2MM **Privately Held**
WEB: www.cefilter.com
SIC: 3679 8742 2741 Electronic circuits; foreign trade consultant; miscellaneous publishing

(G-15904)
CONCEPTS IN WOOD OF CNY
4021 New Court Ave (13206-1640)
PHONE 315 463-8084
Fax: 315 463-1157
David Fuleihan, *President*
EMP: 25
SQ FT: 16,000
SALES (est): 3.4MM **Privately Held**
SIC: 2521 2511 2431 Cabinets, office: wood; filing cabinets (boxes), office: wood; wood household furniture; millwork

(G-15905)
CONSTAS PRINTING CORPORATION
Also Called: Taylor Copy Services
1120 Burnet Ave (13203-3210)
PHONE 315 474-2176
Fax: 315 474-2079
Diane M Brindak, *Ch of Bd*
Diane Constas, *President*
Claudia Constas, *Vice Pres*
EMP: 7
SQ FT: 2,400
SALES (est): 750K **Privately Held**
SIC: 2752 7334 Commercial printing, offset; photocopying & duplicating services

(G-15906)
COOKIE CONNECTION INC
705 Park Ave (13204-2223)
PHONE 315 422-2253
Kathleen Sniezak, *President*
Elizabeth Johnson, *Vice Pres*
EMP: 5
SQ FT: 1,500
SALES (est): 229.8K **Privately Held**
SIC: 2051 Bakery: wholesale or wholesale/retail combined

(G-15907)
COOPER & CLEMENT INC
1840 Lemoyne Ave (13208-1367)
PHONE 315 454-8135
Fax: 315 455-9490
John Clement, *President*
Inga Clement, *Vice Pres*
Ole Westergaard, *Vice Pres*
EMP: 29
SQ FT: 35,000
SALES (est): 4.6MM **Privately Held**
SIC: 2759 2396 Promotional printing; automotive & apparel trimmings

(G-15908)
COOPER CROUSE-HINDS LLC (DH)
Also Called: Cooper Crouse Hinds Elec Pdts
1201 Wolf St (13208-1376)
P.O. Box 4999 (13221-4999)
PHONE 315 477-7000
Fax: 315 477-5118
Alexander M Cutler, *CEO*
Grant L Gawronski, *President*
John Dinger, *Vice Pres*
Hugh Goodridge, *Vice Pres*
Barbara Hapner, *Vice Pres*
▲ **EMP:** 500
SQ FT: 1,000,000
SALES (est): 123MM **Privately Held**
WEB: www.coopercrouse-hinds.com
SIC: 3699 Fire control or bombing equipment, electronic
HQ: Eaton Corporation
1000 Eaton Blvd
Cleveland OH 44122
216 523-5000

(G-15909)
COOPER INDUSTRIES LLC
Also Called: Cooper Molded Products
Wolf & 7th North St (13208)
P.O. Box 4999 (13221-4999)
PHONE 315 477-7000
Christopher Cooney, *Vice Pres*
Hays Lengyel, *Vice Pres*
Nancy Gianni, *Project Mgr*
Pat Blincoe, *Engineer*
Darren Rutland, *Sales Mgr*
EMP: 22 **Privately Held**
SIC: 3646 3648 3613 5063 Commercial indusl & institutional electric lighting fixtures; lighting equipment; switchgear & switchgear accessories; electrical supplies; electrical equipment & supplies; construction machinery
HQ: Cooper Industries, Llc
600 Travis St Ste 5400
Houston TX 77002
713 209-8400

(G-15910)
COUNTERTOPS & CABINETS INC
4073 New Court Ave (13206-1646)
PHONE 315 433-1038
Emil Henry, *President*
Nick Henry, *Admin Sec*
EMP: 5
SQ FT: 3,200
SALES (est): 752K **Privately Held**
WEB: www.cnytops.com
SIC: 2541 1799 Counter & sink tops; counter top installation

(G-15911)
CREATIVE LAMINATES INC
4003 Eastbourne Dr (13206-1631)
PHONE 315 463-7580
Fax: 315 463-0509
Dennis N Brackly, *President*
Melody Brough, *Manager*
EMP: 19
SQ FT: 12,000
SALES (est): 100K **Privately Held**
WEB: www.creativelaminates.com
SIC: 2431 Millwork

(G-15912)
CRITICAL LINK LLC
6712 Brooklawn Pkwy # 203 (13211-2110)
PHONE 315 425-4045
Neha Chopra, *Project Mgr*
Anna Higgs, *Production*
Tom Catalino, *Engineer*
Dave Stehlik, *Engineer*
Tim Iskander, *Senior Engr*
EMP: 20
SQ FT: 8,000
SALES (est): 6MM **Privately Held**
SIC: 3571 8711 Electronic computers; engineering services

(G-15913)
CRUCIBLE INDUSTRIES LLC
575 State Fair Blvd (13209-1560)
PHONE 800 365-1180
James Beckman, *President*
Lorna Carpenter, *Vice Pres*
Lorna E Carpenter, *Vice Pres*
Joe Nadzan, *Vice Pres*
Heath Reimers, *Engineer*
◆ **EMP:** 290
SALES (est): 92MM **Privately Held**
SIC: 3312 Bars, iron: made in steel mills

(G-15914)
CRYOMECH INC
113 Falso Dr (13211-2106)
PHONE 315 455-2555
Fax: 315 455-2544
Peter Gifford, *President*
Rudolph Capella, *General Mgr*
Rich Dausman, *COO*
Elizabeth Murphy, *Opers Mgr*
Lindsay Hoage, *Production*
▲ **EMP:** 100
SQ FT: 24,000
SALES (est): 35.5MM **Privately Held**
WEB: www.cryomech.com
SIC: 3559 Cryogenic machinery, industrial

(G-15915)
CUMMINS NORTHEAST LLC
6193 Eastern Ave (13211-2208)
PHONE 315 437-2296
Fax: 315 437-6596
Robin Riewaldt, *Opers-Prdtn-Mfg*
EMP: 36
SQ FT: 13,760
SALES (corp-wide): 19.1B **Publicly Held**
SIC: 3519 5013 Internal combustion engines; automotive engines & engine parts
HQ: Cummins Northeast Llc
30 Braintree Hill Park # 101
Braintree MA 02184

(G-15916)
CUSTOM SHEET METAL CORP
1 General Motors Dr Ste 5 (13206-1122)
PHONE 315 463-9105
Fax: 315 463-6664
Wilson C Brown, *President*
Shaun Mills, *Manager*
EMP: 8
SQ FT: 5,000
SALES (est): 1.2MM **Privately Held**
SIC: 3444 Sheet metal specialties, not stamped

(G-15917)
CYANDIA INC
843 Malden Rd (13211-1327)
PHONE 315 679-4268
Michael Wetzer, *CEO*
Christine Wetzer, *Vice Pres*
EMP: 15
SQ FT: 4,800
SALES (est): 1.2MM **Privately Held**
SIC: 7372 Prepackaged Software As A Services

(G-15918)
D & D MOTOR SYSTEMS INC
215 Park Ave (13204-2459)
PHONE 315 701-0861
Mike Dearoff, *President*
Eric Dearoff, *Vice Pres*
Eric Dieroff, *Vice Pres*
Jeff Boylan, *Manager*
▲ **EMP:** 20
SALES (est): 5.3MM **Privately Held**
WEB: www.ddmotorsystems.com
SIC: 3621 Motors & generators

(G-15919)
D N GANNON FABRICATING INC
404 Wavel St (13206-1728)
P.O. Box 6572 (13217-6572)
PHONE 315 463-7466
Fax: 315 432-8110
Frank Deuel, *President*
John Noel, *Vice Pres*
EMP: 5
SQ FT: 15,000
SALES: 500K **Privately Held**
SIC: 3441 Fabricated structural metal

(G-15920)
DAILY ORANGE CORPORATION
744 Ostrom Ave (13210-2942)
PHONE 315 443-2314
Dave Seal, *Editor*
Nancy Peck, *Adv Dir*
Peter Waack, *Manager*
Trevor Hass, *Relations*
EMP: 50
SALES (est): 359.6K **Privately Held**
WEB: www.dailyorange.com
SIC: 2711 Newspapers: publishing only, not printed on site

(G-15921)
DARCO MANUFACTURING INC
6756 Thompson Rd (13211-2122)
P.O. Box 6304 (13217-6304)
PHONE 315 432-8905
Fax: 315 432-9241
David A Redding, *President*
Laura Miller, *General Mgr*
Tom Benack, *Senior Mgr*
Bob Dewey, *Supervisor*
Keith Woodard, *Supervisor*
EMP: 42

▲ = Import ▼ = Export
◆ = Import/Export

GEOGRAPHIC SECTION

SQ FT: 22,000
SALES (est): 10.5MM Privately Held
SIC: 3599 Machine shop, jobbing & repair

(G-15922)
DAVID FEHLMAN
Also Called: Rollers Unlimited
6729 Pickard Dr (13211-2123)
P.O. Box 5059 (13220-5059)
PHONE 315 455-8888
Fax: 315 454-8600
David Fehlman, *Owner*
EMP: 5
SQ FT: 3,200
SALES (est): 341.9K **Privately Held**
SIC: 3599 3562 3366 3312 Machine & other job shop work; ball & roller bearings; copper foundries; blast furnaces & steel mills; synthetic rubber; platemaking services

(G-15923)
DECORATED COOKIE COMPANY LLC
314 Lakeside Rd (13209-9729)
PHONE 315 487-2111
Peter Hess, *Mng Member*
EMP: 30
SQ FT: 13,000
SALES (est): 4.8MM **Privately Held**
SIC: 2052 Cookies

(G-15924)
DEPENDABLE TOOL & DIE CO INC
129 Dwight Park Cir # 2 (13209-1010)
PHONE 315 453-5696
Fax: 315 453-2810
Anthony D Dantuono, *President*
Maria Ancona, *VP Sls/Mktg*
Lorraine Ryan, *Manager*
Andrea Tarolli, *Admin Sec*
EMP: 8
SQ FT: 20,000
SALES (est): 740K **Privately Held**
SIC: 3599 Machine shop, jobbing & repair

(G-15925)
DUPLI GRAPHICS CORPORATION (HQ)
Also Called: Dupli Envelope & Graphics
6761 Thompson Rd (13211-2119)
P.O. Box 11500 (13218-1500)
PHONE 315 234-7286
J Kemper Matt, *Ch of Bd*
J Kemper Matt Jr, *President*
Thomas Booth, *Vice Pres*
Rob Slate, *Opers Mgr*
Todd Luchsinger, *CFO*
EMP: 117
SQ FT: 150,000
SALES (est): 23.2MM
SALES (corp-wide): 32MM **Privately Held**
WEB: www.duplionline.com
SIC: 2759 2752 Commercial printing; envelopes: printing; commercial printing, lithographic
PA: Matt Industries Inc.
  6761 Thompson Rd
  Syracuse NY 13211
  315 472-1316

(G-15926)
DUPLI GRAPHICS CORPORATION
Grafek Direct
Dupli Park Dr (13218)
P.O. Box 11500 (13218-1500)
PHONE 315 422-4732
Kemper J Matt, *President*
Fred Kocher, *Sales Mgr*
EMP: 8
SALES (corp-wide): 32MM **Privately Held**
WEB: www.duplionline.com
SIC: 2759 2752 Envelopes: printing; commercial printing, offset
HQ: Dupli Graphics Corporation
  6761 Thompson Rd
  Syracuse NY 13211
  315 234-7286

(G-15927)
DYNAMIC HYBIRDS INC
1201 E Fayette St Ste 11 (13210-1933)
PHONE 315 426-8110
Don Hazelmyer, *President*
EMP: 7
SQ FT: 2,500
SALES (est): 1MM **Privately Held**
WEB: www.hybridcircuit.com
SIC: 3679 Electronic circuits

(G-15928)
EAGLE MEDIA PARTNERS LP (PA)
Also Called: Eagle Newspapers
2501 James St Ste 100 (13206-2996)
PHONE 315 434-8889
H Douglas Barclay, *Partner*
Edward S Green, *Partner*
Stewart Hancock, *Partner*
David Northrup, *Partner*
David Tyler, *Editor*
EMP: 33
SQ FT: 7,000
SALES (est): 3.3MM **Privately Held**
WEB: www.cnylink.com
SIC: 2711 Commercial printing & newspaper publishing combined

(G-15929)
EASTWOOD LITHO INC
4020 New Court Ave (13206-1663)
P.O. Box 131 (13206-0131)
PHONE 315 437-2626
Fax: 315 432-9227
Justin F Mohr, *CEO*
Mark J Mohr, *President*
Betty E Mohr, *Vice Pres*
Patrick H Mohr, *Treasurer*
Mark Lowry, *Manager*
EMP: 30
SQ FT: 15,000
SALES (est): 4.8MM **Privately Held**
WEB: www.eastwoodlitho.com
SIC: 2759 2752 2791 2789 Letterpress printing; commercial printing, lithographic; typesetting; bookbinding & related work

(G-15930)
EATON CORPORATION
Also Called: Ephesus Lighting
125 E Jefferson St (13202-2020)
PHONE 315 579-2872
EMP: 30 **Privately Held**
SIC: 3645 Fluorescent lighting fixtures, residential
HQ: Eaton Corporation
  1000 Eaton Blvd
  Cleveland OH 44122
  216 523-5000

(G-15931)
EATON CROUSE-HINDS
500 7th North St (13208-1369)
PHONE 315 477-7000
Scott Hearn, *Principal*
EMP: 200
SALES (est): 16.7MM **Privately Held**
SIC: 3699 Electrical equipment & supplies

(G-15932)
EATONS CROUSE HINDS BUSINESS
1201 Wolf St (13208-1375)
PHONE 315 477-7000
Jacquiline Townshend, *Sales Mgr*
Kathleen Mills, *Manager*
EMP: 17
SALES (est): 2.9MM **Privately Held**
SIC: 3625 Motor controls & accessories

(G-15933)
ELIZABETH WOOD
Also Called: Endoscopic Procedure Center
4900 Broad Rd (13215-2265)
PHONE 315 492-5470
Elizabeth Wood, *President*
EMP: 5
SALES (est): 841K **Privately Held**
SIC: 3845 Endoscopic equipment, electromedical

(G-15934)
ELTON EL MANTLE INC
6072 Court Street Rd (13206-1711)
P.O. Box 3166 (13220-3166)
PHONE 315 432-9067
Elton Mantle, *President*
EMP: 5
SALES (est): 388K **Privately Held**
SIC: 3621 Motors, electric

(G-15935)
EMPIRE BREWING COMPANY INC
120 Walton St (13202-1571)
PHONE 315 925-8308
David Katleski, *President*
Lisa Shoen, *Human Res Dir*
Monica Palmer, *Mktg Dir*
Olivia Cerio, *Marketing Mgr*
Kelly Joyce, *Merchandise Mgr*
EMP: 64
SALES (est): 3MM **Privately Held**
SIC: 2082 5812 Ale (alcoholic beverage); American restaurant

(G-15936)
EMPIRE DIVISION INC
201 Kirkpatrick St # 207 (13208-2075)
PHONE 315 476-6273
Vincent Williams, *President*
EMP: 72
SQ FT: 9,000
SALES (est): 5MM **Privately Held**
SIC: 3589 3621 5063 5064 Vacuum cleaners & sweepers, electric: industrial; water purification equipment, household type; motors, electric; motors, electric; vacuum cleaners, household; water purification equipment; cleaning equipment & supplies; motors, electric; water purification equipment

(G-15937)
EPHESUS LIGHTING INC
125 E Jefferson St Lbby 1 (13202-2135)
PHONE 315 579-2873
Amy Casper, *CEO*
Mike Lorenz, *President*
Michael Lorenz, *COO*
Mike Quijano, *Sales Dir*
John Kindon, *Accounts Mgr*
▲ **EMP:** 30
SALES (est): 2.8MM **Privately Held**
SIC: 3645 Fluorescent lighting fixtures, residential
HQ: Eaton Corporation
  1000 Eaton Blvd
  Cleveland OH 44122
  216 523-5000

(G-15938)
ERHARD & GILCHER INC
235 Cortland Ave (13202-3825)
P.O. Box 84 (13209-0084)
PHONE 315 474-1072
Fax: 315 475-0751
Peter Coyne, *President*
Rosemary Coyne, *Corp Secy*
Lance McGee, *Vice Pres*
EMP: 35 EST: 1913
SQ FT: 25,000
SALES (est): 3.6MM **Privately Held**
SIC: 2789 Bookbinding & related work

(G-15939)
EVERGREEN CORP CENTRAL NY
Also Called: Evergreen Manufacturing
235 Cortland Ave (13202-3825)
PHONE 315 454-4175
Fax: 315 454-4177
Rene Musso, *President*
EMP: 18
SQ FT: 4,500
SALES (est): 2.9MM **Privately Held**
SIC: 3544 2759 Paper cutting dies; commercial printing

(G-15940)
EXCEL ALUMINUM PRODUCTS INC
563 N Salina St (13208-2530)
PHONE 315 471-0925
Frank Tafel Jr, *President*
Raymond Tafel, *Admin Sec*
EMP: 5
SQ FT: 2,000
SALES: 250K **Privately Held**
SIC: 3442 5031 Storm doors or windows, metal; windows; doors

(G-15941)
FALSO INDUSTRIES INC
Also Called: Falso Metal Fabricating
4100 New Court Ave (13206-1698)
PHONE 315 463-0266
Fax: 315 463-5193
Raymond Falso, *President*
Dean Sharron, *General Mgr*
Richard Iorio, *Corp Secy*
Norb Kieffer, *Plant Mgr*
Dennis McGough, *Manager*
EMP: 20
SQ FT: 19,000
SALES (est): 4.4MM **Privately Held**
WEB: www.falsoindustries.com
SIC: 3469 Metal stampings

(G-15942)
FAYETTE STREET COATINGS INC (DH)
Also Called: Strathmore Products, Inc.
1970 W Fayette St (13204-1740)
P.O. Box 151 (13201-0151)
PHONE 315 488-5401
Fax: 315 488-2715
Eric T Burr, *Ch of Bd*
Liza Adamitz, *Purch Mgr*
Jim Rogers, *Research*
Suzanne Stewart, *Human Res Mgr*
Tom Bilodeau, *Sales Mgr*
EMP: 6
SQ FT: 50,000
SALES (est): 7.9MM
SALES (corp-wide): 9.1MM **Publicly Held**
WEB: www.publicsafety.com
SIC: 2851 Paints & allied products
HQ: The Whitmore Manufacturing Company
  930 Whitmore Dr
  Rockwall TX 75087
  972 771-1000

(G-15943)
FELDMEIER EQUIPMENT INC (PA)
6800 Townline Rd (13211-1325)
P.O. Box 474 (13211-0474)
PHONE 315 823-2000
Fax: 315 454-3701
Robert E Feldmeier, *CEO*
Jean Jackson, *Vice Pres*
James Hulbert, *Project Mgr*
Ron Lamanna, *Purch Mgr*
Anders Nelson, *Engineer*
EMP: 100 EST: 1953
SQ FT: 60,000
SALES (est): 90.5MM **Privately Held**
WEB: www.feldmeier.com
SIC: 3443 Fabricated plate work (boiler shop)

(G-15944)
FUTON CITY DISCOUNTERS INC
Also Called: Sleep Master
6361 Thompson Rd (13206-1448)
PHONE 315 437-1328
Fax: 315 446-1342
Charles Vanpatten, *President*
EMP: 18
SALES (est): 3.4MM **Privately Held**
SIC: 2599 5712 Factory furniture & fixtures; furniture stores

(G-15945)
G A BRAUN INC
461 E Brighton Ave (13210-4143)
P.O. Box 3029 (13220-3029)
PHONE 315 475-3123
Fax: 315 475-4130
Steve Bregande, *Principal*
Jeffrey Hohman, *Project Mgr*
Debbie Currie, *Materials Mgr*
Ed Bidwell, *Purchasing*
Matt Gallagher, *Natl Sales Mgr*
EMP: 25
SALES (corp-wide): 26.4MM **Privately Held**
SIC: 3582 Commercial laundry equipment

Syracuse - Onondaga County (G-15946)

GEOGRAPHIC SECTION

PA: G. A. Braun, Inc.
79 General Irwin Blvd
North Syracuse NY 13212
315 475-3123

(G-15946)
G C HANFORD MANUFACTURING CO (PA)
Also Called: Hanford Pharmaceuticals
304 Oneida St (13202-3433)
P.O. Box 1017 (13201-1017)
PHONE................................315 476-7418
Fax: 315 476-7434
George R Hanford, *Principal*
Joseph J Heath, *Principal*
Peter Ward, *Principal*
Bill Snook, *Opers Mgr*
Chad Garrick, *Production*
EMP: 230 EST: 1846
SQ FT: 80,000
SALES (est): 54.7MM **Privately Held**
WEB: www.hanford.com
SIC: 2834 2833 5122 Penicillin preparations; antibiotics; pharmaceuticals

(G-15947)
GARDALL SAFE CORPORATION
219 Lamson St Ste 1 (13206-2879)
P.O. Box 240 (13206-0240)
PHONE................................315 432-9115
Fax: 315 434-9422
Edward Baroody, *Ch of Bd*
Kris Ruffos, *Purch Mgr*
David A Patton, *Treasurer*
David A Ptton, *Treasurer*
Jim Riccardi, *Accounting Dir*
◆ EMP: 25 EST: 1950
SQ FT: 85,000
SALES (est): 5MM **Privately Held**
WEB: www.gardall.com
SIC: 3499 Safes & vaults, metal

(G-15948)
GARDNER DNVER OBERDORFER PUMPS
5900 Firestone Dr (13206-1103)
PHONE................................315 437-0361
Robin Watkins, *Principal*
Michael Walker, *Chief Mktg Ofcr*
▲ EMP: 30
SQ FT: 50,000
SALES (est): 5.4MM
SALES (corp-wide): 2.1B **Privately Held**
SIC: 3561 Pumps & pumping equipment
HQ: Gardner Denver, Inc.
222 E Erie St Ste 500
Milwaukee WI 53202
414 212-4700

(G-15949)
GEAR MOTIONS INCORPORATED (PA)
Also Called: Nixon Gear
1750 Milton Ave (13209-1626)
PHONE................................315 488-0100
Fax: 315 488-0196
Samuel R Haines, *President*
Dean Burroes, *President*
Ron Wright, *Sales Engr*
EMP: 50
SQ FT: 45,000
SALES (est): 18.4MM **Privately Held**
WEB: www.gearmotions.com
SIC: 3462 Gears, forged steel

(G-15950)
GENERAL ELECTRIC COMPANY
5990 E Molloy Rd (13211-2130)
PHONE................................315 456-3304
Matthew J Battle, *Branch Mgr*
Jeff Martin, *Info Tech Mgr*
EMP: 20
SQ FT: 8,000
SALES (corp-wide): 117.3B **Publicly Held**
SIC: 7694 Electric motor repair
PA: General Electric Company
41 Farnsworth St
Boston MA 02210
617 443-3000

(G-15951)
GENERATION POWER LLC
238 W Division St (13204-1412)
PHONE................................315 234-2451
Steve Starrantino, *Vice Pres*
Frank Besio, *Manager*
Darren Otis, *Manager*
Bob Zywicki,
Jay Bernhardt,
EMP: 9
SALES: 1.8MM **Privately Held**
SIC: 3621 Motors & generators

(G-15952)
GEORGE RETZOS
Also Called: Columbus Baking Co
502 Pearl St (13203-1702)
PHONE................................315 422-2913
James Retzos, *Owner*
EMP: 5 EST: 1934
SALES (est): 457.5K **Privately Held**
SIC: 2051 Bread, all types (white, wheat, rye, etc): fresh or frozen

(G-15953)
GIOVANNI FOOD CO INC (PA)
6050 Court Street Rd (13206-1711)
PHONE................................315 463-7770
Mary Dement, *Chairman*
Louis J Dement, *Vice Pres*
Tim Budd, *Plant Mgr*
Richard G Latimer, *Plant Mgr*
John Dunn, *Production*
◆ EMP: 70
SQ FT: 25,000
SALES (est): 15.7MM **Privately Held**
WEB: www.giovannifoods.com
SIC: 2033 Tomato products: packaged in cans, jars, etc.

(G-15954)
GREENLEAF CABINET MAKERS LLC
6691 Pickard Dr (13211-2114)
PHONE................................315 432-4600
Gerard Davis, *Mng Member*
Kevin Davis, *Manager*
Dave Morrison, *Manager*
EMP: 10 EST: 2001
SQ FT: 3,000
SALES (est): 1.2MM **Privately Held**
SIC: 2541 Wood partitions & fixtures

(G-15955)
H C YOUNG TOOL & MACHINE CO
3700 New Court Ave (13206-1674)
PHONE................................315 463-0663
Fax: 315 463-0663
Gordon K Young, *President*
EMP: 5 EST: 1935
SQ FT: 1,000
SALES (est): 553K **Privately Held**
WEB: www.hcyoung.com
SIC: 3599 Machine shop, jobbing & repair

(G-15956)
HANGER PRSTHETCS & ORTHO INC
910 Erie Blvd E Ste 3 (13210-1060)
PHONE................................315 472-5200
Roy Ostrander, *Manager*
EMP: 5
SALES (corp-wide): 500.5MM **Privately Held**
SIC: 3842 Limbs, artificial
HQ: Hanger Prosthetics & Orthotics, Inc.
10910 Main Dr
Austin TX 78758
512 777-3800

(G-15957)
HARRISON BAKERY WEST
1306 W Genesee St (13204-2184)
PHONE................................315 422-1468
Fax: 315 422-4083
James Rothfeld, *President*
Michael Rothfeld, *Vice Pres*
EMP: 30
SQ FT: 15,000
SALES (est): 5.2MM **Privately Held**
SIC: 2051 5461 Bread, all types (white, wheat, rye, etc): fresh or frozen; cakes, bakery: except frozen; doughnuts, except frozen; bread; cakes; doughnuts

(G-15958)
HART RIFLE BARREL INC
1680 Jamesville Ave (13210-4236)
P.O. Box 182, La Fayette (13084-0182)
PHONE................................315 677-9841
Fax: 315 677-9610
Jack Sutton, *Partner*
James Hart, *Partner*
EMP: 7 EST: 1955
SQ FT: 2,000
SALES: 750K **Privately Held**
WEB: www.hartbarrels.com
SIC: 3484 Rifles or rifle parts, 30 mm. & below

(G-15959)
HERALD NEWSPAPERS COMPANY INC (DH)
Also Called: Herald Journal, The
220 S Warren St (13202-1676)
PHONE................................315 470-0011
Fax: 315 470-3030
Tim Kennedy, *President*
Steve Billmyer, *Editor*
Don Cazentre, *Editor*
Mike Grogan, *Editor*
Toni Guidice, *Editor*
EMP: 612
SQ FT: 50,000
SALES (est): 383.8MM
SALES (corp-wide): 322.5MM **Privately Held**
WEB: www.post-standard.com
SIC: 2711 Newspapers, publishing & printing

(G-15960)
HOLISTIC BLENDS INC
6726 Townline Rd Stop 1 (13211-1915)
PHONE................................315 468-4300
Sherry Brescia, *President*
EMP: 8
SALES (est): 892.9K **Privately Held**
SIC: 2834 Vitamin, nutrient & hematinic preparations for human use

(G-15961)
HY-GRADE METAL PRODUCTS CORP
906 Burnet Ave (13203-3206)
PHONE................................315 475-4221
Fax: 315 472-3101
Michael Donegan, *President*
EMP: 7 EST: 1918
SQ FT: 10,000
SALES (est): 495K **Privately Held**
WEB: www.hy-grademetal.com
SIC: 3469 Spinning metal for the trade

(G-15962)
INDEPENDENT FIELD SVC LLC (PA)
6744 Pickard Dr (13211-2115)
PHONE................................315 559-9243
Aaron Barbaro, *Owner*
EMP: 6
SQ FT: 8,000
SALES (est): 1.2MM **Privately Held**
SIC: 3621 Power generators

(G-15963)
INGLIS CO INC
116 Granger St (13202-2315)
P.O. Box 401, Manlius (13104-0401)
PHONE................................315 475-1315
Kenneth Abramson, *President*
Anthony River, *Vice Pres*
EMP: 7
SQ FT: 5,000
SALES (est): 772.6K **Privately Held**
SIC: 2893 2851 5084 Printing ink; paints & paint additives; lacquers, varnishes, enamels & other coatings; removers & cleaners; paint spray equipment, industrial

(G-15964)
J & J PRINTING INC (PA)
500 Cambridge Ave (13208-1415)
PHONE................................315 458-7411
Fax: 315 454-0912
Matthew Joseph Farr, *President*
Charlie Dalley, *General Mgr*
Betty Farr, *Vice Pres*
EMP: 8 EST: 1969
SQ FT: 3,000
SALES (est): 799.8K **Privately Held**
SIC: 2752 Commercial printing, offset

(G-15965)
JACOBS WOODWORKING LLC
801 W Fayette St (13204-2805)
PHONE................................315 427-8999
Jacob Gerros, *Mng Member*
EMP: 7
SALES (est): 632.5K **Privately Held**
SIC: 2431 Millwork

(G-15966)
JAQUITH INDUSTRIES INC
600 E Brighton Ave (13210-4248)
P.O. Box 780 (13205-0780)
PHONE................................315 478-5700
Fax: 315 478-5707
D Scott Jaquith, *President*
Rob Loughlin, *General Mgr*
Bill Schai, *VP Sales*
Mark Peck, *Manager*
Richard Parks, *CTO*
◆ EMP: 50
SQ FT: 120,000
SALES: 10.1MM **Privately Held**
WEB: www.jaquith.com
SIC: 3312 3648 3728 3444 Blast furnaces & steel mills; lighting equipment; aircraft parts & equipment; sheet metal-work; fabricated plate work (boiler shop); manufactured hardware (general)

(G-15967)
JOHN A EBERLY INC
136 Beattie St (13224-1102)
P.O. Box 8047 (13217-8047)
PHONE................................315 449-3034
John Lee, *President*
EMP: 7
SQ FT: 6,000
SALES (est): 1.1MM **Privately Held**
WEB: www.jaeberly.com
SIC: 3421 5084 Scissors, shears, clippers, snips & similar tools; textile machinery & equipment

(G-15968)
JOHN F KRELL JR
Also Called: Syracuse Hvac
4046 W Seneca Trpk (13215)
PHONE................................315 492-3201
John F Krell, *Partner*
Andrew Krell, *Partner*
EMP: 5
SALES (est): 440K **Privately Held**
SIC: 3585 Heating & air conditioning combination units

(G-15969)
JOHNSTON DANDY COMPANY
Cook, E F Co
100 Dippold Ave (13208-1320)
PHONE................................315 455-5773
Fax: 315 454-9357
Michael Myers, *General Mgr*
Donald Wilson, *Purch Mgr*
Don Wilson, *Purchasing*
Kimberly Pinkham, *Controller*
EMP: 7
SQ FT: 12,540
SALES (corp-wide): 6.7MM **Privately Held**
WEB: www.johnstondandy.com
SIC: 3547 3554 Rolling mill machinery; paper industries machinery
PA: Johnston Dandy Company
148 Main St
Lincoln ME 04457
207 794-6571

(G-15970)
JORDON BOX COMPANY INC
Also Called: Jordan Box Co
140 Dickerson St (13202-2309)
P.O. Box 1054 (13201-1054)
PHONE................................315 422-3419
Fax: 315 422-0318
Rick Casper, *President*
EMP: 20
SQ FT: 30,000
SALES: 700K **Privately Held**
WEB: www.jordanboxco.com
SIC: 2652 Setup paperboard boxes

▲ = Import ▼ = Export
◆ = Import/Export

GEOGRAPHIC SECTION

Syracuse - Onondaga County (G-15994)

(G-15971)
JPW STRUCTURAL CONTRACTING INC
Also Called: Jpw Riggers & Erectors
6376 Thompson Rd (13206-1406)
PHONE..................................315 432-1111
Fax: 315 432-8202
John P Wozniczka III, *Ch of Bd*
Patricia Wozniczka, *Corp Secy*
Jeffery Exner, *Vice Pres*
Jody Wozniczka, *Vice Pres*
Jody Wozniczka, *Opers Mgr*
EMP: 25
SQ FT: 70,000
SALES (est): 9.2MM **Privately Held**
SIC: 3441 Fabricated structural metal

(G-15972)
K&G OF SYRACUSE INC
2500 Erie Blvd E (13224-1110)
PHONE..................................315 446-1921
Karamjit Grewal, *Principal*
EMP: 5
SALES (est): 526.1K **Privately Held**
SIC: 3578 Automatic teller machines (ATM)

(G-15973)
KILIAN MANUFACTURING CORP (HQ)
1728 Burnet Ave (13206-3340)
P.O. Box 6974 (13217-6974)
PHONE..................................315 432-0700
Fax: 315 432-1312
Michael L Hurt, *Ch of Bd*
Christopher H Lake, *President*
William Duff, *General Mgr*
Lorenzo Spinelli, *Plant Mgr*
Keith Austin, *Purchasing*
▲ EMP: 100 EST: 1921
SQ FT: 100,000
SALES (est): 79.8MM
SALES (corp-wide): 746.6MM **Publicly Held**
SIC: 3562 3429 Ball bearings & parts; manufactured hardware (general)
PA: Altra Industrial Motion Corp.
300 Granite St Ste 201
Braintree MA 02184
781 917-0600

(G-15974)
KINANECO INC (PA)
Also Called: Kinaneco Printing Systems
2925 Milton Ave (13209-2519)
PHONE..................................315 468-6201
Fax: 315 468-6202
Greg Kinane, *Chairman*
Peter T Kinane, *Chairman*
Paul Manganiello, *Office Mgr*
EMP: 20 EST: 1973
SQ FT: 6,000
SALES (est): 4MM **Privately Held**
WEB: www.kinaneco.com
SIC: 2752 2759 2754 7311 Commercial printing, offset; business forms: printing; color printing, gravure; advertising agencies

(G-15975)
KNISE & KRICK INC
324 Pearl St (13203-1998)
PHONE..................................315 422-3516
Fax: 315 422-3594
John P Extrom, *President*
Terry Bunch, *Vice Pres*
EMP: 20 EST: 1926
SQ FT: 30,000
SALES (est): 3.7MM **Privately Held**
WEB: www.knisekrick.com
SIC: 3544 Jigs & fixtures

(G-15976)
LEMOYNE MACHINE PRODUCTS CORP
106 Evelyn Ter (13208-1321)
PHONE..................................315 454-0708
Marvin Kisselstein, *President*
Robert Grandinetti, *Vice Pres*
EMP: 5
SQ FT: 5,000
SALES (est): 643.1K **Privately Held**
SIC: 3562 Ball & roller bearings

(G-15977)
LIBERTY FOOD AND FUEL
1131 N Salina St (13208-2027)
PHONE..................................315 299-4039
Anwa Nagnaji, *Manager*
EMP: 6
SALES (est): 803.6K **Privately Held**
SIC: 2869 Fuels

(G-15978)
LIFT SAFE - FUEL SAFE INC
212 W Seneca Tpke (13205-2709)
PHONE..................................315 423-7702
Daniel Sorber, *CEO*
EMP: 10
SALES (est): 1.4MM **Privately Held**
SIC: 2869 Fuels

(G-15979)
LINDE GAS NORTH AMERICA LLC
Also Called: Lifegas
147 Midler Park Dr (13206-1817)
PHONE..................................315 431-4081
Fax: 315 431-4082
Richard Kelley, *Branch Mgr*
Dick Kelly, *Manager*
EMP: 19
SALES (corp-wide): 19.2B **Privately Held**
SIC: 2813 Nitrogen; oxygen, compressed or liquefied
HQ: Linde Gas North America Llc
575 Mountain Ave
New Providence NJ 07974
908 464-8100

(G-15980)
LOCKHEED MARTIN CORPORATION
6060 Tarbell Rd (13206-1301)
PHONE..................................315 456-6604
Mark Schmidt, *Branch Mgr*
EMP: 45
SALES (corp-wide): 46.1B **Publicly Held**
WEB: www.lockheedmartin.com
SIC: 3812 Sonar systems & equipment; radar systems & equipment
PA: Lockheed Martin Corporation
6801 Rockledge Dr
Bethesda MD 20817
301 897-6000

(G-15981)
LOCKHEED MARTIN INTEGRATED
497 Electronics Pkwy (13221)
P.O. Box 4840 (13221-4840)
PHONE..................................315 456-3333
Richard J Masi, *President*
Kenneth George, *Personnel Exec*
Ronald Pacini, *Info Tech Dir*
Keith Speidel, *Technical Staff*
David Svendsen, *Data Proc Exec*
EMP: 26
SALES (corp-wide): 46.1B **Publicly Held**
SIC: 3577 Data conversion equipment, media-to-media: computer
HQ: Lockheed Martin Integrated Systems, Inc.
6801 Rockledge Dr
Bethesda MD 20817
856 486-5000

(G-15982)
LOUIS IANNETTONI
1841 Lemoyne Ave (13208-1328)
PHONE..................................315 454-3231
Louis Iannettoni, *Owner*
Jim Iannettoni, *Vice Pres*
EMP: 65
SALES (est): 4.5MM **Privately Held**
SIC: 3363 Aluminum die-castings

(G-15983)
M & W ALUMINUM PRODUCTS INC
321 Wavel St (13206-1726)
PHONE..................................315 414-0005
Uriah P Montclair, *President*
EMP: 16
SQ FT: 12,330
SALES (est): 2.7MM **Privately Held**
WEB: www.mwalum.com
SIC: 3465 Body parts, automobile: stamped metal

(G-15984)
MATT INDUSTRIES INC (PA)
Also Called: Grphics Grafek
6761 Thompson Rd (13211-2119)
P.O. Box 11500 (13218-1500)
PHONE..................................315 472-1316
J Kemper Matt, *President*
David Martin, *Division Mgr*
Thomas Booth, *Vice Pres*
John Mather, *Vice Pres*
J Kemper Matt Jr, *Vice Pres*
EMP: 120
SQ FT: 150,000
SALES (est): 32MM **Privately Held**
SIC: 2759 5112 Envelopes: printing; envelopes

(G-15985)
MELOON FOUNDRIES LLC
1841 Lemoyne Ave (13208-1389)
PHONE..................................315 454-3231
Fax: 315 454-8559
Robert Evans, *President*
Raymond King, *Division Mgr*
Cecelia Bleich, *Office Mgr*
EMP: 42
SQ FT: 90,000
SALES (est): 10.5MM
SALES (corp-wide): 23.3MM **Privately Held**
SIC: 3365 3366 3291 Aluminum foundries; copper foundries; brass foundry; bronze foundry; abrasive products
HQ: Evans Industries, Inc.
200 Rnmiance Ctr Ste 3150
Detroit MI 48243
313 259-2266

(G-15986)
METALICO ALUMINUM RECOVERY INC
6223 Thompson Rd (13206-1405)
P.O. Box 88, East Syracuse (13057-0088)
PHONE..................................315 463-9292
Fax: 315 463-9290
Carlos E Aguero, *President*
Dennis Flanagan, *General Mgr*
Michael J Drury, *COO*
Arnold S Graber, *Exec VP*
David Delbianco, *Vice Pres*
▲ EMP: 40
SALES (est): 14.2MM
SALES (corp-wide): 476MM **Privately Held**
SIC: 3341 5093 Aluminum smelting & refining (secondary); scrap & waste materials
PA: Metalico, Inc.
135 Dermody St
Cranford NJ 07016
908 497-9610

(G-15987)
MIDDLE AGES BREWING COMPANY
120 Wilkinson St Ste 3 (13204-2490)
PHONE..................................315 476-4250
Fax: 315 476-4264
Mary Rubenstein, *President*
Marc Rubenstein, *Treasurer*
▲ EMP: 6
SQ FT: 10,000
SALES (est): 450K **Privately Held**
SIC: 2082 Beer (alcoholic beverage)

(G-15988)
MIDGLEY PRINTING CORP
433 W Onondaga St Ste B (13202-3277)
PHONE..................................315 475-1864
Fax: 315 475-8325
Lena Midgley, *President*
David Midgley, *Vice Pres*
Robert Midgley, *Vice Pres*
Walter Midgley, *Vice Pres*
John Midgley, *Treasurer*
EMP: 9 EST: 1955
SQ FT: 10,000
SALES (est): 830K **Privately Held**
SIC: 2752 2759 2791 2789 Commercial printing, lithographic; letterpress printing; typesetting; bookbinding & related work

(G-15989)
MIDSTATE PRINTING CORP
230 Ainsley Dr (13210-4203)
PHONE..................................315 475-4101
Fax: 315 475-5129
John Williams III, *Ch of Bd*
Bob Williams, *Vice Pres*
Robert Williams, *Vice Pres*
Thomas Keehfus, *CFO*
Lynn Wilber, *Sales Staff*
EMP: 49
SQ FT: 28,000
SALES (est): 12.9MM **Privately Held**
WEB: www.midstateprinting.com
SIC: 2752 Commercial printing, offset

(G-15990)
MIDSTATE SPRING INC
Also Called: Syracuse Midstate Spring
4054 New Court Ave (13206-1639)
P.O. Box 850 (13206-0850)
PHONE..................................315 437-2623
Fax: 315 437-0796
Walter Melnikow, *President*
John Kirby, *General Mgr*
Paul S Bernet, *Vice Pres*
Richard Raus, *Plant Mgr*
Keith Miller, *Opers Staff*
▲ EMP: 41
SQ FT: 13,000
SALES (est): 10MM **Privately Held**
WEB: www.midstatespring.com
SIC: 3493 3495 Steel springs, except wire; wire springs

(G-15991)
MINIMILL TECHNOLOGIES INC
5792 Widewaters Pkwy # 1 (13214-1847)
PHONE..................................315 692-4557
Kamala G Rajan, *President*
Joseph Gasperetti, *Senior VP*
Srinivasan Balaji, *Vice Pres*
Donnie Parks, *Vice Pres*
George Rice, *Vice Pres*
EMP: 14
SALES: 6MM **Privately Held**
SIC: 2621 Paper mills

(G-15992)
MITTEN MANUFACTURING INC
5960 Court Street Rd (13206-1706)
PHONE..................................315 437-7564
John P Mitten Jr, *CEO*
Jack Mitten, *Principal*
Ron Pfaff, *Systs Engr*
Tim Reiss, *Manager*
EMP: 40
SALES (est): 5.2MM **Privately Held**
SIC: 3999 Atomizers, toiletry

(G-15993)
MONAGHAN MEDICAL CORPORATION
Also Called: Sales & Marketing Office
327 W Fayette St Ste 212 (13202-1331)
PHONE..................................315 472-2136
Michael Amato, *Vice Pres*
EMP: 8
SALES (corp-wide): 11.7MM **Privately Held**
WEB: www.monaghanmed.com
SIC: 3842 Respiratory protection equipment, personal
PA: Monaghan Medical Corporation
5 Latour Ave Ste 1600
Plattsburgh NY 12901
518 561-7330

(G-15994)
MUENCH-KREUZER CANDLE COMPANY (PA)
Also Called: Emkay Candle Company
617 Hiawatha Blvd E (13208-1228)
PHONE..................................315 471-4515
Fax: 315 471-4581
John P Brogan, *Ch of Bd*
Shawn Lynch, *Purchasing*
Greg Kiesinger, *VP Mktg*
▲ EMP: 80
SQ FT: 100,000
SALES (est): 9.9MM **Privately Held**
WEB: www.emkaycandle.com
SIC: 3999 Candles

Syracuse - Onondaga County (G-15995) — GEOGRAPHIC SECTION

(G-15995)
MUZET INC
104 S Main St (13212-3104)
PHONE...............................315 452-0050
Fax: 315 452-1996
Frank Crawford, *Manager*
EMP: 10
SALES (corp-wide): 2.4MM **Privately Held**
SIC: 3931 Musical instruments
PA: Muzet Inc
   219 W Commercial St
   East Rochester NY 14445
   585 586-5320

(G-15996)
N E CONTROLS LLC
7048 Interstate Island Rd (13209-9712)
PHONE...............................315 626-2480
Evan Weaver, *Engineer*
Harvey Stone, *VP Sales*
Brad Stone-Sales, *Sales Mgr*
Al Weaver,
Herb Smith,
EMP: 12
SQ FT: 6,000
SALES: 950K **Privately Held**
WEB: www.necontrols.com
SIC: 3625 5084 Control equipment, electric; industrial machinery & equipment

(G-15997)
NEPTUNE SOFT WATER INC
1201 E Fayette St Ste 6 (13210-1896)
PHONE...............................315 446-5151
Fax: 315 445-9094
William Olivieri, *President*
EMP: 15 EST: 1963
SQ FT: 4,500
SALES (est): 2.4MM **Privately Held**
SIC: 3589 5999 5074 Water treatment equipment, industrial; water purification equipment, household type; water purification equipment; water purification equipment

(G-15998)
NEW YORK MARKING DEVICES CORP (PA)
Also Called: Jessel Marking Equipment
2207 Teall Ave (13206-1544)
P.O. Box 234 (13206-0234)
PHONE...............................315 463-8641
Fax: 315 463-8363
Joseph L Stummer Jr, *President*
Amy Stummer, *Vice Pres*
Ellen Stummer, *Vice Pres*
Peter J Stummer, *Vice Pres*
Nick Posiko, *Director*
EMP: 7
SQ FT: 7,800
SALES: 2.5MM **Privately Held**
WEB: www.nymarking.com
SIC: 3953 Marking devices

(G-15999)
NOLL REYNOLDS MET FABRICATION
554 E Brighton Ave Ste 1 (13210-4265)
PHONE...............................315 422-3333
Kurt Noll, *Owner*
Tarren Reynolds, *Principal*
EMP: 7
SALES: 750K **Privately Held**
SIC: 3499 Furniture parts, metal

(G-16000)
NOVANTA INC
Also Called: Photo Research
7279 William Barry Blvd (13212-3349)
PHONE...............................818 341-5151
EMP: 24
SALES (corp-wide): 373.6MM **Publicly Held**
SIC: 3827 Optical instruments & lenses
PA: Novanta Inc.
   125 Middlesex Tpke
   Bedford MA 01730
   781 266-5700

(G-16001)
OBERDORFER PUMPS INC
5900 Firestone Dr (13206-1103)
PHONE...............................315 437-0361
Fax: 315 463-9561
Kevin Digney, *CEO*
Timothy C Brown, *President*
Phillip J Stuecker, *Vice Pres*
EMP: 43
SQ FT: 46,000
SALES (est): 10.1MM
SALES (corp-wide): 2.1B **Privately Held**
WEB: www.oberdorfer-pumps.com
SIC: 3561 Pumps & pumping equipment; industrial pumps & parts
HQ: Gardner Denver, Inc.
   222 E Erie St Ste 500
   Milwaukee WI 53202
   414 212-4700

(G-16002)
OESTREICH METAL WORKS INC
6131 Court Street Rd (13206-1302)
PHONE...............................315 463-4268
Fax: 315 463-4459
Steve Tallman, *President*
EMP: 5
SQ FT: 4,000
SALES (est): 580.1K **Privately Held**
SIC: 3564 Blowing fans: industrial or commercial; ventilating fans: industrial or commercial; exhaust fans: industrial or commercial

(G-16003)
OMEGA FURNITURE MANUFACTURING
102 Wavel St (13206-1303)
PHONE...............................315 463-7428
Fax: 315 463-8740
George Sakellariou, *President*
EMP: 12
SQ FT: 10,000
SALES: 600K **Privately Held**
WEB: www.omegafmi.com
SIC: 2521 5712 Wood office furniture; furniture stores

(G-16004)
ONEIDA AIR SYSTEMS INC
1001 W Fayette St Ste 2a (13204-2873)
PHONE...............................315 476-5151
Fax: 315 476-5044
Robert Witter, *President*
Jen McManus, *Controller*
Jeffrey Hill, *Manager*
▼ EMP: 50
SQ FT: 60,000
SALES (est): 13.3MM **Privately Held**
WEB: www.oneida-air.com
SIC: 3553 3564 Woodworking machinery; purification & dust collection equipment

(G-16005)
OPTOGENICS OF SYRACUSE INC
2840 Erie Blvd E (13224-1304)
P.O. Box 4894 (13221-4894)
PHONE...............................315 446-3000
Fax: 315 446-5742
Robert Cotran, *President*
Ronald Cotran, *Vice Pres*
Sheri Niedens, *Human Res Mgr*
EMP: 85
SQ FT: 7,000
SALES (est): 11MM
SALES (corp-wide): 88.1MM **Privately Held**
WEB: www.optogenics.com
SIC: 3851 Eyeglasses, lenses & frames
HQ: Essilor Of America, Inc.
   13555 N Stemmons Fwy
   Dallas TX 75234
   214 496-4000

(G-16006)
P C I PAPER CONVERSIONS INC (PA)
3584 Walters Rd (13209-9700)
PHONE...............................315 437-1641
Fax: 315 437-3634
Lloyd M Withers, *President*
Darcy Lewis, *General Mgr*
Matthew Withers, *Vice Pres*
Raymond Ryan, *Treasurer*
Cynthia Callahan, *Controller*
▲ EMP: 120 EST: 1973
SQ FT: 121,500
SALES (est): 27.1MM **Privately Held**
WEB: www.riverleaf.com
SIC: 2679 2678 2672 Paper products, converted; stationery products; coated & laminated paper

(G-16007)
P C I PAPER CONVERSIONS INC
Stik-Withit Printworks
6761 Thompson Rd (13211-2119)
PHONE...............................315 703-8300
Howard Kaye, *Managing Dir*
EMP: 100
SALES (corp-wide): 27.1MM **Privately Held**
SIC: 2891 Adhesives & sealants
PA: P. C. I. Paper Conversions, Inc.
   3584 Walters Rd
   Syracuse NY 13209
   315 437-1641

(G-16008)
P C I PAPER CONVERSIONS INC
Coated Products Division
6761 Thompson Rd (13211-2119)
PHONE...............................315 634-3317
Howard Kaye, *Managing Dir*
Theresa Brown, *Mfg Mgr*
Tim Byrne, *Sales Mgr*
Al Amezaga, *Officer*
EMP: 25
SALES (corp-wide): 27.1MM **Privately Held**
SIC: 2891 Adhesives & sealants
PA: P. C. I. Paper Conversions, Inc.
   3584 Walters Rd
   Syracuse NY 13209
   315 437-1641

(G-16009)
P C I PAPER CONVERSIONS INC
Notes
6761 Thompson Rd (13211-2119)
PHONE...............................315 437-1641
EMP: 10
SALES (corp-wide): 27.1MM **Privately Held**
SIC: 2679 Novelties, paper: made from purchased material
PA: P. C. I. Paper Conversions, Inc.
   3584 Walters Rd
   Syracuse NY 13209
   315 437-1641

(G-16010)
PARATORE SIGNS INC
1551 Brewerton Rd (13208-1403)
PHONE...............................315 455-5551
Fax: 315 455-5920
John Paratore, *CEO*
Valoree Paratore, *VP Sls/Mktg*
Paige J Paratore, *Treasurer*
EMP: 6 EST: 1950
SQ FT: 13,000
SALES (est): 845.6K **Privately Held**
WEB: www.paratoresigns.com
SIC: 2759 7389 Screen printing; sign painting & lettering shop

(G-16011)
PASS & SEYMOUR INC (DH)
50 Boyd Ave (13209-2313)
P.O. Box 4822 (13221-4822)
PHONE...............................315 468-6211
Fax: 315 468-8388
Halsey Cook, *CEO*
Steve Schoffstall, *Principal*
Robert P Smith, *Exec VP*
Phil Leroux, *Senior VP*
Patrick Davin, *Vice Pres*
◆ EMP: 353 EST: 1901
SQ FT: 300,000
SALES (est): 333.8MM
SALES (corp-wide): 21.1MM **Privately Held**
WEB: www.passandseymour.com
SIC: 3643 5731 Current-carrying wiring devices; consumer electronic equipment
HQ: Legrand Holding, Inc.
   60 Woodlawn St
   West Hartford CT 06110
   860 233-6251

(G-16012)
PILKINGTON NORTH AMERICA INC
6412 Deere Rd Ste 1 (13206-1133)
PHONE...............................315 438-3341
EMP: 225
SALES (corp-wide): 5.3B **Privately Held**
SIC: 3211 Flat glass
HQ: Pilkington North America, Inc.
   811 Madison Ave Fl 1
   Toledo OH 43604
   419 247-4955

(G-16013)
PINOS PRESS INC
201 E Jefferson St (13202-2644)
PHONE...............................315 935-0110
Maria Marzocchi, *President*
Michael Marzocchi, *Vice Pres*
EMP: 6
SQ FT: 15,000
SALES: 467K **Privately Held**
SIC: 2079 Olive oil

(G-16014)
PRINTING PRMTNAL SOLUTIONS LLC
Also Called: Printing Promotional Solutions
2320 Milton Ave Ste 5 (13209-2197)
PHONE...............................315 474-1110
Todd Ruetsch,
EMP: 17
SALES (est): 2.9MM **Privately Held**
SIC: 2759 Commercial printing

(G-16015)
PRINTWORKS PRINTING & DESIGN
5982 E Molloy Rd (13211-2130)
PHONE...............................315 433-8587
Fax: 315 433-5102
Michael Kinsella, *President*
EMP: 5
SALES (est): 475K **Privately Held**
SIC: 2759 Commercial printing

(G-16016)
R K B OPTO-ELECTRONICS INC (PA)
6677 Moore Rd (13211-2112)
PHONE...............................315 455-6636
Fax: 315 455-8216
Bruce Dobbie, *President*
William Dobbie, *Chairman*
Sonhui Dobbie, *Purchasing*
Alex Fern Ndez, *Sales Dir*
Chris Wu, *Sales Dir*
EMP: 10
SQ FT: 12,500
SALES (est): 1.6MM **Privately Held**
WEB: www.rkbopto.com
SIC: 3823 3825 Industrial instrmnts msrmnt display/control process variable; instruments to measure electricity

(G-16017)
RAM FABRICATING LLC
412 Wavel St (13206-1728)
PHONE...............................315 437-6654
Charlie Meakin, *Vice Pres*
Brian Garrett, *QA Dir*
Mike Skowron, *Research*
Drew Lopitz, *Accounts Mgr*
Don Riggs, *Manager*
EMP: 30
SQ FT: 15,000
SALES (est): 7.2MM **Privately Held**
SIC: 3498 Tube fabricating (contract bending & shaping)

(G-16018)
RAULLI AND SONS INC (PA)
213 Teall Ave (13210-1291)
PHONE...............................315 479-6693
Fax: 315 479-5514
Richie Raulli, *President*
Paul Raulli, *Corp Secy*
Thomas Raulli, *Vice Pres*
Debbie Kuepper, *Manager*
EMP: 60
SQ FT: 40,000

▲ = Import ▼ = Export ◆ = Import/Export

GEOGRAPHIC SECTION

Syracuse - Onondaga County (G-16045)

SALES (est): 19.9MM **Privately Held**
WEB: www.raulliandsons.com
SIC: **3441** 3446 Fabricated structural metal; architectural metalwork; gates, ornamental metal; railings, prefabricated metal; stairs, staircases, stair treads: prefabricated metal

(G-16019)
RAULLI AND SONS INC
660 Burnet Ave (13203-2404)
PHONE................................315 474-1370
Fax: 315 478-4030
Dennis Raulli, *Manager*
EMP: 15
SQ FT: 9,276
SALES (corp-wide): 19.9MM **Privately Held**
WEB: www.raulliandsons.com
SIC: **3446** Stairs, staircases, stair treads: prefabricated metal
PA: Raulli And Sons, Inc.
   213 Teall Ave
   Syracuse NY 13210
   315 479-6693

(G-16020)
RAULLI AND SONS INC
920 Canal St (13210-1204)
PHONE................................315 479-2515
Joseph Ruscitto, *Branch Mgr*
EMP: 30
SALES (corp-wide): 19.9MM **Privately Held**
SIC: **3291** Abrasive metal & steel products
PA: Raulli And Sons, Inc.
   213 Teall Ave
   Syracuse NY 13210
   315 479-6693

(G-16021)
RB WOODCRAFT INC
1860 Erie Blvd E Ste 1 (13210-1255)
PHONE................................315 474-2429
Fax: 315 474-2734
Raymond A Brooks, *President*
Matthew Bush, *Engineer*
Dave Nicoll, *Engineer*
Joseph P McGlynn, *Human Res Dir*
EMP: 50
SQ FT: 40,000
SALES (est): 12.5MM **Privately Held**
WEB: www.rbwoodcraft.com
SIC: **2431** Millwork; interior & ornamental woodwork & trim

(G-16022)
REHABLITATION TECH OF SYRACUSE
Also Called: Rehab Tech
1101 Erie Blvd E Ste 209 (13210-1144)
PHONE................................315 426-9920
Michael T Hall, *President*
Theresa Hall, *Vice Pres*
EMP: 5
SQ FT: 3,000
SALES (est): 692.7K **Privately Held**
SIC: **3842** Orthopedic appliances; prosthetic appliances

(G-16023)
REVONATE MANUFACTURING LLC
7401 Round Pond Rd (13212-2515)
PHONE................................315 433-1160
Jeff Purdy, *Controller*
Kevin P Conley,
EMP: 50
SALES (est): 553.2K **Privately Held**
SIC: **3571** Electronic computers

(G-16024)
ROBOSHOP INC
226 Midler Park Dr (13206-1819)
PHONE................................315 437-6454
Frank Giovinazzo, *President*
Matthew Eddy, *Vice Pres*
EMP: 7 EST: 1997
SQ FT: 4,500
SALES (est): 500K **Privately Held**
SIC: **3599** Custom machinery

(G-16025)
ROBS CYCLE SUPPLY
613 Wolf St (13208-1141)
PHONE................................315 292-6878
Robert Woodward, *President*
EMP: 9
SALES (est): 1MM **Privately Held**
SIC: **3751** Motorcycles & related parts

(G-16026)
ROTH GLOBAL PLASTICS INC
Also Called: Fralo
1 General Motors Dr (13206-1117)
P.O. Box 245 (13211-0245)
PHONE................................315 475-0100
Fax: 315 475-0200
Jochen Drewniok, *Ch of Bd*
Joseph Brown, *Senior VP*
Theresa Lauer, *Senior VP*
John Pezzi, *Vice Pres*
Linda Good, *Buyer*
▲ EMP: 20
SQ FT: 100,000
SALES (est): 5MM **Privately Held**
WEB: www.fralo.net
SIC: **3089** Septic tanks, plastic

(G-16027)
ROYAL ADHESIVES & SEALANTS LLC
Also Called: Advanced Polymers Intl
3584 Walters Rd Rsd (13209-9700)
PHONE................................315 451-1755
Fax: 315 451-9442
Ted Clark, *CEO*
EMP: 15
SALES (corp-wide): 547.6MM **Privately Held**
SIC: **2891** Adhesives & sealants
PA: Royal Adhesives And Sealants Llc
   2001 W Washington St
   South Bend IN 46628
   574 246-5000

(G-16028)
SAAKSHI INC
Also Called: North Salina Cigar Store
851 N Salina St (13208-2512)
PHONE................................315 475-3988
Fax: 315 426-1143
Jay Vave, *Principal*
EMP: 6
SALES (est): 914.8K **Privately Held**
SIC: **3999** Cigarette & cigar products & accessories

(G-16029)
SABRE ENTERPRISES INC
1813 Lemoyne Ave (13208-1328)
P.O. Box 68 (13211-0068)
PHONE................................315 430-3127
Bob Dumas, *President*
Gerald Vecchiarelli, *Vice Pres*
Scott Wilkinson, *Treasurer*
John White, *Admin Sec*
EMP: 7 EST: 2009
SQ FT: 10,000
SALES (est): 535.7K **Privately Held**
SIC: **3711** Snow plows (motor vehicles), assembly of

(G-16030)
SAGELIFE PARENTING LLC
Also Called: Sagemylife
235 Harrison St Ste 2 (13202-3119)
PHONE................................315 299-5713
Glenna Crooks, *CEO*
Nancy Bloeser, *General Mgr*
EMP: 5 EST: 2014
SQ FT: 34,000
SALES (est): 171.3K **Privately Held**
SIC: **2741**

(G-16031)
SANDYS BUMPER MART INC
120 Wall St (13204-2182)
PHONE................................315 472-8149
Sandor Bozo, *President*
Romana Bozo, *Vice Pres*
EMP: 7 EST: 1970
SQ FT: 10,500
SALES (est): 808.3K **Privately Held**
SIC: **3471** Electroplating of metals or formed products

(G-16032)
SCANCORP INC
1840 Lemoyne Ave (13208-1329)
PHONE................................315 454-5596
Fax: 315 454-8903
John Clement, *President*
Ole Westergaard, *Vice Pres*
Jody Coleman, *Manager*
EMP: 16
SQ FT: 35,000
SALES (est): 1.3MM **Privately Held**
WEB: www.scancorp.com
SIC: **2759** Promotional printing

(G-16033)
SCHILLING FORGE INC
606 Factory Ave (13208-1437)
PHONE................................315 454-4421
Fax: 315 455-8115
Brent A Driscoll, *CEO*
James E Stitt, *Ch of Bd*
Douglas S Pelsue, *President*
John W Whepley, *Corp Secy*
Linda Roby, *Controller*
▲ EMP: 26 EST: 1975
SQ FT: 30,000
SALES (est): 4MM
SALES (corp-wide): 155.4MM **Privately Held**
WEB: www.schillingforge.com
SIC: **3841** 3843 3462 3423 Surgical instruments & apparatus; dental equipment & supplies; iron & steel forgings; hand & edge tools; cutlery
PA: Cutco Corporation
   1116 E State St
   Olean NY 14760
   716 372-3111

(G-16034)
SCHNEIDER BROTHERS CORPORATION
7371 Eastman Rd (13212-2504)
PHONE................................315 458-8369
Fax: 315 458-0358
William D Schneider, *President*
Chris C Schneider, *Corp Secy*
Robert Schneider, *Vice Pres*
Julie Schneider, *Manager*
Joe T Timmons, *Manager*
EMP: 35
SQ FT: 11,000
SALES (est): 7.2MM **Privately Held**
SIC: **3441** Fabricated structural metal

(G-16035)
SCIENTIFIC TOOL CO INC (PA)
101 Arterial Rd (13206-1585)
PHONE................................315 431-4243
Fax: 315 431-4247
Duane Krull, *President*
Chuck Gorman, *President*
Dave Spies, *Vice Pres*
▲ EMP: 18
SQ FT: 16,000
SALES (est): 3.2MM **Privately Held**
SIC: **3599** Machine shop, jobbing & repair

(G-16036)
SEAL & DESIGN INC
Higbee Division
6741 Thompson Rd (13211-2119)
PHONE................................315 432-8021
EMP: 40
SALES (corp-wide): 40.6MM **Privately Held**
SIC: **3053** Gaskets & sealing devices
PA: Seal & Design Inc.
   4015 Casillio Pkwy
   Clarence NY 14031
   716 759-2222

(G-16037)
SELFLOCK SCREW PRODUCTS CO INC
Also Called: SSP
461 E Brighton Ave (13210-4143)
PHONE................................315 541-4464
Fax: 315 475-1093
David M Freund, *President*
Daniel H Kuhns, *Vice Pres*
EMP: 30 EST: 1920
SQ FT: 50,000
SALES (est): 8.1MM **Privately Held**
WEB: www.selflockscrew.com
SIC: **3451** 3541 Screw machine products; machine tools, metal cutting type

(G-16038)
SENECA SIGNS LLC
102 Headson Dr (13214-1102)
PHONE................................315 446-9420
Steve Warner, *Mng Member*
EMP: 7
SALES (est): 41.7K **Privately Held**
WEB: www.signartwork.com
SIC: **3993** Signs & advertising specialties

(G-16039)
SHARENET INC
920 Spencer St (13204-1243)
PHONE................................315 477-1100
Ray Davis, *President*
EMP: 6
SALES (est): 1.5MM **Privately Held**
SIC: **3578** Automatic teller machines (ATM)

(G-16040)
SHENFIELD STUDIO LLC
Also Called: Shenfeld Studio Tile
6361 Thompson Rd Stop 12 (13206-1412)
PHONE................................315 436-8869
Robert C Shenfeld, *Mng Member*
EMP: 10
SALES: 930K **Privately Held**
SIC: **3292** Floor tile, asphalt

(G-16041)
SIGN A RAMA OF SYRACUSE
Also Called: Sign-A-Rama
3060 Erie Blvd E Ste 1 (13224-1404)
PHONE................................315 446-9420
Steve Werner, *Partner*
EMP: 9
SALES (est): 740.9K **Privately Held**
SIC: **3993** Signs & advertising specialties

(G-16042)
SPAULDING LAW PRINTING INC
231 Walton St Ste 103 (13202-1230)
PHONE................................315 422-4805
Alexander Douglas, *President*
EMP: 3
SQ FT: 1,000
SALES: 1MM **Privately Held**
SIC: **2759** Commercial printing

(G-16043)
SPECIALTY WLDG & FABG NY INC (PA)
1025 Hiawatha Blvd E (13208-1359)
P.O. Box 145 (13211-0145)
PHONE................................315 426-1807
Fax: 315 426-1805
Michael P Murphy, *Ch of Bd*
Randal Stier, *President*
Jack Griffiths, *Vice Pres*
Bill Colclough, *Research*
Leslie McNeil, *Controller*
EMP: 61
SQ FT: 135,000
SALES (est): 26.3MM **Privately Held**
WEB: www.specweld.com
SIC: **3441** Fabricated structural metal

(G-16044)
SRCTEC LLC
Also Called: SRC Tec, Inc.
5801 E Taft Rd Ste 7 (13212-3273)
PHONE................................315 452-8700
Drew James, *President*
Deborah Sabella, *Treasurer*
Robert Young, *Accountant*
Dan Andress, *Info Tech Mgr*
Michele Nellenback, *Info Tech Mgr*
EMP: 150
SALES (est): 31.1MM
SALES (corp-wide): 153.2MM **Privately Held**
WEB: www.srctecinc.com
SIC: **3812** Antennas, radar or communications
PA: Src, Inc.
   7502 Round Pond Rd
   North Syracuse NY 13212
   315 452-8000

(G-16045)
STEPS PLUS INC
6375 Thompson Rd (13206-1495)
PHONE................................315 432-0885
Fax: 315 432-0612
Richard R Kopp, *Ch of Bd*

Syracuse - Onondaga County (G-16046)

Judy Taylor, *Vice Pres*
Robert H Kopp, *Treasurer*
Brian Deacan, *Manager*
Vitalie Donescu, *CTO*
EMP: 100
SQ FT: 18,000
SALES (est): 14.2MM **Privately Held**
WEB: www.steps-plus.com
SIC: 3446 Architectural metalwork

(G-16046)
STERI-PHARMA LLC
429 S West St (13202-2326)
PHONE...................................315 473-7180
Andrew Mather, *Prdtn Mgr*
Nick Walip, *Branch Mgr*
Yasser Alejo, *Manager*
John Connelly, *Senior Mgr*
Mark Sweeney, *Director*
EMP: 14
SQ FT: 775
SALES (corp-wide): 20MM **Privately Held**
WEB: www.hanford.com
SIC: 2834 Pharmaceutical preparations
PA: Steri-Pharma, Llc
    120 N State Rt 17
    Paramus NJ 07652
    201 857-8210

(G-16047)
SYRACO PRODUCTS INC
Also Called: Syracuse Stamping Company
1054 S Clinton St (13202-3409)
PHONE...................................800 581-5555
Fax: 315 474-8876
Fred V Honnold, *Ch of Bd*
Elizabeth Hartnett, *Treasurer*
Steve Qigley, *Finance Dir*
EMP: 40 EST: 1993
SQ FT: 103,000
SALES (est): 8.6MM **Privately Held**
WEB: www.syraco.com
SIC: 3429 3491 2655 Manufactured hardware (general); industrial valves; spools, fiber: made from purchased material

(G-16048)
SYRACUSE CASING CO INC
528 Erie Blvd W (13204-2423)
PHONE...................................315 475-0309
Fax: 315 475-8536
Peter Frey Jr, *President*
Christine Frey, *Corp Secy*
▲ EMP: 16
SQ FT: 150,000
SALES (est): 1.7MM **Privately Held**
SIC: 2013 Sausages & other prepared meats; prepared pork products from purchased pork

(G-16049)
SYRACUSE CATHOLIC PRESS ASSN
Also Called: Catholic Sun, The
421 S Warren St Fl 2 (13202-2640)
P.O. Box 511 (13201-0511)
PHONE...................................315 422-8153
Fax: 315 422-7549
Rev Donald Bourgeois, *Manager*
Doug Ross, *Manager*
L D Costanza, *Associate*
EMP: 6
SALES: 850K **Privately Held**
SIC: 2711 Newspapers

(G-16050)
SYRACUSE COMPUTER FORMS INC
Also Called: Hansen & Hansen Qulty Prtg Div
216 Burnet Ave (13203-2335)
P.O. Box 6761 (13217-6761)
PHONE...................................315 478-0108
Fax: 315 475-7234
Ted Hansen, *CEO*
Michael Hansen, *President*
Ric Clark, *Prdtn Mgr*
Toni Hansen, *Treasurer*
Mary Hansen, *Admin Sec*
EMP: 20
SQ FT: 38,172
SALES (est): 3.3MM **Privately Held**
WEB: www.hansenqp.com
SIC: 2761 2752 2796 2791 Computer forms, manifold or continuous; commercial printing, lithographic; commercial printing, offset; platemaking services; typesetting

(G-16051)
SYRACUSE CULTURAL WORKERS PRJ
400 Lodi St (13203-2069)
P.O. Box 6367 (13217-6367)
PHONE...................................315 474-1132
Fax: 315 475-1277
Teresa Florack, *Principal*
John Faley, *Business Mgr*
Marie Summerwood, *Mktg Coord*
Karen Kerney, *Director*
Dick Cool, *Co-Director*
▲ EMP: 10
SQ FT: 1,800
SALES (est): 780K **Privately Held**
WEB: www.syracuseculturalworkers.com
SIC: 2732 5961 Books: printing & binding; pamphlets: printing & binding, not published on site; books, mail order (except book clubs); mail order house

(G-16052)
SYRACUSE HEAT TREATING CORP
7055 Interstate Island Rd (13209-9750)
PHONE...................................315 451-0000
Fax: 315 451-3895
John H Mac Allister, *Ch of Bd*
George Stupp, *Vice Pres*
John Macallister, *CFO*
EMP: 23
SQ FT: 30,000
SALES (est): 6MM **Privately Held**
WEB: www.syracuseheattreating.com
SIC: 3398 Metal heat treating; brazing (hardening) of metal

(G-16053)
SYRACUSE INDUSTRIAL SLS CO LTD
1850 Lemoyne Ave (13208-1282)
PHONE...................................315 478-5751
Fax: 315 472-0855
EMP: 11
SQ FT: 4,500
SALES (est): 1.8MM **Privately Held**
SIC: 2431 5251 Mfg Millwork Ret Hardware

(G-16054)
SYRACUSE PROSTHETIC CENTER INC
1124 E Fayette St (13210-1922)
PHONE...................................315 476-9697
Fax: 315 476-9694
John Tyo, *President*
Sheila Harrington, *Vice Pres*
EMP: 5
SQ FT: 2,000
SALES (est): 500K **Privately Held**
WEB: www.cnyprocenter.com
SIC: 3842 Surgical appliances & supplies

(G-16055)
SYRACUSE UNIVERSITY PRESS INC
621 Skytop Rd Ste 110 (13244-0001)
PHONE...................................315 443-5534
Victoria Lane, *Design Engr*
Theresa A Litz, *Sls & Mktg Exec*
Enid Darby, *Supervisor*
Alice Pfeiffer, *Director*
Rosemary Rainbow, *Administration*
▲ EMP: 21
SALES (est): 2.4MM
SALES (corp-wide): 704.4MM **Privately Held**
SIC: 2731 Books: publishing only
PA: Syracuse University
    900 S Crouse Ave Ste 620
    Syracuse NY 13244
    315 443-1870

(G-16056)
TER-EL ENGRAVING CO INC
2611 Court St (13208-3292)
PHONE...................................315 455-5597
Fax: 315 455-8915
John Green, *President*
EMP: 5
SQ FT: 2,000
SALES (est): 360K **Privately Held**
SIC: 2759 7389 3479 5094 Screen printing; sign painting & lettering shop; engraving jewelry silverware, or metal; trophies; trophies & plaques

(G-16057)
TERRELLS POTATO CHIP CO INC
218 Midler Park Dr (13206-1819)
PHONE...................................315 437-2786
Fax: 315 437-2069
Jack Terrell, *President*
Jim Cashin, *Division Mgr*
Jane Kelsey, *Office Mgr*
Brenda Terrell, *Admin Sec*
EMP: 70 EST: 1946
SQ FT: 30,000
SALES (est): 12.2MM **Privately Held**
SIC: 2096 5145 Potato chips & other potato-based snacks; popcorn & supplies; pretzels; potato chips

(G-16058)
THERMOPATCH CORPORATION (PA)
2204 Erie Blvd E (13224-1100)
P.O. Box 8007 (13217-8007)
PHONE...................................315 446-8110
Fax: 315 445-8046
Tom Depuit, *Ch of Bd*
Edward Gublo, *Opers Staff*
Mark Matteson, *Production*
Vic Simons, *Purch Mgr*
E Zeltmann, *Research*
EMP: 100
SQ FT: 52,000
SALES (est): 34.5MM **Privately Held**
WEB: www.thermopatch.com
SIC: 3953 3582 7359 Figures (marking devices), metal; drycleaning equipment & machinery, commercial; laundry equipment leasing

(G-16059)
TOMPKINS SRM LLC
Also Called: Tomkins USA
623 Oneida St (13202-3414)
PHONE...................................315 422-8763
Mike Mosher, *General Mgr*
William Savage,
EMP: 6
SQ FT: 31,705
SALES (est): 1MM **Privately Held**
SIC: 3559 Sewing machines & attachments, industrial

(G-16060)
TONY BAIRD ELECTRONICS INC
407 S Warren St Ste 200 (13202-4772)
PHONE...................................315 422-4430
Tony Jeffrey Baird, *CEO*
Khaliph A Bey, *Manager*
Sal Damelio, *Manager*
Robert Leuzzi, *Manager*
B J Meltzie, *Manager*
EMP: 4
SQ FT: 1,060
SALES (est): 1.4MM **Privately Held**
WEB: tonybairdelectronics.com
SIC: 3679 5999 Harness assemblies for electronic use: wire or cable; liquid crystal displays (LCD); audio-visual equipment & supplies

(G-16061)
TRI KOLOR PRINTING & STY
1035 Montgomery St (13202-3507)
P.O. Box 669 (13201-0669)
PHONE...................................315 474-6753
Fax: 315 478-6723
Charles De Wolf, *Owner*
Shannon Brown, *Supervisor*
Jim Verrette, *Supervisor*
Mike Albanese, *Representative*
EMP: 10
SQ FT: 12,000
SALES: 580K **Privately Held**
SIC: 2752 2759 2791 7336 Commercial printing, offset; letterpress printing; typesetting; graphic arts & related design

(G-16062)
TV GUILFOIL & ASSOCIATES INC (PA)
121 Dwight Park Cir (13209-1005)
P.O. Box 187, Solvay (13209-0187)
PHONE...................................315 453-0920
Fax: 315 453-5091
Phillip H Allen III, *President*
Tim Allen, *Admin Sec*
▲ EMP: 7
SQ FT: 10,000
SALES (est): 816.6K **Privately Held**
WEB: www.tvguilfoil.com
SIC: 3999 Candles

(G-16063)
UNIMAR INC
3195 Vickery Rd (13212-4574)
PHONE...................................315 699-4400
Michael Marley, *President*
Beth Andrews, *General Mgr*
Thad Fink, *General Mgr*
Michelle Bovee, *Accountant*
Chris Phelps, *Sales Staff*
◆ EMP: 14
SQ FT: 21,000
SALES (est): 6.5MM **Privately Held**
SIC: 3625 5084 5063 Relays & industrial controls; controlling instruments & accessories; lighting fixtures, commercial & industrial

(G-16064)
UPSTATE PRINTING INC
433 W Onondaga St (13202-3209)
PHONE...................................315 475-6140
Fax: 315 475-0169
Jack Rotondo, *President*
Debi Rotondo, *Treasurer*
EMP: 14
SALES (est): 2.1MM **Privately Held**
SIC: 2752 Commercial printing, lithographic

(G-16065)
US BEVERAGE NET INC
225 W Jefferson St (13202-2457)
PHONE...................................315 579-2025
Mark Young, *President*
Sundar Ravindran, *Info Tech Dir*
Thomas Young, *Director*
EMP: 12
SALES (est): 1.2MM **Privately Held**
SIC: 3556 7371 Beverage machinery; custom computer programming services

(G-16066)
VEHICLE SAFETY DEPT
5801 E Taft Rd Ste 4 (13212-3273)
PHONE...................................315 458-6683
Fax: 315 458-8468
James Donnery, *Manager*
EMP: 18
SALES (est): 1.4MM **Privately Held**
SIC: 3714 Sanders, motor vehicle safety

(G-16067)
VERTEX INNOVATIVE SOLUTIONS IN
6671 Commerce Blvd (13211-2211)
PHONE...................................315 437-6711
Paul Snow, *Chairman*
Bill Roberge, *Sales Associate*
EMP: 22
SALES (est): 4MM **Privately Held**
SIC: 3648 Lighting equipment

(G-16068)
WARD SALES CO INC
1117 W Fayette St Ste 1 (13204-2733)
PHONE...................................315 476-5276
Fax: 315 476-2056
Richard Hayko, *President*
Joseph Hayko, *Vice Pres*
EMP: 6 EST: 1939
SQ FT: 30,000
SALES (est): 648.6K **Privately Held**
WEB: www.wardsalescompany.com
SIC: 2261 3953 3942 5199 Screen printing of cotton broadwoven fabrics; screens, textile printing; stuffed toys, including animals; advertising specialties

GEOGRAPHIC SECTION

(G-16069)
WEATHER PRODUCTS CORPORATION
Also Called: Dynamic Pak
102 W Division St Fl 1 (13204-1456)
PHONE.................................315 474-8593
Fax: 315 474-8795
W Davies Birchenough Jr, *Ch of Bd*
Herman Garcia, *Vice Pres*
EMP: 8
SQ FT: 30,000
SALES (est): 1.4MM **Privately Held**
SIC: 3089 7389 Thermoformed finished plastic products; packaging & labeling services; labeling bottles, cans, cartons, etc.

(G-16070)
WESTROCK - SOLVAY LLC (DH)
53 Indl Dr (13204)
PHONE.................................315 484-9050
Fax: 315 484-9434
Peter Tantalo, *General Mgr*
Tom Stigers, *Vice Pres*
George Turner, *Vice Pres*
Matt Wadach, *Purch Mgr*
Cris Machano, *Controller*
▲ **EMP:** 150
SQ FT: 300,000
SALES (est): 78.1MM
SALES (corp-wide): 11.3B **Publicly Held**
WEB: www.solvaypaperboard.com
SIC: 2631 Container board
HQ: Westrock Rkt Company
504 Thrasher St
Norcross GA 30071
770 448-2193

(G-16071)
WESTROCK CP LLC
53 Industrial Dr (13204-1035)
PHONE.................................315 484-9050
EMP: 86
SALES (corp-wide): 11.3B **Publicly Held**
SIC: 2631 Container board
HQ: Westrock Cp, Llc
504 Thrasher St
Norcross GA 30071

(G-16072)
WESTROCK RKT COMPANY
53 Indl Dr (13204)
PHONE.................................770 448-2193
Jeff Locke, *Opers Mgr*
Diana Gardner, *Purch Mgr*
Matthew Wadach, *Purch Mgr*
Robert Murphy, *Engineer*
Peter Tantalo, *Human Res Mgr*
EMP: 162
SALES (corp-wide): 11.3B **Publicly Held**
WEB: www.rocktenn.com
SIC: 2631 Folding boxboard
HQ: Westrock Rkt Company
504 Thrasher St
Norcross GA 30071
770 448-2193

(G-16073)
WIZARD EQUIPMENT INC
Also Called: Bob's Signs
10 Dwight Park Dr Ste 3 (13209-1098)
PHONE.................................315 414-9999
Bob Reilly, *President*
Robert Barnes, *Vice Pres*
EMP: 5
SALES: 200K **Privately Held**
SIC: 3993 Signs & advertising specialties

(G-16074)
WOLFF & DUNGEY INC
325 Temple St (13202-3417)
P.O. Box 3673 (13220-3673)
PHONE.................................315 475-2105
Fax: 315 475-8369
Maurice Birchmeyer, *CEO*
Charles M Reschke, *Vice Pres*
John Birchmeyer, *Admin Sec*
EMP: 30
SQ FT: 20,000
SALES (est): 4.5MM **Privately Held**
SIC: 3365 3543 Aluminum foundries; industrial patterns

(G-16075)
WOOD ETC INC
1175 State Fair Blvd # 3 (13209-1082)
PHONE.................................315 484-9663
Fax: 315 484-9098
Kathleen Schmidt, *President*
Arnold Schmidt, *Vice Pres*
Jesse Schmidt, *Vice Pres*
EMP: 18
SQ FT: 30,000
SALES (est): 2.4MM **Privately Held**
SIC: 2521 2599 2434 Cabinets, office: wood; cabinets, factory; wood kitchen cabinets

Taberg
Oneida County

(G-16076)
TYCO SIMPLEXGRINNELL
4057 Wilson Rd E (13471-2037)
PHONE.................................315 337-6333
EMP: 92
SALES (corp-wide): 954.1MM **Privately Held**
SIC: 3569 Sprinkler systems, fire: automatic
PA: Tyco Simplexgrinnell
1501 Nw 51st St
Boca Raton FL 33431
561 988-3658

Tallman
Rockland County

(G-16077)
KRAMARTRON PRECISION INC
2 Spook Rock Rd Unit 107 (10982)
PHONE.................................845 368-3668
Brian Kramer, *President*
EMP: 5 **EST:** 1974
SQ FT: 3,000
SALES: 500K **Privately Held**
SIC: 3599 Machine shop, jobbing & repair

Tappan
Rockland County

(G-16078)
AG TECH WELDING CORP
238 Oak Tree Rd (10983-2812)
PHONE.................................845 398-0005
Martin De Joia, *President*
Agnes De Joia, *Corp Secy*
EMP: 6
SQ FT: 5,000
SALES (est): 52K **Privately Held**
SIC: 3599 1799 Machine shop, jobbing & repair; welding on site

(G-16079)
CARIBBEAN FOODS DELIGHT INC
117 Route 303 Ste B (10983-2136)
PHONE.................................845 398-3000
Fax: 845 398-3001
Vincent Hosang, *President*
Jeanette Hosang, *Vice Pres*
Raquel Pasquel, *Safety Mgr*
Raquel Pascual, *Purch Dir*
Sheila Desir, *Purch Agent*
◆ **EMP:** 80
SQ FT: 100,000
SALES (est): 17.5MM **Privately Held**
WEB: www.caribbeanfoodsdelights.com
SIC: 2013 2011 Frozen meats from purchased meat; meat packing plants

(G-16080)
EN TECH CORP
375 Western Hwy (10983-1317)
PHONE.................................845 398-0776
EMP: 10
SALES (corp-wide): 6.4MM **Privately Held**
SIC: 3321 Gray & ductile iron foundries

PA: En Tech Corp
91 Ruckman Rd
Closter NJ 07624
718 389-2058

(G-16081)
NATIONWIDE CUSTOM SERVICES
Also Called: Custom Studio Division
77 Main St (10983-2400)
PHONE.................................845 365-0414
Fax: 845 365-0864
Norman Shaifer, *President*
Helen Newman, *Vice Pres*
Grant Venneo, *Manager*
EMP: 8 **EST:** 1961
SQ FT: 2,000
SALES (est): 590K **Privately Held**
SIC: 2731 8661 Books: publishing & printing; religious organizations

(G-16082)
PULMUONE FOODS USA INC
30 Rockland Park Ave (10983-2629)
PHONE.................................845 365-3300
Fax: 845 365-3311
Chang Hwang, *Branch Mgr*
Christine Lee, *Manager*
EMP: 25
SALES (corp-wide): 50.6MM **Privately Held**
SIC: 2024 Tofu desserts, frozen
HQ: Pulmuone Foods Usa, Inc.
2315 Moore Ave
Fullerton CA 92833
714 578-2800

(G-16083)
RJ HARVEY INSTRUMENT CORP
Also Called: Romark Diagnostics
11 Jane St (10983-2503)
PHONE.................................845 359-3943
Fax: 845 359-0264
Robert Maines, *President*
Angelo D'Imperio, *Vice Pres*
EMP: 10
SQ FT: 3,600
SALES (est): 940K **Privately Held**
WEB: www.rjharveyinst.com
SIC: 3841 3829 Diagnostic apparatus, medical; measuring & controlling devices

Tarrytown
Westchester County

(G-16084)
AEROLASE CORPORATION
777 Old Saw Mill River Rd # 2 (10591-6700)
PHONE.................................914 345-8300
Pavel Efremkin, *CEO*
Joseph Hurley, *COO*
Ryan McFadden, *Project Engr*
Jennifer Edson, *Sales Mgr*
Kim Asack, *Regl Sales Mgr*
EMP: 100
SQ FT: 3,000
SALES (est): 14.8MM **Privately Held**
WEB: www.friendlylight.com
SIC: 3841 Surgical lasers

(G-16085)
ALPHA-EN CORPORATION (PA)
120 White Plains Rd (10591-5526)
PHONE.................................914 418-2000
Jerry I Feldman, *Ch of Bd*
Steven M Payne, *President*
George McKeegan, *Exec VP*
Emilie Bodoin, *Director*
EMP: 14 **EST:** 1997
SQ FT: 4,000
SALES (est): 593.4K **Publicly Held**
SIC: 2819 6794 Lithium compounds, inorganic; patent buying, licensing, leasing

(G-16086)
AMPACET CORPORATION (PA)
660 White Plains Rd # 360 (10591-5171)
PHONE.................................914 631-6600
Fax: 914 631-0556
Robert A Defalco, *Ch of Bd*
Giuseppe Giusto, *General Mgr*
Alvaro Mendoza, *General Mgr*
Tom Phiffer, *Business Mgr*
Howard England, *Senior VP*
◆ **EMP:** 948
SQ FT: 36,000
SALES (est): 619.7MM **Privately Held**
WEB: www.ampacet.com
SIC: 3087 Custom compound purchased resins

(G-16087)
BASF CORPORATION
540 White Plains Rd (10591-5103)
P.O. Box 2005 (10591-9005)
PHONE.................................914 785-2000
Stephen Zlock, *Business Mgr*
Loretta Czereeki, *Vice Pres*
Eric Finkelman, *Vice Pres*
Linda Repaci, *Vice Pres*
John Murnane, *Safety Dir*
EMP: 400
SALES (corp-wide): 75.6B **Privately Held**
WEB: www.cibasc.com
SIC: 2869 2819 2899 2843 Industrial organic chemicals; industrial inorganic chemicals; antifreeze compounds; surface active agents; pharmaceutical preparations; vitamin preparations; agricultural chemicals
HQ: Basf Corporation
100 Park Ave
Florham Park NJ 07932
973 245-6000

(G-16088)
BASF CORPORATION
560 White Plains Rd (10591-5113)
PHONE.................................973 245-6000
Stefan Koenig, *Branch Mgr*
EMP: 5
SALES (corp-wide): 75.6B **Privately Held**
WEB: www.cibasc.com
SIC: 2819 Industrial inorganic chemicals
HQ: Basf Corporation
100 Park Ave
Florham Park NJ 07932
973 245-6000

(G-16089)
CROSS BORDER TRANSACTIONS LLC
4 Emerald Woods (10591-6236)
PHONE.................................914 631-0878
Donald Scherer, *CEO*
EMP: 5 **EST:** 2015
SALES (est): 117.2K **Privately Held**
SIC: 7372 Business oriented computer software

(G-16090)
FOSECO INC
777 Old Saw Mill River Rd (10591-6717)
PHONE.................................914 345-4760
EMP: 10
SALES (corp-wide): 2.3B **Privately Held**
SIC: 2899 3569 Mfg Exorterneic Compunds Fluxes And Ceramic Filters
HQ: Foseco, Inc.
20200 Sheldon Rd
Cleveland OH 44142
440 826-4548

(G-16091)
INNOWAVE RF LLC
520 White Plains Rd (10591-5102)
PHONE.................................914 230-4060
Kartik Jayaraman, *CEO*
Priya Ravisekar, *President*
Archana RAO, *Director*
EMP: 5
SALES (est): 600.2K **Privately Held**
SIC: 3679 Microwave components

(G-16092)
ITALMATCH USA CORPORATION
660 White Plains Rd # 510 (10591-5187)
PHONE.................................732 383-8309
Foort De Jong, *CEO*
▲ **EMP:** 12
SQ FT: 1,600
SALES: 22MM **Privately Held**
SIC: 2899 Chemical preparations
HQ: Italmatch Chemicals Spa
Via Pietro Chiesa 7/13
Genova GE 16149
010 642-081

(PA)=Parent Co (HQ)=Headquarters (DH)=Div Headquarters
✪ = New Business established in last 2 years

Tarrytown - Westchester County (G-16093)

(G-16093)
KRAFT HEINZ FOODS COMPANY
555 S Broadway (10591-6301)
PHONE..................914 335-2500
Fax: 914 335-8968
Jean Spence, *Vice Pres*
Ruben Desai, *Opers Staff*
Ralph Warren, *Opers Staff*
Kristin Mooney, *Senior Engr*
Stella Marinelli, *Manager*
EMP: 610
SALES (corp-wide): 210.8B **Publicly Held**
WEB: www.kraftfoods.com
SIC: 2099 2095 2086 2043 Food preparations; roasted coffee; bottled & canned soft drinks; cereal breakfast foods
HQ: Heinz Kraft Foods Company
1 Ppg Pl Ste 3200
Pittsburgh PA 15222
412 456-5700

(G-16094)
MAIN STREET SWEETS
35 Main St (10591-3627)
PHONE..................914 332-5757
Merlina Bertolacci, *Partner*
EMP: 10 **EST:** 2008
SALES (est): 520K **Privately Held**
SIC: 2024 Ice cream & frozen desserts

(G-16095)
MARSHALL CAVENDISH CORP
Also Called: Benchmark Books
99 White Plains Rd (10591-5502)
PHONE..................914 332-8888
Fax: 914 332-1082
Richard Farley, *President*
Mindy Pang, *Editor*
Dovan Chia, *Sales Executive*
Benedict Boo, *Manager*
Lee C Peng, *Info Tech Mgr*
▲ **EMP:** 40
SQ FT: 30,000
SALES (est): 4.9MM
SALES (corp-wide): 1.5B **Privately Held**
WEB: www.marshallcavendish.com
SIC: 2731 Books: publishing only
HQ: Marshall Cavendish Limited
32-38 Saffron Hill
London

(G-16096)
MEDTECH PRODUCTS INC (HQ)
Also Called: New Skin
660 White Plains Rd (10591-5139)
PHONE..................914 524-6810
Matthew Mannelly, *President*
Timothy J Connors, *Exec VP*
Jean A Boyko PHD, *Senior VP*
John Parkinson, *Senior VP*
Samuel C Cowley, *Vice Pres*
▲ **EMP:** 16
SQ FT: 7,000
SALES (est): 25.3MM
SALES (corp-wide): 806.2MM **Publicly Held**
SIC: 2841 2834 Soap & other detergents; pharmaceutical preparations
PA: Prestige Brands Holdings, Inc.
660 White Plains Rd
Tarrytown NY 10591
914 524-6800

(G-16097)
MICRO POWDERS INC (PA)
Also Called: M P I
580 White Plains Rd # 400 (10591-5198)
PHONE..................914 332-6400
Fax: 914 332-6093
James Strauss, *President*
Phyllis Strauss, *Admin Sec*
◆ **EMP:** 26
SQ FT: 2,500
SALES (est): 8.1MM **Privately Held**
WEB: www.micropowders.com
SIC: 3952 3555 2899 2893 Wax, artists'; printing trades machinery; chemical preparations; printing ink; cyclic crudes & intermediates; specialty cleaning, polishes & sanitation goods

(G-16098)
MOMENTIVE PERFORMANCE MTLS INC
Also Called: OSI Specialties
769 Old Saw Mill River Rd (10591-6732)
PHONE..................914 784-4807
Michael Pigeon, *Manager*
EMP: 80
SALES (corp-wide): 2.2B **Privately Held**
WEB: www.gewaterford.com
SIC: 2843 2099 2821 8731 Surface active agents; emulsifiers, food; plastics materials & resins; commercial physical research; chemical preparations
HQ: Momentive Performance Materials Inc.
260 Hudson River Rd
Waterford NY 12188
518 237-3330

(G-16099)
OPEN-XCHANGE INC
303 S Broadway Ste 224 (10591-5410)
P.O. Box 143, Ardsley On Hudson (10503-0143)
PHONE..................914 332-5720
Richard Seibt, *Ch of Bd*
Rafael Laguna, *President*
Carsten Dirks, *COO*
Robert Krulcik, *Senior VP*
Monika Schroeder, *CFO*
EMP: 10
SALES (est): 798K **Privately Held**
SIC: 2741 Guides: publishing & printing

(G-16100)
POLICY ADM SOLUTIONS INC
505 White Plains Rd (10591-5101)
PHONE..................914 332-4320
Peter Pantelides, *President*
EMP: 45
SALES (est): 7.5MM **Privately Held**
SIC: 3571 Mainframe computers

(G-16101)
PRESTIGE BRANDS HOLDINGS INC (PA)
660 White Plains Rd (10591-5139)
PHONE..................914 524-6800
Ronald M Lombardi, *President*
Timothy J Connors, *Exec VP*
Jean A Boyko, *Senior VP*
Christopher Heye, *Senior VP*
John F Parkinson, *Senior VP*
EMP: 65
SALES: 806.2MM **Publicly Held**
SIC: 2834 2841 Pharmaceutical preparations; soap & other detergents; detergents, synthetic organic or inorganic alkaline

(G-16102)
RAUCH INDUSTRIES INC
828 S Broadway (10591-6600)
PHONE..................704 867-5333
Bruce Charbeck, *Branch Mgr*
EMP: 36
SALES (corp-wide): 62.6MM **Privately Held**
SIC: 3231 Christmas tree ornaments: made from purchased glass
PA: Rauch Industries, Inc.
2408 Forbes Rd
Gastonia NC 28056
704 867-5333

(G-16103)
REGENERON PHARMACEUTICALS INC (PA)
777 Old Saw Mill River Rd # 10 (10591-6707)
PHONE..................914 847-7000
Fax: 914 345-7544
P Roy Vagelos, *Ch of Bd*
Leonard S Schleifer, *President*
Neil Stahl, *Exec VP*
Michael Aberman, *Senior VP*
Joseph J Larosa, *Senior VP*
EMP: 277
SQ FT: 1,108,000
SALES: 4.1B **Publicly Held**
WEB: www.regeneron.com
SIC: 2834 Pharmaceutical preparations

(G-16104)
REGENRON HLTHCARE SLUTIONS INC
745 Old Saw Mill River Rd (10591-6701)
PHONE..................914 847-7000
Robert Terifay, *General Mgr*
David Robinson, *Vice Pres*
Melissa Giliberti, *Systems Staff*
Joseph Larosa, *Admin Sec*
EMP: 603
SALES (est): 14.4MM **Privately Held**
SIC: 2834 Pharmaceutical preparations

(G-16105)
SIEMENS HLTHCARE DGNOSTICS INC
511 Benedict Ave (10591-5005)
PHONE..................914 631-0475
Timothy Adams, *Director*
EMP: 39
SALES (corp-wide): 83.5B **Privately Held**
WEB: www.dpcweb.com
SIC: 2835 8734 In vitro & in vivo diagnostic substances; veterinary diagnostic substances; forensic laboratory
HQ: Siemens Healthcare Diagnostics Inc.
511 Benedict Ave
Tarrytown NY 10591
914 631-8000

(G-16106)
SNEAKY CHEF FOODS LLC
520 White Plains Rd (10591-5102)
PHONE..................914 301-3277
Missy Chase Lapine, *CEO*
Craig Herman, *Publisher*
Helen Spanjer, *COO*
Laurence Chase, *Vice Pres*
▲ **EMP:** 10 **EST:** 2012
SALES (est): 1MM **Privately Held**
SIC: 2033 2099 Spaghetti & other pasta sauce: packaged in cans, jars, etc.; peanut butter

(G-16107)
SPIC AND SPAN COMPANY
660 White Plains Rd (10591-5191)
PHONE..................914 524-6823
Matthew M Mannelly, *CEO*
Mark Pettie, *Ch of Bd*
Peter Anderson, *CFO*
Harris Semegram, *Director*
EMP: 12 **EST:** 2000
SQ FT: 6,000
SALES (est): 2.5MM
SALES (corp-wide): 806.2MM **Publicly Held**
SIC: 2842 Cleaning or polishing preparations
PA: Prestige Brands Holdings, Inc.
660 White Plains Rd
Tarrytown NY 10591
914 524-6800

(G-16108)
TARRYTOWN BAKERY INC
150 Wildey St (10591-2910)
PHONE..................914 631-0209
Michael J Birrittella, *President*
EMP: 10
SQ FT: 5,000
SALES (est): 996.1K **Privately Held**
WEB: www.plazaview.com
SIC: 2051 5461 Bread, all types (white, wheat, rye, etc): fresh or frozen; bakeries

(G-16109)
TRADEPAQ CORPORATION
220 White Plains Rd # 360 (10591-7800)
PHONE..................914 332-9174
Elena Serova, *Technical Mgr*
Donald Gross, *Branch Mgr*
EMP: 11
SALES (corp-wide): 6MM **Privately Held**
WEB: www.tradepaq.com
SIC: 7372 Prepackaged software
PA: Tradepaq Corporation
33 Maiden Ln Fl 8
New York NY

(G-16110)
VALAD ELECTRIC HEATING CORP
160 Wildey St Ste 1 (10591-2915)
P.O. Box 577 (10591-0577)
PHONE..................914 631-4927
Fax: 845 634-4395
Arthur Cecchini, *Ch of Bd*
Lauren Cecchini, *Corp Secy*
Arthur Cecchini Jr, *Vice Pres*
Tim James, *Production*
Lauren Cecchini Janes, *Treasurer*
EMP: 12 **EST:** 1941
SQ FT: 35,000
SALES (est): 3.1MM **Privately Held**
WEB: www.valadelectric.com
SIC: 3634 Heaters, space electric; electric household cooking appliances

(G-16111)
VALID ELECTRIC CORP
160 Wildey St Ste 1 (10591-2915)
P.O. Box 577 (10591-0577)
PHONE..................914 631-9436
Arthur L Cecchini, *President*
Arthur Cechini, *President*
EMP: 25 **EST:** 1981
SALES (est): 2.8MM **Privately Held**
SIC: 3634 Heaters, space electric; electric household cooking appliances

(G-16112)
YES DENTAL LABORATORY INC
155 White Plains Rd # 223 (10591-5523)
PHONE..................914 333-7550
Robin Michaels, *President*
Evan Krouse, *Vice Pres*
Karen Lariccia, *Controller*
Irving Maldonado, *Master*
EMP: 25
SALES (est): 3.6MM **Privately Held**
SIC: 3843 Teeth, artificial (not made in dental laboratories)

(G-16113)
ZIP-JACK INDUSTRIES LTD
Also Called: Zip Jack Custom Umbrellas
73 Carrollwood Dr (10591-5210)
PHONE..................914 592-2000
Fax: 914 592-3023
Emanuel Dubinsky, *President*
Martha Dubinsky, *Vice Pres*
Charlotte L Dubinsky, *Treasurer*
▲ **EMP:** 25 **EST:** 1950
SQ FT: 20,000
SALES (est): 2MM **Privately Held**
WEB: www.zipjack.com
SIC: 3999 5699 Garden umbrellas; umbrellas

Thiells
Rockland County

(G-16114)
STEEL TECH SA LLC
7 Hillside Dr (10984-1431)
P.O. Box 361 (10984-0361)
PHONE..................845 786-3691
Allen Klein,
EMP: 5
SALES: 430K **Privately Held**
SIC: 3441 Fabricated structural metal

Thompsonville
Sullivan County

(G-16115)
MONTICELLO BLACK TOP CORP
80 Patio Dr (12784)
P.O. Box 95 (12784-0095)
PHONE..................845 434-7280
Joseph Gottlieb, *President*
EMP: 5 **EST:** 1964
SQ FT: 4,000
SALES (est): 729.9K **Privately Held**
SIC: 2951 5032 Concrete, asphaltic (not from refineries); sand, construction; gravel

▲ = Import ▼ = Export
◆ = Import/Export

Thornwood
Westchester County

(G-16116)
AUTOMATED CONTROL LOGIC INC
Also Called: Acl
578 Commerce St (10594-1327)
PHONE 914 769-8880
Fax: 203 769-2753
Preston Bruenn, *President*
EMP: 12
SALES (est): 3.4MM **Privately Held**
WEB: www.automatedcontrollogic.com
SIC: 3674 3825 1711 Solid state electronic devices; test equipment for electronic & electrical circuits; heating & air conditioning contractors

(G-16117)
CARL ZEISS INC (DH)
1 Zeiss Dr (10594-1996)
P.O. Box 5943, New York (10087-5943)
PHONE 914 747-1800
Fax: 914 681-7409
Cheryl Sarli, *President*
Edward Mancini, *Managing Dir*
Dr Michael Kaschke, *Principal*
Bernd Ayernschmalz, *Editor*
Kenner Eric, *Business Mgr*
▲ **EMP:** 120
SQ FT: 124,000
SALES (est): 319.5MM **Privately Held**
SIC: 3827 5049 3829 5084 Optical instruments & apparatus; optical goods; measuring & controlling devices; instruments & control equipment; analytical instruments
HQ: Carl Zeiss Ag
Carl-Zeiss-Str. 22
Oberkochen 73447
736 420-0

(G-16118)
COMMERCE OFFSET LTD
657 Commerce St (10594-1399)
PHONE 914 769-6671
Fax: 914 769-7845
EMP: 5
SQ FT: 8,400
SALES (est): 540K **Privately Held**
SIC: 2752 Lithographic Commercial Printing

(G-16119)
DIRECT OIL LLC
10 Saint Charles Dr Ste 9 (10594-1055)
PHONE 914 495-3073
Gloria Ferraro, *Owner*
EMP: 5
SALES (est): 464.6K **Privately Held**
SIC: 1389 Oil field services

(G-16120)
FENBAR PRCISION MACHINISTS INC
633 Commerce St (10594-1302)
PHONE 914 769-5506
Fax: 914 769-5602
Leonard Vallender, *President*
Gloria Vallender, *Corp Secy*
Mike Allen, *Plant Mgr*
Louanne Gambino, *Manager*
EMP: 18
SQ FT: 6,500
SALES (est): 3.3MM **Privately Held**
WEB: www.fenbar.com
SIC: 3599 Machine shop, jobbing & repair

(G-16121)
HOUGHTON MIFFLIN HARCOURT PUBG
28 Claremont Ave (10594-1042)
PHONE 914 747-2709
Glenn Polin, *Owner*
EMP: 124
SALES (corp-wide): 1.4B **Publicly Held**
WEB: www.hmco.com
SIC: 2731 Books: publishing only
HQ: Houghton Mifflin Harcourt Publishing Company
222 Berkeley St
Boston MA 02116
617 351-5000

(G-16122)
THORNWOOD PRODUCTS LTD
Also Called: All Star Fabricators
401 Claremont Ave Ste 7 (10594-1038)
PHONE 914 769-9161
Fax: 914 747-4038
Les Vissers, *President*
Peter Cuneo, *Vice Pres*
EMP: 30
SALES (est): 3.7MM **Privately Held**
SIC: 2599 1799 Cabinets, factory; counter top installation

Three Mile Bay
Jefferson County

(G-16123)
ST LAWRENCE LUMBER INC
27140 County Route 57 (13693-7205)
PHONE 315 649-2990
Gregory L Hoppel, *President*
Julie Hoppel, *Vice Pres*
EMP: 7
SALES: 1MM **Privately Held**
WEB: www.stlawrencelumber.com
SIC: 2421 Sawmills & planing mills, general

Ticonderoga
Essex County

(G-16124)
ADIRONDACK MEAT COMPANY INC
30 Commerce Dr (12883-3823)
PHONE 518 585-2333
Peter Ward, *President*
Denise Ward, *Vice Pres*
Joshua Titus, *Office Mgr*
Taylor Ward, *Asst Mgr*
EMP: 13 **EST:** 2012
SALES (est): 1.9MM **Privately Held**
SIC: 2011 2013 Hides, cured or uncured: from carcasses slaughtered on site; sausages & other prepared meats

(G-16125)
ADIRONDACK WASTE MGT INC
Also Called: Adirondack Sanitary Service
963 New York State 9n (12883)
PHONE 518 585-2224
Fax: 518 585-2224
R D Seargent Condit, *President*
Cindy Condit, *Vice Pres*
Doran Rockhill, *Treasurer*
EMP: 7
SQ FT: 1,000
SALES: 300K **Privately Held**
SIC: 2842 Sanitation preparations

(G-16126)
INTERNATIONAL PAPER COMPANY
568 Shore Airport Rd (12883-2890)
PHONE 518 585-6761
Fax: 518 585-5358
Kevin Harkonen, *Plant Mgr*
Eugene Fox, *Engineer*
Chris Mallon, *Branch Mgr*
Joseph Hooker, *Manager*
Calvin Staudt, *Systems Mgr*
EMP: 650
SQ FT: 1,920
SALES (corp-wide): 22.3B **Publicly Held**
WEB: www.internationalpaper.com
SIC: 2621 Paper mills
PA: International Paper Company
6400 Poplar Ave
Memphis TN 38197
901 419-9000

(G-16127)
LIBBYS BAKERY CAFE LLC
92 Montcalm St (12883-1352)
P.O. Box 61 (12883-0061)
PHONE 603 918-8825
Andrew Rasmus, *Principal*
Claire Brown, *Principal*
Katherine Lewis, *Principal*
EMP: 5
SALES (est): 381K **Privately Held**
SIC: 2051 Cakes, pies & pastries

(G-16128)
SPECIALTY MINERALS INC
35 Highland St (12883-1520)
PHONE 518 585-7982
Fax: 518 585-7930
Elaine Bertrand, *General Mgr*
Robert Dorr, *Plant Mgr*
EMP: 6
SALES (corp-wide): 1.8B **Publicly Held**
WEB: www.specialtyminerals.com
SIC: 2819 Industrial inorganic chemicals
HQ: Specialty Minerals Inc.
622 3rd Ave Fl 38
New York NY 10017
212 878-1800

(G-16129)
TICONDEROGA MCH & WLDG CORP
55 Race Track Rd (12883-4003)
PHONE 518 585-7444
EMP: 5 **EST:** 1954
SQ FT: 980
SALES (est): 36.3K **Privately Held**
SIC: 3599 Machine Shop

Tillson
Ulster County

(G-16130)
WINERACKSCOM INC
819 Route 32 (12486-1724)
PHONE 845 658-7181
Michael Babcock, *President*
Howard Babcock, *Vice Pres*
Shannon Rahe, *Manager*
EMP: 26 **EST:** 1990
SQ FT: 20,000
SALES (est): 4.1MM **Privately Held**
SIC: 2541 Wood partitions & fixtures

Tomkins Cove
Rockland County

(G-16131)
TILCON NEW YORK INC
Fort Of Elm (10986)
P.O. Box 217 (10986-0217)
PHONE 845 942-0602
Rich Moon, *Superintendent*
Nathalie Boboshko, *Credit Mgr*
EMP: 22
SQ FT: 2,184
SALES (corp-wide): 25.3B **Privately Held**
WEB: www.tilconny.com
SIC: 1442 Sand mining; gravel & pebble mining
HQ: Tilcon New York Inc.
162 Old Mill Rd
West Nyack NY 10994
845 358-4500

Tonawanda
Erie County

(G-16132)
3M COMPANY
305 Sawyer Ave (14150-7718)
PHONE 716 876-1596
Douglas Lane, *Plant Mgr*
Roy Zimmerman, *Plant Mgr*
Ed Pietti, *Foreman/Supr*
Doug Diemert, *Engineer*
Kathren Kaspar, *Project Engr*
EMP: 400
SALES (corp-wide): 30.2B **Publicly Held**
WEB: www.mmm.com
SIC: 3089 2823 Sponges, plastic; cellulosic manmade fibers
PA: 3m Company
3m Center Bldg 22011w02
Saint Paul MN 55144
651 733-1110

(G-16133)
54321 US INC (DH)
295 Fire Tower Dr (14150-5833)
PHONE 716 695-0258
Morris Goodman, *President*
Ted Wise, *Treasurer*
▲ **EMP:** 10
SALES (est): 1.8MM
SALES (corp-wide): 268.4MM **Privately Held**
WEB: www.54321answer.com
SIC: 3842 Sponges, surgical; surgical appliances & supplies
HQ: Pharmascience Inc
6111 Av Royalmount Bureau 100
Montreal QC H4P 2
514 340-1114

(G-16134)
ACE SPECIALTY CO INC
695 Ensminger Rd (14150-6698)
PHONE 716 874-3670
Fax: 716 876-7418
Patrick J Allen, *President*
Patti Post, *Office Mgr*
EMP: 9 **EST:** 1947
SQ FT: 25,000
SALES: 1.1MM **Privately Held**
WEB: www.acespecialtycompany.com
SIC: 3544 Special dies & tools

(G-16135)
ADAMS SFC INC (HQ)
225 E Park Dr (14150-7813)
P.O. Box 963, Buffalo (14240-0963)
PHONE 716 877-2608
Jack H Berg, *President*
Scott Kroon, *Research*
Paul Macpherson, *Engineer*
Michael Cataffo, *Regl Sales Mgr*
Serge Arutunjan, *Executive*
▲ **EMP:** 40
SQ FT: 39,152
SALES (est): 5.9MM
SALES (corp-wide): 47MM **Privately Held**
WEB: www.pacerpumps.com
SIC: 3569 3563 Filters, general line: industrial; vacuum (air extraction) systems, industrial
PA: Service Filtration Corp.
2900 Macarthur Blvd
Northbrook IL 60062
847 509-2900

(G-16136)
AIRSYS TECHNOLOGIES LLC
79 Fillmore Ave (14150-2335)
PHONE 716 694-6390
Michael Burns,
Ted Arts,
John Richmond,
EMP: 6
SALES: 3MM **Privately Held**
SIC: 3677 3585 Filtration devices, electronic; heating & air conditioning combination units

(G-16137)
ALRY TOOL AND DIE CO INC
386 Fillmore Ave (14150-2417)
P.O. Box 43 (14151-0043)
PHONE 716 693-2419
Fax: 716 693-5971
Michael J Allen, *President*
Daniel T Allen, *Corp Secy*
Francis D Allen Jr, *Vice Pres*
Thomas Allen, *Vice Pres*
Patricia King, *Manager*
EMP: 20 **EST:** 1944
SQ FT: 23,500
SALES (est): 2.3MM **Privately Held**
WEB: www.alry.com
SIC: 3462 3544 Machinery forgings, ferrous; dies & die holders for metal cutting, forming, die casting

Tonawanda - Erie County (G-16138)

(G-16138)
AMERICAN SECURITIES LLC
Also Called: Fiberfrax Manufacturing
330 Fire Tower Dr (14150-5834)
PHONE...................................716 696-3012
EMP: 50 Publicly Held
SIC: 3297 3299 3296 Nonclay refractories; ceramic fiber; mineral wool
PA: American Securities Llc
  299 Park Ave Fl 34
  New York NY 10171

(G-16139)
ANDERSON EQUIPMENT COMPANY
2140 Military Rd (14150-6002)
PHONE...................................716 877-1992
David McDermott, Inv Control Mgr
Don Geis, Financial Exec
John Park, Manager
John Zappia, Info Tech Dir
EMP: 70
SALES (corp-wide): 101.4MM Privately Held
SIC: 3531 Construction machinery
PA: Anderson Equipment Company
  1000 Washington Pike
  Bridgeville PA 15017
  412 343-2300

(G-16140)
ARROW GRINDING INC
525 Vicke St Tonaw Ctr (14150)
PHONE...................................716 693-3333
John C Goller, President
Kathy Goller, Corp Secy
EMP: 25
SQ FT: 25,000
SALES (est): 4.1MM Privately Held
SIC: 3599 Machine shop, jobbing & repair

(G-16141)
AVANTI U S A LTD
412 Young St (14150-4037)
PHONE...................................716 695-5800
Fax: 716 695-0855
G J Caruso, Principal
Gregory J Van Norman, Vice Pres
A P Caruso, Controller
EMP: 15
SQ FT: 4,863
SALES (est): 1.4MM Privately Held
SIC: 3842 2386 3089 Surgical appliances & supplies; garments, leather; injection molding of plastics

(G-16142)
AWNINGS PLUS INC
363 Delaware St (14150-3951)
PHONE...................................716 693-3690
Fax: 716 693-3767
Dan R Gagliardo, President
EMP: 15
SQ FT: 20,000
SALES (est): 1.1MM Privately Held
WEB: www.awningsplus.com
SIC: 2394 1799 Awnings, fabric: made from purchased materials; awning installation

(G-16143)
B & W HEAT TREATING COMPANY
2780 Kenmore Ave (14150-7775)
PHONE...................................716 876-8184
Clifford Calvello, President
EMP: 8
SQ FT: 14,000
SALES (est): 1.3MM Privately Held
SIC: 3398 3471 Metal heat treating; cleaning, polishing & finishing

(G-16144)
BCO INDUSTRIES WESTERN NY INC
77 Oriskany Dr (14150-6722)
P.O. Box 100 (14151-0100)
PHONE...................................716 877-2800
Janet Soltzman, President
Douglas Saltzman, President
Theresa Subsara, Bookkeeper
EMP: 31
SALES (est): 4.5MM Privately Held
WEB: www.bcoworld.com
SIC: 2759 2791 Thermography; visiting cards (including business): printing; facsimile letters: printing; stationery: printing; typesetting

(G-16145)
BIMBO BAKERIES USA INC
Also Called: Best Foods Baking Group
1960 Niagara Falls Blvd (14150-5542)
PHONE...................................716 692-9140
Catherine E Irish, Branch Mgr
EMP: 5
SALES (corp-wide): 13B Privately Held
WEB: www.gwbakeries.com
SIC: 2051 Bread, cake & related products
HQ: Bimbo Bakeries Usa, Inc
  255 Business Center Dr # 200
  Horsham PA 19044
  215 347-5500

(G-16146)
BONCRAFT INC
777 E Park Dr (14150-6708)
PHONE...................................716 662-9720
Fax: 716 662-9578
Timothy Bubar, CEO
James Bubar Jr, President
Bryan McMullen, Prdtn Mgr
Mike Ruda, Maint Spvr
Robert Reis, Opers Staff
EMP: 75 EST: 1952
SQ FT: 20,400
SALES (est): 9.3MM Privately Held
WEB: www.boncraft.com
SIC: 2752 2791 2789 Commercial printing, lithographic; typesetting; bookbinding & related work

(G-16147)
BOULEVARD PRINTING
1330 Niagara Falls Blvd # 2 (14150-8900)
PHONE...................................716 837-3800
Fax: 716 837-0500
John Battistella, Owner
EMP: 6
SALES (est): 620.2K Privately Held
SIC: 2752 Commercial printing, lithographic

(G-16148)
BRIGHTON TOOL & DIE DESIGNERS (PA)
Also Called: Brighton Design
463 Brighton Rd (14150-6966)
PHONE...................................716 876-0879
Fax: 716 876-8341
Chris Banas, President
Chris Eanas, President
EMP: 15
SQ FT: 2,000
SALES (est): 1.7MM Privately Held
SIC: 3544 Special dies & tools

(G-16149)
BROTHERS-IN-LAWN PROPERTY
176 Vulcan (14150)
PHONE...................................716 279-6191
EMP: 9 EST: 2012
SALES (est): 783.8K Privately Held
SIC: 3711 0781 Snow plows (motor vehicles), assembly of; landscape services

(G-16150)
BULOW & ASSOCIATES INC
317 Wheeler St (14150-3828)
P.O. Box 35 (14151-0035)
PHONE...................................716 838-0298
Fax: 716 838-0299
William A Bulow, President
William A Bulow, President
Dennis Wilcox, Vice Pres
Neal Wilcox, Admin Sec
EMP: 5
SALES: 100K Privately Held
SIC: 3993 Signs & advertising specialties

(G-16151)
CENTRAL REDE SIGN CO INC
317 Wheeler St (14150-3828)
PHONE...................................716 213-0797
Neal Wilcox, Principal
EMP: 5
SALES (est): 776.1K Privately Held
SIC: 3993 Signs & advertising specialties

(G-16152)
CENTRISOURCE INC
777 E Park Dr (14150-6708)
PHONE...................................716 871-1105
Fax: 716 505-4354
David Zenger, President
Joseph Zenger, Treasurer
EMP: 5
SALES (est): 440K Privately Held
SIC: 2732 Book printing

(G-16153)
CLIFFORD H JONES INC
608 Young St (14150-4195)
PHONE...................................716 693-2444
Fax: 716 693-2598
Phillip Jones, President
David Jones, Vice Pres
Jamie Mawson, Opers Mgr
EMP: 15
SQ FT: 18,000
SALES (est): 4MM Privately Held
WEB: www.chjones.com
SIC: 3544 3089 Forms (molds), for foundry & plastics working machinery; injection molding of plastics

(G-16154)
COCA-COLA BTLG CO BUFFALO INC
200 Milens Rd (14150-6795)
PHONE...................................716 874-4610
Fax: 716 874-7739
John F Bitzer III, President
Rick Horn Jr, General Mgr
Horn Rick, Sls & Mktg Exec
Flora Torina, Controller
David Moden, Manager
▲ EMP: 170
SQ FT: 75,000
SALES (est): 682.8K
SALES (corp-wide): 298.7MM Privately Held
SIC: 2086 Bottled & canned soft drinks
PA: Abarta, Inc.
  200 Alpha Dr
  Pittsburgh PA 15238
  412 963-6226

(G-16155)
DIGITAL INSTRUMENTS INC
580 Ensminger Rd (14150-6668)
PHONE...................................716 874-5848
Fax: 716 874-5954
John Swanson, President
Amy Betz, Office Mgr
Randy Bogdan, Data Proc Dir
▲ EMP: 10
SQ FT: 6,000
SALES (est): 1.8MM Privately Held
WEB: www.digitalinstruments.com
SIC: 3625 Relays & industrial controls; industrial controls: push button, selector switches, pilot

(G-16156)
E B TROTTNOW MACHINE SPC
330 E Niagara St (14150-1218)
P.O. Box 29 (14151-0029)
PHONE...................................716 694-0600
Fax: 716 694-0742
Mary Pietsch, President
EMP: 18 EST: 1948
SQ FT: 55,000
SALES (est): 3.2MM Privately Held
SIC: 3599 Machine shop, jobbing & repair

(G-16157)
E I DU PONT DE NEMOURS & CO
River Rd & Sheridan Dr (14150)
PHONE...................................716 879-4507
EMP: 182
SALES (corp-wide): 25.1B Publicly Held
WEB: www.dupont.com
SIC: 2879 Agricultural chemicals
PA: E. I. Du Pont De Nemours And Company
  974 Centre Rd
  Wilmington DE 19805
  302 774-1000

(G-16158)
E-ZOIL PRODUCTS INC
234 Fillmore Ave (14150-2340)
PHONE...................................716 213-0103
Glenn Miller, President
Christopher Miller, Vice Pres
Arnette Rauh, Office Mgr
EMP: 25
SQ FT: 10,000
SALES (est): 6.1MM Privately Held
WEB: www.ezoil.com
SIC: 2911 Fuel additives

(G-16159)
EMULSO CORP
2750 Kenmore Ave (14150-7707)
PHONE...................................716 854-2889
William Breeser, President
Brian Williams, Opers Dir
EMP: 6
SQ FT: 30,000
SALES (est): 550K Privately Held
WEB: www.emulso.com
SIC: 2842 2841 5087 Waxes for wood, leather & other materials; furniture polish or wax; soap: granulated, liquid, cake, flaked or chip; janitors' supplies

(G-16160)
FCMP INC
230 Fire Tower Dr (14150-5832)
PHONE...................................716 692-4623
David Callendrier, President
Toni Clark, Manager
▲ EMP: 17 EST: 2000
SQ FT: 20,000
SALES (est): 3.8MM Privately Held
WEB: www.fcmp.com
SIC: 3714 3592 Bearings, motor vehicle; pistons & piston rings

(G-16161)
FIBER LAMINATIONS LIMITED
Also Called: C/O M&M Fowarding
600 Main St (14150-3723)
PHONE...................................716 692-1825
Fax: 716 692-0056
William Neal, Branch Mgr
EMP: 10
SALES (corp-wide): 3.4MM Privately Held
SIC: 3089 Automotive parts, plastic
PA: Fibre Laminations Ltd
  651 Burlington St E
  Hamilton ON L8L 4
  905 312-9152

(G-16162)
FIRST SOURCE LLC
Also Called: Mayfair Sales
100 Pirson Pkwy (14150-6727)
P.O. Box 40, Buffalo (14217-0040)
PHONE...................................716 877-0800
Fax: 716 877-0385
Steve Kottakis, Exec VP
Steve Tzetzo, Opers Mgr
Dave Malabar, Warehouse Mgr
Mike Pulli, Controller
Lisa Brick, Human Res Mgr
EMP: 100 Privately Held
SIC: 2064 Candy & other confectionery products
PA: First Source, Llc
  3612 La Grange Pkwy
  Toano VA 23168

(G-16163)
FLETCHER ENTERPRISES INC
Also Called: Fastsigns
2865 Sheridan Dr (14150-9420)
PHONE...................................716 837-7446
Fax: 716 837-7449
Mary Ellen Fletcher, President
EMP: 5
SALES (est): 420K Privately Held
SIC: 3993 Signs & advertising specialties

(G-16164)
FMC CORPORATION
Also Called: F M C Peroxygen Chemicals Div
78 Sawyer Ave Ste 1 (14150-7751)
PHONE...................................716 879-0400
Fax: 716 879-0474
Greg Campo, Engineer
James Heigl, Engineer
Edward Rzadkiwwicz, Engineer

GEOGRAPHIC SECTION

Tonawanda - Erie County (G-16188)

Moragas Joan, *Sales Dir*
Robert Service, *Manager*
EMP: 200
SALES (corp-wide): 3.2B **Publicly Held**
WEB: www.fmc.com
SIC: 2869 Industrial organic chemicals
PA: Fmc Corporation
  2929 Walnut St
  Philadelphia PA 19104
  215 299-6000

(G-16165)
GERALD FRD PACKG DISPLAY LLC (PA)
550 Fillmore Ave (14150-2509)
PHONE 716 692-2705
Fax: 716 692-5458
Val Racine, *Controller*
Val Sracine, *Mng Member*
▲ **EMP:** 14 **EST:** 1946
SQ FT: 50,000
SALES (est): 2.3MM **Privately Held**
SIC: 2542 Counters or counter display cases: except wood

(G-16166)
GREAT LAKES GEAR CO INC
126 E Niagara St Ste 2 (14150-1215)
PHONE 716 694-0715
Fax: 716 694-7241
Donald Eggleston, *President*
Robert Rees, *President*
Timothy Rees, *Vice Pres*
Susan Guenther, *Human Res Dir*
Mathew Dubin, *Information Mgr*
EMP: 8
SQ FT: 4,500
SALES: 900K **Privately Held**
SIC: 3462 Gears, forged steel

(G-16167)
GREAT LAKES METAL TREATING
300 E Niagara St (14150-1218)
P.O. Box 118 (14151-0118)
PHONE 716 694-1240
Thomas Snyder, *President*
EMP: 10
SQ FT: 18,000
SALES (est): 879K **Privately Held**
SIC: 3398 Metal heat treating

(G-16168)
GREEN BUFFALO FUEL LLC
Also Called: Gbf
720 Riverview Blvd (14150-7824)
PHONE 716 768-0600
Peter Coleman, *CEO*
Brendan Neill, *Marketing Staff*
EMP: 10 **EST:** 2012
SALES (est): 790K **Privately Held**
SIC: 1311 1321 Natural gas production; butane (natural) production

(G-16169)
GREIF INC
2122 Colvin Blvd (14150-6908)
PHONE 716 836-4200
Alco Drost, *Opers Mgr*
Pat Wolfe, *Maint Spvr*
Clinton Gathins, *Opers-Prdtn-Mfg*
Brian Ellis, *Purch Mgr*
Doug Lingrel, *Financial Exec*
EMP: 70
SALES (corp-wide): 3.6B **Publicly Held**
WEB: www.greif.com
SIC: 2655 Drums, fiber: made from purchased material
PA: Greif, Inc.
  425 Winter Rd
  Delaware OH 43015
  740 549-6000

(G-16170)
HDM HYDRAULICS LLC
125 Fire Tower Dr (14150-5880)
PHONE 716 694-8004
William Anderson, *President*
Ron Wojthkowski, *Controller*
Heckman Barry, *CTO*
▲ **EMP:** 100
SQ FT: 46,560

SALES (est): 30.5MM
SALES (corp-wide): 619.1MM **Privately Held**
WEB: www.ligonindustries.com
SIC: 3511 Hydraulic turbine generator set units, complete
PA: Ligon Industries, Llc
  1927 1st Ave N Ste 500
  Birmingham AL 35203
  205 322-3302

(G-16171)
HEBELER CORPORATION (PA)
2000 Military Rd (14150-6704)
PHONE 716 873-9300
Fax: 716 873-7538
Ken Snyder, *President*
John Coleman, *Chairman*
Zeke Gray, *Project Mgr*
Gino Kellerhouse, *Project Mgr*
Nick Leibring, *Project Mgr*
▲ **EMP:** 140 **EST:** 1929
SQ FT: 100,000
SALES (est): 36.4MM **Privately Held**
WEB: www.hebeler.com
SIC: 3599 Custom machinery

(G-16172)
HERR MANUFACTURING CO INC
17 Pearce Ave (14150-6711)
PHONE 716 754-4341
Fax: 716 874-6066
Bruce Mc Lean, *President*
Rick Wahl, *Sales Staff*
EMP: 25 **EST:** 1913
SALES (est): 3.1MM **Privately Held**
SIC: 3552 Textile machinery

(G-16173)
IMA LIFE NORTH AMERICA INC
2175 Military Rd (14150-6001)
PHONE 716 695-6354
Giovanni Pecchioli, *President*
Sergio Marzo, *Corp Secy*
Jose Ruiz, *Exec VP*
Laura Opera, *Vice Pres*
Ernesto Renzi, *Vice Pres*
◆ **EMP:** 150
SQ FT: 43,000
SALES (est): 70MM **Privately Held**
SIC: 2834 Druggists' preparations (pharmaceuticals)
HQ: I.M.A. Industria Macchine Automatiche Spa
  Via Bruno Tosarelli 182/184
  Castenaso BO 40055
  051 651-4111

(G-16174)
INTEGUMENT TECHNOLOGIES INC
72 Pearce Ave (14150-6711)
PHONE 716 873-1199
Fax: 716 873-1303
Terrence G Vargo, *President*
Jennifer Smyth, *Marketing Staff*
EMP: 16
SALES (est): 2.4MM **Privately Held**
WEB: www.integument.com
SIC: 3081 Unsupported plastics film & sheet

(G-16175)
KELLER TECHNOLOGY CORPORATION (PA)
2320 Military Rd (14150-6005)
P.O. Box 103, Buffalo (14217-0103)
PHONE 716 693-3840
Fax: 716 693-0512
Michael A Keller, *Ch of Bd*
Arthur Keller Jr, *Ch of Bd*
Peter Keller, *Vice Pres*
Michael Daigler, *Engineer*
Peter Dennison, *Engineer*
▲ **EMP:** 175 **EST:** 1947
SQ FT: 200,000
SALES (est): 62.6MM **Privately Held**
WEB: www.kellertechnology.com
SIC: 3599 Custom machinery

(G-16176)
LAFARGE NORTH AMERICA INC
4001 River Rd (14150-6513)
PHONE 716 876-8788
Mark Joslin, *Branch Mgr*
EMP: 13

SALES (corp-wide): 23.4B **Privately Held**
SIC: 1422 Crushed & broken limestone
HQ: Lafarge North America Inc.
  8700 W Bryn Mawr Ave LI
  Chicago IL 60631
  703 480-3600

(G-16177)
LORNAMEAD INC
175 Cooper Ave (14150-6656)
PHONE 716 874-7190
James Carney, *VP Opers*
EMP: 76 **Privately Held**
SIC: 2844 Hair preparations, including shampoos
HQ: Lornamead, Inc
  1359 Broadway Fl 17
  New York NY 10018
  914 630-7733

(G-16178)
MAGAZINES & BROCHURES INC
Also Called: Labels X Press
245 Cooper Ave Ste 108 (14150-6642)
PHONE 716 875-9699
Fax: 716 875-9996
Craig Boggs, *President*
Scott Boggs, *Treasurer*
EMP: 5
SALES (est): 750K **Privately Held**
WEB: www.labelsxpress.com
SIC: 2759 2752 Commercial printing; commercial printing, lithographic

(G-16179)
MANTH MFG INC
131 Fillmore Ave (14150-2337)
P.O. Box 866 (14151-0866)
PHONE 716 693-6525
Fax: 716 693-6560
Duane Manth, *President*
EMP: 35
SQ FT: 14,000
SALES: 1.9MM **Privately Held**
SIC: 3599 Machine shop, jobbing & repair

(G-16180)
MAY TOOL & DIE INC
9 Hackett Dr (14150-3797)
PHONE 716 695-1033
Fax: 716 695-1090
Martin J May, *President*
Frederick J May, *Vice Pres*
Joseph O May, *Vice Pres*
Mary Kreher, *Admin Sec*
EMP: 5 **EST:** 1970
SQ FT: 8,000
SALES: 500K **Privately Held**
SIC: 3544 Special dies & tools

(G-16181)
MIDLAND MACHINERY CO INC
101 Cranbrook Road Ext Exd (14150-4110)
PHONE 716 692-1200
Fax: 716 692-1206
Barre W Banks, *President*
Lalit Kumar, *Engineer*
Dave Reinard, *Engineer*
Darrell Banks, *Sls & Mktg Exec*
EMP: 62
SQ FT: 15,000
SALES (est): 15MM **Privately Held**
WEB: www.midlandmachinery.com
SIC: 3531 Asphalt plant, including gravel-mix type

(G-16182)
MODU-CRAFT INC (PA)
276 Creekside Dr (14150-1435)
PHONE 716 694-0709
Fax: 716 694-0709
Kenneth Babka, *President*
EMP: 5
SQ FT: 30,000
SALES: 1MM **Privately Held**
SIC: 3821 2599 2542 Laboratory furniture; factory furniture & fixtures; partitions & fixtures, except wood

(G-16183)
MORNINGSTAR CONCRETE PRODUCTS
528 Young St (14150-4107)
PHONE 716 693-4020
Fax: 716 693-4021
Juanita Morningstar, *President*

Ray D Morningstar, *Vice Pres*
EMP: 14 **EST:** 1913
SQ FT: 120,000
SALES (est): 1.7MM **Privately Held**
WEB: www.morningstarturf.com
SIC: 3271 Blocks, concrete or cinder: standard

(G-16184)
NEW YORK IMAGING SERVICE INC
255 Cooper Ave (14150-6641)
PHONE 716 834-8022
Rob Muzzio, *Branch Mgr*
EMP: 11
SALES (corp-wide): 14.2MM **Privately Held**
SIC: 3844 X-ray apparatus & tubes
PA: New York Imaging Service Inc.
  1 Dalfonso Rd
  Newburgh NY 12550
  845 561-6947

(G-16185)
NIABRAZE LLC
675 Ensminger Rd (14150-6609)
PHONE 716 447-1082
Fax: 716 447-1084
Albert Bluemle Sr, *President*
Dave Gardner, *Opers Mgr*
Thomas Bluemle, *Treasurer*
EMP: 14
SALES (est): 2.2MM **Privately Held**
SIC: 3421 3425 Cutlery; saw blades for hand or power saws

(G-16186)
NIAGARA BLOWER COMPANY (DH)
91 Sawyer Ave (14150-7716)
PHONE 800 426-5169
Fax: 716 875-1077
Peter G Demakos, *President*
Craig D Boyce, *VP Opers*
Robert Smith, *VP Opers*
Tim Howard, *Production*
Michael Mauro, *Production*
▼ **EMP:** 120 **EST:** 1904
SQ FT: 60,000
SALES (est): 38.4MM
SALES (corp-wide): 4.5B **Privately Held**
WEB: www.niagarablower.com
SIC: 3585 Refrigeration & heating equipment; air conditioning units, complete: domestic or industrial; humidifying equipment, except portable
HQ: Alfa Laval Us Holding Inc
  5400 Intl Trade Dr
  Richmond VA 23231
  804 222-5300

(G-16187)
NOCO INCORPORATED (PA)
2440 Sheridan Dr Ste 202 (14150-9416)
PHONE 716 833-6626
James D Newman, *Ch of Bd*
R J Stapell, *Ch of Bd*
Michael Newman, *Exec VP*
Michael L Bradley, *CFO*
Scott Ernst, *Director*
EMP: 5
SQ FT: 15,000
SALES (est): 403.2MM **Privately Held**
SIC: 2992 6719 5172 4924 Lubricating oils & greases; investment holding companies, except banks; petroleum products; natural gas distribution

(G-16188)
NORTH DELAWARE PRINTING INC
645 Delaware St Ste 1 (14150-5390)
PHONE 716 692-0576
Michael J Brown, *President*
Steven Brown, *Vice Pres*
EMP: 9
SQ FT: 3,200
SALES (est): 1.4MM **Privately Held**
WEB: www.northdelawareprinting.com
SIC: 2752 7334 Commercial printing, lithographic; photocopying & duplicating services

Tonawanda - Erie County (G-16189) — GEOGRAPHIC SECTION

(G-16189)
ODEN MACHINERY INC (PA)
199 Fire Tower Dr (14150-5813)
PHONE..................716 874-3000
Ronald Sarto, *CEO*
Tony Fwedersky, *President*
Gregory E Simsa, *CFO*
EMP: 20
SQ FT: 25,000
SALES: 4.5MM **Privately Held**
SIC: 3823 Thermometers, filled system: industrial process type

(G-16190)
OPTICS PLUS INC
4291 Delaware Ave (14150-6129)
PHONE..................716 744-2636
Forrest Reukauf, *Principal*
▲ **EMP:** 9
SALES (est): 1.1MM **Privately Held**
SIC: 3827 Optical instruments & lenses

(G-16191)
PADDOCK CHEVROLET GOLF DOME
175 Brompton Rd (14150-4534)
PHONE..................716 504-4059
Fax: 716 504-4060
Jeff Rainey, *Director*
EMP: 25
SALES (est): 2.1MM **Privately Held**
WEB: www.tonawanda.ny.us
SIC: 3949 7999 Driving ranges, golf, electronic; tennis services & professionals

(G-16192)
PDM STUDIOS INC
510 Main St (14150-3853)
PHONE..................716 694-8337
Paul Michalski, *President*
Samantha Crocker, *Admin Asst*
EMP: 6
SALES (est): 519.3K **Privately Held**
SIC: 2759 Screen printing

(G-16193)
PINE PHARMACEUTICALS LLC
100 Colvin Woods Pkwy (14150-6974)
PHONE..................716 248-1025
Alfonse Muto, *Principal*
EMP: 5
SALES (est): 960.9K **Privately Held**
SIC: 2834 Druggists' preparations (pharmaceuticals)

(G-16194)
PRAXAIR INC
175 E Park Dr (14150-7891)
P.O. Box 44 (14151-0044)
PHONE..................716 879-2000
Fax: 716 879-4719
Joel Emmet, *Principal*
Tim Howley, *Senior VP*
Dennis Conroy, *Vice Pres*
William Therrien, *Vice Pres*
Karen Ginnane, *Plant Mgr*
EMP: 15
SALES (corp-wide): 10.7B **Publicly Held**
SIC: 2819 Industrial inorganic chemicals
PA: Praxair, Inc.
  39 Old Ridgebury Rd
  Danbury CT 06810
  203 837-2000

(G-16195)
PRAXAIR INC
135 E Park Dr (14150-7844)
PHONE..................716 879-4000
John Lewendowski, *Principal*
EMP: 50
SALES (corp-wide): 10.7B **Publicly Held**
SIC: 2813 Industrial gases
PA: Praxair, Inc.
  39 Old Ridgebury Rd
  Danbury CT 06810
  203 837-2000

(G-16196)
R J REYNOLDS TOBACCO COMPANY
275 Cooper Ave Ste 116 (14150-6643)
PHONE..................716 871-1553
Tracy Wozniak, *Principal*
EMP: 226

SALES (corp-wide): 10.6B **Publicly Held**
SIC: 2111 Cigarettes
HQ: R. J. Reynolds Tobacco Company
  401 N Main St
  Winston Salem NC 27101
  336 741-5000

(G-16197)
S R INSTRUMENTS INC (PA)
600 Young St (14150-4188)
PHONE..................716 693-5977
Fax: 716 693-5854
John Siegel, *President*
Brandon Darnell, *Engineer*
Teresa Eyring, *Sls & Mktg Exec*
Peter Adolf, *Human Res Mgr*
Janelle Heimgartner, *Accounts Mgr*
EMP: 48
SQ FT: 25,000
SALES (est): 6.9MM **Privately Held**
WEB: www.srinstruments.com
SIC: 3825 3596 Measuring instruments & meters, electric; weighing machines & apparatus

(G-16198)
SAFESPAN PLATFORM SYSTEMS INC
237 Fillmore Ave (14150-2339)
PHONE..................716 694-1100
Lambros Apostolopoulos, *President*
Thomas Lauber, *Executive*
EMP: 40 **Privately Held**
SIC: 3312 Slabs, steel; structural shapes & pilings, steel
PA: Safespan Platform Systems, Inc.
  252 Fillmore Ave
  Tonawanda NY 14150

(G-16199)
SAFESPAN PLATFORM SYSTEMS INC (PA)
252 Fillmore Ave (14150-2408)
PHONE..................716 694-3332
Fax: 716 694-1100
Lambros Aposto, *CEO*
Chris Herpin, *Project Mgr*
Jacque Austin, *Facilities Mgr*
David Malcolm, *VP Sales*
Scott Krieger, *Info Tech Mgr*
▲ **EMP:** 60
SQ FT: 6,400
SALES (est): 21.1MM **Privately Held**
SIC: 3446 1799 Architectural metalwork; scaffolds, mobile or stationary: metal; rigging & scaffolding; scaffolding construction

(G-16200)
SCHWABEL FABRICATING CO INC (PA)
349 Sawyer Ave (14150-7796)
PHONE..................716 876-2086
Fax: 716 876-5042
Gerald Schwabel, *President*
Paul Schwabel, *Vice Pres*
Dave Purcell, *Director*
William Schwabel, *Admin Sec*
EMP: 23
SQ FT: 30,000
SALES (est): 3.3MM **Privately Held**
WEB: www.schwabelfab.com
SIC: 3443 3599 3552 Heat exchangers, plate type; vessels, process or storage (from boiler shops): metal plate; tanks, standard or custom fabricated: metal plate; machine shop, jobbing & repair; textile machinery

(G-16201)
SCIENTIFICS DIRECT INC
532 Main St (14150-3853)
PHONE..................716 773-7500
Linda Nogle, *General Mgr*
EMP: 14 **EST:** 2012
SALES (est): 2MM **Privately Held**
SIC: 3229 Scientific glassware

(G-16202)
SERVICE FILTRATION CORP
225 E Park Dr (14150-7813)
P.O. Box 963, Buffalo (14240-0963)
PHONE..................716 877-2608
EMP: 30

SALES (corp-wide): 47MM **Privately Held**
WEB: www.pacerpumps.com
SIC: 3569 3677 Filters, general line: industrial; filtration devices, electronic
PA: Service Filtration Corp.
  2900 Macarthur Blvd
  Northbrook IL 60062
  847 509-2900

(G-16203)
SNYDER INDUSTRIES INC (PA)
340 Wales Ave (14150-2513)
P.O. Box 586, North Tonawanda (14120-0586)
PHONE..................716 694-1240
Fax: 716 693-4623
Thomas W Snyder, *Ch of Bd*
Thomas Dunch, *Vice Pres*
Charlie Rudolph, *Vice Pres*
Marie Snyder, *Vice Pres*
Joe Colombo, *Purchasing*
EMP: 55
SQ FT: 24,000
SALES (est): 15.3MM **Privately Held**
WEB: www.snyderindustriesinc.com
SIC: 3599 Machine shop, jobbing & repair

(G-16204)
SURE FLOW EQUIPMENT INC
250 Cooper Ave Ste 102 (14150-6633)
P.O. Box 321 (14151-0321)
PHONE..................800 263-8251
John Wordsworth, *President*
EMP: 50
SALES (est): 14MM **Privately Held**
SIC: 3494 5072 Valves & pipe fittings; hardware

(G-16205)
SWIFT RIVER ASSOCIATES INC (PA)
4051 River Rd (14150-6513)
PHONE..................716 875-0902
Kenneth Rawe Sr, *President*
Tony Pariso, *Corp Secy*
Carmen Pariso, *Vice Pres*
Kenneth Rawe Jr, *Vice Pres*
EMP: 7
SALES (est): 667.3K **Privately Held**
SIC: 2951 Concrete, asphaltic (not from refineries)

(G-16206)
TONAWANDA COKE CORPORATION (PA)
3875 River Rd (14150-6591)
P.O. Box 5007 (14151-5007)
PHONE..................716 876-6222
Fax: 716 876-4400
J D Crane, *CEO*
Ugene Wilkowski, *General Mgr*
Christian Kaderabeck, *QC Mgr*
Ken Thrun, *Project Engr*
Michael Durkin, *CFO*
▲ **EMP:** 100
SQ FT: 150,000
SALES (est): 34.7MM **Privately Held**
WEB: www.tonawandacoke.com
SIC: 3312 Coke produced in chemical recovery coke ovens

(G-16207)
TONAWANDA LIMB & BRACE INC
545 Delaware St (14150-5301)
PHONE..................716 695-1131
Fax: 716 695-0016
Robert Catipovic, *President*
Richard C Catipovic, *Vice Pres*
Nancy Sardina, *Manager*
EMP: 5
SQ FT: 14,000
SALES (est): 616.6K **Privately Held**
SIC: 3842 Prosthetic appliances

(G-16208)
TREEHOUSE PRIVATE BRANDS INC
570 Fillmore Ave (14150-2509)
PHONE..................716 693-4715
EMP: 175
SALES (corp-wide): 3.2B **Publicly Held**
SIC: 2052 Cookies

HQ: Treehouse Private Brands, Inc.
  800 Market St
  Saint Louis MO 63101
  314 877-7300

(G-16209)
TREYCO PRODUCTS CORP
131 Fillmore Ave (14150-2396)
P.O. Box 866 (14151-0866)
PHONE..................716 693-6525
Duane Manth, *President*
▲ **EMP:** 5 **EST:** 1961
SQ FT: 10,000
SALES: 520.8K **Privately Held**
WEB: www.treyco.com
SIC: 3421 Scissors, shears, clippers, snips & similar tools; shears, hand; clippers, fingernail & toenail; snips, tinners'

(G-16210)
UNIFRAX I LLC
Fiberfrax Manufacturing
360 Fire Tower Dr (14150-5893)
PHONE..................716 696-3000
Scott Penman, *Production*
Justin Coburn, *Production*
John Di Matteo, *Engineer*
Barbara Chasser, *Personnel*
William Hanley, *CTO*
EMP: 165 **Publicly Held**
WEB: www.insulfrax.com
SIC: 3297 3299 3296 Nonclay refractories; ceramic fiber; mineral wool
HQ: Unifrax I Llc
  600 Rverwalk Pkwy Ste 120
  Tonawanda NY 14150

(G-16211)
UNIFRAX I LLC (HQ)
600 Rverwalk Pkwy Ste 120 (14150)
PHONE..................716 768-6500
David E Brooks, *President*
Kevin J Gorman, *Senior VP*
Kevin O'Gorman, *Vice Pres*
Brian Mellett, *Engineer*
Jason Pischka, *Engineer*
◆ **EMP:** 110
SALES (est): 436.2MM **Publicly Held**
WEB: www.insulfrax.com
SIC: 3299 Ceramic fiber

(G-16212)
UOP LLC
175 E Park Dr (14150-7844)
P.O. Box 986 (14151-0986)
PHONE..................716 879-7600
Charles J Schorr, *General Mgr*
EMP: 20
SALES (corp-wide): 38.5B **Publicly Held**
WEB: www.uop.com
SIC: 2819 Catalysts, chemical
HQ: Uop Llc
  25 E Algonquin Rd
  Des Plaines IL 60016
  847 391-2000

(G-16213)
WASHINGTON MILLS TONAWANDA INC (HQ)
1000 E Niagara St (14150-1306)
PHONE..................716 693-4550
Ronald Campbell, *Chairman*
Kersi Dordi, *Vice Pres*
Armand Ladage, *Vice Pres*
Melvin Dashineau, *QC Dir*
Michael Pagano, *CFO*
▲ **EMP:** 30
SQ FT: 273,000
SALES (est): 41MM
SALES (corp-wide): 170.9MM **Privately Held**
WEB: www.exolon.com
SIC: 3291 Abrasive products; aluminum oxide (fused) abrasives; silicon carbide abrasive
PA: Washington Mills Group, Inc.
  20 N Main St
  North Grafton MA 01536
  508 839-6511

(G-16214)
WGB INDUSTRIES INC
233 Fillmore Ave Ste 23 (14150-2316)
PHONE..................716 693-5527
Daniel Woodward, *President*
Daniel R Woodward, *President*

GEOGRAPHIC SECTION
Troy - Rensselaer County (G-16237)

Renee Gagnon, *Manager*
Erik Woodward, *Manager*
EMP: 16
SQ FT: 6,000
SALES: 1MM **Privately Held**
SIC: 3363 Aluminum die-castings

(G-16215)
WINTERS INSTRUMENTS INC (HQ)
Also Called: Winters Instruments
600 Ensminger Rd (14150-6637)
PHONE..................281 880-8607
Fax: 716 874-8800
Jeffrey Smith, *President*
Brian McClure, *Exec VP*
Brad Taylor, *VP Mfg*
John Bernotas, *Regl Sales Mgr*
Christopher Olsen, *Regl Sales Mgr*
▲ **EMP:** 45
SQ FT: 10,000
SALES (est): 4.4MM
SALES (corp-wide): 4.7MM **Privately Held**
SIC: 3823 5084 Industrial instrmnts msrmnt display/control process variable; instruments & control equipment
PA: Winters Instruments Ltd
121 Railside Rd
North York ON M3A 1
416 444-2345

(G-16216)
WSF INDUSTRIES INC
7 Hackett Dr (14150-3798)
P.O. Box 400, Buffalo (14217-0400)
PHONE..................716 692-4930
Fax: 716 692-4135
John Hettrick Jr, *CEO*
Gary Fornasiero, *President*
Nancy Warner, *Purch Agent*
Curtis Smith, *QC Mgr*
Chuck Becker, *Design Engr*
EMP: 25 **EST:** 1941
SQ FT: 66,000
SALES: 1.7MM **Privately Held**
WEB: www.wsf-inc.com
SIC: 3443 Autoclaves, industrial

(G-16217)
ZENGER GROUP INC
777 E Park Dr (14150-6708)
PHONE..................716 871-1058
Stephen Zenger, *Principal*
EMP: 44
SALES (est): 3.7MM
SALES (corp-wide): 19.3MM **Privately Held**
SIC: 2752 Commercial printing, lithographic
PA: Zenger Group Inc.
777 E Park Dr
Tonawanda NY 14150
716 871-1058

Troy
Albany County

(G-16218)
ALBANY NIPPLE AND PIPE MFG
60 Cohoes Ave Ste 100a (12183-1518)
PHONE..................518 270-2162
Fax: 518 270-2169
Robert Moss, *President*
Mark Wentland, *Info Tech Dir*
EMP: 20
SALES (est): 2.9MM **Privately Held**
SIC: 3498 Fabricated pipe & fittings

(G-16219)
CRYSTAL IS INC
70 Cohoes Ave Ste 1b (12183-1531)
PHONE..................518 271-7375
Fax: 518 271-7394
Larry Felton, *CEO*
Steven Berger, *President*
Jordan Therese, *Senior VP*
Keith Evans, *Vice Pres*
Shwan Gibb, *Vice Pres*
EMP: 45
SQ FT: 10,500
SALES (est): 10.2MM
SALES (corp-wide): 16.5B **Privately Held**
WEB: www.crystal-is.com
SIC: 3679 Electronic crystals
PA: Asahi Kasei Corporation
1-105, Kandajimbocho
Chiyoda-Ku TKY 101-0
332 963-000

(G-16220)
HONEYWELL INTERNATIONAL INC
3 Tibbits Ave (12183-1433)
PHONE..................518 270-0200
Gary Andrews, *Purch Mgr*
Patricia Marzinsky, *Finance Mgr*
Alicia McKinney, *Human Res Dir*
Twila Harrison, *Human Res Mgr*
Steve Kratz, *Branch Mgr*
EMP: 80
SALES (corp-wide): 38.5B **Publicly Held**
WEB: www.honeywell.com
SIC: 3052 Air line or air brake hose, rubber or rubberized fabric
PA: Honeywell International Inc.
115 Tabor Rd
Morris Plains NJ 07950
973 455-2000

(G-16221)
KAYS CAPS INC (PA)
65 Arch St (12183-1599)
PHONE..................518 273-6079
Fax: 518 791-8529
Roberta Fine, *Ch of Bd*
EMP: 8
SQ FT: 1,000
SALES (est): 608.1K **Privately Held**
WEB: www.kayscaps.com
SIC: 2353 Uniform hats & caps

(G-16222)
LONG ISLAND PIPE SUPPLY INC
60 Cohoes Ave (12183-1555)
PHONE..................518 270-2159
Fax: 518 270-8384
Bob Moss, *President*
EMP: 6
SALES (corp-wide): 59.7MM **Privately Held**
SIC: 3498 Fabricated pipe & fittings
PA: Long Island Pipe Supply Inc
586 Commercial Ave
Garden City NY 11530
516 222-8008

(G-16223)
SEALY MATTRESS CO ALBANY INC
30 Veterans Memorial Dr (12183-1517)
PHONE..................518 880-1600
Fax: 518 880-1600
David J McIiquham, *President*
Gregg Tanis, *Superintendent*
Bill Oryell, *Maint Spvr*
Caroline Feester, *Human Res Dir*
Tom Bartnicki, *Accounts Mgr*
EMP: 300
SQ FT: 265,000
SALES (est): 45.4MM
SALES (corp-wide): 3.1B **Publicly Held**
SIC: 2515 Mattresses, innerspring or box spring
HQ: Sealy Mattress Company
1 Office Parkway Rd
Trinity NC 27370
336 861-3500

Troy
Rensselaer County

(G-16224)
A I T COMPUTERS INC
157 Hoosick St (12180-2375)
PHONE..................518 266-9010
Fax: 518 266-9012
Ahmed Ali, *President*
EMP: 3
SQ FT: 2,000
SALES: 1MM **Privately Held**
WEB: www.aitcomputers.com
SIC: 3577 5734 Computer peripheral equipment; computer & software stores

(G-16225)
APPRENDA INC (PA)
433 River St Fl 4 (12180-2250)
PHONE..................518 383-2130
Sinclair Schuller, *CEO*
Matthew Ammerman, *Vice Pres*
Rakesh Malhotra, *Vice Pres*
Abraham Sultan, *Vice Pres*
Andrew Harris, *QA Dir*
EMP: 66 **EST:** 2007
SALES (est): 11.8MM **Privately Held**
SIC: 7372 Prepackaged software

(G-16226)
ARDEX COSMETICS OF AMERICA
744 Pawling Ave (12180-6212)
PHONE..................518 283-6700
Nubar Sukljian, *President*
▲ **EMP:** 20
SQ FT: 250,000
SALES (est): 2.1MM **Privately Held**
SIC: 2844 Cosmetic preparations

(G-16227)
BATTERY ENERGY STORAGE SYSTEMS
Also Called: Besstech
291 River St Ste 318 (12180-3218)
PHONE..................518 256-7029
Bruce Toyama, *Vice Pres*
Brian Butcher,
Benjamin Backes,
Fernando Gomez-Baquero,
Jae Ho Lee,
EMP: 6
SALES (est): 553.5K **Privately Held**
SIC: 3691 Storage batteries

(G-16228)
BROWN PRINTERS OF TROY INC
Also Called: Brown Printing Co
363 5th Ave (12182-3119)
P.O. Box 388 (12182-0388)
PHONE..................518 235-4080
Fax: 518 235-0884
John H Parry III, *President*
Dawn Parry, *Vice Pres*
Patti Kane, *Office Mgr*
EMP: 14
SQ FT: 9,000
SALES (est): 1.5MM **Privately Held**
WEB: www.brownprinters.com
SIC: 2752 Commercial printing, offset

(G-16229)
CHARLES V WEBER MACHINE SHOP
Also Called: Weber's Mach Shop
2 Campbell Ave (12180-6004)
PHONE..................518 272-8033
Fax: 518 272-8034
Charles H Weber, *President*
EMP: 5 **EST:** 1942
SQ FT: 8,800
SALES (est): 603.5K **Privately Held**
SIC: 3599 Machine shop, jobbing & repair

(G-16230)
CHART INC
Also Called: Clever Fellows I
302 10th St (12180-1617)
PHONE..................518 272-3565
Fax: 518 272-3582
Sam Thomas, *CEO*
John Corey, *President*
EMP: 12
SALES (corp-wide): 1B **Publicly Held**
SIC: 3599 3621 3585 Custom machinery; electric motor & generator parts; parts for heating, cooling & refrigerating equipment
HQ: Chart Inc
407 7th St Nw
New Prague MN 56071
952 758-4484

(G-16231)
CHOPPY V M & SONS LLC
Also Called: V M Choppy & Sons
4 Van Buren St (12180-5550)
PHONE..................518 266-1444
Vincent J Choppy, *Purchasing*
Anne F Choppy, *Mng Member*
Vincent M Choppy,
EMP: 30
SQ FT: 35,000
SALES (est): 5.2MM **Privately Held**
WEB: www.vmchoppyandsons.com
SIC: 3444 Sheet metal specialties, not stamped

(G-16232)
COOKIE FACTORY LLC
520 Congress St (12180-4332)
PHONE..................518 268-1060
Fax: 518 268-1063
Chris Alverino,
EMP: 40
SALES (est): 6MM **Privately Held**
SIC: 2052 Cookies

(G-16233)
DEAKON HOMES AND INTERIORS
Also Called: Troy Cabinet Manufacturing Div
16 Industrial Park Rd (12180-6197)
PHONE..................518 271-0342
Diane F Decurtis, *President*
John De Curtis, *General Mgr*
Margo Jordan, *Bookkeeper*
EMP: 15
SQ FT: 7,000
SALES (est): 1.6MM **Privately Held**
WEB: www.troycabinet.com
SIC: 2434 2541 1521 2522 Wood kitchen cabinets; wood partitions & fixtures; general remodeling, single-family houses; office furniture, except wood; wood office furniture; wood household furniture

(G-16234)
DOWD - WITBECK PRINTING CORP
Also Called: SCHENECTADY HERALD PRINTING CO
599 Pawling Ave (12180-5823)
PHONE..................518 274-2421
Toll Free:..................877 -
Denise Padula, *President*
John E Hupe, *Vice Pres*
Steve Bowes, *Production*
Debbie Goode, *Human Res Mgr*
Chip Kress, *Sales Staff*
EMP: 18
SQ FT: 10,200
SALES: 1.9MM **Privately Held**
WEB: www.alchar.com
SIC: 2752 2796 2791 2789 Commercial printing, offset; platemaking services; typesetting; bookbinding & related work; commercial art & graphic design

(G-16235)
FLOAT TECH INC
216 River St Ste 1 (12180-3848)
PHONE..................518 266-0964
Cecilia Domingos, *President*
Harald Warelius, *Managing Dir*
EMP: 6
SALES (est): 480K **Privately Held**
SIC: 2385 Waterproof outerwear

(G-16236)
GEORGE M DUJACK
Also Called: Du Serv Development Co
80 Town Office Rd (12180-8817)
PHONE..................518 279-1303
George M Dujack, *Owner*
EMP: 5 **EST:** 1973
SALES: 400K **Privately Held**
SIC: 2821 Silicone resins

(G-16237)
GURLEY PRECISION INSTRS INC
514 Fulton St (12180-3315)
PHONE..................518 272-6300
O Patrick Brady, *Ch of Bd*
Rick Evans, *Vice Pres*
Yuiry Benderskiy, *Mfg Dir*
Tom Reed, *Safety Mgr*
Evan Defilippo, *Engineer*
EMP: 105
SQ FT: 78,000

Troy - Rensselaer County (G-16238)

SALES (est): 30MM **Privately Held**
WEB: www.gurley.com
SIC: 3827 3824 3829 3823 Optical instruments & lenses; water meters; physical property testing equipment; industrial instrmnts msrmnt display/control process variable; semiconductors & related devices; radio & TV communications equipment

(G-16238)
HAMILTON PRINTING COMPANY INC
22 Hamilton Ave (12180-7863)
PHONE.............................518 732-2161
Fax: 518 732-7714
John Paeglow, *CEO*
William Greenawalt, *Vice Pres*
Brian F Payne, *Vice Pres*
Mike Hart, *VP Finance*
▲ EMP: 140 **EST**: 1912
SQ FT: 100,000
SALES (est): 19.6MM **Privately Held**
WEB: www.hamprint.com
SIC: 2732 2789 Books: printing & binding; binding only: books, pamphlets, magazines, etc.

(G-16239)
HOFFMANS TRADE GROUP LLC
64 2nd St (12180-3927)
PHONE.............................518 250-5556
Gael Coakley,
▼ EMP: 6
SALES (est): 680K **Privately Held**
SIC: 3255 Plastic refractories

(G-16240)
INDUSTRIAL TOOL & DIE CO INC
14 Industrial Park Rd (12180-6197)
PHONE.............................518 273-7383
Paul V Cacciotti, *President*
Loretta Williams, *Finance Mgr*
Denise Blaire, *Office Mgr*
EMP: 14
SQ FT: 17,000
SALES (est): 1.4MM **Privately Held**
SIC: 3544 Special dies, tools, jigs & fixtures

(G-16241)
INTERNTNAL ELCTRONIC MCHS CORP
Also Called: I E M
850 River St (12180-1239)
PHONE.............................518 268-1636
Zack Mian, *President*
Andy Palmer, *Prdtn Mgr*
Peter Hayes, *Engineer*
Bill Peabody, *Design Engr*
Valerie Alexander, *Manager*
◆ EMP: 27
SQ FT: 35,000
SALES (est): 6.8MM **Privately Held**
WEB: www.iem.net
SIC: 3825 8711 Instruments to measure electricity; engineering services

(G-16242)
MATERIALS RECOVERY COMPANY
8000 Main St (12180-5963)
P.O. Box 11150, Albany (12211-0150)
PHONE.............................518 274-3681
Fax: 518 274-3976
James Ricardi, *Owner*
Marc Perez, *Manager*
▼ EMP: 16
SALES (est): 1.4MM **Privately Held**
WEB: www.mrecovery.com
SIC: 3559 Recycling machinery

(G-16243)
NIBBLE INC BAKING CO
451 Broadway Apt 5 (12180-3355)
PHONE.............................518 334-3950
EMP: 8
SALES (est): 481.6K **Privately Held**
SIC: 2051 Bread, cake & related products

(G-16244)
NORTHEAST PALLET & CONT CO INC
1 Mann Ave Bldg 300 (12180-5547)
P.O. Box 151 (12181-0151)
PHONE.............................518 271-0535
James F Price, *President*
EMP: 16
SQ FT: 18,000
SALES (est): 790K **Privately Held**
SIC: 2449 2448 Rectangular boxes & crates, wood; pallets, wood

(G-16245)
OLD WORLD PROVISIONS INC (PA)
12 Industrial Park Rd (12180-6197)
PHONE.............................518 465-7306
Mark Shuket, *Ch of Bd*
Pat Overbaugh, *Office Mgr*
EMP: 33
SQ FT: 9,000
SALES (est): 5.7MM **Privately Held**
SIC: 2011 Meat packing plants

(G-16246)
PB MAPINFO CORPORATION
1 Global Vw (12180-8371)
PHONE.............................518 285-6000
Murray Martin, *CEO*
John E O'Hara, *Ch of Bd*
Michael J Hickey, *COO*
Brian Lants, *Senior VP*
Barret Johnson, *Vice Pres*
EMP: 903
SQ FT: 150,000
SALES (est): 552.1K
SALES (corp-wide): 3.5B **Publicly Held**
WEB: www.mapinfo.com
SIC: 7372 Business oriented computer software
PA: Pitney Bowes Inc.
   3001 Summer St
   Stamford CT 06905
   203 356-5000

(G-16247)
PERROTTAS BAKERY INC
766 Pawling Ave (12180-6294)
PHONE.............................518 283-4711
Charles A Perrotta, *President*
Louis Perrotta, *Corp Secy*
EMP: 9 **EST**: 1962
SQ FT: 5,000
SALES (est): 897.8K **Privately Held**
SIC: 2051 5461 Bakery: wholesale or wholesale/retail combined; bakeries

(G-16248)
PITNEY BOWES SOFTWARE INC
Also Called: Thompson Group
1 Global Vw (12180-8371)
PHONE.............................518 272-0014
John Hobson, *General Mgr*
Michael Cooper, *General Mgr*
Nathan Lobban, *Accounting Dir*
Alex Yamane, *Info Tech Mgr*
EMP: 14
SALES (corp-wide): 3.5B **Publicly Held**
WEB: www.mapinfo.com
SIC: 7372 7371 Business oriented computer software; computer software development & applications
HQ: Pitney Bowes Software Inc.
   1 Global Vw
   Troy NY 12180
   855 839-5119

(G-16249)
PLACID BAKER
250 Broadway (12180-3235)
PHONE.............................518 326-2657
Margaret Obert, *Principal*
EMP: 8
SALES (est): 588.5K **Privately Held**
SIC: 2051 Cakes, bakery: except frozen

(G-16250)
RAITH AMERICA INC
Also Called: Vistec Lithography
300 Jordan Rd (12180-8346)
PHONE.............................518 874-3000
Rainer Schmid, *Branch Mgr*
EMP: 33

SALES (corp-wide): 25MM **Privately Held**
SIC: 2752 Color lithography
PA: Raith America, Inc.
   1377 Long Island Motor P Ste 101
   Islandia NY 11749
   518 874-3020

(G-16251)
ROSS VALVE MFG
75 102nd St (12180-1125)
PHONE.............................518 274-0961
EMP: 6
SALES (est): 611.7K **Privately Held**
SIC: 3494 Valves & pipe fittings

(G-16252)
S/N PRECISION ENTERPRISES INC
Also Called: Pacamor/Kubar Bearings
145 Jordan Rd Ste 1 (12180-8390)
PHONE.............................518 283-8002
Augustine J Sperrazza Jr, *CEO*
Edward Osta, *Exec VP*
Steve Angrisano, *Controller*
Chris Lake, *Manager*
EMP: 45
SQ FT: 13,250
SALES (est): 11.1MM **Privately Held**
WEB: www.pacamor.com
SIC: 3562 Ball bearings & parts

(G-16253)
SCRIVEN DUPLICATING SERVICE
Also Called: Scriven Press
100 Eastover Rd (12182-1108)
PHONE.............................518 233-8180
Fax: 518 233-8780
Kevin Rafferty, *President*
Brian Rafferty, *Vice Pres*
EMP: 6
SQ FT: 4,800
SALES (est): 750K **Privately Held**
SIC: 2752 Photo-offset printing

(G-16254)
SIGN STUDIO INC
1 Ingalls Ave (12180-1220)
PHONE.............................518 266-0877
Ronald Levesque, *CEO*
Jazmin Low, *Executive Asst*
EMP: 12
SQ FT: 2,500
SALES (est): 1.1MM **Privately Held**
SIC: 3993 Signs & advertising specialties

(G-16255)
SILVER GRIFFIN INC
691 Hoosick Rd (12180-8818)
PHONE.............................518 272-7771
Fax: 518 272-7773
Paul Noonan, *President*
EMP: 15
SALES (est): 870K **Privately Held**
SIC: 2759 7299 7334 Commercial printing; wedding chapel, privately operated; ; photocopying & duplicating services

(G-16256)
STANDARD MANUFACTURING CO INC (PA)
Also Called: Sportsmaster Apparel
750 2nd Ave (12182-2290)
P.O. Box 380 (12182-0380)
PHONE.............................518 235-2200
Fax: 518 235-2668
George Arakelian, *CEO*
Dorothy King, *Corp Secy*
Christian Arakelian, *Vice Pres*
Thomas Thalmann, *Controller*
George Bean, *Info Tech Mgr*
▲ EMP: 65
SQ FT: 250,000
SALES (est): 8MM **Privately Held**
SIC: 2337 2339 2329 Jackets & vests, except fur & leather: women's; women's & misses' outerwear; jackets (suede, leatherette, etc.), sport: men's & boys'; men's & boys' leather, wool & down-filled outerwear

(G-16257)
SUNWARD ELECTRONICS INC
Also Called: Dog Guard
258 Broadway Ste 2a (12180-3235)
Rural Route 258 Broadw (12180)
PHONE.............................518 687-0030
Fax: 518 687-0037
Rose Watkins, *President*
William Drew, *General Mgr*
Richard Dawson, *Marketing Staff*
EMP: 11
SQ FT: 5,000
SALES (est): 1.8MM **Privately Held**
WEB: www.teacherspetproducts.com
SIC: 3496 3612 Fencing, made from purchased wire; transformers, except electric

(G-16258)
TROY BOILER WORKS INC
2800 7th Ave (12180-1587)
PHONE.............................518 274-2650
Fax: 518 274-5454
Louis E Okonski, *President*
John E Okonski Sr, *President*
Brian Maxwell, *General Mgr*
Richard Okonski, *Corp Secy*
EMP: 50 **EST**: 1863
SQ FT: 25,000
SALES (est): 14.3MM **Privately Held**
WEB: www.troyboilerworks.com
SIC: 3443 7699 Vessels, process or storage (from boiler shops): metal plate; tanks, standard or custom fabricated: metal plate; boiler & boiler shop work; boiler repair shop

(G-16259)
VICARIOUS VISIONS INC
350 Jordan Rd (12180-8352)
PHONE.............................518 283-4090
Karthik Bala, *CEO*
Guha Bala, *President*
Steve Derrick, *Manager*
Jesse Sparhawk, *Associate*
EMP: 60
SQ FT: 5,751
SALES (est): 3.3MM
SALES (corp-wide): 4.6B **Publicly Held**
WEB: www.vvisions.com
SIC: 7372 Prepackaged software
PA: Activision Blizzard, Inc.
   3100 Ocean Park Blvd
   Santa Monica CA 90405
   310 255-2000

(G-16260)
VISTEC LITHOGRAPHY INC
300 Jordan Rd (12180-8346)
PHONE.............................518 874-3184
Ken Diekroeger, *President*
Susan Adams, *Manager*
Steve Casella, *Info Tech Mgr*
EMP: 15
SALES (est): 1.5MM **Privately Held**
WEB: www.vistectlithography.com
SIC: 3674 Semiconductors & related devices

(G-16261)
VITA RARA INC
Also Called: Enable Labs
415 River St Ste 4 (12180-2834)
PHONE.............................518 369-7356
Mark Menard, *President*
John Fitzpatrick, *Opers Staff*
Ken Crandall, *Manager*
EMP: 5
SALES: 750K **Privately Held**
WEB: www.vitarara.net
SIC: 7372 Business oriented computer software

(G-16262)
WANT-AD DIGEST INC
Also Called: Classified Advertising
870 Hoosick Rd Ste 1 (12180-6622)
PHONE.............................518 279-1181
William Engelke, *President*
Rose Engelke, *Vice Pres*
Paul Engelke, *Office Mgr*
Rose Hastings, *Director*
EMP: 18
SQ FT: 2,000

GEOGRAPHIC SECTION

SALES (est): 131.7K **Privately Held**
WEB: www.wantaddigest.com
SIC: 2741 5521 Directories: publishing & printing; used car dealers

(G-16263)
WEIGHING & SYSTEMS TECH INC
274 2nd St (12180-4616)
PHONE..................................518 274-2797
Julie Jensen, *President*
EMP: 7
SALES (corp-wide): 695K **Privately Held**
SIC: 3596 Weighing machines & apparatus
PA: Weighing & Systems Technology, Inc.
4558 Morgan Pl
Liverpool NY 13090
315 451-7940

(G-16264)
WELDCOMPUTER CORPORATION
105 Jordan Rd Ste 1 (12180-7612)
PHONE..................................518 283-2897
Fax: 518 283-2907
Robert Cohen, *President*
Dr Keith Strain, *Vice Pres*
Lisa Matter, *Manager*
EMP: 13
SQ FT: 4,000
SALES (est): 1.5MM **Privately Held**
WEB: www.weldcomputer.com
SIC: 3625 Control equipment, electric

Trumansburg
Tompkins County

(G-16265)
EAGLE ENVELOPE COMPANY INC
1891 State Route 96 3 (14886-9143)
P.O. Box 236, Ithaca (14851-0236)
PHONE..................................607 387-3195
Fax: 607 387-3196
J Kemper Matt Sr, *CEO*
Richard Spingarn, *President*
EMP: 9
SQ FT: 3,000
SALES (est): 1.2MM
SALES (corp-wide): 32MM **Privately Held**
WEB: www.eagleprint.com
SIC: 2759 Commercial printing; envelopes; printing
HQ: Dupli Graphics Corporation
6761 Thompson Rd
Syracuse NY 13211
315 234-7286

(G-16266)
FLO-TECH ORTHOTIC & PROSTHETIC
7325 Hulseyville Rd (14886)
P.O. Box 462 (14886-0462)
PHONE..................................607 387-3070
Fax: 607 387-3176
Robert N Brown Sr, *CEO*
Kathleen Brown, *President*
Gary Gridley, *General Mgr*
EMP: 8
SALES (est): 900K **Privately Held**
WEB: www.1800flo-tech.com
SIC: 3842 Prosthetic appliances

(G-16267)
FORCE DYNAMICS INC
4995 Voorheis Rd (14886-9435)
PHONE..................................607 546-5023
Micheal D Wiernicki, *Principal*
EMP: 19
SALES (est): 2.4MM **Privately Held**
WEB: www.force-dynamics.com
SIC: 3559 Special industry machinery

(G-16268)
WASHBURN MANUFACTURING TECH
9828 State Route 96 (14886-9327)
PHONE..................................607 387-3991
Thomas Washburn, *President*
EMP: 8
SQ FT: 2,000

SALES: 1MM **Privately Held**
SIC: 3599 Custom machinery

Tuckahoe
Westchester County

(G-16269)
AUTOMTIVE UPHL CNVERTIBLE TOPS
170 Marbledale Rd (10707-3118)
PHONE..................................914 961-4242
Fax: 914 961-5155
Frank Ackermann, *President*
Ron Ackermann, *Vice Pres*
EMP: 5
SQ FT: 5,000
SALES (est): 370K **Privately Held**
SIC: 2394 2399 Convertible tops, canvas or boat: from purchased materials; automotive covers, except seat & tire covers

(G-16270)
GLOBAL FOOD SOURCE & CO INC
114 Carpenter Ave (10707-2104)
PHONE..................................914 320-9615
Albert J Savarese, *President*
Teresa Belvedere, *Vice Pres*
▲ EMP: 4
SALES: 5MM **Privately Held**
SIC: 2032 Canned specialties

(G-16271)
MEDI-RAY INC
150 Marbledale Rd (10707-3197)
PHONE..................................877 898-3003
Fax: 914 337-4620
Ralph F Farella, *President*
Barry N Dansky, *Treasurer*
Diane Smith, *Manager*
▲ EMP: 63
SQ FT: 23,000
SALES (est): 11.5MM **Privately Held**
WEB: www.mediray.com
SIC: 3412 3842 5063 7623 Metal barrels, drums & pails; orthopedic appliances; electrical apparatus & equipment; refrigeration service & repair; nonferrous foundries; nonferrous rolling & drawing

(G-16272)
STOFFEL POLYGON SYSTEMS INC
199 Marbledale Rd (10707-3117)
PHONE..................................914 961-2000
Fax: 914 961-7231
John F Stoffel, *President*
Arlene M Gruber, *Admin Sec*
EMP: 10
SQ FT: 22,180
SALES (est): 1.2MM **Privately Held**
WEB: www.stoffelpolygon.com
SIC: 3462 Iron & steel forgings

Tully
Onondaga County

(G-16273)
APPLIED CONCEPTS INC
397 State Route 281 (13159-2486)
P.O. Box 1175 (13159-1175)
PHONE..................................315 696-6676
Fax: 315 696-9923
Gary Nelson, *Ch of Bd*
Gary W Nelson, *Ch of Bd*
Stephen C Soos, *Vice Pres*
Brian X Poole, *Opers Staff*
Jim Canale, *Engineer*
EMP: 28
SQ FT: 16,000
SALES (est): 4.4MM **Privately Held**
WEB: www.acipower.com
SIC: 3679 Power supplies, all types: static

(G-16274)
BARBER & DELINE ENRGY SVCS LLC
10 Community Dr (13159)
P.O. Box 616 (13159-0616)
PHONE..................................315 696-8961

Eva Deline, *Mng Member*
EMP: 10
SALES (est): 755.2K **Privately Held**
SIC: 1381 1389 Drilling oil & gas wells; drilling water intake wells; service well drilling; spudding in oil & gas wells; construction, repair & dismantling services

(G-16275)
BARBER & DELINE LLC
995 State Route 11a (13159-2426)
PHONE..................................607 749-2619
Frank Lap, *Manager*
Eva Deline,
EMP: 10
SQ FT: 3,000
SALES (est): 2.7MM **Privately Held**
WEB: www.barber-deline.com
SIC: 1381 1781 Drilling oil & gas wells; water well drilling

(G-16276)
HANCOCK MANUFACTURING CORP
7693 State Route 281 (13159-2501)
P.O. Box 310 (13159-0310)
PHONE..................................315 696-8906
Fax: 315 696-8995
Harold F Brown, *President*
Margaret K Brown, *Vice Pres*
Dawn Harris, *Manager*
EMP: 5
SQ FT: 6,000
SALES (est): 506.3K **Privately Held**
SIC: 3599 Machine shop, jobbing & repair

Tupper Lake
Franklin County

(G-16277)
LIZOTTE LOGGING INC
50 Haymeadow Rd (12986-1069)
PHONE..................................518 359-2200
Fax: 518 359-9253
Jeannel Lizotte, *President*
Cynthia Lizotte, *Admin Sec*
EMP: 15
SALES (est): 2MM **Privately Held**
SIC: 2411 Logging camps & contractors

(G-16278)
PAUL J MITCHELL LOGGING INC
15 Mitchell Ln (12986-1056)
PHONE..................................518 359-7029
Fax: 518 359-3707
Paul J Mitchell, *President*
Mary Michell, *Admin Sec*
EMP: 26
SQ FT: 7,000
SALES (est): 3.6MM **Privately Held**
SIC: 2411 Logging camps & contractors

(G-16279)
RICHARDS LOGGING LLC
201 State Route 3 (12986-7705)
PHONE..................................518 359-2775
Fax: 518 359-2779
Bruce Richards, *Mng Member*
Lawrence Richards,
EMP: 15
SALES (est): 1.5MM **Privately Held**
SIC: 2411 Logging camps & contractors

(G-16280)
TRILAKE THREE PRESS CORP
136 Park St (12986-1818)
PHONE..................................518 359-2462
Dan McClelland, *President*
Judy McClelland, *Vice Pres*
Chantel Skiff, *Advt Staff*
John Morris, *Director*
EMP: 6
SQ FT: 3,500
SALES (est): 340K **Privately Held**
SIC: 2711 Newspapers, publishing & printing

(G-16281)
TUPPER LAKE FREE PRESS INC
136 Park St (12986-1818)
PHONE..................................518 359-2166
M D McClelland, *President*

Daniel Mc Celland, *President*
Sue Mitchell, *Advt Staff*
John A H Morris, *Director*
EMP: 6
SQ FT: 3,000
SALES (est): 280K **Privately Held**
SIC: 2711 Newspapers: publishing only, not printed on site

(G-16282)
TUPPER LAKE HARDWOODS INC
167 Pitchfork Pond Rd (12986-1047)
P.O. Box 748 (12986-0748)
PHONE..................................518 359-8248
Fax: 518 259-8337
Greg Paneaudeau, *President*
Robert Gibeault, *General Mgr*
EMP: 32 EST: 1994
SQ FT: 21,356
SALES (est): 3.8MM **Privately Held**
SIC: 2421 2426 Sawmills & planing mills, general; hardwood dimension & flooring mills

Tuxedo Park
Orange County

(G-16283)
I & I SYSTEMS
66 Table Rock Rd (10987-4720)
PHONE..................................845 753-9126
Shan Custello, *President*
EMP: 7
SALES (est): 701.6K **Privately Held**
SIC: 3953 Letters (marking devices), metal

(G-16284)
INTERNATIONAL PAPER COMPANY
1422 Long Meadow Rd (10987-3500)
PHONE..................................845 986-6409
Virginia Rizzo, *Manager*
Donald G Scott, *Systems Mgr*
David Eurich, *Gnrl Med Prac*
EMP: 140
SALES (corp-wide): 22.3B **Publicly Held**
WEB: www.internationalpaper.com
SIC: 2621 8731 Paper mills; commercial physical research
PA: International Paper Company
6400 Poplar Ave
Memphis TN 38197
901 419-9000

Ulster Park
Ulster County

(G-16285)
DYNO NOBEL INC
161 Ulster Ave (12487-5019)
PHONE..................................845 338-2144
Margie Seeger, *Production*
Margaret Seeger, *Opers-Prdtn-Mfg*
Frank Knapp, *Purchasing*
Tom Gaffney, *Human Res Dir*
Fred Jardinico, *Manager*
EMP: 55
SALES (corp-wide): 2.6B **Privately Held**
SIC: 2892 3489 Explosives; ordnance & accessories
HQ: Dyno Nobel Inc.
2795 E Cottonwood Pkwy # 500
Salt Lake City UT 84121
801 364-4800

(G-16286)
MORESCA CLOTHING AND COSTUME
361 Union Center Rd (12487-5232)
PHONE..................................845 331-6012
Lena Dun, *President*
EMP: 10
SQ FT: 11,000
SALES (est): 1.4MM **Privately Held**
WEB: www.moresca.com
SIC: 2389 5699 5136 5137 Costumes; costumes, masquerade or theatrical; men's & boys' clothing; women's & children's clothing

Unadilla - Otsego County (G-16287)

Unadilla
Otsego County

(G-16287)
AMES COMPANIES INC
196 Clifton St (13849-2418)
P.O. Box 644 (13849-0644)
PHONE...........................607 369-9595
Fax: 607 369-9595
Jay Gerber, *Controller*
Alexander Miller, *Branch Mgr*
EMP: 61
SQ FT: 25,000
SALES (corp-wide): 2B **Publicly Held**
WEB: www.ames.com
SIC: 3423 Garden & farm tools, including shovels
HQ: The Ames Companies Inc
465 Railroad Ave
Camp Hill PA 17011
717 737-1500

Uniondale
Nassau County

(G-16288)
AITHACA CHEMICAL CORP
50 Charles Lindbergh Blvd # 400 (11553-3626)
PHONE...........................516 229-2330
Fax: 516 229-2350
Eric Kastens, *President*
EMP: 10
SQ FT: 300
SALES: 1.3MM **Privately Held**
WEB: www.aithaca.com
SIC: 2819 5169 Chemicals, high purity: refined from technical grade; chemicals & allied products

(G-16289)
AWAP INC
Also Called: Aftermarket Whl Autobody Parts
982 Front St Unit A (11553-1640)
PHONE...........................516 481-4070
Huguette Raphael, *President*
EMP: 7
SALES (est): 624.1K **Privately Held**
SIC: 3131 Body parts, shoe outers

(G-16290)
CAMBRIDGE WHOS WHO PUBG INC (PA)
498 Rxr Plz Fl 4 (11556-0400)
PHONE...........................516 833-8440
Mitchel Robbins, *CEO*
Randy Narod, *President*
Nicole Fogarty, *Editor*
Eric Lee, *COO*
Stephanie Alex, *Asst Director*
EMP: 45
SALES (est): 20.3MM **Privately Held**
SIC: 2741 8748 Miscellaneous publishing; business consulting

(G-16291)
COTY US LLC
726 Eab Plz (11556-0726)
PHONE...........................212 389-7000
Rich Garzon, *Branch Mgr*
EMP: 284 **Publicly Held**
SIC: 2844 Perfumes & colognes; cosmetic preparations
HQ: Coty Us Llc
350 5th Ave Fl C1700
New York NY 10118
212 389-7000

(G-16292)
ELIZABETH WILSON
Also Called: Elizabeth's
579 Edgemere Ave (11553-2517)
PHONE...........................516 486-2157
Elizabeth Wilson, *Owner*
EMP: 4
SQ FT: 1,200
SALES: 2.2MM **Privately Held**
WEB: www.elizabethwilson.com
SIC: 2339 Aprons, except rubber or plastic: women's, misses', juniors'

(G-16293)
FEI COMMUNICATIONS INC
55 Charles Lindbergh Blvd (11553-3689)
PHONE...........................516 794-4500
Martin B Bloch, *President*
Harry Newman, *Vice Pres*
EMP: 180
SALES (est): 25.2MM
SALES (corp-wide): 60.3MM **Publicly Held**
WEB: www.freqelec.com
SIC: 3679 Electronic circuits
PA: Frequency Electronics, Inc.
55 Charles Lindbergh Blvd # 2
Uniondale NY 11553
516 794-4500

(G-16294)
FEI-ZYFER INC
55 Charles Lindbergh Blvd (11553-3689)
PHONE...........................714 933-4045
EMP: 8
SALES (corp-wide): 60.3MM **Publicly Held**
SIC: 3663 Antennas, transmitting & communications
HQ: Fei-Zyfer, Inc.
7321 Lincoln Way
Garden Grove CA 92841
714 933-4000

(G-16295)
FREQUENCY ELECTRONICS INC (PA)
55 Charles Lindbergh Blvd # 2 (11553-3699)
PHONE...........................516 794-4500
Fax: 516 794-4340
Joseph P Franklin, *Ch of Bd*
Martin B Bloch, *President*
James Davis, *President*
Steven Strang, *President*
Nick Bainlardi, *Business Mgr*
EMP: 277 EST: 1961
SALES: 60.3MM **Publicly Held**
WEB: www.freqelec.com
SIC: 3825 3812 3669 3679 Elapsed time meters, electronic; frequency meters: electrical, mechanical & electronic; search & detection systems & instruments; detection apparatus: electronic/magnetic field, light/heat; intercommunication systems, electric; microwave components

(G-16296)
HEARST BUSINESS MEDIA (HQ)
Also Called: F C W Division
50 Charles Lindbergh Blvd # 100 (11553-3600)
PHONE...........................516 227-1300
Rich Malloch, *CEO*
Kathy Chacana, *VP Human Res*
EMP: 97
SALES (est): 7.5MM
SALES (corp-wide): 4.9B **Privately Held**
SIC: 2721 2741 Magazines: publishing only, not printed on site; directories: publishing only, not printed on site
PA: The Hearst Corporation
300 W 57th St Fl 42
New York NY 10019
212 649-2000

(G-16297)
JPM AND ASSOCIATES
639 Nostrand Ave (11553-3026)
PHONE...........................516 483-4699
Sterling Michel, *Vice Pres*
EMP: 10
SALES (est): 860K **Privately Held**
SIC: 7372 Application computer software

(G-16298)
LOCKHEED MARTIN CORPORATION
55 Charles Lindbergh Blvd # 1 (11553-3682)
PHONE...........................516 228-2000
John Piccirillo, *Managing Dir*
Hugh Rice, *Research*
Joseph Cappiello, *Engineer*
Michael Chen, *Engineer*
Vincent Benischek, *Senior Engr*
EMP: 225
SALES (corp-wide): 46.1B **Publicly Held**
WEB: www.lockheedmartin.com
SIC: 3571 Electronic computers
PA: Lockheed Martin Corporation
6801 Rockledge Dr
Bethesda MD 20817
301 897-6000

(G-16299)
SOLAR THIN FILMS INC (PA)
Also Called: Stf
1136 Rxr Plz (11556-1100)
PHONE...........................516 341-7787
Jim Solano, *CEO*
James J Solano Jr, *CEO*
▲ EMP: 16
SALES (est): 3.6MM **Publicly Held**
SIC: 3674 Photovoltaic devices, solid state

(G-16300)
TDK USA CORPORATION (HQ)
455 Rxr Plz (11556-3811)
PHONE...........................516 535-2600
Francis J Sweeney Jr, *Ch of Bd*
Tom Kossmann, *Vice Pres*
Susan Sparks, *Vice Pres*
Iesha Brown, *Administration*
◆ EMP: 68
SQ FT: 60,000
SALES (est): 286MM
SALES (corp-wide): 9.8B **Privately Held**
SIC: 3679 8741 Recording & playback apparatus, including phonograph; administrative management; financial management for business
PA: Tdk Corporation
3-9-1, Shibaura
Minato-Ku TKY 108-0
368 527-300

(G-16301)
VALLE SIGNS AND AWNINGS
889 Nassau Rd (11553-3131)
PHONE...........................516 408-3440
Fax: 516 408-3441
Oscar Valle, *Owner*
EMP: 10
SALES (est): 878.7K **Privately Held**
SIC: 3993 Signs & advertising specialties

Unionville
Orange County

(G-16302)
ROYAL FIREWORKS PRINTING CO
First Ave (10988)
P.O. Box 399 (10988-0399)
PHONE...........................845 726-3333
Thomas Kemnitz, *President*
EMP: 13
SQ FT: 66,000
SALES (est): 1.1MM **Privately Held**
SIC: 2732 5942 Book printing; book stores

Upper Jay
Essex County

(G-16303)
AMSTUTZE WOODWORKING (PA)
246 Springfield Rd (12987-3200)
PHONE...........................518 946-8206
Steve Amstutz, *Principal*
EMP: 5
SALES (est): 456.5K **Privately Held**
SIC: 2431 Millwork

Utica
Oneida County

(G-16304)
A & P MASTER IMAGES
205 Water St (13502-3101)
PHONE...........................315 793-1934
Amanda L Potter, *Owner*
Howard A Potter, *Co-Owner*
EMP: 15
SALES (est): 321.7K **Privately Held**
SIC: 2759 Promotional printing

(G-16305)
ADVANCE ENERGY SYSTEMS NY LLC
17 Tilton Rd (13501-6411)
PHONE...........................315 735-5125
Duane Farr, *President*
EMP: 5
SALES (est): 649.2K **Privately Held**
SIC: 3699 High-energy particle physics equipment

(G-16306)
AEROMED INC
1821 Broad St Ste 1 (13501-1115)
P.O. Box 768, Amsterdam (12010-0768)
PHONE...........................518 843-9144
William E Palmer, *President*
EMP: 5
SALES (est): 721.5K **Privately Held**
WEB: www.aeromed.com
SIC: 3564 Air purification equipment

(G-16307)
ANRITSU INSTRUMENTS COMPANY
421 Broad St Ste 14 (13501-1210)
PHONE...........................315 797-4449
Takanori Sumi, *President*
Lars Pedersen, *Vice Pres*
Frank Tiernan, *Vice Pres*
Kevin Germaine, *Mfg Mgr*
John Butler, *Engineer*
EMP: 50
SQ FT: 60,000
SALES (est): 5.4MM
SALES (corp-wide): 816.4MM **Privately Held**
WEB: www.nettest.com
SIC: 3229 Fiber optics strands
HQ: Anritsu U.S. Holding, Inc.
490 Jarvis Dr
Morgan Hill CA 95037
408 778-2000

(G-16308)
AUSTIN MOHAWK AND COMPANY LLC
2175 Beechgrove Pl (13501-1705)
PHONE...........................315 793-3000
Hayes Barnard, *General Mgr*
John B Millet, *Plant Mgr*
Ted Flint, *Safety Mgr*
Katherine McDonald, *Controller*
Timothy Teeter, *VP Sales*
▲ EMP: 29
SQ FT: 20,000
SALES: 5.5MM **Privately Held**
WEB: www.austinmohawk.com
SIC: 3448 3444 Prefabricated metal buildings; canopies, sheet metal

(G-16309)
BAGEL GROVE INC
5 Burrstone Rd (13502-5405)
PHONE...........................315 724-8015
Matthew Grove, *President*
Anna Grove, *Vice Pres*
EMP: 25
SQ FT: 2,600
SALES: 450K **Privately Held**
WEB: www.bagelgrove.com
SIC: 2051 5149 5461 Bagels, fresh or frozen; crackers, cookies & bakery products; bagels

(G-16310)
BRODOCK PRESS INC (PA)
502 Court St Ste G (13502-4233)
PHONE...........................315 735-9577
Fax: 315 624-0597
Craig S Brodock, *Chairman*
Dave Storey, *Vice Pres*
Donald Weagley, *Vice Pres*
Bryan Brodock, *VP Opers*
Thomas Excell, *Accounts Exec*
EMP: 74 EST: 1960
SQ FT: 80,000
SALES: 12MM **Privately Held**
WEB: www.brodock.com
SIC: 2759 2752 2791 2789 Letterpress printing; commercial printing, lithographic; typesetting; bookbinding & related work

▲ = Import ▼ = Export
◆ = Import/Export

Utica - Oneida County (G-16335)

(G-16311)
CLARA PAPA
Also Called: Kennel Klub
1323 Blandina St 1 (13501-1915)
PHONE..................................315 733-2660
Clara Papa, *Owner*
EMP: 5
SQ FT: 15,000
SALES (est): 237.2K **Privately Held**
SIC: 3999 5199 Pet supplies; pet supplies

(G-16312)
CNY BUSINESS SOLUTIONS
502 Court St Ste 206 (13502-0001)
PHONE..................................315 733-5031
Wendy Aiello, *Principal*
EMP: 5 EST: 2010
SALES (est): 468.2K **Privately Held**
SIC: 3577 Printers & plotters

(G-16313)
COLLINITE CORPORATION
1520 Lincoln Ave (13502-5200)
PHONE..................................315 732-2282
Fax: 315 732-2816
Michael Taylor, *President*
Chris Curley, *Manager*
Ronald Yoddow, *Manager*
Christine Taylor, *Admin Sec*
EMP: 5 EST: 1912
SQ FT: 6,000
SALES (est): 831.5K **Privately Held**
WEB: www.collinite.com
SIC: 2842 5087 5169 5999 Cleaning or polishing preparations; polishing preparations & related products; janitors' supplies; waxes, except petroleum; cleaning equipment & supplies; mail order house

(G-16314)
CONMED ANDOVER MEDICAL INC (HQ)
525 French Rd Ste 3 (13502-5994)
PHONE..................................315 797-8375
Fax: 315 732-5267
Joseph J Corasanti, *CEO*
EMP: 12
SALES (est): 4.7MM
SALES (corp-wide): 719.1MM **Publicly Held**
SIC: 3845 Electromedical apparatus
PA: Conmed Corporation
525 French Rd Ste 3
Utica NY 13502
315 797-8375

(G-16315)
CONMED CORPORATION
Endoscopic Technologies Div
525 French Rd (13502-5994)
PHONE..................................315 797-8375
Robert Shaw Jr, *Plant Mgr*
Dennis Werger, *Manager*
Mike Giordano, *IT/INT Sup*
EMP: 83
SALES (corp-wide): 719.1MM **Publicly Held**
SIC: 3845 8731 3841 Electromedical equipment; commercial physical research; surgical & medical instruments
PA: Conmed Corporation
525 French Rd Ste 3
Utica NY 13502
315 797-8375

(G-16316)
CONMED CORPORATION (PA)
525 French Rd Ste 3 (13502-5994)
PHONE..................................315 797-8375
Fax: 315 797-0321
Mark E Tryniski, *Ch of Bd*
Curt Hartman, *President*
Curt R Hartman, *President*
Richard Turner, *COO*
Daniel Jones, *Counsel*
◆ EMP: 277
SQ FT: 500,000
SALES: 719.1MM **Publicly Held**
SIC: 3845 3841 Electromedical apparatus; electrocardiographs; patient monitoring apparatus; surgical instruments & apparatus; trocars; suction therapy apparatus; probes, surgical

(G-16317)
CRANESVILLE BLOCK CO INC
Also Called: Cranesville Concrete Co
895 Catherine St (13501-1409)
PHONE..................................315 732-2135
Fax: 315 732-8418
John Abdo, *District Mgr*
Mark Smith, *Branch Mgr*
EMP: 25
SQ FT: 3,462
SALES (corp-wide): 41.2MM **Privately Held**
SIC: 3273 Ready-mixed concrete
PA: Cranesville Block Co., Inc.
1250 Riverfront Ctr
Amsterdam NY 12010
518 684-6000

(G-16318)
CRITICAL IMAGING LLC
2428 Chenango Rd (13502-5909)
PHONE..................................315 732-5020
Harold Wood, *Electrical Engi*
Donna Palmieri, *Finance*
Richard Evans,
EMP: 23
SALES (est): 3.9MM **Privately Held**
WEB: www.infraredcomponents.com
SIC: 3861 Cameras, still & motion picture (all types)

(G-16319)
CYBERSPORTS INC (PA)
11 Avery Pl (13502-5401)
PHONE..................................315 737-7150
Todd Hobin, *President*
Candice Hobin, *Vice Pres*
EMP: 7
SALES (est): 726.3K **Privately Held**
WEB: www.cybersportsinc.com
SIC: 7372 Prepackaged software

(G-16320)
DACOBE ENTERPRISES LLC
325 Lafayette St (13502-4228)
PHONE..................................315 368-0093
Dan Beal, *President*
Geoff Thorp, *Vice Pres*
EMP: 10
SQ FT: 250
SALES: 5MM **Privately Held**
SIC: 3089 Plastic processing

(G-16321)
DARMAN MANUFACTURING CO INC
1410 Lincoln Ave (13502-5019)
PHONE..................................315 724-9632
Fax: 315 724-8099
Pamela Darman, *CEO*
Gilbert Jones, *CFO*
Cynthia J Lane, *Treasurer*
James Henrickson, *CTO*
Michael Swiercz, *CTO*
▼ EMP: 16 EST: 1936
SQ FT: 20,800
SALES: 1.9MM **Privately Held**
WEB: www.darmanco.com
SIC: 3088 Plastics plumbing fixtures

(G-16322)
DEIORIO FOODS INC (PA)
Also Called: De Iorio's Bakery
2200 Bleecker St (13501-1739)
PHONE..................................315 732-7612
Fax: 315 724-6964
Robert J Ragusa, *CEO*
Richard Viti, *President*
Michelle Burnett, *General Mgr*
Larry Evans, *Vice Pres*
Robert Horth, *Vice Pres*
EMP: 25 EST: 1924
SALES (est): 17.9MM **Privately Held**
WEB: www.deiorios.com
SIC: 2053 Frozen bakery products, except bread

(G-16323)
DICO PRODUCTS CORPORATION
200 Seward Ave (13502-5750)
PHONE..................................315 797-0470
Bradford Lees Divine, *President*
Dan Beligel, *Treasurer*
▲ EMP: 15

SALES (est): 1.2MM **Privately Held**
WEB: www.dicoproducts.com
SIC: 3496 3429 3291 2392 Hardware cloth, woven wire; manufactured hardware (general); abrasive products; household furnishings

(G-16324)
DIMANCO INC (PA)
Also Called: Divine Bros
200 Seward Ave (13502-5750)
PHONE..................................315 797-0470
Fax: 315 797-0058
B Lees Divine, *President*
Thomas B Dalton, *COO*
Brian Carpenter, *Plant Mgr*
Mike Plescia, *Purch Mgr*
Thomas Banks, *CFO*
▲ EMP: 3
SQ FT: 170,000
SALES (est): 28.4MM **Privately Held**
WEB: www.dimanco.com
SIC: 3291 3562 Buffing or polishing wheels, abrasive or nonabrasive; casters

(G-16325)
DINOS SAUSAGE & MEAT CO INC
722 Catherine St (13501-1304)
PHONE..................................315 732-2661
Fax: 315 732-3094
Anthony Ferrucci, *President*
Carman Bossone, *Manager*
EMP: 11
SQ FT: 6,300
SALES (est): 1.7MM **Privately Held**
SIC: 2013 Sausages & other prepared meats; sausages & related products, from purchased meat; prepared beef products from purchased beef

(G-16326)
DIVA FARMS LTD
1301 Broad St (13501-1605)
PHONE..................................315 735-4397
Margherita Schuller, *President*
EMP: 7
SQ FT: 2,000
SALES (est): 550K **Privately Held**
SIC: 2099 Seasonings & spices

(G-16327)
DIVINE BROTHERS COMPANY
Also Called: Dico Products
200 Seward Ave (13502-5750)
PHONE..................................315 797-0470
Bradford W Divine, *President*
Charles H Divine, *Vice Pres*
Thomas Banks, *CFO*
Michael Plecia, *Director*
◆ EMP: 112 EST: 1892
SQ FT: 112,000
SALES (est): 9.8MM
SALES (corp-wide): 28.4MM **Privately Held**
WEB: www.divinebrothers.com
SIC: 3291 2899 2891 2819 Buffing or polishing wheels, abrasive or nonabrasive; chemical preparations; adhesives & sealants; industrial inorganic chemicals
PA: Dimanco Inc.
200 Seward Ave
Utica NY 13502
315 797-0470

(G-16328)
ECR INTERNATIONAL INC (PA)
Also Called: Utica Boilers
2201 Dwyer Ave (13501-1101)
P.O. Box 4729 (13504-4729)
PHONE..................................315 797-1310
Fax: 315 797-3762
Ronald J Passafaro, *Ch of Bd*
Timothy R Reed, *President*
Earle C Reed, *Vice Chairman*
James Benson, *Vice Pres*
Paul Totaro, *Vice Pres*
◆ EMP: 100 EST: 1928
SQ FT: 190,000
SALES (est): 119MM **Privately Held**
WEB: www.ecrinternational.com
SIC: 3433 3444 3443 Boilers, low-pressure heating: steam or hot water; sheet metalwork; fabricated plate work (boiler shop)

(G-16329)
ELG UTICA ALLOYS HOLDINGS INC
91 Wurz Ave (13502-2533)
PHONE..................................315 733-0475
Anthony Moreno, *President*
EMP: 8
SALES (est): 719.1K
SALES (corp-wide): 4B **Privately Held**
SIC: 3599 Industrial machinery
HQ: Elg Utica Alloys International Gmbh
Kremerskamp 16
Duisburg
203 450-10

(G-16330)
FALVO MANUFACTURING CO INC
20 Harbor Point Rd (13502-2502)
PHONE..................................315 738-7682
Eugene T Falvo, *President*
EMP: 15
SQ FT: 26,000
SALES (est): 1.5MM **Privately Held**
SIC: 2441 2512 2522 2541 Packing cases, wood: nailed or lock corner; upholstered household furniture; office cabinets & filing drawers: except wood; store fixtures, wood

(G-16331)
FARRINGTON PACKAGING CORP
2007 Beechgrove Pl (13501-1703)
PHONE..................................315 733-4600
Raymond Mele, *President*
Gerard Morrissey, *Controller*
Kevin Siembab, *Sales Mgr*
Bill Richardson, *Manager*
Bill Richa, *Info Tech Dir*
EMP: 40
SALES (est): 5MM **Privately Held**
SIC: 2631 2541 Packaging board; wood partitions & fixtures

(G-16332)
FEDERAL SHEET METAL WORKS INC
1416 Dudley Ave (13501-4611)
P.O. Box 273 (13503-0273)
PHONE..................................315 735-4730
Fax: 315 735-0729
Leonard A Capuana, *President*
Michael Capuana, *Treasurer*
EMP: 12
SQ FT: 7,500
SALES: 1.5MM **Privately Held**
SIC: 3444 Sheet metalwork

(G-16333)
FOURTEEN ARNOLD AVE CORP
Also Called: Progress Industries Sales
14 Arnold Ave (13502-5602)
PHONE..................................315 272-1700
Fax: 315 735-4800
Angela Van Derhoof, *President*
Russell Bell, *Manager*
James Coffin, *Business Dir*
EMP: 15
SALES: 277K **Privately Held**
SIC: 3565 Packing & wrapping machinery

(G-16334)
G W CANFIELD & SON INC
600 Plant St (13502-4712)
PHONE..................................315 735-5522
Fax: 315 735-4945
Mark W Canfield, *President*
Anne C Kuhn, *Vice Pres*
EMP: 6
SQ FT: 5,000
SALES (est): 931.8K **Privately Held**
WEB: www.gwcanfield.com
SIC: 2752 Commercial printing, lithographic; commercial printing, offset

(G-16335)
GAMETIME SPORTSWEAR PLUS LLC
1206 Belle Ave (13501-2614)
PHONE..................................315 724-5893
Michael Macchione,
EMP: 6
SQ FT: 3,200

Utica - Oneida County (G-16336) GEOGRAPHIC SECTION

SALES (est): 460K **Privately Held**
SIC: 2329 5699 Men's & boys' sportswear & athletic clothing; sports apparel

(G-16336)
GATEHOUSE MEDIA LLC
Also Called: Observer Dispatch
350 Willowbrook Office Pa (13501)
PHONE...................................315 792-5000
Fax: 315 792-4973
Donna Donnovan, *Principal*
Matt Becker, *Editor*
Rob Booth, *Editor*
Barbara Laible, *Editor*
Marty Lyons, *Editor*
EMP: 38
SALES (corp-wide): 1.2B **Publicly Held**
WEB: www.gatehousemedia.com
SIC: 2711 Newspapers
HQ: Gatehouse Media, Llc
   175 Sullys Trl Ste 300
   Pittsford NY 14534
   585 598-0030

(G-16337)
H F BROWN MACHINE CO INC
708 State St (13502-3458)
PHONE...................................315 732-6129
James F Chubbuck, *President*
Joseph Chubbuck, *Vice Pres*
George Chubbuck, *Treasurer*
EMP: 10 EST: 1946
SQ FT: 26,000
SALES (est): 1.3MM **Privately Held**
SIC: 3599 Machine shop, jobbing & repair

(G-16338)
HPK INDUSTRIES LLC
1208 Broad St (13501-1604)
P.O. Box 4682 (13504-4682)
PHONE...................................315 724-0196
Fax: 315 724-0197
Mike Liberatore, *Director*
Michael A Liberatore,
▲ EMP: 15
SQ FT: 11,000
SALES (est): 1.2MM **Privately Held**
WEB: www.hpkindustries.com
SIC: 2389 5131 Disposable garments & accessories; piece goods & notions

(G-16339)
HUMAN ELECTRONICS INC
155 Genesee St (13501-2105)
PHONE...................................315 724-9850
Philip Szeliga, *President*
EMP: 5 EST: 1999
SQ FT: 16,000
SALES (est): 595.7K **Privately Held**
WEB: www.humanelectronics.com
SIC: 3571 4813 Electronic computers; telephone communication, except radio

(G-16340)
HUMAN TECHNOLOGIES CORPORATION
Also Called: Graphtex A Div of Htc
2260 Dwyer Ave (13501-1193)
PHONE...................................315 735-3532
Fax: 315 735-2699
Tom Keller, *Manager*
Richard E Sebastian, *Manager*
Michael Kowiatek, *Info Tech Mgr*
EMP: 10
SQ FT: 7,600
SALES (corp-wide): 17.3MM **Privately Held**
WEB: www.htcorp.net
SIC: 2396 2759 2395 Screen printing on fabric articles; screen printing; embroidery products, except schiffli machine
PA: Human Technologies Corporation
   2260 Dwyer Ave
   Utica NY 13501
   315 735-3532

(G-16341)
IDG LLC
Also Called: Microfoam
31 Faass Ave (13502-3350)
PHONE...................................315 797-1000
Fax: 315 724-8427
Kevin Sharrow, *Manager*
Steve Bednarz, *Manager*
Scott Ingersoll, *Manager*
Mark Ingersoll, *Director*

Don Polak, *Executive*
EMP: 49
SALES (corp-wide): 199.4MM **Privately Held**
SIC: 3069 Rolls, solid or covered rubber
HQ: Idg, Llc
   1480 Gould Dr
   Cookeville TN 38506
   931 432-4000

(G-16342)
INDIUM CORPORATION OF AMERICA
1676 Lincoln Ave (13502-5398)
PHONE...................................315 793-8200
Fax: 315 793-8907
Ning Lee, *Vice Pres*
John Sovinsky, *Opers Staff*
Geoff Beckwith, *Engineer*
Leslie Schenk, *CFO*
Brad Anderson, *Controller*
EMP: 30
SQ FT: 31,210
SALES (corp-wide): 215.1MM **Privately Held**
WEB: www.indium.com
SIC: 3356 2899 Solder: wire, bar, acid core, & rosin core; chemical preparations
PA: Indium Corporation Of America
   34 Robinson Rd
   Clinton NY 13323
   800 446-3486

(G-16343)
INDIUM CORPORATION OF AMERICA
111 Business Park Dr (13502-6303)
PHONE...................................315 381-2330
Anthony Lanza, *Engineer*
EMP: 38
SALES (corp-wide): 215.1MM **Privately Held**
SIC: 3356 Solder: wire, bar, acid core, & rosin core
PA: Indium Corporation Of America
   34 Robinson Rd
   Clinton NY 13323
   800 446-3486

(G-16344)
INFRARED COMPONENTS CORP
2306 Bleecker St (13501-1746)
PHONE...................................315 732-1544
Thomas Clynne, *President*
Don Darling, *Plant Mgr*
Dick Evans, *Sales Staff*
EMP: 20
SQ FT: 17,000
SALES (est): 3.1MM **Privately Held**
SIC: 3812 Infrared object detection equipment; detection apparatus: electronic/magnetic field, light/heat

(G-16345)
INTERNATIONAL PAPER COMPANY
50 Harbor Point Rd (13502-2502)
PHONE...................................315 797-5120
EMP: 160
SALES (corp-wide): 22.3B **Publicly Held**
SIC: 2621 Paper mills
PA: International Paper Company
   6400 Poplar Ave
   Memphis TN 38197
   901 419-9000

(G-16346)
KELLY FOUNDRY & MACHINE CO
300 Hubbell St Ste 308 (13501-1404)
PHONE...................................315 732-8313
Fax: 315 732-8364
Geogia M Kelley, *President*
Marsha J Kelly, *Corp Secy*
James S Kelly III, *Vice Pres*
Mark James Kelly, *Vice Pres*
EMP: 48 EST: 1892
SQ FT: 14,632
SALES (est): 7.5MM **Privately Held**
WEB: www.kellyfoundry.com
SIC: 3369 3999 3953 Nonferrous foundries; plaques, picture, laminated; marking devices

(G-16347)
METAL SOLUTIONS INC
1821 Broad St Ste 5 (13501-1115)
PHONE...................................315 732-6271
Joseph Cattadoris Jr, *President*
Cathy Cattadoris, *Vice Pres*
John Kulis, *Shareholder*
EMP: 50 EST: 1954
SQ FT: 110,000
SALES (est): 13MM **Privately Held**
WEB: www.nhsmetal.com
SIC: 3444 Sheet metalwork

(G-16348)
MILLENNIUM ANTENNA CORP
1001 Broad St Ste 401 (13501-1545)
PHONE...................................315 798-9374
David Schroeter, *President*
Paul King, *Manager*
EMP: 10
SQ FT: 2,000
SALES (est): 950K **Privately Held**
WEB: www.millenniumantenna.com
SIC: 3663 8711 8731 Antennas, transmitting & communications; engineering services; electronic research

(G-16349)
MOBILE MINI INC
2222 Oriskany St W Ste 3 (13502-2925)
PHONE...................................315 732-4555
Marc Allen, *Branch Mgr*
EMP: 10
SALES (corp-wide): 530.7MM **Publicly Held**
WEB: www.mobilemini.com
SIC: 3448 3441 3412 7359 Prefabricated metal buildings; fabricated structural metal; metal barrels, drums & pails; equipment rental & leasing
PA: Mobile Mini, Inc.
   4646 E Van Buren St # 400
   Phoenix AZ 85008
   480 894-6311

(G-16350)
MUNSON MACHINERY COMPANY INC
210 Seward Ave (13502-5750)
PHONE...................................315 797-0090
Fax: 315 797-5582
Charles H Divine, *CEO*
Robert Batson, *Engineer*
Dan Simmons, *Design Engr*
Nicholas Rubyor, *Regl Sales Mgr*
Antonio Sanchez, *Sales Engr*
▲ EMP: 40 EST: 1828
SQ FT: 45,000
SALES (est): 12.5MM
SALES (corp-wide): 28.4MM **Privately Held**
WEB: www.munsonmachinery.com
SIC: 3532 3531 3559 3541 Crushing, pulverizing & screening equipment; mixers: ore, plaster, slag, sand, mortar, etc.; refinery, chemical processing & similar machinery; machine tools, metal cutting type; buffing & polishing machines; grinding machines, metalworking; metalworking machinery
PA: Dimanco Inc.
   200 Seward Ave
   Utica NY 13502
   315 797-0470

(G-16351)
NATHAN STEEL CORP
36 Wurz Ave (13502-2534)
P.O. Box 299 (13503-0299)
PHONE...................................315 797-1335
Fax: 315 797-1536
Edward Kowalsky, *President*
Wade Wells, *Warehouse Mgr*
Helen Evans, *Manager*
Peter Morgan, *Manager*
EMP: 15
SQ FT: 12,000
SALES (est): 4.1MM **Privately Held**
SIC: 3441 5051 Fabricated structural metal; steel

(G-16352)
NORTH COUNTRY BOOKS INC
220 Lafayette St (13502-4312)
PHONE...................................315 735-4877
Fax: 315 738-4342

Robert Igoe, *President*
EMP: 5
SQ FT: 5,000
SALES: 1.1MM **Privately Held**
WEB: www.northcountrybooks.com
SIC: 2732 5192 Books: printing only; books

(G-16353)
NOVA HEALTH SYSTEMS INC
1001 Broad St Ste 3 (13501-1546)
P.O. Box 4335 (13504-4335)
PHONE...................................315 798-9018
Fax: 315 798-9337
Wade Abraham, *President*
▲ EMP: 6
SQ FT: 4,000
SALES (est): 400K **Privately Held**
WEB: www.novahealthsystems.com
SIC: 3842 5047 Surgical appliances & supplies; medical & hospital equipment

(G-16354)
OHIO BAKING COMPANY INC
Also Called: Spano's Bread
10585 Cosby Manor Rd (13502-1207)
PHONE...................................315 724-2033
Fax: 315 735-7419
Joseph A Spano, *President*
EMP: 20 EST: 1930
SQ FT: 4,000
SALES (est): 3.5MM **Privately Held**
SIC: 2041 2051 5149 5461 Pizza dough, prepared; pizza mixes; bread, all types (white, wheat, rye, etc): fresh or frozen; bakery products; bakeries

(G-16355)
ORBCOMM INC
125 Business Park Dr (13502-6304)
PHONE...................................703 433-6396
EMP: 7
SALES (corp-wide): 178.2MM **Publicly Held**
SIC: 3663 Satellites, communications
PA: Orbcomm Inc.
   395 W Passaic St Ste 3
   Rochelle Park NJ 07662
   703 433-6361

(G-16356)
PRINT SHOPPE
311 Turner St Ste 310 (13501-1766)
PHONE...................................315 792-9585
Fax: 315 368-0064
Steven Finch, *Partner*
Thomas Stewart, *Partner*
EMP: 7
SALES (est): 725.4K **Privately Held**
SIC: 2759 Screen printing

(G-16357)
ROBERT BOSCH LLC
2118 Beechgrove Pl (13501-1706)
PHONE...................................315 733-3312
EMP: 25
SALES (corp-wide): 268.9MM **Privately Held**
SIC: 3841 Mfg Surgical/Medical Instruments
HQ: Robert Bosch Llc
   2800 S 25th Ave
   Broadview IL 60155
   708 865-5200

(G-16358)
SCOOBY RENDERING & INC
Also Called: Scooby Dog Food
1930 Oriskany St W (13502-2920)
PHONE...................................315 793-1014
Fax: 315 793-0043
Michael P Dote, *President*
EMP: 5
SQ FT: 3,000
SALES (est): 654.4K **Privately Held**
SIC: 2047 Dog food

(G-16359)
SHIPRITE SOFTWARE INC
1312 Genesee St (13502-4700)
PHONE...................................315 733-6191
J Mark Ford, *President*
EMP: 9
SQ FT: 8,400

GEOGRAPHIC SECTION

Valley Cottage - Rockland County (G-16386)

SALES (est): 939.3K **Privately Held**
SIC: 7372 7334 7359 Prepackaged software; photocopying & duplicating services; shipping container leasing

(G-16360)
STURGES MANUFACTURING CO INC
2030 Sunset Ave (13502-5500)
P.O. Box 59 (13503-0059)
PHONE..................................315 732-6159
Fax: 315 732-2314
Bruce T Brach, *General Mgr*
Tyler Griffith, *Vice Pres*
Norma Jean Rice, *Vice Pres*
Norma Rice, *QC Mgr*
Sharon Bubb, *Manager*
▲ **EMP:** 75 **EST:** 1909
SQ FT: 58,000
SALES (est): 16.8MM **Privately Held**
WEB: www.sturgesmfg.com
SIC: 2241 Strapping webs; webbing, woven

(G-16361)
T C PETERS PRINTING CO INC
2336 W Whitesboro St (13502-3235)
PHONE..................................315 724-4149
Fax: 315 738-8983
Richard Peters, *CEO*
Douglas Peters, *President*
EMP: 9
SQ FT: 13,200
SALES (est): 1.3MM **Privately Held**
SIC: 2752 Commercial printing, offset

(G-16362)
USA SEWING INC
901 Broad St Ste 2 (13501-1500)
PHONE..................................315 792-8017
John D Inserra, *President*
Lisa Bates, *Manager*
EMP: 49
SALES (est): 3.8MM **Privately Held**
SIC: 3151 Leather gloves & mittens

(G-16363)
UTICA CUTLERY COMPANY
Also Called: Walco Stainless
820 Noyes St (13502-5053)
P.O. Box 10527 (13502)
PHONE..................................315 733-4663
Fax: 315 733-6602
A Edward Allen Jr, *Ch of Bd*
David S Allen, *Ch of Bd*
Phil Benbenek, *Exec VP*
Roy Gonzales, *Vice Pres*
David Barr, *Engineer*
◆ **EMP:** 60
SQ FT: 90,000
SALES (est): 14.3MM **Privately Held**
WEB: www.kutmaster.com
SIC: 3914 3421 5023 5072 Flatware, stainless steel; cutlery, stainless steel; knives: butchers', hunting, pocket, etc.; stainless steel flatware; cutlery

(G-16364)
UTICA METAL PRODUCTS INC
1526 Lincoln Ave (13502-5298)
PHONE..................................315 732-6163
Fax: 315 732-0234
Charles J Fields, *Ch of Bd*
Monte L Craig, *Vice Ch of Bd*
Robert Moore, *COO*
Justin Shade, *Engineer*
Lou Rabbia, *Controller*
EMP: 73
SQ FT: 30,000
SALES (est): 13.8MM **Privately Held**
WEB: www.uticametals.com
SIC: 3465 3471 Automotive stampings; hub caps, automobile: stamped metal; anodizing (plating) of metals or formed products

Valhalla
Westchester County

(G-16365)
CHESTER SHRED-IT/WEST
420 Columbus Ave Ste 202 (10595-1382)
PHONE..................................914 347-4460

Greg Brophy, *President*
EMP: 20
SALES (est): 2.1MM **Privately Held**
SIC: 3589 Shredders, industrial & commercial

(G-16366)
CONSTRUCTION TECHNOLOGY INC (PA)
400 Columbus Ave Ste 110s (10595-3320)
PHONE..................................914 747-8900
Richard Levine, *President*
Deborah Jillson, *Exec Dir*
EMP: 5
SQ FT: 1,000
SALES (est): 2MM **Privately Held**
SIC: 7372 Prepackaged software

(G-16367)
EPOCH MICROELECTRONICS INC
420 Columbus Ave Ste 204 (10595-1382)
PHONE..................................914 332-8570
Ken Suyama, *President*
Aleksander Dec, *Vice Pres*
Sachiko Tokai, *Manager*
EMP: 9
SALES (est): 1.1MM **Privately Held**
WEB: www.epochmicro.com
SIC: 3825 Integrated circuit testers

(G-16368)
LEGACY VALVE LLC
14 Railroad Ave (10595-1609)
P.O. Box 107 (10595-0107)
PHONE..................................914 403-5075
EMP: 12
SALES (est): 2.4MM **Privately Held**
SIC: 3494 Pipe fittings

(G-16369)
PEPSICO
100 Summit Lake Dr # 103 (10595-2318)
PHONE..................................914 801-1500
Rene Lammers, *COO*
Heidi Dubois, *Counsel*
Larry D Thompson, *Exec VP*
Patricia Delease, *Production*
Nicolas Nicolaou, *CFO*
EMP: 31
SALES (est): 4.8MM **Privately Held**
SIC: 2086 Carbonated soft drinks, bottled & canned

(G-16370)
PEPSICO INC
100 E Stevens Ave (10595-1299)
PHONE..................................914 742-4500
Fax: 914 749-3330
Noel E Anderson, *Vice Pres*
Lee French, *Project Mgr*
Onna Burleson, *Research*
Raymond McGarvey, *Research*
Kevin Doyle, *Engineer*
EMP: 380
SALES (corp-wide): 63B **Publicly Held**
WEB: www.pepsico.com
SIC: 2086 Carbonated soft drinks, bottled & canned
PA: Pepsico, Inc.
  700 Anderson Hill Rd
  Purchase NY 10577
  914 253-2000

(G-16371)
PRESBREY-LELAND INC
Also Called: Presbrey- Leland Memorials
250 Lakeview Ave (10595-1618)
PHONE..................................914 949-2264
Fax: 914 949-7846
Nancy Dylan, *President*
EMP: 5 **EST:** 1982
SALES (est): 630.2K **Privately Held**
SIC: 3272 5999 Monuments, concrete; monuments, finished to custom order; monuments & tombstones

(G-16372)
RUHLE COMPANIES INC
Also Called: Farrand Controls Division
99 Wall St (10595-1462)
PHONE..................................914 287-4000
Fax: 914 761-0405
Frank S Ruhle, *Ch of Bd*
Robert E Ruhle, *Exec VP*
Tom Lavacca, *Mfg Spvr*

Richard Babcock, *Production*
William Moore, *QC Mgr*
EMP: 50
SQ FT: 33,000
SALES (est): 9.2MM **Privately Held**
WEB: www.ruhle.com
SIC: 3679 3625 3577 3674 Transducers, electrical; control equipment, electric; computer peripheral equipment; semiconductors & related devices; radio & TV communications equipment; motors & generators

(G-16373)
VTB HOLDINGS INC (HQ)
100 Summit Lake Dr (10595-1339)
PHONE..................................914 345-2255
Juergen Stark, *CEO*
John Hanson, *CFO*
EMP: 6
SALES (est): 207.1MM **Publicly Held**
SIC: 3651 Sound reproducing equipment

Valley Cottage
Rockland County

(G-16374)
ACCESS 24
570 Kings Hwy Fl 4 (10989-1231)
PHONE..................................845 358-5397
John Sindelar, *Owner*
EMP: 6
SALES (est): 600K **Privately Held**
SIC: 3661 Telephones & telephone apparatus

(G-16375)
AERO HEALTHCARE (US) LLC
616 Corporate Way Ste 6 (10989-2047)
PHONE..................................855 225-2376
Brian Parker, *General Mgr*
EMP: 5
SALES (est): 829.5K **Privately Held**
SIC: 3842 5099 Bandages & dressings; tape, adhesive: medicated or non-medicated; lifesaving & survival equipment (non-medical)

(G-16376)
AREMCO PRODUCTS INC
707 Executive Blvd Ste B (10989-2025)
P.O. Box 517 (10989-0517)
PHONE..................................845 268-0039
Peter Schwartz, *President*
David Heinl, *Manager*
Esther Schwartz, *Admin Sec*
▲ **EMP:** 15
SQ FT: 15,500
SALES: 3.9MM **Privately Held**
WEB: www.aremco.com
SIC: 3559 2891 2952 3253 Refinery, chemical processing & similar machinery; adhesives; cement, except linoleum & tile; coating compounds, tar; ceramic wall & floor tile

(G-16377)
CEROVENE INC (PA)
612 Corporate Way Ste 10 (10989-2027)
PHONE..................................845 267-2055
Manish Shah, *President*
Ray Difalco, *Vice Pres*
Lisa Rinaldi, *Manager*
EMP: 10
SQ FT: 40,000
SALES: 8MM **Privately Held**
WEB: www.cerovene.com
SIC: 2834 Pharmaceutical preparations

(G-16378)
FIRST SBF HOLDING INC (PA)
Also Called: Gevril
9 Pinecrest Rd Ste 101 (10989-1443)
PHONE..................................845 425-9882
Samuel Friedman, *President*
Steven Pachtinger, *Vice Pres*
Rachel Itzkowitz, *Bookkeeper*
▲ **EMP:** 5
SALES: 16.1MM **Privately Held**
WEB: www.gevril.com
SIC: 3873 Watches & parts, except crystals & jewels

(G-16379)
INNOTECH GRAPHIC EQP CORP
614 Corporate Way Ste 5 (10989-2026)
PHONE..................................845 268-6900
EMP: 8
SQ FT: 7,500
SALES (est): 800K **Privately Held**
SIC: 3555 5084 Mfg Printing Trades Machinery Whol Industrial Equipment

(G-16380)
LANDMARK GROUP INC
Also Called: National Ramp
709 Executive Blvd Ste A (10989-2024)
PHONE..................................845 358-0350
Garth Walker, *Ch of Bd*
EMP: 33
SALES (est): 8.1MM **Privately Held**
SIC: 3448 Ramps: prefabricated metal

(G-16381)
LEXAR GLOBAL LLC
711 Executive Blvd Ste K (10989-2006)
PHONE..................................845 352-9700
Guy Jacobs, *President*
▲ **EMP:** 9
SQ FT: 18,000
SALES: 4.9MM **Privately Held**
SIC: 3555 Printing trade parts & attachments

(G-16382)
MOUNT VERNON MACHINE INC
614 Corporate Way Ste 8 (10989-2026)
PHONE..................................845 268-9400
Fax: 845 268-9486
Karl Wallburg, *President*
EMP: 20
SQ FT: 16,000
SALES (est): 2.2MM **Privately Held**
WEB: www.mountvernonmachine.com
SIC: 3599 3555 Machine & other job shop work; printing trades machinery

(G-16383)
MP DISPLAYS LLC
704 Executive Blvd Ste 1 (10989-2010)
PHONE..................................845 268-4113
Michael Parkes, *Mng Member*
Marilyn Glisci, *Manager*
▲ **EMP:** 9
SQ FT: 5,300
SALES (est): 1.7MM **Privately Held**
WEB: www.mpdisplays.com
SIC: 2653 3577 Display items, corrugated: made from purchased materials; display items, solid fiber: made from purchased materials; graphic displays, except graphic terminals

(G-16384)
PRAXAIR INC
614 Corporate Way Ste 4 (10989-2026)
PHONE..................................845 267-2337
Robert Berkey, *Branch Mgr*
EMP: 20
SALES (corp-wide): 10.7B **Publicly Held**
SIC: 2813 Industrial gases
PA: Praxair, Inc.
  39 Old Ridgebury Rd
  Danbury CT 06810
  203 837-2000

(G-16385)
RAPHA PHARMACEUTICALS INC
616 Corporate Way (10989-2044)
PHONE..................................956 229-0049
Michael Shoffner, *Vice Pres*
EMP: 8 **EST:** 2015
SALES (est): 510K **Privately Held**
SIC: 2834 Pharmaceutical preparations

(G-16386)
REAL CO INC
616 Corporate Way (10989-2044)
PHONE..................................347 433-8549
Raphaele Chartrand, *Principal*
Muhammad Elkateb, *COO*
EMP: 8 **EST:** 2014
SALES (est): 235.3K **Privately Held**
SIC: 2044 2099 2899 Rice milling; sugar; salt

Valley Cottage - Rockland County (G-16387)

GEOGRAPHIC SECTION

(G-16387)
ROSSI TOOL & DIES INC
161 Route 303 (10989-1922)
PHONE.................................845 267-8246
Fax: 845 268-4966
James Veltidi, *President*
EMP: 6
SQ FT: 4,000
SALES (est): 697.2K **Privately Held**
SIC: 3544 3599 Dies & die holders for metal cutting, forming, die casting; machine shop, jobbing & repair

(G-16388)
SCIENTA PHARMACEUTICALS LLC
612 Corporate Way Ste 9 (10989-2027)
PHONE.................................845 589-0774
EMP: 5
SQ FT: 2,000
SALES (est): 320K **Privately Held**
SIC: 2834 Mfg Pharmaceutical Preparations

(G-16389)
STAR PRESS PEARL RIVER INC
614 Corporate Way Ste 8 (10989-2026)
PHONE.................................845 268-2294
Marino Nicolich, *President*
EMP: 6 EST: 1969
SALES (est): 1MM **Privately Held**
SIC: 2752 2759 Commercial printing, lithographic; letterpress printing

(G-16390)
STATEWIDE FIREPROOF DOOR CO
178 Charles Blvd (10989-2437)
PHONE.................................845 268-6043
Fax: 718 596-4591
Joseph Caneiro, *President*
Carmen Caraballo, *Bookkeeper*
EMP: 11 EST: 1965
SQ FT: 11,000
SALES (est): 1.1MM **Privately Held**
SIC: 3442 Fire doors, metal

(G-16391)
STROMBERG BRAND CORPORATION
Also Called: Stormberg Brand
12 Ford Products Rd (10989-1238)
PHONE.................................914 739-7410
Richard Stromberg, *CEO*
Helen Stromberg, *President*
EMP: 10
SQ FT: 9,000
SALES (est): 600K **Privately Held**
WEB: www.strombergbrand.com
SIC: 2759 Screen printing

(G-16392)
SUPPLYNET INC (PA)
706 Executive Blvd Ste B (10989-2039)
PHONE.................................845 267-2655
Fax: 845 267-2420
Robert Berkey, *President*
Marcia Kalmus, *Accountant*
EMP: 5
SQ FT: 7,500
SALES: 7.3MM **Privately Held**
WEB: www.thesupplynet.com
SIC: 3678 Electronic connectors

(G-16393)
THOR MARKETING CORP
616 Corporate Way Ste 2 (10989-2047)
PHONE.................................201 247-7103
Igor Poluyko, *CEO*
EMP: 8 EST: 2015
SQ FT: 5,800
SALES (est): 299.7K **Privately Held**
SIC: 2392 Blankets, comforters & beddings

(G-16394)
UNIVERSAL STRAPPING INC
630 Corporate Way (10989-2002)
PHONE.................................845 268-2500
Fax: 845 268-7999
Sol Oberlander, *President*
Gedalia Oberlander, *Corp Secy*
▲ EMP: 20
SQ FT: 100,000

SALES (est): 3.9MM **Privately Held**
WEB: www.universalstrapping.com
SIC: 3089 Bands, plastic

(G-16395)
ZEO HEALTH LTD
159 Route 303 (10989-1922)
PHONE.................................845 353-5185
Micah Portney, *President*
EMP: 16
SQ FT: 5,000
SALES: 500K **Privately Held**
SIC: 2834 Vitamin, nutrient & hematinic preparations for human use

Valley Falls
Rensselaer County

(G-16396)
STEPHEN BADER COMPANY INC
10 Charles St (12185-3437)
P.O. Box 297 (12185-0297)
PHONE.................................518 753-4456
Fax: 518 753-4962
Daniel W Johnson, *President*
Rosemarie Johnson, *Vice Pres*
Carrie Johnson, *Admin Sec*
▼ EMP: 10 EST: 1951
SQ FT: 14,000
SALES (est): 1.5MM **Privately Held**
WEB: www.stephenbader.com
SIC: 3541 Grinding machines, metalworking

Valley Stream
Nassau County

(G-16397)
5TH AVENUE CHOCOLATIERE LTD
396 Rockaway Ave (11581-1938)
PHONE.................................516 561-1570
Joseph E Whaley, *Branch Mgr*
EMP: 10
SALES (corp-wide): 1.6MM **Privately Held**
SIC: 2064 5441 2066 Candy & other confectionery products; candy; chocolate & cocoa products
PA: 5th Avenue Chocolatiere Ltd
114 Church St
Freeport NY 11520
212 935-5454

(G-16398)
ADC INDUSTRIES INC (PA)
181a E Jamaica Ave (11580-6069)
PHONE.................................516 596-1304
Joseph Mannino, *President*
Jennifer Krific, *Manager*
EMP: 25
SQ FT: 2,000
SALES: 4.5MM **Privately Held**
WEB: www.airlockdoor.com
SIC: 3491 Valves, automatic control

(G-16399)
AIR GOAL INTL USA INC
30 W Merrick Rd (11580-5719)
PHONE.................................718 656-5880
Henry Siu, *President*
EMP: 11
SALES (est): 610K **Privately Held**
SIC: 2448 Cargo containers, wood & wood with metal

(G-16400)
ANSA SYSTEMS OF USA INC
145 Hook Creek Blvd B6a1 (11581-2293)
PHONE.................................516 887-6855
John Olusoga, *President*
Fola Olusoga, *Office Mgr*
◆ EMP: 5
SALES: 500K **Privately Held**
SIC: 7372 Prepackaged software

(G-16401)
AUTOMATED OFFICE SYSTEMS INC
Also Called: Aos
71 S Central Ave (11580-5495)
PHONE.................................516 396-5555
Larry Sachs, *President*
Kirill Khazan, *Manager*
EMP: 10
SQ FT: 5,000
SALES (est): 537.2K **Privately Held**
WEB: www.aosdata.com
SIC: 7372 Business oriented computer software

(G-16402)
BRAUN BROTHERS BRUSHES INC
35 4th St (11581-1231)
P.O. Box 96 (11582-0096)
PHONE.................................631 667-2179
Fax: 516 825-2222
James Braun, *President*
Pamela Sue Gagas, *Purch Mgr*
EMP: 5 EST: 1946
SQ FT: 1,400
SALES (est): 524.5K **Privately Held**
WEB: www.braunbrosbrushes.com
SIC: 3991 5085 Brushes, household or industrial; brushes, industrial

(G-16403)
CITY REAL ESTATE BOOK INC
9831 S Franklin Ave (11580)
PHONE.................................516 593-2949
Charles Danas, *President*
EMP: 8
SALES: 500K **Privately Held**
SIC: 2721 Magazines: publishing & printing

(G-16404)
CLIQUE APPAREL INC
2034 Green Acres Mall (11581-1545)
PHONE.................................516 375-7969
Naveen Shikapuri, *Ch of Bd*
EMP: 3 EST: 2011
SQ FT: 3,000
SALES: 1MM **Privately Held**
SIC: 2329 Knickers, dress (separate): men's & boys'

(G-16405)
ELLIS PRODUCTS CORP (PA)
Also Called: Style Plus Hosiery Mills
628 Golf Dr (11581-3550)
PHONE.................................516 791-3732
Seymour Ellis, *President*
EMP: 4 EST: 1954
SALES (est): 6.1MM **Privately Held**
SIC: 2251 3944 Women's hosiery, except socks; panty hose; electronic game machines, except coin-operated

(G-16406)
FACILAMATIC INSTRUMENT CORP
39 Clinton Ave (11580-6024)
PHONE.................................516 825-6300
Fax: 516 825-6324
Dennis West, *President*
John E Bergquist, *Vice Pres*
EMP: 15
SQ FT: 15,000
SALES: 1.8MM **Privately Held**
SIC: 3812 Aircraft/aerospace flight instruments & guidance systems; gyro gimbals; gyrocompasses; gyropilots

(G-16407)
GLOBAL PAYMENT TECH INC
20 E Sunrise Hwy (11581-1260)
PHONE.................................516 887-0700
Fax: 516 256-1620
Sue Comple, *Human Res Mgr*
Stephen Katz, *Branch Mgr*
EMP: 10
SALES (corp-wide): 11MM **Publicly Held**
WEB: www.gptx.com
SIC: 3581 Mechanisms & parts for automatic vending machines
PA: Global Payment Technologies, Inc.
170 Wilbur Pl Ste 600
Bohemia NY 11716
631 563-2500

(G-16408)
HETEROCHEMICAL CORPORATION
111 E Hawthorne Ave (11580-6319)
PHONE.................................516 561-8225
Fax: 516 561-8413
Lynne Galler, *President*
Beatrice Galler, *Corp Secy*
Raymond Berruti, *Vice Pres*
EMP: 10 EST: 1946
SQ FT: 18,000
SALES (est): 876.5K **Privately Held**
SIC: 2899 Chemical preparations

(G-16409)
HIGH PERFORMANCE SFTWR USA INC
Also Called: Zuant
145 Hook Creek Blvd (11581-2299)
PHONE.................................866 616-4958
Pete Gillett, *Director*
EMP: 30
SALES (est): 119.6K **Privately Held**
SIC: 7372 Prepackaged software

(G-16410)
JERRYS BAGELS
Also Called: Jerry's Bagels & Bakery
951 Rosedale Rd (11581-2318)
PHONE.................................516 791-0063
Jerry Jacobs, *Owner*
EMP: 8
SALES (est): 571.4K **Privately Held**
SIC: 2051 Bakery: wholesale or wholesale/retail combined

(G-16411)
L M N PRINTING COMPANY INC
23 W Merrick Rd Ste A (11580-5757)
P.O. Box 696 (11582-0696)
PHONE.................................516 285-8526
Fax: 516 285-9268
Nora Aly, *President*
Noreen Carro, *Vice Pres*
EMP: 25
SQ FT: 5,200
SALES (est): 4.3MM **Privately Held**
WEB: www.lmnprinting.com
SIC: 2752 2791 Commercial printing, offset; typesetting

(G-16412)
LELAB DENTAL LABORATORY INC
Also Called: Le Lab
550 W Merrick Rd Ste 8 (11580-5101)
PHONE.................................516 561-5050
Edmond Mardirossia, *President*
Maronlyn Mardirossian, *Vice Pres*
EMP: 5
SQ FT: 1,000
SALES (est): 676.4K **Privately Held**
SIC: 3843 Dental equipment & supplies

(G-16413)
MICHAEL FIORE LTD
126 E Fairview Ave (11580-5930)
PHONE.................................516 561-8238
Michael Fiore, *President*
EMP: 6
SQ FT: 6,000
SALES: 2MM **Privately Held**
SIC: 3545 Machine tool accessories

(G-16414)
MUSICAL LINKS PRODUCTION LLC
Also Called: Mind Music Production
91 S Montague St (11580-5224)
PHONE.................................516 996-1522
Donald Levy, *Mng Member*
Sharon Perez,
EMP: 5
SALES: 50K **Privately Held**
SIC: 2741 7929 7389 Miscellaneous publishing; entertainment service; music recording producer

(G-16415)
NEW YORK CHOCOLATIER INC
396 Rockaway Ave (11581-1938)
PHONE.................................516 561-1570
Joseph E Whaley, *President*
John E Whaley, *Vice Pres*
EMP: 8

▲ = Import ▼ = Export
◆ = Import/Export

GEOGRAPHIC SECTION

Vestal - Broome County (G-16442)

SQ FT: 7,000
SALES (est): 773K
SALES (corp-wide): 1.6MM Privately Held
SIC: 2066 Chocolate & cocoa products
PA: 5th Avenue Chocolatiere Ltd
114 Church St
Freeport NY 11520
212 935-5454

(G-16416)
NEW YORK HEALTH CARE INC (PA)
20 E Sunrise Hwy Ste 201 (11581-1257)
PHONE................................718 375-6700
▲ EMP: 2
SQ FT: 6,000
SALES (est): 145.9MM Publicly Held
SIC: 2834 8082 Mfg Pharmaceuticals & Home Healthcare Services

(G-16417)
ONE IN A MILLION INC
51 Franklin Ave (11580-2847)
P.O. Box 234111, Great Neck (11023-4111)
PHONE................................516 829-1111
Sasan Shavanson, *President*
Yaso Soleimani, *Admin Sec*
EMP: 6
SQ FT: 2,000
SALES (est): 800K Privately Held
SIC: 2759 5112 2284 Screen printing; stationery; embroidery thread

(G-16418)
PARNASA INTERNATIONAL INC
Also Called: C-Air International
181 S Franklin Ave # 400 (11581-1138)
PHONE................................516 394-0400
Glenn Schacher, *President*
Lucille Schacher, *Admin Sec*
▲ EMP: 8
SALES (est): 520K Privately Held
SIC: 2099 Food preparations

(G-16419)
PRECISELED INC
52 Railroad Ave (11580-6031)
PHONE................................516 418-5337
Daniel Machlis, *Principal*
EMP: 5 EST: 2015
SQ FT: 7,000
SALES (est): 312K Privately Held
SIC: 3645 3646 Residential lighting fixtures; garden, patio, walkway & yard lighting fixtures; electric; commercial indusl & institutional electric lighting fixtures

(G-16420)
PRECISION TL DIE & STAMPING CO
Also Called: G & W Tool & Die Co
68 Franklin Ave (11580-2845)
PHONE................................516 561-0041
Fax: 516 561-5197
William Heath, *President*
Deborah Bruno, *Office Mgr*
EMP: 10 EST: 1955
SQ FT: 6,000
SALES: 900K Privately Held
SIC: 3469 3544 Metal stampings; special dies & tools

(G-16421)
PRO METAL OF NY CORP
814 W Merrick Rd (11580-4829)
PHONE................................516 285-0440
Michael Marin, *President*
EMP: 5
SALES (est): 625.7K Privately Held
SIC: 3585 1761 Heating & air conditioning combination units; sheet metalwork

(G-16422)
PSG INNOVATIONS INC
924 Kilmer Ln (11581-3130)
PHONE................................917 299-8986
Philip Green, *CEO*
EMP: 15 EST: 2010
SQ FT: 2,500
SALES: 16MM Privately Held
SIC: 3648 Flashlights

(G-16423)
RAYS ITALIAN BAKERY INC
Also Called: Roma Ray Bakery
45 Railroad Ave (11580-6030)
PHONE................................516 825-9170
Fax: 516 599-9340
Robert Degiovanni, *President*
Vincent Giovanni, *Vice Pres*
Dario Degiovanni, *Admin Sec*
EMP: 12
SQ FT: 10,000
SALES (est): 1.2MM Privately Held
SIC: 2051 Bread, cake & related products

(G-16424)
READY TO ASSEMBLE COMPANY INC
Also Called: Debra Fisher
115 S Corona Ave (11580-6217)
PHONE................................516 825-4397
Bruce Wulwick, *CEO*
Phyllis Wulwick, *Treasurer*
EMP: 20
SALES (est): 2.1MM Privately Held
SIC: 2519 7389 Household furniture, except wood or metal: upholstered;

(G-16425)
ROMA BAKERY INC
45 Railroad Ave (11580-6030)
PHONE................................516 825-9170
Jacoui Digiovanni, *President*
EMP: 17
SQ FT: 10,000
SALES (est): 1.2MM Privately Held
SIC: 2051 Bread, cake & related products

(G-16426)
ROSS-ELLIS LTD
67 Irving Pl (11580-4754)
PHONE................................212 260-9200
Nina Sheldon, *CEO*
EMP: 5
SALES (est): 376.8K Privately Held
SIC: 2759 Commercial printing

(G-16427)
SENERA CO INC
834 Glenridge Ave (11581-3019)
PHONE................................516 639-3774
Seema Gupta, *President*
EMP: 10
SALES: 100K Privately Held
SIC: 3674 Switches, silicon control

(G-16428)
SOUTH SHORE READY MIX INC
116 E Hawthorne Ave (11580-6331)
PHONE................................516 872-3049
Joseph Dilemme, *President*
EMP: 5
SQ FT: 10,000
SALES (est): 712.7K Privately Held
SIC: 3273 Ready-mixed concrete

(G-16429)
TASTE AND SEE ENTRMT INC
Also Called: Taqa Entertainment
255 Dogwood Rd (11580-4039)
P.O. Box 367 (11582-0367)
PHONE................................516 285-3010
Barry Whipple, *CEO*
Patricia Whipple, *General Mgr*
EMP: 5
SALES (est): 863.1K Privately Held
SIC: 3652 7812 5734 7832 Pre-recorded records & tapes; motion picture & video production; computer & software stores; motion picture theaters, except drive-in; record & prerecorded tape stores

(G-16430)
TOTAL DNTL IMPLANT SLTIONS LLC
Also Called: Tag Dental Implant Solutions
260 W Sunrise Hwy (11581-1011)
PHONE................................212 877-3777
Ariel Goldschlag,
EMP: 5
SALES: 750K Privately Held
SIC: 3843 Dental equipment & supplies

(G-16431)
UNIVERSAL 3D INNOVATION INC
1085 Rockaway Ave (11581-2137)
PHONE................................516 837-9423
Tomer Yariz, *President*
Adam Gansky, *Marketing Staff*
Noa Gansky, *Manager*
EMP: 10
SQ FT: 5,000
SALES: 2.5MM Privately Held
SIC: 3993 Signs, not made in custom sign painting shops

Van Hornesville
Herkimer County

(G-16432)
OGD V-HVAC INC
174 Pumkinhook Rd (13475)
P.O. Box Ogd (13475-0160)
PHONE................................315 858-1002
Ormonde G Drham III, *President*
Linda Bowers, *Administration*
EMP: 20
SALES: 400K Privately Held
SIC: 3999 Manufacturing industries

Vernon
Oneida County

(G-16433)
CHEPAUME INDUSTRIES LLC
6201 Cooper St (13476-4022)
PHONE................................315 829-6400
Fax: 315 768-0270
Chester Poplaski,
Melissa Foppes,
EMP: 6
SQ FT: 17,114
SALES (est): 569.1K Privately Held
WEB: www.chepaume.com
SIC: 3479 Coating electrodes

(G-16434)
FOUR DIRECTIONS INC
4677 State Route 5 (13476-3525)
PHONE................................315 829-8388
Peter Wiezalis, *Director*
Kelli Bradley, *Administration*
EMP: 20
SALES (est): 805.5K
SALES (corp-wide): 226.2MM Privately Held
WEB: www.fourdirectionsmedia.com
SIC: 2711 Newspapers: publishing only, not printed on site
HQ: Oneida Nation Enterprises, Llc
5218 Patrick Rd
Verona NY 13478
315 361-7711

(G-16435)
HP HOOD LLC
19 Ward St (13476-4415)
P.O. Box 930 (13476-0930)
PHONE................................315 829-3339
Fax: 315 829-3108
Phil Campbell, *Plant Mgr*
Howard Holdridge, *QC Dir*
EMP: 100
SQ FT: 800
SALES (corp-wide): 1.9B Privately Held
WEB: www.hphood.com
SIC: 2836 2026 Culture media; fluid milk
PA: Hp Hood Llc
6 Kimball Ln Ste 400
Lynnfield MA 01940
617 887-8441

(G-16436)
J H RHODES COMPANY INC
10 Ward St (13476-4416)
PHONE................................315 829-3600
J Rhodes, *Principal*
Richard Greabell, *QC Mgr*
EMP: 11
SALES (corp-wide): 58.6MM Privately Held
SIC: 3674 Semiconductors & related devices
HQ: J H Rhodes Company Inc.
4809 E Thistle Landing Dr
Phoenix AZ

Vernon Center
Oneida County

(G-16437)
MCDONOUGH HARDWOODS LTD
6426 Skinner Rd (13477-3840)
PHONE................................315 829-3449
Daniel McDonough, *CEO*
James McDonough, *Treasurer*
EMP: 25
SALES (est): 1MM Privately Held
SIC: 2421 Sawmills & planing mills, general

Vestal
Broome County

(G-16438)
ACTION GRAPHICS SERVICES INC
Also Called: AGS
1908 Vestal Pkwy E (13850-1956)
PHONE................................607 785-1951
Fax: 607 785-9662
Michael Wilson, *Director*
EMP: 10
SQ FT: 5,000
SALES (est): 950.2K Privately Held
SIC: 2752 5943 7334 Commercial printing, offset; office forms & supplies; school supplies; photocopying & duplicating services

(G-16439)
ADVANCED MTL ANALYTICS LLC
85 Murray Hl Rd Ste 2115 (13850)
PHONE................................321 684-0528
Swastisharan Dey,
EMP: 5
SQ FT: 500
SALES (est): 350K Privately Held
SIC: 3826 Analytical instruments

(G-16440)
BARNEY & DICKENSON INC (PA)
520 Prentice Rd (13850-2197)
PHONE................................607 729-1536
Fax: 607 797-3931
Robert S Murphy Jr, *President*
Mary M Harrison, *Vice Pres*
Brian Taylor, *Engineer*
EMP: 44
SQ FT: 100,000
SALES (est): 6.1MM Privately Held
SIC: 3273 5032 Ready-mixed concrete; concrete mixtures; sand, construction; gravel

(G-16441)
BIMBO BAKERIES USA INC
Also Called: Stroehmann Bakeries 90
1624 Castle Gardens Rd (13850-1102)
PHONE................................800 856-8544
Michael Hicks, *Area Mgr*
Bruce Gross, *Manager*
EMP: 20
SALES (corp-wide): 13B Privately Held
SIC: 2051 5149 Breads, rolls & buns; groceries & related products
HQ: Bimbo Bakeries Usa, Inc
255 Business Center Dr # 200
Horsham PA 19044
215 347-5500

(G-16442)
BOB MURPHY INC
3127 Vestal Rd (13850-2109)
PHONE................................607 729-3553
Fax: 607 770-8064

Vestal - Broome County (G-16443)

Robert S Murphy Jr, *President*
Mary Murphy Harrison, *Vice Pres*
EMP: 17
SQ FT: 130,000
SALES: 2MM **Privately Held**
SIC: 3441 5031 Fabricated structural metal; building materials, exterior; building materials, interior

(G-16443)
C & C READY-MIX CORPORATION (PA)
3112 Vestal Rd (13850-2110)
P.O. Box 157 (13851-0157)
PHONE..................607 797-5108
Fax: 607 770-1940
Nicholas D Cerretani Jr, *President*
Nichols Cerretani Jr, *President*
Anthony Cerretani, *Vice Pres*
Lanny Kipp, *Sales Mgr*
EMP: 25
SQ FT: 1,500
SALES: 5.3MM **Privately Held**
WEB: www.ccreadymix.com
SIC: 3273 2951 Ready-mixed concrete; asphalt & asphaltic paving mixtures (not from refineries)

(G-16444)
CARR COMMUNICATIONS GROUP LLC
Also Called: Carr Printing
513 Prentice Rd (13850-2105)
P.O. Box 8409, Endwell (13762-8409)
PHONE..................607 748-0481
Holly Reyan, *General Mgr*
Kris Osborn, *Purchasing*
Marilyn Maney, *Financial Exec*
Dorothy Wells, *Human Resources*
Mike Zeitz, *Sales Staff*
EMP: 18
SQ FT: 11,000
SALES: 1.5MM **Privately Held**
SIC: 2752 Commercial printing, offset

(G-16445)
CHROMANANOTECH LLC
85 Murray Hill Rd (13850)
PHONE..................607 239-9626
William Bernier,
EMP: 5 **EST:** 2014
SQ FT: 100
SALES (est): 299.1K **Privately Held**
SIC: 2899 Household tints or dyes

(G-16446)
DEAN MANUFACTURING INC
413 Commerce Rd (13850-2238)
PHONE..................607 770-1300
Fax: 607 770-1309
Karl E Hughes Jr, *President*
EMP: 10
SALES (est): 921.8K **Privately Held**
WEB: www.centerlessgrinder.com
SIC: 3546 7389 Grinders, portable: electric or pneumatic; grinding, precision: commercial or industrial

(G-16447)
DETEKION SECURITY SYSTEMS INC
200 Plaza Dr Ste 1 (13850-3680)
PHONE..................607 729-7179
James Walsh, *President*
Alexander Haker, *Vice Pres*
Kevin Kelly, *Engineer*
Baruch Koren, *VP Sls/Mktg*
Bill Walsh, *Accounts Mgr*
EMP: 18
SQ FT: 7,200
SALES (est): 3.7MM **Privately Held**
SIC: 3699 5063 1731 Security control equipment & systems; burglar alarm systems; fire detection & burglar alarm systems specialization

(G-16448)
GANNETT CO INC
Also Called: Binghamton Press
4421 Vestal Pkwy E (13850-3556)
P.O. Box 1270, Binghamton (13902-1270)
PHONE..................607 798-1234
Fax: 607 352-2645
Sherman Bodner, *President*
Richard J Romano, *Personnel*
Jodie Riesbeck, *Adv Dir*
Sharon A Houghton, *Marketing Mgr*
Donna Bell, *Director*
EMP: 77
SQ FT: 100,498
SALES (corp-wide): 5.7B **Publicly Held**
WEB: www.gannett.com
SIC: 2711 Newspapers
PA: Gannett Co., Inc.
7950 Jones Branch Dr
Mc Lean VA 22102
703 854-6000

(G-16449)
GREAT AMERICAN INDUSTRIES INC (DH)
300 Plaza Dr (13850-3647)
PHONE..................607 729-9331
Fax: 607 798-1079
Burton I Koffman, *Ch of Bd*
Richard E Koffman, *Senior VP*
Bert Kaufman, *Manager*
Stphen Fisher,
Paul Garginkle,
◆ **EMP:** 1 **EST:** 1928
SQ FT: 2,000
SALES: 97.8MM
SALES (corp-wide): 4MM **Privately Held**
SIC: 3086 5031 5074 3442 Plastics foam products; building materials, interior; plumbing fittings & supplies; metal doors, sash & trim; metal doors; wet suits, rubber; watersports equipment & supplies; diving equipment & supplies
HQ: Public Loan Company Inc
300 Plaza Dr
Vestal NY 13850
607 584-5274

(G-16450)
K HEIN MACHINES INC
341 Vestal Pkwy E (13850-1631)
PHONE..................607 748-1546
Fax: 607 748-0734
Walter C Hein Sr, *CEO*
W Charles Hein Jr, *President*
Steven W Hein, *Vice Pres*
EMP: 9
SQ FT: 15,000
SALES (est): 537.3K **Privately Held**
WEB: www.kheinmachines.com
SIC: 3599 Machine shop, jobbing & repair

(G-16451)
NATIONAL PIPE & PLASTICS INC (PA)
Also Called: Nppi
3421 Vestal Rd (13850-2188)
PHONE..................607 729-9381
Fax: 607 729-6130
David J Culbertson, *CEO*
Farouk Aziz, *General Mgr*
Charles E Miller, *Vice Pres*
Matt Siegel, *Vice Pres*
Debbie Belknap, *Purch Dir*
◆ **EMP:** 170
SQ FT: 157,000
SALES (est): 92.9MM **Privately Held**
WEB: www.nationalpipe.com
SIC: 3084 Plastics pipe

(G-16452)
NORANDEX INC VESTAL
2300 Vestal Rd (13850-1989)
PHONE..................607 786-0778
Fax: 607 786-0814
Richard Riesen, *Principal*
EMP: 6
SALES (est): 832.2K **Privately Held**
SIC: 3442 5031 5211 Screens, window, metal; windows; lumber & other building materials

(G-16453)
SPST INC
Also Called: Embroidery Screen Prtg Netwrk
119b Rano Blvd (13850-2729)
PHONE..................607 798-6952
James Porter, *President*
EMP: 5
SALES (est): 450K **Privately Held**
SIC: 2759 Screen printing

(G-16454)
SUPERIOR PRINT ON DEMAND
165 Charles St (13850-2431)
PHONE..................607 240-5231
Jeff Valent, *Principal*
EMP: 5
SALES (est): 447.9K **Privately Held**
SIC: 2752 2759 7389 Offset & photolithographic printing; financial note & certificate printing & engraving; personal service agents, brokers & bureaus

(G-16455)
TRUEBITE INC
Also Called: Fotofiles
2590 Glenwood Rd (13850-6115)
PHONE..................607 785-7664
Edward J Calafut, *President*
◆ **EMP:** 23
SQ FT: 6,000
SALES (est): 4.5MM **Privately Held**
WEB: www.truebite.com
SIC: 3499 3674 Magnets, permanent: metallic; photoelectric magnetic devices

(G-16456)
VESTAL ASPHALT INC (PA)
201 Stage Rd (13850-1608)
PHONE..................607 785-3393
Fax: 607 785-3396
Neil I Guiles, *President*
Garrett Guiles, *VP Opers*
Kim Hickok, *Office Mgr*
Timothy Howell, *Manager*
Joann Juliussen, *Manager*
EMP: 14
SQ FT: 3,000
SALES (est): 3.6MM **Privately Held**
WEB: www.vestalasphalt.com
SIC: 2951 Asphalt & asphaltic paving mixtures (not from refineries)

(G-16457)
XEKU CORPORATION
2520 Vestal Pkwy E222 (13850-2078)
PHONE..................607 761-1447
Charles S Jakaitis, *Principal*
EMP: 12
SALES (est): 830K **Privately Held**
SIC: 3829 Measuring & controlling devices

Victor
Ontario County

(G-16458)
331 HOLDING INC
Also Called: U S TEC
100 Rawson Rd Ste 205 (14564-1100)
PHONE..................585 924-1740
Fax: 585 924-7498
William M Thompson, *President*
Dominic Piazza, *Treasurer*
Linda Stellman, *Controller*
EMP: 32
SALES (est): 4MM **Privately Held**
WEB: www.ustecnet.com
SIC: 3699 7373 1731 Electrical equipment & supplies; computer integrated systems design; electrical work

(G-16459)
ADVANCED INTERCONNECT MFG INC (HQ)
Also Called: A I M
780 Canning Pkwy (14564-8983)
PHONE..................585 742-2220
John Durst, *President*
Diane Pepe, *Treasurer*
Gretchen Dunfey, *Human Res Mgr*
Shawn Hodgeman, *Manager*
Jon Martin, *Manager*
▲ **EMP:** 62
SQ FT: 50,000
SALES (est): 14MM
SALES (corp-wide): 93MM **Privately Held**
SIC: 3679 Harness assemblies for electronic use: wire or cable
PA: Floturn, Inc.
4236 Thunderbird Ln
West Chester OH 45014
513 860-8040

(G-16460)
AMERICAN SPORTS MEDIA
106 Cobblestone Court Dr # 323 (14564-1045)
PHONE..................585 924-4250
David Aultman, *Principal*
EMP: 8
SALES (est): 513K **Privately Held**
SIC: 2711 Newspapers, publishing & printing

(G-16461)
AVCOM OF VIRGINIA INC
Also Called: Ramsey Electronics
590 Fishers Station Dr (14564-9744)
PHONE..................585 924-4560
Jay Evans, *Ch of Bd*
John G Ramsey, *President*
EMP: 53
SQ FT: 10,000
SALES (est): 6.9MM
SALES (corp-wide): 30MM **Privately Held**
WEB: www.brynavon.com
SIC: 3825 5961 8331 3651 Test equipment for electronic & electrical circuits; catalog & mail-order houses; job training & vocational rehabilitation services; household audio & video equipment
PA: Brynavon Group, Inc
2000 Montgomery Ave
Villanova PA 19085
610 525-2102

(G-16462)
BIOREM ENVIRONMENTAL INC
100 Rawson Rd Ste 230 (14564-1177)
PHONE..................585 924-2220
Fax: 585 924-8280
Peter Bruijns, *CEO*
Rick Williams, *Prdtn Mgr*
Brian Jensen, *Engineer*
Dean Parker, *Sales Mgr*
Patrick Barr, *Manager*
▲ **EMP:** 40
SALES: 8.2MM
SALES (corp-wide): 9.3MM **Privately Held**
SIC: 3822 Electric air cleaner controls, automatic
HQ: Biorem Technologies Inc
7496 Wellington Road 34
Guelph ON
519 767-9100

(G-16463)
BIOWORKS INC (PA)
100 Rawson Rd Ste 205 (14564-1100)
PHONE..................585 924-4362
Bill Foster, *President*
John Applegate, *Production*
Tina Buerkle, *Purchasing*
Chris Hayes, *Engineer*
Doug Oneil, *Controller*
▲ **EMP:** 3
SQ FT: 1,380
SALES (est): 4MM **Privately Held**
WEB: www.bioworksinc.com
SIC: 2879 Fungicides, herbicides

(G-16464)
BRISTOL INSTRUMENTS INC
50 Victor Heights Pkwy (14564-9010)
PHONE..................585 924-2620
Brian Samoriski, *President*
Michael Houk, *Vice Pres*
John Theodorsen, *Vice Pres*
Peter Battisti, *CFO*
Sam Algera, *Manager*
EMP: 6
SQ FT: 2,000
SALES (est): 700K **Privately Held**
WEB: www.bristol-inst.com
SIC: 3826 Analytical instruments

(G-16465)
BUCKEYE CORRUGATED INC
Also Called: Koch Container Div
797 Old Dutch Rd (14564-8972)
PHONE..................585 924-1600
Fax: 585 924-7040
Robert Harris, *President*
Karen Schafer, *Safety Dir*
Philip Trautman, *Prdtn Mgr*
EMP: 80

▲ = Import ▼ = Export
◆ = Import/Export

SALES (corp-wide): 196.7MM **Privately Held**
WEB: www.buckeyecorrugated.com
SIC: 2653 3993 Boxes, corrugated: made from purchased materials; signs & advertising specialties
PA: Buckeye Corrugated, Inc
 822 Kumho Dr Ste 400
 Fairlawn OH 44333
 330 576-0590

(G-16466)
CHARLES A ROGERS ENTPS INC
Also Called: Car Engineering and Mfg
51 Victor Heights Pkwy (14564-8926)
P.O. Box 627 (14564-0627)
PHONE..........................585 924-6400
Fax: 585 924-6408
Charles A Rogers, *CEO*
Yvette Rogers Pagano, *President*
Brian Rumsey, *Vice Pres*
John Alliet, *Engineer*
Cheryl Hixon, *Office Mgr*
EMP: 45
SQ FT: 40,000
SALES (est): 20.4MM **Privately Held**
WEB: www.car-eng.com
SIC: 3469 3549 3544 Stamping metal for the trade; metalworking machinery; special dies & tools

(G-16467)
CLEARCOVE SYSTEMS INC
7910 Rae Blvd (14564-8933)
PHONE..........................585 734-3012
Gregory Westbrook, *CEO*
Gary Miller, *President*
Terry Wright, *Chief Engr*
EMP: 10 **EST:** 2014
SQ FT: 750
SALES (est): 2.2MM **Privately Held**
SIC: 3589 Sewage & water treatment equipment

(G-16468)
COACH INC
7979 Pittsford Victor Rd (14564)
PHONE..........................585 425-7720
Fax: 585 425-9678
Kelly Lazore, *Manager*
EMP: 15
SALES (corp-wide): 4.4B **Publicly Held**
WEB: www.coach.com
SIC: 3171 Handbags, women's
PA: Coach, Inc.
 10 Hudson Yards
 New York NY 10001
 212 594-1850

(G-16469)
CONSTELLATION BRANDS INC (PA)
207 High Point Dr # 100 (14564-1061)
PHONE..........................585 678-7100
Richard Sands, *Ch of Bd*
Robert Sands, *President*
F Paul Hetterich, *President*
John A Wright, *President*
William F Hackett, *Chairman*
◆ **EMP:** 95
SALES: 6.5B **Publicly Held**
WEB: www.cbrands.com
SIC: 2084 5182 5181 2082 Wines, brandy & brandy spirits; wine & distilled beverages; wine; neutral spirits; beer & other fermented malt liquors; beer (alcoholic beverage); distilled & blended liquors; concentrates, drink

(G-16470)
COOPERVISION INC
209 High Point Dr (14564-1061)
PHONE..........................585 385-6810
Crispin Simon, *CEO*
Thomas Barrett, *Engineer*
Oscar Morales, *Engineer*
Albert Clough, *CFO*
Nick William, *Finance*
▲ **EMP:** 250
SQ FT: 35,000
SALES (est): 31.2MM
SALES (corp-wide): 1.8B **Publicly Held**
WEB: www.coopervision.com
SIC: 3851 Contact lenses

HQ: Coopervision, Inc.
 209 High Point Dr
 Victor NY 14564
 585 385-6810

(G-16471)
COOPERVISION INC (HQ)
Also Called: Ocular Sciences A Coopervision
209 High Point Dr (14564-1061)
PHONE..........................585 385-6810
Thomas Bender, *Ch of Bd*
Bob Ferrigno, *President*
Andrew Sedweg, *President*
Steve Hill, *General Mgr*
Steve Mathieson, *Managing Dir*
▲ **EMP:** 65
SQ FT: 20,000
SALES: 329.5MM
SALES (corp-wide): 1.8B **Publicly Held**
SIC: 3851 Contact lenses
PA: The Cooper Companies Inc
 6140 Stoneridge Mall Rd # 590
 Pleasanton CA 94588
 925 460-3600

(G-16472)
DAY AUTOMATION SYSTEMS INC (PA)
7931 Rae Blvd (14564-9017)
PHONE..........................585 924-4630
Eric J Orban, *CEO*
Bob Ormsby, *Business Mgr*
Robert Ormsby, *Vice Pres*
Laird Updyke, *Project Mgr*
Jeremy Ryan, *Opers Mgr*
EMP: 74
SALES (est): 25.6MM **Privately Held**
WEB: www.dayasi.com
SIC: 3822 Temperature controls, automatic

(G-16473)
DICE AMERICA INC
7676 Netlink Dr (14564-9419)
P.O. Box 360 (14564-0360)
PHONE..........................585 869-6200
Jeff Shufelt, *President*
EMP: 8
SALES: 650K **Privately Held**
WEB: www.diceamerica.com
SIC: 2821 Plastics materials & resins

(G-16474)
ELECTRICAL CONTROLS LINK
100 Rawson Rd Ste 220 (14564-1100)
PHONE..........................585 924-7010
Jim Flynn, *Controller*
EMP: 42
SALES (est): 3.2MM **Privately Held**
WEB: www.han-tek.com
SIC: 3829 Measuring & controlling devices

(G-16475)
ENETICS INC
830 Canning Pkwy (14564-8940)
PHONE..........................585 924-5010
Fax: 585 924-7271
William C Bush, *President*
Travis Downs, *Opers Mgr*
Michael Wowzynski, *Engineer*
Thomas Jacobson, *Software Engr*
EMP: 6
SQ FT: 6,000
SALES (est): 1MM **Privately Held**
WEB: www.enetics.com
SIC: 3625 Relays & industrial controls

(G-16476)
EXHIBITS & MORE
7615 Omnitech Pl Ste 4a (14564-9767)
PHONE..........................585 924-4040
Fax: 585 924-4056
Brian Pitre, *Principal*
EMP: 5
SALES (est): 209.5K **Privately Held**
SIC: 2711 5999 7319 Newspapers, publishing & printing; miscellaneous retail stores; display advertising service

(G-16477)
FLEX ENTERPRISES INC
820 Canning Pkwy (14564-8940)
PHONE..........................585 742-1000
Fax: 585 742-1037
Linda Murphy, *CEO*
Guy Murphy, *President*
▲ **EMP:** 30

SQ FT: 15,000
SALES (est): 5.1MM **Privately Held**
WEB: www.flexenterprises.com
SIC: 3052 5085 Rubber & plastics hose & beltings; industrial supplies; hose, belting & packing; gaskets

(G-16478)
FLIGHTLINE ELECTRONICS INC (DH)
Also Called: Ultra Elec Flightline Systems
7625 Omnitech Pl (14564-9816)
PHONE..........................585 742-5340
Fax: 585 742-5397
Paul Fardellone, *President*
Tom Cooper, *President*
Carlos Santiago, *Principal*
Anthony Diduro, *Vice Pres*
Kelly Selner, *Purch Mgr*
EMP: 100
SQ FT: 33,000
SALES (est): 80.9MM
SALES (corp-wide): 1.1B **Privately Held**
WEB: www.ultra-fei.com
SIC: 3812 Search & navigation equipment
HQ: Ultra Electronics Defense Inc.
 4101 Smith School Rd
 Austin TX 78744
 512 327-6795

(G-16479)
GOOD HEALTH HEALTHCARE NEWSPPR
106 Cobblestone Court Dr (14564-1045)
PHONE..........................585 421-8109
Fax: 585 421-8129
Wagner Dotto, *Owner*
EMP: 10
SALES (est): 293.7K **Privately Held**
WEB: www.cnyhealth.com
SIC: 2711 Newspapers: publishing only, not printed on site

(G-16480)
GORBEL INC
600 Fishers Run (14564-9732)
PHONE..........................800 821-0086
Brian Reh, *President*
Bruce Stevenson, *Facilities Mgr*
Krista Compton, *Buyer*
Jim Gill, *QC Mgr*
Keith Buddendeck, *Engineer*
EMP: 14 **EST:** 2011
SALES (est): 1.6MM **Privately Held**
SIC: 3536 Hoists, cranes & monorails

(G-16481)
HUNTER MACHINE INC
6551 Anthony Dr (14564-1400)
P.O. Box 50 (14564-0050)
PHONE..........................585 924-7480
Fax: 585 924-8305
John D Vouros, *President*
Lynne Vouros, *Accountant*
EMP: 20
SQ FT: 11,600
SALES: 5MM **Privately Held**
WEB: www.hmicncmachining.com
SIC: 3599 Machine & other job shop work

(G-16482)
INDUSTRIAL INDXING SYSTEMS INC
626 Fishers Run (14564-9732)
PHONE..........................585 924-9181
Fax: 585 924-2169
William Schnaufer, *President*
Jon Cassano, *Vice Pres*
Chris Draper, *Purch Agent*
Debbie Seibert, *Purchasing*
Peter Drexel, *Engineer*
EMP: 22 **EST:** 1977
SQ FT: 13,000
SALES (est): 4.9MM **Privately Held**
WEB: www.iis-servo.com
SIC: 3625 Relays & industrial controls

(G-16483)
JOHN RAMSEY ELEC SVCS LLC
Also Called: Jre Test
7940 Rae Blvd (14564-8933)
PHONE..........................585 298-9596
Donna Dedes, *General Mgr*
John G Ramsey,
Bruce Sidari,

EMP: 8
SALES: 2.8MM **Privately Held**
SIC: 3825 Instruments to measure electricity

(G-16484)
JOHNSON CONTROLS INC
7612 Main Street Fishers (14564-9601)
PHONE..........................585 924-9346
Fax: 585 924-7086
Todd Mancuso, *Sales Executive*
Joe Knight, *Manager*
EMP: 37 **Privately Held**
SIC: 3822 Temperature controls, automatic
HQ: Johnson Controls, Inc.
 5757 N Green Bay Ave
 Milwaukee WI 53209
 414 524-1200

(G-16485)
JRE TEST LLC
7940 Rae Blvd (14564-8933)
P.O. Box 182, Mendon (14506-0182)
PHONE..........................585 298-9736
Donna Dedes, *Opers Mgr*
Bruce Sidari, *Mng Member*
John Ramsey,
EMP: 7
SQ FT: 2,000
SALES: 2.8MM **Privately Held**
SIC: 3825 Test equipment for electronic & electric measurement

(G-16486)
KIRTAS INC
Also Called: Kirtas Technologies, Inc.
7620 Omnitech Pl Ste 1 (14564-9428)
P.O. Box 119, Bolton MA (01740-0119)
PHONE..........................585 924-2420
Fax: 585 924-2441
Robb Richardson, *CEO*
▼ **EMP:** 27
SQ FT: 12,000
SALES (est): 4.6MM
SALES (corp-wide): 557.9K **Privately Held**
WEB: www.kirtastech.com
SIC: 3678 Electronic connectors
PA: Ristech Information Systems Inc
 5115 Harvester Rd Unit 8
 Burlington ON
 905 631-7451

(G-16487)
L-3 COMMUNICATIONS CORPORATION (DH)
Also Called: L-3 Cmmunications Corp Gcs Div
7640 Omnitech Pl (14564-9429)
PHONE..........................585 742-9100
Michael Strianese, *CEO*
Lawrence V Blerkom, *Vice Pres*
Kurt Lieberman, *Vice Pres*
Jim Pokora, *Vice Pres*
Lawrence Van Blerkom, *Vice Pres*
EMP: 138
SALES (est): 24.4MM
SALES (corp-wide): 10.4B **Publicly Held**
WEB: www.globalcoms.com
SIC: 3663 4899 Radio & TV communications equipment; satellites, communications; space satellite communications equipment; satellite earth stations
HQ: L-3 Communications Corporation
 600 3rd Ave
 New York NY 10016
 212 697-1111

(G-16488)
LIFETIME STAINLESS STEEL CORP
7387 Ny 96 850 (14564)
PHONE..........................585 924-9393
Stephen Foti, *President*
EMP: 6
SALES: 900K **Privately Held**
SIC: 3263 Cookware, fine earthenware

(G-16489)
LOGICAL CONTROL SOLUTIONS INC
829 Phillips Rd Ste 100 (14564-9431)
PHONE..........................585 424-5340
James Urbanczyk, *President*
Scott Janowski, *Engineer*

Victor - Ontario County (G-16490) — GEOGRAPHIC SECTION

EMP: 18
SQ FT: 45,000
SALES (est): 3.8MM **Privately Held**
SIC: 3822 Temperature controls, automatic

(G-16490)
MAGNET-NDCTIVE SYSTEMS LTD USA
Also Called: Ultra Electronics Inc
7625 Omnitech Pl (14564-9816)
PHONE.................585 924-4000
Russell Greenway, *President*
Bill Gill, *Treasurer*
Colin Frame, *Software Engr*
Nancy Como, *Admin Sec*
▲ **EMP:** 22
SQ FT: 10,000
SALES: 5.6MM
SALES (corp-wide): 1.1B **Privately Held**
SIC: 3663 Receiver-transmitter units (transceiver)
HQ: Ultra Electronics Inc
   107 Church Hill Rd
   Sandy Hook CT 06482
   203 270-3695

(G-16491)
MINITEC FRAMING SYSTEMS LLC
100 Rawson Rd Ste 228 (14564-1151)
PHONE.................585 924-4690
Fax: 585 924-4821
Susan Gijanto-Paeth, *General Mgr*
Susan Paeth, *General Mgr*
Mike Taylor, *Sales Engr*
Andrew Moles,
▲ **EMP:** 14
SQ FT: 40,000
SALES (est): 3.5MM **Privately Held**
SIC: 3354 Aluminum extruded products

(G-16492)
NEW SCALE TECHNOLOGIES INC
121 Victor Heights Pkwy (14564-8938)
PHONE.................585 924-4450
Fax: 585 924-4468
David Henderson, *CEO*
Ted Franceschi, *President*
Jeff Kramer, *Vice Pres*
Allison Leet, *Vice Pres*
Daniele Piazza, *Vice Pres*
EMP: 35
SQ FT: 15,000
SALES (est): 8.8MM **Privately Held**
WEB: www.newscaletech.com
SIC: 3827 Optical alignment & display instruments

(G-16493)
NEWTEX INDUSTRIES INC (PA)
8050 Victor Mendon Rd (14564-9109)
PHONE.................585 924-9135
Fax: 585 924-4645
Jerome Joliet, *CEO*
Douglas Bailey, *President*
Mat Krempl, *VP Opers*
Sean Leavy, *Mfg Mgr*
Harkirat Dhaliwal, *Engineer*
▲ **EMP:** 45 **EST:** 1978
SQ FT: 103,000
SALES: 9MM **Privately Held**
WEB: www.newtex.com
SIC: 2221 2295 2241 Fiberglass fabrics; coated fabrics, not rubberized; narrow fabric mills

(G-16494)
NEXT STEP PUBLISHING INC
Also Called: Next Step Magazine, The
2 W Main St Ste 200 (14564-1153)
PHONE.................585 742-1260
Fax: 585 742-1263
David Mammano, *President*
Laura Sestito, *Editor*
Vincent Crapanzano, *Vice Pres*
Diana Fisher, *Marketing Staff*
Jason Bullock, *Director*
EMP: 15
SQ FT: 1,500
SALES (est): 2.9MM **Privately Held**
SIC: 2721 8748 Periodicals; business consulting

(G-16495)
PACE WINDOW AND DOOR CORP (PA)
Also Called: Pace Window & Door
7224 State Route 96 (14564-9754)
PHONE.................585 924-8350
Fax: 716 942-4837
Robert Mehalso, *Ch of Bd*
Steven Abramson, *President*
Sara Colunio, *Purch Mgr*
Mark Jacobs, *Controller*
Jody Taubenfeld, *Finance*
EMP: 50
SQ FT: 21,000
SALES (est): 8.7MM **Privately Held**
WEB: www.pacewindows.com
SIC: 3089 1751 Plastic hardware & building products; window & door (prefabricated) installation

(G-16496)
PREMIER PACKAGING CORPORATION
6 Framark Dr (14564-1136)
P.O. Box 352 (14564-0352)
PHONE.................585 924-8460
Fax: 585 924-8753
Robert B Bzdick, *President*
Joan T Bzdick, *Treasurer*
Chris Winfield, *Sales Mgr*
Norman Trumbley, *Manager*
EMP: 32
SQ FT: 40,000
SALES (est): 5.4MM
SALES (corp-wide): 18.2MM **Publicly Held**
WEB: www.premiercustompkg.com
SIC: 2657 2675 2653 Folding paperboard boxes; die-cut paper & board; envelopes
PA: Document Security Systems Inc
   200 Canal View Blvd # 300
   Rochester NY 14623
   585 325-3610

(G-16497)
PROGRESSIVE MCH & DESIGN LLC (PA)
Also Called: Pmd
727 Rowley Rd (14564-9728)
PHONE.................585 924-5250
Fax: 585 924-3580
Timothy Lochner, *General Mgr*
Walter Halfmann, *Project Mgr*
Joseph Costello, *Opers Mgr*
Bruce Allison, *Safety Mgr*
Lori Herold, *Purch Agent*
EMP: 110
SQ FT: 26,000
SALES (est): 39MM **Privately Held**
WEB: www.pmdautomation.com
SIC: 3599 Machine & other job shop work

(G-16498)
RAMSEY ELECTRONICS LLC
590 Fishers Station Dr (14564-9744)
PHONE.................585 924-4560
Fax: 585 924-4555
Michael Leo, *General Mgr*
Richard Oddo, *CFO*
EMP: 20
SALES (est): 5.7MM **Privately Held**
SIC: 3825 Test equipment for electronic & electric measurement

(G-16499)
RAPID PRINT AND MARKETING INC
8 High St (14564-1105)
PHONE.................585 924-1520
Fax: 585 924-1584
David Gaudieri, *Owner*
EMP: 5
SQ FT: 3,000
SALES (est): 480K **Privately Held**
SIC: 2752 7334 Commercial printing, lithographic; commercial printing, offset; photocopying & duplicating services

(G-16500)
REDCOM LABORATORIES INC
1 Redcom Ctr (14564-9785)
PHONE.................585 924-6567
Fax: 585 924-6572
Klaus Gueldenpfennig, *President*
Charles Breidenstein, *President*
Larry Vuksanic, *President*
Dinah Weisberg, *Vice Pres*
John Mueller, *Project Mgr*
▲ **EMP:** 200 **EST:** 1978
SQ FT: 140,000
SALES (est): 55.7MM **Privately Held**
WEB: www.redcom.com
SIC: 3661 8748 Switching equipment, telephone; communications consulting

(G-16501)
SENSOR FILMS INCORPORATED
687 Rowley Rd (14564-9728)
PHONE.................585 738-3500
Peter Hessney, *Principal*
EMP: 25
SALES (est): 1.6MM **Privately Held**
SIC: 3699 Sound signaling devices, electrical

(G-16502)
SERVICE EDUCATION INCORPORATED
790 Canning Pkwy Ste 1 (14564-9019)
PHONE.................585 264-9240
Terence Wolfe, *President*
EMP: 6
SQ FT: 2,100
SALES (est): 300K **Privately Held**
WEB: www.serviceed.com
SIC: 2741 Technical manuals: publishing & printing

(G-16503)
SURMOTECH LLC
7676 Netlink Dr (14564-9419)
PHONE.................585 742-1220
Fax: 585 742-1221
Jerry F Valentine, *CEO*
Arthur Kaempffe, *Vice Pres*
Vince Andrews, *Opers Staff*
Steven Faulkner, *Opers Staff*
David Rizzo, *Opers Staff*
EMP: 100
SQ FT: 20,000
SALES (est): 33.7MM **Privately Held**
WEB: www.surmotech.com
SIC: 3679 Electronic circuits

(G-16504)
SYCAMORE HILL DESIGNS INC
7585 Modock Rd (14564-9104)
PHONE.................585 820-7322
Frank Vallone, *President*
EMP: 5
SALES (est): 300K **Privately Held**
SIC: 3484 Small arms

(G-16505)
SYRACUSA SAND AND GRAVEL INC
1389 Malone Rd (14564-9147)
P.O. Box 2 (14564-0002)
PHONE.................585 924-7146
Scott Syracusa, *President*
Mark Syracusa, *Vice Pres*
EMP: 10
SQ FT: 1,000
SALES (est): 1.6MM **Privately Held**
SIC: 1442 Construction sand mining; gravel mining

(G-16506)
TEKNIC INC
115 Victor Heights Pkwy (14564-8938)
PHONE.................585 784-7454
Alan Fullerton, *CEO*
Thomas Bucella, *Ch of Bd*
David Sewhuk, *President*
Warren Bod, *Exec VP*
Mark Deangelo, *Engineer*
▲ **EMP:** 35
SQ FT: 10,000
SALES (est): 5.8MM **Privately Held**
WEB: www.teknic.com
SIC: 3625 Motor controls & accessories

(G-16507)
TELOG INSTRUMENTS INC
830 Canning Pkwy (14564-8940)
PHONE.................585 742-3000
Fax: 585 742-3006
Barry L Ceci, *President*
Greg Desantis, *Vice Pres*
Carlton Quallo, *Vice Pres*
Charlene Donofrio, *Buyer*
Everett Lago, *Engineer*
EMP: 30
SQ FT: 20,000
SALES: 5.7MM
SALES (corp-wide): 2.2B **Publicly Held**
WEB: www.telog.com
SIC: 3829 3823 Measuring & controlling devices; industrial instrmnts msrmnt display/control process variable
PA: Trimble Inc.
   935 Stewart Dr
   Sunnyvale CA 94085
   408 481-8000

(G-16508)
THE CALDWELL MANUFACTURING CO
Advantage Mfg
Holland Industrial Park (14564)
PHONE.................585 352-2803
Michelle McCorry, *Manager*
EMP: 30
SALES (corp-wide): 50MM **Privately Held**
SIC: 3495 Wire springs
PA: The Caldwell Manufacturing Company
   2605 Manitou Rd Ste 100
   Rochester NY 14624
   585 352-3790

(G-16509)
TRIAD NETWORK TECHNOLOGIES
75b Victor Heights Pkwy (14564-8926)
PHONE.................585 924-8505
Fax: 585 924-8507
Pete Sweltz, *President*
Frank Carusone, *Vice Pres*
Don Munn, *Accounts Exec*
Michelle Carusone, *Office Mgr*
EMP: 20
SQ FT: 3,500
SALES (est): 3.3MM **Privately Held**
WEB: www.triadnt.com
SIC: 2298 Cable, fiber

(G-16510)
VICTOR INSULATORS INC
280 Maple Ave (14564-1385)
PHONE.................585 924-2127
Fax: 585 924-7906
Ira Knickerbocker, *Ch of Bd*
Andrew E Schwalm, *President*
Chris Rishel, *Safety Mgr*
Robert Dowdle, *Traffic Mgr*
Peggy Volpe, *Purchasing*
▲ **EMP:** 105
SQ FT: 327,000
SALES: 17MM **Privately Held**
WEB: www.victorinsulatorsinc.com
SIC: 3264 Insulators, electrical: porcelain

(G-16511)
VORTEK TEL 87724633365859
7200 Rawson Rd (14564-9101)
PHONE.................585 924-5000
Scott Seeman, *President*
Matt Courtney, *Regl Sales Mgr*
EMP: 30
SALES (est): 3.2MM
SALES (corp-wide): 615.9MM **Publicly Held**
WEB: www.hoffend.net
SIC: 3536 5084 Hoists; hoists
PA: Daktronics, Inc.
   201 Daktronics Dr
   Brookings SD 57006
   605 692-0200

(G-16512)
W STUART SMITH INC
Also Called: Heritage Packaging
625 Fishers Run (14564-8905)
PHONE.................585 742-3310
Fax: 585 742-3311
William S Smith, *Ch of Bd*
Kristin J Smith, *Vice Pres*
Randy Demkowicz, *Engineer*
Evan Smith, *Controller*
Scott Floyd, *Sales Engr*
◆ **EMP:** 40
SQ FT: 50,000
SALES (est): 8.6MM **Privately Held**
WEB: www.heritagepackaging.com
SIC: 3086 Packaging & shipping materials, foamed plastic

(G-16513)
WASHER SOLUTIONS INC
760 Canning Pkwy Ste A (14564-9018)
PHONE..................................585 742-6388
Mickie T Pitts, *CEO*
EMP: 10 **EST:** 2001
SQ FT: 1,200
SALES (est): 2.2MM **Privately Held**
WEB: www.washersolutions.com
SIC: 3519 Gas engine rebuilding

(G-16514)
WILLIAMSON LAW BOOK CO
790 Canning Pkwy Ste 2 (14564-9019)
PHONE..................................585 924-3400
Fax: 585 924-4153
Greg Chwiecko, *President*
Thomas Osborne, *Treasurer*
EMP: 12 **EST:** 1870
SQ FT: 10,800
SALES (est): 1.2MM **Privately Held**
WEB: www.wlbonline.org
SIC: 2761 7371 Manifold business forms; computer software development

(G-16515)
ZUMIEZ INC
769 Eastview Mall (14564-1037)
PHONE..................................585 425-8720
Sean Larkin, *Branch Mgr*
EMP: 15
SALES (corp-wide): 804.1MM **Publicly Held**
SIC: 3949 Sporting & athletic goods
PA: Zumiez Inc.
   4001 204th St Sw
   Lynnwood WA 98036
   425 551-1500

Voorheesville
Albany County

(G-16516)
ATLAS COPCO COMPTEC LLC (HQ)
46 School Rd (12186-9696)
PHONE..................................518 765-3344
Fax: 518 765-3357
Peter Wagner, *President*
Weston Greenman, *General Mgr*
Holly Simboli, *Principal*
Bill Volk, *Plant Mgr*
Charles Batcher, *Opers Mgr*
◆ **EMP:** 330 **EST:** 1970
SQ FT: 100,000
SALES (est): 122MM
SALES (corp-wide): 11.7B **Privately Held**
WEB: www.atlascopco-act.com
SIC: 3563 Air & gas compressors including vacuum pumps
PA: Atlas Copco Ab
   Sickla Industrivag 3
   Nacka 131 5
   874 380-00

(G-16517)
RFB ASSOCIATES INC
Also Called: Bruno Associates
11 Drywall Ln (12186-3007)
P.O. Box 14825, Albany (12212-4825)
PHONE..................................518 271-0551
Robert Bruno Sr, *President*
Sean P Bruno Sr, *Principal*
EMP: 8
SALES (est): 1.5MM **Privately Held**
SIC: 3559 3569 3565 3552 Automotive related machinery; assembly machines, non-metalworking; packaging machinery; textile machinery

(G-16518)
SPAULDING & ROGERS MFG INC
3252 New Scotland Rd (12186-4332)
PHONE..................................518 768-2070
Fax: 518 768-2240
Huck Spaulding, *Ch of Bd*
Josephine Spaulding, *President*
Jon Schwalb, *Consultant*
▲ **EMP:** 70
SALES (est): 9.9MM **Privately Held**
WEB: www.spaulding-rogers.com
SIC: 3952 Artists' equipment

(G-16519)
STANDARD STEEL FABRICATORS
Dutch Hill Rd (12186)
P.O. Box 404 (12186-0404)
PHONE..................................518 765-4820
David Meixner, *President*
EMP: 18
SALES (est): 3.1MM **Privately Held**
SIC: 3441 Fabricated structural metal

Waccabuc
Westchester County

(G-16520)
MANN CONSULTANTS LLC
67 Chapel Rd (10597-1001)
PHONE..................................914 763-0512
Stuart Mann,
Jeffrey Mandelbaum,
EMP: 22
SALES (est): 1MM **Privately Held**
SIC: 2253 2329 T-shirts & tops, knit; men's & boys' sportswear & athletic clothing

Waddington
St. Lawrence County

(G-16521)
STRUCTURAL WOOD CORPORATION
Also Called: Roll Lock Truss
243 Lincoln Ave (13694-3203)
P.O. Box 339 (13694-0339)
PHONE..................................315 388-4442
Michael McGee, *CEO*
Peter Rieter, *President*
Jim Lyon, *Finance Mgr*
Jim Lion, *Finance*
Bernard Shorett, *Sales Mgr*
EMP: 32
SQ FT: 20,000
SALES (est): 5.3MM **Privately Held**
WEB: www.rolllocktruss.com
SIC: 2439 5031 5211 Structural wood members; doors & windows; lumber & other building materials

Wading River
Suffolk County

(G-16522)
A I P PRINTING & STATIONERS
Also Called: Airport Printing & Stationers
6198 N Country Rd (11792-1625)
PHONE..................................631 929-5529
George A Waldemar, *President*
Chris Waldemar, *Sales Mgr*
Debra Waldemar, *Administration*
EMP: 8
SALES (est): 760K **Privately Held**
SIC: 2752 Lithographing on metal

(G-16523)
L T SALES CORP
Also Called: Lam Tech
Northside Rd (11792)
P.O. Box 637, Shoreham (11786-0637)
PHONE..................................631 886-1390
Carol Scalia, *President*
EMP: 10
SALES (est): 716.7K **Privately Held**
WEB: www.ltimage.com
SIC: 2759 Commercial printing

(G-16524)
LO-CO FUEL CORP
10 Stephen Dr (11792-2126)
PHONE..................................631 929-5086
Michael Lopez, *Principal*
EMP: 5
SALES (est): 664.9K **Privately Held**
SIC: 2869 Fuels

(G-16525)
SAFEGUARD INC
578 Sound Ave (11792)
P.O. Box 922 (11792-0922)
PHONE..................................631 929-3273
Charlie Zimmerman, *President*
EMP: 15
SALES (est): 2.5MM **Privately Held**
SIC: 2899 Fire retardant chemicals

(G-16526)
SPLIT ROCK TRADING CO INC
22 Creek Rd (11792-2501)
P.O. Box 841, Shoreham (11786-0841)
PHONE..................................631 929-3261
Jim Loscalzo, *President*
Peggy Vonbernewitz, *Corp Secy*
EMP: 7
SQ FT: 13,000
SALES: 480K **Privately Held**
WEB: www.splitrockvideo.com
SIC: 3499 5012 5013 5531 Novelties & specialties, metal; automobiles; motorcycles; automotive supplies & parts; automotive accessories; automobiles, new & used; motorcycles

(G-16527)
SWISS SPECIALTIES INC
15 Crescent Ct (11792-3004)
PHONE..................................631 567-8800
Fax: 631 567-8850
Daniel J George, *President*
EMP: 14
SQ FT: 5,000
SALES: 1.9MM **Privately Held**
SIC: 3541 Screw machines, automatic

(G-16528)
THERMO FISHER SCIENTIFIC INC
2800 Veterans Hwy (11792)
PHONE..................................631 648-4040
EMP: 307
SALES (corp-wide): 16.9B **Publicly Held**
WEB: www.thermo.com
SIC: 3826 Analytical instruments
PA: Thermo Fisher Scientific Inc.
   168 3rd Ave
   Waltham MA 02451
   781 622-1000

Wainscott
Suffolk County

(G-16529)
MAPEASY INC
54 Industrial Rd (11975-2001)
P.O. Box 80 (11975-0080)
PHONE..................................631 537-6213
Fax: 631 537-4541
Gary Bradhering, *President*
Chris Harris, *Vice Pres*
▲ **EMP:** 12
SQ FT: 11,000
SALES (est): 1MM **Privately Held**
WEB: www.mapeasy.com
SIC: 2741 4724 Maps: publishing & printing; travel agencies

Walden
Orange County

(G-16530)
AMPAC PAPER LLC (DH)
30 Coldenham Rd (12586-2036)
P.O. Box 271 (12586-0271)
PHONE..................................845 778-5511
John Q Baumann, *Ch of Bd*
Robert Tillis, *President*
Leland Lewis, *Chairman*
Robert De Gregorio, *Senior VP*
Robert D Gregorio, *Senior VP*
▲ **EMP:** 522
SQ FT: 200,000
SALES (est): 103.5MM
SALES (corp-wide): 1.2B **Privately Held**
WEB: www.ampaconline.com
SIC: 2674 2621 5162 Shopping bags: made from purchased materials; paper mills; plastics materials

(G-16531)
C & C ATHLETIC INC
Also Called: Viking Jackets & Athletic Wear
11 Myrtle Ave (12586-2340)
PHONE..................................845 713-4670
Andrea Conklin, *President*
EMP: 5
SQ FT: 4,000
SALES (est): 460K **Privately Held**
WEB: www.vikingathletic.com
SIC: 2759 2339 Screen printing; athletic clothing: women's, misses' & juniors'

(G-16532)
CALFONEX COMPANY
121 Orchard St (12586-1707)
PHONE..................................845 778-2212
Terrance Donovan, *Owner*
EMP: 15
SALES (est): 836.8K **Privately Held**
SIC: 2899 Chemical preparations

(G-16533)
DWYER FARM LLC
40 Bowman Ln (12586-2100)
PHONE..................................914 456-2742
Brian Dwyer, *Principal*
Christopher Dwyer, *Principal*
Jeannie Dwyer, *Principal*
Joseph Dwyer, *Principal*
Mel Dwyer, *Principal*
EMP: 6
SALES (est): 185.1K **Privately Held**
SIC: 2026 Farmers' cheese

(G-16534)
PACIFIC DIE CAST INC
Also Called: Qssi
827 Route 52 Ste 2 (12586-2747)
PHONE..................................845 778-6374
Fax: 845 778-6380
Melissa Durant, *Principal*
EMP: 14
SALES (corp-wide): 14.5MM **Privately Held**
SIC: 3544 Special dies & tools
PA: Pacific Die Cast, Inc.
   12802 Commodity Pl
   Tampa FL 33626
   813 316-2221

(G-16535)
ROMAR CONTRACTING INC
630 State Route 52 (12586-2709)
P.O. Box 658 (12586-0658)
PHONE..................................845 778-2737
Rod Winchell, *President*
EMP: 5
SALES: 500K **Privately Held**
SIC: 3441 Fabricated structural metal

(G-16536)
SPENCE ENGINEERING COMPANY INC
Also Called: Nicholson Steam Trap
150 Coldenham Rd (12586-2909)
PHONE..................................845 778-5566
Fax: 845 778-1072
A William Higgins, *Ch of Bd*
David A Bloss Sr, *President*
Alan R Carlsen, *Vice Pres*
Douglas Frank, *Vice Pres*
Kenneth Smith, *Vice Pres*
▲ **EMP:** 150
SQ FT: 79,000
SALES (est): 33.2MM
SALES (corp-wide): 656.2MM **Publicly Held**
WEB: www.spenceengineering.com
SIC: 3491 3444 3822 3612 Pressure valves & regulators, industrial; metal ventilating equipment; auto controls regulating residntl & coml environmt & applncs; transformers, except electric; valves & pipe fittings
PA: Circor International, Inc.
   30 Corporate Dr Ste 200
   Burlington MA 01803
   781 270-1200

Walden - Orange County (G-16537)

(G-16537)
TILCON NEW YORK INC
272 Berea Rd (12586-2906)
PHONE 845 778-5591
Reinis Siplls, *Branch Mgr*
EMP: 27
SALES (corp-wide): 25.3B **Privately Held**
WEB: www.tilconny.com
SIC: 1429 Trap rock, crushed & broken-quarrying; dolomitic marble, crushed & broken-quarrying
HQ: Tilcon New York Inc.
162 Old Mill Rd
West Nyack NY 10994
845 358-4500

(G-16538)
WALLKILL LODGE NO 627 F&AM
61 Main St (12586-1824)
P.O. Box 311 (12586-0311)
PHONE 845 778-7148
Mark Balck, *President*
EMP: 14
SQ FT: 7,326
SALES (est): 600K **Privately Held**
SIC: 2711 Newspapers

Wales Center
Erie County

(G-16539)
AM BICKFORD INC
12318 Big Tree Rd (14169)
P.O. Box 201 (14169-0201)
PHONE 716 652-1590
Fax: 585 652-2046
John Bickford, *President*
Laureen Stevenson, *Sales Mgr*
Jane Keohane, *Sales Staff*
EMP: 12
SQ FT: 5,000
SALES: 2MM **Privately Held**
WEB: www.ambickford.com
SIC: 3841 Surgical & medical instruments

(G-16540)
HALE ELECTRICAL DIST SVCS INC
12088 Big Tree Rd (14169)
P.O. Box 221 (14169-0221)
PHONE 716 818-7595
David Neveaux, *President*
EMP: 6
SQ FT: 6,000
SALES: 1.5MM **Privately Held**
SIC: 3612 Distribution transformers, electric

Wallkill
Ulster County

(G-16541)
ARTCRAFT BUILDING SERVICES
85 Old Hoagerburgh Rd (12589-3419)
PHONE 845 895-3893
Pasqual J Petrucci, *President*
Janice A Petrucci, *Vice Pres*
EMP: 5
SQ FT: 3,000
SALES (est): 734K **Privately Held**
SIC: 3537 Platforms, stands, tables, pallets & similar equipment; dollies (hand or power trucks), industrial except mining

(G-16542)
CATSMO CORP
Also Called: Solex Catsmo Fine Foods
25 Myers Rd (12589-3516)
PHONE 845 895-2296
Fax: 845 895-1232
Robert Simon, *President*
Melissa Basso, *Principal*
David Simon, *Principal*
Rose-Line Simon, *Vice Pres*
▲ EMP: 12 EST: 1995
SQ FT: 15,000
SALES (est): 2.2MM **Privately Held**
WEB: www.catsmo.com
SIC: 2091 Salmon, smoked

(G-16543)
FAIR-RITE PRODUCTS CORP (PA)
1 Commercial Row (12589-4438)
P.O. Box 288 (12589-0288)
PHONE 845 895-2055
Fax: 845 895-2629
Richard Parker, *Ch of Bd*
Carole U Parker, *President*
Larry Surrells, *Division Mgr*
Carol Rapp, *General Mgr*
Mike Eanni, *Purchasing*
▲ EMP: 125 EST: 1952
SQ FT: 80,000
SALES (est): 29.2MM **Privately Held**
WEB: www.fair-rite.com
SIC: 3679 Cores, magnetic

(G-16544)
JAMES B CROWELL & SONS INC
242 Lippincott Rd (12589-3643)
PHONE 845 895-3464
Fax: 845 895-9701
James Crowell III, *President*
Wendy Sutherland, *Vice Pres*
▲ EMP: 9 EST: 1872
SQ FT: 4,800
SALES (est): 1MM **Privately Held**
SIC: 3544 Industrial molds

(G-16545)
RICHTER METALCRAFT CORPORATION
Also Called: Charles Richter
80 Cottage St (12589-3128)
P.O. Box 297 (12589-0297)
PHONE 845 895-2025
David Richter, *President*
Carol Morgan, *Vice Pres*
Carl Ulrich, *Maint Spvr*
Louise Tancriedi, *Admin Sec*
EMP: 35 EST: 1934
SQ FT: 50,000
SALES (est): 4MM **Privately Held**
WEB: www.charlesrichter.com
SIC: 3469 Metal stampings; stamping metal for the trade; spinning metal for the trade

(G-16546)
SELECT-TECH INC
3050 State Route 208 (12589-4431)
P.O. Box 259 (12589-0259)
PHONE 845 895-8111
Fax: 845 895-8112
William Diener, *President*
Thomas Diener, *Treasurer*
▲ EMP: 5
SQ FT: 25,000
SALES: 600K **Privately Held**
WEB: www.select-tech.com
SIC: 3291 Abrasive products

Walton
Delaware County

(G-16547)
BEYOND DESIGN INC
807 Pines Brook Rd (13856-2381)
PHONE 607 865-7487
Barbara A Salvatore, *President*
EMP: 7
SALES (est): 638.4K **Privately Held**
SIC: 3299 Architectural sculptures: gypsum, clay, papier mache, etc.

(G-16548)
KRAFT HEINZ FOODS COMPANY
261 Delaware St (13856-1099)
PHONE 607 865-7131
Fax: 607 865-5830
Cynthia Waggoner, *Opers-Prdtn-Mfg*
Claudia Gonus, *Manager*
Keith Ormsby, *Executive*
Frank Silfee, *Maintence Staff*
EMP: 200
SALES (corp-wide): 210.8B **Publicly Held**
WEB: www.kraftfoods.com
SIC: 2026 2022 Fermented & cultured milk products; cheese, natural & processed
HQ: Heinz Kraft Foods Company
1 Ppg Pl Ste 3200
Pittsburgh PA 15222
412 456-5700

(G-16549)
NORTHEAST FABRICATORS LLC
30-35 William St (13856-1497)
P.O. Box 65 (13856-0065)
PHONE 607 865-4031
Steve Schick, *Purch Mgr*
Judy Beardslee, *Human Res Mgr*
Kathy Cole, *Office Mgr*
William Brodeur,
John Phraner,
EMP: 70 EST: 1997
SQ FT: 80,000
SALES (est): 20.6MM **Privately Held**
SIC: 3444 3441 Sheet metalwork; fabricated structural metal

Walworth
Wayne County

(G-16550)
MEDCO MACHINE LLC
2320 Walworth Marion Rd (14568-9501)
P.O. Box 454 (14568-0454)
PHONE 315 986-2109
Mark Medyn,
EMP: 6
SQ FT: 4,800
SALES: 700K **Privately Held**
SIC: 3599 Machine shop, jobbing & repair

(G-16551)
ROCHESTER ASPHALT MATERIALS
Also Called: Dolomite Group
1200 Atlantic Ave (14568-9792)
PHONE 315 524-4619
Harvey Smeatin, *Manager*
EMP: 7
SALES (corp-wide): 25.3B **Privately Held**
SIC: 3531 Asphalt plant, including gravel-mix type
HQ: Rochester Asphalt Materials Inc
1150 Penfield Rd
Rochester NY 14625
585 381-7010

(G-16552)
SOFTWARE & GENERAL SERVICES CO
Also Called: S and G Imaging
1365 Fairway 5 Cir (14568-9444)
PHONE 315 986-4184
John Larysz, *Owner*
EMP: 6
SALES (est): 480K **Privately Held**
WEB: www.softwareandgeneral.com
SIC: 7372 Prepackaged software

Wantagh
Nassau County

(G-16553)
1/2 OFF CARDS WANTAGH INC
1162 Wantagh Ave (11793-2110)
PHONE 516 809-9832
Steven Bodenstein, *CEO*
EMP: 5
SALES (est): 390K **Privately Held**
SIC: 2771 Greeting cards

(G-16554)
BNC COMMODITIES INC
3671 Orchard Rd (11793-3130)
P.O. Box 748, Amagansett (11930-0748)
PHONE 631 872-8041
Brett Frankel, *President*
EMP: 10
SQ FT: 2,200
SALES (est): 764.4K **Privately Held**
SIC: 2091 Fish & seafood cakes: packaged in cans, jars, etc.

(G-16555)
CHRISTOPHER ANTHONY PUBG CO
Also Called: Christiny
2225 Wantagh Ave (11793-3917)
PHONE 516 826-9205
Anthony Fannin, *President*
Jo Ann Fannin, *Admin Sec*
▼ EMP: 19 EST: 1978
SQ FT: 6,000
SALES: 2.5MM **Privately Held**
WEB: www.christony.com
SIC: 2741 Catalogs: publishing only, not printed on site

(G-16556)
GREENVALE BAGEL INC
3060 Merrick Rd (11793-4395)
PHONE 516 221-8221
Cesidia Facchini, *President*
Claudio Facchini, *Corp Secy*
Ralph Facchini, *Vice Pres*
EMP: 30
SQ FT: 1,200
SALES (est): 1.5MM **Privately Held**
SIC: 2051 Bagels, fresh or frozen; bakery: wholesale or wholesale/retail combined

(G-16557)
HERSHEY KISS 203 INC
3536 Bunker Ave (11793-3439)
PHONE 516 503-3740
Brian Deluca, *Chairman*
EMP: 5 EST: 2010
SALES (est): 252.5K **Privately Held**
SIC: 2066 Chocolate & cocoa products

(G-16558)
LIFESCAN INC
15 Tardy Ln N (11793-1928)
PHONE 516 557-2693
Debra Podgurski, *Director*
EMP: 258
SALES (corp-wide): 70B **Publicly Held**
SIC: 2835 Blood derivative diagnostic agents
HQ: Lifescan, Inc.
965 Chesterbrook Blvd
Chesterbrook PA 19087
800 227-8862

(G-16559)
LIGHT DENTAL LABS INC
1939 Wantagh Ave Unit A (11793-3949)
PHONE 516 785-7730
Fax: 516 785-7731
Frank Tomasino, *President*
EMP: 5
SALES: 750K **Privately Held**
SIC: 3843 Dental equipment & supplies

(G-16560)
MORTGAGE PRESS LTD
1220 Wantagh Ave (11793-2202)
PHONE 516 409-1400
Russell Sickmen, *CEO*
Joel M Berman, *President*
Andrew Berman, *Exec VP*
EMP: 22
SQ FT: 4,000
SALES (est): 1.3MM **Privately Held**
WEB: www.mortgagepress.com
SIC: 2711 2741 Newspapers; miscellaneous publishing

(G-16561)
NBETS CORPORATION
Also Called: Wantagh 5 & 10
1901 Wantagh Ave (11793-3930)
PHONE 516 785-1259
Fax: 516 785-1294
John Norris, *Ch of Bd*
EMP: 8 EST: 2010
SALES (est): 680K **Privately Held**
SIC: 2392 Household furnishings

(G-16562)
R M F HEALTH MANAGEMENT L L C
Also Called: Professional Health Imaging
3361 Park Ave (11793-3735)
PHONE 718 854-5400
Syndney Bernstein, *Executive*
Robyn Feldstein,
EMP: 21

▲ = Import ▼ = Export
◆ = Import/Export

GEOGRAPHIC SECTION

SQ FT: 9,600
SALES (est): 3.2MM **Privately Held**
SIC: 3844 X-ray apparatus & tubes; nuclear irradiation equipment

(G-16563)
ROYAL LINE LLC
3351 Park Ave (11793-3716)
PHONE 800 516-7450
Scott Simon,
▲ **EMP:** 10 **EST:** 2008
SALES (est): 1MM **Privately Held**
SIC: 3432 3634 Plumbers' brass goods: drain cocks, faucets, spigots, etc.; electric housewares & fans

(G-16564)
WANTAGH COMPUTER CENTER
10 Stanford Ct (11793-1863)
PHONE 516 826-2189
Sidney B Nudelman, *CEO*
EMP: 14
SQ FT: 4,000
SALES (est): 1.5MM **Privately Held**
SIC: 3577 3571 Computer peripheral equipment; electronic computers
PA: S B Nudelman Inc
10 Stanford Ct
Wantagh NY 11793
516 826-2189

(G-16565)
ZUCKERBAKERS INC
2845 Jerusalem Ave (11793-2016)
PHONE 516 785-6900
Andrew Greenstein, *Principal*
EMP: 11
SALES (est): 1.2MM **Privately Held**
SIC: 2051 Bread, cake & related products

Wappingers Falls
Dutchess County

(G-16566)
DRA IMAGING PC
169 Myers Corners Rd # 250 (12590-3868)
PHONE 845 296-1057
Richard Friedland, *CEO*
EMP: 27
SALES (est): 5.1MM **Privately Held**
SIC: 3844 X-ray apparatus & tubes

(G-16567)
FLAVORMATIC INDUSTRIES INC
90 Brentwood Dr (12590)
PHONE 845 297-9100
Fax: 845 297-2881
Judith Back, *President*
Ron Back, *Exec VP*
Ronald Back, *Exec VP*
Robert Back, *Vice Pres*
Richard Febles, *Opers Staff*
▼ **EMP:** 20 **EST:** 1887
SQ FT: 21,000
SALES (est): 5.1MM **Privately Held**
WEB: www.flavormatic.com
SIC: 2087 5169 2844 Beverage bases, concentrates, syrups, powders & mixes; beverage bases; extracts, flavoring; essential oils; perfumes, natural or synthetic

(G-16568)
FRESH HARVEST INCORPORATED
1574 Route 9 (12590-2846)
PHONE 845 296-1024
EMP: 12
SALES (est): 2.5MM **Privately Held**
SIC: 3556 Bakery machinery

(G-16569)
G BOPP USA INC
4 Bill Horton Way (12590-2018)
P.O. Box 393, Hopewell Junction (12533-0393)
PHONE 845 296-1065
Andrew Moss, *General Mgr*
George Baker, *COO*
▲ **EMP:** 7
SALES (est): 1MM **Privately Held**
SIC: 3496 Wire cloth & woven wire products

PA: G. Bopp & Co Ag
Bachmannweg 21
ZUrich ZH
443 776-666

(G-16570)
GEM REPRODUCTION SERVICES CORP
Also Called: Signal Graphics Printing
1299 Route 9 Ste 105 (12590-4918)
PHONE 845 298-0172
Fax: 845 298-0307
Gary Mensching, *President*
Elizabeth Mensching, *Admin Sec*
EMP: 5
SQ FT: 3,300
SALES (est): 956.9K **Privately Held**
SIC: 2752 2759 Commercial printing, offset; commercial printing

(G-16571)
GLAXOSMITHKLINE LLC
6 Alpert Dr (12590-4602)
PHONE 845 797-3259
EMP: 26
SALES (corp-wide): 36B **Privately Held**
SIC: 2834 Pharmaceutical preparations
HQ: Glaxosmithkline Llc
5 Crescent Dr
Philadelphia PA 19112
215 751-4000

(G-16572)
HIGHLAND VALLEY SUPPLY INC
30 Airport Dr (12590-6164)
PHONE 845 849-2863
Raymond Marsella, *President*
David Caparaso, *Vice Pres*
EMP: 15
SQ FT: 11,000
SALES (est): 4MM **Privately Held**
WEB: www.highlandvalleysupply.com
SIC: 3644 Electric conduits & fittings

(G-16573)
HUDSON VALLEY LIGHTING INC
151 Airport Dr (12590-6161)
P.O. Box 10775, Newburgh (12552-0775)
PHONE 845 561-0300
Fax: 845 561-6848
David Littman, *President*
Brent Fields, *Vice Pres*
◆ **EMP:** 75 **EST:** 1960
SQ FT: 65,000
SALES (est): 18MM **Privately Held**
WEB: www.hudsonvalleylighting.com
SIC: 3646 3645 Commercial indusl & institutional electric lighting fixtures; residential lighting fixtures

(G-16574)
JPMORGAN CHASE & CO
1460 Route 9 (12590-4425)
PHONE 845 298-2461
Rick Mendes, *Branch Mgr*
EMP: 12
SALES (corp-wide): 101B **Publicly Held**
SIC: 3644 Insulators & insulation materials, electrical
PA: Jpmorgan Chase & Co.
270 Park Ave Fl 38
New York NY 10017
212 270-6000

(G-16575)
MONEAST INC
Also Called: Sir Speedy
1708 Route 9 (12590-1350)
PHONE 845 298-8898
David Monto, *President*
Randall J Easter, *Treasurer*
Mary Alice Monto, *Admin Sec*
EMP: 6
SQ FT: 2,800
SALES (est): 750K **Privately Held**
SIC: 2752 2791 2789 Commercial printing, lithographic; typesetting; bookbinding & related work

(G-16576)
SONNEMAN-A WAY OF LIGHT
151 Airport Dr (12590-6161)
P.O. Box 7458, Newburgh (12550)
PHONE 845 926-5469
Sonny Park, *Owner*

◆ **EMP:** 5
SALES (est): 800.2K **Privately Held**
SIC: 3646 Commercial indusl & institutional electric lighting fixtures

(G-16577)
THINK GREEN JUNK REMOVAL INC
29 Meadow Wood Ln (12590-5937)
PHONE 845 297-7771
George Makris, *Owner*
EMP: 7
SALES (est): 842.5K **Privately Held**
SIC: 3089 Garbage containers, plastic

(G-16578)
WAPPINGERS FALLS SHOPPER INC
Also Called: Beacon Press News
84 E Main St (12590-2504)
PHONE 845 297-3723
Fax: 845 297-6810
Albert M Osten, *President*
Curtis Schmidt, *General Mgr*
Pat Roza, *Director*
Jothi Vaidyalingan, *Director*
EMP: 50 **EST:** 1959
SQ FT: 12,000
SALES (est): 3.8MM **Privately Held**
SIC: 2711 2752 Newspapers: publishing only, not printed on site; commercial printing, lithographic

Warnerville
Schoharie County

(G-16579)
ZMZ MFG INC
300 Mickle Hollow Rd (12187-2507)
PHONE 518 234-4336
Lisa Zaba Miller, *Principal*
EMP: 8
SALES (est): 704.5K **Privately Held**
SIC: 3999 Manufacturing industries

Warrensburg
Warren County

(G-16580)
NORTHEASTERN PRODUCTS CORP (PA)
Also Called: Nepco
115 Sweet Rd (12885-4754)
P.O. Box 98 (12885-0098)
PHONE 518 623-3161
Fax: 518 623-3803
Paul Schiavi, *CEO*
Gary Schiavi, *President*
Mark Stauber, *Plant Mgr*
Lee Schiavi, *Exec Dir*
EMP: 23
SQ FT: 2,400
SALES (est): 11MM **Privately Held**
WEB: www.nep-co.com
SIC: 2493 Reconstituted wood products

(G-16581)
TUMBLEHOME BOATSHOP
684 State Route 28 (12885-5301)
PHONE 518 623-5050
Reuben Smith, *Owner*
EMP: 6
SALES (est): 534.6K **Privately Held**
SIC: 3732 Boat building & repairing

Warsaw
Wyoming County

(G-16582)
FAIRVIEW PAPER BOX CORP
200 Allen St (14569-1562)
PHONE 585 786-5230
Fax: 585 786-5711
Donald Zaas, *Ch of Bd*
Joel Zaas, *President*
Mark Cassese, *COO*
John L Asimakopoulos, *CFO*

EMP: 27
SQ FT: 55,000
SALES: 6.8MM
SALES (corp-wide): 65MM **Privately Held**
WEB: www.boxit.com
SIC: 2652 Setup paperboard boxes
PA: The Apex Paper Box Company
5601 Walworth Ave
Cleveland OH 44102
216 631-4000

(G-16583)
MORTON BUILDINGS INC
5616 Route 20a E (14569-9302)
PHONE 585 786-8191
Fax: 585 786-5116
John Edmunds, *Opers-Prdtn-Mfg*
EMP: 40
SQ FT: 5,122
SALES (corp-wide): 490.8MM **Privately Held**
WEB: www.mortonbuildings.com
SIC: 3448 5039 Prefabricated metal buildings; prefabricated structures
PA: Morton Buildings, Inc.
252 W Adams St
Morton IL 61550
309 263-7474

(G-16584)
UNIDEX CORPORATION WESTERN NY
2416 State Route 19 N (14569-9336)
PHONE 585 786-3170
Fax: 585 786-3223
Arthur Crater, *President*
Don Cunningham, *General Mgr*
Susan M Gardner, *Vice Pres*
Thomas Baldwin, *Treasurer*
EMP: 16
SQ FT: 21,000
SALES (est): 3.5MM **Privately Held**
WEB: www.unidex-inc.com
SIC: 3549 Assembly machines, including robotic

(G-16585)
UPSTATE DOOR INC
26 Industrial St (14569-1550)
PHONE 585 786-3880
Robert J Fontaine, *CEO*
Brock Beckstrand, *Safety Mgr*
Craig Smith, *Engineer*
Matt Nelson, *Controller*
Jason Hurley, *Sales Mgr*
▲ **EMP:** 75
SQ FT: 55,000
SALES: 7.6MM **Privately Held**
WEB: www.upstatedoor.com
SIC: 2431 Interior & ornamental woodwork & trim

Warwick
Orange County

(G-16586)
AMERICAN TOWMAN NETWORK INC
Also Called: American Towman Expeditions
7 West St (10990-1447)
PHONE 845 986-4546
Fax: 845 986-5181
Steven L Calitri, *President*
Brendan Dooley, *Editor*
Henri Calitri, *Manager*
EMP: 12
SALES (est): 940K **Privately Held**
WEB: www.towman.com
SIC: 2721 7549 Periodicals; towing services; towing service, automotive

(G-16587)
DANGELO HOME COLLECTIONS INC
Also Called: Victoria Dngelo Intr Cllctions
39 Warwick Tpke (10990-3632)
P.O. Box 271 (10990-0271)
PHONE 917 267-8920
Victoria D'Angelo, *President*
Stuart Morrison, *Vice Pres*
▲ **EMP:** 7
SQ FT: 16,000

Warwick - Orange County (G-16588)

SALES: 750K **Privately Held**
WEB: www.dangelohome.com
SIC: 2431 Woodwork, interior & ornamental

(G-16588)
DIGITAL UNITED COLOR PRTG INC
Also Called: Warwick Press
33 South St (10990-1624)
P.O. Box 708 (10990-0708)
PHONE.................................845 986-9846
Scott J Lieberman, *Ch of Bd*
EMP: 11
SALES (est): 1.5MM **Privately Held**
SIC: 2752 Color lithography

(G-16589)
DREAM GREEN PRODUCTIONS
Also Called: Dream Fabric Printing
39 Warwick Tpke (10990-3632)
P.O. Box 271 (10990-0271)
PHONE.................................917 267-8920
Victoria D'Angelo, *Principal*
EMP: 5
SALES (est): 220K **Privately Held**
SIC: 2399 Fabricated textile products

(G-16590)
GARDEN STATE SHAVINGS INC
16 Almond Tree Ln (10990-2442)
PHONE.................................845 544-2835
Kimberlee Martin, *CEO*
Barry Luyster, *Vice Pres*
▼ EMP: 15
SQ FT: 60,000
SALES (est): 1.4MM **Privately Held**
SIC: 2421 Sawdust, shavings & wood chips

(G-16591)
KECK GROUP INC (PA)
314 State Route 94 S (10990-3379)
PHONE.................................845 988-5757
Fax: 845 343-0428
Robert Koeck, *CEO*
Terry Yungman, *Manager*
Frederick Keck, *Executive*
EMP: 12
SQ FT: 20,000
SALES (est): 1.1MM **Privately Held**
WEB: www.keckgroup.com
SIC: 2531 Pews, church

(G-16592)
KINGS QUARTET CORP
270 Kings Hwy (10990-3417)
PHONE.................................845 986-9090
Gary Bernstein, *President*
David Bernstein, *Treasurer*
Bernard Bernstein, *Admin Sec*
Kenneth Bernstein, *Admin Sec*
EMP: 5
SALES (est): 309.8K **Privately Held**
SIC: 2435 Plywood, hardwood or hardwood faced

(G-16593)
KNG CONSTRUCTION CO INC
19 Silo Ln (10990-2872)
PHONE.................................212 595-1451
Mark V Azzopardi, *President*
EMP: 10
SALES (est): 1.1MM **Privately Held**
SIC: 2431 1542 1521 Woodwork, interior & ornamental; commercial & office buildings, renovation & repair; general remodeling, single-family houses

(G-16594)
MECHANICAL RUBBER PDTS CO INC
Also Called: Minisink Rubber
77 Forester Ave Ste 1 (10990-1107)
P.O. Box 593 (10990-0593)
PHONE.................................845 986-2271
Fax: 845 986-0399
Cedric Glasper, *President*
Bill Thomas, *General Mgr*
Dan Wayman, *COO*
Nicole Cosimano, *Purchasing*
Walter Kielb, *Sales Mgr*
EMP: 15
SQ FT: 53,000

SALES (est): 3.1MM **Privately Held**
SIC: 3061 3089 Mechanical rubber goods; molding primary plastic

(G-16595)
MEECO SULLIVAN LLC
3 Chancellor Ln (10990-3411)
PHONE.................................800 232-3625
EMP: 225
SQ FT: 50,000
SALES: 22MM **Privately Held**
SIC: 2499 4493 Mfg Wood Products Marina Operation

(G-16596)
TRACK 7 INC
3 Forester Ave (10990-1129)
PHONE.................................845 544-1810
Betsy Mitchell, *Principal*
EMP: 6
SALES (est): 990.8K **Privately Held**
SIC: 2653 Corrugated & solid fiber boxes

(G-16597)
TRANSPRTTION COLLABORATIVE INC
Also Called: Trans Tech Bus
7 Lake Station Rd (10990-3426)
PHONE.................................845 988-2333
Danny Daniels, *President*
EMP: 42
SALES (est): 9.2MM **Privately Held**
SIC: 3711 Motor vehicles & car bodies

Washingtonville
Orange County

(G-16598)
BRISTOL GIFT CO INC
8 North St (10992-1113)
PHONE.................................845 496-2821
Fax: 845 496-2859
Matthew A Ropiecki Sr, *President*
Ellen Martarano, *Corp Secy*
Matthew J Ropiecki Jr, *Vice Pres*
EMP: 15
SQ FT: 7,000
SALES (est): 2.3MM **Privately Held**
WEB: www.bristolgift.net
SIC: 3499 Picture frames, metal

(G-16599)
BROTHERHOOD AMER OLDEST WNERY
Also Called: Vinevrest Co
100 Brotherhood Plaza Dr (10992-2262)
P.O. Box 190 (10992-0190)
PHONE.................................845 496-3661
Fax: 845 496-8720
Hernan Donoso, *President*
Cesar Baeza, *Corp Secy*
Laura Auld, *Controller*
Carol Tepper, *Manager*
Robert Liberto, *Director*
▲ EMP: 35
SALES (est): 8.3MM **Privately Held**
WEB: www.brotherhoodwinery.net
SIC: 2084 Wines

Wassaic
Dutchess County

(G-16600)
PAWLING CORPORATION
Also Called: Standard Products Division
32 Nelson Hill Rd (12592-2121)
P.O. Box 200 (12592-0200)
PHONE.................................845 373-9300
Fax: 845 373-7827
Greg Holen, *Vice Pres*
Ron Peck, *Purch Mgr*
Tony Baruffo, *Engineer*
Timothy Daley, *Engineer*
Eric Hall, *Engineer*
EMP: 65

SALES (corp-wide): 42MM **Privately Held**
WEB: www.pawling.com
SIC: 3061 3446 2273 Mechanical rubber goods; architectural metalwork; carpets & rugs
PA: Pawling Corporation
157 Charles Colman Blvd
Pawling NY 12564
845 855-1000

(G-16601)
PRESRAY CORPORATION
Also Called: Door Dam
32 Nelson Hill Rd (12592-2121)
P.O. Box 200 (12592-0200)
PHONE.................................845 373-9300
Theodore C Hollander, *Ch of Bd*
Jason Smith, *President*
Kevin Harris, *General Mgr*
Jered Tuberville, *Opers Mgr*
Michael McGregor, *Controller*
▲ EMP: 25 EST: 1955
SQ FT: 50,000
SALES (est): 6.1MM
SALES (corp-wide): 42MM **Privately Held**
WEB: www.presray.com
SIC: 3442 Metal doors
PA: Pawling Corporation
157 Charles Colman Blvd
Pawling NY 12564
845 855-1000

(G-16602)
WALL PROTECTION PRODUCTS LLC
Also Called: Wallguard.com
32 Nelson Hill Rd (12592-2121)
P.O. Box 1109, Dover Plains (12522-1109)
PHONE.................................877 943-6826
Fax: 845 373-7761
Rose Davis, *General Mgr*
Ralph Skokan, *CFO*
Rose Benson, *Manager*
Sandra M McKeever, *Info Tech Mgr*
EMP: 30
SALES (est): 3.1MM **Privately Held**
SIC: 3069 Rubber floor coverings, mats & wallcoverings

Water Mill
Suffolk County

(G-16603)
CAR DOCTOR MOTOR SPORTS LLC
Also Called: Car Doctor, The
610 Scuttle Hole Rd (11976-2520)
P.O. Box 1384, Amagansett (11930-1384)
PHONE.................................631 537-1548
Ryan Pilla, *Owner*
EMP: 6
SALES (est): 450K **Privately Held**
SIC: 3949 Cartridge belts, sporting type

(G-16604)
DEERFIELD MILLWORK INC
58 Deerfield Rd Unit 2 (11976-2151)
PHONE.................................631 726-9663
Keith Dutcher, *President*
Michelle Dutcher, *Finance*
Adam Schmidt, *Manager*
Jeanette Camara, *Info Tech Dir*
EMP: 11
SQ FT: 5,000
SALES (est): 1.4MM **Privately Held**
WEB: www.deerfieldmillwork.com
SIC: 2431 8712 Millwork; architectural services

(G-16605)
DUCK WALK VINYARDS
231 Montauk Hwy (11976-2639)
P.O. Box 962 (11976-0962)
PHONE.................................631 726-7555
Fax: 631 726-4395
Herodotus Damianos, *President*
Alexander Damianos, *Vice Pres*
EMP: 20
SQ FT: 22,470

SALES (est): 1.6MM **Privately Held**
WEB: www.duckwalk.com
SIC: 2084 Wines

(G-16606)
WALPOLE WOODWORKERS INC
779 Montauk Hwy (11976-2607)
P.O. Box 1281 (11976-1281)
PHONE.................................631 726-2859
Fax: 631 726-2861
Lou Maglio, *President*
EMP: 8
SALES (corp-wide): 103.2MM **Privately Held**
WEB: www.walpolewoodworkers.com
SIC: 2499 5211 5712 2452 Fencing, wood; fencing; outdoor & garden furniture; prefabricated wood buildings; prefabricated metal buildings; wood household furniture
PA: Walpole Woodworkers, Inc.
767 East St
Walpole MA 02081
508 668-2800

(G-16607)
WONDER NATURAL FOODS CORP (PA)
30 Blank Ln (11976-2134)
PHONE.................................631 726-4433
Lloyd Lasdon, *CEO*
Stuart Lasdon, *COO*
▲ EMP: 6
SQ FT: 3,000
SALES (est): 1.1MM **Privately Held**
WEB: www.peanutwonder.com
SIC: 2099 Peanut butter

Waterford
Saratoga County

(G-16608)
CASCADES TSSUE GROUP-SALES INC
148 Hudson River Rd (12188-1908)
PHONE.................................518 238-1900
Andre Lair, *Manager*
EMP: 100
SALES (corp-wide): 2.9B **Privately Held**
SIC: 2676 Towels, napkins & tissue paper products
HQ: Cascades Tissue Group-Sales Inc.
148 Hudson River Rd
Waterford NY 12188
819 363-5100

(G-16609)
CASCADES TSSUE GROUP-SALES INC (HQ)
148 Hudson River Rd (12188-1908)
P.O. Box 369 (12188-0369)
PHONE.................................819 363-5100
Fax: 518 238-1919
Daniel Morneau, *President*
Gary A Hayden, *Chairman*
Maryse Fernet, *Vice Pres*
Stephanie Croto, *Controller*
▲ EMP: 40
SALES (est): 32.6MM
SALES (corp-wide): 2.9B **Privately Held**
SIC: 2621 Absorbent paper
PA: Cascades Inc
404 Boul Marie-Victorin
Kingsey Falls QC J0A 1
819 363-5100

(G-16610)
CASCADES USA INC
148 Hudson River Rd (12188-1908)
PHONE.................................518 880-3632
Guy Prenevost, *Principal*
▲ EMP: 48
SALES (est): 10.4MM **Privately Held**
SIC: 2653 Corrugated & solid fiber boxes

(G-16611)
EVONIK CORPORATION
7 Schoolhouse Ln (12188-1931)
P.O. Box 188 (12188-0188)
PHONE.................................518 233-7090
Fax: 518 237-0478

Ralf Duessel, *Manager*
Mike Slingerland, *Manager*
John Gocha, *Maintence Staff*
EMP: 32
SALES (corp-wide): 2.3B **Privately Held**
SIC: 2869 Industrial organic chemicals
HQ: Evonik Corporation
  299 Jefferson Rd
  Parsippany NJ 07054
  973 929-8000

(G-16612)
HALFMOON TOWN WATER DEPARTMENT
8 Brookwood Rd (12188-1206)
PHONE..............................518 233-7489
Fax: 518 233-1705
Frank Tironi, *Director*
EMP: 9 **EST:** 2007
SALES (est): 603.6K **Privately Held**
SIC: 2899 Water treating compounds

(G-16613)
MAXIMUM SECURITY PRODUCTS CORP
Also Called: Hillside Iron Works
3 Schoolhouse Ln (12188-1931)
PHONE..............................518 233-1800
Fax: 518 233-8069
Joseph Burch, *President*
Harold Hatfield, *Corp Secy*
Robert Magee, *Vice Pres*
▲ **EMP:** 50
SQ FT: 100,000
SALES (est): 12MM **Privately Held**
WEB: www.maximumsecuritycorp.com
SIC: 3446 3499 2542 2531 Architectural metalwork; stairs, fire escapes, balconies, railings & ladders; fences, gates, posts & flagpoles; fire- or burglary-resistive products; partitions & fixtures, except wood; public building & related furniture

(G-16614)
MILLWOOD INC
430 Hudson River Rd (12188-1916)
PHONE..............................518 233-1475
Mike Cusack, *Branch Mgr*
EMP: 17 **Privately Held**
SIC: 3565 5084 Packaging machinery; packaging machinery & equipment
PA: Millwood, Inc.
  3708 International Blvd
  Vienna OH 44473

(G-16615)
MOMENTIVE PERFORMANCE MTLS INC
260 Hudson River Rd (12188-1910)
PHONE..............................614 986-2495
Steve Delarge, *Opers Staff*
EMP: 1500 **Privately Held**
WEB: www.gewaterford.com
SIC: 2869 Silicones
PA: Momentive Performance Materials Inc.
  180 E Broad St
  Columbus OH 43215

(G-16616)
MOMENTIVE PERFORMANCE MTLS INC (DH)
260 Hudson River Rd (12188-1910)
PHONE..............................518 237-3330
John G Boss, *President*
Nathan E Fisher, *Exec VP*
Craig R Branchfield, *Vice Pres*
Gary Grace, *Engineer*
Erick R Asmussen, *CFO*
◆ **EMP:** 20
SALES: 2.2B **Privately Held**
WEB: www.gewaterford.com
SIC: 2869 3479 3679 Silicones; coating of metals with silicon; electronic crystals; quartz crystals, for electronic application
HQ: Mpm Intermediate Holdings Inc.
  260 Hudson River Rd
  Waterford NY 12188
  518 237-3330

(G-16617)
MPM HOLDINGS INC (PA)
260 Hudson River Rd (12188-1910)
PHONE..............................518 237-3330
John G Boss, *President*
Douglas A Johns, *Exec VP*

John D Moran, *Senior VP*
George F Knight, *Vice Pres*
Brian D Berger, *CFO*
EMP: 5
SALES (est): 2.2B **Privately Held**
SIC: 2869 3479 3679 Silicones; coating of metals with silicon; electronic crystals; quartz crystals, for electronic application

(G-16618)
MPM INTERMEDIATE HOLDINGS INC (HQ)
260 Hudson River Rd (12188-1910)
PHONE..............................518 237-3330
John G Boss, *President*
Brian D Berger, *CFO*
EMP: 2 **EST:** 2014
SALES (est): 2.2B **Privately Held**
SIC: 2869 3479 3679 Silicones; coating of metals with silicon; electronic crystals; quartz crystals, for electronic application
PA: Mpm Holdings Inc
  260 Hudson River Rd
  Waterford NY 12188
  518 237-3330

(G-16619)
MPM SILICONES LLC
Also Called: Momentive
260 Hudson River Rd (12188-1910)
PHONE..............................518 233-3330
Fax: 518 233-2515
Rick Schumacher, *Vice Pres*
Michael Fackelman, *Engineer*
Tom Yarmowich, *Project Engr*
Brian D Berger, *CFO*
Matthew Haley, *Program Mgr*
EMP: 4600
SALES (est): 203.5MM
SALES (corp-wide): 2.2B **Privately Held**
SIC: 2869 Silicones
HQ: Momentive Performance Materials Inc.
  260 Hudson River Rd
  Waterford NY 12188
  518 237-3330

(G-16620)
ROBERTS NICHOLS FIRE APPARATUS
3 Industry Dr (12188-1935)
PHONE..............................518 431-1945
Harry Roberts, *CEO*
EMP: 9
SALES (est): 1.2MM **Privately Held**
SIC: 3711 Motor vehicles & car bodies

(G-16621)
SOFT-TEX INTERNATIONAL INC
Also Called: Soft-Tex Manufacturing Co
428 Hudson River Rd (12188-1916)
P.O. Box 278 (12188-0278)
PHONE..............................518 235-3645
T Arthur Perry, *President*
Robert O'Connell, *Exec VP*
Jeff Chilton, *Senior VP*
Keith Bolton, *Vice Pres*
Harold J Perry Jr, *Vice Pres*
▲ **EMP:** 90
SQ FT: 120,000
SALES (est): 22.5MM **Privately Held**
WEB: www.bedpillows.com
SIC: 2392 Cushions & pillows

(G-16622)
STEPPING STONES ONE DAY SIGNS
105 Broad St (12188-2313)
P.O. Box 128 (12188-0128)
PHONE..............................518 237-5774
Fax: 518 237-1410
John Matson, *President*
Paul Matson, *Vice Pres*
EMP: 5
SQ FT: 3,000
SALES (est): 517.4K **Privately Held**
SIC: 3993 Signs & advertising specialties

(G-16623)
URSULA OF SWITZERLAND INC (PA)
Also Called: Ursula Company Store
31 Mohawk Ave (12188-2290)
PHONE..............................518 237-2580
Fax: 518 237-3038
Ursula G Rickenbacher, *President*

Lou Pingatore, *COO*
Douglas Randancco, *Vice Pres*
Beth Easly, *Purchasing*
Meinrad Rickenbacher, *Treasurer*
EMP: 22 **EST:** 1965
SQ FT: 35,000
SALES (est): 3.5MM **Privately Held**
WEB: www.ursula.com
SIC: 2335 2337 2331 Gowns, formal; ensemble dresses: women's, misses' & juniors'; women's & misses' suits & coats; women's & misses' blouses & shirts

Waterloo
Seneca County

(G-16624)
EVANS CHEMETICS LP
228 E Main St (13165-1534)
PHONE..............................315 539-9221
Fax: 315 539-9627
Barb Guthrie, *Purch Mgr*
Jeff Mooneyhan, *Engineer*
Pat Wrobel, *Engineer*
Virginia Slowik, *Marketing Staff*
Frank Dipasquale, *Branch Mgr*
EMP: 55
SALES (corp-wide): 29.7MM **Privately Held**
WEB: www.evanschemetics.com
SIC: 2899 Acids
PA: Evans Chemetics Lp
  Glenpointe Center West 4
  Teaneck NJ 07666
  732 635-0100

(G-16625)
FINGER LAKES CONVEYORS INC
2359 State Route 414 E (13165-9633)
PHONE..............................315 539-9246
Fax: 315 539-0879
Michael J Gelder, *Ch of Bd*
Nancy Gelder, *Vice Pres*
EMP: 9
SQ FT: 37,000
SALES: 823K **Privately Held**
WEB: www.flconveyors.com
SIC: 3499 1796 Fire- or burglary-resistive products; machinery installation

(G-16626)
FRAZIER INDUSTRIAL COMPANY
1291 Waterloo Geneva Rd (13165-1201)
PHONE..............................315 539-9256
Staci Predicho, *Human Resources*
EMP: 55
SQ FT: 62,116
SALES (corp-wide): 254.6MM **Privately Held**
WEB: www.ecologic.com
SIC: 2542 3441 Pallet racks: except wood; fabricated structural metal
PA: Frazier Industrial Company
  91 Fairview Ave
  Long Valley NJ 07853
  908 876-3001

(G-16627)
GHARANA INDUSTRIES LLC
Also Called: Ganesh Foods
61 Swift St (13165-1124)
PHONE..............................315 651-4004
◆ **EMP:** 6
SQ FT: 122,000
SALES (est): 420K **Privately Held**
SIC: 2022 Mfg Cheese

(G-16628)
GUESS INC
655 State Route 318 # 96 (13165-5632)
PHONE..............................315 539-5634
Lisa Kuney, *Principal*
EMP: 25
SALES (corp-wide): 2.2B **Publicly Held**
SIC: 2325 Men's & boys' jeans & dungarees
PA: Guess , Inc.
  1444 S Alameda St
  Los Angeles CA 90021
  213 765-3100

(G-16629)
HAMPSHIRE CHEMICAL CORP
228 E Main St (13165-1529)
P.O. Box 700 (13165-0700)
PHONE..............................315 539-9221
Richard Babiarz, *Partner*
Gary Horvath, *QC Dir*
Lori Bentley, *Human Res Mgr*
EMP: 100
SALES (corp-wide): 48.7B **Publicly Held**
SIC: 2869 2899 2819 Industrial organic chemicals; chemical preparations; industrial inorganic chemicals
HQ: Hampshire Chemical Corp
  2 E Spit Brook Rd
  Nashua NH

(G-16630)
MARROS EQUIPMENT & TRUCKS
2354 State Route 414 (13165-8473)
PHONE..............................315 539-8702
John Marro Jr, *President*
EMP: 14 **EST:** 1946
SQ FT: 14,400
SALES (est): 1.4MM **Privately Held**
SIC: 3713 3536 Truck bodies (motor vehicles); hoists

(G-16631)
PETER PRODUCTIONS DEVIVI INC
2494 Kingdom Rd (13165-9400)
PHONE..............................315 568-8484
Fax: 315 568-6041
Peter Devivi, *President*
EMP: 10
SQ FT: 9,000
SALES (est): 1.3MM **Privately Held**
WEB: www.tapertite.com
SIC: 2431 Millwork

(G-16632)
ZYP PRECISION LLC
1098 Birdsey Rd (13165-9404)
PHONE..............................315 539-3667
Edward Huff,
EMP: 5
SALES (est): 412K **Privately Held**
SIC: 3541 Lathes, metal cutting & polishing

Watertown
Jefferson County

(G-16633)
A & K EQUIPMENT INCORPORATED
407 Sherman St (13601-3958)
PHONE..............................705 428-3573
Jim Lowe, *President*
Kevin Lowe, *Principal*
Cathy Lowe, *Corp Secy*
Andrew Lowe, *Vice Pres*
EMP: 5
SALES (est): 387.1K **Privately Held**
SIC: 3596 5046 Scales & balances, except laboratory; scales, except laboratory

(G-16634)
ALLIED MOTION TECHNOLOGIES INC
Also Called: Stature Electric
22543 Fisher Rd (13601-1090)
P.O. Box 6660 (13601-6660)
PHONE..............................315 782-5910
Bill Stout, *General Mgr*
Lenissa Chenoweth, *Materials Mgr*
Todd Gardner, *Materials Mgr*
Jon Richards, *Materials Mgr*
Ron Wenzen, *Branch Mgr*
EMP: 200
SALES (corp-wide): 232.4MM **Publicly Held**
WEB: www.alliedmotion.com
SIC: 3621 3546 Electric motor & generator parts; motors, electric; power-driven handtools
PA: Allied Motion Technologies Inc.
  495 Commerce Dr Ste 3
  Amherst NY 14228
  716 242-8634

Watertown - Jefferson County (G-16635)

(G-16635)
ATOMIC SIGNWORKS
1040 Bradley St Ste 3 (13601-1224)
P.O. Box 6103 (13601-6103)
PHONE...............................315 779-7446
Fax: 315 779-7479
Daniel Gill, *Owner*
EMP: 5
SALES: 250K Privately Held
WEB: www.atomicsignworks.com
SIC: 3993 Signs & advertising specialties

(G-16636)
BARRETT PAVING MATERIALS INC
26572 State Route 37 (13601-5789)
PHONE...............................315 788-2037
Fax: 315 786-0748
Sylvain Gross, *General Mgr*
Patrick O'Bryan, *General Mgr*
Dave Putnam, *Plant Supt*
Scott Zellar, *Safety Mgr*
Scott Lockerbie, *Site Mgr*
EMP: 12
SQ FT: 820
SALES (corp-wide): 84.5MM Privately Held
WEB: www.barrettpaving.com
SIC: 3273 2951 1611 Ready-mixed concrete; asphalt paving mixtures & blocks; highway & street construction
HQ: Barrett Paving Materials Inc.
3 Becker Farm Rd Ste 307
Roseland NJ 07068
973 533-1001

(G-16637)
BIMBO BAKERIES USA INC
144 Eastern Blvd (13601-3132)
PHONE...............................315 785-7060
George Weston, *Branch Mgr*
EMP: 18
SALES (corp-wide): 13B Privately Held
WEB: www.gwbakeries.com
SIC: 2051 Bread, cake & related products
HQ: Bimbo Bakeries Usa, Inc
255 Business Center Dr # 200
Horsham PA 19044
215 347-5500

(G-16638)
BIMBO BAKERIES USA INC
1100 Water St (13601-2146)
PHONE...............................315 782-4189
Rick Kimbell, *Manager*
EMP: 165
SALES (corp-wide): 13B Privately Held
SIC: 2051 Bread, cake & related products
HQ: Bimbo Bakeries Usa, Inc
255 Business Center Dr # 200
Horsham PA 19044
215 347-5500

(G-16639)
BLACK RIVER BREWING CO INC
500 Newell St (13601-2428)
PHONE...............................315 755-2739
Michael Niezabytoski, *Owner*
EMP: 5
SALES (est): 330.7K Privately Held
SIC: 2082 Malt beverages

(G-16640)
BOTTLING GROUP LLC
Also Called: Pepsi Beverages Company
1035 Bradley St (13601-1248)
PHONE...............................315 788-6751
Fax: 315 788-6756
Eric Foss, *CEO*
Dan Wiseman, *General Mgr*
Darel Jones, *Info Tech Dir*
Lewis Hatch, *Info Tech Mgr*
Winnie Parker, *Administration*
EMP: 39 EST: 1999
SALES (est): 4MM Privately Held
SIC: 2086 Carbonated soft drinks, bottled & canned

(G-16641)
CAR-FRESHNER CORPORATION (HQ)
Also Called: Little Trees
21205 Little Tree Dr (13601-5861)
P.O. Box 719 (13601-0719)
PHONE...............................315 788-6250
Fax: 315 788-7467
Richard O Flechtner, *Chairman*
Daniel Estal, *VP Mfg*
Richard Stancato, *Opers Mgr*
Amber Geidel, *Safety Mgr*
Brandy Taylor, *Purch Agent*
◆ EMP: 250 EST: 1952
SQ FT: 30,000
SALES (est): 75.6MM Privately Held
WEB: www.little-trees.com
SIC: 2842 Deodorants, nonpersonal

(G-16642)
CAR-FRESHNER CORPORATION
22569 Fisher Cir (13601-1058)
P.O. Box 719 (13601-0719)
PHONE...............................315 788-6250
Fax: 315 782-0140
Robert Swank, *Principal*
Walter Humphrey, *Engineer*
Theresa Jewett, *Human Resources*
Daniel Shepherd, *Sales Mgr*
Travis Washburn, *Sales Mgr*
EMP: 59 Privately Held
WEB: www.little-trees.com
SIC: 2842 Specialty cleaning, polishes & sanitation goods
HQ: Car-Freshner Corporation
21205 Little Tree Dr
Watertown NY 13601
315 788-6250

(G-16643)
CHAPIN WATERMATICS INC
740 Water St (13601-2154)
PHONE...............................315 782-1170
Fax: 315 782-1490
Narinder Gupta, *CEO*
William Chapin, *President*
Carson Lennox, *Plant Mgr*
Jeff Herron, *Prdtn Mgr*
Laura Tousant, *Treasurer*
◆ EMP: 80 EST: 1935
SQ FT: 40,000
SALES (est): 10.3MM Privately Held
WEB: www.chapindrip.com
SIC: 3052 3523 Plastic hose; fertilizing, spraying, dusting & irrigation machinery
HQ: Jain America Foods, Inc.
1819 Walcutt Rd Ste 1
Columbus OH 43228
614 850-9400

(G-16644)
CHRISTIAN BUS ENDEAVORS INC (PA)
Also Called: Coughlin Printing Group
210 Court St Ste 10 (13601-4546)
PHONE...............................315 788-8560
Michael A Biolsi, *President*
Brian Peck, *Principal*
Gary Ingram, *Corp Secy*
Dan Kelebes, *Manager*
EMP: 10
SALES (est): 1.2MM Privately Held
WEB: www.amfcoughlin.com
SIC: 2759 7374 Commercial printing; computer graphics service

(G-16645)
CLEMENTS BURRVILLE SAWMILL
18181 Van Allen Rd N (13601-5711)
PHONE...............................315 782-4549
Fax: 315 782-4549
Philip Clement, *President*
Betty Clement, *Vice Pres*
EMP: 9
SQ FT: 8,820
SALES: 700K Privately Held
SIC: 2448 2426 2421 Pallets, wood; hardwood dimension & flooring mills; sawmills & planing mills, general

(G-16646)
COCA-COLA REFRESHMENTS USA INC
22614 County Route 51 (13601-5064)
PHONE...............................315 785-8907
Fax: 315 785-6841
Jess Duck, *Manager*
EMP: 33
SALES (corp-wide): 44.2B Publicly Held
WEB: www.cokecce.com
SIC: 2086 Bottled & canned soft drinks
HQ: Coca-Cola Refreshments Usa, Inc.
2500 Windy Ridge Pkwy Se
Atlanta GA 30339
770 989-3000

(G-16647)
COUGHLIN PRINTING GROUP
Also Called: A M F/Coughlin Printing
210 Court St Ste 10 (13601-4546)
PHONE...............................315 788-8560
Fax: 315 836-0043
Doug Bockstanz, *President*
Brian Peck, *General Mgr*
William Barden, *Vice Pres*
Nance Bockstanz, *Vice Pres*
Gary Ingram, *Vice Pres*
EMP: 7
SQ FT: 1,500
SALES (est): 880.8K Privately Held
SIC: 2752 Commercial printing, lithographic; commercial printing, offset

(G-16648)
CURRENT APPLICATIONS INC
275 Bellew Ave S (13601-2381)
P.O. Box 321 (13601-0321)
PHONE...............................315 788-4689
George M Anderson, *President*
Roger Snyder, *Corp Secy*
Christopher Gilbert, *Vice Pres*
Robert Olin, *Vice Pres*
▲ EMP: 49
SQ FT: 20,000
SALES (est): 10.4MM Privately Held
WEB: www.currentapps.com
SIC: 3621 Motors, electric

(G-16649)
CYCLOTHERM OF WATERTOWN INC
787 Pearl St (13601-9111)
PHONE...............................315 782-1100
Charles E Stafford, *President*
EMP: 25
SQ FT: 20,000
SALES (est): 605K Privately Held
SIC: 3443 3554 Boiler shop products: boilers, smokestacks, steel tanks; paper industries machinery

(G-16650)
DOCO QUICK PRINT INC
808 Huntington St (13601-2864)
PHONE...............................315 782-6623
Fax: 315 782-6623
Dan Osborne, *President*
Carolyn Osborne, *Treasurer*
EMP: 6
SQ FT: 3,000
SALES (est): 750K Privately Held
SIC: 2752 Commercial printing, offset

(G-16651)
E AND V ENERGY CORPORATION
22925 State Route 12 (13601-5034)
PHONE...............................315 786-2067
Fax: 315 786-0733
Bill Austin, *Branch Mgr*
EMP: 18
SALES (corp-wide): 19.7MM Privately Held
SIC: 2911 Still oil
PA: E. And V. Energy Corporation
2737 Erie Dr
Weedsport NY 13166
315 594-8076

(G-16652)
GERTRUDE HAWK CHOCOLATES INC
21182 Salmon Run Mall Loo (13601-2248)
EMP: 20
SALES (corp-wide): 240.6MM Privately Held
SIC: 2064 Mfg Candy/Confectionery
PA: Gertrude Hawk Chocolates, Inc.
9 Keystone Industrial Par
Dunmore PA 18512
570 342-7556

(G-16653)
HANSON AGGREGATES PA LLC
25133 Nys Rt 3 (13601-1718)
P.O. Box 130 (13601-0130)
PHONE...............................315 782-2300
Dan O'Connor, *Manager*
Roger Hutchinson, *Manager*
EMP: 10
SALES (corp-wide): 14.4B Privately Held
SIC: 1442 5032 Gravel mining; stone, crushed or broken
HQ: Hanson Aggregates Pennsylvania, Llc
7660 Imperial Way
Allentown PA 18195
610 366-4626

(G-16654)
HENDERSON PRODUCTS INC
Also Called: Henderson Truck Equipment
22686 Fisher Rd Ste A (13601-1088)
PHONE...............................315 785-0994
Dave O'Brien, *Manager*
Dave Obrien, *Manager*
EMP: 22 Publicly Held
WEB: www.henderson-mfg.com
SIC: 3822 Ice maker controls
HQ: Henderson Products, Inc.
1085 S 3rd St
Manchester IA 52057
563 927-2828

(G-16655)
JEFFERSON CONCRETE CORP
22850 County Route 51 (13601-5081)
PHONE...............................315 788-4171
Mark Thompson, *CEO*
Barbara Belcher, *Human Res Dir*
Mark Losee, *Sales Staff*
Donna Borkland, *Manager*
EMP: 55 EST: 1930
SQ FT: 37,000
SALES (est): 9.8MM Privately Held
WEB: www.jeffconcrete.com
SIC: 3272 Manhole covers or frames, concrete; septic tanks, concrete; tanks, concrete; burial vaults, concrete or precast terrazzo

(G-16656)
JOHN VESPA INC (PA)
Also Called: Vespa Sand & Stone
19626 Overlook Dr (13601-5443)
PHONE...............................315 788-6330
Fax: 315 788-7360
John Vespa Jr, *President*
Dorothy Vespa, *Admin Sec*
EMP: 13 EST: 1941
SQ FT: 2,400
SALES: 1.5MM Privately Held
SIC: 1422 1442 Crushed & broken limestone; construction sand mining; gravel mining

(G-16657)
KENAL SERVICES CORP
Also Called: Metal Man Services
1109 Water St (13601-2147)
PHONE...............................315 788-9226
Fax: 315 788-9440
Kenneth Moseley, *President*
Michael Vecchio, *CFO*
Victor Scott, *Manager*
EMP: 7
SQ FT: 15,272
SALES: 600K Privately Held
WEB: www.metalmanservices.com
SIC: 3446 Architectural metalwork

(G-16658)
KENT NUTRITION GROUP INC
810 Waterman Dr (13601-2371)
PHONE...............................315 788-0032
Fax: 315 788-6033
Brad Coolidge, *Opers-Prdtn-Mfg*
Jeremy Ruckman, *QA Dir*
Dave Moorhead, *Engineer*
Bob Spindell, *Systems Staff*
EMP: 10
SQ FT: 13,608
SALES (corp-wide): 578.7MM Privately Held
WEB: www.blueseal.com
SIC: 2048 Prepared feeds

HQ: Kent Nutrition Group, Inc.
1600 Oregon St
Muscatine IA 52761
866 647-1212

(G-16659)
KNORR BRAKE HOLDING CORP (DH)
748 Starbuck Ave (13601-1620)
PHONE..................................315 786-5356
Heinz Hermann Thiele, *President*
Jerry Autry, *Senior Mgr*
Dawn Wetzel, *Admin Asst*
▲ EMP: 1
SALES (est): 1.3B **Privately Held**
SIC: 3743 5013 Railroad equipment; motor vehicle supplies & new parts
HQ: Knorr-Bremse Ag
Moosacher Str. 80
Munchen 80809
893 547-0

(G-16660)
KNORR BRAKE TRUCK SYSTEMS CO (DH)
Also Called: New York Air Brake
748 Starbuck Ave (13601-1620)
P.O. Box 6760 (13601-6760)
PHONE..................................315 786-5200
Peter Riedlinger, *Vice Ch Bd*
Heinz Hermann Thiele, *President*
Mike Hawthorne, *President*
Scott Burkhart, *Vice Pres*
Kishor Pendse, *Vice Pres*
▲ EMP: 445
SQ FT: 250,000
SALES (est): 1.1B **Privately Held**
SIC: 3743 Brakes, air & vacuum: railway
HQ: Knorr Brake Holding Corporation
748 Starbuck Ave
Watertown NY 13601
315 786-5356

(G-16661)
KNOWLTON TECHNOLOGIES LLC
213 Factory St (13601-2748)
PHONE..................................315 782-0600
Frederick G Rudmann, *CEO*
James Ganter, *Exec VP*
James Lee, *Vice Pres*
Nick Cassoni, *Plant Mgr*
John Connor, *Plant Mgr*
◆ EMP: 130
SQ FT: 287,000
SALES (est): 70.8MM
SALES (corp-wide): 9.6B **Publicly Held**
SIC: 2621 Filter paper; specialty papers
PA: Eastman Chemical Company
200 S Wilcox Dr
Kingsport TN 37660
423 229-2000

(G-16662)
LCO DESTINY LLC
Also Called: Timeless Frames
22476 Fisher Rd (13601-1090)
P.O. Box 28 (13601-0028)
PHONE..................................315 782-3302
Fax: 315 782-4825
Kevin Davis, *Opers Staff*
Sandy Durgan, *Opers Staff*
Greg Gaston, *CFO*
Jackie George, *Human Res Dir*
Kay Kwenski, *Natl Sales Mgr*
▲ EMP: 300
SQ FT: 235,000
SALES (est): 41.3MM **Privately Held**
WEB: www.timelessframes.com
SIC: 2499 Picture & mirror frames, wood

(G-16663)
LERAY HOMES INC
22732 Duffy Rd (13601-1794)
PHONE..................................315 788-6087
Daniel Tontarski, *President*
Geraldine Tontarski, *Admin Sec*
EMP: 5
SQ FT: 169
SALES: 4MM **Privately Held**
SIC: 3441 Building components, structural steel

(G-16664)
MARTINS DENTAL STUDIO
Also Called: Martin Dental Studio
162 Sterling St (13601-3311)
P.O. Box 228 (13601-0228)
PHONE..................................315 788-0800
Richard Martin Jr, *President*
EMP: 7
SQ FT: 1,400
SALES (est): 951.7K **Privately Held**
SIC: 3843 8072 Teeth, artificial (not made in dental laboratories); dental laboratories

(G-16665)
NEW YORK AIR BRAKE LLC (DH)
748 Starbuck Ave (13601-1620)
P.O. Box 6760 (13601-6760)
PHONE..................................315 786-5219
Fax: 315 786-5676
Heinz Thiele, *Ch of Bd*
Frank Henderson, *President*
J Paul Morgan, *President*
Marshall G Beck, *Senior VP*
Eric Wright, *Engineer*
▲ EMP: 176
SALES: 22.5MM **Privately Held**
SIC: 3743 Brakes, air & vacuum: railway
HQ: Knorr Brake Holding Corporation
748 Starbuck Ave
Watertown NY 13601
315 786-5356

(G-16666)
NORTH COUNTRY WELDING INC
904 Leray St (13601-1315)
PHONE..................................315 788-9718
Fax: 315 788-7182
Timothy Shawl, *President*
EMP: 6
SQ FT: 3,000
SALES (est): 695.7K **Privately Held**
SIC: 7692 Welding repair

(G-16667)
NORTHERN AWNING & SIGN COMPANY
Also Called: N A S C O
22891 County Route 51 (13601-5005)
PHONE..................................315 782-8515
Fax: 315 782-4859
Michael Fitzgerald, *President*
Donna Yang, *Treasurer*
EMP: 5
SQ FT: 4,000
SALES (est): 543.7K **Privately Held**
WEB: www.nascosigns.com
SIC: 2394 3993 3444 Canvas & related products; awnings, fabric: made from purchased materials; signs & advertising specialties; sheet metalwork

(G-16668)
NORTHERN NY NEWSPAPERS CORP
Also Called: Watertown Daily Times
260 Washington St (13601-4669)
PHONE..................................315 782-1000
Fax: 315 661-2520
John B Johnson Jr, *CEO*
Harold B Johnson II, *President*
Amy Durant, *Editor*
Ken Eysaman, *Editor*
Rich Fyle, *Editor*
EMP: 210
SQ FT: 30,000
SALES (est): 13.2MM
SALES (corp-wide): 32MM **Privately Held**
WEB: www.lowville.com
SIC: 2711 2752 Newspapers; commercial printing, lithographic
PA: Johnson Newspaper Corporation
260 Washington St
Watertown NY
315 782-1000

(G-16669)
PACKAGING CORPORATION AMERICA
Also Called: Pca/Watertown 393
20400 Old Rome State Rd (13601-5514)
PHONE..................................315 785-9083
Fax: 315 786-8796
Beth Hogue, *Manager*
EMP: 15
SALES (corp-wide): 5.7B **Publicly Held**
WEB: www.packagingcorp.com
SIC: 2653 Boxes, corrugated: made from purchased materials
PA: Packaging Corporation Of America
1955 W Field Ct
Lake Forest IL 60045
847 482-3000

(G-16670)
PETRE ALII PETROLEUM
Also Called: Express Mart
1268 Arsenal St (13601-2214)
PHONE..................................315 785-1037
EMP: 6
SALES: 200K **Privately Held**
SIC: 2911 Petroleum Refiner

(G-16671)
SEMCO CERAMICS INC (HQ)
363 Eastern Blvd (13601-3140)
PHONE..................................315 782-3000
Alfred E Calligaris, *President*
Tony Marra, *Vice Pres*
Joe Branch, *CFO*
Douglas E Miller, *Asst Controller*
EMP: 3
SQ FT: 30,000
SALES (est): 4.9MM
SALES (corp-wide): 189.4MM **Privately Held**
SIC: 3253 3251 Ceramic wall & floor tile; structural brick & blocks
PA: The Stebbins Engineering And Manufacturing Company
363 Eastern Blvd
Watertown NY 13601
315 782-3000

(G-16672)
STATURE ELECTRIC INC
22543 Fisher Rd (13601-1090)
P.O. Box 6660 (13601-6660)
PHONE..................................315 782-5910
Fax: 315 782-1917
Roger Ormsby, *President*
Michael Weaver, *QC Mgr*
Lori Ruckar, *Manager*
▲ EMP: 332
SQ FT: 112,000
SALES (est): 51.6MM
SALES (corp-wide): 232.4MM **Publicly Held**
WEB: www.statureelectric.com
SIC: 3621 3546 Electric motor & generator parts; motors, electric; power-driven handtools
PA: Allied Motion Technologies Inc.
495 Commerce Dr Ste 3
Amherst NY 14228
716 242-8634

(G-16673)
TAYLOR CONCRETE PRODUCTS INC
20475 Old Rome Rd (13601-5509)
PHONE..................................315 788-2191
Thomas O'Connor, *President*
Ellen O'Connor, *Vice Pres*
Richard O'Connor, *Vice Pres*
Terri Ganter, *Accountant*
Carmen Tufo, *Sales Associate*
EMP: 21 EST: 1932
SQ FT: 2,500
SALES: 4.1MM **Privately Held**
WEB: www.taylorconcrete.com
SIC: 3271 5032 5211 3272 Blocks, concrete or cinder: standard; concrete & cinder block; concrete & cinder block; concrete products

(G-16674)
UNITED STATES DEPT OF ARMY
Also Called: Dol Avim
Mnns Crners Rd Bldg P2050 (13602)
PHONE..................................315 772-7538
Lloyd H Garnsey, *Manager*
EMP: 240 **Publicly Held**
SIC: 3357 9711 Aircraft wire & cable, non-ferrous; Army;
HQ: United States Department Of The Army
1400 Defense Pentagon
Washington DC 20310
703 695-1717

(G-16675)
WATERTOWN CONCRETE INC
24471 State Route 12 (13601-5784)
PHONE..................................315 788-1040
Fax: 315 788-2649
Joseph Belcher, *President*
Jason Belcher, *Vice Pres*
Chris Gregory, *Finance Mgr*
Bill Hallon, *Sales Mgr*
EMP: 16
SQ FT: 10,000
SALES (est): 2MM **Privately Held**
SIC: 3273 Ready-mixed concrete

(G-16676)
ZIEGLER TRUCK & DIESL REPR INC
22249 Fabco Rd (13601-1775)
PHONE..................................315 782-7278
Charles E Ziegler, *President*
Helen Ziegler, *Admin Sec*
EMP: 5
SALES: 425K **Privately Held**
SIC: 3531 Construction machinery

Waterville
Oneida County

(G-16677)
CENTER STATE PROPANE LLC (PA)
1130 Mason Rd (13480-2102)
PHONE..................................315 841-4044
Karen Kelly, *Manager*
James Wratten,
Mike Buell,
EMP: 4
SALES (est): 1.1MM **Privately Held**
SIC: 1321 Butane (natural) production

(G-16678)
F & R ENTERPRISES INC (PA)
Also Called: Pumilia's Pizza Shell
1594 State Route 315 (13480-1516)
P.O. Box 345 (13480-0345)
PHONE..................................315 841-8189
John Pumilia, *President*
Richard Viti, *CFO*
EMP: 6
SALES (est): 1MM **Privately Held**
SIC: 2038 Pizza, frozen

Watervliet
Albany County

(G-16679)
BIGBEE STEEL AND TANK COMPANY
Also Called: New York Tank Co
958 19th St (12189-1752)
PHONE..................................518 273-0801
Fax: 518 273-1365
Chad O'Brien, *Plant Mgr*
Steven Mapes, *Finance Mgr*
Tim Duffy, *Credit Mgr*
Tim Silvi, *Manager*
EMP: 25
SALES (corp-wide): 44.8MM **Privately Held**
WEB: www.highlandtank.com
SIC: 3443 3714 Farm storage tanks, metal plate; motor vehicle parts & accessories
PA: Bigbee Steel And Tank Company Inc
4535 Elizabethtown Rd
Manheim PA 17545
814 893-5701

(G-16680)
BONDED CONCRETE INC (PA)
303 Watervliet Shaker Rd (12189-3424)
P.O. Box 189 (12189-0189)
PHONE..................................518 273-5800
Fax: 518 273-0848
Salvatore O Clemente, *Ch of Bd*
Thomas A Clemente, *President*
Philip Clemente, *Vice Pres*
Scott Face, *Safety Dir*
Jude Clemente, *Treasurer*
EMP: 25 EST: 1964
SQ FT: 10,000

Watervliet - Albany County (G-16681)

SALES: 10.8MM **Privately Held**
WEB: www.bondedconcrete.com
SIC: 3273 Ready-mixed concrete

(G-16681)
CARDISH MACHINE WORKS INC
7 Elm St (12189-1826)
PHONE 518 273-2329
Fax: 518 273-0016
Eugene J Cardish Jr, *President*
Charles Cardish, *Vice Pres*
EMP: 33 EST: 1933
SALES: 6.3MM **Privately Held**
WEB: www.cardishmachineworks.com
SIC: 3599 Machine shop, jobbing & repair

(G-16682)
CLEVELAND POLYMER TECH LLC (PA)
125 Monroe St Bldg 125 (12189-4019)
P.O. Box 9340, Schenectady (12309-0340)
PHONE 518 326-9146
Sam McLafferty, *CEO*
Harry Adler, *Plant Mgr*
Michele Kennedy, *Office Mgr*
Jen Angelopoulos,
Panos Angelopoulos,
EMP: 8
SQ FT: 3,000
SALES (est): 1.5MM **Privately Held**
SIC: 3499 Machine bases, metal

(G-16683)
COMFORTEX CORPORATION (DH)
Also Called: Comfortex Window Fashions
21 Elm St (12189-1770)
PHONE 518 273-3333
Fax: 518 273-4079
Thomas Marusak, *President*
Suk-Joung Kahng, *Principal*
Brandon Smith, *Prdtn Mgr*
Pat Harris, *Warehouse Mgr*
Tanya Knower, *Production*
▲ EMP: 231
SQ FT: 100,000
SALES (est): 53.4MM **Privately Held**
WEB: www.comfortex.com
SIC: 2591 Window blinds; window shades
HQ: Hunter Douglas Inc.
  1 Blue Hill Plz Ste 1569
  Pearl River NY 10965
  845 664-7000

(G-16684)
EXTREME MOLDING LLC
25 Gibson St Ste 2 (12189-3375)
PHONE 518 326-9319
Fax: 518 266-6263
Lynn Momrow,
Joanne Moon,
▲ EMP: 25
SQ FT: 13,500
SALES: 4MM **Privately Held**
WEB: www.extrememolding.com
SIC: 3089 Injection molding of plastics

(G-16685)
GENERAL BUSINESS SUPPLY INC
Also Called: Tech Valley Printing
2550 9th Ave (12189-1962)
PHONE 518 720-3939
Fax: 518 720-3929
John Smith, *President*
EMP: 55
SALES (est): 5.3MM **Privately Held**
SIC: 2759 2752 Business forms: printing; commercial printing, offset

(G-16686)
HARTCHROM INC
25 Gibson St Ste 1 (12189-3342)
PHONE 518 880-0411
Fax: 518 880-0450
Edgar Oehler, *CEO*
Michael Flaherty, *General Mgr*
EMP: 18 EST: 2001
SQ FT: 33,000

SALES: 4.9MM
SALES (corp-wide): 962.7MM **Privately Held**
WEB: www.hartchrom.com
SIC: 3471 3541 Plating & polishing; anodizing (plating) of metals or formed products; grinding, polishing, buffing, lapping & honing machines
PA: Afg Arbonia-Forster-Holding Ag
  Amriswilerstrasse 50
  Arbon TG
  714 474-141

(G-16687)
LWA WORKS INC
2622 7th Ave Ste 50s (12189-1963)
PHONE 518 271-8360
Lance Weinheimer, *President*
▲ EMP: 5
SALES (est): 500K **Privately Held**
WEB: www.lanartworks.com
SIC: 3599 Machine shop, jobbing & repair

(G-16688)
SAINT-GOBAIN ABRASIVES INC
Also Called: Coated Abrasive Division
2600 10th Ave (12189-1766)
PHONE 518 266-2200
Paul Valle, *Vice Pres*
Pat Acker, *Purch Agent*
Judy Alison, *Manager*
John Snyder, *MIS Mgr*
Frederick Villoutreix, *MIS Mgr*
EMP: 400
SQ FT: 1,880
SALES (corp-wide): 189MM **Privately Held**
WEB: www.sgabrasives.com
SIC: 3291 Abrasive products
HQ: Saint-Gobain Abrasives, Inc.
  1 New Bond St
  Worcester MA 01606
  508 795-5000

(G-16689)
STRECKS INC
Also Called: Streck's Machinery
800 1st St (12189-3501)
PHONE 518 273-4410
Lloyd Demaranville, *President*
Christine Demaranville, *Vice Pres*
Emmy Obrien, *Treasurer*
▲ EMP: 20 EST: 1952
SQ FT: 50,000
SALES (est): 3.3MM **Privately Held**
SIC: 3599 7692 7629 Machine shop, jobbing & repair; welding repair; electrical repair shops

(G-16690)
TROY INDUSTRIAL SOLUTIONS (PA)
70 Cohoes Rd (12189-1829)
PHONE 518 272-4920
Fax: 518 272-0531
Jason W Smith, *Ch of Bd*
David R Barcomb, *General Mgr*
Doug Gerrity, *Sales Mgr*
Doug Rogers, *Manager*
Ron Sievert, *Manager*
EMP: 67
SQ FT: 55,000
SALES (est): 17.8MM **Privately Held**
WEB: www.troybelting.com
SIC: 7694 3052 5084 5085 Electric motor repair; rubber & plastics hose & beltings; industrial machinery & equipment; industrial supplies; conveyors & conveying equipment; motors & generators

(G-16691)
UTILITY SYSTEMS TECH INC
70 Cohoes Rd (12189-1829)
P.O. Box 110, Latham (12110-0110)
PHONE 518 326-4142
Robert Degeneff, *President*
Mark Degeneffe, *General Mgr*
David Wightman, *General Mgr*
Jeff Foran, *Engineer*
Hung Nguyen, *Engineer*
EMP: 13
SALES (est): 2.7MM **Privately Held**
WEB: www.ustpower.com
SIC: 3643 Current-carrying wiring devices

(G-16692)
WICKED SMART LLC
700 5th Ave (12189-3610)
PHONE 518 459-2855
Todd Van Epps, *Mng Member*
Marcie Van Epps,
EMP: 15
SALES: 1.1MM **Privately Held**
SIC: 2396 2395 Screen printing on fabric articles; embroidery & art needlework

Watkins Glen
Schuyler County

(G-16693)
BMS MANUFACTURING CO INC
2857 County Line Rd (14891-9615)
PHONE 607 535-2426
Fax: 607 535-9793
William C Meehan Jr, *CEO*
EMP: 45 EST: 1977
SQ FT: 50,000
SALES (est): 7.4MM **Privately Held**
WEB: www.bmsmanufacturing.com
SIC: 7692 3599 3441 Welding repair; machine & other job shop work; fabricated structural metal

(G-16694)
CARGILL INCORPORATED
518 E 4th St (14891-1219)
PHONE 607 535-6300
Fax: 607 535-6348
Rene Osorio, *Marketing Staff*
Greg Meyer, *Manager*
Jameson Becker, *Manager*
Michael Schmit, *MIS Mgr*
EMP: 93
SQ FT: 10,840
SALES (corp-wide): 107.1B **Privately Held**
WEB: www.cargill.com
SIC: 2899 Salt
PA: Cargill, Incorporated
  15407 Mcginty Rd W
  Wayzata MN 55391
  952 742-7575

(G-16695)
LAKEWOOD VINEYARDS INC
4024 State Route 14 (14891-9630)
PHONE 607 535-9252
Fax: 607 535-6656
Christopher Lamont Stamp, *President*
David A Stamp, *Vice Pres*
Beverly Stamp, *Treasurer*
Teresa Knapp, *Shareholder*
Michael E Stamp, *Shareholder*
▲ EMP: 12
SQ FT: 7,500
SALES (est): 930K **Privately Held**
WEB: www.lakewoodvineyards.com
SIC: 2084 Wines

(G-16696)
SKYLARK PUBLICATIONS LTD
Also Called: Hi-Lites
217 N Franklin St (14891-1201)
PHONE 607 535-9866
Damir Lazaric, *Managing Prtnr*
Flyod Vlajic, *Partner*
Millie Gernold, *Sales Mgr*
Bridgette Goodman, *Software Engr*
EMP: 5
SQ FT: 3,184
SALES (est): 360K **Privately Held**
SIC: 2741 Shopping news: publishing only, not printed on site

(G-16697)
SUIT-KOTE CORPORATION
Also Called: Central Asphalt
20 Fairgrounds Ln (14891-1632)
PHONE 607 535-2743
Kevin Suits, *Branch Mgr*
EMP: 30
SQ FT: 11,524
SALES (corp-wide): 278.7MM **Privately Held**
WEB: www.suit-kote.com
SIC: 2951 1611 2952 Asphalt paving mixtures & blocks; highway & street construction; asphalt felts & coatings

PA: Suit-Kote Corporation
  1911 Lorings Crossing Rd
  Cortland NY 13045
  607 753-1100

(G-16698)
US SALT LLC
Salt Point Rd (14891)
P.O. Box 110 (14891-0110)
PHONE 607 535-2721
Fax: 607 535-2953
Traver Bob, *Safety Dir*
Bob Traver, *Safety Dir*
Sue Oliver, *QA Dir*
Alan Parry, *Manager*
Susan Forshee, *Manager*
EMP: 100
SALES (corp-wide): 2.6B **Publicly Held**
SIC: 2899 Salt
HQ: Us Salt, Llc
  2 Brush Creek Blvd
  Kansas City MO 64112
  816 842-8181

Waverly
Tioga County

(G-16699)
CHARM MFG CO INC
Also Called: Charm Pools
251 State Route 17c (14892-9507)
P.O. Box 294 (14892-0294)
PHONE 607 565-8161
Fax: 607 565-3212
Jane Spicer, *President*
Linda Spicer, *Corp Secy*
Kay Onofre, *Vice Pres*
Richard Spicer, *Vice Pres*
EMP: 50
SQ FT: 50,000
SALES: 2.1MM **Privately Held**
WEB: www.charmpools.com
SIC: 3949 5091 5999 Swimming pools, except plastic; hot tubs; spa equipment & supplies; hot tub & spa chemicals, equipment & supplies; sauna equipment & supplies

(G-16700)
CHEMITE INC
407 County Road 60 (14892-9833)
P.O. Box 271 (14892-0271)
PHONE 607 529-3218
George D Howell, *President*
Jana Howell, *Vice Pres*
Tim Gable, *Purch Mgr*
Eric Howell, *Shareholder*
Jennifer Morehead, *Shareholder*
EMP: 9
SQ FT: 38,000
SALES: 2.8MM **Privately Held**
WEB: www.chemiteinc.com
SIC: 2841 Soap & other detergents

(G-16701)
DORY ENTERPRISES INC
184 State Route 17c (14892-9504)
P.O. Box 389 (14892-0389)
PHONE 607 565-7079
Fax: 607 565-4794
Robert Rynone, *President*
Frederick Douglas, *Sales Staff*
Jackie Cole, *Office Mgr*
EMP: 10
SQ FT: 3,000
SALES: 1.2MM **Privately Held**
SIC: 2653 5113 Corrugated boxes, partitions, display items, sheets & pad; bags, paper & disposable plastic

(G-16702)
GRANITE WORKS LLC
133 William Donnelly (14892-1547)
PHONE 607 565-7012
Rai Leigh, *Sales Staff*
Mary Wilcox, *Manager*
Fred Elias, *Admin Mgr*
Jason Vandyk,
▲ EMP: 20
SALES (est): 3.3MM **Privately Held**
SIC: 3281 Curbing, granite or stone

▲ = Import ▼ = Export
◆ = Import/Export

GEOGRAPHIC SECTION

(G-16703)
HANCOR INC
1 William Donnly Inds (14892-1599)
PHONE.....................607 565-3033
Fax: 607 565-2339
Dave Markie, *Manager*
EMP: 80
SALES (corp-wide): 1.2B **Publicly Held**
SIC: 3082 3084 Tubes, unsupported plastic; plastics pipe
HQ: Hancor, Inc.
4640 Trueman Blvd
Hilliard OH 43026
614 658-0050

(G-16704)
LEPRINO FOODS COMPANY
400 Leprino Ave (14892-1351)
PHONE.....................570 888-9658
Fax: 570 888-6612
Dave Fitzgerald, *Financial Exec*
Neil Brown, *Manager*
EMP: 230
SALES (corp-wide): 1.9B **Privately Held**
WEB: www.leprinofoods.com
SIC: 2022 Cheese, natural & processed
PA: Leprino Foods Company
1830 W 38th Ave
Denver CO 80211
303 480-2600

(G-16705)
PREMIUM VALVE SERVICES LLC
685 Broad Street Ext (14892-9322)
PHONE.....................607 565-7571
Richard Carling, *Branch Mgr*
EMP: 5
SALES (corp-wide): 22.8MM **Privately Held**
SIC: 3592 Valves
HQ: Premium Valve Services, L.L.C.
260 N Sam Houston Pkwy E
Houston TX 77060
281 457-2565

(G-16706)
RYNONE MANUFACTURING CORP
229 Howard St (14892-1519)
PHONE.....................607 565-8187
Fax: 607 565-2905
Chuck Lawson, *Manager*
EMP: 15
SALES (corp-wide): 38.9MM **Privately Held**
WEB: www.rynone.com
SIC: 3089 Plastic containers, except foam
PA: Rynone Manufacturing Corp.
N Thomas Ave
Sayre PA 18840
570 888-5272

(G-16707)
RYNONE PACKAGING CORP
184 State Route 17c (14892-9504)
P.O. Box 389 (14892-0389)
PHONE.....................607 565-8173
Robert F Rynone, *Ch of Bd*
▼ **EMP:** 8
SALES (est): 1.1MM **Privately Held**
SIC: 2671 Packaging paper & plastics film, coated & laminated

Wawarsing
Ulster County

(G-16708)
PRECISION MACHINING AND MFG
190 Port Ben Rd (12489)
P.O. Box 104 (12489-0104)
PHONE.....................845 647-5380
Nick Gajdcz, *President*
Wasyl Gajdycz, *President*
Lisia Gajdycz, *Admin Sec*
EMP: 5 **EST:** 1956
SQ FT: 6,500
SALES: 270K **Privately Held**
SIC: 3544 Special dies & tools

Wayland
Steuben County

(G-16709)
BELANGERS GRAVEL & STONE INC
10184 State Route 21 (14572-9544)
PHONE.....................585 728-3906
Norb Belanger, *Ch of Bd*
EMP: 6
SALES (est): 550.3K **Privately Held**
SIC: 1442 Construction sand & gravel

(G-16710)
GUNLOCKE COMPANY LLC (HQ)
1 Gunlocke Dr (14572-9515)
PHONE.....................585 728-5111
Fax: 585 728-8353
Diane Deleo, *General Mgr*
Jason Thomas, *Business Mgr*
Michael Moffett, *Mfg Dir*
Christopher Harrison, *Opers Staff*
Clarence L Burkey, *Treasurer*
▲ **EMP:** 197
SQ FT: 720,000
SALES (est): 131.6MM
SALES (corp-wide): 2.3B **Publicly Held**
WEB: www.gunlocke.com
SIC: 2521 Wood office furniture
PA: Hni Corporation
408 E 2nd St
Muscatine IA 52761
563 272-7400

(G-16711)
SPECIALTY SERVICES
Also Called: Accent Printing &GRaphics
2631e Naples St (14572)
P.O. Box 397 (14572-0397)
PHONE.....................585 728-5650
Fax: 585 728-5782
Randall Bergvall, *Owner*
EMP: 5
SQ FT: 12,000
SALES (est): 432.4K **Privately Held**
SIC: 2541 2431 Display fixtures, wood; millwork

Wayne
Schuyler County

(G-16712)
NEW MARKET PRODUCTS CO INC
9671 Back St (14893)
P.O. Box 135 (14893-0135)
PHONE.....................607 292-6226
Fax: 607 293-6858
Gary Oborne, *President*
EMP: 12 **EST:** 1967
SQ FT: 10,500
SALES (est): 740K **Privately Held**
WEB: www.nmpco.com
SIC: 3545 Tool holders

Webster
Monroe County

(G-16713)
ASHLY AUDIO INC
847 Holt Rd Ste 1 (14580-9193)
PHONE.....................585 872-0010
Fax: 585 872-0739
David Parse, *CEO*
J P Boucher, *General Mgr*
William Thompson, *Chairman*
John Sexton, *Vice Pres*
John Passaniti, *Engineer*
▲ **EMP:** 42
SQ FT: 25,000
SALES (est): 11.4MM **Privately Held**
WEB: www.ashly.com
SIC: 3651 3663 Household audio equipment; radio & TV communications equipment

(G-16714)
CALVARY DESIGN TEAM INC (PA)
Also Called: CALVARY AUTOMATION SYSTEMS
855 Publishers Pkwy (14580-2587)
PHONE.....................585 347-6127
Fax: 585 321-5054
Mark Chaney, *President*
Jim Diederich, *Business Mgr*
Jose Oliver, *Business Mgr*
Craig Witt, *Business Mgr*
Steve Hakes, *Mfg Dir*
▲ **EMP:** 200
SQ FT: 375,000
SALES: 65.4MM **Privately Held**
WEB: www.calvauto.com
SIC: 3599 8711 Custom machinery; mechanical engineering; industrial engineers

(G-16715)
CDA MACHINE INC
514 Vosburg Rd (14580-1043)
PHONE.....................585 671-5959
Fax: 585 671-5903
William Crosby, *President*
Laurie Maggio, *Office Mgr*
EMP: 9
SQ FT: 13,400
SALES (est): 1MM **Privately Held**
WEB: www.cdamachine.com
SIC: 3599 Machine shop, jobbing & repair

(G-16716)
CGS FABRICATION LLC
855 Publishers Pkwy Ste 3 (14580-2587)
PHONE.....................585 347-6127
Mark Chaney, *Owner*
EMP: 15 **EST:** 2012
SALES: 21.6MM **Privately Held**
SIC: 3469 Machine parts, stamped or pressed metal

(G-16717)
CLARK RIGGING & RENTAL CORP
680 Basket Rd (14580-9764)
PHONE.....................585 265-2910
David Clark, *Branch Mgr*
Dave Baran, *Manager*
Paul Goodman, *Manager*
EMP: 11
SALES (corp-wide): 7.5MM **Privately Held**
SIC: 3731 Marine rigging
PA: Clark Rigging & Rental Corp
500 Ohio St
Lockport NY 14094
716 433-4600

(G-16718)
CLASSIC AUTOMATION LLC (PA)
800 Salt Rd (14580-9666)
PHONE.....................585 241-6010
Margaret Nichols, *Vice Pres*
Christine Damato, *Marketing Staff*
Matt Marshall, *Info Tech Mgr*
Julius Mushi, *Web Dvlpr*
Fritz Ruebeck,
EMP: 40
SQ FT: 17,000
SALES: 10MM **Privately Held**
SIC: 3823 Controllers for process variables, all types; boiler controls: industrial, power & marine type

(G-16719)
CLINTON SIGNS INC
1407 Empire Blvd (14580-2101)
PHONE.....................585 482-1620
Fax: 585 482-3384
Michael S Mammano III, *President*
Kim Mammano, *Controller*
EMP: 6 **EST:** 1938
SQ FT: 5,700
SALES: 400K **Privately Held**
WEB: www.clintonsigns.com
SIC: 3993 7389 1799 7336 Electric signs; sign painting & lettering shop; sign installation & maintenance; commercial art & graphic design

(G-16720)
DATA-PAC MAILING SYSTEMS CORP
1217 Bay Rd Ste 12 (14580-1958)
PHONE.....................585 671-0210
Fax: 585 671-1409
Richard A Yankloski, *President*
Ana Yankloski, *Vice Pres*
Keith Yankloski, *Prdtn Mgr*
Jason Brown, *Info Tech Mgr*
Wayne Wilkerson, *Technology*
EMP: 10
SQ FT: 3,000
SALES (est): 2.5MM **Privately Held**
WEB: www.data-pac.com
SIC: 3571 Electronic computers

(G-16721)
DIGITAL HOME CREATIONS INC
350 Shadowbrook Dr (14580-9108)
PHONE.....................585 576-7070
Ryan J Hills, *CEO*
EMP: 5
SALES: 1.4MM **Privately Held**
SIC: 3491 3651 Automatic regulating & control valves; household audio & video equipment

(G-16722)
EAST SIDE MACHINE INC
625 Phillips Rd (14580-9786)
PHONE.....................585 265-4560
Fax: 585 265-4569
Paul Derleth, *President*
Lou Rossetti, *Vice Pres*
Pat Latona, *Office Mgr*
EMP: 26
SQ FT: 16,000
SALES (est): 5.9MM **Privately Held**
WEB: www.esm1.com
SIC: 3545 Precision tools, machinists'

(G-16723)
EMPIRE STATE WEEKLIES INC
Also Called: Wayne County Mail
46 North Ave (14580-3008)
PHONE.....................585 671-1533
Fax: 585 671-7067
David Young, *President*
EMP: 20
SQ FT: 5,100
SALES (est): 1.4MM **Privately Held**
WEB: www.empirestateweeklies.com
SIC: 2711 Job printing & newspaper publishing combined

(G-16724)
GRIFFIN MANUFACTURING COMPANY
1656 Ridge Rd (14580-3697)
P.O. Box 308 (14580-0308)
PHONE.....................585 265-1991
Fax: 585 265-2621
Angelo Papia, *President*
Darryl Papia, *Vice Pres*
Gary Papia, *Vice Pres*
Terry Papia, *Vice Pres*
Kristin Papia, *Office Mgr*
EMP: 20 **EST:** 1946
SQ FT: 6,000
SALES (est): 3.7MM **Privately Held**
WEB: www.grifhold.com
SIC: 3545 Machine tool accessories

(G-16725)
JOHNSON CONTROLS INC
237 Birch Ln (14580-1301)
PHONE.....................585 671-1930
Peter Baranello, *Manager*
EMP: 25 **Privately Held**
SIC: 2531 Seats, automobile
HQ: Johnson Controls, Inc.
5757 N Green Bay Ave
Milwaukee WI 53209
414 524-1200

(G-16726)
KAL MANUFACTURING CORPORATION
657 Basket Rd (14580-9764)
PHONE.....................585 265-4310
Fax: 585 265-4854
Alan Liwush, *CEO*
Richard Liwush, *Ch of Bd*
Tim Lindsay, *Sales Mgr*

Webster - Monroe County (G-16727)

Brian Hooker, *Manager*
Erika Muscato, *Manager*
EMP: 37 **EST:** 1943
SQ FT: 50,000
SALES (est): 9.1MM **Privately Held**
WEB: www.kal-mfg.com
SIC: 3444 3845 3599 3441 Sheet metalwork; electromedical equipment; machine & other job shop work; fabricated structural metal

(G-16727)
MIKE WILKE
Also Called: Winton Paving
851 Rolins Run (14580-8423)
PHONE.................585 482-5230
Mike Wilke, *Owner*
EMP: 5
SALES (est): 576.3K **Privately Held**
SIC: 3531 Paving breakers

(G-16728)
OPTICOOL SOLUTIONS LLC
Also Called: Opticool Technologies
855 Publishers Pkwy (14580-2587)
PHONE.................585 347-6127
David Brown, *Director*
EMP: 21
SALES (est): 5.7MM **Privately Held**
SIC: 3585 Parts for heating, cooling & refrigerating equipment

(G-16729)
PLANAR OPTICS INC
858 Hard Rd (14580-8950)
PHONE.................585 671-0100
Fax: 585 671-1303
Horst Koch, *President*
Otto Wolsgoot, *Vice Pres*
EMP: 7
SQ FT: 5,400
SALES (est): 983.1K **Privately Held**
SIC: 3827 Optical instruments & lenses

(G-16730)
PRACTICAL INSTRUMENT ELEC INC
Also Called: Pie
82 E Main St Ste 3 (14580-3243)
PHONE.................585 872-9350
Ronald P Clarridge, *CEO*
EMP: 10
SALES (est): 1.2MM **Privately Held**
WEB: www.piecal.com
SIC: 3825 Instruments to measure electricity; engine electrical test equipment

(G-16731)
R D SPECIALTIES INC
560 Salt Rd (14580-9718)
PHONE.................585 265-0220
Fax: 585 265-1132
Douglas R Krasucki, *President*
Jim Mottlet, *Opers Staff*
Grace Krasucki, *Treasurer*
EMP: 15
SQ FT: 8,000
SALES (est): 1.1MM **Privately Held**
WEB: www.rdspecialties.com
SIC: 3312 Bar, rod & wire products

(G-16732)
R P M MACHINE CO
755 Gravel Rd (14580-1715)
PHONE.................585 671-3744
Timothy Mangus, *Partner*
Richard P Mangus, *Partner*
EMP: 5
SALES: 160K **Privately Held**
SIC: 3451 Screw machine products

(G-16733)
RADAX INDUSTRIES INC
700 Basket Rd Ste A (14580-9757)
PHONE.................585 265-2055
Fax: 585 265-0072
Rocco Sacco, *Ch of Bd*
Richard Sacco, *President*
Barbara Sacco, *Treasurer*
Jefferson Treadwell, *Sales Mgr*
Amy Years Formicola, *Admin Sec*
EMP: 27
SQ FT: 55,000
SALES (est): 6.2MM **Privately Held**
WEB: www.radax.com
SIC: 3452 Screws, metal

(G-16734)
SCHUTT CIDER MILL
1063 Plank Rd (14580-9399)
PHONE.................585 872-2924
Martin Schutt, *Owner*
EMP: 10
SQ FT: 3,308
SALES (est): 765.8K **Privately Held**
WEB: www.schuttsapplemill.com
SIC: 2099 5499 5149 Cider, nonalcoholic; juices, fruit or vegetable; juices

(G-16735)
SICK INC
Lazerdata Division
855 Publishers Pkwy (14580-2587)
P.O. Box 448 (14580-0448)
PHONE.................585 347-2000
EMP: 50 **Privately Held**
SIC: 3599 Mfg General Industrial Machinery
HQ: Sick, Inc
6900 W 110th St
Minneapolis MN 55438
952 941-6780

(G-16736)
STUDCO BUILDING SYSTEMS US LLC
1700 Boulter Indus Park (14580-9763)
PHONE.................585 545-3000
Joan Congdon, *Accounts Mgr*
Allan Parr, *Mng Member*
▲ **EMP:** 30
SQ FT: 65,000
SALES (est): 9.2MM **Privately Held**
WEB: www.studcosystems.com
SIC: 3444 Studs & joists, sheet metal

(G-16737)
TRICON MACHINE LLC
820 Coventry Dr (14580-8422)
PHONE.................585 671-0679
Gary German,
EMP: 7
SQ FT: 10,000
SALES: 1MM **Privately Held**
WEB: www.triconmachine.com
SIC: 3599 Custom machinery

(G-16738)
TRIDENT PRECISION MFG INC
734 Salt Rd (14580-9718)
PHONE.................585 265-2010
Fax: 585 265-2304
Nicholas Juskiw, *President*
Dan Nuijens, *Plant Mgr*
Peter Collins, *Opers Mgr*
Kelly Brayer, *Purch Agent*
Diane Cialini, *Buyer*
▲ **EMP:** 95
SQ FT: 60,000
SALES (est): 37.4MM **Privately Held**
WEB: www.tridentprecision.com
SIC: 3469 3545 3569 7373 Stamping metal for the trade; machine tool accessories; assembly machines, non-metalworking; computer-aided design (CAD) systems service; computer-aided manufacturing (CAM) systems service; laser welding, drilling & cutting equipment; sheet metalwork

(G-16739)
UNISEND LLC
249 Gallant Fox Ln (14580-9034)
PHONE.................585 414-9575
Sheikh Wasim Khaled, *Principal*
Steve Muratore, *Principal*
EMP: 5 **EST:** 2012
SALES (est): 347.4K **Privately Held**
SIC: 3822 Building services monitoring controls, automatic

(G-16740)
UNISTEL LLC
860 Hard Rd (14580-8825)
PHONE.................585 341-4600
Ana Nikolovska, *Principal*
Sankar Sewnauth,
◆ **EMP:** 99
SALES: 2MM **Privately Held**
SIC: 3999 Manufacturing industries

(G-16741)
WEBSTER ONTRIO WLWRTH PNNYSVER
164 E Main St (14580-3230)
P.O. Box 1135 (14580-7835)
PHONE.................585 265-3620
Fax: 585 265-3882
Geoffrey Mohr, *Partner*
Mary Jill Mohr, *Partner*
EMP: 12
SQ FT: 1,000
SALES (est): 770.7K **Privately Held**
WEB: www.websterpennysaver.com
SIC: 2711 Newspapers

(G-16742)
WEBSTER PRINTING CORPORATION
46 North Ave (14580-3008)
PHONE.................585 671-1533
W David Young, *President*
Leslie Young, *Admin Sec*
EMP: 18
SQ FT: 2,500
SALES (est): 1.5MM **Privately Held**
SIC: 2759 2791 2789 2752 Newspapers: printing; typesetting; bookbinding & related work; commercial printing, lithographic

(G-16743)
XEROX CORPORATION
800 Phillips Rd Ste 20599 (14580-9791)
PHONE.................585 422-4564
Fax: 585 265-5722
Bernard Blocchi, *General Mgr*
Patricia Cusick, *Vice Pres*
Scott Frame, *Vice Pres*
Robert Wagner, *Vice Pres*
Peter Zehler, *Vice Pres*
EMP: 700
SALES (corp-wide): 18B **Publicly Held**
WEB: www.xerox.com
SIC: 3861 Reproduction machines & equipment
PA: Xerox Corporation
45 Glover Ave Ste 700
Norwalk CT 06850
203 968-3000

(G-16744)
XEROX CORPORATION
800 Phillips Rd (14580-9791)
PHONE.................585 423-5090
Fax: 585 423-4848
Pankaj Kalra, *General Mgr*
Dan Banaszak, *VP Mfg*
Janel Draz, *Project Mgr*
Haik Jermakyan, *Engineer*
Manuel Ortiz, *Engineer*
EMP: 75
SALES (corp-wide): 18B **Publicly Held**
WEB: www.xerox.com
SIC: 3861 Photographic equipment & supplies
PA: Xerox Corporation
45 Glover Ave Ste 700
Norwalk CT 06850
203 968-3000

(G-16745)
ZOMEGA TERAHERTZ CORPORATION
806 Admiralty Way (14580-3912)
PHONE.................585 347-4337
Thomas Tongue, *CEO*
Wendy Zhang, *CFO*
EMP: 15
SALES (est): 3MM **Privately Held**
SIC: 3829 Measuring & controlling devices

Weedsport
Cayuga County

(G-16746)
BARBER WELDING INC
Also Called: Alpha Boats Unlimited
2517 Rte 31 W (13166)
P.O. Box 690 (13166-0690)
PHONE.................315 834-6645
Stephen L Walczyk, *President*
Dave Dunham, *Plant Mgr*
▲ **EMP:** 20
SQ FT: 18,000
SALES (est): 2.6MM **Privately Held**
WEB: www.barberweldinginc.com
SIC: 7692 3441 Welding repair; fabricated structural metal

Wellsburg
Chemung County

(G-16747)
ELMIRA GRINDING WORKS INC
311 Main St (14894-9781)
PHONE.................607 734-1579
Fax: 607 734-7593
Jon Bauer, *President*
Kim Hancock, *Manager*
EMP: 10 **EST:** 1964
SQ FT: 7,500
SALES: 500K **Privately Held**
SIC: 3541 3451 Grinding, polishing, buffing, lapping & honing machines; screw machine products

Wellsville
Allegany County

(G-16748)
ARVOS HOLDING LLC (HQ)
Also Called: Alison US LLC
3020 Truax Rd (14895-9531)
PHONE.................585 596-2501
David Breckinridge, *President*
Ludger Heuberg, *CFO*
EMP: 6
SALES (est): 265.6MM **Privately Held**
SIC: 3494 Steam fittings & specialties
PA: Arvos Holding Gmbh
Ellenbacher Str. 10
Kassel
622 175-3210

(G-16749)
ARVOS INC (DH)
Also Called: Air Preheater
3020 Truax Rd (14895-9531)
P.O. Box 372 (14895-0372)
PHONE.................585 593-2700
David Breckinridge, *President*
Ludger Heuberg, *CFO*
Guillaume Boutillot, *Marketing Staff*
EMP: 277
SALES (est): 265.6MM **Privately Held**
SIC: 3443 Fabricated plate work (boiler shop); air preheaters, nonrotating: plate type
HQ: Arvos Holding Llc
3020 Truax Rd
Wellsville NY 14895
585 596-2501

(G-16750)
CURRENT CONTROLS INC
353 S Brooklyn Ave (14895-1446)
PHONE.................585 593-1544
Fax: 585 593-1713
Robert Landon, *President*
Carl Baxter, *Engineer*
Jeremy McNaughton, *Engineer*
Angela Dunham, *Office Mgr*
Bruce McNaughton, *Manager*
EMP: 150
SQ FT: 25,000
SALES (est): 30.6MM **Privately Held**
WEB: www.currentcontrols.com
SIC: 3612 Control transformers

(G-16751)
DRESSER-RAND LLC
Dresser-Rand, Siemens
37 Coats St (14895-1003)
PHONE.................585 596-3100
Terah Soule, *Business Mgr*
Clay Hale, *CFO*
Doug Martin, *Manager*
Amit Shah, *Info Tech Mgr*
Shawn Holmes, *Administration*
EMP: 650

▲ = Import ▼ = Export
◆ = Import/Export

SALES (corp-wide): 83.5B **Privately Held**
WEB: www.dresser-rand.com
SIC: **3491** 3511 Industrial valves; turbines & turbine generator sets; turbines & turbine generator sets & parts
HQ: Dresser-Rand Llc
1200 W Sam Houston Pkwy N
Houston TX 77043
713 354-6100

(G-16752)
GENESEE METAL PRODUCTS INC
106 Railroad Ave (14895-1143)
PHONE..................................585 968-6000
Fax: 585 968-7000
Michael P Oleksiak, *President*
EMP: 20
SQ FT: 28,000
SALES (est): 3.2MM **Privately Held**
SIC: **3449** Miscellaneous metalwork

(G-16753)
LUFKIN INDUSTRIES LLC
2475 Tarantine Blvd (14895-9687)
PHONE..................................585 593-7930
Tom Shoup, *Engineer*
John Nicoles, *Branch Mgr*
EMP: 50
SALES (corp-wide): 117.3B **Publicly Held**
SIC: **3561** Pumps & pumping equipment; pumps, oil well & field
HQ: Lufkin Industries, Llc
601 S Raguet St
Lufkin TX 75904
936 634-2211

(G-16754)
MATTESON LOGGING INC
2808 Beech Hill Rd (14895-9779)
PHONE..................................585 593-3037
Brian Matteson, *President*
Pammy Matteson, *Vice Pres*
EMP: 5
SALES (est): 411.3K **Privately Held**
SIC: **2411** Logging camps & contractors

(G-16755)
NORTHERN LIGHTS ENTPS INC
Also Called: Northern Lights Candles
3474 Andover Rd (14895-9525)
PHONE..................................585 593-1200
Fax: 585 593-6481
Andrew Glanzman, *President*
Jeannie Skiffington, *Principal*
Christina Glanzman, *Vice Pres*
Leslie Belsito, *Buyer*
Tanya Verdsley, *Credit Mgr*
◆ EMP: 120 EST: 1977
SQ FT: 20,000
SALES (est): 15.3MM **Privately Held**
WEB: www.northernlightscandles.com
SIC: **3999** 5999 Candles; candle shops

(G-16756)
RELEASE COATINGS NEW YORK INC
125 S Brooklyn Ave (14895-1453)
PHONE..................................585 593-2335
Fax: 585 593-4912
Ralph A Naples, *President*
Dennis T Harris, *Vice Pres*
EMP: 5
SQ FT: 7,200
SALES (est): 1MM **Privately Held**
SIC: **2822** Synthetic rubber

(G-16757)
SANDLE CUSTOM BEARING CORP
1110 State Route 19 (14895-9120)
PHONE..................................585 593-7000
Fax: 585 593-7027
Eric Sandle, *President*
Lisa Lindsay, *Manager*
Nancy Reiman, *Manager*
Diana Sandle, *Admin Sec*
▼ EMP: 9
SQ FT: 4,000
SALES (est): 1.6MM **Privately Held**
SIC: **3562** Ball & roller bearings

(G-16758)
SENECA MEDIA INC
Also Called: Wellsville Daily Reporter
159 N Main St (14895-1149)
PHONE..................................585 593-5300
Oak Duke, *Branch Mgr*
EMP: 12
SALES (corp-wide): 6.2MM **Privately Held**
WEB: www.eveningtribune.com
SIC: **2711** Newspapers: publishing only, not printed on site
PA: Seneca Media Inc
32 Broadway Mall
Hornell NY 14843
607 324-1425

(G-16759)
SIEMENS GOVERNMENT TECH INC
Also Called: Dresser Rand, Si
37 Coats St (14895-1003)
P.O. Box 592 (14895-0592)
PHONE..................................585 593-1234
Fax: 585 593-5815
Jason Mattison, *Project Mgr*
Catherine Kinnicutt, *Warehouse Mgr*
Joe Lamberson, *Engineer*
John Meehan, *Engineer*
Joe Menichino, *Engineer*
EMP: 250
SALES (corp-wide): 83.5B **Privately Held**
WEB: www.dresser-rand.com
SIC: **3511** Turbines & turbine generator sets; turbines & turbine generator sets & parts
HQ: Siemens Government Technologies, Inc.
2231 Crystal Dr Ste 700
Arlington VA 22202
703 860-1574

West Babylon
Suffolk County

(G-16760)
110 SAND COMPANY
170 Cabot St (11704-1102)
PHONE..................................631 694-2822
Fax: 631 249-4126
Chester Broman, *President*
EMP: 9
SALES (est): 1.4MM **Privately Held**
SIC: **1442** Sand mining

(G-16761)
110 SAND COMPANY
170 Cabot St (11704-1102)
PHONE..................................631 694-2822
Tom Murphy, *Manager*
EMP: 17
SALES (corp-wide): 8.3MM **Privately Held**
SIC: **1442** Construction sand & gravel
PA: 110 Sand Company
136 Spagnoli Rd
Melville NY 11747
631 694-2822

(G-16762)
A-MARK MACHINERY CORP
101 Lamar St (11704-1301)
PHONE..................................631 643-6300
Fax: 631 643-9069
Marcel Edelstein, *President*
Shelly Edelstein, *Corp Secy*
Paul Schwartz, *Vice Pres*
EMP: 15
SQ FT: 24,000
SALES (est): 5.7MM **Privately Held**
SIC: **3555** Printing trades machinery

(G-16763)
A-QUICK BINDERY LLC
30 Gleam St Unit C (11704-1207)
PHONE..................................631 491-1110
Fax: 631 491-0388
Nick Koutsoliontos, *Owner*
John Liontos,
EMP: 5
SALES (est): 440K **Privately Held**
SIC: **2789** Bookbinding & related work

(G-16764)
ABERDEEN BLOWER & SHTMTL WORKS
401 Columbus Ave (11704-5541)
P.O. Box 1134 (11704-0134)
PHONE..................................631 661-6100
Fax: 631 661-0624
Peter Levine, *President*
John Rolleri, *Partner*
EMP: 7
SALES (est): 1.5MM **Privately Held**
SIC: **3444** Sheet metalwork

(G-16765)
ADCOMM GRAPHICS INC
21 Lamar St (11704-1301)
PHONE..................................212 645-1298
Guy Leibstein, *President*
Raymond Muccioli, *Vice Pres*
Nancy Leibstein, *Controller*
Paul Leibstein, *Admin Sec*
EMP: 25
SQ FT: 5,000
SALES (est): 2.1MM **Privately Held**
SIC: **2741** 7336 Miscellaneous publishing; graphic arts & related design

(G-16766)
ADVANCE PRECISION INDUSTRIES
9 Mahan St Unit A (11704-1319)
PHONE..................................631 491-0910
Fax: 631 491-0911
Anton Korconkiewicz, *President*
EMP: 6
SQ FT: 4,000
SALES (est): 396K **Privately Held**
SIC: **3599** Machine shop, jobbing & repair

(G-16767)
AIRCRAFT FINISHING CORP (PA)
100 Field St Unit A (11704-5550)
PHONE..................................631 422-5000
Fax: 631 422-0815
Sam Serigano, *President*
John Serigano, *Vice Pres*
Kathleen Serigano, *Treasurer*
Ann Serigano, *Admin Sec*
EMP: 16
SQ FT: 18,000
SALES (est): 2.4MM **Privately Held**
SIC: **3471** 3479 Plating of metals or formed products; painting of metal products

(G-16768)
ALLMETAL CHOCOLATE MOLD CO INC
135 Dale St (11704-1103)
PHONE..................................631 752-2888
Fax: 718 752-2885
Joseph Micelli, *President*
Teresa Puma, *Office Mgr*
John Micelli, *Admin Sec*
EMP: 10 EST: 1947
SQ FT: 10,000
SALES (est): 1.2MM **Privately Held**
WEB: www.micelli.com
SIC: **3544** Industrial molds

(G-16769)
AMACON CORPORATION
49 Alder St Unit A (11704-1093)
PHONE..................................631 293-1888
Fax: 631 293-1868
Costas Antoniou, *President*
Ted Antoniou, *Vice Pres*
Henry Mancura, *Vice Pres*
Donald O'Day, *Vice Pres*
Donald Oday, *Vice Pres*
EMP: 11
SALES (est): 1.1MM **Privately Held**
WEB: www.amacon.com
SIC: **3599** Machine shop, jobbing & repair

(G-16770)
AMERICAN ACRYLIC CORPORATION
400 Sheffield Ave (11704-5333)
PHONE..................................631 422-2200
Fax: 631 422-2811
Mandell Ziegler, *CEO*
Thomas C Ziegler, *President*
Ken Bauhof, *General Mgr*
Jennifer Meaney, *General Mgr*
Charlie Ziegler, *Treasurer*
◆ EMP: 20
SQ FT: 20,000
SALES: 1.8MM **Privately Held**
WEB: www.americanacrylic.com
SIC: **3083** 3081 2821 Laminated plastics plate & sheet; unsupported plastics film & sheet; plastics materials & resins

(G-16771)
AMERICAN METAL SPINNING PDTS
21 Eads St (11704-1125)
PHONE..................................631 454-6276
Fax: 516 454-4867
Clark Morse, *President*
Michelle Morse, *Office Mgr*
EMP: 9
SQ FT: 8,000
SALES (est): 726K **Privately Held**
WEB: www.amermetalspinning.com
SIC: **3469** Spinning metal for the trade

(G-16772)
AUTOMATION SOURCE TECHNOLOGIES (PA)
21 Otis St Unit B (11704-1440)
PHONE..................................631 643-1678
Peter Dougherty,
▲ EMP: 9 EST: 2012
SALES (est): 2MM **Privately Held**
SIC: **3621** Phase or rotary converters (electrical equipment)

(G-16773)
BABYLON IRON WORKS INC
205 Edison Ave (11704-1030)
PHONE..................................631 643-3311
Fax: 631 253-0950
Raymond Zahralban, *President*
EMP: 16
SQ FT: 14,000
SALES (est): 3.2MM **Privately Held**
SIC: **3446** Architectural metalwork

(G-16774)
BARTOLOMEO PUBLISHING INC
Also Called: Northport Printing
100 Cabot St Unit A (11704-1133)
PHONE..................................631 420-4949
Dan Bartolomeo, *President*
Patricia Bartolomeo, *Vice Pres*
EMP: 5
SQ FT: 17,200
SALES: 1.5MM **Privately Held**
SIC: **2759** 2752 Commercial printing; letterpress printing; flexographic printing; commercial printing, offset

(G-16775)
BEAM MANUFACTURING CORP
Also Called: Sigro Precision
107 Otis St Unit A (11704-1444)
PHONE..................................631 253-2724
Fax: 631 253-2246
Ernie Lampeter, *President*
EMP: 6
SQ FT: 4,000
SALES (est): 856K **Privately Held**
SIC: **3599** Machine shop, jobbing & repair

(G-16776)
BROOKVALE RECORDS INC
Also Called: Looney Tunes CD Store
31 Brookvale Ave (11704-7901)
PHONE..................................631 587-7722
Kral Groger, *President*
EMP: 11
SALES (est): 950K **Privately Held**
SIC: **2782** Record albums

(G-16777)
BSD TOP DIRECT INC
68 Route 109 (11704-6208)
PHONE..................................646 468-0156
Elisha Mishael, *CEO*
EMP: 5 EST: 2012
SALES (est): 330K **Privately Held**
SIC: **2096** Potato chips & similar snacks

(G-16778)
BURTON INDUSTRIES INC
243 Wyandanch Ave Ste A (11704-1593)
PHONE..................................631 643-6660

West Babylon - Suffolk County (G-16779)

Fax: 631 643-6665
Charles Seelinger, *CEO*
Richard Santos, *President*
Dariusz Siniakowicz, *Exec VP*
Warren Hartman, *Vice Pres*
Thomas Seelinger, *Vice Pres*
EMP: 35
SQ FT: 38,000
SALES (est): 8.6MM Privately Held
WEB: www.burtonheat.com
SIC: 3398 Metal heat treating

(G-16779)
BUSINESS CARD EXPRESS INC
300 Farmingdale Rd (11704)
PHONE.................................631 669-3400
Fax: 631 669-1222
William Richards, *President*
Jerry Peirano, *Treasurer*
EMP: 40
SQ FT: 11,000
SALES (est): 5.4MM Privately Held
SIC: 2759 2752 Thermography; commercial printing, lithographic

(G-16780)
C J & C SHEET METAL CORP
433 Falmouth Rd (11704-5654)
PHONE.................................631 376-9425
James Thurau, *President*
EMP: 12
SALES (est): 970K Privately Held
SIC: 3444 Sheet metalwork

(G-16781)
CENTURY READY MIX INC
615 Cord Ave (11704)
P.O. Box 1065 (11704-0065)
PHONE.................................631 888-2200
Nicolina Nicolia, *President*
Liliana Legarreta, *Accountant*
EMP: 6
SALES (est): 510K Privately Held
SIC: 3273 5039 Ready-mixed concrete; mobile homes

(G-16782)
CHECK-MATE INDUSTRIES INC
370 Wyandanch Ave (11704-1524)
PHONE.................................631 491-1777
Fax: 631 491-1745
Regina M Vieweg, *CEO*
Lucille Scavone, *Admin Asst*
Jacquilene Santaro, *Legal Staff*
EMP: 45
SQ FT: 23,000
SALES (est): 11.6MM Privately Held
SIC: 3469 Metal stampings

(G-16783)
CHEM-TAINER INDUSTRIES INC (PA)
Also Called: Todd Enterprises
361 Neptune Ave (11704-5800)
PHONE.................................631 422-8300
Fax: 631 661-8923
Stuart Pivar, *Ch of Bd*
James Glen, *President*
Robert Trivone, *Exec VP*
Anthony Lamb, *Vice Pres*
Joe Maiello, *Vice Pres*
◆ **EMP:** 50 **EST:** 1961
SQ FT: 20,000
SALES (est): 56MM Privately Held
WEB: www.chemtainer.com
SIC: 3089 Plastic containers, except foam

(G-16784)
CHURCH BULLETIN INC
200 Dale St (11704-1124)
P.O. Box 1659, Massapequa (11758-0911)
PHONE.................................631 249-4994
Fax: 631 293-8354
George Keenan Jr, *President*
EMP: 15
SALES (est): 1.5MM Privately Held
WEB: www.thechurchbulletininc.com
SIC: 2741 Business service newsletters; publishing & printing

(G-16785)
COMPUTERIZED METAL BENDING SER
91 Cabot St Unit A (11704-1132)
PHONE.................................631 249-1177
Kenneth Rosner, *President*
EMP: 16 **EST:** 2010
SALES (est): 1.2MM Privately Held
SIC: 3441 Fabricated structural metal

(G-16786)
CUSTOM FRAME & MOLDING CO
97 Lamar St 101 (11704-1308)
PHONE.................................631 491-9091
Nick Maminakis, *President*
Dr Steven Lewen, *Vice Pres*
Michelle Lewen, *Admin Sec*
EMP: 12
SQ FT: 15,000
SALES (est): 1.5MM Privately Held
SIC: 3499 Picture frames, metal

(G-16787)
CUSTOM METAL INCORPORATED
Also Called: Custom Metal Fabrication
72 Otis St (11704-1406)
PHONE.................................631 643-4075
Stephen Pratt, *President*
Nancy Pratt, *Corp Secy*
Jackie Smith, *Office Mgr*
EMP: 11
SQ FT: 11,300
SALES: 1.4MM Privately Held
WEB: www.custommetalfabrication.com
SIC: 3469 Machine parts, stamped or pressed metal

(G-16788)
DBS INTERIORS CORP
Also Called: Island Interiors
81 Otis St (11704-1405)
P.O. Box 1780 (11704-0780)
PHONE.................................631 491-3013
Fax: 631 491-4112
Robert Laurie, *President*
Ed Bundock, *Vice Pres*
Richard Mills, *Purch Agent*
John Bemonte, *Marketing Mgr*
Susan Laurie, *Office Mgr*
EMP: 12
SQ FT: 7,000
SALES: 2MM Privately Held
SIC: 2519 2541 2517 2511 Furniture, household: glass, fiberglass & plastic; wood partitions & fixtures; wood television & radio cabinets; wood household furniture; wood kitchen cabinets; millwork

(G-16789)
DISPLAY COMPONENTS MFG INC
Also Called: D C M
267 Edison Ave (11704-1020)
PHONE.................................631 420-0600
Fax: 516 420-1049
James P Devine III, *President*
Julie Braga, *Controller*
Barbara Jones, *Manager*
Donna Devine, *Admin Sec*
EMP: 30
SQ FT: 25,000
SALES (est): 5.1MM Privately Held
WEB: www.displaycomponents.com
SIC: 2542 Fixtures: display, office or store: except wood

(G-16790)
EAST CAST CLOR COMPOUNDING INC
Also Called: Linli Color
15 Kean St (11704-1208)
PHONE.................................631 491-9000
Fax: 631 491-9008
George Benz, *CEO*
Tony Arra, *President*
Kevin Rigoulot, *General Mgr*
Jon Shuman, *Vice Pres*
EMP: 9
SQ FT: 10,000
SALES (est): 1.6MM Privately Held
WEB: www.linlicolor.com
SIC: 2865 3089 Dyes & pigments; extruded finished plastic products

(G-16791)
FAMOUS BOX SCOOTER CO
75 Rogers Ct (11704-6540)
PHONE.................................631 943-2013
Charles Rubino, *Owner*
EMP: 5
SALES (est): 217.8K Privately Held
SIC: 3944 Scooters, children's

(G-16792)
FLEXENE CORP
Also Called: Edge-Craft Process Co
108 Lamar St (11704-1312)
P.O. Box 1457 (11704-0457)
PHONE.................................631 491-0580
Kurt Godigkeit, *President*
Walter Ploeger, *Manager*
EMP: 20 **EST:** 1946
SQ FT: 11,000
SALES (est): 2.3MM Privately Held
WEB: www.flexenedgecraft.com
SIC: 2269 Finishing plants

(G-16793)
GAMMA ENTERPRISES LLC
Also Called: Gamma Lab
113 Alder St (11704-1001)
PHONE.................................631 755-1080
Clifford Morgan, *CEO*
▼ **EMP:** 30
SQ FT: 19,000
SALES (est): 7.9MM Privately Held
SIC: 2834 Vitamin, nutrient & hematinic preparations for human use

(G-16794)
GREAT EASTERN PASTA WORKS LLC
Also Called: Pasta People
385 Sheffield Ave (11704-5326)
PHONE.................................631 956-0889
Kambiz Morakkabi,
EMP: 20
SQ FT: 1,500
SALES (est): 2.1MM Privately Held
SIC: 2099 5149 Pasta, uncooked: packaged with other ingredients; pasta & rice

(G-16795)
ISOLATION DYNAMICS CORP
Also Called: Idc
66 Otis St Unit A (11704-1427)
P.O. Box 361, Merrick (11566-0361)
PHONE.................................631 491-5670
Fax: 516 785-6484
Max Borrasso, *President*
EMP: 20
SQ FT: 4,000
SALES (est): 3.4MM Privately Held
WEB: www.isolator.com
SIC: 3493 Steel springs, except wire

(G-16796)
ISOLATION TECHNOLOGY INC
73 Nancy St Unit A (11704-1428)
P.O. Box 460, Massapequa (11758-0460)
PHONE.................................631 253-3314
Fax: 631 253-3316
Bob Grefe, *President*
Robert Joyner, *Corp Secy*
▲ **EMP:** 6
SQ FT: 4,000
SALES (est): 1.2MM Privately Held
WEB: www.isolationtech.com
SIC: 3699 Electric sound equipment

(G-16797)
J & T METAL PRODUCTS CO INC
89 Eads St (11704-1105)
PHONE.................................631 226-7400
Thomas Lander, *President*
EMP: 20 **EST:** 1964
SQ FT: 18,000
SALES (est): 1.9MM Privately Held
SIC: 3443 Industrial vessels, tanks & containers; tanks, standard or custom fabricated: metal plate

(G-16798)
J C INDUSTRIES INC
89 Eads St (11704-1186)
PHONE.................................631 420-1920
Fax: 516 420-0467
Joseph V Celano, *Ch of Bd*
James Celano, *Vice Pres*
Durwood Woodall, *Vice Pres*
Steve Erwin, *Accountant*
EMP: 30 **EST:** 1973
SQ FT: 14,000
SALES (est): 5.7MM Privately Held
WEB: www.jcindustries.com
SIC: 3411 Metal cans

(G-16799)
J T D STAMPING CO INC
403 Wyandanch Ave (11704-1599)
PHONE.................................631 643-4144
Fax: 631 643-4016
Giovanni Bianco, *President*
Aldo D'Adamo, *Vice Pres*
Aldo Dadamo, *Vice Pres*
Tania Malbonavo, *Bookkeeper*
EMP: 39
SQ FT: 20,000
SALES: 3.5MM Privately Held
WEB: www.jtdstamping.com
SIC: 3452 Spring washers, metal

(G-16800)
JALEX INDUSTRIES LTD
86 Nancy St (11704-1404)
PHONE.................................631 491-5072
Fax: 631 491-5201
Alexander Jedynski, *President*
Richard Goldsmith, *Vice Pres*
Michele Jedynski, *Vice Pres*
Woon Lee, *Engineer*
EMP: 15
SQ FT: 7,000
SALES (est): 1.8MM Privately Held
SIC: 3541 Machine tools, metal cutting type

(G-16801)
JAVIN MACHINE CORP
31 Otis St (11704-1405)
PHONE.................................631 643-3322
Fax: 631 643-3340
Geri Spiezio, *CEO*
Vincent Spiezio, *President*
Carol Bertolo, *Office Mgr*
EMP: 15
SQ FT: 16,000
SALES (est): 2.8MM Privately Held
WEB: www.javinmachine.net
SIC: 3599 Machine shop, jobbing & repair

(G-16802)
JF MACHINE SHOP INC
89 Otis St Unit A (11704-1442)
PHONE.................................631 491-7273
Fax: 631 491-7221
Anthony Schiavone, *President*
EMP: 10
SQ FT: 9,000
SALES (est): 1.6MM Privately Held
WEB: www.jfmachine.com
SIC: 3599 Machine shop, jobbing & repair

(G-16803)
JOHNNYS MACHINE SHOP
81 Mahan St (11704-1303)
PHONE.................................631 338-9733
Juan Campos, *Owner*
EMP: 5
SALES: 200K Privately Held
SIC: 3599 Machine & other job shop work; machine shop, jobbing & repair

(G-16804)
KESSLER THERMOMETER CORP
40 Gleam St (11704-1205)
PHONE.................................631 841-5500
Fax: 631 841-5553
Robert Peyser, *President*
▲ **EMP:** 9
SALES (est): 1.1MM Privately Held
SIC: 3823 Thermometers, filled system: industrial process type

(G-16805)
KING ALBUM INC
20 Kean St (11704-1209)
PHONE.................................631 253-9500
Warren King, *President*
EMP: 20
SQ FT: 7,700
SALES: 2.2MM Privately Held
SIC: 2782 Albums

▲ = Import ▼ = Export
◆ = Import/Export

West Babylon - Suffolk County (G-16833)

(G-16806)
L K MANUFACTURING CORP
56 Eads St (11704-1106)
P.O. Box 167, Huntington Station (11746-0137)
PHONE.................................631 243-6910
Fax: 516 420-9506
Robert Lutzker, *President*
Kay Kelly, *Vice Pres*
Samuel Martin, *Vice Pres*
EMP: 22
SQ FT: 15,000
SALES (est): 1.6MM **Privately Held**
WEB: www.lkmfg.com
SIC: 3089 5065 Kitchenware, plastic; electronic parts & equipment

(G-16807)
LETTERAMA INC (PA)
111 Cabot St (11704-1100)
PHONE.................................516 349-0800
Mark Costa, *President*
Kevin Hardiman, *Controller*
▼ **EMP:** 7 **EST:** 1959
SQ FT: 30,000
SALES: 3MM **Privately Held**
SIC: 3993 Signs & advertising specialties

(G-16808)
M T D CORPORATION
41 Otis St (11704-1405)
PHONE.................................631 491-3905
Matthew Turnbull, *President*
Michael Deletto, *Vice Pres*
Lisa Muford, *Bookkeeper*
EMP: 10
SQ FT: 6,500
SALES (est): 1.2MM **Privately Held**
WEB: www.makeupart.net
SIC: 2521 2511 Wood office furniture; wood household furniture

(G-16809)
MATRIX MACHINING CORP
69 B Nancy St Unit h (11704)
PHONE.................................631 643-6690
Fax: 631 643-2310
Joseph Abdale, *President*
Ray Abdale, *Corp Secy*
EMP: 6
SQ FT: 4,700
SALES (est): 999.8K **Privately Held**
SIC: 3599 Machine shop, jobbing & repair

(G-16810)
MATRIX RAILWAY CORP
69 Nancy St Unit A (11704-1425)
PHONE.................................631 643-1483
Nelson Rivas, *Ch of Bd*
▲ **EMP:** 9
SQ FT: 4,000
SALES (est): 870K **Privately Held**
WEB: www.matrixrailway.com
SIC: 3621 Railway motors & control equipment, electric

(G-16811)
MILLWRIGHT WDWRK INSTALLETION
991 Peconic Ave (11704-5629)
PHONE.................................631 587-2635
Fax: 631 587-1573
Martin Sherlock, *President*
Peggy Mauro, *Office Mgr*
Jim Orlando, *Executive*
EMP: 20
SQ FT: 16,000
SALES (est): 2.1MM **Privately Held**
SIC: 2431 1751 Millwork; finish & trim carpentry

(G-16812)
MONO PLATE INC
15 Otis St (11704-1446)
PHONE.................................631 643-3100
Michael Bader, *President*
Harvey Bader, *Vice Pres*
EMP: 8
SALES: 1.5MM **Privately Held**
WEB: www.stampingground.com
SIC: 3559 Rubber working machinery, including tires

(G-16813)
MPI CONSULTING INCORPORATED
Also Called: Wal Machine
87 Jersey St (11704-1206)
PHONE.................................631 253-2377
Fax: 631 253-2286
William A Toscano, *CEO*
Jennifer Luizzi, *Vice Pres*
EMP: 20 **EST:** 1966
SQ FT: 8,000
SALES: 7MM **Privately Held**
SIC: 3429 Aircraft hardware

(G-16814)
MPI CONSULTING INCORPORATED
Also Called: Wal Machine
87 Jersey St (11704-1206)
PHONE.................................631 253-2377
William Toscano, *President*
EMP: 3 **EST:** 2011
SQ FT: 12,000
SALES: 5MM **Privately Held**
SIC: 3365 Aerospace castings, aluminum

(G-16815)
NASSAU TOOL WORKS INC
34 Lamar St (11704-1309)
PHONE.................................631 643-0420
Fax: 631 643-3432
Vincent Di Carlo Jr, *President*
Robert Hunt, *Corp Secy*
Elona Maturo, *Manager*
Lucille Mamouzelos, *Info Tech Mgr*
EMP: 50
SQ FT: 60,000
SALES (est): 10.9MM
SALES (corp-wide): 80.4MM **Publicly Held**
SIC: 3728 3599 Aircraft parts & equipment; aircraft landing assemblies & brakes; machine shop, jobbing & repair
PA: Air Industries Group
       360 Motor Pkwy Ste 100
       Hauppauge NY 11788
       631 881-4920

(G-16816)
NEWMAT NORTHEAST CORP
81b Mahan St (11704-1303)
PHONE.................................631 253-9277
Timothy T Greco, *President*
EMP: 11
SQ FT: 8,000
SALES (est): 2.5MM **Privately Held**
SIC: 2821 1742 Polyvinyl chloride resins (PVC); acoustical & ceiling work

(G-16817)
OUR TERMS FABRICATORS INC
48 Cabot St (11704-1109)
PHONE.................................631 752-1517
John Friese, *President*
Greg D'Arrigo, *Vice Pres*
Terry Connolly, *Manager*
EMP: 32
SQ FT: 18,000
SALES (est): 4.5MM **Privately Held**
WEB: www.ourtermsfabricators.com
SIC: 3231 Furniture tops, glass: cut, beveled or polished

(G-16818)
PEYSER INSTRUMENT CORPORATION
Also Called: Chase Instrument Co
40 Gleam St (11704-1205)
PHONE.................................631 841-3600
Fax: 516 841-5553
Robert Peyser, *President*
Leonard Peyser, *Vice Pres*
John Lewis, *Executive*
▲ **EMP:** 20
SQ FT: 1,500
SALES (est): 2.8MM **Privately Held**
SIC: 3829 5049 Hydrometers, except industrial process type; analytical instruments

(G-16819)
QUALITY SAW & KNIFE INC
115 Otis St (11704-1429)
PHONE.................................631 491-4747
Fredrick Luberto, *President*
Paul Siegfried, *Vice Pres*
EMP: 10
SQ FT: 3,000
SALES (est): 800K **Privately Held**
SIC: 3425 7699 Saw blades, chain type; saw blades for hand or power saws; knife, saw & tool sharpening & repair

(G-16820)
R & J DISPLAYS INC
96 Otis St (11704-1430)
PHONE.................................631 491-3500
Fax: 631 491-8566
Lance Landau, *President*
Phyllis Lazar, *Office Mgr*
EMP: 30
SQ FT: 20,000
SALES (est): 3.2MM **Privately Held**
SIC: 3993 Displays & cutouts, window & lobby

(G-16821)
RGH ASSOCIATES INC
Also Called: Richards Screw Machine
86 Nancy St (11704-1404)
PHONE.................................631 643-1111
Richard Honan, *President*
Richard Goldsmith, *Corp Secy*
EMP: 19
SQ FT: 7,200
SALES (est): 6.5MM **Privately Held**
SIC: 3599 Machine shop, jobbing & repair

(G-16822)
RICHARD MANNO & COMPANY INC
42 Lamar St (11704-1302)
PHONE.................................631 643-2200
Fax: 631 643-2215
Vincent Manno, *President*
Ilian Dimitrov, *General Mgr*
Vincent Chiappone, *Exec VP*
Jason Wagner, *Exec VP*
Christine Burns, *Vice Pres*
▲ **EMP:** 54
SQ FT: 18,000
SALES (est): 11.2MM **Privately Held**
WEB: www.richardmanno.com
SIC: 3599 Machine shop, jobbing & repair

(G-16823)
ROSE GRAPHICS LLC
109 Kean St (11704-1208)
PHONE.................................516 547-6142
Jeannie Bissert, *Manager*
Anthony F Severino,
EMP: 10
SQ FT: 8,000
SALES (est): 2MM **Privately Held**
SIC: 2759 Commercial printing

(G-16824)
S & D WELDING CORP
Also Called: S&D Welding
229 Edison Ave Ste A (11704-1042)
PHONE.................................631 454-0383
Fax: 516 454-0802
Mark Dubicki, *President*
Lucia Dubicki, *Treasurer*
EMP: 5
SALES: 275K **Privately Held**
SIC: 7692 1799 5046 Welding repair; welding on site; commercial cooking & food service equipment

(G-16825)
SAGE KNITWEAR INC
103 Jersey St Unit D (11704-1219)
P.O. Box 748231, Rego Park (11374-8231)
PHONE.................................718 628-7902
Payam Ebrani, *President*
EMP: 5
SQ FT: 3,500
SALES (est): 604.1K **Privately Held**
SIC: 2253 Sweaters & sweater coats, knit; dresses, knit; skirts, knit

(G-16826)
SAV THERMO INC
133 Cabot St (11704-1101)
PHONE.................................631 249-9444
Vincent Caputi, *President*
Anthony Bangaroo, *Vice Pres*
EMP: 10
SQ FT: 10,000
SALES (est): 1.6MM **Privately Held**
SIC: 3089 Trays, plastic

(G-16827)
SINN- TECH INDUSTRIES INC
48 Gleam St (11704-1205)
PHONE.................................631 643-1171
Fax: 631 643-1176
Daniel Tierney, *Owner*
Robert Becker, *Director*
EMP: 10
SQ FT: 7,000
SALES (est): 1MM **Privately Held**
WEB: www.sinn-tech.com
SIC: 3545 Machine tool accessories

(G-16828)
SINN-TECH INDUSTRIES INC
48 Gleam St (11704-1205)
PHONE.................................631 643-1171
Daniel Tierney, *President*
EMP: 8 **EST:** 2015
SALES (est): 311.7K **Privately Held**
SIC: 3449 Miscellaneous metalwork

(G-16829)
SONAER INC
68 Lamar St Unit D (11704-1316)
PHONE.................................631 756-4780
Donald Cierco, *Ch of Bd*
Donald Ciervo, *Ch of Bd*
EMP: 8
SQ FT: 3,000
SALES (est): 1.1MM **Privately Held**
WEB: www.sonozap.com
SIC: 3679 Electronic circuits

(G-16830)
SONICOR INC
82 Otis St (11704-1406)
PHONE.................................631 920-6555
Michael J Parker, *President*
Edmond J Parker, *Vice Pres*
Lewis Levy, *Project Engr*
Augusto D' Agostino, *Manager*
Augusto Dagostino, *Info Tech Mgr*
▲ **EMP:** 12 **EST:** 1966
SQ FT: 3,500
SALES (est): 2.4MM **Privately Held**
WEB: www.sonicor.com
SIC: 3569 3559 3554 3699 Separators for steam, gas, vapor or air (machinery); electroplating machinery & equipment; paper mill machinery: plating, slitting, waxing, etc.; welding machines & equipment, ultrasonic; cleaning equipment, ultrasonic, except medical & dental; medical cleaning equipment, ultrasonic

(G-16831)
SPECIALTY BLDG SOLUTIONS INC
Eads St Ste 165a (11704)
PHONE.................................631 393-6918
John Pearson, *Owner*
Jeanne Demaio, *Office Mgr*
EMP: 8 **EST:** 2009
SALES (est): 594.4K **Privately Held**
SIC: 3479 Coating or wrapping steel pipe

(G-16832)
STERLING TOGGLE INC
99 Mahan St (11704-1303)
PHONE.................................631 491-0500
Fax: 631 491-3401
William Horne Jr, *President*
Susan Horne, *Vice Pres*
Debra Irving, *Vice Pres*
EMP: 12
SALES (est): 1.3MM **Privately Held**
WEB: www.sterlingtoggle.com
SIC: 3555 Printing trades machinery

(G-16833)
STRAHL & PITSCH INC
230 Great East Neck Rd (11704-7602)
P.O. Box 1098 (11704-0098)
PHONE.................................631 669-0175
Fax: 631 587-9120
William France, *Ch of Bd*
William Deluca, *President*
Roger McKenna, *General Mgr*
Hans Kestler, *Vice Pres*
Bill Schnabel, *Plant Mgr*
◆ **EMP:** 40 **EST:** 1904

West Babylon - Suffolk County (G-16834)

SALES (est): 19.2MM **Privately Held**
WEB: www.spwax.com
SIC: 2842 Waxes for wood, leather & other materials

(G-16834)
SUPER WEB INC
97 Lamar St (11704-1308)
PHONE..................................631 643-9100
Fax: 631 643-9069
Marcel Edelstein, *Ch of Bd*
Paul Schwartz, *Vice Pres*
Tom Simon, *Sales Mgr*
Shelly Edelstein, *Admin Sec*
▲ EMP: 30
SQ FT: 27,000
SALES (est): 8MM **Privately Held**
WEB: www.superwebusa.com
SIC: 3555 5084 Printing trades machinery; printing trades machinery, equipment & supplies

(G-16835)
SWEET TOOTH ENTERPRISES LLC
Also Called: Micelli Chocolate Mold Co
135 Dale St (11704-1103)
PHONE..................................631 752-2888
Tim Goddeau, *Opers Mgr*
Paul Hamilton,
EMP: 20
SALES (est): 4.6MM **Privately Held**
SIC: 3089 Molding primary plastic

(G-16836)
TRIANGLE GRINDING MACHINE CORP
66 Nancy St Unit A (11704-1436)
PHONE..................................631 643-3636
Santo Turano, *President*
Domingo Turano, *Vice Pres*
George Turano, *Vice Pres*
EMP: 5
SQ FT: 800
SALES (est): 606.7K **Privately Held**
SIC: 3599 Machine shop, jobbing & repair

(G-16837)
US ELECTROPLATING CORP
100 Field St Unit A (11704-1294)
PHONE..................................631 293-1998
Fax: 516 293-7742
Robert Birmbaum, *President*
EMP: 6 EST: 1971
SQ FT: 3,000
SALES (est): 520K **Privately Held**
SIC: 3471 Plating of metals or formed products; polishing, metals or formed products

(G-16838)
VANDILAY INDUSTRIES INC
Also Called: Dualtron Manufacturing
60 Bell St Unit A (11704-1038)
PHONE..................................631 226-3064
Don Ehrlich, *President*
Chris Schleimer, *Vice Pres*
EMP: 22 EST: 1997
SQ FT: 22,000
SALES (est): 3.9MM **Privately Held**
WEB: www.dualtron.com
SIC: 3545 Machine tool accessories

(G-16839)
VILLAGE VIDEO PRODUCTIONS INC
Also Called: Village Video News
107 Alder St (11704-1001)
PHONE..................................631 752-9311
Robert Wolf, *President*
EMP: 6
SQ FT: 2,000
SALES (est): 876.3K **Privately Held**
WEB: www.vvn.com
SIC: 3663 Satellites, communications

(G-16840)
WEICRO GRAPHICS INC
Also Called: Able Printing
95 Mahan St (11704-1303)
PHONE..................................631 253-3360
Fax: 631 253-3369
Sanford Weiss, *President*
Lucyna Mleczko, *Vice Pres*
EMP: 22

SQ FT: 5,500
SALES (est): 3.2MM **Privately Held**
WEB: www.lemontreestationery.com
SIC: 2752 2759 Commercial printing, offset; commercial printing

West Burlington
Otsego County

(G-16841)
CONTROL LOGIC CORPORATION
2533 State Highway 80 (13482-9717)
PHONE..................................607 965-6423
Fax: 607 965-6426
Randy Holdredge, *President*
Joanne Holdredge, *Admin Sec*
EMP: 6
SALES (est): 460K **Privately Held**
WEB: www.controllogic.com
SIC: 3577 Printers, computer

West Chazy
Clinton County

(G-16842)
R & S MACHINE CENTER INC
Also Called: R&S Machine
44 Academy St (12992-3535)
PHONE..................................518 563-4016
Robert Davenport, *President*
EMP: 10
SQ FT: 7,000
SALES (est): 1.9MM **Privately Held**
SIC: 3599 5051 Machine shop, jobbing & repair; steel

West Edmeston
Madison County

(G-16843)
SCULLY SANITATION
11146 Skaneateles Tpke (13485-3060)
PHONE..................................315 899-8996
Timothy Scully, *Partner*
Kevin Scully, *Partner*
EMP: 8
SALES (est): 300K **Privately Held**
SIC: 2842 Sanitation preparations, disinfectants & deodorants

West Falls
Erie County

(G-16844)
BUTTERWOOD DESSERTS INC
Also Called: Swamp Island Dessert Co
1863 Davis Rd (14170-9701)
PHONE..................................716 652-0131
Fax: 585 652-1759
Bill Panzica, *President*
Carolyn Panzica, *Principal*
EMP: 40
SQ FT: 15,000
SALES (est): 3.4MM **Privately Held**
SIC: 2099 2053 2052 Desserts, ready-to-mix; frozen bakery products, except bread; pastries (danish): frozen; cookies & crackers

(G-16845)
TEAM FABRICATION INC
1055 Davis Rd (14170-9734)
P.O. Box 32 (14170-0032)
PHONE..................................716 655-4038
Robert Hopkins, *President*
William Emhof, *Director*
EMP: 8
SQ FT: 2,376
SALES (est): 1.4MM **Privately Held**
WEB: www.teamfabrication.com
SIC: 3441 Fabricated structural metal

West Haverstraw
Rockland County

(G-16846)
POLANCO MILLS WOODWORK
132 E Railroad Ave (10993-1418)
PHONE..................................845 271-3639
Richard Mills, *Vice Pres*
EMP: 6
SALES (est): 433.3K **Privately Held**
SIC: 2499 Wood products

(G-16847)
VIN-CLAIR INC
Also Called: Vin-Clair Bindery
132 E Railroad Ave (10993-1418)
PHONE..................................845 429-4998
Lou Maiello, *President*
Florence Maiello, *Vice Pres*
Claire Blaha, *Bookkeeper*
EMP: 10
SQ FT: 17,000
SALES (est): 58.1K **Privately Held**
SIC: 2789 Bookbinding & related work

(G-16848)
YOUR FURNITURE DESIGNERS INC
Also Called: Yfd Cabinetry
118 E Railroad Ave (10993-1416)
PHONE..................................845 947-3046
Jose A Mata, *President*
Cristina Matha, *Manager*
EMP: 5
SALES (est): 725.4K **Privately Held**
SIC: 2511 2521 2434 2542 Wood household furniture; wood bedroom furniture; kitchen & dining room furniture; wood office furniture; wood kitchen cabinets; vanities, bathroom: wood; shelving, office & store: except wood

West Hempstead
Nassau County

(G-16849)
ARTISAN WOODWORKING LTD
Also Called: Artisan Custom Interiors
163 Hempstead Tpke (11552-1622)
PHONE..................................516 486-0818
Michael Aiello, *President*
Janet Aiello, *Corp Secy*
EMP: 6
SQ FT: 6,500
SALES (est): 590K **Privately Held**
WEB: www.artisancustominteriors.com
SIC: 2511 Wood household furniture

(G-16850)
AUTOMOTION PARKING SYSTEMS LLC
411 Hempstead Tpke # 200 (11552-1350)
PHONE..................................516 565-5600
Perry Finkelman, *Managing Dir*
Jeffrey Hyde, *Vice Pres*
Jordan Rinzler, *Vice Pres*
Daniel McCrossin, *Opers Mgr*
ARI Milstein, *Exec Dir*
EMP: 2
SQ FT: 1,000
SALES (est): 2.1MM **Privately Held**
SIC: 3559 Parking facility equipment & supplies

(G-16851)
CENTAR FUEL CO INC
700 Nassau Blvd (11552-3531)
PHONE..................................516 538-2424
John Skei, *Principal*
EMP: 5 EST: 2007
SALES (est): 563.8K **Privately Held**
SIC: 2869 Fuels

(G-16852)
D-BEST EQUIPMENT CORP
77 Hempstead Gardens Dr (11552-2643)
PHONE..................................516 358-0965
Marc Cali, *CEO*
EMP: 22

SALES (est): 4.5MM **Privately Held**
SIC: 2869 Enzymes

(G-16853)
GARDEN CITY PRINTERS & MAILERS
144 Cherry Valley Ave (11552-1213)
PHONE..................................516 485-1600
Joseph Grzymalski, *President*
Patricia Grzymalski, *Vice Pres*
▲ EMP: 14
SQ FT: 10,000
SALES (est): 1.1MM **Privately Held**
SIC: 2752 7331 Commercial printing, lithographic; mailing service

(G-16854)
GENESIS ONE UNLIMITED
Also Called: Eb Automation Industries
600 Pinebrook Ave (11552-4225)
PHONE..................................516 208-5863
Earl Birkett, *Principal*
EMP: 6
SALES (est): 250K **Privately Held**
SIC: 2759 3497 Imprinting; gold foil or leaf

(G-16855)
INDEPENDENT HOME PRODUCTS LLC
59 Hempstead Gardens Dr (11552-2641)
PHONE..................................718 541-1256
Abbie Spetner, *Principal*
Yale Lipschik, *CFO*
▲ EMP: 22
SALES (est): 3.4MM **Privately Held**
SIC: 3088 3431 Hot tubs, plastic or fiberglass; bathtubs: enameled iron, cast iron or pressed metal

(G-16856)
INTERNTONAL CONSMR CONNECTIONS
Also Called: Wilson Picture Frames
5 Terminal Rd Unit A (11552-1151)
PHONE..................................516 481-3438
Fax: 516 538-1938
Mark Sternberg, *President*
Alan Kohn, *Shareholder*
EMP: 12
SQ FT: 5,000
SALES (est): 750K **Privately Held**
SIC: 2499 7699 Picture & mirror frames, wood; picture framing, custom

(G-16857)
J GIMBEL INC
275 Hempstead Tpke Ste A (11552-1540)
PHONE..................................718 296-5200
Fax: 718 296-6188
Jackie Sherman, *President*
Leonard Gimbel, *Vice Pres*
Lorie Gimbel, *Treasurer*
EMP: 20
SQ FT: 17,000
SALES (est): 2.2MM **Privately Held**
WEB: www.rollershades.com
SIC: 2591 Blinds vertical; window shades

(G-16858)
KONRAD PROSTHETICS & ORTHOTICS (PA)
596 Jennings Ave (11552-3706)
PHONE..................................516 485-9164
Fax: 516 485-9170
Kurt Konrad, *President*
Elsbeth Konrad, *Corp Secy*
EMP: 6
SQ FT: 200
SALES (est): 733K **Privately Held**
SIC: 3842 7352 5999 Surgical appliances & supplies; invalid supplies rental; artificial limbs

(G-16859)
MAGIC TECH CO LTD
401 Hempstead Tpke (11552-1311)
PHONE..................................516 539-7944
EMP: 5
SALES (est): 440K **Privately Held**
SIC: 3699 5065 Mfg And Dist Karoke Machines

GEOGRAPHIC SECTION

West Henrietta - Monroe County (G-16884)

(G-16860)
MULTITONE FINISHING CO INC
56 Hempstead Gardens Dr (11552-2642)
PHONE...................................516 485-1043
Fax: 516 485-1043
Edward Mc Carthy, *President*
Harvey Pollack, *Vice Pres*
EMP: 8 **EST:** 1963
SQ FT: 4,700
SALES (est): 660K **Privately Held**
SIC: 3471 Finishing, metals or formed products

(G-16861)
MUTUAL ENGRAVING COMPANY INC
511 Hempstead Ave Ste 13 (11552-2738)
P.O. Box 129 (11552-0129)
PHONE...................................516 489-0534
Fax: 516 486-2926
Salvatore Forelli, *President*
Robert Forelli, *Vice Pres*
Emma Cooper, *Project Mgr*
John Battaglia, *Mfg Staff*
Lou Ewanitsko, *Treasurer*
EMP: 65 **EST:** 1939
SQ FT: 15,000
SALES (est): 7MM **Privately Held**
WEB: www.mutualengraving.com
SIC: 2754 2796 2791 2752 Stationery: gravure printing; platemaking services; typesetting; commercial printing, lithographic

(G-16862)
PROFESSIONAL REMODELERS INC
340 Hempstead Ave Unit A (11552-2061)
PHONE...................................516 565-9300
Thomas Stallone, *President*
Marlyn Prousard, *Manager*
EMP: 5
SALES (est): 486.2K **Privately Held**
SIC: 1389 Construction, repair & dismantling services

(G-16863)
STONE EXPO & CABINETRY LLC
7 Terminal Rd (11552-1105)
PHONE...................................516 292-2988
Annie Liu, *Manager*
▲ **EMP:** 16
SALES (est): 2MM **Privately Held**
SIC: 2434 2542 Wood kitchen cabinets; counters or counter display cases: except wood

(G-16864)
US PUMP CORP
707 Woodfield Rd (11552-3826)
PHONE...................................516 303-7799
Nissim Isaacson, *Ch of Bd*
▲ **EMP:** 5
SALES (est): 727.2K **Privately Held**
SIC: 1381 1241 Drilling water intake wells; redrilling oil & gas wells; mining services: lignite

West Henrietta
Monroe County

(G-16865)
ALL AMERICAN PRECISION TL MOLD
Also Called: All American Mold
1325 John St (14586-9121)
PHONE...................................585 436-3080
Fax: 585 436-8183
Mike Veltri, *President*
EMP: 12
SQ FT: 17,000
SALES (est): 1.4MM **Privately Held**
WEB: www.all-americanmold.com
SIC: 3089 3544 Plastic processing; industrial molds

(G-16866)
ALSTOM TRANSPORTATION INC
1025 John St Ste 100h (14586-9781)
PHONE...................................800 717-4477
EMP: 7

SALES (est): 2.6MM **Privately Held**
SIC: 3669 Transportation signaling devices

(G-16867)
AMERICAN FILTRATION TECH INC
100 Thruway Park Dr (14586-9798)
PHONE...................................585 359-4130
Fax: 585 359-4782
Richard Felber, *President*
Brian Felber, *Purch Agent*
Amy Colf, *Admin Mgr*
EMP: 13
SQ FT: 36,000
SALES (est): 3.3MM **Privately Held**
SIC: 3569 3564 Filters; blowers & fans

(G-16868)
APOLLO OPTICAL SYSTEMS INC
925 John St (14586-9780)
PHONE...................................585 272-6170
G Michael Morris, *CEO*
Daniel McGarry, *President*
Claude Tribastone, *President*
Gwen Murphy, *QC Mgr*
Richard Young, *Engineer*
EMP: 38
SALES (est): 9MM **Privately Held**
WEB: www.apollooptical.com
SIC: 3827 Optical instruments & lenses

(G-16869)
APPAIRENT TECHNOLOGIES INC (PA)
150 Lucius Gordon Dr (14586-9687)
PHONE...................................585 214-2460
Fax: 585 214-2461
Chris O'Donnell, *CEO*
Jim Allen, *President*
Rick Alvin, *Vice Pres*
EMP: 5
SQ FT: 2,500
SALES (est): 1.2MM **Privately Held**
WEB: www.appairent.com
SIC: 3663 Radio broadcasting & communications equipment

(G-16870)
B C MANUFACTURING INC
100 Thruway Park Dr (14586-9798)
PHONE...................................585 482-1080
Fax: 585 482-2658
Bob Collins, *President*
EMP: 5
SQ FT: 5,500
SALES (est): 800.5K **Privately Held**
SIC: 3599 Machine shop, jobbing & repair

(G-16871)
BRANDYS MOLD AND TOOL CTR LTD (PA)
10 Riverton Way (14586-9754)
PHONE...................................585 334-8333
Fax: 585 334-2005
Michaela Perkins, *President*
Dan Morse, *General Mgr*
Franz Brandstetter, *Vice Pres*
EMP: 15
SALES (est): 1.5MM **Privately Held**
SIC: 3089 Plastic processing

(G-16872)
BRINKMAN PRECISION INC
Also Called: B P I
100 Park Centre Dr (14586-9688)
PHONE...................................585 429-5001
Andrew J Laniak, *CEO*
Robert J Brinkman, *Ch of Bd*
Kevin Orlop, *Prdtn Mgr*
Bob Coffey, *QC Mgr*
Paul Francia, *Engineer*
EMP: 85
SALES (est): 16MM
SALES (corp-wide): 81.2MM **Privately Held**
WEB: www.brinkmanprecision.com
SIC: 3324 5047 Aerospace investment castings, ferrous; medical equipment & supplies
PA: Brinkman International Group, Inc.
167 Ames St
Rochester NY 14611
585 429-5000

(G-16873)
COHBER PRESS INC (PA)
Also Called: Kodak Gallery - Cohber
1000 John St (14586-9757)
P.O. Box 93100, Rochester (14692-7300)
PHONE...................................585 475-9100
Fax: 585 475-9406
Eric C Webber, *President*
Howard Buzz, *Chairman*
Dan Mahany, *COO*
Chris Bowen, *Vice Pres*
John Giblin, *VP Sales*
EMP: 88 **EST:** 1925
SQ FT: 49,000
SALES (est): 15.5MM **Privately Held**
WEB: www.cohber.com
SIC: 2752 2791 2789 Commercial printing, offset; photo-offset printing; typesetting; bookbinding & related work

(G-16874)
COOPERVISION INC
180 Thruway Park Dr (14586-9798)
PHONE...................................585 385-6810
Michelle McDonagh, *Director*
EMP: 660
SALES (corp-wide): 1.8B **Publicly Held**
SIC: 3851 Contact lenses
HQ: Coopervision, Inc.
209 High Point Dr
Victor NY 14564
585 385-6810

(G-16875)
DELPHI AUTOMOTIVE SYSTEMS LLC
5500 W Henrietta Rd (14586-9701)
PHONE...................................585 359-6000
Bruce Gardephe, *Engineer*
Joseph Kazour, *Engineer*
Lee Markle, *Engineer*
Walter Cossa, *Project Engr*
Jim Zizzleman, *Manager*
EMP: 209 **Privately Held**
WEB: www.delphiauto.com
SIC: 3714 Motor vehicle parts & accessories
HQ: Delphi Automotive Systems, Llc
5725 Delphi Dr
Troy MI 48098
248 813-2000

(G-16876)
DELPHI AUTOMOTIVE SYSTEMS LLC
5500 W Henrietta Rd (14586-9701)
PHONE...................................585 359-6000
Jim Zizleman, *Manager*
EMP: 600 **Privately Held**
WEB: www.delphiauto.com
SIC: 3714 8731 3694 3564 Motor vehicle parts & accessories; commercial physical research; engine electrical equipment; blowers & fans
HQ: Delphi Automotive Systems, Llc
5725 Delphi Dr
Troy MI 48098
248 813-2000

(G-16877)
DELPHI AUTOMOTIVE SYSTEMS LLC
Also Called: Delphi Powertrain Systems
5500 W Henrietta Rd (14586-9701)
PHONE...................................585 359-6000
Walter Piock, *Branch Mgr*
EMP: 38 **Privately Held**
SIC: 3714 Motor vehicle parts & accessories
HQ: Delphi Automotive Systems, Llc
5725 Delphi Dr
Troy MI 48098
248 813-2000

(G-16878)
FORTEQ NORTH AMERICA INC
150 Park Centre Dr (14586-9688)
PHONE...................................585 427-9410
Martin Van Manen, *CEO*
Rune Bakke, *Principal*
Joseph Buonocure, *Principal*
Willaim Banks, *Vice Pres*
Joerge Hotz, *Plant Mgr*
▲ **EMP:** 70
SQ FT: 29,000

SALES (est): 27.4MM **Privately Held**
SIC: 3089 Plastic containers, except foam
PA: Transmission Technology Holding Ag
C/O Bar & Karrer
Zug ZG
582 615-900

(G-16879)
GENESEE METAL STAMPINGS INC
975 John St (14586-9780)
PHONE...................................585 475-0450
Fax: 585 475-0469
Gerard Caschette, *Principal*
John Cook, *Manager*
EMP: 5
SALES (est): 574.8K **Privately Held**
SIC: 3469 Stamping metal for the trade

(G-16880)
GEOSPATIAL SYSTEMS INC (DH)
150 Lucius Gordon Dr # 211 (14586-9687)
PHONE...................................585 427-8310
Maxime Elbaz, *President*
William Kent PHD, *Vice Pres*
Steven Randy Olson, *Vice Pres*
Matt Kremens, *Engineer*
Robert Delach, *CFO*
EMP: 11
SQ FT: 3,000
SALES (est): 1.1MM
SALES (corp-wide): 2.3B **Publicly Held**
SIC: 3861 Aerial cameras
HQ: Teledyne Optech Incorporated
300 Interchange Way
Vaughan ON L4K 5
905 660-0808

(G-16881)
HAMMER PACKAGING CORP (PA)
200 Lucius Gordon Dr (14586-9685)
P.O. Box 22678, Rochester (14692-2678)
PHONE...................................585 424-3880
James E Hammer, *President*
Jason Hammer, *Vice Pres*
Marty Karpie, *Vice Pres*
Louis Lovoli, *Vice Pres*
Tom Mason, *Vice Pres*
▲ **EMP:** 255 **EST:** 1912
SQ FT: 92,000
SALES: 119.2MM **Privately Held**
WEB: www.hammerpackaging.com
SIC: 2759 Labels & seals: printing

(G-16882)
HEALTH CARE ORIGINALS INC
150 Lucius Gordon Dr (14586-9687)
PHONE...................................585 967-1398
Jared Dwarika, *Co-Owner*
EMP: 5
SALES (est): 273.1K **Privately Held**
SIC: 3845 8731 Electromedical apparatus; medical research, commercial

(G-16883)
KATIKATI INC
150 Lucius Gordon Dr (14586-9687)
PHONE...................................585 678-1764
Prathap James Ambaichelvan, *CEO*
Sanjay Hiranandani, *COO*
Allyson Hiranandani, *Vice Pres*
EMP: 5
SALES (est): 251K **Privately Held**
SIC: 3714 5013 8733 Motor vehicle electrical equipment; testing equipment, electrical: automotive; research institute

(G-16884)
MICROGEN SYSTEMS INC
150 Lucius Gordon Dr # 117 (14586-9687)
PHONE...................................585 214-2426
Robert Andosca, *CEO*
Evan Grundman, *Electrical Engi*
Michael Perrotta, *CFO*
EMP: 8
SQ FT: 3,000
SALES (est): 627K **Privately Held**
SIC: 3676 Electronic resistors

West Henrietta - Monroe County (G-16885)

(G-16885)
MOFFETT TURF EQUIPMENT INC
33 Thruway Park Dr (14586-9795)
PHONE 585 334-0100
Fax: 585 334-6332
Thomas Houseknecht, *President*
Ben Mancuso, *Vice Pres*
Patty Nicosia, *Controller*
EMP: 35 EST: 2010
SQ FT: 45,000
SALES: 3MM **Privately Held**
SIC: 3523 Turf equipment, commercial

(G-16886)
ORAFOL AMERICAS INC
200 Park Centre Dr (14586-9674)
PHONE 585 272-0290
Fax: 585 272-0313
Bryan K Parks, *Branch Mgr*
Dave Jacob, *Manager*
EMP: 23
SALES (corp-wide): 573MM **Privately Held**
SIC: 3827 5048 Optical instruments & lenses; optometric equipment & supplies
HQ: Orafol Americas Inc.
   120 Darling Dr
   Avon CT 06001
   860 223-9297

(G-16887)
ORAFOL DISPLAY OPTICS INC (DH)
Also Called: Reflexite Display Optics
200 Park Centre Dr (14586-9674)
PHONE 585 647-1140
Fax: 585 254-4940
Bryan Parks, *President*
Chris Frank, *Engrg Mgr*
Phil Ferrari, *Treasurer*
Terry Edom, *Human Res Mgr*
▲ EMP: 41
SQ FT: 44,000
SALES (est): 57.3MM
SALES (corp-wide): 573MM **Privately Held**
WEB: www.display-optics.com
SIC: 3827 3229 Lenses, optical: all types except ophthalmic; pressed & blown glass
HQ: Orafol Americas Inc.
   120 Darling Dr
   Avon CT 06001
   860 223-9297

(G-16888)
OUTDOOR GROUP LLC
1325 John St (14586-9121)
PHONE 585 201-5358
EMP: 150 EST: 2012
SALES (est): 16.4MM **Privately Held**
SIC: 3949 Archery equipment, general

(G-16889)
OVITZ CORPORATION
150 Lucius Gordon Dr # 115 (14586-9687)
PHONE 585 474-4695
Joseph Rosenshein, *Principal*
Joung Yoon Kim, *Principal*
Walter Rusnak, *Principal*
EMP: 9
SQ FT: 1,000
SALES (est): 530K **Privately Held**
SIC: 3841 Diagnostic apparatus, medical

(G-16890)
PERFECT FORM MANUFACTURING LLC
1325 John St (14586-9121)
PHONE 585 500-5923
Marcia Koch, *General Mgr*
Greg Steil,
Dylan Bates,
Peter Crawford,
Matthew Kruger,
EMP: 5
SQ FT: 3,200
SALES (est): 52.5K **Privately Held**
SIC: 3949 Bows, archery

(G-16891)
PHARMADVA LLC
150 Lucius Gordon Dr # 209 (14586-9687)
PHONE 585 469-1410
Fax: 585 292-5787

Joshua Eddy, *Finance Mgr*
Jonathan Sacks, *Mng Member*
Duane Girdner,
EMP: 6
SQ FT: 6,400
SALES: 80K **Privately Held**
SIC: 3845 Electromedical equipment

(G-16892)
POLYSHOT CORPORATION
75 Lucius Gordon Dr (14586-9682)
PHONE 585 292-5010
Fax: 585 292-5015
Douglas C Hepler, *President*
Jason Burns, *Engineer*
Dave Porter,
▲ EMP: 20
SQ FT: 13,000
SALES (est): 4.8MM **Privately Held**
WEB: www.polyshot.com
SIC: 3442 Metal doors, sash & trim; molding, trim & stripping

(G-16893)
ROCHESTER PRECISION OPTICS LLC
Also Called: R P O
850 John St (14586-9748)
PHONE 585 292-5450
William Hurley, *CEO*
Robert Benson, *Engineer*
Rick Berg, *Engineer*
Bill Strong, *Engineer*
Brian Vogler, *Engineer*
◆ EMP: 190
SQ FT: 104,500
SALES (est): 51.4MM **Privately Held**
WEB: www.rpoptics.com
SIC: 3827 Lenses, optical: all types except ophthalmic; lens mounts; lens grinding equipment, except ophthalmic; optical elements & assemblies, except ophthalmic

(G-16894)
SEMANS ENTERPRISES INC
Also Called: New Cov Manufacturing
25 Hendrix Rd Ste E (14586-9205)
PHONE 585 444-0097
Fax: 585 328-4332
William A Semans II, *Ch of Bd*
Carol Maue- Semans, *Vice Pres*
EMP: 19
SQ FT: 10,000
SALES: 1.8MM **Privately Held**
SIC: 3449 Miscellaneous metalwork

(G-16895)
SIMPORE INC
150 Lucius Gordon Dr # 121 (14586-9687)
PHONE 585 748-5980
Richard D Richmond, *Ch of Bd*
Thomas Gaborski, *President*
Christopher Striemer, *Vice Pres*
James Roussie, *VP Opers*
Nick Cobb, *Sales Mgr*
EMP: 7
SQ FT: 400
SALES (est): 520K **Privately Held**
WEB: www.simpore.com
SIC: 3821 Laboratory equipment: fume hoods, distillation racks, etc.

(G-16896)
SWAGELOK WESTERN NY
10 Thruway Park Dr (14586-9702)
PHONE 585 359-8470
EMP: 5
SALES (est): 569.2K **Privately Held**
SIC: 3823 Mfg Process Control Instruments

(G-16897)
TELEDYNE OPTECH INC
150 Lucius Gordon Dr # 215 (14586-9687)
PHONE 585 427-8310
Maxime Elbaz, *President*
Michel Stanier, *Exec VP*
Paul Larocque, *Vice Pres*
Ed Sluys, *Vice Pres*
Deborah Harradine, *Info Tech Mgr*
EMP: 18
SALES (est): 2.9MM
SALES (corp-wide): 2.3B **Publicly Held**
SIC: 3699 3845 Laser systems & equipment; laser systems & equipment, medical

HQ: Teledyne Optech Incorporated
   300 Interchange Way
   Vaughan ON L4K 5
   905 660-0808

(G-16898)
VUZIX CORPORATION (PA)
25 Hendrix Rd Ste A (14586-9205)
PHONE 585 359-5900
Fax: 585 359-4172
Paul J Travers, *President*
Devrin Talen, *Electrical Engi*
Grant Russell, *CFO*
Brian Degus, *Info Tech Mgr*
EMP: 24 EST: 1997
SQ FT: 29,000
SALES: 2.7MM **Publicly Held**
WEB: www.icuiti.com
SIC: 3577 Computer peripheral equipment

(G-16899)
VWR EDUCATION LLC
Ward's Natural Science
5100 W Henrietta Rd (14586-9729)
PHONE 585 359-2502
Michael Harvey, *Maint Spvr*
Susan Bernholdt, *Human Res Dir*
Janice Gaub, *Marketing Staff*
Kathy Smith, *Programmer Anys*
Cindy Kent, *Executive*
EMP: 250
SALES (corp-wide): 4.3B **Publicly Held**
SIC: 2741 3821 5049 5192 Miscellaneous publishing; laboratory apparatus & furniture; scientific & engineering equipment & supplies; books, periodicals & newspapers
HQ: Vwr Education, Llc
   777 E Park Dr
   Tonawanda NY 14150
   800 242-2042

(G-16900)
WAVODYNE THERAPEUTICS INC
150 Lucius Gordon Dr (14586-9687)
PHONE 954 632-6630
James New, *CEO*
EMP: 2 EST: 2015
SQ FT: 200
SALES: 500MM **Privately Held**
SIC: 2834 Druggists' preparations (pharmaceuticals)

West Hurley
Ulster County

(G-16901)
ANATOLI INC
43 Basin Rd Ste 11 (12491-5201)
PHONE 845 334-9000
Fax: 845 334-9099
Kostas Michalopoulos, *President*
Joan Ramos, *Admin Sec*
EMP: 16
SQ FT: 4,300
SALES (est): 1.4MM **Privately Held**
SIC: 3911 3961 5094 Jewelry, precious metal; costume jewelry; jewelry

West Islip
Suffolk County

(G-16902)
ACT COMMUNICATIONS GROUP INC
170 Higbie Ln (11795-3238)
PHONE 631 669-2403
Fax: 631 669-7768
Richard Carpenter, *President*
Robert Carpenter, *Vice Pres*
Larry Boyd, *Manager*
Angie Carpenter, *Director*
EMP: 18
SQ FT: 1,000
SALES (est): 1.5MM **Privately Held**
WEB: www.actcommgroup.com
SIC: 2791 2752 7311 Typesetting; commercial printing, offset; advertising agencies

(G-16903)
ACTION BULLET RESISTANT
263 Union Blvd (11795-3007)
PHONE 631 422-0888
Leonard J Simonetti, *President*
Jeff Farinacci, *Project Mgr*
Brian Sweeney, *Controller*
Edward Simonetti, *Sales Mgr*
Trish Simonetti, *Manager*
EMP: 12
SQ FT: 14,000
SALES (est): 2.2MM **Privately Held**
WEB: www.actionbullet.co
SIC: 3442 Window & door frames

(G-16904)
DFCI SOLUTIONS INC (PA)
425 Union Blvd (11795-3183)
PHONE 631 669-0494
Michael Knight, *Ch of Bd*
Stephen Meshover, *President*
Olivia Marie, *Vice Pres*
Ken Schurmann, *Production*
Laure Giannizzero, *Buyer*
EMP: 47 EST: 1936
SQ FT: 37,100
SALES (est): 3.5MM **Privately Held**
WEB: www.dfcis.com
SIC: 3429 Metal fasteners

(G-16905)
JEM TOOL & DIE CORP
81 Paris Ct (11795-2815)
PHONE 631 539-8734
Fax: 516 249-8370
Roy Stevens, *President*
Bill Jimenez, *Vice Pres*
Sylvia Goodwin, *Bookkeeper*
EMP: 10 EST: 1961
SQ FT: 8,000
SALES (est): 1.2MM **Privately Held**
SIC: 3545 Machine tool attachments & accessories

(G-16906)
SECUREVUE INC
28 Trues Dr (11795-5139)
PHONE 631 587-5850
Donald Softness, *President*
EMP: 5
SQ FT: 1,000
SALES: 500K **Privately Held**
WEB: www.securevue.net
SIC: 3699 Security devices

(G-16907)
SPC MARKETING COMPANY
Also Called: Meat Industry Newsletter
191 Norma Ave (11795-1510)
P.O. Box 221, Brightwaters (11718-0221)
PHONE 631 661-2727
Stephen R Flanagan, *Owner*
EMP: 5
SQ FT: 1,200
SALES (est): 412.5K **Privately Held**
SIC: 2721 Periodicals: publishing only

(G-16908)
V A P TOOL & DYE
436 W 4th St (11795-2414)
PHONE 631 587-5262
Victor Pons, *Owner*
EMP: 7
SQ FT: 4,700
SALES (est): 400K **Privately Held**
SIC: 3599 Machine shop, jobbing & repair

West Monroe
Oswego County

(G-16909)
AMERITOOL MFG LLC
20 Milo Dr (13167-3264)
PHONE 315 668-2172
Gerald Beck, *Principal*
EMP: 5
SALES (est): 460.7K **Privately Held**
SIC: 3999 Manufacturing industries

▲ = Import ▼ = Export
◆ = Import/Export

GEOGRAPHIC SECTION

West Sand Lake - Rensselaer County (G-16932)

West Nyack
Rockland County

(G-16910)
AMP-LINE CORP
3 Amethyst Ct (10994-1142)
PHONE..................845 623-3288
Guosen Luo, *President*
EMP: 10
SALES (est): 1.3MM **Privately Held**
SIC: 3699 Pulse amplifiers

(G-16911)
ANGEL MEDIA AND PUBLISHING
Also Called: Rockland Review Publishing
26 Snake Hill Rd (10994-1625)
PHONE..................845 727-4949
Fax: 845 727-4944
Joseph Miele, *President*
Joseph Neile, *Publisher*
Arnold Heydt, *Vice Pres*
Mary Cortes, *Manager*
EMP: 6 EST: 1976
SALES (est): 404K **Privately Held**
WEB: www.rocklandreviewnews.com
SIC: 2711 Newspapers

(G-16912)
BEL-BEE PRODUCTS INCORPORATED
100 Snake Hill Rd Ste 1 (10994-1627)
PHONE..................845 353-0300
Vincent Belmont, *Ch of Bd*
Frank Lightfoot, *Safety Mgr*
Joanne Belmont, *Controller*
Herbert Giller, *Manager*
EMP: 15
SQ FT: 25,000
SALES (est): 3.4MM **Privately Held**
WEB: www.bel-bee.com
SIC: 3469 Metal stampings

(G-16913)
BILLY BEEZ USA LLC
1282 Palisades Center Dr (10994-6202)
PHONE..................845 915-4709
EMP: 19
SALES (corp-wide): 14.2MM **Privately Held**
SIC: 3949 5137 7999 Playground equipment; women's & children's dresses, suits, skirts & blouses; amusement ride
PA: Billy Beez Usa, Llc
3 W 35th St Fl 3
New York NY 10001
646 606-2249

(G-16914)
BYLADA FOODS LLC
250 W Nyack Rd Ste 110 (10994-1745)
PHONE..................845 623-1300
Meade Bradshaw, *Branch Mgr*
EMP: 53
SALES (corp-wide): 10.1MM **Privately Held**
SIC: 2099 Food preparations
PA: Bylada Foods Llc
140 W Commercial Ave
Moonachie NJ 07074
201 933-7474

(G-16915)
CROTON WATCH CO INC
250 W Nyack Rd Ste 114 (10994-1745)
PHONE..................800 443-7639
David Mermelstein, *Ch of Bd*
Avrami Mermelstein, *COO*
Lynn Friedman, *Controller*
Karene Lynen, *Cust Svc Dir*
▲ EMP: 26
SQ FT: 18,000
SALES (est): 4.8MM **Privately Held**
WEB: www.crotonwatch.com
SIC: 3873 Watches & parts, except crystals & jewels

(G-16916)
ELECTRONIC BUSINESS TECH
Also Called: Progressive Accounting
199 Van Houten Flds (10994-2531)
PHONE..................845 353-8549
Julian C Papp, *President*
Nick Feinberg,
EMP: 10
SQ FT: 3,000
SALES (est): 900K **Privately Held**
WEB: www.progressiveaccounting.com
SIC: 7372 Prepackaged software

(G-16917)
GANNETT STLLITE INFO NTWRK LLC
1 Crosfield Ave (10994-2222)
PHONE..................845 578-2300
Tony Davenport, *Branch Mgr*
EMP: 30
SALES (corp-wide): 5.7B **Publicly Held**
WEB: www.usatoday.com
SIC: 2711 2752 Newspapers: publishing only, not printed on site; commercial printing, lithographic
HQ: Gannett Satellite Information Network, Llc
7950 Jones Branch Dr
Mc Lean VA 22102
703 854-6000

(G-16918)
GENERAL BEARING CORPORATION (DH)
44 High St (10994-2702)
PHONE..................845 358-6000
Fax: 845 358-7414
David L Gussack, *CEO*
Thomas J Uhlig, *President*
Joseph Hoo, *Vice Pres*
Corby W Self, *Vice Pres*
David Passariello, *Plant Mgr*
▲ EMP: 120 EST: 1958
SQ FT: 190,000
SALES (est): 126.9MM
SALES (corp-wide): 8.7B **Privately Held**
WEB: www.generalbearing.com
SIC: 3562 Ball & roller bearings; ball bearings & parts; roller bearings & parts
HQ: Skf Usa Inc.
890 Forty Foot Rd
Lansdale PA 19446
267 436-6000

(G-16919)
INTERCOS AMERICA INC
11 Centerock Rd (10994-2214)
PHONE..................845 732-3900
EMP: 8
SALES (corp-wide): 41.1MM **Privately Held**
SIC: 2844 Cosmetic preparations
HQ: Intercos America, Inc.
200 N Route 303
Congers NY 10920
845 268-4400

(G-16920)
JOURNAL NEWS
200 N Route 303 (10994-1619)
PHONE..................845 578-2324
Fax: 845 578-2477
John Humenn, *Sales/Mktg Dir*
Minnie Stanley, *Human Res Mgr*
Suzan Clarke, *Relations*
EMP: 5
SALES (est): 293.3K **Privately Held**
SIC: 2711 Newspapers, publishing & printing

(G-16921)
MAINLY MONOGRAMS INC
Also Called: Mercury Apparel
260 W Nyack Rd Ste 1 (10994-1750)
PHONE..................845 624-4923
Dan Alexander Sr, *CEO*
Dan Alexander Jr, *CFO*
Zaharo Ula Alexander, *Treasurer*
Judy Creek, *Office Mgr*
EMP: 45
SQ FT: 19,000
SALES (est): 4.7MM **Privately Held**
SIC: 2395 7336 5611 5621 Embroidery products, except schiffli machine; silk screen design; clothing, sportswear, men's & boys'; women's sportswear; gifts & novelties

(G-16922)
NICE-PAK PRODUCTS INC
100 Brookhill Dr (10994-2133)
PHONE..................845 353-6090
Jennifer Thriston, *Manager*
EMP: 25
SALES (corp-wide): 440.6MM **Privately Held**
SIC: 2621 Towels, tissues & napkins: paper & stock; sanitary tissue paper
PA: Nice-Pak Products, Inc.
2 Nice Pak Park
Orangeburg NY 10962
845 365-2772

(G-16923)
PEARL RIVER PASTRIES LLC
Also Called: Pearl River Pastry Chocolates
389 W Nyack Rd (10994-1723)
PHONE..................845 735-5100
Steve Pierson, *VP Sales*
Renae Goyette, *Branch Mgr*
Joseph Koffman, *Mng Member*
John Slootmaker, *Manager*
Martin Koffman,
EMP: 50
SQ FT: 10,000
SALES: 7MM **Privately Held**
SIC: 2053 5441 Pastries (danish): frozen; candy, nut & confectionery stores

(G-16924)
PEARSON EDUCATION INC
59 Brookhill Dr (10994-2122)
PHONE..................201 236-7000
Michael Schuering, *Exec VP*
Cheryl Gayser, *Human Res Mgr*
EMP: 14
SALES (corp-wide): 7.7B **Privately Held**
WEB: www.phgenit.com
SIC: 2721 2731 Periodicals; book publishing
HQ: Pearson Education, Inc.
1 Lake St
Upper Saddle River NJ 07458
201 236-7000

(G-16925)
PLASTIC-CRAFT PRODUCTS CORP
744 W Nyack Rd (10994-1998)
P.O. Box K (10994-0713)
PHONE..................845 358-3010
Fax: 845 358-3007
Young Nguyen, *General Mgr*
Mark Brecher, *Chairman*
Nancy Brecher, *Treasurer*
EMP: 28 EST: 1939
SQ FT: 30,000
SALES (est): 7.4MM **Privately Held**
SIC: 3089 5162 Plastic processing; plastics materials & basic shapes

(G-16926)
SIMILARWEB INC
251 W Nyack Rd (10994-1724)
PHONE..................347 685-5422
Jason Schwartz, *CFO*
EMP: 18
SALES (est): 387.5K **Privately Held**
SIC: 7372 Prepackaged software

(G-16927)
STEVEN MADDEN LTD
1661 Palisades Center Dr (10994-6206)
PHONE..................845 348-7026
Steve Madden, *Branch Mgr*
EMP: 75
SALES (corp-wide): 1.4B **Publicly Held**
SIC: 3143 Men's footwear, except athletic
PA: Steven Madden, Ltd.
5216 Barnett Ave
Long Island City NY 11104
718 446-1800

(G-16928)
TILCON NEW YORK INC (DH)
Also Called: Totowa Asphalt
162 Old Mill Rd (10994-1406)
PHONE..................845 358-4500
Fax: 845 480-3128
Christopher J Madden, *Ch of Bd*
John Cooney Jr, *President*
Sean Osullivan, *Vice Pres*
Dan Batelli, *Transptn Dir*
Jeff Russell, *Plant Mgr*
▲ EMP: 270 EST: 1964
SALES (est): 294.1MM
SALES (corp-wide): 25.3B **Privately Held**
WEB: www.tilconny.com
SIC: 1429 Trap rock, crushed & broken-quarrying; dolomitic marble, crushed & broken-quarrying
HQ: Tilcon Inc.
301 Hartford Ave
Newington CT 06111
860 223-3651

(G-16929)
TILCON NEW YORK INC
1 Crusher Rd (10994-1601)
PHONE..................845 358-3100
Bernardo Culnes, *Branch Mgr*
EMP: 65
SALES (corp-wide): 25.3B **Privately Held**
WEB: www.tilconny.com
SIC: 1429 1442 1423 Trap rock, crushed & broken-quarrying; dolomitic marble, crushed & broken-quarrying; construction sand & gravel; crushed & broken granite
HQ: Tilcon New York Inc.
162 Old Mill Rd
West Nyack NY 10994
845 358-4500

West Point
Orange County

(G-16930)
PENN ENTERPRISES INC
845 Washington Rd (10996-1111)
PHONE..................845 446-0765
Joseph Fotovich, *Principal*
Russell Williams, *Project Mgr*
EMP: 13
SALES (corp-wide): 7.5MM **Privately Held**
WEB: www.pennenterprises.com
SIC: 3633 Household laundry equipment
PA: Penn Enterprises, Inc
5260 S Stonehaven Dr
Springfield MO 65809
417 379-5889

West Sand Lake
Rensselaer County

(G-16931)
BONDED CONCRETE INC
Rr 43 (12196)
PHONE..................518 674-2854
Tom Coemente, *President*
EMP: 10
SALES (corp-wide): 10.8MM **Privately Held**
WEB: www.bondedconcrete.com
SIC: 3273 Ready-mixed concrete
PA: Bonded Concrete, Inc.
303 Watervliet Shaker Rd
Watervliet NY 12189
518 273-5800

(G-16932)
TROY SAND & GRAVEL CO INC
Rr 43 (12196)
P.O. Box 489 (12196-0489)
PHONE..................518 674-2854
Fax: 518 674-3309
Jude Clemente, *President*
EMP: 15
SALES (corp-wide): 22.1MM **Privately Held**
SIC: 1442 5032 Construction sand & gravel; stone, crushed or broken
PA: Troy Sand & Gravel Co., Inc.
34 Grange Rd
West Sand Lake NY 12196
518 273-5800

West Sayville
Suffolk County

(G-16933)
ACCUCUT INC
120 Easy St (11796-1238)
PHONE.................631 567-2868
Dan Carbone, *CEO*
Joanne Caruso, *Administration*
EMP: 5
SALES: 370K **Privately Held**
SIC: 3441 Fabricated structural metal

(G-16934)
DOR-A-MAR CANVAS PRODUCTS CO
182 Cherry Ave (11796-1200)
PHONE.................631 750-9202
Fax: 631 750-9203
Thomas Degirolamo, *President*
Nancy Dolan, *Office Mgr*
Kenneth Degirolamo, *Manager*
EMP: 18 **EST:** 1959
SQ FT: 6,000
SALES: 1.5MM **Privately Held**
WEB: www.doramar.com
SIC: 2394 Canvas & related products

(G-16935)
FIRE ISLAND SEA CLAM CO INC
132 Atlantic Ave (11796-1904)
P.O. Box 2124, Montauk (11954-0905)
PHONE.................631 589-2199
Fax: 631 589-0515
John Kingston, *President*
Jean Kingston, *Admin Sec*
EMP: 3 **EST:** 1977
SQ FT: 3,500
SALES: 10MM **Privately Held**
WEB: www.fireislandassn.org
SIC: 2431 5812 Moldings, wood: unfinished & prefinished; seafood restaurants

(G-16936)
KUSSMAUL ELECTRONICS CO INC
170 Cherry Ave (11796-1200)
P.O. Box 147, Lynnfield MA (01940-0147)
PHONE.................631 218-0298
Fax: 631 244-9009
Thomas H Nugentul, *Ch of Bd*
Marilyn Kussmaul, *Vice Pres*
Ernest Kussmaul, *Engineer*
Phil Sgroi, *Engineer*
Louise Adler, *Accounting Mgr*
◆ **EMP:** 50
SQ FT: 30,000
SALES (est): 11.8MM **Privately Held**
WEB: www.maul.com
SIC: 3629 3625 Battery chargers, rectifying or nonrotating; control equipment, electric
PA: Mission Critical Electronics, Inc.
2200 Ross Ave Ste 4050
Dallas TX 75201

(G-16937)
PECK & HALE LLC
180 Division Ave (11796-1303)
PHONE.................631 589-2510
Fax: 631 589-2925
John Szeglin, *President*
Dan Becker, *General Mgr*
Jose Diaz-Bujan, *Opers Mgr*
Jose Diaz Bujan, *Opers Staff*
David Mazzara, *Purch Agent*
◆ **EMP:** 40 **EST:** 1946
SQ FT: 27,000
SALES (est): 10.2MM **Privately Held**
WEB: www.peckhale.com
SIC: 3743 3462 3496 Railroad equipment; iron & steel forgings; miscellaneous fabricated wire products

West Seneca
Erie County

(G-16938)
ABI PACKAGING INC
1703 Union Rd (14224-2060)
PHONE.................716 677-2900
Roger Severson, *CEO*
Barb Thurber, *Manager*
EMP: 20
SALES (est): 1.6MM **Privately Held**
SIC: 3086 Plastics foam products

(G-16939)
BIG DATA BIZVIZ LLC
1075 East And West Rd (14224-3669)
PHONE.................716 803-2367
Avin Jain, *CEO*
Rajesh Thanki, *CEO*
EMP: 2
SALES (est): 1.7MM **Privately Held**
SIC: 7372 Business oriented computer software

(G-16940)
BUFFALO HEARG & SPEECH
1026 Union Rd (14224-3445)
PHONE.................716 558-1105
Joe Cozzo, *CEO*
EMP: 45
SALES (corp-wide): 349.7K **Privately Held**
SIC: 3842 Hearing aids
PA: Buffalo Hearing And Speech Center Foundation, Inc.
50 E North St
Buffalo NY 14203
716 885-8318

(G-16941)
BUFFALO METAL FORMING INC
21 Creekview Dr (14224-2406)
PHONE.................716 856-4575
Fax: 716 856-4575
Al Fleischauer, *President*
EMP: 8
SQ FT: 13,500
SALES: 750K **Privately Held**
SIC: 3444 3441 Sheet metalwork; fabricated structural metal

(G-16942)
CONSUMERS BEVERAGES INC
1375 Union Rd (14224-2936)
PHONE.................716 675-4934
Fax: 716 675-4934
Tony Kiminski, *Manager*
Kevin Frankey, *Manager*
EMP: 8
SALES (corp-wide): 21.6MM **Privately Held**
WEB: www.consumerbeverages.com
SIC: 2086 Bottled & canned soft drinks
PA: Consumers Beverages, Inc.
2230 S Park Ave
Buffalo NY
716 826-9200

(G-16943)
EBENEZER RAILCAR SERVICES INC
1005 Indian Church Rd (14224-1305)
P.O. Box 363, Buffalo (14224-0363)
PHONE.................716 674-5650
Fax: 716 674-8703
Jeffrey F Schmarje, *President*
David P Egner, *Vice Pres*
Bob Wingels, *Vice Pres*
Robert Wingels, *Vice Pres*
Janet Jemiolo, *Accounts Mgr*
EMP: 50 **EST:** 1981
SQ FT: 30,000
SALES (est): 17.3MM
SALES (corp-wide): 39MM **Privately Held**
WEB: www.ersindustries.com
SIC: 3743 4789 Railroad equipment; railroad car repair
PA: Ers Industries, Inc.
1005 Indian Church Rd
West Seneca NY 14224
716 675-2040

(G-16944)
ELITE MEDICAL SUPPLY OF NY
1900 Ridge Rd (14224-3332)
PHONE.................716 712-0881
Fax: 716 712-0882
Elwira Kulawik, *Principal*
EMP: 6
SALES (est): 550K **Privately Held**
SIC: 3841 Medical instruments & equipment, blood & bone work

(G-16945)
FIVE STAR INDUSTRIES INC
114 Willowdale Dr (14224-3571)
PHONE.................716 674-2589
Fax: 716 897-5107
Greg Vastola, *President*
Joel Long, *Vice Pres*
EMP: 27
SQ FT: 10,000
SALES (est): 4.4MM **Privately Held**
SIC: 3444 3599 Sheet metalwork; machine shop, jobbing & repair

(G-16946)
GEMCOR AUTOMATION LLC
100 Gemcor Dr (14224-2055)
PHONE.................716 674-9300
Fax: 716 674-3171
William Mangus, *CEO*
Tony Goddard, *COO*
Michael Kwietniak, *Purch Mgr*
Gary Riehle, *Engineer*
Wayne Piacente, *CFO*
EMP: 87
SQ FT: 90,000
SALES (est): 28.3MM **Privately Held**
SIC: 3542 Spinning, spline rolling & winding machines

(G-16947)
GORDEN AUTOMOTIVE EQUIPMENT
60 N America Dr (14224-2225)
PHONE.................716 674-2700
Richard Deney, *President*
Thomas Gormley, *Exec VP*
Herman Deney, *Vice Pres*
Michael Russo, *Treasurer*
Joel Deney, *Manager*
EMP: 10
SALES (est): 978K **Privately Held**
SIC: 3599 Machine shop, jobbing & repair

(G-16948)
GRIFFIN AUTOMATION INC
240 Westminster Rd (14224-1930)
P.O. Box 183, Buffalo (14224-0183)
PHONE.................716 674-2300
Fax: 716 674-2309
Jerald Bidlack, *COO*
John Shephard, *COO*
John Shepphard, *Accounting Mgr*
Frederick McGee, *Human Res Dir*
EMP: 25
SQ FT: 40,000
SALES: 2.5MM **Privately Held**
WEB: www.griffinautomation.com
SIC: 3569 Assembly machines, non-metalworking

(G-16949)
INTERNATIONAL CONTROL PRODUCTS
Also Called: ICP
1700 Union Rd Ste 2 (14224-2052)
PHONE.................716 558-4400
Fax: 716 558-0118
Stephen Gill, *President*
Kevin Gill, *Vice Pres*
Tracey Pacanowski, *Admin Sec*
EMP: 10
SQ FT: 5,000
SALES: 1.6MM **Privately Held**
WEB: www.icproducts.net
SIC: 3621 Electric motor & generator auxiliary parts

(G-16950)
KATHERINE BLIZNIAK (PA)
525 Bullis Rd (14224-2511)
PHONE.................716 674-8545
Katherine Blizniak, *President*
EMP: 6

SALES (est): 619.1K **Privately Held**
SIC: 3732 5091 Boat building & repairing; boat accessories & parts

(G-16951)
KEMPER SYSTEM AMERICA INC (DH)
1200 N America Dr (14224-5303)
PHONE.................716 558-2971
Richard Doornink, *Managing Dir*
Jim Horsley, *Opers Mgr*
Christian Schaefer, *CFO*
Brett Steinberg, *Natl Sales Mgr*
Jeff Younger, *Accounts Exec*
▲ **EMP:** 25
SQ FT: 45,000
SALES (est): 10.7MM
SALES (corp-wide): 298MM **Privately Held**
WEB: www.kempersystem.net
SIC: 2899 Chemical preparations
HQ: Kemper System Gmbh & Co. Kg
Hollandische Str. 32-36
Vellmar 34246
561 829-50

(G-16952)
MAYER BROS APPLE PRODUCTS INC (PA)
3300 Transit Rd (14224-2525)
PHONE.................716 668-1787
John A Mayer, *Ch of Bd*
James Kalec, *Sales Mgr*
Samantha Burris, *Manager*
Garrett Mayer, *Manager*
Russell Wright, *Manager*
▲ **EMP:** 95 **EST:** 1852
SQ FT: 2,800
SALES (est): 28.4MM **Privately Held**
WEB: www.mayerbros.com
SIC: 2033 2086 5499 5963 Fruit juices: fresh; pasteurized & mineral waters, bottled & canned; juices, fruit or vegetable; bottled water delivery

(G-16953)
SE-MAR ELECTRIC CO INC
101 South Ave (14224-2090)
PHONE.................716 674-7404
Fax: 716 674-3878
Robert Haungs, *President*
John Simson, *Principal*
Nancy J Haungs, *Treasurer*
▲ **EMP:** 20
SQ FT: 30,000
SALES: 5.1MM **Privately Held**
SIC: 3613 5571 Control panels, electric; motorcycles

(G-16954)
SENECA WEST PRINTING INC
860 Center Rd (14224-2207)
PHONE.................716 675-8010
Fax: 716 675-4637
Charles Pohlman, *President*
Charles Pohlman Jr, *Vice Pres*
Karen Pohlman, *Office Mgr*
EMP: 6 **EST:** 1965
SQ FT: 4,000
SALES (est): 789.3K **Privately Held**
SIC: 2752 2759 Lithographing on metal; letterpress printing

(G-16955)
X-PRESS SIGNS INC
1780 Union Rd Ste 1 (14224-2026)
PHONE.................716 677-0880
Richard A Johnson Jr, *President*
Darin Spalti, *Vice Pres*
EMP: 6
SALES (est): 554.6K **Privately Held**
SIC: 3993 Signs & advertising specialties

(G-16956)
YOST NEON DISPLAYS INC
20 Ransier Dr (14224-2230)
PHONE.................716 674-6780
Michael Yost, *President*
Deborah Yost, *Vice Pres*
EMP: 5
SALES (est): 475.4K **Privately Held**
WEB: www.yostneon.com
SIC: 3993 1751 Neon signs; cabinet building & installation

GEOGRAPHIC SECTION

West Winfield
Herkimer County

(G-16957)
CHRISTIAN FABRICATION LLC
122 South St (13491-2827)
PHONE..................................315 822-0135
Jamie Christian, *Mng Member*
Jeffery Maine, *Officer*
EMP: 3
SQ FT: 1,296
SALES: 1.5MM **Privately Held**
SIC: 3441 7353 Fabricated structural metal; heavy construction equipment rental

(G-16958)
DANBURY CREEK INC
67 South St (13491-2822)
PHONE..................................315 822-5640
Shawn Wilcox, *CEO*
EMP: 6
SQ FT: 11,000
SALES (est): 540K **Privately Held**
WEB: www.danburycreek.com
SIC: 2431 Panel work, wood

(G-16959)
PRECISIONMATICS CO INC
Also Called: Helmer Avenue
1 Helmer Ave (13491)
P.O. Box 250 (13491-0250)
PHONE..................................315 822-6324
Fax: 315 822-6944
Laslo Pustay, *Ch of Bd*
Judy Williams, *QC Mgr*
John Pustay, *Treasurer*
Steven Pustay, *Admin Sec*
EMP: 50
SQ FT: 22,000
SALES (est): 9.3MM **Privately Held**
WEB: www.precisionmatics.com
SIC: 3599 Machine shop, jobbing & repair

Westbury
Nassau County

(G-16960)
ACCURATE WELDING SERVICE INC
Also Called: Accurate Welding Svce
615 Main St (11590-4903)
PHONE..................................516 333-1730
Fax: 516 333-1773
Joseph Titone, *President*
Charles Titone Jr, *Vice Pres*
EMP: 5
SQ FT: 5,800
SALES: 300K **Privately Held**
SIC: 3599 7692 3446 Machine shop, jobbing & repair; welding repair; architectural metalwork

(G-16961)
ADVANCED FROZEN FOODS INC
28 Urban Ave (11590-4822)
P.O. Box 887 (11590-0887)
PHONE..................................516 333-6344
Roy Tuccillo, *President*
▲ **EMP:** 50
SALES (est): 9.3MM **Privately Held**
SIC: 2015 Poultry slaughtering & processing

(G-16962)
ADVANCED SURFACE FINISHING
111 Magnolia Ave (11590-4719)
PHONE..................................516 876-9710
Fax: 516 334-6039
Peter Tobias, *President*
Barbara Maini, *Office Mgr*
EMP: 25
SQ FT: 15,000
SALES: 1.8MM **Privately Held**
WEB: www.advancedsurfacefinishing.com
SIC: 3479 Painting, coating & hot dipping

(G-16963)
AIRNET COMMUNICATIONS CORP
Also Called: Airnet North Division
609 Cantiague Rock Rd # 5 (11590-1721)
PHONE..................................516 338-0008
Louis Pryce, *Manager*
EMP: 15
SALES (corp-wide): 39.6MM **Privately Held**
WEB: www.airnetcom.com
SIC: 3663 Radio & TV communications equipment
HQ: Airnet Communications Corporation
295 North Dr Ste G
Melbourne FL 32934
321 984-1990

(G-16964)
ALEXIS & GIANNI RETAIL INC
Also Called: L I Fur Factory & Salon
405 Union Ave (11590-3232)
PHONE..................................516 334-3877
Frank Stiller, *President*
Alexis Petras, *Vice Pres*
EMP: 11
SQ FT: 8,000
SALES (est): 857.8K **Privately Held**
SIC: 2371 7219 5632 Fur goods; fur garment cleaning, repairing & storage; furriers

(G-16965)
ALL TYPE SCREW MACHINE PDTS
Also Called: Skelton Screw Products Co
100 New York Ave (11590-4909)
PHONE..................................516 334-5100
Fax: 516 997-6732
Eileen Sinn, *President*
EMP: 6
SQ FT: 5,000
SALES: 300K **Privately Held**
SIC: 3451 Screw machine products

(G-16966)
AMERICAN LINEAR MANUFACTURERS (PA)
629 Main St (11590-4923)
PHONE..................................516 333-1351
Frank Tabone, *President*
EMP: 10
SQ FT: 2,000
SALES: 4.3MM **Privately Held**
SIC: 3545 3599 Machine tool accessories; custom machinery

(G-16967)
AMERICAN OFFICE SUPPLY INC
400 Post Ave Ste 105 (11590-2226)
PHONE..................................516 294-9444
Fax: 516 248-3585
Joseph Caldwell, *President*
Jospeh Caldwell, *President*
Jeff Moore, *Manager*
EMP: 11
SALES (est): 1.5MM **Privately Held**
WEB: www.aoslink.com
SIC: 2759 5943 Commercial printing; stationery stores

(G-16968)
AN EXCELSIOR ELEVATOR CORP
640 Main St Unit 2 (11590-4937)
PHONE..................................516 408-3070
Fax: 516 479-1800
Eric Petzold, *CEO*
Nancy Snyder, *Manager*
EMP: 16
SALES (est): 3.4MM **Privately Held**
SIC: 3534 5084 7699 Elevators & equipment; elevators; elevators: inspection, service & repair

(G-16969)
ARKWIN INDUSTRIES INC (HQ)
686 Main St (11590-5093)
PHONE..................................516 333-2640
Fax: 516 333-4187
William Maglio, *Ch of Bd*
Daniel Berlin, *President*
Laurie Pickering, *General Mgr*
Richard Vonsalzen, *General Mgr*
Frank Robilotto, *Chairman*
EMP: 276 **EST:** 1951
SQ FT: 110,000
SALES (est): 70.3MM
SALES (corp-wide): 2.7B **Publicly Held**
WEB: www.arkwin.com
SIC: 3728 Aircraft parts & equipment
PA: Transdigm Group Incorporated
1301 E 9th St Ste 3000
Cleveland OH 44114
216 706-2960

(G-16970)
ATLAS GRAPHICS INC
567 Main St (11590-4811)
PHONE..................................516 997-5527
Fax: 516 408-3000
Joy Newell, *President*
EMP: 5 **EST:** 1947
SQ FT: 3,000
SALES: 300K **Privately Held**
WEB: www.atlasgraphics.com
SIC: 2796 Photoengraving plates, linecuts or halftones

(G-16971)
AVANEL INDUSTRIES INC
121 Hopper St (11590-4803)
PHONE..................................516 333-0990
Fax: 516 334-2666
Ingo Kurth, *President*
Chris Kurth, *Vice Pres*
EMP: 12
SQ FT: 8,500
SALES: 1.5MM **Privately Held**
WEB: www.avanelindustries.com
SIC: 3825 5049 Test equipment for electronic & electric measurement; scientific & engineering equipment & supplies

(G-16972)
CAB-NETWORK INC
Also Called: Four Quarter
1500 Shames Dr Unit B (11590-1772)
PHONE..................................516 334-8666
Fax: 516 334-8988
Martin Chin, *President*
Patrick Chin, *Treasurer*
EMP: 6
SQ FT: 11,000
SALES: 975K **Privately Held**
SIC: 2511 Kitchen & dining room furniture

(G-16973)
CARTER PRECISION METALS LLC
99 Urban Ave (11590-4800)
PHONE..................................516 333-1917
Frank Carter, *Managing Dir*
EMP: 9
SALES (est): 544.5K **Privately Held**
WEB: www.emtmfg.com
SIC: 3599 3365 Machine & other job shop work; aluminum foundries

(G-16974)
CENTRAL ISLAND JUICE CORP
128 Magnolia Ave (11590-4720)
P.O. Box 498, West Hempstead (11552-0498)
PHONE..................................516 338-8301
Jules Saunder, *President*
Robert Ciolino, *Vice Pres*
Nancy Decrescenzo, *Manager*
EMP: 10
SQ FT: 21,000
SALES (est): 1.4MM **Privately Held**
SIC: 2033 Fruit juices: fresh

(G-16975)
COMPUTER INSTRUMENTS CORP
963a Brush Hollow Rd (11590-1710)
PHONE..................................516 876-8400
Fax: 516 876-9153
Elsa Markovits Wilen, *President*
Don Wilen, *Vice Pres*
EMP: 40 **EST:** 1950
SQ FT: 20,000
SALES (est): 6.2MM **Privately Held**
WEB: www.computerinstruments.com
SIC: 3812 3823 3824 3829 Search & navigation equipment; industrial flow & liquid measuring instruments; fluid meters & counting devices; integrating & totalizing meters for gas & liquids; measuring & controlling devices; aircraft & motor vehicle measurement equipment

(G-16976)
DEPENDABLE ACME THREADED PDTS
167 School St (11590-3371)
PHONE..................................516 338-4700
Fax: 516 997-5464
Annette Farragher, *President*
Magdalene Vogric, *Corp Secy*
EMP: 6 **EST:** 1958
SQ FT: 3,000
SALES: 500K **Privately Held**
WEB: www.dependableacme.com
SIC: 3452 Nuts, metal

(G-16977)
DIONICS-USA INC
96b Urban Ave (11590-4823)
PHONE..................................516 997-7474
Bernard Kravitz, *President*
Kenneth Davis, *Director*
EMP: 7
SALES (est): 1MM **Privately Held**
SIC: 3674 Semiconductors & related devices; integrated circuits; semiconductor networks, etc.; hybrid integrated circuits; photovoltaic devices, solid state

(G-16978)
DONMAR PRINTING CO
363 Union Ave (11590-3231)
PHONE..................................516 280-2239
Sanford Scharf, *President*
EMP: 10
SALES: 251.8K **Privately Held**
SIC: 2752 Commercial printing, lithographic

(G-16979)
E B B GRAPHICS INC
Also Called: Sir Speedy
75 State St (11590-5004)
PHONE..................................516 750-5510
Jack Bloom, *President*
James Cirillo, *General Mgr*
Brandon Bloom, *Principal*
Adrienne Bloom, *Vice Pres*
EMP: 10
SQ FT: 1,000
SALES (est): 1.3MM **Privately Held**
WEB: www.sirspeedyny.net
SIC: 2791 2789 2752 Typesetting; bookbinding & related work; commercial printing, lithographic; commercial printing, offset

(G-16980)
EAST HILLS INSTRUMENT INC
60 Shames Dr Unit B (11590-1767)
PHONE..................................516 621-8686
Cary Ratner, *CEO*
Rosemarie Larose, *Bookkeeper*
Corey Goldstein, *Accounts Exec*
EMP: 19
SQ FT: 10,000
SALES (est): 3.8MM **Privately Held**
SIC: 3821 3823 3824 3825 Laboratory measuring apparatus; industrial instrmnts msrmnt display/control process variable; fluid meters & counting devices; instruments to measure electricity; analytical instruments; measuring & controlling devices

(G-16981)
EI ELECTRONICS INC
Also Called: Electro Industries
1800 Shames Dr (11590-1730)
PHONE..................................516 334-0870
Fax: 516 338-4741
Erran Kagan, *Ch of Bd*
Gangaram Kubal, *Buyer*
James Kearney, *Design Engr*
Sean Bell, *Regl Sales Mgr*
Andrew Werner, *Software Engr*
EMP: 10

Westbury - Nassau County (G-16982)

SALES (est): 1.6MM **Privately Held**
SIC: 3825 Meters: electric, pocket, portable, panelboard, etc.

(G-16982)
EMITLED INC
Also Called: Led Next
2300 Shames Dr (11590-1748)
PHONE................516 531-3533
Asi Levy, *President*
EMP: 5
SALES (est): 530K **Privately Held**
SIC: 3641 Electric light bulbs, complete

(G-16983)
EXECUTIVE BUSINESS MEDIA INC
Also Called: EBM
825 Old Country Rd (11590-5589)
PHONE................516 334-3030
Fax: 516 334-3059
Murray Greenwald, *President*
Helen Scheller, *Chairman*
Fred Schane, *Vice Pres*
Katherine Youssis, *Accountant*
Dick Moran, *Sales Mgr*
EMP: 50
SQ FT: 4,100
SALES (est): 32.1MM **Privately Held**
WEB: www.ebmpubs.com
SIC: 2721 Magazines: publishing only, not printed on site

(G-16984)
FABRIC QUILTERS UNLIMITED INC
1400 Shames Dr (11590-1780)
PHONE................516 333-2866
Fax: 516 333-4016
John Brunning, *President*
Karen Brunning, *Marketing Staff*
EMP: 25 EST: 1959
SQ FT: 7,500
SALES: 1.7MM **Privately Held**
SIC: 2392 2391 2591 Bedspreads & bed sets: made from purchased materials; comforters & quilts: made from purchased materials; draperies, plastic & textile: from purchased materials; window blinds; window shades

(G-16985)
FEINSTEIN IRON WORKS INC
990 Brush Hollow Rd (11590-1783)
PHONE................516 997-8300
Fax: 718 335-3243
Daniel Feinstein, *CEO*
Howard Feinstein, *President*
Murray Gold, *Vice Pres*
EMP: 32 EST: 1931
SQ FT: 45,000
SALES (est): 8.5MM **Privately Held**
WEB: www.feinsteinironworks.com
SIC: 3441 Fabricated structural metal

(G-16986)
FOUR K MACHINE SHOP INC
54 Brooklyn Ave (11590-4902)
PHONE................516 997-0752
Fax: 516 997-2547
Aaron Feder, *President*
Steven Braverman, *Corp Secy*
Joe Roysman, *Vice Pres*
EMP: 6
SQ FT: 5,000
SALES (est): 700K **Privately Held**
SIC: 3599 Machine shop, jobbing & repair

(G-16987)
G & G C MACHINE & TOOL CO INC
18 Sylvester St (11590-4911)
PHONE................516 873-0999
Fax: 516 873-0986
George Christoforou, *President*
Georgia Christoforou, *Vice Pres*
Anthony Marino, *Manager*
EMP: 7
SQ FT: 8,200
SALES (est): 1MM **Privately Held**
SIC: 3599 Machine & other job shop work

(G-16988)
G A RICHARDS & CO INC
18 Sylvester St (11590-4791)
PHONE................516 334-5412
Fax: 516 334-6730
Benjamin Jankowski, *President*
Edward Kaider, *Vice Pres*
Paul Meeter, *Buyer*
Christeena Taylor, *QC Mgr*
Tony Miliusis, *Engineer*
EMP: 12
SQ FT: 5,500
SALES (est): 1.4MM **Privately Held**
SIC: 3469 Machine parts, stamped or pressed metal

(G-16989)
G FRIED CARPERT SERVICE
Also Called: G Fried Carpet and Design Ctr
800 Old Country Rd (11590-5419)
PHONE................516 333-3900
Wendy Fried, *President*
Phillip Ferrall, *Vice Pres*
EMP: 20
SALES (est): 1.4MM **Privately Held**
SIC: 2392 Linings, carpet: textile, except felt

(G-16990)
GARY ROTH & ASSOCIATES LTD
1400 Old Country Rd # 305 (11590-5119)
PHONE................516 333-1000
Gary Roth, *Partner*
EMP: 30
SALES (est): 4MM **Privately Held**
SIC: 3578 8742 Billing machines; management consulting services

(G-16991)
GENERAL CRYOGENIC TECH LLC
400 Shames Dr (11590-1753)
PHONE................516 334-8200
J Hanny Ruddy,
Ralph Cohan,
Peter Dahal,
EMP: 10
SALES: 1.4MM **Privately Held**
SIC: 3559 Cryogenic machinery, industrial

(G-16992)
H FREUND WOODWORKING CO INC
589 Main St (11590-4900)
PHONE................516 334-3774
Fax: 516 334-2179
Frank Freund, *President*
Hubert Freund Jr, *Vice Pres*
EMP: 15 EST: 1962
SQ FT: 13,000
SALES: 1.2MM **Privately Held**
SIC: 2521 Wood office furniture

(G-16993)
HALCYON BUSINESS PUBLICATIONS
Also Called: Area Development Magazine
400 Post Ave Ste 304 (11590-2226)
PHONE................516 338-0900
Fax: 516 338-0100
Dennis Shea, *President*
Dennis J Shea, *President*
Richard Bodo, *Vice Pres*
Jacqueline Mauro, *Controller*
Laura McCool, *Finance Dir*
EMP: 16
SQ FT: 3,700
SALES (est): 2.4MM **Privately Held**
WEB: www.locationusa.com
SIC: 2721 Magazines: publishing only, not printed on site

(G-16994)
HARPER PRODUCTS LTD
Also Called: Pencoa
117 State St (11590-5022)
P.O. Box 692 (11590-0692)
PHONE................516 997-2330
Fax: 516 333-3947
Robert Perlmutter, *CEO*
Rick Perlmutter, *President*
Karen Miller, *Vice Pres*
Helen Perlmutter, *Vice Pres*
Larry Sitten, *Vice Pres*
▲ EMP: 106
SQ FT: 30,000
SALES (est): 14.9MM **Privately Held**
SIC: 3951 Mfg Pens/Mechanical Pencils

(G-16995)
IMPERIAL INSTRUMENT CORP
Also Called: Imperial Instrmnt & Mach
18 Sylvester St (11590-4911)
PHONE................516 739-6644
Andre Cassata, *President*
EMP: 7 EST: 1956
SQ FT: 5,000
SALES (est): 400K **Privately Held**
SIC: 3599 Machine shop, jobbing & repair

(G-16996)
IMPRESS GRAPHIC TECHNOLOGIES
141 Linden Ave (11590-3227)
P.O. Box 13187, Hauppauge (11788-0577)
PHONE................516 781-0845
Darlene Bifone, *President*
John P Bifone, *Vice Pres*
▲ EMP: 12
SQ FT: 7,500
SALES (est): 1.4MM **Privately Held**
SIC: 2759 Commercial printing

(G-16997)
J B TOOL & DIE CO INC
629 Main St (11590-4923)
PHONE................516 333-1480
Fax: 516 333-1729
Frank Tabone, *President*
Joseph Tabone, *Vice Pres*
EMP: 28 EST: 1946
SQ FT: 14,000
SALES: 2MM **Privately Held**
WEB: www.jbtool-die.com
SIC: 3599 3544 Machine shop, jobbing & repair; special dies, tools, jigs & fixtures

(G-16998)
JOHN HASSALL LLC (HQ)
609 Cantiague Rock Rd # 1 (11590-1721)
PHONE................516 334-6200
Fax: 516 222-1911
Monty Gillespie, *President*
Bernie McAteer, *Prdtn Mgr*
Gina Hicks, *Purch Agent*
Danielle Martin, *Purch Agent*
Philip Bilello, *VP Finance*
EMP: 83
SQ FT: 65,000
SALES (est): 18MM
SALES (corp-wide): 109.4MM **Privately Held**
SIC: 3452 3399 Rivets, metal; metal fasteners
PA: Novaria Group, L.L.C.
6300 Ridglea Pl Ste 800
Fort Worth TX 76116
817 381-3810

(G-16999)
JOHN HASSALL LLC
Also Called: Sky Aerospace Products
609 Cantiague Rock Rd # 1 (11590-1721)
PHONE................323 869-0150
Monty Gillespie, *President*
Jack Wilson, *VP Opers*
Song Kim, *Engineer*
Michelle Allen, *Controller*
Lorraine Faber, *Human Res Mgr*
▼ EMP: 75
SQ FT: 17,000
SALES: 4.8MM
SALES (corp-wide): 109.4MM **Privately Held**
WEB: www.skymfg.net
SIC: 3452 Bolts, nuts, rivets & washers
HQ: John Hassall, Llc
609 Cantiague Rock Rd # 1
Westbury NY 11590
516 334-6200

(G-17000)
JUDITH LEWIS PRINTER INC
1915 Ladenburg Dr (11590-5917)
PHONE................516 997-7777
Judith Lewis, *President*
EMP: 6
SQ FT: 2,000
SALES (est): 460K **Privately Held**
SIC: 2752 2759 Commercial printing, offset; letterpress printing

(G-17001)
KAS DIRECT LLC
Also Called: Babyganics
1600 Stewart Ave Ste 411 (11590-6654)
PHONE................516 934-0541
Kevin Schwartz, *CEO*
Mark Ellis, *CFO*
EMP: 50 EST: 2008
SQ FT: 15,000
SALES (est): 15.6MM
SALES (corp-wide): 4.3B **Privately Held**
SIC: 2676 Infant & baby paper products
PA: S. C. Johnson & Son, Inc.
1525 Howe St
Racine WI 53403
262 260-2000

(G-17002)
KEMP METAL PRODUCTS INC
2300 Shames Dr (11590-1748)
PHONE................516 997-8860
Fax: 516 334-7188
Mark Raskin, *President*
Richard Raskin, *Corp Secy*
Scott Raskin, *Vice Pres*
EMP: 30
SQ FT: 10,000
SALES (est): 9.6MM **Privately Held**
WEB: www.kempmetalproducts.com
SIC: 3915 Jewelry parts, unassembled

(G-17003)
KENWIN SALES CORP
Also Called: Levitt Industrial Textile
1100 Shames Dr (11590-1765)
P.O. Box 7150, Hicksville (11802-7150)
PHONE................516 933-7553
Beth Foley, *CEO*
Andrew Kanter, *President*
EMP: 8
SQ FT: 2,000
SALES (est): 1MM **Privately Held**
WEB: www.levitttextiles.com
SIC: 3965 Fasteners

(G-17004)
KPP LTD
Also Called: Admor Blinds & Window Fashion
81 Urban Ave (11590-4821)
PHONE................516 338-5201
Fax: 516 338-4256
Michael Parker, *President*
Dan Kossman, *Vice Pres*
Rita Parker, *Treasurer*
EMP: 7
SQ FT: 1,700
SALES (est): 650K **Privately Held**
WEB: www.admorblinds.com
SIC: 2591 7641 Blinds vertical; reupholstery & furniture repair

(G-17005)
LIBERTY BRASS TURNING CO INC
1200 Shames Dr Unit C (11590-1766)
PHONE................718 784-2911
Fax: 718 784-2038
David Zuckerwise, *CEO*
Peter Zuckerwise, *President*
Marshall Johnson, *Safety Mgr*
Barry Bogel, *CFO*
Erica Iwanowski, *Info Tech Mgr*
EMP: 45 EST: 1919
SQ FT: 20,000
SALES (est): 12.9MM **Privately Held**
WEB: www.libertybrass.com
SIC: 3451 3429 3432 Screw machine products; manufactured hardware (general); plumbing fixture fittings & trim

(G-17006)
LONG ISLAND COMPOST CORP
100 Urban Ave (11590-4823)
PHONE................516 334-6600
Fax: 516 289-1077
Charles Vigliotti, *CEO*
Ed Warner, *Plant Mgr*
Arnold Vigliotti, *Shareholder*
Dominic Vigliotti, *Shareholder*
EMP: 120
SALES (est): 30MM **Privately Held**
WEB: www.licompost.com
SIC: 2875 Compost

▲ = Import ▼ = Export
◆ = Import/Export

GEOGRAPHIC SECTION
Westbury - Nassau County (G-17033)

(G-17007)
LOTUS APPAREL DESIGNS INC
661 Oakwood Ct (11590-5926)
PHONE..................................646 236-9363
Fang Mercedes, *President*
Rey Mercedez, *Owner*
EMP: 2
SALES: 1.3MM **Privately Held**
SIC: 2339 7389 Service apparel, washable: women's;

(G-17008)
LOVE UNLIMITED NY INC
762 Summa Ave (11590-5011)
PHONE..................................718 359-8500
Tom Terrino, *CEO*
Allison Bizinsky, *Manager*
EMP: 45
SQ FT: 25,000
SALES (est): 7.7MM **Privately Held**
WEB: www.mbslove.com
SIC: 2759 2752 Decals: printing; commercial printing, lithographic

(G-17009)
MATCH EYEWEAR LLC
1600 Shames Dr (11590-1761)
PHONE..................................516 877-0170
Fax: 516 877-0160
Shawn Chesanek, *Regl Sales Mgr*
Jonathan Pratt,
Ethan Goodman,
▲ EMP: 35
SQ FT: 17,000
SALES (est): 4.2MM **Privately Held**
WEB: www.floateyewear.com
SIC: 3229 3827 5995 Optical glass; optical instruments & lenses; optical goods stores

(G-17010)
MATERIAL MEASURING CORPORATION
121 Hopper St (11590-4803)
PHONE..................................516 334-6167
Fax: 516 334-2667
Ingo O Kurth, *President*
EMP: 5 EST: 1977
SALES: 340K **Privately Held**
SIC: 3821 Laboratory equipment: fume hoods, distillation racks, etc.

(G-17011)
METPAR CORP
95 State St (11590-5006)
P.O. Box 1873 (11590-9065)
PHONE..................................516 333-2600
Fax: 516 333-2618
Ronald S Mondolino, *President*
Jimmy Fallarino, *Mfg Mgr*
Vincent Salierno, *Site Mgr*
Howard Young, *Purch Mgr*
Dave Vera, *Purchasing*
▲ EMP: 80 EST: 1952
SQ FT: 65,000
SALES (est): 25.4MM **Privately Held**
WEB: www.metpar.com
SIC: 3431 3088 Metal sanitary ware; toilet fixtures, plastic

(G-17012)
MILLER & WEBER INC
507 Davie St (11590-5955)
PHONE..................................718 821-7110
Fax: 718 821-1673
Deanne Miller, *President*
▲ EMP: 22 EST: 1941
SQ FT: 5,000
SALES (est): 3.5MM **Privately Held**
WEB: www.millerweber.com
SIC: 3829 8734 3823 Measuring & controlling devices; thermometers, liquid-in-glass & bimetal type; hydrometers, except industrial process type; testing laboratories; industrial instrmnts msrmnt display/control process variable

(G-17013)
MONTERO INTERNATIONAL INC
Also Called: Pardazzio Uomo
149 Sullivan Ln Unit 1 (11590-3387)
PHONE..................................212 695-1787
Raymond Hagigi, *President*
▲ EMP: 6
SQ FT: 7,500

SALES (est): 682.1K **Privately Held**
SIC: 2329 2325 Shirt & slack suits: men's, youths' & boys'; men's & boys' dress slacks & shorts

(G-17014)
NEW YORK READY MIX INC
Also Called: Commercial Concrete
120 Rushmore St (11590-4816)
PHONE..................................516 338-6969
Rick Cerrone, *President*
Ron Notaroantonio, *Vice Pres*
EMP: 5
SQ FT: 4,000
SALES (est): 615.7K **Privately Held**
SIC: 3271 Blocks, concrete or cinder: standard

(G-17015)
P & L DEVELOPMENT LLC
200 Hicks St (11590-3323)
PHONE..................................516 986-1700
Mitchell Singer, *Branch Mgr*
EMP: 88
SALES (corp-wide): 272.5MM **Privately Held**
SIC: 2834 Pharmaceutical preparations
PA: P & L Development, Llc
 200 Hicks St
 Westbury NY 11590
 516 986-1700

(G-17016)
P & L DEVELOPMENT LLC
Also Called: Pl Developments New York
275 Grand Blvd Unit 1 (11590-3570)
PHONE..................................516 986-1700
EMP: 88
SALES (corp-wide): 275.9MM **Privately Held**
SIC: 2834 Pharmaceutical preparations
PA: P & L Development, Llc
 200 Hicks St
 Westbury NY 11590
 516 986-1700

(G-17017)
P & L DEVELOPMENT LLC (PA)
Also Called: Pl Developments
200 Hicks St (11590-3323)
PHONE..................................516 986-1700
Mitchell Singer, *Ch of Bd*
Evan Singer, *President*
Tom Crowe, *COO*
John Francis, *Senior VP*
Dana S Toops, *Senior VP*
EMP: 58
SALES (est): 275.9MM **Privately Held**
WEB: www.pldevelopments.com
SIC: 2834 Pharmaceutical preparations

(G-17018)
PARFUSE CORP
62 Kinkel St (11590-4915)
PHONE..................................516 997-1795
Fax: 516 997-5047
Angelina J Paris, *President*
Amy Kuna, *Corp Secy*
Donald A Paris, *Vice Pres*
EMP: 35
SQ FT: 10,000
SALES (est): 3.9MM **Privately Held**
SIC: 7692 3398 3341 Brazing; metal heat treating; secondary nonferrous metals

(G-17019)
PNI CAPITAL PARTNERS
1400 Old Country Rd # 103 (11590-5119)
PHONE..................................516 466-7120
Michael Packman, *Ch of Bd*
EMP: 7
SALES (est): 698.6K **Privately Held**
SIC: 3452 Pins

(G-17020)
POWER SCRUB IT INC
Also Called: Alltec Products
75 Urban Ave (11590-4829)
PHONE..................................516 997-2500
Louis Mangione, *President*
Joseph Berdis, *Manager*
EMP: 13
SALES (est): 1.8MM **Privately Held**
SIC: 3589 High pressure cleaning equipment

(G-17021)
PRECISION MECHANISMS CORP
50 Bond St (11590-5002)
PHONE..................................516 333-5955
Fax: 516 333-5956
Daniel Z Petrasek, *President*
Emilia Petrasek, *Vice Pres*
David Jones, *Manager*
Bob Lacock, *Manager*
Steve Newbould, *Manager*
EMP: 30 EST: 1957
SQ FT: 5,000
SALES (est): 6.3MM **Privately Held**
WEB: www.precisionmechanisms.com
SIC: 3566 3625 3593 3545 Speed changers, drives & gears; relays & industrial controls; fluid power cylinders & actuators; machine tool accessories

(G-17022)
PRINCE OF THE SEA LTD
28 Urban Ave (11590-4822)
P.O. Box 887 (11590-0887)
PHONE..................................516 333-6344
Roy Tuccillo, *President*
EMP: 33
SQ FT: 11,000
SALES (est): 2.9MM **Privately Held**
SIC: 2092 Fish, fresh: prepared; fish, frozen: prepared

(G-17023)
PROCOMPONENTS INC (PA)
Also Called: P C I Manufacturing Div
900 Merchants Concourse (11590-5142)
PHONE..................................516 683-0909
Fax: 516 683-1919
Barry Reed Lubman, *President*
Alan Lubman, *Corp Secy*
Mitchel Laurence, *Vice Pres*
Mitchel Lubman, *Vice Pres*
EMP: 25
SALES (est): 3.6MM **Privately Held**
SIC: 3672 3674 8711 Printed circuit boards; semiconductors & related devices; consulting engineer

(G-17024)
R C HENDERSON STAIR BUILDERS
100 Summa Ave (11590-5000)
PHONE..................................516 876-9898
Fax: 516 876-9899
Richard Henderson, *President*
Jason Henderson, *Vice Pres*
Julie Henderson, *Treasurer*
EMP: 10
SQ FT: 8,000
SALES: 1MM **Privately Held**
SIC: 2431 Staircases, stairs & railings; stair railings, wood

(G-17025)
S & B MACHINE WORKS INC
111 New York Ave (11590-4924)
PHONE..................................516 997-2666
Eileen Sinn, *CEO*
Frederick Sinn Jr, *President*
Doris Reeder, *Manager*
EMP: 23
SQ FT: 10,000
SALES (est): 4.7MM **Privately Held**
WEB: www.sbmachineworks.com
SIC: 3444 3599 Sheet metalwork; machine shop, jobbing & repair

(G-17026)
SENTINEL PRINTING INC
Also Called: Sir Speedy
75 State St (11590-5004)
PHONE..................................516 334-7400
Fax: 516 921-5070
Steve Ross, *President*
EMP: 5
SQ FT: 2,200
SALES (est): 500K **Privately Held**
SIC: 2759 2791 2789 2752 Envelopes: printing; stationery: printing; business forms: printing; typesetting; bookbinding & related work; commercial printing, lithographic

(G-17027)
SPECTRONICS CORPORATION
956 Brush Hollow Rd (11590-1714)
PHONE..................................516 333-4840

Fax: 516 333-4859
William B Cooper, *Ch of Bd*
Jonathan D Cooper, *President*
Limin Chen, *Vice Pres*
Richard Cooper, *Vice Pres*
John Duerr, *Vice Pres*
▲ EMP: 190 EST: 1950
SQ FT: 98,000
SALES (est): 60.2MM **Privately Held**
WEB: www.spectroline.com
SIC: 3646 3544 Fluorescent lighting fixtures, commercial; special dies, tools, jigs & fixtures

(G-17028)
STRATHMORE DIRECTORIES LTD
Also Called: Strathmore Publications
26 Bond St (11590-5002)
PHONE..................................516 997-2525
Fax: 516 997-8639
Jack Pizzo, *President*
Karla Osuna, *Chief*
Sandra Marshall, *Admin Sec*
EMP: 25
SALES (est): 2.6MM **Privately Held**
WEB: www.strathmore-ltd.com
SIC: 2721 2741 Trade journals: publishing & printing; miscellaneous publishing

(G-17029)
TAPEMAKER SALES CO INC
48 Urban Ave (11590-4822)
PHONE..................................516 333-0592
Fax: 516 333-0643
Arthur Brandwein, *President*
Helena Brandwein, *Corp Secy*
Mordy Brandwein, *Vice Pres*
Alexander Melamed, *Manager*
Yehuda Gartenlaub, *Director*
EMP: 8
SQ FT: 11,100
SALES (est): 560K **Privately Held**
SIC: 2759 Labels & seals: printing

(G-17030)
TEE PEE AUTO SALES CORP
Also Called: Tri-State Towing Equipment NY
52 Swan St (11590)
PHONE..................................516 338-9333
Tom Decillis, *President*
Peter Pizzo, *Vice Pres*
Tracy Decillis, *Office Mgr*
EMP: 10
SALES (est): 1.1MM **Privately Held**
SIC: 3711 Truck & tractor truck assembly

(G-17031)
TEMPO INDUSTRIES INC
90 Hopper St (11590-4802)
PHONE..................................516 334-6900
Stuart Braunstein, *President*
Jade Beetle, *Principal*
▲ EMP: 1
SALES: 1MM **Privately Held**
SIC: 3993 7389 Advertising novelties; telephone services

(G-17032)
TISHCON CORP (PA)
30 New York Ave (11590-4907)
P.O. Box 331 (11590-0300)
PHONE..................................516 333-3056
Fax: 516 997-1052
Raj K Chopra, *Ch of Bd*
Vipin Patel, *President*
Kamal Chopra, *Senior VP*
Latish Amin, *Mfg Dir*
Hemant Pandit, *Safety Mgr*
▲ EMP: 125 EST: 1977
SALES (est): 59MM **Privately Held**
WEB: www.qgel.com
SIC: 2834 Vitamin preparations; pills, pharmaceutical

(G-17033)
TISHCON CORP
Also Called: Geotec
30 New York Ave (11590-4907)
P.O. Box 331 (11590-0300)
PHONE..................................516 333-3056
Raj Chopra, *Manager*
EMP: 150

Westbury - Nassau County (G-17034)

SALES (corp-wide): 59MM **Privately Held**
WEB: www.qgel.com
SIC: 2834 Pharmaceutical preparations
PA: Tishcon Corp.
30 New York Ave
Westbury NY 11590
516 333-3056

(G-17034)
TISHCON CORP
41 New York Ave (11590-4908)
PHONE................516 333-3050
Raj Chopra, *Branch Mgr*
EMP: 150
SALES (corp-wide): 59MM **Privately Held**
SIC: 2834 Pharmaceutical preparations
PA: Tishcon Corp.
30 New York Ave
Westbury NY 11590
516 333-3056

(G-17035)
TISHCON CORP
36 New York Ave (11590-4907)
PHONE................516 333-3050
Hemant Pandit, *Safety Mgr*
EMP: 150
SALES (corp-wide): 59MM **Privately Held**
WEB: www.qgel.com
SIC: 2834 Vitamin preparations; pills, pharmaceutical
PA: Tishcon Corp.
30 New York Ave
Westbury NY 11590
516 333-3056

(G-17036)
TRIUM STRS-LG ISLD LLC
717 Main St (11590-5021)
PHONE................516 997-5757
Alex Shkoditch, *Manager*
Leonard Gross,
EMP: 99
SALES (est): 24.5MM **Privately Held**
SIC: 3721 Aircraft

(G-17037)
TRIUMPH GROUP INC
Also Called: Triumph Structures-Long Island
717 Main St (11590-5021)
PHONE................516 997-5757
William Gross, *President*
Jolis Rodriguez, *Manager*
EMP: 62
SALES (corp-wide): 3.8B **Publicly Held**
WEB: www.triumphgrp.com
SIC: 3724 Aircraft engines & engine parts
PA: Triumph Group, Inc.
899 Cassatt Rd Ste 210
Berwyn PA 19312
610 251-1000

(G-17038)
TWIN COUNTY RECYCLING CORP (PA)
113 Magnolia Ave (11590-4719)
PHONE................516 827-6900
Fax: 516 827-5906
Carlos Lizza, *President*
Frank Lizza Jr, *Controller*
EMP: 13
SQ FT: 2,000
SALES (est): 1.2MM **Privately Held**
WEB: www.twincountyunitedway.com
SIC: 2951 4953 5032 Asphalt paving mixtures & blocks; recycling, waste materials; aggregate

(G-17039)
UTILITY MANUFACTURING CO INC
700 Main St (11590-5020)
PHONE................516 997-6300
Fax: 516 997-6345
Wilbur Kranz, *CEO*
Audie Kranz, *President*
Mark Sophie, *Accountant*
Caroline Costas, *Executive*
EMP: 30
SQ FT: 44,000
SALES (est): 7MM **Privately Held**
WEB: www.utilitychemicals.com
SIC: 2899 2891 Chemical preparations; adhesives & sealants

(G-17040)
VALPLAST INTERNATIONAL CORP
200 Shames Dr (11590-1784)
PHONE................516 442-3923
Peter S Nagy, *President*
Peter Nagy, *Vice Pres*
Shabab Rahman, *Marketing Staff*
Daniel Irazary, *Manager*
Victor Sala, *Manager*
▲ EMP: 11
SQ FT: 10,500
SALES: 2.5MM **Privately Held**
WEB: www.valplast.com
SIC: 3559 3843 Plastics working machinery; dental equipment & supplies

(G-17041)
VESCOM STRUCTURAL SYSTEMS INC
Also Called: Tms Development
100 Shames Dr Unit 1 (11590-1741)
PHONE................516 876-8100
Joel Person, *President*
EMP: 10
SALES (est): 740K **Privately Held**
WEB: www.vescomstructures.com
SIC: 3299 Floor composition, magnesite

Westerlo
Albany County

(G-17042)
HANNAY REELS INC
553 State Route 143 (12193-2618)
PHONE................518 797-3791
Fax: 518 797-3259
Eric A Hannay, *CEO*
Roger A Hannay, *Ch of Bd*
Marcia Casullo, *General Mgr*
Elaine Hannay Gruener, *Vice Pres*
David G Hannay, *Vice Pres*
◆ EMP: 147 EST: 1933
SQ FT: 196,840
SALES (est): 46MM **Privately Held**
WEB: www.hannay.com
SIC: 3569 3499 Firehose equipment: driers, rack & reels; reels, cable: metal

Westernville
Oneida County

(G-17043)
G J OLNEY INC
9057 Dopp Hill Rd (13486-2301)
PHONE................315 827-4208
G Joseph Olney, *President*
David Olney, *Vice Pres*
EMP: 20 EST: 1917
SQ FT: 4,000
SALES (est): 4.1MM **Privately Held**
SIC: 3556 Food products machinery

Westfield
Chautauqua County

(G-17044)
20 BLISS ST INC
61 E Main St (14787-1305)
PHONE................716 326-2790
Ralph Wilson, *President*
Janice Wilson, *Vice Pres*
EMP: 5
SALES: 200K **Privately Held**
SIC: 1321 Natural gasoline production

(G-17045)
A TRUSTED NAME INC
35 Franklin St (14787-1039)
PHONE................716 326-7400
Jeff Gerdy, *President*
EMP: 12
SQ FT: 4,000
SALES (est): 810K **Privately Held**
WEB: www.atrustedname.com
SIC: 2395 5199 5941 Decorative & novelty stitching, for the trade; advertising specialties; sporting goods & bicycle shops

(G-17046)
BETTER BAKED FOODS INC
25 Jefferson St (14787-1010)
P.O. Box D (14787)
PHONE................716 326-4651
Fax: 716 326-4693
Rodney Bloomquist, *Plant Mgr*
Greg Leone, *Facilities Mgr*
Jerry Pacinelli, *Manager*
Bob Brown, *Maintence Staff*
EMP: 100
SQ FT: 66,400
SALES (corp-wide): 153MM **Privately Held**
WEB: www.betterbaked.com
SIC: 2051 Bread, cake & related products
HQ: Better Baked Foods, Inc.
56 Smedley St
North East PA 16428
814 725-8778

(G-17047)
CROWN HILL STONE INC
59 Franklin St (14787-1037)
P.O. Box 76, Stow (14785-0076)
PHONE................716 326-4601
Fax: 716 326-4600
Geoffrey Turner, *President*
Jeannette Turner, *Corp Secy*
Sue Zanghi, *Sales Mgr*
Donna Arnold, *Manager*
EMP: 32
SQ FT: 1,296
SALES (est): 3.7MM **Privately Held**
SIC: 3272 3281 Building stone, artificial: concrete; fireplace & chimney material: concrete; cut stone & stone products

(G-17048)
NATIONAL GRAPE COOP ASSN INC (PA)
2 S Portage St (14787-1400)
PHONE................716 326-5200
Fax: 716 326-5111
Randolph Graham, *President*
Joseph C Falcone, *Vice Pres*
Harold Smith, *Vice Pres*
Timothy A Buss, *CPA*
Linda G Greenberg, *Manager*
◆ EMP: 20
SQ FT: 50,000
SALES: 608.4MM **Privately Held**
SIC: 2033 2037 Fruit juices: packaged in cans, jars, etc.; fruit juices: concentrated, hot pack; tomato juice: packaged in cans, jars, etc.; jams, jellies & preserves: packaged in cans, jars, etc.; frozen fruits & vegetables; fruit juices, frozen; fruit juice concentrates, frozen

(G-17049)
QUALITY GUIDES
Also Called: Westfield Publication
39 E Main St (14787-1303)
P.O. Box 38 (14787-0038)
PHONE................716 326-3163
Ogden Newspapers, *Owner*
Melissa Bramer, *Exec Dir*
Maureen Delbalso, *Executive*
EMP: 7
SALES (est): 290.9K **Privately Held**
SIC: 2711 Newspapers

(G-17050)
RENOLD HOLDINGS INC (DH)
Also Called: Renold Ajax
100 Bourne St (14787-9706)
PHONE................716 326-3121
Mike Conley, *President*
Carl Cain, *Design Engr*
Wincent Woodeard, *Controller*
▲ EMP: 2
SQ FT: 100,000
SALES (est): 34.8MM
SALES (corp-wide): 239.2MM **Privately Held**
WEB: www.renoldajax.com
SIC: 3568 5085 Power transmission equipment; couplings, shaft: rigid, flexible, universal joint, etc.; power transmission equipment & apparatus
HQ: Renold International Holdings Limited
Renold House
Manchester M22 5
161 498-4500

(G-17051)
RENOLD INC
100 Bourne St (14787-9706)
P.O. Box A (14787)
PHONE................716 326-3121
Fax: 716 326-6121
Mike Conley, *Ch of Bd*
Susan Miller, *Mfg Dir*
Robert Macko, *Purchasing*
Dave Adams, *Regl Sales Mgr*
Jeff Powell, *Regl Sales Mgr*
▲ EMP: 100 EST: 1920
SQ FT: 100,000
SALES (est): 34.3MM
SALES (corp-wide): 239.2MM **Privately Held**
WEB: www.renoldajax.com
SIC: 3568 3535 3566 Power transmission equipment; couplings, shaft: rigid, flexible, universal joint, etc.; conveyors & conveying equipment; belt conveyor systems, general industrial use; speed changers, drives & gears
HQ: Renold Holdings Inc.
100 Bourne St
Westfield NY 14787
716 326-3121

(G-17052)
WAFFENBAUCH USA
165 Academy St (14787-1308)
PHONE................716 326-4508
Sam Villafrank, *CEO*
EMP: 48
SALES: 250K **Privately Held**
SIC: 1382 Oil & gas exploration services

(G-17053)
WELCH FOODS INC A COOPERATIVE
2 S Portage St (14787-1492)
PHONE................716 326-5252
David Moore, *General Mgr*
Robert W McMillin, *Principal*
Tim S Hilaire, *Vice Pres*
Vivian Tseng, *Vice Pres*
Thomas M Curtin, *Manager*
EMP: 175
SALES (corp-wide): 608.4MM **Privately Held**
WEB: www.welchs.com
SIC: 2033 Fruit juices: packaged in cans, jars, etc.
HQ: Welch Foods Inc., A Cooperative
300 Baker Ave Ste 101
Concord MA 01742
978 371-1000

(G-17054)
WELCH FOODS INC A COOPERATIVE
100 N Portage St (14787-1092)
PHONE................716 326-3131
Fax: 716 326-5451
Wilson Haller, *Branch Mgr*
EMP: 26
SALES (corp-wide): 608.4MM **Privately Held**
WEB: www.welchs.com
SIC: 2033 Canned fruits & specialties
HQ: Welch Foods Inc., A Cooperative
300 Baker Ave Ste 101
Concord MA 01742
978 371-1000

(G-17055)
WINE GROUP INC
Also Called: Mogen David Winegroup
85 Bourne St (14787-9706)
PHONE................716 326-3151
Fax: 716 326-4442
Eugene Schwartz, *Vice Pres*
Jean Schwartz, *Manager*

EMP: 60
SQ FT: 83,120
SALES (corp-wide): 100.5MM **Privately Held**
SIC: 2084 Wines
HQ: The Wine Group Inc
17000 E State Highway 120
Ripon CA 95366
209 599-4111

Westhampton
Suffolk County

(G-17056)
DAVE SANDEL CRANES INC
56 S Country Rd (11977-1314)
PHONE..................................631 325-5588
David Sandel, *President*
EMP: 7
SALES: 1MM **Privately Held**
SIC: 3531 Cranes

(G-17057)
HAMPTON SAND CORP
1 High St (11977)
P.O. Box 601, Speonk (11972-0601)
PHONE..................................631 325-5533
Barbara Dawson, *President*
Stan Warshaw, *Manager*
EMP: 8
SQ FT: 1,000
SALES (est): 1.2MM **Privately Held**
SIC: 1442 5261 5032 4953 Sand mining; gravel mining; top soil; brick, stone & related material; recycling, waste materials

Westhampton Beach
Suffolk County

(G-17058)
FRAME WORKS AMERICA INC
Also Called: Spectaculars
146 Mill Rd (11978-2345)
PHONE..................................631 288-1300
William Vetri, *President*
EMP: 40
SQ FT: 1,500
SALES: 3MM **Privately Held**
SIC: 3851 Eyeglasses, lenses & frames

(G-17059)
MICHAEL K LENNON INC
Also Called: Pine Barrens Printing
851 Riverhead Rd (11978-1210)
P.O. Box 704, Westhampton (11977-0704)
PHONE..................................631 288-5200
Fax: 631 288-1036
Michael K Lennon, *President*
Tom Lennon, *CFO*
EMP: 30
SQ FT: 11,000
SALES (est): 4.9MM **Privately Held**
WEB: www.pinebarrensprinting.com
SIC: 2752 Commercial printing, lithographic

(G-17060)
SHUGAR PUBLISHING
Also Called: Qsr Medical Communications
99b Main St (11978-2607)
PHONE..................................631 288-4404
Fax: 631 288-4435
Vivian Mahl, *President*
C S Pithumoni, *Editor*
Dorine Kitay, *Manager*
EMP: 8
SQ FT: 250
SALES: 1.5MM **Privately Held**
WEB: www.practicalgastro.com
SIC: 2721 Periodicals: publishing only

(G-17061)
SOUTHAMPTON TOWN NEWSPAPERS
Also Called: Western Edition
12 Mitchell Rd (11978-2609)
P.O. Box 1071 (11978-7071)
PHONE..................................631 288-1100
Cailin Brophy, *Editor*
Magaret Halsey, *Treasurer*
Frank Costanca, *Manager*

EMP: 10
SALES (corp-wide): 3.9MM **Privately Held**
WEB: www.southamptonpress.com
SIC: 2711 Newspapers
PA: Southampton Town Newspapers Inc
135 Windmill Ln
Southampton NY 11968
631 283-4100

Westmoreland
Oneida County

(G-17062)
MOHAWK METAL MFG & SLS
4901 State Route 233 (13490-1309)
PHONE..................................315 853-7663
William F Schrock, *Principal*
EMP: 5
SQ FT: 20,000
SALES: 2.5MM **Privately Held**
SIC: 2421 Building & structural materials, wood

(G-17063)
PERSONAL GRAPHICS CORPORATION
5123 State Route 233 (13490-1311)
PHONE..................................315 853-3421
Fax: 315 853-2696
Paul Hillman, *President*
EMP: 7
SQ FT: 7,000
SALES: 380K **Privately Held**
SIC: 2759 Screen printing

(G-17064)
RISING STARS SOCCER CLUB CNY
4980 State Route 233 (13490-1308)
P.O. Box 423, Rome (13442-0423)
PHONE..................................315 381-3096
Frank Conestabile, *Owner*
EMP: 10
SALES (est): 494.4K **Privately Held**
SIC: 3949 Sporting & athletic goods

(G-17065)
SHAFER & SONS
Also Called: Storage Sheds
4932 State Route 233 (13490-1308)
PHONE..................................315 853-5285
John H Shafer, *Partner*
Jason Shafer, *Partner*
Joe Shafer, *Partner*
Kathleen Shafer, *Partner*
EMP: 5
SQ FT: 8,000
SALES (est): 570K **Privately Held**
WEB: www.ssheds.com
SIC: 2452 5039 Prefabricated buildings, wood; prefabricated buildings

(G-17066)
SIERSON CRANE & WELDING INC
4822 State Route 233 (13490-1306)
PHONE..................................315 723-6914
Mitchell R Sierson, *President*
EMP: 6
SALES (est): 691.8K **Privately Held**
SIC: 3531 Cranes

Westport
Essex County

(G-17067)
CHAMPLAIN VALLEY MILLING CORP
6679 Main St (12993-2005)
P.O. Box 454 (12993-0454)
PHONE..................................518 962-4711
Fax: 518 962-8799
Samuel M Sherman, *President*
Derinda Sherman, *Vice Pres*
Ayra Pettit, *Treasurer*
EMP: 9
SQ FT: 9,500
SALES (est): 1.5MM **Privately Held**
SIC: 2041 Flour & other grain mill products

Westtown
Orange County

(G-17068)
FROST PUBLICATIONS INC
55 Laurel Hill Dr (10998-3921)
P.O. Box 178 (10998-0178)
PHONE..................................845 726-3232
Don Frost, *Owner*
EMP: 5
SALES (est): 417.9K **Privately Held**
SIC: 2721 1521 Periodicals: publishing & printing; single-family housing construction

(G-17069)
GARRISON WOODWORKING INC
226 Hoslers Rd (10998-3527)
P.O. Box 916, Port Jervis (12771-0916)
PHONE..................................845 726-3525
James W Boyd, *President*
Charles O'Neill, *Treasurer*
EMP: 10
SQ FT: 2,400
SALES (est): 845.1K **Privately Held**
SIC: 2434 2431 Wood kitchen cabinets; millwork

(G-17070)
GRANT-NOREN
83 Ridge Rd (10998-2602)
PHONE..................................845 726-4281
Daniel Grant, *Partner*
Ingela Noren, *Partner*
EMP: 5
SALES: 180K **Privately Held**
SIC: 2499 Picture & mirror frames, wood

White Lake
Sullivan County

(G-17071)
SUTPHEN CORPORATION
30 Sutphen Pl Fl 2 (12786-5517)
P.O. Box 16 (12786-0016)
PHONE..................................845 583-4720
Caryl Rhandy, *Branch Mgr*
EMP: 20
SALES (corp-wide): 52.1MM **Privately Held**
WEB: www.sutpheneast.com
SIC: 3711 Fire department vehicles (motor vehicles), assembly of
PA: The Sutphen Corporation
6450 Eiterman Rd
Dublin OH 43016
800 726-7030

White Plains
Westchester County

(G-17072)
A & C/FURIA ELECTRIC MOTORS
75 Lafayette Ave (10603-1613)
PHONE..................................914 949-0585
Fax: 914 949-8034
Andrew Cerone, *President*
EMP: 11
SQ FT: 5,000
SALES (est): 880K **Privately Held**
SIC: 7694 7699 5999 5251 Electric motor repair; pumps & pumping equipment repair; compressor repair; motors, electric; pumps & pumping equipment; fans, electric

(G-17073)
ACRS INC
1311 Mmroneck Ave Ste 260 (10605)
PHONE..................................914 288-8100
Kenneth F Bernstein, *Ch of Bd*
EMP: 10
SALES (est): 884.9K **Privately Held**
SIC: 1231 Anthracite mining

(G-17074)
ALAMAR PRINTING INC
Also Called: PIP Printing
190 E Post Rd Frnt 1 (10601-4918)
PHONE..................................914 993-9007
Fax: 914 993-0029
Mary Jane Goldman, *President*
Scott Annicelli, *CFO*
EMP: 10
SQ FT: 6,500
SALES (est): 1.7MM **Privately Held**
SIC: 2752 2754 Commercial printing, offset; business form & card printing, gravure; promotional printing, gravure; stationery & invitation printing, gravure

(G-17075)
ALCONOX INC
30 Glenn St Ste 309 (10603-3252)
PHONE..................................914 948-4040
Fax: 914 948-4088
Rhoda Schemin, *President*
Elliot Lebowitz, *COO*
Jill Zisnan, *Vice Pres*
Andrew Jacobson, *Engineer*
Malcolm McLaughlin, *Sls & Mktg Exec*
EMP: 6 EST: 1946
SQ FT: 4,000
SALES (est): 1.5MM **Privately Held**
WEB: www.alconox.com
SIC: 2841 Detergents, synthetic organic or inorganic alkaline

(G-17076)
AMENDOLA MBL & STONE CTR INC
560 Tarrytown Rd (10607-1316)
PHONE..................................914 997-7968
Fax: 914 946-3128
Sergio Amendola, *President*
Joseph Amendola, *Vice Pres*
Maria Amendola, *Admin Sec*
▲ EMP: 62
SQ FT: 3,500
SALES (est): 7.3MM **Privately Held**
SIC: 3281 2493 5999 5211 Granite, cut & shaped; marbleboard (stone face hard board); stones, crystalline: rough; tile, ceramic

(G-17077)
AMERICAN INTL MEDIA LLC
Also Called: Rugby Magazine
11 Martine Ave Ste 870 (10606-4025)
PHONE..................................845 359-4225
Ajon Prusmack, *Principal*
Morrin Burnett, *Controller*
EMP: 10
SQ FT: 3,000
SALES (est): 890K **Privately Held**
SIC: 2721 Magazines: publishing & printing

(G-17078)
ANBECK INC
75 S Broadway Fl 4 (10601-4413)
PHONE..................................518 907-0308
Taylor Davis, *President*
Spencer Uba, *Vice Pres*
EMP: 8 EST: 2015
SALES (est): 260.1K **Privately Held**
SIC: 7372 7371 Application computer software; custom computer programming services

(G-17079)
APPLE PRESS
23 Harrison Blvd (10604-1901)
PHONE..................................914 723-6660
Jody Majthenyi, *Owner*
EMP: 7
SQ FT: 4,800
SALES (est): 450K **Privately Held**
SIC: 2752 7334 Commercial printing, offset; photocopying & duplicating services

(G-17080)
ARTYARNS
70 Westmoreland Ave (10606-2315)
PHONE..................................914 428-0333
Fax: 914 220-0152
Elliot Schreier, *President*
Iris Schreier, *Vice Pres*
EMP: 8

White Plains - Westchester County (G-17081)

SALES (est): 904.4K **Privately Held**
WEB: www.artyarns.com
SIC: 2269 Dyeing: raw stock yarn & narrow fabrics

(G-17081)
BAIRNCO CORPORATION (DH)
1133 Westchester Ave N-222 (10604-3516)
PHONE.....................914 461-1300
Glen M Kassan, *Ch of Bd*
John J Quicke, *President*
Ken Bayne, *CFO*
Lawrence C Maingot, *CFO*
Michele Giglletta, *Manager*
◆ **EMP:** 20 **EST:** 1981
SQ FT: 11,000
SALES (est): 68.4MM
SALES (corp-wide): 782MM **Publicly Held**
WEB: www.bairnco.com
SIC: 2821 3556 Plastics materials & resins; meat, poultry & seafood processing machinery; slicers, commercial, food

(G-17082)
BAKER PRODUCTS INC
5 Oakley Rd (10606-3701)
PHONE.....................212 459-2323
Jeff Brown, *President*
▲ **EMP:** 6
SQ FT: 1,500
SALES: 1.2MM **Privately Held**
SIC: 3111 3172 Case leather; cosmetic bags

(G-17083)
BALLANTRAE LITHOGRAPHERS INC
96 Wayside Dr (10607-2726)
PHONE.....................914 592-3275
Fax: 914 347-7573
Steve Quagliano, *President*
Ralph Bocchimuzzo, *Vice Pres*
Rocco Quagliano, *Treasurer*
EMP: 6
SQ FT: 5,000
SALES (est): 610K **Privately Held**
SIC: 2752 Commercial printing, lithographic; commercial printing, offset

(G-17084)
BEACON PRESS INC
32 Cushman Rd (10606-3706)
PHONE.....................212 691-5050
Kenneth B Weiner, *President*
EMP: 4 **EST:** 1913
SQ FT: 3,000
SALES: 2MM **Privately Held**
WEB: www.beaconpress.com
SIC: 2752 Commercial printing, offset

(G-17085)
BENFIELD CONTROL SYSTEMS INC
25 Lafayette Ave (10603-1613)
PHONE.....................914 948-6660
Fax: 914 948-5145
Daniel J McLaughlin, *President*
Dominic Devito, *Managing Dir*
Roy C Kohli, *Chairman*
Miguel Guerrero, *Project Engr*
William Roloff, *CFO*
EMP: 10
SALES (est): 4.5MM
SALES (corp-wide): 281.4MM **Privately Held**
WEB: www.benfieldcontrolsystems.com
SIC: 3613 8711 Control panels, electric; engineering services
PA: H.H. Benfield Electric Supply Company, Inc.
25 Lafayette Ave
White Plains NY 10603
914 948-6660

(G-17086)
BOTTLING GROUP LLC
Also Called: Pepsi Beverages Company
1111 Westchester Ave (10604-3525)
PHONE.....................800 789-2626
Fax: 914 767-1954
James B Lindsey Jr, *President*
Graig Reese, *General Mgr*
Marjorie Lindsey, *Corp Secy*
Dick Graeber, *Vice Pres*
Joe Fonseca, *Plant Mgr*

EMP: 400
SQ FT: 1,000,000
SALES (est): 127MM
SALES (corp-wide): 63B **Publicly Held**
SIC: 2086 Carbonated beverages, nonalcoholic: bottled & canned; soft drinks: packaged in cans, bottles, etc.
HQ: Pepsi-Cola Bottling Group
1111 Westchester Ave
White Plains NY 10604
914 767-6000

(G-17087)
BOTTLING GROUP LLC (HQ)
Also Called: Pepsi Beverages Company
1111 Westchester Ave (10604-3525)
PHONE.....................914 767-6000
Albert P Carey, *CEO*
Zein Abdalla, *President*
Joanna Sweet, *Administration*
Saad Abdul-Latif,
Debra Crew,
◆ **EMP:** 4
SALES (est): 7B
SALES (corp-wide): 63B **Publicly Held**
WEB: www.bottlinggroup.com
SIC: 2086 Bottled & canned soft drinks; carbonated soft drinks, bottled & canned; carbonated beverages, nonalcoholic: bottled & canned
PA: Pepsico, Inc.
700 Anderson Hill Rd
Purchase NY 10577
914 253-2000

(G-17088)
BRISTOL/WHITE PLAINS
305 North St (10605-2208)
PHONE.....................914 681-1800
EMP: 10
SALES (est): 1.3MM **Privately Held**
SIC: 2621 Bristols

(G-17089)
BUNGE LIMITED FINANCE CORP
50 Main St (10606-1901)
PHONE.....................914 684-2800
Adam Johnson, *General Mgr*
Brian Zachman, *Principal*
Ian Messmore, *Project Mgr*
Vicente Neto, *Project Mgr*
Oana Radeanu, *Project Mgr*
EMP: 165
SALES (est): 61MM **Privately Held**
SIC: 2079 Edible fats & oils
PA: Bunge Limited
C/O Conyers, Dill & Pearman
Hamilton
441 295-1422

(G-17090)
BYRAM CONCRETE & SUPPLY LLC
145 Virginia Rd (10603-2232)
PHONE.....................914 682-4477
Fax: 914 682-4486
John R Percham, *Principal*
EMP: 11
SALES (est): 1.2MM **Privately Held**
SIC: 3273 Ready-mixed concrete

(G-17091)
C P CHEMICAL CO INC
25 Home St (10606-2306)
PHONE.....................914 428-2517
Fax: 914 428-2517
Walter Hasselman Jr, *President*
Kim Couch, *Office Mgr*
EMP: 5
SQ FT: 20,000
SALES: 900K **Privately Held**
WEB: www.tripolymer.com
SIC: 3086 2899 2873 Insulation or cushioning material, foamed plastic; foam charge mixtures; fertilizers: natural (organic), except compost

(G-17092)
CAMEO PROCESS CORP
15 Stewart Pl Apt 7g (10603-3808)
PHONE.....................914 948-0082
Fax: 914 948-0083
Edwin Goldstein, *President*
S G Goldstein, *Treasurer*
EMP: 2

SALES: 6MM **Privately Held**
SIC: 2671 Resinous impregnated paper for packaging

(G-17093)
CLASSIC COLLECTIONS FINE ART
20 Haarlem Ave Ste 408 (10603-2233)
PHONE.....................914 591-4500
Larry Tolchin, *President*
EMP: 6
SQ FT: 5,000
SALES (est): 596K **Privately Held**
SIC: 2741 Art copy: publishing only, not printed on site

(G-17094)
CN GROUP INCORPORATED
76 Mamaroneck Ave (10601-4217)
PHONE.....................914 358-5690
Jerry Duenas, *President*
EMP: 910
SALES (est): 53.9MM **Privately Held**
SIC: 3089 3841 2821 Automotive parts, plastic; surgical & medical instruments; plastics materials & resins

(G-17095)
COMBE INCORPORATED (PA)
1101 Westchester Ave (10604-3503)
PHONE.....................914 694-5454
Fax: 914 694-1926
Dominic Demain, *President*
Richard G Powers, *President*
Christopher B Combe, *Principal*
Jerome S Darby, *Senior VP*
Dominic P Demain, *Senior VP*
▼ **EMP:** 240 **EST:** 1949
SQ FT: 68,000
SALES (est): 140MM **Privately Held**
WEB: www.combe.com
SIC: 2841 2834 Soap & other detergents; soap: granulated, liquid, cake, flaked or chip; pharmaceutical preparations

(G-17096)
CONNECTICUT BUS SYSTEMS LLC
Also Called: CBS
108 Corporate Park Dr # 118 (10604-3801)
PHONE.....................914 696-1900
Fax: 914 696-1234
Jay Cartisnao, *Principal*
EMP: 8
SALES (corp-wide): 18B **Publicly Held**
WEB: www.cbs-blooms.com
SIC: 7372 Business oriented computer software
HQ: Connecticut Business Systems Llc
100 Great Meadow Rd
Wethersfield CT 06109
860 667-2900

(G-17097)
COPY STOP INC
Also Called: L K Printing
50 Main St Ste 32 (10606-1920)
PHONE.....................914 428-5188
Fax: 914 428-8907
Richard Koh, *President*
Josh Green, *Manager*
EMP: 5
SQ FT: 800
SALES (est): 790.2K **Privately Held**
SIC: 2752 Commercial printing, lithographic

(G-17098)
DANONE NUTRICIA EARLY
100 Hillside Ave (10603-2861)
PHONE.....................914 872-8556
Luciana Nunez, *General Mgr*
EMP: 20
SQ FT: 30,000
SALES (est): 1.3MM **Privately Held**
SIC: 2023 Canned baby formula

(G-17099)
DAVID YURMAN ENTERPRISES LLC
125 Westchester Ave # 1060 (10601-4546)
PHONE.....................914 539-4444
Liz Candela, *Sales Associate*
Cara Scalfani, *Director*
EMP: 9

SALES (corp-wide): 268.2MM **Privately Held**
SIC: 3911 Jewelry, precious metal
PA: David Yurman Enterprises Llc
24 Vestry St
New York NY 10013
212 896-1550

(G-17100)
DEBT RESOLVE INC
1133 Westchester Ave S-223 (10604-3545)
PHONE.....................914 949-5500
Stanley E Freimuth, *CEO*
William M Mooney Jr, *Ch of Bd*
Rene A Samson, *Vice Pres*
Ren Samson, *Manager*
EMP: 3
SALES (est): 5.7MM **Privately Held**
WEB: www.debtresolve.com
SIC: 7372 7322 Business oriented computer software; collection agency, except real estate

(G-17101)
DISNEY PUBLISHING WORLDWIDE (DH)
44 Brad Ln (10605-4802)
PHONE.....................212 633-4400
R Russell Hampton Jr, *Chairman*
Robert W Hernandez, *Senior VP*
Bill Greenbaum, *Controller*
▲ **EMP:** 100
SALES (est): 34.2MM **Publicly Held**
SIC: 2721 Periodicals
HQ: Disney Enterprises, Inc.
500 S Buena Vista St
Burbank CA 91521
818 560-1000

(G-17102)
DYNATIC SOLUTIONS INC
1 Water St Ste 225 (10601-1010)
PHONE.....................914 358-9599
Mu James Yang, *President*
EMP: 6
SALES (est): 894.6K **Privately Held**
SIC: 3825 Test equipment for electronic & electric measurement

(G-17103)
EFFICIENCY PRINTING CO INC
126 S Lexington Ave (10606-2510)
P.O. Box 157, Valhalla (10595-0157)
PHONE.....................914 949-8611
Fax: 914 949-8516
James Franzese, *President*
Maurice P Franzese Jr, *Treasurer*
EMP: 13 **EST:** 1944
SQ FT: 5,000
SALES (est): 1.4MM **Privately Held**
SIC: 2752 2759 Commercial printing, lithographic; commercial printing, offset; letterpress printing

(G-17104)
ELECTRO PLATING SERVICE INC
127 Oakley Ave (10601-3903)
PHONE.....................914 948-3777
Fax: 914 948-1627
Julian Galperin, *President*
EMP: 12 **EST:** 1930
SQ FT: 27,000
SALES: 353.8K **Privately Held**
WEB: www.smithwarren.com
SIC: 3471 Electroplating of metals or formed products

(G-17105)
ESCHOLAR LLC
222 Bloomingdale Rd # 107 (10605-1517)
PHONE.....................914 989-2900
Shawn Bay, *CEO*
Wolf Boehme, *President*
Sue Holden, *Vice Pres*
EMP: 11
SQ FT: 2,500
SALES (est): 1MM **Privately Held**
WEB: www.escholar.com
SIC: 3695 5045 Computer software tape & disks: blank, rigid & floppy; computer software

▲ = Import ▼ =Export
◆ =Import/Export

GEOGRAPHIC SECTION

White Plains - Westchester County (G-17128)

(G-17106)
ETHIS COMMUNICATIONS INC
44 Church St Ste 200 (10601-1919)
PHONE 212 791-1440
Fax: 212 791-4980
David Kellner, *Owner*
Ying Guo, *Editor*
Mike Smolinsky, *Editor*
Adam Gundaker, *COO*
Lindsay Hermanson, *Prdtn Mgr*
EMP: 7
SALES (est): 1MM **Privately Held**
SIC: 2741 Miscellaneous publishing

(G-17107)
EXCELL PRINT & PROMOTIONS INC
50 Main St Ste 100 (10606-1901)
PHONE 914 437-8668
David Quas, *President*
EMP: 8
SALES (est): 586.6K **Privately Held**
SIC: 2759 7389 Promotional printing;

(G-17108)
F-O-R SOFTWARE LLC (PA)
Also Called: Two-Four Software
10 Bank St Ste 830 (10606-1952)
PHONE 914 220-8800
Stephen Fry, *Managing Dir*
John Feeney, *Director*
Kevin Ouderkirk,
Brian McLaughlin, *Analyst*
John Flowers,
EMP: 21
SQ FT: 2,100
SALES (est): 3.9MM **Privately Held**
WEB: www.twofour.com
SIC: 7372 Prepackaged software

(G-17109)
FARMERS HUB LLC
8 Francine Ct (10607-1201)
PHONE 646 380-6770
Oseovbie Imoukhuede, *Vice Pres*
Hamilton Martin, *Vice Pres*
EMP: 6
SALES (est): 185.1K **Privately Held**
SIC: 2099 Tea blending

(G-17110)
FORDHAM MARBLE CO INC
45 Crane Ave (10603-3702)
PHONE 914 682-6699
Mario Serdo, *President*
EMP: 15
SALES (est): 1.2MM **Privately Held**
SIC: 3272 3281 Art marble, concrete; cut stone & stone products

(G-17111)
GARRETT J CRONIN
Also Called: Minute Man Printing Company
1 Stuart Way (10607-1805)
PHONE 914 761-9299
Garrett J Cronin, *Principal*
EMP: 5 **EST:** 2010
SALES (est): 179.9K **Privately Held**
SIC: 2759 7389 Commercial printing;

(G-17112)
GAS RECOVERY SYSTEMS LLC (HQ)
Also Called: Gas Recovery Systems Illinois
1 N Lexington Ave Ste 620 (10601-1721)
PHONE 914 421-4903
Thomas Gesicki, *President*
Anthony Albao, *Vice Pres*
Peter Anderson, *Controller*
Carlo Fidani, *Director*
EMP: 12
SQ FT: 2,500
SALES (est): 30.7MM
SALES (corp-wide): 175.8MM **Privately Held**
SIC: 1389 Removal of condensate gasoline from field (gathering) lines
PA: Fortistar Llc
1 N Lexington Ave Ste 620
White Plains NY 10601
914 421-4900

(G-17113)
GEMINI MANUFACTURING LLC
Also Called: Jet Line
56 Lafayette Ave Ste 380 (10603-1684)
P.O. Box 869, Mahopac (10541-0869)
PHONE 914 375-0855
Jon Granek, *Regl Sales Mgr*
Eric Levin, *Mng Member*
▲ **EMP:** 160
SQ FT: 100,000
SALES (est): 15.8MM **Privately Held**
WEB: www.jetlinepromo.com
SIC: 2754 Promotional printing, gravure

(G-17114)
GREAT BRANDS OF EUROPE INC
Also Called: Lu Biscuits
100 Hillside Ave Fl 3 (10603-2862)
PHONE 914 872-8804
David McLean, *Business Mgr*
Joe Porter, *Business Mgr*
Regi Sanders, *Business Mgr*
Elio Pacheco, *Vice Pres*
Tony Cicio, *Vice Pres*
▲ **EMP:** 6
SALES (est): 400K **Privately Held**
WEB: www.danone.fr
SIC: 2052 Cookies & crackers

(G-17115)
GROWTH PRODUCTS LTD
80 Lafayette Ave (10603-1603)
PHONE 914 428-1316
Clare Reinbergen, *Ch of Bd*
Jason Gray, *Sales Mgr*
Armand Mallory, *Executive Asst*
Mary Aronis, *Administration*
▼ **EMP:** 50
SALES (est): 10.7MM **Privately Held**
SIC: 2873 Nitrogenous fertilizers

(G-17116)
HAIGHTS CROSS OPERATING CO (HQ)
10 New King St Ste 102 (10604-1208)
PHONE 914 289-9400
Peter J Quandt, *Ch of Bd*
Linda Koons, *Exec VP*
Kevin M Mc Aliley, *Exec VP*
Mark Kurtz, *Vice Pres*
Paul J Crecca, *CFO*
EMP: 20
SALES (est): 74.3MM
SALES (corp-wide): 99.1MM **Privately Held**
SIC: 2731 Book publishing
PA: Haights Cross Communications, Inc.
136 Madison Ave Fl 8
New York NY 10016
212 209-0500

(G-17117)
HANDCRAFT CABINETRY INC
230 Ferris Ave Ste 1 (10603-3461)
PHONE 914 681-9437
Michael Ford, *President*
EMP: 9
SQ FT: 4,000
SALES (est): 1.4MM **Privately Held**
WEB: www.handcraftcabinetry.com
SIC: 2517 Home entertainment unit cabinets, wood

(G-17118)
HANDY & HARMAN (DH)
1133 Westchester Ave N-222 (10604-3571)
PHONE 914 461-1300
Jeffrey A Svoboda, *President*
Paul E Dixon, *Senior VP*
James McCabe, *Senior VP*
Paul W Bucha, *Vice Pres*
Robert A Davidow, *Vice Pres*
◆ **EMP:** 20
SQ FT: 17,000
SALES (est): 351.3MM
SALES (corp-wide): 782MM **Publicly Held**
SIC: 3356 3399 3341 3317 Precious metals; gold & gold alloy: rolling, drawing or extruding; silver & silver alloy: rolling, drawing or extruding; gold & gold alloy bars, sheets, strip, etc.; powder, metal; flakes, metal; silver powder; secondary precious metals; gold smelting & refining (secondary); silver smelting & refining (secondary); steel pipe & tubes; tubing, mechanical or hypodermic sizes: cold drawn stainless; wire products, ferrous/iron: made in wiredrawing plants; cable, steel: insulated or armored
HQ: Handy & Harman Ltd.
1133 Westchester Ave N-222
White Plains NY 10604
914 461-1300

(G-17119)
HANDY & HARMAN GROUP LTD (DH)
1133 Westchester Ave N-222 (10604-3571)
PHONE 914 461-1300
Warren G Lichtenstein, *Chairman*
James F McCabe, *CFO*
EMP: 17
SALES: 559.4MM
SALES (corp-wide): 782MM **Publicly Held**
SIC: 3462 Turbine engine forgings, ferrous
HQ: Handy & Harman Ltd.
1133 Westchester Ave N-222
White Plains NY 10604
914 461-1300

(G-17120)
HANDY & HARMAN LTD (HQ)
Also Called: Hnh
1133 Westchester Ave N-222 (10604-3571)
PHONE 914 461-1300
Fax: 914 696-8684
Jack L Howard, *CEO*
Warren G Lichtenstein, *Ch of Bd*
William T Fejes Jr, *Senior VP*
Jeffrey A Svoboda, *Senior VP*
Douglas B Woodworth, *CFO*
▼ **EMP:** 799
SALES: 649.4MM
SALES (corp-wide): 782MM **Publicly Held**
WEB: www.whxcorp.com
SIC: 3339 3011 3312 Precious metals; tire & inner tube materials & related products; wire products, steel or iron
PA: Sph Group Holdings Llc
590 Madison Ave Fl 32
New York NY 10022
212 520-2300

(G-17121)
HOGIL PHARMACEUTICAL CORP
237 Mmaroneck Ave Ste 207 (10605)
PHONE 914 681-1800
David Trager, *President*
Howard Wendy, *Chairman*
Suzanne Sabatino, *COO*
Joann Hyppelite, *Manager*
▲ **EMP:** 10
SQ FT: 3,500
SALES (est): 1.9MM **Privately Held**
WEB: www.hogil.com
SIC: 2834 3841 5047 5122 Pharmaceutical preparations; surgical & medical instruments; medical & hospital equipment; drugs, proprietaries & sundries

(G-17122)
HORNELL BREWING CO INC
222 Bloomingdale Rd Ste 4 (10605-1513)
PHONE 914 597-7911
John M Ferolito, *President*
EMP: 5
SALES (est): 273.8K **Privately Held**
SIC: 2082 Malt beverages

(G-17123)
HTF COMPONENTS INC
134 Bowbell Rd (10607-1141)
PHONE 914 703-6795
Fred Silva, *President*
Michael C Silva, *Vice Pres*
Tracy Silva, *Manager*
EMP: 9
SQ FT: 1,545
SALES (est): 1.5MM **Privately Held**
WEB: www.htfcomponents.com
SIC: 3699 5065 Electrical equipment & supplies; electronic parts & equipment

(G-17124)
INTERSTATE THERMOGRAPHERS CORP
70 Westmoreland Ave (10606-2315)
PHONE 914 948-1745
Fax: 914 948-0577
Juan Carlos Cardoso, *President*
Claudio Cardoso, *Vice Pres*
Ella Bradshaw, *Office Mgr*
EMP: 4
SALES (est): 1MM **Privately Held**
SIC: 2759 2752 Thermography; commercial printing, offset

(G-17125)
ITT LLC (HQ)
1133 Westchester Ave N-100 (10604-3543)
PHONE 914 641-2000
Fax: 914 616-2950
Frank T Macinnis, *Ch of Bd*
Denise L Ramos, *President*
Farrokh Batliwala, *President*
Aris C Chicles, *President*
Luca Savi, *President*
◆ **EMP:** 450 **EST:** 1920
SALES (est): 4.6B
SALES (corp-wide): 2.4B **Publicly Held**
WEB: www.ittind.com
SIC: 3594 3625 3823 3812 Fluid power pumps & motors; control equipment, electric; fluidic devices, circuits & systems for process control; radar systems & equipment
PA: Itt Inc.
1133 Westchester Ave N-100
White Plains NY 10604
914 641-2000

(G-17126)
ITT AEROSPACE CONTROLS LLC
4 W Red Oak Ln (10604-3603)
PHONE 914 641-2000
Menotti Lombardi, *Mng Member*
Ken I Bianchi, *Program Mgr*
Kathleen Tolar, *Admin Sec*
EMP: 6
SALES (est): 1MM **Privately Held**
SIC: 3625 Motor controls & accessories

(G-17127)
ITT FLUID TECHNOLOGY CORP (DH)
1133 Westcstr Ave N100 Ste N (10604)
PHONE 914 641-2000
Henry Driesse, *President*
Colin Sabol, *Vice Pres*
Clara Barone, *Marketing Mgr*
◆ **EMP:** 450
SALES (est): 1B
SALES (corp-wide): 2.4B **Publicly Held**
WEB: www.ittresourcecenter.com
SIC: 3494 3594 3561 Valves & pipe fittings; fluid power pumps & motors; pumps & pumping equipment
HQ: Itt, Llc
1133 Westchester Ave N-100
White Plains NY 10604
914 641-2000

(G-17128)
ITT INC (PA)
1133 Westchester Ave N-100 (10604-3543)
PHONE 914 641-2000
Frank T Macinnis, *Ch of Bd*
Denise L Ramos, *President*
Victoria L Creamer, *Senior VP*
Steven C Giuliano, *Vice Pres*
Thomas M Scalera, *CFO*
EMP: 5 **EST:** 1920
SALES: 2.4B **Publicly Held**
SIC: 3594 3625 3823 3812 Fluid power pumps & motors; control equipment, electric; fluidic devices, circuits & systems for process control; radar systems & equipment

White Plains - Westchester County (G-17129)

(G-17129)
ITT INDUSTRIES HOLDINGS INC (DH)
1133 Westchester Ave N-100 (10604-3543)
PHONE..............................914 641-2000
Mary Beth Gustafsson, *President*
Steve Giuliano, *Senior VP*
Daryl Bowker, *Vice Pres*
Michael Savinelli, *Vice Pres*
Thomas Scalera, *CFO*
EMP: 8 **EST:** 2004
SALES (est): 1.8MM
SALES (corp-wide): 2.4B **Publicly Held**
SIC: 2611 4731 Pulp mills; freight consolidation
HQ: International Standard Electric Corporation
 1105 N Market St Ste 1217
 Wilmington DE 19801
 302 427-3769

(G-17130)
JOURNAL NEWS
1133 Westchester Ave N-110 (10604-3516)
PHONE..............................914 694-5000
George Troyano, *President*
EMP: 6
SALES (est): 180.7K **Privately Held**
SIC: 2711 Newspapers, publishing & printing

(G-17131)
KINRO MANUFACTURING INC (DH)
200 Mmaroneck Ave Ste 301 (10601)
PHONE..............................817 483-7791
Jason Lippert, *President*
Scott Mereness, *Vice Pres*
Gary McPhail, *CFO*
▲ **EMP:** 1 **EST:** 1997
SALES (est): 130MM
SALES (corp-wide): 1.4B **Publicly Held**
SIC: 3442 Metal doors, sash & trim
HQ: Kinro Manufacturing, Inc.
 3501 County Road 6 E
 Elkhart IN 46514
 574 535-1125

(G-17132)
L K PRINTING CORP
Also Called: Royal Press
50 Main St Ste 32 (10606-1920)
PHONE..............................914 761-1944
Richard Koh, *President*
Josh Greene, *Vice Pres*
Josh Green, *Manager*
EMP: 6
SQ FT: 1,200
SALES: 700K **Privately Held**
SIC: 2752 Commercial printing, offset

(G-17133)
L S Z INC
Also Called: Alconox
30 Glenn St Ste 309 (10603-3252)
PHONE..............................914 948-4040
Elliot Lebowitz, *CEO*
EMP: 8
SALES (est): 773.3K **Privately Held**
WEB: www.ledizolv.com
SIC: 2841 Detergents, synthetic organic or inorganic alkaline

(G-17134)
LSIL & CO INC
Also Called: Lori Silverman Shoes
2 Greene Ln (10605-5111)
PHONE..............................914 761-0998
Lori Silverman, *President*
EMP: 5
SALES (est): 386.5K **Privately Held**
SIC: 3144 5661 Boots, canvas or leather: women's; women's shoes

(G-17135)
LYDIA H SOIFER & ASSOC INC
Also Called: Soifer Center, The
1025 Westchester Ave (10604-3508)
PHONE..............................914 683-5401
Fax: 914 683-5431
Lydia H Soifer, *President*
Lydia Sorfer, *President*
Allison Sidel, *Psychologist*
Heather Ironside M S, *Director*
EMP: 10

SALES (est): 1MM **Privately Held**
SIC: 3841 Diagnostic apparatus, medical

(G-17136)
MEASUREMENT INCORPORATED
7-11 S Broadway Ste 402 (10601-3546)
PHONE..............................914 682-1969
Sara Silver, *Research*
EMP: 21
SALES (corp-wide): 83MM **Privately Held**
SIC: 2759 Commercial printing
PA: Measurement Incorporated
 423 Morris St
 Durham NC 27701
 919 683-2413

(G-17137)
META-THERM CORP
Also Called: Bio-Nutritional Products
70 W Red Oak Ln (10604-3602)
PHONE..............................914 697-4840
Murray Flashner, *President*
▲ **EMP:** 15
SQ FT: 15,000
SALES: 4MM **Privately Held**
SIC: 2099 Food preparations

(G-17138)
MICROSOFT CORPORATION
125 Westchester Ave (10601-4522)
PHONE..............................914 323-2150
EMP: 599
SALES (corp-wide): 85.3B **Publicly Held**
SIC: 7372 Prepackaged software
PA: Microsoft Corporation
 1 Microsoft Way
 Redmond WA 98052
 425 882-8080

(G-17139)
NATIONAL HEALTH PROM ASSOC
711 Westchester Ave # 301 (10604-3539)
PHONE..............................914 421-2525
Fax: 914 683-6998
Gilbert J Botvin, *President*
David Tomko, *Trustee*
Thomas Papini, *Controller*
Monica Mitchell, *Accounting Mgr*
Stephanie Phillips,
EMP: 22
SQ FT: 120,000
SALES (est): 1.7MM **Privately Held**
SIC: 2741 Miscellaneous publishing

(G-17140)
NESTLE USA INC
1311 Mmroneck Ave Ste 350 (10605)
PHONE..............................914 272-4021
David Rosenbluth, *Principal*
EMP: 139
SALES (corp-wide): 88.3B **Privately Held**
SIC: 2023 Evaporated milk
HQ: Nestle Usa, Inc.
 800 N Brand Blvd
 Glendale CA 91203
 818 549-6000

(G-17141)
NEW ENGLAND RECLAMATION INC
20 Haarlem Ave (10603-2223)
PHONE..............................914 949-2000
Janet Peckham, *Ch of Bd*
John Peckham, *President*
James V De Forest, *Exec VP*
Thomas Vitti, *Treasurer*
EMP: 15
SALES (est): 1.6MM
SALES (corp-wide): 192MM **Privately Held**
WEB: www.peckham.com
SIC: 3399 Metal powders, pastes & flakes
PA: Peckham Industries, Inc.
 20 Haarlem Ave Ste 200
 White Plains NY 10603
 914 949-2000

(G-17142)
NINE WEST GROUP INC (HQ)
1129 Westchester Ave (10604-3505)
PHONE..............................800 999-1877
Fax: 914 640-2417

Kathy Nedorostek, *CEO*
Ron Dente, *Senior VP*
Nina Weigner, *Senior VP*
Vicky Christakos, *Vice Pres*
Patrick McLaughlin, *Vice Pres*
EMP: 1
SALES (est): 75MM
SALES (corp-wide): 2.6B **Privately Held**
SIC: 3144 Boots, canvas or leather: women's
PA: Nine West Holdings, Inc.
 180 Rittenhouse Cir
 Bristol PA 19007
 215 785-4000

(G-17143)
OSAKA GAS ENERGY AMERICA CORP
1 N Lexington Ave Ste 504 (10601-1724)
PHONE..............................914 253-5500
Shojiro Oka, *Principal*
Tatsuro Tsukamoto, *Business Mgr*
John Drake, *Vice Pres*
Bette Jacques, *Human Res Dir*
Yukinori Yamamoto, *Manager*
▲ **EMP:** 21
SALES (est): 527K
SALES (corp-wide): 11.3B **Privately Held**
SIC: 2911 Gases & liquefied petroleum gases
PA: Osaka Gas Co., Ltd.
 4-1-2, Hiranomachi, Chuo-Ku
 Osaka OSK 541-0
 662 054-537

(G-17144)
PARAMOUNT CORD & BRACKETS
6 Tournament Dr (10605-5121)
PHONE..............................212 325-9100
Fax: 718 325-9814
Gary Rosenkranz, *President*
EMP: 4
SQ FT: 8,000
SALES (est): 640K **Privately Held**
WEB: www.pccords.com
SIC: 2211 Corduroys, cotton; basket weave fabrics, cotton

(G-17145)
PATTERSON BLACKTOP CORP (HQ)
20 Haarlem Ave (10603-2223)
PHONE..............................914 949-2000
John Peckham, *President*
Janet G Peckham, *President*
John R Peckham, *President*
James V De Forest, *Exec VP*
Thomas Vitti, *Treasurer*
EMP: 30
SALES (est): 2.6MM
SALES (corp-wide): 192MM **Privately Held**
SIC: 2951 Asphalt paving mixtures & blocks
PA: Peckham Industries, Inc.
 20 Haarlem Ave Ste 200
 White Plains NY 10603
 914 949-2000

(G-17146)
PATTERSON MATERIALS CORP (HQ)
20 Haarlem Ave (10603-2223)
PHONE..............................914 949-2000
Janet G Peckham, *Co-President*
John R Peckham, *Co-President*
James V De Forest, *Exec VP*
EMP: 19
SQ FT: 15,000
SALES (est): 2.6MM
SALES (corp-wide): 192MM **Privately Held**
SIC: 2951 Asphalt paving mixtures & blocks
PA: Peckham Industries, Inc.
 20 Haarlem Ave Ste 200
 White Plains NY 10603
 914 949-2000

(G-17147)
PEARSON LONGMAN LLC (DH)
10 Bank St Ste 1030 (10606-1952)
PHONE..............................212 641-2400
Jeff Taylor, *President*

Roger A Brown, *Vice Pres*
John Stallon, *Vice Pres*
Thomas Wharton, *Vice Pres*
Herbert Yeates, *Treasurer*
EMP: 40
SALES (est): 151.4MM
SALES (corp-wide): 6.7B **Privately Held**
SIC: 2731 2711 Books: publishing & printing; newspapers, publishing & printing
HQ: Pearson Inc.
 330 Hudson St Fl 9
 New York NY 10013
 212 641-2400

(G-17148)
PECKHAM INDUSTRIES INC (PA)
20 Haarlem Ave Ste 200 (10603-2223)
PHONE..............................914 949-2000
Fax: 914 949-2075
John R Peckham, *President*
Gary W Metcalf, *Vice Pres*
Joseph Wildermuth, *Vice Pres*
Darryl Crespino, *Plant Mgr*
Lou Merkle, *Safety Mgr*
▲ **EMP:** 30 **EST:** 1924
SQ FT: 15,000
SALES (est): 192MM **Privately Held**
WEB: www.peckham.com
SIC: 2951 Concrete, asphaltic (not from refineries)

(G-17149)
PECKHAM MATERIALS CORP (HQ)
20 Haarlem Ave Ste 200 (10603-2223)
PHONE..............................914 686-2045
John R Peckham, *President*
Gary Metcalf, *Vice Pres*
Peter Simoneau, *Vice Pres*
John Giorgianne, *Plant Mgr*
Matt Rice, *Plant Mgr*
EMP: 100
SQ FT: 5,000
SALES (est): 20.2MM
SALES (corp-wide): 192MM **Privately Held**
SIC: 2951 1611 5032 Asphalt & asphaltic paving mixtures (not from refineries); concrete, asphaltic (not from refineries); highway & street paving contractor; paving mixtures
PA: Peckham Industries, Inc.
 20 Haarlem Ave Ste 200
 White Plains NY 10603
 914 949-2000

(G-17150)
PENTON BUSINESS MEDIA INC
Fleet Owner Magazine
707 Westchester Ave # 101 (10604-3102)
PHONE..............................914 949-8500
Paul Kisseberth, *Branch Mgr*
EMP: 14
SALES (corp-wide): 348.9MM **Privately Held**
SIC: 2731 Book publishing
HQ: Penton Business Media, Inc.
 9800 Metcalf Ave
 Shawnee Mission KS 66212
 913 341-1300

(G-17151)
PEPSI-COLA BOTTLING GROUP (DH)
Also Called: Pepsico
1111 Westchester Ave (10604-4000)
PHONE..............................914 767-6000
Sean Bishop, *President*
Jenny Nelson, *General Mgr*
Mike Satterfield, *District Mgr*
Dick W Boyce, *Senior VP*
Jeff Campbell, *Senior VP*
◆ **EMP:** 2
SALES (est): 240.9MM
SALES (corp-wide): 63B **Publicly Held**
SIC: 2086 Carbonated soft drinks, bottled & canned
HQ: Pepsi-Cola Metropolitan Bottling Company, Inc.
 1111 Westchester Ave
 White Plains NY 10604
 914 767-6000

GEOGRAPHIC SECTION

White Plains - Westchester County (G-17175)

(G-17152)
PEPSI-COLA METRO BTLG CO INC (HQ)
Also Called: Pepsico
1111 Westchester Ave (10604-4000)
PHONE.................................914 767-6000
Fax: 914 767-1075
Philip A Marineau, *President*
Christine Oconnell, *Publisher*
Robert Carl Biggart, *Chairman*
Lenny Sorbara, *Business Mgr*
Dick W Boyce, *Senior VP*
◆ **EMP:** 5
SQ FT: 100,000
SALES (est): 26.7B
SALES (corp-wide): 63B **Publicly Held**
WEB: www.joy-of-cola.com
SIC: 2086 2087 Carbonated soft drinks, bottled & canned; syrups, drink
PA: Pepsico, Inc.
  700 Anderson Hill Rd
  Purchase NY 10577
  914 253-2000

(G-17153)
PEPSI-COLA OPERATING COMPANY (HQ)
1111 Westchester Ave (10604-4000)
PHONE.................................914 767-6000
John Kayhill, *President*
Steve Schuckenbrock, *CIO*
Vicky Kurak, *Analyst*
EMP: 38
SALES (est): 19.6MM
SALES (corp-wide): 63B **Publicly Held**
SIC: 2086 Bottled & canned soft drinks
PA: Pepsico, Inc.
  700 Anderson Hill Rd
  Purchase NY 10577
  914 253-2000

(G-17154)
PEPSICO INC
1111 Westchester Ave (10604-4000)
PHONE.................................914 253-2000
EMP: 309
SALES (corp-wide): 63B **Publicly Held**
SIC: 2096 Potato chips & similar snacks
PA: Pepsico, Inc.
  700 Anderson Hill Rd
  Purchase NY 10577
  914 253-2000

(G-17155)
PEPSICO INC
150 Airport Rd Hngr V (10604-1219)
PHONE.................................914 253-3474
Archie Walker, *Branch Mgr*
Robert A Baldwin, *Manager*
EMP: 28
SALES (corp-wide): 63B **Publicly Held**
WEB: www.pepsico.com
SIC: 2096 Carbonated soft drinks, bottled & canned
PA: Pepsico, Inc.
  700 Anderson Hill Rd
  Purchase NY 10577
  914 253-2000

(G-17156)
PEPSICO INC
1111 Westchester Ave (10604-3525)
PHONE.................................914 767-6976
Jim Dohr, *Principal*
Neal Bronzo, *Vice Pres*
EMP: 58
SALES (corp-wide): 63B **Publicly Held**
SIC: 2096 Potato chips & similar snacks
PA: Pepsico, Inc.
  700 Anderson Hill Rd
  Purchase NY 10577
  914 253-2000

(G-17157)
PEPSICO WORLD TRADING CO INC
1111 Westchester Ave (10604-4000)
PHONE.................................914 767-6000
Chris Adamski, *President*
EMP: 6
SALES (est): 321.6K
SALES (corp-wide): 63B **Publicly Held**
SIC: 2086 Carbonated soft drinks, bottled & canned

PA: Pepsico, Inc.
  700 Anderson Hill Rd
  Purchase NY 10577
  914 253-2000

(G-17158)
PETER PAUPER PRESS INC
202 Mmaroneck Ave Ste 400 (10601)
PHONE.................................914 681-0144
Fax: 914 681-0389
Laurence Beilenson, *President*
Evelyn Beilenson, *Principal*
Nick Beilenson, *Principal*
Carole Brown, *Production*
Claudine Gandolfi, *Sales Mgr*
▲ **EMP:** 25 **EST:** 1982
SQ FT: 4,004
SALES (est): 3.2MM **Privately Held**
WEB: www.peterpauper.com
SIC: 2731 Books: publishing only

(G-17159)
PFIZER INC
4 Martine Ave (10606-4016)
PHONE.................................914 437-5868
EMP: 146
SALES (corp-wide): 49.6B **Publicly Held**
SIC: 2834 Mfg Pharmaceutical Medicinal Preparations
PA: Pfizer Inc.
  235 E 42nd St
  New York NY 10017
  212 733-2323

(G-17160)
PLASTICYCLE CORPORATION (PA)
245 Main St Ste 430 (10601-2425)
PHONE.................................914 997-6882
Anthony R Corso, *Ch of Bd*
Anthony Corso, *Vice Pres*
Tony Corso, *Human Res Mgr*
Mike Tukav, *Manager*
EMP: 40
SQ FT: 40,000
SALES (est): 6.8MM **Privately Held**
SIC: 3089 Plastic processing

(G-17161)
PREMIER WOODCRAFT LTD
277 Martine Ave 214 (10601-3401)
PHONE.................................610 383-6624
Fax: 610 383-4172
Joseph J Arena, *President*
Eric Svalgard, *Vice Pres*
Greg Nelms, *Controller*
Anna Arena, *Admin Sec*
EMP: 40
SQ FT: 30,000
SALES (est): 3.7MM **Privately Held**
SIC: 2511 2522 2521 2434 Wood household furniture; office furniture, except wood; wood office furniture; wood kitchen cabinets

(G-17162)
READENT INC
Also Called: Jazzles
445 Hamilton Ave Ste 1102 (10601-1832)
PHONE.................................212 710-3004
Andrew Squire, *CEO*
Len Smith, *Manager*
◆ **EMP:** 11
SQ FT: 2,500
SALES (est): 720K **Privately Held**
SIC: 3999 3944 Education aids, devices & supplies; games, toys & children's vehicles

(G-17163)
REEBOK INTERNATIONAL LTD
125 Westchester Ave (10601-4522)
PHONE.................................914 948-3719
EMP: 205
SALES (corp-wide): 18.1B **Privately Held**
SIC: 3149 Children's footwear, except athletic
HQ: Reebok International Ltd.
  1895 J W Foster Blvd
  Canton MA 02021
  781 401-5000

(G-17164)
S & H UNIFORM CORP
1 Aqueduct Rd (10606-1003)
PHONE.................................914 937-6800

Rhoda Ross, *CEO*
Glen Ross, *President*
Dan Berkowitz, *Manager*
Bobbie Marko, *Manager*
▼ **EMP:** 65
SQ FT: 50,000
SALES (est): 10.7MM **Privately Held**
WEB: www.sandhuniforms.com
SIC: 2326 7389 Men's & boys' work clothing; telemarketing services

(G-17165)
S D WARREN COMPANY
925 Westchester Ave # 115 (10604-3507)
PHONE.................................914 696-5544
Brent Demichael, *Branch Mgr*
EMP: 60
SALES (corp-wide): 420.6MM **Privately Held**
SIC: 2679 Paper products, converted
HQ: S. D. Warren Company
  255 State St Fl 4
  Boston MA 02109
  617 423-7300

(G-17166)
SABRA DIPPING COMPANY LLC (DH)
777 Westchester Ave Fl 3 (10604-3520)
PHONE.................................914 372-3900
Fax: 718 204-0417
Shali Shalit-Shoval, *CEO*
Luciano Lopez-May, *Exec VP*
Paul Parker, *Vice Pres*
Doug Pearson, *Vice Pres*
Brandon Williams, *Safety Dir*
▲ **EMP:** 75
SALES (est): 183.8MM **Privately Held**
SIC: 2035 Spreads, sandwich: salad dressing base
HQ: Strauss Group Ltd
  49 Hasivim
  Petah Tikva 49595
  528 288-922

(G-17167)
SAFE FLIGHT INSTRUMENT CORP
20 New King St (10604-1204)
PHONE.................................914 220-1125
Fax: 914 946-7882
Randall Greene, *President*
Joe Wilson, *Vice Pres*
Dick Smith, *Plant Mgr*
Greg Tassio, *Prdtn Mgr*
Victor Falcaro, *Purch Mgr*
EMP: 150 **EST:** 1946
SQ FT: 42,600
SALES (est): 36MM **Privately Held**
WEB: www.safeflight.com
SIC: 3812 7699 Aircraft flight instruments; aircraft control systems, electronic; aircraft flight instrument repair

(G-17168)
SOFTLINK INTERNATIONAL
297 Knollwood Rd Ste 301 (10607-1849)
PHONE.................................914 574-8197
Prakash S Kamat, *CEO*
Sunil Nikhar, *President*
Praveen Lobo, *Vice Pres*
EMP: 45
SQ FT: 1,200
SALES (est): 872.9K **Privately Held**
WEB: www.softlinkinternational.com
SIC: 7372 Prepackaged software

(G-17169)
STARFIRE HOLDING CORPORATION (PA)
445 Hamilton Ave Ste 1210 (10601-1833)
PHONE.................................914 614-7000
Carl Celian Icahn, *Ch of Bd*
Keith Cozza, *Vice Pres*
EMP: 50
SALES (est): 1.4B **Privately Held**
SIC: 3743 4741 4789 Freight cars & equipment; rental of railroad cars; railroad car repair

(G-17170)
STARFUELS INC (HQ)
50 Main St (10606-1901)
PHONE.................................914 289-4800
Robert Ryneveld, *Managing Dir*

Dennis Gormley, *CTO*
EMP: 3 **EST:** 2012
SALES: 21.5MM
SALES (corp-wide): 1MM **Privately Held**
SIC: 3339 2911 1241 Precious metals; oils, fuel; coal mining services
PA: Starcommodities, Inc.
  285 Grand Ave Bldg 3
  Englewood NJ 07631
  201 685-0400

(G-17171)
STEEL EXCEL INC (HQ)
1133 Westchester Ave N-222 (10604-3516)
PHONE.................................914 461-1300
Jack L Howard, *CEO*
Ken Foulke, *Business Mgr*
Thomas Flageollet, *Vice Pres*
Ahmet Houssein, *Vice Pres*
John J Lazlo, *Vice Pres*
▲ **EMP:** 88
SALES: 132.6MM
SALES (corp-wide): 782MM **Publicly Held**
WEB: www.adaptec.com
SIC: 1389 7353 7032 Oil & gas wells: building, repairing & dismantling; oil field equipment, rental or leasing; sporting & recreational camps
PA: Sph Group Holdings Llc
  590 Madison Ave Fl 32
  New York NY 10022
  212 520-2300

(G-17172)
STUDIO FUN INTERNATIONAL INC
44 S Broadway Fl 7 (10601-4417)
PHONE.................................914 238-1000
Harold Clark, *President*
William Magill, *Vice Pres*
Cassie McCann, *Marketing Mgr*
Jennifer Fifield, *Director*
Debra Polansky, *Director*
▲ **EMP:** 30
SALES (est): 6MM
SALES (corp-wide): 1.7B **Privately Held**
WEB: www.rd.com
SIC: 2731 Book publishing
PA: Trusted Media Brands, Inc.
  750 3rd Ave Fl 3
  New York NY 10017
  914 238-1000

(G-17173)
SUNDANCE ENTERPRISES INC (DH)
Also Called: Sundance Solutions
79 Primrose St (10606-1632)
PHONE.................................914 946-2942
Fax: 914 946-2955
William J Purdy, *CEO*
Robert Purdy, *President*
Roger Kurtin, *General Mgr*
Paula Jones, *Finance Mgr*
Ellen Henson, *Accounts Mgr*
▲ **EMP:** 4
SALES (est): 5.9MM
SALES (corp-wide): 4.7B **Privately Held**
SIC: 3841 5999 Diagnostic apparatus, medical; medical apparatus & supplies
HQ: Molnlycke Health Care Ab
  Gamlestadsvagen 3c
  Goteborg 415 0
  317 223-000

(G-17174)
SYMBIO TECHNOLOGIES LLC
333 Mamaroneck Ave (10605-1440)
PHONE.................................914 576-1205
Boyoung Kwon, *Opers Mgr*
Diane Romm, *Marketing Staff*
Lew Tischler, *Manager*
Gideon Romm, *CTO*
Roger Del Russo,
EMP: 7
SALES (est): 1.1MM **Privately Held**
WEB: www.symbio-technologies.com
SIC: 3575 Computer terminals

(G-17175)
TALBOTS INC
125 Westchester Ave # 2460 (10601-4541)
PHONE.................................914 328-1034
Hana Haughton, *Manager*
Sharon See, *Manager*

White Plains - Westchester County (G-17176)

EMP: 7
SALES (corp-wide): 1.3B Privately Held
SIC: 3961 Costume jewelry
HQ: The Talbots Inc
1 Talbots Dr Ste 1
Hingham MA 02043
781 749-7600

(G-17176)
TELEMERGENCY LTD
3 Quincy Ln (10605-5431)
PHONE..................914 629-4222
Elliot I Baum, President
▲ EMP: 5
SQ FT: 1,400
SALES (est): 530K Privately Held
WEB: www.telemergency300.com
SIC: 3669 Emergency alarms

(G-17177)
TENSA SOFTWARE
66 Greenvale Cir (10607-1602)
PHONE..................914 686-5376
Dilib Kha, Owner
EMP: 10
SALES (est): 602.5K Privately Held
SIC: 7372 Prepackaged software

(G-17178)
THE DANNON COMPANY INC (HQ)
100 Hillside Ave Fl 3 (10603-2863)
P.O. Box 5004 (10602-5004)
PHONE..................914 872-8400
Gustavo Valle, CEO
Steve Holmes, General Mgr
Didier Menu, General Mgr
Thomas Kunz, Principal
Frank Riboud, Chairman
◆ EMP: 6
SQ FT: 35,000
SALES (est): 777MM
SALES (corp-wide): 528.4MM Privately Held
WEB: www.dannon.com
SIC: 2026 Yogurt
PA: Danone
17 Boulevard Haussmann
Paris Cedex 09 75439
149 485-000

(G-17179)
VDO LAB INC
400 Tarrytown Rd (10607-1314)
PHONE..................914 949-1741
Fax: 914 949-5743
Hussein Jaffer, President
Mustafe Hirji, Vice Pres
Ahled Hirji, Admin Sec
EMP: 5
SQ FT: 2,110
SALES (est): 559.2K Privately Held
SIC: 3695 Video recording tape, blank

(G-17180)
VIBRA TECH INDUSTRIES INC
126 Oakley Ave (10601-3904)
PHONE..................914 946-1916
Kenneth Strati, President
Cheryl Sieland, Office Mgr
EMP: 11 EST: 1962
SQ FT: 12,000
SALES: 730K Privately Held
SIC: 3471 Finishing, metals or formed products

(G-17181)
WATKINS WELDING AND MCH SP INC
87 Westmoreland Ave (10606-2316)
PHONE..................914 949-6168
Fax: 914 949-8165
Charles G Watkins, President
Inge Watkins, Treasurer
EMP: 7 EST: 1948
SQ FT: 1,850
SALES: 300K Privately Held
SIC: 7692 3599 Welding repair; machine shop, jobbing & repair

(G-17182)
WAYNE PRINTING INC
Also Called: Wayne Printing & Lithographic
70 W Red Oak Ln Fl 4 (10604-3602)
PHONE..................914 761-2400
Fax: 914 761-2710

Jeffrey Wayne, President
EMP: 10 EST: 1946
SQ FT: 1,000
SALES: 1.5MM Privately Held
WEB: www.wayneprinting.com
SIC: 2752 Commercial printing, offset

(G-17183)
WESTCHESTER LAW JOURNAL INC
Also Called: Wlj Printers
199 Main St Ste 301 (10601-3206)
PHONE..................914 948-0715
Fax: 914 948-3014
Lyle Salmon, President
▲ EMP: 5
SQ FT: 1,350
SALES (est): 580K Privately Held
WEB: www.westchesterlawjournal.com
SIC: 2721 7389 Trade journals: publishing only, not printed on site; legal & tax services

(G-17184)
WESTCHESTER MAILING SERVICE
Also Called: Westmail Press
39 Westmoreland Ave Fl 2 (10606-1937)
PHONE..................914 948-1116
Fax: 914 948-9317
George Lusk, President
EMP: 30
SQ FT: 15,000
SALES (est): 2.9MM Privately Held
SIC: 2752 7331 2791 2789 Commercial printing, offset; mailing service; typesetting; bookbinding & related work

(G-17185)
WESTCHESTER WINE WAREHOUSE LLC
53 Tarrytown Rd Ste 1 (10607-1655)
PHONE..................914 824-1400
Fax: 914 824-1401
Ben Khurana,
Rude Seleimi,
EMP: 15
SALES (est): 2.2MM Privately Held
WEB: www.westchesterwine.com
SIC: 2084 2389 Wines; cummerbunds

(G-17186)
WESTFAIR COMMUNICATIONS INC
Also Called: Westchester County Bus Jurnl
3 Westchester Park Dr G7 (10604-3420)
PHONE..................914 694-3600
Fax: 914 694-3680
Dolores Delbello, CEO
Bill Fallon, Editor
Marcia Pflug, Accounts Mgr
Konstantine Wells, Accounts Exec
Susan Barbash, Manager
EMP: 35
SALES (est): 2MM Privately Held
SIC: 2711 2721 Newspapers: publishing only, not printed on site; periodicals

(G-17187)
WHITE PLAINS RUBBER STAMP NAME
39 Westmrland Ave Ste 105 (10606)
P.O. Box 184, Hopewell Junction (12533-0184)
PHONE..................914 949-1900
Fax: 914 949-2328
Justin Wyka, President
EMP: 6
SQ FT: 1,500
SALES: 300K Privately Held
SIC: 3479 3953 Name plates: engraved, etched, etc.; marking devices

(G-17188)
XEROX CORPORATION
8 Hangar Rd (10604-1310)
PHONE..................914 397-1319
Paul Yuhasz, Manager
Brien Zimmermann, Manager
EMP: 23
SALES (corp-wide): 18B Publicly Held
WEB: www.xerox.com
SIC: 3861 Photographic equipment & supplies

PA: Xerox Corporation
45 Glover Ave Ste 700
Norwalk CT 06850
203 968-3000

Whitehall
Washington County

(G-17189)
ADIRONDACK NATURAL STONE LLC
8986 State Route 4 (12887-1800)
P.O. Box 225 (12887-0225)
PHONE..................518 499-0602
Fax: 518 499-0602
Andre Hagadorn, Owner
Greg Cummings, Sales Staff
◆ EMP: 35
SALES (est): 12.4MM Privately Held
WEB: www.adirondacknaturalstone.com
SIC: 1411 Granite, dimension-quarrying

(G-17190)
MAPLEWOOD ICE CO INC
9785 State Route 4 (12887-2317)
P.O. Box 62 (12887-0062)
PHONE..................518 499-2345
Fax: 518 499-2347
David O Wood, President
Donna Wood, Corp Secy
Douglas Wood, Vice Pres
Thomas Pomaineille, Safety Dir
EMP: 30
SQ FT: 6,000
SALES (est): 5.6MM Privately Held
SIC: 2097 5078 Manufactured ice; refrigeration equipment & supplies

(G-17191)
VERMONT STRUCTURAL SLATE CO
Buckley Rd (12887)
PHONE..................518 499-1912
Robert Tucker, Manager
EMP: 12
SALES (corp-wide): 10.4MM Privately Held
WEB: www.vermontstructuralslate.com
SIC: 3281 Cut stone & stone products
PA: Vermont Structural Slate Co Inc
3 Prospect St
Fair Haven VT 05743
802 265-4933

Whitesboro
Oneida County

(G-17192)
COLLEGE CALENDAR COMPANY
148 Clinton St (13492-2501)
PHONE..................315 768-8242
Carter Reul, Owner
Steve Tibits, Manager
EMP: 10
SALES: 850K Privately Held
SIC: 2721 Periodicals

(G-17193)
EVERSAN INC
34 Main St Ste 3 (13492-1039)
PHONE..................315 736-3967
Fax: 315 736-4058
Mustafa Evke, CEO
Allan R Roberts, Vice Pres
Michele Moran, Director
EMP: 14
SALES (est): 2.9MM Privately Held
WEB: www.eversan.com
SIC: 3625 3674 3993 Timing devices, electronic; microprocessors; scoreboards, electric

(G-17194)
QUALITY COMPONENTS FRAMING SYS
44 Mohawk St Bldg 10 (13492-1232)
PHONE..................315 768-1167
Fax: 315 768-3056
Daniel R Webb, President

EMP: 13
SQ FT: 30,000
SALES (est): 1.6MM Privately Held
WEB: www.qcwallpanels.com
SIC: 3253 Clay wall & floor tile

(G-17195)
S R SLOAN INC (PA)
8111 Halsey Rd (13492-3707)
P.O. Box 560, New Hartford (13413-0560)
PHONE..................315 736-7730
Fax: 315 732-5315
Sheldon R Sloan, CEO
Stephen R Sloan, President
Will Compton, Opers Mgr
Melissa Cummings, CFO
Mike Jones, Med Doctor
EMP: 85 EST: 1960
SQ FT: 60,000
SALES (est): 17.4MM Privately Held
WEB: www.srsloan.com
SIC: 2431 2439 Staircases & stairs, wood; trusses, wooden roof

(G-17196)
TELECOMMUNICATION CONCEPTS
Also Called: T C I
329 Oriskany Blvd (13492-1424)
PHONE..................315 736-8523
Don Ryan, President
EMP: 5
SALES (est): 737.9K Privately Held
WEB: www.telecommunicationconcepts.com
SIC: 3661 1731 Telephones & telephone apparatus; telephone & telephone equipment installation

(G-17197)
TURBINE ENGINE COMP UTICA
2 Halsey Rd (13492-3401)
PHONE..................315 768-8070
Fax: 315 768-8014
Rob Cohen, President
Mike Finley, Plant Mgr
Mike Findlay, Facilities Mgr
Marc Paglialonga, QC Mgr
Matt Biesel, Engineer
EMP: 1300
SQ FT: 250,000
SALES (est): 212.8MM
SALES (corp-wide): 249.4MM Privately Held
SIC: 3724 3511 3429 3842 Aircraft engines & engine parts; turbines & turbine generator sets & parts; clamps, couplings, nozzles & other metal hose fittings; surgical appliances & supplies; guided missile & space vehicle parts & auxiliary equipment
PA: U C A Holdings, Inc.
1 W Pack Sq Ste 305
Asheville NC 28801
828 210-8120

(G-17198)
WHITESBORO SPRING & ALIGNMENT (PA)
Also Called: Whitesboro Spring Svce
247 Oriskany Blvd (13492-1596)
PHONE..................315 736-4441
Fax: 315 736-4459
Stewart Wattenbe Jr, President
Melanie Wattenbe, CFO
EMP: 11
SQ FT: 2,500
SALES (est): 1.1MM Privately Held
SIC: 3493 7539 7538 Leaf springs: automobile, locomotive, etc.; brake repair, automotive; general automotive repair shops

Whitestone
Queens County

(G-17199)
ANTICO CASALE USA LLC
1244 Clintonville St 2c (11357-1849)
PHONE..................914 760-1100
Gerard Ambrosio,
Gaetano De Luca,
Fiori Franzese,
Gianluca Nastro,

▲ = Import ▼ = Export
◆ = Import/Export

GEOGRAPHIC SECTION

Williamson - Wayne County (G-17225)

EMP: 4
SQ FT: 800
SALES: 2.6MM **Privately Held**
SIC: 2032 Italian foods: packaged in cans, jars, etc.

(G-17200)
APHRODITIES
2007 Francis Lewis Blvd (11357-3930)
PHONE..................................718 224-1774
John Milonas, *Owner*
EMP: 8
SALES (est): 774.8K **Privately Held**
SIC: 2051 5812 Bread, cake & related products; coffee shop; cafe

(G-17201)
ATLAS FENCE & RAILING CO INC
Also Called: Atlas Fence Co
15149 7th Ave (11357-1236)
PHONE..................................718 767-2200
Toll Free:...................................866 -
Tom Pappas, *President*
Mike Pigone, *Controller*
Josephine USS, *Office Mgr*
EMP: 20
SQ FT: 12,000
SALES (est): 4.9MM **Privately Held**
SIC: 3446 2499 3089 Fences, gates, posts & flagpoles; fences or posts, ornamental iron or steel; fencing, docks & other outdoor wood structural products; fences, gates & accessories: plastic

(G-17202)
BA SPORTS NUTRITION LLC
Also Called: Body Armour
1720 Whitestone Expy # 401 (11357-3065)
PHONE..................................310 424-5077
Lance Collins, *Mng Member*
Carole Oziel, *Manager*
EMP: 292
SALES (est): 15.5MM **Privately Held**
SIC: 2086 Fruit drinks (less than 100% juice): packaged in cans, etc.

(G-17203)
BERARDI BAKERY INC
15045 12th Rd (11357-1809)
PHONE..................................718 746-9529
Vito Berardi, *President*
EMP: 7
SQ FT: 2,800
SALES (est): 490K **Privately Held**
SIC: 2051 Bakery: wholesale or wholesale/retail combined

(G-17204)
CARAVELLA FOOD CORP
16611 Cryders Ln (11357-2832)
PHONE..................................646 552-0455
Tatiana Odato, *President*
Danny Odato, *Vice Pres*
◆ EMP: 12
SQ FT: 3,500
SALES (est): 536.4K **Privately Held**
SIC: 3556 Oilseed crushing & extracting machinery

(G-17205)
CREATIVE WINDOW FASHIONS INC
315 Cresthaven Ln (11357-1148)
PHONE..................................718 746-5817
Steven Lepow, *President*
Meri Gregurovic, *Corp Secy*
EMP: 100
SQ FT: 120,000
SALES (est): 7.5MM **Privately Held**
WEB: www.creativewindowfashions.net
SIC: 2258 Curtains & curtain fabrics, lace

(G-17206)
CROWN AIRCRAFT LIGHTING INC
1021 Clintonville St # 4 (11357-1845)
P.O. Box 570432 (11357-0432)
PHONE..................................718 767-3410
Fax: 718 352-2305
Michelle Virgilio, *President*
EMP: 9
SQ FT: 4,000
SALES (est): 877.3K **Privately Held**
SIC: 3728 Aircraft parts & equipment

(G-17207)
FRENZ GROUP LLC
14932 3rd Ave (11357-1139)
PHONE..................................212 465-0908
Chariklia Varellas, *Mng Member*
Tracy Latteri, *Manager*
▲ EMP: 5
SQ FT: 1,300
SALES (est): 676.3K **Privately Held**
WEB: www.frenzgroup.com
SIC: 3171 Handbags, women's

(G-17208)
HARRIS CORPORATION
1902 Whitestone Expy # 204 (11357-3059)
PHONE..................................718 767-1100
Dominic Catinella, *Manager*
EMP: 18
SALES (corp-wide): 7.4B **Publicly Held**
SIC: 3663 5065 Radio & TV communications equipment; telephone equipment
PA: Harris Corporation
   1025 W Nasa Blvd
   Melbourne FL 32919
   321 727-9100

(G-17209)
HENGYUAN COPPER USA INC
14107 20th Ave Ste 506 (11357-3045)
PHONE..................................718 357-6666
Zhifu Yan, *President*
EMP: 8
SALES (est): 857.9K **Privately Held**
SIC: 3331 Refined primary copper products
PA: Shandong Hengyuan Copper Industry Co.,Ltd.
   Shuixidong, East Fifth Road, North Of Huaihe Rd., Dongying Distr
   Dongying
   546 810-9555

(G-17210)
JENMAR DOOR & GLASS INC
15038 12th Ave (11357-1808)
PHONE..................................718 767-7900
Alan Risi, *Principal*
EMP: 5 EST: 2015
SQ FT: 12,000
SALES (est): 243.2K **Privately Held**
SIC: 3442 Metal doors

(G-17211)
LONG ISLAND FIREPROOF DOOR
Also Called: LI Fireproof Door
1105 Clintonville St (11357-1813)
P.O. Box 570171 (11357-0171)
PHONE..................................718 767-8800
Fax: 718 746-6065
Nick Parise, *Branch Mgr*
EMP: 50
SQ FT: 23,136
SALES (corp-wide): 29MM **Privately Held**
SIC: 3442 3429 7699 5211 Fire doors, metal; manufactured hardware (general); door & window repair; door & window products; door frames, all materials
PA: Long Island Fireproof Door, Inc
   5 Harbor Park Dr Ste 1
   Port Washington NY 11050
   516 390-6800

(G-17212)
NEW YORK DIGITAL PRINT CENTER
15050 14th Rd Ste 1 (11357-2607)
PHONE..................................718 767-1953
Fax: 718 353-7103
Joann Derasmo, *President*
Robert D'Erasmo, *Manager*
EMP: 6
SALES (est): 610K **Privately Held**
SIC: 2752 Commercial printing, lithographic

(G-17213)
PEPPERMINTS SALON INC
15722 Powells Cove Blvd (11357-1332)
PHONE..................................718 357-6304
Evangelia Parlionas, *President*
Felicia Diaram, *Manager*
Margarita Parlionas, *Admin Sec*
EMP: 10

SALES (est): 1.1MM **Privately Held**
SIC: 2844 Cosmetic preparations

(G-17214)
SECURITY DEFENSE SYSTEM
15038 12th Ave (11357-1808)
PHONE..................................718 357-6200
Millie Risi, *President*
Alan Risi, *Consultant*
EMP: 8
SQ FT: 8,000
SALES: 11.5MM **Privately Held**
SIC: 3699 7382 Security devices; protective devices, security

(G-17215)
TOCARE LLC
Also Called: Whitestone Pharmacy
15043b 14th Ave Fl 1 (11357-1864)
PHONE..................................718 767-0618
Roberto Viola,
Nella Viola,
EMP: 8
SALES (est): 962.8K **Privately Held**
SIC: 2834 5122 Pharmaceutical preparations; pharmaceuticals

(G-17216)
TRIBCO LLC
Also Called: Queens Tribune
15050 14th Rd Ste 2 (11357-2607)
PHONE..................................718 357-7400
Fax: 212 357-9417
Laura Chamberlin, *General Mgr*
Bruce Adler, *Editor*
Joshua Dake, *Prdtn Mgr*
Paul Mastronardi, *CFO*
Bob Borkenstein, *Controller*
EMP: 44
SQ FT: 2,000
SALES (est): 3MM **Privately Held**
WEB: www.queenstribune.com
SIC: 2711 Newspapers: publishing only, not printed on site

(G-17217)
TRIBOROUGH ELECTRIC
15044 11th Ave (11357-1806)
PHONE..................................718 321-2144
Peter Gargiulo, *Principal*
EMP: 7
SALES (est): 1MM **Privately Held**
SIC: 3699 Electrical equipment & supplies

(G-17218)
WORLD JOURNAL LLC (HQ)
14107 20th Ave Fl 2 (11357-6093)
PHONE..................................718 746-8889
Fax: 718 746-5972
Jacob MA, *Ch of Bd*
Pily Wang, *Vice Ch Bd*
Corinna Chang, *Accounts Exec*
Sandra Lee, *Accounts Exec*
James Yam, *Accounts Exec*
▲ EMP: 150
SQ FT: 50,000
SALES (est): 52.1MM **Privately Held**
WEB: www.wjnews.net
SIC: 2711 Newspapers: publishing only, not printed on site
PA: Cooper Investors Inc.
   14107 20th Ave Ste 602
   Flushing NY 11357
   718 767-8895

Whitney Point
Broome County

(G-17219)
ADVANCED GRAPHICS COMPANY
2607 Main St (13862-2223)
P.O. Box 311 (13862-0311)
PHONE..................................607 692-7875
Rosemarie Fralick, *Owner*
▼ EMP: 10 EST: 1957
SQ FT: 5,000
SALES (est): 931.9K **Privately Held**
SIC: 2672 3479 2759 Labels (unprinted), gummed: made from purchased materials; name plates: engraved, etched, etc.; screen printing

(G-17220)
POINT CANVAS COMPANY INC
5952 State Route 26 (13862-1211)
PHONE..................................607 692-4381
Lori Warfield, *President*
Sharon Dahulich, *Vice Pres*
Wayne Dahulich, *Treasurer*
Danny Warfield, *Admin Sec*
EMP: 5
SALES: 75K **Privately Held**
SIC: 2394 2395 5199 Canvas & related products; embroidery & art needlework; canvas products

Wht Sphr Spgs
Sullivan County

(G-17221)
KLEIN & SONS LOGGING INC
3114 State Route 52 (12787-5802)
PHONE..................................845 292-6682
Fax: 845 292-5849
Ronald Klein, *President*
Dale Klein, *Admin Sec*
EMP: 18
SQ FT: 3,900
SALES (est): 2.3MM **Privately Held**
SIC: 2411 Logging camps & contractors

Williamson
Wayne County

(G-17222)
DR PEPPER SNAPPLE GROUP INC
Also Called: Mott's
4363 State Route 104 (14589-9332)
PHONE..................................315 589-4911
Stephen Taylor, *Opers Mgr*
Frederick M Dale, *Opers Staff*
Jeffrey N Glahn, *Chief Engr*
Anthony Rozada, *Regl Sales Mgr*
Jack Manganello, *Accounts Exec*
EMP: 250
SALES (corp-wide): 6.2B **Publicly Held**
WEB: www.maunalai.com
SIC: 2086 2087 2084 Soft drinks: packaged in cans, bottles, etc.; flavoring extracts & syrups; wines, brandy & brandy spirits
PA: Dr Pepper Snapple Group, Inc.
   5301 Legacy Dr
   Plano TX 75024
   972 673-7000

(G-17223)
FINGER LAKES TRELLIS SUPPLY
4041a Railroad Ave (14589-9391)
PHONE..................................315 904-4007
Todd Smith, *Owner*
Susana Catlin, *Principal*
▲ EMP: 5
SALES (est): 722.6K **Privately Held**
SIC: 2431 5211 Trellises, wood; doors, storm: wood or metal

(G-17224)
LAGONER FARMS INC
6954 Tuckahoe Rd (14589-9590)
PHONE..................................315 589-4899
Mark Lagoner, *President*
Dianna Lagoner, *Admin Sec*
EMP: 52
SQ FT: 8,000
SALES: 1.5MM **Privately Held**
SIC: 2033 0191 Fruits: packaged in cans, jars, etc.; general farms, primarily crop

(G-17225)
SALMON CREEK CABINETRY INC
6687 Salmon Creek Rd (14589-9557)
PHONE..................................315 589-5419
Charles Ciurca, *President*
EMP: 21
SALES (est): 1.5MM **Privately Held**
SIC: 2434 Wood kitchen cabinets

Williamson - Wayne County (G-17226)

(G-17226)
THATCHER COMPANY NEW YORK INC
4135 Rte 104 (14589)
P.O. Box 118 (14589-0118)
PHONE..................................315 589-9330
Craig N Thatcher, *President*
Chris Pavlick, *General Mgr*
J Christopher Pavlick, *Vice Pres*
Gavin Lapray, *Credit Mgr*
Gail Peacock, *Credit Mgr*
▲ **EMP:** 45
SALES (est): 11.8MM
SALES (corp-wide): 89.5MM **Privately Held**
SIC: 2819 5169 Industrial inorganic chemicals; chemicals & allied products
PA: Thatcher Group, Inc
  1905 W Fortune Rd
  Salt Lake City UT 84104
  801 972-4587

(G-17227)
TRIHEX MANUFACTURING INC
6708 Pound Rd (14589-9751)
PHONE..................................315 589-9331
Fax: 315 589-2024
Roger Lester, *President*
Dina Lester, *Manager*
EMP: 6 EST: 1979
SQ FT: 12,000
SALES: 600K **Privately Held**
SIC: 3451 3452 Screw machine products; bolts, nuts, rivets & washers

Williamstown
Oswego County

(G-17228)
C G & SON MACHINING INC
87 Nichols Rd (13493-2415)
PHONE..................................315 964-2430
Brian Gardner, *CEO*
EMP: 5
SALES: 703.6K **Privately Held**
SIC: 7692 Welding repair

(G-17229)
WARES OF WOOD
259 Cc Rd (13493-3314)
PHONE..................................315 964-2983
Fax: 315 964-2653
Mike Engst, *Owner*
EMP: 24
SQ FT: 24,000
SALES: 625K **Privately Held**
WEB: www.waresofwood.com
SIC: 2521 2541 Cabinets, office: wood; store fixtures, wood

Williamsville
Erie County

(G-17230)
17 BAKERS LLC
8 Los Robles St (14221-6719)
PHONE..................................844 687-6836
Anthony Habib, *CEO*
Anthony Habibm, *CEO*
Ashley Battaglia, *Principal*
EMP: 10 EST: 2015
SALES (est): 311.7K **Privately Held**
SIC: 2052 Bakery products, dry

(G-17231)
ALETHEAS CHOCOLATES INC (PA)
8301 Main St (14221-6139)
PHONE..................................716 633-8620
Gust E Tassy, *President*
Dean Tassy, *Vice Pres*
Nick Malgiieri, *Accounting Mgr*
EMP: 21
SQ FT: 10,000
SALES (est): 2.1MM **Privately Held**
WEB: www.aletheas.com
SIC: 2066 Chocolate

(G-17232)
ALEXANDRIA PROFESSIONAL LLC
15 Lawrence Bell Dr (14221-7075)
PHONE..................................800 957-8427
Lina Kennedy, *Branch Mgr*
EMP: 9
SALES (corp-wide): 329.1K **Privately Held**
SIC: 2844 Toilet preparations
PA: 938023 Ontario Inc
  149 King St
  Port Colborne ON L3K 4
  289 478-1040

(G-17233)
ASHTON-POTTER USA LTD
Also Called: Hig Capital
10 Curtwright Dr (14221-7072)
PHONE..................................716 633-2000
Fax: 716 633-2525
Miles S Nadal, *Ch of Bd*
Barry Switzer, *President*
Joe Sheeran, *Senior VP*
Kelly Smith, *Senior VP*
Bob Morreale, *Vice Pres*
▲ **EMP:** 170
SQ FT: 104,000
SALES (est): 28.2MM
SALES (corp-wide): 2.2B **Privately Held**
WEB: www.ashtonpotter.com
SIC: 2754 2759 Trading stamps: gravure printing; trading stamps: printing
PA: H.I.G. Capital, L.L.C.
  1450 Brickell Ave Fl 31
  Miami FL 33131
  305 379-2322

(G-17234)
AT&T CORP
8200 Transit Rd Ste 200 (14221-2820)
PHONE..................................716 639-0673
Tonnie Logan, *Manager*
EMP: 6
SALES (corp-wide): 146.8B **Publicly Held**
WEB: www.att.com
SIC: 3663 Mobile communication equipment
HQ: At&T Corp.
  1 At&T Way
  Bedminster NJ 07921
  800 403-3302

(G-17235)
BEE PUBLICATIONS INC
Also Called: Amherst Bee
5564 Main St (14221-5410)
PHONE..................................716 632-4700
Fax: 716 633-8601
Trey Measer, *President*
George J Measer III, *President*
Michael Measer, *Vice Pres*
Cynthia Guszik, *Sales Mgr*
Carl Kraft, *Accounts Exec*
EMP: 55
SQ FT: 3,000
SALES: 3.1MM **Privately Held**
WEB: www.beenews.com
SIC: 2711 Newspapers: publishing only, not printed on site

(G-17236)
BROETJE AUTOMATION-USA INC
165 Lawrence Bell Dr # 116 (14221-7900)
PHONE..................................716 204-8640
Ken Benczkowski, *President*
Jeremy Harris, *General Mgr*
Laura Ballard, *Manager*
EMP: 120
SQ FT: 200,000
SALES (est): 24MM
SALES (corp-wide): 1.2MM **Privately Held**
SIC: 3365 Aerospace castings, aluminum
HQ: Broetje-Automation Gmbh
  Am Autobahnkreuz 14
  Rastede 26180
  440 296-60

(G-17237)
CABOODLE PRINTING INC
1975 Wehrle Dr Ste 120 (14221-7022)
PHONE..................................716 693-6000
John Doyle, *President*
Gary Wodarczak, *Vice Pres*
EMP: 6
SALES (est): 985.9K **Privately Held**
WEB: www.caboodleprinting.com
SIC: 2752 Commercial printing, lithographic

(G-17238)
CANADA GOOSE US INC
300 International Dr (14221-5781)
PHONE..................................303 832-7097
EMP: 6
SALES (est): 564.1K
SALES (corp-wide): 138.6K **Privately Held**
SIC: 2339 2337 Women's & misses' outerwear; women's & misses' suits & coats
PA: Canada Goose Holdings Inc
  250 Bowie Ave
  Toronto ON M6E 4
  888 668-0625

(G-17239)
CLOUD TORONTO INC
1967 Wehrle Dr Ste 1 (14221-8452)
PHONE..................................408 569-4542
Adam Noop, *Owner*
EMP: 10
SALES: 2.5MM **Privately Held**
SIC: 3679 Electronic circuits

(G-17240)
DAWN FOOD PRODUCTS INC
160 Lawrence Bell Dr # 120 (14221-7897)
PHONE..................................716 830-8214
EMP: 107
SALES (corp-wide): 2B **Privately Held**
SIC: 2045 Doughnut mixes, prepared: from purchased flour
HQ: Dawn Food Products, Inc.
  3333 Sargent Rd
  Jackson MI 49201
  517 789-4400

(G-17241)
ELASTOMERS INC
2095 Wehrle Dr (14221-7097)
PHONE..................................716 633-4883
Fax: 716 633-4461
Robert J Kunkel Sr, *President*
Robert J Kunkel Jr, *Vice Pres*
EMP: 8
SQ FT: 12,250
SALES: 700K **Privately Held**
SIC: 2821 Elastomers, nonvulcanizable (plastics)

(G-17242)
ENGINEERED PLASTICS INC
300 International Dr # 100 (14221-5783)
PHONE..................................800 682-2525
Ken Szekely, *President*
Ken Lawrence, *Vice Pres*
▲ **EMP:** 20
SQ FT: 2,000
SALES (est): 3.5MM **Privately Held**
SIC: 3996 Tile, floor: supported plastic

(G-17243)
FRITO-LAY NORTH AMERICA INC
25 Curtwright Dr (14221-7073)
PHONE..................................716 631-2360
Kert King, *General Mgr*
Jeff Quinn, *Safety Mgr*
David Bogart, *Director*
EMP: 80
SALES (corp-wide): 63B **Publicly Held**
WEB: www.fritolay.com
SIC: 2096 Corn chips & other corn-based snacks
HQ: Frito-Lay North America, Inc.
  7701 Legacy Dr
  Plano TX 75024

(G-17244)
GENERAL WELDING & FABG INC
4545 Transit Rd (14221-6012)
PHONE..................................716 568-7958
EMP: 7
SALES (corp-wide): 5.3MM **Privately Held**
SIC: 7692 Welding repair
PA: General Welding & Fabricating, Inc.
  991 Maple Rd
  Elma NY 14059
  716 652-0033

(G-17245)
GLOBALQUEST SOLUTIONS INC
2805 Wehrle Dr Ste 11 (14221-7383)
PHONE..................................716 601-3524
Fax: 716 601-3527
Aaron Fox, *President*
Chris Lorenz, *Sales Executive*
Denise Sisti, *Manager*
Michael Morlock, *CTO*
Tom Orschek, *Director*
EMP: 12
SQ FT: 2,000
SALES (est): 3.2MM **Privately Held**
WEB: www.globalquestinc.com
SIC: 7372 Business oriented computer software

(G-17246)
GOODWILL INDS WSTN NY INC
4311 Transit Rd (14221-7231)
PHONE..................................716 633-3305
Tammy Smith, *General Mgr*
EMP: 18
SALES (corp-wide): 8.3MM **Privately Held**
SIC: 3999 Barber & beauty shop equipment
PA: Goodwill Industries Of Western New York, Inc.
  1119 William St
  Buffalo NY 14206
  716 854-3494

(G-17247)
HOLLAND MANUFACTURING INC
415 Lawrence Bell Dr # 6 (14221-7805)
P.O. Box 525, Lancaster (14086-0525)
PHONE..................................716 685-4129
EMP: 6
SALES (est): 388.6K **Privately Held**
SIC: 3999 Manufacturing industries

(G-17248)
LEGAL SERVICING LLC
2801 Wehrle Dr Ste 5 (14221-7381)
PHONE..................................716 565-9300
EMP: 7
SALES (est): 593.4K **Privately Held**
SIC: 1389 Roustabout service

(G-17249)
ORTHO DENT LABORATORY INC
6325 Sheridan Dr (14221-4848)
PHONE..................................716 839-1900
James Wright, *President*
Michael Wright, *Manager*
EMP: 14
SQ FT: 1,000
SALES (est): 1.4MM **Privately Held**
WEB: www.wlof.net
SIC: 3843 Orthodontic appliances

(G-17250)
ORTHO-CLINICAL DIAGNOSTICS INC
15 Limestone Dr (14221-7051)
PHONE..................................716 631-1281
Sue Riester, *Branch Mgr*
EMP: 37
SQ FT: 5,600
SALES (corp-wide): 1B **Privately Held**
WEB: www.orthoclinical.com
SIC: 2835 Blood derivative diagnostic agents
PA: Ortho-Clinical Diagnostics, Inc.
  1001 Us Highway 202
  Raritan NJ 08869
  908 218-8000

(G-17251)
SCHMITT SALES INC
Also Called: Robo Self Serve
5095 Main St (14221-5203)
PHONE..................................716 632-8595
Joe Betts, *Manager*
EMP: 8
SQ FT: 2,347

GEOGRAPHIC SECTION

SALES (corp-wide): 99.9MM **Privately Held**
WEB: www.schmittsales.com
SIC: 1389 Gas field services
PA: Schmitt Sales, Inc.
2101 Saint Ritas Ln
Buffalo NY 14221
716 639-1500

(G-17252)
SENECA RESOURCES CORPORATION
165 Lawrence Bell Dr (14221-7900)
PHONE.................716 630-6750
Fax: 716 630-6777
Scott Brown, *Principal*
Jonathan Wilkins, *Manager*
EMP: 18
SALES (corp-wide): 1.7B **Publicly Held**
WEB: www.srcx.com
SIC: 1382 Oil & gas exploration services
HQ: Seneca Resources Corporation
1201 Louisiana St Ste 400
Houston TX 77002
713 654-2600

(G-17253)
SIMULATED SURGICAL SYSTEMS LLC
Also Called: Ross
5225 Shrdan Dr Tkf Suites (14221)
PHONE.................716 633-7216
David Grant, *Sales Dir*
Mark S Kan,
EMP: 5
SALES (est): 992.2K **Privately Held**
SIC: 3841 Surgical & medical instruments

(G-17254)
SOLMAC INC
1975 Wehrle Dr Ste 130 (14221-7022)
PHONE.................716 630-7061
Borris Soldo, *President*
John Barrett, *General Mgr*
EMP: 9
SALES (est): 1.5MM **Privately Held**
SIC: 3599 Machine shop, jobbing & repair

(G-17255)
SRC LIQUIDATION COMPANY
435 Lawrence Bell Dr # 4 (14221-8440)
PHONE.................716 631-3900
EMP: 5 **Publicly Held**
SIC: 2754 Printing
PA: Src Liquidation Company
600 Albany St
Dayton OH 45417
937 221-1000

(G-17256)
SUCCESSWARE INC
8860 Main St 102 (14221-7640)
PHONE.................716 565-2338
Fax: 716 565-2328
Phil Di RE, *President*
Roy Powell, *Treasurer*
Timothy McGuire, *Sales Dir*
Gerri Di RE, *Admin Asst*
EMP: 15
SQ FT: 1,600
SALES (est): 1.1MM
SALES (corp-wide): 46.7B **Privately Held**
WEB: www.successware21.com
SIC: 7372 Prepackaged software
HQ: Clockwork Home Services, Inc.
50 Central Ave Ste 920
Sarasota FL 34236
941 366-9692

(G-17257)
TEALEAFS
5416 Main St (14221-5362)
PHONE.................716 688-8022
Sydney Hoffman, *Owner*
EMP: 5
SALES (est): 397.4K **Privately Held**
SIC: 2087 Beverage bases

(G-17258)
TOWN OF AMHERST
Also Called: Park's Department
450 Maple Rd (14221-3162)
PHONE.................716 631-7113
Fax: 716 631-7240
Dan Raily, *Manager*
EMP: 40
SQ FT: 15,600 **Privately Held**
WEB: www.apdny.org
SIC: 2531 9111 Picnic tables or benches, park; mayors' offices
PA: Town Of Amherst
5583 Main St Ste 1
Williamsville NY 14221
716 631-7082

(G-17259)
WEST SENECA BEE INC
5564 Main St (14221-5410)
PHONE.................716 632-4700
Trey Measer, *President*
EMP: 60
SQ FT: 4,500
SALES (est): 1.5MM **Privately Held**
SIC: 2711 Newspapers

Williston Park
Nassau County

(G-17260)
ALLOYD ASSOCIATION INC
78 Sherman Ave (11596-2314)
PHONE.................516 248-8835
Lloyd Seigel, *President*
Floyd Seagull, *President*
EMP: 7
SALES (est): 525.2K **Privately Held**
SIC: 3431 Plumbing fixtures: enameled iron cast iron or pressed metal

(G-17261)
GREENWAY CABINETRY INC
485 Willis Ave (11596-1725)
PHONE.................516 877-0009
Frank Tommasini, *President*
David Kolodny, *Office Mgr*
EMP: 10
SALES (est): 630K **Privately Held**
SIC: 2434 Wood kitchen cabinets

(G-17262)
SCHARF AND BREIT INC
2 Hillside Ave Ste F (11596-2335)
PHONE.................516 282-0287
Christopher Aives, *President*
K Rasmussen, *Assistant VP*
EMP: 50
SQ FT: 22,000
SALES (est): 3.5MM **Privately Held**
SIC: 2329 Sweaters & sweater jackets: men's & boys'

(G-17263)
T RS GREAT AMERICAN REST
17 Hillside Ave (11596-2303)
PHONE.................516 294-1680
Fax: 516 294-1885
Patrick Miele, *President*
EMP: 10
SALES (est): 943.3K **Privately Held**
SIC: 2035 Seasonings & sauces, except tomato & dry

Willsboro
Essex County

(G-17264)
COMMONWEALTH HOME FASHION INC
31 Station Rd (12996)
P.O. Box 339 (12996-0339)
PHONE.................514 384-8290
Fax: 518 963-8146
Harvey Levenson, *President*
Bill Clay, *Plant Mgr*
Bill McClay, *Plant Mgr*
Susan Trombly, *Executive*
▲ EMP: 90
SQ FT: 151,000
SALES (est): 10.4MM
SALES (corp-wide): 10MM **Privately Held**
WEB: www.comhomfash.com
SIC: 2259 Curtains & bedding, knit
PA: Decors De Maison Commonwealth Inc
8800 Boul Pie-Ix
Montreal QC H1Z 3
514 384-8290

(G-17265)
GENERAL COMPOSITES INC
39 Myers Way (12996-4539)
PHONE.................518 963-7333
Joseph M Callahan Jr, *CEO*
Jeffrey G Allott, *Ch of Bd*
Mimi Lane, *Plant Mgr*
Daniel Albert, *Controller*
Allison Whalen, *Office Mgr*
▲ EMP: 41
SQ FT: 40,000
SALES (est): 7.7MM **Privately Held**
WEB: www.generalcomposites.com
SIC: 3089 8711 Synthetic resin finished products; consulting engineer

(G-17266)
PRIVA USA INC
39 Myers Way (12996-4539)
PHONE.................518 963-4074
Michael Rattner, *President*
EMP: 7
SALES (est): 590K **Privately Held**
SIC: 2299 Textile goods

Wilmington
Essex County

(G-17267)
ADIRONDACK CHOCOLATE CO LTD (PA)
Also Called: Candy Man
5680 Ny State Rte 86 (12997)
PHONE.................518 946-7270
Joe Dougherty, *President*
EMP: 9 EST: 1962
SQ FT: 800
SALES (est): 1.1MM **Privately Held**
WEB: www.candymanonline.com
SIC: 2066 5441 Chocolate candy, solid; candy

Wilson
Niagara County

(G-17268)
LYNX PRODUCT GROUP LLC
650 Lake St (14172-9600)
PHONE.................716 751-3100
Fax: 716 751-3101
Dawn Coe, *Purchasing*
Renee Moshier, *Office Mgr*
Donald Basil,
David T Beckinghausen,
Mark M Misso,
EMP: 38
SQ FT: 28,000
SALES (est): 9.3MM **Privately Held**
WEB: www.lynxpg.com
SIC: 3582 Washing machines, laundry: commercial, incl. coin-operated

(G-17269)
VALAIR INC
87 Harbor St (14172-9749)
P.O. Box 27 (14172-0027)
PHONE.................716 751-9480
Fax: 716 751-9491
Donald E Sinclair Jr, *Ch of Bd*
John Sinclair, *President*
Linda J Sinclair, *Corp Secy*
EMP: 12
SQ FT: 4,000
SALES (est): 1.7MM **Privately Held**
SIC: 3599 Machine shop, jobbing & repair

(G-17270)
WOODCOCK BROTHERS BREWING COMP
638 Lake St (14172-9600)
P.O. Box 66 (14172-0066)
PHONE.................716 333-4000
Tim Woodcock, *President*
EMP: 9
SALES (est): 959.8K **Privately Held**
SIC: 2082 Malt beverages

Wilton
Saratoga County

(G-17271)
TECH VALLEY TECHNOLOGIES INC
267 Ballard Rd Ste 2 (12831-1594)
PHONE.................518 584-8899
Bruce Hodge, *President*
Susan Spadaro, *Accountant*
EMP: 10
SQ FT: 7,000
SALES: 2MM **Privately Held**
WEB: www.techvalleytech.com
SIC: 3812 Defense systems & equipment

Windsor
Broome County

(G-17272)
DEVONIAN STONE NEW YORK INC
463 Atwell Hill Rd (13865-3623)
PHONE.................607 655-2600
Fax: 607 655-2623
Robert Bellospirito, *President*
Tim Hertzog, *Controller*
▲ EMP: 28
SQ FT: 7,000
SALES: 2.1MM **Privately Held**
WEB: www.devonianstone.com
SIC: 3281 1459 Cut stone & stone products; stoneware clay mining

(G-17273)
WINDSOR UNITED INDUSTRIES LLC
10 Park St (13865)
PHONE.................607 655-3300
Dennis Garges,
EMP: 40
SALES (est): 3.2MM **Privately Held**
SIC: 2499 Decorative wood & woodwork

Wingdale
Dutchess County

(G-17274)
HUNT COUNTRY FURNITURE INC (PA)
19 Dog Tail Corners Rd (12594-1218)
PHONE.................845 832-6601
Todd Gazzoli, *General Mgr*
Randy Williams, *Chairman*
▲ EMP: 80
SQ FT: 60,000
SALES (est): 9.7MM **Privately Held**
WEB: www.huntcountryfurniture.com
SIC: 2511 2599 Chairs, household, except upholstered: wood; restaurant furniture, wood or metal

(G-17275)
WESTCHESTER MODULAR HOMES INC
30 Reagans Mill Rd (12594-1101)
PHONE.................845 832-9400
Fax: 845 832-6698
Charles W Hatcher, *President*
Zachary Revella, *Purch Agent*
Grover Greiner, *Manager*
EMP: 125
SQ FT: 104,000
SALES (est): 20.9MM **Privately Held**
WEB: www.westchestermodular.com
SIC: 2452 Modular homes, prefabricated, wood

Wolcott
Wayne County

(G-17276)
BURNETT CONCRETE
PRODUCTS INC
5941 Auburn St (14590-9721)
P.O. Box 207 (14590-0207)
PHONE..................................315 594-2242
Joseph Burnett, *President*
EMP: 5
SQ FT: 10,000
SALES (est): 676.7K **Privately Held**
SIC: 3272 Concrete products

(G-17277)
CAHOON FARMS INC
10951 Lummisville Rd (14590-9549)
P.O. Box 190 (14590-0190)
PHONE..................................315 594-8081
Fax: 315 594-1678
Donald D Cahoon Jr, *President*
William Cahoon, *Vice Pres*
Dave Green, *Opers Staff*
Sheila Rigerman, *QC Mgr*
Jolene Green, *Controller*
EMP: 35
SQ FT: 44,000
SALES (est): 9.8MM **Privately Held**
SIC: 2033 0723 2037 0175 Fruit juices: fresh; fruit (fresh) packing services; frozen fruits & vegetables; deciduous tree fruits

(G-17278)
CARBALLO CONTRACT
MACHINING
Also Called: C C M
6205 Lake Ave (14590-1040)
PHONE..................................315 594-2511
Jeannie Brockmyer, *Owner*
Bryan Brockmyre, *Opers Staff*
EMP: 5
SQ FT: 3,000
SALES (est): 360K **Privately Held**
WEB: www.ccmprecision.biz
SIC: 3599 Machine & other job shop work

(G-17279)
EAGLE WELDING MACHINE
13458 Ridge Rd (14590-9602)
PHONE..................................315 594-1845
Gary Buckalew, *Owner*
EMP: 9
SALES: 1MM **Privately Held**
SIC: 7692 Welding repair

(G-17280)
MARSHALL INGREDIENTS LLC
5786 Limekiln Rd (14590-9354)
PHONE..................................800 796-9353
EMP: 6
SALES (corp-wide): 787.7K **Privately Held**
SIC: 2034 Fruits, dried or dehydrated, except freeze-dried
PA: Marshall Ingredients Llc
   5740 Limekiln Rd
   Wolcott NY

(G-17281)
WAYUGA COMMUNITY
NEWSPAPERS
Also Called: Waguya News
12039 E Main St (14590-1021)
PHONE..................................315 594-2506
Louis Brach, *Publisher*
Bill Bender, *Accounts Exec*
Chuck Palermo, *Manager*
EMP: 6
SQ FT: 5,004
SALES (corp-wide): 2.5MM **Privately Held**
WEB: www.wayuga.com
SIC: 2711 4225 Newspapers, publishing & printing; general warehousing
PA: Wayuga Community Newspapers Inc
   6784 Main St
   Red Creek NY 13283
   315 754-6229

Woodbury
Nassau County

(G-17282)
ARIZONA BEVERAGE COMPANY
LLC (HQ)
Also Called: Arizona Beverages USA
60 Crossways Park Dr W # 400
(11797-2018)
PHONE..................................516 812-0300
Jim Dar, *Vice Pres*
John Gabella, *Sales Mgr*
Ali Carbone, *Marketing Staff*
Mark Striegel, *Marketing Staff*
Anthony Galeno, *Office Mgr*
▼ EMP: 3
SALES (est): 2.6MM
SALES (corp-wide): 67.8MM **Privately Held**
SIC: 2086 Iced tea & fruit drinks, bottled & canned
PA: Hornell Brewing Co., Inc.
   60 Crossways Park Dr W # 400
   Woodbury NY 11797
   516 812-0300

(G-17283)
CLEVER DEVICES LTD (PA)
300 Crossways Park Dr (11797-2035)
PHONE..................................516 433-6100
Frank Ingrassia, *CEO*
Darryl Curtis, *President*
Amy Miller, *Managing Dir*
Andrew Stanton, *COO*
Buddy Coleman, *Exec VP*
EMP: 43
SQ FT: 10,000
SALES (est): 18.7MM **Privately Held**
WEB: www.cleverdevices.net
SIC: 3679 3663 Recording & playback apparatus, including phonograph; radio & TV communications equipment

(G-17284)
COMPOSITECH LTD
4 Fairbanks Blvd (11797-2604)
PHONE..................................516 835-1458
Jonas Medney, *Ch of Bd*
Christopher F Johnson, *President*
Richard Depoto, *Vice Pres*
Ralph W Segalowitz, *Vice Pres*
Samuel S Gross, *Treasurer*
EMP: 110
SQ FT: 33,000
SALES (est): 11.5MM **Privately Held**
WEB: www.compositech.com
SIC: 3674 6794 Semiconductors & related devices; patent owners & lessors

(G-17285)
E & W MANUFACTURING CO INC
15 Pine Dr (11797-1509)
PHONE..................................516 367-8571
Elliot Wald, *President*
EMP: 21
SQ FT: 15,000
SALES (est): 1.7MM **Privately Held**
SIC: 3991 Paint brushes

(G-17286)
F & V DISTRIBUTION COMPANY
LLC
1 Arizona Plz (11797-1125)
PHONE..................................516 812-0393
Don Vultaggio, *Principal*
EMP: 5 **Privately Held**
SIC: 2086 Iced tea & fruit drinks, bottled & canned
PA: F & V Distribution Company, Llc
   60 Crossways Park Dr W # 400
   Woodbury NY 11797

(G-17287)
GEM MINE CORP
84 Cypress Dr (11797-1523)
PHONE..................................516 367-1075
Fax: 212 391-5645
Camillo Pizzo, *President*
Bob D'Ambrosio, *Finance*
EMP: 7
SALES (est): 644.8K **Privately Held**
SIC: 3911 Jewelry, precious metal

(G-17288)
GLOBAL VIDEO LLC (HQ)
Also Called: Guidance Channel
1000 Woodbury Rd Ste 1 (11797-2530)
PHONE..................................516 222-2600
David Rust, *President*
EMP: 60
SALES (est): 17.1MM
SALES (corp-wide): 1.6B **Publicly Held**
WEB: www.sunburstvm.com
SIC: 2741 5961 5092 6719 Catalogs: publishing & printing; book club, mail order; educational toys; investment holding companies, except banks
PA: School Specialty, Inc.
   W6316 Design Dr
   Greenville WI 54942
   920 734-5712

(G-17289)
HARMAN INTERNATIONAL INDS
INC
Also Called: Consumer Audio Facility
210 Crossways Park Dr (11797-2048)
PHONE..................................516 496-3400
Robert Hessler, *COO*
Lalit Panda, *Vice Pres*
John Busch, *Engineer*
Terrie Woods, *Engineer*
Humberto Forcell, *Marketing Staff*
EMP: 130
SALES (corp-wide): 6.9B **Publicly Held**
WEB: www.harman.com
SIC: 3651 Household audio & video equipment
PA: Harman International Industries Incorporated
   400 Atlantic St Ste 15
   Stamford CT 06901
   203 328-3500

(G-17290)
HOWARD CHARLES INC
180 Froehlich Farm Blvd (11797-2923)
P.O. Box 544, Mahopac (10541-0544)
PHONE..................................917 902-6934
Charles Breslin, *Principal*
EMP: 8
SALES (est): 780K **Privately Held**
SIC: 3089 Plastic kitchenware, tableware & houseware

(G-17291)
LENCORE ACOUSTICS CORP
(PA)
1 Crossways Park Dr W (11797-2014)
PHONE..................................516 682-9292
Fax: 516 682-4785
Jack D Leonard, *Ch of Bd*
Tim Deblaey, *Vice Pres*
Jonathan Leonard, *Vice Pres*
Lori Jewell, *Project Mgr*
Cheryl McLaughlin, *Bookkeeper*
EMP: 10
SQ FT: 2,200
SALES (est): 5.9MM **Privately Held**
WEB: www.lencore.com
SIC: 3446 Partitions & supports/studs, including accoustical systems; acoustical suspension systems, metal

(G-17292)
LI SCRIPT LLC
333 Crossways Park Dr (11797-2066)
PHONE..................................631 321-3850
Fax: 631 321-3859
Michael Shamalov, *Owner*
EMP: 32
SALES (est): 7.3MM **Privately Held**
SIC: 2752 Commercial printing, lithographic

(G-17293)
LINDEN CARE LLC (PA)
Also Called: Linden Pro Care
130 Crossways Park Dr # 101
(11797-2046)
PHONE..................................516 221-7600
John Steinberg, *Partner*
Mark Schmier, *Finance Dir*
Hunter Plotsker, *Accounts Mgr*
Jordan Blue, *Sales Staff*
Matt Pellicane, *Sales Executive*
EMP: 8
SQ FT: 4,000
SALES (est): 2.9MM **Privately Held**
SIC: 2834 Pharmaceutical preparations

(G-17294)
MANHATTAN MILLING & DRYING
CO
78 Pond Rd (11797-1616)
PHONE..................................516 496-1041
John Mc Auley, *President*
Robert Mc Auley, *Treasurer*
EMP: 20
SQ FT: 37,500
SALES (est): 1.1MM **Privately Held**
SIC: 2099 Spices, including grinding

(G-17295)
PHOTO INDUSTRY INC
Also Called: Pemystifying Diital
7600 Jericho Tpke Ste 301 (11797-1705)
PHONE..................................516 364-0016
Fax: 516 364-0140
Allan Lavine, *President*
Jerry Grossman, *Vice Pres*
EMP: 10
SQ FT: 1,200
SALES (est): 980K **Privately Held**
SIC: 2721 Magazines: publishing only, not printed on site

(G-17296)
PROVIDENT FUEL INC
4 Stillwell Ln (11797-1104)
PHONE..................................516 224-4427
Douglas Robalino, *Principal*
EMP: 9
SALES (est): 1.2MM **Privately Held**
SIC: 2869 Fuels

(G-17297)
RAYTECH CORPORATION (HQ)
97 Froehlich Farm Blvd (11797-2903)
PHONE..................................718 259-7388
Larry W Singleton, *President*
Howard Mandell, *CFO*
Alfred Klee, *Internal Med*
EMP: 9
SQ FT: 7,000
SALES (est): 102.8MM
SALES (corp-wide): 112.6MM **Privately Held**
WEB: www.raytech.com
SIC: 3499 Friction material, made from powdered metal
PA: Raytech Corp Asbestos Personal Injury Settlement Trust
   190 Willis Ave
   Mineola NY 11501
   516 747-0300

(G-17298)
RESEARCH FRONTIERS INC
(PA)
240 Crossways Park Dr (11797-2033)
PHONE..................................516 364-1902
Fax: 516 364-3798
Robert L Saxe, *Ch of Bd*
Joseph M Harary, *President*
Michael R Lapointe, *Vice Pres*
Steven M Slovak, *Vice Pres*
Seth L Van Voorhees, *CFO*
EMP: 12 EST: 1930
SQ FT: 9,500
SALES: 2MM **Publicly Held**
WEB: www.refr-spd.com
SIC: 3829 Measuring & controlling devices

(G-17299)
ROYAL PAINT ROLLER CORP
Also Called: Royal Paint Roller Mfg
1 Harvard Dr (11797-3302)
PHONE..................................516 367-4370
Randy Boritz, *President*
Gloria Boritz, *Admin Sec*
EMP: 25 EST: 1968
SQ FT: 23,000
SALES (est): 2MM **Privately Held**
SIC: 3991 Paint rollers

(G-17300)
SORFIN YOSHIMURA IC DISC
LTD
100 Crossways Park Dr W # 200
(11797-2012)
PHONE..................................516 802-4600
Paul Fink, *President*

▲ = Import ▼ = Export
◆ = Import/Export

GEOGRAPHIC SECTION

Manny Prieto, *Vice Pres*
Yasmine Sanders, *Manager*
▲ **EMP:** 7
SALES (est): 1.9MM **Privately Held**
SIC: 3825 Battery testers, electrical

(G-17301)
STAR X-RAY CO INC
2 Sheffield HI (11797-2420)
PHONE.................................631 842-3010
Eric Rosen, *President*
Judith Rosen, *Corp Secy*
Steven Rosen, *Vice Pres*
Timothy O'Connor, *QC Mgr*
▲ **EMP:** 32
SQ FT: 14,500
SALES (est): 4.5MM **Privately Held**
WEB: www.starxray.com
SIC: 3844 5047 X-ray apparatus & tubes; hospital equipment & furniture; dental equipment & supplies; medical equipment & supplies

(G-17302)
VEECO INSTRUMENTS INC
100 Sunnyside Blvd Ste B (11797-2925)
PHONE.................................516 677-0200
Fax: 516 349-9079
Edward Braun, *President*
Keith Johnson, *President*
Robert W Bradshaw, *Senior VP*
Peter Collingwood, *Senior VP*
Bill Miller, *Senior VP*
EMP: 230
SALES (corp-wide): 477MM **Publicly Held**
WEB: www.veeco.com
SIC: 3826 3823 Analytical instruments; industrial instrmnts msrmnt display/control process variable
PA: Veeco Instruments Inc.
1 Terminal Dr
Plainview NY 11803
516 677-0200

(G-17303)
WIN-HOLT EQUIPMENT CORP (PA)
Also Called: Win-Holt Equipment Group
20 Crossways Park Dr N # 205 (11797-2007)
PHONE.................................516 222-0335
Fax: 516 222-0538
Jonathan J Holtz, *CEO*
Dominick Scarfogliero, *President*
Courtney Guerrero, *General Mgr*
Jose Ponce, *COO*
Jane Dunstatter, *Opers Mgr*
▲ **EMP:** 45
SQ FT: 10,000
SALES (est): 88.1MM **Privately Held**
WEB: www.winholt.com
SIC: 2099 Food preparations

(G-17304)
WOODBURY SYSTEMS GROUP INC
30 Glenn Dr (11797-2104)
P.O. Box 346, Plainview (11803-0346)
PHONE.................................516 364-2653
William L Fitzgerald, *President*
Deirdre Volpe, *Vice Pres*
EMP: 6
SALES: 792.5K **Privately Held**
WEB: www.woodsysgrp.com
SIC: 7372 Prepackaged software

Woodhaven
Queens County

(G-17305)
COMCO PLASTICS INC
9831 Jamaica Ave (11421-2213)
PHONE.................................718 849-9000
Fax: 718 441-1538
Michael French, *President*
Jack Russo, *General Mgr*
Wayne Fleming, *QC Mgr*
Jason Romano, *Sales Executive*
▲ **EMP:** 37 **EST:** 1956
SQ FT: 20,000

SALES: 4.3MM **Privately Held**
WEB: www.comcoplastics.com
SIC: 3082 3081 Rods, unsupported plastic; unsupported plastics film & sheet

(G-17306)
JO-VIN DECORATORS INC
9423 Jamaica Ave (11421-2287)
PHONE.................................718 441-9350
Fax: 718 441-1447
Vincent Pappalando, *Ch of Bd*
Annamarie Silberswig, *Manager*
Leo Pappalardo, *Admin Sec*
EMP: 40 **EST:** 1956
SQ FT: 20,000
SALES (est): 4.7MM **Privately Held**
WEB: www.jo-vin.com
SIC: 2391 2299 2392 2394 Curtains & draperies; tops & top processing, manmade or other fiber; bedspreads & bed sets: made from purchased materials; shades, canvas: made from purchased materials

(G-17307)
LATINO SHOW MAGAZINE INC
8025 88th Rd (11421-2423)
PHONE.................................718 709-1151
Cesar Florez, *Publisher*
EMP: 5
SALES (est): 216.8K **Privately Held**
SIC: 2721 Magazines: publishing & printing

(G-17308)
STEINDL CAST STONE CO INC
9107 76th St (11421-2817)
PHONE.................................718 296-8530
John Steindl Jr, *President*
James Steindl, *Vice Pres*
EMP: 6 **EST:** 1928
SQ FT: 2,800
SALES: 500K **Privately Held**
WEB: www.steindlcaststone.com
SIC: 3272 Cast stone, concrete

Woodhull
Steuben County

(G-17309)
OWLETTS SAW MILLS
4214 Cook Rd (14898-9630)
PHONE.................................607 525-6340
Walt Owlett, *Owner*
EMP: 5
SALES (est): 269.8K **Privately Held**
SIC: 2421 Sawmills & planing mills, general

Woodmere
Nassau County

(G-17310)
ALLIED PHARMACY PRODUCTS INC
544 Green Pl (11598-1923)
PHONE.................................516 374-8862
Stuart Meadow, *Principal*
EMP: 5
SALES (est): 605.1K **Privately Held**
SIC: 2834 5047 Pharmaceutical preparations; medical & hospital equipment

(G-17311)
BENISHTY BROTHERS CORP
233 Mosher Ave (11598-1655)
PHONE.................................646 339-9991
EMP: 5
SALES (est): 283K **Privately Held**
SIC: 3524 Lawn & garden mowers & accessories

(G-17312)
CINDERELLAS SWEETS LTD
Also Called: Shabtai Gourmet
874 Lakeside Dr (11598-1916)
PHONE.................................516 374-7976
Cynthia Itzkowitz, *President*
Andrew Itzkowitz, *Vice Pres*
Sid Itzkowitz, *Prdtn Mgr*
EMP: 27

SALES (est): 1.3MM **Privately Held**
SIC: 2051 Bakery: wholesale or wholesale/retail combined

(G-17313)
GLASGOW PRODUCTS INC
886 Lakeside Dr (11598-1916)
PHONE.................................516 374-5937
Fax: 516 561-8891
Paul J Glasgow, *President*
Dorothy Glasgow, *Treasurer*
EMP: 25
SQ FT: 3,000
SALES (est): 3.4MM **Privately Held**
WEB: www.glasgowproducts.com
SIC: 3535 8711 Conveyors & conveying equipment; consulting engineer

(G-17314)
SPANCRAFT LTD
920 Railroad Ave (11598-1697)
PHONE.................................516 295-0055
Fax: 516 569-3333
Philip A Engel, *President*
Steven Engel, *Vice Pres*
◆ **EMP:** 10
SALES (est): 1.1MM **Privately Held**
WEB: www.spancraft.com
SIC: 2519 Household furniture, except wood or metal: upholstered

Woodridge
Sullivan County

(G-17315)
PROFESSIONAL CAB DETAILING CO
Also Called: Procab
Navograrsky Rd (12789)
P.O. Box 727 (12789-0727)
PHONE.................................845 436-7282
Keith Bahr-Tioson, *Owner*
EMP: 10
SQ FT: 15,000
SALES (est): 600K **Privately Held**
WEB: www.procab.com
SIC: 2511 2431 Kitchen & dining room furniture; millwork

Woodside
Queens County

(G-17316)
A SUNSHINE GLASS & ALUMINUM
2901 Brooklyn Queens Expy (11377-1242)
PHONE.................................718 932-8080
Fax: 718 932-6028
Scong Lee, *Principal*
Chris Lee, *Manager*
Julie Kim, *Admin Sec*
EMP: 20
SALES (est): 1.8MM **Privately Held**
SIC: 3211 5023 Flat glass; glassware

(G-17317)
ATHENS IRON FABRICATION INC
Also Called: Athens Welding Iron Works Co
3435 56th St (11377-2121)
PHONE.................................718 424-7799
Fax: 718 803-3927
Vasilios Agapakis, *President*
EMP: 10
SALES (est): 680K **Privately Held**
SIC: 7692 1799 Welding repair; ornamental metal work

(G-17318)
AXEL PLASTICS RES LABS INC
5820 Broadway (11377-2132)
P.O. Box 770855 (11377-0855)
PHONE.................................718 672-8300
Fax: 718 565-7447
Frank Axel, *CEO*
Jake Axel, *President*
Barbara Axel, *Corp Secy*
Leslie Feldman, *CFO*
Glenn Pfister, *Sales Dir*
▼ **EMP:** 32
SQ FT: 4,500

SALES (est): 9.9MM **Privately Held**
WEB: www.axelplast.com
SIC: 2821 2992 Plastics materials & resins; lubricating oils & greases

(G-17319)
BALDWIN RIBBON & STAMPING CORP
3956 63rd St (11377-3649)
PHONE.................................718 335-6700
Fax: 718 478-3449
Ronald Steinberg, *President*
EMP: 15 **EST:** 1946
SQ FT: 5,000
SALES (est): 2MM **Privately Held**
SIC: 2399 3999 Emblems, badges & insignia; military insignia

(G-17320)
BIELECKY BROS INC (PA)
5022 72nd St (11377-6084)
PHONE.................................718 424-4764
Edwood Bielecky, *President*
Ray Hassan, *Controller*
Anthony Malkun, *Sales Staff*
Peter Bielecky, *Admin Sec*
EMP: 22
SQ FT: 24,000
SALES: 3.3MM **Privately Held**
WEB: www.bieleckybrothers.com
SIC: 2519 Rattan furniture: padded or plain; wicker & rattan furniture

(G-17321)
C & T TOOL & INSTRUMENT CO
Also Called: C&T Tool & Instrmnt
4125 58th St (11377-4748)
PHONE.................................718 429-1253
Constantine Tsamis, *Chairman*
EMP: 24
SQ FT: 1,690
SALES (est): 2.2MM **Privately Held**
SIC: 3599 3542 3444 3441 Machine shop, jobbing & repair; machine tools, metal forming type; sheet metalwork; fabricated structural metal

(G-17322)
C L PRECISION MACHINE & TL CO
5015 70th St (11377-6020)
PHONE.................................718 651-8475
Fax: 718 651-8475
George Lolis, *President*
EMP: 5
SQ FT: 1,200
SALES: 250K **Privately Held**
SIC: 3599 Machine shop, jobbing & repair

(G-17323)
CAR-GO INDUSTRIES INC (PA)
5007 49th St (11377-7335)
PHONE.................................718 472-1443
Drori Benman, *President*
EMP: 8
SQ FT: 5,000
SALES (est): 9.3MM **Privately Held**
SIC: 3714 Motor vehicle parts & accessories

(G-17324)
CODY PRINTING CORP
3728 56th St (11377-2438)
PHONE.................................718 651-8854
Kyu Hwang, *CEO*
Kyung Shin, *President*
EMP: 9
SQ FT: 3,000
SALES (est): 990K **Privately Held**
WEB: www.codyprinting.com
SIC: 2752 Commercial printing, lithographic

(G-17325)
DAMIANOU SPORTSWEAR INC
6001 31st Ave Ste 2 (11377-1205)
PHONE.................................718 204-5600
Fax: 718 204-5081
Paul Damianou, *President*
Pat Damianou, *Corp Secy*
Elenitsa Damianou, *Vice Pres*
DOE Chand, *Controller*
EMP: 62
SQ FT: 24,000

Woodside - Queens County (G-17326)

GEOGRAPHIC SECTION

SALES (est): 5.5MM **Privately Held**
SIC: 2335 Women's, juniors' & misses' dresses

(G-17326)
DOMOTECK INTERIORS INC
2430 Brooklyn Queens Expy # 1 (11377-7825)
PHONE.................................718 433-4300
Raja Mustafa, *President*
Konstantinos Mabrikos, *Vice Pres*
Angela Mathews, *Manager*
EMP: 5
SQ FT: 5,000
SALES: 500K **Privately Held**
SIC: 1411 Limestone & marble dimension stone; argillite, dimension-quarrying

(G-17327)
ECUADOR NEWS INC
6403 Roosevelt Ave Fl 2 (11377-3643)
PHONE.................................718 205-7014
Fax: 718 205-2250
Edgar Arboleda, *President*
Marcelo Arboleda, *Exec Dir*
EMP: 15
SALES (est): 570K **Privately Held**
WEB: www.ecuadornews.net
SIC: 2711 Newspapers

(G-17328)
FIRECOM INC (PA)
Also Called: Bio Service
3927 59th St (11377-3435)
PHONE.................................718 899-6100
Paul Mendez, *Ch of Bd*
Howard Kogan, *COO*
Howard L Kogen, *COO*
Antoine J Sayour, *Senior VP*
Dale Fergus, *Vice Pres*
EMP: 130 EST: 1978
SQ FT: 16,000
SALES (est): 53.7MM **Privately Held**
SIC: 3669 1799 Fire detection systems, electric; fire escape installation

(G-17329)
FIRST LINE PRINTING INC
3728 56th St (11377-2438)
PHONE.................................718 606-0860
Salvador Torres, *President*
Sergio Torres, *Manager*
EMP: 10
SALES: 4MM **Privately Held**
SIC: 2752 Commercial printing, lithographic

(G-17330)
FURNITURE DSIGN BY KNOSSOS INC
2430 Bklyn Qns Expy Ste 3 (11377-7825)
PHONE.................................718 729-0404
Steve Tepelidis, *Ch of Bd*
George Despo, *President*
Satyabrata Chowdhury, *Bookkeeper*
EMP: 24
SQ FT: 23,185
SALES: 2.5MM **Privately Held**
SIC: 2499 Decorative wood & woodwork

(G-17331)
GENESIS ELECTRICAL MOTORS
Also Called: Genesis Electl Motor
6010 32nd Ave (11377-2019)
PHONE.................................718 274-7030
Hercules Minnelli, *President*
Beatrice Minnelli, *Corp Secy*
EMP: 5
SQ FT: 4,000
SALES (est): 864.9K **Privately Held**
SIC: 7694 Electric motor repair

(G-17332)
GLOBE ELECTRONIC HARDWARE INC
3424 56th St (11377-2122)
P.O. Box 770727 (11377-0727)
PHONE.................................718 457-0303
Caroline Dennehy, *President*
Paul Murphy, *COO*
M Dennehy, *Vice Pres*
Patrick M Dennehy, *Vice Pres*
EMP: 14 EST: 1976
SQ FT: 8,800
SALES (est): 930K **Privately Held**
WEB: www.globelectronics.com
SIC: 3451 5072 Screw machine products; hardware

(G-17333)
INTERNATIONAL CREATIVE MET INC
Also Called: I C M
3728 61st St (11377-2538)
P.O. Box 770661 (11377-0661)
PHONE.................................718 424-8179
Setrak Onnik Agonian, *President*
▼ EMP: 14
SQ FT: 8,000
SALES (est): 1.2MM **Privately Held**
WEB: www.icmetal.com
SIC: 3446 3599 Architectural metalwork; machine shop, jobbing & repair

(G-17334)
KETCHAM PUMP CO INC
3420 64th St (11377-2398)
PHONE.................................718 457-0800
Fax: 718 672-1408
Stuart Hruska, *President*
B Tonry, *Manager*
EMP: 15 EST: 1903
SQ FT: 10,000
SALES (est): 3.5MM **Privately Held**
SIC: 3561 Pumps & pumping equipment

(G-17335)
KLEER - VIEW INDEX CO INC
6938 Garfield Ave (11377-6027)
PHONE.................................718 896-3800
Fax: 718 275-9704
Ezio Battaglini, *President*
George Lolis, *Engineer*
David Battaglini, *Shareholder*
Domenica Battaglini, *Shareholder*
EMP: 5 EST: 1948
SQ FT: 6,000
SALES (est): 410K **Privately Held**
SIC: 3089 5112 Closures, plastic; stationery & office supplies

(G-17336)
MC COY TOPS AND INTERIORS INC
Also Called: Mc Coy Tops and Covers
6914 49th Ave (11377-6002)
PHONE.................................718 458-5800
John Proimos, *President*
EMP: 8
SQ FT: 6,000
SALES (est): 740K **Privately Held**
SIC: 2399 2394 Seat covers, automobile; convertible tops, canvas or boat: from purchased materials

(G-17337)
METALOCKE INDUSTRIES INC
3202 57th St (11377-1919)
PHONE.................................718 267-9200
Fax: 718 267-9300
Tom Sadi, *President*
Tanveer Sadiq, *Vice Pres*
Ramona Sadig, *Asst Office Mgr*
EMP: 6 EST: 1936
SQ FT: 10,000
SALES: 630K **Privately Held**
SIC: 2431 Doors & door parts & trim, wood

(G-17338)
METRO MACHINING & FABRICATING
3234 61st St (11377-2030)
PHONE.................................718 545-0104
Nicholas Dorazio, *President*
EMP: 7
SALES (est): 570K **Privately Held**
SIC: 3599 Machine shop, jobbing & repair

(G-17339)
MULTI TECH ELECTRIC
2526 50th St (11377-7823)
PHONE.................................718 606-2695
Mario Torres, *Vice Pres*
Laurie Torres, *Administration*
EMP: 10
SALES (est): 740K **Privately Held**
SIC: 3699 Electrical equipment & supplies

(G-17340)
NATIONAL ELEV CAB & DOOR CORP
Also Called: Necd
5315 37th Ave (11377-2474)
PHONE.................................718 478-5900
Fax: 718 478-0087
Harold Friedman, *CEO*
John Ferella, *President*
Jeffrey Friedman, *Exec VP*
George Karazim, *Plant Mgr*
Dave Talcott, *CFO*
▲ EMP: 50 EST: 1930
SQ FT: 30,000
SALES (est): 16.8MM **Privately Held**
WEB: www.necd.com
SIC: 3534 Elevators & equipment

(G-17341)
NORTH AMERICAN MBL SYSTEMS INC
3354 62nd St (11377-2236)
PHONE.................................718 898-8700
Thomas Crowley, *President*
Connor Crowley, *Owner*
EMP: 33
SALES (est): 5.9MM **Privately Held**
SIC: 3663 Radio broadcasting & communications equipment

(G-17342)
NYC TRADE PRINTERS CORP
3245 62nd St (11377-2031)
PHONE.................................718 606-0610
Ely Toledo, *President*
Felix Toledo, *Manager*
EMP: 12
SQ FT: 5,000
SALES (est): 1.5MM **Privately Held**
SIC: 2711 Commercial printing & newspaper publishing combined

(G-17343)
ORTHOPEDIC TREATMENT FACILITY
4906 Queens Blvd (11377-4462)
PHONE.................................718 898-7326
Gary Marano, *President*
Anthony Marano, *Vice Pres*
EMP: 8
SQ FT: 2,800
SALES: 700K **Privately Held**
SIC: 3842 Limbs, artificial; braces, orthopedic

(G-17344)
PACEMAKER PACKAGING CORP
7200 51st Rd (11377-7631)
PHONE.................................718 458-1188
Fax: 718 429-2907
Emil Romotzki, *President*
Michele Romotzki, *Manager*
Helga Romotzki, *Admin Sec*
EMP: 10 EST: 1964
SQ FT: 7,000
SALES (est): 1.8MM **Privately Held**
SIC: 3565 Packaging machinery

(G-17345)
PALMBAY LTD
3739 58th St (11377-2408)
PHONE.................................718 424-3388
Fax: 718 396-4488
Wenchao Tao, *President*
EMP: 6
SQ FT: 20,000
SALES (est): 690K **Privately Held**
WEB: www.disposablewear.com
SIC: 2384 2252 Robes & dressing gowns; slipper socks

(G-17346)
PFEIL & HOLING INC
5815 Northern Blvd (11377-2297)
PHONE.................................718 545-4600
Sy Stricker, *President*
Margo Stricker, *Corp Secy*
Erica Romanoff, *Manager*
◆ EMP: 75 EST: 1923
SQ FT: 50,000
SALES (est): 13.3MM **Privately Held**
WEB: www.cakedeco.com
SIC: 2064 5046 5999 Cake ornaments, confectionery; bakery equipment & supplies; cake decorating supplies

(G-17347)
PIEMONTE HOME MADE RAVIOLI CO (PA)
Also Called: Piemonte Company
3436 65th St (11377-2329)
PHONE.................................718 429-1972
Fax: 718 429-6076
Mario Bertorelli, *President*
Flavio Bertorelli, *Vice Pres*
▲ EMP: 16 EST: 1945
SQ FT: 14,000
SALES (est): 1.6MM **Privately Held**
WEB: www.piemonteravioli.com
SIC: 2098 5812 Macaroni products (e.g. alphabets, rings & shells), dry; noodles (e.g. egg, plain & water), dry; spaghetti, dry; eating places

(G-17348)
PLAYBILL INCORPORATED
3715 61st St (11377-2593)
PHONE.................................718 335-4033
Lewis Cole, *Finance Other*
Laura Goldman, *Manager*
EMP: 20
SALES (corp-wide): 21.6MM **Privately Held**
SIC: 2789 Bookbinding & repairing: trade, edition, library, etc.
PA: Playbill Incorporated
729 7th Ave Fl 4
New York NY 10019
212 557-5757

(G-17349)
RE 99 CENTS INC
4905 Roosevelt Ave (11377-4457)
PHONE.................................718 639-2325
EMP: 6 EST: 2009
SALES (est): 492.6K **Privately Held**
SIC: 3643 Mfg Conductive Wiring Devices

(G-17350)
RED WHITE & BLUE ENTPS CORP
3443 56th St (11377-2121)
PHONE.................................718 565-8080
Vasilios Katranis, *President*
EMP: 5
SALES (est): 529.9K **Privately Held**
SIC: 2521 5712 2541 2434 Wood office filing cabinets & bookcases; customized furniture & cabinets; table or counter tops, plastic laminated; wood kitchen cabinets

(G-17351)
ROBERT-MASTERS CORP
3217 61st St (11377-2029)
PHONE.................................718 545-1030
Roberto C Orellana, *President*
▲ EMP: 7
SQ FT: 10,000
SALES (est): 915.9K **Privately Held**
SIC: 3442 Rolling doors for industrial buildings or warehouses, metal

(G-17352)
SAFEWORKS LLC
Also Called: Spider
3030 60th St Ste 1 (11377-1234)
PHONE.................................800 696-5577
Fax: 718 326-9835
Valerie Pierce, *Owner*
David Herdrich, *Manager*
EMP: 18
SALES (corp-wide): 105.4MM **Privately Held**
WEB: www.safeworks.com
SIC: 3446 7629 7353 Scaffolds, mobile or stationary: metal; electrical equipment repair, high voltage; heavy construction equipment rental
HQ: Safeworks, Llc
365 Upland Dr
Tukwila WA 98188
206 575-6445

(G-17353)
SPAETH DESIGN INC
6006 37th Ave (11377-2541)
PHONE.................................718 606-9685
Sandra L Spaeth, *President*
David Spaeth, *Chairman*
Dorothy Spaeth, *Corp Secy*
Tim Scalia, *Controller*

▲ = Import ▼ = Export
◆ = Import/Export

GEOGRAPHIC SECTION

▲ EMP: 35 EST: 1945
SQ FT: 27,000
SALES (est): 7.6MM Privately Held
WEB: www.spaethdesign.com
SIC: 2653 Display items, corrugated: made from purchased materials

(G-17354)
SPECTRUM ON BROADWAY
6106 34th Ave (11377-2228)
PHONE.....................................718 932-5388
Fax: 718 932-0150
Harvey Brooks, *President*
Michael Gyscek, *Vice Pres*
Joseph Morra, *Vice Pres*
EMP: 12
SALES (est): 1.9MM Privately Held
WEB: www.spectrumsignsinc.com
SIC: 3993 Signs & advertising specialties

(G-17355)
SPECTRUM SIGNS INC
6106 34th Ave (11377-2228)
PHONE.....................................631 756-1010
Harvey Brooks, *President*
Michael Gyscek, *Vice Pres*
Joseph Morra, *Vice Pres*
Joseph Dimaggio, *VP Human Res*
EMP: 45
SQ FT: 20,000
SALES (est): 5.7MM Privately Held
SIC: 3993 Electric signs; signs, not made in custom sign painting shops

(G-17356)
STAINLESS METALS INC
6001 31st Ave Ste 1 (11377-1205)
PHONE.....................................718 784-1454
Fred Meier, *President*
Dan Meier, *Vice Pres*
EMP: 11 EST: 1927
SQ FT: 14,000
SALES (est): 1.4MM Privately Held
WEB: www.stainlessmetals.com
SIC: 3443 3431 Tanks, standard or custom fabricated: metal plate; sinks: enameled iron, cast iron or pressed metal

(G-17357)
SUPER-TEK PRODUCTS INC
2544 Borough Pl (11377-7815)
PHONE.....................................718 278-7900
Fax: 718 204-6013
Dianne Herbert, *General Mgr*
Harry Paullison, *General Mgr*
John Garuti Jr, *Chairman*
Diane Burmeister, *Vice Pres*
Harry Paulson, *Vice Pres*
▲ EMP: 45 EST: 1959
SQ FT: 45,000
SALES (est): 14.4MM Privately Held
WEB: www.super-tek.com
SIC: 2891 Adhesives & sealants; epoxy adhesives; adhesives, plastic

(G-17358)
SYNERGX SYSTEMS INC (HQ)
3927 59th St (11377-3435)
PHONE.....................................516 433-4700
Paul Mendez, *President*
Denise Hajek, *Purch Agent*
John A Poserina, *CFO*
Chris Anzalone, *Sales Mgr*
Vincent Milanesi, *Sales Mgr*
EMP: 89
SQ FT: 16,400
SALES (est): 18.8MM
SALES (corp-wide): 53.7MM Privately Held
WEB: www.synergxsystems.com
SIC: 3669 7382 Emergency alarms; fire alarm apparatus, electric; fire detection systems, electric; transportation signaling devices; security systems services; burglar alarm maintenance & monitoring
PA: Firecom, Inc.
3927 59th St
Woodside NY 11377
718 899-6100

(G-17359)
UTLEYS INCORPORATED
3123 61st St (11377-1222)
PHONE.....................................718 956-1661
Fax: 718 956-4414
George Utley III, *President*
John Utley, *Vice Pres*
Jane DOE, *Admin Asst*
EMP: 45
SQ FT: 6,500
SALES: 7MM Privately Held
WEB: www.utleys.com
SIC: 3565 Packaging machinery

(G-17360)
VERNON PLATING WORKS INC
3318 57th St (11377-2298)
PHONE.....................................718 639-1124
Fax: 718 458-2040
Kenneth Abrahami, *CEO*
Alan Hyman, *President*
EMP: 15
SQ FT: 20,000
SALES (est): 1.2MM Privately Held
SIC: 3471 Electroplating of metals or formed products

(G-17361)
VISUAL MILLWORK & FIXTURE MFG
2515 50th St (11377-7809)
PHONE.....................................718 267-7800
Mario Fichera Jr, *CEO*
Roy White, *CFO*
EMP: 60
SQ FT: 50,000
SALES: 6MM Privately Held
WEB: www.visualdisplayinc.com
SIC: 2542 Office & store showcases & display fixtures

Woodstock
Ulster County

(G-17362)
CUSTOM PATCHES INC
1760 Glasco Tpke (12498-2136)
P.O. Box 22, Mount Marion (12456-0022)
PHONE.....................................845 679-6320
Sophia Preza, *President*
Kari Gilbert, *Manager*
EMP: 35
SALES: 500K Privately Held
SIC: 2395 Pleating & stitching

(G-17363)
INNOVATIVE PDTS OF AMER INC
Also Called: I P A
234 Tinker St (12498-1126)
PHONE.....................................845 679-4500
Peter Vinci, *President*
Vince Mow, *President*
Jennifer Vinci, *Treasurer*
Munmun Khan, *Associate*
▲ EMP: 32
SQ FT: 18,000
SALES: 9.6MM Privately Held
WEB: www.ipatools.com
SIC: 3569 Lubrication equipment, industrial

(G-17364)
MARSHA FLEISHER
Also Called: Loominus Handwoven
18 Tinker St (12498-1233)
PHONE.....................................845 679-6500
Marsha Fleisher, *Owner*
Andrea Rose, *General Mgr*
EMP: 10
SALES (est): 808.6K Privately Held
SIC: 2282 5632 2211 Weaving yarn: throwing & twisting; women's accessory & specialty stores; broadwoven fabric mills, cotton

(G-17365)
ROTRON INCORPORATED (HQ)
Also Called: Ametek Rotron
55 Hasbrouck Ln (12498-1894)
PHONE.....................................845 679-2401
Fax: 845 679-1870
Robert J Vogel, *President*
Michael Denicola, *Vice Pres*
Kenneth Berryann, *Mfg Staff*
Debbie Brooks, *Senior Buyer*
Steve Johnson, *Purchasing*
▲ EMP: 300
SQ FT: 110,000
SALES (est): 181.6MM
SALES (corp-wide): 3.9B Publicly Held
WEB: www.rotronmilaero.com
SIC: 3564 Blowers & fans
PA: Ametek, Inc.
1100 Cassatt Rd
Berwyn PA 19312
610 647-2121

(G-17366)
ROTRON INCORPORATED
Also Called: Ametek Rotron
9 Hasbrouck Ln (12498-1807)
PHONE.....................................845 679-2401
Charles Lohwasser, *Principal*
EMP: 44
SALES (corp-wide): 3.9B Publicly Held
SIC: 3564 Blowers & fans
HQ: Rotron Incorporated
55 Hasbrouck Ln
Woodstock NY 12498
845 679-2401

Woodville
Jefferson County

(G-17367)
RURAL HILL SAND AND GRAV CORP
10262 County Route 79 (13650-2028)
P.O. Box 128, Belleville (13611-0128)
PHONE.....................................315 846-5212
Fax: 315 846-5033
David Staie, *President*
EMP: 12 EST: 1956
SQ FT: 1,000
SALES (est): 1.7MM Privately Held
SIC: 1442 3273 Construction sand mining; gravel mining; ready-mixed concrete

Worcester
Otsego County

(G-17368)
FRITO-LAY NORTH AMERICA INC
10 Main St (12197-3507)
PHONE.....................................607 397-1008
EMP: 92
SALES (corp-wide): 63B Publicly Held
SIC: 2099 5141 Food preparations; groceries, general line
HQ: Frito-Lay North America, Inc.
7701 Legacy Dr
Plano TX 75024

Wyandanch
Suffolk County

(G-17369)
ACCRA SHEETMETAL LLC
1359 Straight Path (11798-4336)
P.O. Box 1219 (11798-0219)
PHONE.....................................631 920-2087
Orlando Stokes,
EMP: 7
SQ FT: 4,000
SALES: 500K Privately Held
SIC: 3444 Sheet metalwork

(G-17370)
ADVANCE GRAFIX EQUIPMENT INC
150 Wyandanch Ave (11798-4436)
PHONE.....................................917 202-4593
Bally Mohan, *President*
EMP: 4
SALES: 1.2MM Privately Held
SIC: 3555 Printing presses

(G-17371)
C & N PACKAGING INC
Also Called: Suffolk Molds
105 Wyandanch Ave (11798-4441)
PHONE.....................................631 491-1400
Alain Mutschler, *CEO*
Daniel Slavinsky, *General Mgr*
Brooks Markert, *Vice Pres*
Brett Torngren, *Vice Pres*
Eileen Sable, *Accounts Mgr*
▲ EMP: 79
SQ FT: 32,000
SALES (est): 24.3MM
SALES (corp-wide): 6.4MM Privately Held
WEB: www.cnpkg.com
SIC: 3089 Closures, plastic
HQ: Mar-Lee Companies, Inc.
180 Authority Dr
Fitchburg MA 01420
978 343-9600

(G-17372)
CANNOLI FACTORY INC
75 Wyandanch Ave (11798-4441)
PHONE.....................................631 643-2700
Fax: 631 643-2777
Michael Zucaro, *President*
▲ EMP: 50
SQ FT: 30,000
SALES (est): 9.5MM Privately Held
SIC: 2051 5149 Pastries, e.g. danish: except frozen; bakery products

(G-17373)
COBBLESTONE BAKERY CORP
39 Wyandanch Ave (11798-4441)
PHONE.....................................631 491-3777
Frank Laferlita, *CEO*
Michael Laferlita, *Admin Sec*
EMP: 40
SQ FT: 20,000
SALES (est): 495K Privately Held
SIC: 2053 5149 Pies, bakery: frozen; crackers, cookies & bakery products

(G-17374)
CORINTHIAN CAST STONE INC
115 Wyandanch Ave (11798-4441)
PHONE.....................................631 920-2340
Jason Hirschhorn, *Ch of Bd*
Jason Duran, *Controller*
Johnathan Foy, *Sales Executive*
▲ EMP: 47 EST: 1998
SQ FT: 20,000
SALES (est): 16.8MM Privately Held
WEB: www.corinthiancaststone.com
SIC: 3272 Stone, cast concrete

(G-17375)
ENTERPRISE CONTAINER LLC
44 Island Container Plz (11798-2200)
PHONE.....................................631 253-4400
Edward Berkowitz, *Branch Mgr*
EMP: 20
SALES (corp-wide): 2.1MM Privately Held
SIC: 2653 Corrugated boxes, partitions, display items, sheets & pad; boxes, corrugated: made from purchased materials; pads, solid fiber: made from purchased materials
PA: Enterprise Container Llc
575 N Midland Ave
Saddle Brook NJ 07663
201 797-7200

(G-17376)
ISLAND CONTAINER CORP
44 Island Container Plz (11798-2229)
PHONE.....................................631 253-4400
Fax: 631 253-4410
Edward Berkowitz, *Ch of Bd*
Rochelle Berkowitz, *Corp Secy*
Gary Berkowitz, *Vice Pres*
Robert Jeffreys, *Vice Pres*
Gregg Austin, *Engineer*
EMP: 100 EST: 1956
SQ FT: 108,000
SALES (est): 32.2MM Privately Held
WEB: www.islandcontainer.com
SIC: 2653 Boxes, corrugated: made from purchased materials

(G-17377)
T G M PRODUCTS INC
90 Wyandanch Ave Unit E (11798-4458)
PHONE.....................................631 491-0515
Thomas G Miller, *President*
EMP: 6
SALES (est): 610K Privately Held
SIC: 3841 Surgical instruments & apparatus

Wyandanch - Suffolk County (G-17378)

(G-17378)
WELD-BUILT BODY CO INC
276 Long Island Ave (11798-3199)
PHONE..............................631 643-9700
Fax: 631 491-4728
Joseph Milan, *President*
Diana Nelson, *Vice Pres*
Harry Brown, *Director*
EMP: 30 EST: 1949
SQ FT: 55,000
SALES: 2.1MM Privately Held
WEB: www.weldbuilt.com
SIC: 3713 Truck bodies (motor vehicles); car carrier bodies

Wynantskill
Rensselaer County

(G-17379)
CASCADES TISSUE GROUP - NY INC
148 Hudson River Rd (12198)
PHONE..............................518 238-1900
Suzanne Blanchet, *CEO*
Alaine Lemaire, *Ch of Bd*
Jean Jobin, *President*
Allan Hogg, *Vice Pres*
Sophia Ferraro, *Technical Staff*
EMP: 175
SQ FT: 700,000
SALES: 120MM
SALES (corp-wide): 2.9B Privately Held
SIC: 2679 Pressed fiber & molded pulp products except food products
PA: Cascades Inc
   404 Boul Marie-Victorin
   Kingsey Falls QC J0A 1
   819 363-5100

Wyoming
Wyoming County

(G-17380)
MARKIN TUBING LP (PA)
1 Markin Ln (14591)
P.O. Box 242 (14591-0242)
PHONE..............................585 495-6211
Fax: 585 495-6482
Maurice J Cunniffe, *Partner*
Allen I Skott, *Partner*
William Carter, *Partner*
John W Dyke, *Partner*
Dan Cunniffe, *COO*
▼ EMP: 89
SQ FT: 250,000
SALES (est): 18.1MM Privately Held
SIC: 3317 Tubes, wrought: welded or lock joint

(G-17381)
MARKIN TUBING INC
Pearl Creek Rd (14591)
PHONE..............................585 495-6211
Barton P Dambra, *President*
Maurice Cunnife, *Chairman*
Arthur A Smith, *Vice Pres*
EMP: 150
SALES (est): 20.7MM Privately Held
WEB: www.markintubing.com
SIC: 3317 3312 Tubes, wrought: welded or lock joint; structural shapes & pilings, steel

(G-17382)
TEXAS BRINE COMPANY LLC
Also Called: Plant Office
1346 Saltvale Rd (14591-9511)
PHONE..............................585 495-6228
Ted Grabowski, *President*
Sandra Wilkinson, *Office Mgr*
Matt Slezak, *Manager*
EMP: 8
SALES (corp-wide): 376.6MM Privately Held
SIC: 2819 Brine
HQ: Texas Brine Company, Llc
   4800 San Felipe St
   Houston TX 77056
   713 877-2700

(G-17383)
TMP TECHNOLOGIES INC
Also Called: Advanced Rubber Products
6110 Lamb Rd (14591-9754)
PHONE..............................585 495-6231
Fax: 585 495-6526
Holly Mitchell, *General Mgr*
Eric Snyder, *Prdtn Mgr*
Susan Lee, *Purch Agent*
Tim Stothers, *Sales Staff*
Robert Flowers, *Manager*
EMP: 60
SALES (corp-wide): 21.8MM Privately Held
WEB: www.tmptech.com
SIC: 3069 Medical & laboratory rubber sundries & related products
PA: Tmp Technologies, Inc.
   1200 Northland Ave
   Buffalo NY 14215
   716 895-6100

Yaphank
Suffolk County

(G-17384)
AARCO PRODUCTS INC
21 Old Dock Rd (11980-9734)
PHONE..............................631 924-5461
Fax: 631 924-5843
George M Demartino, *Ch of Bd*
Scott Schillinger, *General Mgr*
Theresa Ben AVI, *Accounts Mgr*
David Ciancio, *Administration*
▲ EMP: 15 EST: 1975
SQ FT: 10,000
SALES (est): 4.1MM Privately Held
WEB: www.aarcoproducts.com
SIC: 2493 2542 Bulletin boards, wood; office & store showcases & display fixtures

(G-17385)
ALTERNATIVE SERVICE INC
111 Old Dock Rd (11980-9613)
PHONE..............................631 345-9500
Russell Drake, *President*
John Cochrane, *Vice Pres*
▲ EMP: 15
SQ FT: 15,000
SALES (est): 1.4MM Privately Held
SIC: 3444 5084 7699 3541 Sheet metalwork; industrial machine parts; industrial machinery & equipment repair; machine tools, metal cutting type

(G-17386)
AMERICAN ELECTRONIC PRODUCTS
Also Called: A E P
86 Horseblock Rd Unit F (11980-9743)
PHONE..............................631 924-1299
Fax: 631 924-5910
Robert Gazza, *President*
Warren Azzinaro, *Vice Pres*
EMP: 15
SQ FT: 6,000
SALES (est): 1.7MM Privately Held
SIC: 2899 Ink or writing fluids

(G-17387)
CABLES UNLIMITED INC
3 Old Dock Rd (11980-9702)
PHONE..............................631 563-6363
Darren Clark, *President*
Scott Johnson, *Manager*
EMP: 40
SQ FT: 12,000
SALES: 7.5MM
SALES (corp-wide): 32.8MM Publicly Held
WEB: www.cables-unlimited.com
SIC: 3679 5063 Harness assemblies for electronic use: wire or cable; electronic wire & cable
PA: Rf Industries, Ltd.
   7610 Miramar Rd Ste 6000
   San Diego CA 92126
   858 549-6340

(G-17388)
CHIPLOGIC INC
14a Old Dock Rd (11980-9701)
PHONE..............................631 617-6317
Harry Perry, *President*
Mamie Perweiler, *Manager*
EMP: 10
SQ FT: 3,500
SALES (est): 1.4MM Privately Held
SIC: 3679 Electronic circuits

(G-17389)
COSA XENTAUR CORPORATION (PA)
84 Horseblock Rd Unit G (11980-9742)
PHONE..............................631 345-3434
Fax: 631 924-7337
Christoph Mueller, *CEO*
W Craig Allshouse, *President*
Charles Hunt, *Regional Mgr*
Joe Burton, *Purch Mgr*
Matt Ketcham, *Purchasing*
▲ EMP: 10 EST: 1969
SQ FT: 4,500
SALES (est): 13.3MM Privately Held
WEB: www.cosa-instrument.com
SIC: 3823 Computer interface equipment for industrial process control

(G-17390)
EMS DEVELOPMENT CORPORATION (DH)
Also Called: Ultra Electronics, Ems
95 Horseblock Rd Unit 2 (11980-2301)
PHONE..............................631 924-4736
Fax: 631 345-6216
Peter A Crawford, *President*
Charles Coakley, *Plant Mgr*
Ellen Kren, *Purch Mgr*
Carol Haunstein, *QC Mgr*
Chris Geraghty, *Engineer*
▲ EMP: 60 EST: 1972
SQ FT: 60,000
SALES (est): 24.4MM
SALES (corp-wide): 1.1B Privately Held
WEB: www.ultra-ems.com
SIC: 3825 3613 3677 3621 Instruments to measure electricity; time switches, electrical switchgear apparatus; switchgear & switchgear accessories; electronic coils, transformers & other inductors; electric motor & generator parts; rectifiers (electrical apparatus)
HQ: Ultra Electronics Defense Inc.
   4101 Smith School Rd
   Austin TX 78744
   512 327-6795

(G-17391)
EMS DEVELOPMENT CORPORATION
95 Horseblock Rd Unit 2a (11980-2301)
PHONE..............................631 345-6200
Peter Crawford, *President*
EMP: 90
SALES (corp-wide): 1.1B Privately Held
SIC: 3675 3677 3577 3612 Electronic capacitors; electronic coils, transformers & other inductors; computer peripheral equipment; power & distribution transformers
HQ: Ems Development Corporation
   95 Horseblock Rd Unit 2
   Yaphank NY 11980
   631 924-4736

(G-17392)
EMTRON HYBRIDS INC
86 Horseblock Rd Unit G (11980-9743)
PHONE..............................631 924-9668
Fax: 631 924-0637
Damian Emery, *President*
EMP: 20
SQ FT: 6,000
SALES (est): 2.8MM Privately Held
WEB: www.emtronhybrids.com
SIC: 3674 2396 Hybrid integrated circuits; automotive & apparel trimmings

(G-17393)
FRAMERICA CORPORATION
2 Todd Ct (11980-2101)
P.O. Box 699 (11980-0699)
PHONE..............................631 650-1000
Eugene Eichner, *President*
Gordon Van Vechten, *Corp Secy*
Josh Eichner, *Senior VP*
Michael Filan, *Controller*
Catherine Michael, *Credit Mgr*
◆ EMP: 100
SQ FT: 100,000
SALES (est): 32.9MM Privately Held
WEB: www.framerica.com
SIC: 2499 5023 Picture frame molding, finished; frames & framing, picture & mirror

(G-17394)
H B MILLWORK INC
9 Old Dock Rd (11980-9702)
PHONE..............................631 924-4195
Fax: 631 924-1421
Timothy Hollowell, *Principal*
EMP: 6
SALES (corp-wide): 1.9MM Privately Held
WEB: www.hbmillwork.com
SIC: 2431 Millwork
PA: H B Millwork Inc
   500 Long Island Ave
   Medford NY 11763
   631 289-8086

(G-17395)
HI-TEMP SPECIALTY METALS INC
355 Sills Rd (11980)
P.O. Box 159 (11980-0159)
PHONE..............................631 775-8750
Joseph Smokovich, *President*
Shirley Kam, *Vice Pres*
Evan Smokovich, *Vice Pres*
Lawrence P Stryker, *Vice Pres*
Alex Liu, *Opers Mgr*
▲ EMP: 17
SQ FT: 25,000
SALES (est): 10MM Privately Held
WEB: www.hi-tempmetals.com
SIC: 1081 Exploration, metal mining

(G-17396)
L D FLECKEN INC
11 Old Dock Rd Unit 11 (11980-9622)
PHONE..............................631 777-4881
Leo D Flecken, *President*
Debbie Siderine, *Office Mgr*
EMP: 13
SQ FT: 8,000
SALES (est): 1.5MM Privately Held
WEB: www.ldflecken.com
SIC: 3499 Metal household articles

(G-17397)
LYNTRONICS INC
7 Old Dock Rd Unit 1 (11980-9637)
PHONE..............................631 205-1061
Fax: 631 205-1072
Anthony Vigliotti, *President*
EMP: 20
SQ FT: 12,000
SALES (est): 2.5MM Privately Held
SIC: 3679 5063 Harness assemblies for electronic use: wire or cable; batteries, dry cell

(G-17398)
NANOPROBES INC
95 Horseblock Rd Unit 1 (11980-2301)
PHONE..............................631 205-9490
Fax: 631 205-9493
James Hainfeld, *President*
Wenqiu Liu, *General Mgr*
Fred Furuya, *Vice Pres*
Ping Lin, *Research*
Deepali Mitra, *Research*
EMP: 14
SALES: 250K Privately Held
WEB: www.nanoprobes.com
SIC: 2836 Biological products, except diagnostic

(G-17399)
RUGA GRINDING & MFG CORP
84 Horseblock Rd Unit A (11980-9742)
PHONE..............................631 924-5067
Fax: 631 924-3091
Harry Gaenzle, *President*
Ronnie Ganzle, *Treasurer*
Joie Cascillo, *Admin Sec*
EMP: 8
SQ FT: 5,000
SALES (est): 800K Privately Held
SIC: 3599 Machine shop, jobbing & repair

GEOGRAPHIC SECTION

Yonkers - Westchester County (G-17426)

(G-17400)
SCOTTS COMPANY LLC
Also Called: Vigliotti's Great Garden
445 Horseblock Rd (11980-9629)
PHONE..................................631 289-7444
Fax: 631 289-1077
Charles Vigliotti, *President*
Richard Schwerer, *Manager*
Michelle Bunch, *Manager*
EMP: 20
SALES (corp-wide): 19.8MM **Privately Held**
WEB: www.licompost.com
SIC: 2875 5261 5083 2421 Compost; fertilizer; landscaping equipment; sawmills & planing mills, general
PA: Long Island Compost Corp.
100 Urban Ave
Westbury NY 11590
516 334-6600

(G-17401)
SEARLES GRAPHICS INC (PA)
56 Old Dock Rd (11980-9701)
PHONE..................................631 345-2202
Fax: 631 345-0975
Kenneth Searles, *President*
Richard Searles, *Vice Pres*
Gary Lorandini, *Prdtn Mgr*
Leigh Searles, *Treasurer*
Ted Demaio, *Manager*
EMP: 10
SALES (est): 2.8MM **Privately Held**
WEB: www.searlesgraphics.com
SIC: 2752 Commercial printing, offset

(G-17402)
SHAD INDUSTRIES INC
7 Old Dock Rd Unit 1 (11980-9637)
PHONE..................................631 504-6028
Lenore A Veltry, *President*
EMP: 5
SALES (est): 491.4K **Privately Held**
SIC: 3692 Primary batteries, dry & wet

(G-17403)
SOKOLIN LLC (PA)
Also Called: Sokolin Wine
445 Sills Rd Unit K (11980)
PHONE..................................631 537-4434
Fax: 631 537-4435
Daron Watson, *Sales Staff*
David Smydo, *Mng Member*
Dave Sokolin,
EMP: 24 EST: 1934
SQ FT: 15,000
SALES (est): 2MM **Privately Held**
SIC: 2084 Wines

(G-17404)
SWITCHES AND SENSORS INC
86 Horseblock Rd Unit J (11980-9743)
PHONE..................................631 924-2167
Joe Calvitto, *President*
Rudolph Baldeo, *Engineer*
EMP: 10
SQ FT: 6,200
SALES (est): 1.5MM **Privately Held**
SIC: 3625 Switches, electronic applications

(G-17405)
TRIBOLOGY INC
Also Called: Tech Lube
35 Old Dock Rd (11980-9702)
PHONE..................................631 345-3000
Fax: 631 345-3001
William Krause, *President*
Lee Day, *Persnl Mgr*
Paul Anderson, *Mktg Dir*
Terence Tierney, *Executive*
Bill Krause, *Administration*
▲ EMP: 25
SQ FT: 21,000
SALES (est): 5.8MM **Privately Held**
WEB: www.techlube.com
SIC: 2992 2842 Lubricating oils & greases; specialty cleaning, polishes & sanitation goods

(G-17406)
TURBO PLASTICS CORP INC
18 Old Dock Rd 20 (11980-9701)
PHONE..................................631 345-9768
Arthur Anderson, *President*
EMP: 15

SALES: 1.1MM **Privately Held**
SIC: 3089 Injection molding of plastics

(G-17407)
TWIN PANE INSULATED GL CO INC
86 Horseblock Rd Unit D (11980-9743)
P.O. Box 279 (11980-0279)
PHONE..................................631 924-1060
Fax: 631 924-1096
William F Willett, *President*
Rachel Willett, *Treasurer*
Marjorie Mayor, *Officer*
EMP: 15
SQ FT: 11,000
SALES (est): 3MM **Privately Held**
SIC: 3211 5039 Construction glass; glass construction materials

(G-17408)
W J ALBRO MACHINE WORKS INC
Also Called: Albro Gear & Instrument
86 Horseblock Rd Unit L (11980-9743)
PHONE..................................631 345-0657
Fax: 631 345-0663
Kevin Albro, *President*
William Albro, *Vice Pres*
William Ambro Jr, *Treasurer*
EMP: 9
SQ FT: 2,000
SALES: 775K **Privately Held**
SIC: 3599 3728 3621 3566 Custom machinery; gears, aircraft power transmission; aircraft propellers & associated equipment; motors & generators; speed changers, drives & gears; iron & steel forgings

(G-17409)
XENTAUR CORPORATION
84 Horseblock Rd Unit G (11980-9742)
PHONE..................................631 345-3434
Fax: 631 345-5349
Christopher Mueller, *CEO*
Craig Allshouse, *President*
Laura Patanella, *Buyer*
Susanne Muessig, *Office Mgr*
Nyle Nims, *Manager*
EMP: 23
SALES (est): 6MM **Privately Held**
WEB: www.xentaur.com
SIC: 3823 Industrial instrmnts msrmnt display/control process variable

Yonkers
Westchester County

(G-17410)
ALETEIA USA INC
86 Main St Ste 303 (10701-8805)
PHONE..................................914 502-1855
Axel D'Epinay, *CFO*
EMP: 5
SQ FT: 900
SALES (est): 130.5K **Privately Held**
SIC: 2741

(G-17411)
ALLCOM ELECTRIC CORP
104 Crescent Pl (10704-2519)
PHONE..................................914 803-0433
Anna Protosanousis, *Principal*
EMP: 7 EST: 2009
SALES (est): 1MM **Privately Held**
SIC: 3699 Electrical equipment & supplies

(G-17412)
ALTMAN STAGE LIGHTING CO INC
Also Called: Altman Lighting
57 Alexander St (10701-2714)
PHONE..................................914 476-7987
Fax: 914 963-7304
Robert Altman, *Ch of Bd*
Dwarak Parvatum, *COO*
Susan Fry, *Exec VP*
Randall Altman, *Vice Pres*
Derek Lubsen, *Vice Pres*
▲ EMP: 125 EST: 1953
SQ FT: 75,000

SALES (est): 44.7MM **Privately Held**
WEB: www.altmanlighting.com
SIC: 3648 3646 Stage lighting equipment; commercial indusl & institutional electric lighting fixtures

(G-17413)
AMERICAN CANVAS BINDERS CORP
430 Nepperhan Ave (10701-6601)
PHONE..................................914 969-0300
Richard Maslowski, *President*
EMP: 6
SQ FT: 10,000
SALES (est): 450K **Privately Held**
SIC: 2241 Narrow fabric mills

(G-17414)
APF MANAGEMENT COMPANY LLC
60 Fullerton Ave (10704-1097)
PHONE..................................914 665-5400
EMP: 110
SALES (est): 8.8MM **Privately Held**
SIC: 3231 Framed mirrors

(G-17415)
APF MANUFACTURING COMPANY LLC (PA)
Also Called: Apf Munn Master Frame Makers
60 Fullerton Ave (10704-1097)
PHONE..................................914 963-6300
Oudit Harbhajan,
EMP: 30 EST: 2014
SQ FT: 52,000
SALES (est): 1.8MM **Privately Held**
SIC: 2499 3231 Picture & mirror frames, wood; framed mirrors

(G-17416)
ARTISTIC INNOVATION INC
540 Nepperhan Ave Ste 566 (10701-6611)
PHONE..................................914 968-3021
Fax: 914 968-3046
Daniel Doernberg, *President*
EMP: 12
SQ FT: 2,000
SALES: 350K **Privately Held**
WEB: www.artisticinnovation.com
SIC: 3479 Painting of metal products; enameling, including porcelain, of metal products; varnishing of metal products

(G-17417)
ASR GROUP INTERNATIONAL INC (DH)
1 Federal St (10705-1079)
P.O. Box 509 (10702-0509)
PHONE..................................914 963-2400
Antonio Contreras Jr, *Co-President*
Antonio L Contreras Jr, *Co-President*
Luis Fernandez, *Co-President*
Gregory A Maitner, *Vice Pres*
Armando A Tabernilla, *Vice Pres*
◆ EMP: 250
SQ FT: 385,000
SALES (est): 111.5MM
SALES (corp-wide): 1.1B **Privately Held**
WEB: www.tasrc.com
SIC: 2062 Cane sugar refining; granulated cane sugar from purchased raw sugar or syrup
HQ: Florida Crystals Corporation
1 N Clematis St Ste 200
West Palm Beach FL 33401
561 655-6303

(G-17418)
ATLANTIC SCALE COMPANY INC
31 Fullerton Ave (10704-1005)
PHONE..................................914 664-4403
Fax: 914 969-2225
Fred Algieri, *Branch Mgr*
EMP: 5
SALES (corp-wide): 26.8MM **Privately Held**
SIC: 3545 Scales, measuring (machinists' precision tools)
PA: Atlantic Scale Company, Inc.
136 Washington Ave
Nutley NJ 07110
973 661-7090

(G-17419)
BARTIZAN DATA SYSTEMS LLC
217 Riverdale Ave (10705-1131)
PHONE..................................914 965-7977
Joanna Stasuk, *Mktg Dir*
Lewis C Hoff,
Elizabeth Mazei,
EMP: 25
SQ FT: 43,000
SALES (est): 2.5MM **Privately Held**
WEB: www.bartizan.com
SIC: 3555 Printing trades machinery; engraving machinery & equipment, except plates

(G-17420)
BELMAY HOLDING CORPORATION
Also Called: Scent 2 Market
1 Odell Plz Ste 123 (10701-6800)
PHONE..................................914 376-1515
Fax: 914 376-1784
Theodore Kesten, *CEO*
Tim Fawcett, *Managing Dir*
Greg Banwer, *Vice Pres*
Eileen Hedrick, *Vice Pres*
Brent Pope, *Vice Pres*
◆ EMP: 25 EST: 1967
SQ FT: 26,000
SALES (est): 10.7MM **Privately Held**
WEB: www.belmay.com
SIC: 2844 Hair preparations, including shampoos

(G-17421)
BIOINS INC
1767 Central Park Ave # 258 (10710-2828)
PHONE..................................646 457-8117
EMP: 9
SALES (est): 1.2MM **Privately Held**
SIC: 3821 Laboratory apparatus & furniture

(G-17422)
BRUCCI LTD
861 Nepperhan Ave (10703-2013)
PHONE..................................914 965-0707
Fax: 914 965-1965
Murray Bober, *Ch of Bd*
Howard Marcus, *Vice Pres*
Allan Shapiro, *Treasurer*
EMP: 25
SQ FT: 10,800
SALES (est): 4.8MM **Privately Held**
SIC: 2844 5399 Cosmetic preparations; warehouse club stores

(G-17423)
CAROLINAS DESSERTS INC
1562 Central Park Ave (10710-6001)
PHONE..................................914 779-4000
EMP: 8
SALES (est): 587.4K **Privately Held**
SIC: 2051 Bakery: wholesale or wholesale/retail combined

(G-17424)
CAROLYN RAY INC
578 Nepperhan Ave Ste C10 (10701-6670)
PHONE..................................914 476-0619
Fax: 914 476-0677
Carolyn Ray, *President*
EMP: 6
SALES (est): 687.9K **Privately Held**
WEB: www.carolynray.com
SIC: 2261 Finishing plants, cotton

(G-17425)
CASA NUEVA CUSTOM FURNISHING
510 Nepperhan Ave (10701-6602)
PHONE..................................914 476-2272
Fax: 914 476-0560
Antonio Figueroa, *President*
EMP: 7
SQ FT: 12,500
SALES: 1.2MM **Privately Held**
SIC: 3553 Furniture makers' machinery, woodworking

(G-17426)
CDNV WOOD CARVING FRAMES INC (PA)
498 Nepperhan Ave (10701-6604)
PHONE..................................914 375-3447
Fax: 914 375-3726

Yonkers - Westchester County (G-17427)

Cristobal S Venegas, *President*
David Venegas, *Vice Pres*
▲ **EMP:** 18
SALES (est): 1.3MM **Privately Held**
WEB: www.cdnv.com
SIC: 2499 Picture & mirror frames, wood

(G-17427)
CEP TECHNOLOGIES CORPORATION (PA)
763 Saw Mill River Rd (10710-4001)
PHONE 914 968-4100
Fax: 914 968-4151
Kenneth W Kaufman, *President*
Francine Kaufman, *Vice Pres*
Michael Wagner, *Vice Pres*
John Rossi, *Opers Mgr*
Lisa Gilbert, *Human Res Dir*
▲ **EMP:** 40 **EST:** 1960
SQ FT: 22,000
SALES (est): 7.5MM **Privately Held**
SIC: 3469 Metal stampings

(G-17428)
CLOVER WIRE FORMING CO INC
1021 Saw Mill River Rd (10710-3292)
PHONE 914 375-0400
Fax: 914 375-0406
George Margareten, *President*
▲ **EMP:** 30 **EST:** 1957
SQ FT: 35,000
SALES (est): 6MM **Privately Held**
WEB: www.cloverwire.com
SIC: 3496 3316 Miscellaneous fabricated wire products; cold finishing of steel shapes

(G-17429)
CONSUMERS UNION US INC (PA)
Also Called: Consumer Reports
101 Truman Ave (10703-1057)
PHONE 914 378-2000
Fax: 914 378-2904
Diane Archer, *Ch of Bd*
Walter D Bristol, *Ch of Bd*
James Guest, *President*
Marta Tellado, *President*
Jeff Bartlett, *Editor*
EMP: 400 **EST:** 1936
SQ FT: 180,000
SALES: 263MM **Privately Held**
SIC: 2741 2721 7389 Miscellaneous publishing; magazines: publishing only, not printed on site; fund raising organizations

(G-17430)
COSTELLO BROS PETROLEUM CORP (PA)
990 Mclean Ave Ste 3 (10704-4180)
PHONE 914 237-3189
Fax: 914 237-1806
Frank Costello, *President*
Kristopher Costello, *Vice Pres*
EMP: 6 **EST:** 1972
SQ FT: 1,200
SALES (est): 670.6K **Privately Held**
SIC: 2999 5983 Fuel briquettes & waxes; fuel oil dealers

(G-17431)
CREATIVE CABINETRY CORPORATION
42 Morsemere Pl (10701-1511)
PHONE 914 963-6061
Karl Melnychuk, *President*
Francis Melnychuk, *Admin Sec*
EMP: 5
SQ FT: 6,000
SALES: 400K **Privately Held**
SIC: 2522 2521 Cabinets, office: except wood; cabinets, office: wood

(G-17432)
CREATIVE SOLUTIONS GROUP INC (PA)
Also Called: Diam International
555 Tuckahoe Rd (10710-5709)
PHONE 914 771-4200
Edward Winder, *CEO*
Williaml Ecker, *Ch of Bd*
Jorg Niederhufner, *Opers Staff*
Lori Dvizac, *Purch Mgr*
▲ **EMP:** 500

SALES (est): 93.9MM **Privately Held**
WEB: www.diam-int.com
SIC: 3993 Displays & cutouts, window & lobby

(G-17433)
CROWN SIGN SYSTEMS INC
7 Odell Plz Ste 140 (10701-1407)
PHONE 914 375-2118
Michelle Strum, *President*
Tamara Crewa, *Project Mgr*
Carolyn Cohen, *Manager*
EMP: 11
SALES (est): 1.6MM **Privately Held**
SIC: 3993 Signs & advertising specialties

(G-17434)
DALEE BOOKBINDING CO INC
Also Called: Creations In Canvas
129 Clinton Pl (10701-4719)
PHONE 914 965-1660
Fax: 914 965-1802
David Hutter, *President*
Danae Carter, *Manager*
EMP: 16 **EST:** 1965
SQ FT: 12,000
SALES (est): 1MM **Privately Held**
WEB: www.daleebook.com
SIC: 2789 2782 Bookbinding & related work; blankbooks

(G-17435)
DAYLEEN INTIMATES INC
Also Called: Dominique Intimate Apparel
540 Nepperhan Ave (10701-6630)
PHONE 914 969-5900
Mike Chernoff, *President*
▲ **EMP:** 24
SQ FT: 20,000
SALES (est): 6MM **Privately Held**
SIC: 2341 4225 Women's & children's undergarments; general warehousing & storage

(G-17436)
DIMAIO MILLWORK CORPORATION
12 Bright Pl (10705-1342)
PHONE 914 476-1937
Ralph Dimaio Jr, *President*
Sal Fino, *Project Mgr*
Dom Capogna, *Prdtn Mgr*
Rosemary Perrone, *Bookkeeper*
EMP: 35
SQ FT: 20,000
SALES (est): 6.4MM **Privately Held**
WEB: www.dimaiomillwork.com
SIC: 2521 Wood office furniture

(G-17437)
DOLLAR POPULAR INC
473 S Broadway (10705-3249)
P.O. Box 312150, Jamaica (11431-2150)
PHONE 914 375-0361
Muhammad Irfan, *Ch of Bd*
EMP: 8
SALES (est): 648.6K **Privately Held**
SIC: 3643 Outlets, electric: convenience

(G-17438)
ECKER WINDOW CORP
1 Odell Plz (10701-1402)
PHONE 914 776-0000
Fax: 914 776-0030
Robert Ecker, *CEO*
Howard Ecker, *Vice Pres*
Bryce Evadne, *Manager*
Ebrahim Miandoabi, *Manager*
Steven Frigand, *Director*
EMP: 100
SQ FT: 5,000
SALES (est): 22.3MM **Privately Held**
SIC: 2431 1751 Windows & window parts & trim, wood; window & door installation & erection

(G-17439)
ECONOCRAFT WORLDWIDE MFG INC
56 Worth St Frnt Unit (10701-5508)
PHONE 914 966-2280
Fax: 718 585-0788
Shlomo Malki, *President*
Eran Malki, *Vice Pres*
Amir Malki, *Admin Sec*
▼ **EMP:** 5

SQ FT: 27,000
SALES (est): 907.3K **Privately Held**
WEB: www.econocraft.com
SIC: 3589 Car washing machinery

(G-17440)
ELECTRONIC DEVICES INC (HQ)
Also Called: Electronic Devices Inc
21 Gray Oaks Ave (10710-3205)
PHONE 914 965-4400
Fax: 914 965-5531
Jimmy Huang, *President*
Nancy Alcantara, *General Mgr*
Donald Bedell, *Vice Pres*
Steven Huang, *Vice Pres*
Henry Kolokowsky, *Vice Pres*
▲ **EMP:** 30
SQ FT: 45,000
SALES (est): 1.2MM **Privately Held**
WEB: www.edidiodes.com
SIC: 3674 5065 Rectifiers, solid state; diodes, solid state (germanium, silicon, etc.); solid state electronic devices; electronic parts & equipment
PA: North Technology Inc
 161 Tices Ln
 East Brunswick NJ 08816
 732 390-2828

(G-17441)
EMPIRE OPEN MRI
1915 Central Park Ave # 25 (10710-2949)
PHONE 914 961-1777
Michael Singer, *Owner*
EMP: 6
SALES (est): 523K **Privately Held**
SIC: 3845 Ultrasonic scanning devices, medical

(G-17442)
EXCELSIOR PACKAGING GROUP INC
159 Alexander St (10701-2596)
P.O. Box 863 (10702-0863)
PHONE 914 968-1300
Ronnie Shemesh, *CEO*
Charlie Lynch, *Prdtn Mgr*
John Gonnella, *Technical Mgr*
◆ **EMP:** 200
SQ FT: 100,000
SALES (est): 65.8MM **Privately Held**
SIC: 2673 2759 3089 Cellophane bags, unprinted: made from purchased materials; bag, wrapper & seal printing & engraving; laminating of plastic

(G-17443)
FABRIC CONCEPTS FOR INDUSTRY
Also Called: Awning Man, The
354 Ashburton Ave (10701-6014)
PHONE 914 375-2565
Fax: 914 375-1459
Daniel Burke, *President*
EMP: 17
SALES (est): 1.5MM **Privately Held**
SIC: 2394 Awnings, fabric: made from purchased materials

(G-17444)
FITZGERALD PUBLISHING CO INC
Also Called: Golden Legacy Ilstrd Histry
1853 Central Park Ave # 8 (10710-2948)
PHONE 914 793-5016
Bertram Fitzgerald, *President*
Jeanette Fitzgerald, *Vice Pres*
EMP: 5
SALES: 300K **Privately Held**
SIC: 2741 Miscellaneous publishing

(G-17445)
FLEETCOM INC
1081 Yonkers Ave (10704-3123)
PHONE 914 776-5582
Mike Rosenzweig, *President*
Joe Gomez, *Manager*
EMP: 15 **EST:** 1984
SALES (est): 1.1MM **Privately Held**
SIC: 3663 Radio broadcasting & communications equipment

(G-17446)
FOWLER ROUTE CO INC
25 Sunnyside Dr (10705-1763)
PHONE 917 653-4640
EMP: 12
SALES (corp-wide): 5.9MM **Privately Held**
SIC: 3582 Commercial laundry equipment
PA: Fowler Route Co., Inc.
 565 Rahway Ave
 Union NJ 07083
 908 686-3400

(G-17447)
GANNETT STLLITE INFO NTWRK INC
Also Called: Herald Statesman
1 Odell Plz (10701-1402)
PHONE 914 965-5000
Fax: 914 694-5382
John Gambrill, *Branch Mgr*
EMP: 50
SALES (corp-wide): 5.7B **Publicly Held**
WEB: www.usatoday.com
SIC: 2711 Newspapers: publishing only, not printed on site
HQ: Gannett Satellite Information Network, Llc
 7950 Jones Branch Dr
 Mc Lean VA 22102
 703 854-6000

(G-17448)
GOLDEN RENEWABLE ENERGY LLC
700 Nepperhan Ave (10703-2312)
PHONE 914 920-9800
Franklin Canosa, *CFO*
Christina Vlassis, *Human Res Mgr*
Nicholas Canosa,
Jason Provost,
EMP: 5
SALES: 950K **Privately Held**
SIC: 2869 Fuels

(G-17449)
GOTHAM PEN CO INC
Also Called: Gotham Pen and Pencil
1 Roundtop Rd (10710-2327)
PHONE 212 675-7904
Fax: 718 294-6699
Marshall Futterman, *President*
▲ **EMP:** 22 **EST:** 1955
SQ FT: 15,000
SALES (est): 2.5MM **Privately Held**
SIC: 3951 3952 2796 Ball point pens & parts; pencils & pencil parts, mechanical; markers, soft tip (felt, fabric, plastic, etc.); pencils & leads, including artists'; engraving on copper, steel, wood or rubber: printing plates

(G-17450)
GRAPHITE METALLIZING CORP (PA)
Also Called: Graphalloy
1050 Nepperhan Ave (10703-1432)
PHONE 914 968-8400
Fax: 914 968-8468
Eben T Walker, *Ch of Bd*
Rohit Masih, *Engineer*
Mark R Grammer, *CFO*
Eric Ford, *Sales Dir*
Greg Danilek, *Sales Engr*
◆ **EMP:** 94 **EST:** 1913
SQ FT: 95,000
SALES (est): 71.3MM **Privately Held**
WEB: www.graphalloy.com
SIC: 3624 Carbon & graphite products; brushes & brush stock contacts, electric

(G-17451)
GREYSTON BAKERY INC
104 Alexander St (10701-2535)
PHONE 914 375-1510
Fax: 914 375-1514
Michael Brady, *Ch of Bd*
Julius Walls, *President*
Joan Cotter, *Vice Pres*
Harry Kraklow, *Plant Mgr*
Rodney Johnson, *Prdtn Mgr*
◆ **EMP:** 130
SQ FT: 10,000

▲ = Import ▼ = Export
◆ = Import/Export

SALES (est): 1.7MM
SALES (corp-wide): 1.9MM **Privately Held**
WEB: www.greystonbakery.com
SIC: 2051 Cakes, pies & pastries
PA: Greyston Foundation Inc.
21 Park Ave
Yonkers NY 10703
914 376-3900

(G-17452)
HANA SHEET METAL INC
9 Celli Pl 11 (10701-4805)
P.O. Box 156, Atlantic Beach (11509-0156)
PHONE..................................914 377-0773
Awni A Hana, *Ch of Bd*
EMP: 8
SALES (est): 940K **Privately Held**
SIC: 3444 Sheet metalwork

(G-17453)
HEMISPHERE NOVELTIES INC
167 Saw Mill River Rd 3c (10701-6621)
P.O. Box 1240 (10703-8240)
PHONE..................................914 378-4100
Fax: 914 378-4091
Max Wolfeld, *President*
Jeffrey Wolfeld, *Corp Secy*
◆ EMP: 25
SQ FT: 12,000
SALES (est): 3.5MM **Privately Held**
WEB: www.hemispherenovelties.com
SIC: 3172 3965 5091 5131 Personal leather goods; fasteners, buttons, needles & pins; fishing tackle; buttons; belt & buckle assembly kits

(G-17454)
HORNE ORGANIZATION INC (PA)
15 Arthur Pl (10701-1702)
PHONE..................................914 572-1330
Leon H Horne Jr, *President*
Jackie Arce, *Office Mgr*
EMP: 10
SQ FT: 1,500
SALES (est): 2.6MM **Privately Held**
SIC: 2752 7336 Commercial printing, lithographic; graphic arts & related design

(G-17455)
HUDSON SCENIC STUDIO INC (PA)
130 Fernbrook St (10705-1764)
PHONE..................................914 375-0900
Fax: 914 378-9134
Neil Mazzella, *CEO*
John C Boyd, *Vice Pres*
Joanne Veneziano, *Administration*
▼ EMP: 125
SQ FT: 56,000
SALES (est): 21.2MM **Privately Held**
WEB: www.hudsonscenic.com
SIC: 3999 Theatrical scenery

(G-17456)
ITR INDUSTRIES INC (PA)
441 Saw Mill River Rd (10701-4913)
PHONE..................................914 964-7063
Mario F Rolla, *Ch of Bd*
Adrienne Rola, *President*
Peter M Rolla, *President*
▲ EMP: 21
SALES (est): 169.4MM **Privately Held**
SIC: 3431 3429 3446 3088 Shower stalls, metal; manufactured hardware (general); architectural metalwork; shower stalls, fiberglass & plastic

(G-17457)
J KENDALL LLC
Also Called: J K Fertility
71 Belvedere Dr (10705-2813)
PHONE..................................646 739-4956
Fax: 718 634-0348
Julius K Smalls, *CEO*
EMP: 5
SALES (est): 370K **Privately Held**
SIC: 2759 Screen printing

(G-17458)
JENRAY PRODUCTS INC
252 Lake Ave Fl 2a (10701-5706)
PHONE..................................914 375-5596
Fax: 914 375-2096
Raymond D'Urso, *President*
▲ EMP: 26 EST: 1999

SQ FT: 22,000
SALES (est): 3.3MM **Privately Held**
SIC: 3999 Sprays, artificial & preserved

(G-17459)
KAWASAKI RAIL CAR INC (DH)
29 Wells Ave Bldg 4 (10701-8815)
PHONE..................................914 376-4700
Fax: 914 376-4779
Hiroji Iwasaki, *CEO*
Yuichi Yamamoto, *President*
Steven Vangellow, *General Mgr*
Yoshinori Kanehana, *Exec VP*
K Matsufuji, *Vice Pres*
▲ EMP: 230
SQ FT: 28,000
SALES (est): 67.3MM
SALES (corp-wide): 13.1B **Privately Held**
SIC: 3743 Railroad equipment, except locomotives; railway motor cars; train cars & equipment, freight or passenger
HQ: Kawasaki Motors Manufacturing Corp., U.S.A.
6600 Nw 27th St
Lincoln NE 68524
402 476-6600

(G-17460)
KIMBER MFG INC
16 Harrison Ave (10705-2606)
PHONE..................................914 965-0753
Leslie Edelman, *Owner*
EMP: 5
SALES (corp-wide): 92.3MM **Privately Held**
SIC: 3599 Machine shop, jobbing & repair
PA: Kimber Mfg., Inc.
1 Lawton St
Yonkers NY 10705
914 964-0771

(G-17461)
KIMBER MFG INC (PA)
1 Lawton St (10705-2617)
PHONE..................................914 964-0771
Leslie Edelmen, *Ch of Bd*
Abdool Jamal, *Managing Dir*
Doron Segal, *Vice Pres*
Robert Nemergut, *Mfg Dir*
Kieran Kelly, *Mfg Mgr*
▲ EMP: 220
SQ FT: 50,000
SALES (est): 92.3MM **Privately Held**
WEB: www.kimbermfg.com
SIC: 3599 Machine shop, jobbing & repair

(G-17462)
LIGHTING BY DOM YONKERS INC
Also Called: Sparkle Light Manufacturing
253 S Broadway (10705-1351)
PHONE..................................914 968-8700
Fax: 914 968-8716
Dominick Di Gennaro Jr, *President*
Dominick Di Di Gennaro, *Personnel Exec*
EMP: 5 EST: 1979
SQ FT: 5,000
SALES (est): 640K **Privately Held**
SIC: 3646 Commercial indusl & institutional electric lighting fixtures

(G-17463)
M SANTOLIQUIDO CORP
Also Called: San Signs & Awnings
925 Saw Mill River Rd (10710-3238)
PHONE..................................914 375-6674
Fax: 914 375-6689
Michael Santoliquido, *President*
Lucille Santoliquido, *Vice Pres*
Lucille Liquido, *Director*
EMP: 11 EST: 1995
SQ FT: 10,000
SALES (est): 1MM **Privately Held**
WEB: www.sansigns.com
SIC: 3993 Signs & advertising specialties

(G-17464)
MAGNIFICAT INC
86 Main St Ste 303 (10701-8805)
P.O. Box 822 (10702-0822)
PHONE..................................914 502-1820
Gerber Contreras, *Opers Mgr*
Axel Depinay, *Info Tech Mgr*
Fleurus Mame,
Axel D'Epinay,
▲ EMP: 18

SALES (est): 2.2MM
SALES (corp-wide): 1.7MM **Privately Held**
SIC: 2721 Periodicals
PA: Magnificat Films
10 Rue De Penthievre
Paris

(G-17465)
MARBLE WORKS INC
660 Saw Mill River Rd (10710-4009)
PHONE..................................914 376-3653
Fax: 914 376-6938
Sabo Barmaksiz, *President*
Aldo Turelli, *General Mgr*
Rumeldo Turolliis, *Manager*
▲ EMP: 30
SALES (est): 3.4MM **Privately Held**
SIC: 3281 Granite, cut & shaped; marble, building: cut & shaped

(G-17466)
MARPLEX FURNITURE CORPORATION
167 Saw Mill Rver Rd Fl 1 (10701)
PHONE..................................914 969-7755
Fax: 914 969-1200
Peter Bizzarro, *President*
EMP: 5
SQ FT: 13,000
SALES (est): 494.4K **Privately Held**
SIC: 2541 Display fixtures, wood

(G-17467)
MICROMOLD PRODUCTS INC
7 Odell Plz 133 (10701-1407)
PHONE..................................914 969-2850
Fax: 914 969-2736
Arthur Lukach, *Ch of Bd*
Justin Lukach, *President*
Frank Pino, *Human Resources*
Tricia Lombardo, *Sales Staff*
Monique Nunn, *Sales Staff*
EMP: 25 EST: 1954
SQ FT: 13,000
SALES (est): 5.3MM **Privately Held**
WEB: www.micromold.com
SIC: 3089 3494 3053 3084 Plastic containers, except foam; valves & pipe fittings; gaskets, packing & sealing devices; plastics pipe; steel pipe & tubes; fabricated pipe & fittings

(G-17468)
MIRROR-TECH MANUFACTURING CO
286 Nepperhan Ave (10701-3403)
PHONE..................................914 965-1232
Richard Cleary, *President*
EMP: 16 EST: 1961
SQ FT: 7,000
SALES (est): 750K **Privately Held**
SIC: 3231 Mirrored glass; mirrors, truck & automobile: made from purchased glass

(G-17469)
OCTOPUS ADVANCED SYSTEMS INC
27 Covington Rd (10710-3515)
PHONE..................................914 771-6110
Nikolai Prokhorenkov, *Ch of Bd*
EMP: 1
SALES (est): 2MM **Privately Held**
SIC: 3669 Emergency alarms

(G-17470)
ON LINE POWER TECHNOLOGIES
113 Sunnyside Dr (10705-2830)
PHONE..................................914 968-4440
Linda Hack, *President*
Bruce Hack, *Vice Pres*
EMP: 2
SALES (est): 10MM **Privately Held**
SIC: 3568 5063 7389 Power transmission equipment; electrical apparatus & equipment;

(G-17471)
ORZA BAKERY INC
261 New Main St Ste 263 (10701-4103)
PHONE..................................914 965-5736
Fax: 914 965-2017
Vital Tovar, *President*
Ubaldo Tovar, *Vice Pres*

EMP: 17
SQ FT: 8,000
SALES (est): 3MM **Privately Held**
SIC: 2051 Breads, rolls & buns

(G-17472)
OTIS ELEVATOR COMPANY
1 Odell Plz Ste 120 (10701-1415)
PHONE..................................914 375-7800
Fax: 914 375-7830
Marc Zolle, *Manager*
EMP: 12
SALES (corp-wide): 56.1B **Publicly Held**
WEB: www.otis.com
SIC: 3534 Elevators & equipment
HQ: Otis Elevator Company
10 Farm Springs Rd
Farmington CT 06032
860 676-6000

(G-17473)
OUREM IRON WORKS INC
498 Nepperhan Ave Ste 5 (10701-6604)
PHONE..................................914 476-4856
Arthur Viera, *President*
Yvette Matos, *Office Mgr*
Marco Vivanco, *Manager*
EMP: 12 EST: 1977
SQ FT: 25,000
SALES (est): 2.6MM **Privately Held**
SIC: 3446 1799 Fences or posts, ornamental iron or steel; fence construction

(G-17474)
P PASCAL INC
Also Called: P Pascal Coffee Roasters
960 Nepperhan Ave (10703-1726)
P.O. Box 347 (10703-0347)
PHONE..................................914 969-7933
Fax: 914 969-8248
Dean Pialtos, *President*
James Ranni, *Corp Secy*
Barbara Pialtos, *Vice Pres*
Charles Pialtos, *Vice Pres*
Olla Naber, *Admin Sec*
EMP: 27
SQ FT: 15,000
SALES (est): 4MM **Privately Held**
SIC: 2095 Roasted coffee

(G-17475)
PANE DORO
166 Ludlow St (10705-1036)
PHONE..................................914 964-0043
Roger Nehme, *Owner*
EMP: 15
SALES (est): 1.1MM **Privately Held**
SIC: 2051 Cakes, bakery: except frozen

(G-17476)
PENNYSAVER GROUP INC
80 Alexander St (10701-2715)
PHONE..................................914 966-1400
Fax: 914 966-1486
Ed Levitt, *Manager*
Charol Russo, *Manager*
EMP: 10
SALES (corp-wide): 7.6MM **Privately Held**
WEB: www.nysaver.com
SIC: 2711 Newspapers, publishing & printing
PA: Pennysaver Group Inc.
510 Fifth Ave
Pelham NY
914 592-5222

(G-17477)
PIETRO DEMARCO IMPORTERS INC
1185 Saw Mill River Rd # 4 (10710-3241)
PHONE..................................914 969-3201
Pietro Demarco, *President*
Anthony Demarco, *Vice Pres*
▲ EMP: 10
SALES (est): 1.2MM **Privately Held**
SIC: 2079 Olive oil

(G-17478)
POMPIAN MANUFACTURING CO INC
280 Nepperhan Ave (10701-3403)
PHONE..................................914 476-7076
Fax: 914 476-7095
EMP: 8
SQ FT: 10,000

Yonkers - Westchester County (G-17479)

SALES: 900K **Privately Held**
SIC: 3645 5063 Mfg & Whol Electrical Equipment & Electronic Ballast

(G-17479)
PREPAC DESIGNS INC
25 Abner Pl (10704-3015)
PHONE 914 524-7800
Manuel Mendez, *President*
Maggie Cott, *Vice Pres*
Patti Miranda, *Credit Mgr*
Ilene Greenberg, *Sales Staff*
▲ **EMP:** 5
SQ FT: 1,500
SALES: 2.5MM **Privately Held**
WEB: www.designerschoiceline.com
SIC: 3161 Luggage

(G-17480)
PROMED PRODUCTS INC
500 Nepperhan Ave (10701-6654)
PHONE 800 993-4010
Fax: 718 993-4016
Michael Feinkind, *President*
Irving Wolintz, *Accountant*
▲ **EMP:** 6
SQ FT: 12,000
SALES (est): 682.7K **Privately Held**
WEB: www.pro-medusa.com
SIC: 3842 Supports: abdominal, ankle, arch, kneecap, etc.

(G-17481)
ROBERT VIGGIANI
Also Called: Irv & Vic Sportswear Co
37 Vredenburgh Ave Ste B (10704-2150)
PHONE 914 423-4046
Fax: 914 423-4047
Robert Viggiani, *Owner*
EMP: 5
SQ FT: 975
SALES (est): 464.2K **Privately Held**
SIC: 2329 5699 Riding clothes.; men's, youths' & boys'; riding apparel

(G-17482)
RUMSEY CORP
Also Called: B2b Cleaning Services
15 Rumsey Rd (10705-1623)
PHONE 914 751-3640
Anna Negron, *President*
EMP: 6
SALES (est): 300K **Privately Held**
SIC: 3672 7349 Printed circuit boards; building & office cleaning services; office cleaning or charring; cleaning service, industrial or commercial; window cleaning

(G-17483)
SAW MILL WOODWORKING INC
1900 Central Park Ave (10710-2901)
PHONE 914 963-1841
Donald Beniamino, *President*
EMP: 5
SQ FT: 18,000
SALES (est): 403.4K **Privately Held**
SIC: 2541 Cabinets, except refrigerated: show, display, etc.: wood

(G-17484)
SKIL-CARE CORPORATION
29 Wells Ave Bldg 4 (10701-8815)
PHONE 914 963-2040
Fax: 914 963-2567
Martin Prenskean, *Ch of Bd*
Arnold Silverman, *President*
Stephen Warhaftig, *Vice Pres*
▲ **EMP:** 125 **EST:** 1978
SQ FT: 55,000
SALES (est): 18.9MM **Privately Held**
WEB: www.skilcare.com
SIC: 3842 2392 2241 Wheelchairs; household furnishings; narrow fabric mills

(G-17485)
STANSON AUTOMATED LLC
145 Saw Mill River Rd # 2 (10701-6615)
PHONE 866 505-7826
Stewart Iskowitz, *Mng Member*
Joel Iskowitz, *Mng Member*
EMP: 10
SALES (est): 910K **Privately Held**
SIC: 3578 Automatic teller machines (ATM)

(G-17486)
STAR DESK PAD CO INC
60 Mclean Ave (10705-2317)
PHONE 914 963-9400
Fax: 914 963-2580
Sidney Newman, *President*
▲ **EMP:** 45 **EST:** 1946
SQ FT: 60,000
SALES: 2.4MM **Privately Held**
WEB: www.stardesk.com
SIC: 3199 3999 Desk sets, leather; desk pads, except paper

(G-17487)
STEWART EFI LLC
630 Central Park Ave (10704-2018)
PHONE 914 965-0816
Philip Rejeski, *Opers Staff*
Philip Rezvik, *Branch Mgr*
EMP: 78
SALES (corp-wide): 68MM **Privately Held**
WEB: www.stewartefi.com
SIC: 3469 Metal stampings
PA: Stewart Efi, Llc
  45 Old Waterbury Rd
  Thomaston CT 06787
  860 283-8213

(G-17488)
SWAROVSKI NORTH AMERICA LTD
6080 Mall Walk (10704-1223)
PHONE 914 423-4132
EMP: 7
SALES (corp-wide): 4.2B **Privately Held**
SIC: 3961 Costume jewelry
HQ: Swarovski North America Limited
  1 Kenney Dr
  Cranston RI 02920
  401 463-6400

(G-17489)
T C DUNHAM PAINT COMPANY INC
581 Saw Mill River Rd (10701-4924)
PHONE 914 969-4202
Fax: 914 969-3990
Isaac Schwartz, *Ch of Bd*
Eoy Fisch, *Vice Pres*
Eli Fish, *Manager*
Dunham Yossy, *Manager*
EMP: 25
SQ FT: 5,000
SALES: 12MM **Privately Held**
WEB: www.dunhampaint.com
SIC: 2851 Paints & allied products

(G-17490)
TODD SYSTEMS INC
50 Ash St (10701-3900)
PHONE 914 963-3400
K H Todd, *CEO*
Kenneth Todd, *President*
Ruthann Todd, *Vice Pres*
▼ **EMP:** 60 **EST:** 1964
SQ FT: 25,000
SALES (est): 9.7MM **Privately Held**
WEB: www.toddsystems.com
SIC: 3677 Electronic transformers

(G-17491)
TOPPS-ALL PRODUCTS OF YONKERS
148 Ludlow St Ste 2 (10705-7014)
PHONE 914 968-4226
Fax: 914 968-9883
Edward J Bolwell Jr, *President*
EMP: 15 **EST:** 1939
SALES: 2.5MM **Privately Held**
SIC: 2842 Cleaning or polishing preparations; automobile polish

(G-17492)
TOY ADMIRATION CO INC
60 Mclean Ave (10705-2317)
PHONE 914 963-9400
Fax: 914 963-2580
Sidney Newman, *President*
Alice Newman, *Treasurer*
EMP: 30 **EST:** 1945
SQ FT: 60,000
SALES: 2MM **Privately Held**
SIC: 3942 5945 Dolls, except stuffed toy animals; hobby, toy & game shops

(G-17493)
TWO RIVERS COMPUTING INC
976 Mclean Ave (10704-4105)
P.O. Box 498 (10702-0498)
PHONE 914 968-9239
Gus Horowitz, *President*
Suzanne Haig, *Vice Pres*
EMP: 6
SALES (est): 398.1K **Privately Held**
SIC: 7372 Prepackaged software

(G-17494)
VALENTI NECKWEAR CO INC
540 Nepperhan Ave Ste 564 (10701-6611)
PHONE 914 969-0700
Albert Valentine, *President*
EMP: 8
SALES: 250K **Privately Held**
WEB: www.valentineckwear.com
SIC: 2323 2339 Men's & boys' neckwear; neckwear & ties: women's, misses' & juniors'

(G-17495)
VALEO
4 Executive Plz Ste 114 (10701-6803)
PHONE 800 634-2704
Brian Anderson, *President*
Alexandre Depraete, *Project Mgr*
Cheryl Cash, *Prdtn Mgr*
Cedrick Woods, *Site Mgr*
Leon Lane, *Opers Spvr*
EMP: 9
SALES (est): 610K **Privately Held**
SIC: 2399 5091 5099 Glove mending on factory basis; fitness equipment & supplies; safety equipment & supplies

(G-17496)
VINYLINE WINDOW AND DOOR INC
636 Saw Mill River Rd (10710-4009)
PHONE 914 476-3500
Fax: 914 476-3506
Carmen Cangialosi, *President*
Henry Nagani, *Owner*
Robert Gramagila, *Vice Pres*
EMP: 10
SQ FT: 10,000
SALES: 600K **Privately Held**
SIC: 3089 Windows, plastic

(G-17497)
VIOLIFE LLC
1 Executive Blvd Ste 4 (10701-6823)
PHONE 914 207-1820
Joel Pinsky, *Ch of Bd*
Jonathan Pinsky, *Ch of Bd*
Richard Walter, *Vice Pres*
Steven Raptis, *Controller*
Sara Elder, *Sales Staff*
▲ **EMP:** 5
SQ FT: 2,500
SALES (est): 660K **Privately Held**
SIC: 3991 Toothbrushes, except electric

(G-17498)
WHEEL & TIRE DEPOT EX CORP
584 Yonkers Ave (10704-2637)
PHONE 914 375-2100
Jose Calderon, *Manager*
EMP: 8
SALES (est): 1.2MM **Privately Held**
SIC: 3312 Wheels

(G-17499)
WHITNEY BOIN STUDIO INC
42 Warburton Ave Ste 1 (10701-2786)
PHONE 914 377-4385
Whitney Boin, *President*
Theresa Boin, *Vice Pres*
Olympia Meccia, *Opers Mgr*
EMP: 6
SALES (est): 820.9K **Privately Held**
WEB: www.whitneyboinstudio.com
SIC: 3911 Jewelry apparel

(G-17500)
WINESOFT INTERNATIONAL CORP
503 S Broadway Ste 220 (10705-6202)
PHONE 914 400-6247
Marco Vicens, *Manager*
EMP: 6

SALES (est): 251.8K **Privately Held**
WEB: www.winesoftusa.com
SIC: 7372 Application computer software

(G-17501)
YEWTREE MILLWORKS CORP
372 Ashburton Ave (10701-6015)
PHONE 914 320-5851
Keith Murphy, *President*
EMP: 5
SALES (est): 242K **Privately Held**
SIC: 2851 Paints & allied products

(G-17502)
YONKERS CABINETS INC
1179 Yonkers Ave (10704-3210)
PHONE 914 668-2133
Wai Hing Yip, *Owner*
EMP: 8
SALES (est): 839K **Privately Held**
SIC: 2434 Wood kitchen cabinets

(G-17503)
YONKERS TIME PUBLISHING CO
Also Called: Martinelli Publications
40 Larkin Plz (10701-2748)
PHONE 914 965-4000
Fax: 914 965-2892
Franchesca Martinelli, *Owner*
EMP: 15 **EST:** 1934
SQ FT: 6,000
SALES (est): 520K **Privately Held**
WEB: www.martinellipublications.com
SIC: 2711 Newspapers: publishing only, not printed on site

(G-17504)
YONKERS WHL BEER DISTRS INC
424 Riverdale Ave (10705-2908)
PHONE 914 963-8600
Fax: 914 963-7739
Richard McDine, *Owner*
EMP: 5
SALES (est): 343.8K **Privately Held**
SIC: 2082 Beer (alcoholic beverage)

York
Livingston County

(G-17505)
DAVIS TRAILER WORLD LLC
Also Called: Davis Trlr World & Cntry Mall
1640 Main St (14592)
P.O. Box 260 (14592-0260)
PHONE 585 538-6640
Marsha Kingdon, *Bookkeeper*
Dean Davis,
Susan Davis,
EMP: 10 **EST:** 1987
SALES: 3MM **Privately Held**
WEB: www.davistrailerworld.com
SIC: 3715 Truck trailers

Yorktown Heights
Westchester County

(G-17506)
ADVANCED TCHNCAL SOLUTIONS INC
Also Called: Ats
2986 Navajo Rd Ste 100 (10598-1834)
P.O. Box 28 (10598-0028)
PHONE 914 214-8230
Joe Yaniv, *President*
David Wright, *VP Opers*
▲ **EMP:** 10
SQ FT: 2,000
SALES: 5MM **Privately Held**
SIC: 3569 5049 Lubrication equipment, industrial; engineers' equipment & supplies

(G-17507)
BULLETIN BOARDS & DIRCTRY PDTS
2986 Navajo Rd Ste 1 (10598-1800)
PHONE 914 248-8008
Fax: 914 248-5150
Charles Kranz, *President*
Jerry Martin, *Vice Pres*

Esther Glickman, *Admin Sec*
EMP: 15 **EST:** 1921
SQ FT: 40,000
SALES (est): 1.6MM **Privately Held**
SIC: 2493 Bulletin boards, wood; bulletin boards, cork

(G-17508)
BUSINESS MANAGEMENT SYSTEMS
Also Called: Fisau
2404 Loring Pl (10598-3721)
PHONE...............................914 245-8558
Zak Kogan, *CEO*
Leonid Kogan, *President*
Mark Milyavsky, *Vice Pres*
Richard Eigen, *Consultant*
Scott Oldham, *Director*
EMP: 11
SALES (est): 1.4MM **Privately Held**
WEB: www.fisau.com
SIC: 7372 Prepackaged software

(G-17509)
CHASE MEDIA GROUP
1520 Front St (10598-4638)
PHONE...............................914 962-3871
David Cohen, *Controller*
Cynthia Cusumano, *Human Resources*
Chris Longo, *Sales Dir*
Donald Hosmer, *Accounts Exec*
Tom Kelly, *Accounts Exec*
EMP: 15
SALES (est): 738.8K **Privately Held**
SIC: 2711 Newspapers: publishing only, not printed on site

(G-17510)
CROWN DELTA CORPORATION
1550 Front St (10598-4638)
PHONE...............................914 245-8910
Fax: 914 245-8912
Anthony P Konopka, *President*
Richard Bartkus, *Vice Pres*
Mark Konopka, *Opers Mgr*
Kevin Konopka, *Opers Staff*
Anthony J Konopka, *CFO*
▲ **EMP:** 35
SQ FT: 30,000
SALES (est): 10.6MM **Privately Held**
WEB: www.crowndelta.com
SIC: 2869 Silicones

(G-17511)
GAME SPORTSWEAR LTD (PA)
1401 Front St (10598-4639)
PHONE...............................914 962-1701
Fax: 914 892-2411
Enrico Genovese, *President*
Leslie Tandler, *Vice Pres*
Gina M Furano, *Treasurer*
Jennifer Lopez, *Sales Staff*
Virginia Genovese, *Admin Sec*
▲ **EMP:** 25
SQ FT: 76,000
SALES (est): 18.2MM **Privately Held**
SIC: 2253 2339 Knit outerwear mills; women's & misses' outerwear

(G-17512)
MAKARENKO STUDIOS INC
2984 Saddle Ridge Dr (10598-2327)
PHONE...............................914 968-7673
Boris Makarenko, *President*
Sviatoslaw Makarenko, *Treasurer*
EMP: 5 **EST:** 1976
SALES (est): 290K **Privately Held**
SIC: 3231 1542 Stained glass: made from purchased glass; religious building construction

(G-17513)
MEGA GRAPHICS INC
1725 Front St Ste 1 (10598-4651)
PHONE...............................914 962-1402
Robert Pierro, *Principal*
EMP: 5
SALES (est): 425.7K **Privately Held**
SIC: 2759 Commercial printing

(G-17514)
NORTHERN TIER PUBLISHING CORP
Also Called: North County News
1520 Front St (10598-4638)
PHONE...............................914 962-4748

Fax: 914 962-6763
John Chase, *President*
Jean Secor, *Vice Pres*
Rick Pezzullo, *Advt Staff*
Carla Chase, *Admin Sec*
EMP: 11
SQ FT: 2,000
SALES (est): 722K **Privately Held**
SIC: 2711 Newspapers: publishing only, not printed on site

(G-17515)
PARACE BIONICS LLC
276 Landmark Ct (10598-4131)
PHONE...............................877 727-2231
Vandette Carter, *CEO*
EMP: 5
SALES (est): 343.3K **Privately Held**
SIC: 3841 Surgical & medical instruments

(G-17516)
PIC NIC LLC
123 Holmes Ct (10598-2820)
PHONE...............................914 245-6500
Rick Rezzenico, *Partner*
EMP: 8
SALES (est): 893.8K **Privately Held**
SIC: 3556 Ice cream manufacturing machinery

(G-17517)
Q OMNI INC
1994 Commerce St (10598-4412)
PHONE...............................914 962-2726
Kwan Lee, *Owner*
EMP: 6
SALES (est): 542.4K **Privately Held**
SIC: 3582 Drycleaning equipment & machinery, commercial

(G-17518)
RICHARD ANTHONY CORP
Also Called: Richard Anthony Custom Mllwk
1500 Front St Ste 12 (10598-4648)
PHONE...............................914 922-7141
Richard Scavelli, *CEO*
Angela Desiena, *Vice Pres*
EMP: 28
SALES (est): 3.2MM **Privately Held**
SIC: 2431 Millwork

(G-17519)
SHOP SMART CENTRAL INC
Also Called: Chase Press
1520 Front St (10598-4638)
PHONE...............................914 962-3871
Carla Chase, *President*
Rose Mary, *Human Res Mgr*
Amy Bambace, *Accounts Exec*
Tatianna Simone, *Sales Staff*
Jim Brennan, *Supervisor*
EMP: 7
SALES (est): 599.5K **Privately Held**
SIC: 2741 Business service newsletters: publishing & printing

(G-17520)
SIGNS INK LTD
3255 Crompond Rd (10598-3605)
PHONE...............................914 739-9059
Fax: 914 739-9728
Dick Hederson, *President*
Matthew Beachak, *Vice Pres*
Timothy Beachak, *Sales Staff*
Steve Chester, *Sales Staff*
Jim Polinsky, *Manager*
EMP: 10
SQ FT: 1,000
SALES (est): 1.5MM **Privately Held**
SIC: 3993 Signs & advertising specialties

(G-17521)
WOODTRONICS INC
1661 Front St Ste 3 (10598-4650)
PHONE...............................914 962-5205
Fax: 914 962-6114
Jan Efraimsen, *President*
EMP: 5
SQ FT: 4,500
SALES (est): 510K **Privately Held**
SIC: 2499 Decorative wood & woodwork

(G-17522)
YORKTOWN PRINTING CORP
1520 Front St (10598-4697)
PHONE...............................914 962-2526

Fax: 914 962-4820
John W Chase, *President*
Laura Lampel, *Admin Mgr*
EMP: 150
SQ FT: 80,000
SALES (est): 17.8MM **Privately Held**
WEB: www.yzipmail.com
SIC: 2752 Commercial printing, lithographic

Yorkville
Oneida County

(G-17523)
O W HUBBELL & SONS INC
Also Called: Hubbell Galvanising
5124 Commercial Dr (13495-1109)
P.O. Box 37, New York Mills (13417-0037)
PHONE...............................315 736-8311
Fax: 315 736-0381
Allen W Hubbell, *Ch of Bd*
Jock Hubbell, *President*
Vinnie Pham, *Accountant*
James Delude, *Human Resources*
Emmite White, *Human Resources*
▲ **EMP:** 35 **EST:** 1925
SQ FT: 8,000
SALES (est): 5.4MM
SALES (corp-wide): 6.4MM **Privately Held**
WEB: www.hubbellgalvanizing.com
SIC: 3479 Galvanizing of iron, steel or end-formed products
PA: W Hubbell & Sons Inc
5124 Commercial Dr
Yorkville NY 13495
315 736-8311

(G-17524)
ORISKANY MANUFACTURING LLC
2 Wurz Ave (13495-1118)
PHONE...............................315 732-4962
Michael Fitzgerald, *CEO*
EMP: 14 **EST:** 2009
SALES (est): 2.6MM **Privately Held**
SIC: 3999 Manufacturing industries

(G-17525)
ORISKANY MFG TECH LLC
Also Called: Omt
2 Wurz Ave (13495-1118)
PHONE...............................315 732-4962
Fax: 315 732-6165
Stephen Palmieri, *Production*
Thomas Dutcher, *Purch Mgr*
James Caraco, *Engineer*
David Pelligrini, *Marketing Staff*
Debbie Ashe, *Manager*
▲ **EMP:** 30
SQ FT: 30,000
SALES (est): 8.6MM **Privately Held**
WEB: www.oriskanymfg.com
SIC: 3441 3317 Fabricated structural metal; welded pipe & tubes

(G-17526)
OTIS ELEVATOR COMPANY
5172 Commercial Dr (13495-1110)
PHONE...............................315 736-0167
Fax: 315 736-1580
Kerry Greer, *Sales/Mktg Mgr*
EMP: 12
SALES (corp-wide): 56.1B **Publicly Held**
WEB: www.otis.com
SIC: 3534 7699 Elevators & equipment; elevators: inspection, service & repair
HQ: Otis Elevator Company
10 Farm Springs Rd
Farmington CT 06032
860 676-6000

(G-17527)
VICKS LITHOGRAPH & PRTG CORP (PA)
5166 Commercial Dr (13495-1173)
P.O. Box 270 (13495-0270)
PHONE...............................315 272-2401
Fax: 315 736-1901
Dwight E Vicks III, *Ch of Bd*
Dwight E Vicks III, *Ch of Bd*
Frances Driscoll, *General Mgr*
Dwight E Vicks Jr, *Chairman*

Leo McStoy, *Controller*
EMP: 110
SQ FT: 130,000
SALES (est): 22MM **Privately Held**
SIC: 2732 2789 2752 Books: printing only; bookbinding & related work; commercial printing, lithographic

(G-17528)
VICKS LITHOGRAPH & PRTG CORP
5210 Commercial Dr (13495-1111)
P.O. Box 270 (13495-0270)
PHONE...............................315 736-9344
Frank Driscoll, *Manager*
EMP: 130
SALES (corp-wide): 22MM **Privately Held**
SIC: 2732 2752 Book printing; commercial printing, lithographic
PA: Vicks Lithograph & Printing Corp.
5166 Commercial Dr
Yorkville NY 13495
315 272-2401

(G-17529)
W HUBBELL & SONS INC (PA)
5124 Commercial Dr (13495-1109)
P.O. Box 37, New York Mills (13417-0037)
PHONE...............................315 736-8311
Allen W Hubbell, *Principal*
Allen W Hubbel, *Principal*
Steve Mulvihill, *Principal*
EMP: 6
SQ FT: 8,000
SALES (est): 6.4MM **Privately Held**
SIC: 3479 Galvanizing of iron, steel or end-formed products

(G-17530)
WAYNES WELDING INC (PA)
66 Calder Ave (13495-1601)
PHONE...............................315 768-6146
Fax: 315 768-2785
Wayne A Ramsey, *President*
Keith Ives, *Sales Staff*
Joyce Smith, *Manager*
EMP: 20
SQ FT: 9,000
SALES (est): 1.9MM **Privately Held**
SIC: 7692 3599 Welding repair; machine shop, jobbing & repair

Youngstown
Niagara County

(G-17531)
KINETIC FUEL TECHNOLOGY INC
Also Called: Kinetic Laboratories
1205 Balmer Rd (14174-9773)
PHONE...............................716 745-1461
Fax: 716 745-1468
Timothy M Booth, *Ch of Bd*
Eric Fragale, *President*
EMP: 5
SQ FT: 4,500
SALES: 1.2MM **Privately Held**
SIC: 2911 Fuel additives

SIC INDEX

Standard Industrial Classification Alphabetical Index

SIC NO	PRODUCT

A

- 3291 Abrasive Prdts
- 2891 Adhesives & Sealants
- 3563 Air & Gas Compressors
- 3585 Air Conditioning & Heating Eqpt
- 3721 Aircraft
- 3724 Aircraft Engines & Engine Parts
- 3728 Aircraft Parts & Eqpt, NEC
- 2812 Alkalies & Chlorine
- 3363 Aluminum Die Castings
- 3354 Aluminum Extruded Prdts
- 3365 Aluminum Foundries
- 3355 Aluminum Rolling & Drawing, NEC
- 3353 Aluminum Sheet, Plate & Foil
- 3483 Ammunition, Large
- 3826 Analytical Instruments
- 2077 Animal, Marine Fats & Oils
- 1231 Anthracite Mining
- 2389 Apparel & Accessories, NEC
- 2387 Apparel Belts
- 3446 Architectural & Ornamental Metal Work
- 7694 Armature Rewinding Shops
- 3292 Asbestos products
- 2952 Asphalt Felts & Coatings
- 3822 Automatic Temperature Controls
- 3581 Automatic Vending Machines
- 3465 Automotive Stampings
- 2396 Automotive Trimmings, Apparel Findings, Related Prdts

B

- 2673 Bags: Plastics, Laminated & Coated
- 2674 Bags: Uncoated Paper & Multiwall
- 3562 Ball & Roller Bearings
- 2836 Biological Prdts, Exc Diagnostic Substances
- 2782 Blankbooks & Looseleaf Binders
- 3312 Blast Furnaces, Coke Ovens, Steel & Rolling Mills
- 3564 Blowers & Fans
- 3732 Boat Building & Repairing
- 3452 Bolts, Nuts, Screws, Rivets & Washers
- 2732 Book Printing, Not Publishing
- 2789 Bookbinding
- 2731 Books: Publishing & Printing
- 3131 Boot & Shoe Cut Stock & Findings
- 2342 Brassieres, Girdles & Garments
- 2051 Bread, Bakery Prdts Exc Cookies & Crackers
- 3251 Brick & Structural Clay Tile
- 3991 Brooms & Brushes
- 3995 Burial Caskets
- 2021 Butter

C

- 3578 Calculating & Accounting Eqpt
- 2064 Candy & Confectionery Prdts
- 2033 Canned Fruits, Vegetables & Preserves
- 2032 Canned Specialties
- 2394 Canvas Prdts
- 3624 Carbon & Graphite Prdts
- 3955 Carbon Paper & Inked Ribbons
- 3592 Carburetors, Pistons, Rings & Valves
- 2273 Carpets & Rugs
- 2823 Cellulosic Man-Made Fibers
- 3241 Cement, Hydraulic
- 3253 Ceramic Tile
- 2043 Cereal Breakfast Foods
- 2022 Cheese
- 1479 Chemical & Fertilizer Mining
- 2899 Chemical Preparations, NEC
- 2067 Chewing Gum
- 2361 Children's & Infants' Dresses & Blouses
- 3261 China Plumbing Fixtures & Fittings
- 3262 China, Table & Kitchen Articles
- 2066 Chocolate & Cocoa Prdts
- 2111 Cigarettes
- 2121 Cigars
- 2257 Circular Knit Fabric Mills
- 3255 Clay Refractories
- 1459 Clay, Ceramic & Refractory Minerals, NEC
- 1241 Coal Mining Svcs
- 3479 Coating & Engraving, NEC
- 2095 Coffee
- 3316 Cold Rolled Steel Sheet, Strip & Bars
- 3582 Commercial Laundry, Dry Clean & Pressing Mchs
- 2759 Commercial Printing
- 2754 Commercial Printing: Gravure
- 2752 Commercial Printing: Lithographic
- 3646 Commercial, Indl & Institutional Lighting Fixtures
- 3669 Communications Eqpt, NEC
- 3577 Computer Peripheral Eqpt, NEC
- 3572 Computer Storage Devices
- 3575 Computer Terminals
- 3271 Concrete Block & Brick
- 3272 Concrete Prdts
- 3531 Construction Machinery & Eqpt
- 1442 Construction Sand & Gravel
- 2679 Converted Paper Prdts, NEC
- 3535 Conveyors & Eqpt
- 2052 Cookies & Crackers
- 3366 Copper Foundries
- 1021 Copper Ores
- 2298 Cordage & Twine
- 2653 Corrugated & Solid Fiber Boxes
- 3961 Costume Jewelry & Novelties
- 2261 Cotton Fabric Finishers
- 2211 Cotton, Woven Fabric
- 2074 Cottonseed Oil Mills
- 3466 Crowns & Closures
- 1311 Crude Petroleum & Natural Gas
- 1423 Crushed & Broken Granite
- 1422 Crushed & Broken Limestone
- 1429 Crushed & Broken Stone, NEC
- 3643 Current-Carrying Wiring Devices
- 2391 Curtains & Draperies
- 3087 Custom Compounding Of Purchased Plastic Resins
- 3281 Cut Stone Prdts
- 3421 Cutlery
- 2865 Cyclic-Crudes, Intermediates, Dyes & Org Pigments

D

- 3843 Dental Eqpt & Splys
- 2835 Diagnostic Substances
- 2675 Die-Cut Paper & Board
- 3544 Dies, Tools, Jigs, Fixtures & Indl Molds
- 1411 Dimension Stone
- 2047 Dog & Cat Food
- 3942 Dolls & Stuffed Toys
- 2591 Drapery Hardware, Window Blinds & Shades
- 2381 Dress & Work Gloves
- 2034 Dried Fruits, Vegetables & Soup
- 1381 Drilling Oil & Gas Wells

E

- 3263 Earthenware, Whiteware, Table & Kitchen Articles
- 3634 Electric Household Appliances
- 3641 Electric Lamps
- 3694 Electrical Eqpt For Internal Combustion Engines
- 3629 Electrical Indl Apparatus, NEC
- 3699 Electrical Machinery, Eqpt & Splys, NEC
- 3845 Electromedical & Electrotherapeutic Apparatus
- 3313 Electrometallurgical Prdts
- 3675 Electronic Capacitors
- 3677 Electronic Coils & Transformers
- 3679 Electronic Components, NEC
- 3571 Electronic Computers
- 3678 Electronic Connectors
- 3676 Electronic Resistors
- 3471 Electroplating, Plating, Polishing, Anodizing & Coloring
- 3534 Elevators & Moving Stairways
- 3431 Enameled Iron & Metal Sanitary Ware
- 2677 Envelopes
- 2892 Explosives

F

- 2241 Fabric Mills, Cotton, Wool, Silk & Man-Made
- 3499 Fabricated Metal Prdts, NEC
- 3498 Fabricated Pipe & Pipe Fittings
- 3443 Fabricated Plate Work
- 3069 Fabricated Rubber Prdts, NEC
- 3441 Fabricated Structural Steel
- 2399 Fabricated Textile Prdts, NEC
- 2295 Fabrics Coated Not Rubberized
- 2297 Fabrics, Nonwoven
- 3523 Farm Machinery & Eqpt
- 3965 Fasteners, Buttons, Needles & Pins
- 2875 Fertilizers, Mixing Only
- 2655 Fiber Cans, Tubes & Drums
- 2091 Fish & Seafoods, Canned & Cured
- 2092 Fish & Seafoods, Fresh & Frozen
- 3211 Flat Glass
- 2087 Flavoring Extracts & Syrups
- 2045 Flour, Blended & Prepared
- 2041 Flour, Grain Milling
- 3824 Fluid Meters & Counters
- 3593 Fluid Power Cylinders & Actuators
- 3594 Fluid Power Pumps & Motors
- 3492 Fluid Power Valves & Hose Fittings
- 2657 Folding Paperboard Boxes
- 3556 Food Prdts Machinery
- 2099 Food Preparations, NEC
- 3149 Footwear, NEC
- 2053 Frozen Bakery Prdts
- 2037 Frozen Fruits, Juices & Vegetables
- 2038 Frozen Specialties
- 2371 Fur Goods
- 2599 Furniture & Fixtures, NEC

G

- 3944 Games, Toys & Children's Vehicles
- 3524 Garden, Lawn Tractors & Eqpt
- 3053 Gaskets, Packing & Sealing Devices
- 2369 Girls' & Infants' Outerwear, NEC
- 3221 Glass Containers
- 3231 Glass Prdts Made Of Purchased Glass
- 1041 Gold Ores
- 3321 Gray Iron Foundries
- 2771 Greeting Card Publishing
- 3769 Guided Missile/Space Vehicle Parts & Eqpt, NEC
- 3761 Guided Missiles & Space Vehicles
- 2861 Gum & Wood Chemicals
- 3275 Gypsum Prdts

H

- 3423 Hand & Edge Tools
- 3425 Hand Saws & Saw Blades
- 3171 Handbags & Purses
- 3429 Hardware, NEC
- 2426 Hardwood Dimension & Flooring Mills
- 2435 Hardwood Veneer & Plywood
- 2353 Hats, Caps & Millinery
- 3433 Heating Eqpt
- 3536 Hoists, Cranes & Monorails
- 2252 Hosiery, Except Women's
- 2251 Hosiery, Women's Full & Knee Length
- 2392 House furnishings: Textile
- 3142 House Slippers
- 3639 Household Appliances, NEC
- 3651 Household Audio & Video Eqpt
- 3631 Household Cooking Eqpt
- 2519 Household Furniture, NEC
- 3633 Household Laundry Eqpt
- 3632 Household Refrigerators & Freezers
- 3635 Household Vacuum Cleaners

I

- 2097 Ice
- 2024 Ice Cream
- 2819 Indl Inorganic Chemicals, NEC
- 3823 Indl Instruments For Meas, Display & Control
- 3569 Indl Machinery & Eqpt, NEC
- 3567 Indl Process Furnaces & Ovens
- 3537 Indl Trucks, Tractors, Trailers & Stackers
- 2813 Industrial Gases
- 2869 Industrial Organic Chemicals, NEC
- 3543 Industrial Patterns
- 1446 Industrial Sand
- 3491 Industrial Valves
- 2816 Inorganic Pigments
- 3825 Instrs For Measuring & Testing Electricity
- 3519 Internal Combustion Engines, NEC
- 3462 Iron & Steel Forgings
- 1011 Iron Ores

J

- 3915 Jewelers Findings & Lapidary Work
- 3911 Jewelry: Precious Metal

K

- 2253 Knit Outerwear Mills
- 2254 Knit Underwear Mills
- 2259 Knitting Mills, NEC

L

- 3821 Laboratory Apparatus & Furniture
- 2258 Lace & Warp Knit Fabric Mills
- 3952 Lead Pencils, Crayons & Artist's Mtrls
- 2386 Leather & Sheep Lined Clothing
- 3151 Leather Gloves & Mittens
- 3199 Leather Goods, NEC
- 3111 Leather Tanning & Finishing
- 3648 Lighting Eqpt, NEC

SIC INDEX

SIC NO	PRODUCT
3274	Lime
3996	Linoleum & Hard Surface Floor Coverings, NEC
2085	Liquors, Distilled, Rectified & Blended
2411	Logging
2992	Lubricating Oils & Greases
3161	Luggage

M

SIC NO	PRODUCT
2098	Macaroni, Spaghetti & Noodles
3545	Machine Tool Access
3541	Machine Tools: Cutting
3542	Machine Tools: Forming
3599	Machinery & Eqpt, Indl & Commercial, NEC
3322	Malleable Iron Foundries
2083	Malt
2082	Malt Beverages
2761	Manifold Business Forms
3999	Manufacturing Industries, NEC
3953	Marking Devices
2515	Mattresses & Bedsprings
3829	Measuring & Controlling Devices, NEC
3586	Measuring & Dispensing Pumps
2011	Meat Packing Plants
3568	Mechanical Power Transmission Eqpt, NEC
2833	Medicinal Chemicals & Botanical Prdts
2329	Men's & Boys' Clothing, NEC
2323	Men's & Boys' Neckwear
2325	Men's & Boys' Separate Trousers & Casual Slacks
2321	Men's & Boys' Shirts
2311	Men's & Boys' Suits, Coats & Overcoats
2322	Men's & Boys' Underwear & Nightwear
2326	Men's & Boys' Work Clothing
3143	Men's Footwear, Exc Athletic
3412	Metal Barrels, Drums, Kegs & Pails
3411	Metal Cans
3442	Metal Doors, Sash, Frames, Molding & Trim
3497	Metal Foil & Leaf
3398	Metal Heat Treating
2514	Metal Household Furniture
1081	Metal Mining Svcs
1099	Metal Ores, NEC
3469	Metal Stampings, NEC
3549	Metalworking Machinery, NEC
2026	Milk
2023	Milk, Condensed & Evaporated
2431	Millwork
3296	Mineral Wool
3295	Minerals & Earths: Ground Or Treated
3532	Mining Machinery & Eqpt
3496	Misc Fabricated Wire Prdts
2741	Misc Publishing
3449	Misc Structural Metal Work
1499	Miscellaneous Nonmetallic Mining
2451	Mobile Homes
3061	Molded, Extruded & Lathe-Cut Rubber Mechanical Goods
3716	Motor Homes
3714	Motor Vehicle Parts & Access
3711	Motor Vehicles & Car Bodies
3751	Motorcycles, Bicycles & Parts
3621	Motors & Generators
3931	Musical Instruments

N

SIC NO	PRODUCT
1321	Natural Gas Liquids
2711	Newspapers: Publishing & Printing
2873	Nitrogenous Fertilizers
3297	Nonclay Refractories
3644	Noncurrent-Carrying Wiring Devices
3364	Nonferrous Die Castings, Exc Aluminum
3463	Nonferrous Forgings
3369	Nonferrous Foundries: Castings, NEC
3357	Nonferrous Wire Drawing
3299	Nonmetallic Mineral Prdts, NEC
1481	Nonmetallic Minerals Svcs, Except Fuels

O

SIC NO	PRODUCT
2522	Office Furniture, Except Wood
3579	Office Machines, NEC
1382	Oil & Gas Field Exploration Svcs
1389	Oil & Gas Field Svcs, NEC
3533	Oil Field Machinery & Eqpt
3851	Ophthalmic Goods
3827	Optical Instruments
3489	Ordnance & Access, NEC
3842	Orthopedic, Prosthetic & Surgical Appliances/Splys

P

SIC NO	PRODUCT
3565	Packaging Machinery
2851	Paints, Varnishes, Lacquers, Enamels
2671	Paper Coating & Laminating for Packaging
2672	Paper Coating & Laminating, Exc for Packaging
3554	Paper Inds Machinery
2621	Paper Mills
2631	Paperboard Mills
2542	Partitions & Fixtures, Except Wood
2951	Paving Mixtures & Blocks
3951	Pens & Mechanical Pencils
2844	Perfumes, Cosmetics & Toilet Preparations
2721	Periodicals: Publishing & Printing
3172	Personal Leather Goods
2879	Pesticides & Agricultural Chemicals, NEC
2911	Petroleum Refining
2834	Pharmaceuticals
3652	Phonograph Records & Magnetic Tape
2874	Phosphatic Fertilizers
3861	Photographic Eqpt & Splys
2035	Pickled Fruits, Vegetables, Sauces & Dressings
3085	Plastic Bottles
3086	Plastic Foam Prdts
3083	Plastic Laminated Plate & Sheet
3084	Plastic Pipe
3088	Plastic Plumbing Fixtures
3089	Plastic Prdts
3082	Plastic Unsupported Profile Shapes
3081	Plastic Unsupported Sheet & Film
2821	Plastics, Mtrls & Nonvulcanizable Elastomers
2796	Platemaking & Related Svcs
2395	Pleating & Stitching For The Trade
3432	Plumbing Fixture Fittings & Trim, Brass
3264	Porcelain Electrical Splys
2096	Potato Chips & Similar Prdts
3269	Pottery Prdts, NEC
2015	Poultry Slaughtering, Dressing & Processing
3546	Power Hand Tools
3612	Power, Distribution & Specialty Transformers
3448	Prefabricated Metal Buildings & Cmpnts
2452	Prefabricated Wood Buildings & Cmpnts
7372	Prepackaged Software
2048	Prepared Feeds For Animals & Fowls
3229	Pressed & Blown Glassware, NEC
3692	Primary Batteries: Dry & Wet
3399	Primary Metal Prdts, NEC
3339	Primary Nonferrous Metals, NEC
3334	Primary Production Of Aluminum
3331	Primary Smelting & Refining Of Copper
3672	Printed Circuit Boards
2893	Printing Ink
3555	Printing Trades Machinery & Eqpt
2999	Products Of Petroleum & Coal, NEC
2531	Public Building & Related Furniture
2611	Pulp Mills
3561	Pumps & Pumping Eqpt

R

SIC NO	PRODUCT
3663	Radio & T V Communications, Systs & Eqpt, Broadcast/Studio
3671	Radio & T V Receiving Electron Tubes
3743	Railroad Eqpt
3273	Ready-Mixed Concrete
2493	Reconstituted Wood Prdts
3695	Recording Media
3625	Relays & Indl Controls
3645	Residential Lighting Fixtures
2044	Rice Milling
2384	Robes & Dressing Gowns
3547	Rolling Mill Machinery & Eqpt
3351	Rolling, Drawing & Extruding Of Copper
3356	Rolling, Drawing-Extruding Of Nonferrous Metals
3021	Rubber & Plastic Footwear
3052	Rubber & Plastic Hose & Belting

S

SIC NO	PRODUCT
2068	Salted & Roasted Nuts & Seeds
2656	Sanitary Food Containers
2676	Sanitary Paper Prdts
2013	Sausages & Meat Prdts
2421	Saw & Planing Mills
3596	Scales & Balances, Exc Laboratory
2397	Schiffli Machine Embroideries
3451	Screw Machine Prdts
3812	Search, Detection, Navigation & Guidance Systs & Instrs
3341	Secondary Smelting & Refining Of Nonferrous Metals
3674	Semiconductors
3589	Service Ind Machines, NEC
2652	Set-Up Paperboard Boxes
3444	Sheet Metal Work
3731	Shipbuilding & Repairing
2079	Shortening, Oils & Margarine
3993	Signs & Advertising Displays
2262	Silk & Man-Made Fabric Finishers
2221	Silk & Man-Made Fiber
1044	Silver Ores
3914	Silverware, Plated & Stainless Steel Ware
3484	Small Arms
3482	Small Arms Ammunition
2841	Soap & Detergents
2086	Soft Drinks
2436	Softwood Veneer & Plywood
2075	Soybean Oil Mills
2842	Spec Cleaning, Polishing & Sanitation Preparations
3559	Special Ind Machinery, NEC
2429	Special Prdt Sawmills, NEC
3566	Speed Changers, Drives & Gears
3949	Sporting & Athletic Goods, NEC
2678	Stationery Prdts
3511	Steam, Gas & Hydraulic Turbines & Engines
3325	Steel Foundries, NEC
3324	Steel Investment Foundries
3317	Steel Pipe & Tubes
3493	Steel Springs, Except Wire
3315	Steel Wire Drawing & Nails & Spikes
3691	Storage Batteries
3259	Structural Clay Prdts, NEC
2439	Structural Wood Members, NEC
2063	Sugar, Beet
2061	Sugar, Cane
2062	Sugar, Cane Refining
2843	Surface Active & Finishing Agents, Sulfonated Oils
3841	Surgical & Medical Instrs & Apparatus
3613	Switchgear & Switchboard Apparatus
2824	Synthetic Organic Fibers, Exc Cellulosic
2822	Synthetic Rubber (Vulcanizable Elastomers)

T

SIC NO	PRODUCT
3795	Tanks & Tank Components
3661	Telephone & Telegraph Apparatus
2393	Textile Bags
2269	Textile Finishers, NEC
2299	Textile Goods, NEC
3552	Textile Machinery
2284	Thread Mills
2296	Tire Cord & Fabric
3011	Tires & Inner Tubes
2141	Tobacco Stemming & Redrying
2131	Tobacco, Chewing & Snuff
3799	Transportation Eqpt, NEC
3792	Travel Trailers & Campers
3713	Truck & Bus Bodies
3715	Truck Trailers
2791	Typesetting

U

SIC NO	PRODUCT
1094	Uranium, Radium & Vanadium Ores

V

SIC NO	PRODUCT
3494	Valves & Pipe Fittings, NEC
2076	Vegetable Oil Mills
3647	Vehicular Lighting Eqpt

W

SIC NO	PRODUCT
3873	Watch & Clock Devices & Parts
2385	Waterproof Outerwear
3548	Welding Apparatus
7692	Welding Repair
2046	Wet Corn Milling
2084	Wine & Brandy
3495	Wire Springs
2331	Women's & Misses' Blouses
2335	Women's & Misses' Dresses
2339	Women's & Misses' Outerwear, NEC
2337	Women's & Misses' Suits, Coats & Skirts
3144	Women's Footwear, Exc Athletic
2341	Women's, Misses' & Children's Underwear & Nightwear
2441	Wood Boxes
2449	Wood Containers, NEC
2511	Wood Household Furniture
2512	Wood Household Furniture, Upholstered
2434	Wood Kitchen Cabinets
2521	Wood Office Furniture
2448	Wood Pallets & Skids
2499	Wood Prdts, NEC
2491	Wood Preserving
2517	Wood T V, Radio, Phono & Sewing Cabinets
2541	Wood, Office & Store Fixtures
3553	Woodworking Machinery
2231	Wool, Woven Fabric

X

SIC NO	PRODUCT
3844	X-ray Apparatus & Tubes

Y

SIC NO	PRODUCT
2281	Yarn Spinning Mills
2282	Yarn Texturizing, Throwing, Twisting & Winding Mills

SIC INDEX

Standard Industrial Classification Numerical Index

SIC NO	PRODUCT

10 METAL MINING
1011 Iron Ores
1021 Copper Ores
1041 Gold Ores
1044 Silver Ores
1081 Metal Mining Svcs
1094 Uranium, Radium & Vanadium Ores
1099 Metal Ores, NEC

12 COAL MINING
1231 Anthracite Mining
1241 Coal Mining Svcs

13 OIL AND GAS EXTRACTION
1311 Crude Petroleum & Natural Gas
1321 Natural Gas Liquids
1381 Drilling Oil & Gas Wells
1382 Oil & Gas Field Exploration Svcs
1389 Oil & Gas Field Svcs, NEC

14 MINING AND QUARRYING OF NONMETALLIC MINERALS, EXCEPT FUELS
1411 Dimension Stone
1422 Crushed & Broken Limestone
1423 Crushed & Broken Granite
1429 Crushed & Broken Stone, NEC
1442 Construction Sand & Gravel
1446 Industrial Sand
1459 Clay, Ceramic & Refractory Minerals, NEC
1479 Chemical & Fertilizer Mining
1481 Nonmetallic Minerals Svcs, Except Fuels
1499 Miscellaneous Nonmetallic Mining

20 FOOD AND KINDRED PRODUCTS
2011 Meat Packing Plants
2013 Sausages & Meat Prdts
2015 Poultry Slaughtering, Dressing & Processing
2021 Butter
2022 Cheese
2023 Milk, Condensed & Evaporated
2024 Ice Cream
2026 Milk
2032 Canned Specialties
2033 Canned Fruits, Vegetables & Preserves
2034 Dried Fruits, Vegetables & Soup
2035 Pickled Fruits, Vegetables, Sauces & Dressings
2037 Frozen Fruits, Juices & Vegetables
2038 Frozen Specialties
2041 Flour, Grain Milling
2043 Cereal Breakfast Foods
2044 Rice Milling
2045 Flour, Blended & Prepared
2046 Wet Corn Milling
2047 Dog & Cat Food
2048 Prepared Feeds For Animals & Fowls
2051 Bread, Bakery Prdts Exc Cookies & Crackers
2052 Cookies & Crackers
2053 Frozen Bakery Prdts
2061 Sugar, Cane
2062 Sugar, Cane Refining
2063 Sugar, Beet
2064 Candy & Confectionery Prdts
2066 Chocolate & Cocoa Prdts
2067 Chewing Gum
2068 Salted & Roasted Nuts & Seeds
2074 Cottonseed Oil Mills
2075 Soybean Oil Mills
2076 Vegetable Oil Mills
2077 Animal, Marine Fats & Oils
2079 Shortening, Oils & Margarine
2082 Malt Beverages
2083 Malt
2084 Wine & Brandy
2085 Liquors, Distilled, Rectified & Blended
2086 Soft Drinks
2087 Flavoring Extracts & Syrups
2091 Fish & Seafoods, Canned & Cured
2092 Fish & Seafoods, Fresh & Frozen
2095 Coffee
2096 Potato Chips & Similar Prdts
2097 Ice
2098 Macaroni, Spaghetti & Noodles
2099 Food Preparations, NEC

21 TOBACCO PRODUCTS
2111 Cigarettes
2121 Cigars
2131 Tobacco, Chewing & Snuff
2141 Tobacco Stemming & Redrying

22 TEXTILE MILL PRODUCTS
2211 Cotton, Woven Fabric
2221 Silk & Man-Made Fiber
2231 Wool, Woven Fabric
2241 Fabric Mills, Cotton, Wool, Silk & Man-Made
2251 Hosiery, Women's Full & Knee Length
2252 Hosiery, Except Women's
2253 Knit Outerwear Mills
2254 Knit Underwear Mills
2257 Circular Knit Fabric Mills
2258 Lace & Warp Knit Fabric Mills
2259 Knitting Mills, NEC
2261 Cotton Fabric Finishers
2262 Silk & Man-Made Fabric Finishers
2269 Textile Finishers, NEC
2273 Carpets & Rugs
2281 Yarn Spinning Mills
2282 Yarn Texturizing, Throwing, Twisting & Winding Mills
2284 Thread Mills
2295 Fabrics Coated Not Rubberized
2296 Tire Cord & Fabric
2297 Fabrics, Nonwoven
2298 Cordage & Twine
2299 Textile Goods, NEC

23 APPAREL AND OTHER FINISHED PRODUCTS MADE FROM FABRICS AND SIMILAR MATERIAL
2311 Men's & Boys' Suits, Coats & Overcoats
2321 Men's & Boys' Shirts
2322 Men's & Boys' Underwear & Nightwear
2323 Men's & Boys' Neckwear
2325 Men's & Boys' Separate Trousers & Casual Slacks
2326 Men's & Boys' Work Clothing
2329 Men's & Boys' Clothing, NEC
2331 Women's & Misses' Blouses
2335 Women's & Misses' Dresses
2337 Women's & Misses' Suits, Coats & Skirts
2339 Women's & Misses' Outerwear, NEC
2341 Women's, Misses' & Children's Underwear & Nightwear
2342 Brassieres, Girdles & Garments
2353 Hats, Caps & Millinery
2361 Children's & Infants' Dresses & Blouses
2369 Girls' & Infants' Outerwear, NEC
2371 Fur Goods
2381 Dress & Work Gloves
2384 Robes & Dressing Gowns
2385 Waterproof Outerwear
2386 Leather & Sheep Lined Clothing
2387 Apparel Belts
2389 Apparel & Accessories, NEC
2391 Curtains & Draperies
2392 House furnishings: Textile
2393 Textile Bags
2394 Canvas Prdts
2395 Pleating & Stitching For The Trade
2396 Automotive Trimmings, Apparel Findings, Related Prdts
2397 Schiffli Machine Embroideries
2399 Fabricated Textile Prdts, NEC

24 LUMBER AND WOOD PRODUCTS, EXCEPT FURNITURE
2411 Logging
2421 Saw & Planing Mills
2426 Hardwood Dimension & Flooring Mills
2429 Special Prdt Sawmills, NEC
2431 Millwork
2434 Wood Kitchen Cabinets
2435 Hardwood Veneer & Plywood
2436 Softwood Veneer & Plywood
2439 Structural Wood Members, NEC
2441 Wood Boxes
2448 Wood Pallets & Skids
2449 Wood Containers, NEC
2451 Mobile Homes
2452 Prefabricated Wood Buildings & Cmpnts
2491 Wood Preserving
2493 Reconstituted Wood Prdts
2499 Wood Prdts, NEC

25 FURNITURE AND FIXTURES
2511 Wood Household Furniture
2512 Wood Household Furniture, Upholstered
2514 Metal Household Furniture
2515 Mattresses & Bedsprings
2517 Wood T V, Radio, Phono & Sewing Cabinets
2519 Household Furniture, NEC
2521 Wood Office Furniture
2522 Office Furniture, Except Wood
2531 Public Building & Related Furniture
2541 Wood, Office & Store Fixtures
2542 Partitions & Fixtures, Except Wood
2591 Drapery Hardware, Window Blinds & Shades
2599 Furniture & Fixtures, NEC

26 PAPER AND ALLIED PRODUCTS
2611 Pulp Mills
2621 Paper Mills
2631 Paperboard Mills
2652 Set-Up Paperboard Boxes
2653 Corrugated & Solid Fiber Boxes
2655 Fiber Cans, Tubes & Drums
2656 Sanitary Food Containers
2657 Folding Paperboard Boxes
2671 Paper Coating & Laminating for Packaging
2672 Paper Coating & Laminating, Exc for Packaging
2673 Bags: Plastics, Laminated & Coated
2674 Bags: Uncoated Paper & Multiwall
2675 Die-Cut Paper & Board
2676 Sanitary Paper Prdts
2677 Envelopes
2678 Stationery Prdts
2679 Converted Paper Prdts, NEC

27 PRINTING, PUBLISHING, AND ALLIED INDUSTRIES
2711 Newspapers: Publishing & Printing
2721 Periodicals: Publishing & Printing
2731 Books: Publishing & Printing
2732 Book Printing, Not Publishing
2741 Misc Publishing
2752 Commercial Printing: Lithographic
2754 Commercial Printing: Gravure
2759 Commercial Printing
2761 Manifold Business Forms
2771 Greeting Card Publishing
2782 Blankbooks & Looseleaf Binders
2789 Bookbinding
2791 Typesetting
2796 Platemaking & Related Svcs

28 CHEMICALS AND ALLIED PRODUCTS
2812 Alkalies & Chlorine
2813 Industrial Gases
2816 Inorganic Pigments
2819 Indl Inorganic Chemicals, NEC
2821 Plastics, Mtrls & Nonvulcanizable Elastomers
2822 Synthetic Rubber (Vulcanizable Elastomers)
2823 Cellulosic Man-Made Fibers
2824 Synthetic Organic Fibers, Exc Cellulosic
2833 Medicinal Chemicals & Botanical Prdts
2834 Pharmaceuticals
2835 Diagnostic Substances
2836 Biological Prdts, Exc Diagnostic Substances
2841 Soap & Detergents
2842 Spec Cleaning, Polishing & Sanitation Preparations
2843 Surface Active & Finishing Agents, Sulfonated Oils
2844 Perfumes, Cosmetics & Toilet Preparations
2851 Paints, Varnishes, Lacquers, Enamels
2861 Gum & Wood Chemicals
2865 Cyclic-Crudes, Intermediates, Dyes & Org Pigments
2869 Industrial Organic Chemicals, NEC
2873 Nitrogenous Fertilizers
2874 Phosphatic Fertilizers
2875 Fertilizers, Mixing Only
2879 Pesticides & Agricultural Chemicals, NEC
2891 Adhesives & Sealants
2892 Explosives
2893 Printing Ink
2899 Chemical Preparations, NEC

29 PETROLEUM REFINING AND RELATED INDUSTRIES
2911 Petroleum Refining
2951 Paving Mixtures & Blocks
2952 Asphalt Felts & Coatings
2992 Lubricating Oils & Greases
2999 Products Of Petroleum & Coal, NEC

30 RUBBER AND MISCELLANEOUS PLASTICS PRODUCTS
3011 Tires & Inner Tubes
3021 Rubber & Plastic Footwear
3052 Rubber & Plastic Hose & Belting
3053 Gaskets, Packing & Sealing Devices
3061 Molded, Extruded & Lathe-Cut Rubber Mechanical Goods
3069 Fabricated Rubber Prdts, NEC
3081 Plastic Unsupported Sheet & Film
3082 Plastic Unsupported Profile Shapes

SIC INDEX

SIC NO	PRODUCT
3083	Plastic Laminated Plate & Sheet
3084	Plastic Pipe
3085	Plastic Bottles
3086	Plastic Foam Prdts
3087	Custom Compounding Of Purchased Plastic Resins
3088	Plastic Plumbing Fixtures
3089	Plastic Prdts

31 LEATHER AND LEATHER PRODUCTS

SIC NO	PRODUCT
3111	Leather Tanning & Finishing
3131	Boot & Shoe Cut Stock & Findings
3142	House Slippers
3143	Men's Footwear, Exc Athletic
3144	Women's Footwear, Exc Athletic
3149	Footwear, NEC
3151	Leather Gloves & Mittens
3161	Luggage
3171	Handbags & Purses
3172	Personal Leather Goods
3199	Leather Goods, NEC

32 STONE, CLAY, GLASS, AND CONCRETE PRODUCTS

SIC NO	PRODUCT
3211	Flat Glass
3221	Glass Containers
3229	Pressed & Blown Glassware, NEC
3231	Glass Prdts Made Of Purchased Glass
3241	Cement, Hydraulic
3251	Brick & Structural Clay Tile
3253	Ceramic Tile
3255	Clay Refractories
3259	Structural Clay Prdts, NEC
3261	China Plumbing Fixtures & Fittings
3262	China, Table & Kitchen Articles
3263	Earthenware, Whiteware, Table & Kitchen Articles
3264	Porcelain Electrical Splys
3269	Pottery Prdts, NEC
3271	Concrete Block & Brick
3272	Concrete Prdts
3273	Ready-Mixed Concrete
3274	Lime
3275	Gypsum Prdts
3281	Cut Stone Prdts
3291	Abrasive Prdts
3292	Asbestos products
3295	Minerals & Earths: Ground Or Treated
3296	Mineral Wool
3297	Nonclay Refractories
3299	Nonmetallic Mineral Prdts, NEC

33 PRIMARY METAL INDUSTRIES

SIC NO	PRODUCT
3312	Blast Furnaces, Coke Ovens, Steel & Rolling Mills
3313	Electrometallurgical Prdts
3315	Steel Wire Drawing & Nails & Spikes
3316	Cold Rolled Steel Sheet, Strip & Bars
3317	Steel Pipe & Tubes
3321	Gray Iron Foundries
3322	Malleable Iron Foundries
3324	Steel Investment Foundries
3325	Steel Foundries, NEC
3331	Primary Smelting & Refining Of Copper
3334	Primary Production Of Aluminum
3339	Primary Nonferrous Metals, NEC
3341	Secondary Smelting & Refining Of Nonferrous Metals
3351	Rolling, Drawing & Extruding Of Copper
3353	Aluminum Sheet, Plate & Foil
3354	Aluminum Extruded Prdts
3355	Aluminum Rolling & Drawing, NEC
3356	Rolling, Drawing-Extruding Of Nonferrous Metals
3357	Nonferrous Wire Drawing
3363	Aluminum Die Castings
3364	Nonferrous Die Castings, Exc Aluminum
3365	Aluminum Foundries
3366	Copper Foundries
3369	Nonferrous Foundries: Castings, NEC
3398	Metal Heat Treating
3399	Primary Metal Prdts, NEC

34 FABRICATED METAL PRODUCTS, EXCEPT MACHINERY AND TRANSPORTATION EQUIPMENT

SIC NO	PRODUCT
3411	Metal Cans
3412	Metal Barrels, Drums, Kegs & Pails
3421	Cutlery
3423	Hand & Edge Tools
3425	Hand Saws & Saw Blades
3429	Hardware, NEC
3431	Enameled Iron & Metal Sanitary Ware
3432	Plumbing Fixture Fittings & Trim, Brass
3433	Heating Eqpt
3441	Fabricated Structural Steel
3442	Metal Doors, Sash, Frames, Molding & Trim
3443	Fabricated Plate Work
3444	Sheet Metal Work
3446	Architectural & Ornamental Metal Work
3448	Prefabricated Metal Buildings & Cmpnts
3449	Misc Structural Metal Work
3451	Screw Machine Prdts
3452	Bolts, Nuts, Screws, Rivets & Washers
3462	Iron & Steel Forgings
3463	Nonferrous Forgings
3465	Automotive Stampings
3466	Crowns & Closures
3469	Metal Stampings, NEC
3471	Electroplating, Plating, Polishing, Anodizing & Coloring
3479	Coating & Engraving, NEC
3482	Small Arms Ammunition
3483	Ammunition, Large
3484	Small Arms
3489	Ordnance & Access, NEC
3491	Industrial Valves
3492	Fluid Power Valves & Hose Fittings
3493	Steel Springs, Except Wire
3494	Valves & Pipe Fittings, NEC
3495	Wire Springs
3496	Misc Fabricated Wire Prdts
3497	Metal Foil & Leaf
3498	Fabricated Pipe & Pipe Fittings
3499	Fabricated Metal Prdts, NEC

35 INDUSTRIAL AND COMMERCIAL MACHINERY AND COMPUTER EQUIPMENT

SIC NO	PRODUCT
3511	Steam, Gas & Hydraulic Turbines & Engines
3519	Internal Combustion Engines, NEC
3523	Farm Machinery & Eqpt
3524	Garden, Lawn Tractors & Eqpt
3531	Construction Machinery & Eqpt
3532	Mining Machinery & Eqpt
3533	Oil Field Machinery & Eqpt
3534	Elevators & Moving Stairways
3535	Conveyors & Eqpt
3536	Hoists, Cranes & Monorails
3537	Indl Trucks, Tractors, Trailers & Stackers
3541	Machine Tools: Cutting
3542	Machine Tools: Forming
3543	Industrial Patterns
3544	Dies, Tools, Jigs, Fixtures & Indl Molds
3545	Machine Tool Access
3546	Power Hand Tools
3547	Rolling Mill Machinery & Eqpt
3548	Welding Apparatus
3549	Metalworking Machinery, NEC
3552	Textile Machinery
3553	Woodworking Machinery
3554	Paper Inds Machinery
3555	Printing Trades Machinery & Eqpt
3556	Food Prdts Machinery
3559	Special Ind Machinery, NEC
3561	Pumps & Pumping Eqpt
3562	Ball & Roller Bearings
3563	Air & Gas Compressors
3564	Blowers & Fans
3565	Packaging Machinery
3566	Speed Changers, Drives & Gears
3567	Indl Process Furnaces & Ovens
3568	Mechanical Power Transmission Eqpt, NEC
3569	Indl Machinery & Eqpt, NEC
3571	Electronic Computers
3572	Computer Storage Devices
3575	Computer Terminals
3577	Computer Peripheral Eqpt, NEC
3578	Calculating & Accounting Eqpt
3579	Office Machines, NEC
3581	Automatic Vending Machines
3582	Commercial Laundry, Dry Clean & Pressing Mchs
3585	Air Conditioning & Heating Eqpt
3586	Measuring & Dispensing Pumps
3589	Service Ind Machines, NEC
3592	Carburetors, Pistons, Rings & Valves
3593	Fluid Power Cylinders & Actuators
3594	Fluid Power Pumps & Motors
3596	Scales & Balances, Exc Laboratory
3599	Machinery & Eqpt, Indl & Commercial, NEC

36 ELECTRONIC AND OTHER ELECTRICAL EQUIPMENT AND COMPONENTS, EXCEPT COMPUTER

SIC NO	PRODUCT
3612	Power, Distribution & Specialty Transformers
3613	Switchgear & Switchboard Apparatus
3621	Motors & Generators
3624	Carbon & Graphite Prdts
3625	Relays & Indl Controls
3629	Electrical Indl Apparatus, NEC
3631	Household Cooking Eqpt
3632	Household Refrigerators & Freezers
3633	Household Laundry Eqpt
3634	Electric Household Appliances
3635	Household Vacuum Cleaners
3639	Household Appliances, NEC
3641	Electric Lamps
3643	Current-Carrying Wiring Devices
3644	Noncurrent-Carrying Wiring Devices
3645	Residential Lighting Fixtures
3646	Commercial, Indl & Institutional Lighting Fixtures
3647	Vehicular Lighting Eqpt
3648	Lighting Eqpt, NEC
3651	Household Audio & Video Eqpt
3652	Phonograph Records & Magnetic Tape
3661	Telephone & Telegraph Apparatus
3663	Radio & T V Communications, Systs & Eqpt, Broadcast/Studio
3669	Communications Eqpt, NEC
3671	Radio & T V Receiving Electron Tubes
3672	Printed Circuit Boards
3674	Semiconductors
3675	Electronic Capacitors
3676	Electronic Resistors
3677	Electronic Coils & Transformers
3678	Electronic Connectors
3679	Electronic Components, NEC
3691	Storage Batteries
3692	Primary Batteries: Dry & Wet
3694	Electrical Eqpt For Internal Combustion Engines
3695	Recording Media
3699	Electrical Machinery, Eqpt & Splys, NEC

37 TRANSPORTATION EQUIPMENT

SIC NO	PRODUCT
3711	Motor Vehicles & Car Bodies
3713	Truck & Bus Bodies
3714	Motor Vehicle Parts & Access
3715	Truck Trailers
3716	Motor Homes
3721	Aircraft
3724	Aircraft Engines & Engine Parts
3728	Aircraft Parts & Eqpt, NEC
3731	Shipbuilding & Repairing
3732	Boat Building & Repairing
3743	Railroad Eqpt
3751	Motorcycles, Bicycles & Parts
3761	Guided Missiles & Space Vehicles
3769	Guided Missile/Space Vehicle Parts & Eqpt, NEC
3792	Travel Trailers & Campers
3795	Tanks & Tank Components
3799	Transportation Eqpt, NEC

38 MEASURING, ANALYZING AND CONTROLLING INSTRUMENTS; PHOTOGRAPHIC, MEDICAL AN

SIC NO	PRODUCT
3812	Search, Detection, Navigation & Guidance Systs & Instrs
3821	Laboratory Apparatus & Furniture
3822	Automatic Temperature Controls
3823	Indl Instruments For Meas, Display & Control
3824	Fluid Meters & Counters
3825	Instrs For Measuring & Testing Electricity
3826	Analytical Instruments
3827	Optical Instruments
3829	Measuring & Controlling Devices, NEC
3841	Surgical & Medical Instrs & Apparatus
3842	Orthopedic, Prosthetic & Surgical Appliances/Splys
3843	Dental Eqpt & Splys
3844	X-ray Apparatus & Tubes
3845	Electromedical & Electrotherapeutic Apparatus
3851	Ophthalmic Goods
3861	Photographic Eqpt & Splys
3873	Watch & Clock Devices & Parts

39 MISCELLANEOUS MANUFACTURING INDUSTRIES

SIC NO	PRODUCT
3911	Jewelry: Precious Metal
3914	Silverware, Plated & Stainless Steel Ware
3915	Jewelers Findings & Lapidary Work
3931	Musical Instruments
3942	Dolls & Stuffed Toys
3944	Games, Toys & Children's Vehicles
3949	Sporting & Athletic Goods, NEC
3951	Pens & Mechanical Pencils
3952	Lead Pencils, Crayons & Artist's Mtrls
3953	Marking Devices
3955	Carbon Paper & Inked Ribbons
3961	Costume Jewelry & Novelties
3965	Fasteners, Buttons, Needles & Pins
3991	Brooms & Brushes
3993	Signs & Advertising Displays
3995	Burial Caskets
3996	Linoleum & Hard Surface Floor Coverings, NEC
3999	Manufacturing Industries, NEC

73 BUSINESS SERVICES

SIC NO	PRODUCT
7372	Prepackaged Software

76 MISCELLANEOUS REPAIR SERVICES

SIC NO	PRODUCT
7692	Welding Repair
7694	Armature Rewinding Shops

SIC SECTION

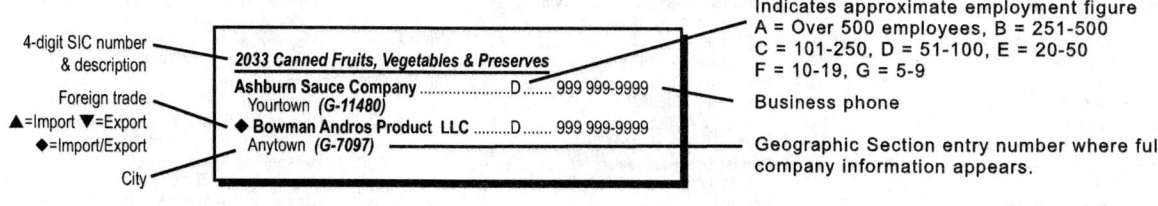

4-digit SIC number & description
Foreign trade
▲=Import ▼=Export
◆=Import/Export
City

Indicates approximate employment figure
A = Over 500 employees, B = 251-500
C = 101-250, D = 51-100, E = 20-50
F = 10-19, G = 5-9

Business phone

Geographic Section entry number where full company information appears.

See footnotes for symbols and codes identification.

- The SIC codes in this section are from the latest Standard Industrial Classification manual published by the U.S. Government's Office of Management and Budget. For more information regarding SICs, see the Explanatory Notes.
- Companies may be listed under multiple classifications.

10 METAL MINING

1011 Iron Ores
Essar Steel Minnesota LLC.................G...... 212 292-2600
  New York *(G-10063)*

1021 Copper Ores
Global Gold Corporation......................F...... 914 925-0020
  Rye *(G-15058)*

1041 Gold Ores
Andes Gold Corporation......................D...... 212 541-2495
  New York *(G-9152)*
▲ Capital Gold Corporation..................G...... 212 668-0842
  New York *(G-9519)*
Global Gold Corporation......................F...... 914 925-0020
  Rye *(G-15058)*
Gncc Capital Inc.................................G...... 702 951-9793
  New York *(G-10325)*

1044 Silver Ores
Global Gold Corporation......................F...... 914 925-0020
  Rye *(G-15058)*
Rochester Silver Works LLC................E...... 585 477-9501
  Rochester *(G-14647)*

1081 Metal Mining Svcs
◆ Coremet Trading Inc........................G...... 212 964-3600
  New York *(G-9724)*
▲ Hi-Temp Specialty Metals Inc...........F...... 631 775-8750
  Yaphank *(G-17395)*

1094 Uranium, Radium & Vanadium Ores
Global Gold Corporation......................F...... 914 925-0020
  Rye *(G-15058)*

1099 Metal Ores, NEC
◆ Alcoa Inc..D...... 212 836-2674
  New York *(G-9077)*
American Douglas Metals Inc.............F...... 716 856-3170
  Buffalo *(G-2807)*

12 COAL MINING

1231 Anthracite Mining
Acrs Inc..F...... 914 288-8100
  White Plains *(G-17073)*
Puglisi & Co.......................................G...... 212 300-2285
  New York *(G-11749)*

1241 Coal Mining Svcs
Desku Group Inc................................G...... 646 436-1464
  Brooklyn *(G-1858)*
Dowa International Corp....................F...... 212 697-3217
  New York *(G-9917)*
Lessoilcom..G...... 516 319-5052
  Franklin Square *(G-5364)*
Randgold Resources Ltd...................G...... 212 815-2129
  New York *(G-11801)*
Starfuels Inc.......................................G...... 914 289-4800
  White Plains *(G-17170)*
Trimet Coal LLC................................E...... 718 951-3654
  Brooklyn *(G-2681)*
▲ US Pump Corp................................G...... 516 303-7799
  West Hempstead *(G-16864)*

13 OIL AND GAS EXTRACTION

1311 Crude Petroleum & Natural Gas
Chanse Petroleum Corporation...........G...... 212 682-3789
  New York *(G-9579)*
China N E Petro Holdings Ltd..............A...... 212 307-3568
  New York *(G-9600)*
County Energy Corp...........................G...... 718 626-7000
  Brooklyn *(G-1808)*
Dlh Energy Service LLC....................G...... 716 410-0028
  Lakewood *(G-7291)*
East Resources Inc............................G...... 716 373-0944
  Allegany *(G-200)*
Flownet LLC......................................G...... 716 685-4036
  Lancaster *(G-7316)*
Green Buffalo Fuel LLC.....................F...... 716 768-0600
  Tonawanda *(G-16168)*
▲ Hess Corporation............................B...... 212 997-8500
  New York *(G-10464)*
Hess Energy Exploration Ltd..............G...... 732 750-6500
  New York *(G-10465)*
Hess Explrtion Prod Hldngs Ltd..........G...... 732 750-6000
  New York *(G-10466)*
Hess Pipeline Corporation.................B...... 212 997-8500
  New York *(G-10468)*
Hess Tioga Gas Plant LLC.................C...... 212 997-8500
  New York *(G-10469)*
Ipp Energy LLC..................................G...... 607 773-3307
  Binghamton *(G-928)*
Kimmeridge Energy MGT Co LLC.....G...... 646 517-7252
  New York *(G-10848)*
Lukoil Americas Corporation.............C...... 212 421-4141
  New York *(G-11061)*
MRC Global (us) Inc..........................F...... 607 739-8575
  Horseheads *(G-6585)*
Reserve Gas Company Inc................G...... 716 937-9484
  Alden *(G-182)*
Resource PTRlm&ptrochmcl Intl.......E...... 212 537-3856
  New York *(G-11842)*
Rocket Tech Fuel Corp......................F...... 516 810-8947
  Bay Shore *(G-737)*
Speedway LLC..................................F...... 631 738-2536
  Lake Grove *(G-7266)*
Stedman Energy Inc..........................G...... 716 789-3018
  Mayville *(G-8219)*
Talisman Energy USA Inc.................G...... 607 562-4000
  Horseheads *(G-6595)*

1321 Natural Gas Liquids
20 Bliss St Inc...................................G...... 716 326-2790
  Westfield *(G-17044)*
Aggressive Energy LLC.....................E...... 718 836-9222
  Brooklyn *(G-1570)*
Blue Rhino Global Sourcing Inc........E...... 516 752-0670
  Melville *(G-8298)*
Center State Propane LLC...............G...... 315 841-4044
  Waterville *(G-16677)*
Green Buffalo Fuel LLC.....................F...... 716 768-0600
  Tonawanda *(G-16168)*
Nfe Management LLC.......................F...... 212 798-6100
  New York *(G-11423)*
Paraco Gas Corporation....................G...... 845 279-8414
  Brewster *(G-1225)*
Paraco Gas Corporation....................F...... 800 647-4427
  Rye Brook *(G-15073)*
Western Oil and Gas JV Inc..............G...... 914 967-4758
  Rye *(G-15069)*

1381 Drilling Oil & Gas Wells
Alden Aurora Gas Company Inc.........G...... 716 937-9484
  Alden *(G-174)*
Barber & Deline Enrgy Svcs LLC......F...... 315 696-8961
  Tully *(G-16274)*
Barber & Deline LLC.........................F...... 607 749-2619
  Tully *(G-16275)*
Copper Ridge Oil Inc........................G...... 716 372-4021
  Jamestown *(G-6984)*
Geotechnical Drilling Inc...................D...... 516 616-6055
  Mineola *(G-8512)*
Joycharge Inc....................................D...... 646 321-1127
  New York *(G-10774)*
Lenape Energy Inc............................G...... 585 344-1200
  Alexander *(G-187)*
Lukoil North America LLC.................E...... 212 421-4141
  New York *(G-11062)*
Schneider Amalco Inc.......................F...... 917 470-9674
  New York *(G-11991)*
Steel Partners Holdings LP...............E...... 212 520-2300
  New York *(G-12189)*
U S Energy Development Corp..........D...... 716 636-0401
  Getzville *(G-5605)*
▲ US Pump Corp................................G...... 516 303-7799
  West Hempstead *(G-16864)*
Western Oil and Gas JV Inc..............G...... 914 967-4758
  Rye *(G-15069)*

1382 Oil & Gas Field Exploration Svcs
Able Environmental Services............G...... 631 567-6585
  Bohemia *(G-1003)*
Aegis Oil Limited Ventures LLC........F...... 646 233-4900
  New York *(G-9051)*
America Capital Energy Corp............G...... 212 983-8316
  New York *(G-9112)*
▲ Aquifer Drilling & Testing Inc..........D...... 516 616-6026
  Mineola *(G-8495)*
▲ Aterra Exploration LLC....................E...... 212 315-0030
  New York *(G-9248)*
Bistate Oil Management Corp...........F...... 212 935-4110
  New York *(G-9405)*
East Resources Inc............................G...... 716 373-0944
  Allegany *(G-200)*
Elliott Associates LP.........................E...... 212 586-9431
  New York *(G-10011)*
FT Seismic Support Inc....................C...... 607 527-8595
  Corning *(G-3972)*
Hess Energy Exploration Ltd..............G...... 732 750-6500
  New York *(G-10465)*
Hess Explrtion Prod Hldngs Ltd..........G...... 732 750-6000
  New York *(G-10466)*
JP Oil Group Inc................................G...... 607 563-1360
  Sidney *(G-15440)*
KKR Ntral Rsources Fund I-A LP......F...... 212 750-8300
  New York *(G-10857)*
Lenape Energy Inc............................G...... 585 344-1200
  Alexander *(G-187)*
Lenape Resources Inc.......................F...... 585 344-1200
  Alexander *(G-188)*
Mac Fadden Holdings Inc..................E...... 212 614-3980
  New York *(G-11081)*
Madoff Energy III LLC.......................G...... 212 744-1918
  New York *(G-11095)*
Mep Alaska LLC................................G...... 646 535-9005
  Brooklyn *(G-2297)*
Native Amercn Enrgy Group Inc.......G...... 718 408-2323
  Forest Hills *(G-5325)*
Norse Energy Corp USA...................G...... 716 568-2048
  Buffalo *(G-3094)*

Occidental Energy Mktg Inc....G....212 632-4950
New York (G-11493)
Range Rsurces - Appalachia LLC....E....716 753-3385
Mayville (G-8218)
Schlumberger Technology Corp....C....607 378-0200
Horseheads (G-6592)
Seneca Resources Corporation....F....716 630-6750
Williamsville (G-17252)
Smith International Inc....D....212 350-9400
New York (G-12105)
Somerset Production Co LLC....G....716 932-6480
Buffalo (G-3189)
▲ Springfield Oil Services Inc....F....914 315-6812
Harrison (G-5991)
Springfield Oil Services Inc....G....516 482-5995
Great Neck (G-5841)
U S Energy Development Corp....D....716 636-0401
Getzville (G-5605)
Unco United Oil Holdings LLC....F....212 481-1003
New York (G-12448)
Waffenbauch USA....E....716 326-4508
Westfield (G-17052)
Warren Energy Services LLC....F....212 697-9660
New York (G-12591)
Wellspring Omni Holdings Corp....A....212 318-9800
New York (G-12610)

1389 Oil & Gas Field Svcs, NEC

A & Mt Realty Group LLC....F....718 974-5871
Brooklyn (G-1528)
◆ Acu Rite Companies Inc....G....716 661-1700
Jamestown (G-6968)
Ah Elctronic Test Eqp Repr Ctr....F....631 234-8979
Central Islip (G-3484)
Alba Fuel Corp....G....718 931-1700
Bronx (G-1266)
Alice Perkins....G....716 378-5100
Salamanca (G-15099)
Arm Construction Company Inc....G....646 235-6520
East Elmhurst (G-4388)
Babula Construction Inc....G....716 681-0886
Lancaster (G-7305)
Barber & Deline Enrgy Svcs LLC....F....315 696-8961
Tully (G-16274)
Bass Oil & Chemical Llc....F....718 628-4444
Brooklyn (G-1671)
Bluebar Oil Co Inc....F....315 245-4328
Blossvale (G-997)
Case Brothers Inc....G....716 925-7172
Limestone (G-7450)
Cotton Well Drilling Co Inc....G....716 672-2788
Sheridan (G-15400)
Darrell Mitchell....G....646 659-7075
Arverne (G-425)
Dimension Development Corp....G....718 361-8825
Long Island City (G-7716)
Direct Oil LLC....G....914 495-3073
Thornwood (G-16119)
Essar Americas....G....212 292-2600
New York (G-10062)
Fame Construction Inc....E....718 626-1000
Astoria (G-442)
Five Star Field Services....G....347 446-6816
Brooklyn (G-1978)
Gas Field Specialists Inc....D....716 378-6422
Horseheads (G-6579)
Gas Recovery Systems LLC....F....914 421-4903
White Plains (G-17112)
Gotham Energy 360 LLC....F....917 338-1023
New York (G-10340)
I & S of NY Inc....F....716 373-7001
Allegany (G-202)
Iron Eagle Group Inc....E....888 481-4445
New York (G-10662)
Jay Little Oil Well Servi....G....716 925-8905
Limestone (G-7451)
Jemcap Servicing LLC....G....212 213-9353
New York (G-10718)
Legal Servicing LLC....G....716 565-9300
Williamsville (G-17248)
Lenape Energy Inc....G....585 344-1200
Alexander (G-187)
Marcellus Energy Services LLC....E....607 236-0038
Candor (G-3378)
Mep Alaska LLC....G....646 535-9005
Brooklyn (G-2297)
Metro Group Inc....D....718 392-3616
Long Island City (G-7811)
Northeastern Air Quality Inc....F....518 857-3641
Albany (G-110)
Occhioerosso John....F....718 541-7025
Staten Island (G-15718)
P & C Gas Measurements Service....F....716 257-3412
Cattaraugus (G-3438)
Petro Inc....G....516 686-1717
Plainview (G-13629)
Petro Inc....G....516 686-1900
Hicksville (G-6387)
Prefab Construction Inc....F....631 821-9613
Sound Beach (G-15513)
Professional Remodelers Inc....G....516 565-9300
West Hempstead (G-16862)
Rpc Inc....E....347 873-3935
Elmont (G-4728)
Sabre Energy Services LLC....F....518 514-1572
Slingerlands (G-15478)
Schaap Brothers....G....518 459-2220
Albany (G-133)
Schlumberger Technology Corp....C....607 378-0200
Horseheads (G-6592)
Schmitt Sales Inc....G....716 632-8595
Williamsville (G-17251)
Schneider Amalco Inc....F....917 470-9674
New York (G-11991)
Smith International Inc....D....212 350-9400
New York (G-12105)
Sovereign Servicing System LLC....F....914 779-1400
Bronxville (G-1503)
Speedway LLC....F....718 815-6897
Staten Island (G-15736)
▲ Steel Excel Inc....D....914 461-1300
White Plains (G-17171)
Superior Energy Services Inc....G....716 483-0100
Jamestown (G-7035)
T A S Sales Service LLC....G....518 234-4919
Cobleskill (G-3739)
Terra Enrgy Resource Tech Inc....F....212 286-9197
New York (G-12302)
Tutor Perini Corporation....B....646 473-2924
New York (G-12429)
U S Energy Development Corp....D....716 636-0401
Getzville (G-5605)
Wellspring Omni Holdings Corp....A....212 318-9800
New York (G-12610)

14 MINING AND QUARRYING OF NONMETALLIC MINERALS, EXCEPT FUELS

1411 Dimension Stone

◆ Adirondack Natural Stone LLC....E....518 499-0602
Whitehall (G-17189)
Alice Perkins....G....716 378-5100
Salamanca (G-15099)
Cold Spring Granite Company....E....518 647-8191
Au Sable Forks (G-475)
Dominic De Nigris Inc....E....718 597-4460
Bronx (G-1316)
Domoteck Interiors Inc....G....718 433-4300
Woodside (G-17326)
Finger Lakes Stone Co Inc....F....607 273-4646
Ithaca (G-6842)
Hadeka Stone Corp....G....518 282-9605
Hampton (G-5959)
Hillburn Granite Company Inc....G....845 357-8900
Hillburn (G-6415)
▲ Hilltop Slate Inc....E....518 642-1453
Middle Granville (G-8399)
Imerys Usa Inc....F....315 287-0780
Gouverneur (G-5746)
▲ Minerals Technologies Inc....E....212 878-1800
New York (G-11276)
▲ New York Quarries Inc....F....518 756-3138
Alcove (G-172)
Suffolk Granite Manufacturing....E....631 226-4774
Lindenhurst (G-7486)
Vermont Multicolor Slate....G....518 642-2400
Middle Granville (G-8402)

1422 Crushed & Broken Limestone

Barrett Paving Materials Inc....F....315 737-9471
Clayville (G-3686)
Cobleskill Stone Products Inc....F....518 299-3066
Prattsville (G-13945)
Cobleskill Stone Products Inc....F....518 295-7121
Schoharie (G-15316)
Cobleskill Stone Products Inc....F....518 234-0221
Cobleskill (G-3735)
Cobleskill Stone Products Inc....F....607 637-4271
Hancock (G-5962)
Dolomite Products Company Inc....E....315 524-1998
Rochester (G-14316)
Graymont Materials (ny) Inc....E....518 891-0236
Saranac Lake (G-15138)
Hanson Aggregates PA Inc....E....315 858-1100
Jordanville (G-7132)
Hanson Aggregates PA Inc....F....518 568-2444
Saint Johnsville (G-15094)
Hanson Aggregates PA LLC....E....315 469-5501
Jamesville (G-7049)
Hanson Aggregates PA LLC....E....315 685-3321
Skaneateles (G-15463)
Hanson Aggregates PA LLC....F....315 393-3743
Ogdensburg (G-13115)
Hanson Aggregates PA LLC....E....585 624-1220
Honeoye Falls (G-6530)
Hanson Aggregates PA LLC....F....315 821-7222
Oriskany Falls (G-13318)
Hanson Aggregates PA LLC....E....315 789-6202
Oaks Corners (G-13070)
Infinity Architectual Systems....F....716 882-2321
Buffalo (G-3007)
Jml Quarries Inc....E....845 932-8206
Cochecton (G-3741)
John Vespa Inc....F....315 788-6330
Watertown (G-16656)
Lafarge North America Inc....F....716 876-8788
Tonawanda (G-16176)
Lilac Quarries LLC....G....607 867-4016
Mount Upton (G-8658)
Patterson Materials Corp....E....845 832-6000
New Windsor (G-8947)
Schaefer Entps of Deposit....E....607 467-4990
Deposit (G-4280)
Shelby Crushed Stone Inc....F....585 798-4501
Medina (G-8281)
◆ Specialty Minerals Inc....E....212 878-1800
New York (G-12152)

1423 Crushed & Broken Granite

Suffolk Granite Manufacturing....E....631 226-4774
Lindenhurst (G-7486)
Tilcon New York Inc....D....845 358-3100
West Nyack (G-16929)

1429 Crushed & Broken Stone, NEC

Barrett Paving Materials Inc....F....315 737-9471
Clayville (G-3686)
Cayuga Crushed Stone Inc....E....607 533-4273
Lansing (G-7348)
County Line Stone Co Inc....E....716 542-5435
Akron (G-21)
Dolomite Products Company Inc....E....585 586-2568
Penfield (G-13498)
Graymont Materials (ny) Inc....D....518 561-5321
Plattsburgh (G-13665)
Hanson Aggregates PA LLC....F....315 393-3743
Ogdensburg (G-13115)
Hanson Aggregates PA LLC....F....315 821-7222
Oriskany Falls (G-13318)
Highland Sand & Gravel Inc....F....845 928-2221
Highland Mills (G-6412)
Masten Enterprises LLC....D....845 932-8206
Cochecton (G-3742)
Peckham Materials Corp....E....518 747-3353
Hudson Falls (G-6649)
Rock Iroquois Products Inc....E....585 637-6834
Brockport (G-1247)
Shelby Crushed Stone Inc....F....585 798-4501
Medina (G-8281)
▲ Tilcon New York Inc....B....845 358-4500
West Nyack (G-16928)
Tilcon New York Inc....E....845 778-5591
Walden (G-16537)
Tilcon New York Inc....D....845 638-3594
Haverstraw (G-6241)
Tilcon New York Inc....D....845 480-3249
Flushing (G-5301)
Tilcon New York Inc....D....845 615-0216
Goshen (G-5740)
Tilcon New York Inc....D....845 457-3158
Montgomery (G-8603)
Tilcon New York Inc....D....845 358-3100
West Nyack (G-16929)

1442 Construction Sand & Gravel

110 Sand Company....E....631 694-2822
Melville (G-8286)

110 Sand Company .... G 631 694-2822
  West Babylon (G-16760)
110 Sand Company .... F 631 694-2822
  West Babylon (G-16761)
A Colarusso and Son Inc .... E 518 828-3218
  Hudson (G-6603)
Barrett Paving Materials Inc .... G 607 723-5367
  Binghamton (G-890)
Belangers Gravel & Stone Inc .... G 585 728-3906
  Wayland (G-16709)
Bonsal American Inc .... E 631 208-8073
  Calverton (G-3286)
Buffalo Crushed Stone Inc .... G 716 566-9636
  Franklinville (G-5368)
Buffalo Crushed Stone Inc .... G 607 587-8102
  Alfred Station (G-196)
Callanan Industries Inc .... G 845 331-6868
  Kingston (G-7182)
Central Dover Development .... G 917 709-3266
  Dover Plains (G-4314)
Chenango Asphalt Products .... F 607 334-3117
  Norwich (G-13021)
Country Side Sand & Gravel .... G 716 988-3271
  Collins (G-3815)
Country Side Sand & Gravel .... F 716 988-3271
  South Dayton (G-15519)
Dalrymple Grav & Contg Co Inc .... F 607 739-0391
  Pine City (G-13550)
Dalrymple Grav & Contg Co Inc .... E 607 529-3235
  Chemung (G-3594)
Dalrymple Holding Corp .... G 607 737-6200
  Pine City (G-13551)
Dicks Concrete Co Inc .... E 845 374-5966
  New Hampton (G-8799)
Diehl Development Inc .... G 585 494-2920
  Bergen (G-845)
E F Lippert Co Inc .... F 716 373-1100
  Allegany (G-199)
E Tetz & Sons Inc .... D 845 692-4486
  Middletown (G-8437)
Eagle Harbor Sand & Gravel Inc .... G 585 798-4501
  Albion (G-164)
East Coast Mines Ltd .... E 631 653-5445
  East Quogue (G-4450)
Elam Sand & Gravel Corp .... E 585 657-8000
  Bloomfield (G-987)
Frew Run Gravel Products Inc .... G 716 569-4712
  Frewsburg (G-5450)
Genoa Sand & Gravel Lnsg .... G 607 533-4551
  Freeville (G-5436)
Greenebuild LLC .... F 917 562-0556
  Brooklyn (G-2053)
H L Robinson Sand & Gravel .... F 607 659-5153
  Candor (G-3377)
Hampton Sand Corp .... G 631 325-5533
  Westhampton (G-17057)
Hanson Aggregates East LLC .... G 315 536-9391
  Penn Yan (G-13513)
Hanson Aggregates East LLC .... E 315 548-2911
  Phelps (G-13533)
Hanson Aggregates PA Inc .... E 315 858-1100
  Jordanville (G-7132)
Hanson Aggregates PA Inc .... F 518 568-2444
  Saint Johnsville (G-15094)
Hanson Aggregates PA LLC .... E 585 624-1220
  Honeoye Falls (G-6530)
Hanson Aggregates PA LLC .... E 315 469-5501
  Jamesville (G-7049)
Hanson Aggregates PA LLC .... E 315 685-3321
  Skaneateles (G-15463)
Hanson Aggregates PA LLC .... F 315 782-2300
  Watertown (G-16653)
Hanson Aggregates PA LLC .... F 315 821-7222
  Oriskany Falls (G-13318)
Hanson Aggregates PA LLC .... E 315 789-6202
  Oaks Corners (G-13070)
Hanson Aggregates PA LLC .... E 585 624-3800
  Honeoye Falls (G-6529)
Hanson Aggregates PA LLC .... E 585 436-3250
  Rochester (G-14421)
I A Construction Corporation .... G 716 933-8787
  Portville (G-13875)
John Vespa Inc .... E 315 788-6330
  Watertown (G-16656)
Johnson S Sand Gravel Inc .... G 315 771-1450
  La Fargeville (G-7237)
Knight Sttlement Sand Grav LLC .... E 607 776-2048
  Bath (G-659)
Lafarge North America Inc .... E 716 651-9235
  Lancaster (G-7322)

Lafarge North America Inc .... E 518 756-5000
  Ravena (G-14023)
Lazarek Inc .... G 315 343-1242
  Oswego (G-13334)
Little Valley Sand & Gravel .... G 716 938-6676
  Little Valley (G-7511)
McEwan Trucking & Grav Produc .... G 716 609-1828
  East Concord (G-4385)
Milestone Construction Corp .... G 718 459-8500
  Rego Park (G-14037)
▲ New York Sand & Stone LLC .... G 718 596-2897
  Maspeth (G-8157)
Northeast Solite Corporation .... E 845 246-2177
  Mount Marion (G-8652)
Palumbo Sand & Gravel Company .... E 845 832-3356
  Dover Plains (G-4317)
R G King General Construction .... G 315 583-3560
  Adams Center (G-4)
R J Valente Gravel Inc .... E 518 279-1001
  Cropseyville (G-4060)
Rd2 Construction & Dem LLC .... F 718 980-1650
  Staten Island (G-15728)
Republic Construction Co Inc .... G 914 235-3654
  New Rochelle (G-8924)
Robinson Concrete Inc .... E 315 253-6666
  Auburn (G-516)
Rock Mountain Farms Inc .... G 845 647-9084
  Ellenville (G-4638)
Ruby Engineering LLC .... E 646 391-4600
  Brooklyn (G-2516)
Rural Hill Sand and Grav Corp .... F 315 846-5212
  Woodville (G-17367)
Rush Gravel Corp .... G 585 533-1740
  Honeoye Falls (G-6536)
Seneca Stone Corporation .... E 607 737-6200
  Pine City (G-13552)
Seven Springs Gravel Pdts LLC .... G 585 343-4336
  Batavia (G-647)
Shelby Crushed Stone Inc .... F 585 798-4501
  Medina (G-8281)
Smith Sand & Gravel Inc .... G 315 673-4124
  Marcellus (G-8089)
Sparrow Mining Co .... G 718 519-6600
  Bronx (G-1460)
Speyside Holdings LLC .... E 845 928-2221
  Highland Mills (G-6414)
Syracusa Sand and Gravel Inc .... F 585 924-7146
  Victor (G-16505)
Syracuse Sand & Gravel LLC .... G 315 548-8207
  Fulton (G-5475)
Tilcon New York Inc .... E 845 942-0602
  Tomkins Cove (G-16131)
Tilcon New York Inc .... D 845 358-3100
  West Nyack (G-16929)
Titus Mountain Sand & Grav LLC .... G 518 483-3740
  Malone (G-8018)
Tri City Highway Products Inc .... E 607 722-2967
  Binghamton (G-957)
Tri-City Highway Products Inc .... E 518 294-9964
  Richmondville (G-14090)
Troy Sand & Gravel Co Inc .... F 518 674-2854
  West Sand Lake (G-16932)
United Materials LLC .... G 716 662-0564
  Orchard Park (G-13301)
US Allegro Inc .... E 347 408-6601
  Maspeth (G-8174)

1446 Industrial Sand

◆ American Minerals Inc .... F 646 747-4222
  New York (G-9125)
New Jersey Pulverizing Co Inc .... G 516 921-9595
  Syosset (G-15832)
Precision Elctro Mnrl Pmco Inc .... E 716 284-2484
  Niagara Falls (G-12863)
St Silicones Inc .... G 518 664-0745
  Mechanicville (G-8231)

1459 Clay, Ceramic & Refractory Minerals, NEC

▲ Applied Minerals Inc .... E 212 226-4265
  New York (G-9184)
Callahan & Nannini Quarry Inc .... G 845 496-4323
  Salisbury Mills (G-15112)
▲ Devonian Stone New York Inc .... E 607 655-2600
  Windsor (G-17272)
Grosso Materials Inc .... F 845 361-5211
  Montgomery (G-8594)

1479 Chemical & Fertilizer Mining

American Rock Salt Company LLC .... E 585 991-6878
  Retsof (G-14054)
Morton Salt Inc .... F 585 493-2511
  Silver Springs (G-15451)

1481 Nonmetallic Minerals Svcs, Except Fuels

▲ Crystal Ceres Industries Inc .... D 716 283-0445
  Niagara Falls (G-12808)

1499 Miscellaneous Nonmetallic Mining

Avs Gem Stone Corp .... G 212 944-6380
  New York (G-9282)
◆ Barton Mines Company LLC .... C 518 798-5462
  Glens Falls (G-5672)
▲ Capital Gold Corporation .... G 212 668-0842
  New York (G-9519)
Didco Inc .... F 212 997-5022
  Rego Park (G-14032)
▲ Double Star USA Inc .... E 212 929-2210
  Brooklyn (G-1874)
Gemfields USA Incorporated .... E 212 398-5400
  New York (G-10267)
Hargrave Development .... F 716 877-7880
  Kenmore (G-7147)
Herkimer Diamond Mines Inc .... E 315 891-7355
  Herkimer (G-6302)
Kotel Importers Inc .... F 212 245-6200
  New York (G-10881)
Ray Griffiths Inc .... G 212 689-7209
  New York (G-11805)
Romance & Co Inc .... G 212 382-0337
  New York (G-11912)
Signature Diamond Entps LLC .... E 212 869-5115
  New York (G-12072)

20 FOOD AND KINDRED PRODUCTS

2011 Meat Packing Plants

A To Z Kosher Meat Products Co .... E 718 384-7400
  Brooklyn (G-1535)
Adirondack Meat Company Inc .... F 518 585-2333
  Ticonderoga (G-16124)
Bliss-Poston The Second Wind .... G 212 481-1055
  New York (G-9416)
◆ Caribbean Foods Delight Inc .... D 845 398-3000
  Tappan (G-16079)
Chefs Delight Packing Co .... F 718 388-8581
  Brooklyn (G-1776)
▼ Crescent Duck Farm Inc .... E 631 722-8700
  Aquebogue (G-384)
Delft Blue LLC .... C 315 768-7100
  New York Mills (G-12720)
▲ Domestic Casing Co .... G 718 522-1902
  Brooklyn (G-1872)
◆ DRG New York Holdings Corp .... D 914 668-9000
  Mount Vernon (G-8677)
Fairbank Reconstruction Corp .... D 800 628-3276
  Ashville (G-429)
Frank Wardynski & Sons Inc .... E 716 854-6083
  Buffalo (G-2955)
◆ Globex Kosher Foods Inc .... E 718 630-5555
  Brooklyn (G-2029)
Gold Medal Packing Inc .... D 315 337-1911
  Oriskany (G-13310)
Hilltown Pork Inc .... F 518 781-4050
  Canaan (G-3331)
Huda Kawshai LLC .... G 929 255-7009
  Jamaica (G-6920)
Ives Farm Market .... G 315 592-4880
  Fulton (G-5463)
Joel Kiryas Meat Market Corp .... G 845 782-9194
  Monroe (G-8557)
Kamerys Wholesale Meats Inc .... G 716 372-6756
  Olean (G-13149)
Martin D Whitbeck .... G 607 746-7642
  Delhi (G-4240)
Old World Provisions Inc .... E 518 465-7306
  Troy (G-16245)
Orleans Custom Packing Inc .... G 585 314-8227
  Holley (G-6490)
▼ Robert & William Inc .... G 631 727-5780
  Riverhead (G-14154)
▲ Sahlen Packing Company Inc .... D 716 852-8677
  Buffalo (G-3175)
Sam A Lupo & Sons Inc .... G 607 748-1141
  Endicott (G-4828)

Employee Codes: A=Over 500 employees, B=251-500
C=101-250, D=51-100, E=20-50, F=10-19, G=5-9

20 FOOD AND KINDRED PRODUCTS

Side Hill Farmers Coop Inc ....G....... 315 447-4693
  Canastota (G-3373)
The Smoke House of Catskills..............G....... 845 246-8767
  Saugerties (G-15197)
Tri-Town Packing Corp ....F....... 315 389-5101
  Brasher Falls (G-1174)
We Work 877 673-6628
  New York (G-12600)

2013 Sausages & Meat Prdts

Adirondack Meat Company Inc ....F....... 518 585-2333
  Ticonderoga (G-16124)
◆ Alle Processing Corp ....C....... 718 894-2000
  Maspeth (G-8115)
Alps Provision Co Inc ....E....... 718 721-4477
  Astoria (G-433)
Arnolds Meat Food Products ....E....... 718 384-8071
  Brooklyn (G-1629)
Atlantic Pork & Provisions Inc............E....... 718 272-9550
  Jamaica (G-6895)
Bianca Burgers LLC ....F....... 516 764-9591
  Rockville Centre (G-14788)
Big Johns Adirondack Inc ....G....... 518 587-3680
  Saratoga Springs (G-15145)
Birds Eye Holdings Inc ....A....... 585 383-1850
  Rochester (G-14232)
Brooklyn Bangers LLC ....F....... 718 875-3535
  Brooklyn (G-1721)
Brooklyn Casing Co Inc ....G....... 718 522-0866
  Brooklyn (G-1723)
Buffalo Provisions Co Inc ....F....... 718 292-4300
  Elmsford (G-4658)
Camellia General Provision Co............F....... 716 893-5352
  Buffalo (G-2865)
◆ Caribbean Foods Delight Inc..........D....... 845 398-3000
  Tappan (G-16079)
▲ Cibao Meat Products Inc ....D....... 718 993-5072
  Bronx (G-1298)
De Ans Pork Products Inc ....E....... 718 788-2464
  Brooklyn (G-1846)
Dinos Sausage & Meat Co Inc ....F....... 315 732-2661
  Utica (G-16325)
▲ Domestic Casing Co ....F....... 718 522-1902
  Brooklyn (G-1872)
Elmgang Enterprises I Inc ....F....... 212 868-4142
  New York (G-10012)
Fairbank Reconstruction Corp ....D....... 800 628-3276
  Ashville (G-429)
Frank Wardynski & Sons Inc ....E....... 716 854-6083
  Buffalo (G-2955)
Freirich Julian Co Inc ....E....... 718 361-9111
  Long Island City (G-7746)
▲ Hansel n Gretel Brand Inc ....C....... 718 326-0041
  Glendale (G-5656)
Hanzlian Sausage Incorporated ....G....... 716 891-5247
  Cheektowaga (G-3574)
Hilltown Pork Inc ....F....... 518 781-4050
  Canaan (G-3331)
Holy Cow Kosher LLC ....G....... 347 788-8620
  Spring Valley (G-15589)
Jacks Gourmet LLC ....F....... 718 954-4681
  Brooklyn (G-2129)
Lancaster Quality Pork Inc ....F....... 718 439-8822
  Brooklyn (G-2194)
Marathon Enterprises Inc ....D....... 718 665-2560
  Bronx (G-1385)
Milan Provision Co Inc ....F....... 718 899-7678
  Corona (G-4003)
Mineo & Sapio Meats Inc ....F....... 716 884-2398
  Buffalo (G-3067)
▲ Niagara Tying Service Inc ....E....... 716 825-0066
  Buffalo (G-3092)
Picone Meat Specialties Ltd...............F....... 914 381-3002
  Mamaroneck (G-8267)
Pork King Sausage Inc ....E....... 718 542-2810
  Bronx (G-1432)
▲ Prime Food Processing Corp ....D....... 718 963-2323
  Brooklyn (G-2441)
Provisionaire & Co LLC ....F....... 315 491-8240
  New York (G-11741)
▲ Rapa Independent North America ..G....... 518 561-0513
  Plattsburgh (G-13694)
Rapacki & Sons ....F....... 516 538-3939
  Lindenhurst (G-7480)
Reliable Brothers Inc ....F....... 518 273-6732
  Green Island (G-5861)
Rosina Food Products Inc ....C....... 716 668-0123
  Buffalo (G-3165)
Rosina Holding Inc ....G....... 716 668-0123
  Buffalo (G-3166)

Salarinos Italian Foods Inc ....F....... 315 697-9766
  Canastota (G-11985)
Schaller Manufacturing Corp..............D....... 718 721-5480
  New York (G-11986)
Schonwetter Enterprises Inc ....E....... 518 237-0171
  Cohoes (G-7433)
Schrader Meat Market ....F....... 607 869-6328
  Romulus (G-14842)
▲ Sun Ming Jan Inc ....F....... 718 418-8221
  Brooklyn (G-2619)
▲ Syracuse Casing Co Inc ....F....... 315 475-0309
  Syracuse (G-16048)
Tower Isles Frozen Foods Ltd ....D....... 718 495-2626
  Brooklyn (G-2671)
Tyson Deli Inc ....B....... 716 826-6400
  Buffalo (G-3228)
White Eagle Packing Co Inc ....F....... 518 374-4366
  Schenectady (G-15313)
Zweigles Inc...D....... 585 546-1740
  Rochester (G-14776)

2015 Poultry Slaughtering, Dressing & Processing

▲ Advanced Frozen Foods Inc ....E....... 516 333-6344
  Westbury (G-16961)
◆ Alle Processing Corp ....C....... 718 894-2000
  Maspeth (G-8115)
Alta Group Inc ....F....... 905 262-5707
  Lewiston (G-7433)
Campanellis Poultry Farm Inc ....G....... 845 482-2222
  Bethel (G-860)
▼ Crescent Duck Farm Inc ....E....... 631 722-8700
  Aquebogue (G-384)
Egg Low Farms Inc ....F....... 607 674-4653
  Sherburne (G-15391)
Goya Foods Inc ....D....... 716 549-0076
  Angola (G-380)
▲ Hansel n Gretel Brand Inc ....C....... 718 326-0041
  Glendale (G-5656)
Hlw Acres LLC ....G....... 585 591-0795
  Attica (G-473)
◆ Hoskie Co Inc ....D....... 718 628-8672
  Brooklyn (G-2088)
Hudson Valley Foie Gras LLC ....F....... 845 292-2500
  Ferndale (G-5171)
JW Consulting Inc ....G....... 845 325-7070
  Monroe (G-8558)
▲ K&Ns Foods Usa LLC ....E....... 315 598-8080
  Fulton (G-5465)
MB Food Processing Inc ....B....... 845 436-5001
  South Fallsburg (G-15520)
Murray Bresky Consultants Ltd ....B....... 845 436-5001
  South Fallsburg (G-15521)
Ready Egg Farms Inc ....F....... 607 674-4653
  Sherburne (G-15394)
Sing Ah Poultry ....G....... 718 625-7253
  Brooklyn (G-2564)
Vineland Kosher Poultry Inc ....F....... 718 921-1347
  Brooklyn (G-2728)
Wendels Poultry Farm ....G....... 716 592-2299
  East Concord (G-4386)

2021 Butter

Canalside Creamery Inc ....G....... 716 695-2876
  North Tonawanda (G-12965)
◆ O-At-Ka Milk Products Coop Inc......B....... 585 343-0536
  Batavia (G-644)
Pure Ghee Inc......................................G....... 718 224-7399
  Flushing (G-5285)

2022 Cheese

Agri-Mark Inc ....D....... 518 497-6644
  Chateaugay (G-3556)
Artisanal Brands Inc ....E....... 914 441-3591
  Bronxville (G-1498)
Castelli America LLC ....D....... 716 782-2101
  Ashville (G-426)
Cemac Foods Corp ....F....... 914 835-0526
  Harrison (G-5978)
Cheese Experts USA Ltd Lblty ....G....... 908 275-3889
  Staten Island (G-15658)
Crosswinds Farm & Creamery ....F....... 607 327-0363
  Ovid (G-13345)
Emkay Trading Corp ....F....... 914 592-9000
  Elmsford (G-4748)
Emkay Trading Corp ....E....... 585 492-3800
  Arcade (G-392)
Empire Cheese Inc ....C....... 585 968-1552
  Cuba (G-4069)

▲ Euphrates Inc ....D....... 518 762-3488
  Johnstown (G-7111)
F Cappiello Dairy Pdts Inc ....E....... 518 374-5064
  Schenectady (G-15254)
Four Fat Fowl Inc ....E....... 518 733-5230
  Stephentown (G-15757)
Friendship Dairies LLC ....C....... 585 973-3031
  Friendship (G-5452)
◆ Gharana Industries LLC ....G....... 315 651-4004
  Waterloo (G-16627)
Great Lakes Cheese NY Inc ....D....... 315 232-4511
  Adams (G-3)
▲ Habco Corp ....G....... 631 789-1400
  Amityville (G-291)
HP Hood LLC ....D....... 607 295-8134
  Arkport (G-410)
Hudson Valley Creamery LLC ....F....... 518 851-2570
  Hudson (G-6618)
Instantwhip of Buffalo Inc ....E....... 716 892-7031
  Buffalo (G-3010)
J Kraft Microscopy Svcs Inc ....G....... 716 592-4402
  Springville (G-15613)
Kraft Heinz Foods Company ....B....... 315 376-6575
  Lowville (G-7938)
Kraft Heinz Foods Company ....C....... 607 527-4584
  Campbell (G-3329)
Kraft Heinz Foods Company ....B....... 607 527-4584
  Campbell (G-3330)
Kraft Heinz Foods Company ....C....... 607 865-7131
  Walton (G-16548)
Kutters Cheese Factory Inc ....E....... 585 599-3693
  Corfu (G-3956)
Lactalis American Group Inc ....D....... 716 827-2622
  Buffalo (G-3042)
◆ Lactalis American Group Inc ....B....... 716 823-6262
  Buffalo (G-3043)
Leprino Foods Company ....C....... 570 888-9658
  Waverly (G-16704)
Losurdo Foods Inc ....C....... 315 344-2444
  Heuvelton (G-6305)
▼ Mongiello Sales Inc ....G....... 845 436-4200
  Hurleyville (G-6731)
Mongiellos Itln Cheese Spc LLC ....C....... 845 436-4200
  Hurleyville (G-6732)
▲ Noga Dairies Inc ....F....... 516 293-5448
  Farmingdale (G-5066)
Original Hrkmer Cnty Chese Inc ....D....... 315 895-7428
  Ilion (G-6743)
Pecoraro Dairy Products Inc...............G....... 718 388-2379
  Brooklyn (G-2411)
Rainbeau Ridge Farm ....G....... 914 234-2197
  Bedford Hills (G-806)
Red Creek Cold Storage LLC ....G....... 315 576-2069
  Red Creek (G-14025)
Sandvoss Farms LLC ....G....... 585 297-7044
  East Bethany (G-4383)
Sorrento Lactalis Incorporated ....G....... 716 823-6262
  Buffalo (G-3193)
▲ Taam-Tov Foods Inc ....G....... 718 788-8880
  Brooklyn (G-2641)
▼ World Cheese Co Inc ....F....... 718 965-1700
  Brooklyn (G-2765)

2023 Milk, Condensed & Evaporated

Alpina Foods Inc ....F....... 855 886-1914
  Batavia (G-621)
Baby Central LLC ....G....... 718 372-2229
  Brooklyn (G-1660)
Century Tom Inc ....G....... 347 654-3179
  College Point (G-3780)
Danone Nutricia Early..........................E....... 914 872-8556
  White Plains (G-17098)
Dynatabs LLC.......................................F....... 718 376-6084
  Brooklyn (G-1888)
El-Gen LLC ....G....... 631 218-3400
  Bohemia (G-1064)
Eximus Connections Corporation ....G....... 631 421-1700
  Huntington Station (G-6703)
Friendship Dairies LLC ....C....... 585 973-3031
  Friendship (G-5452)
FriesIndcmpina Ingrdnts N Amer ....E....... 607 746-0196
  Delhi (G-4239)
▼ GNI Commerce Inc ....G....... 347 275-1155
  Brooklyn (G-2033)
◆ Hain Celestial Group Inc ....C....... 516 587-5000
  New Hyde Park (G-8837)
Infant Formula Laboratory Svc ....F....... 718 257-3000
  Brooklyn (G-2105)
▼ Kerry Inc ....D....... 607 334-1700
  Norwich (G-13029)

SIC SECTION
20 FOOD AND KINDRED PRODUCTS

Makers Nutrition LLC E 631 456-5397
Hauppauge *(G-6125)*
◆ Nationwide Dairy Inc G 347 689-8148
Brooklyn *(G-2352)*
Nestle Usa Inc C 914 272-4021
White Plains *(G-17140)*
Nutra Solutions USA Inc E 631 392-1900
Deer Park *(G-4183)*
◆ O-At-Ka Milk Products Coop Inc B 585 343-0536
Batavia *(G-644)*
Omilk LLC G 646 530-2908
Brooklyn *(G-2391)*
Physiologics LLC F 800 765-6775
Ronkonkoma *(G-14969)*
◆ Rich Products Corporation A 716 878-8422
Buffalo *(G-3157)*
Solivaira Specialties Inc D 716 693-4009
North Tonawanda *(G-12996)*
▼ Sugar Foods Corporation E 212 753-6900
New York *(G-12227)*
Upstate Niagara Coop Inc C 716 892-2121
Buffalo *(G-3238)*
Vitakem Nutraceutical Inc C 631 956-8343
Smithtown *(G-15502)*
Vitamin Power Incororated G 631 676-5790
Hauppauge *(G-6228)*

2024 Ice Cream

▲ Allied Food Products Inc F 718 230-4227
Brooklyn *(G-1590)*
Berrywild G 212 686-5848
New York *(G-9368)*
Bleecker Pastry Tartufo Inc G 718 937-9830
Long Island City *(G-7689)*
Blue Marble Ice Cream F 718 858-5551
Brooklyn *(G-1701)*
Blue Pig Ice Cream Factory G 914 271-3850
Croton On Hudson *(G-4062)*
Byrne Dairy Inc E 315 475-2111
Syracuse *(G-15879)*
Byrne Dairy Inc B 315 475-2121
La Fayette *(G-7241)*
Carols Polar Parlor G 315 468-3404
Syracuse *(G-15885)*
Clinton Creamery Inc F 917 324-9699
Laurelton *(G-7386)*
▲ Crepini LLC E 347 422-0829
Brooklyn *(G-1817)*
▼ Crowley Foods Inc E 800 637-0019
Binghamton *(G-904)*
Delicioso Coco Helado Inc F 718 292-1930
Bronx *(G-1314)*
Df Mavens Inc E 347 813-4705
Astoria *(G-437)*
Elegant Desserts By Metro Inc F 718 388-1323
Brooklyn *(G-1912)*
Ffc Holding Corp Subsidiaries F 716 366-5400
Dunkirk *(G-4342)*
▼ Fieldbrook Foods Corporation C 716 366-5400
Dunkirk *(G-4343)*
Four Brothers Italian Bakery G 914 741-5434
Hawthorne *(G-6246)*
Fresh Ice Cream Company LLC F 347 603-6021
Brooklyn *(G-2006)*
G Pesso & Sons Inc G 718 224-9130
Bayside *(G-771)*
GM Ice Cream Inc G 646 236-7383
Queens Village *(G-13977)*
▲ Grom Columbus LLC G 212 974-3444
New York *(G-10369)*
HP Hood LLC A 607 772-6580
Binghamton *(G-922)*
Ice Cream Man Inc E 518 692-8382
Greenwich *(G-5890)*
JMS Ices Inc F 718 448-0853
Staten Island *(G-15692)*
Jones Humdinger F 607 771-6501
Binghamton *(G-932)*
Kozy Shack Enterprises LLC C 516 870-3000
Hicksville *(G-6360)*
Lasalle Brands Inc F 718 542-0900
Bronx *(G-1378)*
Lickity Splits G 585 345-6091
Batavia *(G-641)*
Longfords Ice Cream Ltd F 914 935-9469
Port Chester *(G-13752)*
Macadoodles G 607 652-9019
Stamford *(G-15625)*
▲ Macedonia Ltd F 718 462-3596
Brooklyn *(G-2250)*
Main Street Sweets F 914 332-5757
Tarrytown *(G-16094)*
Mamas G 518 399-2828
Burnt Hills *(G-3267)*
Marina Ice Cream G 718 235-3000
Brooklyn *(G-2270)*
Marvel Dairy Whip Inc G 516 889-4232
Lido Beach *(G-7442)*
Mexicone G 315 591-1971
Mexico *(G-8397)*
Moonlight Creamery G 585 223-0880
Fairport *(G-4864)*
MSQ Corporation G 718 465-0900
Queens Village *(G-13982)*
My Most Favorite Food G 212 580-5130
New York *(G-11331)*
Ninas Custard E 716 636-0345
Getzville *(G-5601)*
Nutrifast LLC F 347 671-3181
New York *(G-11474)*
NY Froyo LLC G 516 312-4588
Deer Park *(G-4184)*
▲ Olympic Ice Cream Co Inc E 718 849-6200
Richmond Hill *(G-14077)*
Olympic Ice Cream Co Inc E 718 849-6200
Jamaica *(G-6936)*
Original Fowlers Choclat Inc G 716 668-2113
Cheektowaga *(G-3584)*
Paleteria Fernandez Inc E 914 315-1598
Mamaroneck *(G-8041)*
▲ Perrys Ice Cream Company Inc B 716 542-5492
Akron *(G-27)*
Phyljohn Distributors Inc F 518 459-2775
Albany *(G-120)*
Piazzas Ice Cream Ice Hse Inc F 718 818-8811
Staten Island *(G-15721)*
◆ Pop Bar LLC G 212 255-4874
New York *(G-11683)*
Primo Frozen Desserts Inc G 718 252-2312
Brooklyn *(G-2442)*
Pulmuone Foods Usa Inc E 845 365-3300
Tappan *(G-16082)*
Purity Ice Cream Co Inc F 607 272-1545
Ithaca *(G-6872)*
Quaker Bonnet Inc G 716 885-7208
Buffalo *(G-3146)*
▼ Quality Dairy Farms Inc E 315 942-2611
Boonville *(G-1168)*
Scoops R US Incorporated G 212 730-7959
New York *(G-12005)*
Smartys Corner G 607 239-5276
Endicott *(G-4829)*
▲ Soft Serve Apple LLC E 646 442-8002
New York *(G-12115)*
Soft Serve Fruit Co LLC E 646 442-8002
New York *(G-12116)*
▲ Spatula LLC F 917 582-8684
New York *(G-12151)*
Stewarts Processing Corp D 518 581-1200
Ballston Spa *(G-610)*
▲ Sweet Melodys LLC E 716 580-3227
East Amherst *(G-4362)*
Swirl Bliss LLC G 516 867-9475
North Baldwin *(G-12910)*
Tia Lattrell G 845 373-9494
Amenia *(G-217)*
▲ TLC-Lc Inc E 212 756-8900
New York *(G-12355)*
Twisters G 585 346-3730
Livonia *(G-7565)*
Van Alphen & Doran Corp G 518 782-9242
Latham *(G-7382)*
Van Leeuwen Artisan Ice Cream G 718 701-1630
Brooklyn *(G-2719)*
Victory Garden G 212 206-7273
New York *(G-12540)*
Washburns Dairy Inc E 518 725-0629
Gloversville *(G-5728)*
Wicked Spoon Inc F 646 335-2890
New York *(G-12630)*
Zings Company LLC G 631 454-0339
Farmingdale *(G-5145)*

2026 Milk

Bliss Foods Inc G 212 732-8888
New York *(G-9414)*
Bliss Foods Inc F 212 732-8888
New York *(G-9415)*
Byrne Dairy Inc B 315 475-2121
La Fayette *(G-7241)*
▲ Chobani LLC C 607 337-1246
Norwich *(G-13024)*
Chobani LLC A 607 847-6181
New Berlin *(G-8779)*
▼ Crowley Foods Inc E 800 637-0019
Binghamton *(G-904)*
▲ Currant Company LLC G 845 266-8999
Staatsburg *(G-15617)*
Dairy Farmers America Inc E 816 801-6440
East Syracuse *(G-4522)*
Dean Foods Company D 315 452-5001
East Syracuse *(G-4525)*
Dwyer Farm LLC G 914 456-2742
Walden *(G-16533)*
Elmhurst Dairy Inc C 718 526-3442
Jamaica *(G-6910)*
Emkay Trading Corp E 585 492-3800
Arcade *(G-392)*
◆ Fage USA Dairy Industry Inc B 518 762-5912
Johnstown *(G-7112)*
◆ Fage USA Holdings G 518 762-5912
Johnstown *(G-7113)*
Finger Lakes Cheese Trail F 607 857-5726
Odessa *(G-13108)*
▼ Hanan Products Company Inc E 516 938-1000
Hicksville *(G-6354)*
HP Hood LLC D 607 295-8134
Arkport *(G-410)*
HP Hood LLC C 315 363-3870
Oneida *(G-13157)*
HP Hood LLC B 315 658-2132
La Fargeville *(G-7236)*
HP Hood LLC B 518 218-9097
Albany *(G-89)*
HP Hood LLC A 607 772-6580
Binghamton *(G-922)*
HP Hood LLC D 315 829-3339
Vernon *(G-16435)*
Instantwhip of Buffalo Inc E 716 892-7031
Buffalo *(G-3010)*
Kesso Foods Inc G 718 777-5303
East Elmhurst *(G-4393)*
Kong Kee Food Corp E 718 937-2746
Long Island City *(G-7783)*
Kraft Heinz Foods Company C 607 865-7131
Walton *(G-16548)*
Kraft Heinz Foods Company B 607 527-4584
Campbell *(G-3330)*
Maple Hill Creamery LLC E 518 758-7777
Stuyvesant *(G-15782)*
Midland Farms Inc E 518 436-7038
Menands *(G-8376)*
Mualema LLC G 609 820-6098
New York *(G-11321)*
▲ Noga Dairies Inc F 516 293-5448
Farmingdale *(G-5066)*
◆ O-At-Ka Milk Products Coop Inc B 585 343-0536
Batavia *(G-644)*
P & F Bakers Inc G 516 931-6821
Hicksville *(G-6382)*
Purity Ice Cream Co Inc F 607 272-1545
Ithaca *(G-6872)*
Saputo Dairy Foods Usa LLC D 607 746-2141
Delhi *(G-4242)*
Steuben Foods Incorporated C 716 655-4000
Elma *(G-4656)*
Steuben Foods Incorporated F 718 291-3333
Jamaica *(G-6952)*
Stewarts Processing Corp D 518 581-1200
Ballston Spa *(G-610)*
◆ The Dannon Company Inc G 914 872-8400
White Plains *(G-17178)*
Upstate Niagara Coop Inc D 716 892-3156
Buffalo *(G-3237)*
Upstate Niagara Coop Inc C 585 458-1880
Rochester *(G-14748)*
Upstate Niagara Coop Inc E 716 484-7178
Jamestown *(G-7041)*
Upstate Niagara Coop Inc D 315 389-5111
North Lawrence *(G-12935)*
Upstate Niagara Coop Inc C 716 892-2121
Buffalo *(G-3238)*
Whitney Foods Inc F 718 291-3333
Jamaica *(G-6964)*
Yo Fresh Inc E 845 634-1616
New City *(G-8796)*
Yo Fresh Inc E 518 982-0659
Clifton Park *(G-3712)*

SIC

Employee Codes: A=Over 500 employees, B=251-500
C=101-250, D=51-100, E=20-50, F=10-19, G=5-9
2017 Harris
New York Manufacturers Directory
711

2032 Canned Specialties

▲ A & G Food Distributors LLC ....G 917 939-3457
Bayside *(G-762)*

Antico Casale Usa LLC ....G 914 760-1100
Whitestone *(G-17199)*

◆ Beech-Nut Nutrition Company ....B 518 839-0300
Amsterdam *(G-335)*

Borgattis Ravioli Egg Noodles ....G 718 367-3799
Bronx *(G-1287)*

Delicious Foods Inc ....F 718 446-9352
Corona *(G-3997)*

◆ Eve Sales Corp ....F 718 589-6800
Bronx *(G-1328)*

▲ Global Food Source & Co Inc ....G 914 320-9615
Tuckahoe *(G-16270)*

Goya Foods Inc ....D 716 549-0076
Angola *(G-380)*

Grandma Browns Beans Inc ....F 315 963-7221
Mexico *(G-8395)*

▲ Iberia Foods Corp ....D 718 272-8900
Brooklyn *(G-2094)*

Indira Foods Inc ....F 718 343-1500
Floral Park *(G-5208)*

Marketplace Slutions Group LLC ....E 631 868-0111
Holbrook *(G-6461)*

Morris Kitchen Inc ....F 646 413-5186
Brooklyn *(G-2334)*

Novartis Corporation ....E 212 307-1122
New York *(G-11462)*

Phillip Juan ....G 800 834-4543
Staten Island *(G-15720)*

◆ Sahadi Fine Foods Inc ....E 718 369-0100
Brooklyn *(G-2530)*

Sangster Foods Inc ....F 212 993-9129
Brooklyn *(G-2532)*

Steuben Foods Incorporated ....F 718 291-3333
Jamaica *(G-6952)*

2033 Canned Fruits, Vegetables & Preserves

Amiram Dror Inc ....F 212 979-9505
Brooklyn *(G-1611)*

▲ Apple & Eve LLC ....D 516 621-1122
Port Washington *(G-13800)*

Beths Farm Kitchen ....G 518 799-3414
Stuyvesant Falls *(G-15783)*

Birds Eye Holdings Inc ....A 585 383-1850
Rochester *(G-14232)*

◆ Brooklyn Btlg Milton NY Inc ....C 845 795-2171
Milton *(G-8482)*

Cahoon Farms Inc ....E 315 594-8081
Wolcott *(G-17277)*

▼ Carriage House Companies Inc ....A 716 672-4321
Fredonia *(G-5371)*

Central Island Juice Corp ....F 516 338-8301
Westbury *(G-16974)*

Cheribundi Inc ....E 800 699-0460
Geneva *(G-5573)*

◆ Cliffstar LLC ....A 716 366-6100
Dunkirk *(G-4337)*

Club 1100 ....G 585 235-3478
Rochester *(G-14280)*

◆ Dells Maraschino Cherries Inc ....E 718 624-4380
Brooklyn *(G-1851)*

Eleanors Best ....F 845 809-5621
Garrison *(G-5554)*

Fresh Fanatic Inc ....G 516 521-6574
Brooklyn *(G-2005)*

▼ Fruitcrown Products Corp ....E 631 694-5800
Farmingdale *(G-4994)*

◆ Giovanni Food Co Inc ....D 315 463-7770
Syracuse *(G-15953)*

Glk Foods LLC ....E 585 289-4414
Shortsville *(G-15433)*

◆ Global Natural Foods Inc ....E 845 439-3292
Livingston Manor *(G-7562)*

Goya Foods Inc ....D 716 549-0076
Angola *(G-380)*

Green Valley Foods LLC ....G 315 926-4280
Marion *(G-8094)*

Hc Brill Co Inc ....G 716 685-4000
Lancaster *(G-7319)*

Jets Lefrois Corp ....G 585 637-5003
Brockport *(G-1245)*

Kaltech Food Packaging Inc ....E 845 856-1210
Port Jervis *(G-13787)*

Kensington & Sons LLC ....E 646 450-5735
New York *(G-10835)*

▲ L and S Packing Co ....D 631 845-1717
Farmingdale *(G-5030)*

Lagoner Farms Inc ....D 315 589-4899
Williamson *(G-17224)*

▲ Levindi ....F 212 572-7000
New York *(G-10978)*

Lidestri Foods Inc ....E 585 458-8335
Rochester *(G-14480)*

▲ Lidestri Foods Inc ....B 585 377-7700
Fairport *(G-4861)*

Life Juice Brands LLC ....G 585 944-7982
Pittsford *(G-13567)*

Lollipop Tree Inc ....E 845 471-8733
Auburn *(G-506)*

▲ Mayer Bros Apple Products Inc ....D 716 668-1787
West Seneca *(G-16952)*

Mizkan America Inc ....D 585 765-9171
Lyndonville *(G-7968)*

Morris Kitchen Inc ....F 646 413-5186
Brooklyn *(G-2334)*

◆ Motts LLP ....C 972 673-8088
Elmsford *(G-4767)*

◆ National Grape Coop Assn Inc ....E 716 326-5200
Westfield *(G-17048)*

▼ Old Dutch Mustard Co Inc ....G 516 466-0522
Great Neck *(G-5825)*

Private Lbel Fods Rchester Inc ....E 585 254-9205
Rochester *(G-14602)*

▲ Sbk Preserves Inc ....E 800 773-7378
Bronx *(G-1448)*

◆ Seneca Foods Corporation ....E 315 926-8100
Marion *(G-8099)*

Seneca Foods Corporation ....C 315 781-8733
Geneva *(G-5585)*

Seneca Foods Corporation ....F 315 926-4277
Marion *(G-8101)*

Seneca Foods Corporation ....E 585 658-2211
Leicester *(G-7422)*

▲ Sneaky Chef Foods LLC ....F 914 301-3277
Tarrytown *(G-16106)*

Spf Holdings II LLC ....F 212 750-8300
New York *(G-12161)*

US Juice Partners LLC ....G 516 621-1122
Port Washington *(G-13870)*

▲ Victoria Fine Foods LLC ....D 718 649-1635
Brooklyn *(G-2725)*

Vincents Food Corp ....F 516 481-3544
Carle Place *(G-3397)*

Welch Foods Inc A Cooperative ....C 716 326-5252
Westfield *(G-17053)*

Welch Foods Inc A Cooperative ....E 716 326-3131
Westfield *(G-17054)*

Wolfgang B Gourmet Foods Inc ....F 518 719-1727
Catskill *(G-3435)*

2034 Dried Fruits, Vegetables & Soup

▲ Allied Food Products Inc ....F 718 230-4227
Brooklyn *(G-1590)*

◆ Associated Brands Inc ....B 585 798-3475
New York *(G-9238)*

Goya Foods Inc ....D 716 549-0076
Angola *(G-380)*

◆ Hain Celestial Group Inc ....C 516 587-5000
New Hyde Park *(G-8837)*

Interntional Gourmet Soups Inc ....E 212 768-7687
Staten Island *(G-15688)*

Marshall Ingredients LLC ....G 800 796-9353
Wolcott *(G-17280)*

▲ Peeled Inc ....G 212 706-2001
Brooklyn *(G-2412)*

◆ Settons Intl Foods Inc ....E 631 543-8090
Commack *(G-3842)*

Shoreline Fruit LLC ....D 585 765-2639
Lyndonville *(G-7969)*

▲ Wm E Martin and Sons Co Inc ....E 516 605-2444
Roslyn *(G-15024)*

2035 Pickled Fruits, Vegetables, Sauces & Dressings

Allen Pickle Works Inc ....F 516 676-0640
Glen Cove *(G-5610)*

American Specialty Mfg Co ....F 585 544-5600
Rochester *(G-14199)*

Baldwin Richardson Foods Co ....C 315 986-2727
Macedon *(G-7983)*

Batampte Pickle Products Inc ....D 718 251-2100
Brooklyn *(G-1673)*

Birds Eye Holdings Inc ....A 585 383-1850
Rochester *(G-14232)*

Bushwick Kitchen LLC ....G 917 297-1045
Brooklyn *(G-1739)*

Carriage House Companies Inc ....C 716 673-1000
Dunkirk *(G-4334)*

▼ Carriage House Companies Inc ....A 716 672-4321
Fredonia *(G-5371)*

▲ Classic Cooking LLC ....D 718 439-0200
Jamaica *(G-6905)*

Elwood International Inc ....F 631 842-6600
Copiague *(G-3899)*

French Associates Inc ....F 718 387-9880
Fresh Meadows *(G-5440)*

Glk Foods LLC ....E 585 289-4414
Shortsville *(G-15433)*

▲ Gold Pure Food Products Co Inc ....D 516 483-5600
Hempstead *(G-6272)*

Goya Foods Inc ....D 716 549-0076
Angola *(G-380)*

Gravymaster Inc ....E 203 453-1893
Canajoharie *(G-3332)*

Heintz & Weber Co Inc ....G 716 852-7171
Buffalo *(G-2993)*

Instantwhip of Buffalo Inc ....E 716 892-7031
Buffalo *(G-3010)*

Jets Lefrois Corp ....G 585 637-5003
Brockport *(G-1245)*

Kensington & Sons LLC ....E 646 450-5735
New York *(G-10835)*

▲ L and S Packing Co ....D 631 845-1717
Farmingdale *(G-5030)*

Lollipop Tree Inc ....E 845 471-8733
Auburn *(G-506)*

Lucinas Gourmet Food Inc ....G 646 835-9784
Brooklyn *(G-2239)*

▲ Mandarin Soy Sauce Inc ....E 845 343-1505
Middletown *(G-8449)*

▲ Metzger Speciality Brands ....G 212 957-0055
New York *(G-11244)*

Mizkan America Inc ....D 585 765-9171
Lyndonville *(G-7968)*

Mizkan Americas Inc ....F 585 798-5720
Medina *(G-8278)*

▲ Moldova Pickles & Salads Inc ....G 718 284-2220
Brooklyn *(G-2330)*

▼ Old Dutch Mustard Co Inc ....G 516 466-0522
Great Neck *(G-5825)*

▲ Rob Salamida Company Inc ....F 607 729-4868
Johnson City *(G-7105)*

▲ Sabra Dipping Company LLC ....D 914 372-3900
White Plains *(G-17166)*

Sassy Sauce Inc ....G 585 621-1050
Rochester *(G-14669)*

Sum Sum LLC ....G 516 812-3959
Oceanside *(G-13099)*

T RS Great American Rest ....F 516 294-1680
Williston Park *(G-17263)*

▲ Twin Marquis Inc ....D 718 386-6868
Brooklyn *(G-2691)*

United Farm Processing Corp ....C 718 933-6060
Bronx *(G-1485)*

United Pickle Products Corp ....E 718 933-6060
Bronx *(G-1486)*

▲ Victoria Fine Foods LLC ....D 718 649-1635
Brooklyn *(G-2725)*

◆ Wanjashan International LLC ....F 845 343-1505
Middletown *(G-8469)*

Whalens Horseradish Products ....G 518 587-6404
Galway *(G-5484)*

2037 Frozen Fruits, Juices & Vegetables

Atlantic Farm & Food Inc ....F 718 441-3152
Richmond Hill *(G-14066)*

Birds Eye Foods Inc ....G 716 988-3218
South Dayton *(G-15517)*

Blend Smoothie Bar ....G 845 568-7366
New Windsor *(G-8933)*

Cahoon Farms Inc ....E 315 594-8081
Wolcott *(G-17277)*

Cheribundi Inc ....E 800 699-0460
Geneva *(G-5573)*

▲ Classic Cooking LLC ....D 718 439-0200
Jamaica *(G-6905)*

▲ Dynamic Health Labs Inc ....E 718 858-0100
Brooklyn *(G-1886)*

◆ Global Natural Foods Inc ....E 845 439-3292
Livingston Manor *(G-7562)*

Hain Blueprint Inc ....E 212 414-5741
New Hyde Park *(G-8836)*

▲ Levindi ....F 212 572-7000
New York *(G-10978)*

▲ Metzger Speciality Brands ....G 212 957-0055
New York *(G-11244)*

◆ National Grape Coop Assn Inc .... E 716 326-5200
  Westfield (G-17048)
◆ Pepsico Inc .... A 914 253-2000
  Purchase (G-13966)
▲ Prime Food Processing Corp .... D 718 963-2323
  Brooklyn (G-2441)
Pura Fruta LLC .... F 415 279-5727
  Long Island City (G-7850)
◆ Seneca Foods Corporation .... E 315 926-8100
  Marion (G-8099)
T & Smoothie Inc .... G 631 804-6653
  Patchogue (G-13436)
Tami Great Food Corp .... G 845 352-7901
  Monsey (G-8584)
World Waters LLC .... E 212 905-2393
  New York (G-12663)
Zoe Sakoutis LLC .... F 212 414-5741
  New York (G-12717)

2038 Frozen Specialties

◆ Alle Processing Corp .... C 718 894-2000
  Maspeth (G-8115)
▲ America NY RI Wang Fd Group Co ... E 718 628-8999
  Maspeth (G-8117)
▲ Classic Cooking LLC .... D 718 439-0200
  Jamaica (G-6905)
Codinos Limited Inc .... E 518 372-3308
  Schenectady (G-15244)
D R M Management Inc .... E 716 668-0333
  Depew (G-4254)
Delicious Foods Inc .... F 718 446-9352
  Corona (G-3997)
Dufour Pastry Kitchens Inc .... E 718 402-8800
  Bronx (G-1318)
▲ Dvash Foods Inc .... F 845 578-1959
  Monsey (G-8571)
F & R Enterprises Inc .... G 315 841-8189
  Waterville (G-16678)
Finger Food Products Inc .... E 716 297-4888
  Niagara Falls (G-12822)
▲ Freeze-Dry Foods Inc .... E 585 589-6399
  Albion (G-165)
Hong Hop Co Inc .... E 212 962-1735
  New York (G-10502)
▲ Julians Recipe LLC .... G 888 640-8880
  Brooklyn (G-2159)
Juno Chefs .... D 845 294-5400
  Goshen (G-5735)
Kraft Heinz Foods Company .... B 585 226-4400
  Avon (G-540)
Les Chateaux De France Inc .... E 516 239-6795
  Inwood (G-6760)
▲ Milmar Food Group II LLC .... C 845 294-5400
  Goshen (G-5738)
Peak Holdings LLC .... A 212 583-5000
  New York (G-11588)
Salarinos Italian Foods Inc .... F 315 697-9766
  Canastota (G-3372)
▲ Seviroli Foods Inc .... C 516 222-6220
  Garden City (G-5532)
Tami Great Food Corp .... G 845 352-7901
  Monsey (G-8584)
▲ Tuv Taam Corp .... E 718 855-2207
  Brooklyn (G-2689)

2041 Flour, Grain Milling

ADM Milling Co .... D 716 849-7333
  Buffalo (G-2797)
Archer-Daniels-Midland Company ...... E 518 828-4691
  Hudson (G-6605)
Archer-Daniels-Midland Company ...... D 518 828-4691
  Hudson (G-6606)
Ardent Mills LLC .... D 518 447-1700
  Albany (G-49)
◆ Birkett Mills .... G 315 536-3311
  Penn Yan (G-13506)
Birkett Mills .... E 315 536-4112
  Penn Yan (G-13507)
Cargill Incorporated .... G 716 665-6570
  Kennedy (G-7153)
Champlain Valley Milling Corp .... G 518 962-4711
  Westport (G-17067)
Cochecton Mills Inc .... E 845 932-8282
  Cochecton (G-3740)
Frozen Pastry Products Corp .... E 845 364-9833
  Spring Valley (G-15586)
General Mills Inc .... E 716 856-6060
  Buffalo (G-2969)
Losurdo Foods Inc .... E 518 842-1500
  Amsterdam (G-355)

Ohio Baking Company Inc .... E 315 724-2033
  Utica (G-16354)
Western Blending Inc .... E 518 356-6650
  Schenectady (G-15312)

2043 Cereal Breakfast Foods

◆ Associated Brands Inc .... B 585 798-3475
  New York (G-9238)
Avas Corporation .... G 203 470-3587
  New York (G-9275)
Chia Usa LLC .... F 212 226-7512
  New York (G-9593)
Gabila Food Products Inc .... E 631 789-2220
  Copiague (G-3902)
General Mills Inc .... D 716 856-6060
  Buffalo (G-2970)
Group International LLC .... G 718 475-8805
  Flushing (G-5245)
Kellogg Company .... E 315 452-0310
  North Syracuse (G-12951)
Kellogg Company .... A 845 365-5284
  Orangeburg (G-13233)
Kraft Heinz Foods Company .... G 914 335-2500
  Tarrytown (G-16093)
Muesli Fusion Inc .... F 716 984-0855
  Rochester (G-14524)
◆ Pepsico Inc .... A 914 253-2000
  Purchase (G-13966)
Sangster Foods Inc .... F 212 993-9129
  Brooklyn (G-2532)
Sanzdranz LLC .... G 518 894-8625
  Delmar (G-4246)
Sanzdranz LLC .... G 518 894-8625
  Schenectady (G-15292)

2044 Rice Milling

▼ Gassho Body & Mind Inc .... G 518 695-9991
  Schuylerville (G-15320)
Real Co Inc .... G 347 433-8549
  Valley Cottage (G-16386)

2045 Flour, Blended & Prepared

Aryzta LLC .... D 585 235-8160
  Rochester (G-14214)
▲ Bektrom Foods Inc .... E 516 802-3800
  Syosset (G-15813)
Cohens Bakery Inc .... E 716 892-8149
  Buffalo (G-2879)
Dawn Food Products Inc .... C 716 830-8214
  Williamsville (G-17240)
Elis Bread (eli Zabar) Inc .... F 212 772-2011
  New York (G-10005)
Lollipop Tree Inc .... G 845 471-8733
  Auburn (G-506)
▲ Mastroianni Bros Inc .... E 518 355-5310
  Schenectady (G-15277)
New Hope Mills Inc .... F 315 252-2676
  Auburn (G-509)
Peak Holdings LLC .... A 212 583-5000
  New York (G-11588)
Tosca Brick Oven Pizza Real .... G 718 430-0026
  Bronx (G-1473)
Western Blending Inc .... E 518 356-6650
  Schenectady (G-15312)

2046 Wet Corn Milling

Anthony Gigi Inc .... G 860 984-1943
  Shirley (G-15412)
Archer-Daniels-Midland Company ...... G 585 346-2311
  Lakeville (G-7282)
▲ Sweetwater Energy Inc .... G 585 647-5760
  Rochester (G-14708)

2047 Dog & Cat Food

▲ Colgate-Palmolive Company .... A 212 310-2000
  New York (G-9667)
Dog Good Products LLC .... G 212 789-7000
  New York (G-9895)
Hills Pet Products Inc .... G 212 310-2000
  New York (G-10477)
Hound & Gatos Pet Foods Corp .... G 212 618-1917
  New York (G-10517)
Nestle Purina Petcare Company .... B 716 366-8080
  Dunkirk (G-4345)
◆ Pet Proteins LLC .... G 888 293-1029
  New York (G-11629)
Robert Abady Dog Food Co Ltd .... F 845 473-1900
  Poughkeepsie (G-13928)

Scooby Rendering & Inc .... G 315 793-1014
  Utica (G-16358)

2048 Prepared Feeds For Animals & Fowls

Archer-Daniels-Midland Company ...... D 716 849-7333
  Buffalo (G-2819)
Bailey Boonville Mills Inc .... E 315 942-2131
  Boonville (G-1162)
Baker Commodities Inc .... E 585 482-1880
  Rochester (G-14222)
Cargill Incorporated .... E 315 622-3533
  Liverpool (G-7515)
Central Garden & Pet Company .... G 631 451-8021
  Selden (G-15349)
Central Garden & Pet Company .... G 212 877-1270
  New York (G-9564)
Cochecton Mills Inc .... E 845 932-8282
  Cochecton (G-3740)
Commodity Resource Corporation ..... F 585 538-9500
  Caledonia (G-3278)
Gramco Inc .... G 716 592-2845
  Springville (G-15611)
Grandma Maes Cntry Nturals LLC ...... G 212 348-8171
  New York (G-10350)
Heath Manufacturing Company .... G 800 444-3140
  Batavia (G-638)
J & M Feed Corporation .... G 631 281-2152
  Shirley (G-15421)
Kent Nutrition Group Inc .... E 315 788-0032
  Watertown (G-16658)
Lowville Farmers Coop Inc .... E 315 376-6587
  Lowville (G-7939)
Narrowsburg Feed & Grain Co .... F 845 252-3936
  Narrowsburg (G-8768)
Nutra-Vet Research Corp .... F 845 473-1900
  Poughkeepsie (G-13923)
Pace Manufacturing Company .... G 607 936-0431
  Painted Post (G-13392)
Pine Tree Farms Inc .... E 607 532-4312
  Interlaken (G-6749)
Scotts Feed Inc .... E 518 483-3110
  Malone (G-8015)
Southern States Coop Inc .... F 315 438-4500
  East Syracuse (G-4566)
Veterinary Biochemical Ltd .... G 845 473-1900
  Poughkeepsie (G-13939)
Wagners LLC .... G 516 933-6580
  Jericho (G-7090)

2051 Bread, Bakery Prdts Exc Cookies & Crackers

3 Bears Gluten Free Bakery .... F 315 323-0277
  Potsdam (G-13876)
3rd Avenue Doughnut Inc .... F 718 748-3294
  Brooklyn (G-1516)
40 Street Baking Inc .... C 212 683-4700
  Brooklyn (G-1518)
527 Franco Bakery Corporation .... G 718 993-4200
  Bronx (G-1250)
999 Bagels Inc .... G 718 915-0742
  Brooklyn (G-1524)
A & M Appel Distributing Inc .... G 516 735-1172
  Massapequa (G-8176)
A Angonoa Inc .... D 718 762-4466
  College Point (G-3773)
A T A Bagel Shoppe Inc .... G 718 352-4948
  Bayside (G-764)
Addeo Bakers Inc .... F 718 367-8316
  Bronx (G-1263)
Aladdin Bakers Inc .... C 718 499-1818
  Brooklyn (G-1574)
Alicias Bakery Inc .... G 914 235-4689
  New Rochelle (G-8885)
Allies GF Goodies LLC .... F 516 216-1719
  Hicksville (G-6321)
▲ Alrajs Inc .... E 631 225-0300
  Lindenhurst (G-7452)
Always Baked Fresh .... G 631 648-0811
  Holbrook (G-6431)
American Vintage Wine Biscuit .... G 718 361-1003
  Long Island City (G-7657)
Amincor Inc .... C 347 821-3452
  New York (G-9136)
Amiram Dror Inc .... F 212 979-9505
  Brooklyn (G-1611)
▲ Amy Scherber Inc .... F 212 462-4338
  New York (G-9142)
Andrew Sapienza Bakery Inc .... E 516 437-1715
  Elmont (G-4715)

Employee Codes: A=Over 500 employees, B=251-500
C=101-250, D=51-100, E=20-50, F=10-19, G=5-9

20 FOOD AND KINDRED PRODUCTS SIC SECTION

Aphrodities ....G.... 718 224-1774
Whitestone (G-17200)
Aryzta LLC ....C.... 585 235-8160
Rochester (G-14215)
Aryzta LLC ....D.... 585 235-8160
Rochester (G-14214)
B & D Enterprises of Utica ....D.... 315 735-3311
New Hartford (G-8801)
B Cake NY LLC ....G.... 347 787-7199
Brooklyn (G-1658)
Bagel Club Inc ....F.... 718 423-6106
Bayside (G-767)
Bagel Grove Inc ....E.... 315 724-8015
Utica (G-16309)
Bagel Land ....E.... 585 442-3080
Rochester (G-14220)
Bagel Lites LLC ....G.... 855 813-7888
Long Island City (G-7680)
Bagelovers Inc ....F.... 607 844-3683
Dryden (G-4320)
▼ Bagels By Bell Ltd ....E.... 718 272-2780
Brooklyn (G-1663)
Baked Cupcakery ....G.... 716 773-2050
Grand Island (G-5752)
Bakerly LLC ....G.... 212 220-3901
Brooklyn (G-1665)
Bakery & Coffee Shop ....G.... 315 287-1829
Gouverneur (G-5742)
▲ Bauli USA Inc ....G.... 646 380-1891
New York (G-9334)
Berardi Bakery Inc ....G.... 718 746-9529
Whitestone (G-17203)
Better Baked Foods Inc ....D.... 716 326-4651
Westfield (G-17046)
Bien Cuit LLC ....G.... 718 852-0200
Brooklyn (G-1693)
Bimbo Bakeries ....G.... 631 274-4906
Deer Park (G-4108)
Bimbo Bakeries ....G.... 800 289-7876
Olean (G-13135)
Bimbo Bakeries ....F.... 518 463-2221
Albany (G-56)
Bimbo Bakeries Usa Inc ....G.... 716 692-9140
Tonawanda (G-16145)
Bimbo Bakeries Usa Inc ....G.... 718 601-1561
Bronx (G-1284)
Bimbo Bakeries Usa Inc ....G.... 718 545-0291
Long Island City (G-7685)
Bimbo Bakeries Usa Inc ....C.... 716 372-8444
Olean (G-13136)
Bimbo Bakeries Usa Inc ....F.... 516 887-1024
Lynbrook (G-7947)
Bimbo Bakeries Usa Inc ....F.... 315 379-9069
Canton (G-3380)
Bimbo Bakeries Usa Inc ....E.... 516 877-2850
Mineola (G-8498)
Bimbo Bakeries Usa Inc ....C.... 718 463-6300
Maspeth (G-8121)
Bimbo Bakeries Usa Inc ....C.... 631 274-4906
Bay Shore (G-676)
Bimbo Bakeries Usa Inc ....D.... 315 253-9782
Auburn (G-484)
Bimbo Bakeries Usa Inc ....F.... 518 489-4053
Albany (G-57)
Bimbo Bakeries Usa Inc ....E.... 203 531-2311
Bay Shore (G-677)
Bimbo Bakeries Usa Inc ....F.... 716 706-0450
Lancaster (G-7306)
Bimbo Bakeries Usa Inc ....F.... 315 785-7060
Watertown (G-16637)
Bimbo Bakeries Usa Inc ....D.... 845 568-0943
Newburgh (G-12751)
Bimbo Bakeries Usa Inc ....E.... 800 856-8544
Vestal (G-16441)
Bimbo Bakeries Usa Inc ....C.... 315 782-4189
Watertown (G-16638)
Bimbo Bakeries Usa Inc ....F.... 845 294-5282
Goshen (G-5731)
▲ Bimbo Foods Bakeries Inc ....C.... 631 273-6000
Bay Shore (G-678)
Blackbirds Brooklyn LLC ....E.... 917 362-4080
Brooklyn (G-1700)
Blondie S Bakeshop Inc ....G.... 631 424-4545
Centerport (G-3475)
Bread Factory LLC ....E.... 914 637-8150
New Rochelle (G-8889)
Bread Market Cafe ....G.... 212 768-9292
New York (G-9457)
Brighton Bakery ....G.... 315 475-2948
Syracuse (G-15874)
Brooklyn Sweet Spot Inc ....G.... 718 522-2577
Brooklyn (G-1733)
Butter Cooky Bakery ....G.... 516 354-3831
Floral Park (G-5196)
▲ Cannoli Factory Inc ....E.... 631 643-2700
Wyandanch (G-17372)
Caputo Bakery Inc ....G.... 718 875-6871
Brooklyn (G-1756)
Carmine Street Bagels Inc ....F.... 212 691-3041
Staten Island (G-15656)
Carolinas Desserts Inc ....G.... 914 779-4000
Yonkers (G-17423)
Carter Street Bakery Inc ....G.... 585 749-7104
Rochester (G-14261)
Chambord LLC ....E.... 718 859-1110
Brooklyn (G-1772)
Charlotte Neuville Design LLC ....G.... 646 530-4570
Brooklyn (G-1775)
Chocnyc LLC ....G.... 917 804-4848
New York (G-9604)
Cinderellas Sweets Ltd ....E.... 516 374-7976
Woodmere (G-17312)
Circle 5 Deli Corp ....G.... 718 525-5687
Jamaica (G-6902)
City Bakery Inc ....E.... 212 366-1414
New York (G-9628)
Coccadotts Inc ....F.... 518 438-4937
Albany (G-69)
Cohens Bakery Inc ....E.... 716 892-8149
Buffalo (G-2879)
Commitment 2000 Inc ....E.... 716 439-1206
Buffalo (G-2883)
Cookie Connection Inc ....G.... 315 422-2253
Syracuse (G-15906)
Costanzos Bakery Inc ....C.... 716 656-9093
Buffalo (G-2891)
Creative Relations LLC ....G.... 212 462-4392
New York (G-9751)
Cupcake Contessas Corporation ....G.... 516 307-1222
North Bellmore (G-12919)
Cuzins Duzin Corp ....G.... 347 724-6200
Kew Gardens (G-7160)
D-Lite Donuts ....G.... 718 626-5953
Astoria (G-436)
Daly Meghan ....F.... 347 699-3259
Brooklyn (G-1836)
Damascus Bakery Inc ....C.... 718 855-1456
Brooklyn (G-1837)
Delicias Andinas Food Corp ....E.... 718 416-2922
Flushing (G-5237)
Dipaolo Baking Co Inc ....D.... 585 303-5013
Rochester (G-14310)
Duane Park Patisserie Inc ....F.... 212 274-8447
New York (G-9934)
Eileens Special Cheesecake ....G.... 212 966-5585
New York (G-9990)
Enterprise Bagels Inc ....F.... 845 896-3823
Fishkill (G-5183)
Ericeira Inc ....G.... 516 294-4034
Mineola (G-8510)
Famous Doughnuts Inc ....G.... 716 834-6356
Buffalo (G-2944)
FB Sale LLC ....G.... 315 986-9999
Macedon (G-7987)
Felix Roma & Sons Inc ....D.... 607 748-3336
Endicott (G-4808)
▲ Ferrara Bakery & Cafe Inc ....D.... 212 226-6150
New York (G-10154)
Flour Power Bakery Cafe ....G.... 917 747-6895
Livingston Manor (G-7561)
Food Gems Ltd ....E.... 718 296-7788
Ozone Park (G-13379)
Fotis Oneonta Italian Bakery ....G.... 607 432-3871
Oneonta (G-13186)
Fratellis LLC ....E.... 607 722-5663
Binghamton (G-915)
Fritters & Buns Inc ....G.... 845 227-6609
Hopewell Junction (G-6550)
Fung Wong Bakery Inc ....E.... 212 267-4037
New York (G-10224)
Gabila & Sons Mfg Inc ....E.... 631 789-2220
Copiague (G-3901)
Geddes Bakery Co Inc ....E.... 315 437-8084
North Syracuse (G-12945)
Gennaris Itln French Bky Inc ....G.... 516 997-8968
Carle Place (G-3389)
George Retzos ....G.... 315 422-2913
Syracuse (G-15952)
Giovanni Bakery Corp ....F.... 212 695-4296
New York (G-10300)
Glenn Wayne Wholesale Bky Inc ....D.... 631 289-9200
Bohemia (G-1073)
▼ Gluten Free Bake Shop Inc ....E.... 845 782-5307
Mountainville (G-8747)
Golden Glow Cookie Co Inc ....E.... 718 379-6223
Bronx (G-1345)
Good Bread Bakery ....F.... 914 939-3900
Port Chester (G-13748)
Gourmet Toast Corp ....G.... 718 852-4536
Brooklyn (G-2044)
Grannys Kitchens LLC ....B.... 315 735-5000
Frankfort (G-5354)
Great American Dessert Co LLC ....D.... 718 894-3494
Maspeth (G-8141)
Greenvale Bagel Inc ....E.... 516 221-8221
Wantagh (G-16556)
◆ Greyston Bakery Inc ....C.... 914 375-1510
Yonkers (G-17451)
Grimaldis Home Bread Inc ....D.... 718 497-1425
Ridgewood (G-14109)
H & S Edible Products Corp ....E.... 914 413-3489
Mount Vernon (G-8688)
H H B Bakery of Little Neck ....G.... 718 631-7004
Flushing (G-5246)
Hagadah Passover Bakery ....G.... 718 638-1589
Brooklyn (G-2062)
Hahns Old Fashioned Cake Co ....F.... 631 249-3456
Farmingdale (G-5005)
Hana Pastries Inc ....G.... 718 369-7593
Brooklyn (G-2065)
Harrison Bakery West ....E.... 315 422-1468
Syracuse (G-15957)
▲ Heidelberg Group Inc ....E.... 315 866-0999
Herkimer (G-6301)
Herris Gourmet Inc ....G.... 917 578-2308
Brooklyn (G-2078)
Highway Bagels Corp ....G.... 347 350-6493
Brooklyn (G-2080)
Jarets Stuffed Cupcakes ....G.... 607 658-9096
Endicott (G-4814)
Jerrys Bagels ....G.... 516 791-0063
Valley Stream (G-16410)
Jim Romas Bakery Inc ....E.... 607 748-7425
Endicott (G-4817)
▲ JJ Cassone Bakery Inc ....B.... 914 939-1568
Port Chester (G-13750)
Jonathan Lord Corp ....F.... 631 563-4445
Bohemia (G-1085)
Juniors Cheesecake Inc ....G.... 718 852-5257
Brooklyn (G-2160)
King Cracker Corp ....F.... 516 539-9251
Hempstead (G-6277)
Kossars Bialys LLC ....G.... 212 473-4810
New York (G-10879)
Kossars On Grand LLC ....F.... 212 473-4810
New York (G-10880)
L American Ltd ....F.... 716 372-9480
Olean (G-13150)
La Calenita Bakery & Cafeteria ....G.... 718 205-8273
Elmhurst (G-4663)
La Prima Bakery Inc ....F.... 718 584-4442
Bronx (G-1377)
Ladybird Bakery Inc ....G.... 718 499-8108
Brooklyn (G-2190)
Larosa Cupcakes ....G.... 347 866-3920
Staten Island (G-15697)
Libbys Bakery Cafe LLC ....G.... 603 918-8825
Ticonderoga (G-16127)
Lillys Homestyle Bakeshop Inc ....D.... 718 491-2904
Brooklyn (G-2222)
Ljmm Inc ....E.... 845 454-5876
Poughkeepsie (G-13912)
M & M Bagel Corp ....F.... 516 295-1222
Cedarhurst (G-3459)
Mac Crete Corporation ....F.... 718 932-1803
Long Island City (G-7798)
Made Close LLC ....G.... 917 837-1357
Brooklyn (G-2252)
Magnolia Operating LLC ....E.... 212 265-2777
New York (G-11108)
Make My Cake II Inc ....G.... 212 234-2344
New York (G-11117)
▲ Mastroianni Bros Inc ....E.... 518 355-5310
Schenectady (G-15277)
Maxwell Bakery Inc ....E.... 718 498-2200
Brooklyn (G-2286)
McKee Foods Corporation ....A.... 631 979-9364
Hauppauge (G-6128)
Mds Hot Bagels Deli Inc ....G.... 718 438-5650
Brooklyn (G-2289)

SIC SECTION 20 FOOD AND KINDRED PRODUCTS

Megamatt Inc F 516 536-3541 Rockville Centre *(G-14794)*

Melita Corp C 718 392-7280 Bronx *(G-1390)*

Millers Bulk Food and Bakery G 585 798-9700 Medina *(G-8277)*

Miss Grimble Associates Inc F 718 665-2253 Bronx *(G-1399)*

Modern Itln Bky of W Babylon C 631 589-7300 Oakdale *(G-13059)*

Mollys Cupcakes New York G 212 255-5441 New York *(G-11295)*

Mother Mousse Ltd G 718 983-8366 Staten Island *(G-15709)*

New Hope Mills Mfg Inc E 315 252-2676 Auburn *(G-510)*

New Mount Pleasant Bakery E 518 374-7577 Schenectady *(G-15281)*

New Star Bakery E 718 961-8868 Flushing *(G-5271)*

Nibble Inc Baking Co G 518 334-3950 Troy *(G-16243)*

Niebylski Bakery Inc G 718 721-5152 Astoria *(G-450)*

▼ **Nightingale Food Entps Inc** G 347 577-1630 New York *(G-11429)*

Nildas Desserts Limited F 845 454-5876 Poughkeepsie *(G-13922)*

Ohio Baking Company Inc E 315 724-2033 Utica *(G-16354)*

▲ **Old Poland Foods LLC** F 718 486-7700 Brooklyn *(G-2388)*

Operative Cake Corp E 718 278-5600 Bronx *(G-1417)*

Orza Bakery Inc F 914 965-5736 Yonkers *(G-17471)*

Ossining Bakery Lmp Inc G 914 941-2654 Ossining *(G-13324)*

OWayne Enterprises Inc E 718 326-2200 Maspeth *(G-8162)*

Oz Baking Company Ltd G 516 466-5114 Great Neck *(G-5827)*

▲ **Palagonia Bakery Co Inc** D 718 272-5400 Brooklyn *(G-2402)*

Pane DOro F 914 964-0043 Yonkers *(G-17475)*

Paris Baguette G 718 961-0404 Flushing *(G-5278)*

Parkway Bread Distributors Inc G 845 362-1221 Pomona *(G-13732)*

Peking Food LLC E 718 628-8080 Brooklyn *(G-2413)*

Perrottas Bakery Inc G 518 283-4711 Troy *(G-16247)*

Pesces Bakery Inc G 845 246-4730 Saugerties *(G-15191)*

Placid Baker G 518 326-2657 Troy *(G-16249)*

Presser Kosher Baking Corp E 718 375-5088 Brooklyn *(G-2439)*

Quaker Bonnet Inc G 716 885-7208 Buffalo *(G-3146)*

R & H Baking Co Inc E 718 852-1768 Brooklyn *(G-2470)*

Rambachs International Bakery F 518 563-1721 Plattsburgh *(G-13693)*

Rapacki & Sons F 516 538-3939 Lindenhurst *(G-7480)*

Rays Italian Bakery Inc F 516 825-9170 Valley Stream *(G-16423)*

▲ **Rays Restaurant & Bakery Inc** G 718 441-7707 Jamaica *(G-6945)*

Reisman Bros Bakery Inc F 718 331-1975 Brooklyn *(G-2488)*

Richard Engdal Baking Corp F 914 777-9600 Mamaroneck *(G-8044)*

Rm Bakery LLC E 718 472-3036 Maspeth *(G-8168)*

Rock Hill Bakehouse Ltd E 518 743-1627 Gansevoort *(G-5489)*

Rockland Bakery Inc D 845 623-5800 Nanuet *(G-8761)*

Roma Bakery Inc F 516 825-9170 Valley Stream *(G-16425)*

Roslyn Bread Company Inc E 516 625-1470 Roslyn Heights *(G-15031)*

Royal Caribbean Jamaican Bky E 914 668-6868 Mount Vernon *(G-8727)*

◆ **Royal Sweet Bakery Inc** F 718 567-7770 Brooklyn *(G-2514)*

Ruthys Cheesecake Rugelach Bky F 212 463-8800 New York *(G-11938)*

Saint Honore Pastry Shop Inc G 516 767-2555 Port Washington *(G-13861)*

Sandford Blvd Donuts Inc G 914 663-7708 Mount Vernon *(G-8730)*

Sapienza Pastry Inc E 516 352-5232 Elmont *(G-4729)*

▲ **Satispie LLC** E 716 982-4600 Rochester *(G-14670)*

Scaife Enterprises Inc F 585 454-5231 Rochester *(G-14672)*

Settepani Inc E 718 349-6524 Brooklyn *(G-2545)*

Slims Bagels Unlimited Inc E 718 229-1140 Oakland Gardens *(G-13067)*

Smith Street Bread Co LLC F 718 797-9712 Brooklyn *(G-2573)*

Soutine Inc G 212 496-1450 New York *(G-12145)*

Stebe Shcjhjff F 839 383-9833 Poughkeepsie *(G-13935)*

Sugarbear Cupcakes G 917 698-9005 Jamaica *(G-6953)*

▲ **Sullivan St Bky - Hlls Kit Inc** E 212 265-5580 New York *(G-12228)*

Sunrise Baking Co LLC C 718 499-0800 Brooklyn *(G-2621)*

Sunrise Bkg Acquisition Co LLC D 718 499-0800 Brooklyn *(G-2622)*

Sunshine Distribution Corp G 888 506-7051 New York *(G-12238)*

T&B Bakery Corp G 646 642-4300 Maspeth *(G-8172)*

Tarrytown Bakery Inc F 914 631-0209 Tarrytown *(G-16108)*

Tates Wholesale LLC C 631 780-6511 East Moriches *(G-4431)*

Tilaros Bakery Inc G 716 488-3209 Jamestown *(G-7038)*

Triboro Bagel Co Inc E 718 359-9245 Flushing *(G-5303)*

Two Sisters Kiev Bakery Inc G 718 769-2626 Brooklyn *(G-2692)*

Two Sisters Kiev Bakery Inc F 718 627-5438 Brooklyn *(G-2693)*

Uncle Wallys LLC E 631 205-0455 Shirley *(G-15430)*

Valencia Bakery Inc E 718 991-6400 Bronx *(G-1487)*

Village Lantern Baking Corp G 631 225-1690 Lindenhurst *(G-7494)*

Voila Sweets LLC B 718 366-1100 Brooklyn *(G-2734)*

Waldorf Bakers Inc F 718 665-2253 Bronx *(G-1492)*

▲ **Wenner Bread Products Inc** B 800 869-6262 Bayport *(G-761)*

Zaro Bake Shop Inc C 718 993-7327 Bronx *(G-1497)*

Zuckerbakers Inc F 516 785-6900 Wantagh *(G-16565)*

2052 Cookies & Crackers

17 Bakers LLC F 844 687-6836 Williamsville *(G-17230)*

212kiddish Inc G 718 705-7227 Brooklyn *(G-1512)*

AAA Noodle Products Mfg G 212 431-4090 New York *(G-8999)*

▲ **Alrajs Inc** E 631 225-0300 Lindenhurst *(G-7452)*

▲ **Aron Streit Inc** E 212 475-7000 New York *(G-9205)*

Aryzta LLC C 585 235-8160 Rochester *(G-14215)*

Biscuits & Bath Companies LLC E 212 401-3022 New York *(G-9404)*

Butterwood Desserts Inc E 716 652-0131 West Falls *(G-16844)*

Chipita America Inc E 845 292-2540 Ferndale *(G-5168)*

City Baking LLC G 718 392-8514 Long Island City *(G-7698)*

Cone Buddy System Inc F 585 427-9940 Rochester *(G-14285)*

Cookie Factory LLC E 518 268-1060 Troy *(G-16232)*

Cookie Pnache By Bet The Bread G 212 757-4145 New York *(G-9715)*

Cookies United LLC C 631 581-4000 Islip *(G-6807)*

Cooking With Chef Michelle LLC G 516 662-2324 Calverton *(G-3289)*

D F Stauffer Biscuit Co Inc E 585 968-2700 Cuba *(G-4068)*

Danny Macaroons Inc G 260 622-8463 New York *(G-9805)*

Decorated Cookie Company LLC E 315 487-2111 Syracuse *(G-15923)*

Doreen Chrysler F 607 257-2241 Ithaca *(G-6838)*

▲ **Elenis Nyc Inc** E 718 361-8136 Long Island City *(G-7729)*

Falcones Cookie Land Ltd G 718 236-4200 Brooklyn *(G-1955)*

Golden Glow Cookie Co Inc E 718 379-6223 Bronx *(G-1345)*

▲ **Great Brands of Europe Inc** G 914 872-8804 White Plains *(G-17114)*

Jonathan Lord Corp F 631 563-4445 Bohemia *(G-1085)*

▲ **Kaltec Food Packaging Inc** E 845 856-9888 Port Jervis *(G-13786)*

Keebler Company F 585 948-8010 Oakfield *(G-13065)*

Keebler Company E 631 234-3700 Hauppauge *(G-6103)*

Keebler Company E 518 464-1051 Albany *(G-94)*

Keebler Company E 845 365-5200 Orangeburg *(G-13232)*

▼ **La Vita Health Foods Ltd** G 845 368-4101 Suffern *(G-15793)*

Ladybird Bakery Inc G 718 499-8108 Brooklyn *(G-2190)*

▲ **Larte Del Gelato Inc** G 212 366-0570 New York *(G-10930)*

Linden Cookies Inc E 845 268-5050 Congers *(G-3859)*

Lloyd Price Icon Food Brands F 914 764-8624 Pound Ridge *(G-13944)*

Makkos of Brooklyn Ltd D 718 366-9800 Brooklyn *(G-2255)*

Maurybakes LLC E 646 722-6570 New York *(G-11182)*

McDuffies of Scotland Inc E 716 759-8510 Clarence *(G-3664)*

My Most Favorite Food G 212 580-5130 New York *(G-11331)*

New Mount Pleasant Bakery E 518 374-7577 Schenectady *(G-15281)*

One Girl Cookies Ltd F 212 675-4996 Brooklyn *(G-2392)*

Pdi Cone Co Inc D 716 825-8750 Buffalo *(G-3116)*

◆ **Pepsico Inc** A 914 253-2000 Purchase *(G-13966)*

Quaker Bonnet Inc G 716 885-7208 Buffalo *(G-3146)*

Sapienza Pastry Inc E 516 352-5232 Elmont *(G-4729)*

Treehouse Private Brands Inc C 716 693-4715 Tonawanda *(G-16208)*

U Serve Brands Inc G 212 286-2403 New York *(G-12439)*

United Baking Co Inc F 631 413-5116 Central Islip *(G-3513)*

United Baking Co Inc G 631 205-0455 Shirley *(G-15431)*

Wonton Food Inc E 718 784-8178 Long Island City *(G-7926)*

▲ **Wonton Food Inc** C 718 628-6868 Brooklyn *(G-2763)*

Zaro Bake Shop Inc C 718 993-7327 Bronx *(G-1497)*

2053 Frozen Bakery Prdts

Brooklyn Baby Cakes Inc G 917 334-2518 Brooklyn *(G-1720)*

Butterwood Desserts Inc E 716 652-0131 West Falls *(G-16844)*

▲ **Circle Peak Capital MGT LLC** E 646 230-8812 New York *(G-9620)*

Cobblestone Bakery Corp E 631 491-3777 Wyandanch *(G-17373)*

Culinary Arts Specialties Inc D 716 656-8943 Cheektowaga *(G-3566)*

Deiorio Foods Inc E 315 732-7612 Utica *(G-16322)*

Employee Codes: A=Over 500 employees, B=251-500 C=101-250, D=51-100, E=20-50, F=10-19, G=5-9

2017 Harris New York Manufacturers Directory

715

20 FOOD AND KINDRED PRODUCTS

Dufour Pastry Kitchens Inc ....E 718 402-8800
  Bronx *(G-1318)*
Fratellis LLC ....E 607 722-5663
  Binghamton *(G-915)*
Grannys Kitchens LLC ....B 315 735-5000
  Frankfort *(G-5354)*
Ko Fro Foods Inc ....E 718 972-6480
  Brooklyn *(G-2177)*
Liddabit Sweets ....G 917 912-1370
  Brooklyn *(G-2217)*
▼ Love & Quiches Ltd ....C 516 623-8800
  Freeport *(G-5409)*
Micosta Enterprises Inc ....G 518 822-9708
  Hudson *(G-6627)*
Pearl River Pastries LLC 845 735-5100
  West Nyack *(G-16923)*
◆ R E Rich Family Holding Corp ....D 716 878-8000
  Buffalo *(G-3152)*
◆ Rich Products Corporation ....A 716 878-8422
  Buffalo *(G-3157)*
Sugar & Plumm Upper West LLC ....D 201 334-1600
  New York *(G-12226)*
▲ Wenner Bread Products Inc ....B 800 869-6262
  Bayport *(G-761)*

2061 Sugar, Cane

▲ Supreme Chocolatier LLC ....E 718 761-9600
  Staten Island *(G-15744)*

2062 Sugar, Cane Refining

◆ Asr Group International Inc ....C 914 963-2400
  Yonkers *(G-17417)*
Cane Sugar LLC ....G 212 329-2695
  New York *(G-9513)*
▲ Sweeteners Plus Inc ....D 585 728-3770
  Lakeville *(G-7286)*

2063 Sugar, Beet

Beets Love Production LLC ....E 585 270-2471
  Rochester *(G-14228)*

2064 Candy & Confectionery Prdts

5th Avenue Chocolatiere Ltd ....F 516 561-1570
  Valley Stream *(G-16397)*
▲ 5th Avenue Chocolatiere Ltd ....G 212 935-5454
  Freeport *(G-5379)*
Aigner Chocolates Inc 718 544-1850
  Forest Hills *(G-5320)*
▲ Alrajs Inc ....E 631 225-0300
  Lindenhurst *(G-7452)*
Amiram Dror Inc ....F 212 979-9505
  Brooklyn *(G-1611)*
C Howard Company Inc ....G 631 286-7940
  Bellport *(G-827)*
▼ Calico Cottage Inc ....E 631 841-2100
  Amityville *(G-278)*
▲ Chocolat Moderne LLC ....G 212 229-4797
  New York *(G-9605)*
Chocolate Pizza Company Inc ....F 315 673-4098
  Marcellus *(G-8087)*
Chocolations LLC ....G 914 777-3600
  Mamaroneck *(G-8028)*
▲ Chocomaker Inc ....G 716 877-3146
  Buffalo *(G-2873)*
Custom Candy Concepts Inc ....F 516 824-3228
  Inwood *(G-6754)*
Dilese International Inc ....F 716 855-3500
  Buffalo *(G-2915)*
Dylans Candy Bar Inc 212 620-2700
  New York *(G-9946)*
Eatingevolved LLC ....F 631 675-2440
  Setauket *(G-15376)*
◆ Fairbanks Mfg LLC ....C 845 341-0002
  Middletown *(G-8440)*
Fine and Raw Chocolate ....G 718 366-3633
  Brooklyn *(G-1971)*
First Source LLC ....D 716 877-0800
  Tonawanda *(G-16162)*
Gertrude Hawk Chocolates Inc ....E
  Watertown *(G-16652)*
Glennys Inc ....G 516 377-1400
  Brooklyn *(G-2026)*
▲ Godiva Chocolatier Inc ....E 212 984-5900
  New York *(G-10326)*
Gravymaster Inc ....E 203 453-1893
  Canajoharie *(G-3332)*
Handsome Dans LLC ....G 917 965-2499
  New York *(G-10405)*

Hedonist Artisan Chocolates ....F 585 461-2815
  Rochester *(G-14432)*
Hercules Candy Co 315 463-4339
  East Syracuse *(G-4537)*
Hudson Valley Chocolatier Inc ....F 845 831-8240
  Beacon *(G-785)*
▼ In Room Plus Inc ....E 716 838-9433
  Buffalo *(G-3005)*
Jo-Mart Candies Corp ....F 718 375-1277
  Brooklyn *(G-2143)*
Joseph Shalhoub & Son Inc 718 871-6300
  Brooklyn *(G-2150)*
▲ Joyva Corp ....D 718 497-0170
  Brooklyn *(G-2154)*
Keep Healthy Inc ....F 631 651-9090
  Northport *(G-13013)*
Lady-N-Th-wndow Chocolates Inc ......F 631 549-1059
  Huntington *(G-6666)*
◆ Lanco Corporation ....C 631 231-2300
  Ronkonkoma *(G-14929)*
Little Bird Chocolates Inc ....G 646 620-6395
  Massapequa *(G-8180)*
Momn Pops Inc ....E 845 567-0640
  Cornwall *(G-3988)*
▲ Mrchocolatecom LLC ....F 718 875-9772
  Brooklyn *(G-2341)*
▲ N Make Mold Inc ....E 716 854-6050
  Buffalo *(G-3080)*
▼ Naples Vly Mrgers Acqstons LLC ....G 585 490-1339
  Naples *(G-8767)*
Noras Candy Shop ....F 315 337-4530
  Rome *(G-14825)*
Nycjbs LLC ....F 212 533-1888
  New York *(G-11481)*
OH How Cute Inc ....G 347 838-6031
  Staten Island *(G-15719)*
Papa Bubble ....G 212 966-2599
  New York *(G-11562)*
◆ Pfeil & Holing Inc ....D 718 545-4600
  Woodside *(G-17346)*
Premium Sweets USA Inc ....G 718 739-6000
  Jamaica *(G-6940)*
▲ Rajbhog Foods Inc ....E 718 358-5105
  Flushing *(G-5287)*
◆ Richardson Brands Company ....C 518 673-3553
  Canajoharie *(G-3333)*
Robert Pikcilingis 518 355-1860
  Altamont *(G-211)*
Roger L Urban Inc 716 693-5391
  North Tonawanda *(G-12992)*
Salty Road Inc ....G 347 673-3925
  Brooklyn *(G-2531)*
◆ Satin Fine Foods Inc ....F 845 469-1034
  Chester *(G-3615)*
▲ Scaccianoce Inc ....F 718 991-4462
  Bronx *(G-1449)*
Seaward Candies 585 638-6761
  Holley *(G-6492)*
▲ Settons Intl Foods Inc ....E 631 543-8090
  Commack *(G-3842)*
▲ Simply Natural Foods LLC ....E 631 543-9600
  Commack *(G-3843)*
Steve & Andys Organics Inc ....G 718 499-7933
  New York *(G-12199)*
Stones Homemade Candies Inc 315 343-8401
  Oswego *(G-13342)*
◆ Sweetworks Inc ....C 716 634-4545
  Buffalo *(G-3205)*
▲ Tomric Systems Inc ....G 716 854-6050
  Buffalo *(G-3221)*
Valenti Distributing 716 824-2304
  Blasdell *(G-968)*
▲ Vidal Candies USA Inc ....F 609 781-8169
  New York *(G-12541)*
◆ Vigneri Chocolate Inc ....G 585 254-6160
  Rochester *(G-14753)*
Wellspring Corp ....G 212 529-5454
  New York *(G-12609)*
Worlds Finest Chocolate Inc ....C 718 332-2442
  Brooklyn *(G-2767)*

2066 Chocolate & Cocoa Prdts

▲ 5th Avenue Chocolatiere Ltd ....G 212 935-5454
  Freeport *(G-5379)*
5th Avenue Chocolatiere Ltd ....F 516 561-1570
  Valley Stream *(G-16397)*
Adirondack Chocolate Co Ltd ....G 518 946-7270
  Wilmington *(G-17267)*
Aigner Chocolates Inc ....G 718 544-1850
  Forest Hills *(G-5320)*

Aletheas Chocolates Inc ....E 716 633-8620
  Williamsville *(G-17231)*
Amiram Dror Inc ....F 212 979-9505
  Brooklyn *(G-1611)*
◆ Associated Brands Inc ....B 585 798-3475
  New York *(G-9238)*
Big Heart Pet Brands 716 891-6566
  Buffalo *(G-2842)*
Cemoi Inc 212 583-4920
  New York *(G-9560)*
Choco Peanuts Inc 716 998-2353
  Buffalo *(G-2871)*
Chocolate By Design Inc 631 737-0082
  Ronkonkoma *(G-14887)*
Chocolate Pizza Company Inc ....F 315 673-4098
  Marcellus *(G-8087)*
▲ Chocomize Inc 718 729-3264
  Long Island City *(G-7697)*
Commodore Chocolatier USA Inc ......F 845 561-3960
  Newburgh *(G-12753)*
Ctac Holdings LLC ....E 212 924-2280
  Brooklyn *(G-1823)*
Dilese International Inc ....F 716 855-3500
  Buffalo *(G-2915)*
Dolce Vite International LLC 713 962-5767
  Brooklyn *(G-1870)*
Doma Marketing Inc ....G 516 684-1111
  Port Washington *(G-13811)*
Eating Evolved Inc 516 510-2601
  East Setauket *(G-4480)*
Emvi Inc 518 883-5111
  Broadalbin *(G-1241)*
Encore Chocolates Inc ....G 585 266-2970
  Rochester *(G-14350)*
▲ Ernex Corporation Inc 718 951-2251
  Brooklyn *(G-1933)*
Gnosis Chocolate Inc 646 688-5549
  Long Island City *(G-7751)*
▲ Godiva Chocolatier Inc 212 984-5900
  New York *(G-10326)*
Godiva Chocolatier Inc ....E 718 271-3603
  Elmhurst *(G-4661)*
Godiva Chocolatier Inc 718 677-1452
  Brooklyn *(G-2036)*
Godiva Chocolatier Inc 212 809-8990
  New York *(G-10327)*
Greenwood Winery LLC ....E 315 432-8132
  East Syracuse *(G-4534)*
H Fox & Co Inc ....E 718 385-4600
  Brooklyn *(G-2059)*
Hershey Kiss 203 Inc 516 503-3740
  Wantagh *(G-16557)*
▲ Jacques Torres Chocolate LLC 212 414-2462
  New York *(G-10693)*
Jo-Mart Candies Corp ....F 718 375-1277
  Brooklyn *(G-2143)*
▲ Joyva Corp ....D 718 497-0170
  Brooklyn *(G-2154)*
Lady-N-Th-wndow Chocolates Inc ......F 631 549-1059
  Huntington *(G-6666)*
◆ Lanco Corporation ....C 631 231-2300
  Ronkonkoma *(G-14929)*
Landies Candies Co Inc ....F 716 834-8212
  Buffalo *(G-3046)*
Le Chocolat LLC 845 352-8301
  Monsey *(G-8572)*
▲ Le Chocolate of Rockland LLC ......E 845 533-4125
  Suffern *(G-15794)*
Lindt & Sprungli (usa) Inc ....G 212 582-3047
  New York *(G-11000)*
▲ Madelaine Chocolate Novlt Inc ......D 718 945-1500
  Rockaway Beach *(G-14782)*
Madisons Delight LLC ....E 718 720-8900
  Staten Island *(G-15702)*
Mast Brothers Inc 718 388-2625
  Brooklyn *(G-2280)*
▲ Max Brenner Union Square LLC ....G 646 467-8803
  New York *(G-11186)*
Mbny LLC ....F 646 467-8810
  New York *(G-11192)*
Micosta Enterprises Inc ....G 518 822-9708
  Hudson *(G-6627)*
Momn Pops Inc ....E 845 567-0640
  Cornwall *(G-3988)*
New York Chocolatier Inc ....G 516 561-1570
  Valley Stream *(G-16415)*
Nibmor Project LLC ....F 718 374-5091
  Great Neck *(G-5823)*
Noras Candy Shop ....F 315 337-4530
  Rome *(G-14825)*

Parkside Candy Co Inc ....F 716 833-7540
Buffalo *(G-3114)*
▲ Prime Marketing and Sales LLC ....G 888 802-3836
New York *(G-11707)*
▲ Reserve Confections Inc ....F 845 371-7744
Monsey *(G-8578)*
Robert Pikcilingis ....F 518 355-1860
Altamont *(G-211)*
Roger L Urban Inc ....E 716 693-5391
North Tonawanda *(G-12992)*
◆ Settons Intl Foods Inc ....E 631 543-8090
Commack *(G-3842)*
▲ Simply Natural Foods LLC ....E 631 543-9600
Commack *(G-3843)*
◆ Simplycultivated Group LLC ....G 646 389-0682
Horseheads *(G-6594)*
▲ Superior Confections Inc ....D 718 698-3300
Staten Island *(G-15743)*
▲ Sweetriot Inc ....G 212 431-7468
New York *(G-12254)*
◆ Sweetworks Inc ....C 716 634-4545
Buffalo *(G-3205)*
The Chocolate Shop ....G 716 882-5055
Buffalo *(G-3215)*
Yes Were Nuts Ltd ....G 516 374-1940
Hewlett *(G-6317)*

2067 Chewing Gum

▲ Ford Gum & Machine Company Inc .D 716 542-4561
Akron *(G-22)*
Simply Gum Inc ....F 917 721-8032
New York *(G-12083)*
◆ Sweetworks Inc ....C 716 634-4545
Buffalo *(G-3205)*

2068 Salted & Roasted Nuts & Seeds

◆ American Almond Pdts Co Inc ....E 718 875-8310
Brooklyn *(G-1599)*
Choco Peanuts Inc ....G 716 998-2353
Buffalo *(G-2871)*
Our Daily Eats LLC ....F 518 810-8412
Albany *(G-113)*
▲ Peeled Inc ....G 212 706-2001
Brooklyn *(G-2412)*
◆ Sahadi Fine Foods Inc ....E 718 369-0100
Brooklyn *(G-2530)*
▲ Scaccianoce Inc ....F 718 991-4462
Bronx *(G-1449)*
◆ Settons Intl Foods Inc ....E 631 543-8090
Commack *(G-3842)*
▼ Sugar Foods Corporation ....E 212 753-6900
New York *(G-12227)*
Whitsons Food Svc Bronx Corp ....B 631 424-2700
Islandia *(G-6804)*

2074 Cottonseed Oil Mills

Perimondo LLC ....G 212 749-0721
New York *(G-11618)*

2075 Soybean Oil Mills

Cayuga Enterprise 21 ....G 607 441-9166
Manlius *(G-8069)*

2076 Vegetable Oil Mills

▲ Jax Coco USA LLC ....G 347 688-8198
New York *(G-10703)*

2077 Animal, Marine Fats & Oils

Baker Commodities Inc ....E 585 482-1880
Rochester *(G-14222)*

2079 Shortening, Oils & Margarine

▲ Bonelli Foods LLC ....G 212 346-0942
New York *(G-9436)*
Bunge Limited Finance Corp ....C 914 684-2800
White Plains *(G-17089)*
C B S Food Products Corp ....F 718 452-2500
Brooklyn *(G-1743)*
Consumer Flavoring Extract Co ....F 718 435-0201
Brooklyn *(G-1798)*
F Olivers LLC ....G 585 244-2585
Rochester *(G-14367)*
▲ Healthy Brand Oil Corp ....E 718 937-0806
Long Island City *(G-7757)*
▼ Kerry Inc ....D 607 334-1700
Norwich *(G-13029)*
L LLC ....E 716 885-3918
Buffalo *(G-3039)*
▲ Pietro Demarco Importers Inc ....F 914 969-3201
Yonkers *(G-17477)*
Pinos Press Inc ....G 315 935-0110
Syracuse *(G-16013)*

2082 Malt Beverages

Anheuser-Busch LLC ....C 315 638-0365
Baldwinsville *(G-566)*
Anheuser-Busch LLC ....C 212 573-8800
New York *(G-9159)*
Anheuser-Busch Companies LLC ....G 718 589-2610
Bronx *(G-1276)*
Anheuser-Busch Inbev Fin Inc ....G 212 573-8800
New York *(G-9160)*
Barrier Brewing Company LLC ....G 516 316-4429
Long Beach *(G-7638)*
Black River Brewing Co Inc ....G 315 755-2739
Watertown *(G-16639)*
Brazen Street LLC ....E 516 305-7951
Brooklyn *(G-1713)*
▲ Brewery Ommegang Ltd ....E 607 286-4144
Cooperstown *(G-3883)*
▲ Castle Brands Inc ....D 646 356-0200
New York *(G-9542)*
Catskill Mtn Brewing Co Inc ....D 845 256-1700
New Paltz *(G-8874)*
◆ Constellation Brands Inc ....D 585 678-7100
Victor *(G-16469)*
Coopers Cave Ale Co S-Corp ....F 518 792-0007
Glens Falls *(G-5676)*
Cooperstown Brewing Co LLC ....G 607 286-9330
Milford *(G-8473)*
Custom Brewcrafters Inc ....F 585 624-4386
Honeoye Falls *(G-6526)*
Decrescente Distributing Co ....D 518 664-9866
Mechanicville *(G-8226)*
Duvel Mortgage USA Inc ....G 607 267-6121
Cooperstown *(G-3885)*
Empire Brewing Company Inc ....D 315 925-8308
Syracuse *(G-15935)*
▲ High Falls Brewing Company LLC ...C 585 546-1030
Rochester *(G-14434)*
High Falls Operating Co LLC ....A 585 546-1030
Rochester *(G-14435)*
Hoptron Brewtique ....G 631 438-0296
Patchogue *(G-13422)*
Hornell Brewing Co Inc ....G 914 597-7911
White Plains *(G-17122)*
Horseheads Brewing Inc ....G 607 734-8055
Lowman *(G-7934)*
Hyde Park Brewing Co Inc ....E 845 229-8277
Hyde Park *(G-6734)*
Indian Ladder Farmstead Brewer ....G 518 577-1484
Altamont *(G-208)*
Ithaca Beer Company Inc ....E 607 272-1305
Ithaca *(G-6853)*
Keegan Ales LLC ....F 845 331-2739
Kingston *(G-7192)*
Keuka Brewing Co LLC ....G 607 868-4648
Hammondsport *(G-5957)*
▲ Labatt USA LLC ....D 716 604-1050
Buffalo *(G-3041)*
Long Ireland Brewing LLC ....G 631 403-4303
Riverhead *(G-14147)*
▲ Mad Scntsts Brwing Prtners LLC ....E 347 766-2739
Brooklyn *(G-2251)*
▲ Marnier-Lapostolle Inc ....D 212 207-4350
New York *(G-11164)*
▲ Middle Ages Brewing Company ....G 315 476-4250
Syracuse *(G-15987)*
Millercoors LLC ....E 585 385-0670
Pittsford *(G-13570)*
Montauk Brewing Company Inc ....F 631 668-8471
Montauk *(G-8589)*
Newburgh Brewing Company LLC ....F 845 569-2337
Newburgh *(G-12769)*
▼ North American Breweries Inc ....F 585 546-1030
Rochester *(G-14539)*
North Amrcn Brwries Hldngs LLC ....E 585 546-1030
Rochester *(G-14542)*
▲ North Country Malt Supply LLC ....G 518 298-2300
Champlain *(G-3545)*
Olde Saratoga Brewing ....F 518 581-0492
Saratoga Springs *(G-15165)*
Paradox Brewery LLC ....G 518 351-5036
Schroon Lake *(G-15318)*
Rising Sons 6 Brewing Coinc ....G 607 368-4836
Corning *(G-3979)*
Uptown Local ....F 212 988-1704
New York *(G-12475)*
Vanberg & Dewulf Co Inc ....G 607 547-8184
Cooperstown *(G-3886)*
Wagner Vineyards & Brewing Co ....E 607 582-6574
Lodi *(G-7636)*
Woodcock Brothers Brewing Comp ....G 716 333-4000
Wilson *(G-17270)*
Yonkers Whl Beer Distrs Inc ....G 914 963-8600
Yonkers *(G-17504)*

2083 Malt

▲ Great Western Malting Co ....G 800 496-7732
Champlain *(G-3541)*

2084 Wine & Brandy

Americana Vineyards & Winery ....F 607 387-6801
Interlaken *(G-6746)*
Anyelas Vineyards LLC ....F 315 685-3797
Skaneateles *(G-15455)*
Arrowhead Spring Vineyards LLC ....G 716 434-8030
Lockport *(G-7570)*
Atwater Estate Vineyards LLC ....E 607 546-8463
Burdett *(G-3264)*
Billsboro Winery ....G 315 789-9538
Geneva *(G-5570)*
Brooklyn Winery ....F 347 763-1506
Brooklyn *(G-1734)*
▲ Brotherhood Amer Oldest Wnery ....E 845 496-3661
Washingtonville *(G-16599)*
Casa Larga Vineyards ....G 585 223-4210
Fairport *(G-4850)*
Casa Larga Vineyards ....G 585 223-4210
Fairport *(G-4851)*
Cascade Mountain Winery & Rest ....F 845 373-9021
Amenia *(G-215)*
▲ Cava Spiliadis USA ....E 212 247-8214
New York *(G-9551)*
Chautauqua Wine Company Inc ....G 716 934-9463
Silver Creek *(G-15447)*
Clinton Vineyards Inc ....G 845 266-5372
Clinton Corners *(G-3724)*
Cobblestone Frm Winery Vinyrd ....F 315 549-1004
Romulus *(G-14841)*
◆ Constellation Brands Inc ....D 585 678-7100
Victor *(G-16469)*
Constellation Brands Inc ....E 585 393-4880
Canandaigua *(G-3339)*
Constellation Brands Smo LLC ....G 585 396-7161
New York *(G-9707)*
Constellation Brands US Oprs ....A 585 396-7600
Canandaigua *(G-3340)*
◆ Constellation Brands US Oprs ....B 585 396-7600
Canandaigua *(G-3341)*
Coyote Moon LLC ....F 315 686-5600
Clayton *(G-3685)*
▼ Cruzin Management Inc ....E 212 641-8700
New York *(G-9761)*
Deer Run Enterprises Inc ....G 585 346-0850
Geneseo *(G-5565)*
Di Borghese Castello LLC ....F 631 734-5111
Cutchogue *(G-4071)*
▲ Dorset Farms Inc ....F 631 734-6010
Peconic *(G-13470)*
Dr Pepper Snapple Group Inc ....C 315 589-4911
Williamson *(G-17222)*
▲ Dreyfus Ashby Inc ....E 212 818-0770
New York *(G-9929)*
Duck Walk Vinyards ....E 631 726-7555
Water Mill *(G-16605)*
Dutch Spirits LLC ....F 518 398-1022
Pine Plains *(G-13555)*
Dutchess Wines LLC ....G 845 876-1319
Rhinebeck *(G-14056)*
▲ Eagle Crest Vineyard LLC ....G 585 346-5760
Conesus *(G-3850)*
East Branch Winery Inc ....G 607 292-3999
Dundee *(G-4326)*
▲ East End Vineyards LLC ....G 718 468-0500
Queens Village *(G-13976)*
Edrington Group Usa LLC ....E 212 352-6000
New York *(G-9983)*
Fox Run Vineyards Inc ....F 315 536-4616
Penn Yan *(G-13512)*
Frank Wines Inc ....G 646 765-6637
New York *(G-10203)*
Freedom Run Winery Inc ....G 716 433-4136
Lockport *(G-7587)*
▲ Gabriella Importers Inc ....G 212 579-3945
Bohemia *(G-1070)*
Gabriella Importers Inc ....F 212 579-3945
New York *(G-10238)*

Employee Codes: A=Over 500 employees, B=251-500
C=101-250, D=51-100, E=20-50, F=10-19, G=5-9
2017 Harris
New York Manufacturers Directory
717

20 FOOD AND KINDRED PRODUCTS SIC SECTION

Glenora Wine Cellars Inc........E....... 607 243-9500
Dundee *(G-4328)*
Grapes & Grains........G....... 518 283-9463
Rensselaer *(G-14046)*
Greenwood Winery LLC........E....... 315 432-8132
East Syracuse *(G-4534)*
Hazlitts 1852 Vineyards Inc........E....... 607 546-9463
Hector *(G-6257)*
▲ **Hermann J Wiemer Vineyard**........G....... 607 243-7971
Dundee *(G-4329)*
Heron Hill Vineyards Inc........E....... 607 868-4241
Hammondsport *(G-5956)*
Hickory Road Land Co LLC........G....... 607 243-9114
Dundee *(G-4330)*
Hoffman & Hoffman........G....... 315 536-4773
Penn Yan *(G-13514)*
Hosmer Inc........F....... 888 467-9463
Ovid *(G-13346)*
Hunt Country Vineyards........E....... 315 595-2812
Branchport *(G-1172)*
▲ **J Petrocelli Wine Cellars LLC**........E....... 631 765-1100
Peconic *(G-13471)*
Joseph Zakon Winery Ltd........G....... 718 604-1430
Brooklyn *(G-2151)*
▲ **Konstantin D FRAnk& Sons Vini**......E....... 607 868-4884
Hammondsport *(G-5958)*
L & D Acquisition LLC........F....... 585 531-9000
Naples *(G-8765)*
Lafayette Chateau........E....... 607 546-2062
Hector *(G-6258)*
▲ **Lakewood Vineyards Inc**........F....... 607 535-9252
Watkins Glen *(G-16695)*
Lamoreaux Landing WI........D....... 607 582-6162
Lodi *(G-7635)*
▲ **Levindi**........F....... 212 572-7000
New York *(G-10978)*
Lieb Cellars LLC........E....... 631 298-1942
Mattituck *(G-8207)*
Lucas Vineyards & Winery........F....... 607 532-4825
Interlaken *(G-6748)*
Malina Management Company Inc........E....... 607 535-9614
Montour Falls *(G-8610)*
Merritt Estate Winery Inc........F....... 716 965-4800
Forestville *(G-5334)*
▲ **Millbrook Winery Inc**........F....... 845 677-8383
Millbrook *(G-8478)*
Montezuma Winery LLC........G....... 315 568-8190
Seneca Falls *(G-15366)*
Mount Gay Rum........G....... 212 399-4200
New York *(G-11312)*
Negys New Land Vinyrd Winery........G....... 315 585-4432
Geneva *(G-5583)*
▲ **North House Vineyards Inc**........G....... 631 779-2817
Jamesport *(G-6966)*
Olde Chtqua Vneyards Ltd Lblty........F....... 716 792-2749
Portland *(G-13873)*
▲ **Paumanok Vineyards Ltd**........E....... 631 722-8800
Aquebogue *(G-385)*
Pellegrini Vineyards LLC........G....... 631 734-4111
Cutchogue *(G-4072)*
Pindar Vineyards LLC........E....... 631 734-6200
Peconic *(G-13472)*
▲ **Pinnacle Wine Vault LLC**........G....... 212 736-0040
New York *(G-11665)*
Prejean Winery Inc........F....... 315 536-7524
Penn Yan *(G-13516)*
▲ **Premium Wine Group LLC**........E....... 631 298-1900
Mattituck *(G-8209)*
Pugliese Vineyards Inc........G....... 631 734-4057
Cutchogue *(G-4073)*
Quinn and Co of NY Ltd........E....... 212 868-1900
New York *(G-11774)*
Red Newt Cellars Inc........F....... 607 546-4100
Hector *(G-6260)*
Red Tail Ridge Inc........G....... 315 536-4580
Penn Yan *(G-13517)*
Rock Stream Vineyards........G....... 607 243-8322
Rock Stream *(G-14779)*
Royal Wine Corporation........F....... 845 236-4000
Marlboro *(G-8106)*
Sheldrake Point Vineyard LLC........F....... 607 532-8967
Ovid *(G-13348)*
▲ **Shinn Winery LLC**........G....... 631 804-0367
Mattituck *(G-8210)*
SMK Wines & Liquors LLC........G....... 212 685-7651
New York *(G-12106)*
Sokolin LLC........E....... 631 537-4434
Yaphank *(G-17403)*
▲ **Solstars Inc**........G....... 212 605-0430
New York *(G-12126)*
Spanish Artisan Wine Group LLC........G....... 914 414-6982
Patterson *(G-13444)*
Standing Stone Vineyards........G....... 607 582-6051
Hector *(G-6261)*
Swedish Hill Vineyard Inc........D....... 607 403-0029
Romulus *(G-14844)*
Thirsty Owl Wine Company........G....... 607 869-5805
Ovid *(G-13349)*
Thousand Islands Winery LLC........E....... 315 482-9306
Alexandria Bay *(G-192)*
Tickle Hill Winery........G....... 607 546-7740
Hector *(G-6262)*
Trader Joes Company........E....... 212 529-6326
New York *(G-12388)*
Vedell North Fork LLC........G....... 631 323-3526
Cutchogue *(G-4074)*
▲ **Vindagra USA Incorporated**........G....... 516 605-1960
Hicksville *(G-6398)*
Wagner Vineyards & Brewing Co........E....... 607 582-6574
Lodi *(G-7636)*
Westchester Wine Warehouse LLC........F....... 914 824-1400
White Plains *(G-17185)*
Wine Group Inc........D....... 716 326-3151
Westfield *(G-17055)*
Wine Market........G....... 516 328-8800
New Hyde Park *(G-8872)*
Wine Services Inc........G....... 631 722-3800
Riverhead *(G-14160)*
▲ **Wolffer Estate Vineyard Inc**........E....... 631 537-5106
Sagaponack *(G-15082)*
Woodbury Vineyards Inc........G....... 716 679-9463
Fredonia *(G-5377)*

2085 Liquors, Distilled, Rectified & Blended

Braided Oak Spirits LLC........F....... 845 381-1525
Middletown *(G-8429)*
▲ **Castle Brands Inc**........D....... 646 356-0200
New York *(G-9542)*
◆ **Constellation Brands Inc**........D....... 585 678-7100
Victor *(G-16469)*
▼ **Cruzin Management Inc**........E....... 212 641-8700
New York *(G-9761)*
Dutch Spirits LLC........F....... 518 398-1022
Pine Plains *(G-13555)*
Evolution Spirits Inc........G....... 917 543-7880
New York *(G-10094)*
Finger Lakes Distilling........F....... 607 546-5510
Burdett *(G-3265)*
Honeoye Falls Distillery LLC........F....... 201 780-4618
Honeoye Falls *(G-6531)*
▲ **Leblon Holdings LLC**........E....... 212 741-2675
New York *(G-10953)*
Leblon LLC........F....... 954 649-0148
New York *(G-10954)*
▲ **Leblon LLC**........E....... 786 281-5672
New York *(G-10955)*
▲ **Levindi**........F....... 212 572-7000
New York *(G-10978)*
Long Island Spirits Inc........F....... 631 630-9322
Calverton *(G-3292)*
Madison County Distillery LLC........G....... 315 391-6070
Cazenovia *(G-3448)*
▲ **Marnier-Lapostolle Inc**........D....... 212 207-4350
New York *(G-11164)*
Mount Gay Rum........G....... 212 399-4200
New York *(G-11312)*
◆ **Pernod Ricard Usa LLC**........D....... 914 848-4800
New York *(G-11621)*
Prohibition Distillery LLC........G....... 917 685-8989
Roscoe *(G-15011)*
Riazul Imports LLC........F....... 713 894-9177
New York *(G-11860)*
▲ **Russian Standard Vodka USA Inc**....G....... 212 679-1894
New York *(G-11937)*
▲ **Sovereign Brands LLC**........G....... 212 343-8366
New York *(G-12146)*
▲ **Tuthilltown Spirits LLC**........F....... 845 255-1527
Gardiner *(G-5551)*

2086 Soft Drinks

3v Company Inc........E....... 718 858-7333
Brooklyn *(G-1517)*
▲ **Adirondack Beverage Co Inc**........A....... 518 370-3621
Schenectady *(G-15227)*
American Bottling Company........F....... 516 714-0002
Ronkonkoma *(G-14868)*
Ariesun Inc........E....... 866 274-3049
Mount Vernon *(G-8663)*
▼ **Arizona Beverage Company LLC**.....G....... 516 812-0300
Woodbury *(G-17282)*
Ba Sports Nutrition LLC........B....... 310 424-5077
Whitestone *(G-17202)*
Beverage Works Incorporated........G....... 718 834-0500
Brooklyn *(G-1691)*
Beverage Works Nj Inc........E....... 631 293-3501
Farmingdale *(G-4953)*
Beverage Works Ny Inc........E....... 718 812-2034
Brooklyn *(G-1692)*
Big Geyser Inc........G....... 631 549-4940
Melville *(G-8297)*
▲ **Blue Star Beverages Corp**........G....... 718 381-3535
Brooklyn *(G-1704)*
Borabora Fruit Juices Inc........G....... 845 795-1027
Highland *(G-6403)*
Bottling Group LLC........E....... 315 788-6751
Watertown *(G-16640)*
Bottling Group LLC........B....... 800 789-2626
White Plains *(G-17086)*
◆ **Bottling Group LLC**........G....... 914 767-6000
White Plains *(G-17087)*
▲ **Boylan Bottling Co Inc**........E....... 800 289-7978
New York *(G-9447)*
▲ **Brands Within Reach LLC**........E....... 847 720-9090
Mamaroneck *(G-8025)*
Brave Chefs Incorporated........G....... 347 956-5905
Little Neck *(G-7507)*
◆ **Brooklyn Btlg Milton NY Inc**........C....... 845 795-2171
Milton *(G-8482)*
Cheribundi Inc........E....... 800 699-0460
Geneva *(G-5573)*
Chohehco LLC........G....... 315 420-4624
Skaneateles *(G-15457)*
◆ **Cliffstar LLC**........A....... 716 366-6100
Dunkirk *(G-4337)*
Clintons Ditch Coop Co Inc........C....... 315 699-2695
Cicero *(G-3643)*
Coca-Cola Bottling Co of NY........F....... 518 459-2010
Albany *(G-68)*
Coca-Cola Bottling Company........E....... 518 483-0422
Malone *(G-8008)*
▲ **Coca-Cola Btlg Co Buffalo Inc**........C....... 716 874-4610
Tonawanda *(G-16154)*
Coca-Cola Btlg Co of NY Inc........F....... 845 562-3037
New Windsor *(G-8936)*
Coca-Cola Btlg Co of NY Inc........C....... 718 326-3334
Maspeth *(G-8122)*
Coca-Cola Btlg Co of NY Inc........F....... 914 592-4574
Elmsford *(G-4741)*
Coca-Cola Btlg Co of NY Inc........F....... 315 457-9221
Syracuse *(G-15900)*
Coca-Cola Btlg Co of NY Inc........E....... 718 416-7575
Maspeth *(G-8123)*
Coca-Cola Btlg Co of NY Inc........E....... 631 434-3535
Hauppauge *(G-6048)*
Coca-Cola Btlg Co of NY Inc........F....... 718 420-6800
Staten Island *(G-15660)*
Coca-Cola Btlg Co of NY Inc........F....... 914 789-1580
Elmsford *(G-4742)*
Coca-Cola Refreshments USA Inc........E....... 718 401-5200
Bronx *(G-1301)*
Coca-Cola Refreshments USA Inc........E....... 315 785-8907
Watertown *(G-16646)*
Coca-Cola Refreshments USA Inc........G....... 914 592-0806
Hawthorne *(G-6245)*
Consumers Beverages Inc........E....... 716 837-3087
Buffalo *(G-2887)*
Consumers Beverages Inc........G....... 716 675-4934
West Seneca *(G-16942)*
Cornell Beverages Inc........F....... 718 381-3000
Brooklyn *(G-1804)*
Crystal Rock LLC........E....... 716 626-7460
Buffalo *(G-2894)*
Doheny Nice and Easy........G....... 518 793-1733
Glens Falls *(G-5677)*
Dr Pepper Snapple Group Inc........C....... 315 589-4911
Williamson *(G-17222)*
Dr Pepper Snapple Group Inc........D....... 914 846-2300
Elmsford *(G-4747)*
Dr Pepper Snapple Group Inc........G....... 718 246-6200
Brooklyn *(G-1877)*
East Coast Cultures LLC........F....... 917 261-3010
Kingston *(G-7188)*
▼ **Energy Brands Inc**........D....... 212 545-6000
New York *(G-10037)*
F & V Distribution Company LLC........G....... 516 812-0393
Woodbury *(G-17286)*
Fancy Flamingo LLC........G....... 516 209-7306
New York *(G-10134)*
Framedcom........E....... 212 400-2200
New York *(G-10197)*

SIC SECTION 20 FOOD AND KINDRED PRODUCTS

Gangi Distributors Inc F 718 442-5745 Staten Island *(G-15676)*

General Cinema Bevs of Ohio A 914 767-6000 Somers *(G-15509)*

Global Brands Inc G 845 358-1212 Nyack *(G-13052)*

▲ **Goodo Beverage Company** F 347 226-9996 Bronx *(G-1346)*

Grayhawk Leasing LLC G 914 767-6000 Somers *(G-15510)*

◆ **Hain Celestial Group Inc** C 516 587-5000 New Hyde Park *(G-8837)*

Heart of Tea F 917 725-3164 New York *(G-10450)*

Hmo Beverage Corp G 917 371-6100 Brooklyn *(G-2081)*

Hydrive Energy G 914 925-9100 Rye *(G-15060)*

Johnnie Ryan Co Inc F 716 282-1606 Niagara Falls *(G-12838)*

Juices Enterprises Inc G 718 953-1860 Brooklyn *(G-2158)*

Just Beverages LLC G 480 388-1133 Glens Falls *(G-5683)*

Kraft Heinz Foods Company A 914 335-2500 Tarrytown *(G-16093)*

La Cola 1 Inc G 917 509-6669 New York *(G-10907)*

Let Water Be Water LLC G 212 627-2630 New York *(G-10976)*

▲ **Levindi** F 212 572-7000 New York *(G-10978)*

Linda Wine & Spirit G 718 703-5707 Brooklyn *(G-2225)*

▲ **Liquid Management Partners LLC** F 516 775-5050 New Hyde Park *(G-8846)*

Load/N/Go Beverage Corp F 585 218-4019 Rochester *(G-14481)*

Long Island Brand Bevs LLC D 855 542-2832 Long Island City *(G-7794)*

Long Island Iced Tea Corp E 855 542-2832 Hicksville *(G-6365)*

Manhattan Special Bottling F 718 388-4144 Brooklyn *(G-2261)*

▲ **Mayer Bros Apple Products Inc** D 716 668-1787 West Seneca *(G-16952)*

Meadowbrook Distributing Corp D 516 226-9000 Garden City *(G-5520)*

Mnm Service Distributors Inc G 914 337-5268 Bronxville *(G-1501)*

Monfefo LLC G 347 779-2600 Brooklyn *(G-2331)*

N Y Winstons Inc G 212 665-3166 New York *(G-11337)*

Nantucket Allserve Inc B 914 612-4000 Elmsford *(G-4770)*

New York Bottling Co Inc F 718 963-3232 Bronx *(G-1408)*

▲ **New York Spring Water Inc** E 212 777-4649 New York *(G-11408)*

▲ **Nirvana Inc** C 315 942-4900 Forestport *(G-5331)*

Pepsi Beverages Co G 518 782-2150 Latham *(G-7374)*

Pepsi Bottling Holdings Inc F 800 433-2652 Purchase *(G-13963)*

Pepsi Bottling Ventures LLC D 631 772-6144 Patchogue *(G-13432)*

Pepsi Bottling Ventures LLC E 631 226-9000 Amityville *(G-321)*

Pepsi Btlg Group Globl Fin LLC G 914 767-6000 Somers *(G-15511)*

Pepsi Cola Buffalo Btlg Corp B 716 684-2800 Cheektowaga *(G-3585)*

Pepsi Lipton Tea Partnership E 914 253-2000 Purchase *(G-13964)*

▲ **Pepsi-Cola Allied Bottlers** A 518 783-8811 Latham *(G-7375)*

Pepsi-Cola Bottling Co NY Inc B 718 649-2465 College Point *(G-3800)*

Pepsi-Cola Bottling Co NY Inc E 914 699-2600 Mount Vernon *(G-8714)*

Pepsi-Cola Bottling Co NY Inc G 718 786-8550 Maspeth *(G-8165)*

Pepsi-Cola Bottling Co NY Inc D 718 892-1570 Bronx *(G-1424)*

Pepsi-Cola Bottling Co NY Inc B 718 392-1000 College Point *(G-3801)*

◆ **Pepsi-Cola Bottling Group** G 914 767-6000 White Plains *(G-17151)*

◆ **Pepsi-Cola Metro Btlg Co Inc** G 914 767-6000 White Plains *(G-17152)*

Pepsi-Cola Metro Btlg Co Inc E 914 253-2000 Purchase *(G-13965)*

Pepsi-Cola Metro Btlg Co Inc D 607 795-1399 Horseheads *(G-6587)*

Pepsi-Cola Newburgh Btlg Inc C 845 562-5400 Newburgh *(G-12774)*

Pepsi-Cola Operating Company E 914 767-6000 White Plains *(G-17153)*

Pepsico F 419 252-0247 Hawthorne *(G-6252)*

Pepsico E 914 801-1500 Valhalla *(G-16369)*

Pepsico Inc B 914 742-4500 Valhalla *(G-16370)*

Pepsico Inc A 914 253-2000 Purchase *(G-13967)*

Pepsico Inc F 914 253-2713 Purchase *(G-13968)*

◆ **Pepsico Inc** A 914 253-2000 Purchase *(G-13966)*

Pepsico Capital Resources Inc G 914 253-2000 Purchase *(G-13969)*

Pepsico World Trading Co Inc G 914 767-6000 White Plains *(G-17157)*

Purely Maple LLC F 203 997-9309 New York *(G-11753)*

▲ **Quench It Inc** E 845 462-5400 Poughkeepsie *(G-13927)*

Rochester Coca Cola Bottling E 607 739-5678 Horseheads *(G-6591)*

Rochester Coca Cola Bottling D 585 546-3900 Rochester *(G-14638)*

Saratoga Spring Water Company E 518 584-6363 Saratoga Springs *(G-15171)*

Save More Beverage Corp G 518 371-2520 Halfmoon *(G-5916)*

Shopping Center Wine & Liquor G 914 528-1600 Mohegan Lake *(G-8544)*

Snapp Too Enterprise G 718 224-5252 Flushing *(G-5293)*

Snapple G 914 846-2300 Elmsford *(G-4786)*

Stewarts Processing Corp D 518 581-1200 Ballston Spa *(G-610)*

Street King LLC G 212 400-2200 New York *(G-12212)*

Superleaf LLC G 607 280-9198 Brooklyn *(G-2629)*

Switch Beverage Company LLC F 203 202-7383 Port Washington *(G-13867)*

Treo Brands LLC G 914 341-1850 Harrison *(G-5992)*

Tumeric Healing Entps Inc F 508 364-7597 New York *(G-12422)*

Water Resources Group LLC G 631 824-9088 Cold Spring Harbor *(G-3771)*

2087 Flavoring Extracts & Syrups

3v Company Inc E 718 858-7333 Brooklyn *(G-1517)*

Agua Enerviva LLC F 516 597-5440 Bethpage *(G-864)*

◆ **American Almond Pdts Co Inc** E 718 875-8310 Brooklyn *(G-1599)*

Baldwin Richardson Foods Co C 315 986-2727 Macedon *(G-7983)*

Better Fresh Corp G 718 628-3682 Brooklyn *(G-1690)*

▲ **Boylan Bottling Co Inc** E 800 289-7978 New York *(G-9447)*

▲ **Buffalo Blends Inc** E 716 825-4422 Buffalo *(G-2849)*

▼ **Carriage House Companies Inc** A 716 672-4321 Fredonia *(G-5371)*

▲ **Citrus and Allied Essences Ltd** E 516 354-1200 Floral Park *(G-5200)*

◆ **Constellation Brands Inc** D 585 678-7100 Victor *(G-16469)*

Consumer Flavoring Extract Co F 718 435-0201 Brooklyn *(G-1798)*

Craftmaster Flavor Technology F 631 789-8607 Amityville *(G-283)*

Danisco US Inc D 585 277-4300 Rochester *(G-14301)*

◆ **Delbia Do Company Inc** G 718 585-2226 Bronx *(G-1312)*

Delbia Do Company Inc F 718 585-2226 Bronx *(G-1313)*

Dr Pepper Snapple Group Inc C 315 589-4911 Williamson *(G-17222)*

DSM Nutritional Products LLC C 518 372-5155 Glenville *(G-5701)*

▼ **Flavormatic Industries Inc** E 845 297-9100 Wappingers Falls *(G-16567)*

◆ **Fortitech Inc** C 518 372-5155 Schenectady *(G-15255)*

H Fox & Co Inc E 718 385-4600 Brooklyn *(G-2059)*

Iff International Inc E 212 765-5500 New York *(G-10560)*

◆ **Interntnal Flvors Frgrnces Inc** C 212 765-5500 New York *(G-10639)*

◆ **Motts LLP** C 972 673-8088 Elmsford *(G-4767)*

Mr Smoothie G 845 296-1686 Poughkeepsie *(G-13919)*

Natural Organics Laboratories B 631 957-5600 Amityville *(G-315)*

Osf Flavors Inc F 860 298-8350 New York *(G-11531)*

Pepsi-Cola Bottling Co NY Inc F 718 392-1000 New York *(G-11611)*

◆ **Pepsi-Cola Metro Btlg Co Inc** G 914 767-6000 White Plains *(G-17152)*

◆ **Pepsico Inc** A 914 253-2000 Purchase *(G-13966)*

◆ **Star Kay White Inc** D 845 268-2600 Congers *(G-3860)*

Synergy Flavors NY Company LLC G 585 232-6648 Rochester *(G-14711)*

Tealeafs G 716 688-8022 Williamsville *(G-17257)*

Torre Products Co Inc G 212 925-8989 New York *(G-12375)*

◆ **Virginia Dare Extract Co Inc** C 718 788-6320 Brooklyn *(G-2729)*

Wynn Starr Flavors Inc E 845 584-3080 Congers *(G-3863)*

2091 Fish & Seafoods, Canned & Cured

AA USA Trading Inc G 917 586-2573 Brooklyn *(G-1544)*

◆ **Acme Smoked Fish Corp** D 954 942-5598 Brooklyn *(G-1557)*

▲ **Banner Smoked Fish Inc** E 718 449-1992 Brooklyn *(G-1666)*

Blue Ocean Food Trading Inc G 718 689-4290 Brooklyn *(G-1702)*

BNC Commodities Inc F 631 872-8041 Wantagh *(G-16554)*

▲ **Catsmo Corp** F 845 895-2296 Wallkill *(G-16542)*

Deelka Vision Corp E 718 937-4121 Sunnyside *(G-15806)*

▲ **Diamond Seafoods LLC** G 503 351-3240 Port Washington *(G-13809)*

Harbors Maine Lobster LLC E 516 775-2400 New Hyde Park *(G-8839)*

▲ **Premium Ocean LLC** F 917 231-1061 Bronx *(G-1435)*

Samaki Inc G 845 858-1012 Port Jervis *(G-13791)*

Sangster Foods Inc F 212 993-9129 Brooklyn *(G-2532)*

2092 Fish & Seafoods, Fresh & Frozen

6th Ave Gourmet Inc G 845 782-9067 Monroe *(G-8547)*

▲ **Foo Yuan Food Products Co Inc** G 212 925-2840 Long Island City *(G-7744)*

Montauk Inlet Seafood Inc G 631 668-3419 Montauk *(G-8590)*

Oceans Cuisine Ltd F 631 209-9200 Ridge *(G-14092)*

Peak Holdings LLC A 212 583-5000 New York *(G-11588)*

Prince of The Sea Ltd E 516 333-6344 Westbury *(G-17022)*

◆ **Rich Products Corporation** A 716 878-8422 Buffalo *(G-3157)*

2095 Coffee

▲ **Bh Coffee Company LLC** D 914 377-2500 Elmsford *(G-4736)*

Birch Guys LLC G 917 763-0751 Long Island City *(G-7686)*

BK Associates Intl Inc F 607 432-1499 Oneonta *(G-13173)*

S I C

Employee Codes: A=Over 500 employees, B=251-500 C=101-250, D=51-100, E=20-50, F=10-19, G=5-9

20 FOOD AND KINDRED PRODUCTS — SIC SECTION

Cafe Kubal	F	315 278-2812
Syracuse (G-15882)

Caranda Emporium LLC ... 212 866-7100
New York (G-9521)

◆ Coffee Holding Co Inc ... D ... 718 832-0800
Staten Island (G-15661)

Death Wish Coffee Company LLC ... F ... 518 400-1050
Round Lake (G-15037)

▲ Eldorado Coffee Roasters Ltd ... D ... 718 418-4100
Maspeth (G-8137)

Empire Coffee Company Inc ... E ... 914 934-1100
Port Chester (G-13745)

Fal Coffee Inc ... F ... 718 305-4255
Brooklyn (G-1954)

G & M Roaster ... G ... 718 984-5235
Staten Island (G-15675)

Gillies Coffee Company ... E ... 718 499-7766
Brooklyn (G-2024)

Gorilla Coffee Inc ... G ... 718 230-3244
Brooklyn (G-2041)

Irving Farm Coffee Co Inc ... G ... 212 206-0707
New York (G-10664)

John A Vassilaros & Son Inc ... E ... 718 886-4140
Flushing (G-5257)

Joseph H Navaie ... F ... 607 936-9030
Corning (G-3974)

Kraft Heinz Foods Company ... A ... 914 335-2500
Tarrytown (G-16093)

Maidstone Coffee Co ... F ... 585 272-1040
Rochester (G-14491)

Monkey Joe Roasting Company ... G ... 845 331-4598
Kingston (G-7202)

New York Gourmet Coffee Inc ... G ... 631 254-0076
Bay Shore (G-722)

▲ Orens Daily Roast Inc ... G ... 212 348-5400
New York (G-11526)

P Pascal Inc ... E ... 914 969-7933
Yonkers (G-17474)

▲ Paul De Lima Company Inc ... D ... 315 457-3725
Liverpool (G-7540)

Paul De Lima Company Inc ... E ... 315 457-3725
Cicero (G-3650)

▲ Paul Delima Coffee Company ... E ... 315 457-3725
Cicero (G-3651)

▲ Regal Trading Inc ... E ... 914 694-6100
Purchase (G-13970)

▲ S J McCullagh Inc ... E ... 716 856-3473
Buffalo (G-3172)

Sangster Foods Inc ... F ... 212 993-9129
Brooklyn (G-2532)

Star Mountain JFK Inc ... G ... 718 553-6787
Jamaica (G-6951)

Vega Coffee Inc ... G ... 415 881-7969
New York (G-12514)

▲ White Coffee Corp ... D ... 718 204-7900
Astoria (G-462)

2096 Potato Chips & Similar Prdts

Birds Eye Holdings Inc ... A ... 585 383-1850
Rochester (G-14232)

BSD Top Direct Inc ... G ... 646 468-0156
West Babylon (G-16777)

▲ Emmi USA Inc ... F ... 845 268-9990
Orangeburg (G-13225)

Frito-Lay North America Inc ... D ... 716 631-2360
Williamsville (G-17243)

Frito-Lay North America Inc ... E ... 585 343-5456
Batavia (G-633)

Frito-Lay North America Inc ... D ... 607 775-7000
Binghamton (G-916)

Glennys Inc ... G ... 516 377-1400
Brooklyn (G-2026)

◆ Hain Celestial Group Inc ... C ... 516 587-5000
New Hyde Park (G-8837)

◆ Ideal Snacks Corporation ... C ... 845 292-7000
Liberty (G-7437)

◆ Pepsico Inc ... A ... 914 253-2000
Purchase (G-13966)

Pepsico Inc ... B ... 914 253-2000
White Plains (G-17154)

Pepsico Inc ... E ... 914 253-3474
White Plains (G-17155)

Pepsico Inc ... D ... 914 767-6976
White Plains (G-17156)

Pupellos Organic Chips Inc ... F ... 718 710-9154
Oakdale (G-13061)

Robs Really Good LLC ... F ... 516 671-4411
Sea Cliff (G-15342)

◆ Simplycultivated Group LLC ... G ... 646 389-0682
Horseheads (G-6594)

▲ Snack Innovations Inc ... E ... 718 509-9366
Brooklyn (G-2574)

Snacks On 48 Inc ... G ... 347 663-1100
Brooklyn (G-2575)

Switch Beverage Company LLC ... F ... 203 202-7383
Port Washington (G-13867)

Terrells Potato Chip Co Inc ... D ... 315 437-2786
Syracuse (G-16057)

▲ TLC-Lc Inc ... E ... 212 756-8900
New York (G-12355)

Tortilleria Chinantla Inc ... E ... 718 302-0101
Brooklyn (G-2668)

2097 Ice

Adirondack Ice & Air Inc ... F ... 518 483-4340
Malone (G-8005)

Arctic Glacier Minnesota Inc ... E ... 585 388-0080
Fairport (G-4842)

Arctic Glacier Newburgh Inc ... G ... 718 456-2013
Brooklyn (G-1623)

Arctic Glacier Newburgh Inc ... F ... 845 561-0549
Newburgh (G-12750)

Arctic Glacier PA Inc ... E ... 610 494-8200
Fairport (G-4843)

Arctic Glacier Texas Inc ... E ... 215 283-0326
Fairport (G-4844)

Arctic Glacier USA ... E ... 215 283-0326
Fairport (G-4845)

Clayville Ice Co Inc ... G ... 315 839-5405
Clayville (G-3687)

Henry Newman LLC ... E ... 607 273-8512
Ithaca (G-6847)

Huntington Ice & Cube Corp ... F ... 718 456-2013
Brooklyn (G-2091)

Mamitas Ices Ltd ... F ... 718 738-3238
Ozone Park (G-13383)

Maplewood Ice Co Inc ... E ... 518 499-2345
Whitehall (G-17190)

South Shore Ice Co Inc ... F ... 516 379-2056
Roosevelt (G-15009)

2098 Macaroni, Spaghetti & Noodles

AAA Noodle Products Mfg ... G ... 212 431-4090
New York (G-8999)

Bedessee Imports Ltd ... E ... 718 272-1300
Brooklyn (G-1676)

Borgattis Ravioli Egg Noodles ... G ... 718 367-3799
Bronx (G-1287)

Canton Noodle Corporation ... G ... 212 226-3276
New York (G-9515)

Cassinelli Food Products Inc ... G ... 718 274-4881
Long Island City (G-7695)

Dairy Maid Raviolo Mfg ... F ... 718 449-2620
Brooklyn (G-1835)

Deer Park Macaroni Co Inc ... G ... 631 667-4600
Deer Park (G-4128)

Deer Park Macaroni Co Inc ... F ... 631 667-4600
Deer Park (G-4129)

Hong Hop Co Inc ... E ... 212 962-1735
New York (G-10502)

Momofuku 171 First Avenue LLC ... D ... 212 777-7773
New York (G-11297)

Nodus Noodle Corporation ... G ... 718 309-3725
Sunnyside (G-15808)

Noodle Education Inc ... E ... 646 289-7800
New York (G-11451)

▲ Piemonte Home Made Ravioli Co ... F ... 718 429-1972
Woodside (G-17347)

Piemonte Home Made Ravioli Co ... G ... 212 226-0475
New York (G-11660)

Queen Ann Macaroni Mfg Co Inc ... F ... 718 256-1061
Brooklyn (G-2466)

Raffettos Corp ... E ... 212 777-1261
New York (G-11785)

Ravioli Store Inc ... G ... 718 729-9300
Long Island City (G-7858)

▲ Twin Marquis Inc ... D ... 718 386-6868
Brooklyn (G-2691)

Wing Heung Noodle Inc ... F ... 212 966-7496
New York (G-12643)

Wing Kei Noodle Inc ... F ... 212 226-1644
New York (G-12644)

Wonton Food Inc ... F ... 212 677-8865
New York (G-12654)

Yum Yum Noodle Bar ... G ... 845 679-7992
Kingston (G-7226)

2099 Food Preparations, NEC

212kiddish Inc ... G ... 718 705-7227
Brooklyn (G-1512)

3v Company Inc ... E ... 718 858-7333
Brooklyn (G-1517)

ABC Peanut Butter LLC ... B ... 212 661-6886
New York (G-9002)

Ahhmigo LLC ... F ... 212 315-1818
New York (G-9061)

▲ Amalfi Ingredients LLC ... G ... 631 392-1526
Deer Park (G-4095)

◆ American Almond Pdts Co Inc ... E ... 718 875-8310
Brooklyn (G-1599)

Armour Bearer Group Inc ... G ... 646 812-4487
Arverne (G-424)

Aromasong Usa Inc ... F ... 718 838-9669
Brooklyn (G-1630)

Aryzta LLC ... D ... 585 235-8160
Rochester (G-14214)

◆ Associated Brands Inc ... B ... 585 798-3475
New York (G-9238)

Bainbridge & Knight LLC ... E ... 212 986-5100
New York (G-9307)

Baldwin Richardson Foods Co ... C ... 315 986-2727
Macedon (G-7983)

▲ Barilla America Ny Inc ... C ... 585 226-5600
Avon (G-539)

Beak & Skiff Cider Mill Inc ... E ... 315 677-5105
La Fayette (G-7239)

Bektrom Foods Inc ... E ... 516 802-3800
Syosset (G-15814)

▲ Bektrom Foods Inc ... E ... 516 802-3800
Syosset (G-15813)

Bel Americas Inc ... G ... 646 454-8220
New York (G-9347)

Blue Tortilla LLC ... G ... 631 451-0100
Selden (G-15348)

▲ Bombay Kitchen Foods Inc ... F ... 516 767-7401
Port Washington (G-13802)

Brightline Ventures I LLC ... E ... 212 626-6829
New York (G-9461)

Broome County ... E ... 607 785-9567
Endicott (G-4797)

Buna Besta Tortillas ... G ... 347 987-3995
Brooklyn (G-1737)

Butterwood Desserts Inc ... E ... 716 652-0131
West Falls (G-16844)

Bylada Foods LLC ... D ... 845 623-1300
West Nyack (G-16914)

▼ Carriage House Companies Inc ... A ... 716 672-4321
Fredonia (G-5371)

Casablanca Foods LLC ... G ... 212 317-1111
New York (G-9540)

◆ Castella Imports Inc ... C ... 631 231-5500
Hauppauge (G-6040)

Chan & Chan (usa) Corp ... G ... 718 388-9633
Brooklyn (G-1773)

Chan Kee Dried Bean Curd Inc ... G ... 718 622-0820
Brooklyn (G-1774)

▲ Chemicolloid Laboratories Inc ... F ... 516 747-2666
New Hyde Park (G-8821)

Child Nutrition Prog Dept Ed ... E ... 212 371-1000
New York (G-9594)

▲ China Huaren Organic Pdts Inc ... G ... 212 232-0120
New York (G-9597)

Chopt Creative Salad Co LLC ... F ... 646 374-0386
New York (G-9606)

Cookiebaker LLC ... G ... 716 878-8000
Buffalo (G-2889)

D R M Management Inc ... E ... 716 668-0333
Depew (G-4254)

Deedee Desserts LLC ... G ... 716 627-2330
Lake View (G-7279)

Diva Farms Ltd ... G ... 315 735-4397
Utica (G-16326)

▲ Dundee Foods LLC ... F ... 585 377-7700
Fairport (G-4855)

Event Services Corporation ... G ... 315 488-9357
Solvay (G-15508)

Fanshawe Foods LLC ... F ... 212 757-3130
New York (G-10135)

▲ Far Eastern Coconut Company ... F ... 631 851-8800
Central Islip (G-3496)

Farmers Hub LLC ... G ... 646 380-6770
White Plains (G-17109)

▲ Flaum Appetizing Corp ... E ... 718 821-1970
Brooklyn (G-1984)

Fleischmanns Vinegar Co Inc ... E ... 315 587-4414
North Rose (G-12936)

Frito-Lay North America Inc ... D ... 607 397-1008
Worcester (G-17368)

Frito-Lay North America Inc ... D ... 607 775-7000
Binghamton (G-916)

Frozen Food Partners LLC ....G....... 203 661-7500
  New York (G-10214)
Gillies Coffee Company ....E...... 718 499-7766
  Brooklyn (G-2024)
▼ Glenn Foods Inc ....F...... 516 377-1400
  Freeport (G-5402)
▲ Gold Pure Food Products Co Inc .....D...... 516 483-5600
  Hempstead (G-6272)
Golden Taste Inc ....E...... 845 356-4133
  Spring Valley (G-15587)
▲ Gourmet Boutique LLC ....C...... 718 977-1200
  Jamaica (G-6916)
Gourmet Crafts Inc ....F...... 718 372-0505
  Brooklyn (G-2043)
▲ Gourmet Guru Inc ....E...... 718 842-2828
  Bronx (G-1347)
Gourmet Toast Corp ....F...... 718 852-4536
  Brooklyn (G-2044)
Gravymaster Inc ....E...... 203 453-1893
  Canajoharie (G-3332)
Great Eastern Pasta Works LLC ....E...... 631 956-0889
  West Babylon (G-16794)
H & S Edible Products Corp ....E...... 914 413-3489
  Mount Vernon (G-8688)
Hong Hop Co Inc ....E...... 212 962-1735
  New York (G-10502)
HP Hood LLC ....D...... 607 295-8134
  Arkport (G-410)
Instantwhip of Buffalo Inc ....G...... 716 892-7031
  Buffalo (G-3010)
▲ Johns Ravioli Company Inc ....F...... 914 576-7030
  New Rochelle (G-8915)
▲ Joyva Corp ....D...... 718 497-0170
  Brooklyn (G-2154)
Kale Factory Inc ....G...... 917 363-6361
  Brooklyn (G-2166)
Kerry Inc ....E...... 845 584-3080
  Congers (G-3858)
▼ Kerry Inc ....D...... 607 334-1700
  Norwich (G-13029)
▲ Kozy Shack Enterprises LLC ....C...... 516 870-3000
  Hicksville (G-6359)
Kozy Shack Enterprises LLC ....C...... 516 870-3000
  Hicksville (G-6360)
Kraft Heinz Foods Company ....A...... 914 335-2500
  Tarrytown (G-16093)
Kraft Heinz Foods Company 585 226-4400
  Avon (G-540)
La Escondida Inc ....G...... 845 562-1387
  Newburgh (G-12765)
▲ La Flor Products Company Inc .....E...... 631 851-9601
  Hauppauge (G-6111)
La Regina Di San Marzano Inc 212 269-4202
  New York (G-10910)
Labella Pasta Inc ....G...... 845 331-9130
  Kingston (G-7195)
Lakeside Cider Mill Farm Inc ....G...... 518 399-8359
  Ballston Lake (G-582)
▲ Lams Foods Inc ....F...... 718 217-0476
  Queens Village (G-13981)
Land OLakes Inc ....G...... 516 681-2980
  Hicksville (G-6362)
▲ Larte Del Gelato Inc ....G...... 212 366-0570
  New York (G-10930)
Lollipop Tree Inc ....E...... 845 471-8733
  Auburn (G-506)
M & M Food Products Inc ....F...... 718 821-1970
  Brooklyn (G-2244)
Maizteca Foods Inc ....E...... 718 641-3933
  South Richmond Hill (G-15534)
Majani Tea Company 817 896-5720
  New York (G-11114)
Mandalay Food Products Inc ....G...... 718 230-3370
  Brooklyn (G-2257)
Manhattan Milling & Drying Co ....E...... 516 496-1041
  Woodbury (G-17294)
▲ Maramont Corporation ....B...... 718 439-8900
  Brooklyn (G-2265)
▲ Martens Country Kit Pdts LLC ....F...... 315 776-8821
  Port Byron (G-13734)
▲ Mediterrean Dyro Company ....E...... 718 786-4888
  Long Island City (G-7809)
Merb LLC ....G...... 631 393-3621
  Farmingdale (G-5048)
▲ Meta-Therm Corp ....F...... 914 697-4840
  White Plains (G-17137)
Mighty Quinns Barbeque LLC ....E...... 973 777-8340
  New York (G-11261)
Milnot Holding Corporation ....G...... 518 839-0300
  Amsterdam (G-357)

Mizkan America Inc ....D...... 585 765-9171
  Lyndonville (G-7968)
Mizkan Americas Inc ....F...... 585 798-5720
  Medina (G-8278)
Mizkan Americas Inc ....F...... 315 483-6944
  Sodus (G-15503)
Moira New Hope Food Pantry ....E...... 518 529-6524
  Moira (G-8546)
Momentive Performance Mtls Inc ....D...... 914 784-4807
  Tarrytown (G-16098)
Mondelez Global LLC ....F...... 585 345-3300
  Batavia (G-642)
Morris Kitchen Inc ....F...... 646 413-5186
  Brooklyn (G-2334)
▲ Natural Lab Inc ....G...... 718 321-8848
  Flushing (G-5270)
Naturally Free Food Inc ....G...... 631 361-9710
  Smithtown (G-15492)
New York Ravioli Pasta Co Inc ....E...... 516 270-2852
  New Hyde Park (G-8851)
▲ Old Dutch Mustard Co Inc ....G...... 516 466-0522
  Great Neck (G-5825)
Omg Desserts Inc ....F...... 585 698-1561
  Rochester (G-14548)
▲ Once Again Nut Butter Collectv ......D...... 585 468-2535
  Nunda (G-13041)
Original Hrkmer Cnty Chese Inc ....D...... 315 895-7428
  Ilion (G-6740)
P-Hgh 2 Co Inc ....F...... 954 534-6058
  Buffalo (G-3109)
Pane Vita LLC ....F...... 888 509-3310
  Rochester (G-14570)
▲ Parnasa International Inc 516 394-0400
  Valley Stream (G-16418)
Peaceful Valley Maple Farm 518 762-0491
  Johnstown (G-7119)
Peak Holdings LLC ....A...... 212 583-5000
  New York (G-11588)
Pelican Bay Ltd ....F...... 718 729-9300
  Long Island City (G-7838)
Pellicano Specialty Foods Inc ....F...... 716 822-2366
  Buffalo (G-3117)
Pennant Ingredients Inc ....D...... 585 235-8160
  Rochester (G-14575)
Purespice LLC ....G...... 617 549-8400
  Hopewell Junction (G-6558)
▲ Raw Indulgence Ltd 866 498-4671
  Hawthorne (G-6253)
Rawpothecary Inc 917 783-7770
  Brooklyn (G-2479)
Real Co Inc ....G...... 347 433-8549
  Valley Cottage (G-16386)
Redland Foods Corp ....F...... 716 288-9061
  Cheektowaga (G-3589)
◆ Rich Products Corporation ....A...... 716 878-8422
  Buffalo (G-3157)
▲ Rob Salamida Company Inc ....F...... 607 729-4868
  Johnson City (G-7105)
Sabra Dipping Company LLC ....F...... 516 249-0151
  Farmingdale (G-5107)
Salvador Colletti Blank ....G...... 718 217-6725
  Douglaston (G-4310)
Sapienza Pastry Inc ....E...... 516 352-5232
  Elmont (G-4729)
Schutt Cider Mill ....F...... 585 872-2924
  Webster (G-16734)
▲ Seasons Soyfood Inc ....G...... 718 797-9896
  Brooklyn (G-2542)
◆ Settons Intl Foods Inc ....E...... 631 543-8090
  Commack (G-3842)
Sfoglini LLC ....F...... 646 872-1035
  Brooklyn (G-2546)
▲ Sneaky Chef Foods LLC ....F...... 914 301-3277
  Tarrytown (G-16106)
▲ SOS Chefs of New York Inc ....F...... 212 505-5813
  New York (G-12139)
Spf Holdings II LLC ....F...... 212 750-8300
  New York (G-12161)
▲ Steinway Pasta & Gelati Inc ....F...... 718 246-5414
  Brooklyn (G-2607)
▼ Sugar Foods Corporation ....E...... 212 753-6900
  New York (G-12227)
Sugar Shack Desert Company Inc ....G...... 518 523-7540
  Lake Placid (G-7276)
Terrace Management Inc ....E...... 914 737-0400
  Cortlandt Manor (G-4054)
Tortilla Heaven Inc ....E...... 845 339-1550
  Kingston (G-7217)
▲ Tuv Taam Corp ....F...... 718 855-2207
  Brooklyn (G-2689)

▲ Twin Marquis Inc ....D...... 718 386-6868
  Brooklyn (G-2691)
▲ U S Sugar Co Inc ....E...... 716 828-1170
  Buffalo (G-3229)
UFS Industries Inc ....D...... 718 822-1100
  Mount Vernon (G-8744)
Ultra Thin Ready To Bake Pizza ....E...... 516 679-6655
  New Hyde Park (G-8868)
▲ Victoria Fine Foods LLC ....D...... 718 649-1635
  Brooklyn (G-2725)
▲ VIP Foods Inc ....E...... 718 821-5330
  Ridgewood (G-14131)
Whitsons Food Svc Bronx Corp ....B...... 631 424-2700
  Islandia (G-6804)
▲ Win-Holt Equipment Corp ....G...... 516 222-0335
  Woodbury (G-17303)
▲ Wm E Martin and Sons Co Inc ....E...... 516 605-2444
  Roslyn (G-15024)
▲ Wonder Natural Foods Corp ....G...... 631 726-4433
  Water Mill (G-16607)
Wonton Food Inc ....E...... 718 784-8178
  Long Island City (G-7926)
▲ Wonton Food Inc ....C...... 718 628-6868
  Brooklyn (G-2763)
Wonton Food Inc ....F...... 212 677-8865
  New York (G-12654)

21 TOBACCO PRODUCTS

2111 Cigarettes

East End ....F...... 716 532-2622
  Collins (G-3816)
Jacobs Tobacco Company ....E...... 518 358-4948
  Hogansburg (G-6428)
Juicy Vapor LLC ....F...... 855 525-8429
  Amherst (G-248)
◆ Philip Morris Intl Inc ....C...... 917 663-2000
  New York (G-11645)
PMI Global Services Inc ....E...... 917 663-2000
  New York (G-11679)
R J Reynolds Tobacco Company ....C...... 716 871-1553
  Tonawanda (G-16196)
Revolution Vapor LLC ....G...... 518 627-4133
  Amsterdam (G-367)
Schweitzer-Mauduit Intl Inc ....C...... 518 329-4222
  Ancram (G-375)
▲ Seneca Manufacturing Company ...G...... 716 945-4400
  Salamanca (G-15106)
Seneca Nation Enterprise ....F...... 716 934-7430
  Irving (G-6765)
Vector Group Ltd ....B...... 212 409-2800
  New York (G-12512)

2121 Cigars

American Cigar ....G...... 718 969-0008
  Fresh Meadows (G-5438)
Davidoff Gneva Madison Ave Inc ....G...... 212 751-9060
  New York (G-9828)
Mafco Consolidated Group Inc ....F...... 212 572-8600
  New York (G-11096)
Martinez Hand Made Cigars ....G...... 212 239-4049
  New York (G-11169)

2131 Tobacco, Chewing & Snuff

Elab Smokers Boutique ....G...... 585 865-4513
  Rochester (G-14343)
Mafco Consolidated Group Inc ....F...... 212 572-8600
  New York (G-11096)
National Tobacco Company LP ....F...... 212 253-8185
  New York (G-11353)

2141 Tobacco Stemming & Redrying

Schweitzer-Mauduit Intl Inc ....C...... 518 329-4222
  Ancram (G-375)

22 TEXTILE MILL PRODUCTS

2211 Cotton, Woven Fabric

1510 Associates LLC ....G...... 212 828-8720
  New York (G-8960)
A and J Apparel Corp ....G...... 212 398-8899
  New York (G-8983)
A3 Apparel LLC ....G...... 888 403-9669
  New York (G-8997)
Advanced Fashions Technology ....G...... 212 221-0606
  New York (G-9044)
Alessi International Limited ....F...... 516 676-8841
  Glen Cove (G-5609)

Employee Codes: A=Over 500 employees, B=251-500
C=101-250, D=51-100, E=20-50, F=10-19, G=5-9

▲ **Ann Gish Inc** ..... G 212 969-9200
New York *(G-9163)*

▲ **Apollo Apparel Group LLC** ..... F 212 398-6585
New York *(G-9175)*

▲ **AV Denim Inc** ..... E 212 764-6668
New York *(G-9270)*

Avitto Leather Goods Inc ..... G 212 219-7501
New York *(G-9279)*

▲ **Axis Na LLC** ..... F 212 840-4005
New York *(G-9284)*

Bandier Corp ..... F 212 242-5400
New York *(G-9313)*

◆ **Basileus Company LLC** ..... F 315 963-3516
Manlius *(G-8067)*

◆ **Benartex Inc** ..... E 212 840-3250
New York *(G-9357)*

▲ **Beyond Loom Inc** ..... G 212 575-3100
New York *(G-9383)*

Bill Blass Group LLC ..... F 212 689-8957
New York *(G-9396)*

Blu Sand LLC ..... G 212 564-1147
New York *(G-9419)*

Brooklyn Denim Co ..... F 718 782-2600
Brooklyn *(G-1725)*

▲ **Brunschwig & Fils LLC** ..... F 800 538-1880
Bethpage *(G-865)*

◆ **Cai Inc** ..... G 212 819-0008
New York *(G-9497)*

Charming Fashion Inc ..... G 212 730-2872
New York *(G-9584)*

Creation Baumann USA Inc ..... E 516 764-7431
Rockville Centre *(G-14790)*

Designway Ltd ..... G 212 254-2220
New York *(G-9858)*

▲ **Equipment Apparel LLC** ..... D 212 502-1890
New York *(G-10053)*

Fab Industries Corp ..... E 516 498-3200
Great Neck *(G-5809)*

Fashion Apparel Industries ..... F 212 704-0800
New York *(G-10140)*

▲ **French Accnt Rugs & Tapestries** ..... G 212 686-6097
New York *(G-10207)*

Geordie Magee Uphl & Canvas ..... G 315 676-7679
Brewerton *(G-1203)*

◆ **Gerli & Co Inc** ..... E 212 213-1919
New York *(G-10286)*

Gotham T-Shirt Corp ..... G 516 676-0900
Sea Cliff *(G-15341)*

Haleys Comet Seafood Corp ..... E 212 571-1828
New York *(G-10397)*

Hanesbrands Inc ..... G 212 576-9300
New York *(G-10406)*

Harley Robert D Company Ltd ..... G 212 947-1872
New York *(G-10413)*

Hmx LLC ..... D 212 682-9073
New York *(G-10490)*

▲ **Horizon Apparel Mfg Inc** ..... G 516 361-4878
Atlantic Beach *(G-469)*

Internationl Studios Inc ..... G 212 819-1616
New York *(G-10638)*

Joy of Learning ..... G 718 443-6463
Brooklyn *(G-2152)*

▲ **Jrg Apparel Group Company Ltd** ..... G 212 997-0900
New York *(G-10775)*

Knightly Endeavors ..... F 845 340-0949
Kingston *(G-7194)*

▲ **L Allmeier** ..... G 212 243-7390
New York *(G-10900)*

▲ **La Lame Inc** ..... G 212 921-9770
New York *(G-10909)*

◆ **Lydall Performance Mtl Inc** ..... C 518 273-6320
Green Island *(G-5859)*

▲ **Magic Brands International LLC** ..... F 212 563-4999
New York *(G-11103)*

Marsha Fleisher ..... F 845 679-6500
Woodstock *(G-17364)*

▼ **Mason Contract Products LLC** ..... D 516 328-6900
New Hyde Park *(G-8848)*

Meder Textile Co Inc ..... G 516 883-0409
Port Washington *(G-13840)*

Medline Industries Inc ..... B 845 344-3301
Middletown *(G-8450)*

Mgk Group Inc ..... E 212 989-2732
New York *(G-11246)*

Michael Stuart Inc ..... E 718 821-0704
Brooklyn *(G-2309)*

▲ **Min Run (usa) Inc** ..... G 646 331-1018
Port Washington *(G-13845)*

N Y Contract Seating Inc ..... G 718 417-9298
Maspeth *(G-8152)*

Navas Designs Inc ..... E 818 988-9050
New York *(G-11359)*

▲ **Neilson International Inc** ..... G 631 454-0400
Farmingdale *(G-5064)*

Nochairs Inc ..... G 917 748-8731
New York *(G-11449)*

▲ **Northpoint Trading Inc** ..... F 212 481-8001
New York *(G-11460)*

▲ **Northwest Company LLC** ..... D 516 484-6996
Roslyn *(G-15022)*

Obvious Inc ..... E 212 278-0007
New York *(G-11492)*

Paramount Cord & Brackets ..... G 212 325-9100
White Plains *(G-17144)*

Perfect Print Inc ..... E 718 832-5280
Brooklyn *(G-2417)*

▲ **Phoenix Usa LLC** ..... G 646 351-6598
New York *(G-11652)*

▲ **Refuel Inc** ..... G 917 645-2974
New York *(G-11818)*

▲ **Renaissnce Crpt Tapestries Inc** ..... F 212 696-0080
New York *(G-11831)*

▲ **Richloom Home Fashions Corp** ..... F 212 685-5400
New York *(G-11871)*

▲ **Scalamandre Wallpaper Inc** ..... B 631 467-8800
Hauppauge *(G-6185)*

SD Eagle Global Inc ..... G 516 822-1778
Jericho *(G-7086)*

Shahin Designs Ltd ..... G 212 737-7225
New York *(G-12039)*

Shindo Usa Inc ..... G 212 868-9311
New York *(G-12051)*

▲ **Sita Finishing Inc** ..... F 718 417-5295
Brooklyn *(G-2567)*

Sky Laundromat Inc ..... F 718 639-7070
Jamaica *(G-6949)*

Star Draperies Inc ..... F 631 756-7121
Farmingdale *(G-5114)*

▲ **Taikoh USA Inc** ..... F 646 556-6652
New York *(G-12273)*

▲ **US Design Group Ltd** ..... F 212 354-4070
New York *(G-12485)*

Versailles Drapery Upholstery ..... F 212 533-2059
Long Island City *(G-7914)*

Wallace Home Design Ctr ..... G 631 765-3890
Southold *(G-15561)*

◆ **Westpoint Home LLC** ..... A 212 930-2074
New York *(G-12615)*

Westpoint International Inc ..... F 212 930-2044
New York *(G-12616)*

▲ **Xing Lin USA Intl Corp** ..... G 212 947-4846
New York *(G-12678)*

2221 Silk & Man-Made Fiber

A B C Elastic Corp ..... G 718 388-2953
Brooklyn *(G-1531)*

Albany International Corp ..... C 518 445-2200
Rensselaer *(G-14042)*

▲ **Ann Gish Inc** ..... G 212 969-9200
New York *(G-9163)*

Apex Texicon Inc ..... E 516 239-4400
New York *(G-9173)*

Art People Inc ..... G 212 431-4865
New York *(G-9212)*

▲ **Beyond Loom Inc** ..... G 212 575-3100
New York *(G-9383)*

▲ **Concepts Nyc Inc** ..... E 212 244-1033
New York *(G-9693)*

Creation Baumann USA Inc ..... E 516 764-7431
Rockville Centre *(G-14790)*

Eastern Silk Mills Inc ..... G 212 730-1300
New York *(G-9966)*

Ess Bee Industries Inc ..... E 718 894-5202
Brooklyn *(G-1936)*

◆ **Fabric Resources Intl Ltd** ..... F 516 829-4550
Great Neck *(G-5810)*

◆ **Fiber Glass Industries Inc** ..... D 518 842-4000
Amsterdam *(G-345)*

Fiber Glass Industries Inc ..... D 518 843-3533
Amsterdam *(G-346)*

Fibrix LLC ..... E 716 683-4100
Depew *(G-4257)*

▲ **Frp Apparel Group LLC** ..... G 212 695-8000
New York *(G-10215)*

◆ **Gerli & Co Inc** ..... E 212 213-1919
New York *(G-10286)*

Greenbuds LLC ..... G 718 483-9212
Brooklyn *(G-2052)*

Himatsingka America Inc ..... E 212 252-0802
New York *(G-10479)*

Himatsingka Holdings NA Inc ..... G 212 545-8929
New York *(G-10480)*

Intertex USA Inc ..... F 212 279-3601
New York *(G-10641)*

◆ **Ivi Services Inc** ..... D 607 729-5111
Binghamton *(G-929)*

▲ **Jag Manufacturing Inc** ..... E 518 762-9558
Johnstown *(G-7116)*

Jakob Schlaepfer Inc ..... G 212 221-2323
New York *(G-10696)*

JM Manufacturer Inc ..... G 212 869-0626
New York *(G-10742)*

Judscott Handprints Ltd ..... F 914 347-5515
Elmsford *(G-4759)*

Kragel Co Inc ..... G 716 648-1344
Hamburg *(G-5932)*

▲ **La Lame Inc** ..... G 212 921-9770
New York *(G-10909)*

▼ **Laregence Inc** ..... E 212 736-2548
New York *(G-10928)*

Mgk Group Inc ..... E 212 989-2732
New York *(G-11246)*

National Contract Industries ..... G 212 249-0045
New York *(G-11347)*

▲ **New York Poplin LLC** ..... G 718 768-3296
Brooklyn *(G-2366)*

▲ **Newtex Industries Inc** ..... E 585 924-9135
Victor *(G-16493)*

Pierce Arrow Drapery Mfg ..... G 716 876-3023
Buffalo *(G-3125)*

▲ **Polytex Inc** ..... D 716 549-5100
Angola *(G-381)*

▲ **Richloom Home Fashions Corp** ..... F 212 685-5400
New York *(G-11871)*

▲ **Scalamandre Silks Inc** ..... D 212 980-3888
New York *(G-11982)*

Scalamandre Silks Inc ..... D 212 376-2900
New York *(G-11983)*

▲ **Scalamandre Wallpaper Inc** ..... B 631 467-8800
Hauppauge *(G-6185)*

Scent-Sation Inc ..... D 718 672-4300
Queens Village *(G-13983)*

Schneider Mills Inc ..... F 212 768-7500
New York *(G-11994)*

◆ **Simplicity Creative Group Inc** ..... A 212 686-7676
New York *(G-12082)*

◆ **Springfield LLC** ..... E 516 861-6250
Jericho *(G-7089)*

Stern & Stern Industries Inc ..... D 607 324-4485
Hornell *(G-6567)*

Superior Fiber Mills Inc ..... E 718 782-7500
Brooklyn *(G-2628)*

Tli Import Inc ..... G 917 578-4568
Brooklyn *(G-2661)*

Toltec Fabrics Inc ..... C 212 706-9310
New York *(G-12358)*

Toray Industries Inc ..... G 212 697-8150
New York *(G-12373)*

◆ **Unique Quality Fabrics Inc** ..... G 845 343-3070
Middletown *(G-8468)*

▲ **US Home Textiles Group LLC** ..... G 212 768-3030
New York *(G-12487)*

◆ **Westpoint Home LLC** ..... A 212 930-2074
New York *(G-12615)*

White Plains Drapery Uphl Inc ..... E 914 381-0908
Mamaroneck *(G-8050)*

▲ **Zorlu USA Inc** ..... F 212 689-4622
New York *(G-12719)*

2231 Wool, Woven Fabric

▲ **Acker & Ll Mills Corporation** ..... G 212 307-7247
New York *(G-9017)*

▲ **Beyond Loom Inc** ..... G 212 575-3100
New York *(G-9383)*

◆ **Citisource Industries Inc** ..... E 212 683-1033
New York *(G-9625)*

Eldeen Clothing Inc ..... F 212 719-9190
New York *(G-9994)*

Equissentials LLC ..... F 607 432-2856
Oneonta *(G-13185)*

◆ **Fabric Resources Intl Ltd** ..... F 516 829-4550
Great Neck *(G-5810)*

Hawkins Fabrics Inc ..... E 518 773-9550
Gloversville *(G-5714)*

Interaxissourcingcom Inc ..... E 212 905-6001
New York *(G-10623)*

▲ **Light House Hill Marketing** ..... F 212 354-1338
New York *(G-10990)*

▲ **Loomstate LLC** ..... E 212 219-2300
New York *(G-11031)*

▲ Matt Textile Inc ....G.... 212 967-6010
New York (G-11180)
Nazim Izzak Inc ....G.... 212 920-5546
Long Island City (G-7821)
▲ Oakhurst Partners LLC ....G.... 212 502-3220
New York (G-11490)
▲ Pinder International Inc ....G.... 631 273-0324
Hauppauge (G-6164)
▲ Scalamandre Wallpaper Inc ....B.... 631 467-8800
Hauppauge (G-6185)
▲ Warren Corporation ....C.... 860 684-2766
New York (G-12590)
Woolmark Americas Inc ....G.... 347 767-3160
New York (G-12657)
▲ Yarnz International Inc ....G.... 212 868-5883
New York (G-12689)

2241 Fabric Mills, Cotton, Wool, Silk & Man-Made

Albany International Corp ....C.... 518 445-2200
Rensselaer (G-14042)
Ambind Corp ....G.... 716 836-4365
Buffalo (G-2805)
American Canvas Binders Corp ....G.... 914 969-0300
Yonkers (G-17413)
▲ American Trim Mfg Inc ....E.... 518 239-8151
Durham (G-4355)
▲ Bardwil Industries Inc ....G.... 212 944-1870
New York (G-9317)
Breton Industries Inc ....D.... 518 842-3030
Amsterdam (G-336)
Champion Zipper Corp ....G.... 212 239-0414
New York (G-9576)
▲ Colonial Tag & Label Co Inc ....F.... 516 482-0508
Great Neck (G-5799)
▲ Danray Textiles Corp ....F.... 212 354-5213
New York (G-9807)
Depot Label Company Inc ....G.... 631 467-2952
Patchogue (G-13418)
Eiseman-Ludmar Co Inc ....F.... 516 932-6990
Hicksville (G-6343)
▲ Essential Ribbons Inc ....G.... 212 967-4173
New York (G-10065)
▲ Fashion Ribbon Co Inc ....E.... 718 482-0100
Long Island City (G-7738)
H Group ....F.... 212 719-5500
New York (G-10389)
Imperial-Harvard Label Co ....F.... 212 736-8420
New York (G-10574)
Itc Mfg Group Inc ....F.... 212 684-3696
New York (G-10669)
▲ J & M Textile Co Inc ....F.... 212 268-8000
New York (G-10674)
Jakob Schlaepfer Inc ....G.... 212 221-2323
New York (G-10696)
▲ La Lame Inc ....G.... 212 921-9770
New York (G-10909)
Label Source Inc ....G.... 212 244-1403
New York (G-10911)
◆ Labels Inter-Global Inc ....F.... 212 398-0006
New York (G-10912)
Labeltex Mills Inc ....G.... 212 279-6165
New York (G-10913)
Marketing Action Xecutives Inc ....G.... 212 971-9155
New York (G-11159)
▲ Mergence Studios Ltd ....F.... 212 288-5616
Hauppauge (G-6133)
New Classic Trade Inc ....G.... 347 822-9052
Jamaica (G-6934)
New York Binding Co Inc ....E.... 718 729-2454
Long Island City (G-7825)
▲ Newtex Industries Inc ....E.... 585 924-9135
Victor (G-16493)
▲ R-Pac International Corp ....E.... 212 465-1818
New York (G-11783)
▲ Scalamandre Silks Inc ....D.... 212 980-3888
New York (G-11982)
▲ Schoen Trimming & Cord Co Inc ....F.... 212 255-3949
New York (G-11996)
◆ Simplicity Creative Group Inc ....A.... 212 686-7676
New York (G-12082)
▲ Skil-Care Corporation ....C.... 914 963-2040
Yonkers (G-17484)
Sml USA Inc ....E.... 212 736-8800
New York (G-12107)
Solstiss Inc ....G.... 212 719-9194
New York (G-12127)
▲ Sturges Manufacturing Co Inc ....D.... 315 732-6159
Utica (G-16360)
Tamber Knits Inc ....E.... 212 730-1121
New York (G-12275)
Triangle Label Tag Inc ....G.... 718 875-3030
Brooklyn (G-2679)
Valley Industrial Products Inc ....E.... 631 385-9300
Huntington (G-6689)

2251 Hosiery, Women's Full & Knee Length

Brach Knitting Mills Inc ....F.... 845 651-4450
Florida (G-5210)
▲ Classic Hosiery Inc ....E.... 845 342-6661
Middletown (G-8431)
Ellis Products Corp ....G.... 516 791-3732
Valley Stream (G-16405)
▲ Fine Sheer Industries Inc ....F.... 212 594-4224
New York (G-10164)
◆ Gina Group LLC ....E.... 212 947-2445
New York (G-10298)
▲ Horizon Imports Inc ....D.... 212 239-8660
New York (G-10506)
▼ Hot Sox Company Incorporated ....E.... 212 957-2000
New York (G-10514)
▲ Leg Resource Inc ....E.... 212 736-4574
New York (G-10961)

2252 Hosiery, Except Women's

▲ Ace Drop Cloth Canvas Pdts Inc ....E.... 718 731-1550
Bronx (G-1260)
▲ Ashko Group LLC ....F.... 212 594-6050
New York (G-9229)
Customize Elite Socks LLC ....G.... 212 533-8551
New York (G-9772)
Etc Hosiery & Underwear Ltd ....G.... 212 947-5151
New York (G-10076)
▲ Fine Sheer Industries Inc ....F.... 212 594-4224
New York (G-10164)
Galiva Inc ....G.... 903 600-5755
Brooklyn (G-2012)
Gbg Socks LLC ....E.... 646 839-7000
New York (G-10253)
◆ Gina Group LLC ....E.... 212 947-2445
New York (G-10298)
▲ Haddad Hosiery LLC ....G.... 212 251-0022
New York (G-10394)
▲ High Point Design LLC ....F.... 212 354-2400
New York (G-10472)
▲ Horizon Imports Inc ....D.... 212 239-8660
New York (G-10506)
▼ Hot Sox Company Incorporated ....E.... 212 957-2000
New York (G-10514)
J T Enterprises LLC ....G.... 716 433-9368
Lockport (G-7594)
La Strada Dance Footwear Inc ....G.... 631 242-1401
Deer Park (G-4163)
▲ Leadertex Intl Inc ....E.... 212 563-2242
New York (G-10947)
▲ Leg Resource Inc ....E.... 212 736-4574
New York (G-10961)
Look By M Inc ....G.... 212 213-4019
New York (G-11028)
New Hampton Creations Inc ....G.... 212 244-7474
New York (G-11389)
Palmbay Ltd ....G.... 718 424-3388
Woodside (G-17345)
Richard Edelson ....G.... 914 428-7573
Hartsdale (G-5999)
Socks and More of NY Inc ....G.... 718 769-1785
Brooklyn (G-2577)
Socks For Everyone Inc ....G.... 347 754-0210
Fresh Meadows (G-5445)
Spartan Brands Inc ....F.... 212 340-0320
New York (G-12150)
Sticky Socks LLC ....G.... 212 541-5927
New York (G-12205)
▲ You and ME Legwear LLC ....F.... 212 279-9292
New York (G-12698)
Z Best Printing Inc ....F.... 631 595-1400
Deer Park (G-4230)

2253 Knit Outerwear Mills

▲ 180s LLC ....E.... 410 534-6320
New York (G-8961)
79 Metro Ltd ....G.... 212 944-4030
New York (G-8980)
A & B Finishing Inc ....E.... 718 522-4702
Brooklyn (G-1525)
Accurate Knitting Corp ....G.... 646 552-2216
Brooklyn (G-1551)
Alpha Knitting Mills Inc ....F.... 718 628-6300
Brooklyn (G-1594)
American T Shirts Inc ....G.... 212 563-7125
New York (G-9129)
Andrea Strongwater ....G.... 212 873-0905
New York (G-9154)
▲ Asian Global Trading Corp ....F.... 718 786-0998
Long Island City (G-7672)
▲ B & B Sweater Mills Inc ....F.... 718 456-8693
Brooklyn (G-1655)
Beachbuttons LLC ....G.... 917 306-9369
New York (G-9338)
▲ Betsy & Adam Ltd ....E.... 212 302-3750
New York (G-9378)
▲ Binghamton Knitting Co Inc ....E.... 607 722-6941
Binghamton (G-892)
Blueberry Knitting Inc ....G.... 718 599-6520
Brooklyn (G-1705)
Central Mills Inc ....C.... 212 221-0748
New York (G-9565)
▲ Charter Ventures LLC ....F.... 212 868-0222
New York (G-9585)
◆ Domani Fashions Corp ....G.... 718 797-0505
Brooklyn (G-1871)
▲ Dressy Tessy Inc ....G.... 212 869-0750
New York (G-9927)
E I Du Pont De Nemours & Co ....E.... 716 876-4420
Buffalo (G-2924)
Elegant Headwear Co Inc ....G.... 212 695-8520
New York (G-9998)
▲ Emerald Holdings Inc ....G.... 718 797-4404
Brooklyn (G-1918)
Endres Knitwear Co Inc ....G.... 718 933-8687
Bronx (G-1326)
Fashion Avenue Knits Inc ....F.... 718 456-9000
New York (G-10142)
Fast-Trac Entertainment Ltd ....G.... 888 758-8886
New York (G-10146)
Freedom Rains Inc ....G.... 646 710-4512
New York (G-10206)
Gabani Inc ....G.... 631 283-4930
Southampton (G-15544)
▲ GAME Sportswear Ltd ....E.... 914 962-1701
Yorktown Heights (G-17511)
▲ Gce International Inc ....D.... 212 704-4800
New York (G-10259)
▲ Gildan Apparel USA Inc ....D.... 212 476-0341
New York (G-10295)
▲ Golden Leaves Knitwear Inc ....E.... 718 875-8235
Brooklyn (G-2038)
Grand Processing Inc ....E.... 718 388-0600
Brooklyn (G-2048)
Great Adirondack Yarn Company ....F.... 518 843-3381
Amsterdam (G-349)
▲ Hamil America Inc ....F.... 212 244-2645
New York (G-10400)
Hania By Anya Cole LLC ....G.... 212 302-3550
New York (G-10408)
▲ Hertling Trousers Inc ....E.... 718 784-6100
Brooklyn (G-2079)
IaM Maliamills LLC ....G.... 805 845-2137
Brooklyn (G-2093)
Imperial Sweater Mills Inc ....G.... 718 871-4414
Brooklyn (G-2100)
J & E Talit Inc ....G.... 718 850-1333
Richmond Hill (G-14076)
Jeric Knit Wear ....G.... 631 979-8827
Smithtown (G-15490)
Jfs Inc ....F.... 646 264-1200
New York (G-10730)
Julia Knit Inc ....G.... 718 848-1900
Ozone Park (G-13381)
K & S Childrens Wear Inc ....E.... 718 624-0006
Brooklyn (G-2162)
▲ Kc Collections LLC ....G.... 212 302-4412
New York (G-10826)
KD Dids Inc ....G.... 718 402-2012
Bronx (G-1369)
Keryakos Inc ....F.... 518 344-7092
Schenectady (G-15272)
Knit Illustrated Inc ....E.... 212 268-9054
New York (G-10862)
Knit Resource Center Ltd ....G.... 212 221-1990
New York (G-10863)
Lids Corporation ....G.... 518 459-7060
Albany (G-97)
▲ Lloyds Fashions Inc ....D.... 631 435-3353
Brentwood (G-1190)
Lynch Knitting Mills Inc ....E.... 718 821-3436
Brooklyn (G-2241)
▲ M A M Knitting Mills Corp ....E.... 800 570-0093
Brooklyn (G-2246)

Employee Codes: A=Over 500 employees, B=251-500
C=101-250, D=51-100, E=20-50, F=10-19, G=5-9
2017 Harris
New York Manufacturers Directory
723

▲ M B M Manufacturing Inc ....F 718 769-4148
Brooklyn *(G-2248)*
Machinit Inc ....G 631 454-9297
Farmingdale *(G-5039)*
Mann Consultants LLC ....E 914 763-0512
Waccabuc *(G-16520)*
Manrico Usa Inc ....G 212 794-4200
New York *(G-11139)*
Marble Knits Inc ....E 718 237-7990
Brooklyn *(G-2266)*
Mars Fashions Inc ....E 718 402-2200
Bronx *(G-1387)*
Matchables Inc ....F 718 389-9318
Brooklyn *(G-2282)*
Mdj Sales Associates Inc ....G 914 420-5897
Mamaroneck *(G-8039)*
Mongru Neckwear Inc ....E 718 706-0406
Long Island City *(G-7816)*
Native Textiles Inc ....G 212 951-5100
New York *(G-11354)*
New York Knitting Processor ....G 718 366-3469
Ridgewood *(G-14115)*
New York Sweater Company Inc ....E 845 629-9533
New York *(G-11409)*
North Star Knitting Mills Inc ....G 718 894-4848
Glendale *(G-5660)*
NY Denim Inc ....F 212 764-6668
New York *(G-11477)*
Phillips-Van Heusen Europe ....F 212 381-3500
New York *(G-11649)*
Premier Knits Ltd ....F 718 323-8264
Ozone Park *(G-13384)*
◆ Pvh Corp ....D 212 381-3500
New York *(G-11756)*
Rags Knitwear Ltd ....F 718 782-8417
Brooklyn *(G-2473)*
◆ Ralph Lauren Corporation ....B 212 318-7000
New York *(G-11792)*
S & T Knitting Co Inc ....E 607 722-7558
Conklin *(G-3874)*
S & V Knits Inc ....E 631 752-1595
Farmingdale *(G-5106)*
S & W Knitting Mills Inc ....E 718 237-2416
Brooklyn *(G-2524)*
Sage Knitwear Inc ....G 718 628-7902
West Babylon *(G-16825)*
Sares International Inc ....E 718 366-8412
Brooklyn *(G-2533)*
Sarug Inc ....D 718 339-2791
Brooklyn *(G-2534)*
Sarug Inc ....G 718 381-7300
Ridgewood *(G-14123)*
▲ Summit Apparel Inc ....F 631 213-8299
Hauppauge *(G-6202)*
Sweater Brand Inc ....G 718 797-0505
Brooklyn *(G-2635)*
▲ T & R Knitting Mills Inc ....E 718 497-4017
Glendale *(G-5665)*
T & R Knitting Mills Inc ....F 212 840-8665
New York *(G-12265)*
Tomas Maier ....G 212 988-8686
New York *(G-12364)*
▲ United Knitwear International ....G 212 354-2920
New York *(G-12465)*
Unlimited Jeans Co Inc ....G 212 661-6355
New York *(G-12472)*
Warm ....G 212 925-1200
New York *(G-12585)*
Warnaco Inc ....F 718 722-3000
Brooklyn *(G-2744)*
Winter Water Factory ....G 646 387-3247
Brooklyn *(G-2761)*
WR Design Corp ....E 212 354-9000
New York *(G-12669)*

2254 Knit Underwear Mills

▲ Balanced Tech Corp ....E 212 768-8330
New York *(G-9309)*
In Toon Amkor Fashions Inc ....E 718 937-4546
Long Island City *(G-7765)*
Jockey International Inc ....E 212 840-4900
New York *(G-10746)*
Jockey International Inc ....E 518 761-0965
Lake George *(G-7261)*
▲ Komar Kids LLC ....F 212 725-1500
New York *(G-10873)*
Maidenform LLC ....F 201 436-9200
New York *(G-11110)*
Native Textiles Inc ....G 212 951-5100
New York *(G-11354)*

Spartan Brands Inc ....F 212 340-0320
New York *(G-12150)*

2257 Circular Knit Fabric Mills

A-One Moving & Storage Inc ....E 718 266-6002
Brooklyn *(G-1541)*
Apex Aridyne Corp ....G 516 239-4400
Inwood *(G-6750)*
Apex Texicon Inc ....E 516 239-4400
New York *(G-9173)*
Cap USA Jerseyman Harlem Inc ....G 212 222-7942
New York *(G-9517)*
Gehring Tricot Corporation ....C 315 429-8551
Dolgeville *(G-4305)*
Hill Knitting Mills Inc ....E 718 846-5000
Richmond Hill *(G-14075)*
Lemral Knitwear Inc ....D 718 210-0175
Brooklyn *(G-2210)*
▲ Lifestyle Design Usa Ltd ....G 212 279-9400
New York *(G-10988)*
S & W Knitting Mills Inc ....E 718 237-2416
Brooklyn *(G-2524)*

2258 Lace & Warp Knit Fabric Mills

Apex Aridyne Corp ....G 516 239-4400
Inwood *(G-6750)*
Apex Texicon Inc ....E 516 239-4400
New York *(G-9173)*
▲ Binghamton Knitting Co Inc ....E 607 722-6941
Binghamton *(G-892)*
Creative Window Fashions Inc ....D 718 746-5817
Whitestone *(G-17205)*
Eagle Lace Dyeing Corp ....F 212 947-2712
New York *(G-9958)*
Fab Industries Corp ....E 516 498-3200
Great Neck *(G-5809)*
▲ Gehring Tricot Corporation ....D 315 429-8551
Garden City *(G-5507)*
Gehring Tricot Corporation ....C 315 429-8551
Dolgeville *(G-4305)*
George Knitting Mills Corp ....G 212 242-3300
New York *(G-10282)*
Helmont Mills Inc ....G 518 568-7913
Saint Johnsville *(G-15095)*
Hosel & Ackerson Inc ....G 212 575-1490
New York *(G-10509)*
Hudson Fabrics LLC ....F 518 671-6100
Hudson *(G-6617)*
▲ Ipm US Inc ....G 212 481-7967
New York *(G-10655)*
◆ Klauber Brothers Inc ....E 212 686-2531
New York *(G-10859)*
Litchfield Fabrics of NC ....G 518 773-9500
Gloversville *(G-5717)*
Mary Bright Inc ....G 212 677-1970
New York *(G-11172)*
Mohawk Fabric Company Inc ....F 518 842-3090
Amsterdam *(G-358)*
Orbit Industries LLC ....F 914 244-1500
Mount Kisco *(G-8638)*
Solstiss Inc ....G 212 719-9194
New York *(G-12127)*
Somerset Dyeing & Finishing ....E 518 773-7383
Gloversville *(G-5720)*
▲ Somerset Industries Inc ....E 518 773-7383
Gloversville *(G-5721)*
Sunwin Global Industry Inc ....G 646 370-6196
New York *(G-12239)*
Super-Trim Inc ....E 212 255-2370
New York *(G-12241)*
▲ Thompson Packaging Novlt Inc ....G 212 686-4242
New York *(G-12327)*
▲ Veratex Inc ....F 212 683-9300
New York *(G-12520)*

2259 Knitting Mills, NEC

▲ Bank-Miller Co Inc ....E 914 227-9357
Pelham *(G-13489)*
▲ Commonwealth Home Fashion Inc ....D 514 384-8290
Willsboro *(G-17264)*
Hawkins Fabrics Inc ....E 518 773-9550
Gloversville *(G-5714)*
Hofset Fabrics Ltd ....G 718 522-6228
Brooklyn *(G-2082)*
Maidenform LLC ....F 201 436-9200
New York *(G-11110)*
Nochairs Inc ....G 917 748-8731
New York *(G-11449)*
Sextet Fabrics Inc ....F 516 593-0608
East Rockaway *(G-4470)*

2261 Cotton Fabric Finishers

All About Art Inc ....F 718 321-0755
Flushing *(G-5225)*
B & K Dye Cutting Inc ....G 718 497-5216
Brooklyn *(G-1656)*
Basiloff LLC ....G 646 671-0353
New York *(G-9331)*
Carolyn Ray Inc ....G 914 476-0619
Yonkers *(G-17424)*
Central Textiles Inc ....F 212 213-8740
New York *(G-9566)*
D & R Silk Screening Ltd ....F 631 234-7464
Central Islip *(G-3494)*
Dyenamix Inc ....G 212 941-6642
New York *(G-9945)*
Dynamic Screenprinting ....G 518 487-4256
Albany *(G-74)*
Judscott Handprints Ltd ....F 914 347-5515
Elmsford *(G-4759)*
Lee Dyeing Company NC Inc ....F 518 736-5232
Johnstown *(G-7118)*
Loremanss Embroidery Engrav ....F 518 834-9205
Keeseville *(G-7139)*
Marcel Finishing Corp ....E 718 381-2889
Plainview *(G-13618)*
Mountain T-Shirts Inc ....G 518 943-4533
Catskill *(G-3432)*
Printery ....G 315 253-7403
Auburn *(G-514)*
Prismatic Dyeing & Finshg Inc ....D 845 561-1800
Newburgh *(G-12775)*
Reynolds Drapery Service Inc ....F 315 845-8632
Newport *(G-12792)*
▲ Santee Print Works ....F 212 997-1570
New York *(G-11969)*
▲ Seo Ryung Inc ....F 718 321-0755
Flushing *(G-5291)*
Steve Poli Sales ....G 315 487-0394
Camillus *(G-3324)*
Tramwell Inc ....G 315 789-2762
Geneva *(G-5587)*
Ward Sales Co Inc ....G 315 476-5276
Syracuse *(G-16068)*
Z Best Printing Inc ....F 631 595-1400
Deer Park *(G-4230)*

2262 Silk & Man-Made Fabric Finishers

American Spray-On Corp ....E 212 929-2100
New York *(G-9128)*
▲ Ann Gish Inc ....G 212 969-9200
New York *(G-9163)*
▲ Beckmann Converting Inc ....E 518 842-0073
Amsterdam *(G-334)*
Central Textiles Inc ....F 212 213-8740
New York *(G-9566)*
Dyenamix Inc ....G 212 941-6642
New York *(G-9945)*
Eastern Silk Mills Inc ....G 212 730-1300
New York *(G-9966)*
Efs Designs ....G 718 852-9511
Brooklyn *(G-1906)*
◆ Fabric Resources Intl Ltd ....F 516 829-4550
Great Neck *(G-5810)*
▲ Gehring Tricot Corporation ....D 315 429-8551
Garden City *(G-5507)*
Intertex USA Inc ....F 212 279-3601
New York *(G-10641)*
Judscott Handprints Ltd ....F 914 347-5515
Elmsford *(G-4759)*
Knucklehead Embroidery Inc ....G 607 797-2725
Johnson City *(G-7098)*
Marcel Finishing Corp ....E 718 381-2889
Plainview *(G-13618)*
▲ Mv Corp Inc ....C 631 273-8020
Bay Shore *(G-720)*
Prismatic Dyeing & Finshg Inc ....D 845 561-1800
Newburgh *(G-12775)*
▲ Raxon Fabrics Corp ....F 212 532-6816
New York *(G-11804)*
Rescuestuff Inc ....G 718 318-7570
Peekskill *(G-13480)*
Screen Gems Inc ....G 845 561-0036
New Windsor *(G-8953)*
Toltec Fabrics Inc ....C 212 706-9310
New York *(G-12358)*
Valley Stream Sporting Gds Inc ....E 516 593-7800
Lynbrook *(G-7966)*

SIC SECTION
22 TEXTILE MILL PRODUCTS

2269 Textile Finishers, NEC
American Country Quilts & Lin ....G 631 283-5466
  Southampton *(G-15538)*
Artyarns ....G 914 428-0333
  White Plains *(G-17080)*
Ben-Sak Textile Inc ....G 212 279-5122
  New York *(G-9356)*
China Ting Fashion Group (usa) ....G 212 716-1600
  New York *(G-9602)*
▲ Duck River Textiles Inc ....G 212 679-2980
  New York *(G-9936)*
Flexene Corp ....E 631 491-0580
  West Babylon *(G-16792)*
Hosel & Ackerson Inc ....G 212 575-1490
  New York *(G-10509)*
▲ Majestic Rayon Corporation ....E 212 929-6443
  New York *(G-11115)*
Marcel Finishing Corp ....E 718 381-2889
  Plainview *(G-13618)*
National Spinning Co Inc ....E 212 382-6400
  New York *(G-11351)*
Newcastle Fabrics Corp ....G 718 388-6600
  Brooklyn *(G-2369)*
◆ Paxar Corporation ....E 845 398-3229
  Orangeburg *(G-13238)*
Prismatic Dyeing & Finshg Inc ....D 845 561-1800
  Newburgh *(G-12775)*
Skin Prints Inc ....G 845 920-8756
  Pearl River *(G-13466)*
Sml USA Inc ....E 212 736-8800
  New York *(G-12107)*

2273 Carpets & Rugs
Aladdin Manufacturing Corp ....C 212 561-8715
  New York *(G-9069)*
Auto-Mat Company Inc ....E 516 938-7373
  Hicksville *(G-6325)*
Bloomsburg Carpet Inds Inc ....G 212 688-7447
  New York *(G-9417)*
▲ Carpet Fabrications Intl ....E 914 381-6060
  Mamaroneck *(G-8026)*
Edward Fields Incorporated ....F 212 310-0400
  New York *(G-9985)*
▲ Elizabeth Eakins Inc ....F 212 628-1950
  New York *(G-10008)*
▲ Excellent Art Mfg Corp ....F 718 388-7075
  Inwood *(G-6756)*
Interfaceflor LLC ....E 212 686-8284
  New York *(G-10627)*
Lanes Flr Cvrngs Intriors Inc ....E 212 532-5200
  New York *(G-10926)*
▲ Loom Concepts LLC ....E 212 813-9586
  New York *(G-11030)*
Lorena Canals USA Inc ....G 844 567-3622
  Hastings On Hudson *(G-6005)*
Mannington Mills Inc ....G 212 251-0290
  New York *(G-11137)*
▲ Mark Nelson Designs LLC ....F 646 422-7020
  New York *(G-11156)*
Mgk Group Inc ....E 212 989-2732
  New York *(G-11246)*
Michaelian & Kohlberg Inc ....G 212 431-9009
  New York *(G-11251)*
▲ Northpoint Trading Inc ....E 212 481-8001
  New York *(G-11460)*
Odegard Inc ....F 212 545-0069
  Long Island City *(G-7828)*
Pawling Corporation ....D 845 373-9300
  Wassaic *(G-16600)*
▲ Renaissnce Crpt Tapestries Inc ....F 212 696-0080
  New York *(G-11831)*
Rosecore Division ....F 516 504-4530
  Great Neck *(G-5835)*
Safavieh Inc ....B 516 945-1900
  Port Washington *(G-13860)*
▲ Scalamandre Silks Inc ....D 212 980-3888
  New York *(G-11982)*
Shaw Contract Flrg Svcs Inc ....G 212 953-7429
  New York *(G-12047)*
Shyam Ahuja Limited ....G 212 644-5910
  New York *(G-12057)*
▲ Sunrise Tile Inc ....G 718 939-0538
  Flushing *(G-5299)*
Tandus Centiva Inc ....C 212 206-7170
  New York *(G-12279)*
Tdg Operations LLC ....G 212 779-4300
  New York *(G-12284)*
Tiger 21 LLC ....G 212 360-1700
  New York *(G-12337)*

Tsar USA LLC ....F 646 415-7968
  New York *(G-12415)*
Wells Rugs Inc ....G 516 676-2056
  Glen Cove *(G-5631)*

2281 Yarn Spinning Mills
Advanced Yarn Technologies Inc ....E 518 239-6600
  Durham *(G-4354)*
▲ Colortex Inc ....G 212 564-2000
  New York *(G-9676)*
Great Adirondack Yarn Company ....F 518 843-3381
  Amsterdam *(G-349)*
Missiontex Inc ....G 718 532-9053
  Brooklyn *(G-2322)*
National Spinning Co Inc ....E 212 382-6400
  New York *(G-11351)*
Printz and Patternz LLC ....G 518 944-6020
  Schenectady *(G-15286)*
St Regis Sportswear Ltd ....G 518 725-6767
  Gloversville *(G-5722)*
◆ Ultrafab Inc ....C 585 924-2186
  Farmington *(G-5158)*
▼ United Thread Mills Corp ....G 516 536-3900
  Oceanside *(G-13102)*

2282 Yarn Texturizing, Throwing, Twisting & Winding Mills
▲ La Lame Inc ....G 212 921-9770
  New York *(G-10909)*
▲ Majestic Rayon Corporation ....E 212 929-6443
  New York *(G-11115)*
Marsha Fleisher ....F 845 679-6500
  Woodstock *(G-17364)*

2284 Thread Mills
Albany International Corp ....C 607 749-7226
  Homer *(G-6515)*
American Quality Embroidery ....E 631 467-3200
  Ronkonkoma *(G-14869)*
One In A Million Inc ....G 516 829-1111
  Valley Stream *(G-16417)*
▼ United Thread Mills Corp ....G 516 536-3900
  Oceanside *(G-13102)*

2295 Fabrics Coated Not Rubberized
A-One Laminating Corp ....G 718 266-6002
  Brooklyn *(G-1540)*
A-One Moving & Storage Inc ....E 718 266-6002
  Brooklyn *(G-1541)*
Architectural Fiberglass Corp ....E 631 842-4772
  Copiague *(G-3892)*
▲ Beckmann Converting Inc ....E 518 842-0073
  Amsterdam *(G-334)*
Breton Industries Inc ....D 518 842-3030
  Amsterdam *(G-336)*
▲ Chemprene Inc ....C 845 831-2800
  Beacon *(G-782)*
▲ Chemprene Holding Inc ....C 845 831-2800
  Beacon *(G-783)*
Co2 Textiles LLC ....G 212 269-2222
  New York *(G-9650)*
▲ Comfort Care Textiles Inc ....E 631 543-0531
  Commack *(G-3828)*
▲ Eurotex Inc ....F 716 205-8861
  Niagara Falls *(G-12816)*
◆ Fabric Resources Intl Ltd ....F 516 829-4550
  Great Neck *(G-5810)*
◆ GE Polymershapes ....F 516 433-4092
  Hicksville *(G-6347)*
GM Insulation Corp ....F 516 354-6000
  Elmont *(G-4721)*
▲ Imperial Laminators Co Inc ....F 718 272-9500
  Brooklyn *(G-2098)*
Kiltronx Enviro Systems LLC ....E 239 273-8870
  New York *(G-10844)*
New York Cutting & Gumming Co ......E 212 563-4146
  Middletown *(G-8454)*
▲ Newtex Industries Inc ....E 585 924-9135
  Victor *(G-16493)*
▼ Perry Plastics Inc ....F 718 747-5600
  Flushing *(G-5281)*
Piedmont Plastics Inc ....G 518 724-0563
  Albany *(G-121)*
Precision Cstm Coatings I LLC ....C 212 868-5770
  New York *(G-11695)*
▲ Tonoga Inc ....C 518 658-3202
  Petersburg *(G-13528)*
▲ Tpi Industries LLC ....E 845 692-2820
  Middletown *(G-8465)*

2296 Tire Cord & Fabric
Albany International Corp ....C 518 445-2230
  Menands *(G-8365)*
DC Fabrication & Welding Inc ....G 845 295-0215
  Ferndale *(G-5169)*
Designatronics Incorporated ....B 516 328-3300
  New Hyde Park *(G-8826)*
Haines Equipment Inc ....E 607 566-8531
  Avoca *(G-537)*
York Industries Inc ....E 516 746-3736
  Garden City Park *(G-5546)*

2297 Fabrics, Nonwoven
Albany International Corp ....C 518 445-2200
  Rensselaer *(G-14042)*
▲ Fabrication Enterprises Inc ....E 914 591-9300
  Elmsford *(G-4753)*
▲ Imperial Laminators Co Inc ....F 718 272-9500
  Brooklyn *(G-2098)*
▲ Legendary Auto Interiors Ltd ....E 315 331-1212
  Newark *(G-12734)*
Mgk Group Inc ....E 212 989-2732
  New York *(G-11246)*
▲ Saint-Gobain Adfors Amer Inc ....D 716 775-3900
  Grand Island *(G-5768)*
Saint-Gobain Adfors Amer Inc ....D 585 589-4401
  Albion *(G-170)*

2298 Cordage & Twine
▲ A & A Line & Wire Corp ....F 718 456-2657
  Maspeth *(G-8110)*
Albany International Corp ....C 607 749-7226
  Homer *(G-6515)*
All-Lifts Incorporated ....E 518 465-3461
  Albany *(G-44)*
Cables and Chips Inc ....E 212 619-3132
  New York *(G-9493)*
▲ Continental Cordage Corp ....D 315 655-9800
  Cazenovia *(G-3443)*
Cortland Company Inc ....C 607 753-8276
  Cortland *(G-4017)*
◆ Fiber Instrument Sales Inc ....C 315 736-2206
  Oriskany *(G-13309)*
Fiberone LLC ....F 315 434-8877
  East Syracuse *(G-4529)*
▲ Gladding Braided Products LLC .....E 315 653-7211
  South Otselic *(G-15531)*
Sampo Inc ....E 315 896-2606
  Barneveld *(G-617)*
▲ Schoen Trimming & Cord Co Inc ....F 212 255-3949
  New York *(G-11996)*
◆ Simplicity Creative Group Inc ....A 212 686-7676
  New York *(G-12082)*
T M International LLC ....G 718 842-0949
  Bronx *(G-1471)*
Triad Network Technologies ....E 585 924-8505
  Victor *(G-16509)*

2299 Textile Goods, NEC
A Thousand Cranes Inc ....F 212 724-9596
  New York *(G-8993)*
▲ Ace Drop Cloth Canvas Pdts Inc ....E 718 731-1550
  Bronx *(G-1260)*
Alok Inc ....G 212 643-4360
  New York *(G-9097)*
▲ Arabella Textiles LLC ....G 212 679-0611
  New York *(G-9189)*
Architectural Textiles USA Inc ....E 212 213-6972
  New York *(G-9196)*
▲ Benson Mills Inc ....E 718 236-6743
  Brooklyn *(G-1684)*
Blc Textiles Inc ....E 516 791-4500
  Mineola *(G-8499)*
Copen United LLC ....E 212 819-0008
  New York *(G-9718)*
Courtaulds Textiles Ltd ....F 212 946-8000
  New York *(G-9737)*
▲ David King Linen Inc ....E 718 241-7298
  Brooklyn *(G-1842)*
Dean Trading Corp ....F 718 485-0600
  Brooklyn *(G-1847)*
Federal Prison Industries ....D 518 897-4000
  Ray Brook *(G-14024)*
▲ Feldman Company Inc ....F 212 966-1303
  New York *(G-10150)*
Fibrix LLC ....E 716 683-4100
  Depew *(G-4257)*
Fil Doux Inc ....F 212 202-1459
  Brooklyn *(G-1969)*

Employee Codes: A=Over 500 employees, B=251-500
C=101-250, D=51-100, E=20-50, F=10-19, G=5-9

▲ Gappa Textiles Inc ... F ... 212 481-7100
New York *(G-10247)*
Ghani Textiles Inc ... G ... 718 859-4561
Brooklyn *(G-2023)*
▲ Global Resources Sg Inc ... F ... 212 686-1411
New York *(G-10320)*
Ino-Tex LLC ... G ... 212 400-2205
New York *(G-10606)*
◆ Ivi Services Inc ... D ... 607 729-5111
Binghamton *(G-929)*
▲ James Thompson & Company Inc ... G ... 212 686-4242
New York *(G-10698)*
Jo-Vin Decorators Inc ... E ... 718 441-9350
Woodhaven *(G-17306)*
Jonice Industries ... G ... 516 640-4283
Hempstead *(G-6276)*
▲ K F I Inc ... G ... 516 546-2904
Roosevelt *(G-15006)*
Kiltronx Enviro Systems LLC ... C ... 917 971-7177
Hauppauge *(G-6104)*
▲ La Lame Inc ... G ... 212 921-9770
New York *(G-10909)*
▲ Lintex Linens Inc ... B ... 212 679-8046
New York *(G-11003)*
▲ Manrico Usa Inc ... G ... 212 794-4200
New York *(G-11140)*
Navy Plum LLC ... G ... 845 641-7441
Monsey *(G-8576)*
Novita Fabrics Furnishing Corp ... F ... 516 299-4500
Glen Cove *(G-5623)*
Priva USA Inc ... G ... 518 963-4074
Willsboro *(G-17266)*
Return Textiles LLC ... G ... 646 408-0108
New York *(G-11847)*
Rovel Manufacturing Co Inc ... G ... 516 365-2752
Roslyn *(G-15023)*
S Hellerman Inc ... F ... 718 622-2995
Brooklyn *(G-2526)*
◆ Sabbsons International Inc ... F ... 718 360-1947
Brooklyn *(G-2528)*
▼ Shannon Entps Wstn NY Inc ... D ... 716 693-7954
North Tonawanda *(G-12993)*
Simple Elegance New York Inc ... F ... 718 360-1947
Brooklyn *(G-2562)*
Sivko Furs Inc ... G ... 607 698-4827
Canisteo *(G-3379)*
Solivaira Specialties Inc ... D ... 716 693-4009
North Tonawanda *(G-12996)*
◆ Solvaira Specialties Inc ... C ... 716 693-4040
North Tonawanda *(G-12997)*
▲ Soundcoat Company Inc ... D ... 631 242-2200
Deer Park *(G-4212)*
Southern Adrndck Fbr Prdcrs CP ... G ... 518 692-2700
Greenwich *(G-5893)*
Superior Fiber Mills Inc ... E ... 718 782-7500
Brooklyn *(G-2628)*
Thistle Hill Weavers ... G ... 518 284-2729
Cherry Valley *(G-3597)*
▼ TRM Linen Inc ... G ... 718 686-6075
Brooklyn *(G-2683)*
Vincent Manufacturing Co Inc ... F ... 315 823-0280
Little Falls *(G-7506)*
▲ Yankee Corp ... F ... 718 589-1377
Bronx *(G-1495)*

23 APPAREL AND OTHER FINISHED PRODUCTS MADE FROM FABRICS AND SIMILAR MATERIAL

2311 Men's & Boys' Suits, Coats & Overcoats

▲ Adrian Jules Ltd ... D ... 585 342-5886
Rochester *(G-14174)*
▲ Advance Apparel Intl Inc ... G ... 212 944-0984
New York *(G-9034)*
Allytex LLC ... G ... 518 376-7539
Ballston Spa *(G-591)*
◆ Amerimade Coat Inc ... G ... 212 216-0925
New York *(G-9133)*
Bestec Concept Inc ... G ... 718 937-5848
Long Island City *(G-7683)*
Bindle and Keep ... G ... 917 740-5002
Brooklyn *(G-1699)*
▲ Blueduck Trading Ltd ... G ... 212 268-3122
New York *(G-9424)*
Canali USA Inc ... G ... 212 767-0205
New York *(G-9510)*
▲ Check Group LLC ... D ... 212 221-4700
New York *(G-9587)*
▲ Christian Casey LLC ... E ... 212 500-2200
New York *(G-9608)*
Christian Casey LLC ... E ... 212 500-2200
New York *(G-9609)*
▲ Concorde Apparel Company LLC ... G ... 212 307-7848
New York *(G-9695)*
Crisada Inc ... G ... 718 729-9730
Long Island City *(G-7707)*
Donna Karan Company LLC ... C ... 212 789-1500
New York *(G-9900)*
▲ Donna Karan Company LLC ... B ... 212 789-1500
New York *(G-9901)*
Elite Uniforms Ltd ... G ... 516 487-5481
Great Neck *(G-5805)*
▲ Excelled Shpskin Lea Coat Corp ... F ... 212 594-5843
New York *(G-10103)*
▲ G-III Apparel Group Ltd ... C ... 212 403-0500
New York *(G-10234)*
Giliberto Designs Inc ... E ... 212 695-0216
New York *(G-10296)*
▲ Great 4 Image ... E ... 518 424-2058
Rensselaer *(G-14047)*
▲ Hana Sportswear Inc ... E ... 315 639-6332
Dexter *(G-4285)*
Hickey Freeman Tailored CL Inc ... E ... 585 467-7240
Rochester *(G-14433)*
◆ Hugo Boss Usa Inc ... D ... 212 940-0600
New York *(G-10528)*
J & X Production ... F ... 646 366-8288
New York *(G-10675)*
John Kochis Custom Designs ... G ... 212 244-6046
New York *(G-10749)*
▲ L Allmeier ... G ... 212 243-7390
New York *(G-10900)*
▲ L F Fashion Orient Intl Co Ltd ... G ... 917 667-3398
New York *(G-10901)*
▲ M Hidary & Co Inc ... D ... 212 736-6540
New York *(G-11073)*
▲ Manchu New York Inc ... G ... 212 921-5050
New York *(G-11125)*
▲ Martin Greenfield Clothiers ... C ... 718 497-5480
Brooklyn *(G-2277)*
Med-Eng LLC ... E ... 315 713-0103
Ogdensburg *(G-13119)*
▲ Mv Corp Inc ... C ... 631 273-8020
Bay Shore *(G-720)*
▲ Occunomix International LLC ... E ... 631 741-1940
Port Jeff STA *(G-13769)*
Otex Protective Inc ... G ... 585 232-7160
Rochester *(G-14559)*
Pat & Rose Dress Inc ... D ... 212 279-1357
New York *(G-11578)*
▲ Philipp Plein Madison Ave LLC ... F ... 212 644-3304
New York *(G-11646)*
Primo Coat Corp ... E ... 718 349-2070
Long Island City *(G-7847)*
Proper Cloth LLC ... G ... 646 964-4221
New York *(G-11736)*
◆ Ralph Lauren Corporation ... B ... 212 318-7000
New York *(G-11792)*
▲ Roth Clothing Co Inc ... G ... 718 384-4927
Brooklyn *(G-2508)*
Royal Clothing Corp ... G ... 718 436-5841
Brooklyn *(G-2510)*
▲ Saint Laurie Ltd ... E ... 212 643-1916
New York *(G-11954)*
▲ Shane Tex Inc ... F ... 516 486-7522
Hempstead *(G-6287)*
Strong Group Inc ... G ... 516 766-6300
Oceanside *(G-13097)*
Therese The Childrens Collectn ... G ... 518 346-2315
Schenectady *(G-15305)*
Tom James Company ... F ... 212 581-6968
New York *(G-12361)*
Tom James Company ... F ... 212 593-0204
New York *(G-12362)*
Uniforms By Park Coats Inc ... E ... 718 499-1182
Brooklyn *(G-2698)*
▲ Urban Textiles Inc ... F ... 212 777-1900
New York *(G-12481)*
Vf Imagewear Inc ... E ... 718 352-2363
Bayside *(G-778)*
Woodmere Fabrics Inc ... G ... 212 695-0144
New York *(G-12656)*
Wp Lavori USA Inc ... G ... 718 855-4295
Brooklyn *(G-2769)*
◆ Wp Lavori USA Inc ... G ... 212 244-6074
New York *(G-12668)*
▲ Xmh-Hfi Inc ... A ... 585 467-7240
Rochester *(G-14772)*
Yong Ji Productions Inc ... E ... 917 559-4616
Corona *(G-4010)*

2321 Men's & Boys' Shirts

Americo Group Inc ... F ... 212 563-2700
New York *(G-9130)*
▲ Americo Group Inc ... D ... 212 563-2700
New York *(G-9131)*
Arthur Gluck Shirtmakers Inc ... F ... 212 755-8165
Brooklyn *(G-1636)*
▲ Ben Wachter Associates Inc ... G ... 212 736-4064
New York *(G-9354)*
▲ Bowe Industries Inc ... D ... 718 441-6464
Glendale *(G-5646)*
Bowe Industries Inc ... D ... 718 441-6464
Glendale *(G-5647)*
▲ Check Group LLC ... D ... 212 221-4700
New York *(G-9587)*
▲ Christian Casey LLC ... E ... 212 500-2200
New York *(G-9608)*
Christian Casey LLC ... E ... 212 500-2200
New York *(G-9609)*
Colony Holdings Intl LLC ... F ... 212 868-2800
New York *(G-9671)*
Cyberlimit Inc ... F ... 212 840-9597
New York *(G-9775)*
◆ Donna Karan International Inc ... A ... 212 789-1500
New York *(G-9902)*
Donna Karan International Inc ... G ... 212 768-5800
New York *(G-9903)*
Ferris USA LLC ... G ... 617 895-8102
New York *(G-10155)*
◆ Garan Incorporated ... C ... 212 563-1292
New York *(G-10248)*
▼ Garan Manufacturing Corp ... G ... 212 563-2000
New York *(G-10249)*
Gbg National Brands Group LLC ... G ... 646 839-7000
New York *(G-10252)*
Gce International Inc ... D ... 773 263-1210
New York *(G-10261)*
◆ Great Universal Corp ... F ... 917 302-0065
New York *(G-10359)*
Groupe 16sur20 LLC ... F ... 212 625-1620
New York *(G-10372)*
◆ Haddad Bros Inc ... F ... 212 563-2117
New York *(G-10393)*
Ibrands International LLC ... F ... 212 354-1330
New York *(G-10547)*
Interbrand LLC ... G ... 212 840-9595
New York *(G-10624)*
Jacks and Jokers 52 LLC ... G ... 917 740-2595
New York *(G-10687)*
Jordache Enterprises Inc ... D ... 212 944-1330
New York *(G-10760)*
◆ Jordache Enterprises Inc ... C ... 212 643-8400
New York *(G-10761)*
Just Brass Inc ... G ... 212 724-5447
New York *(G-10792)*
▲ Kt Group Inc ... G ... 212 760-2500
New York *(G-10892)*
Lt2 LLC ... E ... 212 684-1510
New York *(G-11056)*
M S B International Ltd ... F ... 212 302-5551
New York *(G-11076)*
Miltons of New York Inc ... G ... 212 997-3359
New York *(G-11272)*
▲ Mulitex Usa Inc ... G ... 212 398-0440
New York *(G-11323)*
▲ Nat Nast Company Inc ... G ... 212 575-1186
New York *(G-11341)*
Oxford Industries Inc ... F ... 212 840-2288
New York *(G-11541)*
Perry Ellis International Inc ... F ... 212 536-5400
New York *(G-11622)*
◆ Perry Ellis Menswear LLC ... C ... 212 221-7500
New York *(G-11624)*
Phillips-Van Heusen Europe ... F ... 212 381-3500
New York *(G-11649)*
◆ Pvh Corp ... D ... 212 381-3500
New York *(G-11756)*
Pvh Corp ... G ... 845 561-0233
New Windsor *(G-8949)*
Pvh Corp ... G ... 631 254-8200
Deer Park *(G-4195)*
Pvh Corp ... G ... 212 719-2600
New York *(G-11759)*
Ralph Lauren Corporation ... F ... 212 421-1570
New York *(G-11793)*
◆ Ralph Lauren Corporation ... B ... 212 318-7000
New York *(G-11792)*

23 APPAREL AND OTHER FINISHED PRODUCTS MADE FROM FABRICS AND SIMILAR MATERIAL

▲ Roffe Accessories Inc .... F 212 213-1440
  New York *(G-11903)*
Saad Collection Inc .... F 212 937-0341
  New York *(G-11949)*
▲ Schwartz Textile Converting Co ..... E 718 499-8243
  Brooklyn *(G-2537)*
Sifonya Inc .... G 212 620-4512
  New York *(G-12065)*
▲ Sue & Sam Co Inc .... E 718 436-1672
  Brooklyn *(G-2618)*
◆ Warnaco Inc .... B 212 287-8000
  New York *(G-12587)*
Warnaco Inc .... F 718 722-3000
  Brooklyn *(G-2744)*
Whittall & Shon .... G 212 594-2626
  New York *(G-12629)*
Yale Trouser Corporation .... F 516 255-0700
  Oceanside *(G-13107)*

2322 Men's & Boys' Underwear & Nightwear

Apparel Partnership Group LLC ..... G 212 302-7722
  New York *(G-9178)*
Becks Classic Mfg Inc .... D 631 435-3800
  Brentwood *(G-1178)*
▲ Check Group LLC .... D 212 221-4700
  New York *(G-9587)*
▲ Christian Casey LLC .... E 212 500-2200
  New York *(G-9608)*
Christian Casey LLC .... E 212 500-2200
  New York *(G-9609)*
▲ Comme-Ci Comme-CA AP Group .... E 631 300-1035
  Hauppauge *(G-6050)*
▲ Solo Licensing Corp .... G 212 244-5505
  New York *(G-12125)*
▲ Tommy John Inc .... E 800 708-3490
  New York *(G-12366)*
◆ Twist Intimate Group LLC .... G 212 695-5990
  New York *(G-12433)*
◆ Warnaco Group Inc .... D 212 287-8000
  New York *(G-12586)*
◆ Warnaco Inc .... B 212 287-8000
  New York *(G-12587)*
Warnaco Inc .... F 718 722-3000
  Brooklyn *(G-2744)*
▲ Waterbury Garment LLC .... E 212 725-1500
  New York *(G-12597)*
▲ Wickers Sportswear Inc .... G 631 543-1700
  Commack *(G-3848)*

2323 Men's & Boys' Neckwear

Countess Mara Inc .... G 212 768-7300
  New York *(G-9735)*
Fogel Neckwear Corp .... D 212 686-7673
  New York *(G-10184)*
J M C Bow Co Inc .... F 718 686-8110
  Brooklyn *(G-2125)*
JS Blank & Co Inc .... E 212 689-4835
  New York *(G-10776)*
MANE Enterprises Inc .... D 718 472-4955
  Long Island City *(G-7801)*
Mongru Neckwear Inc .... E 718 706-0406
  Long Island City *(G-7816)*
◆ Perry Ellis Menswear LLC .... C 212 221-7500
  New York *(G-11624)*
◆ Ralph Lauren Corporation .... B 212 318-7000
  New York *(G-11792)*
Randa Accessories Lea Gds LLC ...... D 212 354-5100
  New York *(G-11799)*
▲ Roffe Accessories Inc .... F 212 213-1440
  New York *(G-11903)*
S Broome and Co Inc .... D 718 663-6800
  Long Island City *(G-7870)*
▲ Selini Neckwear Inc .... E 212 268-5488
  New York *(G-12026)*
▲ Tie King Inc .... E 718 768-8484
  Brooklyn *(G-2659)*
Tie King Inc .... G 212 714-9511
  New York *(G-12336)*
Tie View Neckwear Co Inc .... E 718 853-4156
  Brooklyn *(G-2660)*
Valenti Neckwear Co Inc .... G 914 969-0700
  Yonkers *(G-17494)*
W B Bow Tie Corp .... F 212 683-6130
  New York *(G-12572)*
◆ Warnaco Inc .... B 212 287-8000
  New York *(G-12587)*
Wetherall Contracting NY Inc .... G 718 894-7011
  Middle Village *(G-8417)*

2325 Men's & Boys' Separate Trousers & Casual Slacks

▲ Adrian Jules Ltd .... D 585 342-5886
  Rochester *(G-14174)*
Bruno & Canio Ltd .... E 845 624-3060
  Nanuet *(G-8753)*
▲ C E Chquie Ltd .... G 212 268-0006
  New York *(G-9490)*
▲ Check Group LLC .... D 212 221-4700
  New York *(G-9587)*
▲ Christian Casey LLC .... E 212 500-2200
  New York *(G-9608)*
Christian Casey LLC .... E 212 500-2200
  New York *(G-9609)*
Donna Karan Company LLC .... C 212 789-1500
  New York *(G-9900)*
▲ Donna Karan Company LLC .... B 212 789-1500
  New York *(G-9901)*
◆ Donna Karan International Inc ..... E 212 789-1500
  New York *(G-9902)*
Donna Karan International Inc .... G 212 768-5800
  New York *(G-9903)*
Gbg Denim Usa LLC .... G 646 839-7000
  Plattsburgh *(G-13663)*
Groupe 16sur20 LLC .... F 212 625-1620
  New York *(G-10372)*
Guess Inc .... E 845 928-3930
  Central Valley *(G-3524)*
Guess Inc .... E 315 539-5634
  Waterloo *(G-16628)*
Guess Inc .... E 212 286-9856
  New York *(G-10379)*
Guess Inc .... E 716 298-3561
  Niagara Falls *(G-12830)*
▲ Hertling Trousers Inc .... E 718 784-6100
  Brooklyn *(G-2079)*
Hot Kiss Inc .... G 212 730-0404
  New York *(G-10512)*
◆ Hugo Boss Usa Inc .... D 212 940-0600
  New York *(G-10528)*
▲ Int Trading USA LLC .... C 212 760-2338
  New York *(G-10614)*
Jordache Enterprises Inc .... D 212 944-1330
  New York *(G-10760)*
◆ Jordache Enterprises Inc .... C 212 643-8400
  New York *(G-10761)*
Kalikow Brothers LP .... E 212 643-0315
  New York *(G-10804)*
Kaltex America Inc .... F 212 971-0575
  New York *(G-10806)*
Levi Strauss & Co .... F 212 944-8555
  New York *(G-10977)*
Levi Strauss & Co .... F 917 213-6263
  Flushing *(G-5265)*
Lucky Brand Dungarees LLC .... E 631 350-7358
  Huntington Station *(G-6715)*
▲ M Hidary & Co Inc .... D 212 736-6540
  New York *(G-11073)*
M S B International Ltd .... F 212 302-5551
  New York *(G-11076)*
▲ Martin Greenfield Clothiers .... C 718 497-5480
  Brooklyn *(G-2277)*
Messex Group Inc .... G 646 229-2582
  New York *(G-11240)*
Miltons of New York Inc .... G 212 997-3359
  New York *(G-11272)*
▲ Montero International Inc .... G 212 695-1787
  Westbury *(G-17013)*
▲ Mulitex Usa Inc .... G 212 398-0440
  New York *(G-11323)*
▲ One Jeanswear Group Inc .... E 212 835-2500
  New York *(G-11506)*
Pat & Rose Dress Inc .... D 212 279-1357
  New York *(G-11578)*
Perry Ellis International Inc .... F 212 536-5400
  New York *(G-11622)*
◆ Perry Ellis Menswear LLC .... C 212 221-7500
  New York *(G-11624)*
Primo Coat Corp .... E 718 349-2070
  Long Island City *(G-7847)*
◆ Ralph Lauren Corporation .... B 212 318-7000
  New York *(G-11792)*
◆ Ryba General Merchandise Inc .... G 718 522-2028
  Brooklyn *(G-2519)*
Sean John Clothing Inc .... E 212 500-2200
  New York *(G-12010)*
Sean John Clothing Inc .... E 212 500-2200
  New York *(G-12011)*
▲ Xmh-Hfi Inc .... A 585 467-7240
  Rochester *(G-14772)*

Yale Trouser Corporation .... F 516 255-0700
  Oceanside *(G-13107)*

2326 Men's & Boys' Work Clothing

5 Star Apparel LLC .... G 212 563-1233
  New York *(G-8977)*
▲ Ace Drop Cloth Canvas Pdts Inc .... E 718 731-1550
  Bronx *(G-1260)*
▲ Adar Medical Uniform LLC .... G 718 935-1197
  Brooklyn *(G-1560)*
AKOS Group Ltd .... E 212 683-4747
  New York *(G-9067)*
American Apparel Ltd .... G 516 504-4559
  Great Neck *(G-5790)*
Badgley Mischka Licensing LLC ..... E 212 921-1585
  New York *(G-9301)*
▲ Bangla Clothing USA Inc .... G 201 679-2615
  New York *(G-9314)*
Beardslee Realty .... E 516 747-5557
  Mineola *(G-8497)*
▲ Bespoke Apparel Inc .... E 212 382-0330
  New York *(G-9372)*
▲ Best Medical Wear Ltd .... G 718 858-5544
  Brooklyn *(G-1688)*
Bestec Concept Inc .... E 718 937-5848
  Long Island City *(G-7683)*
▲ Billion Tower Intl LLC .... F 212 220-0608
  New York *(G-9397)*
Broadway Knitting Mills Inc .... G 716 692-4421
  North Tonawanda *(G-12961)*
▲ Courage Clothing Co Inc .... F 212 354-5690
  New York *(G-9736)*
Dalcom USA Ltd .... F 516 466-7733
  Great Neck *(G-5802)*
David Christy .... G 607 863-4610
  Cincinnatus *(G-3653)*
Doral Apparel Group Inc .... G 917 208-5652
  New York *(G-9908)*
▲ Du Monde Trading Inc .... E 212 944-1306
  New York *(G-9933)*
▲ E J Manufacturing Inc .... G 516 313-9380
  Merrick *(G-8384)*
▲ Eighteen Liana Trading Inc .... E 718 369-4247
  New York *(G-9989)*
Enzo Manzoni LLC .... G 212 464-7000
  Brooklyn *(G-1928)*
Ferris USA LLC .... E 617 895-8102
  New York *(G-10155)*
◆ HC Contracting Inc .... D 212 643-9292
  New York *(G-10433)*
Hillary Merchant Inc .... G 646 575-9242
  New York *(G-10476)*
Intermedia Outdoors Inc .... D 212 852-6600
  New York *(G-10629)*
Intrigue Concepts Inc .... G 800 424-8170
  Roosevelt *(G-15005)*
Joseph Abboud Manufacturing ..... G 212 586-9140
  New York *(G-10764)*
Kimmiekakes LLC .... F 212 946-0311
  New York *(G-10849)*
Kollage Work Too Ltd .... G 212 695-1821
  New York *(G-10872)*
Lady Brass Co Inc .... G 516 887-8040
  Hewlett *(G-6308)*
Medline Industries Inc .... B 845 344-3301
  Middletown *(G-8450)*
▲ Mesh LLC .... E 646 839-7000
  New York *(G-11237)*
New York Hospital Disposable .... E 718 384-1620
  Brooklyn *(G-2365)*
Norcorp Inc .... E 914 666-1310
  Mount Kisco *(G-8637)*
▲ Occunomix International LLC ..... E 631 741-1940
  Port Jeff STA *(G-13769)*
▲ Penfli Industries Inc .... F 212 947-6080
  Great Neck *(G-5830)*
Rag & Bone Industries LLC .... D 212 249-3331
  New York *(G-11786)*
▲ Rag & Bone Industries LLC .... D 212 278-8214
  New York *(G-11787)*
Richard Manufacturing Co Inc ...... G 718 254-0958
  Brooklyn *(G-2493)*
▲ Ruleville Manufacturing Co Inc .... G 212 695-1620
  New York *(G-11935)*
▼ S & H Uniform Corp .... D 914 937-6800
  White Plains *(G-17164)*
Sarar Usa Inc .... G 845 928-8874
  Central Valley *(G-3526)*
Starmark Apparel Inc .... E 212 967-6347
  New York *(G-12187)*

Employee Codes: A=Over 500 employees, B=251-500
C=101-250, D=51-100, E=20-50, F=10-19, G=5-9

23 APPAREL AND OTHER FINISHED PRODUCTS MADE FROM FABRICS AND SIMILAR MATERIAL SIC SECTION

Stealth Inc.......F....... 718 252-7900
Brooklyn *(G-2602)*
▲ Ventura Enterprise Co Inc.......E....... 212 391-0170
New York *(G-12517)*
Vf Imagewear Inc.......E....... 718 352-2363
Bayside *(G-778)*

2329 Men's & Boys' Clothing, NEC

Adpro Sports Inc.......D....... 716 854-5116
Buffalo *(G-2798)*
▲ Alexander Wang Incorporated.......D....... 212 532-3103
New York *(G-9083)*
All Net Ltd.......F....... 516 504-4559
Great Neck *(G-5788)*
◆ Alleson of Rochester Inc.......D....... 585 272-0630
Rochester *(G-14187)*
Alleson of Rochester Inc.......E....... 315 789-8464
Geneva *(G-5569)*
▲ Alpha 6 Distributions LLC.......F....... 516 801-8290
Locust Valley *(G-7628)*
▲ American Challenge Enterprises.......G....... 631 595-7171
New Hyde Park *(G-8815)*
Apogee Retail NY.......G....... 516 731-1727
Levittown *(G-7423)*
Bandit International Ltd.......F....... 718 402-2100
Bronx *(G-1280)*
▲ Beluga Inc.......E....... 212 594-5511
New York *(G-9353)*
◆ Benetton Trading Usa Inc.......G....... 212 593-0290
New York *(G-9359)*
Bernette Apparel LLC.......F....... 212 279-5526
New York *(G-9366)*
Bert Wassererman.......G....... 212 759-5210
New York *(G-9369)*
▲ Big Idea Brands LLC.......F....... 212 938-0270
New York *(G-9394)*
Billion Tower USA LLC.......G....... 212 220-0608
New York *(G-9398)*
Brigantine Inc.......G....... 212 354-8550
New York *(G-9459)*
Broadway Knitting Mills Inc.......G....... 716 692-4421
North Tonawanda *(G-12961)*
Broken Threads Inc.......G....... 212 730-4351
New York *(G-9468)*
▲ Brunschwig & Fils LLC.......F....... 800 538-1880
Bethpage *(G-865)*
By Robert James.......G....... 212 253-2121
New York *(G-9485)*
▲ C E Chquie Ltd.......G....... 212 268-0006
New York *(G-9490)*
Caroda Inc.......E....... 212 630-9986
New York *(G-9528)*
Central Mills Inc.......C....... 212 221-0748
New York *(G-9565)*
City Jeans Inc.......G....... 718 239-5353
Bronx *(G-1300)*
Clique Apparel Inc.......G....... 516 375-7969
Valley Stream *(G-16404)*
Columbia Sportswear Company.......C....... 631 274-6091
Deer Park *(G-4119)*
▲ Comme-Ci Comme-CA AP Group.......E....... 631 300-1035
Hauppauge *(G-6050)*
Continental Knitting Mills.......G....... 631 242-5330
Deer Park *(G-4120)*
▲ Cotton Emporium Inc.......G....... 718 894-3365
Glendale *(G-5650)*
Cotton Express Inc.......E....... 212 921-4588
New York *(G-9729)*
Cougar Sport Inc.......F....... 212 947-3054
New York *(G-9732)*
Craftatlantic LLC.......F....... 646 726-4205
New York *(G-9744)*
▲ David Peyser Sportswear Inc.......C....... 631 231-7788
Bay Shore *(G-691)*
David Peyser Sportswear Inc.......E....... 212 695-7716
New York *(G-9821)*
▲ Endurance LLC.......E....... 212 719-2500
New York *(G-10033)*
Eon Collections.......E....... 212 695-1263
New York *(G-10048)*
◆ Eternal Fortune Fashion LLC.......F....... 212 965-5322
New York *(G-10077)*
Ferris USA LLC.......G....... 617 895-8102
New York *(G-10155)*
Feyem USA Inc.......G....... 845 363-6253
Brewster *(G-1219)*
▲ Fieldston Clothes Inc.......G....... 212 354-8550
New York *(G-10161)*
▲ G-III Apparel Group Ltd.......C....... 212 403-0500
New York *(G-10234)*
Gametime Sportswear Plus LLC.......G....... 315 724-5893
Utica *(G-16335)*
▲ Gemtex Inc.......G....... 212 302-0102
New York *(G-10270)*
◆ General Sportwear Company Inc.......G....... 212 764-5820
New York *(G-10274)*
Groupe 16sur20 LLC.......F....... 212 625-1620
New York *(G-10372)*
Haculla Nyc Inc.......F....... 718 886-3163
Fresh Meadows *(G-5441)*
Hansae Co Ltd.......G....... 212 354-6690
New York *(G-10410)*
▼ Herman Kay Company Ltd.......C....... 212 239-2025
New York *(G-10462)*
◆ Hf Mfg Corp.......G....... 212 594-9142
New York *(G-10470)*
Hockey Facility.......G....... 518 452-7396
Albany *(G-87)*
House Pearl Fashions (us) Ltd.......F....... 212 840-3183
New York *(G-10521)*
▲ I Spiewak & Sons Inc.......E....... 212 695-1620
New York *(G-10542)*
▲ Icer Sports LLC.......F....... 212 221-4700
New York *(G-10552)*
Ifg Corp.......C....... 212 629-9600
New York *(G-10561)*
Ifg Corp.......G....... 212 239-8615
New York *(G-10562)*
Jacob Hidary Foundation Inc.......F....... 212 736-6540
New York *(G-10691)*
▲ JD Class Inc.......G....... 212 764-6663
New York *(G-10710)*
John Varvatos Company.......E....... 212 812-8000
New York *(G-10754)*
Joseph (uk) Inc.......G....... 212 570-0077
New York *(G-10763)*
Just Bottoms & Tops Inc.......F....... 212 564-3202
New York *(G-10791)*
Kicks Closet Sportswear Inc.......G....... 347 577-0857
Bronx *(G-1372)*
▲ Kidz World Inc.......F....... 212 563-4949
New York *(G-10843)*
▲ King Sales Inc.......F....... 718 301-9862
Brooklyn *(G-2173)*
▲ Komar Luxury Brands.......G....... 646 472-0060
New York *(G-10875)*
▲ Lakeview Sportswear Corp.......G....... 347 663-9519
Brooklyn *(G-2192)*
Linder New York LLC.......F....... 646 678-5819
New York *(G-10998)*
▲ London Paris Ltd.......G....... 718 564-4793
Brooklyn *(G-2234)*
Luxe Imagine Consulting LLC.......G....... 212 273-9770
New York *(G-11066)*
▲ M A M Knitting Mills Corp.......E....... 800 570-0093
Brooklyn *(G-2246)*
▲ M Hidary & Co Inc.......D....... 212 736-6540
New York *(G-11073)*
Maiyet Inc.......G....... 646 602-0000
New York *(G-11113)*
Mann Consultants LLC.......E....... 914 763-0512
Waccabuc *(G-16520)*
Mayberry Shoe Company Inc.......G....... 315 692-4086
Manlius *(G-8074)*
▲ Mee Accessories LLC.......C....... 917 262-1000
New York *(G-11218)*
▲ Miss Group.......G....... 212 391-2535
New York *(G-11281)*
▲ Montero International Inc.......G....... 212 695-1787
Westbury *(G-17013)*
▲ Must USA Inc.......G....... 212 391-8288
New York *(G-11328)*
▲ Nautica International Inc.......D....... 212 541-5757
New York *(G-11358)*
▲ Nepenthes America Inc.......G....... 212 343-4262
New York *(G-11368)*
▲ Nevaeh Jeans Company.......G....... 845 641-4255
New York *(G-11377)*
Nine West Holdings Inc.......G....... 212 575-2571
New York *(G-11438)*
▲ North American Mills Inc.......F....... 212 695-6146
New York *(G-11456)*
Nyc Idol Apparel Inc.......G....... 212 997-9797
New York *(G-11479)*
On The Double Inc.......G....... 518 431-3571
Germantown *(G-5591)*
▲ One Step Up Ltd.......D....... 212 398-1110
New York *(G-11508)*
Oxford Industries Inc.......E....... 212 247-7712
New York *(G-11540)*
P & I Sportswear Inc.......G....... 718 934-4587
New York *(G-11546)*
Piaget.......F....... 212 355-6444
New York *(G-11656)*
Pride & Joys Inc.......F....... 212 594-9820
New York *(G-11704)*
Ps38 LLC.......F....... 212 819-1123
New York *(G-11742)*
Pti-Pacific Inc.......G....... 212 414-8495
New York *(G-11744)*
Pvh Corp.......G....... 212 381-3800
New York *(G-11757)*
R J Liebe Athletic Company.......D....... 585 237-6111
Perry *(G-13525)*
▲ Rainforest Inc.......F....... 212 575-7620
New York *(G-11790)*
◆ Ralph Lauren Corporation.......B....... 212 318-7000
New York *(G-11792)*
▲ Ramsbury Property Us Inc.......F....... 212 223-6250
New York *(G-11796)*
Robert Viggiani.......G....... 914 423-4046
Yonkers *(G-17481)*
Rp55 Inc.......G....... 212 840-4035
New York *(G-11929)*
▲ Ruleville Manufacturing Co Inc.......G....... 212 695-1620
New York *(G-11935)*
S & S Fashions Inc.......G....... 718 328-0001
Bronx *(G-1443)*
S & W Knitting Mills Inc.......E....... 718 237-2416
Brooklyn *(G-2524)*
Sanctuary Brands LLC.......G....... 212 704-4014
New York *(G-11964)*
Sandy Dalal Ltd.......G....... 212 532-5822
New York *(G-11967)*
▼ Sb Corporation.......G....... 212 822-3166
New York *(G-11979)*
Scharf and Breit Inc.......E....... 516 282-0287
Williston Park *(G-17262)*
▲ Schwartz Textile Converting Co.......E....... 718 499-8243
Brooklyn *(G-2537)*
◆ Sister Sister Inc.......G....... 212 629-9600
New York *(G-12087)*
▲ Standard Manufacturing Co Inc.......D....... 518 235-2200
Troy *(G-16256)*
▲ Sterling Possessions Ltd.......G....... 212 594-0418
New York *(G-12197)*
Swimwear Anywhere Inc.......E....... 845 858-4141
Port Jervis *(G-13794)*
Tamka Sport LLC.......G....... 718 224-7820
Douglaston *(G-4313)*
Tbhl International LLC.......F....... 212 799-2007
New York *(G-12282)*
▼ Tibana Finishing Inc.......E....... 718 417-5375
Ridgewood *(G-14127)*
▲ Tillsonburg Company USA Inc.......E....... 267 994-8096
New York *(G-12341)*
Under Armour Inc.......E....... 518 761-6787
Lake George *(G-7264)*
Uniqlo USA LLC.......F....... 877 486-4756
New York *(G-12460)*
Valley Stream Sporting Gds Inc.......E....... 516 593-7800
Lynbrook *(G-7966)*
▲ Versailles Industries LLC.......G....... 212 792-9615
New York *(G-12524)*
Vf Outdoor Inc.......E....... 718 698-6215
Staten Island *(G-15753)*
Vf Outdoor LLC.......E....... 845 928-4900
Central Valley *(G-3528)*
Viewsport Inc.......G....... 585 738-6803
Penfield *(G-13505)*
◆ Warnaco Group Inc.......D....... 212 287-8000
New York *(G-12586)*
◆ Warnaco Inc.......B....... 212 287-8000
New York *(G-12587)*
Warnaco Inc.......F....... 718 722-3000
Brooklyn *(G-2744)*
Warrior Sports Inc.......G....... 315 536-0937
Penn Yan *(G-13523)*

2331 Women's & Misses' Blouses

18 Rocks LLC.......E....... 631 465-9990
Melville *(G-8287)*
79 Metro Ltd.......G....... 212 944-4030
New York *(G-8980)*
Agi Brooks Production Co Inc.......F....... 212 268-1533
New York *(G-9056)*
▲ Alexander Wang Incorporated.......D....... 212 532-3103
New York *(G-9083)*
▲ Alfred Dunner Inc.......D....... 212 478-4300
New York *(G-9084)*

SIC SECTION
23 APPAREL AND OTHER FINISHED PRODUCTS MADE FROM FABRICS AND SIMILAR MATERIAL

Alvin Valley Direct LLC ....F 212 392-4725
New York *(G-9106)*
Amerex Corporation ....G 212 221-3151
New York *(G-9111)*
▲ Anna Sui Corp ....E 212 768-1951
New York *(G-9164)*
Apparel Group Ltd ....E 212 328-1200
New York *(G-9177)*
▲ Ben Wachter Associates Inc ....G 212 736-4064
New York *(G-9354)*
▲ Bernard Chaus Inc ....D 212 354-1280
New York *(G-9364)*
Bernard Chaus Inc ....C 646 562-4700
New York *(G-9365)*
▲ Bowe Industries Inc ....D 718 441-6464
Glendale *(G-5646)*
Brach Knitting Mills Inc ....F 845 651-4450
Florida *(G-5210)*
Brooke Leigh Ltd ....F 212 736-9098
New York *(G-9469)*
▲ Courage Clothing Co Inc ....F 212 354-5690
New York *(G-9736)*
Cyberlimit Inc ....F 212 840-9597
New York *(G-9775)*
▲ Cynthia Rowley Inc ....F 212 242-3803
New York *(G-9777)*
Donna Karan Company LLC ....C 212 789-1500
New York *(G-9900)*
▲ Donna Karan Company LLC ....B 212 789-1500
New York *(G-9901)*
◆ Donna Karan International Inc .....A 212 789-1500
New York *(G-9902)*
Donna Karan International Inc ....G 212 768-5800
New York *(G-9903)*
Elie Tahari Ltd ....F 212 398-2622
New York *(G-10001)*
Elie Tahari Ltd ....D 212 763-2000
New York *(G-10003)*
Embassy Apparel Inc ....F 212 768-8330
New York *(G-10019)*
Feyem USA Inc ....G 845 363-6253
Brewster *(G-1219)*
Fourtys Ny Inc ....F 212 382-0301
New York *(G-10193)*
FSI - New York Inc ....G 212 730-9545
New York *(G-10216)*
Fuller Sportswear Co Inc ....G 516 773-3353
Great Neck *(G-5814)*
Gabrielle Andra ....G 212 366-9624
New York *(G-10239)*
◆ Garan Incorporated ....C 212 563-1292
New York *(G-10248)*
▼ Garan Manufacturing Corp ....G 212 563-2000
New York *(G-10249)*
▲ Gce International Inc ....D 212 704-4800
New York *(G-10259)*
Geoffrey Beene Inc ....E 212 371-5570
New York *(G-10279)*
▲ Gildan Apparel USA Inc ....D 212 476-0341
New York *(G-10295)*
Glamourpuss Nyc LLC ....G 212 722-1370
New York *(G-10306)*
▲ Golden Horse Enterprise NY Inc ..G 212 594-3339
New York *(G-10331)*
Hansae Co Ltd ....G 212 354-6690
New York *(G-10410)*
▲ Icer Sports LLC ....F 212 221-4700
New York *(G-10552)*
▲ Ind Rev LLC ....F 212 221-4700
New York *(G-10585)*
▲ International Direct Group Inc .....E 212 921-9036
New York *(G-10634)*
▲ Jeanjer LLC ....A 212 944-1330
New York *(G-10716)*
Jordache Enterprises Inc ....D 212 944-1330
New York *(G-10760)*
◆ Jordache Enterprises Inc ....C 212 643-8400
New York *(G-10761)*
▲ Kate Spade & Company ....B 212 354-4900
New York *(G-10816)*
▼ Krasner Group Inc ....G 212 268-4100
New York *(G-10886)*
Ksk International Inc ....G 212 354-7770
New York *(G-10891)*
◆ Land n Sea Inc ....D 212 703-2980
New York *(G-10923)*
Lea & Viola Inc ....G 646 918-6866
New York *(G-10945)*
▲ Liberty Apparel Company Inc ......E 718 625-4000
New York *(G-10984)*

Lt2 LLC ....E 212 684-1510
New York *(G-11056)*
M S B International Ltd ....F 212 302-5551
New York *(G-11076)*
▲ Maggy London International Ltd ..D 212 944-7199
New York *(G-11102)*
Melwood Partners Inc ....G 516 307-8030
Garden City *(G-5521)*
▲ Mulitex Usa Inc ....G 212 398-0440
New York *(G-11323)*
▼ Necessary Objects Ltd ....E 212 334-9888
New York *(G-11365)*
▲ Nyc Knitwear Inc ....G 212 840-1313
New York *(G-11480)*
Orchard Apparel Group Ltd ....G 212 268-8701
New York *(G-11523)*
Orchid Manufacturing Co Inc ....F 212 840-5700
New York *(G-11524)*
Paddy Lee Fashions Inc ....F 718 786-6020
Long Island City *(G-7833)*
Pat & Rose Dress Inc ....D 212 279-1357
New York *(G-11578)*
▲ Permit Fashion Group Inc ....E 212 912-0988
New York *(G-11620)*
Phillips-Van Heusen Europe ....E 212 381-3500
New York *(G-11649)*
Plugg LLC ....F 212 840-6655
New York *(G-11678)*
◆ Pvh Corp ....D 212 381-3500
New York *(G-11756)*
Pvh Corp ....E 212 719-2600
New York *(G-11759)*
▲ Ramy Brook LLC ....E 212 744-2789
New York *(G-11797)*
▲ Raven New York LLC ....G 212 584-9690
New York *(G-11803)*
▲ Rhoda Lee Inc ....D 212 840-5700
New York *(G-11859)*
▲ Rio Apparel USA Inc ....G 212 869-9150
New York *(G-11875)*
Rio Garment SA ....A 212 822-3182
New York *(G-11876)*
Robert Danes Danes Inc ....G 212 226-1351
New York *(G-11889)*
▲ S & S Manufacturing Co Inc ....D 212 444-6000
New York *(G-11943)*
Saad Collection Inc ....F 212 937-0341
New York *(G-11949)*
Soho Apparel Ltd ....G 212 840-1109
New York *(G-12118)*
Spencer AB Inc ....G 646 831-3728
New York *(G-12160)*
Stitch & Couture Inc ....E 212 947-9204
New York *(G-12206)*
▲ Style Partners Inc ....F 212 904-1499
New York *(G-12223)*
T Rj Shirts Inc ....G 347 642-3071
East Elmhurst *(G-4399)*
Tahari ASL LLC ....B 212 763-2800
New York *(G-12272)*
▼ Tibana Finishing Inc ....E 718 417-5375
Ridgewood *(G-14127)*
▲ Triumph Apparel Corporation .....E 212 302-2606
New York *(G-12407)*
Turn On Products Inc ....F 212 764-4545
New York *(G-12427)*
▲ Turn On Products Inc ....D 212 764-2121
New York *(G-12426)*
Ursula of Switzerland Inc ....E 518 237-2580
Waterford *(G-16623)*
Vanity Room Inc ....F 212 921-7154
New York *(G-12503)*
▲ Ventura Enterprise Co Inc ....E 212 391-0170
New York *(G-12517)*
Westside Clothing Co Inc ....G 212 273-9898
New York *(G-12619)*
Yeohlee Inc ....F 212 631-8099
New York *(G-12690)*

2335 Women's & Misses' Dresses

18 Rocks LLC ....E 631 465-9990
Melville *(G-8287)*
▲ A & M Rosenthal Entps Inc ....E 646 638-9600
New York *(G-8981)*
Agi Brooks Production Co Inc ....F 212 268-1533
New York *(G-9056)*
Allison Che Fashion Inc ....E 212 391-1433
New York *(G-9091)*
Alvina Vlenta Couture Collectn ......F 212 921-7058
New York *(G-9107)*

Alvina Vlenta Couture Collectn ......G 212 921-7058
New York *(G-9108)*
Amsale Aberra LLC ....E 212 695-5936
New York *(G-9140)*
▲ Anna Sui Corp ....E 212 768-1951
New York *(G-9164)*
Arcangel Inc ....G 347 771-0789
New York *(G-9194)*
Arteast LLC ....E 212 965-8787
New York *(G-9216)*
B S J Limited ....E 212 764-4600
New York *(G-9291)*
▲ B S J Limited ....A 212 221-8403
New York *(G-9292)*
▲ Bangla Clothing USA Inc ....G 201 679-2615
New York *(G-9314)*
Bari-Jay Fashions Inc ....E 212 921-1551
New York *(G-9321)*
▲ Bernard Chaus Inc ....D 212 354-1280
New York *(G-9364)*
Birnbaum & Bullock Ltd ....E 212 242-2914
New York *(G-9403)*
▲ Bms Designs Inc ....F 718 828-5792
Bronx *(G-1285)*
Brides Inc ....G 718 435-6092
Brooklyn *(G-1714)*
▲ Cachet Industries Inc ....E 212 944-2188
New York *(G-9495)*
Carol Peretz ....F 516 248-6300
Mineola *(G-8501)*
▲ Cheri Pink Inc ....E 212 869-1948
New York *(G-9590)*
China Ting Fashion Group (usa) ...G 212 716-1600
New York *(G-9602)*
Christian Siriano Holdings LLC ......E 212 695-5494
New York *(G-9611)*
▲ Christos Inc ....E 212 921-0025
New York *(G-9614)*
▲ Couture Inc ....E 212 921-1166
New York *(G-9738)*
Crisada Inc ....G 718 729-9730
Long Island City *(G-7707)*
Csco LLC ....E 212 221-5100
New York *(G-9762)*
CTS LLC ....E 212 278-0058
New York *(G-9763)*
▲ Cynthia Rowley Inc ....F 212 242-3803
New York *(G-9777)*
D J Night Ltd ....E 212 302-9050
New York *(G-9783)*
Dalma Dress Mfg Co Inc ....E 212 391-8296
Greenvale *(G-5880)*
Damianou Sportswear Inc ....D 718 204-5600
Woodside *(G-17325)*
▲ Dave & Johnny Ltd ....E 212 302-9050
New York *(G-9816)*
Diamond Bridal Collection Ltd ....E 212 302-0210
New York *(G-9870)*
Donna Karan Company LLC ....C 212 789-1500
New York *(G-9900)*
Donna Karan Company LLC ....C 716 297-0752
Niagara Falls *(G-12811)*
▲ Donna Karan Company LLC ......B 212 789-1500
New York *(G-9901)*
◆ Donna Karan International Inc ....A 212 789-1500
New York *(G-9902)*
Donna Karan International Inc ....G 212 768-5800
New York *(G-9903)*
Elana Laderos Ltd ....F 212 764-0840
New York *(G-9993)*
Elizabeth Fillmore LLC ....G 212 647-0863
New York *(G-10009)*
Everlasting Memories ....G 716 833-1111
Blasdell *(G-962)*
Fashion Deli Inc ....F 818 772-5637
New York *(G-10144)*
▲ Faviana International Inc ....E 212 594-4422
New York *(G-10147)*
Forever Yours Intl Corp ....E 516 443-2743
Saint James *(G-15089)*
Four Seasons Fashion Mfg Inc ....E 212 947-6820
New York *(G-10192)*
G-III Apparel Group Ltd ....E 212 403-0500
New York *(G-10235)*
Geoffrey Beene Inc ....E 212 371-5570
New York *(G-10279)*
Haddad Bros Inc ....E 718 377-5505
Brooklyn *(G-2061)*
▲ Halmode Apparel Inc ....A 212 819-9114
New York *(G-10398)*

Employee Codes: A=Over 500 employees, B=251-500
C=101-250, D=51-100, E=20-50, F=10-19, G=5-9

2017 Harris
New York Manufacturers Directory

23 APPAREL AND OTHER FINISHED PRODUCTS MADE FROM FABRICS AND SIMILAR MATERIAL

Haute By Blair Stanley LLC .... G 212 557-7868
 New York (G-10426)
▲ I S C A Corp .... F 212 719-5123
 New York (G-10541)
▲ Icer Scrubs LLC .... F 212 221-4700
 New York (G-10551)
Infinity Sourcing Services LLC .... G 212 868-2900
 New York (G-10594)
J R Nites .... G 212 354-9670
 New York (G-10682)
Jaclyn Inc .... F 212 736-5657
 New York (G-10689)
▲ Jiranimo Industries Ltd .... F 212 921-5106
 New York (G-10737)
▼ Jim Couture Inc .... D 212 921-7058
 New York (G-10741)
▲ Jlnw Inc .... D 212 719-4666
 Long Island City (G-7771)
▲ Jon Teri Sports Inc .... E 212 398-0657
 New York (G-10756)
▲ Jovani Fashion Ltd .... E 212 279-0222
 New York (G-10772)
▲ Judys Group Inc .... E 212 921-0515
 New York (G-10779)
▲ Jump Design Group Inc .... C 212 869-3300
 New York (G-10786)
▲ Karen Miller Ltd .... F 212 819-9550
 New York (G-10811)
◆ Kasper Group LLC .... C 212 354-4311
 New York (G-10815)
▲ Kelly Grace Corp .... D 212 704-9603
 New York (G-10830)
▼ Krasner Group Inc .... G 212 268-4100
 New York (G-10886)
▲ L F Fashion Orient Intl Co Ltd .... G 917 667-3398
 New York (G-10901)
Lavish Layette Inc .... G 516 256-9130
 Cedarhurst (G-3458)
▲ Lily & Taylor Inc .... F 212 564-5459
 New York (G-10997)
◆ Lm Mignon LLC .... F 212 730-9221
 New York (G-11017)
▲ Lou Sally Fashions Corp .... E 212 354-9670
 New York (G-11047)
Lou Sally Fashions Corp .... E 212 354-1283
 New York (G-11048)
Lovely Bride LLC .... G 212 924-2050
 New York (G-11054)
Melwood Partners Inc .... G 516 307-8030
 Garden City (G-5521)
▲ Michael Vollbracht LLC .... F 212 753-0123
 New York (G-11250)
▲ Millennium Productions Inc .... F 212 944-6203
 New York (G-11267)
▲ Milliore Fashion Inc .... G 212 302-0001
 New York (G-11270)
▲ Mp Holdings Inc .... F 212 465-6800
 New York (G-11313)
▼ Necessary Objects Ltd .... E 212 334-9888
 New York (G-11365)
▲ Paris Wedding Center Corp .... G 347 368-4085
 Flushing (G-5279)
▲ Paris Wedding Center Corp .... E 212 267-8088
 New York (G-11573)
Parsley Apparel Corp .... E 631 981-7181
 Ronkonkoma (G-14965)
Pat & Rose Dress Inc .... D 212 279-1357
 New York (G-11578)
Patra Ltd .... F 212 764-6575
 New York (G-11580)
Patra Ltd .... F 212 764-6575
 New York (G-11581)
▲ Patra Ltd .... E 212 764-6575
 New York (G-11582)
Paula Varsalona Inc .... G 212 570-9100
 New York (G-11586)
▲ Phoebe Company LLC .... D 212 302-5556
 New York (G-11650)
PJ Designs Inc .... E 212 355-3100
 New York (G-11671)
Plugg LLC .... F 212 840-6655
 New York (G-11678)
▲ Product Development Intl LLC .... G 212 279-6170
 New York (G-11727)
▲ Pronovias USA Inc .... E 212 897-6393
 New York (G-11733)
Quality Pattern Corp .... D 212 704-0355
 New York (G-11768)
▲ R & M Richards Inc .... D 212 921-8820
 New York (G-11781)

Ralph Lauren Corporation .... F 212 221-7751
 New York (G-11795)
▲ Raven New York LLC .... G 212 584-9690
 New York (G-11803)
Rogan LLC .... G 212 680-1407
 New York (G-11904)
▲ Rogan LLC .... E 646 496-9339
 New York (G-11905)
◆ Ronni Nicole Group LLC .... E 212 764-1000
 New York (G-11913)
Selia Yang Inc .... G 212 480-4252
 New York (G-12025)
Sg Nyc LLC .... E 310 210-1837
 New York (G-12034)
▲ Shane Tex Inc .... F 516 486-7522
 Hempstead (G-6287)
Skinz Inc .... E 516 593-3139
 Lynbrook (G-7962)
Spencer AB Inc .... G 646 831-3728
 New York (G-12160)
▲ SSG Fashions Ltd .... G 212 221-0933
 New York (G-12179)
Stitch & Couture Inc .... E 212 947-9204
 New York (G-12206)
Studio Krp LLC .... F 310 589-5777
 New York (G-12220)
▲ Style Partners Inc .... F 212 904-1499
 New York (G-12223)
Tabrisse Collections Inc .... F 212 921-1014
 New York (G-12270)
Tahari ASL LLC .... B 212 763-2800
 New York (G-12272)
Texport Fabrics Corp .... F 212 226-6066
 New York (G-12305)
Therese The Childrens Collectn .... G 518 346-2315
 Schenectady (G-15305)
▲ Thread LLC .... G 212 414-8844
 New York (G-12332)
Tom & Linda Platt Inc .... F 212 221-7208
 New York (G-12359)
Turn On Products Inc .... F 212 764-4545
 New York (G-12427)
Ursula of Switzerland Inc .... E 518 237-2580
 Waterford (G-16623)
Vanity Room Inc .... F 212 921-7154
 New York (G-12503)
▲ Vera Wang Group LLC .... C 212 575-6400
 New York (G-12518)
▲ Wear Abouts Apparel Inc .... F 212 827-0888
 New York (G-12602)
▲ Worth Collection Ltd .... F 212 268-0312
 New York (G-12665)
Yeohlee Inc .... F 212 631-8099
 New York (G-12690)

2337 Women's & Misses' Suits, Coats & Skirts

2h International Corp .... G 347 623-9380
 Forest Hills (G-5319)
79 Metro Ltd .... G 212 944-4030
 New York (G-8980)
▲ Adar Medical Uniform LLC .... G 718 935-1197
 Brooklyn (G-1560)
Adrienne Landau Designs Inc .... F 212 695-8362
 New York (G-9031)
▲ Age Manufacturers Inc .... D 718 927-0048
 Brooklyn (G-1569)
Agi Brooks Production Co Inc .... F 212 268-1533
 New York (G-9056)
▲ Alfred Dunner Inc .... D 212 478-4300
 New York (G-9084)
◆ Amerimade Coat Inc .... G 212 216-0925
 New York (G-9133)
▲ Anna Sui Corp .... E 212 768-1951
 New York (G-9164)
Bestec Concept Inc .... G 718 937-5848
 Long Island City (G-7683)
Bindle and Keep 917 740-5002
 Brooklyn (G-1699)
▲ Blatt Searle & Company Ltd .... E 212 730-7717
 Long Island City (G-7688)
Brooke Leigh Ltd .... F 212 736-9098
 New York (G-9469)
Bruno & Canio Ltd .... E 845 624-3060
 Nanuet (G-8753)
Canada Goose Us Inc 303 832-7097
 Williamsville (G-17238)
▼ Carolina Herrera Ltd .... E 212 944-4757
 New York (G-9535)

Chancelle Suits Inc .... F 212 921-5300
 New York (G-9578)
▲ Cheri Pink Inc .... F 212 869-1948
 New York (G-9590)
▲ Countess Corporation .... G 212 869-7070
 New York (G-9734)
Donna Karan Company LLC .... F 212 372-6500
 New York (G-9899)
Donna Karan Company LLC .... C 212 789-1500
 New York (G-9900)
▲ Donna Karan Company LLC .... B 212 789-1500
 New York (G-9901)
◆ Donna Karan International Inc .... A 212 789-1500
 New York (G-9902)
Donna Karan International Inc .... F 212 768-5800
 New York (G-9903)
Elie Tahari Ltd .... D 212 398-2622
 New York (G-10002)
Elie Tahari Ltd .... D 631 329-8883
 East Hampton (G-4410)
Elie Tahari Ltd .... D 973 671-6300
 New York (G-10004)
Elie Tahari Ltd .... D 212 763-2000
 New York (G-10003)
Elie Tahari Ltd .... F 212 398-2622
 New York (G-10001)
▲ Excelled Shpskin Lea Coat Corp .... F 212 594-5843
 New York (G-10103)
Four Seasons Fashion Mfg Inc .... E 212 947-6820
 New York (G-10192)
▲ G-III Apparel Group Ltd .... C 212 403-0500
 New York (G-10234)
G-III Leather Fashions Inc .... C 212 403-0500
 New York (G-10236)
G18 Corporation .... F 212 869-0010
 New York (G-10237)
Geoffrey Beene Inc .... E 212 371-5570
 New York (G-10279)
▲ Global Gold Inc .... E 212 239-4657
 New York (G-10318)
▲ Harrison Sportswear Inc .... F 212 391-1051
 New York (G-10418)
▼ Herman Kay Company Ltd .... F 212 239-2025
 New York (G-10462)
◆ Hugo Boss Usa Inc .... D 212 940-0600
 New York (G-10528)
◆ Item-Eyes Inc .... D 631 321-0923
 New York (G-10670)
◆ J Percy For Mrvin Rchards Ltd .... E 212 944-5300
 New York (G-10680)
▲ Jeanjer LLC .... A 212 944-1330
 New York (G-10716)
▲ Jon Teri Sports Inc .... E 212 398-0657
 New York (G-10756)
▲ Judys Group Inc .... E 212 921-0515
 New York (G-10779)
Julia Jordan Corporation .... F 646 214-3090
 New York (G-10782)
Kayo of California .... G 212 354-6336
 New York (G-10823)
Lady Brass Co Inc .... G 516 887-8040
 Hewlett (G-6308)
▲ Levy Group Inc .... C 212 398-0707
 New York (G-10979)
▲ Lf Outerwear LLC .... D 212 239-2025
 New York (G-10981)
▲ Lily & Taylor Inc .... F 212 564-5459
 New York (G-10997)
Linrich Designs Inc .... G 212 382-2257
 New York (G-11002)
▲ Maggy Boutique Ltd .... E 212 997-5222
 New York (G-11101)
▲ Marlou Garments Inc .... F 516 739-7100
 New Hyde Park (G-8847)
Miny Group Inc .... D 212 925-6722
 New York (G-11279)
▲ Mp Studio Inc .... G 212 302-5666
 New York (G-11314)
Nine West Holdings Inc .... C 212 642-3860
 New York (G-11440)
Nine West Holdings Inc .... F 212 968-1521
 New York (G-11442)
Nyc Idol Apparel Inc .... G 212 997-9797
 New York (G-11479)
Pat & Rose Dress Inc .... D 212 279-1357
 New York (G-11578)
▲ Permit Fashion Group Inc .... G 212 912-0988
 New York (G-11620)
▲ Philipp Plein Madison Ave LLC .... F 212 644-3304
 New York (G-11646)

SIC SECTION 23 APPAREL AND OTHER FINISHED PRODUCTS MADE FROM FABRICS AND SIMILAR MATERIAL

Pleating Plus Ltd......F....... 201 863-2991
Orangeburg *(G-13240)*
Primo Coat Corp......E....... 718 349-2070
Long Island City *(G-7847)*
▲ **R & M Richards Inc**......D....... 212 921-8820
New York *(G-11781)*
▲ **Rhoda Lee Inc**......D....... 212 840-5700
New York *(G-11859)*
▲ **Saint Laurie Ltd**......E....... 212 643-1916
New York *(G-11954)*
▲ **Shane Tex Inc**......F....... 516 486-7522
Hempstead *(G-6287)*
▲ **Standard Manufacturing Co Inc**......D....... 518 235-2200
Troy *(G-16256)*
▲ **Style Partners Inc**......F....... 212 904-1499
New York *(G-12223)*
Tenby LLC......C....... 646 863-5890
New York *(G-12300)*
Terrapin Station Ltd......F....... 716 874-6677
Buffalo *(G-3214)*
Theory LLC......D....... 212 762-2300
New York *(G-12313)*
Theory LLC......G....... 212 879-0265
New York *(G-12314)*
Theory LLC......G....... 631 204-0231
Southampton *(G-15553)*
▲ **Tiger Fashion Inc**......E....... 212 244-1175
New York *(G-12338)*
▲ **Tiger J LLC**......E....... 212 764-5624
New York *(G-12339)*
Travis Ayers Inc......E....... 212 921-5165
New York *(G-12394)*
Turn On Products Inc......F....... 212 764-4545
New York *(G-12427)*
Uniforms By Park Coats Inc......E....... 718 499-1182
Brooklyn *(G-2698)*
Uniqlo USA LLC......F....... 877 486-4756
New York *(G-12460)*
Ursula of Switzerland Inc......E....... 518 237-2580
Waterford *(G-16623)*
View Collections Inc......F....... 212 944-4030
New York *(G-12542)*
Yeohlee Inc......F....... 212 631-8099
New York *(G-12690)*
Zaralo LLC......G....... 212 764-4590
New York *(G-12704)*

2339 Women's & Misses' Outerwear, NEC

▲ **31 Phillip Lim LLC**......E....... 212 354-6540
New York *(G-8972)*
525 America LLC......G....... 212 840-1313
New York *(G-8978)*
◆ **5th & Ocean Clothing Inc**......C....... 716 604-9000
Buffalo *(G-2790)*
▲ **6th Avenue Showcase Inc**......G....... 212 382-0400
New York *(G-8979)*
A & B Finishing Inc......E....... 718 522-4702
Brooklyn *(G-1525)*
◆ **A H Schreiber Co Inc**......D....... 212 594-7234
New York *(G-8989)*
▲ **Accessory Street LLC**......F....... 212 686-8990
New York *(G-9012)*
Adpro Sports Inc......D....... 716 854-5116
Buffalo *(G-2798)*
Aerobic Wear Inc......G....... 631 673-1830
Huntington Station *(G-6693)*
▲ **Age Manufacturers Inc**......D....... 718 927-0048
Brooklyn *(G-1569)*
AKOS Group Ltd......E....... 212 683-4747
New York *(G-9067)*
▲ **Alfred Dunner Inc**......D....... 212 478-4300
New York *(G-9084)*
◆ **Alleson of Rochester Inc**......D....... 585 272-0630
Rochester *(G-14187)*
Alleson of Rochester Inc......E....... 315 789-8464
Geneva *(G-5569)*
▲ **Alpha 6 Distributions LLC**......F....... 516 801-8290
Locust Valley *(G-7628)*
▲ **Amber Bever Inc**......G....... 212 391-4911
New York *(G-9109)*
American Apparel Trading Corp......G....... 212 764-5990
New York *(G-9114)*
▲ **American Challenge Enterprises**......G....... 631 595-7171
New Hyde Park *(G-8815)*
▲ **Angel-Made In Heaven Inc**......G....... 212 869-5678
New York *(G-9157)*
Angel-Made In Heaven Inc......G....... 718 832-4778
Brooklyn *(G-1612)*
▲ **Anna Sui Corp**......E....... 212 768-1951
New York *(G-9164)*
▲ **Argee America Inc**......G....... 212 768-9840
New York *(G-9199)*
Aura International Mfg Inc......G....... 212 719-1418
New York *(G-9262)*
▲ **Avalin LLC**......F....... 212 842-2286
New York *(G-9273)*
AZ Yashir Bapaz Inc......G....... 212 947-7357
New York *(G-9285)*
B Tween LLC......F....... 212 819-9040
New York *(G-9294)*
Bag Bazaar Ltd......E....... 212 689-3508
New York *(G-9304)*
▲ **Bagznyc Corp**......F....... 212 643-8202
New York *(G-9305)*
Bam Sales LLC......G....... 212 781-3000
New York *(G-9311)*
Bandit International Ltd......F....... 718 402-2100
Bronx *(G-1280)*
Bands N Bows......G....... 718 984-4316
Staten Island *(G-15643)*
▲ **Bank-Miller Co Inc**......E....... 914 227-9357
Pelham *(G-13489)*
▲ **Bernard Chaus Inc**......D....... 212 354-1280
New York *(G-9364)*
Bernard Chaus Inc......C....... 646 562-4700
New York *(G-9365)*
Bestec Concept Inc......G....... 718 937-5848
Long Island City *(G-7683)*
▲ **Bh Brand Inc**......E....... 212 239-1635
New York *(G-9386)*
Big Bang Clothing Inc......G....... 212 221-0379
New York *(G-9393)*
Blue Cast Denim Co Inc......E....... 212 719-1182
Huntington *(G-6657)*
▲ **Blueduck Trading Ltd**......G....... 212 268-3122
New York *(G-9424)*
Brigantine Inc......G....... 212 354-8550
New York *(G-9459)*
Brooke Leigh Ltd......F....... 212 736-9098
New York *(G-9469)*
C & C Athletic Inc......G....... 845 713-4670
Walden *(G-16531)*
Canada Goose Us Inc......G....... 303 832-7097
Williamsville *(G-17238)*
▲ **Carolina Amato Inc**......G....... 212 768-9095
New York *(G-9534)*
▼ **Carolina Herrera Ltd**......E....... 212 944-5757
New York *(G-9535)*
Casuals Etc Inc......D....... 212 838-1319
New York *(G-9544)*
▲ **Cathy Daniels Ltd**......E....... 212 354-8000
New York *(G-9550)*
◆ **Central Apparel Group Ltd**......F....... 212 868-6505
New York *(G-9562)*
Central Mills Inc......C....... 212 221-0748
New York *(G-9565)*
▲ **Cheri Pink Inc**......E....... 212 869-1948
New York *(G-9590)*
China Ting Fashion Group (usa)......G....... 212 716-1600
New York *(G-9602)*
▲ **Chloe International Inc**......F....... 212 730-6661
New York *(G-9603)*
▲ **Christina Sales Inc**......F....... 212 391-0710
New York *(G-9612)*
▲ **City Sites Sportswear Inc**......E....... 718 375-2990
Brooklyn *(G-1785)*
▲ **Collection Xiix Ltd**......F....... 212 686-8990
New York *(G-9670)*
▲ **Comint Apparel Group LLC**......F....... 212 947-7474
New York *(G-9683)*
▲ **Comme-Ci Comme-CA AP Group**......E....... 631 300-1035
Hauppauge *(G-6050)*
Consolidated Fashion Corp......G....... 212 719-3000
New York *(G-9705)*
Continental Knitting Mills......G....... 631 242-5330
Deer Park *(G-4120)*
▲ **Cynthia Rowley Inc**......F....... 212 242-3803
New York *(G-9777)*
▲ **Daily Wear Sportswear Corp**......G....... 718 972-0533
Brooklyn *(G-1834)*
Dalma Dress Mfg Co Inc......E....... 212 391-8296
Greenvale *(G-5880)*
Dana Michele LLC......G....... 917 757-7777
New York *(G-9798)*
Dani II Inc......F....... 212 869-5999
New York *(G-9802)*
Danice Stores Inc......F....... 212 665-0389
New York *(G-9803)*
▲ **Design For All LLC**......E....... 212 523-0021
New York *(G-9852)*
Designs By Lanie Inc......G....... 718 945-4221
Rockaway Beach *(G-14781)*
▲ **DFA New York LLC**......E....... 212 523-0021
New York *(G-9866)*
Dianos Kathryn Designs......G....... 212 267-1584
New York *(G-9874)*
DMD International Ltd......D....... 212 944-7300
New York *(G-9890)*
Donna Karan Company LLC......C....... 212 789-1500
New York *(G-9900)*
▲ **Donna Karan Company LLC**......B....... 212 789-1500
New York *(G-9901)*
◆ **Donna Karan International Inc**......A....... 212 789-1500
New York *(G-9902)*
Donna Karan International Inc......G....... 212 768-5800
New York *(G-9903)*
Doral Apparel Group Inc......G....... 917 208-5652
New York *(G-9908)*
Double Take Fashions Inc......G....... 718 832-9000
Brooklyn *(G-1875)*
▼ **Dr Jayscom**......F....... 888 437-5297
New York *(G-9922)*
▲ **Drew Philips Corp**......G....... 212 354-0095
New York *(G-9928)*
▲ **Du Monde Trading Inc**......E....... 212 944-1306
New York *(G-9933)*
▲ **Eileen Fisher Inc**......C....... 914 591-5700
Irvington *(G-6768)*
El-La Design Inc......G....... 212 382-1080
New York *(G-9992)*
Elie Tahari Ltd......F....... 212 398-2622
New York *(G-10001)*
Elie Tahari Ltd......D....... 212 398-2622
New York *(G-10002)*
Elizabeth Gillett Ltd......G....... 212 629-7993
New York *(G-10010)*
Elizabeth Wilson......G....... 516 486-2157
Uniondale *(G-16292)*
▲ **Emerald Holdings Inc**......G....... 718 797-4404
Brooklyn *(G-1918)*
▲ **F & J Designs Inc**......G....... 212 302-8755
New York *(G-10114)*
▲ **Fad Inc**......E....... 631 385-2460
Huntington *(G-6661)*
Falls Manufacturing Inc......G....... 518 672-7189
Philmont *(G-13540)*
Fashion Ave Sweater Knits LLC......D....... 212 302-8282
New York *(G-10141)*
▲ **Feldman Manufacturing Corp**......D....... 718 433-1700
Long Island City *(G-7739)*
▲ **Fieldston Clothes Inc**......G....... 212 354-8550
New York *(G-10161)*
First Love Fashions LLC......F....... 212 256-1089
New York *(G-10168)*
Four Dee Inc......D....... 718 615-1695
Brooklyn *(G-2000)*
Four Seasons Fashion Mfg Inc......E....... 212 947-6820
New York *(G-10192)*
▲ **French Atmosphere Inc**......G....... 516 371-9100
New York *(G-10208)*
Fusion Pro Performance Ltd......F....... 917 833-0761
New York *(G-10226)*
▲ **G-III Apparel Group Ltd**......C....... 212 403-0500
New York *(G-10234)*
G-III Leather Fashions Inc......E....... 212 403-0500
New York *(G-10236)*
▲ **GAME Sportswear Ltd**......E....... 914 962-1701
Yorktown Heights *(G-17511)*
◆ **Garan Incorporated**......C....... 212 563-1292
New York *(G-10248)*
▼ **Garan Manufacturing Corp**......G....... 212 563-2000
New York *(G-10249)*
Gbg Denim Usa LLC......G....... 646 839-7000
Plattsburgh *(G-13663)*
Gbg West LLC......C....... 646 839-7000
New York *(G-10257)*
Geoffrey Beene Inc......E....... 212 371-5570
New York *(G-10279)*
▲ **Gfb Fashions Ltd**......F....... 212 239-9230
New York *(G-10288)*
Giulietta LLC......G....... 212 334-1859
New York *(G-10301)*
▲ **GMC Mercantile Corp**......F....... 212 498-9488
New York *(G-10324)*
▲ **Golden Leaves Knitwear Inc**......E....... 718 875-8235
Brooklyn *(G-2038)*
▲ **Golden Season Fashion USA Inc**......F....... 212 268-6048
New York *(G-10335)*
▲ **Great Wall Corp**......C....... 212 704-4372
Long Island City *(G-7754)*

SIC

Employee Codes: A=Over 500 employees, B=251-500
C=101-250, D=51-100, E=20-50, F=10-19, G=5-9
2017 Harris
New York Manufacturers Directory
731

23 APPAREL AND OTHER FINISHED PRODUCTS MADE FROM FABRICS AND SIMILAR MATERIAL

▲ Halmode Apparel Inc ....A 212 819-9114
New York (G-10398)
▼ Hana Sportswear Inc ....E 315 639-6332
Dexter (G-4285)
▲ HB Athletic Inc..........................F 914 560-8422
New Rochelle (G-8910)
◆ HC Contracting Inc....................D 212 643-9292
New York (G-10433)
Hearts of Palm LLC......................E 212 944-6660
New York (G-10451)
Hearts of Palm LLC......................D 212 944-6660
New York (G-10452)
▼ Herman Kay Company Ltd ....C 212 239-2025
New York (G-10462)
Hoehn Inc ....F 518 463-8900
Albany (G-88)
▲ Hot Line Industries Inc ....F 516 764-0400
Plainview (G-13605)
▲ Hot Shot Hk LLC......................E 212 921-1111
New York (G-10513)
House Pearl Fashions (us) Ltd .....F 212 840-3183
New York (G-10521)
▲ I ABC Corporation....................E 315 639-3100
Dexter (G-4286)
Idra Alta Moda LLC......................F 914 644-8202
New York (G-10558)
Ifg Corp ....C 212 629-9600
New York (G-10561)
▲ Ikeddi Enterprises Inc ....F 212 302-7644
New York (G-10565)
Ikeddi Enterprises Inc ....G 212 302-7644
New York (G-10566)
In Moda com Inc ....E 718 788-4466
New York (G-10578)
▲ Int Trading USA LLC ....C 212 760-2338
New York (G-10614)
▲ Intriguing Threads Apparel Inc ...F 212 768-8733
New York (G-10647)
Isabel Toledo Enterprises Inc ......G 212 685-0948
New York (G-10666)
◆ Item-Eyes Inc ....D 631 321-0923
New York (G-10670)
J & E Talit Inc ....G 718 850-1333
Richmond Hill (G-14076)
◆ J Percy For Mrvin Rchards Ltd ....E 212 944-5300
New York (G-10680)
▲ Jacques Moret Inc....................C 212 354-2400
New York (G-10692)
Jaxis Inc ....G 212 302-7611
Brooklyn (G-2135)
Jaya Apparel Group LLC ....F 212 764-4980
New York (G-10705)
▲ Jeanjer LLC ....A 212 944-1330
New York (G-10716)
▲ JEnvie Sport Inc ....G 212 967-2322
New York (G-10720)
Jesse Joeckel ....G 631 668-2772
Montauk (G-8588)
▲ Jlnw Inc ....D 212 719-4666
Long Island City (G-7771)
◆ Joe Benbasset Inc...................E 212 268-4920
New York (G-10747)
Jomat New York Inc ....E 718 369-7641
Brooklyn (G-2146)
▲ Jonathan Michael Coat Corp ....G 212 239-9230
New York (G-10758)
▲ Jonden Manufacturing Co Inc ...G 516 442-4895
New York (G-10759)
Jonden Manufacturing Co Inc .....F 718 369-4925
Oceanside (G-13083)
Jordache Enterprises Inc ....D 212 944-1330
New York (G-10760)
◆ Jordache Enterprises Inc ....C 212 643-8400
New York (G-10761)
Joseph Abboud Manufacturing ...G 212 586-9140
New York (G-10764)
▲ Jsc Designs Ltd ....E 212 302-1001
New York (G-10778)
▲ Judys Group Inc ....E 212 921-0515
New York (G-10779)
Just Bottoms & Tops Inc ....F 212 564-3202
New York (G-10791)
▼ K T P Design Co Inc ....F 212 481-6613
New York (G-10797)
Kaltex America Inc ....F 212 971-0575
New York (G-10806)
Karen Kane Inc ....F 212 827-0980
New York (G-10810)
Kasper Group LLC ....F 212 354-4311
New York (G-10814)

▲ Katz Martell Fashion Trdg Intl ...G 212 840-0070
New York (G-10819)
Kayo of California ....F 212 354-6336
New York (G-10823)
▲ Kicks Closet Sportswear Inc....G 347 577-0857
Bronx (G-1372)
Koral Industries............................F 212 719-0392
New York (G-10876)
▼ Krasner Group Inc ....G 212 268-4100
New York (G-10886)
Ksk International Inc ....G 212 354-7770
New York (G-10891)
▲ Lahoya Enterprise Inc ....E 718 886-8799
College Point (G-3794)
▲ Lai Apparel Design Inc............G 212 382-1075
New York (G-10918)
◆ Land n Sea Inc ....D 212 703-2980
New York (G-10923)
Lavish Layette Inc........................G 516 256-9130
Cedarhurst (G-3458)
Lea Apparel Inc ....G 718 418-2800
Glendale (G-5657)
Leesa Designs Ltd ....G 631 261-3991
Centerport (G-3478)
◆ Leggiadro International Inc .....E 212 997-8766
New York (G-10962)
Lemral Knitwear Inc.....................D 718 210-0175
Brooklyn (G-2210)
▲ Leslie Stuart Co Inc ....E 212 629-4551
New York (G-10975)
Lgb Inc ....E 212 278-8280
New York (G-10982)
▲ Liberty Apparel Company Inc ...G 212 221-0101
New York (G-10983)
▲ Liberty Apparel Company Inc ...E 718 625-4000
New York (G-10984)
Life Style Design Group ....E 212 391-8666
New York (G-10987)
Light Inc ....G 212 629-1095
New York (G-10991)
▲ Lily & Taylor Inc ....F 212 564-5459
New York (G-10997)
Linrich Designs Inc......................G 212 382-2257
New York (G-11002)
▲ Liquid Knits Inc ....F 718 706-6600
Long Island City (G-7791)
Lotus Apparel Designs Inc..........G 646 236-9363
Westbury (G-17007)
Luxe Imagine Consulting LLC ....G 212 273-9770
New York (G-11066)
▲ M A M Knitting Mills Corp ....E 800 570-0093
Brooklyn (G-2246)
Machinit Inc ....G 631 454-9297
Farmingdale (G-5039)
▲ Mag Brands LLC ....D 212 629-9600
New York (G-11097)
▲ Maggy Boutique Ltd ....F 212 997-5222
New York (G-11101)
▲ Main Street Fashions Inc........F 212 764-2613
New York (G-11112)
Maiyet Inc.....................................G 646 602-0000
New York (G-11113)
Malia Mills Inc..............................F 212 354-4200
Brooklyn (G-2256)
▲ Manchu New York Inc ....F 212 921-5050
New York (G-11125)
Manchu Times Fashion Inc.........G 212 921-5050
New York (G-11126)
▲ Mango Usa Inc.........................E 718 998-6050
Brooklyn (G-2258)
Marcasiano Inc ....G 212 614-9412
New York (G-11144)
▲ Marconi Intl USA Co Ltd ....G 212 391-2626
New York (G-11146)
Marina Holding Corp ....F 718 646-9283
Brooklyn (G-2269)
Mars Fashions Inc.......................E 718 402-2200
Bronx (G-1387)
Max Leon Inc ....F 845 928-8201
Central Valley (G-3525)
Mayberry Shoe Company Inc .....G 315 692-4086
Manlius (G-8074)
▲ Medi-Tech International Corp ...G 800 333-0109
Brooklyn (G-2291)
▲ Meryl Diamond Ltd ....E 212 730-0333
New York (G-11236)
Meskita Lifestyle Brands LLC ....E 212 695-5054
New York (G-11238)
Michael Feldman Inc...................D 718 433-1700
Long Island City (G-7812)

Miguelina Inc................................F 212 925-0320
New York (G-11262)
◆ Mikael Aghal LLC ....F 212 596-4010
New York (G-11263)
▲ Millennium Productions Inc ....F 212 944-6203
New York (G-11267)
Miltons of New York Inc...............F 212 997-3359
New York (G-11272)
MISS Sportswear Inc ....G 212 391-2535
Brooklyn (G-2320)
▲ MISS Sportswear Inc ....G 212 391-2535
New York (G-11283)
MISS Sportswear Inc ....E 718 369-6012
Brooklyn (G-2321)
▲ Moes Wear Apparel Inc...........F 718 940-1597
Brooklyn (G-2328)
Morelle Products Ltd ....G 212 391-8070
New York (G-11304)
▲ Mv Corp Inc ....C 631 273-8020
Bay Shore (G-720)
Mynt 1792 LLC.............................F 212 249-4562
New York (G-11333)
▲ Mystic Inc.................................D 212 239-2025
New York (G-11334)
▼ Necessary Objects Ltd ....E 212 334-9888
New York (G-11365)
▲ New Concepts of New York LLC ...E 212 695-4999
New York (G-11381)
▲ New York Accessory Group Inc ......G 212 532-7911
New York (G-11395)
New York Knitting Processor......G 718 366-3469
Ridgewood (G-14115)
Nine West Holdings Inc ....G 212 642-3860
New York (G-11436)
Nine West Holdings Inc ....G 212 221-6376
New York (G-11437)
Nine West Holdings Inc ....G 215 785-4000
New York (G-11439)
Nine West Holdings Inc ....G 212 575-2571
New York (G-11438)
Nine West Holdings Inc ....G 212 642-3860
New York (G-11441)
Nine West Holdings Inc ....G 212 822-1300
New York (G-11443)
Nlhe LLC ....E 212 594-0012
New York (G-11445)
▲ Noah Enterprises Ltd...............G 212 736-2888
New York (G-11448)
Ocean Waves Swim LLC ....G 212 967-4481
New York (G-11494)
▲ ODY Accessories Inc ....E 212 239-0580
New York (G-11496)
On The Double Inc ....G 518 431-3571
Germantown (G-5591)
▲ One Jeanswear Group Inc ....E 212 835-2500
New York (G-11506)
▲ One Mountain Imports LLC .....G 212 643-0805
New York (G-11507)
▲ One Step Up Ltd ....D 212 398-1110
New York (G-11508)
Only Hearts Ltd ....F 718 783-3218
New York (G-11511)
▲ Outerstuff LLC ....E 212 594-9700
New York (G-11536)
P & I Sportswear Inc ....G 718 934-4587
New York (G-11546)
Pacific Alliance Usa Inc ....G 336 500-8184
New York (G-11551)
▲ Pacific Alliance Usa Inc ....E 646 839-7000
New York (G-11552)
Paddy Lee Fashions Inc ....F 718 786-6020
Long Island City (G-7833)
Park Avenue Sportswear Ltd ......F 718 369-0520
Brooklyn (G-2408)
Pat & Rose Dress Inc..................D 212 279-1357
New York (G-11578)
▲ Penfli Industries Inc ....F 212 947-6080
Great Neck (G-5830)
▲ Permit Fashion Group Inc ....G 212 912-0988
New York (G-11620)
Perry Ellis International Inc.........F 212 536-5499
New York (G-11623)
Petrunia LLC................................G 607 277-1930
Ithaca (G-6869)
PLC Apparel LLC ....G 212 239-3434
New York (G-11676)
Pleating Plus Ltd ....F 201 863-2991
Orangeburg (G-13240)
Plugg LLC.....................................F 212 840-6655
New York (G-11678)

SIC SECTION — 23 APPAREL AND OTHER FINISHED PRODUCTS MADE FROM FABRICS AND SIMILAR MATERIAL

▲ Popnyc 1 LLC .... G 646 684-4600
  New York (G-11684)
Pride & Joys Inc .... F 212 594-9820
  New York (G-11704)
Primo Coat Corp .... E 718 349-2070
  Long Island City (G-7847)
Pti-Pacific Inc .... G 212 414-8495
  New York (G-11744)
Pvh Corp .... D 212 502-6300
  New York (G-11758)
Pvh Corp .... G 212 381-3800
  New York (G-11757)
RAK Finishing Corp .... E 718 416-4242
  Howard Beach (G-6598)
Ralph Lauren Corporation .... G 917 934-4200
  New York (G-11794)
▲ Ramsbury Property Us Inc .... F 212 223-6250
  New York (G-11796)
▲ RD Intrntnl Style .... G 212 382-2360
  New York (G-11810)
Rene Portier Inc .... G 718 853-7896
  Brooklyn (G-2492)
▲ Republic Clothing Corporation ..... E 212 719-3000
  New York (G-11836)
Republic Clothing Group Inc .... C 212 719-3000
  New York (G-11837)
▲ Rhoda Lee Inc .... D 212 840-5700
  New York (G-11859)
▲ Richard Leeds Intl Inc .... D 212 532-4546
  New York (G-11862)
Richard Manufacturing Co Inc .... G 718 254-0958
  Brooklyn (G-2493)
▲ Ritchie Corp .... F 212 768-0083
  New York (G-11880)
Rmll Corp .... G 212 719-4666
  New York (G-11885)
Robespierre Inc .... G 212 764-8810
  New York (G-11892)
▲ Robespierre Inc .... E 212 594-0012
  New York (G-11893)
Rogers Group Inc .... E 212 643-9292
  New York (G-11907)
▲ Rvc Enterprises LLC .... E 212 391-4600
  New York (G-11939)
▲ S & S Manufacturing Co Inc .... D 212 444-6000
  New York (G-11943)
S & V Knits Inc .... E 631 752-1595
  Farmingdale (G-5106)
S & W Knitting Mills Inc .... E 718 237-2416
  Brooklyn (G-2524)
S Broome and Co Inc .... D 718 663-6800
  Long Island City (G-7870)
S2 Sportswear Inc .... F 347 335-0713
  Brooklyn (G-2527)
Salisbury Sportswear Inc .... E 516 221-9519
  Bellmore (G-821)
▲ Sam Hee International Inc .... G 212 594-7815
  New York (G-11961)
▲ Sarina Accessories LLC .... E 212 239-8106
  New York (G-11973)
▲ Sea Waves Inc .... F 516 766-4201
  Oceanside (G-13096)
Senneth LLC .... G 347 232-3170
  Monsey (G-8582)
▲ Sensational Collection Inc .... G 212 840-7388
  New York (G-12029)
Shirl-Lynn of New York .... F 315 363-5898
  Oneida (G-13167)
▲ Smooth Industries Incorporated . E 212 869-1080
  New York (G-12109)
Snowman .... G 212 239-8818
  New York (G-12113)
Sophiexx Corporation .... G 917 963-5339
  Flushing (G-5294)
Spectrum Apparel Inc .... D 212 239-2025
  New York (G-12157)
▲ SRP Apparel Group Inc .... G 212 764-4810
  New York (G-12176)
Ssa Trading Ltd .... F 646 465-9500
  New York (G-12178)
▲ SSG Fashions Ltd .... G 212 221-0933
  New York (G-12179)
St John .... G 718 720-8367
  Staten Island (G-15737)
St John .... G 718 771-4541
  Brooklyn (G-2595)
▲ Standard Manufacturing Co Inc .. D 518 235-2200
  Troy (G-16256)
Steilmann European Selections ...... D 914 997-0015
  Port Chester (G-13759)

▲ Sterling Possessions Ltd .... G 212 594-0418
  New York (G-12197)
Stony Apparel Corp .... G 212 391-0022
  New York (G-12209)
▲ Street Beat Sportswear Inc .... F 718 302-1500
  Brooklyn (G-2610)
▲ Sunynams Fashions Ltd .... G 212 268-5200
  New York (G-12240)
▲ Survival Inc .... G 631 385-5060
  Centerport (G-3481)
Swatfame Inc .... G 212 944-8022
  New York (G-12251)
◆ Swimwear Anywhere Inc .... D 631 420-1400
  Farmingdale (G-5121)
Swimwear Anywhere Inc .... E 845 858-4141
  Port Jervis (G-13794)
Tahari ASL LLC .... E 212 763-2800
  New York (G-12272)
▲ Tailored Sportsman LLC .... E 646 366-8733
  New York (G-12274)
Tamka Sport LLC .... G 718 224-7820
  Douglaston (G-4313)
Tbhl International LLC .... F 212 799-2007
  New York (G-12282)
Texwood Inc (u S A) .... G 212 262-8383
  New York (G-12306)
▲ THE Design Group Inc .... F 212 681-1548
  New York (G-12309)
▲ Tiger J LLC .... E 212 764-5624
  New York (G-12339)
▲ Tillsonburg Company USA Inc ... E 267 994-8096
  New York (G-12341)
Toni Industries Inc .... E 212 921-0700
  Great Neck (G-5845)
▼ TR Designs Inc .... E 212 398-9300
  New York (G-12387)
▲ Turn On Products Inc .... D 212 764-2121
  New York (G-12426)
Turn On Products Inc .... G 212 764-4545
  New York (G-12427)
▲ Urban Apparel Group Inc .... E 212 947-7009
  New York (G-12478)
▲ Uspa Accessories LLC .... C 212 868-2590
  New York (G-12492)
Valenti Neckwear Co Inc .... G 914 969-0700
  Yonkers (G-17494)
▲ Venus Manufacturing Co Inc ...... D 315 639-3100
  Dexter (G-4287)
Vf Imagewear Inc .... E 718 352-2363
  Bayside (G-778)
Vf Outdoor LLC .... E 845 928-4900
  Central Valley (G-3528)
Vf Sportswear Inc .... E 212 541-5757
  New York (G-12532)
◆ Warnaco Group Inc .... D 212 287-8000
  New York (G-12586)
Warrior Sports Inc .... G 315 536-0937
  Penn Yan (G-13523)
▲ West Pacific Enterprises Corp ... G 212 564-6800
  New York (G-12613)
▲ White Gate Holdings Inc .... E 212 564-3266
  New York (G-12625)
Yigal-Azrouel Inc .... E 212 302-1194
  New York (G-12691)
▲ Z-Ply Corp .... E 212 398-7011
  New York (G-12701)
▼ Zar Group LLC .... C 212 944-2510
  New York (G-12703)
◆ Zg Apparel Group LLC .... E 646 930-1113
  New York (G-12711)
Zia Power Inc .... E 845 661-8388
  New York (G-12712)
▲ Zoomers Inc .... E 718 369-2656
  Brooklyn (G-2782)

2341 Women's, Misses' & Children's Underwear & Nightwear

Allure Fashions Inc .... G 516 829-2470
  Great Neck (G-5789)
▲ Ann Gish Inc .... G 212 969-9200
  New York (G-9163)
Apparel Partnership Group LLC ..... G 212 302-7722
  New York (G-9178)
▲ Ariela and Associates Intl LLC ... C 212 683-4131
  New York (G-9202)
Becks Classic Mfg Inc .... D 631 435-3800
  Brentwood (G-1178)
Beverly Creations Inc .... F 800 439-6855
  New York (G-9381)

▲ Carole Hchman Design Group Inc .. C 918 423-3535
  New York (G-9533)
▲ Comme-Ci Comme-CA AP Group .. E 631 300-1035
  Hauppauge (G-6050)
▲ Dayleen Intimates Inc .... E 914 969-5900
  Yonkers (G-17435)
Enticing Lingerie Inc .... E 718 998-8625
  Brooklyn (G-1927)
Faye Bernard Loungewear .... G 718 951-7245
  Brooklyn (G-1962)
▲ Gia Lingerie Inc .... E 212 448-0918
  New York (G-10292)
▲ Handcraft Manufacturing Corp ... E 212 251-0022
  New York (G-10404)
▲ Intimateco LLC .... G 212 239-4411
  New York (G-10644)
▲ Kokin Inc .... E 212 643-8225
  New York (G-10870)
▲ Komar Layering LLC .... E 212 725-1500
  New York (G-10874)
▲ Komar Luxury Brands .... G 646 472-0060
  New York (G-10875)
Lady Ester Lingerie Corp .... E 212 689-1729
  New York (G-10914)
Loungehouse LLC .... E 646 524-2965
  New York (G-11052)
Luxerdame Co Inc .... E 718 752-9800
  Long Island City (G-7796)
Maidenform LLC .... C 718 494-0268
  Staten Island (G-15703)
Mrt Textile Inc .... E 800 674-1073
  New York (G-11318)
Natori Company Incorporated .... E 212 532-7796
  New York (G-11356)
▲ Natori Company Incorporated ... E 212 532-7796
  New York (G-11355)
Only Hearts Ltd .... E 718 783-3218
  New York (G-11511)
▲ Richard Leeds Intl Inc .... D 212 532-4546
  New York (G-11862)
Sidney A Bush Co .... E 718 742-9629
  Bronx (G-1453)
▲ Solo Licensing Corp .... G 212 244-5505
  New York (G-12125)
Vanity Fair Brands LP .... E 212 548-1548
  New York (G-12502)
Wacoal International Corp .... D 212 532-6100
  New York (G-12576)
◆ Warnaco Group Inc .... D 212 287-8000
  New York (G-12586)
◆ Warnaco Inc .... B 212 287-8000
  New York (G-12587)
Warnaco Inc .... F 718 722-3000
  Brooklyn (G-2744)
▲ Waterbury Garment LLC .... E 212 725-1500
  New York (G-12597)
▲ Wickers Sportswear Inc .... G 631 543-1700
  Commack (G-3848)

2342 Brassieres, Girdles & Garments

Burlen Corp .... F 212 684-0052
  New York (G-9480)
▲ Carole Hchman Design Group Inc .. C 918 423-3535
  New York (G-9533)
▲ Cupid Foundations Inc .... D 212 686-6224
  New York (G-9767)
Deunall Corporation .... E 516 667-8875
  Levittown (G-7427)
E P Sewing Pleating Inc .... E 212 967-2575
  New York (G-9951)
East Coast Molders Inc .... C 516 240-6000
  Oceanside (G-13078)
Edith Lances Corp .... E 212 683-1990
  New York (G-9981)
Enticing Lingerie Inc .... E 718 998-8625
  Brooklyn (G-1927)
Higgins Supply Company Inc .... D 607 836-6474
  Mc Graw (G-8222)
Luxerdame Co Inc .... E 718 752-9800
  Long Island City (G-7796)
▲ New York Elegance Entps Inc .... F 212 685-3088
  New York (G-11400)
▲ Prime Garments Inc .... F 212 354-7294
  New York (G-11706)
▼ Rago Foundations LLC .... D 718 728-8436
  Astoria (G-454)
Sensual Inc .... E 212 869-1450
  New York (G-12030)
▲ Valmont Inc .... E 212 685-1653
  New York (G-12496)

Employee Codes: A=Over 500 employees, B=251-500
C=101-250, D=51-100, E=20-50, F=10-19, G=5-9

23 APPAREL AND OTHER FINISHED PRODUCTS MADE FROM FABRICS AND SIMILAR MATERIAL SIC SECTION

Wacoal America Inc ... C ... 718 794-1032
Bronx (G-1491)
Wacoal America Inc ... E ... 212 743-9600
New York (G-12575)
◆ Warnaco Group Inc ... D ... 212 287-8000
New York (G-12586)
◆ Warnaco Inc ... B ... 212 287-8000
New York (G-12587)
Warnaco Inc ... F ... 718 722-3000
Brooklyn (G-2744)

2353 Hats, Caps & Millinery

▲ A-1 Skull Cap Corp ... E ... 718 633-9333
Brooklyn (G-1539)
Albrizio Inc ... G ... 212 719-5290
Brooklyn (G-1577)
Athletic Cap Co Inc ... E ... 718 398-1300
Staten Island (G-15641)
Bonk Sam Unforms Civilian Cap ... E ... 718 585-0665
Bronx (G-1286)
▲ Cookies Inc ... A ... 646 452-5552
New York (G-9716)
Dorel Hat Co ... E ... 845 831-5231
Beacon (G-784)
▲ Flexfit Llc ... D ... 516 932-8800
Hicksville (G-6344)
Gce International Inc ... F ... 212 868-0500
New York (G-10260)
Genesco Inc ... G ... 585 227-3080
Rochester (G-14393)
Hankin Brothers Cap Co ... F ... 716 892-8840
Buffalo (G-2987)
◆ Hat Attack Inc ... E ... 718 994-1000
Bronx (G-1351)
Kays Caps Inc ... G ... 518 273-6079
Troy (G-16221)
▲ Kim Eugenia Inc ... G ... 212 674-1345
New York (G-10845)
▲ Kingform Cap Company Inc ... D ... 516 822-2501
Hicksville (G-6358)
▲ Kokin Inc ... E ... 212 643-8225
New York (G-10870)
▲ Kraft Hat Manufacturers Inc ... D ... 845 735-6200
Pearl River (G-13461)
▲ Lenore Marshall Inc ... G ... 212 947-5945
New York (G-10967)
Lids Corporation ... E ... 718 338-7790
Brooklyn (G-2218)
▲ Lloyds Fashions Inc ... D ... 631 435-3353
Brentwood (G-1190)
Makins Hats Ltd ... G ... 212 594-6666
New York (G-11119)
Matthews Hats ... G ... 718 859-4683
Brooklyn (G-2285)
Mega Power Sports Corporation ... G ... 212 627-3380
New York (G-11220)
New ERA Cap Co Inc ... B ... 716 604-9000
Buffalo (G-3084)
▲ New ERA Cap Co Inc ... C ... 716 604-9000
Buffalo (G-3085)
New ERA Cap Co Inc ... G ... 716 549-0445
Derby (G-4284)
Paletot Ltd ... F ... 212 268-3774
New York (G-11555)
Room At The Top Inc ... G ... 718 257-0766
Brooklyn (G-2505)
Tanen Cap Co ... F ... 212 254-7100
Brooklyn (G-2645)
Therese The Childrens Collectn ... G ... 518 346-2315
Schenectady (G-15305)
Twins Enterprise Inc ... G ... 631 368-4702
Commack (G-3844)
▲ W & M Headwear Co Inc ... E ... 718 768-2222
Brooklyn (G-2739)
Whittall & Shon ... G ... 212 594-2626
New York (G-12629)

2361 Children's & Infants' Dresses & Blouses

▲ Bonpoint Inc ... E ... 212 246-3291
New York (G-9437)
▲ Bowe Industries Inc ... D ... 718 441-6464
Glendale (G-5646)
Brooke Maya Inc ... E ... 212 279-2340
New York (G-9470)
Carters Inc ... G ... 315 637-3128
Fayetteville (G-5163)
Carters Inc ... G ... 718 980-1759
Staten Island (G-15657)
Carters Inc ... G ... 631 549-6781
Huntington Station (G-6699)
▲ Consolidated Childrens AP Inc ... G ... 212 239-8615
New York (G-9703)
Cream Bebe ... F ... 917 578-2088
Brooklyn (G-1813)
E-Play Brands LLC ... G ... 212 563-2646
New York (G-9955)
◆ Garan Incorporated ... C ... 212 563-1292
New York (G-10248)
▼ Garan Manufacturing Corp ... G ... 212 563-2000
New York (G-10249)
Gce International Inc ... F ... 212 868-0500
New York (G-10260)
◆ General Sportwear Company Inc ... G ... 212 764-5820
New York (G-10274)
▼ Gerson & Gerson Inc ... D ... 212 244-6775
New York (G-10287)
▲ Grand Knitting Mills Inc ... E ... 631 226-5000
Amityville (G-290)
◆ Great Universal Corp ... F ... 917 302-0065
New York (G-10359)
Haddad Bros Inc ... E ... 718 377-5505
Brooklyn (G-2061)
◆ Haddad Bros Inc ... F ... 212 563-2117
New York (G-10393)
Hard Ten Clothing Inc ... G ... 212 302-1321
New York (G-10412)
▲ JM Originals Inc ... C ... 845 647-3003
Ellenville (G-4634)
Jordache Enterprises Inc ... D ... 212 944-1330
New York (G-10760)
◆ Jordache Enterprises Inc ... C ... 212 643-8400
New York (G-10761)
◆ Land n Sea Inc ... D ... 212 703-2980
New York (G-10923)
Lollipops Inc ... E ... 845 352-8642
Monsey (G-8573)
▲ Manchu New York Inc ... G ... 212 921-5050
New York (G-11125)
Michael Stuart Inc ... E ... 718 821-0704
Brooklyn (G-2309)
Rosenau Beck Inc ... F ... 212 279-6202
New York (G-11918)
▲ S & C Bridals LLC ... G ... 212 789-7000
New York (G-11942)
▲ Silly Phillie Creations Inc ... E ... 718 492-6300
Brooklyn (G-2556)
Sports Products America LLC ... E ... 212 594-5511
New York (G-12168)
▲ Star Childrens Dress Co Inc ... D ... 212 244-1390
New York (G-12184)
Steve Zinn ... F ... 718 746-8551
Flushing (G-5298)
▲ Sue & Sam Co Inc ... E ... 718 436-1672
Brooklyn (G-2618)
Thats My Girl Inc ... G ... 212 695-0020
Brooklyn (G-2655)
ZIC Sportswear Inc ... E ... 718 361-9022
Long Island City (G-7933)
▲ Zinnias Inc ... F ... 718 746-8551
Bellerose (G-812)

2369 Girls' & Infants' Outerwear, NEC

Aerobic Wear Inc ... G ... 631 673-1830
Huntington Station (G-6693)
◆ Amerimade Coat Inc ... G ... 212 216-0925
New York (G-9133)
Baby Uv/Kids Uv Inc ... F ... 917 301-9020
Brooklyn (G-1661)
▲ Babyfair Inc ... E ... 212 736-7989
New York (G-9299)
◆ Best Brands Consumer Pdts Inc ... G ... 212 684-7456
New York (G-9373)
Detour Apparel Inc ... G ... 212 221-3265
New York (G-9861)
▲ Devil Dog Manufacturing Co Inc ... G ... 845 647-4411
Ellenville (G-4633)
◆ Domani Fashions Corp ... G ... 718 797-0505
Brooklyn (G-1871)
E-Play Brands LLC ... G ... 212 563-2646
New York (G-9955)
▲ Fine Sheer Industries Inc ... F ... 212 594-4224
New York (G-10164)
Franco Apparel Group Inc ... D ... 212 967-7272
New York (G-10200)
◆ Garan Incorporated ... C ... 212 563-1292
New York (G-10248)
▼ Garan Manufacturing Corp ... G ... 212 563-2000
New York (G-10249)
◆ General Sportwear Company Inc ... G ... 212 764-5820
New York (G-10274)
▼ Gerson & Gerson Inc ... D ... 212 244-6775
New York (G-10287)
Haddad Bros Inc ... E ... 718 377-5505
Brooklyn (G-2061)
▲ Ideal Creations Inc ... E ... 212 563-5928
New York (G-10555)
▲ In Mocean Group LLC ... D ... 732 960-2415
New York (G-10577)
▲ Isfel Co Inc ... G ... 212 736-6216
New York (G-10667)
▲ Jeanjer LLC ... A ... 212 944-1330
New York (G-10716)
Jgx LLC ... G ... 212 575-1244
New York (G-10731)
▲ Jj Basics LLC ... E ... 212 768-4779
New York (G-10739)
▲ JM Originals Inc ... C ... 845 647-3003
Ellenville (G-4634)
Jomat New York Inc ... E ... 718 369-7641
Brooklyn (G-2146)
Jordache Enterprises Inc ... D ... 212 944-1330
New York (G-10760)
◆ Jordache Enterprises Inc ... C ... 212 643-8400
New York (G-10761)
K & S Childrens Wear Inc ... E ... 718 624-0006
Brooklyn (G-2162)
Kahn-Lucas-Lancaster Inc ... D ... 212 239-2407
New York (G-10801)
◆ Land n Sea Inc ... D ... 212 703-2980
New York (G-10923)
▲ Liberty Apparel Company Inc ... E ... 718 625-4000
New York (G-10984)
◆ Lollytogs Ltd ... D ... 212 502-6000
New York (G-11024)
▲ M Hidary & Co Inc ... D ... 212 736-6540
New York (G-11073)
Michael Stuart Inc ... E ... 718 821-0704
Brooklyn (G-2309)
Miltons of New York Inc ... G ... 212 997-3359
New York (G-11272)
▲ Outerstuff LLC ... E ... 212 594-9700
New York (G-11536)
◆ Oxygen Inc ... G ... 516 433-1144
Hicksville (G-6380)
Pink Crush LLC ... G ... 718 788-6978
New York (G-11664)
Pti-Pacific Inc ... G ... 212 414-8495
New York (G-11744)
Rogers Group Inc ... E ... 212 643-9292
New York (G-11907)
▼ S Rothschild & Co Inc ... C ... 212 354-8550
New York (G-11947)
Sch Dpx Corporation ... G ... 917 405-5377
New York (G-11985)
▲ Silly Phillie Creations Inc ... E ... 718 492-6300
Brooklyn (G-2556)
◆ Sister Sister Inc ... G ... 212 629-9600
New York (G-12087)
Sleepy Head Inc ... F ... 718 237-9655
Brooklyn (G-2570)
Swatfame Inc ... G ... 212 944-8022
New York (G-12251)
Therese The Childrens Collectn ... G ... 518 346-2315
Schenectady (G-15305)
◆ Warnaco Group Inc ... D ... 212 287-8000
New York (G-12586)
▲ Waterbury Garment LLC ... E ... 212 725-1500
New York (G-12597)
Yigal-Azrouel Inc ... E ... 212 302-1194
New York (G-12691)
▲ Z-Ply Corp ... E ... 212 398-7011
New York (G-12701)
ZIC Sportswear Inc ... E ... 718 361-9022
Long Island City (G-7933)
▲ Zinnias Inc ... F ... 718 746-8551
Bellerose (G-812)

2371 Fur Goods

Alexis & Gianni Retail Inc ... F ... 516 334-3877
Westbury (G-16964)
▲ Anage Inc ... F ... 212 944-6533
New York (G-9144)
Anastasia First International ... F ... 212 868-9241
New York (G-9149)
Anastasia Furs International ... G ... 212 868-9241
New York (G-9150)
Arbeit Bros Inc ... G ... 212 736-9761
New York (G-9190)
Avante ... G ... 516 782-4888
Great Neck (G-5793)

SIC SECTION — 23 APPAREL AND OTHER FINISHED PRODUCTS MADE FROM FABRICS AND SIMILAR MATERIAL

B Smith Furs Inc .... F 212 967-5290
New York *(G-9293)*

◆ Best Brands Consumer Pdts Inc .... G 212 684-7456
New York *(G-9373)*

Blum & Fink Inc .... F 212 695-2606
New York *(G-9426)*

CPT Usa LLC .... E 212 575-1616
New York *(G-9741)*

▲ Dennis Basso Couture Inc .... F 212 794-4500
New York *(G-9846)*

Fox Unlimited Inc .... G 212 736-3071
New York *(G-10195)*

Georgy Creative Fashions Inc .... G 212 279-4885
New York *(G-10284)*

◆ J Percy For Mrvin Rchards Ltd .... E 212 944-5300
New York *(G-10680)*

Jerry Sorbara Furs Inc .... F 212 594-3897
New York *(G-10721)*

◆ Kaitery Furs Ltd .... G 718 204-1396
Long Island City *(G-7778)*

Miller & Berkowitz Ltd .... F 212 244-5459
New York *(G-11268)*

Mink Mart Inc .... G 212 868-2785
New York *(G-11278)*

Moschos Furs Inc .... G 212 244-0255
New York *(G-11309)*

N Pologeorgis Furs Inc .... F 212 563-2250
New York *(G-11335)*

Samuel Schulman Furs Inc .... E 212 736-5550
New York *(G-11963)*

Sekas International Ltd .... F 212 629-6095
New York *(G-12021)*

▲ Stallion Inc .... E 718 706-0111
Long Island City *(G-7882)*

Stefan Furs Inc .... G 212 594-2788
New York *(G-12191)*

Steves Original Furs Inc .... E 212 967-8007
New York *(G-12203)*

Superior Furs Inc .... F 516 365-4123
Manhasset *(G-8065)*

Tom Moriber Furs Inc .... F 212 244-2180
New York *(G-12363)*

USA Furs By George Inc .... G 212 643-1415
New York *(G-12490)*

Xanadu .... G 212 465-0580
New York *(G-12674)*

2381 Dress & Work Gloves

Falls Manufacturing Inc .... G 518 672-7189
Philmont *(G-13540)*

◆ Fownes Brothers & Co Inc .... E 212 683-0150
New York *(G-10194)*

Fownes Brothers & Co Inc .... E 518 752-4411
Gloversville *(G-5711)*

Gce International Inc .... F 212 868-0500
New York *(G-10260)*

▲ Manzella Knitting .... G 716 825-0808
Orchard Park *(G-13281)*

2384 Robes & Dressing Gowns

▲ Carole Hchman Design Group Inc .... C 918 423-3535
New York *(G-9533)*

Jisan Trading Corporation .... E 212 244-1269
New York *(G-10738)*

▲ Komar Luxury Brands .... G 646 472-0060
New York *(G-10875)*

Lady Ester Lingerie Corp .... E 212 689-1729
New York *(G-10914)*

Mata Fashions LLC .... G 917 716-7894
New York *(G-11176)*

▲ Natori Company Incorporated .... D 212 532-7796
New York *(G-11355)*

Palmbay Ltd .... G 718 424-3388
Woodside *(G-17345)*

▲ Richard Leeds Intl Inc .... D 212 532-4546
New York *(G-11862)*

Sketch Studio Trading Inc .... G 212 244-2875
New York *(G-12090)*

2385 Waterproof Outerwear

A W R Group Inc .... F 718 729-0412
Long Island City *(G-7644)*

▲ Alpha 6 Distributions LLC .... F 516 801-8290
Locust Valley *(G-7628)*

▲ Cheri Mon Baby LLC .... G 212 354-5511
Brooklyn *(G-1777)*

▲ Essex Manufacturing Inc .... D 212 239-0080
New York *(G-10066)*

Float Tech Inc .... G 518 266-0964
Troy *(G-16235)*

▲ Hercules Group Inc .... E 212 813-8000
Port Washington *(G-13821)*

▲ Levy Group Inc .... C 212 398-0707
New York *(G-10979)*

▲ Top Fortune Usa Ltd .... G 516 608-2694
Lynbrook *(G-7965)*

2386 Leather & Sheep Lined Clothing

▲ Andrew M Schwartz LLC .... G 212 391-7070
New York *(G-9155)*

Avanti U S A Ltd .... F 716 695-5800
Tonawanda *(G-16141)*

Cockpit Usa Inc .... F 212 575-1616
New York *(G-9661)*

▲ Cockpit Usa Inc .... F 212 575-1616
New York *(G-9662)*

Cockpit Usa Inc .... F 908 558-9704
New York *(G-9663)*

▲ Dada Group US Inc .... G 631 888-0818
Bayside *(G-769)*

▲ Excelled Shpskin Lea Coat Corp .... F 212 594-5843
New York *(G-10103)*

▲ G-III Apparel Group Ltd .... C 212 403-0500
New York *(G-10234)*

G-III Leather Fashions Inc .... E 212 403-0500
New York *(G-10236)*

Georgy Creative Fashions Inc .... G 212 279-4885
New York *(G-10284)*

▼ Gloria Apparel Inc .... F 212 947-0869
New York *(G-10322)*

▲ J Lowy Co .... G 718 338-7324
Brooklyn *(G-2124)*

◆ J Percy For Mrvin Rchards Ltd .... E 212 944-5300
New York *(G-10680)*

Lost Worlds Inc .... G 212 923-3423
New York *(G-11045)*

Louis Schwartz .... G 845 356-6624
Spring Valley *(G-15593)*

Studio One Leather Design Inc .... F 212 760-1701
New York *(G-12221)*

▲ US Authentic LLC .... G 914 767-0295
Katonah *(G-7134)*

2387 Apparel Belts

Barrera Jose & Maria Co Ltd .... E 212 239-1994
New York *(G-9325)*

◆ Coach Inc .... B 212 594-1850
New York *(G-9656)*

▲ Coach Stores Inc .... A 212 643-9727
New York *(G-9659)*

▲ Courtlandt Boot Jack Co Inc .... E 718 445-6200
Flushing *(G-5235)*

▲ Daniel M Friedman & Assoc Inc .... E 212 695-5545
New York *(G-9804)*

Dynasty Belts Inc .... E 516 625-6280
New Hyde Park *(G-8829)*

Gbg USA Inc .... D 646 839-7083
New York *(G-10254)*

Gbg USA Inc .... E 212 615-3400
New York *(G-10255)*

Gbg USA Inc .... E 212 290-8041
New York *(G-10256)*

Nassau Suffolk Brd of Womens .... E 631 666-8835
Bay Shore *(G-721)*

▲ New Classic Inc .... F 718 609-1100
Long Island City *(G-7823)*

P M Belts Usa Inc .... E 800 762-3580
Brooklyn *(G-2401)*

◆ Perry Ellis Menswear LLC .... C 212 221-7500
New York *(G-11624)*

Queue Solutions LLC .... F 631 750-6440
Bohemia *(G-1125)*

Randa Accessories Lea Gds LLC .... D 212 354-5100
New York *(G-11799)*

Sandy Duftler Designs Ltd .... F 516 379-3084
North Baldwin *(G-12908)*

Sh Leather Novelty Company .... G 718 387-7742
Brooklyn *(G-2547)*

Sibeau Handbags Inc .... E 212 686-0210
New York *(G-12059)*

▲ Trafalgar Company LLC .... G 212 768-8800
New York *(G-12390)*

Universal Elliot Corp .... G 212 736-8877
New York *(G-12471)*

Walco Leather Co Inc .... E 212 243-2244
New York *(G-12577)*

Xinya International Trading Co .... G 212 216-9681
New York *(G-12679)*

2389 Apparel & Accessories, NEC

▲ A Lunt Design Inc .... F 716 662-0781
Orchard Park *(G-13250)*

▲ Adf Accessories Inc .... G 516 450-5755
Lynbrook *(G-7943)*

▲ Apollo Apparel Group LLC .... F 212 398-6585
New York *(G-9175)*

Barbara Matera Ltd .... D 212 475-5006
New York *(G-9315)*

▲ Bh Brand Inc .... E 212 239-1635
New York *(G-9386)*

Brooklyn Denim Co .... F 718 782-2600
Brooklyn *(G-1725)*

Carelli Costumes Inc .... E 212 765-6166
New York *(G-9524)*

▲ Carter Enterprises LLC .... E 718 853-5052
Brooklyn *(G-1760)*

Club Monaco US Inc .... G 212 886-2660
New York *(G-9647)*

▲ Cortland Industries Inc .... F 212 575-2710
New York *(G-9728)*

Costume Armour Inc .... F 845 534-9120
Cornwall *(G-3987)*

Costume Culture By Franco LLC .... F 718 821-7100
Glendale *(G-5649)*

Craft Clerical Clothes Inc .... G 212 764-6122
New York *(G-9743)*

Creative Costume Co .... G 212 564-5552
New York *(G-9748)*

Crosswinds Sourcing LLC .... G 646 438-6904
New York *(G-9757)*

Cygnet Studio Inc .... F 646 450-4550
New York *(G-9776)*

D-C Theatricks .... G 716 847-0180
Buffalo *(G-2900)*

Danny R Couture Corp .... G 212 594-1095
New York *(G-9806)*

David & Young Co Inc .... G 212 594-6034
New York *(G-9818)*

Davis .... G 716 833-4678
Buffalo *(G-2903)*

Diamond Collection LLC .... E 718 846-1008
Richmond Hill *(G-14071)*

▲ Dreamwave LLC .... E 212 594-4250
New York *(G-9925)*

▲ Dvf Studio LLC .... D 212 741-6607
New York *(G-9942)*

Eric Winterling Inc .... E 212 629-7686
New York *(G-10056)*

▼ Euroco Costumes Inc .... G 212 629-9665
New York *(G-10085)*

▲ Fetherston Design Group LLC .... E 212 643-7537
New York *(G-10156)*

Foot Locker Retail Inc .... G 516 827-5306
Hicksville *(G-6345)*

▲ Gce International Inc .... D 212 704-4800
New York *(G-10259)*

▲ HB Athletic Inc .... F 914 560-8422
New Rochelle *(G-8910)*

Hoehn Inc .... F 518 463-8900
Albany *(G-88)*

▲ Hpk Industries LLC .... F 315 724-0196
Utica *(G-16338)*

Hudson Dying & Finishing LLC .... E 518 752-4389
Gloversville *(G-5716)*

Intercotton Company Inc .... G 212 265-3809
New York *(G-10626)*

Izquierdo Studios Ltd .... F 212 807-9757
New York *(G-10671)*

J & C Finishing .... E 718 456-1087
Ridgewood *(G-14110)*

J M B Apparel Designer Group .... G 212 764-8410
New York *(G-10679)*

J M C Bow Co Inc .... F 718 686-8110
Brooklyn *(G-2125)*

Jersey Express Inc .... F 716 834-6151
Buffalo *(G-3018)*

▲ Jimeale Incorporated .... G 917 686-5383
New York *(G-10735)*

▲ JM Studio Inc .... F 646 546-5514
New York *(G-10743)*

Jmk Enterprises LLC .... G 845 634-8100
New City *(G-8786)*

John Kristiansen New York Inc .... F 212 388-1097
New York *(G-10750)*

Jonathan Meizler LLC .... G 212 213-2977
New York *(G-10757)*

▲ Joseph Industries Inc .... G 212 764-0010
New York *(G-10765)*

Employee Codes: A=Over 500 employees, B=251-500
C=101-250, D=51-100, E=20-50, F=10-19, G=5-9

2017 Harris
New York Manufacturers Directory

735

23 APPAREL AND OTHER FINISHED PRODUCTS MADE FROM FABRICS AND SIMILAR MATERIAL SIC SECTION

◆ **Kidz Concepts LLC** ....D 212 398-1110
New York *(G-10842)*
Kiton Building Corp ....E 212 486-3224
New York *(G-10855)*
Koon Enterprises LLC ....G 718 886-3163
Fresh Meadows *(G-5442)*
Kww Productions Corp ....F 212 398-8181
New York *(G-10896)*
▼ **Lakeland Industries Inc** ....C 631 981-9700
Ronkonkoma *(G-14928)*
Lakeview Innovations Inc ....F 212 502-6702
New York *(G-10920)*
Linder New York LLC ....F 646 678-5819
New York *(G-10998)*
M2 Fashion Group Holdings Inc ....G 917 208-2948
New York *(G-11080)*
Miles Alexander LLC ....F 516 937-5262
Hicksville *(G-6372)*
Moresca Clothing and Costume ....F 845 331-6012
Ulster Park *(G-16286)*
My Hanky Inc ....F 646 321-0869
Brooklyn *(G-2344)*
▲ **New York Accessory Group Inc** ....E 212 532-7911
New York *(G-11395)*
New York Hospital Disposable ....E 718 384-1620
Brooklyn *(G-2365)*
▲ **New York Popular Inc** ....D 718 499-2020
Brooklyn *(G-2367)*
Nmny Group LLC ....E 212 944-6500
New York *(G-11447)*
NY 1 Art Gallery Inc ....G 917 698-0626
New Hyde Park *(G-8852)*
▲ **NY Orthopedic Usa Inc** ....D 718 852-5330
Brooklyn *(G-2382)*
P B O E Pwred By Our Envmt Inc ....G 917 803-9474
Brooklyn *(G-2400)*
Parsons-Meares Ltd ....D 212 242-3378
Long Island City *(G-7834)*
Patient-Wear LLC ....G 914 740-7770
Bronx *(G-1422)*
◆ **Perry Ellis Menswear LLC** ....C 212 221-7500
New York *(G-11624)*
▲ **Ppr Direct Marketing LLC** ....G 718 965-8600
Brooklyn *(G-2433)*
RA Newhouse Inc ....D 516 248-6670
Mineola *(G-8532)*
Rainforest Apparel LLC ....G 212 840-0880
New York *(G-11789)*
Randa Accessories Lea Gds LLC ....D 212 354-5100
New York *(G-11799)*
Reiss Ltd ....G 212 488-2411
New York *(G-11822)*
Ribz LLC ....G 212 764-9595
New York *(G-11861)*
▲ **Rjm2 Ltd** ....G 212 944-1660
New York *(G-11884)*
Robert Miller Associates LLC ....F 718 392-1640
Long Island City *(G-7862)*
▲ **Rose Solomon Co** ....E 718 855-1788
Brooklyn *(G-2506)*
▲ **Rosetti Handbags and ACC** ....E 212 273-3765
New York *(G-11919)*
▲ **Roth Clothing Co Inc** ....G 718 384-4927
Brooklyn *(G-2508)*
◆ **Rubies Costume Company Inc** ....B 718 846-1008
Richmond Hill *(G-14081)*
Rubies Costume Company Inc ....D 631 777-3300
Bay Shore *(G-741)*
Rubies Costume Company Inc ....C 718 441-0834
Richmond Hill *(G-14082)*
Rubies Costume Company Inc ....C 631 951-3688
Bay Shore *(G-742)*
Rubies Costume Company Inc ....E 516 326-1500
Melville *(G-8354)*
Rubies Costume Company Inc ....C 718 846-1008
Richmond Hill *(G-14083)*
Rubies Masquerade Company LLC ....G 718 846-1008
Richmond Hill *(G-14084)*
▲ **S & B Fashion Inc** ....G 718 482-1386
Long Island City *(G-7869)*
Schneeman Studio Limited ....G 212 244-3330
New York *(G-11990)*
◆ **Shamron Mills Ltd** ....G 212 354-0430
New York *(G-12041)*
South Central Boyz ....G 718 496-7270
Brooklyn *(G-2586)*
▲ **Swank Inc** ....B 212 867-2600
New York *(G-12248)*
▲ **Timeless Fashions LLC** ....G 212 730-9328
New York *(G-12351)*
Tr Apparel LLC ....E 310 595-4337
New York *(G-12385)*
Tr Apparel LLC ....G 646 358-3888
New York *(G-12386)*
▲ **Trafalgar Company LLC** ....G 212 768-8800
New York *(G-12390)*
Twcc Product and Sales ....E 212 614-9364
New York *(G-12432)*
▲ **Ufo Contemporary Inc** ....F 212 226-5400
New York *(G-12444)*
Unified Inc led ....F 646 370-4650
New York *(G-12453)*
Warner ....G 716 446-0663
Buffalo *(G-3248)*
Westchester Wine Warehouse LLC ....F 914 824-1400
White Plains *(G-17185)*
Zam Barrett Dialogue Inc ....G 646 649-0140
Brooklyn *(G-2780)*

2391 Curtains & Draperies

A Schneller Sons Inc ....F 212 695-9440
New York *(G-8992)*
Abalene Decorating Services ....E 718 782-2000
New York *(G-9000)*
Anthony Lawrence of New York ....E 212 206-8820
Long Island City *(G-7661)*
Associated Drapery & Equipment ....F 516 671-5245
Monroe *(G-8548)*
▲ **Baby Signature Inc** ....G 212 686-1700
New York *(G-9298)*
◆ **Belle Maison USA Ltd** ....E 718 805-0200
Richmond Hill *(G-14068)*
Bettertex Inc ....F 212 431-3373
New York *(G-9379)*
▲ **Bramson House Inc** ....C 516 764-5006
Freeport *(G-5390)*
C & G of Kingston Inc ....D 845 331-0148
Kingston *(G-7180)*
Cabriole Designs Inc ....G 212 593-4528
New York *(G-9494)*
◆ **County Draperies Inc** ....E 845 342-9009
Middletown *(G-8433)*
Deangelis Ltd ....E 212 348-8225
New York *(G-9833)*
Decorative Novelty Co Inc ....F 718 965-8600
Brooklyn *(G-1849)*
Delta Upholsterers Inc ....E 212 489-3308
New York *(G-9841)*
Drapery Industries Inc ....F 585 232-2992
Rochester *(G-14318)*
Fabric Quilters Unlimited Inc ....E 516 333-2866
Westbury *(G-16984)*
Henry B Urban Inc ....E 212 489-3308
New York *(G-10457)*
J Edlin Interiors Ltd ....F 212 243-2111
New York *(G-10677)*
Jo-Vin Decorators Inc ....E 718 441-9350
Woodhaven *(G-17306)*
Laminated Window Products Inc ....F 631 242-6883
Bay Shore *(G-710)*
▼ **Laregence Inc** ....E 212 736-2548
New York *(G-10928)*
◆ **Louis Hornick & Co Inc** ....G 212 679-2448
New York *(G-11049)*
Majestic Curtains LLC ....G 718 898-0774
Elmhurst *(G-4664)*
▼ **Mason Contract Products LLC** ....D 516 328-6900
New Hyde Park *(G-8848)*
McCarroll Uphl Designs LLC ....G 518 828-0500
Hudson *(G-6625)*
▲ **Mistdoda Inc** ....E 919 735-7111
New York *(G-11284)*
▲ **Mutual Sales Corp** ....E 718 361-8373
Long Island City *(G-7817)*
Northast Coml Win Trtments Inc ....D 845 331-0148
Kingston *(G-7203)*
▲ **Revman International Inc** ....E 212 894-3100
New York *(G-11854)*
Reynolds Drapery Service Inc ....F 315 845-8632
Newport *(G-12792)*
▲ **Richloom Fabrics Corp** ....F 212 685-5400
New York *(G-11869)*
▲ **Richloom Fabrics Group Inc** ....G 212 685-5400
New York *(G-11870)*
▲ **Richloom Home Fashions Corp** ....F 212 685-5400
New York *(G-11871)*
▲ **Royal Home Fashions Inc** ....G 212 689-7222
New York *(G-11924)*
Seaway Mats Inc ....G 518 483-2560
Malone *(G-8016)*
Showeray Co ....D 718 965-3633
Brooklyn *(G-2551)*
Shyam Ahuja Limited ....G 212 644-5910
New York *(G-12057)*
Terbo Ltd ....G 718 847-2860
Richmond Hill *(G-14087)*
Wayne Decorators Inc ....G 718 529-4200
Jamaica *(G-6963)*
Wcd Window Coverings Inc ....E 845 336-4511
Lake Katrine *(G-7271)*
White Plains Drapery Uphl Inc ....E 914 381-0908
Mamaroneck *(G-8050)*
White Workroom Inc ....G 212 941-5910
New York *(G-12627)*
▲ **Wildcat Territory Inc** ....F 718 361-6726
Long Island City *(G-7921)*

2392 House furnishings: Textile

AEP Environmental LLC ....F 716 446-0739
Buffalo *(G-2801)*
▲ **Alen Sands York Associates Ltd** ....F 212 563-6305
New York *(G-9080)*
Alexandra Ferguson LLC ....G 718 788-7768
Brooklyn *(G-1581)*
Allied Down Products Inc ....G 718 389-5454
Brooklyn *(G-1589)*
Anhui Skyworth LLC ....D 917 940-6903
Hempstead *(G-6264)*
▲ **Ann Gish Inc** ....G 212 969-9200
New York *(G-9163)*
▲ **Area Inc** ....G 212 924-7084
New York *(G-9198)*
▲ **Arlee Home Fashions Inc** ....D 212 213-0425
New York *(G-9203)*
▲ **Baby Signature Inc** ....G 212 686-1700
New York *(G-9298)*
▲ **Bardwil Industries Inc** ....G 212 944-1870
New York *(G-9317)*
◆ **Belle Maison USA Ltd** ....E 718 805-0200
Richmond Hill *(G-14068)*
Benson Sales Co Inc ....F 718 236-6743
Brooklyn *(G-1685)*
▲ **Bramson House Inc** ....C 516 764-5006
Freeport *(G-5390)*
▲ **Broder Mfg Inc** ....G 718 366-1667
Brooklyn *(G-1718)*
C & G of Kingston Inc ....D 845 331-0148
Kingston *(G-7180)*
▲ **Caddy Concepts Inc** ....F 516 570-6279
Great Neck *(G-5795)*
▲ **Catalina Products Corp** ....E 718 336-8288
Brooklyn *(G-1764)*
▲ **Cathay Home Inc** ....E 212 213-0988
New York *(G-9548)*
▲ **Continental Quilting Co Inc** ....E 718 499-9100
Brooklyn *(G-1800)*
◆ **County Draperies Inc** ....E 845 342-9009
Middletown *(G-8433)*
▼ **Cpac Inc** ....E 585 382-3223
Leicester *(G-7420)*
▲ **Creative Home Furnishings** ....G 631 582-8000
Central Islip *(G-3492)*
Creative Scents USA Inc ....G 718 522-5901
Brooklyn *(G-1816)*
▲ **Dico Products Corporation** ....F 315 797-0470
Utica *(G-16323)*
Elegant Linen Inc ....E 718 871-3535
Brooklyn *(G-1913)*
Ess Bee Industries Inc ....E 718 894-5202
Brooklyn *(G-1936)*
▲ **Excellent Art Mfg Corp** ....F 718 388-7075
Inwood *(G-6756)*
EY Industries Inc ....F 718 624-9122
Brooklyn *(G-1947)*
Fabric Quilters Unlimited Inc ....E 516 333-2866
Westbury *(G-16984)*
G Fried Carpet Service ....E 516 333-3900
Westbury *(G-16989)*
Handy Laundry Products Corp ....G 800 263-5973
Airmont *(G-15)*
Henry B Urban Inc ....E 212 489-3308
New York *(G-10457)*
◆ **Himatsingka America Inc** ....E 212 545-8929
New York *(G-10478)*
Hollander HM Fshons Hldngs LLC ....F 212 575-0400
New York *(G-10498)*
Hollander Sleep Products LLC ....D 212 575-0400
New York *(G-10499)*
Home Fashions Intl LLC ....F 212 684-0091
New York *(G-10501)*

SIC

SIC SECTION 23 APPAREL AND OTHER FINISHED PRODUCTS MADE FROM FABRICS AND SIMILAR MATERIAL

◆ Indigo Home Inc G 212 684-4146 New York (G-10589)
◆ Ingenious Designs LLC C 631 254-3376 Ronkonkoma (G-14912)
Jay Import Company Inc E 212 683-2727 New York (G-10704)
Jdt International LLC G 212 400-7570 New York (G-10712)
Jo-Vin Decorators Inc E 718 441-9350 Woodhaven (G-17306)
◆ Josie Accessories Inc D 212 889-6376 New York (G-10768)
▲ Kaltex North America Inc F 212 894-3200 New York (G-10807)
▲ Kim Seybert Inc F 212 564-7850 New York (G-10846)
▲ Kravet Fabrics Inc D 516 293-2000 Bethpage (G-869)
◆ Madison Industries Inc F 212 679-5110 New York (G-11094)
McCarroll Uphl Designs LLC G 518 828-0500 Hudson (G-6625)
Medline Industries Inc B 845 344-3301 Middletown (G-8450)
Mgk Group Inc E 212 989-2732 New York (G-11246)
Michael Stuart Inc E 718 821-0704 Brooklyn (G-2309)
Moga Trading Company Inc G 718 760-2966 Corona (G-4004)
▲ National Wire & Metal Tech Inc E 716 661-9180 Jamestown (G-7021)
▲ Nationwide Tarps Incorporated D 518 843-1545 Amsterdam (G-361)
Nbets Corporation G 516 785-1259 Wantagh (G-16561)
▲ Nl Shoes and Bags LLC G 212 594-0012 New York (G-11444)
▲ Northpoint Trading Inc F 212 481-8001 New York (G-11460)
▲ NY Cutting Inc G 845 368-1459 Airmont (G-17)
Paramount Textiles Inc F 212 966-1040 New York (G-11570)
▲ Perfex Corporation F 315 826-3600 Poland (G-13727)
▲ Place Vendome Holding Co Inc G 212 696-0765 Bronx (G-1428)
Premier Skirting Products Inc F 516 239-6581 Lawrence (G-7397)
Prime Feather Industries Ltd F 718 326-8701 Suffern (G-15798)
▲ Q Squared Design LLC E 212 686-8860 New York (G-11763)
▲ R & M Industries Inc F 212 366-6414 New York (G-11780)
Repellem Consumer Pdts Corp F 631 273-3992 Islandia (G-6802)
▲ Revman International Inc E 212 894-3100 New York (G-11854)
▲ Richloom Corp F 212 685-5400 New York (G-11868)
▲ Richloom Fabrics Corp F 212 685-5400 New York (G-11869)
▲ Richloom Fabrics Group Inc G 212 685-5400 New York (G-11870)
▲ Royal Copenhagen Inc F 845 454-4442 Poughkeepsie (G-13929)
▲ Royal Home Fashions Inc G 212 689-7222 New York (G-11924)
Scent-Sation Inc D 718 672-4300 Queens Village (G-13983)
Showeray Co D 718 965-3633 Brooklyn (G-2551)
▲ Silly Phillie Creations Inc E 718 492-6300 Brooklyn (G-2556)
▲ Skil-Care Corporation C 914 963-2040 Yonkers (G-17484)
▲ Sleeping Partners Intl Inc F 212 254-1515 Brooklyn (G-2569)
Smith & Johnson Dry Goods G 212 951-7067 New York (G-12103)
▲ Soft-Tex International Inc D 518 235-3645 Waterford (G-16621)
State Bags LLC F 617 895-8532 New York (G-12188)
▲ Stuart Weitzman LLC E 212 823-9560 New York (G-12218)
▲ Such Intl Incorporation G 212 686-9888 Setauket (G-15380)
◆ Sunham Home Fashions LLC D 212 695-1218 New York (G-12236)
Superior Decorators Inc F 718 381-4793 Glendale (G-5664)
Sure Fit Inc E 212 395-9340 New York (G-12244)
Tablecloths For Granted Ltd F 518 370-5481 Schenectady (G-15303)
Terbo Ltd G 718 847-2860 Richmond Hill (G-14087)
▲ Thompson Packaging Novlt Inc G 212 686-4242 New York (G-12327)
Thor Marketing Corp G 201 247-7103 Valley Cottage (G-16393)
▲ Twinny Products Inc F 718 592-7500 Corona (G-4008)
▲ University Table Cloth Company F 845 371-3876 Spring Valley (G-15606)
Wayne Decorators Inc G 718 529-4200 Jamaica (G-6963)
▲ Wildcat Territory Inc F 718 361-6726 Long Island City (G-7921)
William Harvey Studio Inc G 718 599-4343 Brooklyn (G-2753)
Xpresspa Holdings LLC F 212 750-9595 New York (G-12683)

2393 Textile Bags

▲ Ace Drop Cloth Canvas Pdts Inc E 718 731-1550 Bronx (G-1260)
Advanced Medical Mfg Corp E 845 369-7535 Suffern (G-15784)
▲ Aka Sport Inc F 631 858-9888 Dix Hills (G-4289)
Carry Hot Inc F 212 279-7535 New York (G-9537)
Clear Edge Crosible Inc D 315 685-3466 Skaneateles Falls (G-15467)
GPM Associates LLC G 585 359-1770 Rush (G-15050)
GPM Associates LLC E 585 335-3940 Dansville (G-4077)
▲ H G Maybeck Co Inc E 718 297-4410 Jamaica (G-6918)
▲ Health Matters America Inc F 716 235-8772 Buffalo (G-2992)
◆ Ivi Services Inc D 607 729-5111 Binghamton (G-929)
▲ Jag Manufacturing Inc E 518 762-9558 Johnstown (G-7116)
Jakes Sneakers Inc G 718 233-1132 Brooklyn (G-2134)
Johnson Outdoors Inc C 607 779-2200 Binghamton (G-931)
Kragel Co Inc G 716 648-1344 Hamburg (G-5932)
▲ Kush Oasis Enterprises LLC G 516 513-1316 Syosset (G-15827)
Mgk Group Inc E 212 989-2732 New York (G-11246)
Paulpac LLC G 631 283-7610 Southampton (G-15548)
Redco Foods Inc D 315 823-1300 Little Falls (G-7504)
▼ Select Fabricators Inc F 585 393-0650 Canandaigua (G-3357)
▲ Twinny Products Inc F 718 592-7500 Corona (G-4008)
Wayne Decorators Inc G 718 529-4200 Jamaica (G-6963)

2394 Canvas Prdts

125-127 Main Street Corp F 631 477-1500 Greenport (G-5876)
Abble Awning Co Inc G 516 822-1200 Bethpage (G-862)
▲ Ace Canvas & Tent Corp F 631 648-0614 Ronkonkoma (G-14848)
▲ Ace Drop Cloth Canvas Pdts Inc E 718 731-1550 Bronx (G-1260)
Acme Awning Co Inc F 718 409-1881 Bronx (G-1262)
▼ Air Structures Amercn Tech Inc E 914 937-4500 Port Chester (G-13737)
Allen Boat Co Inc G 716 842-0800 Buffalo (G-2802)
Anchor Canvas LLC G 631 265-5602 Smithtown (G-15483)
Automtive Uphl Cnvertible Tops G 914 961-4242 Tuckahoe (G-16269)
Awning Mart Inc G 315 699-5928 Cicero (G-3642)
Awnings Plus Inc F 716 693-3690 Tonawanda (G-16142)
Breton Industries Inc D 518 842-3030 Amsterdam (G-336)
Broadway Neon Sign Corp F 908 241-4177 Ronkonkoma (G-14881)
Brock Awnings Ltd F 631 765-5200 Hampton Bays (G-5960)
C E King & Sons Inc G 631 324-4944 East Hampton (G-4406)
Canvas Products Company Inc F 516 742-1058 Mineola (G-8500)
Capitol Awning Co Inc F 212 505-1717 Jamaica (G-6900)
Classic Awnings Inc F 716 649-0390 Hamburg (G-5920)
Coverall Manufacturing G 315 652-2731 Baldwinsville (G-568)
▲ Covergrip Corporation G 855 268-3747 Bohemia (G-1041)
▲ Custom Canvas Manufacturing Co E 716 852-6372 Buffalo (G-2897)
▲ Custom European Imports Inc E 845 357-5718 Sloatsburg (G-15480)
▲ Dhs Systems LLC F 845 359-6066 Orangeburg (G-13224)
Di Sanos Creative Canvas Inc G 315 894-3137 Frankfort (G-5351)
Dor-A-Mar Canvas Products Co F 631 750-9202 West Sayville (G-16934)
Doyle-Hild Sailmakers G 718 885-2255 Bronx (G-1317)
▲ Durasol Systems Inc D 845 610-1100 Chester (G-3605)
Fabric Concepts For Industry F 914 375-2565 Yonkers (G-17443)
Haarstick Sailmakers Inc F 585 342-5200 Rochester (G-14418)
▲ Jag Manufacturing Inc E 518 762-9558 Johnstown (G-7116)
Jamestown Awning Inc G 716 483-1435 Jamestown (G-7005)
Jo-Vin Decorators Inc E 718 441-9350 Woodhaven (G-17306)
Johnson Outdoors Inc C 607 779-2200 Binghamton (G-931)
Kohler Awning Inc E 716 685-3333 Buffalo (G-3036)
Kragel Co Inc G 716 648-1344 Hamburg (G-5932)
Kraus & Sons Inc F 212 620-0408 New York (G-10887)
Laminated Window Products Inc F 631 242-6883 Bay Shore (G-710)
Lanza Corp G 914 937-6360 Port Chester (G-13751)
▲ Leiter Sukkahs Inc G 718 436-0303 Brooklyn (G-2209)
M & M Canvas & Awnings Inc G 631 424-5370 Islandia (G-6800)
Mauceri Sign Inc F 718 656-7700 Jamaica (G-6929)
Mc Coy Tops and Interiors Inc G 718 458-5800 Woodside (G-17336)
▼ Melbourne C Fisher Yacht Sails G 631 673-5055 Huntington Station (G-6716)
▼ Meyco Products Inc E 631 421-9800 Melville (G-8336)
▲ Nationwide Tarps Incorporated D 518 843-1545 Amsterdam (G-361)
Northern Awning & Sign Company G 315 782-8515 Watertown (G-16667)
Perma Tech Inc E 716 854-0707 Buffalo (G-3122)
Point Canvas Company Inc G 607 692-4381 Whitney Point (G-17220)
Quantum Sails Rochester LLC G 585 342-5200 Rochester (G-14615)
Reid K Dalland G 845 687-8728 Stone Ridge (G-15765)
Sausbiers Awning Shop Inc G 518 828-3748 Hudson (G-6633)
▼ Select Fabricators Inc F 585 393-0650 Canandaigua (G-3357)
Service Canvas Co Inc F 716 853-0558 Buffalo (G-3182)
Steinway Awning II LLC G 718 729-2965 Astoria (G-459)

Employee Codes: A=Over 500 employees, B=251-500 C=101-250, D=51-100, E=20-50, F=10-19, G=5-9

23 APPAREL AND OTHER FINISHED PRODUCTS MADE FROM FABRICS AND SIMILAR MATERIAL SIC SECTION

TG Peppe Inc ... G ... 516 239-7852
Lawrence *(G-7401)*

Toptec Products LLC ... F ... 631 421-9800
Melville *(G-8361)*

Ulmer Sales LLC ... F ... 718 885-1700
Bronx *(G-1484)*

Utility Canvas Inc ... G ... 845 255-9290
Gardiner *(G-5552)*

Vinyl Works Inc ... E ... 518 786-1200
Latham *(G-7383)*

▲ Y & A Trading Inc ... F ... 718 436-6333
Brooklyn *(G-2772)*

2395 Pleating & Stitching For The Trade

A Garys Treasures ... F ... 518 383-1171
Clifton Park *(G-3693)*

A Trusted Name Inc ... F ... 716 326-7400
Westfield *(G-17045)*

Acme Pleating & Fagoting Corp ... F ... 212 674-3737
New York *(G-9018)*

▲ Active World Solutions Inc ... G ... 718 922-9404
Brooklyn *(G-1559)*

Aditiany Inc ... G ... 212 997-8440
New York *(G-9028)*

All About Art Inc ... F ... 718 321-0755
Flushing *(G-5225)*

All American Awards Inc ... F ... 631 567-2025
Bohemia *(G-1011)*

American Country Quilts & Lin ... G ... 631 283-5466
Southampton *(G-15538)*

American Quality Embroidery ... G ... 631 467-3200
Ronkonkoma *(G-14869)*

Arena Graphics Inc ... G ... 516 767-5108
Port Washington *(G-13801)*

Athletic Cap Co Inc ... E ... 718 398-1300
Staten Island *(G-15641)*

Atlantic Coast Embroidery Inc ... G ... 631 283-2175
Southampton *(G-15539)*

Clinton Clrs & EMB Shoppe Inc ... G ... 315 853-8421
Clinton *(G-3718)*

Clpa Embroidery ... G ... 516 409-0002
Bellmore *(G-816)*

Control Research Inc ... G ... 631 225-1111
Amityville *(G-282)*

Custom Patches Inc ... E ... 845 679-6320
Woodstock *(G-17362)*

Design Archives Inc ... G ... 212 768-0617
New York *(G-9851)*

Dirt T Shirts Inc ... E ... 845 336-4230
Kingston *(G-7187)*

▲ Eagle Regalia Co Inc ... F ... 845 425-2245
Spring Valley *(G-15582)*

East Coast Embroidery Ltd ... G ... 631 254-3878
Deer Park *(G-4133)*

Eiseman-Ludmar Co Inc ... F ... 516 932-6990
Hicksville *(G-6343)*

Expressions Punching & Digitiz ... G ... 718 291-1177
Jamaica *(G-6911)*

F X Graphix Inc ... G ... 716 871-1511
Buffalo *(G-2943)*

Gildan Apparel USA Inc ... G ... 716 759-6273
Clarence *(G-3662)*

Glenda Inc ... G ... 718 442-8981
Staten Island *(G-15678)*

▲ Holland & Sherry Inc ... E ... 212 542-8410
New York *(G-10497)*

Hosel & Ackerson Inc ... G ... 212 575-1490
New York *(G-10509)*

Human Technologies Corporation ... F ... 315 735-3532
Utica *(G-16340)*

Instant Monogramming Inc ... G ... 585 654-5550
Rochester *(G-14450)*

▲ Jomar Industries Inc ... E ... 845 357-5773
Airmont *(G-16)*

Kabrics ... G ... 607 962-6344
Corning *(G-3975)*

Karishma Fashions Inc ... G ... 718 565-5404
Jackson Heights *(G-6888)*

Kevin J Kassman ... G ... 585 529-4245
Rochester *(G-14469)*

Knucklehead Embroidery Inc ... G ... 607 797-2725
Johnson City *(G-7098)*

Loremanss Embroidery Engrav ... F ... 518 834-9205
Keeseville *(G-7139)*

Mainly Monograms Inc ... E ... 845 624-4923
West Nyack *(G-16921)*

Milaaya Inc ... G ... 212 764-6386
New York *(G-11265)*

Monte Goldman Embroidery Co ... F ... 212 874-5397
New York *(G-11301)*

Mrinalini Inc ... G ... 646 510-2747
New York *(G-11316)*

Northeast Stitches & Ink Inc ... E ... 518 798-5549
South Glens Falls *(G-15528)*

▲ NY Embroidery Inc ... E ... 516 822-6456
Hicksville *(G-6378)*

On The Job Embroidery & AP ... G ... 914 381-3556
Mamaroneck *(G-8040)*

Pass Em-Entries Inc ... F ... 718 392-0100
Long Island City *(G-7835)*

Penn & Fletcher Inc ... F ... 212 239-6868
Long Island City *(G-7839)*

Pink Inc ... E ... 212 352-8282
New York *(G-11663)*

Planet Embroidery ... F ... 718 381-4827
Ridgewood *(G-14118)*

Pleating Plus Ltd ... F ... 201 863-2991
Orangeburg *(G-13240)*

Point Canvas Company Inc ... G ... 607 692-4381
Whitney Point *(G-17220)*

Pro Lettering LLC ... G ... 607 484-0255
Endicott *(G-4826)*

Quist Industries Ltd ... F ... 718 243-2800
Brooklyn *(G-2468)*

Rescuestuff Inc ... G ... 718 318-7570
Peekskill *(G-13480)*

River Rat Design ... F ... 315 393-4770
Ogdensburg *(G-13121)*

Ross L Sports Screening Inc ... F ... 716 824-5350
Buffalo *(G-3167)*

Round Top Knit & Screening ... G ... 518 622-3600
Round Top *(G-15040)*

Royal Tees Inc ... G ... 845 357-9448
Suffern *(G-15800)*

Sand Hill Industries Inc ... G ... 518 885-7991
Ballston Spa *(G-608)*

Screen Gems Inc ... G ... 845 561-0036
New Windsor *(G-8953)*

Screen The World Inc ... F ... 631 475-0023
Holtsville *(G-6508)*

▲ Seo Ryung Inc ... F ... 718 321-0755
Flushing *(G-5291)*

Shykat Promotions ... G ... 866 574-2757
Forestville *(G-5336)*

Stanley Pleating Stitching Co ... E ... 718 392-2417
Long Island City *(G-7886)*

Stephen M Kiernan ... E ... 716 836-6300
Buffalo *(G-3196)*

Stucki Embroidery Works Inc ... F ... 845 657-2308
Boiceville *(G-1158)*

Stylist Pleating Corp ... F ... 718 384-8181
Brooklyn *(G-2617)*

Todd Walbridge ... G ... 585 254-3018
Rochester *(G-14727)*

U All Inc ... E ... 518 438-2558
Albany *(G-144)*

U S Embroidery Inc ... F ... 718 585-9662
Bronx *(G-1483)*

Uniform Namemakers Inc ... F ... 716 626-5474
Buffalo *(G-3232)*

Verdonette Inc ... G ... 212 719-2003
New York *(G-12521)*

Vogue Too Plting Stitching EMB ... F ... 212 354-1022
New York *(G-12565)*

Voyager Emblems Inc ... C ... 416 255-3421
Buffalo *(G-3245)*

Wicked Smart LLC ... F ... 518 459-2855
Watervliet *(G-16692)*

2396 Automotive Trimmings, Apparel Findings, Related Prdts

Acorn Products Corp ... F ... 315 894-4868
Ilion *(G-6739)*

Albert Siy ... G ... 718 359-0389
Flushing *(G-5224)*

American Spray-On Corp ... E ... 212 929-2100
New York *(G-9128)*

Amoseastern Apparel Inc ... F ... 212 921-1859
New York *(G-9138)*

Angel Textiles Inc ... G ... 212 532-0900
New York *(G-9156)*

Apple Imprints Apparel Inc ... E ... 716 893-1130
Buffalo *(G-2817)*

▲ Apsco Sports Enterprises Inc ... D ... 718 965-9500
Brooklyn *(G-1620)*

Aro-Graph Corporation ... G ... 315 463-8693
Syracuse *(G-15857)*

Art Flag Company Inc ... F ... 212 334-1890
New York *(G-9210)*

▲ Artistic Ribbon Novelty Co Inc ... E ... 212 255-4224
New York *(G-9220)*

Athletic Cap Co Inc ... E ... 718 398-1300
Staten Island *(G-15641)*

Barnaby Prints Inc ... F ... 845 477-2501
Greenwood Lake *(G-5896)*

Bondy Printing Corp ... G ... 631 242-1510
Bay Shore *(G-679)*

Bpe Studio Inc ... G ... 212 868-9896
New York *(G-9448)*

C H Thompson Company Inc ... D ... 607 724-1094
Binghamton *(G-901)*

◆ Cai Inc ... G ... 212 819-0008
New York *(G-9497)*

Casual Friday Inc ... F ... 585 544-9470
Rochester *(G-14262)*

Coe Displays Inc ... G ... 718 937-5658
Long Island City *(G-7702)*

Cooper & Clement Inc ... E ... 315 454-8135
Syracuse *(G-15907)*

Creative Images & Applique ... D ... 718 821-8700
Maspeth *(G-8126)*

D & R Silk Screening Ltd ... F ... 631 234-7464
Central Islip *(G-3494)*

Decal Makers Inc ... E ... 516 221-7200
Bellmore *(G-817)*

Dirt T Shirts Inc ... E ... 845 336-4230
Kingston *(G-7187)*

Eagle Finishing ... E ... 718 497-7875
Brooklyn *(G-1896)*

Eagle Lace Dyeing Corp ... F ... 212 947-2712
New York *(G-9958)*

▲ Empire Bias Binding Co Inc ... F ... 718 545-0300
Long Island City *(G-7730)*

Emtron Hybrids Inc ... E ... 631 924-9668
Yaphank *(G-17392)*

Flp Group LLC ... F ... 315 252-7583
Auburn *(G-496)*

▲ Freeport Screen & Stamping ... E ... 516 379-0330
Freeport *(G-5401)*

Galli Shirts and Sports AP ... G ... 845 226-7305
Stormville *(G-15779)*

Hollywood Advertising Banners ... E ... 631 842-3000
Copiague *(G-3906)*

Human Technologies Corporation ... F ... 315 735-3532
Utica *(G-16340)*

Ihd Motorsports LLC ... F ... 979 690-1669
Binghamton *(G-925)*

Irene Cerone ... G ... 315 668-2899
Brewerton *(G-1204)*

J M L Productions Inc ... D ... 718 643-1674
Brooklyn *(G-2126)*

Jack J Florio Jr ... G ... 716 434-9123
Lockport *(G-7595)*

Kenmar Shirts Inc ... E ... 718 824-3880
Bronx *(G-1371)*

Kevin J Kassman ... G ... 585 529-4245
Rochester *(G-14469)*

L I C Screen Printing Inc ... E ... 516 546-7289
Merrick *(G-8387)*

▲ Legendary Auto Interiors Ltd ... E ... 315 331-1212
Newark *(G-12734)*

Lending Trimming Co Inc ... D ... 212 242-7502
New York *(G-10965)*

Loremanss Embroidery Engrav ... F ... 518 834-9205
Keeseville *(G-7139)*

Mart-Tex Athletics Inc ... E ... 631 454-9583
Farmingdale *(G-5043)*

Mas Cutting Inc ... G ... 212 869-0826
New York *(G-11173)*

Master Craft Finishers Inc ... E ... 631 586-0540
Deer Park *(G-4171)*

Master Image Printing Inc ... G ... 914 347-4400
Elmsford *(G-4763)*

Mountain T-Shirts Inc ... G ... 518 943-4533
Catskill *(G-3432)*

New York Binding Co Inc ... E ... 718 729-2454
Long Island City *(G-7825)*

Northeast Stitches & Ink Inc ... E ... 518 798-5549
South Glens Falls *(G-15528)*

▲ Pangea Brands LLC ... G ... 617 638-0001
New York *(G-11559)*

Pangea Brands LLC ... G ... 617 638-0001
New York *(G-11560)*

Park Avenue Imprints LLC ... G ... 716 822-5737
Buffalo *(G-3113)*

Patrick Rohan ... G ... 718 781-2573
Monticello *(G-8607)*

Paula Varsalona Ltd ... F ... 212 570-9100
New York *(G-11586)*

SIC SECTION

24 LUMBER AND WOOD PRODUCTS, EXCEPT FURNITURE

▲ Perfect Shoulder Company Inc .... E 914 699-8100
Mount Vernon *(G-8715)*
▲ Phoenix Ribbon Co Inc .... G 212 239-0155
New York *(G-11651)*
Polkadot Usa Inc .... G 914 835-3697
Mamaroneck *(G-8043)*
Printz and Patternz LLC .... G 518 944-6020
Schenectady *(G-15286)*
Rainbow Lettering .... G 607 732-5751
Elmira *(G-4699)*
Randy Sixberry .... G 315 265-6211
Potsdam *(G-13883)*
Round Top Knit & Screening .... G 518 622-3600
Round Top *(G-15040)*
Sellco Industries Inc .... E 607 756-7594
Cortland *(G-4045)*
◆ Simplicity Creative Group Inc .... A 212 686-7676
New York *(G-12082)*
Solidus Industries Inc .... D 607 749-4540
Homer *(G-6522)*
Special Tees .... E 718 980-0987
Staten Island *(G-15735)*
Starline Usa Inc .... C 716 773-0100
Grand Island *(G-5770)*
Todd Walbridge .... G 585 254-3018
Rochester *(G-14727)*
U All Inc .... E 518 438-2558
Albany *(G-144)*
Wicked Smart LLC .... F 518 459-2855
Watervliet *(G-16692)*
Zan Optics Products Inc .... E 718 435-0533
Brooklyn *(G-2781)*

2397 Schiffli Machine Embroideries

American Images Inc .... F 716 825-8888
Buffalo *(G-2808)*
Rmb Embroidery Service .... G 585 271-5560
Rochester *(G-14629)*

2399 Fabricated Textile Prdts, NEC

AAa Amercn Flag Dctg Co Inc .... G 212 279-4644
New York *(G-8998)*
Ace Banner & Flag Company .... F 212 620-9111
New York *(G-9014)*
▲ American Leather Specialties .... D 800 556-6488
Brooklyn *(G-1603)*
American Puff Corp .... D 516 379-1300
Freeport *(G-5387)*
Arista Flag Corporation .... F 845 246-7700
Saugerties *(G-15180)*
Art Flag Company Inc .... F 212 334-1890
New York *(G-9210)*
Automtve Uphl Cnvertible Tops .... G 914 961-4242
Tuckahoe *(G-16269)*
Baldwin Ribbon & Stamping Corp .... F 718 335-6700
Woodside *(G-17319)*
Becks Classic Mfg Inc .... D 631 435-3800
Brentwood *(G-1178)*
▲ Big Apple Sign Corp .... E 212 629-3650
New York *(G-9392)*
Big Apple Sign Corp .... E 631 342-0303
Islandia *(G-6788)*
Breton Industries Inc .... D 518 842-3030
Amsterdam *(G-336)*
▲ Caldeira USA Inc .... G 212 532-2292
New York *(G-9499)*
City Signs Inc .... G 718 375-5933
Brooklyn *(G-1784)*
Davis Restraint Systems Inc .... F 631 563-1500
Bohemia *(G-1051)*
Dkm Sales LLC .... E 716 893-7777
Buffalo *(G-2916)*
Dream Green Productions .... G 917 267-8920
Warwick *(G-16589)*
▲ Eagle Regalia Co Inc .... F 845 425-2245
Spring Valley *(G-15582)*
Hampton Transport Inc .... F 631 716-4445
Coram *(G-3943)*
◆ HMS Productions Inc .... D 212 719-9190
New York *(G-10489)*
Hollywood Banners Inc .... E 631 842-3000
Copiague *(G-3907)*
Jeans Inc .... G 646 223-1122
New York *(G-10717)*
Kamali Group Inc .... G 516 627-4000
Great Neck *(G-5819)*
Koring Bros Inc .... G 888 233-1292
New Rochelle *(G-8916)*
Kraus & Sons Inc .... F 212 620-0408
New York *(G-10887)*

Mama Luca Production Inc .... G 212 582-9700
New York *(G-11123)*
Mc Coy Tops and Interiors Inc .... G 718 458-5800
Woodside *(G-17336)*
▲ National Flag & Display Co Inc .... E 212 228-6600
New York *(G-11348)*
National Military Industries .... G 908 782-1646
Palenville *(G-13397)*
National Parachute Industries .... E 908 782-1646
Palenville *(G-13398)*
Osprey Boat .... G 631 331-4153
Mount Sinai *(G-8656)*
▲ Paragon Corporation .... F 516 484-6090
Port Washington *(G-13855)*
▲ Penthouse Manufacturing Co Inc .... B 516 379-1300
Freeport *(G-5418)*
▲ Radio Circle Realty Inc .... G 914 241-8742
Mount Kisco *(G-8642)*
Regal Emblem Co Inc .... F 212 925-8833
New York *(G-11819)*
Saratoga Horseworks Ltd .... E 518 843-6756
Amsterdam *(G-368)*
Sellco Industries Inc .... E 607 756-7594
Cortland *(G-4045)*
Skd Tactical Inc .... G 845 897-2889
Highland Falls *(G-6410)*
▼ Stidd Systems Inc .... E 631 477-2400
Greenport *(G-5877)*
Stonegate Stabless .... G 518 746-7133
Fort Edward *(G-5346)*
▲ Triple E Manufacturing .... F 716 761-6996
Sherman *(G-15403)*
Valeo .... G 800 634-2704
Yonkers *(G-17495)*
Yoland Corporation .... E 718 499-4803
Brooklyn *(G-2776)*

24 LUMBER AND WOOD PRODUCTS, EXCEPT FURNITURE

2411 Logging

3b Timber Company Inc .... G 315 942-6580
Boonville *(G-1161)*
Attica Package Company Inc .... F 585 591-0510
Attica *(G-472)*
▼ B & B Forest Products Ltd .... F 518 622-0811
Cairo *(G-3270)*
Baker Logging & Firewood .... G 585 374-5733
Naples *(G-8764)*
Central Timber Co Inc .... G 518 638-6338
Granville *(G-5773)*
Chad Pierson .... G 518 251-0186
Bakers Mills *(G-557)*
Chip It All Ltd .... G 631 473-2040
Port Jefferson *(G-13774)*
Clearlake Land Co Inc .... G 315 848-2427
Star Lake *(G-15628)*
Couture Logging Inc .... G 607 753-6445
Cortland *(G-4023)*
Couture Timber Harvesting .... G 607 836-4719
Mc Graw *(G-8221)*
Daniel & Lois Lyndaker Logging .... G 315 346-6527
Castorland *(G-3423)*
Davis Logging & Lumber .... G 315 245-1040
Camden *(G-3314)*
Decker Forest Products Inc .... G 607 563-2345
Sidney *(G-15438)*
Donald Snyder Jr .... F 315 265-4485
Potsdam *(G-13878)*
Ed Beach Forest Management .... G 607 538-1745
Bloomville *(G-994)*
Farney Tree & Excavation LLC .... G 315 783-1161
Croghan *(G-4058)*
Finger Lakes Timber Co Inc .... G 585 346-2990
Livonia *(G-7564)*
George Chilson Logging .... G 607 732-1558
Elmira *(G-4686)*
GL & RL Logging Inc .... F 518 883-3936
Broadalbin *(G-1242)*
Guldenschuh Logging & Lbr LLC .... G 585 538-4750
Caledonia *(G-3280)*
Harris Logging Inc .... E 518 792-1083
Queensbury *(G-13998)*
Homer Logging Contractor .... G 607 753-8553
Homer *(G-6520)*
J & S Logging Inc .... E 315 262-2112
South Colton *(G-15515)*
Kapstone Container Corporation .... D 518 842-2450
Amsterdam *(G-352)*

Kevin Regan Logging Ltd .... G 315 245-3890
Camden *(G-3317)*
Klein & Sons Logging Inc .... F 845 292-6682
Wht Sphr Spgs *(G-17221)*
Lizotte Logging Inc .... F 518 359-2200
Tupper Lake *(G-16277)*
Lyndaker Timber Harvesting LLC .... F 315 346-1328
Castorland *(G-3424)*
Matteson Logging Inc .... G 585 593-3037
Wellsville *(G-16754)*
Mountain Forest Products Inc .... G 518 597-3674
Crown Point *(G-4067)*
Murray Logging LLC .... G 518 834-7372
Keeseville *(G-7140)*
Northern Timber Harvesting LLC .... F 585 233-7330
Alfred Station *(G-197)*
P H Gucker Inc .... G 518 834-9501
Keeseville *(G-7141)*
Paul J Mitchell Logging Inc .... E 518 359-7029
Tupper Lake *(G-16278)*
Peters Inc .... G 607 637-5470
Hancock *(G-5966)*
Richard Bauer Logging .... G 585 343-4149
Alexander *(G-190)*
Richards Logging LLC .... F 518 359-2775
Tupper Lake *(G-16279)*
Robert W Butts Logging Co .... G 518 643-2897
Peru *(G-13527)*
Robert W Still .... F 315 942-5594
Ava *(G-531)*
Russell Bass .... G 607 637-5253
Hancock *(G-5967)*
Schaefer Logging Inc .... F 607 467-4990
Deposit *(G-4281)*
Seaway Timber Harvesting Inc .... D 315 769-5970
Massena *(G-8200)*
Smoothbore International Inc .... G 315 754-8124
Red Creek *(G-14026)*
Snyder Logging .... G 315 265-1462
Potsdam *(G-13884)*
Tim Cretin Logging & Sawmill .... F 315 946-4476
Lyons *(G-7976)*
Timothy L Simpson .... G 518 234-1401
Sharon Springs *(G-15385)*
Tonche Timber LLC .... G 845 389-3489
Amsterdam *(G-370)*
Van Cpeters Logging Inc .... G 607 637-3574
Hancock *(G-5968)*
Wadsworth Logging Inc .... F 518 863-6870
Gloversville *(G-5727)*
Wagner Logging LLC .... G 607 467-2347
Masonville *(G-8109)*
William Ward Logging .... F 518 946-7826
Jay *(G-7055)*

2421 Saw & Planing Mills

A D Bowman & Son Lumber Co .... E 607 692-2595
Castle Creek *(G-3417)*
Adams Lumber Co Inc .... F 716 358-2815
Cattaraugus *(G-3436)*
Angelica Forest Products Inc .... G 585 466-3205
Angelica *(G-376)*
Axtell Bradtke Lumber Co .... G 607 265-3850
Masonville *(G-8107)*
B & B Lumber Company Inc .... D 315 492-1786
Jamesville *(G-7045)*
B & J Lumber Co Inc .... G 518 677-3845
Cambridge *(G-3304)*
Baillie Lumber Co LP .... E 315 942-5284
Boonville *(G-1163)*
Bissel-Babcock Millwork Inc .... F 716 761-6976
Sherman *(G-15401)*
Bono Sawdust Supply Co Inc .... G 718 446-1374
Corona *(G-3993)*
Brookside Lumber Inc .... F 315 497-0937
Moravia *(G-8616)*
Capital Sawmill Service .... G 518 479-0729
Nassau *(G-8770)*
Carlson Wood Products Inc .... G 716 287-2923
Sinclairville *(G-15452)*
Casters Custom Sawing .... F 315 387-5104
Sandy Creek *(G-15131)*
Clements Burrville Sawmill .... G 315 782-4549
Watertown *(G-16645)*
Cote Hardwood Products Inc .... F 607 898-5737
Locke *(G-7568)*
Crawford Furniture Mfg Corp .... C 716 483-2102
Jamestown *(G-6985)*
Dansville Logging & Lumber .... E 585 335-5879
Dansville *(G-4076)*

Employee Codes: A=Over 500 employees, B=251-500
C=101-250, D=51-100, E=20-50, F=10-19, G=5-9

24 LUMBER AND WOOD PRODUCTS, EXCEPT FURNITURE

Donver Incorporated .... F 716 945-1910
  Kill Buck *(G-7166)*
Embassy Millwork Inc .... F 518 839-0965
  Amsterdam *(G-344)*
Farney Lumber Corporation .... F 315 346-6013
  Lowville *(G-7936)*
▼ Garden State Shavings Inc .... F 845 544-2835
  Warwick *(G-16590)*
◆ GM Palmer Inc .... F 585 492-2990
  Arcade *(G-393)*
Great Jones Lumber Corp .... F 212 254-5560
  New York *(G-10357)*
Greater Niagara Bldg Ctr Inc .... F 716 299-0543
  Niagara Falls *(G-12827)*
Greene Lumber Co LP .... E 607 278-6101
  Davenport *(G-4080)*
Gutchess Freedom Inc .... D 716 492-2824
  Freedom *(G-5378)*
▼ Gutchess Lumber Co Inc .... C 607 753-3393
  Cortland *(G-4030)*
Hawkeye Forest Products LP .... F 608 534-6156
  Hamburg *(G-5928)*
Hennig Custom Woodwork Corp ..... G 516 536-3460
  Oceanside *(G-13080)*
▼ J & J Log & Lumber Corp .... D 845 832-6535
  Dover Plains *(G-4315)*
J A Yansick Lumber Co Inc .... E 585 492-4312
  Arcade *(G-395)*
Jdlr Enterprises LLC .... G 315 813-2911
  Sherrill *(G-15406)*
Johnston Forest Products Inc .... G 607 363-2947
  East Branch *(G-4384)*
L J Valente Inc .... G 518 674-3750
  Averill Park *(G-535)*
Lyons & Sullivan Inc .... G 518 584-1523
  Saratoga Springs *(G-15162)*
Machina Deus Lex Inc .... G 917 577-0972
  Jamaica *(G-6926)*
Mallery Lumber LLC .... F 607 622-2236
  Hancock *(G-5965)*
McDonough Hardwoods Ltd .... E 315 829-3449
  Vernon Center *(G-16437)*
Meltz Lumber Co of Mellenville ...... E 518 672-7021
  Hudson *(G-6626)*
Mettowee Lumber & Plastics Co .... C 518 642-1100
  Granville *(G-5777)*
Mohawk Metal Mfg & Sls .... G 315 853-7663
  Westmoreland *(G-17062)*
Owletts Saw Mills .... G 607 525-6340
  Woodhull *(G-17309)*
▼ PA Pellets LLC .... F 814 848-9970
  Pittsford *(G-13572)*
Pallets Inc .... E 518 747-4177
  Fort Edward *(G-5343)*
PDJ Inc .... E 315 655-8824
  Cazenovia *(G-3450)*
Petteys Lumber .... G 518 792-5943
  Fort Ann *(G-5337)*
Piccini Industries Ltd .... E 845 365-0614
  Orangeburg *(G-13239)*
Potter Lumber Co Inc .... E 716 373-1260
  Allegany *(G-203)*
Rudy Stempel & Family Sawmill ..... G 518 872-0431
  East Berne *(G-4381)*
Russell Bass .... F 607 637-5253
  Hancock *(G-5967)*
S Donadic Woodworking Inc .... D 718 361-9888
  Sunnyside *(G-15809)*
▼ Salamanca Lumber Company Inc ..E 716 945-4810
  Salamanca *(G-15104)*
Saw Mill Pediatrics Pllc .... G 914 449-6064
  Pleasantville *(G-13720)*
Scotts Company LLC .... E 631 289-7444
  Yaphank *(G-17400)*
Simplicity Bandsaw Inc .... G 716 557-8805
  Hinsdale *(G-6424)*
Spiegel Woodworks Inc .... F 845 336-8090
  Kingston *(G-7211)*
St Lawrence Lumber Inc .... G 315 649-2990
  Three Mile Bay *(G-16123)*
Swanson Lumber .... G 716 499-1726
  Gerry *(G-5593)*
▲ Tri-State Brick & Stone NY Inc .... D 212 366-0300
  New York *(G-12402)*
Tupper Lake Hardwoods Inc .... F 518 359-8248
  Tupper Lake *(G-16282)*
Upstate Increte Incorporated .... G 585 254-2010
  Rochester *(G-14747)*
Urrey Lumber .... G 518 827-4851
  Middleburgh *(G-8419)*

Wagner Millwork Inc .... D 607 687-5362
  Owego *(G-13361)*
Weather Tight Exteriors .... G 631 375-5108
  Ridge *(G-14095)*
Wolski Wood Works Inc .... G 718 577-9816
  Flushing *(G-5308)*
Wyde Lumber .... F 845 513-5571
  Monticello *(G-8608)*

2426 Hardwood Dimension & Flooring Mills

A D Bowman & Son Lumber Co ..... E 607 692-2595
  Castle Creek *(G-3417)*
Artistic Frame Corp .... C 212 289-2100
  New York *(G-9219)*
B & B Lumber Company Inc .... D 315 492-1786
  Jamesville *(G-7045)*
Carlson Wood Products Inc .... G 716 287-2923
  Sinclairville *(G-15452)*
Cassadaga Designs Inc .... G 716 595-3030
  Cassadaga *(G-3414)*
Clements Burrville Sawmill .... G 315 782-4549
  Watertown *(G-16645)*
Custom Woodwork Ltd .... F 631 727-5260
  Riverhead *(G-14140)*
Designer Hardwood Flrg CNY Inc .. F 315 207-0044
  Oswego *(G-13329)*
Donver Incorporated .... F 716 945-1910
  Kill Buck *(G-7166)*
Empire Exhibits & Displays Inc ..... G 518 266-9362
  Mechanicville *(G-8227)*
Fibron Products Inc .... E 716 886-2378
  Buffalo *(G-2947)*
▼ Fitzpatrick and Weller Inc .... F 716 699-2393
  Ellicottville *(G-4641)*
Fountain Tile Outlet Inc .... G 718 927-4555
  Brooklyn *(G-1999)*
Guldenschuh Logging & Lbr LLC ... E 585 538-4750
  Caledonia *(G-3280)*
▼ Gutchess Lumber Co Inc .... C 607 753-3393
  Cortland *(G-4030)*
H B Millwork Inc .... F 631 289-8086
  Medford *(G-8246)*
Horizon Floors I LLC .... E 212 509-9686
  New York *(G-10505)*
▼ J & J Log & Lumber Corp .... D 845 832-6535
  Dover Plains *(G-4315)*
J A Yansick Lumber Co Inc .... E 585 492-4312
  Arcade *(G-395)*
Jim Quinn .... F 518 356-0398
  Schenectady *(G-15270)*
▲ Legno Veneto USA .... E 716 651-9169
  Depew *(G-4261)*
Madison & Dunn .... G 585 563-7760
  Rochester *(G-14488)*
Mason Carvings Inc .... G 716 664-9402
  Jamestown *(G-7017)*
Mm of East Aurora LLC .... F 716 651-9663
  Buffalo *(G-3069)*
◆ MP Caroll Inc .... F 716 683-8520
  Cheektowaga *(G-3579)*
Mullican Flooring LP .... F 716 537-2642
  Holland *(G-6482)*
North Hudson Woodcraft Corp ...... E 315 429-3105
  Dolgeville *(G-4306)*
▼ Norton-Smith Hardwoods Inc ..... G 716 945-0346
  Salamanca *(G-15103)*
Petteys Lumber .... G 518 792-5943
  Fort Ann *(G-5337)*
Potter Lumber Co Inc .... E 716 373-1260
  Allegany *(G-203)*
▼ Potter Lumber Co LLC .... D 814 438-7888
  Hamburg *(G-5936)*
Premier Hardwood Products Inc ... E 315 492-1786
  Jamesville *(G-7050)*
Randolph Dimension Corporation . F 716 358-6901
  Randolph *(G-14017)*
Revival Industries Inc .... E 315 868-1085
  Ilion *(G-6745)*
S Donadic Woodworking Inc .... D 718 361-9888
  Sunnyside *(G-15809)*
Sirianni Hardwoods Inc .... E 607 962-4688
  Painted Post *(G-13394)*
Tectonic Flooring USA LLC .... D 212 686-2700
  New York *(G-12292)*
Tupper Lake Hardwoods Inc .... E 518 359-8248
  Tupper Lake *(G-16282)*
Vitobob Furniture Inc .... G 516 676-1696
  Long Island City *(G-7916)*
▼ Wagner Hardwoods LLC .... C 607 594-3321
  Cayuta *(G-3440)*

Wagner Hardwoods LLC .... C 607 594-3321
  Cayuta *(G-3441)*
Wagner Millwork Inc .... D 607 687-5362
  Owego *(G-13361)*
Wood Floor Expo Inc .... G 212 472-0671
  New York *(G-12655)*
Wrights Hardwoods Inc .... E 716 595-2345
  Cassadaga *(G-3415)*

2429 Special Prdt Sawmills, NEC

RWS Manufacturing Inc .... G 518 361-1657
  Queensbury *(G-14009)*

2431 Millwork

A Losee & Sons .... G 516 676-3060
  Glen Cove *(G-5608)*
A W Hamel Stair Mfg Inc .... F 518 346-3031
  Schenectady *(G-15226)*
Ace Fire Door Corp .... E 718 901-0001
  Bronx *(G-1261)*
Adams Interior Fabrications .... F 631 249-8282
  Massapequa *(G-8177)*
Adirondack Stairs Inc .... F 845 246-2525
  Saugerties *(G-15178)*
▲ Adriatic Wood Products Inc .... E 718 922-4621
  Brooklyn *(G-1563)*
American Wood Column Corp .... G 718 782-3163
  Brooklyn *(G-1610)*
Amity Woodworking Inc .... G 631 598-7000
  Amityville *(G-275)*
Amstutze Woodworking .... G 518 946-8206
  Upper Jay *(G-16303)*
Apollo Windows & Doors Inc .... F 718 386-3326
  Brooklyn *(G-1617)*
Architctral Mllwk Installation .... E 631 499-0755
  East Northport *(G-4433)*
Artistic Ironworks Inc .... G 631 665-4285
  Bay Shore *(G-672)*
Atlantic Stairs Corp .... G 718 417-8818
  Brooklyn *(G-1647)*
▲ Attica Millwork Inc .... F 585 591-2333
  Attica *(G-471)*
Auburn Custom Millwork Inc .... G 315 253-3843
  Auburn *(G-478)*
Bator Bintor Inc .... F 347 546-6503
  Brooklyn *(G-1674)*
Bauerschmidt & Sons Inc .... D 718 528-3500
  Jamaica *(G-6898)*
Beaver Creek Industries Inc .... G 607 545-6382
  Canaseraga *(G-3362)*
Bennett Stair Company Inc .... G 518 384-1554
  Ballston Lake *(G-580)*
Bloch Industries LLC .... D 585 334-9600
  Rochester *(G-14235)*
Blooming Grove Stair Co .... F 845 783-4245
  Monroe *(G-8550)*
Blooming Grove Stair Co .... G 845 791-4016
  Monticello *(G-8604)*
BNC Innovative Woodworking ...... F 718 277-2800
  Brooklyn *(G-1706)*
Braga Woodworks .... G 845 342-4636
  Middletown *(G-8428)*
Brauen Construction .... G 585 492-0042
  Arcade *(G-390)*
Broadway Neon Sign Corp .... F 908 241-4177
  Ronkonkoma *(G-14881)*
▲ Burt Millwork Corporation .... E 718 257-4601
  Brooklyn *(G-1738)*
Capital District Stairs Inc .... G 518 383-2449
  Halfmoon *(G-5909)*
Capital Kit Cab & Door Mfrs .... G 718 886-0303
  College Point *(G-3779)*
Carob Industries Inc .... F 631 225-0900
  Lindenhurst *(G-7459)*
◆ Case Group LLC .... E 518 720-3100
  Green Island *(G-5854)*
Chautauqua Woods Corp .... G 716 366-3808
  Dunkirk *(G-4336)*
Christiana Millwork Inc .... G 315 492-9099
  Jamesville *(G-7046)*
▲ City Store Gates Mfg Corp .... E 718 939-9700
  College Point *(G-3781)*
Clearwood Custom Carpentry and .G 315 432-8422
  East Syracuse *(G-4518)*
Columbus Woodworking Inc .... G 607 674-4546
  Sherburne *(G-15390)*
Concepts In Wood of CNY .... E 315 463-8084
  Syracuse *(G-15904)*
Conley Caseworks Inc .... G 716 655-5830
  Elma *(G-4647)*

Cousins Furniture & Hm Imprvs............E....... 631 254-3752
Deer Park *(G-4121)*
Craftsmen Woodworkers Ltd................E....... 718 326-3350
Maspeth *(G-8125)*
Creative Laminates Inc...........................F....... 315 463-7580
Syracuse *(G-15911)*
Crown Mill Work Corp...........................G....... 845 371-2200
Monsey *(G-8570)*
Crown Woodworking Corp.....................G....... 718 974-6415
Brooklyn *(G-1820)*
Cuccio-Zanetti Inc..................................G....... 518 587-1363
Middle Grove *(G-8404)*
▲ **Custom Door & Mirror Inc**.................E....... 631 414-7725
Farmingdale *(G-4970)*
Custom Stair & Millwork Co...................G....... 315 839-5793
Sauquoit *(G-15199)*
Custom Wood Inc....................................G....... 718 927-4700
Brooklyn *(G-1828)*
D K P Wood Railings & Stairs................F....... 631 665-8656
Bay Shore *(G-690)*
D R Cornue Woodworks..........................G....... 315 655-9463
Cazenovia *(G-3444)*
Danbury Creek Inc..................................G....... 315 822-5640
West Winfield *(G-16958)*
▲ **DAngelo Home Collections Inc**.........G....... 917 267-8920
Warwick *(G-16587)*
Dbs Interiors Corp..................................F....... 631 491-3013
West Babylon *(G-16788)*
DC Contracting & Building Corp...........F....... 631 385-1117
Huntington Station *(G-6701)*
Deer Pk Stair Bldg Mllwk Inc.................E....... 631 363-5000
Blue Point *(G-998)*
Deerfield Millwork Inc.............................F....... 631 726-9663
Water Mill *(G-16604)*
Dorm Company Corporation..................G....... 502 551-6195
Clarence *(G-3657)*
Duncan & Son Carpentry Inc.................E....... 914 664-4311
Mount Vernon *(G-8678)*
Ecker Window Corp................................D....... 914 776-0000
Yonkers *(G-17438)*
Ed Negron Fine Woodworking...............G....... 718 246-1016
Brooklyn *(G-1902)*
Efj Inc..D....... 518 234-4799
Cobleskill *(G-3737)*
EM Pfaff & Son Inc................................F....... 607 739-3691
Horseheads *(G-6575)*
Empire Building Products Inc...............G....... 518 695-6094
Schuylerville *(G-15319)*
▲ **Fancy Windows & Doors Mfg Corp**..G....... 718 366-7800
Brooklyn *(G-1957)*
▲ **Fantasy Furniture Inc**.......................E....... 718 386-8078
Ridgewood *(G-14106)*
Fenway Holdings LLC............................E....... 212 757-0606
New York *(G-10153)*
▲ **Finger Lakes Trellis Supply**.............G....... 315 904-4007
Williamson *(G-17223)*
Fire Island Sea Clam Co Inc..................G....... 631 589-2199
West Sayville *(G-16935)*
Five Star Millwork LLC...........................F....... 845 920-0247
Pearl River *(G-13456)*
Fontrick Door Inc....................................E....... 585 345-6032
Batavia *(G-632)*
Funda-Mantels LLC................................G....... 631 399-3223
Mastic *(G-8203)*
G & G Window Repair Inc......................F....... 585 334-3370
Rush *(G-15048)*
Garrison Woodworking Inc....................F....... 845 726-3525
Westtown *(G-17069)*
Grace Ryan & Magnus Mllwk LLC.........D....... 914 665-0902
Mount Vernon *(G-8686)*
◆ **Griffon Corporation**...........................E....... 212 957-5000
New York *(G-10363)*
H B Millwork Inc......................................F....... 631 289-8086
Medford *(G-8246)*
H B Millwork Inc......................................G....... 631 924-4195
Yaphank *(G-17394)*
Highland Organization Corp..................E....... 631 991-3240
Deer Park *(G-4150)*
I Meglio Corp...E....... 631 617-6900
Brentwood *(G-1184)*
▲ **Ideal Wood Products Inc**...................E....... 315 823-1124
Little Falls *(G-7501)*
Ignelzi Interiors Inc.................................E....... 718 464-0279
Queens Village *(G-13979)*
Inform Studio Inc.....................................F....... 718 401-6149
Bronx *(G-1362)*
Island Stairs Corp...................................G....... 347 645-0560
Staten Island *(G-15689)*
Island Street Lumber Co Inc..................G....... 716 692-4127
North Tonawanda *(G-12978)*

J Percoco Industries Inc.........................G....... 631 312-4572
Bohemia *(G-1079)*
◆ **J Zeluck Inc**..E....... 718 251-8060
Brooklyn *(G-2128)*
Jackson Woodworks Inc.........................G....... 518 651-2032
Brainardsville *(G-1171)*
Jacobs Woodworking LLC......................G....... 315 427-8999
Syracuse *(G-15965)*
Jays Furniture Products Inc..................E....... 716 876-8854
Buffalo *(G-3015)*
JEm Wdwkg & Cabinets Inc...................F....... 518 828-5361
Hudson *(G-6620)*
John Langenbacher Co Inc.....................E....... 718 328-0141
Bronx *(G-1368)*
KB Millwork Inc.......................................G....... 516 280-2183
Levittown *(G-7429)*
Kelly Window Systems Inc.....................E....... 631 420-8500
Farmingdale *(G-5026)*
Kng Construction Co Inc........................F....... 212 595-1451
Warwick *(G-16593)*
Krefab Corporation.................................F....... 631 842-5151
Copiague *(G-3909)*
L Builders Supply Inc.............................B....... 518 355-7190
Schenectady *(G-15275)*
Lasser Products Incorporated...............G....... 585 249-5180
Rochester *(G-14475)*
Living Doors Inc......................................F....... 631 924-5393
Medford *(G-8253)*
M & D Millwork LLC................................F....... 631 789-1439
Amityville *(G-307)*
Mack Wood Working................................G....... 845 657-6625
Shokan *(G-15432)*
Marretti USA Inc......................................G....... 212 255-5565
New York *(G-11165)*
Medina Millworks LLC............................G....... 585 798-2969
Medina *(G-8276)*
Mestel Brothers Stairs & Rails...............C....... 516 496-4127
Syosset *(G-15828)*
Metalocke Industries Inc........................G....... 718 267-9200
Woodside *(G-17337)*
Metropolitan Fine Mllwk Corp................F....... 914 669-4900
North Salem *(G-12939)*
Michael Bernstein Design Assoc...........E....... 718 456-9277
Brooklyn *(G-2308)*
Michbi Doors Inc.....................................D....... 631 231-9050
Brentwood *(G-1192)*
Midwood Signs & Design Inc..................G....... 718 499-9041
Brooklyn *(G-2312)*
Millco Woodworking LLC........................F....... 585 526-6844
Hall *(G-5917)*
▲ **Miller Blaker Inc**.................................D....... 718 665-3930
Bronx *(G-1398)*
Millwright Wdwrk Installetion................E....... 631 587-2635
West Babylon *(G-16811)*
Mind Designs Inc....................................G....... 631 563-3644
Farmingville *(G-5160)*
Monroe Stair Products Inc......................E....... 845 783-4245
Monroe *(G-8563)*
Monroe Stair Products Inc......................G....... 845 791-4016
Monticello *(G-8606)*
Ne & Ws Inc..G....... 718 326-4699
Maspeth *(G-8154)*
▲ **Nordic Interior Inc**...............................C....... 718 456-7000
Maspeth *(G-8159)*
North Fork Wood Works Inc....................F....... 631 255-4028
Mattituck *(G-8208)*
Northern Forest Pdts Co Inc...................G....... 315 942-6955
Boonville *(G-1166)*
Old World Mouldings Inc.........................G....... 631 563-8660
Bohemia *(G-1113)*
Overhead Door Corporation...................D....... 518 828-7652
Hudson *(G-6629)*
Paul David Enterprises Inc.....................G....... 646 667-5530
New York *(G-11584)*
Pella Corporation....................................B....... 516 385-3622
Albertson *(G-158)*
Pella Corporation....................................B....... 516 385-3622
Albertson *(G-159)*
Pella Corporation....................................B....... 607 223-2023
Johnson City *(G-7100)*
Pella Corporation....................................B....... 607 231-8550
Johnson City *(G-7101)*
Pella Corporation....................................B....... 607 231-8550
Johnson City *(G-7102)*
Pella Corporation....................................B....... 607 238-2812
Johnson City *(G-7103)*
Pella Corporation....................................B....... 607 238-2812
Johnson City *(G-7104)*
Pella Corporation....................................C....... 631 208-0710
Calverton *(G-3294)*

Peter Productions Devivi Inc.................F....... 315 568-8484
Waterloo *(G-16631)*
▲ **Pgs Millwork Inc**..................................D....... 212 244-6610
New York *(G-11642)*
Piccini Industries Ltd.............................E....... 845 365-0614
Orangeburg *(G-13239)*
Professional Cab Detailing Co...............F....... 845 436-7282
Woodridge *(G-17315)*
Props Displays & Interiors......................F....... 212 620-3840
New York *(G-11737)*
Quaker Millwork & Lumber Inc..............E....... 716 662-3388
Orchard Park *(G-13293)*
▲ **Quality Millwork Corp**.........................E....... 718 892-2250
Bronx *(G-1438)*
Quality Stair Builders Inc.......................F....... 631 694-0711
Farmingdale *(G-5093)*
R C Henderson Stair Builders................F....... 516 876-9898
Westbury *(G-17024)*
Randolph Dimension Corporation.........F....... 716 358-6901
Randolph *(G-14017)*
RB Woodcraft Inc....................................E....... 315 474-2429
Syracuse *(G-16021)*
Red Tail Moulding & Mllwk LLC..............G....... 516 852-4613
Center Moriches *(G-3468)*
Richard Anthony Corp............................E....... 914 922-7141
Yorktown Heights *(G-17518)*
Rj Millworkers Inc...................................E....... 607 433-0525
Oneonta *(G-13193)*
Rochester Colonial Mfg Corp................D....... 585 254-8191
Rochester *(G-14639)*
Rochester Lumber Company..................E....... 585 924-7171
Farmington *(G-5155)*
Rockaway Stairs Ltd...............................G....... 718 945-0047
Far Rockaway *(G-4924)*
Roode Hoek & Co Inc..............................F....... 718 522-5921
Brooklyn *(G-2504)*
Royal Windows Mfg Corp.......................E....... 631 435-8888
Bay Shore *(G-740)*
Royalton Millwork & Design...................G....... 716 439-4092
Lockport *(G-7613)*
Russin Lumber Corp...............................F....... 845 457-4000
Newburgh *(G-12778)*
S Donadic Woodworking Inc..................D....... 718 361-9888
Sunnyside *(G-15809)*
S R Sloan Inc...D....... 315 736-7730
Whitesboro *(G-17195)*
Scanga Woodworking Corp....................E....... 845 265-9115
Cold Spring *(G-3766)*
Select Interior Door Ltd..........................E....... 585 535-9900
North Java *(G-12934)*
Shawmut Woodworking & Sup Inc........G....... 212 920-8900
New York *(G-12048)*
Siegfrieds Basement Inc.........................F....... 212 629-3523
New York *(G-12061)*
Specialty Services...................................G....... 585 728-5650
Wayland *(G-16711)*
Spiegel Woodworks Inc...........................F....... 845 336-8090
Kingston *(G-7211)*
SSP Window Cleaning Corp....................F....... 917 750-2619
Brooklyn *(G-2594)*
Stairworld Inc..G....... 718 441-9722
Richmond Hill *(G-14085)*
Stated Island Stair Inc............................G....... 718 317-9276
Staten Island *(G-15738)*
Staten Island Stair Inc............................G....... 718 317-9276
Staten Island *(G-15740)*
Stealth Archtctral Windows Inc.............F....... 718 821-6666
Brooklyn *(G-2601)*
Syracuse Industrial Sls Co Ltd...............F....... 315 478-5751
Syracuse *(G-16053)*
TDS Woodworking Inc............................F....... 718 442-5298
Staten Island *(G-15745)*
Three R Enterprises Inc..........................E....... 585 254-5050
Rochester *(G-14725)*
Tiedemann Waldemar Inc.......................F....... 716 875-5665
Buffalo *(G-3218)*
Unadilla Silo Company Inc.....................D....... 607 369-9341
Sidney *(G-15444)*
Unicenter Millwork Inc............................G....... 716 741-8201
Clarence Center *(G-3681)*
United Rockland Holding Co Inc............E....... 845 357-1900
Suffern *(G-15802)*
Universal Custom Millwork Inc...............D....... 518 330-6622
Amsterdam *(G-372)*
▲ **Upstate Door Inc**..................................D....... 585 786-3880
Warsaw *(G-16585)*
Urban Woodworks Ltd.............................G....... 718 827-1570
Brooklyn *(G-2711)*
Vander Heyden Woodworking................G....... 212 242-0525
New York *(G-12500)*

S
I
C

Employee Codes: A=Over 500 employees, B=251-500
C=101-250, D=51-100, E=20-50, F=10-19, G=5-9
2017 Harris
New York Manufacturers Directory
741

24 LUMBER AND WOOD PRODUCTS, EXCEPT FURNITURE

Wagner Millwork Inc ....D...... 607 687-5362
  Owego (G-13361)
Window Technologies LLC ....F...... 402 464-0202
  New York (G-12640)
Wolfe Lumber Mill Inc ....G...... 716 772-7750
  Gasport (G-5560)
Wood Innovations of Suffolk ....G...... 631 698-2345
  Medford (G-8263)
Xylon Industries Inc ....G...... 631 293-4717
  Farmingdale (G-5144)
Yesteryears Vintage Doors LLC 315 324-5250
  Hammond (G-5952)
Zanzano Woodworking Inc ....F...... 914 725-6025
  Scarsdale (G-15225)

2434 Wood Kitchen Cabinets

Able Kitchen ....F...... 877 268-1264
  Cedarhurst (G-3455)
Acme Kitchenettes Corp ....E...... 518 828-4191
  Hudson (G-6604)
▲ Aki Cabinets Inc ....F...... 718 721-2541
  Astoria (G-432)
Amoroso Wood Products Co Inc ....G...... 631 249-4998
  Melville (G-8294)
Andike Millwork Inc ....G...... 718 894-1796
  Maspeth (G-8118)
▲ Artone LLC ....D...... 716 664-2232
  Jamestown (G-6972)
Atlantic States Distributing ....G...... 518 427-6364
  Menands (G-8368)
Auburn-Watson Corp ....F...... 716 876-8000
  Depew (G-4247)
Bauerschmidt & Sons Inc ....G...... 718 528-3500
  Jamaica (G-6898)
Bloch Industries LLC ....D...... 585 334-9600
  Rochester (G-14235)
Cabinet Shapes Corp ....F...... 718 784-6255
  Long Island City (G-7691)
Cabinetry By Tbr Inc ....G...... 516 365-8500
  Manhasset (G-8055)
Cabinets By Stanley Inc ....G...... 718 222-5861
  Brooklyn (G-1747)
Cambridge Kitchens Mfg Inc ....F...... 516 935-5100
  Hicksville (G-6329)
Candlelight Cabinetry Inc ....C...... 716 434-2114
  Lockport (G-7575)
Capital Kit Cab & Door Mfrs ....G...... 718 886-0303
  College Point (G-3779)
Carefree Kitchens Inc ....G...... 631 567-2120
  Holbrook (G-6436)
Carlos & Alex Atelier Inc ....G...... 718 441-8911
  Richmond Hill (G-14070)
Casa Collection Inc ....G...... 718 694-0272
  Brooklyn (G-1762)
▲ Catskill Craftsmen Inc ....D...... 607 652-7321
  Stamford (G-15624)
Cbc Custom Millwork Inc ....F...... 718 499-6742
  Brooklyn (G-1765)
Central Kitchen Corp ....F...... 631 283-1029
  Southampton (G-15541)
Chicone Builders LLC ....F...... 607 535-6540
  Montour Falls (G-8609)
Classic Cabinets ....F...... 845 357-4331
  Suffern (G-15787)
Clearwood Custom Carpentry and ..E...... 315 432-8422
  East Syracuse (G-4518)
Commercial Millworks Inc ....G...... 315 475-7479
  Syracuse (G-15902)
Cosmopolitan Cabinet Company ...G...... 631 467-4960
  Ronkonkoma (G-14890)
▼ Craft Custom Woodwork Co Inc ..F...... 718 821-2162
  Maspeth (G-8124)
Creative Cabinet Corp America .....F...... 631 751-5768
  Stony Brook (G-15769)
Custom CAS Inc ....E...... 718 726-3575
  Long Island City (G-7708)
Custom Woodcraft LLC ....F...... 315 843-4234
  Munnsville (G-8750)
D & M Custom Cabinets Inc ....F...... 516 678-2818
  Oceanside (G-13075)
Dak Mica and Wood Products ....G...... 631 467-0749
  Ronkonkoma (G-14892)
Dbs Interiors Corp ....F...... 631 491-3013
  West Babylon (G-16788)
Deakon Homes and Interiors ....F...... 518 271-0342
  Troy (G-16233)
Di Fiore and Sons Custom Wdwkg ..G...... 718 278-1663
  Long Island City (G-7715)
EC Wood & Company Inc ....F...... 718 388-2287
  Deer Park (G-4135)

EM Pfaff & Son Inc ....F...... 607 739-3691
  Horseheads (G-6575)
Enterprise Wood Products Inc ......F...... 718 853-9243
  Brooklyn (G-1926)
European Craft Inc ....G...... 516 313-2243
  Great Neck (G-5806)
Fantasy Home Improvement Corp ...G...... 718 277-4021
  Brooklyn (G-1958)
Fina Cabinet Corp ....G...... 718 409-2900
  Mount Vernon (G-8681)
Fra-Rik Formica Fabg Co Inc ....F...... 718 597-3335
  Bronx (G-1337)
Garrison Woodworking Inc ....F...... 845 726-3525
  Westtown (G-17069)
▲ Glissade New York LLC ....E...... 631 756-4800
  Farmingdale (G-4999)
Greenway Cabinetry Inc ....F...... 516 877-0009
  Williston Park (G-17261)
Hearth Cabinets and More Ltd .....G...... 315 641-1197
  Liverpool (G-7521)
Hendrickson Custom Cabinetry ....F...... 718 401-0137
  Bronx (G-1356)
Hollywood Cabinets Co ....G...... 516 354-0857
  Elmont (G-4722)
Home Ideal Inc ....G...... 718 762-8998
  Flushing (G-5251)
Ignelzi Interiors Inc ....E...... 718 464-0279
  Queens Village (G-13979)
Infinity Design LLC ....F...... 718 416-3853
  Maspeth (G-8145)
J Percoco Industries Inc ....G...... 631 312-4572
  Bohemia (G-1079)
Jordache Woodworking Corp ....F...... 718 349-3373
  Brooklyn (G-2147)
K-Binet Inc ....F...... 845 348-1149
  Blauvelt (G-972)
▲ Kalnitz Kitchens Inc ....G...... 716 684-1700
  Buffalo (G-3026)
▲ Kw Distributors Group Inc ....F...... 718 843-3500
  Ozone Park (G-13382)
▲ Legacy Furniture Inc ....F...... 718 527-5331
  Monroe (G-8560)
Little Wolf Cabinet Shop Inc ....E...... 212 734-1116
  New York (G-11013)
Longo Commercial Cabinets Inc ...E...... 631 225-4290
  Lindenhurst (G-7469)
Lyn Jo Kitchens Inc ....G...... 718 336-6060
  Brooklyn (G-2240)
▲ Material Process Systems Inc ..F...... 718 302-3081
  Brooklyn (G-2283)
Matteo & Antonio Bartolotta ....F...... 315 252-2220
  Auburn (G-508)
McGraw Wood Products LLC ....G...... 607 836-6465
  Mc Graw (G-8223)
Mega Cabinets Inc ....E...... 631 789-4112
  Amityville (G-311)
Methods Tooling & Mfg Inc ....F...... 845 246-7100
  Mount Marion (G-8651)
▲ Metro Kitchens Corp ....F...... 718 434-1166
  Brooklyn (G-2305)
Michael Bernstein Design Assoc ...E...... 718 456-9277
  Brooklyn (G-2308)
Michael P Mmarr ....G...... 315 623-9380
  Constantia (G-3881)
Millco Woodworking LLC ....F...... 585 526-6844
  Hall (G-5917)
Modern Cabinet Company Inc .....E...... 845 473-4900
  Poughkeepsie (G-13917)
▲ N Y Elli Design Corp ....F...... 718 228-0014
  Maspeth (G-8153)
Nagad Cabinets Inc ....G...... 718 382-7200
  Brooklyn (G-2347)
Neo Cabinetry LLC ....F...... 718 403-0456
  Brooklyn (G-2356)
▲ New York Vanity and Mfg Co ....F...... 718 417-1010
  Freeport (G-5415)
NY Cabinet Factory Inc ....F...... 718 256-6541
  Brooklyn (G-2381)
▲ Pgs Millwork Inc ....D...... 212 244-6610
  New York (G-11642)
Piccini Industries Ltd ....E...... 845 365-0614
  Orangeburg (G-13239)
Precision Dental Cabinets Inc ......F...... 631 543-3870
  Smithtown (G-15495)
Premier Woodcraft Ltd ....E...... 610 383-6624
  White Plains (G-17161)
Premium Woodworking LLC ....G...... 718 782-7747
  Brooklyn (G-2438)
R & M Thermofoil Doors Inc ....G...... 718 206-4991
  Jamaica (G-6943)

Ralph Payne ....G...... 718 222-4200
  Brooklyn (G-2477)
Red White & Blue Entps Corp ....G...... 718 565-8080
  Woodside (G-17350)
Ribble Lumber Inc ....G...... 315 536-6221
  Penn Yan (G-13518)
Royal Custom Cabinets ....G...... 315 376-6042
  Lowville (G-7942)
S & V Custom Furniture Mfg ....F...... 516 746-8299
  Mineola (G-8536)
S Donadic Woodworking Inc ....D...... 718 361-9888
  Sunnyside (G-15809)
▲ Salko Kitchens Inc ....F...... 845 565-4420
  New Windsor (G-8952)
Salmon Crek Cabinetry Inc ....E...... 315 589-5419
  Williamson (G-17225)
Serway Bros Inc ....G...... 315 337-0601
  Rome (G-14836)
Sherry-Mica Products Inc ....G...... 631 471-7513
  Ronkonkoma (G-14985)
Silva Cabinetry Inc ....E...... 914 737-7697
  Buchanan (G-2787)
▲ Stone Expo & Cabinetry LLC ....F...... 516 292-2988
  West Hempstead (G-16863)
Upstate Cabinet Co Inc ....F...... 585 429-5090
  Rochester (G-14746)
Viola Cabinet Corporation ....G...... 716 284-6327
  Niagara Falls (G-12888)
▲ W Designe Inc ....E...... 914 736-1058
  Peekskill (G-13484)
White House Cabinet Shop LLC ...G...... 607 674-9358
  Sherburne (G-15399)
William Brooks Woodworking ....F...... 718 495-9767
  Brooklyn (G-2752)
▲ Win Wood Cabinetry Inc ....G...... 516 304-2216
  Greenvale (G-5883)
Wood Etc Inc ....F...... 315 484-9663
  Syracuse (G-16075)
Yonkers Cabinets Inc ....G...... 914 668-2133
  Yonkers (G-17502)
Your Furniture Designers Inc ....G...... 845 947-3046
  West Haverstraw (G-16848)
Your Way Custom Cabinets Inc ....G...... 914 371-1870
  Mount Vernon (G-8746)

2435 Hardwood Veneer & Plywood

Geonex International Corp ....G...... 212 473-4555
  New York (G-10280)
Kings Quartet Corp ....F...... 845 986-9090
  Warwick (G-16592)
Northeast Panel & Truss LLC ....E...... 845 339-3656
  Kingston (G-7205)
Shepards Sawmill ....G...... 585 638-5664
  Holley (G-6493)
Sure-Lock Industries LLC ....F...... 315 207-0044
  Oswego (G-13343)
▲ Veneer One Inc ....E...... 516 536-6480
  Oceanside (G-13103)

2436 Softwood Veneer & Plywood

H B Millwork Inc ....F...... 631 289-8086
  Medford (G-8246)

2439 Structural Wood Members, NEC

Architctral Mllwk Installation ....E...... 631 499-0755
  East Northport (G-4433)
Empire Building Products Inc ....G...... 518 695-6094
  Schuylerville (G-15319)
Faulkner Truss Company Inc ....G...... 315 536-8894
  Dresden (G-4319)
Harvest Homes Inc ....E...... 518 895-2341
  Delanson (G-4233)
L Builders Supply Inc ....B...... 518 355-7190
  Schenectady (G-15275)
New England Barns Inc ....E...... 631 445-1461
  Southold (G-15560)
Niagara Truss & Pallet LLC ....F...... 716 433-5400
  Lockport (G-7607)
Northeast Panel & Truss LLC ....E...... 845 339-3656
  Kingston (G-7205)
P & R Truss Co ....G...... 716 496-5484
  Chaffee (G-3535)
Pdj Components Inc ....G...... 845 469-9191
  Chester (G-3611)
Proof Industries Inc ....G...... 631 694-7663
  Farmingdale (G-5090)
Railtech Composites Inc ....F...... 518 324-6190
  Plattsburgh (G-13692)
Rochester Lumber Company ....E...... 585 924-7171
  Farmington (G-5155)

24 LUMBER AND WOOD PRODUCTS, EXCEPT FURNITURE

S R Sloan Inc .... D 315 736-7730
  Whitesboro *(G-17195)*
Steele Truss Company Inc .... E 518 562-4663
  Plattsburgh *(G-13698)*
Stephenson Lumber Company Inc .... G 518 548-7521
  Speculator *(G-15563)*
Structural Wood Corporation .... E 315 388-4442
  Waddington *(G-16521)*
Timber Frames Inc .... G 585 374-6405
  Canandaigua *(G-3359)*
Ufp New York LLC .... G 315 381-5093
  Clinton *(G-3723)*
Ufp New York LLC .... E 716 496-5484
  Chaffee *(G-3536)*
Ufp New York LLC .... E 518 828-2888
  Hudson *(G-6637)*
Ufp New York LLC .... E 607 563-1556
  Sidney *(G-15443)*
Unadilla Silo Company Inc .... D 607 369-9341
  Sidney *(G-15444)*
Wt Motto Building Products 315 457-2211
  Liverpool *(G-7557)*

2441 Wood Boxes

Abbot & Abbot Box Corp .... F 888 930-5972
  Long Island City *(G-7646)*
Bragley Mfg Co Inc .... E 718 622-7469
  Brooklyn *(G-1712)*
Bristol Boarding Inc .... G 585 271-7860
  Rochester *(G-14247)*
Falvo Manufacturing Co Inc .... F 315 738-7682
  Utica *(G-16330)*
Fca LLC .... G 518 756-9655
  Coeymans *(G-3745)*
Great Lakes Specialites .... E 716 672-4622
  Fredonia *(G-5374)*
M &L Industry of NY Inc .... G 845 827-6255
  Highland Mills *(G-6413)*
McGraw Wood Products LLC ..... E 607 836-6465
  Mc Graw *(G-8223)*
McIntosh Box & Pallet Co Inc ...... F 315 789-8750
  Geneva *(G-5582)*
McIntosh Box & Pallet Co Inc ..... D 315 675-8511
  Bernhards Bay *(G-858)*
McIntosh Box & Pallet Co Inc ..... E 315 446-9350
  Rome *(G-14820)*
Norjac Boxes Inc .... E 631 842-1300
  Copiague *(G-3916)*
Philpac Corporation .... E 716 875-8005
  Buffalo *(G-3124)*
Quality Woodworking Corp .... F 718 875-3437
  Brooklyn *(G-2464)*
Reuter Pallet Pkg Sys Inc .... G 845 457-9937
  Montgomery *(G-8602)*
Technical Packaging Inc .... F 516 223-2300
  Baldwin *(G-562)*

2448 Wood Pallets & Skids

219 South West .... G 315 474-2065
  Syracuse *(G-15844)*
A D Bowman & Son Lumber Co ..... E 607 692-2595
  Castle Creek *(G-3417)*
Abbot & Abbot Box Corp .... F 888 930-5972
  Long Island City *(G-7646)*
Air Goal Intl USA Inc .... F 718 656-5880
  Valley Stream *(G-16399)*
▲ Airline Container Services .... G 516 371-4125
  Lido Beach *(G-7439)*
B & B Lumber Company Inc ...... D 315 492-1786
  Jamesville *(G-7045)*
Berry Industrial Group Inc .... G 845 353-8338
  Nyack *(G-13045)*
Best Pallet & Crate LLC .... G 518 438-2945
  Albany *(G-55)*
Chemung Cty Assc Retrd Ctzns ..... C 607 734-6151
  Elmira *(G-4675)*
Clements Burrville Sawmill .... G 315 782-4549
  Watertown *(G-16645)*
▼ Concord Express Cargo Inc .... G 718 276-7200
  Jamaica *(G-6906)*
Crawford Furniture Mfg Corp ..... C 716 483-2102
  Jamestown *(G-6985)*
Curran Renewable Energy LLC .... E 315 769-2000
  Massena *(G-8193)*
Custom Shipping Products Inc .... F 716 355-4437
  Clymer *(G-3733)*
D & F Pallet Inc .... F 716 672-2984
  Fredonia *(G-5372)*
Dimensional Mills Inc .... G 518 746-1047
  Hudson Falls *(G-6640)*

Dwa Pallet Inc .... G 518 746-1047
  Hudson Falls *(G-6641)*
Essex Box & Pallet Co Inc .... E 518 834-7279
  Keeseville *(G-7137)*
Four-Way Pallet Corp .... E 631 351-3401
  Huntington Station *(G-6706)*
G & H Wood Products LLC .... F 716 372-5510
  Olean *(G-13148)*
Great Lakes Specialites .... E 716 672-4622
  Fredonia *(G-5374)*
Just Wood Pallets Inc .... G 718 644-7013
  New Windsor *(G-8940)*
Lindley Wood Works Inc .... F 607 523-7786
  Lindley *(G-7496)*
McIntosh Box & Pallet Co Inc ..... D 315 675-8511
  Bernhards Bay *(G-858)*
McIntosh Box & Pallet Co Inc ..... F 315 789-8750
  Geneva *(G-5582)*
McIntosh Box & Pallet Co Inc ..... E 315 446-9350
  Rome *(G-14820)*
Nefab Packaging North East LLC ..... E 518 346-9105
  Scotia *(G-15328)*
Neville Mfg Svc & Dist Inc .... F 716 834-3038
  Cheektowaga *(G-3582)*
North Shore Pallet Inc .... G 631 673-4700
  Huntington Station *(G-6719)*
Northeast Pallet & Cont Co Inc .... F 518 271-0535
  Troy *(G-16244)*
Orleans Pallet Company Inc .... E 585 589-0781
  Albion *(G-167)*
Pallet Division Inc .... G 585 328-3780
  Rochester *(G-14568)*
Pallet Services Inc .... E 585 647-4020
  Rochester *(G-14569)*
Pallets Inc .... E 518 747-4177
  Fort Edward *(G-5343)*
Pallets R US Inc .... E 631 758-2360
  Bellport *(G-837)*
Paul Bunyan Products Inc .... E 315 696-6164
  Cortland *(G-4039)*
Peco Pallet Inc .... E 914 376-5444
  Irvington *(G-6776)*
Peter C Herman Inc .... E 315 926-4100
  Marion *(G-8098)*
Pooran Pallet Inc .... G 718 938-7970
  Bronx *(G-1431)*
Reuter Pallet Pkg Sys Inc .... G 845 457-9937
  Montgomery *(G-8602)*
Sanjay Pallets Inc .... G 347 590-2485
  Bronx *(G-1447)*
▼ Sg Blocks Inc .... G 212 520-6218
  New York *(G-12033)*
Shepards Sawmill .... G 585 638-5664
  Holley *(G-6493)*
Steven Coffey Pallet S Inc .... G 585 261-6783
  Rochester *(G-14704)*
Vansantis Development Inc .... E 315 461-0113
  Liverpool *(G-7554)*
Wolfe Lumber Mill Inc .... G 716 772-7750
  Gasport *(G-5560)*

2449 Wood Containers, NEC

Abbot & Abbot Box Corp .... F 888 930-5972
  Long Island City *(G-7646)*
David Isseks & Sons Inc .... E 212 966-8694
  New York *(G-9820)*
Essex Box & Pallet Co Inc .... E 518 834-7279
  Keeseville *(G-7137)*
Great Lakes Specialites .... E 716 672-4622
  Fredonia *(G-5374)*
Northeast Pallet & Cont Co Inc .... F 518 271-0535
  Troy *(G-16244)*
Pluribus Products Inc .... E 718 852-1614
  Brooklyn *(G-2427)*
R D A Container Corporation ..... E 585 247-2323
  Gates *(G-5563)*
Rosenwach Tank Co Inc .... E 212 972-4411
  Astoria *(G-455)*
Wolfe Lumber Mill Inc .... G 716 772-7750
  Gasport *(G-5560)*

2451 Mobile Homes

All Star Carts & Vehicles Inc ...... D 631 666-5581
  Bay Shore *(G-668)*
American Home Mfg LLC .... D 718 855-0617
  New York *(G-9120)*
Champion Home Builders Inc .... C 315 841-4122
  Sangerfield *(G-15132)*
Leatherstocking Mobile Home PA ..... G 315 839-5691
  Sauquoit *(G-15200)*

Sonic Boom Inc .... F 212 242-2852
  New York *(G-12129)*
Sterling Building Systems .... G 716 685-0505
  Depew *(G-4275)*

2452 Prefabricated Wood Buildings & Cmpnts

Alta Industries Ltd .... F 845 586-3336
  Halcottsville *(G-5904)*
Best Mdlr HMS Afrbe P Q& S In ..... F 631 204-0049
  Southampton *(G-15540)*
Bill Lake Homes Construction .... D 518 673-2424
  Sprakers *(G-15577)*
Cort Contracting .... F 845 758-1190
  Red Hook *(G-14028)*
Duro-Shed Inc .... E 585 344-0800
  Buffalo *(G-2921)*
Eastern Exterior Wall 631 589-3880
  Bohemia *(G-1061)*
Energy Panel Structures Inc .... G 315 923-7777
  Clyde *(G-3726)*
Energy Panel Structures Inc .... G 585 343-1777
  Batavia *(G-630)*
Energy Panel Structures Inc .... G 518 355-6708
  Schenectady *(G-15251)*
Harvest Homes Inc .... E 518 895-2341
  Delanson *(G-4233)*
Historical Soc of Mddltown Walk ..... G 845 342-0941
  Middletown *(G-8444)*
Jabo Agricultural Inc .... E 631 475-1800
  Patchogue *(G-13424)*
Lapp Management Corp 607 243-5141
  Himrod *(G-6422)*
Northern Design & Bldg Assoc .... E 518 747-2200
  Queensbury *(G-14006)*
Pine Ridge Log HM Restorations ..... F 315 387-3360
  Lacona *(G-7251)*
Roscoe Brothers Inc .... F 607 844-3750
  Dryden *(G-4322)*
Shafer & Sons 315 853-5285
  Westmoreland *(G-17065)*
◆ Shelter Enterprises Inc .... D 518 237-4100
  Cohoes *(G-3758)*
Solid Bilt Construction .... G 315 893-1738
  Madison *(G-7994)*
Walpole Woodworkers Inc .... G 631 726-2859
  Water Mill *(G-16606)*
Westchester Modular Homes Inc ..... G 845 832-9400
  Wingdale *(G-17275)*
Whitley East LLC .... D 718 403-0050
  Brooklyn *(G-2748)*
Wood Tex Products LLC .... D 607 243-5141
  Himrod *(G-6423)*

2491 Wood Preserving

Bestway Enterprises Inc .... E 607 753-8261
  Cortland *(G-4012)*
Bestway of New York Inc .... G 607 753-8261
  Cortland *(G-4013)*
▲ Colorspec Coatings Intl Inc ..... F 631 472-8251
  Holbrook *(G-6440)*
Donver Incorporated .... F 716 945-1910
  Kill Buck *(G-7166)*
Genesee Reserve Buffalo LLC ..... E 716 824-3116
  Buffalo *(G-2973)*
Northeast Treaters Inc .... E 518 945-2660
  Athens *(G-464)*
Northeast Treaters NY LLC .... E 518 945-2660
  Athens *(G-465)*
◆ Osmose Holdings Inc .... A 716 882-5905
  Depew *(G-4267)*
Wego International Floors LLC ..... F 516 487-3510
  Great Neck *(G-5849)*

2493 Reconstituted Wood Prdts

▲ Aarco Products Inc .... F 631 924-5461
  Yaphank *(G-17384)*
▲ Amendola MBL & Stone Ctr Inc ..... D 914 997-7968
  White Plains *(G-17076)*
Bedford Wdwrk Instllations Inc ..... G 914 764-9434
  Bedford *(G-796)*
Bulletin Boards & Dirctry Pdts .... F 914 248-8008
  Yorktown Heights *(G-17507)*
▲ Continental Buchanan LLC ..... D 703 480-3800
  Buchanan *(G-2785)*
Hi-Temp Fabrication Inc .... F 716 852-5655
  Buffalo *(G-2995)*
Niagara Fiberboard Inc .... E 716 434-8881
  Lockport *(G-7605)*

Employee Codes: A=Over 500 employees, B=251-500
C=101-250, D=51-100, E=20-50, F=10-19, G=5-9

Northeastern Products Corp E 518 623-3161
Warrensburg *(G-16580)*
Zircar Refr Composites Inc F 845 651-2200
Florida *(G-5217)*

2499 Wood Prdts, NEC

A Van Hoek Woodworking Limited G 718 599-4388
Brooklyn *(G-1536)*
◆ Aakron Rule Corp C 716 542-5483
Akron *(G-19)*
Aakron Rule Corp D 716 542-5483
Akron *(G-20)*
▲ Abbott Industries Inc E 718 291-0800
Jamaica *(G-6891)*
AC Moore Incorporated G 516 796-5831
Bethpage *(G-863)*
Aces Over Eights Inc G 585 292-9690
Rochester *(G-14169)*
Adams Interior Fabrications F 631 249-8282
Massapequa *(G-8177)*
Aid Wood Working F 631 244-7768
Bohemia *(G-1010)*
Air Chex Equipment Corp G 845 358-8179
Nyack *(G-13043)*
▲ Amci Ltd D 718 937-5858
Long Island City *(G-7656)*
American Woods & Veneers Works E 718 937-2195
Long Island City *(G-7659)*
Andike Millwork Inc G 718 894-1796
Maspeth *(G-8118)*
Apf Manufacturing Company LLC E 914 963-6300
Yonkers *(G-17415)*
Architectural Dctg Co LLC E 845 483-1340
Poughkeepsie *(G-13888)*
Architectural Enhancements Inc F 845 343-9663
Middletown *(G-8426)*
Art Essentials of New York G 845 368-1100
Airmont *(G-12)*
Atelier Viollet Corp G 718 782-1727
Brooklyn *(G-1644)*
Atlas Fence & Railing Co Inc E 718 767-2200
Whitestone *(G-17201)*
Babcock Co Inc E 607 776-3341
Bath *(G-653)*
▲ Brooks Woodworking Inc F 914 666-2029
Mount Kisco *(G-8623)*
Budd Woodwork Inc F 718 389-1110
Brooklyn *(G-1736)*
Cabinet Shapes Corp F 718 784-6255
Long Island City *(G-7691)*
▲ Canova Inc F 212 352-3582
New York *(G-9514)*
▲ Catskill Craftsmen Inc D 607 652-7321
Stamford *(G-15624)*
▲ Cdnv Wood Carving Frames Inc F 914 375-3447
Yonkers *(G-17426)*
▲ Cffco USA Inc G 718 747-1118
Jericho *(G-7061)*
▼ Cfp Purchasing Inc G 705 806-0383
Flushing *(G-5231)*
▲ Channel Manufacturing Inc E 516 944-6271
Port Washington *(G-13804)*
Charles Freihofer Baking Co G 518 463-2221
Albany *(G-63)*
Cherry Creek Woodcraft Inc E 716 988-3211
South Dayton *(G-15518)*
▲ Cowee Forest Products Inc E 518 658-2233
Berlin *(G-855)*
Craz Woodworking Assoc Inc F 631 205-1890
Bellport *(G-828)*
Daniel Demarco and Assoc Inc E 631 598-7000
Amityville *(G-284)*
Designs By Robert Scott Inc E 718 609-2535
Brooklyn *(G-1857)*
Di Fiore and Sons Custom Wdwkg G 718 278-1663
Long Island City *(G-7715)*
Di Vico Craft Products Ltd G 845 265-9390
Cold Spring *(G-3762)*
Drummond Framing Inc F 212 647-1701
New York *(G-9932)*
Ed Negron Fine Woodworking G 718 246-1016
Brooklyn *(G-1902)*
◆ Enchante Accessories Inc C 212 689-6008
New York *(G-10029)*
Encore Retail Systems Inc F 718 385-3443
Brooklyn *(G-1923)*
Essex Box & Pallet Co Inc E 518 834-7279
Keeseville *(G-7137)*
▲ FG Galassi Moulding Co Inc G 845 258-2100
Goshen *(G-5734)*
Fibron Products Inc E 716 886-2378
Buffalo *(G-2947)*
Frame Shoppe & Art Gallery G 516 365-6014
Manhasset *(G-8060)*
◆ Framerica Corporation D 631 650-1000
Yaphank *(G-17393)*
▲ Fred M Lawrence Co Inc E 718 786-7227
Bay Shore *(G-701)*
Furniture Dsign By Knossos Inc E 718 729-0404
Woodside *(G-17330)*
Galas Framing Services F 718 706-0007
Long Island City *(G-7747)*
General Art Company Inc F 212 255-1298
New York *(G-10272)*
▲ Globus Cork Inc F 347 963-4059
Bronx *(G-1344)*
Grant-Noren G 845 726-4281
Westtown *(G-17070)*
Graphics Slution Providers Inc G 845 677-5088
Lagrangeville *(G-7253)*
Green Renewable Inc E 518 658-2233
Berlin *(G-856)*
Hennig Custom Woodwork Corp G 516 536-3460
Oceanside *(G-13080)*
House of Heydenryk Jr Inc F 212 206-9611
New York *(G-10518)*
Hubray Inc F 800 645-2855
North Baldwin *(G-12907)*
▲ Imperial Frames & Albums LLC G 718 832-9793
Brooklyn *(G-2097)*
Innova Interiors Inc E 718 401-2122
Bronx *(G-1363)*
Interntonal Consmr Connections F 516 481-3438
West Hempstead *(G-16856)*
Interstate Wood Products Inc E 631 842-4488
Amityville *(G-296)*
James King Woodworking Inc G 518 761-6091
Queensbury *(G-14000)*
Jeffrey John G 631 842-2850
Amityville *(G-299)*
Jordache Woodworking Corp F 718 349-3373
Brooklyn *(G-2147)*
Julius Lowy Frame Restoring Co E 212 861-8585
New York *(G-10785)*
K & B Woodworking Inc G 518 634-7253
Cairo *(G-3274)*
Lanwood Industries Inc E 718 786-3000
Bay Shore *(G-711)*
Lanza Corp G 914 937-6360
Port Chester *(G-13751)*
▲ Lco Destiny LLC B 315 782-3302
Watertown *(G-16662)*
Long Lumber and Supply Corp F 518 439-1661
Slingerlands *(G-15477)*
M & R Woodworking & Finishing G 718 486-5480
Brooklyn *(G-2245)*
▲ M A Moslow & Bros Inc E 716 896-2950
Buffalo *(G-3052)*
McGraw Wood Products LLC E 607 836-6465
Mc Graw *(G-8223)*
McIntosh Box & Pallet Co Inc E 315 446-9350
Rome *(G-14820)*
Meeco Sullivan LLC C 800 232-3625
Warwick *(G-16595)*
▲ N Sketch Build Inc G 800 975-0597
Fishkill *(G-5187)*
▲ North American Enclosures Inc E 631 234-9500
Central Islip *(G-3507)*
Northern Forest Pdts Co Inc G 315 942-6955
Boonville *(G-1166)*
P B & H Moulding Corporation E 315 455-1756
Fayetteville *(G-5166)*
Pdj Components Inc E 845 469-9191
Chester *(G-3611)*
Pella Corporation C 631 208-0710
Calverton *(G-3294)*
▲ Pgs Millwork Inc D 212 244-6610
New York *(G-11642)*
Picture Perfect Framing G 718 851-1884
Brooklyn *(G-2418)*
Polanco Mills Woodwork G 845 271-3639
West Haverstraw *(G-16846)*
Premium Mulch & Materials Inc F 631 320-3666
Coram *(G-3949)*
Prime Wood Products G 518 792-1407
Queensbury *(G-14008)*
▲ Putnam Rolling Ladder Co Inc F 212 226-5147
New York *(G-11755)*
Putnam Rolling Ladder Co Inc F 718 381-8219
Brooklyn *(G-2459)*
Quattro Frameworks Inc F 718 361-2620
Long Island City *(G-7855)*
Quebracho Inc G 718 326-3605
Brooklyn *(G-2465)*
▲ R P M Industries Inc E 315 255-1105
Auburn *(G-515)*
Regence Picture Frames Inc E 718 779-0888
Lynbrook *(G-7959)*
Revival Industries Inc F 315 868-1085
Ilion *(G-6745)*
Richard Rothbard Inc G 845 355-2300
Slate Hill *(G-15474)*
Rose Fence Inc F 516 223-0777
Baldwin *(G-561)*
Ryers Creek Corp E 607 523-6617
Corning *(G-3980)*
Sky Frame & Art Inc E 212 925-7856
New York *(G-12095)*
▲ Structural Industries Inc C 631 471-5200
Bohemia *(G-1137)*
Superior Wood Turnings F 716 483-1254
Jamestown *(G-7037)*
T Eason Land Surveyor G 631 474-2200
Port Jeff STA *(G-13772)*
Thomas Matthews Wdwkg Ltd F 631 287-3657
Southampton *(G-15554)*
Thomas Matthews Wdwkg Ltd G 631 287-2023
Southampton *(G-15555)*
Ultimate Styles of America F 631 254-0219
Bay Shore *(G-753)*
▲ Unisource Food Eqp Systems Inc G 516 681-0537
Holbrook *(G-6479)*
Walpole Woodworkers Inc G 631 726-2859
Water Mill *(G-16606)*
Wholesale Mulch & Sawdust Inc G 607 687-2637
Owego *(G-13362)*
Windsor United Industries LLC E 607 655-3300
Windsor *(G-17273)*
Wood Innovations of Suffolk G 631 698-2345
Medford *(G-8263)*
Woodmotif Inc F 516 564-8325
Hempstead *(G-6289)*
Woodtronics Inc G 914 962-5205
Yorktown Heights *(G-17521)*
▲ York Ladder Inc G 718 784-6666
Long Island City *(G-7930)*

25 FURNITURE AND FIXTURES

2511 Wood Household Furniture

A & S Woodworking Inc G 518 821-0832
Hudson *(G-6602)*
A-1 Manhattan Custom Furn Inc G 212 750-9800
Island Park *(G-6777)*
American Epoxy and Metal Inc G 718 828-7828
Scarsdale *(G-15216)*
Anthony Lawrence of New York E 212 206-8820
Long Island City *(G-7661)*
Arthur Brown W Mfg Co F 631 243-5594
Deer Park *(G-4102)*
▲ Arthur Lauer Inc E 845 255-7871
Gardiner *(G-5547)*
Artisan Woodworking Ltd G 516 486-0818
West Hempstead *(G-16849)*
Atelier Viollet Corp G 718 782-1727
Brooklyn *(G-1644)*
▲ Auratic USA Incorporated G 212 684-8888
New York *(G-9264)*
Bel Art International E 718 402-2100
Bronx *(G-1282)*
▲ Benchmark Furniture Mfg D 718 257-4707
Brooklyn *(G-1681)*
Black River Valley Wdwkg LLC G 315 376-8405
Castorland *(G-3421)*
Brueton Industries Inc D 516 379-3400
Freeport *(G-5391)*
◆ Bush Industries Inc C 716 665-2000
Jamestown *(G-6978)*
Cab-Network Inc G 516 334-8666
Westbury *(G-16972)*
Carlos & Alex Atelier Inc E 718 441-8911
Richmond Hill *(G-14070)*
Carver Creek Enterprises Inc G 585 657-7511
Bloomfield *(G-983)*
Cassadaga Designs Inc G 716 595-3030
Cassadaga *(G-3414)*
▲ Catskill Craftsmen Inc D 607 652-7321
Stamford *(G-15624)*
▲ Charles H Beckley Inc F 718 665-2218
Bronx *(G-1297)*

S I C

SIC SECTION 25 FURNITURE AND FIXTURES

Comerford Hennessy At Home Inc ....G....... 631 537-6200
Bridgehampton *(G-1233)*
▲ Community Products LLC ....C....... 845 658-8799
Rifton *(G-14132)*
Concepts In Wood of CNY ....E....... 315 463-8084
Syracuse *(G-15904)*
Conesus Lake Association Inc ....E....... 585 346-6864
Lakeville *(G-7283)*
Cousins Furniture & Hm Imprvs ....E....... 631 254-3752
Deer Park *(G-4121)*
Crawford Furniture Mfg Corp ....C....... 716 483-2102
Jamestown *(G-6985)*
Custom Display Manufacture ....G....... 516 783-6491
North Bellmore *(G-12920)*
Custom Woodcraft LLC ....F....... 315 843-4234
Munnsville *(G-8750)*
D & W Design Inc ....E....... 845 343-3366
Middletown *(G-8435)*
David Sutherland Showrooms - N ....G....... 212 871-9717
New York *(G-9823)*
Dbs Interiors Corp ....F....... 631 491-3013
West Babylon *(G-16788)*
Dcl Furniture Manufacturing ....E....... 516 248-2683
Mineola *(G-8505)*
Deakon Homes and Interiors ....F....... 518 271-0342
Troy *(G-16233)*
Designs By Robert Scott Inc ....E....... 718 609-2535
Brooklyn *(G-1857)*
Dessin/Fournir Inc ....F....... 212 758-0844
New York *(G-9859)*
▲ Dinette Depot Ltd ....D....... 516 515-9623
Brooklyn *(G-1865)*
Ducduc LLC ....F....... 212 226-1868
New York *(G-9935)*
▲ Dune Inc ....G....... 212 925-6171
New York *(G-9938)*
E-One Inc ....D....... 716 646-6790
Hamburg *(G-5921)*
East End Country Kitchens Inc ....F....... 631 727-2258
Calverton *(G-3290)*
▲ Eclectic Cntract Furn Inds Inc ....F....... 212 967-5504
New York *(G-9976)*
El Greco Woodworking Inc ....E....... 716 483-0315
Jamestown *(G-6991)*
Emilia Interiors Inc ....F....... 718 629-4202
Brooklyn *(G-1920)*
▲ Ercole Nyc Inc ....F....... 212 675-2218
Brooklyn *(G-1932)*
Eugenia Selective Living Inc ....F....... 631 277-1461
Islip *(G-6808)*
Eurocraft Custom Furniture ....G....... 718 956-0600
Long Island City *(G-7732)*
Falcon Chair and Table Inc ....E....... 716 664-7136
Falconer *(G-4897)*
Feinkind Inc ....G....... 800 289-6136
Irvington *(G-6769)*
Fenix Furniture Co ....E....... 631 273-3500
Bay Shore *(G-700)*
▲ Fiber-Seal of New York Inc ....G....... 212 888-5580
New York *(G-10157)*
Final Dimension Inc ....G....... 718 786-0100
Maspeth *(G-8139)*
Fine Arts Furniture Inc ....G....... 212 744-9139
Long Island City *(G-7740)*
▲ Forecast Consoles Inc ....E....... 631 253-9000
Hauppauge *(G-6079)*
Franz Fischer Inc ....F....... 718 821-1300
Brooklyn *(G-2003)*
Fred Schulz Inc ....G....... 845 724-3409
Poughquag *(G-13941)*
French & Itln Furn Craftsmen ....G....... 718 599-5000
Brooklyn *(G-2004)*
Furniture Doctor Inc ....G....... 585 657-6941
Bloomfield *(G-988)*
Glendale Architectural WD Pdts ....E....... 718 326-2700
Glendale *(G-5654)*
▼ Hard Manufacturing Co Inc ....D....... 716 893-1800
Buffalo *(G-2988)*
▼ Harden Furniture Inc ....C....... 315 675-3600
Mc Connellsville *(G-8220)*
Hayman-Chaffey Designs Inc ....F....... 212 889-7771
New York *(G-10428)*
Henry B Urban Inc ....E....... 212 489-3308
New York *(G-10457)*
▲ Hunt Country Furniture Inc ....D....... 845 832-6601
Wingdale *(G-17274)*
Icon Design LLC ....E....... 585 768-6040
Le Roy *(G-7409)*
Innovant Inc ....G....... 212 929-4883
New York *(G-10603)*

Inova LLC ....E....... 212 932-0366
New York *(G-10608)*
Inter Craft Custom Furniture ....G....... 718 278-2573
Astoria *(G-445)*
J Percoco Industries Inc ....G....... 631 312-4572
Bohemia *(G-1079)*
K & B Woodworking Inc ....G....... 518 634-7253
Cairo *(G-3274)*
Kazac Inc ....G....... 631 249-7299
Farmingdale *(G-5024)*
Kittinger Company Inc ....E....... 716 876-1000
Buffalo *(G-3033)*
Knoll Inc ....D....... 917 359-8620
New York *(G-10864)*
▲ L& JG Stickley Incorporated ....A....... 315 682-5500
Manlius *(G-8073)*
Lanoves Inc ....G....... 718 384-1880
Brooklyn *(G-2195)*
Lemode Concepts Inc ....G....... 631 841-0796
Amityville *(G-305)*
Little Wolf Cabinet Shop Inc ....E....... 212 734-1116
New York *(G-11013)*
Long Lumber and Supply Corp ....F....... 518 439-1661
Slingerlands *(G-15477)*
▲ M & C Furniture ....G....... 718 422-2136
Brooklyn *(G-2242)*
M T D Corporation ....F....... 631 491-3905
West Babylon *(G-16808)*
Machias Furniture Factory Inc ....G....... 716 353-8687
Machias *(G-7993)*
◆ Mackenzie-Childs LLC ....C....... 315 364-7567
Aurora *(G-530)*
Manchester Wood Inc ....C....... 518 642-9518
Granville *(G-5776)*
McGraw Wood Products LLC ....E....... 607 836-6465
Mc Graw *(G-8223)*
Mica International Ltd ....F....... 516 378-3400
Freeport *(G-5413)*
New Day Woodwork Inc ....E....... 718 275-1721
Glendale *(G-5659)*
Nicholas Dfine Furn Decorators ....F....... 914 245-8982
Bronx *(G-1411)*
▲ Offi & Company ....G....... 800 958-6334
Corning *(G-3977)*
▲ Patrick Mackin Custom Furn ....G....... 718 237-2592
Brooklyn *(G-2409)*
Petro Moore Manufacturing Corp ....G....... 718 784-2516
Long Island City *(G-7841)*
Piccini Industries Ltd ....E....... 845 365-0614
Orangeburg *(G-13239)*
▼ Pillow Perfections Ltd Inc ....G....... 718 383-2259
Brooklyn *(G-2420)*
Premier Woodcraft Ltd ....E....... 610 383-6624
White Plains *(G-17161)*
◆ Premiere Living Products LLC ....F....... 631 873-4337
Dix Hills *(G-4295)*
Professional Cab Detailing Co ....F....... 845 436-7282
Woodridge *(G-17315)*
Raff Enterprises ....G....... 518 218-7883
Albany *(G-126)*
Recycled Brooklyn Group LLC ....F....... 917 902-0662
Brooklyn *(G-2485)*
▼ Reis D Furniture Mfg ....E....... 516 248-5676
Mineola *(G-8534)*
◆ Renco Group Inc ....G....... 212 541-6000
New York *(G-11832)*
▲ Royal Jamestown Furniture Inc ....E....... 716 664-5260
Jamestown *(G-7026)*
Sitecraft Inc ....G....... 718 729-4900
Astoria *(G-457)*
Sleep Care Enterprises Inc ....G....... 631 246-9000
Stony Brook *(G-15771)*
Stillwater Wood & Iron ....G....... 518 664-4501
Stillwater *(G-15761)*
▲ Sundown Ski & Sport Shop Inc ....E....... 631 737-8600
Lake Grove *(G-7267)*
Universal Designs Inc ....G....... 718 721-1111
Long Island City *(G-7910)*
Wallace Home Design Ctr ....G....... 631 765-3890
Southold *(G-15561)*
Walpole Woodworkers Inc ....G....... 631 726-2859
Water Mill *(G-16606)*
Walter P Sauer LLC ....E....... 718 937-0600
Brooklyn *(G-2743)*
William Somerville Maintenance ....D....... 212 534-4600
New York *(G-12636)*
Woodmotif Inc ....F....... 516 564-8325
Hempstead *(G-6289)*
Your Furniture Designers Inc ....G....... 845 947-3046
West Haverstraw *(G-16848)*

2512 Wood Household Furniture, Upholstered

A Schneller Sons Inc ....F....... 212 695-9440
New York *(G-8992)*
▲ Arthur Lauer Inc ....E....... 845 255-7871
Gardiner *(G-5547)*
▲ Artone LLC ....D....... 716 664-2232
Jamestown *(G-6972)*
August Studios ....G....... 718 706-6487
Long Island City *(G-7678)*
▲ Avanti Furniture Corp ....F....... 516 293-8220
Farmingdale *(G-4949)*
▲ Classic Sofa Ltd ....D....... 212 620-0485
New York *(G-9637)*
Deangelis Ltd ....E....... 212 348-8225
New York *(G-9833)*
Delta Upholsterers Inc ....E....... 212 489-3308
New York *(G-9841)*
Doreen Interiors Ltd ....E....... 212 255-9008
New Hyde Park *(G-8828)*
Elan Upholstery Inc ....F....... 631 563-0650
Bohemia *(G-1065)*
Falvo Manufacturing Co Inc ....F....... 315 738-7682
Utica *(G-16330)*
▲ Fiber-Seal of New York Inc ....G....... 212 888-5580
New York *(G-10157)*
Furniture By Craftmaster Ltd ....G....... 631 750-0658
Bohemia *(G-1069)*
H & H Furniture Co ....G....... 718 850-5252
Jamaica *(G-6917)*
Hallagan Manufacturing Co Inc ....D....... 315 331-4640
Newark *(G-12731)*
▼ Harden Furniture Inc ....C....... 315 675-3600
Mc Connellsville *(G-8220)*
Henry B Urban Inc ....E....... 212 489-3308
New York *(G-10457)*
Jackson Dakota Inc ....F....... 718 786-8600
Long Island City *(G-7769)*
▲ Jackson Dakota Inc ....G....... 212 838-9444
New York *(G-10688)*
Jays Furniture Products Inc ....E....... 716 876-8854
Buffalo *(G-3015)*
Kittinger Company Inc ....E....... 716 876-1000
Buffalo *(G-3033)*
◆ Mackenzie-Childs LLC ....C....... 315 364-7567
Aurora *(G-530)*
Matteo & Antonio Bartolotta ....F....... 315 252-2220
Auburn *(G-508)*
Mazza Classics Incorporated ....G....... 631 390-9060
Farmingdale *(G-5046)*
McCarroll Uphl Designs LLC ....G....... 518 828-0500
Hudson *(G-6625)*
Nicholas Dfine Furn Decorators ....F....... 914 245-8982
Bronx *(G-1411)*
Pheonix Custom Furniture Ltd ....E....... 212 727-2648
Long Island City *(G-7842)*
Princeton Upholstery Co Inc ....D....... 845 343-2196
Middletown *(G-8458)*
Rob Herschenfeld Design Inc ....F....... 718 456-6801
Brooklyn *(G-2499)*
▲ Royal Jamestown Furniture Inc ....E....... 716 664-5260
Jamestown *(G-7026)*
Simon S Decorating Inc ....G....... 718 339-2931
Brooklyn *(G-2561)*
▲ Slava Industries Incorporated ....G....... 718 499-4850
Brooklyn *(G-2568)*
▲ Smith & Watson ....E....... 212 686-6444
New York *(G-12104)*
Sofa Doctor Inc ....G....... 718 292-6300
Bronx *(G-1458)*
Two Worlds Arts Ltd ....G....... 212 929-2210
Brooklyn *(G-2694)*
Versailles Drapery Upholstery ....F....... 212 533-2059
Long Island City *(G-7914)*
Walco Leather Co Inc ....E....... 212 243-2244
New York *(G-12577)*
Wallace Home Design Ctr ....G....... 631 765-3890
Southold *(G-15561)*
Yepes Fine Furniture ....E....... 718 383-0221
Brooklyn *(G-2774)*

2514 Metal Household Furniture

▲ American Best Cabinets Inc ....E....... 845 369-6666
Suffern *(G-15785)*
Brueton Industries Inc ....D....... 516 379-3400
Freeport *(G-5391)*
▲ Charles P Rogers Brass Beds ....F....... 212 675-4400
New York *(G-9582)*
▲ CIDC Corp ....F....... 718 342-5820
Brooklyn *(G-1780)*

SIC

Employee Codes: A=Over 500 employees, B=251-500
C=101-250, D=51-100, E=20-50, F=10-19, G=5-9
2017 Harris
New York Manufacturers Directory
745

D & W Design Inc ....E 845 343-3366
Middletown (G-8435)
◆ Embassy Dinettes Inc ....G 631 253-2292
Deer Park (G-4138)
F&M Ornamental Designs LLC ....G 212 353-2600
New York (G-10117)
▲ F&M Ornamental Designs LLC ....F 908 241-7776
New York (G-10118)
Furniture Doctor Inc ....G 585 657-6941
Bloomfield (G-988)
▲ Glissade New York LLC ....E 631 756-4800
Farmingdale (G-4999)
▼ Hard Manufacturing Co Inc ....D 716 893-1800
Buffalo (G-2988)
▲ Hellas Stone Inc ....G 718 545-4716
Astoria (G-444)
▲ Majestic Home Imprvs Distr ....G 718 853-5079
Brooklyn (G-2253)
Manhattan Cabinets Inc ....G 212 548-2436
New York (G-11127)
Meeker Sales Corp ....G 718 384-5400
Brooklyn (G-2293)
Methods Tooling & Mfg Inc ....E 845 246-7100
Mount Marion (G-8651)
▲ NK Medical Products Inc ....G 716 759-7200
Amherst (G-254)
◆ Novum Medical Products Inc ....F 716 759-7200
Amherst (G-255)
Precision Orna Ir Works Inc ....G 718 379-5200
Bronx (G-1433)
◆ Renco Group Inc ....G 212 541-6000
New York (G-11832)
Royal Metal Products Inc ....E 518 966-4442
Surprise (G-15811)
▲ Slava Industries Incorporated ....G 718 499-4850
Brooklyn (G-2568)
Steelcraft Manufacturing Co ....F 718 277-2404
Brooklyn (G-2603)

2515 Mattresses & Bedsprings

◆ Brook North Farms Inc ....F 315 834-9390
Auburn (G-487)
▲ Charles H Beckley Inc ....F 718 665-2218
Bronx (G-1297)
▲ Comfort Bedding Inc ....E 718 485-7662
Brooklyn (G-1794)
Dixie Foam Ltd ....G 212 645-8999
Brooklyn (G-1867)
Duxiana Dux Bed ....G 212 755-2600
New York (G-9941)
E & G Bedding Corp ....E 718 369-1092
Brooklyn (G-1889)
▼ Hard Manufacturing Co Inc ....D 716 893-1800
Buffalo (G-2988)
▼ Ideal Manufacturing Inc ....E 585 872-7190
East Rochester (G-4462)
Jamestown Mattress Co ....E 716 665-2247
Jamestown (G-7010)
KKR Millennium GP LLC ....A 212 750-8300
New York (G-10856)
◆ M R C Industries Inc ....C 516 328-6900
Port Washington (G-13839)
Mattress Factory ....G 718 760-4202
Corona (G-4002)
Metro Mattress Corp ....E 716 205-2300
Niagara Falls (G-12847)
▲ Otis Bedding Mfg Co Inc ....E 716 825-2599
Buffalo (G-3105)
◆ Quality Foam Inc ....F 718 381-3644
Brooklyn (G-2461)
Rollers Inc ....G 716 837-0700
Buffalo (G-3164)
▲ Royal Bedding Co Buffalo Inc ....E 716 895-1414
Buffalo (G-3168)
Sealy Mattress Co Albany Inc ....B 518 880-1600
Troy (G-16223)
Sleep Improvement Center Inc ....F 516 536-5799
Rockville Centre (G-14798)
▲ Steinbock-Braff Inc ....E 718 972-6500
Brooklyn (G-2606)
▲ VSM Investors LLC ....G 212 351-1600
New York (G-12571)
Zzz Mattress Manufacturing ....E 718 454-1468
Saint Albans (G-15085)

2517 Wood T V, Radio, Phono & Sewing Cabinets

Cleary Custom Cabinets Inc ....F 516 939-2475
Hicksville (G-6333)
Dbs Interiors Corp ....F 631 491-3013
West Babylon (G-16788)
Handcraft Cabinetry Inc ....G 914 681-9437
White Plains (G-17117)
Loffreno Cstm Interiors Contg ....E 718 981-0319
Staten Island (G-15699)
Time Base Corporation ....E 631 293-4068
Edgewood (G-4617)
▲ W Designe Inc ....E 914 736-1058
Peekskill (G-13484)

2519 Household Furniture, NEC

3phase Industries LLC ....G 347 763-2942
Brooklyn (G-1515)
Albert Menin Interiors Ltd ....F 212 876-3041
Bronx (G-1267)
Anandamali Inc ....F 212 343-8964
New York (G-9147)
Bielecky Bros Inc ....E 718 424-4764
Woodside (G-17320)
▲ Comely International Trdg Inc ....G 212 683-1240
New York (G-9682)
Culin/Colella Inc ....G 914 698-7727
Mamaroneck (G-8031)
Dbs Interiors Corp ....F 631 491-3013
West Babylon (G-16788)
Eugenia Selective Living Inc ....F 631 277-1461
Islip (G-6808)
Harome Designs LLC ....E 631 864-1900
Commack (G-3834)
▲ Holland & Sherry Inc ....E 212 542-8410
New York (G-10497)
▲ L& JG Stickley Incorporated ....A 315 682-5500
Manlius (G-8073)
Matthew Shively LLC ....G 914 937-3531
Port Chester (G-13754)
Mbh Furniture Innovations Inc ....G 845 354-8202
Spring Valley (G-15595)
Ololo Inc ....G 877 701-0110
Brooklyn (G-2390)
Ready To Assemble Company Inc ....E 516 825-4397
Valley Stream (G-16424)
Rent-A-Center Inc ....G 718 322-2400
Jamaica (G-6947)
◆ Spancraft Ltd ....F 516 295-0055
Woodmere (G-17314)
▲ Vondom LLC ....G 212 207-3252
New York (G-12569)

2521 Wood Office Furniture

▲ A G Master Crafts Ltd ....F 516 745-6262
Garden City (G-5492)
A Schneller Sons Inc ....F 212 695-9440
New York (G-8992)
▲ Artistic Products LLC ....E 631 435-0200
Hauppauge (G-6026)
▲ Artone LLC ....D 716 664-2232
Jamestown (G-6972)
B D B Typewriter Supply Works ....E 718 232-4800
Brooklyn (G-1659)
Bauerschmidt & Sons Inc ....D 718 528-3500
Jamaica (G-6898)
Bloch Industries LLC ....D 585 334-9600
Rochester (G-14235)
Brueton Industries Inc ....D 516 379-3400
Freeport (G-5391)
◆ Bush Industries Inc ....C 716 665-2000
Jamestown (G-6978)
▼ Ccn International Inc ....D 315 789-4400
Geneva (G-5572)
Centre Interiors Wdwkg Co Inc ....E 718 323-1343
Ozone Park (G-13376)
Chicone Builders LLC ....G 607 535-6540
Montour Falls (G-8609)
Commercial Display Design LLC ....F 607 336-7353
Norwich (G-13025)
Concepts In Wood of CNY ....E 315 463-8084
Syracuse (G-15904)
▼ Craft Custom Woodwork Co Inc ....F 718 821-2162
Maspeth (G-8124)
Creative Cabinetry Corporation ....G 914 963-6061
Yonkers (G-17431)
Culin/Colella Inc ....G 914 698-7727
Mamaroneck (G-8031)
DAF Office Networks Inc ....F 315 699-7070
Cicero (G-3644)
Dates Weiser Furniture Corp ....D 716 891-1700
Buffalo (G-2902)
Davinci Designs Inc ....F 631 595-1095
Deer Park (G-4126)
Dcl Furniture Manufacturing ....E 516 248-2683
Mineola (G-8505)
Deakon Homes and Interiors ....F 518 271-0342
Troy (G-16233)
Den-Jo Woodworking Corp ....F 718 388-2287
Brooklyn (G-1854)
Designs By Robert Scott Inc ....E 718 609-2535
Brooklyn (G-1857)
Dimaio Millwork Corporation ....E 914 476-1937
Yonkers (G-17436)
Divine Art Furniture Inc ....G 718 834-0111
Brooklyn (G-1866)
▲ E-Systems Group LLC ....E 607 775-1100
Conklin (G-3868)
Eugenia Selective Living Inc ....F 631 277-1461
Islip (G-6808)
Exhibit Corporation America ....E 718 937-2600
Long Island City (G-7734)
F E Hale Mfg Co ....D 315 894-5490
Frankfort (G-5352)
Fina Cabinet Corp ....G 718 409-2900
Mount Vernon (G-8681)
▲ Forecast Consoles Inc ....E 631 253-9000
Hauppauge (G-6079)
Furniture By Craftmaster Ltd ....G 631 750-0658
Bohemia (G-1069)
Glendale Architectural WD Pdts ....E 718 326-2700
Glendale (G-5654)
▲ Gunlocke Company LLC ....C 585 728-5111
Wayland (G-16710)
H Freund Woodworking Co Inc ....F 516 334-3774
Westbury (G-16992)
▼ Harden Furniture Inc ....C 315 675-3600
Mc Connellsville (G-8220)
Heartwood Specialties Inc ....G 607 654-0102
Hammondsport (G-5955)
Hni Corporation ....C 212 683-2232
New York (G-10491)
◆ Humanscale Corporation ....E 212 725-4749
New York (G-10531)
Innovant Inc ....D 212 929-4883
New York (G-10602)
Interior Solutions of Wny LLC ....G 716 332-0372
Buffalo (G-3011)
Kazac Inc ....G 631 249-7299
Farmingdale (G-5024)
Kittinger Company Inc ....E 716 876-1000
Buffalo (G-3033)
Knoll Inc ....D 917 359-8620
New York (G-10864)
Krefab Corporation ....F 631 842-5151
Copiague (G-3909)
▲ Lake Country Woodworkers Ltd ....E 585 374-6353
Naples (G-8766)
Little Wolf Cabinet Shop Inc ....E 212 734-1116
New York (G-11013)
Loffreno Cstm Interiors Contg ....E 718 981-0319
Staten Island (G-15699)
Longo Commercial Cabinets Inc ....E 631 225-4290
Lindenhurst (G-7469)
M T D Corporation ....F 631 491-3905
West Babylon (G-16808)
▲ Manhattan Comfort Inc ....E 888 230-2225
Brooklyn (G-2259)
Materials Design Workshop ....F 718 893-1954
Bronx (G-1389)
Matteo & Antonio Bartolotta ....F 315 252-2220
Auburn (G-508)
▲ Miller Blaker Inc ....D 718 665-3930
Bronx (G-1398)
Millers Millworks Inc ....E 585 494-1420
Bergen (G-850)
▲ N Y Elli Design Corp ....F 718 228-0014
Maspeth (G-8153)
New Dimensions Office Group ....D 718 387-0995
Brooklyn (G-2361)
Nicholas Dfine Furn Decorators ....F 914 245-8982
Bronx (G-1411)
Omega Furniture Manufacturing ....F 315 463-7428
Syracuse (G-16003)
Pheonix Custom Furniture Ltd ....E 212 727-2648
Long Island City (G-7842)
Piccini Industries Ltd ....E 845 365-0614
Orangeburg (G-13239)
▲ Poppin Inc ....D 212 391-7200
New York (G-11685)
Premier Woodcraft Ltd ....E 610 383-6624
White Plains (G-17161)
▲ Prince Seating Corp ....E 718 363-2300
Brooklyn (G-2444)

SIC SECTION

25 FURNITURE AND FIXTURES

Princeton Upholstery Co Inc..................D.... 845 343-2196
 Middletown (G-8458)
Red White & Blue Entps Corp................G.... 718 565-8080
 Woodside (G-17350)
Riverfront Costume Design ....G.... 716 693-2501
 North Tonawanda (G-12990)
Saraval Industries ....G.... 516 768-9033
 Nyack (G-13053)
Stylecraft Interiors Inc ....F.... 516 487-2133
 Great Neck (G-5843)
▲ Technology Desking Inc.......................E.... 212 257-6998
 New York (G-12290)
Three R Enterprises Inc.........................E.... 585 254-5050
 Rochester (G-14725)
Universal Designs Inc............................G.... 718 721-1111
 Long Island City (G-7910)
▲ Upstate Office Liquidators Inc.............F.... 607 722-9234
 Johnson City (G-7106)
Wares of Wood ....E.... 315 964-2983
 Williamstown (G-17229)
Wood Etc Inc ....F.... 315 484-9663
 Syracuse (G-16075)
Woodmotif Inc...F.... 516 564-8325
 Hempstead (G-6289)
Your Furniture Designers Inc................G.... 845 947-3046
 West Haverstraw (G-16848)

2522 Office Furniture, Except Wood

3phase Industries LLC ....G.... 347 763-2942
 Brooklyn (G-1515)
Able Steel Equipment Co Inc ....F.... 718 361-9240
 Long Island City (G-7647)
Afco Systems Inc...................................C.... 631 424-3935
 Farmingdale (G-4931)
Allcraft Fabricators Inc..........................D.... 631 951-4100
 Hauppauge (G-6015)
Aronowitz Metal Works ....G.... 845 356-1660
 Monsey (G-8568)
▲ Artone LLC...D.... 716 664-2232
 Jamestown (G-6972)
Aztec Industries Inc...............................G.... 631 585-1331
 Ronkonkoma (G-14875)
Brueton Industries Inc...........................G.... 516 379-3400
 Freeport (G-5391)
Creative Cabinetry Corporation............G.... 914 963-6061
 Yonkers (G-17431)
▲ Davies Office Refurbishing Inc ....C.... 518 426-7188
 Albany (G-71)
Davinci Designs Inc...............................F.... 631 595-1095
 Deer Park (G-4126)
Dcl Furniture Manufacturing.................E.... 516 248-2683
 Mineola (G-8505)
Deakon Homes and Interiors ....F.... 518 271-0342
 Troy (G-16233)
▲ E-Systems Group LLC.........................E.... 607 775-1100
 Conklin (G-3868)
Eugenia Selective Living Inc................F.... 631 277-1461
 Islip (G-6808)
Exhibit Corporation America ....E.... 718 937-2600
 Long Island City (G-7734)
Falvo Manufacturing Co Inc ....E.... 315 738-7682
 Utica (G-16330)
▲ Forecast Consoles Inc........................E.... 631 253-9000
 Hauppauge (G-6079)
◆ Hergo Ergonomic Support..................E.... 718 894-0639
 Maspeth (G-8143)
Hudson Valley Office Furn Inc.............G.... 845 565-6673
 Newburgh (G-12763)
Integrated Tech Support Svcs ....G.... 718 454-2497
 Saint Albans (G-15084)
Keilhauer..F.... 646 742-0192
 New York (G-10829)
Kimball Office Inc..................................E.... 212 753-6161
 New York (G-10847)
Knoll Inc ....D.... 917 359-8620
 New York (G-10864)
Larson Metal Manufacturing Co ....G.... 716 665-6807
 Jamestown (G-7016)
▲ Lucia Group Inc...................................G.... 631 392-4900
 Deer Park (G-4168)
▲ Natural Stone & Cabinet Inc...............G.... 718 388-2988
 Brooklyn (G-2353)
New Dimensions Office Group ....D.... 718 387-0995
 Brooklyn (G-2361)
▲ Nova Metal Inc ....G.... 718 981-4000
 Staten Island (G-15717)
Piccini Industries Ltd............................E.... 845 365-0614
 Orangeburg (G-13239)
▲ Poppin Inc..D.... 212 391-7200
 New York (G-11685)

Premier Woodcraft Ltd ....E.... 610 383-6624
 White Plains (G-17161)
▲ Prince Seating Corp............................E.... 718 363-2300
 Brooklyn (G-2444)
Riverfront Costume Design ....G.... 716 693-2501
 North Tonawanda (G-12990)
Royal Metal Products Inc ....E.... 518 966-4442
 Surprise (G-15811)
Saturn Sales Inc....................................E.... 519 658-5125
 Niagara Falls (G-12874)
Schwab Corp..C.... 812 547-2956
 Rochester (G-14676)
Schwab Corp..E.... 585 381-4900
 Rochester (G-14675)
Seating Inc...G.... 800 468-2475
 Nunda (G-13042)
▼ Ulrich Planfiling Eqp Corp..................E.... 716 763-1815
 Lakewood (G-7295)
▲ Vitra Inc...F.... 212 463-5700
 New York (G-12558)
Workplace Interiors LLC ....F.... 585 425-7420
 Fairport (G-4887)
X F Inc ....F.... 212 244-2240
 Brooklyn (G-2770)

2531 Public Building & Related Furniture

Able Steel Equipment Co Inc ....F.... 718 361-9240
 Long Island City (G-7647)
American Bptst Chrches Mtro NY ....G.... 212 870-3195
 New York (G-9115)
Artistry in Wood of Syracuse................F.... 315 431-4022
 East Syracuse (G-4506)
▲ Artone LLC...D.... 716 664-2232
 Jamestown (G-6972)
B/E Aerospace Inc ....E.... 631 563-6400
 Bohemia (G-1022)
B/E Aerospace Inc ....C.... 631 589-0877
 Bohemia (G-1023)
Chair Factory...E.... 718 363-2383
 Brooklyn (G-1771)
E & D Specialty Stands Inc ....E.... 716 337-0161
 North Collins (G-12928)
East/West Industries Inc ....E.... 631 981-5900
 Ronkonkoma (G-14896)
▲ Forecast Consoles Inc........................E.... 631 253-9000
 Hauppauge (G-6079)
Hartford Hwy Dept.................................G.... 315 724-0654
 New Hartford (G-8806)
Jays Furniture Products Inc ....E.... 716 876-8854
 Buffalo (G-3015)
Jcdecaux Mallscape LLC ....G.... 646 834-1200
 New York (G-10709)
Johnson Controls Inc ....D.... 518 884-8313
 Ballston Spa (G-600)
Johnson Controls Inc ....E.... 585 671-1930
 Webster (G-16725)
Johnson Controls Inc ....E.... 585 724-2232
 Rochester (G-14464)
Keck Group Inc ....F.... 845 988-5757
 Warwick (G-16591)
▲ Maximum Security Products Corp .....E.... 518 233-1800
 Waterford (G-16613)
Maxsecure Systems Inc ....G.... 800 657-4336
 Buffalo (G-3059)
▲ N Y Elli Design Corp ....E.... 718 228-0014
 Maspeth (G-8153)
Pluribus Products Inc...........................E.... 718 852-1614
 Brooklyn (G-2427)
Readyjet Technical Svcs Inc................F.... 518 705-4019
 Johnstown (G-7124)
Rosenwach Tank Co Inc ....E.... 212 972-4411
 Astoria (G-455)
Ry-Lecia Inc...G.... 631 244-0011
 Bohemia (G-1127)
Seating Inc...E.... 800 468-2475
 Nunda (G-13042)
Steeldeck Ny Inc....................................F.... 718 599-3700
 Brooklyn (G-2604)
▲ Studio 21 LA Inc..................................E.... 718 965-6579
 Brooklyn (G-2612)
◆ Testori Interiors Inc ....E.... 518 298-4400
 Champlain (G-3546)
Town of Amherst ....E.... 716 631-7113
 Williamsville (G-17258)
Tymor Park...G.... 845 724-5691
 Lagrangeville (G-7260)
▲ Unifor Inc...F.... 212 673-3434
 New York (G-12455)

2541 Wood, Office & Store Fixtures

16 Tons Inc...E.... 718 418-8446
 Brooklyn (G-1511)
Abaco Steel Products Inc.....................G.... 631 589-1800
 Bohemia (G-1002)
▲ Abbott Industries Inc ....E.... 718 291-0800
 Jamaica (G-6891)
All Merchandise Display Corp ....G.... 718 257-2221
 Highland Mills (G-6411)
Allegany Laminating and Supply ....G.... 716 372-2424
 Allegany (G-198)
Alrod Associates Inc ....F.... 631 981-2193
 Ronkonkoma (G-14866)
Arcy Plastic Laminates Inc ....E.... 518 235-0753
 Albany (G-48)
▲ Array Marketing Group Inc.................E.... 212 750-3367
 New York (G-9208)
▲ Artone LLC...D.... 716 664-2232
 Jamestown (G-6972)
Auburn Custom Millwork Inc ....G.... 315 253-3843
 Auburn (G-478)
Auratic Inc..G.... 914 413-8154
 New York (G-9263)
Bator Bintor Inc ....F.... 347 546-6503
 Brooklyn (G-1674)
Bauerschmidt & Sons Inc ....D.... 718 528-3500
 Jamaica (G-6898)
Bloch Industries LLC ....D.... 585 334-9600
 Rochester (G-14235)
Champion Millwork Inc ....E.... 315 463-0711
 Syracuse (G-15892)
CNA Specialties Inc..............................G.... 631 567-7929
 Sayville (G-15206)
Contempra Design Inc..........................G.... 718 984-8586
 Staten Island (G-15662)
Countertops & Cabinets Inc.................G.... 315 433-1038
 Syracuse (G-15910)
Creative Counter Tops Inc ....F.... 845 471-6480
 Poughkeepsie (G-13894)
Custom Countertops Inc ....G.... 716 685-2871
 Depew (G-4253)
Custom Design Kitchens Inc...............F.... 518 355-4446
 Duanesburg (G-4325)
Custom Wood Inc ....G.... 718 927-4700
 Brooklyn (G-1828)
▲ David Flatt Furniture Ltd ....F.... 718 937-7944
 Long Island City (G-7710)
Dbs Interiors Corp ....E.... 631 491-3013
 West Babylon (G-16788)
Deakon Homes and Interiors ....F.... 518 271-0342
 Troy (G-16233)
Delocon Wholesale Inc.........................E.... 716 592-2711
 Springville (G-15609)
E F Thresh Inc.......................................G.... 315 437-7301
 East Syracuse (G-4526)
Empire Archtctural Systems Inc..........E.... 518 773-5109
 Johnstown (G-7110)
Empire Fabricators Inc.........................G.... 585 235-3050
 Rochester (G-14346)
Encore Retail Systems Inc ....E.... 718 385-3443
 Brooklyn (G-1923)
Evans & Paul Unlimited Corp ....E.... 212 255-7272
 New York (G-10088)
Falvo Manufacturing Co Inc ....E.... 315 738-7682
 Utica (G-16330)
Farrington Packaging Corp..................E.... 315 733-4600
 Utica (G-16331)
Fina Cabinet Corp ....G.... 718 409-2900
 Mount Vernon (G-8681)
Fleetwood Cabinet Co Inc ....E.... 516 379-2139
 Brooklyn (G-1986)
▲ Forecast Consoles Inc........................E.... 631 253-9000
 Hauppauge (G-6079)
Frank J Martello....................................G.... 585 235-2780
 Rochester (G-14381)
Gaughan Construction Corp................G.... 718 850-9577
 Richmond Hill (G-14074)
▲ Gotham City Industries Inc ....E.... 985 851-5474
 Scarsdale (G-15217)
Greenleaf Cabinet Makers LLC ....F.... 315 432-4600
 Syracuse (G-15954)
▲ Hamlet Products Inc ....F.... 914 665-0307
 Mount Vernon (G-8689)
Heartwood Specialties Inc ....G.... 607 654-0102
 Hammondsport (G-5955)
Home Ideal Inc.......................................E.... 718 762-8998
 Flushing (G-5251)
Home4u Inc..G.... 347 262-7214
 Brooklyn (G-2086)

Employee Codes: A=Over 500 employees, B=251-500
C=101-250, D=51-100, E=20-50, F=10-19, G=5-9

2017 Harris
New York Manufacturers Directory

25 FURNITURE AND FIXTURES

Hunter Metal Industries Inc ....D....... 631 475-5900
  East Patchogue (G-4448)
▲ Icestone LLC ....E....... 718 624-4900
  Brooklyn (G-2095)
▲ Industrial Support Inc ....D....... 716 662-2954
  Buffalo (G-3006)
Integrated Wood Components Inc ....E....... 607 467-1739
  Deposit (G-4278)
Inter State Laminates Inc ....E....... 518 283-8355
  Poestenkill (G-13724)
J M P Display Fixture Co Inc ....G....... 718 649-0333
  Brooklyn (G-2127)
Johnny Mica Inc ....G....... 631 225-5213
  Lindenhurst (G-7466)
Joseph Fedele ....G....... 718 448-3658
  Staten Island (G-15694)
◆ Karp Associates Inc ....D....... 631 768-8300
  Melville (G-8332)
Kitchen Specialty Craftsmen ....G....... 607 739-0833
  Elmira (G-4693)
Koeppels Kustom Kitchens Inc ....G....... 518 489-0092
  Albany (G-96)
L & J Interiors Inc ....E....... 631 218-0838
  Bohemia (G-1089)
L Builders Supply Inc ....B....... 518 355-7190
  Schenectady (G-15275)
▲ Leo D Bernstein & Sons Inc ....E....... 212 337-9578
  New York (G-10968)
Lif Distributing Inc ....F....... 631 630-6900
  Islandia (G-6799)
◆ Lifestyle-Trimco ....E....... 718 257-9101
  Brooklyn (G-2219)
Little Wolf Cabinet Shop Inc ....E....... 212 734-1116
  New York (G-11013)
Longo Commercial Cabinets Inc ....E....... 631 225-4290
  Lindenhurst (G-7469)
▲ Madjek Inc ....D....... 631 842-4475
  Amityville (G-308)
◆ Marietta Corporation ....B....... 607 753-6746
  Cortland (G-4033)
Marplex Furniture Corporation ....G....... 914 969-7755
  Yonkers (G-17466)
Metropolitan Granite & MBL Inc ....G....... 585 342-7020
  Rochester (G-14505)
Mg Concepts (de) LLC ....G....... 631 608-8090
  Amityville (G-313)
Michael P Mmarr ....G....... 315 623-9380
  Constantia (G-3881)
▲ New Business Solutions Inc ....E....... 631 789-1500
  Amityville (G-316)
New Dimensions Office Group ....D....... 718 387-0995
  Brooklyn (G-2361)
Nlr Counter Tops LLC ....G....... 347 295-0410
  New York (G-11446)
P & B Woodworking Inc ....F....... 845 744-2508
  Pine Bush (G-13549)
Pine Hill Fabricators ....G....... 716 823-2474
  Buffalo (G-3127)
Precision Built Tops LLC ....G....... 607 336-5417
  Norwich (G-13035)
Premier Fixtures LLC ....D....... 631 236-4100
  Hauppauge (G-6170)
▲ Premier Woodworking Inc ....E....... 631 236-4100
  Hauppauge (G-6171)
R H Guest Incorporated ....G....... 718 675-7600
  Brooklyn (G-2471)
Rasjada Enterprises Ltd ....F....... 631 242-1055
  Bay Shore (G-732)
Red White & Blue Entps Corp ....G....... 718 565-8080
  Woodside (G-17350)
Ridge Cabinet & Showcase Inc ....E....... 585 663-0560
  Rochester (G-14626)
Rochester Countertop Inc ....F....... 585 338-2260
  Rochester (G-14640)
Saw Mill Woodworking Inc ....G....... 914 963-1841
  Yonkers (G-17483)
Serway Bros Inc ....E....... 315 337-0601
  Rome (G-14836)
Sharonana Enterprises Inc ....E....... 631 875-5619
  Coram (G-3950)
Solid Surfaces Inc ....E....... 585 292-5340
  Rochester (G-14692)
▲ Space-Craft Worldwide Inc ....E....... 631 603-3000
  Edgewood (G-4612)
Specialty Services ....G....... 585 728-5650
  Wayland (G-16711)
Steelcraft Manufacturing Co ....F....... 718 277-2404
  Brooklyn (G-2603)
Steeldeck Ny Inc ....F....... 718 599-3700
  Brooklyn (G-2604)

Stein Industries Inc ....E....... 631 789-2222
  Amityville (G-325)
Stereo Advantage Inc ....F....... 716 656-7161
  Cheektowaga (G-3590)
Telesca-Heyman Inc ....F....... 212 534-3442
  New York (G-12296)
Three R Enterprises Inc ....F....... 585 254-5050
  Rochester (G-14725)
Total Display Solutions Inc ....F....... 607 724-9999
  Binghamton (G-956)
Triad Counter Corp ....E....... 631 750-0615
  Bohemia (G-1146)
Unico Inc..F....... 845 562-9255
  Newburgh (G-12782)
Universal Designs Inc ....G....... 718 721-1111
  Long Island City (G-7910)
Vitarose Corp of America ....G....... 718 951-9700
  Brooklyn (G-2733)
Wares of Wood ....E....... 315 964-2983
  Williamstown (G-17229)
Wilbedone Inc ....E....... 607 756-8813
  Cortland (G-4047)
Wilsonart Intl Holdings LLC ....E....... 516 935-6980
  Bethpage (G-879)
Wineracksscom Inc ....E....... 845 658-7181
  Tillson (G-16130)
Wolak Inc ....G....... 315 839-5366
  Clayville (G-3691)

2542 Partitions & Fixtures, Except Wood

260 Oak Street Inc ....G....... 877 852-4676
  Buffalo (G-2788)
▲ Aarco Products Inc ....F....... 631 924-5461
  Yaphank (G-17384)
Abaco Steel Products Inc ....G....... 631 589-1800
  Bohemia (G-1002)
▲ Abbott Industries Inc ....E....... 718 291-0800
  Jamaica (G-6891)
Able Steel Equipment Co Inc ....F....... 718 361-9240
  Long Island City (G-7647)
Air Crafters Inc ....C....... 631 471-7788
  Ronkonkoma (G-14857)
All American Metal Corporation ....G....... 516 223-1760
  Freeport (G-5383)
All American Metal Corporation ....E....... 516 623-0222
  Freeport (G-5384)
All Racks Industries Inc ....E....... 212 244-1069
  New York (G-9085)
Alrod Associates Inc ....F....... 631 981-2193
  Ronkonkoma (G-14866)
American Standard Mfg Inc ....E....... 518 868-2512
  Central Bridge (G-3482)
ASAP Rack Rental Inc ....G....... 718 499-4495
  Brooklyn (G-1638)
◆ Avf Inc ....F....... 951 360-7111
  Buffalo (G-2827)
Bobrick Washroom Equipment Inc ......D....... 518 877-7444
  Clifton Park (G-3697)
▲ Bridge Metal Industries LLC ....C....... 914 663-9200
  Mount Vernon (G-8667)
Clark Specialty Co Inc ....E....... 607 776-3193
  Bath (G-655)
Custom Fixtures Inc ....G....... 718 965-1141
  Brooklyn (G-1825)
Dakota Systems Mfg Corp ....G....... 631 249-5811
  Farmingdale (G-4973)
Data Control Inc ....G....... 585 265-2980
  Ontario (G-13199)
Dejah Associates Inc ....E....... 631 265-2185
  Bay Shore (G-694)
Display Components Mfg Inc ....E....... 631 420-0600
  West Babylon (G-16789)
▲ Display Technologies LLC ....D....... 718 321-3100
  New Hyde Park (G-8827)
▲ E-Systems Group LLC ....E....... 607 775-1100
  Conklin (G-3868)
Eazy Movements ....G....... 716 837-2083
  Buffalo (G-2931)
Evans & Paul LLC ....E....... 516 576-0800
  Plainview (G-13600)
Exclusive Designs ....E....... 516 378-5258
  Freeport (G-5396)
▲ Fixture Hardware Mfg Corp ....E....... 718 499-9422
  Brooklyn (G-1980)
Four S Showcase Manufacturing ....G....... 718 649-4900
  Brooklyn (G-2001)
Frazier Industrial Company ....D....... 315 539-9256
  Waterloo (G-16626)
▼ Gaylord Bros Inc ....F....... 315 457-5070
  North Syracuse (G-12944)

▲ Gerald Frd Packg Display LLC ....F....... 716 692-2705
  Tonawanda (G-16165)
▲ Glaro Inc ....D....... 631 234-1717
  Hauppauge (G-6085)
▲ Glasbau Hahn America LLC ....G....... 845 566-3331
  Newburgh (G-12759)
◆ Global Steel Products Corp ....C....... 631 586-3455
  Deer Park (G-4147)
▲ Hamlet Products Inc ....F....... 914 665-0307
  Mount Vernon (G-8689)
Hawver Display Inc ....E....... 585 544-2290
  Rochester (G-14430)
◆ Hergo Ergonomic Support ....E....... 718 894-0639
  Maspeth (G-8143)
Hunter Metal Industries Inc ....D....... 631 475-5900
  East Patchogue (G-4448)
▲ Inscape (new York) Inc ....D....... 716 665-6210
  Falconer (G-4902)
Jack Luckner Steel Shelving Co ....D....... 718 363-0500
  Maspeth (G-8147)
Joldeson One Aerospace Inds ....D....... 718 848-7396
  Ozone Park (G-13380)
▲ Knickerbocker Partition Corp ....E....... 516 546-0550
  Freeport (G-5406)
▲ La Mar Lighting Co Inc ....D....... 631 777-7700
  Farmingdale (G-5032)
Ledan Inc ....E....... 631 239-1226
  Northport (G-13014)
◆ Lifestyle-Trimco ....E....... 718 257-9101
  Brooklyn (G-2219)
Locker Masters Inc ....E....... 518 288-3203
  Granville (G-5774)
▲ Lucia Group Inc ....G....... 631 392-4900
  Deer Park (G-4168)
Manhattan Display Inc ....G....... 718 392-1365
  Long Island City (G-7802)
▲ Mass Mdsg Self Selection Eqp ....E....... 631 234-3300
  Bohemia (G-1102)
▲ Maximum Security Products Corp ...E....... 518 233-1800
  Waterford (G-16613)
Mechtronics Corporation ....E....... 845 831-9300
  Beacon (G-787)
Mega Vision Inc ....E....... 718 228-1065
  Brooklyn (G-2295)
▲ Millennium Stl Rack Rntals Inc ......G....... 212 594-2190
  Brooklyn (G-2316)
▲ Milton Merl & Associates Inc ....E....... 212 634-9292
  New York (G-11271)
▲ Mobile Media Inc ....E....... 845 744-8080
  Pine Bush (G-13548)
Modern Craft Bar Rest Equip ....G....... 631 226-5647
  Lindenhurst (G-7473)
Modu-Craft Inc ....G....... 716 694-0709
  Tonawanda (G-16182)
Nationwide Exhibitor Svcs Inc ....F....... 631 467-2034
  Central Islip (G-3505)
▲ New Business Solutions Inc ....E....... 631 789-1500
  Amityville (G-316)
▲ Parabit Systems Inc ....E....... 516 378-4800
  Roosevelt (G-15008)
R H Guest Incorporated ....G....... 718 675-7600
  Brooklyn (G-2471)
S & K Counter Tops Inc ....G....... 716 662-7986
  Orchard Park (G-13296)
Steven Kraus Associates Inc ....G....... 631 923-2033
  Huntington (G-6682)
▲ Stone Expo & Cabinetry LLC ....F....... 516 292-2988
  West Hempstead (G-16863)
▲ Sturdy Store Displays Inc ....E....... 718 389-9919
  Brooklyn (G-2616)
Ted-Steel Industries Ltd ....G....... 212 279-3878
  New York (G-12293)
Traco Manufacturing Inc ....G....... 585 343-2434
  Batavia (G-651)
Tri-Boro Shlving Prtition Corp ....F....... 434 315-5600
  Ridgewood (G-14129)
Tri-Boro Shlving Prtition Corp ....F....... 718 782-8527
  Ridgewood (G-14130)
Trylon Wire & Metal Works Inc ....E....... 718 542-4472
  Bronx (G-1481)
Visual Millwork & Fixture Mfg ....D....... 718 267-7800
  Woodside (G-17361)
Yaloz Mould & Die Co Inc ....E....... 718 389-1131
  Brooklyn (G-2773)
Your Furniture Designers Inc ....G....... 845 947-3046
  West Haverstraw (G-16848)

SIC SECTION

2591 Drapery Hardware, Window Blinds & Shades

Company	Code	Phone
Abalene Decorating Services — New York (G-9000)	E	718 782-2000
Blinds To Go (us) Inc — Staten Island (G-15648)	E	718 477-9523
▲ Blindtek Designer Systems Inc — Elmsford (G-4737)	F	914 347-7100
▲ Comfortex Corporation — Watervliet (G-16683)	C	518 273-3333
D & D Window Tech Inc — New York (G-9782)	G	212 308-2822
Designers Touch Inc — Long Beach (G-7639)	G	718 641-3718
Drapery Industries Inc — Rochester (G-14318)	F	585 232-2992
Evolve Guest Controls LLC — Port Washington (G-13814)	F	855 750-9090
Fabric Quilters Unlimited Inc — Westbury (G-16984)	E	516 333-2866
Geigtech East Bay LLC — New York (G-10264)	F	844 543-4437
◆ Hunter Douglas Inc — Pearl River (G-13460)	D	845 664-7000
Hunter Douglas Inc — New York (G-10533)	C	212 588-0564
Instant Verticals Inc — Farmingdale (G-5012)	F	631 501-0001
J Gimbel Inc — West Hempstead (G-16857)	E	718 296-5200
KPP Ltd — Westbury (G-17004)	E	516 338-5201
▲ Levolor Window Furnishings Inc — Pearl River (G-13462)	B	845 664-7000
▼ Manhattan Shade & Glass Co Inc — New York (G-11133)	D	212 288-5616
McCarroll Uphl Designs LLC — Hudson (G-6625)	E	518 828-0500
◆ Mechoshade Systems Inc — Long Island City (G-7808)	C	718 729-2020
Nu Ways Inc — Rochester (G-14546)	G	585 254-7510
◆ P E Guerin — New York (G-11548)	D	212 243-5270
Pj Decorators Inc — East Meadow (G-4427)	E	516 735-9693
Solar Screen Co Inc — Corona (G-4007)	G	718 592-8222
Tentina Window Fashions Inc — Lindenhurst (G-7490)	C	631 957-9585
Vertical Research Partners LLC — New York (G-12530)	F	212 257-6499
Wcd Window Coverings Inc — Lake Katrine (G-7271)	E	845 336-4511
Window Workshops Inc — Buffalo (G-3257)	F	716 876-9981
◆ Windowcraft Inc — Garden City Park (G-5544)	F	516 294-3580
Windowtex Inc — Garden City Park (G-5545)	G	877 294-3580

2599 Furniture & Fixtures, NEC

Company	Code	Phone
A-Plus Restaurant Equipment — Brooklyn (G-1542)	F	718 522-2656
▲ Adirondack Scenic Inc — Argyle (G-409)	D	518 638-8000
▲ AFC Industries Inc — College Point (G-3777)	D	347 532-1200
All Star Carts & Vehicles Inc — Bay Shore (G-668)	D	631 666-5581
▲ Arper USA Inc — New York (G-9207)	G	212 647-8900
Artistry In Wood of Syracuse — East Syracuse (G-4506)	F	315 431-4022
Brandt Equipment LLC — Bronx (G-1288)	G	718 994-0800
Carts Mobile Food Eqp Corp — Brooklyn (G-1761)	F	718 788-5540
Creative Stone & Cabinets — Selden (G-15350)	G	631 772-6548
Dellet Industries Inc — Brooklyn (G-1850)	F	718 965-0101
Dine Rite Seating Products Inc — Lindenhurst (G-7462)	E	631 592-8126
Durall Dolly LLC — Brooklyn (G-1883)	F	802 728-7122
Evans & Paul LLC — Plainview (G-13600)	E	516 576-0800
Excel Commercial Seating — Lindenhurst (G-7464)	E	828 428-8338
Futon City Discounters Inc — Syracuse (G-15944)	F	315 437-1328
G Z G Rest & Kit Met Works — Brooklyn (G-2011)	F	718 788-8621
Halfway House LLC — Elizabethtown (G-4628)	G	518 873-2198
▼ Hard Manufacturing Co Inc — Buffalo (G-2988)	D	716 893-1800
▲ Hunt Country Furniture Inc — Wingdale (G-17274)	D	845 832-6601
Inova LLC — Altamont (G-209)	F	518 861-3400
Interiors-Pft Inc — Long Island City (G-7767)	E	212 244-9600
J P Installations Warehouse — New Rochelle (G-8914)	F	914 576-3188
Kedco Inc — Farmingdale (G-5025)	F	516 454-7800
Kinfolk Studios Inc — Brooklyn (G-2171)	F	347 799-2946
Kinplex Corp — Edgewood (G-4604)	E	631 242-4800
L & D Manufacturing Corp — Bronx (G-1375)	G	718 665-5226
Lafayette Pub Inc — New York (G-10915)	E	212 925-4242
▲ Lb Furniture Industries LLC — Hudson (G-6624)	C	518 828-1501
Maxsun Corporation — Maspeth (G-8151)	F	718 418-6800
Modern Craft Bar Rest Equip — Lindenhurst (G-7473)	F	631 226-5647
Modu-Craft Inc — North Tonawanda (G-12982)	F	716 694-0709
Modu-Craft Inc — Tonawanda (G-16182)	F	716 694-0709
Monroe Table Company Inc — Salamanca (G-15102)	F	716 945-7700
▲ N3a Corporation — Inwood (G-6762)	F	516 284-6799
▲ NK Medical Products Inc — Amherst (G-254)	G	716 759-7200
◆ Novum Medical Products Inc — Amherst (G-255)	F	716 759-7200
▼ Porta Decor — Hicksville (G-6390)	F	516 826-6900
R V H Estates Inc — Mount Vernon (G-8724)	G	914 664-9888
▲ Ramler International Ltd — Syosset (G-15836)	E	516 353-3106
Restaurant 570 8th Avenue LLC — New York (G-11844)	F	646 722-8191
Rollhaus Seating Products Inc — Long Island City (G-7863)	F	718 729-9111
Sandys Deli Inc — Rouses Point (G-15044)	G	518 297-6951
Smart Space Products LLC — New York (G-12101)	F	877 777-2441
▼ Starliner Shipping & Travel — Brooklyn (G-2600)	F	718 385-1515
T O Gronlund Company Inc — New York (G-12268)	F	212 679-3535
T-Company LLC — Smithtown (G-15500)	F	646 290-6365
Thornwood Products Ltd — Thornwood (G-16122)	E	914 769-9161
▲ VSM Investors LLC — New York (G-12571)	F	212 351-1600
W&P Design LLC — Brooklyn (G-2741)	G	434 806-1443
Wood Etc Inc — Syracuse (G-16075)	F	315 484-9663

26 PAPER AND ALLIED PRODUCTS

2611 Pulp Mills

Company	Code	Phone
Advanced Recovery & Recycl LLC — Baldwinsville (G-565)	F	315 450-3301
Andritz Inc — Glens Falls (G-5670)	E	518 745-2988
APC Paper Company Inc — Norfolk (G-12897)	D	315 384-4225
▲ Cenibra Inc — New York (G-9561)	G	212 818-8242
Central Nat Pulp & Ppr Sls Inc — Purchase (G-13955)	A	914 696-9000
Georgia-Pacific Corrugated LLC — Batavia (G-635)	D	585 343-3800
Harvest Technologies Inc — Ballston Spa (G-599)	G	518 899-7124
International Paper Company — Conklin (G-3869)	C	607 775-1550
ITT Engineered Valves LLC — Seneca Falls (G-15363)	E	662 257-6982
ITT Industries Holdings Inc — White Plains (G-17129)	G	914 641-2000
Norton Pulpstones Incorporated — Lockport (G-7608)	G	716 433-9400
Owasco Recycling Center — Auburn (G-512)	G	315 252-0332
Parsons & Whittemore Inc — Port Chester (G-13756)	E	914 937-9009
Parsons Whittemore Entps Corp — Port Chester (G-13757)	E	914 937-9009
R D S Mountain View Trucking — Little Falls (G-7503)	G	315 823-4265
Recommunity Recycling — Beacon (G-789)	B	845 926-1071
Sierra Processing LLC — Schenectady (G-15297)	F	518 433-0020
Suffolk Indus Recovery Corp — Coram (G-3951)	D	631 732-6403

2621 Paper Mills

Company	Code	Phone
A-One Laminating Corp — Brooklyn (G-1540)	G	718 266-6002
Albany International Corp — Menands (G-8365)	C	518 445-2230
▲ Ampac Paper LLC — Walden (G-16530)	A	845 778-5511
Andex Corp — Rochester (G-14204)	E	585 328-3790
APC Paper Company Inc — Norfolk (G-12897)	D	315 384-4225
Atlas Recycling LLC — New York (G-9257)	G	212 925-3280
▼ Automation Papers Inc — Syracuse (G-15862)	G	315 432-0565
Batavia Legal Printing Inc — Le Roy (G-7403)	G	585 768-2100
▲ Bigrow Paper Mfg Corp — Brooklyn (G-1695)	F	718 624-4439
Bristol Core Inc — Canandaigua (G-3336)	F	585 919-0302
Bristol/White Plains — White Plains (G-17088)	F	914 681-1800
BSD Aluminum Foil LLC — Brooklyn (G-1735)	E	347 689-3875
Burrows Paper Corporation — Lyons Falls (G-7977)	E	315 348-8491
Burrows Paper Corporation — Little Falls (G-7497)	D	315 823-2300
Burrows Paper Corporation — Little Falls (G-7498)	D	315 823-2300
▲ Carta Usa LLC — Rochester (G-14260)	E	585 436-3012
▲ Cascades Tssue Group-Sales Inc — Waterford (G-16609)	E	819 363-5100
Chem-Puter Friendly Inc — Mount Sinai (G-8654)	E	631 331-2259
Citigroup Inc — New York (G-9624)	C	212 816-6000
Clearwater Paper Corporation — Gouverneur (G-5744)	D	315 287-1200
▲ Cottrell Paper Company Inc — Rock City Falls (G-14777)	E	518 885-1702
▲ Crosstex International Inc — Hauppauge (G-6058)	D	631 582-6777
Datagraphic Business Systems — Brentwood (G-1180)	F	516 485-9069
Donald Bruhnke — New York (G-9897)	F	212 600-1260
Donne Dieu — New York (G-9905)	G	212 226-0573
Dunmore Corporation — Brewster (G-1217)	G	845 279-5061
Dunn Paper - Natural Dam Inc — Gouverneur (G-5745)	D	315 287-1200
Euro Fine Paper Inc — Garden City (G-5503)	G	516 238-5253
Fibercel Packaging LLC — Portville (G-13874)	E	716 933-8703
Fibermark North America Inc — Brownville (G-2783)	D	315 782-5800
▲ Flower Cy Tissue Mills Co Inc — Rochester (G-14376)	E	585 458-9200
▲ Freeport Paper Industries Inc — Central Islip (G-3497)	D	631 851-1555
▲ Galison Publishing LLC — New York (G-10240)	E	212 354-8840

Employee Codes: A=Over 500 employees, B=251-500, C=101-250, D=51-100, E=20-50, F=10-19, G=5-9

Georgia-Pacific LLC ... A ... 518 561-3500
Plattsburgh *(G-13664)*

Gratitude & Company Inc ... G ... 607 277-3188
Ithaca *(G-6845)*

Hollingsworth & Vose Company ... C ... 518 695-8000
Greenwich *(G-5889)*

Huhtamaki Inc ... A ... 315 593-5311
Fulton *(G-5461)*

International Paper Company ... A ... 518 585-6761
Ticonderoga *(G-16126)*

International Paper Company ... C ... 845 986-6409
Tuxedo Park *(G-16284)*

International Paper Company ... C ... 607 775-1550
Conklin *(G-3869)*

International Paper Company ... C ... 315 797-5120
Utica *(G-16345)*

▲ Irving Consumer Products Inc ... B ... 518 747-4151
Fort Edward *(G-5342)*

Kapstone Container Corporation ... D ... 518 842-2450
Amsterdam *(G-352)*

◆ Knowlton Technologies LLC ... C ... 315 782-0600
Watertown *(G-16661)*

◆ Lenaro Paper Co Inc ... F ... 631 439-8800
Central Islip *(G-3502)*

Lion Die-Cutting Co Inc ... E ... 718 383-8841
Brooklyn *(G-2229)*

Minimill Technologies Inc ... F ... 315 692-4557
Syracuse *(G-15991)*

Mohawk Fine Papers Inc ... E ... 518 237-1741
Cohoes *(G-3752)*

▲ Mohawk Fine Papers Inc ... B ... 518 237-1740
Cohoes *(G-3751)*

National Paper Converting Inc ... G ... 607 687-6049
Owego *(G-13356)*

◆ Nice-Pak Products Inc ... B ... 845 365-2772
Orangeburg *(G-13236)*

Nice-Pak Products Inc ... E ... 845 353-6090
West Nyack *(G-16922)*

North End Paper Co Inc ... G ... 315 593-8100
Fulton *(G-5471)*

▲ NY Cutting Inc ... G ... 845 368-1459
Airmont *(G-17)*

▼ Omniafiltra LLC ... E ... 315 346-7300
Beaver Falls *(G-795)*

Pactiv LLC ... G ... 585 394-1525
Canandaigua *(G-3351)*

Palisades Paper Inc ... G ... 845 354-0333
Spring Valley *(G-15597)*

▲ Paper Solutions Inc ... F ... 718 499-4226
Brooklyn *(G-2404)*

◆ Plastirun Corporation ... E ... 631 273-2626
Brentwood *(G-1193)*

▼ Potsdam Specialty Paper Inc ... D ... 315 265-4000
Potsdam *(G-13881)*

▲ Precare Corp ... G ... 631 667-1055
Hauppauge *(G-6168)*

◆ Precision Charts Inc ... E ... 631 244-8295
Bohemia *(G-1120)*

◆ Professional Disposables Inc ... A ... 845 365-1700
Orangeburg *(G-13244)*

Refill Services LLC ... G ... 607 369-5864
Sidney *(G-15441)*

Sabin Robbins Paper Company ... E ... 513 874-5270
New York *(G-11950)*

Sca Tissue North America LLC ... E ... 518 692-8434
Greenwich *(G-5892)*

Sca Tissue North America LLC ... C ... 518 583-2785
Saratoga Springs *(G-15172)*

▲ Scalamandre Wallpaper Inc ... B ... 631 467-8800
Hauppauge *(G-6185)*

Schweitzer-Mauduit Intl Inc ... C ... 518 329-4222
Ancram *(G-375)*

Stephen Singer Pattern Co Inc ... F ... 212 947-2902
New York *(G-12196)*

Summit Financial Printing LLC ... E ... 212 913-0510
New York *(G-12233)*

▲ T & L Trading Co ... G ... 718 782-5550
Brooklyn *(G-2637)*

Tag Envelope Co Inc ... E ... 718 389-6844
College Point *(G-3809)*

United Data Forms Inc ... F ... 631 218-0104
Bohemia *(G-1151)*

Verso Corporation ... B ... 212 599-2700
New York *(G-12526)*

Verso Paper Management LP ... A ... 781 320-8660
New York *(G-12527)*

Verso Paper Management LP ... G ... 212 599-2700
New York *(G-12528)*

2631 Paperboard Mills

Alpine Paper Box Co Inc ... E ... 718 345-4040
Brooklyn *(G-1595)*

◆ American Wire Tie Inc ... E ... 716 337-2412
North Collins *(G-12926)*

Base Container Inc ... F ... 718 636-2004
Brooklyn *(G-1669)*

▲ Burt Rigid Box Inc ... F ... 607 433-2510
Oneonta *(G-13176)*

Cascades Cntnerboard Packg Inc ... C ... 716 285-3681
Niagara Falls *(G-12801)*

▲ Cascades Cntnerboard Packg Inc ... C ... 450 923-3031
Niagara Falls *(G-12802)*

▼ Continental Kraft Corp ... G ... 516 681-9090
Jericho *(G-7063)*

Di Domenico Packaging Co Inc ... G ... 718 727-5454
Staten Island *(G-15665)*

Enterprise Folding Box Co Inc ... E ... 716 876-6421
Buffalo *(G-2941)*

Farrington Packaging Corp ... E ... 315 733-4600
Utica *(G-16331)*

Fibermark North America Inc ... D ... 315 782-5800
Brownville *(G-2783)*

▲ Greenpac Mill LLC ... D ... 716 299-0560
Niagara Falls *(G-12829)*

Interface Performance Mtls Inc ... D ... 518 686-3400
Hoosick Falls *(G-6540)*

International Paper Company ... C ... 607 775-1550
Conklin *(G-3869)*

Kapstone Container Corporation ... D ... 518 842-2450
Amsterdam *(G-352)*

M&F Stringing LLC ... E ... 914 664-1600
Mount Vernon *(G-8703)*

Ms Paper Products Co Inc ... G ... 718 624-0248
Brooklyn *(G-2342)*

Multi Packaging Solutions Inc ... D ... 812 422-4104
Hicksville *(G-6376)*

Niagara Fiberboard Inc ... E ... 716 434-8881
Lockport *(G-7605)*

Pactiv LLC ... E ... 585 248-1213
Pittsford *(G-13573)*

Paper Box Corp ... D ... 212 226-7490
New York *(G-11563)*

Pdf Seal Incorporated ... E ... 631 595-7035
Deer Park *(G-4188)*

Pkg Group ... G ... 212 965-0112
New York *(G-11672)*

Prestige Box Corporation ... E ... 516 773-3115
Great Neck *(G-5833)*

Professional Packg Svcs Inc ... E ... 518 677-5100
Eagle Bridge *(G-4357)*

◆ Royal Industries Inc ... E ... 718 369-3046
Brooklyn *(G-2511)*

Small Packages Inc ... G ... 845 255-7710
New Paltz *(G-8878)*

Solomon Schwimmer ... G ... 718 625-5719
Brooklyn *(G-2583)*

▲ Tin Box Company of America Inc ... E ... 631 845-1600
Farmingdale *(G-5132)*

▲ Westrock - Solvay Llc ... C ... 315 484-9050
Syracuse *(G-16070)*

Westrock CP LLC ... D ... 315 484-9050
Syracuse *(G-16071)*

Westrock Mwv LLC ... C ... 212 688-5000
New York *(G-12618)*

Westrock Rkt Company ... C ... 770 448-2193
Syracuse *(G-16072)*

2652 Set-Up Paperboard Boxes

A Fleisig Paper Box Corp ... F ... 212 226-7490
New York *(G-8986)*

American Package Company Inc ... E ... 718 389-4444
Brooklyn *(G-1605)*

▲ Brick & Ballerstein Inc ... D ... 718 497-1400
Ridgewood *(G-14103)*

Burt Rigid Box Inc ... D ... 607 433-2510
Oneonta *(G-13175)*

Clarke-Boxit Corporation ... G ... 716 487-1950
Jamestown *(G-6980)*

Drescher Paper Box Inc ... F ... 716 854-0288
Buffalo *(G-2918)*

Earlville Paper Box Co Inc ... E ... 315 691-2131
Earlville *(G-4360)*

▲ F M Howell & Company ... D ... 607 734-6291
Elmira *(G-4684)*

Fairview Paper Box Corp ... E ... 585 786-5230
Warsaw *(G-16582)*

Friedel Paper Box & Converting ... G ... 315 437-3325
Baldwinsville *(G-569)*

Jordon Box Company Inc ... E ... 315 422-3419
Syracuse *(G-15970)*

Ketchum Manufacturing Co Inc ... F ... 518 696-3331
Lake Luzerne *(G-7272)*

Lionel Habas Associates Inc ... F ... 212 860-8454
New York *(G-11005)*

Parlor City Paper Box Co Inc ... D ... 607 772-0600
Binghamton *(G-941)*

▲ Paul T Freund Corporation ... D ... 315 597-4873
Palmyra *(G-13413)*

Prestige Box Corporation ... E ... 516 773-3115
Great Neck *(G-5833)*

Propak Inc ... G ... 518 677-5100
Eagle Bridge *(G-4358)*

Pure Trade Us Inc ... E ... 212 256-1600
New York *(G-11751)*

▲ Seneca FLS Spc & Logistics Co ... D ... 315 568-4139
Seneca Falls *(G-15370)*

West Gluers ... G ... 631 232-1235
Hauppauge *(G-6233)*

2653 Corrugated & Solid Fiber Boxes

Action Rack Display Mfg ... F ... 718 257-7111
Brooklyn *(G-1558)*

Ares Printing and Packg Corp ... C ... 718 858-8760
Brooklyn *(G-1625)*

▼ Arma Container Corp ... E ... 631 254-1200
Deer Park *(G-4101)*

Bellotti Packaging Inc ... F ... 315 433-0131
East Syracuse *(G-4510)*

Buckeye Corrugated Inc ... G ... 315 437-1181
Syracuse *(G-15876)*

Buckeye Corrugated Inc ... D ... 585 924-1600
Victor *(G-16465)*

Burt Rigid Box Inc ... D ... 607 433-2510
Oneonta *(G-13175)*

Calpac Incorporated ... F ... 631 789-0502
Amityville *(G-279)*

▲ Cascades Cntnerboard Packg Inc ... C ... 450 923-3031
Niagara Falls *(G-12802)*

▲ Cascades USA Inc ... E ... 518 880-3632
Waterford *(G-16610)*

Cattaraugus Containers Inc ... E ... 716 676-2000
Franklinville *(G-5369)*

▲ Color Carton Corp ... D ... 718 665-0840
Bronx *(G-1302)*

Displays & Beyond Inc ... F ... 718 805-7786
Glendale *(G-5651)*

Dory Enterprises Inc ... F ... 607 565-7079
Waverly *(G-16701)*

Enterprise Container LLC ... E ... 631 253-4400
Wyandanch *(G-17375)*

Fennell Industries LLC ... E ... 607 733-6693
Elmira *(G-4685)*

Fiber USA Corp ... G ... 718 888-1512
Flushing *(G-5241)*

Gavin Mfg Corp ... E ... 631 467-0040
Farmingdale *(G-4997)*

▲ General Die and Die Cutng Inc ... D ... 516 665-3584
Roosevelt *(G-15004)*

▲ General Fibre Products Corp ... D ... 516 358-7500
New Hyde Park *(G-8835)*

Georgia-Pacific LLC ... C ... 518 346-6151
Schenectady *(G-15264)*

Inner-Pak Container Inc ... F ... 631 289-9700
Patchogue *(G-13423)*

International Paper Company ... C ... 585 663-1000
Rochester *(G-14452)*

International Paper Company ... F ... 716 852-2144
Buffalo *(G-3012)*

International Paper Company ... D ... 518 372-6461
Glenville *(G-5702)*

International Paper Company ... C ... 607 775-1550
Conklin *(G-3869)*

Island Container Corp ... D ... 631 253-4400
Wyandanch *(G-17376)*

Jamestown Cont of Rochester ... D ... 585 254-9190
Rochester *(G-14460)*

▼ Jamestown Container Corp ... D ... 716 665-4623
Falconer *(G-4904)*

Kapstone Container Corporation ... D ... 518 842-2450
Amsterdam *(G-352)*

Key Container Corp ... G ... 631 582-3847
East Islip *(G-4417)*

Lakeside Container Corp ... F ... 518 561-6150
Plattsburgh *(G-13675)*

Land Packaging Corp ... F ... 914 472-5976
Scarsdale *(G-15220)*

Lee Philips Packaging Inc ... F ... 631 580-3306
Ronkonkoma *(G-14931)*

SIC SECTION
26 PAPER AND ALLIED PRODUCTS

M C Packaging Corporation ....E 631 643-3763
  Babylon *(G-550)*
Mechtronics Corporation ....E 845 831-9300
  Beacon *(G-787)*
Mkt329 Inc ....F 631 249-5500
  Farmingdale *(G-5059)*
▲ Mp Displays LLC ....G 845 268-4113
  Valley Cottage *(G-16383)*
▲ Niagara Sheets LLC ....D 716 692-1129
  North Tonawanda *(G-12983)*
Norampac New England Inc ....C 860 923-9563
  Schenectady *(G-15282)*
Norampac New York City Inc ....C 718 340-2100
  Maspeth *(G-8158)*
Norampac Schenectady Inc ....C 518 346-6151
  Schenectady *(G-15283)*
▲ Orcon Industries Corp ....E 585 768-7000
  Le Roy *(G-7417)*
Packaging Corporation America ....C 315 457-6780
  Liverpool *(G-7538)*
Packaging Corporation America ....F 315 785-9083
  Watertown *(G-16669)*
Pactiv LLC ....C 315 457-6780
  Liverpool *(G-7539)*
Pactiv LLC ....E 585 248-1213
  Pittsford *(G-13573)*
Parlor City Paper Box Co Inc ....D 607 772-0600
  Binghamton *(G-941)*
Philpac Corporation ....E 716 875-8005
  Buffalo *(G-3124)*
President Cont Group II LLC ....E 845 516-1600
  Middletown *(G-8457)*
Prestige Box Corporation ....E 516 773-3115
  Great Neck *(G-5833)*
Professional Packg Svcs Inc ....E 518 677-5100
  Eagle Bridge *(G-4357)*
R D A Container Corporation ....E 585 247-2323
  Gates *(G-5563)*
▲ Seneca FLS Spc & Logistics Co .....D 315 568-4139
  Seneca Falls *(G-15370)*
▲ Spaeth Design Inc ....E 718 606-9685
  Woodside *(G-17353)*
▲ Specialized Packg Group Inc ....G 315 638-4355
  Baldwinsville *(G-575)*
Specialized Packg Radisson LLC ....C 315 638-4355
  Baldwinsville *(G-576)*
Star Corrugated Box Co Inc ....G 718 386-3200
  Flushing *(G-5296)*
Syracuse Corrugated Box Corp ....F 315 437-9901
  East Syracuse *(G-4570)*
Technical Library Service Inc ....F 212 219-0770
  Brooklyn *(G-2649)*
Technical Packaging Inc ....F 516 223-2300
  Baldwin *(G-562)*
Track 7 Inc ....G 845 544-1810
  Warwick *(G-16596)*
Valentine Packaging Corp ....F 718 418-6000
  Maspeth *(G-8175)*
WA Packaging LLC ....E 518 724-6466
  Schenectady *(G-15311)*
Westrock - Southern Cont LLC ....C 315 487-6111
  Camillus *(G-3327)*
Westrock Cp LLC ....C 770 448-2193
  New Hartford *(G-8813)*
Westrock CP LLC ....C 716 694-1000
  North Tonawanda *(G-13006)*
Westrock CP LLC ....C 716 692-6510
  North Tonawanda *(G-13007)*
Westrock Rkt Company ....C 330 296-5155
  Deer Park *(G-4226)*
Westrock Rkt Company ....C 770 448-2193
  Camillus *(G-3328)*

2655 Fiber Cans, Tubes & Drums

Acran Spill Containment Inc ....G 631 841-2300
  Amityville *(G-274)*
American Intrmdal Cont Mfg LLC ....G 631 774-6790
  Hauppauge *(G-6022)*
Caraustar Industries Inc ....G 716 874-0393
  Buffalo *(G-2867)*
Carthage Fibre Drum Inc ....F 315 493-2730
  Carthage *(G-3408)*
Consolidated Container Co LLC ....C 585 262-6470
  Rochester *(G-14288)*
▲ Custom Manufacturing Inc ....G 607 569-2738
  Hammondsport *(G-5954)*
◆ Diemolding Corporation ....G 315 697-2221
  Canastota *(G-3367)*
Diemolding Corporation ....G 315 697-2221
  Canastota *(G-3368)*

Greif Inc ....D 716 836-4200
  Tonawanda *(G-16169)*
Industrial Paper Tube Inc ....F 718 893-5000
  Bronx *(G-1361)*
Kuraray America Inc ....E 212 986-2230
  New York *(G-10893)*
Philpac Corporation ....E 716 875-8005
  Buffalo *(G-3124)*
▲ Skydyne Company ....D 845 858-6400
  Port Jervis *(G-13793)*
Syraco Products Inc ....E 800 581-5555
  Syracuse *(G-16047)*

2656 Sanitary Food Containers

◆ Amscan Inc ....C 914 345-2020
  Elmsford *(G-4732)*
Amscan Inc ....D 845 469-9116
  Chester *(G-3599)*
Amscan Inc ....D 845 782-0490
  Harriman *(G-5970)*
Apexx Omni-Graphics Inc ....D 718 326-3330
  Maspeth *(G-8119)*
Consolidated Container Co LLC ....C 585 262-6470
  Rochester *(G-14288)*
International Paper Company ....C 607 775-1550
  Conklin *(G-3869)*
▲ Last Straw Inc ....E 516 371-2727
  Lawrence *(G-7393)*
Pactiv LLC ....C 518 562-6101
  Plattsburgh *(G-13684)*
◆ Plastirun Corporation ....E 631 273-2626
  Brentwood *(G-1193)*
▲ Sqp Inc ....C 518 831-6800
  Schenectady *(G-15299)*

2657 Folding Paperboard Boxes

Abbot & Abbot Box Corp ....F 888 930-5972
  Long Island City *(G-7646)*
Alpha Packaging Industries Inc ....E 718 267-4115
  Long Island City *(G-7654)*
▲ Arkay Packaging Corporation ....E 631 273-2000
  Hauppauge *(G-6024)*
Burt Rigid Box Inc ....D 607 433-2510
  Oneonta *(G-13175)*
Cattaraugus Containers Inc ....E 716 676-2000
  Franklinville *(G-5369)*
▲ Climax Manufacturing Company ....C 315 376-8000
  Carthage *(G-3412)*
Climax Manufacturing Company ....C 315 376-8000
  Castorland *(G-3422)*
Climax Packaging Inc ....C 315 376-8000
  Lowville *(G-7935)*
▲ Color Carton Corp ....D 718 665-0840
  Bronx *(G-1302)*
Designers Folding Box Corp ....E 716 853-5141
  Buffalo *(G-2910)*
Diamond Packaging Holdings LLC ....G 585 334-8030
  Rochester *(G-14306)*
Disc Graphics Inc ....C 631 300-1129
  Hauppauge *(G-6063)*
▲ Disc Graphics Inc ....B 631 234-1400
  Hauppauge *(G-6064)*
▲ F M Howell & Company ....D 607 734-6291
  Elmira *(G-4684)*
Flower City Printing Inc ....E 585 663-9000
  Rochester *(G-14374)*
Gavin Mfg Corp ....E 631 467-0040
  Farmingdale *(G-4997)*
▼ Gaylord Bros Inc ....D 315 457-5070
  North Syracuse *(G-12944)*
▲ HSM Packaging Corporation ....D 315 476-7996
  Liverpool *(G-7523)*
▲ Knoll Printing & Packaging Inc ....E 516 621-0100
  Syosset *(G-15826)*
M C Packaging Corporation ....E 631 643-3763
  Babylon *(G-550)*
▼ Mod-Pac Corp ....C 716 873-0640
  Buffalo *(G-3071)*
Multi Packg Solutions Intl Ltd ....G 646 885-0005
  New York *(G-11325)*
▲ Novel Box Company Ltd ....E 718 965-2222
  Brooklyn *(G-2377)*
Pactiv LLC ....C 518 562-6101
  Plattsburgh *(G-13684)*
Paper Box Corp ....D 212 226-7490
  New York *(G-11563)*
Premier Packaging Corporation ....E 585 924-8460
  Victor *(G-16496)*
Prestige Box Corporation ....E 516 773-3115
  Great Neck *(G-5833)*

▲ Specialized Packg Group Inc ....G 315 638-4355
  Baldwinsville *(G-575)*
Specialized Packg Radisson LLC ....C 315 638-4355
  Baldwinsville *(G-576)*
▲ Standard Group ....E 718 335-5500
  East Elmhurst *(G-4397)*
▲ Standard Group LLC ....C 718 507-6430
  East Elmhurst *(G-4398)*
Viking Industries Inc ....D 845 883-6325
  New Paltz *(G-8882)*
Visitainer Corp ....E 718 636-0300
  Brooklyn *(G-2731)*

2671 Paper Coating & Laminating for Packaging

▲ Allen-Bailey Tag & Label Inc ....D 585 538-2324
  Caledonia *(G-3276)*
◆ Allied Converters Inc ....E 914 235-1585
  New Rochelle *(G-8886)*
▲ American Packaging Corporation ...C 585 254-9500
  Rochester *(G-14198)*
Anasia Inc ....E 718 588-1407
  Bronx *(G-1275)*
Apexx Omni-Graphics Inc ....D 718 326-3330
  Maspeth *(G-8119)*
Ares Box LLC ....E 718 858-8760
  Brooklyn *(G-1624)*
Bemis Company Inc ....C 631 794-2900
  Edgewood *(G-4594)*
Berry Plastics Corporation ....B 315 986-6270
  Macedon *(G-7984)*
Cameo Process Corp ....E 914 948-0082
  White Plains *(G-17092)*
CCL Label Inc ....C 716 852-2155
  Buffalo *(G-2868)*
Classic Labels Inc ....E 631 467-2300
  Patchogue *(G-13417)*
Colad Group LLC ....D 716 961-1776
  Buffalo *(G-2880)*
Cove Point Holdings LLC ....F 212 599-3388
  New York *(G-9740)*
Craft Packaging Inc ....G 718 633-4045
  Brooklyn *(G-1811)*
De Luxe Packaging Corp ....E 416 754-4633
  Saugerties *(G-15183)*
Depot Label Company Inc ....C 631 467-2952
  Patchogue *(G-13418)*
Ecoplast & Packaging LLC ....E 718 996-0800
  Brooklyn *(G-1901)*
▲ F M Howell & Company ....D 607 734-6291
  Elmira *(G-4684)*
▲ Folene Packaging LLC ....E 917 626-6740
  Brooklyn *(G-1992)*
▲ General Fibre Products Corp ....D 516 358-7500
  New Hyde Park *(G-8835)*
General Trade Mark La ....E 718 979-7261
  Staten Island *(G-15677)*
Idesco Corp ....F 212 889-2530
  New York *(G-10557)*
International Paper Company ....C 585 663-1000
  Rochester *(G-14452)*
▲ K Sidrane Inc ....E 631 393-6974
  Farmingdale *(G-5021)*
▲ Kal Pac Corp ....F 845 457-7013
  Montgomery *(G-8597)*
Mason Transparent Package Inc ....E 718 792-6000
  Bronx *(G-1388)*
Multi Packaging Solutions Inc ....C 516 488-2000
  Hicksville *(G-6375)*
◆ Multi Packaging Solutions Inc ....E 646 885-0157
  New York *(G-11324)*
Nameplate Mfrs of Amer ....E 631 752-0055
  Farmingdale *(G-5061)*
Nova Packaging Ltd Inc ....G 914 232-8406
  Katonah *(G-7133)*
▲ Packstar Group Inc ....D 716 853-1688
  Buffalo *(G-3111)*
▲ Pactech Packaging LLC ....D 585 458-8008
  Rochester *(G-14566)*
Pactiv LLC ....C 518 562-6101
  Plattsburgh *(G-13684)*
Paperworks Industries Inc ....F 913 621-0922
  Baldwinsville *(G-573)*
Patco Tapes Inc ....G 718 497-1527
  Maspeth *(G-8164)*
Penta-Tech Coated Products LLC ......F 315 986-4098
  Macedon *(G-7989)*
Pliant LLC ....B 315 986-6286
  Macedon *(G-7990)*

Pregis LLC .... D 518 743-3100
Glens Falls *(G-5697)*

◆ **Print Pack Inc** .... C 404 460-7000
Farmingdale *(G-5088)*

▲ **Printex Packaging Corporation** .... D 631 234-4300
Islandia *(G-6801)*

◆ **Quality Circle Products Inc** .... D 914 736-6600
Montrose *(G-8614)*

▲ **RMS Packaging Inc** .... F 914 205-2070
Peekskill *(G-13481)*

▼ **Rynone Packaging Corp** .... G 607 565-8173
Waverly *(G-16707)*

Saint-Gobain Prfmce Plas Corp .... C 518 642-2200
Granville *(G-5781)*

Sealed Air Corporation .... C 518 370-1693
Schenectady *(G-15295)*

▲ **Shaant Industries Inc** .... E 716 366-3654
Dunkirk *(G-4350)*

Smart USA Inc .... E 718 416-4400
Glendale *(G-5663)*

▲ **Time Release Sciences Inc** .... E 716 823-4580
Buffalo *(G-3219)*

◆ **Transcntinental Ultra Flex Inc** .... B 718 272-9100
Brooklyn *(G-2674)*

▲ **Tri-Plex Packaging Corporation** .... E 212 481-6070
New York *(G-12401)*

▲ **Universal Packg Systems Inc** .... A 631 543-2277
Commack *(G-3845)*

Valley Industrial Products Inc .... E 631 385-9300
Huntington *(G-6689)*

◆ **Vitex Packaging Group Inc** .... F 212 265-6575
New York *(G-12557)*

W E W Container Corporation .... E 718 827-8150
Brooklyn *(G-2740)*

Westrock Mwv LLC .... C 212 688-5000
New York *(G-12618)*

2672 Paper Coating & Laminating, Exc for Packaging

3 Star Papers Limited .... F 718 499-5481
Brooklyn *(G-1514)*

A-One Laminating Corp .... G 718 266-6002
Brooklyn *(G-1540)*

▲ **Adchem Corp** .... C 631 727-6000
Riverhead *(G-14137)*

Adflex Corporation .... E 585 454-2950
Rochester *(G-14173)*

▼ **Advanced Graphics Company** .... F 607 692-7875
Whitney Point *(G-17219)*

Albany International Corp .... D 518 447-6400
Menands *(G-8366)*

▲ **Allen-Bailey Tag & Label Inc** .... D 585 538-2324
Caledonia *(G-3276)*

Avery Dennison Corporation .... C 845 680-3873
Orangeburg *(G-13220)*

Avery Dennison Corporation .... C 626 304-2000
New York *(G-9276)*

C & R De Santis Inc .... E 718 447-5076
Staten Island *(G-15653)*

CCL Label Inc .... C 716 852-2155
Buffalo *(G-2868)*

Classic Labels Inc .... E 631 467-2300
Patchogue *(G-13417)*

Cove Point Holdings LLC .... F 212 599-3388
New York *(G-9740)*

Cytec Industries Inc .... D 716 372-9650
Olean *(G-13142)*

D W S Associates Inc .... E 631 667-6616
Deer Park *(G-4125)*

Dunmore Corporation .... D 845 279-5061
Brewster *(G-1217)*

Eis Inc .... D 585 426-5330
Rochester *(G-14341)*

Fibermark North America Inc .... C 315 376-3571
Lowville *(G-7937)*

Greenbush Tape & Label Inc .... E 518 465-2389
Albany *(G-83)*

Itac Label & Tag Corp .... G 718 625-2148
Brooklyn *(G-2119)*

▲ **K Sidrane Inc** .... E 631 393-6974
Farmingdale *(G-5021)*

▲ **Kleen Stik Industries Inc** .... F 718 984-5031
Staten Island *(G-15696)*

Label Gallery Inc .... E 607 334-3244
Norwich *(G-13030)*

Label Makers Inc .... E 631 319-6329
Bohemia *(G-1090)*

Liberty Label Mfg Inc .... F 631 737-2365
Holbrook *(G-6457)*

◆ **Merco Hackensack Inc** .... G 845 357-3699
Hillburn *(G-6416)*

Micro Essential Laboratory .... E 718 338-3618
Brooklyn *(G-2310)*

Miken Companies Inc .... D 716 668-6311
Buffalo *(G-3065)*

▲ **Mohawk Fine Papers Inc** .... B 518 237-1740
Cohoes *(G-3751)*

New York Cutting & Gumming Co .... E 212 563-4146
Middletown *(G-8454)*

Oaklee International Inc .... D 631 436-7900
Ronkonkoma *(G-14958)*

▲ **Overnight Labels Inc** .... E 631 242-4240
Deer Park *(G-4186)*

▲ **P C I Paper Conversions Inc** .... C 315 437-1641
Syracuse *(G-16006)*

Paris Art Label Co Inc .... D 631 467-2300
Patchogue *(G-13429)*

Patco Tapes Inc .... G 718 497-1527
Maspeth *(G-8164)*

Princeton Label & Packaging .... E 609 490-0800
Patchogue *(G-13433)*

▲ **Rochester 100 Inc** .... C 585 475-0200
Rochester *(G-14633)*

▲ **S & S Prtg Die-Cutting Co Inc** .... F 718 388-8990
Brooklyn *(G-2522)*

Stoney Croft Converters Inc .... F 718 608-9800
Staten Island *(G-15741)*

Syracuse Label Co Inc .... D 315 422-1037
Liverpool *(G-7550)*

T L F Graphics Inc .... D 585 272-5500
Rochester *(G-14716)*

▲ **Tape-It Inc** .... E 631 243-4100
Bay Shore *(G-750)*

▲ **Tri Star Label Inc** .... G 914 237-4800
Mount Vernon *(G-8740)*

▲ **Tri-Flex Label Corp** .... E 631 293-0411
Farmingdale *(G-5133)*

Triangle Label Tag Inc .... G 718 875-3030
Brooklyn *(G-2679)*

Valley Industrial Products Inc .... E 631 385-9300
Huntington *(G-6689)*

2673 Bags: Plastics, Laminated & Coated

Adart Polyethylene Bag Mfg .... G 516 932-1001
Plainview *(G-13576)*

▲ **Aladdin Packaging LLC** .... D 631 273-4747
Hauppauge *(G-6014)*

Alco Plastics Inc .... E 716 683-3020
Lancaster *(G-7301)*

◆ **Allied Converters Inc** .... E 914 235-1585
New Rochelle *(G-8886)*

▲ **Amby International Inc** .... G 718 645-0964
Brooklyn *(G-1597)*

▲ **American Packaging Corporation** .... C 585 254-9500
Rochester *(G-14198)*

◆ **API Industries Inc** .... B 845 365-2200
Orangeburg *(G-13218)*

API Industries Inc .... C 845 365-2200
Orangeburg *(G-13219)*

Bag Arts The Art Packaging LLC .... G 212 684-7020
New York *(G-9303)*

Baggu .... G 347 457-5266
Brooklyn *(G-1664)*

▲ **Bags Unlimited Inc** .... E 585 436-6282
Rochester *(G-14221)*

▲ **Basic Ltd** .... E 718 438-5576
Brooklyn *(G-1670)*

▲ **Bison Bag Co Inc** .... D 716 434-4380
Lockport *(G-7572)*

Capitol Poly Corp .... E 718 855-6000
Brooklyn *(G-1755)*

Clear View Bag Company Inc .... C 518 458-7153
Albany *(G-64)*

Colden Closet LLC .... G 716 713-6125
East Aurora *(G-4368)*

Connover Packaging Inc .... G 585 377-2510
East Rochester *(G-4456)*

Courier Packaging Inc .... E 718 349-2390
Brooklyn *(G-1809)*

Craft Pak Inc .... G 718 257-2700
Staten Island *(G-15663)*

Craft-Pak Inc .... F 718 763-0700
Brooklyn *(G-1812)*

Ecoplast & Packaging LLC .... G 718 996-0800
Brooklyn *(G-1901)*

Edco Supply Corporation .... D 718 788-8108
Brooklyn *(G-1903)*

Excellent Poly Inc .... F 718 768-6555
Brooklyn *(G-1943)*

◆ **Excelsior Packaging Group Inc** .... C 914 968-1300
Yonkers *(G-17442)*

Filmpak Extrusion LLC .... D 631 293-6767
Melville *(G-8319)*

▲ **Fortune Poly Products Inc** .... F 718 361-0767
Jamaica *(G-6912)*

▼ **Franklin Poly Film Inc** .... E 718 492-3523
Brooklyn *(G-2002)*

Garb-O-Liner Inc .... G 914 235-1585
New Rochelle *(G-8904)*

Golden Group International Ltd .... G 845 440-1025
Patterson *(G-13440)*

▲ **H G Maybeck Co Inc** .... E 718 297-4410
Jamaica *(G-6918)*

◆ **Ivi Services Inc** .... D 607 729-5111
Binghamton *(G-929)*

Jad Corp of America .... E 718 762-8900
College Point *(G-3792)*

▲ **Jay Bags Inc** .... G 845 459-6500
Spring Valley *(G-15590)*

▲ **JM Murray Center Inc** .... C 607 756-9913
Cortland *(G-4031)*

JM Murray Center Inc .... C 607 756-0246
Cortland *(G-4032)*

▲ **Josh Packaging Inc** .... E 631 822-1660
Hauppauge *(G-6102)*

Kemco Sales LLC .... F 203 762-1902
East Rochester *(G-4463)*

▲ **Maco Bag Corporation** .... C 315 226-1000
Newark *(G-12735)*

◆ **Magcrest Packaging Inc** .... G 845 425-0451
Monsey *(G-8574)*

Manhattan Poly Bag Corporation .... E 917 689-7549
Brooklyn *(G-2260)*

Mason Transparent Package Inc .... E 718 792-6000
Bronx *(G-1388)*

Metpak Inc .... G 917 309-0196
Brooklyn *(G-2304)*

Metro Lining Company .... G 718 383-2700
Brooklyn *(G-2306)*

▲ **Metropolitan Packg Mfg Corp** .... E 718 383-2700
Brooklyn *(G-2307)*

Milla Global Inc .... G 516 488-3601
Brooklyn *(G-2315)*

Mint-X Products Corporation .... F 877 646-8224
College Point *(G-3798)*

Modern Plastic Bags Mfg Inc .... G 718 237-2985
Brooklyn *(G-2327)*

▲ **Nap Industries Inc** .... D 718 625-4948
Brooklyn *(G-2348)*

▲ **New York Packaging Corp** .... D 516 746-0600
New Hyde Park *(G-8850)*

▲ **New York Packaging II LLC** .... C 516 746-0600
Garden City *(G-5523)*

▲ **Noteworthy Industries Inc** .... C 518 842-2662
Amsterdam *(G-364)*

Nova Packaging Ltd Inc .... E 914 232-8406
Katonah *(G-7133)*

▲ **Pacific Poly Product Corp** .... F 718 786-7129
Long Island City *(G-7832)*

◆ **Pack America Corp** .... G 212 508-6666
New York *(G-11554)*

Pactiv LLC .... C 518 793-2524
Glens Falls *(G-5695)*

Paradise Plastics LLC .... E 718 788-3733
Brooklyn *(G-2405)*

▲ **Paramount Equipment Inc** .... E 631 981-4422
Ronkonkoma *(G-14964)*

▲ **Poly Craft Industries Corp** .... E 631 630-6731
Hauppauge *(G-6166)*

◆ **Poly-Pak Industries Inc** .... B 631 293-6767
Melville *(G-8348)*

Polyseal Packaging Corp .... E 718 792-5530
Bronx *(G-1429)*

▲ **Primo Plastics Inc** .... E 718 349-1000
Brooklyn *(G-2443)*

▲ **Protective Lining Corp** .... D 718 854-3838
Brooklyn *(G-2456)*

Rainbow Poly Bag Co Inc .... E 718 386-3500
Brooklyn *(G-2476)*

▲ **Rege Inc** .... F 845 565-7772
New Windsor *(G-8950)*

Repellem Consumer Pdts Corp .... F 631 273-3992
Islandia *(G-6802)*

Rtr Bag & Co Ltd .... G 212 620-0011
New York *(G-11932)*

Salerno Plastic Film .... G 518 563-3636
Plattsburgh *(G-13695)*

▼ **Select Fabricators Inc** .... F 585 393-0650
Canandaigua *(G-3357)*

SIC SECTION 26 PAPER AND ALLIED PRODUCTS

Star Poly Bag Inc ... F ... 718 384-3130 Brooklyn *(G-2599)*

Summit Promotions LLC ... F ... 631 952-1570 Bay Shore *(G-748)*

Supreme Poly Plastics Inc ... E ... 718 456-9300 Brooklyn *(G-2632)*

▲ T M I Plastics Industries Inc ... F ... 718 383-0363 Brooklyn *(G-2638)*

▲ Tai Seng ... G ... 718 399-6311 Brooklyn *(G-2644)*

Technipoly Manufacturing Inc ... E ... 718 383-0363 Brooklyn *(G-2650)*

▲ Thompson Packaging Novlt Inc ... G ... 212 686-4242 New York *(G-12327)*

▲ Trinity Packaging Corporation ... E ... 914 273-4111 Armonk *(G-422)*

United Plastics Inc ... G ... 718 389-2255 Brooklyn *(G-2701)*

◆ Vitex Packaging Group Inc ... F ... 212 265-6575 New York *(G-12557)*

W E W Container Corporation ... E ... 718 827-8150 Brooklyn *(G-2740)*

▲ Wally Packaging Inc ... G ... 718 377-5323 Brooklyn *(G-2742)*

2674 Bags: Uncoated Paper & Multiwall

333 J & M Food Corp ... F ... 718 381-1493 Ridgewood *(G-14096)*

▲ American Packaging Corporation ... C ... 585 254-9500 Rochester *(G-14198)*

▲ Ampac Paper LLC ... A ... 845 778-5511 Walden *(G-16530)*

APC Paper Company Inc ... D ... 315 384-4225 Norfolk *(G-12897)*

Bag Arts The Art Packaging LLC ... G ... 212 684-7020 New York *(G-9303)*

▲ Custom Eco Friendly LLC ... G ... 347 227-0229 Roslyn *(G-15018)*

Kapstone Container Corporation ... D ... 518 842-2450 Amsterdam *(G-352)*

Lin Jin Feng ... G ... 718 232-3039 Brooklyn *(G-2223)*

Polyseal Packaging Corp ... E ... 718 792-5530 Bronx *(G-1429)*

▲ R P Fedder Corp ... E ... 585 288-1600 Rochester *(G-14618)*

Rtr Bag & Co Ltd ... G ... 212 620-0011 New York *(G-11932)*

Shalam Imports Inc ... F ... 718 686-6271 Brooklyn *(G-2548)*

2675 Die-Cut Paper & Board

Able National Corp ... E ... 718 386-8801 Brooklyn *(G-1549)*

All Out Die Cutting Inc ... E ... 718 346-6666 Brooklyn *(G-1587)*

Allied Sample Card Co Inc ... E ... 718 238-0523 Brooklyn *(G-1591)*

American Dsplay Die Ctters Inc ... E ... 212 645-1274 New York *(G-9117)*

Art Industries of New York ... E ... 212 633-9200 New York *(G-9211)*

Baseline Graphics Inc ... F ... 585 223-0153 Fairport *(G-4847)*

▲ Borden & Riley Paper Co Inc ... E ... 718 454-9494 Hollis *(G-6494)*

Dia ... G ... 212 675-4097 New York *(G-9867)*

▲ General Die and Die Cutng Inc ... D ... 516 665-3584 Roosevelt *(G-15004)*

▲ General Fibre Products Corp ... D ... 516 358-7500 New Hyde Park *(G-8835)*

Glens Falls Business Forms Inc ... F ... 518 798-6643 Queensbury *(G-13996)*

Hubray Inc ... F ... 800 645-2855 North Baldwin *(G-12907)*

▼ Kleer-Fax Inc ... D ... 631 225-1100 Amityville *(G-303)*

Leather Indexes Corp ... D ... 516 827-1900 Hicksville *(G-6363)*

Lion Die-Cutting Co Inc ... E ... 718 383-8841 Brooklyn *(G-2229)*

Manufacturers Indexing Pdts ... G ... 631 271-0956 Halesite *(G-5905)*

Mid Island Die Cutting Corp ... C ... 631 293-0180 Farmingdale *(G-5053)*

Miken Companies Inc ... D ... 716 668-6311 Buffalo *(G-3065)*

New Horizon Graphics Inc ... E ... 631 231-8055 Hauppauge *(G-6147)*

New York Cutting & Gumming Co ... E ... 212 563-4146 Middletown *(G-8454)*

Norampac New York City Inc ... C ... 718 340-2100 Maspeth *(G-8158)*

▲ Orange Die Cutting Corp ... C ... 845 562-0900 Newburgh *(G-12772)*

▲ Paperworld Inc ... E ... 516 221-2702 Bellmore *(G-819)*

Precision Diecutting Inc ... G ... 315 776-8465 Port Byron *(G-13736)*

Premier Packaging Corporation ... E ... 585 924-8460 Victor *(G-16496)*

▲ S & S Prtg Die-Cutting Co Inc ... F ... 718 388-8990 Brooklyn *(G-2522)*

Spectrum Prtg Lithography Inc ... F ... 212 255-3131 New York *(G-12158)*

Ums Manufacturing LLC ... F ... 518 562-2410 Plattsburgh *(G-13705)*

▲ Welsh Gold Stampers Inc ... E ... 718 984-5031 Staten Island *(G-15754)*

2676 Sanitary Paper Prdts

◆ Amscan Inc ... C ... 914 345-2020 Elmsford *(G-4732)*

Attends Healthcare Inc ... A ... 212 338-5100 New York *(G-9259)*

Becks Classic Mfg Inc ... D ... 631 435-3800 Brentwood *(G-1178)*

◆ Bentley Manufacturing Inc ... G ... 212 714-1800 New York *(G-9361)*

Cascades Tssue Group-Sales Inc ... D ... 518 238-1900 Waterford *(G-16608)*

▲ Cellu Tissue - Long Island LLC ... C ... 631 232-2626 Central Islip *(G-3489)*

▲ Crosstex International Inc ... D ... 631 582-6777 Hauppauge *(G-6058)*

Deluxe Packaging Corp ... F ... 845 246-6090 Saugerties *(G-15184)*

◆ First Quality Products Inc ... F ... 516 829-4949 Great Neck *(G-5812)*

▲ Florelle Tissue Corporation ... E ... 647 997-7405 Brownville *(G-2784)*

Georgia-Pacific LLC ... A ... 518 561-3500 Plattsburgh *(G-13664)*

Kas Direct LLC ... E ... 516 934-0541 Westbury *(G-17001)*

▲ Maxim Hygiene Products Inc ... F ... 516 621-3323 Mineola *(G-8523)*

Monthly Gift Inc ... G ... 888 444-9661 New York *(G-11302)*

▲ Mr Disposable Inc ... F ... 718 388-8574 Brooklyn *(G-2339)*

▲ N3a Corporation ... D ... 516 284-6799 Inwood *(G-6762)*

◆ Nice-Pak Products Inc ... B ... 845 365-2772 Orangeburg *(G-13236)*

Precare Corp ... G ... 631 524-5171 Hauppauge *(G-6167)*

▲ Precare Corp ... G ... 631 667-1055 Hauppauge *(G-6168)*

Procter & Gamble Company ... C ... 646 885-4201 New York *(G-11726)*

◆ Professional Disposables Inc ... A ... 845 365-1700 Orangeburg *(G-13244)*

▲ Rochester Midland Corporation ... C ... 585 336-2200 Rochester *(G-14643)*

▲ Select Products Holdings LLC ... E ... 855 777-3532 Huntington *(G-6681)*

▲ Sqp Inc ... C ... 518 831-6800 Schenectady *(G-15299)*

▲ US Alliance Paper Inc ... C ... 631 254-3030 Edgewood *(G-4619)*

Waymor1 Inc ... E ... 518 677-8511 Cambridge *(G-3311)*

2677 Envelopes

Apec Paper Industries Ltd ... G ... 212 730-0088 New York *(G-9172)*

Buffalo Envelope Inc ... F ... 716 686-0100 Depew *(G-4249)*

▲ Cambridge-Pacific Inc ... E ... 518 677-5988 Cambridge *(G-3305)*

Cenveo Inc ... D ... 716 662-2800 Orchard Park *(G-13260)*

Cenveo Inc ... F ... 716 686-0100 Depew *(G-4252)*

Conformer Products Inc ... F ... 516 504-6300 Great Neck *(G-5800)*

CPW Direct Mail Group LLC ... E ... 631 588-6565 Farmingdale *(G-4964)*

East Cast Envlope Graphics LLC ... E ... 718 326-2424 Maspeth *(G-8135)*

Jacmax Industries LLC ... G ... 718 439-3743 Brooklyn *(G-2130)*

▼ Kleer-Fax Inc ... D ... 631 225-1100 Amityville *(G-303)*

Mercury Envelope Co Inc ... D ... 516 678-6744 Rockville Centre *(G-14795)*

Old Ue LLC ... B ... 718 707-0700 Long Island City *(G-7829)*

◆ Poly-Pak Industries Inc ... B ... 631 293-6767 Melville *(G-8348)*

Premier Packaging Corporation ... E ... 585 924-8460 Victor *(G-16496)*

▲ Rochester 100 Inc ... C ... 585 475-0200 Rochester *(G-14633)*

Westrock Mwv LLC ... C ... 212 688-5000 New York *(G-12618)*

X-L Envelope and Printing Inc ... F ... 716 852-2135 Buffalo *(G-3258)*

2678 Stationery Prdts

Allen William & Company Inc ... C ... 212 675-6461 Glendale *(G-5644)*

▲ Anne Taintor Inc ... G ... 718 483-9312 Brooklyn *(G-1613)*

Bak USA Technologies Corp ... E ... 716 248-2704 Buffalo *(G-2831)*

▲ Cos TEC Manufacturing Corp ... G ... 631 589-7170 Bohemia *(G-1039)*

Duck Flats Pharma ... G ... 315 689-3407 Elbridge *(G-4625)*

▲ Dynamic Intl Mfrs & Distrs Inc ... F ... 347 993-1914 Suffern *(G-15788)*

▲ General Diaries Corporation ... F ... 516 371-2244 Inwood *(G-6758)*

▲ Innovative Designs LLC ... E ... 212 695-0892 New York *(G-10605)*

▲ International Design Assoc Ltd ... G ... 212 687-0333 New York *(G-10633)*

▼ Kleer-Fax Inc ... D ... 631 225-1100 Amityville *(G-303)*

Leather Indexes Corp ... D ... 516 827-1900 Hicksville *(G-6363)*

▲ Moleskine America Inc ... E ... 646 461-3018 New York *(G-11294)*

▲ P C I Paper Conversions Inc ... C ... 315 437-1641 Syracuse *(G-16006)*

Paper Magic Group Inc ... B ... 631 521-3682 New York *(G-11564)*

▲ USA Custom Pad Corp ... E ... 607 563-9550 Sidney *(G-15445)*

Westrock Mwv LLC ... C ... 212 688-5000 New York *(G-12618)*

2679 Converted Paper Prdts, NEC

Accent Label & Tag Co Inc ... G ... 631 244-7066 Ronkonkoma *(G-14847)*

Adelphi Paper Hangings ... G ... 518 284-9066 Sharon Springs *(G-15382)*

▲ Aigner Label Holder Corp ... F ... 845 562-4510 New Windsor *(G-8930)*

▲ Allen-Bailey Tag & Label Inc ... D ... 585 538-2324 Caledonia *(G-3276)*

◆ Allied Converters Inc ... E ... 914 235-1585 New Rochelle *(G-8886)*

Apexx Omni-Graphics Inc ... D ... 718 326-3330 Maspeth *(G-8119)*

▼ Auto Data Systems Inc ... F ... 631 831-7427 Deer Park *(G-4104)*

▼ Avco Industries Inc ... F ... 631 851-1555 Central Islip *(G-3486)*

Beetins Wholesale Inc ... F ... 718 524-0899 Staten Island *(G-15645)*

Best Time Processor LLC ... G ... 917 455-4126 Richmond Hill *(G-14069)*

Cascades Tissue Group - NY Inc ... C ... 518 238-1900 Wynantskill *(G-17379)*

▲ CCT (us) Inc ... F ... 716 297-7509 Niagara Falls *(G-12803)*

▲ Deltacraft Paper Company LLC ... C ... 716 856-5135 Buffalo *(G-2906)*

Depot Label Company Inc ... G ... 631 467-2952 Patchogue *(G-13418)*

Eagles Nest Holdings LLC ... E ... 513 874-5270 New York *(G-9959)*

Emergent Power Inc ... G ... 201 441-3590 Latham *(G-7362)*

▲ Felix Schoeller North Amer Inc ... C ... 315 298-5133 Pulaski *(G-13946)*

Employee Codes: A=Over 500 employees, B=251-500 C=101-250, D=51-100, E=20-50, F=10-19, G=5-9

2017 Harris New York Manufacturers Directory

753

Flavor Paper Ltd ....F 718 422-0230
Brooklyn *(G-1985)*
▲ Gardei Industries LLC ....F 716 693-7100
North Tonawanda *(G-12973)*
Gavin Mfg Corp ....E 631 467-0040
Farmingdale *(G-4997)*
▼ Gaylord Bros Inc ....D 315 457-5070
North Syracuse *(G-12944)*
▲ General Fibre Products Corp ....D 516 358-7500
New Hyde Park *(G-8835)*
Gerald McGlone ....G 518 482-2613
Colonie *(G-3820)*
◆ Global Tissue Group Inc ....E 631 924-3019
Medford *(G-8245)*
▲ Graphic Cntrls Acqisition Corp ....B 716 853-7500
Buffalo *(G-2978)*
Graphic Controls Holdings Inc ....F 716 853-7500
Buffalo *(G-2979)*
Greenfiber Albany Inc ....E 518 842-1470
Gloversville *(G-5712)*
Howard J Moore Company Inc ....E 631 351-8467
Plainview *(G-13606)*
Interface Performance Mtls ....F 315 346-3100
Beaver Falls *(G-794)*
▲ Interntnal Bus Cmmncations Inc ....E 516 352-4505
New Hyde Park *(G-8842)*
Jerry Tomaselli ....F 718 965-1400
Brooklyn *(G-2137)*
▲ K Sidrane Inc ....E 631 393-6974
Farmingdale *(G-5021)*
▲ Katz Group Americas Inc ....E 716 995-3071
Sanborn *(G-15122)*
Larkin Anya Ltd ....G 718 361-1827
Long Island City *(G-7788)*
▲ Lulu DK LLC ....G 212 223-4234
New York *(G-11063)*
▲ M C Packaging Corporation ....E 631 414-7840
Farmingdale *(G-5038)*
M C Packaging Corporation ....E 631 643-3763
Babylon *(G-550)*
▲ Marketing Group International ....G 631 754-8095
Northport *(G-13016)*
Master Image Printing Inc ....G 914 347-4400
Elmsford *(G-4763)*
Mid-York Press Inc ....D 607 674-4491
Sherburne *(G-15393)*
Millcraft Paper Company ....E 716 856-5135
Buffalo *(G-3066)*
National Advertising & Prtg ....G 212 629-7650
New York *(G-11346)*
Northeastern Paper Corp ....G 631 659-3634
Huntington *(G-6670)*
▲ Noteworthy Industries Inc ....C 518 842-2662
Amsterdam *(G-364)*
▲ P C I Paper Conversions Inc ....C 315 437-1641
Syracuse *(G-16006)*
P C I Paper Conversions Inc ....F 315 437-1641
Syracuse *(G-16009)*
◆ Pack America Corp ....G 212 508-6666
New York *(G-11554)*
▲ Paperworld Inc ....E 516 221-2702
Bellmore *(G-819)*
▲ Paradigm Mktg Consortium Inc ....E 516 677-6012
Syosset *(G-15835)*
▼ Pkk Inc ....E 716 257-3451
Cattaraugus *(G-3439)*
▲ Plug Power Inc ....B 518 782-7700
Latham *(G-7377)*
Precision Label Corporation ....F 631 270-4490
Farmingdale *(G-5087)*
Quadra Flex Corp ....G 607 758-7066
Cortland *(G-4042)*
◆ Quality Circle Products Inc ....D 914 736-6600
Montrose *(G-8614)*
RB Converting Inc ....G 607 777-1325
Binghamton *(G-945)*
S D Warren Company ....D 914 696-5544
White Plains *(G-17165)*
▲ Shell Containers Inc (ny) ....E 516 352-4505
New Hyde Park *(G-8861)*
Sml USA Inc ....E 212 736-8800
New York *(G-12107)*
Soavedra Masonry Inc ....G 347 695-5254
Harrison *(G-5990)*
▲ Specialty Quality Packg LLC ....D 914 580-3200
Scotia *(G-15331)*
Stanley Paper Co Inc ....F 518 489-1131
Albany *(G-136)*
Stickershopcom Inc ....G 631 563-4323
Holbrook *(G-6474)*
Stoney Croft Converters Inc ....F 718 608-9800
Staten Island *(G-15741)*
Sunnyside Decorative Prints Co ....G 516 671-1935
Glen Cove *(G-5630)*
Tag Envelope Co Inc ....E 718 389-6844
College Point *(G-3809)*
▲ Tri-Flex Label Corp ....E 631 293-0411
Farmingdale *(G-5133)*
▲ Tri-Seal International Inc ....G 845 353-3300
Blauvelt *(G-978)*
▲ Trinity Packaging Corporation ....E 914 273-4111
Armonk *(G-422)*
▼ VIP Paper Trading Inc ....E 212 382-4642
New York *(G-12546)*
▲ Waymor1 Inc ....D 518 677-8511
Cambridge *(G-3310)*
Waymor1 Inc ....E 518 677-8511
Cambridge *(G-3311)*
Web-Tech Packaging Inc ....F 716 684-4520
Lancaster *(G-7347)*
Winghing 8 Ltd ....G 718 439-0021
Brooklyn *(G-2760)*

27 PRINTING, PUBLISHING, AND ALLIED INDUSTRIES

2711 Newspapers: Publishing & Printing

21st Century Fox America Inc ....D 212 852-7000
New York *(G-8967)*
21st Century Fox America Inc ....G 845 735-1116
Pearl River *(G-13454)*
50+ Lifestyle ....G 631 286-0058
Bellport *(G-824)*
◆ A C J Communications Inc ....F 631 587-5612
Babylon *(G-544)*
A Zimmer Ltd ....D 315 422-7011
Syracuse *(G-15845)*
Adirondack Publishing Co Inc ....E 518 891-2600
Saranac Lake *(G-15134)*
Advance Magazine Publs Inc ....C 212 450-7000
New York *(G-9040)*
Advertiser Publications Inc ....F 845 783-1111
Chester *(G-3598)*
▲ Afro Times Newspaper ....F 718 636-9500
Brooklyn *(G-1568)*
After 50 Inc ....G 716 832-9300
Lancaster *(G-7299)*
Albany Catholic Press Assoc ....G 518 453-6688
Albany *(G-38)*
Albany Student Press Inc ....E 518 442-5665
Albany *(G-43)*
Albion-Holley Pennysaver Inc ....D 585 589-5641
Albion *(G-161)*
Algemeiner Journal Inc ....G 718 771-0400
Brooklyn *(G-1583)*
All Island Media Inc ....C 631 698-8400
Edgewood *(G-4592)*
All Island Media Inc ....E 516 942-8400
Hicksville *(G-6319)*
Alm Media LLC ....B 212 457-9400
New York *(G-9095)*
Alm Media Holdings Inc ....B 212 457-9400
New York *(G-9096)*
Almanac ....G 845 334-8206
Kingston *(G-7176)*
American City Bus Journals Inc ....E 716 541-1654
Buffalo *(G-2806)*
American Media Inc ....D 212 545-4800
New York *(G-9124)*
American Sports Media ....G 585 924-4250
Victor *(G-16460)*
American Sports Media LLC ....G 585 377-9636
Rochester *(G-14200)*
Amnews Corporation ....E 212 932-7400
New York *(G-9137)*
Angel Media and Publishing ....G 845 727-4949
West Nyack *(G-16911)*
Angie Mangino ....G 347 489-4009
Staten Island *(G-15638)*
Angola Pennysaver Inc ....F 716 549-1164
Angola *(G-379)*
AR Publishing Company Inc ....F 212 482-0303
New York *(G-9188)*
Architects Newspaper LLC ....F 212 966-0630
New York *(G-9195)*
Artvoice ....F 716 881-6604
Buffalo *(G-2820)*
Asahi Shimbun America Inc ....F 212 398-0257
New York *(G-9225)*
Aspect Printing Inc ....E 347 789-4284
Brooklyn *(G-1640)*
Auburn Publishing Co ....D 315 253-5311
Auburn *(G-480)*
Bangla Patrika Inc ....G 718 482-9923
Long Island City *(G-7681)*
Bee Publications Inc ....D 716 632-4700
Williamsville *(G-17235)*
Belsito Communications Inc ....F 845 534-9700
New Windsor *(G-8932)*
▼ Best Line Inc ....G 917 670-6210
Staten Island *(G-15646)*
Beth Kobliner Company LLC ....G 212 501-8407
New York *(G-9376)*
Bizeventz Inc ....G 315 579-3901
Syracuse *(G-15871)*
Bleezarde Publishing Inc ....G 518 756-2030
Ravena *(G-14020)*
Blue and White Publishing Inc ....F 215 431-3339
New York *(G-9420)*
Boonville Herald Inc ....G 315 942-4449
Boonville *(G-1164)*
Bornomala USA Inc ....G 347 753-2355
Jackson Heights *(G-6887)*
Bradford Publications Inc ....C 716 373-2500
Olean *(G-13137)*
Brasilans Press Pblcations Inc ....E 212 764-6161
New York *(G-9456)*
Brooklyn Journal Publications ....E 718 422-7400
Brooklyn *(G-1729)*
Brooklyn Rail Inc ....F 718 349-8427
Brooklyn *(G-1730)*
Buffalo Law Journal ....G 716 541-1600
Buffalo *(G-2853)*
Buffalo News Inc ....A 716 849-4401
Buffalo *(G-2857)*
Buffalo Standard Printing Corp ....F 716 835-9454
Buffalo *(G-2860)*
Bureau of National Affairs Inc ....E 212 687-4530
New York *(G-9479)*
Business First of New York ....E 716 854-5822
Buffalo *(G-2862)*
Business First of New York ....E 518 640-6800
Latham *(G-7357)*
Business Journals ....F 212 790-5100
New York *(G-9483)*
Camden News Inc ....G 315 245-1849
Camden *(G-3312)*
Canandaigua Msgnr Incorported ....D 585 394-0770
Canandaigua *(G-3337)*
Canarsie Courier Inc ....F 718 257-0600
Brooklyn *(G-1752)*
Capital Region Wkly Newspapers ....E 518 877-7160
Albany *(G-60)*
Carefree Daily Money Managemen ....G 631 751-1281
Setauket *(G-15375)*
Carib News Inc ....F 212 944-1991
New York *(G-9525)*
Catskill Delaware Publications ....F 845 887-5200
Callicoon *(G-3284)*
Catskill Mountain Publishing ....F 845 586-2601
Arkville *(G-411)*
Cdc Publishing LLC ....E 215 579-1695
Morrisville *(G-8619)*
Chase Media Group ....F 914 962-3871
Yorktown Heights *(G-17509)*
Chester West County Press ....G 914 684-0006
Mount Vernon *(G-8671)*
China Daily Distribution Corp ....F 212 537-8888
New York *(G-9596)*
China Newsweek Corporation ....F 212 481-2510
New York *(G-9601)*
▲ Chinese Medical Report Inc ....G 718 359-5676
Flushing *(G-5232)*
Christian Press Inc ....G 718 886-4400
Flushing *(G-5233)*
Chronicle Express ....F 315 536-4422
Penn Yan *(G-13508)*
Citizen Publishing Corp ....F 845 627-1414
Nanuet *(G-8754)*
City Newspaper ....G 585 244-3329
Rochester *(G-14276)*
Clarion Publications Inc ....F 585 243-3530
Geneseo *(G-5564)*
Classic News ....G 718 698-5256
Staten Island *(G-15659)*
CNY Business Review Inc ....F 315 472-3104
Syracuse *(G-15898)*
Colors Fashion Inc ....F 212 629-0401
New York *(G-9675)*

S I C

Community Media Group LLC ....F 518 439-4949
Delmar *(G-4244)*
Community Media LLC ....E 212 229-1890
New York *(G-9689)*
Community News Group LLC ....C 718 260-2500
Brooklyn *(G-1796)*
Community Newspaper Group LLC ....F 607 432-1000
Oneonta *(G-13181)*
Community Newspaper Group LLC ....E 518 565-4114
Plattsburgh *(G-13660)*
Community Newsppr Holdings Inc ....E 585 798-1400
Medina *(G-8269)*
Community Newsppr Holdings Inc ....D 716 693-1000
Niagara Falls *(G-12805)*
Community Newsppr Holdings Inc ....D 716 282-2311
Niagara Falls *(G-12806)*
Community Newsppr Holdings Inc ....E 716 439-9222
Lockport *(G-7577)*
Copia Interactive LLC ....E 212 481-0520
New York *(G-9719)*
Cortland Standard Printing Co ....D 607 756-5665
Cortland *(G-4022)*
Courier-Life Inc ....C 718 260-2500
Brooklyn *(G-1810)*
Crain News Service ....G 212 254-0890
New York *(G-9746)*
CT Publications Co ....G 718 592-2196
Corona *(G-3996)*
Daily Cornell Sun ....E 607 273-0746
Ithaca *(G-6836)*
Daily Freeman ....F 845 331-5000
Kingston *(G-7186)*
Daily Gazette Company ....B 518 374-4141
Schenectady *(G-15246)*
Daily Gazette Company ....C 518 395-3060
Schenectady *(G-15247)*
Daily Mail & Greene Cnty News ....F 518 943-2100
Catskill *(G-3427)*
Daily Muse Inc ....F 646 861-0284
New York *(G-9789)*
▲ Daily News LP ....A 212 210-2100
New York *(G-9790)*
Daily Orange Corporation ....E 315 443-2314
Syracuse *(G-15920)*
Daily Racing Form ....F 212 514-2180
New York *(G-9791)*
Daily Record ....F 585 232-2035
Rochester *(G-14299)*
Daily World Press Inc ....F 212 922-9201
New York *(G-9793)*
Dale Press Inc ....E 718 543-6200
Bronx *(G-1310)*
Danet Inc ....F 718 266-4444
Brooklyn *(G-1838)*
Dans Paper Inc ....D 631 537-0500
Southampton *(G-15542)*
Das Yidishe Licht Inc ....G 718 387-3166
Brooklyn *(G-1840)*
Dbg Media ....G 718 599-6828
Brooklyn *(G-1845)*
Delaware County Times Inc ....G 607 746-2176
Delhi *(G-4237)*
Denton Publications Inc ....D 518 873-6368
Elizabethtown *(G-4626)*
Denton Publications Inc ....E 518 561-9680
Plattsburgh *(G-13661)*
Der Blatt Inc ....F 845 783-1148
Monroe *(G-8553)*
Der Yid Inc ....E 718 797-3900
Brooklyn *(G-1856)*
Digital First Media LLC ....E 212 257-7212
New York *(G-9877)*
Digital One USA Inc ....F 718 396-4890
Flushing *(G-5238)*
Division Street News Corp ....F 518 234-2515
Cobleskill *(G-3736)*
Document Journal Inc ....G 917 287-2141
New York *(G-9894)*
DOT Publishing ....F 315 593-2510
Fulton *(G-5456)*
▲ Dow Jones & Company Inc ....B 609 627-2999
New York *(G-9913)*
Dow Jones & Company Inc ....C 212 597-5600
New York *(G-9914)*
Dow Jones & Company Inc ....E 212 597-5983
New York *(G-9915)*
Dray Enterprises Inc ....F 585 768-2201
Le Roy *(G-7406)*
E W Smith Publishing Co ....F 845 562-1218
New Windsor *(G-8937)*

Eagle Media Partners LP ....E 315 434-8889
Syracuse *(G-15928)*
East Hampton Ind News Inc ....E 631 324-2500
East Hampton *(G-4408)*
East Hampton Star Inc ....E 631 324-0002
East Hampton *(G-4409)*
Ecclesiastical Communications ....F 212 688-2399
New York *(G-9974)*
Economist Newspaper NA Inc ....F 212 554-0676
New York *(G-9980)*
Ecuador News Inc ....F 718 205-7014
Woodside *(G-17327)*
El Aguila ....G 212 410-2450
New York *(G-9991)*
El Diario LLC ....C 212 807-4600
Brooklyn *(G-1908)*
Empire Publishing Inc ....F 516 829-4000
Far Rockaway *(G-4921)*
Empire State Weeklies Inc ....E 585 671-1533
Webster *(G-16723)*
Epoch Times International Inc ....G 212 239-2808
New York *(G-10050)*
Event Journal Inc ....G 516 470-1811
Bethpage *(G-866)*
Evercore Partners Svcs E LLC ....A 212 857-3100
New York *(G-10090)*
Exhibits & More ....G 585 924-4040
Victor *(G-16476)*
Expositor Newspapers Inc ....G 585 427-2468
Rochester *(G-14365)*
▲ Fairchild Publications Inc ....A 212 630-4000
New York *(G-10128)*
Finger Lakes Media Inc ....F 607 243-7600
Dundee *(G-4327)*
Finger Lakes Printing Co Inc ....E 315 789-3333
Geneva *(G-5576)*
Fire Island Tide Publication ....F 631 567-7470
Sayville *(G-15210)*
Firefighters Journal ....E 718 391-0283
Long Island City *(G-7741)*
Five Islands Publishing Inc ....F 631 583-5345
Bronx *(G-1332)*
Four Directions Inc ....E 315 829-8388
Vernon *(G-16434)*
▲ Francepress LLC ....G 646 202-9828
New York *(G-10198)*
Fredonia Pennysaver Inc ....G 716 679-1509
Fredonia *(G-5373)*
Freetime Magazine Inc ....G 585 473-2266
Rochester *(G-14382)*
French Morning LLC ....G 646 290-7463
New York *(G-10209)*
▲ FT Publications Inc ....D 212 641-6500
New York *(G-10218)*
FT Publications Inc ....E 212 641-2420
New York *(G-10219)*
Fulton Newspapers Inc ....E 315 598-6397
Fulton *(G-5457)*
Gallagher Printing Inc ....E 716 873-2434
Buffalo *(G-2962)*
Gannett Co Inc ....E 516 484-7510
Port Washington *(G-13818)*
Gannett Co Inc ....D 585 232-7100
Rochester *(G-14387)*
Gannett Co Inc ....G 585 924-3406
Farmington *(G-5151)*
Gannett Co Inc ....D 607 798-1234
Vestal *(G-16448)*
Gannett Co Inc ....E 914 278-9315
New Rochelle *(G-8903)*
Gannett Co Inc ....G 585 346-4150
Lakeville *(G-7284)*
Gannett Stllite Info Ntwrk Inc ....E 914 965-5000
Yonkers *(G-17447)*
Gannett Stllite Info Ntwrk Inc ....D 585 798-1400
Medina *(G-8272)*
Gannett Stllite Info Ntwrk Inc ....F 914 381-3400
Mamaroneck *(G-8035)*
Gannett Stllite Info Ntwrk LLC ....E 845 578-2300
West Nyack *(G-16917)*
Gannett Stllite Info Ntwrk LLC ....C 845 454-2000
Poughkeepsie *(G-13900)*
▲ Gatehouse Media LLC ....D 585 598-0030
Pittsford *(G-13561)*
Gatehouse Media LLC ....E 315 792-5000
Utica *(G-16336)*
Gatehouse Media LLC ....G 607 776-2121
Bath *(G-656)*
Gatehouse Media LLC ....F 315 866-2220
Herkimer *(G-6300)*

Gatehouse Media LLC ....D 607 936-4651
Corning *(G-3973)*
Gatehouse Media LLC ....D 585 394-0770
Canandaigua *(G-3347)*
Gatehouse Media LLC ....C 607 324-1425
Hornell *(G-6564)*
Gatehouse Media MO Holdings ....G 530 846-3661
Pittsford *(G-13562)*
Gatehuse Media PA Holdings Inc ....D 585 598-0030
Pittsford *(G-13563)*
Gateway Newspapers Inc ....G 845 628-8400
Mahopac *(G-7996)*
General Media Strategies Inc ....G 212 586-4141
New York *(G-10273)*
Gleaner Company Ltd ....F 718 657-0788
Jamaica *(G-6915)*
Glens Falls Newspapers Inc ....G 518 792-3131
Glens Falls *(G-5680)*
Good Health Healthcare Newsppr ....F 585 421-8109
Victor *(G-16479)*
Great North Road Media Inc ....F 646 619-1355
New York *(G-10358)*
Guidance Group Inc ....F 631 756-4618
Melville *(G-8325)*
▲ Hagedorn Communications Inc ....D 914 636-7400
New Rochelle *(G-8906)*
Haitian Times Inc ....G 718 230-8700
New Rochelle *(G-8907)*
Hamodia Corp ....F 718 853-9094
Brooklyn *(G-2064)*
Hearst Business Media Corp ....F 631 650-4441
Great River *(G-5851)*
▲ Hearst Corporation ....A 212 649-2000
New York *(G-10438)*
Hearst Corporation ....A 518 454-5694
Albany *(G-86)*
Hearst Corporation ....E 212 649-2275
New York *(G-10447)*
Hellenic Corporation ....F 212 986-6881
New York *(G-10455)*
Herald Newspapers Company Inc ....A 315 470-0011
Syracuse *(G-15959)*
Herald Press Inc ....G 718 784-5255
Long Island City *(G-7758)*
Herald Publishing Company LLC ....G 315 470-2022
New York *(G-10460)*
Hickville Illustrated News ....D 516 747-8282
Mineola *(G-8513)*
High Ridge News LLC ....G 718 548-7412
Bronx *(G-1357)*
Highline Media LLC ....C 859 692-2100
New York *(G-10475)*
Hispanic Com Pub Inc ....F 718 224-5863
Bayside *(G-772)*
Holdens Screen Supply Corp ....G 212 627-2727
New York *(G-10495)*
Home Reporter Inc ....E 718 238-6600
Brooklyn *(G-2085)*
Hudson Valley Black Press ....G 845 562-1313
Newburgh *(G-12762)*
Huersch Marketing Group LLC ....G 518 874-1045
Green Island *(G-5857)*
Hyatt Times Square New York ....F 212 398-2158
New York *(G-10536)*
IMG The Daily ....G 212 541-5640
New York *(G-10572)*
▲ Impremedia LLC ....D 212 807-4785
Brooklyn *(G-2101)*
India Abroad Publications Inc ....D 212 929-1727
New York *(G-10588)*
Indian Time ....F 518 358-9531
Hogansburg *(G-6427)*
Informa Uk Ltd ....G 646 957-8966
New York *(G-10597)*
Investment News ....E 212 210-0100
New York *(G-10650)*
Investmentwires Inc ....G 212 331-8995
New York *(G-10651)*
Investors Business Daily Inc ....F 212 626-7676
New York *(G-10652)*
Irish Echo Newspaper Corp ....F 212 482-4818
New York *(G-10660)*
Irish Tribune Inc ....F 212 684-3366
New York *(G-10661)*
Ithaca Journal News Co Inc ....E 607 272-2321
Ithaca *(G-6854)*
Jewish Journal ....G 718 630-9350
Brooklyn *(G-2140)*
Jewish Press Inc ....C 718 330-1100
Brooklyn *(G-2141)*

Employee Codes: A=Over 500 employees, B=251-500
C=101-250, D=51-100, E=20-50, F=10-19, G=5-9
2017 Harris
New York Manufacturers Directory
755

27 PRINTING, PUBLISHING, AND ALLIED INDUSTRIES SIC SECTION

Jewish Week Inc E 212 921-7822
New York *(G-10727)*
Jobs Weekly Inc F 716 648-5627
Hamburg *(G-5929)*
John Lor Publishing Ltd E 631 475-1000
Patchogue *(G-13425)*
Johnson Acquisition Corp F 518 828-1616
Hudson *(G-6622)*
Johnson Newspaper Corporation E 518 483-4700
Malone *(G-8011)*
Journal News G 914 694-5000
White Plains *(G-17130)*
Journal News G 845 578-2324
West Nyack *(G-16920)*
Journal Register Company D 212 257-7212
New York *(G-10770)*
Journal Register Company D 518 584-4242
Saratoga Springs *(G-15161)*
Journal Register Company E 212 257-7212
New York *(G-10771)*
Kch Publications Inc E 516 671-2360
Glen Cove *(G-5619)*
▲ **Korea Central Daily News Inc** D 718 361-7700
Long Island City *(G-7784)*
▲ **Korea Times New York Inc** D 718 784-4526
Long Island City *(G-7785)*
Korea Times New York Inc G 718 729-5555
Long Island City *(G-7786)*
Korea Times New York Inc G 718 961-7979
Flushing *(G-5262)*
L & M Publications Inc E 516 378-3133
Garden City *(G-5513)*
Latin Business Chronicle G 305 441-0002
New York *(G-10932)*
▲ **Lebhar-Friedman Inc** E 212 756-5000
New York *(G-10951)*
Lebhar-Friedman Inc C 212 756-5000
New York *(G-10952)*
Lee Enterprises Incorporated C 518 792-3131
Glens Falls *(G-5686)*
Lee Newspapers Inc G 518 673-3237
Palatine Bridge *(G-13395)*
Lee Publications Inc D 518 673-3237
Palatine Bridge *(G-13396)*
Ll Community Newspapers Inc G 516 747-8282
Mineola *(G-8520)*
Life Time Fitness Inc G 914 290-5100
Harrison *(G-5987)*
Litmor Publishing Corp F 516 931-0012
Hicksville *(G-6364)*
Livingston County News G 585 243-1234
Geneseo *(G-5566)*
Lmg National Publishing Inc E 585 598-6874
Fairport *(G-4862)*
Local Media Group Inc E 845 341-1100
Middletown *(G-8446)*
Local Media Group Inc B 845 341-1100
Middletown *(G-8447)*
Local Media Group Inc D 845 341-1100
Middletown *(G-8448)*
Local Media Group Inc F 845 794-3712
Monticello *(G-8605)*
Local Media Group Inc F 845 340-4910
Kingston *(G-7197)*
Long Island Business News E 631 737-1700
Ronkonkoma *(G-14933)*
Long Island Catholic Newspaper E 516 594-1212
Roosevelt *(G-15007)*
Long Island Cmnty Nwsppers Inc D 516 482-4490
Mineola *(G-8522)*
Long Island Cmnty Nwsppers Inc F 631 427-7000
Huntington *(G-6668)*
Long Islander Newspapers LLC G 631 427-7000
Huntington *(G-6669)*
Louis Vuitton North Amer Inc G 212 644-2574
New York *(G-11051)*
Lowville Newspaper Corporation G 315 376-3525
Lowville *(G-7940)*
Made Fresh Daily G 212 285-2253
New York *(G-11092)*
Main Street Connect LLC F 203 803-4110
Armonk *(G-417)*
Malone Newspapers Corp E 518 483-2000
Malone *(G-8014)*
Manchester Newspaper Inc E 518 642-1234
Granville *(G-5775)*
Manhattan Media LLC E 212 268-8600
New York *(G-11130)*
Manhattan Times Inc F 212 569-5800
New York *(G-11134)*

Mark I Publications Inc E 718 205-8000
Rego Park *(G-14035)*
Market Place Publications E 516 997-7909
Carle Place *(G-3395)*
Markets Media LLC G 646 442-4646
New York *(G-11162)*
Massapequa Post E 516 798-5100
Massapequa Park *(G-8188)*
Melmont Fine Pringng/Graphics G 516 939-2253
Bethpage *(G-874)*
Mendon Hnoye FLS Lima Sentinel G 585 624-5470
Honeoye Falls *(G-6534)*
Merchandiser Inc G 315 462-6411
Clifton Springs *(G-3714)*
Mexico Independent Inc E 315 963-3763
Mexico *(G-8396)*
Miami Media LLC F 212 268-8600
New York *(G-11247)*
Mid-York Press Inc D 607 674-4491
Sherburne *(G-15393)*
Midway News Inc G 212 628-3009
New York *(G-11260)*
Ming Pao (new York) Inc F 212 334-2220
New York *(G-11277)*
Ming Pao (new York) Inc D 718 786-2888
Long Island City *(G-7813)*
Minority Reporter Inc G 585 225-3628
Rochester *(G-14515)*
Moneypaper Inc F 914 925-0022
Rye *(G-15064)*
Moneysaver Advertising Inc F 585 593-1275
Bolivar *(G-1160)*
Mortgage Press Ltd E 516 409-1400
Wantagh *(G-16560)*
Nassau County Publications G 516 481-5400
Hempstead *(G-6283)*
▲ **National Herald Inc** E 718 784-5255
Long Island City *(G-7820)*
National Parts Peddler Newsppr G 315 699-7583
Cicero *(G-3649)*
Neighbor Newspapers G 631 226-2636
Farmingdale *(G-5063)*
Neighbor To Neighbor News Inc G 585 492-2525
Arcade *(G-397)*
New Berlin Gazette E 607 847-6131
Norwich *(G-13031)*
New Living Inc G 631 751-8819
Patchogue *(G-13428)*
New Media Investment Group Inc B 212 479-3160
New York *(G-11391)*
New Ski Inc E 607 277-7000
Ithaca *(G-6867)*
New York Cvl Srvc Emplys Pblsh F 212 962-2690
New York *(G-11398)*
New York Daily Challenge Inc F 718 636-9500
Brooklyn *(G-2364)*
New York Daily News G 212 248-2100
New York *(G-11399)*
▲ **New York IL Bo Inc** F 718 961-1538
Flushing *(G-5272)*
New York Observer Llc D 212 887-8460
New York *(G-11405)*
New York Press Inc E 212 268-8600
New York *(G-11406)*
▲ **New York Times Company** B 212 556-1234
New York *(G-11410)*
New York Times Company F 718 281-7000
Flushing *(G-5273)*
New York Times Company F 212 556-4300
New York *(G-11411)*
New York University E 212 998-4300
New York *(G-11412)*
New York1 News Operations F 212 379-3311
New York *(G-11413)*
News Communications Inc F 212 689-2500
New York *(G-11415)*
News Corporation C 212 416-3400
New York *(G-11416)*
News India Usa LLC G 212 675-7515
New York *(G-11417)*
News India USA Inc F 212 675-7515
New York *(G-11418)*
News of The Highlands Inc F 845 534-7771
Cornwall *(G-3990)*
News Report Inc E 718 851-6607
Brooklyn *(G-2370)*
Newsday LLC B 631 843-4050
Melville *(G-8341)*
Newsday LLC C 631 843-3135
Melville *(G-8342)*

Newspaper Association Amer Inc E 212 856-6300
New York *(G-11420)*
Newspaper Delivery Solutions G 718 370-1111
Staten Island *(G-15710)*
Newspaper Publisher LLC F 607 775-0472
Conklin *(G-3871)*
Newspaper Times Union F 518 454-5676
Albany *(G-108)*
Nick Lugo Inc F 212 348-2100
New York *(G-11426)*
Nikkei America Inc E 212 261-6200
New York *(G-11432)*
Nikkei Visual Images Amer Inc G 212 261-6200
New York *(G-11433)*
Nordic Press Inc G 212 686-3356
New York *(G-11452)*
North Country This Week G 315 265-1000
Potsdam *(G-13880)*
Northern NY Newspapers Corp C 315 782-1000
Watertown *(G-16668)*
Northern Tier Publishing Corp F 914 962-4748
Yorktown Heights *(G-17514)*
▲ **Noticia Hispanoamericana Inc** E 516 223-5678
Baldwin *(G-560)*
Novoye Rsskoye Slovo Pubg Corp D 646 460-4566
Brooklyn *(G-2378)*
Nyc Community Media LLC F 212 229-1890
Brooklyn *(G-2384)*
Nyc Trade Printers Corp F 718 606-0610
Woodside *(G-17342)*
Nyp Holdings Inc D 718 260-2500
Brooklyn *(G-2385)*
▲ **Nyp Holdings Inc** A 212 997-9272
New York *(G-11485)*
Nyt Capital LLC F 212 556-1234
New York *(G-11488)*
Oak Lone Publishing Co Inc E 518 792-1126
Glens Falls *(G-5693)*
Observer Daily Sunday Newsppr D 716 366-3000
Dunkirk *(G-4346)*
Ogden Newspapers Inc C 716 487-1111
Jamestown *(G-7022)*
Oneida Publications Inc E 315 363-5100
Oneida *(G-13163)*
Ottaway Newspapers Inc F 845 343-2181
Middletown *(G-8455)*
Outlook Newspaper E 845 356-6261
Suffern *(G-15796)*
Owego Pennysaver Press Inc F 607 687-2434
Owego *(G-13358)*
Page Front Group Inc G 716 823-8222
Lackawanna *(G-7246)*
Panagraphics Inc G 716 312-8088
Orchard Park *(G-13287)*
Patchogue Advance Inc E 631 475-1000
Patchogue *(G-13430)*
▲ **Peace Times Weekly Inc** G 718 762-6500
Flushing *(G-5280)*
▼ **Pearson Inc** D 212 641-2400
New York *(G-11594)*
Pearson Longman LLC E 212 641-2400
White Plains *(G-17147)*
Pennysaver Group Inc F 914 966-1400
Yonkers *(G-17476)*
Pipe Dream E 607 777-2515
Binghamton *(G-943)*
Post Community Media LLC C 518 374-4141
Saratoga Springs *(G-15167)*
Post Journal F 716 487-1111
Jamestown *(G-7023)*
Prometheus International Inc F 718 472-0700
Long Island City *(G-7848)*
Prospect News F 212 374-2800
New York *(G-11738)*
Publishing Group America Inc F 646 658-0550
New York *(G-11747)*
Putnam Cnty News Recorder LLC F 845 265-2468
Cold Spring *(G-3764)*
Quality Guides G 716 326-3163
Westfield *(G-17049)*
R W Publications Div of Wtrhs E 716 714-5620
Elma *(G-4653)*
R W Publications Div of Wtrhs E 716 714-5620
Elma *(G-4654)*
Realtimetraderscom E 716 632-6600
Buffalo *(G-3155)*
Record G 518 270-1200
Saratoga Springs *(G-15169)*
Record Advertiser E 716 693-1000
North Tonawanda *(G-12988)*

SIC SECTION 27 PRINTING, PUBLISHING, AND ALLIED INDUSTRIES

Record Review LLC ....F 914 244-0533
Bedford Hills (G-807)
Rheinwald Printing Co Inc ....F 585 637-5100
Brockport (G-1246)
Richner Communications Inc ....C 516 569-4000
Garden City (G-5529)
Richner Communications Inc ....G 516 569-4000
Lawrence (G-7399)
Ridgewood Times Prtg & Pubg ....E 718 821-7500
Ridgewood (G-14122)
Right World View ....E 914 406-2994
Purchase (G-13971)
Rizzoli Intl Publications Inc................F 212 308-2000
New York (G-11883)
Rochester Business Journal ....E 585 546-8303
Rochester (G-14636)
Rochester Catholic Press ....F 585 529-9530
Rochester (G-14637)
Rochester Democrat & Chronicle................E 585 232-7100
Rochester (G-14641)
Rocket Communications Inc................F 716 873-2594
Buffalo (G-3162)
Royal News Corp ....F 212 564-8972
New York (G-11926)
Ruby Newco LLC ....G 212 852-7000
New York (G-11933)
Russkaya Reklama Inc ....E 718 769-3000
Brooklyn (G-2518)
S G New York LLC................F 631 698-8400
Edgewood (G-4610)
S G New York LLC................E 631 665-4000
Bohemia (G-1128)
S I Communications Inc ....F 914 725-2500
Scarsdale (G-15222)
Sag Harbor Express................G 631 725-1700
Sag Harbor (G-15079)
Salamanca Press Penny Saver................E 716 945-1500
Salamanca (G-15105)
Sample News Group LLC ....D 315 343-3800
Oswego (G-13340)
Satellite Network Inc................F 718 336-2698
Brooklyn (G-2536)
Sb New York Inc ....D 212 457-7790
New York (G-11980)
Schneps Publications Inc ....E 718 224-5863
Bayside (G-775)
Seabay Media Holdings LLC................G 212 457-7790
New York (G-12009)
Second Amendment Foundation................G 716 885-6408
Buffalo (G-3180)
Seneca County Area Shopper ....G 607 532-4333
Ovid (G-13347)
Seneca Media Inc ....D 607 324-1425
Hornell (G-6566)
Seneca Media Inc ....F 585 593-5300
Wellsville (G-16758)
Service Advertising Group Inc ....F 718 361-6161
Long Island City (G-7875)
◆ Shelter Island Reporter Inc................G 631 749-1000
Shelter Island (G-15388)
Sing Tao Newspapers NY Ltd ....F 212 431-9030
Brooklyn (G-2565)
Sing Tao Newspapers NY Ltd ....E 718 821-0123
Brooklyn (G-2566)
▲ Sing Tao Newspapers NY Ltd ....E 212 699-3800
New York (G-12084)
Smithtown News Inc ....E 631 265-2100
Smithtown (G-15498)
South Shore Tribune Inc ....G 516 431-5628
Island Park (G-6784)
Southampton Town Newspapers ....E 631 283-4100
Southampton (G-15552)
Southampton Town Newspapers ....F 631 288-1100
Westhampton Beach (G-17061)
Spartacist Publishing Co ....E 212 732-7860
New York (G-12148)
Spartan Publishing Inc................F 716 664-7373
Jamestown (G-7029)
Spectator Publishing Co Inc................E 212 854-9550
New York (G-12155)
Sports Pblications Prod NY LLC ....D 212 366-7700
New York (G-12167)
Sports Reporter Inc ....G 212 737-2750
New York (G-12169)
Spring Publishing Corporation................G 718 782-0881
Brooklyn (G-2592)
Ssrja LLC ....F 718 725-7020
Jamaica (G-6950)
▲ St Lawrence County Newspapers ....D 315 393-1003
Ogdensburg (G-13122)
Star Community Pubg Group LLC ....C 631 843-4050
Melville (G-8357)
Star Sports Corp ....E 516 773-4075
Great Neck (G-5842)
Star-Gazette Fund Inc................C 607 734-5151
Elmira (G-4702)
Steffen Publishing Inc ....D 315 865-4100
Holland Patent (G-6488)
Stratconglobal Inc................G 212 989-2355
New York (G-12211)
Straus Communications................F 845 782-4000
Chester (G-3616)
Straus Newspapers Inc ....E 845 782-4000
Chester (G-3617)
Stuart Communications Inc ....F 845 252-7414
Narrowsburg (G-8769)
Sun-Times Media Group Inc ....E 716 945-1644
Salamanca (G-15110)
Syracuse Catholic Press Assn ....G 315 422-8153
Syracuse (G-16049)
Tablet Publishing Company Inc................E 718 965-7333
Brooklyn (G-2643)
Tefft Publishers Inc................G 518 692-9290
Greenwich (G-5894)
Tegna Inc ....C 716 849-2222
Buffalo (G-3212)
Tenney Media Group................D 315 853-5569
Clinton (G-3722)
The Earth Times Foundation ....G 718 297-0488
Brooklyn (G-2656)
The Sandhar Corp................G 718 523-0819
Jamaica (G-6958)
Thestreet Inc................D 212 321-5000
New York (G-12316)
Thousand Islands Printing Co................G 315 482-2581
Alexandria Bay (G-191)
Times Beacon Record Newspapers ......F 631 331-1154
East Setauket (G-4494)
Times Review Newspaper Corp................E 631 354-8031
Mattituck (G-8211)
Tioga County Courier ....G 607 687-0108
Owego (G-13360)
Tompkins Weekly Inc................G 607 539-7100
Ithaca (G-6878)
Tri-Town News Inc................E 607 561-3515
Sidney (G-15442)
Tri-Village Publishers Inc ....D 518 843-1100
Amsterdam (G-371)
Tribco LLC ....E 718 357-7400
Whitestone (G-17216)
Tribune Entertainment Co Del ....E 203 866-2204
New York (G-12404)
Tricycle Foundation Inc................G 800 873-9871
New York (G-12405)
Trilake Three Press Corp................G 518 359-2462
Tupper Lake (G-16280)
Tupper Lake Free Press Inc ....G 518 359-2166
Tupper Lake (G-16281)
Ubm Inc................A 212 600-3000
New York (G-12440)
Ubm LLC................F 516 562-5000
New York (G-12442)
Ubm LLC................A 516 562-5085
New York (G-12441)
Ulster County Press Office ....G 845 687-4480
High Falls (G-6402)
Ulster Publishing Co Inc ....E 845 334-8205
Kingston (G-7219)
Ulster Publishing Co Inc ....F 845 255-7005
New Paltz (G-8881)
Unified Media Inc ....F 917 595-2710
New York (G-12454)
Urdu Times ....G 718 297-8700
Jamaica (G-6961)
US Hispanic Media Inc................G 212 885-8000
Brooklyn (G-2713)
USA Today International Corp ....G 703 854-3400
New York (G-12491)
Vnovom Svete ....G 212 302-9480
New York (G-12562)
Vpj Publication Inc................E 718 845-3221
Howard Beach (G-6600)
Vus Is Neias LLC................G 347 627-3999
Brooklyn (G-2738)
W H White Publications Inc................G 914 725-2500
Dobbs Ferry (G-4304)
W M T Publications Inc................F 585 244-3329
Rochester (G-14755)
Wallkill Lodge No 627 F&Am ....F 845 778-7148
Walden (G-16538)
Wallkill Valley Publications ....E 845 561-0170
Newburgh (G-12786)
Wappingers Falls Shopper Inc ....E 845 297-3723
Wappingers Falls (G-16578)
Wave Publishing Co Inc ....F 718 634-4000
Rockaway Beach (G-14783)
Wayuga Community Newspapers ....E 315 754-6229
Red Creek (G-14027)
Wayuga Community Newspapers ....G 315 594-2506
Wolcott (G-17281)
Webster Ontrio Wlwrth Pnnysver................F 585 265-3620
Webster (G-16741)
Weekly Ajkal ....F 718 565-2100
Jackson Heights (G-6889)
Weekly Business News Corp................G 212 689-5888
New York (G-12603)
Weisbeck Publishing Printing ....G 716 937-9226
Alden (G-186)
West Publishing Corporation ....E 212 922-1920
New York (G-12614)
West Seneca Bee Inc ....D 716 632-4700
Williamsville (G-17259)
Westbury Times ....D 516 747-8282
Mineola (G-8539)
Westfair Communications Inc ....E 914 694-3600
White Plains (G-17186)
Westmore News Inc ....G 914 939-6864
Port Chester (G-13761)
Westside News Inc................F 585 352-3411
Spencerport (G-15574)
William B Collins Company ....D 518 773-8272
Gloversville (G-5729)
William Boyd Printing Co Inc................C 518 339-5832
Latham (G-7385)
William J Kline & Son Inc ....D 518 843-1100
Amsterdam (G-374)
Williamsburg Bulletin ....G 718 387-0123
Brooklyn (G-2755)
Wolfe Publications Inc................C 585 394-0770
Canandaigua (G-3360)
Workers Vanguard ....E 212 732-7862
New York (G-12658)
▲ World Journal LLC ....C 718 746-8889
Whitestone (G-17218)
World Journal LLC ....E 718 445-2277
Flushing (G-5310)
World Journal LLC ....F 718 871-5000
Brooklyn (G-2766)
▲ Yated Neeman Inc ....F 845 369-1600
Monsey (G-8586)
Yoga In Daily Life - NY Inc................G 718 539-8548
College Point (G-3811)
Yonkers Time Publishing Co ....F 914 965-4000
Yonkers (G-17503)
Zenith Color Comm Group Inc................E 212 989-4400
Long Island City (G-7932)

2721 Periodicals: Publishing & Printing

21st Century Fox America Inc ....D 212 447-4600
New York (G-8968)
21st Century Fox America Inc ....D 212 852-7000
New York (G-8967)
▲ 2600 Enterprises Inc ....F 631 474-2677
Saint James (G-15086)
A Guideposts Church Corp................C 212 251-8100
New York (G-8988)
Academy of Political Science ....G 212 870-2500
New York (G-9008)
Access Intelligence LLC................A 212 204-4269
New York (G-9009)
Adirondack Life Inc................F 518 946-2191
Jay (G-7054)
Advance Magazine Publs Inc ....D 212 286-2860
New York (G-9036)
▲ Advance Magazine Publs Inc ....A 212 286-2860
New York (G-9037)
Advance Magazine Publs Inc................D 212 790-4422
New York (G-9038)
Advance Magazine Publs Inc ....D 212 286-2860
New York (G-9039)
Advance Magazine Publs Inc................C 212 450-7000
New York (G-9040)
Advance Magazine Publs Inc ....D 212 697-0126
New York (G-9041)
Advanced Research Media Inc ....F 631 751-9696
East Setauket (G-4474)
Adventure Publishing Group ....E 212 575-4510
New York (G-9049)
▲ Alcoholics Anonymous Grapevine...F 212 870-3400
New York (G-9078)

S I C

27 PRINTING, PUBLISHING, AND ALLIED INDUSTRIES SIC SECTION

Alm Media LLC ... B ... 212 457-9400 New York *(G-9095)*
Alm Media Holdings Inc ... B ... 212 457-9400 New York *(G-9096)*
▲ Alpha Media Group Inc ... B ... 212 302-2626 New York *(G-9099)*
America Press Inc ... E ... 212 581-4640 New York *(G-9113)*
American Graphic Design Awards ... G ... 212 696-4380 New York *(G-9118)*
▲ American Inst Chem Engineers ... D ... 646 495-1355 New York *(G-9121)*
American Institute Physics Inc ... C ... 516 576-2410 Melville *(G-8293)*
American Intl Media LLC ... F ... 845 359-4225 White Plains *(G-17077)*
American Jewish Committee ... G ... 212 891-1400 New York *(G-9122)*
American Jewish Congress Inc ... E ... 212 879-4500 New York *(G-9123)*
American Towman Network Inc ... F ... 845 986-4546 Warwick *(G-16586)*
AMG Supply Company LLC ... E ... 212 790-6370 New York *(G-9135)*
Analysts In Media (aim) Inc ... E ... 212 488-1777 New York *(G-9145)*
Animal Fair Media Inc ... F ... 212 629-0392 New York *(G-9162)*
Annointed Buty Ministries LLC ... G ... 646 867-3796 Brooklyn *(G-1614)*
Archaelogy Magazine ... E ... 718 472-3050 Long Island City *(G-7666)*
Archie Comic Publications Inc ... D ... 914 381-5155 Pelham *(G-13488)*
Art & Understanding Inc ... G ... 518 426-9010 Albany *(G-50)*
Arthur Frommer Magazines LLC ... F ... 646 695-6739 New York *(G-9217)*
▲ Artnews Ltd ... F ... 212 398-1690 New York *(G-9223)*
Aspen Publishers Inc ... A ... 212 771-0600 New York *(G-9235)*
Aspire One Communications LLC ... F ... 201 281-2998 Cornwall *(G-3986)*
Associated Bus Publications Co ... E ... 212 490-3999 New York *(G-9239)*
Association For Cmpt McHy Inc ... D ... 212 869-7440 New York *(G-9240)*
Athlon Spt Communications Inc ... E ... 212 478-1910 New York *(G-9250)*
Atlantic Monthly Group Inc ... E ... 202 266-7000 New York *(G-9251)*
Backstage LLC ... E ... 212 493-4243 Brooklyn *(G-1662)*
Barsky Ventures LLC ... G ... 212 265-8890 New York *(G-9327)*
Baywood Publishing Company ... G ... 631 691-1270 Amityville *(G-277)*
▲ Bazaar ... G ... 212 903-5497 New York *(G-9336)*
Beauty Fashion Inc ... E ... 212 840-8800 New York *(G-9340)*
Bedford Freeman & Worth ... C ... 212 576-9400 New York *(G-9342)*
Bedford Communications Inc ... E ... 212 807-8220 New York *(G-9344)*
Beer Marketers Insights Inc ... G ... 845 507-0040 Suffern *(G-15786)*
Bellerophon Publications Inc ... E ... 212 627-9977 New York *(G-9351)*
Berger & Wild LLC ... G ... 646 415-8459 New York *(G-9363)*
Bernhard Arnold & Company Inc ... G ... 212 907-1500 New York *(G-9367)*
▲ Bertelsmann Inc ... E ... 212 782-1000 New York *(G-9370)*
Bertelsmann Pubg Group Inc ... A ... 212 782-1000 New York *(G-9371)*
▲ Beverage Media Group Inc ... F ... 212 571-3232 New York *(G-9380)*
Binah Magazines Corp ... G ... 718 305-5200 Brooklyn *(G-1698)*
BJ Magazines Inc ... G ... 212 367-9705 New York *(G-9407)*
Blackbook Media Corp ... E ... 212 334-1800 New York *(G-9410)*
Blue Horizon Media Inc ... F ... 212 661-7878 New York *(G-9421)*
Bnei Aram Soba Inc ... F ... 718 645-4460 Brooklyn *(G-1707)*
Boardman Simons Publishing ... E ... 212 620-7200 New York *(G-9432)*
Bondi Digital Publishing LLC ... G ... 212 405-1655 New York *(G-9435)*
Boy Scouts of America ... G ... 212 532-0985 New York *(G-9446)*
Brant Art Publications Inc ... E ... 212 941-2800 New York *(G-9454)*
▲ Brant Publications Inc ... E ... 212 941-2800 New York *(G-9455)*
Brownstone Publishers Inc ... E ... 212 473-8200 New York *(G-9474)*
Buffalo Spree Publishing Inc ... G ... 585 413-0040 Rochester *(G-14249)*
Buffalo Spree Publishing Inc ... E ... 716 783-9119 Buffalo *(G-2859)*
Business Tech Communications ... F ... 516 354-5205 Garden City *(G-5498)*
Bust Inc ... G ... 212 675-1707 Brooklyn *(G-1741)*
Bz Media LLC ... F ... 631 421-4158 Melville *(G-8299)*
C Q Communications Inc ... E ... 516 681-2922 Hicksville *(G-6328)*
Cambridge University Press ... D ... 212 337-5000 New York *(G-9507)*
Capco Marketing ... F ... 315 699-1687 Baldwinsville *(G-567)*
Capital Reg Wkly Newsppr Group ... F ... 518 674-2841 Averill Park *(G-533)*
Carol Group Ltd ... G ... 212 505-2030 New York *(G-9532)*
Cdc Publishing LLC ... E ... 215 579-1695 Morrisville *(G-8619)*
Center For Inquiry Inc ... F ... 716 636-4869 Amherst *(G-231)*
Cfo Publishing LLC ... E ... 212 459-3004 New York *(G-9572)*
Choice Magazine Listening Inc ... G ... 516 883-8280 Port Washington *(G-13805)*
City and State Ny LLC ... E ... 212 268-0442 New York *(G-9627)*
City Real Estate Book Inc ... G ... 516 593-2949 Valley Stream *(G-16403)*
Civil Svc Rtred Employees Assn ... F ... 718 937-0290 Long Island City *(G-7699)*
Clarion Publications Inc ... F ... 585 243-3530 Geneseo *(G-5564)*
◆ Clp Pb LLC ... E ... 212 340-8100 New York *(G-9646)*
▲ CMX Media LLC ... E ... 917 793-5831 New York *(G-9649)*
CNY Business Review Inc ... F ... 315 472-3104 Syracuse *(G-15898)*
College Calendar Company ... F ... 315 768-8242 Whitesboro *(G-17192)*
Commentary Inc ... F ... 212 891-1400 New York *(G-9684)*
Commonweal Foundation Inc ... F ... 212 662-4200 New York *(G-9687)*
Complex Media Inc ... G ... 917 793-5831 New York *(G-9692)*
Conde Nast ... E ... 212 630-3642 New York *(G-9696)*
Conde Nast International Inc ... D ... 212 286-2860 New York *(G-9697)*
Conference Board Inc ... C ... 212 759-0900 New York *(G-9699)*
Congress For Jewish Culture ... G ... 212 505-8040 New York *(G-9700)*
Consumers Union US Inc ... B ... 914 378-2000 Yonkers *(G-17429)*
Continuity Publishing Inc ... F ... 212 869-4170 New York *(G-9710)*
Convenience Store News ... G ... 214 217-7800 New York *(G-9713)*
Cornell University ... E ... 607 254-2473 Ithaca *(G-6834)*
Crain Communications Inc ... C ... 212 210-0100 New York *(G-9745)*
Crain News Service ... G ... 212 254-0890 New York *(G-9746)*
Crains New York Business ... E ... 212 210-0250 New York *(G-9747)*
Credit Union Journal Inc ... G ... 212 803-8200 New York *(G-9753)*
▲ Daily Beast Company LLC ... D ... 212 445-4600 New York *(G-9788)*
Data Key Communication LLC ... F ... 315 445-2347 Fayetteville *(G-5164)*
▲ Davis Ziff Publishing Inc ... D ... 212 503-3500 New York *(G-9829)*
Davler Media Group LLC ... E ... 212 315-0800 New York *(G-9830)*
Delaware County Times Inc ... G ... 607 746-2176 Delhi *(G-4237)*
Demos Medical Publishing LLC ... F ... 516 889-1791 New York *(G-9844)*
Dennis Publishing Inc ... D ... 646 717-9500 New York *(G-9847)*
Denton Publications Inc ... E ... 518 561-9680 Plattsburgh *(G-13661)*
▲ Departures Magazine ... E ... 212 382-5600 New York *(G-9849)*
Discover Media LLC ... E ... 212 624-4800 New York *(G-9883)*
▲ Disney Publishing Worldwide ... D ... 212 633-4400 White Plains *(G-17101)*
Dissent Magazine ... F ... 212 316-3120 New York *(G-9885)*
Distinction Magazine Inc ... E ... 631 843-3522 Melville *(G-8311)*
Dj Publishing Inc ... E ... 516 767-2500 Port Washington *(G-13810)*
Doctorow Communications Inc ... F ... 845 708-5166 New City *(G-8783)*
Dotto Wagner ... G ... 315 342-8020 Oswego *(G-13330)*
▲ Dow Jones & Company Inc ... B ... 609 627-2999 New York *(G-9913)*
Dow Jones & Company Inc ... E ... 212 597-5983 New York *(G-9915)*
Dow Jones Aer Company Inc ... A ... 212 416-2000 New York *(G-9916)*
Downtown Media Group LLC ... F ... 646 723-4510 New York *(G-9919)*
Ducts Webzine Association ... F ... 718 383-6728 Brooklyn *(G-1882)*
E W Williams Publications ... G ... 212 661-1516 New York *(G-9953)*
Earl G Graves Pubg Co Inc ... D ... 212 242-8000 New York *(G-9960)*
EC Publications Inc ... F ... 212 728-1844 New York *(G-9973)*
Economist Intelligence Unit NA ... D ... 212 554-0600 New York *(G-9978)*
▲ Economist Newspaper Group Inc ... C ... 212 541-0500 New York *(G-9979)*
Eidosmedia Inc ... F ... 646 795-2100 New York *(G-9988)*
Elmont North Little League ... G ... 516 775-8210 Elmont *(G-4719)*
Envy Publishing Group Inc ... G ... 212 253-9874 New York *(G-10047)*
Equal Opprtnity Pblcations Inc ... F ... 631 421-9421 Melville *(G-8314)*
▲ Essence Communications Inc ... C ... 212 522-1212 New York *(G-10064)*
Et Publishing Intl LLC ... F ... 212 838-7220 New York *(G-10075)*
Excelsior Publications ... G ... 607 746-7600 Delhi *(G-4238)*
Executive Business Media Inc ... E ... 516 334-3030 Westbury *(G-16983)*
▲ Faces Magazine Inc ... F ... 201 843-4004 Poughkeepsie *(G-13898)*
Fahy-Williams Publishing Inc ... F ... 315 781-6820 Geneva *(G-5575)*
▲ Fairchild Publications Inc ... A ... 212 630-4000 New York *(G-10128)*
Fairchild Publishing LLC ... G ... 212 286-3897 New York *(G-10129)*
Family Publishing Group Inc ... E ... 914 381-7474 Mamaroneck *(G-8034)*
Fashion Calendar International ... G ... 212 289-0420 New York *(G-10143)*
Forum Publishing Co ... G ... 631 754-5000 Centerport *(G-3476)*
Foundation For Cultural Review ... G ... 212 247-6980 New York *(G-10191)*
Francis Emory Fitch Inc ... E ... 212 619-3800 New York *(G-10199)*
Fridge Magazine Inc ... G ... 212 997-7673 New York *(G-10211)*
Frontiers Unlimited Inc ... G ... 631 283-4663 Southampton *(G-15543)*
Frost Publications Inc ... G ... 845 726-3232 Westtown *(G-17068)*
▲ Frozen Food Digest Inc ... G ... 212 557-8600 New York *(G-10213)*

SIC SECTION
27 PRINTING, PUBLISHING, AND ALLIED INDUSTRIES

Fun Media Inc ....E 646 472-0135
New York *(G-10223)*
Genomeweb LLC ....F 212 651-5636
New York *(G-10278)*
Getting The Word Out Inc ....G 518 891-9352
Saranac Lake *(G-15137)*
Glamour Magazine ....G 212 286-2860
New York *(G-10305)*
Global Entity Media Inc ....G 631 580-7772
Ronkonkoma *(G-14905)*
Global Finance Magazine ....G 212 447-7900
New York *(G-10314)*
Global Finance Media Inc ....F 212 447-7900
New York *(G-10315)*
Golden Owl Publishing Company ....G 914 962-6911
New York *(G-10333)*
▲ Golfing Magazine ....G 516 822-5446
Hicksville *(G-6352)*
Good Times Magazine ....G 516 280-2100
Carle Place *(G-3390)*
Government Data Publication ....E 347 789-8719
Brooklyn *(G-2045)*
Grants Financial Publishing ....F 212 809-7994
New York *(G-10352)*
▲ Graphis Inc ....F 212 532-9387
New York *(G-10354)*
Gruner + Jahr Prtg & Pubg Co ....C 212 463-1000
New York *(G-10375)*
◆ Gruner + Jahr USA Group Inc ....B 866 323-9336
New York *(G-10376)*
Guernica ....F 914 414-7318
Brooklyn *(G-2055)*
Guilford Publications Inc ....D 212 431-9800
New York *(G-10382)*
H F W Communications Inc ....F 315 703-7979
East Syracuse *(G-4535)*
H W Wilson Company Inc ....B 718 588-8635
Bronx *(G-1350)*
Halcyon Business Publications ....F 516 338-0900
Westbury *(G-16993)*
Hammer Communications Inc ....F 631 261-5806
Northport *(G-13012)*
Hamptons Magazine ....E 631 283-7125
Southampton *(G-15545)*
Hamptons Media LLC ....G 631 283-6900
Southampton *(G-15546)*
Hamptons Media LLC ....E 646 835-5211
New York *(G-10403)*
Harpers Magazine Foundation ....E 212 420-5720
New York *(G-10417)*
Hart Energy Publishing Lllp ....G 212 621-4621
New York *(G-10422)*
Hatherleigh Company Ltd ....G 607 538-1092
Hobart *(G-6425)*
Haymarket Group Ltd ....F 212 239-0855
New York *(G-10429)*
▲ Haymarket Media Inc ....C 646 638-6000
New York *(G-10430)*
Healthy Way of Life Magazine ....G 718 616-1681
Brooklyn *(G-2070)*
Hearst Bus Communications Inc ....G 212 649-2000
New York *(G-10435)*
Hearst Business Media ....D 516 227-1300
Uniondale *(G-16296)*
Hearst Business Media Corp ....G 631 650-6151
Great River *(G-5850)*
Hearst Business Media Corp ....F 631 650-4441
Great River *(G-5851)*
Hearst Business Publishing Inc ....F 212 969-7500
New York *(G-10436)*
▲ Hearst Corporation ....A 212 649-2000
New York *(G-10438)*
Hearst Corporation ....E 212 649-3100
New York *(G-10439)*
Hearst Corporation ....E 212 903-5366
New York *(G-10440)*
Hearst Corporation ....D 516 382-4580
New York *(G-10442)*
Hearst Corporation ....A 518 454-5694
Albany *(G-86)*
Hearst Corporation ....D 212 649-4271
New York *(G-10444)*
Hearst Corporation ....D 212 204-4300
New York *(G-10445)*
Hearst Corporation ....D 212 903-5000
New York *(G-10446)*
Hearst Corporation ....E 212 649-2275
New York *(G-10447)*
▲ Hearst Holdings Inc ....F 212 649-2000
New York *(G-10449)*

Hello and Hola Media Inc ....E 212 807-4795
Brooklyn *(G-2072)*
Herman Hall Communications ....F 718 941-1879
Brooklyn *(G-2077)*
Highline Media LLC ....C 859 692-2100
New York *(G-10475)*
▲ Historic TW Inc ....D 212 484-8000
New York *(G-10484)*
▲ Hnw Inc ....F 212 258-9215
New York *(G-10492)*
Holmes Group The Inc ....G 212 333-2300
New York *(G-10500)*
Homesell Inc ....F 718 514-0346
Staten Island *(G-15684)*
Hotelinteractive Inc ....F 631 424-7755
Smithtown *(G-15488)*
Human Life Foundation Inc ....G 212 685-5210
New York *(G-10529)*
▲ Humana Press Inc ....E 212 460-1500
New York *(G-10530)*
I On Youth ....G 716 832-6509
Buffalo *(G-3001)*
Icarus Enterprises Inc ....G 917 969-4461
New York *(G-10550)*
Icd Publications Inc ....E 631 246-9300
Islandia *(G-6796)*
Imek Media LLC ....E 212 422-9000
New York *(G-10570)*
Impressions Inc ....G 212 594-5954
New York *(G-10575)*
Index Magazine ....G 212 243-1428
New York *(G-10587)*
Industry Forecast ....G 914 244-8617
Mount Kisco *(G-8630)*
Ink Publishing Corporation ....G 347 294-1220
Brooklyn *(G-2106)*
Institute of Electrical and El ....E 212 705-8900
New York *(G-10612)*
Institutional Invester ....G 212 224-3300
New York *(G-10613)*
Intelligne The Ftr Cmptng Nwsl ....F 212 222-1123
New York *(G-10619)*
Intellitravel Media Inc ....F 646 695-6700
New York *(G-10620)*
Intercultural Alliance Artists ....G 917 406-1202
Flushing *(G-5253)*
Interhellenic Publishing Inc ....G 212 967-5016
New York *(G-10628)*
International Center For Postg ....G 607 257-5860
Ithaca *(G-6851)*
International Data Group Inc ....E 212 331-7883
New York *(G-10632)*
Interntnl Publcatns Media Grup ....G 917 604-9602
New York *(G-10640)*
Interview Inc ....E 212 941-2900
New York *(G-10642)*
Irish America Inc ....E 212 725-2993
New York *(G-10659)*
Japan America Learning Ctr Inc ....F 914 723-7600
Scarsdale *(G-15218)*
▲ Jobson Medical Information LLC ....C 212 274-7000
New York *(G-10745)*
Kbs Communications LLC ....F 212 765-7124
New York *(G-10825)*
Keller International Pubg LLC ....E 516 829-9210
Port Washington *(G-13832)*
▼ L F International Inc ....D 212 756-5000
New York *(G-10902)*
L I F Publishing Corp ....E 631 345-5200
Shirley *(G-15422)*
L Magazine LLC ....F 212 807-1254
Brooklyn *(G-2186)*
Lagardere North America Inc ....E 212 477-7373
New York *(G-10916)*
▲ Latina Media Ventures LLC ....E 212 642-0200
New York *(G-10933)*
Latino Show Magazine Inc ....G 718 709-1151
Woodhaven *(G-17307)*
Laurtom Inc ....E 914 273-2233
Mount Kisco *(G-8634)*
Leadership Directories Inc ....E 212 627-4140
New York *(G-10946)*
▲ Lebhar-Friedman Inc ....E 212 756-5000
New York *(G-10951)*
Lebhar-Friedman Inc ....C 212 756-5000
New York *(G-10952)*
Locations Magazine ....G 212 288-4745
New York *(G-11019)*
Lockwood Trade Journal Co Inc ....E 212 391-2060
Long Island City *(G-7793)*

Long Island Catholic Newspaper ....E 516 594-1212
Roosevelt *(G-15007)*
Los Angeles Mag Holdg Co Inc ....E 212 456-7777
New York *(G-11044)*
Ltb Media (usa) Inc ....D 212 447-9555
New York *(G-11057)*
Lucky Magazine ....F 212 286-6220
New York *(G-11058)*
Luminary Publishing Inc ....F 845 334-8600
Kingston *(G-7199)*
Luria Communications Inc ....G 631 329-4922
East Hampton *(G-4413)*
M Shanken Communications Inc ....C 212 684-4224
New York *(G-11077)*
Mac Fadden Holdings Inc ....E 212 614-3980
New York *(G-11081)*
▲ Macfadden Cmmnctions Group LLC ....C 212 979-4800
New York *(G-11083)*
Macmillan Holdings LLC ....G 212 576-9428
New York *(G-11087)*
Mag Inc ....E 607 257-6970
Ithaca *(G-6858)*
Magazine I Spectrum E ....E 212 419-7555
New York *(G-11098)*
▲ Magnificat Inc ....F 914 502-1820
Yonkers *(G-17464)*
Manhattan Media LLC ....E 212 268-8600
New York *(G-11130)*
Mann Publications Inc ....E 212 840-6266
New York *(G-11135)*
Mansueto Ventures LLC ....C 212 389-5300
New York *(G-11142)*
▲ Marie Claire USA ....D 212 841-8493
New York *(G-11150)*
Maritime Activity Reports ....E 212 477-6700
New York *(G-11153)*
▲ Mark Levine ....F 212 677-4457
New York *(G-11155)*
Marketing Edge ....G 212 790-1512
New York *(G-11160)*
▲ Martha Stewart Living ....B 212 827-8000
New York *(G-11166)*
▲ Martha Stewart Living Omni LLC ....B 212 827-8000
New York *(G-11167)*
Martinelli Holdings LLC ....E 302 504-1361
Rye *(G-15062)*
▲ Marvel Entertainment LLC ....C 212 576-4000
New York *(G-11170)*
Mary Ann Liebert Inc ....D 914 740-2100
New Rochelle *(G-8917)*
Mass Appeal Magazine ....G 718 858-0979
Brooklyn *(G-2279)*
Mathisen Ventures Inc ....G 212 986-1025
New York *(G-11179)*
▲ McCall Pattern Company ....C 212 465-6800
New York *(G-11195)*
McCarthy LLC ....F 646 862-5354
New York *(G-11196)*
McMahon Publishing Company ....D 212 957-5300
New York *(G-11202)*
Med Reviews LLC ....E 212 239-5860
New York *(G-11206)*
Media Press Corp ....E 212 791-6347
New York *(G-11208)*
Medikidz Usa Inc ....G 646 895-9319
New York *(G-11216)*
Meredith Corporation ....C 212 557-6600
New York *(G-11228)*
Meredith Corporation ....F 212 499-2000
New York *(G-11229)*
Meredith Corporation ....D 515 284-2157
New York *(G-11230)*
Mergent Inc ....B 212 413-7700
New York *(G-11231)*
Metrosource Publishing Inc ....F 212 691-5127
New York *(G-11242)*
Miami Media LLC ....F 212 268-8600
New York *(G-11247)*
Mishpacha Magazine Inc ....G 718 686-9339
Brooklyn *(G-2319)*
Modern Farmer Media Inc ....F 518 828-7447
Hudson *(G-6628)*
Morris Communications Co LLC ....E 212 620-9580
New York *(G-11307)*
Music & Sound Retailer Inc ....E 516 767-2500
Port Washington *(G-13847)*
Nation Company LP ....E 212 209-5400
New York *(G-11344)*
Nation Magazine ....E 212 209-5400
New York *(G-11345)*

S I C

Employee Codes: A=Over 500 employees, B=251-500
C=101-250, D=51-100, E=20-50, F=10-19, G=5-9
2017 Harris
New York Manufacturers Directory
759

National Marketing Services ....F 516 942-9595
Roslyn Heights *(G-15030)*
National Prof Resources ....E 914 937-8879
Port Chester *(G-13755)*
National Review Inc ....E 212 679-7330
New York *(G-11350)*
▼ **Nature America Inc** ....B 212 726-9200
New York *(G-11357)*
▲ **NBM Publishing Inc** ....G 212 643-5407
New York *(G-11363)*
NCM Publishers Inc ....G 212 691-9100
New York *(G-11364)*
Nervecom Inc ....F 212 625-9914
New York *(G-11369)*
New Art Publications Inc ....F 718 636-9100
Brooklyn *(G-2359)*
New Hope Media LLC ....G 646 366-0830
New York *(G-11390)*
New York Media LLC ....C 212 508-0700
New York *(G-11403)*
Newbay Media LLC ....F 516 944-5940
Port Washington *(G-13848)*
Newsgraphics of Delmar Inc ....E 518 439-5363
Delmar *(G-4245)*
Next Step Publishing Inc ....F 585 742-1260
Victor *(G-16494)*
Niche Media Holdings LLc ....E 702 990-2500
New York *(G-11424)*
Nickelodeon Magazines Inc ....G 212 541-1949
New York *(G-11427)*
▲ **Nihao Media LLC** ....G 609 903-4264
New York *(G-11430)*
Njf Publishing Corp ....G 631 345-5200
Shirley *(G-15427)*
▲ **Northeast Group** ....D 518 563-8214
Plattsburgh *(G-13682)*
Northside Media Group LLC ....F 917 318-6513
Brooklyn *(G-2375)*
Northside Media Group LLC ....E 917 318-6513
Brooklyn *(G-2376)*
Nova Science Publishers Inc ....F 631 231-7269
Hauppauge *(G-6149)*
Nsgv Inc ....E 212 367-3167
New York *(G-11466)*
Nsgv Inc ....E 212 367-4118
New York *(G-11467)*
Nsgv Inc ....E 212 367-3100
New York *(G-11468)*
Nyemac Inc ....G 631 668-1303
Montauk *(G-8591)*
Nylon LLc ....E 212 226-6454
New York *(G-11482)*
Nylon Media Inc ....E 212 226-6454
New York *(G-11483)*
Nyrev Inc ....E 212 757-8070
New York *(G-11486)*
Odyssey Mag Pubg Group Inc ....C 212 545-4800
New York *(G-11497)*
Paper Publishing Company Inc ....E 212 226-4405
New York *(G-11565)*
Parade Publications Inc ....D 212 450-7000
New York *(G-11568)*
Parents Guide Network Corp ....E 212 213-8840
New York *(G-11571)*
Pati Inc ....F 718 244-6788
Jamaica *(G-6938)*
Pearson Education Inc ....F 201 236-7000
West Nyack *(G-16924)*
▲ **Penhouse Media Group Inc** ....C 212 702-6000
New York *(G-11607)*
▲ **Penton Media Inc** ....B 212 204-4200
New York *(G-11608)*
Penton Media Inc ....G 212 204-4200
New York *(G-11609)*
Periodical Services Co Inc ....F 518 822-9300
Hudson *(G-6630)*
Photo Industry Inc ....F 516 364-0016
Woodbury *(G-17295)*
Playbill Incorporated ....E 212 557-5757
New York *(G-11674)*
Pointwise Information Service ....F 315 457-4111
Liverpool *(G-7542)*
Preparatory Magazine Group ....D 718 761-4800
Staten Island *(G-15724)*
Prescribing Reference Inc ....D 646 638-6000
New York *(G-11699)*
Primedia Special Interest Publ ....D 212 726-4300
New York *(G-11709)*
Professnal Spt Pblications Inc ....D 212 697-1460
New York *(G-11728)*
Professnal Spt Pblications Inc ....D 516 327-9500
Elmont *(G-4727)*
Psychonomic Society Inc ....E 512 381-1494
New York *(G-11743)*
Public Relations Soc Amer Inc ....E 212 460-1400
New York *(G-11746)*
Pwxyz LLC ....G 212 377-5500
New York *(G-11761)*
Q Communications Inc ....G 212 594-6520
New York *(G-11762)*
Quest Media Llc ....F 646 840-3404
New York *(G-11772)*
Ragozin Data ....E 212 674-3123
Long Island City *(G-7856)*
Ralph Martinelli ....E 914 345-3055
Elmsford *(G-4775)*
Ramholtz Publishing Inc ....D 718 761-4800
Staten Island *(G-15727)*
Rd Publications Inc ....C 914 238-1000
Pleasantville *(G-13717)*
Readers Dgest Latinoamerica SA ....B 914 238-1000
Pleasantville *(G-13718)*
Readers Digest Assn Incthe ....F 414 423-0100
New York *(G-11811)*
Readers Digest Assn Incthe ....F 914 238-1000
Mount Kisco *(G-8644)*
Real Est Book of Long Island ....F 516 364-5000
Syosset *(G-15837)*
Real Estate Media Inc ....E 212 929-6976
New York *(G-11813)*
Redbook Magazine ....F 212 649-3331
New York *(G-11815)*
◆ **Relx Inc** ....E 212 309-8100
New York *(G-11826)*
Relx Inc ....E 212 463-6644
New York *(G-11827)*
Relx Inc ....B 212 633-3900
New York *(G-11828)*
Res Media Group Inc ....F 212 320-3750
New York *(G-11838)*
Retail Management Pubg Inc ....F 212 981-0217
New York *(G-11845)*
Rfp LLC ....E 212 838-7733
New York *(G-11855)*
Risk Society Management Pubg ....E 212 286-9364
New York *(G-11879)*
Rnd Enterprises Inc ....F 212 627-0165
New York *(G-11886)*
Rodale Inc ....B 212 697-2040
New York *(G-11900)*
Rolling Stone Magazine ....G 212 484-1616
New York *(G-11909)*
Romantic Times Inc ....F 718 237-1097
Brooklyn *(G-2503)*
Ross Communications Associates ....F 631 393-5089
Melville *(G-8353)*
Rough Draft Publishing LLC ....F 212 741-4773
New York *(G-11920)*
Rsl Media LLC ....G 212 307-6760
New York *(G-11931)*
Ruby Newco LLC ....G 212 852-7000
New York *(G-11933)*
Rye Record ....G 914 713-3213
Rye *(G-15067)*
Sandow Media LLC ....F 646 805-0200
New York *(G-11966)*
Saveur Magazine ....E 212 219-7400
New York *(G-11977)*
Schnell Publishing Company Inc ....F 212 791-4200
New York *(G-11995)*
▲ **Scholastic Corporation** ....G 212 343-6100
New York *(G-11997)*
▲ **Scholastic Inc** ....A 800 724-6527
New York *(G-11998)*
▲ **Securities Data Publishing Inc** ....G 212 631-1411
New York *(G-12014)*
Security Letter ....G 212 348-1553
New York *(G-12015)*
Shoreline Publishing Inc ....G 914 738-7869
Pelham *(G-13494)*
Shugar Publishing ....G 631 288-4404
Westhampton Beach *(G-17060)*
Simmons-Boardman Pubg Corp ....G 212 620-7200
New York *(G-12078)*
Sky Art Media Inc ....G 917 355-9022
New York *(G-12094)*
Small Business Advisors Inc ....F 516 374-1387
Atlantic Beach *(G-470)*
Smart & Strong LLC ....E 212 938-2051
New York *(G-12100)*
Smooth Magazine ....F 212 925-1150
New York *(G-12110)*
Society For The Study ....G 212 822-8806
New York *(G-12114)*
Sound Communications Inc ....E 516 767-2500
Port Washington *(G-13866)*
▲ **Source Media Inc** ....B 212 803-8200
New York *(G-12143)*
Spc Marketing Company ....G 631 661-2727
West Islip *(G-16907)*
Spin Magazine Media ....G 212 231-7400
New York *(G-12163)*
▲ **Sports Illustrated For Kids** ....E 212 522-1212
New York *(G-12166)*
Spotlight Publications LLC ....G 914 345-9473
Elmsford *(G-4787)*
Springer Adis Us LLC ....E 212 460-1500
New York *(G-12171)*
Springer Healthcare LLC ....E 212 460-1500
New York *(G-12173)*
Springer Publishing Co LLC ....E 212 431-4370
New York *(G-12174)*
◆ **Springer Scnce + Bus Media LLC** ....C 781 871-6600
New York *(G-12175)*
Standard Analytics Io Inc ....G 917 882-5422
New York *(G-12181)*
Staten Island Parent Magazine ....G 718 761-4800
Staten Island *(G-15739)*
Steffen Publishing Inc ....D 315 865-4100
Holland Patent *(G-6488)*
Strathmore Directories Ltd ....E 516 997-2525
Westbury *(G-17028)*
Stuff Magazine ....G 212 302-2626
New York *(G-12222)*
Suburban Publishing Inc ....F 845 463-0542
Poughkeepsie *(G-13936)*
Suffolk Community Council Inc ....G 631 434-9277
Deer Park *(G-4214)*
Summit Professional Networks ....D 212 557-7480
New York *(G-12234)*
Surface Magazine ....E 646 805-0200
New York *(G-12246)*
Sussex Publishers Inc ....E 212 260-7210
New York *(G-12247)*
Swaps Monitor Publications Inc ....F 212 742-8550
New York *(G-12249)*
Swift Fulfillment Services ....G 516 593-1198
Lynbrook *(G-7964)*
T V Trade Media Inc ....F 212 288-3933
New York *(G-12269)*
Techweb LLC ....F 516 562-5000
Manhasset *(G-8066)*
Teen Fire Magazine ....G 646 415-3703
New York *(G-12294)*
Testa Communications Inc ....E 516 767-2500
Port Washington *(G-13868)*
The PRS Group Inc ....F 315 431-0511
East Syracuse *(G-4571)*
Thestreet Inc ....D 212 321-5000
New York *(G-12316)*
Thomas International Pubg Co ....G 212 613-3441
New York *(G-12320)*
Thomas Publishing Company LLC ....G 212 695-0500
New York *(G-12323)*
Thomas Publishing Company LLC ....G 212 290-7297
New York *(G-12324)*
Thomas Publishing Company LLC ....B 212 695-0500
New York *(G-12321)*
Thomson Rters Tax Accnting Inc ....D 212 367-6300
New York *(G-12330)*
Time Inc ....E 212 522-1212
New York *(G-12343)*
Time Inc ....E 212 522-1633
New York *(G-12344)*
◆ **Time Inc** ....A 212 522-1212
New York *(G-12345)*
Time Inc ....E 212 522-0361
New York *(G-12346)*
▲ **Time Inc Affluent Media Group** ....B 212 382-5600
New York *(G-12347)*
▲ **Time Out New York Partners LP** ....D 646 432-3000
New York *(G-12348)*
Time Warner Companies Inc ....D 212 484-8000
New York *(G-12350)*
TMC Usa LLC ....G 518 587-8920
Saratoga Springs *(G-15175)*
Towse Publishing Co ....F 914 235-3095
New Rochelle *(G-8925)*
Trader Interntnal Publications ....G 914 631-6856
Sleepy Hollow *(G-15475)*

S I C

Trans-High Corporation E 212 387-0500
New York *(G-12391)*

▲ **Trend Pot Inc** E 212 431-9970
New York *(G-12397)*

◆ **Trusted Media Brands Inc** A 914 238-1000
New York *(G-12413)*

Trusted Media Brands Inc F 646 293-6025
New York *(G-12414)*

TV Guide Magazine LLC G 212 852-7500
New York *(G-12430)*

▲ **TV Guide Magazine Group Inc** D 212 852-7500
New York *(G-12431)*

▲ **U S Japan Publication NY Inc** G 212 252-8833
New York *(G-12438)*

Ubm Inc A 212 600-3000
New York *(G-12440)*

Ubm LLC A 516 562-5085
New York *(G-12441)*

Ubm LLC F 516 562-5000
New York *(G-12442)*

Ulster Publishing Co Inc E 845 334-8205
Kingston *(G-7219)*

Universal Cmmncations of Miami C 212 986-5100
New York *(G-12469)*

Uptown Media Group LLC E 212 360-5073
New York *(G-12476)*

Urban Racercom G 718 279-2202
Bayside *(G-777)*

Urbandaddy Inc F 212 929-7905
New York *(G-12482)*

US China Magazine E 212 663-4333
New York *(G-12484)*

US Frontline News Inc E 212 922-9090
New York *(G-12486)*

▲ **US News & World Report Inc** C 212 716-6800
New York *(G-12488)*

US Weekly LLC D 212 484-1616
New York *(G-12489)*

Value Line Inc D 212 907-1500
New York *(G-12497)*

Value Line Publishing LLC C 212 907-1500
New York *(G-12498)*

◆ **Vanity Fair** F 212 286-6052
New York *(G-12501)*

Vending Times Inc F 516 442-1850
Rockville Centre *(G-14802)*

Veranda Publications Inc G 212 903-5206
New York *(G-12519)*

Vibe Media Group LLC D 212 448-7300
New York *(G-12536)*

Vickers Stock Research Corp E 212 425-7500
New York *(G-12537)*

Virtual Urth F 914 793-1269
Bronxville *(G-1504)*

▲ **Visionaire Publishing LLC** E 646 434-6091
New York *(G-12553)*

Vogue Magazine D 212 286-2860
New York *(G-12564)*

Wall Street Reporter Magazine D 212 363-2600
New York *(G-12581)*

Wallkill Valley Publications E 845 561-0170
Newburgh *(G-12786)*

Watch Journal LLC G 212 229-1500
New York *(G-12593)*

Weider Publications LLC C 212 545-4800
New York *(G-12604)*

Welcome Magazine Inc F 716 839-3121
Amherst *(G-272)*

▲ **Wenner Media LLC** C 212 484-1616
New York *(G-12611)*

▲ **Westchester Law Journal Inc** G 914 948-0715
White Plains *(G-17183)*

Western New York Family Mag G 716 836-3486
Buffalo *(G-3253)*

Westfair Communications Inc E 914 694-3600
White Plains *(G-17186)*

Wine & Spirits Magazine Inc G 212 695-4660
New York *(G-12641)*

▲ **Wine On Line International** G 212 755-4363
New York *(G-12642)*

Winsight LLC G 646 708-7309
New York *(G-12648)*

Womens E News Inc G 212 244-1720
New York *(G-12653)*

Working Mother Media Inc D 212 351-6400
New York *(G-12659)*

World Business Media LLC F 212 344-0759
Massapequa Park *(G-8191)*

World Guide Publishing E 800 331-7840
New York *(G-12662)*

Wsn Inc G 212 924-7620
New York *(G-12670)*

Yale Robbins Inc D 212 683-5700
New York *(G-12687)*

2731 Books: Publishing & Printing

450 Ridge St Inc G 716 754-2789
Lewiston *(G-7432)*

▲ **Abbeville Press Inc** E 212 366-5585
New York *(G-9001)*

Adir Publishing Co F 718 633-9437
Brooklyn *(G-1562)*

Ai Entertainment Holdings LLC F 212 247-6400
New York *(G-9063)*

Aip Publishing LLC C 516 576-2200
Melville *(G-8290)*

▲ **Alba House Publishers** E 718 698-2759
Staten Island *(G-15633)*

Alfred Publishing Co Inc D 315 736-1572
Oriskany *(G-13303)*

▲ **Allworth Communications Inc** F 212 777-8395
New York *(G-9094)*

Alm Media LLC B 212 457-9400
New York *(G-9095)*

Alm Media Holdings Inc B 212 457-9400
New York *(G-9096)*

Amereon Ltd G 631 298-5100
Mattituck *(G-8206)*

▲ **American Inst Chem Engineers** D 646 495-1355
New York *(G-9121)*

American Institute Physics Inc C 516 576-2410
Melville *(G-8293)*

Amherst Media Inc G 716 874-4450
Buffalo *(G-2809)*

▼ **Amsco School Publications Inc** D 212 886-6500
New York *(G-9141)*

Annuals Publishing Co Inc G 212 505-0950
New York *(G-9165)*

▲ **Anthroposophic Press Inc** G 518 851-2054
Clifton Park *(G-3695)*

Apollo Investment Fund VII LP G 212 515-3200
New York *(G-9176)*

Arbor Books Inc E 201 236-9990
New York *(G-9191)*

Aspen Publishers Inc A 212 771-0600
New York *(G-9235)*

▲ **Assouline Publishing Inc** G 212 989-6769
New York *(G-9241)*

▲ **Ateres Publishing & Bk Bindery** F 718 935-9355
Brooklyn *(G-1645)*

Atlas & Company LLC G 212 234-3100
New York *(G-9254)*

◆ **Barrons Educational Series Inc** D 631 434-3311
Hauppauge *(G-6032)*

Baywood Publishing Company G 631 691-1270
Amityville *(G-277)*

Bear Port Publishing Company F 212 337-8577
New York *(G-9339)*

Beauty Fashion Inc E 212 840-8800
New York *(G-9340)*

Bedford Freeman & Worth C 212 576-9400
New York *(G-9342)*

Bedford Freeman & Worth D 212 375-7000
New York *(G-9343)*

Bedrock Communications G 212 532-4150
New York *(G-9345)*

▲ **Benchmark Education Co LLC** D 914 637-7200
New Rochelle *(G-8888)*

▲ **Bertelsmann Inc** E 212 782-1000
New York *(G-9370)*

Bertelsmann Pubg Group Inc A 212 782-1000
New York *(G-9371)*

Binghamton University D 607 777-2316
Binghamton *(G-896)*

Birchbrook Press G 607 746-7453
Delhi *(G-4236)*

▲ **Bloomsbury Publishing Inc** D 212 419-5300
New York *(G-9418)*

Bmg Rights Management (us) LLC E 212 561-3000
New York *(G-9430)*

Boardman Simons Publishing E 212 620-7200
New York *(G-9432)*

▲ **Bobley-Harmann Corporation** G 516 433-3800
Ronkonkoma *(G-14880)*

Booklinks Publishing Svcs LLC G 718 852-2116
Brooklyn *(G-1709)*

Booklyn Artists Alliance G 718 383-9621
Brooklyn *(G-1710)*

Boydell & Brewer Inc F 585 275-0419
Rochester *(G-14243)*

▲ **Bright Kids Nyc Inc** E 917 539-4575
New York *(G-9460)*

British American Publishing D 518 786-6000
Latham *(G-7356)*

Brown Publishing Network Inc G 212 682-3330
New York *(G-9472)*

▼ **Burns Archive Photographic Dis** G 212 889-1938
New York *(G-9481)*

Byliner Inc E 415 680-3608
New York *(G-9488)*

Callaway Arts & Entrmt Inc F 212 798-3168
New York *(G-9502)*

Cambridge University Press D 212 337-5000
New York *(G-9507)*

Campus Course Paks Inc G 516 877-3967
Garden City *(G-5499)*

Canopy Books LLC G 516 354-4888
Floral Park *(G-5198)*

Castle Connolly Medical Ltd E 212 367-8400
New York *(G-9543)*

CB Publishing LLC G 516 354-4888
Floral Park *(G-5199)*

CCC Publications Inc G 718 306-1008
Brooklyn *(G-1767)*

▲ **Central Cnfrnce of Amrcn Rbbis** F 212 972-3636
New York *(G-9563)*

Chain Store Age Magazine G 212 756-5000
New York *(G-9574)*

Christian Book Publishing E 646 559-2533
New York *(G-9607)*

▼ **Church Publishing Incorporated** G 212 592-1800
New York *(G-9615)*

Cinderella Press Ltd G 212 431-3130
New York *(G-9616)*

▲ **Clarkson N Potter Inc** F 212 782-9000
New York *(G-9635)*

Codesters Inc G 646 232-1025
New York *(G-9664)*

▲ **Columbia University Press Inc** E 212 459-0600
New York *(G-9678)*

Columbia University Press Inc E 212 459-0600
New York *(G-9679)*

Columbia University Press Inc E 212 459-0600
New York *(G-9680)*

Conde Nast E 212 630-3642
New York *(G-9696)*

Confrtrnity of Prescious Blood G 718 436-1120
Brooklyn *(G-1797)*

Congress For Jewish Culture G 212 505-8040
New York *(G-9700)*

Continuum Intl Pubg Group Inc F 646 649-4215
New York *(G-9712)*

Cornell University D 607 277-2338
Ithaca *(G-6833)*

Cornell University G 607 255-0897
Ithaca *(G-6835)*

Crabtree Publishing Inc E 212 496-5040
New York *(G-9742)*

Cross Border Usa Inc G 212 425-9649
New York *(G-9756)*

D C I Technical Inc F 516 355-0464
Franklin Square *(G-5362)*

Daheshist Publishing Co Ltd F 212 581-8360
New York *(G-9787)*

▲ **Davis Ziff Publishing Inc** D 212 503-3500
New York *(G-9829)*

Definition Press Inc F 212 777-4490
New York *(G-9836)*

Delaney Books Inc F 516 921-8888
Syosset *(G-15819)*

Demos Medical Publishing LLC F 516 889-1791
New York *(G-9844)*

Divine Phoenix LLC A 585 737-1482
Skaneateles *(G-15459)*

▲ **Dorling Kindersley Publishing** D 212 213-4800
New York *(G-9910)*

Dreams To Print G 718 483-8020
Brooklyn *(G-1879)*

Dwj Books LLC G 631 899-4500
Sag Harbor *(G-15078)*

E W Williams Publications G 212 661-1516
New York *(G-9953)*

Eagle Art Publishing Inc G 212 685-7411
New York *(G-9957)*

Editions Schellmann Inc G 212 219-1821
New York *(G-9982)*

Edwin Mellen Press Inc E 716 754-2796
Lewiston *(G-7434)*

Eleanor Ettinger Inc E 212 925-7474
New York *(G-9995)*

SIC

27 PRINTING, PUBLISHING, AND ALLIED INDUSTRIES SIC SECTION

Elsevier Engineering Info Inc................E....... 201 356-6800
New York (G-10014)
▲ Entertainment Weekly Inc ....C....... 212 522-5600
New York (G-10044)
F P H Communications..........................G....... 212 528-1728
New York (G-10116)
Faces Magazine Inc ....D....... 845 454-7420
Poughkeepsie (G-13899)
▲ Facts On File Inc ....D....... 212 967-8800
New York (G-10126)
▲ Fairchild Publications Inc ....A....... 212 630-4000
New York (G-10128)
Family Publishing Group Inc ....E....... 914 381-7474
Mamaroneck (G-8034)
▲ Farrar Straus and Giroux LLC ....E....... 212 741-6900
New York (G-10138)
Feminist Press Inc ....G....... 212 817-7929
New York (G-10152)
Folio Graphics Co Inc............................G....... 718 763-2076
Brooklyn (G-1993)
▲ Foxhill Press Inc ....E....... 212 995-9620
New York (G-10196)
Frank Merriwell Inc ....F....... 516 921-8888
Syosset (G-15823)
Franklin Report LLC ....G....... 212 639-9100
New York (G-10204)
Future Us Inc..D....... 844 779-2822
New York (G-10228)
Ggp Publishing Inc ....F....... 914 834-8896
Harrison (G-5984)
▲ Gildan Media Corp ....F....... 718 459-6299
Flushing (G-5243)
Government Data Publication................E....... 347 789-8719
Brooklyn (G-2045)
Gq Magazine...G....... 212 286-2860
New York (G-10344)
Grand Central Publishing......................C....... 212 364-1200
New York (G-10347)
▲ Graphis Inc ....F....... 212 532-9387
New York (G-10354)
Grey House Publishing Inc ....E....... 845 483-3535
Poughkeepsie (G-13904)
Grey House Publishing Inc ....E....... 518 789-8700
Amenia (G-216)
Grolier International Inc ....G....... 212 343-6100
New York (G-10368)
Guilford Publications Inc ....D....... 212 431-9800
New York (G-10382)
H W Wilson Company Inc.......................B....... 718 588-8635
Bronx (G-1350)
▲ Hachette Book Group Inc.................B....... 212 364-1200
New York (G-10391)
▲ Haights Cross Cmmnications Inc.....E....... 212 209-0500
New York (G-10395)
Haights Cross Operating Co..................E....... 914 289-9400
White Plains (G-17116)
Harpercollins Publishers LLC................E....... 212 553-4200
New York (G-10415)
Harpercollins Publishers LLC................D....... 212 207-7000
New York (G-10416)
▲ Harry N Abrams Incorporated..........D....... 212 206-7715
New York (G-10419)
Harvard University Press ....D....... 212 337-0280
New York (G-10425)
◆ Hazan Cohen Group LLC ....F....... 646 827-0030
New York (G-10432)
Hdt Group LLC ....G....... 914 490-2107
New York (G-10434)
Hearst Business Media Corp ....F....... 631 650-4441
Great River (G-5851)
▲ Hearst Corporation ....A....... 212 649-2000
New York (G-10438)
Hearst Corporation.................................E....... 212 649-2275
New York (G-10447)
▲ Helvetica Press Incorporated ....G....... 212 737-1857
New York (G-10456)
▲ Henry Holt and Company LLC..........D....... 646 307-5095
New York (G-10459)
Highline Media LLC................................C....... 859 692-2100
New York (G-10475)
▲ Hippocrene Books Inc.......................G....... 212 685-4371
New York (G-10482)
▲ Holiday House Inc.............................F....... 212 688-0085
New York (G-10496)
Houghton Mifflin Harcourt Pubg ....E....... 212 420-5800
New York (G-10515)
Houghton Mifflin Harcourt Pubg ....C....... 914 747-2709
Thornwood (G-16121)
▲ Hudson Park Press Inc.....................G....... 212 929-8898
New York (G-10526)
▲ Humana Press Inc..............................E....... 212 460-1500
New York (G-10530)
Iat Interactive LLC.................................E....... 914 273-2233
Mount Kisco (G-8628)
Incisive Rwg Inc.....................................C....... 212 457-9400
New York (G-10581)
Infobase Publishing Company ....G....... 212 967-8800
New York (G-10595)
Interntnl Publcatns Media Grup............G....... 917 604-9602
New York (G-10640)
James Morgan Publishing ....G....... 212 655-5470
New York (G-10697)
Jim Henson Company Inc......................E....... 212 794-2400
New York (G-10733)
John Wiley & Sons Inc ....D....... 845 457-6250
Montgomery (G-8596)
▲ Jonathan David Publishers Inc.........F....... 718 456-8611
Middle Village (G-8413)
▲ Judaica Press Inc..............................G....... 718 972-6202
Brooklyn (G-2156)
▲ Juris Publishing Inc...........................E....... 631 351-5430
Huntington (G-6665)
▲ K T A V Publishing House Inc...........F....... 201 963-9524
Brooklyn (G-2165)
Kensington Publishing Corp ....D....... 212 407-1500
New York (G-10836)
▲ Klutz ....E....... 650 687-2600
New York (G-10860)
Kobalt Music Pubg Amer Inc ....D....... 212 247-6204
New York (G-10865)
▲ Kodansha USA Inc.............................G....... 917 322-6200
New York (G-10867)
▲ Le Book Publishing Inc ....G....... 212 334-5252
New York (G-10940)
Learningexpress LLC ....E....... 646 274-6454
New York (G-10948)
▲ Lee & Low Books Incorporated ....F....... 212 779-4400
New York (G-10957)
Legal Strategies Inc...............................G....... 516 377-3940
Merrick (G-8389)
Lexis Publishing ....C....... 518 487-3000
Menands (G-8373)
▼ Library Tales Publishing Inc ....G....... 347 394-2629
New York (G-10985)
Lippincott Massie McQuilkin L ....F....... 212 352-2055
New York (G-11006)
▲ Literary Classics of US......................F....... 212 308-3360
New York (G-11008)
Little Bee Books Inc...............................G....... 212 321-0237
New York (G-11011)
Liveright Publishing Corp......................G....... 212 354-5500
New York (G-11015)
Living Well Innovations Inc...................G....... 646 517-3200
Hauppauge (G-6113)
Looseleaf Law Publications Inc............F....... 718 359-5559
Flushing (G-5268)
M&M Printing Inc....................................F....... 516 796-3020
Carle Place (G-3394)
M/B Midtown LLC...................................F....... 212 477-2495
New York (G-11079)
Macmillan College Pubg Co Inc............F....... 212 702-2000
New York (G-11086)
▲ Macmillan Publishers Inc ....A....... 646 307-5151
New York (G-11088)
◆ Macmillan Publishing Group LLC.....E....... 212 674-5151
New York (G-11089)
▲ Malhame Publs & Importers Inc ....E....... 631 694-8600
Bohemia (G-1101)
▲ Marshall Cavendish Corp..................E....... 914 332-8888
Tarrytown (G-16095)
▲ Martha Stewart Living........................B....... 212 827-8000
New York (G-11166)
Mary Ann Liebert Inc ....D....... 914 740-2100
New Rochelle (G-8917)
Mathisen Ventures Inc...........................G....... 212 986-1025
New York (G-11179)
▲ McBooks Press Inc ....G....... 607 272-2114
Ithaca (G-6859)
▲ McCall Pattern Company...................C....... 212 465-6800
New York (G-11195)
McGraw-Hill Glbl Edctn Hldngs.............D....... 646 766-2000
New York (G-11198)
McGraw-Hill School Education H ....B....... 646 766-2000
New York (G-11199)
McGraw-Hill School Educatn LLC ....A....... 646 766-2060
New York (G-11200)
Mediaplanet Publishing Hse Inc............E....... 646 922-1409
New York (G-11211)
Medikidz Usa Inc ....G....... 646 895-9319
New York (G-11216)
Meegenius Inc ....G....... 212 283-7285
New York (G-11219)
▲ Melcher Media Inc ....F....... 212 727-2322
New York (G-11222)
Meredith Corporation ....D....... 515 284-2157
New York (G-11230)
Merkos Llnyonei Chinuch Inc ....E....... 718 778-0226
Brooklyn (G-2300)
▲ Mesorah Publications Ltd ....E....... 718 921-9000
Brooklyn (G-2302)
Metro Creative Graphics Inc ....E....... 212 947-5100
New York (G-11241)
Micro Publishing Inc...............................G....... 212 533-9180
New York (G-11253)
Modern Language Assn Amer Inc ....C....... 646 576-5000
New York (G-11288)
▲ Monacelli Press LLC..........................G....... 212 229-9925
New York (G-11298)
▲ Mondo Publishing Inc.......................E....... 212 268-3560
New York (G-11299)
▲ Monthly Review Foundation Inc ....G....... 212 691-2555
New York (G-11303)
▲ Moznaim Publishing Co Inc ....G....... 718 853-0525
Brooklyn (G-2337)
▲ Mud Puddle Books Inc ....G....... 212 647-9168
New York (G-11322)
◆ Multi Packaging Solutions Inc ....E....... 646 885-0157
New York (G-11324)
N A R Associates Inc ....G....... 845 557-8713
Barryville (G-620)
National Learning Corp ....F....... 516 921-8888
Syosset (G-15830)
Nationwide Custom Services.................G....... 845 365-0414
Tappan (G-16081)
Natural E Creative LLC ....F....... 516 488-1143
New Hyde Park (G-8849)
▲ NBM Publishing Inc ....G....... 212 643-5407
New York (G-11363)
New City Press Inc..................................G....... 845 229-0335
Hyde Park (G-6735)
New Directions Publishing.....................F....... 212 255-0230
New York (G-11384)
New Press..E....... 212 629-8802
New York (G-11392)
New York Legal Publishing....................G....... 518 459-1100
Menands (G-8377)
New York Qrtrly Foundation Inc ....F....... 917 843-8825
Brooklyn (G-2368)
Newkirk Products Inc ....C....... 518 862-3200
Albany (G-107)
News Corporation...................................C....... 212 416-3400
New York (G-11416)
News India USA Inc ....F....... 212 675-7515
New York (G-11418)
North Shore Home Improver..................F....... 631 474-2824
Port Jeff STA (G-13767)
▲ North-South Books Inc......................E....... 212 706-4545
New York (G-11459)
Nova Science Publishers Inc ....F....... 631 231-7269
Hauppauge (G-6149)
Omniumedia LLC ....G....... 516 593-2735
Elmont (G-4725)
Options Publishing LLC ....F....... 603 429-2698
New York (G-11518)
Other Press LLC......................................G....... 212 414-0054
New York (G-11534)
Oxford Book Company Inc.....................C....... 212 227-2120
New York (G-11538)
◆ Oxford University Press LLC ....B....... 212 726-6000
New York (G-11542)
Oxford University Press LLC ....G....... 212 726-6000
New York (G-11543)
Ozmodyl Ltd ....G....... 212 226-0622
New York (G-11545)
P J D Publications Ltd ....G....... 516 626-0650
New Hyde Park (G-8855)
Pace Walkers of America Inc ....F....... 631 444-2147
Port Jefferson (G-13778)
▲ Palgrave Macmillan Ltd ....G....... 646 307-5028
New York (G-11556)
▲ Papercutz Inc.....................................G....... 646 559-4681
New York (G-11566)
▲ Parachute Publishing LLC ....E....... 212 337-6743
New York (G-11567)
Pearson Education Inc ....E....... 845 340-8700
Kingston (G-7206)
Pearson Education Inc ....F....... 212 782-3337
New York (G-11591)
Pearson Education Inc ....E....... 212 366-2000
New York (G-11592)

S I C

Pearson Education Inc ... F ... 201 236-7000
West Nyack *(G-16924)*

◆ Pearson Education Holdings Inc ... A ... 201 236-6716
New York *(G-11593)*

▼ Pearson Inc ... D ... 212 641-2400
New York *(G-11594)*

Pearson Longman LLC ... C ... 917 981-2200
New York *(G-11595)*

Pearson Longman LLC ... E ... 212 641-2400
White Plains *(G-17147)*

Penguin Random House LLC ... E ... 212 782-1000
New York *(G-11603)*

Penguin Random House LLC ... B ... 212 782-9000
New York *(G-11604)*

Penguin Random House LLC ... A ... 212 572-6162
New York *(G-11605)*

Penguin Random House LLC ... A ... 212 782-9000
New York *(G-11606)*

Penguin Random House LLC ... C ... 212 366-2377
Albany *(G-117)*

Penton Business Media Inc ... F ... 914 949-8500
White Plains *(G-17150)*

Peri-Facts Academy ... G ... 585 275-6037
Rochester *(G-14577)*

Peter Lang Publishing Inc ... F ... 212 647-7700
New York *(G-11631)*

▲ Peter Mayer Publishers Inc ... F ... 212 673-2210
New York *(G-11632)*

▲ Peter Pauper Press Inc ... E ... 914 681-0144
White Plains *(G-17158)*

Petersons Nelnet LLC ... C ... 609 896-1800
Albany *(G-118)*

▲ Phaidon Press Inc ... E ... 212 652-5400
New York *(G-11643)*

▲ Philipp Feldheim Inc ... G ... 845 356-2282
Nanuet *(G-8760)*

Picador USA ... F ... 646 307-5629
New York *(G-11658)*

Poetry Mailing List Marsh Hawk ... G ... 516 766-1891
Oceanside *(G-13090)*

Poets House Inc ... F ... 212 431-7920
New York *(G-11680)*

Preserving Chrstn Publications ... G ... 315 942-6617
Boonville *(G-1167)*

▲ Prestel Publishing Inc ... G ... 212 995-2720
New York *(G-11701)*

Primedia Special Interest Publ ... D ... 212 726-4300
New York *(G-11709)*

▲ Princton Archtctural Press LLC ... E ... 212 995-9620
New York *(G-11714)*

Pro Publica Inc ... D ... 212 514-5250
New York *(G-11725)*

Project Energy Savers LLC ... F ... 718 596-4231
Brooklyn *(G-2454)*

▲ Prometheus Books Inc ... E ... 716 691-2158
Amherst *(G-258)*

PSR Press Ltd ... F ... 716 754-2266
Lewiston *(G-7435)*

Pwxyz LLC ... G ... 212 377-5500
New York *(G-11761)*

▲ Quarto Group Inc ... E ... 212 779-0700
New York *(G-11770)*

Rapid Intellect Group Inc ... F ... 518 929-3210
Chatham *(G-3559)*

Readers Dgest Yung Fmilies Inc ... E ... 914 238-1000
Pleasantville *(G-13719)*

Reading Room Inc ... G ... 212 463-1029
New York *(G-11812)*

Relx Inc ... C ... 607 772-2600
Conklin *(G-3873)*

◆ Relx Inc ... E ... 212 309-8100
New York *(G-11826)*

Repertoire International De Ll ... E ... 212 817-1990
New York *(G-11835)*

Research Centre of Kabbalah ... G ... 718 805-0380
Richmond Hill *(G-14079)*

▲ Richard C Owen Publishers Inc ... F ... 914 232-3903
Somers *(G-15512)*

▲ Rizzoli Intl Publications Inc ... E ... 212 387-3400
New York *(G-11881)*

Rizzoli Intl Publications Inc ... F ... 212 387-3572
New York *(G-11882)*

▲ Rosen Publishing Group Inc ... C ... 212 777-3017
New York *(G-11917)*

▲ Ryland Peters & Small Inc ... G ... 646 791-5410
New York *(G-11941)*

S P Books Inc ... G ... 212 431-5011
New York *(G-11946)*

Samuel French Inc ... E ... 212 206-8990
New York *(G-11962)*

▲ Scholastic Corporation ... G ... 212 343-6100
New York *(G-11997)*

▲ Scholastic Inc ... A ... 800 724-6527
New York *(G-11998)*

Scholastic Inc ... E ... 212 343-6100
New York *(G-11999)*

Scholium International Inc ... G ... 516 883-8032
Port Washington *(G-13863)*

Second Chance Press Inc ... G ... 631 725-1101
Sag Harbor *(G-15081)*

▲ Seven Stories Press Inc ... G ... 212 226-8760
New York *(G-12032)*

▲ Sheridan House Inc ... G ... 914 725-5431
Scarsdale *(G-15223)*

Simmons-Boardman Pubg Corp ... G ... 212 620-7200
New York *(G-12078)*

Simon & Schuster Inc ... D ... 212 698-7000
New York *(G-12079)*

Simon Schuster Digital Sls Inc ... D ... 212 698-4391
New York *(G-12081)*

Six Boro Publishing ... G ... 347 589-6756
New York *(G-12089)*

▲ Skyhorse Publishing Inc ... E ... 212 643-6816
New York *(G-12096)*

Soho Press Inc ... G ... 212 260-1900
New York *(G-12119)*

Soul Journ LLC ... F ... 646 823-9882
New York *(G-12142)*

Spartacist Publishing Co ... E ... 212 732-7860
New York *(G-12148)*

Springer Adis Us LLC ... E ... 212 460-1500
New York *(G-12171)*

Springer Customer Svc Ctr LLC ... B ... 212 460-1500
New York *(G-12172)*

Springer Publishing Co LLC ... E ... 212 431-4370
New York *(G-12174)*

◆ Springer Scnce + Bus Media LLC ... C ... 781 871-6600
New York *(G-12175)*

▲ Square One Publishers Inc ... F ... 516 535-2010
Garden City Park *(G-5542)*

Stanley M Indig ... G ... 718 692-0648
Brooklyn *(G-2597)*

Station Hill of Barrytown ... G ... 845 758-5293
Barrytown *(G-619)*

Steffen Publishing Inc ... D ... 315 865-4100
Holland Patent *(G-6488)*

STf Services Inc ... E ... 315 463-8506
East Syracuse *(G-4567)*

Stonesong Press LLC ... G ... 212 929-4600
New York *(G-12208)*

Storybooks Forever ... F ... 716 822-7845
Buffalo *(G-3198)*

▲ Studio Fun International Inc ... E ... 914 238-1000
White Plains *(G-17172)*

Sweet Mouth Inc ... E ... 800 433-7758
New York *(G-12253)*

▲ Syracuse University Press Inc ... E ... 315 443-5534
Syracuse *(G-16055)*

T G S Inc ... G ... 516 629-6905
Locust Valley *(G-7634)*

Targum Press USA Inc ... G ... 248 355-2266
Brooklyn *(G-2646)*

Teachers College Columbia Univ ... E ... 212 678-3929
New York *(G-12287)*

Teasurebox Publishing LLC ... G ... 718 506-4354
Jamaica *(G-6955)*

Thornwillow Press Ltd ... G ... 212 980-0738
New York *(G-12331)*

Time Home Entertainment Inc ... E ... 212 522-1212
New York *(G-12342)*

Time Inc ... E ... 212 522-1212
New York *(G-12343)*

Tom Doherty Associates Inc ... E ... 212 388-0100
New York *(G-12360)*

◆ Trusted Media Brands Inc ... A ... 914 238-1000
New York *(G-12413)*

Trusted Media Brands Inc ... F ... 646 293-6025
New York *(G-12414)*

Turtle Pond Publications LLC ... G ... 212 579-4393
New York *(G-12428)*

▲ Unisystems Inc ... E ... 212 826-0850
New York *(G-12463)*

▲ United Synggue Cnsrvtive Jdism ... E ... 212 533-7800
New York *(G-12467)*

▲ Vaad LHafotzas Sichoes ... F ... 718 778-5436
Brooklyn *(G-2715)*

▲ Vandam Inc ... F ... 212 929-0416
New York *(G-12499)*

▲ Vantage Press Inc ... E ... 212 736-1767
New York *(G-12504)*

Vaultcom Inc ... E ... 212 366-4212
New York *(G-12511)*

Verso Inc ... G ... 718 246-8160
Brooklyn *(G-2723)*

▲ W W Norton & Company Inc ... C ... 212 354-5500
New York *(G-12573)*

W W Norton & Company Inc ... G ... 212 354-5500
New York *(G-12574)*

▲ Waldman Publishing Corporation ... F ... 212 730-9590
New York *(G-12579)*

Warodean Corporation ... G ... 718 359-5559
Flushing *(G-5307)*

Westsea Publishing Co Inc ... G ... 631 420-1110
Farmingdale *(G-5143)*

Whittier Publications Inc ... G ... 516 432-8120
Oceanside *(G-13106)*

◆ William H Sadlier Inc ... C ... 212 233-3646
New York *(G-12634)*

William S Hein & Co Inc ... D ... 716 882-2600
Getzville *(G-5606)*

William S Hein & Co Inc ... D ... 716 882-2600
Buffalo *(G-3256)*

Windows Media Publishing LLC ... E ... 917 732-7892
Brooklyn *(G-2759)*

Wolters Kluwer US Inc ... F ... 212 894-8920
New York *(G-12652)*

Wolters Kluwer US Inc ... E ... 631 517-8060
Babylon *(G-553)*

Woodward/White Inc ... F ... 718 509-6082
Brooklyn *(G-2764)*

Wordwise Inc ... G ... 914 232-5366
Katonah *(G-7135)*

▲ Workman Publishing Co Inc ... C ... 212 254-5900
New York *(G-12660)*

Workman Publishing Co Inc ... C ... 212 254-5900
New York *(G-12661)*

Worth Publishers Inc ... C ... 212 475-6000
New York *(G-12666)*

▲ YS Publishing Co Inc ... G ... 212 682-9360
New York *(G-12699)*

Zinepak LLC ... F ... 212 706-8621
New York *(G-12713)*

Zola Books Inc ... E ... 917 822-4950
New York *(G-12718)*

2732 Book Printing, Not Publishing

450 Ridge St Inc ... G ... 716 754-2789
Lewiston *(G-7432)*

B-Squared Inc ... E ... 212 777-2044
New York *(G-9296)*

Bedford Freeman & Worth ... C ... 212 576-9400
New York *(G-9342)*

Bmg Printing and Promotion LLC ... G ... 631 231-9200
Bohemia *(G-1026)*

Book1one LLC ... G ... 585 458-2101
Rochester *(G-14242)*

Bridge Enterprises Inc ... G ... 718 625-6622
Brooklyn *(G-1715)*

Cct Inc ... G ... 212 532-3355
New York *(G-9552)*

Centrisource Inc ... G ... 716 871-1105
Tonawanda *(G-16152)*

E Graphics Corporation ... G ... 718 486-9767
Brooklyn *(G-1892)*

Electronic Printing Inc ... G ... 631 218-2200
Bohemia *(G-1066)*

Experiment LLC ... G ... 212 889-1659
New York *(G-10108)*

Flare Multicopy Corp ... E ... 718 258-8860
Brooklyn *(G-1982)*

Hachette Book Group USA Inc ... E ... 212 364-1200
New York *(G-10392)*

▲ Hamilton Printing Company Inc ... C ... 518 732-2161
Troy *(G-16238)*

▲ Hudson Valley Paper Works Inc ... F ... 845 569-8883
Newburgh *(G-12764)*

In-House Inc ... F ... 718 445-9007
College Point *(G-3787)*

◆ Kravitz Design Inc ... G ... 212 625-1644
New York *(G-10889)*

▲ Literary Classics of US ... F ... 212 308-3360
New York *(G-11008)*

▲ Logical Operations Inc ... C ... 585 350-7000
Rochester *(G-14482)*

North Country Books Inc ... G ... 315 735-4877
Utica *(G-16352)*

Printing Factory LLC ... F ... 718 451-0500
Brooklyn *(G-2447)*

Promotional Sales Books LLC ... G ... 212 675-0364
New York *(G-11731)*

S
I
C

Employee Codes: A=Over 500 employees, B=251-500
C=101-250, D=51-100, E=20-50, F=10-19, G=5-9

2017 Harris
New York Manufacturers Directory

763

27 PRINTING, PUBLISHING, AND ALLIED INDUSTRIES

▲ R D Manufacturing Corp.................G...... 914 238-1000
  Pleasantville *(G-13716)*
Royal Fireworks Printing Co................F...... 845 726-3333
  Unionville *(G-16302)*
Steffen Publishing Inc.....................D...... 315 865-4100
  Holland Patent *(G-6488)*
▼ Sterling Pierce Company Inc............E...... 516 593-1170
  East Rockaway *(G-4471)*
Stop Entertainment Inc....................F...... 212 242-7867
  Monroe *(G-8564)*
▲ Syracuse Cultural Workers Prj.........F...... 315 474-1132
  Syracuse *(G-16051)*
The Nugent Organization Inc..............F...... 212 645-6600
  Oceanside *(G-13101)*
Tobay Printing Co Inc.....................E...... 631 842-3300
  Copiague *(G-3934)*
▼ Twp America Inc.........................E...... 212 274-8090
  New York *(G-12435)*
Vicks Lithograph & Prtg Corp..............C...... 315 272-2401
  Yorkville *(G-17527)*
Vicks Lithograph & Prtg Corp..............C...... 315 736-9344
  Yorkville *(G-17528)*
Willis Mc Donald Co Inc...................F...... 212 366-1526
  New York *(G-12638)*
Worzalla Publishing Company..............C...... 212 967-7909
  New York *(G-12667)*

2741 Misc Publishing

▲ 212 Media LLC...........................E...... 212 710-3092
  New York *(G-8966)*
Abkco Music & Records Inc................E...... 212 399-0300
  New York *(G-9004)*
ABRA Media Inc............................G...... 518 398-1010
  Pine Plains *(G-13554)*
Absolute Color Corporation................G...... 212 868-0404
  New York *(G-9007)*
Adcomm Graphics Inc.....................E...... 212 645-1298
  West Babylon *(G-16765)*
Add Associates Inc........................G...... 315 449-3474
  Cicero *(G-3641)*
Adirondack Pennysaver Inc...............E...... 518 563-0100
  Plattsburgh *(G-13650)*
Affluent Design Inc........................F...... 631 655-2556
  Mastic Beach *(G-8204)*
Ai Media Group Inc........................F...... 212 660-2400
  New York *(G-9064)*
Albany Student Press Inc..................E...... 518 442-5665
  Albany *(G-43)*
Albion-Holley Pennysaver Inc.............D...... 585 589-5641
  Albion *(G-161)*
Aleteia Usa Inc.............................. 914 502-1855
  Yonkers *(G-17410)*
▼ Alfred Mainzer Inc......................E...... 718 392-4200
  Long Island City *(G-7650)*
All Times Publishing LLC..................E...... 315 422-7011
  Syracuse *(G-15847)*
Alley Music Corp...........................E...... 212 779-7977
  New York *(G-9088)*
Alm Media LLC............................B...... 212 457-9400
  New York *(G-9095)*
Alm Media Holdings Inc..................B...... 212 457-9400
  New York *(G-9096)*
American Hsptals Patient Guide.........F...... 518 346-1099
  Schenectady *(G-15230)*
American Media Inc......................D...... 212 545-4800
  New York *(G-9124)*
Amy Pak Publishing Inc..................G...... 585 964-8188
  Holley *(G-6489)*
An Group Inc..............................G...... 631 549-4090
  Melville *(G-8295)*
Answer Printing Inc........................F...... 212 922-2922
  New York *(G-9166)*
AR Media Inc..............................E...... 212 352-0731
  New York *(G-9187)*
ARC Music Corporation...................F...... 212 492-9414
  New York *(G-9192)*
Argus Media Inc...........................F...... 646 376-6130
  New York *(G-9201)*
Art Asiapacific Publishing LLC............G...... 212 255-6003
  New York *(G-9209)*
Aspen Publishers Inc.....................A...... 212 771-0600
  New York *(G-9235)*
Atlas Music Publishing LLC...............G...... 646 502-5170
  New York *(G-9255)*
Auto Market Publications Inc............G...... 631 667-0500
  Deer Park *(G-4105)*
Avalon Copy Centers Amer Inc..........D...... 315 471-3333
  Syracuse *(G-15863)*
Avalon Copy Centers Amer Inc..........E...... 716 995-7777
  Buffalo *(G-2825)*

Award Publishing Limited.................G...... 212 246-0405
  New York *(G-9283)*
Badoud Communications Inc............C...... 315 472-7821
  Syracuse *(G-15866)*
Bdg Media Inc.............................B...... 917 951-9768
  New York *(G-9337)*
▲ Black Book Photography Inc..........F...... 212 979-6700
  New York *(G-9409)*
Blood Moon Productions Ltd............G...... 718 556-9410
  Staten Island *(G-15649)*
▲ Boosey & Hawkes Inc.................E...... 212 358-5300
  New York *(G-9439)*
Bourne Music Publishers.................F...... 212 391-4300
  New York *(G-9444)*
Brownstone Publishers Inc..............E...... 212 473-8200
  New York *(G-9474)*
Bucket Links LLC........................G...... 212 290-2900
  New York *(G-9475)*
Bulkley Dunton...........................E...... 212 863-1800
  New York *(G-9477)*
Burdick Publications Inc.................G...... 315 685-9500
  Skaneateles *(G-15456)*
Business Directory Inc...................F...... 718 486-8099
  Brooklyn *(G-1740)*
Byliner Inc.................................. 415 680-3608
  New York *(G-9488)*
◆ Bys Publishing LLC....................G...... 315 655-9431
  Cazenovia *(G-3442)*
▲ C F Peters Corp........................E...... 718 416-7800
  Glendale *(G-5648)*
Cambridge Info Group Inc...............F...... 301 961-6700
  New York *(G-9506)*
Cambridge Whos Who Pubg Inc........E...... 516 833-8440
  Uniondale *(G-16290)*
Carbert Music Inc.........................E...... 212 725-9277
  New York *(G-9523)*
Carl Fischer LLC..........................E...... 212 777-0900
  New York *(G-9526)*
Castle Connolly Medical Ltd............E...... 212 367-8400
  New York *(G-9543)*
Catholic News Publishing Co............F...... 914 632-7771
  Mamaroneck *(G-8027)*
Cayuga Press Cortland Inc..............E...... 888 229-8421
  East Syracuse *(G-4516)*
Ceo Cast Inc..............................F...... 212 732-4300
  New York *(G-9570)*
Charing Cross Music Inc.................G...... 212 541-7571
  New York *(G-9580)*
Cherry Lane Magazine LLC..............D...... 212 561-3000
  New York *(G-9591)*
▼ Christopher Anthony Pubg Co........E...... 516 826-9205
  Wantagh *(G-16555)*
Church Bulletin Inc........................F...... 631 249-4994
  West Babylon *(G-16784)*
City of New York..........................E...... 718 965-8787
  Brooklyn *(G-1782)*
▲ City Post Express Inc..................G...... 718 995-8690
  Jamaica *(G-6904)*
Classic Collections Fine Art..............E...... 914 591-4500
  White Plains *(G-17093)*
Classpass Inc..............................E...... 646 701-2172
  New York *(G-9638)*
Clearstep Technologies LLC.............G...... 315 952-3628
  Camillus *(G-3322)*
Coastal Publications Inc..................F...... 631 725-1700
  Sag Harbor *(G-15076)*
Color Unlimited Inc.......................G...... 212 802-7547
  New York *(G-9673)*
Communications & Energy Corp........F...... 315 446-5723
  Syracuse *(G-15903)*
Community Cpons Frnchising Inc......E...... 516 277-1968
  Glen Cove *(G-5613)*
Community Newsppr Holdings Inc....D...... 716 282-2311
  Niagara Falls *(G-12806)*
Complete Publishing Solutions..........G...... 212 242-7321
  New York *(G-9691)*
Comps Inc.................................F...... 516 676-0400
  Glen Cove *(G-5614)*
Consumers Union US Inc................B...... 914 378-2000
  Yonkers *(G-17429)*
Cornell University.........................G...... 607 255-0897
  Ithaca *(G-6835)*
Couture Press............................E...... 310 734-4831
  New York *(G-9739)*
Custom Publishing Group Ltd..........G...... 212 840-8800
  New York *(G-9770)*
D C I Technical Inc.......................F...... 516 355-0464
  Franklin Square *(G-5362)*
▼ Daily Racing Form Inc.................C...... 212 366-7600
  New York *(G-9792)*

Dailycandy Inc..............................E...... 646 230-8719
  New York *(G-9794)*
Dapper Dads Inc..........................G...... 917 903-8045
  Brooklyn *(G-1839)*
Dayton T Brown Inc......................B...... 631 589-6300
  Bohemia *(G-1052)*
Desi Talk LLC.............................F...... 212 675-7515
  New York *(G-9850)*
Dex Media Inc............................E...... 603 263-2811
  Buffalo *(G-2911)*
Dex Media Inc............................E...... 315 251-3300
  Buffalo *(G-2912)*
Directory Major Malls Inc................G...... 845 348-7000
  Nyack *(G-13049)*
◆ DK Publishing..........................F...... 212 366-2000
  New York *(G-9888)*
Dlc Comprehensive Medical PC........F...... 718 857-1200
  Brooklyn *(G-1868)*
Dohnsco Inc..............................G...... 516 773-4800
  Manhasset *(G-8059)*
Downtown Music LLC...................E...... 212 625-2980
  New York *(G-9920)*
Draper Associates Incorporated.......F...... 212 255-2727
  New York *(G-9924)*
Dwell Life Inc..............................E...... 212 382-2010
  New York *(G-9943)*
East Meet East Inc........................ 650 450-4446
  New York *(G-9963)*
Eastern Harbor Media....................G...... 212 725-9260
  New York *(G-9964)*
Easy Book Publishing Inc................G...... 518 459-6281
  Albany *(G-75)*
Economy 24/7 Inc........................E...... 917 403-8876
  Brooklyn *(G-1900)*
Educa Publishing Inc.....................G...... 516 472-0678
  Great Neck *(G-5804)*
Elsevier Engineering Info Inc...........E...... 201 356-6800
  New York *(G-10014)*
◆ Elsevier Inc.............................B...... 212 633-3773
  New York *(G-10015)*
Energy Intelligence Group Inc..........E...... 212 532-1112
  New York *(G-10038)*
Enjoy City North Inc.....................F...... 607 584-5061
  Binghamton *(G-913)*
Entrainant Inc.............................G...... 212 946-4724
  New York *(G-10045)*
Epost International Inc..................G...... 212 352-9390
  New York *(G-10051)*
Equityarcade LLC........................G...... 678 232-1301
  Brooklyn *(G-1931)*
Ethis Communications Inc..............G...... 212 791-1440
  White Plains *(G-17106)*
Euphorbia Productions Ltd.............G...... 212 533-1700
  New York *(G-10082)*
▲ Experiment Publishing LLC..........G...... 212 889-1273
  New York *(G-10109)*
F+w Media Inc...........................E...... 212 447-1400
  New York *(G-10119)*
Family Publications Ltd..................F...... 212 947-2177
  New York *(G-10133)*
Fantasy Sports Media Group Inc......E...... 416 917-6002
  New York *(G-10137)*
▲ Fashiondex Inc........................G...... 914 271-6121
  New York *(G-10145)*
Federated Media Publishing LLC......G...... 917 677-7976
  New York *(G-10149)*
Fidazzel Inc................................G...... 917 557-3860
  Bronx *(G-1330)*
Finger Lakes Massage Group..........F...... 607 272-9024
  Ithaca *(G-6841)*
First Games Publr Netwrk Inc..........D...... 212 983-0501
  New York *(G-10166)*
Fischler Hockey Service.................F...... 212 749-4152
  New York *(G-10172)*
Fitzgerald Publishing Co Inc...........G...... 914 793-5016
  Yonkers *(G-17444)*
Food52 Inc................................G...... 718 596-5560
  Brooklyn *(G-1994)*
Fordham University......................F...... 718 817-4795
  Bronx *(G-1335)*
▲ Foundation Center Inc...............C...... 212 620-4230
  New York *(G-10190)*
Franklin-Douglas Inc.....................F...... 516 883-0121
  Port Washington *(G-13816)*
Fredonia Pennysaver Inc................G...... 716 679-1509
  Fredonia *(G-5373)*
Freeville Publishing Co Inc..............F...... 607 844-9119
  Freeville *(G-5435)*
Froebe Group LLC......................G...... 646 649-2150
  New York *(G-10212)*

SIC SECTION 27 PRINTING, PUBLISHING, AND ALLIED INDUSTRIES

▲ G Schirmer Inc ....G....212 254-2100
New York (G-10232)
G Schirmer Inc ....E....845 469-4699
Chester (G-3607)
Gametime Media Inc ....G....212 860-2090
New York (G-10246)
Gannett Co Inc ....D....607 352-2702
Johnson City (G-7093)
Gds Publishing Inc ....F....212 796-2000
New York (G-10262)
Gen Publishing Inc ....D....914 834-3880
New Rochelle (G-8905)
Genius Media Group Inc ....F....509 670-7502
Brooklyn (G-2020)
Global Grind Digital ....E....212 840-9399
New York (G-10319)
Global Video LLC ....D....516 222-2600
Woodbury (G-17288)
Golden Eagle Marketing LLC ....G....212 726-1242
New York (G-10330)
Golf Directories USA Inc ....G....516 365-5351
Manhasset (G-8061)
Gooding & Associates Inc ....F....631 749-3313
Shelter Island (G-15387)
Government Data Publication ....E....347 789-8719
Brooklyn (G-2045)
Grant Hamilton ....F....716 652-0320
East Aurora (G-4371)
Greater Rchster Advertiser Inc ....E....585 385-1974
East Rochester (G-4460)
Grey House Publishing Inc ....E....518 789-8700
Amenia (G-216)
Grey House Publishing Inc ....E....845 483-3535
Poughkeepsie (G-13904)
Gruner & Jahr USA ....F....212 782-7870
New York (G-10374)
Guest Informat LLC ....F....212 557-3010
New York (G-10380)
Guilford Publications Inc ....D....212 431-9800
New York (G-10382)
Haines Publishing Inc ....E....315 252-2178
Auburn (G-499)
Hampton Press Incorporated ....G....646 638-3800
New York (G-10402)
Harpercollins ....G....212 207-7000
New York (G-10414)
Hart Energy Publishing Lllp ....G....212 621-4621
New York (G-10422)
◆ Hazan Cohen Group LLC ....F....646 827-0030
New York (G-10432)
Hearst Business Media ....D....516 227-1300
Uniondale (G-16296)
Hearst Communications Inc ....F....212 649-2000
New York (G-10437)
Hearst Corporation ....E....212 830-2980
New York (G-10443)
Hearst Digital Studios Inc ....E....212 969-7552
New York (G-10448)
Helium Media Inc ....G....917 596-4081
New York (G-10454)
Hibert Publishing LLC ....F....914 381-7474
Rye (G-15059)
▲ Hibu Inc ....C....516 730-1900
East Meadow (G-4425)
Highline Media LLC ....C....859 692-2100
New York (G-10475)
▲ Historic TW Inc ....D....212 484-8000
New York (G-10484)
History Publishing Company LLC ....G....845 398-8161
Palisades (G-13401)
Hola Publishing Co ....G....718 424-3129
Long Island City (G-7761)
Home Service Publications ....G....914 238-1000
Pleasantville (G-13714)
▲ Humana Press Inc ....E....212 460-1500
New York (G-10530)
Humor Rainbow Incorporated ....E....646 402-9113
New York (G-10532)
▲ Iahcp Inc ....E....631 650-2499
Islip (G-6809)
Ibt Media Inc ....E....646 867-7100
New York (G-10548)
Ideas International Inc ....E....914 937-4302
Rye Brook (G-15071)
Infoservices International ....F....631 549-1805
Cold Spring Harbor (G-3769)
Integrated Copyright Group ....E....615 329-3999
New York (G-10615)
Intuition Publishing Limited ....G....212 838-7115
New York (G-10648)

Israeli Yellow Pages ....E....718 520-1000
Kew Gardens (G-7162)
Jackdaw Publications ....F....914 962-6911
Amawalk (G-214)
Jewish Heritage For Blind ....G....718 338-4999
Brooklyn (G-2139)
▲ Jobson Medical Information LLC ....C....212 274-7000
New York (G-10745)
▲ John Szoke Graphics Inc ....G....212 219-8300
New York (G-10753)
Johnny Bienstock Music ....E....212 779-7977
New York (G-10755)
Kalel Partners LLC ....F....347 561-7804
Flushing (G-5258)
Kendor Music Inc ....F....716 492-1254
Delevan (G-4235)
Korangy Publishing Inc ....D....212 260-1332
New York (G-10877)
Korean Yellow Pages ....F....718 461-0073
Flushing (G-5263)
Kraus Organization Limited ....G....212 686-5411
New York (G-10888)
Kyra Communications Corp ....F....516 783-6244
Seaford (G-15344)
L & L Trucking Inc ....E....315 339-2550
Rome (G-14818)
Lagunatic Music & Filmworks ....F....212 353-9600
New York (G-10917)
Language and Graphics Inc ....G....212 315-5266
New York (G-10927)
Largo Music Inc ....G....212 756-5080
New York (G-10929)
Leadership Directories Inc ....E....212 627-4140
New York (G-10946)
Learnvest Inc ....E....212 675-6711
New York (G-10949)
Ledes Group Inc ....F....212 840-8800
New York (G-10956)
Lefrak Entertainment Co Ltd ....G....212 586-3600
New York (G-10960)
Lightbulb Press Inc ....E....212 485-8800
New York (G-10993)
Lino Press Inc ....E....718 665-2625
Bronx (G-1383)
Llcs Publishing Corp ....F....718 569-2703
Brooklyn (G-2232)
London Theater News Ltd ....F....212 517-8608
New York (G-11025)
Lucky Peach LLC ....G....212 228-0031
New York (G-11059)
Ludlow Music Inc ....F....212 594-9795
New York (G-11060)
Luminary Publishing Inc ....F....845 334-8600
Kingston (G-7199)
Macmillan Academic Pubg Inc ....F....212 226-1476
New York (G-11085)
Mailers-Pblsher Wlfare Tr Fund ....G....212 869-5986
New York (G-11111)
▲ Mapeasy Inc ....F....631 537-6213
Wainscott (G-16529)
▲ Marian Goodman Gallery Inc ....E....212 977-7160
New York (G-11149)
Marketresearchcom Inc ....F....212 807-2600
New York (G-11161)
Mary Ann Liebert Inc ....D....914 740-2100
New Rochelle (G-8917)
Mathisen Ventures Inc ....G....212 986-1025
New York (G-11179)
Maximillion Communications LLC ....D....212 564-3945
New York (G-11188)
▲ McCall Pattern Company ....C....212 465-6800
New York (G-11195)
▲ Media Transcripts Inc ....E....212 362-1481
New York (G-11209)
Media Trust LLC ....G....212 802-1162
New York (G-11210)
Medical Daily Inc ....E....646 867-7100
New York (G-11213)
Medical Information Systems ....G....516 621-7200
Port Washington (G-13842)
Mens Journal LLC ....D....212 484-1616
New York (G-11225)
Merchant Publishing Inc ....F....212 691-6666
New York (G-11227)
Merrill Corporation Inc ....D....212 620-5600
New York (G-11234)
Metro Group Inc ....G....716 434-4055
Lockport (G-7601)
Mexico Independent Inc ....E....315 963-3763
Mexico (G-8396)

Michael Karp Music Inc ....G....212 840-3285
New York (G-11249)
Millennium Medical Publishing ....F....212 995-2211
New York (G-11266)
Mindbodygreen LLC ....E....347 529-6952
Brooklyn (G-2317)
Minyanville Media Inc ....E....212 991-6200
New York (G-11280)
Mom Dad Publishing Inc ....E....646 476-9170
New York (G-11296)
▲ Monthly Review Foundation Inc ....G....212 691-2555
New York (G-11303)
Morey Publishing ....E....516 284-3300
Farmingdale (G-5060)
Mortgage Press Ltd ....E....516 409-1400
Wantagh (G-16560)
Mosby Holdings Corp ....G....212 309-8100
New York (G-11308)
Mt Morris Shopper Inc ....G....585 658-3520
Mount Morris (G-8653)
Mtm Publishing Inc ....G....212 242-6930
New York (G-11320)
Multi-Health Systems Inc ....D....800 456-3003
Cheektowaga (G-3580)
▲ Music Sales Corporation ....G....212 254-2100
New York (G-11327)
Musical Links Production LLC ....G....516 996-1522
Valley Stream (G-16414)
My Publisher Inc ....G....212 935-5215
New York (G-11332)
Narratively Inc ....E....203 536-0332
Brooklyn (G-2349)
National Health Prom Assoc ....E....914 421-2525
White Plains (G-17139)
National Rding Styles Inst Inc ....F....516 921-5500
Syosset (G-15831)
Neff Holding Company ....G....914 595-8200
Armonk (G-418)
Network Journal Inc ....G....212 962-3791
New York (G-11375)
New Direct Product Corp ....G....212 929-0515
New York (G-11383)
New York Legal Publishing ....G....518 459-1100
Menands (G-8377)
Newbay Media LLC ....F....516 944-5940
Port Washington (G-13848)
▲ Nihao Media LLC ....G....609 903-4264
New York (G-11430)
Nimbletv Inc ....F....646 502-7010
New York (G-11434)
Nybg ....G....718 817-8700
Bronx (G-1414)
O Val Nick Music Co Inc ....G....212 873-2179
New York (G-11489)
Oakwood Publishing Co ....G....516 482-7720
Great Neck (G-5824)
One Story Inc ....G....917 816-3659
Brooklyn (G-2393)
Online Publishers Association ....E....646 473-1000
New York (G-11510)
Open-Xchange Inc ....F....914 332-5720
Tarrytown (G-16099)
Openroad Integrated Media Inc ....E....212 691-0900
New York (G-11515)
Options Publishing LLC ....F....603 429-2698
New York (G-11518)
▲ Osprey Publishing Inc ....G....212 419-5300
New York (G-11533)
Outlook Newspaper ....E....845 356-6261
Suffern (G-15796)
Outreach Publishing Corp ....G....718 773-0525
Brooklyn (G-2399)
Pace Editions Inc ....E....212 421-3237
New York (G-11549)
Pace Editions Inc ....G....212 675-7431
New York (G-11550)
Paragon Publishing Inc ....G....718 302-2093
Brooklyn (G-2406)
▲ Peer International Corp ....E....212 265-3910
New York (G-11596)
Peermusic III Ltd ....G....212 265-3910
New York (G-11598)
Peermusic Ltd ....F....212 265-3910
New York (G-11599)
Per Annum Inc ....E....212 647-8700
New York (G-11612)
Petersons Nelnet LLC ....C....609 896-1800
Albany (G-118)
Phillifox Music ....F....646 260-9300
New York (G-11648)

SIC

Employee Codes: A=Over 500 employees, B=251-500
C=101-250, D=51-100, E=20-50, F=10-19, G=5-9
2017 Harris
New York Manufacturers Directory
765

27 PRINTING, PUBLISHING, AND ALLIED INDUSTRIES SIC SECTION

Playlife LLC ....G.... 646 207-9082
New York (G-11675)
Portfolio Media Inc ....C.... 646 783-7100
New York (G-11687)
Press Express ....G.... 914 592-3790
Elmsford (G-4773)
Primary Wave Publishing LLC ....G.... 212 661-6990
New York (G-11705)
Princess Music Publishing Co ....E.... 212 586-0240
New York (G-11712)
Professnal Spt Pblications Inc ....F.... 516 327-9500
Elmont (G-4726)
Publishers Clearing House LLC ....E.... 516 249-4063
Melville (G-8350)
Quality Pattern Corp ....D.... 212 704-0355
New York (G-11768)
Qworldstar Inc ....G.... 212 768-4500
New York (G-11778)
R W Publications Div of Wtrhs ....E.... 716 714-5620
Elma (G-4653)
Record Press Inc ....G.... 212 619-4949
New York (G-11814)
Redspring Communications Inc ....E.... 518 587-0547
Saratoga Springs (G-15170)
Regan Arts LLC ....F.... 646 488-6613
New York (G-11820)
Reliable Press II Inc ....F.... 718 840-5812
Brooklyn (G-2489)
Renegade Nation Online LLC ....G.... 212 868-9000
New York (G-11834)
Repertoire International De Ll ....E.... 212 817-1990
New York (G-11835)
Reservoir Media Management Inc ....F.... 212 675-0541
New York (G-11839)
Retirement Insiders ....G.... 631 751-1329
Setauket (G-15378)
Rheinwald Printing Co Inc ....F.... 585 637-5100
Brockport (G-1246)
Riot New Media Group Inc ....G.... 604 700-4896
Brooklyn (G-2495)
Rockefeller University ....G.... 212 327-8568
New York (G-11897)
Rolling Stone Magazine ....G.... 212 484-1616
New York (G-11909)
Rosemont Press Incorporated ....G.... 212 239-4770
Deer Park (G-4201)
▲ Rough Guides US Ltd ....D.... 212 414-3635
New York (G-11921)
Royalty Network Inc ....G.... 212 967-4300
New York (G-11928)
Rsl Media LLC ....G.... 212 307-6760
New York (G-11931)
S G New York LLC ....E.... 631 665-4000
Bohemia (G-1128)
Sacks and Company New York ....G.... 212 741-1000
New York (G-11952)
Sag Harbor Express ....G.... 631 725-1700
Sag Harbor (G-15079)
Sagelife Parenting LLC ....G.... 315 299-5713
Syracuse (G-16030)
Salamanca Press Penny Saver ....E.... 716 945-1500
Salamanca (G-15105)
◆ Scepter Publishers ....G.... 212 354-0670
New York (G-11984)
Scholastic Inc ....D.... 212 343-7100
New York (G-12000)
Screen Gems-EMI Music Inc ....D.... 212 786-8000
New York (G-12007)
Seabay Media Holdings LLC ....G.... 212 457-7790
New York (G-12009)
Selby Marketing Associates Inc ....F.... 585 377-0750
Fairport (G-4876)
Select Information Exchange ....F.... 212 496-6435
New York (G-12023)
Sentinel Printing Services Inc ....D.... 845 562-1218
New Windsor (G-8954)
Sephardic Yellow Pages ....E.... 718 998-0299
Brooklyn (G-2543)
Service Advertising Group Inc ....F.... 718 361-6161
Long Island City (G-7875)
Service Education Incorporated ....G.... 585 264-9240
Victor (G-16502)
Seymour Science LLC ....G.... 516 699-8404
Great Neck (G-5840)
▲ Shapiro Bernstein & Co Inc ....F.... 212 588-0878
New York (G-12044)
Sharedbook Inc ....E.... 646 442-8840
New York (G-12045)
Shop Smart Central Inc ....G.... 914 962-3871
Yorktown Heights (G-17519)
▲ Sing Tao Newspapers NY Ltd ....E.... 212 699-3800
New York (G-12084)
Skylark Publications Ltd ....G.... 607 535-9866
Watkins Glen (G-16696)
Slosson Edctl Publications Inc ....F.... 716 652-0930
East Aurora (G-4379)
Sneaker News Inc ....G.... 347 687-1588
New York (G-12111)
Social Science Electronic Pubg ....F.... 585 442-8170
Rochester (G-14690)
Soho Editions Inc ....E.... 914 591-5100
Mohegan Lake (G-8545)
◆ Sony Music Holdings Inc ....A.... 212 833-8000
New York (G-12137)
▲ Sony/Atv Music Publishing LLC ....E.... 212 833-7730
New York (G-12138)
Southampton Town Newspapers ....E.... 631 283-4100
Southampton (G-15552)
Space 150 ....C.... 612 332-6458
Brooklyn (G-2587)
Spinmedia Group Inc ....D.... 646 274-9110
New York (G-12164)
Spirit Music Group Inc ....E.... 212 533-7672
New York (G-12165)
Standard Analytics Io Inc ....G.... 917 882-5422
New York (G-12181)
Statebook LLC ....G.... 845 383-1991
Kingston (G-7212)
Stephen Singer Pattern Co Inc ....F.... 212 947-2902
New York (G-12196)
STf Services Inc ....E.... 315 463-8506
East Syracuse (G-4567)
Straight Arrow Publishing Co ....C.... 212 484-1616
New York (G-12210)
Strathmore Directories Ltd ....E.... 516 997-2525
Westbury (G-17028)
Student Lifeline Inc ....E.... 516 327-0800
Franklin Square (G-5367)
Summit Communications ....G.... 914 273-5504
Armonk (G-420)
Super Express USA Pubg Corp ....F.... 212 227-5800
Richmond Hill (G-14086)
Supermedia LLC ....D.... 212 513-9700
New York (G-12243)
Tablet Publishing Company Inc ....E.... 718 965-7333
Brooklyn (G-2643)
Taylor & Francis Group LLC ....C.... 212 216-7800
New York (G-12281)
▲ Te Neues Publishing Company ....F.... 212 627-9090
New York (G-12285)
Tenney Media Group ....D.... 315 853-5569
Clinton (G-3722)
Thehuffingtonpostcom Inc ....E.... 212 245-7844
New York (G-12311)
Theskimm Inc ....F.... 212 228-4628
New York (G-12315)
Thomas Publishing Company LLC ....B.... 212 695-0500
New York (G-12321)
Thomas Publishing Company LLC ....D.... 212 629-2127
New York (G-12322)
Thomson Reuters Corporation ....F.... 212 393-9461
New York (G-12328)
▲ Thomson Reuters Corporation ....A.... 646 223-4000
New York (G-12329)
Time Warner Companies Inc ....D.... 212 484-8000
New York (G-12350)
Total Webcasting Inc ....G.... 845 883-0909
New Paltz (G-8879)
Trader Interntnal Publications ....G.... 914 631-6856
Sleepy Hollow (G-15475)
Trading Edge Ltd ....G.... 347 699-7079
Ridgewood (G-14128)
Treiman Publications Corp ....G.... 607 657-8473
Berkshire (G-854)
Tribune Entertainment Co Del ....E.... 203 866-2204
New York (G-12404)
Tribune Media Services Inc ....B.... 518 792-9914
Queensbury (G-14013)
▲ Triumph Learning LLC ....E.... 212 652-0200
New York (G-12408)
◆ Trusted Media Brands Inc ....A.... 914 238-1000
New York (G-12413)
Turbo Express Inc ....G.... 718 723-3686
Jamaica (G-6960)
Two Palms Press Inc ....F.... 212 965-8598
New York (G-12434)
Ubm Inc ....A.... 212 600-3000
New York (G-12440)
Ucc Guide Inc ....F.... 518 434-0909
Albany (G-145)
Underline Communications LLC ....F.... 212 994-4340
New York (G-12449)
Unify360 LLC ....G.... 718 213-7687
Hollis (G-6499)
▲ Universal Edition Inc ....D.... 917 213-2177
New York (G-12470)
Urban Mapping Inc ....F.... 415 946-8170
New York (G-12480)
▲ USA Custom Pad Corp ....E.... 607 563-9550
Sidney (G-15445)
Value Line Inc ....D.... 212 907-1500
New York (G-12497)
▲ Vandam Inc ....F.... 212 929-0416
New York (G-12499)
Vending Times Inc ....F.... 516 442-1850
Rockville Centre (G-14802)
Vendome Group LLC ....D.... 646 795-3899
New York (G-12516)
Verse Music Group LLC ....G.... 212 564-0977
New York (G-12525)
Viamedia Corporation ....G.... 718 485-7792
Brooklyn (G-2724)
Vidbolt Inc ....G.... 716 560-8944
Buffalo (G-3242)
Viewfinder Inc ....G.... 212 831-0939
New York (G-12543)
Vincys Printing Ltd ....F.... 518 355-4363
Schenectady (G-15309)
Visant Secondary Holdings Corp ....G.... 914 595-8200
Armonk (G-423)
VWR Education LLC ....C.... 585 359-2502
West Henrietta (G-16899)
Want-Ad Digest Inc ....F.... 518 279-1181
Troy (G-16262)
▼ Warner Music Inc ....D.... 212 275-2000
New York (G-12589)
Watchanish LLC ....F.... 917 558-0404
New York (G-12594)
Wayuga Community Newspapers ....E.... 315 754-6229
Red Creek (G-14027)
Welcome Rain Publishers LLC ....G.... 212 686-1909
New York (G-12606)
Wmg Acquisition Corp ....F.... 212 275-2000
New York (G-12650)
▲ Won & Lee Inc ....E.... 516 222-0712
Garden City (G-5538)
Worldscale Association NYC ....G.... 212 422-2786
New York (G-12664)
Yam TV LLC ....G.... 917 932-5418
New York (G-12688)
Yellow Pages Inc ....G.... 845 639-6060
New City (G-8795)
Zazoom LLC ....F.... 212 321-2100
New York (G-12706)

2752 Commercial Printing: Lithographic

2 1 2 Postcards Inc ....E.... 212 767-8227
New York (G-8962)
2 X 4 Inc ....E.... 212 647-1170
New York (G-8963)
21st Century Fox America Inc ....D.... 212 852-7000
New York (G-8967)
3g Graphics LLC ....G.... 716 634-2585
Amherst (G-218)
450 Ridge St Inc ....G.... 716 754-2789
Lewiston (G-7432)
514 Adams Corporation ....G.... 516 352-6948
Franklin Square (G-5359)
518 Prints LLC ....G.... 518 674-5346
Averill Park (G-532)
6727 11th Ave Corp ....F.... 718 837-8787
Brooklyn (G-1521)
A & D Offset Printers Ltd ....G.... 516 746-2476
Mineola (G-8486)
A & M Litho Inc ....E.... 516 342-9727
Bethpage (G-861)
A C Envelope Inc ....G.... 516 420-0646
Farmingdale (G-4926)
▲ A Esteban & Company Inc ....E.... 212 989-7000
New York (G-8984)
A Esteban & Company Inc ....E.... 212 714-2227
New York (G-8985)
A I P Printing & Stationers ....G.... 631 929-5529
Wading River (G-16522)
A Q P Inc ....G.... 585 256-1690
Rochester (G-14161)
ABC Check Printing Corp ....F.... 718 855-4702
Brooklyn (G-1546)
Academy Printing Services Inc ....G.... 631 765-3346
Southold (G-15557)

Accuprint G 518 456-2431 Albany *(G-34)*
Ace Printing & Publishing Inc F 718 939-0040 Flushing *(G-5221)*
Act Communications Group Inc F 631 669-2403 West Islip *(G-16902)*
Action Graphics Services Inc F 607 785-1951 Vestal *(G-16438)*
Ad Vantage Press G 212 941-8355 New York *(G-9023)*
Adirondack Publishing Co Inc E 518 891-2600 Saranac Lake *(G-15134)*
Ads-N-Color Inc E 718 797-0900 Brooklyn *(G-1564)*
Advanced Business Group Inc F 212 398-1010 New York *(G-9042)*
Advanced Digital Printing LLC E 718 649-1500 New York *(G-9043)*
Advantage Press Inc F 518 584-3405 Saratoga Springs *(G-15142)*
Advantage Printing Inc F 718 820-0688 Kew Gardens *(G-7158)*
▲ **Advantage Quick Print Inc** G 212 989-5644 New York *(G-9047)*
Advertising Lithographers F 212 966-7771 New York *(G-9050)*
Agrecolor Inc F 516 741-8700 Mineola *(G-8491)*
Ahw Printing Corp F 516 536-3600 Oceanside *(G-13072)*
Alamar Printing Inc F 914 993-9007 White Plains *(G-17074)*
Albany Letter Shop Inc G 518 434-1172 Albany *(G-39)*
Albert Siy G 718 359-0389 Flushing *(G-5224)*
Aldine Inc (ny) D 212 226-2870 New York *(G-9079)*
Alexander Polakovich G 718 229-6200 Bayside *(G-766)*
All Color Business Spc Ltd G 516 420-0649 Deer Park *(G-4091)*
All Color Offset Printers Inc G 516 420-0649 Farmingdale *(G-4936)*
All Ready Inc G 607 722-0826 Conklin *(G-3864)*
All Time Products Inc G 718 464-1400 Queens Village *(G-13974)*
Allen William & Company Inc C 212 675-6461 Glendale *(G-5644)*
Allied Reproductions Inc E 212 255-2472 New York *(G-9090)*
Allstatebannerscom Corporation G 718 300-1256 Long Island City *(G-7652)*
Alpha Printing Corp F 315 454-5507 Syracuse *(G-15851)*
Alpina Color Graphics Inc G 212 285-2700 New York *(G-9100)*
Alpina Copyworld Inc F 212 683-3511 New York *(G-9101)*
Alpine Business Group Inc G 212 989-4198 New York *(G-9102)*
Amax Printing Inc F 718 384-8600 Maspeth *(G-8116)*
American Business Forms Inc D 716 836-5111 Amherst *(G-223)*
American Icon Industries Inc G 845 561-1299 Newburgh *(G-12749)*
American Print Solutions Inc E 718 246-7800 Brooklyn *(G-1606)*
Amsterdam Printing & Litho Inc G 518 792-6501 Queensbury *(G-13987)*
Amsterdam Printing & Litho Inc F 518 842-6000 Amsterdam *(G-332)*
Amsterdam Printing & Litho Inc E 518 842-6000 Amsterdam *(G-333)*
▲ **Anne Taintor Inc** G 718 483-9312 Brooklyn *(G-1613)*
Answer Printing Inc F 212 922-2922 New York *(G-9166)*
Apple Press G 914 723-6660 White Plains *(G-17079)*
Arcade Inc A 212 541-2600 New York *(G-9193)*
Ares Printing and Packg Corp C 718 858-8760 Brooklyn *(G-1625)*
Argo Envelope Corp D 718 729-2700 Long Island City *(G-7667)*
Argo Lithographers Inc E 718 729-2700 Long Island City *(G-7669)*
Arista Innovations Inc E 516 746-2262 Mineola *(G-8496)*
Arnold Printing Corp F 607 272-7800 Ithaca *(G-6819)*
Arnold Taylor Printing Inc G 516 781-0564 Bellmore *(G-813)*
Aro-Graph Corporation G 315 463-8693 Syracuse *(G-15857)*
Art Digital Technologies LLC F 646 649-4820 Brooklyn *(G-1634)*
Art Scroll Printing Corp F 212 929-2413 New York *(G-9214)*
Artina Group Inc E 914 592-1850 Elmsford *(G-4734)*
Artscroll Printing Corp E 212 929-2413 New York *(G-9224)*
Asn Inc E 718 894-0800 Maspeth *(G-8120)*
Atlantic Color Corp E 631 345-3800 Shirley *(G-15413)*
Atlas Print Solutions Inc E 212 949-8775 New York *(G-9256)*
Automatic Press Inc G 212 924-5573 New York *(G-9267)*
Avm Printing Inc F 631 351-1331 Hauppauge *(G-6030)*
▲ **Avon Reproductions Inc** E 631 273-2400 Hauppauge *(G-6031)*
B & P Jays Inc G 716 668-8408 Buffalo *(G-2830)*
B D B Typewriter Supply Works E 718 232-4800 Brooklyn *(G-1659)*
Badoud Communications Inc C 315 472-7821 Syracuse *(G-15866)*
Bajan Group Inc G 518 464-2884 Latham *(G-7355)*
Ballantrae Lithographers Inc G 914 592-3275 White Plains *(G-17083)*
Barone Offset Printing Corp G 212 989-5500 Mohegan Lake *(G-8543)*
Bartolomeo Publishing Inc G 631 420-4949 West Babylon *(G-16774)*
Batavia Press LLC E 585 343-4429 Batavia *(G-624)*
Bates Jackson Engraving Co Inc E 716 854-3000 Buffalo *(G-2834)*
Baum Christine and John Corp G 585 621-8910 Rochester *(G-14224)*
Beacon Press Inc G 212 691-5050 White Plains *(G-17084)*
Beastons Budget Printing G 585 244-2721 Rochester *(G-14227)*
Beehive Press Inc G 718 654-1200 Bronx *(G-1281)*
Bel Aire Offset Corp G 718 539-8333 Flushing *(G-5229)*
▲ **Benchemark Printing Inc** D 518 393-1361 Schenectady *(G-15234)*
Benchmark Graphics Ltd F 212 683-1711 New York *(G-9358)*
Benjamin Printing Inc F 315 788-7922 Adams *(G-2)*
Bennett Multimedia Inc F 718 629-1454 Brooklyn *(G-1682)*
Bennett Printing Corporation F 718 629-1454 Brooklyn *(G-1683)*
Bernard Hall G 585 425-3340 Fairport *(G-4848)*
Bevilacque Group LLC F 212 414-8858 New York *(G-9382)*
▲ **Beyer Graphics Inc** D 631 543-3900 Commack *(G-3824)*
Billing Coding and Prtg Inc G 718 827-9409 Brooklyn *(G-1697)*
Bishop Print Shop Inc G 607 965-8155 Edmeston *(G-4622)*
Bittner Company LLC F 585 214-1790 Rochester *(G-14233)*
Bk Printing Inc G 315 565-5396 East Syracuse *(G-4511)*
Bluesoho G 646 805-2583 New York *(G-9425)*
Bmg Printing and Promotion LLC G 631 231-9200 Bohemia *(G-1026)*
Boka Printing Inc G 607 725-3235 Binghamton *(G-898)*
Boncraft Inc D 716 662-9720 Tonawanda *(G-16146)*
Bondy Printing Corp G 631 242-1510 Bay Shore *(G-679)*
Boulevard Printing G 716 837-3800 Tonawanda *(G-16147)*
Boxcar Press Incorporated E 315 473-0930 Syracuse *(G-15873)*
BP Beyond Printing Inc G 516 328-2700 Hempstead *(G-6266)*
▼ **BP Digital Imaging LLC** G 607 753-0022 Cortland *(G-4016)*
Brennans Quick Print Inc G 518 793-4999 Glens Falls *(G-5673)*
Bridge Printing Inc G 212 243-5390 Long Island City *(G-7690)*
Brodock Press Inc D 315 735-9577 Utica *(G-16310)*
Brooks Litho Digital Group Inc G 631 789-4500 Deer Park *(G-4112)*
Brown Printers of Troy Inc F 518 235-4080 Troy *(G-16228)*
Brown Printing Company E 212 782-7800 New York *(G-9471)*
Brownstone Capitl Partners LLC G 212 889-0069 New York *(G-9473)*
Business Card Express Inc E 631 669-3400 West Babylon *(G-16779)*
C & R De Santis Inc E 718 447-5076 Staten Island *(G-15653)*
C K Printing G 718 965-0388 Brooklyn *(G-1744)*
C To C Design & Print Inc F 631 885-4020 Ronkonkoma *(G-14882)*
Caboodle Printing Inc G 716 693-6000 Williamsville *(G-17237)*
Cadmus Journal Services Inc G 212 736-2002 New York *(G-9496)*
Cadmus Journal Services Inc D 607 762-5365 Conklin *(G-3866)*
Canaan Printing Inc F 718 729-3100 Bayside *(G-768)*
Canandaigua Msgnr Incorporated D 585 394-0770 Canandaigua *(G-3337)*
Canastota Publishing Co Inc G 315 697-9010 Canastota *(G-3365)*
Candid Litho Printing Ltd D 212 431-3800 Long Island City *(G-7693)*
Canfield & Tack Inc D 585 235-7710 Rochester *(G-14257)*
Canyon Publishing Inc F 212 334-0227 New York *(G-9516)*
Capital Dst Print & Imaging G 518 456-6773 Schenectady *(G-15238)*
Carges Entps of Canandaigua G 585 394-2600 Canandaigua *(G-3338)*
Carlara Group Ltd G 914 769-2020 Pleasantville *(G-13712)*
Carnels Printing Inc G 516 883-3355 Port Washington *(G-13803)*
Carr Communications Group LLC F 607 748-0481 Vestal *(G-16444)*
Castlereagh Printcraft Inc D 516 623-1728 Freeport *(G-5392)*
Cathedral Corporation C 315 338-0021 Rome *(G-14808)*
Catskill Delaware Publications F 845 887-5200 Callicoon *(G-3284)*
Cayuga Press Cortland Inc E 888 229-8421 East Syracuse *(G-4516)*
▲ **Cazar Printing & Advertising** G 718 446-4606 Corona *(G-3994)*
Cds Productions Inc F 518 385-8255 Schenectady *(G-15241)*
Cedar West Inc G 631 467-1444 Ronkonkoma *(G-14886)*
Cenveo Inc F 716 686-0100 Depew *(G-4252)*
Chakra Communications Inc E 607 748-7491 Endicott *(G-4798)*
Chakra Communications Inc E 716 505-7300 Lancaster *(G-7309)*
Challenge Graphics Svcs Inc E 631 586-0171 Deer Park *(G-4115)*
Chan Luu LLC E 212 398-3163 New York *(G-9577)*
Chenango Union Printing Inc G 607 334-2112 Norwich *(G-13022)*
Cherry Lane Lithographing Corp E 516 293-9294 Plainview *(G-13587)*
▲ **China Imprint LLC** G 585 563-3391 Rochester *(G-14274)*
Chromagraphics Press Inc G 631 367-6160 Melville *(G-8302)*

Employee Codes: A=Over 500 employees, B=251-500
C=101-250, D=51-100, E=20-50, F=10-19, G=5-9
2017 Harris
New York Manufacturers Directory
767

27 PRINTING, PUBLISHING, AND ALLIED INDUSTRIES SIC SECTION

Company	Location	Size	Phone
Cilyox Inc	Buffalo (G-2874)	F	716 853-3809
Circle Press Inc	New York (G-9621)	D	212 924-4277
Clarsons Corp	Rochester (G-14278)	F	585 235-8775
Classic Color Graphics Inc	Hicksville (G-6330)	G	516 822-9090
Classic Color Graphics Inc	Hicksville (G-6331)	G	516 822-9090
Cody Printing Corp	Woodside (G-17324)	G	718 651-8854
Coe Displays Inc	Long Island City (G-7702)	G	718 937-5658
Cohber Press Inc	West Henrietta (G-16873)	D	585 475-9100
Colad Group LLC	Buffalo (G-2880)	D	716 961-1776
Color Card LLC	Central Islip (G-3491)	F	631 232-1300
▲ Color Carton Corp	Bronx (G-1302)	D	718 665-0840
Color-Aid Corporation	Hudson Falls (G-6639)	G	212 673-5500
Colorfast	New York (G-9674)	F	212 929-2440
Colorfully Yours Inc	Bay Shore (G-687)	F	631 242-8600
Combine Graphics Corp	Forest Hills (G-5322)	G	212 695-4044
Commerce Offset Ltd	Thornwood (G-16118)	G	914 769-6671
Commercial Press Inc	Canton (G-3381)	G	315 274-0028
Commercial Print & Imaging	Buffalo (G-2882)	E	716 597-0100
Community Media LLC	New York (G-9689)	E	212 229-1890
Community Newspaper Group LLC	Oneonta (G-13181)	F	607 432-1000
Compass Printing Plus	Saranac Lake (G-15135)	F	518 891-7050
Compass Printing Plus	Saranac Lake (G-15136)	G	518 523-3308
Complemar Print LLC	Buffalo (G-2884)	F	716 875-7238
Composite Forms Inc	Port Chester (G-13740)	F	914 937-1808
Compucolor Associates Inc	New Hyde Park (G-8823)	E	516 358-0000
▲ Concept Printing Inc	Nyack (G-13047)	G	845 353-4040
Conkur Printing Co Inc	New York (G-9701)	E	212 541-5980
Consolidated Color Press Inc	New York (G-9704)	F	212 929-8197
Constas Printing Corporation	Syracuse (G-15905)	G	315 474-2176
Copy Stop Inc	White Plains (G-17097)	G	914 428-5188
Coral Color Process Ltd	Commack (G-3829)	E	631 543-5200
▲ Coral Graphic Services Inc	Hicksville (G-6335)	C	516 576-2100
Coral Graphic Services Inc	Hicksville (G-6336)	C	516 576-2100
Cosmos Communications Inc	Long Island City (G-7705)	C	718 482-1800
Coughlin Printing Group	Watertown (G-16647)	G	315 788-8560
Courier Printing Corp	Deposit (G-4277)	E	607 467-2191
Craig Envelope Corp	Long Island City (G-7706)	E	718 786-4277
Crawford Print Shop Inc	Addison (G-5)	G	607 359-4970
Create-A-Card Inc	Saint James (G-15087)	G	631 584-2273
Creative Forms Inc	New York (G-9749)	G	212 431-7540
Creative Printing Corp	New York (G-9750)	G	212 226-3870
Cronin Enterprises Inc	Elmsford (G-4745)	G	914 345-9600
D G M Graphics Inc	Merrick (G-8383)	F	516 223-2220
Daily Record	Rochester (G-14299)	F	585 232-2035
Dan Trent Company Inc	Buffalo (G-2901)	G	716 822-1422
Dani Lu Inc	Latham (G-7360)	E	518 782-5411
Dark Star Lithograph Corp	New City (G-8782)	G	845 634-3780
Datorib Inc	Selden (G-15351)	G	631 698-6222
David Helsing	Horseheads (G-6573)	G	607 796-2681
Dawn Paper Co Inc	East Rockaway (G-4469)	F	516 596-9110
Dealer-Presscom Inc	Bohemia (G-1053)	G	631 589-0434
Deanco Digital Printing LLC	Sunnyside (G-15805)	F	212 371-2025
Decal Makers Inc	Bellmore (G-817)	E	516 221-7200
Decal Techniques Inc	Bay Shore (G-692)	G	631 491-1800
Delaware Graphics LLC	Lake View (G-7280)	G	716 627-7582
Dell Communications Inc	New York (G-9840)	G	212 989-3434
Delta Press Inc	High Falls (G-6400)	E	212 989-3445
Denton Advertising Inc	Bohemia (G-1055)	F	631 586-4333
Denton Publications Inc	Elizabethtown (G-4626)	D	518 873-6368
Dependable Lithographers Inc	Long Island City (G-7712)	F	718 472-4200
Design Distributors Inc	Deer Park (G-4130)	D	631 242-2000
Design Lithographers Inc	New York (G-9853)	F	212 645-8900
Design Printing Corp	Farmingdale (G-4975)	G	631 753-9801
Designlogocom Inc	New York (G-9856)	G	212 564-0200
Dick Bailey Service Inc	Brooklyn (G-1863)	F	718 522-4363
Digital Color Concepts Inc	New York (G-9875)	E	212 989-4888
Digital Imaging Tech LLC	Ballston Spa (G-593)	G	518 885-4400
Digital United Color Prtg Inc	Warwick (G-16588)	F	845 986-9846
Dispatch Graphics Inc	New York (G-9884)	F	212 307-5943
Distinctive Printing Inc	New York (G-9886)	G	212 727-3000
Diversified Envelope Ltd	Rochester (G-14312)	F	585 615-4697
Division Street News Corp	Cobleskill (G-3736)	F	518 234-2515
Doco Quick Print Inc	Watertown (G-16650)	G	315 782-6623
Donmar Printing Co	Westbury (G-16978)	F	516 280-2239
▲ Donnelley Financial LLC	New York (G-9906)	B	212 425-0298
Dovelin Printing Company Inc	Brooklyn (G-1876)	F	718 302-3951
Dowd - Witbeck Printing Corp	Troy (G-16234)	F	518 274-2421
DP Murphy Co Inc	Deer Park (G-4132)	D	631 673-9400
Dual Print & Mail LLC	Grand Island (G-5754)	G	716 775-8001
Dual Print & Mail LLC	Cheektowaga (G-3568)	D	716 684-3825
Dupli Graphics Corporation	Syracuse (G-15925)	C	315 234-7286
Dupli Graphics Corporation	Syracuse (G-15926)	G	315 422-4732
E & J Offset Inc	Mount Vernon (G-8680)	G	718 663-8850
E B B Graphics Inc	Westbury (G-16979)	F	516 750-5510
E L Smith Printing Co Inc	New City (G-8784)	E	201 373-0111
E W Smith Publishing Co	New Windsor (G-8937)	F	845 562-1218
Eagle Graphics Inc	Rochester (G-14324)	G	585 244-5006
East Coast Thermographers Inc	College Point (G-3782)	E	718 321-3211
East Ridge Quick Print	Rochester (G-14325)	F	585 266-4911
Eastern Hills Printing	Clarence (G-3659)	G	716 741-3300
Eastside Printers	East Syracuse (G-4527)	F	315 437-6515
Eastwood Litho Inc	Syracuse (G-15929)	E	315 437-2626
Echo Appellate Press Inc	Long Beach (G-7640)	G	516 432-3601
Edgian Press Inc	Hicksville (G-6342)	G	516 931-2114
Edwards Graphic Co Inc	Bronx (G-1325)	G	718 548-6858
Efficiency Printing Co Inc	White Plains (G-17103)	F	914 949-8611
Eleanor Ettinger Inc	New York (G-9995)	E	212 925-7474
Elmat Quality Printing Ltd	Cedarhurst (G-3456)	F	516 569-5722
Empire Press Co	Brooklyn (G-1921)	G	718 756-9500
Engrav-O-Type Press Inc	Rochester (G-14351)	F	585 262-7590
Entermarket	Mount Kisco (G-8627)	G	914 437-7268
Enterprise Press Inc	New York (G-10043)	C	212 741-2111
Evolution Impressions Inc	Rochester (G-14361)	D	585 473-6600
Excel Graphics Services Inc	New York (G-10101)	F	212 929-2183
Excelsior Graphics Inc	New York (G-10104)	G	212 730-6200
Executive Prtg & Direct Mail	Elmsford (G-4752)	G	914 592-3200
F & B Photo Offset Co Inc	Island Park (G-6779)	G	516 431-5433
F & D Services Inc	Staten Island (G-15672)	F	718 984-1635
F & T Graphics Inc	Hauppauge (G-6075)	F	631 643-1000
F J Remey Co Inc	Mineola (G-8511)	E	516 741-5112
F5 Networks Inc	New York (G-10122)	G	888 882-7535
Falconer Printing & Design Inc	Falconer (G-4899)	F	716 665-2121
Fambus Inc	Endicott (G-4807)	G	607 785-3700
Fao Printing	Brooklyn (G-1959)	F	718 282-3310
Farthing Press Inc	Buffalo (G-2945)	G	716 852-4674
Fasprint	Malone (G-8009)	G	518 483-4631
Federal Envelope Inc	New York (G-10148)	F	212 243-8380
Final Touch Printing Inc	Spring Valley (G-15585)	F	845 352-2677
Finer Touch Printing Corp	Port Washington (G-13815)	F	516 944-8000
First Displays Inc	Long Island City (G-7742)	F	347 642-5972
First Line Printing Inc	Woodside (G-17329)	F	718 606-0860
Fitch Graphics Ltd	New York (G-10175)	E	212 619-3800
▲ Five Star Prtg & Mailing Svcs	New York (G-10176)	F	212 929-0300
Fiveboro Printing & Supplies	Brooklyn (G-1979)	G	718 431-9500
Flare Multicopy Corp	Brooklyn (G-1982)	E	718 258-8860
Flower City Printing Inc	Rochester (G-14375)	G	585 512-1235
Flower City Printing Inc	Rochester (G-14374)	C	585 663-9000
Flp Group LLC	Auburn (G-496)	F	315 252-7583
▲ Flynns Inc	New York (G-10182)	E	212 339-8700
Fort Orange Press Inc	Albany (G-81)	E	518 489-3233
Forward Enterprises Inc	Rochester (G-14379)	F	585 235-7670
Francis Emory Fitch Inc	New York (G-10199)	E	212 619-3800
▼ Franklin Printing Group Ltd	Cedarhurst (G-3457)	G	516 569-1248
Frederick Coon Inc	Elma (G-4648)	E	716 683-6812
Freeville Publishing Co Inc	Freeville (G-5435)	F	607 844-9119

SIC SECTION — 27 PRINTING, PUBLISHING, AND ALLIED INDUSTRIES

Company	Code	Phone
Fulton Newspapers Inc — Fulton *(G-5457)*	E	315 598-6397
Fx Silk Screen Printing I — Rochester *(G-14385)*	E	585 266-6773
G & P Printing Inc — New York *(G-10229)*	G	212 274-8092
G W Canfield & Son Inc — Utica *(G-16334)*	E	315 735-5522
Gallagher Printing Inc — Buffalo *(G-2962)*	E	716 873-2434
▲ Gallant Graphices Ltd Inc — Stanfordville *(G-15627)*	E	845 868-1166
Gannett Stllite Info Ntwrk LLC — West Nyack *(G-16917)*	E	845 578-2300
▲ Garden City Printers & Mailers — West Hempstead *(G-16853)*	F	516 485-1600
Gatehouse Media LLC — Canandaigua *(G-3347)*	D	585 394-0770
Gateway Prtg & Graphics Inc — Hamburg *(G-5926)*	E	716 823-3873
Gazette Press Inc — Rye *(G-15056)*	E	914 963-8300
Gbv Promotions Inc — Bay Shore *(G-702)*	F	631 231-7300
Gem Reproduction Services Corp — Wappingers Falls *(G-16570)*	G	845 298-0172
Gemson Graphics Inc — Albertson *(G-154)*	G	516 873-8400
General Business Supply Inc — Watervliet *(G-16685)*	D	518 720-3939
Geneva Printing Company Inc — Geneva *(G-5579)*	G	315 789-8191
Genie Instant Printing Co Inc — New York *(G-10277)*	F	212 575-8258
Glens Falls Printing LLC — Glens Falls *(G-5681)*	F	518 793-0555
Global Graphics Inc — Flushing *(G-5244)*	G	718 939-4967
Gmp LLC — Port Chester *(G-13747)*	D	914 939-0571
Gn Printing — Long Island City *(G-7750)*	E	718 784-1713
Golos Printing Inc — Elmira Heights *(G-4710)*	G	607 732-1896
Gotham Ink Corp — Syosset *(G-15825)*	G	516 677-1969
Government Data Publication — Brooklyn *(G-2045)*	E	347 789-8719
GPM Associates LLC — Dansville *(G-4077)*	E	585 335-3940
Grand Meridian Printing Inc — Long Island City *(G-7752)*	E	718 937-3888
Grand Prix Litho Inc — Holbrook *(G-6449)*	E	631 242-4182
Graphic Artisan Ltd — Suffern *(G-15790)*	G	845 368-1700
▲ Graphic Cntrls Acqisition Corp — Buffalo *(G-2978)*	B	716 853-7500
Graphic Controls Holdings Inc — Buffalo *(G-2979)*	E	716 853-7500
Graphic Dimensions Press Inc — Brooklyn *(G-2049)*	F	718 252-4003
Graphic Fabrications Inc — Rockville Centre *(G-14791)*	G	516 763-3222
Graphicomm Inc — Niagara Falls *(G-12826)*	G	716 283-0830
Graphics of Utica — Remsen *(G-14040)*	G	315 797-4868
Graphics Plus Printing Inc — Cortland *(G-4029)*	E	607 299-0500
Great Eastern Color Lith — Poughkeepsie *(G-13903)*	D	845 454-7420
Great Impressions Inc — New York *(G-10356)*	F	212 989-8555
Green Girl Prtg & Msgnr Inc — New York *(G-10360)*	G	212 575-0357
Greenwood Graphics Inc — Hicksville *(G-6353)*	F	516 822-4856
Grover Cleveland Press Inc — Amherst *(G-244)*	F	716 564-2222
Guaranteed Printing Svc Co Inc — Long Island City *(G-7755)*	E	212 929-2410
H T L & S Ltd — Brooklyn *(G-2060)*	F	718 435-4474
Haig Press Inc — Hauppauge *(G-6088)*	E	631 582-5800
Hamptons Magazine — Southampton *(G-15545)*	E	631 283-7125
Harmon and Castella Printing — Poughkeepsie *(G-13905)*	F	845 471-9163
Hearst Corporation — Albany *(G-86)*	A	518 454-5694
Hempstead Sentinel Inc — Hempstead *(G-6273)*	F	516 486-5000
Heritage Printing Center — Plattsburgh *(G-13669)*	G	518 563-8240
Hl Speed Envelope Co Inc — Mount Vernon *(G-8690)*	F	718 617-1600
Hill Crest Press — Catskill *(G-3429)*	G	518 943-0671
Hillside Printing Inc — Jamaica *(G-6919)*	F	718 658-6719
Hks Printing Company Inc — New York *(G-10487)*	F	212 675-2529
▲ Hooek Produktion Inc — New York *(G-10503)*	G	212 367-9111
Horne Organization Inc — Yonkers *(G-17454)*	F	914 572-1330
Hospitality Graphics Inc — New York *(G-10510)*	G	212 643-6700
Huckleberry Inc — Hauppauge *(G-6096)*	F	631 630-5450
Hudson Envelope Corporation — New York *(G-10525)*	E	212 473-6666
▲ Hudson Park Press Inc — New York *(G-10526)*	F	212 929-8898
Hudson Printing Co Inc — New York *(G-10527)*	E	718 937-8600
Hugh F McPherson Inc — Cheektowaga *(G-3575)*	G	716 668-6107
Hunt Graphics Inc — Coram *(G-3944)*	F	631 751-5349
I 2 Print Inc — Long Island City *(G-7762)*	F	718 937-8800
Impala Press Ltd — Ronkonkoma *(G-14911)*	G	631 588-4262
In-House Inc — College Point *(G-3787)*	F	718 445-9007
In-Step Marketing Inc — New York *(G-10579)*	F	212 797-3450
Industrial Color Inc — New York *(G-10591)*	G	212 334-4667
Ink Well — Brooklyn *(G-2107)*	G	718 253-9736
Ink-It Printing Inc — College Point *(G-3788)*	G	718 229-5590
Instant Again LLC — Rochester *(G-14449)*	E	585 436-8003
Instant Stream Inc — New York *(G-10611)*	F	917 438-7182
International Newsppr Prtg Co — Glen Head *(G-5635)*	E	516 626-6095
Interstate Litho Corp — Brentwood *(G-1185)*	D	631 232-6025
Interstate Thermographers Corp — White Plains *(G-17124)*	G	914 948-1745
Iron Horse Graphics Ltd — Bridgehampton *(G-1234)*	F	631 537-3400
Iver Printing Inc — Flushing *(G-5255)*	G	718 275-2070
J & J Printing Inc — Syracuse *(G-15964)*	G	315 458-7411
J A T Printing Inc — Huntington *(G-6664)*	G	631 427-1155
J F B & Sons Lithographers — Lake Ronkonkoma *(G-7278)*	D	631 467-1444
J P Printing Inc — Farmingdale *(G-5015)*	G	516 293-6110
J V Haring & Son — Staten Island *(G-15691)*	F	718 720-1947
Jack J Florio Jr — Lockport *(G-7595)*	G	716 434-9123
Jacobs Press Inc — Auburn *(G-503)*	F	315 252-4861
Jam Printing Publishing Inc — Elmsford *(G-4758)*	G	914 345-8400
James Conolly Printing Co — Rochester *(G-14459)*	E	585 426-4150
Jane Lewis — Binghamton *(G-930)*	G	607 722-0584
Japan Printing & Graphics Inc — New York *(G-10700)*	G	212 406-2905
JDS Graphics Inc — New York *(G-10711)*	F	973 330-3300
Jfb Print Solutions Inc — Lido Beach *(G-7441)*	G	631 694-8300
Johnnys Ideal Printing Co — Hudson *(G-6621)*	G	518 828-6666
Jon Lyn Ink Inc — Merrick *(G-8386)*	G	516 546-2312
◆ Joseph Paul — Brooklyn *(G-2149)*	G	718 693-4269
Judith Lewis Printer Inc — Westbury *(G-17000)*	G	516 997-7777
Jurist Company Inc — Long Island City *(G-7774)*	G	212 243-8008
Kader Lithograph Company Inc — Long Island City *(G-7777)*	G	917 664-4380
Kaleidoscope Imaging Inc — New York *(G-10802)*	E	212 631-9947
Karr Graphics Corp — Long Island City *(G-7779)*	E	718 784-9390
Kas-Ray Industries Inc — New York *(G-10812)*	E	212 620-3144
Kaufman Brothers Printing — New York *(G-10820)*	G	212 563-1854
Kaymil Printing Company Inc — New York *(G-10812)*	G	212 594-3718
Keeners East End Litho Inc — East Hampton *(G-4412)*	G	631 324-8565
Keller Bros & Miller Inc — Buffalo *(G-3028)*	G	716 854-2374
Kent Associates Inc — New York *(G-10837)*	G	212 675-0722
Kenyon Press Inc — Sherburne *(G-15392)*	E	607 674-9066
Key Brand Entertainment Inc — New York *(G-10839)*	C	212 966-5400
Kim Jae Printing Co Inc — Roslyn Heights *(G-15028)*	G	212 691-6289
Kimsco Business Systems Inc — Lynbrook *(G-7952)*	G	516 599-5658
Kinaneco Inc — Syracuse *(G-15974)*	E	315 468-6201
King Lithographers Inc — Mount Vernon *(G-8698)*	E	914 667-4200
Kingsbury Printing Co Inc — Queensbury *(G-14002)*	G	518 747-6606
▲ Kling Magnetics Inc — Chatham *(G-3558)*	E	518 392-4000
Knickerbocker Graphics Svcs — New York *(G-10861)*	F	212 244-7485
Kolcorp Industries Ltd — New York *(G-10871)*	E	212 354-0400
◆ Kwik Ticket Inc — Brooklyn *(G-2183)*	F	718 421-3800
L & K Graphics Inc — Deer Park *(G-4161)*	G	631 667-2269
L I F Publishing Corp — Shirley *(G-15422)*	E	631 345-5200
L K Printing Corp — White Plains *(G-17132)*	G	914 761-1944
L Loy Press Inc — Buffalo *(G-3040)*	G	716 634-5966
L M N Printing Company Inc — Valley Stream *(G-16411)*	E	516 285-8526
Label Gallery Inc — Norwich *(G-13030)*	E	607 334-3244
Lake Placid Advertisers Wkshp — Lake Placid *(G-7275)*	E	518 523-3359
Laser Printer Checks Corp — Monroe *(G-8559)*	G	845 782-5837
Laumont Labs Inc — New York *(G-10936)*	E	212 664-0595
Leader Printing Inc — Merrick *(G-8388)*	F	516 546-1544
Lee Printing Inc — Brooklyn *(G-2205)*	G	718 237-1651
Lehmann Printing Company Inc — New York *(G-10963)*	G	212 929-2395
Leigh Scott Enterprises Inc — Bellerose *(G-810)*	G	718 343-5440
Lennons Litho Inc — Herkimer *(G-6304)*	F	315 866-3156
Leonard Martin Bus Systems — New City *(G-8787)*	G	845 638-9350
Levon Graphics Corp — Farmingdale *(G-5035)*	D	631 753-2022
LI Script LLC — Woodbury *(G-17292)*	G	631 321-3850
Liberty Label Mfg Inc — Holbrook *(G-6457)*	F	631 737-2365
Litho Partners Inc — New York *(G-11009)*	E	212 627-9225
Lithomatic Business Forms Inc — New York *(G-11010)*	G	212 255-6700
Litmor Publishing Corp — Hicksville *(G-6364)*	F	516 931-0012
Lmg National Publishing Inc — Fairport *(G-4862)*	E	585 598-6874

Employee Codes: A=Over 500 employees, B=251-500
C=101-250, D=51-100, E=20-50, F=10-19, G=5-9

27 PRINTING, PUBLISHING, AND ALLIED INDUSTRIES

Company	Code	Phone
Loudon Ltd — East Northport (G-4441)	G	631 757-4447
Louis Heindl & Son Inc — Rochester (G-14483)	G	585 454-5080
Love Unlimited NY Inc — Westbury (G-17008)	E	718 359-8500
Lynmar Printing Corp — Amityville (G-306)	G	631 957-8500
▲ M L Design Inc — New York (G-11075)	G	212 233-0213
M T M Printing Co Inc — College Point (G-3796)	F	718 353-3297
Madison Printing Corp — Ithaca (G-6857)	G	607 273-3535
Magazines & Brochures Inc — Tonawanda (G-16178)	G	716 875-9699
Magjak Printing Corporation — Port Chester (G-13753)	G	914 939-8800
Malone Industrial Press Inc — Malone (G-8013)	G	518 483-5880
Manifestation-Glow Press Inc — Fresh Meadows (G-5444)	G	718 380-5259
Mansfield Press Inc — New York (G-11141)	F	212 265-5411
Marcal Printing Inc — Hicksville (G-6367)	G	516 942-9500
Marcy Printing Inc — Brooklyn (G-2268)	G	718 935-9100
Mark T Westinghouse — Catskill (G-3431)	G	518 678-3262
Marketshare LLC — Brentwood (G-1191)	G	631 273-0598
Marks Corpex Banknote Co — Bay Shore (G-715)	G	631 968-0277
Marlow Printing Co Inc — Brooklyn (G-2274)	E	718 625-4949
▼ Marsid Group Ltd — Carle Place (G-3396)	G	516 334-1603
Mason & Gore Inc — Rye (G-15063)	E	914 921-1025
Master Image Printing Inc — Elmsford (G-4763)	G	914 347-4400
Mc Squared Nyc Inc — New York (G-11193)	F	212 947-2260
McG Graphics Inc — Dix Hills (G-4294)	G	631 499-0730
Mdi Holdings LLC — New York (G-11203)	A	212 559-1127
Mdr Printing Corp — Manhasset (G-8062)	G	516 627-3221
▲ Medallion Associates Inc — New York (G-11207)	E	212 929-9130
▲ Mercury Print Productions Inc — Rochester (G-14504)	C	585 458-7900
Merrill New York Company Inc — New York (G-11235)	C	212 229-6500
Messenger Press — Ballston Spa (G-603)	G	518 885-9231
Mib Industries Inc — Ridgewood (G-14114)	E	718 497-2200
Michael K Lennon Inc — Westhampton Beach (G-17059)	E	631 288-5200
Mickelberry Communications Inc — New York (G-11252)	G	212 832-0303
Microera Printers Inc — Rochester (G-14509)	E	585 783-1300
Mid Atlantic Graphics Corp — Shirley (G-15425)	E	631 345-3800
Mid-York Press Inc — Sherburne (G-15393)	D	607 674-4491
Middletown Press — Middletown (G-8451)	G	845 343-1895
Midgley Printing Corp — Syracuse (G-15988)	G	315 475-1864
Midstate Printing Corp — Syracuse (G-15989)	E	315 475-4101
Mikam Graphics LLC — New York (G-11264)	D	212 684-9393
Miken Companies Inc — Buffalo (G-3065)	D	716 668-6311
Miller Enterprises CNY Inc — Manlius (G-8075)	G	315 682-4999
Miller Printing & Litho Inc — Amsterdam (G-356)	G	518 842-0001
▲ Mines Press Inc — Cortlandt Manor (G-4052)	C	914 788-1800
Minuteman Press Inc — Nanuet (G-8759)	G	845 623-2277
Minuteman Press Intl Inc — Jamaica (G-6932)	G	718 343-5440
Mitchell Prtg & Mailing Inc — Oswego (G-13335)	F	315 343-3531
MJB Printing Corp — Islip (G-6811)	G	631 581-0177
Mod-Pac Corp — Buffalo (G-3072)	D	716 447-9013
Monarch Graphics Inc — Central Islip (G-3504)	F	631 232-1300
Moneast Inc — Wappingers Falls (G-16575)	G	845 298-8898
Monte Press Inc — Bronx (G-1403)	G	718 325-4999
Mooney-Keehley Inc — Rochester (G-14521)	G	585 271-1573
Moore Printing Company Inc — Canandaigua (G-3349)	G	585 394-1533
Multimedia Services Inc — Corning (G-3976)	G	607 936-3186
Multiple Imprssons of Rchester — Rochester (G-14525)	G	585 546-1160
Mutual Engraving Company Inc — West Hempstead (G-16861)	D	516 489-0534
Myrtle Leola Inc — Hempstead (G-6281)	G	516 228-2312
Nameplate Mfrs of Amer — Farmingdale (G-5061)	E	631 752-0055
Nash Printing Inc — Plainview (G-13623)	F	516 935-4567
National Reproductions Inc — New York (G-11349)	E	212 619-3800
NCR Corporation — Ithaca (G-6866)	G	607 273-5310
Nesher Printing Inc — New York (G-11371)	G	212 760-2521
New Goldstar 1 Printing Corp — New York (G-11388)	G	212 343-3909
New Horizon Graphics Inc — Hauppauge (G-6147)	E	631 231-8055
New York Digital Print Center — Whitestone (G-17212)	G	718 767-1953
New York Press & Graphics Inc — Albany (G-106)	F	518 489-7089
New York Typing & Printing Co — Forest Hills (G-5327)	G	718 268-7900
Newburgh Envelope Corp — Newburgh (G-12770)	G	845 566-4211
Newport Graphics Inc — New York (G-11414)	E	212 924-2600
Newsgraphics of Delmar Inc — Delmar (G-4245)	E	518 439-5363
North Delaware Printing Inc — Tonawanda (G-16188)	G	716 692-0576
Northeast Commercial Prtg Inc — Albany (G-109)	G	518 459-5047
▲ Northeast Prtg & Dist Co Inc — Plattsburgh (G-13683)	E	518 563-8214
Northern NY Newspapers Corp — Watertown (G-16668)	C	315 782-1000
Observer Daily Sunday Newsppr — Dunkirk (G-4346)	D	716 366-3000
Office Grabs NY Inc — Brooklyn (G-2386)	G	212 444-1331
▼ Official Offset Corporation — Amityville (G-317)	E	631 957-8500
Old Ue LLC — Long Island City (G-7829)	B	718 707-0700
Olympic Press Inc — New York (G-11502)	F	212 242-4934
Orbis Brynmore Lithographics — New York (G-11522)	G	212 987-2100
Orffeo Printing & Imaging Inc — Lancaster (G-7328)	G	716 681-5757
▲ Orlandi Inc — Farmingdale (G-5071)	D	631 756-0110
Orlandi Inc — Farmingdale (G-5072)	E	631 756-0110
Ozipko Enterprises Inc — Rochester (G-14560)	G	585 424-6940
P & W Press Inc — New York (G-11547)	E	646 486-3417
P D R Inc — Plainview (G-13626)	G	516 829-5300
Pace Editions Inc — New York (G-11550)	G	212 675-7431
Paladino Prtg & Graphics Inc — Flushing (G-5277)	G	718 279-6000
Pama Enterprises Inc — Great Neck (G-5828)	G	516 504-6300
▲ Panther Graphics Inc — Rochester (G-14571)	E	585 546-7163
◆ Paper House Productions Inc — Saugerties (G-15190)	E	845 246-7261
Parkside Printing Co Inc — Jericho (G-7081)	F	516 933-5423
Parrinello Printing Inc — Buffalo (G-3115)	F	716 633-7780
Patrick Ryans Modern Press — Albany (G-114)	F	518 434-2921
▲ Paul Michael Group Inc — Ronkonkoma (G-14966)	G	631 585-5700
◆ Paxar Corporation — Orangeburg (G-13238)	E	845 398-3229
Paya Printing of NY Inc — Albertson (G-157)	G	516 625-8346
PDM Litho Inc — Long Island City (G-7836)	E	718 301-1740
Peachtree Enterprises Inc — Long Island City (G-7837)	E	212 989-3445
Perception Imaging Inc — Holbrook (G-6466)	F	631 676-5262
Perfect Forms and Systems Inc — Smithtown (G-15494)	F	631 462-1100
Persch Service Print Inc — Dunkirk (G-4347)	G	716 366-2677
Petcap Press Corporation — Long Island City (G-7840)	E	718 609-0910
Petit Printing Corp — Getzville (G-5603)	G	716 871-9490
Phoenix Graphics Inc — Rochester (G-14582)	E	585 232-4040
Photo Agents Ltd — Huntington (G-6674)	G	631 421-0258
Pic A Poc Enterprises Inc — Ronkonkoma (G-14970)	G	631 981-2094
Pine Bush Printing Co Inc — Albany (G-122)	G	518 456-2431
Pioneer Printers Inc — North Tonawanda (G-12986)	F	716 693-7100
Platinum Printing & Graphics — Farmingdale (G-5082)	G	631 249-3325
Play-It Productions Inc — Port Washington (G-13856)	F	212 695-6530
Pollack Graphics Inc — New York (G-11681)	G	212 727-8400
Pop Printing Incorporated — Brooklyn (G-2429)	F	212 808-7800
Positive Print Litho Offset — New York (G-11689)	E	212 431-4850
Post Community Media LLC — Saratoga Springs (G-15167)	E	518 374-4141
Post Road — New York (G-11690)	F	203 545-2122
Pre Cycled Inc — Brewster (G-1227)	G	845 278-7611
Precision Envelope Co Inc — Farmingdale (G-5086)	G	631 694-3990
Preebro Printing — Brooklyn (G-2437)	F	718 633-7300
Press of Fremont Payne Inc — New York (G-11700)	G	212 966-6570
Presstek Printing LLC — Rochester (G-14599)	F	585 266-2770
Prestige Envelope & Lithograph — Merrick (G-8391)	F	631 521-7043
Prestone Press LLC — Long Island City (G-7845)	C	347 468-7900
Pricet Printing — Cazenovia (G-3451)	G	315 655-0369
Print & Graphics Group — Clifton Park (G-3704)	G	518 371-4649
Print Bear LLC — New York (G-11715)	G	518 703-6098
▲ Print Better Inc — Ridgewood (G-14119)	G	347 348-1841
Print By Premier LLC — New York (G-11716)	G	212 947-1365
Print Center Inc — Cold Spring Harbor (G-3770)	G	718 643-9559
Print Cottage LLC — Massapequa Park (G-8189)	F	516 369-1749
Print Management Group Corp — New York (G-11718)	G	212 213-1555
Print Market Inc — Deer Park (G-4193)	G	631 940-8181
▲ Print Media Inc — New York (G-11719)	D	212 563-4040
Print On Demand Initiative Inc — Rochester (G-14600)	F	585 239-6044
Print Shop — Horseheads (G-6589)	G	607 734-4937

Company	Employees	Phone	Location
Print Solutions Plus Inc	G	315 234-3801	Liverpool (G-7545)
Printcorp Inc	E	631 696-0641	Ronkonkoma (G-14971)
Printech Business Systems Inc	F	212 290-2542	New York (G-11720)
Printers 3 Inc	F	631 351-1331	Hauppauge (G-6172)
Printing Resources Inc	E	518 482-2470	Albany (G-124)
Printing Sales Group Limited	E	718 258-8860	Brooklyn (G-2449)
Printing Spectrum Inc	F	631 689-1010	East Setauket (G-4490)
Printing X Press Ions	G	631 242-1992	Dix Hills (G-4296)
Printinghouse Press Ltd	G	212 719-0990	New York (G-11722)
Printroc Inc	F	585 461-2556	Rochester (G-14601)
Printutopia	F	718 788-1545	Brooklyn (G-2451)
Printz and Patternz LLC	G	518 944-6020	Schenectady (G-15286)
Pro Printing	G	516 561-9700	Lynbrook (G-7957)
Professional Solutions Print	G	631 231-9300	Hauppauge (G-6174)
Profile Printing & Graphics	G	631 273-2727	Hauppauge (G-6175)
Progressive Color Graphics	E	212 292-8787	Great Neck (G-5834)
Progressive Graphics & Prtg	G	315 331-3635	Newark (G-12741)
Prompt Printing Inc	G	631 454-6524	Farmingdale (G-5089)
Pronto Printer	G	914 737-0800	Cortlandt Manor (G-4053)
Psychonomic Society Inc	E	512 381-1494	New York (G-11743)
Quad/Graphics Inc	B	212 672-1300	New York (G-11764)
Quad/Graphics Inc	E	718 706-7600	Long Island City (G-7851)
Quad/Graphics Inc	A	518 581-4000	Saratoga Springs (G-15168)
Quad/Graphics Inc	A	212 206-5535	New York (G-11765)
Quad/Graphics Inc	A	212 741-1001	New York (G-11766)
Quadrangle Quickprints Ltd	G	631 694-4464	Melville (G-8351)
Quality Graphics Tri State	G	845 735-2523	Pearl River (G-13465)
Quantum Color Inc	E	716 283-8700	Niagara Falls (G-12865)
Quicker Printer Inc	G	607 734-8622	Elmira (G-4698)
Quickprint	G	585 394-2600	Canandaigua (G-3356)
R & J Graphics Inc	F	631 293-6611	Farmingdale (G-5095)
R & L Press Inc	G	718 447-8557	Staten Island (G-15726)
R D Printing Associates Inc	F	631 390-5964	Farmingdale (G-5096)
▲ R Hochman Papers Incorporated	F	516 466-6414	Brooklyn (G-2472)
Raith America Inc	E	518 874-3000	Troy (G-16250)
Rapid Print and Marketing Inc	G	585 924-1520	Victor (G-16499)
Rapid Rays Printing & Copying	G	716 852-0550	Buffalo (G-3153)
Rapid Reproductions LLC	G	607 843-2221	Oxford (G-13364)
Rapid Service Engraving Co	G	716 896-4555	Buffalo (G-3154)
Rasco Graphics Inc	G	212 206-0447	New York (G-11802)
Ready Check Glo Inc	G	516 547-1849	East Northport (G-4444)
Redi Records Payroll	F	718 854-6990	Brooklyn (G-2486)
Reflex Offset Inc	G	516 746-4142	Deer Park (G-4199)
Register Graphics Inc	E	716 358-2921	Randolph (G-14018)
REM Printing Inc	G	518 438-7338	Albany (G-128)
Remsen Graphics Corp	G	718 643-7500	Brooklyn (G-2491)
Resonant Legal Media LLC	E	212 687-7100	New York (G-11840)
Resonant Legal Media LLC	D	800 781-3591	New York (G-11841)
Rgm Signs Inc	G	718 442-0598	Staten Island (G-15732)
Rheinwald Printing Co Inc	F	585 637-5100	Brockport (G-1246)
Richard Ruffner	F	631 234-4600	Central Islip (G-3509)
RIT Printing Corp	F	631 586-6220	Bay Shore (G-735)
Rmd Holding Inc	G	845 628-0030	Mahopac (G-8001)
Rmf Print Management Group	F	716 683-4351	Depew (G-4273)
Robert Portegello Graphics	G	718 241-8118	Brooklyn (G-2500)
Robert Tabatznik Assoc Inc	F	845 336-4555	Kingston (G-7209)
Rosemont Press Incorporated	E	212 239-4770	New York (G-11915)
Rosen Mandell & Immerman Inc	E	212 691-2277	New York (G-11916)
Royal Tees Inc	G	845 357-9448	Suffern (G-15800)
Rv Printing	G	631 567-8658	Holbrook (G-6469)
Ry-Gan Printing Inc	G	585 482-7770	Rochester (G-14663)
Ryan Printing Inc	E	845 535-3235	Blauvelt (G-974)
Sammba Printing Inc	G	516 944-4449	Port Washington (G-13862)
Sample News Group LLC	D	315 343-3800	Oswego (G-13340)
Sand Hill Industries Inc	G	518 885-7991	Ballston Spa (G-608)
▲ Sanford Printing Inc	G	718 461-1202	Flushing (G-5290)
Scotti Graphics Inc	E	212 367-9602	Long Island City (G-7872)
Scriven Duplicating Service	G	518 233-8180	Troy (G-16253)
SDS Business Cards Inc	F	516 747-3131	Syosset (G-15839)
Seaboard Graphic Services LLC	E	315 652-4200	Liverpool (G-7547)
Searles Graphics Inc	F	631 345-2202	Yaphank (G-17401)
Security Offset Services Inc	G	631 944-6031	Huntington (G-6680)
Seifert Graphics Inc	F	315 736-2744	Oriskany (G-13313)
Select-A-Form Inc	D	631 981-3076	Holbrook (G-6470)
Seneca West Printing Inc	G	716 675-8010	West Seneca (G-16954)
Sentinel Printing Inc	G	516 334-7400	Westbury (G-17026)
Shield Press Inc	G	212 431-7489	New York (G-12050)
Shipman Printing Inds Inc	E	716 504-7700	Niagara Falls (G-12876)
Shipmtes/Printmates Holdg Corp	D	518 370-1158	Scotia (G-15330)
Shoreline Publishing Inc	G	914 738-7869	Pelham (G-13494)
Sign World Inc	E	212 619-9000	Brooklyn (G-2554)
Sizzal LLC	E	212 354-6123	Long Island City (G-7878)
Sloane Design Inc	G	212 539-0184	New York (G-12099)
Source Envelope Inc	G	866 284-0707	Farmingdale (G-5111)
Source One Promotional Product	G	516 208-6996	Merrick (G-8393)
South Bridge Press Inc	G	212 233-4047	New York (G-12144)
Spectrum Graphics & Print	F	845 473-4400	Poughkeepsie (G-13933)
Spectrum Prtg Lithography Inc	F	212 255-3131	New York (G-12158)
Speedcard Inc	G	631 472-1904	Holbrook (G-6473)
Speedway Press Inc	G	315 343-3531	Oswego (G-13341)
▲ Spring Printing Inc	F	718 797-2818	Brooklyn (G-2591)
St Gerard Enterprises Inc	F	631 473-2003	Port Jeff STA (G-13770)
St James Printing Inc	G	631 981-2095	Ronkonkoma (G-14989)
▲ St Lawrence County Newspapers	D	315 393-1003	Ogdensburg (G-13122)
St Vincent Press Inc	F	585 325-5320	Rochester (G-14699)
▲ Standwill Packaging Inc	E	631 752-1236	Farmingdale (G-5113)
Star Press Pearl River Inc	G	845 268-2294	Valley Cottage (G-16389)
▲ Star Quality Printing Inc	F	631 273-1900	Hauppauge (G-6200)
Steffen Publishing Inc	D	315 865-4100	Holland Patent (G-6488)
Sterling North America Inc	E	631 243-6933	Hauppauge (G-6201)
▼ Sterling Pierce Company Inc	E	516 593-1170	East Rockaway (G-4471)
Sterling United Inc	G	716 835-9290	Amherst (G-262)
Steval Graphics Concepts Inc	F	516 576-0220	Plainview (G-13636)
Stevens Bandes Graphics Corp	F	212 675-1128	New York (G-12202)
Stevenson Printing Co Inc	G	516 676-1233	Glen Cove (G-5629)
Stony Brook University	E	631 632-6434	Stony Brook (G-15772)
Stony Point Graphics Ltd	G	845 786-3322	Stony Point (G-15777)
Stubbs Printing Inc	G	315 769-8641	Massena (G-8201)
Studley Printing & Publishing	F	518 563-1414	Plattsburgh (G-13701)
Stylistic Press Inc	F	212 675-0797	New York (G-12225)
Suffolk Copy Center Inc	G	631 665-0570	Bay Shore (G-745)
Summit Graphics	G	716 433-1014	Lockport (G-7615)
Summit Print & Mail LLC	G	716 433-1014	Lockport (G-7616)
Sun Printing Incorporated	E	607 337-3034	Norwich (G-13037)
Superior Print On Demand	G	607 240-5231	Vestal (G-16454)
Syracuse Computer Forms Inc	E	315 478-0108	Syracuse (G-16050)
Sz - Design & Print Inc	F	845 352-0395	Monsey (G-8583)
T C Peters Printing Co Inc	G	315 724-4149	Utica (G-16361)
Taylor	G	518 954-2832	Amsterdam (G-369)
Technipoly Manufacturing Inc	E	718 383-0363	Brooklyn (G-2650)
▲ Tele-Pak Inc	E	845 426-2300	Monsey (G-8585)
Teller Printing Corp	G	718 486-3662	Brooklyn (G-2653)
The Kingsbury Printing Co Inc	G	518 747-6606	Hudson Falls (G-6650)
The Nugent Organization Inc	F	212 645-6600	Oceanside (G-13101)
Thomas Group Inc	F	212 947-6400	New York (G-12319)
Three Star Offset Printing	F	516 867-8223	Freeport (G-5431)
Tobay Printing Co Inc	E	631 842-3300	Copiague (G-3934)
Tom & Jerry Printcraft Forms	E	914 777-7468	Mamaroneck (G-8048)
Top Copi Reproductions Inc	F	212 571-4141	New York (G-12368)
▲ Toppan Printing Co Amer Inc	E	212 975-9060	New York (G-12370)
Torsaf Printers Inc	G	516 569-5577	Hewlett (G-6314)
Total Concept Graphic Inc	G	212 229-2626	New York (G-12378)
Tovie Asarese Royal Prtg Co	G	716 885-7692	Buffalo (G-3223)
Trade Mark Graphics Inc	G	718 306-0001	Brooklyn (G-2673)
Transaction Printer Group	G	607 274-2500	Ithaca (G-6881)

SIC

Employee Codes: A=Over 500 employees, B=251-500
C=101-250, D=51-100, E=20-50, F=10-19, G=5-9

◆ Transcntinental Ultra Flex Inc ... B ... 718 272-9100
Brooklyn *(G-2674)*
Transcontinental Printing GP ... G ... 716 626-3078
Amherst *(G-267)*
Tremont Offset Inc ... G ... 718 892-7333
Bronx *(G-1474)*
Tri Kolor Printing & Sty ... F ... 315 474-6753
Syracuse *(G-16061)*
Tri-Lon Clor Lithographers Ltd ... E ... 212 255-6140
New York *(G-12400)*
Tri-Star Offset Corp ... E ... 718 894-5555
Maspeth *(G-8173)*
Tri-Town News Inc ... E ... 607 561-3515
Sidney *(G-15442)*
Triad Printing Inc ... G ... 845 343-2722
Middletown *(G-8466)*
Tripi Engraving Co Inc ... E ... 718 383-6500
Brooklyn *(G-2682)*
Tropp Printing Corp ... G ... 212 233-4519
New York *(G-12409)*
Troy Sign & Printing ... G ... 718 994-4482
Bronx *(G-1479)*
Tucker Printers Inc ... D ... 585 359-3030
Henrietta *(G-6298)*
▲ Twenty-First Century Press Inc ... F ... 716 837-0800
Buffalo *(G-3227)*
Twin Counties Pro Printers Inc ... F ... 518 828-3278
Hudson *(G-6636)*
Unicom Graphic Communications ... G ... 212 221-2456
New York *(G-12452)*
Unique Printing Company LLC ... G ... 718 386-2519
Flushing *(G-5305)*
Upstate Printing Inc ... F ... 315 475-6140
Syracuse *(G-16064)*
V & J Graphics Inc ... G ... 315 363-1933
Oneida *(G-13169)*
V C N Group Ltd Inc ... G ... 516 223-4812
North Baldwin *(G-12911)*
Valentine Printing Corp ... G ... 718 444-4400
Brooklyn *(G-2716)*
Vanguard Graphics LLC ... C ... 607 272-1212
Ithaca *(G-6882)*
▲ Variable Graphics LLC ... G ... 212 691-2323
New York *(G-12505)*
Vectra Inc ... G ... 718 361-1000
Long Island City *(G-7911)*
Veterans Offset Printing Inc ... G ... 585 288-2900
Rochester *(G-14752)*
Viatech Pubg Solutions Inc ... E ... 631 968-8500
Bay Shore *(G-754)*
Vic-Gina Printing Company Inc ... G ... 914 636-0200
New Rochelle *(G-8927)*
Vicks Lithograph & Prtg Corp ... C ... 315 736-9344
Yorkville *(G-17528)*
Vicks Lithograph & Prtg Corp ... C ... 315 272-2401
Yorkville *(G-17527)*
Vincys Printing Ltd ... F ... 518 355-4363
Schenectady *(G-15309)*
VIP Printing ... G ... 718 641-9361
Howard Beach *(G-6599)*
▲ Virgil Mountain Inc ... G ... 212 378-0007
New York *(G-12547)*
Vivona Business Printers Inc ... G ... 516 496-3453
Syosset *(G-15842)*
Wall Street Business Pdts Inc ... E ... 212 563-4014
New York *(G-12580)*
Wallkill Valley Publications ... E ... 845 561-0170
Newburgh *(G-12786)*
Walnut Printing Inc ... G ... 718 707-0100
Long Island City *(G-7917)*
Wappingers Falls Shopper Inc ... E ... 845 297-3723
Wappingers Falls *(G-16578)*
Warren Printing Inc ... F ... 212 627-5000
Long Island City *(G-7918)*
Wayne Printing Inc ... F ... 914 761-2400
White Plains *(G-17182)*
Webb-Mason Inc ... E ... 716 276-8792
Buffalo *(G-3250)*
Webster Printing Corporation ... F ... 585 671-1533
Webster *(G-16742)*
Weeks & Reichel Printing Inc ... G ... 631 589-1443
Sayville *(G-15215)*
Weicro Graphics Inc ... E ... 631 253-3360
West Babylon *(G-16840)*
Westchester Mailing Service ... E ... 914 948-1116
White Plains *(G-17184)*
Westmore Litho Corp ... G ... 718 361-9403
Long Island City *(G-7920)*
Westprint Inc ... G ... 212 989-3805
New York *(G-12617)*
Westypo Printers Inc ... G ... 914 737-7394
Peekskill *(G-13487)*
William Boyd Printing Co Inc ... C ... 518 339-5832
Latham *(G-7385)*
William Charles Prtg Co Inc ... E ... 516 349-0900
Plainview *(G-13646)*
William J Kline & Son Inc ... D ... 518 843-1100
Amsterdam *(G-374)*
William J Ryan ... G ... 585 392-6200
Hilton *(G-6421)*
Wilson Press LLC ... E ... 315 568-9693
Seneca Falls *(G-15372)*
Winner Press Inc ... E ... 718 937-7715
Long Island City *(G-7924)*
Winson Surnamer Inc ... G ... 718 729-8787
Long Island City *(G-7925)*
▲ Won & Lee Inc ... E ... 516 222-0712
Garden City *(G-5538)*
Woodbury Printing Plus + Inc ... G ... 845 928-6610
Central Valley *(G-3529)*
Worldwide Ticket Craft ... D ... 516 538-6200
Merrick *(G-8394)*
Wynco Press One Inc ... G ... 516 354-6145
Glen Oaks *(G-5641)*
X Myles Mar Inc ... E ... 212 683-2015
New York *(G-12673)*
X-L Envelope and Printing Inc ... F ... 716 852-2135
Buffalo *(G-3258)*
Yorktown Printing Corp ... C ... 914 962-2526
Yorktown Heights *(G-17522)*
Zacmel Graphics LLC ... G ... 631 944-6031
Huntington *(G-6692)*
Zenger Group Inc ... E ... 716 871-1058
Tonawanda *(G-16217)*
Zenger Partners LLC ... E ... 716 876-2284
Kenmore *(G-7152)*

2754 Commercial Printing: Gravure

Adflex Corporation ... E ... 585 454-2950
Rochester *(G-14173)*
Advanced Printing New York Inc ... G ... 212 840-8108
New York *(G-9045)*
Alamar Printing Inc ... F ... 914 993-9007
White Plains *(G-17074)*
Alfa Card Inc ... G ... 718 326-7107
Glendale *(G-5643)*
▲ American Packaging Corporation ... C ... 585 254-9500
Rochester *(G-14198)*
American Print Solutions Inc ... G ... 718 208-2309
Brooklyn *(G-1607)*
▲ Ashton-Potter USA Ltd ... C ... 716 633-2000
Williamsville *(G-17233)*
Benton Announcements Inc ... F ... 716 836-4100
Buffalo *(G-2839)*
C C Industries Inc ... F ... 518 581-7633
Saratoga Springs *(G-15146)*
Clarion Publications Inc ... F ... 585 243-3530
Geneseo *(G-5564)*
▲ Clintrak Clinical Labeling S ... D ... 631 467-3900
Bohemia *(G-1034)*
Color Industries LLC ... G ... 718 392-8301
Long Island City *(G-7703)*
Copy Corner Inc ... G ... 718 388-4545
Brooklyn *(G-1803)*
Dijifi LLC ... F ... 646 519-2447
Brooklyn *(G-1864)*
Ecoplast & Packaging LLC ... G ... 718 996-0800
Brooklyn *(G-1901)*
▲ Gemini Manufacturing LLC ... C ... 914 375-0855
White Plains *(G-17113)*
▼ Gooding Co Inc ... E ... 716 434-5501
Lockport *(G-7592)*
◆ Gruner + Jahr USA Group Inc ... B ... 866 323-9336
New York *(G-10376)*
Image Sales & Marketing Inc ... G ... 516 238-7023
Massapequa Park *(G-8186)*
Jack J Florio Jr ... G ... 716 434-9123
Lockport *(G-7595)*
Janco Press Inc ... F ... 631 563-3003
Bohemia *(G-1081)*
Karr Graphics Corp ... E ... 718 784-9390
Long Island City *(G-7779)*
Kinaneco Inc ... E ... 315 468-6201
Syracuse *(G-15974)*
Krepe Kraft Inc ... B ... 716 826-7086
Buffalo *(G-3037)*
Lane Park Graphics Inc ... G ... 914 273-5898
Patterson *(G-13442)*
Leonardo Printing Corp ... G ... 914 664-7890
Mount Vernon *(G-8700)*
Liberty Label Mfg Inc ... F ... 631 737-2365
Holbrook *(G-6457)*
Mastro Graphic Arts Inc ... E ... 585 436-7570
Rochester *(G-14499)*
McG Graphics Inc ... G ... 631 499-0730
Dix Hills *(G-4294)*
Mod-Pac Corp ... D ... 716 447-9013
Buffalo *(G-3072)*
Mrs John L Strong & Co LLC ... F ... 212 838-3775
New York *(G-11317)*
Mutual Engraving Company Inc ... D ... 516 489-0534
West Hempstead *(G-16861)*
Niagara Label Company Inc ... F ... 716 542-3000
Akron *(G-25)*
Paya Printing of NY Inc ... G ... 516 625-8346
Albertson *(G-157)*
Sommer and Sons Printing Inc ... F ... 716 822-4311
Buffalo *(G-3190)*
SRC Liquidation Company ... G ... 716 631-3900
Williamsville *(G-17255)*
▲ Tele-Pak Inc ... E ... 845 426-2300
Monsey *(G-8585)*
Trust of Colum Unive In The Ci ... F ... 212 854-2793
New York *(G-12412)*
◆ Vitex Packaging Group Inc ... F ... 212 265-6575
New York *(G-12557)*

2759 Commercial Printing

2 1 2 Postcards Inc ... E ... 212 767-8227
New York *(G-8962)*
4 Over 4com Inc ... G ... 718 932-2700
Astoria *(G-431)*
461 New Lots Avenue LLC ... G ... 347 303-9305
Brooklyn *(G-1519)*
5 Stars Printing Corp ... F ... 718 461-4612
Flushing *(G-5220)*
6727 11th Ave Corp ... F ... 718 837-8787
Brooklyn *(G-1521)*
A & A Graphics Inc II ... G ... 516 735-0078
Seaford *(G-15343)*
A & P Master Images ... F ... 315 793-1934
Utica *(G-16304)*
A C Envelope Inc ... G ... 516 420-0646
Farmingdale *(G-4926)*
▲ A Graphic Printing Inc ... G ... 212 233-9696
New York *(G-8987)*
A M & J Digital ... G ... 518 434-2579
Menands *(G-8363)*
A Tradition of Excellence Inc ... G ... 845 638-4595
New City *(G-8781)*
◆ Abigal Press Inc ... D ... 718 641-5350
Ozone Park *(G-13375)*
Academy Printing Services Inc ... G ... 631 765-3346
Southold *(G-15557)*
Accel Printing & Graphics ... G ... 914 241-3369
Mount Kisco *(G-8621)*
Actioncraft Products Inc ... G ... 516 883-6423
Port Washington *(G-13795)*
▲ Active World Solutions Inc ... G ... 718 922-9404
Brooklyn *(G-1559)*
Adco Innvtive Prmtnal Pdts Inc ... G ... 716 805-1076
East Aurora *(G-4364)*
Adflex Corporation ... E ... 585 454-2950
Rochester *(G-14173)*
Adirondack Pennysaver Inc ... E ... 518 563-0100
Plattsburgh *(G-13650)*
Advance Finance Group LLC ... D ... 212 630-5900
New York *(G-9035)*
▼ Advanced Graphics Company ... F ... 607 692-7875
Whitney Point *(G-17219)*
Albert Siy ... G ... 718 359-0389
Flushing *(G-5224)*
Aldine Inc (ny) ... D ... 212 226-2870
New York *(G-9079)*
▲ Allsafe Technologies Inc ... D ... 716 691-0400
Amherst *(G-222)*
Alpina Copyworld Inc ... F ... 212 683-3511
New York *(G-9101)*
Alpine Business Group Inc ... G ... 212 989-4198
New York *(G-9102)*
▲ Alvin J Bart & Sons Inc ... C ... 718 417-1300
Glendale *(G-5645)*
Always Printing ... G ... 914 481-5209
Port Chester *(G-13739)*
AMA Precision Screening Inc ... F ... 585 293-0820
Churchville *(G-3633)*
Amax Printing Inc ... F ... 718 384-8600
Maspeth *(G-8116)*
◆ American Casting and Mfg Corp ... D ... 800 342-0333
Plainview *(G-13581)*

American Office Supply Inc ....F 516 294-9444
Westbury *(G-16967)*
Amerikom Group Inc ....D 212 675-1329
New York *(G-9132)*
Amsterdam Printing & Litho Inc ....F 518 792-6501
Queensbury *(G-13988)*
Ansun Graphics Inc ....F 315 437-6869
Syracuse *(G-15854)*
Apple Enterprises Inc ....E 718 361-2200
Long Island City *(G-7662)*
April Printing Co Inc ....F 212 685-7455
New York *(G-9185)*
Arca Ink ....G 518 798-0100
Queensbury *(G-13991)*
Arena Graphics Inc ....G 516 767-5108
Port Washington *(G-13801)*
Argo Envelope Corp ....D 718 729-2700
Long Island City *(G-7667)*
Argo Lithographers Inc ....E 718 729-2700
Long Island City *(G-7669)*
Arista Innovations Inc ....E 516 746-2262
Mineola *(G-8496)*
▲ Artistic Typography Corp ....G 212 463-8880
New York *(G-9221)*
Artistics Printing Corp ....G 516 561-2121
Franklin Square *(G-5360)*
Artscroll Printing Corp ....E 212 929-2413
New York *(G-9224)*
▲ Ashton-Potter USA Ltd ....C 716 633-2000
Williamsville *(G-17233)*
Asn Inc ....E 718 894-0800
Maspeth *(G-8120)*
Aspect Printing Inc ....E 347 789-4284
Brooklyn *(G-1640)*
Astro Label & Tag Ltd ....G 718 435-4474
Brooklyn *(G-1641)*
Atlantic Coast Embroidery Inc ....G 631 283-2175
Southampton *(G-15539)*
▲ Bags Unlimited Inc ....E 585 436-6282
Rochester *(G-14221)*
Balajee Enterprises Inc ....G 212 629-6150
New York *(G-9308)*
Barnaby Prints Inc ....F 845 477-2501
Greenwood Lake *(G-5896)*
Barnett Paul Inc ....E 212 673-3250
New York *(G-9322)*
Bartolomeo Publishing Inc ....G 631 420-4949
West Babylon *(G-16774)*
Baseline Graphics Inc ....F 585 223-0153
Fairport *(G-4847)*
Batavia Press LLC ....E 585 343-4429
Batavia *(G-624)*
Bates Jackson Engraving Co Inc ....E 716 854-3000
Buffalo *(G-2834)*
Bco Industries Western NY Inc ....E 716 877-2800
Tonawanda *(G-16144)*
BDR Creative Concepts Inc ....F 516 942-7768
Farmingdale *(G-4951)*
Bedford Freeman & Worth ....C 212 576-9400
New York *(G-9342)*
Beebie Printing & Art Agcy Inc ....G 518 725-4528
Gloversville *(G-5708)*
Beis Moshiach Inc ....E 718 778-8000
Brooklyn *(G-1679)*
▲ Benchemark Printing Inc ....D 518 393-1361
Schenectady *(G-15234)*
Berkshire Business Forms Inc ....F 518 828-2600
Hudson *(G-6610)*
Bestype Digital Imaging LLC ....F 212 966-6886
New York *(G-9374)*
Bfc Print Network Inc ....G 716 838-4532
Amherst *(G-228)*
Bidpress LLC ....G 267 973-8876
New York *(G-9389)*
▲ Big Apple Sign Corp ....E 212 629-3650
New York *(G-9392)*
Bizbash Media Inc ....E 646 638-3600
New York *(G-9406)*
▲ Bobley-Harmann Corporation ....G 516 433-3800
Ronkonkoma *(G-14880)*
Body Builders Inc ....G 718 492-7997
Brooklyn *(G-1708)*
Bondy Printing Corp ....G 631 242-1510
Bay Shore *(G-679)*
BP Beyond Printing Inc ....G 516 328-2700
Hempstead *(G-6266)*
Bradley Marketing Group Inc ....G 212 967-6100
New York *(G-9449)*
Brodock Press Inc ....D 315 735-9577
Utica *(G-16310)*

Brooks Litho Digital Group Inc ....G 631 789-4500
Deer Park *(G-4112)*
Buffalo Newspress Inc ....C 716 852-1600
Buffalo *(G-2858)*
Burr & Son Inc ....G 315 446-1550
Syracuse *(G-15877)*
Business Card Express Inc ....E 631 669-3400
West Babylon *(G-16779)*
C & C Athletic Inc ....G 845 713-4670
Walden *(G-16531)*
C F Print Ltd Inc ....F 631 567-2110
Deer Park *(G-4113)*
Cama Graphics Inc ....F 718 707-9747
Long Island City *(G-7692)*
Candid Worldwide LLC ....G 212 799-5300
Long Island City *(G-7694)*
▲ Casual Home Worldwide Inc ....G 631 789-2999
Amityville *(G-280)*
▲ Century Direct LLC ....C 212 763-0600
Islandia *(G-6789)*
Cenveo Inc ....F 716 686-0100
Depew *(G-4252)*
Chakra Communications Inc ....E 607 748-7491
Endicott *(G-4798)*
Check-O-Matic Inc ....G 845 781-7675
Monroe *(G-8552)*
Chenango Union Printing Inc ....G 607 334-2112
Norwich *(G-13022)*
Christian Bus Endeavors Inc ....F 315 788-8560
Watertown *(G-16644)*
Chroma Communications Inc ....G 631 289-8871
Medford *(G-8240)*
CHv Printed Company ....F 516 997-1101
East Meadow *(G-4419)*
Citiforms Inc ....G 212 334-9671
New York *(G-9623)*
Classic Album ....E 718 388-2818
Brooklyn *(G-1786)*
Classic Labels Inc ....E 631 467-2300
Patchogue *(G-13417)*
Clear Channel Outdoor Inc ....F 212 812-0000
New York *(G-9641)*
Colad Group LLC ....D 716 961-1776
Buffalo *(G-2880)*
Colonial Label Systems Inc ....E 631 254-0111
Bay Shore *(G-685)*
▲ Colonial Tag & Label Co Inc ....F 516 482-0508
Great Neck *(G-5799)*
Color Card LLC ....F 631 232-1300
Central Islip *(G-3491)*
Comgraph Sales Service ....G 716 601-7243
Elma *(G-4646)*
Commercial Press Inc ....G 315 274-0028
Canton *(G-3381)*
Control Research Inc ....G 631 225-1111
Amityville *(G-282)*
Cooper & Clement Inc ....E 315 454-8135
Syracuse *(G-15907)*
Copy Color Inc ....F 212 889-6202
New York *(G-9720)*
Copy Room Inc ....F 212 371-8600
New York *(G-9721)*
Copy X/Press Ltd ....D 631 585-2200
Ronkonkoma *(G-14888)*
CPW Direct Mail Group LLC ....E 631 588-6565
Farmingdale *(G-4964)*
Craig Envelope Corp ....E 718 786-4277
Long Island City *(G-7706)*
Create-A-Card Inc ....G 631 584-2273
Saint James *(G-15087)*
Crisray Printing Corp ....E 631 293-3770
Farmingdale *(G-4965)*
Curtis Prtg Co The Del Press ....G 518 477-4820
East Greenbush *(G-4402)*
Custom Prtrs Guilderland Inc ....F 518 456-2811
Guilderland *(G-5902)*
Custom Sportswear Corp ....G 914 666-9200
Bedford Hills *(G-800)*
D B F Associates ....G 718 328-0005
Bronx *(G-1307)*
D G M Graphics Inc ....F 516 223-2220
Merrick *(G-8383)*
DArcy Printing and Lithog ....G 212 924-1554
New York *(G-9809)*
Dash Printing Inc ....G 212 643-8534
New York *(G-9812)*
Data Flow Inc ....G 631 436-9200
Medford *(G-8242)*
▲ Data Palette Info Svcs LLC ....D 718 433-1060
Port Washington *(G-13807)*

De La Rue North America Inc ....G 518 463-7621
Albany *(G-72)*
Delft Printing Inc ....G 716 683-1100
Lancaster *(G-7311)*
Dental Tribune America LLC ....F 212 244-7181
New York *(G-9848)*
Design Distributors Inc ....D 631 242-2000
Deer Park *(G-4130)*
Design Printing Corp ....G 631 753-9801
Farmingdale *(G-4975)*
DEW Graphics Inc ....E 212 727-8820
New York *(G-9865)*
Diamond Inscription Tech ....F 646 366-7944
New York *(G-9873)*
Digital Evolution Inc ....E 212 732-2722
New York *(G-9876)*
Digital Print Services ....G 877 832-1200
Buffalo *(G-2914)*
Direct Print Inc ....F 212 987-6003
New York *(G-9882)*
Dit Prints Incorporated ....G 518 885-4400
Ballston Spa *(G-594)*
Diversified Envelope Ltd ....F 585 615-4697
Rochester *(G-14312)*
Division Den-Bar Enterprises ....G 914 381-2220
Mamaroneck *(G-8033)*
Dkm Sales LLC ....E 716 893-7777
Buffalo *(G-2916)*
Doctor Print Inc ....E 631 873-4560
Hauppauge *(G-6066)*
Doremus FP LLC ....E 212 366-3800
New York *(G-9909)*
▲ Drns Corp ....F 718 369-4530
Brooklyn *(G-1881)*
Dupli Graphics Corporation ....C 315 234-7286
Syracuse *(G-15925)*
Dupli Graphics Corporation ....G 315 422-4732
Syracuse *(G-15926)*
Dutchess Plumbing & Heating ....G 845 889-8255
Staatsburg *(G-15618)*
Dynamic Packaging Inc ....F 718 388-0800
Brooklyn *(G-1887)*
E&I Printing ....F 212 206-0506
New York *(G-9954)*
Eagle Envelope Company Inc ....G 607 387-3195
Trumansburg *(G-16265)*
Eaglesome Graphics Inc ....F 716 665-1116
Jamestown *(G-6989)*
East Coast Thermographers Inc ....E 718 321-3211
College Point *(G-3782)*
Eastwood Litho Inc ....E 315 437-2626
Syracuse *(G-15929)*
Edgian Press Inc ....G 516 931-2114
Hicksville *(G-6342)*
Efficiency Printing Co Inc ....F 914 949-8611
White Plains *(G-17103)*
Efs Designs ....G 718 852-9511
Brooklyn *(G-1906)*
Ehs Group LLC ....G 914 937-6162
Port Chester *(G-13744)*
Elm Graphics Inc ....G 315 737-5984
New Hartford *(G-8803)*
Endeavor Printing LLC ....G 718 570-2720
Long Island City *(G-7731)*
Enterprise Press Inc ....C 212 741-2111
New York *(G-10043)*
Evenhouse Printing ....G 716 649-2666
Hamburg *(G-5925)*
Evergreen Corp Central NY ....F 315 454-4175
Syracuse *(G-15939)*
Excell Print & Promotions Inc ....G 914 437-8668
White Plains *(G-17107)*
Excellent Printing Inc ....G 718 384-7272
Brooklyn *(G-1944)*
◆ Excelsior Packaging Group Inc ....C 914 968-1300
Yonkers *(G-17442)*
Excelsus Solutions LLC ....E 585 533-0003
Rochester *(G-14363)*
Exotic Print and Paper Inc ....F 212 807-0465
New York *(G-10107)*
▲ Expedi-Printing Inc ....C 516 513-0919
Great Neck *(G-5807)*
Eye Graphics & Printing Inc ....F 718 488-0606
Brooklyn *(G-1948)*
F & B Photo Offset Co Inc ....G 516 431-5433
Island Park *(G-6779)*
F A Printing ....G 212 974-5982
New York *(G-10115)*
Fairmount Press ....G 212 255-2300
New York *(G-10130)*

Employee Codes: A=Over 500 employees, B=251-500
C=101-250, D=51-100, E=20-50, F=10-19, G=5-9

2017 Harris
New York Manufacturers Directory

773

27 PRINTING, PUBLISHING, AND ALLIED INDUSTRIES

Company	Col	Phone
Falconer Printing & Design Inc	F	716 665-2121
Falconer (G-4899)		
Farthing Press Inc	G	716 852-4674
Buffalo (G-2945)		
Federal Envelope Inc	F	212 243-8380
New York (G-10148)		
Fedex Office & Print Svcs Inc	G	718 982-5223
Staten Island (G-15673)		
Fineline Thermographers Inc	G	718 643-1100
Brooklyn (G-1972)		
First2print Inc	G	212 868-6886
New York (G-10169)		
◆ Flexo Transparent Inc	C	716 825-7710
Buffalo (G-2951)		
Flp Group LLC	F	315 252-7583
Auburn (G-496)		
Force Digital Media Inc	G	631 243-0243
Deer Park (G-4143)		
Forward Enterprises Inc	F	585 235-7670
Rochester (G-14379)		
Franklin Packaging Inc	G	631 582-8900
Northport (G-13011)		
Fred Weidner & Son Printers	G	212 964-8676
New York (G-10205)		
Frederick Coon Inc	G	716 683-6812
Elma (G-4648)		
▲ Freeport Screen & Stamping	E	516 379-0330
Freeport (G-5401)		
Freeville Publishing Co Inc	F	607 844-9119
Freeville (G-5435)		
Fresh Prints LLC	E	917 826-2752
New York (G-10210)		
Fulcrum Promotions & Prtg LLC	G	203 909-6362
New York (G-10221)		
G&J Graphics Inc	G	718 409-9874
Bronx (G-1340)		
▲ Gallant Graphices Ltd Inc	E	845 868-1166
Stanfordville (G-15627)		
Garrett J Cronin	G	914 761-9299
White Plains (G-17111)		
Gary Stock Corporation	G	914 276-2700
Croton Falls (G-4061)		
▲ Gatehouse Media LLC	D	585 598-0030
Pittsford (G-13561)		
Gazette Press Inc	E	914 963-8300
Rye (G-15056)		
GE Healthcare Fincl Svcs Inc	G	212 713-2000
New York (G-10263)		
Gem Reproduction Services Corp	G	845 298-0172
Wappingers Falls (G-16570)		
Gem West Inc	G	631 567-4228
Patchogue (G-13420)		
Gemson Graphics Inc	G	516 873-8400
Albertson (G-154)		
General Business Supply Inc	D	518 720-3939
Watervliet (G-16685)		
General Trade Mark La	E	718 979-7261
Staten Island (G-15677)		
Genesis One Unlimeted	G	516 208-5863
West Hempstead (G-16854)		
Genie Instant Printing Co Inc	F	212 575-8258
New York (G-10277)		
Golos Printing Inc	G	607 732-1896
Elmira Heights (G-4710)		
▲ Gould J Perfect Screen Prtrs	F	607 272-0099
Ithaca (G-6844)		
Grado Group Inc	G	718 556-4200
Staten Island (G-15680)		
Grand Meridian Printing Inc	E	718 937-3888
Long Island City (G-7752)		
Graph-Tex Inc	G	607 756-7791
Cortland (G-4027)		
Graph-Tex Inc	G	607 756-1875
Cortland (G-4028)		
Graphic Lab Inc	E	212 682-1815
New York (G-10353)		
Graphic Printing	G	718 701-4433
Bronx (G-1348)		
Graphics 247 Corp	G	718 729-2470
Long Island City (G-7753)		
Graphics Plus Printing Inc	F	607 299-0500
Cortland (G-4029)		
Greenbush Tape & Label Inc	E	518 465-2389
Albany (G-83)		
Grover Cleveland Press Inc	F	716 564-2222
Amherst (G-244)		
Gruber Display Co Inc	F	718 882-8220
Bronx (G-1349)		
H T L & S Ltd	F	718 435-4474
Brooklyn (G-2060)		
Haig Press Inc	E	631 582-5800
Hauppauge (G-6088)		
▲ Hammer Packaging Corp	B	585 424-3880
West Henrietta (G-16881)		
Handone Studios Inc	G	585 421-8175
Fairport (G-4857)		
Hanson Sign & Screen Process	E	716 484-8564
Falconer (G-4901)		
Harmon and Castella Printing	F	845 471-9163
Poughkeepsie (G-13905)		
Hart Reproduction Services	G	212 704-0556
New York (G-10423)		
Hearst Corporation	B	212 767-5800
New York (G-10441)		
Herrmann Group LLC	G	716 876-9798
Kenmore (G-7148)		
HI Speed Envelope Co Inc	E	718 617-1600
Mount Vernon (G-8690)		
Hi-Tech Packg World-Wide LLC	F	845 947-1912
New Windsor (G-8939)		
Hill Crest Press	G	518 943-0671
Catskill (G-3429)		
Horace J Metz	F	716 873-9103
Kenmore (G-7149)		
Hospitality Inc	E	212 268-1930
New York (G-10511)		
Hudson Envelope Corporation	E	212 473-6666
New York (G-10525)		
Human Technologies Corporation	F	315 735-3532
Utica (G-16340)		
▲ I N K T Inc	E	212 957-2700
New York (G-10540)		
Idc Printing & Sty Co Inc	G	516 599-0400
Lynbrook (G-7951)		
Image Typography Inc	F	631 218-6932
Holbrook (G-6450)		
▲ Impress Graphic Technologies	F	516 781-0845
Westbury (G-16996)		
Impressive Imprints	F	716 692-0905
North Tonawanda (G-12977)		
Imtech Graphics Inc	F	212 282-7010
New York (G-10576)		
Incodema3d LLC	F	607 269-4390
Ithaca (G-6849)		
Industrial Test Eqp Co Inc	E	516 883-6423
Port Washington (G-13824)		
Info Label Inc	F	518 664-0791
Halfmoon (G-5911)		
Integrated Graphics Inc	G	212 592-5600
New York (G-10616)		
Interstate Thermographers Corp	G	914 948-1745
White Plains (G-17124)		
Iron Horse Graphics Ltd	G	631 537-3400
Bridgehampton (G-1234)		
Island Silkscreen Inc	G	631 757-4567
East Northport (G-4437)		
Issacs Yisroel	G	718 851-7430
Brooklyn (G-2117)		
Itc Mfg Group Inc	F	212 684-3696
New York (G-10669)		
J Kendall LLC	G	646 739-4956
Yonkers (G-17457)		
J M L Productions Inc	D	718 643-1674
Brooklyn (G-2126)		
J N White Associates Inc	D	585 237-5191
Perry (G-13524)		
Jack J Florio Jr	G	716 434-9123
Lockport (G-7595)		
Janco Press Inc	F	631 563-3003
Bohemia (G-1081)		
Japan Printing & Graphics Inc	G	212 406-2905
New York (G-10700)		
Joed Press	G	212 243-3620
New York (G-10748)		
John Auguliaro Printing Co	G	718 382-5283
Brooklyn (G-2145)		
Johnnys Ideal Printing Co	G	518 828-6666
Hudson (G-6621)		
▲ Jomar Industries Inc	E	845 357-5773
Airmont (G-16)		
Jomart Associates Inc	E	212 627-2153
Islandia (G-6798)		
Jon Lyn Ink Inc	G	516 546-2312
Merrick (G-8386)		
Judith Lewis Printer Inc	G	516 997-7777
Westbury (G-17000)		
K & B Stamping Co Inc	G	914 664-8555
Mount Vernon (G-8696)		
Kallen Corp	E	212 242-1470
New York (G-10805)		
Karr Graphics Corp	E	718 784-9390
Long Island City (G-7779)		
▲ Kates Paperie Ltd	G	212 966-3904
New York (G-10817)		
Kaufman Brothers Printing	G	212 563-1854
New York (G-10820)		
Kaymil Printing Company Inc	G	212 594-3718
New York (G-10822)		
▲ Kenan International Trading	G	718 672-4922
Corona (G-4000)		
Kenmar Shirts Inc	E	718 824-3880
Bronx (G-1371)		
Key Computer Svcs of Chelsea	D	212 206-8060
New York (G-10840)		
Kim Jae Printing Co Inc	G	212 691-6289
Roslyn Heights (G-15028)		
Kinaneco Inc	E	315 468-6201
Syracuse (G-15974)		
Knucklehead Embroidery Inc	G	607 797-2725
Johnson City (G-7098)		
Kroger Packaging Inc	G	631 249-6690
Farmingdale (G-5029)		
Kurrier Inc	G	718 389-3018
Brooklyn (G-2181)		
L & M Uniserv Corp	G	718 854-3700
Brooklyn (G-2185)		
L I C Screen Printing Inc	E	516 546-7289
Merrick (G-8387)		
L Loy Press Inc	G	716 634-5966
Buffalo (G-3040)		
L T Sales Corp	F	631 886-1390
Wading River (G-16523)		
◆ Labels Inter-Global Inc	F	212 398-0006
New York (G-10912)		
Lake Placid Advertisers Wkshp	E	518 523-3359
Lake Placid (G-7275)		
LAM Western New York Inc	G	716 856-0308
Buffalo (G-3045)		
Landlord Guard Inc	F	212 695-6505
New York (G-10924)		
Lauricella Press Inc	E	516 931-5906
Brentwood (G-1189)		
Lennons Litho Inc	F	315 866-3156
Herkimer (G-6304)		
Leo Paper Inc	G	917 305-0708
New York (G-10970)		
Levon Graphics Corp	D	631 753-2022
Farmingdale (G-5035)		
Lifeforms Printing	G	716 685-4500
Depew (G-4263)		
Linco Printing Inc	E	718 937-5141
Long Island City (G-7789)		
Linda Campbell	G	718 994-4026
Bronx (G-1382)		
Linden Forms & Systems Inc	E	212 219-1100
Brooklyn (G-2226)		
Lion In The Sun Park Slope Ltd	G	718 369-4006
Brooklyn (G-2230)		
Logomax Inc	G	631 420-0484
Farmingdale (G-5036)		
Loremanss Embroidery Engrav	F	518 834-9205
Keeseville (G-7139)		
Louis Heindl & Son Inc	G	585 454-5080
Rochester (G-14483)		
Love Unlimited NY Inc	E	718 359-8500
Westbury (G-17008)		
M C Packaging Corporation	E	631 643-3763
Babylon (G-550)		
M T M Printing Co Inc	F	718 353-3297
College Point (G-3796)		
Magazines & Brochures Inc	G	716 875-9699
Tonawanda (G-16178)		
Makerbot Industries LLC	G	347 457-5758
New York (G-11118)		
Malone Industrial Press Inc	E	518 483-5880
Malone (G-8013)		
Mark T Westinghouse	G	518 678-3262
Catskill (G-3431)		
Marlow Printing Co Inc	E	718 625-4949
Brooklyn (G-2274)		
Mason Transparent Package Inc	E	718 792-6000
Bronx (G-1388)		
Maspeth Press Inc	G	718 429-2363
Maspeth (G-8149)		
Master Image Printing Inc	G	914 347-4400
Elmsford (G-4763)		
▲ Mastercraft Decorators Inc	E	585 223-5150
Fairport (G-4863)		
Mastro Graphic Arts Inc	E	585 436-7570
Rochester (G-14499)		

Matt Industries Inc ......C 315 472-1316
Syracuse *(G-15984)*
Matthew-Lee Corporation ......F 631 226-0100
Lindenhurst *(G-7471)*
McAuliffe Paper Inc ......E 315 453-2222
Liverpool *(G-7534)*
Measurement Incorporated ......E 914 682-1969
White Plains *(G-17136)*
▲ **Medallion Associates Inc** ......E 212 929-9130
New York *(G-11207)*
Media Signs LLC ......G 718 252-7575
Brooklyn *(G-2292)*
Mega Graphics Inc ......G 914 962-1402
Yorktown Heights *(G-17513)*
▲ **Menu Solutions Inc** ......D 718 575-5160
Bronx *(G-1391)*
Merchandiser Inc ......G 315 462-6411
Clifton Springs *(G-3714)*
Merlin Printing Inc ......E 631 842-6666
Amityville *(G-312)*
Merrill Communications LLC ......G 212 620-5600
New York *(G-11232)*
Merrill Corporation ......D 917 934-7300
New York *(G-11233)*
Merrill New York Company Inc ......C 212 229-6500
New York *(G-11235)*
Metro Creative Graphics Inc ......E 212 947-5100
New York *(G-11241)*
Middletown Press ......G 845 343-1895
Middletown *(G-8451)*
Midgley Printing Corp ......G 315 475-1864
Syracuse *(G-15988)*
Miken Companies Inc ......D 716 668-6311
Buffalo *(G-3065)*
Mimeocom Inc ......B 212 847-3000
New York *(G-11273)*
▲ **Mines Press Inc** ......C 914 788-1800
Cortlandt Manor *(G-4052)*
Mini Graphics Inc ......D 516 223-6464
Hauppauge *(G-6139)*
Mixture Screen Printing ......G 845 561-2857
Newburgh *(G-12767)*
▼ **Mod-Pac Corp** ......C 716 873-0640
Buffalo *(G-3071)*
Moore Printing Company Inc ......G 585 394-1533
Canandaigua *(G-3349)*
Mpe Graphics Inc ......F 631 582-8900
Bohemia *(G-1106)*
◆ **Multi Packaging Solutions Inc** ......E 646 885-0157
New York *(G-11324)*
▲ **Mv Corp Inc** ......C 631 273-8020
Bay Shore *(G-720)*
Nathan Printing Express Inc ......G 914 472-0914
Scarsdale *(G-15221)*
New Art Signs Co Inc ......G 718 443-0900
Glen Head *(G-5637)*
▲ **New Deal Printing Corp** ......G 718 729-5800
New York *(G-11382)*
New York Christan Times Inc ......G 718 638-6397
Brooklyn *(G-2363)*
New York Legal Publishing ......G 518 459-1100
Menands *(G-8377)*
New York Sample Card Co Inc ......E 212 242-1242
New York *(G-11407)*
Newport Business Solutions Inc ......F 631 319-6129
Bohemia *(G-1110)*
Niagara Label Company Inc ......F 716 542-3000
Akron *(G-25)*
Niagara Sample Book Co Inc ......F 716 284-6151
Niagara Falls *(G-12850)*
Noble Checks Inc ......G 212 537-6241
Brooklyn *(G-2373)*
Nomad Editions LLC ......F 212 918-0992
Bronxville *(G-1502)*
North American DF Inc ......G 718 698-2500
Staten Island *(G-15711)*
North American Graphics Inc ......F 212 725-2200
New York *(G-11455)*
North Six Inc ......F 212 463-7227
New York *(G-11458)*
Northwind Graphics ......G 518 899-9651
Ballston Spa *(G-605)*
Nys Nyu-Cntr Intl Cooperation ......E 212 998-3680
New York *(G-11487)*
One In A Million Inc ......G 516 829-1111
Valley Stream *(G-16417)*
Ontario Label Graphics Inc ......F 716 434-8505
Lockport *(G-7609)*
Origin Press Inc ......G 516 746-2262
Mineola *(G-8530)*
P & W Press Inc ......E 646 486-3417
New York *(G-11547)*
Pace Editions Inc ......G 212 675-7431
New York *(G-11550)*
Paratore Signs Inc ......G 315 455-5551
Syracuse *(G-16010)*
Patrick Rohan ......G 718 781-2573
Monticello *(G-8607)*
Patrick Ryans Modern Press ......F 518 434-2921
Albany *(G-114)*
Paulin Investment Company ......E 631 957-8500
Amityville *(G-320)*
PBR Graphics Inc ......G 518 458-2909
Albany *(G-115)*
PDM Studios Inc ......G 716 694-8337
Tonawanda *(G-16192)*
PDQ Shipping Services ......G 845 255-5500
New Paltz *(G-8877)*
Penny Lane Printing Inc ......D 585 226-8111
Avon *(G-542)*
Personal Graphics Corporation ......G 315 853-3421
Westmoreland *(G-17063)*
Peter Papastrat ......G 607 723-8112
Binghamton *(G-942)*
Photo Agents Ltd ......G 631 421-0258
Huntington *(G-6674)*
Pierrepont Visual Graphics ......G 585 305-9672
Rochester *(G-14585)*
▲ **Poly-Flex Corp** ......F 631 586-9500
Edgewood *(G-4607)*
Pony Farm Press & Graphics ......G 607 432-9020
Oneonta *(G-13192)*
Precision Envelope Co Inc ......G 631 694-3990
Farmingdale *(G-5086)*
Precision Label Corporation ......F 631 270-4490
Farmingdale *(G-5087)*
Premier Ink Systems Inc ......E 845 782-5802
Harriman *(G-5973)*
Presstek Printing LLC ......F 585 266-2770
Rochester *(G-14599)*
Print City Corp ......F 212 487-9778
New York *(G-11717)*
▲ **Print House Inc** ......D 718 443-7500
Brooklyn *(G-2445)*
Print Mall ......G 718 437-7700
Brooklyn *(G-2446)*
◆ **Print Pack Inc** ......C 404 460-7000
Farmingdale *(G-5088)*
Print Shoppe ......G 315 792-9585
Utica *(G-16356)*
Printech Business Systems Inc ......F 212 290-2542
New York *(G-11720)*
Printed Image ......G 716 821-1880
Buffalo *(G-3137)*
Printery ......G 516 922-3250
Oyster Bay *(G-13373)*
Printfacility Inc ......G 212 349-4009
New York *(G-11721)*
Printing Max New York Inc ......G 718 692-1400
Brooklyn *(G-2448)*
Printing Prmtnal Solutions LLC ......F 315 474-1110
Syracuse *(G-16014)*
Printing Resources Inc ......E 518 482-2470
Albany *(G-124)*
Printout Copy Corp ......E 718 855-4040
Brooklyn *(G-2450)*
Printworks Printing & Design ......G 315 433-8587
Syracuse *(G-16015)*
Priority Printing Entps Inc ......F 646 285-0684
New York *(G-11723)*
Proof 7 Ltd ......F 212 680-1843
New York *(G-11735)*
▲ **Publimax Printing Corp** ......G 718 366-7133
Ridgewood *(G-14121)*
Quadra Flex Corp ......G 607 758-7066
Cortland *(G-4042)*
Quality Graphics West Seneca ......G 716 668-4528
Cheektowaga *(G-3588)*
Quality Impressions Inc ......G 646 613-0002
New York *(G-11767)*
Quality Offset LLC ......G 347 342-4660
Long Island City *(G-7854)*
Quist Industries Ltd ......F 718 243-2800
Brooklyn *(G-2468)*
R & M Graphics of New York ......F 212 929-0294
New York *(G-11779)*
▲ **R D Manufacturing Corp** ......G 914 238-1000
Pleasantville *(G-13716)*
Rainbow Lettering ......G 607 732-5751
Elmira *(G-4699)*
Regal Screen Printing Intl ......G 845 356-8181
Spring Valley *(G-15601)*
Republican Registrar Inc ......G 315 497-1551
Moravia *(G-8617)*
Rfn Inc ......F 516 764-5100
Bay Shore *(G-733)*
Richard Ruffner ......F 631 234-4600
Central Islip *(G-3509)*
Richs Sttches EMB Screenprint ......G 845 621-2175
Mahopac *(G-8000)*
▼ **Rike Enterprises Inc** ......F 631 277-8338
Islip *(G-6812)*
RIT Printing Corp ......F 631 586-6220
Bay Shore *(G-735)*
River & Sound Publication LLC ......G 631 225-7100
Copiague *(G-3923)*
Rose Graphics LLC ......F 516 547-6142
West Babylon *(G-16823)*
Ross-Ellis Ltd ......G 212 260-9200
Valley Stream *(G-16426)*
Round Top Knit & Screening ......G 518 622-3600
Round Top *(G-15040)*
Royal Tees Inc ......G 845 357-9448
Suffern *(G-15800)*
RR Donnelley & Sons Company ......F 716 763-2613
Lakewood *(G-7294)*
RR Donnelley & Sons Company ......D 518 438-9722
Albany *(G-129)*
RR Donnelley & Sons Company ......G 646 755-8125
New York *(G-11930)*
S & S Graphics Inc ......F 914 668-4230
Mount Vernon *(G-8728)*
▲ **S & S Prtg Die-Cutting Co Inc** ......F 718 388-8990
Brooklyn *(G-2522)*
S L C Industries Incorporated ......F 607 775-2299
Binghamton *(G-948)*
Salamanca Press Penny Saver ......E 716 945-1500
Salamanca *(G-15105)*
Sammba Printing Inc ......G 516 944-4449
Port Washington *(G-13862)*
Sand Hill Industries Inc ......G 518 885-7991
Ballston Spa *(G-608)*
Scan-A-Chrome Color Inc ......G 631 532-6146
Copiague *(G-3925)*
Scancorp Inc ......F 315 454-5596
Syracuse *(G-16032)*
Scotti Graphics Inc ......E 212 367-9602
Long Island City *(G-7872)*
Screen The World Inc ......F 631 475-0023
Holtsville *(G-6508)*
SDS Business Cards Inc ......F 516 747-3131
Syosset *(G-15839)*
Select-A-Form Inc ......D 631 981-3076
Holbrook *(G-6470)*
Seneca West Printing Inc ......G 716 675-8010
West Seneca *(G-16954)*
Sentinel Printing Inc ......G 516 334-7400
Westbury *(G-17026)*
Sephardic Yellow Pages ......E 718 998-0299
Brooklyn *(G-2543)*
Seri Systems Inc ......E 585 272-5515
Rochester *(G-14682)*
Shapeways Inc ......D 914 356-5816
New York *(G-12043)*
Sharp Printing Inc ......G 716 731-3994
Sanborn *(G-15127)*
Shipman Printing Inds Inc ......E 716 504-7700
Niagara Falls *(G-12876)*
Shore Line Monogramming Inc ......F 914 698-8000
Mamaroneck *(G-8047)*
Short Run Forms Inc ......D 631 567-7171
Bohemia *(G-1133)*
Shykat Promotions ......G 866 574-2757
Forestville *(G-5336)*
Sign Shop Inc ......G 631 226-4145
Copiague *(G-3928)*
Silk Screen Art Inc ......F 518 762-8423
Johnstown *(G-7126)*
Silver Griffin Inc ......F 518 272-7771
Troy *(G-16255)*
◆ **Sino Printing Inc** ......F 212 334-6896
New York *(G-12086)*
Soho Letterpress Inc ......F 718 788-2518
Brooklyn *(G-2578)*
Solarz Bros Printing Corp ......G 718 383-1330
Brooklyn *(G-2582)*
Source Envelope Inc ......G 866 284-0707
Farmingdale *(G-5111)*
Spaulding Law Printing Inc ......G 315 422-4805
Syracuse *(G-16042)*

Employee Codes: A=Over 500 employees, B=251-500
C=101-250, D=51-100, E=20-50, F=10-19, G=5-9
2017 Harris
New York Manufacturers Directory
775

27 PRINTING, PUBLISHING, AND ALLIED INDUSTRIES

Spectrum Prtg Lithography Inc ....F 212 255-3131
  New York (G-12158)
Speedy Enterprise of USA Corp ....G 718 463-3000
  Flushing (G-5295)
Spst Inc ....G 607 798-6952
  Vestal (G-16453)
St James Printing Inc ....G 631 981-2095
  Ronkonkoma (G-14989)
▲ Standwill Packaging Inc ....E 631 752-1236
  Farmingdale (G-5113)
Star Press Pearl River Inc 845 268-2294
  Valley Cottage (G-16389)
Starcraft Press Inc ....G 718 383-6700
  Long Island City (G-7887)
Starfire Printing Inc ....G 631 736-1495
  Holtsville (G-6509)
Stellar Printing Inc ....D 718 361-1600
  Long Island City (G-7890)
Stony Point Graphics Ltd ....G 845 786-3322
  Stony Point (G-15777)
Stromberg Brand Corporation ....F 914 739-7410
  Valley Cottage (G-16391)
Structured 3d Inc ....G 346 704-2614
  Amityville (G-326)
Superior Print On Demand ....G 607 240-5231
  Vestal (G-16454)
Swift Multigraphics LLC ....G 585 442-8000
  Rochester (G-14709)
Syracuse Label Co Inc ....D 315 422-1037
  Liverpool (G-7550)
▲ Syracuse Letter Company Inc ....F 315 476-8328
  Bridgeport (G-1237)
T L F Graphics Inc ....G 585 272-5500
  Rochester (G-14716)
T S O General Corp ....E 631 952-5320
  Brentwood (G-1195)
T&K Printing Inc ....F 718 439-9454
  Brooklyn (G-2640)
T-Base Communications USA Inc ....E 315 713-0013
  Ogdensburg (G-13123)
Table Tops Paper Corp ....G 718 598-7832
  Brooklyn (G-2642)
▲ Tape Printers Inc ....F 631 249-5585
  Farmingdale (G-5125)
Tapemaker Sales Co Inc 516 333-0592
  Westbury (G-17029)
Tapemaker Supply Company LLC ....G 914 693-3407
  Hartsdale (G-6001)
Tara Rific Screen Printing Inc ....G 718 583-6864
  Bronx (G-1472)
Tcmf Inc ....D 607 724-1094
  Binghamton (G-954)
▲ Tele-Pak Inc ....E 845 426-2300
  Monsey (G-8585)
Ter-El Engraving Co Inc ....G 315 455-5597
  Syracuse (G-16056)
The Gramecy Group ....G 518 348-1325
  Clifton Park (G-3710)
Thomson Press (india) Limited ....G 646 318-0369
  Long Island City (G-7901)
Todd Walbridge 585 254-3018
  Rochester (G-14727)
Top Copi Reproductions Inc ....F 212 571-4141
  New York (G-12368)
Toppan Vite (new York) Inc 212 596-7747
  New York (G-12371)
Toprint Ltd ....G 718 439-0469
  Brooklyn (G-2667)
Total Solution Graphics Inc ....G 718 706-1540
  Long Island City (G-7903)
Tovie Asarese Royal Prtg Co 716 885-7692
  Buffalo (G-3223)
◆ Transcntinental Ultra Flex Inc ....B 718 272-9100
  Brooklyn (G-2674)
Tri Kolor Printing & Sty ....F 315 474-6753
  Syracuse (G-16061)
Tri-Lon Clor Lithographers Ltd ....E 212 255-6140
  New York (G-12400)
Triangle Label Tag Inc ....G 718 875-3030
  Brooklyn (G-2679)
Tripi Engraving Co Inc ....E 718 383-6500
  Brooklyn (G-2682)
U All Inc 518 438-2558
  Albany (G-144)
United Graphics Inc ....E 716 871-2600
  Buffalo (G-3234)
United Print Group Inc ....F 718 392-4242
  Long Island City (G-7908)
▲ Universal Screening Associates ....F 718 232-2744
  Brooklyn (G-2708)

Unlimited Ink Inc ....E 631 582-0696
  Hauppauge (G-6221)
▲ USA Custom Pad Corp ....G 607 563-9550
  Sidney (G-15445)
Varick Street Litho Inc ....G 646 843-0800
  New York (G-12506)
Venus Printing Company ....F 212 967-8900
  Hewlett (G-6316)
Veterans Offset Printing Inc ....G 585 288-2900
  Rochester (G-14752)
Viking Athletics Ltd ....E 631 957-8000
  Lindenhurst (G-7492)
◆ Vitex Packaging Group Inc ....F 212 265-6575
  New York (G-12557)
Voss Signs LLC ....E 315 682-6418
  Manlius (G-8076)
W N Vanalstine & Sons Inc ....D 518 237-1436
  Cohoes (G-3761)
Webster Printing Corporation ....F 585 671-1533
  Webster (G-16742)
Weeks & Reichel Printing Inc ....G 631 589-1443
  Sayville (G-15215)
Weicro Graphics Inc ....E 631 253-3360
  West Babylon (G-16840)
▲ Welsh Gold Stampers Inc 718 984-5031
  Staten Island (G-15754)
Were Forms Inc 585 482-4400
  Rochester (G-14761)
Westprint Inc ....F 212 989-3805
  New York (G-12617)
Westypo Printers Inc ....G 914 737-7394
  Peekskill (G-13487)
Wheeler/Rinstar Ltd ....F 212 244-1130
  New York (G-12622)
Willco Fine Art Ltd ....F 718 935-9567
  New York (G-12632)
William Charles Prtg Co Inc ....E 516 349-0900
  Plainview (G-13646)
William J Ryan ....G 585 392-6200
  Hilton (G-6421)
Willis Mc Donald Co Inc ....F 212 366-1526
  New York (G-12638)
Wilson Press LLC ....E 315 568-9693
  Seneca Falls (G-15372)
▲ Won & Lee Inc ....F 516 222-0712
  Garden City (G-5538)
Worldwide Ticket Craft ....D 516 538-6200
  Merrick (G-8394)
X Myles Mar Inc 212 683-2015
  New York (G-12673)
X Press Screen Printing ....G 716 679-7788
  Dunkirk (G-4353)
XI Graphics Inc ....E 212 929-8700
  New York (G-12680)
Xpress Printing Inc ....G 516 605-1000
  Plainview (G-13647)
▲ Zacks Enterprises Inc ....E 800 366-4924
  Orangeburg (G-13248)
Zan Optics Products Inc ....E 718 435-0533
  Brooklyn (G-2781)

2761 Manifold Business Forms

▲ Abra-Ka-Data Systems Ltd ....E 631 667-5550
  Deer Park (G-4086)
Amsterdam Printing & Litho Inc ....F 518 842-6000
  Amsterdam (G-332)
Amsterdam Printing & Litho Inc ....E 518 842-6000
  Amsterdam (G-331)
Bmg Printing and Promotion LLC ....G 631 231-9200
  Bohemia (G-1026)
Boces Business Office 607 763-3300
  Binghamton (G-897)
Five Boro Holding LLC ....F 718 431-9500
  Brooklyn (G-1977)
Gateway Prtg & Graphics Inc ....F 716 823-3873
  Hamburg (G-5926)
Idc Printing & Sty Co Inc ....G 516 599-0400
  Lynbrook (G-7951)
Linden Forms & Systems Inc ....E 212 219-1100
  Brooklyn (G-2226)
Maggio Data Forms Printing Ltd ....C 631 348-0343
  Hauppauge (G-6124)
Marcy Business Forms Inc ....G 718 935-9100
  Brooklyn (G-2267)
◆ Multi Packaging Solutions Inc ....E 646 885-0157
  New York (G-11324)
P P I Business Forms Inc ....G 716 825-1241
  Buffalo (G-3107)
Resonant Legal Media LLC ....D 800 781-3591
  New York (G-11841)

Richard Ruffner ....F 631 234-4600
  Central Islip (G-3509)
▲ Rmf Printing Technologies Inc ....E 716 683-7500
  Lancaster (G-7339)
RR Donnelley & Sons Company ....D 716 773-0647
  Grand Island (G-5766)
RR Donnelley & Sons Company ....D 716 773-0300
  Grand Island (G-5767)
Select-A-Form Inc ....D 631 981-3076
  Holbrook (G-6470)
▲ Specialized Printed Forms Inc ....E 585 538-2381
  Caledonia (G-3282)
Standard Register Inc ....F 937 221-1303
  Melville (G-8356)
Syracuse Computer Forms Inc ....E 315 478-0108
  Syracuse (G-16050)
Williamson Law Book Co ....F 585 924-3400
  Victor (G-16514)

2771 Greeting Card Publishing

1/2 Off Cards Wantagh Inc ....G 516 809-9832
  Wantagh (G-16553)
▲ Anne Taintor Inc ....G 718 483-9312
  Brooklyn (G-1613)
Avanti Press Inc ....E 212 414-1025
  New York (G-9274)
Massimo Friedman Inc ....E 716 836-0408
  Buffalo (G-3057)
◆ Paper House Productions Inc ....E 845 246-7261
  Saugerties (G-15190)
Paper Magic Group Inc ....B 631 521-3682
  New York (G-11564)
▲ Quotable Cards Inc ....E 212 420-7552
  New York (G-11776)
Schurman Retail Group ....E 212 206-0067
  New York (G-12002)

2782 Blankbooks & Looseleaf Binders

ABC Check Printing Corp ....F 718 855-4702
  Brooklyn (G-1546)
Acco Brands ....E 607 561-5515
  Sidney (G-15434)
Acco Brands USA LLC ....C 847 541-9500
  Ogdensburg (G-13109)
▲ Albumx Corp ....D 914 939-6878
  Port Chester (G-13738)
Brewer-Cantelmo Co Inc ....E 212 244-4600
  New York (G-9458)
Brookvale Records Inc ....F 631 587-7722
  West Babylon (G-16776)
Classic Album ....E 718 388-2818
  Brooklyn (G-1786)
▲ Classic Album LLC ....D 718 388-2818
  Brooklyn (G-1787)
Colad Group LLC ....D 716 961-1776
  Buffalo (G-2880)
Consolidated Loose Leaf Inc ....G 212 924-5800
  New York (G-9706)
Dalee Bookbinding Co Inc ....F 914 965-1660
  Yonkers (G-17434)
▲ Datamax International Inc ....E 212 693-0933
  New York (G-9815)
Deluxe Corporation ....B 845 362-4054
  Spring Valley (G-15580)
Deluxe Corporation ....B 212 472-7222
  New York (G-9842)
▲ Dickard Widder Industries Inc ....C 718 326-3700
  Maspeth (G-8131)
Dorose Novelty Co Inc ....F 718 451-3088
  East Elmhurst (G-4391)
Federal Sample Card Corp ....D 718 458-1344
  Elmhurst (G-4660)
Foster - Gordon Manufacturing ....G 631 589-6776
  Bohemia (G-1068)
▲ General Diaries Corporation ....F 516 371-2244
  Inwood (G-6758)
GPM Associates LLC ....E 585 335-3940
  Dansville (G-4077)
◆ Graphic Image Incorporated ....C 631 249-9600
  Melville (G-8324)
King Album Inc 631 253-9500
  West Babylon (G-16805)
Lanwood Industries Inc ....E 718 786-3000
  Bay Shore (G-711)
Leather Craftsmen Inc ....D 631 752-9000
  Farmingdale (G-5034)
Leather Indexes Corp ....D 516 827-1900
  Hicksville (G-6363)
▲ Mypublisher Inc ....F 914 773-4312
  Elmsford (G-4768)

2017 Harris
New York Manufacturers Directory

- **New York Sample Card Co Inc** ....E.... 212 242-1242 — New York *(G-11407)*
- **Niagara Sample Book Co Inc** ....F.... 716 284-6151 — Niagara Falls *(G-12850)*
- ▲ **Quo Vadis Editions Inc** ....E.... 716 648-2602 — Hamburg *(G-5939)*
- ▲ **Quotable Cards Inc** ....G.... 212 420-7552 — New York *(G-11776)*
- **Renegade Nation Ltd** ....F.... 212 868-9000 — New York *(G-11833)*
- ▲ **Roger Michael Press Inc** ....F.... 732 752-0800 — Brooklyn *(G-2502)*
- **Sellco Industries Inc** ....E.... 607 756-7594 — Cortland *(G-4045)*
- **Simon & Simon LLC** ....G.... 202 419-0490 — New York *(G-12080)*
- **Tm Music Inc** ....F.... 212 471-4000 — New York *(G-12356)*
- **Tommy Boy Entertainment LLC** ....F.... 212 388-8300 — New York *(G-12365)*
- **Wmg Acquisition Corp** ....F.... 212 275-2000 — New York *(G-12650)*

2789 Bookbinding

- **514 Adams Corporation** ....G.... 516 352-6948 — Franklin Square *(G-5359)*
- **A-1 Products Inc** ....G.... 718 789-1818 — Brooklyn *(G-1538)*
- **A-Quick Bindery LLC** ....G.... 631 491-1110 — West Babylon *(G-16763)*
- **Agrecolor Inc** ....F.... 516 741-8700 — Mineola *(G-8491)*
- **Arcade Bookbinding Corp** ....E.... 718 366-8484 — Ridgewood *(G-14100)*
- **Argo Lithographers Inc** ....E.... 718 729-2700 — Long Island City *(G-7669)*
- **Arista Innovations Inc** ....E.... 516 746-2262 — Mineola *(G-8496)*
- ▲ **Ateres Publishing & Bk Bindery** ....F.... 718 935-9355 — Brooklyn *(G-1645)*
- **Baum Christine and John Corp** ....G.... 585 621-8910 — Rochester *(G-14224)*
- **Beastons Budget Printing** ....G.... 585 244-2721 — Rochester *(G-14227)*
- ▲ **Benchemark Printing Inc** ....D.... 518 393-1361 — Schenectady *(G-15234)*
- **Bernard Hall** ....G.... 585 425-3340 — Fairport *(G-4848)*
- ▲ **Beyer Graphics Inc** ....D.... 631 543-3900 — Commack *(G-3824)*
- **Bg Bindery Inc** ....G.... 631 767-4242 — Long Island City *(G-7684)*
- **Boncraft Inc** ....D.... 716 662-9720 — Tonawanda *(G-16146)*
- **Bondy Printing Corp** ....G.... 631 242-1510 — Bay Shore *(G-679)*
- **Brodock Press Inc** ....D.... 315 735-9577 — Utica *(G-16310)*
- **Brooks Litho Digital Group Inc** ....G.... 631 789-4500 — Deer Park *(G-4112)*
- **Bruce Woehr** ....F.... 585 654-6746 — Rochester *(G-14248)*
- **C & C Bindery Co Inc** ....E.... 631 752-7078 — Farmingdale *(G-4954)*
- **C & H Cstm Bkbinding Embossing** ....G.... 800 871-8980 — Medford *(G-8237)*
- **Carlara Group Ltd** ....G.... 914 769-2020 — Pleasantville *(G-13712)*
- **Carnels Printing Inc** ....G.... 516 883-3355 — Port Washington *(G-13803)*
- **Castlereagh Printcraft Inc** ....D.... 516 623-1728 — Freeport *(G-5392)*
- **Chakra Communications Inc** ....E.... 607 748-7491 — Endicott *(G-4798)*
- **Challenge Graphics Svcs Inc** ....E.... 631 586-0171 — Deer Park *(G-4115)*
- **Classic Album** ....E.... 718 388-2818 — Brooklyn *(G-1786)*
- **Cohber Press Inc** ....D.... 585 475-9100 — West Henrietta *(G-16873)*
- **Copy Corner Inc** ....G.... 718 388-4545 — Brooklyn *(G-1803)*
- **Copy Room Inc** ....F.... 212 371-8600 — New York *(G-9721)*
- **Cosmos Communications Inc** ....C.... 718 482-1800 — Long Island City *(G-7705)*
- **D G M Graphics Inc** ....F.... 516 223-2220 — Merrick *(G-8383)*
- **Dalee Bookbinding Co Inc** ....F.... 914 965-1660 — Yonkers *(G-17434)*
- **David Helsing** ....G.... 607 796-2681 — Horseheads *(G-6573)*
- **Dependable Lithographers Inc** ....F.... 718 472-4200 — Long Island City *(G-7712)*
- **Design Printing Corp** ....G.... 631 753-9801 — Farmingdale *(G-4975)*
- **Dispatch Graphics Inc** ....F.... 212 307-5943 — New York *(G-9884)*
- **Division Den-Bar Enterprises** ....G.... 914 381-2220 — Mamaroneck *(G-8033)*
- **Dowd - Witbeck Printing Corp** ....F.... 518 274-2421 — Troy *(G-16234)*
- **DP Murphy Co Inc** ....D.... 631 673-9400 — Deer Park *(G-4132)*
- **E B B Graphics Inc** ....F.... 516 750-5510 — Westbury *(G-16979)*
- **E L Smith Printing Co Inc** ....E.... 201 373-0111 — New City *(G-8784)*
- **Eastside Printers** ....F.... 315 437-6515 — East Syracuse *(G-4527)*
- **Eastwood Litho Inc** ....E.... 315 437-2626 — Syracuse *(G-15929)*
- **Erhard & Gilcher Inc** ....E.... 315 474-1072 — Syracuse *(G-15938)*
- **Flare Multicopy Corp** ....E.... 718 258-8860 — Brooklyn *(G-1982)*
- **Flp Group LLC** ....F.... 315 252-7583 — Auburn *(G-496)*
- **Foster - Gordon Manufacturing** ....G.... 631 589-6776 — Bohemia *(G-1068)*
- **Fulton Newspapers Inc** ....E.... 315 598-6397 — Fulton *(G-5457)*
- **Gateway Prtg & Graphics Inc** ....E.... 716 823-3873 — Hamburg *(G-5926)*
- **Gazette Press Inc** ....E.... 914 963-8300 — Rye *(G-15056)*
- **Gerald Frd Packg Display LLC** ....F.... 716 692-2705 — North Tonawanda *(G-12974)*
- **Gild-Rite Inc** ....G.... 631 752-9000 — Farmingdale *(G-4998)*
- **Gold Pride Press Inc** ....E.... 585 224-8800 — Rochester *(G-14411)*
- **Graphicomm Inc** ....G.... 716 283-0830 — Niagara Falls *(G-12826)*
- **Haig Press Inc** ....E.... 631 582-5800 — Hauppauge *(G-6088)*
- ▲ **Hamilton Printing Company Inc** ....C.... 518 732-2161 — Troy *(G-16238)*
- **Hudson Printing Co Inc** ....E.... 718 937-8600 — New York *(G-10527)*
- **In-House Inc** ....F.... 718 445-9007 — College Point *(G-3787)*
- **Interstate Litho Corp** ....D.... 631 232-6025 — Brentwood *(G-1185)*
- ▲ **J Mackenzie Ltd** ....E.... 585 321-1770 — Rochester *(G-14456)*
- **Jack J Florio Jr** ....G.... 716 434-9123 — Lockport *(G-7595)*
- **James Conolly Printing Co** ....E.... 585 426-4150 — Rochester *(G-14459)*
- **Jane Lewis** ....G.... 607 722-0584 — Binghamton *(G-930)*
- **Johnnys Ideal Printing Co** ....G.... 518 828-6666 — Hudson *(G-6621)*
- **Jon Lyn Ink Inc** ....G.... 516 546-2312 — Merrick *(G-8386)*
- **Kader Lithograph Company Inc** ....C.... 917 664-4380 — Long Island City *(G-7777)*
- **Kaufman Brothers Printing** ....G.... 212 563-1854 — New York *(G-10820)*
- **King Lithographers Inc** ....E.... 914 667-4200 — Mount Vernon *(G-8698)*
- **L Loy Press Inc** ....G.... 716 634-5966 — Buffalo *(G-3040)*
- **Louis Heindl & Son Inc** ....G.... 585 454-5080 — Rochester *(G-14483)*
- ▲ **Melcher Media Inc** ....F.... 212 727-2322 — New York *(G-11222)*
- ▲ **Mercury Print Productions Inc** ....C.... 585 458-7900 — Rochester *(G-14504)*
- **Mid Island Group** ....E.... 631 293-0180 — Farmingdale *(G-5054)*
- **Mid-Island Bindery Inc** ....E.... 631 293-0180 — Farmingdale *(G-5055)*
- **Midgley Printing Corp** ....G.... 315 475-1864 — Syracuse *(G-15988)*
- ▲ **Mines Press Inc** ....C.... 914 788-1800 — Cortlandt Manor *(G-4052)*
- **Moneast Inc** ....G.... 845 298-8898 — Wappingers Falls *(G-16575)*
- **Multiple Imprssons of Rchester** ....G.... 585 546-1160 — Rochester *(G-14525)*
- **Mutual Library Bindery Inc** ....E.... 315 455-6638 — East Syracuse *(G-4551)*
- **Newport Graphics Inc** ....E.... 212 924-2600 — New York *(G-11414)*
- **On The Spot Binding Inc** ....E.... 718 497-2200 — Ridgewood *(G-14117)*
- **Ozipko Enterprises Inc** ....G.... 585 424-6740 — Rochester *(G-14560)*
- **Piroke Trade Inc** ....G.... 646 515-1537 — Brooklyn *(G-2423)*
- **Playbill Incorporated** ....E.... 718 335-4033 — Woodside *(G-17348)*
- **Prestige Envelope & Lithograph** ....F.... 631 521-7043 — Merrick *(G-8391)*
- **Printech Business Systems Inc** ....F.... 212 290-2542 — New York *(G-11720)*
- **Printing Resources Inc** ....E.... 518 482-2470 — Albany *(G-124)*
- **Pro Printing** ....G.... 516 561-9700 — Lynbrook *(G-7957)*
- **Progressive Graphics & Prtg** ....G.... 315 331-3635 — Newark *(G-12741)*
- **Prompt Bindery Co Inc** ....F.... 212 675-5181 — New York *(G-11732)*
- **Psychonomic Society Inc** ....E.... 512 381-1494 — New York *(G-11743)*
- **Quad/Graphics Inc** ....A.... 518 581-4000 — Saratoga Springs *(G-15168)*
- **Quality Bindery Service Inc** ....E.... 716 883-5185 — Buffalo *(G-3147)*
- **Reynolds Book Bindery LLC** ....F.... 607 772-8937 — Binghamton *(G-946)*
- **Richard Ruffner** ....F.... 631 234-4600 — Central Islip *(G-3509)*
- **Riverside Mfg Acquisition LLC** ....C.... 585 458-2090 — Rochester *(G-14627)*
- **Rmd Holding Inc** ....G.... 845 628-0030 — Mahopac *(G-8001)*
- ▲ **Roger Michael Press Inc** ....F.... 732 752-0800 — Brooklyn *(G-2502)*
- **Rosemont Press Incorporated** ....E.... 212 239-4770 — New York *(G-11915)*
- **Rosen Mandell & Immerman Inc** ....E.... 212 691-2277 — New York *(G-11916)*
- **Sentinel Printing Inc** ....G.... 516 334-7400 — Westbury *(G-17026)*
- **Shipman Printing Inds Inc** ....E.... 716 504-7700 — Niagara Falls *(G-12876)*
- **Spectrum Prtg Lithography Inc** ....F.... 212 255-3131 — New York *(G-12158)*
- ▼ **Sterling Pierce Company Inc** ....E.... 516 593-1170 — East Rockaway *(G-4471)*
- **Thomas Group Inc** ....F.... 212 947-6400 — New York *(G-12319)*
- **Tobay Printing Co Inc** ....E.... 631 842-3300 — Copiague *(G-3934)*
- **Tom & Jerry Printcraft Forms** ....E.... 914 777-7468 — Mamaroneck *(G-8048)*
- **Tri-Lon Clor Lithographers Ltd** ....E.... 212 255-6140 — New York *(G-12400)*
- ▲ **Twenty-First Century Press Inc** ....F.... 716 837-0800 — Buffalo *(G-3227)*
- **Vicks Lithograph & Prtg Corp** ....C.... 315 272-2401 — Yorkville *(G-17527)*
- **Vin-Clair Inc** ....F.... 845 429-4998 — West Haverstraw *(G-16847)*
- **Webster Printing Corporation** ....F.... 585 671-1533 — Webster *(G-16742)*
- ▲ **Welsh Gold Stampers Inc** ....E.... 718 984-5031 — Staten Island *(G-15754)*
- **Westchester Mailing Service** ....E.... 914 948-1116 — White Plains *(G-17184)*
- **Whitford Development Inc** ....F.... 631 471-7711 — Port Jefferson *(G-13780)*
- **William Charles Prtg Co Inc** ....E.... 516 349-0900 — Plainview *(G-13646)*
- **Wilson Press LLC** ....E.... 315 568-9693 — Seneca Falls *(G-15372)*
- ▲ **Won & Lee Inc** ....E.... 516 222-0712 — Garden City *(G-5538)*
- **Wynco Press One Inc** ....G.... 516 354-6145 — Glen Oaks *(G-5641)*
- **X Myles Mar Inc** ....E.... 212 683-2015 — New York *(G-12673)*
- **Zan Optics Products Inc** ....E.... 718 435-0533 — Brooklyn *(G-2781)*
- **Zenger Partners LLC** ....E.... 716 876-2284 — Kenmore *(G-7152)*

Employee Codes: A=Over 500 employees, B=251-500
C=101-250, D=51-100, E=20-50, F=10-19, G=5-9
2017 Harris
New York Manufacturers Directory
777

27 PRINTING, PUBLISHING, AND ALLIED INDUSTRIES

2791 Typesetting

514 Adams Corporation ....G....... 516 352-6948
  Franklin Square *(G-5359)*
Act Communications Group Inc ....F....... 631 669-2403
  West Islip *(G-16902)*
Agrecolor Inc..............................F....... 516 741-8700
  Mineola *(G-8491)*
Alabaster Group Inc.....................G....... 516 867-8223
  Freeport *(G-5382)*
Albion-Holley Pennysaver Inc ......D....... 585 589-5641
  Albion *(G-161)*
All Ready Inc ....G....... 607 722-0826
  Conklin *(G-3864)*
Arista Innovations Inc ....E....... 516 746-2262
  Mineola *(G-8496)*
▲ Art Resources Transfer Inc ....G....... 212 255-2919
  New York *(G-9213)*
▲ Artistic Typography Corp...........G....... 212 463-8880
  New York *(G-9221)*
Artscroll Printing Corp..................E....... 212 929-2413
  New York *(G-9224)*
Bates Jackson Engraving Co Inc .E....... 716 854-3000
  Buffalo *(G-2834)*
Baum Christine and John Corp ....G....... 585 621-8910
  Rochester *(G-14224)*
Bco Industries Western NY Inc ....E....... 716 877-2800
  Tonawanda *(G-16144)*
Beastons Budget Printing ....G....... 585 244-2721
  Rochester *(G-14227)*
Beehive Press Inc ....G....... 718 654-1200
  Bronx *(G-1281)*
▲ Benchemark Printing Inc...........D....... 518 393-1361
  Schenectady *(G-15234)*
Bernard Hall................................G....... 585 425-3340
  Fairport *(G-4848)*
▲ Beyer Graphics Inc...................D....... 631 543-3900
  Commack *(G-3824)*
Boncraft Inc.................................D....... 716 662-9720
  Tonawanda *(G-16146)*
Bondy Printing Corp.....................G....... 631 242-1510
  Bay Shore *(G-679)*
Brodock Press Inc ....D....... 315 735-9577
  Utica *(G-16310)*
Brooks Litho Digital Group Inc .....G....... 631 789-4500
  Deer Park *(G-4112)*
Bytheway Publishing Services .....F....... 607 334-8365
  Norwich *(G-13020)*
Carlara Group Ltd ....G....... 914 769-2020
  Pleasantville *(G-13712)*
Carnels Printing Inc.....................G....... 516 883-3355
  Port Washington *(G-13803)*
Castlereagh Printcraft Inc ....D....... 516 623-1728
  Freeport *(G-5392)*
Cds Productions Inc ....F....... 518 385-8255
  Schenectady *(G-15241)*
Chakra Communications Inc ......E....... 716 505-7300
  Lancaster *(G-7309)*
Chakra Communications Inc ......E....... 607 748-7491
  Endicott *(G-4798)*
Challenge Graphics Svcs Inc .....E....... 631 586-0171
  Deer Park *(G-4115)*
Clarsons Corp ....F....... 585 235-8775
  Rochester *(G-14278)*
Cohber Press Inc ....D....... 585 475-9100
  West Henrietta *(G-16873)*
Consolidated Color Press Inc......F....... 212 929-8197
  New York *(G-9704)*
Cortland Standard Printing Co ....G....... 607 756-5665
  Cortland *(G-4022)*
Cosmos Communications Inc ....C....... 718 482-1800
  Long Island City *(G-7705)*
Csw Inc ....F....... 585 247-4010
  Rochester *(G-14293)*
D G M Graphics Inc.....................G....... 516 223-2220
  Merrick *(G-8383)*
Desktop Publishing Concepts .....F....... 631 752-1934
  Farmingdale *(G-4976)*
Digital Color Concepts Inc ....E....... 212 989-4888
  New York *(G-9875)*
Digital Page LLC ....F....... 518 446-9129
  Albany *(G-73)*
Dispatch Graphics Inc.................F....... 212 307-5943
  New York *(G-9884)*
Dowd - Witbeck Printing Corp ....F....... 518 274-2421
  Troy *(G-16234)*
DP Murphy Co Inc ....D....... 631 673-9400
  Deer Park *(G-4132)*
Draper Associates Incorporated .F....... 212 255-2727
  New York *(G-9924)*

E B B Graphics Inc......................F....... 516 750-5510
  Westbury *(G-16979)*
Eastwood Litho Inc ....E....... 315 437-2626
  Syracuse *(G-15929)*
Empire Press Co ....G....... 718 756-9500
  Brooklyn *(G-1921)*
Falconer Printing & Design Inc ...F....... 716 665-2121
  Falconer *(G-4899)*
Flare Multicopy Corp ....E....... 718 258-8860
  Brooklyn *(G-1982)*
Flp Group LLC ....F....... 315 252-7583
  Auburn *(G-496)*
Fort Orange Press Inc ....E....... 518 489-3233
  Albany *(G-81)*
Fulton Newspapers Inc................E....... 315 598-6397
  Fulton *(G-5457)*
▲ Gallant Graphices Ltd Inc ....E....... 845 868-1166
  Stanfordville *(G-15627)*
Gateway Prtg & Graphics Inc......E....... 716 823-3873
  Hamburg *(G-5926)*
Gazette Press Inc ....E....... 914 963-8300
  Rye *(G-15056)*
▲ Gg Design and Printing ....G....... 718 321-3220
  New York *(G-10289)*
Graphic Fabrications Inc.............G....... 516 763-3222
  Rockville Centre *(G-14791)*
Graphicomm Inc..........................G....... 716 283-0830
  Niagara Falls *(G-12826)*
Grid Typographic Services Inc ....F....... 212 627-0303
  New York *(G-10362)*
Hamptons Magazine ....E....... 631 283-7125
  Southampton *(G-15545)*
Hks Printing Company Inc ....F....... 212 675-2529
  New York *(G-10487)*
Hugh F McPherson Inc ....G....... 716 668-6107
  Cheektowaga *(G-3575)*
In-House Inc ....F....... 718 445-9007
  College Point *(G-3787)*
Interstate Litho Corp....................D....... 631 232-6025
  Brentwood *(G-1185)*
Jack J Florio Jr............................G....... 716 434-9123
  Lockport *(G-7595)*
James Conolly Printing Co ....E....... 585 426-4150
  Rochester *(G-14459)*
Jane Lewis..................................G....... 607 722-0584
  Binghamton *(G-930)*
Johnnys Ideal Printing Co...........F....... 518 828-6666
  Hudson *(G-6621)*
Jon Lyn Ink Inc ....G....... 516 546-2312
  Merrick *(G-8386)*
L Loy Press Inc ....G....... 716 634-5966
  Buffalo *(G-3040)*
L M N Printing Company Inc ....E....... 516 285-8526
  Valley Stream *(G-16411)*
Lake Placid Advertisers Wkshp ..E....... 518 523-3359
  Lake Placid *(G-7275)*
Leigh Scott Enterprises Inc ....G....... 718 343-5440
  Bellerose *(G-810)*
Litmor Publishing Corp ....F....... 516 931-0012
  Hicksville *(G-6364)*
Loudon Ltd ....G....... 631 757-4447
  East Northport *(G-4441)*
Louis Heindl & Son Inc ....G....... 585 454-5080
  Rochester *(G-14483)*
▲ Medallion Associates Inc ....E....... 212 929-9130
  New York *(G-11207)*
▲ Mercury Print Productions Inc...C....... 585 458-7900
  Rochester *(G-14504)*
Midgley Printing Corp..................G....... 315 475-1864
  Syracuse *(G-15988)*
▲ Mines Press Inc........................C....... 914 788-1800
  Cortlandt Manor *(G-4052)*
Moneast Inc ....G....... 845 298-8898
  Wappingers Falls *(G-16575)*
Multiple Imprssons of Rchester ...G....... 585 546-1160
  Rochester *(G-14525)*
Mutual Engraving Company Inc ..D....... 516 489-0534
  West Hempstead *(G-16861)*
News India USA Inc ....F....... 212 675-7515
  New York *(G-11418)*
Newspaper Publisher LLC ....F....... 607 775-0472
  Conklin *(G-3871)*
▼ Official Offset Corporation........E....... 631 957-8500
  Amityville *(G-317)*
Ozipko Enterprises Inc................G....... 585 424-6740
  Rochester *(G-14560)*
P D R Inc ....G....... 516 829-5300
  Plainview *(G-13626)*
Panagraphics Inc ....G....... 716 312-8088
  Orchard Park *(G-13287)*

Patrick Ryans Modern Press ....F....... 518 434-2921
  Albany *(G-114)*
Prestige Envelope & Lithograph ..F....... 631 521-7043
  Merrick *(G-8391)*
Printery ....G....... 516 922-3250
  Oyster Bay *(G-13373)*
Printing Resources Inc ....E....... 518 482-2470
  Albany *(G-124)*
Pro Printing ....G....... 516 561-9700
  Lynbrook *(G-7957)*
Progressive Graphics & Prtg ......G....... 315 331-3635
  Newark *(G-12741)*
Publishing Synthesis Ltd ....G....... 212 219-0135
  New York *(G-11748)*
Quad/Graphics Inc ....A....... 518 581-4000
  Saratoga Springs *(G-15168)*
Quicker Printer Inc......................G....... 607 734-8622
  Elmira *(G-4698)*
Rmd Holding Inc ....G....... 845 628-0030
  Mahopac *(G-8001)*
Rubber Stamps Inc ....E....... 212 675-1180
  Mineola *(G-8535)*
Scotti Graphics Inc ....E....... 212 367-9602
  Long Island City *(G-7872)*
Sentinel Printing Inc ....G....... 516 334-7400
  Westbury *(G-17026)*
Stone Crest Industries Inc ....G....... 607 652-2665
  Stamford *(G-15626)*
Syracuse Computer Forms Inc ...G....... 315 478-0108
  Syracuse *(G-16050)*
Thomas Group Inc ....F....... 212 947-6400
  New York *(G-12319)*
Times Review Newspaper Corp ..E....... 631 354-8031
  Mattituck *(G-8211)*
Tobay Printing Co Inc ....E....... 631 842-3300
  Copiague *(G-3934)*
Tom & Jerry Printcraft Forms ......E....... 914 777-7468
  Mamaroneck *(G-8048)*
Torsaf Printers Inc ....G....... 516 569-5577
  Hewlett *(G-6314)*
Tri Kolor Printing & Sty................F....... 315 474-6753
  Syracuse *(G-16061)*
Tri-Lon Clor Lithographers Ltd ....E....... 212 255-6140
  New York *(G-12400)*
Tripi Engraving Co Inc ....E....... 718 383-6500
  Brooklyn *(G-2682)*
Voss Signs LLC ....G....... 315 682-6418
  Manlius *(G-8076)*
Wallkill Valley Publications ....E....... 845 561-0170
  Newburgh *(G-12786)*
Webster Printing Corporation ......F....... 585 671-1533
  Webster *(G-16742)*
Westchester Mailing Service ....G....... 914 948-1116
  White Plains *(G-17184)*
Wilson Press LLC ....E....... 315 568-9693
  Seneca Falls *(G-15372)*
Woodbury Printing Plus + Inc......G....... 845 928-6610
  Central Valley *(G-3529)*
Worldwide Ticket Craft ....D....... 516 538-6200
  Merrick *(G-8394)*
Wynco Press One Inc ....G....... 516 354-6145
  Glen Oaks *(G-5641)*
X Myles Mar Inc ....E....... 212 683-2015
  New York *(G-12673)*
Zenger Partners LLC ....E....... 716 876-2284
  Kenmore *(G-7152)*

2796 Platemaking & Related Svcs

Absolute Color Corporation.........G....... 212 868-0404
  New York *(G-9007)*
Adflex Corporation ....E....... 585 454-2950
  Rochester *(G-14173)*
Aldine Inc (ny) ....D....... 212 226-2870
  New York *(G-9079)*
Allstate Sign & Plaque Corp ....F....... 631 242-2828
  Deer Park *(G-4093)*
Atlas Graphics Inc ....G....... 516 997-5527
  Westbury *(G-16970)*
Chakra Communications Inc ......E....... 716 505-7300
  Lancaster *(G-7309)*
Charles Henricks Inc ....F....... 212 243-5800
  New York *(G-9581)*
Circle Press Inc ....D....... 212 924-4277
  New York *(G-9621)*
Csw Inc ....F....... 585 247-4010
  Rochester *(G-14293)*
▲ Custom House Engravers Inc ...G....... 631 567-3004
  Bohemia *(G-1046)*
D & A Offset Services Inc ....F....... 212 924-0612
  New York *(G-9780)*

SIC SECTION

28 CHEMICALS AND ALLIED PRODUCTS

David Fehlman ....G...... 315 455-8888
  Syracuse *(G-15922)*
Dowd - Witbeck Printing Corp ....F...... 518 274-2421
  Troy *(G-16234)*
Eastern Color Stripping Inc ....F...... 631 563-3700
  Bohemia *(G-1060)*
▲ Gallant Graphices Ltd Inc ....E...... 845 868-1166
  Stanfordville *(G-15627)*
Gazette Press Inc ....E...... 914 963-8300
  Rye *(G-15056)*
▲ Gotham Pen Co Inc ....E...... 212 675-7904
  Yonkers *(G-17449)*
Karr Graphics Corp ....E...... 718 784-9390
  Long Island City *(G-7779)*
Koehlr-Gibson Mkg Graphics Inc ....E...... 716 838-5960
  Buffalo *(G-3035)*
Kristen Graphics Inc ....F...... 212 929-2183
  New York *(G-10890)*
Lane Park Litho Plate ....E...... 212 255-9100
  New York *(G-10925)*
Lazer Incorporated ....E...... 336 744-8047
  Rochester *(G-14476)*
Leo P Callahan Inc ....F...... 607 797-7314
  Binghamton *(G-933)*
Lgn Materials & Solutions ....F...... 888 414-0005
  Mount Vernon *(G-8701)*
Micro Publishing Inc ....G...... 212 533-9180
  New York *(G-11253)*
Miroddi Imaging Inc ....G...... 516 624-6898
  Oyster Bay *(G-13372)*
Mutual Engraving Company Inc ....D...... 516 489-0534
  West Hempstead *(G-16861)*
P & H Thermotech Inc ....G...... 585 624-1310
  Lima *(G-7447)*
Rapid Service Engraving Co ....G...... 716 896-4555
  Buffalo *(G-3154)*
▲ Rigidized Metals Corporation ....E...... 716 849-4703
  Buffalo *(G-3158)*
Rotation Dynamics Corporation ....E...... 585 352-9023
  Spencerport *(G-15573)*
Syracuse Computer Forms Inc ....E...... 315 478-0108
  Syracuse *(G-16050)*
Tobay Printing Co Inc ....E...... 631 842-3300
  Copiague *(G-3934)*
Torch Graphics Inc ....E...... 212 679-4334
  New York *(G-12374)*
Tripi Engraving Co Inc ....E...... 718 383-6500
  Brooklyn *(G-2682)*
▲ Welsh Gold Stampers Inc ....E...... 718 984-5031
  Staten Island *(G-15754)*
Wilcro Inc ....G...... 716 632-4204
  Buffalo *(G-3254)*

28 CHEMICALS AND ALLIED PRODUCTS

2812 Alkalies & Chlorine

Chemours Company Fc LLC ....E...... 716 278-5100
  Niagara Falls *(G-12804)*
Church & Dwight Co Inc ....F...... 518 887-5109
  Schenectady *(G-15242)*
Indian Springs Mfg Co Inc ....F...... 315 635-6101
  Baldwinsville *(G-570)*
Occidental Chemical Corp ....E...... 716 278-7795
  Niagara Falls *(G-12855)*
Occidental Chemical Corp ....E...... 716 773-8100
  Grand Island *(G-5765)*
Occidental Chemical Corp ....C...... 716 278-7794
  Niagara Falls *(G-12856)*
Olin Chlor Alkali Logistics ....C...... 716 278-6411
  Niagara Falls *(G-12857)*

2813 Industrial Gases

Air Products and Chemicals Inc ....D...... 518 463-4273
  Glenmont *(G-5666)*
Air Products and Chemicals Inc ....G...... 585 798-2324
  Medina *(G-8264)*
Airgas Inc ....E...... 585 436-7780
  Rochester *(G-14182)*
Airgas Inc ....F...... 518 690-0068
  Albany *(G-36)*
Airgas USA LLC ....E...... 315 433-1295
  Syracuse *(G-15846)*
Airgas USA LLC ....F...... 585 436-7781
  Rochester *(G-14183)*
Fountainhead Group Inc ....C...... 708 598-7100
  New York Mills *(G-12724)*
Linde Gas North America LLC ....E......
  Cohoes *(G-3749)*

Linde Gas North America LLC ....F...... 866 543-3427
  Cheektowaga *(G-3578)*
Linde Gas North America LLC ....F...... 315 431-4081
  Syracuse *(G-15979)*
Linde LLC ....E...... 716 847-0748
  Buffalo *(G-3048)*
Linde LLC ....D...... 518 439-8187
  Feura Bush *(G-5172)*
Linde Merchant Production Inc ....G...... 315 593-1360
  Fulton *(G-5469)*
Matheson Tri-Gas Inc ....F...... 518 203-5003
  Cohoes *(G-3750)*
Matheson Tri-Gas Inc ....F...... 518 439-0362
  Feura Bush *(G-5173)*
Neon ....F...... 212 727-5628
  New York *(G-11367)*
▼ Oxair Ltd ....F...... 716 298-8288
  Niagara Falls *(G-12858)*
Praxair Inc ....E...... 845 267-2337
  Valley Cottage *(G-16384)*
Praxair Inc ....E...... 716 649-1600
  Hamburg *(G-5937)*
Praxair Inc ....E...... 518 482-4360
  Albany *(G-123)*
Praxair Inc ....E...... 716 286-4600
  Niagara Falls *(G-12861)*
Praxair Inc ....C...... 845 359-4200
  Orangeburg *(G-13241)*
Praxair Inc ....E...... 716 879-4000
  Tonawanda *(G-16195)*
Praxair Distribution Inc ....G...... 315 457-5821
  Liverpool *(G-7543)*
Praxair Distribution Inc ....F...... 315 735-6153
  Marcy *(G-8092)*

2816 Inorganic Pigments

▲ Applied Minerals Inc ....E...... 212 226-4265
  New York *(G-9184)*
BASF Beauty Care Solutions LLC ....F...... 631 689-0200
  Stony Brook *(G-15766)*
BASF Corporation ....B...... 914 737-2554
  Peekskill *(G-13473)*
Deluxe Paint ....F...... 718 768-9494
  Brooklyn *(G-1853)*
▲ Heany Industries Inc ....D...... 585 889-2700
  Scottsville *(G-15336)*

2819 Indl Inorganic Chemicals, NEC

Aithaca Chemical Corp ....F...... 516 229-2330
  Uniondale *(G-16288)*
Akzo Nobel Chemicals LLC ....C...... 914 674-5008
  Dobbs Ferry *(G-4300)*
Alpha-En Corporation ....F...... 914 418-2000
  Tarrytown *(G-16085)*
Ames Goldsmith Corp ....E...... 518 792-7435
  Glens Falls *(G-5669)*
Anchor Commerce Trading Corp ....G...... 516 881-3485
  Atlantic Beach *(G-468)*
Arkema Inc ....C...... 585 243-6359
  Piffard *(G-13546)*
Auterra Inc ....D...... 518 382-9600
  Schenectady *(G-15232)*
BASF Corporation ....G...... 973 245-6000
  Tarrytown *(G-16088)*
BASF Corporation ....B...... 914 788-1627
  Peekskill *(G-13474)*
BASF Corporation ....B...... 212 450-8280
  New York *(G-9329)*
BASF Corporation ....C...... 631 689-0200
  East Setauket *(G-4478)*
BASF Corporation ....B...... 914 785-2000
  Tarrytown *(G-16087)*
Benzsay & Harrison Inc ....G...... 518 895-2311
  Delanson *(G-4231)*
◆ Buffalo Tungsten Inc ....D...... 716 759-6353
  Depew *(G-4251)*
Byk USA Inc ....E...... 845 469-5800
  Chester *(G-3602)*
Calgon Carbon Corporation ....G...... 716 531-9113
  North Tonawanda *(G-12964)*
Carbide-Usa LLC ....G...... 607 331-9353
  Elmira *(G-4674)*
Carbon Activated Corporation ....G...... 716 662-2005
  Orchard Park *(G-13258)*
▼ Cerion Energy Inc ....E...... 585 271-5630
  Rochester *(G-14268)*
Cerion LLC ....F...... 585 271-5630
  Rochester *(G-14269)*
Chemours Company Fc LLC ....E...... 716 278-5100
  Niagara Falls *(G-12804)*

Chemtrade Chemicals US LLC ....E...... 315 430-7650
  Syracuse *(G-15893)*
Chemtrade Chemicals US LLC ....G...... 315 478-2323
  Syracuse *(G-15894)*
Danisco US Inc ....D...... 585 277-4300
  Rochester *(G-14301)*
◆ Divine Brothers Company ....E...... 315 797-0470
  Utica *(G-16327)*
▲ Dynasty Chemical Corp ....E...... 518 463-1146
  Menands *(G-8370)*
E I Du Pont De Nemours & Co ....E...... 585 339-4200
  Rochester *(G-14323)*
Emco Chemical (usa) Corp ....E...... 718 797-3652
  Brooklyn *(G-1916)*
◆ Esm Group Inc ....F...... 716 446-8985
  Amherst *(G-240)*
Esm Special Metals & Tech Inc ....E...... 716 446-8914
  Amherst *(G-242)*
Ferro Corporation ....E...... 585 586-8770
  East Rochester *(G-4458)*
Ferro Corporation ....C...... 315 536-3357
  Penn Yan *(G-13509)*
Ferro Electronics Materials ....C...... 716 278-9400
  Niagara Falls *(G-12821)*
FMC Corporation ....E...... 716 735-3761
  Middleport *(G-8421)*
▲ Germanium Corp America Inc ....F...... 315 853-4900
  Clinton *(G-3719)*
Hampshire Chemical Corp ....D...... 315 539-9221
  Waterloo *(G-16629)*
Incitec Pivot Limited ....G...... 212 238-3010
  New York *(G-10582)*
Innovative Municipal Pdts US ....E...... 800 387-5777
  Glenmont *(G-5668)*
Interstate Chemical Co Inc ....F...... 585 344-2822
  Batavia *(G-640)*
Isonics Corporation ....G...... 212 356-7400
  New York *(G-10668)*
▲ Kowa American Corporation ....F...... 212 303-7800
  New York *(G-10882)*
Lakeshore Carbide Inc ....G...... 716 462-4349
  Lake View *(G-7281)*
Lawn Elements Inc ....G...... 631 656-9711
  Holbrook *(G-6456)*
▼ Meliorum Technologies Inc ....G...... 585 313-0616
  Rochester *(G-14503)*
▲ Minerals Technologies Inc ....E...... 212 878-1800
  New York *(G-11276)*
Moog Inc ....D...... 716 731-6300
  Niagara Falls *(G-12848)*
Multisorb Tech Intl LLC ....G...... 716 824-8900
  Buffalo *(G-3078)*
Multisorb Technologies Inc ....G...... 716 668-4191
  Cheektowaga *(G-3581)*
Multisorb Technologies Inc ....E...... 716 656-1402
  Buffalo *(G-3079)*
Next Potential LLC ....G...... 401 742-5190
  New York *(G-11422)*
Niagara Refining LLC ....E...... 716 706-1400
  Depew *(G-4266)*
◆ North American Hoganas Inc ....E...... 716 285-3451
  Niagara Falls *(G-12851)*
Oneh2 Inc ....G...... 703 862-9656
  Hector *(G-6259)*
Poly Scientific R&D Corp ....E...... 631 586-0400
  Bay Shore *(G-725)*
▲ Polyset Company Inc ....E...... 518 664-6000
  Mechanicville *(G-8229)*
Praxair Inc ....F...... 716 879-2000
  Tonawanda *(G-16194)*
Precision Elctro Mnrl Pmco Inc ....E...... 716 284-2484
  Niagara Falls *(G-12863)*
Prince Mineral Holding Corp ....G...... 646 747-4222
  New York *(G-11710)*
PVS Chemical Solutions Inc ....D...... 716 825-5762
  Buffalo *(G-3142)*
PVS Technologies Inc ....E...... 716 825-5762
  Buffalo *(G-3143)*
S E A Supplies Ltd ....F...... 516 694-6677
  Plainview *(G-13633)*
Sabre Energy Services LLC ....F...... 518 514-1572
  Slingerlands *(G-15478)*
Scientific Polymer Products ....G...... 585 265-0413
  Ontario *(G-13214)*
Signa Chemistry Inc ....F...... 212 933-4101
  New York *(G-12071)*
Somerville Acquisitions Co Inc ....F...... 845 856-5261
  Huguenot *(G-6651)*
Somerville Tech Group Inc ....D...... 908 782-9500
  Huguenot *(G-6652)*

Employee Codes: A=Over 500 employees, B=251-500
C=101-250, D=51-100, E=20-50, F=10-19, G=5-9

2017 Harris
New York Manufacturers Directory

Specialty Minerals Inc .... G 518 585-7982
Ticonderoga (G-16128)
◆ Specialty Minerals Inc .... E 212 878-1800
New York (G-12152)
◆ Summit Research Labs Inc .... C 845 856-5261
Huguenot (G-6653)
▼ Tangram Company LLC .... E 631 758-0460
Holtsville (G-6511)
Texas Brine Company LLC .... G 585 495-6228
Wyoming (G-17382)
▲ Thatcher Company New York Inc ..... E 315 589-9330
Williamson (G-17226)
Tibro Water Technologies Ltd .... F 647 426-3415
Sherrill (G-15409)
Transport National Dev Inc .... E 716 662-0270
Orchard Park (G-13300)
UOP LLC .... E 716 879-7600
Tonawanda (G-16212)
US Peroxide .... G 716 775-5585
Grand Island (G-5772)
◆ Vanchlor Company Inc .... F 716 434-2624
Lockport (G-7624)
Vanchlor Company Inc .... F 716 434-2624
Lockport (G-7625)
◆ Vandemark Chemical Inc .... D 716 433-6764
Lockport (G-7626)
▲ VWR Chemicals LLC .... E 518 297-4444
Rouses Point (G-15045)
◆ Washington Mills Elec Mnrls .... D 716 278-6600
Niagara Falls (G-12890)

2821 Plastics, Mtrls & Nonvulcanizable Elastomers

◆ Adam Scott Designs Inc .... E 212 420-8866
New York (G-9024)
Alco Industries Inc .... E 740 254-4311
Round Lake (G-15036)
◆ American Acrylic Corporation .... E 631 422-2200
West Babylon (G-16770)
American Epoxy and Metal Inc .... G 718 828-7828
Scarsdale (G-15216)
▼ Ashley Resin Corp .... G 718 851-8111
Brooklyn (G-1639)
▲ Astro Chemical Company Inc .... E 518 399-5338
Ballston Lake (G-579)
Atc Plastics LLC .... E 212 375-2515
New York (G-9245)
▼ Axel Plastics RES Labs Inc .... E 718 672-8300
Woodside (G-17318)
◆ Bairnco Corporation .... E 914 461-1300
White Plains (G-17081)
Bamberger Polymers Intl Corp .... F 516 622-3600
Jericho (G-7060)
▲ Barrett Bronze Inc .... E 914 699-6060
Mount Vernon (G-8665)
Belsul America Corp .... F 212 520-1827
New York (G-9352)
Ccmi Inc .... G 315 781-3270
Geneva (G-5571)
Clarence Resins and Chemicals .... G 716 406-9804
Clarence Center (G-3673)
CN Group Incorporated .... A 914 358-5690
White Plains (G-17094)
▲ Coda Resources Ltd .... D 718 649-1666
Brooklyn (G-1790)
Craftech .... D 518 828-5011
Chatham (G-3557)
Creations In Lucite Inc .... G 718 871-2000
Brooklyn (G-1814)
Cytec Industries Inc .... D 716 372-9650
Olean (G-13142)
▼ Cytec Olean Inc .... D 716 372-9650
Olean (G-13143)
▲ De Witt Plastics Inc .... F 315 255-1209
Auburn (G-492)
Dice America Inc .... G 585 869-6200
Victor (G-16473)
Durez Corporation .... F 716 286-0100
Niagara Falls (G-12812)
E I Du Pont De Nemours & Co .... E 716 876-4420
Buffalo (G-2924)
Elastomers Inc .... G 716 633-4883
Williamsville (G-17241)
Empire Plastics Inc .... E 607 754-9132
Endwell (G-4835)
Endurart Inc .... E 212 473-7000
New York (G-10034)
Everfab Inc .... D 716 655-1550
East Aurora (G-4370)
Exxonmobil Chemical Company .... C 315 966-1000
Macedon (G-7986)
▲ Fougera Pharmaceuticals Inc .... C 631 454-7677
Melville (G-8321)
◆ GE Plastics .... G 518 475-5011
Selkirk (G-15355)
General Vy-Coat LLC .... E 718 266-6002
Brooklyn (G-2019)
George M Dujack .... G 518 279-1303
Troy (G-16236)
Hanet Plastics Usa Inc .... G 518 324-5850
Plattsburgh (G-13668)
Hexion Inc .... E 518 792-8040
South Glens Falls (G-15525)
Hutchinson Industries Inc .... E 716 852-1435
Buffalo (G-2998)
Imperial Polymers Inc .... G 718 387-4741
Brooklyn (G-2099)
International Casein Corp Cal .... G 516 466-4363
Great Neck (G-5816)
▲ John C Dolph Company Inc .... E 732 329-2333
Schenectady (G-15271)
▲ Jrlon Inc .... D 315 597-4067
Palmyra (G-13409)
Kent Chemical Corporation .... E 212 521-1700
New York (G-10838)
Macneil Polymers Inc .... F 716 681-7755
Buffalo (G-3054)
Majestic Mold & Tool Inc .... F 315 695-2079
Phoenix (G-13542)
Manufacturers Indexing Pdts .... G 631 271-0956
Halesite (G-5905)
Maviano Corp .... G 845 494-2598
Monsey (G-8575)
▲ MB Plastics Inc .... F 718 523-1180
Greenlawn (G-5874)
▼ Meliorum Technologies Inc .... G 585 313-0616
Rochester (G-14503)
◆ Mitsui Chemicals America Inc .... E 914 253-0777
Rye Brook (G-15072)
Momentive Performance Mtls Inc .... D 914 784-4807
Tarrytown (G-16098)
▲ Nationwide Tarps Incorporated .... D 518 843-1545
Amsterdam (G-361)
Newmat Northeast Corp .... F 631 253-9277
West Babylon (G-16816)
Parker-Hannifin Corporation .... E 315 926-4211
Marion (G-8097)
Pawling Corporation .... C 845 855-1000
Pawling (G-13451)
Perfect Poly Inc .... E 631 265-0539
Nesconset (G-8777)
Plaslok Corp .... E 716 681-7755
Buffalo (G-3128)
Plexi Craft Quality Products .... F 212 924-3244
New York (G-11677)
Polycast Industries Inc .... G 631 595-2530
Bay Shore (G-726)
PPG Architectural Finishes Inc .... C 607 334-9951
Norwich (G-13034)
▲ Queen City Manufacturing Inc .... G 716 877-1102
Buffalo (G-3149)
Rodgard Corporation .... E 716 852-1435
Buffalo (G-3163)
Sabic Innovative Plas US LLC .... B 518 475-5011
Selkirk (G-15358)
▲ Saga International Recycl LLC .... G 718 621-5900
Brooklyn (G-2529)
Saint-Gobain Prfmce Plas Corp .... C 518 686-7301
Hoosick Falls (G-6545)
Saint-Gobain Prfmce Plas Corp .... C 518 642-2200
Granville (G-5781)
▲ SC Medical Overseas Inc .... G 516 935-8500
Jericho (G-7085)
Solid Surfaces Inc .... E 585 292-5340
Rochester (G-14692)
Telechemische Inc .... G 845 561-3237
Newburgh (G-12781)
▼ Terphane Holdings LLC .... G 585 657-5800
Bloomfield (G-990)
◆ Terphane Inc .... D 585 657-5800
Bloomfield (G-991)
▼ Tmp Technologies Inc .... D 716 895-6100
Buffalo (G-3220)
◆ Toray Holding (usa) Inc .... E 212 697-8150
New York (G-12372)
Toray Industries Inc .... G 212 697-8150
New York (G-12373)
▲ Transpo Industries Inc .... E 914 636-1000
New Rochelle (G-8926)
Tri-Seal Holdings Inc .... D 845 353-3300
Blauvelt (G-977)
Unico Inc .... F 845 562-9255
Newburgh (G-12782)
Wilsonart Intl Holdings LLC .... E 516 935-6980
Bethpage (G-879)
WR Smith & Sons Inc .... G 845 620-9400
Nanuet (G-8763)

2822 Synthetic Rubber (Vulcanizable Elastomers)

Canton Bio-Medical Inc .... E 518 283-5963
Poestenkill (G-13722)
David Fehlman .... G 315 455-8888
Syracuse (G-15922)
▲ Depco Inc .... F 631 582-1995
Hauppauge (G-6061)
▲ Dynax Corporation .... G 914 764-0202
Pound Ridge (G-13943)
Hilord Chemical Corporation .... E 631 234-7373
Hauppauge (G-6094)
▲ Integrated Liner Tech Inc .... E 518 621-7422
Rensselaer (G-14048)
Liberty Tire Recycling LLC .... E 716 433-7370
Lockport (G-7597)
Release Coatings New York Inc .... G 585 593-2335
Wellsville (G-16756)
Silicone Products & Technology .... C 716 684-1155
Lancaster (G-7343)
▲ Specialty Silicone Pdts Inc .... E 518 885-8826
Ballston Spa (G-609)
Vasquez Tito .... F 212 944-0441
New York (G-12510)

2823 Cellulosic Man-Made Fibers

3M Company .... B 716 876-1596
Tonawanda (G-16132)
Cytec Industries Inc .... D 716 372-9650
Olean (G-13142)
E I Du Pont De Nemours & Co .... E 716 876-4420
Buffalo (G-2924)
Solivaira Specialties Inc .... D 716 693-4009
North Tonawanda (G-12996)
◆ Solvaira Specialties Inc .... C 716 693-4040
North Tonawanda (G-12997)

2824 Synthetic Organic Fibers, Exc Cellulosic

Dal-Tile Corporation .... G 718 894-9574
Maspeth (G-8128)
▲ Dynax Corporation .... G 914 764-0202
Pound Ridge (G-13943)
Fibrix LLC .... E 716 683-4100
Depew (G-4257)
Solid Surface Acrylics LLC .... F 716 743-1870
North Tonawanda (G-12995)
Solutia Business Entps Inc .... F 314 674-1000
New York (G-12128)
◆ Stein Fibers Ltd .... F 518 489-5700
Albany (G-137)
Vybion Inc .... F 607 266-0860
Ithaca (G-6884)

2833 Medicinal Chemicals & Botanical Prdts

Abh Natures Products Inc .... E 631 249-5783
Edgewood (G-4589)
▼ Ajes Pharmaceuticals LLC .... E 631 608-1728
Copiague (G-3891)
Albany Molecular Research Inc .... F 518 433-7700
Rensselaer (G-14043)
Albany Molecular Research Inc .... F 518 512-2000
Rensselaer (G-14044)
Alo Acquisition LLC .... G 518 464-0279
Albany (G-45)
Alphabet Holding Company Inc .... E 631 200-2000
Ronkonkoma (G-14865)
▲ Amri Rensselaer .... A 518 512-2000
Albany (G-47)
Asept Pak Inc .... E 518 651-2026
Malone (G-8007)
◆ Bio-Botanica Inc .... D 631 231-0987
Hauppauge (G-6034)
Biotemper .... G 516 302-7985
Carle Place (G-3387)
Collaborative Laboratories .... D 631 689-0200
East Setauket (G-4479)
Cosmic Enterprise .... G 718 342-6257
Brooklyn (G-1807)

28 CHEMICALS AND ALLIED PRODUCTS

G C Hanford Manufacturing Co .... C 315 476-7418
  Syracuse *(G-15946)*
GE Healthcare Inc .... F 516 626-2799
  Port Washington *(G-13819)*
▲ Gemini Pharmaceuticals Inc .... C 631 543-3334
  Commack *(G-3833)*
Good Earth Inc .... G 716 684-8111
  Lancaster *(G-7317)*
Healthee Endeavors Inc .... G 718 653-5499
  Bronx *(G-1353)*
Healthy N Fit Intl Inc .... F 914 271-6040
  Croton On Hudson *(G-4064)*
Immudyne Inc .... F 914 244-1777
  Mount Kisco *(G-8629)*
Kannalife Sciences Inc .... G 516 669-3219
  Lloyd Harbor *(G-7567)*
Lee Yuen Fung Trading Co Inc .... F 212 594-9595
  New York *(G-10959)*
▲ Mercer Milling Co .... E 315 701-1334
  Liverpool *(G-7535)*
▲ Natural Organics Inc .... C 631 293-0030
  Melville *(G-8339)*
Nbty Inc .... F 631 200-2000
  Bayport *(G-759)*
Nbty Inc .... F 631 244-2065
  Ronkonkoma *(G-14951)*
Nbty Inc .... F 518 452-5813
  Albany *(G-105)*
Nbty Inc .... D 631 244-2021
  Ronkonkoma *(G-14952)*
◆ Nbty Inc .... A 631 200-2000
  Ronkonkoma *(G-14953)*
Nbty Inc .... D 631 200-7338
  Ronkonkoma *(G-14954)*
Nbty Inc .... F 631 588-3492
  Holbrook *(G-6464)*
▲ Nbty Manufacturing LLC .... E 631 567-9500
  Ronkonkoma *(G-14955)*
Nutraqueen LLC .... F 347 368-6568
  New York *(G-11473)*
Nutrascience Labs Inc .... E 631 247-0660
  Farmingdale *(G-5068)*
Only Natural Inc .... F 516 897-7001
  Island Park *(G-6783)*
◆ Pfizer Inc .... A 212 733-2323
  New York *(G-11636)*
Pfizer Overseas LLC .... G 212 733-2323
  New York *(G-11641)*
Princeton Sciences .... G 845 368-1214
  Airmont *(G-18)*
Proper Chemical Ltd .... G 631 420-8000
  Farmingdale *(G-5091)*
Regeneron Pharmaceuticals Inc .... E 518 488-6000
  Rensselaer *(G-14050)*
Regeneron Pharmaceuticals Inc .... E 518 488-6000
  Rensselaer *(G-14051)*
Setauket Manufacturing Co .... G 631 231-7272
  Ronkonkoma *(G-14984)*
Stauber Prfmce Ingredients Inc .... G 845 651-4443
  Florida *(G-5215)*
▲ Ucb Pharma Inc .... B 919 767-2555
  Rochester *(G-14739)*
Vitalize Labs LLC .... G 212 966-6130
  New York *(G-12556)*
Vitamix Laboratories Inc .... E 631 465-9245
  Commack *(G-3847)*
Wacf Enterprise Inc .... E 631 745-5841
  Northport *(G-13018)*
▲ Wellquest International Inc .... G 212 689-9094
  New York *(G-12608)*

2834 Pharmaceuticals

3v Company Inc .... E 718 858-7333
  Brooklyn *(G-1517)*
5th Avenue Pharmacy Inc .... G 718 439-8585
  Brooklyn *(G-1520)*
872 Hunts Point Pharmacy Inc .... G 718 991-3519
  Bronx *(G-1251)*
888 Pharmacy Inc .... F 718 871-8833
  Brooklyn *(G-1523)*
A & Z Pharmaceutical Inc .... D 631 952-3802
  Hauppauge *(G-6006)*
◆ A & Z Pharmaceutical Inc .... C 631 952-3800
  Hauppauge *(G-6007)*
Abraxis Bioscience LLC .... G 716 773-0800
  Grand Island *(G-5750)*
▲ Acorda Therapeutics Inc .... B 914 347-4300
  Ardsley *(G-403)*
Actavis Laboratories Ny Inc .... D 631 693-8000
  Copiague *(G-3889)*

Actinium Pharmaceuticals Inc .... F 732 243-9495
  New York *(G-9021)*
Advance Pharmaceutical Inc .... E 631 981-4600
  Holtsville *(G-6500)*
▲ Affymax Inc .... G 650 812-8700
  New York *(G-9054)*
Aiping Pharmaceutical Inc .... G 631 952-3802
  Hauppauge *(G-6012)*
▲ Alfred Khalily Inc .... F 516 504-0059
  Great Neck *(G-5787)*
Allied Pharmacy Products Inc .... F 516 374-8862
  Woodmere *(G-17310)*
Altaire Pharmaceuticals Inc .... C 631 722-5988
  Aquebogue *(G-383)*
American Bio Medica Corp .... D 518 758-8158
  Kinderhook *(G-7167)*
American Hormones Inc .... F 845 471-7272
  Poughkeepsie *(G-13886)*
American Regent Inc .... B 631 924-4000
  Shirley *(G-15411)*
Amneal Pharmaceuticals LLC .... E 908 231-1911
  Brookhaven *(G-1505)*
▲ Amneal Pharmaceuticals NY LLC .... E 631 952-0214
  Brookhaven *(G-1506)*
Anacor Pharmaceuticals Inc .... C 212 733-2323
  New York *(G-9143)*
Angiogenex Inc .... G 347 468-6799
  Aquebogue *(G-9158)*
Anima Mundi Herbals LLC .... G 415 279-5727
  Long Island City *(G-7660)*
Anterios Inc .... G 212 303-1683
  New York *(G-9167)*
Aoi Pharma Inc .... F 212 531-5970
  New York *(G-9171)*
Apothecus Pharmaceutical Corp .... F 516 624-8200
  Oyster Bay *(G-13366)*
Ark Sciences Inc .... G 646 943-1520
  Islandia *(G-6787)*
Asence Inc .... E 347 335-2606
  New York *(G-9226)*
Atlantic Essential Pdts Inc .... D 631 434-8333
  Hauppauge *(G-6027)*
Auven Therapeutics MGT LP .... F 212 616-4000
  New York *(G-9269)*
Auxilium Pharmaceuticals Inc .... F 484 321-2022
  Rye *(G-15054)*
Azurrx Biopharma Inc .... F 646 699-7855
  Brooklyn *(G-1654)*
Barc Usa Inc .... E 516 719-1052
  New Hyde Park *(G-8818)*
Barr Laboratories Inc .... C 845 362-1100
  Pomona *(G-13728)*
BASF Corporation .... B 914 785-2000
  Tarrytown *(G-16087)*
Bausch & Lomb Holdings Inc .... G 585 338-6000
  New York *(G-9335)*
◆ Bausch & Lomb Incorporated .... B 585 338-6000
  Rochester *(G-14225)*
Beyondspring Phrmceuticals Inc .... F 646 305-6387
  New York *(G-9385)*
Bi Nutraceuticals Inc .... D 631 232-1105
  Central Islip *(G-3488)*
Bicon Pharmaceutical Inc .... F 631 593-4199
  Deer Park *(G-4107)*
◆ Bio-Botanica Inc .... D 631 231-0987
  Hauppauge *(G-6034)*
▲ Biospecifics Technologies Corp .... G 516 593-7000
  Lynbrook *(G-7948)*
Bli International Inc .... C 631 940-9000
  Deer Park *(G-4109)*
◆ Bristol-Myers Squibb Company .... A 212 546-4000
  New York *(G-9464)*
Bristol-Myers Squibb Company .... E 315 432-2000
  East Syracuse *(G-4512)*
Bristol-Myers Squibb Company .... C 516 832-2191
  Garden City *(G-5497)*
Bronson Nutritionals LLC .... E 631 750-0000
  Hauppauge *(G-6038)*
Campbell Alliance Group Inc .... E 212 377-2740
  New York *(G-9509)*
Cancer Targeting Systems .... G 212 965-4534
  New York *(G-9511)*
Cellvation Inc .... G 212 554-4520
  New York *(G-9556)*
Central Islip Pharmacy Inc .... G 631 234-6039
  Central Islip *(G-3490)*
Century Grand Inc .... F 212 925-3838
  New York *(G-9569)*
Cerovene Inc .... F 845 359-1101
  Orangeburg *(G-13221)*

Cerovene Inc .... F 845 267-2055
  Valley Cottage *(G-16377)*
Chartwell Pharma Nda B2 Holdin .... G 845 268-5000
  Congers *(G-3854)*
Chartwell Pharmaceuticals LLC .... D 845 268-5000
  Congers *(G-3855)*
Cleveland Biolabs Inc .... E 716 849-6810
  Buffalo *(G-2876)*
Cognigen Corporation .... D 716 633-3463
  Buffalo *(G-2878)*
▼ Combe Incorporated .... C 914 694-5454
  White Plains *(G-17095)*
Container Tstg Solutions LLC .... F 716 487-3300
  Jamestown *(G-6983)*
Container Tstg Solutions LLC .... F 716 487-3300
  Sinclairville *(G-15453)*
Contract Pharmacal Corp .... E 631 231-4610
  Hauppauge *(G-6052)*
Contract Pharmacal Corp .... C 631 231-4610
  Hauppauge *(G-6053)*
Contract Pharmacal Corp .... E 631 231-4610
  Hauppauge *(G-6054)*
Contract Pharmacal Corp .... D 631 231-4610
  Hauppauge *(G-6055)*
Contract Pharmacal Corp .... C 631 231-4610
  Hauppauge *(G-6056)*
Contract Pharmacal Corp .... F 631 231-4610
  Hauppauge *(G-6057)*
Contract Phrmctcals Ltd Nagara .... C 716 887-3400
  Buffalo *(G-2888)*
Cortice Biosciences Inc .... F 646 747-9090
  New York *(G-9727)*
▲ CRS Nuclear Services LLC .... F 716 810-0688
  Cheektowaga *(G-3565)*
▲ Danbury Pharma LLC .... F 716 393-6333
  Farmingdale *(G-4974)*
Delcath Systems Inc .... E 212 489-2100
  New York *(G-9838)*
Dipexium Pharmaceuticals Inc .... G 212 269-2834
  New York *(G-9881)*
Dr Reddys Laboratories NY Inc .... F 518 827-7702
  Middleburgh *(G-8418)*
Drt Laboratories LLC .... G 845 547-2034
  Airmont *(G-14)*
◆ DSM Nutritional Products LLC .... B 518 372-5155
  Schenectady *(G-15249)*
DSM Nutritional Products LLC .... C 518 372-5155
  Glenville *(G-5701)*
Durata Therapeutics Inc .... G 646 871-6400
  New York *(G-9940)*
Eckerson Drugs Inc .... F 845 352-1800
  Spring Valley *(G-15583)*
▼ Edlaw Pharmaceuticals Inc .... E 631 454-6888
  Farmingdale *(G-4985)*
Eli Lilly and Company .... F 516 622-2244
  New Hyde Park *(G-8832)*
▲ Encysive Pharmaceuticals Inc .... E 212 733-2323
  New York *(G-10031)*
Enumeral Biomedical Corp .... G 347 227-4787
  New York *(G-10046)*
Enzo Life Sciences Inc .... E 631 694-7070
  Farmingdale *(G-4988)*
◆ Enzo Life Sciences Intl Inc .... E 610 941-0430
  Farmingdale *(G-4989)*
Eon Labs Inc .... F 516 478-9700
  New Hyde Park *(G-8833)*
▲ Epic Pharma LLC .... C 718 276-8600
  Laurelton *(G-7387)*
Erika T Schwartz MD PC .... G 212 873-3420
  New York *(G-10058)*
▲ FB Laboratories Inc .... E 631 750-0000
  Hauppauge *(G-6076)*
Flushing Pharmacy Inc .... C 718 260-8999
  Brooklyn *(G-1989)*
▲ Forest Laboratories LLC .... C 212 421-7850
  New York *(G-10185)*
Forest Laboratories LLC .... D 212 421-7850
  Hauppauge *(G-6080)*
Forest Laboratories LLC .... E 631 858-6010
  Commack *(G-3831)*
◆ Fortitech Inc .... C 518 372-5155
  Schenectady *(G-15255)*
Fortress Biotech Inc .... F 781 652-4500
  New York *(G-10187)*
▲ Fougera Pharmaceuticals Inc .... C 631 454-7677
  Melville *(G-8321)*
Fougera Pharmaceuticals Inc .... C 631 454-7677
  Hicksville *(G-6346)*
Freeda Vitamins Inc .... E 718 433-4337
  Long Island City *(G-7745)*

Employee Codes: A=Over 500 employees, B=251-500
C=101-250, D=51-100, E=20-50, F=10-19, G=5-9

Fresenius Kabi Usa LLC........B....... 716 773-0053
Grand Island *(G-5758)*
Fresenius Kabi USA LLC........E....... 716 773-0800
Grand Island *(G-5759)*
▲ **Futurebiotics LLC**........E....... 631 273-6300
Hauppauge *(G-6082)*
G C Hanford Manufacturing Co........C....... 315 476-7418
Syracuse *(G-15946)*
G S W Worldwide LLC........D....... 646 437-4800
New York *(G-10231)*
▼ **Gamma Enterprises LLC**........E....... 631 755-1080
West Babylon *(G-16793)*
▲ **Geritrex LLC**........E....... 914 668-4003
Mount Vernon *(G-8682)*
Geritrex Holdings Inc........G....... 914 668-4003
Mount Vernon *(G-8683)*
Glaxosmithkline LLC........E....... 845 341-7590
Montgomery *(G-8593)*
Glaxosmithkline LLC........E....... 845 797-3259
Wappingers Falls *(G-16571)*
Glaxosmithkline LLC........E....... 585 738-9025
Rochester *(G-14406)*
Glaxosmithkline LLC........E....... 716 913-5679
Buffalo *(G-2975)*
Glaxosmithkline LLC........D....... 518 239-6901
East Durham *(G-4387)*
Glaxosmithkline LLC........E....... 518 852-9637
Mechanicville *(G-8228)*
Global Alliance For Tb........E....... 212 227-7540
New York *(G-10310)*
Greentree Pharmacy Inc........F....... 718 768-2700
Brooklyn *(G-2054)*
Guosa Life Sciences Inc........F....... 516 481-1540
North Baldwin *(G-12906)*
H & C Chemists Inc........F....... 212 535-1700
New York *(G-10385)*
▲ **H W Naylor Co Inc**........F....... 607 263-5145
Morris *(G-8618)*
Healthone Pharmacy Inc........F....... 718 495-9015
Brooklyn *(G-2069)*
▲ **Hi-Tech Pharmacal Co Inc**........B....... 631 789-8228
Amityville *(G-294)*
▲ **Hogil Pharmaceutical Corp**........F....... 914 681-1800
White Plains *(G-17121)*
Holistic Blends Inc........G....... 315 468-4300
Syracuse *(G-15960)*
Hospira Inc........C....... 716 684-9400
Buffalo *(G-2997)*
Ibio Inc........G....... 302 355-0650
New York *(G-10545)*
◆ **Ima Life North America Inc**........C....... 716 695-6354
Tonawanda *(G-16173)*
Immune Pharmaceuticals Inc........F....... 646 440-9310
New York *(G-10573)*
Innovative Labs LLC........D....... 631 231-5522
Hauppauge *(G-6097)*
▼ **Intellicell Biosciences Inc**........G....... 646 576-8700
New York *(G-10617)*
Intercept Pharmaceuticals Inc........D....... 646 747-1000
New York *(G-10625)*
International Life Science........G....... 631 549-0471
Huntington *(G-6663)*
▲ **Intra-Cellular Therapies Inc**........E....... 212 923-3344
New York *(G-10645)*
Invagen Pharmaceuticals Inc........C....... 631 949-6367
Central Islip *(G-3499)*
▲ **Invagen Pharmaceuticals Inc**........B....... 631 231-3233
Hauppauge *(G-6099)*
Ip Med Inc........G....... 516 766-3800
Oceanside *(G-13082)*
Izun Pharmaceuticals Corp........G....... 212 618-6357
New York *(G-10672)*
Jerome Stvens Phrmcuticals Inc........F....... 631 567-1113
Bohemia *(G-1082)*
▲ **JRS Pharma LP**........E....... 845 878-8300
Patterson *(G-13441)*
▲ **Kabco Pharmaceuticals Inc**........G....... 631 842-3600
Amityville *(G-300)*
Kadmon Corporation LLC........G....... 212 308-6000
New York *(G-10799)*
Kadmon Holdings Inc........C....... 212 308-6000
New York *(G-10800)*
Kannalife Sciences Inc........G....... 516 669-3219
Lloyd Harbor *(G-7567)*
Kbl Healthcare LP........G....... 212 319-5555
New York *(G-10824)*
Kent Chemical Corporation........E....... 212 521-1700
New York *(G-10838)*
Kingston Pharma LLC........G....... 315 705-4019
Massena *(G-8197)*

▲ **Klg Usa LLC**........A....... 845 856-5311
Port Jervis *(G-13788)*
Linden Care LLC........G....... 516 221-7600
Woodbury *(G-17293)*
Lion Biotechnologies Inc........F....... 212 946-4856
New York *(G-11004)*
▲ **Liptis Pharmaceuticals USA Inc**........A....... 845 627-0260
Spring Valley *(G-15592)*
LNK International Inc........D....... 631 435-3500
Hauppauge *(G-6114)*
LNK International Inc........D....... 631 435-3500
Hauppauge *(G-6115)*
LNK International Inc........D....... 631 435-3500
Hauppauge *(G-6116)*
LNK International Inc........D....... 631 543-3787
Hauppauge *(G-6117)*
LNK International Inc........D....... 631 435-3500
Hauppauge *(G-6118)*
LNK International Inc........D....... 631 231-3415
Hauppauge *(G-6119)*
LNK International Inc........D....... 631 231-4020
Hauppauge *(G-6120)*
▲ **Lotta Luv Beauty LLC**........F....... 646 786-2847
New York *(G-11046)*
▲ **Luitpold Pharmaceuticals Inc**........B....... 631 924-4000
Shirley *(G-15423)*
Macrochem Corporation........G....... 212 514-8094
New York *(G-11090)*
Mallinckrodt LLC........A....... 607 538-9124
Hobart *(G-6426)*
▲ **Marco Hi-Tech JV LLC**........G....... 212 798-8114
New York *(G-11145)*
◆ **Marietta Corporation**........B....... 607 753-6746
Cortland *(G-4033)*
Marken LLP........G....... 631 396-7454
Farmingdale *(G-5041)*
Maxus Pharmaceuticals Inc........F....... 631 249-0003
Farmingdale *(G-5045)*
Medek Laboratories Inc........E....... 845 943-4988
Monroe *(G-8562)*
▲ **Medtech Products Inc**........F....... 914 524-6810
Tarrytown *(G-16096)*
◆ **Mentholatum Company**........E....... 716 677-2500
Orchard Park *(G-13284)*
▲ **Mercer Milling Co**........E....... 315 701-1334
Liverpool *(G-7535)*
Mesoblast Inc........G....... 212 880-2060
New York *(G-11239)*
Mskcc Rmipc........F....... 212 639-6212
New York *(G-11319)*
Nanorx Inc........G....... 914 671-0224
Chappaqua *(G-3553)*
Natural Organics Labroratories........B....... 631 957-5600
Amityville *(G-315)*
Natures Bounty Inc........F....... 631 567-9500
Bohemia *(G-1108)*
▲ **Natures Bounty Inc**........A....... 631 580-6137
Ronkonkoma *(G-14950)*
▲ **Natures Value Inc**........C....... 631 846-2500
Coram *(G-3946)*
ND Labs Inc........F....... 516 612-4900
Lynbrook *(G-7955)*
Neurotrope Inc........G....... 973 242-0005
Irvington *(G-6774)*
▲ **New York Health Care Inc**........G....... 718 375-6700
Valley Stream *(G-16416)*
▲ **Norwich Pharmaceuticals Inc**........B....... 607 335-3000
Norwich *(G-13033)*
Novartis Corporation........E....... 212 307-1122
New York *(G-11462)*
Novartis Corporation........C....... 845 368-6000
Suffern *(G-15795)*
Novartis Corporation........D....... 718 276-8600
Laurelton *(G-7388)*
Novartis Pharmaceuticals Corp........G....... 718 276-8600
Laurelton *(G-7389)*
Noven Pharmaceuticals Inc........E....... 212 682-4420
New York *(G-11464)*
Nutra-Scientifics LLC........G....... 917 238-8510
Pomona *(G-13731)*
Nutraceutical Wellness LLC........G....... 888 454-3320
New York *(G-11472)*
Nutrascience Labs Inc........E....... 631 247-0660
Farmingdale *(G-5068)*
NV Prrcone MD Cosmeceuticals........G....... 212 734-2537
New York *(G-11475)*
NY Phrmacy Compounding Ctr Inc........G....... 201 403-5151
Astoria *(G-451)*
Ohr Pharmaceutical Inc........F....... 212 682-8452
New York *(G-11498)*

Oligomerix Inc........G....... 914 997-8877
New York *(G-11500)*
Ony Inc........E....... 716 636-9096
Amherst *(G-257)*
Ony Inc Baird Researchpark........E....... 716 636-9096
Buffalo *(G-3102)*
Opthotech Corp........F....... 212 845-8200
New York *(G-11517)*
Organic Frog Inc........G....... 516 897-0369
Hauppauge *(G-6156)*
OSI Pharmaceuticals LLC........D....... 631 847-0175
Farmingdale *(G-5073)*
▼ **OSI Pharmaceuticals LLC**........G....... 631 962-2000
Farmingdale *(G-5074)*
P & L Development LLC........D....... 516 986-1700
Westbury *(G-17015)*
P & L Development LLC........D....... 516 986-1700
Westbury *(G-17016)*
P & L Development LLC........D....... 516 986-1700
Westbury *(G-17017)*
Pace Up Pharmaceuticals LLC........G....... 631 450-4495
Lindenhurst *(G-7478)*
▲ **Pall Corporation**........A....... 516 484-5400
Port Washington *(G-13852)*
▲ **Par Pharmaceutical Inc**........B....... 845 425-7100
Spring Valley *(G-15598)*
Par Phrmceutical Companies Inc........E....... 845 573-5500
Chestnut Ridge *(G-3624)*
Par Sterile Products LLC........E....... 845 573-5500
Chestnut Ridge *(G-3625)*
Perrigo Company........E....... 718 960-9900
Bronx *(G-1425)*
Perrigo New York Inc........F....... 718 901-2800
Bronx *(G-1426)*
▲ **Perrigo New York Inc**........B....... 718 960-9900
Bronx *(G-1427)*
▲ **Pfizer HCP Corporation**........F....... 212 733-2323
New York *(G-11635)*
◆ **Pfizer Inc**........A....... 212 733-2323
New York *(G-11636)*
Pfizer Inc........B....... 518 297-6611
Rouses Point *(G-15042)*
Pfizer Inc........C....... 914 437-5868
White Plains *(G-17159)*
Pfizer Inc........C....... 937 746-3603
New York *(G-11637)*
Pfizer Inc........D....... 212 733-6276
New York *(G-11638)*
Pfizer Inc........C....... 804 257-2000
New York *(G-11639)*
Pfizer Inc........C....... 212 733-2323
New York *(G-11640)*
Pfizer Overseas LLC........G....... 212 733-2323
New York *(G-11641)*
Pharbest Pharmaceuticals Inc........E....... 631 249-5130
Farmingdale *(G-5077)*
▲ **Pharmaceutic Labs LLC**........F....... 518 608-1060
Albany *(G-119)*
Pharmalife Inc........G....... 631 249-4040
Farmingdale *(G-5078)*
▲ **Pharmavantage LLC**........G....... 631 321-8171
Babylon *(G-551)*
Phoenix Laboratories Inc........C....... 516 822-1230
Farmingdale *(G-5079)*
Pine Pharmaceuticals LLC........G....... 716 248-1025
Tonawanda *(G-16193)*
Pituitary Society........F....... 212 263-6772
New York *(G-11669)*
Polygen Pharmaceuticals Inc........E....... 631 392-4044
Edgewood *(G-4608)*
Precision Pharma Services Inc........C....... 631 752-7314
Melville *(G-8349)*
Prestige Brands Holdings Inc........D....... 914 524-6800
Tarrytown *(G-16101)*
▲ **Prime Pack LLC**........F....... 732 253-7734
New York *(G-11708)*
Progenics Pharmaceuticals Inc........D....... 646 975-2500
New York *(G-11729)*
Purine Pharma LLC........E....... 315 705-4030
Massena *(G-8199)*
▲ **Purity Products Inc**........D....... 516 767-1967
Plainview *(G-13631)*
Quadpharma LLC........G....... 877 463-7823
Clarence *(G-3670)*
Quality Nature Inc........G....... 718 484-4666
Brooklyn *(G-2462)*
Quogue Capital LLC........G....... 212 554-4475
New York *(G-11775)*
R J S Direct Marketing Inc........F....... 631 667-5768
Deer Park *(G-4197)*

SIC

SIC SECTION

28 CHEMICALS AND ALLIED PRODUCTS

Randob Labs Ltd..................................G.... 845 534-2197
  Cornwall *(G-3991)*
Rapha Pharmaceuticals Inc ....G.... 956 229-0049
  Valley Cottage *(G-16385)*
Regeneron Pharmaceuticals Inc ....B.... 914 847-7000
  Tarrytown *(G-16103)*
Regenron Hlthcare Slutions Inc ....A.... 914 847-7000
  Tarrytown *(G-16104)*
Relmada Therapeutics Inc ....E.... 646 677-3853
  New York *(G-11825)*
Retrophin LLC ....G.... 212 983-1310
  New York *(G-11846)*
Rij Pharmaceutical Corporation ....E.... 845 692-5799
  Middletown *(G-8459)*
Rls Holdings Inc.................................G.... 716 418-7274
  Clarence *(G-3671)*
♦ Rohto USA Inc ....G.... 716 677-2500
  Orchard Park *(G-13295)*
Ropack USA Inc ....F.... 631 482-7777
  Commack *(G-3840)*
S1 Biopharma Inc ....G.... 201 839-0941
  New York *(G-11948)*
▲ Safetec of America Inc....................D.... 716 895-1822
  Buffalo *(G-3173)*
Salutem Group LLC ....G.... 347 620-2640
  New York *(G-11960)*
Saptalis Pharmaceuticals LLC ....F.... 631 231-2751
  Hauppauge *(G-6184)*
Saratoga Pharmaceuticals Inc ....F.... 518 894-1875
  Clifton Park *(G-3706)*
Satnam Distributors LLC.....................G.... 516 802-0600
  Jericho *(G-7084)*
Scarguard Labs LLC ....F.... 516 482-8050
  Great Neck *(G-5839)*
Sciarra Laboratories Inc......................G.... 516 933-7853
  Hicksville *(G-6393)*
Sciegen Pharmaceuticals Inc ....E.... 631 434-2723
  Hauppauge *(G-6186)*
▲ Sciegen Pharmaceuticals Inc ....C.... 631 434-2723
  Hauppauge *(G-6187)*
Scienta Pharmaceuticals LLC.............G.... 845 589-0774
  Valley Cottage *(G-16388)*
Seidlin Consulting ....G.... 212 496-2043
  New York *(G-12020)*
Shrineeta Pharmacy ....G.... 212 234-7959
  New York *(G-12055)*
Shrineeta Pharmacy Inc ....E.... 212 234-7959
  New York *(G-12056)*
Siga Technologies Inc ....E.... 212 672-9100
  New York *(G-12066)*
▲ Silarx Pharmaceuticals Inc ....E.... 845 352-4020
  Carmel *(G-3405)*
Silver Oak Pharmacy Inc.....................G.... 718 922-3400
  Brooklyn *(G-2557)*
Sincerus LLC ....G.... 800 419-2804
  Brooklyn *(G-2563)*
Skills Alliance Inc................................G.... 646 492-5300
  New York *(G-12091)*
Skincare Products Inc ....G.... 917 837-5255
  New York *(G-12093)*
Spirit Pharmaceuticals LLC ....G.... 215 943-4000
  Centereach *(G-3473)*
Spri Clinical Trials................................F.... 718 616-2400
  Brooklyn *(G-2590)*
Stemline Therapeutics Inc ....E.... 646 502-2311
  New York *(G-12193)*
Steri-Pharma LLC ....F.... 315 473-7180
  Syracuse *(G-16046)*
Sterrx LLC ....E.... 518 324-7879
  Plattsburgh *(G-13699)*
Sterrx LLC ....F.... 518 324-7879
  Plattsburgh *(G-13700)*
Strativa Pharmaceuticals ....F.... 201 802-4000
  Spring Valley *(G-15602)*
Sunquest Pharmaceuticals Inc...........F.... 855 478-6779
  Syosset *(G-15840)*
Synergy Pharmaceuticals Inc ....E.... 212 297-0020
  New York *(G-12262)*
Syntho Pharmaceuticals Inc ....G.... 631 755-9898
  Farmingdale *(G-5122)*
▲ Tg Therapeutics Inc ....E.... 212 554-4484
  New York *(G-12307)*
▲ Time-Cap Laboratories Inc ....C.... 631 753-9090
  Farmingdale *(G-5131)*
▲ Tishcon Corp ....C.... 516 333-3056
  Westbury *(G-17032)*
Tishcon Corp......................................C.... 516 333-3056
  Westbury *(G-17033)*
Tishcon Corp......................................C.... 516 333-3050
  Westbury *(G-17034)*

Tishcon Corp......................................C.... 516 333-3050
  Westbury *(G-17035)*
▼ Tmp Technologies Inc ....D.... 716 895-6100
  Buffalo *(G-3220)*
Tocare LLC ....G.... 718 767-0618
  Whitestone *(G-17215)*
Tongli Pharmaceuticals USA Inc ....F.... 212 842-8837
  Flushing *(G-5302)*
Tonix Phrmceuticals Holdg Corp ....F.... 212 980-9155
  New York *(G-12367)*
▲ Topiderm Inc....................................C.... 631 226-7979
  Amityville *(G-329)*
▲ Topix Pharmaceuticals Inc ....E.... 631 225-5757
  Amityville *(G-330)*
Transparency Life Sciences LLC.........F.... 862 252-1216
  New York *(G-12393)*
Triceutical Inc ....F.... 631 249-0003
  Bronx *(G-1477)*
▲ Ucb Pharma Inc..............................B.... 919 767-2555
  Rochester *(G-14739)*
▼ Unipharm Inc ....E.... 212 564-3634
  New York *(G-12459)*
♦ United-Guardian Inc ....E.... 631 273-0900
  Hauppauge *(G-6220)*
Unither Manufacturing LLC.................C.... 585 475-9000
  Rochester *(G-14743)*
▼ Velocity Pharma LLC ....G.... 631 393-2905
  Farmingdale *(G-5137)*
▼ Venus Pharmaceuticals Intl Inc ....F.... 631 249-4140
  Hauppauge *(G-6223)*
Very Best Irtj ....F.... 914 271-6585
  Croton On Hudson *(G-4066)*
Vida-Blend LLC..................................E.... 518 627-4138
  Amsterdam *(G-373)*
Viropro Inc..E.... 650 300-5190
  New York *(G-12548)*
▲ Vita-Nat Inc ....G.... 631 293-6000
  Farmingdale *(G-5138)*
Vitalis LLC ....G.... 646 831-7338
  New York *(G-12555)*
♦ Vitane Pharmaceuticals Inc ....E.... 845 267-6700
  Congers *(G-3862)*
Wavodyne Therapeutics Inc ....G.... 954 632-6630
  West Henrietta *(G-16900)*
Wellmill LLC ....F.... 631 465-9245
  Farmingdale *(G-5142)*
Wyeth Holdings LLC ....D.... 845 602-5000
  Pearl River *(G-13469)*
♦ Wyeth LLC.......................................A.... 973 660-5000
  New York *(G-12671)*
X-Gen Pharmaceuticals Inc................G.... 607 562-2700
  Big Flats *(G-883)*
X-Gen Pharmaceuticals Inc................E.... 631 261-8188
  Elmira *(G-4707)*
X-Gen Pharmaceuticals Inc................E.... 607 562-2700
  Horseheads *(G-6596)*
Xstelos Holdings Inc...........................G.... 212 729-4962
  New York *(G-12684)*
Ys Marketing Inc.................................F.... 718 778-6080
  Brooklyn *(G-2778)*
Zenith Solutions..................................G.... 718 575-8570
  Flushing *(G-5312)*
Zeo Health Ltd ....F.... 845 353-5185
  Valley Cottage *(G-16395)*
Zinerva Pharmaceuticals LLC ....G.... 630 729-4184
  Clarence Center *(G-3682)*
▲ Zitomer LLC ....G.... 212 737-5560
  New York *(G-12715)*

2835 Diagnostic Substances

Alere Inc..B.... 516 767-1112
  Port Washington *(G-13798)*
Bella International Inc..........................G.... 716 484-0102
  Jamestown *(G-6973)*
Biochemical Diagnostics Inc...............E.... 631 595-9200
  Edgewood *(G-4595)*
▲ Biopool Us Inc.................................E.... 716 483-3851
  Oceanside *(G-6974)*
▲ Chembio Diagnostic Systems Inc....C.... 631 924-1135
  Medford *(G-8238)*
▲ Chembio Diagnostics Inc................E.... 631 924-1135
  Medford *(G-8239)*
▲ Clark Laboratories Inc ....G.... 716 483-3851
  Jamestown *(G-6979)*
Danisco US Inc...................................D.... 585 256-5200
  Rochester *(G-14300)*
Darmiyan LLC.....................................G.... 917 689-0389
  New York *(G-9810)*
Dnano Inc..G.... 607 316-3694
  Ithaca *(G-6837)*

♦ E-Z-Em Inc.......................................E.... 609 524-2864
  Melville *(G-8313)*
Eagle International LLC ....G.... 917 282-2536
  Nanuet *(G-8756)*
Enzo Life Sciences Inc ....E.... 631 694-7070
  Farmingdale *(G-4988)*
Gotham Veterinary Center PC............E.... 212 222-1900
  New York *(G-10341)*
Immco Diagnostics Inc ....G.... 716 691-6955
  Buffalo *(G-3003)*
Immco Diagnostics Inc ....D.... 716 691-6911
  Buffalo *(G-3004)*
Kannalife Sciences Inc ....G.... 516 669-3219
  Lloyd Harbor *(G-7567)*
Ken-Ton Open Mri PC ....G.... 716 876-7000
  Kenmore *(G-7150)*
Lesanne Life Sciences LLC ....G.... 914 234-0860
  Bedford *(G-797)*
Lifelink Monitoring Corp ....F.... 845 336-2098
  Bearsville *(G-792)*
Lifescan Inc...B.... 516 557-2693
  Wantagh *(G-16558)*
Northeast Doulas ....G.... 845 621-0654
  Mahopac *(G-7999)*
Ortho-Clinical Diagnostics Inc.............E.... 716 631-1281
  Williamsville *(G-17250)*
Ortho-Clinical Diagnostics Inc.............E.... 585 453-3000
  Rochester *(G-14556)*
Siemens Hlthcare Dgnostics Inc ....E.... 914 631-0475
  Tarrytown *(G-16105)*
Ufc Biotechnology ....F.... 716 777-3776
  Amherst *(G-269)*
▲ Welch Allyn Inc................................A.... 315 685-4100
  Skaneateles Falls *(G-15472)*
Working Family Solutions Inc..............G.... 845 802-6182
  Saugerties *(G-15198)*

2836 Biological Prdts, Exc Diagnostic Substances

▲ Acorda Therapeutics Inc ....B.... 914 347-4300
  Ardsley *(G-403)*
Advance Biofactures Corp..................E.... 516 593-7000
  Lynbrook *(G-7944)*
♦ AG Biotech Inc................................G.... 585 346-0020
  Livonia *(G-7563)*
▲ Akshar Extracts Inc.........................G.... 631 588-9727
  Ronkonkoma *(G-14858)*
Albany Molecular Research Inc...........E.... 518 512-2234
  Albany *(G-40)*
♦ Albany Molecular Research Inc ......C.... 518 512-2000
  Albany *(G-41)*
Angus Chemical Company ....F.... 716 283-1434
  Niagara Falls *(G-12796)*
AV Therapeutics Inc............................E.... 917 497-5523
  New York *(G-9271)*
C T M Industries Ltd............................E.... 718 479-3300
  Jamaica *(G-6899)*
Coral Blood Service ....F.... 800 483-4888
  Elmsford *(G-4743)*
Cypress Bioscience Inc......................F.... 858 452-2323
  New York *(G-9778)*
D C I Plasma Center Inc.....................G.... 914 241-1646
  Mount Kisco *(G-8625)*
Debmar-Mercury ....G.... 212 669-5025
  New York *(G-9834)*
♦ DSM Nutritional Products LLC.........B.... 518 372-5155
  Schenectady *(G-15249)*
▲ Ecological Laboratories Inc ....F.... 516 823-3441
  Lynbrook *(G-7950)*
HP Hood LLC......................................D.... 315 829-3339
  Vernon *(G-16435)*
Instrumentation Laboratory Co ....C.... 845 680-0028
  Orangeburg *(G-13231)*
International Aids Vaccine Ini..............C.... 212 847-1111
  New York *(G-10630)*
Ip Med Inc ....G.... 516 766-3800
  Oceanside *(G-13082)*
Kadmon Holdings Inc ....C.... 212 308-6000
  New York *(G-10800)*
Lake Immunogenics Inc ....F.... 585 265-1973
  Ontario *(G-13205)*
Life Technologies Corporation ....D.... 716 774-6700
  Grand Island *(G-5762)*
Man of World......................................D.... 212 915-0017
  New York *(G-11124)*
Nanoprobes Inc...................................F.... 631 205-9490
  Yaphank *(G-17398)*
Nelco Laboratories Inc........................E.... 631 242-0082
  Deer Park *(G-4178)*

Employee Codes: A=Over 500 employees, B=251-500
C=101-250, D=51-100, E=20-50, F=10-19, G=5-9

28 CHEMICALS AND ALLIED PRODUCTS

Nxxi Inc .... F 914 701-4500
  Purchase (G-13962)
Oligomerix Inc .... G 914 997-8877
  New York (G-11500)
Omrix Biopharmaceuticals Inc .... C 908 218-0707
  New York (G-11503)
Rentschler Biotechnologie GMBH ...... G 631 656-7137
  Hauppauge (G-6177)
Roar Biomedical Inc .... G 631 591-2749
  Calverton (G-3297)
Siga Technologies Inc .... E 212 672-9100
  New York (G-12066)
Stemcultures LLC 518 621-0848
  Rensselaer (G-14052)
Synergy Pharmaceuticals Inc .... G 212 227-8611
  New York (G-12261)
Turing Pharmaceuticals LLC .... E 646 356-5577
  New York (G-12425)
Wyeth Holdings LLC .... D 845 602-5000
  Pearl River (G-13469)
◆ Wyeth LLC .... A 973 660-5000
  New York (G-12671)
▼ Zeptometrix Corporation .... E 716 882-0920
  Buffalo (G-3262)

2841 Soap & Detergents

Alabu Inc .... G 518 665-0411
  Mechanicville (G-8224)
Alconox Inc .... G 914 948-4040
  White Plains (G-17075)
Aura Detergent LLC .... F 718 824-2162
  Bronx (G-1278)
▼ Baums Castorine Company Inc ...... G 315 336-8154
  Rome (G-14805)
Bfma Holding Corporation .... G 607 753-6746
  Cortland (G-4014)
Chemite Inc .... G 607 529-3218
  Waverly (G-16700)
Cleanse TEC .... E 718 346-9111
  Brooklyn (G-1788)
▲ Colgate-Palmolive Company .... A 212 310-2000
  New York (G-9667)
Colgate-Palmolive Nj Inc .... A 212 310-2000
  New York (G-9669)
▼ Combe Incorporated .... C 914 694-5454
  White Plains (G-17095)
Cosco Enterprises Inc .... F 718 383-4488
  Ridgewood (G-14104)
▼ Cpac Inc .... E 585 382-3223
  Leicester (G-7420)
▲ Crosstex International Inc .... D 631 582-6777
  Hauppauge (G-6058)
Ecolab Inc .... F 716 683-6298
  Cheektowaga (G-3569)
Emulso Corp .... G 716 854-2889
  Tonawanda (G-16159)
Enviro Service & Supply Corp .... F 347 838-6500
  Staten Island (G-15671)
Gfl USA Inc .... G 917 297-8701
  Brooklyn (G-2022)
Glissen Chemical Co Inc .... E 718 436-4200
  Brooklyn (G-2028)
Greenmaker Industries LLC .... F 866 684-7800
  Farmingdale (G-5002)
▲ H & H Laboratories Inc .... F 718 624-8041
  Brooklyn (G-2057)
H & H Laboratories Inc .... G 718 624-8041
  Brooklyn (G-2058)
▲ Ilex Consumer Pdts Group LLC ..... F 410 897-0701
  Irvington (G-6772)
Jayen Chemical Supplies Inc .... G 516 933-3311
  Plainview (G-13611)
◆ King Research Inc .... E 718 788-0122
  Brooklyn (G-2172)
L S Z Inc .... G 914 948-4040
  White Plains (G-17133)
Marietta Corporation .... B 607 753-0982
  Cortland (G-4034)
Maybelline Inc .... A 212 885-1310
  New York (G-11190)
▲ Medtech Products Inc .... F 914 524-6810
  Tarrytown (G-16096)
Monroe Fluid Technology Inc .... G 585 392-3434
  Hilton (G-6418)
Prestige Brands Holdings Inc .... D 914 524-6800
  Tarrytown (G-16101)
Pro-Line Solutions Inc .... G 914 664-0002
  Mount Vernon (G-8719)
▲ Robert Racine .... E 518 677-0224
  Cambridge (G-3309)
Ronbar Laboratories Inc .... F 718 937-6755
  Long Island City (G-7864)
S & S Soap Co Inc .... E 718 585-2900
  Bronx (G-1444)
Sabon Management LLC .... F 212 982-0968
  New York (G-11951)
Schneider M Soap & Chemical Co .... G 718 389-1000
  Ridgewood (G-14124)
Sunfeather Natural Soap Co Inc .... G 315 265-1776
  Potsdam (G-13885)
▲ T S Pink Corp .... F 607 432-1100
  Oneonta (G-13194)

2842 Spec Cleaning, Polishing & Sanitation Preparations

Adirondack Waste MGT Inc .... G 518 585-2224
  Ticonderoga (G-16125)
▲ Aireactor Inc .... F 718 326-2433
  Maspeth (G-8113)
American Wax Company Inc .... F 718 392-8080
  Long Island City (G-7658)
Arrow Chemical Corp .... F 516 377-7770
  Freeport (G-5389)
ATW Resources LLC .... G 212 994-0600
  New York (G-9261)
▲ Bennett Manufacturing Co Inc .... C 716 937-9161
  Alden (G-175)
Bono Sawdust Supply Co Inc .... G 718 446-1374
  Corona (G-3993)
Caltex International Ltd .... E 315 425-1040
  Syracuse (G-15883)
◆ Car-Freshner Corporation .... C 315 788-6250
  Watertown (G-16641)
Car-Freshner Corporation .... D 315 788-6250
  Watertown (G-16642)
Castoleum Corporation .... F 914 664-5877
  Mount Vernon (G-8670)
Chem-Puter Friendly Inc .... E 631 331-2259
  Mount Sinai (G-8654)
▲ Chemclean Corporation .... E 718 525-4500
  Jamaica (G-6901)
City of New York .... C 718 236-2693
  Brooklyn (G-1783)
Clean All of Syracuse LLC .... G 315 472-9189
  Syracuse (G-15897)
Cleanse TEC .... E 718 346-9111
  Brooklyn (G-1788)
▲ Colgate-Palmolive Company .... A 212 310-2000
  New York (G-9667)
Collinite Corporation .... G 315 732-2282
  Utica (G-16313)
Comfort Wax Incorporated .... F 718 204-7028
  Astoria (G-434)
Connie French Cleaners Inc .... G 516 487-1343
  Great Neck (G-5801)
Connies Laundry .... G 716 822-2800
  Buffalo (G-2886)
Conrad Blasius Equipment Co .... G 516 753-1200
  Plainview (G-13590)
County Waste Management Inc .... G 914 592-5007
  Harrison (G-5981)
▼ Cpac Inc .... E 585 382-3223
  Leicester (G-7420)
▲ Crescent Marketing Inc .... C 716 337-0145
  North Collins (G-12927)
▲ Crosstex International Inc .... D 631 582-6777
  Hauppauge (G-6058)
Emulso Corp .... G 716 854-2889
  Tonawanda (G-16159)
Enviro Service & Supply Corp .... F 347 838-6500
  Staten Island (G-15671)
FBC Chemical Corporation .... G 716 681-1581
  Lancaster (G-7315)
Finger Lakes Chemicals Inc .... E 585 454-4760
  Rochester (G-14370)
Four Sasons Multi-Services Inc .... G 347 843-6262
  Bronx (G-1336)
George Basch Co Inc .... F 516 378-8100
  North Bellmore (G-12921)
▲ Gliptone Manufacturing Inc .... F 631 285-7250
  Ronkonkoma (G-14904)
Greenmaker Industries LLC .... F 866 684-7800
  Farmingdale (G-5002)
Griffin Chemical Company LLC .... G 716 693-2465
  North Tonawanda (G-12976)
Grillbot LLC .... G 646 258-5639
  New York (G-10364)
James Richard Specialty Chem .... G 914 478-7500
  Hastings On Hudson (G-6004)
◆ King Research Inc .... E 718 788-0122
  Brooklyn (G-2172)
Laundress Inc .... F 212 209-0074
  New York (G-10937)
Lb Laundry Inc .... G 347 399-8030
  Flushing (G-5264)
Mdi Holdings LLC .... A 212 559-1127
  New York (G-11203)
◆ Micro Powders Inc .... E 914 332-6400
  Tarrytown (G-16097)
Mirandy Products Ltd .... E 516 489-6800
  South Hempstead (G-15530)
Noble Pine Products Co Inc .... G 914 664-5877
  Mount Vernon (G-8710)
Nuvite Chemical Compounds Corp .... F 718 383-8351
  Brooklyn (G-2380)
Olin Chlor Alkali Logistics .... C 716 278-6411
  Niagara Falls (G-12857)
P S M Group Inc .... E 716 532-6686
  Forestville (G-5335)
Premier Brands of America Inc .... E 718 325-3000
  Mount Vernon (G-8718)
▲ Premier Brands of America Inc ..... C 914 667-6200
  Mount Vernon (G-8717)
▲ Progressive Products LLC .... G 914 417-6022
  Rye Brook (G-15074)
▲ Rochester Midland Corporation ..... C 585 336-2200
  Rochester (G-14643)
Royce Associates A Ltd Partnr .... E 516 367-6298
  Jericho (G-7083)
▲ Safetec of America Inc .... D 716 895-1822
  Buffalo (G-3173)
Scully Sanitation .... G 315 899-8996
  West Edmeston (G-16843)
Sensor & Decontamination Inc .... F 301 526-8389
  Binghamton (G-950)
Simply Amazing Enterprises Inc .... G 631 503-6452
  Melville (G-8355)
Solvents Company Inc .... F 631 595-9300
  Kingston (G-7210)
Spic and Span Company .... G 914 524-6823
  Tarrytown (G-16107)
Spongebath LLC .... G 917 475-1347
  Astoria (G-458)
Spray Nine Corporation .... D 800 477-7299
  Johnstown (G-7128)
◆ Strahl & Pitsch Inc .... E 631 669-0175
  West Babylon (G-16833)
◆ Synco Chemical Corporation .... E 631 567-5300
  Bohemia (G-1140)
Tjb Sunshine Enterprises .... F 518 384-6483
  Ballston Lake (G-588)
Topps-All Products of Yonkers .... F 914 968-4226
  Yonkers (G-17491)
▲ Tribology Inc .... E 631 345-3000
  Yaphank (G-17405)
TWI-Laq Industries Inc .... E 718 638-5860
  Bronx (G-1482)
U S Plychmical Overseas Corp .... E 845 356-5530
  Chestnut Ridge (G-3627)
◆ Us Nonwovens Corp .... C 631 952-0100
  Brentwood (G-1199)
US Polychemical Holding Corp .... E 845 356-5530
  Spring Valley (G-15607)
▲ Walter G Legge Company Inc .... G 914 737-5040
  Peekskill (G-13485)
Wedding Gown Preservation Co .... D 607 748-7999
  Endicott (G-4834)

2843 Surface Active & Finishing Agents, Sulfonated Oils

▲ Androme Leather Inc .... F 518 773-7945
  Gloversville (G-5706)
BASF Corporation .... B 914 785-2000
  Tarrytown (G-16087)
Bigsky Technologies LLC .... G 585 218-9499
  Rochester (G-14231)
Comander Terminals LLC .... F 516 922-7600
  Oyster Bay (G-13368)
Halmark Architectural Finshg .... E 718 272-1831
  Brooklyn (G-2063)
Momentive Performance Mtls Inc ...... D 914 784-4807
  Tarrytown (G-16098)
Suit-Kote Corporation .... F 716 683-8850
  Buffalo (G-3200)

SIC SECTION
28 CHEMICALS AND ALLIED PRODUCTS

2844 Perfumes, Cosmetics & Toilet Preparations

▲ **3lab Inc** .... F 201 567-9100
New York *(G-8974)*

Abbe Laboratories Inc .... F 631 756-2223
Farmingdale *(G-4929)*

AEP Environmental LLC .... F 716 446-0739
Buffalo *(G-2801)*

Alan F Bourguet .... F 516 883-4315
Port Washington *(G-13797)*

▲ **Albion Cosmetics Inc** .... G 212 869-1052
New York *(G-9075)*

Alexandria Professional LLC .... G 800 957-8427
Williamsville *(G-17232)*

◆ **All Cultures Inc** .... E 631 293-3143
Greenlawn *(G-5872)*

▲ **Allan John Company** .... F 212 940-2210
New York *(G-9086)*

◆ **Apple Beauty Inc** .... G 646 832-3051
New York *(G-9182)*

▲ **Ardex Cosmetics of America** .... E 518 283-6700
Troy *(G-16226)*

Aromasong Usa Inc .... F 718 838-9669
Brooklyn *(G-1630)*

◆ **Avon Products Inc** .... C 212 282-5000
New York *(G-9281)*

Avon Products Inc .... F 716 572-4842
Buffalo *(G-2828)*

Bare Escentuals Inc .... G 646 537-0070
New York *(G-9319)*

▲ **Becca Inc** .... F 646 568-6250
New York *(G-9341)*

Bellarno International Ltd .... G 212 302-4107
New York *(G-9349)*

◆ **Belmay Holding Corporation** .... E 914 376-1515
Yonkers *(G-17420)*

◆ **Bio-Botanica Inc** .... D 631 231-0987
Hauppauge *(G-6034)*

▲ **Bobbi Brown Prof Cosmt Inc** .... E 646 613-6500
New York *(G-9433)*

▲ **Borghese Inc** .... E 212 659-5318
New York *(G-9441)*

British Science Corporation .... G 212 980-8700
Staten Island *(G-15652)*

Brucci Ltd .... E 914 965-0707
Yonkers *(G-17422)*

▲ **Bycmac Corp** .... E 845 255-0884
Gardiner *(G-5548)*

▲ **California Fragrance Company** .... E 631 424-4023
Huntington Station *(G-6698)*

Cassini Parfums Ltd .... G 212 753-7540
New York *(G-9541)*

▲ **China Huaren Organic Pdts Inc** .... G 212 232-0120
New York *(G-9597)*

◆ **Christian Dior Perfumes LLC** .... E 212 931-2200
New York *(G-9610)*

Clark Botanicals Inc .... F 914 826-4319
Bronxville *(G-1499)*

Clinique Services Inc .... G 212 572-4200
New York *(G-9643)*

Colgat-Plmolive Centl Amer Inc .... G 212 310-2000
New York *(G-9666)*

▲ **Colgate-Palmolive Company** .... A 212 310-2000
New York *(G-9667)*

Colgate-Palmolive Company .... B 718 506-3961
Queens Village *(G-13975)*

Colgate-Palmolive Globl Trdg .... G 212 310-2000
New York *(G-9668)*

Collaborative Laboratories .... D 631 689-0200
East Setauket *(G-4479)*

Common Sense Natural Soap .... E 518 677-0224
Cambridge *(G-3306)*

Conopco Inc .... E 585 647-8322
Rochester *(G-14287)*

◆ **Coty Inc** .... D 212 389-7300
New York *(G-9730)*

▲ **Coty US LLC** .... C 212 389-7000
New York *(G-9731)*

Coty US LLC .... B 212 389-7000
Uniondale *(G-16291)*

▼ **Cpac Inc** .... E 585 382-3223
Leicester *(G-7420)*

Delbia Do Company Inc .... F 718 585-2226
Bronx *(G-1313)*

◆ **Delbia Do Company Inc** .... G 718 585-2226
Bronx *(G-1312)*

▲ **Dermatech Labs Inc** .... F 631 225-1700
Lindenhurst *(G-7461)*

Distribio USA LLC .... G 212 989-6077
New York *(G-9887)*

Doctor Bronze Solar Potions .... E 516 775-4974
Elmont *(G-4718)*

▼ **Dr Miracles Inc** .... F 212 481-3584
Purchase *(G-13956)*

Drt Laboratories LLC .... G 845 547-2034
Airmont *(G-14)*

◆ **EL Erman International Ltd** .... G 212 444-9440
Brooklyn *(G-1909)*

Elias Fragrances Inc .... F 718 693-6400
Rye Brook *(G-15070)*

▲ **Elite Parfums Ltd** .... D 212 983-2640
New York *(G-10007)*

Epic Beauty Co LLC .... G 212 327-3059
New York *(G-10049)*

◆ **Essie Cosmetics Ltd** .... D 212 818-1500
New York *(G-10067)*

Estee Lauder Companies Inc .... A 917 606-3240
New York *(G-10068)*

Estee Lauder Companies Inc .... A 212 572-4200
New York *(G-10069)*

◆ **Estee Lauder Companies Inc** .... A 212 572-4200
New York *(G-10070)*

Estee Lauder Companies Inc .... A 212 572-4015
Melville *(G-8315)*

Estee Lauder Companies Inc .... A 646 602-7590
New York *(G-10071)*

▲ **Estee Lauder Inc** .... A 212 572-4200
New York *(G-10072)*

Estee Lauder Inc .... D 631 531-1000
Melville *(G-8316)*

Estee Lauder Inc .... C 631 454-7000
Melville *(G-8317)*

Estee Lauder Inc .... D 212 756-4800
New York *(G-10073)*

▲ **Estee Lauder International Inc** .... G 212 572-4200
New York *(G-10074)*

◆ **Eternal Love Parfums Corp** .... G 516 921-6100
Syosset *(G-15821)*

Ex-It Medical Devices Inc .... G 212 653-0637
New York *(G-10098)*

Exquis LLC .... F 845 537-5380
Harriman *(G-5971)*

▲ **F L Demeter Inc** .... E 516 487-5187
Great Neck *(G-5808)*

▼ **Flavormatic Industries Inc** .... E 845 297-9100
Wappingers Falls *(G-16567)*

FMC International Ltd .... G 914 935-0918
Port Chester *(G-13746)*

▲ **Forsythe Cosmetic Group Ltd** .... D 516 239-4200
Freeport *(G-5400)*

▲ **Four Paws Products Ltd** .... D 631 436-7421
Ronkonkoma *(G-14902)*

▲ **Fragrance Acquisitions LLC** .... D 845 534-9172
Newburgh *(G-12755)*

Fragrance Outlet Inc .... F 845 928-1408
Central Valley *(G-3523)*

Fsr Beauty Ltd .... G 212 447-0036
New York *(G-10217)*

Fusion Brands America Inc .... E 212 269-1387
New York *(G-10225)*

▼ **Gassho Body & Mind Inc** .... G 518 695-9991
Schuylerville *(G-15320)*

Gfl USA Inc .... G 917 297-8701
Brooklyn *(G-2022)*

Glacee Skincare LLC .... G 212 690-7632
New York *(G-10304)*

Good Home Co Inc .... G 212 352-1509
New York *(G-10337)*

▲ **H & H Laboratories Inc** .... F 718 624-8041
Brooklyn *(G-2057)*

H & H Laboratories Inc .... G 718 624-8041
Brooklyn *(G-2058)*

◆ **Hain Celestial Group Inc** .... C 516 587-5000
New Hyde Park *(G-8837)*

Hair Ventures LLC .... F 718 664-7689
Irvington *(G-6771)*

Hax Pherceuticals Inc .... G 212 401-8695
New York *(G-10427)*

Hogan Flavors & Fragrances .... E 212 598-4310
New York *(G-10493)*

Iff International Inc .... E 212 765-5500
New York *(G-10560)*

▲ **Innovative Cosmtc Concepts LLC** .... G 212 391-8110
New York *(G-10604)*

▲ **Inter Parfums Inc** .... D 212 983-2640
New York *(G-10621)*

Intercos America Inc .... G 845 732-3900
West Nyack *(G-16919)*

◆ **Interntnal Flvors Frgrnces Inc** .... C 212 765-5500
New York *(G-10639)*

▲ **Jackel Inc** .... D 908 359-2039
New York *(G-10686)*

◆ **Jean Philippe Fragrances LLC** .... D 212 983-2640
New York *(G-10714)*

Jean Pierre Inc .... F 718 440-7349
New York *(G-10715)*

JP Filling Inc .... D 845 534-4793
Mountainville *(G-8748)*

Judith N Graham Inc .... G 914 921-5446
Rye *(G-15061)*

June Jacobs Labs LLC .... D 212 471-4830
New York *(G-10788)*

Kantian Skincare LLC .... G 631 780-4711
Smithtown *(G-15491)*

Kind Group LLC .... G 212 645-0800
New York *(G-10850)*

◆ **King Research Inc** .... E 718 788-0122
Brooklyn *(G-2172)*

▲ **Klg Usa LLC** .... A 845 856-5311
Port Jervis *(G-13788)*

▲ **Lady Burd Exclusive Cosmt Inc** .... C 631 454-0444
Farmingdale *(G-5033)*

Le Labo Inc .... E 212 532-7206
New York *(G-10942)*

Le Labo Inc .... E 646 719-1740
Brooklyn *(G-2201)*

Lechler Laboratories Inc .... E 845 426-6800
Spring Valley *(G-15591)*

Liddell Corporation .... F 716 297-8557
Niagara Falls *(G-12842)*

Lord & Berry North America Ltd .... G 516 745-0088
Garden City *(G-5517)*

LOreal Usa Inc .... B 212 818-1500
New York *(G-11035)*

LOreal Usa Inc .... B 917 606-9554
New York *(G-11036)*

LOreal Usa Inc .... E 212 389-4201
New York *(G-11037)*

LOreal Usa Inc .... G 212 984-4704
New York *(G-11038)*

LOreal Usa Inc .... B 646 658-5477
New York *(G-11039)*

▲ **LOreal USA Products Inc** .... G 732 873-3520
New York *(G-11040)*

Lornamead Inc .... D 716 874-7190
Tonawanda *(G-16177)*

◆ **Lornamead Inc** .... D 914 630-7733
New York *(G-11043)*

Malin + Goetz Inc .... F 212 244-7771
New York *(G-11121)*

▲ **Mana Products Inc** .... B 718 361-2550
Long Island City *(G-7799)*

Mana Products Inc .... B 718 361-5204
Long Island City *(G-7800)*

◆ **Marietta Corporation** .... B 607 753-6746
Cortland *(G-4033)*

Marvellissima Intl Ltd .... G 212 682-7306
New York *(G-11171)*

Maybelline Inc .... A 212 885-1310
New York *(G-11190)*

▲ **Mehron Inc** .... E 845 426-1700
Chestnut Ridge *(G-3623)*

◆ **Mentholatum Company** .... E 716 677-2500
Orchard Park *(G-13284)*

Mountain Gift and Powder Co .... G 518 327-3516
Paul Smiths *(G-13448)*

▲ **MZB Accessories LLC** .... D 718 472-7500
Long Island City *(G-7818)*

Nature Only Inc .... G 917 922-6539
Forest Hills *(G-5326)*

Naturpathica Holistic Hlth Inc .... D 631 329-8792
East Hampton *(G-4414)*

New Avon LLC .... A 212 282-8500
New York *(G-11380)*

▲ **Newburgh Distribution Corp** .... G 845 561-6330
New Windsor *(G-8945)*

Oasis Cosmetic Labs Inc .... F 631 758-0038
Holtsville *(G-6505)*

Olan Laboratories Inc .... G 631 582-2006
Hauppauge *(G-6151)*

▲ **Paula Dorf Cosmetics Inc** .... E 212 582-0073
New York *(G-11585)*

Peppermints Salon Inc .... F 718 357-6304
Whitestone *(G-17213)*

▲ **Perfume Americana Inc** .... G 212 683-8029
New York *(G-11615)*

▼ **Perfume Amrcana Whlesalers Inc** .... F 212 683-8029
New York *(G-11616)*

▲ **Perfumers Workshop Intl Ltd** .... G 212 644-8950
New York *(G-11617)*

SIC

Employee Codes: A=Over 500 employees, B=251-500
C=101-250, D=51-100, E=20-50, F=10-19, G=5-9
2017 Harris
New York Manufacturers Directory
785

28 CHEMICALS AND ALLIED PRODUCTS

▲ Peter Thomas Roth Labs LLC .... E 212 581-5800
   New York (G-11633)
Plastic & Reconstructive Svcs .... G 914 584-5605
   Mount Kisco (G-8640)
Precision Cosmetics Mfg Co .... G 914 667-1200
   Mount Vernon (G-8716)
Procter & Gamble Company .... C 646 885-4201
   New York (G-11726)
Professional Buty Holdings Inc .... F 631 787-8576
   Hauppauge (G-6173)
▲ PS Pibbs Inc .... E 718 445-8046
   Flushing (G-5284)
▲ Puig Usa Inc .... F 212 271-5940
   New York (G-11750)
Pureology Research LLC .... F 212 984-4360
   New York (G-11754)
Quality King Distributors Inc .... C 631 439-2027
   Ronkonkoma (G-14973)
Quip Nyc Inc .... G 703 615-1076
   Brooklyn (G-2467)
Redken 5th Avenue Nyc LLC .... E 212 984-5113
   New York (G-11816)
Rev Holdings Inc .... A 212 527-4000
   New York (G-11848)
Revlon Inc .... E 212 527-6330
   New York (G-11850)
▲ Revlon Inc .... B 212 527-4000
   New York (G-11851)
▲ Revlon Consumer Products Corp .... B 212 527-4000
   New York (G-11852)
▲ Revlon Holdings Inc .... D 212 527-4000
   New York (G-11853)
RGI Group Incorporated .... E 212 527-4000
   New York (G-11858)
Rimmel Inc .... G 212 479-4300
   New York (G-11873)
▲ Robell Research Inc .... G 212 755-6577
   New York (G-11888)
▲ Robert Racine .... E 518 677-0224
   Cambridge (G-3309)
Sally Beauty Supply LLC .... G 716 831-3286
   Amherst (G-260)
Salonclick LLC .... F 718 643-6793
   New York (G-11959)
Scent-A-Vision Inc .... E 631 424-4905
   Huntington Station (G-6722)
Selective Beauty Corporation .... F 585 336-7600
   New York (G-12024)
◆ Shiseido Americas Corporation .... G 212 805-2300
   New York (G-12054)
▼ Skin Atelier Inc .... F 845 294-1202
   Goshen (G-5739)
Skin Nutrition Intl Inc .... E 212 231-8355
   New York (G-12092)
Sml Acquisition LLC .... C 914 592-3130
   Elmsford (G-4785)
▼ Soft Sheen Products Inc .... E 212 818-1500
   New York (G-12117)
▲ Solabia USA Inc .... D 212 847-2397
   New York (G-12120)
St Tropez Inc .... G 800 366-6383
   New York (G-12180)
▲ Sundial Brands LLC .... C 631 842-8800
   Amityville (G-327)
Sundial Group LLC .... G 631 842-8800
   Farmingdale (G-5118)
Symrise Inc .... E 845 469-7675
   Chester (G-3618)
Takasago Intl Corp USA .... D 845 751-0799
   Harriman (G-5975)
▲ Temptu Inc .... E 212 675-4000
   New York (G-12299)
Temptu Inc .... G 718 937-9503
   Long Island City (G-7899)
▲ Thompson Ferrier LLC .... E 212 244-2212
   New York (G-12326)
▲ Tish & Snookys NYC Inc .... F 718 937-6055
   Long Island City (G-7902)
▲ Topiderm Inc .... C 631 226-7979
   Amityville (G-329)
Tula Life LLC .... G 201 895-3309
   New York (G-12421)
◆ United-Guardian Inc .... E 631 273-0900
   Hauppauge (G-6220)
▲ Universal Packg Systems Inc .... A 631 543-2477
   Commack (G-3845)
▼ Value Fragrances Inc .... G 845 294-5726
   Goshen (G-5741)
▲ Verla International Ltd .... B 845 561-2440
   New Windsor (G-8957)

▲ Victoria Albi Intl Inc .... F 212 689-2600
   New York (G-12539)
Xania Labs Inc .... G 718 361-2550
   Long Island City (G-7928)
▼ Yours Trading Inc .... G 718 539-0088
   College Point (G-3812)
▼ Yoyo Lip Gloss Inc .... F 718 357-6304
   Astoria (G-463)
▲ Zela International Co .... E 518 436-1833
   Albany (G-151)
Zotos International Inc .... B 315 781-3207
   Geneva (G-5589)

2851 Paints, Varnishes, Lacquers, Enamels

A & B Color Corp (del) .... G 718 441-5482
   Kew Gardens (G-7157)
Absolute Coatings Inc .... E 914 636-0700
   New Rochelle (G-8884)
Amsterdam Color Works Inc .... F 718 231-8626
   Bronx (G-1274)
▲ Angiotech Biocoatings Corp .... E 585 321-1130
   Henrietta (G-6292)
Anthony River Inc .... F 315 475-1315
   Syracuse (G-15855)
Atc Plastics LLC .... E 212 375-2515
   New York (G-9245)
Atlas Coatings Group Corp .... D 718 469-8787
   Brooklyn (G-1648)
B & F Architectural Support Gr .... E 212 279-6488
   New York (G-9287)
Barson Composites Corporation .... E 516 752-7882
   Old Bethpage (G-13126)
Benjamin Moore & Co .... E 518 736-1723
   Johnstown (G-7108)
Cytec Industries Inc .... D 716 372-9650
   Olean (G-13142)
Delta Polymers Inc .... G 631 254-6240
   Bay Shore (G-695)
Deluxe Paint .... F 718 768-9494
   Brooklyn (G-1853)
Designer Epoxy Finishes Inc .... E 646 943-6044
   Melville (G-8310)
▲ Emco Finishing Products Inc .... G 716 483-1176
   Jamestown (G-6993)
◆ Enecon Corporation .... D 516 349-0022
   Medford (G-8243)
Eric S Turner & Company Inc .... F 914 235-7114
   New Rochelle (G-8898)
▲ Excel Paint Applicators Inc .... E 347 221-1968
   Inwood (G-6755)
Farrow and Ball Inc .... F 212 752-5544
   New York (G-10139)
Fayette Street Coatings Inc .... G 315 488-5401
   Syracuse (G-15942)
Fayette Street Coatings Inc .... F 315 488-5401
   Liverpool (G-7519)
▲ Fougera Pharmaceuticals Inc .... C 631 454-7677
   Melville (G-8321)
G & M Dege Inc .... F 631 475-1450
   East Patchogue (G-4447)
Gabriela Systems Ltd .... G 631 225-7952
   Lindenhurst (G-7465)
Garco Manufacturing Corp Inc .... G 718 287-3330
   Brooklyn (G-2013)
General Coatings Tech Inc .... E 718 821-1232
   Ridgewood (G-14108)
General Vy-Coat LLC .... E 718 266-6002
   Brooklyn (G-2070)
▲ Heany Industries Inc .... D 585 889-2700
   Scottsville (G-15336)
Industrial Finishing Products .... F 718 342-4871
   Brooklyn (G-2104)
Inglis Co Inc .... G 315 475-1315
   Syracuse (G-15963)
Inhance Technologies LLC .... F 716 825-9031
   Buffalo (G-3009)
Insulating Coatings Corp .... F 607 723-1727
   Binghamton (G-927)
▲ John C Dolph Company Inc .... E 732 329-2333
   Schenectady (G-15271)
▲ Jrlon Inc .... D 315 597-4067
   Palmyra (G-13409)
Liberty Panel Center Inc .... F 718 647-2763
   Brooklyn (G-2216)
Masterdisk Corporation .... F 212 541-5022
   Elmsford (G-4764)
Mercury Paint Corporation .... D 718 469-8787
   Brooklyn (G-2298)
Musicskins LLC .... F 646 827-4271
   Brooklyn (G-2343)

Nautical Marine Paint Corp .... E 718 462-7000
   Brooklyn (G-2354)
Nochem Paint Stripping Inc .... G 631 563-2750
   Blue Point (G-999)
Nortek Powder Coating LLC .... F 315 337-2339
   Rome (G-14826)
◆ Paint Over Rust Products Inc .... E 914 636-0700
   New Rochelle (G-8919)
▲ Peter Kwasny Inc .... G 727 641-1462
   Hauppauge (G-6161)
Rapid Removal LLC .... F 716 665-4663
   Falconer (G-4909)
Reddi Car Corp .... E 631 589-3141
   Sayville (G-15214)
Robert Greenburg .... G 845 586-2226
   Margaretville (G-8093)
Royce Associates A Ltd Partnr .... E 516 367-6298
   Jericho (G-7083)
Si Group Inc .... C 518 347-4200
   Rotterdam Junction (G-15035)
◆ Si Group Inc .... C 518 347-4200
   Schenectady (G-15296)
▲ Sml Brothers Holding Corp .... D 718 402-2000
   Bronx (G-1457)
Starlite Pnt & Varnish Co Inc .... G 718 292-6420
   Bronx (G-1464)
T C Dunham Paint Company Inc .... E 914 969-4202
   Yonkers (G-17489)
▼ T J Ronan Paint Corp .... E 718 292-1100
   Bronx (G-1470)
◆ Talyarps Corporation .... D 914 699-3030
   Pelham (G-13496)
Talyarps Corporation .... E 914 699-3030
   Mount Vernon (G-8735)
▼ Uc Coatings Corporation .... E 716 833-9366
   Buffalo (G-3230)
Yewtree Millworks Corp .... G 914 320-5851
   Yonkers (G-17501)

2861 Gum & Wood Chemicals

Gumbusters .... G 866 846-8486
   Brooklyn (G-2056)
Naval Stores Co .... F 914 664-5877
   Mount Vernon (G-8709)
Ocip Holding LLC .... G 646 589-6180
   New York (G-11495)
Prismatic Dyeing & Finshg Inc .... D 845 561-1800
   Newburgh (G-12775)
▼ Tioga Hardwoods Inc .... G 607 657-8686
   Berkshire (G-853)
Westrock Mwv LLC .... C 212 688-5000
   New York (G-12618)

2865 Cyclic-Crudes, Intermediates, Dyes & Org Pigments

Chemours Company Fc LLC .... E 716 278-5100
   Niagara Falls (G-12804)
Crowley Tar Products Co Inc .... G 212 682-1200
   New York (G-9758)
Deep Dyeing Inc .... F 718 418-7187
   Manhasset (G-8058)
Durez Corporation .... F 716 286-0100
   Niagara Falls (G-12812)
East Cast Clor Compounding Inc .... G 631 491-9000
   West Babylon (G-16790)
F M Group Inc .... F 845 589-0102
   Congers (G-3856)
◆ Jos H Lowenstein and Sons Inc .... D 718 218-8013
   Brooklyn (G-2148)
▲ LTS (chemical) Inc .... G 845 494-2940
   Orangeburg (G-13234)
Magic Tank LLC .... G 877 646-2442
   New York (G-11106)
◆ Micro Powders Inc .... E 914 332-6400
   Tarrytown (G-16097)
◆ Mitsui Chemicals America Inc .... E 914 253-0777
   Rye Brook (G-15072)
Naval Stores Co .... F 914 664-5877
   Mount Vernon (G-8709)
Novartis Corporation .... E 212 307-1122
   New York (G-11462)
Premier Brands of America Inc .... E 718 325-3000
   Mount Vernon (G-8718)
Rand Machine Products Inc .... G 716 985-4681
   Sinclairville (G-15454)
◆ Si Group Inc .... C 518 347-4200
   Schenectady (G-15296)
▲ Sml Brothers Holding Corp .... D 718 402-2000
   Bronx (G-1457)

2869 Industrial Organic Chemicals, NEC

A and L Home Fuel LLC....F....607 638-1994
Schenevus (G-15314)
◆ Agrasun Inc....F....305 377-3337
New York (G-9059)
Aj Greentech Holdings Ltd....G....718 395-8706
Flushing (G-5223)
Akzo Nobel Chemicals LLC....G....716 778-8554
Burt (G-3268)
Akzo Nobel Chemicals LLC....F....914 674-5432
Dobbs Ferry (G-4301)
Akzo Nobel Functional Chem LLC....D....845 276-8200
Brewster (G-1208)
Ames Goldsmith Corp....E....518 792-7435
Glens Falls (G-5669)
Arcadia Chem Preservative LLC....G....516 466-5258
Great Neck (G-5791)
Arkema Inc....C....585 243-6359
Piffard (G-13546)
Avstar Fuel Systems Inc....G....315 255-1955
Auburn (G-483)
◆ Balchem Corporation....B....845 326-5600
New Hampton (G-8797)
Bamboo Global Industries....G....973 943-1878
New York (G-9312)
BASF Corporation....C....631 380-2490
Stony Brook (G-15767)
BASF Corporation....B....518 465-6534
Rensselaer (G-14045)
BASF Corporation....B....914 785-2000
Tarrytown (G-16087)
Brockyn Corporation....F....631 244-2770
Bohemia (G-1027)
Buell Fuel LLC....F....315 841-3000
Deansboro (G-4084)
Caltex International Ltd....E....315 425-1040
Syracuse (G-15883)
CAM Fuel Inc....G....718 246-4306
Brooklyn (G-1750)
Castle Fuels Corporation....E....914 381-6600
Harrison (G-5977)
Centar Fuel Co Inc....G....516 538-2424
West Hempstead (G-16851)
China Ruitai Intl Holdings Ltd....G....718 740-2278
Hollis (G-6495)
Classic Flavors Fragrances Inc....G....212 777-0004
New York (G-9636)
Collaborative Laboratories....D....631 689-0200
East Setauket (G-4479)
Comax Aromatics Corporation....E....631 249-0505
Melville (G-8304)
▲ Comax Manufacturing Corp....D....631 249-0505
Melville (G-8305)
Comboland Packing Corp....D....718 858-4200
Brooklyn (G-1793)
Consolidated Edison Co NY Inc....C....914 933-2936
Rye (G-15055)
Craftmaster Flavor Technology....F....631 789-8607
Amityville (G-283)
▲ Crown Delta Corporation....E....914 245-8910
Yorktown Heights (G-17510)
◆ Cumberland Packing Corp....B....718 858-4200
Brooklyn (G-1824)
D-Best Equipment Corp....E....516 358-0965
West Hempstead (G-16852)
Dancker Sellew & Douglas Inc....G....908 231-1600
East Syracuse (G-4523)
Danisco US Inc....D....585 256-5200
Rochester (G-14300)
Degennaro Fuel Service LLC....G....518 239-6350
Medusa (G-8285)
Dib Managmnt Inc....F....718 439-8190
Brooklyn (G-1862)
Eastman Chemical Company....D....585 722-2905
Rochester (G-14326)
Economy Energy LLC....G....845 222-3384
Peekskill (G-13476)
Enviro Service & Supply Corp....F....347 838-6500
Staten Island (G-15671)
Euro Fuel Co....G....914 424-5052
Patterson (G-13439)
Evonik Corporation....E....518 233-7090
Waterford (G-16611)
Family Fuel Co Inc....G....718 232-2009
Brooklyn (G-1956)
Fire Island Fuel....G....631 772-1482
Shirley (G-15418)
Flavors Holdings Inc....G....212 572-8677
New York (G-10178)
FMC Corporation....C....716 879-0400
Tonawanda (G-16164)
Friendly Fuel Incorporated....G....518 581-7036
Saratoga Springs (G-15153)
Friendly Star Fuel Inc....G....718 369-8801
Brooklyn (G-2007)
Fuel Energy Services USA Ltd....E....607 846-2650
Horseheads (G-6578)
Fuel Tank Environmental....G....631 902-1408
Centerport (G-3477)
Full Motion Beverage Inc....G....631 585-1100
Plainview (G-13603)
Givaudan Fragrances Corp....C....212 649-8800
New York (G-10302)
Golden Renewable Energy LLC....G....914 920-9800
Yonkers (G-17448)
Hampshire Chemical Corp....D....315 539-9221
Waterloo (G-16629)
Henpecked Husband Farms Corp....G....631 728-2800
Speonk (G-15575)
Hexion Inc....E....518 792-8040
South Glens Falls (G-15525)
Hudson Technologies Company....E....845 735-6000
Pearl River (G-13459)
▼ International Mtls & Sups Inc....G....518 834-9899
Keeseville (G-7138)
◆ Interntnal Flvors Frgrnces Inc....C....212 765-5500
New York (G-10639)
▲ Islechem LLC....E....716 773-8618
Grand Island (G-5761)
Jmg Fuel Inc....G....631 579-4319
Ronkonkoma (G-14920)
◆ Jos H Lowenstein and Sons Inc....D....718 218-8013
Brooklyn (G-2148)
JRs Fuels Inc....G....518 622-9939
Cairo (G-3273)
Kent Chemical Corporation....E....212 521-1700
New York (G-10838)
Kore Infrastructure LLC....G....646 532-9060
Glen Cove (G-5620)
Leroux Fuels....G....518 563-3653
Plattsburgh (G-13676)
Liberty Food and Fuel....G....315 299-4039
Syracuse (G-15977)
Lift Safe - Fuel Safe Inc....F....315 423-7702
Syracuse (G-15978)
Lo-Co Fuel Corp....G....631 929-5086
Wading River (G-16524)
Logo....G....212 846-2568
New York (G-11022)
Mafco Consolidated Group Inc....F....212 572-8600
New York (G-11096)
▲ Marval Industries Inc....D....914 381-2400
Mamaroneck (G-8038)
MNS Fuel Corp....F....516 735-3835
Ronkonkoma (G-14945)
Molecular Glasses Inc....G....585 210-2861
Rochester (G-14519)
Momentive Performance Mtls Inc....A....614 986-2495
Waterford (G-16615)
◆ Momentive Performance Mtls Inc....E....518 237-3330
Waterford (G-16616)
Momentive Prfmce Mtls Holdings....A....518 533-4600
Albany (G-102)
Morgan Fuel & Heating Co Inc....E....845 856-7831
Port Jervis (G-13789)
Morgan Fuel & Heating Co Inc....E....845 246-4931
Saugerties (G-15188)
Morgan Fuel & Heating Co Inc....E....845 626-7766
Kerhonkson (G-7156)
Mpm Holdings Inc....G....518 237-3330
Waterford (G-16617)
Mpm Intermediate Holdings Inc....G....518 237-3330
Waterford (G-16618)
Mpm Silicones LLC....A....518 233-3330
Waterford (G-16619)
N & L Fuel Corp....G....718 863-3538
Bronx (G-1404)
North East Fuel Group Inc....G....718 984-6774
Staten Island (G-15714)
Northeastern Fuel Corp....G....917 560-6241
Staten Island (G-15715)
Northeastern Fuel NY Inc....G....718 761-5360
Staten Island (G-15716)
Oak-Bark Corporation....G....518 372-5691
Scotia (G-15329)
Patdan Fuel Corporation....G....718 326-3668
Middle Village (G-8416)
Poly Scientific R&D Corp....E....631 586-0400
Bay Shore (G-725)
Polymer Slutions Group Fin LLC....G....212 771-1717
New York (G-11682)
Provident Fuel Inc....G....516 224-4427
Woodbury (G-17296)
Quality Fuel 1 Corporation....G....631 392-4090
North Babylon (G-12903)
Remsen Fuel Inc....G....718 984-9551
Staten Island (G-15730)
▲ Rose Solomon Co....E....718 855-1788
Brooklyn (G-2506)
Royce Associates A Ltd Partnr....G....516 367-6298
Jericho (G-7083)
S&B Alternative Fuels Inc....G....631 585-6637
Lake Grove (G-7265)
Smith & Sons Fuels Inc....G....518 661-6112
Mayfield (G-8214)
Solvents Company Inc....F....631 595-9300
Kingston (G-7210)
Southbay Fuel Injectors....G....516 442-4707
Rockville Centre (G-14800)
▲ Specialty Silicone Pdts Inc....E....518 885-8826
Ballston Spa (G-609)
Spot Certified Inc....G....212 643-6770
Brooklyn (G-2589)
▼ Sugar Foods Corporation....E....212 753-6900
New York (G-12227)
Sundial Fragrances & Flavors....E....631 842-8800
Amityville (G-328)
Symrise Inc....E....646 459-5000
New York (G-12258)
Symrise Inc....E....845 469-7675
Chester (G-3618)
Telechemische Inc....G....845 561-3237
Newburgh (G-12781)
▲ Twin Lake Chemical Inc....F....716 433-3824
Lockport (G-7622)
Unified Solutions For Clg Inc....F....718 782-8800
Brooklyn (G-2697)
▲ United Biochemicals LLC....D....716 731-5161
Sanborn (G-15128)
Wecare Organics LLC....E....315 689-1937
Jordan (G-7131)
Western New York Energy LLC....E....585 798-9693
Medina (G-8284)
York Fuel Incorporated....G....718 951-0202
Brooklyn (G-2777)
Zymtrnix Catalytic Systems Inc....G....918 694-8206
Ithaca (G-6886)

2873 Nitrogenous Fertilizers

Agrium Advanced Tech US Inc....F....631 286-0598
Bohemia (G-1009)
C P Chemical Co Inc....G....914 428-2517
White Plains (G-17091)
▼ Growth Products Ltd....E....914 428-1316
White Plains (G-17115)
Ocip Holding LLC....G....646 589-6180
New York (G-11495)
Rt Solutions LLC....G....585 245-3456
Rochester (G-14662)
Scotts Company LLC....G....631 478-6843
Hauppauge (G-6188)

2874 Phosphatic Fertilizers

International Ord Tech Inc....D....716 664-1100
Jamestown (G-7003)
Mdi Holdings LLC....A....212 559-1127
New York (G-11203)
Occidental Chemical Corp....G....716 694-3827
North Tonawanda (G-12984)
Occidental Chemical Corp....C....716 278-7794
Niagara Falls (G-12856)

2875 Fertilizers, Mixing Only

Carolina Eastern-Vail Inc....E....518 854-9785
Salem (G-15111)
Commodity Resource Corporation....F....585 538-9500
Caledonia (G-3278)
Growmark Fs LLC....F....585 538-2186
Caledonia (G-3279)
Long Island Compost Corp....C....516 334-6600
Westbury (G-17006)
Lowville Farmers Coop Inc....E....315 376-6587
Lowville (G-7939)
Scotts Company LLC....E....631 289-7444
Yaphank (G-17400)

S I C

Employee Codes: A=Over 500 employees, B=251-500
C=101-250, D=51-100, E=20-50, F=10-19, G=5-9
2017 Harris
New York Manufacturers Directory
787

2879 Pesticides & Agricultural Chemicals, NEC

Agrochem Inc ....E 518 226-4850
Saratoga Springs *(G-15143)*

Alco Industries Inc ....E 740 254-4311
Round Lake *(G-15036)*

◆ AP&g Co Inc ....D 718 492-3648
Brooklyn *(G-1615)*

BASF Corporation ....B 914 785-2000
Tarrytown *(G-16087)*

▲ Bioworks Inc ....G 585 924-4362
Victor *(G-16463)*

E I Du Pont De Nemours & Co ....C 718 761-0043
Staten Island *(G-15668)*

E I Du Pont De Nemours & Co ....C 716 879-4507
Tonawanda *(G-16157)*

FMC Corporation ....E 716 735-3761
Middleport *(G-8421)*

G & S Farm & Home Inc ....G 716 542-9922
Akron *(G-23)*

Island Marketing Corp ....G 516 739-0500
Mineola *(G-8517)*

Noble Pine Products Co Inc ....F 914 664-5877
Mount Vernon *(G-8710)*

Novartis Corporation ....E 212 307-1122
New York *(G-11462)*

2891 Adhesives & Sealants

Able National Corp ....E 718 386-8801
Brooklyn *(G-1549)*

Adirondack Spclty Adhsives Inc ....F 518 869-5736
Albany *(G-35)*

Advanced Polymer Solutions LLC ....G 516 621-5800
Port Washington *(G-13796)*

All Out Die Cutting Inc ....E 718 346-6666
Brooklyn *(G-1587)*

Alney Group Ltd ....G 631 242-9100
Deer Park *(G-4094)*

▲ Angiotech Biocoatings Corp ....E 585 321-1130
Henrietta *(G-6292)*

▲ Aremco Products Inc ....F 845 268-0039
Valley Cottage *(G-16376)*

◆ Beacon Adhesives Inc ....E 914 699-3400
Mount Vernon *(G-8666)*

Best Adhesives Company Inc ....G 718 417-3800
Ridgewood *(G-14102)*

Classic Labels Inc ....E 631 467-2300
Patchogue *(G-13417)*

▲ Continental Buchanan LLC ....D 703 480-3800
Buchanan *(G-2785)*

▲ Deal International Inc ....E 585 288-4444
Rochester *(G-14304)*

◆ Divine Brothers Company ....C 315 797-0470
Utica *(G-16327)*

Hercules Incorporated ....G 718 383-1717
Brooklyn *(G-2075)*

Hercules Incorporated ....G 315 461-4730
Liverpool *(G-7522)*

Hexion Inc ....E 518 792-8040
South Glens Falls *(G-15525)*

Hudson Industries Corporation ....E 518 762-4638
Johnstown *(G-7115)*

J M Canty Inc ....E 716 625-4227
Lockport *(G-7593)*

Northern Adhesives Inc ....E 718 388-5834
Brooklyn *(G-2374)*

P C I Paper Conversions Inc ....D 315 703-8300
Syracuse *(G-16007)*

P C I Paper Conversions Inc ....E 315 634-3317
Syracuse *(G-16008)*

Polycast Industries Inc ....G 631 595-2530
Bay Shore *(G-726)*

▲ Polyset Company Inc ....E 518 664-6000
Mechanicville *(G-8229)*

PPG Architectural Finishes Inc ....G 585 271-1363
Rochester *(G-14590)*

R-Co Products Corporation ....F 800 854-7657
Lakewood *(G-7293)*

Ran Mar Enterprises Ltd ....F 631 666-4754
Bay Shore *(G-731)*

Royal Adhesives & Sealants LLC ....F 315 451-1755
Syracuse *(G-16027)*

▲ Saint Gobain Grains & Powders ....A 716 731-8200
Niagara Falls *(G-12870)*

Saint-Gobain Prfmce Plas Corp ....C 518 642-2200
Granville *(G-5781)*

Solenis ....G 212 772-0560
New York *(G-12122)*

Solenis ....G 212 204-6679
New York *(G-12123)*

Solenis ....G 212 362-1759
New York *(G-12124)*

▲ Super-Tek Products Inc ....E 718 278-7900
Woodside *(G-17357)*

Utility Manufacturing Co Inc ....E 516 997-6300
Westbury *(G-17039)*

◆ Vitex Packaging Group Inc ....F 212 265-6575
New York *(G-12557)*

Walsh & Hughes Inc ....G 631 427-5904
Huntington Station *(G-6728)*

Wild Works Incorporated ....G 716 891-4197
Albany *(G-150)*

2892 Explosives

Dyno Nobel Inc ....D 845 338-2144
Ulster Park *(G-16285)*

Maxam North America Inc ....G 313 322-8651
Ogdensburg *(G-13118)*

2893 Printing Ink

Atlas Coatings Corp ....D 718 402-2000
Bronx *(G-1277)*

Bishop Print Shop Inc ....G 607 965-8155
Edmeston *(G-4622)*

▲ Calchem Corporation ....G 631 423-5696
Ronkonkoma *(G-14883)*

Flint Group Incorporated ....E 585 458-1223
Rochester *(G-14373)*

Gotham Ink & Color Co Inc ....E 845 947-4000
Stony Point *(G-15774)*

▲ Image Specialists Inc ....F 631 475-0867
Saint James *(G-15090)*

Inglis Co Inc ....G 315 475-1315
Syracuse *(G-15963)*

Intrinsiq Materials Inc ....G 585 301-4432
Rochester *(G-14454)*

◆ Micro Powders Inc ....E 914 332-6400
Tarrytown *(G-16097)*

Millennium Rmnfctred Toner Inc ....F 718 585-9887
Bronx *(G-1397)*

▲ Specialty Ink Co Inc ....F 631 586-3666
Blue Point *(G-1000)*

▼ Standard Screen Supply Corp ....F 212 627-2727
New York *(G-12182)*

Wikoff Color Corporation ....F 585 458-0653
Rochester *(G-14763)*

2899 Chemical Preparations, NEC

Aiping Pharmaceutical Inc ....G 631 952-3802
Hauppauge *(G-6012)*

Akzo Nobel Chemicals LLC ....G 716 778-8554
Burt *(G-3268)*

Akzo Nobel Chemicals LLC ....C 914 674-5008
Dobbs Ferry *(G-4300)*

Alco Industries Inc ....E 740 254-4311
Round Lake *(G-15036)*

▲ Alonzo Fire Works Display Inc ....G 518 664-9994
Mechanicville *(G-8225)*

American Electronic Products ....F 631 924-1299
Yaphank *(G-17386)*

Anabec Inc ....G 716 759-1674
Clarence *(G-3655)*

▲ Aufhauser Corporation ....F 516 694-8696
Plainview *(G-13584)*

◆ Balchem Corporation ....B 845 326-5600
New Hampton *(G-8797)*

Barson Composites Corporation ....E 516 752-7882
Old Bethpage *(G-13126)*

BASF Corporation ....B 914 785-2000
Tarrytown *(G-16087)*

Bass Oil Company Inc ....E 718 628-4444
Brooklyn *(G-1672)*

▼ Bcp Ingredients Inc ....D 845 326-5600
New Hampton *(G-8798)*

Beyond Beauty Basics LLC ....F 516 731-7100
Levittown *(G-7425)*

▲ Bonide Products Inc ....C 315 736-8231
Oriskany *(G-13304)*

▲ C & A Service Inc ....G 516 354-1200
Floral Park *(G-5197)*

C P Chemical Co Inc ....G 914 428-2517
White Plains *(G-17091)*

Calfonex Company ....F 845 778-2212
Walden *(G-16532)*

Cargill Incorporated ....D 607 535-6300
Watkins Glen *(G-16694)*

Chromananotech LLC ....G 607 239-9626
Vestal *(G-16445)*

▲ Citrus and Allied Essences Ltd ....E 516 354-1200
Floral Park *(G-5200)*

Classic Flavors Fragrances Inc ....G 212 777-0004
New York *(G-9636)*

Coventya Inc ....G 315 768-6635
Oriskany *(G-13306)*

Crystal Fusion Tech Inc ....F 631 253-9800
Farmingdale *(G-4966)*

Cytec Industries Inc ....D 716 372-9650
Olean *(G-13142)*

Danisco US Inc ....D 585 256-5200
Rochester *(G-14300)*

◆ Divine Brothers Company ....C 315 797-0470
Utica *(G-16327)*

E I Du Pont De Nemours & Co ....E 585 339-4200
Rochester *(G-14323)*

▲ Ecological Laboratories Inc ....F 516 823-3441
Lynbrook *(G-7950)*

Engineering Maint Pdts Inc ....F 516 624-9774
Oyster Bay *(G-13369)*

Evans Chemetics LP ....D 315 539-9221
Waterloo *(G-16624)*

F M Group Inc ....F 845 589-0102
Congers *(G-3856)*

Fantasy Fireworks Display ....G 518 664-1809
Stillwater *(G-15759)*

▼ FCC Acquisition LLC ....E 716 282-1399
Niagara Falls *(G-12818)*

◆ Fireworks By Grucci Inc ....E 631 286-0088
Bellport *(G-831)*

▼ Fitzsimmons Systems Inc ....F 315 214-7010
Cazenovia *(G-3445)*

Foseco Inc ....F 914 345-4760
Tarrytown *(G-16090)*

Fppf Chemical Co Inc ....G 716 856-9607
Buffalo *(G-2954)*

▲ Geliko LLC ....E 212 876-5620
New York *(G-10265)*

Gordon Fire Equipment LLC ....G 845 691-5700
Highland *(G-6404)*

▲ Greenfield Manufacturing Inc ....F 518 581-2368
Saratoga Springs *(G-15156)*

Halfmoon Town Water Department ....G 518 233-7489
Waterford *(G-16612)*

Hampshire Chemical Corp ....D 315 539-9221
Waterloo *(G-16629)*

Hanson Aggregates PA LLC ....F 585 436-3250
Rochester *(G-14421)*

Heterochemical Corporation ....F 516 561-8225
Valley Stream *(G-16408)*

Horizon Power Source LLC ....E 877 240-0580
Glen Cove *(G-5618)*

▼ I A S National Inc ....E 631 423-6900
Huntington Station *(G-6710)*

▼ Ics Penetron International Ltd ....F 631 928-8282
East Setauket *(G-4485)*

Indium Corporation of America ....E 315 793-8200
Utica *(G-16342)*

Instrumentation Laboratory Co ....C 845 680-0028
Orangeburg *(G-13231)*

International Fire-Shield Inc ....F 315 255-1006
Auburn *(G-501)*

◆ Island Pyrochemical Inds Corp ....F 516 746-2100
Mineola *(G-8519)*

▲ Italmatch USA Corporation ....F 732 383-8309
Tarrytown *(G-16092)*

Johnson Manufacturing Company ....F 716 881-3030
Buffalo *(G-3021)*

▲ Kemper System America Inc ....E 716 558-2971
West Seneca *(G-16951)*

Kent Chemical Corporation ....E 212 521-1700
New York *(G-10838)*

Luxfer Magtech Inc ....D 631 727-8600
Riverhead *(G-14149)*

Mdi Holdings LLC ....A 212 559-1127
New York *(G-11203)*

◆ Micro Powders Inc ....E 914 332-6400
Tarrytown *(G-16097)*

Momentive Performance Mtls Inc ....D 914 784-4807
Tarrytown *(G-16098)*

Monroe Fluid Technology Inc ....E 585 392-3434
Hilton *(G-6418)*

Nalco Company LLC ....E 518 796-1985
Saratoga Springs *(G-15163)*

Octagon Process LLC ....G 845 680-8800
Orangeburg *(G-13237)*

Pure Kemika LLC ....G 718 745-2200
Flushing *(G-5286)*

PVS Chemical Solutions Inc ....D 716 825-5762
Buffalo *(G-3142)*

▲ Pyrotechnique By Grucci Inc ....E 540 639-8800
Bellport *(G-840)*

S
I
C

Real Co Inc .... G 347 433-8549
Valley Cottage *(G-16386)*
Reddi Car Corp .... G 631 589-3141
Sayville *(G-15214)*
Reliance Fluid Tech LLC .... E 716 332-0988
Niagara Falls *(G-12867)*
▲ **Rochester Midland Corporation** .... C 585 336-2200
Rochester *(G-14643)*
Roto Salt Company Inc .... E 315 536-3742
Penn Yan *(G-13519)*
Royce Associates A Ltd Partnr .... G 516 367-6298
Jericho *(G-7083)*
Safeguard Inc .... F 631 929-3273
Wading River *(G-16525)*
Solvents Company Inc .... F 631 595-9300
Kingston *(G-7210)*
▲ **Specialty Ink Co Inc** .... F 631 586-3666
Blue Point *(G-1000)*
◆ **Specialty Minerals Inc** .... E 212 878-1800
New York *(G-12152)*
Spectra Color Corp .... F 631 563-4828
Holbrook *(G-6472)*
▼ **Supresta US LLC** .... E 914 674-9434
Ardsley *(G-406)*
▲ **Tam Ceramics LLC** .... D 716 278-9480
Niagara Falls *(G-12881)*
▼ **Tangram Company LLC** .... E 631 758-0460
Holtsville *(G-6511)*
Technic Inc .... F 516 349-0700
Plainview *(G-13638)*
Topaz Industries Inc .... F 631 207-0700
Holtsville *(G-6513)*
Torre Products Co Inc .... G 212 925-8989
New York *(G-12375)*
US Salt LLC .... D 607 535-2721
Watkins Glen *(G-16698)*
Utility Manufacturing Co Inc .... E 516 997-6300
Westbury *(G-17039)*
Venue Graphics Supply Inc .... F 718 361-1690
Long Island City *(G-7913)*
Water Wise of America Inc .... G 585 232-1210
Rochester *(G-14756)*
Water Wise of America Inc .... G 585 232-1210
Rochester *(G-14757)*
◆ **Watson Bowman Acme Corp** .... D 716 691-8162
Amherst *(G-271)*
Wyeth Holdings LLC .... D 845 602-5000
Pearl River *(G-13469)*
Yiwen Usa Inc .... F 212 370-0828
New York *(G-12693)*
▲ **Young Explosives Corp** .... D 585 394-1783
Canandaigua *(G-3361)*
Yr Blanc & Co LLC .... G 716 800-3999
Buffalo *(G-3261)*
▲ **Zircar Ceramics Inc** .... E 845 651-6600
Florida *(G-5216)*

29 PETROLEUM REFINING AND RELATED INDUSTRIES

2911 Petroleum Refining

209 Discount Oil .... E 845 386-2090
Middletown *(G-8424)*
Algafuel America .... G 516 295-2257
Hewlett *(G-6307)*
▲ **C & A Service Inc** .... G 516 354-1200
Floral Park *(G-5197)*
California Petro Trnspt Corp .... G 212 302-5151
New York *(G-9500)*
▲ **Citrus and Allied Essences Ltd** .... E 516 354-1200
Floral Park *(G-5200)*
E and V Energy Corporation .... F 315 786-2067
Watertown *(G-16651)*
E-Zoil Products Inc .... E 716 213-0103
Tonawanda *(G-16158)*
Enertech Labs Inc .... G 716 332-9074
Buffalo *(G-2938)*
Ergun Inc .... G 631 721-0049
Roslyn Heights *(G-15025)*
Fppf Chemical Co Inc .... G 716 856-9607
Buffalo *(G-2954)*
Global Earth Energy .... G 716 332-7150
Buffalo *(G-2976)*
Green Global Energy Inc .... G 716 501-9770
Niagara Falls *(G-12828)*
Heat USA II LLC .... F 212 254-4328
College Point *(G-3786)*
Heat USA II LLC .... E 212 564-4328
New York *(G-10453)*
▲ **Hess Corporation** .... B 212 997-8500
New York *(G-10464)*
Hess Oil Virgin Island Corp .... A 212 997-8500
New York *(G-10467)*
Hess Pipeline Corporation .... B 212 997-8500
New York *(G-10468)*
Hudson Energy Services LLC .... G 630 300-0013
Suffern *(G-15791)*
Hygrade Fuel Inc .... G 516 741-0723
Mineola *(G-8514)*
◆ **Industrial Raw Materials LLC** .... F 212 688-8080
Plainview *(G-13607)*
Kent Chemical Corporation .... E 212 521-1700
New York *(G-10838)*
Kinetic Fuel Technology Inc .... G 716 745-1461
Youngstown *(G-17531)*
▲ **Koster Keunen Waxes Ltd** .... F 631 589-0400
Sayville *(G-15212)*
Naval Stores Co .... F 914 664-5877
Mount Vernon *(G-8709)*
Northern Biodiesel Inc .... G 585 545-4534
Ontario *(G-13206)*
▲ **Osaka Gas Energy America Corp** .... E 914 253-5500
White Plains *(G-17143)*
Performance Diesel Service LLC .... F 315 854-5269
Plattsburgh *(G-13686)*
Petre Alii Petroleum .... G 315 785-1037
Watertown *(G-16670)*
R H Crown Co Inc .... E 518 762-4589
Johnstown *(G-7123)*
Ringhoff Fuel Inc .... G 631 878-0663
East Moriches *(G-4430)*
Solvents Company Inc .... F 631 595-9300
Kingston *(G-7210)*
Starfuels Inc .... G 914 289-4800
White Plains *(G-17170)*
Suit-Kote Corporation .... D 585 268-7127
Belmont *(G-843)*
▼ **Summit Lubricants Inc** .... E 585 815-0798
Batavia *(G-649)*
Tri-State Biodiesel LLC .... D 718 860-6600
Bronx *(G-1476)*

2951 Paving Mixtures & Blocks

A Colarusso and Son Inc .... E 518 828-3218
Hudson *(G-6603)*
Albany Asp & Aggregates Corp .... E 518 436-8916
Albany *(G-37)*
All Phases Asp & Ldscpg Dsgn .... F 631 588-1372
Ronkonkoma *(G-14862)*
Alliance Paving Materials Inc .... G 315 337-0795
Rome *(G-14803)*
Amfar Asphalt Corp .... G 631 269-9660
Kings Park *(G-7169)*
Atlas Bituminous Co Inc .... F 315 457-2394
Syracuse *(G-15860)*
Barrett Paving Materials Inc .... E 315 353-6611
Norwood *(G-13040)*
Barrett Paving Materials Inc .... G 607 723-5367
Binghamton *(G-890)*
Barrett Paving Materials Inc .... F 315 737-9471
Clayville *(G-3686)*
Barrett Paving Materials Inc .... F 315 788-2037
Watertown *(G-16636)*
Bross Quality Paving .... G 845 532-7116
Ellenville *(G-4632)*
C & C Ready-Mix Corporation .... E 607 797-5108
Vestal *(G-16443)*
C & C Ready-Mix Corporation .... F 607 687-1690
Owego *(G-13351)*
Callanan Industries Inc .... E 845 457-3158
Montgomery *(G-8592)*
▲ **Callanan Industries Inc** .... C 518 374-2222
Schenectady *(G-15236)*
Callanan Industries Inc .... E 845 331-6868
Kingston *(G-7182)*
Canal Asphalt Inc .... F 914 667-8500
Mount Vernon *(G-8669)*
Cobleskill Stone Products Inc .... F 607 432-8321
Oneonta *(G-13180)*
Cobleskill Stone Products Inc .... F 607 637-4271
Hancock *(G-5962)*
Cofire Paving Corporation .... E 718 463-1403
Flushing *(G-5234)*
Cold Mix Manufacturing Corp .... F 718 463-1444
Mount Vernon *(G-8673)*
Cosmicoat of Wny Inc .... G 716 772-2644
Gasport *(G-5556)*
Deans Paving Inc .... G 315 736-7601
Marcy *(G-8091)*
Dolomite Products Company Inc .... E 315 524-1998
Rochester *(G-14316)*
Dolomite Products Company Inc .... F 607 324-3636
Hornell *(G-6561)*
Dolomite Products Company Inc .... E 585 586-2568
Penfield *(G-13498)*
Dolomite Products Company Inc .... F 585 768-7295
Le Roy *(G-7405)*
Dolomite Products Company Inc .... F 585 352-0460
Spencerport *(G-15569)*
G&G Sealcoating and Paving Inc .... E 585 787-1500
Ontario *(G-13202)*
Gernatt Asphalt Products Inc .... E 716 532-3371
Collins *(G-3817)*
Gernatt Asphalt Products Inc .... G 716 496-5111
Springville *(G-15610)*
Grace Associates Inc .... G 718 767-9000
Harrison *(G-5986)*
Graymont Materials (ny) Inc .... G 518 873-2275
Lewis *(G-7431)*
Graymont Materials (ny) Inc .... D 518 561-5321
Plattsburgh *(G-13665)*
Graymont Materials Inc .... E 518 561-5200
Plattsburgh *(G-13667)*
Hanson Aggregates East LLC .... E 585 343-1787
Stafford *(G-15621)*
Hanson Aggregates PA LLC .... E 585 624-3800
Honeoye Falls *(G-6529)*
J Pahura Contractors .... G 585 589-5793
Albion *(G-166)*
Jamestown Macadam Inc .... F 716 664-5108
Jamestown *(G-7009)*
Jet-Black Sealers Inc .... G 716 891-4197
Buffalo *(G-3019)*
John T Montecalvo Inc .... G 631 325-1492
Speonk *(G-15576)*
Kal-Harbour Inc .... F 518 266-0690
Albany *(G-93)*
King Road Materials Inc .... E 518 381-9995
Schenectady *(G-15273)*
King Road Materials Inc .... F 518 382-5354
Schenectady *(G-15274)*
Kings Park Asphalt Corporation .... G 631 269-9774
Hauppauge *(G-6105)*
Lafarge North America Inc .... E 518 756-5000
Ravena *(G-14023)*
Monticello Black Top Corp .... G 845 434-7280
Thompsonville *(G-16115)*
Morlyn Asphalt Corp .... G 845 888-2695
Cochecton *(G-3743)*
Narde Paving Company Inc .... E 607 737-7177
Elmira *(G-4696)*
▲ **Nicolia Concrete Products Inc** .... D 631 669-0700
Lindenhurst *(G-7476)*
Northern Bituminous Mix Inc .... G 315 598-2141
Fulton *(G-5472)*
▲ **Package Pavement Company Inc** .... D 845 221-2224
Stormville *(G-15780)*
Pallette Stone Corporation .... E 518 584-2421
Gansevoort *(G-5487)*
Parks Paving & Sealing Inc .... F 315 737-5761
Sauquoit *(G-15201)*
Patterson Blacktop Corp .... E 914 949-2000
White Plains *(G-17145)*
Patterson Materials Corp .... F 914 949-2000
White Plains *(G-17146)*
Pavco Asphalt Inc .... E 631 289-3223
Holtsville *(G-6506)*
▲ **Peckham Industries Inc** .... E 914 949-2000
White Plains *(G-17148)*
Peckham Industries Inc .... F 518 943-0155
Catskill *(G-3433)*
Peckham Industries Inc .... F 518 893-2176
Greenfield Center *(G-5871)*
Peckham Industries Inc .... G 518 945-1120
Athens *(G-466)*
Peckham Materials Corp .... D 914 686-2045
White Plains *(G-17149)*
Peckham Materials Corp .... E 518 945-1120
Athens *(G-467)*
Peckham Materials Corp .... F 518 494-2313
Chestertown *(G-3622)*
Peckham Materials Corp .... E 518 747-3353
Hudson Falls *(G-6649)*
Posillico Materials LLC .... F 631 249-1872
Farmingdale *(G-5084)*
Prima Asphalt and Concrete .... F 631 289-3223
Holtsville *(G-6507)*
PSI Transit Mix Corp .... G 631 382-7930
Smithtown *(G-15496)*

SIC

Employee Codes: A=Over 500 employees, B=251-500
C=101-250, D=51-100, E=20-50, F=10-19, G=5-9
2017 Harris
New York Manufacturers Directory
789

R Schleider Contracting Corp................G....... 631 269-4249
Kings Park (G-7174)
Rason Asphalt Inc..................................G....... 631 293-6210
Farmingdale (G-5097)
Rason Asphalt Inc..................................G....... 516 671-1500
Glen Cove (G-5626)
Rason Asphalt Inc..................................G....... 516 239-7880
Lawrence (G-7398)
Rochester Asphalt Materials..................G....... 585 381-7010
Rochester (G-14634)
Rock Iroquois Products Inc ....F....... 585 381-7010
Rochester (G-14655)
Seabreeze Pavement of Ny LLC ....G....... 585 338-2333
Rochester (G-14679)
Sheldon Slate Products Co Inc..............E....... 518 642-1280
Middle Granville (G-8401)
▲ Suit-Kote Corporation ....C....... 607 753-1100
Cortland (G-4046)
Suit-Kote Corporation ....F....... 315 735-8501
Oriskany (G-13314)
Suit-Kote Corporation ....E....... 585 473-6321
Rochester (G-14706)
Suit-Kote Corporation ....E....... 607 535-2743
Watkins Glen (G-16697)
Suit-Kote Corporation ....E....... 716 664-3750
Jamestown (G-7033)
Swift River Associates Inc ....G....... 716 875-0902
Tonawanda (G-16205)
Thalle Industries Inc...............................E....... 914 762-3415
Briarcliff Manor (G-1231)
Tri City Highway Products Inc...............E....... 607 722-2967
Binghamton (G-957)
Tri-City Highway Products Inc...............E....... 518 294-9964
Richmondville (G-14090)
Twin County Recycling Corp ....F....... 516 827-6900
Westbury (G-17038)
Ultimate Pavers Corp..............................E....... 917 417-2652
Staten Island (G-15750)
▲ Unilock New York Inc.........................G....... 845 278-6700
Brewster (G-1229)
Universal Ready Mix Inc.........................G....... 516 746-4535
New Hyde Park (G-8871)
Vestal Asphalt Inc ....F....... 607 785-3393
Vestal (G-16456)
Zielinskis Asphalt Inc ....F....... 315 306-4057
Oriskany Falls (G-13319)

S
I
C

2952 Asphalt Felts & Coatings

▲ Aremco Products Inc.........................F....... 845 268-0039
Valley Cottage (G-16376)
Barrett Paving Materials Inc...................E....... 315 353-6611
Norwood (G-13040)
Callanan Industries Inc...........................E....... 845 457-3158
Montgomery (G-8592)
Johns Manville Corporation...................E....... 518 565-3000
Plattsburgh (G-13673)
K-D Stone Inc ....F....... 518 642-2082
Middle Granville (G-8400)
◆ Marathon Roofing Products Inc........F....... 716 685-3340
Orchard Park (G-13282)
Peckham Materials Corp ....E....... 518 747-3353
Hudson Falls (G-6649)
▲ Polyset Company Inc.........................E....... 518 664-6000
Mechanicville (G-8229)
Savage & Son Installations LLC............E....... 585 342-7533
Rochester (G-14671)
Sheldon Slate Products Co Inc..............E....... 518 642-1280
Middle Granville (G-8401)
Spray-Tech Finishing Inc ....F....... 716 664-6317
Jamestown (G-7030)
Suit-Kote Corporation ....E....... 607 535-2743
Watkins Glen (G-16697)
Texture Plus Inc ....E....... 631 218-9200
Bohemia (G-1143)
Tntpaving...G....... 607 372-4911
Endicott (G-4831)

2992 Lubricating Oils & Greases

▼ Axel Plastics RES Labs Inc..............E....... 718 672-8300
Woodside (G-17318)
▲ Battenfeld Grease Oil Corp NY.........E....... 716 695-2100
North Tonawanda (G-12960)
▼ Battenfeld-American Inc...................E....... 716 822-8410
Buffalo (G-2835)
▼ Baums Castorine Company Inc.......G....... 315 336-8154
Rome (G-14805)
Bestline International RES Inc..............G....... 518 631-2177
Schenectady (G-15235)
▲ Black Bear Company Inc..................E....... 718 784-7330
Long Island City (G-7687)
▲ Blaser Production Inc.......................F....... 845 294-3200
Goshen (G-5732)
◆ Blaser Swisslube Holding Corp........F....... 845 294-3200
Goshen (G-5733)
Castoleum Corporation..........................F....... 914 664-5877
Mount Vernon (G-8670)
Chemlube International LLC ....F....... 914 381-5800
Harrison (G-5979)
◆ Chemlube Marketing Inc...................F....... 914 381-5800
Harrison (G-5980)
◆ Finish Line Technologies Inc ....E....... 631 666-7300
Hauppauge (G-6077)
Industrial Oil Tank Service.....................F....... 315 736-6080
Oriskany (G-13311)
▲ Inland Vacuum Industries Inc ....F....... 585 293-3330
Churchville (G-3638)
▲ Interdynamics.....................................F....... 914 241-1423
Mount Kisco (G-8631)
▲ Loobrica International Corp.............G....... 347 997-0296
Staten Island (G-15700)
Mdi Holdings LLC ....A....... 212 559-1127
New York (G-11203)
Monroe Fluid Technology Inc ....E....... 585 392-3434
Hilton (G-6418)
Noco Incorporated..................................G....... 716 833-6626
Tonawanda (G-16187)
Oil and Lubricant Depot LLC ....F....... 718 258-9220
Amityville (G-318)
▲ Ore-Lube Corporation ....F....... 631 205-0030
Bellport (G-836)
Polycast Industries Inc...........................G....... 631 595-2530
Bay Shore (G-726)
Safety-Kleen Systems Inc ....F....... 716 855-2212
Buffalo (G-3174)
▲ Specialty Silicone Pdts Inc ....E....... 518 885-8826
Ballston Spa (G-609)
Tallmans Express Lube..........................G....... 315 266-1033
New Hartford (G-8812)
▲ Tribology Inc......................................E....... 631 345-3000
Yaphank (G-17405)

2999 Products Of Petroleum & Coal, NEC

▲ Cooks Intl Ltd Lblty Co......................G....... 212 741-4407
New York (G-9717)
Costello Bros Petroleum Corp..............G....... 914 237-3189
Yonkers (G-17430)
Hh Liquidating Corp ....A....... 646 282-2500
New York (G-10471)
▲ Premier Ingridients Inc......................G....... 516 641-6763
Great Neck (G-5832)

30 RUBBER AND MISCELLANEOUS PLASTICS PRODUCTS

3011 Tires & Inner Tubes

East Coast Intl Tire Inc...........................F....... 718 386-9088
Maspeth (G-8136)
▼ Handy & Harman Ltd ....A....... 914 461-1300
White Plains (G-17120)
McCarthy Tire Svc Co NY Inc................F....... 518 449-5185
Menands (G-8375)
New York CT Loc246 Seiu Wel BF.........G....... 212 233-0616
New York (G-11397)
Roli Retreads Inc....................................E....... 631 694-7670
Farmingdale (G-5102)
Sph Group Holdings LLC.......................G....... 212 520-2300
New York (G-12162)

3021 Rubber & Plastic Footwear

▲ Anthony L & S LLC ....G....... 212 386-7245
New York (G-9168)
Crocs Inc..F....... 212 362-1655
New York (G-9755)
Crocs Inc..F....... 845 928-3002
Central Valley (G-3521)
Deckers Outdoor Corporation ....B....... 212 486-2509
New York (G-9835)
▲ Detny Footwear Inc............................G....... 212 423-1040
New York (G-9860)
Homegrown For Good LLC....................F....... 857 540-6361
New Rochelle (G-8912)
Inkkas LLC...G....... 646 845-9803
New York (G-10600)
Little Eric Shoes On Madison ....G....... 212 717-1513
New York (G-11012)
▲ Mango Usa Inc...................................E....... 718 998-6050
Brooklyn (G-2258)
Nike Inc ....E....... 212 226-5433
New York (G-11431)
Nike Inc ....E....... 631 242-3014
Deer Park (G-4181)
Nike Inc ....E....... 631 960-0184
Islip Terrace (G-6815)
Skechers USA Inc ....F....... 718 585-3024
Bronx (G-1456)
▲ Steven Madden Retail Inc.................F....... 718 446-1800
Long Island City (G-7893)
▲ Timing Group LLC ....F....... 646 878-2600
New York (G-12353)
Vans Inc ....F....... 631 724-1011
Lake Grove (G-7268)
Vans Inc ....F....... 718 349-2311
Brooklyn (G-2720)
Wallico Shoes Corp ....G....... 212 826-7171
New York (G-12583)

3052 Rubber & Plastic Hose & Belting

▲ Anchor Tech Products Corp ....E....... 914 592-0240
Elmsford (G-4733)
▲ Bedgevant Inc ....G....... 718 492-0297
Brooklyn (G-1678)
Cataract Hose Co ....E....... 914 941-9019
Ossining (G-13321)
◆ Chapin Watermatics Inc....................D....... 315 782-1170
Watertown (G-16643)
Deer Park Driveshaft & Hose ....G....... 631 667-4091
Deer Park (G-4127)
▲ Flex Enterprises Inc..........................E....... 585 742-1000
Victor (G-16477)
Habasit America Inc...............................D....... 716 824-8484
Buffalo (G-2984)
▲ Hitachi Cable America Inc.................F....... 914 694-9200
Purchase (G-13957)
Honeywell International Inc ....D....... 518 270-0200
Troy (G-16220)
▲ Mason Industries Inc ....C....... 631 348-0282
Hauppauge (G-6126)
▲ Mercer Rubber Co..............................C....... 631 348-0282
Hauppauge (G-6132)
Moreland Hose & Belting Corp..............G....... 631 563-7071
Oakdale (G-13060)
▲ Peraflex Hose Inc...............................F....... 716 876-8806
Buffalo (G-3120)
▲ Sampla Belting North Amer LLC ......E....... 716 667-7450
Lackawanna (G-7249)
▲ Standard Motor Products Inc...........B....... 718 392-0200
Long Island City (G-7884)
▲ Superflex Ltd ....E....... 718 768-1400
Brooklyn (G-2625)
Tl Group Auto Systems LLC ....G....... 315 568-7042
Seneca Falls (G-15371)
Troy Industrial Solutions........................D....... 518 272-4920
Watervliet (G-16690)
Van Slyke Belting LLC............................G....... 518 283-5479
Poestenkill (G-13726)
WF Lake Corp..E....... 518 798-9934
Queensbury (G-14014)

3053 Gaskets, Packing & Sealing Devices

A L Sealing...G....... 315 699-6900
Chittenango (G-3629)
▲ Allstate Gasket & Packing Inc..........F....... 631 254-4050
Deer Park (G-4092)
American Sealing Technology...............F....... 631 254-0019
Deer Park (G-4097)
Apex Packing & Rubber Co Inc ....F....... 631 420-8150
Farmingdale (G-4943)
Apple Rubber Products Inc....................C....... 716 684-7649
Lancaster (G-7304)
▲ Bag Arts Ltd.......................................G....... 212 684-7020
New York (G-9302)
Boonville Manufacturing Corp...............G....... 315 942-4368
Boonville (G-1165)
Commercial Gaskets New York ....F....... 212 244-8130
New York (G-9685)
▲ Everlast Seals and Supply LLC ....F....... 718 388-7373
Brooklyn (G-1941)
Frank Lowe Rbr & Gasket Co Inc ....E....... 631 777-2707
Shirley (G-15419)
Gaddis Industrial Equipment..................F....... 516 759-3100
Locust Valley (G-7631)
Garlock Sealing Tech LLC......................A....... 315 597-4811
Palmyra (G-13407)
GM Components Holdings LLC ....D....... 716 439-2402
Lockport (G-7591)
Hollingsworth & Vose Company............C....... 518 695-8000
Greenwich (G-5889)
Interface Performance Mtls Inc.............C....... 315 592-8100
Fulton (G-5462)

Interface Performance Mtls Inc..........D....... 518 686-3400
  Hoosick Falls (G-6540)
John Crane Inc..........................D....... 315 593-6237
  Fulton (G-5464)
▲ Make-Waves Instrument Corp..........E....... 716 681-7524
  Depew (G-4264)
Micromold Products Inc..................F....... 914 969-2850
  Yonkers (G-17467)
◆ Noroc Enterprises Inc.................E....... 718 585-3230
  Bronx (G-1412)
Premier Fixtures LLC...................D....... 631 236-4100
  Hauppauge (G-6170)
▲ Prince Rubber & Plas Co Inc..........E....... 225 272-1653
  Buffalo (G-3136)
Quick Cut Gasket & Rubber..............F....... 716 684-8628
  Lancaster (G-7335)
▲ S A S Industries Inc..................F....... 631 727-1441
  Manorville (G-8080)
Schlegel Electronic Mtls Inc...........F....... 585 295-2030
  Rochester (G-14673)
◆ Schlegel Systems Inc..................C....... 585 427-7200
  Rochester (G-14674)
Seal & Design Inc......................E....... 315 432-8021
  Syracuse (G-16036)
Sealcraft Industries Inc...............F....... 718 517-2000
  Brooklyn (G-2541)
SKF USA Inc............................D....... 716 661-2600
  Jamestown (G-7028)
Technical Packaging Inc................F....... 516 223-2300
  Baldwin (G-562)
Temper Corporation.....................D....... 518 853-3467
  Fonda (G-5317)
Thermal Foams/Syracuse Inc.............E....... 315 699-8734
  Cicero (G-3652)
Unique Packaging Corporation...........G....... 514 341-5872
  Champlain (G-3548)
USA Sealing Inc........................E....... 716 288-9952
  Cheektowaga (G-3592)
Web Seal Inc...........................E....... 585 546-1320
  Rochester (G-14758)
Xto Incorporated.......................D....... 315 451-7807
  Liverpool (G-7558)

3061 Molded, Extruded & Lathe-Cut Rubber Mechanical Goods

Apple Rubber Products Inc..............C....... 716 684-7649
  Lancaster (G-7304)
Bridgestone APM Company................D....... 419 423-9552
  Sanborn (G-15114)
▲ Camso Manufacturing Usa Ltd..........D....... 518 561-7528
  Plattsburgh (G-13657)
Delford Industries Inc.................D....... 845 342-3901
  Middletown (G-8436)
Finzer Holding LLC.....................E....... 315 597-1147
  Palmyra (G-13406)
Mechanical Rubber Pdts Co Inc..........F....... 845 986-2271
  Warwick (G-16594)
▲ Moldtech Inc..........................E....... 716 685-3344
  Lancaster (G-7327)
Ms Spares LLC..........................G....... 607 223-3024
  Clay (G-3683)
Pawling Corporation....................C....... 845 855-1000
  Pawling (G-13451)
Pawling Corporation....................D....... 845 373-9300
  Wassaic (G-16600)
Pawling Engineered Pdts Inc............E....... 845 855-1000
  Pawling (G-13452)
Pexco LLC..............................E....... 518 792-1199
  Glens Falls (G-5696)
Pilot Products Inc.....................F....... 718 728-2141
  Long Island City (G-7843)
R & A Industrial Products..............G....... 716 823-4300
  Buffalo (G-3150)
The Centro Company Inc.................G....... 914 533-2200
  South Salem (G-15537)
▲ Triangle Rubber Co Inc...............E....... 631 589-9400
  Bohemia (G-1147)

3069 Fabricated Rubber Prdts, NEC

◆ Adam Scott Designs Inc................E....... 212 420-8866
  New York (G-9024)
Advanced Back Technologies.............G....... 631 231-0076
  Hauppauge (G-6009)
▲ Apple Rubber Products Inc............E....... 716 684-6560
  Lancaster (G-7303)
Apple Rubber Products Inc..............C....... 716 684-7649
  Lancaster (G-7304)
Buffalo Lining & Fabricating...........G....... 716 883-6500
  Buffalo (G-2854)
▼ Cementex Latex Corp..................F....... 212 741-1770
  New York (G-9558)
Certified Health Products Inc..........E....... 718 339-7498
  Brooklyn (G-1770)
▲ Chamberlin Rubber Company Inc........E....... 585 427-7780
  Rochester (G-14270)
▲ Chemprene Inc........................C....... 845 831-2800
  Beacon (G-782)
▲ Chemprene Holding Inc................C....... 845 831-2800
  Beacon (G-783)
Continental Latex Corp.................F....... 718 783-7883
  Brooklyn (G-1799)
Enbi Indiana Inc.......................E....... 585 647-1627
  Rochester (G-14349)
Enviroform Recycled Pdts Inc...........G....... 315 789-1810
  Geneva (G-5574)
Eraser Company Inc.....................G....... 315 454-3237
  Mattydale (G-8212)
Finzer Holding LLC.....................E....... 315 597-1147
  Palmyra (G-13406)
Foam Products Inc......................E....... 718 292-4830
  Bronx (G-1334)
Geri-Gentle Corporation................G....... 917 804-7807
  Brooklyn (G-2021)
◆ Great American Industries Inc........E....... 607 729-9331
  Vestal (G-16449)
▲ Hampton Art LLC......................E....... 631 924-1335
  Medford (G-8247)
Idg LLC................................G....... 315 797-1000
  Utica (G-16341)
Impladent Ltd..........................G....... 718 465-1810
  Jamaica (G-6921)
Inflation Systems Inc..................G....... 914 381-8070
  Mamaroneck (G-8036)
Jamestown Scientific Inds LLC..........G....... 716 665-3224
  Jamestown (G-7012)
Kelson Products Inc....................G....... 716 825-2585
  Orchard Park (G-13277)
Kiklord LLC............................G....... 917 859-1700
  Long Beach (G-7641)
Le Chameau USA Inc.....................G....... 646 356-0460
  New York (G-10941)
Life Medical Technologies LLC..........F....... 845 894-2121
  Hopewell Junction (G-6556)
◆ Magic Touch Icewares Intl............E....... 212 794-2852
  New York (G-11107)
▲ Mam USA Corporation..................F....... 914 269-2500
  Purchase (G-13961)
▲ Mason Industries Inc.................C....... 631 348-0282
  Hauppauge (G-6126)
▲ Mercer Rubber Co.....................C....... 631 348-0282
  Hauppauge (G-6132)
Millhouse 1889 Inc.....................E....... 631 259-4777
  Northport (G-13017)
▲ Moldtech Inc.........................E....... 716 685-3344
  Lancaster (G-7327)
Newyork Pedorthic Associates...........E....... 718 236-7700
  Brooklyn (G-2371)
▲ Package Print Technologies...........E....... 716 871-9905
  Buffalo (G-3110)
Par-Foam Products Inc..................E....... 716 855-2066
  Buffalo (G-3112)
Pawling Corporation....................C....... 845 855-1000
  Pawling (G-13451)
▲ Power Up Manufacturing Inc...........E....... 716 876-4890
  Buffalo (G-3131)
▲ Prince Rubber & Plas Co Inc.........E....... 225 272-1653
  Buffalo (G-3136)
Remedies Surgical Supplies.............G....... 718 599-5301
  Brooklyn (G-2490)
Rotation Dynamics Corporation..........F....... 585 352-9023
  Spencerport (G-15573)
Rubber Stamps Inc......................E....... 212 675-1180
  Mineola (G-8535)
▼ Rubberform Recycled Pdts LLC.........F....... 716 478-0404
  Lockport (G-7614)
◆ Schlegel Systems Inc.................C....... 585 427-7200
  Rochester (G-14674)
SD Christie Associates Inc.............G....... 914 734-1800
  Peekskill (G-13482)
Seaway Mats Inc........................G....... 518 483-2560
  Malone (G-8016)
Short Jj Associates Inc................F....... 315 986-3511
  Macedon (G-7991)
Tire Conversion Tech Inc...............E....... 518 372-1600
  Latham (G-7379)
▼ Tmp Technologies Inc.................E....... 716 895-6100
  Buffalo (G-3220)
Tmp Technologies Inc...................D....... 585 495-6231
  Wyoming (G-17383)
▼ Traffic Logix Corporation............G....... 866 915-6449
  Spring Valley (G-15603)
▲ Triangle Rubber Co Inc...............E....... 631 589-9400
  Bohemia (G-1147)
▲ Turner Bellows Inc...................E....... 585 235-4456
  Rochester (G-14735)
Vehicle Manufacturers Inc..............E....... 631 851-1700
  Hauppauge (G-6222)
Wall Protection Products LLC...........E....... 877 943-6826
  Wassaic (G-16602)
Zylon Corporation......................F....... 845 425-9469
  Monsey (G-8587)

3081 Plastic Unsupported Sheet & Film

▲ Ace Canvas & Tent Corp...............F....... 631 648-0614
  Ronkonkoma (G-14848)
◆ American Acrylic Corporation.........E....... 631 422-2200
  West Babylon (G-16770)
◆ API Industries Inc...................B....... 845 365-2200
  Orangeburg (G-13218)
API Industries Inc.....................C....... 845 365-2200
  Orangeburg (G-13219)
▲ Astra Products Inc...................G....... 631 464-4747
  Copiague (G-3895)
Berry Plastics Corporation.............B....... 315 986-6270
  Macedon (G-7984)
Bfgg Investors Group LLC...............E....... 585 424-3456
  Rochester (G-14230)
Clear View Bag Company Inc.............C....... 518 458-7153
  Albany (G-64)
▲ Comco Plastics Inc...................E....... 718 849-9000
  Woodhaven (G-17305)
Curbell Incorporated...................G....... 315 434-7240
  East Syracuse (G-4520)
D Bag Lady Inc.........................G....... 585 425-8095
  Fairport (G-4853)
Dunmore Corporation....................D....... 845 279-5061
  Brewster (G-1217)
Ecoplast & Packaging LLC...............E....... 718 996-0800
  Brooklyn (G-1901)
Edco Supply Corporation................D....... 718 788-8108
  Brooklyn (G-1903)
Excellent Poly Inc.....................F....... 718 768-6555
  Brooklyn (G-1943)
Farber Plastics Inc....................E....... 516 378-4860
  Freeport (G-5397)
Farber Trucking Corp...................E....... 516 378-4860
  Freeport (G-5398)
▲ Favorite Plastic Corp................C....... 718 253-7000
  Brooklyn (G-1961)
▼ Franklin Poly Film Inc...............E....... 718 492-3523
  Brooklyn (G-2002)
Great Lakes Plastics Co Inc............E....... 716 896-3100
  Buffalo (G-2981)
Integument Technologies Inc............F....... 716 873-1199
  Tonawanda (G-16174)
◆ Island Pyrochemical Inds Corp........F....... 516 746-2100
  Mineola (G-8519)
Kent Chemical Corporation..............E....... 212 521-1700
  New York (G-10838)
Kings Film & Sheet Inc.................E....... 718 624-7510
  Brooklyn (G-2175)
Knf Clean Room Products Corp...........E....... 631 588-7000
  Ronkonkoma (G-14923)
▲ Knoll Printing & Packaging Inc.......E....... 516 621-0100
  Syosset (G-15826)
Latham International Inc...............F....... 518 346-5292
  Schenectady (G-15276)
◆ Latham International Inc.............G....... 518 783-7776
  Latham (G-7368)
▲ Maco Bag Corporation.................C....... 315 226-1000
  Newark (G-12735)
Msi Inc................................F....... 845 639-6683
  New City (G-8788)
▲ Nationwide Tarps Incorporated........D....... 518 843-1545
  Amsterdam (G-361)
Nova Packaging Ltd Inc.................E....... 914 232-8406
  Katonah (G-7133)
Nuhart & Co Inc........................G....... 718 383-8484
  Brooklyn (G-2379)
Oaklee International Inc...............D....... 631 436-7900
  Ronkonkoma (G-14958)
Orafol Americas Inc....................E....... 585 272-0309
  Henrietta (G-6297)
Pace Polyethylene Mfg Co Inc...........E....... 914 381-3000
  Harrison (G-5988)
Pacific Designs Intl Inc...............G....... 718 364-2867
  Bronx (G-1419)
▲ Plascal Corp.........................E....... 516 249-2200
  Farmingdale (G-5081)

30 RUBBER AND MISCELLANEOUS PLASTICS PRODUCTS SIC SECTION

Pliant LLC ....B 315 986-6286
Macedon *(G-7990)*
Pocono Pool Products-North ....E 518 283-1023
Rensselaer *(G-14049)*
▲ **Potential Poly Bag Inc** ....G 718 258-0800
Brooklyn *(G-2430)*
▲ **Precision Packaging Pdts Inc** ....C 585 638-8200
Holley *(G-6491)*
R & F Boards & Dividers Inc ....G 718 331-1529
Brooklyn *(G-2469)*
Rainbow Poly Bag Co Inc ....E 718 386-3500
Brooklyn *(G-2476)*
Robeco/Ascot Products Inc ....G 516 248-1521
Garden City *(G-5530)*
▲ **Royal Plastics Corp** ....F 718 647-7500
Brooklyn *(G-2513)*
Sand Hill Industries Inc ....G 518 885-7991
Ballston Spa *(G-608)*
▲ **Scapa North America** ....E 315 413-1111
Liverpool *(G-7546)*
Sentinel Products Corp ....F 518 568-7036
Saint Johnsville *(G-15098)*
▲ **Shaant Industries Inc** ....E 716 366-3654
Dunkirk *(G-4350)*
◆ **Swimline Corp** ....E 631 254-2155
Edgewood *(G-4613)*
▲ **Top Quality Products Inc** ....G 212 213-1988
New York *(G-12369)*
Toray Industries Inc ....G 212 697-8150
New York *(G-12373)*
Tri-Seal Holdings Inc ....D 845 353-3300
Blauvelt *(G-977)*
▲ **Turner Bellows Inc** ....E 585 235-4456
Rochester *(G-14735)*
Vinyl Materials Inc ....E 631 586-9444
Deer Park *(G-4224)*

3082 Plastic Unsupported Profile Shapes

Chelsea Plastics Inc ....F 212 924-4530
New York *(G-9589)*
▲ **Comco Plastics Inc** ....E 718 849-9000
Woodhaven *(G-17305)*
▲ **Finger Lakes Extrusion Corp** ....E 585 905-0632
Canandaigua *(G-3346)*
▼ **Franklin Poly Film Inc** ....E 718 492-3523
Brooklyn *(G-2002)*
Great Lakes Plastics Co Inc ....E 716 896-3100
Buffalo *(G-2981)*
Hancor Inc ....D 607 565-3033
Waverly *(G-16703)*
Howard J Moore Company Inc ....E 631 351-8467
Plainview *(G-13606)*
◆ **Mitsui Chemicals America Inc** ....E 914 253-0777
Rye Brook *(G-15072)*
▲ **Ontario Plastics Inc** ....E 585 663-2644
Rochester *(G-14550)*

3083 Plastic Laminated Plate & Sheet

▼ **ADC Acquisition Company** ....E 518 377-6471
Niskayuna *(G-12893)*
Advanced Assembly Services Inc ....G 716 217-8144
Angola *(G-378)*
Advanced Structures Corp ....F 631 667-5000
Deer Park *(G-4088)*
Allred & Associates Inc ....E 315 252-2559
Elbridge *(G-4624)*
◆ **American Acrylic Corporation** ....E 631 422-2200
West Babylon *(G-16770)*
Anthony River Inc ....F 315 475-1315
Syracuse *(G-15855)*
Architctral Dsign Elements LLC ....G 718 218-7800
Brooklyn *(G-1621)*
▲ **Blue Sky Plastic Production** ....F 718 366-3966
Brooklyn *(G-1703)*
▲ **Clear Cast Technologies Inc** ....E 914 945-0848
Ossining *(G-13322)*
Composite Systems & Tech LLC ....G 716 491-8490
Massena *(G-8192)*
Displays By Rioux Inc ....G 315 458-3639
North Syracuse *(G-12941)*
▲ **Favorite Plastic Corp** ....C 718 253-7000
Brooklyn *(G-1961)*
◆ **Griffon Corporation** ....E 212 957-5000
New York *(G-10363)*
▲ **Inland Paper Products Corp** ....E 718 827-8150
Brooklyn *(G-2108)*
Inter State Laminates Inc ....E 518 283-8355
Poestenkill *(G-13724)*
Iridium Industries Inc ....E 516 504-9700
Great Neck *(G-5817)*
Jaguar Industries Inc ....F 845 947-1800
Haverstraw *(G-6237)*
Jay Moulding Corporation ....F 518 237-4200
Cohoes *(G-3748)*
▲ **La Mart Manufacturing Corp** ....G 718 384-6917
Brooklyn *(G-2188)*
Lawrence Packaging Inc ....G 516 420-1930
Plainview *(G-13615)*
◆ **Nalge Nunc International Corp** ....A 585 586-8800
Rochester *(G-14527)*
Norton Performance Plas Corp ....G 518 642-2200
Granville *(G-5779)*
Solid Surface Acrylics Inc ....F 716 743-1870
North Tonawanda *(G-12994)*
Strux Corp ....E 516 768-3969
Lindenhurst *(G-7485)*
Synthetic Textiles Inc ....G 716 842-2598
Buffalo *(G-3206)*
▲ **Unico Special Products Inc** ....E 845 562-9255
Newburgh *(G-12783)*

3084 Plastic Pipe

▲ **Advanced Distribution System** ....D 845 848-2357
Palisades *(G-13400)*
▲ **BMC LLC** ....E 716 681-7755
Buffalo *(G-2844)*
Hancor Inc ....D 607 565-3033
Waverly *(G-16703)*
Micromold Products Inc ....E 914 969-2850
Yonkers *(G-17467)*
◆ **National Pipe & Plastics Inc** ....C 607 729-9381
Vestal *(G-16451)*
North American Pipe Corp ....F 516 338-2863
Jericho *(G-7079)*
▲ **Prince Rubber & Plas Co Inc** ....E 225 272-1653
Buffalo *(G-3136)*

3085 Plastic Bottles

▲ **Alphamed Bottles Inc** ....F 631 275-5042
Hauppauge *(G-6017)*
▼ **Capitol Plastic Products Inc** ....C 518 627-0051
Amsterdam *(G-338)*
Capitol Plastic Products LLC ....G 518 627-0051
Amsterdam *(G-339)*
◆ **Chapin International Inc** ....C 585 343-3140
Batavia *(G-627)*
◆ **Chapin Manufacturing Inc** ....C 585 343-3140
Batavia *(G-628)*
Cortland Plastics Intl LLC ....E 607 662-0120
Cortland *(G-4020)*
David Johnson ....F 315 493-4735
Carthage *(G-3413)*
Intrapac International Corp ....C 518 561-2030
Plattsburgh *(G-13671)*
Kybod Group LLC ....G 408 306-1657
New York *(G-10897)*
◆ **Nalge Nunc International Corp** ....A 585 586-8800
Rochester *(G-14527)*
Pvc Container Corporation ....C 518 672-7721
Philmont *(G-13541)*
Samco Scientific Corporation ....C 800 522-3359
Rochester *(G-14666)*
▲ **Vista Packaging Inc** ....E 718 854-9200
Brooklyn *(G-2732)*
Weber Intl Packg Co LLC ....D 518 561-8282
Plattsburgh *(G-13707)*
World Company ....G 718 551-8282
Flushing *(G-5309)*

3086 Plastic Foam Prdts

24 Seven Enterprises Inc ....G 845 563-9033
New Windsor *(G-8928)*
ABI Packaging Inc ....E 716 677-2900
West Seneca *(G-16938)*
Advanced Plstic Fbrctions Corp ....G 631 231-4466
Hauppauge *(G-6010)*
Arm Rochester Inc ....F 585 354-5077
Rochester *(G-14210)*
Berry Plastics Corporation ....B 315 986-6270
Macedon *(G-7984)*
▲ **Burnett Process Inc** ....G 585 254-8080
Rochester *(G-14252)*
C P Chemical Co Inc ....G 914 428-2517
White Plains *(G-17091)*
Calpac Incorporated ....F 631 789-0502
Amityville *(G-279)*
▲ **Cellect LLC** ....C 508 744-6906
Saint Johnsville *(G-15092)*
▲ **Cellect Plastics LLC** ....D 518 568-7036
Saint Johnsville *(G-15093)*
Chesu Inc ....F 239 564-2803
East Hampton *(G-4407)*
▲ **Chocolate Delivery Systems Inc** ....D 716 854-6050
Buffalo *(G-2872)*
Curbell Plastics Inc ....F 585 426-1690
Rochester *(G-14295)*
Dura Foam Inc ....E 718 894-2488
Maspeth *(G-8133)*
First Qlty Packg Solutions LLC ....F 516 829-3030
Great Neck *(G-5811)*
Foam Products Inc ....E 718 292-4830
Bronx *(G-1334)*
General Vy-Coat LLC ....E 718 266-6002
Brooklyn *(G-2019)*
◆ **Great American Industries Inc** ....G 607 729-9331
Vestal *(G-16449)*
Hopp Companies Inc ....F 516 358-4170
New Hyde Park *(G-8841)*
Hunter Panels LLC ....D 386 753-0786
Montgomery *(G-8595)*
▲ **Interntnal Bus Cmmncations Inc** ....E 516 352-4505
New Hyde Park *(G-8842)*
▼ **Jamestown Container Corp** ....D 716 665-4623
Falconer *(G-4904)*
Jem Container Corp ....F 516 349-7770
Plainview *(G-13612)*
▲ **Knoll Printing & Packaging Inc** ....E 516 621-0100
Syosset *(G-15826)*
Lamar Plastics Packaging Ltd ....D 516 378-2500
Freeport *(G-5408)*
◆ **Latham International Inc** ....G 518 783-7776
Latham *(G-7368)*
Latham Pool Products Inc ....E 260 432-8731
Latham *(G-7370)*
Lewis & Myers Inc ....G 585 494-1410
Bergen *(G-848)*
New York State Foam Enrgy LLC ....G 845 534-4656
Cornwall *(G-3989)*
▲ **Orcon Industries Corp** ....D 585 768-7000
Le Roy *(G-7417)*
Par-Foam Products Inc ....C 716 855-2066
Buffalo *(G-3112)*
Philpac Corporation ....E 716 875-8005
Buffalo *(G-3124)*
Pliant LLC ....B 315 986-6286
Macedon *(G-7990)*
▲ **Printex Packaging Corporation** ....D 631 234-4300
Islandia *(G-6801)*
Professional Packg Svcs Inc ....E 518 677-5100
Eagle Bridge *(G-4357)*
R D A Container Corporation ....E 585 247-2323
Gates *(G-5563)*
Rimco Plastics Corp ....E 607 739-3864
Horseheads *(G-6590)*
Saint-Gobain Prfmce Plas Corp ....C 518 642-2200
Granville *(G-5781)*
Sealed Air Corporation ....C 518 370-1693
Schenectady *(G-15294)*
Sealed Air Corporation ....C 518 370-1693
Schenectady *(G-15295)*
▲ **Shell Containers Inc (ny)** ....E 516 352-4505
New Hyde Park *(G-8861)*
◆ **Shelter Enterprises Inc** ....D 518 237-4100
Cohoes *(G-3758)*
▲ **Skd Distribution Corp** ....E 718 525-6000
Jericho *(G-7088)*
Snow Craft Co Inc ....E 516 739-1399
New Hyde Park *(G-8862)*
▲ **Soundcoat Company Inc** ....D 631 242-2200
Deer Park *(G-4212)*
Stephen Gould Corporation ....G 212 497-8180
New York *(G-12195)*
Strux Corp ....E 516 768-3969
Lindenhurst *(G-7485)*
Technical Packaging Inc ....F 516 223-2300
Baldwin *(G-562)*
▲ **Thermal Foams/Syracuse Inc** ....G 716 874-6474
Buffalo *(G-3216)*
▼ **Tmp Technologies Inc** ....D 716 895-6100
Buffalo *(G-3220)*
TSS Foam Industries Corp ....F 585 538-2321
Caledonia *(G-3283)*
◆ **W Stuart Smith Inc** ....E 585 742-3310
Victor *(G-16512)*
Walnut Packaging Inc ....E 631 293-3836
Farmingdale *(G-5140)*

SIC

SIC SECTION

30 RUBBER AND MISCELLANEOUS PLASTICS PRODUCTS

3087 Custom Compounding Of Purchased Plastic Resins

Company	Emp	Phone
Advance Chemicals Usa Inc	G	718 633-1030
Brooklyn *(G-1565)*		
◆ Ampacet Corporation	A	914 631-6600
Tarrytown *(G-16086)*		
Atc Plastics LLC	E	212 375-2515
New York *(G-9245)*		
Lahr Recycling & Resins Inc	F	585 425-8608
Fairport *(G-4860)*		
▲ Marval Industries Inc	D	914 381-2400
Mamaroneck *(G-8038)*		
▲ Polyset Company Inc	E	518 664-6000
Mechanicville *(G-8229)*		
▲ Si Group Inc	C	518 347-4200
Schenectady *(G-15296)*		
◆ Solepoxy Inc	D	716 372-6300
Olean *(G-13153)*		

3088 Plastic Plumbing Fixtures

Company	Emp	Phone
Allegany Laminating and Supply	G	716 372-2424
Allegany *(G-198)*		
An-Cor Industrial Plastics Inc	D	716 695-3141
North Tonawanda *(G-12954)*		
Bow Industrial Corporation	D	518 561-0190
Champlain *(G-3538)*		
D & M Enterprises Incorporated	G	914 937-6430
Port Chester *(G-13741)*		
▼ Darman Manufacturing Coinc	F	315 724-9632
Utica *(G-16321)*		
Gms Hicks Street Corporation	E	718 858-1010
Brooklyn *(G-2032)*		
▲ Independent Home Products LLC	E	718 541-1256
West Hempstead *(G-16855)*		
▲ ITR Industries Inc	E	914 964-7063
Yonkers *(G-17456)*		
▲ Metpar Corp	D	516 333-2600
Westbury *(G-17011)*		
On Point Reps Inc	G	518 258-2268
Montgomery *(G-8599)*		
▲ Quality Enclosures Inc	E	631 234-0115
Central Islip *(G-3508)*		

3089 Plastic Prdts

Company	Emp	Phone
3M Company	B	716 876-1596
Tonawanda *(G-16132)*		
A & G Heat Sealing	G	631 724-7764
Smithtown *(G-15481)*		
▲ A R Arena Products Inc	E	585 277-1680
Rochester *(G-14162)*		
A R V Precision Mfg Inc	G	631 293-9643
Farmingdale *(G-4927)*		
A-1 Products Inc	G	718 789-1818
Brooklyn *(G-1538)*		
▲ Abbott Industries Inc	E	718 291-0800
Jamaica *(G-6891)*		
▲ Abr Molding Andy LLC	F	212 576-1821
Ridgewood *(G-14098)*		
▲ Accessory Corporation	A	212 391-8607
New York *(G-9010)*		
Ace Molding & Tool Inc	G	631 567-2355
Bohemia *(G-1007)*		
Acme Awning Co Inc	F	718 409-1881
Bronx *(G-1262)*		
▲ Adirondack Plas & Recycl Inc	E	518 746-9212
Argyle *(G-408)*		
Albany International Corp	C	607 749-7226
Homer *(G-6515)*		
▲ Albea Cosmetics America Inc	E	212 371-5100
New York *(G-9073)*		
▲ Albest Metal Stamping Corp	D	718 388-6000
Brooklyn *(G-1576)*		
All American Precision Tl Mold	F	585 436-3080
West Henrietta *(G-16865)*		
▲ Allen Field Co Inc	F	631 665-2782
Brightwaters *(G-1238)*		
▲ Alliance Precision Plas Corp	E	585 426-5310
Rochester *(G-14189)*		
Alliance Precision Plas Corp	E	585 426-5310
Rochester *(G-14190)*		
▲ Allsafe Technologies Inc	D	716 691-0400
Amherst *(G-222)*		
Alpha Incorporated	G	718 765-1614
Brooklyn *(G-1593)*		
Aluminum Injection Mold Co LLC	G	585 502-6087
Le Roy *(G-7402)*		
Amadeo Serrano	G	516 608-8359
Freeport *(G-5386)*		
Amcor Rigid Plastics Usa LLC	E	716 366-2440
Dunkirk *(G-4331)*		
◆ American Casting and Mfg Corp	D	800 342-0333
Plainview *(G-13581)*		
American Casting and Mfg Corp	G	516 349-7010
Plainview *(G-13582)*		
▼ American Intl Trimming	E	718 369-9643
Brooklyn *(G-1602)*		
American Package Company Inc	E	718 389-4444
Brooklyn *(G-1605)*		
American Visuals Inc	G	631 694-6104
Farmingdale *(G-4941)*		
◆ Amscan Inc	C	914 345-2020
Elmsford *(G-4732)*		
An-Cor Industrial Plastics Inc	D	716 695-3141
North Tonawanda *(G-12954)*		
Anka Tool & Die Inc	E	845 268-4116
Congers *(G-3851)*		
▲ Anna Young Assoc Ltd	C	516 546-4400
Freeport *(G-5388)*		
Apexx Omni-Graphics Inc	D	718 326-3330
Maspeth *(G-8119)*		
Aquarium Pump & Piping Systems	F	631 567-5555
Sayville *(G-15203)*		
▼ Armstrong Mold Corporation	E	315 437-1517
East Syracuse *(G-4504)*		
Armstrong Mold Corporation	D	315 437-1517
East Syracuse *(G-4505)*		
Associated Materials LLC	F	631 467-4535
Ronkonkoma *(G-14873)*		
Atlas Fence & Railing Co Inc	E	718 767-2200
Whitestone *(G-17201)*		
▲ Autronic Plastics Inc	D	516 333-7577
Central Islip *(G-3485)*		
Avanti U S A Ltd	F	716 695-5800
Tonawanda *(G-16141)*		
Aztec Tool Co Inc	E	631 243-1144
Edgewood *(G-4593)*		
▲ Baird Mold Making Inc	G	631 667-0322
Bay Shore *(G-674)*		
▲ Baralan Usa Inc	E	718 849-5768
Richmond Hill *(G-14067)*		
Barton Tool Inc	G	716 665-2801
Falconer *(G-4892)*		
Benners Gardens LLC	F	518 828-1055
Hudson *(G-6609)*		
Berry Plastics Corporation	C	315 484-0397
Solvay *(G-15506)*		
Berry Plastics Group Inc	F	716 366-2112
Dunkirk *(G-4332)*		
▲ Billie-Ann Plastics Pkg Corp	E	718 497-3409
Brooklyn *(G-1696)*		
Binghamton Precision Tool Inc	F	607 772-6021
Binghamton *(G-894)*		
▼ Bo-Mer Plastics LLC	E	315 252-7216
Auburn *(G-486)*		
Bragley Mfg Co Inc	E	718 622-7469
Brooklyn *(G-1712)*		
◆ Braiform Enterprises Inc	E	800 738-7396
New York *(G-9450)*		
Brandys Mold and Tool Ctr Ltd	F	585 334-8333
West Henrietta *(G-16871)*		
Buffalo Polymer Processors Inc	E	716 537-3153
Holland *(G-6480)*		
Burnham Polymeric Inc	G	518 792-3040
Fort Edward *(G-5340)*		
Buttons & Trimcom Inc	F	212 868-1971
New York *(G-9484)*		
C & M Products Inc	G	315 471-3303
Syracuse *(G-15880)*		
▲ C & N Packaging Inc	D	631 491-1400
Wyandanch *(G-17371)*		
▲ Cambridge Security Seals LLC	E	845 520-4111
Pomona *(G-13729)*		
Capco Wai Shing LLC	G	212 268-1976
New York *(G-9518)*		
Capitol Cups Inc	E	518 627-0051
Amsterdam *(G-337)*		
Captive Plastics LLC	F	716 366-2112
Dunkirk *(G-4333)*		
Carolina Precision Plas LLC	D	631 981-0743
Ronkonkoma *(G-14885)*		
Cast-All Corporation	E	516 741-4025
Mineola *(G-8502)*		
Cast-All Corporation	E	516 741-4025
Mineola *(G-8503)*		
Cdj Stamping Inc	G	585 224-8120
Rochester *(G-14263)*		
▼ Cementex Latex Corp	F	212 741-1770
New York *(G-9558)*		
Centro Inc	B	212 791-9450
New York *(G-9567)*		
▲ Century Mold Company Inc	D	585 352-8600
Rochester *(G-14266)*		
▲ Century Mold Mexico LLC	G	585 352-8600
Rochester *(G-14267)*		
Certainteed Corporation	B	716 827-7560
Buffalo *(G-2870)*		
▲ Champlain Plastics Inc	D	518 297-3700
Rouses Point *(G-15041)*		
◆ Chem-Tainer Industries Inc	E	631 422-8300
West Babylon *(G-16783)*		
Chem-Tek Systems Inc	F	631 253-3010
Bay Shore *(G-683)*		
Chenango Valley Tech Inc	E	607 674-4115
Sherburne *(G-15389)*		
▲ Chocolate Delivery Systems Inc	D	716 854-6050
Buffalo *(G-2872)*		
Christi Plastics Inc	G	585 436-8510
Rochester *(G-14275)*		
Cjk Manufacturing LLC	F	585 663-6370
Rochester *(G-14277)*		
Clifford H Jones Inc	F	716 693-2444
Tonawanda *(G-16153)*		
CN Group Incorporated	A	914 358-5690
White Plains *(G-17094)*		
▲ Colonie Plastics Corp	C	631 434-6969
Bay Shore *(G-686)*		
Color Craft Finishing Corp	E	631 563-3230
Bohemia *(G-1038)*		
Commodore Machine Co Inc	F	585 657-6916
Bloomfield *(G-984)*		
▲ Commodore Plastics LLC	E	585 657-7777
Bloomfield *(G-985)*		
▼ Confer Plastics Inc	C	800 635-3213
North Tonawanda *(G-12967)*		
Consolidated Container Co LLC	F	585 343-9351
Batavia *(G-629)*		
Continental Latex Corp	F	718 783-7883
Brooklyn *(G-1799)*		
CPI of Falconer Inc	E	716 664-4444
Falconer *(G-4894)*		
Craftech	D	518 828-5011
Chatham *(G-3557)*		
Craftech Industries Inc	D	518 828-5001
Hudson *(G-6611)*		
▲ Crown Industries Inc	F	973 672-2277
New York *(G-9759)*		
Cs Manufacturing Limited	E	607 587-8154
Alfred *(G-193)*		
▲ CSP Technologies Inc	E	518 627-0051
Amsterdam *(G-342)*		
CT Industrial Supply Co Inc	F	718 417-3226
Brooklyn *(G-1822)*		
▲ Cubbies Unlimited Corporation	F	631 586-8572
Deer Park *(G-4124)*		
▲ Currier Plastics Inc	D	315 255-1779
Auburn *(G-490)*		
▲ Custom Door & Mirror Inc	E	631 414-7725
Farmingdale *(G-4970)*		
▲ Custom House Engravers Inc	G	631 567-3004
Bohemia *(G-1046)*		
Custom Lucite Creations Inc	F	718 871-2000
Brooklyn *(G-1827)*		
▲ Cy Plastics Works Inc	F	585 229-2555
Honeoye *(G-6523)*		
Dacobe Enterprises LLC	F	315 368-0093
Utica *(G-16320)*		
Dawnex Industries Inc	F	718 384-0199
Brooklyn *(G-1844)*		
Di Domenico Packaging Co Inc	F	718 727-5454
Staten Island *(G-15665)*		
Diamond Packaging Holdings LLC	C	585 334-8030
Rochester *(G-14306)*		
Displays By Rioux Inc	G	315 458-3639
North Syracuse *(G-12941)*		
Dortronics Systems Inc	E	631 725-0505
Sag Harbor *(G-15077)*		
Dpi of Rochester LLC	G	585 325-3610
Rochester *(G-14317)*		
Dutchland Plastics Corp	C	315 280-0247
Sherrill *(G-15405)*		
◆ E & T Plastic Mfg Co Inc	D	718 729-6226
Long Island City *(G-7722)*		
▲ E-Z Ware Dishes Inc	G	718 376-3244
Brooklyn *(G-1895)*		
East Cast Clor Compounding Inc	G	631 491-9000
West Babylon *(G-16790)*		
East Pattern & Model Corp	E	585 461-3240
Fairport *(G-4856)*		

Employee Codes: A=Over 500 employees, B=251-500
C=101-250, D=51-100, E=20-50, F=10-19, G=5-9

30 RUBBER AND MISCELLANEOUS PLASTICS PRODUCTS SIC SECTION

Eastern Enterprise Corp .... F 718 727-8600
Staten Island (G-15670)

Eastern Industrial Steel Corp .... G 845 639-9749
New City (G-8785)

Eck Plastic Arts Inc .... E 607 722-3227
Binghamton (G-909)

Egli Machine Company Inc .... E 607 563-3663
Sidney (G-15439)

▲ Elara Fdsrvice Disposables LLC ...... G 516 470-1523
Jericho (G-7066)

Em-Kay Molds Inc .... G 716 895-6180
Buffalo (G-2935)

▲ Engineered Composites Inc .... E 716 362-0295
Buffalo (G-2939)

Engineered Molding Tech LLC .... F 518 482-2004
Albany (G-78)

▲ Epp Team Inc .... D 585 454-4995
Rochester (G-14354)

Ernie Green Industries Inc .... D 585 295-8951
Rochester (G-14356)

Ernie Green Industries Inc .... C 585 647-2300
Rochester (G-14357)

Ernie Green Industries Inc .... D 585 647-2300
Rochester (G-14358)

▲ Etna Products Co Inc .... F 212 989-7591
New York (G-10078)

▲ Eugene G Danner Mfg Inc .... E 631 234-5261
Central Islip (G-3495)

Euro Woodworking Inc .... G 718 246-9172
Brooklyn (G-1938)

Europrojects Intl Inc .... G 917 262-0795
New York (G-10086)

Everblock Systems LLC .... G 844 422-5625
New York (G-10089)

◆ Excelsior Packaging Group Inc .... C 914 968-1300
Yonkers (G-17442)

▲ Extreme Molding LLC .... E 518 326-9319
Watervliet (G-16684)

Faro Industries Inc .... F 585 647-6000
Rochester (G-14368)

Fei Products LLC .... E 716 693-6230
North Tonawanda (G-12972)

▲ Felchar Manufacturing Corp .... A 607 723-3106
Binghamton (G-914)

Fiber Laminations Limited .... F 716 692-1825
Tonawanda (G-16161)

▲ Fibre Materials Corp .... E 516 349-1660
Plainview (G-13602)

▲ Finger Lakes Extrusion Corp .... E 585 905-0632
Canandaigua (G-3346)

Form A Rockland Plastics Inc .... G 315 848-3300
Cranberry Lake (G-4057)

Form-Tec Inc .... E 516 867-0200
Freeport (G-5399)

Formatix Corp .... E 631 467-3399
Ronkonkoma (G-14901)

Formed Plastics Inc .... D 516 334-2300
Carle Place (G-3388)

▲ Forteq North America Inc .... D 585 427-9410
West Henrietta (G-16878)

Frisch Plastics Corp .... E 973 685-5936
Hartsdale (G-5998)

G and G Service .... G 518 785-9247
Latham (G-7363)

G N R Plastics Inc .... G 631 724-8758
Smithtown (G-15487)

▲ Gagne Associates Inc .... E 800 800-5954
Johnson City (G-7092)

▲ Galt Industries Inc .... G 212 758-0770
New York (G-10243)

Gantz-Newman LLC .... F 631 249-0680
Farmingdale (G-4996)

▲ Gary Plastic Packaging Corp .... B 718 893-2200
Bronx (G-1341)

Gen-West Associates LLC .... G 315 255-1779
Auburn (G-497)

▲ General Composites Inc .... E 518 963-7333
Willsboro (G-17265)

▲ Genesee Precision Inc .... E 585 344-0385
Batavia (G-634)

Genpak LLC .... C 845 343-7971
Middletown (G-8442)

◆ Germanow-Simon Corporation .... E 585 232-1440
Rochester (G-14399)

Gifford Group Inc .... F 212 569-8500
New York (G-10293)

Global Marine Power Inc .... E 631 208-2933
Calverton (G-3291)

Global Security Tech LLC .... F 917 838-4507
New York (G-10321)

GPM Associates LLC .... E 585 335-3940
Dansville (G-4077)

▲ Great Pacific Entps US Inc .... E 518 761-2593
Glens Falls (G-5682)

GSE Composites Inc .... F 631 389-1300
Hauppauge (G-6087)

H & H Hulls Inc .... G 518 828-1339
Hudson (G-6616)

H Risch Inc .... D 585 442-0110
Rochester (G-14415)

Hall Construction Pdts & Svcs .... G 518 747-7047
Hudson Falls (G-6647)

▲ Hamlet Products Inc .... F 914 665-0307
Mount Vernon (G-8689)

▲ Hanger Headquarters LLC .... G 212 391-8607
New York (G-10407)

▲ Hansa Plastics Inc .... F 631 269-9050
Kings Park (G-7171)

Harbec Inc .... D 585 265-0010
Ontario (G-13203)

Hart To Hart Industries Inc .... G 716 492-2709
Chaffee (G-3534)

Hlp Klearfold Packaging Pdts .... F 718 554-3271
New York (G-10488)

Home and Above LLC .... F 914 220-3451
Brooklyn (G-2084)

Howard Charles Inc .... G 917 902-6934
Woodbury (G-17290)

Iadc Inc .... F 718 238-0623
Staten Island (G-15686)

Ilion Plastics Inc .... F 315 894-4868
Ilion (G-6741)

Illinois Tool Works Inc .... D 860 435-2574
Millerton (G-8479)

Imco Inc .... E 585 352-7810
Spencerport (G-15570)

Imperial Polymers Inc .... G 718 387-4741
Brooklyn (G-2099)

Industrial Paper Tube Inc .... F 718 893-5000
Bronx (G-1361)

◆ Ingenious Designs LLC .... C 631 254-3376
Ronkonkoma (G-14912)

Inhance Technologies LLC .... E 716 825-9031
Buffalo (G-3009)

▼ Innovative Plastics Corp .... C 845 359-7500
Orangeburg (G-13230)

Inteva Products LLC .... B 248 655-8886
New York (G-10643)

Iridium Industries Inc .... E 516 504-9700
Great Neck (G-5817)

▲ ISO Plastics Corp .... D 914 663-8300
Mount Vernon (G-8694)

J M R Plastics Corporation .... G 718 898-9825
Middle Village (G-8412)

J T Systematic .... G 607 754-0929
Endwell (G-4836)

▲ J-Trend Systems Inc .... G 646 688-3272
New York (G-10683)

Jamestown Mvp LLC .... G 716 846-1418
Falconer (G-4906)

Jamestown Plastics Inc .... E 716 792-4144
Brocton (G-1249)

Joe Pietryka Incorporated .... D 845 855-1201
Pawling (G-13450)

Johnson Manufacturing Co .... G 631 472-1184
Bayport (G-758)

JSM Vinyl Products Inc .... F 516 775-4520
New Hyde Park (G-8844)

K & H Industries Inc .... F 716 312-0088
Hamburg (G-5930)

K & H Industries Inc .... E 716 312-0088
Hamburg (G-5931)

K & H Precision Products Inc .... E 585 624-4894
Honeoye Falls (G-6532)

K2 Plastics Inc .... G 585 494-2727
Bergen (G-847)

▲ Kasson & Keller Inc .... A 518 853-3421
Fonda (G-5315)

Kc Tag Co .... G 518 842-6666
Amsterdam (G-353)

▲ Kelta Inc .... E 631 789-5000
Edgewood (G-4602)

Kenney Manufacturing Displays .... F 631 231-5563
Brentwood (G-1188)

Kernow North America .... F 585 586-3590
Pittsford (G-13566)

Kleer - View Index Co Inc .... G 718 896-3800
Woodside (G-17335)

▼ Kleer-Fax Inc .... D 631 225-1100
Amityville (G-303)

▲ Kling Magnetics Inc .... E 518 392-4000
Chatham (G-3558)

◆ Kobe Steel USA Holdings Inc .... G 212 751-9400
New York (G-10866)

▲ Koonichi Inc .... G 718 886-8338
Fresh Meadows (G-5443)

L I C Screen Printing Inc .... E 516 546-7289
Merrick (G-8387)

L K Manufacturing Corp .... E 631 243-6910
West Babylon (G-16806)

Leidel Corporation .... E 631 244-0900
Bohemia (G-1093)

M & M Molding Corp .... C 631 582-1900
Central Islip (G-3503)

M I T Poly-Cart Corp .... G 212 724-7290
New York (G-11074)

▲ Macauto Usa Inc .... E 585 342-2060
Rochester (G-14485)

▲ Major-IPC Inc .... G 845 292-2200
Liberty (G-7438)

Markwik Corp .... F 516 470-1990
Hicksville (G-6370)

▲ Marval Industries Inc .... D 914 381-2400
Mamaroneck (G-8038)

Master Molding Inc .... F 631 694-1444
Farmingdale (G-5044)

Md4 Holdings Inc .... F 315 434-1869
East Syracuse (G-4549)

Mechanical Rubber Pdts Co Inc .... F 845 986-2271
Warwick (G-16594)

Memory Protection Devices Inc .... F 631 293-5891
Farmingdale (G-5047)

▲ Mercury Plastics Corp .... E 718 498-5400
Brooklyn (G-2299)

▲ Metal Cladding Inc .... D 716 434-5513
Lockport (G-7600)

Methodsourcing Corp .... F 914 217-7276
Elmsford (G-4765)

Metropltan Data Sltons MGT Inc .... F 516 586-5520
Farmingdale (G-5051)

Mettowee Lumber & Plastics Co .... C 518 642-1100
Granville (G-5777)

Mgs Mfg Group Inc .... D 716 684-9400
Buffalo (G-3063)

Micromold Products Inc .... E 914 969-2850
Yonkers (G-17467)

Micron Powder Industries LLC .... F 718 851-0011
Brooklyn (G-2311)

Midbury Industries Inc .... F 516 868-0600
Freeport (G-5414)

Miller Technology Inc .... G 631 694-2224
Farmingdale (G-5056)

Milne Mfg Inc .... F 716 772-2536
Gasport (G-5559)

Minico Industries Inc .... G 631 595-1455
Bay Shore (G-719)

▲ Mirage Moulding Mfg Inc .... F 631 843-6168
Farmingdale (G-5057)

▲ Mold-A-Matic Corporation .... E 607 433-2121
Oneonta (G-13189)

◆ Mold-Rite Plastics LLC .... C 518 561-1812
Plattsburgh (G-13678)

Molding Decor Inc .... G 718 377-2930
Brooklyn (G-2329)

▲ Monarch Plastics Inc .... E 716 569-2175
Frewsburg (G-5451)

▲ Msi-Molding Solutions Inc .... E 315 736-2412
Rome (G-14822)

◆ Multi Packaging Solutions Inc .... E 646 885-0157
New York (G-11324)

◆ Nalge Nunc International Corp .... A 585 586-8800
Rochester (G-14527)

Natech Plastics Inc .... E 631 580-3506
Ronkonkoma (G-14949)

▲ Nathan Boning Co LLC .... G 212 244-4781
New York (G-11342)

New York Cutting & Gumming Co .... E 212 563-4146
Middletown (G-8454)

New York Manufactured Products .... F 585 254-9353
Rochester (G-14532)

Niagara Fiberglass Inc .... E 716 822-3921
Buffalo (G-3087)

◆ Nordon Inc .... D 585 546-6200
Rochester (G-14538)

▲ Northeast Windows Usa Inc .... E 516 378-6577
Merrick (G-8390)

Norwesco Inc .... F 607 687-8081
Owego (G-13357)

▲ Novel Box Company Ltd .... E 718 965-2222
Brooklyn (G-2377)

S I C

30 RUBBER AND MISCELLANEOUS PLASTICS PRODUCTS

▲ Novelty Crystal Corp ....E...... 718 458-6700
  Long Island City *(G-7826)*
Ocala Group LLC ....F...... 516 233-2750
  New Hyde Park *(G-8853)*
▲ Oneida Molded Plastics LLC......C...... 315 363-7990
  Oneida *(G-13161)*
Oneida Molded Plastics LLC..........D...... 315 363-7990
  Oneida *(G-13162)*
Oneonta Fence ....G...... 607 433-6707
  Oneonta *(G-13190)*
▲ Ontario Plastics Inc ....E...... 585 663-2644
  Rochester *(G-14550)*
P & M Safe America LLC ....F...... 718 292-6363
  Bronx *(G-1418)*
P M Plastics Inc ....E...... 716 662-1255
  Orchard Park *(G-13286)*
P V C Molding Technologies ....E...... 315 331-1212
  Newark *(G-12740)*
Pace Window and Door Corp ....E...... 585 924-8350
  Victor *(G-16495)*
Pactiv Corporation ....C...... 518 743-3100
  Glens Falls *(G-5694)*
Pactiv LLC ....G...... 847 482-2000
  Canandaigua *(G-3352)*
Pactiv LLC ....C...... 518 562-6120
  Plattsburgh *(G-13685)*
Pactiv LLC ....C...... 585 393-3229
  Canandaigua *(G-3353)*
Pactiv LLC ....A...... 585 393-3149
  Canandaigua *(G-3354)*
Pactiv LLC ....C...... 518 793-2524
  Glens Falls *(G-5695)*
Patmian LLC ....B...... 212 758-0770
  New York *(G-11579)*
Pawling Corporation ....C...... 845 855-1000
  Pawling *(G-13451)*
Pawling Engineered Pdts Inc........C...... 845 855-1000
  Pawling *(G-13452)*
Peconic Plastics Inc ....F...... 631 653-3676
  Quogue *(G-14015)*
▲ Pelican Products Co Inc ....E...... 718 860-3220
  Bronx *(G-1423)*
Peninsula Plastics Ltd ....D...... 716 854-3050
  Buffalo *(G-3118)*
Performance Advantage Co Inc...F...... 716 683-7413
  Lancaster *(G-7332)*
Perma Tech Inc ....E...... 716 854-0707
  Buffalo *(G-3122)*
Philcom Limited ....D...... 716 875-8005
  Buffalo *(G-3123)*
Phoenix Services Group LLC .....E...... 518 828-6611
  Hudson *(G-6631)*
Pii Holdings Inc ....G...... 716 876-9951
  Buffalo *(G-3126)*
Piper Plastics Corp ....E...... 631 842-6889
  Copiague *(G-3918)*
Plascoline Inc ....F...... 917 410-5754
  New York *(G-11673)*
Plastic Solutions Inc ....E...... 631 234-9013
  Bayport *(G-760)*
Plastic Sys/Gr Bflo Inc ....G...... 716 835-7555
  Buffalo *(G-3129)*
Plastic Works ....G...... 914 576-2050
  New Rochelle *(G-8920)*
Plastic-Craft Products Corp ....E...... 845 358-3010
  West Nyack *(G-16925)*
Plasticware LLC ....F...... 845 267-0790
  Monsey *(G-8577)*
Plasticycle Corporation ....E...... 914 997-6882
  White Plains *(G-17160)*
◆ PMI Industries LLC ....E...... 585 464-8050
  Rochester *(G-14586)*
Polymer Conversions Inc............D...... 716 662-8550
  Orchard Park *(G-13290)*
Polymer Engineered Pdts Inc .....D...... 585 426-1811
  Rochester *(G-14588)*
▲ Powertex Inc ....E...... 518 297-4000
  Rouses Point *(G-15043)*
▲ Ppr Direct Inc ....F...... 718 965-8600
  Brooklyn *(G-2432)*
▲ Precision Techniques Inc ....D...... 718 991-1440
  Bronx *(G-1434)*
Prestige Hangers Str Fixs Corp ...G...... 718 522-6777
  Brooklyn *(G-2440)*
▲ Prime Marketing and Sales LLC ...G...... 888 802-3836
  New York *(G-11707)*
Primoplast Inc ....F...... 631 750-0680
  Bohemia *(G-1121)*
▲ Prince Rubber & Plas Co Inc .....E...... 225 272-1653
  Buffalo *(G-3136)*

▲ Printex Packaging Corporation ....D...... 631 234-4300
  Islandia *(G-6801)*
◆ Protective Industries Inc ....C...... 716 876-9951
  Buffalo *(G-3139)*
Protective Industries Inc ....C...... 716 876-9855
  Buffalo *(G-3140)*
Pulse Plastics Products Inc ....E...... 718 328-5224
  Bronx *(G-1436)*
Pvc Container Corporation ....C...... 518 672-7721
  Philmont *(G-13541)*
Pylantis New York LLC ....E...... 310 429-5911
  Groton *(G-5901)*
▲ Q Squared Design LLC ....E...... 212 686-8860
  New York *(G-11763)*
Quality Lineals Usa Inc................G...... 516 378-6577
  Merrick *(G-8392)*
Quoin LLC ....A...... 914 967-9400
  Rye *(G-15066)*
▲ R P M Industries Inc ....E...... 315 255-1105
  Auburn *(G-515)*
▲ Rainbow Plastics Inc ....F...... 718 218-7288
  Brooklyn *(G-2475)*
Richlar Industries Inc ....F...... 315 463-5144
  East Syracuse *(G-4559)*
Rimco Plastics Corp ....E...... 607 739-3864
  Horseheads *(G-6590)*
Robinson Knife ....F...... 716 685-6300
  Buffalo *(G-3161)*
Rochling Advent Tool & Mold LP ..E...... 585 254-2000
  Rochester *(G-14654)*
▲ Roth Global Plastics Inc ....E...... 315 475-0100
  Syracuse *(G-16026)*
◆ Royal Industries Inc ....E...... 718 369-3046
  Brooklyn *(G-2511)*
Royce Associates A Ltd Partnr ...G...... 516 367-6298
  Jericho *(G-7083)*
▲ Rui Xing International Trdg Co ...G...... 516 298-2667
  Hicksville *(G-6391)*
Russell Plastics Tech Co Inc ....C...... 631 963-8602
  Lindenhurst *(G-7481)*
Rynone Manufacturing Corp ......F...... 607 565-8187
  Waverly *(G-16706)*
Sabic Innovative Plastics ....E...... 713 448-7474
  East Greenbush *(G-4404)*
Saint-Gobain Prfmce Plas Corp....E...... 518 283-5963
  Poestenkill *(G-13725)*
SAV Thermo Inc ....F...... 631 249-9444
  West Babylon *(G-16826)*
◆ Schlegel Systems Inc ....C...... 585 427-7200
  Rochester *(G-14674)*
Seal Reinforced Fiberglass Inc ...E...... 631 842-2230
  Copiague *(G-3926)*
Seal Reinforced Fiberglass Inc ...G...... 631 842-2230
  Copiague *(G-3927)*
Seaway Mats Inc ....G...... 518 483-2560
  Malone *(G-8016)*
Shamrock Plastics & Tool Inc .....G...... 585 328-6040
  Rochester *(G-14683)*
Sigma Worldwide LLC ....E...... 646 217-0629
  New York *(G-12067)*
Silgan Plastics LLC ....C...... 315 536-5690
  Penn Yan *(G-13521)*
Silvatrim Corp ....E...... 212 675-0933
  New York *(G-12075)*
▲ Skd Distribution Corp ....E...... 718 525-6000
  Jericho *(G-7088)*
Sky Dive ....D...... 845 858-6400
  Port Jervis *(G-13792)*
▲ Sonoco-Crellin Inc ....C...... 518 392-2000
  Chatham *(G-3560)*
▲ Sonoco-Crellin Intl Inc ....B...... 518 392-2000
  Chatham *(G-4561)*
▲ Southern Tier Plastics Inc ....D...... 607 723-2601
  Binghamton *(G-952)*
Space Age Plstic Fbrcators Inc ...F...... 718 324-4062
  Bronx *(G-1459)*
Space Sign ....F...... 718 961-1112
  College Point *(G-3808)*
Spotless Plastics (usa) Inc..........E...... 631 951-9000
  Hauppauge *(G-6198)*
Staroba Plastics Inc ....C...... 716 537-3153
  Holland *(G-6484)*
▲ Sterling Molded Products Inc ....E...... 845 344-4546
  Middletown *(G-8463)*
Streamline Plastics Co Inc ....E...... 718 401-4000
  Bronx *(G-1466)*
▲ Structural Industries Inc ....C...... 631 471-5200
  Bohemia *(G-1137)*
Stuart Mold & Manufacturing .....F...... 716 488-9765
  Falconer *(G-4914)*

Summit Manufacturing ....G...... 631 952-1570
  Bay Shore *(G-746)*
Summit Manufacturing ....E...... 631 952-1570
  Bay Shore *(G-747)*
Superior Plus Cnstr Pdts Corp ....F...... 315 463-5144
  East Syracuse *(G-4569)*
Supreme Poultry Inc ....G...... 718 472-0300
  Long Island City *(G-7897)*
▲ Surprise Plastics Inc ....E...... 718 492-6355
  Brooklyn *(G-2634)*
Sweet Tooth Enterprises LLC .....E...... 631 752-2888
  West Babylon *(G-16835)*
Syntec Technologies Inc ....E...... 585 768-2513
  Rochester *(G-14712)*
▲ Syracuse Plastics LLC ....C...... 315 637-9881
  Liverpool *(G-7551)*
T A Tool & Molding Inc ....E...... 631 293-0172
  Farmingdale *(G-5123)*
Termatec Molding Inc ....E...... 315 483-4150
  Sodus *(G-15505)*
◆ Tessy Plastics Corp ....B...... 315 689-3924
  Skaneateles *(G-15466)*
Teva Womens Health Inc ....F...... 716 693-6230
  North Tonawanda *(G-13002)*
▲ Thermold Corporation ....C...... 315 697-3924
  Canastota *(G-3374)*
Think Green Junk Removal Inc ...G...... 845 297-7771
  Wappingers Falls *(G-16577)*
▲ Tii Technologies Inc ....E...... 516 364-9300
  Edgewood *(G-4616)*
Titherington Design & Mfg ....F...... 518 324-2205
  Plattsburgh *(G-13704)*
▲ Toolroom Express Inc ....D...... 607 723-5373
  Conklin *(G-3876)*
Toray Industries Inc ....G...... 212 697-8150
  New York *(G-12373)*
▲ Transpo Industries Inc ....E...... 914 636-1000
  New Rochelle *(G-8926)*
Tri-State Window Factory Corp ...D...... 631 667-8600
  Deer Park *(G-4218)*
Trimac Molding Services ....G...... 607 967-2900
  Bainbridge *(G-555)*
Tulip Molded Plastics Corp ....D...... 716 282-1261
  Niagara Falls *(G-12885)*
Tully Products Inc ....G...... 716 773-3166
  Grand Island *(G-5771)*
Turbo Plastics Corp Inc ....F...... 631 345-9768
  Yaphank *(G-17406)*
▲ TVI Imports LLC ....G...... 631 793-3077
  Massapequa Park *(G-8190)*
◆ Ultrafab Inc ....C...... 585 924-2186
  Farmington *(G-5158)*
Unifab Inc ....E...... 585 235-1760
  Rochester *(G-14742)*
Unifuse LLC ....F...... 845 889-4000
  Staatsburg *(G-15619)*
United Plastics Inc ....G...... 718 389-2255
  Brooklyn *(G-2701)*
▲ Universal Strapping Inc ....E...... 845 268-2500
  Valley Cottage *(G-16394)*
Usheco Inc ....F...... 845 658-9200
  Kingston *(G-7223)*
▲ Van Blarcom Closures Inc.........C...... 718 855-3810
  Brooklyn *(G-2718)*
Viapack Inc ....F...... 718 729-5500
  Long Island City *(G-7915)*
◆ Viele Manufacturing Corp ....B...... 718 893-2200
  Bronx *(G-1490)*
Villeroy & Boch Usa Inc..............G...... 212 213-8149
  New York *(G-12545)*
Vinyl Materials Inc......................E...... 631 586-9444
  Deer Park *(G-4224)*
Vinyline Window and Door Inc ...F...... 914 476-3500
  Yonkers *(G-17496)*
Visitainer Corp ....E...... 718 636-0300
  Brooklyn *(G-2731)*
Vitarose Corp of America ....G...... 718 951-9700
  Brooklyn *(G-2733)*
▲ W Kintz Plastics Inc ....C...... 518 296-8513
  Howes Cave *(G-6601)*
Weather Products Corporation ...G...... 315 474-8593
  Syracuse *(G-16069)*
Window Tech Systems Inc ....E...... 518 899-9000
  Ballston Spa *(G-611)*
Zan Optics Products Inc.............E...... 718 435-0533
  Brooklyn *(G-2781)*
Zone Fabricators Inc...................F...... 718 272-0200
  Ozone Park *(G-13388)*

Employee Codes: A=Over 500 employees, B=251-500
C=101-250, D=51-100, E=20-50, F=10-19, G=5-9

31 LEATHER AND LEATHER PRODUCTS

3111 Leather Tanning & Finishing

A-1 Products Inc .... G 718 789-1818
  Brooklyn *(G-1538)*
◆ Adam Scott Designs Inc .... E 212 420-8866
  New York *(G-9024)*
▲ Androme Leather Inc .... F 518 773-7945
  Gloversville *(G-5706)*
▲ Arrow Leather Finishing Inc .... E 518 762-3121
  Johnstown *(G-7107)*
▲ Aston Leather Inc .... G 212 481-2760
  New York *(G-9242)*
▲ Baker Products Inc .... G 212 459-2323
  White Plains *(G-17082)*
C & H Cstm Bkbinding Embossing ...... G 800 871-8980
  Medford *(G-8237)*
▲ Cejon Inc .... E 201 437-8788
  New York *(G-9554)*
▲ Colonial Tanning Corporation .... E 518 725-7171
  Gloversville *(G-5709)*
▲ Corium Corporation .... F 914 381-0100
  Mamaroneck *(G-8030)*
▲ Edsim Leather Co Inc .... F 212 695-8500
  New York *(G-9984)*
Givi Inc .... G 212 586-5029
  New York *(G-10303)*
Graphic Image Associates LLC .... D 631 249-9600
  Melville *(G-8323)*
◆ Graphic Image Incorporated .... C 631 249-9600
  Melville *(G-8324)*
Hastings Hide Inc .... G 516 295-2400
  Lawrence *(G-7391)*
◆ Hat Attack Inc .... E 718 994-1000
  Bronx *(G-1351)*
Hohenforst Splitting Co Inc .... G 518 725-0012
  Gloversville *(G-5715)*
John Gailer Inc .... E 212 243-5662
  Long Island City *(G-7772)*
Justin Gregory Inc .... G 631 249-5187
  Farmingdale *(G-5020)*
Kamali Group Inc .... G 516 627-4000
  Great Neck *(G-5819)*
▲ Legendary Auto Interiors Ltd .... E 315 331-1212
  Newark *(G-12734)*
Mohawk River Leather Works .... F 518 853-3900
  Fultonville *(G-5480)*
▲ Pacific Worldwide Inc .... F 212 502-3360
  New York *(G-11553)*
▲ Pan American Leathers Inc .... G 978 741-4150
  New York *(G-11558)*
▲ Pearl Leather Finishers Inc .... D 518 762-4543
  Johnstown *(G-7120)*
▲ Pearl Leather Group LLC .... E 516 627-4047
  Great Neck *(G-5829)*
▲ Pearl Meadow Stables Inc .... C 518 762-7733
  Johnstown *(G-7121)*
▲ Rainbow Leather Inc .... F 718 939-8762
  College Point *(G-3804)*
▲ Simco Leather Corporation .... E 518 762-7100
  Johnstown *(G-7127)*
▲ Street Smart Designs Inc .... G 646 865-0056
  New York *(G-12213)*
System of AME Binding .... F 631 390-8560
  Central Islip *(G-3512)*
Tandy Leather Factory Inc .... G 845 480-3588
  Nyack *(G-13054)*
▲ Trebbianno LLC .... D 212 868-2770
  New York *(G-12396)*
Vic Demayos Inc .... G 845 626-4343
  Accord *(G-1)*
Walco Leather Co Inc .... G 212 243-2244
  New York *(G-12577)*
◆ Wood & Hyde Leather Co Inc .... F 518 725-7105
  Gloversville *(G-5730)*

3131 Boot & Shoe Cut Stock & Findings

▲ Age Manufacturers Inc .... D 718 927-0048
  Brooklyn *(G-1569)*
Awap Inc .... G 516 481-4070
  Uniondale *(G-16289)*
Counter Evolution .... G 212 647-7505
  New York *(G-9733)*
Custom Countertops Inc .... G 716 646-1579
  Orchard Park *(G-13268)*
Custom Countertops Inc .... G 716 685-2871
  Depew *(G-4253)*
Custom Design Kitchens Inc .... F 518 355-4446
  Duanesburg *(G-4325)*
Golden Pacific Lxj Inc .... G 267 975-6537
  New York *(G-10334)*
MBA Orthotics Inc .... G 631 392-4755
  Bay Shore *(G-716)*
▲ Premier Brands of America Inc .... C 914 667-6200
  Mount Vernon *(G-8717)*
Priscilla Quart Co Firts .... G 516 365-2755
  Manhasset *(G-8064)*
Rand Luxury Inc .... G 212 655-4505
  New York *(G-11798)*
▲ Randall Loeffler Inc .... F 212 226-8787
  New York *(G-11800)*
Tread Quarters .... G 800 876-6676
  Rochester *(G-14730)*
U-Lace LLC .... G 716 848-0939
  Rochester *(G-14738)*
Upper 90 Soccer & Sport .... G 718 643-0167
  Brooklyn *(G-2710)*
Upper East Vereniary Center .... G 212 369-8387
  New York *(G-12473)*
Upper Manhattan Arts Project .... G 914 980-9805
  Ardsley *(G-407)*
Upper Ninty LLC .... G 646 863-3105
  New York *(G-12474)*

3142 House Slippers

RG Barry Corporation .... F 212 244-3145
  New York *(G-11856)*

3143 Men's Footwear, Exc Athletic

Air Skate & Air Jump Corp .... F 212 967-1201
  Brooklyn *(G-1572)*
▲ Bm America LLC .... E 201 438-7733
  New York *(G-9427)*
◆ Coach Inc .... B 212 594-1850
  New York *(G-9656)*
▲ Detny Footwear Inc .... G 212 423-1040
  New York *(G-9860)*
▲ GH Bass & Co .... B 212 381-3900
  New York *(G-10290)*
◆ Jerry Miller Molded Shoes Inc .... F 716 881-3920
  Buffalo *(G-3017)*
Kcp Holdco Inc .... A 212 265-1500
  New York *(G-10827)*
Kenneth Cole Productions LP .... E 212 265-1500
  New York *(G-10832)*
▲ Kenneth Cole Productions Inc .... B 212 265-1500
  New York *(G-10833)*
Lake View Manufacturing LLC .... F 315 364-7892
  King Ferry *(G-7168)*
▲ Neumann Jutta New York Inc .... F 212 982-7048
  New York *(G-11376)*
Nicholas Kirkwood LLC .... G 646 559-5239
  New York *(G-11425)*
▲ NY Accessory Group Ltd Lblty .... G 212 989-6350
  New York *(G-11476)*
▲ Pedifix Inc .... E 845 277-2850
  Brewster *(G-1226)*
Phillips-Van Heusen Europe .... F 212 381-3500
  New York *(G-11649)*
◆ Pvh Corp .... D 212 381-3500
  New York *(G-11756)*
Rockport Company LLC .... D 631 243-0418
  Deer Park *(G-4200)*
Rockport Company LLC .... G 718 271-3627
  Elmhurst *(G-4666)*
Steven Madden Ltd .... D 845 348-7026
  West Nyack *(G-16927)*
Steven Madden Ltd .... E 212 736-3283
  New York *(G-12200)*
◆ Steven Madden Ltd .... B 718 446-1800
  Long Island City *(G-7892)*
T O Dey Service Corp .... F 212 683-6300
  New York *(G-12267)*
▲ Tic TAC Toes Mfg Corp .... D 518 773-8187
  Gloversville *(G-5726)*
Tru Mold Shoes Inc .... E 716 881-4484
  Buffalo *(G-3226)*

3144 Women's Footwear, Exc Athletic

Akh Group LLC .... G 646 320-8720
  New York *(G-9066)*
◆ Alpargatas Usa Inc .... E 646 277-7171
  New York *(G-9098)*
Attitudes Footwear Inc .... G 212 754-9113
  New York *(G-9260)*
◆ Coach Inc .... B 212 594-1850
  New York *(G-9656)*
▲ Detny Footwear Inc .... G 212 423-1040
  New York *(G-9860)*
▲ Everlast Worldwide Inc .... E 212 239-0990
  New York *(G-10093)*
▲ GH Bass & Co .... B 212 381-3900
  New York *(G-10425)*
◆ Jerry Miller Molded Shoes Inc .... F 716 881-3920
  Buffalo *(G-3017)*
▲ Kenneth Cole Productions Inc .... B 212 265-1500
  New York *(G-10833)*
Lake View Manufacturing LLC .... F 315 364-7892
  King Ferry *(G-7168)*
Lsil & Co Inc .... G 914 761-0998
  White Plains *(G-17134)*
▲ Mango Usa Inc .... E 718 998-6050
  Brooklyn *(G-2258)*
▲ Neumann Jutta New York Inc .... F 212 982-7048
  New York *(G-11376)*
Nicholas Kirkwood LLC .... G 646 559-5239
  New York *(G-11425)*
▲ Nine West Footwear Corporation .... B 800 999-1877
  New York *(G-11435)*
Nine West Group Inc .... G 800 999-1877
  White Plains *(G-17142)*
▲ Pedifix Inc .... E 845 277-2850
  Brewster *(G-1226)*
▼ Right Fit Shoes LLC .... G 212 575-9445
  New York *(G-11872)*
▲ SM New York .... F 718 446-1800
  Long Island City *(G-7880)*
Steven Madden Ltd .... D 718 446-1800
  New York *(G-12201)*
◆ Steven Madden Ltd .... B 718 446-1800
  Long Island City *(G-7892)*
T O Dey Service Corp .... F 212 683-6300
  New York *(G-12267)*
▲ Tic TAC Toes Mfg Corp .... D 518 773-8187
  Gloversville *(G-5726)*
Tru Mold Shoes Inc .... G 716 881-4484
  Buffalo *(G-3226)*

3149 Footwear, NEC

Custom Sports Lab Inc .... G 212 832-1648
  New York *(G-9771)*
▲ Everlast Worldwide Inc .... E 212 239-0990
  New York *(G-10093)*
▲ GH Bass & Co .... B 212 381-3900
  New York *(G-10290)*
Kicks Closet Sportswear Inc .... G 347 577-0857
  Bronx *(G-1372)*
La Strada Dance Footwear Inc .... G 631 242-1401
  Deer Park *(G-4163)*
▲ Mango Usa Inc .... E 718 998-6050
  Brooklyn *(G-2258)*
Mayberry Shoe Company Inc .... G 315 692-4086
  Manlius *(G-8074)*
McM Products USA Inc .... E 646 756-4090
  New York *(G-11201)*
Reebok International Ltd .... C 914 948-3719
  White Plains *(G-17163)*
Reebok International Ltd .... C 718 370-0471
  Staten Island *(G-15729)*
▲ SM New York .... F 718 446-1800
  Long Island City *(G-7880)*
◆ Steven Madden Ltd .... B 718 446-1800
  Long Island City *(G-7892)*
▲ Vsg International LLC .... G 718 300-8171
  Brooklyn *(G-2737)*

3151 Leather Gloves & Mittens

American Target Marketing Inc .... E 518 725-4369
  Gloversville *(G-5705)*
▲ Fieldtex Products Inc .... C 585 427-2940
  Rochester *(G-14369)*
◆ Fownes Brothers & Co Inc .... E 212 683-0150
  New York *(G-10194)*
Fownes Brothers & Co Inc .... E 518 752-4411
  Gloversville *(G-5711)*
Protech (llc) .... E 518 725-7785
  Gloversville *(G-5719)*
Samco LLC .... E 518 725-4705
  Johnstown *(G-7125)*
USA Sewing Inc .... E 315 792-8017
  Utica *(G-16362)*
▲ Worldwide Protective Pdts LLC .... C 877 678-4568
  Hamburg *(G-5946)*

3161 Luggage

▲ 212 Biz LLC .... G 212 391-4444
  New York *(G-8964)*

SIC SECTION

32 STONE, CLAY, GLASS, AND CONCRETE PRODUCTS

◆ Adam Scott Designs Inc ....E...... 212 420-8866
New York (G-9024)
▲ Aka Sport Inc ....F...... 631 858-9888
Dix Hills (G-4289)
▲ Ameribag Outdoors ....E...... 845 339-4082
Kingston (G-7177)
Atlantic Specialty Co Inc ....E...... 845 356-2502
Monsey (G-8569)
Barclay Brown Corp ....F...... 718 376-7166
Brooklyn (G-1668)
Bragley Mfg Co Inc ....E...... 718 622-7469
Brooklyn (G-1712)
Calvin Klein Inc ....E...... 212 292-9000
New York (G-9505)
▲ Carry-All Canvas Bag Co Inc ....G...... 718 375-4230
Brooklyn (G-1759)
▲ Coach Stores Inc ....A...... 212 643-9727
New York (G-9659)
◆ Dlx Industries Inc ....D...... 718 272-9420
Brooklyn (G-1869)
Donna Morgan LLC ....E...... 212 575-2550
New York (G-9904)
Ead Cases ....F...... 845 343-2111
Middletown (G-8438)
Fibre Case & Novelty Co Inc ....E...... 212 254-6060
New York (G-10158)
▲ Fieldtex Products Inc ....C...... 585 427-2940
Rochester (G-14369)
◆ Fish & Crown Ltd ....D...... 212 707-9603
New York (G-10173)
▲ Golden Bridge Group Inc ....E...... 718 335-8882
Elmhurst (G-4662)
Goyard Inc ....E...... 212 813-0005
New York (G-10343)
Junk In My Trunk Inc ....E...... 631 420-5865
Farmingdale (G-5019)
Lo & Sons Inc ....F...... 917 775-4025
Brooklyn (G-2233)
▲ Merzon Leather Co Inc ....C...... 718 782-6260
Brooklyn (G-2301)
▲ Prepac Designs Inc ....G...... 914 524-7800
Yonkers (G-17479)
Progressive Fibre Products Co ....E...... 212 566-2720
New York (G-11730)
Randa Accessories Lea Gds LLC ......D...... 212 354-5100
New York (G-11799)
Rhino Trunk & Case Inc ....F...... 585 244-4553
Rochester (G-14624)
▲ Roadie Products Inc ....E...... 631 567-8588
Holbrook (G-6468)
▼ Rose Trunk Mfg Co Inc ....F...... 516 766-6686
Oceanside (G-13093)
◆ Royal Industries Inc ....E...... 718 369-3046
Brooklyn (G-2511)
Sigma Worldwide LLC ....E...... 646 217-0629
New York (G-12067)
Sky Dive ....D...... 845 858-6400
Port Jervis (G-13792)
▲ Three Point Ventures LLC ....F...... 585 697-3444
Rochester (G-14724)
▲ Trafalgar Company LLC ....G...... 212 768-8800
New York (G-12390)
▲ Trunk & Trolley LLC ....G...... 212 947-9001
New York (G-12411)
Tumi Inc ....C...... 212 447-8747
New York (G-12423)
Tumi Inc ....C...... 212 742-8020
New York (G-12424)
Xstatic Pro Inc ....F...... 718 237-2299
Brooklyn (G-2771)

3171 Handbags & Purses

▲ Ahq LLC ....E...... 212 328-1560
New York (G-9062)
Akh Group LLC ....G...... 646 320-8720
New York (G-9066)
Atalla Handbags Inc ....G...... 718 965-5500
Brooklyn (G-1643)
▲ Bagznyc Corp ....F...... 212 643-8202
New York (G-9305)
▲ Baikal Inc ....D...... 212 239-4650
New York (G-9306)
Coach Inc ....F...... 212 581-4115
New York (G-9651)
Coach Inc ....F...... 718 760-0624
Elmhurst (G-4659)
Coach Inc ....F...... 585 425-7720
Victor (G-16468)
Coach Inc ....F...... 212 245-4148
New York (G-9652)

Coach Inc ....E...... 212 473-6925
New York (G-9653)
Coach Inc ....F...... 212 754-0041
New York (G-9654)
Coach Inc ....F...... 212 675-6403
New York (G-9655)
◆ Coach Inc ....B...... 212 594-1850
New York (G-9656)
Coach Leatherware Intl ....G...... 212 594-1850
New York (G-9657)
▲ Coach Services Inc ....E...... 212 594-1850
New York (G-9658)
▲ Coach Stores Inc ....A...... 212 643-9727
New York (G-9659)
Deux Lux Inc ....E...... 212 620-0801
New York (G-9863)
▲ Essex Manufacturing Inc ....E...... 212 239-0080
New York (G-10066)
Formart Corp ....F...... 212 819-1819
New York (G-10186)
▲ Frenz Group LLC ....E...... 212 465-0908
Whitestone (G-17207)
Kcp Holdco Inc ....A...... 212 265-1500
New York (G-10827)
▲ Kenneth Cole Productions Inc ....E...... 212 265-1500
New York (G-10833)
▲ Latique Handbags and ACC LLC ....F...... 212 564-2914
New York (G-10934)
McM Products USA Inc ....E...... 646 756-4090
New York (G-11201)
▲ Nine West Footwear Corporation ..B...... 800 999-1877
New York (G-11435)
Pure Trade Us Inc ....F...... 212 256-1600
New York (G-11751)
Quilted Koala Ltd ....F...... 800 223-5678
New York (G-11773)
◆ Renco Group Inc ....G...... 212 541-6000
New York (G-11832)
▲ Roadie Products Inc ....E...... 631 567-8588
Holbrook (G-6468)
▲ Rodem Incorporated ....F...... 212 779-7122
New York (G-11901)
Sibeau Handbags Inc ....E...... 212 686-0210
New York (G-12059)
▲ Stuart Weitzman LLC ....E...... 212 823-9560
New York (G-12218)

3172 Personal Leather Goods

American Puff Corp ....D...... 516 379-1300
Freeport (G-5387)
Astucci US Ltd ....F...... 718 752-9700
Long Island City (G-7674)
▲ Astucci US Ltd ....G...... 212 725-3171
New York (G-9243)
Atlantic Specialty Co Inc ....E...... 845 356-2502
Monsey (G-8569)
▲ Baker Products Inc ....E...... 212 459-2323
White Plains (G-17082)
Baublebar Inc ....D...... 646 664-4803
New York (G-9333)
◆ Coach Inc ....B...... 212 594-1850
New York (G-9656)
▲ Coach Stores Inc ....A...... 212 643-9727
New York (G-9659)
▲ Datamax International Inc ....E...... 212 693-0933
New York (G-9815)
Elco Manufacturing Co Inc ....F...... 516 767-3577
Port Washington (G-13813)
▲ Excelled Shpskin Lea Coat Corp ....F...... 212 594-5843
New York (G-10103)
Fahrenheit NY Inc ....E...... 212 354-6554
New York (G-10127)
Form A Rockland Plastics Inc ....G...... 315 848-3300
Cranberry Lake (G-4057)
Grownbeans Inc ....G...... 212 989-3486
New York (G-10373)
▲ Helgen Industries Inc ....C...... 631 841-6300
Amityville (G-293)
◆ Hemisphere Novelties Inc ....E...... 914 378-4100
Yonkers (G-17453)
House of Portfolios Co Inc ....G...... 212 206-7323
New York (G-10519)
House of Portfolios Co Inc ....G...... 212 206-7323
New York (G-10520)
International Time Products ....G...... 516 931-0005
Jericho (G-7073)
Just Brass Inc ....G...... 212 724-5447
New York (G-10792)
K Displays ....F...... 718 854-6045
Brooklyn (G-2163)

L Y Z Creations Ltd Inc ....E...... 718 768-2977
Brooklyn (G-2187)
Leather Artisan ....G...... 518 359-3102
Childwold (G-3628)
◆ Leather Impact Inc ....G...... 212 382-2788
New York (G-10950)
◆ M G New York Inc ....F...... 212 371-5566
New York (G-11070)
▲ Merzon Leather Co Inc ....C...... 718 782-6260
Brooklyn (G-2301)
Montana Global LLC ....G...... 212 213-1572
Jamaica (G-6933)
▲ Neumann Jutta New York Inc ....F...... 212 982-7048
New York (G-11376)
▲ Penthouse Manufacturing Co Inc ....B...... 516 379-1300
Freeport (G-5418)
Randa Accessories Lea Gds LLC ......D...... 212 354-5100
New York (G-11799)
Roma Industries LLC ....G...... 212 268-0723
New York (G-11910)
Sibeau Handbags Inc ....E...... 212 686-0210
New York (G-12059)
Slim Line Case Co Inc ....F...... 585 546-3639
Rochester (G-14689)
▲ Trafalgar Company LLC ....G...... 212 768-8800
New York (G-12390)
Unique Packaging Corporation ....G...... 514 341-5872
Champlain (G-3548)
Walco Leather Co Inc ....E...... 212 243-2244
New York (G-12577)

3199 Leather Goods, NEC

112 Jerome Dreyfuss LLC ....G...... 212 334-6920
New York (G-8958)
Adirondack Leather Pdts Inc ....F...... 607 547-5798
Fly Creek (G-5313)
Art Craft Leather Goods Inc ....E...... 718 257-7401
Brooklyn (G-1633)
▲ Courtlandt Boot Jack Co Inc ....E...... 718 445-6200
Flushing (G-5235)
Dog Good Products LLC ....G...... 212 789-7000
New York (G-9895)
▲ Dvf Studio LLC ....D...... 212 741-6607
New York (G-9942)
East West Global Sourcing Inc ....G...... 917 887-2286
Brooklyn (G-1897)
Equicenter Inc ....E...... 585 742-2522
Honeoye Falls (G-6527)
Fahrenheit NY Inc ....E...... 212 354-6554
New York (G-10127)
▼ Finger Lakes Lea Crafters LLC ....F...... 315 252-4107
Auburn (G-494)
▲ Fiorentina LLC ....E...... 516 208-5448
Merrick (G-8385)
▲ Helgen Industries Inc ....C...... 631 841-6300
Amityville (G-293)
Import-Export Corporation ....F...... 718 707-0880
Long Island City (G-7764)
Kamali Leather Corp ....G...... 518 762-2522
Johnstown (G-7117)
Leather Outlet ....G...... 518 668-0328
Lake George (G-7262)
Max 200 Performance Dog Eqp ....E...... 315 776-9588
Port Byron (G-13735)
McM Products USA Inc ....E...... 646 756-4090
New York (G-11201)
▲ Perrone Leather LLC ....D...... 518 853-4300
Fultonville (G-5482)
▲ Sampla Belting North Amer LLC ....E...... 716 667-7450
Lackawanna (G-7249)
▲ Star Desk Pad Co Inc ....E...... 914 963-9400
Yonkers (G-17486)
▲ Tucano Usa Inc ....G...... 212 966-9211
New York (G-12419)
◆ Unique Overseas Inc ....G...... 516 466-9792
Great Neck (G-5846)
Walco Leather Co Inc ....E...... 212 243-2244
New York (G-12577)

32 STONE, CLAY, GLASS, AND CONCRETE PRODUCTS

3211 Flat Glass

A Sunshine Glass & Aluminum ....E...... 718 932-8080
Woodside (G-17316)
Corning Incorporated ....E...... 607 974-8496
Corning (G-3967)
Corning Incorporated ....D...... 315 379-3200
Canton (G-3382)

Employee Codes: A=Over 500 employees, B=251-500
C=101-250, D=51-100, E=20-50, F=10-19, G=5-9

Corning Incorporated ....G.... 607 974-6729
Painted Post (G-13391)
Europrojects Intl Inc ....G.... 917 262-0795
New York (G-10086)
Express Building Supply Inc ....E.... 516 608-0379
Oceanside (G-13079)
Farley Windows Inc ....G.... 315 764-1111
Massena (G-8194)
Glass Apps LLC ....F.... 310 987-1536
New York (G-10307)
▲ Global Glass Corp ....G.... 516 681-2309
Hicksville (G-6350)
Guardian Industries Corp ....B.... 315 787-7000
Geneva (G-5580)
▲ Hecht & Sohn Glass Co Inc ....G.... 718 782-8295
Brooklyn (G-2071)
Lafayette Mirror & Glass Co ....G.... 718 768-0660
New Hyde Park (G-8845)
▲ Lazer Marble & Granite Corp ....G.... 718 859-9644
Brooklyn (G-2197)
▼ Manhattan Shade & Glass Co Inc ....D.... 212 288-5616
New York (G-11133)
Pilkington North America Inc ....C.... 315 438-3341
Syracuse (G-16012)
RG Glass Creations Inc ....E.... 212 675-0030
New York (G-11857)
Saxon Glass Technologies Inc ....F.... 607 587-9630
Alfred (G-194)
▲ Schott Corporation ....D.... 914 831-2200
Elmsford (G-4778)
Schott Gemtron Corporation ....C.... 423 337-3522
Elmsford (G-4779)
Schott Government Services LLC ....G.... 703 418-1409
Elmsford (G-4780)
▲ Schott Solar Pv Inc ....G.... 888 457-6527
Elmsford (G-4782)
South Seneca Vinyl LLC ....G.... 315 585-6050
Romulus (G-14843)
▼ Stefan Sydor Optics Inc ....E.... 585 271-7300
Rochester (G-14702)
Strong Tempering GL Indust LLC ....F.... 718 765-0007
Brooklyn (G-2611)
Tempco Glass Fabrication LLC ....G.... 718 461-6888
Flushing (G-5300)
Tower Insulating Glass LLC ....E.... 516 887-3300
North Bellmore (G-12923)
Twin Pane Insulated GL Co Inc ....F.... 631 924-1060
Yaphank (G-17407)
Window-Fix Inc ....E.... 718 854-3475
Brooklyn (G-2757)
▲ Zered Inc ....F.... 718 353-7464
College Point (G-3813)

3221 Glass Containers

Anchor Glass Container Corp ....B.... 607 737-1933
Elmira Heights (G-4708)
▲ Baralan Usa Inc ....E.... 718 849-5768
Richmond Hill (G-14067)
Certainteed Corporation ....C.... 716 823-3684
Lackawanna (G-7243)
▲ Glopak USA Corp ....F.... 347 869-9252
College Point (G-3784)
Glopak USA Corp ....D.... 516 433-3214
Hicksville (G-6351)
Intrapac International Corp ....C.... 518 561-2030
Plattsburgh (G-13671)
▲ Lidestri Foods Inc ....B.... 585 377-7700
Fairport (G-4861)
◆ Liquor Bottle Packg Intl Inc ....G.... 212 922-2813
New York (G-11007)
Oliveplaste LLC ....E.... 315 356-2670
Rome (G-14828)
Owens-Brockway Glass Cont Inc ....C.... 315 258-3211
Auburn (G-513)
Pennsauken Packing Company LLC ....F.... 585 377-7700
Fairport (G-4869)
▲ Rocco Bormioli Glass Co Inc ....E.... 212 719-0606
New York (G-11896)
▲ Saint Gobain Grains & Powders ....A.... 716 731-8200
Niagara Falls (G-12870)
▲ Schott Corporation ....D.... 914 831-2200
Elmsford (G-4778)
▲ SGD North America ....E.... 212 753-4200
New York (G-12035)
Vivreau Advanced Water Systems ....F.... 212 502-3749
New York (G-12559)

3229 Pressed & Blown Glassware, NEC

Anritsu Instruments Company ....E.... 315 797-4449
Utica (G-16307)
Architectural Glass Inc ....F.... 845 831-3116
Beacon (G-781)
▲ Art and Cook Inc ....F.... 718 567-7778
Brooklyn (G-1631)
▼ Bedford Downing Glass ....G.... 718 418-6409
Brooklyn (G-1677)
Biolitec Inc ....E.... 413 525-0600
New York (G-9402)
Bronx Wstchester Tempering Inc ....E.... 914 663-9400
Mount Vernon (G-8668)
Co-Optics America Lab Inc ....E.... 607 432-0557
Oneonta (G-13179)
◆ Corning Incorporated ....A.... 607 974-9000
Corning (G-3962)
Corning Incorporated ....D.... 607 974-9000
Corning (G-3963)
Corning Incorporated ....E.... 607 974-1274
Painted Post (G-13390)
Corning Incorporated ....E.... 607 974-9000
Corning (G-3964)
Corning Incorporated ....D.... 315 379-3200
Canton (G-3382)
Corning Incorporated ....E.... 607 433-3100
Oneonta (G-13182)
Corning Incorporated ....E.... 607 974-0206
Big Flats (G-880)
Corning Incorporated ....E.... 607 248-1200
Corning (G-3965)
Corning Incorporated ....B.... 607 974-0206
Big Flats (G-881)
Corning Incorporated ....G.... 607 974-4488
Corning (G-3966)
Corning Incorporated ....G.... 607 974-6729
Painted Post (G-13391)
▼ Corning International Corp ....G.... 607 974-9000
Corning (G-3968)
Corning Specialty Mtls Inc ....G.... 607 974-9000
Corning (G-3970)
Corning Tropel Corporation ....C.... 585 377-3200
Fairport (G-4852)
◆ Corning Vitro Corporation ....A.... 607 974-8605
Corning (G-3971)
▲ Daylight Technology USA Inc ....G.... 973 255-8100
Maspeth (G-8129)
◆ Depp Glass Inc ....F.... 718 784-8500
Long Island City (G-7713)
Eye Deal Eyewear Inc ....G.... 716 297-1500
Niagara Falls (G-12817)
Formcraft Display Products ....G.... 914 632-1410
New Rochelle (G-8900)
◆ Germanow-Simon Corporation ....E.... 585 232-1440
Rochester (G-14399)
▲ Gillinder Brothers Inc ....D.... 845 856-5375
Port Jervis (G-13785)
Glassart Inc ....G.... 607 739-3939
Millport (G-8481)
Glasteel Parts & Services Inc ....E.... 585 235-1010
Rochester (G-14405)
▲ Goodlite Products Inc ....F.... 718 697-7502
Brooklyn (G-2040)
▲ Gray Glass Inc ....E.... 718 217-2943
Queens Village (G-13978)
Ion Optics Inc ....F.... 518 339-6853
Albany (G-90)
▲ Jinglebell Inc ....G.... 914 219-5395
Armonk (G-416)
◆ King Research Inc ....E.... 718 788-0122
Brooklyn (G-2172)
Led Lumina USA LLC ....G.... 631 750-4433
Bohemia (G-1091)
◆ Lighting Holdings Intl LLC ....F.... 845 306-1850
Purchase (G-13960)
Mata Ig ....G.... 212 979-7921
New York (G-11177)
▲ Match Eyewear LLC ....E.... 516 877-0170
Westbury (G-17009)
Navitar Inc ....D.... 585 359-4000
Rochester (G-14530)
New York Energy Synthetics Inc ....G.... 212 634-4787
New York (G-11401)
▲ Orafol Display Optics Inc ....E.... 585 647-1140
West Henrietta (G-16887)
Owens Corning Sales LLC ....B.... 518 475-3600
Feura Bush (G-5174)
▲ Pasabahce USA ....G.... 212 683-1600
New York (G-11577)
Photonic Controls LLC ....F.... 607 562-4585
Horseheads (G-6588)
R Bruce Mapes ....F.... 518 761-2020
Glens Falls (G-5698)
Saint-Gobain Prfmce Plas Corp ....C.... 518 686-7301
Hoosick Falls (G-6544)
Schott Corporation ....D.... 315 255-2791
Auburn (G-517)
▲ Schott Corporation ....D.... 914 831-2200
Elmsford (G-4778)
Scientifics Direct Inc ....F.... 716 773-7500
Tonawanda (G-16201)
▲ Semrok Inc ....D.... 585 594-7050
Rochester (G-14681)
▲ Sleepy Hollow Chimney Sup Ltd ....F.... 631 231-2333
Brentwood (G-1194)
Somers Stain Glass Inc ....F.... 631 586-7772
Deer Park (G-4211)
▼ Stefan Sydor Optics Inc ....E.... 585 271-7300
Rochester (G-14702)
◆ Volpi Manufacturing USA Co Inc ....E.... 315 255-1737
Auburn (G-527)

3231 Glass Prdts Made Of Purchased Glass

▲ Ad Notam LLC ....F.... 631 951-2020
Hauppauge (G-6008)
Adirondack Stained Glass Works ....G.... 518 725-0387
Gloversville (G-5704)
Apf Management Company LLC ....C.... 914 665-5400
Yonkers (G-17414)
Apf Manufacturing Company LLC ....E.... 914 963-6300
Yonkers (G-17415)
Batavia Precision Glass LLC ....G.... 585 343-6050
Buffalo (G-2833)
Benson Industries Inc ....F.... 212 779-3230
New York (G-9360)
C B Management Services Inc ....F.... 845 735-2300
Pearl River (G-13455)
▲ Campus Crafts Inc ....G.... 585 328-6780
Rochester (G-14256)
▲ Carvart Glass Inc ....F.... 212 675-0030
New York (G-9538)
Chapman Stained Glass Studio ....G.... 518 449-5552
Albany (G-62)
Community Glass Inc ....G.... 607 737-8860
Elmira (G-4676)
◆ Depp Glass Inc ....F.... 718 784-8500
Long Island City (G-7713)
▲ Dundy Glass & Mirror Corp ....E.... 718 723-5800
Springfield Gardens (G-15608)
Dunlea Whl GL & Mirror Inc ....G.... 914 664-5277
Mount Vernon (G-8679)
Executive Mirror Doors Inc ....G.... 631 234-1090
Ronkonkoma (G-14899)
Exquisite Glass & Stone Inc ....G.... 718 937-9266
Astoria (G-441)
Farley Windows Inc ....G.... 315 764-1111
Massena (G-8194)
Flickinger Glassworks Inc ....G.... 718 875-1531
Brooklyn (G-1987)
G & M Clearview Inc ....G.... 845 781-4877
Monroe (G-8555)
▲ Glassfab Inc ....E.... 585 262-4000
Rochester (G-14404)
▲ Global Glass Corp ....G.... 516 681-2309
Hicksville (G-6350)
▲ Gmd Industries Inc ....G.... 718 445-8779
College Point (G-3785)
Granville Glass & Granite ....G.... 518 812-0492
Hudson Falls (G-6645)
▲ Gray Glass Inc ....E.... 718 217-2943
Queens Village (G-13978)
▲ Hecht & Sohn Glass Co Inc ....G.... 718 782-8295
Brooklyn (G-2071)
Immco Diagnostics Inc ....G.... 716 691-6955
Buffalo (G-3003)
Immco Diagnostics Inc ....D.... 716 691-6911
Buffalo (G-3004)
▲ Jimmy Crystal New York Co Ltd ....E.... 212 594-0858
New York (G-10736)
▲ Jinglebell Inc ....G.... 914 219-5395
Armonk (G-416)
▲ Kasson & Keller Inc ....A.... 518 853-3421
Fonda (G-5315)
Lafayette Mirror & Glass Co ....G.... 718 768-0660
New Hyde Park (G-8845)
Lalique North America Inc ....E.... 212 355-6550
New York (G-10922)
Makarenko Studios Inc ....G.... 914 968-7673
Yorktown Heights (G-17512)
Michbi Doors Inc ....D.... 631 231-9050
Brentwood (G-1192)
Mirror-Tech Manufacturing Co ....F.... 914 965-1232
Yonkers (G-17468)

Mri Northtowns Group PC ......F 716 836-4646
Buffalo (G-3076)
Oldcastle Building Envelope ......G 212 957-5400
New York (G-11499)
Oldcastle Buildingenvelope Inc ......C 631 234-2200
Hauppauge (G-6152)
Oneida International Inc ......G 315 361-3000
Oneida (G-13160)
Oneida Silversmiths Inc ......G 315 361-3000
Oneida (G-13164)
Our Terms Fabricators Inc ......E 631 752-1517
West Babylon (G-16817)
Pal Manufacturing Corp ......E 516 937-1990
Hicksville (G-6384)
Potters Industries LLC ......E 315 265-4920
Potsdam (G-13882)
Prisma Glass & Mirror Inc ......G 718 366-7191
Ridgewood (G-14120)
▲ Quality Enclosures Inc ......E 631 234-0115
Central Islip (G-3508)
Rauch Industries Inc ......E 704 867-5333
Tarrytown (G-16102)
Rn Furniture Corp ......G 347 960-9622
Richmond Hill (G-14080)
Rochester Colonial Mfg Corp ......D 585 254-8191
Rochester (G-14639)
◆ Rochester Insulated Glass Inc ......D 585 289-3611
Manchester (G-8052)
Rohlfs Stined Leaded GL Studio ......E 914 699-4848
Mount Vernon (G-8726)
▲ Rosco Inc ......C 718 526-2601
Jamaica (G-6948)
Royal Metal Products Inc ......E 518 966-4442
Surprise (G-15811)
Select Interior Door Ltd ......E 585 535-9900
North Java (G-12934)
Somers Stain Glass Inc ......F 631 586-7772
Deer Park (G-4211)
▲ Stark Aquarium Products Co Inc ......E 718 445-5357
Flushing (G-5297)
▲ Sunborn Swiss Watches LLC ......G 516 967-8836
New Hyde Park (G-8864)
Sunburst Studios Inc ......G 718 768-6360
Brooklyn (G-2620)
▲ Swift Glass Co Inc ......D 607 733-7166
Elmira Heights (G-4714)
Taylor Made Group LLC ......D 518 725-0681
Gloversville (G-5724)
▲ Taylor Products Inc ......G 518 773-9312
Gloversville (G-5725)
TEC Glass & Inst LLC ......G 315 926-7639
Marion (G-8102)
Unico Inc ......F 845 562-9255
Newburgh (G-12782)
Upstate Insulated Glass Inc ......G 315 475-4960
Central Square (G-3519)
Vitarose Corp of America ......G 718 951-9700
Brooklyn (G-2733)
Vitrix Inc ......G 607 936-8707
Corning (G-3984)

3241 Cement, Hydraulic

Ciment St-Laurent Inc ......C 518 943-4040
Catskill (G-3426)
Euro Gear (usa) Inc ......G 518 578-1775
Plattsburgh (G-13662)
Graymont Materials (ny) Inc ......G 518 873-2275
Lewis (G-7431)
Hanson Aggregates New York LLC ......F 716 665-4620
Jamesville (G-7047)
Lafarge Building Materials Inc ......F 518 756-5000
Ravena (G-14022)
Lafarge North America Inc ......E 716 651-9235
Lancaster (G-7322)
Lafarge North America Inc ......G 716 854-5791
Buffalo (G-3044)
Lafarge North America Inc ......E 716 772-2621
Lockport (G-7596)
Lafarge North America Inc ......E 716 297-3031
Niagara Falls (G-12841)
Lafarge North America Inc ......D 914 930-3027
Buchanan (G-2786)
Lafarge North America Inc ......E 518 756-5000
Ravena (G-14023)
▲ Lehigh Cement Company ......C 518 792-1137
Glens Falls (G-5687)
Lehigh Cement Company LLC ......E 518 792-1137
Glens Falls (G-5688)
Pallette Stone Corporation ......E 518 584-2421
Gansevoort (G-5487)

3251 Brick & Structural Clay Tile

Certified Flameproofing Corp ......G 631 265-4824
Smithtown (G-15484)
Everblock Systems LLC ......G 844 422-5625
New York (G-10089)
◆ Noroc Enterprises Inc ......E 718 585-3230
Bronx (G-1412)
Semco Ceramics Inc ......G 315 782-3000
Watertown (G-16671)
▲ Stone and Bath Gallery ......G 718 438-4500
Brooklyn (G-2609)

3253 Ceramic Tile

▲ Aremco Products Inc ......F 845 268-0039
Valley Cottage (G-16376)
Artsaics Studios Inc ......G 631 254-2558
Deer Park (G-4103)
Dal-Tile Corporation ......G 914 835-1801
Harrison (G-5982)
▲ Ercole Nyc Inc ......F 212 675-2218
Brooklyn (G-1932)
▲ Hastings Tile & Bath Inc ......F 516 379-3500
Ronkonkoma (G-14910)
▲ Lazer Marble & Granite Corp ......G 718 859-9644
Brooklyn (G-2197)
Merola Sales Company Inc ......E 800 963-7652
Glendale (G-5658)
NY Tilemakers ......G 989 278-8453
Brooklyn (G-2383)
Quality Components Framing Sys ......F 315 768-1167
Whitesboro (G-17194)
Quemere International ......G 914 934-8366
Port Chester (G-13758)
Semco Ceramics Inc ......G 315 782-3000
Watertown (G-16671)
Tile Shop Inc ......G 585 424-2180
Rochester (G-14726)

3255 Clay Refractories

Filtros Ltd ......E 585 586-8770
East Rochester (G-4459)
▼ Hoffmans Trade Group LLC ......G 518 250-5556
Troy (G-16239)
◆ Saint-Gobain Strl Ceramics ......A 716 278-6233
Niagara Falls (G-12873)
Upstate Refractory Svcs Inc ......E 315 331-2955
Newark (G-12746)

3259 Structural Clay Prdts, NEC

▲ American Chimney Supplies Inc ......G 631 434-2020
Hauppauge (G-6020)
Bistrian Cement Corporation ......F 631 324-1123
East Hampton (G-4405)
▲ Boston Valley Pottery Inc ......D 716 649-7490
Orchard Park (G-13254)
Chimney Doctors Americas Corp ......G 631 868-3586
Bayport (G-757)
Lenon Models Inc ......G 212 229-1581
New York (G-10966)

3261 China Plumbing Fixtures & Fittings

▼ AMG Global LLC ......G 212 689-6008
New York (G-9134)
Gamma Products Inc ......D 845 562-3332
New Windsor (G-8938)
▲ Larcent Enterprises Inc ......E 845 562-3332
New Windsor (G-8941)
▲ Stone and Bath Gallery ......G 718 438-4500
Brooklyn (G-2609)

3262 China, Table & Kitchen Articles

Carmona Nyc LLC ......G 718 227-6662
Rego Park (G-14031)
Jill Fagin Enterprises Inc ......G 212 674-9383
New York (G-10732)
◆ Korin Japanese Trading Corp ......E 212 587-7021
New York (G-10878)
Oneida International Inc ......G 315 361-3000
Oneida (G-13160)
Oneida Silversmiths Inc ......G 315 361-3000
Oneida (G-13164)
Swissmar Inc ......G 905 764-1121
Niagara Falls (G-12879)

3263 Earthenware, Whiteware, Table & Kitchen Articles

Ceramica Varm ......G 914 381-6215
New Rochelle (G-8892)
▲ Green Wave International Inc ......G 718 499-3371
Brooklyn (G-2051)
▲ Jill Fenichell Inc ......G 718 237-2490
Brooklyn (G-2142)
◆ Korin Japanese Trading Corp ......E 212 587-7021
New York (G-10878)
Lifetime Stainless Steel Corp ......G 585 924-9393
Victor (G-16488)
◆ Mackenzie-Childs LLC ......C 315 364-7567
Aurora (G-530)
Williams-Sonoma Stores Inc ......F 212 633-2203
New York (G-12637)

3264 Porcelain Electrical Splys

▲ Arnold Magnetic Tech Corp ......C 585 385-9010
Rochester (G-14211)
▲ Cetek Inc ......E 845 452-3510
Poughkeepsie (G-13892)
Corning Incorporated ......E 607 974-1274
Painted Post (G-13390)
Eneflux Armtek Magnetics Inc ......G 516 576-3434
Medford (G-8244)
Ferro Electronics Materials ......C 716 278-9400
Niagara Falls (G-12821)
◆ Ferro Electronics Materials ......G 315 536-3357
Penn Yan (G-13510)
Ferro Electronics Materials ......C 315 536-3357
Penn Yan (G-13511)
Filtros Ltd ......E 585 586-8770
East Rochester (G-4459)
◆ Hitachi Metals America Ltd ......E 914 694-9200
Purchase (G-13959)
◆ Hoosier Magnetics Inc ......D 315 393-1813
Ogdensburg (G-13116)
Lapp Insulator Company LLC ......F 585 768-6221
Le Roy (G-7411)
▲ Lapp Insulators LLC ......C 585 768-6221
Le Roy (G-7412)
▲ Victor Insulators Inc ......C 585 924-2127
Victor (G-16510)

3269 Pottery Prdts, NEC

American Country Quilts & Lin ......G 631 283-5466
Southampton (G-15538)
Konstantinos Floral Decorators ......G 718 434-3603
Brooklyn (G-2180)
Make Holding LLC ......E 646 313-1957
New York (G-11116)
▲ Saint Gobain Grains & Powders ......A 716 731-8200
Niagara Falls (G-12870)
▲ Saint-Gbain Advnced Crmics LLC ......C 716 278-6066
Niagara Falls (G-12871)
Schiller Stores Inc ......G 845 928-4316
Central Valley (G-3527)

3271 Concrete Block & Brick

Ace Cntracting Consulting Corp ......G 631 567-4752
Bohemia (G-1006)
All American Concrete Corp ......G 718 497-3301
Brooklyn (G-1584)
All County Block & Supply Corp ......G 631 589-3675
Bohemia (G-1012)
Arnan Development Corp ......D 607 432-6641
Oneonta (G-13171)
Barrasso & Sons Trucking Inc ......E 631 581-0360
Islip Terrace (G-6814)
▲ Belden Brick Sales & Svc Inc ......F 212 686-3939
New York (G-9348)
Brickit ......E 631 727-8977
Hauppauge (G-6037)
Chimney Doctors Americas Corp ......G 631 868-3586
Bayport (G-757)
Colonie Block and Supply Co ......G 518 869-8411
Colonie (G-3819)
Cossitt Concrete Products Inc ......F 315 824-2700
Hamilton (G-5947)
▲ Cranesville Block Co Inc ......E 518 684-6000
Amsterdam (G-341)
Cranesville Block Co Inc ......E 315 773-2296
Felts Mills (G-5167)
Creative Yard Designs Inc ......G 315 706-6143
Manlius (G-8070)
Crest Haven Precast Inc ......G 518 483-4750
Burke (G-3266)
Dicks Concrete Co Inc ......E 845 374-5966
New Hampton (G-8799)
Duke Concrete Products Inc ......E 518 793-7743
Queensbury (G-13995)
Edgewood Industries Inc ......G 516 227-2447
Garden City (G-5501)

Employee Codes: A=Over 500 employees, B=251-500
C=101-250, D=51-100, E=20-50, F=10-19, G=5-9
2017 Harris
New York Manufacturers Directory
799

Everblock Systems LLC G 844 422-5625
New York *(G-10089)*
Felicetti Concrete Products G 716 284-5740
Niagara Falls *(G-12819)*
▼ **Fort Miller Service Corp** F 518 695-5000
Greenwich *(G-5888)*
▼ **Get Real Surfaces Inc** F 845 337-4483
Poughkeepsie *(G-13901)*
Gone South Concrete Block Inc E 315 598-2141
Fulton *(G-5459)*
Grace Associates Inc G 718 767-9000
Harrison *(G-5986)*
Grandview Block & Supply Co E 518 346-7981
Schenectady *(G-15265)*
Great American Awning & Patio F 518 899-2300
Ballston Spa *(G-598)*
Hanson Aggregates New York LLC G 607 276-5881
Almond *(G-204)*
▲ **Imperia Masonry Supply Corp** E 914 738-0900
Pelham *(G-13492)*
Jenna Concrete Corporation E 718 842-5250
Bronx *(G-1366)*
Jenna Harlem River Inc G 718 842-5997
Bronx *(G-1367)*
Lafarge North America Inc E 518 756-5000
Ravena *(G-14023)*
Lage Industries Corporation F 718 342-3400
Brooklyn *(G-2191)*
Modern Block LLC G 315 923-7443
Clyde *(G-3729)*
Montfort Brothers Inc E 845 896-6694
Fishkill *(G-5186)*
Morningstar Concrete Products F 716 693-4020
Tonawanda *(G-16183)*
New York Ready Mix Inc G 516 338-6969
Westbury *(G-17014)*
▲ **Nicolia Concrete Products Inc** D 631 669-0700
Lindenhurst *(G-7476)*
Northeast Mesa LLC G 845 878-9344
Carmel *(G-3402)*
Palumbo Block Co Inc E 845 832-6100
Dover Plains *(G-4316)*
Phelps Cement Products Inc E 315 548-9415
Phelps *(G-13535)*
Radiation Shielding Systems F 888 631-2278
Suffern *(G-15799)*
Riefler Concrete Products LLC C 716 649-3260
Hamburg *(G-5940)*
Smithtown Concrete Products F 631 265-1815
Saint James *(G-15091)*
Suffolk Cement Products Inc E 631 727-2317
Calverton *(G-3300)*
Superior Block Corp F 718 421-0900
Brooklyn *(G-2626)*
Taylor Concrete Products Inc E 315 788-2191
Watertown *(G-16673)*
Tros Lanscaping Supply Company F 518 783-6954
Cohoes *(G-3759)*
Unilock Ltd E 716 822-6074
Buffalo *(G-3233)*
▲ **Unilock New York Inc** G 845 278-6700
Brewster *(G-1229)*

3272 Concrete Prdts

A & R Concrete Products LLC E 845 562-0640
New Windsor *(G-8929)*
Access Products Inc G 800 679-4022
Buffalo *(G-2795)*
Accurate Precast F 718 345-2910
Brooklyn *(G-1552)*
▲ **Afco Precast Sales Corp** D 631 924-7114
Middle Island *(G-8405)*
▲ **Alp Stone Inc** F 718 706-6166
Long Island City *(G-7653)*
▲ **American Chimney Supplies Inc** G 631 434-2020
Hauppauge *(G-6020)*
Arnan Development Corp D 607 432-6641
Oneonta *(G-13171)*
Baliva Concrete Products Inc G 585 328-8442
Rochester *(G-14223)*
Barrett Paving Materials Inc F 315 737-9471
Clayville *(G-3686)*
Beck Vault Company G 315 337-7590
Rome *(G-14806)*
Binghamton Burial Vault Co Inc F 607 722-4931
Binghamton *(G-891)*
Binghamton Precast & Sup Corp E 607 722-0334
Binghamton *(G-893)*
Bistrian Cement Corporation F 631 324-1123
East Hampton *(G-4405)*
Buffalo Crushed Stone Inc E 716 826-7310
Buffalo *(G-2850)*
Burnett Concrete Products Inc G 315 594-2242
Wolcott *(G-17276)*
Callanan Industries Inc E 315 697-9569
Canastota *(G-3364)*
▲ **Callanan Industries Inc** C 518 374-2222
Schenectady *(G-15236)*
Callanan Industries Inc E 845 331-6868
Kingston *(G-7182)*
▲ **Castek Inc** G 914 636-1000
New Rochelle *(G-8891)*
Chim-Cap Corp E 631 454-7576
Farmingdale *(G-4958)*
Chimney Doctors Americas Corp G 631 868-3586
Bayport *(G-757)*
City Mason Corp F 718 658-3796
Jamaica *(G-6903)*
▲ **Coastal Pipeline Products Corp** E 631 369-4000
Calverton *(G-3288)*
▲ **Copeland Coating Company Inc** F 518 766-2932
Nassau *(G-8771)*
Coral Cast LLC E 516 349-1300
Plainview *(G-13592)*
▲ **Corinthian Cast Stone Inc** E 631 920-2340
Wyandanch *(G-17374)*
Cossitt Concrete Products Inc F 315 824-2700
Hamilton *(G-5947)*
Crown Hill Stone Inc E 716 326-4601
Westfield *(G-17047)*
David Kucera Inc E 845 255-1044
Gardiner *(G-5549)*
Diamond Precast Products Inc F 631 874-3777
Center Moriches *(G-3464)*
Dillner Precast Inc G 631 421-9130
Huntington Station *(G-6702)*
Dillner Precast Inc G 631 421-9130
Lloyd Harbor *(G-7566)*
Doric Vault of Wny Inc F 716 828-1776
Buffalo *(G-2917)*
Duranm Inc G 914 774-3367
Cortlandt Manor *(G-4049)*
Dynasty Metal Works Inc G 631 284-3719
Riverhead *(G-14141)*
East Main Associates D 585 624-1990
Lima *(G-7444)*
▲ **Eaton Brothers Corp** G 716 649-8250
Hamburg *(G-5922)*
Elderlee Incorporated C 315 789-6670
Oaks Corners *(G-13069)*
Express Concrete Inc G 631 273-4224
Brentwood *(G-1183)*
Fordham Marble Co Inc F 914 682-6699
White Plains *(G-17110)*
Foro Marble Co Inc E 718 852-2322
Brooklyn *(G-1996)*
▲ **Fort Miller Group Inc** B 518 695-5000
Greenwich *(G-5887)*
▼ **Fort Miller Service Corp** F 518 695-5000
Greenwich *(G-5888)*
Galle & Zinter Inc G 716 833-4212
Buffalo *(G-2963)*
Gamble & Gamble Inc G 716 731-3239
Sanborn *(G-15120)*
Geotech Associates Ltd G 631 286-0251
Brookhaven *(G-1507)*
▼ **Get Real Surfaces Inc** F 845 337-4483
Poughkeepsie *(G-13901)*
Glens Falls Ready Mix Inc F 518 793-1695
Queensbury *(G-13997)*
Glenwood Cast Stone Inc G 718 859-6500
Brooklyn *(G-2027)*
Grace Associates Inc G 718 767-9000
Harrison *(G-5986)*
Graymont Materials (ny) Inc G 518 483-2671
Malone *(G-8010)*
Graymont Materials (ny) Inc G 518 873-2275
Lewis *(G-7431)*
Great ATL Pr-Cast Con Statuary G 718 948-5677
Staten Island *(G-15682)*
Guardian Concrete Inc F 518 372-0080
Schenectady *(G-15267)*
H F Cary & Sons G 607 598-2563
Lockwood *(G-7627)*
Hanson Aggregates East LLC G 716 372-1574
Allegany *(G-201)*
Healthy Basement Systems LLC F 516 650-9046
Medford *(G-8249)*
▲ **Heidenhain International Inc** C 716 661-1700
Jamestown *(G-6999)*
Ideal Burial Vault Company G 585 599-2242
Corfu *(G-3955)*
Island Ready Mix Inc E 631 874-3777
Center Moriches *(G-3467)*
Jab Concrete Supply Corp E 718 842-5250
Bronx *(G-1364)*
Jefferson Concrete Corp D 315 788-4171
Watertown *(G-16655)*
Jenna Concrete Corporation E 718 842-5250
Bronx *(G-1366)*
Jenna Harlem River Inc G 718 842-5997
Bronx *(G-1367)*
John E Potente & Sons Inc G 516 935-8585
Hicksville *(G-6357)*
▲ **Key Cast Stone Company Inc** E 631 789-2145
Amityville *(G-302)*
Lafarge North America Inc E 518 756-5000
Ravena *(G-14023)*
Lakelands Concrete Pdts Inc E 585 624-1990
Lima *(G-7445)*
Lhv Precast Inc E 845 336-8880
Kingston *(G-7196)*
Long Island Geotech G 631 473-1044
Port Jefferson *(G-13776)*
Long Island Green Guys G 631 664-4306
Riverhead *(G-14148)*
Long Island Precast Inc E 631 286-0240
Brookhaven *(G-1508)*
M K Ulrich Construction Inc F 716 893-5777
Buffalo *(G-3053)*
Meditub Incorporated F 866 633-4882
Lawrence *(G-7395)*
Mid-Hudson Concrete Pdts Inc G 845 265-3141
Cold Spring *(G-3763)*
Milano Granite and Marble Corp F 718 477-7200
Staten Island *(G-15706)*
▲ **Nicolia Concrete Products Inc** D 631 669-0700
Lindenhurst *(G-7476)*
Northeast Concrete Pdts Inc F 518 563-0700
Plattsburgh *(G-13681)*
▲ **NY Tempering LLC** G 718 326-8989
Maspeth *(G-8160)*
Oldcastle Precast Inc F 518 767-2116
South Bethlehem *(G-15514)*
Oldcastle Precast Inc E 518 767-2112
Selkirk *(G-15356)*
Oneida Sales & Service Inc F 716 270-0433
Lackawanna *(G-7245)*
P J R Industries Inc E 716 825-9300
Buffalo *(G-3106)*
Pelkowski Precast Corp F 631 269-5727
Kings Park *(G-7173)*
Preload Concrete Structures E 631 231-8100
Hauppauge *(G-6169)*
Presbrey-Leland Inc G 914 949-2264
Valhalla *(G-16371)*
Quikrete Companies Inc E 716 213-2027
Lackawanna *(G-7247)*
Rain Catchers Seamless Gutters G 516 520-1956
Bethpage *(G-878)*
Riefler Concrete Products LLC C 716 649-3260
Hamburg *(G-5940)*
Robert M Vault G 315 243-1447
Bridgeport *(G-1236)*
Robinson Concrete Inc E 315 253-6666
Auburn *(G-516)*
Roman Stone Construction Co E 631 667-0566
Bay Shore *(G-738)*
▲ **Royal Marble & Granite Inc** G 516 536-5900
Oceanside *(G-13094)*
St Raymond Monument Co G 718 824-3600
Bronx *(G-1462)*
Stag Brothers Cast Stone Co G 718 629-0975
Brooklyn *(G-2596)*
Steindl Cast Stone Co Inc G 718 296-8530
Woodhaven *(G-17308)*
Suffolk Cement Precast Inc G 631 727-4432
Calverton *(G-3299)*
▲ **Suhor Industries Inc** F 585 377-5100
Fairport *(G-4883)*
Suhor Industries Inc G 716 483-6818
Jamestown *(G-7032)*
Sunnycrest Inc E 315 252-7214
Auburn *(G-521)*
Superior Aggragates Supply LLC E 516 333-2923
Lindenhurst *(G-7488)*
Superior Walls Upstate NY Inc D 585 624-9390
Lima *(G-7449)*
Superior Wlls of Hdson Vly Inc E 845 485-4033
Poughkeepsie *(G-13937)*

SIC SECTION — 32 STONE, CLAY, GLASS, AND CONCRETE PRODUCTS

Taylor Concrete Products Inc ... E ... 315 788-2191
Watertown *(G-16673)*
Towne House Restorations Inc ... G ... 718 497-9200
Long Island City *(G-7904)*
▲ Transpo Industries Inc ... E ... 914 636-1000
New Rochelle *(G-8926)*
▲ Unilock New York Inc ... G ... 845 278-6700
Brewster *(G-1229)*
Universal Step Inc ... G ... 315 437-7611
East Syracuse *(G-4577)*
Vault Wo ... G ... 212 281-1723
Brooklyn *(G-2721)*
▲ Walter G Legge Company Inc ... G ... 914 737-5040
Peekskill *(G-13485)*
Wel Made Enterprises Inc ... F ... 631 752-1238
Farmingdale *(G-5141)*
Woodards Concrete Products Inc ... E ... 845 361-3471
Bullville *(G-3263)*
▲ Woodside Granite Industries ... G ... 585 589-6500
Albion *(G-171)*

3273 Ready-Mixed Concrete

A-1 Transitmix Inc ... F ... 718 292-3200
Bronx *(G-1256)*
Advanced Ready Mix Corp ... F ... 718 497-5020
Brooklyn *(G-1566)*
All American Transit Mix Corp ... G ... 718 417-3654
Brooklyn *(G-1585)*
Atlas Concrete Batching Corp ... D ... 718 523-3000
Jamaica *(G-6896)*
Atlas Transit Mix Corp ... C ... 718 523-3000
Jamaica *(G-6897)*
Barney & Dickenson Inc ... E ... 607 729-1536
Vestal *(G-16440)*
Barrett Paving Materials Inc ... F ... 315 788-2037
Watertown *(G-16636)*
Best Concrete Mix Corp ... E ... 718 463-5500
Flushing *(G-5230)*
Bonded Concrete Inc ... E ... 518 273-5800
Watervliet *(G-16680)*
Bonded Concrete Inc ... F ... 518 674-2854
West Sand Lake *(G-16931)*
▲ Brewster Transit Mix Corp ... E ... 845 279-3738
Brewster *(G-1213)*
Brewster Transit Mix Corp ... E ... 845 279-3738
Brewster *(G-1214)*
Byram Concrete & Supply LLC ... F ... 914 682-4477
White Plains *(G-17090)*
C & C Ready-Mix Corporation ... E ... 607 797-5108
Vestal *(G-16443)*
C & C Ready-Mix Corporation ... F ... 607 687-1690
Owego *(G-13351)*
Capital Concrete Inc ... G ... 716 648-8001
Hamburg *(G-5919)*
Casa Redimix Concrete Corp ... F ... 718 589-1555
Bronx *(G-1291)*
Ccz Ready Mix Concrete Corp ... G ... 516 579-7352
Levittown *(G-7426)*
Cemex Cement Inc ... D ... 212 317-6000
New York *(G-9559)*
Century Ready Mix Inc ... G ... 631 888-2200
West Babylon *(G-16781)*
Champion Materials Inc ... G ... 315 493-2654
Carthage *(G-3410)*
Champion Materials Inc ... E ... 315 493-2654
Carthage *(G-3411)*
Chenango Concrete Corp ... F ... 518 294-9964
Richmondville *(G-14089)*
Clark Concrete Co Inc ... G ... 315 478-4101
Syracuse *(G-15896)*
Classic Concrete Corp ... F ... 516 822-1800
Hicksville *(G-6332)*
Clemente Latham Concrete Corp ... D ... 518 374-2222
Schenectady *(G-15243)*
Cobleskill Red E Mix & Supply ... F ... 518 234-2015
Amsterdam *(G-340)*
Corona Ready Mix Inc ... F ... 718 271-5940
Corona *(G-3995)*
Cortland Ready Mix Inc ... F ... 607 753-3063
Cortland *(G-4021)*
Cossitt Concrete Products Inc ... F ... 315 824-2700
Hamilton *(G-5947)*
Costanza Ready Mix Inc ... G ... 516 334-7788
North Bellmore *(G-12918)*
Cranesville Block Co Inc ... E ... 315 732-2135
Utica *(G-16317)*
Cranesville Block Co Inc ... E ... 845 292-1585
Liberty *(G-7436)*
Cranesville Block Co Inc ... E ... 845 896-5687
Fishkill *(G-5182)*
Cranesville Block Co Inc ... E ... 845 331-1775
Kingston *(G-7185)*
Cranesville Block Co Inc ... G ... 315 384-4000
Norfolk *(G-12898)*
▲ Cranesville Block Co Inc ... E ... 518 684-6000
Amsterdam *(G-341)*
Cranesville Block Co Inc ... E ... 315 773-2296
Felts Mills *(G-5167)*
Custom Mix Concrete Inc ... G ... 607 737-0281
Coopers Plains *(G-3882)*
Custom Mix Concrete Inc ... G ... 607 737-0281
Chemung *(G-3593)*
Custom Mix Inc ... F ... 516 797-7090
Massapequa Park *(G-8185)*
Dalrymple Grav & Contg Co Inc ... F ... 607 739-0391
Pine City *(G-13550)*
Dalrymple Holding Corp ... E ... 607 737-6200
Pine City *(G-13551)*
Deer Park Sand & Gravel Corp ... E ... 631 586-2323
Bay Shore *(G-693)*
Dicks Concrete Co Inc ... E ... 845 374-5966
New Hampton *(G-8799)*
Dunkirk Construction Products ... G ... 716 366-5220
Dunkirk *(G-4338)*
E Tetz & Sons Inc ... D ... 845 692-4486
Middletown *(G-8437)*
East Coast Spring Mix Inc ... G ... 845 355-1215
New Hampton *(G-8800)*
Electric City Concrete Co Inc ... E ... 518 887-5560
Amsterdam *(G-343)*
Empire Transit Mix Inc ... E ... 718 384-3000
Brooklyn *(G-1922)*
F H Stickles & Son Inc ... F ... 518 851-9048
Livingston *(G-7560)*
Ferrara Bros Bldg Mtls Corp ... E ... 718 939-3030
Flushing *(G-5240)*
Fulmont Ready-Mix Company Inc ... F ... 518 887-5560
Amsterdam *(G-347)*
G & J Rdymx & Masnry Sup Inc ... F ... 718 454-0800
Hollis *(G-6497)*
Glens Falls Ready Mix Inc ... G ... 518 793-1695
Amsterdam *(G-348)*
Glens Falls Ready Mix Inc ... F ... 518 793-1695
Queensbury *(G-13997)*
Grandview Concrete Corp ... E ... 518 346-7981
Schenectady *(G-15266)*
Graymont Materials (ny) Inc ... F ... 315 265-8036
Plattsburgh *(G-13666)*
Graymont Materials (ny) Inc ... D ... 518 561-5321
Plattsburgh *(G-13665)*
Graymont Materials (ny) Inc ... G ... 518 873-2275
Lewis *(G-7431)*
Greco Bros Rdymx Con Co Inc ... G ... 718 855-6271
Brooklyn *(G-2050)*
Haley Concrete Inc ... F ... 716 492-0849
Delevan *(G-4234)*
Hanson Aggregates East LLC ... F ... 585 344-1810
Batavia *(G-637)*
Hanson Aggregates East LLC ... F ... 585 798-0762
Medina *(G-8274)*
Hanson Aggregates East LLC ... F ... 716 372-1574
Falconer *(G-4900)*
Hanson Aggregates East LLC ... E ... 315 548-2911
Phelps *(G-13533)*
Hanson Aggregates New York LLC ... F ... 716 665-4620
Jamestown *(G-6998)*
Hanson Aggregates New York LLC ... F ... 585 638-5841
Pavilion *(G-13449)*
Hanson Aggregates New York LLC ... C ... 315 469-5501
Jamesville *(G-7048)*
Inwood Material ... F ... 516 371-1842
Inwood *(G-6759)*
Island Ready Mix Inc ... E ... 631 874-3777
Center Moriches *(G-3467)*
James Town Macadam Inc ... D ... 716 665-4504
Falconer *(G-4903)*
Jenna Concrete Corporation ... E ... 718 842-5250
Bronx *(G-1366)*
Jenna Harlem River Inc ... G ... 718 842-5997
Bronx *(G-1367)*
Jet Redi Mix Concrete Inc ... F ... 631 580-3640
Ronkonkoma *(G-14919)*
King Road Materials Inc ... F ... 518 382-5354
Albany *(G-95)*
Kings Park Ready Mix Corp ... F ... 631 269-4330
Kings Park *(G-7172)*
Lafarge North America Inc ... E ... 518 756-5000
Ravena *(G-14023)*
Lazarek Inc ... G ... 315 343-1242
Oswego *(G-13334)*
Lehigh Cement Company ... E ... 518 943-5940
Catskill *(G-3430)*
Lewbro Ready Mix Inc ... G ... 315 497-0498
Groton *(G-5899)*
Manitou Concrete ... D ... 585 424-6040
Rochester *(G-14492)*
Manzione Ready Mix Corp ... G ... 718 628-3837
Brooklyn *(G-2264)*
Mastro Concrete Inc ... G ... 718 528-6788
Rosedale *(G-15014)*
N Y Western Concrete Corp ... G ... 585 343-6850
Batavia *(G-643)*
New Atlantic Ready Mix Corp ... G ... 718 812-0739
Hollis *(G-6498)*
Nex-Gen Ready Mix Corp ... G ... 347 231-0073
Bronx *(G-1410)*
Nicolia Ready Mix Inc ... E ... 631 669-7000
Lindenhurst *(G-7477)*
Northern Ready-Mix Inc ... F ... 315 598-2141
Fulton *(G-5473)*
Oldcastle Precast Inc ... F ... 518 767-2116
South Bethlehem *(G-15514)*
Oneida Sales & Service Inc ... F ... 716 270-0433
Lackawanna *(G-7245)*
Otsego Ready Mix Inc ... F ... 607 432-3400
Oneonta *(G-13191)*
Precision Ready Mix Inc ... G ... 718 658-5600
Jamaica *(G-6939)*
Presti Ready Mix Concrete Inc ... G ... 516 378-6006
Freeport *(G-5419)*
Quality Ready Mix Inc ... F ... 516 437-0100
New Hyde Park *(G-8857)*
Queens Ready Mix Inc ... G ... 718 526-4919
Jamaica *(G-6942)*
Quikrete Companies Inc ... E ... 315 673-2020
Marcellus *(G-8088)*
Residential Fences Corp ... E ... 631 205-9758
Ridge *(G-14094)*
Richmond Ready Mix Corp ... G ... 917 731-8400
Staten Island *(G-15733)*
Riefler Concrete Products LLC ... C ... 716 649-3260
Hamburg *(G-5940)*
Robinson Concrete Inc ... E ... 315 253-6666
Auburn *(G-516)*
Robinson Concrete Inc ... F ... 315 492-6200
Jamesville *(G-7051)*
Robinson Concrete Inc ... F ... 315 676-4662
Brewerton *(G-1205)*
Rochester Asphalt Materials ... D ... 585 924-7360
Farmington *(G-5154)*
Rochester Asphalt Materials ... G ... 585 381-7010
Rochester *(G-14634)*
Rock Iroquois Products Inc ... F ... 585 381-7010
Rochester *(G-14655)*
Rural Hill Sand and Grav Corp ... F ... 315 846-5212
Woodville *(G-17367)*
Russian Mix Inc ... G ... 347 385-7198
Brooklyn *(G-2517)*
Saunders Concrete Co Inc ... F ... 607 756-7905
Cortland *(G-4044)*
Scara-Mix Inc ... E ... 718 442-7357
Staten Island *(G-15734)*
Seville Central Mix Corp ... G ... 516 868-3000
Freeport *(G-5426)*
Seville Central Mix Corp ... D ... 516 293-6190
Old Bethpage *(G-13130)*
Seville Central Mix Corp ... E ... 516 239-8333
Lawrence *(G-7400)*
South Shore Ready Mix Inc ... G ... 516 872-3049
Valley Stream *(G-16428)*
Star Ready Mix East Inc ... F ... 631 289-8787
East Hampton *(G-4416)*
Star Ready Mix Inc ... F ... 631 289-8787
Medford *(G-8260)*
Stephen Miller Gen Contrs Inc ... E ... 518 661-5601
Gloversville *(G-5723)*
Suffolk Cement Products Inc ... E ... 631 727-2317
Calverton *(G-3300)*
Sullivan Concrete Inc ... F ... 845 888-2235
Cochecton *(G-3744)*
T Mix Inc ... G ... 646 379-6814
Brooklyn *(G-2639)*
TEC - Crete Transit Mix Corp ... E ... 718 657-6880
Ridgewood *(G-14126)*
Thousand Island Ready Mix Con ... G ... 315 686-3203
La Fargeville *(G-7238)*
Torrington Industries Inc ... G ... 315 676-4662
Central Square *(G-3518)*
United Materials LLC ... D ... 716 683-1432
North Tonawanda *(G-13004)*

SIC

Employee Codes: A=Over 500 employees, B=251-500
C=101-250, D=51-100, E=20-50, F=10-19, G=5-9

2017 Harris
New York Manufacturers Directory
801

United Materials LLC ....E ....716 731-2332 Sanborn *(G-15129)*
United Materials LLC ....G ....716 662-0564 Orchard Park *(G-13301)*
United Transit Mix Inc ....F ....718 416-3400 Brooklyn *(G-2703)*
US Concrete Inc ....E ....718 853-4644 Roslyn Heights *(G-15034)*
US Concrete Inc ....E ....718 438-6800 Brooklyn *(G-2712)*
W F Saunders & Sons Inc ....F ....315 469-3217 Nedrow *(G-8773)*
Watertown Concrete Inc ....F ....315 788-1040 Watertown *(G-16675)*

3274 Lime

Masick Soil Conservation Co ....F ....518 827-5354 Schoharie *(G-15317)*
▲ **Minerals Technologies Inc** ....E ....212 878-1800 New York *(G-11276)*

3275 Gypsum Prdts

▲ **Continental Buchanan LLC** ....D ....703 480-3800 Buchanan *(G-2785)*
East Pattern & Model Corp ....E ....585 461-3240 Fairport *(G-4856)*
Empire Gypsum Pdts & Sup Corp ....G ....914 592-8141 Elmsford *(G-4749)*
Henderson Hbr Prfrmg Arts Assn ....F ....315 938-7333 Henderson Harbor *(G-6291)*
Lafarge North America Inc ....D ....914 930-3027 Buchanan *(G-2786)*
United States Gypsum Company ....C ....585 948-5221 Oakfield *(G-13066)*

3281 Cut Stone Prdts

Adirondack Precision Cut Stone ....F ....518 681-3060 Queensbury *(G-13986)*
Alart Inc ....G ....212 840-1508 New York *(G-9071)*
▲ **Amendola MBL & Stone Ctr Inc** ....D ....914 997-7968 White Plains *(G-17076)*
American Bluestone LLC ....F ....607 369-2235 Sidney *(G-15435)*
Aurora Stone Group LLC ....F ....315 471-6869 East Syracuse *(G-4508)*
▲ **Barra & Trumbore Inc** ....G ....845 626-5442 Kerhonkson *(G-7154)*
Busch Products Inc ....E ....315 474-8422 Syracuse *(G-15878)*
Callanan Industries Inc ....E ....845 331-6868 Kingston *(G-7182)*
Capital Stone LLC ....G ....518 382-7588 Schenectady *(G-15239)*
Capital Stone Saratoga LLC ....G ....518 226-8677 Saratoga Springs *(G-15147)*
Crown Hill Stone Inc ....E ....716 326-4601 Westfield *(G-17047)*
Dalrymple Holding Corp ....E ....607 737-6200 Pine City *(G-13551)*
Denton Stoneworks Inc ....F ....516 746-1500 Garden City Park *(G-5539)*
▲ **Devonian Stone New York Inc** ....E ....607 655-2600 Windsor *(G-17272)*
Dicamillo Marble and Granite ....E ....845 878-0078 Patterson *(G-13437)*
◆ **Domenick Denigris Inc** ....E ....718 823-2264 Bronx *(G-1315)*
Dominic De Nigris Inc ....E ....718 597-4460 Bronx *(G-1316)*
▲ **European Marble Works Co Inc** ....F ....718 387-9778 Garden City *(G-5504)*
▲ **Evergreen Slate Company Inc** ....D ....518 642-2530 Middle Granville *(G-8398)*
First Presbyterian Church ....G ....315 252-3861 Auburn *(G-495)*
Fordham Marble Co Inc ....F ....914 682-6699 White Plains *(G-17110)*
▲ **Gdi Custom Marble & Granite** ....F ....718 996-9100 Brooklyn *(G-2018)*
Geneva Granite Co Inc ....F ....315 789-8142 Geneva *(G-5578)*
▲ **Glen Plaza Marble & Gran Inc** ....G ....516 671-1100 Glen Cove *(G-5617)*
▲ **Granite & Marble Works Inc** ....E ....518 584-2800 Gansevoort *(G-5486)*
Granite Tops Inc ....E ....914 699-2909 Mount Vernon *(G-8687)*
▲ **Granite Works LLC** ....E ....607 565-7012 Waverly *(G-16702)*
Graymont Materials Inc ....E ....518 561-5200 Plattsburgh *(G-13667)*
Hanson Aggregates East LLC ....F ....315 493-3721 Great Bend *(G-5783)*
Hanson Aggregates PA LLC ....E ....315 789-6202 Oaks Corners *(G-13070)*
House of Stone Inc ....G ....845 782-7271 Monroe *(G-8556)*
▲ **Icestone LLC** ....E ....718 624-4900 Brooklyn *(G-2095)*
▲ **International Stone Accessrs** ....G ....718 522-5399 Brooklyn *(G-2111)*
▲ **Italian Marble & Granite Inc** ....F ....716 741-1800 Clarence Center *(G-3676)*
Jamestown Kitchen & Bath Inc ....G ....716 665-2299 Jamestown *(G-7008)*
▲ **Joseph Corcoran Marble Inc** ....G ....631 423-8712 Huntington Station *(G-6713)*
▲ **Lace Marble & Granite Inc** ....G ....718 854-9028 Brooklyn *(G-2189)*
Marble Doctors LLC ....E ....203 628-8339 New York *(G-11143)*
▲ **Marble Works Inc** ....E ....914 376-3653 Yonkers *(G-17465)*
Masonville Stone Incorporated ....G ....607 265-3597 Masonville *(G-8108)*
MCM Natural Stone Inc ....F ....585 586-6510 Rochester *(G-14502)*
▲ **Minerals Technologies Inc** ....E ....212 878-1800 New York *(G-11276)*
Monroe Industries Inc ....G ....585 226-8230 Avon *(G-541)*
New York Marble and Stone Corp ....F ....718 729-7272 Maspeth *(G-8156)*
▲ **New York Quarries Inc** ....F ....518 756-3138 Alcove *(G-172)*
North American Slate Inc ....G ....518 642-1702 Granville *(G-5778)*
North American Stone Inc ....G ....585 266-4020 Rochester *(G-14541)*
North Shore Monuments Inc ....G ....516 759-2156 Glen Head *(G-5639)*
Northeast Solite Corporation ....E ....845 246-2177 Mount Marion *(G-8652)*
Pallette Stone Corporation ....E ....518 584-2421 Gansevoort *(G-5487)*
PR & Stone & Tile Inc ....G ....718 383-1115 Brooklyn *(G-2434)*
Premier Group NY ....F ....212 229-1200 New York *(G-11698)*
Puccio Design International ....F ....516 248-6426 Garden City *(G-5528)*
Rivera ....G ....718 458-1488 Flushing *(G-5288)*
Rock Iroquois Products Inc ....F ....585 381-7010 Rochester *(G-14655)*
Roto Salt Company Inc ....E ....315 536-3742 Penn Yan *(G-13519)*
▲ **Royal Marble & Granite Inc** ....G ....516 536-5900 Oceanside *(G-13094)*
Salsburg Dimensional Stone ....F ....631 653-6790 Brookhaven *(G-1510)*
Sanford Stone LLC ....E ....607 467-1313 Deposit *(G-4279)*
Seneca Stone Corporation ....F ....315 549-8253 Fayette *(G-5162)*
Seneca Stone Corporation ....G ....607 737-6200 Pine City *(G-13552)*
Sheldon Slate Products Co Inc ....E ....518 642-1280 Middle Granville *(G-8401)*
Suffolk Granite Manufacturing ....E ....631 226-4774 Lindenhurst *(G-7486)*
Thalle Industries Inc ....E ....914 762-3415 Briarcliff Manor *(G-1231)*
▲ **Unilock New York Inc** ....G ....845 278-6700 Brewster *(G-1229)*
Unique MBL Gran Orgnztion Corp ....G ....718 482-0440 Long Island City *(G-7907)*
Vermont Natural Stoneworks ....E ....518 642-2460 Middle Granville *(G-8403)*
Vermont Structural Slate Co ....F ....518 499-1912 Whitehall *(G-17191)*
W F Saunders & Sons Inc ....F ....315 469-3217 Nedrow *(G-8773)*
White Plains Marble Inc ....G ....914 347-6000 Elmsford *(G-4794)*

3291 Abrasive Prdts

09 Flshy Bll/Dsert Sunrise LLC ....G ....518 583-6638 Saratoga Springs *(G-15140)*
American Douglas Metals Inc ....F ....716 856-3170 Buffalo *(G-2807)*
▲ **Barker Brothers Incorporated** ....D ....718 456-6400 Ridgewood *(G-14101)*
◆ **Barton Mines Company LLC** ....C ....518 798-5462 Glens Falls *(G-5672)*
Bedrock Landscaping Mtls Corp ....G ....631 587-4950 Babylon *(G-546)*
▲ **Buffalo Abrasives Inc** ....E ....716 693-3856 North Tonawanda *(G-12962)*
Charles A Hones Inc ....G ....607 273-5720 Ithaca *(G-6832)*
Conrad Blasius Equipment Co ....G ....516 753-1200 Plainview *(G-13590)*
▲ **Datum Alloys Inc** ....G ....607 239-6274 Endicott *(G-4800)*
▲ **Dedeco International Sales Inc** ....E ....845 887-4840 Long Eddy *(G-7642)*
▲ **Dico Products Corporation** ....F ....315 797-0470 Utica *(G-16323)*
▲ **Dimanco Inc** ....G ....315 797-0470 Utica *(G-16324)*
◆ **Divine Brothers Company** ....C ....315 797-0470 Utica *(G-16327)*
▼ **EAC Holdings of NY Corp** ....E ....716 822-2500 Buffalo *(G-2925)*
◆ **Electro Abrasives LLC** ....E ....716 822-2500 Buffalo *(G-2933)*
Eraser Company Inc ....C ....315 454-3237 Mattydale *(G-8212)*
Global Abrasive Products Inc ....E ....716 438-0047 Lockport *(G-7588)*
Imerys Fsed Mnrl Ngara FLS Inc ....G ....716 286-1234 Niagara Falls *(G-12833)*
▲ **Imerys Fsed Mnrl Ngara FLS Inc** ....E ....716 286-1250 Niagara Falls *(G-12834)*
Jta USA Inc ....G ....718 722-0902 Brooklyn *(G-2155)*
Malyn Industrial Ceramics Inc ....G ....716 741-1510 Clarence Center *(G-3679)*
Meloon Foundries LLC ....E ....315 454-3231 Syracuse *(G-15985)*
◆ **Pellets LLC** ....G ....716 693-1750 North Tonawanda *(G-12985)*
▲ **Precision Abrasives Corp** ....E ....716 826-5833 Orchard Park *(G-13291)*
Precision Elctro Mnrl Pmco Inc ....E ....716 284-2484 Niagara Falls *(G-12863)*
Raulli and Sons Inc ....E ....315 479-2515 Syracuse *(G-16020)*
Saint-Gbain Advnced Crmics LLC ....E ....716 691-2000 Amherst *(G-259)*
Saint-Gobain Abrasives Inc ....B ....518 266-2200 Watervliet *(G-16688)*
▲ **Select-Tech Inc** ....G ....845 895-8111 Wallkill *(G-16546)*
Smm - North America Trade Corp ....G ....212 604-0710 New York *(G-12108)*
Sunbelt Industries Inc ....F ....315 823-2947 Little Falls *(G-7505)*
◆ **Uneeda Enterprizes Inc** ....C ....877 863-3321 Spring Valley *(G-15605)*
Warren Cutlery Corp ....F ....845 876-3444 Rhinebeck *(G-14060)*
◆ **Washington Mills Elec Mnrls** ....D ....716 278-6600 Niagara Falls *(G-12890)*
▲ **Washington Mills Tonawanda Inc** ....E ....716 693-4550 Tonawanda *(G-16213)*

3292 Asbestos products

▲ **Allied Tile Mfg Corp** ....G ....718 647-2200 Brooklyn *(G-1592)*
Regional MGT & Consulting Inc ....F ....718 599-3718 Brooklyn *(G-2487)*
Shenfield Studio LLC ....F ....315 436-8869 Syracuse *(G-16040)*

3295 Minerals & Earths: Ground Or Treated

A&B Conservation LLC ....G ....845 282-7272 Monsey *(G-8566)*
Allied Aero Services Inc ....G ....631 277-9368 Brentwood *(G-1175)*
DSM Nutritional Products LLC ....C ....518 372-5155 Glenville *(G-5701)*
◆ **Fortitech Inc** ....C ....518 372-5155 Schenectady *(G-15255)*
▲ **Mineralbious Corp** ....F ....516 498-9715 Port Washington *(G-13846)*
▲ **Minerals Technologies Inc** ....E ....212 878-1800 New York *(G-11276)*

SIC SECTION
33 PRIMARY METAL INDUSTRIES

Company	Emp Code	Phone
Norlite Corporation	B	518 235-0030
Cohoes (G-3754)		
Northeast Solite Corporation	E	845 246-2646
Saugerties (G-15189)		
Northeast Solite Corporation	E	845 246-2177
Mount Marion (G-8652)		
▲ Opta Minerals	F	905 689-7361
Buffalo (G-3103)		
Oro Avanti Inc	G	516 487-5185
Great Neck (G-5826)		
▼ Prince Minerals LLC	D	646 747-4222
New York (G-11711)		
Skyline LLC	E	631 403-4131
East Setauket (G-4492)		

3296 Mineral Wool

Company	Emp Code	Phone
American Securities LLC	E	716 696-3012
Tonawanda (G-16138)		
▲ Burnett Process Inc	G	585 254-8080
Rochester (G-14252)		
Elliot Industries Inc	G	716 287-3100
Ellington (G-4644)		
Lencore Acoustics Corp	F	315 384-9114
Norfolk (G-12899)		
Mecho Systems	F	718 729-8373
Long Island City (G-7807)		
Owens Corning Sales LLC	B	518 475-3600
Feura Bush (G-5174)		
Richlar Industries Inc	F	315 463-5144
East Syracuse (G-4559)		
▲ Soundcoat Company Inc	D	631 242-2200
Deer Park (G-4212)		
▲ Ssf Production LLC	F	518 324-3407
Plattsburgh (G-13697)		
Superior Plus Cnstr Pdts Corp	F	315 463-5144
East Syracuse (G-4569)		
Unifrax Corporation	E	716 278-3800
Niagara Falls (G-12886)		
Unifrax I LLC	C	716 696-3000
Tonawanda (G-16210)		

3297 Nonclay Refractories

Company	Emp Code	Phone
American Securities LLC	E	716 696-3012
Tonawanda (G-16138)		
◆ Ask Chemicals Hi-Tech LLC	D	607 587-9146
Alfred Station (G-195)		
▲ Blasch Precision Ceramics Inc	D	518 436-1263
Menands (G-8369)		
Capitol Restoration Corp	G	516 783-1425
North Bellmore (G-12915)		
▲ Ceramaterials LLC	G	518 701-6722
Port Jervis (G-13781)		
Filtros Ltd	E	585 586-8770
East Rochester (G-4459)		
Global Alumina Corporation	G	212 351-0000
New York (G-10311)		
Global Alumina Services Co	B	212 309-8060
New York (G-10312)		
Hanyan & Higgins Company Inc	G	315 769-8838
Massena (G-8196)		
◆ Monofrax LLC	C	716 483-7200
Falconer (G-4907)		
▼ Rembar Company LLC	E	914 693-2620
Dobbs Ferry (G-4302)		
Roccera LLC	F	585 426-0887
Rochester (G-14632)		
Saint-Gobain Dynamics Inc	F	716 278-6007
Niagara Falls (G-12872)		
▲ Silicon Carbide Products Inc	E	607 562-8599
Horseheads (G-6593)		
Surmet Ceramics Corporation	F	716 875-4091
Buffalo (G-3204)		
Unifrax I LLC	C	716 696-3000
Tonawanda (G-16210)		
▲ Zircar Refr Composites Inc	G	845 651-4481
Florida (G-5218)		
Zircar Zirconia Inc	E	845 651-3040
Florida (G-5219)		

3299 Nonmetallic Mineral Prdts, NEC

Company	Emp Code	Phone
American Crmic Process RES LLC	G	315 828-6268
Phelps (G-13529)		
American Securities LLC	E	716 696-3012
Tonawanda (G-16138)		
American Wood Column Corp	G	718 782-3163
Brooklyn (G-1610)		
Argosy Ceramic Arospc Mtls LLC	F	212 268-0003
New York (G-9200)		
B & R Promotional Products	G	212 563-0040
New York (G-9288)		
▲ Barrett Bronze Inc	E	914 699-6060
Mount Vernon (G-8665)		
Beyond Design Inc	G	607 865-7487
Walton (G-16547)		
Brooklyn Remembers Inc	F	718 491-1705
Brooklyn (G-1731)		
▲ Cetek Inc	E	845 452-3510
Poughkeepsie (G-13892)		
▲ Design Research Ltd	C	212 228-7675
New York (G-9854)		
Dream Statuary Inc	G	718 647-2024
Brooklyn (G-1878)		
Elliot Gantz & Company Inc	E	631 249-0680
Farmingdale (G-4987)		
Enrg Inc	F	716 873-2939
Buffalo (G-2940)		
Essex Works Ltd	F	718 495-4575
Brooklyn (G-1937)		
Everblock Systems LLC	G	844 422-5625
New York (G-10089)		
▲ Foster Reeve & Associates Inc	G	718 609-0090
Brooklyn (G-1998)		
Fra-Rik Formica Fabg Co Inc	G	718 597-3335
Bronx (G-1337)		
Gallery 91	G	212 966-3722
New York (G-10242)		
Halo Associates	G	212 691-9549
New York (G-10399)		
▲ Heany Industries Inc	D	585 889-2700
Scottsville (G-15336)		
Jonas Louis Paul Studios Inc	G	518 851-2211
Hudson (G-6623)		
Kodiak Studios Inc	G	718 769-5399
Brooklyn (G-2178)		
▲ Reliance Mica Co Inc	G	718 788-0282
Rockaway Park (G-14787)		
▲ S & J Trading Inc	G	718 347-1323
Floral Park (G-5209)		
▲ Starfire Systems Inc	F	518 899-9336
Schenectady (G-15300)		
Studio Associates of New York	G	212 268-1163
New York (G-12219)		
▲ Ufx Holding I Corporation	G	212 644-5900
New York (G-12445)		
Ufx Holding II Corporation	G	212 644-5900
New York (G-12446)		
Unifrax Holding Co	G	212 644-5900
New York (G-12456)		
◆ Unifrax I LLC	C	716 768-6500
Tonawanda (G-16211)		
Unifrax I LLC	C	716 696-3000
Tonawanda (G-16210)		
Vescom Structural Systems Inc	F	516 876-8100
Westbury (G-17041)		

33 PRIMARY METAL INDUSTRIES

3312 Blast Furnaces, Coke Ovens, Steel & Rolling Mills

Company	Emp Code	Phone
A-1 Iron Works Inc	G	718 927-4766
Brooklyn (G-1537)		
Albaluz Films LLC	G	347 613-2321
New York (G-9072)		
▲ Allvac	F	716 433-4411
Lockport (G-7569)		
▲ American Chimney Supplies Inc	G	631 434-2020
Hauppauge (G-6020)		
Artistic Ironworks Inc	G	631 665-4285
Bay Shore (G-672)		
B H M Metal Products Co	G	845 292-5297
Kauneonga Lake (G-7136)		
Baker Tool & Die	G	716 694-2025
North Tonawanda (G-12958)		
Baker Tool & Die & Die	G	716 694-2025
North Tonawanda (G-12959)		
Belmet Products Inc	E	718 542-8220
Bronx (G-1283)		
Bonura and Sons Iron Works	F	718 381-4100
Franklin Square (G-5361)		
Bryant Manufacturing Wny Inc	G	716 894-8282
Buffalo (G-2847)		
China Industrial Steel Inc	G	646 328-1502
New York (G-9598)		
Coventry Manufacturing Co Inc	E	914 668-2212
Mount Vernon (G-8674)		
◆ Crucible Industries LLC	B	800 365-1180
Syracuse (G-15913)		
Cs Manufacturing Limited	E	607 587-8154
Alfred (G-193)		
DAgostino Iron Works Inc	G	585 235-8850
Rochester (G-14298)		
Dakota Systems Mfg Corp	G	631 249-5811
Farmingdale (G-4973)		
David Fehlman	G	315 455-8888
Syracuse (G-15922)		
▲ Dunkirk Specialty Steel LLC	C	716 366-1000
Dunkirk (G-4340)		
Elderlee Incorporated	C	315 789-6670
Oaks Corners (G-13069)		
Fuller Tool Incorporated	F	315 891-3183
Newport (G-12790)		
Hallock Fabricating Corp	G	631 727-2441
Riverhead (G-14144)		
▼ Handy & Harman Ltd	A	914 461-1300
White Plains (G-17120)		
Hitachi Metals America Ltd	E	914 694-9200
Purchase (G-13958)		
Hmi Metal Powders	C	315 839-5421
Clayville (G-3688)		
▲ Homogeneous Metals Inc	D	315 839-5421
Clayville (G-3689)		
Image Iron Works Inc	G	718 592-8276
Corona (G-3998)		
◆ Jaquith Industries Inc	E	315 478-5700
Syracuse (G-15966)		
Jfe Engineering Corporation	F	212 310-9320
New York (G-10728)		
Jfe Steel America Inc	G	212 310-9320
New York (G-10729)		
▲ Juniper Elbow Co Inc	C	718 326-2546
Middle Village (G-8414)		
Kenbenco Inc	F	845 246-3066
Saugerties (G-15186)		
Lino International Inc	G	516 482-7100
Great Neck (G-5821)		
▲ Mardek LLC	G	585 735-9333
Pittsford (G-13569)		
Markin Tubing LP	F	585 495-6211
Buffalo (G-3056)		
Markin Tubing Inc	C	585 495-6211
Wyoming (G-17381)		
Matrix Steel Company Inc	F	718 381-6800
Brooklyn (G-2284)		
N C Iron Works Inc	G	718 633-4660
Brooklyn (G-2346)		
◆ Niagara Specialty Metals Inc	E	716 542-5552
Akron (G-26)		
Nitro Wheels Inc	F	716 337-0709
North Collins (G-12930)		
▲ Nucor Steel Auburn Inc	B	315 253-4561
Auburn (G-511)		
Pecker Iron Works LLC	G	914 665-0100
Mount Kisco (G-8639)		
Qsf Inc	G	585 247-6200
Gates (G-5562)		
R D Specialties Inc	F	585 265-0220
Webster (G-16731)		
Recon Construction Corp	E	718 939-1305
Little Neck (G-7509)		
◆ Renco Group Inc	G	212 541-6000
New York (G-11832)		
Republic Steel Inc	B	716 827-2800
Blasdell (G-965)		
Rochester Structural LLC	F	585 436-1250
Rochester (G-14651)		
Safespan Platform Systems Inc	E	716 694-1100
Tonawanda (G-16198)		
Sims Group USA Holdings Corp	D	718 786-6031
Long Island City (G-7877)		
Sph Group Holdings LLC	G	212 520-2300
New York (G-12162)		
Spin-Rite Corporation	F	585 266-5200
Rochester (G-14695)		
Standex Air Dist Pdts Inc	E	585 798-0300
Medina (G-8283)		
Tdy Industries LLC	E	716 433-4411
Lockport (G-7617)		
TI Group Auto Systems LLC	G	315 568-7042
Seneca Falls (G-15371)		
▲ Tonawanda Coke Corporation	D	716 876-6222
Tonawanda (G-16206)		
Tri Valley Iron Inc	F	845 365-1013
Palisades (G-13403)		
Universal Stainless & Alloy	C	716 366-1000
Dunkirk (G-4352)		
Vell Company Inc	G	845 365-1013
Palisades (G-13404)		
▲ Viraj - USA Inc	G	516 280-8380
Garden City (G-5535)		

Employee Codes: A=Over 500 employees, B=251-500
C=101-250, D=51-100, E=20-50, F=10-19, G=5-9

33 PRIMARY METAL INDUSTRIES

Wheel & Tire Depot Ex Corp .... G 914 375-2100
 Yonkers *(G-17498)*

3313 Electrometallurgical Prdts

◆ CCA Holding Inc .... C 716 446-8800
 Amherst *(G-230)*
 Globe Metallurgical Inc .... D 716 804-0862
 Niagara Falls *(G-12825)*
▲ Golden Egret LLC .... G 516 922-2839
 East Norwich *(G-4446)*
◆ Medima LLC .... C 716 741-0400
 Clarence *(G-3666)*
 Thyssenkrupp Materials NA Inc .... G 212 972-8800
 New York *(G-12335)*

3315 Steel Wire Drawing & Nails & Spikes

▲ Able Industries Inc .... F 914 739-5685
 Cortlandt Manor *(G-4048)*
▲ Aerospace Wire & Cable Inc .... E 718 358-2345
 College Point *(G-3776)*
 Alexscoe LLC .... E 315 463-9207
 East Syracuse *(G-4500)*
◆ American Wire Tie Inc .... E 716 337-2412
 North Collins *(G-12926)*
 Bekaert Corporation .... E 716 830-1321
 Amherst *(G-227)*
▲ Braun Horticulture Inc .... G 716 282-6101
 Niagara Falls *(G-12798)*
 CFS Enterprises Inc .... E 718 585-0500
 Bronx *(G-1295)*
▲ Cobra Manufacturing Corp .... G 845 514-2505
 Lake Katrine *(G-7269)*
◆ Continental Cordage Corp .... D 315 655-9800
 Cazenovia *(G-3443)*
◆ Dragon Trading Inc .... G 212 717-1496
 New York *(G-9923)*
▲ Dsr International Corp .... G 631 427-2600
 Great Neck *(G-5803)*
 E B Iron Art LLC .... F 716 876-7510
 Buffalo *(G-2923)*
 EB Acquisitions LLC .... D 212 355-3310
 New York *(G-9971)*
 Forsyth Industries Inc .... E 716 652-1070
 Buffalo *(G-2953)*
◆ Handy & Harman .... E 914 461-1300
 White Plains *(G-17118)*
 Hanes Supply Inc .... E 518 438-0139
 Albany *(G-84)*
 Hitachi Metals America Ltd .... E 914 694-9200
 Purchase *(G-13958)*
◆ Hohmann & Barnard Inc .... E 631 234-0600
 Hauppauge *(G-6095)*
▲ Island Industries Corp .... G 631 451-8825
 Coram *(G-3945)*
▲ Lee Spring Company LLC .... C 718 362-5183
 Brooklyn *(G-2206)*
 Liberty Fabrication Inc .... G 718 495-5735
 Brooklyn *(G-2215)*
 Master-Halco Inc .... F 631 585-8150
 Ronkonkoma *(G-14939)*
 Northeast Wire and Cable Co .... G 716 297-8483
 Niagara Falls *(G-12852)*
▲ Nupro Technologies LLC .... F 412 422-5922
 Canandaigua *(G-3350)*
 Omega Wire Inc .... D 315 689-7115
 Jordan *(G-7130)*
 Oneonta Fence .... G 607 433-6707
 Oneonta *(G-13190)*
▲ Owl Wire & Cable LLC .... C 315 697-2011
 Canastota *(G-3370)*
▲ Qmc Technologies Inc .... F 716 681-0810
 Depew *(G-4271)*
▲ Rolling Gate Supply Corp .... E 718 366-5258
 Glendale *(G-5661)*
 Rose Fence Inc .... F 516 223-0777
 Baldwin *(G-561)*
 Sheltred Wkshp For Dsabled Inc .... C 607 722-2364
 Binghamton *(G-951)*
 Sigmund Cohn Corp .... D 914 664-5300
 Mount Vernon *(G-8734)*
 Spectrum Cable Corporation .... G 585 235-7714
 Rochester *(G-14694)*
▲ Styles Manufacturing Corp .... F 516 763-5303
 Oceanside *(G-13098)*
▲ Tappan Wire & Cable Inc .... C 845 353-9000
 Blauvelt *(G-976)*
 Technical Wldg Fabricators LLC .... F 518 463-2229
 Albany *(G-140)*
 Web Associates Inc .... G 716 883-3377
 Buffalo *(G-3249)*

3316 Cold Rolled Steel Sheet, Strip & Bars

Aero-Data Metal Crafters Inc .... C 631 471-7733
 Ronkonkoma *(G-14856)*
▲ Clover Wire Forming Co Inc .... E 914 375-0400
 Yonkers *(G-17428)*
◆ Gibraltar Industries Inc .... D 716 826-6500
 Buffalo *(G-2974)*
 Hitachi Metals America Ltd .... E 914 694-9200
 Purchase *(G-13958)*
 Niagara Lasalle Corporation .... D 716 827-7010
 Buffalo *(G-3089)*
 Northeast Cnstr Inds Inc .... F 845 565-1000
 Montgomery *(G-8598)*
◆ Renco Group Inc .... G 212 541-6000
 New York *(G-11832)*
 Sunlight US Co Inc .... G 716 826-6500
 Buffalo *(G-3201)*
 Worthington Industries Inc .... D 315 336-5500
 Rome *(G-14840)*

3317 Steel Pipe & Tubes

Coventry Manufacturing Co Inc .... E 914 668-2212
 Mount Vernon *(G-8674)*
◆ Davidson Corporation .... G 718 439-6300
 Brooklyn *(G-1843)*
◆ Handy & Harman .... E 914 461-1300
 White Plains *(G-17118)*
 Liberty Pipe Incorporated .... G 516 747-2472
 Mineola *(G-8521)*
▼ Markin Tubing LP .... D 585 495-6211
 Wyoming *(G-17380)*
 Markin Tubing LP .... F 585 495-6211
 Buffalo *(G-3056)*
 Markin Tubing Inc .... C 585 495-6211
 Wyoming *(G-17381)*
 McHone Industries Inc .... D 716 945-3380
 Salamanca *(G-15101)*
 Micromold Products Inc .... E 914 969-2850
 Yonkers *(G-17467)*
◆ Oriskany Mfg Tech LLC .... E 315 732-4962
 Yorkville *(G-17525)*
 Stony Brook Mfg Co Inc .... E 631 369-9530
 Calverton *(G-3298)*
▲ Super Steelworks Corporation .... G 718 386-4770
 Deer Park *(G-4215)*
 TI Group Auto Systems LLC .... G 315 568-7042
 Seneca Falls *(G-15371)*
▼ Tricon Piping Systems Inc .... F 315 655-4178
 Canastota *(G-3375)*
▲ Welded Tube Usa Inc .... D 716 828-1111
 Lackawanna *(G-7250)*

3321 Gray Iron Foundries

Acme Nipple Mfg Co Inc .... G 716 873-7491
 Buffalo *(G-2796)*
 Auburn Foundry Inc .... F 315 253-4441
 Auburn *(G-479)*
 Cpp - Guaymas .... C 315 687-0014
 Chittenango *(G-3631)*
◆ Dragon Trading Inc .... G 212 717-1496
 New York *(G-9923)*
 En Tech Corp .... F 845 398-0776
 Tappan *(G-16080)*
◆ Hitachi Metals America Ltd .... E 914 694-9200
 Purchase *(G-13959)*
 Jamestown Iron Works Inc .... F 716 665-2818
 Falconer *(G-4905)*
 Matrix Steel Company Inc .... G 718 381-6800
 Brooklyn *(G-2284)*
 McWane Inc .... B 607 734-2211
 Elmira *(G-4694)*
▲ Noresco Industrial Group Inc .... E 516 759-3355
 Glen Cove *(G-5622)*
 Oneida Foundries Inc .... E 315 363-4570
 Oneida *(G-13159)*
 Penner Elbow Company Inc .... F 718 526-9000
 Elmhurst *(G-4665)*
 S M S C Inc .... G 315 942-4394
 Boonville *(G-1169)*
▲ Staub Usa Inc .... G 914 747-0300
 Pleasantville *(G-13721)*

3322 Malleable Iron Foundries

Eastern Company .... D 315 468-6251
 Solvay *(G-15507)*
 Emcom Industries Inc .... G 716 852-3711
 Buffalo *(G-2936)*
▲ Noresco Industrial Group Inc .... E 516 759-3355
 Glen Cove *(G-5622)*

▲ Plattco Corporation .... E 518 563-4640
 Plattsburgh *(G-13687)*

3324 Steel Investment Foundries

Brinkman Precision Inc .... D 585 429-5001
 West Henrietta *(G-16872)*
 Consoldted Precision Pdts Corp .... B 315 687-0014
 Chittenango *(G-3630)*
 Cpp-Syracuse Inc .... E 315 687-0014
 Chittenango *(G-3632)*
 Cs Manufacturing Limited .... E 607 587-8154
 Alfred *(G-193)*
 Jbf Stainless LLC .... E 315 569-2800
 Cazenovia *(G-3446)*
 Quality Castings Inc .... E 732 409-3203
 Long Island City *(G-7853)*
 Worldwide Resources Inc .... F 718 760-5000
 Brooklyn *(G-2768)*

3325 Steel Foundries, NEC

A & V Castings Inc .... G 212 997-0042
 New York *(G-8982)*
 American Foundrymens Society .... D 315 468-6251
 Syracuse *(G-15853)*
 Amt Incorporated .... E 518 284-2910
 Sharon Springs *(G-15383)*
 Brinkman Intl Group Inc .... E 585 429-5000
 Rochester *(G-14245)*
 C J Winter Machine Tech .... E 585 429-5000
 Rochester *(G-14254)*
 Eastern Industrial Steel Corp .... G 845 639-9749
 New City *(G-8785)*
▲ Pcore Electric Company Inc .... D 585 768-1200
 Le Roy *(G-7418)*
 Steel Craft Rolling Door .... F 631 608-8662
 Copiague *(G-3929)*

3331 Primary Smelting & Refining Of Copper

Hengyuan Copper USA Inc .... G 718 357-6666
 Whitestone *(G-17209)*
 Sherburne Metal Sales Inc .... F 607 674-4441
 Sherburne *(G-15395)*
◆ Tecnofil Chenango SAC .... E 607 674-4441
 Sherburne *(G-15398)*

3334 Primary Production Of Aluminum

◆ Alcoa Inc .... D 212 836-2674
 New York *(G-9077)*
 Greene Brass & Alum Fndry LLC .... G 607 656-4204
 Bloomville *(G-996)*

3339 Primary Nonferrous Metals, NEC

▲ AAA Catalytic Recycling Inc .... F 631 920-7944
 Farmingdale *(G-4928)*
 Ames Goldsmith Corp .... E 518 792-7435
 Glens Falls *(G-5669)*
 Billanti Casting Co Inc .... E 516 775-4800
 New Hyde Park *(G-8819)*
 Doral Refining Corp .... E 516 223-3684
 Freeport *(G-5394)*
 Eco-Bat America LLC .... C 845 692-4414
 Middletown *(G-8439)*
 Euro Pacific Precious Metals .... E 212 481-0310
 New York *(G-10084)*
 General Refining & Smelting .... G 516 538-4747
 Hempstead *(G-6270)*
 General Refining Corporation .... G 516 538-4747
 Hempstead *(G-6271)*
 Globe Metallurgical Inc .... D 716 804-0862
 Niagara Falls *(G-12825)*
 Goldmark Products Inc .... E 631 777-3343
 Farmingdale *(G-5001)*
▼ Handy & Harman Ltd .... A 914 461-1300
 White Plains *(G-17120)*
 Hh Liquidating Corp .... A 646 282-2500
 New York *(G-10471)*
 Marina Jewelry Co Inc .... G 212 354-5027
 New York *(G-11152)*
▲ Materion Advanced Materials .... C 800 327-1355
 Buffalo *(G-3058)*
▲ Medima LLC .... C 716 741-0400
 Clarence *(G-3666)*
 Rochester Silver Works LLC .... G 585 743-1610
 Rochester *(G-14648)*
 RS Precision Industries Inc .... E 631 420-0424
 Farmingdale *(G-5105)*
 S & W Metal Trading Corp .... G 212 719-5070
 New York *(G-11944)*

SIC SECTION — 33 PRIMARY METAL INDUSTRIES

Sabin Metal Corporation ....C....... 585 538-2194
 Scottsville *(G-15339)*
▲ Saes Smart Materials Inc ....E....... 315 266-2026
 New Hartford *(G-8810)*
Sigmund Cohn Corp ....D....... 914 664-5300
 Mount Vernon *(G-8734)*
Sph Group Holdings LLC ....G....... 212 520-2300
 New York *(G-12162)*
Starfuels Inc ....G....... 914 289-4800
 White Plains *(G-17170)*
Tdy Industries LLC ....E....... 716 433-4411
 Lockport *(G-7617)*
▲ Umicore Technical Materials ....C....... 518 792-7700
 Glens Falls *(G-5699)*
Umicore USA Inc ....E....... 919 874-7171
 Glens Falls *(G-5700)*
Wallace Refiners Inc ....G....... 212 391-2649
 New York *(G-12582)*
Zerovalent Nanometals Inc ....G....... 585 298-8592
 Rochester *(G-14774)*

3341 Secondary Smelting & Refining Of Nonferrous Metals

Advanced Precision Technology ......F....... 845 279-3540
 Brewster *(G-1207)*
Amt Incorporated ....E....... 518 284-2910
 Sharon Springs *(G-15383)*
Ben Weitsman of Albany LLC ....E....... 518 462-4444
 Albany *(G-53)*
Cora Materials Corp ....F....... 516 488-6300
 New Hyde Park *(G-8824)*
Eco-Bat America LLC ....C....... 845 692-4414
 Middletown *(G-8439)*
Encore Refining and Recycling ....G....... 631 319-1910
 Holbrook *(G-6446)*
General Refining & Smelting ....G....... 516 538-4747
 Hempstead *(G-6270)*
▲ Germanium Corp America Inc ....F....... 315 853-4900
 Clinton *(G-3719)*
◆ Handy & Harman ....E....... 914 461-1300
 White Plains *(G-17118)*
Island Recycling Corp ....G....... 631 234-6688
 Central Islip *(G-3500)*
Karbra Company ....C....... 212 736-9300
 New York *(G-10809)*
▲ Metalico Aluminum Recovery Inc ..E....... 315 463-9292
 Syracuse *(G-15986)*
Parfuse Corp ....E....... 516 997-1795
 Westbury *(G-17018)*
Pluribus Products Inc ....E....... 718 852-1614
 Brooklyn *(G-2427)*
S & W Metal Trading Corp ....G....... 212 719-5070
 New York *(G-11944)*
▲ Sabin Metal Corporation ....F....... 631 329-1695
 East Hampton *(G-4415)*
Sabin Metal Corporation ....C....... 585 538-2194
 Scottsville *(G-15339)*
Scepter Inc ....E....... 315 568-4225
 Seneca Falls *(G-15367)*
Sims Group USA Holdings Corp ......D....... 718 786-6031
 Long Island City *(G-7877)*
Special Metals Corporation ....D....... 716 366-5663
 Dunkirk *(G-4351)*

3351 Rolling, Drawing & Extruding Of Copper

Aurubis Buffalo Inc ....F....... 716 879-6700
 Buffalo *(G-2822)*
▲ Aurubis Buffalo Inc ....B....... 716 879-6700
 Buffalo *(G-2823)*
Camden Wire Co Inc ....A....... 315 245-3800
 Camden *(G-3313)*
▲ Continental Cordage Corp ....D....... 315 655-9800
 Cazenovia *(G-3443)*
International Wire Group ....G....... 315 245-3800
 Camden *(G-3315)*
Luvata Heat Transfer Solutions ......G....... 716 879-6700
 Buffalo *(G-3051)*
◆ Milward Alloys Inc ....E....... 716 434-5536
 Lockport *(G-7602)*
Omega Wire Inc ....D....... 315 689-7115
 Jordan *(G-7130)*
▲ Omega Wire Inc ....B....... 315 245-3800
 Camden *(G-3318)*
▲ Owi Corporation ....G....... 315 245-4305
 Camden *(G-3319)*
Performance Wire & Cable Inc ....F....... 315 245-2594
 Camden *(G-3320)*
Sherburne Metal Sales Inc ....F....... 607 674-4441
 Sherburne *(G-15395)*

3353 Aluminum Sheet, Plate & Foil

Alcoa Fastening Systems ....G....... 585 368-5049
 Rochester *(G-14185)*
◆ Alcoa Inc ....D....... 212 836-2674
 New York *(G-9077)*
◆ Alufoil Products Co Inc ....F....... 631 231-4141
 Hauppauge *(G-6018)*
American Douglas Metals Inc ....F....... 716 856-3170
 Buffalo *(G-2807)*
BSD Aluminum Foil LLC ....E....... 347 689-3875
 Brooklyn *(G-1735)*
Hadco Metal Trading Co LLC ....G....... 631 270-9724
 Melville *(G-8326)*
Novelis Corporation ....B....... 315 342-1036
 Oswego *(G-13337)*
Novelis Corporation ....B....... 315 349-0121
 Oswego *(G-13338)*
▲ USA Foil Inc ....E....... 631 234-5252
 Brentwood *(G-1200)*

3354 Aluminum Extruded Prdts

◆ A-Fab Initiatives Inc ....G....... 716 877-5257
 Buffalo *(G-2793)*
Alumi-Tech LLC ....G....... 585 663-7010
 Penfield *(G-13497)*
Amt Incorporated ....E....... 518 284-2910
 Sharon Springs *(G-15383)*
Constellium ....E....... 212 675-5087
 New York *(G-9708)*
▼ Flagpoles Incorporated ....E....... 631 751-5500
 East Setauket *(G-4483)*
▲ Itts Industrial Inc ....G....... 718 605-6934
 Staten Island *(G-15690)*
▼ J Sussman Inc ....E....... 718 297-0228
 Jamaica *(G-6922)*
Jem Threading Specialties Inc ......G....... 718 665-3341
 Bronx *(G-1365)*
▲ Keymark Corporation ....A....... 518 853-3421
 Fonda *(G-5316)*
▲ Minitec Framing Systems LLC ....F....... 585 924-4690
 Victor *(G-16491)*
North American Pipe Corp ....F....... 516 338-2863
 Jericho *(G-7079)*
▼ North Coast Outfitters Ltd ....E....... 631 727-5580
 Riverhead *(G-14150)*
Pioneer Window Holdings Inc ....E....... 518 762-5526
 Johnstown *(G-7122)*
Swiss Tool Corporation ....E....... 631 842-7766
 Copiague *(G-3931)*

3355 Aluminum Rolling & Drawing, NEC

Irtronics Instruments Inc ....F....... 914 693-6291
 Ardsley *(G-405)*
▲ N A Alumil Corporation ....G....... 718 355-9393
 Long Island City *(G-7819)*
Novelis Corporation ....F....... 315 349-0121
 Oswego *(G-13339)*
▲ SI Partners Inc ....G....... 516 433-1415
 Hicksville *(G-6394)*

3356 Rolling, Drawing-Extruding Of Nonferrous Metals

▲ Aufhauser Corporation ....F....... 516 694-8696
 Plainview *(G-13584)*
Aufhauser Manufacturing Corp ....E....... 516 694-8696
 Plainview *(G-13585)*
Braze Alloy Inc ....G....... 718 815-5757
 Staten Island *(G-15651)*
Cathay Resources Inc ....G....... 516 922-2839
 East Norwich *(G-4445)*
▲ Continental Cordage Corp ....D....... 315 655-9800
 Cazenovia *(G-3443)*
Cpp-Syracuse Inc ....E....... 315 687-0014
 Chittenango *(G-3632)*
Eco-Bat America LLC ....C....... 845 692-4414
 Middletown *(G-8439)*
◆ Handy & Harman ....E....... 914 461-1300
 White Plains *(G-17118)*
Hh Liquidating Corp ....A....... 646 282-2500
 New York *(G-10471)*
▲ Indium Corporation of America ......E....... 800 446-3486
 Clinton *(G-3720)*
Indium Corporation of America ......E....... 315 793-8200
 Utica *(G-16342)*
Indium Corporation of America ......E....... 315 381-2330
 Utica *(G-16343)*
Jewelers Solder Supply Inc ....F....... 718 637-1256
 Brooklyn *(G-2138)*
▲ Medi-Ray Inc ....D....... 877 898-3003
 Tuckahoe *(G-16271)*
▲ Nationwide Precision Pdts Corp .....B....... 585 272-7100
 Rochester *(G-14529)*
Nickel Group LLC ....G....... 212 706-7906
 Rockaway Park *(G-14786)*
▼ Prince Minerals LLC ....D....... 646 747-4222
 New York *(G-11711)*
RB Diamond Inc ....G....... 212 398-4560
 New York *(G-11809)*
▼ Selectrode Industries Inc ....D....... 631 547-5470
 Huntington Station *(G-6723)*
Sigmund Cohn Corp ....D....... 914 664-5300
 Mount Vernon *(G-8734)*
Special Metals Corporation ....D....... 315 798-2900
 New Hartford *(G-8811)*
Titanium Dem Remediation Group ..F....... 716 433-4100
 Lockport *(G-7619)*

3357 Nonferrous Wire Drawing

Cable Your World Inc ....G....... 631 509-1180
 Port Jeff STA *(G-13764)*
Caldwell Bennett Inc ....E....... 315 337-8540
 Oriskany *(G-13305)*
Camden Wire Co Inc ....A....... 315 245-3800
 Camden *(G-3313)*
Colonial Wire & Cable Co Inc ....D....... 631 234-8500
 Hauppauge *(G-6049)*
▲ Continental Cordage Corp ....G....... 315 655-9800
 Cazenovia *(G-3443)*
▲ Convergent Cnnctivity Tech Inc .....G....... 845 651-5250
 Florida *(G-5211)*
Corning Cable Systems Cr Un ....G....... 607 974-9000
 Corning *(G-3960)*
Corning Inc ....E....... 607 974-9000
 Corning *(G-3961)*
Corning Incorporated ....G....... 646 521-9600
 New York *(G-9726)*
Corning Incorporated ....G....... 607 974-6729
 Painted Post *(G-13391)*
◆ Corning Incorporated ....A....... 607 974-9000
 Corning *(G-3962)*
Corning Incorporated ....E....... 607 248-1200
 Corning *(G-3965)*
Corning Optcal Cmmncations LLC .F....... 607 974-7543
 Corning *(G-3969)*
Corning Specialty Mtls Inc ....G....... 607 974-9000
 Corning *(G-3970)*
County WD Applnc & TV Srvc of ....F....... 585 328-7417
 Rochester *(G-14290)*
▲ Fiberdyne Labs Inc ....D....... 315 895-8470
 Frankfort *(G-5353)*
▲ International Wire Group Inc ....B....... 315 245-2000
 Camden *(G-3316)*
Jaguar Industries Inc ....F....... 845 947-1800
 Haverstraw *(G-6237)*
Kris-Tech Wire Company Inc ....E....... 315 339-5268
 Rome *(G-14817)*
◆ Leviton Manufacturing Co Inc ....B....... 631 812-6000
 Melville *(G-8334)*
▲ Monroe Cable Company Inc ....C....... 845 692-2800
 Middletown *(G-8452)*
▲ Rdi Inc ....F....... 914 773-1000
 Mount Kisco *(G-8643)*
Rockland Insulated Wire Cable .....G....... 845 429-3103
 Haverstraw *(G-6239)*
Siemens Corporation ....F....... 202 434-7800
 New York *(G-12062)*
Siemens USA Holdings Inc ....B....... 212 258-4000
 New York *(G-12064)*
Sinclair Technologies Inc ....F....... 716 874-3682
 Hamburg *(G-5942)*
Steelflex Electro Corp ....D....... 516 226-4466
 Lindenhurst *(G-7483)*
▲ Tappan Wire & Cable Inc ....C....... 845 353-9000
 Blauvelt *(G-976)*
TLC-The Light Connection Inc ....D....... 315 736-7384
 Oriskany *(G-13317)*
United States Dept of Army ....C....... 315 772-7538
 Watertown *(G-16674)*
▲ United Wire Technologies Inc ....F....... 315 675-3558
 Cleveland *(G-3692)*
Universal Builders Supply Inc ....F....... 845 758-8801
 Red Hook *(G-14030)*
▲ Whirlwind Music Distrs Inc ....D....... 585 663-8820
 Rochester *(G-14762)*

3363 Aluminum Die Castings

▲ Albest Metal Stamping Corp ....D....... 718 388-6000
 Brooklyn *(G-1576)*

Employee Codes: A=Over 500 employees, B=251-500
C=101-250, D=51-100, E=20-50, F=10-19, G=5-9

Crown Die Casting Corp....E.... 914 667-5400
Mount Vernon *(G-8675)*
Greene Brass & Alum Fndry LLC....G.... 607 656-4204
Bloomville *(G-996)*
▲ Greenfield Industries Inc....D.... 516 623-9230
Freeport *(G-5404)*
ITT Corporation....D.... 914 641-2000
Seneca Falls *(G-15361)*
ITT Corporation....D.... 315 568-2811
Seneca Falls *(G-15362)*
▼ Jamestown Bronze Works Inc....G.... 716 665-2302
Jamestown *(G-7006)*
Louis Iannettoni....D.... 315 454-3231
Syracuse *(G-15982)*
▲ Pinnacle Manufacturing Co Inc....E.... 585 343-5664
Batavia *(G-645)*
Tpi Arcade Inc....D.... 585 492-0122
Arcade *(G-401)*
WGB Industries Inc....F.... 716 693-5527
Tonawanda *(G-16214)*

3364 Nonferrous Die Castings, Exc Aluminum

▲ Albest Metal Stamping Corp....D.... 718 388-6000
Brooklyn *(G-1576)*
◆ American Casting and Mfg Corp....D.... 800 342-0333
Plainview *(G-13581)*
American Casting and Mfg Corp....G.... 516 349-7010
Plainview *(G-13582)*
Cast-All Corporation....E.... 516 741-4025
Mineola *(G-8503)*
Cast-All Corporation....E.... 516 741-4025
Mineola *(G-8502)*
Crown Die Casting Corp....E.... 914 667-5400
Mount Vernon *(G-8675)*
Crown Novelty Works Inc....G.... 631 253-0949
Melville *(G-8308)*
Greenfield Die Casting Corp....E.... 516 623-9230
Freeport *(G-5403)*
Mar-A-Thon Filters Inc....G.... 631 957-4774
Lindenhurst *(G-7470)*
▲ Pinnacle Manufacturing Co Inc....E.... 585 343-5664
Batavia *(G-645)*
Thomas Foundry LLC....G.... 315 361-9048
Oneida *(G-13168)*

3365 Aluminum Foundries

Airflex Industrial Inc....E.... 631 752-1234
Farmingdale *(G-4933)*
Amt Incorporated....E.... 518 284-2910
Sharon Springs *(G-15383)*
▼ Armstrong Mold Corporation....E.... 315 437-1517
East Syracuse *(G-4504)*
Armstrong Mold Corporation....D.... 315 437-1517
East Syracuse *(G-4505)*
◆ August Thomsen Corp....E.... 516 676-7100
Glen Cove *(G-5611)*
▼ Auto-Mate Technologies LLC....F.... 631 727-8886
Riverhead *(G-14139)*
Broetje Automation-Usa Inc....C.... 716 204-8640
Williamsville *(G-17236)*
Carter Precision Metals LLC....G.... 516 333-1917
Westbury *(G-16973)*
Charles Lay....F.... 607 432-4518
Oneonta *(G-13177)*
Charles Lay....G.... 607 656-4204
Greene *(G-5862)*
Consoldted Precision Pdts Corp....B.... 315 687-0014
Chittenango *(G-3630)*
Corbett Stves Pttern Works Inc....E.... 585 546-7109
Rochester *(G-14289)*
Crown Die Casting Corp....E.... 914 667-5400
Mount Vernon *(G-8675)*
E M T Manufacturing Inc....F.... 516 333-1917
East Meadow *(G-4422)*
East Pattern & Model Corp....E.... 585 461-3240
Fairport *(G-4856)*
Eastern Castings Co....F.... 518 677-5610
Cambridge *(G-3307)*
Eastern Strategic Materials....E.... 212 332-1619
New York *(G-9967)*
Har-Son Mfg Inc....F.... 716 532-2641
Gowanda *(G-5748)*
◆ Hitachi Metals America Ltd....E.... 914 694-9200
Purchase *(G-13959)*
J & J Bronze & Aluminum Cast....E.... 718 383-2111
Brooklyn *(G-2121)*
Massena Metals Inc....F.... 315 769-3846
Massena *(G-8198)*

Meloon Foundries LLC....E.... 315 454-3231
Syracuse *(G-15985)*
Micro Instrument Corp....D.... 585 458-3150
Rochester *(G-14507)*
◆ Milward Alloys Inc....E.... 716 434-5536
Lockport *(G-7602)*
Mpi Consulting Incorporated....G.... 631 253-2377
West Babylon *(G-16814)*
Pyrotek Incorporated....D.... 607 756-3050
Cortland *(G-4041)*
Smart USA Inc....E.... 718 416-4400
Glendale *(G-5663)*
Taylor Metalworks Inc....C.... 716 662-3113
Orchard Park *(G-13298)*
Townline Machine Co Inc....F.... 315 462-3413
Clifton Springs *(G-3716)*
Wolff & Dungey Inc....E.... 315 475-2105
Syracuse *(G-16074)*

3366 Copper Foundries

Amt Incorporated....E.... 518 284-2910
Sharon Springs *(G-15383)*
Argos Inc....E.... 845 528-0576
Putnam Valley *(G-13973)*
Art Bedi-Makky Foundry Corp....G.... 718 383-4191
Brooklyn *(G-1632)*
Charles Lay....F.... 607 432-4518
Oneonta *(G-13177)*
Charles Lay....G.... 607 656-4204
Greene *(G-5862)*
David Fehlman....G.... 315 455-8888
Syracuse *(G-15922)*
▲ Eastern Finding Corp....F.... 516 747-6640
New Hyde Park *(G-8830)*
Excalbur Brnze Sculpture Fndry....E.... 718 366-3444
Brooklyn *(G-1942)*
J & J Bronze & Aluminum Cast....E.... 718 383-2111
Brooklyn *(G-2121)*
Meloon Foundries LLC....E.... 315 454-3231
Syracuse *(G-15985)*
▲ Modern Art Foundry Inc....E.... 718 728-2030
Astoria *(G-449)*
Omega Wire Inc....E.... 315 337-4300
Rome *(G-14829)*
Omega Wire Inc....D.... 315 689-7115
Jordan *(G-7130)*
▲ Rodeo of NY Inc....E.... 212 730-0744
New York *(G-11902)*

3369 Nonferrous Foundries: Castings, NEC

Allstar Casting Corporation....E.... 212 563-0909
New York *(G-9092)*
Argos Inc....E.... 845 528-0576
Putnam Valley *(G-13973)*
Buffalo Metal Casting Co Inc....E.... 716 874-6211
Buffalo *(G-2855)*
▲ Cardona Industries USA Ltd....G.... 516 466-5200
Great Neck *(G-5796)*
Carrera Casting Corp....C.... 212 382-3296
New York *(G-9536)*
Cast-All Corporation....E.... 516 741-4025
Mineola *(G-8502)*
City Casting Corp....G.... 212 938-0511
New York *(G-9629)*
Controlled Castings Corp....E.... 516 349-1718
Plainview *(G-13591)*
Cpp-Syracuse Inc....E.... 315 687-0014
Chittenango *(G-3632)*
Crown Die Casting Corp....E.... 914 667-5400
Mount Vernon *(G-8675)*
General Motors LLC....B.... 315 764-2000
Massena *(G-8195)*
Globalfoundries US Inc....C.... 518 305-9013
Malta *(G-8019)*
Globalfoundries US Inc....F.... 408 462-3900
Ballston Spa *(G-597)*
Greenfield Die Casting Corp....E.... 516 623-9230
Freeport *(G-5403)*
J & J Bronze & Aluminum Cast....E.... 718 383-2111
Brooklyn *(G-2121)*
▼ Jamestown Bronze Works Inc....G.... 716 665-2302
Jamestown *(G-7006)*
K & H Precision Products Inc....E.... 585 624-4894
Honeoye Falls *(G-6532)*
Karbra Company....C.... 212 736-9300
New York *(G-10809)*
Kelly Foundry & Machine Co....E.... 315 732-8313
Utica *(G-16346)*
Lamothermic Corp....D.... 845 278-6118
Brewster *(G-1222)*

▲ Medi-Ray Inc....D.... 877 898-3003
Tuckahoe *(G-16271)*
Miller Technology Inc....G.... 631 694-2224
Farmingdale *(G-5056)*
▲ Plattco Corporation....E.... 518 563-4640
Plattsburgh *(G-13687)*
Quality Castings Inc....E.... 732 409-3203
Long Island City *(G-7853)*
Summit Aerospace Inc....G.... 718 433-1326
Long Island City *(G-7895)*
Wemco Casting LLC....D.... 631 563-8050
Bohemia *(G-1156)*
▲ Zierick Manufacturing Corp....D.... 800 882-8020
Mount Kisco *(G-8648)*

3398 Metal Heat Treating

A1 International Heat Treating....G.... 718 863-5552
Bronx *(G-1257)*
Aterian Investment Partners LP....F.... 212 547-2806
New York *(G-9247)*
B & W Heat Treating Company....G.... 716 876-8184
Tonawanda *(G-16143)*
Bodycote Thermal Proc Inc....E.... 585 436-7876
Rochester *(G-14240)*
Bsv Metal Finishers Inc....E.... 585 349-7072
Spencerport *(G-15567)*
Buffalo Armory LLC....G.... 716 935-6346
Buffalo *(G-2848)*
Burke Frging Heat Treating Inc....E.... 585 235-6060
Rochester *(G-14251)*
Burton Industries Inc....E.... 631 643-6660
West Babylon *(G-16778)*
Captech Industries LLC....G.... 347 374-1182
Rome *(G-14807)*
Cpp - Steel Treaters....E.... 315 736-3081
Oriskany *(G-13307)*
Elmira Heat Treating Inc....E.... 607 734-1577
Elmira *(G-4682)*
Expedient Heat Treating Corp....G.... 716 433-1177
North Tonawanda *(G-12970)*
◆ Gibraltar Industries Inc....D.... 716 826-6500
Buffalo *(G-2974)*
Graywood Companies Inc....E.... 585 254-7000
Rochester *(G-14413)*
Great Lakes Metal Treating....F.... 716 694-1240
Tonawanda *(G-16167)*
Hercules Heat Treating Corp....E.... 718 625-1266
Brooklyn *(G-2074)*
Hi-Temp Brazing Inc....E.... 631 491-4917
Deer Park *(G-4148)*
International Ord Tech Inc....D.... 716 664-1100
Jamestown *(G-7003)*
Jasco Heat Treating Inc....E.... 585 388-0071
Fairport *(G-4859)*
Metal Improvement Company LLC....F.... 631 567-2610
Bay Shore *(G-717)*
Metal Improvement Company LLC....D.... 607 533-7000
Lansing *(G-7349)*
Milgo Industrial Inc....D.... 718 388-6476
Brooklyn *(G-2313)*
Milgo Industrial Inc....G.... 718 387-0406
Brooklyn *(G-2314)*
Modern Heat Trting Forging Inc....F.... 716 884-2176
Buffalo *(G-3073)*
Parfuse Corp....E.... 516 997-1795
Westbury *(G-17018)*
Rochester Steel Treating Works....F.... 585 546-3348
Rochester *(G-14650)*
Sunlight US Co Inc....G.... 716 826-6500
Buffalo *(G-3201)*
Syracuse Heat Treating Corp....E.... 315 451-0000
Syracuse *(G-16052)*

3399 Primary Metal Prdts, NEC

Advantech Industries Inc....C.... 585 247-0701
Rochester *(G-14181)*
Ames Advanced Materials Corp....D.... 518 792-5808
South Glens Falls *(G-15522)*
Ames Goldsmith Corp....E.... 518 792-7435
Glens Falls *(G-5669)*
Bridge Components Inc....G.... 716 731-1184
Sanborn *(G-15113)*
◆ Buffalo Tungsten Inc....D.... 716 759-6353
Depew *(G-4251)*
Cintube Ltd....F.... 518 324-3333
Plattsburgh *(G-13659)*
▲ Cws Powder Coatings Company LP G.... 845 398-2911
Blauvelt *(G-970)*
◆ Handy & Harman....E.... 914 461-1300
White Plains *(G-17118)*

Hje Company Inc ... G ... 518 792-8733
Queensbury *(G-13999)*
HK Metal Trading Ltd ... G ... 212 868-3333
New York *(G-10486)*
▲ **Imerys Steelcasting Usa Inc** ... D ... 716 278-1634
Niagara Falls *(G-12835)*
John Hassall LLC ... D ... 516 334-6200
Westbury *(G-16998)*
New England Reclamation Inc ... F ... 914 949-2000
White Plains *(G-17141)*
New Project LLC ... G ... 718 788-3444
Brooklyn *(G-2362)*
Oerlikon Metco (us) Inc ... F ... 716 270-2228
Amherst *(G-256)*
Pmb Precision Products Inc ... F ... 631 491-6753
North Babylon *(G-12902)*
Reed Systems Ltd ... F ... 845 647-3660
Ellenville *(G-4637)*
▼ **Rembar Company LLC** ... E ... 914 693-2620
Dobbs Ferry *(G-4302)*
Specialty Fabricators ... F ... 631 256-6982
Oakdale *(G-13062)*
Tam Ceramics Group of Ny LLC ... D ... 716 278-9400
Niagara Falls *(G-12880)*
◆ **Universal Metals Inc** ... G ... 516 829-0896
Great Neck *(G-5847)*

34 FABRICATED METAL PRODUCTS, EXCEPT MACHINERY AND TRANSPORTATION EQUIPMENT

3411 Metal Cans

Anheuser-Busch Companies LLC ... G ... 718 589-2610
Bronx *(G-1276)*
Ardagh Metal Packaging USA Inc ... C ... 607 584-3300
Conklin *(G-3865)*
Ball Metal Beverage Cont Corp ... C ... 845 692-3800
Middletown *(G-8427)*
Ball Metal Beverage Cont Corp ... C ... 518 587-6030
Saratoga Springs *(G-15144)*
Brakewell Stl Fabricators Inc ... E ... 845 469-9131
Chester *(G-3601)*
Cmc-Kuhnke Inc ... F ... 518 694-3310
Albany *(G-65)*
Crown Cork & Seal Usa Inc ... C ... 845 343-9586
Middletown *(G-8434)*
Erie Engineered Products Inc ... E ... 716 206-0204
Lancaster *(G-7314)*
◆ **Genpak LLC** ... E ... 518 798-9511
Glens Falls *(G-5679)*
J C Industries Inc ... E ... 631 420-1920
West Babylon *(G-16798)*
Marley Spoon Inc ... G ... 646 934-6970
New York *(G-11163)*
Metal Container Corporation ... C ... 845 567-1500
New Windsor *(G-8943)*
Seneca Foods Corporation ... D ... 315 926-0531
Marion *(G-8100)*
Silgan Containers Mfg Corp ... C ... 315 946-4826
Lyons *(G-7975)*
Sky Dive ... D ... 845 858-6400
Port Jervis *(G-13792)*

3412 Metal Barrels, Drums, Kegs & Pails

Abbot & Abbot Box Corp ... F ... 888 930-5972
Long Island City *(G-7646)*
Erie Engineered Products Inc ... E ... 716 206-0204
Lancaster *(G-7314)*
▲ **Medi-Ray Inc** ... D ... 877 898-3003
Tuckahoe *(G-16271)*
Mobile Mini Inc ... F ... 315 732-4555
Utica *(G-16349)*
Sky Dive ... D ... 845 858-6400
Port Jervis *(G-13792)*
Westrock - Southern Cont LLC ... C ... 315 487-6111
Camillus *(G-3327)*
Westrock CP LLC ... C ... 716 694-1000
North Tonawanda *(G-13006)*

3421 Cutlery

Advanced Machine Design Co Inc ... E ... 716 826-2000
Buffalo *(G-2800)*
BSD Aluminum Foil LLC ... E ... 347 689-3875
Brooklyn *(G-1735)*
▲ **Cutco Cutlery Corporation** ... B ... 716 372-3111
Olean *(G-13141)*
Gibar Inc ... C ... 315 452-5656
Cicero *(G-3646)*
▲ **Great American Tool Co Inc** ... G ... 716 646-5700
Hamburg *(G-5927)*
Home and Above LLC ... F ... 914 220-3451
Brooklyn *(G-2084)*
Inquiring Minds Inc ... G ... 845 246-5775
Saugerties *(G-15185)*
John A Eberly Inc ... G ... 315 449-3034
Syracuse *(G-15967)*
▲ **Klein Cutlery LLC** ... D ... 585 928-2500
Bolivar *(G-1159)*
◆ **Korin Japanese Trading Corp** ... E ... 212 587-7021
New York *(G-10878)*
▼ **Lifetime Brands Inc** ... B ... 516 683-6000
Garden City *(G-5514)*
Mpdraw LLC ... E ... 212 228-8383
New York *(G-11315)*
Niabraze LLC ... F ... 716 447-1082
Tonawanda *(G-16185)*
▲ **Novelty Crystal Corp** ... E ... 718 458-6700
Long Island City *(G-7826)*
Oneida International Inc ... G ... 315 361-3000
Oneida *(G-13160)*
Oneida Silversmiths Inc ... G ... 315 361-3000
Oneida *(G-13164)*
◆ **Ontario Knife Company** ... D ... 716 676-5527
Franklinville *(G-5370)*
Palladia Inc ... C ... 212 206-3669
New York *(G-11557)*
Ratan Ronkonkoma ... G ... 631 588-6800
Ronkonkoma *(G-14977)*
Rev Holdings Inc ... A ... 212 527-4000
New York *(G-11848)*
▲ **Revlon Consumer Products Corp** ... B ... 212 527-4000
New York *(G-11852)*
▲ **Revlon Holdings Inc** ... D ... 212 527-4000
New York *(G-11853)*
RGI Group Incorporated ... E ... 212 527-4000
New York *(G-11858)*
▲ **Schilling Forge Inc** ... E ... 315 454-4421
Syracuse *(G-16033)*
Schrader Meat Market ... F ... 607 869-6328
Romulus *(G-14842)*
Servotronics Inc ... C ... 716 655-5990
Elma *(G-4655)*
Sherrill Manufacturing Inc ... C ... 315 280-0727
Sherrill *(G-15407)*
Starfire Swords Ltd Inc ... E ... 607 589-7244
Spencer *(G-15564)*
▲ **Treyco Products Corp** ... G ... 716 693-6525
Tonawanda *(G-16209)*
◆ **Utica Cutlery Company** ... D ... 315 733-4663
Utica *(G-16363)*
Warren Cutlery Corp ... F ... 845 876-3444
Rhinebeck *(G-14060)*
Woods Knife Corporation ... E ... 516 798-4972
Massapequa *(G-8184)*

3423 Hand & Edge Tools

▲ **Allway Tools Inc** ... D ... 718 792-3636
Bronx *(G-1269)*
Ames Companies Inc ... E ... 607 739-4544
Pine Valley *(G-13556)*
Ames Companies Inc ... D ... 607 369-9595
Unadilla *(G-16287)*
Best Way Tools By Anderson Inc ... G ... 631 586-4702
Deer Park *(G-4106)*
Boucheron Joaillerie USA Inc ... G ... 212 715-7330
New York *(G-9442)*
Circo File Corp ... G ... 516 922-1848
Oyster Bay *(G-13367)*
Classic Tool Design Inc ... E ... 845 562-8700
New Windsor *(G-8935)*
Clopay Ames True Tmper Hldng ... F ... 516 938-5544
Jericho *(G-7062)*
Coastel Cable Tools Inc ... E ... 315 471-5361
Syracuse *(G-15899)*
▲ **Dead Ringer LLC** ... G ... 585 355-4685
Rochester *(G-14303)*
▲ **Design Source By Lg Inc** ... E ... 212 274-0022
New York *(G-9855)*
▲ **Dresser-Argus Inc** ... G ... 718 643-1540
Brooklyn *(G-1880)*
Edward C Lyons Company Inc ... G ... 718 515-5361
Bronx *(G-1323)*
Edward C Muller Corp ... F ... 718 881-7270
Bronx *(G-1324)*
Empire Devleopment ... G ... 716 789-2097
Mayville *(G-8215)*
Gei International Inc ... E ... 315 463-9261
East Syracuse *(G-4533)*
Huron Tl & Cutter Grinding Co ... E ... 631 420-7000
Farmingdale *(G-5008)*
▲ **Hydramec Inc** ... E ... 585 593-5190
Scio *(G-15321)*
◆ **Ivy Classic Industries Inc** ... E ... 914 632-8200
New Rochelle *(G-8913)*
▲ **Lancaster Knives Inc** ... E ... 716 683-5050
Lancaster *(G-7323)*
Metro City Group Inc ... G ... 516 781-2500
Bellmore *(G-818)*
▲ **North Pk Innovations Group Inc** ... G ... 716 699-2031
Ellicottville *(G-4643)*
Nyc District Council Ubcja ... G ... 212 366-7500
New York *(G-11478)*
Robinson Tools LLC ... G ... 585 586-5432
Penfield *(G-13503)*
Royal Molds Inc ... F ... 718 382-7686
Brooklyn *(G-2512)*
▲ **Schilling Forge Inc** ... E ... 315 454-4421
Syracuse *(G-16033)*
▲ **Snyder Manufacturing Inc** ... E ... 716 945-0354
Salamanca *(G-15107)*
◆ **Swimline International Corp** ... C ... 631 254-2155
Edgewood *(G-4614)*
The Swatch Group U S Inc ... G ... 212 297-9192
New York *(G-12310)*
▲ **U S Air Tool Co Inc** ... F ... 631 471-3300
Ronkonkoma *(G-14994)*
Wall Tool & Tape Corp ... E ... 718 641-6813
Ozone Park *(G-13386)*
Winters Railroad Service Inc ... G ... 716 337-2668
North Collins *(G-12932)*
Woods Knife Corporation ... E ... 516 798-4972
Massapequa *(G-8184)*
York Industries Inc ... E ... 516 746-3736
Garden City Park *(G-5546)*

3425 Hand Saws & Saw Blades

▲ **Allway Tools Inc** ... D ... 718 792-3636
Bronx *(G-1269)*
◆ **Amana Tool Corp** ... D ... 631 752-1300
Farmingdale *(G-4939)*
▲ **Diamond Saw Works Inc** ... E ... 716 496-7417
Chaffee *(G-3532)*
Dinosaw Inc ... E ... 518 828-9942
Hudson *(G-6612)*
Niabraze LLC ... F ... 716 447-1082
Tonawanda *(G-16185)*
Quality Saw & Knife Inc ... F ... 631 491-4747
West Babylon *(G-16819)*
▼ **Suffolk McHy & Pwr Tl Corp** ... G ... 631 289-7153
Patchogue *(G-13435)*

3429 Hardware, NEC

A & L Doors & Hardware LLC ... F ... 718 585-8400
Bronx *(G-1252)*
Advantage Wholesale Supply LLC ... D ... 718 839-3499
Brooklyn *(G-1567)*
American Casting and Mfg Corp ... G ... 516 349-7010
Plainview *(G-13582)*
Amertac Holdings Inc ... G ... 610 336-1330
Monsey *(G-8567)*
Barry Industries Inc ... F ... 212 242-5200
New York *(G-9326)*
Bfg Marine Inc ... F ... 631 586-5500
Bay Shore *(G-675)*
Boa Security Technologies Corp ... G ... 516 576-0295
Huntington *(G-6658)*
Boehm Surgical Instrument ... F ... 585 436-6584
Rochester *(G-14241)*
Cast-All Corporation ... E ... 516 741-4025
Mineola *(G-8502)*
▲ **City Store Gates Mfg Corp** ... E ... 718 939-9700
College Point *(G-3781)*
▲ **Classic Brass Inc** ... D ... 716 763-1400
Lakewood *(G-7288)*
▲ **Crest Lock Co Inc** ... F ... 718 345-9898
Brooklyn *(G-1818)*
D Best Service Co Inc ... G ... 718 972-6133
Brooklyn *(G-1829)*
Daniel Demarco and Assoc Inc ... E ... 631 598-7000
Amityville *(G-284)*
▲ **Decorative Hardware** ... F ... 914 238-5251
Chappaqua *(G-3551)*
▲ **Delta Lock Company LLC** ... F ... 631 238-7035
Bohemia *(G-1054)*
Designatronics Incorporated ... B ... 516 328-3300
New Hyde Park *(G-8826)*
Dfci Solutions Inc ... E ... 631 669-0494
West Islip *(G-16904)*

S I C

Employee Codes: A=Over 500 employees, B=251-500
C=101-250, D=51-100, E=20-50, F=10-19, G=5-9
2017 Harris
New York Manufacturers Directory
807

34 FABRICATED METAL PRODUCTS, EXCEPT MACHINERY AND TRANSPORTATION EQUIPMENT SIC SECTION

▲ **Dico Products Corporation** ....F 315 797-0470
Utica *(G-16323)*
Dortronics Systems Inc ....E 631 725-0505
Sag Harbor *(G-15077)*
Dover Marine Mfg & Sup Co Inc ....G 631 667-4300
Deer Park *(G-4131)*
▲ **Dreamseats LLC** ....E 631 656-1066
Commack *(G-3830)*
Eaton Electric Holdings LLC ....C 607 756-2821
Cortland *(G-4025)*
Eazy Locks LLC ....G 718 327-7770
Far Rockaway *(G-4920)*
▲ **ER Butler & Co Inc** ....E 212 925-3565
New York *(G-10055)*
Excelco Developments Inc ....E 716 934-2651
Silver Creek *(G-15448)*
Fastener Dimensions Inc ....E 718 847-6321
Ozone Park *(G-13378)*
▲ **Fixture Hardware Mfg Corp** ....E 718 499-9422
Brooklyn *(G-1980)*
G Marks Hdwr Liquidating Corp ....D 631 225-5400
Amityville *(G-288)*
▲ **H A Guden Company Inc** ....E 631 737-2900
Ronkonkoma *(G-14908)*
Industrial Electronic Hardware ....D 718 492-4440
Brooklyn *(G-2103)*
Ingham Industries Inc ....G 631 242-2493
Holbrook *(G-6451)*
▲ **ITR Industries Inc** ....E 914 964-7063
Yonkers *(G-17456)*
◆ **Jaquith Industries Inc** ....E 315 478-5700
Syracuse *(G-15966)*
Kelley Bros Llc ....G 315 852-3302
De Ruyter *(G-4081)*
▲ **Kenstan Lock & Hardware Co Inc** ....E 631 423-1977
Plainview *(G-13614)*
▲ **Key High Vacuum Products Inc** ....E 631 584-5959
Nesconset *(G-8775)*
▲ **Kilian Manufacturing Corp** ....D 315 432-0700
Syracuse *(G-15973)*
Kyntec Corporation ....G 716 810-6956
Buffalo *(G-3038)*
▲ **Legendary Auto Interiors Ltd** ....E 315 331-1212
Newark *(G-12734)*
Liberty Brass Turning Co Inc ....E 718 784-2911
Westbury *(G-17005)*
Lightron Corporation ....G 516 938-5544
Jericho *(G-7075)*
Long Island Fireproof Door ....E 718 767-8800
Whitestone *(G-17211)*
▲ **Magnetic Aids Inc** ....G 845 863-1400
Newburgh *(G-12766)*
Morgik Metal Designs ....F 212 463-0304
New York *(G-11305)*
Mpi Consulting Incorporated ....E 631 253-2377
West Babylon *(G-16813)*
Nanz Custom Hardware Inc ....D 212 367-7000
New York *(G-11340)*
Nanz Custom Hardware Inc ....D 212 367-7000
Deer Park *(G-4176)*
◆ **Napco Security Tech Inc** ....B 631 842-9400
Amityville *(G-314)*
▲ **Nielsen Hardware Corporation** ....E 607 821-1475
Binghamton *(G-940)*
◆ **Northknight Logistics Inc** ....F 716 283-3090
Niagara Falls *(G-12853)*
▲ **Orbital Holdings Inc** ....E 951 360-7100
Buffalo *(G-3104)*
◆ **P & F Industries Inc** ....C 631 694-9800
Melville *(G-8346)*
◆ **P E Guerin** ....D 212 243-5270
New York *(G-11548)*
Pinquist Tool & Die Co Inc ....E 718 389-3900
Lynbrook *(G-7956)*
Pk30 System LLC ....F 212 473-8050
Stone Ridge *(G-15764)*
▲ **Progressive Hardware Co Inc** ....G 631 445-1826
East Northport *(G-4443)*
Real Design Inc ....F 315 429-3071
Dolgeville *(G-4308)*
▲ **Rize Enterprises LLC** ....G 631 249-9000
Bay Shore *(G-736)*
▲ **RKI Building Spc Co Inc** ....G 718 728-7788
College Point *(G-3805)*
Rollson Inc ....E 631 423-9578
Huntington *(G-6678)*
▲ **Rosco Inc** ....C 718 526-2601
Jamaica *(G-6948)*
▲ **Safe Skies LLC** ....G 888 632-5027
New York *(G-11953)*
◆ **Samscreen Inc** ....E 607 722-3979
Conklin *(G-3875)*
Southco Inc ....B 585 624-2545
Honeoye Falls *(G-6537)*
▼ **Stidd Systems Inc** ....E 631 477-2400
Greenport *(G-5877)*
Syraco Products Inc ....E 800 581-5555
Syracuse *(G-16047)*
▼ **Tattersall Industries LLC** ....E 518 381-4270
Schenectady *(G-15304)*
Taylor Made Group LLC ....D 518 725-0681
Gloversville *(G-5724)*
Tools & Stamping Corp ....G 718 392-4040
Brooklyn *(G-2663)*
Trico Manufacturing Corp ....G 718 349-6565
Brooklyn *(G-2680)*
Turbine Engine Comp Utica ....A 315 768-8070
Whitesboro *(G-17197)*
▲ **United Metal Industries Inc** ....G 516 354-6800
New Hyde Park *(G-8869)*
Water Street Brass Corporation ....E 716 763-0059
Lakewood *(G-7296)*
▲ **Weber-Knapp Company** ....C 716 484-9135
Jamestown *(G-7043)*
William H Jackson Company ....G 718 784-4482
Long Island City *(G-7923)*
▲ **Wolo Mfg Corp** ....E 631 242-0333
Deer Park *(G-4228)*
Yaloz Mould & Die Co Inc ....E 718 389-1131
Brooklyn *(G-2773)*
York Industries Inc ....E 516 746-3736
Garden City Park *(G-5546)*

3431 Enameled Iron & Metal Sanitary Ware

▼ **Advance Tabco Inc** ....D 631 242-8270
Edgewood *(G-4591)*
Alloyd Association Inc ....G 516 248-8835
Williston Park *(G-17260)*
CNA Specialties Inc ....G 631 567-7929
Sayville *(G-15206)*
▲ **Independent Home Products LLC** ....E 718 541-1256
West Hempstead *(G-16855)*
▲ **ITR Industries Inc** ....E 914 964-7063
Yonkers *(G-17456)*
Kenbenco Inc ....F 845 246-3066
Saugerties *(G-15186)*
Ketcham Medicine Cabinets ....E 631 615-6151
Ronkonkoma *(G-14922)*
Kohler Co ....E 212 529-2800
New York *(G-10869)*
▲ **Kraus USA Inc** ....F 516 621-1300
Port Washington *(G-13835)*
▲ **Metpar Corp** ....D 516 333-2600
Westbury *(G-17011)*
Porcelain Refinishing Corp ....F 516 352-4841
Flushing *(G-5283)*
▲ **Sola Home Expo Inc** ....G 718 646-3383
Brooklyn *(G-2579)*
Stainless Metals Inc ....F 718 784-1454
Woodside *(G-17356)*
Unico Inc ....F 845 562-9255
Newburgh *(G-12782)*
Vanity Fair Bathmart Inc ....F 718 584-6700
Bronx *(G-1488)*
▲ **Watermark Designs Holdings Ltd** ....D 718 257-2800
Brooklyn *(G-2745)*

3432 Plumbing Fixture Fittings & Trim, Brass

A B S Brass Products Inc ....F 718 497-2115
Brooklyn *(G-1532)*
Acme Parts Inc ....E 718 649-1750
Brooklyn *(G-1556)*
Artys Sprnklr Svc Instllation ....F 516 538-4371
East Meadow *(G-4418)*
Coronet Parts Mfg Co Inc ....E 718 649-1750
Brooklyn *(G-1805)*
Coronet Parts Mfg Co Inc ....E 718 649-1750
Brooklyn *(G-1806)*
Diamond Brass Corp ....G 718 418-3871
Brooklyn *(G-1859)*
▲ **ER Butler & Co Inc** ....E 212 925-3565
New York *(G-10055)*
G Sicuranza Ltd ....G 516 759-0259
Glen Cove *(G-5616)*
Giagni Enterprises LLC ....G 914 699-6500
Mount Vernon *(G-8684)*
Giagni International Corp ....G 914 699-6500
Mount Vernon *(G-8685)*
Hanco Metal Products Inc ....F 212 787-5992
Brooklyn *(G-2066)*
▲ **I W Industries Inc** ....C 631 293-9494
Melville *(G-8330)*
▲ **Jacknob International Ltd** ....D 631 546-6560
Hauppauge *(G-6101)*
L A S Replacement Parts Inc ....F 718 583-4700
Bronx *(G-1376)*
Liberty Brass Turning Co Inc ....E 718 784-2911
Westbury *(G-17005)*
Malyn Industrial Ceramics Inc ....G 716 741-1510
Clarence Center *(G-3679)*
Mark Posner ....G 718 258-6241
Brooklyn *(G-2272)*
Martin Brass Works Inc ....G 718 523-3146
Jamaica *(G-6928)*
◆ **P E Guerin** ....D 212 243-5270
New York *(G-11548)*
Roccera LLC ....F 585 426-0887
Rochester *(G-14632)*
▲ **Royal Line LLC** ....F 800 516-7450
Wantagh *(G-16563)*
Toto USA Inc ....G 917 237-0665
New York *(G-12380)*
Toto USA Inc ....G 770 282-8686
New York *(G-12381)*
▲ **Watermark Designs Holdings Ltd** ....D 718 257-2800
Brooklyn *(G-2745)*

3433 Heating Eqpt

A Nuclimate Qulty Systems Inc ....F 315 431-0226
East Syracuse *(G-4498)*
American Comfort Direct LLC ....E 201 364-8309
New York *(G-9116)*
Atlantis Energy Systems Inc ....G 916 438-2930
Poughkeepsie *(G-13890)*
Atlantis Solar Inc ....F 916 226-9183
Potsdam *(G-13877)*
Best Boilers Inc ....F 718 372-4210
Brooklyn *(G-1687)*
Biotech Energy Inc ....G 800 340-1387
Plattsburgh *(G-13654)*
Carrier Corporation ....B 315 432-6000
Syracuse *(G-15888)*
▲ **Chentronics Corporation** ....E 607 334-5531
Norwich *(G-13023)*
▲ **CIDC Corp** ....F 718 342-5820
Brooklyn *(G-1780)*
▲ **Dyson-Kissner-Moran Corp** ....E 212 661-4600
Poughkeepsie *(G-13896)*
Economy Pump & Motor Repair ....G 718 433-2600
Astoria *(G-438)*
◆ **ECR International Inc** ....D 315 797-1310
Utica *(G-16328)*
ECR International Inc ....C 716 366-5500
Dunkirk *(G-4341)*
▲ **Embassy Industries Inc** ....C 631 435-0209
Hauppauge *(G-6071)*
Empire Industrial Burner Svc ....F 631 242-4619
Deer Park *(G-4139)*
Fedders Islandaire Inc ....D 631 471-2900
East Setauket *(G-4482)*
Fisonic Corp ....G 212 732-3777
Long Island City *(G-7743)*
▲ **Fisonic Corp** ....F 716 763-0295
New York *(G-10174)*
◆ **Flynn Burner Corporation** ....E 914 636-1320
New Rochelle *(G-8899)*
Frederick Cowan & Company Inc ....F 631 369-0360
Riverhead *(G-14143)*
▲ **Fulton Heating Solutions Inc** ....D 315 298-5121
Pulaski *(G-13949)*
▼ **Fulton Volcanic Inc** ....D 315 298-5121
Pulaski *(G-13950)*
▲ **Hawkencatskills LLC** ....G 518 966-8900
Greenville *(G-5885)*
I-Evolve Techonology Services ....F 801 566-5268
Amherst *(G-245)*
Integrated Solar Tech LLC ....G 914 249-9364
Port Chester *(G-13749)*
▲ **Juniper Elbow Co Inc** ....C 718 326-2546
Middle Village *(G-8414)*
Jus-Sar Fuel Inc ....G 845 791-8900
Harris *(G-5976)*
Marathon Heater Co Inc ....G 607 657-8113
Richford *(G-14063)*
◆ **Mx Solar USA LLC** ....C 732 356-7300
New York *(G-11330)*
Nanopv Corporation ....C 609 851-3666
Liverpool *(G-7536)*
New Energy Systems Group ....C 917 573-0302
New York *(G-11385)*

S I C

SIC SECTION — 34 FABRICATED METAL PRODUCTS, EXCEPT MACHINERY AND TRANSPORTATION EQUIPMENT

Company	Code	Phone
O C P Inc, Farmingdale (G-5069)	E	516 679-2000
▲ Omega Heater Company Inc, Ronkonkoma (G-14959)	D	631 588-8820
▲ Original Convector Specialist, Brooklyn (G-2395)	G	718 342-5820
▲ Prism Solar Technologies Inc, Highland (G-6407)	E	845 883-4200
▲ RE Hansen Industries Inc, East Setauket (G-4491)	C	631 471-2900
Real Goods Solar Inc, New City (G-8791)	C	845 708-0800
▲ Roberts-Gordon LLC, Buffalo (G-3160)	D	716 852-4400
Rockmills Steel Products Corp, Maspeth (G-8169)	F	718 366-8300
▲ Slant/Fin Corporation, Greenvale (G-5881)	B	516 484-2600
Solar Energy Systems LLC, Brooklyn (G-2580)	F	718 389-1545
▼ Stephen Hanley, Long Island City (G-7891)	D	718 729-3360
Unilux Advanced Mfg LLC, Schenectady (G-15308)	E	518 344-7490
Vincent Genovese, Mastic Beach (G-8205)	G	631 281-8170

3441 Fabricated Structural Steel

Company	Code	Phone
760 NI Holdings, Buffalo (G-2791)	E	716 821-1391
▲ A & T Iron Works Inc, New Rochelle (G-8883)	E	914 632-8992
◆ A-Fab Initiatives Inc, Buffalo (G-2793)	F	716 877-5257
A/C Design & Fabrication Corp, Staten Island (G-15632)	G	718 227-8100
AAA Welding and Fabrication of, Rochester (G-14163)	G	585 254-2830
Abalon Precision Mfg Corp, Mount Vernon (G-8659)	F	718 589-5682
Abalon Precision Mfg Corp, Mount Vernon (G-8660)	F	718 589-5682
Acadia Stairs, Fishkill (G-5180)	G	845 765-8600
Accucut Inc, West Sayville (G-16933)	G	631 567-2868
Achilles Construction Co Inc, Mount Vernon (G-8662)	G	718 389-4717
Ackroyd Metal Fabricators Inc, Menands (G-8364)	F	518 434-1281
Adsco Manufacturing Corp, Buffalo (G-2799)	D	716 827-5450
Advanced Thermal Systems Inc, Lancaster (G-7298)	E	716 681-1800
Advantage Machining Inc, Niagara Falls (G-12795)	F	716 731-6418
Aero-Data Metal Crafters Inc, Ronkonkoma (G-14856)	C	631 471-7733
Airflex Corp, Farmingdale (G-4932)	D	631 752-1219
Aldo Frustacci Iron Works Inc, Brooklyn (G-1578)	F	718 768-0707
All-City Metal Inc, Maspeth (G-8114)	E	718 937-3975
Alp Steel Corp, Buffalo (G-2804)	E	716 854-3030
American Aerogel Corporation, Rochester (G-14196)	E	585 328-2140
Apollo Steel Corporation, Niagara Falls (G-12797)	F	716 283-8758
Asp Industries Inc, Rochester (G-14217)	E	585 254-9130
Atlantis Equipment Corporation, Stephentown (G-15756)	F	518 733-5910
B H M Metal Products Co, Kauneonga Lake (G-7136)	G	845 292-5297
B P Nash Co Inc, East Syracuse (G-4509)	F	315 445-1310
▲ Barber Welding Inc, Weedsport (G-16746)	E	315 834-6645
Barker Steel LLC, Albany (G-52)	E	518 465-6221
Barry Steel Fabrication Inc, Lockport (G-7571)	F	716 433-2144
Bear Metal Works Inc, Buffalo (G-2836)	F	716 824-4530
▲ Bennett Manufacturing Co Inc, Alden (G-175)	C	716 937-9161
Bereza Iron Works Inc, Rochester (G-14229)	F	585 254-6311
Blackstone Advanced Tech LLC, Jamestown (G-6975)	C	716 665-5410
Bms Manufacturing Co Inc, Watkins Glen (G-16693)	E	607 535-2426
Bob Murphy Inc, Vestal (G-16442)	F	607 729-3553
Bombardier Transportation, Hornell (G-6560)	D	607 324-0216
Bombardier Trnsp Holdings USA, Bath (G-654)	D	607 776-4791
Bristol Metals Inc, Bloomfield (G-982)	F	585 657-7665
Buffalo Metal Forming Inc, West Seneca (G-16941)	G	716 856-4575
Burnt Hills Fabricators Inc, Ballston Spa (G-592)	F	518 885-1115
C & C Custom Metal Fabricators, Hauppauge (G-6039)	G	631 235-9646
C & C Metal Fabrications Inc, Fulton (G-5453)	F	315 598-7607
C & T Tool & Instrument Co, Woodside (G-17321)	E	718 429-1253
Cameron Bridge Works LLC, Elmira (G-4672)	E	607 734-9456
▲ Cameron Mfg & Design Inc, Horseheads (G-6571)	C	607 739-3606
Carpenter Industries Inc, Syracuse (G-15886)	F	315 463-4284
Castle Harvester Co Inc, Seneca Castle (G-15359)	F	585 526-5884
CBM Fabrications Inc, Ballston Lake (G-581)	F	518 399-8023
Chautauqua Machine Spc LLC, Ashville (G-427)	F	716 782-3276
Christian Fabrication LLC, West Winfield (G-16957)	G	315 822-0135
Cives Corporation, Gouverneur (G-5743)	C	315 287-2200
Cobbe Industries Inc, Gerry (G-5592)	E	716 287-2661
Cobra Operating Industries LLC, Afton (G-9)	G	607 639-1700
Columbia Metal Fabricators, Port Jeff STA (G-13765)	G	631 476-7527
Computerized Metal Bending Ser, West Babylon (G-16785)	F	631 249-1177
Cottonwood Metals Inc, Bohemia (G-1040)	E	646 807-8674
County Fabricators, Pleasantville (G-13713)	F	914 741-0219
Cyncal Steel Fabricators Inc, Bay Shore (G-689)	F	631 254-5600
D N Gannon Fabricating Inc, Syracuse (G-15919)	G	315 463-7466
Dennies Manufacturing Inc, Canandaigua (G-3342)	E	585 393-4646
Diversified Manufacturing Inc, Lancaster (G-7312)	F	716 681-7670
Donald Stefan, Chaffee (G-3533)	G	716 492-1110
Dynasty Metal Works Inc, Riverhead (G-14141)	G	631 284-3719
E & Y General Cnstr Co Inc, Staten Island (G-15667)	F	718 567-7011
E B Atlas Steel Corp, Buffalo (G-2922)	F	716 876-0900
Eastern Manufacturing Inc, Clarence Center (G-3674)	F	716 741-4572
Eastern Welding Inc, Riverhead (G-14142)	G	631 727-0306
Elevator Accessories Mfg, Peekskill (G-13477)	G	914 739-7004
Elmira Metal Works Inc, Elmira (G-4683)	G	607 734-9813
Empire Industrial Systems Corp, Bay Shore (G-699)	F	631 242-4619
Empire Metal Fabricators Inc, Rochester (G-14347)	G	585 288-2140
Eps Iron Works Inc, Mineola (G-8509)	G	516 294-5840
Erie Engineered Products Inc, Lackawanna (G-7314)	E	716 206-0204
Everfab Inc, East Aurora (G-4370)	D	716 655-1550
Excel Industries Inc, Clarence (G-3681)	E	716 542-5468
Farmingdale Iron Works Inc, Farmingdale (G-4991)	G	631 249-5995
Feinstein Iron Works Inc, Westbury (G-16985)	E	516 997-8300
Fence Plaza Corp, Brooklyn (G-1966)	G	718 469-2200
Five Corners Repair Inc, Bliss (G-980)	F	585 322-7369
▼ Flagpoles Incorporated, East Setauket (G-4483)	D	631 751-5500
▲ Fort Miller Group Inc, Greenwich (G-5887)	B	518 695-5000
Frazier Industrial Company, Waterloo (G-16626)	D	315 539-9256
Fred A Nudd Corporation, Ontario (G-13201)	E	315 524-2531
Gasport Welding & Fabg Inc, Gasport (G-5557)	F	716 772-7205
George Industries LLC, Endicott (G-4810)	C	607 748-3371
◆ Gibraltar Industries Inc, Buffalo (G-2974)	F	716 826-6500
Glenridge Fabricators Inc, Glendale (G-5655)	F	718 456-2297
Hallock Fabricating Corp, Riverhead (G-14144)	E	631 727-2441
Hansen Steel, Farmington (G-5152)	E	585 398-2020
Homer Iron Works LLC, Homer (G-6519)	E	607 749-3963
Hudson Steel Fabricators, Rochester (G-14440)	E	585 454-3923
Industrial Fabricating Corp, East Syracuse (G-4539)	E	315 437-3353
▲ Industrial Support Inc, Buffalo (G-3006)	D	716 662-2954
▲ Inscape (new York) Inc, Falconer (G-4902)	D	716 665-6210
Irony Limited Inc, East Hampton (G-4411)	G	631 329-4065
Irv Schroder & Sons Inc, Stottville (G-15781)	E	518 828-0194
Irving Woodlands LLC, Conklin (G-3870)	E	607 723-4862
J F M Sheet Metal Inc, Ronkonkoma (G-14916)	G	631 737-8494
J M Haley Corp, Farmingdale (G-5013)	D	631 845-5200
Jaab Precision Inc, Ronkonkoma (G-14918)	G	631 218-3725
James Woerner Inc, Farmingdale (G-5016)	G	631 454-9330
Jbs LLC, Scotia (G-15327)	E	518 346-0001
Jentsch & Co Inc, Buffalo (G-3016)	G	716 852-4111
Joy Edward Company, East Syracuse (G-4547)	E	315 474-3360
Jpw Structural Contracting Inc, Syracuse (G-15971)	E	315 432-1111
K & E Fabricating Co Inc, Buffalo (G-3023)	G	716 829-1829
Kal Manufacturing Corporation, Webster (G-16726)	E	585 265-4310
KDO Industries Inc, Amityville (G-301)	G	631 608-4612
King Steel Iron Work Corp, Brooklyn (G-2174)	F	718 384-7500
Kleinfelder John, Mayville (G-8216)	G	716 753-3163
Knj Fabricators LLC, Bronx (G-1374)	F	347 234-6985
Koenig Iron Works Inc, Long Island City (G-7782)	E	718 433-0900
Kryten Iron Works Inc, Hawthorne (G-6249)	G	914 345-0990
Kuno Steel Products Corp, Hicksville (G-6361)	F	516 938-8500
Leading Edge Fabrication, Deer Park (G-4164)	G	631 274-9797
Leray Homes Inc, Watertown (G-16663)	G	315 788-6087
Lindenhurst Fabricators Inc, Lindenhurst (G-7467)	G	631 226-3737
Linita Design & Mfg Corp, Lackawanna (G-7244)	E	716 566-7753
▲ M & L Steel & Ornamental Iron, Staten Island (G-15701)	F	718 816-8660
▲ Mageba USA LLC, New York (G-11099)	E	212 317-1991
▲ Major-IPC Inc, Liberty (G-7438)	G	845 292-2200
▲ Marex Aquisition Corp, Rochester (G-14497)	C	585 458-3940

Employee Codes: A=Over 500 employees, B=251-500, C=101-250, D=51-100, E=20-50, F=10-19, G=5-9

34 FABRICATED METAL PRODUCTS, EXCEPT MACHINERY AND TRANSPORTATION EQUIPMENT SIC SECTION

Marovato Industries Inc .... F 718 389-0800
Brooklyn *(G-2275)*

▲ Mason Industries Inc .... C 631 348-0282
Hauppauge *(G-6126)*

Maspeth Steel Fabricators Inc .... G 718 361-9192
Long Island City *(G-7804)*

Maspeth Welding Inc .... E 718 497-5430
Maspeth *(G-8150)*

Metal Concepts .... G 845 592-1863
Beacon *(G-788)*

Metal Crafts Inc .... G 718 443-3333
Brooklyn *(G-2303)*

Metal Fab LLC .... G 607 775-3200
Binghamton *(G-936)*

Metal Works of NY Inc .... G 718 525-9440
Jamaica *(G-6930)*

Miller Metal Fabricating Inc .... G 585 359-3400
Rochester *(G-14514)*

Miscellnous Ir Fabricators Inc .... E 518 355-1822
Schenectady *(G-15280)*

Mobile Mini Inc .... F 315 732-4555
Utica *(G-16349)*

▼ Monarch Metal Fabrication Inc .... G 631 563-8967
Bohemia *(G-1105)*

Mount Vernon Iron Works Inc .... G 914 668-7064
Mount Vernon *(G-8708)*

Nathan Steel Corp .... F 315 797-1335
Utica *(G-16351)*

Nci Group Inc .... D 315 339-1245
Rome *(G-14824)*

New Vision Industries Inc .... F 607 687-7700
Endicott *(G-4820)*

New York Manufactured Products .... F 585 254-9353
Rochester *(G-14532)*

North E Rggers Erectors NY Inc .... E 518 842-6377
Amsterdam *(G-362)*

▲ North Eastern Fabricators Inc .... E 718 542-0450
New York *(G-11457)*

Northeast Fabricators LLC .... D 607 865-4031
Walton *(G-16549)*

Oehlers Wldg & Fabrication Inc .... F 716 821-1800
Buffalo *(G-3098)*

Orange County Ironworks LLC .... E 845 769-3000
Montgomery *(G-8600)*

▲ Oriskany Mfg Tech LLC .... E 315 732-4962
Yorkville *(G-17525)*

P & H Inc .... E 631 231-7660
Hauppauge *(G-6157)*

P K G Equipment Incorporated .... E 585 436-4650
Rochester *(G-14564)*

Patsy Strocchia & Sons Iron Wo .... F 516 625-8800
Albertson *(G-156)*

Pcx Aerostructures LLC .... E 631 249-7901
Ronkonkoma *(G-14967)*

Pcx Aerostructures LLC .... E 631 467-2632
Farmingdale *(G-5075)*

Peralta Metal Works Inc .... G 718 649-8661
Brooklyn *(G-2416)*

Perma Tech Inc .... E 716 854-0707
Buffalo *(G-3122)*

▲ Pierce Industries LLC .... E 585 458-0888
Rochester *(G-14584)*

Port Authority of NY & NJ .... D 718 390-2534
Staten Island *(G-15723)*

Portfab LLC .... E 718 542-3600
Amityville *(G-322)*

Precision Metals Corp .... E 631 586-5032
Bay Shore *(G-727)*

Precision Polish LLC .... E 315 894-3792
Frankfort *(G-5356)*

Prime Materials Recovery Inc .... G 315 697-5251
Canastota *(G-3371)*

▲ Productand Design Inc .... F 718 858-2440
Brooklyn *(G-2452)*

R & J Sheet Metal Distrs Inc .... G 518 433-1525
Albany *(G-125)*

R&S Steel LLC .... E 315 281-0123
Rome *(G-14831)*

▲ Ramsey Charles Company .... F 845 338-1464
Kingston *(G-7208)*

Raulli and Sons Inc .... D 315 479-6693
Syracuse *(G-16018)*

REO Welding Inc .... F 518 238-1022
Cohoes *(G-3756)*

▲ Risa Management Corp .... E 718 361-2606
Maspeth *(G-8167)*

Riverside Iron LLC .... F 315 535-4864
Gouverneur *(G-5747)*

RJ Precision LLC .... G 585 768-8030
Stafford *(G-15622)*

▲ Robert E Derecktor Inc .... D 914 698-0962
Mamaroneck *(G-8045)*

Romar Contracting Inc .... G 845 778-2737
Walden *(G-16535)*

Roth Design & Consulting Inc .... E 718 209-0193
Brooklyn *(G-2509)*

Rothe Welding Inc .... G 845 246-3051
Saugerties *(G-15193)*

Rs Automation .... F 585 589-0199
Albion *(G-169)*

▲ Rus Industries Inc .... E 716 284-7828
Niagara Falls *(G-12869)*

Schenectady Steel Co Inc .... D 518 355-3220
Schenectady *(G-15293)*

Schenectady Steel Co Inc .... E 607 275-0086
Ithaca *(G-6875)*

Schneider Brothers Corporation .... E 315 458-8369
Syracuse *(G-16034)*

Schuler-Subra Inc .... G 716 893-3100
Buffalo *(G-3177)*

▲ Seibel Modern Mfg & Wldg Corp .... D 716 683-1536
Lancaster *(G-7342)*

Sentry Metal Blast Inc .... E 716 285-5241
Niagara Falls *(G-12875)*

Sherco Services LLC .... F 516 676-3028
Glen Cove *(G-5627)*

Silverstone Shtmtl Fbrications .... G 718 422-0380
Brooklyn *(G-2559)*

Specialty Steel Fabg Corp .... F 718 893-6326
Bronx *(G-1461)*

Specialty Wldg & Fabg NY Inc .... D 315 426-1807
Syracuse *(G-16043)*

Standard Ascnsion Towers Group .... D 716 681-2222
Depew *(G-4274)*

Standard Steel Fabricators .... F 518 765-4820
Voorheesville *(G-16519)*

Steel Tech SA LLC .... G 845 786-3691
Thiells *(G-16114)*

▲ Stone Bridge Iron and Stl Inc .... D 518 695-3752
Gansevoort *(G-5490)*

▼ Stone Well Bodies & Mch Inc .... F 315 497-3512
Genoa *(G-5590)*

STS Steel Inc .... D 518 370-2693
Schenectady *(G-15301)*

Sunlight US Co Inc .... G 716 826-6500
Buffalo *(G-3201)*

Supreme Steel Inc .... F 631 884-1320
Lindenhurst *(G-7489)*

Team Fabrication Inc .... G 716 655-4038
West Falls *(G-16845)*

Titan Steel Corp .... F 315 656-7046
Kirkville *(G-7229)*

Triboro Iron Works Inc .... G 718 361-9600
Long Island City *(G-7906)*

Triton Builders Inc .... E 631 841-2534
Amityville *(G-331)*

Tropical Driftwood Originals .... G 516 623-0980
Roosevelt *(G-15010)*

Tymetal Corp .... E 518 692-9930
Greenwich *(G-5895)*

Ulster Precision Inc .... E 845 338-0995
Kingston *(G-7218)*

United Iron Inc .... E 914 667-5700
Mount Vernon *(G-8745)*

United Structure Solution Inc .... F 347 227-7526
New York *(G-12466)*

Universal Metal Works LLC .... F 315 598-7607
Fulton *(G-5476)*

▲ Vance Metal Fabricators Inc .... D 315 789-5626
Geneva *(G-5588)*

Vulcan Iron Works Inc .... G 631 395-6846
Manorville *(G-8082)*

Vulcraft of New York Inc .... C 607 529-9000
Chemung *(G-3595)*

Ward Steel Company Inc .... E 315 451-4566
Liverpool *(G-7555)*

◆ Watson Bowman Acme Corp .... D 716 691-8162
Amherst *(G-271)*

Welding Metallurgy Inc .... E 631 253-0500
Hauppauge *(G-6231)*

Whitacre Engineering Company .... G 315 622-1075
Liverpool *(G-7556)*

Wilston Enterprises Inc .... F 716 483-1411
Jamestown *(G-7044)*

Winters Railroad Service Inc .... G 716 337-2668
North Collins *(G-12932)*

3442 Metal Doors, Sash, Frames, Molding & Trim

A & L Doors & Hardware LLC .... F 718 585-8400
Bronx *(G-1252)*

▲ A & S Window Associates Inc .... E 718 275-7900
Glendale *(G-5642)*

A G M Deco Inc .... F 718 624-6200
Brooklyn *(G-1533)*

▲ A G M Deco Inc .... F 718 624-6200
Brooklyn *(G-1534)*

Accurate Metal Weather Strip .... G 914 668-6042
Mount Vernon *(G-8661)*

Ace Fire Door Corp .... E 718 901-0001
Bronx *(G-1261)*

▲ Acme Architectural Pdts Inc .... D 718 384-7800
Brooklyn *(G-1555)*

Action Bullet Resistant .... F 631 422-0888
West Islip *(G-16903)*

Air Tite Manufacturing Inc .... C 516 897-0295
Long Beach *(G-7637)*

All United Window Corp .... E 718 624-0490
Brooklyn *(G-1588)*

Alpine Overhead Doors Inc .... E 631 456-7800
East Setauket *(G-4475)*

Altype Fire Door Corp .... G 718 292-3500
Bronx *(G-1271)*

▲ Alumil Fabrication Inc .... F 845 469-2874
Newburgh *(G-12748)*

Amarr Company .... F 585 426-8290
Rochester *(G-14195)*

American Rolling Door Ltd .... G 718 273-0485
Staten Island *(G-15637)*

American Steel Gate Corp .... G 718 291-4050
Jamaica *(G-6893)*

Assa Abloy Entrance Systems US .... E 315 492-6600
East Syracuse *(G-4507)*

▲ Bison Steel Incorporated .... G 716 683-0900
Depew *(G-4248)*

Brooklyn Store Front Co Inc .... G 718 384-4372
Brooklyn *(G-1732)*

▲ Champion Aluminum Corp .... C 631 656-3424
Hauppauge *(G-6042)*

Corkhill Manufacturing Co Inc .... G 718 528-7413
Jamaica *(G-6907)*

D D & L Inc .... F 607 729-9131
Binghamton *(G-906)*

Dawson Metal Company Inc .... C 716 664-3811
Jamestown *(G-6987)*

Dayton Industries Inc .... E 718 542-8144
Bronx *(G-1311)*

Deronde Doors and Frames Inc .... F 716 895-8888
Buffalo *(G-2908)*

Dural Door Company Inc .... F 718 729-1333
Long Island City *(G-7720)*

Eastern Storefronts & Mtls Inc .... F 631 471-7065
Ronkonkoma *(G-14897)*

Elegant Entries Inc .... F 631 595-1000
Syosset *(G-15820)*

◆ Ellison Bronze Inc .... D 716 665-6522
Falconer *(G-4895)*

Empire Archtctural Systems Inc .... E 518 773-5109
Johnstown *(G-7110)*

Excel Aluminum Products Inc .... G 315 471-0925
Syracuse *(G-15940)*

F A Alpine Windows Mfg .... F 845 469-5700
Chester *(G-3606)*

Gamma North Corporation .... E 716 902-5100
Alden *(G-178)*

General Fire-Proof Door Corp .... E 718 893-5500
Bronx *(G-1342)*

◆ Global Steel Products Corp .... C 631 586-3455
Deer Park *(G-4147)*

◆ Great American Industries Inc .... G 607 729-9331
Vestal *(G-16449)*

◆ Griffon Corporation .... E 212 957-5000
New York *(G-10363)*

Grover Aluminum Products Inc .... E 631 475-3500
Patchogue *(G-13421)*

Gscp Emax Acquisition LLC .... G 212 902-1000
New York *(G-10378)*

▲ Hopes Windows Inc .... C 716 665-5124
Jamestown *(G-7000)*

I Fix Screen .... G 631 421-1938
Centereach *(G-3471)*

▲ Inscape (new York) Inc .... D 716 665-6210
Falconer *(G-4902)*

Inter-Fence Co Inc .... E 718 939-9700
College Point *(G-3789)*

Interntional Fireprof Door Inc .... F 718 783-1310
Brooklyn *(G-2112)*

▲ **Interstate Window Corporation** D 631 231-0800
Brentwood *(G-1186)*
▼ **J Sussman Inc** E 718 297-0228
Jamaica *(G-6922)*
▲ **Jaidan Industries Inc** F 516 944-3650
Port Washington *(G-13827)*
Jenmar Door & Glass Inc G 718 767-7900
Whitestone *(G-17210)*
▲ **Karey Kassl Corp** E 516 349-8484
Plainview *(G-13613)*
◆ **Karp Associates Inc** D 631 768-8300
Melville *(G-8332)*
▲ **Kasson & Keller Inc** A 518 853-3421
Fonda *(G-5315)*
Kelly Window Systems Inc E 631 420-8500
Farmingdale *(G-5026)*
▲ **Kinro Manufacturing Inc** G 817 483-7791
White Plains *(G-17131)*
L & L Overhead Garage Doors G 718 721-2518
Long Island City *(G-7787)*
Lif Industries Inc D 516 390-6800
Port Washington *(G-13837)*
Long Island Fireproof Door E 718 767-8800
Whitestone *(G-17211)*
▼ **M & D Installers Inc** E 718 782-6978
Brooklyn *(G-2243)*
Markar Architectural Products G 716 685-4104
Lancaster *(G-7326)*
Master Window & Door Corp F 718 782-5407
Brooklyn *(G-2281)*
▲ **McKeon Rolling Stl Door Co Inc** E 631 803-3000
Bellport *(G-834)*
Mercury Lock and Door Service E 718 542-7048
Bronx *(G-1392)*
Metalline Fire Door Co Inc E 718 583-2320
Bronx *(G-1393)*
Michbi Doors Inc D 631 231-9050
Brentwood *(G-1192)*
Milanese Commercial Door LLC F 518 658-0398
Berlin *(G-857)*
Milgo Industrial Inc D 718 388-6476
Brooklyn *(G-2313)*
Milgo Industrial Inc G 718 387-0406
Brooklyn *(G-2314)*
New Bgnnngs Win Door Dstrs LLC F 845 214-0698
Poughkeepsie *(G-13920)*
Norandex Inc Vestal G 607 786-0778
Vestal *(G-16452)*
▼ **North American Door Corp** F 518 566-0161
Plattsburgh *(G-13680)*
▲ **Optimum Window Mfg Corp** E 845 647-1900
Ellenville *(G-4636)*
Overhead Door Corporation D 518 828-7652
Hudson *(G-6629)*
Pal Manufacturing Corp E 516 937-1990
Hicksville *(G-6384)*
Pioneer Window Holdings Inc F 516 822-7000
Hicksville *(G-6388)*
Pioneer Window Holdings Inc E 518 762-5526
Johnstown *(G-7122)*
Pk30 System LLC F 212 473-8050
Stone Ridge *(G-15764)*
▲ **Polyshot Corporation** E 585 292-5010
West Henrietta *(G-16892)*
▲ **Presray Corporation** E 845 373-9300
Wassaic *(G-16601)*
Raydoor Inc G 212 421-0641
New York *(G-11807)*
Renewal By Andersen LLC E 631 843-1716
Farmingdale *(G-5098)*
▲ **Robert-Masters Corp** G 718 545-1030
Woodside *(G-17351)*
Rochester Colonial Mfg Corp D 585 254-8191
Rochester *(G-14639)*
Rochester Lumber Company E 585 924-7171
Farmington *(G-5155)*
Rohlfs Stined Leaded GL Studio E 914 699-4848
Mount Vernon *(G-8726)*
Roly Door Sales Inc G 716 877-1515
Hamburg *(G-5941)*
Schwab Corp E 585 381-4900
Rochester *(G-14675)*
Shade & Shutter Systems of NY G 631 208-0275
Southampton *(G-15551)*
Slanto Manufacturing Inc E 516 759-5721
Glen Cove *(G-5628)*
Statewide Fireproof Door Co F 845 268-6043
Valley Cottage *(G-16390)*
Steelmasters Inc E 718 498-2854
Brooklyn *(G-2605)*
Sunrise Door Solutions G 631 464-4139
Copiague *(G-3930)*
Superior Stl Door Trim Co Inc F 716 665-3256
Jamestown *(G-7036)*
Supreme Fire-Proof Door Co Inc F 718 665-4224
Bronx *(G-1468)*
Texas Home Security Inc E 516 747-2100
New Hyde Park *(G-8865)*
Thermal Tech Doors Inc E 516 745-0100
Garden City *(G-5534)*
Thompson Overhead Door Co Inc F 718 788-2470
Brooklyn *(G-2658)*
Trulite Louvre Corp E 516 756-1850
Old Bethpage *(G-13131)*
▲ **United Steel Products Inc** D 718 478-5330
Corona *(G-4009)*
Universal Fire Proof Door E 718 455-8442
Brooklyn *(G-2706)*
Vr Containment LLC G 917 972-3441
Fresh Meadows *(G-5447)*
Window Rama Enterprises Inc G 631 462-9054
Commack *(G-3849)*
Window Tech Systems Inc E 518 899-9000
Ballston Spa *(G-611)*
Windowman Inc (usa) G 718 246-2626
Brooklyn *(G-2758)*

3443 Fabricated Plate Work

828 Express Inc G 917 577-9019
Staten Island *(G-15629)*
▲ **A K Allen Co Inc** C 516 747-5450
Mineola *(G-8488)*
A L Eastmond & Sons Inc D 718 378-3000
Bronx *(G-1254)*
▲ **Aavid Niagara LLC** F 716 297-0652
Niagara Falls *(G-12794)*
▲ **Acro Industries Inc** C 585 254-3661
Rochester *(G-14171)*
▲ **Aerco International Inc** C 845 580-8000
Blauvelt *(G-969)*
Aero-Data Metal Crafters Inc C 631 471-7733
Ronkonkoma *(G-14856)*
All-State Diversified Pdts Inc E 315 472-4728
Syracuse *(G-15848)*
Alliance Innovative Mfg Inc E 716 822-1626
Lackawanna *(G-7242)*
▲ **Allstate Gasket & Packing Inc** F 631 254-4050
Deer Park *(G-4092)*
American Boiler Tank Wldg Inc E 518 463-5012
Albany *(G-46)*
◆ **American Precision Inds Inc** C 716 691-9100
Amherst *(G-224)*
Ametek Inc C 516 832-7710
Garden City *(G-5494)*
▼ **Amherst Stnless Fbrication LLC** E 716 691-7012
Amherst *(G-225)*
API Heat Transfer Company G 716 684-6700
Buffalo *(G-2816)*
API Heat Transfer Inc C 585 496-5755
Arcade *(G-387)*
Arvos Inc B 585 593-2700
Wellsville *(G-16749)*
Atlantic Industrial Tech Inc E 631 234-3131
Shirley *(G-15414)*
Aurora Indus Machining Inc E 716 826-7911
Orchard Park *(G-13252)*
Bellmore Steel Products Corp F 516 785-9667
Bellmore *(G-815)*
Bigbee Steel and Tank Company E 518 273-0801
Watervliet *(G-16679)*
Blackstone Advanced Tech LLC C 716 665-5410
Jamestown *(G-6975)*
Bos-Hatten Inc F 716 662-7030
Orchard Park *(G-13253)*
Breton Industries Inc D 518 842-3030
Amsterdam *(G-336)*
Bridgehampton Steel & Wldg Inc F 631 537-2486
Bridgehampton *(G-1232)*
Bruce Pierce G 716 731-9310
Sanborn *(G-15115)*
▼ **Buflovak LLC** E 716 895-2100
Buffalo *(G-2861)*
Byelocorp Scientific Inc E 212 785-2580
New York *(G-9686)*
C & F Fabricators & Erectors G 607 432-3520
Colliersville *(G-3814)*
Cardinal Tank Corp E 718 625-4350
Brooklyn *(G-1757)*
▲ **Charles Ross & Son Company** D 631 234-0500
Hauppauge *(G-6044)*
▲ **Cigar Box Studios Inc** F 845 236-9283
Marlboro *(G-8105)*
CMS Heat Transfer Division Inc E 631 968-0084
Bohemia *(G-1037)*
Contech Engnered Solutions LLC F 716 870-9091
Orchard Park *(G-13265)*
▼ **Costanzos Welding Inc** E 716 282-0845
Niagara Falls *(G-12807)*
Crown Tank Company LLC G 855 276-9682
Horseheads *(G-6572)*
Curtiss-Wright Flow Control G 845 382-6918
Lake Katrine *(G-7270)*
Cyclotherm of Watertown Inc E 315 782-1100
Watertown *(G-16649)*
David Isseks & Sons Inc E 212 966-8694
New York *(G-9820)*
Direkt Force LLC E 716 652-3022
East Aurora *(G-4369)*
Doyle & Roth Mfg Co Inc F 212 269-7840
New York *(G-9921)*
ECR International Inc C 716 366-5500
Dunkirk *(G-4341)*
◆ **ECR International Inc** D 315 797-1310
Utica *(G-16328)*
Empire Industrial Systems Corp F 631 242-4619
Bay Shore *(G-699)*
Endicott Precision Inc C 607 754-7076
Endicott *(G-4803)*
Energy Nuclear Operations E 315 342-0055
Oswego *(G-13331)*
Erie Engineered Products Inc E 716 206-0204
Lancaster *(G-7314)*
Exergy LLC E 516 832-9300
Garden City *(G-5505)*
Expert Industries Inc E 718 434-6060
Brooklyn *(G-1946)*
Feldmeier Equipment Inc D 315 823-2000
Syracuse *(G-15943)*
Feldmeier Equipment Inc D 315 823-2000
Little Falls *(G-7499)*
Feldmeier Equipment Inc C 315 823-2000
Little Falls *(G-7500)*
Fluid Handling LLC C 716 897-2800
Cheektowaga *(G-3570)*
Fross Industries Inc E 716 297-0652
Niagara Falls *(G-12823)*
Fuel Efficiency LLC G 315 923-2511
Clyde *(G-3727)*
▲ **Fulton Boiler Works Inc** D 315 298-5121
Pulaski *(G-13947)*
Fulton Boiler Works Inc C 315 298-5121
Pulaski *(G-13948)*
Gasport Welding & Fabg Inc F 716 772-7205
Gasport *(G-5557)*
General Oil Equipment Co Inc E 716 691-7012
Amherst *(G-243)*
Glenridge Fabricators Inc F 718 456-2297
Glendale *(G-5655)*
◆ **Global Steel Products Corp** C 631 586-3455
Deer Park *(G-4147)*
◆ **Graham Corporation** B 585 343-2216
Batavia *(G-636)*
Hyperbaric Technologies Inc G 518 842-3030
Amsterdam *(G-350)*
Industrial Fabricating Corp E 315 437-8234
East Syracuse *(G-4540)*
Inex Inc G 716 537-2270
Holland *(G-6481)*
J & T Metal Products Co Inc E 631 226-7400
West Babylon *(G-16797)*
J M Canty Inc E 716 625-4227
Lockport *(G-7593)*
J W Stevens Co Inc G 315 472-6311
East Syracuse *(G-4545)*
◆ **Jaquith Industries Inc** E 315 478-5700
Syracuse *(G-15966)*
John R Robinson Inc E 718 786-6088
Long Island City *(G-7773)*
Joshua Liner Gallery LLC F 212 244-7415
New York *(G-10767)*
Kintex Inc D 716 297-0652
Niagara Falls *(G-12839)*
Lane Enterprises Inc F 607 776-3366
Bath *(G-660)*
▲ **Lifetime Chimney Supply LLC** G 516 576-8144
Plainview *(G-13616)*
Manhattan Cooling Towers Inc F 212 279-1045
New York *(G-11128)*
▲ **Marex Aquisition Corp** C 585 458-3940
Rochester *(G-14497)*

S I C

Employee Codes: A=Over 500 employees, B=251-500
C=101-250, D=51-100, E=20-50, F=10-19, G=5-9
2017 Harris
New York Manufacturers Directory
811

Marine Boiler & Welding Inc ....F 718 378-1900
Bronx *(G-1386)*

Methods Tooling & Mfg Inc ....E 845 246-7100
Mount Marion *(G-8651)*

Metrofab Pipe Incorporated ....F 516 349-7373
Plainview *(G-13619)*

Miller Metal Fabricating Inc ....G 585 359-3400
Rochester *(G-14514)*

Modutank Inc ....F 718 392-1112
Long Island City *(G-7815)*

Mono-Systems Inc ....E 716 821-1344
Buffalo *(G-3074)*

▲ **Motivair Corporation** ....E 716 691-9222
Amherst *(G-252)*

Mount Kisco Transfer Stn Inc ....G 914 666-6350
Mount Kisco *(G-8635)*

Nitram Energy Inc ....E 716 662-6540
Orchard Park *(G-13285)*

North American Svcs Group LLC ....F 518 885-1820
Ballston Spa *(G-604)*

Perforated Screen Surfaces ....E 866 866-8690
Conklin *(G-3872)*

▲ **Pfaudler US Inc** ....C 585 235-1000
Rochester *(G-14579)*

Roemac Industrial Sales Inc ....G 716 692-7332
North Tonawanda *(G-12991)*

Rosenwach Tank Co Inc ....E 212 972-4411
Astoria *(G-455)*

Ross Metal Fabricators Inc ....E 631 586-7000
Deer Park *(G-4202)*

Saraga Industries Corp ....G 631 842-4049
Amityville *(G-324)*

Sargent Manufacturing Inc ....G 212 722-7000
New York *(G-11972)*

Schwabel Fabricating Co Inc ....E 716 876-2086
Tonawanda *(G-16200)*

▲ **Seibel Modern Mfg & Wldg Corp** ....D 716 683-1536
Lancaster *(G-7342)*

▲ **Slant/Fin Corporation** ....B 516 484-2600
Greenvale *(G-5881)*

Slantco Manufacturing Inc ....G 516 484-2600
Greenvale *(G-5882)*

SPX Corporation ....E 631 249-7900
Ronkonkoma *(G-14988)*

SPX Corporation ....B 585 436-5550
Rochester *(G-14697)*

Stainless Metals Inc ....F 718 784-1454
Woodside *(G-17356)*

▲ **Stavo Industries Inc** ....F 845 331-4552
Kingston *(G-7213)*

Steelways Inc ....E 845 562-0860
Newburgh *(G-12780)*

Stutzman Management Corp ....F 800 735-2013
Lancaster *(G-7344)*

Supreme Boilers Inc ....G 718 342-2220
Brooklyn *(G-2631)*

Taylor Tank Company Inc ....E 718 434-1300
Brooklyn *(G-2647)*

Themis Chimney Inc ....F 718 937-4716
Brooklyn *(G-2657)*

Thermotech Corp ....G 716 823-3311
Buffalo *(G-3217)*

Troy Boiler Works Inc ....E 518 274-2650
Troy *(G-16258)*

Trulite Louvre Corp ....E 516 756-1850
Old Bethpage *(G-13131)*

United Wind Inc ....F 800 268-9896
Brooklyn *(G-2704)*

Vette Corp New York ....D 585 265-0330
Ontario *(G-13216)*

◆ **Vship Co** ....F 718 706-8566
Astoria *(G-460)*

Water Cooling Corp ....G 718 723-6500
Rosedale *(G-15015)*

Wayne Integrated Tech Corp ....E 631 242-0213
Edgewood *(G-4620)*

Wsf Industries Inc ....E 716 692-4930
Tonawanda *(G-16216)*

▲ **Yula Corporation** ....E 718 991-0900
Bronx *(G-1496)*

Zone Fabricators Inc ....F 718 272-0200
Ozone Park *(G-13388)*

3444 Sheet Metal Work

303 Contracting Inc ....E 716 896-2122
Orchard Park *(G-13249)*

A & L Shtmtl Fabrications Corp ....E 718 842-1600
Bronx *(G-1253)*

Aabco Sheet Metal Co Inc ....D 718 821-1166
Ridgewood *(G-14097)*

Abdo Shtmtl & Fabrication Inc ....G 315 894-4664
Frankfort *(G-5349)*

Aberdeen Blower & Shtmtl Works ....G 631 661-6100
West Babylon *(G-16764)*

Accra Sheetmetal LLC ....G 631 920-2087
Wyandanch *(G-17369)*

Accurate Specialty Metal Fabri ....E 718 418-6895
Middle Village *(G-8409)*

▲ **Acme Architectural Pdts Inc** ....D 718 384-7800
Brooklyn *(G-1555)*

▲ **Acro Industries Inc** ....C 585 254-3661
Rochester *(G-14171)*

Acro-Fab Ltd ....E 315 564-6688
Hannibal *(G-5969)*

Advanced Precision Technology ....F 845 279-3540
Brewster *(G-1207)*

Advantech Industries Inc ....C 585 247-0701
Rochester *(G-14181)*

Aero Trades Mfg Corp ....E 516 746-3360
Mineola *(G-8489)*

Aero-Data Metal Crafters Inc ....C 631 471-7733
Ronkonkoma *(G-14856)*

Aeroduct Inc ....E 516 248-9550
Mineola *(G-8490)*

Afco Systems Inc ....C 631 424-3935
Farmingdale *(G-4931)*

Air Louver & Damper Inc ....E 718 392-3232
Maspeth *(G-8112)*

Air Louver & Damper Inc ....F 718 392-3232
Long Island City *(G-7649)*

Aj Genco Mch Sp McHy Rdout Svc ....F 716 664-4925
Falconer *(G-4889)*

Aldo Frustacci Iron Works Inc ....F 718 768-0707
Brooklyn *(G-1578)*

Aleta Industries Inc ....F 718 349-0040
Brooklyn *(G-1580)*

Alfred B Parella ....G 518 872-1238
Altamont *(G-206)*

Alkemy Machine LLC ....G 585 436-8730
Rochester *(G-14186)*

All Around Spiral Inc ....G 631 588-0220
Ronkonkoma *(G-14860)*

All Island Blower & Shtmtl ....F 631 567-7070
Bohemia *(G-1013)*

All Star Carts & Vehicles Inc ....D 631 666-5581
Bay Shore *(G-668)*

▲ **Allen Machine Products Inc** ....E 631 630-8800
Hauppauge *(G-6016)*

Alliance Welding & Steel Fabg ....F 516 775-7600
Floral Park *(G-5191)*

Allure Metal Works Inc ....F 631 588-0220
Ronkonkoma *(G-14864)*

Alnik Service Corporation ....G 516 873-7300
New Hyde Park *(G-8814)*

Alpine Machine Inc ....F 607 272-1344
Ithaca *(G-6818)*

▲ **Alternative Service Inc** ....F 631 345-9500
Yaphank *(G-17385)*

Amsco Inc ....F 716 823-4213
Buffalo *(G-2811)*

Apparatus Mfg Inc ....G 845 471-5116
Poughkeepsie *(G-13887)*

▲ **Arcadia Mfg Group Inc** ....E 518 434-6213
Green Island *(G-5853)*

Arcadia Mfg Group Inc ....G 518 434-6213
Menands *(G-8367)*

Architctral Shetmetal Pdts Inc ....G 518 381-6144
Scotia *(G-15323)*

Arlan Damper Corporation ....E 631 589-7431
Bohemia *(G-1019)*

Art Form Sheet Metal Fabricato ....G 718 728-0111
Long Island City *(G-7670)*

Art Precision Metal Products ....F 631 842-8889
Copiague *(G-3894)*

▲ **Ascension Industries Inc** ....D 716 693-9381
North Tonawanda *(G-12956)*

Asm USA Inc ....G 212 925-2906
New York *(G-9233)*

Asp Industries Inc ....E 585 254-9130
Rochester *(G-14217)*

Atlantis Equipment Corporation ....F 518 733-5910
Stephentown *(G-15756)*

Atlas Sign ....G 718 604-7446
Brooklyn *(G-1649)*

Auburn Tank & Manufacturing Co ....F 315 255-2788
Auburn *(G-481)*

▲ **Austin Mohawk and Company LLC** ....E 315 793-3000
Utica *(G-16308)*

Auto Body Services LLC ....F 631 431-4640
Lindenhurst *(G-7455)*

Avalanche Fabrication Inc ....F 585 545-4000
Ontario *(G-13196)*

◆ **B & B Sheet Metal Inc** ....E 718 433-2501
Long Island City *(G-7679)*

B & H Precision Fabricators ....F 631 563-9620
Bohemia *(G-1021)*

Banner Metalcraft Inc ....D 631 563-7303
Ronkonkoma *(G-14878)*

Bargold Storage Systems LLC ....E 718 247-7000
Long Island City *(G-7682)*

Batavia Enclosures Inc ....G 585 344-1797
Arcade *(G-388)*

Berjen Metal Industries Ltd ....G 631 673-7979
Huntington *(G-6656)*

Best Tinsmith Supply Inc ....G 518 863-2541
Northville *(G-13019)*

Blackstone Advanced Tech LLC ....C 716 665-5410
Jamestown *(G-6975)*

Blackstone Business Entps Inc ....C 716 665-5410
Jamestown *(G-6976)*

Boss Precision Ltd ....D 585 352-7070
Spencerport *(G-15566)*

Broadway Neon Sign Corp ....F 908 241-4177
Ronkonkoma *(G-14881)*

Brothers Roofing Supplies Co ....E 718 779-0280
East Elmhurst *(G-4389)*

Buffalo Metal Forming Inc ....G 716 856-4575
West Seneca *(G-16941)*

C & T Tool & Instrument Co ....E 718 429-1253
Woodside *(G-17321)*

C J & C Sheet Metal Corp ....F 631 376-9425
West Babylon *(G-16780)*

▲ **Cannon Industries Inc** ....D 585 254-8080
Rochester *(G-14258)*

CBM Fabrications Inc ....E 518 399-8023
Ballston Lake *(G-581)*

Center Sheet Metal Inc ....C 718 378-4476
Bronx *(G-1293)*

▲ **Cetek Inc** ....E 845 452-3510
Poughkeepsie *(G-13892)*

Chamtek Mfg Inc ....E 585 328-4900
Rochester *(G-14272)*

Cherry Holding Ltd ....G 516 679-3748
North Bellmore *(G-12916)*

Choppy V M & Sons LLC ....E 518 266-1444
Troy *(G-16231)*

Citros Building Materials Co ....E 718 779-0727
East Elmhurst *(G-4390)*

City Cooling Enterprises Inc ....G 718 331-7400
Brooklyn *(G-1781)*

Clark Specialty Co Inc ....E 607 776-3193
Bath *(G-655)*

Construction Parts Whse Inc ....G 315 445-1310
East Syracuse *(G-4519)*

CPI Industries Inc ....D 631 909-3434
Manorville *(G-8078)*

Craft-Tech Mfg Corp ....G 631 563-4949
Bohemia *(G-1042)*

Crown Die Casting Corp ....E 914 667-5400
Mount Vernon *(G-8675)*

Custom Sheet Metal Contg LLC ....F 716 896-2122
Buffalo *(G-2898)*

Custom Sheet Metal Corp ....G 315 463-9105
Syracuse *(G-15916)*

Cutting Edge Metal Works ....E 631 981-8333
Holtsville *(G-6503)*

Cw Metals Inc ....E 917 416-7906
Long Island City *(G-7709)*

D & G Sheet Metal Co Inc ....F 718 326-9111
Maspeth *(G-8127)*

D and D Sheet Metal Corp ....F 718 465-7585
Jamaica *(G-6909)*

Dart Awning Inc ....F 718 945-4224
Freeport *(G-5393)*

Dawson Metal Company Inc ....C 716 664-3811
Jamestown *(G-6987)*

Dayton T Brown Inc ....B 631 589-6300
Bohemia *(G-1052)*

Delta Sheet Metal Corp ....C 718 429-5805
Long Island City *(G-7711)*

Dimar Manufacturing Corp ....C 716 759-0351
Clarence *(G-3656)*

▲ **Dj Acquisition Management Corp** ....D 585 265-3000
Ontario *(G-13200)*

Doortec Archtctural Met GL LLC ....E 718 567-2730
Brooklyn *(G-1873)*

DOT Tool Co Inc ....G 607 724-7001
Binghamton *(G-908)*

Dundas-Jafine Inc ....E 716 681-9690
Alden *(G-177)*

SIC SECTION — 34 FABRICATED METAL PRODUCTS, EXCEPT MACHINERY AND TRANSPORTATION EQUIPMENT

Dynasty Stainless Steel & Meta............E 718 205-6623
Maspeth *(G-8134)*
E G M Restaurant Equipment Mfg..........G....... 718 782-9800
Brooklyn *(G-1891)*
◆ **ECR International Inc**.........................D....... 315 797-1310
Utica *(G-16328)*
Elderlee Incorporated............................C....... 315 789-6670
Oaks Corners *(G-13069)*
Elevator Accessories Mfg.......................F 914 739-7004
Peekskill *(G-13477)*
Elmsford Sheet Metal Works Inc............D....... 914 739-6300
Cortlandt Manor *(G-4050)*
Empire Air Specialties Inc.......................E 518 689-4440
Albany *(G-77)*
Empire Ventilation Eqp Co Inc...............F 718 728-2143
Florida *(G-5212)*
Endicott Precision Inc............................C....... 607 754-7076
Endicott *(G-4803)*
Engineering Mfg Tech LLC......................D 607 754-7111
Endicott *(G-4805)*
Expert Industries Inc..............................E 718 434-6060
Brooklyn *(G-1946)*
F M L Industries Inc...............................G....... 607 749-7273
Homer *(G-6517)*
Federal Sheet Metal Works Inc..............F 315 735-4730
Utica *(G-16332)*
Five Star Awnings Inc..............................F 718 860-6070
Ridgewood *(G-14107)*
Five Star Industries Inc...........................E 716 674-2589
West Seneca *(G-16945)*
Franchet Metal Craft Inc..........................G....... 718 658-6400
Jamaica *(G-6913)*
Fred A Nudd Corporation........................E 315 524-2531
Ontario *(G-13201)*
Genesee Building Products LLC...........G....... 585 548-2726
Stafford *(G-15620)*
GM Sheet Metal Inc.................................F 718 349-2830
Brooklyn *(G-2031)*
Goergen-Mackwirth Co Inc......................E 716 874-4800
Buffalo *(G-2977)*
Golden Group International Ltd.............G....... 845 440-1025
Patterson *(G-13440)*
Gottlieb Schwartz Family........................E 718 761-2010
Staten Island *(G-15679)*
Greene Technologies Inc........................D....... 607 656-4166
Greene *(G-5866)*
Gt Innovations LLC..................................G....... 585 739-7659
Churchville *(G-3637)*
H & M Leasing Corp.................................G....... 631 225-5246
Copiague *(G-3904)*
Hana Sheet Metal Inc...............................G....... 914 377-0773
Yonkers *(G-17452)*
Hansen Steel..E 585 398-2020
Farmington *(G-5152)*
Harbor Elc Fabrication Tls Inc...............E 914 636-4400
New Rochelle *(G-8909)*
Hart To Hart Industries Inc.....................G....... 716 492-2709
Chaffee *(G-3534)*
Hatfield Metal Fab Inc.............................E 845 454-9078
Poughkeepsie *(G-13906)*
◆ **Hergo Ergonomic Support**...................E 718 894-0639
Maspeth *(G-8143)*
Hermann Gerdens Inc...............................G....... 631 841-3132
Copiague *(G-3905)*
Hi-Tech Industries NY Inc........................E 607 217-7361
Johnson City *(G-7094)*
Hrd Metal Products Inc............................G....... 631 243-6700
Deer Park *(G-4151)*
◆ **Hunter Douglas Inc**...............................D....... 845 664-7000
Pearl River *(G-13460)*
I Rauchs Sons Inc.....................................E 718 507-8844
East Elmhurst *(G-4392)*
IEC Electronics Corp................................B 585 647-1760
Rochester *(G-14444)*
Illinois Tool Works Inc...............................E 607 770-4945
Binghamton *(G-926)*
Imperial Damper & Louver Co.................E 718 731-3800
Bronx *(G-1360)*
▼ **Incodema Inc**..E 607 277-7070
Ithaca *(G-6848)*
Industrial Fabricating Corp......................E 315 437-3353
East Syracuse *(G-4539)*
Intellimetal Inc...D....... 585 424-3260
Rochester *(G-14451)*
Interior Metals...E 718 439-7324
Brooklyn *(G-2110)*
Jamestown Advanced Pdts Corp...........E 716 483-3406
Jamestown *(G-7004)*
◆ **Jaquith Industries Inc**...........................E 315 478-5700
Syracuse *(G-15966)*
Jar Metals Inc...F 845 425-8901
Nanuet *(G-8758)*
Joe P Industries Inc...................................F 631 293-7889
Farmingdale *(G-5018)*
▲ **Juniper Elbow Co Inc**............................C....... 718 326-2546
Middle Village *(G-8414)*
K Barthelmes Mfg Co Inc.........................F 585 328-8140
Rochester *(G-14466)*
Kal Manufacturing Corporation..............E 585 265-4310
Webster *(G-16726)*
Karo Sheet Metal Inc.................................E 718 542-8420
Brooklyn *(G-2169)*
Ke Durasol Awnings Inc.............................G....... 845 610-1100
Chester *(G-3609)*
▲ **Kenan International Trading**...............G....... 718 672-4922
Corona *(G-4000)*
Ksm Group Ltd...G....... 716 751-6006
Newfane *(G-12787)*
▲ **Lambro Industries Inc**.............................D....... 631 842-8088
Amityville *(G-304)*
Lane Enterprises Inc...................................E 518 885-4385
Ballston Spa *(G-601)*
Leader Sheet Metal Inc...............................F 347 271-4961
Bronx *(G-1379)*
Liffey Sheet Metal Corp.............................F....... 347 381-1134
Brooklyn *(G-2220)*
Lotus Awnings Enterprises Inc...............G....... 718 965-4824
Brooklyn *(G-2237)*
M&G Duravent Inc..F 518 463-7284
Albany *(G-98)*
Maloya Laser Inc...E 631 543-2327
Commack *(G-3837)*
Manufacturing Resources Inc..................E 631 481-0041
Rochester *(G-14493)*
▲ **Marex Aquisition Corp**...........................C....... 585 458-3940
Rochester *(G-14497)*
Mariah Metal Products Inc........................G....... 516 938-9783
Hicksville *(G-6368)*
Mason Scott Industries LLC......................F 516 349-1800
Roslyn Heights *(G-15029)*
▲ **McAlpin Industries Inc**...........................C....... 585 266-3060
Rochester *(G-14500)*
McHone Industries Inc................................D....... 716 945-3380
Salamanca *(G-15101)*
MD International Industries......................E 631 254-3100
Deer Park *(G-4173)*
Mega Vision Inc..E 718 228-1065
Brooklyn *(G-2295)*
Merz Metal & Machine Corp......................E 716 893-7786
Buffalo *(G-3062)*
Metal Solutions Inc.......................................E 315 732-6271
Utica *(G-16347)*
Metalsmith Inc..G....... 631 467-1500
Holbrook *(G-6463)*
Methods Tooling & Mfg Inc........................E 845 246-7100
Mount Marion *(G-8651)*
Metro Duct Systems Inc...............................F 718 278-4294
Long Island City *(G-7810)*
Middleby Corporation..................................E 631 226-6688
Lindenhurst *(G-7472)*
▼ **Monarch Metal Fabrication Inc**............G....... 631 563-8967
Bohemia *(G-1105)*
Ms Spares LLC..G....... 607 223-3024
Clay *(G-3683)*
N & L Instruments Inc..................................F 631 471-4000
Ronkonkoma *(G-14948)*
Nci Group Inc..D....... 315 339-1245
Rome *(G-14824)*
Nelson Air Device Corporation..................C....... 718 729-3801
Maspeth *(G-8155)*
▼ **North Coast Outfitters Ltd**....................E 631 727-5580
Riverhead *(G-14150)*
Northeast Fabricators LLC.........................D....... 607 865-4031
Walton *(G-16549)*
Northern Awning & Sign Company...........G....... 315 782-8515
Watertown *(G-16667)*
Olympic Manufacturing Inc.........................E 631 231-8900
Hauppauge *(G-6153)*
Omc Inc...C....... 718 731-5001
Bronx *(G-1416)*
P R B Metal Products Inc.............................F 631 467-1800
Ronkonkoma *(G-14961)*
Pal Aluminum Inc..G....... 516 937-1990
Hicksville *(G-6383)*
Pal Aluminum Inc..E 718 262-0091
Jamaica *(G-6937)*
Pathfinder Industries Inc.............................E 315 593-2483
Fulton *(G-5474)*
PDQ Manufacturing Co Inc.........................E 845 889-3123
Rhinebeck *(G-14057)*
Penasack Machine Company Inc...............E 585 589-7044
Albion *(G-168)*
Penner Elbow Company Inc..........................F 718 526-9000
Elmhurst *(G-4665)*
Pirnat Precise Metals Inc.............................G....... 631 293-9169
Farmingdale *(G-5080)*
Plattsburgh Sheet Metal Inc........................G....... 518 561-4930
Plattsburgh *(G-13688)*
Precision Fabrication LLC............................G....... 585 591-3449
Attica *(G-474)*
Precision Metals Corp..................................E 631 586-5032
Bay Shore *(G-727)*
Precision Mtal Fabricators Inc....................F 718 832-9805
Brooklyn *(G-2435)*
Precision Systems Mfg Inc..........................E 315 451-3480
Liverpool *(G-7544)*
Product Integration & Mfg Inc.....................E 585 436-6260
Rochester *(G-14605)*
Prokosch and Sonn Sheet Metal.................E 845 562-4211
Newburgh *(G-12776)*
Protofast Holding Corp.................................G....... 631 753-2549
Copiague *(G-3920)*
Radiation Shielding Systems........................F 888 631-2278
Suffern *(G-15799)*
Rami Sheet Metal Inc.....................................G....... 845 426-2948
Spring Valley *(G-15600)*
Rand Products Manufacturing Co...............G....... 518 374-9871
Schenectady *(G-15288)*
Rayco Manufacturing Co Inc........................F 516 431-2006
Jamaica *(G-6944)*
Read Manufacturing Company Inc.............E 631 567-4487
Holbrook *(G-6467)*
Reynolds Manufacturing Inc........................F 607 562-8936
Big Flats *(G-882)*
▲ **Rigidized Metals Corporation**..................E 716 849-4703
Buffalo *(G-3158)*
▲ **Robert E Derecktor Inc**..............................D....... 914 698-0962
Mamaroneck *(G-8045)*
Rochester Colonial Mfg Corp.......................D....... 585 254-8191
Rochester *(G-14639)*
Rollson Inc..E 631 423-9578
Huntington *(G-6678)*
Royal Metal Products Inc..............................E 518 966-4442
Surprise *(G-15811)*
S & B Machine Works Inc.............................E 516 997-2666
Westbury *(G-17025)*
S & T Machine Inc..F 718 272-2484
Brooklyn *(G-2523)*
Savaco Inc...G....... 716 751-9455
Newfane *(G-12788)*
Service Mfg Group Inc...................................E 716 893-1482
Buffalo *(G-3184)*
Service Mfg Group Inc...................................F 716 893-1482
Buffalo *(G-3183)*
Shanghai Stove Inc...F 718 599-4583
Brooklyn *(G-2550)*
Solidus Industries Inc...................................D....... 607 749-4540
Homer *(G-6522)*
Space Sign...F....... 718 961-1112
College Point *(G-3808)*
▲ **Spence Engineering Company Inc**...C....... 845 778-5566
Walden *(G-16536)*
Standard Industrial Works Inc......................F 631 888-0130
Bay Shore *(G-744)*
Standex Air Dist Pdts Inc...............................E 585 798-0300
Medina *(G-8283)*
Steel Sales Inc..E 607 674-6363
Sherburne *(G-15397)*
Steel Work Inc..G....... 585 232-1555
Rochester *(G-14701)*
Steelcraft Manufacturing Co..........................F 718 277-2404
Brooklyn *(G-2603)*
Sterling Industries Inc.....................................E 631 753-3070
Farmingdale *(G-5117)*
▲ **Studco Building Systems US LLC**....E 585 545-3000
Webster *(G-16736)*
Superior Elec Enclosure Inc...........................G....... 718 797-9090
Brooklyn *(G-2627)*
Superior Exteriors of Buffalo..........................F 716 873-1000
Buffalo *(G-3203)*
T Lemme Mechanical Inc................................E 518 436-4136
Menands *(G-8379)*
Tatra Mfg Corporation.....................................F....... 631 691-1184
Copiague *(G-3932)*
▲ **TCS Industries Inc**..D....... 585 426-1160
Rochester *(G-14718)*
Technimetal Precision Inds..............................E 631 231-8900
Hauppauge *(G-6210)*
Themis Chimney Inc..F 718 937-4716
Brooklyn *(G-2657)*

Employee Codes: A=Over 500 employees, B=251-500
C=101-250, D=51-100, E=20-50, F=10-19, G=5-9

2017 Harris
New York Manufacturers Directory

813

34 FABRICATED METAL PRODUCTS, EXCEPT MACHINERY AND TRANSPORTATION EQUIPMENT SIC SECTION

Tri-Metal Industries Inc....E....716 691-3323
Amherst *(G-268)*
Tri-State Metals LLC....F....914 347-8157
Elmsford *(G-4789)*
▲ Tri-Technologies Inc....E....914 699-2001
Mount Vernon *(G-8741)*
▲ Trident Precision Mfg Inc....D....585 265-2010
Webster *(G-16738)*
Tripar Manufacturing Co Inc....G....631 563-0855
Bohemia *(G-1148)*
Truform Manufacturing Corp....D....585 458-1090
Rochester *(G-14734)*
Trylon Wire & Metal Works Inc....E....718 542-4472
Bronx *(G-1481)*
Ulster Precision Inc....E....845 338-0995
Kingston *(G-7218)*
▼ Ultimate Prcision Met Pdts Inc....D....631 249-9441
Farmingdale *(G-5136)*
Unadilla Silo Company Inc....D....607 369-9341
Sidney *(G-15444)*
United Sheet Metal Corp....E....718 482-1197
Long Island City *(G-7909)*
Universal Precision Corp....E....585 321-9760
Rochester *(G-14744)*
Universal Shielding Corp....E....631 667-7900
Deer Park *(G-4219)*
▲ Vance Metal Fabricators Inc....D....315 789-5626
Geneva *(G-5588)*
Vin Mar Precision Metal Inc....F....631 563-6608
Copiague *(G-3937)*
Vitarose Corp of America....G....718 951-9700
Brooklyn *(G-2733)*
▲ Voss Manufacturing Inc....D....716 731-5062
Sanborn *(G-15130)*
▲ Wainland Inc....E....718 626-2233
Astoria *(G-461)*
Wayne Integrated Tech Corp....E....631 242-0213
Edgewood *(G-4620)*
Wenig Corporation....E....718 542-3600
Bronx *(G-1493)*
Wg Sheet Metal Corp....G....718 235-3093
Brooklyn *(G-2746)*
William Kanes Mfg Corp....G....718 346-1515
Brooklyn *(G-2754)*
◆ Worksman Trading Corp....E....718 322-2000
Ozone Park *(G-13387)*
▲ Zahk Sales Inc....G....631 348-9300
Islandia *(G-6805)*

3446 Architectural & Ornamental Metal Work

786 Iron Works Corp....G....718 418-4808
Brooklyn *(G-1522)*
▲ A & T Iron Works Inc....E....914 632-8992
New Rochelle *(G-8883)*
A1 Ornamental Iron Works Inc....G....718 265-3055
Brooklyn *(G-1543)*
Aca Quality Building Pdts LLC....E....718 991-2423
Bronx *(G-1259)*
Accurate Welding Service Inc....G....516 333-1730
Westbury *(G-16960)*
▲ Acme Architectural Pdts Inc....D....718 384-7800
Brooklyn *(G-1555)*
Aero-Data Metal Crafters Inc....C....631 471-7733
Ronkonkoma *(G-14856)*
Airflex Industrial Inc....E....631 752-1234
Farmingdale *(G-4933)*
Airflex Industrial Inc....D....631 752-1234
Farmingdale *(G-4934)*
Aldo Frustacci Iron Works Inc....F....718 768-0707
Brooklyn *(G-1578)*
Aldos Iron Works Inc....G....718 834-0408
Brooklyn *(G-1579)*
All American Metal Corporation....E....516 623-0222
Freeport *(G-5384)*
All American Stairs & Railing....F....718 441-8400
Richmond Hill *(G-14065)*
All Metal Specialties Inc....E....716 664-6009
Jamestown *(G-6969)*
▲ Allied Bronze Corp (del Corp)....E....646 421-6400
New York *(G-9089)*
Alpha Iron Works LLC....F....585 424-7260
Rochester *(G-14193)*
▲ Arcadia Mfg Group Inc....E....518 434-6213
Green Island *(G-5853)*
Arcadia Mfg Group Inc....G....518 434-6213
Menands *(G-8367)*
Armento Incorporated....G....716 875-2423
Kenmore *(G-7145)*
Artistic Ironworks Inc....G....631 665-4285
Bay Shore *(G-672)*

Atlas Fence & Railing Co Inc....E....718 767-2200
Whitestone *(G-17201)*
Babylon Iron Works Inc....F....631 643-3311
West Babylon *(G-16773)*
Beeche Systems Corp....D....518 381-6000
Scotia *(G-15324)*
Bobrick Washroom Equipment Inc....D....518 877-7444
Clifton Park *(G-3697)*
Bracci Ironworks Inc....F....718 629-2374
Brooklyn *(G-1711)*
C & F Iron Works Inc....F....914 592-2450
Elmsford *(G-4738)*
C & F Steel Corp....F....914 592-3928
Elmsford *(G-4739)*
Cabezon Design Group Inc....G....718 488-9868
Brooklyn *(G-1746)*
Caliper Architecture PC....G....718 302-2427
Brooklyn *(G-1748)*
Caliperstudio Co....G....718 302-3504
Brooklyn *(G-1749)*
▲ City Store Gates Mfg Corp....E....718 939-9700
College Point *(G-3781)*
Creative Metal Fabricators....G....631 567-2266
Bohemia *(G-1043)*
Custom Design Metals Inc....G....631 563-2444
Bohemia *(G-1045)*
D V S Iron & Aluminum Works....G....718 768-7961
Brooklyn *(G-1832)*
Duke of Iron Inc....G....631 543-3600
Smithtown *(G-15486)*
E & J Iron Works Inc....E....718 665-6040
Bronx *(G-1320)*
E F Iron Works & Construction....G....631 242-4766
Bay Shore *(G-698)*
▲ E S P Metal Crafts Inc....G....718 381-2443
Brooklyn *(G-1893)*
Ej Group Inc....G....315 699-2601
Cicero *(G-3645)*
Elevator Accessories Mfg....F....914 739-7004
Peekskill *(G-13477)*
Enterprise Metalworks Inc....G....718 328-9331
Bronx *(G-1327)*
Fence Plaza Corp....G....718 469-2200
Brooklyn *(G-1966)*
▲ Fixture Hardware Mfg Corp....E....718 499-9422
Brooklyn *(G-1980)*
Fjs Industries Inc....F....917 428-3797
Brooklyn *(G-1981)*
▼ Flagpoles Incorporated....D....631 751-5500
East Setauket *(G-4483)*
Flushing Iron Weld Inc....E....718 359-2208
Flushing *(G-5242)*
Forest Iron Works Inc....G....516 671-4229
Locust Valley *(G-7630)*
G C D M Ironworks Inc....E....914 347-2058
Elmsford *(G-4754)*
▲ Giumenta Corp....E....718 832-1200
Brooklyn *(G-2025)*
◆ Global Steel Products Corp....C....631 586-3455
Deer Park *(G-4147)*
Grillmaster Inc....E....718 272-9191
Howard Beach *(G-6597)*
Hi-Tech Metals Inc....E....718 894-1212
Maspeth *(G-8144)*
Imperial Damper & Louver Co....E....718 731-3800
Bronx *(G-1360)*
Inter-Fence Co Inc....E....718 939-9700
College Point *(G-3789)*
▼ International Creative Met Inc....F....718 424-8179
Woodside *(G-17333)*
Iron Art Inc....G....914 592-7977
Elmsford *(G-4757)*
Iron Worker....F....516 338-2756
Smithtown *(G-15489)*
Irony Limited Inc....G....631 329-4065
East Hampton *(G-4411)*
▲ ITR Industries Inc....E....914 964-7063
Yonkers *(G-17456)*
Jamaica Iron Works Inc....F....718 657-4849
Jamaica *(G-6923)*
Jamestown Fab Stl & Sup Inc....G....716 665-2227
Jamestown *(G-7007)*
▲ Jaxson Rollforming Inc....E....631 842-7775
Amityville *(G-298)*
Jerry Cardullo Iron Works Inc....F....631 242-8881
Bay Shore *(G-709)*
▲ Jonathan Metal & Glass Ltd....D....718 846-8000
Jamaica *(G-6924)*
Kammetal Inc....F....718 625-2628
Brooklyn *(G-2167)*

Kammetal Inc....F....718 722-9991
Brooklyn *(G-2168)*
Kenal Services Corp....G....315 788-9226
Watertown *(G-16657)*
Kendi Iron Works Inc....G....718 821-2722
Brooklyn *(G-2170)*
▼ Keuka Studios Inc....G....585 624-5960
Rush *(G-15051)*
Kleinfelder John....G....716 753-3163
Mayville *(G-8216)*
Kms Contracting Inc....F....718 495-6500
Brooklyn *(G-2176)*
Koenig Iron Works Inc....E....718 433-0900
Long Island City *(G-7782)*
Kryten Iron Works Inc....G....914 345-0990
Hawthorne *(G-6249)*
Lencore Acoustics Corp....F....516 682-9292
Woodbury *(G-17291)*
Lopopolo Iron Works Inc....G....718 339-0572
Brooklyn *(G-2236)*
M B C Metal Inc....F....718 384-6713
Brooklyn *(G-2247)*
Martin Chafkin....G....718 383-1155
Brooklyn *(G-2276)*
Martin Orna Ir Works II Inc....G....516 354-3923
Elmont *(G-4723)*
▲ Material Process Systems Inc....F....718 302-3081
Brooklyn *(G-2283)*
▲ Maximum Security Products Corp....E....518 233-1800
Waterford *(G-16613)*
McAllisters Precision Wldg Inc....F....518 221-3455
Menands *(G-8374)*
▲ Melto Metal Products Co Inc....E....516 546-8866
Freeport *(G-5412)*
Mestel Brothers Stairs & Rails....C....516 496-4127
Syosset *(G-15828)*
Metalworks Inc....E....718 319-0011
Bronx *(G-1394)*
▼ Metro Door Inc....D....631 277-6490
Great River *(G-5852)*
Milgo Industrial Inc....D....718 388-6476
Brooklyn *(G-2313)*
Milgo Industrial Inc....G....718 387-0406
Brooklyn *(G-2314)*
▲ Mison Concepts Inc....G....516 933-8000
Hicksville *(G-6373)*
▲ Modern Art Foundry Inc....E....718 728-2030
Astoria *(G-449)*
Moon Gates Company....G....718 426-0023
East Elmhurst *(G-4395)*
Morgik Metal Designs....F....212 463-0304
New York *(G-11305)*
Moro Corporation....E....607 724-4241
Binghamton *(G-937)*
New Dimensions Office Group....D....718 387-0995
Brooklyn *(G-2361)*
New England Tool Co Ltd....G....845 651-7550
Florida *(G-5214)*
▲ Old Dutchmans Wrough Iron Inc....G....716 688-2034
Getzville *(G-5602)*
Oldcastle Precast Inc....F....518 767-2116
South Bethlehem *(G-15514)*
Ornametal Inc....G....845 562-5151
Newburgh *(G-12773)*
Ourem Iron Works Inc....F....914 476-4856
Yonkers *(G-17473)*
▲ Paley Studios Ltd....F....585 232-5260
Rochester *(G-14567)*
▲ Paragon Aquatics....E....845 452-5500
Lagrangeville *(G-7257)*
Pawling Corporation....D....845 373-9300
Wassaic *(G-16600)*
Peconic Ironworks Ltd....F....631 204-0323
Southampton *(G-15549)*
Pk30 System LLC....F....212 473-8050
Stone Ridge *(G-15764)*
▲ Pole-Tech Co Inc....F....631 689-5525
East Setauket *(G-4489)*
Railings By New Star Brass....E....516 358-1153
Brooklyn *(G-2474)*
Raulli and Sons Inc....F....315 474-1370
Syracuse *(G-16019)*
Raulli and Sons Inc....D....315 479-6693
Syracuse *(G-16018)*
Raulli Iron Works Inc....F....315 337-8070
Rome *(G-14832)*
Riverside Iron LLC....F....315 535-4864
Gouverneur *(G-5747)*
Rollson Inc....E....631 423-9578
Huntington *(G-6678)*

SIC SECTION
34 FABRICATED METAL PRODUCTS, EXCEPT MACHINERY AND TRANSPORTATION EQUIPMENT

Royal Metal Products Inc ....E 518 966-4442
Surprise (G-15811)
▲ S A Baxter LLC ....G...... 845 469-7995
Chester (G-3614)
S R S Inc ....E 732 548-6630
Maspeth (G-8170)
▲ Safespan Platform Systems Inc ....D 716 694-3332
Tonawanda (G-16199)
Safeworks LLC ....F 800 696-5577
Woodside (G-17352)
Sh Ironworks Inc ....G...... 917 907-0507
Flushing (G-5292)
▲ Shanker Industries Inc ....G...... 631 940-9889
Deer Park (G-4209)
Stain Rail Systems Inc ....F 732 548-6630
Maspeth (G-8171)
Steel Sales Inc ....E 607 674-6363
Sherburne (G-15397)
Steel Work Inc ....G...... 585 232-1555
Rochester (G-14701)
Steps Plus Inc ....D 315 432-0885
Syracuse (G-16045)
Studio 40 Inc ....E 212 420-8631
Brooklyn (G-2613)
Studio Dellarte ....G...... 718 599-3715
Brooklyn (G-2614)
Superior Metal & Woodwork Inc ....E 631 465-9004
Farmingdale (G-5119)
Tee Pee Fence and Railing ....F 718 658-8323
Jamaica (G-6957)
◆ Tensator Inc ....D 631 666-0300
Bay Shore (G-751)
Tonys Ornamental Ir Works Inc ....E 315 337-3730
Rome (G-14838)
Tri State Shearing Bending Inc ....F 718 485-2200
Brooklyn (G-2677)
Triple H Construction Inc ....E 516 280-8252
East Meadow (G-4428)
Tropical Driftwood Originals ....G...... 516 623-0980
Roosevelt (G-15010)
Tymetal Corp ....E 518 692-9930
Greenwich (G-5895)
United Iron Inc ....E 914 667-5700
Mount Vernon (G-8745)
Universal Steel Fabricators ....F 718 342-0782
Brooklyn (G-2709)
Village Wrought Iron Inc ....G...... 315 683-5589
Fabius (G-4841)
Vr Containment LLC ....G...... 917 972-3441
Fresh Meadows (G-5447)
Waverly Iron Corp ....E 631 732-2800
Medford (G-8262)
West End Iron Works Inc ....G...... 518 456-1105
Albany (G-149)
Z-Studios Dsign Fbrication LLC ....G...... 347 512-4210
Brooklyn (G-2779)

3448 Prefabricated Metal Buildings & Cmpnts

All American Building ....G...... 607 797-7123
Binghamton (G-885)
▲ Austin Mohawk and Company LLC .E 315 793-3000
Utica (G-16308)
◆ Birdair Inc ....D 716 633-9500
Amherst (G-229)
Deraffele Mfg Co Inc ....E 914 636-6850
New Rochelle (G-8894)
Energy Panel Structures Inc ....G...... 315 923-7777
Clyde (G-3726)
Energy Panel Structures Inc ....G...... 585 343-1777
Batavia (G-630)
Energy Panel Structures Inc ....G...... 518 355-6708
Schenectady (G-15251)
▲ Fillmore Greenhouses Inc ....E 585 567-2678
Portageville (G-13872)
▲ Framing Technology Inc ....E 585 464-8470
Rochester (G-14380)
Guardian Booth LLC ....F 844 992-6684
Spring Valley (G-15588)
Landmark Group Inc ....E 845 358-0350
Valley Cottage (G-16380)
Latium USA Trading LLC ....D 631 563-4000
Holbrook (G-6455)
Man Products Inc ....E 631 789-6500
Farmingdale (G-5040)
Metadure Defense & SEC LLC ....F 631 249-2141
Farmingdale (G-5049)
▼ Metallic Ladder Mfg Corp ....F 716 358-6201
Randolph (G-14016)

Metals Building Products ....E 844 638-2527
Holbrook (G-6462)
Mobile Mini Inc ....F 315 732-4555
Utica (G-16349)
Mobile Mini Inc ....E 631 543-4900
Commack (G-3838)
Morton Buildings Inc ....E 585 786-8191
Warsaw (G-16583)
Nci Group Inc ....D 315 339-1245
Rome (G-14824)
Overhead Door Corporation ....D 518 828-7652
Hudson (G-6629)
Pei Liquidation Company ....F 518 489-5101
Albany (G-116)
Pei Liquidation Company ....F 315 431-4697
East Syracuse (G-4554)
Precision Fabrication LLC ....E 585 591-3449
Attica (G-474)
Qub9 Inc ....G...... 585 484-1808
Rochester (G-14616)
Sunbilt Solar Pdts By Sussman ....D 718 297-0228
Jamaica (G-6954)
T Shore Products Ltd ....G...... 315 252-9174
Auburn (G-522)
Universal Shielding Corp ....E 631 667-7900
Deer Park (G-4219)
Veerhouse Voda Haiti LLC ....G...... 917 353-5944
New York (G-12513)
Walpole Woodworkers Inc ....G...... 631 726-2859
Water Mill (G-16606)

3449 Misc Structural Metal Work

A&B McKeon Glass Inc ....G...... 718 525-2152
Staten Island (G-15631)
▲ Abasco Inc ....E 716 649-4790
Hamburg (G-5918)
Accurate Metal Weather Strip ....G...... 914 668-6042
Mount Vernon (G-8661)
Agl Industries Inc ....E 718 326-7597
Maspeth (G-8111)
AM Architectural Metal & Glass ....E 845 942-8848
Garnerville (G-5553)
Arista Steel Designs Corp ....E 718 965-7077
Brooklyn (G-1627)
▲ Baco Enterprises Inc ....D 718 589-6225
Bronx (G-1279)
Barker Steel LLC ....E 518 465-6221
Albany (G-52)
City Evolutionary ....G...... 718 861-7585
Bronx (G-1299)
Coral Management Corp ....G...... 718 893-9286
Bronx (G-1304)
Designs By Novello Inc ....G...... 914 934-7711
Port Chester (G-13742)
▲ Dimension Fabricators Inc ....E 518 374-1936
Schenectady (G-15248)
Empire Metal Finishing Inc ....E 718 545-6700
Astoria (G-440)
Fala Technologies Inc ....E 845 336-4000
Kingston (G-7189)
Ferro Fabricators Inc ....E 718 851-4027
Brooklyn (G-1967)
GCM Metal Industries Inc ....F 718 386-4059
Brooklyn (G-2015)
Genesee Metal Products Inc ....E 585 968-6000
Wellsville (G-16752)
Halmark Architectural Finshg ....E 718 272-1831
Brooklyn (G-2063)
Harbor Wldg & Fabrication Corp .....F 631 667-1880
Bay Shore (G-704)
▲ Inscape (new York) Inc ....D 716 665-6210
Falconer (G-4902)
Integrity Tool Incorporated ....F 315 524-4409
Ontario (G-13204)
Janed Enterprises ....F 631 694-4494
Farmingdale (G-5017)
Klein Reinforcing Services Inc ....F 585 352-9433
Spencerport (G-15571)
Kraman Iron Works Inc ....F 212 460-8400
New York (G-10885)
▲ Lakeside Capital Corporation ....E 716 664-2555
Jamestown (G-7015)
Lane Enterprises Inc ....E 518 885-4385
Ballston Spa (G-601)
▲ Longstem Organizers Inc ....G...... 914 777-2174
Jefferson Valley (G-7057)
▲ Metal Products Intl LLC ....G...... 716 215-1930
Niagara Falls (G-12846)
New York Steel Services Co ....G...... 718 291-7770
Jamaica (G-6935)

Orange County Ironworks LLC ....E 845 769-3000
Montgomery (G-8600)
▲ Orbital Holdings Inc ....E 951 360-7100
Buffalo (G-3104)
▲ Paragon Aquatics ....E 845 452-5500
Lagrangeville (G-7257)
Pierce Steel Fabricators ....F 716 372-7652
Olean (G-13152)
Ppi Corp ....E 585 880-7277
Geneseo (G-5567)
▲ Risa Management Corp ....E 718 361-2606
Maspeth (G-8167)
Riverside Iron LLC ....E 315 535-4864
Gouverneur (G-5747)
▲ Rolite Mfg Inc ....E 716 683-0259
Lancaster (G-7340)
▲ Rollform of Jamestown Inc ....F 716 665-5310
Jamestown (G-7025)
Semans Enterprises Inc ....F 585 444-0097
West Henrietta (G-16894)
Signature Metal MBL Maint LLC ......D 718 292-8280
Bronx (G-1455)
Sims Steel Corporation ....E 631 587-8670
Lindenhurst (G-7482)
Sinn-Tech Industries Inc ....G...... 631 643-1171
West Babylon (G-16828)
▲ Siw Inc ....F 631 888-0130
Bay Shore (G-743)
Sky Dive ....D 845 858-6400
Port Jervis (G-13792)
Steel Sales Inc ....E 607 674-6363
Sherburne (G-15397)
Tebbens Steel LLC ....F 631 208-8330
Calverton (G-3301)
Tonys Ornamental Ir Works Inc ....E 315 337-3730
Rome (G-14838)
Torino Industrial Inc ....F 631 509-1640
Bellport (G-842)
▲ Tough Trac Inc ....G...... 631 504-6700
Medford (G-8261)
United Iron Inc ....E 914 667-5700
Mount Vernon (G-8745)
Wide Flange Inc ....F 718 492-8705
Brooklyn (G-2749)

3451 Screw Machine Prdts

Acme Precision Screw Pdts Inc ....F 585 328-2028
Rochester (G-14170)
Albert Gates Inc ....D 585 594-9401
North Chili (G-12924)
All Type Screw Machine Pdts ....G...... 516 334-5100
Westbury (G-16965)
▲ Anderson Precision Inc ....D 716 484-1148
Jamestown (G-6971)
Andros Manufacturing Corp ....F 585 663-5700
Rochester (G-14205)
Brinkman Intl Group Inc ....E 585 429-5000
Rochester (G-14245)
Broda Machine Co Inc ....F 716 297-3221
Niagara Falls (G-12799)
C R C Manufacturing Inc ....E 585 254-8820
Rochester (G-14255)
C&C Automatics Inc ....E 315 331-1436
Newark (G-12730)
Century Metal Parts Corp ....E 631 667-0800
Bay Shore (G-682)
Craftech Industries Inc ....D 518 828-5001
Hudson (G-6611)
Curtis Screw Co Inc ....E 716 898-7800
Buffalo (G-2896)
Elmira Grinding Works Inc ....F 607 734-1579
Wellsburg (G-16747)
Emory Machine & Tool Co Inc ....E 585 436-9610
Farmington (G-5150)
Five Star Tool Co Inc ....E 585 328-9580
Rochester (G-14372)
Globe Electronic Hardware Inc ....E 718 457-0303
Woodside (G-17332)
Gsp Components Inc ....D 585 436-3377
Rochester (G-14414)
Hanco Metal Products Inc ....F 212 787-5992
Brooklyn (G-2066)
▲ I W Industries Inc ....C 631 293-9494
Melville (G-8330)
J & J Swiss Precision Inc ....E 631 243-5584
Deer Park (G-4154)
Jordan Products Inc ....E 585 385-7777
Penfield (G-13500)
Kaddis Manufacturing Corp ....G...... 585 624-3070
Honeoye Falls (G-6533)

Employee Codes: A=Over 500 employees, B=251-500
C=101-250, D=51-100, E=20-50, F=10-19, G=5-9

34 FABRICATED METAL PRODUCTS, EXCEPT MACHINERY AND TRANSPORTATION EQUIPMENT SIC SECTION

Kathleen B Mead ....G....... 585 247-0146
Rochester *(G-14468)*
Ktd Screw Machine Inc ....G....... 631 243-6861
Deer Park *(G-4160)*
Lexington Machining LLC ....D....... 585 235-0880
Rochester *(G-14478)*
Lexington Machining LLC ....C....... 585 235-0880
Rochester *(G-14479)*
Liberty Brass Turning Co Inc ....E....... 718 784-2911
Westbury *(G-17005)*
M Manastrip-M Corporation ....G....... 518 664-2089
Clifton Park *(G-3699)*
Manacraft Precision Inc ....F....... 914 654-0967
Pelham *(G-13493)*
Manth-Brownell Inc ....C....... 315 687-7263
Kirkville *(G-7227)*
Marmach Machine Inc ....G....... 585 768-8800
Le Roy *(G-7414)*
Micro Threaded Products Inc ....G....... 585 288-0080
Rochester *(G-14508)*
Miggins Screw Products Inc ....G....... 845 279-2307
Brewster *(G-1224)*
Muller Tool Inc ....E....... 716 895-3658
Buffalo *(G-3077)*
Multimatic Products Inc ....D....... 800 767-7633
Ronkonkoma *(G-14947)*
▲ Murphy Manufacturing Co Inc ....G....... 585 223-0100
Fairport *(G-4865)*
Norwood Screw Machine Parts ....F....... 516 481-6644
Mineola *(G-8528)*
Precision Machine Tech LLC ....D....... 585 467-1840
Rochester *(G-14595)*
R P M Machine Co ....G....... 585 671-3744
Webster *(G-16732)*
Ranney Precision ....F....... 716 731-6418
Niagara Falls *(G-12866)*
Selflock Screw Products Co Inc ....E....... 315 541-4464
Syracuse *(G-16037)*
▲ Supply Technologies (ny) ....F....... 212 966-3310
Albany *(G-139)*
Supreme Screw Products Inc ....F....... 718 293-6600
Plainview *(G-13637)*
T & L Automatics Inc ....C....... 585 647-3717
Rochester *(G-14715)*
TAC Screw Products Inc ....F....... 585 663-5840
Rochester *(G-14717)*
Taylor Metalworks Inc ....C....... 716 662-3113
Orchard Park *(G-13298)*
Teale Machine Company Inc ....D....... 585 244-6700
Rochester *(G-14719)*
▲ Thuro Metal Products Inc ....E....... 631 435-0444
Brentwood *(G-1196)*
Thuro Metal Products Inc ....F....... 631 435-0444
Brentwood *(G-1197)*
Townline Machine Co Inc ....F....... 315 462-3413
Clifton Springs *(G-3716)*
▲ Tri-Technologies Inc ....E....... 914 699-2001
Mount Vernon *(G-8741)*
Trihex Manufacturing Inc ....G....... 315 589-9331
Williamson *(G-17227)*
Triple Point Manufacturing ....G....... 631 218-4988
Bohemia *(G-1149)*
Umbro Machine & Tool Co Inc ....F....... 845 876-4669
Rhinebeck *(G-14059)*
Vanguard Metals Inc ....F....... 631 234-6500
Central Islip *(G-3514)*
Verns Machine Co Inc ....E....... 315 926-4223
Marion *(G-8103)*

3452 Bolts, Nuts, Screws, Rivets & Washers

▲ American Pride Fasteners LLC ....E....... 631 940-8292
Bay Shore *(G-670)*
Anthony Manno & Co Inc ....G....... 631 445-1834
Deer Park *(G-4099)*
▲ Baco Enterprises Inc ....D....... 718 589-6225
Bronx *(G-1279)*
Buckley Qc Fasteners Inc ....E....... 716 662-1490
Orchard Park *(G-13255)*
Craftech Industries Inc ....D....... 518 828-5001
Hudson *(G-6611)*
Cwr Manufacturing Corporation ....D....... 315 437-1032
East Syracuse *(G-4521)*
Dependable Acme Threaded Pdts ....G....... 516 338-4700
Westbury *(G-16976)*
Fastener Dimensions Inc ....E....... 718 847-6321
Ozone Park *(G-13378)*
Huck International Inc ....C....... 845 331-7300
Kingston *(G-7191)*
J T D Stamping Co Inc ....E....... 631 643-4144
West Babylon *(G-16799)*
Jem Threading Specialties Inc ....G....... 718 665-3341
Bronx *(G-1365)*
John F Rafter Inc ....G....... 716 992-3425
Eden *(G-4587)*
John Hassall LLC ....D....... 516 334-6200
Westbury *(G-16998)*
▼ John Hassall LLC ....D....... 323 869-0150
Westbury *(G-16999)*
Kinemotive Corporation ....E....... 631 249-6440
Farmingdale *(G-5028)*
LD McCauley LLC ....C....... 716 662-6744
Orchard Park *(G-13280)*
▲ Marksmen Manufacturing Corp ....E....... 800 305-6942
Deer Park *(G-4170)*
Pin Pharma Inc ....G....... 212 543-2583
New York *(G-11661)*
Pin Pretty Inc ....G....... 718 887-5290
Brooklyn *(G-2421)*
Pins N Needles ....G....... 212 535-6222
New York *(G-11666)*
Pni Capital Partners ....G....... 516 466-7120
Westbury *(G-17019)*
Radax Industries Inc ....E....... 585 265-2055
Webster *(G-16733)*
Rochester Stampings Inc ....F....... 585 467-5241
Rochester *(G-14649)*
Schaefer Machine Co Inc ....E....... 516 248-6880
Mineola *(G-8537)*
Sesco Industries Inc ....F....... 718 939-5137
College Point *(G-3807)*
Simon Defense Inc ....G....... 516 217-6000
Middle Island *(G-8408)*
Socket Products Mfg Corp ....G....... 631 232-9870
Islandia *(G-6803)*
Southco Inc ....B....... 585 624-2545
Honeoye Falls *(G-6537)*
Superior Washer & Gasket Corp ....D....... 631 273-8282
Hauppauge *(G-6203)*
▲ Supply Technologies (ny) ....F....... 212 966-3310
Albany *(G-139)*
▲ Tamperproof Screw Company Inc ....F....... 516 931-1616
Hicksville *(G-6397)*
Teka Precision Inc ....G....... 845 753-1900
Nyack *(G-13055)*
Treo Industries Inc ....G....... 631 737-4022
Bohemia *(G-1145)*
Trihex Manufacturing Inc ....G....... 315 589-9331
Williamson *(G-17227)*
▲ Zierick Manufacturing Corp ....D....... 800 882-8020
Mount Kisco *(G-8648)*

3462 Iron & Steel Forgings

Alry Tool and Die Co Inc ....E....... 716 693-2419
Tonawanda *(G-16137)*
▲ Ball Chain Mfg Co Inc ....D....... 914 664-7500
Mount Vernon *(G-8664)*
▲ Biltron Automotive Products ....E....... 631 928-8613
Port Jeff STA *(G-13763)*
Borgwarner Ithaca LLC ....B....... 607 257-6700
Ithaca *(G-6825)*
▲ Borgwarner Morse TEC Inc ....B....... 607 257-6700
Ithaca *(G-6826)*
Borgwarner Morse TEC Inc ....D....... 607 257-6700
Ithaca *(G-6828)*
Burke Frging Heat Treating Inc ....E....... 585 235-6060
Rochester *(G-14251)*
Columbus McKinnon Corporation ....D....... 716 689-5400
Getzville *(G-5596)*
▲ Crown Industrial ....G....... 607 745-8709
Cortland *(G-4024)*
Delaware Valley Forge Inc ....E....... 716 447-9140
Buffalo *(G-2905)*
▲ Designatronics Incorporated ....G....... 516 328-3300
New Hyde Park *(G-8825)*
◆ Dragon Trading Inc ....G....... 212 717-1496
New York *(G-9923)*
Eaton Electric Holdings LLC ....C....... 607 756-2821
Cortland *(G-4025)*
▲ Firth Rixson Inc ....D....... 585 328-1383
Rochester *(G-14371)*
Gear Motions Incorporated ....E....... 716 885-1080
Buffalo *(G-2967)*
Gear Motions Incorporated ....E....... 315 488-0100
Syracuse *(G-15949)*
General Motors LLC ....A....... 716 879-5000
Buffalo *(G-2971)*
Great Lakes Gear Co Inc ....G....... 716 694-0715
Tonawanda *(G-16166)*
Handy & Harman Group Ltd ....F....... 914 461-1300
White Plains *(G-17119)*
◆ Hohmann & Barnard Inc ....E....... 631 234-0600
Hauppauge *(G-6095)*
Hohmann & Barnard Inc ....E....... 518 357-9757
Schenectady *(G-15268)*
Ieh FM Holdings LLC ....E....... 212 702-4300
New York *(G-10559)*
▲ Jrlon Inc ....D....... 315 597-4067
Palmyra *(G-13409)*
Kurz and Zobel Inc ....G....... 585 254-9060
Rochester *(G-14472)*
Mattessich Iron LLC ....G....... 315 409-8496
Baldwinsville *(G-571)*
Metrofab Pipe Incorporated ....F....... 516 349-7373
Plainview *(G-13619)*
Paul & Franza LLC ....F....... 718 342-8106
Brooklyn *(G-2410)*
◆ Peck & Hale LLC ....E....... 631 589-2510
West Sayville *(G-16937)*
Perfect Gear & Instrument ....F....... 516 328-3330
New Hyde Park *(G-8856)*
Perfect Gear & Instrument ....E....... 516 873-6122
Garden City Park *(G-5541)*
Pro-Gear Co Inc ....G....... 716 684-3811
Buffalo *(G-3138)*
Riley Gear Corporation ....E....... 716 694-0900
North Tonawanda *(G-12989)*
S R & R Industries Inc ....G....... 845 692-8329
Middletown *(G-8461)*
▲ Schilling Forge Inc ....E....... 315 454-4421
Syracuse *(G-16033)*
▲ Secs Inc ....E....... 914 667-5600
Mount Vernon *(G-8731)*
Secs Inc ....E....... 914 667-5600
Mount Vernon *(G-8732)*
Special Metals Corporation ....D....... 716 366-5663
Dunkirk *(G-4351)*
Stoffel Polygon Systems Inc ....F....... 914 961-2000
Tuckahoe *(G-16272)*
Superior Motion Controls Inc ....E....... 516 420-2921
Farmingdale *(G-5120)*
Superite Gear Instr of Hppauge ....G....... 631 234-0100
Hauppauge *(G-6204)*
Trojan Steel ....G....... 518 686-7426
Hoosick Falls *(G-6546)*
Viking Iron Works Inc ....F....... 845 471-5010
Poughkeepsie *(G-13940)*
▲ Vulcan Steam Forging Co ....E....... 716 875-3680
Buffalo *(G-3246)*
W J Albro Machine Works Inc ....G....... 631 345-0657
Yaphank *(G-17408)*
York Industries Inc ....E....... 516 746-3736
Garden City Park *(G-5546)*

3463 Nonferrous Forgings

▲ Hammond & Irving Inc ....D....... 315 253-6265
Auburn *(G-500)*
▲ N F & M International Inc ....D....... 516 997-4212
Jericho *(G-7077)*
Penn State Metal Fabri ....G....... 718 786-8814
Brooklyn *(G-2415)*
Special Metals Corporation ....D....... 716 366-5663
Dunkirk *(G-4351)*

3465 Automotive Stampings

Albert Kemperle Inc ....E....... 718 629-1084
Brooklyn *(G-1575)*
American Blvd Auto Sups Inc ....G....... 718 328-1984
Bronx *(G-1272)*
Automotive LLC ....F....... 248 728-8642
Batavia *(G-623)*
Ford Motor Company ....B....... 716 821-4000
Buffalo *(G-2952)*
Kustom Korner ....F....... 716 646-0173
Hamburg *(G-5933)*
M & W Aluminum Products Inc ....F....... 315 414-0005
Syracuse *(G-15983)*
P R B Metal Products Inc ....F....... 631 467-1800
Ronkonkoma *(G-14961)*
▲ Racing Industries Inc ....E....... 631 905-0100
Calverton *(G-3296)*
Utica Metal Products Inc ....D....... 315 732-6163
Utica *(G-16364)*

3466 Crowns & Closures

Reynolds Packaging McHy Inc ....D....... 716 358-6451
Falconer *(G-4910)*
▲ Van Blarcom Closures Inc ....C....... 718 855-3810
Brooklyn *(G-2718)*

S I C

3469 Metal Stampings, NEC

4m Precision Industries Inc ... D ... 315 252-8415
Auburn *(G-476)*
▲ A-1 Stamping & Spinning Corp ... F ... 718 388-2626
Rockaway Park *(G-14784)*
Able National Corp ... E ... 718 386-8801
Brooklyn *(G-1549)*
Acme Archictectural Products ... B ... 718 360-0700
Brooklyn *(G-1554)*
Acme Kitchenettes Corp ... E ... 518 828-4191
Hudson *(G-6604)*
▲ Acro Industries Inc ... C ... 585 254-3661
Rochester *(G-14171)*
Action Machined Products Inc ... F ... 631 842-2333
Copiague *(G-3890)*
Advanced Structures Corp ... F ... 631 667-5000
Deer Park *(G-4088)*
Afco Systems Inc ... C ... 631 424-3935
Farmingdale *(G-4931)*
▲ Ajl Manufacturing Inc ... C ... 585 254-1128
Rochester *(G-14184)*
▲ Albest Metal Stamping Corp ... D ... 718 388-6000
Brooklyn *(G-1576)*
All Out Die Cutting Inc ... E ... 718 346-6666
Brooklyn *(G-1587)*
▲ Allen Machine Products Inc ... E ... 631 630-8800
Hauppauge *(G-6016)*
▲ Allied Metal Spinning Corp ... D ... 718 893-3300
Bronx *(G-1268)*
Alton Manufacturing Inc ... D ... 585 458-2600
Rochester *(G-14194)*
American Metal Spinning Pdts ... G ... 631 454-6276
West Babylon *(G-16771)*
American Mtal Stmping Spinning ... F ... 718 384-1500
Brooklyn *(G-1604)*
Arnell Inc ... G ... 516 486-7098
Hempstead *(G-6265)*
▼ Arro Tool & Die Inc ... F ... 716 763-6203
Lakewood *(G-7287)*
Art Precision Metal Products ... F ... 631 842-8889
Copiague *(G-3894)*
B & R Tool Inc ... G ... 718 948-2729
Staten Island *(G-15642)*
B H M Metal Products Co ... G ... 845 292-5297
Kauneonga Lake *(G-7136)*
Bailey Manufacturing Co LLC ... E ... 716 965-2731
Forestville *(G-5333)*
Barnes Group Inc ... G ... 315 457-9200
Syracuse *(G-15867)*
Bel-Bee Products Incorporated ... F ... 845 353-0300
West Nyack *(G-16912)*
Belmet Products Inc ... E ... 718 542-8220
Bronx *(G-1283)*
Belrix Industries Inc ... G ... 716 821-5964
Buffalo *(G-2837)*
Bowen Products Corporation ... G ... 315 498-4481
Nedrow *(G-8772)*
Brach Machine Inc ... F ... 585 343-9134
Batavia *(G-626)*
Bridgeport Metalcraft Inc ... G ... 315 623-9597
Constantia *(G-3880)*
Bryant Machine Co Inc ... F ... 716 894-8282
Buffalo *(G-2846)*
C & H Precision Tools Inc ... E ... 631 758-3806
Holtsville *(G-6502)*
▲ Cameo Metal Products Inc ... E ... 718 788-1106
Brooklyn *(G-1751)*
▲ Cannon Industries Inc ... D ... 585 254-8080
Rochester *(G-14258)*
▲ Cep Technologies Corporation ... E ... 914 968-4100
Yonkers *(G-17427)*
Cgs Fabrication LLC ... F ... 585 347-6127
Webster *(G-16716)*
▲ Chamart Exclusives Inc ... G ... 914 345-3870
Elmsford *(G-4740)*
Charles A Rogers Entps Inc ... E ... 585 924-6400
Victor *(G-16466)*
Check-Mate Industries Inc ... E ... 631 491-1777
West Babylon *(G-16782)*
Chivvis Enterprises Inc ... F ... 631 842-9055
Copiague *(G-3897)*
Cnc Manufacturing Corp ... E ... 718 728-6800
Long Island City *(G-7701)*
Cobbe Industries Inc ... E ... 716 287-2661
Gerry *(G-5592)*
▲ Coda Resources Ltd ... D ... 718 649-1666
Brooklyn *(G-1790)*
Colonial Precision Machinery ... G ... 631 249-0738
Farmingdale *(G-4960)*

Compar Manufacturing Corp ... E ... 212 304-2777
New York *(G-9690)*
Corbett Stves Pttern Works Inc ... E ... 585 546-7109
Rochester *(G-14289)*
◆ Corning Vitro Corporation ... A ... 607 974-8605
Corning *(G-3971)*
▲ Creative Design and Mch Inc ... E ... 845 778-9001
Rock Tavern *(G-14780)*
Crosby Company ... E ... 716 852-3522
Buffalo *(G-2893)*
Custom Metal Incorporated ... F ... 631 643-4075
West Babylon *(G-16787)*
D-K Manufacturing Corp ... E ... 315 592-4327
Fulton *(G-5455)*
Dayton Industries Inc ... E ... 718 542-8144
Bronx *(G-1311)*
Dayton Rogers New York LLC ... D ... 585 349-4040
Rochester *(G-14302)*
Die-Matic Products LLC ... E ... 516 433-7900
Plainview *(G-13597)*
▼ Dunkirk Metal Products Wny LLC ... E ... 716 366-2555
Dunkirk *(G-4339)*
Eaton Electric Holdings LLC ... C ... 607 756-2821
Cortland *(G-4025)*
Electric Motors and Pumps Inc ... G ... 718 935-9118
Brooklyn *(G-1910)*
Endicott Precision Inc ... C ... 607 754-7076
Endicott *(G-4803)*
Engineering Mfg Tech LLC ... D ... 607 754-7111
Endicott *(G-4805)*
Erdle Perforating Holdings Inc ... D ... 585 247-4700
Rochester *(G-14355)*
Fabrication Specialties Corp ... G ... 631 242-0326
Deer Park *(G-4141)*
Falso Industries Inc ... E ... 315 463-0266
Syracuse *(G-15941)*
▼ Feldware Inc ... E ... 718 372-0486
Brooklyn *(G-1965)*
Forkey Construction & Fabg Inc ... E ... 607 849-4879
Cortland *(G-4026)*
Forsyth Industries Inc ... E ... 716 652-1070
Buffalo *(G-2953)*
▲ Freeport Screen & Stamping ... E ... 516 379-0330
Freeport *(G-5401)*
G A Richards & Co Inc ... F ... 516 334-5412
Westbury *(G-16988)*
▲ Gasser & Sons Inc ... C ... 631 543-6600
Commack *(G-3832)*
Gay Sheet Metal Dies Inc ... G ... 716 877-0208
Buffalo *(G-2966)*
Gem Metal Spinning & Stamping ... G ... 718 729-7014
Long Island City *(G-7749)*
Genesee Metal Stampings Inc ... G ... 585 475-0450
West Henrietta *(G-16879)*
German Machine & Assembly Inc ... E ... 585 546-4200
Rochester *(G-14398)*
◆ Gleason Works ... A ... 585 473-1000
Rochester *(G-14408)*
Great Lakes Pressed Steel Corp ... E ... 716 885-4037
Buffalo *(G-2982)*
Greene Technologies Inc ... D ... 607 656-4166
Greene *(G-5866)*
Hy-Grade Metal Products Corp ... G ... 315 475-4221
Syracuse *(G-15961)*
▲ Hyman Podrusnick Co Inc ... G ... 718 853-4502
Brooklyn *(G-2092)*
International Ord Tech Inc ... D ... 716 664-1100
Jamestown *(G-7003)*
▲ Interplex Industries Inc ... F ... 718 961-6212
College Point *(G-3790)*
J P Machine Products Inc ... F ... 631 249-9229
Farmingdale *(G-5014)*
Johnson & Hoffman LLC ... D ... 516 742-3333
Carle Place *(G-3392)*
K Tooling LLC ... F ... 607 637-3781
Hancock *(G-5964)*
▲ Kerns Manufacturing Corp ... C ... 718 784-4044
Long Island City *(G-7780)*
▼ Koch Metal Spinning Co Inc ... D ... 716 835-3631
Buffalo *(G-3034)*
◆ Korin Japanese Trading Corp ... E ... 212 587-7021
New York *(G-10878)*
Lamparts Co Inc ... F ... 914 723-8986
Mount Vernon *(G-8699)*
▲ Lancaster Knives Inc ... E ... 716 683-5050
Lancaster *(G-7323)*
▲ Lb Furniture Industries LLC ... C ... 518 828-1501
Hudson *(G-6624)*
Long Island Metalform Inc ... F ... 631 242-9088
Deer Park *(G-4167)*

M F Manufacturing Enterprises ... G ... 516 822-5135
Hicksville *(G-6366)*
Maehr Industries Inc ... G ... 631 924-1661
Bellport *(G-833)*
▲ Magic Novelty Co Inc ... E ... 212 304-2777
New York *(G-11104)*
Mantel & Mantel Stamping Corp ... G ... 631 467-1916
Ronkonkoma *(G-14937)*
▲ Marex Aquisition Corp ... C ... 585 458-3940
Rochester *(G-14497)*
Matov Industries Inc ... E ... 718 392-5060
Long Island City *(G-7806)*
McHone Industries Inc ... D ... 716 945-3380
Salamanca *(G-15101)*
Mega Tool & Mfg Corp ... E ... 607 734-8398
Elmira *(G-4695)*
Nash Metalware Co Inc ... F ... 315 339-5794
Rome *(G-14823)*
National Computer & Electronic ... G ... 631 242-7222
Deer Park *(G-4177)*
National Die & Button Mould Co ... E ... 201 939-7800
Brooklyn *(G-2350)*
▲ National Wire & Metal Tech Inc ... E ... 716 661-9180
Jamestown *(G-7021)*
▲ Novel Box Company Ltd ... E ... 718 965-2222
Brooklyn *(G-2377)*
▲ OEM Solutions Inc ... G ... 716 864-9324
Clarence *(G-3667)*
▲ Oxo International Inc ... C ... 212 242-3333
New York *(G-11544)*
P R B Metal Products Inc ... F ... 631 467-1800
Ronkonkoma *(G-14961)*
▲ P&G Metal Components Corp ... D ... 716 896-7900
Buffalo *(G-3108)*
Pall Corporation ... A ... 607 753-6041
Cortland *(G-4035)*
Pervi Precision Company ... G ... 631 589-5557
Bohemia *(G-1117)*
Precision Photo-Fab Inc ... D ... 716 821-9393
Buffalo *(G-3133)*
Precision Tl Die & Stamping Co ... F ... 516 561-0041
Valley Stream *(G-16420)*
Premier Metals Group ... E ... 585 436-4020
Rochester *(G-14597)*
▲ Progressus Company Inc ... F ... 516 255-0245
Rockville Centre *(G-14796)*
Pronto Tool & Die Co Inc ... E ... 631 981-8920
Ronkonkoma *(G-14972)*
Quality Metal Stamping LLC ... G ... 516 255-9000
Rockville Centre *(G-14797)*
R G Flair Co Inc ... E ... 631 586-7311
Bay Shore *(G-730)*
Rayco Manufacturing Co Inc ... F ... 516 431-2006
Jamaica *(G-6944)*
Reynolds Manufacturing Inc ... F ... 607 562-8936
Big Flats *(G-882)*
Richter Metalcraft Corporation ... E ... 845 895-2025
Wallkill *(G-16545)*
▲ Rigidized Metals Corporation ... E ... 716 849-4703
Buffalo *(G-3158)*
Rochester Stampings Inc ... F ... 585 467-5241
Rochester *(G-14649)*
▲ Rolite Mfg Inc ... E ... 716 683-0259
Lancaster *(G-7340)*
Russco Metal Spinning Co Inc ... F ... 516 872-6055
Oceanside *(G-13095)*
▲ S & S Prtg Die-Cutting Co Inc ... F ... 718 388-8990
Brooklyn *(G-2522)*
S D Z Metal Spinning Stamping ... F ... 718 778-3600
Brooklyn *(G-2525)*
Schiller Stores Inc ... G ... 631 208-9400
Riverhead *(G-14155)*
Seneca Ceramics Corp ... G ... 315 781-0100
Phelps *(G-13536)*
Sharon Manufacturing Co Inc ... G ... 631 242-8870
Deer Park *(G-4210)*
Sharon Metal Stamping Corp ... G ... 718 828-4510
Bronx *(G-1451)*
Simplex Manufacturing Co Inc ... F ... 315 252-7524
Auburn *(G-519)*
Smithers Tools & Mch Pdts Inc ... D ... 845 876-3063
Rhinebeck *(G-14058)*
Solidus Industries Inc ... D ... 607 749-4540
Homer *(G-6522)*
Square Stamping Mfg Corp ... E ... 315 896-2641
Barneveld *(G-618)*
▼ Stampcrete International Ltd ... E ... 315 451-2837
Liverpool *(G-7549)*
▲ Stamped Fittings Inc ... E ... 607 733-9988
Elmira Heights *(G-4713)*

Employee Codes: A=Over 500 employees, B=251-500
C=101-250, D=51-100, E=20-50, F=10-19, G=5-9
2017 Harris
New York Manufacturers Directory
817

34 FABRICATED METAL PRODUCTS, EXCEPT MACHINERY AND TRANSPORTATION EQUIPMENT

▲ Stever-Locke Industries Inc ....G 585 624-3450
  Honeoye Falls (G-6538)
Stewart Efi LLC ....D 914 965-0816
  Yonkers (G-17487)
Superior Washer & Gasket Corp ....D 631 273-8282
  Hauppauge (G-6203)
Surving Studios ....F 845 355-1430
  Middletown (G-8464)
Tooling Enterprises Inc ....F 716 842-0445
  Buffalo (G-3222)
Tools & Stamping Corp ....G 718 392-4040
  Brooklyn (G-2663)
Toronto Metal Spinning and Ltg ....E 905 793-1174
  Niagara Falls (G-12883)
▲ Tri-Technologies Inc ....G 914 699-2001
  Mount Vernon (G-8741)
▲ Trident Precision Mfg Inc ....D 585 265-2010
  Webster (G-16738)
TRW Automotive Inc ....B 315 255-3311
  Auburn (G-525)
TRW Automotive US LLC ....C 315 255-3311
  Auburn (G-526)
▲ Twinco Mfg Co Inc ....E 631 231-0022
  Hauppauge (G-6219)
▼ Ultimate Prcision Met Pdts Inc ....D 631 249-9441
  Farmingdale (G-5136)
Universal Shielding Corp ....E 631 667-7900
  Deer Park (G-4219)
V Lake Industries Inc ....G 716 885-9141
  Buffalo (G-3239)
Vanity Fair Bathmart Inc ....F 718 584-6700
  Bronx (G-1488)
Village Metals Inc ....G 585 271-1250
  Rochester (G-14754)
Volkert Precision Tech Inc ....G 718 464-9500
  Queens Village (G-13984)
Vosky Precision Machining Corp ....F 631 737-3200
  Ronkonkoma (G-15000)
W & H Stampings Inc ....E 631 234-6161
  Hauppauge (G-6229)
Web Associates Inc ....G 716 883-3377
  Buffalo (G-3149)
Welding Metallurgy Inc ....D 631 253-0500
  Hauppauge (G-6232)
Wessie Machine Inc ....G 315 926-4060
  Marion (G-8104)
Wilmax Usa LLC ....F 917 388-2790
  New York (G-12639)
WR Smith & Sons Inc ....G 845 620-9400
  Nanuet (G-8763)
Zeta Machine Corp ....G 631 471-8832
  Ronkonkoma (G-15002)

3471 Electroplating, Plating, Polishing, Anodizing & Coloring

21st Century Finishes Inc ....F 516 221-7000
  North Bellmore (G-12914)
Abetter Processing Corp ....F 718 252-2223
  Brooklyn (G-1547)
Able Anodizing Corp ....F 718 252-0660
  Brooklyn (G-1548)
ABS Metal Corp ....G 646 302-9018
  Hewlett (G-6306)
Aircraft Finishing Corp ....F 631 422-5000
  West Babylon (G-16767)
Airmarine Electroplating Corp ....F 516 623-4406
  Freeport (G-5381)
Anthony River Inc ....F 315 475-1315
  Syracuse (G-15855)
Astro Electroplating Inc ....E 631 968-0656
  Bay Shore (G-673)
B & W Heat Treating Company ....G 716 876-8184
  Tonawanda (G-16143)
Barnes Metal Finishing Inc ....F 585 798-4817
  Medina (G-8265)
▲ Berkman Bros Inc ....E 718 782-1827
  Brooklyn (G-1686)
Bfg Manufacturing Services Inc .....F 716 362-0888
  Buffalo (G-2841)
Buffalo Metal Finishing Co ....F 716 883-2751
  Buffalo (G-2856)
C H Thompson Company Inc ....D 607 724-1094
  Binghamton (G-901)
Carpenter Industries Inc ....F 315 463-4284
  Syracuse (G-15886)
Coating Technology Inc ....E 585 546-7170
  Rochester (G-14282)
Control Electropolishing Corp ....F 718 858-6634
  Brooklyn (G-1801)

D & I Finishing Inc ....G 631 471-3034
  Bohemia (G-1048)
D & W Enterprises LLC ....F 585 590-6727
  Medina (G-8270)
Dan Kane Plating Co Inc ....F 212 675-4947
  New York (G-9797)
Dura Spec Inc ....F 718 526-3053
  North Baldwin (G-12904)
Eastside Oxide Co ....E 607 734-1253
  Elmira (G-4680)
Electro Plating Service Inc ....F 914 948-3777
  White Plains (G-17104)
Empire Metal Finishing Inc ....E 718 545-6700
  Astoria (G-440)
▼ Epner Technology Incorporated ...E 718 782-5948
  Brooklyn (G-1929)
Epner Technology Incorporated .....E 718 782-8722
  Brooklyn (G-1930)
Eric S Turner & Company Inc ....F 914 235-7114
  New Rochelle (G-8898)
▲ Ever-Nu-Metal Products Inc ....E 646 423-5833
  Brooklyn (G-1939)
F & H Metal Finishing Co Inc ....F 585 798-2151
  Medina (G-8271)
Fallon Inc ....E 718 326-7226
  Maspeth (G-8138)
Finest Cc Corp ....G 917 574-4525
  Bronx (G-1331)
First Impressions Finishing ....G 631 467-2244
  Ronkonkoma (G-14900)
Frontier Plating ....F 716 896-2811
  Buffalo (G-2959)
G J C Ltd Inc ....E 607 770-4500
  Binghamton (G-917)
Galmer Inc ....G 718 392-4609
  Long Island City (G-7748)
General Galvanizing Sup Co Inc ......E 718 589-4300
  Bronx (G-1343)
General Plating LLC ....E 585 423-0830
  Rochester (G-14391)
Genesee Vly Met Finshg Co Inc ......E 585 232-4412
  Rochester (G-14395)
Greene Technologies Inc ....D 607 656-4166
  Greene (G-5866)
Halmark Architectural Finshg ....E 718 272-1831
  Brooklyn (G-2063)
Hartchrom Inc ....F 518 880-0411
  Watervliet (G-16686)
Harvard Maintenance Inc ....A 212 682-2617
  New York (G-10424)
▲ I W Industries Inc ....G 631 293-9494
  Melville (G-8330)
▲ Interplex Industries Inc ....F 718 961-6212
  College Point (G-3790)
John Larocca & Son Inc ....G 631 423-5256
  Huntington Station (G-6712)
Kent Electro-Plating Corp ....F 718 358-9599
  Dix Hills (G-4292)
Key Tech Finishing ....E 716 832-1232
  Buffalo (G-3029)
▲ Keymark Corporation ....A 518 853-3421
  Fonda (G-5316)
Keystone Corporation ....E 716 832-1232
  Buffalo (G-3031)
L W S Inc ....F 631 580-0472
  Ronkonkoma (G-14925)
Lws Precision Deburring Inc ....F 631 580-0472
  Ronkonkoma (G-14935)
Maracle Industrial Finshg Co ....E 585 387-9077
  Rochester (G-14495)
Master Craft Finishers Inc ....E 631 586-0540
  Deer Park (G-4171)
McAlpin Industries Inc ....E 585 544-5335
  Rochester (G-14501)
Metal Man Restoration ....F 914 662-4218
  Mount Vernon (G-8704)
Mid Hudson Plating Inc ....G 845 849-1277
  Poughkeepsie (G-13916)
Multitone Finishing Co Inc ....G 516 485-1043
  West Hempstead (G-16860)
▲ Nas CP Corp ....D 718 961-6757
  College Point (G-3799)
Nassau Chromium Plating Co Inc ...F 516 746-6666
  Mineola (G-8526)
North East Finishing Co Inc ....F 631 789-8000
  Copiague (G-3917)
Northeast Paving Concepts LLC .....E 518 477-1338
  East Schodack (G-4473)
Oerlikon Balzers Coating USA ....E 716 564-8557
  Buffalo (G-3099)

P3 Technologies ....G 585 730-7340
  Rochester (G-14565)
Paradigm Group LLC ....F 718 860-1538
  Bronx (G-1420)
Praxair Surface Tech Inc ....C 845 398-8322
  Orangeburg (G-13242)
▲ Precious Plate Inc ....D 716 283-0690
  Niagara Falls (G-12862)
Products Superb Inc ....E 315 923-7057
  Clyde (G-3731)
Programatic Platers Inc ....E 718 721-4330
  East Elmhurst (G-4396)
Psb Ltd ....E 585 654-7078
  Rochester (G-14607)
Rainbow Powder Coating Corp ....G 631 586-4019
  Deer Park (G-4198)
Rayco of Schenectady Inc ....E 518 212-5113
  Amsterdam (G-366)
Reynolds Tech Fabricators Inc ....E 315 437-0532
  East Syracuse (G-4558)
Rochester Overnight Pltg LLC ....D 585 328-4590
  Rochester (G-14645)
Saccomize Inc ....G 818 287-3000
  Bronx (G-1446)
Sandys Bumper Mart Inc ....E 315 472-8149
  Syracuse (G-16031)
Sas Maintenance Services Inc ......F 718 837-2124
  Brooklyn (G-2535)
Sherrill Manufacturing Inc ....C 315 280-0727
  Sherrill (G-15407)
Silverman & Gorf Inc ....E 718 625-1309
  Brooklyn (G-2558)
Surface Finish Technology ....E 607 732-2909
  Elmira (G-4703)
T & M Plating Inc ....E 212 967-1110
  New York (G-12264)
Tcmf Inc ....D 607 724-1094
  Binghamton (G-954)
Thomas Foundry LLC ....E 315 361-9048
  Oneida (G-13168)
Tripp Plating Works Inc ....G 716 894-2424
  Buffalo (G-3225)
Tronic Plating Co Inc ....F 516 293-7883
  Farmingdale (G-5135)
Tropical Driftwood Originals ....E 516 623-0980
  Roosevelt (G-15010)
Tru-Tone Metal Products Inc ....E 718 386-5960
  Brooklyn (G-2686)
US Electroplating Corp ....G 631 293-1998
  West Babylon (G-16837)
Utica Metal Products Inc ....D 315 732-6163
  Utica (G-16364)
Vernon Plating Works Inc ....F 718 639-1124
  Woodside (G-17360)
Vibra Tech Industries Inc ....F 914 946-1916
  White Plains (G-17180)
▲ Victoria Plating Co Inc ....D 718 589-1550
  Bronx (G-1489)
West Falls Machine Co Inc ....F 716 655-0440
  East Aurora (G-4380)
Wilco Finishing Corp ....E 718 417-6405
  Brooklyn (G-2751)

3479 Coating & Engraving, NEC

Accurate Pnt Powdr Coating Inc .....F 585 235-1650
  Rochester (G-14167)
Advanced Coating Service LLC ......G 585 247-3970
  Rochester (G-14176)
Advanced Coating Techniques ....E 631 643-4555
  Babylon (G-545)
▼ Advanced Graphics Company ......F 607 692-7875
  Whitney Point (G-17219)
Advanced Lamp Coatings Corp ......E 631 585-5505
  Ronkonkoma (G-14853)
Advanced Surface Finishing ....E 516 876-9710
  Westbury (G-16962)
Aircraft Finishing Corp ....F 631 422-5000
  West Babylon (G-16767)
All Spec Finishing Inc ....E 607 770-9174
  Binghamton (G-886)
▲ Angiotech Biocoatings Corp ....E 585 321-1130
  Henrietta (G-6292)
Applause Coating LLC ....F 631 231-5223
  Brentwood (G-1176)
Artistic Innovation Inc ....F 914 968-3021
  Yonkers (G-17416)
Ascribe Inc ....E 585 413-0298
  Rochester (G-14216)
Ashburns Inc ....G 212 227-5692
  New York (G-9227)

SIC SECTION 34 FABRICATED METAL PRODUCTS, EXCEPT MACHINERY AND TRANSPORTATION EQUIPMENT

Barson Composites Corporation .... E 516 752-7882
Old Bethpage *(G-13126)*
▲ **Berkman Bros Inc** .... E 718 782-1827
Brooklyn *(G-1686)*
Buffalo Finishing Works Inc .... G 716 893-5266
Buffalo *(G-2851)*
Buffalo Metal Finishing Co .... G 716 883-2751
Buffalo *(G-2856)*
C & M Products Inc .... G 315 471-3303
Syracuse *(G-15880)*
C H Thompson Company Inc .... D 607 724-1094
Binghamton *(G-901)*
Chepaume Industries LLC .... G 315 829-6400
Vernon *(G-16433)*
Chromalloy Gas Turbine LLC .... E 845 692-8912
Middletown *(G-8430)*
Clad Metal Specialties Inc .... F 631 666-7750
Bay Shore *(G-684)*
Cnv Architectural Coatings Inc .... G 718 418-9584
Brooklyn *(G-1789)*
Color Craft Finishing Corp .... F 631 563-3230
Bohemia *(G-1038)*
Color ME Mine .... F 585 383-8420
Rochester *(G-14283)*
▲ **Custom House Engravers Inc** .... G 631 567-3004
Bohemia *(G-1046)*
Custom Laser Inc .... E 716 434-8600
Lockport *(G-7578)*
D & I Finishing Inc .... G 631 471-3034
Bohemia *(G-1048)*
Deloka LLC .... G 315 946-6910
Lyons *(G-7972)*
Duzmor Painting Inc .... G 585 768-4760
Le Roy *(G-7407)*
Dynocoat Inc .... F 631 244-9344
Holbrook *(G-6444)*
Eastern Silver of Boro Park .... G 718 854-5600
Brooklyn *(G-1899)*
▲ **Electronic Coating Tech Inc** .... F 518 688-2048
Cohoes *(G-3747)*
Elegance Coating Ltd .... E 386 668-8379
Champlain *(G-3540)*
Everlasting Images .... G 607 785-8743
Endicott *(G-4806)*
F & H Metal Finishing Co Inc .... F 585 798-2151
Medina *(G-8271)*
▲ **Fougera Pharmaceuticals Inc** .... C 631 454-7677
Melville *(G-8321)*
▲ **Frontier Ht-Dip Glvanizing Inc** .... F 716 875-2091
Buffalo *(G-2957)*
Future Spray Finishing Co .... G 631 242-6252
Deer Park *(G-4146)*
Greene Technologies Inc .... D 607 656-4166
Greene *(G-5866)*
Harold Wood Co Inc .... G 716 873-1535
Buffalo *(G-2990)*
Hatfield Metal Fab Inc .... E 845 454-9078
Poughkeepsie *(G-13906)*
▲ **Heany Industries Inc** .... D 585 889-2700
Scottsville *(G-15336)*
Hilord Chemical Corporation .... E 631 234-7373
Hauppauge *(G-6094)*
Hitemco Medical Applications .... C 516 752-7882
Old Bethpage *(G-13128)*
Hudson Valley Coatings LLC .... G 845 398-1778
Congers *(G-3857)*
Industrial Paint Services Corp .... F 607 687-0107
Owego *(G-13352)*
Isoflux Incorporated .... G 585 349-0640
Rochester *(G-14455)*
▼ **Jamestown Bronze Works Inc** .... G 716 665-2302
Jamestown *(G-7006)*
▲ **Jrlon Inc** .... D 315 597-4067
Palmyra *(G-13409)*
▲ **Keymark Corporation** .... A 518 853-3421
Fonda *(G-5316)*
Kwong CHI Metal Fabrication .... G 718 369-6429
Brooklyn *(G-2184)*
▲ **Lodolce Machine Co Inc** .... E 845 246-7017
Saugerties *(G-15187)*
Mac Artspray Finishing Corp .... F 718 649-3800
Brooklyn *(G-2249)*
Master Craft Finishers Inc .... E 631 586-0540
Deer Park *(G-4171)*
McHugh Painting Co Inc .... F 716 741-8077
Clarence *(G-3665)*
▲ **Metal Cladding Inc** .... D 716 434-5513
Lockport *(G-7600)*
Metal Finishing Supply Inc .... G 315 655-8068
Canastota *(G-3369)*
Modern Coating and Research .... F 315 597-3517
Palmyra *(G-13411)*
◆ **Momentive Performance Mtls Inc** .... E 518 237-3330
Waterford *(G-16616)*
Momentive Prfmce Mtls Holdings .... A 518 533-4600
Albany *(G-102)*
Monroe County Auto Svcs Inc .... E 585 764-3741
Rochester *(G-14520)*
Mpm Holdings Inc .... G 518 237-3330
Waterford *(G-16617)*
Mpm Intermediate Holdings Inc .... G 518 237-3330
Waterford *(G-16618)*
Nameplate Mfrs of Amer .... E 631 752-0055
Farmingdale *(G-5061)*
NC Industries Inc .... F 248 528-5200
Buffalo *(G-3082)*
Newchem Inc .... E 315 331-7680
Newark *(G-12738)*
▲ **O W Hubbell & Sons Inc** .... E 315 736-8311
Yorkville *(G-17523)*
Oerlikon Balzers Coating USA .... E 716 564-8557
Buffalo *(G-3099)*
Paradigm Group LLC .... G 718 860-1538
Bronx *(G-1420)*
Piper Plastics Corp .... E 631 842-6889
Copiague *(G-3918)*
Precision Design Systems Inc .... E 585 426-4500
Rochester *(G-14592)*
Precision Laser Technology LLC .... F 585 458-6208
Rochester *(G-14594)*
Pro-Teck Coating Inc .... F 716 537-2619
Holland *(G-6483)*
▲ **Qualicoat Inc** .... D 585 293-2650
Churchville *(G-3640)*
R S T Cable and Tape Inc .... G 631 981-0096
Ronkonkoma *(G-14976)*
R Spoor Finishing Corp .... F 607 748-5905
Endicott *(G-4827)*
Rayana Designs Inc .... E 718 786-2040
Long Island City *(G-7859)*
Read Manufacturing Company Inc .... E 631 567-4487
Holbrook *(G-6467)*
Rims Like New Inc .... F 845 537-0396
Middletown *(G-8460)*
Sentry Metal Blast Inc .... E 716 285-5241
Niagara Falls *(G-12875)*
Sequa Corporation .... E 201 343-1122
Orangeburg *(G-13247)*
Solidus Industries Inc .... D 607 749-4540
Homer *(G-6522)*
Specialty Bldg Solutions Inc .... G 631 393-6918
West Babylon *(G-16831)*
Steel Partners Holdings LP .... E 212 520-2300
New York *(G-12189)*
Stuart-Dean Co Inc .... F 718 472-1326
Long Island City *(G-7894)*
▲ **Superior Metals & Processing** .... G 718 545-7500
Long Island City *(G-7896)*
Swain Technology Inc .... F 585 889-2786
Scottsville *(G-15340)*
Tailored Coatings Inc .... E 716 893-4869
Buffalo *(G-3209)*
Tcmf Inc .... D 607 724-1094
Binghamton *(G-954)*
Ter-El Engraving Co Inc .... G 315 455-5597
Syracuse *(G-16056)*
The Gramecy Group .... G 518 348-1325
Clifton Park *(G-3710)*
Tj Powder Coaters LLC .... G 607 724-4779
Binghamton *(G-955)*
Trojan Metal Fabrication Inc .... E 631 968-5040
Bay Shore *(G-752)*
▲ **Turbine Arfoil Cating Repr LLC** .... C 845 692-8912
Middletown *(G-8467)*
W Hubbell & Sons Inc .... G 315 736-8311
Yorkville *(G-17529)*
W W Custom Clad Inc .... D 518 673-3322
Canajoharie *(G-3334)*
White Plains Rubber Stamp Name .... G 914 949-1900
White Plains *(G-17187)*

3482 Small Arms Ammunition

Benjamin Sheridan Corporation .... G 585 657-6161
Bloomfield *(G-981)*
CIC International Ltd .... D 212 213-0089
Brooklyn *(G-1779)*
▲ **Crosman Corporation** .... E 585 657-6161
Bloomfield *(G-986)*
Crosman Corporation .... E 585 398-3920
Farmington *(G-5148)*

3483 Ammunition, Large

CIC International Ltd .... D 212 213-0089
Brooklyn *(G-1779)*
Circor Aerospace Inc .... D 631 737-1900
Hauppauge *(G-6045)*

3484 Small Arms

Benjamin Sheridan Corporation .... G 585 657-6161
Bloomfield *(G-981)*
▲ **Crosman Corporation** .... E 585 657-6161
Bloomfield *(G-986)*
Crosman Corporation .... E 585 398-3920
Farmington *(G-5148)*
Dan Wesson Corp .... F 607 336-1174
Norwich *(G-13026)*
Hart Rifle Barrel Inc .... G 315 677-9841
Syracuse *(G-15958)*
Kyntec Corporation .... G 716 810-6956
Buffalo *(G-3038)*
Oriskany Arms Inc .... G 315 737-2196
Oriskany *(G-13312)*
Redding-Hunter Inc .... E 607 753-3331
Cortland *(G-4043)*
Remington Arms Company LLC .... A 315 895-3482
Ilion *(G-6744)*
Sycamore Hill Designs Inc .... G 585 820-7322
Victor *(G-16504)*
▲ **Tri-Technologies Inc** .... E 914 699-2001
Mount Vernon *(G-8741)*

3489 Ordnance & Access, NEC

CIC International Ltd .... D 212 213-0089
Brooklyn *(G-1779)*
Dyno Nobel Inc .... D 845 338-2144
Ulster Park *(G-16285)*
▼ **Island Ordnance Systems LLC** .... F 516 746-2100
Mineola *(G-8518)*
Magellan Aerospace NY Inc .... C 718 699-4000
Corona *(G-4001)*
◆ **Mil-Spec Industries Corp** .... G 516 625-5787
Glen Cove *(G-5621)*

3491 Industrial Valves

ADC Industries Inc .... E 516 596-1304
Valley Stream *(G-16398)*
▲ **Air System Products Inc** .... F 716 683-0435
Lancaster *(G-7300)*
Byelocorp Scientific Inc .... E 212 785-2580
New York *(G-9486)*
Caithness Equities Corporation .... E 212 599-2112
New York *(G-9498)*
◆ **Curtiss-Wright Flow Ctrl Corp** .... C 631 293-3800
Farmingdale *(G-4968)*
Curtiss-Wright Flow Ctrl Corp .... C 631 293-3800
Farmingdale *(G-4969)*
Digital Home Creations Inc .... G 585 576-7070
Webster *(G-16721)*
Doyle & Roth Mfg Co Inc .... F 212 269-7840
New York *(G-9921)*
Dresser-Rand LLC .... A 585 596-3100
Wellsville *(G-16751)*
▲ **Flomatic Corporation** .... E 518 761-9797
Glens Falls *(G-5678)*
Flow-Safe Inc .... E 716 662-2585
Orchard Park *(G-13270)*
J H Buscher Inc .... G 716 667-2003
Orchard Park *(G-13276)*
▲ **John N Fehlinger Co Inc** .... F 212 233-5656
New York *(G-10752)*
McWane Inc .... B 607 734-2211
Elmira *(G-4694)*
▲ **Murphy Manufacturing Co Inc** .... G 585 223-0100
Fairport *(G-4865)*
▲ **Plattco Corporation** .... E 518 563-4640
Plattsburgh *(G-13687)*
◆ **Precision Valve & Automtn Inc** .... C 518 371-2684
Cohoes *(G-3755)*
▲ **Spence Engineering Company Inc** ... C 845 778-5566
Walden *(G-16536)*
Syraco Products Inc .... E 800 581-5555
Syracuse *(G-16047)*
▲ **Total Energy Fabrication Corp** .... G 580 363-1500
North Salem *(G-12940)*
◆ **Town Food Service Eqp Co Inc** .... F 718 388-5650
Brooklyn *(G-2672)*
Trac Regulators Inc .... E 914 699-9352
Mount Vernon *(G-8739)*
Tyco Simplexgrinnell .... E 315 437-9664
East Syracuse *(G-4574)*

S I C

Employee Codes: A=Over 500 employees, B=251-500
C=101-250, D=51-100, E=20-50, F=10-19, G=5-9
2017 Harris
New York Manufacturers Directory
819

34 FABRICATED METAL PRODUCTS, EXCEPT MACHINERY AND TRANSPORTATION EQUIPMENT

▲ William E Williams Valve Corp .... E 718 392-1660
Long Island City (G-7922)

3492 Fluid Power Valves & Hose Fittings

▲ A K Allen Co Inc .... C 516 747-5450
Mineola (G-8488)
Aalborg Instrs & Contrls Inc .... D 845 398-3160
Orangeburg (G-13217)
▲ Aerco International Inc .... C 845 580-8000
Blauvelt (G-969)
▲ BW Elliott Mfg Co LLC .... B 607 772-0404
Binghamton (G-900)
Direkt Force LLC .... E 716 652-3022
East Aurora (G-4369)
Dmic Inc .... F 716 743-4360
North Tonawanda (G-12969)
Dsti Inc .... G 716 557-2362
Olean (G-13145)
Dynamic Sealing Tech Inc .... G 716 376-0708
Olean (G-13146)
◆ Eastport Operating Partners LP .... G 212 387-8791
New York (G-9969)
▲ Key High Vacuum Products Inc .... E 631 584-5959
Nesconset (G-8775)
Kinemotive Corporation .... E 631 249-6440
Farmingdale (G-5028)
▲ KSA Manufacturing LLC .... F 315 488-0809
Camillus (G-3323)
Lourdes Industries Inc .... D 631 234-6600
Hauppauge (G-6121)
Moog Inc .... B 716 655-3000
East Aurora (G-4375)
◆ Moog Inc .... A 716 652-2000
Elma (G-4651)
Own Instrument Inc .... F 914 668-6546
Mount Vernon (G-8712)
Servotronics Inc .... C 716 655-5990
Elma (G-4655)
▲ Steel & Obrien Mfg Inc .... D 585 492-5800
Arcade (G-400)
Tactair Fluid Controls Inc .... C 315 451-3928
Liverpool (G-7552)
Upstate Tube Inc .... G 315 488-5636
Camillus (G-3326)
Young & Franklin Inc .... D 315 457-3110
Liverpool (G-7559)

3493 Steel Springs, Except Wire

Angelica Spring Company Inc .... F 585 466-7892
Angelica (G-377)
Chet Kruszkas Service Inc .... F 716 662-7450
Orchard Park (G-13261)
Isolation Dynamics Corp .... E 631 491-5670
West Babylon (G-16795)
▲ Lee Spring Company LLC .... C 718 362-5183
Brooklyn (G-2206)
▲ Midstate Spring Inc .... E 315 437-2623
Syracuse (G-15990)
▲ Newport Magnetics Inc .... G 315 845-8878
Newport (G-12791)
Temper Corporation .... E 518 853-3467
Fonda (G-5317)
Whitesboro Spring & Alignment .... F 315 736-4441
Whitesboro (G-17198)
Whiting Door Mfg Corp .... D 716 542-3070
Akron (G-31)

3494 Valves & Pipe Fittings, NEC

▲ A K Allen Co Inc .... C 516 747-5450
Mineola (G-8488)
Aalborg Instrs & Contrls Inc .... D 845 398-3160
Orangeburg (G-13217)
Advanced Thermal Systems Inc .... E 716 681-1800
Lancaster (G-7298)
▲ Anderson Precision Inc .... F 716 484-1148
Jamestown (G-6971)
Arvos Holding LLC .... G 585 596-2501
Wellsville (G-16748)
◆ Curtiss-Wright Flow Ctrl Corp .... C 631 293-3800
Farmingdale (G-4968)
▼ Delaware Mfg Inds Corp .... D 716 743-4360
North Tonawanda (G-12968)
▼ Devin Mfg Inc .... F 585 496-5770
Arcade (G-391)
Eaton Electric Holdings LLC .... C 607 756-2821
Cortland (G-4025)
▲ Everflow Supplies Inc .... E 908 436-1100
Brooklyn (G-1940)
▲ Flomatic Corporation .... E 518 761-9797
Glens Falls (G-5678)

Ford Regulator Valve Corp .... G 718 497-3255
Brooklyn (G-1995)
◆ ITT Fluid Technology Corp .... B 914 641-2000
White Plains (G-17127)
J H Robotics Inc .... E 607 729-3758
Johnson City (G-7096)
▲ Key High Vacuum Products Inc .... E 631 584-5959
Nesconset (G-8775)
Kingston Hoops Summer .... G 845 401-6830
Kingston (G-7193)
Lance Valves .... G 716 681-5825
Lancaster (G-7324)
Legacy Valve LLC .... E 914 403-5075
Valhalla (G-16368)
Lemode Plumbing & Heating .... E 718 545-3336
Astoria (G-447)
M Manastrip-M Corporation .... G 518 664-2089
Clifton Park (G-3699)
▲ Make-Waves Instrument Corp .... E 716 681-7524
Depew (G-4264)
Martin Brass Works Inc .... E 718 523-3146
Jamaica (G-6928)
Micromold Products Inc .... E 914 969-2850
Yonkers (G-17467)
Rand Machine Products Inc .... D 716 665-5217
Falconer (G-4908)
Ross Valve Mfg .... E 518 274-0961
Troy (G-16251)
Sigmamotor Inc .... E 716 735-3115
Middleport (G-8423)
Smiths Gas Service Inc .... G 518 438-0400
Albany (G-134)
▲ Spence Engineering Company Inc ... C 845 778-5566
Walden (G-16536)
▲ Steel & Obrien Mfg Inc .... D 585 492-5800
Arcade (G-400)
Sure Flow Equipment Inc .... E 800 263-8251
Tonawanda (G-16204)
▲ Total Piping Solutions Inc .... E 716 372-0160
Olean (G-13154)
▲ United Pipe Nipple Co Inc .... C 516 295-2468
Hewlett (G-6315)
Venco Sales Inc .... E 631 754-0782
Huntington (G-6691)
▲ William E Williams Valve Corp .... E 718 392-1660
Long Island City (G-7922)

3495 Wire Springs

Ajax Wire Specialty Co Inc .... F 516 935-2333
Hicksville (G-6318)
Barnes Group Inc .... G 315 457-9200
Syracuse (G-15867)
Commerce Spring Corp .... F 631 293-4844
Farmingdale (G-4961)
Commercial Communications LLC ...... G 845 343-9078
Middletown (G-8432)
Fennell Spring Company LLC .... D 607 739-3541
Horseheads (G-6577)
Kinemotive Corporation .... E 631 249-6440
Farmingdale (G-5028)
▲ Lee Spring Company LLC .... C 718 362-5183
Brooklyn (G-2206)
Lee Spring LLC .... E 718 236-2222
Brooklyn (G-2207)
▲ Midstate Spring Inc .... E 315 437-2623
Syracuse (G-15990)
▼ Pullman Mfg Corporation .... G 585 334-1350
Rochester (G-14608)
Teka Precision Inc .... G 845 753-1900
Nyack (G-13055)
◆ The Caldwell Manufacturing Co .... D 585 352-3790
Rochester (G-14721)
The Caldwell Manufacturing Co 585 352-2803
Victor (G-16508)
Unimex Corporation .... D 212 755-8800
New York (G-12458)
Unimex Corporation .... C 718 236-2222
Brooklyn (G-2699)

3496 Misc Fabricated Wire Prdts

369 River Road Inc .... E 716 694-5001
North Tonawanda (G-12953)
▲ Abbott Industries Inc .... E 718 291-0800
Jamaica (G-6891)
▲ Aeroflex Incorporated .... E 516 694-6700
Plainview (G-13578)
▲ Albest Metal Stamping Corp .... D 718 388-6000
Brooklyn (G-1576)
All-Lifts Incorporated .... E 518 465-3461
Albany (G-44)

▲ American Intl Trimming .... G 718 369-9643
Brooklyn (G-1602)
▲ American Wire Tie Inc .... E 716 337-2412
North Collins (G-12926)
Angelica Spring Company Inc .... F 585 466-7892
Angelica (G-377)
Bayshore Wire Products Corp .... F 631 451-8825
Coram (G-3941)
▲ Better Wire Products Inc .... E 716 883-3377
Buffalo (G-2840)
◆ Brook North Farms Inc .... F 315 834-9390
Auburn (G-487)
Cable Management Solutions Inc .... E 631 674-0004
Bay Shore (G-680)
▲ Chemprene Inc .... C 845 831-2800
Beacon (G-782)
▲ Chemprene Holding Inc .... C 845 831-2800
Beacon (G-783)
▲ Clover Wire Forming Co Inc .... E 914 375-0400
Yonkers (G-17428)
▼ Cobra Systems Inc .... F 845 338-6675
Bloomington (G-993)
◆ Columbus McKinnon Corporation ...... C 716 689-5400
Getzville (G-5595)
Columbus McKinnon Corporation .... C 716 689-5400
Getzville (G-5597)
Columbus McKinnon Corporation .... C 716 689-5400
Getzville (G-5598)
Compar Manufacturing Corp .... E 212 304-2777
New York (G-9690)
▲ Continental Cordage Corp .... D 315 655-9800
Cazenovia (G-3443)
▲ Cuba Specialty Mfg Co Inc .... F 585 567-4176
Fillmore (G-5175)
Cuddeback Machining Inc .... E 585 392-5889
Hilton (G-6417)
▲ Dico Products Corporation .... D 315 797-0470
Utica (G-16323)
Engineering Mfg Tech LLC .... D 607 754-7111
Endicott (G-4805)
Eraser Company Inc .... C 315 454-3237
Mattydale (G-8212)
Flanagans Creative Disp Inc .... E 845 858-2542
Port Jervis (G-13784)
Flatcut LLC .... G 212 542-5732
Brooklyn (G-1983)
▲ G Bopp USA Inc .... G 845 296-1065
Wappingers Falls (G-16569)
Greene Technologies Inc .... F 607 656-4166
Greene (G-5866)
Habasit America Inc .... D 716 824-8484
Buffalo (G-2984)
Hitachi Metals America Ltd .... D 914 694-9200
Purchase (G-13958)
◆ Hohmann & Barnard Inc .... E 631 234-0600
Hauppauge (G-6095)
Hohmann & Barnard Inc .... E 518 357-9757
Schenectady (G-15268)
Interstate Wood Products Inc .... E 631 842-4488
Amityville (G-296)
J Davis Manufacturing Co Inc .... E 315 337-7574
Rome (G-14816)
Joldeson One Aerospace Inds .... D 718 848-7396
Ozone Park (G-13380)
Kehr-Buffalo Wire Frame Co Inc .... E 716 897-2288
Buffalo (G-3027)
▲ Lubow Machine Corp .... F 631 226-1700
Copiague (G-3911)
Lyn Jo Enterprises Ltd .... G 716 753-2776
Mayville (G-8217)
▲ Magic Novelty Co Inc .... E 212 304-2777
New York (G-11104)
◆ Nexans Energy USA Inc .... C 845 469-2141
Chester (G-3610)
Nyc Fireplaces & Kitchens .... G 718 326-4328
Maspeth (G-8161)
Oneida Sales & Service Inc .... E 716 822-8205
Buffalo (G-3101)
◆ Peck & Hale LLC .... E 631 589-2510
West Sayville (G-16937)
Quality Industrial Services .... F 716 667-7703
Orchard Park (G-13294)
Reelcology Inc .... F 845 258-1880
Pine Island (G-13553)
◆ Renco Group Inc .... E 212 541-6000
New York (G-11832)
▲ Rose Fence Inc .... E 516 223-0777
Freeport (G-5423)
Rose Fence Inc .... D 516 790-2308
Halesite (G-5906)

SIC SECTION 34 FABRICATED METAL PRODUCTS, EXCEPT MACHINERY AND TRANSPORTATION EQUIPMENT

Rose Fence Inc ....F 516 223-0777
Baldwin *(G-561)*
SCI Bore Inc ....G 212 674-7128
New York *(G-12003)*
▼ Selectrode Industries Inc ....D 631 547-5470
Huntington Station *(G-6723)*
Sigmund Cohn Corp ....D 914 664-5300
Mount Vernon *(G-8734)*
Sinclair International Company ....E 518 798-2361
Queensbury *(G-14012)*
Star Wire Mesh Fabricators ....G 212 831-4133
New York *(G-12185)*
Sunward Electronics Inc ....F 518 687-0030
Troy *(G-16257)*
Teka Precision Inc ....G 845 753-1900
Nyack *(G-13055)*
Trimtec Inc ....G 516 783-5428
Seaford *(G-15347)*
Trylon Wire & Metal Works Inc ....E 718 542-4472
Bronx *(G-1481)*
Ultra Clarity Corp ....G 719 470-1010
Spring Valley *(G-15604)*
Utility Engineering Co ....F 845 735-8900
Pearl River *(G-13468)*
▲ Weico Wire & Cable Inc ....E 631 254-2970
Edgewood *(G-4621)*

3497 Metal Foil & Leaf

◆ Alufoil Products Co Inc ....F 631 231-4141
Hauppauge *(G-6018)*
▲ American Packaging Corporation ....C 585 254-9500
Rochester *(G-14198)*
De Luxe Packaging Corp ....E 416 754-4633
Saugerties *(G-15183)*
Genesis One Unlimeted ....G 516 208-5863
West Hempstead *(G-16854)*
Oak-Mitsui Inc ....D 518 686-8060
Hoosick Falls *(G-6542)*
▲ Oak-Mitsui Technologies LLC ....E 518 686-4961
Hoosick Falls *(G-6543)*
Pactiv LLC ....C 518 793-2524
Glens Falls *(G-5695)*
Quick Roll Leaf Mfg Co Inc ....E 845 457-1500
Montgomery *(G-8601)*
Steel Partners Holdings LP ....E 212 520-2300
New York *(G-12189)*
Thermal Process Cnstr Co ....E 631 293-6400
Farmingdale *(G-5129)*
Tri-State Food Jobbers Inc ....G 718 921-1211
Brooklyn *(G-2678)*
◆ Vitex Packaging Group Inc ....F 212 265-6575
New York *(G-12557)*

3498 Fabricated Pipe & Pipe Fittings

Accord Pipe Fabricators Inc ....E 718 657-3900
Jamaica *(G-6892)*
Advanced Thermal Systems Inc ....E 716 681-1800
Lancaster *(G-7298)*
Albany Nipple and Pipe Mfg ....E 518 270-2162
Troy *(G-16218)*
▲ Arcadia Mfg Group Inc ....E 518 434-6213
Green Island *(G-5853)*
Arcadia Mfg Group Inc ....G 518 434-6213
Menands *(G-8367)*
▲ Cobey Inc ....D 716 362-9550
Buffalo *(G-2877)*
Coventry Manufacturing Co Inc ....E 914 668-2212
Mount Vernon *(G-8674)*
Cwr Manufacturing Corporation ....D 315 437-1032
East Syracuse *(G-4521)*
D & G Welding Inc ....G 716 873-3088
Buffalo *(G-2899)*
Daikin Applied Americas Inc ....D 315 253-2771
Auburn *(G-491)*
Falcon Perspectives Inc ....G 718 706-9168
Long Island City *(G-7737)*
▲ Fixture Hardware Mfg Corp ....E 718 499-9422
Brooklyn *(G-1980)*
Flatcut LLC ....G 212 542-5732
Brooklyn *(G-1983)*
Greene Technologies Inc ....D 607 656-4166
Greene *(G-5866)*
H & H Metal Specialty Inc ....E 716 665-2110
Jamestown *(G-6997)*
J D Steward Inc ....G 718 358-0169
Flushing *(G-5256)*
James Woerner Inc ....G 631 454-9330
Farmingdale *(G-5016)*
▲ Juniper Elbow Co Inc ....C 718 326-2546
Middle Village *(G-8414)*
▲ Juniper Industries Florida Inc ....G 718 326-2546
Middle Village *(G-8415)*
▲ Leo International Inc ....E 718 290-8005
Brooklyn *(G-2213)*
◆ Leroy Plastics Inc ....D 585 768-8158
Le Roy *(G-7413)*
Long Island Pipe Supply Inc ....G 718 456-7877
Flushing *(G-5267)*
Long Island Pipe Supply Inc ....G 518 270-2159
Troy *(G-16222)*
Long Island Pipe Supply Inc ....E 516 222-8008
Garden City *(G-5516)*
M Manastrip-M Corporation ....G 518 664-2089
Clifton Park *(G-3699)*
Met Weld International LLC ....D 518 765-2318
Altamont *(G-210)*
Micromold Products Inc ....E 914 969-2850
Yonkers *(G-17467)*
Ram Fabricating LLC ....E 315 437-6654
Syracuse *(G-16017)*
Rochester Tube Fabricators ....G 585 254-0290
Rochester *(G-14653)*
▲ Spinco Metal Products Inc ....D 315 331-6285
Newark *(G-12743)*
Standex Air Dist Pdts Inc ....E 585 798-0300
Medina *(G-8283)*
Star Tubing Corp ....G 716 483-1703
Jamestown *(G-7031)*
Tag Flange & Machining Inc ....G 516 536-1300
Oceanside *(G-13100)*
Truly Tubular Fitting Corp ....F 914 664-8686
Mount Vernon *(G-8742)*
Tube Fabrication Company Inc ....F 716 673-1871
Fredonia *(G-5375)*
Wedco Fabrications Inc ....G 718 852-6330
College Point *(G-3810)*

3499 Fabricated Metal Prdts, NEC

901 D LLC ....E 845 369-1111
Airmont *(G-11)*
▲ A - Mic Corporation ....F 909 598-1814
Niagara Falls *(G-12793)*
A D Mfg Corp ....F 516 352-6161
Floral Park *(G-5189)*
▲ Access Display Group Inc ....F 516 678-7772
Freeport *(G-5380)*
Albany Mtal Fbrcation Holdings ....G 518 463-5161
Albany *(G-42)*
Alpine Paper Box Co Inc ....E 718 345-4040
Brooklyn *(G-1595)*
American Standard Mfg Inc ....E 518 868-2512
Central Bridge *(G-3482)*
Aquarium Pump & Piping Systems ....F 631 567-5555
Sayville *(G-15203)*
▲ Arnold Magnetic Tech Corp ....C 585 385-9010
Rochester *(G-14211)*
Atech-Seh Metal Fabricator ....E 716 895-8888
Buffalo *(G-2821)*
Backyard Fence Inc ....F 518 452-9496
Albany *(G-51)*
Brakewell Stl Fabricators Inc ....E 845 469-9131
Chester *(G-3601)*
Bristol Gift Co Inc ....F 845 496-2821
Washingtonville *(G-16598)*
Brooklyn Cstm Met Fbrction Inc ....G 718 499-1573
Brooklyn *(G-1724)*
Brzozka Industries Inc ....F 631 588-8164
Holbrook *(G-6434)*
Buttons & Trimcom Inc ....F 212 868-1971
New York *(G-9484)*
C & M Products Inc ....G 315 471-3303
Syracuse *(G-15880)*
▲ Carpentier Industries LLC ....F 585 385-5550
East Rochester *(G-4455)*
CC Family LLC ....F 516 666-8116
Brooklyn *(G-1766)*
◆ Chapin International Inc ....C 585 343-3140
Batavia *(G-627)*
◆ Chapin Manufacturing Inc ....C 585 343-3140
Batavia *(G-628)*
▲ Classic Medallics Inc ....E 718 392-5410
Mount Vernon *(G-8672)*
Cleveland Polymer Tech LLC ....G 518 326-9146
Watervliet *(G-16682)*
Consolidated Barricades Inc ....G 518 922-7944
Fultonville *(G-5478)*
Criterion Bell & Specialty ....E 718 788-2600
Brooklyn *(G-1819)*
▲ Crown Industries Inc ....F 973 672-2277
New York *(G-9759)*
Crystalizations Systems Inc ....F 631 467-0090
Holbrook *(G-6441)*
Custom Frame & Molding Co ....F 631 491-9091
West Babylon *(G-16786)*
Di Highway Sign Structure Corp ....E 315 736-8312
New York Mills *(G-12721)*
Dimar Manufacturing Corp ....C 716 759-0351
Clarence *(G-3656)*
Dobrin Industries Inc ....G 800 353-2229
Lockport *(G-7581)*
Elias Artmetal Inc ....F 516 873-7501
Mineola *(G-8507)*
Empire Metal Finishing Inc ....E 718 545-6700
Astoria *(G-440)*
Fabritex Inc ....G 706 376-6584
New York *(G-10124)*
Factory East ....E 718 280-1558
Brooklyn *(G-1952)*
Finger Lakes Conveyors Inc ....G 315 539-9246
Waterloo *(G-16625)*
Frame Shoppe & Art Gallery ....G 516 365-6014
Manhasset *(G-8060)*
Galmer Ltd ....G 718 392-4609
Long Island City *(G-7748)*
◆ Gardall Safe Corporation ....E 315 432-9115
Syracuse *(G-15947)*
▲ Garment Care Systems LLC ....G 518 674-1826
Averill Park *(G-534)*
Gcm Steel Products Inc ....F 718 386-3346
Brooklyn *(G-2016)*
◆ Gibraltar Industries Inc ....D 716 826-6500
Buffalo *(G-2974)*
◆ Hannay Reels Inc ....C 518 797-3791
Westerlo *(G-17042)*
Hatfield Metal Fab Inc ....E 845 454-9078
Poughkeepsie *(G-13906)*
▲ Icestone LLC ....E 718 624-4900
Brooklyn *(G-2095)*
▲ Inter Pacific Consulting Corp ....G 718 460-2787
Flushing *(G-5252)*
James D Rubino Inc ....E 631 244-8730
Bohemia *(G-1080)*
JE Monahan Fabrications LLC ....F 518 761-0414
Queensbury *(G-14001)*
▼ Jordan Panel Systems Corp ....E 631 754-4900
East Northport *(G-4439)*
▲ Kefa Industries Group Inc ....G 718 568-9297
Rego Park *(G-14034)*
Kwong CHI Metal Fabrication ....G 718 369-6429
Brooklyn *(G-2184)*
L D Flecken Inc ....F 631 777-4881
Yaphank *(G-17396)*
Machinery Mountings Inc ....F 631 851-0480
Hauppauge *(G-6123)*
Magnaworks Technology Inc ....G 631 218-3431
Bohemia *(G-1100)*
▲ Magnetic Aids Inc ....G 845 863-1400
Newburgh *(G-12766)*
▲ Materion Brewster LLC ....D 845 279-0900
Brewster *(G-1223)*
▲ Maximum Security Products Corp ....E 518 233-1800
Waterford *(G-16613)*
McD Metals LLC ....F 518 456-9694
Albany *(G-100)*
▼ Metallic Ladder Mfg Corp ....F 716 358-6201
Randolph *(G-14016)*
MMC Magnetics Corp ....F 631 435-9888
Hauppauge *(G-6141)*
National Maint Contg Corp ....D 716 285-1583
Niagara Falls *(G-12849)*
New Dimension Awards Inc ....G 718 236-8200
Brooklyn *(G-2360)*
New York Manufactured Products ....F 585 254-9353
Rochester *(G-14532)*
Noll Reynolds Met Fabrication ....G 315 422-3333
Syracuse *(G-15999)*
▲ Nrd LLC ....E 716 773-7634
Grand Island *(G-5764)*
PBL Industries Corp ....F 631 979-4266
Smithtown *(G-15493)*
Peak Motion Inc ....G 716 534-4925
Clarence *(G-3668)*
▲ Peelle Company ....G 631 231-6000
Hauppauge *(G-6159)*
Petro Moore Manufacturing Corp ....G 718 784-2516
Long Island City *(G-7841)*
Picture Perfect Framing ....G 718 851-1884
Brooklyn *(G-2418)*
▲ Polymag Inc ....E 631 286-4111
Bellport *(G-839)*

SIC

Employee Codes: A=Over 500 employees, B=251-500
C=101-250, D=51-100, E=20-50, F=10-19, G=5-9
2017 Harris
New York Manufacturers Directory
821

34 FABRICATED METAL PRODUCTS, EXCEPT MACHINERY AND TRANSPORTATION EQUIPMENT

▲ Precision Magnetics LLC .... E 585 385-9010
  Rochester *(G-14596)*
Precision Spclty Fbrctions LLC .... E 716 824-2108
  Buffalo *(G-3134)*
Range Repair Warehouse .... G 585 235-0980
  Penfield *(G-13502)*
Raytech Corp Asbestos Personal 516 747-0300
  Mineola *(G-8533)*
Raytech Corporation .... G 718 259-7388
  Woodbury *(G-17297)*
Reelcology Inc .... F 845 258-1880
  Pine Island *(G-13553)*
Romac Electronics Inc .... E 516 349-7900
  Plainview *(G-13632)*
▲ Rush Gold Manufacturing Ltd ...... D 516 781-3155
  Bellmore *(G-820)*
▲ Saratoga Trunk and Furniture ..... F 518 463-3252
  Albany *(G-130)*
Schwab Corp .... E 585 381-4900
  Rochester *(G-14675)*
Schwab Corp .... C 812 547-2956
  Rochester *(G-14676)*
▲ Sono-Tek Corporation .... D 845 795-2020
  Milton *(G-8484)*
Split Rock Trading Co Inc .... G 631 929-3261
  Wading River *(G-16526)*
▲ Structural Industries Inc .... C 631 471-5200
  Bohemia *(G-1137)*
▲ Stylebuilt Accessories Inc .... F 917 439-0578
  East Rockaway *(G-4472)*
Sunlight US Co Inc .... G 716 826-6500
  Buffalo *(G-3201)*
▲ Technomag Inc .... G 631 246-6142
  East Setauket *(G-4493)*
Thyssenkrupp Materials NA Inc 212 972-8800
  New York *(G-12335)*
Total Metal Resource .... F 718 384-7818
  Brooklyn *(G-2669)*
Trine Rolled Moulding Corp .... E 718 828-5200
  Bronx *(G-1478)*
◆ Truebite Inc .... E 607 785-7664
  Vestal *(G-16455)*
Ulster County Iron Works LLC 845 255-0003
  New Paltz *(G-8880)*
Win-Holt Equipment Corp 516 222-0433
  Garden City *(G-5537)*
▲ Wtbi Inc .... G 631 547-1993
  Huntington Station *(G-6729)*

35 INDUSTRIAL AND COMMERCIAL MACHINERY AND COMPUTER EQUIPMENT

3511 Steam, Gas & Hydraulic Turbines & Engines

Atlantic Projects Company Inc .... F 518 878-2065
  Clifton Park *(G-3696)*
Awr Energy Inc .... F 585 469-7750
  Plattsburgh *(G-13652)*
Beowawe Binary LLC .... E 646 829-3900
  New York *(G-9362)*
▲ Cooper Turbocompressor Inc ..... B 716 896-6600
  Buffalo *(G-2890)*
▲ Corfu Machine Inc .... E 585 418-4083
  Corfu *(G-3953)*
Dresser-Rand Group Inc .... D 716 375-3000
  Olean *(G-13144)*
Dresser-Rand LLC .... A 585 596-3100
  Wellsville *(G-16751)*
Frontier Hydraulics Corp .... F 716 694-2070
  Buffalo *(G-2958)*
▲ Gas Turbine Controls Corp 914 693-0830
  Hawthorne *(G-6247)*
GE Global Research .... G 518 387-5000
  Niskayuna *(G-12894)*
GE Transportation Eng Systems .... F 518 258-9276
  Schenectady *(G-15256)*
General Electric Company .... B 518 385-2211
  Schenectady *(G-15258)*
General Electric Company .... B 518 385-3716
  Schenectady *(G-15259)*
General Electric Company .... B 203 373-2756
  Schenectady *(G-15260)*
General Electric Company .... B 518 385-2211
  Schenectady *(G-15261)*
General Electric Company 315 456-7901
  Liverpool *(G-7520)*

General Electric Company .... B 518 387-5000
  Schenectady *(G-15262)*
General Electric Company .... G 518 385-3439
  Schenectady *(G-15263)*
General Electric Company .... A 518 385-4022
  Schenectady *(G-15257)*
General Electric Company .... E 518 385-7620
  Niskayuna *(G-12895)*
▲ Hdm Hydraulics LLC .... D 716 694-8004
  Tonawanda *(G-16170)*
Ingersoll-Rand Company .... E 716 896-6600
  Buffalo *(G-3008)*
▲ Mannesmann Corporation .... D 212 258-4000
  New York *(G-11136)*
Mission Critical Energy Inc .... G 716 276-8465
  Getzville *(G-5600)*
Omega Industries & Development .. E 516 349-8010
  Plainview *(G-13625)*
Siemens Government Tech Inc ...... C 585 593-1234
  Wellsville *(G-16759)*
Signa Chemistry Inc .... F 212 933-4101
  New York *(G-12071)*
▲ Stork H & E Turbo Blading Inc ... C 607 277-4968
  Ithaca *(G-6876)*
Tgp Flying Cloud Holdings LLC ..... E 646 829-3900
  New York *(G-12308)*
Turbine Engine Comp Utica .... A 315 768-8070
  Whitesboro *(G-17197)*
Turbo Machined Products LLC ...... E 315 895-3010
  Frankfort *(G-5358)*
Tuthill Corporation .... B 631 727-1097
  Riverhead *(G-14158)*
Weaver Wind Energy LLC .... G 607 379-9463
  Freeville *(G-5437)*
Wind Products Inc 212 292-3135
  Brooklyn *(G-2756)*
Worldwide Gas Turbine Pdts Inc ... G 518 877-7200
  Clifton Park *(G-3711)*

3519 Internal Combustion Engines, NEC

AB Engine .... G 518 557-3510
  Latham *(G-7351)*
Briggs & Stratton Corporation .... F 315 495-0100
  Sherrill *(G-15404)*
Briggs & Stratton Corporation .... C 315 495-0100
  Munnsville *(G-8749)*
Cummins - Allison Corp .... D 718 263-2482
  Kew Gardens *(G-7159)*
◆ Cummins Inc .... D 716 456-2676
  Lakewood *(G-7289)*
Cummins Inc .... A 716 456-2111
  Lakewood *(G-7290)*
Cummins Inc .... B 812 377-5000
  Jamestown *(G-6986)*
Cummins Inc .... B 718 892-2400
  Bronx *(G-1306)*
Cummins Northeast LLC .... E 315 437-2296
  Syracuse *(G-15915)*
D & W Diesel Inc .... F 518 437-1300
  Latham *(G-7359)*
Jack W Miller .... G 585 538-2399
  Scottsville *(G-15337)*
▲ Mannesmann Corporation .... D 212 258-4000
  New York *(G-11136)*
Omega Industries & Development .. E 516 349-8010
  Plainview *(G-13625)*
Perkins International Inc .... G 309 675-1000
  Buffalo *(G-3121)*
Washer Solutions Inc .... F 585 742-6388
  Victor *(G-16513)*

3523 Farm Machinery & Eqpt

Asp Blade Intrmdate Hldngs Inc .... G 212 476-8000
  New York *(G-9234)*
Bdp Industries Inc .... E 518 695-6851
  Greenwich *(G-5886)*
◆ Chapin Manufacturing Inc .... C 585 343-3140
  Batavia *(G-628)*
◆ Chapin Watermatics Inc .... D 315 782-1170
  Watertown *(G-16643)*
Don Beck Inc .... G 585 493-3040
  Castile *(G-3416)*
Eastern Welding Inc .... G 631 727-0306
  Riverhead *(G-14142)*
◆ Fountainhead Group Inc .... C 315 736-0037
  New York Mills *(G-12722)*
Good Earth Organics Corp .... E 716 684-8111
  Lancaster *(G-7318)*
Haines Equipment Inc .... E 607 566-8531
  Avoca *(G-537)*

House of The Foaming Case Inc ... G 718 454-0101
  Saint Albans *(G-15083)*
Moffett Turf Equipment Inc 585 334-0100
  West Henrietta *(G-16885)*
▲ Oxbo International Corporation .. D 585 548-2665
  Byron *(G-3269)*
P & D Equipment Sales LLC 585 343-2394
  Alexander *(G-189)*
Plant-Tech2o Inc 516 483-7845
  Hempstead *(G-6285)*
Renaldos Sales and Service Ctr 716 337-3760
  North Collins *(G-12931)*
Richard Stewart 518 632-5363
  Hartford *(G-5996)*
Road Cases USA Inc 631 563-0633
  Bohemia *(G-1126)*
Westmoor Ltd .... F 315 363-1500
  Sherrill *(G-15410)*
Zappala Farms AG Systems Inc 315 626-6293
  Cato *(G-3425)*

3524 Garden, Lawn Tractors & Eqpt

Benishty Brothers Corp .... G 646 339-9991
  Woodmere *(G-17311)*
Briggs & Stratton Corporation .... C 315 495-0100
  Munnsville *(G-8749)*
Cazenovia Equipment Co Inc .... G 315 736-0898
  Clinton *(G-3717)*
◆ Chapin International Inc .... C 585 343-3140
  Batavia *(G-627)*
◆ Chapin Manufacturing Inc .... C 585 343-3140
  Batavia *(G-628)*
Clopay Ames True Tmper Hldng ... F 516 938-5544
  Jericho *(G-7062)*
▲ Eaton Brothers Corp .... G 716 649-8250
  Hamburg *(G-5922)*
Fradan Manufacturing Corp .... F 914 632-3653
  New Rochelle *(G-8902)*
◆ Kadco Auto Inc 518 661-6068
  Mayfield *(G-8213)*
Real Bark Mulch LLC 518 747-3650
  Fort Edward *(G-5345)*
Rhett M Clark Inc 585 538-9570
  Caledonia *(G-3281)*
Saxby Implement Corp .... F 585 624-2938
  Mendon *(G-8382)*
Victoire Latam Asset MGT LLC ...... F 212 319-6550
  New York *(G-12538)*

3531 Construction Machinery & Eqpt

▲ AAAA York Inc .... F 718 784-6666
  Long Island City *(G-7645)*
Air-Flo Mfg Co Inc .... D 607 733-8284
  Elmira *(G-4670)*
Anderson Equipment Company ..... D 716 877-1992
  Tonawanda *(G-16139)*
Applied Technology Mfg Corp .... E 607 687-2200
  Owego *(G-13350)*
Asp Blade Intrmdate Hldngs Inc .... G 212 476-8000
  New York *(G-9234)*
▲ BW Elliott Mfg Co LLC .... B 607 772-0404
  Binghamton *(G-900)*
Capitol Eq 2 LLC .... G 518 886-8341
  Saratoga Springs *(G-15148)*
CCS Machinery Inc .... F 631 968-0900
  Bay Shore *(G-681)*
Ceno Technologies Inc .... G 716 885-5050
  Buffalo *(G-2869)*
Cives Corporation .... D 315 543-2321
  Harrisville *(G-5995)*
Cooper Industries LLC .... E 315 477-7000
  Syracuse *(G-15909)*
Crane Equipment & Service Inc .... G 716 689-5400
  Amherst *(G-235)*
Dave Sandel Cranes Inc .... G 631 325-5588
  Westhampton *(G-17056)*
Diamond Coring & Cutting Inc ..... G 718 381-4545
  Maspeth *(G-8130)*
◆ Dover Global Holdings Inc .... E 212 922-1640
  New York *(G-9912)*
Drillco National Group Inc .... E 718 726-9801
  Long Island City *(G-7718)*
Eric S Hapeman 716 731-5416
  Niagara Falls *(G-12815)*
ET Oakes Corporation .... E 631 630-9837
  Hauppauge *(G-6074)*
G C Castings Inc .... F 607 432-4518
  Oneonta *(G-13187)*
Gei International Inc .... E 315 463-9261
  East Syracuse *(G-4533)*

Hansteel (usa) Inc.....G..... 212 226-0105
New York *(G-10411)*
Highway Garage.....G..... 518 568-2837
Saint Johnsville *(G-15096)*
Industrial Handling Svcs Inc.....G..... 518 399-0488
Alplaus *(G-205)*
Kinedyne Inc.....F..... 716 667-6833
Orchard Park *(G-13278)*
▲ Kinshofer Usa Inc.....F..... 716 731-4333
Sanborn *(G-15123)*
Kyntec Corporation.....G..... 716 810-6956
Buffalo *(G-3038)*
Line Ward Corporation.....G..... 716 675-7373
Buffalo *(G-3049)*
Lomin Construction Company.....G..... 516 759-5734
Glen Head *(G-5636)*
Mettle Concept Inc.....G..... 888 501-0680
New York *(G-11243)*
Midland Machinery Co Inc.....D..... 716 692-1200
Tonawanda *(G-16181)*
Mike Wilke.....G..... 585 482-5230
Webster *(G-16727)*
▲ Munson Machinery Company Inc.....E..... 315 797-0090
Utica *(G-16350)*
New Eagle Silo Corp.....G..... 585 492-1300
Arcade *(G-398)*
Oneida Sales & Service Inc.....E..... 716 822-8205
Buffalo *(G-3101)*
Oneida Sales & Service Inc.....F..... 716 270-0433
Lackawanna *(G-7245)*
▲ Oswald Manufacturing Co Inc.....E..... 516 883-8850
Port Washington *(G-13849)*
◆ Ozteck Industries Inc.....E..... 516 883-8857
Port Washington *(G-13850)*
Park Ave Bldg & Roofg Sups LLC.....E..... 718 403-0100
Brooklyn *(G-2407)*
Patterson Blacktop Corp.....G..... 845 628-3425
Carmel *(G-3403)*
Pauls Rods & Restos Inc.....G..... 631 665-7637
Deer Park *(G-4187)*
Peckham Materials Corp.....E..... 518 747-3353
Hudson Falls *(G-6649)*
Penn Can Equipment Corporation.....G..... 315 378-0337
Lyons *(G-7974)*
Penn State Metal Fabri.....G..... 718 786-8814
Brooklyn *(G-2415)*
Pier-Tech Inc.....E..... 516 442-5420
Oceanside *(G-13089)*
▲ Precision Product Inc.....G..... 718 852-7127
Brooklyn *(G-2436)*
Presti Ready Mix Concrete Inc.....G..... 516 378-6006
Freeport *(G-5419)*
Primoplast Inc.....F..... 631 750-0680
Bohemia *(G-1121)*
Pro-Tech Wldg Fabrication Inc.....E..... 585 436-9855
Rochester *(G-14603)*
▲ Professional Pavers Corp.....E..... 718 784-7853
Rego Park *(G-14039)*
Railworks Transit Systems Inc.....E..... 212 502-7900
New York *(G-11788)*
Rapistak Corporation.....G..... 716 822-2804
Blasdell *(G-964)*
Rochester Asphalt Materials.....G..... 315 524-4619
Walworth *(G-16551)*
S R & R Industries Inc.....G..... 845 692-8329
Middletown *(G-8461)*
▲ Schutte-Buffalo Hammermill LLC.....E..... 716 855-1202
Buffalo *(G-3178)*
Seville Central Mix Corp.....D..... 516 293-6190
Old Bethpage *(G-13130)*
Sierson Crane & Welding Inc.....G..... 315 723-6914
Westmoreland *(G-17066)*
T S P Corp.....F..... 585 768-6769
Le Roy *(G-7419)*
Technopaving New York Inc.....G..... 631 351-6472
Huntington Station *(G-6725)*
Town of Ohio.....E..... 315 392-2055
Forestport *(G-5332)*
Vanhouten Motorsports.....G..... 315 387-6312
Lacona *(G-7252)*
X-Treme Ready Mix Inc.....G..... 718 739-3384
Jamaica *(G-6965)*
Ziegler Truck & Diesl Repr Inc.....G..... 315 782-7278
Watertown *(G-16676)*

3532 Mining Machinery & Eqpt

American Material Processing.....G..... 315 318-0017
Clifton Springs *(G-3713)*
▲ Drillco Equipment Co Inc.....E..... 718 777-5986
Long Island City *(G-7717)*
Flatcut LLC.....G..... 212 542-5732
Brooklyn *(G-1983)*
Gbt Global.....E..... 718 593-9698
New York *(G-10258)*
Lawson M Whiting Inc.....G..... 315 986-3064
Macedon *(G-7988)*
▲ Munson Machinery Company Inc.....E..... 315 797-0090
Utica *(G-16350)*
Universal Metal Fabricators.....F..... 845 331-8248
Kingston *(G-7221)*

3533 Oil Field Machinery & Eqpt

Anchor Commerce Trading Corp.....G..... 516 881-3485
Atlantic Beach *(G-468)*
Basin Holdings US LLC.....E..... 212 695-7376
New York *(G-9332)*
◆ Blue Tee Corp.....G..... 212 598-0880
New York *(G-9422)*
◆ Derrick Corporation.....C..... 716 683-9010
Buffalo *(G-2909)*
Derrick Corporation.....C..... 716 685-4892
Cheektowaga *(G-3567)*
▲ Desmi-Afti Inc.....E..... 716 662-0632
Orchard Park *(G-13269)*
Schlumberger Technology Corp.....C..... 607 378-0200
Horseheads *(G-6592)*
Smith International Inc.....F..... 585 265-2330
Ontario *(G-13215)*

3534 Elevators & Moving Stairways

◆ A & D Entrances LLC.....F..... 718 989-2441
Jamaica *(G-6890)*
Access Elevator & Lift Inc.....G..... 716 483-3696
Jamestown *(G-6967)*
◆ Allround Logistics Inc.....G..... 718 544-8945
Forest Hills *(G-5321)*
An Excelsior Elevator Corp.....F..... 516 408-3070
Westbury *(G-16968)*
Ankom Development LLC.....G..... 315 986-1937
Macedon *(G-7980)*
Bhi Elevator Cabs Inc.....F..... 516 431-5665
Island Park *(G-6778)*
Big Apple Elevtr Srv & Consult.....G..... 212 279-0700
New York *(G-9391)*
CEC Elevator Cab Corp.....D..... 718 328-3632
Bronx *(G-1292)*
◆ Dover Global Holdings Inc.....E..... 212 922-1640
New York *(G-9912)*
Dural Door Company Inc.....F..... 718 729-1333
Long Island City *(G-7720)*
E Z Entry Doors Inc.....F..... 716 434-3440
Lockport *(G-7583)*
Eag Electric Inc.....G..... 201 376-5103
Staten Island *(G-15669)*
Eazylift Albany LLC.....G..... 518 452-6929
Latham *(G-7361)*
Elevator Accessories Mfg.....F..... 914 739-7004
Peekskill *(G-13477)*
Elevator Ventures Corporation.....D..... 212 375-1900
Ozone Park *(G-13377)*
Herbert Wolf Corp.....G..... 212 242-0300
New York *(G-10461)*
Interface Products Co Inc.....G..... 631 242-4605
Bay Shore *(G-707)*
Island Custom Stairs Inc.....G..... 631 205-5335
Medford *(G-8251)*
Keystone Iron & Wire Works Inc.....G..... 718 392-1616
Long Island City *(G-7781)*
Kinglift Elevator Inc.....G..... 917 923-3517
New York *(G-10854)*
▲ Monitor Elevator Products LLC.....D..... 631 543-4334
Hauppauge *(G-6143)*
▲ National Elev Cab & Door Corp.....E..... 718 478-5900
Woodside *(G-17340)*
Otis Elevator Company.....F..... 315 736-0167
Yorkville *(G-17526)*
Otis Elevator Company.....E..... 917 339-9600
New York *(G-11535)*
Otis Elevator Company.....F..... 914 375-7800
Yonkers *(G-17472)*
Otis Elevator Company.....E..... 518 426-4006
Albany *(G-112)*
Palmer Industries Inc.....G..... 607 754-8741
Endicott *(G-4822)*
Rokon Tech LLC.....G..... 718 429-0729
Elmhurst *(G-4667)*
S & H Enterprises Inc.....G..... 888 323-8755
Queensbury *(G-14010)*
Schindler Elevator Corporation.....C..... 212 708-1000
New York *(G-11987)*
Schindler Elevator Corporation.....C..... 718 417-3131
Glendale *(G-5662)*
Schindler Elevator Corporation.....D..... 516 860-1321
Hicksville *(G-6392)*
Schindler Elevator Corporation.....E..... 800 225-3123
New York *(G-11988)*
▲ Sgl Services Corp.....F..... 718 630-0392
New York *(G-12036)*
Thyssenkrupp Elevator Corp.....D..... 212 268-2020
New York *(G-12334)*
Velis Associates Inc.....G..... 631 225-4220
Lindenhurst *(G-7491)*

3535 Conveyors & Eqpt

4695 Main Street Snyder Inc.....G..... 716 833-3270
Buffalo *(G-2789)*
American Material Processing.....G..... 315 318-0017
Clifton Springs *(G-3713)*
▲ Chemprene Inc.....C..... 845 831-2800
Beacon *(G-782)*
▲ Chemprene Holding Inc.....C..... 845 831-2800
Beacon *(G-783)*
◆ Columbus McKinnon Corporation.....C..... 716 689-5400
Getzville *(G-5595)*
Columbus McKinnon Corporation.....C..... 716 689-5400
Getzville *(G-5597)*
Columbus McKinnon Corporation.....C..... 716 689-5400
Getzville *(G-5598)*
▲ Dairy Conveyor Corp.....D..... 845 278-7878
Brewster *(G-1215)*
▲ Desmi-Afti Inc.....E..... 716 662-0632
Orchard Park *(G-13269)*
General Splice Corporation.....G..... 914 271-5131
Croton On Hudson *(G-4063)*
Glasgow Products Inc.....E..... 516 374-5937
Woodmere *(G-17313)*
▲ Greenbelt Industries Inc.....E..... 800 668-1114
Buffalo *(G-2983)*
Haines Equipment Inc.....E..... 607 566-8531
Avoca *(G-537)*
Hohl Machine & Conveyor Co Inc.....E..... 716 882-7210
Buffalo *(G-2996)*
▼ I J White Corporation.....D..... 631 293-3788
Farmingdale *(G-5009)*
International Robotics Inc.....F..... 914 630-1060
Larchmont *(G-7350)*
▲ J D Handling Systems Inc.....F..... 518 828-9676
Ghent *(G-5607)*
Joldeson One Aerospace Inds.....D..... 718 848-7396
Ozone Park *(G-13380)*
Northeast Conveyors Inc.....F..... 585 768-8912
Lima *(G-7446)*
Noto Industrial Corp.....G..... 631 736-7600
Coram *(G-3948)*
Raymond Corporation.....E..... 315 643-5000
East Syracuse *(G-4557)*
◆ Raymond Corporation.....A..... 607 656-2311
Greene *(G-5869)*
Re-Al Industrial Corp.....G..... 716 542-4556
Akron *(G-28)*
▲ Renold Inc.....D..... 716 326-3121
Westfield *(G-17051)*
▲ Rlp Holdings Inc.....G..... 716 852-0832
Buffalo *(G-3159)*
Rota Pack Inc.....F..... 631 274-1037
Farmingdale *(G-5103)*
Service Specialties Inc.....G..... 716 822-7706
Buffalo *(G-3185)*
Shako Inc.....G..... 315 437-1294
East Syracuse *(G-4563)*
Speedways Conveyors Inc.....E..... 716 893-2222
Buffalo *(G-3195)*
Troy Industrial Solutions.....D..... 518 272-4920
Watervliet *(G-16690)*
United Rbotic Integrations LLC.....G..... 716 683-8334
Alden *(G-185)*
▲ Ward Industrial Equipment Inc.....G..... 716 856-6966
Buffalo *(G-3247)*

3536 Hoists, Cranes & Monorails

◆ Columbus McKinnon Corporation.....C..... 716 689-5400
Getzville *(G-5595)*
Columbus McKinnon Corporation.....D..... 716 689-5400
Amherst *(G-234)*
Columbus McKinnon Corporation.....C..... 716 689-5400
Getzville *(G-5597)*
Columbus McKinnon Corporation.....C..... 716 689-5400
Getzville *(G-5598)*
Debrucque Cleveland Tramrail S.....G..... 315 697-5160
Canastota *(G-3366)*

SIC

Employee Codes: A=Over 500 employees, B=251-500
C=101-250, D=51-100, E=20-50, F=10-19, G=5-9
2017 Harris
New York Manufacturers Directory
823

Dun-Rite Spclized Carriers LLC ... F ... 718 991-1100 — Bronx *(G-1319)*
▲ Gorbel Inc ... C ... 585 924-6262 — Fishers *(G-5178)*
Gorbel Inc ... D ... 585 924-6262 — Fishers *(G-5179)*
Gorbel Inc ... F ... 800 821-0086 — Victor *(G-16480)*
Kleinfelder John ... G ... 716 753-3163 — Mayville *(G-8216)*
Konecranes Inc ... F ... 585 359-4450 — Henrietta *(G-6295)*
▲ Mannesmann Corporation ... D ... 212 258-4000 — New York *(G-11136)*
Marros Equipment & Trucks ... F ... 315 539-8702 — Waterloo *(G-16630)*
▲ Mohawk Resources Ltd ... D ... 518 842-1431 — Amsterdam *(G-359)*
Reimann & Georger Corporation ... E ... 716 895-1156 — Buffalo *(G-3156)*
T Shore Products Ltd ... G ... 315 252-9174 — Auburn *(G-522)*
Thego Corporation ... G ... 631 776-2472 — Bellport *(G-841)*
▼ US Hoists Corp ... G ... 631 472-3030 — Calverton *(G-3302)*
Vortek Tel 87724633365859 ... E ... 585 924-5000 — Victor *(G-16511)*

3537 Indl Trucks, Tractors, Trailers & Stackers

Arlington Equipment Corp ... G ... 518 798-5867 — Queensbury *(G-13992)*
Arpac LLC ... F ... 315 471-5103 — Syracuse *(G-15858)*
Artcraft Building Services ... G ... 845 895-3893 — Wallkill *(G-16541)*
ASAP Rack Rental Inc ... G ... 718 499-4495 — Brooklyn *(G-1638)*
Atlantic Engineer Products LLC ... E ... 518 822-1800 — Hudson *(G-6607)*
B & J Delivers Inc ... G ... 631 524-5550 — Brentwood *(G-1177)*
▲ Channel Manufacturing Inc ... E ... 516 944-6271 — Port Washington *(G-13804)*
◆ Columbus McKinnon Corporation ... C ... 716 689-5400 — Getzville *(G-5595)*
Columbus McKinnon Corporation ... C ... 716 689-5400 — Getzville *(G-5597)*
Columbus McKinnon Corporation ... C ... 716 689-5400 — Getzville *(G-5598)*
▲ Continental Lift Truck Inc ... F ... 718 738-4738 — South Ozone Park *(G-15532)*
Crown Equipment Corporation ... D ... 516 822-5100 — Hicksville *(G-6338)*
▼ Devin Mfg Inc ... F ... 585 496-5770 — Arcade *(G-391)*
Dl Manufacturing Inc ... E ... 315 432-8977 — North Syracuse *(G-12942)*
◆ Ducon Technologies Inc ... F ... 631 694-1700 — New York *(G-9937)*
Ducon Technologies Inc ... E ... 631 420-4900 — Farmingdale *(G-4979)*
E-One Inc ... D ... 716 646-6790 — Hamburg *(G-5921)*
Elramida Holdings Inc ... F ... 646 280-0503 — Brooklyn *(G-1915)*
Jamestown Industrial Trcks Inc ... F ... 716 893-6105 — Buffalo *(G-3014)*
Jasper Transport LLC ... G ... 315 729-5760 — Penn Yan *(G-13515)*
◆ Koke Inc ... E ... 800 535-5303 — Queensbury *(G-14003)*
Meteor Express Inc ... F ... 718 551-9177 — Jamaica *(G-6931)*
Mettler-Toledo Inc ... C ... 607 257-6000 — Ithaca *(G-6860)*
Mil & Mir Steel Products Co ... G ... 718 328-7596 — Bronx *(G-1396)*
Palpross Incorporated ... F ... 845 469-2188 — Selkirk *(G-15357)*
Pb08 Inc ... G ... 347 866-7353 — Hicksville *(G-6385)*
Railex Corp ... D ... 518 347-6040 — Schenectady *(G-15287)*
◆ Raymond Consolidated Corp ... C ... 800 235-7200 — Greene *(G-5868)*
◆ Raymond Corporation ... A ... 607 656-2311 — Greene *(G-5869)*
Raymond Corporation ... C ... 607 656-2311 — East Syracuse *(G-4555)*
Raymond Corporation ... B ... 315 463-5000 — East Syracuse *(G-4556)*
Raymond Corporation ... E ... 315 643-5000 — East Syracuse *(G-4557)*
Raymond Sales Corporation ... G ... 607 656-2311 — Greene *(G-5870)*
Speedways Conveyors Inc ... E ... 716 893-2222 — Buffalo *(G-3195)*
Stanley Industrial Eqp LLC ... G ... 315 656-8733 — Kirkville *(G-7228)*
Ward Lafrance Truck Corp ... F ... 518 893-1865 — Saratoga Springs *(G-15176)*
Win-Holt Equipment Corp ... C ... 516 222-0433 — Garden City *(G-5537)*

3541 Machine Tools: Cutting

Abtex Corporation ... E ... 315 536-7403 — Dresden *(G-4318)*
Adria Machine & Tool Inc ... G ... 585 889-3360 — Scottsville *(G-15332)*
Advanced Machine Design Co Inc ... E ... 716 826-2000 — Buffalo *(G-2800)*
Alpine Machine Inc ... F ... 607 272-1344 — Ithaca *(G-6818)*
▲ Alternative Service Inc ... F ... 631 345-9500 — Yaphank *(G-17385)*
Alton Manufacturing Inc ... D ... 585 458-2600 — Rochester *(G-14194)*
▲ Ascension Industries Inc ... D ... 716 693-9381 — North Tonawanda *(G-12956)*
Aztec Mfg of Rochester ... G ... 585 352-8152 — Spencerport *(G-15565)*
▲ Baldwin Machine Works Inc ... G ... 631 842-9110 — Copiague *(G-3896)*
▲ Brinkman Products Inc ... B ... 585 235-4545 — Rochester *(G-14246)*
Coastel Cable Tools Inc ... E ... 315 471-5361 — Syracuse *(G-15899)*
Connex Grinding & Machining ... G ... 315 946-4340 — Lyons *(G-7971)*
Crowley Fabg Machining Co Inc ... G ... 607 484-0299 — Endicott *(G-4799)*
Dinosaw Inc ... E ... 518 828-9942 — Hudson *(G-6612)*
East Coast Tool & Mfg ... G ... 716 826-5183 — Buffalo *(G-2927)*
Elmira Grinding Works Inc ... F ... 607 734-1579 — Wellsburg *(G-16747)*
Five Star Tool Co Inc ... E ... 585 328-9580 — Rochester *(G-14372)*
Gallery of Machines LLC ... G ... 607 849-6028 — Marathon *(G-8083)*
Gb Aero Engine LLC ... B ... 914 925-9600 — Rye *(G-15057)*
Genco John ... G ... 716 483-5446 — Jamestown *(G-6994)*
◆ Gleason Corporation ... A ... 585 473-1000 — Rochester *(G-14407)*
◆ Gleason Works ... A ... 585 473-1000 — Rochester *(G-14408)*
Graywood Companies Inc ... E ... 585 254-7000 — Rochester *(G-14413)*
H S Assembly Inc ... G ... 585 266-4287 — Rochester *(G-14416)*
Halpern Tool Corp ... G ... 914 633-0038 — New Rochelle *(G-8908)*
◆ Hardinge Inc ... C ... 607 734-2281 — Elmira *(G-4688)*
Hartchrom Inc ... F ... 518 880-0411 — Watervliet *(G-16686)*
High Speed Hammer Company Inc ... F ... 585 266-4287 — Rochester *(G-14436)*
IPC/Razor LLC ... D ... 212 551-4500 — New York *(G-10654)*
Ish Precision Machine Corp ... F ... 718 436-8858 — Brooklyn *(G-2116)*
J Vogler Enterprise LLC ... F ... 585 247-1625 — Rochester *(G-14457)*
Jalex Industries Ltd ... F ... 631 491-5072 — West Babylon *(G-16800)*
Johnson Mch & Fibr Pdts Co Inc ... F ... 716 665-2003 — Jamestown *(G-7014)*
◆ Kps Capital Partners LP ... E ... 212 338-5100 — New York *(G-10883)*
Kyocera Precision Tools Inc ... F ... 607 687-0012 — Owego *(G-13353)*
▲ Lancaster Knives Inc ... E ... 716 683-5050 — Lancaster *(G-7323)*
Link Group Inc ... F ... 718 567-7082 — Brooklyn *(G-2228)*
Lk Industries Inc ... G ... 716 941-9202 — Glenwood *(G-5703)*
▲ Lubow Machine Corp ... F ... 631 226-1700 — Copiague *(G-3911)*
▲ Montrose Equipment Sales Inc ... F ... 718 388-7446 — Brooklyn *(G-2332)*
Mortech Industries Inc ... G ... 845 628-6138 — Mahopac *(G-7998)*
Multimatic Products Inc ... D ... 800 767-7633 — Ronkonkoma *(G-14947)*
▲ Munson Machinery Company Inc ... E ... 315 797-0090 — Utica *(G-16350)*
Myles Tool Company Inc ... E ... 716 731-1300 — Sanborn *(G-15124)*
Nifty Bar Grinding & Cutting ... E ... 585 381-0450 — Penfield *(G-13501)*
▼ Omega Consolidated Corporation ... E ... 585 392-9262 — Hilton *(G-6419)*
P & R Industries Inc ... E ... 585 266-6725 — Rochester *(G-14562)*
▲ Parlec Inc ... C ... 585 425-4400 — Fairport *(G-4868)*
Ppi Corp ... E ... 585 880-7277 — Geneseo *(G-5567)*
▲ Precise Tool & Mfg Inc ... D ... 585 247-0700 — Rochester *(G-14591)*
Producto Corporation ... C ... 716 484-7131 — Jamestown *(G-7024)*
R Steiner Technologies Inc ... E ... 585 425-5912 — Fairport *(G-4875)*
Rapid Precision Machining Inc ... D ... 585 467-0780 — Rochester *(G-14620)*
▲ Rush Machinery Inc ... G ... 585 554-3070 — Rushville *(G-15053)*
▲ S & S Machinery Corp ... E ... 718 492-7400 — Brooklyn *(G-2520)*
S & S Machinery Corp ... E ... 718 492-7400 — Brooklyn *(G-2521)*
Selflock Screw Products Co Inc ... E ... 315 541-4464 — Syracuse *(G-16037)*
Seneca Falls Capital Inc ... G ... 315 568-5804 — Seneca Falls *(G-15368)*
Seneca Falls Machine Tool Co ... D ... 315 568-5804 — Seneca Falls *(G-15369)*
▲ Simmons Machine Tool Corp ... C ... 518 462-5431 — Menands *(G-8378)*
▼ Stephen Bader Company Inc ... F ... 518 753-4456 — Valley Falls *(G-16396)*
Superior Motion Controls Inc ... E ... 516 420-2921 — Farmingdale *(G-5120)*
Swiss Specialties Inc ... F ... 631 567-8800 — Wading River *(G-16527)*
Teka Precision Inc ... G ... 845 753-1900 — Nyack *(G-13055)*
Transport National Dev Inc ... E ... 716 662-0270 — Orchard Park *(G-13299)*
Truemade Products Inc ... G ... 631 981-4755 — Ronkonkoma *(G-14993)*
Verns Machine Co Inc ... E ... 315 926-4223 — Marion *(G-8103)*
Welch Machine Inc ... G ... 585 647-3578 — Rochester *(G-14759)*
▼ World LLC ... F ... 631 940-9121 — Deer Park *(G-4229)*
Zwack Incorporated ... E ... 518 733-5135 — Stephentown *(G-15758)*
Zyp Precision LLC ... G ... 315 539-3667 — Waterloo *(G-16632)*

3542 Machine Tools: Forming

Adaptive Mfg Tech Inc ... E ... 631 580-5400 — Ronkonkoma *(G-14850)*
Advanced Engineered Products ... F ... 631 435-3535 — Bay Shore *(G-666)*
Advanced Machine Design Co Inc ... E ... 716 826-2000 — Buffalo *(G-2800)*
Advantage Metalwork Finshg LLC ... D ... 585 454-0160 — Rochester *(G-14180)*
Alcoa Inc ... F ... 716 358-6451 — Falconer *(G-4890)*
American Racing Headers Inc ... E ... 631 608-1427 — Deer Park *(G-4096)*
Austin Industries Inc ... G ... 585 589-1353 — Albion *(G-162)*
Bars Precision Inc ... F ... 585 742-6380 — Fairport *(G-4846)*
Bdp Industries Inc ... E ... 518 695-6851 — Greenwich *(G-5886)*

SIC SECTION

35 INDUSTRIAL AND COMMERCIAL MACHINERY AND COMPUTER EQUIPMENT

Company	Code	Phone
Brinkman Intl Group Inc — Rochester (G-14245)	G	585 429-5000
Buffalo Machine Tls of Niagara — Lockport (G-7574)	F	716 201-1310
C & T Tool & Instrument Co — Woodside (G-17321)	E	718 429-1253
C J Winter Machine Tech — Rochester (G-14254)	F	585 429-5000
Commodore Manufacutring Corp — Brooklyn (G-1795)	E	718 788-2600
◆ Dover Global Holdings Inc — New York (G-9912)	E	212 922-1640
◆ Ecko Fin & Tooling Inc — Jamestown (G-6990)	F	716 487-0200
Gemcor Automation LLC — West Seneca (G-16946)	D	716 674-9300
▲ Gh Induction Atmospheres LLC — Rochester (G-14402)	E	585 368-2120
High Speed Hammer Company Inc — Rochester (G-14436)	F	585 266-4287
▲ Hydramec Inc — Scio (G-15321)	F	585 593-5190
◆ Kobe Steel USA Holdings Inc — New York (G-10866)	G	212 751-9400
Lourdes Systems Inc — Hauppauge (G-6122)	F	631 234-7077
▲ Lubow Machine Corp — Copiague (G-3911)	F	631 226-1700
Manhasset Tool & Die Co Inc — Lancaster (G-7325)	F	716 684-6066
Miller Mechanical Services Inc — Glens Falls (G-5690)	F	518 792-0430
▼ Mpi Incorporated — Poughkeepsie (G-13918)	D	845 471-7630
Precision Eforming LLC — Cortland (G-4040)	F	607 753-7730
Prim Hall Enterprises Inc — Plattsburgh (G-13691)	F	518 561-7408
Producto Corporation — Jamestown (G-7024)	C	716 484-7131
Raloid Tool Co Inc — Mechanicville (G-8230)	F	518 664-4261
Schaefer Machine Co Inc — Mineola (G-8537)	E	516 248-6880
Servotec Usa LLC — Hudson (G-6634)	G	518 671-6120
▼ Smart High Voltage Solutions — Bohemia (G-1135)	F	631 563-6724
Special Metals Corporation — Dunkirk (G-4351)	D	716 366-5663
▲ Standard Paper Box Machine Co — Bronx (G-1463)	E	718 328-3300
▲ Strippit Inc — Akron (G-29)	C	716 542-5500
Taumel Metalforming Corp — Patterson (G-13445)	G	845 878-3100
▲ Trueforge Global McHy Corp — Rockville Centre (G-14801)	G	516 825-7040
▲ U S Air Tool Co Inc — Ronkonkoma (G-14994)	F	631 471-3300
Uhmac Inc — Holland (G-6485)	F	716 537-2343
Vader Systems LLC — East Amherst (G-4363)	G	716 636-1742
▼ Win Set Technologies LLC — Centereach (G-3474)	F	631 234-7077

3543 Industrial Patterns

Company	Code	Phone
A & T Tooling LLC — Lancaster (G-7297)	G	716 601-7299
▼ Armstrong Mold Corporation — East Syracuse (G-4504)	E	315 437-1517
Armstrong Mold Corporation — East Syracuse (G-4505)	D	315 437-1517
Bianca Group Ltd — New York (G-9388)	G	212 768-3011
City Pattern Shop Inc — Syracuse (G-15895)	F	315 463-5239
G Haynes Holdings Inc — Bloomville (G-995)	G	607 538-1160
IBlt Inc — New York (G-10546)	E	212 768-0292
K & H Precision Products Inc — Honeoye Falls (G-6532)	E	585 624-4894
Southern Tier Patterns — Elmira (G-4701)	G	607 734-1265
Studio One Leather Design Inc — New York (G-12221)	F	212 760-1701
W N R Pattern & Tool Inc — Lancaster (G-7346)	G	716 681-9334

Company	Code	Phone
Wolff & Dungey Inc — Syracuse (G-16074)	E	315 475-2105

3544 Dies, Tools, Jigs, Fixtures & Indl Molds

Company	Code	Phone
A & D Tool Inc — Dix Hills (G-4288)	G	631 243-4339
Aaron Tool & Mold Inc — Rochester (G-14164)	E	585 426-5100
▲ Accede Mold & Tool Co Inc — Rochester (G-14165)	D	585 254-6490
Accurate Tool & Die LLC — Rochester (G-14168)	F	585 254-2830
Ace Specialty Co Inc — Tonawanda (G-16134)	G	716 874-3670
▲ Advanced Mold & Tooling Inc — Rochester (G-14179)	E	585 426-2110
All American Precision Tl Mold — West Henrietta (G-16865)	F	585 436-3080
All Out Die Cutting Inc — Brooklyn (G-1587)	E	718 346-6666
▲ Alliance Precision Plas Corp — Rochester (G-14189)	C	585 426-5310
Alliance Precision Plas Corp — Rochester (G-14190)	E	585 426-5310
Allmetal Chocolate Mold Co Inc — West Babylon (G-16768)	F	631 752-2888
▲ Allstate Tool and Die Inc — Rochester (G-14191)	D	585 426-0400
Alry Tool and Die Co Inc — Tonawanda (G-16137)	F	716 693-2419
Alton Manufacturing Inc — Rochester (G-14194)	D	585 458-2600
▲ Amada Tool America Inc — Batavia (G-622)	D	585 344-3900
American Dies Inc — Brooklyn (G-1601)	F	718 387-1900
American Dsplay Die Ctters Inc — New York (G-9117)	E	212 645-1274
American Orthotic Lab Co Inc — College Point (G-3778)	E	718 961-6487
Amsco Inc — Buffalo (G-2811)	F	716 823-4213
Anka Tool & Die Inc — Congers (G-3851)	E	845 268-4116
Arnell Inc — Hempstead (G-6265)	G	516 486-7098
▼ Arro Tool & Die Inc — Lakewood (G-7287)	F	716 763-6203
Art Precision Metal Products — Copiague (G-3894)	F	631 842-8889
Artisan Management Group Inc — Frewsburg (G-5448)	G	716 569-4094
▲ Ascension Industries Inc — North Tonawanda (G-12956)	D	716 693-9381
Bennett Die & Tool Inc — Horseheads (G-6570)	E	607 739-5629
Bennett Die & Tool Inc — Ithaca (G-6821)	F	607 273-2836
Bill Shea Enterprises Inc — Batavia (G-625)	F	585 343-2284
Binghamton Precision Tool Inc — Binghamton (G-894)	G	607 772-6021
Blue Chip Mold Inc — Rochester (G-14236)	F	585 647-1790
Brayley Tool & Machine Inc — Rochester (G-14244)	G	585 342-7190
Brighton Tool & Die Designers — Tonawanda (G-16148)	F	716 876-0879
Carbaugh Tool Company Inc — Elmira (G-4673)	E	607 739-3293
▲ Century Mold Company Inc — Rochester (G-14266)	D	585 352-8600
Chamtek Mfg Inc — Rochester (G-14272)	E	585 328-4900
Charles A Rogers Entps Inc — Victor (G-16466)	E	585 924-6400
Chenango Valley Tech Inc — Sherburne (G-15389)	E	607 674-4115
Clifford H Jones Inc — Tonawanda (G-16153)	F	716 693-2444
Coil Stamping Inc — Holbrook (G-6439)	F	631 588-3040
Cosmo Electronic Machine Corp — Farmingdale (G-4962)	E	631 249-2535
Cuddeback Machining Inc — Hilton (G-6417)	G	585 392-5889
Custom Molding Solutions Inc — Churchville (G-3635)	E	585 293-1702
▲ Cy Plastics Works Inc — Honeoye (G-6523)	G	585 229-2555

Company	Code	Phone
▲ D Maldari & Sons Inc — Brooklyn (G-1830)	E	718 499-3555
Dewes Gumbs Die Co Inc — Long Island City (G-7714)	G	718 784-9755
▲ Diemax of Rochester Inc — Rochester (G-14307)	F	585 288-3912
Dixon Tool and Manufacturing — Rochester (G-14313)	F	585 235-1352
DOT Tool Co Inc — Binghamton (G-908)	G	607 724-7001
Dynamic Dies Inc — Rochester (G-14322)	F	585 247-4010
East Pattern & Model Corp — Fairport (G-4856)	F	585 461-3240
▲ Eberhardt Enterprises Inc — Rochester (G-14340)	F	585 458-7681
▼ Eden Tool & Die Inc — Eden (G-4586)	F	716 992-4240
Egli Machine Company Inc — Sidney (G-15439)	E	607 563-3663
Electro Form Corp — Binghamton (G-910)	F	607 722-6404
Electronic Die Corp — Brooklyn (G-1911)	F	718 455-3200
Enhanced Tool Inc — Amherst (G-239)	F	716 691-5200
Etna Tool & Die Corporation — New York (G-10079)	F	212 475-4350
Everfab Inc — East Aurora (G-4370)	D	716 655-1550
Evergreen Corp Central NY — Syracuse (G-15939)	F	315 454-4175
Fuller Tool Incorporated — Newport (G-12790)	F	315 891-3183
G N R Plastics Inc — Smithtown (G-15487)	F	631 724-8758
Gatti Tool & Mold Inc — Rochester (G-14388)	F	585 328-1350
Gay Sheet Metal Dies Inc — Buffalo (G-2966)	F	716 877-0208
▲ General Die and Die Cutng Inc — Roosevelt (G-15004)	D	516 665-3584
▲ Genesee Precision Inc — Batavia (G-634)	F	585 344-0385
Globmarble LLC — Brooklyn (G-2030)	G	347 717-4088
Graywood Companies Inc — Rochester (G-14413)	E	585 254-7000
Great Lakes Pressed Steel Corp — Buffalo (G-2982)	E	716 885-4037
HNST Mold Inspections LLC — Nanuet (G-8757)	G	845 215-9258
Hy-Tech Mold Inc — Rochester (G-14441)	F	585 247-2450
▲ Hytech Tool & Die Inc — Jamestown (G-7001)	F	716 488-2796
Industrial Tool & Die Co Inc — Troy (G-16240)	F	518 273-7383
Intek Precision — Churchville (G-3639)	G	585 293-0853
Inter Molds Inc — Bay Shore (G-706)	G	631 667-8580
Intri-Cut Inc — Amherst (G-247)	F	716 691-5200
J B Tool & Die Co Inc — Westbury (G-16997)	E	516 333-1480
J T Systematic — Endwell (G-4836)	G	607 754-0929
James B Crowell & Sons Inc — Wallkill (G-16544)	G	845 895-3464
James Wire Die Co — Ilion (G-6742)	F	315 894-3233
Jmt Program Leadership Group — Rochester (G-14463)	G	585 217-1134
K & H Precision Products Inc — Honeoye Falls (G-6532)	E	585 624-4894
K D M Die Company Inc — Buffalo (G-3024)	F	716 828-9000
Keyes Machine Works Inc — Gates (G-5561)	G	585 426-5059
Knise & Krick Inc — Syracuse (G-15975)	E	315 422-3516
▲ Light Waves Concept Inc — New York (G-10992)	F	212 677-6400
Long Island Tool & Die Inc — Copiague (G-3910)	F	631 225-0600
M J M Tooling Corp — Bronx (G-1384)	G	718 292-3590
Machine Tool Specialty — Cicero (G-3648)	G	315 699-5287

Employee Codes: A=Over 500 employees, B=251-500
C=101-250, D=51-100, E=20-50, F=10-19, G=5-9

2017 Harris
New York Manufacturers Directory

825

35 INDUSTRIAL AND COMMERCIAL MACHINERY AND COMPUTER EQUIPMENT SIC SECTION

Machinecraft Inc.....E..... 585 436-1070
Rochester *(G-14486)*
Magnus Precision Mfg Inc.....D..... 315 548-8032
Phelps *(G-13534)*
Manhasset Tool & Die Co Inc.....F..... 716 684-6066
Lancaster *(G-7325)*
▲ **Mannesmann Corporation**.....D..... 212 258-4000
New York *(G-11136)*
Mantel & Mantel Stamping Corp.....G..... 631 467-1916
Ronkonkoma *(G-14937)*
Manufacturers Tool & Die Co.....G..... 585 352-1080
Spencerport *(G-15572)*
May Tool & Die Inc.....G..... 716 695-1033
Tonawanda *(G-16180)*
Mega Tool & Mfg Corp.....E..... 607 734-8398
Elmira *(G-4695)*
Micro Instrument Corp.....D..... 585 458-3150
Rochester *(G-14507)*
Micron Inds Rochester Inc.....G..... 585 247-6130
Rochester *(G-14512)*
Moldcraft Inc.....E..... 716 684-1126
Depew *(G-4265)*
Ms Machining Inc.....G..... 607 723-1105
Binghamton *(G-938)*
Multifold Die Ctng Finshg Corp.....G..... 631 232-1235
Hauppauge *(G-6144)*
Mustang-Major Tool & Die Co.....G..... 716 992-9200
Eden *(G-4588)*
▲ **Nas CP Corp**.....D..... 718 961-6757
College Point *(G-3799)*
National Steel Rule Die Inc.....F..... 718 402-1396
Bronx *(G-1407)*
Niagara Fiberglass Inc.....E..... 716 822-3921
Buffalo *(G-3087)*
Niagara Punch & Die Corp.....G..... 716 896-7619
Buffalo *(G-3090)*
▼ **Nicoform Inc**.....F..... 585 454-5530
Rochester *(G-14537)*
Nijon Tool Co Inc.....F..... 631 242-3434
Deer Park *(G-4180)*
◆ **Nordon Inc**.....D..... 585 546-6200
Rochester *(G-14538)*
Northern Design Inc.....G..... 716 652-7071
East Aurora *(G-4378)*
P & H Machine Shop Inc.....G..... 585 247-5500
Rochester *(G-14561)*
P & R Industries Inc.....E..... 585 266-6725
Rochester *(G-14562)*
P & R Industries Inc.....F..... 585 544-1811
Rochester *(G-14563)*
P Tool & Die Co Inc.....E..... 585 889-1340
North Chili *(G-12925)*
▲ **P&G Metal Components Corp**.....D..... 716 896-7900
Buffalo *(G-3108)*
Pacific Die Cast Inc.....F..... 845 778-6374
Walden *(G-16534)*
Palma Tool & Die Company Inc.....E..... 716 681-4685
Lancaster *(G-7329)*
Paragon Steel Rule Dies Inc.....F..... 585 254-3395
Rochester *(G-14572)*
Patmian LLC.....B..... 212 758-0770
New York *(G-11579)*
Peak Motion Inc.....G..... 716 534-4925
Clarence *(G-3668)*
Phelinger Tool & Die Corp.....G..... 716 685-1780
Alden *(G-181)*
Pivot Punch Corporation.....D..... 716 625-8000
Lockport *(G-7610)*
Plastic Solutions Inc.....E..... 631 234-9013
Bayport *(G-760)*
◆ **PMI Industries LLC**.....E..... 585 464-8050
Rochester *(G-14586)*
Ppi Corp.....E..... 585 880-7277
Geneseo *(G-5567)*
Precise Punch Corporation.....F..... 716 625-8000
Lockport *(G-7611)*
▲ **Precision Grinding & Mfg Corp**.....C..... 585 458-4300
Rochester *(G-14593)*
Precision Machining and Mfg.....G..... 845 647-5380
Wawarsing *(G-16708)*
Precision Systems Mfg Inc.....E..... 315 451-3480
Liverpool *(G-7544)*
Precision Tl Die & Stamping Co.....F..... 516 561-0041
Valley Stream *(G-16420)*
Prime Tool & Die LLC.....G..... 607 334-5435
Norwich *(G-13036)*
Producto Corporation.....C..... 716 484-7131
Jamestown *(G-7024)*
Pronto Tool & Die Co Inc.....E..... 631 981-8920
Ronkonkoma *(G-14972)*
Prototype Manufacturing Corp.....F..... 716 695-1700
North Tonawanda *(G-12987)*
Quality Lineals Usa Inc.....E..... 516 378-6577
Freeport *(G-5421)*
Raloid Tool Co Inc.....F..... 518 664-4261
Mechanicville *(G-8230)*
Ram Precision Tool Inc.....G..... 716 759-8722
Lancaster *(G-7336)*
Rand Machine Products Inc.....D..... 716 665-5217
Falconer *(G-4908)*
Rand Machine Products Inc.....G..... 716 985-4681
Sinclairville *(G-15454)*
Rid Lom Precision Mfg.....E..... 585 594-8600
Rochester *(G-14625)*
Rochester Stampings Inc.....F..... 585 467-5241
Rochester *(G-14649)*
Rochester Tool and Mold Inc.....F..... 585 464-9336
Rochester *(G-14652)*
Rochling Advent Tool & Mold LP.....E..... 585 254-2000
Rochester *(G-14654)*
Roman Malakov Diamonds Ltd.....G..... 212 944-8500
New York *(G-11911)*
Romold Inc.....F..... 585 529-4440
Rochester *(G-14658)*
Rossi Tool & Dies Inc.....G..... 845 267-8246
Valley Cottage *(G-16387)*
Royal Molds Inc.....F..... 718 382-7686
Brooklyn *(G-2512)*
S B Whistler & Sons Inc.....E..... 585 798-3000
Medina *(G-8280)*
Saturn Industries Inc.....E..... 518 828-9956
Hudson *(G-6632)*
Sb Molds LLC.....D..... 845 352-3700
Monsey *(G-8581)*
Sharon Metal Stamping Corp.....G..... 718 828-4510
Bronx *(G-1451)*
Silicone Products & Technology.....C..... 716 684-1155
Lancaster *(G-7343)*
▲ **Spectronics Corporation**.....C..... 516 333-4840
Westbury *(G-17027)*
Stamp Rite Tool & Die Inc.....G..... 718 752-0334
Long Island City *(G-7883)*
Star Mold Co Inc.....G..... 631 694-2283
Farmingdale *(G-5115)*
▲ **Strippit Inc**.....C..... 716 542-5500
Akron *(G-29)*
Stuart Tool & Die Inc.....E..... 716 488-1975
Falconer *(G-4915)*
Synergy Tooling Systems Inc.....E..... 716 834-4457
Amherst *(G-264)*
Syntec Technologies Inc.....F..... 585 464-9336
Rochester *(G-14713)*
T A Tool & Molding Inc.....F..... 631 293-0172
Farmingdale *(G-5123)*
Thayer Tool & Die Inc.....F..... 716 782-4841
Ashville *(G-430)*
Tips & Dies Inc.....F..... 315 337-4161
Rome *(G-14837)*
Tooling Enterprises Inc.....F..... 716 842-0445
Buffalo *(G-3222)*
Tools & Stamping Corp.....G..... 718 392-4040
Brooklyn *(G-2663)*
Trinity Tools Inc.....E..... 716 694-1111
North Tonawanda *(G-13003)*
Turning Point Tool LLC.....G..... 585 288-7380
Rochester *(G-14736)*
▼ **Ultimate Prcision Met Pdts Inc**.....D..... 631 249-9441
Farmingdale *(G-5136)*
Universal Tooling Corporation.....F..... 716 985-4691
Gerry *(G-5594)*
▲ **Van Thomas Inc**.....E..... 585 426-1414
Rochester *(G-14751)*
W N R Pattern & Tool Inc.....G..... 716 681-9334
Lancaster *(G-7346)*
Xli Corporation.....D..... 585 436-2250
Rochester *(G-14771)*
Z Works Inc.....G..... 631 750-0612
Bohemia *(G-1157)*

3545 Machine Tool Access

Advance D Tech Inc.....F..... 845 534-8248
Cornwall *(G-3985)*
Ale-Techniques Inc.....F..... 845 687-7200
High Falls *(G-6399)*
American Linear Manufacturers.....F..... 516 333-1351
Westbury *(G-16966)*
Atlantic Scale Company Inc.....G..... 914 664-4403
Yonkers *(G-17418)*
Atwood Tool & Machine Inc.....E..... 607 648-6543
Chenango Bridge *(G-3596)*
B & B Precision Mfg Inc.....E..... 585 226-6226
Avon *(G-538)*
▲ **Baldwin Machine Works Inc**.....G..... 631 842-9110
Copiague *(G-3896)*
Bdp Industries Inc.....E..... 518 695-6851
Greenwich *(G-5886)*
Bnm Product Service.....G..... 631 750-1586
Holbrook *(G-6432)*
Boro Park Cutting Tool Corp.....E..... 718 720-0610
Staten Island *(G-15650)*
Brinkman Intl Group Inc.....G..... 585 429-5000
Rochester *(G-14245)*
C J Winter Machine Tech.....F..... 585 429-5000
Rochester *(G-14254)*
▲ **Champion Cutting Tool Corp**.....E..... 516 536-8200
Rockville Centre *(G-14789)*
Circo File Corp.....G..... 516 922-1848
Oyster Bay *(G-13367)*
▲ **Curran Manufacturing Corp**.....E..... 631 273-1010
Hauppauge *(G-6059)*
Curran Manufacturing Corp.....E..... 631 273-1010
Hauppauge *(G-6060)*
Custom Service Solutions Inc.....G..... 585 637-3760
Brockport *(G-1243)*
▲ **Designatronics Incorporated**.....G..... 516 328-3300
New Hyde Park *(G-8825)*
Dinosaw Inc.....E..... 518 828-9942
Hudson *(G-6612)*
Dock Hardware Incorporated.....F..... 585 266-7920
Rochester *(G-14314)*
Dorsey Metrology Intl Inc.....E..... 845 229-2929
Poughkeepsie *(G-13895)*
▲ **Drill America Inc**.....G..... 516 764-5700
Oceanside *(G-13077)*
Drt Power Systems LLC - Lane.....D..... 585 247-5940
Rochester *(G-14319)*
Dura-Mill Inc.....E..... 518 899-2255
Ballston Spa *(G-595)*
East Side Machine Inc.....E..... 585 265-4560
Webster *(G-16722)*
Egli Machine Company Inc.....E..... 607 563-3663
Sidney *(G-15439)*
Everfab Inc.....D..... 716 655-1550
East Aurora *(G-4370)*
▲ **F W Roberts Mfg Co Inc**.....F..... 716 434-3555
Lockport *(G-7585)*
Flashflo Manufacturing Inc.....F..... 716 826-9500
Buffalo *(G-2948)*
Flashflo Manufacturing Inc.....G..... 716 840-9594
Buffalo *(G-2949)*
▲ **Flexbar Machine Corporation**.....E..... 631 582-8440
Islandia *(G-6793)*
Fred M Velepec Co Inc.....E..... 718 821-6636
Glendale *(G-5653)*
Fronhofer Tool Company Inc.....E..... 518 692-2496
Cossayuna *(G-4055)*
▲ **Gardei Industries LLC**.....F..... 716 693-7100
North Tonawanda *(G-12973)*
Garey Mfg & Design Corp.....G..... 315 463-5306
East Syracuse *(G-4532)*
Genesee Manufacturing Co Inc.....G..... 585 266-3201
Rochester *(G-14394)*
Genius Tools Americas Corp.....F..... 716 662-6872
Orchard Park *(G-13272)*
◆ **Germanow-Simon Corporation**.....E..... 585 232-1440
Rochester *(G-14399)*
Graywood Companies Inc.....E..... 585 254-7000
Rochester *(G-14413)*
Griffin Manufacturing Company.....E..... 585 265-1991
Webster *(G-16724)*
◆ **Hardinge Inc**.....C..... 607 734-2281
Elmira *(G-4688)*
▲ **Heidenhain International Inc**.....C..... 716 661-1700
Jamestown *(G-6999)*
Hubbard Tool and Die Corp.....E..... 315 337-7840
Rome *(G-14815)*
Huron Tl & Cutter Grinding Co.....E..... 631 420-7000
Farmingdale *(G-5008)*
▼ **Innex Industries Inc**.....E..... 585 247-3575
Rochester *(G-14448)*
Innovative Automation Inc.....F..... 631 439-3300
Farmingdale *(G-5011)*
J H Robotics Inc.....E..... 607 729-3758
Johnson City *(G-7096)*
JD Tool Inc.....G..... 607 786-3129
Endicott *(G-4816)*
Jem Tool & Die Corp.....F..... 631 539-8734
West Islip *(G-16905)*
JW Burg Machine & Tool Inc.....G..... 716 434-0015
Clarence Center *(G-3678)*

SIC

◆ Kps Capital Partners LP ....E 212 338-5100
New York (G-10883)
▲ Lancaster Knives Inc ....E 716 683-5050
Lancaster (G-7323)
Linde LLC ....D 716 773-7552
Grand Island (G-5763)
Lovejoy Chaplet Corporation ....E 518 686-5232
Hoosick Falls (G-6541)
▲ M & S Precision Machine Co LLC ....F 518 747-1193
Queensbury (G-14004)
Macinnes Tool Corporation ....E 585 467-1920
Rochester (G-14487)
▲ Make-Waves Instrument Corp ....E 716 681-7524
Depew (G-4264)
Mausner Equipment Co Inc ....C 631 689-7358
Setauket (G-15377)
Melland Gear Instr of Huppauge ....E 631 234-0100
Hauppauge (G-6130)
Methods Tooling & Mfg Inc ....E 845 246-7100
Mount Marion (G-8651)
▲ Mibro Group ....D 716 631-5713
Buffalo (G-3064)
Michael Fiore Ltd ....G 516 561-8238
Valley Stream (G-16413)
◆ Micro Centric Corporation ....E 800 573-1139
Plainview (G-13621)
Miller Metal Fabricating Inc ....G 585 359-3400
Rochester (G-14514)
Morgood Tools Inc ....D 585 436-8828
Rochester (G-14522)
Myles Tool Company Inc ....E 716 731-1300
Sanborn (G-15124)
NC Industries Inc ....F 248 528-5200
Buffalo (G-3082)
New Market Products Co Inc ....F 607 292-6226
Wayne (G-16712)
Northeastern Water Jet Inc ....F 518 843-4988
Amsterdam (G-363)
Northfeld Precision Instr Corp ....E 516 431-1112
Island Park (G-6782)
Novatech Inc ....E 716 892-6682
Cheektowaga (G-3583)
▲ Park Enterprises Rochester Inc ....C 585 546-4200
Rochester (G-14573)
▲ Parlec Inc ....C 585 425-4400
Fairport (G-4868)
▲ Ppi Corp ....D 585 243-0300
Geneseo (G-5568)
▲ Precision Grinding & Mfg Corp ....C 585 458-4300
Rochester (G-14593)
Precision Mechanisms Corp ....E 516 333-5955
Westbury (G-17021)
▲ Production Metal Cutting Inc ....F 585 458-7136
Rochester (G-14606)
Robert J Faraone ....G 585 232-7160
Rochester (G-14630)
Rochling Advent Tool & Mold LP ....E 585 254-2000
Rochester (G-14654)
Ross JC Inc ....G 716 439-1161
Lockport (G-7612)
Rota File Corporation ....E 516 496-7200
Syosset (G-15838)
S & R Tool Inc ....G 585 346-2029
Lakeville (G-7285)
▲ S & S Machinery Corp ....E 718 492-7400
Brooklyn (G-2520)
S S Precision Gear & Instr ....G 718 457-7474
Corona (G-4006)
Safina Center ....G 808 888-9440
Stony Brook (G-15770)
Schenck Corporation ....D 631 242-4010
Deer Park (G-4205)
▲ Schenck Trebel Corp ....D 631 242-4397
Deer Park (G-4206)
Scomac Inc ....F 585 494-2200
Bergen (G-852)
Seneca Falls Machine Tool Co ....D 315 568-5804
Seneca Falls (G-15369)
Sinn- Tech Industries Inc ....F 631 643-1171
West Babylon (G-16827)
Socket Products Mfg Corp ....G 631 232-9870
Islandia (G-6803)
Steiner Technologies Inc ....F 585 425-5910
Fairport (G-4880)
Streamline Precision Inc ....G 585 421-9050
Fairport (G-4881)
Streamline Precision Inc ....G 585 421-9050
Fairport (G-4882)
▲ Strippit Inc ....C 716 542-5500
Akron (G-29)

Superior Tool Co Inc ....F 716 692-3900
North Tonawanda (G-12998)
▲ Thuro Metal Products Inc ....E 631 435-0444
Brentwood (G-1196)
Transport National Dev Inc ....E 716 662-0270
Orchard Park (G-13300)
▲ Trident Precision Mfg Inc ....D 585 265-2010
Webster (G-16738)
Trinity Tools Inc ....E 716 694-1111
North Tonawanda (G-13003)
▲ Truebite Inc ....F 607 786-3184
Endicott (G-4832)
Universal Tooling Corporation ....F 716 985-4691
Gerry (G-5594)
Vandilay Industries Inc ....E 631 226-3064
West Babylon (G-16838)
Velmex Inc ....E 585 657-6151
Bloomfield (G-992)
▲ Willemin Macodel Incorporated ....F 914 345-3504
Hawthorne (G-6256)
Xactra Technologies Inc ....D 585 426-2030
Rochester (G-14767)

3546 Power Hand Tools

Allied Motion Technologies Inc ....C 315 782-5910
Watertown (G-16634)
▲ Awt Supply Corp ....G 516 437-9105
Elmont (G-4717)
Black & Decker (us) Inc ....B 914 235-6300
Brewster (G-1212)
Black & Decker (us) Inc ....G 716 884-6220
Buffalo (G-2843)
Black & Decker (us) Inc ....G 631 952-2008
Hauppauge (G-6035)
Dean Manufacturing Inc ....F 607 770-1300
Vestal (G-16446)
▲ Dynabrade Inc ....C 716 631-0100
Clarence (G-3658)
▲ Great American Tool Co Inc ....G 716 646-5700
Hamburg (G-5927)
Huck International Inc ....C 845 331-7300
Kingston (G-7191)
◆ Ivy Classic Industries Inc ....E 914 632-8200
New Rochelle (G-8913)
Kelley Farm & Garden Inc ....E 518 234-2332
Cobleskill (G-3738)
▲ Meritool LLC ....F 716 699-6005
Ellicottville (G-4642)
New York Industrial Works Inc ....G 718 292-0615
Bronx (G-1409)
◆ P & F Industries Inc ....C 631 694-9800
Melville (G-8346)
Rbhammers Corp ....F 845 353-5042
Blauvelt (G-973)
Reimann & Georger Corporation ....E 716 895-1156
Buffalo (G-3156)
▲ Stature Electric Inc ....B 315 782-5910
Watertown (G-16672)
▼ Stephen Hanley ....D 718 729-3360
Long Island City (G-7891)

3547 Rolling Mill Machinery & Eqpt

Anthony Manufacturing Inc ....G 631 957-9424
Lindenhurst (G-7454)
Eaton Electric Holdings LLC ....C 607 756-2821
Cortland (G-4025)
◆ Ivy Classic Industries Inc ....E 914 632-8200
New Rochelle (G-8913)
Johnston Dandy Company ....G 315 455-5773
Syracuse (G-15969)
▲ Mannesmann Corporation ....D 212 258-4000
New York (G-11136)
Polymag Tek Inc ....F 585 235-8390
Rochester (G-14587)

3548 Welding Apparatus

Apogee Translite Inc ....E 631 254-6975
Deer Park (G-4100)
▲ Lubow Machine Corp ....F 631 226-1700
Copiague (G-3911)
McAllisters Precision Wldg Inc ....F 518 221-3455
Menands (G-8374)
Riverview Industries Inc ....G 845 265-5284
Cold Spring (G-3765)
▲ Vante Inc ....F 716 778-7691
Newfane (G-12789)

3549 Metalworking Machinery, NEC

Advanced Machine Design Co Inc ....E 716 826-2000
Buffalo (G-2800)
▲ Alliance Automation Systems ....C 585 426-2700
Rochester (G-14188)
▲ Autostat Corporation ....F 516 379-9447
Roosevelt (G-15003)
▲ Bartell Machinery Systems LLC ....C 315 336-7600
Rome (G-14804)
Carpenter Manufacturing Co ....E 315 682-9176
Manlius (G-8068)
Charles A Rogers Entps Inc ....E 585 924-6400
Victor (G-16466)
Duall Finishing Inc ....G 716 827-1707
Buffalo (G-2920)
Eraser Company Inc ....C 315 454-3237
Mattydale (G-8212)
▲ Esm II Inc ....E 716 446-8888
Amherst (G-241)
▲ Expert Metal Slitters Corp ....G 718 361-2735
Long Island City (G-7736)
◆ Hardinge Inc ....C 607 734-2281
Elmira (G-4688)
Hje Company Inc ....G 518 792-8733
Queensbury (G-13999)
▲ Hover-Davis Inc ....C 585 352-9590
Rochester (G-14439)
Manufacturing Resources Inc ....E 631 481-0041
Rochester (G-14493)
▲ MGS Manufacturing Inc ....E 315 337-3350
Rome (G-14821)
▲ Mold-A-Matic Corporation ....E 607 433-2121
Oneonta (G-13189)
Mono-Systems Inc ....E 716 821-1344
Buffalo (G-3074)
▲ Munson Machinery Company Inc ....E 315 797-0090
Utica (G-16350)
Pace Technology Inc ....E 631 981-2400
Ronkonkoma (G-14963)
Pems Tool & Machine Inc ....E 315 823-3595
Little Falls (G-7502)
Precision Systems Mfg Inc ....E 315 451-3480
Liverpool (G-7544)
▲ Reelex Packaging Solutions Inc ....E 845 878-7878
Patterson (G-13443)
Riverside Machinery Company ....E 718 492-7400
Brooklyn (G-2498)
▲ S & S Machinery Corp ....E 718 492-7400
Brooklyn (G-2520)
S & S Machinery Corp ....E 718 492-7400
Brooklyn (G-2521)
Serge Duct Designs Inc ....E 718 783-7799
Brooklyn (G-2544)
▲ Strippit Inc ....C 716 542-5500
Akron (G-29)
◆ Tessy Plastics Corp ....B 315 689-3924
Skaneateles (G-15466)
Unidex Corporation Western NY ....F 585 786-3170
Warsaw (G-16584)
Vader Systems LLC ....G 716 636-1742
East Amherst (G-4363)
▲ Van Blarcom Closures Inc ....C 718 855-3810
Brooklyn (G-2718)
▲ Voss Manufacturing Inc ....D 716 731-5062
Sanborn (G-15130)
Xto Incorporated ....D 315 451-7807
Liverpool (G-7558)

3552 Textile Machinery

Aglika Trade LLC ....F 727 424-1944
Middle Village (G-8410)
Angel Textiles Inc ....G 212 532-0900
New York (G-9156)
Big Apple Sign Corp ....E 631 342-0303
Islandia (G-6788)
Chroma Logic ....G 716 736-2458
Ripley (G-14135)
Corbertex LLC ....G 212 971-0008
New York (G-9723)
◆ Eastman Machine Company ....C 716 856-2200
Buffalo (G-2929)
EMC Fintech ....F 716 488-9071
Falconer (G-4896)
Herr Manufacturing Co Inc ....E 716 754-4341
Tonawanda (G-16172)
Herrmann Group LLC ....G 716 876-9798
Kenmore (G-7148)
Mjk Cutting Inc ....F 718 384-7613
Brooklyn (G-2323)

S
I
C

Employee Codes: A=Over 500 employees, B=251-500
C=101-250, D=51-100, E=20-50, F=10-19, G=5-9
2017 Harris
New York Manufacturers Directory
827

Mohawk Valley Knt McHy Co Inc ... F ... 315 736-3038
New York Mills *(G-12726)*
Rfb Associates Inc ... G ... 518 271-0551
Voorheesville *(G-16517)*
Schwabel Fabricating Co Inc ... E ... 716 876-2086
Tonawanda *(G-16200)*
Screen Team Inc ... F ... 718 786-2424
Long Island City *(G-7873)*
▲ Sharmeen Textile Inc ... G ... 646 298-5757
New York *(G-12046)*
Simtec Industries Corporation ... G ... 631 293-0080
Farmingdale *(G-5109)*
Thread Check Inc ... D ... 631 231-1515
Hauppauge *(G-6214)*
Viewsport Inc ... G ... 585 738-6803
Penfield *(G-13505)*

3553 Woodworking Machinery

Cannonsville Lumber Inc ... G ... 607 467-3380
Deposit *(G-4276)*
Casa Nueva Custom Furnishing ... G ... 914 476-2272
Yonkers *(G-17425)*
▲ Cem Machine Inc ... E ... 315 493-4258
Carthage *(G-3409)*
Corbett Stves Pttern Works Inc ... E ... 585 546-7109
Rochester *(G-14289)*
Downtown Interiors Inc ... F ... 212 337-0230
New York *(G-9918)*
◆ Hardinge Inc ... C ... 607 734-2281
Elmira *(G-4688)*
▼ James L Taylor Mfg Co ... E ... 845 452-3780
Poughkeepsie *(G-13909)*
James L Taylor Mfg Co ... G ... 845 452-3780
Poughkeepsie *(G-13910)*
▲ Merritt Machinery LLC ... E ... 716 434-5558
Lockport *(G-7599)*
▼ Oneida Air Systems Inc ... E ... 315 476-5151
Syracuse *(G-16004)*
Paratus Industries Inc ... E ... 716 826-2000
Orchard Park *(G-13288)*
Phoenix Wood Wrights Ltd ... F ... 631 727-9691
Riverhead *(G-14151)*
US Sander LLC ... G ... 518 875-9157
Esperance *(G-4839)*

3554 Paper Inds Machinery

Automecha International Ltd ... E ... 607 843-2235
Oxford *(G-13363)*
Cyclotherm of Watertown Inc ... E ... 315 782-1100
Watertown *(G-16649)*
▲ F W Roberts Mfg Co Inc ... F ... 716 434-3555
Lockport *(G-7585)*
Friedel Paper Box & Converting ... G ... 315 437-3325
Baldwinsville *(G-569)*
GL&v USA Inc ... D ... 518 747-2444
Hudson Falls *(G-6643)*
▲ GL&v USA Inc ... D ... 518 747-2444
Hudson Falls *(G-6644)*
Haanen Packard Machinery Inc ... G ... 518 747-2330
Hudson Falls *(G-6646)*
Interntnal Strpping Diecutting ... G ... 718 383-7720
Brooklyn *(G-2113)*
Jacob Inc ... E ... 646 450-3067
Brooklyn *(G-2131)*
Johnston Dandy Company ... G ... 315 455-5773
Syracuse *(G-15969)*
Kadant Inc ... F ... 518 793-8801
Glens Falls *(G-5684)*
Lake Image Systems Inc ... F ... 585 321-3630
Henrietta *(G-6296)*
Richlar Industries Inc ... F ... 315 463-5144
East Syracuse *(G-4559)*
Rsb Associates Inc ... F ... 518 281-5067
Altamont *(G-212)*
Sinclair International Company ... E ... 518 798-2361
Queensbury *(G-14012)*
▲ Sonicor Inc ... F ... 631 920-6555
West Babylon *(G-16830)*
▲ Standard Paper Box Machine Co ... E ... 718 328-3300
Bronx *(G-1463)*
Superior Plus Cnstr Pdts Corp ... F ... 315 463-5144
East Syracuse *(G-4569)*
Verso Corporation ... B ... 212 599-2700
New York *(G-12526)*

3555 Printing Trades Machinery & Eqpt

A C Envelope Inc ... G ... 516 420-0646
Farmingdale *(G-4926)*
A-Mark Machinery Corp ... F ... 631 643-6300
West Babylon *(G-16762)*
Advance Grafix Equipment Inc ... G ... 917 202-4593
Wyandanch *(G-17370)*
Anand Printing Machinery Inc ... G ... 631 667-3079
Deer Park *(G-4098)*
Apexx Omni-Graphics Inc ... D ... 718 326-3330
Maspeth *(G-8119)*
▲ Awt Supply Corp ... G ... 516 437-9105
Elmont *(G-4717)*
Bartizan Data Systems LLC ... E ... 914 965-7977
Yonkers *(G-17419)*
▲ Bmp America Inc ... C ... 585 798-0950
Medina *(G-8267)*
C M E Corp ... F ... 315 451-7101
Syracuse *(G-15881)*
Castlereagh Printcraft Inc ... D ... 516 623-1728
Freeport *(G-5392)*
Copier & Printer Supply LLC ... G ... 585 329-1077
Mendon *(G-8380)*
Copy4les Inc ... F ... 212 487-9778
New York *(G-9722)*
Csw Inc ... F ... 585 247-4010
Rochester *(G-14293)*
Daige Products Inc ... F ... 516 621-2100
Albertson *(G-153)*
Davis International Inc ... G ... 585 421-8175
Fairport *(G-4854)*
Exacta LLC ... G ... 716 406-2303
Clarence Center *(G-3675)*
▲ Halm Industries Co Inc ... D ... 516 676-6700
Glen Head *(G-5632)*
Halm Instrument Co Inc ... D ... 516 676-6700
Glen Head *(G-5633)*
◆ Hodgins Engraving Co Inc ... D ... 585 343-4444
Batavia *(G-639)*
▲ Impressions International Inc ... G ... 585 442-5240
Rochester *(G-14447)*
Innotech Graphic Eqp Corp ... G ... 845 268-6900
Valley Cottage *(G-16379)*
◆ International Imaging Mtls Inc ... B ... 716 691-6333
Amherst *(G-246)*
▲ Lexar Global LLC ... G ... 845 352-9700
Valley Cottage *(G-16381)*
Mekatronics Incorporated ... E ... 516 883-6805
Port Washington *(G-13844)*
◆ Micro Powders Inc ... E ... 914 332-6400
Tarrytown *(G-16097)*
Mount Vernon Machine Inc ... E ... 845 268-9400
Valley Cottage *(G-16382)*
Newport Business Solutions Inc ... F ... 631 319-6129
Bohemia *(G-1110)*
▲ Package Print Technologies ... E ... 716 871-9905
Buffalo *(G-3110)*
◆ Paxar Corporation ... E ... 845 398-3229
Orangeburg *(G-13238)*
Perretta Graphics Corp ... E ... 845 473-0550
Poughkeepsie *(G-13925)*
Prim Hall Enterprises Inc ... F ... 518 561-7408
Plattsburgh *(G-13691)*
Rollers Inc ... G ... 716 837-0700
Buffalo *(G-3164)*
Rubber Stamps Inc ... E ... 212 675-1180
Mineola *(G-8535)*
Southern Graphic Systems LLC ... E ... 315 695-7079
Phoenix *(G-13544)*
Specilty Bus Mchs Holdings LLC ... E ... 212 587-9600
New York *(G-12154)*
Sterling Toggle Inc ... F ... 631 491-0500
West Babylon *(G-16832)*
▲ Super Web Inc ... E ... 631 643-9100
West Babylon *(G-16834)*
Total Offset Inc ... F ... 212 966-4482
New York *(G-12379)*
Universal Metal Fabricators ... F ... 845 331-8248
Kingston *(G-7221)*
▲ Vits International Inc ... E ... 845 353-5000
Blauvelt *(G-979)*
Voodoo Manufacturing Inc ... G ... 646 893-8366
Brooklyn *(G-2736)*
Woerner Industries Inc ... E ... 585 436-1934
Rochester *(G-14765)*

3556 Food Prdts Machinery

◆ Ag-Pak Inc ... F ... 716 772-2651
Gasport *(G-5555)*
◆ Bairnco Corporation ... E ... 914 461-1300
White Plains *(G-17081)*
Bakers Pride Oven Co Inc ... C ... 914 576-0200
New Rochelle *(G-8887)*
Bari Engineering Corp ... E ... 212 966-2080
New York *(G-9320)*
Blue Toad Hard Cider ... E ... 585 424-5508
Rochester *(G-14237)*
Bonduelle USA Inc ... E ... 585 948-5252
Oakfield *(G-13064)*
Brooklyn Brew Shop LLC ... F ... 718 874-0119
Brooklyn *(G-1722)*
▼ Buflovak LLC ... E ... 716 895-2100
Buffalo *(G-2861)*
C-Flex Bearing Co Inc ... F ... 315 895-7454
Frankfort *(G-5350)*
Cantinafoods Inc ... G ... 716 602-3536
Buffalo *(G-2866)*
◆ Caravella Food Corp ... F ... 646 552-0455
Whitestone *(G-17204)*
Carts Mobile Food Eqp Corp ... E ... 718 788-5540
Brooklyn *(G-1761)*
▲ Chemicolloid Laboratories Inc ... F ... 516 747-2666
New Hyde Park *(G-8821)*
Chester-Jensen Company ... E ... 610 876-6276
Cattaraugus *(G-3437)*
Delaval Inc ... F ... 585 599-4696
Corfu *(G-3954)*
Delsur Parts ... G ... 631 630-1606
Brentwood *(G-1181)*
Desu Machinery Corporation ... D ... 716 681-5798
Depew *(G-4255)*
▲ Elmar Industries Inc ... D ... 716 681-5650
Depew *(G-4256)*
Esquire Mechanical Corp ... G ... 718 625-4006
Brooklyn *(G-1935)*
ET Oakes Corporation ... E ... 631 630-9837
Hauppauge *(G-6074)*
Expert Industries Inc ... E ... 718 434-6060
Brooklyn *(G-1946)*
Feldmeier Equipment Inc ... C ... 315 823-2000
Little Falls *(G-7500)*
Fresh Harvest Incorporated ... F ... 845 296-1024
Wappingers Falls *(G-16568)*
G J Olney Inc ... E ... 315 827-4208
Westernville *(G-17043)*
Goodnature Products Inc ... F ... 716 855-3325
Orchard Park *(G-13273)*
Haines Equipment Inc ... E ... 607 566-8531
Avoca *(G-537)*
Home Maide Inc ... F ... 845 837-1700
Harriman *(G-5972)*
Hotrock Ovens LLC ... F ... 917 224-4342
Red Hook *(G-14029)*
▼ I J White Corporation ... D ... 631 293-3788
Farmingdale *(G-5009)*
Juice Press LLC ... G ... 212 777-0034
New York *(G-10780)*
Kedco Inc ... F ... 516 454-7800
Farmingdale *(G-5025)*
Kinplex Corp ... E ... 631 242-4800
Edgewood *(G-4604)*
Los Olivos Ltd ... F ... 631 773-6439
Farmingdale *(G-5037)*
◆ Ludwig Holdings Corp ... D ... 845 340-9727
Kingston *(G-7198)*
Lyophilization Systems Inc ... G ... 845 338-0456
New Paltz *(G-8876)*
M & E Mfg Co Inc ... D ... 845 331-7890
Kingston *(G-7200)*
Mary F Morse ... G ... 315 866-2741
Mohawk *(G-8542)*
Mohawk Valley Manufacturing ... G ... 315 797-0851
Frankfort *(G-5355)*
◆ National Equipment Corporation ... F ... 718 585-0200
Bronx *(G-1405)*
National Equipment Corporation ... E ... 718 585-0200
Bronx *(G-1406)*
▲ Olmstead Products Corp ... F ... 516 681-3700
Hicksville *(G-6379)*
P & M LLC ... E ... 631 842-2200
Amityville *(G-319)*
Pic Nic LLC ... G ... 914 245-6500
Yorktown Heights *(G-17516)*
Precision Consulting ... G ... 631 727-0847
Riverhead *(G-14152)*
▲ Purvi Enterprises Incorporated ... G ... 347 808-9448
Maspeth *(G-8166)*
Richard H Williams Associates ... G ... 631 751-4156
Setauket *(G-15379)*
Sidco Food Distribution Corp ... F ... 718 733-3939
Bronx *(G-1452)*
▲ Simply Natural Foods LLC ... E ... 631 543-9600
Commack *(G-3843)*
Singlecut Beersmiths LLC ... F ... 718 606-0788
Astoria *(G-456)*

▲ **SPX Flow Tech Systems Inc** ....D....... 716 692-3000
Getzville *(G-5604)*
▲ **Unisource Food Eqp Systems Inc**....G....... 516 681-0537
Holbrook *(G-6479)*
US Beverage Net Inc.............................F....... 315 579-2025
Syracuse *(G-16065)*
▲ **Vr Food Equipment Inc**.....................F....... 315 531-8133
Penn Yan *(G-13522)*
Wilder Manufacturing Co Inc ....D....... 516 222-0433
Garden City *(G-5536)*
Win-Holt Equipment Corp ....C....... 516 222-0433
Garden City *(G-5537)*
Wired Coffee and Bagel Inc ....F....... 518 506-3194
Malta *(G-8022)*
Zahm & Nagel Co Inc.............................G....... 716 833-1532
Holland *(G-6486)*
Zaro Bake Shop Inc ....D....... 212 292-0175
New York *(G-12705)*

3559 Special Ind Machinery, NEC

Accurate McHning Incorporation ....F....... 315 689-1428
Elbridge *(G-4623)*
▲ **Addex Inc**..G....... 781 344-5800
Newark *(G-12729)*
▲ **Adirondack Plas & Recycl Inc**...........E....... 518 746-9212
Argyle *(G-408)*
▼ **Andela Tool & Machine Inc**...............G....... 315 858-0055
Richfield Springs *(G-14061)*
◆ **Arbe Machinery Inc** ....F....... 631 756-2477
Farmingdale *(G-4945)*
▲ **Aremco Products Inc**..........................F....... 845 268-0039
Valley Cottage *(G-16376)*
Automotion Parking Systems LLC........G....... 516 565-5600
West Hempstead *(G-16850)*
B&K Precision Corporation ....G....... 631 369-2665
Manorville *(G-8077)*
Ben Weitsman of Albany LLC................E....... 518 462-4444
Albany *(G-53)*
Blue Star Products Inc ....F....... 631 952-3204
Hauppauge *(G-6036)*
Byfusion Inc ....G....... 347 563-5286
Brooklyn *(G-1742)*
▲ **Cameo Metal Products Inc** ....E....... 718 788-1106
Brooklyn *(G-1751)*
▼ **Caswell Inc** ....F....... 315 946-1213
Lyons *(G-7970)*
▲ **Century-Tech Inc**.................................G....... 718 326-9400
Hempstead *(G-6268)*
▲ **Charles Ross & Son Company** ....D....... 631 234-0500
Hauppauge *(G-6044)*
Cleaning Tech Group LLC......................E....... 716 665-2340
Jamestown *(G-6981)*
Crumbrubber Technology Inc...............F....... 718 468-3988
Hollis *(G-6496)*
▲ **Cryomech Inc** ....D....... 315 455-2555
Syracuse *(G-15914)*
Curtin-Hebert Co Inc.............................F....... 518 725-7157
Gloversville *(G-5710)*
Cvd Equipment Corporation ....E....... 845 246-3631
Saugerties *(G-15182)*
▲ **Cvd Equipment Corporation** ....C....... 631 981-7081
Central Islip *(G-3493)*
▲ **Designatronics Incorporated** ....G....... 516 328-3300
New Hyde Park *(G-8825)*
Digital Matrix Corp.................................E....... 516 481-7990
Farmingdale *(G-4978)*
Eastend Enforcement Products ....G....... 631 878-8424
Center Moriches *(G-3465)*
Eltee Tool & Die Co ....F....... 607 748-4301
Endicott *(G-4801)*
Emhart Glass Manufacturing Inc...........C....... 607 734-3671
Horseheads *(G-6576)*
Esc Control Electronics LLC ....G....... 631 467-5328
Sayville *(G-15207)*
Force Dynamics Inc...............................F....... 607 546-5023
Trumansburg *(G-16267)*
General Cryogenic Tech LLC.................F....... 516 334-8200
Westbury *(G-16991)*
George Ponte Inc ....G....... 914 243-4202
Jefferson Valley *(G-7056)*
◆ **Germanow-Simon Corporation** ....E....... 585 232-1440
Rochester *(G-14399)*
▲ **Glass Star America Inc**......................F....... 631 291-9432
Center Moriches *(G-3466)*
Globalfoundries US Inc ....F....... 512 457-3900
Hopewell Junction *(G-6551)*
Gordon S Anderson Mfg Co...................G....... 845 677-3304
Millbrook *(G-8475)*
Haanen Packard Machinery Inc ....G....... 518 747-2330
Hudson Falls *(G-6646)*
Herbert Jaffe Inc.....................................G....... 718 392-1956
Long Island City *(G-7759)*
▲ **High Frequency Tech Co Inc**.............F....... 631 242-3020
Deer Park *(G-4149)*
◆ **Hitachi Metals America Ltd**...............E....... 914 694-9200
Purchase *(G-13959)*
Ieh FM Holdings LLC ....E....... 212 702-4300
New York *(G-10559)*
Illinois Tool Works Inc ....C....... 716 681-8222
Lancaster *(G-7320)*
▲ **Innovation Associates Inc**.................C....... 607 798-9376
Johnson City *(G-7095)*
Innovative Cleaning Solutions...............G....... 716 731-4408
Sanborn *(G-15121)*
James Morris...E....... 315 824-8519
Hamilton *(G-5948)*
Kabar Manufacturing Corp.....................E....... 631 694-1036
Farmingdale *(G-5023)*
▲ **Kabar Manufacturing Corp**................E....... 631 694-6857
Farmingdale *(G-5022)*
Lam Research Corporation....................E....... 845 896-0606
Fishkill *(G-5185)*
▲ **Maharlika Holdings LLC** ....F....... 631 319-6203
Ronkonkoma *(G-14936)*
▼ **Materials Recovery Company**...........F....... 518 274-3681
Troy *(G-16242)*
Michael Benalt Inc..................................E....... 845 628-1008
Mahopac *(G-7997)*
Mono Plate Inc..G....... 631 643-3100
West Babylon *(G-16812)*
▲ **Multiline Technology Inc** ....C....... 631 249-8300
Ronkonkoma *(G-14946)*
▲ **Munson Machinery Company Inc**....E....... 315 797-0090
Utica *(G-16350)*
◆ **National Equipment Corporation** ......F....... 718 585-0200
Bronx *(G-1405)*
National Equipment Corporation...........E....... 718 585-0200
Bronx *(G-1406)*
Northeast Data Destruction & R ....G....... 845 331-5554
Kingston *(G-7204)*
▲ **Northrock Industries Inc** ....E....... 631 924-6130
Bohemia *(G-1112)*
▲ **Optipro Systems LLC** ....D....... 585 265-0160
Ontario *(G-13208)*
P K G Equipment Incorporated..............E....... 585 436-4650
Rochester *(G-14564)*
Pearl Technologies Inc...........................E....... 315 365-2632
Savannah *(G-15202)*
◆ **Pfaudler Inc**..B....... 585 464-5663
Rochester *(G-14578)*
▲ **Precision Process Inc**.........................D....... 716 731-1587
Niagara Falls *(G-12864)*
▲ **Qes Solutions Inc**................................D....... 585 254-8693
Rochester *(G-14611)*
◆ **Quality Strapping Inc** ....D....... 718 418-1111
Brooklyn *(G-2463)*
▼ **Queenaire Technologies Inc** ....G....... 315 393-5454
Ogdensburg *(G-13120)*
R & B Machinery Corp ....G....... 716 894-3332
Buffalo *(G-3151)*
Reefer Tek Llc..F....... 347 590-1067
Bronx *(G-1440)*
Reynolds Tech Fabricators Inc..............E....... 315 437-0532
East Syracuse *(G-4558)*
Rfb Associates Inc..................................G....... 518 271-0551
Voorheesville *(G-16517)*
Riverview Associates Inc........................F....... 585 235-5980
Rochester *(G-14628)*
Ross Microsystems Inc...........................G....... 845 918-1208
New City *(G-8792)*
Shred Center ....G....... 716 664-3052
Jamestown *(G-7027)*
Silver Creek Enterprises Inc ....G....... 716 934-2611
Silver Creek *(G-15450)*
Sj Associates Inc ....E....... 516 942-3232
Jericho *(G-7087)*
▲ **Sonicor Inc** ....F....... 631 920-6555
West Babylon *(G-16830)*
Spectrum Catalysts Inc..........................G....... 631 560-3683
Central Islip *(G-3511)*
SPX Corporation.....................................E....... 585 279-1216
Rochester *(G-14696)*
Stainless Design Concepts Ltd..............E....... 845 246-3631
Saugerties *(G-15195)*
Standard Ascnsion Towers Group........D....... 716 681-2222
Depew *(G-4274)*
Stephen A Manoogian Inc ....G....... 518 762-2525
Johnstown *(G-7129)*
Surepure Inc..F....... 917 368-8480
New York *(G-12245)*
Technic Inc ....F....... 516 349-0700
Plainview *(G-13638)*
Tokyo Electron America Inc..................G....... 518 289-3100
Malta *(G-8021)*
Tompkins Metal Finishing Inc...............D....... 585 344-2600
Batavia *(G-650)*
Tompkins Srm LLC ....G....... 315 422-8763
Syracuse *(G-16059)*
Ui Acquisition Holding Co......................G....... 607 779-7522
Conklin *(G-3877)*
Ui Holding Company...............................G....... 607 779-7522
Conklin *(G-3878)*
▲ **Ultrepet LLC** ....D....... 781 275-6400
Albany *(G-146)*
▲ **Universal Instruments Corp**..............C....... 800 842-9732
Conklin *(G-3879)*
Universal Thin Film Lab Corp................G....... 845 562-0601
Newburgh *(G-12784)*
▲ **Valplast International Corp** ....F....... 516 442-3923
Westbury *(G-17040)*
▲ **Veeco Instruments Inc**.......................B....... 516 677-0200
Plainview *(G-13644)*
West Metal Works Inc ....E....... 716 895-4900
Buffalo *(G-3252)*
Wilt Industries Inc...................................G....... 518 548-4961
Lake Pleasant *(G-7277)*

3561 Pumps & Pumping Eqpt

Air Flow Pump Corp ....G....... 718 241-2800
Brooklyn *(G-1571)*
▲ **Air Techniques Inc** ....B....... 516 433-7676
Melville *(G-8291)*
▲ **American Ship Repairs Company** ....F....... 718 435-5570
Brooklyn *(G-1609)*
▲ **Armstrong Pumps Inc**........................D....... 716 693-8813
North Tonawanda *(G-12955)*
▲ **Buffalo Pumps Inc** ....C....... 716 693-1850
North Tonawanda *(G-12963)*
Century-Tech Inc.....................................F....... 718 326-9400
Hempstead *(G-6267)*
Curaegis Technologies Inc ....F....... 585 254-1100
Rochester *(G-14294)*
Daikin Applied Americas Inc..................D....... 315 253-2771
Auburn *(G-491)*
▲ **Federal Pump Corporation**................E....... 718 451-2000
Brooklyn *(G-1963)*
Fisonic Corp..G....... 212 732-3777
Long Island City *(G-7743)*
▲ **Fisonic Corp** ....F....... 716 763-0295
New York *(G-10174)*
▲ **Fluid Handling LLC**............................G....... 716 897-2800
Cheektowaga *(G-3571)*
▲ **Gardner Dnver Oberdorfer Pumps**...E....... 315 437-0361
Syracuse *(G-15948)*
Geopump Inc...G....... 585 798-6666
Medina *(G-8273)*
▲ **Goulds Pumps Incorporated**.............A....... 315 568-2811
Seneca Falls *(G-15360)*
Goulds Pumps Incorporated..................B....... 315 258-4949
Auburn *(G-498)*
ITT Corporation.......................................D....... 315 568-2811
Seneca Falls *(G-15362)*
◆ **ITT Fluid Technology Corp** ....B....... 914 641-2000
White Plains *(G-17127)*
ITT Goulds Pumps Inc ....A....... 914 641-2129
Seneca Falls *(G-15364)*
▲ **ITT Water Technology Inc**.................B....... 315 568-2811
Seneca Falls *(G-15365)*
▲ **John N Fehlinger Co Inc**....................F....... 212 233-5656
New York *(G-10752)*
Ketcham Pump Co Inc............................F....... 718 457-0800
Woodside *(G-17334)*
◆ **Liberty Pumps Inc** ....C....... 585 494-1817
Bergen *(G-849)*
Linde LLC ....D....... 716 773-7552
Grand Island *(G-5763)*
Lufkin Industries LLC.............................E....... 585 593-7930
Wellsville *(G-16753)*
▲ **Mannesmann Corporation** ....D....... 212 258-4000
New York *(G-11136)*
McWane Inc ....B....... 607 734-2211
Elmira *(G-4694)*
Oberdorfer Pumps Inc ....E....... 315 437-0361
Syracuse *(G-16001)*
Oyster Bay Pump Works Inc..................F....... 516 922-3789
Hicksville *(G-6381)*
Pentair Water Pool and Spa Inc............E....... 845 452-5500
Lagrangeville *(G-7258)*
▲ **Pulsafeeder Inc** ....C....... 585 292-8000
Rochester *(G-14609)*

S I C

Employee Codes: A=Over 500 employees, B=251-500
C=101-250, D=51-100, E=20-50, F=10-19, G=5-9
2017 Harris
New York Manufacturers Directory
829

▲ **Sihi Pumps Inc** ....E 716 773-6450
Grand Island *(G-5769)*
▲ **Stavo Industries Inc** ....F 845 331-4552
Kingston *(G-7213)*
Trench & Marine Pump Co Inc ....E 212 423-9098
Bronx *(G-1475)*
▲ **Voss Usa Inc** ....C 212 995-2255
New York *(G-12570)*
◆ **Wastecorp Pumps LLC** ....F 888 829-2783
New York *(G-12592)*
Water Cooling Corp ....G 718 723-6500
Rosedale *(G-15015)*
Westmoor Ltd ....F 315 363-1500
Sherrill *(G-15410)*
Xylem Inc ....F 716 862-4123
Seneca Falls *(G-15373)*
Xylem Inc ....C 315 258-4949
Auburn *(G-529)*
Xylem Inc ....B 914 323-5700
Rye Brook *(G-15075)*

3562 Ball & Roller Bearings

A Hyatt Ball Co Ltd ....G 518 747-0272
Fort Edward *(G-5339)*
American Refuse Supply Inc ....G 718 893-8157
Bronx *(G-1273)*
David Fehlman ....G 315 455-8888
Syracuse *(G-15922)*
▲ **Dimanco Inc** ....G 315 797-0470
Utica *(G-16324)*
▲ **General Bearing Corporation** ....C 845 358-6000
West Nyack *(G-16918)*
▲ **Kilian Manufacturing Corp** ....D 315 432-0700
Syracuse *(G-15973)*
Lemoyne Machine Products Corp ....G 315 454-0708
Syracuse *(G-15976)*
▲ **Mageba USA LLC** ....E 212 317-1991
New York *(G-11099)*
▲ **Nes Bearing Company Inc** ....E 716 372-6532
Olean *(G-13151)*
Raydon Precision Bearing Co ....G 516 887-2582
Lynbrook *(G-7958)*
S/N Precision Enterprises Inc ....E 518 283-8002
Troy *(G-16252)*
▼ **Sandle Custom Bearing Corp** ....G 585 593-7000
Wellsville *(G-16757)*
Schatz Bearing Corporation ....D 845 452-6000
Poughkeepsie *(G-13930)*
SKF USA Inc ....D 716 661-2869
Falconer *(G-4912)*
SKF USA Inc ....D 716 661-2600
Jamestown *(G-7028)*
SKF USA Inc ....D 716 661-2600
Falconer *(G-4913)*
Workshop Art Fabrication ....F 845 331-0385
Kingston *(G-7225)*

3563 Air & Gas Compressors

▲ **Adams Sfc Inc** ....E 716 877-2608
Tonawanda *(G-16135)*
▲ **Air Techniques Inc** ....B 516 433-7676
Melville *(G-8291)*
◆ **Atlas Copco Comptec LLC** ....B 518 765-3344
Voorheesville *(G-16516)*
Auburn Vacuum Forming Co Inc ....F 315 253-2440
Auburn *(G-482)*
Auto Body Services LLC ....F 631 431-4640
Lindenhurst *(G-7455)*
Bedford Precision Parts Corp ....E 914 241-2211
Bedford Hills *(G-799)*
Buffalo Compressed Air Inc ....G 716 783-8673
Cheektowaga *(G-3563)*
◆ **Chapin International Inc** ....C 585 343-3140
Batavia *(G-627)*
◆ **Chapin Manufacturing Inc** ....C 585 343-3140
Batavia *(G-628)*
Comairco Equipment Inc ....G 716 656-0211
Cheektowaga *(G-3564)*
▲ **Cooper Turbocompressor Inc** ....B 716 896-6600
Buffalo *(G-2890)*
▲ **Crosman Corporation** ....E 585 657-6161
Bloomfield *(G-986)*
Crosman Corporation ....E 585 398-3920
Farmington *(G-5148)*
▲ **Cyclone Air Power Inc** ....G 718 447-3038
Staten Island *(G-15664)*
Dresser-Rand Group Inc ....D 716 375-3000
Olean *(G-13144)*
Eastern Air Products LLC ....F 716 391-1866
Lancaster *(G-7313)*
Ebara Technologies Inc ....D 845 896-1370
Hopewell Junction *(G-6548)*
▲ **Edwards Vacuum LLC** ....D 800 848-9800
Sanborn *(G-15119)*
◆ **Fountainhead Group Inc** ....C 315 736-0037
New York Mills *(G-12722)*
Fountainhead Group Inc ....E 315 736-0037
New York Mills *(G-12723)*
Fountainhead Group Inc ....C 708 598-7100
New York Mills *(G-12724)*
Gas Tchnlogy Enrgy Cncepts LLC ....G 716 831-9695
Buffalo *(G-2965)*
GM Components Holdings LLC ....B 716 439-2463
Lockport *(G-7590)*
◆ **Graham Corporation** ....B 585 343-2216
Batavia *(G-636)*
Idex Corporation ....G 585 292-8121
Rochester *(G-14443)*
Kinequip Inc ....F 716 694-5000
Buffalo *(G-3032)*
Mahle Indstrbeteiligungen GMBH ....D 716 319-6700
Amherst *(G-250)*
▲ **Precision Plus Vacuum Parts** ....D 716 297-2039
Sanborn *(G-15125)*
Screw Compressor Tech Inc ....F 716 827-6600
Buffalo *(G-3179)*
Spfm Corp ....G 718 788-6800
Brooklyn *(G-2588)*
Turbopro Inc ....G 716 681-8651
Alden *(G-184)*
Vac Air Service Inc ....F 716 665-2206
Jamestown *(G-7042)*

3564 Blowers & Fans

Acme Engineering Products Inc ....E 518 236-5659
Mooers *(G-8615)*
Aeromed Inc ....G 518 843-9144
Utica *(G-16306)*
Air Crafters Inc ....C 631 471-7788
Ronkonkoma *(G-14857)*
Air Engineering Filters Inc ....G 914 238-5945
Chappaqua *(G-3550)*
Air Export Mechanical ....G 917 709-5310
Flushing *(G-5222)*
Air Wave Air Conditioning Co ....E 212 545-1122
Bronx *(G-1265)*
American Filtration Tech Inc ....F 585 359-4130
West Henrietta *(G-16867)*
Ametek Tchnical Indus Pdts Inc ....E 845 246-3401
Saugerties *(G-15179)*
Apgn Inc ....F 518 324-4150
Plattsburgh *(G-13651)*
Applied Safety LLC ....G 718 608-6292
Long Island City *(G-7664)*
▲ **Austin Air Systems Limited** ....D 716 856-3700
Buffalo *(G-2824)*
◆ **Automotive Filters Mfg Inc** ....F 631 435-1010
Bohemia *(G-1020)*
Beecher Emssn Sltn Tchnlgs LLC ....F 607 796-0149
Elmira *(G-4671)*
Beltran Associates Inc ....E 718 252-2996
Brooklyn *(G-1680)*
Brodco Inc ....E 631 842-4477
Lido Beach *(G-7440)*
Buffalo Bioblower Tech LLC ....G 716 625-8618
Lockport *(G-7573)*
▲ **Buffalo Filter LLC** ....D 716 835-7000
Lancaster *(G-7307)*
Camfil USA Inc ....G 518 456-6085
Syracuse *(G-15884)*
▲ **Canarm Ltd** ....G 800 267-4427
Ogdensburg *(G-13113)*
Clean Gas Systems Inc ....E 631 467-1600
Hauppauge *(G-6046)*
Daikin Applied Americas Inc ....D 315 253-2771
Auburn *(G-491)*
Delphi Automotive Systems LLC ....A 585 359-6000
West Henrietta *(G-16876)*
Ducon Technologies Inc ....E 631 420-4900
Farmingdale *(G-4979)*
◆ **Ducon Technologies Inc** ....F 631 694-1700
New York *(G-9937)*
Dundas-Jafine Inc ....E 716 681-9690
Alden *(G-177)*
Filta Clean Co Inc ....E 718 495-3800
Brooklyn *(G-1970)*
Filtros Ltd ....E 585 586-8770
East Rochester *(G-4459)*
▲ **Healthway Home Products Inc** ....E 315 298-2904
Pulaski *(G-13951)*
Healthway Products Company ....E 315 207-1410
Oswego *(G-13332)*
▲ **Hilliard Corporation** ....B 607 733-7121
Elmira *(G-4690)*
Hilliard Corporation ....F 607 733-7121
Elmira *(G-4691)*
▲ **Howden North America Inc** ....D 803 741-2700
Depew *(G-4259)*
Howden North America Inc ....D 716 817-6900
Depew *(G-4260)*
Isolation Systems Inc ....F 716 694-6390
North Tonawanda *(G-12979)*
JT Systems Inc ....F 315 622-1980
Liverpool *(G-7529)*
▲ **Low-Cost Mfg Co Inc** ....G 516 627-3282
Carle Place *(G-3393)*
Moffitt Corporation Inc ....E 585 768-7010
Le Roy *(G-7415)*
Moffitt Fan Corporation ....E 585 768-7010
Le Roy *(G-7416)*
Nexstar Holding Corp ....G 716 929-9000
Amherst *(G-253)*
◆ **North American Filter Corp** ....D 800 265-8943
Newark *(G-12739)*
◆ **Northland Filter Intl LLC** ....E 315 207-1410
Oswego *(G-13336)*
Oestreich Metal Works Inc ....G 315 463-4268
Syracuse *(G-16002)*
▼ **Oneida Air Systems Inc** ....E 315 476-5151
Syracuse *(G-16004)*
Parker-Hannifin Corporation ....D 248 628-6017
Lancaster *(G-7330)*
Phytofilter Technologies Inc ....G 518 507-6399
Saratoga Springs *(G-15166)*
Pliotron Company America LLC ....G 716 298-4457
Niagara Falls *(G-12860)*
▲ **R P Fedder Corp** ....E 585 288-1600
Rochester *(G-14618)*
Rapid Fan & Blower Inc ....F 718 786-2060
Long Island City *(G-7857)*
Roome Technologies Inc ....G 585 229-4437
Honeoye *(G-6524)*
▲ **Rotron Incorporated** ....B 845 679-2401
Woodstock *(G-17365)*
Rotron Incorporated ....E 845 679-2401
Woodstock *(G-17366)*
Sbb Inc ....G 315 422-2376
East Syracuse *(G-4562)*
▲ **Standard Motor Products Inc** ....B 718 392-0200
Long Island City *(G-7884)*
Sullivan Bazinet Bongio Inc ....E 315 437-6500
East Syracuse *(G-4568)*

3565 Packaging Machinery

A & G Heat Sealing ....G 631 724-7764
Smithtown *(G-15481)*
All Packaging McHy & Sups Corp ....F 631 588-7310
Ronkonkoma *(G-14861)*
Automecha International Ltd ....E 607 843-2235
Oxford *(G-13363)*
Brooks Bottling Co LLC ....F 607 432-1782
Oneonta *(G-13174)*
Desu Machinery Corporation ....D 716 681-5798
Depew *(G-4255)*
◆ **Dover Global Holdings Inc** ....E 212 922-1640
New York *(G-9912)*
Feldmeier Equipment Inc ....C 315 823-2000
Little Falls *(G-7500)*
Filling Equipment Co Inc ....F 718 445-2111
College Point *(G-3783)*
Fourteen Arnold Ave Corp ....F 315 272-1700
Utica *(G-16333)*
Haines Equipment Inc ....E 607 566-8531
Avoca *(G-537)*
Hypres Inc ....E 914 592-1190
Elmsford *(G-4756)*
K C Technical Services Inc ....G 631 589-7170
Bohemia *(G-1086)*
▲ **Kabar Manufacturing Corp** ....E 631 694-6857
Farmingdale *(G-5022)*
▼ **Kaps-All Packaging Systems** ....D 631 574-8778
Riverhead *(G-14145)*
Millwood Inc ....F 518 233-1475
Waterford *(G-16614)*
Modern Packaging Inc ....D 631 595-2437
Deer Park *(G-4175)*
◆ **National Equipment Corporation** ....F 718 585-0200
Bronx *(G-1405)*
National Equipment Corporation ....E 718 585-0200
Bronx *(G-1406)*

SIC

35 INDUSTRIAL AND COMMERCIAL MACHINERY AND COMPUTER EQUIPMENT

Niagara Scientific Inc..................D....... 315 437-0821
  East Syracuse *(G-4552)*
▲ Orics Industries Inc......................E....... 718 461-8613
  Farmingdale *(G-5070)*
Overhead Door Corporation............D....... 518 828-7652
  Hudson *(G-6629)*
Pacemaker Packaging Corp..............F....... 718 458-1188
  Woodside *(G-17344)*
▲ Packaging Dynamics Ltd................F....... 631 563-4499
  Bohemia *(G-1114)*
Pb Leiner-USA...................................G....... 516 822-4040
  Plainview *(G-13627)*
Reynolds Packaging McHy Inc.........D....... 716 358-6451
  Falconer *(G-4910)*
Rfb Associates Inc...........................G....... 518 271-0551
  Voorheesville *(G-16517)*
Rota Pack Inc...................................F....... 631 274-1037
  Farmingdale *(G-5103)*
Save O Seal Corporation Inc............G....... 914 592-3031
  Elmsford *(G-4777)*
Sharon Manufacturing Co Inc..........G....... 631 242-8870
  Deer Park *(G-4210)*
Silver Creek Enterprises Inc.............E....... 716 934-2611
  Silver Creek *(G-15450)*
▲ Turbofil Packaging Mchs LLC........F....... 914 239-3878
  Mount Vernon *(G-8743)*
▲ Universal Packg Systems Inc.........A....... 631 543-2277
  Commack *(G-3845)*
Utleys Incorporated.........................E....... 718 956-1661
  Woodside *(G-17359)*
Volckening Inc..................................E....... 718 748-0294
  Brooklyn *(G-2735)*

3566 Speed Changers, Drives & Gears

American Torque Inc........................F....... 718 526-2433
  Jamaica *(G-6894)*
▲ Biltron Automotive Products..........E....... 631 928-8613
  Port Jeff STA *(G-13763)*
▲ Buffalo Gear Inc.............................E....... 716 731-2100
  Sanborn *(G-15116)*
Buffalo Power Elec Ctr De................E....... 716 651-1600
  Depew *(G-4250)*
Danaher Corporation........................G....... 716 691-9100
  Amherst *(G-236)*
Designatronics Incorporated............B....... 516 328-3300
  New Hyde Park *(G-8826)*
Emerson Indus Automtn USA LLC...E....... 716 774-1193
  Grand Island *(G-5756)*
◆ Gleason Works...............................A....... 585 473-1000
  Rochester *(G-14408)*
Harmonic Drive LLC.........................G....... 631 231-6630
  Hauppauge *(G-6089)*
▲ Interparts International Inc............E....... 516 576-2000
  Plainview *(G-13610)*
▲ John G Rubino Inc..........................E....... 315 253-7396
  Auburn *(G-504)*
▲ Jrlon Inc..D....... 315 597-4067
  Palmyra *(G-13409)*
Magna Products Corp......................E....... 585 647-2280
  Rochester *(G-14489)*
McGuigan Inc...................................E....... 631 750-6222
  Bohemia *(G-1103)*
Niagara Gear Corporation................E....... 716 874-3131
  Buffalo *(G-3088)*
▲ Nuttall Gear L L C...........................D....... 716 298-4100
  Niagara Falls *(G-12854)*
Oliver Gear Inc.................................E....... 716 885-1080
  Buffalo *(G-3100)*
◆ Ondrivesus Corp............................E....... 516 771-6777
  Freeport *(G-5416)*
Peerless-Winsmith Inc.....................C....... 716 592-9311
  Springville *(G-15614)*
Perfection Gear Inc..........................C....... 716 592-9310
  Springville *(G-15615)*
Precipart Corporation......................C....... 631 777-8727
  Farmingdale *(G-5085)*
Precision Mechanisms Corp............E....... 516 333-5955
  Westbury *(G-17021)*
▲ Renold Inc......................................D....... 716 326-3121
  Westfield *(G-17051)*
Rochester Gear Inc..........................E....... 585 254-5442
  Rochester *(G-14642)*
W J Albro Machine Works Inc.........G....... 631 345-0657
  Yaphank *(G-17408)*

3567 Indl Process Furnaces & Ovens

Ambrell Inc......................................G....... 585 889-9000
  Scottsville *(G-15333)*
▲ Ameritherm Inc..............................F....... 585 889-0236
  Scottsville *(G-15334)*

◆ API Heat Transf Thermasys Corp....E....... 716 901-8504
  Buffalo *(G-2815)*
▼ Buflovak LLC..................................E....... 716 895-2100
  Buffalo *(G-2861)*
▲ Cooks Intl Ltd Lblty Co...................G....... 212 741-4407
  New York *(G-9717)*
Cosmos Electronic Machine Corp...E....... 631 249-2535
  Farmingdale *(G-4963)*
Easco Boiler Corp.............................E....... 718 378-3000
  Bronx *(G-1322)*
▲ Embassy Industries Inc..................C....... 631 435-0209
  Hauppauge *(G-6071)*
▼ Fulton Volcanic Inc........................D....... 315 298-5121
  Pulaski *(G-13950)*
◆ Harper International Corp...............D....... 716 276-9900
  Buffalo *(G-2991)*
▲ Hpi Co Inc.......................................E....... 718 851-2753
  Brooklyn *(G-2089)*
Igniter Systems Inc..........................E....... 716 542-5511
  Akron *(G-24)*
J H Buhrmaster Company Inc.........G....... 518 843-1700
  Amsterdam *(G-351)*
Linde LLC...D....... 716 773-7552
  Grand Island *(G-5763)*
Parker-Hannifin Corporation............D....... 716 685-4040
  Lancaster *(G-7331)*
Radiant Pro Ltd................................G....... 516 763-5678
  Oceanside *(G-13092)*
▼ Rayco Enterprises Inc....................D....... 716 685-6860
  Lancaster *(G-7337)*
Thermal Process Cnstr Co...............E....... 631 293-6400
  Farmingdale *(G-5129)*
Ultraflex Power Technologies..........G....... 631 467-6814
  Ronkonkoma *(G-14995)*
Vent-A-Kiln Corporation..................D....... 716 876-2023
  Buffalo *(G-3240)*
Vincent Genovese.............................E....... 631 281-8170
  Mastic Beach *(G-8205)*

3568 Mechanical Power Transmission Eqpt, NEC

Advanced Thermal Systems Inc......E....... 716 681-1800
  Lancaster *(G-7298)*
Babbitt Bearings Incorporated........D....... 315 479-6603
  Syracuse *(G-15865)*
Borgwarner Morse TEC Inc.............D....... 607 257-6700
  Ithaca *(G-6828)*
▲ Borgwarner Morse TEC Inc............B....... 607 257-6700
  Ithaca *(G-6826)*
▲ BW Elliott Mfg Co LLC....................B....... 607 772-0404
  Binghamton *(G-900)*
C-Flex Bearing Co Inc.....................F....... 315 895-7454
  Frankfort *(G-5350)*
Champlain Hudson Power Ex Inc....G....... 518 465-0710
  Albany *(G-61)*
▲ Cierra Industries Inc......................F....... 315 252-6630
  Auburn *(G-488)*
◆ Cobham Management Services Inc...A.... 716 662-0006
  Orchard Park *(G-13264)*
Designatronics Incorporated............B....... 516 328-3300
  New Hyde Park *(G-8826)*
Eaw Electronic Systems Inc............G....... 845 471-5290
  Poughkeepsie *(G-13897)*
▲ Fait Usa Inc....................................G....... 215 674-5310
  New York *(G-10131)*
▲ Howden North America Inc............D....... 803 741-2700
  Depew *(G-4259)*
Hudson Power Transmission Co.....G....... 718 622-3869
  Brooklyn *(G-2090)*
Huron TI & Cutter Grinding Co........E....... 631 420-7000
  Farmingdale *(G-5008)*
Kaddis Manufacturing Corp.............G....... 585 624-3070
  Honeoye Falls *(G-6533)*
Kinemotive Corporation...................E....... 631 249-6440
  Farmingdale *(G-5028)*
Liston Manufacturing Inc.................E....... 716 695-2111
  North Tonawanda *(G-12981)*
Ls Power Equity Partners LP...........G....... 212 615-3456
  New York *(G-11055)*
Machine Components Corp............G....... 516 694-7222
  Plainview *(G-13617)*
▼ Magtrol Inc......................................E....... 716 668-5555
  Buffalo *(G-3055)*
Maine Power Express LLC..............G....... 518 465-0710
  Albany *(G-99)*
Metallized Carbon Corporation.......C....... 914 941-3738
  Ossining *(G-13323)*
On Line Power Technologies...........G....... 914 968-4440
  Yonkers *(G-17470)*

▲ Package One Inc............................D....... 518 344-5425
  Schenectady *(G-15285)*
▲ Renold Holdings Inc.......................G....... 716 326-3121
  Westfield *(G-17050)*
▲ Renold Inc......................................D....... 716 326-3121
  Westfield *(G-17051)*
▲ Sepac Inc..E....... 607 732-2030
  Elmira *(G-4700)*
Turnomat Company LLC..................G....... 585 924-1630
  Farmington *(G-5157)*
◆ Watson Bowman Acme Corp..........D....... 716 691-8162
  Amherst *(G-271)*
York Industries Inc..........................E....... 516 746-3736
  Garden City Park *(G-5546)*

3569 Indl Machinery & Eqpt, NEC

▲ Adams Sfc Inc................................E....... 716 877-2608
  Tonawanda *(G-16135)*
▲ Advanced Tchncal Solutions Inc....F....... 914 214-8230
  Yorktown Heights *(G-17506)*
Airsep Corporation...........................D....... 716 691-0202
  Amherst *(G-219)*
▲ Alliance Automation Systems.........C....... 585 426-2700
  Rochester *(G-14188)*
Allied Inspection Services LLC.......F....... 716 489-3199
  Falconer *(G-4891)*
▲ American Felt & Filter Co Inc.........D....... 845 561-3560
  New Windsor *(G-8931)*
American Filtration Tech Inc...........F....... 585 359-4130
  West Henrietta *(G-16867)*
American Material Processing........G....... 315 318-0017
  Clifton Springs *(G-3713)*
◆ Audubon Machinery Corporation...D....... 716 564-5165
  North Tonawanda *(G-12957)*
Automated Cells & Eqp Inc..............E....... 607 936-1341
  Painted Post *(G-13389)*
Bowen Products Corporation..........G....... 315 498-4481
  Nedrow *(G-8772)*
▲ Bullex Inc..F....... 518 689-2023
  Albany *(G-58)*
Burnett Process Inc.........................E....... 585 277-1623
  Rochester *(G-14253)*
Chart Industries Inc.........................D....... 716 691-0202
  Amherst *(G-232)*
Chart Industries Inc.........................D....... 716 691-0202
  Amherst *(G-233)*
Cleaning Tech Group LLC...............E....... 716 665-2340
  Jamestown *(G-6981)*
Crandall Filling Machinery Inc........G....... 716 897-3486
  Buffalo *(G-2892)*
▲ Distech Systems Inc.......................G....... 585 254-7020
  Rochester *(G-14311)*
Drasgow Inc.....................................E....... 585 786-3603
  Gainesville *(G-5483)*
Dynamasters Inc..............................G....... 585 458-9970
  Rochester *(G-14321)*
Eastern Precision Mfg.....................G....... 845 358-1951
  Nyack *(G-13050)*
▼ Filter Tech Inc.................................D....... 315 682-8815
  Manlius *(G-8071)*
▲ Finesse Creations Inc.....................F....... 718 692-2100
  Brooklyn *(G-1973)*
Firematic Supply Co Inc.................E....... 631 924-3181
  East Yaphank *(G-4581)*
Foseco Inc.......................................F....... 914 345-4760
  Tarrytown *(G-16090)*
◆ Fountainhead Group Inc.................C....... 315 736-0037
  New York Mills *(G-12722)*
Gem Fabrication of NC....................G....... 704 278-6713
  Garden City *(G-5508)*
Graver Technologies LLC................E....... 585 624-1330
  Honeoye Falls *(G-6528)*
Griffin Automation Inc.....................E....... 716 674-2300
  West Seneca *(G-16948)*
◆ Guyson Corporation of USa............E....... 518 587-7894
  Saratoga Springs *(G-15157)*
◆ Hannay Reels Inc............................C....... 518 797-3791
  Westerlo *(G-17042)*
▲ Hilliard Corporation........................B....... 607 733-7121
  Elmira *(G-4690)*
Hilliard Corporation.........................F....... 607 733-7121
  Elmira *(G-4691)*
Honeybee Robotics Ltd..................E....... 212 966-0661
  Brooklyn *(G-2087)*
▲ Hubco Inc.......................................D....... 716 683-5940
  Alden *(G-179)*
▲ Innovative Pdts of Amer Inc..........E....... 845 679-4500
  Woodstock *(G-17363)*
Island Automated Gate Co LLC......G....... 631 425-0196
  Huntington Station *(G-6711)*

Employee Codes: A=Over 500 employees, B=251-500
C=101-250, D=51-100, E=20-50, F=10-19, G=5-9

J H Robotics Inc ..... E 607 729-3758
Johnson City *(G-7096)*

Kyntec Corporation ..... G 716 810-6956
Buffalo *(G-3038)*

Lifc Corp ..... G 516 426-5737
Port Washington *(G-13838)*

Long Island Pipe Supply Inc ..... E 516 222-8008
Garden City *(G-5515)*

▲ Lubow Machine Corp ..... F 631 226-1700
Copiague *(G-3911)*

Lydall Performance Mtls Inc ..... F 518 273-6320
Green Island *(G-5860)*

Machine Tool Repair & Sales ..... G 631 580-2550
Holbrook *(G-6460)*

Markpericom ..... G 516 208-6824
Oceanside *(G-13088)*

McHone Industries Inc ..... D 716 945-3380
Salamanca *(G-15101)*

Mep Alaska LLC ..... G 646 535-9005
Brooklyn *(G-2297)*

New Vision Industries Inc ..... F 607 687-7700
Endicott *(G-4820)*

◆ North American Filter Corp ..... D 800 265-8943
Newark *(G-12739)*

▲ Pall Corporation ..... A 516 484-5400
Port Washington *(G-13852)*

Pall Corporation ..... A 607 753-6041
Cortland *(G-4035)*

Parker-Hannifin Corporation ..... D 248 628-6017
Lancaster *(G-7330)*

Peerless Mfg Co ..... E 716 539-7400
Orchard Park *(G-13289)*

Peregrine Industries Inc ..... G 631 838-2870
New York *(G-11614)*

Pyrotek Incorporated ..... E 716 731-3221
Sanborn *(G-15126)*

Quality Manufacturing Sys LLC ..... G 716 763-0988
Lakewood *(G-7292)*

▲ Reliable Autmtc Sprnklr Co Inc ..... B 914 829-2042
Elmsford *(G-4776)*

Rfb Associates Inc ..... G 518 271-0551
Voorheesville *(G-16517)*

▲ SC Supply Chain Management LLC . G 212 344-3322
New York *(G-11981)*

Sentry Automatic Sprinkler ..... F 631 723-3095
Riverhead *(G-14156)*

Service Filtration Corp ..... E 716 877-2608
Tonawanda *(G-16202)*

Sidco Filter Corporation ..... E 585 289-3100
Manchester *(G-8053)*

Sinclair International Company ..... E 518 798-2361
Queensbury *(G-14012)*

▲ Sonicor Inc ..... F 631 920-6555
West Babylon *(G-16830)*

Spaghetti Bridge LLC ..... G 646 369-7505
Scarsdale *(G-15224)*

▲ Stavo Industries Inc ..... F 845 331-4552
Kingston *(G-7213)*

Stavo Industries Inc ..... E 845 331-5389
Kingston *(G-7214)*

▲ Sussman-Automatic Corporation ..... D 718 937-4500
Long Island City *(G-7898)*

▲ Taylor Devices Inc ..... C 716 694-0800
North Tonawanda *(G-13001)*

▲ Trident Precision Mfg Inc ..... D 585 265-2010
Webster *(G-16738)*

Tyco Simplexgrinnell ..... E 315 437-9664
East Syracuse *(G-4574)*

Tyco Simplexgrinnell ..... E 716 483-0079
Jamestown *(G-7040)*

Tyco Simplexgrinnell ..... D 315 337-6333
Taberg *(G-16076)*

Universal Metal Fabricators ..... F 845 331-8248
Kingston *(G-7221)*

Veeco Process Equipment Inc ..... C 516 677-0200
Plainview *(G-13645)*

William R Shoemaker Inc ..... G 716 649-0511
Hamburg *(G-5945)*

3571 Electronic Computers

▲ Alliance Magnetic LLC ..... G 914 944-1690
Ossining *(G-13320)*

Apple Commuter Inc ..... G 917 299-0066
New Hyde Park *(G-8816)*

Apple Healing & Relaxation ..... G 718 278-1089
Long Island City *(G-7663)*

▲ Argon Corp ..... F 516 487-5314
Great Neck *(G-5792)*

Arnouse Digital Devices Corp ..... F 516 673-4444
New Hyde Park *(G-8817)*

B-Reel Inc ..... E 917 388-3836
New York *(G-9295)*

▲ Binghamton Simulator Co Inc ..... E 607 321-2980
Binghamton *(G-895)*

Celoxica Inc ..... G 212 880-2075
New York *(G-9557)*

Computer Conversions Corp ..... E 631 261-3300
East Northport *(G-4434)*

Critical Link LLC ..... E 315 425-4045
Syracuse *(G-15912)*

Data-Pac Mailing Systems Corp ..... F 585 671-0210
Webster *(G-16720)*

Datacom Systems Inc ..... E 315 463-9541
East Syracuse *(G-4524)*

Dees Audio & Vision ..... G 585 719-9256
Rochester *(G-14305)*

▲ Digicom International Inc ..... F 631 249-8999
Farmingdale *(G-4977)*

▲ E-Systems Group LLC ..... E 607 775-1100
Conklin *(G-3868)*

Electronic Systems Inc ..... G 631 589-4389
Holbrook *(G-6445)*

▲ Elo Touch Solutions Inc ..... E 585 427-2802
Rochester *(G-14345)*

Envent Systems Inc ..... G 646 294-6980
Pelham *(G-13491)*

Facsimile Cmmncations Inds Inc ..... D 212 741-6400
New York *(G-10125)*

▲ Flash Ventures Inc ..... F 212 255-7070
New York *(G-10177)*

G S Communications USA Inc ..... E 718 389-7371
Brooklyn *(G-2010)*

Group Enterainment LLC ..... G 212 868-5233
New York *(G-10371)*

H&L Computers Inc ..... E 516 873-8088
Flushing *(G-5247)*

▲ Hand Held Products Inc ..... B 315 554-6000
Skaneateles Falls *(G-15468)*

Hi-Tech Advanced Solutions Inc ..... F 718 926-3488
Forest Hills *(G-5324)*

Human Electronics Inc ..... G 315 724-9850
Utica *(G-16339)*

IBM World Trade Corporation ..... G 914 765-1900
Armonk *(G-413)*

International Bus Mchs Corp ..... A 607 754-9558
Endicott *(G-4813)*

Irpenscom ..... G 585 507-7997
Penfield *(G-13499)*

J & N Computer Services Inc ..... F 585 388-8780
Fairport *(G-4858)*

▲ Kemp Technologies Inc ..... D 917 688-4067
New York *(G-10831)*

Lockheed Martin Corporation ..... C 516 228-2000
Uniondale *(G-16298)*

M&C Associates LLC ..... E 631 467-8760
Bohemia *(G-1098)*

Medsim-Eagle Simulation Inc ..... F 607 658-9354
Endicott *(G-4818)*

N & G of America Inc ..... F 516 428-3414
Plainview *(G-13622)*

N & L Instruments Inc ..... F 631 471-4000
Ronkonkoma *(G-14948)*

NCR Corporation ..... C 516 876-7200
Jericho *(G-7078)*

One Technologies LLC ..... G 718 509-0704
Brooklyn *(G-2394)*

Oracle America Inc ..... D 518 427-9353
Albany *(G-111)*

Oracle America Inc ..... D 585 317-4648
Fairport *(G-4866)*

Pace Technology Inc ..... E 631 981-2400
Ronkonkoma *(G-14963)*

Photon Vision Systems Inc ..... F 607 749-2689
Homer *(G-6521)*

Policy ADM Solutions Inc ..... E 914 332-4320
Tarrytown *(G-16100)*

Qualtronic Devices Inc ..... F 631 360-0859
Smithtown *(G-15497)*

Revonate Manufacturing LLC ..... E 315 433-1160
Syracuse *(G-16023)*

Stargate Computer Corp ..... G 516 474-4799
Port Jeff STA *(G-13771)*

▲ Telxon Corporation ..... E 631 738-2400
Holtsville *(G-6512)*

Todd Enterprises Inc ..... D 516 773-8087
Great Neck *(G-5844)*

▲ Toshiba Amer Info Systems Inc ..... B 949 583-3000
New York *(G-12376)*

◆ Toshiba America Inc ..... E 212 596-0600
New York *(G-12377)*

Transland Sourcing LLC ..... G 718 596-5704
Brooklyn *(G-2675)*

Wantagh Computer Center ..... F 516 826-2189
Wantagh *(G-16564)*

Wilcro Inc ..... G 716 632-4204
Buffalo *(G-3254)*

Yellow E House Inc ..... G 718 888-2000
Flushing *(G-5311)*

3572 Computer Storage Devices

Datalink Computer Products ..... F 914 666-2358
Mount Kisco *(G-8626)*

EMC Corporation ..... E 716 833-5348
Amherst *(G-238)*

EMC Corporation ..... E 585 387-9505
East Rochester *(G-4457)*

Emcs LLC ..... G 716 523-2002
Hamburg *(G-5924)*

Formats Unlimited Inc ..... F 631 249-9200
Deer Park *(G-4144)*

Garland Technology LLC ..... E 716 242-8500
Buffalo *(G-2964)*

Gim Electronics Corp ..... F 516 942-3382
Hicksville *(G-6349)*

Globalfoundries US Inc ..... C 518 305-9013
Malta *(G-8019)*

Matrox Graphics Inc ..... G 518 561-4417
Plattsburgh *(G-13677)*

Quantum Asset Recovery ..... G 716 393-2712
Buffalo *(G-3148)*

Quantum Knowledge LLC ..... G 631 727-6111
Riverhead *(G-14153)*

Quantum Logic Corp ..... G 516 746-1380
New Hyde Park *(G-8858)*

Quantum Performance Company ..... G 518 642-3111
Granville *(G-5780)*

Sale 121 Corp ..... D 240 855-8988
New York *(G-11956)*

◆ Sony Corporation of America ..... C 212 833-8000
New York *(G-12132)*

Todd Enterprises Inc ..... D 516 773-8087
Great Neck *(G-5844)*

▲ Toshiba Amer Info Systems Inc ..... B 949 583-3000
New York *(G-12376)*

William S Hein & Co Inc ..... D 716 882-2600
Getzville *(G-5606)*

3575 Computer Terminals

901 D LLC ..... E 845 369-1111
Airmont *(G-11)*

AG Neovo Professional Inc ..... F 212 647-9080
New York *(G-9055)*

Cine Design Group LLC ..... G 646 747-0734
New York *(G-9617)*

▲ Clayton Dubilier & Rice Fun ..... E 212 407-5200
New York *(G-9640)*

Igt Global Solutions Corp ..... D 518 382-2900
Schenectady *(G-15269)*

Integra Microsystem 1988 Inc ..... G 718 609-6099
Brooklyn *(G-2109)*

International Bus Mchs Corp ..... A 845 433-1234
Poughkeepsie *(G-13907)*

Nu - Communitek LLC ..... F 516 433-3553
Hicksville *(G-6377)*

Orbit International Corp ..... C 631 435-8300
Hauppauge *(G-6154)*

PC Solutions & Consulting ..... G 607 735-0466
Elmira *(G-4697)*

Shadowtv Inc ..... G 212 445-2540
New York *(G-12037)*

Symbio Technologies LLC ..... G 914 576-1205
White Plains *(G-17174)*

▲ Touchstone Technology Inc ..... F 585 458-2690
Rochester *(G-14728)*

Ultra-Scan Corporation ..... F 716 832-6269
Amherst *(G-270)*

Wey Inc ..... G 212 532-3299
New York *(G-12621)*

3577 Computer Peripheral Eqpt, NEC

A I T Computers Inc ..... G 518 266-9010
Troy *(G-16224)*

Aalborg Instrs & Contrls Inc ..... D 845 398-3160
Orangeburg *(G-13217)*

Advanced Barcode Technology ..... F 516 570-8100
Great Neck *(G-5784)*

Aero-Vision Technologies Inc ..... G 631 643-8349
Melville *(G-8289)*

Aeroflex Plainview Inc ..... C 631 231-9100
Hauppauge *(G-6011)*

35 INDUSTRIAL AND COMMERCIAL MACHINERY AND COMPUTER EQUIPMENT

▲ Andrea Electronics Corporation ..... F 631 719-1800
  Bohemia (G-1016)
Annese & Associates Inc ..... G 716 972-0076
  Buffalo (G-2812)
▲ Anorad Corporation ..... C 631 380-2100
  East Setauket (G-4476)
Atlaz International Ltd ..... F 516 239-1854
  Lawrence (G-7390)
Aventura Technologies Inc ..... E 631 300-4000
  Commack (G-3822)
B V M Associates ..... G 631 254-6220
  Shirley (G-15415)
▲ Binghamton Simulator Co Inc ..... E 607 321-2980
  Binghamton (G-895)
Blue Skies ..... G 631 392-1140
  Deer Park (G-4110)
Broadnet Technologies Inc ..... F 315 443-3694
  Syracuse (G-15875)
Brocade Cmmnctions Systems Inc ..... G 212 497-8500
  New York (G-9467)
Cal Blen Electronic Industries ..... F 631 242-6243
  Deer Park (G-4114)
Capture Globa Integ Solut Inc ..... G 718 352-0579
  Bayside Hills (G-779)
Chem-Puter Friendly Inc ..... E 631 331-2259
  Mount Sinai (G-8654)
Chemung Cty Assc Retrd Ctzns ..... C 607 734-6151
  Elmira (G-4675)
Cisco Systems Inc ..... C 212 714-4000
  New York (G-9622)
▲ Clayton Dubilier & Rice Fun ..... E 212 407-5200
  New York (G-9640)
CNy Business Solutions ..... G 315 733-5031
  Utica (G-16312)
Control Logic Corporation ..... G 607 965-6423
  West Burlington (G-16841)
CPW Direct Mail Group LLC ..... E 631 588-6565
  Farmingdale (G-4964)
▲ Data Device Corporation ..... B 631 567-5600
  Bohemia (G-1049)
Datatran Labs Inc ..... G 845 856-4313
  Port Jervis (G-13783)
▲ Dia-Nielsen USA Incorporated ..... G 856 642-9700
  Buffalo (G-2913)
Eastman Kodak Company ..... B 585 724-4000
  Rochester (G-14328)
Ems Development Corporation ..... D 631 345-6200
  Yaphank (G-17391)
Future Star Digatech ..... F 718 666-0350
  Brooklyn (G-2008)
◆ Gasoft Equipment Inc ..... F 845 863-1010
  Newburgh (G-12756)
Glowa Manufacturing Inc ..... E 607 770-0811
  Binghamton (G-919)
Gunther Partners LLC ..... G 212 521-2930
  New York (G-10384)
▲ Hand Held Products Inc ..... B 315 554-6000
  Skaneateles Falls (G-15468)
Hand Held Products Inc ..... F 315 554-6000
  Skaneateles Falls (G-15469)
▲ Hauppauge Computer Works Inc ..... E 631 434-1600
  Hauppauge (G-6090)
▲ Hauppauge Digital Inc ..... F 631 434-1600
  Hauppauge (G-6091)
◆ Hergo Ergonomic Support ..... E 718 894-0639
  Maspeth (G-8143)
Hf Technologies LLC ..... E 585 254-5030
  Hamlin (G-5950)
◆ Hitachi Metals America Ltd ..... E 914 694-9200
  Purchase (G-13959)
HP Inc ..... D 212 835-1640
  New York (G-10523)
◆ Humanscale Corporation ..... E 212 725-4749
  New York (G-10531)
IBM World Trade Corporation ..... G 914 765-1900
  Armonk (G-413)
▲ Inner Workings Inc ..... E 646 352-4394
  New York (G-10601)
Innovative Systems of New York ..... G 516 541-7410
  Massapequa Park (G-8187)
Inpora Technologies LLC ..... D 646 838-2474
  New York (G-10609)
Jadak LLC ..... F 315 701-0678
  North Syracuse (G-12949)
Jadak Technologies Inc ..... D 315 701-0678
  North Syracuse (G-12950)
Juniper Networks Inc ..... A 212 520-3300
  New York (G-10789)
▲ Kantek Inc ..... E 516 594-4600
  Oceanside (G-13084)
Lexmark International Inc ..... E 212 949-1090
  New York (G-10980)
Lockheed Martin Integrated ..... E 315 456-3333
  Syracuse (G-15981)
Lsc Peripherals Incorporated ..... G 631 244-0707
  Bohemia (G-1096)
Luminescent Systems Inc ..... B 716 655-0800
  East Aurora (G-4373)
Macrolink Inc ..... E 631 924-8265
  Medford (G-8255)
Maia Systems LLC ..... E 718 206-0100
  Jamaica (G-6927)
Marco Manufacturing Inc ..... E 845 485-1571
  Poughkeepsie (G-13914)
Mdi Holdings LLC ..... A 212 559-1127
  New York (G-11203)
Medsim-Eagle Simulation Inc ..... F 607 658-9354
  Endicott (G-4818)
Mg Imaging ..... G 212 704-4073
  New York (G-11245)
Mirion Technologies Ist Corp ..... D 607 562-4300
  Horseheads (G-6584)
▲ Mp Displays LLC ..... G 845 268-4113
  Valley Cottage (G-16383)
NCR Corporation ..... C 607 273-5310
  Ithaca (G-6866)
▲ Norazza Inc ..... G 716 706-1160
  Buffalo (G-3093)
Orbit International Corp ..... E 631 435-8300
  Hauppauge (G-6154)
P C Rfrs Radiology ..... E 212 586-5700
  Long Island City (G-7830)
◆ Paxar Corporation ..... E 845 398-3229
  Orangeburg (G-13238)
Pda Panache Corp ..... E 631 776-0523
  Bohemia (G-1116)
Peoples Choice M R I ..... F 716 681-7377
  Buffalo (G-3119)
Perceptive Pixel Inc ..... E 701 367-5845
  New York (G-11613)
Performance Technologies Inc ..... D 585 256-0200
  Rochester (G-14576)
Phoenix Venture Fund LLC ..... E 212 759-1909
  New York (G-11653)
◆ QED Technologies Intl Inc ..... E 585 256-6540
  Rochester (G-14610)
▲ Rdi Inc ..... F 914 773-1000
  Mount Kisco (G-8643)
Redwood Cllaborative Media Inc ..... F 631 393-6051
  Melville (G-8352)
Reliable Elec Mt Vernon Inc ..... E 914 668-4440
  Mount Vernon (G-8725)
Rodale Wireless Inc ..... E 631 231-0044
  Hauppauge (G-6179)
Ruhle Companies Inc ..... E 914 287-4000
  Valhalla (G-16372)
S G I ..... G 917 386-0385
  New York (G-11945)
Saab Sensis Corporation ..... C 315 445-0550
  East Syracuse (G-4561)
Scroll Media Inc ..... G 617 395-8904
  New York (G-12008)
Secuprint Inc ..... F 585 341-3100
  Rochester (G-14680)
Sequential Electronics Systems ..... E 914 592-1345
  Elmsford (G-4783)
▲ Sima Technologies LLC ..... G 412 828-9130
  Hauppauge (G-6191)
◆ Sony Corporation of America ..... C 212 833-8000
  New York (G-12132)
Symbol Technologies LLC ..... F 631 738-2400
  Bohemia (G-1139)
Symbol Technologies LLC ..... G 631 738-3346
  Holtsville (G-6510)
Symbol Technologies LLC ..... F 631 218-3907
  Holbrook (G-6477)
Synaptics Incorporated ..... F 585 899-4300
  Rochester (G-14710)
T&K Printing Inc ..... F 718 439-9454
  Brooklyn (G-2640)
▲ Technomag Inc ..... G 631 246-6142
  East Setauket (G-4493)
Todd Enterprises Inc ..... D 516 773-8087
  Great Neck (G-5844)
Torrent Ems LLC ..... F 716 312-4099
  Lockport (G-7620)
▲ Toshiba Amer Info Systems Inc ..... B 949 583-3000
  New York (G-12376)
Tpg Printers Inc ..... B 607 273-5310
  Ithaca (G-6879)
Transact Technologies Inc ..... D 607 257-8901
  Ithaca (G-6880)
Vader Systems LLC ..... G 716 636-1742
  East Amherst (G-4363)
▲ Vishay Thin Film LLC ..... C 716 283-4025
  Niagara Falls (G-12889)
Vuzix Corporation ..... E 585 359-5900
  West Henrietta (G-16898)
Wantagh Computer Center ..... F 516 826-2189
  Wantagh (G-16564)
▲ Watson Productions LLC ..... F 516 334-9766
  Hauppauge (G-6230)
Welch Allyn Inc ..... A 315 685-4100
  Skaneateles Falls (G-15471)
Wilson & Wilson Group ..... G 212 729-4736
  Forest Hills (G-5330)
X Brand Editions ..... G 718 482-7646
  Long Island City (G-7927)
Xerox Corporation ..... D 516 677-1500
  Melville (G-8362)
Xerox Corporation ..... E 585 423-3538
  Rochester (G-14769)
▲ Z-Axis Inc ..... D 315 548-5000
  Phelps (G-13539)

3578 Calculating & Accounting Eqpt

Gary Roth & Associates Ltd ..... E 516 333-1000
  Westbury (G-16990)
▲ Hand Held Products Inc ..... B 315 554-6000
  Skaneateles Falls (G-15468)
Hopp Companies Inc ..... E 516 358-4170
  New Hyde Park (G-8841)
International Mdse Svcs Inc ..... G 914 699-4000
  Mount Vernon (G-8693)
Jpmorgan Chase Bank Nat Assn ..... G 718 767-3592
  College Point (G-3793)
Jpmorgan Chase Bank Nat Assn ..... G 718 668-0346
  Staten Island (G-15695)
K&G of Syracuse Inc ..... G 315 446-1921
  Syracuse (G-15972)
Kenney Manufacturing Displays ..... F 631 231-5563
  Brentwood (G-1188)
▲ Logic Controls Inc ..... E 516 248-0400
  Bethpage (G-872)
Mid Enterprise Inc ..... G 631 924-3933
  Middle Island (G-8407)
▲ Parabit Systems Inc ..... E 516 378-4800
  Roosevelt (G-15008)
Powa Technologies Inc ..... E 347 344-7848
  New York (G-11691)
Rasa Services Inc ..... G 516 294-4292
  New Hyde Park (G-8859)
Sharenet Inc ..... E 315 477-1100
  Syracuse (G-16039)
Stanson Automated LLC ..... F 866 505-7826
  Yonkers (G-17485)

3579 Office Machines, NEC

Action Technologies Inc ..... G 718 278-1000
  Long Island City (G-7648)
Automecha International Ltd ..... E 607 843-2235
  Oxford (G-13363)
Central Time Clock Inc ..... F 718 784-4900
  Long Island City (G-7696)
Cummins - Allison Corp ..... D 718 263-2482
  Kew Gardens (G-7159)
Dominion Voting Systems Inc ..... F 404 955-9799
  Jamestown (G-6988)
▲ Magnetic Technologies Corp ..... D 585 385-9010
  Rochester (G-14490)
National Time Recording Eqp Co ..... F 212 227-3310
  New York (G-11352)
Neopost USA Inc ..... E 631 435-9100
  Hauppauge (G-6146)
Pitney Bowes Inc ..... E 212 564-7548
  New York (G-11667)
Pitney Bowes Inc ..... E 203 356-5000
  New York (G-11668)
Pitney Bowes Inc ..... E 516 822-0900
  Hicksville (G-6389)
▲ Staplex Company Inc ..... E 718 768-3333
  Brooklyn (G-2598)
Widmer Time Recorder Company ..... F 212 227-0405
  New York (G-12631)

3581 Automatic Vending Machines

American Lckr SEC Systems Inc ..... E 716 699-2773
  Ellicottville (G-4640)
Cubic Trnsp Systems Inc ..... F 212 255-1810
  New York (G-9764)

Employee Codes: A=Over 500 employees, B=251-500
C=101-250, D=51-100, E=20-50, F=10-19, G=5-9

35 INDUSTRIAL AND COMMERCIAL MACHINERY AND COMPUTER EQUIPMENT

Global Payment Tech Inc ....F 516 887-0700
  Valley Stream *(G-16407)*
▲ Global Payment Tech Inc ....E 631 563-2500
  Bohemia *(G-1074)*
L & L Precision Machining ....F 631 462-9587
  East Northport *(G-4440)*
Vengo Inc ....G 866 526-7054
  Long Island City *(G-7912)*

3582 Commercial Laundry, Dry Clean & Pressing Mchs

Fowler Route Co Inc ....F 917 653-4640
  Yonkers *(G-17446)*
▲ G A Braun Inc ....D 315 475-3123
  North Syracuse *(G-12943)*
G A Braun Inc ....E 315 475-3123
  Syracuse *(G-15945)*
Lb Laundry Inc ....G 347 399-8030
  Flushing *(G-5264)*
Lynx Product Group LLC ....E 716 751-3100
  Wilson *(G-17268)*
▼ Maxi Companies Inc ....G 315 446-1002
  De Witt *(G-4083)*
Pressure Washing Services Inc ....G 607 286-7458
  Milford *(G-8474)*
Q Omni Inc ....G 914 962-2726
  Yorktown Heights *(G-17517)*
Thermopatch Corporation ....D 315 446-8110
  Syracuse *(G-16058)*

3585 Air Conditioning & Heating Eqpt

A Nuclimate Qulty Systems Inc ....F 315 431-0226
  East Syracuse *(G-4498)*
A&S Refrigeration Equipment ....G 718 993-6030
  Bronx *(G-1255)*
AC Air Cooling Co Inc ....F 718 933-1011
  Bronx *(G-1258)*
Advance Energy Tech Inc ....E 518 371-2140
  Halfmoon *(G-5908)*
Aeroseal LLC ....F 315 373-0765
  East Syracuse *(G-4499)*
Airsys Technologies LLC ....G 716 694-6390
  Tonawanda *(G-16136)*
▲ Alstrom Corporation ....E 718 824-4901
  Bronx *(G-1270)*
American Refrigeration Inc ....G 212 699-4000
  New York *(G-9127)*
▲ Atmost Refrigeration Co Inc ....G 518 828-2180
  Hudson *(G-6608)*
Balticare Inc ....G 646 380-9470
  New York *(G-9310)*
Besicorp Ltd ....F 845 336-7700
  Kingston *(G-7179)*
Bombardier Trnsp Holdings USA ......D 607 776-4791
  Bath *(G-654)*
Carrier Corporation ....E 315 432-6000
  Syracuse *(G-15887)*
Carrier Corporation ....B 315 463-5744
  East Syracuse *(G-4513)*
Carrier Corporation ....A 315 432-6000
  Syracuse *(G-15889)*
Carrier Corporation ....B 315 432-6000
  East Syracuse *(G-4514)*
Carrier Corporation ....B 315 432-3844
  East Syracuse *(G-4515)*
Carrier Corporation ....B 315 432-6000
  Syracuse *(G-15888)*
Chart Inc ....F 518 272-3565
  Troy *(G-16230)*
Chudnow Manufacturing Co Inc ....E 516 593-4222
  Oceanside *(G-13074)*
Colburns AC Rfrgn ....F 716 569-3695
  Frewsburg *(G-5449)*
▲ Cold Point Corporation ....E 315 339-2331
  Rome *(G-14809)*
▲ Columbia Pool Accessories Inc ....G 718 993-0389
  Bronx *(G-1303)*
Daikin Applied Americas Inc ....D 315 253-2771
  Auburn *(G-491)*
Dundas-Jafine Inc ....E 716 681-9690
  Alden *(G-177)*
◆ Duro Dyne Corporation ....F 631 249-9000
  Farmingdale *(G-4980)*
◆ Duro Dyne Machinery Corp ....E 631 249-9000
  Bay Shore *(G-696)*
▲ Duro Dyne National Corp ....C 631 249-9000
  Bay Shore *(G-697)*
Economy Pump & Motor Repair ....G 718 433-2600
  Astoria *(G-438)*

EMC Fintech ....F 716 488-9071
  Falconer *(G-4896)*
▲ Enviromaster International LLC ....D 315 336-3716
  Rome *(G-14810)*
Environmental Temp Systems LLC ...G 516 640-5818
  Mineola *(G-8508)*
Fedders Islandaire Inc ....D 631 471-2900
  East Setauket *(G-4482)*
Foster Refrigerators Entp ....F 518 671-6036
  Hudson *(G-6614)*
Fts Systems Inc ....D 845 687-5300
  Stone Ridge *(G-15763)*
GM Components Holdings LLC ....B 716 439-2463
  Lockport *(G-7590)*
◆ Graham Corporation ....B 585 343-2216
  Batavia *(G-636)*
Grillmaster Inc ....E 718 272-9191
  Howard Beach *(G-6597)*
Healthway Products Company ....E 315 207-1410
  Oswego *(G-13332)*
▲ Heaven Fresh USA Inc ....G 800 642-0367
  Niagara Falls *(G-12831)*
▲ Hoshizaki Nrtheastern Dist Ctr .....D 516 605-1411
  Plainview *(G-13604)*
▲ Hydro-Air Components Inc ....C 716 827-6510
  Buffalo *(G-3000)*
Ice Air LLC ....E 914 668-4700
  Mount Vernon *(G-8692)*
JE Miller Inc ....E 315 437-6811
  East Syracuse *(G-4546)*
John F Krell Jr ....E 315 492-3201
  Syracuse *(G-15968)*
Kedco Inc ....F 516 454-7800
  Farmingdale *(G-5025)*
Keeler Services ....C 607 776-5757
  Bath *(G-658)*
▲ Klearbar Inc ....G 516 684-9892
  Port Washington *(G-13834)*
Layton Manufacturing Corp ....F 718 498-6000
  Brooklyn *(G-2196)*
Lightron Corporation ....G 516 938-5544
  Jericho *(G-7075)*
M M Tool and Manufacturing ....G 845 691-4140
  Highland *(G-6405)*
Manning Lewis Div Rubicon Inds ......E 908 687-2400
  Brooklyn *(G-2262)*
Marathon Heater Co Inc ....G 607 657-8113
  Richford *(G-14063)*
Max Thermo Corporation ....F 845 294-3640
  Goshen *(G-5737)*
▼ Mgr Equipment Corp ....E 516 239-3030
  Inwood *(G-6761)*
▲ Millrock Technology Inc ....G 845 339-5700
  Kingston *(G-7201)*
Mohawk Cabinet Company Inc ....F 518 725-0645
  Gloversville *(G-5718)*
▲ Motivair Corporation ....E 716 691-9222
  Amherst *(G-252)*
MSP Technologycom LLC ....G 631 424-7542
  Centerport *(G-3480)*
Nationwide Coils Inc ....G 914 277-7396
  Mount Kisco *(G-8636)*
▼ Niagara Blower Company ....C 800 426-5169
  Tonawanda *(G-16186)*
▲ Niagara Dispensing Tech Inc ....F 716 636-9827
  Buffalo *(G-3086)*
Northern Air Systems Inc ....E 585 594-5050
  Rochester *(G-14543)*
Opticool Solutions LLC ....E 585 347-6127
  Webster *(G-16728)*
Parker-Hannifin Corporation ....F 716 685-4040
  Lancaster *(G-7331)*
◆ Pfannenberg Inc ....E 716 685-6866
  Lancaster *(G-7333)*
Pro Metal of NY Corp ....G 516 285-0440
  Valley Stream *(G-16421)*
▲ Rayco Enterprises Inc ....D 716 685-6860
  Lancaster *(G-7337)*
▲ RE Hansen Industries Inc ....C 631 471-2900
  East Setauket *(G-4491)*
Roemac Industrial Sales Inc ....G 716 692-7332
  North Tonawanda *(G-12991)*
▲ Rubicon Industries Corp ....E 718 434-4700
  Brooklyn *(G-2515)*
S & V Restaurant Eqp Mfrs Inc ....E 718 220-1140
  Bronx *(G-1445)*
Siemens Industry Inc ....E 716 568-0983
  Buffalo *(G-3187)*
Solitec Incorporated ....F 315 298-4213
  Pulaski *(G-13952)*

Split Systems Corp ....G 516 223-5511
  North Baldwin *(G-12909)*
▲ Standard Motor Products Inc ....B 718 392-0200
  Long Island City *(G-7884)*
Storflex Holdings Inc ....C 607 962-2137
  Corning *(G-3982)*
Supermarket Equipment Depo Inc ....G 718 665-6200
  Bronx *(G-1467)*
Thomson Industries Inc ....F 716 691-9100
  Amherst *(G-266)*
Trane US Inc ....D 718 721-8844
  Long Island City *(G-7905)*
Trane US Inc ....G 914 593-0303
  Elmsford *(G-4788)*
Trane US Inc ....E 315 234-1500
  East Syracuse *(G-4573)*
Trane US Inc ....E 518 785-1315
  Latham *(G-7380)*
Trane US Inc ....E 585 256-2500
  Rochester *(G-14729)*
Trane US Inc ....E 716 626-1260
  Buffalo *(G-3224)*
Trane US Inc ....E 631 952-9477
  Plainview *(G-13639)*
▲ Transit Air Inc ....F 607 324-0216
  Hornell *(G-6568)*
▲ Universal Coolers Inc ....E 718 788-8621
  Brooklyn *(G-2705)*
Universal Parent and Youth ....F 917 754-2426
  Brooklyn *(G-2707)*
York International Corporation ....D 718 389-4152
  Long Island City *(G-7929)*

3586 Measuring & Dispensing Pumps

Aptargroup Inc ....C 845 639-3700
  Congers *(G-3852)*
▲ Charles Ross & Son Company .....D 631 234-0500
  Hauppauge *(G-6044)*
Economy Pump & Motor Repair ....G 718 433-2600
  Astoria *(G-438)*
▲ Pulsafeeder Inc ....E 585 292-8000
  Rochester *(G-14609)*
Schlumberger Technology Corp ....C 607 378-0200
  Horseheads *(G-6592)*
▲ Valois of America Inc ....C 845 639-3700
  Congers *(G-3861)*

3589 Service Ind Machines, NEC

Abe Pool Service ....G 845 473-7730
  Hyde Park *(G-6733)*
Advance Food Service Co Inc ....E 631 242-4800
  Edgewood *(G-4590)*
▼ Advance Tabco Inc ....D 631 242-8270
  Edgewood *(G-4591)*
American Comfort Direct LLC ....E 201 364-8309
  New York *(G-9116)*
Arpa USA ....G 212 965-4099
  New York *(G-9206)*
◆ Atlantic Ultraviolet Corp ....E 631 234-3275
  Hauppauge *(G-6028)*
▲ Attias Oven Corp ....G 718 499-0145
  Brooklyn *(G-1650)*
Bakers Pride Oven Co Inc ....C 914 576-0200
  New Rochelle *(G-8887)*
◆ Blue Tee Corp ....G 212 598-0880
  New York *(G-9422)*
Business Advisory Services ....G 718 337-3740
  Far Rockaway *(G-4919)*
Carts Mobile Food Eqp Corp ....E 718 788-5540
  Brooklyn *(G-1761)*
Chester Shred-It/West ....G 914 347-4460
  Valhalla *(G-16365)*
City of Kingston ....F 845 331-2490
  Kingston *(G-7184)*
City of Olean ....G 716 376-5694
  Olean *(G-13138)*
City of Oneonta ....G 607 433-3470
  Oneonta *(G-13178)*
Clearcove Systems Inc ....F 585 734-3012
  Victor *(G-16467)*
Commercial Solutions Inc ....F 716 731-5825
  Sanborn *(G-15118)*
Custom Klean Corp ....F 315 865-8101
  Holland Patent *(G-6487)*
Dyna-Vac Equipment Inc ....F 315 865-8084
  Stittville *(G-15762)*
▼ Econocraft Worldwide Mfg Inc .....G 914 966-2280
  Yonkers *(G-17439)*
Empire Division Inc ....D 315 476-6273
  Syracuse *(G-15936)*

SIC SECTION — 35 INDUSTRIAL AND COMMERCIAL MACHINERY AND COMPUTER EQUIPMENT

◆ Environment-One Corporation ....C 518 346-6161
Schenectady *(G-15252)*
Ewt Holdings III Corp ....G 212 644-5900
New York *(G-10096)*
Ferguson Enterprises Inc ....E 800 437-1146
New Hyde Park *(G-8834)*
H2o Solutions Inc ....F 518 527-0915
Stillwater *(G-15760)*
Heliojet Cleaning Tech Inc ....F 585 768-8710
Le Roy *(G-7408)*
Hercules International Inc ....E 631 423-6900
Huntington Station *(G-6708)*
Hobart Corporation ....E 585 427-9000
Rochester *(G-14438)*
▼ I A S National Inc ....E 631 423-6900
Huntington Station *(G-6710)*
IMC Teddy Food Service ....E 631 789-8881
Amityville *(G-295)*
Incorporated Village Garden Cy ....C 516 465-4020
Garden City *(G-5510)*
Integrated Water Management ....G 607 844-4276
Dryden *(G-4321)*
▲ Key High Vacuum Products Inc .....E 631 584-5959
Nesconset *(G-8775)*
▲ Kinplex Corp ....E 631 242-4800
Edgewood *(G-4603)*
Kinplex Corp ....E 631 242-4800
Edgewood *(G-4604)*
Klee Corp ....G 585 272-0320
Rochester *(G-14470)*
◆ Korin Japanese Trading Corp ....E 212 587-7021
New York *(G-10878)*
Liquid Industries Inc ....G 716 628-2999
Niagara Falls *(G-12843)*
Metro Group Inc ....D 718 392-3616
Long Island City *(G-7811)*
Metro Lube ....G 718 947-1167
Rego Park *(G-14036)*
National Vac Envmtl Svcs Corp ....E 518 743-0563
Glens Falls *(G-5691)*
Neptune Soft Water Inc ....F 315 446-5151
Syracuse *(G-15997)*
New Windsor Waste Water Plant ....F 845 561-2550
New Windsor *(G-8944)*
Northeast Water Systems LLC ....G 585 943-9225
Kendall *(G-7144)*
Orege North America Inc ....G 770 862-9388
New York *(G-11525)*
Ossining Village of Inc ....G 914 202-9668
Ossining *(G-13325)*
Oxford Cleaners ....G 212 734-0006
New York *(G-11539)*
Oyster Bay Pump Works Inc ....F 516 922-3789
Hicksville *(G-6381)*
Pathfinder 103 Inc ....G 315 363-4260
Oneida *(G-13165)*
Pentair Water Pool and Spa Inc ....E 845 452-5500
Lagrangeville *(G-7258)*
▲ Pleatco LLC ....D 516 609-0200
Glen Cove *(G-5624)*
Power Scrub It Inc ....E 516 997-2500
Westbury *(G-17020)*
Pure Planet Waters LLC ....F 718 676-7900
Brooklyn *(G-2458)*
R C Kolstad Water Corp ....E 585 216-2230
Ontario *(G-13210)*
▲ R-S Restaurant Eqp Mfg Corp ....E 212 925-0335
New York *(G-11784)*
Richard R Cain Inc ....E 845 229-7410
Hyde Park *(G-6736)*
Roger & Sons Inc ....G 212 226-4734
New York *(G-11906)*
Royal Prestige Lasting Co ....F 516 280-5148
Hempstead *(G-6286)*
Strategies North America Inc ....G 716 945-6053
Salamanca *(G-15108)*
▲ Toga Manufacturing Inc ....G 631 242-4800
Edgewood *(G-4618)*
Vivreau Advanced Water Systems .....F 212 502-3749
New York *(G-12559)*
Water Energy Systems LLC ....G 844 822-7665
New York *(G-12569)*
▲ Water Technologies Inc ....G 315 986-0000
Macedon *(G-7992)*
Water Treatment Services Inc ....G 914 241-2461
Bedford Hills *(G-808)*
Wilder Manufacturing Co Inc ....D 516 222-0433
Garden City *(G-5536)*
Yr Blanc & Co LLC ....G 716 800-3999
Buffalo *(G-3261)*

3592 Carburetors, Pistons, Rings & Valves

▲ Fcmp Inc ....F 716 692-4623
Tonawanda *(G-16160)*
▲ Fuel Systems Solutions Inc ....E 646 502-7170
New York *(G-10220)*
Premium Valve Services LLC ....G 607 565-7571
Waverly *(G-16705)*
Valvetech Inc ....E 315 548-4551
Phelps *(G-13538)*

3593 Fluid Power Cylinders & Actuators

▲ A K Allen Co Inc ....C 516 747-5450
Mineola *(G-8488)*
Actuant Corporation ....E 607 753-8276
Cortland *(G-4011)*
Allenair Corporation ....D 516 747-5450
Mineola *(G-8494)*
▲ Ameritool Mfg Inc ....E 315 668-2172
Central Square *(G-3516)*
Direkt Force LLC ....E 716 652-3022
East Aurora *(G-4369)*
◆ Eastport Operating Partners LP .....G 212 387-8791
New York *(G-9969)*
Hydra Technology Corp ....G 716 896-8316
Buffalo *(G-2999)*
▲ ITT Enidine Inc ....B 716 662-1900
Orchard Park *(G-13275)*
Precision Mechanisms Corp ....E 516 333-5955
Westbury *(G-17021)*
Skytravel (usa) LLC ....F 518 888-2610
Schenectady *(G-15298)*
Springville Mfg Co Inc ....E 716 592-4957
Springville *(G-15616)*
Superior Motion Controls Inc ....E 516 420-2921
Farmingdale *(G-5120)*
Tactair Fluid Controls Inc ....C 315 451-3928
Liverpool *(G-7552)*
Triumph Actuation Systems LLC ....D 516 378-0162
Freeport *(G-5432)*
Young & Franklin Inc ....E 315 457-3110
Liverpool *(G-7559)*

3594 Fluid Power Pumps & Motors

Atlantic Industrial Tech Inc ....E 631 234-3131
Shirley *(G-15414)*
Huck International Inc ....C 845 331-7300
Kingston *(G-7191)*
Hydroacoustics Inc ....F 585 359-1000
Henrietta *(G-6294)*
◆ Itt LLC ....B 914 641-2000
White Plains *(G-17125)*
ITT Corporation ....D 315 568-2811
Seneca Falls *(G-15362)*
◆ ITT Fluid Technology Corp ....B 914 641-2000
White Plains *(G-17127)*
ITT Inc ....B 914 641-2000
White Plains *(G-17128)*
Parker-Hannifin Corporation ....C 585 425-7000
Fairport *(G-4867)*
Trench & Marine Pump Co Inc ....E 212 423-9098
Bronx *(G-1475)*
Triumph Actuation Systems LLC ....D 516 378-0162
Freeport *(G-5432)*

3596 Scales & Balances, Exc Laboratory

A & K Equipment Incorporated ....G 705 428-3573
Watertown *(G-16633)*
Circuits & Systems Inc ....E 516 593-4301
East Rockaway *(G-4468)*
▲ Itin Scale Co Inc ....E 718 336-5900
Brooklyn *(G-2120)*
Measupro Inc ....F 845 425-8777
Spring Valley *(G-15596)*
Mettler-Toledo Inc ....C 607 257-6000
Ithaca *(G-6860)*
S R Instruments Inc ....E 716 693-5977
Tonawanda *(G-16197)*
Scale-Tronix Inc ....F 914 948-8117
Skaneateles *(G-15465)*
Weighing & Systems Tech Inc ....G 518 274-2797
Troy *(G-16263)*

3599 Machinery & Eqpt, Indl & Commercial, NEC

A & G Precision Corp ....F 631 957-5613
Amityville *(G-273)*
A & L Machine Company Inc ....G 631 463-3111
Islandia *(G-6785)*
A and K Machine and Welding ....G 631 231-2552
Bay Shore *(G-663)*
A P Manufacturing ....G 909 228-3049
Bohemia *(G-1001)*
A R V Precision Mfg Inc ....G 631 293-9643
Farmingdale *(G-4927)*
A-Line Technologies Inc ....F 607 772-2439
Binghamton *(G-884)*
Abk Enterprises Inc ....G 631 348-0555
Central Islip *(G-3483)*
Absolute Manufacturing Inc ....G 631 563-7466
Bohemia *(G-1004)*
▲ Accede Mold & Tool Co Inc ....G 585 254-6490
Rochester *(G-14165)*
▲ Accurate Industrial Machining ....E 631 242-0566
Holbrook *(G-6430)*
Accurate Welding Service Inc ....G 516 333-1730
Westbury *(G-16960)*
Acme Industries of W Babylon ....F 631 737-5231
Ronkonkoma *(G-14849)*
▲ Acro Industries Inc ....C 585 254-3661
Rochester *(G-14171)*
Acro-Fab Ltd ....E 315 564-6688
Hannibal *(G-5969)*
Active Manufacturing Inc ....F 607 775-3162
Kirkwood *(G-7230)*
Adaptive Mfg Tech Inc ....E 631 580-5400
Ronkonkoma *(G-14850)*
Addison Precision Mfg Corp ....D 585 254-1386
Rochester *(G-14172)*
Advan-Tech Manufacturing Inc ....E 716 667-1500
Orchard Park *(G-13251)*
Advance Precision Industries ....G 631 491-0910
West Babylon *(G-16766)*
Advanced Aerospace Machining ....G 631 694-7745
Farmingdale *(G-4930)*
Advanced Machine Inc ....F 585 423-8255
Rochester *(G-14178)*
Advanced Mfg Techniques ....G 518 877-8560
Clifton Park *(G-3694)*
Aero Specialties Manufacturing ....F 631 242-7200
Deer Park *(G-4089)*
AG Tech Welding Corp ....G 845 398-0005
Tappan *(G-16078)*
Aj Genco Mch Sp McHy Rdout Svc ...F 716 664-4925
Falconer *(G-4889)*
Akraturn Mfg Inc ....D 607 775-2802
Kirkwood *(G-7231)*
Aljo Precision Products Inc ....E 516 420-4419
Old Bethpage *(G-13124)*
Alkemy Machine LLC ....G 585 436-8730
Rochester *(G-14186)*
Allen Tool Phoenix Inc ....E 315 463-7533
East Syracuse *(G-4501)*
Allied Industrial Products Co ....G 716 664-3893
Jamestown *(G-6970)*
▲ Aloi Solutions LLC ....G 585 292-0920
Rochester *(G-14192)*
▲ Alpha Fasteners Corp ....G 516 867-6188
Freeport *(G-5385)*
Alpha Manufacturing Corp ....F 631 249-3700
Farmingdale *(G-4938)*
Alpine Machine Inc ....F 607 272-1344
Ithaca *(G-6818)*
Altamont Spray Welding Inc ....G 518 861-8870
Altamont *(G-207)*
Amacon Corporation ....E 631 293-1888
West Babylon *(G-16769)*
American Linear Manufacturers ....F 516 333-1351
Westbury *(G-16966)*
◆ American Wire Tie Inc ....E 716 337-2412
North Collins *(G-12926)*
Ancon Gear & Instrument Corp ....F 631 694-5255
Amityville *(G-276)*
▲ Antab Mch Sprfinishing Lab Inc ....G 585 865-8290
Rochester *(G-14207)*
Applied Technology Mfg Corp ....E 607 687-2200
Owego *(G-13350)*
◆ Arbe Machinery Inc ....F 631 756-2477
Farmingdale *(G-4945)*
Archimedes Products Inc ....G 631 589-1215
Bohemia *(G-1018)*
Architectural Coatings Inc ....F 718 418-9584
Brooklyn *(G-1622)*
Argencord Machine Corp Inc ....G 631 842-8990
Copiague *(G-3893)*
Argo General Machine Work Inc ....G 718 392-4605
Long Island City *(G-7668)*
Armstrong Mold Corporation ....D 315 437-1517
East Syracuse *(G-4505)*

Employee Codes: A=Over 500 employees, B=251-500
C=101-250, D=51-100, E=20-50, F=10-19, G=5-9

2017 Harris
New York Manufacturers Directory

835

Arrow Grinding Inc .... E 716 693-3333
Tonawanda (G-16140)
Art Precision Metal Products .... F 631 842-8889
Copiague (G-3894)
Artisan Machining Inc .... G 631 589-1416
Ronkonkoma (G-14872)
Artisan Management Group Inc .... G 716 569-4094
Frewsburg (G-5448)
Astra Tool & Instr Mfg Corp .... E 914 747-3863
Hawthorne (G-6244)
Atlantis Equipment Corporation .... F 518 733-5910
Stephentown (G-15756)
Auburn Bearing & Mfg Inc .... G 315 986-7600
Macedon (G-7982)
AW Mack Manufacturing Co Inc .... F 845 452-4050
Poughkeepsie (G-13891)
B & R Industries Inc .... F 631 736-2275
Medford (G-8235)
B C Manufacturing Inc .... G 585 482-1080
West Henrietta (G-16870)
Babbitt Bearings Inc .... D 315 479-6603
Syracuse (G-15864)
Babbitt Bearings Incorporated .... D 315 479-6603
Syracuse (G-15865)
Badge Machine Products Inc .... E 585 394-0330
Canandaigua (G-3335)
Barton Tool Inc .... G 716 665-2801
Falconer (G-4892)
BEAM Manufacturing Corp .... G 631 253-2724
West Babylon (G-16775)
Belden Manufacturing Inc .... E 607 238-0998
Kirkwood (G-7232)
Bill Shea Enterprises Inc .... F 585 343-2284
Batavia (G-625)
Binghamton Precision Tool Inc .... G 607 772-6021
Binghamton (G-894)
Birch Machine & Tool Inc .... G 716 735-9802
Middleport (G-8420)
Blading Services Unlimited LLC .... F 315 875-5313
Canastota (G-3363)
Blair Cnstr Fabrication Sp .... G 315 253-2321
Auburn (G-485)
Bliss Machine Inc .... F 585 492-5128
Arcade (G-389)
Blue Manufacturing Co Inc .... G 607 796-2463
Millport (G-8480)
Bms Manufacturing Co Inc .... E 607 535-2426
Watkins Glen (G-16693)
Breed Enterprises Inc .... G 585 388-0126
Fairport (G-4849)
Broadalbin Manufacturing Corp .... E 518 883-5313
Broadalbin (G-1240)
Bruce Pierce .... G 716 731-9310
Sanborn (G-15115)
Bryant Machine & Development .... F 716 894-8282
Buffalo (G-2845)
Buxton Machine and Tool Co Inc .... F 716 876-2312
Buffalo (G-2863)
C & H Machining Inc .... F 631 582-6737
Bohemia (G-1030)
C & T Tool & Instrument Co .... E 718 429-1253
Woodside (G-17321)
C L Precision Machine & Tl Co .... G 718 651-8475
Woodside (G-17322)
C R C Manufacturing Inc .... F 585 254-8820
Rochester (G-14255)
▲ Calvary Design Team Inc .... C 585 347-6127
Webster (G-16714)
Canfield Machine & Tool LLC .... E 315 593-8062
Fulton (G-5454)
Capy Machine Shop Inc .... E 631 694-6916
Melville (G-8300)
Carballo Contract Machining .... G 315 594-2511
Wolcott (G-17278)
Carbaugh Tool Company Inc .... E 607 739-3293
Elmira (G-4673)
Cardish Machine Works Inc .... E 518 273-2329
Watervliet (G-16681)
Carter Precision Metals LLC .... G 516 333-1917
Westbury (G-16973)
Casey Machine Co Inc .... D 716 651-0150
Lancaster (G-7308)
Cayuga Tool and Die Inc .... G 607 533-7400
Groton (G-5898)
CBM Fabrications Inc .... E 518 399-8023
Ballston Lake (G-581)
Cda Machine Inc .... G 585 671-5959
Webster (G-16715)
Cdl Manufacturing Inc .... G 585 589-2533
Albion (G-163)
Certified Fabrications Inc .... F 716 731-8123
Sanborn (G-15117)
Certified Prcsion McHining Inc .... G 631 244-3671
Bohemia (G-1032)
▲ Cetek Inc .... E 845 452-3510
Poughkeepsie (G-13892)
Charl Industries Inc .... E 631 234-0100
Hauppauge (G-6043)
Charles V Weber Machine Shop .... G 518 272-8033
Troy (G-16229)
Chart Inc .... F 518 272-3565
Troy (G-16230)
Chautqua Prcsion Machining Inc .... F 716 763-3752
Ashville (G-428)
▲ Chocovision Corporation .... F 845 473-4970
Poughkeepsie (G-13893)
▼ City Gear Inc .... G 914 450-4746
Irvington (G-6767)
Cjn Machinery Corp .... G 631 244-8030
Holbrook (G-6437)
Classic Auto Crafts Inc .... G 518 966-8003
Greenville (G-5884)
Clip Clop International Inc .... F 631 392-1340
Bohemia (G-1035)
Conesus Lake Association Inc .... E 585 346-6864
Lakeville (G-7283)
Conrad Blasius Equipment Co .... G 516 753-1200
Plainview (G-13590)
Converter Design Inc .... G 518 745-7138
Glens Falls (G-5675)
Corbett Stves Pttern Works Inc .... E 585 546-7109
Rochester (G-14289)
Cortland Machine and Tool Co .... F 607 756-5852
Cortland (G-4019)
Courser Inc .... E 607 739-3861
Elmira (G-4677)
Craftsman Manufacturing Co In .... G 585 426-5780
Rochester (G-14291)
▼ Cubitek Inc .... F 631 665-6900
Brentwood (G-1179)
▲ Cyclone Air Power Inc .... G 718 447-3038
Staten Island (G-15664)
D J Crowell Co Inc .... G 716 684-3343
Alden (G-176)
D K Machine Inc .... F 518 747-0626
Fort Edward (G-5341)
D-K Manufacturing Corp .... E 315 592-4327
Fulton (G-5455)
Darco Manufacturing Inc .... E 315 432-8905
Syracuse (G-15921)
Daves Precision Machine Shop .... F 845 626-7263
Kerhonkson (G-7155)
David Fehlman .... G 315 455-8888
Syracuse (G-15922)
Deck Bros Inc .... E 716 852-0262
Buffalo (G-2904)
Delaney Machine Products Ltd .... G 631 225-1032
Lindenhurst (G-7460)
Dennies Manufacturing Inc .... E 585 393-4646
Canandaigua (G-3342)
Denny Machine Co Inc .... D 716 873-6865
Buffalo (G-2907)
Dependable Tool & Die Co Inc .... G 315 453-5696
Syracuse (G-15924)
Dern Moore Machine Company Inc .... G 716 433-6243
Lockport (G-7580)
Derosa Fabrications Inc .... E 631 563-0640
Bohemia (G-1056)
▼ Devin Mfg Inc .... F 585 496-5770
Arcade (G-391)
Dewey Machine & Tool Inc .... G 607 749-3930
Homer (G-6516)
DMD Machining Technology Inc .... G 585 659-8180
Kendall (G-7143)
Dormitory Authority - State NY .... G 631 434-1487
Brentwood (G-1182)
Dougs Machine Shop Inc .... G 585 905-0004
Canandaigua (G-3343)
Duetto Integrated Systems Inc .... F 631 851-0102
Islandia (G-6792)
Dyna-Tech Quality Inc .... G 585 458-9970
Rochester (G-14320)
Dynak Inc .... F 585 271-2255
Churchville (G-3636)
E & R Machine Inc .... E 716 434-6639
Lockport (G-7582)
E B Industries LLC .... E 631 293-8565
Farmingdale (G-4981)
E B Trottnow Machine Spc .... F 716 694-0600
Tonawanda (G-16156)
E J Willis Company Inc .... F 315 891-7602
Middleville (G-8472)
E M T Manufacturing Inc .... F 516 333-1917
East Meadow (G-4422)
▲ Eagle Bridge Machine & Tl Inc .... E 518 686-4541
Eagle Bridge (G-4356)
Eagle Instruments Inc .... G 914 939-6843
Port Chester (G-13743)
Eastern Machine and Electric .... G 716 284-8271
Niagara Falls (G-12813)
Eastern Precision Machining .... G 631 286-4758
Bellport (G-829)
Edr Industries Inc .... F 516 868-1928
Freeport (G-5395)
▲ Edsal Machine Products Inc .... F 718 439-9163
Brooklyn (G-1905)
▲ Edwin J McKenica & Sons Inc .... F 716 823-4646
Buffalo (G-2932)
Efficient Automated Mch Corp .... F 718 937-9393
Long Island City (G-7727)
Ehrlich Enterprises Inc .... F 631 956-0690
Hauppauge (G-6069)
▲ Elg Utica Alloys Inc .... E 315 733-0475
Herkimer (G-6299)
Elg Utica Alloys Holdings Inc .... G 315 733-0475
Utica (G-16329)
Elite Machine Inc .... G 585 289-4733
Manchester (G-8051)
Elite Precise Manufacturer LLC .... G 518 993-3040
Fort Plain (G-5347)
Emcom Industries Inc .... G 716 852-3711
Buffalo (G-2936)
Emory Machine & Tool Co Inc .... E 585 436-9610
Farmington (G-5150)
Empire Plastics Inc .... E 607 754-9132
Endwell (G-4835)
Empro Niagara Inc .... G 716 433-2769
Lockport (G-7584)
Endicott Precision Inc .... C 607 754-7076
Endicott (G-4803)
Engineering Mfg Tech LLC .... D 607 754-7111
Endicott (G-4805)
Estebania Enterprises Inc .... G 585 529-9330
Rochester (G-14359)
ET Oakes Corporation .... E 631 630-9837
Hauppauge (G-6074)
ET Precision Optics Inc .... D 585 254-2560
Rochester (G-14360)
Etna Tool & Die Corporation .... F 212 475-4350
New York (G-10079)
Euro Gear (usa) Inc .... G 518 578-1775
Plattsburgh (G-13662)
Everfab Inc .... D 716 655-1550
East Aurora (G-4370)
Exact Machining & Mfg .... G 585 334-7090
Rochester (G-14362)
Excel Industries Inc .... E 716 542-5468
Clarence (G-3661)
Exigo Precision Inc .... G 585 254-5818
Rochester (G-14364)
Expert Machine Services Inc .... G 718 786-1200
Long Island City (G-7735)
F M L Industries Inc .... G 607 749-7273
Homer (G-6517)
▲ Fairview Fitting & Mfg Inc .... D 716 614-0320
North Tonawanda (G-12971)
Farrant Screw Machine Products .... G 585 457-3213
Java Village (G-7053)
Felton Machine Co Inc .... E 716 215-9001
Niagara Falls (G-12820)
Fenbar Prcision Machinists Inc .... F 914 769-5506
Thornwood (G-16120)
Fermer Precision Inc .... D 315 822-6371
Ilion (G-6740)
Ferraro Manufacturing Company .... G 631 752-1509
Farmingdale (G-4992)
Ferro Machine Co Inc .... G 845 398-3641
Orangeburg (G-13228)
▲ Finesse Creations Inc .... F 718 692-2100
Brooklyn (G-1973)
Five Star Industries Inc .... E 716 674-2589
West Seneca (G-16945)
▲ Flex-Hose Company Inc .... E 315 437-1903
East Syracuse (G-4530)
Forbes Precision Inc .... F 585 865-7069
Rochester (G-14378)
Four K Machine Shop Inc .... G 516 997-0752
Westbury (G-16986)
Frederick Machine Repair Inc .... G 716 332-0104
Buffalo (G-2956)

S I C

836 — 2017 Harris New York Manufacturers Directory

SIC SECTION
35 INDUSTRIAL AND COMMERCIAL MACHINERY AND COMPUTER EQUIPMENT

Company	Code	Phone
Fross Industries Inc, Niagara Falls (G-12823)	E	716 297-0652
Fulton Tool Co Inc, Fulton (G-5458)	E	315 598-2900
Fultonville Machine & Tool Co, Fultonville (G-5479)	F	518 853-4441
Future Screw Machine Pdts Inc, Southold (G-15558)	F	631 765-1610
G & G C Machine & Tool Co Inc, Westbury (G-16987)	G	516 873-0999
Gamma Instrument Co Inc, Hempstead (G-6269)	G	516 486-5526
Gefa Instrument Corp, Old Bethpage (G-13127)	F	516 420-4419
Gem Manufacturing Inc, Rochester (G-14390)	G	585 235-1670
Genco John, Jamestown (G-6994)	G	716 483-5446
General Cutting Inc, Ronkonkoma (G-14903)	F	631 580-5011
Genesis Machining Corp, North Baldwin (G-12905)	F	516 377-1197
Gentner Precision Components, Palmyra (G-13408)	G	315 597-5734
Giuliante Machine Tool Inc, Peekskill (G-13478)	E	914 835-0008
Gli-Dex Sales Corp, North Tonawanda (G-12975)	E	716 692-6501
Global Precision Products Inc, Rush (G-15049)	G	585 334-4640
Globe Grinding Corp, Copiague (G-3903)	F	631 694-1970
Gmr Manufacturing Inc, Central Islip (G-3498)	G	631 582-2600
Gorden Automotive Equipment, West Seneca (G-16947)	F	716 674-2700
▲ Greno Industries Inc, Scotia (G-15325)	G	518 393-4195
Grind, New York (G-10366)	G	646 558-3250
Gullo Machine & Tool Inc, Bloomfield (G-989)	F	585 657-7318
H & H Technologies Inc, Ronkonkoma (G-14907)	E	631 567-3526
H C Young Tool & Machine Co, Syracuse (G-15955)	G	315 463-0663
H F Brown Machine Co Inc, Utica (G-16337)	F	315 732-6129
H T Specialty Inc, Rochester (G-14417)	F	585 458-4060
Hagner Industries Inc, Buffalo (G-2986)	G	716 873-5720
Hallock Fabricating Corp, Riverhead (G-14144)	G	631 727-2441
Hancock Manufacturing Corp, Tully (G-16276)	G	315 696-8906
Har-Son Mfg Inc, Gowanda (G-5748)	F	716 532-2641
Hartman Enterprises Inc, Oneida (G-13156)	D	315 363-7300
Harwitt Industries Inc, Freeport (G-5405)	F	516 623-9787
Haskell Machine & Tool Inc, Homer (G-6518)	F	607 749-2421
▲ Hebeler Corporation, Tonawanda (G-16171)	C	716 873-9300
Herbert Wolf Corp, New York (G-10461)	G	212 242-0300
Herkimer Tool & Machining Corp, Herkimer (G-6303)	F	315 866-2110
Hes Inc, Addison (G-7)	G	607 359-2974
Hi-Tech Cnc Machining Corp, Mount Vernon (G-8691)	G	914 668-5090
Hi-Tech Industries NY Inc, Johnson City (G-7094)	E	607 217-7361
Hoercher Industries Inc, East Rochester (G-4461)	G	585 398-2982
Hohl Machine & Conveyor Co Inc, Buffalo (G-2996)	E	716 882-7210
▲ HSM Machine Works Inc, Medford (G-8250)	E	631 924-6600
Hubbard Tool and Die Corp, Rome (G-14815)	E	315 337-7840
Hunter Machine Inc, Victor (G-16481)	E	585 924-7480
Hw Specialties Co Inc, Bohemia (G-1075)	F	631 589-0745
I D Machine Inc, Elmira (G-4692)	G	607 796-2549
Imperial Instrument Corp, Westbury (G-16995)	G	516 739-6644
Indian Springs Mfg Co Inc, Baldwinsville (G-570)	F	315 635-6101
Industrial Machine & Gear Work, Oceanside (G-13081)	G	516 569-4820
Industrial Precision Pdts Inc, Oswego (G-13333)	F	315 343-4421
Industrial Services of Wny, Niagara Falls (G-12836)	G	716 799-7788
Ingleside Machine Co Inc, Farmington (G-5153)	D	585 924-4363
Interactive Instruments Inc, Scotia (G-15326)	G	518 347-0955
International Climbing Mchs, Ithaca (G-6852)	G	607 288-4001
▼ International Creative Met Inc, Woodside (G-17333)	F	718 424-8179
▲ International Tool & Mch Inc, Rochester (G-14453)	F	585 654-6955
Ironshore Holdings Inc, Liverpool (G-7527)	F	315 457-1052
Island Instrument Corp, Deer Park (G-4153)	G	631 243-0550
Island Machine Inc, Plattsburgh (G-13672)	G	518 562-1232
▲ ISO Plastics Corp, Mount Vernon (G-8694)	D	914 663-8300
J & G Machine & Tool Co Inc, Marion (G-8096)	F	315 310-7130
J & J Swiss Precision Inc, Deer Park (G-4154)	E	631 243-5584
J & J TI Die Mfg & Stampg Corp, Carmel (G-3400)	G	845 228-0242
J & L Precision Co Inc, Le Roy (G-7410)	F	585 768-6388
J B Tool & Die Co Inc, Westbury (G-16997)	E	516 333-1480
J D Cousins Inc, Buffalo (G-3013)	E	716 824-1098
J F Machining Company Inc, Ransomville (G-14019)	F	716 791-3910
J R S Precision Machining, Ronkonkoma (G-14917)	E	631 737-1330
J Soehner Corporation, Rockville Centre (G-14793)	F	516 599-2534
J T Systematic, Endwell (G-4836)	G	607 754-0929
Jack Merkel Inc, Hauppauge (G-6100)	G	631 234-2600
Jacobi Tool & Die Mfg Inc, Medford (G-8252)	G	631 736-5394
▲ Jam Industries Inc, Rochester (G-14458)	E	585 458-9830
Jamar Precision Products Co, Deer Park (G-4155)	G	631 254-0234
Jamestown Iron Works Inc, Falconer (G-4905)	F	716 665-2818
Javcon Machine Inc, Deer Park (G-4157)	G	631 586-1890
Javin Machine Corp, West Babylon (G-16801)	F	631 643-3322
Jet Sew Corporation, Barneveld (G-614)	F	315 896-2683
Jewelers Machinist Co Inc, Babylon (G-549)	G	631 661-5020
JF Machine Shop Inc, West Babylon (G-16802)	F	631 491-7273
John J Mazur Inc, Deer Park (G-4158)	F	631 242-4554
Johnnys Machine Shop, West Babylon (G-16803)	G	631 338-9733
Johnson Mch & Fibr Pdts Co Inc, Jamestown (G-7014)	F	716 665-2003
Johnston Precision Inc, Auburn (G-505)	G	315 253-4181
Jolin Machining Corp, Bohemia (G-1084)	F	631 589-1305
Just In Time Cnc Machining, Dansville (G-4078)	F	585 335-2010
K & H Industries Inc, Hamburg (G-5930)	F	716 312-0088
K & H Precision Products Inc, Honeoye Falls (G-6532)	F	585 624-4894
K D M Die Company Inc, Buffalo (G-3024)	G	716 828-9000
K Hein Machines Inc, Vestal (G-16450)	G	607 748-1546
Kal Manufacturing Corporation, Webster (G-16726)	E	585 265-4310
▲ Keller Technology Corporation, Tonawanda (G-16175)	C	716 693-3840
Kenwell Corporation, Fulton (G-5466)	D	315 592-4263
Keyes Machine Works Inc, Gates (G-5561)	G	585 426-5059
Kimber Mfg Inc, Yonkers (G-17460)	G	914 965-0753
▲ Kimber Mfg Inc, Yonkers (G-17461)	C	914 964-0771
Kimber Mfg Inc, Elmsford (G-4760)	D	406 758-2222
Kinemotive Corporation, Farmingdale (G-5028)	E	631 249-6440
▲ KMA Corporation, Glens Falls (G-5685)	G	518 743-1330
Konar Precision Mfg Inc, Deer Park (G-4159)	G	631 242-4466
Kondor Technologies Inc, Ronkonkoma (G-14924)	F	631 471-8832
Kramartron Precision Inc, Tallman (G-16077)	G	845 368-3668
Kronenberger Mfg Corp, East Rochester (G-4464)	E	585 385-2340
Krug Precision Inc, Port Washington (G-13836)	G	516 944-9350
Kurtz Truck Equipment Inc, Marathon (G-8084)	F	607 849-3468
Kurz and Zobel Inc, Rochester (G-14472)	G	585 254-9060
Kz Precision Inc, Lancaster (G-7321)	G	716 683-3202
L & L Precision Machining, East Northport (G-4440)	F	631 462-9587
L & S Metals Inc, North Tonawanda (G-12980)	E	716 692-6865
L P R Precision Parts & Tls Co, Farmingdale (G-5031)	F	631 293-7334
Labco of Palmyra Inc, Palmyra (G-13410)	G	315 597-5202
Lagasse Works Inc, Lyons (G-7973)	G	315 946-9202
Lagoe-Oswego Corp, Rochester (G-14473)	G	315 343-3160
Lakeside Industries Inc, Bemus Point (G-844)	F	716 386-3031
Lakeside Precision Inc, Dunkirk (G-4344)	F	716 366-5030
Lasticks Aerospace Inc, Bay Shore (G-712)	G	631 242-8484
Leetech Manufacturing Inc, Bohemia (G-1092)	G	631 563-1442
Lewis Machine Co Inc, Brooklyn (G-2214)	G	718 625-0799
Liberty Machine & Tool, Cicero (G-3647)	G	315 699-3242
▲ Linda Tool & Die Corporation, Brooklyn (G-2224)	E	718 522-2066
▲ Lodolce Machine Co Inc, Saugerties (G-15187)	E	845 246-7017
Loughlin Manufacturing Corp, Bohemia (G-1095)	F	631 585-4422
▲ Lwa Works Inc, Watervliet (G-16687)	G	518 271-8360
▲ M & S Precision Machine Co LLC, Queensbury (G-14004)	F	518 747-1193
Macro Tool & Machine Company, Lagrangeville (G-7255)	G	845 223-3824
Maehr Industries Inc, Bellport (G-833)	G	631 924-1661
Magellan Aerospace NY Inc, Bohemia (G-1099)	C	631 589-2440
Malisa Branko Inc, Copiague (G-3912)	G	631 225-9741
Manth Mfg Inc, Tonawanda (G-16179)	E	716 693-6525
Manuf Appld Renova Sys, Corinth (G-3959)	G	518 654-9084
Mar-A-Thon Filters Inc, Lindenhurst (G-7470)	G	631 957-4774
Mardon Tool & Die Co Inc, Rochester (G-14496)	F	585 254-4545
▲ Marksmen Manufacturing Corp, Deer Park (G-4170)	E	800 305-6942
Massapqua Prcsion McHining Ltd, Amityville (G-310)	G	631 789-1485
▲ Master Machine Incorporated, Jamestown (G-7018)	F	716 487-2555
Matic Industries Inc, College Point (G-3797)	D	718 886-5470

Employee Codes: A=Over 500 employees, B=251-500
C=101-250, D=51-100, E=20-50, F=10-19, G=5-9

2017 Harris
New York Manufacturers Directory

35 INDUSTRIAL AND COMMERCIAL MACHINERY AND COMPUTER EQUIPMENT

Matrix Machining Corp .... G 631 643-6690
  West Babylon *(G-16809)*
Mayfair Machine Company Inc .... G 631 981-6644
  Ronkonkoma *(G-14940)*
Mc Ivor Manufacturing Inc .... G 716 825-1808
  Buffalo *(G-3060)*
McGuigan Inc .... E 631 750-6222
  Bohemia *(G-1103)*
Meade Machine Co Inc .... G 315 923-1703
  Clyde *(G-3728)*
Medco Machine LLC .... G 315 986-2109
  Walworth *(G-16550)*
Mega Tool & Mfg Corp .... E 607 734-8398
  Elmira *(G-4695)*
Meridian Manufacturing Inc .... G 518 885-0450
  Ballston Spa *(G-602)*
Metal Parts Manufacturing Inc .... G 315 831-2530
  Remsen *(G-14041)*
Metro Machining & Fabricating .... G 718 545-0104
  Woodside *(G-17338)*
Micro Instrument Corp .... D 585 458-3150
  Rochester *(G-14507)*
Micro-Tech Machine Inc .... E 315 331-6671
  Newark *(G-12737)*
Miles Machine Inc .... G 716 484-6026
  Jamestown *(G-7020)*
Milex Precision Inc .... F 631 595-2393
  Bay Shore *(G-718)*
Miller Technology Inc .... G 631 694-2224
  Farmingdale *(G-5056)*
Minutemen Precsn McHning Tool ...... E 631 467-4900
  Ronkonkoma *(G-14944)*
Mitchell Machine Tool LLC .... G 585 254-7520
  Rochester *(G-14516)*
Modern Packaging Inc .... D 631 595-2437
  Deer Park *(G-4175)*
Modern-TEC Manufacturing Inc .... G 716 625-8700
  Lockport *(G-7603)*
Morco Products Corp .... F 718 853-4005
  Brooklyn *(G-2333)*
Morris Machining Service Inc .... G 585 527-8100
  Rochester *(G-14523)*
Mount Vernon Machine Inc .... E 845 268-9400
  Valley Cottage *(G-16382)*
Ms Machining Inc .... G 607 723-1105
  Binghamton *(G-938)*
Ms Spares LLC .... G 607 223-3024
  Clay *(G-3683)*
Muller Tool Inc .... G 716 895-3658
  Buffalo *(G-3077)*
Nassau Tool Works Inc .... E 631 643-0420
  West Babylon *(G-16815)*
Neptune Machine Inc .... E 718 852-4100
  Brooklyn *(G-2357)*
NET & Die Inc .... E 315 592-4311
  Fulton *(G-5470)*
New Age Precision Tech Inc .... E 631 588-1692
  Ronkonkoma *(G-14956)*
New York State Tool Co Inc .... F 315 737-8985
  Chadwicks *(G-3530)*
Niagara Precision Inc .... E 716 439-0956
  Lockport *(G-7606)*
▼ Nicoform Inc .... F 585 454-5530
  Rochester *(G-14537)*
Nitro Manufacturing LLC .... G 716 646-9900
  North Collins *(G-12929)*
North-East Machine Inc .... G 518 746-1837
  Hudson Falls *(G-6648)*
Northeast Hardware Specialties ...... F 516 487-6868
  Mineola *(G-8527)*
Northern Machining Inc .... F 315 384-3189
  Norfolk *(G-12900)*
O & S Machine & Tool Co Inc .... G 716 941-5542
  Colden *(G-3772)*
Olmstead Machine Inc .... G 315 587-9864
  North Rose *(G-12938)*
Optics Technology Inc .... G 585 586-0950
  Pittsford *(G-13571)*
Otto-Tech Machine Co Inc .... G 845 687-8800
  High Falls *(G-6401)*
▲ P & F Industries of NY Corp .... G 718 894-3501
  Maspeth *(G-8163)*
P T E Inc .... F 516 775-3839
  Floral Park *(G-5206)*
Page Devices Inc .... F 516 735-8376
  Levittown *(G-7430)*
▲ Pall Corporation .... A 516 484-5400
  Port Washington *(G-13852)*
Pall Corporation .... A 607 753-6041
  Cortland *(G-4035)*

Parker Machine Company Inc .... F 518 747-0675
  Fort Edward *(G-5344)*
Parry Machine Co Inc .... G 315 597-5014
  Palmyra *(G-13412)*
Peko Precision Products Inc .... F 585 301-1386
  Rochester *(G-14574)*
Pems Tool & Machine Inc .... E 315 823-3595
  Little Falls *(G-7502)*
Performance Mfg Inc .... F 716 735-3500
  Middleport *(G-8422)*
Pervi Precision Company .... G 631 589-5557
  Bohemia *(G-1117)*
Pgm of New England LLC .... D 585 458-4300
  Rochester *(G-14580)*
Phoenix Mch Pdts of Hauppauge .... G 631 234-0100
  Hauppauge *(G-6163)*
Pol-Tek Industries Ltd .... F 716 823-1502
  Buffalo *(G-3130)*
Port Everglades Machine Works .... F 516 367-2280
  Plainview *(G-13630)*
Port Jervis Machine Corp .... G 845 856-6210
  Port Jervis *(G-13790)*
▼ Posimech Inc .... E 631 924-5959
  Medford *(G-8258)*
Ppi Corp .... E 585 880-7277
  Geneseo *(G-5567)*
Pre-Tech Plastics Inc .... E 518 942-5950
  Mineville *(G-8541)*
Precision Arms Inc .... G 845 225-1130
  Carmel *(G-3404)*
Precision Disc Grinding Corp .... F 516 747-5450
  Mineola *(G-8531)*
Precision Lathe Work Co Inc .... G 845 357-3110
  Suffern *(G-15797)*
Precision Metals Corp .... E 631 586-5032
  Bay Shore *(G-727)*
Precision Systems Mfg Inc .... E 315 451-3480
  Liverpool *(G-7544)*
Precision Tool and Mfg .... E 518 678-3130
  Palenville *(G-13399)*
Precisionmatics Co Inc .... E 315 822-6324
  West Winfield *(G-16959)*
Premier Machining Tech Inc .... G 716 608-1311
  Buffalo *(G-3135)*
Production Milling Company .... G 914 666-0792
  Bedford Hills *(G-805)*
Progressive Mch & Design LLC .... C 585 924-5250
  Victor *(G-16497)*
Progressive Tool Company Inc .... E 607 748-8294
  Endwell *(G-4838)*
Pronto Tool & Die Co Inc .... E 631 981-8920
  Ronkonkoma *(G-14972)*
Proto Machine Inc .... E 631 392-1159
  Bay Shore *(G-729)*
Prz Technologies Inc .... F 716 683-1300
  Lancaster *(G-7334)*
Qta Machining Inc .... F 716 862-8108
  Buffalo *(G-3145)*
Qualified Manufacturing Corp .... F 631 249-4440
  Farmingdale *(G-5092)*
Quality Machining Service Inc .... G 315 736-5774
  New York Mills *(G-12727)*
Qualtech Tool & Machine Inc .... F 585 223-9227
  Fairport *(G-12742)*
R & S Machine Center Inc .... F 518 563-4016
  West Chazy *(G-16842)*
R E F Precision Products .... F 631 242-4471
  Deer Park *(G-4196)*
Rand Machine Products Inc .... D 716 665-5217
  Falconer *(G-4908)*
Redding-Hunter Inc .... E 607 753-3331
  Cortland *(G-4043)*
Reliance Machining Inc .... E 718 784-0314
  Long Island City *(G-7860)*
Ren Tool & Manufacturing Co .... F 518 377-2123
  Schenectady *(G-15290)*
RGH Associates Inc .... F 631 643-1111
  West Babylon *(G-16821)*
▲ Richard Manno & Company Inc ...... D 631 643-2200
  West Babylon *(G-16822)*
Richards Machine Tool Co Inc .... E 716 683-3380
  Lancaster *(G-7338)*
Rick-Mic Industries Inc .... F 631 563-8389
  Ronkonkoma *(G-14979)*
Rinaldi Precision Machine .... F 631 242-4141
  Bay Shore *(G-734)*
Ripley Machine & Tool Co Inc .... F 716 736-3205
  Ripley *(G-14136)*
Riverside Machinery Company .... G 718 492-7400
  Brooklyn *(G-2497)*

Rjs Machine Works Inc .... G 716 826-1778
  Lackawanna *(G-7248)*
Rmw Filtration Products Co LLC ...... G 631 226-9412
  Copiague *(G-3924)*
Roboshop Inc .... G 315 437-6454
  Syracuse *(G-16024)*
Roccera LLC .... F 585 426-0887
  Rochester *(G-14632)*
Rochester Atomated Systems Inc ..... E 585 594-3222
  Rochester *(G-14635)*
Rochester Tool and Mold Inc .... F 585 464-9336
  Rochester *(G-14652)*
Roger Latari .... G 631 580-2422
  Ronkonkoma *(G-14980)*
Rona Precision Inc .... G 631 737-4034
  Ronkonkoma *(G-14981)*
Rossi Tool & Dies Inc .... G 845 267-8246
  Valley Cottage *(G-16387)*
Rozal Industries Inc .... E 631 420-4277
  Farmingdale *(G-5104)*
Rt Machined Specialties .... G 716 731-2055
  Niagara Falls *(G-12868)*
RTD Manufacturing Inc .... G 315 337-3151
  Rome *(G-14835)*
Ruga Grinding & Mfg Corp .... G 631 924-5067
  Yaphank *(G-17399)*
S & B Machine Works Inc .... F 516 997-2666
  Westbury *(G-17025)*
S & H Machine Company Inc .... G 716 834-1194
  Buffalo *(G-3170)*
S R & R Industries Inc .... G 845 692-8329
  Middletown *(G-8461)*
Sal MA Instrument Corp .... G 631 242-2227
  Deer Park *(G-4204)*
Saturn Industries Inc .... E 518 828-9956
  Hudson *(G-6632)*
Schwabel Fabricating Co Inc .... E 716 876-2086
  Tonawanda *(G-16200)*
▲ Scientific Tool Co Inc .... F 315 431-4243
  Syracuse *(G-16035)*
SDJ Machine Shop Inc .... F 585 458-1236
  Rochester *(G-14678)*
Seanair Machine Co Inc .... F 631 694-2820
  Farmingdale *(G-5108)*
Secondary Services Inc .... F 716 896-4000
  Buffalo *(G-3181)*
Seeley Machine Inc .... E 518 798-9510
  Queensbury *(G-14011)*
Semi-Linear Inc .... E 212 243-2108
  New York *(G-12027)*
▲ Service Machine & Tool Company ... E 607 732-0413
  Elmira Heights *(G-4712)*
Shar-Mar Machine Company .... G 631 567-8040
  Bohemia *(G-1132)*
Sick Inc .... E 585 347-2000
  Webster *(G-16735)*
Sigma Manufacturing Inds Inc .... F 718 842-9180
  Bronx *(G-1454)*
Sigmamotor Inc .... E 716 735-3115
  Middleport *(G-8423)*
Smidgens Inc .... G 585 624-1486
  Lima *(G-7448)*
Smith Metal Works Newark Inc .... E 315 331-1651
  Newark *(G-12742)*
Smith Tool & Die Inc .... G 607 674-4165
  Sherburne *(G-15396)*
Smithers Tools & Mch Pdts Inc .... D 845 876-3063
  Rhinebeck *(G-14058)*
Snyder Industries Inc .... D 716 694-1240
  Tonawanda *(G-16203)*
Solmac Inc .... G 716 630-7061
  Williamsville *(G-17254)*
▲ Sotek Inc .... D 716 821-5961
  Blasdell *(G-966)*
Source Technologies .... F 718 708-0305
  Brooklyn *(G-2585)*
Spartan Precision Machining .... E 516 546-5171
  Freeport *(G-5428)*
Springville Mfg Co Inc .... E 716 592-4957
  Springville *(G-15616)*
Stanfordville Mch & Mfg Co Inc ...... D 845 868-2266
  Poughkeepsie *(G-13934)*
Staub Machine Company Inc .... E 716 649-4211
  Hamburg *(G-5944)*
Stephen A Manoogian Inc .... G 518 762-2525
  Johnstown *(G-7129)*
Stony Manufacturing Inc .... G 716 652-6730
  Elma *(G-4657)*
▲ Strecks Inc .... E 518 273-4410
  Watervliet *(G-16689)*

Strong Forge & Fabrication ....E 585 343-5251
Batavia *(G-648)*
Summit Instrument Corp ....G 516 433-0140
Hicksville *(G-6396)*
▲ **Superior Technology Inc** ....E 585 352-6556
Rochester *(G-14707)*
Superior Welding ....G 631 676-2751
Holbrook *(G-6476)*
▲ **Supply Technologies (ny)** ....F 212 966-3310
Albany *(G-139)*
Swissway Inc ....E 631 351-5350
Huntington Station *(G-6724)*
▲ **Sylhan LLC** ....E 631 243-6600
Edgewood *(G-4615)*
Syntec Technologies Inc ....F 585 464-9336
Rochester *(G-14713)*
T M Machine Inc ....G 716 822-0817
Buffalo *(G-3208)*
T R P Machine Inc ....E 631 567-9620
Bohemia *(G-1141)*
Tangent Machine & Tool Corp ....E 631 249-3088
Farmingdale *(G-5124)*
Tarsia Technical Industries ....G 631 231-8322
Hauppauge *(G-6206)*
Taylor Precision Machining ....G 607 535-3101
Montour Falls *(G-8612)*
Ted Westbrook ....G 716 625-4443
Lockport *(G-7618)*
Temrick Inc ....G 631 567-8860
Bohemia *(G-1142)*
Tennyson Machine Co Inc ....F 914 668-5468
Mount Vernon *(G-8737)*
Theodosiou Inc ....G 718 728-6800
Long Island City *(G-7900)*
TI Group Auto Systems LLC ....G 315 568-7042
Seneca Falls *(G-15371)*
Ticonderoga Mch & Wldg Corp ....G 518 585-7444
Ticonderoga *(G-16129)*
Tioga Tool Inc ....F 607 785-6005
Endicott *(G-4830)*
Tobeyco Manufacturing Co Inc ....F 607 962-2446
Corning *(G-3983)*
▲ **Toolroom Express Inc** ....D 607 723-5373
Conklin *(G-3876)*
Towpath Machine Corp ....G 315 252-0112
Auburn *(G-524)*
Trebor Instrument Corp ....G 631 423-7026
Dix Hills *(G-4299)*
Triangle Grinding Machine Corp ....G 631 643-3636
West Babylon *(G-16836)*
Tricon Machine LLC ....G 585 671-0679
Webster *(G-16737)*
Tripar Manufacturing Co Inc ....G 631 563-0855
Bohemia *(G-1148)*
Triple Point Manufacturing ....G 631 218-4988
Bohemia *(G-1149)*
Triplett Machine Inc ....D 315 548-3198
Phelps *(G-13537)*
Triplex Industries Inc ....F 585 621-6920
Rochester *(G-14731)*
Truarc Fabrication ....G 518 691-0430
Gansevoort *(G-5491)*
▲ **Twinco Mfg Co Inc** ....E 631 231-0022
Hauppauge *(G-6219)*
Two Bills Machine & Tool Co ....F 516 437-2585
Floral Park *(G-5207)*
U-Cut Enterprises Inc ....E 315 492-9316
Jamesville *(G-7052)*
Ultra Tool and Manufacturing ....F 585 467-3700
Rochester *(G-14740)*
United Machining Inc ....G 631 589-6751
Bohemia *(G-1152)*
Universal Metal Fabricators ....F 845 331-8248
Kingston *(G-7221)*
▲ **Upturn Industries Inc** ....E 607 967-2923
Bainbridge *(G-556)*
Ushers Machine and Tool Co Inc ....E 518 877-5501
Round Lake *(G-15038)*
V A P Tool & Dye ....G 631 587-5262
West Islip *(G-16908)*
V Lake Industries Inc ....G 716 885-9141
Buffalo *(G-3239)*
Vader Systems LLC ....G 716 636-1742
East Amherst *(G-4363)*
Valair Inc ....F 716 751-9480
Wilson *(G-17269)*
Van Laeken Richard ....G 315 331-0289
Newark *(G-12747)*
▲ **Van Thomas Inc** ....E 585 426-1414
Rochester *(G-14751)*
Vanguard Metals Inc ....F 631 234-6500
Central Islip *(G-3514)*
Verns Machine Co Inc ....E 315 926-4223
Marion *(G-8103)*
Victoria Precision Inc ....G 845 473-9309
Hyde Park *(G-6738)*
Village Decoration Ltd ....E 315 437-2522
East Syracuse *(G-4579)*
Visimetrics Corporation ....G 716 871-7070
Buffalo *(G-3244)*
Vosky Precision Machining Corp ....F 631 737-3200
Ronkonkoma *(G-15000)*
▲ **Voss Manufacturing Inc** ....D 716 731-5062
Sanborn *(G-15130)*
Vytek Inc ....F 631 750-1770
Bohemia *(G-1155)*
W H Jones & Son Inc ....F 716 875-8233
Kenmore *(G-7151)*
W J Albro Machine Works Inc ....G 631 345-0657
Yaphank *(G-17408)*
Walsh & Sons Machine Inc ....G 845 526-0301
Mahopac *(G-8004)*
Washburn Manufacturing Tech ....G 607 387-3991
Trumansburg *(G-16268)*
Watkins Welding and Mch Sp Inc ....G 914 949-6168
White Plains *(G-17181)*
Wayne Integrated Tech Corp ....E 631 242-0213
Edgewood *(G-4620)*
Waynes Welding Inc ....E 315 768-6146
Yorkville *(G-17530)*
Weaver Machine & Tool Co Inc ....F 315 253-4422
Auburn *(G-528)*
◆ **Wendt Corporation** ....D 716 391-1200
Buffalo *(G-3251)*
West Falls Machine Co Inc ....F 716 655-0440
East Aurora *(G-4380)*
▲ **Westchstr Crnkshft Grndng** ....G 718 651-3900
East Elmhurst *(G-4400)*
Wiggby Precision Machine Corp ....E 718 439-6900
Brooklyn *(G-2750)*
Willard Machine ....F 716 885-1630
Buffalo *(G-3255)*
William Kanes Mfg Corp ....G 718 346-1515
Brooklyn *(G-2754)*
William Moon Iron Works Inc ....F 518 943-3861
Catskill *(G-3434)*
Williams Tool Inc ....E 315 737-7226
Chadwicks *(G-3531)*
Winn Manufacturing Inc ....G 518 642-3515
Granville *(G-5782)*
Woods Machine and Tool LLC ....F 607 699-3253
Nichols *(G-12892)*
Wordingham Machine Co Inc ....E 585 924-2294
Rochester *(G-14766)*
Wrightcut EDM & Machine Inc ....G 607 733-5018
Elmira *(G-4706)*
Zip Products Inc ....F 585 482-0044
Rochester *(G-14775)*

36 ELECTRONIC AND OTHER ELECTRICAL EQUIPMENT AND COMPONENTS, EXCEPT COMPUTER

3612 Power, Distribution & Specialty Transformers

Arstan Products International ....F 516 433-1313
Hicksville *(G-6324)*
Berkshire Transformer ....G 631 467-5328
Central Islip *(G-3487)*
Buffalo Power Elec Ctr De ....E 716 651-1600
Depew *(G-4250)*
Cooper Power Systems LLC ....B 716 375-7100
Olean *(G-13140)*
Current Controls Inc ....C 585 593-1544
Wellsville *(G-16750)*
Dyco Electronics Inc ....D 607 324-2030
Hornell *(G-6562)*
Electron Coil Inc ....D 607 336-7414
Norwich *(G-13027)*
Ems Development Corporation ....D 631 345-6200
Yaphank *(G-17391)*
Exxelia-Raf Tabtronics LLC ....E 585 243-4331
Piffard *(G-13547)*
Frederick Cowan & Company Inc ....F 631 369-0360
Riverhead *(G-14143)*
General Electric Company ....A 518 385-4022
Schenectady *(G-15257)*
General Electric Company ....E 518 385-7620
Niskayuna *(G-12895)*
Hale Electrical Dist Svcs Inc ....G 716 818-7595
Wales Center *(G-16540)*
K Road Power Management LLC ....F 212 351-0535
New York *(G-10796)*
Kepco Inc ....E 718 461-7000
Flushing *(G-5259)*
Kepco Inc ....D 718 461-7000
Flushing *(G-5260)*
Kepco Inc ....E 718 461-7000
Flushing *(G-5261)*
Marvel Equipment Corp Inc ....G 718 383-6597
Brooklyn *(G-2278)*
Mitchell Electronics Corp ....E 914 699-3800
Mount Vernon *(G-8707)*
▲ **Niagara Transformer Corp** ....D 716 896-6500
Buffalo *(G-3091)*
▲ **Piller Usa Inc** ....E 845 695-6600
Middletown *(G-8456)*
Precision Electronics Inc ....F 631 842-4900
Copiague *(G-3919)*
Ram Transformer Technologies ....F 914 632-3988
New Rochelle *(G-8922)*
Sag Harbor Industries Inc ....E 631 725-0440
Sag Harbor *(G-15080)*
Schneider Electric It Corp ....F 646 335-0216
New York *(G-11992)*
Schneider Electric Usa Inc ....F 585 377-1313
Penfield *(G-13504)*
Siemens Corporation ....F 202 434-7800
New York *(G-12062)*
Siemens USA Holdings Inc ....B 212 258-4000
New York *(G-12064)*
▲ **Spellman High Vltage Elec Corp** ....B 631 630-3000
Hauppauge *(G-6197)*
▲ **Spence Engineering Company Inc** ....C 845 778-5566
Walden *(G-16536)*
Sunward Electronics Inc ....F 518 687-0030
Troy *(G-16257)*
Switching Power Inc ....D 631 981-7231
Ronkonkoma *(G-14990)*
Telephone Sales & Service Co ....E 212 233-8505
New York *(G-12295)*
Transistor Devices Inc ....E 631 471-7492
Ronkonkoma *(G-14992)*
Veeco Instruments Inc ....C 516 349-8300
Plainview *(G-13643)*

3613 Switchgear & Switchboard Apparatus

▲ **Abasco Inc** ....E 716 649-4790
Hamburg *(G-5918)*
▲ **Alarm Controls Corporation** ....E 631 586-4220
Deer Park *(G-4090)*
All City Switchboard Corp ....E 718 956-7244
Long Island City *(G-7651)*
Allied Circuits LLC ....E 716 551-0285
Buffalo *(G-2803)*
Atlas Switch Co Inc ....E 516 222-6280
Garden City *(G-5495)*
Avanti Control Systems Inc ....G 518 921-4368
Gloversville *(G-5707)*
Benfield Control Systems Inc ....F 914 948-6660
White Plains *(G-17085)*
Boulay Fabrication Inc ....F 315 677-5247
La Fayette *(G-7240)*
C A M Graphics Co Inc ....E 631 842-3400
Farmingdale *(G-4955)*
Claddagh Electronics Ltd ....E 718 784-0571
Long Island City *(G-7700)*
Cooper Industries LLC ....E 315 477-7000
Syracuse *(G-15909)*
Cooper Power Systems LLC ....B 716 375-7100
Olean *(G-13140)*
Custom Controls ....G 315 253-4785
Scipio Center *(G-15322)*
Electric Swtchbard Sltions LLC ....G 718 643-1105
New Hyde Park *(G-8831)*
Electrotech Service Eqp Corp ....E 718 626-7700
Astoria *(G-439)*
Emerson Network Power ....F 607 724-2484
Binghamton *(G-911)*
▲ **Ems Development Corporation** ....D 631 924-4736
Yaphank *(G-17390)*
Inertia Switch Inc ....E 845 359-8300
Orangeburg *(G-13229)*
Junior Achevement of Eastrn NY ....G 518 783-4336
Latham *(G-7366)*
◆ **Leviton Manufacturing Co Inc** ....B 631 812-6000
Melville *(G-8334)*

Employee Codes: A=Over 500 employees, B=251-500
C=101-250, D=51-100, E=20-50, F=10-19, G=5-9
2017 Harris
New York Manufacturers Directory
839

Link Control Systems Inc ....F .... 631 471-3950 Ronkonkoma (G-14932)
▲ Marquardt Switches Inc ....C .... 315 655-8050 Cazenovia (G-3449)
Micro Instrument Corp ....D .... 585 458-3150 Rochester (G-14507)
Odyssey Controls Inc ....G .... 585 548-9800 Bergen (G-851)
Product Station Inc ....F .... 516 942-4220 Jericho (G-7082)
Schneider Electric Usa Inc ....C .... 646 335-0220 New York (G-11993)
▲ Se-Mar Electric Co Inc ....E .... 716 674-7404 West Seneca (G-16953)
Select Controls Inc ....E .... 631 567-9010 Bohemia (G-1131)
Sinclair Technologies Inc ....E .... 716 874-3682 Hamburg (G-5942)
Smith Control Systems Inc ....F .... 518 828-7646 Hudson (G-6635)
Soc America Inc ....F .... 631 472-6666 Ronkonkoma (G-14986)
Switching Power Inc ....D .... 631 981-7231 Ronkonkoma (G-14990)
Trac Regulators Inc ....E .... 914 699-9352 Mount Vernon (G-8739)
▲ Transit Air Inc ....E .... 607 324-0216 Hornell (G-6568)

3621 Motors & Generators

▲ Aeroflex Incorporated ....B .... 516 694-6700 Plainview (G-13578)
Aeroflex Plainview Inc ....B .... 516 694-6700 Plainview (G-13579)
Aeroflex Plainview Inc ....C .... 631 231-9100 Hauppauge (G-6011)
▲ Allied Motion Technologies Inc ....C .... 716 242-8634 Amherst (G-221)
Allied Motion Technologies Inc ....C .... 315 782-5910 Watertown (G-16634)
◆ American Precision Inds Inc ....C .... 716 691-9100 Amherst (G-224)
Ametek Inc ....D .... 607 763-4700 Binghamton (G-888)
Ametek Inc ....D .... 585 263-7700 Rochester (G-14202)
Apogee Power Usa Inc ....F .... 202 746-2890 Hartsdale (G-5997)
▲ Applied Power Systems Inc ....E .... 516 935-2230 Hicksville (G-6322)
▲ ARC Systems Inc ....E .... 631 582-8020 Hauppauge (G-6023)
Auburn Armature Inc ....D .... 315 253-9721 Auburn (G-477)
▲ Automation Source Technologies ....G .... 631 643-1678 West Babylon (G-16772)
Chart Inc ....F .... 518 272-3565 Troy (G-16230)
Chemark International USA Inc ....G .... 631 593-4566 Deer Park (G-4118)
Con Rel Auto Electric Inc ....E .... 518 356-1646 Schenectady (G-15245)
Cummins Inc ....B .... 812 377-5000 Jamestown (G-6986)
▲ Current Applications Inc ....E .... 315 788-4689 Watertown (G-16648)
▲ D & D Motor Systems Inc ....E .... 315 701-0861 Syracuse (G-15918)
Designatronics Incorporated ....B .... 516 328-3300 New Hyde Park (G-8826)
EDP Renewables North Amer LLC ....G .... 518 426-1650 Albany (G-76)
Electron Coil Inc ....D .... 607 336-7414 Norwich (G-13027)
Elton El Mantle Inc ....G .... 315 432-9067 Syracuse (G-15934)
Emes Motor Inc ....G .... 718 387-2445 Brooklyn (G-1919)
Empire Division Inc ....D .... 315 476-6273 Syracuse (G-15936)
▲ Ems Development Corporation ....D .... 631 924-4736 Yaphank (G-17390)
Ener-G Cogen LLC ....G .... 718 551-7170 New York (G-10035)
Ener-G-Rotors Inc ....G .... 518 372-2608 Schenectady (G-15250)
▲ Eni Technology Inc ....B .... 585 427-8300 Rochester (G-14353)
▲ Faradyne Motors LLC ....F .... 315 331-5985 Palmyra (G-13405)
▲ Felchar Manufacturing Corp ....A .... 607 723-3106 Binghamton (G-914)
Franklin Electric Co Inc ....A .... 718 244-7744 Jamaica (G-6914)
▼ Gaffney Kroese Supply Corp ....F .... 516 228-5091 Garden City (G-5506)
General Electric Company ....B .... 518 385-2211 Schenectady (G-15261)
Generation Power LLC ....G .... 315 234-2451 Syracuse (G-15951)
▲ Getec Inc ....F .... 845 292-0800 Ferndale (G-5170)
Got Power Inc ....G .... 631 767-9493 Ronkonkoma (G-14906)
Hes Inc ....G .... 607 359-2974 Addison (G-7)
IEC Holden Corporation ....F .... 518 213-3991 Plattsburgh (G-13670)
Independent Field Svc LLC ....G .... 315 559-9243 Syracuse (G-15962)
Industrial Test Eqp Co Inc ....E .... 516 883-6423 Port Washington (G-13824)
Intelligen Power Systems LLC ....G .... 212 750-0373 Old Bethpage (G-13129)
International Control Products ....F .... 716 558-4400 West Seneca (G-16949)
Island Components Group Inc ....F .... 631 563-4224 Holbrook (G-6453)
▲ John G Rubino Inc ....E .... 315 253-7396 Auburn (G-504)
K Road Moapa Solar LLC ....F .... 212 351-0535 New York (G-10795)
Kaddis Manufacturing Corp ....G .... 585 624-3070 Honeoye Falls (G-6533)
Lcdrives Corp ....F .... 860 712-8926 Potsdam (G-13879)
Magna Products Corp ....E .... 585 647-2280 Rochester (G-14489)
▲ Makerbot Industries LLC ....B .... 347 334-6800 Brooklyn (G-2254)
▲ Matrix Railway Corp ....G .... 631 643-1483 West Babylon (G-16810)
Mks Medical Electronics ....C .... 585 292-7400 Rochester (G-14518)
▲ Modular Devices Inc ....D .... 631 345-3100 Shirley (G-15426)
Nidec Motor Corporation ....F .... 315 434-9303 East Syracuse (G-4553)
▲ Power and Composite Tech LLC ....D .... 518 843-6825 Amsterdam (G-365)
Power Gneration Indus Engs Inc ....F .... 315 633-9389 Bridgeport (G-1235)
Powercomplete LLC ....G .... 212 228-4129 New York (G-11692)
Premco Inc ....F .... 914 636-7095 New Rochelle (G-8921)
Protective Power Systms & Cntr ....F .... 845 773-9016 Poughkeepsie (G-13926)
R M S Motor Corporation ....F .... 607 723-2323 Binghamton (G-944)
Ruhle Companies Inc ....E .... 914 287-4000 Valhalla (G-16372)
Sag Harbor Industries Inc ....E .... 631 725-0440 Sag Harbor (G-15080)
▲ Sima Technologies LLC ....G .... 412 828-9130 Hauppauge (G-6191)
Sopark Corp ....C .... 716 822-0434 Buffalo (G-3191)
▲ Stature Electric Inc ....B .... 315 782-5910 Watertown (G-16672)
Supergen Products LLC ....G .... 315 573-7887 Newark (G-12744)
▲ Taro Manufacturing Company Inc ....F .... 315 252-9430 Auburn (G-523)
Troy Industrial Solutions ....D .... 518 272-4920 Watervliet (G-16690)
▲ Vdc Electronics Inc ....F .... 631 683-5850 Huntington (G-6690)
W J Albro Machine Works Inc ....G .... 631 345-0657 Yaphank (G-17408)
▲ Wind Solutions LLC ....G .... 518 813-8029 Esperance (G-4840)

3624 Carbon & Graphite Prdts

▲ Carbon Graphite Materials Inc ....G .... 716 792-7979 Brocton (G-1248)
▲ Ceramaterials LLC ....G .... 518 701-6722 Port Jervis (G-13781)
Go Blue Technologies Ltd ....G .... 631 404-6285 North Babylon (G-12901)
◆ Graphite Metallizing Corp ....D .... 914 968-8400 Yonkers (G-17450)
Hh Liquidating Corp ....A .... 646 282-2500 New York (G-10471)
J V Precision Inc ....G .... 518 851-3200 Hudson (G-6619)
▲ Kureha Advanced Materials Inc ....F .... 724 295-3352 New York (G-10894)
Metal Coated Fibers Inc ....E .... 518 280-8514 Schenectady (G-15278)
Metallized Carbon Corporation ....C .... 914 941-3738 Ossining (G-13323)
▲ Mwi Inc ....D .... 585 424-4200 Rochester (G-14526)
Pyrotek Incorporated ....E .... 716 731-3221 Sanborn (G-15126)
Saturn Industries Inc ....E .... 518 828-9956 Hudson (G-6632)

3625 Relays & Indl Controls

Addex Inc ....G .... 315 331-7700 Newark (G-12728)
Adeptronics Incorporated ....G .... 631 667-0659 Bay Shore (G-665)
Afi Cybernetics Corporation ....E .... 607 732-3244 Elmira (G-4668)
Air Crafters Inc ....C .... 631 471-7788 Ronkonkoma (G-14857)
▲ Alarm Controls Corporation ....E .... 631 586-4220 Deer Park (G-4090)
◆ Altronix Corp ....D .... 718 567-8181 Brooklyn (G-1596)
◆ American Precision Inds Inc ....C .... 716 691-9100 Amherst (G-224)
▲ Anderson Instrument Co Inc ....D .... 518 922-5315 Fultonville (G-5477)
◆ API Deltran Inc ....C .... 716 691-9100 Amherst (G-226)
Bakery Innovative Tech Corp ....F .... 631 758-3081 Patchogue (G-13415)
Bemco of Western Ny Inc ....G .... 716 823-8400 Buffalo (G-2838)
Bomac Inc ....F .... 315 433-9181 Syracuse (G-15872)
▲ Burgess-Manning Inc ....D .... 716 662-6540 Orchard Park (G-13257)
◆ C D A Inc ....G .... 631 473-1595 Nesconset (G-8774)
Calia Technical Inc ....G .... 718 447-3928 Staten Island (G-15655)
Con Rel Auto Electric Inc ....E .... 518 356-1646 Schenectady (G-15245)
◆ Conic Systems Inc ....F .... 845 856-4053 Port Jervis (G-13782)
Continental Instruments LLC ....E .... 631 842-9400 Amityville (G-281)
▲ Cox & Company Inc ....C .... 212 366-0200 Plainview (G-13593)
Datatran Labs Inc ....G .... 845 856-4313 Port Jervis (G-13783)
Designatronics Incorporated ....B .... 516 328-3300 New Hyde Park (G-8826)
▲ Designatronics Incorporated ....G .... 516 328-3300 New Hyde Park (G-8825)
Deutsch Relays ....F .... 631 342-1700 Hauppauge (G-6062)
▲ Digital Instruments Inc ....F .... 716 874-5848 Tonawanda (G-16155)
Dortronics Systems Inc ....E .... 631 725-0505 Sag Harbor (G-15077)
▲ Dri Relays Inc ....D .... 631 342-1700 Hauppauge (G-6067)
▲ Dyson-Kissner-Moran Corp ....E .... 212 661-4600 Poughkeepsie (G-13896)
Eaton Corporation ....C .... 212 319-2100 New York (G-9970)
Eaton Corporation ....C .... 585 394-1780 Canandaigua (G-3344)
Eaton Corporation ....C .... 516 353-3017 East Meadow (G-4423)
Eaton Corporation ....G .... 716 691-0008 Buffalo (G-2930)
Eaton Hydraulics LLC ....G .... 716 375-7132 Olean (G-13147)
Eatons Crouse Hinds Business ....F .... 315 477-7000 Syracuse (G-15932)
Edo LLC ....C .... 631 630-4000 Amityville (G-287)
Electro-Kinetics Inc ....F .... 845 887-4930 Callicoon (G-3285)

SIC SECTION — 36 ELECTRONIC AND OTHER ELECTRICAL EQUIPMENT AND COMPONENTS, EXCEPT COMPUTER

Electronic Machine Parts LLC .... F 631 434-3700
  Hauppauge (G-6070)
▲ Elevator Systems Inc .... E 516 239-4044
  Garden City (G-5502)
Enetics Inc .... G 585 924-5010
  Victor (G-16475)
Eversan Inc .... F 315 736-3967
  Whitesboro (G-17193)
Exfo Burleigh Pdts Group Inc .... D 585 301-1530
  Canandaigua (G-3345)
Fics Inc .... E 607 359-4474
  Addison (G-6)
Fortitude Industries .... D 607 324-1500
  Hornell (G-6563)
G C Controls Inc .... E 607 656-4117
  Greene (G-5865)
Gemtrol Inc .... G 716 894-0716
  Buffalo (G-2968)
General Control Systems Inc .... E 518 270-8045
  Green Island (G-5855)
General Oil Equipment Co Inc .... E 716 691-7012
  Amherst (G-243)
Goddard Design Co .... G 718 599-0170
  Brooklyn (G-2034)
Harris Corporation .... E 315 838-7000
  Rome (G-14813)
▲ Hasco Componets .... E 516 328-9292
  New Hyde Park (G-8840)
▲ I D E Processes Corporation .... F 718 544-1177
  Kew Gardens (G-7161)
I E D Corp .... F 631 348-0424
  Islandia (G-6795)
▲ ICM Controls Corp .... D 315 233-5266
  North Syracuse (G-12947)
Industrial Indxing Systems Inc .... E 585 924-9181
  Victor (G-16482)
Inertia Switch Inc .... E 845 359-8300
  Orangeburg (G-13229)
▲ Infitec Inc .... D 315 433-1150
  East Syracuse (G-4543)
▲ Interntnal Cntrls Msrmnts Corp .... C 315 233-5266
  North Syracuse (G-12948)
◆ Itt LLC .... B 914 641-2000
  White Plains (G-17125)
ITT Aerospace Controls LLC .... G 914 641-2000
  White Plains (G-17126)
ITT Corporation .... E 585 269-7109
  Hemlock (G-6263)
ITT Corporation .... D 315 258-4904
  Auburn (G-502)
ITT Corporation .... F 914 641-2000
  Seneca Falls (G-15361)
ITT Corporation .... D 315 568-2811
  Seneca Falls (G-15362)
ITT Inc .... G 914 641-2000
  White Plains (G-17128)
JE Miller Inc .... F 315 437-6811
  East Syracuse (G-4546)
Kaman Automation Inc .... G 585 254-8840
  Rochester (G-14467)
▲ Kearney-National Inc .... F 212 661-4600
  New York (G-10828)
◆ Kussmaul Electronics Co Inc .... E 631 218-0298
  West Sayville (G-16936)
L-3 Cmmnctons Ntronix Holdings .... D 212 697-1111
  New York (G-10904)
Linde LLC .... D 716 773-7552
  Grand Island (G-5763)
Logitek Inc .... D 631 567-1100
  Bohemia (G-1094)
Machine Components Corp .... E 516 694-7222
  Plainview (G-13617)
Magnus Precision Mfg Inc .... D 315 548-8032
  Phelps (G-13534)
▼ Magtrol Inc .... E 716 668-5555
  Buffalo (G-3055)
▲ Makerbot Industries LLC .... B 347 334-6800
  Brooklyn (G-2254)
▲ Marine & Indus Hydraulics Inc .... F 914 698-2036
  Mamaroneck (G-8037)
▲ Marquardt Switches Inc .... C 315 655-8050
  Cazenovia (G-3449)
▲ Mason Industries Inc .... C 631 348-0282
  Hauppauge (G-6126)
Mason Industries Inc .... C 631 348-0282
  Hauppauge (G-6127)
Micromod Automation Inc .... E 585 321-9200
  Rochester (G-14510)
▼ Micropen Technologies Corp .... D 585 624-2610
  Honeoye Falls (G-6535)

Moog Inc .... C 716 805-8100
  East Aurora (G-4376)
◆ Moog Inc .... A 716 652-2000
  Elma (G-4651)
▲ Morris Products Inc .... F 518 743-0523
  Queensbury (G-14005)
N E Controls LLC .... F 315 626-2480
  Syracuse (G-15996)
▲ Nas-Tra Automotive Inds Inc .... C 631 225-1225
  Lindenhurst (G-7474)
National Time Recording Eqp Co .... F 212 227-3310
  New York (G-11352)
Nitram Energy Inc .... F 716 662-6540
  Orchard Park (G-13285)
North Point Technologies .... F 607 238-1114
  Johnson City (G-7099)
North Point Technology LLC .... F 866 885-3377
  Endicott (G-4821)
Nsi Industries LLC .... C 800 841-2505
  Mount Vernon (G-8711)
▲ Omntec Mfg Inc .... E 631 981-2001
  Ronkonkoma (G-14960)
Panelogic Inc .... F 607 962-6319
  Corning (G-3978)
Peerless Instrument Co Inc .... E 631 396-6500
  Farmingdale (G-5076)
Powr-UPS Corp .... E 631 345-5700
  Shirley (G-15428)
Precision Electronics Inc .... F 631 842-4900
  Copiague (G-3919)
Precision Mechanisms Corp .... E 516 333-5955
  Westbury (G-17021)
▲ Pulsafeeder Inc .... C 585 292-8000
  Rochester (G-14609)
Rasp Incorporated .... E 518 747-8020
  Gansevoort (G-5488)
▲ Rochester Industrial Ctrl Inc .... D 315 524-4555
  Ontario (G-13212)
Rockwell Automation Inc .... C 585 487-2700
  Rochester (G-14656)
Rotork Controls Inc .... F 585 328-1550
  Rochester (G-14659)
▲ Rotork Controls Inc .... C 585 328-1550
  Rochester (G-14660)
Ruhle Companies Inc .... E 914 287-4000
  Valhalla (G-16372)
◆ Schmersal Inc .... E 914 347-4775
  Hawthorne (G-6254)
Select Controls Inc .... E 631 567-9010
  Bohemia (G-1131)
Sequential Electronics Systems .... E 914 592-1345
  Elmsford (G-4783)
Service Mfg Group Inc .... F 716 893-1482
  Buffalo (G-3183)
▲ Soft-Noze Usa Inc .... G 315 732-2726
  Frankfort (G-5357)
▲ Soundcoat Company Inc .... D 631 242-2200
  Deer Park (G-4212)
Speer Equipment Inc .... G 585 964-2700
  Hamlin (G-5951)
Ssac Inc .... E 800 843-8848
  Baldwinsville (G-577)
▲ Stetron International Inc .... F 716 854-3443
  Buffalo (G-3197)
Switches and Sensors Inc .... F 631 924-2167
  Yaphank (G-17404)
Teale Machine Company Inc .... D 585 244-6700
  Rochester (G-14719)
Techniflo Corporation .... G 716 741-3500
  Clarence Center (G-3680)
▲ Teknic Inc .... E 585 784-7454
  Victor (G-16506)
▲ Tork Inc .... D 914 664-3542
  Mount Vernon (G-8738)
Transistor Devices Inc .... E 631 471-7492
  Ronkonkoma (G-14992)
Trident Valve Actuator Co .... F 914 698-2650
  Mamaroneck (G-8049)
◆ Unimar Inc .... F 315 699-4400
  Syracuse (G-16063)
US Drives Inc .... D 716 731-1606
  Niagara Falls (G-12887)
Vibration & Noise Engrg Corp .... G 716 827-4959
  Orchard Park (G-13302)
▲ Vibration Eliminator Co Inc .... F 631 841-4000
  Copiague (G-3936)
Weldcomputer Corporation .... F 518 283-2897
  Troy (G-16264)
Young & Franklin Inc .... D 315 457-3110
  Liverpool (G-7559)

Zeppelin Electric Company Inc .... G 631 928-9467
  East Setauket (G-4497)

3629 Electrical Indl Apparatus, NEC

▲ Alliance Control Systems Inc .... G 845 279-4430
  Brewster (G-1209)
American Fuel Cell LLC .... G 585 474-3993
  Rochester (G-14197)
Applied Energy Solutions LLC .... E 585 538-3270
  Caledonia (G-3277)
▲ Applied Power Systems Inc .... E 516 935-2230
  Hicksville (G-6322)
C & M Circuits Inc .... E 631 589-0208
  Bohemia (G-1031)
Calibration Technologies Inc .... G 631 676-6133
  Centereach (G-3470)
China Lithium Technologies .... G 212 391-2688
  New York (G-9599)
▲ Curtis Instruments Inc .... C 914 666-2971
  Mount Kisco (G-8624)
Curtis/Palmer Hydroelectric LP .... G 518 654-6297
  Corinth (G-3957)
Cygnus Automation Inc .... E 631 981-0909
  Bohemia (G-1047)
Donald R Husband Inc .... G 607 770-1990
  Johnson City (G-7091)
Eluminocity US Inc .... G 651 528-1165
  New York (G-10016)
▲ Ems Development Corporation .... D 631 924-4736
  Yaphank (G-17390)
Ems Technologies Inc .... D 607 723-3676
  Binghamton (G-912)
Endicott Research Group Inc .... D 607 754-9187
  Endicott (G-4804)
▲ G B International Trdg Co Ltd .... C 607 785-0938
  Endicott (G-4809)
General Electric Company .... E 518 459-4110
  Albany (G-82)
General Electric Company .... E 518 746-5750
  Hudson Falls (G-6642)
GM Components Holdings LLC .... B 716 439-2463
  Lockport (G-7590)
GW Lisk Company Inc .... E 315 548-2165
  Phelps (G-13532)
Key Signals .... G 631 433-2962
  East Moriches (G-4429)
◆ Kussmaul Electronics Co Inc .... E 631 218-0298
  West Sayville (G-16936)
▲ Nrd LLC .... E 716 773-7634
  Grand Island (G-5764)
▲ Tonoga Inc .... E 518 658-3202
  Petersburg (G-13528)
Viking Technologies Ltd .... E 631 957-8000
  Lindenhurst (G-7493)
▲ Walter R Tucker Entps Ltd .... F 607 467-2866
  Deposit (G-4282)

3631 Household Cooking Eqpt

Applince Installation Svc Corp .... E 716 884-7425
  Buffalo (G-2818)
Bakers Pride Oven Co Inc .... C 914 576-0200
  New Rochelle (G-8887)
◆ Korin Japanese Trading Corp .... E 212 587-7021
  New York (G-10878)
▲ Oxo International Inc .... C 212 242-3333
  New York (G-11544)
◆ Toshiba America Inc .... E 212 596-0600
  New York (G-12377)
Unibrands Corporation .... F 212 897-2278
  New York (G-12451)

3632 Household Refrigerators & Freezers

Acme Kitchenettes Corp .... E 518 828-4191
  Hudson (G-6604)
Ae Fund Inc .... E 315 698-7650
  Brewerton (G-1202)
Dover Corporation .... E 212 922-1640
  New York (G-9911)
◆ Felix Storch Inc .... C 718 893-3900
  Bronx (G-1329)
General Electric Company .... A 518 385-4022
  Schenectady (G-15257)
Robin Industries Ltd .... F 718 218-9616
  Brooklyn (G-2501)
Sure-Kol Refrigerator Co Inc .... F 718 625-0601
  Brooklyn (G-2633)

Employee Codes: A=Over 500 employees, B=251-500
C=101-250, D=51-100, E=20-50, F=10-19, G=5-9

3633 Household Laundry Eqpt

AES Electronics Inc....G....212 371-8120
New York (G-9052)
Coinmach Service Corp....A....516 349-8555
Plainview (G-13588)
CSC Serviceworks Inc....E....516 349-8555
Plainview (G-13594)
CSC Serviceworks Holdings....E....516 349-8555
Plainview (G-13595)
Penn Enterprises Inc....F....845 446-0765
West Point (G-16930)
Spin Holdco Inc....G....516 349-8555
Plainview (G-13635)

3634 Electric Household Appliances

▲ Abbott Industries Inc....E....718 291-0800
Jamaica (G-6891)
▲ Advanced Response Corporation....G....212 459-0887
New York (G-9046)
Algonquin Power....G....315 393-5595
Ogdensburg (G-13110)
American Comfort Direct LLC....E....201 364-8309
New York (G-9116)
Dampits International Inc....G....212 581-3047
New York (G-9796)
Emerald Electronics Usa Inc....G....718 872-5544
Brooklyn (G-1917)
▼ Fulton Volcanic Inc....D....315 298-5121
Pulaski (G-13950)
General Elc Capitl Svcs Inc....G....315 554-2000
Skaneateles (G-15461)
Goodnature Products Inc....F....716 855-3325
Orchard Park (G-13273)
Harrys Inc....E....888 212-6855
New York (G-10421)
▲ Heaven Fresh USA Inc....G....800 642-0367
Niagara Falls (G-12831)
Hrg Group Inc....E....212 906-8555
New York (G-10524)
▲ Plus Its Cheap LLC....E....845 233-2435
New City (G-8789)
▲ Quality Life Inc....F....718 939-5787
College Point (G-3803)
Quip Nyc Inc....G....703 615-1076
Brooklyn (G-2467)
Remedies Surgical Supplies....G....718 599-5301
Brooklyn (G-2490)
▲ Royal Line LLC....F....800 516-7450
Wantagh (G-16563)
Schlesinger Siemans Elec LLC....F....718 386-6230
New York (G-11989)
Sundance Industries Inc....G....845 795-5809
Milton (G-8485)
▲ Tactica International Inc....F....212 575-0500
New York (G-12271)
▲ Uniware Houseware Corp....F....631 242-7400
Brentwood (G-1198)
US Health Equipment Company....E....845 658-7576
Kingston (G-7222)
Valad Electric Heating Corp....F....914 631-4927
Tarrytown (G-16110)
Valid Electric Corp....E....914 631-9436
Tarrytown (G-16111)
Vincent Genovese....G....631 281-8170
Mastic Beach (G-8205)

3635 Household Vacuum Cleaners

American Comfort Direct LLC....E....201 364-8309
New York (G-9116)
D & C Cleaning Inc....F....631 789-5659
Copiague (G-3898)
▲ Global Resources Sg Inc....F....212 686-1411
New York (G-10320)
▲ Nationwide Sales and Service....F....631 491-6625
Farmingdale (G-5062)
Tri County Custom Vacuum....G....845 774-7595
Monroe (G-8565)

3639 Household Appliances, NEC

A Gatty Products Inc....G....914 592-3903
Elmsford (G-4731)
▼ Ajmadison Corp....D....718 532-1800
Brooklyn (G-1573)
Barrage....E....212 586-9390
New York (G-9324)
Design Solutions Ll Inc....G....631 656-8700
Saint James (G-15088)
Grillbot LLC....G....646 369-7242
New York (G-10365)
Hobart Corporation....E....631 864-3440
Commack (G-3835)
Jado Sewing Machines Inc....E....718 784-2314
Long Island City (G-7770)
Marine Park Appliances LLC....G....718 513-1808
Brooklyn (G-2271)
Platinum Carting Corp....F....631 649-4322
Bay Shore (G-724)

3641 Electric Lamps

◆ Atlantic Ultraviolet Corp....E....631 234-3275
Hauppauge (G-6028)
Boehm Surgical Instrument....F....585 436-6584
Rochester (G-14241)
Emitted Inc....G....516 531-3533
Westbury (G-16982)
▲ Foscarini Inc....G....212 247-2218
New York (G-10189)
General Electric Company....A....518 385-4022
Schenectady (G-15257)
Goldstar Lighting LLC....F....646 543-6811
New York (G-10336)
K & H Industries Inc....F....716 312-0088
Hamburg (G-5930)
K & H Industries Inc....E....716 312-0088
Hamburg (G-5931)
Kreon Inc....G....516 470-9522
Bethpage (G-870)
▲ La Mar Lighting Co Inc....D....631 777-7700
Farmingdale (G-5032)
▲ Led Waves Inc....F....347 416-6182
Brooklyn (G-2204)
◆ Lighting Holdings Intl LLC....F....845 306-1850
Purchase (G-13960)
▲ Lowel-Light Manufacturing Inc....E....718 921-0600
Brooklyn (G-2238)
Lumia Energy Solutions LLC....G....516 478-5795
Jericho (G-7076)
▲ Make-Waves Instrument Corp....E....716 681-7524
Depew (G-4264)
Oledworks LLC....E....585 287-6802
Rochester (G-14547)
Philips Elec N Amer Corp....C....607 776-3692
Bath (G-661)
Preston Glass Industries Inc....E....718 997-8888
Forest Hills (G-5328)
▲ Ric-Lo Productions Ltd....E....845 469-2285
Chester (G-3613)
▲ Saratoga Lighting Holdings LLC....G....212 906-7800
New York (G-11971)
◆ Satco Products Inc....D....631 243-2022
Edgewood (G-4611)
Siemens Corporation....F....202 434-7800
New York (G-12062)
Siemens USA Holdings Inc....B....212 258-4000
New York (G-12064)
Welch Allyn Inc....A....315 685-4347
Skaneateles Falls (G-15473)
▲ Westron Corporation....E....516 678-2300
Oceanside (G-13105)

3643 Current-Carrying Wiring Devices

Alstom Signaling Inc....E....585 274-8700
Schenectady (G-15229)
Andrew Marc Outlet....G....631 727-2520
Riverhead (G-14138)
Andros Manufacturing Corp....F....585 663-5700
Rochester (G-14205)
Atc Plastics LLC....E....212 375-2515
New York (G-9245)
Automatic Connector Inc....F....631 543-5000
Hauppauge (G-6029)
Bassin Technical Sales Co....E....914 698-9358
Mamaroneck (G-8024)
Belden Inc....B....607 796-5600
Horseheads (G-6569)
Bronx New Way Corp....G....347 431-1385
Bronx (G-1289)
C A M Graphics Co Inc....E....631 842-3400
Farmingdale (G-4955)
Charlton Precision Pdts Inc....G....845 338-2351
Kingston (G-7183)
Command Components Corporation....G....631 666-4411
Bay Shore (G-688)
Cooper Power Systems LLC....B....716 375-7100
Olean (G-13140)
▲ Cox & Company Inc....C....212 366-0200
Plainview (G-13593)
Crown Die Casting Corp....E....914 667-5400
Mount Vernon (G-8675)
▲ Delfingen Us-New York Inc....E....716 215-0300
Niagara Falls (G-12810)
Delta Metal Products Co Inc....E....718 855-4200
Brooklyn (G-1852)
Diversified Electrical Pdts....F....631 567-5710
Bohemia (G-1058)
Dollar Popular Inc....G....914 375-0361
Yonkers (G-17437)
EB Acquisitions LLC....D....212 355-3310
New York (G-9971)
Exxelia-Raf Tabtronics LLC....E....585 243-4331
Piffard (G-13547)
◆ Fiber Instrument Sales Inc....C....315 736-2206
Oriskany (G-13309)
Heary Bros Lghtning Protection....E....716 941-6141
Springville (G-15612)
Inertia Switch Inc....E....845 359-8300
Orangeburg (G-13229)
Jaguar Industries Inc....F....845 947-1800
Haverstraw (G-6237)
Joldeson One Aerospace Inds....D....718 848-7396
Ozone Park (G-13380)
K & H Industries Inc....F....716 312-0088
Hamburg (G-5930)
▲ Kelta Inc....E....631 789-5000
Edgewood (G-4602)
L-3 Communications Corporation....A....631 436-7400
Hauppauge (G-6108)
◆ Leviton Manufacturing Co Inc....B....631 812-6000
Melville (G-8334)
◆ Lighting Holdings Intl LLC....F....845 306-1850
Purchase (G-13960)
Lite Brite Manufacturing Inc....F....718 855-9797
Brooklyn (G-2231)
Lourdes Industries Inc....D....631 234-6600
Hauppauge (G-6121)
▲ MD Electronics of Illinois....D....716 488-0300
Jamestown (G-7019)
▲ Micro Contacts Inc....E....516 433-4830
Hicksville (G-6371)
Mini-Circuits Fort Wayne LLC....B....718 934-4500
Brooklyn (G-2318)
▲ Monarch Electric Products Inc....G....718 583-7996
Bronx (G-1402)
Mono-Systems Inc....E....716 821-1344
Buffalo (G-3074)
▲ NEa Manufacturing Corp....E....516 371-4200
Inwood (G-6763)
Orbit International Corp....C....631 435-8300
Hauppauge (G-6154)
◆ Pass & Seymour Inc....B....315 468-6211
Syracuse (G-16011)
Pei/Genesis Inc....G....631 256-1747
Farmingville (G-5161)
RE 99 Cents Inc....G....718 639-2325
Woodside (G-17349)
Reynolds Packaging McHy Inc....D....716 358-6451
Falconer (G-4910)
Rodale Wireless Inc....E....631 231-0044
Hauppauge (G-6179)
▲ Russell Industries Inc....F....516 536-5000
Lynbrook (G-7960)
Saturn Industries Inc....E....518 828-9956
Hudson (G-6632)
▼ Sector Microwave Inds Inc....D....631 242-2245
Deer Park (G-4208)
Sinclair Technologies Inc....E....716 874-3682
Hamburg (G-5942)
▲ Stever-Locke Industries Inc....G....585 624-3450
Honeoye Falls (G-6538)
▲ Superpower Inc....D....518 346-1414
Schenectady (G-15302)
Switching Power Inc....D....631 981-7231
Ronkonkoma (G-14990)
Swivelier Company Inc....D....845 353-1455
Blauvelt (G-975)
▲ Tappan Wire & Cable Inc....C....845 353-9000
Blauvelt (G-976)
▲ Tii Technologies Inc....E....516 364-9300
Edgewood (G-4616)
Utility Systems Tech Inc....F....518 326-4142
Watervliet (G-16691)
▲ Whirlwind Music Distrs Inc....D....585 663-8820
Rochester (G-14762)
▲ Zierick Manufacturing Corp....D....800 882-8020
Mount Kisco (G-8648)

3644 Noncurrent-Carrying Wiring Devices

Alumiseal Corp....E....518 329-2820
Copake Falls (G-3888)

S I C

SIC SECTION 36 ELECTRONIC AND OTHER ELECTRICAL EQUIPMENT AND COMPONENTS, EXCEPT COMPUTER

Cables and Chips Inc..........E....... 212 619-3132
New York *(G-9493)*
Chase Corporation..........F....... 212 644-7281
New York *(G-9586)*
Chase Corporation..........F....... 631 243-6380
Deer Park *(G-4117)*
Chase Corporation..........F....... 631 827-0476
Northport *(G-13009)*
Complete SEC & Contrls Inc..........F....... 631 421-7200
Huntington Station *(G-6700)*
Delta Metal Products Co Inc..........E....... 718 855-4200
Brooklyn *(G-1852)*
▲ **Gerome Technologies Inc**..........D....... 518 463-1324
Menands *(G-8372)*
Heat and Frost Inslatrs & Asbs..........G....... 718 784-3456
Astoria *(G-443)*
Highland Valley Supply Inc..........F....... 845 849-2863
Wappingers Falls *(G-16572)*
▲ **J H C Fabrications Inc**..........E....... 718 649-0065
Brooklyn *(G-2122)*
Jpmorgan Chase & Co..........F....... 845 298-2461
Wappingers Falls *(G-16574)*
Lapp Insulator Company LLC..........F....... 585 768-6221
Le Roy *(G-7411)*
▲ **Lapp Insulators LLC**..........C....... 585 768-6221
Le Roy *(G-7412)*
Pole Position Raceway..........G....... 716 683-7223
Cheektowaga *(G-3586)*
◆ **Producto Electric Corp**..........E....... 845 359-4900
Orangeburg *(G-13243)*
▲ **Superflex Ltd**..........E....... 718 768-1400
Brooklyn *(G-2625)*
Varflex Corporation..........C....... 315 336-4400
Rome *(G-14839)*
Veja Electronics Inc..........D....... 631 321-6086
Deer Park *(G-4222)*
▲ **Volt Tek Inc**..........F....... 585 377-2050
Fairport *(G-4886)*
▲ **Von Roll Usa Inc**..........C....... 518 344-7100
Schenectady *(G-15310)*
▲ **Zierick Manufacturing Corp**..........D....... 800 882-8020
Mount Kisco *(G-8648)*

3645 Residential Lighting Fixtures

▲ **A-1 Stamping & Spinning Corp**..........F....... 718 388-2626
Rockaway Park *(G-14784)*
◆ **Adesso Inc**..........E....... 212 736-4440
New York *(G-9027)*
Artemis Studios Inc..........D....... 718 788-6022
Brooklyn *(G-1635)*
▲ **Canarm Ltd**..........G....... 800 267-4427
Ogdensburg *(G-13113)*
▲ **Cooper Lighting LLC**..........C....... 516 470-1000
Hicksville *(G-6334)*
Crownlite Mfg Corp..........E....... 631 589-9100
Bohemia *(G-1044)*
Custom Lampshades Inc..........F....... 718 254-0500
Brooklyn *(G-1826)*
David Weeks Studio..........F....... 212 966-3433
New York *(G-9824)*
Decor By Dene Inc..........F....... 718 376-5566
Brooklyn *(G-1848)*
▲ **Dreyfus Ashby Inc**..........E....... 212 818-0770
New York *(G-9929)*
Eaton Corporation..........E....... 315 579-2872
Syracuse *(G-15930)*
▲ **Ephesus Lighting Inc**..........E....... 315 579-2873
Syracuse *(G-15937)*
▲ **ER Butler & Co Inc**..........E....... 212 925-3565
New York *(G-10055)*
Excalbur Brnze Sculpture Fndry..........E....... 718 366-3444
Brooklyn *(G-1942)*
◆ **Hudson Valley Lighting Inc**..........D....... 845 561-0300
Wappingers Falls *(G-16573)*
▲ **Jamaica Lamp Corp**..........E....... 718 776-5039
Queens Village *(G-13980)*
Judis Lampshades Inc..........G....... 917 561-3921
Brooklyn *(G-2157)*
▲ **Lexstar Inc**..........F....... 845 947-1415
Haverstraw *(G-6238)*
▲ **Litelab Corp**..........C....... 716 856-4300
Buffalo *(G-3050)*
Lyric Lighting Ltd Inc..........G....... 718 497-0109
Ridgewood *(G-14113)*
Matov Industries Inc..........E....... 718 392-5060
Long Island City *(G-7806)*
▲ **Modulightor Inc**..........F....... 212 371-0336
New York *(G-11291)*
New Generation Lighting Inc..........F....... 212 966-0328
New York *(G-11387)*
Nulux Inc..........E....... 718 383-1112
Ridgewood *(G-14116)*
Philips Elec N Amer Corp..........C....... 607 776-3692
Bath *(G-661)*
Pompian Manufacturing Co Inc..........G....... 914 476-7076
Yonkers *(G-17478)*
Preciseled Inc..........G....... 516 418-5337
Valley Stream *(G-16419)*
▲ **Prestigeline Inc**..........D....... 631 273-3636
Bay Shore *(G-728)*
▲ **Quality HM Brands Holdings LLC**..........G....... 718 292-2024
Bronx *(G-1437)*
Quoizel Inc..........E....... 631 436-4402
Hauppauge *(G-6176)*
Rapid-Lite Fixture Corporation..........F....... 347 599-2600
Brooklyn *(G-2478)*
Remains Lighting..........E....... 212 675-8051
New York *(G-11829)*
Sandy Littman Inc..........G....... 845 562-1112
Newburgh *(G-12779)*
▲ **Saratoga Lighting Holdings LLC**..........G....... 212 906-7800
New York *(G-11971)*
◆ **Satco Products Inc**..........D....... 631 243-2022
Edgewood *(G-4611)*
Savwatt Usa Inc..........F....... 646 478-2676
New York *(G-11978)*
◆ **Swarovski Lighting Ltd**..........B....... 518 563-7500
Plattsburgh *(G-13702)*
Swarovski Lighting Ltd..........B....... 518 324-6378
Plattsburgh *(G-13703)*
Swivelier Company Inc..........D....... 845 353-1455
Blauvelt *(G-975)*
Tarsier Ltd..........C....... 212 401-6181
New York *(G-12280)*
Tudor Electrical Supply Co Inc..........G....... 212 867-7550
New York *(G-12420)*
Ulster Precision Inc..........E....... 845 338-0995
Kingston *(G-7218)*
▲ **Vision Quest Lighting Inc**..........E....... 631 737-4800
Ronkonkoma *(G-14998)*
Vonn LLC..........F....... 917 572-5000
Forest Hills *(G-5329)*
▲ **Wainland Inc**..........E....... 718 626-2233
Astoria *(G-461)*

3646 Commercial, Indl & Institutional Lighting Fixtures

A & L Lighting Ltd..........F....... 718 821-1188
Medford *(G-8233)*
▲ **A-1 Stamping & Spinning Corp**..........F....... 718 388-2626
Rockaway Park *(G-14784)*
AEP Environmental LLC..........F....... 716 446-0739
Buffalo *(G-2801)*
Al Energy Solutions Led Llc..........E....... 646 380-6670
New York *(G-9068)*
▲ **Altman Stage Lighting Co Inc**..........C....... 914 476-7987
Yonkers *(G-17412)*
▲ **American Scientific Ltg Corp**..........E....... 718 369-1100
Brooklyn *(G-1608)*
Apogee Translite Inc..........E....... 631 254-6975
Deer Park *(G-4100)*
Aquarii Inc..........G....... 315 672-8807
Camillus *(G-3321)*
Aristocrat Lighting Inc..........F....... 718 522-0003
Brooklyn *(G-1628)*
▲ **Arlee Lighting Corp**..........G....... 516 595-8558
Inwood *(G-6751)*
Awaken Led Company..........F....... 802 338-5971
Champlain *(G-3537)*
▲ **Canarm Ltd**..........G....... 800 267-4427
Ogdensburg *(G-13113)*
Cooper Industries LLC..........E....... 315 477-7000
Syracuse *(G-15909)*
▲ **Cooper Lighting LLC**..........C....... 516 470-1000
Hicksville *(G-6334)*
Crownlite Mfg Corp..........E....... 631 589-9100
Bohemia *(G-1044)*
▲ **DAc Lighting Inc**..........E....... 914 698-5959
Mamaroneck *(G-8032)*
▲ **Dreyfus Ashby Inc**..........E....... 212 818-0770
New York *(G-9929)*
Edison Price Lighting Inc..........C....... 718 685-0700
Long Island City *(G-7723)*
Edison Price Lighting Inc..........D....... 718 685-0700
Long Island City *(G-7724)*
Electric Lighting Agencies..........E....... 212 645-4580
New York *(G-9996)*
Electric Lighting Agencies..........E....... 212 645-4580
Jericho *(G-7067)*
Elegance Lighting Ltd..........F....... 631 509-0640
Port Jefferson *(G-13775)*
Energy Conservation & Sup Inc..........F....... 718 855-5888
Brooklyn *(G-1924)*
▲ **Green Energy Concepts Inc**..........G....... 845 238-2574
Chester *(G-3608)*
◆ **Hudson Valley Lighting Inc**..........D....... 845 561-0300
Wappingers Falls *(G-16573)*
◆ **Jesco Lighting Inc**..........E....... 718 366-3211
Port Washington *(G-13828)*
▲ **Jesco Lighting Group LLC**..........E....... 718 366-3211
Port Washington *(G-13829)*
▲ **La Mar Lighting Co Inc**..........D....... 631 777-7700
Farmingdale *(G-5032)*
LDI Lighting Inc..........G....... 718 384-4490
Brooklyn *(G-2198)*
LDI Lighting Inc..........G....... 718 384-4490
Brooklyn *(G-2199)*
▲ **Legion Lighting Co Inc**..........E....... 718 498-1770
Brooklyn *(G-2208)*
▲ **Light Waves Concept Inc**..........F....... 212 677-6400
New York *(G-10992)*
Lighting By Dom Yonkers Inc..........G....... 914 968-8700
Yonkers *(G-17462)*
▲ **Lighting Services**..........D....... 845 942-2800
Stony Point *(G-15776)*
Linear Lighting Corporation..........C....... 718 361-7552
Long Island City *(G-7790)*
Lite Brite Manufacturing Inc..........F....... 718 855-9797
Brooklyn *(G-2231)*
▲ **Lite-Makers Inc**..........E....... 718 739-9300
Jamaica *(G-6925)*
Litelab Corp..........G....... 718 361-6829
Long Island City *(G-7792)*
▲ **Litelab Corp**..........C....... 716 856-4300
Buffalo *(G-3050)*
▲ **LSI Lightron Inc**..........A....... 845 562-5500
New Windsor *(G-8942)*
▲ **Lukas Lighting Inc**..........E....... 800 841-4011
Long Island City *(G-7795)*
Luminatta Inc..........G....... 914 664-3600
Mount Vernon *(G-8702)*
Luminescent Systems Inc..........B....... 716 655-0800
East Aurora *(G-4373)*
▲ **Luxo Corporation**..........F....... 914 345-0067
Elmsford *(G-4761)*
▲ **Magniflood Inc**..........E....... 631 226-1000
Amityville *(G-309)*
Matov Industries Inc..........E....... 718 392-5060
Long Island City *(G-7806)*
▲ **Modulightor Inc**..........F....... 212 371-0336
New York *(G-11291)*
▲ **North American Mfg Entps Inc**..........E....... 718 524-4370
Staten Island *(G-15712)*
North American Mfg Entps Inc..........F....... 718 524-4370
Staten Island *(G-15713)*
Nulux Inc..........E....... 718 383-1112
Ridgewood *(G-14116)*
Oledworks LLC..........E....... 585 287-6802
Rochester *(G-14547)*
Philips Lighting N Amer Corp..........C....... 646 265-7170
New York *(G-11647)*
Preciseled Inc..........G....... 516 418-5337
Valley Stream *(G-16419)*
Primelite Manufacturing Corp..........G....... 516 868-4411
Freeport *(G-5420)*
Rapid-Lite Fixture Corporation..........F....... 347 599-2600
Brooklyn *(G-2478)*
Remains Lighting..........E....... 212 675-8051
New York *(G-11829)*
S E A Supplies Ltd..........F....... 516 694-6677
Plainview *(G-13633)*
Sandy Littman Inc..........G....... 845 562-1112
Newburgh *(G-12779)*
▲ **Saratoga Lighting Holdings LLC**..........G....... 212 906-7800
New York *(G-11971)*
▲ **Savenergy Inc**..........G....... 516 239-1958
Garden City *(G-5531)*
Savwatt Usa Inc..........F....... 646 478-2676
New York *(G-11978)*
▲ **Selux Corporation**..........C....... 845 691-7723
Highland *(G-6408)*
Solarpath Inc..........G....... 201 490-4499
New York *(G-12121)*
◆ **Sonneman-A Way of Light**..........G....... 845 926-5469
Wappingers Falls *(G-16576)*
▲ **Spectronics Corporation**..........C....... 516 333-4840
Westbury *(G-17027)*
Swivelier Company Inc..........D....... 845 353-1455
Blauvelt *(G-975)*

S I C

Employee Codes: A=Over 500 employees, B=251-500
C=101-250, D=51-100, E=20-50, F=10-19, G=5-9
2017 Harris
New York Manufacturers Directory
843

36 ELECTRONIC AND OTHER ELECTRICAL EQUIPMENT AND COMPONENTS, EXCEPT COMPUTER

Trulite Louvre Corp ..... E 516 756-1850
  Old Bethpage (G-13131)
Twinkle Lighting Inc ..... G 718 225-0939
  Flushing (G-5304)
Versaponents Inc ..... F 631 242-3387
  Deer Park (G-4223)
▲ Vision Quest Lighting Inc ..... E 631 737-4800
  Ronkonkoma (G-14998)
Vonn LLC ..... F 917 572-5000
  Forest Hills (G-5329)
Xeleum Lighting LLC ..... F 954 617-8170
  Mount Kisco (G-8647)
▲ Zumtobel Lighting Inc ..... C 845 691-6262
  Highland (G-6409)

3647 Vehicular Lighting Eqpt

Aerospace Lighting Corporation ..... D 631 563-6400
  Bohemia (G-1008)
▲ Astronics Corporation ..... C 716 805-1599
  East Aurora (G-4366)
B/E Aerospace Inc ..... E 631 563-6400
  Bohemia (G-1022)
Licenders ..... G 212 759-5200
  New York (G-10986)
Luminescent Systems Inc ..... B 716 655-0800
  East Aurora (G-4373)
Mega Vations Inc ..... G 718 934-2192
  Brooklyn (G-2294)
▼ Mobile Fleet Inc ..... G 631 206-2920
  Hauppauge (G-6142)
Power and Cnstr Group Inc ..... E 585 889-6020
  Scottsville (G-15338)
Truck-Lite Co LLC ..... D 716 661-1235
  Falconer (G-4916)
Truck-Lite Co LLC ..... E 716 665-2614
  Falconer (G-4917)
◆ Truck-Lite Co LLC ..... B 716 665-6214
  Falconer (G-4918)
▲ Wolo Mfg Corp ..... G 631 242-0333
  Deer Park (G-4228)

3648 Lighting Eqpt, NEC

Acolyte Industries Inc ..... F 212 629-6830
  New York (G-9019)
Al Energy Solutions Led Llc ..... E 646 380-6670
  New York (G-9068)
▲ Altman Stage Lighting Co Inc ..... C 914 476-7987
  Yonkers (G-17412)
▲ CEIT Corp ..... F 518 825-0649
  Plattsburgh (G-13658)
▲ Coldstream Group Inc ..... F 914 698-5959
  Mamaroneck (G-8029)
Cooper Industries LLC ..... E 315 477-7000
  Syracuse (G-15909)
◆ Creative Stage Lighting Co Inc ..... E 518 251-3302
  North Creek (G-12933)
Edison Power & Light Co Inc ..... F 718 522-0002
  Brooklyn (G-1904)
Eluminocity US Inc ..... G 651 528-1165
  New York (G-10016)
▲ Enchante Lites LLC ..... E 212 602-1818
  New York (G-10030)
▲ Expo Furniture Designs Inc ..... F 516 674-1420
  Glen Cove (G-5615)
▲ Fabbian USA Corp ..... F 973 882-3824
  New York (G-10123)
Goddard Design Co ..... F 718 599-0170
  Brooklyn (G-2034)
Gordon S Anderson Mfg Co ..... G 845 677-3304
  Millbrook (G-8475)
Gti Graphic Technology Inc ..... E 845 562-7066
  Newburgh (G-12760)
▲ HB Architectural Lighting Inc ..... F 347 851-4123
  Bronx (G-1352)
Illumination Technologies Inc ..... F 315 463-4673
  East Syracuse (G-4538)
Island Lite Louvers Inc ..... E 631 608-4250
  Amityville (G-297)
J M Canty Inc ..... F 716 625-4227
  Lockport (G-7593)
◆ Jaquith Industries Inc ..... E 315 478-5700
  Syracuse (G-15966)
Jed Lights Inc ..... G 516 812-5001
  Garden City Park (G-5540)
Jt Roselle Lighting & Sup Inc ..... F 914 666-3700
  Mount Kisco (G-8632)
▲ Julian A McDermott Corporation ..... F 718 456-3606
  Ridgewood (G-14111)
▲ La Mar Lighting Co Inc ..... D 631 777-7700
  Farmingdale (G-5032)

Lamparts Co Inc ..... F 914 723-8986
  Mount Vernon (G-8699)
Lbg Acquisition LLC ..... E 212 226-1276
  New York (G-10939)
Light Blue USA LLC ..... G 718 475-2515
  Brooklyn (G-2221)
Lighting Collaborative Inc ..... E 212 253-7220
  New York (G-10995)
Lighting Sculptures Inc ..... F 631 242-3387
  Deer Park (G-4166)
Lindsey Adelman ..... E 718 623-3013
  Brooklyn (G-2227)
Luminescent Systems Inc ..... B 716 655-0800
  East Aurora (G-4373)
Medtek Lighting Corporation ..... G 518 745-7264
  Glens Falls (G-5689)
Methods Tooling & Mfg Inc ..... G 845 246-7100
  Mount Marion (G-8651)
Mjk Enterprises LLC ..... G 917 653-9042
  Brooklyn (G-2324)
Northern Air Technology Inc ..... G 585 594-5050
  Rochester (G-14544)
Nu-Tech Lighting Corp ..... G 212 541-7397
  New York (G-11469)
▲ Olive Led Lighting Inc ..... G 718 746-0830
  Flushing (G-5276)
Outdoor Lightning Perspectives ..... G 631 266-6200
  Huntington (G-6672)
Power and Cnstr Group Inc ..... E 585 889-6020
  Scottsville (G-15338)
Projector Lamp Services LLC ..... F 631 244-0051
  Bohemia (G-1123)
Psg Innovations Inc ..... F 917 299-8986
  Valley Stream (G-16422)
▲ Ric-Lo Productions Ltd ..... E 845 469-2285
  Chester (G-3613)
Rodac USA Corp ..... E 716 741-3931
  Clarence (G-3672)
▲ Saratoga Lighting Holdings LLC ..... G 212 906-7800
  New York (G-11971)
Secret Celebrity Licensing LLC ..... G 212 812-9277
  New York (G-12012)
Sensio America ..... F 877 501-5337
  Saratoga Springs (G-15173)
Serway Bros Inc ..... E 315 337-0601
  Rome (G-14836)
Siemens Electro Industrial Sa ..... A 212 258-4000
  New York (G-12063)
▲ Sir Industries Inc ..... G 631 234-2444
  Hauppauge (G-6192)
▲ Star Headlight Lantern Co Inc ..... C 585 226-9500
  Avon (G-543)
Strider Global LLC ..... G 212 726-1302
  New York (G-12215)
Tarsier Ltd ..... C 212 401-6181
  New York (G-12280)
▲ Tecnolux Incorporated ..... G 718 369-3900
  Brooklyn (G-2651)
▲ Times Square Stage Ltg Co Inc ..... E 845 947-3034
  Stony Point (G-15778)
Truck-Lite Co LLC ..... D 716 661-1235
  Falconer (G-4916)
Truck-Lite Co LLC ..... E 716 665-2614
  Falconer (G-4917)
Unibrands Corporation ..... F 212 897-2278
  New York (G-12451)
▲ USA Illumination Inc ..... E 845 565-8500
  New Windsor (G-8956)
Vertex Innovative Solutions In ..... E 315 437-6711
  Syracuse (G-16067)
Vincent Conigliaro ..... F 845 340-0489
  Kingston (G-7224)
▲ Visual Effects Inc ..... F 718 324-0011
  Jamaica (G-6962)
Vivid Rgb Lighting LLC ..... G 718 635-0817
  Peekskill (G-13483)
William J Blume Worldwide Svcs ..... G 914 723-6185
  Saratoga Springs (G-15177)

3651 Household Audio & Video Eqpt

A and K Global Inc ..... D 718 412-1876
  Bayside (G-763)
▲ Accent Speaker Technology Ltd ..... G 631 738-2540
  Holbrook (G-6429)
▲ Aguilar Amplification LLC ..... F 212 431-9109
  New York (G-9060)
All In Audio Inc ..... F 718 506-0948
  Brooklyn (G-1586)
Amplitech Group Inc ..... G 631 521-7831
  Bohemia (G-1015)

▲ Andrea Electronics Corporation ..... F 631 719-1800
  Bohemia (G-1016)
▲ Ashly Audio Inc ..... E 585 872-0010
  Webster (G-16713)
▲ Audio Technology New York Inc ..... F 718 369-7528
  Brooklyn (G-1653)
Audio Video Invasion Inc ..... F 516 345-2636
  Plainview (G-13583)
▼ Audiosavings Inc ..... F 888 445-1555
  Inwood (G-6752)
Avcom of Virginia Inc ..... D 585 924-4560
  Victor (G-16461)
AVI-Spl Employee ..... B 212 840-4801
  New York (G-9277)
B & H Electronics Corp ..... E 845 782-5000
  Monroe (G-8549)
▲ B & K Components Ltd ..... E 323 776-4277
  Buffalo (G-2829)
Broadcast Manager Inc ..... G 212 509-1200
  New York (G-9465)
Citation Manufacturing Co Inc ..... G 845 425-6868
  Spring Valley (G-15579)
▲ Communication Power Corp ..... E 631 434-7306
  Hauppauge (G-6051)
Convergent Audio Tech Inc ..... G 585 359-2700
  Rush (G-15046)
Covington Sound ..... G 646 256-7486
  Bronx (G-1305)
Data Interchange Systems Inc ..... G 914 277-7775
  Purdys (G-13972)
Digital Home Creations Inc ..... G 585 576-7070
  Webster (G-16720)
G E Inspection Technologies LP ..... C 315 554-2000
  Skaneateles (G-15460)
General Elc Capitl Svcs Inc ..... G 315 554-2000
  Skaneateles (G-15461)
Gilmores Sound Advice Inc ..... F 212 265-4445
  New York (G-10297)
◆ Globa Phoni Compu Techn Solut ..... E 607 257-7279
  Ithaca (G-6843)
▲ Global Market Development Inc ..... E 631 667-1002
  Edgewood (G-4599)
Granada Electronics Inc ..... G 718 387-1157
  Brooklyn (G-2047)
Harman International Inds Inc ..... C 516 496-3400
  Woodbury (G-17289)
Henley Brands LLC ..... F 516 883-8220
  Port Washington (G-13820)
Hope International Productions ..... F 212 247-3188
  New York (G-10504)
Ilab America Inc ..... G 631 615-5053
  Selden (G-15352)
Interaction Insight Corp ..... G 800 285-2950
  New York (G-10622)
◆ Jwin Electronics Corp ..... D 516 626-7188
  Port Washington (G-13831)
▲ Key Digital Systems Inc ..... E 914 667-9700
  Mount Vernon (G-8697)
L A R Electronics Corp ..... E 716 285-0555
  Niagara Falls (G-12840)
L-3 Communications Corporation ..... A 631 436-7400
  Hauppauge (G-6108)
Laird Telemedia ..... C 845 339-9555
  Mount Marion (G-8650)
Lamm Industries Inc ..... G 718 368-0181
  Brooklyn (G-2193)
Masterdisk Corporation ..... F 212 541-5022
  Elmsford (G-4764)
Navitar Inc ..... D 585 359-4000
  Rochester (G-14530)
▲ NEa Manufacturing Corp ..... E 516 371-4200
  Inwood (G-6763)
New Audio LLC ..... E 212 213-6060
  New York (G-11379)
New Wop Records ..... G 631 617-9732
  Deer Park (G-4179)
Nykon Inc ..... G 315 483-0504
  Sodus (G-15504)
Professional Technology Inc ..... G 315 337-4156
  Rome (G-14830)
Pure Acoustics Inc ..... G 718 788-4411
  Brooklyn (G-2457)
Request Inc ..... E 518 899-1254
  Halfmoon (G-5914)
Request Serious Play LLC ..... E 518 899-1254
  Halfmoon (G-5915)
◆ Samson Technologies Corp ..... D 631 784-2200
  Hauppauge (G-6182)
Shyk International Corp ..... G 212 663-3302
  New York (G-12058)

SIC SECTION 36 ELECTRONIC AND OTHER ELECTRICAL EQUIPMENT AND COMPONENTS, EXCEPT COMPUTER

▲ **Sima Technologies LLC**....................G....... 412 828-9130
Hauppauge *(G-6191)*
Sing Trix....................F....... 212 352-1500
New York *(G-12085)*
◆ **Sony Corporation of America**....................C....... 212 833-8000
New York *(G-12132)*
▲ **Sound Video Systems Wny LLC**......F....... 716 684-8200
Buffalo *(G-3194)*
Speaqua Corp....................E....... 516 380-5008
Deer Park *(G-4213)*
Sunshine Distribution Corp....................G....... 888 506-7051
New York *(G-12238)*
Theodore A Rapp Associates....................G....... 845 469-2100
Chester *(G-3620)*
Tkm Technologies Inc....................G....... 631 474-4700
Port Jeff STA *(G-13773)*
◆ **Toshiba America Inc**....................E....... 212 596-0600
New York *(G-12377)*
Touchtunes Music Corporation....................G....... 847 419-3300
New York *(G-12382)*
Tunecore Inc....................E....... 646 651-1060
Brooklyn *(G-2687)*
Video Technology Services Inc....................F....... 516 937-9700
Syosset *(G-15841)*
Vincent Conigliaro....................F....... 845 340-0489
Kingston *(G-7224)*
Vtb Holdings Inc....................G....... 914 345-2255
Valhalla *(G-16373)*
▲ **Whirlwind Music Distrs Inc**....................D....... 585 663-8820
Rochester *(G-14762)*
▲ **Wyrestorm Technologies LLC**....................F....... 518 289-1293
Round Lake *(G-15039)*
▲ **Yorkville Sound Inc**....................G....... 716 297-2920
Niagara Falls *(G-12891)*

3652 Phonograph Records & Magnetic Tape

▲ **A To Z Media Inc**....................F....... 212 260-0237
New York *(G-8994)*
Abkco Music & Records Inc....................E....... 212 399-0300
New York *(G-9004)*
Atlantic Recording Corp....................B....... 212 707-2000
New York *(G-9252)*
▲ **Bertelsmann Inc**....................E....... 212 782-1000
New York *(G-9370)*
Bridge Records Inc....................G....... 914 654-9270
New Rochelle *(G-8890)*
C & C Duplicators Inc....................E....... 631 244-0800
Bohemia *(G-1029)*
Chesky Records Inc....................F....... 212 586-7799
New York *(G-9592)*
Columbia Records Inc....................F....... 212 833-8000
New York *(G-9677)*
Cult Records LLC....................G....... 718 395-2077
New York *(G-9765)*
▲ **Dorling Kindersley Publishing**..........D....... 212 213-4800
New York *(G-9910)*
Eks Manufacturing Inc....................F....... 917 217-0784
Brooklyn *(G-1907)*
Emusiccom Inc....................D....... 212 201-9240
New York *(G-10028)*
Europadisk LLC....................E....... 718 407-7300
Long Island City *(G-7733)*
▲ **Extreme Group Holdings LLC**..........F....... 212 833-8000
New York *(G-10111)*
High Quality Video Inc....................F....... 212 686-9534
New York *(G-10473)*
His Productions USA Inc....................G....... 212 594-3737
New York *(G-10483)*
▲ **Historic TW Inc**....................D....... 212 484-8000
New York *(G-10484)*
Hope International Productions..........F....... 212 247-3188
New York *(G-10504)*
Imago Recording Company....................G....... 212 751-3033
New York *(G-10569)*
John Marshall Sound Inc....................G....... 212 265-6066
New York *(G-10751)*
Lefrak Entertainment Co Ltd....................G....... 212 586-3600
New York *(G-10960)*
Masterdisk Corporation....................F....... 212 541-5022
Elmsford *(G-4764)*
Media Technologies Ltd....................F....... 631 467-7900
Eastport *(G-4584)*
Mmo Music Group Inc....................G....... 914 592-1188
Elmsford *(G-4766)*
Optic Solution LLC....................F....... 518 293-4321
Saranac *(G-15133)*
Peer-Southern Productions Inc..........E....... 212 265-3910
New York *(G-11597)*
Pete Levin Music Inc....................G....... 845 247-9211
Saugerties *(G-15192)*
Pivot Records LLC....................F....... 718 417-1213
Brooklyn *(G-2424)*
▲ **Recorded Anthlogy of Amrcn Mus**...F....... 212 290-1695
Brooklyn *(G-2484)*
Roadrunner Records Inc....................E....... 212 274-7500
New York *(G-11887)*
Side Hustle Music Group LLC....................F....... 800 219-4003
New York *(G-12060)*
▲ **Sony Broadband Entertainment**.......F....... 212 833-6800
New York *(G-12131)*
◆ **Sony Corporation of America**..........C....... 212 833-8000
New York *(G-12132)*
Sony Music Entertainment Inc..........A....... 212 833-8000
New York *(G-12134)*
▲ **Sony Music Entertainment Inc**.........A....... 212 833-8500
New York *(G-12135)*
Sony Music Entertainment Inc..........E....... 212 833-5057
New York *(G-12136)*
◆ **Sony Music Holdings Inc**....................A....... 212 833-8000
New York *(G-12137)*
Sterling Sound Inc....................E....... 212 604-9433
New York *(G-12198)*
Taste and See Entrmt Inc....................G....... 516 285-3010
Valley Stream *(G-16429)*
Time Warner Companies Inc....................D....... 212 484-8000
New York *(G-12350)*
Ulster-Greene County A R C....................G....... 845 331-8451
Kingston *(G-7220)*
Vaire LLC....................G....... 631 271-4933
Huntington Station *(G-6727)*
Warner Music Group Corp....................B....... 212 275-2000
New York *(G-12588)*
▼ **Warner Music Inc**....................D....... 212 275-2000
New York *(G-12589)*
Wea International Inc....................D....... 212 275-1300
New York *(G-12601)*

3661 Telephone & Telegraph Apparatus

ABS Talkx Inc....................G....... 631 254-9100
Bay Shore *(G-664)*
Access 24....................G....... 845 358-5397
Valley Cottage *(G-16374)*
▼ **Aines Manufacturing Corp**....................E....... 631 471-3900
Islip *(G-6806)*
Alcatel-Lucent USA Inc....................D....... 516 349-4900
Plainview *(G-13580)*
Alternative Technology Corp....................G....... 914 478-5900
Hastings On Hudson *(G-6002)*
▲ **Astrocom Electronics Inc**....................D....... 607 432-1930
Oneonta *(G-13172)*
▲ **Audio-Sears Corp**....................D....... 607 652-7305
Stamford *(G-15623)*
▲ **Brook Telephone Mfg & Sup Co**.......F....... 718 449-4222
Brooklyn *(G-1719)*
Call Forwarding Technologies....................G....... 516 621-3600
Greenvale *(G-5879)*
▲ **Clayton Dubilier & Rice Fun**....................E....... 212 407-5200
New York *(G-9640)*
Corning Incorporated....................E....... 607 248-1200
Corning *(G-3965)*
Corning Incorporated....................G....... 607 974-6729
Painted Post *(G-13391)*
◆ **Corning Incorporated**....................A....... 607 974-9000
Corning *(G-3962)*
Data Transmission Essentials....................F....... 516 378-8820
Harrison *(G-5983)*
Eagle Telephonics Inc....................F....... 631 471-3600
Bohemia *(G-1059)*
▲ **ESi Cases & Accessories Inc**..........E....... 212 883-8838
New York *(G-10061)*
◆ **Fiber Instrument Sales Inc**....................C....... 315 736-2206
Oriskany *(G-13309)*
▲ **Fiberall Corp**....................E....... 516 371-5200
Inwood *(G-6757)*
▲ **Fiberwave Corporation**....................C....... 718 802-9011
Brooklyn *(G-1968)*
▲ **Forerunner Technologies Inc**..........E....... 631 337-2100
Bohemia *(G-1067)*
Fujitsu Ntwrk Cmmnications Inc..........F....... 845 731-2000
Pearl River *(G-13457)*
Harris Corporation....................E....... 585 244-5830
Rochester *(G-14427)*
▲ **I D Tel Corp**....................F....... 718 876-6000
Staten Island *(G-15685)*
Interdgital Communications LLC..........C....... 631 622-4000
Melville *(G-8331)*
▲ **Kelta Inc**....................E....... 631 789-5000
Edgewood *(G-4602)*
Kent Optronics Inc....................F....... 845 897-0138
Hopewell Junction *(G-6555)*
L-3 Communications Corporation..........A....... 631 436-7400
Hauppauge *(G-6108)*
Maia Systems LLC....................G....... 718 206-0100
Jamaica *(G-6927)*
▲ **Parabit Systems Inc**....................E....... 516 378-4800
Roosevelt *(G-15008)*
Performance Technologies Inc....................D....... 585 256-0200
Rochester *(G-14576)*
▲ **Powermate Cellular**....................G....... 718 833-9400
Brooklyn *(G-2431)*
Prager Metis Cpas LLC....................F....... 212 972-7555
New York *(G-11693)*
Quality One Wireless LLC....................C....... 631 233-3337
Ronkonkoma *(G-14974)*
R I R Communications Systems..........G....... 718 706-9957
Mount Vernon *(G-8722)*
R I R Communications Systems..........E....... 718 706-9957
Mount Vernon *(G-8723)*
▲ **Redcom Laboratories Inc**....................C....... 585 924-6567
Victor *(G-16500)*
▲ **Rus Industries Inc**....................E....... 716 284-7828
Niagara Falls *(G-12869)*
◆ **Sandstone Technologies Corp**..........G....... 585 785-5537
Rochester *(G-14667)*
Sandstone Technologies Corp....................G....... 585 785-5537
Rochester *(G-14668)*
Shoretel Inc....................G....... 877 654-3573
Rochester *(G-14684)*
Siemens Corporation....................E....... 905 528-8811
Buffalo *(G-3186)*
Siemens Corporation....................F....... 202 434-7800
New York *(G-12062)*
Siemens Industries Inc....................G....... 607 936-9512
Corning *(G-3981)*
Siemens USA Holdings Inc....................B....... 212 258-4000
New York *(G-12064)*
▼ **Splice Technologies Inc**....................G....... 631 924-8108
Manorville *(G-8081)*
Telecommunication Concepts....................G....... 315 736-8523
Whitesboro *(G-17196)*
Telephonics Corporation....................D....... 631 755-7659
Farmingdale *(G-5126)*
▲ **Telephonics Corporation**....................A....... 631 755-7000
Farmingdale *(G-5127)*
Terahertz Technologies Inc....................G....... 315 736-3642
Oriskany *(G-13316)*
▲ **Tii Technologies Inc**....................E....... 516 364-9300
Edgewood *(G-4616)*
▲ **Toshiba Amer Info Systems Inc**........B....... 949 583-3000
New York *(G-12376)*
◆ **Toshiba America Inc**....................E....... 212 596-0600
New York *(G-12377)*

3663 Radio & T V Communications, Systs & Eqpt, Broadcast/Studio

2p Agency Usa Inc....................G....... 212 203-5586
Brooklyn *(G-1513)*
Actv Inc (del Corp)....................D....... 212 995-9500
New York *(G-9022)*
Advanced Comm Solutions....................G....... 914 693-5076
Ardsley *(G-404)*
AG Adriano Goldschmied Inc....................G....... 845 928-8616
Central Valley *(G-3520)*
Airnet Communications Corp....................F....... 516 338-0008
Westbury *(G-16963)*
Amplitech Inc....................G....... 631 521-7738
Bohemia *(G-1014)*
Amplitech Group Inc....................G....... 631 521-7831
Bohemia *(G-1015)*
Anaren Holding Corp....................G....... 212 415-6700
New York *(G-9148)*
▲ **Andrea Electronics Corporation**.......F....... 631 719-1800
Bohemia *(G-1016)*
▲ **Apex Airtronics Inc**....................E....... 718 485-8560
Brooklyn *(G-1616)*
Appairent Technologies Inc....................G....... 585 214-2460
West Henrietta *(G-16869)*
Arcom Automatics LLC....................G....... 315 422-1230
Syracuse *(G-15856)*
Armstrong Transmitter Corp....................F....... 315 673-1269
Marcellus *(G-8086)*
▲ **Arrow-Communication Labs Inc**......B....... 315 422-1230
Syracuse *(G-15859)*
▲ **Ashly Audio Inc**....................E....... 585 872-0010
Webster *(G-16713)*
AT&T Corp....................G....... 716 639-0673
Williamsville *(G-17234)*
AVI-Spl Employee....................B....... 212 840-4801
New York *(G-9277)*

S
I
C

Employee Codes: A=Over 500 employees, B=251-500
C=101-250, D=51-100, E=20-50, F=10-19, G=5-9
2017 Harris
New York Manufacturers Directory
845

36 ELECTRONIC AND OTHER ELECTRICAL EQUIPMENT AND COMPONENTS, EXCEPT COMPUTER

B & H Electronics Corp .... E 845 782-5000
  Monroe (G-8549)
Basil S Kadhim .... G 888 520-5192
  New York (G-9330)
Bayside Beepers & Cellular .... G 718 343-3888
  Glen Oaks (G-5640)
Belden Inc .... B 607 796-5600
  Horseheads (G-6569)
Benchmark Media Systems Inc .... F 315 437-6300
  Syracuse (G-15868)
Bet Networks Incorporated 212 846-8111
  New York (G-9375)
Bullitt Mobile LLC .... D 631 424-1749
  Bohemia (G-1028)
Century Metal Parts Corp .... G 631 667-0800
  Bay Shore (G-682)
Chyronhego Corporation .... D 631 845-2000
  Melville (G-8303)
▼ CJ Component Products LLC ...... G 631 567-3733
  Oakdale (G-13057)
Clever Devices Ltd .... E 516 433-6100
  Woodbury (G-17283)
Click It Inc .... D 631 686-2900
  Hauppauge (G-6047)
▲ Cmb Wireless Group LLC .... C 631 750-4700
  Bohemia (G-1036)
Cntry Cross Communications LLC ... F 386 758-9696
  Jamestown (G-6982)
Commscope Technologies LLC .... F 315 768-3573
  Marcy (G-8090)
▲ Communication Power Corp .... E 631 434-7306
  Hauppauge (G-6051)
▲ Comtech PST Corp .... C 631 777-8900
  Melville (G-8306)
◆ Comtech Telecom Corp .... C 631 962-7000
  Melville (G-8307)
▲ Eagle Comtronics Inc .... C 315 451-3313
  Liverpool (G-7518)
◆ Edo LLC .... E 631 630-4000
  Amityville (G-285)
Edo LLC .... A 631 630-4200
  Amityville (G-286)
Eeg Enterprises Inc .... F 516 293-7472
  Farmingdale (G-4986)
▼ Electro-Metrics Corporation .... E 518 762-2600
  Johnstown (G-7109)
Elite Cellular Accessories Inc .... E 877 390-2502
  Deer Park (G-4136)
▲ Eni Mks Products Group .... F 585 427-8300
  Rochester (G-14352)
▲ Eni Technology Inc .... B 585 427-8300
  Rochester (G-14353)
Evado Filip 917 774-8666
  New York (G-10087)
Fei-Zyfer Inc .... G 714 933-4045
  Uniondale (G-16294)
Fleetcom Inc .... F 914 776-5582
  Yonkers (G-17445)
Flycell Inc .... E 212 400-1212
  New York (G-10181)
Fujitsu Ntwrk Cmmnications Inc ...... F 845 731-2000
  Pearl River (G-13457)
▲ GE Mds LLC .... C 585 242-9600
  Rochester (G-14389)
Geosync Microwave Inc .... G 631 760-5567
  Hauppauge (G-6084)
Global Tower LLC .... G 561 995-0320
  La Fargeville (G-7235)
◆ Globecomm Systems Inc .... C 631 231-9800
  Hauppauge (G-6086)
◆ Griffon Corporation .... F 212 957-5000
  New York (G-10363)
Gurley Precision Instrs Inc .... F 518 272-6300
  Troy (G-16237)
Hamtronics Inc .... G 585 392-9430
  Rochester (G-14419)
▲ Hand Held Products Inc .... B 315 554-6000
  Skaneateles Falls (G-15468)
Harris Corporation .... A 585 244-5830
  Rochester (G-14422)
Harris Corporation .... B 585 244-5830
  Rochester (G-14428)
Harris Corporation .... F 718 767-1100
  Whitestone (G-17208)
Harris Corporation .... B 585 244-5830
  Rochester (G-14429)
Hopewell Precision Inc .... E 845 221-2737
  Hopewell Junction (G-6552)
Icell Inc .... C 516 590-0007
  Hempstead (G-6274)

▲ Icon Enterprises Intl Inc .... E 718 752-9764
  Long Island City (G-7763)
Iheartcommunications Inc .... C 585 454-4884
  Rochester (G-14445)
Iheartcommunications Inc .... E 212 603-4660
  New York (G-10564)
Imagine Communications Corp .... F 212 303-4200
  New York (G-10568)
Instruments For Industry Inc .... E 631 467-8400
  Ronkonkoma (G-14913)
It Commodity Sourcing Inc .... G 718 677-1577
  Brooklyn (G-2118)
▲ John Mezzalingua Assoc LLC ...... C 315 431-7100
  Liverpool (G-7528)
▲ L-3 Cmmnctons Fgn Holdings Inc ... E 212 697-1111
  New York (G-10903)
◆ L-3 Cmmunications Holdings Inc ... D 212 697-1111
  New York (G-10905)
L-3 Communications Corporation ... B 631 231-1700
  Hauppauge (G-6107)
L-3 Communications Corporation ... A 631 436-7400
  Hauppauge (G-6108)
L-3 Communications Corporation ... D 607 721-5465
  Kirkwood (G-7234)
L-3 Communications Corporation ... D 631 231-1700
  Hauppauge (G-6109)
L-3 Communications Corporation ... D 631 436-7400
  Hauppauge (G-6110)
L-3 Communications Corporation ... E 585 742-9100
  Victor (G-16487)
L-3 Communications Corporation ... B 212 697-1111
  New York (G-10906)
Linen Micarta LLC .... F 212 203-5145
  New York (G-11001)
Loral Space & Cmmnctns Holdng .... E 212 697-1105
  New York (G-11032)
Loral Space Communications Inc ... E 212 697-1105
  New York (G-11033)
Loral Spacecom Corporation .... E 212 697-1105
  New York (G-11034)
▲ M&S Accessory Network Corp ..... F 347 492-7790
  New York (G-11078)
▲ Magnet-Ndctive Systems Ltd USA ... E 585 924-4000
  Victor (G-16490)
Maritime Broadband Inc .... E 347 404-6041
  Long Island City (G-7803)
Mark Peri International .... F 516 208-6824
  Oceanside (G-13087)
Millennium Antenna Corp .... F 315 798-9374
  Utica (G-16348)
Mini-Circuits Fort Wayne LLC .... B 718 934-4500
  Brooklyn (G-2318)
Mirion Tech Imaging LLC .... E 607 562-4300
  Horseheads (G-6583)
Mks Medical Electronics .... C 585 292-7400
  Rochester (G-14518)
Motorola Solutions Inc .... E 518 348-0833
  Halfmoon (G-5912)
Motorola Solutions Inc .... C 718 330-2163
  Brooklyn (G-2336)
Motorola Solutions Inc .... E 518 869-9517
  Albany (G-103)
Movin On Sounds and SEC Inc ...... E 516 489-2350
  Franklin Square (G-5365)
Navitar Inc .... D 585 359-4000
  Rochester (G-14530)
NBC Universal LLC .... E 718 482-8310
  Long Island City (G-7822)
North American MBL Systems Inc ... E 718 898-8700
  Woodside (G-17341)
Nycom Business Solutions Inc .... G 516 345-6000
  Franklin Square (G-5366)
Orbcomm Inc .... G 703 433-6396
  Utica (G-16355)
Panvidea Inc .... F 212 967-9613
  New York (G-11561)
Parrys .... F 315 824-0002
  Hamilton (G-5949)
Persistent Systems LLC .... E 212 561-5895
  New York (G-11626)
Quanta Electronics Inc .... F 631 961-9953
  Centereach (G-3472)
▲ Quintel Usa Inc .... E 585 420-8364
  Rochester (G-14617)
Rehabilitation International .... G 212 420-1500
  Jamaica (G-6946)
Rodale Wireless Inc .... E 631 231-0044
  Hauppauge (G-6179)
Ruhle Companies Inc .... E 914 287-4000
  Valhalla (G-16372)

Sartek Industries Inc .... G 631 473-3555
  Port Jefferson (G-13779)
Sdr Technology Inc .... G 716 583-1249
  Alden (G-183)
▲ Sentry Technology Corporation ... F 800 645-4224
  Ronkonkoma (G-14983)
Sequential Electronics Systems ...... E 914 592-1345
  Elmsford (G-4783)
Shoretel Inc .... G 877 654-3573
  Rochester (G-14684)
Silicon Imaging Inc .... C 518 374-3367
  Niskayuna (G-12896)
Sinclair Technologies Inc .... G 716 874-3682
  Hamburg (G-5942)
Specialty Microwave Corp .... F 631 737-2175
  Ronkonkoma (G-14987)
Spectralink Corporation .... D 212 372-6997
  New York (G-12156)
Srtech Industry Corp .... E 718 496-7001
  Oakland Gardens (G-13068)
STI-Co Industries Inc .... E 716 662-2680
  Orchard Park (G-13297)
▲ Telephonics Corporation .... A 631 755-7000
  Farmingdale (G-5127)
▲ Telxon Corporation .... E 631 738-2400
  Holtsville (G-6512)
Times Square Studios Ltd .... C 212 930-7720
  New York (G-12352)
Toura LLC .... F 646 652-8668
  Brooklyn (G-2670)
United Satcom Inc .... G 718 359-4100
  Flushing (G-5306)
◆ Vicon Industries Inc .... C 716 952-2288
  Hauppauge (G-6225)
Village Video Productions Inc .... G 631 752-9311
  West Babylon (G-16839)
▲ W & W Manufacturing Co .... F 516 942-0011
  Deer Park (G-4225)
▲ Whirlwind Music Distrs Inc .... D 585 663-8820
  Rochester (G-14762)
Wireless Communications Inc .... G 845 353-5921
  Nyack (G-13056)
Zetek Corporation .... F 212 668-1485
  New York (G-12710)

3669 Communications Eqpt, NEC

▲ Alarm Controls Corporation .... E 631 586-4220
  Deer Park (G-4090)
All Metro Emrgncy Response Sys ... G 516 750-9100
  Lynbrook (G-7945)
All Products Designs .... G 631 748-6901
  Smithtown (G-15482)
▲ Alstom Signaling Inc .... B 585 783-2000
  Schenectady (G-15228)
Alstom Signaling Inc .... E 585 274-8700
  Schenectady (G-15229)
Alstom Transportation Inc .... G 800 717-4477
  West Henrietta (G-16866)
Andrea Systems LLC .... E 631 390-3140
  Farmingdale (G-4942)
Apex Signal Corporation .... D 631 567-1100
  Bohemia (G-1017)
Apple Core Electronics Inc .... F 718 628-4068
  Brooklyn (G-1618)
AVI-Spl Employee .... B 212 840-4801
  New York (G-9277)
BNo Intl Trdg Co Inc .... G 716 487-1900
  Jamestown (G-6977)
Capstream Technologies LLC .... G 716 945-7100
  Salamanca (G-15100)
Comet Flasher Inc .... G 716 821-9595
  Buffalo (G-2881)
Cq Traffic Control Devices LLC ...... G 518 767-0057
  Selkirk (G-15354)
Curbell Medical Products Inc .... F 716 667-2520
  Orchard Park (G-13266)
▲ Curbell Medical Products Inc .... C 716 667-2520
  Orchard Park (G-13267)
Datasonic Inc .... G 516 248-7330
  East Meadow (G-4421)
Detector Pro .... G 845 635-3488
  Pleasant Valley (G-13711)
Fire Apparatus Service Tech .... G 716 753-3538
  Sherman (G-15402)
Firecom Inc .... C 718 899-6100
  Woodside (G-17328)
Firetronics Inc .... G 516 997-5151
  Jericho (G-7069)
Frequency Electronics Inc .... B 516 794-4500
  Uniondale (G-16295)

Fuel Watchman Sales & Service............F 718 665-6100
Bronx *(G-1338)*
▲ General Traffic Equipment Corp.......F 845 569-9000
Newburgh *(G-12758)*
Goddard Design Co ....G....... 718 599-0170
Brooklyn *(G-2034)*
Harris Corporation ....A 413 263-6200
Rochester *(G-14425)*
Intelligent Traffic Systems ....G....... 631 567-5994
Bohemia *(G-1078)*
▲ Intercall Systems Inc ....E 516 294-4524
Mineola *(G-8516)*
Kentronics Inc..G....... 631 567-5994
Bohemia *(G-1087)*
L & M Welding LLC ....G....... 516 220-1722
Freeport *(G-5407)*
▲ L-3 Cmmnctons Fgn Holdings Inc....E 212 697-1111
New York *(G-10903)*
◆ L-3 Cmmunications Holdings Inc......D........ 212 697-1111
New York *(G-10905)*
L-3 Communications Corporation.........B........ 212 697-1111
New York *(G-10906)*
Lifewatch Inc ....F 800 716-1433
Hewlett *(G-6310)*
Lik LLC...F 516 848-5135
Northport *(G-13015)*
▲ McDowell Research Co Inc ....D....... 315 332-7100
Newark *(G-12736)*
◆ Napco Security Tech Inc ....B 631 842-9400
Amityville *(G-314)*
North Hills Signal Proc Corp..................F 516 682-7740
Syosset *(G-15834)*
▲ Nrd LLC...E 716 773-7634
Grand Island *(G-5764)*
Octopus Advanced Systems Inc ....G....... 914 771-6110
Yonkers *(G-17469)*
Personal Alarm SEC Systems ....F 212 448-1944
New York *(G-11627)*
Power Line Constructors Inc ....E 315 853-6183
Clinton *(G-3721)*
Response Care Inc..................................G....... 585 671-4144
Rochester *(G-14623)*
▼ Roanwell Corporation.........................E 718 401-0288
Bronx *(G-1441)*
Sentry Devices Corp...............................G....... 631 491-3191
Dix Hills *(G-4298)*
Simplexgrinnell LP..................................D....... 585 288-6200
Rochester *(G-14688)*
Simplexgrinnell LP..................................E 518 952-6040
Clifton Park *(G-3708)*
Simplexgrinnell LP..................................G....... 845 774-4120
Harriman *(G-5974)*
Simplexgrinnell LP..................................E 315 437-4660
East Syracuse *(G-4564)*
Simplexgrinnell LP..................................F 607 338-5100
East Syracuse *(G-4565)*
▲ Star Headlight Lantern Co Inc ....C....... 585 226-9500
Avon *(G-543)*
Synergx Systems Inc..............................D....... 516 433-4700
Woodside *(G-17358)*
Telebyte Inc ....E 631 423-3232
Hauppauge *(G-6212)*
▲ Telemergency Ltd ....G....... 914 629-4222
White Plains *(G-17176)*
▲ Telephonics Corporation....................A 631 755-7000
Farmingdale *(G-5127)*
Telephonics Corporation.........................F 631 755-7000
Huntington *(G-6685)*
Telesite USA Inc ....F 631 952-2288
Hauppauge *(G-6213)*
Traffic Lane Closures LLC ....G....... 845 228-6100
Brewster *(G-1228)*
▲ Twinco Mfg Co Inc ....E 631 231-0022
Hauppauge *(G-6219)*
▲ TX Rx Systems Inc..............................C....... 716 549-4700
Angola *(G-382)*
Unibrands Corporation...........................F 212 897-2278
New York *(G-12451)*
Unitone Communication Systems.........G....... 212 777-9090
New York *(G-12468)*
◆ Vicon Industries Inc ....C....... 631 952-2288
Hauppauge *(G-6225)*
▼ Visiontron Corp....................................E 631 582-8600
Hauppauge *(G-6227)*
▲ Werma (usa) Inc ....G....... 315 414-0200
East Syracuse *(G-4580)*
Zetek Corporation...................................F 212 668-1485
New York *(G-12710)*

3671 Radio & T V Receiving Electron Tubes

▲ E-Beam Services Inc..........................G....... 516 622-1422
Hicksville *(G-6341)*
Harris Corporation ....E 585 244-5830
Rochester *(G-14427)*
▲ New Sensor Corporation ....D....... 718 937-8300
Long Island City *(G-7824)*
Passur Aerospace Inc ....G....... 631 589-6800
Bohemia *(G-1115)*
▲ Thomas Electronics Inc......................C....... 315 923-2051
Clyde *(G-3732)*
Y & Z Precision Inc ....F 516 349-8243
Plainview *(G-13648)*

3672 Printed Circuit Boards

◆ A A Technology Inc.............................E 631 913-0400
Ronkonkoma *(G-14845)*
Ace Electronics Inc..................................F 914 773-2000
Hawthorne *(G-6242)*
▲ Advance Circuit Technology Inc.......E 585 328-2000
Rochester *(G-14175)*
▲ Advance Micro Power Corp ....F 631 471-6157
Ronkonkoma *(G-14852)*
Advanced Digital Info Corp.....................E 607 266-4000
Ithaca *(G-6816)*
Advanced Manufacturing Svc Inc ....E 631 676-5210
Ronkonkoma *(G-14854)*
American Quality Technology ....F 607 777-9488
Binghamton *(G-887)*
◆ American Technical Ceramics...........B 631 622-4700
Huntington Station *(G-6695)*
▲ Ansen Corporation..............................G....... 315 393-3573
Ogdensburg *(G-13111)*
Ansen Corporation ....C....... 315 393-3573
Ogdensburg *(G-13112)*
Bryit Group LLC.......................................F 631 563-6603
Holbrook *(G-6433)*
Bsu Inc..E 607 272-8100
Ithaca *(G-6829)*
Buffalo Circuits Inc..................................G....... 716 662-2113
Orchard Park *(G-13256)*
▲ C & D Assembly Inc ....E 607 898-4275
Groton *(G-5897)*
C A M Graphics Co Inc ....E 631 842-3400
Farmingdale *(G-4955)*
Chautauqua Circuits Inc.........................G....... 716 366-5771
Dunkirk *(G-4335)*
Coast To Coast Circuits Inc ....E 585 254-2980
Rochester *(G-14281)*
Cygnus Automation Inc...........................E 631 981-0909
Bohemia *(G-1047)*
Della Systems Inc ....F 631 580-0010
Ronkonkoma *(G-14893)*
Falconer Electronics Inc ....D....... 716 665-4176
Falconer *(G-4898)*
Geometric Circuits Inc.............................D....... 631 249-0230
Holbrook *(G-6448)*
Hazlow Electronics Inc ....E 585 325-5323
Rochester *(G-14431)*
I3 Assemblies Inc ....G....... 607 238-7077
Binghamton *(G-923)*
I3 Electronics Inc ....C....... 866 820-4820
Endicott *(G-4811)*
IEC Electronics Corp ....B 315 331-7742
Newark *(G-12732)*
IEC Electronics Wire Cable Inc.............D....... 585 924-9010
Newark *(G-12733)*
Irtronics Instruments Inc.........................F 914 693-6291
Ardsley *(G-405)*
▲ Isine Inc..G....... 631 913-4400
Ronkonkoma *(G-14914)*
Jabil Circuit Inc ....B 845 471-9237
Poughkeepsie *(G-13908)*
Kendall Circuits Inc ....E 631 473-3636
Mount Sinai *(G-8655)*
Mpl Inc..E 607 266-0480
Ithaca *(G-6864)*
Nationwide Circuits Inc ....E 585 328-0791
Rochester *(G-14528)*
▲ NEa Manufacturing Corp....................E 516 371-4200
Inwood *(G-6763)*
▼ Oakdale Industrial Elec Corp ....F 631 737-4090
Ronkonkoma *(G-14957)*
Ormec Systems Corp ....E 585 385-3520
Rochester *(G-14552)*
▲ Park Electrochemical Corp ....C....... 631 465-3600
Melville *(G-8347)*
Performance Technologies Inc..............D....... 585 256-0200
Rochester *(G-14576)*
Procomponents Inc ....E 516 683-0909
Westbury *(G-17023)*
Rce Manufacturing LLC..........................G....... 631 856-9005
Commack *(G-3839)*
▲ Rochester Industrial Ctrl Inc.............D....... 315 524-4555
Ontario *(G-13212)*
Rumsey Corp...G....... 914 751-3640
Yonkers *(G-17482)*
S K Circuits Inc ....F 703 376-8718
Oneida *(G-13166)*
Sag Harbor Industries Inc ....E 631 725-0440
Sag Harbor *(G-15080)*
Sanmina Corporation ....B 607 689-5000
Owego *(G-13359)*
Sheltred Wkshp For Dsabled Inc...........C....... 607 722-2364
Binghamton *(G-951)*
Sopark Corp ....C....... 716 822-0434
Buffalo *(G-3191)*
▲ Stetron International Inc....................F 716 854-3443
Buffalo *(G-3197)*
▲ Stever-Locke Industries Inc ....G....... 585 624-3450
Honeoye Falls *(G-6538)*
Surf-Tech Manufacturing Corp ....F 631 589-1194
Bohemia *(G-1138)*
TCS Electronics Inc ....E 585 337-4301
Farmington *(G-5156)*
Transistor Devices Inc ....E 631 471-7492
Ronkonkoma *(G-14992)*
Windsor Technology LLC.......................F 585 461-2500
Rochester *(G-14764)*

3674 Semiconductors

Able Electronics Inc................................F 631 924-5386
Bellport *(G-825)*
Accumetrics Inc ....F 716 684-0002
Latham *(G-7352)*
Accumetrics Associates Inc ....F 518 393-2200
Latham *(G-7353)*
▲ Acolyte Technologies Corp...............F 212 629-3239
New York *(G-9020)*
Addmm LLC...F 631 913-4400
Ronkonkoma *(G-14851)*
Advis Inc..G....... 585 568-0100
Caledonia *(G-3275)*
▼ Aeroflex Holding Corp ....E 516 694-6700
Plainview *(G-13577)*
▲ Aeroflex Incorporated.........................B 516 694-6700
Plainview *(G-13578)*
Aeroflex Plainview Inc ....B 516 694-6700
Plainview *(G-13579)*
Aeroflex Plainview Inc ....C....... 631 231-9100
Hauppauge *(G-6011)*
Aljo-Gefa Precision Mfg LLC ....E 516 420-4419
Old Bethpage *(G-13125)*
American Fuel Cell LLC..........................G....... 585 474-3993
Rochester *(G-14197)*
▲ Artemis Inc...G....... 631 232-2424
Hauppauge *(G-6025)*
▲ Atlantis Energy Systems Inc..............F 845 486-4052
Poughkeepsie *(G-13889)*
Atlantis Energy Systems Inc..................G....... 916 438-2930
Poughkeepsie *(G-13890)*
Autodyne Manufacturing Co Inc............F 631 957-5858
Lindenhurst *(G-7456)*
Automated Control Logic Inc.................F 914 769-8880
Thornwood *(G-16116)*
Beech Grove Technology Inc.................G....... 845 223-6844
Hopewell Junction *(G-6547)*
Besicorp Ltd ....F 845 336-7700
Kingston *(G-7179)*
Bga Technology LLC ....F 631 750-4600
Bohemia *(G-1025)*
Bharat Electronics Limited ....G....... 516 248-4021
Garden City *(G-5496)*
CAM Touchview Products Inc................F 631 842-3400
Farmingdale *(G-4956)*
▲ Central Semiconductor Corp............D 631 435-1110
Hauppauge *(G-6041)*
Ceres Technologies Inc ....D....... 845 247-4701
Saugerties *(G-15181)*
Cold Springs R & D Inc..........................F 315 413-1237
Syracuse *(G-15901)*
Compositech Ltd......................................C....... 516 835-1458
Woodbury *(G-17284)*
Convergent Med MGT Svcs LLC ....G....... 718 921-6159
Brooklyn *(G-1802)*
Cooper Power Systems LLC..................B 716 375-7100
Olean *(G-13140)*
Corning Incorporated ....E 607 248-1200
Corning *(G-3965)*

SIC

Employee Codes: A=Over 500 employees, B=251-500
C=101-250, D=51-100, E=20-50, F=10-19, G=5-9

2017 Harris
New York Manufacturers Directory

847

◆ **Corning Incorporated** ...A ... 607 974-9000
Corning *(G-3962)*

Corning Incorporated ...G ... 607 974-6729
Painted Post *(G-13391)*

Corning Specialty Mtls Inc ...G ... 607 974-9000
Corning *(G-3970)*

Crystalonics Inc ...F ... 631 981-6140
Ronkonkoma *(G-14891)*

Curtiss-Wright Controls ...G ... 631 756-4740
Farmingdale *(G-4967)*

Cypress Semiconductor Corp ...F ... 631 261-1358
Northport *(G-13010)*

▲ **Data Device Corporation** ...B ... 631 567-5600
Bohemia *(G-1049)*

▲ **Data Display USA Inc** ...C ... 631 218-2130
Holbrook *(G-6443)*

Dionics-Usa Inc ...G ... 516 997-7474
Westbury *(G-16977)*

DJS Nyc Inc ...G ... 845 445-8618
Spring Valley *(G-15581)*

Dynamic Photography Inc ...G ... 516 381-2951
Roslyn *(G-15019)*

▲ **Electronic Devices Inc** ...E ... 914 965-4400
Yonkers *(G-17440)*

Elite Semi Conductor Products ...G ... 631 884-8400
Lindenhurst *(G-7463)*

Ely Beach Solar LLC ...G ... 718 796-9400
New York *(G-10017)*

Emagin Corporation ...D ... 845 838-7900
Hopewell Junction *(G-6549)*

Emtron Hybrids Inc ...E ... 631 924-9668
Yaphank *(G-17392)*

▲ **Endicott Interconnect Tech Inc** ...A ... 866 820-4820
Endicott *(G-4802)*

Enrg Inc ...F ... 716 873-2939
Buffalo *(G-2940)*

Eversan Inc ...F ... 315 736-3967
Whitesboro *(G-17193)*

Freescale Semiconductor Inc ...G ... 585 425-4000
Pittsford *(G-13560)*

General Microwave Corporation ...F ... 516 802-0900
Syosset *(G-15824)*

General Semiconductor Inc ...G ... 631 300-3818
Hauppauge *(G-6083)*

Globalfoundries US Inc ...F ... 512 457-3900
Hopewell Junction *(G-6551)*

Globalfoundries US Inc ...F ... 408 462-3900
Ballston Spa *(G-597)*

Gs Direct LLC ...G ... 212 902-1000
New York *(G-10377)*

Gurley Precision Instrs Inc ...C ... 518 272-6300
Troy *(G-16237)*

H K Technologies Inc ...G ... 212 779-0100
New York *(G-10390)*

Hi-Tron Semiconductor Corp ...E ... 631 231-1500
Hauppauge *(G-6093)*

◆ **Hipotronics Inc** ...C ... 845 279-8091
Brewster *(G-1220)*

Hisun Optoelectronics Co Ltd ...F ... 718 886-6966
Flushing *(G-5250)*

I E D Corp ...F ... 631 348-0424
Islandia *(G-6795)*

I3 Electronics Inc ...B ... 866 820-4820
Endicott *(G-4812)*

▲ **Ic Technologies LLC** ...G ... 212 966-7895
New York *(G-10549)*

Idalia Solar Technologies LLC ...G ... 212 792-3913
New York *(G-10553)*

Ieh FM Holdings LLC ...E ... 212 702-4300
New York *(G-10559)*

Ilc Holdings Inc ...G ... 631 567-5600
Bohemia *(G-1076)*

▲ **Ilc Industries LLC** ...E ... 631 567-5600
Bohemia *(G-1077)*

▲ **Intech 21 Inc** ...F ... 516 626-7221
Port Washington *(G-13825)*

INTEL Corporation ...D ... 408 765-8080
Getzville *(G-5599)*

International Bus Mchs Corp ...A ... 845 894-2121
Hopewell Junction *(G-6553)*

International Bus Mchs Corp ...E ... 212 324-5000
New York *(G-10631)*

International Bus Mchs Corp ...C ... 800 426-4968
Hopewell Junction *(G-6554)*

▲ **Interplex Industries Inc** ...F ... 718 961-6212
College Point *(G-3790)*

Intex Company Inc ...D ... 718 336-3491
Brooklyn *(G-2114)*

▲ **Isine Inc** ...G ... 631 913-4400
Ronkonkoma *(G-14914)*

Isonics Corporation ...G ... 212 356-7400
New York *(G-10668)*

J H Rhodes Company Inc ...F ... 315 829-3600
Vernon *(G-16436)*

▲ **Lakestar Semi Inc** ...F ... 212 974-6254
New York *(G-10919)*

Lasermax Inc ...D ... 585 272-5420
Rochester *(G-14474)*

◆ **Leviton Manufacturing Co Inc** ...B ... 631 812-6000
Melville *(G-8334)*

Light Blue USA LLC ...G ... 718 475-2515
Brooklyn *(G-2221)*

Lightspin Technologies Inc ...G ... 301 656-7600
Endwell *(G-4837)*

Logitek Inc ...D ... 631 567-1100
Bohemia *(G-1094)*

LSI Computer Systems ...E ... 631 271-0400
Melville *(G-8335)*

M C Products ...E ... 631 471-4070
Holbrook *(G-6459)*

Marcon Services ...G ... 516 223-8019
Freeport *(G-5411)*

▲ **Marktech International Corp** ...E ... 518 956-2980
Latham *(G-7373)*

▲ **Materion Brewster LLC** ...D ... 845 279-0900
Brewster *(G-1223)*

▼ **McG Electronics Inc** ...E ... 631 586-5125
Deer Park *(G-4172)*

Mellanox Technologies Inc ...D ... 408 970-3400
New York *(G-11223)*

Micro Contract Manufacturing ...D ... 631 738-7874
Ronkonkoma *(G-14941)*

▲ **Micro Semicdtr Researches LLC** ...G ... 646 863-6070
New York *(G-11254)*

Microchip Technology Inc ...G ... 631 233-3280
Hauppauge *(G-6136)*

Microchip Technology Inc ...C ... 607 785-5992
Endicott *(G-4819)*

Micromem Technologies ...F ... 212 672-1806
New York *(G-11255)*

Mini-Circuits Fort Wayne LLC ...B ... 718 934-4500
Brooklyn *(G-2318)*

MMC Magnetics Corp ...F ... 631 435-9888
Hauppauge *(G-6141)*

Monolithic Coatings Inc ...G ... 914 621-2765
Sharon Springs *(G-15384)*

▲ **Nationwide Tarps Incorporated** ...D ... 518 843-1545
Amsterdam *(G-361)*

Navitar Inc ...D ... 585 359-4000
Rochester *(G-14530)*

Nsi Industries LLC ...C ... 800 841-2505
Mount Vernon *(G-8711)*

Oledworks LLC ...E ... 585 287-6802
Rochester *(G-14547)*

▲ **Onyx Solar Group LLC** ...G ... 917 951-9732
New York *(G-11513)*

Orbit International Corp ...C ... 631 435-8300
Hauppauge *(G-6154)*

▲ **Park Electrochemical Corp** ...C ... 631 465-3600
Melville *(G-8347)*

▲ **Passive-Plus Inc** ...F ... 631 425-0938
Huntington *(G-6673)*

◆ **Philips Medical Systems Mr** ...B ... 518 782-1122
Latham *(G-7376)*

Piezo Electronics Research ...F ... 845 735-9349
Pearl River *(G-13463)*

Plures Technologies Inc ...G ... 585 905-0554
Canandaigua *(G-3355)*

Procomponents Inc ...E ... 516 683-0909
Westbury *(G-17023)*

Pvi Solar Inc ...G ... 212 280-2100
New York *(G-11760)*

Renewable Energy Inc ...G ... 718 690-2691
Little Neck *(G-7510)*

Riverhawk Company LP ...E ... 315 624-7171
New Hartford *(G-8809)*

▲ **RSM Electron Power Inc** ...D ... 631 586-7600
Deer Park *(G-4203)*

RSM Electron Power Inc ...D ... 631 586-7600
Hauppauge *(G-6181)*

Ruhle Companies Inc ...E ... 914 287-4000
Valhalla *(G-16372)*

S3j Electronics LLC ...E ... 716 206-1309
Lancaster *(G-7341)*

Schott Corporation ...D ... 315 255-2791
Auburn *(G-517)*

Schott Lithotec USA Corp ...D ... 845 463-5300
Elmsford *(G-4781)*

▲ **Schott Solar Pv Inc** ...G ... 888 457-6527
Elmsford *(G-4782)*

Semitronics Corp ...E ... 516 223-0200
Freeport *(G-5425)*

Sencer Inc ...G ... 315 536-3474
Penn Yan *(G-13520)*

Sendyne Corp ...G ... 212 966-0663
New York *(G-12028)*

Senera Co Inc ...F ... 516 639-3774
Valley Stream *(G-16427)*

Silicon Pulsed Power LLC ...G ... 610 407-4700
Clifton Park *(G-3707)*

Sinclair Technologies Inc ...E ... 716 874-3682
Hamburg *(G-5942)*

▲ **Solar Thin Films Inc** ...F ... 516 341-7787
Uniondale *(G-16299)*

▲ **Solartech Renewables LLC** ...F ... 646 675-1853
Poughkeepsie *(G-13931)*

Solid Cell Inc ...G ... 585 426-5000
Rochester *(G-14691)*

Sonotec US Inc ...C ... 631 404-7497
Central Islip *(G-3510)*

▲ **Spectron Glass & Electronics** ...F ... 631 582-5600
Hauppauge *(G-6193)*

▲ **Standard Microsystems Corp** ...C ... 631 435-6000
Hauppauge *(G-6199)*

▲ **Stetron International Inc** ...F ... 716 854-3443
Buffalo *(G-3197)*

▲ **Sumitomo Elc USA Holdings Inc** ...G ... 212 490-6610
New York *(G-12232)*

▼ **Super Conductor Materials Inc** ...F ... 845 368-0240
Suffern *(G-15801)*

Swissbit Na Inc ...G ... 914 935-1400
Port Chester *(G-13760)*

Symwave Inc ...G ... 949 542-4400
Hauppauge *(G-6205)*

Tarsier Ltd ...C ... 212 401-6181
New York *(G-12280)*

▲ **Tel Technology Center Amer LLC** ...E ... 512 424-4200
Albany *(G-141)*

Telephonics Corporation ...E ... 631 549-6000
Huntington *(G-6683)*

Telephonics Tlsi Corp ...C ... 631 470-8854
Huntington *(G-6687)*

Thales Laser SA ...D ... 585 223-2370
Fairport *(G-4884)*

Thermo Cidtec Inc ...E ... 315 451-9410
Liverpool *(G-7553)*

Thermoaura Inc ...F ... 518 880-2125
Albany *(G-142)*

Tlsi Incorporated ...D ... 631 470-8880
Huntington *(G-6688)*

▲ **Tork Inc** ...D ... 914 664-3542
Mount Vernon *(G-8738)*

◆ **Truebite Inc** ...E ... 607 785-7664
Vestal *(G-16455)*

University At Albany ...E ... 518 437-8686
Albany *(G-147)*

Vgg Holding LLC ...G ... 212 415-6700
New York *(G-12533)*

Viking Technologies Ltd ...E ... 631 957-8000
Lindenhurst *(G-7493)*

Vistec Lithography Inc ...F ... 518 874-3184
Troy *(G-16260)*

Widetronix Inc ...G ... 607 330-4752
Ithaca *(G-6885)*

◆ **Yingli Green Enrgy Amricas Inc** ...E ... 888 686-8820
New York *(G-12692)*

▲ **Zastech Inc** ...E ... 516 496-4777
Syosset *(G-15843)*

3675 Electronic Capacitors

American Technical Ceramics ...B ... 631 622-4700
Huntington Station *(G-6696)*

◆ **American Technical Ceramics** ...B ... 631 622-4700
Huntington Station *(G-6695)*

AVX Corporation ...D ... 716 372-6611
Olean *(G-13134)*

▲ **Custom Electronics Inc** ...D ... 607 432-3880
Oneonta *(G-13184)*

Electron Coil Inc ...D ... 607 336-7414
Norwich *(G-13027)*

Ems Development Corporation ...D ... 631 345-6200
Yaphank *(G-17391)*

◆ **Hipotronics Inc** ...C ... 845 279-8091
Brewster *(G-1220)*

Integer Holdings Corporation ...E ... 716 937-5100
Alden *(G-180)*

Kemet Properties LLC ...G ... 718 654-8079
Bronx *(G-1370)*

▲ **Knowles Cazenovia Inc** ...C ... 315 655-8710
Cazenovia *(G-3447)*

SIC SECTION 36 ELECTRONIC AND OTHER ELECTRICAL EQUIPMENT AND COMPONENTS, EXCEPT COMPUTER

▲ **MTK Electronics Inc**...E....631 924-7666
Medford *(G-8256)*
▲ **Passive-Plus Inc**...F....631 425-0938
Huntington *(G-6673)*
▲ **Roberts-Gordon LLC**...D....716 852-4400
Buffalo *(G-3160)*
▲ **Stk Electronics Inc**...E....315 655-8476
Cazenovia *(G-3452)*
Strux Corp...E....516 768-3969
Lindenhurst *(G-7485)*
Tbt Group Inc...F....212 685-1836
New York *(G-12283)*
Traxel Labs Inc...G....631 590-1095
Nesconset *(G-8778)*
▲ **Tronser Inc**...G....315 655-9528
Cazenovia *(G-3453)*
Viking Technologies Ltd...E....631 957-8000
Lindenhurst *(G-7493)*
▲ **Virtue Paintball LLC**...G....631 617-5560
Hauppauge *(G-6226)*
Voltronics LLC...E....410 749-2424
Cazenovia *(G-3454)*

3676 Electronic Resistors

Dahua Electronics Corporation...E....718 886-2188
Flushing *(G-5236)*
Hvr Advnced Pwr Components Inc...F....716 693-4700
Cheektowaga *(G-3576)*
▲ **Kionix Inc**...C....607 257-1080
Ithaca *(G-6856)*
Microgen Systems Inc...G....585 214-2426
West Henrietta *(G-16884)*
▼ **Micropen Technologies Corp**...D....585 624-2610
Honeoye Falls *(G-6535)*
▲ **Passive-Plus Inc**...F....631 425-0938
Huntington *(G-6673)*
▲ **Stetron International Inc**...F....716 854-3443
Buffalo *(G-3197)*
▲ **Virtue Paintball LLC**...G....631 617-5560
Hauppauge *(G-6226)*
Vishay Americas Inc...C....315 938-7575
Henderson *(G-6290)*
▲ **Vishay Thin Film LLC**...C....716 283-4025
Niagara Falls *(G-12889)*

3677 Electronic Coils & Transformers

▲ **Aeroflex Incorporated**...B....516 694-6700
Plainview *(G-13578)*
Airsys Technologies LLC...G....716 694-6390
Tonawanda *(G-16136)*
▲ **All Shore Industries Inc**...F....718 720-0018
Staten Island *(G-15634)*
▲ **Allen Avionics Inc**...E....516 248-8080
Mineola *(G-8493)*
◆ **American Precision Inds Inc**...C....716 691-9100
Amherst *(G-224)*
American Precision Inds Inc...D....716 652-3600
East Aurora *(G-4365)*
American Precision Inds Inc...D....585 496-5755
Arcade *(G-386)*
American Trans-Coil Corp...F....516 922-9640
Oyster Bay *(G-13365)*
▲ **Applied Power Systems Inc**...E....516 935-2230
Hicksville *(G-6322)*
Atlantic Transformer Inc...F....716 795-3258
Barker *(G-612)*
▲ **Bel Transformer Inc**...D....516 239-5777
Inwood *(G-6753)*
Beta Transformer Tech Corp...E....631 244-7393
Bohemia *(G-1024)*
▲ **Bright Way Supply Inc**...F....718 833-2882
Brooklyn *(G-1717)*
Coil-Q Corporation...G....914 779-7109
Bronxville *(G-1500)*
▲ **Data Device Corporation**...B....631 567-5600
Bohemia *(G-1049)*
Electron Coil Inc...D....607 336-7414
Norwich *(G-13027)*
Ems Development Corporation...D....631 345-6200
Yaphank *(G-17391)*
▲ **Ems Development Corporation**...D....631 924-4736
Yaphank *(G-17390)*
▲ **Eni Technology Inc**...B....585 427-8300
Rochester *(G-14353)*
Es Beta Inc...E....631 582-6740
Hauppauge *(G-6073)*
▲ **Esc Control Electronics LLC**...E....631 467-5328
Sayville *(G-15208)*
Exxelia-Raf Tabtronics LLC...E....585 243-4331
Piffard *(G-13547)*
▲ **Fil-Coil (fc) Corp**...E....631 467-5328
Sayville *(G-15209)*
Frequency Selective Networks...F....718 424-7500
Maspeth *(G-8140)*
Fuse Electronics Inc...G....607 352-3222
Kirkwood *(G-7233)*
Gowanda - Bti LLC...D....716 492-4081
Arcade *(G-394)*
▲ **Hammond Manufacturing Co Inc**...F....716 630-7030
Cheektowaga *(G-3573)*
◆ **Hipotronics Inc**...C....845 279-8091
Brewster *(G-1220)*
Island Audio Engineering...G....631 543-2372
Commack *(G-3836)*
M F L B Inc...F....631 254-8300
Bay Shore *(G-714)*
Microwave Filter Company Inc...E....315 438-4700
East Syracuse *(G-4550)*
Mini-Circuits Fort Wayne LLC...B....718 934-4500
Brooklyn *(G-2318)*
▲ **Misonix Inc**...D....631 694-9555
Farmingdale *(G-5058)*
Mitchell Electronics Corp...E....914 699-3800
Mount Vernon *(G-8707)*
Mohawk Electro Techniques Inc...D....315 896-2661
Barneveld *(G-615)*
▲ **MTK Electronics Inc**...E....631 924-7666
Medford *(G-8256)*
▲ **NEa Manufacturing Corp**...E....516 371-4200
Inwood *(G-6763)*
New York Fan Coil LLC...G....646 580-1344
Coram *(G-3947)*
Pall International Corporation...B....516 484-5400
Port Washington *(G-13854)*
▲ **Pall Trinity Micro Corporation**...A....607 753-6041
Cortland *(G-4038)*
Precision Electronics Inc...F....631 842-4900
Copiague *(G-3919)*
Prms Inc...G....631 851-7945
Shirley *(G-15429)*
▲ **Rdi Inc**...F....914 773-1000
Mount Kisco *(G-8643)*
Sag Harbor Industries Inc...E....631 725-0440
Sag Harbor *(G-15080)*
Service Filtration Corp...E....716 877-2608
Tonawanda *(G-16202)*
Tdk-Lambda Americas Inc...F....631 967-3000
Hauppauge *(G-6207)*
▼ **Todd Systems Inc**...D....914 963-3400
Yonkers *(G-17490)*
Tte Filters LLC...G....716 532-2234
Gowanda *(G-5749)*
Urban Technologies Inc...G....716 672-2709
Fredonia *(G-5376)*

3678 Electronic Connectors

Accessories For Electronics...E....631 847-0158
South Hempstead *(G-15529)*
Amphenol Corporation...B....607 563-5364
Sidney *(G-15436)*
Amphenol Corporation...A....607 563-5011
Sidney *(G-15437)*
Automatic Connector Inc...F....631 543-5000
Hauppauge *(G-6029)*
Belden Inc...B....607 796-5600
Horseheads *(G-6569)*
▲ **Casa Innovations Inc**...G....718 965-6600
Brooklyn *(G-1763)*
Deutsch Corporate Inc...F....212 710-5870
New York *(G-9862)*
▲ **EBY Electro Inc**...E....516 576-7777
Plainview *(G-13598)*
▲ **Executive Machines Inc**...E....718 965-6600
Brooklyn *(G-1945)*
▲ **Felchar Manufacturing Corp**...A....607 723-3106
Binghamton *(G-914)*
I Trade Technology Ltd...G....615 348-7233
Suffern *(G-15792)*
Ieh Corporation...C....718 492-4440
Brooklyn *(G-2096)*
▲ **Keystone Electronics Corp**...C....718 956-8900
Astoria *(G-446)*
▼ **Kirtas Inc**...E....585 924-2420
Victor *(G-16486)*
◆ **Leviton Manufacturing Co Inc**...B....631 812-6000
Melville *(G-8334)*
▲ **Mason Industries Inc**...C....631 348-0282
Hauppauge *(G-6126)*
▲ **Mill-Max Mfg Corp**...C....516 922-6000
Oyster Bay *(G-13371)*
Mini-Circuits Fort Wayne LLC...B....718 934-4500
Brooklyn *(G-2318)*
▲ **NEa Manufacturing Corp**...E....516 371-4200
Inwood *(G-6763)*
▲ **Power Connector Inc**...E....631 563-7878
Bohemia *(G-1118)*
▲ **Rdi Inc**...F....914 773-1000
Mount Kisco *(G-8643)*
Resonance Technologies Inc...E....631 237-4901
Ronkonkoma *(G-14978)*
Sitewatch Technology LLC...G....207 778-3246
East Quogue *(G-4452)*
Supplynet Inc...G....845 267-2655
Valley Cottage *(G-16392)*
Sureseal Corporation...G....607 336-6676
Norwich *(G-13038)*
▲ **Taro Manufacturing Company Inc**...F....315 252-9430
Auburn *(G-523)*
▲ **Universal Remote Control Inc**...D....914 630-4343
Harrison *(G-5993)*
▲ **Virtue Paintball LLC**...G....631 617-5560
Hauppauge *(G-6226)*
▲ **Whirlwind Music Distrs Inc**...D....585 663-8820
Rochester *(G-14762)*

3679 Electronic Components, NEC

3835 Lebron Rest Eqp & Sup Inc...E....212 942-8258
New York *(G-8973)*
901 D LLC...E....845 369-1111
Airmont *(G-11)*
▲ **A K Allen Co Inc**...C....516 747-5450
Mineola *(G-8488)*
A R V Precision Mfg Inc...G....631 293-9643
Farmingdale *(G-4927)*
AAR Allen Services Inc...E....516 222-9000
Garden City *(G-5493)*
Accessories For Electronics...E....631 847-0158
South Hempstead *(G-15529)*
Ace Electronics Inc...F....914 773-2000
Hawthorne *(G-6242)*
▲ **Advance Circuit Technology Inc**...E....585 328-2000
Rochester *(G-14175)*
▲ **Advanced Interconnect Mfg Inc**...D....585 742-2220
Victor *(G-16459)*
Aeroflex Plainview Inc...B....516 694-6700
Plainview *(G-13579)*
Aeroflex Plainview Inc...C....631 231-9100
Hauppauge *(G-6011)*
▲ **Albatros North America Inc**...E....518 381-7100
Ballston Spa *(G-590)*
▲ **All Shore Industries Inc**...F....718 720-0018
Staten Island *(G-15634)*
▲ **Allen Avionics Inc**...E....516 248-8080
Mineola *(G-8493)*
Alloy Machine & Tool Co Inc...G....516 593-3445
Lynbrook *(G-7946)*
Altec Datacom LLC...G....631 242-2417
Bay Shore *(G-669)*
American Aerospace Contrls Inc...E....631 694-5100
Farmingdale *(G-4940)*
American Quality Technology...F....607 777-9488
Binghamton *(G-887)*
▲ **Amphenol Intrconnect Pdts Corp**...G....607 754-4444
Endicott *(G-4795)*
Ampro International Inc...G....845 278-4910
Brewster *(G-1210)*
Amron Electronics Inc...E....631 737-1234
Ronkonkoma *(G-14870)*
▲ **Anaren Inc**...B....315 432-8909
East Syracuse *(G-4502)*
Antenna & Radome Res Assoc...E....631 231-8400
Bay Shore *(G-671)*
▲ **Apollo Display Tech Corp**...E....631 580-4360
Ronkonkoma *(G-14871)*
Applied Concepts Inc...E....315 696-6676
Tully *(G-16273)*
▲ **Applied Power Systems Inc**...E....516 935-2230
Hicksville *(G-6322)*
▲ **Apx Technologies Inc**...E....516 433-1313
Hicksville *(G-6323)*
▲ **Arnold-Davis LLC**...C....607 772-1201
Binghamton *(G-889)*
Arstan Products International...F....516 433-1313
Hicksville *(G-6324)*
B H M Metal Products Co...G....845 292-5297
Kauneonga Lake *(G-7136)*
B3cg Interconnect Usa Inc...F....450 491-4040
Plattsburgh *(G-13653)*
Badger Technologies Inc...E....585 869-7101
Farmington *(G-5146)*

S I C

Employee Codes: A=Over 500 employees, B=251-500
C=101-250, D=51-100, E=20-50, F=10-19, G=5-9
2017 Harris
New York Manufacturers Directory
849

36 ELECTRONIC AND OTHER ELECTRICAL EQUIPMENT AND COMPONENTS, EXCEPT COMPUTER

▲ Badger Technologies Inc ....D...... 585 869-7101
  Farmington (G-5147)
BC Systems Inc ....E...... 631 751-9370
  Setauket (G-15374)
Becker Electronics Inc ....D...... 631 619-9100
  Ronkonkoma (G-14879)
▲ Behlman Electronics Inc ....G...... 631 435-0410
  Hauppauge (G-6033)
Berkshire Transformer ....G...... 631 467-5328
  Central Islip (G-3487)
Bryit Group LLC ....F...... 631 563-6603
  Holbrook (G-6433)
Bud Barger Assoc Inc ....G...... 631 696-6703
  Farmingville (G-5159)
C A M Graphics Co Inc ....E...... 631 842-3400
  Farmingdale (G-4955)
Cables Unlimited Inc ....G...... 631 563-6363
  Yaphank (G-17387)
▼ Canfield Electronics Inc ....F...... 631 585-4100
  Lindenhurst (G-7458)
Centroid Inc ....E...... 516 349-0070
  Plainview (G-13586)
Chiplogic Inc ....F...... 631 617-6317
  Yaphank (G-17388)
Clever Devices Ltd ....G...... 845 566-0051
  Newburgh (G-12752)
Clever Devices Ltd ....E...... 516 433-6100
  Woodbury (G-17283)
Cloud Toronto Inc ....F...... 408 569-4542
  Williamsville (G-17239)
Cobham Holdings (us) Inc ....A...... 716 662-0006
  Orchard Park (G-13262)
Cobham Holdings Inc ....F...... 716 662-0006
  Orchard Park (G-13263)
Communications & Energy Corp ....F...... 315 446-5723
  Syracuse (G-15903)
▲ Condor Electronics Corp ....E...... 585 235-1500
  Rochester (G-14284)
Crystal Is Inc ....E...... 518 271-7375
  Troy (G-16219)
D & S Supplies Inc ....F...... 718 721-5256
  Astoria (G-435)
Dimension Technologies Inc ....G...... 585 436-3530
  Rochester (G-14309)
Dortronics Systems Inc ....E...... 631 725-0505
  Sag Harbor (G-15077)
Dynamic Hybirds Inc ....G...... 315 426-8110
  Syracuse (G-15927)
▲ Eastland Electronics Co Inc ....G...... 631 580-3800
  Ronkonkoma (G-14898)
◆ Edo LLC ....G...... 631 630-4000
  Amityville (G-285)
▼ Electronics & Innovation Ltd .....F...... 585 214-0598
  Rochester (G-14344)
Empresas De Manufactura Inc ....C...... 631 240-9251
  East Setauket (G-4481)
Engagement Technology LLC ....F...... 914 591-7600
  Elmsford (G-4750)
▲ Eni Technology Inc ....B...... 585 427-8300
  Rochester (G-14353)
▲ Ergotech Group Inc ....F...... 914 347-3800
  Elmsford (G-4751)
▲ Esc Control Electronics LLC ....E...... 631 467-5328
  Sayville (G-15208)
Espey Mfg & Electronics Corp ....C...... 518 245-4400
  Saratoga Springs (G-15151)
▲ Fair-Rite Products Corp ....C...... 845 895-2055
  Wallkill (G-16543)
Fei Communications Inc ....C...... 516 794-4500
  Uniondale (G-16293)
Felluss Recording ....G...... 212 727-8055
  New York (G-10151)
Fine Sounds Group Inc ....F...... 212 364-0219
  New York (G-10165)
Frequency Electronics Inc ....B...... 516 794-4500
  Uniondale (G-16295)
General Microwave Corporation .....F...... 516 802-0900
  Syosset (G-15824)
Gotenna Inc ....F...... 415 894-2616
  Brooklyn (G-2042)
▲ Grado Laboratories Inc ....F...... 718 435-5340
  Brooklyn (G-2046)
▲ Haynes Roberts Inc ....F...... 212 989-1901
  New York (G-10431)
Hazlow Electronics Inc ....E...... 585 325-5323
  Rochester (G-14431)
◆ Hipotronics Inc ....E...... 845 279-8091
  Brewster (G-1220)
▲ Hs Associates Corp ....G...... 516 496-2940
  Jericho (G-7071)

Hypres Inc ....E...... 914 592-1190
  Elmsford (G-4756)
I3 Cable & Harness LLC ....D...... 607 238-7077
  Binghamton (G-924)
Idt Energy Inc ....E...... 877 887-6866
  Jamestown (G-7002)
IEC Electronics Corp ....B...... 315 331-7742
  Newark (G-12732)
Imrex LLC ....B...... 516 479-3675
  Oyster Bay (G-13370)
Innovative Power Products Inc ......E...... 631 563-0088
  Holbrook (G-6452)
Innowave Rf LLC ....G...... 914 230-4060
  Tarrytown (G-16091)
Interntonal Telecom Components ...F...... 631 243-1444
  Deer Park (G-4152)
Island Circuits International ....G...... 516 625-5555
  College Point (G-3791)
Island Research and Dev Corp ....D...... 631 471-7100
  Ronkonkoma (G-14915)
Jaguar Industries Inc ....E...... 845 947-1800
  Haverstraw (G-6237)
▲ Jenlor Ltd ....F...... 315 637-9080
  Fayetteville (G-5165)
▲ Jet Components Inc ....E...... 631 436-7300
  Islandia (G-6797)
▲ Kearney-National Inc ....F...... 212 661-4600
  New York (G-10828)
▲ Keltron Electronics (de Corp) ....F...... 631 567-6300
  Ronkonkoma (G-14921)
▲ L-3 Cmmnctons Fgn Holdings Inc ....E...... 212 697-1111
  New York (G-10903)
◆ L-3 Cmmunications Holdings Inc ...D...... 212 697-1111
  New York (G-10905)
L-3 Communications Corporation ...E...... 631 289-0363
  Patchogue (G-13427)
L-3 Communications Corporation ...B...... 212 697-1111
  New York (G-10906)
Lexan Industries Inc ....F...... 631 434-7586
  Bay Shore (G-713)
Lighthouse Components ....E...... 917 993-6820
  New York (G-10994)
Logitek Inc ....D...... 631 567-1100
  Bohemia (G-1094)
Lyntronics Inc ....E...... 631 205-1061
  Yaphank (G-17397)
M W Microwave Corp ....F...... 516 295-1814
  Lawrence (G-7394)
Marcon Electronic Systems LLC ....G...... 516 633-6396
  Freeport (G-5410)
Mechanical Pwr Conversion LLC ...G...... 607 766-9620
  Binghamton (G-934)
Mekatronics Incorporated ....E...... 516 883-6805
  Port Washington (G-13844)
Meridian Technologies Inc ....E...... 516 285-1000
  Elmont (G-4724)
▲ Merit Electronic Design Co Inc ...C...... 631 667-9699
  Edgewood (G-4606)
Mezmeriz Inc ....G...... 607 216-8140
  Ithaca (G-6861)
Microwave Circuit Tech Inc ....E...... 631 845-1041
  Farmingdale (G-5052)
Microwave Filter Company Inc ......E...... 315 438-4700
  East Syracuse (G-4550)
▲ Mid Hdson Wkshp For The Dsbled ..E...... 845 471-3820
  Poughkeepsie (G-13915)
Mini-Circuits Fort Wayne LLC ....B...... 718 934-4500
  Brooklyn (G-2318)
Mirion Technologies Ist Corp ....D...... 607 562-4300
  Horseheads (G-6584)
MLS Sales ....G...... 516 681-2736
  Bethpage (G-875)
◆ Momentive Performance Mtls Inc ...E...... 518 237-3330
  Waterford (G-16616)
Mpm Holdings Inc ....G...... 518 237-3330
  Waterford (G-16617)
Mpm Intermediate Holdings Inc .....G...... 518 237-3330
  Waterford (G-16618)
▲ NEa Manufacturing Corp ....E...... 516 371-4200
  Inwood (G-6763)
Nelson Holdings Ltd ....G...... 607 772-1794
  Binghamton (G-939)
New York Digital Corporation ....F...... 631 630-9798
  Huntington Station (G-6718)
▲ North Hills Signal Proc Corp ......G...... 516 682-7700
  Syosset (G-15833)
▼ Oakdale Industrial Elec Corp ......F...... 631 737-4090
  Ronkonkoma (G-14957)
Opus Technology Corporation ....F...... 631 271-1883
  Melville (G-8345)

Orbit International Corp ....C...... 631 435-8300
  Hauppauge (G-6154)
Orbit International Corp ....D...... 631 435-8300
  Hauppauge (G-6155)
Orthogonal ....G...... 585 254-2775
  Rochester (G-14557)
Paal Technologies Inc ....E...... 631 319-6262
  Ronkonkoma (G-14962)
▲ Passive-Plus Inc ....F...... 631 425-0938
  Huntington (G-6673)
Pcb Group Inc ....E...... 716 684-0001
  Depew (G-4268)
Pcb Piezotronics Inc ....B...... 716 684-0003
  Depew (G-4270)
◆ Philips Medical Systems Mr ......B...... 518 782-1122
  Latham (G-7376)
Phoenix Cables Corporation ....C...... 845 691-6253
  Highland (G-6406)
Photonamics Inc ....F...... 585 426-3774
  Rochester (G-14583)
Polycast Industries Inc ....G...... 631 595-2530
  Bay Shore (G-726)
▲ Precision Assembly Tech Inc .....E...... 631 699-9400
  Bohemia (G-1119)
Premier Systems LLC ....E...... 631 587-9700
  Babylon (G-552)
Prime Electronic Components ....F...... 631 254-0101
  Deer Park (G-4192)
Pvi Solar Inc ....E...... 212 280-2100
  New York (G-11760)
▲ Quality Contract Assemblies ....F...... 585 663-9030
  Rochester (G-14612)
R L C Electronics Inc ....D...... 914 241-1334
  Mount Kisco (G-8641)
▲ Rdi Inc ....F...... 914 773-1000
  Mount Kisco (G-8643)
▲ Recom Power Inc ....G...... 718 855-9713
  Brooklyn (G-2483)
Rem-Tronics Inc ....D...... 716 934-2697
  Dunkirk (G-4348)
Rochester Industrial Ctrl Inc ....D...... 315 524-4555
  Ontario (G-13213)
▲ Rochester Industrial Ctrl Inc .....D...... 315 524-4555
  Ontario (G-13212)
Ruhle Companies Inc ....E...... 914 287-4000
  Valhalla (G-16372)
▲ Russell Industries Inc ....F...... 516 536-5000
  Lynbrook (G-7960)
Safe Circuits Inc ....G...... 631 586-3682
  Dix Hills (G-14427)
Sayeda Manufacturing Corp ....F...... 631 345-2525
  Medford (G-8259)
SC Textiles Inc ....G...... 631 944-6262
  Huntington (G-6679)
▲ Scientific Components Corp .....B...... 718 934-4500
  Brooklyn (G-2538)
Scientific Components Corp ....B...... 718 368-2060
  Brooklyn (G-2539)
Secs Inc ....E...... 914 667-5600
  Mount Vernon (G-8732)
▲ Sendec Inc ....C...... 585 425-3390
  Fairport (G-4877)
Sln Group Inc ....G...... 718 677-5969
  Brooklyn (G-2571)
Sonaer Inc ....G...... 631 756-4780
  West Babylon (G-16829)
Sopark Corp ....C...... 716 822-0434
  Buffalo (G-3191)
Space Coast Semiconductor Inc ....F...... 631 414-7131
  Farmingdale (G-5112)
▲ Spectron Glass & Electronics ...F...... 631 582-5600
  Hauppauge (G-6193)
Spectron Systems Technology .....F...... 631 582-5600
  Hauppauge (G-6194)
Spectrum Microwave Inc ....E...... 315 253-6241
  Auburn (G-520)
▲ Stetron International Inc ....F...... 716 854-3443
  Buffalo (G-3197)
Sturges Elec Pdts Co Inc ....E...... 607 844-8604
  Dryden (G-4323)
Sun Circuits International Inc ....B...... 631 240-9251
  Setauket (G-15381)
Superior Motion Controls Inc ....E...... 516 420-2921
  Farmingdale (G-5120)
Surmotech LLC ....D...... 585 742-1220
  Victor (G-16503)
T-S-K Electronics Inc ....E...... 716 693-3916
  North Tonawanda (G-12999)
TCS Electronics Inc ....E...... 585 337-4301
  Farmington (G-5156)

36 ELECTRONIC AND OTHER ELECTRICAL EQUIPMENT AND COMPONENTS, EXCEPT COMPUTER

◆ Tdk USA Corporation .... D 516 535-2600
   Uniondale *(G-16300)*
Telephonics Corporation .... E 631 549-6000
   Huntington *(G-6683)*
▲ Telephonics Corporation .... A 631 755-7000
   Farmingdale *(G-5127)*
Three Five III-V Materials Inc .... F 212 213-8043
   New York *(G-12333)*
Tlsi Incorporated .... D 631 470-8880
   Huntington *(G-6688)*
Tony Baird Electronics Inc .... E 315 422-4430
   Syracuse *(G-16060)*
Torotron Corporation .... G 718 428-6992
   Fresh Meadows *(G-5446)*
▲ Trading Services International ..... F 212 501-0142
   New York *(G-12389)*
Tyco Electronics Corporation .... E 585 785-2500
   Rochester *(G-14737)*
▲ Ultralife Corporation .... B 315 332-7100
   Newark *(G-12745)*
Ultravolt Inc .... D 631 471-4444
   Ronkonkoma *(G-14996)*
Unison Industries LLC .... B 607 335-5000
   Norwich *(G-13039)*
▲ Vestal Electronic Devices LLC .... F 607 773-8461
   Endicott *(G-4833)*
Voices For All LLC .... G 518 261-1664
   Mechanicville *(G-8232)*
W D Technology Inc .... G 914 779-8738
   Eastchester *(G-4583)*
▲ Walter G Legge Company Inc .... G 914 737-5040
   Peekskill *(G-13485)*
Werlatone Inc .... E 845 278-2220
   Patterson *(G-13446)*
Xedit Corp .... G 718 380-1592
   Queens Village *(G-13985)*

3691 Storage Batteries

Amco Intl Mfg & Design Inc .... E 718 388-8668
   Brooklyn *(G-1598)*
Battery Energy Storage Systems ... G 518 256-7029
   Troy *(G-16227)*
▲ Battsco LLC .... E 516 586-6544
   Hicksville *(G-6327)*
Bren-Trnics Batteries Intl Inc .... G 631 499-5155
   Commack *(G-3825)*
Bren-Trnics Batteries Intl LLC .... E 631 499-5155
   Commack *(G-3826)*
▲ Bren-Tronics Inc .... C 631 499-5155
   Commack *(G-3827)*
China Lithium Technologies .... E 212 391-2688
   New York *(G-9599)*
El-Don Battery Post Inc .... G 716 627-3697
   Hamburg *(G-5923)*
Ener1 Inc .... E 212 920-3500
   New York *(G-10036)*
Exide Technologies .... G 585 344-0656
   Batavia *(G-631)*
Hrg Group Inc .... E 212 906-8555
   New York *(G-10524)*
Johnson Controls Inc .... C 585 724-2232
   Rochester *(G-14464)*
New Energy Systems Group .... C 917 573-0302
   New York *(G-11385)*
Synergy Digital .... F 718 643-2742
   Brooklyn *(G-2636)*
▲ Ultralife Corporation .... B 315 332-7100
   Newark *(G-12745)*
▲ W & W Manufacturing Co .... F 516 942-0011
   Deer Park *(G-4225)*

3692 Primary Batteries: Dry & Wet

▲ Bren-Tronics Inc .... C 631 499-5155
   Commack *(G-3827)*
Electrochem Solutions Inc .... E 716 759-5800
   Clarence *(G-3660)*
Empire Scientific .... G 630 510-8636
   Deer Park *(G-4140)*
Shad Industries Inc .... G 631 504-6028
   Yaphank *(G-17402)*
▲ TAe Trans Atlantic Elec Inc .... E 631 595-9206
   Deer Park *(G-4216)*

3694 Electrical Eqpt For Internal Combustion Engines

▲ ARC Systems Inc .... E 631 582-8020
   Hauppauge *(G-6023)*
▲ Autel US Inc .... G 631 923-2620
   Farmingdale *(G-4948)*
Con Rel Auto Electric Inc .... E 518 356-1646
   Schenectady *(G-15245)*
Cummins Inc .... B 812 377-5000
   Jamestown *(G-6986)*
Delphi Automotive Systems LLC ... A 585 359-6000
   West Henrietta *(G-16876)*
Eastern Unit Exch Rmnfacturing .... F 718 739-7113
   Floral Park *(G-5203)*
Eluminocity US Inc .... G 651 528-1165
   New York *(G-10016)*
Eraser Company Inc .... C 315 454-3237
   Mattydale *(G-8212)*
Ieh FM Holdings LLC .... E 212 702-4300
   New York *(G-10559)*
▲ Karlyn Industries Inc .... F 845 351-2249
   Southfields *(G-15556)*
▲ Kearney-National Inc .... E 212 661-4600
   New York *(G-10828)*
◆ Leviton Manufacturing Co Inc .... B 631 812-6000
   Melville *(G-8334)*
▲ Magnum Shielding Corporation .. E 585 381-9957
   Pittsford *(G-13568)*
Martinez Specialties Inc .... G 607 898-3053
   Groton *(G-5900)*
▲ Nas-Tra Automotive Inds Inc ...... C 631 225-1225
   Lindenhurst *(G-7474)*
Prestolite Electric Inc .... C 585 492-2278
   Arcade *(G-399)*
Sopark Corp .... C 716 822-0434
   Buffalo *(G-3191)*
▲ Standard Motor Products Inc ..... B 718 392-0200
   Long Island City *(G-7884)*
▲ Taro Manufacturing Company Inc . F ... 315 252-9430
   Auburn *(G-523)*
▲ Zenith Autoparts Corp .... E 845 344-1382
   Middletown *(G-8471)*
▲ Zierick Manufacturing Corp .... D 800 882-8020
   Mount Kisco *(G-8648)*

3695 Recording Media

Aarfid LLC .... G 716 992-3999
   Eden *(G-4585)*
BMA Media Services Inc .... E 585 385-2060
   Rochester *(G-14238)*
Connectiva Systems Inc .... B 646 722-8741
   New York *(G-9702)*
Continuity Software Inc .... E 646 216-8628
   New York *(G-9711)*
Dm2 Media LLC .... E 646 419-4357
   New York *(G-9889)*
Escholar LLC .... F 914 989-2900
   White Plains *(G-17105)*
Infinite Software Solutions .... F 718 982-1315
   Staten Island *(G-15687)*
John J Richardson .... F 516 538-6339
   Lawrence *(G-7392)*
▲ L & M Optical Disc LLC .... D 718 649-3500
   New York *(G-10899)*
Longtail Studios Inc .... E 646 443-8146
   New York *(G-11027)*
Medicine Rules Inc .... G 631 334-5395
   East Setauket *(G-4486)*
Multi-Health Systems Inc .... D 800 456-3003
   Cheektowaga *(G-3580)*
Next Big Sound Inc .... G 646 657-9837
   New York *(G-11421)*
Orpheo USA Corp .... G 212 464-8255
   New York *(G-11527)*
Phreesia New York .... B 888 654-7473
   New York *(G-11654)*
▲ Professional Tape Corporation ... G 516 656-5519
   Glen Cove *(G-5625)*
◆ Sony Corporation of America .... C 212 833-8000
   New York *(G-12132)*
Sony Dadc US Inc .... B 212 833-8800
   New York *(G-12133)*
▲ Stamper Technology Inc .... G 585 247-8370
   Rochester *(G-14700)*
VDO Lab Inc .... G 914 949-1741
   White Plains *(G-17179)*
West African Movies .... G 718 731-2190
   Bronx *(G-1494)*

3699 Electrical Machinery, Eqpt & Splys, NEC

303 Contracting Inc .... E 716 896-2122
   Orchard Park *(G-13249)*
331 Holding Inc .... E 585 924-1740
   Victor *(G-16458)*
3krf LLC .... G 516 208-6824
   Oceanside *(G-13071)*
A & S Electric .... G 212 228-2030
   Brooklyn *(G-1529)*
Aabacs Group Inc .... F 718 961-3577
   College Point *(G-3774)*
Advance Energy Systems NY LLC . G . 315 735-5125
   Utica *(G-3694)*
Advanced Mfg Techniques .... G 518 877-8560
   Clifton Park *(G-3694)*
Advanced Photonics Inc .... G 631 471-3693
   Ronkonkoma *(G-14855)*
Aeb Sapphire Corp .... G 516 586-8232
   Massapequa *(G-8178)*
▲ Albatros North America Inc .... E 518 381-7100
   Ballston Spa *(G-590)*
Alexy Associates Inc .... E 845 482-3000
   Bethel *(G-859)*
▲ All Shore Industries Inc .... F 718 720-0018
   Staten Island *(G-15634)*
Allcom Electric Corp .... G 914 803-0433
   Yonkers *(G-17411)*
Altaquip LLC .... E 631 580-4740
   Ronkonkoma *(G-14867)*
◆ Altronix Corp .... D 718 567-8181
   Brooklyn *(G-1596)*
American Avionic Tech Corp .... E 631 924-8200
   Medford *(G-8234)*
Amertac Holdings Inc .... C 610 336-1330
   Monsey *(G-8567)*
Ametek Inc .... D 585 263-7700
   Rochester *(G-14202)*
AMP-Line Corp .... F 845 623-3288
   West Nyack *(G-16910)*
Analog Digital Technology LLC ..... C 585 698-1845
   Rochester *(G-14203)*
Assa Abloy Entrance Systems US . E ... 315 492-6600
   East Syracuse *(G-4507)*
▲ Atlantic Electronic Tech LLC ...... G 800 296-2177
   Brooklyn *(G-1646)*
Atlas Switch Co Inc .... E 516 222-6280
   Garden City *(G-5495)*
Audible Difference Inc .... F 212 662-4848
   Brooklyn *(G-1651)*
Audible Difference Inc .... F 212 662-4848
   Brooklyn *(G-1652)*
Avalonics Inc .... G 516 238-7074
   Levittown *(G-7424)*
B & H Electronics Corp .... E 845 782-5000
   Monroe *(G-8549)*
Bare Beauty Laser Hair Removal .. G 718 278-2273
   New York *(G-9318)*
▲ BDB Technologies LLC .... G 800 921-4270
   Brooklyn *(G-1675)*
▲ Binghamton Simulator Co Inc .... E 607 321-2980
   Binghamton *(G-895)*
Bombardier Trnsp Holdings USA .. D 607 776-4791
   Bath *(G-654)*
Branson Ultrasonics Corp .... E 585 624-8000
   Honeoye Falls *(G-6525)*
▲ Bren-Tronics Inc .... C 631 499-5155
   Commack *(G-3827)*
BSC Associates LLC .... F 607 321-2980
   Binghamton *(G-899)*
▲ Buffalo Filter LLC .... D 716 835-7000
   Lancaster *(G-7307)*
C & G Video Systems Inc .... G 315 452-1490
   Liverpool *(G-7513)*
Car Essentials Inc .... E 518 745-1300
   Queensbury *(G-13994)*
▲ Castle Power Solutions LLC ...... G 518 743-1000
   South Glens Falls *(G-15523)*
Cathay Global Co Inc .... G 718 229-0920
   Bayside Hills *(G-780)*
Century Systems Ltd .... G 718 543-5991
   Bronx *(G-1294)*
Ces Industries Inc .... E 631 782-7088
   Islandia *(G-6790)*
Comsec Ventures International ..... G 518 523-1600
   Lake Placid *(G-7273)*
▲ Cooper Crouse-Hinds LLC .... B 315 477-7000
   Syracuse *(G-15908)*
Cooper Industries LLC .... E 315 477-7000
   Syracuse *(G-15909)*
Cooper Power Systems LLC .... B 716 375-7100
   Olean *(G-13140)*
Cooperfriedman Elc Sup Co Inc .... G 718 269-4906
   Long Island City *(G-7704)*
▲ Crysta-Lyn Chemical Company . G 607 296-4721
   Binghamton *(G-905)*
Custom Sound and Video .... E 585 424-5000
   Rochester *(G-14296)*

Employee Codes: A=Over 500 employees, B=251-500
C=101-250, D=51-100, E=20-50, F=10-19, G=5-9

CVI Laser LLC .... D 585 244-7220
Rochester (G-14297)
Da Electric .... E 347 270-3422
Bronx (G-1309)
Dahill Distributors Inc .... G 347 371-9453
Brooklyn (G-1833)
Denmar Electric .... F 845 624-4430
Nanuet (G-8755)
Detekion Security Systems Inc .... F 607 729-7179
Vestal (G-16447)
Dorsey Metrology Intl Inc .... E 845 229-2929
Poughkeepsie (G-13895)
▲ Dyson-Kissner-Moran Corp .... E 212 661-4600
Poughkeepsie (G-13896)
Eastco Manufacturing Corp .... F 914 738-5667
Pelham (G-13490)
Eaton Crouse-Hinds .... C 315 477-7000
Syracuse (G-15931)
Edo LLC .... A 631 630-4200
Amityville (G-286)
Emco Electric Services LLC .... G 212 420-9766
New York (G-10022)
▲ Emcom Inc .... D 315 255-5300
Auburn (G-493)
Empire Plastics Inc .... E 607 754-9132
Endwell (G-4835)
▲ Euchner USA Inc .... F 315 701-0315
East Syracuse (G-4528)
Evergreen High Voltage LLC .... G 281 814-9973
Lake Placid (G-7274)
Exfo Burleigh Pdts Group Inc .... D 585 301-1530
Canandaigua (G-3345)
Eyelock Corporation .... F 914 619-5570
New York (G-10112)
Eyelock LLC .... G 855 393-5625
New York (G-10113)
EZ Lift Operator Corp .... F 845 356-1676
Spring Valley (G-15584)
Fairview Bell and Intercom .... G 718 627-8621
Brooklyn (G-1953)
◆ Fiber Instrument Sales Inc .... C 315 736-2206
Oriskany (G-13309)
Fire Fox Security Corp .... G 917 981-9280
Brooklyn (G-1974)
Forte Network .... E 631 390-9050
East Northport (G-4436)
Full Circle Studios LLC .... G 716 875-7740
Buffalo (G-2960)
FWC Networks Inc .... F 718 408-1558
Brooklyn (G-2009)
G X Electric Corporation .... E 212 921-0400
New York (G-10233)
Gb Group Inc .... G 212 594-3748
New York (G-10251)
General Elc Capitl Svcs Inc .... G 315 554-2000
Skaneateles (G-15461)
▲ Gerome Technologies Inc .... D 518 463-1324
Menands (G-8372)
Green Island Power Authority .... F 518 273-0661
Green Island (G-5856)
Guardian Systems Tech Inc .... F 716 481-5597
East Aurora (G-4372)
▲ Hampton Technologies LLC .... E 631 924-1335
Medford (G-8248)
◆ Hawk-I Security Inc .... G 631 656-1056
Hauppauge (G-6092)
◆ Hergo Ergonomic Support .... E 718 894-0639
Maspeth (G-8143)
Highlander Realty Inc .... E 914 235-8073
New Rochelle (G-8911)
Home Depot USA Inc .... C 845 561-6540
Newburgh (G-12761)
Htf Components Inc .... G 914 703-6795
White Plains (G-17123)
▲ Iba Industrial Inc .... E 631 254-6800
Edgewood (G-4600)
Iconix Inc .... F 516 307-1324
Mineola (G-8515)
Ingham Industries Inc .... G 631 242-2493
Holbrook (G-6451)
Innovative Video Tech Inc .... F 516 840-2587
Hauppauge (G-6098)
▲ Isolation Technology Inc .... G 631 253-3314
West Babylon (G-16796)
Issco Corporation .... E 212 732-8748
Garden City (G-5512)
▲ Itin Scale Co Inc .... E 718 336-5900
Brooklyn (G-2120)
J H M Engineering .... E 718 871-1810
Brooklyn (G-2123)

▲ Kinetic Marketing Inc .... G 212 620-0600
New York (G-10852)
Knf Clean Room Products Corp .... E 631 588-7000
Ronkonkoma (G-14923)
▲ Koregon Enterprises Inc .... G 450 218-6836
Champlain (G-3543)
L-3 Cmmnctons Ntronix Holdings .... D 212 697-1111
New York (G-10904)
L-3 Communications Corporation .... D 607 721-5465
Kirkwood (G-7234)
Laser Consultants Inc .... G 631 423-4905
Huntington (G-6667)
Lasermax Inc .... D 585 272-5420
Rochester (G-14474)
▼ Levition Manufacturing Co .... E 631 812-6000
Melville (G-8333)
Lucas Electric .... G 516 809-8619
Seaford (G-15345)
Lyn Jo Enterprises Ltd .... G 716 753-2776
Mayville (G-8217)
Madison Electric .... F 718 358-4121
Cambria Heights (G-3303)
Magic Tech Co Ltd .... G 516 539-7944
West Hempstead (G-16859)
Manhattan Scientifics Inc .... G 212 541-2405
New York (G-11132)
Manhole Brrier SEC Systems Inc .... E 516 741-1032
Kew Gardens (G-7165)
Manor Electric Supply Corp .... F 347 312-2521
Brooklyn (G-2263)
Manufacturing Solutions Inc .... E 585 235-3320
Rochester (G-14494)
Mitsubishi Elc Pwr Pdts Inc .... G 516 962-2813
Melville (G-8337)
Mkj Communications Corp .... F 212 206-0072
New York (G-11286)
Multi Tech Electric .... F 718 606-2695
Woodside (G-17339)
◆ Napco Security Tech Inc .... B 631 842-9400
Amityville (G-314)
National Security Systems Inc .... E 516 627-2222
Manhasset (G-8063)
Navitar Inc .... D 585 359-4000
Rochester (G-14530)
Nbn Technologies LLC .... G 585 355-5556
Rochester (G-14531)
▲ Ncc Ny LLC .... E 718 943-7000
Brooklyn (G-2355)
News/Sprts Microwave Rentl Inc .... E 619 670-0572
New York (G-11419)
Nk Electric LLC .... G 914 271-0222
Croton On Hudson (G-4065)
Northrop Grumman Intl Trdg Inc .... G 716 626-7233
Buffalo (G-3096)
▲ OEM Solutions Inc .... G 716 864-9324
Clarence (G-3667)
Optimum Applied Systems Inc .... F 845 471-3333
Poughkeepsie (G-13924)
▲ Parabit Systems Inc .... E 516 378-4800
Roosevelt (G-15008)
▲ Piller Usa Inc .... E 845 695-6600
Middletown (G-8456)
Pinpoint Systems Intl Inc .... D 631 775-2100
Bellport (G-838)
▲ Promptus Electronic Hdwr Inc .... E 914 699-4700
Mount Vernon (G-8721)
▲ Protex International Corp .... D 631 563-4250
Bohemia (G-1124)
Rbw Studio LLC .... E 212 388-1621
Brooklyn (G-2481)
Robotic Directions .... G 585 453-9417
Rochester (G-14631)
Rockwell Collins Simulation .... D 607 352-1298
Binghamton (G-947)
Rodale Wireless Inc .... E 631 231-0044
Hauppauge (G-6179)
Ross Electronics Ltd .... E 718 569-6643
Haverstraw (G-6240)
Schuler-Haas Electric Corp .... E 607 936-3514
Painted Post (G-13393)
▲ Scorpion Security Products Inc .... G 607 724-9999
Binghamton (G-949)
Securevue Inc .... G 631 587-5850
West Islip (G-16906)
Security Defense System .... G 718 357-6200
Whitestone (G-17214)
▲ Security Dynamics Inc .... F 631 392-1701
Bohemia (G-1130)
Sensor Films Incorporated .... E 585 738-3500
Victor (G-16501)

▲ Sima Technologies LLC .... G 412 828-9130
Hauppauge (G-6191)
Simulaids Inc .... D 845 679-2475
Saugerties (G-15194)
Skae Power Solutions LLC .... E 845 365-9103
Palisades (G-13402)
Smithers Tools & Mch Pdts Inc .... D 845 876-3063
Rhinebeck (G-14058)
▲ Sonicor Inc .... F 631 920-6555
West Babylon (G-16830)
▲ Spirent Inc .... G 631 208-0680
Riverhead (G-14157)
Striano Electric Co Inc .... E 516 408-4969
Garden City Park (G-5543)
Sunwire Electric Corp .... G 718 456-7500
Brooklyn (G-2623)
T & G Wholesale Electric Corp .... G 585 396-9690
Canandaigua (G-3358)
T Jn Electric .... F 917 560-0981
Mahopac (G-8002)
T Jn Electric Inc .... G 845 628-6970
Mahopac (G-8003)
Tectran Inc .... G 800 776-5549
Cheektowaga (G-3591)
Teledyne Optech Inc .... F 585 427-8310
West Henrietta (G-16897)
Telephonics Corporation .... G 631 470-8838
Huntington (G-6684)
Telephonics Corporation .... D 631 755-7000
Farmingdale (G-5128)
Telephonics Corporation .... D 631 470-8800
Huntington (G-6686)
Teltech Security Corp .... G 718 871-8800
Brooklyn (G-2654)
Tory Electric .... G 914 292-5036
Bedford (G-798)
Triborough Electric .... G 718 321-2144
Whitestone (G-17217)
▲ Trident Precision Mfg Inc .... D 585 265-2010
Webster (G-16738)
Triton Infosys Inc .... E 877 308-2388
New York (G-12406)
U E Systems Incorporated .... E 914 592-1220
Elmsford (G-4790)
Uncharted Play Inc .... E 646 675-7783
New York (G-12447)
United Technologies Corp .... B 866 788-5095
Pittsford (G-13574)
Uptek Solutions .... F 631 256-5565
Bohemia (G-1153)
▲ V E Power Door Co Inc .... E 631 231-4500
Brentwood (G-1201)
Verifyme Inc .... G 212 994-7002
New York (G-12522)
▲ Videotec Security Incorporated .... G 518 825-0020
Plattsburgh (G-13706)
Werner Brothers Electric Inc .... G 518 377-3056
Rexford (G-14055)
Windowman Inc (usa) .... G 718 246-2626
Brooklyn (G-2758)
Wired Up Electric Inc .... G 845 878-3122
Pawling (G-13453)
▲ Z-Axis Inc .... D 315 548-5000
Phelps (G-13539)

37 TRANSPORTATION EQUIPMENT

3711 Motor Vehicles & Car Bodies

AB Fire Inc .... G 917 416-6444
Brooklyn (G-1545)
Air Flow Manufacturing .... F 607 733-8284
Elmira (G-4669)
Antiques & Collectible Autos .... G 716 825-3990
Buffalo (G-2813)
Antonicelli Vito Race Car .... G 716 684-2205
Buffalo (G-2814)
Armor Dynamics Inc .... F 845 658-9200
Kingston (G-7178)
▲ Auto Sport Designs Inc .... F 631 425-1555
Huntington Station (G-6697)
Brothers-In-Lawn Property .... G 716 279-6191
Tonawanda (G-16149)
CIC International Ltd .... D 212 213-0089
Brooklyn (G-1779)
Conti Auto Body Corp .... G 516 921-6435
Syosset (G-15816)
▲ Daimler Buses North Amer Inc .... A 315 768-8101
Oriskany (G-13308)
Dejana Trck Utility Eqp Co LLC .... C 631 544-9000
Kings Park (G-7170)

Dejana Trck Utility Eqp Co LLC ....E 631 549-0944
Huntington *(G-6660)*
Empire Coachworks Intl LLC ....D 732 257-7981
Suffern *(G-15789)*
Fiberglass Replacement Parts..............F 716 893-6471
Buffalo *(G-2946)*
◆ **Global Fire Corporation** ....E 888 320-1799
New York *(G-10316)*
JP Bus & Truck Repair Ltd....................F 516 767-2700
Port Washington *(G-13830)*
▲ **Jtekt Torsen North America** ....F 585 464-5000
Rochester *(G-14465)*
Leonard Bus Sales Inc ....G....... 607 467-3100
Rome *(G-14819)*
Madrid Fire District................................G....... 315 322-4346
Madrid *(G-7995)*
Marcovicci-Wenz Engineering...............G....... 631 467-9040
Ronkonkoma *(G-14938)*
◆ **Medical Coaches Incorporated** ....E 607 432-1333
Oneonta *(G-13188)*
Pcb Coach Builders Corp.......................G....... 718 897-7606
Rego Park *(G-14038)*
Prevost Car US Inc.................................C 518 957-2052
Plattsburgh *(G-13689)*
▲ **Ranger Design Us Inc**........................E 800 565-5321
Ontario *(G-13211)*
Roberts Nichols Fire Apparatus ....G....... 518 431-1945
Waterford *(G-16620)*
Sabre Enterprises Inc............................G....... 315 430-3127
Syracuse *(G-16029)*
Scehenvus Fire Dist...............................D 607 638-9017
Schenevus *(G-15315)*
Smart Systems Inc................................E 607 776-5380
Bath *(G-662)*
Sutphen Corporation.............................E 845 583-4720
White Lake *(G-17071)*
Tee Pee Auto Sales Corp.......................F 516 338-9333
Westbury *(G-17030)*
Tesla Motors Inc....................................A 212 206-1204
New York *(G-12304)*
Transprttion Collaborative Inc...............E 845 988-2333
Warwick *(G-16597)*
Troyer Inc...F 585 352-5590
Rochester *(G-14732)*
Wendys Auto Express Inc......................G....... 845 624-6100
Nanuet *(G-8762)*

3713 Truck & Bus Bodies

▲ **Abasco Inc**..E 716 649-4790
Hamburg *(G-5918)*
Able Weldbuilt Industries Inc.................F 631 643-9700
Deer Park *(G-4085)*
◆ **Brunner International Inc**..................C 585 798-6000
Medina *(G-8268)*
▲ **Concrete Mixer Supplycom Inc** ....G....... 716 375-5565
Olean *(G-13139)*
Conti Auto Body Corp ....G....... 516 921-6435
Syosset *(G-15816)*
▲ **Daimler Buses North Amer Inc** ....A 315 768-8101
Oriskany *(G-13308)*
Demartini Oil Equipment Svc.................G....... 518 463-5752
Glenmont *(G-5667)*
Donver Incorporated..............................F 716 945-1910
Kill Buck *(G-7166)*
Eastern Welding Inc...............................G....... 631 727-0306
Riverhead *(G-14142)*
Ekostinger Inc ....F 585 739-0450
Rochester *(G-14342)*
Fiberglass Replacement Parts..............F 716 893-6471
Buffalo *(G-2946)*
General Welding & Fabg Inc ....G....... 585 697-7660
Rochester *(G-14392)*
Jeffersonville Volunteer ....E 845 482-3110
Jeffersonville *(G-7059)*
Kurtz Truck Equipment Inc ....F 607 849-3468
Marathon *(G-8084)*
Marros Equipment & Trucks ....F 315 539-8702
Waterloo *(G-16630)*
Premium Bldg Components Inc ....E 518 885-0194
Ballston Spa *(G-607)*
Renaldos Sales and Service Ctr............G....... 716 337-3760
North Collins *(G-12931)*
Rexford Services Inc ....G....... 716 366-6671
Dunkirk *(G-4349)*
▲ **Tectran Mfg Inc**..................................D 800 776-5549
Buffalo *(G-3211)*
Unicell Body Company Inc....................E 716 853-8628
Buffalo *(G-3231)*
Unicell Body Company Inc....................F 716 853-8628
Schenectady *(G-15307)*
Unicell Body Company Inc....................F 585 424-2660
Rochester *(G-14741)*
USA Body Inc ....G....... 315 852-6123
De Ruyter *(G-4082)*
Weld-Built Body Co Inc ....E 631 643-9700
Wyandanch *(G-17378)*

3714 Motor Vehicle Parts & Access

4bumpers Llc..F 212 721-9600
New York *(G-8976)*
A-Line Technologies Inc.........................F 607 772-2439
Binghamton *(G-884)*
▲ **Abasco Inc**..E 716 649-4790
Hamburg *(G-5918)*
Agri Services Co ....G....... 716 937-6618
Alden *(G-173)*
Allomatic Products Company................G....... 516 775-0330
Floral Park *(G-5192)*
▲ **Alloy Metal Products LLC**..................F 315 676-2405
Central Square *(G-3515)*
American Auto ACC Incrporation..........E 718 886-6600
Flushing *(G-5226)*
American Engnred Cmponents Inc.......D 516 742-8386
Carle Place *(G-3385)*
American Refuse Supply Inc ....G....... 718 893-8157
Bronx *(G-1273)*
Anchor Commerce Trading Corp ....G....... 516 881-3485
Atlantic Beach *(G-468)*
Apsis USA Inc ....F 631 421-6800
Farmingdale *(G-4944)*
▲ **ARC Remanufacturing Inc**..................D 718 728-0701
Long Island City *(G-7665)*
Auburn Bearing & Mfg Inc......................G....... 315 986-7600
Macedon *(G-7982)*
Automotive Accessories Group ....B 212 736-8100
New York *(G-9268)*
◆ **Automotive Filters Mfg Inc** ....F 631 435-1010
Bohemia *(G-1020)*
Axle Express ....E 518 347-2220
Schenectady *(G-15233)*
▲ **Axle Teknology LLC**...........................G....... 631 423-3044
Huntington *(G-6655)*
Bam Enterprises Inc..............................G....... 716 773-7634
Grand Island *(G-5753)*
Banner Transmission & Eng Co ....F 516 221-9459
Bellmore *(G-814)*
Bigbee Steel and Tank Company ....E 518 273-0801
Watervliet *(G-16679)*
▲ **Biltron Automotive Products** ....E 631 928-8613
Port Jeff STA *(G-13763)*
Borgwarner Inc.......................................E 607 257-1800
Ithaca *(G-6824)*
▲ **Borgwarner Morse TEC Inc**...............B 607 257-6700
Ithaca *(G-6826)*
Borgwarner Morse TEC Inc....................D 607 266-5111
Ithaca *(G-6827)*
Borgwarner Morse TEC Inc....................D 607 257-6700
Cortland *(G-4015)*
Borgwarner Morse TEC Inc....................D 607 257-6700
Ithaca *(G-6828)*
Car-Go Industries Inc ....G....... 718 472-1443
Woodside *(G-17323)*
Classic & Performance Spc ....E 716 759-1800
Lancaster *(G-7310)*
▲ **CRS Remanufacturing Co Inc**.............F 718 739-1720
Jamaica *(G-6908)*
Cubic Trnsp Systems Inc ....F 212 255-1810
New York *(G-9764)*
Cummins Inc ....A 716 456-2111
Lakewood *(G-7290)*
Cummins Inc ....B 812 377-5000
Jamestown *(G-6986)*
Curtis L Maclean L C ....B 716 898-7800
Buffalo *(G-2895)*
▲ **Custom Sitecom LLC**..........................F 631 420-4238
Farmingdale *(G-4971)*
Deer Park Driveshaft & Hose ....G....... 631 667-4091
Deer Park *(G-4127)*
Delphi Automotive LLP ....G....... 716 438-4886
Amherst *(G-237)*
Delphi Automotive Systems LLC ....C 585 359-6000
West Henrietta *(G-16875)*
Delphi Automotive Systems LLC ....A 585 359-6000
West Henrietta *(G-16876)*
Delphi Automotive Systems LLC ....E 585 359-6000
West Henrietta *(G-16877)*
Delphi Thermal Systems ....F 716 439-2454
Lockport *(G-7579)*
Dennys Drive Shaft Service ....G....... 716 875-6640
Kenmore *(G-7146)*
Dmic Inc...F 716 743-4360
North Tonawanda *(G-12969)*
Drive Shaft Shop Inc..............................F 631 348-1818
Hauppauge *(G-6068)*
Electron Top Mfg Co Inc........................E 718 846-7400
Richmond Hill *(G-14072)*
Electronic Machine Parts LLC ....F 631 434-3700
Hauppauge *(G-6070)*
Exten II LLC ....F 716 895-2214
Buffalo *(G-2942)*
▲ **Extreme Auto Accessories Corp** ......F 718 978-6722
South Ozone Park *(G-15533)*
Factory Wheel Warehouse Inc...............G....... 516 605-2131
Plainview *(G-13601)*
▲ **Fast By Gast Inc**..................................G....... 716 773-1536
Grand Island *(G-5757)*
▲ **Fcmp Inc** ....F 716 692-4623
Tonawanda *(G-16160)*
▲ **Fuel Systems Solutions Inc** ....E 646 502-7170
New York *(G-10220)*
General Motors LLC...............................B 315 764-2000
Massena *(G-8195)*
◆ **Gleason Works** ....A 585 473-1000
Rochester *(G-14408)*
GM Components Holdings LLC............C 716 439-2011
Lockport *(G-7589)*
GM Components Holdings LLC............B 585 647-7000
Rochester *(G-14410)*
GM Components Holdings LLC............B 716 439-2463
Lockport *(G-7590)*
▲ **Interparts International Inc**...............E 516 576-2000
Plainview *(G-13610)*
▲ **ITT Enidine Inc** ....B 716 662-1900
Orchard Park *(G-13275)*
Johnson Controls Inc.............................C 585 724-2232
Rochester *(G-14464)*
Jt Precision Inc ....E 716 795-3860
Barker *(G-613)*
▲ **Jtekt Torsen North America** ....F 585 464-5000
Rochester *(G-14465)*
K M Drive Line Inc..................................G....... 718 599-0628
Brooklyn *(G-2164)*
▲ **Karlyn Industries Inc** ....F 845 351-2249
Southfields *(G-15556)*
Katikati Inc..G....... 585 678-1764
West Henrietta *(G-16883)*
▲ **Kearney-National Inc** ....F 212 661-4600
New York *(G-10828)*
▲ **Kerns Manufacturing Corp**..................C 718 784-4044
Long Island City *(G-7780)*
Kurtz Truck Equipment Inc ....F 607 849-3468
Marathon *(G-8084)*
◆ **Lee World Industries LLC**....................C 212 265-8866
New York *(G-10958)*
▼ **Magtrol Inc**...E 716 668-5555
Buffalo *(G-3055)*
Mahle Behr USA Inc...............................B 716 439-2011
Lockport *(G-7598)*
Mahle Industries Incorporated..............F 248 735-3623
Amherst *(G-251)*
Marcovicci-Wenz Engineering...............G....... 631 467-9040
Ronkonkoma *(G-14938)*
▲ **Motor Components LLC** ....D 607 737-8011
Elmira Heights *(G-4711)*
▲ **Nas-Tra Automotive Inds Inc**.............C 631 225-1225
Lindenhurst *(G-7474)*
Nassau Auto Remanufacturer ....G....... 516 485-4500
Hempstead *(G-6282)*
▼ **Norcatec LLC**.......................................E 516 222-7070
Garden City *(G-5524)*
Omega Industries & Development ....E 516 349-8010
Plainview *(G-13625)*
◆ **P & F Industries Inc** ....C 631 694-9800
Melville *(G-8346)*
▲ **Pall Corporation**...................................A 516 484-5400
Port Washington *(G-13852)*
Pall Corporation......................................A 607 753-6041
Cortland *(G-4035)*
Par-Foam Products Inc..........................C 716 855-2066
Buffalo *(G-3112)*
Parker-Hannifin Corporation..................D 248 628-6017
Lancaster *(G-7330)*
▲ **Parts Unlimited Inc** ....D 518 885-7500
Ballston Spa *(G-606)*
Performance Designed By Peters ....F 585 223-9062
Fairport *(G-4870)*
Phillip J Ortiz Manufacturing ....G....... 845 226-7030
Hopewell Junction *(G-6557)*
▲ **Powerflow Inc**.......................................D 716 892-1014
Buffalo *(G-3132)*

Pro Torque ....E 631 218-8700
Bohemia *(G-1122)*
Pro-Value Distribution Inc ....G 585 783-1461
Rochester *(G-14604)*
Protech Automation LLC ....G 585 344-3201
Batavia *(G-646)*
▲ Rosco Inc ....C 718 526-2601
Jamaica *(G-6948)*
◆ Rpb Distributors LLC ....G 914 244-3600
Mount Kisco *(G-8645)*
Secor Marketing Group Inc ....G 914 381-3600
Mamaroneck *(G-8046)*
Smith Metal Works Newark Inc ....E 315 331-1651
Newark *(G-12742)*
▲ Specialty Silicone Pdts Inc ....E 518 885-8826
Ballston Spa *(G-609)*
▲ Standard Motor Products Inc ....B 718 392-0200
Long Island City *(G-7884)*
Temper Corporation ....G 518 853-3467
Fonda *(G-5318)*
Terrys Transmission ....G 315 458-4333
North Syracuse *(G-12952)*
Tesla Motors Inc ....A 212 206-1204
New York *(G-12304)*
TI Group Auto Systems LLC ....G 315 568-7042
Seneca Falls *(G-15371)*
▲ Titanx Engine Cooling Inc ....B 716 665-7129
Jamestown *(G-7039)*
Transcedar Industries Ltd ....G 716 731-6442
Niagara Falls *(G-12884)*
Troyer Inc ....F 585 352-5590
Rochester *(G-14732)*
TRW Automotive Inc ....B 315 255-3311
Auburn *(G-525)*
Vehicle Safety Dept ....F 315 458-6683
Syracuse *(G-16066)*
▼ Whiting Door Mfg Corp ....B 716 542-5427
Akron *(G-30)*
▲ Wolo Mfg Corp ....E 631 242-0333
Deer Park *(G-4228)*
Yomiuri International Inc ....G 212 752-2196
New York *(G-12695)*
Zwack Incorporated ....E 518 733-5135
Stephentown *(G-15758)*

3715 Truck Trailers

◆ Blue Tee Corp ....G 212 598-0880
New York *(G-9422)*
Cross Country Mfg Inc ....F 607 656-4103
Greene *(G-5863)*
Cross Country Mfg Inc ....F 607 656-4103
Greene *(G-5864)*
Davis Trailer World LLC ....F 585 538-6640
York *(G-17505)*
Full Service Auto Body Inc ....F 718 831-9300
Floral Park *(G-5204)*
G L 7 Sales Plus Ltd ....G 631 696-8290
Coram *(G-3942)*
General Welding & Fabg Inc ....G 716 652-0033
Elma *(G-4649)*
Seneca Truck & Trailer Inc ....G 315 781-1100
Geneva *(G-5586)*
▼ Stone Well Bodies & Mch Inc ....F 315 497-3512
Genoa *(G-5590)*

3716 Motor Homes

Authority Transportation Inc ....F 888 933-1268
Dix Hills *(G-4291)*

3721 Aircraft

▲ Aip/Aerospace Holdings LLC ....G 212 916-8142
New York *(G-9065)*
Alliant Tchsystems Oprtons LLC ....E 631 737-6100
Ronkonkoma *(G-14863)*
Altius Aviation LLC ....G 315 455-7555
Syracuse *(G-15852)*
Atk Gasl Inc ....F 631 737-6100
Ronkonkoma *(G-14874)*
Barclay Tagg Racing ....E 631 404-8269
Floral Park *(G-5195)*
Boeing Company ....A 201 259-9400
New York *(G-9434)*
▲ Calspan Corporation ....C 716 631-6955
Buffalo *(G-2864)*
Calspan Corporation ....E 716 236-1040
Niagara Falls *(G-12800)*
CIC International Ltd ....D 212 213-0089
Brooklyn *(G-1779)*
Drone Usa Inc ....G 212 220-8795
New York *(G-9930)*
Grumman Field Support Services ....D 516 575-0574
Bethpage *(G-867)*
▲ Joka Industries Inc ....E 631 589-0444
Bohemia *(G-1083)*
Lesly Enterprise & Associates ....G 631 988-1301
Deer Park *(G-4165)*
Lockheed Martin Corporation ....E 716 297-1000
Niagara Falls *(G-12844)*
Lockheed Martin Corporation ....G 212 953-1510
New York *(G-11020)*
Lockheed Martin Corporation ....E 315 456-1548
Liverpool *(G-7530)*
Lockheed Martin Corporation ....D 315 793-5800
New Hartford *(G-8807)*
Luminati Aerospace LLC ....F 631 574-2616
Calverton *(G-3293)*
M & H Research and Dev Corp ....G 607 734-2346
Beaver Dams *(G-793)*
Moog Inc ....B 716 655-3000
East Aurora *(G-4375)*
Northrop Grumman Systems Corp ....A 516 575-0574
Bethpage *(G-877)*
Northrop Grumman Systems Corp ....D 716 626-4600
Buffalo *(G-3097)*
Northrop Grumman Systems Corp ....G 631 423-1014
Huntington *(G-6671)*
Pro Drones Usa LLC ....F 718 530-3558
New York *(G-11724)*
Sikorsky Aircraft Corporation ....D 585 424-1990
Rochester *(G-14687)*
Trium Strs-Lg Isld LLC ....D 516 997-5757
Westbury *(G-17036)*
Tsc LLC ....G 661 824-6609
New York *(G-12416)*

3724 Aircraft Engines & Engine Parts

Advanced Atomization Tech LLC ....B 315 923-2341
Clyde *(G-3725)*
▲ ARC Systems Inc ....E 631 582-8020
Hauppauge *(G-6023)*
B H Aircraft Company Inc ....D 631 580-9747
Ronkonkoma *(G-14877)*
Chromalloy American LLC ....E 845 230-7355
Orangeburg *(G-13222)*
Chromalloy Gas Turbine LLC ....C 845 359-2462
Orangeburg *(G-13223)*
Chromalloy Gas Turbine LLC ....E 845 692-8912
Middletown *(G-8430)*
Colonial Group LLC ....E 516 349-8010
Plainview *(G-13589)*
▲ Davis Aircraft Products Co Inc ....C 631 563-1500
Bohemia *(G-1050)*
▲ Dyna-Empire Inc ....C 516 222-2700
Garden City *(G-5500)*
Gb Aero Engine LLC ....B 914 925-9600
Rye *(G-15057)*
General Electric Company ....A 518 385-4022
Schenectady *(G-15257)*
General Electric Company ....E 518 385-7620
Niskayuna *(G-12895)*
Honeywell International Inc ....A 315 554-6643
Skaneateles Falls *(G-15470)*
Honeywell International Inc ....A 845 342-4400
Middletown *(G-8445)*
Honeywell International Inc ....A 212 964-5111
Melville *(G-8328)*
Howe Machine & Tool Corp ....F 516 931-5687
Bethpage *(G-868)*
▲ ITT Enidine Inc ....B 716 662-1900
Orchard Park *(G-13275)*
▲ Kerns Manufacturing Corp ....C 718 784-4044
Long Island City *(G-7780)*
Lourdes Industries Inc ....D 631 234-6600
Hauppauge *(G-6121)*
McGuigan Inc ....E 631 750-6222
Bohemia *(G-1103)*
Nell-Joy Industries Inc ....E 631 842-8989
Copiague *(G-3915)*
Omega Industries & Development ....E 516 349-8010
Plainview *(G-13625)*
Sequa Corporation ....E 813 434-4522
Orangeburg *(G-13246)*
SOS International LLC ....E 212 742-2410
New York *(G-12140)*
▲ Therm Incorporated ....C 607 272-8500
Ithaca *(G-6877)*
Triumph Actuation Systems LLC ....D 516 378-0162
Freeport *(G-5432)*
Triumph Group Inc ....D 516 997-5757
Westbury *(G-17037)*
Turbine Engine Comp Utica ....A 315 768-8070
Whitesboro *(G-17197)*
United Technologies Corp ....G 315 432-7849
East Syracuse *(G-4576)*

3728 Aircraft Parts & Eqpt, NEC

Aero Trades Mfg Corp ....E 516 746-3360
Mineola *(G-8489)*
Air Industries Group ....D 631 881-4920
Hauppauge *(G-6013)*
▲ Air Industries Machining Corp ....C 631 968-5000
Bay Shore *(G-667)*
▲ Alcoa Fastening Systems ....C 845 334-7203
Kingston *(G-7175)*
Alken Industries Inc ....D 631 467-2000
Ronkonkoma *(G-14859)*
Alro Machine Tool & Die Co Inc ....F 631 226-5020
Lindenhurst *(G-7453)*
Arkwin Industries Inc ....B 516 333-2640
Westbury *(G-16969)*
Armacel Armor Corporation ....E 805 384-1144
New York *(G-9204)*
▲ Astronics Corporation ....C 716 805-1599
East Aurora *(G-4366)*
Ausco Inc ....D 516 944-9882
Farmingdale *(G-4947)*
B & B Precision Components Inc ....G 631 273-3321
Ronkonkoma *(G-14876)*
B/E Aerospace Inc ....E 631 563-6400
Bohemia *(G-1022)*
Bar Fields Inc ....F 347 587-7795
Brooklyn *(G-1667)*
▲ Blair Industries Inc ....E 631 924-6600
Medford *(G-8236)*
Canfield Aerospace & Mar Inc ....E 631 648-1050
Ronkonkoma *(G-14884)*
Caravan International Corp ....G 212 223-7190
New York *(G-9522)*
Carleton Technologies Inc ....B 716 662-0006
Orchard Park *(G-13259)*
Cellular Empire Inc ....F 347 587-7795
Brooklyn *(G-1768)*
Circor Aerospace Inc ....D 631 737-1900
Hauppauge *(G-6045)*
▲ Cox & Company Inc ....C 212 366-0200
Plainview *(G-13593)*
CPI Aerostructures Inc ....B 631 586-5200
Edgewood *(G-4596)*
Crown Aircraft Lighting Inc ....G 718 767-3410
Whitestone *(G-17206)*
▲ Davis Aircraft Products Co Inc ....C 631 563-1500
Bohemia *(G-1050)*
Design/OI Inc ....F 631 474-5536
Port Jeff STA *(G-13766)*
▲ Dresser-Argus Inc ....G 718 643-1540
Brooklyn *(G-1880)*
Drt Power Systems LLC - Lane ....D 585 247-5940
Rochester *(G-14319)*
Ducommun Aerostructures NY Inc ....B 518 731-2791
Coxsackie *(G-4056)*
▲ Dyna-Empire Inc ....C 516 222-2700
Garden City *(G-5500)*
East/West Industries Inc ....E 631 981-5900
Ronkonkoma *(G-14896)*
Eastern Precision Machining ....G 631 286-4758
Bellport *(G-829)*
◆ Edo LLC ....G 631 630-4000
Amityville *(G-285)*
Engineered Metal Products Inc ....G 631 842-3780
Copiague *(G-3900)*
Enlighten Air Inc ....G 917 656-1248
New York *(G-10041)*
Ensil Technical Services Inc ....E 716 282-1020
Niagara Falls *(G-12814)*
Excelco Developments Inc ....E 716 934-2651
Silver Creek *(G-15448)*
Excelco/Newbrook Inc ....D 716 934-2644
Silver Creek *(G-15449)*
Fluid Mechanisms Hauppauge Inc ....E 631 234-0100
Hauppauge *(G-6078)*
GE Aviation Systems LLC ....C 631 467-5500
Bohemia *(G-1071)*
▲ GKN Aerospace Monitor Inc ....B 562 619-8558
Amityville *(G-289)*
◆ Gleason Works ....A 585 473-1000
Rochester *(G-14408)*
▲ Gny Equipment LLC ....F 631 667-1010
Bay Shore *(G-703)*
Goodrich Corporation ....C 315 838-1200
Rome *(G-14811)*

Handy Tool & Mfg Co Inc....................E....... 718 478-9203
Brooklyn *(G-2068)*
Hicksville Machine Works Corp.............F....... 516 931-1524
Hicksville *(G-6355)*
Honeywell International Inc...................B....... 516 577-2000
Melville *(G-8329)*
▲ **HSM Machine Works Inc**...................E....... 631 924-6600
Medford *(G-8250)*
Jac Usa Inc..G....... 212 841-7430
New York *(G-10685)*
Jamco Aerospace Inc............................E....... 631 586-7900
Deer Park *(G-4156)*
◆ **Jaquith Industries Inc**........................E....... 315 478-5700
Syracuse *(G-15966)*
Joldeson One Aerospace Inds..............D....... 718 848-7396
Ozone Park *(G-13380)*
Lai International Inc.............................D....... 763 780-0060
Green Island *(G-5858)*
Loar Group Inc..C....... 212 210-9348
New York *(G-11018)*
Magellan Aerospace NY Inc...................C....... 718 699-4000
Corona *(G-4001)*
Magellan Aerospace NY Inc...................C....... 631 589-2440
Bohemia *(G-1099)*
MD International Industries...................E....... 631 254-3100
Deer Park *(G-4173)*
Metadure Parts & Sales Inc..................F....... 631 249-2141
Farmingdale *(G-5050)*
◆ **Metal Dynamics Intl Corp**..................G....... 631 231-1153
Hauppauge *(G-6134)*
Milex Precision Inc................................F....... 631 595-2393
Bay Shore *(G-718)*
Min-Max Machine Ltd..............................F....... 631 585-4378
Ronkonkoma *(G-14943)*
Minutemen Precsn McHning Tool..........E....... 631 467-4900
Ronkonkoma *(G-14944)*
◆ **Moog Inc**...A....... 716 652-2000
Elma *(G-4651)*
Nassau Tool Works Inc............................E....... 631 643-0420
West Babylon *(G-16815)*
Norsk Titanium US Inc............................G....... 646 277-7514
New York *(G-11453)*
Omega Industries & Development........E....... 516 349-8010
Plainview *(G-13625)*
Parker-Hannifin Corporation..................C....... 631 231-3737
Clyde *(G-3730)*
▼ **Posimech Inc**..E....... 631 924-5959
Medford *(G-8258)*
Precision Cnc..G....... 631 847-3999
Deer Park *(G-4191)*
▲ **Precision Gear Incorporated**.............C....... 718 321-7200
College Point *(G-3802)*
Reese Manufacturing Inc.......................G....... 631 842-3780
Copiague *(G-3922)*
Ripi Precision Co Inc..............................F....... 631 694-2453
Farmingdale *(G-5100)*
S & L Aerospace Metals LLC..................D....... 718 326-1821
Flushing *(G-5289)*
Santa Fe Manufacturing Corp................G....... 631 234-0100
Hauppauge *(G-6183)*
Servotronics Inc......................................C....... 716 655-5990
Elma *(G-4655)*
▲ **Styles Aviation Inc**.............................G....... 845 677-8185
Lagrangeville *(G-7259)*
▼ **Sumner Industries Inc**........................F....... 631 666-7290
Bay Shore *(G-749)*
Superior Motion Controls Inc................E....... 516 420-2921
Farmingdale *(G-5120)*
Tangent Machine & Tool Corp...............E....... 631 249-3088
Farmingdale *(G-5124)*
Tdl Manufacturing Inc............................F....... 215 538-8820
Hauppauge *(G-6208)*
Tek Precision Co Ltd..............................E....... 631 242-0330
Deer Park *(G-4217)*
Tens Machine Company Inc..................E....... 631 981-0490
Holbrook *(G-6478)*
TPC Inc..G....... 315 438-8605
East Syracuse *(G-4572)*
Triumph Actuation Systems LLC..........D....... 516 378-0162
Freeport *(G-5432)*
US Milpack & Mfg Corp..........................G....... 718 342-1307
Brooklyn *(G-2714)*
Usairports Services Inc..........................E....... 585 527-6835
Rochester *(G-14749)*
Vosky Precision Machining Corp..........F....... 631 737-3200
Ronkonkoma *(G-15000)*
W J Albro Machine Works Inc...............G....... 631 345-0657
Yaphank *(G-17408)*
Wilco Industries Inc................................G....... 631 676-2593
Ronkonkoma *(G-15001)*
Young & Franklin Inc..............................D....... 315 457-3110
Liverpool *(G-7559)*

3731 Shipbuilding & Repairing

Alpha Marine Repair................................E....... 718 816-7150
Staten Island *(G-15636)*
Caddell Dry Dock & Repr Co Inc............C....... 718 442-2112
Staten Island *(G-15654)*
Cgsi Group LLC.......................................F....... 516 986-5503
Bronx *(G-1296)*
Clark Rigging & Rental Corp..................F....... 585 265-2910
Webster *(G-16717)*
◆ **Dragon Trading Inc**............................G....... 212 717-1496
New York *(G-9923)*
Electric Boat Corporation.......................D....... 518 884-1270
Ballston Spa *(G-596)*
Electric Boat Corporation.......................C....... 518 884-1596
Rock City Falls *(G-14778)*
Excelco Developments Inc....................E....... 716 934-2651
Silver Creek *(G-15448)*
Excelco/Newbrook Inc............................D....... 716 934-2644
Silver Creek *(G-15449)*
George G Sharp Inc................................E....... 212 732-2800
New York *(G-10281)*
Godfrey Prpeller Adjusting Svc.............G....... 718 768-3744
Brooklyn *(G-2035)*
Highland Museum & Lighthouse...........F....... 508 487-1121
Cairo *(G-3272)*
Huntington Ingalls Inc............................E....... 518 884-3834
Saratoga Springs *(G-15159)*
May Ship Repair Contg Corp..................E....... 718 442-9700
Staten Island *(G-15705)*
McQuilling Partners Inc..........................E....... 516 227-5718
Garden City *(G-5519)*
▼ **Metalcraft Marine Us Inc**....................F....... 315 501-4015
Cape Vincent *(G-3384)*
▲ **Moran Shipyard Corporation**..............C....... 718 981-5600
Staten Island *(G-15707)*
Moran Towing Corporation.....................G....... 718 981-5600
Staten Island *(G-15708)*
Port Everglades Machine Works...........F....... 516 367-2280
Plainview *(G-13630)*
▲ **Reynolds Shipyard Corporation**.......F....... 718 981-2800
Staten Island *(G-15731)*
▲ **Robert E Derecktor Inc**......................D....... 914 698-0962
Mamaroneck *(G-8045)*
Scarano Boat Building Inc.....................E....... 518 463-3401
Albany *(G-131)*
Standard Ascnsion Towers Group........D....... 716 681-2222
Depew *(G-4274)*
Steelways Inc..E....... 845 562-0860
Newburgh *(G-12780)*
▼ **Stidd Systems Inc**..............................E....... 631 477-2400
Greenport *(G-5877)*
United Ship Repair Inc............................F....... 718 237-2800
Brooklyn *(G-2702)*
Viking Mar Wldg Ship Repr LLC.............F....... 718 758-4116
Brooklyn *(G-2727)*
Weldrite Closures Inc.............................E....... 585 429-8790
Rochester *(G-14760)*

3732 Boat Building & Repairing

Allen Boat Co Inc.....................................G....... 716 842-0800
Buffalo *(G-2802)*
▼ **American Metalcraft Marine**...............G....... 315 686-9891
Clayton *(G-3684)*
▲ **AVS Laminates Inc**.............................E....... 631 286-2136
Bellport *(G-826)*
Cayuga Wooden Boatworks Inc............E....... 315 253-7447
Ithaca *(G-6830)*
Cellboat Development Corp..................G....... 800 973-4659
Melville *(G-8301)*
Coecles Hbr Marina & Boat Yard..........F....... 631 749-0856
Shelter Island *(G-15386)*
Eastern Welding Inc................................G....... 631 727-0306
Riverhead *(G-14142)*
Fantasy Glass Compan...........................G....... 845 786-5818
Stony Point *(G-15773)*
Gar Wood Custom Boats.........................G....... 518 494-2966
Brant Lake *(G-1173)*
Global Marine Power Inc........................E....... 631 208-2933
Calverton *(G-3291)*
▲ **Hacker Boat Company Inc**.................E....... 518 543-6731
Silver Bay *(G-15446)*
Hampton Shipyards Inc..........................F....... 631 653-6777
East Quogue *(G-4451)*
▲ **Jag Manufacturing Inc**........................E....... 518 762-9558
Johnstown *(G-7116)*
Katherine Blizniak...................................G....... 716 674-8545
West Seneca *(G-16950)*
▼ **Marathon Boat Group Inc**...................F....... 607 849-3211
Marathon *(G-8085)*
May Ship Repair Contg Corp..................E....... 718 442-9700
Staten Island *(G-15705)*
▼ **Metalcraft Marine Us Inc**....................F....... 315 501-4015
Cape Vincent *(G-3384)*
Mokai Manufacturing Inc.........................G....... 845 566-8287
Newburgh *(G-12768)*
▲ **Robert E Derecktor Inc**......................D....... 914 698-0962
Mamaroneck *(G-8045)*
Rocking The Boat Inc..............................F....... 718 466-5799
Bronx *(G-1442)*
Scarano Boatbuilding Inc.......................E....... 518 463-3401
Albany *(G-132)*
▼ **Stidd Systems Inc**..............................E....... 631 477-2400
Greenport *(G-5877)*
Superboats Inc..G....... 631 226-1761
Lindenhurst *(G-7487)*
Tumblehome Boatshop...........................G....... 518 623-5050
Warrensburg *(G-16581)*
Wooden Boatworks..................................G....... 631 477-6507
Greenport *(G-5878)*

3743 Railroad Eqpt

Acf Industries Holding Corp..................G....... 212 702-4363
New York *(G-9016)*
Alstom Signaling Inc...............................E....... 585 274-8700
Schenectady *(G-15229)*
Alstom Transportation Inc......................E....... 212 692-5353
New York *(G-9104)*
American Motive Power Inc...................E....... 585 335-3132
Dansville *(G-4075)*
▲ **Bombardier Mass Transit Corp**.........B....... 518 566-0150
Plattsburgh *(G-13655)*
Bombardier Transportation....................D....... 607 324-0216
Hornell *(G-6560)*
Buffalo Investors Corp...........................G....... 212 702-4363
New York *(G-9476)*
CAF Usa Inc...D....... 607 737-3004
Elmira Heights *(G-4709)*
▲ **Cox & Company Inc**...........................C....... 212 366-0200
Plainview *(G-13593)*
▲ **Eagle Bridge Machine & Tl Inc**..........E....... 518 686-4541
Eagle Bridge *(G-4356)*
Ebenezer Railcar Services Inc...............E....... 716 674-5650
West Seneca *(G-16943)*
Era-Contact Usa LLC................................F....... 631 524-5530
Hauppauge *(G-6072)*
General Electric Company......................E....... 845 567-7410
Newburgh *(G-12757)*
Gray Manufacturing Inds LLC................F....... 607 281-1325
Hornell *(G-6565)*
Highcrest Investors LLC.........................D....... 212 702-4323
New York *(G-10474)*
Horne Products Inc..................................G....... 631 293-0773
Farmingdale *(G-5007)*
Hudson Machine Works Inc....................C....... 845 279-1413
Brewster *(G-1221)*
▲ **Kawasaki Rail Car Inc**........................C....... 914 376-4700
Yonkers *(G-17459)*
Knorr Brake Company LLC......................G....... 518 561-1387
Plattsburgh *(G-13674)*
▲ **Knorr Brake Holding Corp**.................G....... 315 786-5356
Watertown *(G-16659)*
▲ **Knorr Brake Truck Systems Co**.........B....... 315 786-5200
Watertown *(G-16660)*
▲ **Koshii Maxelum America Inc**............E....... 845 471-0500
Poughkeepsie *(G-13911)*
▲ **New York Air Brake LLC**......................C....... 315 786-5219
Watertown *(G-16665)*
Niagara Cooler Inc...................................G....... 716 434-1235
Lockport *(G-7604)*
◆ **Peck & Hale LLC**.................................E....... 631 589-2510
West Sayville *(G-16937)*
Rand Machine Products Inc...................D....... 716 665-5217
Falconer *(G-4908)*
Semec Corp...F....... 518 825-0160
Plattsburgh *(G-13696)*
Starfire Holding Corporation.................E....... 914 614-7000
White Plains *(G-17169)*
▲ **Strato Transit Components LLC**......G....... 518 686-4541
Eagle Bridge *(G-4359)*
Transco Railway Products Inc...............E....... 716 824-1219
Blasdell *(G-967)*
▲ **Twinco Mfg Co Inc**..............................E....... 631 231-0022
Hauppauge *(G-6219)*
Westcode Incorporated...........................E....... 607 766-9881
Binghamton *(G-959)*
Westinghouse A Brake Tech Corp.........D....... 518 561-0044
Plattsburgh *(G-13708)*

SIC

Employee Codes: A=Over 500 employees, B=251-500
C=101-250, D=51-100, E=20-50, F=10-19, G=5-9

2017 Harris
New York Manufacturers Directory

855

37 TRANSPORTATION EQUIPMENT

Westinghouse A Brake Tech Corp..........F 914 347-8650
  Elmsford *(G-4793)*

3751 Motorcycles, Bicycles & Parts

▲ East Coast Cycle LLC ....G...... 631 780-5360
  Farmingdale *(G-4983)*
▲ Evelo Inc ....G...... 917 251-8743
  Rockaway Park *(G-14785)*
Golub Corporation ....D...... 518 943-3903
  Catskill *(G-3428)*
Golub Corporation ....D...... 518 899-6063
  Malta *(G-8020)*
Golub Corporation ....D...... 315 363-0679
  Oneida *(G-13155)*
Golub Corporation ....D...... 607 336-2588
  Norwich *(G-13028)*
Golub Corporation ....C...... 518 583-3697
  Saratoga Springs *(G-15154)*
Golub Corporation ....D...... 518 822-0076
  Hudson *(G-6615)*
Golub Corporation ....C...... 607 235-7243
  Binghamton *(G-920)*
Golub Corporation ....C...... 845 344-0327
  Middletown *(G-8443)*
Great American Bicycle LLC ....E...... 518 584-8100
  Saratoga Springs *(G-15155)*
Ihd Motorsports LLC ....F...... 979 690-1669
  Binghamton *(G-925)*
Indian Larry Legacy ....G...... 718 609-9184
  Brooklyn *(G-2102)*
▲ Jetson Electric Bikes LLC ....G...... 908 309-8880
  New York *(G-10722)*
Orange County Choppers Inc ....G...... 845 522-5200
  Newburgh *(G-12771)*
Palmer Industries Inc ....G...... 607 754-1954
  Endicott *(G-4824)*
◆ Piaggio Group Americas Inc ....E...... 212 380-4400
  New York *(G-11657)*
Pidyon Controls Inc ....G...... 212 683-9523
  New York *(G-11659)*
Price Chopper Operating Co ....F...... 518 562-3565
  Plattsburgh *(G-13690)*
Robs Cycle Supply ....G...... 315 292-6878
  Syracuse *(G-16025)*
Social Bicycles Inc ....E...... 917 746-7624
  Brooklyn *(G-2576)*
Sumax Cycle Products Inc ....F...... 315 768-1058
  Oriskany *(G-13315)*
Super Price Chopper Inc ....G...... 716 893-3323
  Buffalo *(G-3202)*
◆ Worksman Trading Corp ....F...... 718 322-2000
  Ozone Park *(G-13387)*

3761 Guided Missiles & Space Vehicles

Drt Power Systems LLC - Lane........D...... 585 247-5940
  Rochester *(G-14319)*
Edo LLC ....A...... 631 630-4200
  Amityville *(G-286)*
Lockheed Martin Corporation ....A...... 315 456-0123
  Liverpool *(G-7531)*
Lockheed Martin Corporation ....A...... 607 751-2000
  Owego *(G-13354)*
Lockheed Martin Corporation ....D...... 607 751-7434
  Owego *(G-13355)*
Lws Precision Deburring Inc ....F...... 631 580-0472
  Ronkonkoma *(G-14935)*

3769 Guided Missile/Space Vehicle Parts & Eqpt, NEC

Gb Aero Engine LLC ....B...... 914 925-9600
  Rye *(G-15057)*
▲ GKN Aerospace Monitor Inc ....B...... 562 619-8558
  Amityville *(G-289)*
▲ L-3 Cmmnctons Fgn Holdings Inc....E...... 212 697-1111
  New York *(G-10903)*
◆ L-3 Cmmunications Holdings Inc.....D...... 212 697-1111
  New York *(G-10905)*
L-3 Communications Corporation .....A...... 631 436-7400
  Hauppauge *(G-6108)*
L-3 Communications Corporation .....B...... 212 697-1111
  New York *(G-10906)*
Lockheed Martin Corporation ....E...... 716 297-1000
  Niagara Falls *(G-12844)*
Magellan Aerospace NY Inc ....C...... 718 699-4000
  Corona *(G-4001)*
◆ Moog Inc ....A...... 716 652-2000
  Elma *(G-4651)*
Saturn Industries Inc ....E...... 518 828-9956
  Hudson *(G-6632)*

Servotronics Inc.................................C...... 716 655-5990
  Elma *(G-4655)*
SKF USA Inc ....D...... 716 661-2869
  Falconer *(G-4912)*
Turbine Engine Comp Utica ....A...... 315 768-8070
  Whitesboro *(G-17197)*
Unison Industries LLC ....B...... 607 335-5000
  Norwich *(G-13039)*

3792 Travel Trailers & Campers

All Star Carts & Vehicles Inc ....D...... 631 666-5581
  Bay Shore *(G-668)*

3795 Tanks & Tank Components

Federal Prison Industries ....C...... 845 386-6819
  Otisville *(G-13344)*
Lourdes Industries Inc ....D...... 631 234-6600
  Hauppauge *(G-6121)*
◆ Tecmotiv (usa) Inc ....E...... 905 669-5911
  Niagara Falls *(G-12882)*

3799 Transportation Eqpt, NEC

Adirondack Power Sports ....G...... 518 481-6269
  Malone *(G-8006)*
Bombardier Trnsp Holdings USA ....D...... 607 776-4791
  Bath *(G-654)*
Bullet Industries Inc..........................G...... 585 352-0836
  Spencerport *(G-15568)*
Clopay Ames True Tmper Hldng ....F...... 516 938-5544
  Jericho *(G-7062)*
▲ Club Protector Inc ....G...... 716 652-4787
  Elma *(G-4645)*
Kens Service & Sales Inc ....F...... 716 683-1155
  Elma *(G-4650)*
Mdek Inc..G...... 347 569-7318
  Brooklyn *(G-2288)*
Performance Custom Trailer...............G...... 518 504-4021
  Lake George *(G-7263)*
Rolling Star Manufacturing Inc..........G...... 315 896-4767
  Barneveld *(G-616)*
Tectran Inc ....G...... 800 776-5549
  Cheektowaga *(G-3591)*
Truxton Corp ....G...... 718 842-6000
  Bronx *(G-1480)*

38 MEASURING, ANALYZING AND CONTROLLING INSTRUMENTS; PHOTOGRAPHIC, MEDICAL AN

3812 Search, Detection, Navigation & Guidance Systs & Instrs

1robotics LLC.....................................G...... 845 369-6770
  Airmont *(G-10)*
901 D LLC ....E...... 845 369-1111
  Airmont *(G-11)*
Accutrak Inc ....F...... 212 925-5330
  New York *(G-9013)*
▲ Aeroflex Incorporated ....B...... 516 694-6700
  Plainview *(G-13578)*
Ametek Inc ....D...... 585 263-7700
  Rochester *(G-14202)*
Amherst Systems Inc ....C...... 716 631-0610
  Buffalo *(G-2810)*
▲ Artemis Inc.......................................G...... 631 232-2424
  Hauppauge *(G-6025)*
Atair Aerospace Inc ....F...... 718 923-1709
  Brooklyn *(G-1642)*
Aventura Technologies Inc ....E...... 631 300-4000
  Commack *(G-3822)*
B & Z Technologies LLC ....G...... 631 675-9666
  East Setauket *(G-4477)*
▲ Bae Systems Controls Inc..............A...... 607 770-2000
  Endicott *(G-4796)*
C Speed LLC ....E...... 315 453-1043
  Liverpool *(G-7514)*
C-Flex Bearing Co Inc.......................F...... 315 895-7454
  Frankfort *(G-5350)*
CIC International Ltd..........................D...... 212 213-0089
  Brooklyn *(G-1779)*
▲ Clayton Dubilier & Rice Fun...........E...... 212 407-5200
  New York *(G-9640)*
Cobham Holdings (us) Inc ....A...... 716 662-0006
  Orchard Park *(G-13262)*
Cobham Holdings Inc........................F...... 716 662-0006
  Orchard Park *(G-13263)*
Computer Instruments Corp ....E...... 516 876-8400
  Westbury *(G-16975)*

▲ Cox & Company Inc ....C...... 212 366-0200
  Plainview *(G-13593)*
Drs-Electronic Warfare & Netwo ....B...... 716 631-6200
  Buffalo *(G-2919)*
▲ Dyna-Empire Inc..............................C...... 516 222-2700
  Garden City *(G-5500)*
Eastern Strategic Materials................E...... 212 332-1619
  New York *(G-9967)*
◆ Edo LLC ....G...... 631 630-4000
  Amityville *(G-285)*
Edo LLC ....A...... 631 630-4200
  Amityville *(G-286)*
Emergency Beacon Corp ....F...... 914 576-2700
  New Rochelle *(G-8896)*
Excelsior Mlt-Cltural Inst Inc.............F...... 706 627-4285
  Flushing *(G-5239)*
Facilamatic Instrument Corp ....F...... 516 825-6300
  Valley Stream *(G-16406)*
Flightline Electronics Inc ....D...... 585 742-5340
  Victor *(G-16478)*
Frequency Electronics Inc ....B...... 516 794-4500
  Uniondale *(G-16295)*
Gryphon Sensors LLC ....F...... 315 452-8810
  North Syracuse *(G-12946)*
Harris Corporation ....A...... 585 269-6600
  Rochester *(G-14423)*
Harris Corporation ....B...... 585 269-5001
  Rochester *(G-14424)*
Harris Corporation ....A...... 585 269-5000
  Rochester *(G-14426)*
Harris Corporation ....C...... 703 668-6239
  Rome *(G-14812)*
Ieh FM Holdings LLC ....E...... 212 702-4300
  New York *(G-10559)*
Inertia Switch Inc ....E...... 845 359-8300
  Orangeburg *(G-13229)*
▲ Inficon Inc ....C...... 315 434-1149
  East Syracuse *(G-4541)*
Infrared Components Corp ....E...... 315 732-1544
  Utica *(G-16344)*
◆ Itt LLC ....B...... 914 641-2000
  White Plains *(G-17125)*
ITT Corporation ....D...... 914 641-2000
  Seneca Falls *(G-15361)*
ITT Corporation ....D...... 315 568-2811
  Seneca Falls *(G-15362)*
ITT Inc ....A...... 914 641-2000
  White Plains *(G-17128)*
Joldeson One Aerospace Inds ....D...... 718 848-7396
  Ozone Park *(G-13380)*
▲ Kerns Manufacturing Corp.............C...... 718 784-4044
  Long Island City *(G-7780)*
Kwadair LLC ....G...... 646 824-2511
  Brooklyn *(G-2182)*
▲ L-3 Cmmnctons Fgn Holdings Inc....E...... 212 697-1111
  New York *(G-10903)*
◆ L-3 Cmmunications Holdings Inc.....D...... 212 697-1111
  New York *(G-10905)*
L-3 Communications Corporation .....B...... 212 697-1111
  New York *(G-10906)*
Laufer Wind Group LLC ....F...... 212 792-3912
  New York *(G-10935)*
Lockheed Martin Corporation ....A...... 607 751-2000
  Owego *(G-13354)*
Lockheed Martin Corporation ....D...... 607 751-7434
  Owego *(G-13355)*
Lockheed Martin Corporation ....E...... 315 456-6604
  Syracuse *(G-15980)*
Lockheed Martin Corporation ....E...... 212 697-1105
  New York *(G-11021)*
Lockheed Martin Corporation ....E...... 716 297-1000
  Niagara Falls *(G-12844)*
Lockheed Martin Corporation ....A...... 315 456-0123
  Liverpool *(G-7531)*
Lockheed Martin Global Inc ....D...... 315 456-2982
  Liverpool *(G-7532)*
Lockheed Martin Overseas ....E...... 315 456-0123
  Liverpool *(G-7533)*
Logitek Inc ....D...... 631 567-1100
  Bohemia *(G-1094)*
Magellan Aerospace NY Inc ....C...... 718 699-4000
  Corona *(G-4001)*
Metro Dynmc Scntific Instr Lab ....F...... 631 842-4300
  Copiague *(G-3914)*
Mirion Technologies Ist Corp ....D...... 607 562-4300
  Horseheads *(G-6584)*
Mod-A-Can Inc....................................E...... 516 931-8545
  Hicksville *(G-6374)*
◆ Moog Inc ....A...... 716 652-2000
  Elma *(G-4651)*

SIC SECTION — 38 MEASURING, ANALYZING AND CONTROLLING INSTRUMENTS; PHOTOGRAPHIC, MEDICAL AN

Moog Inc ..... E 716 687-4778
Elma (G-4652)
Moog Inc ..... B 716 687-5486
East Aurora (G-4377)
▲ **Moor Electronics Inc** ..... G 716 821-5304
Buffalo (G-3075)
New York Nautical Inc ..... G 212 962-4522
New York (G-11404)
Northrop Grumman Corporation ..... A 703 280-2900
Bethpage (G-876)
Norwich Aero Products Inc ..... D 607 336-7636
Norwich (G-13032)
Orthstar Enterprises Inc ..... D 607 562-2100
Horseheads (G-6586)
Penetradar Corporation ..... F 716 731-2629
Niagara Falls (G-12859)
Placemeter Inc ..... G 917 225-4579
Brooklyn (G-2425)
Rodale Wireless Inc ..... E 631 231-0044
Hauppauge (G-6179)
Saab Defense and SEC USA LLC ..... F 315 445-5009
East Syracuse (G-4560)
Safe Flight Instrument Corp ..... C 914 220-1125
White Plains (G-17167)
▼ **Select Fabricators Inc** ..... F 585 393-0650
Canandaigua (G-3357)
Sensormatic Electronics LLC ..... F 718 597-6719
Bronx (G-1450)
Sensormatic Electronics LLC ..... F 845 365-3125
Orangeburg (G-13245)
▲ **Sentry Technology Corporation** ..... E 631 739-2000
Ronkonkoma (G-14982)
▲ **Sentry Technology Corporation** ..... F 800 645-4224
Ronkonkoma (G-14983)
Srctec LLC ..... C 315 452-8700
Syracuse (G-16044)
Systems Drs C3 Inc ..... B 716 631-6200
Buffalo (G-3207)
Tech Valley Technologies Inc ..... F 518 584-8899
Wilton (G-17271)
▲ **Telephonics Corporation** ..... A 631 755-7000
Farmingdale (G-5127)
▼ **Traffic Logix Corporation** ..... G 866 915-6449
Spring Valley (G-15603)
Transistor Devices Inc ..... E 631 471-7492
Ronkonkoma (G-14992)
Tusk Manufacturing Inc ..... E 631 567-3349
Bohemia (G-1150)
U E Systems Incorporated ..... E 914 592-1220
Elmsford (G-4790)
U S Tech Corporation ..... F 315 437-7207
East Syracuse (G-4575)
UNI Source Technology ..... F 514 748-8888
Champlain (G-3547)
Vacuum Instrument Corporation ..... D 631 737-0900
Ronkonkoma (G-14997)
Virtualapt Corp ..... G 917 293-3173
Brooklyn (G-2730)
◆ **VJ Technologies Inc** ..... E 631 589-8800
Bohemia (G-1154)
Woodbine Products Inc ..... E 631 586-3770
Hauppauge (G-6236)
Worldwide Arntcal Cmpnents Inc ..... F 631 842-3780
Copiague (G-3939)
Worldwide Arntcal Cmpnents Inc ..... G 631 842-3780
Copiague (G-3940)

3821 Laboratory Apparatus & Furniture

Adirondack Machine Corporation ..... G 518 792-2258
Hudson Falls (G-6638)
▲ **Air Techniques Inc** ..... B 516 433-7676
Melville (G-8291)
Anaren Microwave Inc ..... C 315 432-8909
East Syracuse (G-4503)
Ankom Technology Corp ..... E 315 986-8090
Macedon (G-7981)
Biodesign Inc of New York ..... F 845 454-6610
Carmel (G-3398)
Bioins Inc ..... G 646 457-8117
Yonkers (G-17421)
Biospherix Ltd ..... E 315 387-3414
Parish (G-13414)
Crystal Linton Technologies ..... F 585 444-8784
Rochester (G-14292)
▲ **Dynamica Inc** ..... G 212 818-1900
New York (G-9948)
East Hills Instrument Inc ..... F 516 621-8686
Westbury (G-16980)
Fts Systems Inc ..... D 845 687-5300
Stone Ridge (G-15763)

◆ **Fungilab Inc** ..... G 631 750-6361
Hauppauge (G-6081)
Healthalliance Hospital ..... G 845 338-2500
Kingston (G-7190)
▲ **Hyman Podrusnick Co Inc** ..... G 718 853-4502
Brooklyn (G-2092)
Instrumentation Laboratory Co ..... C 845 680-0028
Orangeburg (G-13231)
▲ **Integrated Liner Tech Inc** ..... E 518 621-7422
Rensselaer (G-14048)
Integrted Work Envronments LLC ..... G 716 725-5088
East Amherst (G-4361)
▲ **Itin Scale Co Inc** ..... E 718 336-5900
Brooklyn (G-2120)
▲ **J H C Fabrications Inc** ..... E 718 649-0065
Brooklyn (G-2122)
▲ **Jamestown Metal Products LLC** ..... C 716 665-5313
Jamestown (G-7011)
Lab Crafters Inc ..... E 631 471-7755
Ronkonkoma (G-14926)
Lomir Inc ..... F 518 483-7697
Malone (G-8012)
Maripharm Laboratories ..... F 716 984-6520
Niagara Falls (G-12845)
Material Measuring Corporation ..... G 516 334-6167
Westbury (G-17010)
Modu-Craft Inc ..... G 716 694-0709
Tonawanda (G-16182)
Modu-Craft Inc ..... G 716 694-0709
North Tonawanda (G-12982)
◆ **Nalge Nunc International Corp** ..... A 585 586-8800
Rochester (G-14527)
Newport Corporation ..... F 585 248-4246
Rochester (G-14535)
Next Advance Inc ..... F 518 674-3510
Averill Park (G-536)
Radon Testing Corp of America ..... F 914 345-3380
Elmsford (G-4774)
S P Industries Inc ..... D 845 255-5000
Gardiner (G-5550)
▲ **Scientific Industries Inc** ..... E 631 567-4700
Bohemia (G-1129)
Simpore Inc ..... G 585 748-5980
West Henrietta (G-16895)
SPS Medical Supply Corp ..... F 585 968-2377
Cuba (G-4070)
▲ **Staplex Company Inc** ..... E 718 768-3333
Brooklyn (G-2598)
Steriliz LLC ..... G 585 415-5411
Rochester (G-14703)
Techtrade LLC ..... G 212 481-2515
New York (G-12291)
Theta Industries Inc ..... F 516 883-4088
Port Washington (G-13869)
▲ **Vistalab Technologies Inc** ..... E 914 244-6226
Brewster (G-1230)
VWR Education LLC ..... C 585 359-2502
West Henrietta (G-16899)

3822 Automatic Temperature Controls

▲ **A K Allen Co Inc** ..... C 516 747-5450
Mineola (G-8488)
Advantex Solutions Inc ..... G 718 278-2290
Bellerose (G-809)
Air Louver & Damper Inc ..... E 718 392-3232
Maspeth (G-8112)
Air Louver & Damper Inc ..... F 718 392-3232
Long Island City (G-7649)
Airflex Industrial Inc ..... E 631 752-1234
Farmingdale (G-4933)
▲ **Anderson Instrument Co Inc** ..... D 518 922-5315
Fultonville (G-5477)
Automated Bldg MGT Systems Inc ..... E 516 216-5603
Floral Park (G-5194)
Automated Building Controls ..... G 914 381-2860
Mamaroneck (G-8023)
Bilbee Controls Inc ..... F 518 622-3033
Cairo (G-3271)
▲ **Biorem Environmental Inc** ..... E 585 924-2220
Victor (G-16462)
▲ **Bitzer Scroll Inc** ..... D 315 463-2101
Syracuse (G-15870)
Black River Generations LLC ..... E 315 773-2314
Fort Drum (G-5338)
Building Management Assoc Inc ..... E 718 542-4779
Bronx (G-1290)
Care Enterprises Inc ..... G 631 472-8155
Bayport (G-755)
Carrier Corporation ..... B 315 432-6000
Syracuse (G-15888)

Cascade Technical Services LLC ..... F 516 596-6300
Lynbrook (G-7949)
Cascade Technical Services LLC ..... G 518 355-2201
Schenectady (G-15240)
Clean Room Depot Inc ..... F 631 589-3033
Holbrook (G-6438)
▲ **Cox & Company Inc** ..... C 212 366-0200
Plainview (G-13593)
Daikin Applied Americas Inc ..... D 315 253-2771
Auburn (G-491)
Day Automation Systems Inc ..... D 585 924-4630
Victor (G-16472)
E Global Solutions Inc ..... G 516 767-5138
Port Washington (G-13812)
East Hudson Watershed Corp ..... G 845 319-6349
Patterson (G-13438)
Eastern Strategic Materials ..... E 212 332-1619
New York (G-9967)
Evolve Guest Controls LLC ..... F 855 750-9090
Port Washington (G-13814)
Fedders Islandaire Inc ..... D 631 471-2900
East Setauket (G-4482)
Fuel Watchman Sales & Service ..... F 718 665-6100
Bronx (G-1338)
Grillmaster Inc ..... E 718 272-9191
Howard Beach (G-6597)
Heating & Burner Supply Inc ..... G 718 665-0006
Bronx (G-1355)
Henderson Products Inc ..... E 315 785-0994
Watertown (G-16654)
▲ **Infitec Inc** ..... D 315 433-1150
East Syracuse (G-4543)
Intellidyne LLC ..... F 516 676-0777
Plainview (G-13608)
Intrepid Control Service Inc ..... G 718 886-8771
Flushing (G-5254)
Irtronics Instruments Inc ..... F 914 693-6291
Ardsley (G-405)
Johnson Controls Inc ..... E 585 924-9346
Victor (G-16484)
Johnson Controls Inc ..... E 914 593-5200
Hawthorne (G-6248)
Johnson Controls Inc ..... E 716 688-7340
Buffalo (G-3020)
Johnson Controls Inc ..... C 585 724-2232
Rochester (G-14464)
Leo Schultz ..... G 716 969-0945
Cheektowaga (G-3577)
Logical Control Solutions Inc ..... F 585 424-5340
Victor (G-16489)
Long Island Analytical Labs ..... F 631 472-3400
Holbrook (G-6458)
Microb Phase Services ..... F 518 877-8948
Clifton Park (G-3702)
Pii Holdings Inc ..... G 716 876-9951
Buffalo (G-3126)
Protective Industries Inc ..... D 716 876-9951
Buffalo (G-3141)
◆ **Protective Industries Inc** ..... C 716 876-9951
Buffalo (G-3139)
▲ **Pulsafeeder Inc** ..... C 585 292-8000
Rochester (G-14609)
▲ **RE Hansen Industries Inc** ..... C 631 471-2900
East Setauket (G-4491)
Siemens Industry Inc ..... D 716 568-0983
Amherst (G-261)
▲ **Solarwaterway** ..... E 646 387-9346
Brooklyn (G-2581)
▲ **Spence Engineering Company Inc** ... C 845 778-5566
Walden (G-16536)
▲ **Svyz Trading Corp** ..... G 718 220-1140
Bronx (G-1469)
T S B A Group Inc ..... E 718 565-6000
Sunnyside (G-15810)
▲ **Transit Air Inc** ..... E 607 324-0216
Hornell (G-6568)
U S Energy Controls Inc ..... F 718 380-1004
New Hyde Park (G-8867)
Unisend LLC ..... G 585 414-9575
Webster (G-16739)
Virtual Super LLC ..... G 212 685-6400
New York (G-12550)
Zebra Environmental Corp ..... F 516 596-6300
Lynbrook (G-7967)

3823 Indl Instruments For Meas, Display & Control

A C T Associates ..... F 716 759-8348
Clarence (G-3654)

S I C

Employee Codes: A=Over 500 employees, B=251-500
C=101-250, D=51-100, E=20-50, F=10-19, G=5-9
2017 Harris
New York Manufacturers Directory
857

38 MEASURING, ANALYZING AND CONTROLLING INSTRUMENTS; PHOTOGRAPHIC, MEDICAL AN

Aalborg Instrs & Contrls Inc ....D 845 398-3160
  Orangeburg *(G-13217)*
Ametek Inc ....D 585 263-7700
  Rochester *(G-14202)*
Analytical Technology Inc ....F 646 208-4643
  New York *(G-9146)*
Anchor Commerce Trading Corp ....G 516 881-3485
  Atlantic Beach *(G-468)*
▲ Anderson Instrument Co Inc............D 518 922-5315
  Fultonville *(G-5477)*
▲ Applied Power Systems Inc ....E 516 935-2230
  Hicksville *(G-6322)*
Aspex Incorporated ....E 212 966-0410
  New York *(G-9237)*
ATI Trading Inc ....F 718 888-7918
  Flushing *(G-5228)*
Aureonic ....G 518 791-9331
  Gansevoort *(G-5485)*
B Live LLC ....G 212 489-0721
  New York *(G-9290)*
Bae Systems Info & Elec Sys ....F 631 912-1525
  Greenlawn *(G-5873)*
Beauty America LLC ....E 917 744-1430
  Great Neck *(G-5794)*
◆ Blue Tee Corp ....E 212 598-0880
  New York *(G-9422)*
Cal Blen Electronic Industries ....F 631 242-6243
  Deer Park *(G-4114)*
▲ Calibrated Instruments Inc................E 914 741-5700
  Manhasset *(G-8056)*
Cemtrex Inc ....E 631 756-9116
  Farmingdale *(G-4957)*
Ceres Technologies Inc ....D 845 247-4701
  Saugerties *(G-15181)*
Classic Automation LLC ....E 585 241-6010
  Webster *(G-16718)*
Computer Instruments Corp ....E 516 876-8400
  Westbury *(G-16975)*
Conax Technologies LLC ....C 716 684-4500
  Buffalo *(G-2885)*
▲ Cosa Xentaur Corporation ....F 631 345-3434
  Yaphank *(G-17389)*
Cytexone Technology LLC ....G 212 792-6700
  New York *(G-9779)*
Danaher Corporation ....C 516 443-9432
  New York *(G-9799)*
▲ Dau Thrmal Slutions N Amer Inc ....E 585 678-9025
  Macedon *(G-7985)*
◆ Defelsko Corporation ....D 315 393-4450
  Ogdensburg *(G-13114)*
Digital Analysis Corporation ....F 315 685-0760
  Skaneateles *(G-15458)*
Digitronik Dev Labs Inc ....G 585 360-0043
  Rochester *(G-14308)*
Display Logic USA Inc ....F 516 513-1420
  Mineola *(G-8506)*
Diversified Electrical Pdts ....F 631 567-5710
  Bohemia *(G-1058)*
▲ Dyna-Empire Inc ....C 516 222-2700
  Garden City *(G-5500)*
East Hills Instrument Inc ....F 516 621-8686
  Westbury *(G-16980)*
Electrcal Instrumentation Ctrl ....F 518 861-5789
  Delanson *(G-4232)*
Electronic Machine Parts LLC ....F 631 434-3700
  Hauppauge *(G-6070)*
Emerson Electric Co ....E 212 244-2490
  New York *(G-10023)*
Emerson Indus Automtn USA LLC ......E 716 774-1193
  Grand Island *(G-5756)*
Emerson Network Power ....G 516 349-8500
  Plainview *(G-13599)*
Enerac Inc ....F 516 997-1554
  Holbrook *(G-6447)*
Ewt Holdings III Corp ....E 212 644-5900
  New York *(G-10096)*
Fts Systems Inc ....D 845 687-5300
  Stone Ridge *(G-15763)*
Gizmo Products Inc ....G 585 301-0970
  Rochester *(G-14403)*
Gurley Precision Instrs Inc ....C 518 272-6300
  Troy *(G-16237)*
Hades Manufacturing Corp ....F 631 249-4244
  Farmingdale *(G-5204)*
Harris Corporation ....C 703 668-6239
  Rome *(G-14812)*
▲ Heidenhain International Inc ....C 716 661-1700
  Jamestown *(G-6999)*
Herman H Sticht Company Inc ....G 718 852-7602
  Brooklyn *(G-2076)*

▲ Hilliard Corporation ....B 607 733-7121
  Elmira *(G-4690)*
Hilliard Corporation ....F 607 733-7121
  Elmira *(G-4691)*
Industrial Machine Repair ....G 607 272-0717
  Ithaca *(G-6850)*
▲ Inficon Inc ....C 315 434-1149
  East Syracuse *(G-4541)*
Inficon Holding AG ....G 315 434-1100
  East Syracuse *(G-4542)*
▲ Integrated Control Corp ....E 631 673-5100
  Huntington *(G-6662)*
Invensys Systems Inc ....F 214 527-3099
  New York *(G-10649)*
◆ Itt LLC ....B 914 641-2000
  White Plains *(G-17125)*
ITT Corporation ....C 914 641-2000
  Seneca Falls *(G-15361)*
ITT Corporation ....D 315 568-2811
  Seneca Falls *(G-15362)*
ITT Inc ....E 914 641-2000
  White Plains *(G-17128)*
▲ Kessler Thermometer Corp ....C 631 841-5500
  West Babylon *(G-16804)*
▲ Koehler Instrument Company Inc ......D 631 589-3800
  Bohemia *(G-1088)*
Macrolink Inc ....E 631 924-8265
  Medford *(G-8255)*
▼ Magtrol Inc ....E 716 668-5555
  Buffalo *(G-3055)*
Malcon Inc ....F 914 666-7146
  Bedford Hills *(G-804)*
Mark - 10 Corporation ....G 631 842-9200
  Copiague *(G-3913)*
Mausner Equipment Co Inc ....C 631 689-7358
  Setauket *(G-15377)*
Medsafe Systems Inc ....G 516 883-8222
  Port Washington *(G-13843)*
Micromod Automtn & Contrls Inc ......C 585 321-9209
  Rochester *(G-14511)*
▲ Miller & Weber Inc ....E 718 821-7110
  Westbury *(G-17012)*
Mks Instruments Inc ....E 585 292-7472
  Rochester *(G-14517)*
Norwich Aero Products Inc ....D 607 336-7636
  Norwich *(G-13032)*
Nutec Components Inc ....F 631 242-1224
  Deer Park *(G-4182)*
Oden Machinery Inc ....E 716 874-3000
  Tonawanda *(G-16189)*
Ormec Systems Corp ....E 585 385-3520
  Rochester *(G-14552)*
Orthstar Enterprises Inc ....D 607 562-2100
  Horseheads *(G-6586)*
Partlow Corporation ....C 518 922-5315
  Fultonville *(G-5481)*
Pcb Group Inc ....E 716 684-0001
  Depew *(G-4268)*
Pneumercator Company Inc ....E 631 293-8450
  Hauppauge *(G-6165)*
Poseidon Systems LLC ....F 585 239-6025
  Rochester *(G-14589)*
▲ Pulsafeeder Inc ....C 585 292-8000
  Rochester *(G-14609)*
R K B Opto-Electronics Inc ....F 315 455-6636
  Syracuse *(G-16016)*
◆ Rhi US Ltd ....E 716 483-7200
  Falconer *(G-4911)*
Riverhawk Company LP ....C 315 624-7171
  New Hartford *(G-8809)*
Robat Inc ....G 518 812-6244
  Clifton Park *(G-3705)*
Roessel & Co Inc ....G 585 458-5560
  Rochester *(G-14657)*
▲ Rotronic Instrument Corp ....F 631 348-6844
  Hauppauge *(G-6180)*
Rwb Controls Inc ....G 716 897-4341
  Buffalo *(G-3169)*
Select Controls Inc ....E 631 567-9010
  Bohemia *(G-1131)*
Sequential Electronics Systems ....E 914 592-1345
  Elmsford *(G-4783)*
Siemens Industry Inc ....C 631 218-1000
  Bohemia *(G-1134)*
Sixnet LLC ....D 518 877-5173
  Ballston Lake *(G-586)*
▲ Sixnet Holdings LLC ....E 518 877-5173
  Ballston Lake *(G-587)*
Solar Metrology LLC ....G 845 247-4701
  Holbrook *(G-6471)*

Springfield Control Systems ....G 718 631-0870
  Douglaston *(G-4312)*
Swagelok Western NY ....G 585 359-8470
  West Henrietta *(G-16896)*
Taber Acquisition Corp ....D 716 694-4000
  North Tonawanda *(G-13000)*
Tel-Tru Inc ....D 585 295-0225
  Rochester *(G-14720)*
Telog Instruments Inc ....E 585 742-3000
  Victor *(G-16507)*
Thread Check Inc ....D 631 231-1515
  Hauppauge *(G-6214)*
▼ Transtech Systems Inc ....C 518 370-5558
  Latham *(G-7381)*
Vacuum Instrument Corporation ......D 631 737-0900
  Ronkonkoma *(G-14997)*
Veeco Instruments Inc ....C 516 677-0200
  Woodbury *(G-17302)*
Vetra Systems Corporation ....G 631 434-3185
  Hauppauge *(G-6224)*
Viatran Corporation ....E 716 629-3800
  North Tonawanda *(G-13005)*
▲ Weiss Instruments Inc ....D 631 207-1200
  Holtsville *(G-6514)*
▲ Winters Instruments Inc ....E 281 880-8607
  Tonawanda *(G-16215)*
Xentaur Corporation ....F 631 345-3434
  Yaphank *(G-17409)*

3824 Fluid Meters & Counters

Aalborg Instrs & Contrls Inc ....D 845 398-3160
  Orangeburg *(G-13217)*
Cmp Advnced Mech Sltons NY LLC ...G 607 352-1712
  Binghamton *(G-902)*
Computer Instruments Corp ....E 516 876-8400
  Westbury *(G-16975)*
▲ Curtis Instruments Inc ....C 914 666-2971
  Mount Kisco *(G-8624)*
▲ Designatronics Incorporated ....E 516 328-3300
  New Hyde Park *(G-8825)*
East Hills Instrument Inc ....F 516 621-8686
  Westbury *(G-16980)*
Empresas De Manufactura Inc ....C 631 240-9251
  East Setauket *(G-4481)*
Encore Electronics Inc ....E 518 584-5354
  Saratoga Springs *(G-15150)*
◆ Environment-One Corporation ....C 518 346-6161
  Schenectady *(G-15252)*
Flexim Americas Corporation ....F 631 492-2300
  Edgewood *(G-4598)*
G & O Equipment Corp ....G 718 218-7844
  Bronx *(G-1339)*
Gurley Precision Instrs Inc ....C 518 272-6300
  Troy *(G-16237)*
Heat-Timer Corporation ....E 212 481-2020
  Bronx *(G-1354)*
K-Technologies Inc ....E 716 828-4444
  Buffalo *(G-3025)*
Melland Gear Instr of Huppauge ......E 631 234-0100
  Hauppauge *(G-6130)*
Schlumberger Technology Corp ....C 607 378-0200
  Horseheads *(G-6592)*
Siemens Industry Inc ....C 631 231-3600
  Hauppauge *(G-6189)*
SPX Flow Us LLC ....E 585 436-5550
  Rochester *(G-14698)*
Sun Circuits International Inc ....B 631 240-9251
  Setauket *(G-15381)*
Turbo Machined Products LLC ....C 315 895-3010
  Frankfort *(G-5358)*
Vantage Mfg & Assembly LLC ....E 845 471-5290
  Poughkeepsie *(G-13938)*
▲ Walter R Tucker Entps Ltd ....E 607 467-2866
  Deposit *(G-4282)*

3825 Instrs For Measuring & Testing Electricity

Agilent Technologies Inc ....A 877 424-4536
  New York *(G-9057)*
Ah Elctronic Test Eqp Repr Ctr ....F 631 234-8979
  Central Islip *(G-3484)*
Allied Motion Systems Corp ....F 716 691-5868
  Amherst *(G-220)*
▲ Allied Motion Technologies Inc ....C 716 242-8634
  Amherst *(G-221)*
American Quality Technology ....F 607 777-9488
  Binghamton *(G-887)*
Ametek Inc ....D 585 263-7700
  Rochester *(G-14202)*

SIC SECTION 38 MEASURING, ANALYZING AND CONTROLLING INSTRUMENTS; PHOTOGRAPHIC, MEDICAL AN

Anmar Acquisition LLC ......G 585 352-7777
Rochester *(G-14206)*

Apogee Power Usa Inc ......F 202 746-2890
Hartsdale *(G-5997)*

Aurora Technical Services Ltd ......G 716 652-1463
East Aurora *(G-4367)*

Automated Control Logic Inc ......F 914 769-8880
Thornwood *(G-16116)*

Automation Correct LLC ......G 315 299-3589
Syracuse *(G-15861)*

Avanel Industries Inc ......F 516 333-0990
Westbury *(G-16971)*

Avcom of Virginia Inc ......D 585 924-4560
Victor *(G-16461)*

C Speed LLC ......E 315 453-1043
Liverpool *(G-7514)*

C-Flex Bearing Co Inc ......F 315 895-7454
Frankfort *(G-5350)*

Calmetrics Inc ......G 631 580-2522
Holbrook *(G-6435)*

▲ **Cetek Inc** ......E 845 452-3510
Poughkeepsie *(G-13892)*

Cgw Corp ......G 631 472-6600
Bayport *(G-756)*

Clarke Hess Communication RES ......G 631 698-3350
Medford *(G-8241)*

▲ **Clayton Dubilier & Rice Fun** ......E 212 407-5200
New York *(G-9640)*

▲ **Comtech PST Corp** ......C 631 777-8900
Melville *(G-8306)*

▲ **Curtis Instruments Inc** ......C 914 666-2971
Mount Kisco *(G-8624)*

Dynatic Solutions Inc ......G 914 358-9599
White Plains *(G-17102)*

East Hills Instrument Inc ......F 516 621-8686
Westbury *(G-16980)*

Edo LLC ......A 631 630-4200
Amityville *(G-286)*

Edo LLC ......E 631 218-1413
Bohemia *(G-1062)*

El Electronics Inc ......F 516 334-0870
Westbury *(G-16981)*

▲ **Ems Development Corporation** ......D 631 924-4736
Yaphank *(G-17390)*

Enertiv Inc ......G 646 350-3525
New York *(G-10039)*

Epoch Microelectronics Inc ......G 914 332-8570
Valhalla *(G-16367)*

Everest Bbn Inc ......F 212 268-7979
New York *(G-10091)*

Evergreen High Voltage LLC ......G 281 814-9973
Lake Placid *(G-7274)*

Fluid Metering Inc ......E 516 922-6050
Syosset *(G-15822)*

Frequency Electronics Inc ......B 516 794-4500
Uniondale *(G-16295)*

Gcns Technology Group Inc ......F 347 713-8160
Brooklyn *(G-2017)*

General Microwave Corporation ......F 516 802-0900
Syosset *(G-15824)*

Hamilton Marketing Corporation ......G 585 395-0678
Brockport *(G-1244)*

Herman H Sticht Company Inc ......G 718 852-7602
Brooklyn *(G-2076)*

◆ **Hipotronics Inc** ......C 845 279-8091
Brewster *(G-1220)*

▲ **Iet Labs Inc** ......F 516 334-5959
Roslyn Heights *(G-15027)*

International Insurance Soc ......G 212 815-9291
New York *(G-10636)*

◆ **Interntnal Elctronic Mchs Corp** ......E 518 268-1636
Troy *(G-16241)*

▲ **Interplex Industries Inc** ......F 718 961-6212
College Point *(G-3790)*

John Ramsey Elec Svcs LLC ......G 585 298-9596
Victor *(G-16483)*

Jre Test LLC ......G 585 298-9736
Victor *(G-16485)*

Larry Kings Corporation ......G 718 481-8741
Rosedale *(G-15013)*

Lexan Industries Inc ......F 631 434-7586
Bay Shore *(G-713)*

Linde LLC ......D 716 773-7552
Grand Island *(G-5763)*

Logitek Inc ......D 631 567-1100
Bohemia *(G-1094)*

▼ **Ludl Electronic Products Ltd** ......E 914 769-6111
Hawthorne *(G-6250)*

▲ **Macrodyne Inc** ......F 518 383-3800
Clifton Park *(G-3700)*

▲ **Magnetic Analysis Corporation** ......D 914 530-2000
Elmsford *(G-4762)*

▼ **Magtrol Inc** ......E 716 668-5555
Buffalo *(G-3055)*

▲ **Make-Waves Instrument Corp** ......E 716 681-7524
Depew *(G-4264)*

Millivac Instruments Inc ......G 518 355-8300
Schenectady *(G-15279)*

▲ **Nas CP Corp** ......D 718 961-6757
College Point *(G-3799)*

New York Enrgy Synthetics Inc ......G 212 634-4787
New York *(G-11401)*

North Atlantic Industries Inc ......C 631 567-1100
Bohemia *(G-1111)*

Northeast Metrology Corp ......F 716 827-3770
Buffalo *(G-3095)*

Omni-ID Usa Inc ......E 585 697-9913
Rochester *(G-14549)*

Optimized Devices Inc ......F 914 769-6100
Pleasantville *(G-13715)*

Peerless Instrument Co Inc ......C 631 396-6500
Farmingdale *(G-5076)*

Performance Systems Contg Inc ......E 607 277-6240
Ithaca *(G-6868)*

Photonix Technologies Inc ......F 607 786-4600
Endicott *(G-4825)*

Practical Instrument Elec Inc ......F 585 872-9350
Webster *(G-16730)*

Pragmatics Technology Inc ......G 845 795-5071
Milton *(G-8483)*

Precision Filters Inc ......E 607 277-3550
Ithaca *(G-6871)*

Primesouth Inc ......F 585 567-4191
Fillmore *(G-5176)*

▲ **Pulsafeeder Inc** ......C 585 292-8000
Rochester *(G-14609)*

Pulsar Technology Systems Inc ......G 718 361-9292
Long Island City *(G-7849)*

▲ **Quadlogic Controls Corporation** ......D 212 930-9300
Long Island City *(G-7852)*

▲ **Qualitrol Company LLC** ......C 586 643-3717
Fairport *(G-4872)*

Qualitrol Finance Corp ......G 585 586-1515
Fairport *(G-4873)*

R K B Opto-Electronics Inc ......F 315 455-6636
Syracuse *(G-16016)*

Ramsey Electronics LLC ......E 585 924-4560
Victor *(G-16498)*

Rodale Wireless Inc ......E 631 231-0044
Hauppauge *(G-6179)*

S R Instruments Inc ......E 716 693-5977
Tonawanda *(G-16197)*

Schlumberger Technology Corp ......C 607 378-0200
Horseheads *(G-6592)*

Scientific Components Corp ......E 631 243-4901
Deer Park *(G-4207)*

Scj Associates Inc ......E 585 359-0600
Rochester *(G-14677)*

▲ **Sorfin Yoshimura Ic Disc Ltd** ......G 516 802-4600
Woodbury *(G-17300)*

T & C Power Conversion Inc ......F 585 482-5551
Rochester *(G-14714)*

▲ **Teledyne Lecroy Inc** ......C 845 425-2000
Chestnut Ridge *(G-3626)*

Trek Inc ......F 716 438-7555
Lockport *(G-7621)*

◆ **Urban Green Energy Inc** ......E 917 720-5681
New York *(G-12479)*

Viatran Corporation ......E 716 629-3800
North Tonawanda *(G-13005)*

▲ **W & W Manufacturing Co** ......F 516 942-0011
Deer Park *(G-4225)*

W D Technology Inc ......G 914 779-8738
Eastchester *(G-4583)*

▲ **Walter R Tucker Entps Ltd** ......E 607 467-2866
Deposit *(G-4282)*

Xelic Incorporated ......F 585 415-2764
Pittsford *(G-13575)*

▲ **Zumbach Electronics Corp** ......D 914 241-7080
Mount Kisco *(G-8649)*

3826 Analytical Instruments

A S A Precision Co Inc ......G 845 482-4870
Jeffersonville *(G-7058)*

Advanced Mtl Analytics LLC ......G 321 684-0528
Vestal *(G-16439)*

Advion Inc ......E 607 266-9162
Ithaca *(G-6817)*

Applied Image Inc ......E 585 482-0300
Rochester *(G-14209)*

Bristol Instruments Inc ......G 585 924-2620
Victor *(G-16464)*

Brookhaven Instruments Corp ......E 631 758-3200
Holtsville *(G-6501)*

Caltex International Ltd ......E 315 425-1040
Syracuse *(G-15883)*

Cambridge Manufacturing LLC ......G 516 326-1350
New Hyde Park *(G-8820)*

▲ **Carl Zeiss Inc** ......C 914 747-1800
Thornwood *(G-16117)*

Ceres Technologies Inc ......D 845 247-4701
Saugerties *(G-15181)*

Chromosense LLC ......G 347 770-5421
Brooklyn *(G-1778)*

Corning Incorporated ......G 607 974-6729
Painted Post *(G-13391)*

CTB Enterprise LLC ......F 631 563-0088
Holbrook *(G-6442)*

East Coast Envmtl Group Inc ......G 516 352-1946
Farmingdale *(G-4984)*

East Hills Instrument Inc ......F 516 621-8686
Westbury *(G-16980)*

Ewt Holdings III Corp ......G 212 644-5900
New York *(G-10096)*

Exfo Burleigh Pdts Group Inc ......D 585 301-1530
Canandaigua *(G-3345)*

Finger Lakes Radiology LLC ......G 315 787-5399
Geneva *(G-5577)*

Gemprint Corporation ......E 212 997-0007
New York *(G-10269)*

General Microwave Corporation ......F 516 802-0900
Syosset *(G-15824)*

High Voltage Inc ......E 518 329-3275
Copake *(G-3887)*

Islandia Mri Associates PC ......F 631 234-2828
Central Islip *(G-3501)*

Micro Photo Acoustics Inc ......G 631 750-6035
Ronkonkoma *(G-14942)*

▲ **MMC Enterprises Corp** ......G 800 435-1088
Hauppauge *(G-6140)*

▼ **Multiwire Laboratories Ltd** ......G 607 257-3378
Ithaca *(G-6865)*

▲ **Nexgen Enviro Systems Inc** ......G 631 226-2930
Lindenhurst *(G-7475)*

Niagara Scientific Inc ......D 315 437-0821
East Syracuse *(G-4552)*

Novartis Pharmaceuticals Corp ......G 888 669-6682
New York *(G-11463)*

Phymetrix Inc ......G 631 627-3950
Medford *(G-8257)*

Porous Materials Inc ......E 607 257-5544
Ithaca *(G-6870)*

Rheonix Inc ......D 607 257-1242
Ithaca *(G-6873)*

Smartpill Corporation ......E 716 882-0701
Buffalo *(G-3188)*

Spectra Vista Corporation ......G 845 471-7007
Poughkeepsie *(G-13932)*

Thermo Fisher Scientific Inc ......B 631 648-4040
Wading River *(G-16528)*

Thermo Fisher Scientific Inc ......B 585 458-8008
Rochester *(G-14722)*

Thermo Fisher Scientific Inc ......A 585 899-7610
Rochester *(G-14723)*

Tokyo Electron America Inc ......F 518 292-4200
Albany *(G-143)*

Uptek Solutions ......F 631 256-5565
Bohemia *(G-1153)*

Veeco Instruments Inc ......C 516 677-0200
Woodbury *(G-17302)*

3827 Optical Instruments

21st Century Optics Inc ......E 347 527-1079
Long Island City *(G-7643)*

▲ **Advanced Glass Industries Inc** ......D 585 458-8040
Rochester *(G-14177)*

▲ **Aeroflex Incorporated** ......B 516 694-6700
Plainview *(G-13578)*

Aeroflex Plainview Inc ......B 516 694-6700
Plainview *(G-13579)*

▲ **Anorad Corporation** ......C 631 380-2100
East Setauket *(G-4476)*

Apollo Optical Systems Inc ......E 585 272-6170
West Henrietta *(G-16868)*

◆ **Applied Coatings Holding Corp** ......G 585 482-0300
Rochester *(G-14208)*

Applied Image Inc ......E 585 482-0300
Rochester *(G-14209)*

Ariel Optics Inc ......G 585 265-4820
Ontario *(G-13195)*

SIC

Employee Codes: A=Over 500 employees, B=251-500
C=101-250, D=51-100, E=20-50, F=10-19, G=5-9

2017 Harris
New York Manufacturers Directory

859

▼ **Binoptics LLC** .... D 607 257-3200
Ithaca *(G-6823)*

▲ **Carl Zeiss Inc** .... C 914 747-1800
Thornwood *(G-16117)*

CK Coatings .... G 585 502-0425
Le Roy *(G-7404)*

Claude Tribastone Inc .... G 585 265-3776
Ontario *(G-13197)*

Corning Tropel Corporation .... C 585 377-3200
Fairport *(G-4852)*

CVI Laser LLC .... D 585 244-7220
Rochester *(G-14297)*

Dorsey Metrology Intl Inc .... E 845 229-2929
Poughkeepsie *(G-13895)*

▲ **Dynamic Laboratories Inc** .... E 631 231-7474
Ronkonkoma *(G-14895)*

Eele Laboratories LLC .... F 631 244-0051
Bohemia *(G-1063)*

Evergreen Bleachers Inc .... G 518 654-9084
Corinth *(G-3958)*

Exfo Burleigh Pdts Group Inc .... D 585 301-1530
Canandaigua *(G-3345)*

▲ **Genesis Vision Inc** .... E 585 254-0193
Rochester *(G-14397)*

Gradient Lens Corporation .... E 585 235-2620
Rochester *(G-14412)*

Gurley Precision Instrs Inc .... C 518 272-6300
Troy *(G-16237)*

Halo Optical Products Inc .... D 518 773-4256
Gloversville *(G-5713)*

▲ **Hart Specialties Inc** .... D 631 226-5600
Amityville *(G-292)*

Hudson Mirror LLC .... E 914 930-8906
Peekskill *(G-13479)*

▲ **Isp Optics Corporation** .... D 914 591-3070
Irvington *(G-6773)*

▲ **Jml Optical Industries LLC** .... D 585 248-8900
Rochester *(G-14462)*

Keon Optics Inc .... F 845 429-7103
Stony Point *(G-15775)*

Kevin Freeman .... G 631 447-5321
Patchogue *(G-13426)*

Leica Microsystems Inc .... G 716 686-3000
Depew *(G-4262)*

Lens Triptar Co Inc .... G 585 473-4470
Rochester *(G-14477)*

▼ **Lumetrics Inc** .... F 585 214-2455
Rochester *(G-14484)*

Machida Incorporated .... G 845 365-0600
Orangeburg *(G-13235)*

▲ **Match Eyewear LLC** .... E 516 877-0170
Westbury *(G-17009)*

▲ **Meopta USA Inc** .... C 631 436-5900
Hauppauge *(G-6131)*

Metavac LLC .... E 631 207-2344
Holtsville *(G-6504)*

Micatu Inc .... G 888 705-8836
Horseheads *(G-6582)*

Navitar Inc .... D 585 359-4000
Rochester *(G-14530)*

New Scale Technologies Inc .... E 585 924-4450
Victor *(G-16492)*

▲ **Newport Rochester Inc** .... D 585 262-1325
Rochester *(G-14536)*

▲ **Nikon Instruments Inc** .... D 631 547-4200
Melville *(G-8343)*

▲ **North American Enclosures Inc** .... E 631 234-9500
Central Islip *(G-3507)*

Novanta Inc .... E 818 341-5151
Syracuse *(G-16000)*

▲ **Optics Plus Inc** .... G 716 744-2636
Tonawanda *(G-16190)*

Optics Technology Inc .... G 585 586-0950
Pittsford *(G-13571)*

Optimax Systems Inc .... C 585 265-1020
Ontario *(G-13207)*

▲ **Optipro Systems LLC** .... D 585 265-0160
Ontario *(G-13208)*

Orafol Americas Inc .... E 585 272-0290
West Henrietta *(G-16886)*

▲ **Orafol Display Optics Inc** .... E 585 647-1140
West Henrietta *(G-16887)*

Photon Gear Inc .... F 585 265-3360
Ontario *(G-13209)*

Planar Optics Inc .... G 585 671-0100
Webster *(G-16729)*

Plx Inc .... E 631 586-4190
Deer Park *(G-4189)*

▲ **Quality Vision Intl Inc** .... G 585 544-0400
Rochester *(G-14613)*

▲ **Quality Vision Services Inc** .... D 585 544-0450
Rochester *(G-14614)*

Rochester Photonics Corp .... D 585 387-0674
Rochester *(G-14646)*

◆ **Rochester Precision Optics LLC** .... C 585 292-5450
West Henrietta *(G-16893)*

RPC Photonics Inc .... F 585 272-2840
Rochester *(G-14661)*

Santa Fe Manufacturing Corp .... G 631 234-0100
Hauppauge *(G-6183)*

Schott Corporation .... D 315 255-2791
Auburn *(G-517)*

Spectral Systems LLC .... E 845 896-2200
Hopewell Junction *(G-6559)*

Spectrum Thin Films Inc .... E 631 901-1010
Hauppauge *(G-6196)*

▼ **Stefan Sydor Optics Inc** .... E 585 271-7300
Rochester *(G-14702)*

Steven John Opticians .... G 718 543-3336
Bronx *(G-1465)*

Surgical Design Corp .... F 914 273-2445
Armonk *(G-421)*

Synergy Intrntnal Optrnics LLC .... E 631 277-0500
Ronkonkoma *(G-14991)*

▲ **Tele-Vue Optics Inc** .... E 845 469-4551
Chester *(G-3619)*

US Optical LLC .... E 315 463-4800
East Syracuse *(G-4578)*

Va Inc .... E 585 385-5930
Rochester *(G-14750)*

Victory Vision Care Inc .... G 718 622-2020
Brooklyn *(G-2726)*

Videk Inc .... E 585 377-0377
Fairport *(G-4885)*

▲ **Welch Allyn Inc** .... A 315 685-4100
Skaneateles Falls *(G-15472)*

Westchester Technologies Inc .... E 914 736-1034
Peekskill *(G-13486)*

3829 Measuring & Controlling Devices, NEC

Accuvein Inc .... G 816 997-9400
Cold Spring Harbor *(G-3767)*

Analytical Technology Inc .... F 646 208-4643
New York *(G-9146)*

Andor Design Corp .... G 516 364-1619
Syosset *(G-15812)*

Aspex Incorporated .... E 212 966-0410
New York *(G-9237)*

Aurora Technical Services Ltd .... G 716 652-1463
East Aurora *(G-4367)*

Biodesign Inc of New York .... F 845 454-6610
Carmel *(G-3398)*

▲ **Carl Zeiss Inc** .... C 914 747-1800
Thornwood *(G-16117)*

Circor Aerospace Inc .... D 631 737-1900
Hauppauge *(G-6045)*

Climatronics Corp .... F 541 471-7111
Bohemia *(G-1033)*

Computer Instruments Corp .... E 516 876-8400
Westbury *(G-16975)*

Cosense Inc .... E 516 364-9161
Syosset *(G-15817)*

Cubic Trnsp Systems Inc .... F 212 255-1810
New York *(G-9764)*

Dayton T Brown Inc .... B 631 589-6300
Bohemia *(G-1052)*

◆ **Defelsko Corporation** .... D 315 393-4450
Ogdensburg *(G-13114)*

Dispersion Technology Inc .... G 914 241-4777
Bedford Hills *(G-802)*

Dylix Corporation .... E 719 773-2985
Grand Island *(G-5755)*

▲ **Dyna-Empire Inc** .... C 516 222-2700
Garden City *(G-5500)*

▲ **Dynamic Systems Inc** .... E 518 283-5350
Poestenkill *(G-13723)*

East Hills Instrument Inc .... F 516 621-8686
Westbury *(G-16980)*

Eastern Niagra Radiology .... E 716 882-6544
Buffalo *(G-2928)*

Electrical Controls Link .... E 585 924-7010
Victor *(G-16474)*

Electro-Optical Products Corp .... G 718 456-6000
Ridgewood *(G-14105)*

Elsag North America LLC .... G 877 773-5724
Brewster *(G-1218)*

Enerac Inc .... F 516 997-1554
Holbrook *(G-6447)*

Erbessd Reliability LLC .... E 518 874-2700
South Glens Falls *(G-15524)*

▲ **Fougera Pharmaceuticals Inc** .... C 631 454-7677
Melville *(G-8321)*

Freeman Technology Inc .... E 732 829-8345
Bayside *(G-770)*

G E Inspection Technologies LP .... C 315 554-2000
Skaneateles *(G-15460)*

Gei International Inc .... E 315 463-9261
East Syracuse *(G-4533)*

◆ **Germanow-Simon Corporation** .... E 585 232-1440
Rochester *(G-14399)*

◆ **Gleason Corporation** .... A 585 473-1000
Rochester *(G-14407)*

◆ **Gleason Works** .... A 585 473-1000
Rochester *(G-14408)*

Gurley Precision Instrs Inc .... C 518 272-6300
Troy *(G-16237)*

H D M Labs Inc .... G 516 431-8357
Island Park *(G-6780)*

Hci Engineering .... G 315 336-3450
Rome *(G-14814)*

▲ **Helmel Engineering Pdts Inc** .... E 716 297-8644
Niagara Falls *(G-12832)*

Herman H Sticht Company Inc .... G 718 852-7602
Brooklyn *(G-2076)*

▲ **Highway Toll ADM LLC** .... F 516 684-9584
Roslyn Heights *(G-15026)*

◆ **Hipotronics Inc** .... C 845 279-8091
Brewster *(G-1220)*

Imaginant Inc .... E 585 264-0480
Pittsford *(G-13564)*

Industrial Test Eqp Co Inc .... E 516 883-6423
Port Washington *(G-13824)*

▲ **Itin Scale Co Inc** .... E 718 336-5900
Brooklyn *(G-2120)*

James A Staley Co Inc .... F 845 878-3344
Carmel *(G-3401)*

Joerger Enterprises Inc .... G 631 239-5579
East Northport *(G-4438)*

Kem Medical Products Corp .... G 631 454-6565
Farmingdale *(G-5027)*

Kinemotive Corporation .... E 631 249-6440
Farmingdale *(G-5028)*

Kld Labs Inc .... E 631 549-4222
Hauppauge *(G-6106)*

L N D Incorporated .... E 516 678-6141
Oceanside *(G-13085)*

Liberty Controls Inc .... G 718 461-0600
College Point *(G-3795)*

Machine Technology Inc .... G 845 454-4030
Poughkeepsie *(G-13913)*

▲ **Magnetic Analysis Corporation** .... D 914 530-2000
Elmsford *(G-4762)*

▼ **Magtrol Inc** .... E 716 668-5555
Buffalo *(G-3055)*

▲ **Make-Waves Instrument Corp** .... E 716 681-7524
Depew *(G-4264)*

▲ **Mason Industries Inc** .... C 631 348-0282
Hauppauge *(G-6126)*

Mechanical Technology Inc .... E 518 218-2550
Albany *(G-101)*

▲ **Miller & Weber Inc** .... E 718 821-7110
Westbury *(G-17012)*

Mirion Tech Conax Nuclear Inc .... E 716 681-1973
Buffalo *(G-3068)*

Mirion Technologies Ist Corp .... D 607 562-4300
Horseheads *(G-6584)*

MTI Instruments Inc .... F 518 218-2550
Albany *(G-104)*

MTS Systems Corporation .... C 518 899-2140
Ballston Lake *(G-584)*

Nis Manufacturing Inc .... G 518 456-2566
Cohoes *(G-3753)*

Norwich Aero Products Inc .... D 607 336-7636
Norwich *(G-13032)*

Nuclear Diagnostic Pdts NY Inc .... G 516 575-4201
Plainview *(G-13624)*

Orolia Usa Inc .... D 585 321-5800
Rochester *(G-14553)*

Oyster Bay Pump Works Inc .... F 516 922-3789
Hicksville *(G-6381)*

Parker-Hannifin Corporation .... B 631 231-3737
Hauppauge *(G-6158)*

Pcb Piezotronics Inc .... G 716 684-0001
Depew *(G-4269)*

Peerless Instrument Co Inc .... C 631 396-6500
Farmingdale *(G-5076)*

▲ **Peyser Instrument Corporation** .... E 631 841-3600
West Babylon *(G-16818)*

Poseidon Systems LLC .... F 585 239-6025
Rochester *(G-14589)*

SIC SECTION 38 MEASURING, ANALYZING AND CONTROLLING INSTRUMENTS; PHOTOGRAPHIC, MEDICAL AN

Precision Biologics Inc....G....516 482-1200
Great Neck *(G-5831)*
Precision Design Systems Inc....E....585 426-4500
Rochester *(G-14592)*
Research Frontiers Inc....F....516 364-1902
Woodbury *(G-17298)*
Riverhawk Company LP....E....315 624-7171
New Hartford *(G-8809)*
RJ Harvey Instrument Corp....F....845 359-3943
Tappan *(G-16083)*
S P Industries Inc....D....845 255-5000
Gardiner *(G-5550)*
Schenck Corporation....D....631 242-4010
Deer Park *(G-4205)*
▲ **Schenck Trebel Corp**....D....631 242-4397
Deer Park *(G-4206)*
▲ **Schott Corporation**....D....914 831-2200
Elmsford *(G-4778)*
SKF USA Inc....D....716 661-2600
Jamestown *(G-7028)*
▲ **Teledyne Lecroy Inc**....C....845 425-2000
Chestnut Ridge *(G-3626)*
Telog Instruments Inc....E....585 742-3000
Victor *(G-16507)*
Titan Controls Inc....F....516 358-2407
New York *(G-12354)*
U E Systems Incorporated....E....914 592-1220
Elmsford *(G-4790)*
Vacuum Instrument Corporation....D....631 737-0900
Ronkonkoma *(G-14997)*
Vector Magnetics LLC....E....607 273-8351
Ithaca *(G-6883)*
Videk Inc....E....585 377-0377
Fairport *(G-4885)*
◆ **VJ Technologies Inc**....E....631 589-8800
Bohemia *(G-1154)*
Voice Analysis Clinic....G....212 245-3803
New York *(G-12566)*
▲ **Weiss Instruments Inc**....D....631 207-1200
Holtsville *(G-6514)*
Xeku Corporation....F....607 761-1447
Vestal *(G-16457)*
York Industries Inc....E....516 746-3736
Garden City Park *(G-5546)*
Zomega Terahertz Corporation....F....585 347-4337
Webster *(G-16745)*

3841 Surgical & Medical Instrs & Apparatus

Abyrx Inc....F....914 357-2600
Irvington *(G-6766)*
Advantage Plus Diagnostics Inc....G....631 393-5044
Melville *(G-8288)*
Aerolase Corporation....D....914 345-8300
Tarrytown *(G-16084)*
Ala Scientific Instruments Inc....F....631 393-6401
Farmingdale *(G-4935)*
AM Bickford Inc....F....716 652-1590
Wales Center *(G-16539)*
American Bio Medica Corp....D....518 758-8158
Kinderhook *(G-7167)*
◆ **American Diagnostic Corp**....D....631 273-6155
Hauppauge *(G-6021)*
▲ **American Healthcare Supply Inc**....F....212 674-3636
New York *(G-9119)*
Angiodynamics Inc....B....518 792-4112
Glens Falls *(G-5671)*
Angiodynamics Inc....B....518 742-4430
Queensbury *(G-13989)*
Angiodynamics Inc....B....518 975-1400
Queensbury *(G-13990)*
Angiodynamics Inc....B....518 795-1400
Latham *(G-7354)*
Argon Medical Devices Inc....G....585 321-1130
Henrietta *(G-6293)*
Astra Tool & Instr Mfg Corp....E....914 747-3863
Hawthorne *(G-6244)*
Avery Biomedical Devices Inc....F....631 864-1600
Commack *(G-3823)*
◆ **Bausch & Lomb Incorporated**....B....585 338-6000
Rochester *(G-14225)*
Baxter Healthcare Corporation....B....800 356-3454
Medina *(G-8266)*
Beacon Spch Lnge Pthlgy Phys....F....516 626-1635
Roslyn *(G-15016)*
Becton Dickinson and Company....B....845 353-3371
Nyack *(G-13044)*
Biochemical Diagnostics Inc....E....631 595-9200
Edgewood *(G-4595)*
▲ **Biodex Medical Systems Inc**....C....631 924-9000
Shirley *(G-15416)*
Biodex Medical Systems Inc....E....631 924-3146
Shirley *(G-15417)*
Bioresearch Inc....G....212 734-5315
Pound Ridge *(G-13942)*
Boehm Surgical Instrument....F....585 436-6584
Rochester *(G-14241)*
Bovie Medical Corporation....G....727 384-2323
Purchase *(G-13953)*
▲ **Bovie Medical Corporation**....C....914 468-4009
Purchase *(G-13954)*
▲ **Buffalo Filter LLC**....D....716 835-7000
Lancaster *(G-7307)*
Buxton Medical Equipment Corp....E....631 957-4500
Lindenhurst *(G-7457)*
C R Bard Inc....B....518 793-2531
Queensbury *(G-13993)*
C R Bard Inc....A....518 793-2531
Glens Falls *(G-5674)*
Clerio Vision Inc....F....617 216-7881
Rochester *(G-14279)*
CN Group Incorporated....A....914 358-5690
White Plains *(G-17094)*
Cognitiveflow Sensor Tech....G....631 513-9369
Stony Brook *(G-15768)*
◆ **Conmed Corporation**....B....315 797-8375
Utica *(G-16316)*
Conmed Corporation....D....315 797-8375
Utica *(G-16315)*
Corning Tropel Corporation....C....585 377-3200
Fairport *(G-4852)*
Cynosure Inc....G....516 594-3333
Hicksville *(G-6340)*
Daxor Corporation....E....212 244-0555
New York *(G-9831)*
Delcath Systems Inc....E....212 489-2100
New York *(G-9838)*
Derm/Buro Inc....G....516 694-8300
Plainview *(G-13596)*
▲ **Designs For Vision Inc**....C....631 585-3300
Ronkonkoma *(G-14894)*
◆ **E-Z-Em Inc**....E....609 524-2864
Melville *(G-8313)*
▲ **East Coast Orthoic & Pros Cor**....D....516 248-5566
Deer Park *(G-4134)*
Elite Medical Supply of NY....G....716 712-0881
West Seneca *(G-16944)*
▲ **Elliquence LLC**....F....516 277-9000
Baldwin *(G-558)*
▲ **Esc Control Electronics LLC**....E....631 467-5328
Sayville *(G-15208)*
Extek Inc....E....585 533-1672
Rush *(G-15047)*
Eyeglass Service Industries....G....914 666-3150
Bedford Hills *(G-803)*
▲ **Fabrication Enterprises Inc**....E....914 591-9300
Elmsford *(G-4753)*
Flatbush Surgical Supply Co....G....516 775-0507
Elmont *(G-4720)*
▲ **Flexbar Machine Corporation**....E....631 582-8440
Islandia *(G-6793)*
Fluorologic Inc....G....585 248-2796
Pittsford *(G-13559)*
Ftt Medical Inc....G....585 235-1430
Rochester *(G-14384)*
▲ **Gaymar Industries Inc**....B....800 828-7341
Orchard Park *(G-13271)*
▲ **Getinge Usa Inc**....C....585 475-1400
Rochester *(G-14401)*
Gradian Health Systems Inc....G....212 537-0340
New York *(G-10345)*
Greatbatch Inc....D....716 759-5200
Clarence *(G-3663)*
Hanger Inc....F....516 678-3650
Rockville Centre *(G-14792)*
▲ **Harmac Medical Products Inc**....C....716 897-4500
Buffalo *(G-2989)*
▲ **Hogil Pharmaceutical Corp**....F....914 681-1800
White Plains *(G-17121)*
Hub Surgical & Orthopedic Sups....G....718 585-5415
Bronx *(G-1358)*
Huron Tl & Cutter Grinding Co....E....631 420-7000
Farmingdale *(G-5008)*
Hurryworks LLC....D....516 998-4600
Port Washington *(G-13822)*
Incredible Scents Inc....G....516 656-3300
Glen Head *(G-5634)*
Ineedmd Holdings Inc....G....212 256-9669
New York *(G-10592)*
Intersurgical Incorporated....F....315 451-2900
East Syracuse *(G-4544)*
Ip Med Inc....G....516 766-3800
Oceanside *(G-13082)*
J H M Engineering....E....718 871-1810
Brooklyn *(G-2123)*
Ken-Ton Open Mri PC....G....716 876-7000
Kenmore *(G-7150)*
Lake Region Medical Inc....C....716 662-5025
Orchard Park *(G-13279)*
Liberty Install Inc....F....631 651-5655
Centerport *(G-3479)*
Lydia H Soifer & Assoc Inc....F....914 683-5401
White Plains *(G-17135)*
Manhattan Eastside Dev Corp....F....212 305-3275
New York *(G-11129)*
Mdi East Inc....E....518 747-8730
South Glens Falls *(G-15526)*
◆ **Medical Depot Inc**....B....516 998-4600
Port Washington *(G-13841)*
Medical Technology Products....G....631 285-6640
Greenlawn *(G-5875)*
Medipoint Inc....F....516 294-8822
Mineola *(G-8524)*
Medline Industries Inc....B....845 344-3301
Middletown *(G-8450)*
Medsource Technologies LLC....D....716 662-5025
Orchard Park *(G-13283)*
Memory Md Inc....G....917 318-0215
New York *(G-11224)*
Mick Radio Nuclear Instrument....F....718 597-3999
Mount Vernon *(G-8706)*
▲ **Misonix Inc**....D....631 694-9555
Farmingdale *(G-5058)*
Modular Medical Corp....E....718 829-2626
Bronx *(G-1400)*
▲ **Monaghan Medical Corporation**....D....518 561-7330
Plattsburgh *(G-13679)*
◆ **Moog Inc**....A....716 652-2000
Elma *(G-4651)*
N Y B P Inc....G....585 624-2541
Mendon *(G-8381)*
Nano Vibronix Inc....F....516 374-8330
Cedarhurst *(G-3461)*
Nanobionovum LLC....F....518 581-1171
Saratoga Springs *(G-15164)*
▲ **Nasco Enterprises Inc**....G....516 921-9696
Syosset *(G-15829)*
Nasiff Associates Inc....G....315 676-2346
Central Square *(G-3517)*
▲ **Navilyst Medical Inc**....A....800 833-9973
Glens Falls *(G-5692)*
Njr Medical Devices....E....440 258-8204
Cedarhurst *(G-3462)*
▲ **Novamed-Usa Inc**....E....914 789-2100
Elmsford *(G-4771)*
Ocala Group LLC....F....516 233-2750
New Hyde Park *(G-8853)*
Omnicare Anesthesia PC....E....718 433-0044
Astoria *(G-452)*
▲ **Orics Industries Inc**....E....718 461-8613
Farmingdale *(G-5070)*
Ortho Medical Products....F....212 879-3700
New York *(G-11528)*
Ortho-Clinical Diagnostics Inc....F....585 453-5200
Rochester *(G-14554)*
Ortho-Clinical Diagnostics Inc....B....585 453-4771
Rochester *(G-14555)*
Orthocon Inc....E....914 357-2600
Irvington *(G-6775)*
Ovitz Corporation....G....585 474-4695
West Henrietta *(G-16889)*
▲ **P Ryton Corp**....F....718 937-7052
Long Island City *(G-7831)*
Pall Corporation....A....607 753-6041
Cortland *(G-4035)*
▲ **Pall Corporation**....A....516 484-5400
Port Washington *(G-13852)*
Parace Bionics LLC....G....877 727-2231
Yorktown Heights *(G-17515)*
Parkchester Dps LLC....C....718 823-4411
Bronx *(G-1421)*
Peter Digioia....G....516 644-5517
Plainview *(G-13628)*
▼ **Pharma-Smart International Inc**....E....585 427-0730
Rochester *(G-14581)*
Praxis Powder Technology Inc....E....518 812-0112
Queensbury *(G-14007)*
Precimed Inc....E....716 759-5600
Clarence *(G-3669)*
Precision Biologics Inc....G....516 482-1200
Great Neck *(G-5831)*

S I C

Employee Codes: A=Over 500 employees, B=251-500
C=101-250, D=51-100, E=20-50, F=10-19, G=5-9
2017 Harris
New York Manufacturers Directory
861

38 MEASURING, ANALYZING AND CONTROLLING INSTRUMENTS; PHOTOGRAPHIC, MEDICAL AN SIC SECTION

▲ Proactive Medical Products LLC ......G 845 205-6004
Mount Vernon (G-8720)
Professional Medical Devices ......F 914 835-0614
Harrison (G-5989)
Progressive Orthotics Ltd ......G 631 732-5556
Selden (G-15353)
▲ Reichert Inc ......C 716 686-4500
Depew (G-4272)
Repro Med Systems Inc ......D 845 469-2042
Chester (G-3612)
Responselink Inc ......G 518 424-7776
Latham (G-7378)
RJ Harvey Instrument Corp ......F 845 359-3943
Tappan (G-16083)
Robert Bosch LLC ......E 315 733-3312
Utica (G-16357)
▲ Schilling Forge Inc ......E 315 454-4421
Syracuse (G-16033)
Seedlngs Lf Scnce Ventures LLC ......G 917 913-8511
New York (G-12017)
Seneca TEC Inc ......G 585 381-2645
Fairport (G-4878)
▼ Sigma Intl Gen Med Apprtus LLC ......B 585 798-3901
Medina (G-8282)
Simulaids Inc ......D 845 679-2475
Saugerties (G-15194)
Simulated Surgical Systems LLC ......G 716 633-7216
Williamsville (G-17253)
Skyler Brand Ventures LLC ......G 646 979-5904
New York (G-12097)
Solid-Look Corporation ......G 917 683-1780
Douglaston (G-4311)
Sonomed Inc ......E 516 354-0900
New Hyde Park (G-8863)
St Silicones Corporation ......F 518 406-3208
Clifton Park (G-3709)
Stj Enterprises ......D 516 612-0110
Cedarhurst (G-3463)
▲ Sundance Enterprises Inc ......G 914 946-2942
White Plains (G-17173)
Surgical Design Corp ......F 914 273-2445
Armonk (G-421)
T G M Products Inc ......G 631 491-0515
Wyandanch (G-17377)
Tril Inc ......G 631 645-7989
Copiague (G-3935)
▲ Vante Inc ......F 716 778-7691
Newfane (G-12789)
▲ Vasomedical Inc ......E 516 997-4600
Plainview (G-13641)
Vasomedical Solutions Inc ......D 516 997-4600
Plainview (G-13642)
Viterion Corporation ......F 914 333-6033
Elmsford (G-4792)
Vizio Medical Devices LLC ......F 646 845-7382
New York (G-12561)
▲ W A Baum Co Inc ......D 631 226-3940
Copiague (G-3938)
Welch Allyn Inc ......A 315 685-4100
Skaneateles Falls (G-15471)
▲ Welch Allyn Inc ......A 315 685-4100
Skaneateles Falls (G-15472)
Welch Allyn Inc ......A 315 685-4347
Skaneateles Falls (G-15473)
Wyeth Holdings LLC ......D 845 602-5000
Pearl River (G-13469)

3842 Orthopedic, Prosthetic & Surgical Appliances/Splys

▲ 54321 Us Inc ......F 716 695-0258
Tonawanda (G-16133)
Aaaaar Orthopedics Inc ......G 845 278-4938
Brewster (G-1206)
▲ Advanced Enterprises Inc ......F 845 342-1009
Middletown (G-8425)
Advanced Prosthetics Orthotics ......F 516 365-7225
Manhasset (G-8054)
Advantage Orthotics Inc ......G 631 368-1754
East Northport (G-4432)
Aero Healthcare (us) LLC ......G 855 225-2376
Valley Cottage (G-16375)
Agnovos Healthcare LLC ......G 646 502-5860
New York (G-9058)
Aramsco Inc ......F 718 361-7540
Ridgewood (G-14099)
Argon Medical Devices Inc ......G 585 321-1130
Henrietta (G-6293)
Arimed Orthotics Prosthetics P ......F 718 875-8754
Brooklyn (G-1626)
Arimed Orthotics Prosthetics P ......F 718 979-6155
Staten Island (G-15640)
Avanti U S A Ltd ......F 716 695-5800
Tonawanda (G-16141)
Backtech Inc ......G 973 279-0838
New York (G-9300)
Benway-Haworth-Lwlr-Iacosta He ......F 518 432-4070
Albany (G-54)
Bio-Chem Barrier Systems LLC ......G 631 261-2682
Northport (G-13008)
▲ Biodex Medical Systems Inc ......C 631 924-9000
Shirley (G-15416)
Biodex Medical Systems Inc ......E 631 924-3146
Shirley (G-15417)
Bionic Eye Technologies Inc ......G 845 505-5254
Fishkill (G-5181)
Brannock Device Co Inc ......E 315 475-9862
Liverpool (G-7512)
Buffalo Hearg & Speech ......E 716 558-1105
West Seneca (G-16940)
Byer California ......G 212 944-8989
New York (G-9487)
Church Communities NY Inc ......E 518 589-5103
Elka Park (G-4629)
Church Communities NY Inc ......E 518 589-5103
Elka Park (G-4630)
▲ Cirrus Healthcare Products LLC ......E 631 692-7600
Cold Spring Harbor (G-3768)
Cityscape Ob/Gyn PLLC ......F 212 683-3595
New York (G-9632)
▲ Community Products LLC ......C 845 658-8799
Rifton (G-14132)
Community Products LLC ......E 845 658-7720
Chester (G-3603)
Community Products LLC ......F 845 572-3433
Chester (G-3604)
Community Products LLC ......E 518 589-5103
Elka Park (G-4631)
Complete Orthopedic Svcs Inc ......E 516 357-9113
East Meadow (G-4420)
Creative Orthotics Prosthetics ......F 607 734-7215
Elmira (G-4678)
Creative Orthotics Prosthetics ......G 607 771-4672
Binghamton (G-903)
Creative Orthotics Prosthetics ......G 607 431-2526
Oneonta (G-13183)
Crosley Medical Products Inc ......F 631 595-2547
Deer Park (G-4122)
Custom Sports Lab Inc ......G 212 832-1648
New York (G-9771)
▲ Cy Plastics Works Inc ......E 585 229-2555
Honeoye (G-6523)
Depuy Synthes Inc ......C 607 271-2500
Horseheads (G-6574)
Derm/Buro Inc ......G 516 694-8300
Plainview (G-13596)
East Cast Orthtics Prosthetics ......F 716 856-5192
Buffalo (G-2926)
East Coast Orthoic & Pros Cor ......G 212 923-2161
New York (G-9962)
Eis Inc ......D 585 426-5330
Rochester (G-14341)
Elwood Specialty Products Inc ......F 716 877-6622
Buffalo (G-2934)
Eschen Prosthetic & Orthotic L ......E 212 606-1262
New York (G-10059)
▲ Euromed Inc ......D 845 359-4039
Orangeburg (G-13227)
Family Hearing Center ......G 845 897-3059
Fishkill (G-5184)
Far Rockaway Drugs Inc ......F 718 471-2500
Far Rockaway (G-4922)
Fenway Holdings LLC ......E 212 757-0606
New York (G-10153)
Fiber Foot Appliances Inc ......F 631 465-9199
Farmingdale (G-4993)
Fist Inc ......G 718 643-3478
Brooklyn (G-1976)
Flo-Tech Orthotic & Prosthetic ......G 607 387-3070
Trumansburg (G-16266)
Future Mobility Products Inc ......E 716 783-9130
Buffalo (G-2961)
Gadabout USA Wheelchairs Inc ......F 585 338-2110
Rochester (G-14386)
▲ Getinge Sourcing LLC ......C 585 475-1400
Rochester (G-14400)
▲ Getinge Usa Inc ......C 585 475-1400
Rochester (G-14401)
Gfh Orthotic & Prosthetic Labs ......G 631 467-3725
Bohemia (G-1072)
Go Blue Technologies Ltd ......G 631 404-6285
North Babylon (G-12901)
Goldberg Prosthetic & Orthotic ......F 631 689-6606
East Setauket (G-4484)
Grand Slam Holdings LLC ......E 212 583-5000
New York (G-10348)
Great Lakes Orthopedic Labs ......G 716 878-7307
Buffalo (G-2980)
Greatbatch Inc ......D 716 759-5200
Clarence (G-3663)
Green Prosthetics & Orthotics ......G 716 484-1088
Jamestown (G-6996)
▲ Hal-Hen Company Inc ......E 516 294-3200
New Hyde Park (G-8838)
▲ Hand Care Inc ......G 516 747-5649
Roslyn (G-15020)
Hanger Inc ......G 718 575-5504
Forest Hills (G-5323)
Hanger Prsthetcs & Ortho Inc ......F 607 277-6620
Ithaca (G-6846)
Hanger Prsthetcs & Ortho Inc ......G 607 776-8013
Bath (G-657)
Hanger Prsthetcs & Ortho Inc ......D 518 446-1774
Albany (G-85)
Hanger Prsthetcs & Ortho Inc ......G 607 771-4672
Binghamton (G-921)
Hanger Prsthetcs & Ortho Inc ......G 315 472-5200
Syracuse (G-15956)
Hanger Prsthetcs & Ortho Inc ......G 585 292-9510
Rochester (G-14420)
Hanger Prsthetcs & Ortho Inc ......D 607 795-1220
Elmira (G-4687)
Hanger Prsthetcs & Ortho Inc ......G 315 789-4810
Geneva (G-5581)
▲ Harvy Surgical Supply Corp ......E 718 939-1122
Flushing (G-5249)
Hersco-Orthotic Labs Corp ......E 718 391-0416
Long Island City (G-7760)
Higgins Supply Company Inc ......D 607 836-6474
Mc Graw (G-8222)
Howmedica Osteonics Corp ......G 518 783-1880
Latham (G-7364)
Huron Tl & Cutter Grinding Co ......E 631 420-7000
Farmingdale (G-5008)
Instrumentation Laboratory Co ......C 845 680-0028
Orangeburg (G-13231)
J P R Pharmacy Inc ......F 718 327-0600
Far Rockaway (G-4923)
J-K Prosthetics & Orthotics ......E 914 699-2077
Mount Vernon (G-8695)
Kem Medical Products Corp ......G 631 454-6565
Farmingdale (G-5027)
Klemmt Orthotics & Prosthetics ......G 607 770-4400
Johnson City (G-7097)
Konrad Prosthetics & Orthotics ......G 516 485-9164
West Hempstead (G-16858)
▼ Lakeland Industries Inc ......C 631 981-9700
Ronkonkoma (G-14928)
Langer Biomechanics Inc ......D 800 645-5520
Ronkonkoma (G-14930)
Latorre Orthopedic Laboratory ......F 518 786-8655
Latham (G-7372)
Ldc ......G 516 822-2499
Bethpage (G-871)
Lehneis Orthotics Prosthetic ......G 631 360-3859
Hauppauge (G-6112)
Lehneis Orthotics Prosthetic ......G 631 369-3115
Riverhead (G-14146)
Lorelei Orthotics Prosthetics ......G 212 727-2011
New York (G-11041)
M H Mandelbaum Orthotic ......F 631 473-8668
Port Jefferson (G-13777)
Mayflower Splint Co ......E 631 549-5131
Dix Hills (G-4293)
▲ Medi-Ray Inc ......D 877 898-3003
Tuckahoe (G-16271)
▲ Medi-Tech International Corp ......G 800 333-0109
Brooklyn (G-2291)
Medical Acoustics LLC ......F 716 218-7353
Buffalo (G-3061)
Medical Action Industries Inc ......C 631 231-4600
Hauppauge (G-6129)
Medline Industries Inc ......B 845 344-3301
Middletown (G-8450)
Monaghan Medical Corporation ......G 315 472-2136
Syracuse (G-15993)
National Prosthetic Orthot ......G 718 767-8400
Bayside (G-774)
New Dynamics Corporation ......E 845 692-0022
Middletown (G-8453)

S I C

New England Orthotic & Prost ... G ... 212 831-3600
New York *(G-11386)*
New England Orthotic & Prost ... G ... 845 471-7777
Poughkeepsie *(G-13921)*
New York Rhbilitative Svcs LLC ... F ... 516 239-0990
Lawrence *(G-7396)*
Nortech Laboratories Inc ... F ... 631 501-1452
Farmingdale *(G-5067)*
North Shore Orthtics Prsthtics ... G ... 631 928-3040
Port Jeff STA *(G-13768)*
Northwell Health Inc ... A ... 888 387-5811
New York *(G-11461)*
▲ Nova Health Systems Inc ... G ... 315 798-9018
Utica *(G-16353)*
Nucare Pharmacy Inc ... F ... 212 426-9300
New York *(G-11470)*
Nucare Pharmacy West LLC ... F ... 212 462-2525
New York *(G-11471)*
▲ NY Orthopedic Usa Inc ... D ... 718 852-5330
Brooklyn *(G-2382)*
▲ Occunomix International LLC ... E ... 631 741-1940
Port Jeff STA *(G-13769)*
Orcam Inc ... F ... 800 713-3741
Jericho *(G-7080)*
Ortho Medical Products ... F ... 212 879-3700
New York *(G-11528)*
Ortho Rite Inc ... E ... 914 235-9100
New Rochelle *(G-8918)*
Orthocraft Inc ... G ... 718 692-0113
Brooklyn *(G-2396)*
Orthopedic Arts Laboratory Inc ... G ... 718 858-2400
Brooklyn *(G-2397)*
Orthopedic Treatment Facility ... G ... 718 898-7326
Woodside *(G-17343)*
Orthotic & Prosthetic Images ... G ... 516 292-8726
Hempstead *(G-6284)*
Orthotics & Prosthetics Dept ... F ... 585 341-9299
Rochester *(G-14558)*
Overhead Door Corporation ... D ... 518 828-7652
Hudson *(G-6629)*
▲ Pall Biomedical Inc ... C ... 516 484-3600
Port Washington *(G-13851)*
Pall Corporation ... A ... 607 753-6041
Cortland *(G-4035)*
Pall Corporation ... A ... 607 753-6041
Cortland *(G-4036)*
Pall Corporation ... A ... 516 484-2818
Port Washington *(G-13853)*
Pall Corporation ... A ... 607 753-6041
Cortland *(G-4037)*
Palmer Industries Inc ... G ... 607 754-8741
Endicott *(G-4822)*
Palmer Industries Inc ... E ... 607 754-2957
Endicott *(G-4823)*
Palmer Industries Inc ... G ... 607 754-1954
Endicott *(G-4824)*
Paradigm Spine LLC ... E ... 212 367-7274
New York *(G-11569)*
▲ Premier Brands of America Inc ... C ... 914 667-6200
Mount Vernon *(G-8717)*
▲ Proficient Surgical Eqp Inc ... G ... 516 487-1175
Port Washington *(G-13857)*
◆ Profoot Inc ... E ... 718 965-8600
Brooklyn *(G-2453)*
Progressive Orthotics Ltd ... G ... 631 732-5556
Selden *(G-15353)*
Progressive Orthotics Ltd ... F ... 631 447-3860
East Patchogue *(G-4449)*
▲ Promed Products Inc ... G ... 800 993-4010
Yonkers *(G-17480)*
Prosthetic Rehabilitation Ctr ... G ... 845 565-8255
Newburgh *(G-12777)*
Prosthetics By Nelson Inc ... F ... 716 894-6666
Cheektowaga *(G-3587)*
Prosthodontic & Implant Den ... G ... 212 319-6363
New York *(G-11740)*
Rehablitation Tech of Syracuse ... G ... 315 426-9920
Syracuse *(G-16022)*
▲ Robert Busse & Co Inc ... B ... 631 435-4711
Hauppauge *(G-6178)*
Robert Cohen ... G ... 718 789-0996
Ozone Park *(G-13385)*
Rochester Orthopedic Labs ... G ... 585 272-1060
Rochester *(G-14644)*
▲ Roner Inc ... G ... 718 392-6020
Long Island City *(G-7865)*
Roner Inc ... C ... 718 392-6020
Long Island City *(G-7866)*
Sampsons Prsthtic Orthotic Lab ... E ... 518 374-6011
Schenectady *(G-15291)*
Schuster & Richard Labortories ... G ... 718 358-8607
College Point *(G-3806)*
Scientific Plastics Inc ... F ... 212 967-1199
New York *(G-12004)*
◆ Silipos Holding LLC ... E ... 716 283-0700
Niagara Falls *(G-12877)*
▲ Skil-Care Corporation ... C ... 914 963-2040
Yonkers *(G-17484)*
Sontek Industries Inc ... G ... 781 749-3055
New York *(G-12130)*
▲ SPS Medical Supply Corp ... D ... 585 359-0130
Rush *(G-15052)*
SPS Medical Supply Corp ... F ... 585 968-2377
Cuba *(G-4070)*
Stafford Labs Orthotics/Prosth ... F ... 845 692-5227
Middletown *(G-8462)*
Steriliz LLC ... G ... 585 415-5411
Rochester *(G-14703)*
Stj Orthotic Services Inc ... F ... 631 956-0181
Lindenhurst *(G-7484)*
Syracuse Prosthetic Center Inc ... G ... 315 476-9697
Syracuse *(G-16054)*
▲ Tape Systems Inc ... F ... 914 668-3700
Mount Vernon *(G-8736)*
▲ TDS Fitness Equipment ... E ... 607 733-6789
Elmira *(G-4704)*
Todt Hill Audiological Svcs ... G ... 718 816-1952
Staten Island *(G-15749)*
Tonawanda Limb & Brace Inc ... G ... 716 695-1131
Tonawanda *(G-16207)*
Tumble Forms Inc ... E ... 315 429-3101
Dolgeville *(G-4309)*
Turbine Engine Comp Utica ... A ... 315 768-8070
Whitesboro *(G-17197)*
Ultrapedics Ltd ... G ... 718 748-4806
Brooklyn *(G-2696)*
Upstate Medical Solutions Inc ... G ... 716 799-3782
Buffalo *(G-3236)*
Vcp Mobility Inc ... B ... 718 356-7827
Staten Island *(G-15751)*
Venture Respiratory Inc ... F ... 718 437-3633
Brooklyn *(G-2722)*
▲ VSM Investors LLC ... G ... 212 351-1600
New York *(G-12571)*
▲ Widex Usa Inc ... D ... 718 360-1000
Hauppauge *(G-6234)*
William H Shapiro ... G ... 212 263-7037
New York *(G-12635)*
Womens Health Care PC ... G ... 718 850-0009
Richmond Hill *(G-14088)*
Wyeth Holdings LLC ... D ... 845 602-5000
Pearl River *(G-13469)*
Xylon Industries Inc ... G ... 631 293-4717
Farmingdale *(G-5144)*
Y Lift New York LLC ... F ... 212 861-7787
New York *(G-12685)*

3843 Dental Eqpt & Splys

A D K Dental Lab ... G ... 518 563-6093
Plattsburgh *(G-13649)*
A-Implant Dental Lab Corp ... G ... 212 582-4720
New York *(G-8995)*
▲ Air Techniques Inc ... B ... 516 433-7676
Melville *(G-8291)*
American Medical & Dental Sups ... F ... 845 517-5876
Spring Valley *(G-15578)*
Art Dental Laboratory Inc ... G ... 516 437-1882
Floral Park *(G-5193)*
Avalonbay Communities Inc ... E ... 516 484-7766
Glen Cove *(G-5612)*
Boehm Surgical Instrument ... F ... 585 436-6584
Rochester *(G-14241)*
Brandt Equipment LLC ... G ... 718 994-0800
Bronx *(G-1288)*
▲ Buffalo Dental Mfg Co Inc ... E ... 516 496-7200
Syosset *(G-15815)*
Cettel Studio of New York Inc ... G ... 518 494-3622
Chestertown *(G-3621)*
◆ Cmp Industries LLC ... E ... 518 434-3147
Albany *(G-66)*
Cmp Industries LLC ... G ... 518 434-3147
Albany *(G-67)*
▲ Corning Rubber Company Inc ... F ... 631 738-0041
Ronkonkoma *(G-14889)*
Cpac Equipment Inc ... F ... 585 382-3223
Leicester *(G-7421)*
▲ Crosstex International Inc ... D ... 631 582-6777
Hauppauge *(G-6058)*
Cynosure Inc ... G ... 516 594-3333
Hicksville *(G-6340)*
Darby Dental Supply ... G ... 516 688-6421
Jericho *(G-7065)*
▲ Dedeco International Sales Inc ... E ... 845 887-4840
Long Eddy *(G-7642)*
Dmx Enteprise ... F ... 212 481-1010
New York *(G-9891)*
Gac ... G ... 631 357-8600
Islandia *(G-6794)*
Gallery 57 Dental ... E ... 212 246-8700
New York *(G-10241)*
Gan Kavod Inc ... G ... 315 797-3114
New Hartford *(G-8805)*
Glaxosmithkline LLC ... D ... 518 239-6901
East Durham *(G-4387)*
Grasers Dental Ceramics ... G ... 716 649-5100
Orchard Park *(G-13274)*
Henry Schein Inc ... E ... 315 431-0340
East Syracuse *(G-4536)*
Henry Schein Fincl Svcs LLC ... F ... 631 843-5500
Melville *(G-8327)*
Impladent Ltd ... G ... 718 465-1810
Jamaica *(G-6921)*
J H M Engineering ... E ... 718 871-1810
Brooklyn *(G-2123)*
Jeffrey D Menoff ... G ... 716 665-1468
Jamestown *(G-7013)*
▲ JM Murray Center Inc ... C ... 607 756-9913
Cortland *(G-4031)*
JM Murray Center Inc ... C ... 607 756-0246
Cortland *(G-4032)*
Kay See Dental Mfg Co ... F ... 816 842-2817
New York *(G-10821)*
Lelab Dental Laboratory Inc ... G ... 516 561-5050
Valley Stream *(G-16412)*
Light Dental Labs Inc ... G ... 516 785-7730
Wantagh *(G-16559)*
◆ Lornamead Inc ... D ... 914 630-7733
New York *(G-11043)*
Lucas Dental Equipment Co Inc ... F ... 631 244-2807
Bohemia *(G-1097)*
Luitpold Pharmaceuticals Inc ... E ... 631 924-4000
Shirley *(G-15424)*
Marotta Dental Studio Inc ... E ... 631 249-7520
Farmingdale *(G-5042)*
Martins Dental Studio ... G ... 315 788-0800
Watertown *(G-16664)*
Mini-Max Dntl Repr Eqpmnts Inc ... G ... 631 242-0322
Deer Park *(G-4174)*
Nu Life Restorations of L I ... D ... 516 489-5200
Old Westbury *(G-13133)*
Oramaax Dental Products Inc ... F ... 516 771-8514
Freeport *(G-5417)*
Ortho Dent Laboratory Inc ... F ... 716 839-1900
Williamsville *(G-17249)*
Precision Dental Cabinets Inc ... F ... 631 543-3870
Smithtown *(G-15495)*
Precision Dental Ceramics of B ... F ... 716 681-4133
Bowmansville *(G-1170)*
Professional Manufacturers ... F ... 631 586-2440
Deer Park *(G-4194)*
Sabra Dental Products ... G ... 914 945-0836
Ossining *(G-13328)*
Safe-Dent Enterprises LLC ... G ... 845 362-0141
Monsey *(G-8580)*
▲ Schilling Forge Inc ... E ... 315 454-4421
Syracuse *(G-16033)*
◆ Score International ... E ... 407 322-3230
Plainview *(G-13634)*
Sentage Corporation ... E ... 914 664-2200
Mount Vernon *(G-8733)*
Smile Specialists ... F ... 877 337-6135
New York *(G-12102)*
Stylecraft Interiors Inc ... F ... 516 487-2133
Great Neck *(G-5843)*
Temrex Corporation ... E ... 516 868-6221
Freeport *(G-5430)*
Tiger Supply Inc ... G ... 631 293-2700
Farmingdale *(G-5130)*
Total Dntl Implant Sltions LLC ... G ... 212 877-3777
Valley Stream *(G-16430)*
▲ Valplast International Corp ... F ... 516 442-3923
Westbury *(G-17040)*
Vincent Martino Dental Lab ... F ... 716 674-7800
Buffalo *(G-3243)*
Yes Dental Laboratory Inc ... E ... 914 333-7550
Tarrytown *(G-16112)*

3844 X-ray Apparatus & Tubes

◆ AFP Imaging Corporation ... F ... 914 592-6665
Mount Kisco *(G-8622)*

▲ **Air Techniques Inc** ....B 516 433-7676
Melville *(G-8291)*
American Access Care LLC ....F 631 582-9729
Hauppauge *(G-6019)*
▲ **Biodex Medical Systems Inc** ....C 631 924-9000
Shirley *(G-15416)*
▲ **Community Products LLC** ....C 845 658-8799
Rifton *(G-14132)*
Dra Imaging PC ....E 845 296-1057
Wappingers Falls *(G-16566)*
▲ **Flow X Ray Corporation** ....D 631 242-9729
Deer Park *(G-4142)*
Genesis Digital Imaging Inc ....F 310 305-7358
Rochester *(G-14396)*
Mitegen LLC ....G 607 266-8877
Ithaca *(G-6862)*
▼ **Multiwire Laboratories Ltd** ....G 607 257-3378
Ithaca *(G-6865)*
New York Imaging Service Inc ....F 716 834-8022
Tonawanda *(G-16184)*
Phantom Laboratory Inc ....F 518 692-1190
Greenwich *(G-5891)*
Photo Medic Equipment Inc ....D 631 242-6600
Bay Shore *(G-723)*
▲ **Quantum Medical Imaging LLC** ....D 631 567-5800
Ronkonkoma *(G-14975)*
R M F Health Management L L C ....E 718 854-5400
Wantagh *(G-16562)*
▼ **RC Imaging Inc** ....G 585 392-4336
Hilton *(G-6420)*
Siemens Corporation ....F 202 434-7800
New York *(G-12062)*
Siemens USA Holdings Inc ....B 212 258-4000
New York *(G-12064)*
▲ **Star X-Ray Co Inc** ....E 631 842-3010
Woodbury *(G-17301)*
Surescan Corporation ....E 607 321-0042
Binghamton *(G-953)*
◆ **VJ Technologies Inc** ....E 631 589-8800
Bohemia *(G-1154)*
▲ **Wolf X-Ray Corporation** ....D 631 242-9729
Deer Park *(G-4227)*

3845 Electromedical & Electrotherapeutic Apparatus

Advd Heart Phys & Surgs ....F 212 434-3000
New York *(G-9048)*
Argon Medical Devices Inc ....G 585 321-1130
Henrietta *(G-6293)*
▲ **Biofeedback Instrument Corp** ....G 212 222-5665
New York *(G-9401)*
▲ **Buffalo Filter LLC** ....D 716 835-7000
Lancaster *(G-7307)*
C R Bard Inc ....A 518 793-2531
Glens Falls *(G-5674)*
Cardiac Life Products Inc ....G 585 267-7775
East Rochester *(G-4454)*
City Sports Imaging Inc ....E 212 481-3600
New York *(G-9631)*
Complex Biosystems Inc ....G 315 464-8007
Liverpool *(G-7517)*
Conmed Andover Medical Inc ....F 315 797-8375
Utica *(G-16314)*
Conmed Corporation ....D 315 797-8375
Utica *(G-16315)*
◆ **Conmed Corporation** ....B 315 797-8375
Utica *(G-16316)*
Ddc Technologies Inc ....G 516 594-1533
Oceanside *(G-13076)*
Elizabeth Wood ....G 315 492-5470
Syracuse *(G-15933)*
Empire Open Mri ....G 914 961-1777
Yonkers *(G-17441)*
Equivital Inc ....E 646 513-4169
New York *(G-10054)*
Excel Technology Inc ....F 212 355-3400
New York *(G-10102)*
Fonar Corporation ....C 631 694-2929
Melville *(G-8320)*
Forest Medical LLC ....G 315 434-9000
East Syracuse *(G-4531)*
Gary Gelbfish MD ....G 718 258-3004
Brooklyn *(G-2014)*
Global Instrumentation LLC ....F 315 682-0272
Manlius *(G-8072)*
Gravity East Village Inc ....G 212 388-9788
New York *(G-10355)*
Health Care Originals Inc ....G 585 967-1398
West Henrietta *(G-16882)*
Imacor Inc ....E 516 393-0970
Garden City *(G-5509)*
▲ **Infimed Inc** ....D 315 453-4545
Liverpool *(G-7524)*
Infimed Inc ....G 585 383-1710
Pittsford *(G-13565)*
Integrated Medical Devices ....G 315 457-4200
Liverpool *(G-7526)*
J H M Engineering ....E 718 871-1810
Brooklyn *(G-2123)*
Jadak LLC ....F 315 701-0678
North Syracuse *(G-12949)*
Jarvik Heart Inc ....E 212 397-3911
New York *(G-10701)*
Kal Manufacturing Corporation ....E 585 265-4310
Webster *(G-16726)*
Laser and Varicose Vein Trtmnt ....G 718 667-1777
Staten Island *(G-15698)*
Lifesciences Technology Inc ....G 516 569-0085
Hewlett *(G-6309)*
Med Services Inc ....D 631 218-6450
Bohemia *(G-1104)*
▲ **Misonix Inc** ....D 631 694-9555
Farmingdale *(G-5058)*
Motion Intelligence Inc ....G 607 227-4400
Ithaca *(G-6863)*
Nanovibronix Inc ....F 914 233-3004
Elmsford *(G-4769)*
Natus Medical Incorporated ....G 631 457-4430
Hauppauge *(G-6145)*
Netech Corporation ....F 631 531-0100
Farmingdale *(G-5065)*
New York Laser & Aestheticks ....G 516 627-7777
Roslyn *(G-15021)*
New York Marine Elec Inc ....G 631 734-6050
Hampton Bays *(G-5961)*
Nirx Medical Technologies LLC ....F 516 676-6479
Glen Head *(G-5638)*
▲ **Novamed-Usa Inc** ....E 914 789-2100
Elmsford *(G-4771)*
Ocean Cardiac Monitoring ....G 631 777-3700
Deer Park *(G-4185)*
Pharmadva LLC ....G 585 469-1410
West Henrietta *(G-16891)*
◆ **Philips Medical Systems Mr** ....B 518 782-1122
Latham *(G-7376)*
▲ **Photonics Industries Intl Inc** ....D 631 218-2240
Ronkonkoma *(G-14968)*
Ray Medica Inc ....E 952 885-0500
New York *(G-11806)*
▲ **Sonicor Inc** ....F 631 920-6555
West Babylon *(G-16830)*
Sonomed Inc ....E 516 354-0900
New Hyde Park *(G-8863)*
Soterix Medical Inc ....F 888 990-8327
New York *(G-12141)*
Stand Up Mri of Lynbrook PC ....F 516 256-1558
Lynbrook *(G-7963)*
Stj Enterprises ....D 516 612-0110
Cedarhurst *(G-3463)*
Sun Scientific Inc ....G 914 479-5108
Dobbs Ferry *(G-4303)*
Teledyne Optech Inc ....F 585 427-8310
West Henrietta *(G-16897)*
Ultradian Diagnostics LLC ....G 518 618-0046
Rensselaer *(G-14053)*
University of Rochester ....B 585 275-3483
Rochester *(G-14745)*
▲ **Vasomedical Inc** ....E 516 997-4600
Plainview *(G-13641)*
▲ **Vermed Inc** ....D 802 463-9976
Buffalo *(G-3241)*
Visiplex Instruments Corp ....D 845 365-0190
Elmsford *(G-4791)*
▲ **Z-Axis Inc** ....D 315 548-5000
Phelps *(G-13539)*

3851 Ophthalmic Goods

21st Century Optics Inc ....E 347 527-1079
Long Island City *(G-7643)*
Accu Coat Inc ....G 585 288-2330
Rochester *(G-14166)*
Alden Optical Laboratory Inc ....F 716 937-9181
Lancaster *(G-7302)*
Art-Craft Optical Company Inc ....E 585 546-6640
Rochester *(G-14213)*
Bausch & Lomb Holdings Inc ....G 585 338-6000
New York *(G-9335)*
◆ **Bausch & Lomb Incorporated** ....B 585 338-6000
Rochester *(G-14225)*
Bausch & Lomb Incorporated ....B 585 338-6000
Rochester *(G-14226)*
Co-Optics America Lab Inc ....E 607 432-0557
Oneonta *(G-13179)*
Colors In Optics Ltd ....D 718 845-0300
New Hyde Park *(G-8822)*
Coopervision Inc ....A 585 385-6810
West Henrietta *(G-16874)*
Coopervision Inc ....A 585 889-3301
Scottsville *(G-15335)*
▲ **Coopervision Inc** ....C 585 385-6810
Victor *(G-16470)*
▲ **Coopervision Inc** ....D 585 385-6810
Victor *(G-16471)*
▲ **Corinne McCormack Inc** ....F 212 868-7919
New York *(G-9725)*
▲ **Designs For Vision Inc** ....C 631 585-3300
Ronkonkoma *(G-14894)*
Edroy Products Co Inc ....G 845 358-6600
Nyack *(G-13051)*
Empire Optical Inc ....F 585 454-4470
Rochester *(G-14348)*
Equicheck LLC ....G 631 987-6356
Patchogue *(G-13419)*
▲ **Esc Control Electronics LLC** ....E 631 467-5328
Sayville *(G-15208)*
Essilor Laboratories Amer Inc ....E 845 365-6700
Orangeburg *(G-13226)*
Eye Deal Eyewear Inc ....G 716 297-1500
Niagara Falls *(G-12817)*
▲ **Eyeworks Inc** ....G 585 454-4470
Rochester *(G-14366)*
Frame Works America Inc ....E 631 288-1300
Westhampton Beach *(G-17058)*
Glasses USA LLC ....F 212 784-6094
New York *(G-10309)*
Hirsch Optical Corp ....D 516 752-2211
Farmingdale *(G-5006)*
His Vision Inc ....E 585 254-0022
Rochester *(G-14437)*
Humanware USA Inc ....E 800 722-3393
Champlain *(G-3542)*
J I Intrntnal Contact Lens Lab ....G 718 997-1212
Rego Park *(G-14033)*
Kathmando Valley Preservation ....F 212 727-0074
New York *(G-10818)*
Lens Lab ....G 718 379-2020
Bronx *(G-1381)*
Lens Lab Express ....G 718 921-5488
Brooklyn *(G-2211)*
Lens Lab Express of Graham Ave ....G 718 486-0117
Brooklyn *(G-2212)*
Lens Lab Express Southern Blvd ....G 718 626-5184
Astoria *(G-448)*
Mager & Gougelman Inc ....G 212 661-3939
New York *(G-11100)*
Mager & Gougelman Inc ....G 212 661-3939
Hempstead *(G-6278)*
Mager & Gougelman Inc ....G 516 489-0202
Hempstead *(G-6279)*
Mark F Rosenhaft N A O ....G 516 374-1010
Cedarhurst *(G-3460)*
Millbrook Family Eyecare ....G 845 677-5012
Millbrook *(G-8477)*
Modo Retail LLC ....E 212 965-4900
New York *(G-11289)*
▲ **Moscot Wholesale Corp** ....G 212 647-1550
New York *(G-11310)*
North Bronx Retinal & Ophthlmi ....G 347 535-4932
Bronx *(G-1413)*
Oakley Inc ....D 212 575-0960
New York *(G-11491)*
Optika Eyes Ltd ....G 631 567-8852
Sayville *(G-15213)*
▲ **Optisource International Inc** ....E 631 924-8360
Bellport *(G-835)*
Optogenics of Syracuse Inc ....D 315 446-3000
Syracuse *(G-16005)*
▲ **Parker Warby Retail Inc** ....E 646 517-5223
New York *(G-11575)*
Strauss Eye Prosthetics Inc ....G 585 424-1350
Rochester *(G-14705)*
Surgical Design Corp ....F 914 273-2445
Armonk *(G-421)*
▲ **Tri-Supreme Optical LLC** ....D 631 249-2020
Farmingdale *(G-5134)*
Winchester Optical Company ....E 607 734-4251
Elmira *(G-4705)*
Wyeth Holdings LLC ....D 845 602-5000
Pearl River *(G-13469)*

Xinya International Trading Co..............G....... 212 216-9681
New York (G-12679)
▲ Zyloware Corporation........................D....... 914 708-1200
Port Chester (G-13762)

3861 Photographic Eqpt & Splys

▲ Air Techniques Inc...........................B....... 516 433-7676
Melville (G-8291)
Alanelli Psle..G....... 212 828-6600
New York (G-9070)
▲ All-Pro Imaging Corp.........................E....... 516 433-7676
Melville (G-8292)
Apexx Omni-Graphics Inc......................D....... 718 326-3330
Maspeth (G-8119)
Astrodyne Inc...G....... 516 536-5755
Oceanside (G-13073)
AVI-Spl Employee..................................B....... 212 840-4801
New York (G-9277)
Avid Technology Inc..............................E....... 212 983-2424
New York (G-9278)
▲ Bescor Video Accessories Ltd.........F....... 631 420-1717
Farmingdale (G-4952)
▲ Cannon Industries Inc.......................D....... 585 254-8080
Rochester (G-14258)
Carestream Health Inc...........................B....... 585 627-1800
Rochester (G-14259)
◆ Champion Photochemistry Inc..........D....... 585 760-6444
Rochester (G-14271)
Chemung Cty Assc Retrd Ctzns............C....... 607 734-6151
Elmira (G-4675)
▼ Cpac Inc...E....... 585 382-3223
Leicester (G-7420)
Creatron Services Inc.............................E....... 516 437-5119
Floral Park (G-5201)
Critical Imaging LLC..............................E....... 315 732-5020
Utica (G-16318)
▲ Dnp Electronics America LLC..........D....... 212 503-1060
New York (G-9892)
Dolby Laboratories Inc..........................F....... 212 767-1700
New York (G-9896)
Eastchester Photo Services...................G....... 914 961-6596
Eastchester (G-4582)
Eastman Kodak Company......................D....... 585 722-2187
Rochester (G-14327)
Eastman Kodak Company......................B....... 585 724-4000
Rochester (G-14328)
Eastman Kodak Company......................D....... 585 724-5600
Rochester (G-14329)
Eastman Kodak Company......................D....... 585 722-9695
Pittsford (G-13558)
Eastman Kodak Company......................D....... 585 726-6261
Rochester (G-14330)
Eastman Kodak Company......................D....... 585 724-4000
Rochester (G-14331)
Eastman Kodak Company......................F....... 800 698-3324
Rochester (G-14332)
Eastman Kodak Company......................D....... 585 722-4385
Rochester (G-14333)
Eastman Kodak Company......................D....... 585 588-5598
Rochester (G-14334)
Eastman Kodak Company......................C....... 585 726-7000
Rochester (G-14335)
Eastman Kodak Company......................G....... 585 722-4007
Rochester (G-14336)
Eastman Kodak Company......................D....... 585 588-3896
Rochester (G-14337)
Eastman Kodak Company......................E....... 585 724-4000
Rochester (G-14338)
Eastman Park Micrographics Inc..........E....... 866 934-4376
Rochester (G-14339)
Ebsco Industries Inc..............................G....... 585 398-2000
Farmington (G-5149)
Efam Enterprises LLC...........................E....... 718 204-1760
Long Island City (G-7725)
Emda Inc..F....... 631 243-6363
Edgewood (G-4597)
Facsimile Cmmncations Inds Inc..........D....... 212 741-6400
New York (G-10125)
Fluxdata Incorporated............................G....... 800 425-0176
Rochester (G-14377)
▲ Focus Camera Inc...............................C....... 718 437-8800
Brooklyn (G-1990)
Garys Loft..G....... 212 244-0970
New York (G-10250)
Geospatial Systems Inc..........................F....... 585 427-8310
West Henrietta (G-16880)
Gpc International Inc.............................G....... 631 752-9600
Melville (G-8322)
Henrys Deals Inc.....................................E....... 347 821-4685
Brooklyn (G-2073)
Hilord Chemical Corporation.................E....... 631 234-7373
Hauppauge (G-6094)
Jack L Popkin & Co Inc..........................G....... 718 361-6700
Kew Gardens (G-7163)
Just Lamps of New York Inc..................F....... 716 626-2240
Buffalo (G-3022)
Kelmar Systems Inc................................F....... 631 421-1230
Huntington Station (G-6714)
◆ Kodak Alaris Inc..................................B....... 585 290-2891
Rochester (G-14471)
Kogeto Inc...G....... 646 490-8169
New York (G-10868)
▲ Konica Mnolta Sups Mfg USA Inc.....D....... 845 294-8400
Goshen (G-5736)
Kyle Editing LLC....................................G....... 212 675-3464
New York (G-10898)
Labgrafix Printing Inc.............................G....... 516 280-8300
Lynbrook (G-7953)
Lake Image Systems Inc.........................F....... 585 321-3630
Henrietta (G-6296)
▲ Lanel Inc..F....... 516 437-5119
Floral Park (G-5205)
Lasertech Crtridge RE-Builders............G....... 518 373-1246
Clifton Park (G-3698)
▲ Lowel-Light Manufacturing Inc.........E....... 718 921-0600
Brooklyn (G-2238)
Mekatronics Incorporated.......................E....... 516 883-6805
Port Washington (G-13844)
Mirion Technologies Ist Corp.................D....... 607 562-4300
Horseheads (G-6584)
▲ Norazza Inc..G....... 716 706-1160
Buffalo (G-3093)
◆ Printer Components Inc.......................G....... 585 924-5190
Fairport (G-4871)
Qls Solutions Group Inc.........................E....... 716 852-2203
Buffalo (G-3144)
Rear View Safety Inc...............................E....... 855 815-3842
Brooklyn (G-2482)
Rockland Colloid Corp............................G....... 845 359-5559
Piermont (G-13545)
Seneca TEC Inc..G....... 585 381-2645
Fairport (G-4878)
Shelley Promotions Inc...........................G....... 212 924-4987
New York (G-12049)
▲ Sima Technologies LLC.......................G....... 412 828-9130
Hauppauge (G-6191)
Stallion Technologies Inc.......................G....... 315 622-1176
Liverpool (G-7548)
Thermo Cidtec Inc...................................E....... 315 451-9410
Liverpool (G-7553)
Tiffen Acquisition LLC............................F....... 631 273-2500
Hauppauge (G-6215)
▲ Tiffen Acquisition LLC.........................D....... 631 273-2500
Hauppauge (G-6216)
Tiffen Company LLC...............................G....... 631 273-2500
Hauppauge (G-6217)
Toner-N-More Inc....................................G....... 718 232-6200
Brooklyn (G-2662)
Truesense Imaging Inc............................C....... 585 784-5500
Rochester (G-14733)
▲ Turner Bellows Inc...............................E....... 585 235-4456
Rochester (G-14735)
Va Inc...E....... 585 385-5930
Rochester (G-14750)
▲ Vishay Thin Film LLC..........................C....... 716 283-4025
Niagara Falls (G-12889)
Watec America Corporation....................E....... 702 434-6111
Middletown (G-8470)
Xerox Corporation...................................F....... 585 423-4711
Rochester (G-14768)
Xerox Corporation...................................A....... 585 422-4564
Webster (G-16743)
Xerox Corporation...................................B....... 212 716-4000
New York (G-12675)
Xerox Corporation...................................E....... 914 397-1319
White Plains (G-17188)
Xerox Corporation...................................D....... 585 425-6100
Fairport (G-4888)
Xerox Corporation...................................D....... 212 633-8190
New York (G-12676)
Xerox Corporation...................................D....... 212 330-1386
New York (G-12677)
Xerox Corporation...................................E....... 845 918-3147
Suffern (G-15803)
Xerox Corporation...................................D....... 585 423-5090
Webster (G-16744)
Xerox Corporation...................................C....... 585 264-5584
Rochester (G-14770)
Xerox Corporation...................................D....... 716 831-3300
Buffalo (G-3259)

3873 Watch & Clock Devices & Parts

▲ American Time Mfg Ltd......................F....... 585 266-5120
Rochester (G-14201)
◆ Compumatic Time Recorders Inc.....G....... 718 531-5749
North Bellmore (G-12917)
▲ Croton Watch Co Inc..........................E....... 800 443-7639
West Nyack (G-16915)
◆ E Gluck Corporation...........................C....... 718 784-0700
Little Neck (G-7508)
▲ Ewatchfactory Corp............................G....... 212 564-8318
New York (G-10095)
▲ First Sbf Holding Inc..........................G....... 845 425-9882
Valley Cottage (G-16378)
▲ Game Time LLC..................................F....... 914 557-9662
New York (G-10244)
▲ Geneva Watch Company Inc.............E....... 212 221-1177
New York (G-10276)
H Best Ltd...F....... 212 354-2400
New York (G-10387)
Hammerman Bros Inc.............................G....... 212 956-2800
New York (G-10401)
Justa Company..G....... 718 932-6139
Long Island City (G-7775)
Life Watch Technology Inc.....................D....... 917 669-2428
Flushing (G-5266)
▲ M & Co Ltd...G....... 212 414-6400
New York (G-11067)
Marco Moore Inc.....................................D....... 212 575-2090
Great Neck (G-5822)
National Time Recording Eqp Co..........F....... 212 227-3310
New York (G-11352)
Olympic Jewelry Inc...............................G....... 212 768-7004
New York (G-11501)
▲ Pavana USA Inc...................................G....... 646 833-8811
New York (G-11587)
◆ Pedre Corp...E....... 212 868-2935
Hicksville (G-6386)
▲ Precision International Co Inc..........G....... 212 268-9090
New York (G-11697)
Richemont North America Inc...............G....... 212 891-2440
New York (G-11863)
Richemont North America Inc...............G....... 212 644-9500
New York (G-11864)
▲ Sarina Accessories LLC.....................E....... 212 239-8106
New York (G-11973)
▲ Stuhrling Original LLC........................G....... 718 840-5760
Brooklyn (G-2615)
▲ TWI Watches LLC................................E....... 718 663-3969
Brooklyn (G-2690)
Visage Swiss Watch LLC........................G....... 212 594-7991
New York (G-12552)
▲ Watchcraft Inc.....................................G....... 347 531-0382
Long Island City (G-7919)

39 MISCELLANEOUS MANUFACTURING INDUSTRIES

3911 Jewelry: Precious Metal

A & S Fine Jewelry Corp........................G....... 718 243-2201
Brooklyn (G-1530)
A & V Castings Inc.................................G....... 212 997-0042
New York (G-8982)
A Jaffe Inc...C....... 212 843-7464
New York (G-8991)
Abraham Jwly Designers & Mfrs...........F....... 212 944-1149
New York (G-9005)
Abrimian Bros Corp................................F....... 212 382-1106
New York (G-9006)
Adamor Inc..G....... 212 688-8885
New York (G-9025)
AF Design Inc..G....... 347 548-5273
New York (G-9053)
Alart Inc...G....... 212 840-1508
New York (G-9071)
▲ Albea Cosmetics America Inc...........E....... 212 371-5100
New York (G-9073)
Alchemy Simya Inc.................................E....... 646 230-1122
New York (G-9076)
Alex Sepkus Inc......................................F....... 212 391-8466
New York (G-9081)
Alexander Primak Jewelry Inc...............D....... 212 398-0287
New York (G-9082)
▲ Alfred Butler Inc.................................F....... 516 829-7460
Great Neck (G-5786)
All The Rage Inc.....................................G....... 516 605-2001
Hicksville (G-6320)
▲ Almond Jewelers Inc..........................F....... 516 933-6000
Port Washington (G-13799)

S I C

▲ **Alpine Creations Ltd**....G....212 308-9353
New York ***(G-9103)***

Ambras Fine Jewelry Inc....E....718 784-5252
Long Island City ***(G-7655)***

American Craft Jewelers Inc....G....718 972-0945
Brooklyn ***(G-1600)***

American Originals Corporation....G....212 836-4155
New York ***(G-9126)***

Anatoli Inc....F....845 334-9000
West Hurley ***(G-16901)***

Ancient Modern Art LLC....F....212 302-0080
New York ***(G-9151)***

▲ **Anima Group LLC**....G....917 913-2053
New York ***(G-9161)***

Apicella Jewelers Inc....E....212 840-2024
New York ***(G-9174)***

▲ **AR & AR Jewelry Inc**....E....212 764-7916
New York ***(G-9186)***

Arringement International Inc....G....347 323-7974
Flushing ***(G-5227)***

Art-TEC Jewelry Designs Ltd....F....212 719-2941
New York ***(G-9215)***

▲ **Asher Jewelry Company Inc**....D....212 302-6233
New York ***(G-9228)***

Ateret LLC....G....212 819-0777
New York ***(G-9246)***

Atlantic Precious Metal Cast....G....718 937-7100
Long Island City ***(G-7676)***

Atr Jewelry Inc....F....212 819-0075
New York ***(G-9258)***

B K Jewelry Contractor Inc....E....212 398-9093
New York ***(G-9289)***

Barber Brothers Jewelry Mfg....F....212 819-0666
New York ***(G-9316)***

Baroka Creations Inc....G....212 768-0527
New York ***(G-9323)***

Bartholomew Mazza Ltd Inc....E....212 935-4530
New York ***(G-9328)***

Bellataire Diamonds Inc....F....212 687-8881
New York ***(G-9350)***

▲ **BH Multi Com Corp**....E....212 944-0020
New York ***(G-9387)***

Bielka Inc....G....212 980-6841
New York ***(G-9390)***

Billanti Casting Co Inc....E....516 775-4800
New Hyde Park ***(G-8819)***

BJG Services LLC....E....516 592-5692
New York ***(G-9408)***

Bourghol Brothers Inc....G....845 268-9752
Congers ***(G-3853)***

Bral Nader Fine Jewelry Inc....G....800 493-1222
New York ***(G-9452)***

▲ **Brannkey Inc**....D....212 371-1515
New York ***(G-9453)***

Brilliant Jewelers/Mjj Inc....C....212 353-2326
New York ***(G-9462)***

Bristol Seamless Ring Corp....F....212 874-2645
New York ***(G-9463)***

Burke & Bannayan....G....585 723-1010
Rochester ***(G-14250)***

Carlo Monte Designs Inc....G....212 935-5611
New York ***(G-9527)***

▲ **Carol Dauplaise Ltd**....E....212 564-7301
New York ***(G-9529)***

Carol Dauplaise Ltd....E....212 997-5290
New York ***(G-9530)***

Carr Manufacturing Jewelers....G....518 783-6093
Latham ***(G-7358)***

Carvin French Jewelers Inc....E....212 755-6474
New York ***(G-9539)***

Chaindom Enterprises Inc....G....212 719-4778
New York ***(G-9575)***

Chameleon Gems Inc....F....516 829-3333
Great Neck ***(G-5797)***

Charles Perrella Inc....E....845 348-4777
Nyack ***(G-13046)***

▲ **Charles Vaillant Inc**....G....212 752-4832
New York ***(G-9583)***

▲ **Christopher Designs Inc**....E....212 382-1013
New York ***(G-9613)***

▲ **Cigar Oasis Inc**....G....516 520-5258
Farmingdale ***(G-4959)***

▲ **CJ Jewelry Inc**....F....212 719-2464
New York ***(G-9633)***

▲ **Clyde Duneier Inc**....D....212 398-1122
New York ***(G-9648)***

Color Merchants Inc....E....212 682-4788
New York ***(G-9672)***

Concord Jewelry Mfg Co LLC....E....212 719-4030
New York ***(G-9694)***

▲ **Creative Gold LLC**....E....718 686-2225
Brooklyn ***(G-1815)***

Crescent Wedding Rings Inc....G....212 869-8296
New York ***(G-9754)***

Crown Jewelers Intl Inc....G....212 420-7800
New York ***(G-9760)***

▲ **Csi International Inc**....E....716 282-5408
Niagara Falls ***(G-12809)***

D & D Creations Co Inc....G....212 840-1198
New York ***(G-9781)***

D Oro Onofrio Inc....G....718 491-2961
Brooklyn ***(G-1831)***

Danwak Jewelry Corp....G....212 730-4541
New York ***(G-9808)***

Dasan Inc....E....212 244-5410
New York ***(G-9811)***

David Friedman Chain Co Inc....F....212 684-1760
New York ***(G-9819)***

David Howell Product Design....E....914 666-4080
Bedford Hills ***(G-801)***

David S Diamonds Inc....F....212 921-8029
New York ***(G-9822)***

David Weisz & Sons Inc....G....212 840-4747
New York ***(G-9825)***

David Yurman Enterprises LLC....G....914 539-4444
White Plains ***(G-17099)***

◆ **David Yurman Enterprises LLC**....B....212 896-1550
New York ***(G-9826)***

David Yurman Enterprises LLC....G....516 627-1700
Manhasset ***(G-8057)***

David Yurman Enterprises LLC....G....845 928-8660
Central Valley ***(G-3522)***

David Yurman Retail LLC....G....877 226-1400
New York ***(G-9827)***

DBC Inc....D....212 819-1177
New York ***(G-9832)***

Diamond Distributors Inc....G....212 921-9188
New York ***(G-9872)***

Diana Kane Incorporated....G....718 638-6520
Brooklyn ***(G-1860)***

Dimoda Designs Inc....E....212 355-8166
New York ***(G-9880)***

Donna Distefano Ltd....G....212 594-3757
New York ***(G-9898)***

Doris Panos Designs Ltd....G....631 245-0580
Melville ***(G-8312)***

▲ **Duran Jewelry Inc**....G....212 431-1959
New York ***(G-9939)***

Dweck Industries Inc....G....718 615-1695
Brooklyn ***(G-1884)***

▲ **Dynamic Design Group Inc**....F....212 840-9400
New York ***(G-9947)***

E Chabot Ltd....E....212 575-1026
Brooklyn ***(G-1890)***

◆ **E M G Creations Inc**....F....212 643-0960
New York ***(G-9950)***

▲ **Eagle Regalia Co Inc**....F....845 425-2245
Spring Valley ***(G-15582)***

Earring King Jewelry Mfg Inc....G....718 544-7947
New York ***(G-9961)***

Eastern Jewelry Mfg Co Inc....E....212 840-0001
New York ***(G-9965)***

Echo Group Inc....F....917 608-7440
New York ***(G-9975)***

Eclipse Collection Jewelers....F....212 764-6883
New York ***(G-9977)***

Ed Levin Inc....E....518 677-8595
Cambridge ***(G-3308)***

Efron Designs Ltd....G....718 482-8440
Long Island City ***(G-7728)***

Elegant Jewelers Mfg Co Inc....F....212 869-4951
New York ***(G-9999)***

Ema Jewelry Inc....D....212 575-8989
New York ***(G-10018)***

Emsaru USA Corp....G....212 459-9355
New York ***(G-10025)***

Eshel Jewelry Mfg Co Inc....F....212 588-8800
New York ***(G-10060)***

Eternal Line....G....845 856-1999
Sparrow Bush ***(G-15562)***

Euro Bands Inc....F....212 719-9777
New York ***(G-10083)***

F M Abdulky Inc....F....607 272-7373
Ithaca ***(G-6839)***

F M Abdulky Inc....G....607 272-7373
Ithaca ***(G-6840)***

Fam Creations....E....212 869-4833
New York ***(G-10132)***

Fantasia Jewelry Inc....E....212 921-9590
New York ***(G-10136)***

Feldman Jewelry Creations Inc....G....718 438-8895
Brooklyn ***(G-1964)***

First Image Design Corp....E....212 221-8282
New York ***(G-10167)***

Five Star Creations Inc....E....845 783-1187
Monroe ***(G-8554)***

Frank Blancato Inc....F....212 768-1495
New York ***(G-10202)***

Gem Mine Corp....G....516 367-1075
Woodbury ***(G-17287)***

Gem-Bar Setting Inc....G....212 869-9238
New York ***(G-10266)***

Gemoro Inc....G....212 768-8844
New York ***(G-10268)***

Gemveto Jewelry Company Inc....E....212 755-2522
New York ***(G-10271)***

George Lederman Inc....G....212 753-4556
New York ***(G-10283)***

Georland Corporation....G....212 730-4730
New York ***(G-10285)***

Giovane Ltd....E....212 332-7373
New York ***(G-10299)***

Global Gem Corporation....G....212 350-9936
New York ***(G-10317)***

Gold & Diamonds Wholesale Outl....G....718 438-7888
Brooklyn ***(G-2037)***

Goldarama Company Inc....G....212 730-7299
New York ***(G-10328)***

Golden Integrity Inc....E....212 764-6753
New York ***(G-10332)***

Goldmark Products Inc....E....631 777-3343
Farmingdale ***(G-5001)***

Gorga Fehren Fine Jewelry LLC....G....646 861-3595
New York ***(G-10339)***

Gottlieb & Sons Inc....E....212 575-1907
New York ***(G-10342)***

▲ **Gramercy Jewelry Mfg Corp**....E....212 268-0461
New York ***(G-10346)***

Grandeur Creations Inc....G....212 643-1277
New York ***(G-10349)***

▲ **Guild Diamond Products Inc**....F....212 871-0007
New York ***(G-10381)***

Gumuchian Fils Ltd....F....212 593-3118
New York ***(G-10383)***

H & T Goldman Corporation....G....800 822-0272
New York ***(G-10386)***

H C Kionka & Co Inc....F....212 227-3155
New York ***(G-10388)***

Hammerman Bros Inc....G....212 956-2800
New York ***(G-10401)***

Hanna Altinis Co Inc....E....718 706-1134
Long Island City ***(G-7756)***

▲ **Hansa Usa LLC**....E....646 412-6407
New York ***(G-10409)***

▲ **Harry Winston Inc**....C....212 399-1000
New York ***(G-10420)***

Henry Design Studios Inc....G....516 801-2760
Locust Valley ***(G-7632)***

Henry Dunay Designs Inc....E....212 768-9700
New York ***(G-10458)***

▲ **Hjn Inc**....F....212 398-9564
New York ***(G-10485)***

Horo Creations LLC....G....212 719-4818
New York ***(G-10508)***

Houles USA Inc....G....212 935-3900
New York ***(G-10516)***

Hw Holdings Inc....G....212 399-1000
New York ***(G-10534)***

Hy Gold Jewelers Inc....G....212 744-3202
New York ***(G-10535)***

Ilico Jewelry Inc....G....516 482-0201
Great Neck ***(G-5815)***

Imena Jewelry Manufacturer Inc....F....212 827-0073
New York ***(G-10571)***

Incon Gems Inc....F....212 221-8560
New York ***(G-10583)***

▲ **Indonesian Imports Inc**....E....888 800-5899
New York ***(G-10590)***

▲ **Innovative Jewelry Inc**....G....718 408-8950
Bay Shore ***(G-705)***

Inori Jewels....F....347 703-5078
New York ***(G-10607)***

Intentions Jewelry LLC....G....845 226-4650
Lagrangeville ***(G-7254)***

Iradj Moini Couture Ltd....F....212 594-9242
New York ***(G-10656)***

Iridesse Inc....F....212 230-6000
New York ***(G-10658)***

Iriniri Designs Ltd....F....845 469-7934
Sugar Loaf ***(G-15804)***

SIC SECTION 39 MISCELLANEOUS MANUFACTURING INDUSTRIES

J H Jewelry Co Inc ... F ... 212 239-1330
New York (G-10678)
J J Creations Inc ... E ... 718 392-2828
Long Island City (G-7768)
J R Gold Designs Ltd ... F ... 212 922-9292
New York (G-10681)
▲ Jacmel Jewelry Inc ... C ... 718 349-4300
New York (G-10690)
▲ Jacoby Enterprises LLC ... G ... 718 435-0289
Brooklyn (G-2133)
Jaguar Casting Co Inc ... E ... 212 869-0197
New York (G-10694)
Jaguar Jewelry Casting NY Inc ... G ... 212 768-4848
New York (G-10695)
▲ Jane Bohan Inc ... G ... 212 529-6090
New York (G-10699)
Jasani Designs Usa Inc ... G ... 212 257-6465
New York (G-10702)
Jay-Aimee Designs Inc ... C ... 718 609-0333
Hicksville (G-6356)
Jayden Star LLC ... G ... 212 686-0400
New York (G-10706)
▲ JC Crystal Inc ... E ... 212 594-0858
New York (G-10708)
Jean & Alex Jewelry Mfg & Cons ... F ... 212 935-7621
New York (G-10713)
Jeff Cooper Inc ... F ... 516 333-8200
Carle Place (G-3391)
Jewelmak Inc ... E ... 212 398-2999
New York (G-10723)
Jewelry Arts Manufacturing ... E ... 212 382-3583
New York (G-10724)
Jewels By Star Ltd ... E ... 212 308-3490
New York (G-10725)
Jeweltex Mfg Corp ... F ... 212 921-8188
New York (G-10726)
▲ Jimmy Crystal New York Co Ltd ... E ... 212 594-0858
New York (G-10736)
▲ JK Jewelry Inc ... D ... 585 346-3464
Rochester (G-14461)
JK Manufacturing Inc ... G ... 212 683-3535
Locust Valley (G-7633)
Joan Boyce Ltd ... G ... 212 867-7474
New York (G-10744)
Jordan Scott Designs Ltd ... E ... 212 947-4250
New York (G-10762)
▲ Jotaly Inc ... A ... 212 886-6000
New York (G-10769)
JSA Jewelry Inc ... F ... 212 764-4504
New York (G-10777)
Julius Cohen Jewelers Inc ... G ... 212 371-3050
New York (G-10783)
▲ Just Perfect MSP Ltd ... E ... 877 201-0005
New York (G-10793)
▲ Justin Ashley Designs Inc ... G ... 718 707-0200
Long Island City (G-7776)
▲ Justyna Kaminska NY Inc ... G ... 917 423-5527
New York (G-10794)
▲ Kaprielian Enterprises Inc ... D ... 212 645-6623
New York (G-10808)
Karbra Company ... C ... 212 736-9300
New York (G-10809)
Keith Lewis Studio Inc ... G ... 845 339-5629
Rifton (G-14134)
▼ Krasner Group Inc ... G ... 212 268-4100
New York (G-10886)
Kurt Gaum Inc ... F ... 212 719-2836
New York (G-10895)
◆ La Fina Design Inc ... G ... 212 689-6725
New York (G-10908)
Lali Jewelry Inc ... G ... 212 944-2277
New York (G-10921)
▲ Le Hook Rouge LLC ... G ... 212 947-6272
Brooklyn (G-2200)
Le Paveh Ltd ... F ... 212 736-6110
New York (G-10943)
Le Roi Inc ... F ... 315 342-3681
Fulton (G-5468)
▲ Le Vian Corp ... D ... 516 466-7200
Great Neck (G-5820)
Le Vian Corp ... E ... 516 466-7200
New York (G-10944)
Leo Ingwer Inc ... E ... 212 719-1342
New York (G-10969)
Leo Schachter & Co Inc ... D ... 212 688-2000
New York (G-10971)
Leser Enterprises Ltd ... F ... 212 644-8921
New York (G-10973)
Lindsay-Hoenig Ltd ... G ... 212 575-9711
New York (G-10999)
Lokai Holdings LLC ... F ... 646 979-3474
New York (G-11023)
Loremi Jewelry Inc ... E ... 212 840-3429
New York (G-11042)
Louis Tamis & Sons Inc ... E ... 212 684-1760
New York (G-11050)
Love Bright Jewelry Inc ... E ... 516 620-2509
Oceanside (G-13086)
M & S Quality Co Ltd ... F ... 212 302-8757
New York (G-11068)
M A R A Metals Ltd ... G ... 718 786-7868
Long Island City (G-7797)
M H Manufacturing Incorporated ... G ... 212 461-6900
New York (G-11071)
M Heskia Company Inc ... G ... 212 768-1845
New York (G-11072)
Magnum Creation Inc ... F ... 212 642-0993
New York (G-11109)
Manny Grunberg Inc ... E ... 212 302-6173
New York (G-11138)
Marco Moore Inc ... D ... 212 575-2090
Great Neck (G-5822)
Marina Jewelry Co Inc ... G ... 212 354-5027
New York (G-11152)
Mark King Jewelry Inc ... G ... 212 921-0746
New York (G-11154)
Mark Robinson Inc ... G ... 212 223-3515
New York (G-11157)
Markowitz Jewelry Co Inc ... E ... 845 774-1175
Monroe (G-8561)
Marlborough Jewels Inc ... G ... 718 768-2000
Brooklyn (G-2273)
▲ Martin Flyer Incorporated ... E ... 212 840-8899
New York (G-11168)
Master Craft Jewelry Co Inc ... D ... 516 599-1012
Lynbrook (G-7954)
Masterpiece Color LLC ... G ... 917 279-6056
New York (G-11174)
Mavito Fine Jewelry Ltd Inc ... F ... 212 398-9384
New York (G-11185)
Maxine Denker Inc ... G ... 212 689-1440
Staten Island (G-15704)
▲ MB Plastics Inc ... F ... 718 523-1180
Greenlawn (G-5874)
ME & Ro Inc ... G ... 212 431-8744
New York (G-11204)
▲ Mellem Corporation ... F ... 607 723-0001
Binghamton (G-935)
◆ Mer Gems Corp ... G ... 212 714-9129
New York (G-11226)
▲ Mgd Brands Inc ... D ... 516 545-0150
Plainview (G-13620)
Michael Anthony Jewelers LLC ... C ... 914 699-0000
Mount Vernon (G-8705)
Michael Bondanza Inc ... E ... 212 869-0043
New York (G-11248)
Midura Jewels Inc ... G ... 213 265-8090
New York (G-11259)
Milla Global Inc ... G ... 516 488-3601
Brooklyn (G-2315)
Mimi So International LLC ... E ... 212 300-8600
New York (G-11274)
Min Ho Designs Inc ... G ... 212 838-3667
New York (G-11275)
▲ MJM Jewelry Corp ... E ... 212 354-5014
New York (G-11285)
MJM Jewelry Corp ... D ... 718 596-1600
Brooklyn (G-2325)
Monelle Jewelry ... G ... 212 977-9535
New York (G-11300)
Moti Ganz (usa) Inc ... G ... 212 302-0040
New York (G-11311)
▲ MW Samara LLC ... E ... 212 764-3332
New York (G-11329)
Mwsi Inc ... D ... 914 347-4200
Hawthorne (G-6251)
▲ N Y Bijoux Corp ... G ... 212 244-9585
New York (G-11336)
▲ Nicolo Raineri ... G ... 212 925-6128
New York (G-11428)
North American Mint Inc ... G ... 585 654-8500
Rochester (G-14540)
NP Roniet Creations Inc ... G ... 212 302-1847
New York (G-11465)
O C Tanner Company ... G ... 914 921-2025
Rye (G-15065)
O C Tanner Company ... G ... 518 348-2035
Clifton Park (G-3703)
Oscar Heyman & Bros Inc ... E ... 212 593-0400
New York (G-11530)
Osnat Gad Inc ... G ... 212 957-0535
New York (G-11532)
Overnight Mountings Inc ... D ... 516 865-3000
New Hyde Park (G-8854)
▲ Paragon Corporation ... F ... 516 484-6090
Port Washington (G-13855)
Parijat Jewels Inc ... G ... 212 286-2326
New York (G-11572)
Park West Jewelery Inc ... G ... 646 329-6145
New York (G-11574)
Pearl Erwin Inc ... E ... 212 889-7410
New York (G-11589)
Pesselnik & Cohen Inc ... G ... 212 925-0287
New York (G-11628)
Peter Atman Inc ... F ... 212 644-8882
New York (G-11630)
PHC Restoration Holdings LLC ... F ... 212 643-0517
New York (G-11644)
Pin People LLC ... F ... 888 309-7467
Spring Valley (G-15599)
◆ Pink Box Accessories LLC ... G ... 716 777-4477
Brooklyn (G-2422)
Pronto Jewelry Inc ... E ... 212 719-9455
New York (G-11734)
R & R Grosbard Inc ... E ... 212 575-0077
New York (G-11782)
R Klein Jewelry Co Inc ... D ... 516 482-3260
Massapequa (G-8181)
R M Reynolds ... G ... 315 789-7365
Geneva (G-5584)
Rand & Paseka Mfg Co Inc ... E ... 516 867-1500
Freeport (G-5422)
Reinhold Brothers Inc ... E ... 212 867-8310
New York (G-11821)
Renaissance Bijou Ltd ... G ... 212 869-1969
New York (G-11830)
Richards & West Inc ... D ... 585 461-4088
East Rochester (G-4466)
Richline Group Inc ... E ... 212 643-2908
New York (G-11865)
Richline Group Inc ... C ... 212 764-8454
New York (G-11866)
Richline Group Inc ... C ... 914 699-0000
New York (G-11867)
▲ Riva Jewelry Manufacturing Inc ... C ... 718 361-3100
Brooklyn (G-2496)
Robert Bartholomew Ltd ... E ... 516 767-2970
Port Washington (G-13859)
▼ Roberto Coin Inc ... F ... 212 486-4545
New York (G-11891)
Robin Stanley Inc ... G ... 212 871-0007
New York (G-11894)
Roman Malakov Diamonds Ltd ... G ... 212 944-8500
New York (G-11911)
▲ Royal Jewelry Mfg Inc ... E ... 212 302-2500
Great Neck (G-5836)
Royal Miracle Corp ... E ... 212 921-5797
New York (G-11925)
Rubinstein Jewelry Mfg Co ... F ... 718 784-8650
Long Island City (G-7868)
Rudolf Friedman Inc ... F ... 212 869-5070
New York (G-11934)
Rumson Acquisition LLC ... F ... 718 349-4300
New York (G-11936)
▲ Ryan Gems Inc ... E ... 212 697-0149
New York (G-11940)
▲ S & M Ring Corp ... F ... 212 382-0900
Hewlett (G-6312)
S Kashi & Sons Inc ... F ... 212 869-9393
Great Neck (G-5837)
S Scharf Inc ... F ... 516 541-9552
Massapequa (G-8182)
▲ Samuel Aaron Inc ... D ... 718 392-5454
Mount Vernon (G-8729)
▲ Samuel B Collection Inc ... G ... 516 466-1826
Great Neck (G-5838)
Sanoy Inc ... E ... 212 695-6384
New York (G-11968)
Sarkisians Jewelry Co ... G ... 212 869-1060
New York (G-11974)
Satco Castings Service Inc ... E ... 516 354-1500
New Hyde Park (G-8860)
Satellite Incorporated ... G ... 212 221-6687
New York (G-11976)
Scott Kay Inc ... C ... 201 287-0100
New York (G-12006)
▲ Select Jewelry Inc ... D ... 718 784-3626
Long Island City (G-7874)
▲ Shah Diamonds Inc ... F ... 212 888-9393
New York (G-12038)

SIC

Employee Codes: A=Over 500 employees, B=251-500
C=101-250, D=51-100, E=20-50, F=10-19, G=5-9
2017 Harris
New York Manufacturers Directory
867

Shanu Gems Inc ....F.... 212 921-4470
New York *(G-12042)*

Sharodine Inc ....G.... 516 767-3548
Port Washington *(G-13865)*

Shining Creations Inc ....G.... 845 358-4911
New City *(G-8793)*

▲ Shiro Limited ....G.... 212 780-0007
New York *(G-12053)*

Simco Manufacturing Jewelers ....F.... 212 575-8390
New York *(G-12076)*

Simka Diamond Corp ....F.... 212 921-4420
New York *(G-12077)*

Somerset Manufacturers Inc ....E.... 516 626-3832
Roslyn Heights *(G-15033)*

▲ Spark Creations Inc ....F.... 212 575-8385
New York *(G-12147)*

Standard Wedding Band Co ....G.... 516 294-0954
Garden City *(G-5533)*

Stanley Creations Inc ....C.... 718 361-6100
Long Island City *(G-7885)*

Stanmark Jewelry Inc ....G.... 212 730-2557
New York *(G-12183)*

▲ Sterling Possessions Ltd ....G.... 212 594-0418
New York *(G-12197)*

Stone House Associates Inc ....G.... 212 221-7447
New York *(G-12207)*

Sulphur Creations Inc ....G.... 212 719-2223
New York *(G-12229)*

Sumer Gold Ltd ....G.... 212 354-8677
New York *(G-12231)*

Suna Bros Inc ....E.... 212 869-5670
New York *(G-12235)*

Sunrise Jewelers of NY Inc ....G.... 516 541-1302
Massapequa *(G-8183)*

Tambetti Inc ....G.... 212 751-9584
New York *(G-12276)*

Tamsen Z LLC ....G.... 212 292-6412
New York *(G-12277)*

Tanagro Jewelry Corp ....E.... 212 753-2817
New York *(G-12278)*

Technical Service Industries ....E.... 212 719-9800
Jamaica *(G-6956)*

Teena Creations Inc ....G.... 516 867-1500
Freeport *(G-5429)*

Temple St Clair LLC ....E.... 212 219-8664
New York *(G-12298)*

Thomas Sasson Co Inc ....G.... 212 697-4998
New York *(G-12325)*

Tiga Holdings Inc ....E.... 845 838-3000
Beacon *(G-791)*

▲ Trianon Collection Inc ....E.... 212 921-9450
New York *(G-12403)*

▲ Ultra Fine Jewelry Mfg ....E.... 516 349-2848
Plainview *(G-13640)*

▲ UNI Jewelry Inc ....G.... 212 398-1818
New York *(G-12450)*

◆ Unimax Supply Co Inc ....E.... 212 925-1051
New York *(G-12457)*

Unique Designs Inc ....F.... 212 575-7701
New York *(G-12461)*

United Brothers Jewelry Inc ....E.... 212 921-2558
New York *(G-12464)*

Valentin & Kalich Jwly Mfg Ltd ....E.... 212 575-9044
New York *(G-12494)*

Valentine Jewelry Mfg Co Inc ....E.... 212 382-0606
New York *(G-12495)*

▲ Variety Gem Co Inc ....F.... 212 921-1820
Great Neck *(G-5848)*

▲ Verragio Ltd ....E.... 212 868-8181
New York *(G-12523)*

Viktor Gold Enterprise Corp ....G.... 212 768-8885
New York *(G-12544)*

Von Musulin Patricia ....G.... 212 206-8345
New York *(G-12567)*

W & B Mazza & Sons Inc ....E.... 516 379-4130
North Baldwin *(G-12913)*

Walter Edbril Inc ....E.... 212 532-3253
New York *(G-12584)*

Weisco Inc ....F.... 212 575-8989
New York *(G-12605)*

Whitney Boin Studio Inc ....G.... 914 377-4385
Yonkers *(G-17499)*

William Goldberg Diamond Corp ....E.... 212 980-4343
New York *(G-12633)*

Xomox Jewelry Inc ....G.... 212 944-8428
New York *(G-12681)*

▲ Yofah Religious Articles Inc ....F.... 718 435-3288
Brooklyn *(G-2775)*

Yurman Retail Inc ....G.... 888 398-7626
New York *(G-12700)*

▲ Zdny & Co Inc ....F.... 212 354-1233
New York *(G-12707)*

Zeeba Jewelry Mfg Inc ....G.... 212 997-1009
New York *(G-12709)*

Zelman & Friedman Jwly Mfg Co ....E.... 718 349-3400
Long Island City *(G-7931)*

3914 Silverware, Plated & Stainless Steel Ware

All American Awards Inc ....F.... 631 567-2025
Bohemia *(G-1011)*

Atlantic Trophy Co Inc ....G.... 212 684-6020
New York *(G-9253)*

▲ Csi International Inc ....E.... 716 282-5408
Niagara Falls *(G-12809)*

▲ D W Haber & Son Inc ....E.... 718 993-6405
Bronx *(G-1308)*

Denvin Inc ....E.... 718 232-3389
Brooklyn *(G-1855)*

▲ Dwm International Inc ....F.... 646 290-7448
Long Island City *(G-7721)*

Endurart Inc ....E.... 212 473-7000
New York *(G-10034)*

Oneida International Inc ....G.... 315 361-3000
Oneida *(G-13160)*

Oneida Silversmiths Inc ....G.... 315 361-3000
Oneida *(G-13164)*

▼ Quest Bead & Cast Inc ....G.... 212 354-1737
New York *(G-11771)*

R Goldsmith ....F.... 718 239-1396
Bronx *(G-1439)*

Sherrill Manufacturing Inc ....C.... 315 280-0727
Sherrill *(G-15407)*

Silver City Group Inc ....G.... 315 363-0344
Sherrill *(G-15408)*

▲ Studio Silversmiths Inc ....E.... 718 418-6785
Ridgewood *(G-14125)*

Swed Masters Workshop LLC ....F.... 212 644-8822
New York *(G-12252)*

◆ Utica Cutlery Company ....D.... 315 733-4663
Utica *(G-16363)*

Valerie Bohigian ....G.... 914 631-8866
Sleepy Hollow *(G-15476)*

3915 Jewelers Findings & Lapidary Work

A J C Jewelry Contracting Inc ....G.... 212 594-3703
New York *(G-8990)*

A J M Enterprises ....F.... 716 626-7294
Buffalo *(G-2792)*

Ace Diamond Corp ....G.... 212 730-8231
New York *(G-9015)*

Allstar Casting Corporation ....E.... 212 563-0909
New York *(G-9092)*

Ampex Casting Corporation ....F.... 212 719-1318
New York *(G-9139)*

Antwerp Diamond Distributors ....F.... 212 319-3300
New York *(G-9169)*

Antwerp Sales Intl Inc ....F.... 212 354-6515
New York *(G-9170)*

Asa Manufacturing Inc ....E.... 718 853-3033
Brooklyn *(G-1637)*

Asco Castings Inc ....G.... 212 719-9800
Long Island City *(G-7671)*

Asur Jewelry Inc ....G.... 718 472-1687
Long Island City *(G-7675)*

Baroka Creations Inc ....G.... 212 768-0527
New York *(G-9323)*

Boucheron Joaillerie USA Inc ....G.... 212 715-7330
New York *(G-9442)*

Carrera Casting Corp ....C.... 212 382-3296
New York *(G-9536)*

Centurion Diamonds Inc ....G.... 718 946-6918
New York *(G-9568)*

▲ Christopher Designs Inc ....E.... 212 382-1013
New York *(G-9613)*

Classic Creations Inc ....G.... 516 498-1991
Great Neck *(G-5798)*

▲ Creative Tools & Supply Inc ....G.... 212 279-7077
New York *(G-9752)*

D M J Casting Inc ....G.... 212 719-1951
New York *(G-9784)*

D R S Watch Materials ....E.... 212 819-0470
New York *(G-9785)*

Danhier Co LLC ....F.... 212 563-7683
New York *(G-9801)*

Dialase Inc ....G.... 212 575-8833
New York *(G-9868)*

Diamex Inc ....G.... 212 575-8145
New York *(G-9869)*

Diamond Boutique ....G.... 516 444-3373
Port Washington *(G-13808)*

Diamond Constellation Corp ....G.... 212 819-0324
New York *(G-9871)*

Dresdiam Inc ....E.... 212 819-2217
New York *(G-9926)*

Dweck Industries Inc ....E.... 718 615-1695
Brooklyn *(G-1885)*

▲ E Schreiber Inc ....E.... 212 382-0280
New York *(G-9952)*

Elite Group International NY ....F.... 917 334-1919
New York *(G-10006)*

Engelack Gem Corporation ....G.... 212 719-3094
New York *(G-10040)*

Fine Cut Diamonds Corporation ....G.... 212 575-8780
New York *(G-10163)*

Fischer Diamonds Inc ....F.... 212 869-1990
New York *(G-10170)*

▲ Fischler Diamonds Inc ....G.... 212 921-8196
New York *(G-10171)*

Frank Billanti Casting Co Inc ....F.... 212 221-0440
New York *(G-10201)*

Gemini Manufactures ....F.... 716 633-0306
Cheektowaga *(G-3572)*

Goldmark Inc ....E.... 718 438-0295
Brooklyn *(G-2039)*

▲ Guild Diamond Products Inc ....F.... 212 871-0007
New York *(G-10381)*

Hershel Horowitz Corp ....G.... 212 719-1710
New York *(G-10463)*

Ideal Brilliant Co Inc ....F.... 212 840-2044
New York *(G-10554)*

Igc New York Inc ....G.... 212 764-0949
New York *(G-10563)*

Isaac Waldman Inc ....G.... 212 354-8220
New York *(G-10665)*

J A G Diamond Manufacturers ....G.... 212 575-0660
New York *(G-10676)*

Jaguar Casting Co Inc ....E.... 212 869-0197
New York *(G-10694)*

Jewelry Arts Manufacturing ....E.... 212 382-3583
New York *(G-10724)*

Jim Wachtler Inc ....G.... 212 755-4367
New York *(G-10734)*

▲ Julius Klein Group ....E.... 212 719-1811
New York *(G-10784)*

Kaleko Bros ....G.... 212 819-0100
New York *(G-10803)*

▲ Kaprielian Enterprises Inc ....D.... 212 645-6623
New York *(G-10808)*

Karbra Company ....C.... 212 736-9300
New York *(G-10809)*

Kemp Metal Products Inc ....E.... 516 997-8860
Westbury *(G-17002)*

Lazare Kaplan Intl Inc ....D.... 212 972-9700
New York *(G-10938)*

Leo Schachter Diamonds LLC ....D.... 212 688-2000
New York *(G-10972)*

Loremi Jewelry Inc ....E.... 212 840-3429
New York *(G-11042)*

▲ Magic Novelty Co Inc ....E.... 212 304-2777
New York *(G-11104)*

Mavito Fine Jewelry Ltd Inc ....F.... 212 398-9384
New York *(G-11185)*

Max Kahan Inc ....F.... 212 575-4646
New York *(G-11187)*

ME & Ro Inc ....G.... 212 431-8744
New York *(G-11204)*

Miller & Veit Inc ....F.... 212 247-2275
New York *(G-11269)*

Modern Settings LLC ....E.... 631 351-1212
Huntington Station *(G-6717)*

Moishe L Horowitz ....F.... 212 719-4247
New York *(G-11292)*

Moti Ganz (usa) Inc ....G.... 212 302-0040
New York *(G-11311)*

Nathan Berrie & Sons Inc ....G.... 516 432-8500
Island Park *(G-6781)*

New York Findings Corp ....F.... 212 925-5745
New York *(G-11402)*

Nyman Jewelry Inc ....G.... 212 944-1976
New York *(G-11484)*

▲ Perma Glow Ltd Inc ....F.... 212 575-9677
New York *(G-11619)*

Precision Diamond Cutters Inc ....G.... 212 719-4438
New York *(G-11696)*

R G Flair Co Inc ....E.... 631 586-7311
Bay Shore *(G-730)*

Renco Manufacturing Inc ....E.... 718 392-8877
Long Island City *(G-7861)*

SIC SECTION 39 MISCELLANEOUS MANUFACTURING INDUSTRIES

Satco Castings Service Inc ....E 516 354-1500
New Hyde Park *(G-8860)*

▲ Shah Diamonds Inc ....F 212 888-9393
New York *(G-12038)*

Stephen J Lipkins Inc ....G 631 249-8866
Farmingdale *(G-5116)*

Sunshine Diamond Cutter Inc ....G 212 221-1028
New York *(G-12237)*

T M W Diamonds Mfg Co ....G 212 869-8444
New York *(G-12266)*

▲ Touch Adjust Clip Co Inc ....F 631 589-3077
Bohemia *(G-1144)*

▲ Townley Inc ....E 212 779-0544
New York *(G-12383)*

United Gemdiam Inc ....E 718 851-5083
Brooklyn *(G-2700)*

Via America Fine Jewelry Inc ....G 212 302-1218
New York *(G-12535)*

Waldman Alexander M Diamond Co ....E 212 921-8098
New York *(G-12578)*

White Coat Inc ....E 212 575-8880
New York *(G-12624)*

William Goldberg Diamond Corp ....E 212 980-4343
New York *(G-12633)*

◆ Zak Jewelry Tools Inc ....F 212 768-8122
New York *(G-12702)*

Zirconia Creations Intl ....G 212 239-3730
New York *(G-12714)*

3931 Musical Instruments

Albert Augustine Ltd ....D 917 661-0220
New York *(G-9074)*

Barbera Transduser Systems ....F 718 816-3025
Staten Island *(G-15644)*

DAddario & Company Inc ....D 631 439-3300
Melville *(G-8309)*

◆ DAddario & Company Inc ....A 631 439-3300
Farmingdale *(G-4972)*

▲ DAndrea Inc ....E 516 496-2200
Syosset *(G-15818)*

▲ DAngelico Guitars of America ....G 732 380-0995
New York *(G-9800)*

▲ Dimarzio Inc ....E 718 442-6655
Staten Island *(G-15666)*

▲ E & O Mari Inc ....D 845 562-4400
Newburgh *(G-12754)*

Elsener Organ Works Inc ....G 631 254-2744
Deer Park *(G-4137)*

▲ Evans Manufacturing LLC ....D 631 439-3300
Farmingdale *(G-4990)*

Fodera Guitars Inc ....F 718 832-3455
Brooklyn *(G-1991)*

Gluck Orgelbau Inc ....G 212 233-2684
New York *(G-10323)*

▲ Gms Drum Co Inc ....G 516 586-8820
Farmingdale *(G-5000)*

Guitar Specialist Inc ....G 914 533-5589
South Salem *(G-15535)*

▲ Hipshot Products Inc ....F 607 532-9404
Interlaken *(G-6747)*

J D Calato Manufacturing Co ....E 716 285-3546
Niagara Falls *(G-12837)*

Jason Ladanye Guitar Piano & H ....E 518 527-3973
Albany *(G-92)*

Kerner and Merchant ....G 315 463-8023
East Syracuse *(G-4548)*

▲ Leonard Carlson ....G 518 477-4710
East Greenbush *(G-4403)*

▲ Luthier Musical Corp ....G 212 397-6038
New York *(G-11065)*

▲ Mari Strings Inc ....F 212 799-6781
New York *(G-11148)*

Muzet Inc ....F 315 452-0050
Syracuse *(G-15995)*

Nathan Love LLC ....F 212 925-7111
New York *(G-11343)*

▲ New Sensor Corporation ....D 718 937-8300
Long Island City *(G-7824)*

Rico International ....G 818 767-7711
Farmingdale *(G-5099)*

Roli USA Inc ....F 412 600-4840
New York *(G-11908)*

▲ Sadowsky Guitars Ltd ....F 718 433-1990
Long Island City *(G-7871)*

◆ Samson Technologies Corp ....D 631 784-2200
Hauppauge *(G-6182)*

Siegfrieds Call Inc ....G 845 765-2275
Beacon *(G-790)*

Sound Source Inc ....G 585 271-5370
Rochester *(G-14693)*

▲ Steinway Inc ....A 718 721-2600
Long Island City *(G-7888)*

◆ Steinway and Sons ....C 718 721-2600
Long Island City *(G-7889)*

◆ Steinway Musical Instrs Inc ....E 781 894-9770
New York *(G-12192)*

▲ Stuart Spector Designs Ltd ....G 845 246-6124
Saugerties *(G-15196)*

3942 Dolls & Stuffed Toys

◆ ADC Dolls Inc ....C 212 244-4500
New York *(G-9026)*

Beila Group Inc ....F 212 260-1948
New York *(G-9346)*

▲ Best Toy Manufacturing Ltd ....F 718 855-9040
Brooklyn *(G-1689)*

◆ Commonwealth Toy Novelty Inc ....E 212 242-4070
New York *(G-9688)*

Community Products LLC ....E 518 589-5103
Elka Park *(G-4631)*

Cosmetics Plus Ltd ....G 516 768-7250
Amagansett *(G-213)*

Dana Michele LLC ....G 917 757-7777
New York *(G-9798)*

Fierce Fun Toys LLC ....G 646 322-7172
New York *(G-10162)*

▲ Goldberger Company LLC ....F 212 924-1194
New York *(G-10329)*

Jim Henson Company Inc ....E 212 794-2400
New York *(G-10733)*

▲ Jupiter Creations Inc ....G 917 493-9393
New York *(G-10790)*

▲ Lovee Doll & Toy Co Inc ....G 212 242-1545
New York *(G-11053)*

Madame Alexander Doll Co LLC ....D 212 244-4500
New York *(G-11091)*

Mattel Inc ....F 716 714-8514
East Aurora *(G-4374)*

North American Bear Co Inc ....F 212 388-0700
New York *(G-11454)*

▲ Shalom Toy Co Inc ....F 718 499-3770
Brooklyn *(G-2549)*

▲ Tonner Doll Company Inc ....E 845 339-9537
Kingston *(G-7216)*

Toy Admiration Co Inc ....E 914 963-9400
Yonkers *(G-17492)*

Ward Sales Co Inc ....G 315 476-5276
Syracuse *(G-16068)*

▲ Well-Made Toy Mfg Corporation ....E 718 381-4225
Port Washington *(G-13871)*

3944 Games, Toys & Children's Vehicles

212 Db Corp ....E 212 652-5600
New York *(G-8965)*

Alleghany Capital Corporation ....F 212 752-1356
New York *(G-9087)*

▲ ATI Model Products Inc ....E 631 694-7022
Farmingdale *(G-4946)*

▲ Babysafe Usa LLC ....G 877 367-4141
Afton *(G-8)*

▲ Barron Games Intl Co LLC ....F 716 630-0054
Buffalo *(G-2832)*

▲ Buffalo Games Inc ....D 716 827-8393
Buffalo *(G-2852)*

▲ C T A Digital Inc ....E 845 513-0433
Monroe *(G-8551)*

Church Communities NY Inc ....E 518 589-5103
Elka Park *(G-4629)*

Church Communities NY Inc ....E 518 589-5103
Elka Park *(G-4630)*

Compoz A Puzzle Inc ....G 516 883-2311
Port Washington *(G-13806)*

▲ Creative Kids Far East Inc ....C 845 368-0246
Airmont *(G-13)*

▲ Dakott LLC ....G 888 805-6795
New York *(G-9795)*

Dana Michele LLC ....G 917 757-7777
New York *(G-9798)*

▲ Design Works Craft Inc ....G 631 244-5749
Bohemia *(G-1057)*

Drescher Paper Box Inc ....F 716 854-0288
Buffalo *(G-2918)*

▲ E C C Corp ....G 518 873-6494
Elizabethtown *(G-4627)*

Ellis Products Corp ....G 516 791-3732
Valley Stream *(G-16405)*

Everi Games Inc ....G 518 881-1122
Schenectady *(G-15253)*

Famous Box Scooter Co ....G 631 943-2013
West Babylon *(G-16791)*

Gargraves Trackage Corporation ....G 315 483-6577
North Rose *(G-12937)*

▲ Habermaass Corporation ....F 315 685-8919
Skaneateles *(G-15462)*

Jim Henson Company Inc ....E 212 794-2400
New York *(G-10733)*

Joel Zelcer ....F 917 525-6790
Brooklyn *(G-2144)*

▲ Jupiter Creations Inc ....G 917 493-9393
New York *(G-10790)*

Kidtellect Inc ....G 617 803-1456
New York *(G-10841)*

▲ Kling Magnetics Inc ....E 518 392-4000
Chatham *(G-3558)*

Littlebits Electronics Inc ....D 917 464-4577
New York *(G-11014)*

▲ Marvel Entertainment LLC ....C 212 576-4000
New York *(G-11170)*

▲ Master Art Corp ....G 845 362-6430
Spring Valley *(G-15594)*

Master Juvenile Products Inc ....F 845 647-8400
Ellenville *(G-4635)*

Mattel Inc ....F 716 714-8514
East Aurora *(G-4374)*

▲ Mechanical Displays Inc ....G 718 258-5588
Brooklyn *(G-2290)*

▲ Ogosport LLC ....G 718 554-0777
Brooklyn *(G-2387)*

Pidyon Controls Inc ....G 212 683-9523
New York *(G-11659)*

Pride Lines Ltd ....G 631 225-0033
Lindenhurst *(G-7479)*

R F Giardina Co ....F 516 922-1364
Oyster Bay *(G-13374)*

◆ Readent Inc ....F 212 710-3004
White Plains *(G-17162)*

Sandbox Brands Inc ....G 212 647-8877
New York *(G-11965)*

Solowave Design Corp ....G 716 646-3103
Hamburg *(G-5943)*

Spectrum Crafts Inc ....E 631 244-5749
Bohemia *(G-1136)*

Top Race Inc ....G 347 424-5795
Brooklyn *(G-2665)*

Toymax Inc ....G 212 633-6611
New York *(G-12384)*

Tucker Jones House Inc ....E 631 642-9092
East Setauket *(G-4495)*

Vogel Applied Technologies ....G 212 677-3136
New York *(G-12563)*

Way Out Toys Inc ....G 212 689-9094
New York *(G-12599)*

Whats Next Manufacturing Inc ....E 585 492-1014
Arcade *(G-402)*

Wobbleworks Inc ....G 415 987-1534
New York *(G-12651)*

3949 Sporting & Athletic Goods, NEC

A Hyatt Ball Co Ltd ....G 518 747-0272
Fort Edward *(G-5339)*

Absolute Fitness US Corp ....D 732 979-8582
Bayside *(G-765)*

Adirondack Outdoor Center ....G 315 369-2300
Old Forge *(G-13132)*

Adpro Sports Inc ....D 716 854-5116
Buffalo *(G-2798)*

Alternatives For Children ....E 631 271-0777
Dix Hills *(G-4290)*

▲ Apparel Production Inc ....G 212 278-8362
New York *(G-9179)*

▲ Asia Connection LLC ....F 212 369-4644
New York *(G-9231)*

◆ Athalon Sportgear Inc ....G 212 268-8070
New York *(G-9249)*

Azibi Ltd ....F 212 869-6550
New York *(G-9286)*

Bears Management Group Inc ....G 585 624-5694
Lima *(G-7443)*

Billy Beez Usa LLC ....F 315 741-5099
Syracuse *(G-15869)*

Billy Beez Usa LLC ....F 646 606-2249
New York *(G-9399)*

Billy Beez Usa LLC ....F 845 915-4709
West Nyack *(G-16913)*

▼ Blades ....F 212 477-1059
New York *(G-9411)*

Bob Perani Sport Shops Inc ....G 585 427-2930
Rochester *(G-14239)*

Bruynswick Sales Inc ....F 845 789-2049
New Paltz *(G-8873)*

Employee Codes: A=Over 500 employees, B=251-500
C=101-250, D=51-100, E=20-50, F=10-19, G=5-9
2017 Harris
New York Manufacturers Directory
869

Buffalo Sports Inc ..... G 716 826-7700
Blasdell (G-961)
Bungers Surf Shop ..... G 631 244-3646
Sayville (G-15205)
Burnt Mill Smithing ..... G 585 293-2380
Churchville (G-3634)
Burton Corporation ..... D 802 862-4500
Champlain (G-3539)
Car Doctor Motor Sports LLC ..... G 631 537-1548
Water Mill (G-16603)
Cascade Helmets Holdings Inc ..... G 315 453-3073
Liverpool (G-7516)
Central New York Golf Center ..... G 315 463-1200
East Syracuse (G-4517)
▲ Chapman Skateboard Co Inc ..... G 631 321-4773
Deer Park (G-4116)
Charm Mfg Co Inc ..... E 607 565-8161
Waverly (G-16699)
City Sports Inc ..... G 212 730-2009
New York (G-9630)
Cooperstown Bat Co Inc ..... F 607 547-2415
Fly Creek (G-5314)
Cooperstown Bat Co Inc ..... G 607 547-2415
Cooperstown (G-3884)
Copper John Corporation ..... F 315 258-9269
Auburn (G-489)
Cortland Line Mfg LLC ..... E 607 756-2851
Cortland (G-4018)
▲ Cy Plastics Works Inc ..... E 585 229-2555
Honeoye (G-6523)
D Squared Technologies Inc ..... G 516 932-7319
Jericho (G-7064)
▼ Devin Mfg Inc ..... F 585 496-5770
Arcade (G-391)
Eastern Jungle Gym Inc ..... E 845 878-9800
Carmel (G-3399)
Elmira Country Club Inc ..... G 607 734-6251
Elmira (G-4681)
▲ Everlast Sports Mfg Corp ..... E 212 239-0990
New York (G-10092)
▲ Everlast Worldwide Inc ..... E 212 239-0990
New York (G-10093)
▲ Excellent Art Mfg Corp ..... F 718 388-7075
Inwood (G-6756)
Fenway Holdings LLC ..... E 212 757-0606
New York (G-10153)
Fishing Valley LLC ..... G 716 523-6158
Lockport (G-7586)
Fist Inc ..... G 718 643-3478
Brooklyn (G-1976)
Florida North Inc ..... F 518 868-2888
Sloansville (G-15479)
Fly-Tyers Carry-All LLC ..... G 607 821-1460
Charlotteville (G-3555)
◆ Fownes Brothers & Co Inc ..... E 212 683-0150
New York (G-10194)
Fownes Brothers & Co Inc ..... E 518 752-4411
Gloversville (G-5711)
▲ Genetclly Enhnced Athc RES Inc ..... G 631 750-3195
Hicksville (G-6348)
Good Show Sportwear Inc ..... F 212 334-8751
New York (G-10338)
Grace Wheeler ..... G 716 664-6501
Jamestown (G-6995)
Grand Slam Safety LLC ..... G 315 766-7008
Croghan (G-4059)
▼ Gym Store Inc ..... G 718 366-7804
Maspeth (G-8142)
▲ Hana Sportswear Inc ..... E 315 639-6332
Dexter (G-4285)
Hart Sports Inc ..... G 631 385-1805
Huntington Station (G-6707)
Heads & Tails Lure Co ..... G 607 739-7900
Horseheads (G-6580)
Herrmann Group LLC ..... G 716 876-9798
Kenmore (G-7148)
Hinspergers Poly Industries ..... E 585 798-6625
Medina (G-8275)
Hootz Family Bowling Inc ..... F 518 756-4668
Ravena (G-14021)
Hypoxico Inc ..... G 212 972-1009
New York (G-10538)
▲ Imagination Playground LLC ..... G 212 463-0334
New York (G-10567)
◆ Imperial Pools Inc ..... C 518 786-1200
Latham (G-7365)
▲ International Leisure Pdts Inc ..... E 631 254-2155
Edgewood (G-4601)
▲ J R Products Inc ..... G 716 633-7565
Clarence Center (G-3677)
▲ Jag Manufacturing Inc ..... E 518 762-9558
Johnstown (G-7116)
Joe Moro ..... G 607 272-0591
Ithaca (G-6855)
Johnson Outdoors Inc ..... C 607 779-2200
Binghamton (G-931)
Kohlberg Sports Group Inc ..... G 914 241-7430
Mount Kisco (G-8633)
▼ Latham Pool Products Inc ..... C 518 951-1000
Latham (G-7369)
▲ Macgregor Golf North Amer Inc ..... D 646 840-5200
New York (G-11084)
Makiplastic ..... G 716 772-2222
Gasport (G-5558)
Mattel Inc ..... F 716 714-8514
East Aurora (G-4374)
▲ Maverik Lacrosse LLC ..... A 516 213-3050
New York (G-11184)
Michael Britt Inc ..... G 516 248-2010
Mineola (G-8525)
Morris Golf Ventures ..... E 631 283-0559
Southampton (G-15547)
Muscle Sports Products ..... G 631 755-1388
Bohemia (G-1107)
◆ Nalge Nunc International Corp ..... A 585 586-8800
Rochester (G-14527)
▼ North Coast Outfitters Ltd ..... E 631 727-5580
Riverhead (G-14150)
Northern King Lures Inc ..... G 585 865-3373
Rochester (G-14545)
▲ Olympia Sports Company Inc ..... F 914 347-4737
Elmsford (G-4772)
▲ Otis Products Inc ..... C 315 348-4300
Lyons Falls (G-7978)
Outdoor Group LLC ..... C 585 201-5358
West Henrietta (G-16888)
Paddock Chevrolet Golf Dome ..... E 716 504-4059
Tonawanda (G-16191)
▲ Peloton Interactive Inc ..... E 818 571-7236
New York (G-11602)
Perfect Form Manufacturing LLC ..... G 585 500-5923
West Henrietta (G-16890)
Performance Lacrosse Group Inc ..... G 315 453-3073
Liverpool (G-7541)
▲ Physicalmind Institute ..... F 212 343-2150
New York (G-11655)
Pilgrim Surf & Supply ..... G 718 218-7456
Brooklyn (G-2419)
PNC Sports ..... G 516 665-2244
Deer Park (G-4190)
Pocono Pool Products-North ..... E 518 283-1023
Rensselaer (G-14049)
Polytech Pool Mfg Inc ..... F 718 492-8991
Brooklyn (G-2428)
PRC Liquidating Company ..... E 212 823-9626
New York (G-11694)
▲ Premiumbag LLC ..... G 718 657-6219
Jamaica (G-6941)
Pro Hitter Corp ..... F 845 358-8670
New City (G-8790)
Promats Athletics LLC ..... E 607 746-8911
Delhi (G-4241)
▲ Quaker Boy Inc ..... E 716 662-3979
Orchard Park (G-13292)
Qubicaamf Worldwide LLC ..... C 315 376-6541
Lowville (G-7941)
Radar Sports LLC ..... G 516 678-1919
Oceanside (G-13091)
Rawlings Sporting Goods Co Inc ..... D 315 429-8511
Dolgeville (G-4307)
Rising Stars Soccer Club CNY ..... F 315 381-3096
Westmoreland (G-17064)
▲ Rome Specialty Company Inc ..... E 315 337-8200
Rome (G-14834)
Roscoe Little Store Inc ..... G 607 498-5553
Roscoe (G-15012)
Rottkamp Tennis Inc ..... E 631 421-0040
Huntington Station (G-6720)
Sampo Inc ..... E 315 896-2606
Barneveld (G-617)
Sea Isle Custom Rod Builders ..... G 516 868-8855
Freeport (G-5424)
Seaway Mats Inc ..... G 518 483-2560
Malone (G-8016)
Shehawken Archery Co Inc ..... F 607 967-8333
Bainbridge (G-554)
▲ Sky Bounce Ball Company Inc ..... G 516 305-4883
Hewlett (G-6313)
Sportsfield Specialties Inc ..... E 607 746-8911
Delhi (G-4243)
Stephenson Custom Case Company ..... E 905 542-8762
Niagara Falls (G-12878)
◆ Swimline Corp ..... E 631 254-2155
Edgewood (G-4613)
▲ TDS Fitness Equipment ..... E 607 733-6789
Elmira (G-4704)
Tosch Products Ltd ..... G 315 672-3040
Camillus (G-3325)
▲ Vertical Lax Inc ..... G 518 669-3699
Albany (G-148)
Viking Athletics Ltd ..... E 631 957-8000
Lindenhurst (G-7492)
Warrior Sports Inc ..... G 315 536-0937
Penn Yan (G-13523)
Watson Adventures LLC ..... G 212 564-8293
New York (G-12598)
▲ Wilbar International Inc ..... D 631 951-9800
Hauppauge (G-6235)
Xpogo LLC ..... G 717 650-5232
New York (G-12682)
Zumiez Inc ..... F 585 425-8720
Victor (G-16515)

3951 Pens & Mechanical Pencils

▲ A & L Pen Manufacturing Corp ..... D 718 499-8966
Brooklyn (G-1527)
◆ Aakron Rule Corp ..... C 716 542-5483
Akron (G-19)
Effanjay Pens Inc ..... E 212 316-9565
Long Island City (G-7726)
▲ Gotham Pen Co Inc ..... E 212 675-7904
Yonkers (G-17449)
▲ Harper Products Ltd ..... C 516 997-2330
Westbury (G-16994)
Henry Morgan ..... F 718 317-5013
Staten Island (G-15683)
▲ Mark Dri Products Inc ..... C 516 484-6200
Bethpage (G-873)
▲ Mercury Pen Company Inc ..... G 518 899-9653
Ballston Lake (G-583)
▲ Pelican Products Co Inc ..... E 718 860-3220
Bronx (G-1423)
▲ STS Refill America LLC ..... G 516 934-8008
Hicksville (G-6395)

3952 Lead Pencils, Crayons & Artist's Mtrls

◆ Aakron Rule Corp ..... C 716 542-5483
Akron (G-19)
Clapper Hollow Designs Inc ..... E 518 234-9561
Cobleskill (G-3734)
Effanjay Pens Inc ..... E 212 316-9565
Long Island City (G-7726)
Frames Plus Inc ..... F 518 462-1842
Menands (G-8371)
◆ Golden Artist Colors Inc ..... C 607 847-6154
New Berlin (G-8780)
▲ Gotham Pen Co Inc ..... E 212 675-7904
Yonkers (G-17449)
Handmade Frames Inc ..... F 718 782-8364
Brooklyn (G-2067)
Lopez Restorations Inc ..... F 718 383-1555
Brooklyn (G-2235)
◆ Micro Powders Inc ..... E 914 332-6400
Tarrytown (G-16097)
North America Pastel Artists ..... G 718 463-4701
Flushing (G-5274)
▲ R & F Handmade Paints Inc ..... F 845 331-3112
Kingston (G-7207)
Rosendahl Industries Ltd Inc ..... E 718 436-2711
Brooklyn (G-2507)
▲ Simon Liu Inc ..... F 718 567-2011
Brooklyn (G-2560)
▲ Sml Brothers Holding Corp ..... D 718 402-2000
Bronx (G-1457)
▲ Spaulding & Rogers Mfg Inc ..... D 518 768-2070
Voorheesville (G-16518)
Tri Mar Enterprises Inc ..... G 718 418-3644
Brooklyn (G-2676)

3953 Marking Devices

A & M Steel Stamps Inc ..... G 516 741-6223
Mineola (G-8487)
Bianca Group Ltd ..... G 212 768-3011
New York (G-9388)
C M E Corp ..... F 315 451-7101
Syracuse (G-15881)
▲ Cannizzaro Seal & Engraving Co ..... G 718 513-6125
Brooklyn (G-1754)
▼ Crafters Workshop Inc ..... G 914 345-2838
Elmsford (G-4744)

Dab-O-Matic Corp ....D....914 699-7070
Mount Vernon (G-8676)
East Coast Thermographers Inc....E....718 321-3211
College Point (G-3782)
Effanjay Pens Inc....E....212 316-9565
Long Island City (G-7726)
▲ Hampton Art LLC....E....631 924-1335
Medford (G-8247)
▲ Heidenhain International Inc....C....716 661-1700
Jamestown (G-6999)
◆ Hodgins Engraving Co Inc....D....585 343-4444
Batavia (G-639)
I & I Systems....G....845 753-9126
Tuxedo Park (G-16283)
Joseph Treu Successors Inc....G....212 691-7026
New York (G-10766)
Kelly Foundry & Machine Co....E....315 732-8313
Utica (G-16346)
Koehlr-Gibson Mkg Graphics Inc....E....716 838-5960
Buffalo (G-3035)
Krengel Manufacturing Co Inc....F....212 227-1901
Fulton (G-5467)
Long Island Stamp & Seal Co....F....718 628-8550
Ridgewood (G-14112)
Michael Todd Stevens....G....585 436-9957
Rochester (G-14506)
Name Base Inc....G....212 545-1400
New York (G-11338)
New York Marking Devices Corp....G....585 454-5188
Rochester (G-14534)
New York Marking Devices Corp....G....315 463-8641
Syracuse (G-15998)
Rubber Stamp X Press....G....631 423-1322
Huntington Station (G-6721)
Rubber Stamps Inc....E....212 675-1180
Mineola (G-8535)
▲ Specialty Ink Co Inc....F....631 586-3666
Blue Point (G-1000)
▼ Tech Products Inc....E....718 442-4900
Staten Island (G-15748)
Thermopatch Corporation....D....315 446-8110
Syracuse (G-16058)
Ul Corp....G....201 203-4453
Bayside (G-776)
Ulano Product Inc....C....718 622-5200
Brooklyn (G-2695)
▲ United Silicone Inc....D....716 681-8222
Lancaster (G-7345)
United Sttes Brnze Sign of Fla....E....516 352-5155
New Hyde Park (G-8870)
Ward Sales Co Inc....G....315 476-5276
Syracuse (G-16068)
White Plains Rubber Stamp Name....G....914 949-1900
White Plains (G-17187)

3955 Carbon Paper & Inked Ribbons

Guttz Corporation of America....F....914 591-9600
Irvington (G-6770)
Hf Technologies LLC....E....585 254-5030
Hamlin (G-5950)
◆ International Imaging Mtls Inc....B....716 691-6333
Amherst (G-246)
▲ New York Cartridge Exchange....G....212 840-2227
New York (G-11396)
Northeast Toner Inc....G....518 899-5545
Ballston Lake (G-585)
◆ Printer Components Inc....G....585 924-5190
Fairport (G-4871)
Qls Solutions Group Inc....E....716 852-2203
Buffalo (G-3144)
Recharge Net Inc....G....585 546-1060
Rochester (G-14621)
Smartoners Inc....G....718 975-0197
Brooklyn (G-2572)
▲ Summit Technologies LLC....E....631 590-1040
Holbrook (G-6475)

3961 Costume Jewelry & Novelties

Accessory Plays LLC....E....212 564-7301
New York (G-9011)
▲ Alexis Bittar LLC....C....718 422-7580
Brooklyn (G-1582)
◆ Allure Jewelry and ACC LLC....E....646 226-8057
New York (G-9093)
Anatoli Inc....F....845 334-9000
West Hurley (G-16901)
◆ Avon Products Inc....C....212 282-5000
New York (G-9281)
Barrera Jose & Maria Co Ltd....E....212 239-1994
New York (G-9325)
▼ Ben-Amun Co Inc....E....212 944-6480
New York (G-9355)
Beth Ward Studios LLC....F....646 922-7575
New York (G-9377)
Bnns Co Inc....G....212 302-1844
New York (G-9431)
Carol For Eva Graham Inc....G....212 889-8686
New York (G-9531)
Carvin French Jewelers Inc....E....212 755-6474
New York (G-9539)
Catherine Stein Designs Inc....E....212 840-1188
New York (G-9549)
Ciner Manufacturing Co Inc....E....212 947-3770
New York (G-9619)
▲ Columbus Trading Corp....F....212 564-1780
New York (G-9681)
Custom Pins Inc....G....914 690-9378
Elmsford (G-4746)
Dabby-Reid Ltd....F....212 356-0040
New York (G-9786)
Designs On Fifth Ltd....G....212 921-4162
New York (G-9857)
Ema Jewelry Inc....D....212 575-8989
New York (G-10018)
Erickson Beamon Ltd....F....212 643-4810
New York (G-10057)
▲ Eu Design LLC....G....212 420-7788
New York (G-10081)
Fantasia Jewelry Inc....E....212 921-9590
New York (G-10136)
First International USA Ltd....E....718 854-0181
Brooklyn (G-1975)
Five Star Creations Inc....E....845 783-1187
Monroe (G-8554)
Formart Corp....F....212 819-1819
New York (G-10186)
Greenbeads Llc....G....212 327-2765
New York (G-10361)
Grinnell Designs Ltd....E....212 391-5277
New York (G-10367)
Holbrooke Inc....G....646 397-4674
New York (G-10494)
▲ Horly Novelty Co Inc....G....212 226-4800
New York (G-10507)
▲ I Love Accessories Inc....G....212 239-1875
New York (G-10539)
▲ International Inspirations Ltd....E....212 465-8500
New York (G-10635)
▲ J & H Creations Inc....E....212 465-0962
New York (G-10673)
J J Creations Inc....E....718 392-2828
Long Island City (G-7768)
Jay Turoff....F....718 856-7300
Brooklyn (G-2136)
Jaymar Jewelry Co Inc....G....212 564-4788
New York (G-10707)
Jewelry Arts Manufacturing....E....212 382-3583
New York (G-10724)
Jill Fagin Enterprises Inc....G....212 674-9383
New York (G-10732)
Jj Fantasia Inc....G....212 868-1198
New York (G-10740)
Jules Smith Llc....G....718 783-2495
New York (G-10781)
▲ K2 International Corp....G....212 947-1734
New York (G-10798)
Kenneth J Lane Inc....F....212 868-1780
New York (G-10834)
Krainz Creations Inc....E....212 583-1555
New York (G-10884)
Leonore Doskow Inc....E....914 737-1335
Montrose (G-8613)
▲ Lesilu Productions Inc....G....212 947-6419
New York (G-10974)
▲ Mac Swed Inc....G....917 617-3885
New York (G-11082)
▲ Magic Novelty Co Inc....E....212 304-2777
New York (G-11104)
Marlborough Jewels Inc....G....718 768-2000
Brooklyn (G-2273)
Masterpiece Diamonds LLC....F....212 937-0681
New York (G-11175)
▲ Mataci Inc....D....212 502-1899
New York (G-11178)
Maurice Max Inc....E....212 334-6573
New York (G-11181)
Mwsi Inc....D....914 347-4200
Hawthorne (G-6251)
▲ Nes Jewelry Inc....C....212 502-0025
New York (G-11370)
Noir Jewelry LLC....G....212 465-8500
New York (G-11450)
Pearl Erwin Inc....E....212 889-7410
New York (G-11589)
Pearl Erwin Inc....E....212 883-0650
New York (G-11590)
Pepe Creations Inc....F....212 391-1514
New York (G-11610)
Pincharming Inc....F....516 663-5115
Garden City (G-5525)
Reino Manufacturing Co Inc....F....914 636-8990
New Rochelle (G-8923)
▲ Rush Gold Manufacturing Ltd....D....516 781-3155
Bellmore (G-820)
▲ Salmco Jewelry Corp....F....212 695-8792
New York (G-11958)
Sanoy Inc....E....212 695-6384
New York (G-11968)
▲ Sarina Accessories LLC....E....212 239-8106
New York (G-11973)
Shira Accessories Ltd....F....212 594-4455
New York (G-12052)
Steezys LLC....G....646 276-5333
New York (G-12190)
▲ Stephan & Company ACC Ltd....E....212 481-3888
New York (G-12194)
Swarovski North America Ltd....G....914 423-4132
Yonkers (G-17488)
Swarovski North America Ltd....G....212 695-1502
New York (G-12250)
Talbots Inc....G....914 328-1034
White Plains (G-17175)
▲ Toho Shoji (new York) Inc....F....212 868-7466
New York (G-12357)
Top Shelf Jewelry Inc....F....845 647-4661
Ellenville (G-4639)
▲ Tycoon International Inc....G....212 563-7107
New York (G-12436)
◆ Vetta Jewelry Inc....E....212 564-8250
New York (G-12531)
Vitafede....F....213 488-0136
New York (G-12554)
Von Musulin Patricia....G....212 206-8345
New York (G-12567)
Yacoubian Jewelers Inc....E....212 302-6729
New York (G-12686)
Ziva Gem LLC....F....646 416-5828
New York (G-12716)

3965 Fasteners, Buttons, Needles & Pins

▲ American Pride Fasteners LLC....E....631 940-8292
Bay Shore (G-670)
Buttons & Trimcom Inc....F....212 868-1971
New York (G-9484)
Catame Inc....F....213 749-2610
New York (G-9546)
Champion Zipper Corp....G....212 239-0414
New York (G-9576)
▲ Clo-Shure Intl Inc....G....212 268-5029
New York (G-9644)
Columbia Button Nailhead Corp....F....718 386-3414
Brooklyn (G-1792)
Connection Mold Inc....G....585 458-6463
Rochester (G-14286)
CPI of Falconer Inc....E....716 664-4444
Falconer (G-4894)
Cw Fasteners & Zippers Corp....F....212 594-3203
New York (G-9774)
▲ E-Won Industrial Co Inc....E....212 750-9610
New York (G-9956)
▲ Empire State Metal Pdts Inc....E....718 847-1617
Richmond Hill (G-14073)
◆ Emsig Manufacturing Corp....F....718 784-7717
New York (G-10026)
Emsig Manufacturing Corp....F....518 828-7301
Hudson (G-6613)
Emsig Manufacturing Corp....E....718 784-7717
New York (G-10027)
▲ Eu Design LLC....G....212 420-7788
New York (G-10081)
▲ Fasteners Depot LLC....F....718 622-4222
Brooklyn (G-1960)
◆ Hemisphere Novelties Inc....E....914 378-4100
Yonkers (G-17453)
Itc Mfg Group Inc....F....212 684-3696
New York (G-10669)
Jem Threading Specialties Inc....G....718 665-3341
Bronx (G-1365)
▲ Joyce Trimming Inc....G....212 719-3110
New York (G-10773)

S I C

Employee Codes: A=Over 500 employees, B=251-500
C=101-250, D=51-100, E=20-50, F=10-19, G=5-9
2017 Harris
New York Manufacturers Directory
871

Karp Overseas Corporation....E....718 784-2105
Maspeth *(G-8148)*

Kenwin Sales Corp....G....516 933-7553
Westbury *(G-17003)*

Kraus & Sons Inc....F....212 620-0408
New York *(G-10887)*

M H Stryke Co Inc....F....631 242-2660
Deer Park *(G-4169)*

Maxine Denker Inc....G....212 689-1440
Staten Island *(G-15704)*

▲ Mona Slide Fasteners Inc....E....718 325-7700
Bronx *(G-1401)*

▲ Namm Singer Inc....F....212 947-2566
New York *(G-11339)*

National Die & Button Mould Co....E....201 939-7800
Brooklyn *(G-2350)*

Rings Wire Inc....G....212 741-9779
New York *(G-11874)*

▲ Riri USA Inc....G....212 268-3866
New York *(G-11877)*

Tamber Knits Inc....E....212 730-1121
New York *(G-12275)*

3991 Brooms & Brushes

◆ 131-11 Atlantic RE Inc....D....718 441-7700
Richmond Hill *(G-14064)*

Abtex Corporation....E....315 536-7403
Dresden *(G-4318)*

Braun Brothers Brushes Inc....G....631 667-2179
Valley Stream *(G-16402)*

▲ Braun Industries Inc....E....516 741-6000
Albertson *(G-152)*

▲ Brushtech (disc) Inc....F....518 563-8420
Plattsburgh *(G-13656)*

▲ Colgate-Palmolive Company....A....212 310-2000
New York *(G-9667)*

▼ Cpac Inc....E....585 382-3223
Leicester *(G-7420)*

▲ Culicover & Shapiro Inc....G....516 597-4888
Hicksville *(G-6339)*

E & W Manufacturing Co Inc....E....516 367-8571
Woodbury *(G-17285)*

Eraser Company Inc....C....315 454-3237
Mattydale *(G-8212)*

▲ FM Brush Co Inc....C....718 821-5939
Glendale *(G-5652)*

▲ Full Circle Home LLC....G....212 432-0001
New York *(G-10222)*

K & R Allied Inc....F....718 625-6610
Brooklyn *(G-2161)*

▲ Kirschner Brush LLC....F....718 292-1809
Bronx *(G-1373)*

Marketshare LLC....G....631 273-0598
Brentwood *(G-1191)*

Pan American Roller Inc....F....914 762-8700
Ossining *(G-13326)*

▲ Perfex Corporation....F....315 826-3600
Poland *(G-13727)*

Premier Paint Roller Co LLC....F....718 441-7700
Richmond Hill *(G-14078)*

Rossiter & Schmitt Co Inc....G....516 937-3610
Bay Shore *(G-739)*

Royal Paint Roller Corp....E....516 367-4370
Woodbury *(G-17299)*

Teka Fine Line Brushes Inc....G....718 692-2928
Brooklyn *(G-2652)*

▲ Violife LLC....G....914 207-1820
Yonkers *(G-17497)*

Volckening Inc....E....718 748-0294
Brooklyn *(G-2735)*

▲ Walter R Tucker Entps Ltd....E....607 467-2866
Deposit *(G-4282)*

Young & Swartz Inc....F....716 852-2171
Buffalo *(G-3260)*

3993 Signs & Advertising Displays

A B C Mc Cleary Sign Co Inc....F....315 493-3550
Carthage *(G-3407)*

A M S Sign Designs....G....631 467-7722
Centereach *(G-3469)*

◆ Aakron Rule Corp....C....716 542-5483
Akron *(G-19)*

ABC Windows and Signs Corp....F....718 353-6210
College Point *(G-3775)*

Accurate Signs & Awnings Inc....F....718 788-0302
Brooklyn *(G-1553)*

Acme Signs of Baldwinsville....G....315 638-4865
Baldwinsville *(G-564)*

Ad Makers Long Island Inc....F....631 595-9100
Deer Park *(G-4087)*

Adirondack Sign Perfect Inc....G....518 409-7446
Saratoga Springs *(G-15141)*

Adstream America LLC....F....845 496-8283
New York *(G-9032)*

All Signs....G....973 736-2113
Staten Island *(G-15635)*

All Star Awnings & Signs....F....516 742-8469
Mineola *(G-8492)*

Alley Cat Signs Inc....F....631 924-7446
Middle Island *(G-8406)*

Allied Decorations Co Inc....F....315 637-0273
Syracuse *(G-15849)*

Allstate Sign & Plaque Corp....F....631 242-2828
Deer Park *(G-4093)*

American Car Signs Inc....G....518 227-1173
Duanesburg *(G-4324)*

American Visuals Inc....G....631 694-6104
Farmingdale *(G-4941)*

Amsterdam Printing & Litho Inc....F....518 842-6000
Amsterdam *(G-332)*

Amsterdam Printing & Litho Inc....E....518 842-6000
Amsterdam *(G-333)*

Architectural Sign Group Inc....G....516 326-1800
Elmont *(G-4716)*

Art Parts Signs Inc....G....585 381-2134
East Rochester *(G-4453)*

Artkraft Strauss LLC....E....212 265-5155
New York *(G-9222)*

Artscroll Printing Corp....E....212 929-2413
New York *(G-9224)*

Asi Sign Systems Inc....G....646 742-1320
New York *(G-9230)*

Asi Sign Systems Inc....G....716 775-0104
Grand Island *(G-5751)*

Atlantic Steinway Awng II LLC....G....718 729-2965
Long Island City *(G-7677)*

Atomic Signworks....G....315 779-7446
Watertown *(G-16635)*

▲ Azar International Inc....E....845 624-8808
Nanuet *(G-8751)*

▲ B Barine Inc....E....718 499-5650
Brooklyn *(G-1657)*

Bedford Precision Parts Corp....E....914 241-2211
Bedford Hills *(G-799)*

Big Apple Sign Corp....E....631 342-0303
Islandia *(G-6788)*

▲ Big Apple Sign Corp....E....212 629-3650
New York *(G-9392)*

Bmg Printing and Promotion LLC....G....631 231-9200
Bohemia *(G-1026)*

Bridgewater Mdsg Concepts....F....718 383-5500
Brooklyn *(G-1716)*

Broadway Neon Sign Corp....F....908 241-4177
Ronkonkoma *(G-14881)*

Buckeye Corrugated Inc....D....585 924-1600
Victor *(G-16465)*

Bulow & Associates Inc....G....716 838-0298
Tonawanda *(G-16150)*

Cab Signs Inc....E....718 479-2424
Brooklyn *(G-1745)*

Central Rede Sign Co Inc....G....716 213-0797
Tonawanda *(G-16151)*

◆ Chameleon Color Cards Ltd....D....716 625-9452
Lockport *(G-7576)*

Chautauqua Sign Co Inc....G....716 665-2222
Falconer *(G-4893)*

Checklist Boards Corporation....G....585 586-0152
Rochester *(G-14273)*

City Signs Inc....G....718 375-5933
Brooklyn *(G-1784)*

Climax Packaging Inc....C....315 376-8000
Lowville *(G-7935)*

Clinton Signs Inc....G....585 482-1620
Webster *(G-16719)*

Coe Displays Inc....G....718 937-5658
Long Island City *(G-7702)*

Colad Group LLC....D....716 961-1776
Buffalo *(G-2880)*

Colonial Redi Record Corp....E....718 972-7433
Brooklyn *(G-1791)*

Community Products LLC....E....845 658-8351
Rifton *(G-14133)*

▲ Creative Solutions Group Inc....B....914 771-4200
Yonkers *(G-17432)*

▲ Crown Industries Inc....F....973 672-2277
New York *(G-9759)*

Crown Sign Systems Inc....F....914 375-2118
Yonkers *(G-17433)*

Custom Display Manufacture....G....516 783-6491
North Bellmore *(G-12920)*

Decal Makers Inc....E....516 221-7200
Bellmore *(G-817)*

Decree Signs & Graphics Inc....F....973 278-3603
Floral Park *(G-5202)*

Design A Sign of Putnam Inc....G....845 279-5328
Brewster *(G-1216)*

Designplex LLC....G....845 358-6647
Nyack *(G-13048)*

Display Marketing Group Inc....E....631 348-4450
Islandia *(G-6791)*

Display Presentations Ltd....D....631 951-4050
Hauppauge *(G-6065)*

▲ Display Producers Inc....C....718 904-1200
New Rochelle *(G-8895)*

Displays & Beyond Inc....F....718 805-7786
Glendale *(G-5651)*

Dkm Sales LLC....E....716 893-7777
Buffalo *(G-2916)*

▲ DSI Group Inc....C....800 553-2202
Maspeth *(G-8132)*

Dura Engraving Corporation....E....718 706-6400
Long Island City *(G-7719)*

East End Sign Design Inc....G....631 399-2574
Mastic *(G-8202)*

Eastern Concepts Ltd....F....718 472-3377
Sunnyside *(G-15807)*

▼ Eastern Metal of Elmira Inc....D....607 734-2295
Elmira *(G-4679)*

▼ Edge Display Group Entp Inc....F....631 498-1373
Bellport *(G-830)*

Elderlee Incorporated....C....315 789-6670
Oaks Corners *(G-13069)*

Elite Signs Inc....G....718 993-7342
Pomona *(G-13730)*

Eversan Inc....F....315 736-3967
Whitesboro *(G-17193)*

Executive Sign Corp....G....212 397-4050
Cornwall On Hudson *(G-3992)*

Executive Sign Corporation....G....212 397-4050
New York *(G-10106)*

Exhibit Corporation America....E....718 937-2600
Long Island City *(G-7734)*

▲ Faster-Form Corp....D....800 327-3676
New Hartford *(G-8804)*

Fastsigns....F....518 456-7446
Albany *(G-79)*

Flado Enterprises Inc....G....716 668-6400
Depew *(G-4258)*

▲ Flair Display Inc....D....718 324-9330
Bronx *(G-1333)*

Fletcher Enterprises Inc....G....716 837-7446
Tonawanda *(G-16163)*

Flexlume Sign Corporation....G....716 884-2020
Buffalo *(G-2950)*

Forrest Engraving Co Inc....F....845 228-0200
New Rochelle *(G-8901)*

Fortune Sign....G....646 383-8682
Brooklyn *(G-1997)*

▼ Fossil Industries Inc....E....631 254-9200
Deer Park *(G-4145)*

Frank Torrone & Sons Inc....F....718 273-7600
Staten Island *(G-15674)*

G I Certified Inc....G....212 397-1945
New York *(G-10230)*

Gloede Neon Signs Ltd Inc....F....845 471-4366
Poughkeepsie *(G-13902)*

Graphic Signs & Awnings Ltd....G....718 227-6000
Staten Island *(G-15681)*

Graphitek Inc....F....518 686-5966
Hoosick Falls *(G-6539)*

Greyline Signs Inc....G....716 947-4526
Derby *(G-4283)*

Hadley Exhibits Inc....D....716 874-3666
Buffalo *(G-2985)*

Hanson Sign & Screen Process....E....716 484-8564
Falconer *(G-4901)*

Hermosa Corp....E....315 768-4320
New York Mills *(G-12725)*

HI Tech Signs of NY Inc....G....516 794-7880
East Meadow *(G-4424)*

Hollywood Signs Inc....G....917 577-7333
Brooklyn *(G-2083)*

◆ ID Signsystems Inc....E....585 266-5750
Rochester *(G-14442)*

Ideal Signs Inc....G....718 292-9196
Bronx *(G-1359)*

Image360....G....585 272-1234
Rochester *(G-14446)*

Impressive Imprints Inc....G....631 293-6161
Farmingdale *(G-5010)*

▲ **International Bronze Manufac** ... F ... 516 248-3080
Albertson *(G-155)*
▲ **International Patterns Inc** ... D ... 631 952-2000
Plainview *(G-13609)*
Island Nameplate Inc ... G ... 845 651-4005
Florida *(G-5213)*
▲ **Jaf Converters Inc** ... E ... 631 842-3131
Copiague *(G-3908)*
Jal Signs Inc ... F ... 516 536-7280
Baldwin *(G-559)*
Jax Signs and Neon Inc ... G ... 607 727-3420
Endicott *(G-4815)*
Jay Turoff ... F ... 718 856-7300
Brooklyn *(G-2136)*
Jem Sign Corp ... G ... 516 867-4466
Hempstead *(G-6275)*
▲ **Jomar Industries Inc** ... E ... 845 357-5773
Airmont *(G-16)*
Joseph Struhl Co Inc ... F ... 516 741-3660
New Hyde Park *(G-8843)*
JP Signs ... G ... 518 569-3907
Chazy *(G-3562)*
K & B Stamping Co Inc ... G ... 914 664-8555
Mount Vernon *(G-8696)*
Keep America Beautiful Inc ... G ... 518 842-4388
Amsterdam *(G-354)*
▲ **Kenan International Trading** ... G ... 718 672-4922
Corona *(G-4000)*
King Displays Inc ... F ... 212 629-8455
New York *(G-10853)*
▲ **Kling Magnetics Inc** ... E ... 518 392-4000
Chatham *(G-3558)*
◆ **Knr Fragrances & Cosmetics Inc** ... F ... 631 586-8500
Edgewood *(G-4605)*
KP Industries Inc ... F ... 516 679-3161
North Bellmore *(G-12922)*
Kraus & Sons Inc ... F ... 212 620-0408
New York *(G-10887)*
L I C Screen Printing Inc ... E ... 516 546-7289
Merrick *(G-8387)*
L Miller Design Inc ... G ... 631 242-1163
Deer Park *(G-4162)*
L Y Z Creations Ltd Inc ... E ... 718 768-2977
Brooklyn *(G-2187)*
Lamar Plastics Packaging Ltd ... D ... 516 378-2500
Freeport *(G-5408)*
◆ **Lanco Corporation** ... C ... 631 231-2300
Ronkonkoma *(G-14929)*
Lanza Corp ... G ... 914 937-6360
Port Chester *(G-13751)*
▼ **Letterama Inc** ... G ... 516 349-0800
West Babylon *(G-16807)*
Liberty Awnings & Signs Inc ... G ... 347 203-1470
East Elmhurst *(G-4394)*
◆ **Lifestyle-Trimco** ... E ... 718 257-9101
Brooklyn *(G-2219)*
Linear Signs Inc ... F ... 631 532-5330
Lindenhurst *(G-7468)*
M Santoliquido Corp ... F ... 914 375-6674
Yonkers *(G-17463)*
Manhattan Neon Sign Corp ... F ... 212 714-0430
New York *(G-11131)*
Marigold Signs Inc ... F ... 516 433-7446
Hicksville *(G-6369)*
Mastercraft Manufacturing Co ... G ... 718 729-5620
Long Island City *(G-7805)*
Mauceri Sign Inc ... F ... 718 656-7700
Jamaica *(G-6929)*
▲ **Maxworld Inc** ... G ... 212 242-7588
New York *(G-11189)*
Mds USA Inc ... E ... 718 358-5588
Flushing *(G-5269)*
▲ **Mechtronics Corporation** ... E ... 845 231-1400
Beacon *(G-786)*
Mechtronics Corporation ... E ... 845 831-9300
Beacon *(G-787)*
Mekanism Inc ... E ... 212 226-2772
New York *(G-11221)*
Metropolitan Sign & Riggin ... G ... 718 231-0010
Bronx *(G-1395)*
Metropolitan Signs Inc ... G ... 315 638-1448
Baldwinsville *(G-572)*
Midwood Signs & Design Inc ... G ... 718 499-9041
Brooklyn *(G-2312)*
◆ **Millennium Signs & Display Inc** ... E ... 516 292-8000
Hempstead *(G-6280)*
Miller Mohr Display Inc ... G ... 631 941-2769
East Setauket *(G-4487)*
Mixture Screen Printing ... G ... 845 561-2857
Newburgh *(G-12767)*

Modulex New York Inc ... G ... 646 742-1320
New York *(G-11290)*
Mohawk Sign Systems Inc ... E ... 518 842-5303
Amsterdam *(G-360)*
Monasani Signs Inc ... G ... 631 266-2635
East Northport *(G-4442)*
Morris Brothers Sign Svc Inc ... G ... 212 675-9130
New York *(G-11306)*
Motion Message Inc ... F ... 631 924-9500
Manorville *(G-8079)*
Movinads & Signs LLC ... G ... 518 378-3000
Halfmoon *(G-5913)*
Mr Sign Usa Inc ... F ... 718 218-3321
Brooklyn *(G-2340)*
▼ **Mystic Display Co Inc** ... G ... 718 485-2651
Brooklyn *(G-2345)*
Nameplate Mfrs of Amer ... E ... 631 752-0055
Farmingdale *(G-5061)*
Nas Quick Sign Inc ... G ... 716 876-7599
Buffalo *(G-3081)*
National Advertising & Prtg ... G ... 212 629-7650
New York *(G-11346)*
National Prfmce Solutions Inc ... D ... 718 833-4767
Brooklyn *(G-2351)*
Nationwide Exhibitor Svcs Inc ... F ... 631 467-2034
Central Islip *(G-3505)*
New Art Signs Co Inc ... G ... 718 443-0900
Glen Head *(G-5637)*
▲ **New Dimensions Research Corp** ... C ... 631 694-1356
Melville *(G-8340)*
New Kit On The Block ... G ... 631 757-5655
Bohemia *(G-1109)*
New Style Signs Limited Inc ... F ... 212 242-7848
New York *(G-11393)*
▲ **Newline Products Inc** ... E ... 972 881-3318
New Windsor *(G-8946)*
Noel Assoc ... G ... 516 371-5420
Inwood *(G-6764)*
Norampac New York City Inc ... C ... 718 340-2100
Maspeth *(G-8158)*
North Shore Neon Sign Co Inc ... E ... 718 937-4848
Flushing *(G-5275)*
Northeast Promotional Group In ... G ... 518 793-1024
South Glens Falls *(G-15527)*
Northeastern Sign Corp ... G ... 315 265-6657
South Colton *(G-15516)*
Northern Awning & Sign Company ... G ... 315 782-8515
Watertown *(G-16667)*
▲ **Nysco Products LLC** ... D ... 718 792-9000
Bronx *(G-1415)*
Olson Sign Company Inc ... G ... 518 370-2118
Schenectady *(G-15284)*
On The Mark Digital Printing & ... G ... 716 823-3373
Hamburg *(G-5935)*
▲ **Orlandi Inc** ... D ... 631 756-0110
Farmingdale *(G-5071)*
Orlandi Inc ... E ... 631 756-0110
Farmingdale *(G-5072)*
Pama Enterprises Inc ... G ... 516 504-6300
Great Neck *(G-5828)*
Penn Signs Inc ... E ... 718 797-1112
Brooklyn *(G-2414)*
Plasti-Vue Corp ... G ... 718 463-2300
Flushing *(G-5282)*
▲ **Platinum Sales Promotion Inc** ... G ... 718 361-0200
Long Island City *(G-7844)*
Polyplastic Forms Inc ... E ... 631 249-5011
Farmingdale *(G-5083)*
Poncio Signs ... G ... 718 543-4851
Bronx *(G-1430)*
Precision Signscom Inc ... D ... 631 842-5060
Amityville *(G-323)*
Premier Sign Systems LLC ... E ... 585 235-0390
Rochester *(G-14598)*
▲ **Promotional Development Inc** ... D ... 718 485-8550
Brooklyn *(G-2455)*
Props Displays & Interiors ... F ... 212 620-3840
New York *(G-11737)*
Pyx Inc ... G ... 718 469-4253
Brooklyn *(G-2460)*
Qcr Express Corp ... G ... 888 924-5888
Astoria *(G-453)*
Quick Sign F X ... F ... 516 249-6531
Farmingdale *(G-5094)*
Quorum Group LLC ... D ... 585 798-8888
Medina *(G-8279)*
R & J Displays Inc ... E ... 631 491-3500
West Babylon *(G-16820)*
Rapp Signs Inc ... F ... 607 656-8167
Greene *(G-5867)*

Ray Sign Inc ... F ... 518 377-1371
Schenectady *(G-15289)*
Resonant Legal Media LLC ... D ... 800 781-3591
New York *(G-11841)*
Rgm Signs Inc ... G ... 718 442-0598
Staten Island *(G-15732)*
Riverwood Sgns By Dndev Dsigns ... G ... 845 229-0282
Hyde Park *(G-6737)*
Rocket Fuel Inc ... B ... 212 594-8888
New York *(G-11898)*
Rome Sign & Display Co ... G ... 315 336-0550
Rome *(G-14833)*
Rosenwach Tank Co Inc ... F ... 718 274-3250
Long Island City *(G-7867)*
▲ **Royal Promotion Group Inc** ... D ... 212 246-3780
New York *(G-11927)*
Rpf Associates Inc ... G ... 631 462-7446
Commack *(G-3841)*
◆ **Rsquared Ny Inc** ... D ... 631 521-8700
Edgewood *(G-4609)*
Santoro Signs Inc ... G ... 716 895-8875
Buffalo *(G-3176)*
Saxton Corporation ... E ... 518 732-7705
Castleton On Hudson *(G-3420)*
Sellco Industries Inc ... E ... 607 756-7594
Cortland *(G-4045)*
Seneca Signs LLC ... G ... 315 446-9420
Syracuse *(G-16038)*
Sign & Signs ... G ... 718 941-6200
Brooklyn *(G-2552)*
Sign A Rama Inc ... G ... 631 952-3324
Hauppauge *(G-6190)*
Sign A Rama of Syracuse ... G ... 315 446-9420
Syracuse *(G-16041)*
Sign Center Inc ... F ... 212 967-2113
New York *(G-12068)*
Sign Company ... G ... 212 967-2113
New York *(G-12069)*
▲ **Sign Design Group New York Inc** ... F ... 718 392-0779
Long Island City *(G-7876)*
Sign Expo Enterprises ... F ... 212 925-8585
New York *(G-12070)*
Sign Group Inc ... E ... 718 438-7103
Brooklyn *(G-2553)*
Sign Guys LLC ... G ... 315 253-4276
Auburn *(G-518)*
Sign Here Enterprises LLC ... G ... 914 328-3111
Hartsdale *(G-6000)*
Sign Impressions Inc ... G ... 585 723-0420
Rochester *(G-14685)*
Sign Language Inc ... G ... 585 237-2620
Perry *(G-13526)*
Sign Studio Inc ... F ... 518 266-0877
Troy *(G-16254)*
Sign Up Now Inc ... G ... 516 221-3394
Bellmore *(G-822)*
Sign Works Incorporated ... E ... 914 592-0700
Elmsford *(G-4784)*
Sign World Inc ... E ... 212 619-9000
Brooklyn *(G-2554)*
Signature Industries Inc ... F ... 516 679-5177
Freeport *(G-5427)*
Signature Name Plate Co Inc ... G ... 585 321-9960
Rochester *(G-14686)*
▲ **Signs & Decal Corp** ... E ... 718 486-6400
Brooklyn *(G-2555)*
Signs Inc ... G ... 518 483-4759
Malone *(G-8017)*
Signs Ink Ltd ... F ... 914 739-9059
Yorktown Heights *(G-17520)*
Signs of Success Ltd ... E ... 516 295-6000
Lynbrook *(G-7961)*
Smith Graphics Inc ... G ... 631 420-4180
Farmingdale *(G-5110)*
Snyders Neon Displays Inc ... G ... 518 857-4100
Colonie *(G-3821)*
Space Sign ... F ... 718 961-1112
College Point *(G-3808)*
Spanjer Corp ... G ... 347 448-8033
Long Island City *(G-7881)*
Specialty Signs Co Inc ... F ... 212 243-8521
New York *(G-12153)*
Spectrum On Broadway ... F ... 718 932-5388
Woodside *(G-17354)*
Spectrum Signs Inc ... E ... 631 756-1010
Woodside *(G-17355)*
Speedy Sign A Rama USA Inc ... G ... 516 783-1075
Bellmore *(G-823)*
Starlite Media LLC ... G ... 212 909-7700
New York *(G-12186)*

S I C

Employee Codes: A=Over 500 employees, B=251-500
C=101-250, D=51-100, E=20-50, F=10-19, G=5-9
2017 Harris
New York Manufacturers Directory
873

Steel-Brite Ltd ... F ... 631 589-4044
Oakdale (G-13063)

Stepping Stones One Day Signs ... G ... 518 237-5774
Waterford (G-16622)

Strategic Signage Sourcing LLC ... F ... 518 450-1093
Saratoga Springs (G-15174)

Suma Industries Inc ... G ... 646 436-5202
New York (G-12230)

Super Neon Light Co Inc ... G ... 718 236-5667
Brooklyn (G-2624)

T J Signs Unlimited LLC ... E ... 631 273-4800
Islip (G-6813)

▼ Tech Products Inc ... E ... 718 442-4900
Staten Island (G-15748)

▲ Tempo Industries Inc ... G ... 516 334-6900
Westbury (G-17031)

Three Gems Inc ... G ... 516 248-0388
New Hyde Park (G-8866)

Timely Signs Inc ... G ... 516 285-5339
Elmont (G-4730)

Timely Signs of Kingston Inc ... F ... 845 331-8710
Kingston (G-7215)

Todd Walbridge ... G ... 585 254-3018
Rochester (G-14727)

▲ Trans-Lux Corporation ... D ... 800 243-5544
New York (G-12392)

Tru-Art Sign Co Inc ... F ... 718 658-5068
Jamaica (G-6959)

Turoff Tower Graphics Inc ... F ... 718 856-7300
Brooklyn (G-2688)

Ulrich Sign Co Inc ... E ... 716 434-0167
Lockport (G-7623)

Ultimate Signs & Designs Inc ... E ... 516 481-0800
Hempstead (G-6288)

Unique Display Mfg Corp ... G ... 516 546-3800
Freeport (G-5433)

United Print Group Inc ... F ... 718 392-4242
Long Island City (G-7908)

United Sttes Brnze Sign of Fla ... E ... 516 352-5155
New Hyde Park (G-8870)

Universal 3d Innovation Inc ... F ... 516 837-9423
Valley Stream (G-16431)

Universal Signs and Svc Inc ... E ... 631 446-1121
Deer Park (G-4220)

USA Signs of America Inc ... D ... 631 254-6900
Deer Park (G-4221)

Valle Signs and Awnings ... F ... 516 408-3440
Uniondale (G-16301)

Valley Creek Side Inc ... G ... 315 839-5526
Clayville (G-3690)

Vez Inc ... G ... 718 273-7002
Staten Island (G-15752)

Viana Signs Corp ... F ... 516 887-2000
Oceanside (G-13104)

Victory Signs Inc ... G ... 315 762-0220
Canastota (G-3376)

▲ Visual Citi Inc ... C ... 631 482-3030
Lindenhurst (G-7495)

▲ Visual Effects Inc ... F ... 718 324-0011
Jamaica (G-6962)

Visual ID Source Inc ... F ... 516 307-9759
Mineola (G-8538)

Visual Impact Graphics Inc ... G ... 585 548-7118
Batavia (G-652)

Vital Signs & Graphics Co Inc ... G ... 518 237-8372
Cohoes (G-3760)

▲ Von Pok & Chang New York Inc ... G ... 212 599-0556
New York (G-12568)

Voss Signs LLC ... E ... 315 682-6418
Manlius (G-8076)

Wedel Sign Company Inc ... G ... 631 727-4577
Riverhead (G-14159)

Westchester Signs Inc ... G ... 914 666-7446
Mount Kisco (G-8646)

Whispr Group Inc ... F ... 212 924-3979
Brooklyn (G-2747)

Wizard Equipment Inc ... G ... 315 414-9999
Syracuse (G-16073)

Wl Concepts & Production Inc ... G ... 516 538-5300
Freeport (G-5434)

Woodbury Printing Plus + Inc ... G ... 845 928-6610
Central Valley (G-3529)

X-Press Signs Inc ... G ... 716 677-0880
West Seneca (G-16955)

Yellowpagecitycom ... F ... 585 410-6688
Rochester (G-14773)

▲ Yong Xin Kitchen Supplies Inc ... F ... 212 995-8908
New York (G-12696)

Yost Neon Displays Inc ... G ... 716 674-6780
West Seneca (G-16956)

Z-Car-D Corp ... E ... 631 424-2077
Huntington Station (G-6730)

3995 Burial Caskets

Milso Industries Inc ... F ... 631 234-1133
Hauppauge (G-6138)

North Hudson Woodcraft Corp ... E ... 315 429-3105
Dolgeville (G-4306)

3996 Linoleum & Hard Surface Floor Coverings, NEC

East To West Architectral Pdts ... G ... 631 433-9690
East Northport (G-4435)

▲ Engineered Plastics Inc ... E ... 800 682-2525
Williamsville (G-17242)

Heritage Contract Flooring LLC ... E ... 716 853-1555
Buffalo (G-2994)

Signature Systems Group LLC ... G ... 800 569-2751
New York (G-12073)

3999 Manufacturing Industries, NEC

141 Industries LLC ... F ... 978 273-8831
New York (G-8959)

40 North Industries ... E ... 212 821-1600
New York (G-8975)

A & L Asset Management Ltd ... C ... 718 566-1500
Brooklyn (G-1526)

A&M Model Makers LLC ... G ... 626 813-9661
Macedon (G-7979)

Accenta Incorporated ... G ... 716 565-6262
Buffalo (G-2794)

Accessible Bath Tech LLC ... F ... 518 937-1518
Albany (G-33)

Accurate Pnt Powdr Coating Inc ... F ... 585 235-1650
Rochester (G-14167)

Active Manufacturing Inc ... F ... 607 775-3162
Kirkwood (G-7230)

Adel Rootstein (usa) Inc ... E ... 718 499-5650
Brooklyn (G-1561)

Adults and Children With Learn ... E ... 516 593-8230
East Rockaway (G-4467)

AFP Manufacturing Corp ... F ... 516 466-6464
Great Neck (G-5785)

▲ Age Manufacturers Inc ... D ... 718 927-0048
Brooklyn (G-1569)

Air Flow Manufacturing ... F ... 607 733-8284
Elmira (G-4669)

▲ Aloi Solutions LLC ... E ... 585 292-0920
Rochester (G-14192)

▲ Alvanon Inc ... E ... 212 868-4314
New York (G-9105)

▲ American Culture Hair Inc ... E ... 631 242-3142
Huntington Station (G-6694)

Ameritool Mfg LLC ... G ... 315 668-2172
West Monroe (G-16909)

▲ Arcadia Mfg Group Inc ... E ... 518 434-6213
Green Island (G-5853)

Arcadia Mfg Group Inc ... G ... 518 434-6213
Menands (G-8367)

Arnprior Rpid Mfg Slutions Inc ... C ... 585 617-6301
Rochester (G-14212)

Artemis Studios Inc ... D ... 718 788-6022
Brooklyn (G-1635)

Ascribe Inc ... E ... 585 413-0298
Rochester (G-14216)

◆ Astron Candle Manufacturing Co ... G ... 718 728-3330
Long Island City (G-7673)

Atlas Metal Industries Inc ... G ... 607 776-2048
Hammondsport (G-5953)

▲ Avanti Advanced Mfg Corp ... G ... 716 541-8945
Buffalo (G-2826)

B & R Promotional Products ... G ... 212 563-0040
New York (G-9288)

▲ B Barine Inc ... E ... 718 499-5650
Brooklyn (G-1657)

B F G Elcpltg and Mfg Co ... E ... 716 362-0888
Blasdell (G-960)

Balance Enterprises Inc ... G ... 516 822-3183
Hicksville (G-6326)

Baldwin Ribbon & Stamping Corp ... F ... 718 335-6700
Woodside (G-17319)

Bee Green Industries Inc ... G ... 516 334-3525
Carle Place (G-3386)

Best Priced Products Inc ... G ... 914 345-3800
Elmsford (G-4735)

Biocontinuum Group Inc ... G ... 212 406-1060
New York (G-9400)

Blackbox Biometrics Inc ... E ... 585 329-3399
Rochester (G-14234)

Blanche P Field LLC ... E ... 212 355-6616
New York (G-9412)

▲ Blandi Products LLC ... F ... 908 377-2885
New York (G-9413)

▲ Boom LLC ... E ... 646 218-0752
New York (G-9438)

Brooklyn Industries LLC ... F ... 718 788-5250
Brooklyn (G-1726)

Brooklyn Industries LLC ... F ... 718 486-6464
Brooklyn (G-1727)

Brooklyn Industries LLC ... F ... 718 789-2764
Brooklyn (G-1728)

Bullex Inc ... E ... 518 689-2023
Albany (G-59)

Callanan Industries Inc ... G ... 518 382-5354
Schenectady (G-15237)

▲ Candle In The Window Inc ... F ... 718 852-5743
Brooklyn (G-1753)

Candles By Foster ... G ... 914 739-9226
Peekskill (G-13475)

▲ Cathedral Candle Co ... D ... 315 422-9119
Syracuse (G-15890)

▲ Center Line Studios Inc ... F ... 845 534-7143
New Windsor (G-8934)

Chan & Chan (usa) Corp ... G ... 718 388-9633
Brooklyn (G-1773)

◆ Christian Dior Perfumes LLC ... E ... 212 931-2200
New York (G-9610)

Clara Papa ... G ... 315 733-2660
Utica (G-16311)

Commercial Fabrics Inc ... F ... 716 694-0641
North Tonawanda (G-12966)

Copesetic Inc ... F ... 315 684-7780
Morrisville (G-8620)

Costume Armour Inc ... F ... 845 534-9120
Cornwall (G-3987)

Creative Models & Prototypes ... G ... 516 433-6828
Hicksville (G-6337)

Criterion Bell & Specialty ... E ... 718 788-2600
Brooklyn (G-1819)

▼ Crusader Candle Co Inc ... E ... 718 625-0005
Brooklyn (G-1821)

D & M Enterprises Incorporated ... G ... 914 937-6430
Port Chester (G-13741)

▲ Demeo Brothers Inc ... F ... 212 268-1400
New York (G-9843)

Deva Concepts LLC ... E ... 212 343-0344
New York (G-9864)

Diane Studios Inc ... D ... 718 788-6007
Brooklyn (G-1861)

Dj Pirrone Industries Inc ... G ... 518 864-5496
Pattersonville (G-13447)

Dolmen ... F ... 912 596-1537
Conklin (G-3867)

Donorwall Inc ... F ... 212 766-9670
New York (G-9907)

E-Z Global Wholesale Inc ... G ... 888 769-7888
Brooklyn (G-1894)

▲ Eagle Regalia Co Inc ... F ... 845 425-2245
Spring Valley (G-15582)

East Penn Manufacturing Co ... G ... 631 321-7161
Babylon (G-547)

▲ Eastern Feather & Down Corp ... G ... 718 387-4100
Brooklyn (G-1898)

EDM Mfg ... G ... 631 669-1966
Babylon (G-548)

Emerald Models Inc ... G ... 585 584-3739
East Bethany (G-4382)

◆ Eser Realty Corp ... E ... 718 383-0565
Brooklyn (G-1934)

Essex Industries ... G ... 518 942-6671
Mineville (G-8540)

▲ Essex Manufacturing Inc ... D ... 212 239-0080
New York (G-10066)

Eton Institute ... F ... 855 334-3688
New York (G-10080)

Executive Creations Inc ... G ... 212 422-2640
New York (G-10105)

▼ Falk Industries Inc ... F ... 518 725-2777
Johnstown (G-7114)

▲ Faster-Form Corp ... D ... 800 327-3676
New Hartford (G-8804)

Federal Sample Card Corp ... D ... 718 458-1344
Elmhurst (G-4660)

Feraco Industries ... G ... 631 547-8120
Huntington Station (G-6704)

Fingerprint America Inc ... G ... 518 435-1609
Albany (G-80)

◆ Fish & Crown Ltd ... D ... 212 707-9603
New York (G-10173)

Five Star Creations Inc E 845 783-1187
Monroe (G-8554)
▲ Four Paws Products Ltd D 631 436-7421
Ronkonkoma (G-14902)
Freedom Mfg LLC F 518 584-0441
Saratoga Springs (G-15152)
Fun Industries of NY F 631 845-3805
Farmingdale (G-4995)
Genesis Mannequins USA II Inc G 212 505-6600
New York (G-10275)
Givi Inc G 212 586-5029
New York (G-10303)
Global Precision Inds Inc F 585 254-0010
Rochester (G-14409)
Goldmont Enterprises Inc F 212 947-3633
Middle Village (G-8411)
Goodwill Inds of Greater NY C 914 621-0781
Baldwin Place (G-563)
Goodwill Inds Wstn NY Inc F 716 633-3305
Williamsville (G-17246)
Grand Island Animal Hospital E 716 773-7645
Grand Island (G-5760)
▲ Gustbuster Ltd G 631 391-9000
Farmingdale (G-5003)
Hair Color Research Group Inc E 718 445-6026
Flushing (G-5248)
Handmade Frames Inc F 718 782-8364
Brooklyn (G-2067)
Holland Manufacturing Inc G 716 685-4129
Williamsville (G-17247)
◆ Hoskie Co Inc D 718 628-8672
Brooklyn (G-2088)
Hrg Group Inc E 212 906-8555
New York (G-10524)
▼ Hudson Scenic Studio Inc C 914 375-0900
Yonkers (G-17455)
Identfication Data Imaging LLC G 516 484-6500
Port Washington (G-13823)
Image Tech F 716 635-0167
Buffalo (G-3002)
Innovative Industries LLC G 718 784-7300
Long Island City (G-7766)
▲ International Bronze Manufac F 516 248-3080
Albertson (G-155)
▲ International Design Assoc Ltd G 212 687-0333
New York (G-10633)
Iquit Cig LLC G 718 475-1422
Brooklyn (G-2115)
Isco Industries F 502 714-5306
Horseheads (G-6581)
Islip Miniture Golf G 631 940-8900
Bay Shore (G-708)
▲ Ivy Enterprises Inc C 516 621-9779
Port Washington (G-13826)
▲ J & A Usa Inc G 631 243-3336
Brentwood (G-1187)
J & R Unique Giftware E 718 821-0398
Maspeth (G-8146)
J T Systematic G 607 754-0929
Endwell (G-4836)
Jacobs Juice Corp G 646 255-2860
Brooklyn (G-2132)
Jags Manufacturing Network Inc G 631 750-6367
Holbrook (G-6454)
▲ Jamaica Lamp Corp E 718 776-5039
Queens Village (G-13980)
Jason & Jean Products Inc F 718 271-8300
Corona (G-3999)
▲ Jenalex Creative Marketing Inc G 212 935-2266
New York (G-10719)
▲ Jenray Products Inc E 914 375-5596
Yonkers (G-17458)
JG Innovative Industries Inc G 718 784-7300
Kew Gardens (G-7164)
John Gailer Inc E 212 243-5662
Long Island City (G-7772)
John Prior G 516 520-9801
East Meadow (G-4426)
Joya LLC F 718 852-6979
Brooklyn (G-2153)
Jpm Fine Woodworking LLC G 516 236-7605
Jericho (G-7074)
Just Right Carbines LLC G 585 261-5331
Canandaigua (G-3348)
Kafko (us) Corp G 877 721-7665
Latham (G-7367)
Kelly Foundry & Machine Co E 315 732-8313
Utica (G-16346)
Ketchum Manufacturing Co Inc F 518 696-3331
Lake Luzerne (G-7272)
Kevco Industries G 845 255-7407
New Paltz (G-8875)
King Displays Inc F 212 629-8455
New York (G-10853)
▲ Kittywalk Systems Inc G 516 627-8418
Port Washington (G-13833)
▲ Kkw Corp E 631 589-5454
Sayville (G-15211)
▲ Lab-Aids Inc E 631 737-1133
Ronkonkoma (G-14927)
Learnimation G 917 868-7261
Brooklyn (G-2202)
Lemetric Hair Centers Inc F 212 986-5620
New York (G-10964)
Lemon Brothers Foundation Inc F 347 920-2749
Bronx (G-1380)
▲ Leo D Bernstein & Sons Inc E 212 337-9578
New York (G-10968)
Liberty Displays Inc E 716 743-1757
Amherst (G-249)
◆ Lifestyle-Trimco E 718 257-9101
Brooklyn (G-2219)
Lux Mundi Corp G 631 244-4596
Ronkonkoma (G-14934)
M & S Schmalberg Inc F 212 244-2090
New York (G-11069)
M and J Hair Center Inc F 516 872-1010
Garden City (G-5518)
Mack Studios Displays Inc E 315 252-7542
Auburn (G-507)
Malouf Colette Inc F 212 941-9588
New York (G-11122)
Marilyn Model Management Inc F 646 556-7587
New York (G-11151)
Martec Industries F 585 458-3940
Rochester (G-14498)
Martin Chafkin G 718 383-1155
Brooklyn (G-2276)
▲ McGaw Group LLC F 212 876-8822
New York (G-11197)
▲ Meisel-Peskin Co Inc D 718 497-1840
Brooklyn (G-2296)
▲ Mgd Brands Inc D 516 545-0150
Plainview (G-13620)
Miss Jessies LLC G 718 643-9016
New York (G-11282)
Mission Crane Service Inc D 718 937-3333
Long Island City (G-7814)
Mitten Manufacturing Inc E 315 437-7564
Syracuse (G-15992)
▲ Moti Inc F 718 436-4280
Brooklyn (G-2335)
▲ Muench-Kreuzer Candle Company D 315 471-4515
Syracuse (G-15994)
Nationwide Exhibitor Svcs Inc F 631 467-2034
Central Islip (G-3505)
Nitro Manufacturing LLC F 716 646-9900
Hamburg (G-5934)
◆ Northern Lights Entps Inc C 585 593-1200
Wellsville (G-16755)
Northern New York Rural G 518 891-9460
Saranac Lake (G-15139)
Nubian Heritage G 631 265-3551
Hauppauge (G-6150)
O Brien Gere Mfg Inc G 315 437-6100
Liverpool (G-7537)
Ogd V-Hvac Inc E 315 858-1002
Van Hornesville (G-16432)
▲ Ohserase Manufacturing LLC E 518 358-9309
Akwesasne (G-32)
▲ Old Williamsburgh Candle Corp C 718 566-1500
Brooklyn (G-2389)
Oledworks LLC E 585 287-6802
Rochester (G-14547)
Omicron Technologies Inc E 631 434-7697
Holbrook (G-6465)
Oriskany Manufacturing LLC F 315 732-4962
Yorkville (G-17524)
▲ Orlandi Inc D 631 756-0110
Farmingdale (G-5071)
Orlandi Inc E 631 756-0110
Farmingdale (G-5072)
Oso Industries Inc G 917 709-2050
Brooklyn (G-2398)
Our Own Candle Company Inc F 716 769-5000
Findley Lake (G-5177)
Paperworks Industries Inc F 913 621-0922
Baldwinsville (G-573)
▲ Patience Brewster Inc F 315 685-8336
Skaneateles (G-15464)
PCI Industries Corp E 914 662-2700
Mount Vernon (G-8713)
Performance Precision Mfg LLC G 518 993-3033
Fort Plain (G-5348)
Petland Discounts Inc G 516 821-3194
Hewlett (G-6311)
▲ Pets n People Inc G 631 232-1200
Hauppauge (G-6162)
◆ Production Resource Group LLC D 212 589-5400
Armonk (G-419)
Production Resource Group LLC E 845 567-5700
New Windsor (G-8948)
▲ Promotional Development Inc D 718 485-8550
Brooklyn (G-2455)
Props Displays & Interiors F 212 620-3840
New York (G-11737)
▲ PS Pibbs Inc E 718 445-8046
Flushing (G-5284)
Pyrotek Incorporated E 716 731-3221
Sanborn (G-15126)
Qps Die Cutters Finishers Corp E 718 966-1811
Staten Island (G-15725)
Quality Candle Mfg Co Inc F 631 842-8475
Copiague (G-3921)
Quest Manufacturing Inc E 716 312-8000
Hamburg (G-5938)
▲ R V Dow Enterprises Inc F 585 454-5862
Rochester (G-14619)
Ray Gold Shade Inc F 718 377-8892
Brooklyn (G-2480)
◆ Readent Inc F 212 710-3004
White Plains (G-17162)
Remus Industries G 914 906-1544
Ossining (G-13327)
Rockwell Video Solutions LLC F 631 745-0582
Southampton (G-15550)
Rutcarele Inc G 347 830-5353
Corona (G-4005)
Ryers Creek Corp E 607 523-6617
Corning (G-3980)
S & H Enterprises Inc G 888 323-8755
Queensbury (G-14010)
S B Manufacturing LLC F 845 352-3700
Monsey (G-8579)
▲ S M Frank & Company Inc G 914 739-3100
New Windsor (G-8951)
Saakshi Inc G 315 475-3988
Syracuse (G-16028)
▲ Select Industries New York Inc F 800 723-5333
New York (G-12022)
◆ Shake-N-Go Fashion Inc D 516 944-7777
Port Washington (G-13864)
Shapes Etc Inc F 585 335-6619
Dansville (G-4079)
Shyam Ahuja Limited G 212 644-5910
New York (G-12057)
▲ Simcha Candle Co Inc G 845 783-0406
New Windsor (G-8955)
Sonaal Industries Inc G 718 383-3860
Brooklyn (G-2584)
◆ Spartan Brands Inc F 212 340-0320
New York (G-12149)
Spectrum Brands Inc B 631 232-1200
Hauppauge (G-6195)
▲ Star Desk Pad Co Inc E 914 963-9400
Yonkers (G-17486)
Steeldeck Ny Inc F 718 599-3700
Brooklyn (G-2604)
Stiegelbauer Associates Inc E 718 624-0835
Brooklyn (G-2608)
▼ Strategic Mktg Promotions Inc F 845 623-7777
Pearl River (G-13467)
Subcon Industries G 716 945-4430
Salamanca (G-15109)
Supersil LLC D 347 266-9900
Brooklyn (G-2630)
Swift Multigraphics LLC G 585 442-8000
Rochester (G-14709)
▲ Tactica International Inc F 212 575-0500
New York (G-12271)
Teachspin Inc F 716 725-6116
Buffalo (G-3210)
Techgrass F 646 719-2000
New York (G-12288)
▲ Tent and Table Com LLC F 716 570-0258
Buffalo (G-3213)
▲ Thompson Ferrier LLC G 212 244-2212
New York (G-12326)
Tii Industries Inc F 631 789-5000
Copiague (G-3933)

S I C

39 MISCELLANEOUS MANUFACTURING INDUSTRIES SIC SECTION

▲ Topoo Industries Incorporated .... G 718 331-3755
Brooklyn *(G-2666)*
▼ Tri-Force Sales LLC .... E 732 261-5507
New York *(G-12399)*
▲ Tri-Plex Packaging Corporation .... E 212 481-6070
New York *(G-12401)*
Trove Inc .... F 212 268-2046
Brooklyn *(G-2684)*
▲ TV Guilfoil & Associates Inc .... G 315 453-0920
Syracuse *(G-16062)*
Unique Petz LLC .... E 212 714-1800
New York *(G-12462)*
◆ Unistel LLC .... D 585 341-4600
Webster *(G-16740)*
Unlimited Industries Inc .... G 631 666-9483
Brightwaters *(G-1239)*
Uptown Nails LLC .... C 800 748-1881
New York *(G-12477)*
Vali Industries Inc .... F 718 821-5555
Brooklyn *(G-2717)*
▲ Water Splash Inc .... G 800 936-3430
Champlain *(G-3549)*
▲ Welsh Gold Stampers Inc .... E 718 984-5031
Staten Island *(G-15754)*
Woodfalls Industries .... F 518 236-7201
Plattsburgh *(G-13709)*
Zebrowski Industries Inc .... G 716 532-3911
Collins *(G-3818)*
▲ Zip-Jack Industries Ltd .... E 914 592-2000
Tarrytown *(G-16113)*
Zmz Mfg Inc .... G 518 234-4336
Warnerville *(G-16579)*

73 BUSINESS SERVICES

7372 Prepackaged Software

2k Inc .... G 646 536-3007
New York *(G-8969)*
30dc Inc .... G 212 962-4400
New York *(G-8970)*
30dc Inc .... F 212 962-4400
New York *(G-8971)*
6n Systems Inc .... G 518 583-6400
Halfmoon *(G-5907)*
A K A Computer Consulting Inc .... G 718 351-5200
Staten Island *(G-15630)*
A2ia Corp .... G 917 237-0390
New York *(G-8996)*
Aarfid LLC .... G 716 992-3999
Eden *(G-4585)*
Abel Noser Solutions Ltd .... E 646 884-6440
New York *(G-9003)*
Accela Inc .... F 631 563-5005
Ronkonkoma *(G-14846)*
Accelify Solutions LLC .... E 888 922-2354
Brooklyn *(G-1550)*
Adl Data Systems Inc .... E 914 591-1800
Hawthorne *(G-6243)*
Adobe Systems Inc .... E 212 471-0904
New York *(G-9029)*
Adobe Systems Incorporated .... E 212 471-0904
New York *(G-9030)*
Adtech Us Inc .... C 212 402-4840
New York *(G-9033)*
Advanced Cmpt Sftwr Consulting .... G 718 300-3577
Bronx *(G-1264)*
Advanced Comfort Systems Inc .... F 518 884-8444
Ballston Spa *(G-589)*
Amcom Software Inc .... F 212 951-7600
New York *(G-9110)*
Anbeck Inc .... G 518 907-0308
White Plains *(G-17078)*
Andigo New Media Inc .... G 212 727-8445
New York *(G-9153)*
◆ Ansa Systems of USA Inc .... G 516 887-6855
Valley Stream *(G-16400)*
Appboy Inc .... F 504 327-7269
New York *(G-9180)*
Appfigures Inc .... F 212 343-7900
New York *(G-9181)*
Application Security Inc .... D 212 912-4100
New York *(G-9183)*
Apprenda Inc .... D 518 383-2130
Troy *(G-16225)*
Appsbidder Inc .... G 917 880-4269
Brooklyn *(G-1619)*
APS Enterprise Software Inc .... E 631 784-7720
Huntington *(G-6654)*
Archive360 Inc .... E 212 731-2438
New York *(G-9197)*
Arcserve (usa) LLC .... E 866 576-9742
Islandia *(G-6786)*
Articulate Global Inc .... C 800 861-4880
New York *(G-9218)*
Arumai Technologies Inc .... F 914 217-0038
Armonk *(G-412)*
Asite LLC .... D 203 545-3089
New York *(G-9232)*
Aspen Research Group Ltd .... G 212 425-9588
New York *(G-9236)*
Astria Solutions Group LLC .... E 518 346-7799
Schenectady *(G-15231)*
AT&T Corp .... F 212 317-7048
New York *(G-9244)*
Auric Technology LLC .... F 212 573-0911
New York *(G-9265)*
Autodesk Inc .... F 646 613-8680
New York *(G-9266)*
Autodesk Inc .... E 607 257-4280
Ithaca *(G-6820)*
Automated & MGT Solutions LLC .... G 518 283-5352
East Greenbush *(G-4401)*
Automated Office Systems Inc .... F 516 396-5555
Valley Stream *(G-16401)*
Avalanche Studios New York Inc .... D 212 993-6447
New York *(G-9272)*
Avocode Inc .... F 646 934-8410
New York *(G-9280)*
Aycan Medical Systems LLC .... F 585 271-3078
Rochester *(G-14219)*
B601 V2 Inc .... G 646 391-6431
New York *(G-9297)*
Base Systems Inc .... G 845 278-1991
Brewster *(G-1211)*
BEC Acquisition Co LLC .... G 516 986-3050
Melville *(G-8296)*
Beyondly Inc .... F 646 658-3665
New York *(G-9384)*
Big Data Bizviz LLC .... G 716 803-2367
West Seneca *(G-16939)*
Big White Wall Holding Inc .... F 917 281-2649
New York *(G-9395)*
Bigwood Systems Inc .... G 607 257-0915
Ithaca *(G-6822)*
Billing Blocks Inc .... F 718 442-5006
Staten Island *(G-15647)*
Blue Wolf Group LLC .... D 866 455-9653
New York *(G-9423)*
BMC Software Inc .... E 646 452-4100
New York *(G-9428)*
BMC Software Inc .... E 212 730-1389
New York *(G-9429)*
Bootstrap Software .... G 212 871-2020
New York *(G-9440)*
Boundless Spatial Inc .... E 646 831-5531
New York *(G-9443)*
Boxbee Inc .... G 646 612-7839
New York *(G-9445)*
Brainpop LLC .... E 212 574-6017
New York *(G-9451)*
Brainworks Software Dev Corp .... G 631 563-5000
Sayville *(G-15204)*
Brigadoon Software Inc .... G 845 624-0909
Nanuet *(G-8752)*
Broadway Technology LLC .... E 646 912-6450
New York *(G-9466)*
Bull Street LLC .... G 212 495-9855
New York *(G-9478)*
Buncee LLC .... F 631 591-1390
Calverton *(G-3287)*
Business Integrity Inc .... G 718 238-2008
New York *(G-9482)*
Business Management Systems .... F 914 245-8558
Yorktown Heights *(G-17508)*
Byte Consulting Inc .... G 646 500-8606
New York *(G-9489)*
C S I G Inc .... G 845 383-3800
Kingston *(G-7181)*
▼ Ca Inc .... A 800 225-5224
New York *(G-9491)*
Ca Inc .... C 800 225-5224
New York *(G-9492)*
California US Holdings Inc .... A 212 726-6500
New York *(G-9501)*
Callaway Digital Arts Inc .... E 212 675-3050
New York *(G-9503)*
Callidus Software Inc .... F 212 554-7300
New York *(G-9504)*
Caminus Corporation .... D 212 515-3600
New York *(G-9508)*
Candex Solutions Inc .... G 215 650-3214
New York *(G-9512)*
Capital Programs Inc .... G 212 842-4640
New York *(G-9520)*
Careconnector .... G 919 360-2987
Brooklyn *(G-1758)*
Catalyst Group Inc .... G 212 243-7777
New York *(G-9545)*
Catch Ventures Inc .... F 347 620-4351
New York *(G-9547)*
Catholic News Publishing Co .... F 914 632-7771
Mamaroneck *(G-8027)*
Cavalry Solutions .... G 315 422-1699
Syracuse *(G-15891)*
Cbord Group Inc .... C 607 257-2410
Ithaca *(G-6831)*
Cdml Computer Services Ltd .... G 718 428-9063
Fresh Meadows *(G-5439)*
Cegid Corporation .... F 212 757-9038
New York *(G-9553)*
Ceipal LLC .... G 585 351-2934
Rochester *(G-14264)*
Ceipal LLC .... G 585 351-2934
Rochester *(G-14265)*
Cellufun Inc .... E 212 385-2255
New York *(G-9555)*
Celonis Inc .... G 941 615-9670
Brooklyn *(G-1769)*
Ceros Inc .... E 347 744-9250
New York *(G-9571)*
Cgi Technologies Solutions Inc .... F 212 682-7411
New York *(G-9573)*
Checkm8 Inc .... F 212 268-0048
New York *(G-9588)*
Chequedcom Inc .... E 888 412-0699
Saratoga Springs *(G-15149)*
Childrens Progress Inc .... E 212 730-0905
New York *(G-9595)*
Cinedigm Software .... G 212 206-9001
New York *(G-9618)*
Citixsys Technologies Inc .... G 212 745-1365
New York *(G-9626)*
Clarityad Inc .... G 646 397-4198
New York *(G-9634)*
Classroom Inc .... E 212 545-8400
New York *(G-9639)*
▲ Clayton Dubilier & Rice Fun .... E 212 407-5200
New York *(G-9640)*
Clearview Social Inc .... G 801 414-7675
Buffalo *(G-2875)*
Clever Goats Media LLC .... G 917 512-0340
New York *(G-9642)*
Cloud Rock Group LLC .... G 516 967-6023
Roslyn *(G-15017)*
Cloudsense Inc .... G 917 880-6195
New York *(G-9645)*
Coalition On Positive Health .... F 212 633-2500
New York *(G-9660)*
Cognotion Inc .... G 347 692-0640
New York *(G-9665)*
Comet Informatics LLC .... G 585 385-2310
Pittsford *(G-13557)*
Commercehub Inc .... G 518 810-0700
Albany *(G-70)*
Commify Technology .... F 917 603-1822
New York *(G-9686)*
Comprehensive Dental Tech .... G 607 467-4456
Hancock *(G-5963)*
Condeco Software Inc .... E 917 677-7600
New York *(G-9698)*
Connecticut Bus Systems LLC .... G 914 696-1900
White Plains *(G-17096)*
Construction Technology Inc .... G 914 747-8900
Valhalla *(G-16366)*
Contactive Inc .... E 646 476-9059
New York *(G-9709)*
Conversant LLC .... G 212 471-9570
New York *(G-9714)*
Coocoo SMS Inc .... F 646 459-4260
Huntington *(G-6659)*
Cross Border Transactions LLC .... G 914 631-0878
Tarrytown *(G-16089)*
CTI Software Inc .... F 631 253-3550
Deer Park *(G-4123)*
Cuffs Planning & Models Ltd .... G 914 632-1883
New Rochelle *(G-8893)*
Cultureiq Inc .... G 212 755-8633
New York *(G-9766)*
Curaegis Technologies Inc .... F 585 254-1100
Rochester *(G-14294)*

Cureatr Inc ....F 212 203-3927
New York *(G-9768)*
Curemdcom Inc ....B 646 224-2201
New York *(G-9769)*
Customshow Inc ....G 800 255-5303
New York *(G-9773)*
Cyandia Inc ....F 315 679-4268
Syracuse *(G-15917)*
Cybersports Inc ....G 315 737-7150
Utica *(G-16319)*
Dartcom Incorporated ....G 315 790-5456
New Hartford *(G-8802)*
Data Implementation Inc ....G 212 979-2015
New York *(G-9813)*
Datadog Inc ....E 866 329-4466
New York *(G-9814)*
Davel Systems Inc ....G 718 382-6024
Brooklyn *(G-1841)*
Dbase LLC ....G 607 729-0234
Binghamton *(G-907)*
Debt Resolve Inc ....G 914 949-5500
White Plains *(G-17100)*
Defran Systems Inc ....E 212 727-8342
New York *(G-9837)*
Delivery Systems Inc ....F 212 221-7007
New York *(G-9839)*
Deniz Information Systems ....G 212 750-5199
New York *(G-9845)*
Digital Associates LLC ....G 631 983-6075
Smithtown *(G-15485)*
Diligent Board Member Svcs LLC ....E 212 741-8181
New York *(G-9878)*
Diligent Corporation ....C 212 741-8181
New York *(G-9879)*
Do It Different Inc ....G 917 842-0230
New York *(G-9893)*
Document Strategies LLC ....F 585 506-9000
Rochester *(G-14315)*
Dow Jones & Company Inc ....E 212 597-5983
New York *(G-9915)*
Dropcar Inc ....G 212 464-8860
New York *(G-9931)*
Dwnld Inc ....E 484 483-6572
New York *(G-9944)*
Dynamo Development Inc ....G 212 385-1552
New York *(G-9949)*
E H Hurwitz & Associates ....G 718 884-3766
Bronx *(G-1321)*
Eastnets Americas Corp ....F 212 631-0666
New York *(G-9968)*
Ebeling Associates Inc ....F 518 688-8700
Halfmoon *(G-5910)*
EBM Care Inc ....G 212 500-5000
New York *(G-9972)*
Efront Financial Solutions Inc ....E 212 220-0660
New York *(G-9986)*
Eft Energy Inc ....G 212 290-2300
New York *(G-9987)*
Electronic Arts Inc ....G 212 672-0722
New York *(G-9997)*
Electronic Business Tech ....F 845 353-8549
West Nyack *(G-16916)*
Elepath Inc ....G 347 417-4975
Brooklyn *(G-1914)*
Elephant Talk Cmmncations Corp ....B 866 901-3309
New York *(G-10000)*
Elodina Inc ....G 646 402-5202
New York *(G-10013)*
Emblaze Systems Inc ....C 212 371-1100
New York *(G-10020)*
EMC Corporation ....E 212 899-5500
New York *(G-10021)*
EMC Corporation ....E 585 387-9505
East Rochester *(G-4457)*
Empire Innovation Group LLC ....F 716 852-5000
Buffalo *(G-2937)*
Empowrx LLC ....G 212 755-3577
New York *(G-10024)*
Endava Inc ....G 212 920-7240
New York *(G-10032)*
Enterprise Management Tech LLC ....G 212 835-1557
New York *(G-10042)*
Enterprise Network of New York ....F 516 263-0641
Brooklyn *(G-1925)*
Enterprise Tech Group Inc ....F 914 588-0327
New Rochelle *(G-8897)*
Equilend Holdings LLC ....E 212 901-2200
New York *(G-10052)*
Ert Software Inc ....G 845 358-5721
Blauvelt *(G-971)*

Ex El Enterprises Ltd ....F 212 489-4500
New York *(G-10097)*
Exact Solutions Inc ....F 212 707-8627
New York *(G-10099)*
Exacttarget Inc ....G 646 560-2275
New York *(G-10100)*
Exchange My Mail Inc ....F 516 605-1835
Jericho *(G-7068)*
Express Checkout LLC ....G 646 512-2068
New York *(G-10110)*
EZ Newsletter LLC ....F 412 943-7777
Brooklyn *(G-1949)*
EZ Systems US Inc ....C 212 634-6899
Brooklyn *(G-1950)*
F R A M Technologies Inc ....G 718 338-6230
Brooklyn *(G-1951)*
F-O-R Software LLC ....F 212 231-9506
New York *(G-10120)*
F-O-R Software LLC ....E 914 220-8800
White Plains *(G-17108)*
F-O-R Software LLC ....G 212 724-3920
New York *(G-10121)*
▲ Facts On File Inc ....D 212 967-8800
New York *(G-10126)*
Falconstor Software Inc ....F 631 777-5188
Melville *(G-8318)*
Femtech Women Powered Software ....D 516 328-2631
Franklin Square *(G-5363)*
Fidelus Technologies LLC ....D 212 616-7800
New York *(G-10159)*
Fidesa US Corporation ....B 212 269-9000
New York *(G-10160)*
Filestream Inc ....F 516 759-4100
Locust Valley *(G-7629)*
Flexsin ....F 212 470-9279
New York *(G-10179)*
Flextrade Systems Inc ....C 516 627-8993
Great Neck *(G-5813)*
Flogic Inc ....F 914 478-1352
Hastings On Hudson *(G-6003)*
Floored Inc ....F 908 347-5845
New York *(G-10180)*
Fog Creek Software Inc ....G 866 364-2733
New York *(G-10183)*
Formats Unlimited Inc ....F 631 249-9200
Deer Park *(G-4144)*
Forwardlane Inc ....F 310 779-8590
New York *(G-10188)*
Frazer Computing Inc ....E 315 379-3500
Canton *(G-3383)*
Freshop Inc ....F 585 738-6035
Rochester *(G-14383)*
Fuel Data Systems Inc ....G 800 447-7870
Middletown *(G-8441)*
Fusion Telecom Intl Inc ....C 212 201-2400
New York *(G-10227)*
Galaxy Software LLC ....G 631 244-8405
Oakdale *(G-13058)*
Games For Change Inc ....G 212 242-4922
New York *(G-10245)*
Geoweb3d Inc ....G 607 323-1212
Binghamton *(G-918)*
Ghostery Inc ....G 917 262-2530
New York *(G-10291)*
Gifts Software Inc ....E 904 438-6000
New York *(G-10294)*
Glassbox US Inc ....E 917 378-2933
New York *(G-10308)*
Glitnir Ticketing Inc ....G 516 390-5168
Levittown *(G-7428)*
Global Applctions Solution LLC ....G 212 741-9595
New York *(G-10313)*
Globalquest Solutions Inc ....F 716 601-3524
Williamsville *(G-17245)*
Globeop Financial Services LLC ....C 914 670-3600
Harrison *(G-5985)*
Grantoo LLC ....G 646 356-0460
New York *(G-10351)*
Group Commerce Inc ....F 646 346-0598
New York *(G-10370)*
Hailo Network Usa Inc ....G 646 561-8552
New York *(G-10396)*
Happy Software Inc ....G 518 584-4668
Saratoga Springs *(G-15158)*
Health Care Compliance ....E 516 478-4100
Jericho *(G-7070)*
Heartland Commerce Inc ....E 845 920-0800
Pearl River *(G-13458)*
Heineck Associates Inc ....G 631 207-2347
Bellport *(G-832)*

High Performance Sftwr USA Inc ....E 866 616-4958
Valley Stream *(G-16409)*
Hinge Inc ....F 502 445-3111
New York *(G-10481)*
Hovee Inc ....F 646 249-6200
New York *(G-10522)*
Hudson Software Corporation ....E 914 773-0400
Elmsford *(G-4755)*
Huntington Services Inc ....G 516 795-8500
Massapequa *(G-8179)*
Hyperlaw Inc ....F 212 873-6982
New York *(G-10537)*
IAC Search LLC ....E 212 314-7300
New York *(G-10543)*
Iac/Interactivecorp ....C 212 314-7300
New York *(G-10544)*
Identifycom Inc ....G 212 235-0000
New York *(G-10556)*
Inboxmind LLC ....G 646 773-7726
New York *(G-10580)*
Incentivate Health LLC ....G 518 469-8491
Saratoga Springs *(G-15160)*
Incycle Software Corp ....G 212 626-2608
New York *(G-10584)*
Indegy Inc ....E 866 801-5394
New York *(G-10586)*
Infinity Augmented Reality Inc ....G 917 677-2084
New York *(G-10593)*
Info Quick Solutions ....E 315 463-1400
Liverpool *(G-7525)*
Infobase Publishing Company ....G 212 967-8800
New York *(G-10595)*
Infor Global Solutions Inc ....D 646 336-1700
New York *(G-10596)*
Informa Solutions Inc ....E 516 543-3733
Garden City *(G-5511)*
Informatica LLC ....F 212 845-7650
New York *(G-10598)*
Informerly Inc ....G 646 238-7137
New York *(G-10599)*
Innovation MGT Group Inc ....F 800 889-0987
Shirley *(G-15420)*
Inprotopia Corporation ....F 917 338-7501
New York *(G-10610)*
Insight Unlimited Inc ....G 914 861-2090
Chappaqua *(G-3552)*
INTEL Corporation ....D 408 765-8080
Getzville *(G-5599)*
Intellicheck Mobilisa Inc ....E 360 344-3233
Jericho *(G-7072)*
Intelligize Incorporated ....G 571 612-8580
New York *(G-10618)*
International Bus Mchs Corp ....F 914 345-5219
Armonk *(G-414)*
International Bus Mchs Corp ....E 914 499-2000
Armonk *(G-415)*
International MGT Netwrk ....F 646 401-0032
New York *(G-10637)*
Internodal International Inc ....E 631 765-0037
Southold *(G-15559)*
Intralinks Holdings Inc ....E 212 543-7700
New York *(G-10646)*
Invision Inc ....G 212 557-5554
New York *(G-10653)*
Irene Goodman Literary Agency ....G 212 604-0330
New York *(G-10657)*
Irv Inc ....E 212 334-4507
New York *(G-10663)*
Isabella Products Inc ....F 516 699-8404
Great Neck *(G-5818)*
Isimulate LLC ....G 877 947-2831
Albany *(G-91)*
J9 Technologies Inc ....E 412 586-5038
New York *(G-10684)*
Joseph A Filippazzo Software ....G 718 987-1626
Staten Island *(G-15693)*
Jpm and Associates ....F 516 483-4699
Uniondale *(G-16297)*
Jumprope Inc ....G 347 927-5867
New York *(G-10787)*
Kaseya US Sales LLC ....D 415 694-5700
New York *(G-10813)*
Kastor Consulting Inc ....G 718 224-9109
Bayside *(G-773)*
Key Computer Svcs of Chelsea ....D 212 206-8060
New York *(G-10840)*
Keynote Systems Corporation ....G 716 564-1332
Buffalo *(G-3030)*
Kindling Inc ....F 212 400-6296
New York *(G-10851)*

SIC

Employee Codes: A=Over 500 employees, B=251-500
C=101-250, D=51-100, E=20-50, F=10-19, G=5-9
2017 Harris
New York Manufacturers Directory
877

73 BUSINESS SERVICES SIC SECTION

Klara Technologies Inc ....F 844 215-5272
New York *(G-10858)*

Kontrolscan Inc ....G 917 743-0481
Scarsdale *(G-15219)*

Latchable Inc ....E 646 833-0604
New York *(G-10931)*

Latham Software Sciences Inc ....F 518 785-1100
Latham *(G-7371)*

Laurus Development Inc ....F 716 823-1202
Buffalo *(G-3047)*

Learningateway LLC ....G 212 920-7969
Brooklyn *(G-2203)*

Liftforward Inc ....F 917 693-4993
New York *(G-10989)*

Liiiike Shopping Inc ....F 914 271-2001
New York *(G-10996)*

Lincdoc LLC ....G 585 563-1669
East Rochester *(G-4465)*

Livetiles Corp ....F 917 472-7887
New York *(G-11016)*

Lookbooks Media Inc ....F 646 737-3360
New York *(G-11029)*

Luluvise Inc ....E 914 309-7812
New York *(G-11064)*

Madhat Inc ....G 518 947-0732
New York *(G-11093)*

Magic Numbers Inc ....G 646 839-8578
New York *(G-11105)*

Magsoft Corporation ....G 518 877-8390
Clifton Park *(G-3701)*

Maler Technologies Inc ....G 212 391-2070
New York *(G-11120)*

Marcus Goldman Inc ....F 212 431-0707
New York *(G-11147)*

Market Factory Inc ....F 212 625-9988
New York *(G-11158)*

Maven Marketing LLC ....G 615 510-3248
New York *(G-11183)*

Maz Digital Inc ....F 646 692-9799
New York *(G-11191)*

McAfee Inc ....G 646 728-1440
New York *(G-11194)*

Mdcare911 LLC ....G 917 640-4869
Brooklyn *(G-2287)*

Mealplan Corp ....G 909 706-8398
New York *(G-11205)*

Mediapost Communications LLC ....E 212 204-2000
New York *(G-11212)*

Medical Transcription Billing ....A 631 863-1198
New York *(G-11214)*

Medidata Solutions Inc ....B 212 918-1800
New York *(G-11215)*

Medius Software Inc ....F 877 295-0058
New York *(G-11217)*

Meethappy Inc ....F 917 903-0591
Seaford *(G-15346)*

Meta Pharmacy Systems Inc ....E 516 488-6189
Garden City *(G-5522)*

Micro Systems Specialists Inc ....G 845 677-6150
Millbrook *(G-8476)*

Microcad Trning Consulting Inc ....G 617 923-0500
Lagrangeville *(G-7256)*

Microcad Trning Consulting Inc ....G 631 291-9484
Hauppauge *(G-6135)*

Microsoft Corporation ....D 585 240-6037
Rochester *(G-14513)*

Microsoft Corporation ....A 914 323-2150
White Plains *(G-17138)*

Microsoft Corporation ....F 212 245-2100
New York *(G-11256)*

Microsoft Corporation ....D 516 380-1531
Hauppauge *(G-6137)*

Microstrategy Incorporated ....F 888 537-8135
New York *(G-11257)*

Midas Mdici Group Holdings Inc ....G 212 792-0920
New York *(G-11258)*

Mml Software Ltd ....E 631 941-1313
East Setauket *(G-4488)*

Mnn Holding Company LLC ....F 404 558-5251
Brooklyn *(G-2326)*

Mobile Data Systems Inc ....G 631 360-3400
Nesconset *(G-8776)*

Mobile Hatch Inc ....G 212 314-7300
New York *(G-11287)*

Mobileapp Systems LLC ....G 716 667-2780
Buffalo *(G-3070)*

Molabs Inc ....G 310 721-6828
New York *(G-11293)*

Mpr Magazine App Inc ....E 718 403-0303
Brooklyn *(G-2338)*

Multimedia Plus Inc ....F 212 982-3229
New York *(G-11326)*

Nastel Technologies Inc ....D 631 761-9100
Melville *(G-8338)*

Navatar Consulting Group Inc ....E 212 863-9655
New York *(G-11360)*

Navatar Consulting Group Inc ....E 212 863-9655
New York *(G-11361)*

NBC Internet Inc ....B 212 315-9016
New York *(G-11362)*

Nemaris Inc ....E 646 794-8648
New York *(G-11366)*

Nervve Technologies Inc ....E 716 800-2250
Buffalo *(G-3083)*

Netegrity Inc ....C 631 342-6000
Central Islip *(G-3506)*

Netologic Inc ....E 212 269-3796
New York *(G-11372)*

Netsuite Inc ....G 646 652-5700
New York *(G-11373)*

Network Components LLC ....F 212 799-5890
New York *(G-11374)*

Neverware Inc ....F 516 302-3223
New York *(G-11378)*

New Triad For Collaborative ....E 212 873-9610
New York *(G-11394)*

Nikish Software Corp ....G 631 754-1618
Hauppauge *(G-6148)*

Nitel Inc ....G 347 731-1558
Brooklyn *(G-2372)*

Northrop Grumman Systems Corp ....E 315 336-0500
Rome *(G-14827)*

Olympic Software & Consulting ....G 631 351-0655
Melville *(G-8344)*

Omx (us) Inc ....A 646 428-2800
New York *(G-11504)*

On Demand Books LLC ....G 212 966-2222
New York *(G-11505)*

One-Blue LLC ....G 212 223-4380
New York *(G-11509)*

Ontra Presentations LLC ....G 212 213-1315
New York *(G-11512)*

Openfin Inc ....G 917 450-8822
New York *(G-11514)*

Operative Media Inc ....C 212 994-8930
New York *(G-11516)*

Oracle Corporation ....B 516 247-4500
Mineola *(G-8529)*

Oracle Corporation ....B 585 383-1998
Rochester *(G-14551)*

Oracle Corporation ....B 212 508-7700
New York *(G-11519)*

Oracle Corporation ....C 212 508-7700
New York *(G-11520)*

Orangenius Inc ....F 631 742-0648
New York *(G-11521)*

Orthstar Enterprises Inc ....D 607 562-2100
Horseheads *(G-6586)*

Os33 Inc ....G 708 336-3466
New York *(G-11529)*

Overture Media Inc ....G 917 446-7455
New York *(G-11537)*

Pap Chat Inc ....G 516 350-1888
Brooklyn *(G-2403)*

Par Technology Corporation ....D 315 738-0600
New Hartford *(G-8808)*

Parlor Labs Inc ....G 646 217-0918
New York *(G-11576)*

Patient Portal Tech Inc ....F 315 638-2030
Baldwinsville *(G-574)*

Patron Technology Inc ....G 212 271-4328
New York *(G-11583)*

Pb Mapinfo Corporation ....A 518 285-6000
Troy *(G-16246)*

Peer Software Incorporated ....G 631 979-1770
Hauppauge *(G-6160)*

Pefin Technologies LLC ....F 917 715-3720
New York *(G-11600)*

Pegasystems Inc ....E 212 626-6550
New York *(G-11601)*

Perry Street Software Inc ....G 415 935-1429
New York *(G-11625)*

Pexip Inc ....E 703 338-3544
New York *(G-11634)*

Pingmd Inc ....G 212 632-2665
New York *(G-11662)*

Pitney Bowes Software Inc ....F 518 272-0014
Troy *(G-16248)*

Piwik Pro LLC ....E 888 444-0049
New York *(G-11670)*

Platform Experts Inc ....G 646 843-7100
Brooklyn *(G-2426)*

Playfitness Corp ....G 917 497-5443
Staten Island *(G-15722)*

Pocket Solutions Inc ....G 631 355-1073
Brookhaven *(G-1509)*

Poly Software International ....G 845 735-9301
Pearl River *(G-13464)*

Portable Tech Solutions LLC ....F 631 727-8084
Calverton *(G-3295)*

Portfolio Decisionware Inc ....E 212 947-1326
New York *(G-11686)*

Portware LLC ....D 212 425-5233
New York *(G-11688)*

Powa Technologies Inc ....E 347 344-7848
New York *(G-11691)*

Practicepro Software Systems ....G 516 222-0010
Garden City *(G-5526)*

Pretlist ....G 646 368-1849
New York *(G-11702)*

Pricing Engine Inc ....F 917 549-3289
New York *(G-11703)*

Principia Partners LLC ....D 212 480-2270
New York *(G-11713)*

Professional Access LLC ....G 212 432-2844
Chappaqua *(G-3554)*

Proginet Corporation ....E 516 535-3600
Garden City *(G-5527)*

Prospector Network ....E 212 601-2781
New York *(G-11739)*

Pts Financial Technology LLC ....E 844 825-7634
New York *(G-11745)*

Pupa Tek Inc ....G 631 664-7817
Huntington *(G-6675)*

Purebase Networks Inc ....G 646 670-8964
New York *(G-11752)*

Quality and Asrn Tech Corp ....G 646 450-6762
Ridge *(G-14093)*

Quartet Financial Systems Inc ....F 845 358-6071
New York *(G-11769)*

Quovo Inc ....E 646 216-9437
New York *(G-11777)*

Radnor-Wallace ....G 516 767-2131
Port Washington *(G-13858)*

Raleigh and Drake Pbc ....F 212 625-8212
New York *(G-11791)*

Rational Retention LLC ....E 518 489-3000
Albany *(G-127)*

Razorfish LLC ....G 212 798-6600
New York *(G-11808)*

Red Oak Software Inc ....G 585 454-3170
Rochester *(G-14622)*

Reentry Games Inc ....G 646 421-0080
New York *(G-11817)*

Relavis Corporation ....E 212 995-2900
New York *(G-11823)*

Reliant Security ....E 917 338-2200
New York *(G-11824)*

Responcer Inc ....G 917 572-0895
New York *(G-11843)*

Revana Inc ....E 212 244-6137
New York *(G-11849)*

Ringlead Inc ....F 310 906-0545
Huntington *(G-6676)*

Rision Inc ....G 212 987-2628
New York *(G-11878)*

Ritnoa Inc ....E 212 660-2148
Bellerose *(G-811)*

Robert Ehrlich ....G 516 353-4617
New York *(G-11890)*

Robly Digital Marketing LLC ....E 917 238-0730
New York *(G-11895)*

Robocom Us LLC ....F 631 861-2045
Farmingdale *(G-5101)*

Robot Fruit Inc ....F 631 423-7250
Huntington *(G-6677)*

Rockport Pa LLC ....F 212 482-8580
New York *(G-11899)*

Roomactually LLC ....G 646 388-1922
New York *(G-11914)*

Rovi Corporation ....C 212 524-7000
New York *(G-11922)*

Rovi Corporation ....C 212 824-0355
New York *(G-11923)*

RPS Holdings Inc ....E 607 257-7778
Ithaca *(G-6874)*

S C T ....F 585 467-7740
Rochester *(G-14664)*

Safe Passage International Inc ....F 585 292-4910
Rochester *(G-14665)*

Sakonnet Technology LLC ....E 212 849-9267
New York *(G-11955)*
Salentica Systems Inc ....E 212 672-1777
New York *(G-11957)*
San Jae Educational Resou ....G 845 364-5458
Pomona *(G-13733)*
Sapphire Systems Inc ....F 212 905-0100
New York *(G-11970)*
Sas Institute Inc ....F 212 757-3826
New York *(G-11975)*
▲ **Scholastic Corporation** ....G 212 343-6100
New York *(G-11997)*
▲ **Scholastic Inc** ....A 800 724-6527
New York *(G-11998)*
Schoolnet Inc ....C 646 496-9000
New York *(G-12001)*
Sculptgraphicz Inc ....G 646 837-7302
Brooklyn *(G-2540)*
Secured Services Inc ....G 866 419-3900
New York *(G-12013)*
Seed Media Group LLC ....E 646 502-7050
New York *(G-12016)*
Sefaira Inc ....E 855 733-2472
New York *(G-12018)*
Segovia Technology Co ....F 212 868-4412
New York *(G-12019)*
Serendipity Consulting Corp ....F 914 763-8251
South Salem *(G-15536)*
Servicenow Inc ....F 914 318-1168
New York *(G-12031)*
Shake Inc ....F 650 544-5479
New York *(G-12040)*
Shiprite Software Inc ....G 315 733-6191
Utica *(G-16359)*
Shoretel Inc ....G 877 654-3573
Rochester *(G-14684)*
Shritec Consultants Inc ....G 516 621-7072
Albertson *(G-160)*
Siemens Product Life Mgmt Sftw ....E 585 389-8699
Fairport *(G-4879)*
Signpost Inc ....F 646 503-4231
New York *(G-12074)*
Similarweb Inc ....F 347 685-5422
West Nyack *(G-16926)*
Simply Logic Labs LLC ....G 516 626-6228
Roslyn Heights *(G-15032)*
Sitecompli LLC ....F 800 564-1152
New York *(G-12088)*
Skystem LLC ....G 877 778-3320
New York *(G-12098)*
Slyde Inc ....F 917 331-2114
Long Island City *(G-7879)*
Smn Medical PC ....F 844 362-2428
Rye *(G-15068)*
Sneakers Software Inc ....F 800 877-9221
New York *(G-12112)*
Social Bicycles Inc ....E 917 746-7624
Brooklyn *(G-2576)*
Softlink International ....E 914 574-8197
White Plains *(G-17168)*
Software & General Services Co ....G 315 986-4184
Walworth *(G-16552)*
Solve Advisors Inc ....G 646 699-5041
Rockville Centre *(G-14799)*
Somml Health LLC ....G 518 880-2170
Albany *(G-135)*
Soroc Technology Corp ....G 716 849-5913
Buffalo *(G-3192)*
Spektrix Inc ....G 646 741-5110
New York *(G-12159)*
Spring Inc ....G 646 732-0323
New York *(G-12170)*
Squond Inc ....E 718 778-6630
Brooklyn *(G-2593)*
SS&c Technologies Inc ....E 212 503-6400
New York *(G-12177)*
Standardware Inc ....G 914 738-6382
Pelham *(G-13495)*
Sticky ADS TV Inc ....G 646 668-1346
New York *(G-12204)*
Stop N Shop LLC ....G 518 512-9657
Albany *(G-138)*
Strada Soft Inc ....G 718 556-6940
Staten Island *(G-15742)*
Striata Inc ....D 212 918-4677
New York *(G-12214)*
Structured Retail Products ....G 212 224-3692
New York *(G-12216)*
Structuredweb Inc ....E 201 325-3110
New York *(G-12217)*
Styleclick Inc ....D 212 329-0300
New York *(G-12224)*
Successware Inc ....F 716 565-2338
Williamsville *(G-17256)*
Successware Remote LLC ....G 716 842-1439
Buffalo *(G-3199)*
Suite Solutions Inc ....E 716 929-3050
Amherst *(G-263)*
Super Software ....G 845 735-0000
New City *(G-8794)*
Superchat LLC ....G 212 352-8581
New York *(G-12242)*
Sutton Place Software Inc ....G 631 421-1737
Melville *(G-8358)*
Sybase Inc ....D 212 596-1100
New York *(G-12255)*
Symantec Corporation ....D 631 656-0185
Smithtown *(G-15499)*
Symantec Corporation ....D 646 487-6000
New York *(G-12256)*
Symphony Talent LLC ....D 212 999-9000
New York *(G-12257)*
Synced Inc ....G 917 565-5591
New York *(G-12259)*
Synco Technologies Inc ....G 212 255-2031
New York *(G-12260)*
Syntel Inc ....F 212 785-9810
New York *(G-12263)*
Syrasoft LLC ....F 315 708-0341
Baldwinsville *(G-578)*
Systems Trading Inc ....G 718 261-8900
Melville *(G-8359)*
Targetprocess Inc ....F 607 346-0621
Amherst *(G-265)*
Teachergaming LLC ....F 866 644-9323
New York *(G-12286)*
Teachley LLC ....G 347 552-1272
Staten Island *(G-15746)*
Teacup Software Inc ....G 212 563-9288
Brooklyn *(G-2648)*
Team Builders Inc ....F 718 979-1005
Staten Island *(G-15747)*
Technology Crossover MGT VII ....C 212 808-0200
New York *(G-12289)*
Tel Tech International ....E 516 393-5174
Melville *(G-8360)*
Telmar Information Services ....E 212 725-3000
New York *(G-12297)*
Tensa Software ....F 914 686-5376
White Plains *(G-17177)*
Tep Events International Inc ....F 646 393-4723
New York *(G-12301)*
Tequipment Inc ....D 516 922-3508
Huntington Station *(G-6726)*
Terranua US Corp ....F 212 852-9028
New York *(G-12303)*
Theirapp LLC ....E 212 896-1255
New York *(G-12312)*
Thing Daemon Inc ....E 917 696-5794
New York *(G-12317)*
Thinktrek Inc ....F 212 884-8399
New York *(G-12318)*
▲ **Thomson Reuters Corporation** ....A 646 223-4000
New York *(G-12329)*
Tika Mobile Inc ....F 516 635-1696
New York *(G-12340)*
Time To Know Inc ....F 212 230-1210
New York *(G-12349)*
Tootter Inc ....E 212 300-7489
Brooklyn *(G-2664)*
Tpa Computer Corp ....F 877 866-6044
Carmel *(G-3406)*
Trac Medical Solutions Inc ....G 518 346-7799
Schenectady *(G-15306)*
Tradepaq Corporation ....F 914 332-9174
Tarrytown *(G-16109)*
Tradewins Publishing Corp ....G 631 361-6916
Smithtown *(G-15501)*
Transportgistics Inc ....F 631 567-4100
Mount Sinai *(G-8657)*
Treauu Inc ....G 703 731-0196
New York *(G-12395)*
Trendlytics Innvation Labs Inc ....G 415 971-4123
New York *(G-12398)*
Trovvit Inc ....G 718 908-5376
Brooklyn *(G-2685)*
Trueex LLC ....E 646 786-8526
New York *(G-12410)*
Tss-Transport Snltn Sstms ....G 917 267-8534
New York *(G-12417)*
Ttg LLC ....G 917 777-0959
New York *(G-12418)*
Tunaverse Media Inc ....G 631 778-8350
Hauppauge *(G-6218)*
Two Rivers Computing Inc ....G 914 968-9239
Yonkers *(G-17493)*
Tyme Global Technologies LLC ....E 212 796-1950
New York *(G-12437)*
U X World Inc ....G 914 375-6167
Hawthorne *(G-6255)*
Udisense Inc ....G 858 442-9875
New York *(G-12443)*
Ufn LLC ....G 800 533-1787
Fishkill *(G-5188)*
Upstate Records Management LLC ....G 518 834-1144
Keeseville *(G-7142)*
Urthworx Inc ....G 646 373-7535
New York *(G-12483)*
Usq Group LLC ....G 212 777-7751
New York *(G-12493)*
Value Spring Technology Inc ....F 917 705-4658
Harrison *(G-5994)*
Varnish Software Inc ....G 201 857-2832
New York *(G-12507)*
Varonis Systems Inc ....C 877 292-8767
New York *(G-12508)*
Varsity Monitor LLC ....G 212 691-6292
New York *(G-12509)*
Vehicle Tracking Solutions LLC ....E 631 586-7400
Commack *(G-3846)*
Velocity Outsourcing LLC ....E 212 891-4043
New York *(G-12515)*
Vertana Group LLC ....F 646 706-7210
New York *(G-12529)*
Vhx Corporation ....F 347 689-1446
New York *(G-12534)*
Vicarious Visions Inc ....D 518 283-4090
Troy *(G-16259)*
Virtual Frameworks Inc ....F 646 690-8207
New York *(G-12549)*
Virtusphere Inc ....F 607 760-2207
Binghamton *(G-958)*
Virtuvent Inc ....G 646 845-0387
New York *(G-12551)*
Visible Systems Corporation ....E 508 628-1510
Oneida *(G-13170)*
Visual Listing Systems Inc ....G 631 689-7222
East Setauket *(G-4496)*
Vita Rara Inc ....G 518 369-7356
Troy *(G-16261)*
Vizbee Inc ....G 650 787-1424
New York *(G-12560)*
Vormittag Associates Inc ....C 800 824-7776
Ronkonkoma *(G-14999)*
Vortex Ventures Inc ....G 516 946-8345
North Baldwin *(G-12912)*
Wagner Technical Services Inc ....F 845 566-4018
Newburgh *(G-12785)*
Watchitoo Inc ....G 212 354-5888
New York *(G-12595)*
Wercs Ltd ....E 518 640-9200
Latham *(G-7384)*
West Internet Trading Company ....G 415 484-5848
New York *(G-12612)*
Wetpaintcom Inc ....E 206 859-6300
New York *(G-12620)*
Whentech LLC ....F 212 571-0042
New York *(G-12623)*
White Label Partners LLC ....G 917 445-6650
New York *(G-12626)*
Whiteboard Ventures Inc ....F 855 972-6346
New York *(G-12628)*
Winesoft International Corp ....G 914 400-6247
Yonkers *(G-17500)*
Wing Tel Inc ....G 347 508-5802
New York *(G-12645)*
Wink Inc ....E 212 389-1382
New York *(G-12646)*
Wink Labs Inc ....E 916 717-0437
New York *(G-12647)*
Wireless Generation Inc ....G 212 213-8177
Brooklyn *(G-2762)*
Wizq Inc ....F 586 381-9048
New York *(G-12649)*
Woodbury Systems Group Inc ....G 516 364-2653
Woodbury *(G-17304)*
X Function Inc ....E 212 231-0092
New York *(G-12672)*
Xborder Entertainment LLC ....G 518 726-7036
Plattsburgh *(G-13710)*

S I C

Employee Codes: A=Over 500 employees, B=251-500
C=101-250, D=51-100, E=20-50, F=10-19, G=5-9

2017 Harris
New York Manufacturers Directory

879

Ymobiz Inc ....F 917 470-9280
New York (G-12694)
Yooconnect1 LLC ....G 212 726-2062
New York (G-12697)
Ypis of Staten Island Inc ....G 718 815-4557
Staten Island (G-15755)
Zedge Inc ....D 330 577-3424
New York (G-12708)

76 MISCELLANEOUS REPAIR SERVICES

7692 Welding Repair

303 Contracting Inc ....E 716 896-2122
Orchard Park (G-13249)
A & J Machine & Welding Inc ....F 631 845-7586
Farmingdale (G-4925)
AAA Welding and Fabrication of ....G 585 254-2830
Rochester (G-14163)
Accurate Welding Service Inc ....G 516 333-1730
Westbury (G-16960)
Acro-Fab Ltd ....E 315 564-6688
Hannibal (G-5969)
Airweld Inc ....G 631 924-6366
Ridge (G-14091)
Aj Genco Mch Sp McHy Rdout Svc ....F 716 664-4925
Falconer (G-4889)
Allen Tool Phoenix Inc ....E 315 463-7533
East Syracuse (G-4501)
Alliance Services Corp ....F 516 775-7600
Floral Park (G-5190)
Alliance Welding & Steel Fabg ....F 516 775-7600
Floral Park (G-5191)
Alloy Metal Works Inc ....G 631 694-8163
Farmingdale (G-4937)
Alpine Machine Inc ....F 607 272-1344
Ithaca (G-6818)
ARC TEC Wldg & Fabrication Inc ....G 718 982-9274
Staten Island (G-15639)
Athens Iron Fabrication Inc ....F 718 424-7799
Woodside (G-17317)
Atlantis Equipment Corporation ....F 518 733-5910
Stephentown (G-15756)
▲ Barber Welding Inc ....E 315 834-6645
Weedsport (G-16746)
Benemy Welding & Fabrication ....G 315 548-8500
Phelps (G-13530)
Big Apple Welding Supply ....G 718 439-3959
Brooklyn (G-1694)
Bms Manufacturing Co Inc ....E 607 535-2426
Watkins Glen (G-16693)
Bracci Ironworks Inc ....F 718 629-2374
Brooklyn (G-1711)
Brenseke George Wldg Ir Works ....G 631 271-4870
Deer Park (G-4111)
Broadalbin Manufacturing Corp ....E 518 883-5313
Broadalbin (G-1240)
Bruce Pierce ....G 716 731-9310
Sanborn (G-15115)
C G & Son Machining Inc ....G 315 964-2430
Williamstown (G-17228)
CBM Fabrications Inc ....E 518 399-8023
Ballston Lake (G-581)
Certified Fabrications Inc ....F 716 731-8123
Sanborn (G-15117)
Chautauqua Machine Spc LLC ....F 716 782-3276
Ashville (G-427)
Competicion Mower Repair ....G 516 280-6584
Mineola (G-8504)
Cs Automation Inc ....F 315 524-5123
Ontario (G-13198)
Custom Laser Inc ....E 716 434-8600
Lockport (G-7578)
D & G Welding Inc ....G 716 873-3088
Buffalo (G-2899)
Deck Bros Inc ....E 716 852-0262
Buffalo (G-2904)
Dennies Manufacturing Inc ....E 585 393-4646
Canandaigua (G-3342)
Donald Stefan ....G 716 492-1110
Chaffee (G-3533)
Dorgan Welding Service ....G 315 462-9030
Phelps (G-13531)
E B Industries LLC ....E 631 293-8565
Farmingdale (G-4982)
Eagle Welding Machine ....G 315 594-1845
Wolcott (G-17279)
Etna Tool & Die Corporation ....F 212 475-4350
New York (G-10079)
Excelco/Newbrook Inc ....D 716 934-2644
Silver Creek (G-15449)
F M L Industries Inc ....G 607 749-7273
Homer (G-6517)
Flushing Boiler & Welding Co ....G 718 463-1266
Brooklyn (G-1988)
Formac Welding Inc ....G 631 421-5525
Huntington Station (G-6705)
G & C Welding Co Inc ....G 516 883-3228
Port Washington (G-13817)
Gasport Welding & Fabg Inc ....F 716 772-7205
Gasport (G-5557)
Gc Mobile Services Inc ....G 914 736-9730
Cortlandt Manor (G-4051)
Genco John ....G 716 483-5446
Jamestown (G-6994)
General Welding & Fabg Inc ....G 716 652-0033
Elma (G-4649)
General Welding & Fabg Inc ....G 716 568-7958
Williamsville (G-17244)
General Welding & Fabg Inc ....G 716 824-1572
Blasdell (G-963)
General Welding & Fabg Inc ....G 716 681-8200
Buffalo (G-2972)
General Welding & Fabg Inc ....G 716 304-3622
Niagara Falls (G-12824)
Guthrie Heli-ARC Inc ....G 585 548-5053
Bergen (G-846)
Hadfield Inc ....F 631 981-4314
Ronkonkoma (G-14909)
Hadleys Fab-Weld Inc ....G 315 926-5101
Marion (G-8095)
Hansen Steel ....E 585 398-2020
Farmington (G-5152)
Hartman Enterprises Inc ....D 315 363-7300
Oneida (G-13156)
Haskell Machine & Tool Inc ....F 607 749-2421
Homer (G-6518)
Haun Welding Supply Inc ....F 607 846-2289
Elmira (G-4689)
Haun Welding Supply Inc ....G 315 592-5012
Fulton (G-5460)
Homer Iron Works LLC ....G 607 749-3963
Homer (G-6519)
Huntington Welding & Iron ....G 631 423-3331
Huntington Station (G-6709)
In Northeast Precision Welding ....G 518 441-2260
Castleton On Hudson (G-3418)
Ingleside Machine Co Inc ....D 585 924-4363
Farmington (G-5153)
▼ Kon Tat Group Corporation ....G 718 207-5022
Brooklyn (G-2179)
L & S Metals Inc ....E 716 692-6865
North Tonawanda (G-12980)
Lagasse Works Inc ....G 315 946-9202
Lyons (G-7973)
Lagoe-Oswego Corp ....E 315 343-3160
Rochester (G-14473)
Linita Design & Mfg Corp ....E 716 566-7753
Lackawanna (G-7244)
M and M Industrial Welding ....G 631 451-6044
Medford (G-8254)
M M Welding ....E 315 363-3980
Oneida (G-13158)
Maple Grove Corp ....E 585 492-5286
Arcade (G-396)
Maspeth Welding Inc ....E 718 497-5430
Maspeth (G-8150)
Meades Welding and Fabricating ....G 631 581-1555
Islip (G-6810)
Mega Tool & Mfg Corp ....E 607 734-8398
Elmira (G-4695)
Miller Metal Fabricating Inc ....G 585 359-3400
Rochester (G-14514)
▲ Modern Mechanical Fab Inc ....G 518 298-5177
Champlain (G-3544)
Mooradian Hydraulics & Eqp Co ....F 518 766-3866
Castleton On Hudson (G-3419)
Ms Spares LLC ....G 607 223-3024
Clay (G-3683)
New Age Ironworks Inc ....F 718 277-1895
Brooklyn (G-2358)
New York Manufacturing Corp ....G 585 254-9353
Rochester (G-14533)
North Country Welding Inc ....G 315 788-9718
Watertown (G-16666)
NY Iron Inc ....F 718 302-9000
Long Island City (G-7827)
Parfuse Corp ....E 516 997-1795
Westbury (G-17018)
Phillip J Ortiz Manufacturing ....G 845 226-7030
Hopewell Junction (G-6557)
Phoenix Welding & Fabg Inc ....G 315 695-2223
Phoenix (G-13543)
Pro-Tech Wldg Fabrication Inc ....E 585 436-9855
Rochester (G-14603)
Qsf Inc ....G 585 247-6200
Gates (G-5562)
Quality Industrial Services ....F 716 667-7703
Orchard Park (G-13294)
Reliable Welding & Fabrication ....G 631 758-2637
Patchogue (G-13434)
REO Welding Inc ....F 518 238-1022
Cohoes (G-3756)
Rini Tank & Truck Service ....F 718 384-6606
Brooklyn (G-2494)
Rj Welding & Fabricating Inc ....G 315 523-1288
Clifton Springs (G-3715)
Robert M Brown ....F 607 426-6250
Montour Falls (G-8611)
Rothe Welding Inc ....G 845 246-3051
Saugerties (G-15193)
S & D Welding Corp ....G 631 454-0383
West Babylon (G-16824)
S J B Fabrication ....F 716 895-0281
Buffalo (G-3171)
Smithers Tools & Mch Pdts Inc ....D 845 876-3063
Rhinebeck (G-14058)
▲ Strecks Inc ....E 518 273-4410
Watervliet (G-16689)
Tangent Machine & Tool Corp ....E 631 249-3088
Farmingdale (G-5124)
▲ Technapulse LLC ....F 631 234-8700
Hauppauge (G-6209)
▲ Tek Weld ....F 631 694-5503
Hauppauge (G-6211)
Tracey Welding Co Inc ....G 518 756-6309
Coeymans (G-3746)
W R P Welding Ltd ....G 631 249-8859
Farmingdale (G-5139)
Watkins Welding and Mch Sp Inc ....G 914 949-6168
White Plains (G-17181)
Waynes Welding Inc ....E 315 768-6146
Yorkville (G-17530)
Welding and Brazing Svcs Inc ....G 607 397-1009
Richfield Springs (G-14062)
Welding Chapter of New York ....G 212 481-1496
New York (G-12607)
West Metal Works Inc ....E 716 895-4900
Buffalo (G-3252)

7694 Armature Rewinding Shops

A & C/Furia Electric Motors ....F 914 949-0585
White Plains (G-17072)
Accurate Marine Specialties ....G 631 589-5502
Bohemia (G-1005)
Alpha DC Motors Inc ....F 315 432-9039
Syracuse (G-15850)
Auburn Armature Inc ....D 315 253-9721
Auburn (G-477)
Auburn Armature Inc ....E 585 426-4607
Rochester (G-14218)
B & R Electric Motor Inc ....G 631 752-7533
Farmingdale (G-4950)
B J S Electric ....G 845 774-8166
Chester (G-3600)
Bailey Electric Motor Repair ....G 585 542-5902
Corfu (G-3952)
Bayshore Electric Motors ....G 631 475-1397
Patchogue (G-13416)
Daves Electric Motors & Pumps ....G 212 982-2930
New York (G-9817)
Electric Motor Specialty Inc ....G 716 487-1458
Jamestown (G-6992)
Ener-G-Rotors Inc ....G 518 372-2608
Schenectady (G-15250)
General Electric Company ....E 315 456-3304
Syracuse (G-15950)
General Electric Company ....E 518 459-4110
Albany (G-82)
Genesis Electrical Motors ....G 718 274-7030
Woodside (G-17331)
Lawtons Electric Motor Service ....G 315 393-2728
Ogdensburg (G-13117)
Longo New York Inc ....F 212 929-7128
New York (G-11026)
Northeastern Electric Motors ....G 518 793-5939
Hadley (G-5903)
Patchogue Electric Motors Inc ....G 631 475-0117
Patchogue (G-13431)

S I C

76 MISCELLANEOUS REPAIR SERVICES

Premco Inc ....F 914 636-7095
New Rochelle *(G-8921)*

Prime Electric Motors Inc ....G 718 784-1124
Long Island City *(G-7846)*

RC Entps Bus & Trck Inc ....G 518 568-5753
Saint Johnsville *(G-15097)*

Sunset Ridge Holdings Inc ....G 716 487-1458
Jamestown *(G-7034)*

Troy Industrial Solutions ....D 518 272-4920
Watervliet *(G-16690)*

United Richter Electrical Mtrs ....F 716 855-1945
Buffalo *(G-3235)*

ALPHABETIC SECTION

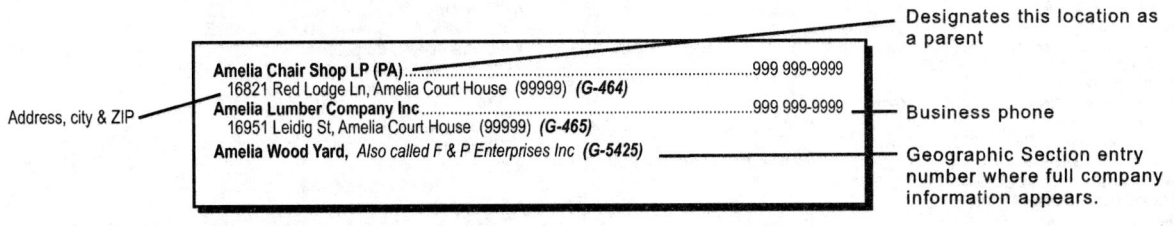

See footnotes for symbols and codes identification.
* Companies listed alphabetically.
* Complete physical or mailing address.

09 FIshy BIl/Dsert Sunrise LLC 518 583-6638
2 Smith Bridge Rd Saratoga Springs (12866) *(G-15140)*
1/2 Off Cards Wantagh Inc 516 809-9832
1162 Wantagh Ave Wantagh (11793) *(G-16553)*
110 Sand Company (PA) 631 694-2822
136 Spagnoli Rd Melville (11747) *(G-8286)*
110 Sand Company 631 694-2822
170 Cabot St West Babylon (11704) *(G-16760)*
110 Sand Company 631 694-2822
170 Cabot St West Babylon (11704) *(G-16761)*
112 Jerome Dreyfuss LLC 212 334-6920
475 Broome St New York (10013) *(G-8958)*
116 26 Street, Brooklyn *Also called Angel-Made In Heaven Inc (G-1612)*
125-127 Main Street Corp 631 477-1500
125 Main St 127 Greenport (11944) *(G-5876)*
131-11 Atlantic RE Inc 718 441-7700
13111 Atlantic Ave Ste 1 Richmond Hill (11418) *(G-14064)*
141 Industries LLC 978 273-8831
300 E 5th St Apt 11 New York (10003) *(G-8959)*
1510 Associates LLC 212 828-8720
1500 Lexington Ave New York (10029) *(G-8960)*
16 Tons Inc 718 418-8446
27 Knickerbocker Ave Brooklyn (11237) *(G-1511)*
17 Bakers LLC 844 687-6836
8 Los Robles St Williamsville (14221) *(G-17230)*
18 Rocks LLC 631 465-9990
290 Spagnoli Rd Melville (11747) *(G-8287)*
180s LLC (HQ) 410 534-6320
1 Liberty Plz New York (10006) *(G-8961)*
1884 Collection, New York *Also called Anima Group LLC (G-9161)*
1gpn, New York *Also called First Games Publr Netwrk Inc (G-10166)*
1robotics LLC 845 369-6770
360 Route 59 Airmont (10952) *(G-10)*
1st Responder Newspaper, New Windsor *Also called Belsito Communications Inc (G-8932)*
2 1 2 Postcards Inc 212 767-8227
121 Varick St Frnt B New York (10013) *(G-8962)*
2 X 4 Inc 212 647-1170
180 Varick St Rm 1518 New York (10014) *(G-8963)*
20 Bliss St Inc 716 326-2790
61 E Main St Westfield (14787) *(G-17044)*
209 Discount Oil 845 386-2090
10 Sands Station Rd Middletown (10940) *(G-8424)*
212 Biz LLC (PA) 212 391-4444
525 Fashion Ave Rm 2301 New York (10018) *(G-8964)*
212 Db Corp 212 652-5600
30 W 22nd St Fl 6 New York (10010) *(G-8965)*
212 Media LLC 212 710-3092
460 Park Ave S Fl 4 New York (10016) *(G-8966)*
212kiddish Inc 718 705-7227
168 Spencer St Brooklyn (11205) *(G-1512)*
219 South West 315 474-2065
219 S West St Syracuse (13202) *(G-15844)*
21st Century Finishes Inc 516 221-7000
1895 Newbridge Rd North Bellmore (11710) *(G-12914)*
21st Century Fox America Inc (HQ) 212 852-7000
1211 Ave Of The Americas New York (10036) *(G-8967)*
21st Century Fox America Inc 212 447-4600
200 Madison Ave Fl 8 New York (10016) *(G-8968)*
21st Century Fox America Inc 845 735-1116
1 Blue Hill Plz Ste 1525 Pearl River (10965) *(G-13454)*
21st Century Optics Inc (HQ) 347 527-1079
4700 33rd St Ste 1r Long Island City (11101) *(G-7643)*
24 Seven Enterprises Inc 845 563-9033
1073 State Route 94 Ste 9 New Windsor (12553) *(G-8928)*
260 Oak Street Inc 877 852-4676
260 Oak St Buffalo (14203) *(G-2788)*
2600 Enterprises Inc 631 474-2677
2 Flowerfield Ste 30 Saint James (11780) *(G-15086)*
2fish 5loaves Comminty Pantry, Arverne *Also called Armour Bearer Group Inc (G-424)*

2h International Corp 347 623-9380
6766 108th St Apt D1 Forest Hills (11375) *(G-5319)*
2k Inc 646 536-3007
622 Broadway Fl 6 New York (10012) *(G-8969)*
2p Agency Usa Inc 212 203-5586
1674 E 22nd St Apt 3a Brooklyn (11229) *(G-1513)*
3 Bears Gluten Free Bakery 315 323-0277
51 Market St Potsdam (13676) *(G-13876)*
3 Star Papers Limited 718 499-5481
67 34th St Unit 4 Brooklyn (11232) *(G-1514)*
30 Degrees Weatherproof, New York *Also called David Peyser Sportswear Inc (G-9821)*
303 Contracting Inc (HQ) 716 896-2122
5486 Powers Rd Orchard Park (14127) *(G-13249)*
30dc Inc (PA) 212 962-4400
80 Broad St Fl 5 New York (10004) *(G-8970)*
30dc Inc 212 962-4400
80 Broad St Fl 5 New York (10004) *(G-8971)*
31 Phillip Lim LLC (PA) 212 354-6540
304 Hudson St Fl 8 New York (10013) *(G-8972)*
3239603400 La Head Quarters, New York *Also called Peer International Corp (G-11596)*
331 Holding Inc 585 924-1740
100 Rawson Rd Ste 205 Victor (14564) *(G-16458)*
333 J & M Food Corp 718 381-1493
333 Seneca Ave Ridgewood (11385) *(G-14096)*
369 River Road Inc 716 694-5001
369 River Rd North Tonawanda (14120) *(G-12953)*
3835 Lebron Rest Eqp & Sup Inc 212 942-8258
3835 9th Ave New York (10034) *(G-8973)*
39th Street Music-Div, New York *Also called Michael Karp Music Inc (G-11249)*
3b Timber Company Inc 315 942-6580
8745 Industrial Dr Boonville (13309) *(G-1161)*
3doodler, New York *Also called Wobbleworks Inc (G-12651)*
3g Graphics LLC 716 634-2585
7138 Transit Rd Amherst (14221) *(G-218)*
3krf LLC 516 208-6824
3516 Hargale Rd Oceanside (11572) *(G-13071)*
3lab Inc 201 567-9100
525 Fashion Ave Rm 2300 New York (10018) *(G-8974)*
3M Company 716 876-1596
305 Sawyer Ave Tonawanda (14150) *(G-16132)*
3phase Industries LLC 347 763-2942
481 Van Buren St Unit 9a Brooklyn (11221) *(G-1515)*
3rd Avenue Doughnut Inc 718 748-3294
7111 3rd Ave Brooklyn (11209) *(G-1516)*
3v Company Inc 718 858-7333
110 Bridge St Ste 3 Brooklyn (11201) *(G-1517)*
4 Over 4com Inc 718 932-2700
1941 46th St Astoria (11105) *(G-431)*
40 North Industries 212 821-1600
9 W 57th St Fl 30 New York (10019) *(G-8975)*
40 Street Baking Inc 212 683-4700
8617 17th Ave Brooklyn (11214) *(G-1518)*
450 Ridge St Inc 716 754-2789
450 Ridge St Lewiston (14092) *(G-7432)*
461 New Lots Avenue LLC 347 303-9305
461 New Lots Ave Brooklyn (11207) *(G-1519)*
4695 Main Street Snyder Inc 716 833-3270
358 Walton Dr Buffalo (14226) *(G-2789)*
4bumpers Llc 212 721-9600
285 New Wstmnster End Ave New York (10023) *(G-8976)*
4m Precision Industries Inc 315 252-8415
4000 Technology Park Blvd Auburn (13021) *(G-476)*
5 Star Apparel LLC 212 563-1233
31 W 34th St Fl 3 New York (10001) *(G-8977)*
5 Stars Printing Corp 718 461-4612
13330 32nd Ave Flushing (11354) *(G-5220)*
50+ Lifestyle 631 286-0058
146 S Country Rd Ste 4 Bellport (11713) *(G-824)*
514 Adams Corporation 516 352-6948
781 Hempstead Tpke Franklin Square (11010) *(G-5359)*

(PA)=Parent Co (HQ)=Headquarters (DH)=Div Headquarters

ALPHABETIC SECTION

518 Prints LLC 518 674-5346
　1548 Burden Lake Rd Ste 4 Averill Park (12018) *(G-532)*
525 America LLC (PA) 212 840-1313
　Seventh Ave Rm 701 New York (10018) *(G-8978)*
527 Franco Bakery Corporation 718 993-4200
　527 E 138th St Bronx (10454) *(G-1250)*
54321 Us Inc (HQ) 716 695-0258
　295 Fire Tower Dr Tonawanda (14150) *(G-16133)*
5th & Ocean Clothing Inc 716 604-9000
　160 Delaware Ave Buffalo (14202) *(G-2790)*
5th Avenue Chocolatiere Ltd 516 561-1570
　396 Rockaway Ave Valley Stream (11581) *(G-16397)*
5th Avenue Chocolatiere Ltd (PA) 212 935-5454
　114 Church St Freeport (11520) *(G-5379)*
5th Avenue Pharmacy Inc 718 439-8585
　4818 5th Ave Ste 1 Brooklyn (11220) *(G-1520)*
6727 11th Ave Corp 718 837-8787
　6727 11th Ave Brooklyn (11219) *(G-1521)*
6n Systems Inc 518 583-6400
　3 Corporate Dr Ste 202 Halfmoon (12065) *(G-5907)*
6th Ave Gourmet Inc 845 782-9067
　51 Forest Rd Unit 116 Monroe (10950) *(G-8547)*
6th Avenue Showcase Inc 212 382-0400
　241 W 37th St Frnt 2 New York (10018) *(G-8979)*
760 NI Holdings 716 821-1391
　760 Northland Ave Buffalo (14211) *(G-2791)*
786 Iron Works Corp 718 418-4808
　50 Morgan Ave Brooklyn (11237) *(G-1522)*
79 Metro Ltd (PA) 212 944-4030
　265 W 37th St Rm 205 New York (10018) *(G-8980)*
828 Express Inc 917 577-9019
　619 Elbe Ave Staten Island (10304) *(G-15629)*
872 Hunts Point Pharmacy Inc 718 991-3519
　872 Hunts Point Ave Bronx (10474) *(G-1251)*
888 Pharmacy Inc 718 871-8833
　4821 8th Ave Brooklyn (11220) *(G-1523)*
901 D LLC 845 369-1111
　360 Route 59 Ste 3 Airmont (10952) *(G-11)*
999 Bagels Inc 718 915-0742
　1410 86th St Brooklyn (11228) *(G-1524)*
A & A Graphics Inc II 516 735-0078
　615 Arlington Dr Seaford (11783) *(G-15343)*
A & A Line & Wire Corp 718 456-2657
　5118 Grand Ave Ste 10 Maspeth (11378) *(G-8110)*
A & B Color Corp (del) (PA) 718 441-5482
　8204 Lefferts Blvd # 356 Kew Gardens (11415) *(G-7157)*
A & B Finishing Inc 718 522-4702
　401 Park Ave Brooklyn (11205) *(G-1525)*
A & C/Furia Electric Motors 914 949-0585
　75 Lafayette Ave White Plains (10603) *(G-17072)*
A & D Entrances LLC 718 989-2441
　11090 Dunkirk St Jamaica (11412) *(G-6890)*
A & D Offset Printers Ltd 516 746-2476
　146 2nd St Apt 3 Mineola (11501) *(G-8486)*
A & D Tool Inc 631 243-4339
　30 Pashen Pl Dix Hills (11746) *(G-4288)*
A & F Trucking & Excavating, Salamanca *Also called Alice Perkins (G-15099)*
A & G Food Distributors LLC 917 939-3457
　21610 47th Ave Apt 3b Bayside (11361) *(G-762)*
A & G Heat Sealing 631 724-7764
　1 Albatross Ln Smithtown (11787) *(G-15481)*
A & G Precision Corp 631 957-5613
　680 Albany Ave Amityville (11701) *(G-273)*
A & J Machine & Welding Inc 631 845-7586
　6040 New Hwy Farmingdale (11735) *(G-4925)*
A & J Washroom Accessories, New Windsor *Also called Gamma Products Inc (G-8938)*
A & K Equipment Incorporated 705 428-3573
　407 Sherman St Watertown (13601) *(G-16633)*
A & L Asset Management Ltd 718 566-1500
　143 Alabama Ave Brooklyn (11207) *(G-1526)*
A & L Doors & Hardware LLC 718 585-8400
　375 E 163rd St Frnt 2 Bronx (10451) *(G-1252)*
A & L Lighting Ltd 718 821-1188
　15 Commercial Blvd Medford (11763) *(G-8233)*
A & L Machine Company Inc 631 463-3111
　200 Blydenburg Rd Ste 9 Islandia (11749) *(G-6785)*
A & L Pen Manufacturing Corp 718 499-8966
　145 12th St Brooklyn (11215) *(G-1527)*
A & L Shtmtl Fabrications Corp 718 842-1600
　1243 Oakpoint Ave Bronx (10474) *(G-1253)*
A & M Appel Distributing Inc 516 735-1672
　500 N Atlanta Ave Massapequa (11758) *(G-8176)*
A & M Home Improvement, Maspeth *Also called Andike Millwork Inc (G-8118)*
A & M Litho Inc 516 342-9727
　4 Hunt Pl Bethpage (11714) *(G-861)*
A & M Rosenthal Entps Inc 646 638-9600
　8 W 38th St Fl 4 New York (10018) *(G-8981)*
A & M Steel Stamps Inc 516 741-6223
　55 Windsor Ave Mineola (11501) *(G-8487)*
A & Mt Realty Group LLC 718 974-5871
　1979 Pacific St Fl 1 Brooklyn (11233) *(G-1528)*
A & P Master Images 315 793-1934
　205 Water St Utica (13502) *(G-16304)*

A & R Concrete Products LLC 845 562-0640
　7 Ruscitti Rd New Windsor (12553) *(G-8929)*
A & S Electric 212 228-2030
　952 Flushing Ave Brooklyn (11206) *(G-1529)*
A & S Fine Jewelry Corp 718 243-2201
　777 Kent Ave Ste 244 Brooklyn (11205) *(G-1530)*
A & S Window Associates Inc 718 275-7900
　8819 76th Ave Glendale (11385) *(G-5642)*
A & S Woodworking Inc 518 821-0832
　9 Partition St Hudson (12534) *(G-6602)*
A & T Iron Works Inc 914 632-8992
　25 Cliff St New Rochelle (10801) *(G-8883)*
A & T Tooling LLC 716 601-7299
　91 Beach Ave Lancaster (14086) *(G-7297)*
A & U America's Aids Magazine, Albany *Also called Art & Understanding Inc (G-50)*
A & V Castings Inc 212 997-0042
　257 W 39th St Fl 16w New York (10018) *(G-8982)*
A & Z Pharmaceutical Inc 631 952-3802
　350 Wireless Blvd Hauppauge (11788) *(G-6006)*
A & Z Pharmaceutical Inc (PA) 631 952-3800
　180 Oser Ave Hauppauge (11788) *(G-6007)*
A - Mic Corporation 909 598-1814
　4600 Witmer Indus Est Niagara Falls (14305) *(G-12793)*
A A C, Farmingdale *Also called American Aerospace Contrls Inc (G-4940)*
A A P C O Screen Prntng/Sprtwr, Binghamton *Also called Peter Papastrat (G-942)*
A A Technology Inc 631 913-0400
　101 Trade Zone Dr Ronkonkoma (11779) *(G-14845)*
A and J Apparel Corp 212 398-8899
　209 W 38th St Rm 1207 New York (10018) *(G-8983)*
A and K Global Inc 718 412-1876
　3312 208th St Bayside (11361) *(G-763)*
A and K Machine and Welding 631 231-2552
　20 Drexel Dr Bay Shore (11706) *(G-663)*
A and L Home Fuel LLC 607 638-1994
　601 Smokey Ave Schenevus (12155) *(G-15314)*
A Angonoa Inc (PA) 718 762-4466
　11505 15th Ave College Point (11356) *(G-3773)*
A B C Elastic Corp 718 388-2953
　889 Metropolitan Ave Brooklyn (11211) *(G-1531)*
A B C Mc Cleary Sign Co Inc 315 493-3550
　40230 State Route 3 Carthage (13619) *(G-3407)*
A B S Brass Products Inc 718 497-2115
　185 Moore St Brooklyn (11206) *(G-1532)*
A C Envelope Inc 516 420-0646
　51 Heisser Ln Ste B Farmingdale (11735) *(G-4926)*
A C J Communications Inc 631 587-5612
　65 Deer Park Ave Ste 2 Babylon (11702) *(G-544)*
A C T Associates 716 759-8348
　10100 Main St Clarence (14031) *(G-3654)*
A Colarusso and Son Inc (PA) 518 828-3218
　91 Newman Rd Hudson (12534) *(G-6603)*
A D Bowman & Son Lumber Co 607 692-2595
　1737 Us Highway 11 Castle Creek (13744) *(G-3417)*
A D C, Hauppauge *Also called American Diagnostic Corp (G-6021)*
A D K Dental Lab. 518 563-6093
　87 Hammond Ln Plattsburgh (12901) *(G-13649)*
A D M, North Tonawanda *Also called Riverfront Costume Design (G-12990)*
A D Mfg Corp 516 352-6161
　24844 Jericho Tpke Floral Park (11001) *(G-5189)*
A D T, Mineola *Also called Aquifer Drilling & Testing Inc (G-8495)*
A Division A & Liquid Systems, North Tonawanda *Also called Buffalo Pumps Inc (G-12963)*
A E C Electrotech, Carle Place *Also called American Engnred Cmponents Inc (G-3385)*
A E P, Yaphank *Also called American Electronic Products (G-17386)*
A Esteban & Company Inc (PA) 212 989-7000
　132 W 36th St Rm 1000 New York (10018) *(G-8984)*
A Esteban & Company Inc 212 714-2227
　132 W 36th St Rm 1000 New York (10018) *(G-8985)*
A Fleisig Paper Box Corp 212 226-7490
　1751 2nd Ave Apt 10a New York (10128) *(G-8986)*
A G I, Rochester *Also called Advanced Glass Industries Inc (G-14177)*
A G M Deco Inc 718 624-6200
　305 Wallabout St 307 Brooklyn (11206) *(G-1533)*
A G M Deco Inc (PA) 718 624-6200
　741 Myrtle Ave Brooklyn (11205) *(G-1534)*
A G Master Crafts Ltd 516 745-6262
　5 South St Ste A Garden City (11530) *(G-5492)*
A Garys Treasures 518 383-1171
　629 Plank Rd Clifton Park (12065) *(G-3693)*
A Gatty Products Inc 914 592-3903
　1 Warehouse Ln Elmsford (10523) *(G-4731)*
A Gatty Svce, Elmsford *Also called A Gatty Products Inc (G-4731)*
A Graphic Printing Inc 212 233-9696
　49 Market St Frnt 2 New York (10002) *(G-8987)*
A Guideposts Church Corp 212 251-8100
　16 E 34th St Fl 21 New York (10016) *(G-8988)*
A H Schreiber Co Inc (PA) 212 594-7234
　460 W 34th St Fl 10 New York (10001) *(G-8989)*
A Hyatt Ball Co Ltd 518 747-0272
　School St Fort Edward (12828) *(G-5339)*
A I M, Victor *Also called Advanced Interconnect Mfg Inc (G-16459)*

ALPHABETIC SECTION
Abalon Precision Mfg Corp (PA)

A I P Printing & Stationers 631 929-5529
6198 N Country Rd Wading River (11792) ***(G-16522)***
A I T Computers Inc 518 266-9010
157 Hoosick St Troy (12180) ***(G-16224)***
A J C Jewelry Contracting Inc 212 594-3703
247 W 30th St Fl 3 New York (10001) ***(G-8990)***
A J Congress, New York *Also called American Jewish Congress Inc* ***(G-9123)***
A J Gnco Mch Shp/Mchnery Rdout, Falconer *Also called Aj Genco Mch Sp McHy Rdout Svc* ***(G-4889)***
A J Hollander Enterprises, Lawrence *Also called Hastings Hide Inc* ***(G-7391)***
A J M Enterprises 716 626-7294
348 Cayuga Rd Buffalo (14225) ***(G-2792)***
A Jaffe Inc 212 843-7464
592 5th Ave Fl 3 New York (10036) ***(G-8991)***
A K A Computer Consulting Inc 718 351-5200
881 Richmond Rd Staten Island (10304) ***(G-15630)***
A K Allen Co Inc 516 747-5450
255 E 2nd St Mineola (11501) ***(G-8488)***
A L Eastmond & Sons Inc (PA) 718 378-3000
1175 Leggett Ave Bronx (10474) ***(G-1254)***
A L Sealing 315 699-6900
2280 Osborne Rd Chittenango (13037) ***(G-3629)***
A Losee & Sons 516 676-3060
68 Landing Rd Glen Cove (11542) ***(G-5608)***
A Lunt Design Inc 716 662-0781
5755 Big Tree Rd Orchard Park (14127) ***(G-13250)***
A M & J Digital 518 434-2579
800 N Pearl St Ste 5 Menands (12204) ***(G-8363)***
A M F/Coughlin Printing, Watertown *Also called Coughlin Printing Group* ***(G-16647)***
A M I, New York *Also called Weider Publications LLC* ***(G-12604)***
A M S Sign Designs 631 467-7722
2360 Middle Country Rd Centereach (11720) ***(G-3469)***
A Nuclimate Qulty Systems Inc 315 431-0226
6295 E Molloy Rd East Syracuse (13057) ***(G-4498)***
A P Manufacturing 909 228-3049
21 Floyds Run Bohemia (11716) ***(G-1001)***
A P S, Hicksville *Also called Applied Power Systems Inc* ***(G-6322)***
A Petteys Lumber, Fort Ann *Also called Petteys Lumber* ***(G-5337)***
A Q P Inc 585 256-1690
2975 Brighton Henrietta T Rochester (14623) ***(G-14161)***
A R Arena Products Inc 585 277-1680
2101 Mount Read Blvd Rochester (14615) ***(G-14162)***
A R V Precision Mfg Inc 631 293-9643
60 Baiting Place Rd Ste B Farmingdale (11735) ***(G-4927)***
A S A Precision Co Inc 845 482-4870
295 Jffersonville N Br Rd Jeffersonville (12748) ***(G-7058)***
A S L, Brooklyn *Also called American Scientific Ltg Corp* ***(G-1608)***
A S P, Albany *Also called Albany Student Press Inc* ***(G-43)***
A Schneller Sons Inc 212 695-9440
129 W 29th St Fl 6 New York (10001) ***(G-8992)***
A Strongwater Designs, New York *Also called Andrea Strongwater* ***(G-9154)***
A Sunshine Glass & Aluminum 718 932-8080
2901 Brooklyn Queens Expy Woodside (11377) ***(G-17316)***
A T A Bagel Shoppe Inc 718 352-4948
20814 Cross Island Pkwy Bayside (11360) ***(G-764)***
A T C, Oyster Bay *Also called American Trans-Coil Corp* ***(G-13365)***
A T M, Hornell *Also called Fortitude Industries* ***(G-6563)***
A Thousand Cranes Inc 212 724-9596
208 W 79th St Apt 2 New York (10024) ***(G-8993)***
A To Z Kosher Meat Products Co 718 384-7400
123 Borinquen Pl Brooklyn (11211) ***(G-1535)***
A To Z Media Inc (PA) 212 260-0237
243 W 30th St Fl 6 New York (10001) ***(G-8994)***
A Tradition of Excellence Inc 845 638-4595
85b Maple Ave New City (10956) ***(G-8781)***
A Trusted Name Inc 716 326-7400
35 Franklin St Westfield (14787) ***(G-17045)***
A V T, New York *Also called AV Therapeutics Inc* ***(G-9271)***
A Van Hoek Woodworking Limited 718 599-4388
71 Montrose Ave Brooklyn (11206) ***(G-1536)***
A W Hamel Stair Mfg Inc 518 346-3031
3111 Amsterdam Rd Schenectady (12302) ***(G-15226)***
A W R Group Inc 718 729-0412
3715 Hunters Point Ave Long Island City (11101) ***(G-7644)***
A W S, Port Chester *Also called D & M Enterprises Incorporated* ***(G-13741)***
A Yashir Bapa, New York *Also called AZ Yashir Bapaz Inc* ***(G-9285)***
A Zimmer Ltd 315 422-7011
W Tenesee St Syracuse (13204) ***(G-15845)***
A&B Conservation LLC 845 282-7272
12 Maple Leaf Rd Monsey (10952) ***(G-8566)***
A&B McKeon Glass Inc 718 525-2152
69 Roff St Staten Island (10304) ***(G-15631)***
A&M Model Makers LLC 626 813-9661
1675 Wayneport Rd Ste 1 Macedon (14502) ***(G-7979)***
A&S Refrigeration Equipment 718 993-6030
557 Longfellow Ave Bronx (10474) ***(G-1255)***
A-1 Iron Works Inc 718 927-4766
2413 Atlantic Ave Brooklyn (11233) ***(G-1537)***
A-1 Manhattan Custom Furn Inc 212 750-9800
4315 Austin Blvd Island Park (11558) ***(G-6777)***
A-1 Products Inc 718 789-1818
165 Classon Ave Brooklyn (11205) ***(G-1538)***
A-1 Skull Cap Corp 718 633-9333
1212 36th St Brooklyn (11218) ***(G-1539)***
A-1 Stamping & Spinning Corp 718 388-2626
225 Beach 143rd St Rockaway Park (11694) ***(G-14784)***
A-1 Transitmix Inc 718 292-3200
431 E 165th St Frnt 1 Bronx (10456) ***(G-1256)***
A-Fab Initiatives Inc 716 877-5257
99 Bud Mil Dr Buffalo (14206) ***(G-2793)***
A-Implant Dental Lab Corp 212 582-4720
10 Park Ave New York (10016) ***(G-8995)***
A-Line Technologies Inc 607 772-2439
197 Corporate Dr Binghamton (13904) ***(G-884)***
A-Mark Machinery Corp 631 643-6300
101 Lamar St West Babylon (11704) ***(G-16762)***
A-One Laminating Corp 718 266-6002
1636 Coney Island Ave 2b Brooklyn (11230) ***(G-1540)***
A-One Moving & Storage Inc 718 266-6002
1725 Avenue M Brooklyn (11230) ***(G-1541)***
A-Plus Restaurant Equipment 718 522-2656
623 Sackett St Brooklyn (11217) ***(G-1542)***
A-Quick Bindery LLC 631 491-1110
30 Gleam St Unit C West Babylon (11704) ***(G-16763)***
A-R Payne Cabinet Comp, Brooklyn *Also called Ralph Payne* ***(G-2477)***
A. Lange & Sohne Corporate, New York *Also called Richemont North America Inc* ***(G-11863)***
A.L. Blades, Hornell *Also called Dolomite Products Company Inc* ***(G-6561)***
A.S.I. Francies Ltd, New York *Also called Antwerp Sales Intl Inc* ***(G-9170)***
A/C Design & Fabrication Corp 718 227-8100
638 Sharrotts Rd Staten Island (10309) ***(G-15632)***
A1 International Heat Treating 718 863-5552
905 Brush Ave Bronx (10465) ***(G-1257)***
A1 Ornamental Iron Works Inc 718 265-3055
61 Jefferson St Brooklyn (11206) ***(G-1543)***
A1 Skullcaps, Brooklyn *Also called A-1 Skull Cap Corp* ***(G-1539)***
A2ia Corp 917 237-0390
24 W 40th St Fl 3 New York (10018) ***(G-8996)***
A3 Apparel LLC 888 403-9669
1407 Broadway Rm 716a New York (10018) ***(G-8997)***
AA USA Trading Inc 917 586-2573
154 42nd St Brooklyn (11232) ***(G-1544)***
AAa Amercn Flag Dctg Co Inc 212 279-4644
36 W 37th St Fl 9 New York (10018) ***(G-8998)***
AAA Catalytic Recycling Inc 631 920-7944
345 Eastern Pkwy Farmingdale (11735) ***(G-4928)***
AAA Noodle Products Mfg 212 431-4090
102 Bowery New York (10013) ***(G-8999)***
AAA Welding and Fabrication of 585 254-2830
1085 Lyell Ave Rochester (14606) ***(G-14163)***
AAAA York Inc 718 784-6666
3720 12th St Long Island City (11101) ***(G-7645)***
Aaaaaa Creative Designs, New York *Also called Paper Box Corp* ***(G-11563)***
Aaaaar Orthopedics Inc 845 278-4938
141 Main St Brewster (10509) ***(G-1206)***
Aabacs Group Inc 718 961-3577
1509 132nd St College Point (11356) ***(G-3774)***
Aabco Sheet Metal Co Inc (PA) 718 821-1166
47 40 Metropolitan Ave Ridgewood (11385) ***(G-14097)***
Aai, Auburn *Also called Auburn Armature Inc* ***(G-477)***
Aai Manufacturing Div, Bronx *Also called Sharon Metal Stamping Corp* ***(G-1451)***
Aakron Rule Corp (PA) 716 542-5483
8 Indianola Ave Akron (14001) ***(G-19)***
Aakron Rule Corp 716 542-5483
2 Oak St Akron (14001) ***(G-20)***
Aalborg Instrs & Contrls Inc 845 398-3160
20 Corporate Dr Orangeburg (10962) ***(G-13217)***
Aand D Maintenance, Bridgehampton *Also called Bridgehampton Steel & Wldg Inc* ***(G-1232)***
AAR Allen Services Inc 516 222-9000
747 Zeckendorf Blvd Garden City (11530) ***(G-5493)***
Aarco Products Inc 631 924-5461
21 Old Dock Rd Yaphank (11980) ***(G-17384)***
Aarfid LLC (PA) 716 992-3999
3780 Yochum Rd Eden (14057) ***(G-4585)***
Aaron Tool & Mold Inc 585 426-5100
620 Trolley Blvd Rochester (14606) ***(G-14164)***
Aatc, Medford *Also called American Avionic Tech Corp* ***(G-8234)***
Aatech, Clyde *Also called Advanced Atomization Tech LLC* ***(G-3725)***
Aavid Niagara LLC (HQ) 716 297-0652
3315 Haseley Dr Niagara Falls (14304) ***(G-12794)***
AB Aerospace, Brooklyn *Also called Cellular Empire Inc* ***(G-1768)***
AB Engine 518 557-3510
4a Northway Ln Latham (12110) ***(G-7351)***
AB Fire Inc 917 416-6444
1554 61st St Brooklyn (11219) ***(G-1545)***
Abaco Steel Products Inc 631 589-1800
1560 Locust Ave Bohemia (11716) ***(G-1002)***
Abalene Decorating Services 718 782-2000
315 W 39th St Rm 611 New York (10018) ***(G-9000)***
Abalon Precision Mfg Corp (PA) 718 589-5682
717 S 3rd Ave Mount Vernon (10550) ***(G-8659)***

ALPHABETIC

Abalon Precision Mfg Corp 718 589-5682
717 S 3rd Ave Mount Vernon (10550) *(G-8660)*
Abasco Inc 716 649-4790
5225 Southwestern Blvd Hamburg (14075) *(G-5918)*
Abbe Laboratories Inc 631 756-2223
1095 Broadhollow Rd Ste E Farmingdale (11735) *(G-4929)*
Abbeville Press Inc 212 366-5585
116 W 23rd St Fl 5 New York (10011) *(G-9001)*
Abbeville Publishing Group, New York *Also called Abbeville Press Inc (G-9001)*
Abble Awning Co Inc 516 822-1200
313 Broadway Ste 315 Bethpage (11714) *(G-862)*
Abbot & Abbot Box Corp 888 930-5972
3711 10th St Long Island City (11101) *(G-7646)*
Abbot & Abbot Packing Service, Long Island City *Also called Abbot & Abbot Box Corp (G-7646)*
Abbot Flag Co Div, Spring Valley *Also called Eagle Regalia Co Inc (G-15582)*
Abbott Industries Inc (PA) 718 291-0800
9525 149th St Jamaica (11435) *(G-6891)*
ABC Casting, Jamaica *Also called Technical Service Industries (G-6956)*
ABC Check Printing Corp 718 855-4702
544 Park Ave Ste 436 Brooklyn (11205) *(G-1546)*
ABC Peanut Butter LLC 212 661-6886
295 Madison Ave Ste 1618 New York (10017) *(G-9002)*
ABC Showerdoors, Brooklyn *Also called All United Window Corp (G-1588)*
ABC Television Network, New York *Also called Times Square Studios Ltd (G-12352)*
ABC Windows and Signs Corp 718 353-6210
12606 18th Ave College Point (11356) *(G-3775)*
Abdo Shtmtl & Fabrication Inc 315 894-4664
4293 Acme Rd Frankfort (13340) *(G-5349)*
Abe Pool Service 845 473-7730
793 Violet Ave Hyde Park (12538) *(G-6733)*
Abel Noser Solutions Ltd 646 884-6440
1 Battery Park Plz # 601 New York (10004) *(G-9003)*
Abercrombie & Fitch, Brooklyn *Also called Apsco Sports Enterprises Inc (G-1620)*
Aberdeen Blower & Shtmtl Works 631 661-6100
401 Columbus Ave West Babylon (11704) *(G-16764)*
Abetter Processing Corp 718 252-2223
984 E 35th St Brooklyn (11210) *(G-1547)*
ABG Accessories, New York *Also called Elegant Headwear Co Inc (G-9998)*
Abh Natures Products Inc 631 249-5783
131 Heartland Blvd Edgewood (11717) *(G-4589)*
ABI Packaging Inc 716 677-2900
1703 Union Rd West Seneca (14224) *(G-16938)*
Abigal Press Inc 718 641-5350
9735 133rd Ave Ozone Park (11417) *(G-13375)*
Abk Enterprises Inc 631 348-0555
403 E Suffolk Ave Central Islip (11749) *(G-3483)*
Abkco Music & Records Inc (PA) 212 399-0300
85 5th Ave Fl 11 New York (10003) *(G-9004)*
Able Anodizing Corp 718 252-0660
1767 Bay Ridge Ave Brooklyn (11204) *(G-1548)*
Able Electronics Inc 631 924-5386
18 Sawgrass Dr Bellport (11713) *(G-825)*
Able Environmental Services 631 567-6585
1599 Ocean Ave Bohemia (11716) *(G-1003)*
Able Industries Inc 914 739-5685
18 Brook Ln Cortlandt Manor (10567) *(G-4048)*
Able Kitchen 877 268-1264
540 Willow Ave Unit B Cedarhurst (11516) *(G-3455)*
Able Kitchen Supplies, Cedarhurst *Also called Able Kitchen (G-3455)*
Able National Corp 718 386-8801
49 Wyckoff Ave Ste 1 Brooklyn (11237) *(G-1549)*
Able Printing, West Babylon *Also called Weicro Graphics Inc (G-16840)*
Able Steel Equipment Co Inc 718 361-9240
5002 23rd St Long Island City (11101) *(G-7647)*
Able Weldbuilt Industries Inc 631 643-9700
1050 Grand Blvd Deer Park (11729) *(G-4085)*
Able Wire Co, Cortlandt Manor *Also called Able Industries Inc (G-4048)*
Abr Molding Andy LLC 212 576-1821
1624 Centre St Ridgewood (11385) *(G-14098)*
ABRA Media Inc 518 398-1010
2773 W Church St Pine Plains (12567) *(G-13554)*
Abra-Ka-Data Systems Ltd 631 667-5550
39 W Jefryn Blvd Ste 1 Deer Park (11729) *(G-4086)*
Abraham Jwly Designers & Mfrs 212 944-1149
37 W 47th St Ste 202 New York (10036) *(G-9005)*
Abraxis Bioscience LLC 716 773-0800
3159 Staley Rd Grand Island (14072) *(G-5750)*
Abrimian Bros Corp 212 382-1106
48 W 48th St Ste 805 New York (10036) *(G-9006)*
ABS Metal Corp 646 302-9018
58 Holly Rd Hewlett (11557) *(G-6306)*
ABS Talkx Inc 631 254-9100
34 Cleveland Ave Bay Shore (11706) *(G-664)*
Absolute Business Products, Port Washington *Also called Jaidan Industries Inc (G-13827)*
Absolute Coatings Inc 914 636-0700
38 Portman Rd New Rochelle (10801) *(G-8884)*
Absolute Color Corporation 212 868-0404
109 W 27th St Frnt 2 New York (10001) *(G-9007)*
Absolute Engineering Company, Bohemia *Also called Absolute Manufacturing Inc (G-1004)*
Absolute Fitness US Corp 732 979-8582
21337 39th Ave Ste 322 Bayside (11361) *(G-765)*
Absolute Manufacturing Inc 631 563-7466
210 Knickerbocker Ave Bohemia (11716) *(G-1004)*
ABT, Great Neck *Also called Advanced Barcode Technology (G-5784)*
Abtex Corporation 315 536-7403
89 Main St Dresden (14441) *(G-4318)*
Abyrx Inc 914 357-2600
1 Bridge St Ste 121 Irvington (10533) *(G-6766)*
AC Air Cooling Co Inc 718 933-1011
1637 Stillwell Ave Bronx (10461) *(G-1258)*
AC Air Cooling Company, Bronx *Also called Air Wave Air Conditioning Co (G-1265)*
AC DC Power Systems & Contrls, Poughkeepsie *Also called Protective Power Systms & Cntr (G-13926)*
AC Moore Incorporated 516 796-5831
3988 Hempstead Tpke Bethpage (11714) *(G-863)*
Aca Quality Building Pdts LLC 718 991-2423
1322 Garrison Ave Bronx (10474) *(G-1259)*
Academy of Political Science 212 870-2500
475 Riverside Dr Ste 1274 New York (10115) *(G-9008)*
Academy Printing Services Inc 631 765-3346
42 Hortons Ln Southold (11971) *(G-15557)*
Acadia Stairs 845 765-8600
73 Route 9 Ste 3 Fishkill (12524) *(G-5180)*
Accede Mold & Tool Co Inc 585 254-6490
1125 Lexington Ave Rochester (14606) *(G-14165)*
Accel Printing & Graphics 914 241-3369
128 Radio Circle Dr Ste 2 Mount Kisco (10549) *(G-8621)*
Accela Inc 631 563-5005
100 Comac St Ste 2 Ronkonkoma (11779) *(G-14846)*
Accelify Solutions LLC 888 922-2354
3611 14th Ave Ste 422 Brooklyn (11218) *(G-1550)*
Accent Label & Tag Co Inc (PA) 631 244-7066
348 Woodlawn Ave Ronkonkoma (11779) *(G-14847)*
Accent Printing &GRaphics, Wayland *Also called Specialty Services (G-16711)*
Accent Speaker Technology Ltd 631 738-2540
1511 Lincoln Ave Holbrook (11741) *(G-6429)*
Accenta Incorporated 716 565-6262
150 Lawrence Bell Dr # 108 Buffalo (14221) *(G-2794)*
Accesory Headquarters, New York *Also called Ahq LLC (G-9062)*
Access 24 845 358-5397
570 Kings Hwy Fl 4 Valley Cottage (10989) *(G-16374)*
Access Display Group Inc 516 678-7772
151 S Main St Freeport (11520) *(G-5380)*
Access Elevator & Lift Inc (PA) 716 483-3696
1209 E 2nd St Jamestown (14701) *(G-6967)*
Access Intelligence LLC 212 204-4269
249 W 17th St New York (10011) *(G-9009)*
Access Products Inc 800 679-4022
241 Main St Ste 100 Buffalo (14203) *(G-2795)*
Accessible Bath Tech LLC 518 937-1518
6 Albright Ave Albany (12203) *(G-33)*
Accessories For Electronics 631 847-0158
620 Mead Ter South Hempstead (11550) *(G-15529)*
Accessory Corporation 212 391-8607
575 8th Ave Fl 16 New York (10018) *(G-9010)*
Accessory Plays LLC 212 564-7301
29 W 36th St New York (10018) *(G-9011)*
Accessory Street LLC 212 686-8990
1370 Broadway New York (10018) *(G-9012)*
Acco Brands 607 561-5515
101 Oneil Rd Sidney (13838) *(G-15434)*
Acco Brands USA LLC 847 541-9500
941 Acco Way Ogdensburg (13669) *(G-13109)*
Acco North America, Ogdensburg *Also called Acco Brands USA LLC (G-13109)*
Accord Pipe Fabricators Inc 718 657-3900
9226 180th St Jamaica (11433) *(G-6892)*
Accounts Payable Department, Ronkonkoma *Also called Nbty Inc (G-14951)*
Accra Sheetmetal LLC 631 920-2087
1359 Straight Path Wyandanch (11798) *(G-17369)*
Accu Coat Inc 585 288-2330
111 Humboldt St Ste 8 Rochester (14609) *(G-14166)*
Accucut Inc 631 567-2868
120 Easy St West Sayville (11796) *(G-16933)*
Accumetrics Inc 716 684-0002
6 British American Blvd # 100 Latham (12110) *(G-7352)*
Accumetrics Associates Inc 518 393-2200
6 British American Blvd # 100 Latham (12110) *(G-7353)*
Accuprint (PA) 518 456-2431
2005 Western Ave Ste 1 Albany (12203) *(G-34)*
Accurate Industrial Machining 631 242-0566
1711 Church St Holbrook (11741) *(G-6430)*
Accurate Knitting Corp 646 552-2216
1478 E 26th St Brooklyn (11210) *(G-1551)*
Accurate Marine Specialties 631 589-5502
2200 Artic Ave Bohemia (11716) *(G-1005)*
Accurate McHning Incorporation 315 689-1428
251 State Route 5 Elbridge (13060) *(G-4623)*
Accurate Metal Weather Strip 914 668-6042
725 S Fulton Ave Mount Vernon (10550) *(G-8661)*
Accurate Pnt Powdr Coating Inc 585 235-1650
606 Hague St Rochester (14606) *(G-14167)*

ALPHABETIC

Accurate Precast ... 718 345-2910
1957 Pitkin Ave Brooklyn (11207) *(G-1552)*
Accurate Signs & Awnings Inc ... 718 788-0302
247 Prospect Ave Ste 2 Brooklyn (11215) *(G-1553)*
Accurate Specialty Metal Fabri ... 718 418-6895
6420 Admiral Ave Middle Village (11379) *(G-8409)*
Accurate Tool & Die LLC ... 585 254-2830
1085 Lyell Ave Rochester (14606) *(G-14168)*
Accurate Welding Service Inc ... 516 333-1730
615 Main St Westbury (11590) *(G-16960)*
Accurate Welding Svce, Westbury *Also called Accurate Welding Service Inc (G-16960)*
Accusonic Products, Edgewood *Also called Global Market Development Inc (G-4599)*
Accutrak Inc ... 212 925-5330
432 Washington St Ste 113 New York (10013) *(G-9013)*
Accuvein Inc (PA) ... 816 997-9400
40 Goose Hill Rd Cold Spring Harbor (11724) *(G-3767)*
Ace, Brooklyn *Also called Montrose Equipment Sales Inc (G-2332)*
Ace Banner & Flag Company ... 212 620-9111
107 W 27th St New York (10001) *(G-9014)*
Ace Banner Flag & Graphics, New York *Also called Ace Banner & Flag Company (G-9014)*
Ace Canvas & Tent Corp ... 631 648-0614
155 Raynor Ave Ronkonkoma (11779) *(G-14848)*
Ace Cntracting Consulting Corp ... 631 567-4752
515 Johnson Ave Bohemia (11716) *(G-1006)*
Ace Diamond Corp ... 212 730-8231
30 W 47th St Ste 808r New York (10036) *(G-9015)*
Ace Drop Cloth Canvas Pdts Inc ... 718 731-1550
4216 Park Ave Bronx (10457) *(G-1260)*
Ace Drop Cloth Co, Bronx *Also called Ace Drop Cloth Canvas Pdts Inc (G-1260)*
Ace Electronics Inc ... 914 773-2000
140 Old Saw Mill Riv Rd Hawthorne (10532) *(G-6242)*
Ace Fire Door Corp ... 718 901-0001
4000 Park Ave Bronx (10457) *(G-1261)*
Ace Manufacturing, Rochester *Also called Jam Industries Inc (G-14458)*
Ace Molding & Tool Inc ... 631 567-2355
51 Floyds Run Bohemia (11716) *(G-1007)*
Ace Printing & Publishing Inc ... 718 939-0040
14951 Roosevelt Ave Flushing (11354) *(G-5221)*
Ace Printing Co, Flushing *Also called Ace Printing & Publishing Inc (G-5221)*
Ace Specialty Co Inc ... 716 874-3670
695 Ensminger Rd Tonawanda (14150) *(G-16134)*
Acec, New York *Also called America Capital Energy Corp (G-9112)*
Aces Over Eights Inc ... 585 292-9690
1100 Jefferson Rd Ste 22 Rochester (14623) *(G-14169)*
Acf Industries Holding Corp (HQ) ... 212 702-4363
767 5th Ave New York (10153) *(G-9016)*
Achilles Construction Co Inc ... 718 389-4717
373 Hayward Ave Mount Vernon (10552) *(G-8662)*
Acj Communications, Massapequa Park *Also called Massapequa Post (G-8188)*
Acker & Ll Mills Corporation ... 212 307-7247
44 W 62nd St Apt 3b New York (10023) *(G-9017)*
Ackroyd Metal Fabricators Inc ... 518 434-1281
966 Broadway Ste 2 Menands (12204) *(G-8364)*
Acl, Thornwood *Also called Automated Control Logic Inc (G-16116)*
ACM, New York *Also called Association For Cmpt McHy Inc (G-9240)*
Acme Architectural Products ... 718 360-0700
513 Porter Ave Brooklyn (11222) *(G-1554)*
Acme Architectural Pdts Inc (PA) ... 718 384-7800
251 Lombardy St Brooklyn (11222) *(G-1555)*
Acme Architectural Walls, Brooklyn *Also called Acme Architectural Pdts Inc (G-1555)*
Acme Awning Co Inc ... 718 409-1881
435 Van Nest Ave Bronx (10460) *(G-1262)*
Acme Engineering Products Inc ... 518 236-5659
2330 State Route 11 Mooers (12958) *(G-8615)*
Acme Industries of W Babylon ... 631 737-5231
125 Gary Way Ste 2 Ronkonkoma (11779) *(G-14849)*
Acme Kitchenettes Corp ... 518 828-4191
4269 Us Route 9 Hudson (12534) *(G-6604)*
Acme Manufacturing Company, Medina *Also called Standex Air Dist Pdts Inc (G-8283)*
Acme Marine, Calverton *Also called US Hoists Corp (G-3302)*
Acme Marine Hoist, Bellport *Also called Thego Corporation (G-841)*
Acme Nipple Mfg Co Inc ... 716 873-7491
1930 Elmwood Ave Buffalo (14207) *(G-2796)*
Acme Office Group, Brooklyn *Also called New Dimensions Office Group (G-2361)*
Acme Parts Inc ... 718 649-1750
901 Elton St Brooklyn (11208) *(G-1556)*
Acme Pleating & Fagoting Corp ... 212 674-3737
147 W 26th St Fl 2 New York (10001) *(G-9018)*
Acme Precision Screw Pdts Inc ... 585 328-2028
623 Glide St Rochester (14606) *(G-14170)*
Acme Signs of Baldwinsville ... 315 638-4865
3 Marble St Baldwinsville (13027) *(G-564)*
Acme Smoked Fish Corp (PA) ... 954 942-5598
30 Gem St 56 Brooklyn (11222) *(G-1557)*
Acolyte Industries Inc ... 212 629-6830
251 W 30th St Ste 12e New York (10001) *(G-9019)*
Acolyte Technologies Corp ... 212 629-3239
44 E 32nd St Rm 901 New York (10016) *(G-9020)*
Acorda Therapeutics Inc (PA) ... 914 347-4300
420 Saw Mill River Rd Ardsley (10502) *(G-403)*
Acorn, New York *Also called Music Sales Corporation (G-11327)*
Acorn Products Corp ... 315 894-4868
27 Pleasant Ave Ilion (13357) *(G-6739)*
Acran Spill Containment Inc (PA) ... 631 841-2300
599 Albany Ave Amityville (11701) *(G-274)*
Acro Industries Inc ... 585 254-3661
554 Colfax St Rochester (14606) *(G-14171)*
Acro-Fab Ltd ... 315 564-6688
55 Rochester St Hannibal (13074) *(G-5969)*
Acrolite, Elbridge *Also called Accurate McHning Incorporation (G-4623)*
Acrs Inc ... 914 288-8100
1311 Mmroneck Ave Ste 260 White Plains (10605) *(G-17073)*
ACS, Ballston Spa *Also called Advanced Comfort Systems Inc (G-589)*
Act Communications Group Inc ... 631 669-2403
170 Higbie Ln West Islip (11795) *(G-16902)*
Actavis Laboratories Ny Inc ... 631 693-8000
33 Ralph Ave Copiague (11726) *(G-3889)*
Actinium Pharmaceuticals Inc ... 732 243-9495
546 5th Ave Fl 14 New York (10036) *(G-9021)*
Action Bullet Resistant ... 631 422-0888
263 Union Blvd West Islip (11795) *(G-16903)*
Action Graphics Services Inc ... 607 785-1951
1908 Vestal Pkwy E Vestal (13850) *(G-16438)*
Action Machined Products Inc ... 631 842-2333
1355 Bangor St Copiague (11726) *(G-3890)*
Action Rack Display Mfg ... 718 257-7111
980 Alabama Ave Brooklyn (11207) *(G-1558)*
Action Technologies Inc ... 718 278-1000
3809 33rd St Apt 1 Long Island City (11101) *(G-7648)*
Actioncraft Products Inc ... 516 883-6423
2 Manhasset Ave Port Washington (11050) *(G-13795)*
Active Business Systems, Long Island City *Also called Action Technologies Inc (G-7648)*
Active Manufacturing Inc ... 607 775-3162
32 Laughlin Rd Kirkwood (13795) *(G-7230)*
Active Process Supply, New York *Also called Standard Screen Supply Corp (G-12182)*
Active World Solutions Inc ... 718 922-9404
609 Fountain Ave Brooklyn (11208) *(G-1559)*
Actuant Corporation ... 607 753-8276
44 River St Cortland (13045) *(G-4011)*
Actv Inc (del Corp) (HQ) ... 212 995-9500
233 Park Ave S Fl 10 New York (10003) *(G-9022)*
Acu Rite Companies Inc ... 716 661-1700
1 Precision Way Jamestown (14701) *(G-6968)*
Ad Makers Long Island Inc ... 631 595-9100
60 E Jefryn Blvd Ste 3 Deer Park (11729) *(G-4087)*
Ad Notam LLC ... 631 951-2020
135 Ricefield Ln Hauppauge (11788) *(G-6008)*
Ad Vantage Press ... 212 941-8355
481 Washington St Fl 7 New York (10013) *(G-9023)*
Adam Scott Designs Inc ... 212 420-8866
118 E 25th St Fl 11 New York (10010) *(G-9024)*
Adamor Inc ... 212 688-8885
17 E 48th St Rm 901 New York (10017) *(G-9025)*
Adams Interior Fabrications ... 631 249-8282
8 Iroquois Pl Massapequa (11758) *(G-8177)*
Adams Lumber Co Inc ... 716 358-2815
6052 Adams Rd Cattaraugus (14719) *(G-3436)*
Adams Press, Franklin Square *Also called 514 Adams Corporation (G-5359)*
Adams Ridge, Lancaster *Also called Markar Architectural Products (G-7326)*
Adams Sfc Inc (HQ) ... 716 877-2608
225 E Park Dr Tonawanda (14150) *(G-16135)*
Adaptive Mfg Tech Inc ... 631 580-5400
181 Remington Blvd Ronkonkoma (11779) *(G-14850)*
Adar Medical Uniform LLC ... 718 935-1197
307 Richardson St Brooklyn (11222) *(G-1560)*
Adart Poly Bag Mfg, Plainview *Also called Adart Polyethylene Bag Mfg (G-13576)*
Adart Polyethylene Bag Mfg ... 516 932-1001
1 W Ames Ct Ste 201 Plainview (11803) *(G-13576)*
ADC Acquisition Company ... 518 377-6471
2 Commerce Park Rd Niskayuna (12309) *(G-12893)*
ADC Dolls Inc ... 212 244-4500
112 W 34th St Ste 1207 New York (10120) *(G-9026)*
ADC Industries Inc (PA) ... 516 596-1304
181a E Jamaica Ave Valley Stream (11580) *(G-16398)*
Adchem Corp (PA) ... 631 727-6000
1852 Old Country Rd Riverhead (11901) *(G-14137)*
Adchem Industries, Riverhead *Also called Adchem Corp (G-14137)*
Adco Innvtive Prmtnal Pdts Inc ... 716 805-1076
574 Main St Ste 301 East Aurora (14052) *(G-4364)*
Adcomm Graphics Inc ... 212 645-1298
21 Lamar St West Babylon (11704) *(G-16765)*
Add Associates Inc ... 315 449-3474
6333 Daedalus Rd Cicero (13039) *(G-3641)*
Addeo Bakers Inc ... 718 367-8316
2372 Hughes Ave Bronx (10458) *(G-1263)*
Addex Inc ... 315 331-7700
251 Murray St Newark (14513) *(G-12728)*
Addex Inc (PA) ... 781 344-5800
251 Murray St Newark (14513) *(G-12729)*
Addison Precision Mfg Corp ... 585 254-1386
500 Avis St Rochester (14615) *(G-14172)*
Additude Magazine, New York *Also called New Hope Media LLC (G-11390)*

ALPHABETIC

ALPHABETIC SECTION

Addmm LLC 631 913-4400
4155 Veterans Memorial Hw Ronkonkoma (11779) *(G-14851)*
Adel Rootstein (usa) Inc 718 499-5650
145 18th St Brooklyn (11215) *(G-1561)*
Adelphi Paper Hangings 518 284-9066
102 Main St Sharon Springs (13459) *(G-15382)*
Adeptronics Incorporated 631 667-0659
281 Skip Ln Ste C Bay Shore (11706) *(G-665)*
Adesso Inc (PA) 212 736-4440
360 W 31st St Rm 909 New York (10001) *(G-9027)*
Adf Accessories Inc 516 450-5755
381 Sunrise Hwy Unit 5r Lynbrook (11563) *(G-7943)*
Adflex Corporation 585 454-2950
300 Ormond St Rochester (14605) *(G-14173)*
Adir Publishing Co 718 633-9437
1212 36th St Brooklyn (11218) *(G-1562)*
Adirondack Beverage Co Inc 518 370-3621
701 Corporation Park Schenectady (12302) *(G-15227)*
Adirondack Chocolate Co Ltd (PA) 518 946-7270
5680 Ny State Rte 86 Wilmington (12997) *(G-17267)*
Adirondack Daily Enterprise, Saranac Lake *Also called Adirondack Publishing Co Inc (G-15134)*
ADIRONDACK EXPLORER, Saranac Lake *Also called Getting The Word Out Inc (G-15137)*
Adirondack Home News, Holland Patent *Also called Steffen Publishing Inc (G-6488)*
Adirondack Ice & Air Inc 518 483-4340
26 Railroad St Malone (12953) *(G-8005)*
Adirondack Leather Pdts Inc 607 547-5798
196 Cemetery Rd Fly Creek (13337) *(G-5313)*
Adirondack Life Inc (PA) 518 946-2191
Rr 9 Box North Jay (12941) *(G-7054)*
Adirondack Life Magazine, Jay *Also called Adirondack Life Inc (G-7054)*
Adirondack Machine Corporation 518 792-2258
84 Boulevard St Hudson Falls (12839) *(G-6638)*
Adirondack Meat Company Inc 518 585-2333
30 Commerce Dr Ticonderoga (12883) *(G-16124)*
Adirondack Natural Stone LLC 518 499-0602
8986 State Route 4 Whitehall (12887) *(G-17189)*
Adirondack Outdoor Center 315 369-2300
2839 State Route 28 Old Forge (13420) *(G-13132)*
Adirondack Pennysaver Inc 518 563-0100
177 Margaret St Plattsburgh (12901) *(G-13650)*
Adirondack Plas & Recycl Inc (PA) 518 746-9212
453 County Route 45 Argyle (12809) *(G-408)*
Adirondack Power Sports 518 481-6269
5378 State Route 37 Malone (12953) *(G-8006)*
Adirondack Precision Cut Stone (PA) 518 681-3060
536 Queensbury Ave Queensbury (12804) *(G-13986)*
Adirondack Publishing Co Inc (HQ) 518 891-2600
54 Broadway Saranac Lake (12983) *(G-15134)*
Adirondack Sanitary Service, Ticonderoga *Also called Adirondack Waste MGT Inc (G-16125)*
Adirondack Scenic Inc 518 638-8000
439 County Route 45 Ste 1 Argyle (12809) *(G-409)*
Adirondack Sign Perfect Inc 518 409-7446
72 Ballston Ave Saratoga Springs (12866) *(G-15141)*
Adirondack Spclty Adhsives Inc 518 869-5736
4258 Albany St Albany (12205) *(G-35)*
Adirondack Stained Glass Works 518 725-0387
29 W Fulton St Ste 6 Gloversville (12078) *(G-5704)*
Adirondack Stairs Inc 845 246-2525
990 Kings Hwy Saugerties (12477) *(G-15178)*
Adirondack Studios, Argyle *Also called Adirondack Scenic Inc (G-409)*
Adirondack Waste MGT Inc 518 585-2224
963 New York State 9n Ticonderoga (12883) *(G-16125)*
Adirondack-Aire, Rome *Also called Cold Point Corporation (G-14809)*
Adirondex, Malone *Also called Adirondack Ice & Air Inc (G-8005)*
Aditiany Inc 212 997-8440
37 W 39th St Rm 1100 New York (10018) *(G-9028)*
Adjustable Shelving, Melville *Also called Karp Associates Inc (G-8332)*
Adl Data Systems Inc 914 591-1800
9 Skyline Dr Ste 4 Hawthorne (10532) *(G-6243)*
ADM, Buffalo *Also called Archer-Daniels-Midland Company (G-2819)*
ADM, Hudson *Also called Archer-Daniels-Midland Company (G-6606)*
ADM, Lakeville *Also called Archer-Daniels-Midland Company (G-7282)*
ADM Milling Co 716 849-7333
250 Ganson St Buffalo (14203) *(G-2797)*
Admor Blinds & Window Fashion, Westbury *Also called KPP Ltd (G-17004)*
Adobe Systems Inc 212 471-0904
1540 Broadway Fl 17 New York (10036) *(G-9029)*
Adobe Systems Incorporated 212 471-0904
8 W 40th St Fl 8 New York (10018) *(G-9030)*
ADOTTA AMERICA, New York *Also called Europrojects Intl Inc (G-10086)*
Adpro Sports Inc 716 854-5116
55 Amherst Villa Rd Buffalo (14225) *(G-2798)*
Adrean Printing, New Rochelle *Also called Vic-Gina Printing Company Inc (G-8927)*
Adria Machine & Tool Inc 585 889-3360
966 North Rd Scottsville (14546) *(G-15332)*
Adrian Jules Ltd 585 342-5886
1392 E Ridge Rd Rochester (14621) *(G-14174)*
Adrian-Jules Custom Tailor, Rochester *Also called Adrian Jules Ltd (G-14174)*

Adriatic Wood Products Inc 718 922-4621
1994 Industrial Park Rd Brooklyn (11207) *(G-1563)*
Adrienne Landau Designs Inc 212 695-8362
519 8th Ave Fl 21 New York (10018) *(G-9031)*
Ads-N-Color Inc 718 797-0900
20 Jay St Ste 530 Brooklyn (11201) *(G-1564)*
Adsco Manufacturing Corp 716 827-5450
4979 Lake Ave Buffalo (14219) *(G-2799)*
Adstream America LLC (HQ) 845 496-8283
845 3rd Ave Fl 6 New York (10022) *(G-9032)*
Adtech, Rochester *Also called Analog Digital Technology LLC (G-14203)*
Adtech Us Inc 212 402-4840
770 Broadway Fl 4 New York (10003) *(G-9033)*
Adults and Children With Learn 516 593-8230
22 Alice Ct East Rockaway (11518) *(G-4467)*
Advan-Tech Manufacturing Inc 716 667-1500
3645 California Rd Orchard Park (14127) *(G-13251)*
Advance Apparel Intl Inc 212 944-0984
265 W 37th St Rm 906 New York (10018) *(G-9034)*
Advance Biofactures Corp 516 593-7000
35 Wilbur St Lynbrook (11563) *(G-7944)*
Advance Chemicals Usa Inc 718 633-1030
1230 57th St Brooklyn (11219) *(G-1565)*
Advance Circuit Technology Inc 585 328-2000
19 Jetview Dr Rochester (14624) *(G-14175)*
Advance Construction Group, New York *Also called B & F Architectural Support Gr (G-9287)*
Advance D Tech Inc 845 534-8248
2 Mill St Stop 19 Cornwall (12518) *(G-3985)*
Advance Energy Systems NY LLC 315 735-5125
17 Tilton Rd Utica (13501) *(G-16305)*
Advance Energy Tech Inc 518 371-2140
1 Solar Dr Halfmoon (12065) *(G-5908)*
Advance Finance Group LLC 212 630-5900
101 Park Ave Frnt New York (10178) *(G-9035)*
Advance Food Service Co Inc 631 242-4800
200 Heartland Blvd Edgewood (11717) *(G-4590)*
Advance Grafix Equipment Inc 917 202-4593
150 Wyandanch Ave Wyandanch (11798) *(G-17370)*
ADVANCE MAGAZINE PUBLISHERS, INC., New York *Also called Advance Magazine Publs Inc (G-9036)*
ADVANCE MAGAZINE PUBLISHERS, INC., New York *Also called Advance Magazine Publs Inc (G-9039)*
Advance Magazine Publs Inc 212 286-2860
1440 Broadway Fl 10 New York (10018) *(G-9036)*
Advance Magazine Publs Inc (HQ) 212 286-2860
1 World Trade Ctr Fl 28 New York (10007) *(G-9037)*
Advance Magazine Publs Inc 212 790-4422
1166 Ave Of The Amrcs 14 New York (10036) *(G-9038)*
Advance Magazine Publs Inc 212 286-2860
1166 Ave Of The Amrcs 1 New York (10036) *(G-9039)*
Advance Magazine Publs Inc 212 450-7000
711 3rd Ave Rm 700 New York (10017) *(G-9040)*
Advance Magazine Publs Inc 212 697-0126
750 3rd Ave Frnt G New York (10017) *(G-9041)*
Advance Micro Power Corp 631 471-6157
2190 Smithtown Ave Ronkonkoma (11779) *(G-14852)*
Advance Pharmaceutical Inc (PA) 631 981-4600
895 Waverly Ave Holtsville (11742) *(G-6500)*
Advance Precision Industries 631 491-0910
9 Mahan St Unit A West Babylon (11704) *(G-16766)*
Advance Pressure Products, Ithaca *Also called Porous Materials Inc (G-6870)*
Advance Tabco Inc (HQ) 631 242-8270
200 Heartland Blvd Edgewood (11717) *(G-4591)*
Advanced Aerospace Machining 631 694-7745
154 Rome St Farmingdale (11735) *(G-4930)*
Advanced Assembly Services Inc 716 217-8144
35 S Main St Angola (14006) *(G-378)*
Advanced Atomization Tech LLC 315 923-2341
124 Columbia St Clyde (14433) *(G-3725)*
Advanced Back Technologies 631 231-0076
89 Ste F Cabot Ct Hauppauge (11788) *(G-6009)*
Advanced Barcode Technology 516 570-8100
175 E Shore Rd Ste 228 Great Neck (11023) *(G-5784)*
Advanced Business Group Inc 212 398-1010
266 W 37th St Fl 15 New York (10018) *(G-9042)*
Advanced Cmpt Sftwr Consulting 718 300-3577
2236 Pearsall Ave Bronx (10469) *(G-1264)*
Advanced Coating Service LLC 585 247-3970
15 Hytec Cir Rochester (14606) *(G-14176)*
Advanced Coating Techniques 631 643-4555
313 Wyandanch Ave Babylon (11704) *(G-545)*
Advanced Coating Technologies, Amherst *Also called Bekaert Corporation (G-227)*
Advanced Comfort Systems Inc 518 884-8444
12b Commerce Dr Ballston Spa (12020) *(G-589)*
Advanced Comm Solutions 914 693-5076
38 Ridge Rd Ardsley (10502) *(G-404)*
Advanced Digital Info Corp 607 266-4000
10 Brown Rd Ithaca (14850) *(G-6816)*
Advanced Digital Printing LLC 718 649-1500
65 W 36th St Fl 11 New York (10018) *(G-9043)*
Advanced Distribution System 845 848-2357
275 Oak Tree Rd Palisades (10964) *(G-13400)*

Advanced Engineered Products 631 435-3535
25 Drexel Dr Bay Shore (11706) ***(G-666)***
Advanced Enterprises Inc 845 342-1009
366 Highland Ave Ext Middletown (10940) ***(G-8425)***
Advanced Fashions Technology 212 221-0606
110 W 40th St Rm 1100 New York (10018) ***(G-9044)***
Advanced Foam Products Div, Buffalo *Also called Tmp Technologies Inc* ***(G-3220)***
Advanced Frozen Foods Inc 516 333-6344
28 Urban Ave Westbury (11590) ***(G-16961)***
Advanced Glass Industries Inc 585 458-8040
1335 Emerson St Rochester (14606) ***(G-14177)***
Advanced Graphics Company 607 692-7875
2607 Main St Whitney Point (13862) ***(G-17219)***
Advanced Interconnect Mfg Inc (HQ) 585 742-2220
780 Canning Pkwy Victor (14564) ***(G-16459)***
Advanced Lamp Coatings Corp 631 585-5505
2165 5th Ave Ronkonkoma (11779) ***(G-14853)***
Advanced Machine Design Co Inc 716 826-2000
45 Roberts Ave Buffalo (14206) ***(G-2800)***
Advanced Machine Inc 585 423-8255
439 Central Ave Ste 108 Rochester (14605) ***(G-14178)***
Advanced Manufacturing Svc Inc 631 676-5210
100 13th Ave Ste 2 Ronkonkoma (11779) ***(G-14854)***
Advanced Medical Mfg Corp 845 369-7535
7-11 Suffern Pl Ste 2 Suffern (10901) ***(G-15784)***
Advanced Mfg Techniques 518 877-8560
453 Kinns Rd Clifton Park (12065) ***(G-3694)***
Advanced Mold & Tooling Inc 585 426-2110
769 Trabold Rd Rochester (14624) ***(G-14179)***
Advanced Mtl Analytics LLC 321 684-0528
85 Murray Hl Rd Ste 2115 Vestal (13850) ***(G-16439)***
Advanced Photonics Inc 631 471-3693
151 Trade Zone Dr Ronkonkoma (11779) ***(G-14855)***
Advanced Plstic Fbrctions Corp 631 231-4466
99 Marcus Blvd Hauppauge (11788) ***(G-6010)***
Advanced Polymer Solutions LLC 516 621-5800
99 Seaview Blvd Ste 1a Port Washington (11050) ***(G-13796)***
Advanced Polymers Intl, Syracuse *Also called Royal Adhesives & Sealants LLC* ***(G-16027)***
Advanced Precision Technology 845 279-3540
577 N Main St Ste 7 Brewster (10509) ***(G-1207)***
Advanced Printing New York Inc 212 840-8108
263 W 38th St New York (10018) ***(G-9045)***
Advanced Prosthetics Orthotics 516 365-7225
50 Maple Pl Manhasset (11030) ***(G-8054)***
Advanced Quickprinting, Rochester *Also called A Q P Inc* ***(G-14161)***
Advanced Ready Mix Corp 718 497-5020
239 Ingraham St Brooklyn (11237) ***(G-1566)***
Advanced Recovery & Recycl LLC 315 450-3301
3475 Linda Ln Baldwinsville (13027) ***(G-565)***
Advanced Research Media Inc 631 751-9696
21 Bennetts Rd Ste 101 East Setauket (11733) ***(G-4474)***
Advanced Response Corporation 212 459-0887
345 W 58th St Apt 11a New York (10019) ***(G-9046)***
Advanced Rubber Products, Wyoming *Also called Tmp Technologies Inc* ***(G-17383)***
Advanced Structures Corp (PA) 631 667-5000
235 W Industry Ct Deer Park (11729) ***(G-4088)***
Advanced Surface Finishing 516 876-9710
111 Magnolia Ave Westbury (11590) ***(G-16962)***
Advanced Tchncal Solutions Inc 914 214-8230
2986 Navajo Rd Ste 100 Yorktown Heights (10598) ***(G-17506)***
Advanced Technology Division, Plainview *Also called Technic Inc* ***(G-13638)***
Advanced Thermal Systems Inc 716 681-1800
15 Enterprise Dr Lancaster (14086) ***(G-7298)***
Advanced Yarn Technologies Inc 518 239-6600
4750 State Hwy 145 Durham (12422) ***(G-4354)***
Advantage Machining Inc 716 731-6418
6421 Wendt Dr Niagara Falls (14304) ***(G-12795)***
Advantage Metalwork Finshg LLC 585 454-0160
1000 University Ave # 700 Rochester (14607) ***(G-14180)***
Advantage Orthotics Inc 631 368-1754
337 Larkfield Rd East Northport (11731) ***(G-4432)***
Advantage Plus Diagnostics Inc 631 393-5044
200 Broadhollow Rd Melville (11747) ***(G-8288)***
Advantage Press Inc 518 584-3405
74 Warren St Saratoga Springs (12866) ***(G-15142)***
Advantage Printing Inc 718 820-0688
12034 Queens Blvd Ste 310 Kew Gardens (11415) ***(G-7158)***
Advantage Quick Print Inc 212 989-5644
30 E 33rd St Frnt B New York (10016) ***(G-9047)***
Advantage Wholesale Supply LLC 718 839-3499
172 Empire Blvd Brooklyn (11225) ***(G-1567)***
Advantage Wood Shop, Cheektowaga *Also called Stereo Advantage Inc* ***(G-3590)***
Advantech Industries Inc 585 247-0701
3850 Buffalo Rd Rochester (14624) ***(G-14181)***
Advantex Solutions Inc 718 278-2290
24845 Jericho Tpke Bellerose (11426) ***(G-809)***
Advd Heart Phys & Surgs 212 434-3000
130 E 77th St Fl 4 New York (10075) ***(G-9048)***
Adventure Publishing Group 212 575-4510
307 7th Ave Rm 1601 New York (10001) ***(G-9049)***
Advertiser, Albany *Also called Capital Region Wkly Newspapers* ***(G-60)***
Advertiser Publications Inc 845 783-1111
148 State Route 17m Chester (10918) ***(G-3598)***
Advertiser, The, Averill Park *Also called Capital Reg Wkly Newsppr Group* ***(G-533)***
Advertising Lithographers 212 966-7771
121 Varick St Fl 9 New York (10013) ***(G-9050)***
Advion Inc (PA) 607 266-9162
10 Brown Rd Ste 101 Ithaca (14850) ***(G-6817)***
Advis Inc 585 568-0100
2218 River Rd Caledonia (14423) ***(G-3275)***
Ae Fund Inc 315 698-7650
5860 Mckinley Rd Brewerton (13029) ***(G-1202)***
Aeb Sapphire Corp 516 586-8232
152 Ontario Ave Massapequa (11758) ***(G-8178)***
Aegis Oil Limited Ventures LLC 646 233-4900
14 Wall St Fl 20 New York (10005) ***(G-9051)***
AEP Environmental LLC 716 446-0739
2495 Main St Ste 230 Buffalo (14214) ***(G-2801)***
Aerco International Inc (HQ) 845 580-8000
100 Oritani Dr Blauvelt (10913) ***(G-969)***
Aero Brand Inks, Blue Point *Also called Specialty Ink Co Inc* ***(G-1000)***
Aero Healthcare (us) LLC 855 225-2376
616 Corporate Way Ste 6 Valley Cottage (10989) ***(G-16375)***
Aero Specialties Manufacturing 631 242-7200
20 Burt Dr Deer Park (11729) ***(G-4089)***
Aero Trades Mfg Corp 516 746-3360
65 Jericho Tpke Mineola (11501) ***(G-8489)***
Aero-Data Metal Crafters Inc 631 471-7733
2085 5th Ave Ronkonkoma (11779) ***(G-14856)***
Aero-Vision Technologies Inc (PA) 631 643-8349
7 Round Tree Dr Melville (11747) ***(G-8289)***
Aerobic Wear Inc 631 673-1830
16 Depot Rd Huntington Station (11746) ***(G-6693)***
Aeroduct Inc 516 248-9550
134 Herricks Rd Mineola (11501) ***(G-8490)***
Aeroflex Holding Corp (HQ) 516 694-6700
35 S Service Rd Plainview (11803) ***(G-13577)***
Aeroflex Incorporated (HQ) 516 694-6700
35 S Service Rd Plainview (11803) ***(G-13578)***
Aeroflex Plainview Inc (HQ) 516 694-6700
35 S Service Rd Plainview (11803) ***(G-13579)***
Aeroflex Plainview Inc 631 231-9100
350 Kennedy Dr Hauppauge (11788) ***(G-6011)***
Aerolase Corporation 914 345-8300
777 Old Saw Mill River Rd # 2 Tarrytown (10591) ***(G-16084)***
Aeromed Inc 518 843-9144
1821 Broad St Ste 1 Utica (13501) ***(G-16306)***
Aeroseal LLC 315 373-0765
6838 Ellicott Dr East Syracuse (13057) ***(G-4499)***
Aerospace Lighting Corporation (HQ) 631 563-6400
355 Knickerbocker Ave Bohemia (11716) ***(G-1008)***
Aerospace Wire & Cable Inc 718 358-2345
12909 18th Ave College Point (11356) ***(G-3776)***
AES Electronics Inc 212 371-8120
135 E 54th St Apt 10j New York (10022) ***(G-9052)***
AF Design Inc 347 548-5273
1239 Broadway Ste 701 New York (10001) ***(G-9053)***
Afab Initiative, Buffalo *Also called American Douglas Metals Inc* ***(G-2807)***
AFC Industries Inc 347 532-1200
1316 133rd Pl Ste 1 College Point (11356) ***(G-3777)***
Afco Modular Enclosure Systems, Farmingdale *Also called Afco Systems Inc* ***(G-4931)***
Afco Precast Sales Corp 631 924-7114
114 Rocky Point Rd Middle Island (11953) ***(G-8405)***
Afco Systems Inc 631 424-3935
200 Finn Ct Ste 1 Farmingdale (11735) ***(G-4931)***
Afe, South Hempstead *Also called Accessories For Electronics* ***(G-15529)***
Aferge Mds, Rochester *Also called GE Mds LLC* ***(G-14389)***
Affco, New Windsor *Also called American Felt & Filter Co Inc* ***(G-8931)***
Affiliated Services Group, Huntington *Also called SC Textiles Inc* ***(G-6679)***
Affluent Design Inc 631 655-2556
48 Biltmore Dr Mastic Beach (11951) ***(G-8204)***
Affymax Inc 650 812-8700
630 5th Ave Ste 2260 New York (10111) ***(G-9054)***
Afi Cybernetics Corporation 607 732-3244
713 Batavia St Elmira (14904) ***(G-4668)***
AFP Imaging Corporation (HQ) 914 592-6665
185 Kisco Ave Ste 202 Mount Kisco (10549) ***(G-8622)***
AFP Industries, Lancaster *Also called Air System Products Inc* ***(G-7300)***
AFP Manufacturing Corp 516 466-6464
9 Park Pl Great Neck (11021) ***(G-5785)***
African American Observer, New York *Also called General Media Strategies Inc* ***(G-10273)***
Afro Times Newspaper 718 636-9500
1195 Atlantic Ave Brooklyn (11216) ***(G-1568)***
After 50 Inc 716 832-9300
5 W Main St Rear Lancaster (14086) ***(G-7299)***
Aftermarket Whl Autobody Parts, Uniondale *Also called Awap Inc* ***(G-16289)***
AG Adriano Goldschmied Inc 845 928-8616
216 Red Apple Ct Central Valley (10917) ***(G-3520)***
AG Biotech Inc 585 346-0020
3578 Shoreline Dr Livonia (14487) ***(G-7563)***
AG Neovo Professional Inc 212 647-9080
156 5th Ave Ste 434 New York (10010) ***(G-9055)***

ALPHABETIC

AG Tech Welding Corp...845 398-0005
  238 Oak Tree Rd Tappan (10983) *(G-16078)*
Ag-Pak Inc...716 772-2651
  8416 Telegraph Rd Gasport (14067) *(G-5555)*
Age Manufacturers Inc......................................718 927-0048
  10624 Avenue D Brooklyn (11236) *(G-1569)*
Age Timberline Mamba, Farmingdale Also called Amana Tool Corp *(G-4939)*
Aggressive Energy LLC......................................718 836-9222
  78 Rapelye St Ste A Brooklyn (11231) *(G-1570)*
Agi Brooks Production Co Inc (PA).....................212 268-1533
  7 E 14th St Apt 615 New York (10003) *(G-9056)*
Agilent Technologies Inc...................................877 424-4536
  399 Park Ave New York (10022) *(G-9057)*
Agl Industries Inc..718 326-7597
  5912 57th St Maspeth (11378) *(G-8111)*
Aglika Trade LLC..727 424-1944
  5905 74th St Middle Village (11379) *(G-8410)*
Agn Professional, New York Also called AG Neovo Professional Inc *(G-9055)*
Agnovos Healthcare LLC..................................646 502-5860
  140 Broadway Fl 46 New York (10005) *(G-9058)*
Agrasun Inc..305 377-3337
  2578 Broadway 117 New York (10025) *(G-9059)*
Agrasun Renewable Energy, New York Also called Agrasun Inc *(G-9059)*
Agrecolor Inc (PA)..516 741-8700
  400 Sagamore Ave Mineola (11501) *(G-8491)*
Agri Services Co...716 937-6618
  13899 North Rd Alden (14004) *(G-173)*
Agri-Mark Inc...518 497-6644
  39 Mccadam Ln Chateaugay (12920) *(G-3556)*
Agricultrure Biological Engrg, Ithaca Also called Cornell University *(G-6835)*
Agrium Advanced Tech US Inc...........................631 286-0598
  165 Orville Dr Bohemia (11716) *(G-1009)*
Agrochem Inc...518 226-4850
  3 Duplainville Rd Saratoga Springs (12866) *(G-15143)*
AGS, Vestal Also called Action Graphics Services Inc *(G-16438)*
Agua Enerviva LLC..516 597-5440
  15 Grumman Rd W Ste 1300 Bethpage (11714) *(G-864)*
Aguilar Amplification LLC.................................212 431-9109
  599 Broadway Fl 7 New York (10012) *(G-9060)*
Agway, Cobleskill Also called Kelley Farm & Garden Inc *(G-3738)*
Agway, Akron Also called G & S Farm & Home Inc *(G-23)*
Ah Elctronic Test Eqp Repr Ctr.........................631 234-8979
  7 Olive St Central Islip (11722) *(G-3484)*
Ahhmigo LLC..212 315-1818
  120 Cent Park S Rm 7c New York (10019) *(G-9061)*
Ahlstrom Kamyr, Glens Falls Also called Andritz Inc *(G-5670)*
Ahq LLC...212 328-1560
  10 W 33rd St Rm 306 New York (10001) *(G-9062)*
Ahw Printing Corp...516 536-3600
  2920 Long Beach Rd Oceanside (11572) *(G-13072)*
Ai Entertainment Holdings LLC (HQ)..................212 247-6400
  730 5th Ave Fl 20 New York (10019) *(G-9063)*
Ai Media Group Inc...212 660-2400
  589 8th Ave Fl 17 New York (10018) *(G-9064)*
Aiche, New York Also called American Inst Chem Engineers *(G-9121)*
Aicm, Hauppauge Also called American Intrmdal Cont Mfg LLC *(G-6022)*
Aid Wood Working..631 244-7768
  1555 Ocean Ave Ste C Bohemia (11716) *(G-1010)*
Aigner Chocolates Inc (PA)...............................718 544-1850
  10302 Metropolitan Ave Forest Hills (11375) *(G-5320)*
Aigner Index,, New Windsor Also called Aigner Label Holder Corp *(G-8930)*
Aigner Label Holder Corp.................................845 562-4510
  218 Mac Arthur Ave New Windsor (12553) *(G-8930)*
Aines Manufacturing Corp................................631 471-3900
  96 E Bayberry Rd Islip (11751) *(G-6806)*
Aip Aerospace, New York Also called Aip/Aerospace Holdings LLC *(G-9065)*
Aip Publishing LLC..516 576-2200
  1305 Walt Whitman Rd # 300 Melville (11747) *(G-8290)*
Aip/Aerospace Holdings LLC (PA).....................212 916-8142
  330 Madison Ave Fl 28 New York (10017) *(G-9065)*
Aiping Pharmaceutical Inc................................631 952-3802
  350w Wireless Blvd Hauppauge (11788) *(G-6012)*
Air Chex Equipment Corp..................................845 358-8179
  50 Lydecker St Nyack (10960) *(G-13043)*
Air Conditioning, Bronx Also called AC Air Cooling Co Inc *(G-1258)*
Air Crafters Inc...631 471-7788
  2085 5th Ave Ronkonkoma (11779) *(G-14857)*
Air Engineering Filters Inc................................914 238-5945
  17 Memorial Dr Chappaqua (10514) *(G-3550)*
Air Export Mechanical......................................917 709-5310
  4108 Parsons Blvd Apt 4r Flushing (11355) *(G-5222)*
Air Flow Manufacturing....................................607 733-8284
  365 Upper Oakwood Ave Elmira (14903) *(G-4669)*
Air Flow Pump Corp..718 241-2800
  8412 Foster Ave Brooklyn (11236) *(G-1571)*
Air Flow Pump Supply, Brooklyn Also called Air Flow Pump Corp *(G-1571)*
Air Goal Intl USA Inc...718 656-5880
  30 W Merrick Rd Valley Stream (11580) *(G-16399)*
Air Industries Group (PA)..................................631 881-4920
  360 Motor Pkwy Ste 100 Hauppauge (11788) *(G-6013)*

Air Industries Machining Corp...........................631 968-5000
  1479 N Clinton Ave Bay Shore (11706) *(G-667)*
Air Louver & Damper Inc...................................718 392-3232
  5670 58th Pl Maspeth (11378) *(G-8112)*
Air Louver & Damper Inc (PA)...........................718 392-3232
  2121 44th Rd Long Island City (11101) *(G-7649)*
Air Preheater, Wellsville Also called Arvos Inc *(G-16749)*
Air Products and Chemicals Inc........................518 463-4273
  461 River Rd Glenmont (12077) *(G-5666)*
Air Products and Chemicals Inc........................585 798-2324
  4141 Bates Rd Medina (14103) *(G-8264)*
Air Skate & Air Jump Corp (PA).........................212 967-1201
  2208 E 5th St Brooklyn (11223) *(G-1572)*
Air Structures Amercn Tech Inc........................914 937-4500
  211 S Ridge St Ste 3 Port Chester (10573) *(G-13737)*
Air System Products Inc...................................716 683-0435
  51 Beach Ave Lancaster (14086) *(G-7300)*
Air Techniques Inc (HQ)....................................516 433-7676
  1295 Walt Whitman Rd Melville (11747) *(G-8291)*
Air Tite Manufacturing Inc................................516 897-0295
  724 Park Pl Ste B Long Beach (11561) *(G-7637)*
Air Wave Air Conditioning Co............................212 545-1122
  1637 Stillwell Ave Bronx (10461) *(G-1265)*
Air-Flo Mfg Co Inc..607 733-8284
  365 Upper Oakwood Ave Elmira (14903) *(G-4670)*
Air-O-Tronics, Cazenovia Also called Stk Electronics Inc *(G-3452)*
Aircraft Finishing Corp (PA)..............................631 422-5000
  100 Field St Unit A West Babylon (11704) *(G-16767)*
Aireactor Inc...718 326-2433
  5 Railroad Pl Maspeth (11378) *(G-8113)*
Airflex Corp..631 752-1219
  965 Conklin St Farmingdale (11735) *(G-4932)*
Airflex Industrial Inc (PA)..................................631 752-1234
  965 Conklin St Farmingdale (11735) *(G-4933)*
Airflex Industrial Inc...631 752-1234
  937 Conklin St Farmingdale (11735) *(G-4934)*
Airgas Inc...585 436-7780
  77 Deep Rock Rd Rochester (14624) *(G-14182)*
Airgas Inc...518 690-0068
  84 Karner Rd Albany (12205) *(G-36)*
Airgas USA LLC..315 433-1295
  121 Boxwood Ln Syracuse (13206) *(G-15846)*
Airgas USA LLC..585 436-7781
  77 Deep Rock Rd Rochester (14624) *(G-14183)*
Airline Container Services................................516 371-4125
  354 Harbor Dr Lido Beach (11561) *(G-7439)*
Airline Container Svces, Lido Beach Also called Airline Container Services *(G-7439)*
Airmarine Electroplating Corp..........................516 623-4406
  388 Woodcleft Ave Freeport (11520) *(G-5381)*
Airnet Communications Corp............................516 338-0008
  609 Cantiague Rock Rd # 5 Westbury (11590) *(G-16963)*
Airnet North Division, Westbury Also called Airnet Communications Corp *(G-16963)*
Airport Press, The, Jamaica Also called Pati Inc *(G-6938)*
Airport Printing & Stationers, Wading River Also called A I P Printing & Stationers *(G-16522)*
Airsep, Amherst Also called Chart Industries Inc *(G-232)*
Airsep, Amherst Also called Chart Industries Inc *(G-233)*
Airsep Corporation...716 691-0202
  260 Creekside Dr Ste 100 Amherst (14228) *(G-219)*
Airsys Technologies Inc....................................716 694-6390
  79 Fillmore Ave Tonawanda (14150) *(G-16136)*
Airtech Lab, Brooklyn Also called Dib Managmnt Inc *(G-1862)*
Airtek, Lancaster Also called Rayco Enterprises Inc *(G-7337)*
Airweld Inc...631 924-6366
  1740 Middle Country Rd Ridge (11961) *(G-14091)*
Aithaca Chemical Corp.....................................516 229-2330
  50 Charles Lindbergh Blvd # 400 Uniondale (11553) *(G-16288)*
Aj Genco Mch Sp McHy Rdout Svc....................716 664-4925
  235 Carter St Falconer (14733) *(G-4889)*
Aj Greentech Holdings Ltd................................718 395-8706
  13620 38th Ave Ste 3g Flushing (11354) *(G-5223)*
Ajax Wire Specialty Co Inc................................516 935-2333
  119 Bloomingdale Rd Hicksville (11801) *(G-6318)*
Ajes Pharmaceuticals LLC................................631 608-1728
  11a Lincoln St Copiague (11726) *(G-3891)*
Ajl Manufacturing Inc.......................................585 254-1128
  100 Holleder Pkwy Rochester (14615) *(G-14184)*
Ajmadison Corp..718 532-1800
  3605 13th Ave Brooklyn (11218) *(G-1573)*
Aka Sport Inc...631 858-9888
  16 Princeton Dr Dix Hills (11746) *(G-4289)*
Akh Group LLC...646 320-8720
  601 W 26th St Rm M228 New York (10001) *(G-9066)*
Akhon Samoy Weekly, Flushing Also called Digital One USA Inc *(G-5238)*
Aki Cabinets Inc...718 721-2541
  2636 2nd St Astoria (11102) *(G-432)*
AKOS Group Ltd..212 683-4747
  315 5th Ave Fl 11 New York (10016) *(G-9067)*
Akraturn Mfg Inc..607 775-2802
  1743 Us Route 11 Kirkwood (13795) *(G-7231)*
Akribos Watches, Brooklyn Also called TWI Watches LLC *(G-2690)*
Akron-Corfu Pennysaver, Elma Also called R W Publications Div of Wtrhs *(G-4653)*

Akshar Extracts Inc 631 588-9727
59 Remington Blvd Ronkonkoma (11779) *(G-14858)*
Akzo Nobel Central Research, Dobbs Ferry *Also called Akzo Nobel Chemicals LLC (G-4300)*
Akzo Nobel Chemicals LLC 914 674-5008
7 Livingstone Ave Dobbs Ferry (10522) *(G-4300)*
Akzo Nobel Chemicals LLC 716 778-8554
2153 Lockport Olcott Rd Burt (14028) *(G-3268)*
Akzo Nobel Chemicals LLC 914 674-5432
9 Livingstone Ave Dobbs Ferry (10522) *(G-4301)*
Akzo Nobel Functional Chem LLC 845 276-8200
281 Fields Ln Brewster (10509) *(G-1208)*
Al Cohens Famous Rye Bread Bky, Buffalo *Also called Cohens Bakery Inc (G-2879)*
Al Energy Solutions Led Llc 646 380-6670
1140 Ave Of The Americas New York (10036) *(G-9068)*
Ala Scientific Instruments Inc 631 393-6401
60 Marine St Ste 1 Farmingdale (11735) *(G-4935)*
Alabaster Group Inc 516 867-8223
188 N Main St Freeport (11520) *(G-5382)*
Alabu Inc 518 665-0411
30 Graves Rd Mechanicville (12118) *(G-8224)*
Alabu Skin Care, Mechanicville *Also called Alabu Inc (G-8224)*
Aladdin Bakers Inc (PA) 718 499-1818
240 25th St Brooklyn (11232) *(G-1574)*
Aladdin Manufacturing Corp 212 561-8715
295 5th Ave Ste 1412 New York (10016) *(G-9069)*
Aladdin Packaging LLC 631 273-4747
115 Engineers Rd Hauppauge (11788) *(G-6014)*
Alamar Printing Inc 914 993-9007
190 E Post Rd Frnt 1 White Plains (10601) *(G-17074)*
Alan F Bourguet 516 883-4315
63 Essex Ct Port Washington (11050) *(G-13797)*
Alanelli Psle 212 828-6600
630 5th Ave New York (10111) *(G-9070)*
Alarm Controls Corporation 631 586-4220
19 Brandywine Dr Deer Park (11729) *(G-4090)*
Alart Inc 212 840-1508
578 5th Ave Unit 33 New York (10036) *(G-9071)*
Alba Fuel Corp 718 931-1700
2135 Wllmsbrdge Rd Fl 2 Bronx (10461) *(G-1266)*
Alba House Publishers 718 698-2759
2187 Victory Blvd Staten Island (10314) *(G-15633)*
Albaluz Films LLC 347 613-2321
954 Lexington Ave New York (10021) *(G-9072)*
Albany Asp & Aggregates Corp 518 436-8916
101 Dunham Dr Albany (12202) *(G-37)*
Albany Catholic Press Assoc 518 453-6688
40 N Main Ave Ste 2 Albany (12203) *(G-38)*
Albany International Corp 518 445-2230
1373 Broadway Menands (12204) *(G-8365)*
Albany International Corp 607 749-7226
156 S Main St Homer (13077) *(G-6515)*
Albany International Corp 518 447-6400
1373 Broadway Menands (12204) *(G-8366)*
Albany International Corp 518 445-2200
253 Troy Rd Rensselaer (12144) *(G-14042)*
Albany Letter Shop Inc 518 434-1172
16 Van Zandt St Ste 20 Albany (12207) *(G-39)*
Albany Molecular Research Inc 518 512-2234
21 Corporate Cir Albany (12203) *(G-40)*
Albany Molecular Research Inc 518 433-7700
81 Columbia Tpke Rensselaer (12144) *(G-14043)*
Albany Molecular Research Inc (PA) 518 512-2000
26 Corporate Cir Albany (12203) *(G-41)*
Albany Molecular Research Inc 518 512-2000
33 Riverside Ave Rensselaer (12144) *(G-14044)*
Albany Mtal Fbrcation Holdings 518 463-5161
67 Henry Johnson Blvd Albany (12210) *(G-42)*
Albany Nipple and Pipe Mfg 518 270-2162
60 Cohoes Ave Ste 100a Troy (12183) *(G-16218)*
Albany Student Press Inc 518 442-5665
1400 Washington Ave Cc329 Albany (12222) *(G-43)*
Albatros North America Inc 518 381-7100
6 Mccrea Hill Rd Ballston Spa (12020) *(G-590)*
Albea Cosmetics America Inc (HQ) 212 371-5100
595 Madison Ave Fl 10 New York (10022) *(G-9073)*
Albert Augustine Ltd 917 661-0220
151 W 26th St Fl 4 New York (10001) *(G-9074)*
Albert Gates Inc 585 594-9401
3434 Union St North Chili (14514) *(G-12924)*
Albert Kemperle Inc 718 629-1084
890 E 51st St Brooklyn (11203) *(G-1575)*
Albert Menin Interiors Ltd 212 876-3041
2417 3rd Ave Fl 3 Bronx (10451) *(G-1267)*
Albert Siy 718 359-0389
13508 Booth Memorial Ave Flushing (11355) *(G-5224)*
Albest Metal Stamping Corp 718 388-6000
1 Kent Ave Brooklyn (11249) *(G-1576)*
Albion Cosmetics Inc 212 869-1052
110 E 42nd St Rm 1506 New York (10017) *(G-9075)*
Albion-Holley Pennysaver Inc 585 589-5641
170 N Main St Albion (14411) *(G-161)*
Albrizio Couture, Brooklyn *Also called Albrizio Inc (G-1577)*
Albrizio Inc 212 719-5290
257 Varet St Ste Mgmt Brooklyn (11206) *(G-1577)*
Albro Gear & Instrument, Yaphank *Also called W J Albro Machine Works Inc (G-17408)*
Albumx Corp 914 939-6878
21 Grace Church St Port Chester (10573) *(G-13738)*
Alcatel-Lucent USA Inc 516 349-4900
1 Fairchild Ct Ste 340 Plainview (11803) *(G-13580)*
Alchemy Simya Inc 646 230-1122
161 Avnue Of The Americas New York (10013) *(G-9076)*
Alco Industries Inc 740 254-4311
2103 Route 9 Round Lake (12151) *(G-15036)*
Alco Plastics Inc 716 683-3020
35 Ward Rd Lancaster (14086) *(G-7301)*
Alco Products Div, Orchard Park *Also called Nitram Energy Inc (G-13285)*
Alco Products USA, Orchard Park *Also called Peerless Mfg Co (G-13289)*
Alcoa Fastening Systems 585 368-5049
181 Mckee Rd Rochester (14611) *(G-14185)*
Alcoa Fastening Systems 845 334-7203
1 Corporate Dr Kingston (12401) *(G-7175)*
Alcoa Fastening Systems Rings, Kingston *Also called Huck International Inc (G-7191)*
Alcoa Inc (PA) 212 836-2674
390 Park Ave Fl 12 New York (10022) *(G-9077)*
Alcoa Inc 716 358-6451
2632 S Work St Ste 24 Falconer (14733) *(G-4890)*
Alcoholics Anonymous Grapevine (PA) 212 870-3400
475 Riverside Dr Ste 1264 New York (10115) *(G-9078)*
Alconox, White Plains *Also called L S Z Inc (G-17133)*
Alconox Inc 914 948-4040
30 Glenn St Ste 309 White Plains (10603) *(G-17075)*
Alden Advertiser, Alden *Also called Weisbeck Publishing Printing (G-186)*
Alden Aurora Gas Company Inc 716 937-9484
13441 Railroad St Alden (14004) *(G-174)*
Alden Optical Laboratory Inc 716 937-9181
6 Lancaster Pkwy Lancaster (14086) *(G-7302)*
Aldine Inc (ny) 212 226-2870
150 Varick St Fl 5 New York (10013) *(G-9079)*
Aldo Frustacci Iron Works Inc 718 768-0707
165 27th St Brooklyn (11232) *(G-1578)*
Aldos Iron Works Inc 718 834-0408
75 Van Brunt St Brooklyn (11231) *(G-1579)*
Ale-Techniques Inc 845 687-7200
2452b Lucas Tpke High Falls (12440) *(G-6399)*
Alen Sands York Associates Ltd 212 563-6305
236 W 26th St Rm 801 New York (10001) *(G-9080)*
Alere Inc 516 767-1112
14 Vanderventer Ave Port Washington (11050) *(G-13798)*
Alessi International Limited 516 676-8841
51 Buckeye Rd Glen Cove (11542) *(G-5609)*
Aleta Industries Inc 718 349-0040
40 Ash St Brooklyn (11222) *(G-1580)*
Aleteia Usa Inc 914 502-1855
86 Main St Ste 303 Yonkers (10701) *(G-17410)*
Aletheas Chocolates Inc (PA) 716 633-8620
8301 Main St Williamsville (14221) *(G-17231)*
Alex Sepkus Inc 212 391-8466
42 W 48th St Ste 501 New York (10036) *(G-9081)*
Alexander Polakovich 718 229-6200
4235 Bell Blvd Bayside (11361) *(G-766)*
Alexander Primak Jewelry Inc 212 398-0287
529 5th Ave Fl 15 New York (10017) *(G-9082)*
Alexander Wang Incorporated (PA) 212 532-3103
386 Broadway Fl 3 New York (10013) *(G-9083)*
Alexandra Ferguson LLC 718 788-7768
34 35th St Unit 6 Brooklyn (11232) *(G-1581)*
Alexandre Furs, New York *Also called Samuel Schulman Furs Inc (G-11963)*
Alexandria Professional LLC 800 957-8427
15 Lawrence Bell Dr Williamsville (14221) *(G-17232)*
Alexandros, New York *Also called Anastasia First International (G-9149)*
Alexandros, New York *Also called Anastasia Furs International (G-9150)*
Alexis & Gianni Retail Inc 516 334-3877
405 Union Ave Westbury (11590) *(G-16964)*
Alexis Bittar LLC (PA) 718 422-7580
45 Main St Ste 725 Brooklyn (11201) *(G-1582)*
Alexscoe LLC 315 463-9207
6852 Manlius Center Rd East Syracuse (13057) *(G-4500)*
Alexy Associates Inc 845 482-3000
86 Jim Stephenson Rd Bethel (12720) *(G-859)*
Alfa Card Inc 718 326-7107
7915 Cooper Ave Glendale (11385) *(G-5643)*
Alfa Chem, Great Neck *Also called Alfred Khalily Inc (G-5787)*
Alfred B Parella 518 872-1238
20 Reservoir Rd Altamont (12009) *(G-206)*
Alfred Butler Inc 516 829-7460
107 Grace Ave Great Neck (11021) *(G-5786)*
Alfred Dunner Inc (PA) 212 478-4300
1411 Broadway Fl 24 New York (10018) *(G-9084)*
Alfred Khalily Inc 516 504-0059
2 Harbor Way Great Neck (11024) *(G-5787)*
Alfred Mainzer Inc (PA) 718 392-4200
2708 40th Ave Long Island City (11101) *(G-7650)*
Alfred Music, Oriskany *Also called Alfred Publishing Co Inc (G-13303)*

ALPHABETIC

Alfred Publishing Co Inc 315 736-1572
123 Dry Rd Oriskany (13424) ***(G-13303)***

Algafuel America 516 295-2257
289 Meadowview Ave Hewlett (11557) ***(G-6307)***

Algemeiner Journal Inc 718 771-0400
508 Montgomery St Brooklyn (11225) ***(G-1583)***

Algonquin Books Chapel Hl Div, New York *Also called Workman Publishing Co Inc* ***(G-12660)***

Algonquin Power 315 393-5595
19 Mill St Ogdensburg (13669) ***(G-13110)***

Ali & Kris, New York *Also called Brooke Leigh Ltd* ***(G-9469)***

Ali Ro, New York *Also called Donna Morgan LLC* ***(G-9904)***

Alice & Trixie, New York *Also called Millennium Productions Inc* ***(G-11267)***

Alice Perkins 716 378-5100
148 Washington St Salamanca (14779) ***(G-15099)***

Alicias Bakery Inc 914 235-4689
498 Main St Ste A New Rochelle (10801) ***(G-8885)***

Alison US LLC, Wellsville *Also called Arvos Holding LLC* ***(G-16748)***

Alison Wine & Vineyard, Rhinebeck *Also called Dutchess Wines LLC* ***(G-14056)***

Aljo Precision Products Inc 516 420-4419
205 Bethpge Sweet Holw Old Bethpage (11804) ***(G-13124)***

Aljo-Gefa Precision Mfg LLC 516 420-4419
205 Bethpage Sweet Holw Old Bethpage (11804) ***(G-13125)***

Alkemy Machine LLC 585 436-8730
1600 Lexington Ave 103c Rochester (14606) ***(G-14186)***

Alken Industries Inc 631 467-2000
2175 5th Ave Ronkonkoma (11779) ***(G-14859)***

All About Art Inc 718 321-0755
4128 Murray St Flushing (11355) ***(G-5225)***

All American Awards Inc 631 567-2025
331 Knickerbocker Ave Bohemia (11716) ***(G-1011)***

All American Building 607 797-7123
109 Crestmont Rd Binghamton (13905) ***(G-885)***

All American Concrete Corp 718 497-3301
239 Ingraham St Brooklyn (11237) ***(G-1584)***

All American Metal Corporation (PA) 516 223-1760
200 Buffalo Ave Freeport (11520) ***(G-5383)***

All American Metal Corporation 516 623-0222
200 Buffalo Ave Freeport (11520) ***(G-5384)***

All American Mold, West Henrietta *Also called All American Precision Tl Mold* ***(G-16865)***

All American Precision Tl Mold 585 436-3080
1325 John St West Henrietta (14586) ***(G-16865)***

All American Stairs & Railing 718 441-8400
13023 91st Ave Richmond Hill (11418) ***(G-14065)***

All American Transit Mix Corp 718 417-3654
46 Knickerbocker Ave Brooklyn (11237) ***(G-1585)***

All American Uniform, Bohemia *Also called All American Awards Inc* ***(G-1011)***

All Around Spiral Inc 631 588-0220
10 Fleetwood Ct Ronkonkoma (11779) ***(G-14860)***

All Cast Foundry, Brooklyn *Also called J & J Bronze & Aluminum Cast* ***(G-2121)***

All City Switchboard Corp 718 956-7244
3541 11th St Long Island City (11106) ***(G-7651)***

All Color Business Spc Ltd 516 420-0649
305 Suburban Ave Deer Park (11729) ***(G-4091)***

All Color Business Specialties, Farmingdale *Also called All Color Offset Printers Inc* ***(G-4936)***

All Color Offset Printers Inc 516 420-0649
51 Henry St Ste A Farmingdale (11735) ***(G-4936)***

All County Block & Supply Corp 631 589-3675
899 Lincoln Ave Bohemia (11716) ***(G-1012)***

All Craft Jewelry Supply, New York *Also called Creative Tools & Supply Inc* ***(G-9752)***

All Cultures Inc 631 293-3143
12 Gates St Greenlawn (11740) ***(G-5872)***

All Gone Restoration, Staten Island *Also called Occhioerosso John* ***(G-15718)***

All In Audio Inc 718 506-0948
5314 16th Ave Ste 83 Brooklyn (11204) ***(G-1586)***

All Island Blower & Shtmtl 631 567-7070
1585 Smithtown Ave Unit C Bohemia (11716) ***(G-1013)***

All Island Media Inc (PA) 631 698-8400
1 Rodeo Dr Edgewood (11717) ***(G-4592)***

All Island Media Inc 516 942-8400
325 Duffy Ave Unit 2 Hicksville (11801) ***(G-6319)***

All Merchandise Display Corp 718 257-2221
4 Pheasant Run Highland Mills (10930) ***(G-6411)***

All Metal Specialties Inc 716 664-6009
300 Livingston Ave Jamestown (14701) ***(G-6969)***

All Metro Emrgncy Response Sys 516 750-9100
50 Broadway Lynbrook (11563) ***(G-7945)***

All Net Ltd 516 504-4559
15 Cuttermill Rd Ste 145 Great Neck (11021) ***(G-5788)***

All Out Die Cutting Inc 718 346-6666
49 Wyckoff Ave Ste 1 Brooklyn (11237) ***(G-1587)***

All Packaging McHy & Sups Corp 631 588-7310
90 13th Ave Unit 11 Ronkonkoma (11779) ***(G-14861)***

All Phases Asp & Ldscpg Dsgn 631 588-1372
60 18th Ave Ronkonkoma (11779) ***(G-14862)***

All Products Designs 631 748-6901
227a Route 111 Smithtown (11787) ***(G-15482)***

All Racks Industries Inc 212 244-1069
361 W 36th St Frnt A New York (10018) ***(G-9085)***

All Ready Inc 607 722-0826
39 Carol Ct Conklin (13748) ***(G-3864)***

All Ready Printing, Conklin *Also called All Ready Inc* ***(G-3864)***

All Shore Industries Inc 718 720-0018
1 Edgewater St Ste 215 Staten Island (10305) ***(G-15634)***

All Signs 973 736-2113
63 Bridgetown St Staten Island (10314) ***(G-15635)***

All Spec Finishing Inc 607 770-9174
219 Clinton St Binghamton (13905) ***(G-886)***

All Star Awnings & Signs 516 742-8469
332 Sagamore Ave Mineola (11501) ***(G-8492)***

All Star Carts & Vehicles Inc 631 666-5581
1565 5th Industrial Ct B Bay Shore (11706) ***(G-668)***

All Star Fabricators, Thornwood *Also called Thornwood Products Ltd* ***(G-16122)***

All The Rage Inc 516 605-2001
147 W Cherry St Unit 1 Hicksville (11801) ***(G-6320)***

All Time Products Inc 718 464-1400
21167 Jamaica Ave Queens Village (11428) ***(G-13974)***

All Times Publishing LLC 315 422-7011
1415 W Genesee St Syracuse (13204) ***(G-15847)***

All Type Screw Machine Pdts 516 334-5100
100 New York Ave Westbury (11590) ***(G-16965)***

All United Window Corp 718 624-0490
85 Classon Ave 97 Brooklyn (11205) ***(G-1588)***

All Weather Outerwear, Brooklyn *Also called Lakeview Sportswear Corp* ***(G-2192)***

All-City Metal Inc 718 937-3975
5435 46th St Maspeth (11378) ***(G-8114)***

All-Lifts Incorporated 518 465-3461
27-39 Thatcher St Albany (12207) ***(G-44)***

All-Pro Imaging Corp 516 433-7676
1295 Walt Whitman Rd Melville (11747) ***(G-8292)***

All-State Diversified Pdts Inc 315 472-4728
8 Dwight Park Dr Syracuse (13209) ***(G-15848)***

All-Tech, Brooklyn *Also called Integra Microsystem 1988 Inc* ***(G-2109)***

Allan John Company 212 940-2210
611 5th Ave Fl 7 New York (10022) ***(G-9086)***

Allcom Electric Corp 914 803-0433
104 Crescent Pl Yonkers (10704) ***(G-17411)***

Allcraft Fabricators Inc 631 951-4100
150 Wireless Blvd Hauppauge (11788) ***(G-6015)***

Alle Processing Corp 718 894-2000
5620 59th St Maspeth (11378) ***(G-8115)***

Allegany Laminating and Supply 716 372-2424
158 W Main St Allegany (14706) ***(G-198)***

Alleghany Capital Corporation (HQ) 212 752-1356
7 Times Square Tower New York (10036) ***(G-9087)***

Allegiant Health, Deer Park *Also called Bli International Inc* ***(G-4109)***

Allegra Print & Imaging, Schenectady *Also called Capital Dst Print & Imaging* ***(G-15238)***

Allen Air, Mineola *Also called A K Allen Co Inc* ***(G-8488)***

Allen Avionics Inc 516 248-8080
255 E 2nd St Mineola (11501) ***(G-8493)***

Allen Boat Co Inc 716 842-0800
370 Babcock St Rear Buffalo (14206) ***(G-2802)***

Allen Field Co Inc 631 665-2782
256 Orinoco Dr Ste A Brightwaters (11718) ***(G-1238)***

Allen Machine Products Inc 631 630-8800
120 Ricefield Ln Ste 100 Hauppauge (11788) ***(G-6016)***

Allen Pickle Works Inc 516 676-0640
36 Garvies Point Rd Glen Cove (11542) ***(G-5610)***

Allen Tool Phoenix Inc 315 463-7533
6821 Ellicott Dr East Syracuse (13057) ***(G-4501)***

Allen William & Company Inc 212 675-6461
7119 80th St Ste 8315 Glendale (11385) ***(G-5644)***

Allen-Bailey Tag & Label Inc (PA) 585 538-2324
3177 Lehigh St Caledonia (14423) ***(G-3276)***

Allenair Corporation 516 747-5450
255 E 2nd St Mineola (11501) ***(G-8494)***

Alleson Athletic, Rochester *Also called Alleson of Rochester Inc* ***(G-14187)***

Alleson of Rochester Inc (PA) 585 272-0630
2921 Brighton Henrietta Rochester (14623) ***(G-14187)***

Alleson of Rochester Inc 315 789-8464
833 Canandaigua Rd Ste 40 Geneva (14456) ***(G-5569)***

Alley Cat Signs Inc 631 924-7446
506 Middle Country Rd Middle Island (11953) ***(G-8406)***

Alley Music Corp 212 779-7977
126 E 38th St New York (10016) ***(G-9088)***

Alliance Automation Systems 585 426-2700
400 Trabold Rd Rochester (14624) ***(G-14188)***

Alliance Control Systems Inc 845 279-4430
577 N Main St Ste 9 Brewster (10509) ***(G-1209)***

Alliance Innovative Mfg Inc 716 822-1626
1 Alliance Dr Lackawanna (14218) ***(G-7242)***

Alliance Magnetic LLC 914 944-1690
100 Executive Blvd # 202 Ossining (10562) ***(G-13320)***

Alliance Paving Materials Inc 315 337-0795
846 Lawrence St Rome (13440) ***(G-14803)***

Alliance Precision Plas Corp (PA) 585 426-5310
1220 Lee Rd Rochester (14606) ***(G-14189)***

Alliance Precision Plas Corp 585 426-5310
105 Elmore Dr Rochester (14606) ***(G-14190)***

Alliance Services Corp 516 775-7600
23 Van Siclen Ave Floral Park (11001) ***(G-5190)***

Alliance Welding & Steel Fabg 516 775-7600
15 Van Siclen Ave Floral Park (11001) *(G-5191)*
Alliant Tchsystems Oprtons LLC 631 737-6100
77 Raynor Ave Ronkonkoma (11779) *(G-14863)*
Allied, Buffalo *Also called Mibro Group (G-3064)*
Allied Aero Services Inc 631 277-9368
506 Grand Blvd Brentwood (11717) *(G-1175)*
Allied Bronze Corp (del Corp) 646 421-6400
32 Avenue Of The Americas New York (10013) *(G-9089)*
Allied Circuits LLC 716 551-0285
22 James E Casey Dr Buffalo (14206) *(G-2803)*
Allied Converters Inc 914 235-1585
64 Drake Ave New Rochelle (10805) *(G-8886)*
Allied Decorations Co Inc 315 637-0273
720 Erie Blvd W Syracuse (13204) *(G-15849)*
Allied Down Products Inc 718 389-5454
84 Oak St Brooklyn (11222) *(G-1589)*
Allied Food Products Inc 718 230-4227
251 Saint Marks Ave Brooklyn (11238) *(G-1590)*
Allied Industrial Products Co 716 664-3893
880 E 2nd St Jamestown (14701) *(G-6970)*
Allied Industries, Jamestown *Also called Allied Industrial Products Co (G-6970)*
Allied Inspection Services LLC 716 489-3199
2020 Allen Street Ext # 120 Falconer (14733) *(G-4891)*
Allied K & R Broom & Brush Co, Brooklyn *Also called K & R Allied Inc (G-2161)*
Allied Metal Spinning Corp 718 893-3300
1290 Viele Ave Bronx (10474) *(G-1268)*
Allied Motion Systems Corp (HQ) 716 691-5868
495 Commerce Dr Ste 3 Amherst (14228) *(G-220)*
Allied Motion Technologies Inc (PA) 716 242-8634
495 Commerce Dr Ste 3 Amherst (14228) *(G-221)*
Allied Motion Technologies Inc 315 782-5910
22543 Fisher Rd Watertown (13601) *(G-16634)*
Allied Orthopedics, Ozone Park *Also called Robert Cohen (G-13385)*
Allied Pharmacy Products Inc 516 374-8862
544 Green Pl Woodmere (11598) *(G-17310)*
Allied Products, New York *Also called Biofeedback Instrument Corp (G-9401)*
Allied Reproductions Inc 212 255-2472
121 Varick St Fl 9 New York (10013) *(G-9090)*
Allied Sample Card Co Inc 718 238-0523
140 58th St Ste 7a Brooklyn (11220) *(G-1591)*
Allied Sign Co, Syracuse *Also called Allied Decorations Co Inc (G-15849)*
Allied Tile Mfg Corp 718 647-2200
2840 Atlantic Ave Ste 3 Brooklyn (11207) *(G-1592)*
Allies GF Goodies LLC 516 216-1719
1b W Village Grn Hicksville (11801) *(G-6321)*
Allison Che Fashion Inc (PA) 212 391-1433
1400 Broadway Lbby 5 New York (10018) *(G-9091)*
Allmetal Chocolate Mold Co Inc 631 752-2888
135 Dale St West Babylon (11704) *(G-16768)*
Allomatic Products Company 516 775-0330
102 Jericho Tpke Ste 104 Floral Park (11001) *(G-5192)*
Alloy Machine & Tool Co Inc 516 593-3445
169 Vincent Ave Lynbrook (11563) *(G-7946)*
Alloy Metal Products LLC 315 676-2405
193 Us Route 11 Central Square (13036) *(G-3515)*
Alloy Metal Works Inc 631 694-8163
146 Verdi St Farmingdale (11735) *(G-4937)*
Alloyd Association Inc 516 248-8835
78 Sherman Ave Williston Park (11596) *(G-17260)*
Allred & Associates Inc 315 252-2559
321 Rte 5 W Elbridge (13060) *(G-4624)*
Allround Logistics Inc (PA) 718 544-8945
7240 Ingram St Forest Hills (11375) *(G-5321)*
Allround Maritime Services, Forest Hills *Also called Allround Logistics Inc (G-5321)*
Allsafe Technologies Inc 716 691-0400
290 Creekside Dr Amherst (14228) *(G-222)*
Allstar Casting Corporation 212 563-0909
240 W 37th St Frnt 7 New York (10018) *(G-9092)*
Allstate Banners, Long Island City *Also called Allstatebannerscom Corporation (G-7652)*
Allstate Gasket & Packing Inc 631 254-4050
31 Prospect Pl Deer Park (11729) *(G-4092)*
Allstate Sign & Plaque Corp 631 242-2828
70 Burt Dr Deer Park (11729) *(G-4093)*
Allstate Tool and Die Inc 585 426-0400
15 Coldwater Cres Rochester (14624) *(G-14191)*
Allstatebannerscom Corporation 718 300-1256
3511 9th St Long Island City (11106) *(G-7652)*
Allstateelectronics, Brooklyn *Also called Henrys Deals Inc (G-2073)*
Allsupermarkets, Ridgewood *Also called 333 J & M Food Corp (G-14096)*
Alltec Products, Westbury *Also called Power Scrub It Inc (G-17020)*
Alltek Labeling Systems, Staten Island *Also called Stoney Croft Converters Inc (G-15741)*
Allure Fashions Inc 516 829-2470
8 Barstow Rd Apt 2e Great Neck (11021) *(G-5789)*
Allure Jewelry and ACC LLC 646 226-8057
15 W 36th St Fl 12 New York (10018) *(G-9093)*
Allure Metal Works Inc 631 588-0220
71 Hoffman Ln Ronkonkoma (11749) *(G-14864)*
Allvac 716 433-4411
695 Ohio St Lockport (14094) *(G-7569)*
Allway Tools Inc 718 792-3636
1255 Seabury Ave Bronx (10462) *(G-1269)*
Allworth Communications Inc 212 777-8395
10 E 23rd St Ste 510 New York (10010) *(G-9094)*
Allworth Press, New York *Also called Allworth Communications Inc (G-9094)*
Allytex LLC 518 376-7539
540 Acland Blvd Ballston Spa (12020) *(G-591)*
Alm Media LLC (HQ) 212 457-9400
120 Broadway Fl 5 New York (10271) *(G-9095)*
Alm Media Holdings Inc (PA) 212 457-9400
120 Broadway Fl 5 New York (10271) *(G-9096)*
Almanac 845 334-8206
322 Wall St Kingston (12401) *(G-7176)*
Almond Group, Port Washington *Also called Almond Jewelers Inc (G-13799)*
Almond Jewelers Inc 516 933-6000
16 S Maryland Ave Port Washington (11050) *(G-13799)*
Almost Famous Clothing, New York *Also called Turn On Products Inc (G-12426)*
Alney Group Ltd 631 242-9100
435 Brook Ave Unit 16 Deer Park (11729) *(G-4094)*
Alnik Service Corporation 516 873-7300
20 Tulip Pl New Hyde Park (11040) *(G-8814)*
Alo Acquisition LLC (HQ) 518 464-0279
26 Corporate Cir Albany (12203) *(G-45)*
Aloi Materials Handling, Rochester *Also called Aloi Solutions LLC (G-14192)*
Aloi Solutions LLC (PA) 585 292-0920
660 W Metro Park Rochester (14623) *(G-14192)*
Alok Inc 212 643-4360
7 W 34th St Ste 79105 New York (10001) *(G-9097)*
Alonzo Fire Works Display Inc (PA) 518 664-9994
12 County Route 75 Mechanicville (12118) *(G-8225)*
Alp Steel Corp 716 854-3030
650 Exchange St Buffalo (14210) *(G-2804)*
Alp Stone Inc 718 706-6166
2520 50th Ave Fl 2 Long Island City (11101) *(G-7653)*
Alpargatas Usa Inc 646 277-7171
33 E 33rd St Rm 501 New York (10016) *(G-9098)*
Alpha 6 Distributions LLC 516 801-8290
11 Oyster Bay Rd Locust Valley (11560) *(G-7628)*
Alpha Boats Unlimited, Weedsport *Also called Barber Welding Inc (G-16746)*
Alpha DC Motors Inc 315 432-9039
5949 E Molloy Rd Syracuse (13211) *(G-15850)*
Alpha Fasteners Corp 516 867-6188
154 E Merrick Rd Freeport (11520) *(G-5385)*
Alpha Incorporated 718 765-1614
265 80th St Brooklyn (11209) *(G-1593)*
Alpha Iron Works LLC 585 424-7260
65 Goodway Dr S Rochester (14623) *(G-14193)*
Alpha Knitting Mills Inc 718 628-6300
41 Varick Ave Ste Mgmt Brooklyn (11237) *(G-1594)*
Alpha Manufacturing Corp 631 249-3700
152 Verdi St Farmingdale (11735) *(G-4938)*
Alpha Marine Repair 718 816-7150
88 Coursen Pl Staten Island (10304) *(G-15636)*
Alpha Media Group Inc (PA) 212 302-2626
415 Madison Ave Fl 3 New York (10017) *(G-9099)*
Alpha Packaging Industries Inc 718 267-4115
2004 33rd St Long Island City (11105) *(G-7654)*
Alpha Printing Corp 315 454-5507
131 Falso Dr Syracuse (13211) *(G-15851)*
Alpha-En Corporation (PA) 914 418-2000
120 White Plains Rd Tarrytown (10591) *(G-16085)*
Alphabet Holding Company Inc (HQ) 631 200-2000
2100 Smithtown Ave Ronkonkoma (11779) *(G-14865)*
AlphaGraphics, Rochester *Also called Bittner Company LLC (G-14233)*
AlphaGraphics, Lake View *Also called Delaware Graphics LLC (G-7280)*
AlphaGraphics, Hempstead *Also called Myrtle Leola Inc (G-6281)*
Alphamed Bottles Inc 631 275-5042
360 Oser Ave Hauppauge (11788) *(G-6017)*
Alpina Color Graphics Inc 212 285-2700
27 Cliff St Rm 502 New York (10038) *(G-9100)*
Alpina Copyworld Inc (PA) 212 683-3511
102 Madison Ave Frnt B New York (10016) *(G-9101)*
Alpina Digital, New York *Also called Alpina Copyworld Inc (G-9101)*
Alpina Foods Inc 855 886-1914
5011 Agpark Dr W Batavia (14020) *(G-621)*
Alpine Business Group Inc (PA) 212 989-4198
30 E 33rd St Frnt B New York (10016) *(G-9102)*
Alpine Creations Ltd 212 308-9353
17 E 48th St Fl 6 New York (10017) *(G-9103)*
Alpine Creative Group, New York *Also called Alpine Business Group Inc (G-9102)*
Alpine Machine Inc 607 272-1344
1616 Trumansburg Rd Ithaca (14850) *(G-6818)*
Alpine Overhead Doors Inc 631 456-7800
8 Hulse Rd Ste 1 East Setauket (11733) *(G-4475)*
Alpine Paper Box Co Inc 718 345-4040
2246 Fulton St Brooklyn (11233) *(G-1595)*
Alps Provision Co Inc 718 721-4477
2270 45th St Astoria (11105) *(G-433)*
Alps Sweet Shop, Beacon *Also called Hudson Valley Chocolatier Inc (G-785)*
Alrajs Inc (PA) 631 225-0300
146 Albany Ave Lindenhurst (11757) *(G-7452)*

ALPHABETIC

Alro Machine Tool & Die Co Inc 631 226-5020
585 W Hoffman Ave Lindenhurst (11757) *(G-7453)*
Alrod Associates Inc 631 981-2193
710 Union Pkwy Ste 9 Ronkonkoma (11779) *(G-14866)*
Alry Tool and Die Co Inc 716 693-2419
386 Fillmore Ave Tonawanda (14150) *(G-16137)*
Alside Supply Center, Ronkonkoma *Also called Associated Materials LLC (G-14873)*
Alstom Signaling Inc (HQ) 585 783-2000
1 River Rd Schenectady (12345) *(G-15228)*
Alstom Signaling Inc 585 274-8700
1 River Rd Schenectady (12345) *(G-15229)*
Alstom Transportation Inc 212 692-5353
641 Lexington Ave Fl 28 New York (10022) *(G-9104)*
Alstom Transportation Inc 800 717-4477
1025 John St Ste 100h West Henrietta (14586) *(G-16866)*
Alstrom Corporation 718 824-4901
1408 Seabury Ave Bronx (10461) *(G-1270)*
Alstrom Trnspt Info Solutions, Schenectady *Also called Alstom Signaling Inc (G-15228)*
Alta Group Inc 905 262-5707
210 S 8th St Lewiston (14092) *(G-7433)*
Alta Industries Ltd 845 586-3336
46966 State Hwy 30 Halcottsville (12438) *(G-5904)*
Alta Log Homes, Halcottsville *Also called Alta Industries Ltd (G-5904)*
Altaire Pharmaceuticals Inc 631 722-5988
311 West Ln Aquebogue (11931) *(G-383)*
Altamont Spray Welding Inc 518 861-8870
133 Lewis Rd Altamont (12009) *(G-207)*
Altaquip LLC 631 580-4740
200 13th Ave Unit 6 Ronkonkoma (11779) *(G-14867)*
Altec Datacom LLC 631 242-2417
70 Corbin Ave Ste I Bay Shore (11706) *(G-669)*
Alternative Service Inc 631 345-9500
111 Old Dock Rd Yaphank (11980) *(G-17385)*
Alternative Technology Corp 914 478-5900
1 North St Ste 1 Hastings On Hudson (10706) *(G-6002)*
Alternatives For Children 631 271-0777
600 S Service Rd Dix Hills (11746) *(G-4290)*
Altius Aviation LLC 315 455-7555
113 Tuskegee Rd Ste 2 Syracuse (13211) *(G-15852)*
Altman Lighting, Yonkers *Also called Altman Stage Lighting Co Inc (G-17412)*
Altman Stage Lighting Co Inc 914 476-7987
57 Alexander St Yonkers (10701) *(G-17412)*
Alton Manufacturing Inc 585 458-2600
825 Lee Rd Rochester (14606) *(G-14194)*
Altro Business Forms Div, New York *Also called New Deal Printing Corp (G-11382)*
Altronix Corp 718 567-8181
140 58th St Bldg A3w Brooklyn (11220) *(G-1596)*
Altum Press, Long Island City *Also called Cama Graphics Inc (G-7692)*
Altype Fire Door Corp 718 292-3500
9 Bruckner Blvd Bronx (10454) *(G-1271)*
Aluf Plastics Division, Orangeburg *Also called API Industries Inc (G-13218)*
Alufoil Products Co Inc 631 231-4141
135 Oser Ave Ste 3 Hauppauge (11788) *(G-6018)*
Alumi-Tech LLC 585 663-7010
1640 Harris Rd Penfield (14526) *(G-13497)*
Alumidock, Randolph *Also called Metallic Ladder Mfg Corp (G-14016)*
Alumil Fabrication Inc 845 469-2874
1900 Corporate Blvd Newburgh (12550) *(G-12748)*
Aluminum Injection Mold Co LLC 585 502-6087
8741 Lake Street Rd Ste 4 Le Roy (14482) *(G-7402)*
Alumiseal Corp 518 329-2820
118 N Mountain Rd Copake Falls (12517) *(G-3888)*
Alvanon Inc 212 868-4314
145 W 30th St Fl 10 New York (10001) *(G-9105)*
Alvin J Bart, Glendale *Also called Allen William & Company Inc (G-5644)*
Alvin J Bart & Sons Inc 718 417-1300
7119 80th St Ste 8315 Glendale (11385) *(G-5645)*
Alvin Valley Direct LLC 212 392-4725
146 W 28th St Apt 5 New York (10001) *(G-9106)*
Alvina Vlenta Couture Collectn 212 921-7058
525 Fashion Ave Rm 1703 New York (10018) *(G-9107)*
Alvina Vlenta Couture Collectn 212 921-7058
225 W 37th St New York (10018) *(G-9108)*
Always Baked Fresh 631 648-0811
331 Dante Ct Ste F Holbrook (11741) *(G-6431)*
Always Printing 914 481-5209
149 Highland St Port Chester (10573) *(G-13739)*
AM Architectural Metal & Glass 845 942-8848
5 Bridge St Garnerville (10923) *(G-5553)*
AM Bickford Inc 716 652-1590
12318 Big Tree Rd Wales Center (14169) *(G-16539)*
AM Display, Highland Mills *Also called All Merchandise Display Corp (G-6411)*
Am-Best Emblems, Boiceville *Also called Stucki Embroidery Works Inc (G-1158)*
Am-Pol Eagle, Buffalo *Also called Buffalo Standard Printing Corp (G-2860)*
AMA Precision Screening Inc 585 293-0820
456 Sanford Rd N Churchville (14428) *(G-3633)*
Amacon Corporation 631 293-1888
49 Alder St Unit A West Babylon (11704) *(G-16769)*
Amada Tool America Inc 585 344-3900
4 Treadeasy Ave Ste A Batavia (14020) *(G-622)*

Amadeo Serrano 516 608-8359
36 Frankel Ave Freeport (11520) *(G-5386)*
Amalfi Ingredients LLC 631 392-1526
94 E Jefryn Blvd Ste H Deer Park (11729) *(G-4095)*
Amana Tool Corp 631 752-1300
120 Carolyn Blvd Farmingdale (11735) *(G-4939)*
Amarr Company 585 426-8290
550 Mile Crssing Blvd 1 Rochester (14624) *(G-14195)*
Amarr Garage Doors, Rochester *Also called Amarr Company (G-14195)*
Amax Industrial Products, Bohemia *Also called Brockyn Corporation (G-1027)*
Amax Printing Inc 718 384-8600
6417 Grand Ave Maspeth (11378) *(G-8116)*
Amazing Meals, Maspeth *Also called Alle Processing Corp (G-8115)*
Amber Bever Inc 212 391-4911
110 W 40th St Rm 204 New York (10018) *(G-9109)*
Ambind Corp 716 836-4365
Cheektowaga Buffalo (14225) *(G-2805)*
Ambras Fine Jewelry Inc 718 784-5252
3100 47th Ave Unit 3 Long Island City (11101) *(G-7655)*
Ambras Fjc, Long Island City *Also called Ambras Fine Jewelry Inc (G-7655)*
Ambrell, Scottsville *Also called Ameritherm Inc (G-15334)*
Ambrell Inc 585 889-9000
39 Main St Ste 1 Scottsville (14546) *(G-15333)*
Amby International Inc 718 645-0964
1460 E 12th St Brooklyn (11230) *(G-1597)*
Amci Ltd 718 937-5858
3302 48th Ave Long Island City (11101) *(G-7656)*
Amco Intl Mfg & Design Inc 718 388-8668
10 Conselyea St Brooklyn (11211) *(G-1598)*
Amcom Software Inc 212 951-7600
256 W 38th St Fl 8 New York (10018) *(G-9110)*
Amcor Rigid Plastics Usa LLC 716 366-2440
1 Cliffstar Ave Dunkirk (14048) *(G-4331)*
Amendola MBL & Stone Ctr Inc 914 997-7968
560 Tarrytown Rd White Plains (10607) *(G-17076)*
Amereon Ltd 631 298-5100
800 Wickham Ave Mattituck (11952) *(G-8206)*
Amerex Corporation 212 221-3151
512 7th Ave Fl 9 New York (10018) *(G-9111)*
Ameri Serv South, Jamestown *Also called Vac Air Service Inc (G-7042)*
Ameribag Outdoors 845 339-4082
5 Ameribag Dr Kingston (12401) *(G-7177)*
America Capital Energy Corp 212 983-8316
405 Lexington Ave Fl 65 New York (10174) *(G-9112)*
America Latina, Port Chester *Also called Westmore News Inc (G-13761)*
America NY Rl Wang Fd Group Co 718 628-8999
5885 58th Ave Maspeth (11378) *(G-8117)*
America Press Inc (PA) 212 581-4640
106 W 56th St New York (10019) *(G-9113)*
American Access Care LLC 631 582-9729
32 Central Ave Hauppauge (11788) *(G-6019)*
American Acrylic Corporation 631 422-2200
400 Sheffield Ave West Babylon (11704) *(G-16770)*
American Aerogel Corporation 585 328-2140
460 Buffalo Rd Ste 200a Rochester (14611) *(G-14196)*
American Aerospace Contrls Inc 631 694-5100
570 Smith St Farmingdale (11735) *(G-4940)*
American Almond Pdts Co Inc (PA) 718 875-8310
103 Walworth St Brooklyn (11205) *(G-1599)*
American Apparel Ltd 516 504-4559
15 Cuttermill Rd Ste 145 Great Neck (11021) *(G-5790)*
American Apparel Trading Corp (PA) 212 764-5990
209 W 38th St Rm 1004 New York (10018) *(G-9114)*
American Attitude, New York *Also called Kww Productions Corp (G-10896)*
American Auto ACC Incrporation (PA) 718 886-6600
3506 Leavitt St Apt Cfc Flushing (11354) *(G-5226)*
American Avionic Tech Corp 631 924-8200
25 Industrial Blvd Medford (11763) *(G-8234)*
American Best Cabinets Inc 845 369-6666
397 Spook Rock Rd Suffern (10901) *(G-15785)*
American Bio Medica Corp (PA) 518 758-8158
122 Smith Rd Kinderhook (12106) *(G-7167)*
American Bluestone LLC 607 369-2235
760 Quarry Rd Sidney (13838) *(G-15435)*
American Blvd Auto Sups Inc 718 328-1984
911 Jennings St Bronx (10460) *(G-1272)*
American Boiler Tank Wldg Inc 518 463-5012
53 Pleasant St Albany (12207) *(G-46)*
American Bottling Company 516 714-0002
2004 Orville Dr N Ronkonkoma (11779) *(G-14868)*
American Bptst Chrches Mtro NY 212 870-3195
527 W 22nd St New York (10011) *(G-9115)*
American Business Forms Inc 716 836-5111
3840 E Robinson Rd # 249 Amherst (14228) *(G-223)*
American Canvas Binders Corp 914 969-0300
430 Nepperhan Ave Yonkers (10701) *(G-17413)*
American Car Signs Inc 518 227-1173
1483 W Duane Lake Rd Duanesburg (12056) *(G-4324)*
American Casting and Mfg Corp (PA) 800 342-0333
51 Commercial St Plainview (11803) *(G-13581)*
American Casting and Mfg Corp 516 349-7010
65 S Terminal Dr Plainview (11803) *(G-13582)*

American Challenge Enterprises 631 595-7171
1804 Plaza Ave Ste 6 New Hyde Park (11040) ***(G-8815)***
American Chimney Supplies Inc 631 434-2020
129 Oser Ave Ste B Hauppauge (11788) ***(G-6020)***
American Cigar 718 969-0008
6940 Fresh Meadow Ln Fresh Meadows (11365) ***(G-5438)***
American City Bus Journals Inc 716 541-1654
465 Main St Ste 100 Buffalo (14203) ***(G-2806)***
American Cleaning Solutions, Long Island City *Also called American Wax Company Inc* ***(G-7658)***
American Comfort Direct LLC 201 364-8309
708 3rd Ave Fl 6 New York (10017) ***(G-9116)***
American Country Quilts & Lin 631 283-5466
134 Mariner Dr Unit C Southampton (11968) ***(G-15538)***
American Craft Jewelers Inc (PA) 718 972-0945
3611 14th Ave Ste 522 Brooklyn (11218) ***(G-1600)***
American Crmic Process RES LLC 315 828-6268
835 Mcivor Rd Phelps (14532) ***(G-13529)***
American Culture, Greenlawn *Also called All Cultures Inc* ***(G-5872)***
American Culture Hair Inc 631 242-3142
159 E 2nd St Huntington Station (11746) ***(G-6694)***
American Diagnostic Corp 631 273-6155
55 Commerce Dr Hauppauge (11788) ***(G-6021)***
American Dies Inc 718 387-1900
37 Provost St Brooklyn (11222) ***(G-1601)***
American Douglas Metals Inc 716 856-3170
99 Bud Mil Dr Buffalo (14206) ***(G-2807)***
American Dsplay Die Ctters Inc 212 645-1274
121 Varick St Rm 301 New York (10013) ***(G-9117)***
American Electronic Products 631 924-1299
86 Horseblock Rd Unit F Yaphank (11980) ***(G-17386)***
American Engnred Cmponents Inc 516 742-8386
40 Voice Rd Carle Place (11514) ***(G-3385)***
American Epoxy and Metal Inc 718 828-7828
83 Cushman Rd Scarsdale (10583) ***(G-15216)***
American Express Publishing, New York *Also called Time Inc Affluent Media Group* ***(G-12347)***
American Felt & Filter Co Inc 845 561-3560
361 Walsh Ave New Windsor (12553) ***(G-8931)***
American Filtration Tech Inc 585 359-4130
100 Thruway Park Dr West Henrietta (14586) ***(G-16867)***
American Foundrymens Society 315 468-6251
3000 Milton Ave Syracuse (13209) ***(G-15853)***
American Fuel Cell LLC 585 474-3993
1200 Ridgeway Ave Ste 123 Rochester (14615) ***(G-14197)***
American Glass Light, Newburgh *Also called Sandy Littman Inc* ***(G-12779)***
American Graphic Design Awards 212 696-4380
89 5th Ave Ste 901 New York (10003) ***(G-9118)***
American Healthcare Supply Inc 212 674-3636
304 Park Ave S New York (10010) ***(G-9119)***
American Heritage Magazine, New York *Also called Nsgv Inc* ***(G-11468)***
American Home Mfg LLC 718 855-0617
302 5th Ave New York (10001) ***(G-9120)***
American Hormones Inc 845 471-7272
69 W Cedar St Ste 2 Poughkeepsie (12601) ***(G-13886)***
American Hose & Hydralics, Bronx *Also called American Refuse Supply Inc* ***(G-1273)***
American Hsptals Patient Guide 518 346-1099
1890 Maxon Rd Ext Schenectady (12308) ***(G-15230)***
American Icon Industries Inc 845 561-1299
392 N Montgomery St Ste 2 Newburgh (12550) ***(G-12749)***
American Images Inc 716 825-8888
25 Imson St Buffalo (14210) ***(G-2808)***
American Inst Chem Engineers (PA) 646 495-1355
120 Wall St Fl 23 New York (10005) ***(G-9121)***
American Institute Physics Inc 516 576-2410
Hntngton Qad Ste 1n1-2 Melville (11747) ***(G-8293)***
American Intl Media LLC 845 359-4225
11 Martine Ave Ste 870 White Plains (10606) ***(G-17077)***
American Intl Trimming 718 369-9643
80 39th St Brooklyn (11232) ***(G-1602)***
American Intrmdal Cont Mfg LLC 631 774-6790
150 Motor Pkwy Ste 401 Hauppauge (11788) ***(G-6022)***
American Jewish Committee 212 891-1400
561 Fashion Ave Fl 16 New York (10018) ***(G-9122)***
American Jewish Congress Inc (PA) 212 879-4500
825 3rd Ave Fl 181800 New York (10022) ***(G-9123)***
American Lckr SEC Systems Inc 716 699-2773
12 Martha St Ellicottville (14731) ***(G-4640)***
American Leather Specialties 800 556-6488
87 34th St Unit 1 Brooklyn (11232) ***(G-1603)***
American Linear Manufacturers (PA) 516 333-1351
629 Main St Westbury (11590) ***(G-16966)***
American Marking Systems, Fulton *Also called Krengel Manufacturing Co Inc* ***(G-5467)***
American Material Processing 315 318-0017
2896 State Route 96 Clifton Springs (14432) ***(G-3713)***
American Media Inc 212 545-4800
4 New York Plz Fl 2 New York (10004) ***(G-9124)***
American Medical & Dental Sups 845 517-5876
100 Red Schoolhouse Rd A6 Spring Valley (10977) ***(G-15578)***
American Metal, Rome *Also called Nash Metalware Co Inc* ***(G-14823)***
American Metal Spinning Pdts 631 454-6276
21 Eads St West Babylon (11704) ***(G-16771)***
American Metalcraft Marine 315 686-9891
690 Riverside Dr Clayton (13624) ***(G-3684)***
American Minerals Inc (HQ) 646 747-4222
21 W 46th St Fl 14 New York (10036) ***(G-9125)***
American Motive Power Inc 585 335-3132
9431 Foster Wheeler Rd Dansville (14437) ***(G-4075)***
American Mtal Stmping Spinning 718 384-1500
1 Nassau Ave Brooklyn (11222) ***(G-1604)***
American Office Supply Inc 516 294-9444
400 Post Ave Ste 105 Westbury (11590) ***(G-16967)***
American Originals Corporation 212 836-4155
1156 Ave Of Ste 710 New York (10036) ***(G-9126)***
American Orthotic Lab Co Inc 718 961-6487
924 118th St College Point (11356) ***(G-3778)***
American Package Company Inc 718 389-4444
226 Franklin St Brooklyn (11222) ***(G-1605)***
American Packaging Corporation (PA) 585 254-9500
777 Driving Park Ave Rochester (14613) ***(G-14198)***
American Precision Inds Inc (HQ) 716 691-9100
45 Hazelwood Dr Amherst (14228) ***(G-224)***
American Precision Inds Inc 716 652-3600
270 Quaker Rd East Aurora (14052) ***(G-4365)***
American Precision Inds Inc 585 496-5755
95 North St Arcade (14009) ***(G-386)***
American Pride Fasteners LLC 631 940-8292
195 S Fehr Way Bay Shore (11706) ***(G-670)***
American Print Solutions Inc 718 246-7800
561 President St Brooklyn (11215) ***(G-1606)***
American Print Solutions Inc (PA) 718 208-2309
2233 Nostrand Ave Ste 7 Brooklyn (11210) ***(G-1607)***
American Printing & Envelope, New York *Also called Apec Paper Industries Ltd* ***(G-9172)***
American Printing and Off Sups, Kingston *Also called Robert Tabatznik Assoc Inc* ***(G-7209)***
American Printing Eqp & Sup, Elmont *Also called Awt Supply Corp* ***(G-4717)***
American Products, Rochester *Also called American Time Mfg Ltd* ***(G-14201)***
American Profile Magazine, New York *Also called Publishing Group America Inc* ***(G-11747)***
American Puff Corp 516 379-1300
225 Buffalo Ave Freeport (11520) ***(G-5387)***
American Quality Embroidery (PA) 631 467-3200
740 Koehler Ave Ronkonkoma (11779) ***(G-14869)***
American Quality Technology 607 777-9488
6 Emma St Binghamton (13905) ***(G-887)***
American Racing Headers Inc 631 608-1427
880 Grand Blvd Deer Park (11729) ***(G-4096)***
American Recreational Products, Bohemia *Also called Ry-Lecia Inc* ***(G-1127)***
American Refrigeration Inc (HQ) 212 699-4000
142 W 57th St Fl 17 New York (10019) ***(G-9127)***
American Refuse Supply Inc 718 893-8157
521 Longfellow Ave Bronx (10474) ***(G-1273)***
American Regent Inc 631 924-4000
5 Ramsey Rd Shirley (11967) ***(G-15411)***
American Regent Laboratories, Shirley *Also called American Regent Inc* ***(G-15411)***
American Rock Salt Company LLC (PA) 585 991-6878
3846 Retsof Rd Retsof (14539) ***(G-14054)***
American Rolling Door Ltd 718 273-0485
40 Dolson Pl Staten Island (10303) ***(G-15637)***
American Scientific Ltg Corp 718 369-1100
25 12th St Ste 4 Brooklyn (11215) ***(G-1608)***
American Sealing Technology 631 254-0019
31 Prospect Pl Deer Park (11729) ***(G-4097)***
American Securities LLC 716 696-3012
330 Fire Tower Dr Tonawanda (14150) ***(G-16138)***
American Ship Repairs Company 718 435-5570
1011 38th St 13 Brooklyn (11219) ***(G-1609)***
American Signcrafters, Islip *Also called T J Signs Unlimited LLC* ***(G-6813)***
American Silk Mills, New York *Also called Gerli & Co Inc* ***(G-10286)***
American Specialty Mfg Co 585 544-5600
272 Hudson Ave Rochester (14605) ***(G-14199)***
American Sports Media 585 924-4250
106 Cobblestone Court Dr # 323 Victor (14564) ***(G-16460)***
American Sports Media LLC (PA) 585 377-9636
2604 Elmwood Ave Ste 343 Rochester (14618) ***(G-14200)***
American Spray-On Corp 212 929-2100
22 W 21st St Fl 2 New York (10010) ***(G-9128)***
American Standard Mfg Inc 518 868-2512
106 Industrial Park Ln Central Bridge (12035) ***(G-3482)***
American Steel Gate Corp 718 291-4050
10510 150th St Jamaica (11435) ***(G-6893)***
American T Shirts Inc 212 563-7125
225 W 39th St Fl 6 New York (10018) ***(G-9129)***
American Target Marketing Inc 518 725-4369
11 Cayadutta St Gloversville (12078) ***(G-5705)***
American Technical Ceramics (HQ) 631 622-4700
1 Norden Ln Huntington Station (11746) ***(G-6695)***
American Technical Ceramics 631 622-4700
17 Stepar Pl Huntington Station (11746) ***(G-6696)***
American Time Mfg Ltd 585 266-5120
1600 N Clinton Ave Ste 1 Rochester (14621) ***(G-14201)***
American Torque Inc 718 526-2433
10522 150th St Jamaica (11435) ***(G-6894)***
American Towman Expeditions, Warwick *Also called American Towman Network Inc* ***(G-16586)***

A L P H A B E T I C

(PA)=Parent Co (HQ)=Headquarters (DH)=Div Headquarters
2017 Harris
New York Manufacturers Directory
895

American Towman Network Inc 845 986-4546
7 West St Warwick (10990) **(G-16586)**
American Trans-Coil Corp 516 922-9640
69 Hamilton Ave Ste 3 Oyster Bay (11771) **(G-13365)**
American Trim Mfg Inc 518 239-8151
4750 State Hwy 145 Durham (12422) **(G-4355)**
American Turf Monthly, Great Neck *Also called Star Sports Corp* **(G-5842)**
American Vintage Wine Biscuit 718 361-1003
4003 27th St Long Island City (11101) **(G-7657)**
American Visual Display, Farmingdale *Also called American Visuals Inc* **(G-4941)**
American Visuals Inc 631 694-6104
90 Gazza Blvd Farmingdale (11735) **(G-4941)**
American Wax Company Inc 718 392-8080
3930 Review Ave Long Island City (11101) **(G-7658)**
American Wire Tie Inc (PA) 716 337-2412
2073 Franklin St North Collins (14111) **(G-12926)**
American Wood Column Corp 718 782-3163
913 Grand St Brooklyn (11211) **(G-1610)**
American Woods & Veneers Works 718 937-2195
4735 27th St Long Island City (11101) **(G-7659)**
Americana Vineyards & Winery 607 387-6801
4367 E Covert Rd Interlaken (14847) **(G-6746)**
Americo Group Inc 212 563-2700
498 7th Ave Fl 8 New York (10018) **(G-9130)**
Americo Group Inc (PA) 212 563-2700
1411 Broadway Fl 2 New York (10018) **(G-9131)**
Amerikom Group Inc 212 675-1329
247 W 30th St Rm 6w New York (10001) **(G-9132)**
Amerimade Coat Inc 212 216-0925
463 Fashion Ave Rm 802 New York (10018) **(G-9133)**
Ameritherm Inc (HQ) 585 889-0236
39 Main St Ste 1 Scottsville (14546) **(G-15334)**
Ameritool Mfg Inc 315 668-2172
64 Corporate Park Dr Central Square (13036) **(G-3516)**
Ameritool Mfg LLC 315 668-2172
20 Milo Dr West Monroe (13167) **(G-16909)**
Amertac Holdings Inc (PA) 610 336-1330
25 Robert Pitt Dr Monsey (10952) **(G-8567)**
Ames Advanced Materials Corp (HQ) 518 792-5808
50 Harrison Ave South Glens Falls (12803) **(G-15522)**
Ames Companies Inc 607 739-4544
114 Smith Rd Pine Valley (14872) **(G-13556)**
Ames Companies Inc 607 369-9595
196 Clifton St Unadilla (13849) **(G-16287)**
Ames Goldsmith Corp 518 792-7435
21 Rogers St Glens Falls (12801) **(G-5669)**
Ametal International, Brooklyn *Also called Kon Tat Group Corporation* **(G-2179)**
Ametek Inc 516 832-7710
300 Endo Blvd Garden City (11530) **(G-5494)**
Ametek Inc 607 763-4700
33 Lewis Rd Ste 6 Binghamton (13905) **(G-888)**
Ametek Inc 585 263-7700
255 Union St N Rochester (14605) **(G-14202)**
Ametek Power Instruments, Rochester *Also called Ametek Inc* **(G-14202)**
Ametek Rotron, Woodstock *Also called Rotron Incorporated* **(G-17365)**
Ametek Rotron, Woodstock *Also called Rotron Incorporated* **(G-17366)**
Ametek Rtron Technical Mtr Div, Saugerties *Also called Ametek Tchnical Indus Pdts Inc* **(G-15179)**
Ametek Tchnical Indus Pdts Inc 845 246-3401
75 North St Saugerties (12477) **(G-15179)**
Amfar Asphalt Corp 631 269-9660
137 Old Northport Rd Kings Park (11754) **(G-7169)**
AMG Global LLC (HQ) 212 689-6008
4 E 34th St New York (10016) **(G-9134)**
AMG Global NY & Enchante ACC, New York *Also called AMG Global LLC* **(G-9134)**
AMG Supply Company LLC 212 790-6370
1166 Av Of The Americas New York (10036) **(G-9135)**
Amherst Bee, Williamsville *Also called Bee Publications Inc* **(G-17235)**
Amherst Media Inc 716 874-4450
175 Rano St Ste 200 Buffalo (14207) **(G-2809)**
Amherst Stnless Fbrication LLC 716 691-7012
60 John Glenn Dr Amherst (14228) **(G-225)**
Amherst Systems Inc (HQ) 716 631-0610
1740 Wehrle Dr Buffalo (14221) **(G-2810)**
AMI, New York *Also called American Media Inc* **(G-9124)**
AMI Brands, Mamaroneck *Also called Brands Within Reach LLC* **(G-8025)**
Amica Magazine, New York *Also called Rizzoli Intl Publications Inc* **(G-11883)**
Amincor Inc 347 821-3452
1350 Ave Of Amrcas Fl 24 New York (10019) **(G-9136)**
Amiram Dror Inc (PA) 212 979-9505
226 India St Brooklyn (11222) **(G-1611)**
Amity Wood Industries, Amityville *Also called Amity Woodworking Inc* **(G-275)**
Amity Woodworking Inc 631 598-7000
25 Greene Ave Amityville (11701) **(G-275)**
Amneal Pharmaceuticals LLC 908 231-1911
50 Horseblock Rd Brookhaven (11719) **(G-1505)**
Amneal Pharmaceuticals NY LLC (HQ) 631 952-0214
50 Horseblock Rd Brookhaven (11719) **(G-1506)**
Amnews Corporation 212 932-7400
2340 Frdrick Duglass Blvd New York (10027) **(G-9137)**
Amoroso Wood Products Co Inc 631 249-4998
462 Old Country Rd Melville (11747) **(G-8294)**
Amoseastern Apparel Inc (PA) 212 921-1859
49 W 38th St Fl 7 New York (10018) **(G-9138)**
AMP-Line Corp 845 623-3288
3 Amethyst Ct West Nyack (10994) **(G-16910)**
Ampac Paper LLC (HQ) 845 778-5511
30 Coldenham Rd Walden (12586) **(G-16530)**
Ampacet Corporation (PA) 914 631-6600
660 White Plains Rd # 360 Tarrytown (10591) **(G-16086)**
Ampaco, Brooklyn *Also called American Package Company Inc* **(G-1605)**
Ampex Casting Corporation 212 719-1318
23 W 47th St Unit 3 New York (10036) **(G-9139)**
Amphenol Aerospace Industrial, Sidney *Also called Amphenol Corporation* **(G-15436)**
Amphenol Corporation 607 563-5364
40-60 Delaware Ave Sidney (13838) **(G-15436)**
Amphenol Corporation 607 563-5011
40-60 Delaware Ave Sidney (13838) **(G-15437)**
Amphenol Intrconnect Pdts Corp (HQ) 607 754-4444
20 Valley St Endicott (13760) **(G-4795)**
Amplitech Inc 631 521-7738
620 Johnson Ave Ste 2 Bohemia (11716) **(G-1014)**
Amplitech Group Inc 631 521-7831
620 Johnson Ave Bohemia (11716) **(G-1015)**
Ampro International Inc 845 278-4910
30 Coventry Ln Brewster (10509) **(G-1210)**
Amri, Rensselaer *Also called Albany Molecular Research Inc* **(G-14044)**
Amri Rensselaer, Rensselaer *Also called Albany Molecular Research Inc* **(G-14043)**
Amri Rensselaer 518 512-2000
26 Corporate Cir Albany (12203) **(G-47)**
Amron Electronics Inc 631 737-1234
160 Gary Way Ronkonkoma (11779) **(G-14870)**
Amsale Aberra LLC 212 695-5936
318 W 39th St Fl 12 New York (10018) **(G-9140)**
Amscan Inc (HQ) 914 345-2020
80 Grasslands Rd Ste 3 Elmsford (10523) **(G-4732)**
Amscan Inc 845 469-9116
47 Elizabeth Dr Chester (10918) **(G-3599)**
Amscan Inc 845 782-0490
2 Commerce Dr S Harriman (10926) **(G-5970)**
Amsco Inc 716 823-4213
925 Bailey Ave Buffalo (14206) **(G-2811)**
Amsco School Publications Inc 212 886-6500
315 Hudson St Fl 5 New York (10013) **(G-9141)**
Amsterdam Color Works Inc 718 231-8626
3326 Merritt Ave Bronx (10475) **(G-1274)**
Amsterdam Oil Heat, Amsterdam *Also called J H Buhrmaster Company Inc* **(G-351)**
Amsterdam Pharmacy, New York *Also called Shrineeta Pharmacy Inc* **(G-12056)**
Amsterdam Printing & Litho Inc 518 792-6501
428 Corinth Rd Queensbury (12804) **(G-13987)**
Amsterdam Printing & Litho Inc 518 842-6000
166 Wallins Corners Rd Amsterdam (12010) **(G-332)**
Amsterdam Printing & Litho Inc 518 842-6000
166 Wallins Corners Rd Amsterdam (12010) **(G-333)**
Amsterdam Printing & Litho Inc 518 792-6501
428 Corinth Rd Queensbury (12804) **(G-13988)**
Amstutze Woodworking (PA) 518 946-8206
246 Springfield Rd Upper Jay (12987) **(G-16303)**
Amt Incorporated 518 284-2910
883 Chestnut St Sharon Springs (13459) **(G-15383)**
Amy Pak Publishing Inc 585 964-8188
3997 Roosevelt Hwy Holley (14470) **(G-6489)**
Amy Scherber Inc (PA) 212 462-4338
75 9th Ave New York (10011) **(G-9142)**
Amy's Bread, New York *Also called Amy Scherber Inc* **(G-9142)**
An Excelsior Elevator Corp 516 408-3070
640 Main St Unit 2 Westbury (11590) **(G-16968)**
An Group Inc 631 549-4090
17 Scott Dr Melville (11747) **(G-8295)**
An-Cor Industrial Plastics Inc 716 695-3141
900 Niagara Falls Blvd North Tonawanda (14120) **(G-12954)**
Anabec Inc 716 759-1674
9393 Main St Clarence (14031) **(G-3655)**
Anacor Acquisition, LLC, Rochester *Also called Anmar Acquisition LLC* **(G-14206)**
Anacor Pharmaceuticals Inc 212 733-2323
235 E 42nd St New York (10017) **(G-9143)**
Anage Inc 212 944-6533
530 Fashion Ave Frnt 5 New York (10018) **(G-9144)**
Analog Digital Technology LLC 585 698-1845
95 Mount Read Blvd # 149 Rochester (14611) **(G-14203)**
Analysts In Media (aim) Inc 212 488-1777
55 Broad St Fl 9 New York (10004) **(G-9145)**
Analytical Technology Inc (PA) 646 208-4643
80 Broad St New York (10004) **(G-9146)**
Analytics Intell, Garden City *Also called Informa Solutions Inc* **(G-5511)**
Anand Printing Machinery Inc 631 667-3079
188 W 16th St Deer Park (11729) **(G-4098)**
Anandamali Inc 212 343-8964
35 N Moore St New York (10013) **(G-9147)**
Anaren Inc (HQ) 315 432-8909
6635 Kirkville Rd East Syracuse (13057) **(G-4502)**

ALPHABETIC

Anaren Holding Corp (PA) 212 415-6700
590 Madison Ave Fl 41 New York (10022) ***(G-9148)***
Anaren Microwave Inc 315 432-8909
6635 Kirkville Rd East Syracuse (13057) ***(G-4503)***
Anasia Inc 718 588-1407
1175 Jerome Ave Bronx (10452) ***(G-1275)***
Anastasia First International 212 868-9241
345 7th Ave Fl 19 New York (10001) ***(G-9149)***
Anastasia Furs International (PA) 212 868-9241
345 7th Ave Fl 19 New York (10001) ***(G-9150)***
Anatoli Inc 845 334-9000
43 Basin Rd Ste 11 West Hurley (12491) ***(G-16901)***
Anbeck Inc 518 907-0308
75 S Broadway Fl 4 White Plains (10601) ***(G-17078)***
Anchor Canvas LLC 631 265-5602
556 W Jericho Tpke Smithtown (11787) ***(G-15483)***
Anchor Commerce Trading Corp 516 881-3485
53 Dutchess Blvd Atlantic Beach (11509) ***(G-468)***
Anchor Glass Container Corp 607 737-1933
151 E Mccanns Blvd Elmira Heights (14903) ***(G-4708)***
Anchor Tech Products Corp 914 592-0240
4 Vernon Ln Ste 2 Elmsford (10523) ***(G-4733)***
Ancient Modern Art LLC 212 302-0080
14 E 17th St Ph 1 New York (10003) ***(G-9151)***
Ancon Gear & Instrument Corp (PA) 631 694-5255
29 Seabro Ave Amityville (11701) ***(G-276)***
Andela Products, Richfield Springs *Also called Andela Tool & Machine Inc* ***(G-14061)***
Andela Tool & Machine Inc 315 858-0055
493 State Route 28 Richfield Springs (13439) ***(G-14061)***
Anderson Equipment Company 716 877-1992
2140 Military Rd Tonawanda (14150) ***(G-16139)***
Anderson Instrument Co Inc (HQ) 518 922-5315
156 Auriesville Rd Fultonville (12072) ***(G-5477)***
Anderson Precision Inc 716 484-1148
20 Livingston Ave Jamestown (14701) ***(G-6971)***
Andes Gold Corporation 212 541-2495
405 Lexington Ave New York (10174) ***(G-9152)***
Andex Corp 585 328-3790
69 Deep Rock Rd Rochester (14624) ***(G-14204)***
Andigo New Media Inc 212 727-8445
150 W 25th St Rm 900 New York (10001) ***(G-9153)***
Andike Millwork Inc (PA) 718 894-1796
5818 64th St Fl 2 Maspeth (11378) ***(G-8118)***
Andor Design Corp 516 364-1619
20 Pond View Dr Syosset (11791) ***(G-15812)***
Andrea Electronics Corporation (PA) 631 719-1800
620 Johnson Ave Ste 1b Bohemia (11716) ***(G-1016)***
Andrea Strongwater 212 873-0905
465 W End Ave New York (10024) ***(G-9154)***
Andrea Systems LLC 631 390-3140
140 Finn Ct Farmingdale (11735) ***(G-4942)***
Andrew M Schwartz LLC 212 391-7070
71 Gansevoort St Ste 2a New York (10014) ***(G-9155)***
Andrew Marc Outlet 631 727-2520
408 Tanger Mall Dr Riverhead (11901) ***(G-14138)***
Andrew Sapienza Bakery Inc 516 437-1715
553 Meacham Ave Elmont (11003) ***(G-4715)***
Andritz Inc 518 745-2988
13 Pruyns Island Dr Glens Falls (12801) ***(G-5670)***
Androme Leather Inc 518 773-7945
21 Foster St Gloversville (12078) ***(G-5706)***
Andros Manufacturing Corp 585 663-5700
30 Hojack Park Rochester (14612) ***(G-14205)***
Angel Media and Publishing 845 727-4949
26 Snake Hill Rd West Nyack (10994) ***(G-16911)***
Angel Textiles Inc 212 532-0900
519 8th Ave Fl 21 New York (10018) ***(G-9156)***
Angel-Made In Heaven Inc (PA) 212 869-5678
525 Fashion Ave Rm 1710 New York (10018) ***(G-9157)***
Angel-Made In Heaven Inc 718 832-4778
116 26th St Brooklyn (11232) ***(G-1612)***
Angelic Gourmet, Naples *Also called Naples Vly Mrgers Acqstons LLC* ***(G-8767)***
Angelica Forest Products Inc 585 466-3205
54 Closser Ave Angelica (14709) ***(G-376)***
Angelica Spring Company Inc 585 466-7892
99 West Ave Angelica (14709) ***(G-377)***
Angie Mangino 347 489-4009
366 Craig Ave Staten Island (10307) ***(G-15638)***
Angie Washroom, New Windsor *Also called Larcent Enterprises Inc* ***(G-8941)***
Angiodynamics Inc 518 792-4112
10 Glens Fls Technical Pa Glens Falls (12801) ***(G-5671)***
Angiodynamics Inc 518 742-4430
543 Queensbury Ave Queensbury (12804) ***(G-13989)***
Angiodynamics Inc 518 975-1400
603 Queensbury Ave Queensbury (12804) ***(G-13990)***
Angiodynamics Inc (PA) 518 795-1400
14 Plaza Dr Latham (12110) ***(G-7354)***
Angiogenex Inc (PA) 347 468-6799
425 Madison Ave Ste 902 New York (10017) ***(G-9158)***
Angiotech Biocoatings Corp 585 321-1130
336 Summit Point Dr Henrietta (14467) ***(G-6292)***
Ango Home, New York *Also called Feldman Company Inc* ***(G-10150)***
Angola Pennysaver Inc 716 549-1164
19 Center St Angola (14006) ***(G-379)***
Angus Buffers & Biochemicals, Niagara Falls *Also called Angus Chemical Company* ***(G-12796)***
Angus Chemical Company 716 283-1434
2236 Liberty Dr Niagara Falls (14304) ***(G-12796)***
Anheuser-Busch LLC 315 638-0365
2885 Belgium Rd Baldwinsville (13027) ***(G-566)***
Anheuser-Busch LLC 212 573-8800
250 Park Ave Fl 2 New York (10177) ***(G-9159)***
Anheuser-Busch Companies LLC 718 589-2610
510 Food Center Dr Bronx (10474) ***(G-1276)***
Anheuser-Busch Inbev Fin Inc 212 573-8800
250 Park Ave New York (10177) ***(G-9160)***
Anhui Skyworth LLC 917 940-6903
44 Kensington Ct Hempstead (11550) ***(G-6264)***
Anima Group LLC 917 913-2053
435 E 79th St Ph H New York (10075) ***(G-9161)***
Anima Mundi Herbals LLC 415 279-5727
2323 Borden Ave Long Island City (11101) ***(G-7660)***
Animal Fair Media Inc 212 629-0392
545 8th Ave Rm 401 New York (10018) ***(G-9162)***
Anka Tool & Die Inc 845 268-4116
150 Wells Ave Congers (10920) ***(G-3851)***
Ankom Development LLC 315 986-1937
2052 Oneil Rd Macedon (14502) ***(G-7980)***
Ankom Technology Corp 315 986-8090
2052 Oneil Rd Macedon (14502) ***(G-7981)***
Anmar Acquisition LLC (HQ) 585 352-7777
35 Vantage Point Dr Rochester (14624) ***(G-14206)***
Ann Gish Inc (PA) 212 969-9200
4 W 20th St New York (10011) ***(G-9163)***
Anna Sui Corp (PA) 212 768-1951
250 W 39th St Fl 15 New York (10018) ***(G-9164)***
Anna Young Assoc Ltd 516 546-4400
100 Doxsee Dr Freeport (11520) ***(G-5388)***
Anne Taintor Inc 718 483-9312
137 Montague St Brooklyn (11201) ***(G-1613)***
Annese & Associates Inc 716 972-0076
500 Corporate Pkwy # 106 Buffalo (14226) ***(G-2812)***
Anni Jewels, New York *Also called Dynamic Design Group Inc* ***(G-9947)***
Annointed Buty Ministries LLC 646 867-3796
1697 E 54th St Brooklyn (11234) ***(G-1614)***
Annuals Publishing Co Inc 212 505-0950
10 E 23rd St Ste 510 New York (10010) ***(G-9165)***
Anorad Corporation 631 380-2100
41 Research Way East Setauket (11733) ***(G-4476)***
Anritsu Instruments Company 315 797-4449
421 Broad St Ste 14 Utica (13501) ***(G-16307)***
Ansa Systems of USA Inc 516 887-6855
145 Hook Creek Blvd B6a1 Valley Stream (11581) ***(G-16400)***
Ansen Corporation (PA) 315 393-3573
100 Chimney Point Dr Ogdensburg (13669) ***(G-13111)***
Ansen Corporation 315 393-3573
100 Chimney Point Dr Ogdensburg (13669) ***(G-13112)***
Ansun Graphics Inc 315 437-6869
6392 Deere Rd Ste 4 Syracuse (13206) ***(G-15854)***
Answer Printing Inc 212 922-2922
505 8th Ave Rm 1101 New York (10018) ***(G-9166)***
Antab Mch Sprfinishing Lab Inc 585 865-8290
46 Latta Rd Rochester (14612) ***(G-14207)***
Antenna & Radome Res Assoc (PA) 631 231-8400
15 Harold Ct Bay Shore (11706) ***(G-671)***
Antenna Products, Amityville *Also called Edo LLC* ***(G-286)***
Anterios Inc 212 303-1683
60 E 42nd St Ste 1160 New York (10165) ***(G-9167)***
Anthony Gigi Inc 860 984-1943
45 Ramsey Rd Unit 28 Shirley (11967) ***(G-15412)***
Anthony L & S LLC (PA) 212 386-7245
500 Fashion Ave Fl 16b New York (10018) ***(G-9168)***
Anthony L&S Footwear Group, New York *Also called Anthony L & S LLC* ***(G-9168)***
Anthony Lawrence of New York 212 206-8820
3233 47th Ave Long Island City (11101) ***(G-7661)***
Anthony Manno & Co Inc 631 445-1834
307 Skidmores Rd Ste 2 Deer Park (11729) ***(G-4099)***
Anthony Manufacturing Inc 631 957-9424
34 Gear Ave Lindenhurst (11757) ***(G-7454)***
Anthony River Inc 315 475-1315
116 Granger St Syracuse (13202) ***(G-15855)***
Anthroposophic Press Inc (PA) 518 851-2054
15 Greenridge Dr Clifton Park (12065) ***(G-3695)***
Antico Casale Usa LLC 914 760-1100
1244 Clintonville St 2c Whitestone (11357) ***(G-17199)***
Antiques & Collectible Autos 716 825-3990
35 Dole St Buffalo (14210) ***(G-2813)***
Anton Community Newspapers, Mineola *Also called Long Island Cmnty Nwsppers Inc* ***(G-8522)***
Antonicelli Vito Race Car 716 684-2205
3883 Broadway St Buffalo (14227) ***(G-2814)***
Antwerp Diamond Distributors 212 319-3300
6 E 45th St Rm 302 New York (10017) ***(G-9169)***

ALPHABETIC

(PA)=Parent Co (HQ)=Headquarters (DH)=Div Headquarters
2017 Harris
New York Manufacturers Directory
897

Antwerp Sales Intl Inc ... 212 354-6515
576 5th Ave New York (10036) ***(G-9170)***
Anvil Knitwear, Inc., New York *Also called Gildan Apparel USA Inc* ***(G-10295)***
Anyelas Vineyards LLC ... 315 685-3797
2433 W Lake Rd Skaneateles (13152) ***(G-15455)***
Aoi Pharma Inc ... 212 531-5970
750 Lexington Ave Fl 20 New York (10022) ***(G-9171)***
Aos, Valley Stream *Also called Automated Office Systems Inc* ***(G-16401)***
AP&g Co Inc ... 718 492-3648
75 E 2nd St Brooklyn (11218) ***(G-1615)***
APC Paper Company Inc ... 315 384-4225
100 Remington Ave Norfolk (13667) ***(G-12897)***
APC-Mge, New York *Also called Schneider Electric It Corp* ***(G-11992)***
Apec Paper Industries Ltd ... 212 730-0088
237 W 37th St Rm 901 New York (10018) ***(G-9172)***
Apex Airtronics Inc (PA) ... 718 485-8560
2465 Atlantic Ave Brooklyn (11207) ***(G-1616)***
Apex Aridyne Corp ... 516 239-4400
168 Doughty Blvd Inwood (11096) ***(G-6750)***
Apex Packing & Rubber Co Inc ... 631 420-8150
1855 New Hwy Ste D Farmingdale (11735) ***(G-4943)***
Apex Signal Corporation ... 631 567-1100
110 Wilbur Pl Bohemia (11716) ***(G-1017)***
Apex Texicon Inc (PA) ... 516 239-4400
295 Madison Ave New York (10017) ***(G-9173)***
Apexx Omni-Graphics Inc ... 718 326-3330
5829 64th St Maspeth (11378) ***(G-8119)***
Apf Management Company LLC ... 914 665-5400
60 Fullerton Ave Yonkers (10704) ***(G-17414)***
Apf Manufacturing Company LLC (PA) ... 914 963-6300
60 Fullerton Ave Yonkers (10704) ***(G-17415)***
Apf Marine Co, Hauppauge *Also called Advanced Plstic Fbrctions Corp* ***(G-6010)***
Apf Munn Master Frame Makers, Yonkers *Also called Apf Manufacturing Company LLC* ***(G-17415)***
Apg Neuros, Plattsburgh *Also called Apgn Inc* ***(G-13651)***
Apgn Inc ... 518 324-4150
160 Banker Rd Plattsburgh (12901) ***(G-13651)***
Aphrodities ... 718 224-1774
2007 Francis Lewis Blvd Whitestone (11357) ***(G-17200)***
API, Central Islip *Also called Autronic Plastics Inc* ***(G-3485)***
API Deltran Inc ... 716 691-9100
45 Hazelwood Dr Amherst (14228) ***(G-226)***
API Heat Transf Thermasys Corp (HQ) ... 716 901-8504
2777 Walden Ave Buffalo (14225) ***(G-2815)***
API Heat Transfer Company (PA) ... 716 684-6700
2777 Walden Ave Ste 1 Buffalo (14225) ***(G-2816)***
API Heat Transfer Inc ... 585 496-5755
91 North St Arcade (14009) ***(G-387)***
API Industries Inc (PA) ... 845 365-2200
2 Glenshaw St Orangeburg (10962) ***(G-13218)***
API Industries Inc ... 845 365-2200
2 Glenshaw St Orangeburg (10962) ***(G-13219)***
API Technologies, Ronkonkoma *Also called Pace Technology Inc* ***(G-14963)***
API Technologies, Fairport *Also called Sendec Corp* ***(G-4877)***
API Technologies Corp, Auburn *Also called Spectrum Microwave Inc* ***(G-520)***
Apicella Jewelers Inc ... 212 840-2024
40 W 39th St Fl 4 New York (10018) ***(G-9174)***
Apogee Power Usa Inc ... 202 746-2890
7 Verne Pl Hartsdale (10530) ***(G-5997)***
Apogee Retail NY ... 516 731-1727
3041 Hempstead Tpke Levittown (11756) ***(G-7423)***
Apogee Translite Inc ... 631 254-6975
593 Acorn St Ste B Deer Park (11729) ***(G-4100)***
Apollo Apparel Group LLC ... 212 398-6585
1407 Broadway Rm 2000 New York (10018) ***(G-9175)***
Apollo Display Tech Corp (PA) ... 631 580-4360
87 Raynor Ave Ste 1 Ronkonkoma (11779) ***(G-14871)***
Apollo Investment Fund VII LP ... 212 515-3200
9 W 57th St Fl 43 New York (10019) ***(G-9176)***
Apollo Jeans, New York *Also called Apollo Apparel Group LLC* ***(G-9175)***
Apollo Lighting and Hasco Ltg, Mount Vernon *Also called Luminatta Inc* ***(G-8702)***
Apollo Optical Systems Inc ... 585 272-6170
925 John St West Henrietta (14586) ***(G-16868)***
Apollo Steel Corporation ... 716 283-8758
4800 Tomson Ave Niagara Falls (14304) ***(G-12797)***
Apollo Windows & Doors Inc ... 718 386-3326
1003 Metropolitan Ave Brooklyn (11211) ***(G-1617)***
Apothecus Pharmaceutical Corp (PA) ... 516 624-8200
220 Townsend Sq Oyster Bay (11771) ***(G-13366)***
Appairent Technologies Inc (PA) ... 585 214-2460
150 Lucius Gordon Dr West Henrietta (14586) ***(G-16869)***
Apparatus Mfg Inc ... 845 471-5116
13 Commerce St Poughkeepsie (12603) ***(G-13887)***
Apparel Group Ltd ... 212 328-1200
469 7th Ave Fl 8 New York (10018) ***(G-9177)***
Apparel Partnership Group LLC ... 212 302-7722
250 W 39th St Rm 701 New York (10018) ***(G-9178)***
Apparel Production Inc ... 212 278-8362
270 W 39th St Rm 1701 New York (10018) ***(G-9179)***
Appboy Inc ... 504 327-7269
263 W 38th St Fl 16 New York (10018) ***(G-9180)***
Appfigures Inc ... 212 343-7900
133 Chrystie St Fl 3 New York (10002) ***(G-9181)***
Applause Coating LLC ... 631 231-5223
8b Grand Blvd Brentwood (11717) ***(G-1176)***
Apple & Eve LLC (HQ) ... 516 621-1122
2 Seaview Blvd Ste 100 Port Washington (11050) ***(G-13800)***
Apple Beauty Inc ... 646 832-3051
214 W 39th St Rm 1006 New York (10018) ***(G-9182)***
Apple Commuter Inc ... 917 299-0066
54 Lake Dr New Hyde Park (11040) ***(G-8816)***
Apple Core Electronics Inc ... 718 628-4068
991 Flushing Ave Brooklyn (11206) ***(G-1618)***
Apple Digital Printing, Long Island City *Also called Apple Enterprises Inc* ***(G-7662)***
Apple Enterprises Inc ... 718 361-2200
1308 43rd Ave Long Island City (11101) ***(G-7662)***
Apple Healing & Relaxation ... 718 278-1089
3114 Broadway Long Island City (11106) ***(G-7663)***
Apple Imprints Apparel Inc ... 716 893-1130
2336 Bailey Ave Buffalo (14211) ***(G-2817)***
Apple Press ... 914 723-6660
23 Harrison Blvd White Plains (10604) ***(G-17079)***
Apple Rubber Products Inc (PA) ... 716 684-6560
310 Erie St Lancaster (14086) ***(G-7303)***
Apple Rubber Products Inc ... 716 684-7649
204 Cemetery Rd Lancaster (14086) ***(G-7304)***
Application Security Inc (HQ) ... 212 912-4100
55 Broad St Rm 10a New York (10004) ***(G-9183)***
Applied Coatings Holding Corp (PA) ... 585 482-0300
1653 E Main St Ste 1 Rochester (14609) ***(G-14208)***
Applied Concepts Inc ... 315 696-6676
397 State Route 281 Tully (13159) ***(G-16273)***
Applied Energy Solutions LLC ... 585 538-3270
1 Technology Pl Caledonia (14423) ***(G-3277)***
Applied Image Inc ... 585 482-0300
1653 E Main St Ste 1 Rochester (14609) ***(G-14209)***
Applied Minerals Inc (PA) ... 212 226-4265
110 Greene St Ste 1101 New York (10012) ***(G-9184)***
Applied Power Systems Inc ... 516 935-2230
124 Charlotte Ave Hicksville (11801) ***(G-6322)***
Applied Safety LLC ... 718 608-6292
4349 10th St Ste 311 Long Island City (11101) ***(G-7664)***
Applied Technology Mfg Corp ... 607 687-2200
71 Temple St Owego (13827) ***(G-13350)***
Applied Terminal Systems, Auburn *Also called Daikin Applied Americas Inc* ***(G-491)***
Applince Installation Svc Corp (PA) ... 716 884-7425
3190 Genesee St Buffalo (14225) ***(G-2818)***
Apprenda Inc (PA) ... 518 383-2130
433 River St Fl 4 Troy (12180) ***(G-16225)***
Apprise Mobile, New York *Also called Theirapp LLC* ***(G-12312)***
Appsbidder Inc ... 917 880-4269
55 Clark St 772 Brooklyn (11201) ***(G-1619)***
April Printing Co Inc ... 212 685-7455
1201 Broadway Ste 403 New York (10001) ***(G-9185)***
APS Enterprise Software Inc ... 631 784-7720
775 Park Ave Huntington (11743) ***(G-6654)***
Apsco Sports Enterprises Inc ... 718 965-9500
50th & 1st Ave Bldg 57 Brooklyn (11232) ***(G-1620)***
Apsis USA Inc ... 631 421-6800
1855 New Hwy Ste B Farmingdale (11735) ***(G-4944)***
Aptar Congers, Congers *Also called Aptargroup Inc* ***(G-3852)***
Aptargroup Inc ... 845 639-3700
250 N Route 303 Congers (10920) ***(G-3852)***
APV Crepaco, Getzville *Also called SPX Flow Tech Systems Inc* ***(G-5604)***
Apx Arstan Products, Hicksville *Also called Arstan Products International* ***(G-6324)***
Apx Technologies Inc ... 516 433-1313
264 Duffy Ave Hicksville (11801) ***(G-6323)***
Aquarii Inc ... 315 672-8807
17 Genesee St Camillus (13031) ***(G-3321)***
Aquarium Pump & Piping Systems ... 631 567-5555
528 Chester Rd Sayville (11782) ***(G-15203)***
Aquifer Drilling & Testing Inc (PA) ... 516 616-6026
75 E 2nd St Mineola (11501) ***(G-8495)***
AR & AR Jewelry Inc ... 212 764-7916
31 W 47th St Fl 15 New York (10036) ***(G-9186)***
AR Media Inc ... 212 352-0731
601 W 26th St Rm 810 New York (10001) ***(G-9187)***
AR Publishing Company Inc ... 212 482-0303
55 Broad St Rm 20b New York (10004) ***(G-9188)***
Arabella Textiles LLC ... 212 679-0611
303 5th Ave Rm 1402 New York (10016) ***(G-9189)***
Aramsco Inc ... 718 361-7540
1819 Flushing Ave Ste 2 Ridgewood (11385) ***(G-14099)***
Arbe Machinery Inc ... 631 756-2477
54 Allen Blvd Farmingdale (11735) ***(G-4945)***
Arbeit Bros Inc ... 212 736-9761
345 7th Ave Fl 20 New York (10001) ***(G-9190)***
Arbor Books Inc ... 201 236-9990
244 Madison Ave New York (10016) ***(G-9191)***
Arbor Valley Flooring, Salamanca *Also called Norton-Smith Hardwoods Inc* ***(G-15103)***
Arborn Printing & Graphics, Mamaroneck *Also called Division Den-Bar Enterprises* ***(G-8033)***
ARC Music Corporation ... 212 492-9414
630 9th Ave Ste 1212 New York (10036) ***(G-9192)***

ALPHABETIC

ARC Remanufacturing Inc..........718 728-0701
1940 42nd St Long Island City (11105) *(G-7665)*
ARC Systems Inc..........631 582-8020
2090 Joshuas Path Hauppauge (11788) *(G-6023)*
ARC TEC Wldg & Fabrication Inc..........718 982-9274
15 Harrison Ave Staten Island (10302) *(G-15639)*
Arca Ink..........518 798-0100
4 Highland Ave Queensbury (12804) *(G-13991)*
Arcade Inc..........212 541-2600
1700 Broadway Fl 25 New York (10019) *(G-9193)*
Arcade Bookbinding Corp..........718 366-8484
801 Wyckoff Ave Ridgewood (11385) *(G-14100)*
Arcade Glass Works, Chaffee *Also called Hart To Hart Industries Inc (G-3534)*
Arcade Herald, Arcade *Also called Neighbor To Neighbor News Inc (G-397)*
Arcadia Chem Preservative LLC..........516 466-5258
100 Great Neck Rd Apt 5b Great Neck (11021) *(G-5791)*
Arcadia Mfg Group Inc (PA)..........518 434-6213
80 Cohoes Ave Green Island (12183) *(G-5853)*
Arcadia Mfg Group Inc..........518 434-6213
1032 Broadway Menands (12204) *(G-8367)*
Arcangel Inc..........347 771-0789
209 W 38th St Rm 1001 New York (10018) *(G-9194)*
Archaelogy Magazine..........718 472-3050
3636 33rd St Ste 301 Long Island City (11106) *(G-7666)*
Archer-Daniels-Midland Company..........716 849-7333
250 Ganson St Buffalo (14203) *(G-2819)*
Archer-Daniels-Midland Company..........518 828-4691
201 State Route 23b Hudson (12534) *(G-6605)*
Archer-Daniels-Midland Company..........518 828-4691
Ste B Rr 23 Hudson (12534) *(G-6606)*
Archer-Daniels-Midland Company..........585 346-2311
3401 Rochester Rd Lakeville (14480) *(G-7282)*
Archie Comic Publications Inc..........914 381-5155
629 Fifth Ave Pelham (10803) *(G-13488)*
Archie Comics Publishers, Pelham *Also called Archie Comic Publications Inc (G-13488)*
Archimedes Products Inc..........631 589-1215
21 Floyds Run Bohemia (11716) *(G-1018)*
Architctral Dsign Elements LLC..........718 218-7800
52 Box St Brooklyn (11222) *(G-1621)*
Architctral Mllwk Installation..........631 499-0755
590 Elwood Rd East Northport (11731) *(G-4433)*
Architctral Shetmetal Pdts Inc..........518 381-6144
1329 Amsterdam Rd Scotia (12302) *(G-15323)*
Architects Newspaper LLC..........212 966-0630
21 Murray St Fl 5 New York (10007) *(G-9195)*
Architectural Coatings Inc..........718 418-9584
538 Johnson Ave Brooklyn (11237) *(G-1622)*
Architectural Dctg Co LLC..........845 483-1340
130 Salt Point Tpke Poughkeepsie (12603) *(G-13888)*
Architectural Enhancements Inc..........845 343-9663
135 Crotty Rd Middletown (10941) *(G-8426)*
Architectural Fiberglass Corp..........631 842-4772
1395 Marconi Blvd Copiague (11726) *(G-3892)*
Architectural Glass Inc..........845 831-3116
71 Maple St Apt 2 Beacon (12508) *(G-781)*
Architectural Sign Group Inc..........516 326-1800
145 Meacham Ave Elmont (11003) *(G-4716)*
Architectural Textiles USA Inc..........212 213-6972
36 E 23rd St Ste F New York (10010) *(G-9196)*
Architex International, New York *Also called Architectural Textiles USA Inc (G-9196)*
Archive360 Inc..........212 731-2438
65 Broadway Fl 23 New York (10006) *(G-9197)*
Arco Pharmaceutical, Ronkonkoma *Also called Nbty Inc (G-14953)*
Arcom Automatics LLC..........315 422-1230
185 Ainsley Dr Syracuse (13210) *(G-15856)*
Arcom Labs, Syracuse *Also called Arrow-Communication Labs Inc (G-15859)*
Arcserve (usa) LLC..........866 576-9742
1 Ca Plz Islandia (11749) *(G-6786)*
Arctic Glacier Minnesota Inc..........585 388-0080
900 Turk Hill Rd Fairport (14450) *(G-4842)*
Arctic Glacier Newburgh Inc..........718 456-2013
335 Moffat St Brooklyn (11237) *(G-1623)*
Arctic Glacier Newburgh Inc (HQ)..........845 561-0549
225 Lake St Newburgh (12550) *(G-12750)*
Arctic Glacier PA Inc..........610 494-8200
900 Turk Hill Rd Fairport (14450) *(G-4843)*
Arctic Glacier Texas Inc..........215 283-0326
900 Turk Hill Rd Fairport (14450) *(G-4844)*
Arctic Glacier USA..........215 283-0326
900 Turk Hill Rd Fairport (14450) *(G-4845)*
Arctix, Locust Valley *Also called Alpha 6 Distributions LLC (G-7628)*
Arcy Plastic Laminates Inc (PA)..........518 235-0753
555 Patroon Creek Blvd Albany (12206) *(G-48)*
Ardagh Metal Packaging USA Inc..........607 584-3300
379 Broome Corporate Pkwy Conklin (13748) *(G-3865)*
Ardent Mills LLC..........518 447-1700
101 Normanskill St Albany (12202) *(G-49)*
Ardex Cosmetics of America..........518 283-6700
744 Pawling Ave Troy (12180) *(G-16226)*
Area Development Magazine, Westbury *Also called Halcyon Business Publications (G-16993)*
Area Inc..........212 924-7084
58 E 11th St Fl 2 New York (10003) *(G-9198)*
Area Warehouse, New York *Also called Area Inc (G-9198)*
Aremco Products Inc..........845 268-0039
707 Executive Blvd Ste B Valley Cottage (10989) *(G-16376)*
Arena Graphics Inc..........516 767-5108
52 Main St Frnt Port Washington (11050) *(G-13801)*
Arena Sports Center, Port Washington *Also called Arena Graphics Inc (G-13801)*
Ares Box LLC..........718 858-8760
63 Flushing Ave Unit 224 Brooklyn (11205) *(G-1624)*
Ares Printing and Packg Corp..........718 858-8760
Brooklyn Navy Yard Bldg Brooklyn (11205) *(G-1625)*
Argee America Inc..........212 768-9840
1400 Broadway Rm 2307 New York (10018) *(G-9199)*
Argee Sportswear, New York *Also called Argee America Inc (G-9199)*
Argencord Machine Corp Inc..........631 842-8990
10 Reith St Copiague (11726) *(G-3893)*
Argo Envelope Corp..........718 729-2700
4310 21st St Long Island City (11101) *(G-7667)*
Argo General Machine Work Inc..........718 392-4605
3816 11th St Long Island City (11101) *(G-7668)*
Argo Lithographers Inc..........718 729-2700
4310 21st St Long Island City (11101) *(G-7669)*
Argon Corp (PA)..........516 487-5314
160 Great Neck Rd Great Neck (11021) *(G-5792)*
Argon Medical Devices Inc..........585 321-1130
336 Summit Point Dr Henrietta (14467) *(G-6293)*
Argos Inc..........845 528-0576
58 Seifert Ln Putnam Valley (10579) *(G-13973)*
Argosy Ceramic Arospc Mtls LLC..........212 268-0003
225 W 34th St Ste 1106 New York (10122) *(G-9200)*
Argus Media Inc..........646 376-6130
500 5th Ave Ste 2410 New York (10110) *(G-9201)*
Arh, Deer Park *Also called American Racing Headers Inc (G-4096)*
Ariel Optics Inc..........585 265-4820
261 David Pkwy Ontario (14519) *(G-13195)*
Ariela and Associates Intl LLC (PA)..........212 683-4131
1359 Broadway Fl 21 New York (10018) *(G-9202)*
Aries Precision Products, Rochester *Also called Estebania Enterprises Inc (G-14359)*
Ariesun Inc..........866 274-3049
160 W 3rd St Mount Vernon (10550) *(G-8663)*
Arimed Orthotics Prosthetics P (PA)..........718 875-8754
302 Livingston St Brooklyn (11217) *(G-1626)*
Arimed Orthotics Prosthetics P..........718 979-6155
235 Dongan Hills Ave 2d Staten Island (10305) *(G-15640)*
Arista Flag Corporation..........845 246-7700
157 W Saugerties Rd Saugerties (12477) *(G-15180)*
Arista Innovations Inc..........516 746-2262
131 Liberty Ave Mineola (11501) *(G-8496)*
Arista Printing, Mineola *Also called Arista Innovations Inc (G-8496)*
Arista Steel Designs Corp..........718 965-7077
788 3rd Ave Brooklyn (11232) *(G-1627)*
Aristocrat Lighting Inc..........718 522-0003
104 Halleck St Brooklyn (11231) *(G-1628)*
Arizona Beverage Company LLC (HQ)..........516 812-0300
60 Crossways Park Dr W # 400 Woodbury (11797) *(G-17282)*
Arizona Beverages USA, Woodbury *Also called Arizona Beverage Company LLC (G-17282)*
Ark Sciences Inc..........646 943-1520
1601 Veterans Hwy Ste 315 Islandia (11749) *(G-6787)*
Arkay Packaging Corporation (PA)..........631 273-2000
100 Marcus Blvd Ste 2 Hauppauge (11788) *(G-6024)*
Arkema Inc..........585 243-6359
3289 Genesee St Piffard (14533) *(G-13546)*
Arkwin Industries Inc (HQ)..........516 333-2640
686 Main St Westbury (11590) *(G-16969)*
Arlan Damper Corporation..........631 589-7431
1598 Lakeland Ave Bohemia (11716) *(G-1019)*
Arlee Group, New York *Also called Arlee Home Fashions Inc (G-9203)*
Arlee Home Fashions Inc (PA)..........212 213-0425
261 5th Ave Fl Mezz New York (10016) *(G-9203)*
Arlee Lighting Corp..........516 595-8558
125 Doughty Blvd Inwood (11096) *(G-6751)*
Arlington Equipment Corp..........518 798-5867
588 Queensbury Ave Queensbury (12804) *(G-13992)*
Arlyn Scales, East Rockaway *Also called Circuits & Systems Inc (G-4468)*
Arm & Hammer, Schenectady *Also called Church & Dwight Co Inc (G-15242)*
Arm Construction Company Inc..........646 235-6520
10001 27th Ave East Elmhurst (11369) *(G-4388)*
Arm Rochester Inc..........585 354-5077
138 Joseph Ave Rochester (14605) *(G-14210)*
Arma Container Corp..........631 254-1200
65 N Industry Ct Deer Park (11729) *(G-4101)*
Armacel Armor Corporation..........805 384-1144
745 5th Ave Fl 7 New York (10151) *(G-9204)*
Armadillo Bar & Grill, Kingston *Also called Tortilla Heaven Inc (G-7217)*
Armento Architectural Arts, Kenmore *Also called Armento Incorporated (G-7145)*
Armento Incorporated..........716 875-2423
1011 Military Rd Kenmore (14217) *(G-7145)*
Armitron Watch Div, Little Neck *Also called E Gluck Corporation (G-7508)*
Armor Dynamics Inc..........845 658-9200
138 Maple Hill Rd Kingston (12401) *(G-7178)*

ALPHABETIC

Armor Tile, Buffalo *Also called Engineered Composites Inc* ***(G-2939)***
Armour Bearer Group Inc............646 812-4487
424 Beach 65th St Arverne (11692) ***(G-424)***
Armstrong Mold Corporation (PA)............315 437-1517
6910 Manlius Center Rd East Syracuse (13057) ***(G-4504)***
Armstrong Mold Corporation............315 437-1517
5860 Fisher Rd East Syracuse (13057) ***(G-4505)***
Armstrong Pumps Inc............716 693-8813
93 East Ave North Tonawanda (14120) ***(G-12955)***
Armstrong Transmitter Corp............315 673-1269
4835 N Street Rd Marcellus (13108) ***(G-8086)***
Arnan Development Corp (PA)............607 432-6641
6459 State Highway 23 Oneonta (13820) ***(G-13171)***
Arnell Inc............516 486-7098
73 High St Hempstead (11550) ***(G-6265)***
Arnold Magnetic Tech Corp (HQ)............585 385-9010
770 Linden Ave Rochester (14625) ***(G-14211)***
Arnold Printing Corp............607 272-7800
604 W Green St Ithaca (14850) ***(G-6819)***
Arnold Taylor Printing Inc............516 781-0564
2218 Brody Ln Bellmore (11710) ***(G-813)***
Arnold-Davis LLC............607 772-1201
187 Indl Pk Dr Binghamton (13904) ***(G-889)***
Arnolds Meat Food Products............718 384-8071
274 Heyward St Brooklyn (11206) ***(G-1629)***
Arnouse Digital Devices Corp............516 673-4444
1983 Marcus Ave Ste 104 New Hyde Park (11042) ***(G-8817)***
Arnprior Rpid Mfg Slutions Inc (PA)............585 617-6301
2400 Mount Read Blvd # 112 Rochester (14615) ***(G-14212)***
Aro-Graph Corporation............315 463-8693
847 North Ave Syracuse (13206) ***(G-15857)***
Aro-Graph Displays, Syracuse *Also called Aro-Graph Corporation* ***(G-15857)***
Aromafloria, Huntington Station *Also called California Fragrance Company* ***(G-6698)***
Aromasong Usa Inc............718 838-9669
35 Frost St Brooklyn (11211) ***(G-1630)***
Aron Streit Inc............212 475-7000
148-154 Rivington St New York (10002) ***(G-9205)***
Aronowitz Metal Works............845 356-1660
5 Edwin Ln Monsey (10952) ***(G-8568)***
Arpa USA............212 965-4099
62 Greene St Frnt 1 New York (10012) ***(G-9206)***
Arpac LLC............315 471-5103
6581 Townline Rd Syracuse (13206) ***(G-15858)***
Arper USA Inc............212 647-8900
476 Broadway Ste 2f New York (10013) ***(G-9207)***
Array Marketing Group Inc (PA)............212 750-3367
200 Madison Ave Ste 2121 New York (10016) ***(G-9208)***
Arringement International Inc............347 323-7974
16015 45th Ave Flushing (11358) ***(G-5227)***
Arro Tool & Die Inc............716 763-6203
4687 Gleason Rd Lakewood (14750) ***(G-7287)***
Arrow Chemical Corp............516 377-7770
28 Rider Pl Freeport (11520) ***(G-5389)***
Arrow Grinding Inc............716 693-3333
525 Vicke St Tonaw Ctr Tonawanda (14150) ***(G-16140)***
Arrow Leather Finishing Inc............518 762-3121
12 W State St Johnstown (12095) ***(G-7107)***
Arrow-Communication Labs Inc............315 422-1230
185 Ainsley Dr Syracuse (13210) ***(G-15859)***
Arrowear Athletic Apparel, Lynbrook *Also called Valley Stream Sporting Gds Inc* ***(G-7966)***
Arrowhead Spring Vineyards LLC............716 434-8030
4746 Townline Rd Lockport (14094) ***(G-7570)***
Arrowpak, Richmond Hill *Also called Baralan Usa Inc* ***(G-14067)***
Arstan Products International............516 433-1313
264 Duffy Ave Hicksville (11801) ***(G-6324)***
Art & Understanding Inc............518 426-9010
25 Monroe St Ste 205 Albany (12210) ***(G-50)***
Art and Cook Inc............718 567-7778
14 C 53rd St Fl 2 Brooklyn (11232) ***(G-1631)***
Art Asiapacific Publishing LLC............212 255-6003
410 W 24th St Apt 14a New York (10011) ***(G-9209)***
Art Bedi-Makky Foundry Corp............718 383-4191
227 India St Ste 31 Brooklyn (11222) ***(G-1632)***
Art Boards, Brooklyn *Also called Patrick Mackin Custom Furn* ***(G-2409)***
Art Craft Leather Goods Inc............718 257-7401
1970 Pitkin Ave Brooklyn (11207) ***(G-1633)***
Art Dental Laboratory Inc............516 437-1882
199 Jericho Tpke Ste 402 Floral Park (11001) ***(G-5193)***
Art Digital Technologies LLC............646 649-4820
85 Debevoise Ave Brooklyn (11222) ***(G-1634)***
Art Essentials of New York (PA)............845 368-1100
25 Church Rd Airmont (10952) ***(G-12)***
Art Flag Company Inc............212 334-1890
8 Jay St Frnt 1 New York (10013) ***(G-9210)***
Art Foam, Lindenhurst *Also called Strux Corp* ***(G-7485)***
Art Form Sheet Metal Fabricato............718 728-0111
2120 45th Rd Long Island City (11101) ***(G-7670)***
Art In America, New York *Also called Brant Art Publications Inc* ***(G-9454)***
Art Industries of New York............212 633-9200
601 W 26th St Rm 1425 New York (10001) ***(G-9211)***
Art Parts Signs Inc............585 381-2134
100 Lincoln Pkwy East Rochester (14445) ***(G-4453)***
Art People Inc............212 431-4865
594 Broadway Rm 1102 New York (10012) ***(G-9212)***
Art Precision Metal Products............631 842-8889
1465 S Strong Ave Copiague (11726) ***(G-3894)***
Art Resources Transfer Inc............212 255-2919
526 W 26th St Rm 614 New York (10001) ***(G-9213)***
Art Scroll Printing Corp............212 929-2413
230 W 41st St Bsmt 1 New York (10036) ***(G-9214)***
Art Supply & Instruments, Brooklyn *Also called Rosendahl Industries Ltd Inc* ***(G-2507)***
Art-Craft Optical Company Inc............585 546-6640
57 Goodway Dr S Rochester (14623) ***(G-14213)***
Art-TEC Jewelry Designs Ltd (PA)............212 719-2941
48 W 48th St Ste 401 New York (10036) ***(G-9215)***
Artcraft Building Services............845 895-3893
85 Old Hoagerburgh Rd Wallkill (12589) ***(G-16541)***
Arteast LLC............212 965-8787
102 Franklin St Fl 4 New York (10013) ***(G-9216)***
Artemis Inc............631 232-2424
36 Central Ave Hauppauge (11788) ***(G-6025)***
Artemis Studios Inc............718 788-6022
34 35th St Ste 2b Brooklyn (11232) ***(G-1635)***
Arthur Brown W Mfg Co............631 243-5594
49 E Industry Ct Ste I Deer Park (11729) ***(G-4102)***
Arthur Frommer Budget Travel, New York *Also called Arthur Frommer Magazines LLC* ***(G-9217)***
Arthur Frommer Magazines LLC............646 695-6739
530 7th Ave Uppr 2 New York (10018) ***(G-9217)***
Arthur Gluck Shirtmakers Inc............212 755-8165
871 E 24th St Brooklyn (11210) ***(G-1636)***
Arthur Invitation, New York *Also called Exotic Print and Paper Inc* ***(G-10107)***
Arthur Lauer Inc............845 255-7871
47 Steves Ln Gardiner (12525) ***(G-5547)***
Articulate Global Inc............800 861-4880
244 5th Ave Ste 2960 New York (10001) ***(G-9218)***
Artina Group Inc............914 592-1850
250 Clearbrook Rd Ste 245 Elmsford (10523) ***(G-4734)***
Artisan Bags, Childwold *Also called Leather Artisan* ***(G-3628)***
Artisan Custom Interiors, West Hempstead *Also called Artisan Woodworking Ltd* ***(G-16849)***
Artisan Machining Inc............631 589-1416
49 Remington Blvd Ronkonkoma (11779) ***(G-14872)***
Artisan Management Group Inc............716 569-4094
39 Venman St Frewsburg (14738) ***(G-5448)***
Artisan Woodworking Ltd............516 486-0818
163 Hempstead Tpke West Hempstead (11552) ***(G-16849)***
Artisanal Brands Inc............914 441-3591
42 Forest Ln Bronxville (10708) ***(G-1498)***
Artistic Frame Corp (PA)............212 289-2100
979 3rd Ave Ste 1705 New York (10022) ***(G-9219)***
Artistic Group, The, New York *Also called Artistic Typography Corp* ***(G-9221)***
Artistic Innovation Inc............914 968-3021
540 Nepperhan Ave Ste 566 Yonkers (10701) ***(G-17416)***
Artistic Ironworks Inc............631 665-4285
94 Saxon Ave Bay Shore (11706) ***(G-672)***
Artistic Products LLC............631 435-0200
125 Commerce Dr Hauppauge (11788) ***(G-6026)***
Artistic Ribbon Novelty Co Inc............212 255-4224
22 W 21st St Fl 3 New York (10010) ***(G-9220)***
Artistic Typography Corp (PA)............212 463-8880
151 W 30th St Fl 8 New York (10001) ***(G-9221)***
Artistics Printing Corp............516 561-2121
746 Franklin Ave Ste 2 Franklin Square (11010) ***(G-5360)***
Artistry In Wood of Syracuse............315 431-4022
6804 Manlius Center Rd # 2 East Syracuse (13057) ***(G-4506)***
Artists, Doo Wop, Deer Park *Also called New Wop Records* ***(G-4179)***
Artkraft Sign, New York *Also called Artkraft Strauss LLC* ***(G-9222)***
Artkraft Strauss LLC............212 265-5155
1776 Broadway Ste 1810 New York (10019) ***(G-9222)***
Artnews Ltd (HQ)............212 398-1690
110 Greene St Ph 2 New York (10012) ***(G-9223)***
Artone Furniture By Design, Jamestown *Also called Artone LLC* ***(G-6972)***
Artone LLC............716 664-2232
1089 Allen St Jamestown (14701) ***(G-6972)***
Artsaics Studios Inc............631 254-2558
1006 Grand Blvd Deer Park (11729) ***(G-4103)***
Artscroll Printing Corp (PA)............212 929-2413
53 W 23rd St Fl 4 New York (10010) ***(G-9224)***
Artube, Great Neck *Also called Iridium Industries Inc* ***(G-5817)***
Artvoice............716 881-6604
810 Main St Buffalo (14202) ***(G-2820)***
Artyarns............914 428-0333
70 Westmoreland Ave White Plains (10606) ***(G-17080)***
Artys Sprnklr Svc Instllation............516 538-4371
448 Cedar Ln East Meadow (11554) ***(G-4418)***
Arumai Technologies Inc (PA)............914 217-0038
175 King St Armonk (10504) ***(G-412)***
Arusha Tanzanite, Great Neck *Also called Le Vian Corp* ***(G-5820)***
Arvos Holding LLC (HQ)............585 596-2501
3020 Truax Rd Wellsville (14895) ***(G-16748)***
Arvos Inc (HQ)............585 593-2700
3020 Truax Rd Wellsville (14895) ***(G-16749)***

ALPHABETIC

Aryzta LLC...585 235-8160
64 Chester St Rochester (14611) ***(G-14214)***
Aryzta LLC...585 235-8160
235 Buffalo Rd Rochester (14611) ***(G-14215)***
Asa Manufacturing Inc...718 853-3033
1352 39th St Brooklyn (11218) ***(G-1637)***
Asahi Shimbun America Inc...212 398-0257
620 8th Ave New York (10018) ***(G-9225)***
ASAP Rack Rental Inc...718 499-4495
33 35th St St5 Brooklyn (11232) ***(G-1638)***
Asavings.com, Brooklyn *Also called Focus Camera Inc* ***(G-1990)***
Ascension Industries Inc (PA)...716 693-9381
1254 Erie Ave North Tonawanda (14120) ***(G-12956)***
Asco Castings Inc (PA)...212 719-9800
3100 47th Ave Ste G Long Island City (11101) ***(G-7671)***
Ascribe Inc...585 413-0298
383 Buell Rd Rochester (14624) ***(G-14216)***
Asence Inc...347 335-2606
65 Broadway Fl 7 New York (10006) ***(G-9226)***
Asept Pak Inc...518 651-2026
64 West St Malone (12953) ***(G-8007)***
Ashburns Inc...212 227-5692
90 John St Rm 409 New York (10038) ***(G-9227)***
Ashburns Engravers, New York *Also called Ashburns Inc* ***(G-9227)***
Asher Collection, New York *Also called Asher Jewelry Company Inc* ***(G-9228)***
Asher Jewelry Company Inc...212 302-6233
48 W 48th St Ste 303 New York (10036) ***(G-9228)***
Ashko Group LLC...212 594-6050
10 W 33rd St Rm 1019 New York (10001) ***(G-9229)***
Ashland Hercules Water Tech, Brooklyn *Also called Hercules Incorporated* ***(G-2075)***
Ashland Hercules Water Tech, Liverpool *Also called Hercules Incorporated* ***(G-7522)***
Ashley Resin Corp...718 851-8111
1171 59th St Brooklyn (11219) ***(G-1639)***
Ashly Audio Inc...585 872-0010
847 Holt Rd Ste 1 Webster (14580) ***(G-16713)***
Ashton-Potter USA Ltd...716 633-2000
10 Curtwright Dr Williamsville (14221) ***(G-17233)***
Asi Sign Systems, New York *Also called Modulex New York Inc* ***(G-11290)***
Asi Sign Systems Inc...646 742-1320
192 Lexington Ave Rm 1002 New York (10016) ***(G-9230)***
Asi Sign Systems Inc...716 775-0104
2957 Alt Blvd Grand Island (14072) ***(G-5751)***
Asia Connection LLC...212 369-4644
200 E 90th St Apt 4h New York (10128) ***(G-9231)***
Asian Global Trading Corp...718 786-0998
3613 36th Ave Ste 2 Long Island City (11106) ***(G-7672)***
Asite LLC...203 545-3089
375 Park Ave Ste 2607 New York (10152) ***(G-9232)***
Ask Chemicals Hi-Tech LLC...607 587-9146
6329 Rte 21 Alfred Station (14803) ***(G-195)***
Asm, Central Bridge *Also called American Standard Mfg Inc* ***(G-3482)***
Asm Mechanical Systems, Ridgewood *Also called Aabco Sheet Metal Co Inc* ***(G-14097)***
Asm USA Inc...212 925-2906
73 Spring St Rm 309 New York (10012) ***(G-9233)***
Asn Inc...718 894-0800
6020 59th Pl Ste 2 Maspeth (11378) ***(G-8120)***
Asp Blade Intrmdate Hldngs Inc (PA)...212 476-8000
299 Park Ave Fl 34 New York (10171) ***(G-9234)***
Asp Industries Inc...585 254-9130
9 Evelyn St Rochester (14606) ***(G-14217)***
Aspect Printing Inc...347 789-4284
904 E 51st St Brooklyn (11203) ***(G-1640)***
Aspen Law & Business, New York *Also called Aspen Publishers Inc* ***(G-9235)***
Aspen Publishers Inc (HQ)...212 771-0600
76 9th Ave Ste 724 New York (10011) ***(G-9235)***
Aspen Research Group Ltd...212 425-9588
17 State St Fl 15 New York (10004) ***(G-9236)***
Aspex Incorporated...212 966-0410
161 Hudson St Apt 1a New York (10013) ***(G-9237)***
Aspire One Communications LLC...201 281-2998
245 Main St Ste 8 Cornwall (12518) ***(G-3986)***
Asr Group International Inc (HQ)...914 963-2400
1 Federal St Yonkers (10705) ***(G-17417)***
Assa Abloy Entrance Systems US...315 492-6600
28 Corporate Cir Ste 1 East Syracuse (13057) ***(G-4507)***
Assembly Equipment Division, Rochester *Also called High Speed Hammer Company Inc* ***(G-14436)***
Associated Brands Inc...585 798-3475
111 8th Ave New York (10011) ***(G-9238)***
Associated Bus Publications Co...212 490-3999
1466 Broadway Ste 910 New York (10036) ***(G-9239)***
Associated Drapery & Equipment...516 671-5245
3 Kosnitz Dr Unit 111 Monroe (10950) ***(G-8548)***
Associated Materials LLC...631 467-4535
1830 Lakeland Ave Ronkonkoma (11779) ***(G-14873)***
Association For Cmpt McHy Inc (PA)...212 869-7440
2 Penn Plz Rm 701 New York (10121) ***(G-9240)***
Assouline Publishing Inc (PA)...212 989-6769
3 Park Ave Fl 27 New York (10016) ***(G-9241)***
Aston Leather Inc...212 481-2760
153 W 27th St Ste 406 New York (10001) ***(G-9242)***
Astor-Honor Division, New York *Also called Beauty Fashion Inc* ***(G-9340)***
Astra Products Inc...631 464-4747
6 Bethpage Rd Copiague (11726) ***(G-3895)***
Astra Tool & Instr Mfg Corp...914 747-3863
369 Bradhurst Ave Hawthorne (10532) ***(G-6244)***
Astria Solutions Group LLC...518 346-7799
2165 Technology Dr Schenectady (12308) ***(G-15231)***
Astro Chemical Company Inc...518 399-5338
3 Mill Rd Ballston Lake (12019) ***(G-579)***
Astro Electroplating Inc...631 968-0656
171 4th Ave Bay Shore (11706) ***(G-673)***
Astro Label & Tag Ltd...718 435-4474
5820 Fort Hamilton Pkwy Brooklyn (11219) ***(G-1641)***
Astrocom Electronics Inc...607 432-1930
115 Dk Lifgren Dr Oneonta (13820) ***(G-13172)***
Astrodyne Inc...516 536-5755
18 Neil Ct Oceanside (11572) ***(G-13073)***
Astron Candle Manufacturing Co...718 728-3330
1125 30th Ave Long Island City (11102) ***(G-7673)***
Astronics Corporation (PA)...716 805-1599
130 Commerce Way East Aurora (14052) ***(G-4366)***
Astucci US Ltd...718 752-9700
4369 9th St Long Island City (11101) ***(G-7674)***
Astucci US Ltd (PA)...212 725-3171
385 5th Ave Rm 1100 New York (10016) ***(G-9243)***
Asur Jewelry Inc...718 472-1687
4709 30th St Ste 403 Long Island City (11101) ***(G-7675)***
AT&T Corp...716 639-0673
8200 Transit Rd Ste 200 Williamsville (14221) ***(G-17234)***
AT&T Corp...212 317-7048
767 5th Ave Fl 12a New York (10153) ***(G-9244)***
Atair Aerospace Inc...718 923-1709
63 Flushing Ave Unit 262 Brooklyn (11205) ***(G-1642)***
Atalla Handbags Inc...718 965-5500
117 57th St Brooklyn (11220) ***(G-1643)***
Atc, Huntington Station *Also called American Technical Ceramics* ***(G-6695)***
Atc Plastics LLC...212 375-2515
555 Madison Ave Fl 5 New York (10022) ***(G-9245)***
Atco EZ Dock, Auburn *Also called Auburn Tank & Manufacturing Co* ***(G-481)***
Atd Precision Machining, Rochester *Also called Allstate Tool and Die Inc* ***(G-14191)***
Atech-Seh Metal Fabricator...716 895-8888
330 Greene St Buffalo (14206) ***(G-2821)***
Ateco Products, Bay Shore *Also called Sumner Industries Inc* ***(G-749)***
Atelier Viollet Corp...718 782-1727
505 Driggs Ave Brooklyn (11211) ***(G-1644)***
Ateres Book Binding, Brooklyn *Also called Ateres Publishing & Bk Bindery* ***(G-1645)***
Ateres Publishing & Bk Bindery...718 935-9355
845 Bedford Ave Brooklyn (11205) ***(G-1645)***
Ateret LLC...212 819-0777
22 W 48th St New York (10036) ***(G-9246)***
Aterian Investment Partners LP (PA)...212 547-2806
11 E 44th St Rm 1803 New York (10017) ***(G-9247)***
Aterra Exploration LLC...212 315-0030
230 W 56th St Apt 53d New York (10019) ***(G-9248)***
Athalon Sportgear Inc...212 268-8070
10 W 33rd St Rm 1012 New York (10001) ***(G-9249)***
Athens Iron Fabrication Inc...718 424-7799
3435 56th St Woodside (11377) ***(G-17317)***
Athens Welding Iron Works Co, Woodside *Also called Athens Iron Fabrication Inc* ***(G-17317)***
Athletic Cap Co Inc...718 398-1300
123 Fields Ave Staten Island (10314) ***(G-15641)***
Athlon Spt Communications Inc...212 478-1910
60 E 42nd St Ste 820 New York (10165) ***(G-9250)***
ATI, Brooklyn *Also called Anne Taintor Inc* ***(G-1613)***
ATI, New York *Also called Analytical Technology Inc* ***(G-9146)***
ATI Model Products Inc (PA)...631 694-7022
180 Smith St Farmingdale (11735) ***(G-4946)***
ATI Specialty Materials, Lockport *Also called Tdy Industries LLC* ***(G-7617)***
ATI Trading Inc...718 888-7918
13631 41st Ave Ste 5a Flushing (11355) ***(G-5228)***
Atis Colojet, Ronkonkoma *Also called Maharlika Holdings LLC* ***(G-14936)***
Atk Gasl Inc...631 737-6100
77 Raynor Ave Ronkonkoma (11779) ***(G-14874)***
Atlantic Business Products, New York *Also called Facsimile Cmmncations Inds Inc* ***(G-10125)***
Atlantic Coast Embroidery Inc...631 283-2175
172 Mariner Dr Southampton (11968) ***(G-15539)***
Atlantic Color Corp...631 345-3800
14 Ramsey Rd Shirley (11967) ***(G-15413)***
Atlantic Electronic Tech LLC...800 296-2177
285 5th Ave Apt 2b Brooklyn (11215) ***(G-1646)***
Atlantic Electronic Technology, Brooklyn *Also called Atlantic Electronic Tech LLC* ***(G-1646)***
Atlantic Engineer Products LLC...518 822-1800
239 State Route 23b Hudson (12534) ***(G-6607)***
Atlantic Essential Pdts Inc...631 434-8333
7 Oser Ave Ste 1 Hauppauge (11788) ***(G-6027)***
Atlantic Farm & Food Inc...718 441-3152
11415 Atlantic Ave Richmond Hill (11418) ***(G-14066)***
Atlantic Industrial Tech Inc...631 234-3131
90 Precision Dr Shirley (11967) ***(G-15414)***

ALPHABETIC

(PA)=Parent Co (HQ)=Headquarters (DH)=Div Headquarters

Atlantic Monthly Group Inc.....202 266-7000
60 Madison Ave New York (10010) ***(G-9251)***
Atlantic Pork & Provisions Inc.....718 272-9550
14707 94th Ave Jamaica (11435) ***(G-6895)***
Atlantic Precious Metal Cast.....718 937-7100
4132 27th St Long Island City (11101) ***(G-7676)***
Atlantic Projects Company Inc.....518 878-2065
5 Southside Dr Ste 11s Clifton Park (12065) ***(G-3696)***
Atlantic Recording Corp (HQ).....212 707-2000
1633 Broadway Lowr 2c1 New York (10019) ***(G-9252)***
Atlantic Records, New York *Also called Atlantic Recording Corp* ***(G-9252)***
Atlantic Scale Company Inc.....914 664-4403
31 Fullerton Ave Yonkers (10704) ***(G-17418)***
Atlantic Specialty Co Inc.....845 356-2502
20 Jeffrey Pl Monsey (10952) ***(G-8569)***
Atlantic Stairs Corp.....718 417-8818
284a Meserole St Brooklyn (11206) ***(G-1647)***
Atlantic States Distributing.....518 427-6364
1325 Broadway Menands (12204) ***(G-8368)***
Atlantic States Kitchens Baths, Menands *Also called Atlantic States Distributing* ***(G-8368)***
Atlantic Steinway Awng II LLC.....718 729-2965
4230 24th St Long Island City (11101) ***(G-7677)***
Atlantic Transformer Inc.....716 795-3258
1674 Quaker Rd Barker (14012) ***(G-612)***
Atlantic Trophy Co Inc.....212 684-6020
866 Avenue Of The America New York (10001) ***(G-9253)***
Atlantic Ultraviolet Corp.....631 234-3275
375 Marcus Blvd Hauppauge (11788) ***(G-6028)***
Atlantic, The, New York *Also called Atlantic Monthly Group Inc* ***(G-9251)***
Atlantis Energy Systems Inc (PA).....845 486-4052
7 Industry St Poughkeepsie (12603) ***(G-13889)***
Atlantis Energy Systems Inc (PA).....916 438-2930
7 Industry St Poughkeepsie (12603) ***(G-13890)***
Atlantis Equipment Corporation (PA).....518 733-5910
16941 Ny 22 Stephentown (12168) ***(G-15756)***
Atlantis Solar and Wind, Potsdam *Also called Atlantis Solar Inc* ***(G-13877)***
Atlantis Solar Inc.....916 226-9183
2302 River Rd Potsdam (13676) ***(G-13877)***
Atlas & Company LLC.....212 234-3100
355 Lexington Ave Fl 6 New York (10017) ***(G-9254)***
Atlas Bituminous Co Inc.....315 457-2394
173 Farrell Rd Syracuse (13209) ***(G-15860)***
Atlas Coatings Corp.....718 402-2000
820 E 140th St Bronx (10454) ***(G-1277)***
Atlas Coatings Group Corp (PA).....718 469-8787
4808 Farragut Rd Brooklyn (11203) ***(G-1648)***
Atlas Concrete Batching Corp.....718 523-3000
9511 147th Pl Jamaica (11435) ***(G-6896)***
Atlas Copco Comptec LLC (HQ).....518 765-3344
46 School Rd Voorheesville (12186) ***(G-16516)***
Atlas Fence, East Syracuse *Also called Alexscoe LLC* ***(G-4500)***
Atlas Fence & Railing Co Inc.....718 767-2200
15149 7th Ave Whitestone (11357) ***(G-17201)***
Atlas Fence Co, Whitestone *Also called Atlas Fence & Railing Co Inc* ***(G-17201)***
Atlas Graphics Inc.....516 997-5527
567 Main St Westbury (11590) ***(G-16970)***
Atlas Metal Industries Inc.....607 776-2048
17 Wheeler Ave Hammondsport (14840) ***(G-5953)***
Atlas Music Publishing LLC (PA).....646 502-5170
6 E 39th St Ste 1104 New York (10016) ***(G-9255)***
Atlas Print Solutions Inc.....212 949-8775
589 8th Ave Fl 4 New York (10018) ***(G-9256)***
Atlas Recycling LLC.....212 925-3280
25 Howard St Fl 2 New York (10013) ***(G-9257)***
Atlas Sign.....718 604-7446
1544 Atlantic Ave Brooklyn (11213) ***(G-1649)***
Atlas Switch Co Inc.....516 222-6280
969 Stewart Ave Garden City (11530) ***(G-5495)***
Atlas Transit Mix Corp.....718 523-3000
9511 147th Pl Jamaica (11435) ***(G-6897)***
Atlaz International Ltd.....516 239-1854
298 Lawrence Ave Unit 1 Lawrence (11559) ***(G-7390)***
Atmost Refrigeration Co Inc (PA).....518 828-2180
793 Route 66 Hudson (12534) ***(G-6608)***
Atomic Signworks.....315 779-7446
1040 Bradley St Ste 3 Watertown (13601) ***(G-16635)***
Atr Jewelry Inc.....212 819-0075
71 W 47th St Ste 402 New York (10036) ***(G-9258)***
Ats, Yorktown Heights *Also called Advanced Tchncal Solutions Inc* ***(G-17506)***
Attends Healthcare Inc.....212 338-5100
200 Park Ave New York (10166) ***(G-9259)***
Attias Oven Corp.....718 499-0145
926 3rd Ave Brooklyn (11232) ***(G-1650)***
Attica Millwork Inc.....585 591-2333
71 Market St Attica (14011) ***(G-471)***
Attica Package Company Inc.....585 591-0510
45 Windsor St Attica (14011) ***(G-472)***
Attitudes Footwear Inc.....212 754-9113
1040 1st Ave Ste 232 New York (10022) ***(G-9260)***
ATW Resources LLC.....212 994-0600
767 3rd Ave Fl 14 New York (10017) ***(G-9261)***
Atwater Estate Vineyards LLC.....607 546-8463
5055 State Route 414 Burdett (14818) ***(G-3264)***
Atwater Foods, Lyndonville *Also called Shoreline Fruit LLC* ***(G-7969)***
Atwood Tool & Machine Inc.....607 648-6543
39 Kattelville Rd Chenango Bridge (13745) ***(G-3596)***
Auburn Armature Inc (PA).....315 253-9721
70 Wright Cir Auburn (13021) ***(G-477)***
Auburn Armature Inc.....585 426-4607
80 Elmgrove Park Rochester (14624) ***(G-14218)***
Auburn Bearing & Mfg Inc.....315 986-7600
4 State Route 350 Macedon (14502) ***(G-7982)***
Auburn Custom Millwork Inc.....315 253-3843
4022 Technology Park Blvd Auburn (13021) ***(G-478)***
Auburn Foundry Inc.....315 253-4441
15 Wadsworth St Auburn (13021) ***(G-479)***
Auburn Leathercrafters, Auburn *Also called Finger Lakes Lea Crafters LLC* ***(G-494)***
Auburn Publishing Co.....315 253-5311
25 Dill St Auburn (13021) ***(G-480)***
Auburn Tank & Manufacturing Co.....315 255-2788
24 Mcmaster St Auburn (13021) ***(G-481)***
Auburn Vacuum Forming Co Inc.....315 253-2440
40 York St Auburn (13021) ***(G-482)***
Auburn-Watson Corp (PA).....716 876-8000
3295 Walden Ave Depew (14043) ***(G-4247)***
Audible Difference Inc.....212 662-4848
193 6th St Brooklyn (11215) ***(G-1651)***
Audible Difference Inc (PA).....212 662-4848
370 State St Brooklyn (11217) ***(G-1652)***
Audible Difference Lnc, Brooklyn *Also called Audible Difference Inc* ***(G-1652)***
Audio Technology New York Inc.....718 369-7528
129 31st St Brooklyn (11232) ***(G-1653)***
Audio Video Invasion Inc.....516 345-2636
53 Werman Ct Plainview (11803) ***(G-13583)***
Audio-Sears Corp.....607 652-7305
2 South St Stamford (12167) ***(G-15623)***
Audiology, Brooklyn *Also called Audio Technology New York Inc* ***(G-1653)***
Audiosavings Inc.....888 445-1555
600 Bayview Ave Ste 200 Inwood (11096) ***(G-6752)***
Audubon Machinery Corporation (PA).....716 564-5165
814 Wurlitzer Dr North Tonawanda (14120) ***(G-12957)***
Aufhauser Corp Canada, Plainview *Also called Aufhauser Manufacturing Corp* ***(G-13585)***
Aufhauser Corporation (PA).....516 694-8696
39 West Mall Plainview (11803) ***(G-13584)***
Aufhauser Manufacturing Corp.....516 694-8696
39 West Mall Plainview (11803) ***(G-13585)***
August Graphics, Bronx *Also called D B F Associates* ***(G-1307)***
August Studios.....718 706-6487
4008 22nd St Fl 3 Long Island City (11101) ***(G-7678)***
August Thomsen Corp.....516 676-7100
36 Sea Cliff Ave Glen Cove (11542) ***(G-5611)***
Augusta Studios, Long Island City *Also called August Studios* ***(G-7678)***
Auntie Anne's, Ithaca *Also called Doreen Chrysler* ***(G-6838)***
Aura Detergent LLC (PA).....718 824-2162
1811 Mayflower Ave Bronx (10461) ***(G-1278)***
Aura Essence, Brooklyn *Also called Candle In The Window Inc* ***(G-1753)***
Aura International Mfg Inc.....212 719-1418
512 Fashion Ave Fl 26 New York (10018) ***(G-9262)***
Aurafin Oroamerica, New York *Also called Richline Group Inc* ***(G-11867)***
Auratic Inc.....914 413-8154
41 Madison Ave Ste 1402 New York (10010) ***(G-9263)***
Auratic USA Incorporated.....212 684-8888
41 Madison Ave Ste 1904 New York (10010) ***(G-9264)***
Aureonic.....518 791-9331
13 Whispering Pines Rd Gansevoort (12831) ***(G-5485)***
Auric Technology LLC.....212 573-0911
330 Madison Ave Fl 6 New York (10017) ***(G-9265)***
Aurora Indus Machining Inc.....716 826-7911
3380 N Benzing Rd Orchard Park (14127) ***(G-13252)***
Aurora Machine, Rochester *Also called Alkemy Machine LLC* ***(G-14186)***
Aurora Sef, Peekskill *Also called RMS Packaging Inc* ***(G-13481)***
Aurora Shoe Company, King Ferry *Also called Lake View Manufacturing LLC* ***(G-7168)***
Aurora Stone Group LLC.....315 471-6869
114 Marcy St East Syracuse (13057) ***(G-4508)***
Aurora Technical Services Ltd.....716 652-1463
11970 Parker Rd East Aurora (14052) ***(G-4367)***
Aurubis Buffalo Inc.....716 879-6700
600 Military Rd Buffalo (14207) ***(G-2822)***
Aurubis Buffalo Inc (HQ).....716 879-6700
70 Sayre St Buffalo (14207) ***(G-2823)***
Ausco Inc.....516 944-9882
425 Smith St Ste 1 Farmingdale (11735) ***(G-4947)***
Austin Air Systems Limited.....716 856-3700
500 Elk St Buffalo (14210) ***(G-2824)***
Austin Industries Inc (PA).....585 589-1353
3871 Oak Orchard Rd Albion (14411) ***(G-162)***
Austin Mohawk and Company LLC.....315 793-3000
2175 Beechgrove Pl Utica (13501) ***(G-16308)***
Autel North America, Farmingdale *Also called Autel US Inc* ***(G-4948)***
Autel US Inc (HQ).....631 923-2620
175 Central Ave Ste 200 Farmingdale (11735) ***(G-4948)***

Auterra Inc............518 382-9600
2135 Technology Dr Schenectady (12308) **(G-15232)**
Authentic Parts, Holbrook *Also called Ingham Industries Inc* **(G-6451)**
Authority On Transportation, Dix Hills *Also called Authority Transportation Inc* **(G-4291)**
Authority Transportation Inc............888 933-1268
167 Oakfield Ave Dix Hills (11746) **(G-4291)**
Auto Body Services LLC............631 431-4640
400 W Hoffman Ave Lindenhurst (11757) **(G-7455)**
Auto Data Labels, Deer Park *Also called Auto Data Systems Inc* **(G-4104)**
Auto Data Systems Inc (PA)............631 831-7427
2000 Deer Park Ave Deer Park (11729) **(G-4104)**
Auto Market Publications Inc............631 667-0500
1641 Deer Park Ave Ste 5 Deer Park (11729) **(G-4105)**
Auto Sport Designs Inc............631 425-1555
203 W Hills Rd Huntington Station (11746) **(G-6697)**
Auto-Mat Company Inc............516 938-7373
69 Hazel St Hicksville (11801) **(G-6325)**
Auto-Mate Technologies LLC............631 727-8886
34 Hinda Blvd Riverhead (11901) **(G-14139)**
Autodesk Inc............646 613-8680
38 W 21st St Fl 9 New York (10010) **(G-9266)**
Autodesk Inc............607 257-4280
2353 N Triphammer Rd Ithaca (14850) **(G-6820)**
Autodyne Manufacturing Co Inc............631 957-5858
200 N Strong Ave Lindenhurst (11757) **(G-7456)**
Automated & MGT Solutions LLC............518 283-5352
743 Columbia Tpke East Greenbush (12061) **(G-4401)**
Automated Bldg MGT Systems Inc (PA)............516 216-5603
54 Cherry Ln Floral Park (11001) **(G-5194)**
Automated Building Controls............914 381-2860
629 N Barry Ave Mamaroneck (10543) **(G-8023)**
Automated Cells & Eqp Inc............607 936-1341
9699 Enterprise Dr Painted Post (14870) **(G-13389)**
Automated Control Logic Inc............914 769-8880
578 Commerce St Thornwood (10594) **(G-16116)**
Automated Dynamics, Niskayuna *Also called ADC Acquisition Company* **(G-12893)**
Automated Office Systems Inc............516 396-5555
71 S Central Ave Valley Stream (11580) **(G-16401)**
Automated Systems Group, Rochester *Also called Micro Instrument Corp* **(G-14507)**
Automatic Bar Machining Co, Rochester *Also called Kathleen B Mead* **(G-14468)**
Automatic Connector Inc............631 543-5000
375 Oser Ave Hauppauge (11788) **(G-6029)**
Automatic Press Inc............212 924-5573
140 W 30th St Frnt 1 New York (10001) **(G-9267)**
Automation Correct LLC............315 299-3589
405 Parrish Ln Syracuse (13205) **(G-15861)**
Automation Papers Inc............315 432-0565
6361 Thompson Rd Stop 1 Syracuse (13206) **(G-15862)**
Automation Source Technologies (PA)............631 643-1678
21 Otis St Unit B West Babylon (11704) **(G-16772)**
Automationcorrect.com, Syracuse *Also called Automation Correct LLC* **(G-15861)**
Automecha International Ltd (PA)............607 843-2235
48 S Canal St Oxford (13830) **(G-13363)**
Automotion Parking Systems LLC............516 565-5600
411 Hempstead Tpke # 200 West Hempstead (11552) **(G-16850)**
Automotive LLC............248 728-8642
4320 Federal Dr Batavia (14020) **(G-623)**
Automotive Accessories Group............212 736-8100
505 8th Ave Rm 12a05 New York (10018) **(G-9268)**
Automotive Filters Mfg Inc............631 435-1010
80a Keyland Ct A Bohemia (11716) **(G-1020)**
Automotive Leather Group, Great Neck *Also called Kamali Group Inc* **(G-5819)**
Automtive Uphl Cnvertible Tops............914 961-4242
170 Marbledale Rd Tuckahoe (10707) **(G-16269)**
Autostat Corporation............516 379-9447
209 Nassau Rd 11 Roosevelt (11575) **(G-15003)**
Autronic Plastics Inc (PA)............516 333-7577
1150 Motor Pkwy Central Islip (11722) **(G-3485)**
Auven Therapeutics MGT LP............212 616-4000
1325 Avenue Of The Americ New York (10019) **(G-9269)**
Auxilium Pharmaceuticals Inc............484 321-2022
70 High St Rye (10580) **(G-15054)**
AV Denim Inc............212 764-6668
230 W 38th St Fl 8r New York (10018) **(G-9270)**
AV Therapeutics Inc............917 497-5523
20 E 68th St Ste 204 New York (10065) **(G-9271)**
Ava Wood Products, Ava *Also called Robert W Still* **(G-531)**
Avalanche Fabrication Inc............585 545-4000
6314 Dean Pkwy Ontario (14519) **(G-13196)**
Avalanche Studios New York Inc............212 993-6447
536 Broadway New York (10012) **(G-9272)**
Avalin LLC............212 842-2286
221 W 37th St Fl 3 New York (10018) **(G-9273)**
Avalon Copy Centers Amer Inc (PA)............315 471-3333
901 N State St Syracuse (13208) **(G-15863)**
Avalon Copy Centers Amer Inc............716 995-7777
741 Main St Buffalo (14203) **(G-2825)**
Avalon Document Services, Syracuse *Also called Avalon Copy Centers Amer Inc* **(G-15863)**
Avalon Document Services, Buffalo *Also called Avalon Copy Centers Amer Inc* **(G-2825)**
Avalonbay Communities Inc............516 484-7766
1100 Avalon Sq Glen Cove (11542) **(G-5612)**
Avalonics Inc............516 238-7074
94 Gardiners Ave Ste 164 Levittown (11756) **(G-7424)**
Avanel Industries Inc............516 333-0990
121 Hopper St Westbury (11590) **(G-16971)**
Avant Garde Screen Printing Co, Flushing *Also called Albert Siy* **(G-5224)**
Avante............516 782-4888
35 Hicks Ln Great Neck (11024) **(G-5793)**
Avanti Advanced Mfg Corp............716 541-8945
673 Ontario St Buffalo (14207) **(G-2826)**
Avanti Control Systems Inc............518 921-4368
1 Hamilton St Fl 2 Gloversville (12078) **(G-5707)**
Avanti Furniture Corp............516 293-8220
497 Main St Farmingdale (11735) **(G-4949)**
Avanti Press Inc............212 414-1025
6 W 18th St Ste 6l New York (10011) **(G-9274)**
Avanti U S A Ltd............716 695-5800
412 Young St Tonawanda (14150) **(G-16141)**
Avas Corporation............203 470-3587
225 W 115th St Apt 3a New York (10026) **(G-9275)**
Avco Industries Inc............631 851-1555
120 Windsor Pl Central Islip (11722) **(G-3486)**
Avcom of Virginia Inc............585 924-4560
590 Fishers Station Dr Victor (14564) **(G-16461)**
Aventura Technologies Inc (PA)............631 300-4000
48 Mall Dr Commack (11725) **(G-3822)**
Avenue Magazine, New York *Also called Manhattan Media LLC* **(G-11130)**
Avery Biomedical Devices Inc............631 864-1600
61 Mall Dr Ste 1 Commack (11725) **(G-3823)**
Avery Dennison, Orangeburg *Also called Paxar Corporation* **(G-13238)**
Avery Dennison Corporation............845 680-3873
524 Route 303 Orangeburg (10962) **(G-13220)**
Avery Dennison Corporation............626 304-2000
218 W 40th St Fl 8 New York (10018) **(G-9276)**
Avf Inc (PA)............951 360-7111
2775 Broadway St Ste 200 Buffalo (14227) **(G-2827)**
AVI, Plainview *Also called Audio Video Invasion Inc* **(G-13583)**
AVI-Spl Employee............212 840-4801
8 W 38th St Rm 1101 New York (10018) **(G-9277)**
Avid Technology Inc............212 983-2424
90 Park Ave New York (10016) **(G-9278)**
Avitto Leather Goods Inc............212 219-7501
424 W Broadway Frnt A New York (10012) **(G-9279)**
Avm Printing Inc............631 351-1331
43 Corporate Dr Hauppauge (11788) **(G-6030)**
Avocode Inc............646 934-8410
55 E 73rd St Apt Gf New York (10021) **(G-9280)**
Avon Press, Hauppauge *Also called Avon Reproductions Inc* **(G-6031)**
Avon Products Inc (PA)............212 282-5000
777 3rd Ave New York (10017) **(G-9281)**
Avon Products Inc............716 572-4842
433 Thorncliff Rd Buffalo (14223) **(G-2828)**
Avon Reproductions Inc............631 273-2400
175 Engineers Rd Hauppauge (11788) **(G-6031)**
Avs Gem Stone Corp............212 944-6380
48 W 48th St Ste 1010 New York (10036) **(G-9282)**
AVS Laminates Inc............631 286-2136
99 Bellport Ave Bellport (11713) **(G-826)**
Avstar Fuel Systems Inc............315 255-1955
15 Brookfield Pl Auburn (13021) **(G-483)**
AVX Corporation............716 372-6611
1695 Seneca Ave Olean (14760) **(G-13134)**
AW Mack Manufacturing Co Inc............845 452-4050
1098 Dutchess Tpke Poughkeepsie (12603) **(G-13891)**
Awaken Led Company............802 338-5971
477 State Route 11 # 1050 Champlain (12919) **(G-3537)**
Awap Inc............516 481-4070
982 Front St Unit A Uniondale (11553) **(G-16289)**
Award Publishing Limited............212 246-0405
40 W 55th St Apt 9b New York (10019) **(G-9283)**
Awning Man, The, Yonkers *Also called Fabric Concepts For Industry* **(G-17443)**
Awning Mart Inc............315 699-5928
5665 State Route 31 Cicero (13039) **(G-3642)**
Awnings Plus Inc............716 693-3690
363 Delaware St Tonawanda (14150) **(G-16142)**
Awr Energy Inc............585 469-7750
35 Melody Ln Plattsburgh (12901) **(G-13652)**
Awt Supply Corp............516 437-9105
153 Meacham Ave Elmont (11003) **(G-4717)**
Axel Plastics RES Labs Inc............718 672-8300
5820 Broadway Woodside (11377) **(G-17318)**
Axis Denim, New York *Also called Axis Na LLC* **(G-9284)**
Axis Na LLC (PA)............212 840-4005
70 W 40th St Fl 11 New York (10018) **(G-9284)**
Axle Express............518 347-2220
729 Broadway Schenectady (12305) **(G-15233)**
Axle Teknology LLC (PA)............631 423-3044
113 Woodbury Rd Huntington (11743) **(G-6655)**
Axtell Bradtke Lumber Co............607 265-3850
113 Beals Pond Rd Masonville (13804) **(G-8107)**
Aycan Medical Systems LLC............585 271-3078
693 East Ave Ste 102 Rochester (14607) **(G-14219)**

AZ Yashir Bapaz Inc 212 947-7357
134 W 37th St New York (10018) **(G-9285)**
Azar Displays, Nanuet *Also called Azar International Inc* **(G-8751)**
Azar International Inc (PA) 845 624-8808
31 W Prospect St Nanuet (10954) **(G-8751)**
Azibi Ltd 212 869-6550
270 W 39th St Rm 1501 New York (10018) **(G-9286)**
Aztec Industries Inc 631 585-1331
200 13th Ave Unit 5 Ronkonkoma (11779) **(G-14875)**
Aztec Mfg of Rochester 585 352-8152
19 Hickory Ln Spencerport (14559) **(G-15565)**
Aztec Tool Co Inc 631 243-1144
180 Rodeo Dr Edgewood (11717) **(G-4593)**
Azurrx Biopharma Inc 646 699-7855
760 Parkside Ave Ste 217 Brooklyn (11226) **(G-1654)**
B & B Forest Products Ltd 518 622-0811
251 Route 145 Cairo (12413) **(G-3270)**
B & B Jewelry Mfg Co, New York *Also called Barber Brothers Jewelry Mfg* **(G-9316)**
B & B Lumber Company Inc (PA) 315 492-1786
4800 Solvay Rd Jamesville (13078) **(G-7045)**
B & B Precision Components Inc 631 273-3321
301 Christopher St # 303 Ronkonkoma (11779) **(G-14876)**
B & B Precision Mfg Inc (PA) 585 226-6226
310 W Main St Avon (14414) **(G-538)**
B & B Sheet Metal Inc 718 433-2501
2540 50th Ave Long Island City (11101) **(G-7679)**
B & B Sweater Mills Inc (PA) 718 456-8693
1160 Flushing Ave Brooklyn (11237) **(G-1655)**
B & D Enterprises of Utica (PA) 315 735-3311
2 Campion Rd Ste 7 New Hartford (13413) **(G-8801)**
B & F Architectural Support Gr 212 279-6488
450 7th Ave Ste 307 New York (10123) **(G-9287)**
B & H Electronics Corp 845 782-5000
308 Museum Village Rd Monroe (10950) **(G-8549)**
B & H Precision Fabricators 631 563-9620
95 Davinci Dr Bohemia (11716) **(G-1021)**
B & J Delivers Inc 631 524-5550
70 Emjay Blvd Bldg D Brentwood (11717) **(G-1177)**
B & J Lumber Co Inc 518 677-3845
1075 State Route 22 Cambridge (12816) **(G-3304)**
B & K Components Ltd 323 776-4277
2100 Old Union Rd Buffalo (14227) **(G-2829)**
B & K Dye Cutting Inc 718 497-5216
245 Varet St Brooklyn (11206) **(G-1656)**
B & P Jays Inc 716 668-8408
19 N Hill Dr Buffalo (14224) **(G-2830)**
B & R Electric Motor Inc 631 752-7533
5919 Central Ave Farmingdale (11735) **(G-4950)**
B & R Industries Inc 631 736-2275
12 Commercial Blvd Medford (11763) **(G-8235)**
B & R Promotional Products 212 563-0040
34 W 120th St Apt 1 New York (10027) **(G-9288)**
B & R Tool Inc 718 948-2729
955 Rensselaer Ave Staten Island (10309) **(G-15642)**
B & S Bialy, Brooklyn *Also called Bagels By Bell Ltd* **(G-1663)**
B & W Heat Treating Company 716 876-8184
2780 Kenmore Ave Tonawanda (14150) **(G-16143)**
B & Z Technologies LLC 631 675-9666
7 Technology Dr East Setauket (11733) **(G-4477)**
B Barine Inc 718 499-5650
145 18th St Brooklyn (11215) **(G-1657)**
B C America, New York *Also called Intertex USA Inc* **(G-10641)**
B C Manufacturing Inc 585 482-1080
100 Thruway Park Dr West Henrietta (14586) **(G-16870)**
B C T, Holbrook *Also called Speedcard Inc* **(G-6473)**
B C T, New York *Also called Great Impressions Inc* **(G-10356)**
B C T, Syosset *Also called SDS Business Cards Inc* **(G-15839)**
B Cake NY LLC 347 787-7199
702 Washington Ave Brooklyn (11238) **(G-1658)**
B D B Typewriter Supply Works 718 232-4800
6215 14th Ave Brooklyn (11219) **(G-1659)**
B F G Elcpltg and Mfg Co 716 362-0888
3949 Jeffrey Blvd Blasdell (14219) **(G-960)**
B H Aircraft Company Inc (PA) 631 580-9747
2230 Smithtown Ave Ronkonkoma (11779) **(G-14877)**
B H M Metal Products Co 845 292-5297
Horseshoe Lake Rd Kauneonga Lake (12749) **(G-7136)**
B J Long Co, Rochester *Also called R V Dow Enterprises Inc* **(G-14619)**
B J S Electric 845 774-8166
1000 Craigville Rd Chester (10918) **(G-3600)**
B K Integrity, New York *Also called Golden Integrity Inc* **(G-10332)**
B K Jewelry Contractor Inc 212 398-9093
71 W 47th St Fl 11 New York (10036) **(G-9289)**
B Live LLC 212 489-0721
347 W 36th St Rm 402 New York (10018) **(G-9290)**
B M P, Medina *Also called Bmp America Inc* **(G-8267)**
B P I, West Henrietta *Also called Brinkman Precision Inc* **(G-16872)**
B P Nash Co Inc 315 445-1310
5841 Butternut Dr East Syracuse (13057) **(G-4509)**
B S C, Binghamton *Also called Binghamton Simulator Co Inc* **(G-895)**
B S J Limited 212 764-4600
1400 Broadway Ste 1702 New York (10018) **(G-9291)**
B S J Limited (PA) 212 221-8403
1375 Broadway Rm 508 New York (10018) **(G-9292)**
B Smith Furs Inc 212 967-5290
224 W 30th St Rm 402 New York (10001) **(G-9293)**
B Tween LLC 212 819-9040
1411 Broadway Rm 2520 New York (10018) **(G-9294)**
B V M Associates 631 254-6220
999-32 Montrell 414 Shirley (11967) **(G-15415)**
B W A, New York *Also called Ben Wachter Associates Inc* **(G-9354)**
B&K Precision Corporation 631 369-2665
31 Oakwood Dr Manorville (11949) **(G-8077)**
B-Reel Inc 917 388-3836
401 Broadway Fl 24 New York (10013) **(G-9295)**
B-Squared Inc 212 777-2044
104 W 29th St Fl 7 New York (10001) **(G-9296)**
B/E Aerospace Inc 631 563-6400
355 Knickerbocker Ave Bohemia (11716) **(G-1022)**
B/E Aerospace Inc 631 589-0877
355 Knickerbocker Ave Bohemia (11716) **(G-1023)**
B2b Cleaning Services, Yonkers *Also called Rumsey Corp* **(G-17482)**
B3cg Interconnect Usa Inc 450 491-4040
1523 Military Tpke # 200 Plattsburgh (12901) **(G-13653)**
B601 V2 Inc 646 391-6431
315 5th Ave Rm 903 New York (10016) **(G-9297)**
Ba Sports Nutrition LLC 310 424-5077
1720 Whitestone Expy # 401 Whitestone (11357) **(G-17202)**
Baar & Beards, New York *Also called Gce International Inc* **(G-10260)**
Babbit Bearings, Syracuse *Also called Babbitt Bearings Inc* **(G-15864)**
Babbitt Bearings Inc (PA) 315 479-6603
734 Burnet Ave Syracuse (13203) **(G-15864)**
Babbitt Bearings Incorporated 315 479-6603
734 Burnet Ave Syracuse (13203) **(G-15865)**
Babcock Co Inc 607 776-3341
36 Delaware Ave Bath (14810) **(G-653)**
Babula Construction Inc 716 681-0886
5136 William St Lancaster (14086) **(G-7305)**
Baby Beluga, New York *Also called Beluga Inc* **(G-9353)**
Baby Central LLC 718 372-2229
2436 Mcdonald Ave Brooklyn (11223) **(G-1660)**
Baby Signature Inc (PA) 212 686-1700
251 5th Ave Fl 2l New York (10016) **(G-9298)**
Baby Uv/Kids Uv Inc 917 301-9020
50th St & 1st Bdg 57 Fl 5 Brooklyn (11232) **(G-1661)**
Babydoll, New York *Also called Mag Brands LLC* **(G-11097)**
Babyfair Inc 212 736-7989
34 W 33rd St Rm 818 New York (10001) **(G-9299)**
Babyganics, Westbury *Also called Kas Direct LLC* **(G-17001)**
Babylon Iron Works Inc 631 643-3311
205 Edison Ave West Babylon (11704) **(G-16773)**
Babysafe Usa LLC 877 367-4141
251 County Road 17 Afton (13730) **(G-8)**
Backstage LLC (PA) 212 493-4243
45 Main St Ste 416 Brooklyn (11201) **(G-1662)**
Backtech Inc 973 279-0838
2 Peter Cooper Rd Apt Mf New York (10010) **(G-9300)**
Backyard Fence Inc 518 452-9496
4204 Albany St Albany (12205) **(G-51)**
Baco Enterprises Inc (PA) 718 589-6225
1190 Longwood Ave Bronx (10474) **(G-1279)**
Badge Machine Products Inc 585 394-0330
2491 Brickyard Rd Canandaigua (14424) **(G-3335)**
Badger Technologies Inc 585 869-7101
5829 County Road 41 Farmington (14425) **(G-5146)**
Badger Technologies Inc (PA) 585 869-7101
5829 County Road 41 Farmington (14425) **(G-5147)**
Badgley Mischka Licensing LLC 212 921-1585
550 7th Ave Fl 22 New York (10018) **(G-9301)**
Badoud Communications Inc 315 472-7821
750 W Genesee St Syracuse (13204) **(G-15866)**
Bae Systems Controls Inc (HQ) 607 770-2000
1098 Clark St Endicott (13760) **(G-4796)**
Bae Systems Info & Elec Sys 631 912-1525
450 Pulaski Rd Greenlawn (11740) **(G-5873)**
Bag Arts Ltd 212 684-7020
20 W 36th St Rm 5r New York (10018) **(G-9302)**
Bag Arts The Art Packaging LLC 212 684-7020
20 W 36th St Fl 5 New York (10018) **(G-9303)**
Bag Bazaar Ltd 212 689-3508
1 E 33rd St Fl 6 New York (10016) **(G-9304)**
Bagel Club, Bayside *Also called A T A Bagel Shoppe Inc* **(G-764)**
Bagel Club Inc 718 423-6106
20521 35th Ave Bayside (11361) **(G-767)**
Bagel Grove Inc 315 724-8015
5 Burrstone Rd Utica (13502) **(G-16309)**
Bagel Land 585 442-3080
1896 Monroe Ave Rochester (14618) **(G-14220)**
Bagel Lites LLC 855 813-7888
240 51st Ave Apt 1f Long Island City (11101) **(G-7680)**
Bagel Oasis, Flushing *Also called Triboro Bagel Co Inc* **(G-5303)**
Bagel Shoppe, The, Fishkill *Also called Enterprise Bagels Inc* **(G-5183)**

ALPHABETIC

Bagelovers Inc 607 844-3683
42 Elm St Dryden (13053) *(G-4320)*
Bagelry, Cedarhurst *Also called M & M Bagel Corp (G-3459)*
Bagels By Bell Ltd 718 272-2780
10013 Foster Ave Brooklyn (11236) *(G-1663)*
Bagels On The Square, Staten Island *Also called Carmine Street Bagels Inc (G-15656)*
Baggu 347 457-5266
109 Ingraham St Brooklyn (11237) *(G-1664)*
Bags Unlimited Inc 585 436-6282
7 Canal St Rochester (14608) *(G-14221)*
Bagznyc Corp 212 643-8202
19 W 34th St Rm 318 New York (10001) *(G-9305)*
Baikal Inc (PA) 212 239-4650
341 W 38th St Fl 3 New York (10018) *(G-9306)*
Bailey Boonville Mills Inc 315 942-2131
123 Mill St Boonville (13309) *(G-1162)*
Bailey Electric Motor Repair 585 542-5902
2186 Main Rd Corfu (14036) *(G-3952)*
Bailey Manufacturing Co LLC 716 965-2731
10987 Bennett State Rd Forestville (14062) *(G-5333)*
Baillie Lumber Co LP 315 942-5284
189 West St Boonville (13309) *(G-1163)*
Bainbridge & Knight LLC 212 986-5100
801 2nd Ave Fl 19 New York (10017) *(G-9307)*
Baird Mold Making Inc 631 667-0322
195 N Fehr Way Ste C Bay Shore (11706) *(G-674)*
Bairnco Corporation (HQ) 914 461-1300
1133 Westchester Ave N-222 White Plains (10604) *(G-17081)*
Bajan Group Inc 518 464-2884
950 New Loudon Rd Ste 280 Latham (12110) *(G-7355)*
Bak USA Technologies Corp 716 248-2704
425 Michigan Ave Ste 4 Buffalo (14203) *(G-2831)*
Baked Cupcakery 716 773-2050
1879 Whitehaven Rd Grand Island (14072) *(G-5752)*
Baker Commodities Inc 585 482-1880
2268 Browncroft Blvd Rochester (14625) *(G-14222)*
Baker Logging & Firewood 585 374-5733
8781 Grlnghuse Atlanta Rd Naples (14512) *(G-8764)*
Baker Products Inc 212 459-2323
5 Oakley Rd White Plains (10606) *(G-17082)*
Baker Tool & Die 716 694-2025
48 Industrial Dr North Tonawanda (14120) *(G-12958)*
Baker Tool & Die & Die 716 694-2025
48 Industrial Dr North Tonawanda (14120) *(G-12959)*
Bakerly LLC (PA) 212 220-3901
81 Prospect St Brooklyn (11201) *(G-1665)*
Bakers of All Nations, Mineola *Also called Ericeira Inc (G-8510)*
Bakers Pride Oven Co Inc 914 576-0200
145 Huguenot St Ste Mz1 New Rochelle (10801) *(G-8887)*
Bakery & Coffee Shop 315 287-1829
274 W Main St Gouverneur (13642) *(G-5742)*
Bakery Associates, Setauket *Also called Richard H Williams Associates (G-15379)*
Bakery Innovative Tech Corp 631 758-3081
139 N Ocean Ave Patchogue (11772) *(G-13415)*
Balajee Enterprises Inc 212 629-6150
150 W 30th St Frnt 2 New York (10001) *(G-9308)*
Balance Enterprises Inc 516 822-3183
12 W Cherry St Hicksville (11801) *(G-6326)*
Balanced Tech Corp 212 768-8330
37 W 37th St Fl 10 New York (10018) *(G-9309)*
Balchem Corporation (PA) 845 326-5600
52 Sunrise Park Rd New Hampton (10958) *(G-8797)*
Baldwin Machine Works Inc 631 842-9110
20 Grant Ave 2040 Copiague (11726) *(G-3896)*
Baldwin Ribbon & Stamping Corp 718 335-6700
3956 63rd St Woodside (11377) *(G-17319)*
Baldwin Richardson Foods Co 315 986-2727
3268 Blue Heron Dr Macedon (14502) *(G-7983)*
Balint Tool, Brooklyn *Also called Tools & Stamping Corp (G-2663)*
Baliva Concrete Products Inc 585 328-8442
245 Paul Rd Rochester (14624) *(G-14223)*
Ball Chain Mfg Co Inc (PA) 914 664-7500
741 S Fulton Ave Mount Vernon (10550) *(G-8664)*
Ball Metal Beverage Cont Corp 845 692-3800
95 Ballard Rd Middletown (10941) *(G-8427)*
Ball Metal Beverage Cont Corp 518 587-6030
11 Adams Rd Saratoga Springs (12866) *(G-15144)*
Ball Metal Beverage Cont Div, Middletown *Also called Ball Metal Beverage Cont Corp (G-8427)*
Ball Metal Beverage Cont Div, Saratoga Springs *Also called Ball Metal Beverage Cont Corp (G-15144)*
Ballantrae Lithographers Inc 914 592-3275
96 Wayside Dr White Plains (10607) *(G-17083)*
Balticare Inc 646 380-9470
501 Fashion Ave Rm 414 New York (10018) *(G-9310)*
Bam Enterprises Inc (PA) 716 773-7634
2243 Corning Rd Grand Island (14072) *(G-5753)*
Bam Sales LLC (PA) 212 781-3000
1407 Broadway Rm 2018 New York (10018) *(G-9311)*
Bamberger Polymers Intl Corp 516 622-3600
2 Jericho Plz Ste 109 Jericho (11753) *(G-7060)*
Bamboo Global Industries 973 943-1878
339 E 58th St Apt 7e New York (10022) *(G-9312)*
Bandier Corp 212 242-5400
960 Park Ave Apt 11b New York (10028) *(G-9313)*
Bandit International Ltd 718 402-2100
600 E 132nd St Bronx (10454) *(G-1280)*
Bands N Bows 718 984-4316
34 Fieldway Ave Staten Island (10308) *(G-15643)*
Bangla Clothing USA Inc (PA) 201 679-2615
262 W 38th St New York (10018) *(G-9314)*
Bangla Patrika Inc 718 482-9923
3806 31st St 2 Long Island City (11101) *(G-7681)*
Bank Displays.com, Deer Park *Also called L Miller Design Inc (G-4162)*
Bank-Miller Co Inc 914 227-9357
333 Fifth Ave Pelham (10803) *(G-13489)*
Banner Metalcraft Inc 631 563-7303
300 Trade Zone Dr Ronkonkoma (11779) *(G-14878)*
Banner Smoked Fish Inc 718 449-1992
2715 W 15th St Brooklyn (11224) *(G-1666)*
Banner Transmission & Eng Co 516 221-9459
2765 Broadway Bellmore (11710) *(G-814)*
Banner Transmissions, Bellmore *Also called Banner Transmission & Eng Co (G-814)*
Bar Fields Inc 347 587-7795
2614 W 13th St Brooklyn (11223) *(G-1667)*
Bara Fashions, Brooklyn *Also called Matchables Inc (G-2282)*
Baralan Usa Inc (HQ) 718 849-5768
12019 89th Ave Richmond Hill (11418) *(G-14067)*
Barbara Matera Ltd 212 475-5006
890 Broadway Fl 5 New York (10003) *(G-9315)*
Barber & Deline Enrgy Svcs LLC 315 696-8961
10 Community Dr Tully (13159) *(G-16274)*
Barber & Deline LLC 607 749-2619
995 State Route 11a Tully (13159) *(G-16275)*
Barber Brothers Jewelry Mfg 212 819-0666
580 5th Ave Ste 725 New York (10036) *(G-9316)*
Barber Welding Inc 315 834-6645
2517 Rte 31 W Weedsport (13166) *(G-16746)*
Barbera Transduser Systems 718 816-3025
21 Louis St Staten Island (10304) *(G-15644)*
Barc Usa Inc 516 719-1052
5 Delaware Dr Ste 2 New Hyde Park (11042) *(G-8818)*
Barclay Brown Corp 718 376-7166
47 Lancaster Ave Brooklyn (11223) *(G-1668)*
Barclay Tagg Racing 631 404-8269
86 Geranium Ave Floral Park (11001) *(G-5195)*
Bardwil Industries Inc (PA) 212 944-1870
1071 Ave Of The Americas New York (10018) *(G-9317)*
Bardwil Linens, New York *Also called Bardwil Industries Inc (G-9317)*
Bare Beauty Laser Hair Removal 718 278-2273
5 E 57th St Fl 6 New York (10022) *(G-9318)*
Bare Escentuals Inc 646 537-0070
1140 3rd Ave New York (10065) *(G-9319)*
Bare Minerals, New York *Also called Bare Escentuals Inc (G-9319)*
Bare Wire Div, Jordan *Also called Omega Wire Inc (G-7130)*
Bare Wire Div, Camden *Also called Omega Wire Inc (G-3318)*
Bare Wire Division, Camden *Also called Owi Corporation (G-3319)*
Bare Wire Division, Camden *Also called International Wire Group Inc (G-3316)*
Bargold Storage Systems LLC 718 247-7000
4141 38th St Long Island City (11101) *(G-7682)*
Bari Engineering Corp 212 966-2080
240 Bowery New York (10012) *(G-9320)*
Bari-Jay Fashions Inc (PA) 212 921-1551
225 W 37th St Fl 7 New York (10018) *(G-9321)*
Barilla America Ny Inc 585 226-5600
100 Horseshoe Blvd Avon (14414) *(G-539)*
Barker Brothers Incorporated 718 456-6400
1666 Summerfield St Ste 1 Ridgewood (11385) *(G-14101)*
Barker Steel LLC 518 465-6221
126 S Port Rd Albany (12202) *(G-52)*
Barnaby Prints Inc (PA) 845 477-2501
673 Jersey Ave Greenwood Lake (10925) *(G-5896)*
Barnes Group Inc 315 457-9200
1225 State Fair Blvd Syracuse (13209) *(G-15867)*
Barnes Metal Finishing Inc 585 798-4817
3932 Salt Works Rd Medina (14103) *(G-8265)*
Barnett Paul Inc 212 673-3250
155 Ave Of The Americas 7 New York (10013) *(G-9322)*
Barney & Dickenson Inc (PA) 607 729-1536
520 Prentice Rd Vestal (13850) *(G-16440)*
Baroka Creations Inc 212 768-0527
36 W 47th St Ste 1402 New York (10036) *(G-9323)*
Barone Offset Printing Corp 212 989-5500
89 Lake Ridge Cv Mohegan Lake (10547) *(G-8543)*
Barr Laboratories Inc 845 362-1100
2 Quaker Rd Pomona (10970) *(G-13728)*
Barra & Trumbore Inc 845 626-5442
40 Old Mine Rd Kerhonkson (12446) *(G-7154)*
Barrage 212 586-9390
401 W 47th St Frnt A New York (10036) *(G-9324)*
Barrasso & Sons Trucking Inc 631 581-0360
160 Floral Park St Islip Terrace (11752) *(G-6814)*

ALPHABETIC

(PA)=Parent Co (HQ)=Headquarters (DH)=Div Headquarters
2017 Harris
New York Manufacturers Directory
905

Barrera Jose & Maria Co Ltd 212 239-1994
29 W 36th St Fl 8 New York (10018) *(G-9325)*
Barrett Bronze Inc 914 699-6060
115 Miller Pl Mount Vernon (10550) *(G-8665)*
Barrett Paving Materials Inc 315 353-6611
Rr 56 Norwood (13668) *(G-13040)*
Barrett Paving Materials Inc 607 723-5367
14 Brandywine St Binghamton (13901) *(G-890)*
Barrett Paving Materials Inc 315 737-9471
363 Rasbach Rd Clayville (13322) *(G-3686)*
Barrett Paving Materials Inc 315 788-2037
26572 State Route 37 Watertown (13601) *(G-16636)*
Barrie House Coffee & Tea, Elmsford *Also called Bh Coffee Company LLC (G-4736)*
Barrier Brewing Company LLC 516 316-4429
612 W Walnut St Long Beach (11561) *(G-7638)*
Barron Games Intl Co LLC 716 630-0054
84 Aero Dr Ste 5 Buffalo (14225) *(G-2832)*
Barrons Educational, Hauppauge *Also called Barrons Educational Series Inc (G-6032)*
Barrons Educational Series Inc (PA) 631 434-3311
250 Wireless Blvd Hauppauge (11788) *(G-6032)*
Barry Industries Inc 212 242-5200
36 W 17th St Frnt 1 New York (10011) *(G-9326)*
Barry Steel Fabrication Inc (PA) 716 433-2144
30 Simonds St Lockport (14094) *(G-7571)*
Barry Supply Co Div, New York *Also called Barry Industries Inc (G-9326)*
Bars Precision Inc 585 742-6380
15 Wind Loft Cir Fairport (14450) *(G-4846)*
Barsky Ventures LLC 212 265-8890
250 W 57th St Ste 2514 New York (10107) *(G-9327)*
Barson Composites Corporation (PA) 516 752-7882
160 Bethpage Sweet Old Bethpage (11804) *(G-13126)*
Bartell Machinery Systems LLC (HQ) 315 336-7600
6321 Elmer Hill Rd Rome (13440) *(G-14804)*
Bartholomew Mazza Ltd Inc 212 935-4530
22 W 48th St Ste 805 New York (10036) *(G-9328)*
Bartizan Data Systems LLC 914 965-7977
217 Riverdale Ave Yonkers (10705) *(G-17419)*
Bartolomeo Publishing Inc 631 420-4949
100 Cabot St Unit A West Babylon (11704) *(G-16774)*
Bartolotta Furniture, Auburn *Also called Matteo & Antonio Bartolotta (G-508)*
Barton International, Glens Falls *Also called Barton Mines Company LLC (G-5672)*
Barton Mines Company LLC (PA) 518 798-5462
6 Warren St Glens Falls (12801) *(G-5672)*
Barton Tool Inc 716 665-2801
1864 Lyndon Blvd Falconer (14733) *(G-4892)*
Basco, Amherst *Also called American Precision Inds Inc (G-224)*
Base Container Inc 718 636-2004
180 Classon Ave Brooklyn (11205) *(G-1669)*
Base Systems Inc 845 278-1991
1606 Route 22 Brewster (10509) *(G-1211)*
Baseline Graphics Inc 585 223-0153
148 Selborne Chase Fairport (14450) *(G-4847)*
BASF Beauty Care Solutions LLC 631 689-0200
50 Health Sciences Dr Stony Brook (11790) *(G-15766)*
BASF Corporation 914 737-2554
1057 Lower South St Peekskill (10566) *(G-13473)*
BASF Corporation 631 380-2490
25 Health Sciences Dr # 220 Stony Brook (11790) *(G-15767)*
BASF Corporation 518 465-6534
70 Riverside Ave Rensselaer (12144) *(G-14045)*
BASF Corporation 914 785-2000
540 White Plains Rd Tarrytown (10591) *(G-16087)*
BASF Corporation 973 245-6000
560 White Plains Rd Tarrytown (10591) *(G-16088)*
BASF Corporation 914 788-1627
1057 Lower South St Peekskill (10566) *(G-13474)*
BASF Corporation 212 450-8280
545 5th Ave Fl 11 New York (10017) *(G-9329)*
BASF Corporation 631 689-0200
361 Sheep Pasture Rd East Setauket (11733) *(G-4478)*
BASF The Chemical Company, East Setauket *Also called BASF Corporation (G-4478)*
Basic Formula, New York *Also called Cougar Sport Inc (G-9732)*
Basic Ltd 718 438-5576
3611 14th Ave Ste B02 Brooklyn (11218) *(G-1670)*
Basil S Kadhim 888 520-5192
280 Madison Ave Rm 912 New York (10016) *(G-9330)*
Basileus Company LLC 315 963-3516
8104 Cazenovia Rd Manlius (13104) *(G-8067)*
Basilio's, Canastota *Also called Salarinos Italian Foods Inc (G-3372)*
Basiloff LLC 646 671-0353
179 Bennett Ave Apt 7f New York (10040) *(G-9331)*
Basin Holdings US LLC (PA) 212 695-7376
200 Park Ave Fl 58 New York (10166) *(G-9332)*
Bass Oil & Chemical Llc 718 628-4444
136 Morgan Ave Brooklyn (11237) *(G-1671)*
Bass Oil Company Inc 718 628-4444
136 Morgan Ave Brooklyn (11237) *(G-1672)*
Bassin Technical Sales Co 914 698-9358
1009 W Boston Post Rd # 2 Mamaroneck (10543) *(G-8024)*
Batampte Pickle Products Inc (PA) 718 251-2100
77 Brooklyn Terminal Mkt Brooklyn (11236) *(G-1673)*
Batavia Enclosures Inc 585 344-1797
636 Main St Arcade (14009) *(G-388)*
Batavia Legal Printing Inc 585 768-2100
7 Bank St Le Roy (14482) *(G-7403)*
Batavia Precision Glass LLC 585 343-6050
231 Currier Ave Buffalo (14212) *(G-2833)*
Batavia Press LLC 585 343-4429
3817 W Main Street Rd Batavia (14020) *(G-624)*
Bates Industries, South Glens Falls *Also called Mdi East Inc (G-15526)*
Bates Jackson Engraving Co Inc 716 854-3000
17 Elm St 21 Buffalo (14203) *(G-2834)*
Bator Bintor Inc 347 546-6503
42 Delevan St Brooklyn (11231) *(G-1674)*
Battenfeld Grease Oil Corp NY 716 695-2100
1174 Erie Ave North Tonawanda (14120) *(G-12960)*
Battenfeld-American Inc 716 822-8410
1575 Clinton St Buffalo (14206) *(G-2835)*
Battery Energy Storage Systems 518 256-7029
291 River St Ste 318 Troy (12180) *(G-16227)*
Battsco LLC 516 586-6544
190 Lauman Ln Unit A Hicksville (11801) *(G-6327)*
Baublebar Inc 646 664-4803
1115 Broadway Fl 5 New York (10010) *(G-9333)*
Bauerschmidt & Sons Inc 718 528-3500
11920 Merrick Blvd Jamaica (11434) *(G-6898)*
Bauli USA Inc 646 380-1891
295 Madison Ave Rm 1705 New York (10017) *(G-9334)*
Baum Christine and John Corp 585 621-8910
1577 W Ridge Rd Rochester (14615) *(G-14224)*
Baums Castorine Company Inc 315 336-8154
200 Matthew St Rome (13440) *(G-14805)*
Bausch & Lomb Holdings Inc (HQ) 585 338-6000
450 Lexington Ave New York (10017) *(G-9335)*
Bausch & Lomb Incorporated (HQ) 585 338-6000
1400 N Goodman St Rochester (14609) *(G-14225)*
Bausch & Lomb Incorporated 585 338-6000
1400 N Goodman St Rochester (14609) *(G-14226)*
Baxter Healthcare Corporation 800 356-3454
711 Park Ave Medina (14103) *(G-8266)*
Bay Sales Company, New York *Also called Salmco Jewelry Corp (G-11958)*
Bayshore Electric Motors 631 475-1397
33 Suffolk Ave Patchogue (11772) *(G-13416)*
Bayshore Motors, Patchogue *Also called Bayshore Electric Motors (G-13416)*
Bayshore Wire Products Corp 631 451-8825
480 Mill Rd Coram (11727) *(G-3941)*
Bayside Beepers & Cellular 718 343-3888
25607 Hillside Ave Glen Oaks (11004) *(G-5640)*
Baywood Publishing Company 631 691-1270
26 Austin Ave Ste 2 Amityville (11701) *(G-277)*
Bazaar 212 903-5497
300 W 57th St Fl 25 New York (10019) *(G-9336)*
BC Systems Inc 631 751-9370
200 N Belle Mead Ave # 2 Setauket (11733) *(G-15374)*
BCM, Mount Vernon *Also called Ball Chain Mfg Co Inc (G-8664)*
Bco Industries Western NY Inc 716 877-2800
77 Oriskany Dr Tonawanda (14150) *(G-16144)*
Bcp Ingredients Inc (HQ) 845 326-5600
52 Sunrise Park Rd New Hampton (10958) *(G-8798)*
Bd Initiative-Hlthcare Wrkr SA, Nyack *Also called Becton Dickinson and Company (G-13044)*
Bd Projects, New York *Also called Architects Newspaper LLC (G-9195)*
BDB Technologies LLC 800 921-4270
768 Bedford Ave Brooklyn (11205) *(G-1675)*
Bdg Media Inc 917 951-9768
158 W 27th St Fl 11 New York (10001) *(G-9337)*
Bdm, Syosset *Also called Buffalo Dental Mfg Co Inc (G-15815)*
Bdp Industries Inc (PA) 518 695-6851
354 State Route 29 Greenwich (12834) *(G-5886)*
BDR Creative Concepts Inc 516 942-7768
141 Central Ave Ste B Farmingdale (11735) *(G-4951)*
Be The Media, New Hyde Park *Also called Natural E Creative LLC (G-8849)*
Beachbuttons LLC 917 306-9369
6 Greene St Apt 4b New York (10013) *(G-9338)*
Beacon, Babylon *Also called A C J Communications Inc (G-544)*
Beacon Adhesives Inc 914 699-3400
125 S Macquesten Pkwy Mount Vernon (10550) *(G-8666)*
Beacon Chemical, Mount Vernon *Also called Beacon Adhesives Inc (G-8666)*
Beacon Newspapers, Hempstead *Also called Nassau County Publications (G-6283)*
Beacon Press Inc 212 691-5050
32 Cushman Rd White Plains (10606) *(G-17084)*
Beacon Press News, Wappingers Falls *Also called Wappingers Falls Shopper Inc (G-16578)*
Beacon Spch Lnge Pthlgy Phys 516 626-1635
1441 Old Northern Blvd Roslyn (11576) *(G-15016)*
Beacon Therapy Services, Roslyn *Also called Beacon Spch Lnge Pthlgy Phys (G-15016)*
Beak & Skiff Cider Mill Inc 315 677-5105
4472 Us Route 20 La Fayette (13084) *(G-7239)*
Beal Blocks, New York *Also called B & R Promotional Products (G-9288)*
BEAM Manufacturing Corp 631 253-2724
107 Otis St Unit A West Babylon (11704) *(G-16775)*
Bear Metal Works Inc 716 824-4350
144 Milton St Buffalo (14210) *(G-2836)*

A
L
P
H
A
B
E
T
I
C

Bear Port Publishing Company....212 337-8577
45 W 21st St 3b New York (10010) *(G-9339)*
Beardslee Realty....516 747-5557
290 E Jericho Tpke Mineola (11501) *(G-8497)*
Bears Management Group Inc....585 624-5694
7577 E Main St Lima (14485) *(G-7443)*
Bears Playgrounds, Lima *Also called Bears Management Group Inc (G-7443)*
Beastons Budget Printing....585 244-2721
1260 Scttsvlle Rd Ste 300 Rochester (14624) *(G-14227)*
Beauty America LLC....917 744-1430
10 Bond St Ste 296 Great Neck (11021) *(G-5794)*
Beauty Fashion Inc....212 840-8800
8 W 38th St Frnt 2 New York (10018) *(G-9340)*
Beaver Creek Industries Inc....607 545-6382
11530 White Rd Canaseraga (14822) *(G-3362)*
Bebop Books, New York *Also called Lee & Low Books Incorporated (G-10957)*
BEC Acquisition Co LLC....516 986-3050
270 Spagnoli Rd Ste 102 Melville (11747) *(G-8296)*
Becca Inc....646 568-6250
142 W 36th St Fl 15 New York (10018) *(G-9341)*
Beck Vault Company....315 337-7590
6648 Shank Ave Rome (13440) *(G-14806)*
Beck, Don, Corfu *Also called Delaval Inc (G-3954)*
Becker Electronics Inc....631 619-9100
50 Alexander Ct Ste 2 Ronkonkoma (11779) *(G-14879)*
Beckmann Converting Inc (PA)....518 842-0073
14 Park Dr Amsterdam (12010) *(G-334)*
Becks Classic Mfg Inc....631 435-3800
50 Emjay Blvd Ste 7 Brentwood (11717) *(G-1178)*
Becton Dickinson and Company....845 353-3371
1 Main St Apt 3307 Nyack (10960) *(G-13044)*
Bedessee Imports Ltd....718 272-1300
140 Varick Ave Brooklyn (11237) *(G-1676)*
Bedford Freeman & Worth (HQ)....212 576-9400
1 New York Plz Ste 4500 New York (10004) *(G-9342)*
Bedford Freeman & Worth....212 375-7000
1 New York Plz Ste 4500 New York (10004) *(G-9343)*
Bedford Communications Inc....212 807-8220
1410 Broadway Frnt 2 New York (10018) *(G-9344)*
Bedford Downing Glass....718 418-6409
220 Ingraham St Ste 2 Brooklyn (11237) *(G-1677)*
Bedford Precision Parts Corp....914 241-2211
290 Adams St Bedford Hills (10507) *(G-799)*
Bedford Pund Rdge Rcord Review, Bedford Hills *Also called Record Review LLC (G-807)*
Bedford Wdwrk Instllations Inc....914 764-9434
200 Pound Ridge Rd Bedford (10506) *(G-796)*
Bedgevant Inc....718 492-0297
200 60th St Brooklyn (11220) *(G-1678)*
Bedrock Communications....212 532-4150
152 Madison Ave Rm 802 New York (10016) *(G-9345)*
Bedrock Landscaping Mtls Corp (PA)....631 587-4950
454 Sunrise Hwy Babylon (11704) *(G-546)*
Bedrock Plus, Babylon *Also called Bedrock Landscaping Mtls Corp (G-546)*
Bee Green Industries Inc....516 334-3525
322 Westbury Ave Carle Place (11514) *(G-3386)*
Bee Publications Inc....716 632-4700
5564 Main St Williamsville (14221) *(G-17235)*
Beebie Printing & Art Agcy Inc....518 725-4528
40 E Pine St Gloversville (12078) *(G-5708)*
Beech Grove Technology Inc....845 223-6844
11 Sandy Pines Blvd Hopewell Junction (12533) *(G-6547)*
Beech-Nut Nutrition Company (HQ)....518 839-0300
1 Nutritious Pl Amsterdam (12010) *(G-335)*
Beeche Systems Corp....518 381-6000
Scotia Glenville Indl Par Scotia (12302) *(G-15324)*
Beecher Emssn Sltn Tchnlgs LLC (PA)....607 796-0149
1580 Lake St Elmira (14901) *(G-4671)*
Beehive Press Inc....718 654-1200
3742 Boston Rd Bronx (10469) *(G-1281)*
Beer Marketers Insights Inc....845 507-0040
49 E Maple Ave Suffern (10901) *(G-15786)*
Beetins Wholesale Inc....718 524-0899
125 Ravenhurst Ave Staten Island (10310) *(G-15645)*
Beets Love Production LLC....585 270-2471
1150 Lee Rd Rochester (14606) *(G-14228)*
Behlman Electronics Inc (HQ)....631 435-0410
80 Cabot Ct Hauppauge (11788) *(G-6033)*
Beila Group Inc....212 260-1948
285 Mott St New York (10012) *(G-9346)*
Beis Moshiach Inc....718 778-8000
744 Eastern Pkwy Brooklyn (11213) *(G-1679)*
Beitals Aquarium Sales & Svc, Pearl River *Also called C B Management Services Inc (G-13455)*
Bekaert Corporation....716 830-1321
6000 N Bailey Ave Ste 9 Amherst (14226) *(G-227)*
Bektrom Foods Inc....516 802-3800
155 Foxhunt Cres Syosset (11791) *(G-15813)*
Bektrom Foods Inc (PA)....516 802-3800
155 Foxhunt Cres Syosset (11791) *(G-15814)*
Bel Aire Offset Corp....718 539-8333
1853 College Point Blvd Flushing (11356) *(G-5229)*
Bel Aire Printing, Flushing *Also called Bel Aire Offset Corp (G-5229)*
Bel Americas Inc....646 454-8220
122 E 42nd St Rm 2715 New York (10168) *(G-9347)*
Bel Art International....718 402-2100
600 E 132nd St Bronx (10454) *(G-1282)*
Bel Transformer Inc (HQ)....516 239-5777
500 Bayview Ave Inwood (11096) *(G-6753)*
Bel-Bee Products Incorporated....845 353-0300
100 Snake Hill Rd Ste 1 West Nyack (10994) *(G-16912)*
Belangers Gravel & Stone Inc....585 728-3906
10184 State Route 21 Wayland (14572) *(G-16709)*
Belden Brick Sales & Svc Inc (HQ)....212 686-3939
333 7th Ave Rm 502 New York (10001) *(G-9348)*
Belden Inc....607 796-5600
224 N Main St Ste 4 Horseheads (14845) *(G-6569)*
Belden Manufacturing Inc....607 238-0998
1813 Us Route 11 Kirkwood (13795) *(G-7232)*
Belden Tri-State Building Mtls, New York *Also called Belden Brick Sales & Svc Inc (G-9348)*
Belfair Draperies, Long Island City *Also called Anthony Lawrence of New York (G-7661)*
BELGIAN BOYS USA, Farmingdale *Also called Merb LLC (G-5048)*
Bell Press, Brooklyn *Also called Graphic Dimensions Press Inc (G-2049)*
Bell-Pac, East Syracuse *Also called Bellotti Packaging Inc (G-4510)*
Bella International Inc....716 484-0102
111 W 2nd St Ste 4000 Jamestown (14701) *(G-6973)*
Bellarno International Ltd....212 302-4107
1140 Ave Of The Americas New York (10036) *(G-9349)*
Bellataire Diamonds Inc....212 687-8881
19 W 44th St Fl 15 New York (10036) *(G-9350)*
Belle Maison USA Ltd....718 805-0200
8950 127th St Richmond Hill (11418) *(G-14068)*
Bellerophon Publications Inc....212 627-9977
205 Lexington Ave Fl 17 New York (10016) *(G-9351)*
Bellevue Builders Supply, Schenectady *Also called L Builders Supply Inc (G-15275)*
Bellini Collections, New York *Also called Formart Corp (G-10186)*
Bellmore Steel Products Corp....516 785-9667
2282 Bellmore Ave Bellmore (11710) *(G-815)*
Bellotti Packaging Inc....315 433-0131
6881 Schuyler Rd East Syracuse (13057) *(G-4510)*
Belmay Holding Corporation....914 376-1515
1 Odell Plz Ste 123 Yonkers (10701) *(G-17420)*
Belmet Products Inc (PA)....718 542-8220
1350 Garrison Ave Bronx (10474) *(G-1283)*
Belrix Industries Inc....716 821-5964
3590 Jeffrey Blvd Buffalo (14219) *(G-2837)*
Belsito Communications Inc....845 534-9700
1 Ardmore St New Windsor (12553) *(G-8932)*
Belsul America Corp....212 520-1827
125 Park Ave Fl 25 New York (10017) *(G-9352)*
Belt Dewatering Press, Greenwich *Also called Bdp Industries Inc (G-5886)*
Belt Maintenance Systems, Buffalo *Also called Rlp Holdings Inc (G-3159)*
Belton Industries, Brooklyn *Also called Filta Clean Co Inc (G-1970)*
Beltran Associates Inc....718 252-2996
1133 E 35th St Ste 1 Brooklyn (11210) *(G-1680)*
Beluga Inc (PA)....212 594-5511
463 7th Ave Fl 4 New York (10018) *(G-9353)*
Bematech, Bethpage *Also called Logic Controls Inc (G-872)*
Bemco of Western Ny Inc....716 823-8400
122 Roberts Ave Buffalo (14206) *(G-2838)*
Bemis Company Inc....631 794-2900
100 Wilshire Blvd Edgewood (11717) *(G-4594)*
Bemis North America, Edgewood *Also called Bemis Company Inc (G-4594)*
Ben Wachter Associates Inc (PA)....212 736-4064
36 W 44th St Ste 700 New York (10036) *(G-9354)*
Ben Weitsman of Albany LLC....518 462-4444
300 Smith Blvd Albany (12202) *(G-53)*
Ben-Amun Co Inc (PA)....212 944-6480
246 W 38th St Fl 12a New York (10018) *(G-9355)*
Ben-Sak Textile Inc....212 279-5122
307 W 38th St 9 New York (10018) *(G-9356)*
Benartex Inc....212 840-3250
132 W 36th St Rm 401 New York (10018) *(G-9357)*
Benchemark Printing Inc....518 393-1361
1890 Maxon Rd Ext Schenectady (12308) *(G-15234)*
Benchers Unlimited, Brooklyn *Also called Issacs Yisroel (G-2117)*
Benchmark Books, Tarrytown *Also called Marshall Cavendish Corp (G-16095)*
Benchmark Education Co LLC (PA)....914 637-7200
145 Huguenot St Fl 8 New Rochelle (10801) *(G-8888)*
Benchmark Furniture Mfg....718 257-4707
300 Dewitt Ave Brooklyn (11236) *(G-1681)*
Benchmark Graphics Ltd....212 683-1711
9 E 37th St Fl 5 New York (10016) *(G-9358)*
Benchmark Media Systems Inc....315 437-6300
203 E Hampton Pl Ste 2 Syracuse (13206) *(G-15868)*
Benedictine Hospital, Kingston *Also called Healthalliance Hospital (G-7190)*
Benemy Welding & Fabrication....315 548-8500
8 Pleasant Ave Phelps (14532) *(G-13530)*
Benetton Services, New York *Also called Ramsbury Property Us Inc (G-11796)*
Benetton Trading Usa Inc (PA)....212 593-0290
601 5th Ave Fl 4 New York (10017) *(G-9359)*
Benfield Control Systems Inc....914 948-6660
25 Lafayette Ave White Plains (10603) *(G-17085)*

ALPHABETIC

(PA)=Parent Co (HQ)=Headquarters (DH)=Div Headquarters

Benishty Brothers Corp 646 339-9991
233 Mosher Ave Woodmere (11598) *(G-17311)*
Benjamin Moore & Co 518 736-1723
Union Ave Ext Johnstown (12095) *(G-7108)*
Benjamin Printing Inc 315 788-7922
60 E Church St Adams (13605) *(G-2)*
Benjamin Sheridan Corporation (HQ) 585 657-6161
7629 State Route 5 And 20 Bloomfield (14469) *(G-981)*
Benners Gardens LLC 518 828-1055
1 Hudson City Ctr Hudson (12534) *(G-6609)*
Bennett Die & Tool Inc 607 739-5629
130 Wygant Rd Horseheads (14845) *(G-6570)*
Bennett Die & Tool Inc 607 273-2836
113 Brewery Ln Ithaca (14850) *(G-6821)*
Bennett Manufacturing Co Inc 716 937-9161
13315 Railroad St Alden (14004) *(G-175)*
Bennett Multimedia Inc 718 629-1454
1087 Utica Ave Brooklyn (11203) *(G-1682)*
Bennett Printing Corporation 718 629-1454
1087 Utica Ave Brooklyn (11203) *(G-1683)*
Bennett Stair Company Inc 518 384-1554
1021 State Route 50 Ballston Lake (12019) *(G-580)*
Bensak, New York Also called Ben-Sak Textile Inc *(G-9356)*
Benson Industries Inc 212 779-3230
192 Lexington Ave Rm 502 New York (10016) *(G-9360)*
Benson Mills Inc 718 236-6743
140 58th St Ste 7j Brooklyn (11220) *(G-1684)*
Benson Sales Co Inc 718 236-6743
6813 20th Ave Brooklyn (11204) *(G-1685)*
Benson Steel Fabricators, Saugerties Also called Kenbenco Inc *(G-15186)*
Bentley Cravats, New York Also called W B Bow Tie Corp *(G-12572)*
Bentley Manufacturing Inc (PA) 212 714-1800
10 W 33rd St Rm 220 New York (10001) *(G-9361)*
Benton Announcements Inc 716 836-4100
3006 Bailey Ave 3010 Buffalo (14215) *(G-2839)*
Bentones Enterprises, New York Also called Hjn Inc *(G-10485)*
Benway-Haworth-Lwlr-Iacosta He 518 432-4070
21 Everett Rd Albany (12205) *(G-54)*
Benzsay & Harrison Inc 518 895-2311
Railroad Ave Delanson (12053) *(G-4231)*
Beowawe Binary LLC 646 829-3900
1095 Avenue Of The Ave New York (10036) *(G-9362)*
Berardi Bakery Inc 718 746-9529
15045 12th Rd Whitestone (11357) *(G-17203)*
Bereza Iron Works Inc 585 254-6311
87 Dewey Ave Rochester (14608) *(G-14229)*
Berger & Wild LLC 646 415-8459
401 Broadway Ste 302 New York (10013) *(G-9363)*
Berjen Metal Industries Ltd 631 673-7979
645 New York Ave Ste 1 Huntington (11743) *(G-6656)*
Berkman Bros Inc 718 782-1827
538 Johnson Ave Brooklyn (11237) *(G-1686)*
Berkshire Business Forms Inc 518 828-2600
829 Route 66 Hudson (12534) *(G-6610)*
Berkshire Transformer (PA) 631 467-5328
77 Windsor Pl Ste 18 Central Islip (11722) *(G-3487)*
Berkshire Weaving, New York Also called Richloom Fabrics Group Inc *(G-11870)*
Bernan Associates, New York Also called Kraus Organization Limited *(G-10888)*
Bernard Chaus Inc (PA) 212 354-1280
530 Fashion Ave Fl 18 New York (10018) *(G-9364)*
Bernard Chaus Inc 646 562-4700
515 7th Ave Ste 18 New York (10018) *(G-9365)*
Bernard Hall 585 425-3340
10 Perinton Hills Mall Fairport (14450) *(G-4848)*
Bernette Apparel LLC 212 279-5526
42 W 39th St Fl 2 New York (10018) *(G-9366)*
Bernhard Arnold & Company Inc (PA) 212 907-1500
485 Lexington Ave Fl 9 New York (10017) *(G-9367)*
Bernstein Display, New York Also called Leo D Bernstein & Sons Inc *(G-10968)*
Berry Industrial Group Inc (PA) 845 353-8338
30 Main St Nyack (10960) *(G-13045)*
Berry Jewelry Company, New York Also called MJM Jewelry Corp *(G-11285)*
Berry Jewelry Company, Brooklyn Also called MJM Jewelry Corp *(G-2325)*
Berry Plastics Corporation 315 484-0397
1500 Milton Ave Solvay (13209) *(G-15506)*
Berry Plastics Corporation 315 986-6270
200 Main St Macedon (14502) *(G-7984)*
Berry Plastics Group Inc 716 366-2112
3565 Chadwick Dr Dunkirk (14048) *(G-4332)*
Berrywild 212 686-5848
200 E 30th St Bsmt New York (10016) *(G-9368)*
Bert Wassererman 212 759-5210
370 Lexington Ave New York (10017) *(G-9369)*
Bertelsmann Inc (HQ) 212 782-1000
1745 Broadway Fl 20 New York (10019) *(G-9370)*
Bertelsmann Pubg Group Inc (HQ) 212 782-1000
1540 Broadway Fl 24 New York (10036) *(G-9371)*
Beryllium Manufacturing, Copiague Also called Worldwide Arntcal Cmpnents Inc *(G-3940)*
Besam Entrance Solutions, East Syracuse Also called Assa Abloy Entrance Systems US *(G-4507)*
Bescor Video Accessories Ltd 631 420-1717
244 Route 109 Farmingdale (11735) *(G-4952)*
Besicorp Ltd (PA) 845 336-7700
1151 Flatbush Rd Kingston (12401) *(G-7179)*
Bespoke Apparel Inc 212 382-0330
214 W 39th St Rm 200b New York (10018) *(G-9372)*
Besstech, Troy Also called Battery Energy Storage Systems *(G-16227)*
Best Adhesives Company Inc 718 417-3800
4702 Metropolitan Ave Ridgewood (11385) *(G-14102)*
Best Boilers Inc 718 372-4210
2402 Neptune Ave Brooklyn (11224) *(G-1687)*
Best Brands Consumer Pdts Inc (PA) 212 684-7456
20 W 33rd St Fl 5 New York (10001) *(G-9373)*
Best Bread, Port Chester Also called Good Bread Bakery *(G-13748)*
Best Concrete Mix Corp 718 463-5500
3510 College Point Blvd Flushing (11354) *(G-5230)*
Best Foods Baking Group, Tonawanda Also called Bimbo Bakeries Usa Inc *(G-16145)*
Best Line Inc 917 670-6210
101 Manila Ave Fl 2 Staten Island (10306) *(G-15646)*
Best Mdlr HMS Afrbe P Q& S In 631 204-0049
495 County Road 39 Southampton (11968) *(G-15540)*
Best Medical Wear Ltd 718 858-5544
21 Hall St Brooklyn (11205) *(G-1688)*
Best Pallet & Crate LLC 518 438-2945
22 Railroad Ave Albany (12205) *(G-55)*
Best Priced Products Inc 914 345-3800
250 Clearbrook Rd Ste 240 Elmsford (10523) *(G-4735)*
Best Time Processor LLC 917 455-4126
8746 Van Wyck Expy Richmond Hill (11418) *(G-14069)*
Best Tinsmith Supply Inc 518 863-2541
4 Zetta Dr Northville (12134) *(G-13019)*
Best Toy Manufacturing Ltd 718 855-9040
43 Hall St Ste B1 Brooklyn (11205) *(G-1689)*
Best Way Tools By Anderson Inc 631 586-4702
171 Brook Ave Deer Park (11729) *(G-4106)*
Bestec Concept Inc 718 937-5848
4310 23rd St Lbby 4 Long Island City (11101) *(G-7683)*
Bestline International RES Inc 518 631-2177
224 State St Schenectady (12305) *(G-15235)*
Bestway Enterprises Inc (PA) 607 753-8261
3877 Luker Rd Cortland (13045) *(G-4012)*
Bestway of New York Inc 607 753-8261
3877 Luker Rd Cortland (13045) *(G-4013)*
Bestype Digital Imaging LLC 212 966-6886
285 W Broadway Frnt A New York (10013) *(G-9374)*
Bet Networks Incorporated 212 846-8111
1540 Broadway Fl 26 New York (10036) *(G-9375)*
Beta Transformer Tech Corp (HQ) 631 244-7393
40 Orville Dr Ste 2 Bohemia (11716) *(G-1024)*
Beth Kobliner Company LLC 212 501-8407
1995 Broadway Ste 1800 New York (10023) *(G-9376)*
Beth Ward Studios LLC 646 922-7575
133 W 25th St Rm 8e New York (10001) *(G-9377)*
Beths Farm Kitchen 518 799-3414
504 Rte 46 Stuyvesant Falls (12174) *(G-15783)*
Betsy & Adam Ltd (PA) 212 302-3750
1400 Broadway Rm 602 New York (10018) *(G-9378)*
Better Baked Foods Inc 716 326-4651
25 Jefferson St Westfield (14787) *(G-17046)*
Better Fresh Corp 718 628-3682
41 Varick Ave Brooklyn (11237) *(G-1690)*
Better Wire Products Inc 716 883-3377
1255 Niagara St Buffalo (14213) *(G-2840)*
Bettertex Inc 212 431-3373
450 Broadway New York (10013) *(G-9379)*
Bettertex Interioirs, New York Also called Bettertex Inc *(G-9379)*
Beval Engine & Machine, Central Islip Also called Abk Enterprises Inc *(G-3483)*
Beverage Media Group Inc (PA) 212 571-3232
152 Madison Ave Rm 600 New York (10016) *(G-9380)*
Beverage Works Incorporated 718 834-0500
70 Hamilton Ave 8 Brooklyn (11231) *(G-1691)*
Beverage Works Nj Inc 631 293-3501
16 Dubon Ct Farmingdale (11735) *(G-4953)*
Beverage Works Ny Inc 718 812-2034
70 Hamilton Ave 8 Brooklyn (11231) *(G-1692)*
Beverly Creations Inc 800 439-6855
40 E 34th St Rm 1403 New York (10016) *(G-9381)*
Bevilacque Group LLC 212 414-8858
250 Hudson St New York (10013) *(G-9382)*
Beyer Graphics Inc 631 543-3900
30 Austin Blvd Ste A Commack (11725) *(G-3824)*
Beyond Beauty Basics LLC 516 731-7100
3359 Hempstead Tpke Levittown (11756) *(G-7425)*
Beyond Design Inc 607 865-7487
807 Pines Brook Rd Walton (13856) *(G-16547)*
Beyond Loom Inc (PA) 212 575-3100
262 W 38th St Rm 203 New York (10018) *(G-9383)*
Beyondly Inc 646 658-3665
20 W 20th St Ste 1004 New York (10011) *(G-9384)*
Beyondspring Phrmceuticals Inc 646 305-6387
28 Liberty St Fl 39 New York (10005) *(G-9385)*
Bfc Print Network Inc (PA) 716 838-4532
455 Commerce Dr Ste 6 Amherst (14228) *(G-228)*

Bfg Manufacturing Services Inc....716 362-0888
3949 Jeffrey Blvd Buffalo (14219) **(G-2841)**
Bfg Marine Inc....631 586-5500
200 Candlewood Rd Bay Shore (11706) **(G-675)**
Bfgg Investors Group LLC....585 424-3456
1900 University Ave Rochester (14610) **(G-14230)**
Bfma Holding Corporation....607 753-6746
37 Huntington St Cortland (13045) **(G-4014)**
Bg Bindery Inc....631 767-4242
3002 48th Ave Long Island City (11101) **(G-7684)**
Bga Technology LLC....631 750-4600
116 Wilbur Pl Bohemia (11716) **(G-1025)**
Bh Brand Inc....212 239-1635
10 W 33rd St Rm 218 New York (10001) **(G-9386)**
Bh Brands, New York *Also called Bh Brand Inc* **(G-9386)**
Bh Coffee Company LLC (PA)....914 377-2500
4 Warehouse Ln Ste 121 Elmsford (10523) **(G-4736)**
BH Multi Com Corp (PA)....212 944-0020
15 W 46th St Fl 6 New York (10036) **(G-9387)**
Bharat Electronics Limited....516 248-4021
53 Hilton Ave Garden City (11530) **(G-5496)**
Bhi Elevator Cabs Inc....516 431-5665
74 Alabama Ave Island Park (11558) **(G-6778)**
Bi Nutraceuticals Inc....631 232-1105
120 Hoffman Ln Central Islip (11749) **(G-3488)**
Bianca Burgers LLC....516 764-9591
15 S Long Beach Rd Rockville Centre (11570) **(G-14788)**
Bianca Group Ltd....212 768-3011
244 W 39th St Fl 4 New York (10018) **(G-9388)**
Bicon Pharmaceutical Inc....631 593-4199
75 N Industry Ct Deer Park (11729) **(G-4107)**
Bidpress LLC....267 973-8876
659 Washington St Apt 5r New York (10014) **(G-9389)**
Bielecky Bros Inc (PA)....718 424-4764
5022 72nd St Woodside (11377) **(G-17320)**
Bielka Inc....212 980-6841
136 E 57th St Ste 907 New York (10022) **(G-9390)**
Bien Cuit LLC....718 852-0200
120 Smith St Brooklyn (11201) **(G-1693)**
Big Apple Elevtr Srv & Consult....212 279-0700
247 W 30th St New York (10001) **(G-9391)**
Big Apple Sign Corp....631 342-0303
3 Oval Dr Islandia (11749) **(G-6788)**
Big Apple Sign Corp (PA)....212 629-3650
247 W 35th St Frnt 1 New York (10001) **(G-9392)**
Big Apple Visual Group, Islandia *Also called Big Apple Sign Corp* **(G-6788)**
Big Apple Visual Group, New York *Also called Big Apple Sign Corp* **(G-9392)**
Big Apple Welding Supply....718 439-3959
236 47th St Brooklyn (11220) **(G-1694)**
Big Bang Clothing Inc....212 221-0379
214 W 39th St Rm 1008 New York (10018) **(G-9393)**
Big Bang Clothing Co, New York *Also called Big Bang Clothing Inc* **(G-9393)**
Big Bear, Buffalo *Also called Stephen M Kiernan* **(G-3196)**
Big City Bagel Lites, Long Island City *Also called Bagel Lites LLC* **(G-7680)**
Big Data Bizviz LLC....716 803-2367
1075 East And West Rd West Seneca (14224) **(G-16939)**
Big Geyser Inc....631 549-4940
150 Broadhollow Rd # 211 Melville (11747) **(G-8297)**
Big Heart Pet Brands....716 891-6566
243 Urban St Buffalo (14211) **(G-2842)**
Big Idea Brands LLC....212 938-0270
1410 Broadway Frnt 4 New York (10018) **(G-9394)**
Big John's Beef Jerky, Saratoga Springs *Also called Big Johns Adirondack Inc* **(G-15145)**
Big Johns Adirondack Inc....518 587-3680
45 N Milton Rd Saratoga Springs (12866) **(G-15145)**
Big White Wall Holding Inc....917 281-2649
41 E 11th St Fl 11 New York (10003) **(G-9395)**
Bigbee Steel and Tank Company....518 273-0801
958 19th St Watervliet (12189) **(G-16679)**
Bigrow Paper Mfg Corp....718 624-4439
930 Bedford Ave Brooklyn (11205) **(G-1695)**
Bigrow Paper Product, Brooklyn *Also called Bigrow Paper Mfg Corp* **(G-1695)**
Bigsky Technologies LLC....585 218-9499
1600 N Clinton Ave Ste 11 Rochester (14621) **(G-14231)**
Bigwood Systems Inc....607 257-0915
35 Thornwood Dr Ste 400 Ithaca (14850) **(G-6822)**
Bilbee Controls Inc....518 622-3033
628 Main St Cairo (12413) **(G-3271)**
Bilinski Sausage Mfg Co, Cohoes *Also called Schonwetter Enterprises Inc* **(G-3757)**
Bill Blass Group LLC....212 689-8957
236 5th Ave Fl 8 New York (10001) **(G-9396)**
Bill Lake Homes Construction....518 673-2424
188 Flanders Rd Sprakers (12166) **(G-15577)**
Bill Shea Enterprises Inc....585 343-2284
8825 Alexander Rd Batavia (14020) **(G-625)**
Billanti Casting Co Inc....516 775-4800
299 S 11th St New Hyde Park (11040) **(G-8819)**
Billanti Jewelry Casting, New Hyde Park *Also called Billanti Casting Co Inc* **(G-8819)**
Billie-Ann Plastics Pkg Corp....718 497-3409
360 Troutman St Brooklyn (11237) **(G-1696)**
Billing Blocks Inc....718 442-5006
147 North Ave Staten Island (10314) **(G-15647)**
Billing Coding and Prtg Inc....718 827-9409
455 Grant Ave Brooklyn (11208) **(G-1697)**
Billion Tower Intl LLC....212 220-0608
989 6th Ave Fl 8 New York (10018) **(G-9397)**
Billion Tower USA LLC....212 220-0608
989 Avenue Of The America New York (10018) **(G-9398)**
Billsboro Winery....315 789-9538
4760 State Route 14 Geneva (14456) **(G-5570)**
Billy Beez Usa LLC....315 741-5099
9090 Destiy Usa Dr L301 Unit L 301 Syracuse (13204) **(G-15869)**
Billy Beez Usa LLC (PA)....646 606-2249
3 W 35th St Fl 3 New York (10001) **(G-9399)**
Billy Beez Usa LLC....845 915-4709
1282 Palisades Center Dr West Nyack (10994) **(G-16913)**
Biltron Automotive Products....631 928-8613
509 Bicycle Path Unit Q Port Jeff STA (11776) **(G-13763)**
Bimbo Bakeries....631 274-4906
955 Grand Blvd Deer Park (11729) **(G-4108)**
Bimbo Bakeries....800 289-7876
111 N 2nd St Olean (14760) **(G-13135)**
Bimbo Bakeries....518 463-2221
78 N Manning Blvd Albany (12206) **(G-56)**
Bimbo Bakeries USA, Bay Shore *Also called Bimbo Foods Bakeries Inc* **(G-678)**
Bimbo Bakeries Usa Inc....716 692-9140
1960 Niagara Falls Blvd Tonawanda (14150) **(G-16145)**
Bimbo Bakeries Usa Inc....718 601-1561
5625 Broadway Frnt 2 Bronx (10463) **(G-1284)**
Bimbo Bakeries Usa Inc....718 545-0291
4011 34th Ave Long Island City (11101) **(G-7685)**
Bimbo Bakeries Usa Inc....716 372-8444
111 N 2nd St Olean (14760) **(G-13136)**
Bimbo Bakeries Usa Inc....516 887-1024
669 Sunrise Hwy Spc 4 Lynbrook (11563) **(G-7947)**
Bimbo Bakeries Usa Inc....315 379-9069
19 Miner St Ste D Canton (13617) **(G-3380)**
Bimbo Bakeries Usa Inc....516 877-2850
12 E Jericho Tpke Mineola (11501) **(G-8498)**
Bimbo Bakeries Usa Inc....718 463-6300
5754 Page Pl Maspeth (11378) **(G-8121)**
Bimbo Bakeries Usa Inc....631 274-4906
1724 5th Ave Bay Shore (11706) **(G-676)**
Bimbo Bakeries Usa Inc....315 253-9782
11 Corcoran Dr Auburn (13021) **(G-484)**
Bimbo Bakeries Usa Inc....518 489-4053
40 Fuller Rd Albany (12205) **(G-57)**
Bimbo Bakeries Usa Inc....203 531-2311
30 Inez Dr Bay Shore (11706) **(G-677)**
Bimbo Bakeries Usa Inc....716 706-0450
2900 Commerce Pkwy Lancaster (14086) **(G-7306)**
Bimbo Bakeries Usa Inc....315 785-7060
144 Eastern Blvd Watertown (13601) **(G-16637)**
Bimbo Bakeries Usa Inc....845 568-0943
98 Scobie Dr Newburgh (12550) **(G-12751)**
Bimbo Bakeries Usa Inc....800 856-8544
1624 Castle Gardens Rd Vestal (13850) **(G-16441)**
Bimbo Bakeries Usa Inc....315 782-4189
1100 Water St Watertown (13601) **(G-16638)**
Bimbo Bakeries Usa Inc....845 294-5282
9 Police Dr Goshen (10924) **(G-5731)**
Bimbo Foods Bakeries Inc (HQ)....631 273-6000
40 Harold Ct Bay Shore (11706) **(G-678)**
Binah Magazines Corp....718 305-5200
207 Foster Ave Brooklyn (11230) **(G-1698)**
Bindle and Keep....917 740-5002
47 Hall St Ste 109 Brooklyn (11205) **(G-1699)**
Binghamton Burial Vault Co Inc....607 722-4931
1114 Porter Ave Binghamton (13901) **(G-891)**
Binghamton Knitting Co Inc....607 722-6941
11 Alice St Binghamton (13904) **(G-892)**
Binghamton Precast & Sup Corp....607 722-0334
18 Phelps St Binghamton (13901) **(G-893)**
Binghamton Precision Tool Inc....607 772-6021
10 Ballard St Binghamton (13904) **(G-894)**
Binghamton Press, Vestal *Also called Gannett Co Inc* **(G-16448)**
Binghamton Simulator Co Inc....607 321-2980
151 Court St Binghamton (13901) **(G-895)**
Binghamton University....607 777-2316
Vestal Pkwy E Binghamton (13901) **(G-896)**
Binoptics LLC (HQ)....607 257-3200
9 Brown Rd Ithaca (14850) **(G-6823)**
Bio Nutrition, Island Park *Also called Only Natural Inc* **(G-6783)**
Bio Service, Woodside *Also called Firecom Inc* **(G-17328)**
Bio-Botanica Inc (PA)....631 231-0987
75 Commerce Dr Hauppauge (11788) **(G-6034)**
Bio-Chem Barrier Systems LLC....631 261-2682
11 W Scudder Pl Northport (11768) **(G-13008)**
Bio-Nutritional Products, White Plains *Also called Meta-Therm Corp* **(G-17137)**
Biochemical Diagnostics Inc....631 595-9200
180 Heartland Blvd Edgewood (11717) **(G-4595)**
Biocontinuum Group Inc....212 406-1060
116 Chambers St New York (10007) **(G-9400)**
Biodesign Inc of New York (PA)....845 454-6610
1 Sunset Rdg Carmel (10512) **(G-3398)**

ALPHABETIC

Biodex Medical Systems Inc (PA) 631 924-9000
20 Ramsey Rd Shirley (11967) ***(G-15416)***
Biodex Medical Systems Inc 631 924-3146
49 Natcon Dr Shirley (11967) ***(G-15417)***
Biodigitalpc, New Hyde Park *Also called Arnouse Digital Devices Corp* ***(G-8817)***
Biofeedback Instrument Corp 212 222-5665
255 W 98th St Apt 3d New York (10025) ***(G-9401)***
Bioinformatics Publishing, New York *Also called Genomeweb LLC* ***(G-10278)***
Bioins Inc 646 457-8117
1767 Central Park Ave # 258 Yonkers (10710) ***(G-17421)***
Biolitec Inc 413 525-0600
110 E 42nd St Rm 1800 New York (10017) ***(G-9402)***
Biologic Solutions, Port Chester *Also called FMC International Ltd* ***(G-13746)***
Biologique Recherche, New York *Also called Distribio USA LLC* ***(G-9887)***
Bionic Eye Technologies Inc 845 505-5254
4 Willow Lake Dr Fishkill (12524) ***(G-5181)***
Biopool Us Inc 716 483-3851
2823 Girts Rd Jamestown (14701) ***(G-6974)***
Biorem Environmental Inc 585 924-2220
100 Rawson Rd Ste 230 Victor (14564) ***(G-16462)***
Bioresearch Inc (PA) 212 734-5315
4 Sunset Ln Pound Ridge (10576) ***(G-13942)***
Biospecifics Technologies Corp (PA) 516 593-7000
35 Wilbur St Lynbrook (11563) ***(G-7948)***
Biospherix Ltd 315 387-3414
25 Union St Parish (13131) ***(G-13414)***
Biospherix Medical, Parish *Also called Biospherix Ltd* ***(G-13414)***
Biotech Energy Inc 800 340-1387
35a Smithfield Blvd Plattsburgh (12901) ***(G-13654)***
Biotech Energy Systems, Plattsburgh *Also called Biotech Energy Inc* ***(G-13654)***
Biotemper 516 302-7985
516 Mineola Ave Carle Place (11514) ***(G-3387)***
Biotemper Plus, Carle Place *Also called Biotemper* ***(G-3387)***
Bioworks Inc (PA) 585 924-4362
100 Rawson Rd Ste 205 Victor (14564) ***(G-16463)***
Birch Coffee, Long Island City *Also called Birch Guys LLC* ***(G-7686)***
Birch Guys LLC 917 763-0751
4035 23rd St Long Island City (11101) ***(G-7686)***
Birch Machine & Tool Inc 716 735-9802
80 Telegraph Rd Middleport (14105) ***(G-8420)***
Birchbrook Impressions, Delhi *Also called Birchbrook Press* ***(G-4236)***
Birchbrook Press 607 746-7453
2309 County Highway 16 Delhi (13753) ***(G-4236)***
Bird Bus Sales, Port Washington *Also called JP Bus & Truck Repair Ltd* ***(G-13830)***
Birdair Inc (HQ) 716 633-9500
65 Lawrence Bell Dr Ste 1 Amherst (14221) ***(G-229)***
Birds Eye Foods Inc 716 988-3218
Mechanic St South Dayton (14138) ***(G-15517)***
Birds Eye Holdings Inc 585 383-1850
90 Linden Park Rochester (14625) ***(G-14232)***
Birkett Mills (PA) 315 536-3311
163 Main St Ste 2 Penn Yan (14527) ***(G-13506)***
Birkett Mills 315 536-4112
163 Main St Ste 3 Penn Yan (14527) ***(G-13507)***
Birnbaum & Bullock Ltd 212 242-2914
151 W 25th St Rm 2a New York (10001) ***(G-9403)***
Birthstone Enterprises, New York *Also called Alchemy Simya Inc* ***(G-9076)***
Biscuits & Bath Companies LLC 212 401-3022
41 W 13th St New York (10011) ***(G-9404)***
Bishop Print Shop Inc 607 965-8155
9 East St Edmeston (13335) ***(G-4622)***
Bison Bag Co Inc 716 434-4380
5404 Crown Dr Lockport (14094) ***(G-7572)***
Bison Iron & Step, Buffalo *Also called M K Ulrich Construction Inc* ***(G-3053)***
Bison Products, Buffalo *Also called Upstate Niagara Coop Inc* ***(G-3237)***
Bison Steel Incorporated 716 683-0900
2 Main St Ste 103 Depew (14043) ***(G-4248)***
Bissel-Babcock Millwork Inc 716 761-6976
3866 Kendrick Rd Sherman (14781) ***(G-15401)***
Bistate Oil Management Corp 212 935-4110
10 E 40th St Rm 2705 New York (10016) ***(G-9405)***
Bistrian Cement Corporation 631 324-1123
225 Springs Fireplace Rd East Hampton (11937) ***(G-4405)***
Bittner Company LLC 585 214-1790
75 Goodway Dr Ste 3 Rochester (14623) ***(G-14233)***
Bitzer Scroll Inc 315 463-2101
6055 Court Street Rd Syracuse (13206) ***(G-15870)***
Bizbash Masterplanner, New York *Also called Bizbash Media Inc* ***(G-9406)***
Bizbash Media Inc (PA) 646 638-3600
8 W 38th St Rm 200 New York (10018) ***(G-9406)***
Bizeventz Inc 315 579-3901
269 W Jefferson St Syracuse (13202) ***(G-15871)***
BJ Magazines Inc 212 367-9705
200 Varick St New York (10014) ***(G-9407)***
BJG Services LLC 516 592-5692
14 Penn Plz New York (10122) ***(G-9408)***
BK Associates Intl Inc 607 432-1499
127 Commerce Rd Oneonta (13820) ***(G-13173)***
Bk Printing Inc 315 565-5396
6507 Basile Rowe East Syracuse (13057) ***(G-4511)***

ALPHABETIC

Black & Decker (us) Inc 914 235-6300
2 Powers Ln Brewster (10509) ***(G-1212)***
Black & Decker (us) Inc 716 884-6220
881 W Delavan Ave Buffalo (14209) ***(G-2843)***
Black & Decker (us) Inc 631 952-2008
180 Oser Ave Ste 100 Hauppauge (11788) ***(G-6035)***
Black Bear Company Inc 718 784-7330
2710 49th Ave Long Island City (11101) ***(G-7687)***
Black Bear Fuels Oil, Harris *Also called Jus-Sar Fuel Inc* ***(G-5976)***
Black Book Photography Inc 212 979-6700
740 Broadway Ste 202 New York (10003) ***(G-9409)***
Black Book, The, New York *Also called Black Book Photography Inc* ***(G-9409)***
Black Enterprise, New York *Also called Earl G Graves Pubg Co Inc* ***(G-9960)***
Black Hound, Brooklyn *Also called Amiram Dror Inc* ***(G-1611)***
Black River Brewing Co Inc 315 755-2739
500 Newell St Watertown (13601) ***(G-16639)***
Black River Generations LLC 315 773-2314
4515 2nd St Fort Drum (13602) ***(G-5338)***
Black River Valley Wdwkg LLC 315 376-8405
4773 State Route 410 Castorland (13620) ***(G-3421)***
Blackbirds Brooklyn LLC 917 362-4080
597 Sackett St Brooklyn (11217) ***(G-1700)***
Blackbook, New York *Also called McCarthy LLC* ***(G-11196)***
Blackbook Media Corp 212 334-1800
32 Union Sq E Ste 4l New York (10003) ***(G-9410)***
Blackbox Biometrics Inc 585 329-3399
125 Tech Park Dr Ste 1131 Rochester (14623) ***(G-14234)***
Blackheart Records, New York *Also called Lagunatic Music & Filmworks* ***(G-10917)***
Blackstone Advanced Tech LLC 716 665-5410
86 Blackstone Ave Jamestown (14701) ***(G-6975)***
Blackstone Business Entps Inc 716 665-5410
100 Blackstone Ave Jamestown (14701) ***(G-6976)***
Blackstone Group, New York *Also called Grand Slam Holdings LLC* ***(G-10348)***
Blackswirl, New York *Also called Robert Ehrlich* ***(G-11890)***
Blades 212 477-1059
659 Broadway New York (10012) ***(G-9411)***
Blading Services Unlimited LLC 315 875-5313
40 Madison Blvd Canastota (13032) ***(G-3363)***
Blair Cnstr Fabrication Sp 315 253-2321
13 Brae Ridge Rd Auburn (13021) ***(G-485)***
Blair Industries Inc (PA) 631 924-6600
3671 Horseblock Rd Medford (11763) ***(G-8236)***
Blair-Hsm, Medford *Also called HSM Machine Works Inc* ***(G-8250)***
Blanche P Field LLC 212 355-6616
155 E 56th St Ph New York (10022) ***(G-9412)***
Blandi Products LLC 908 377-2885
950 3rd Ave Fl 3 New York (10022) ***(G-9413)***
Blasch Precision Ceramics Inc (PA) 518 436-1263
580 Broadway Ste 1 Menands (12204) ***(G-8369)***
Blaser Production Inc 845 294-3200
31 Hatfield Ln Goshen (10924) ***(G-5732)***
Blaser Swisslube Holding Corp (HQ) 845 294-3200
31 Hatfield Ln Goshen (10924) ***(G-5733)***
Blatt Searle & Company Ltd (PA) 212 730-7717
4121 28th St Long Island City (11101) ***(G-7688)***
Blc Textiles Inc 516 791-4500
330 Old Country Rd # 201 Mineola (11501) ***(G-8499)***
Bleecker Pastry Tartufo Inc 718 937-9830
3722 13th St Long Island City (11101) ***(G-7689)***
Bleezarde Publishing Inc 518 756-2030
164 Main St Ravena (12143) ***(G-14020)***
Blend Smoothie Bar 845 568-7366
25 Creamery Dr New Windsor (12553) ***(G-8933)***
Bli International Inc 631 940-9000
75 N Industry Ct Deer Park (11729) ***(G-4109)***
Blinds To Go (us) Inc 718 477-9523
2845 Richmond Ave Staten Island (10314) ***(G-15648)***
Blindtek Designer Systems Inc 914 347-7100
1 Hayes St Elmsford (10523) ***(G-4737)***
Bliss Foods Inc 212 732-8888
275 Greenwich St Frnt 2 New York (10007) ***(G-9414)***
Bliss Foods Inc 212 732-8888
275 Greenwich St Frnt 2 New York (10007) ***(G-9415)***
Bliss Machine Inc 585 492-5128
260 North St Arcade (14009) ***(G-389)***
Bliss-Poston The Second Wind 212 481-1055
928 Broadway Ste 403 New York (10010) ***(G-9416)***
Bloch Industries LLC 585 334-9600
140 Commerce Dr Rochester (14623) ***(G-14235)***
Blondie S Bakeshop Inc 631 424-4545
90 Washington Dr Centerport (11721) ***(G-3475)***
Blood Moon Productions Ltd 718 556-9410
75 Saint Marks Pl Staten Island (10301) ***(G-15649)***
Blooming Grove Stair Co (PA) 845 783-4245
1 Stair Way Monroe (10950) ***(G-8550)***
Blooming Grove Stair Co 845 791-4016
309 E Broadway Monticello (12701) ***(G-8604)***
Bloomsburg Carpet Inds Inc 212 688-7447
49 W 23rd St Fl 4 New York (10010) ***(G-9417)***
Bloomsbury Publishing Inc 212 419-5300
1385 Brdwy Fl 5 New York (10018) ***(G-9418)***
Bloomsbury USA, New York *Also called Bloomsbury Publishing Inc* ***(G-9418)***

ALPHABETIC SECTION Borden & Riley Paper Co Inc

Blu Sand LLC 212 564-1147
589 8th Ave Fl 9 New York (10018) **(G-9419)**
Blue and White Publishing Inc 215 431-3339
425 Riverside Dr Apt 3c New York (10025) **(G-9420)**
Blue Box, Brooklyn *Also called Pink Box Accessories LLC* **(G-2422)**
Blue Boy, Staten Island *Also called Rgm Signs Inc* **(G-15732)**
Blue Cast Denim Co Inc 212 719-1182
10 Blue Grass Ct Huntington (11743) **(G-6657)**
Blue Chip Mold Inc 585 647-1790
95 Lagrange Ave Rochester (14613) **(G-14236)**
Blue Horizon Media Inc (PA) 212 661-7878
11 Park Pl Rm 1508 New York (10007) **(G-9421)**
Blue Manufacturing Co Inc 607 796-2463
3852 Watkins Rd Millport (14864) **(G-8480)**
Blue Marble Ice Cream 718 858-5551
220 36th St Unit 33 Brooklyn (11232) **(G-1701)**
Blue Ocean Food Trading Inc 718 689-4290
5726 1st Ave Ste 12 Brooklyn (11220) **(G-1702)**
Blue Pig Ice Cream Factory 914 271-3850
121 Maple St Croton On Hudson (10520) **(G-4062)**
Blue Rhino Global Sourcing Inc 516 752-0670
10 Hub Dr Ste 101 Melville (11747) **(G-8298)**
Blue Skies 631 392-1140
859 Long Island Ave Deer Park (11729) **(G-4110)**
Blue Sky Plastic Production 718 366-3966
305 Johnson Ave Brooklyn (11206) **(G-1703)**
Blue Star Beverages Corp 718 381-3535
1099 Flushing Ave Brooklyn (11237) **(G-1704)**
Blue Star Products Inc 631 952-3204
355 Marcus Blvd Ste 2 Hauppauge (11788) **(G-6036)**
Blue Stone Press, High Falls *Also called Ulster County Press Office* **(G-6402)**
Blue Tee Corp (PA) 212 598-0880
387 Park Ave S Fl 5 New York (10016) **(G-9422)**
Blue Toad Hard Cider 585 424-5508
120 Mushroom Blvd Rochester (14623) **(G-14237)**
Blue Tortilla LLC 631 451-0100
1070 Middle Country Rd # 4 Selden (11784) **(G-15348)**
Blue Wolf Group LLC (HQ) 866 455-9653
11 E 26th St Fl 21 New York (10010) **(G-9423)**
Bluebar Oil Co Inc 315 245-4328
8446 Mill Pond Way Blossvale (13308) **(G-997)**
Blueberry Knitting Inc (PA) 718 599-6520
138 Ross St Brooklyn (11211) **(G-1705)**
Blueduck Trading Ltd 212 268-3122
463 7th Ave Rm 806 New York (10018) **(G-9424)**
Blueprint Cleanse, New York *Also called Zoe Sakoutis LLC* **(G-12717)**
Bluesoho (PA) 646 805-2583
160 Varick St Fl 2 New York (10013) **(G-9425)**
Blum & Fink Inc 212 695-2606
158 W 29th St Fl 12 New York (10001) **(G-9426)**
Blume Worldwide Services, Saratoga Springs *Also called William J Blume Worldwide Svcs* **(G-15177)**
Bm America LLC (HQ) 201 438-7733
4 W 58th St Fl 10 New York (10019) **(G-9427)**
BMA Media Services Inc 585 385-2060
1655 Lyell Ave Rochester (14606) **(G-14238)**
BMC, Broadalbin *Also called Broadalbin Manufacturing Corp* **(G-1240)**
BMC, Brooklyn *Also called Bridgewater Mdsg Concepts* **(G-1716)**
BMC LLC 716 681-7755
3155 Broadway St Buffalo (14227) **(G-2844)**
BMC Software Inc 646 452-4100
14 E 47th St Fl 3 New York (10017) **(G-9428)**
BMC Software Inc 212 730-1389
1114 Ave Of The Americas New York (10036) **(G-9429)**
Bmg Chrysalis, New York *Also called Bmg Rights Management (us) LLC* **(G-9430)**
Bmg Printing and Promotion LLC 631 231-9200
170 Wilbur Pl Ste 700 Bohemia (11716) **(G-1026)**
Bmg Rights Management (us) LLC (HQ) 212 561-3000
1745 Broadway Fl 19 New York (10019) **(G-9430)**
Bmp America Inc (HQ) 585 798-0950
11625 Maple Ridge Rd Medina (14103) **(G-8267)**
Bms Designs Inc 718 828-5792
1385 Seabury Ave Bronx (10461) **(G-1285)**
Bms Manufacturing Co Inc 607 535-2426
2857 County Line Rd Watkins Glen (14891) **(G-16693)**
BNC Commodities Inc 631 872-8041
3671 Orchard Rd Wantagh (11793) **(G-16554)**
BNC Innovative Woodworking 718 277-2800
555 Liberty Ave Brooklyn (11207) **(G-1706)**
Bnei Aram Soba Inc 718 645-4460
1616 Ocean Pkwy Brooklyn (11223) **(G-1707)**
Bnm Product Service 631 750-1586
1561 Lincoln Ave Holbrook (11741) **(G-6432)**
Bnns Co Inc 212 302-1844
71 W 47th St Ste 600-601 New York (10036) **(G-9431)**
BNo Intl Trdg Co Inc 716 487-1900
505 Chautauqua Ave Jamestown (14701) **(G-6977)**
Bnz Tech, East Setauket *Also called B & Z Technologies LLC* **(G-4477)**
Bo-Mer Plastics LLC 315 252-7216
13 Pulaski St Auburn (13021) **(G-486)**
Boa Security Technologies Corp 516 576-0295
586 New York Ave Unit 3 Huntington (11743) **(G-6658)**
Boardman Simons Publishing (PA) 212 620-7200
55 Broad St Fl 26 New York (10004) **(G-9432)**
Bob Murphy Inc 607 729-3553
3127 Vestal Rd Vestal (13850) **(G-16442)**
Bob Perani Sport Shops Inc 585 427-2930
1225 Jefferson Rd Rochester (14623) **(G-14239)**
Bob's Signs, Syracuse *Also called Wizard Equipment Inc* **(G-16073)**
Bobbi Brown Prof Cosmt Inc 646 613-6500
575 Broadway Fl 4 New York (10012) **(G-9433)**
Bobby Jones Sportswear, Rochester *Also called Xmh-Hfi Inc* **(G-14772)**
Bobley-Harmann Corporation 516 433-3800
200 Trade Zone Dr Unit 2 Ronkonkoma (11779) **(G-14880)**
Bobrick Washroom Equipment Inc 518 877-7444
200 Commerce Dr Clifton Park (12065) **(G-3697)**
Boces Business Office 607 763-3300
435 Glenwood Rd Binghamton (13905) **(G-897)**
Body Armour, Whitestone *Also called Ba Sports Nutrition LLC* **(G-17202)**
Body Builders Inc 718 492-7997
5518 3rd Ave Brooklyn (11220) **(G-1708)**
Bodycote Thermal Proc Inc 585 436-7876
620 Buffalo Rd Rochester (14611) **(G-14240)**
Boehm Surgical Instrument 585 436-6584
966 Chili Ave Ste 3 Rochester (14611) **(G-14241)**
Boeing Company 201 259-9400
304 Park Ave S New York (10010) **(G-9434)**
Boka Printing Inc 607 725-3235
12 Hall St Binghamton (13903) **(G-898)**
Bomac Inc 315 433-9181
6477 Ridings Rd Syracuse (13206) **(G-15872)**
Bomb Magazine, Brooklyn *Also called New Art Publications Inc* **(G-2359)**
Bombardier Mass Transit Corp 518 566-0150
71 Wall St Plattsburgh (12901) **(G-13655)**
Bombardier Transportation 607 324-0216
1 William K Jackson Ln Hornell (14843) **(G-6560)**
Bombardier Trnsp Holdings USA 607 776-4791
7940 State Route 415 Bath (14810) **(G-654)**
Bombay Kitchen Foods Inc 516 767-7401
76 S Bayles Ave Port Washington (11050) **(G-13802)**
Bon Bons Chocolatier, Huntington *Also called Lady-N-Th-wndow Chocolates Inc* **(G-6666)**
Boncraft Inc 716 662-9720
777 E Park Dr Tonawanda (14150) **(G-16146)**
Bonded Concrete Inc (PA) 518 273-5800
303 Watervliet Shaker Rd Watervliet (12189) **(G-16680)**
Bonded Concrete Inc 518 674-2854
Rr 43 West Sand Lake (12196) **(G-16931)**
Bondi Digital Publishing LLC 212 405-1655
88 10th Ave Frnt 6 New York (10011) **(G-9435)**
Bonduelle USA Inc 585 948-5252
40 Stevens St Oakfield (14125) **(G-13064)**
Bondy Printing Corp 631 242-1510
267 W Main St Bay Shore (11706) **(G-679)**
Bonelli Foods LLC 212 346-0942
139 Fulton St Rm 314 New York (10038) **(G-9436)**
Bongenre.com, Brooklyn *Also called Jill Fenichell Inc* **(G-2142)**
Bonide Products Inc 315 736-8231
6301 Sutliff Rd Oriskany (13424) **(G-13304)**
Bonjour For Kids, New York *Also called Consolidated Childrens AP Inc* **(G-9703)**
Bonk Sam Unforms Civilian Cap 718 585-0665
131 Rose Feiss Blvd Fl 2 Bronx (10454) **(G-1286)**
Bonnie J, New York *Also called Sanoy Inc* **(G-11968)**
Bono Sawdust Co, Corona *Also called Bono Sawdust Supply Co Inc* **(G-3993)**
Bono Sawdust Supply Co Inc 718 446-1374
3330 127th Pl Corona (11368) **(G-3993)**
Bonpoint Inc (PA) 212 246-3291
396 W Broadway Apt 3 New York (10012) **(G-9437)**
Bonsal American Inc 631 208-8073
931 Burman Blvd Calverton (11933) **(G-3286)**
Bonura and Sons Iron Works 718 381-4100
957 Lorraine Dr Franklin Square (11010) **(G-5361)**
Book1one LLC 585 458-2101
655 Driving Park Ave Rochester (14613) **(G-14242)**
Booklinks Publishing Svcs LLC 718 852-2116
55 Washington St Ste 253c Brooklyn (11201) **(G-1709)**
Booklyn Artists Alliance 718 383-9621
37 Greenpoint Ave Ste C4 Brooklyn (11222) **(G-1710)**
Boom Creative Development, New York *Also called Boom LLC* **(G-9438)**
Boom LLC 646 218-0752
800 3rd Ave Fl 2 New York (10022) **(G-9438)**
Boonville Herald Inc 315 942-4449
105 E Schuyler St Boonville (13309) **(G-1164)**
Boonville Manufacturing Corp 315 942-4368
13485 State Route 12 Boonville (13309) **(G-1165)**
Boonvlle Hrald Adrndack Turist, Boonville *Also called Boonville Herald Inc* **(G-1164)**
Boosey & Hawkes Inc (HQ) 212 358-5300
229 W 28th St Fl 11 New York (10001) **(G-9439)**
Bootstrap Software 212 871-2020
129 W 29th St Fl 12 New York (10001) **(G-9440)**
Borabora Fruit Juices Inc 845 795-1027
255 Milton Highland (12528) **(G-6403)**
Borden & Riley Paper Co Inc 718 454-9494
18410 Jamaica Ave Ste W3 Hollis (11423) **(G-6494)**

ALPHABETIC

Borgattis Ravioli Egg Noodles 718 367-3799
632 E 187th St Bronx (10458) *(G-1287)*
Borghese Inc (PA) 212 659-5318
3 E 54th St Fl 20 New York (10022) *(G-9441)*
Borgwarner Inc 607 257-1800
780 Warren Rd Ithaca (14850) *(G-6824)*
Borgwarner Ithaca LLC 607 257-6700
800 Warren Rd Ithaca (14850) *(G-6825)*
Borgwarner Morse TEC Inc (HQ) 607 257-6700
800 Warren Rd Ithaca (14850) *(G-6826)*
Borgwarner Morse TEC Inc 607 266-5111
780 Warren Rd Ithaca (14850) *(G-6827)*
Borgwarner Morse TEC Inc 607 257-6700
3690 Luker Rd Cortland (13045) *(G-4015)*
Borgwarner Morse TEC Inc 607 257-6700
781 Warner Rd Ithaca (14850) *(G-6828)*
Bornomala USA Inc 347 753-2355
3766 72nd St Fl 3 Jackson Heights (11372) *(G-6887)*
Boro Park Cutting Tool Corp 718 720-0610
106b Wakefield Ave Staten Island (10314) *(G-15650)*
Boro Park Signs, Brooklyn *Also called Sign Group Inc (G-2553)*
Bos-Hatten Inc 716 662-7030
50 Cobham Dr Orchard Park (14127) *(G-13253)*
Boss Precision Ltd 585 352-7070
2440 S Union St Spencerport (14559) *(G-15566)*
Boss Sauce, Rochester *Also called American Specialty Mfg Co (G-14199)*
Boston Valley Pottery Inc (PA) 716 649-7490
6860 S Abbott Rd Orchard Park (14127) *(G-13254)*
Boston Valley Terra Cotta, Orchard Park *Also called Boston Valley Pottery Inc (G-13254)*
Bottling Group LLC 315 788-6751
1035 Bradley St Watertown (13601) *(G-16640)*
Bottling Group LLC 800 789-2626
1111 Westchester Ave White Plains (10604) *(G-17086)*
Bottling Group LLC (HQ) 914 767-6000
1111 Westchester Ave White Plains (10604) *(G-17087)*
Boucheron Joaillerie USA Inc 212 715-7330
460 Park Ave Fl 12 New York (10022) *(G-9442)*
Boulay Fabrication Inc 315 677-5247
Rr 20 Box West La Fayette (13084) *(G-7240)*
Boulevard Printing 716 837-3800
1330 Niagara Falls Blvd # 2 Tonawanda (14150) *(G-16147)*
Boundless Spatial Inc 646 831-5531
222 Broadway Fl 19 New York (10038) *(G-9443)*
Boundless Technologies, Phelps *Also called Z-Axis Inc (G-13539)*
Bourghol Brothers Inc 845 268-9752
73 Lake Rd Congers (10920) *(G-3853)*
Bourne Co, New York *Also called Bourne Music Publishers (G-9444)*
Bourne Music Publishers 212 391-4300
5 W 37th St Fl 6 New York (10018) *(G-9444)*
Bovie Medical Corporation 727 384-2323
4 Manhattanville Rd Purchase (10577) *(G-13953)*
Bovie Medical Corporation (PA) 914 468-4009
4 Manhattanville Rd # 106 Purchase (10577) *(G-13954)*
Bow Industrial Corporation 518 561-0190
178 W Service Rd Champlain (12919) *(G-3538)*
Bowe Industries Inc (PA) 718 441-6464
8836 77th Ave Glendale (11385) *(G-5646)*
Bowe Industries Inc 718 441-6464
8836 77th Ave Glendale (11385) *(G-5647)*
Bowen Products Corporation 315 498-4481
5084 S Onondaga Rd Nedrow (13120) *(G-8772)*
Boxbee Inc 646 612-7839
134 W 26th St Rm 404 New York (10001) *(G-9445)*
Boxcar Press Incorporated 315 473-0930
509 W Fayette St Ste 135 Syracuse (13204) *(G-15873)*
Boy Scouts of America 212 532-0985
271 Madison Ave Ste 401 New York (10016) *(G-9446)*
Boyd Printing Company, Latham *Also called William Boyd Printing Co Inc (G-7385)*
Boydell & Brewer Inc 585 275-0419
668 Mount Hope Ave Rochester (14620) *(G-14243)*
Boylan Bottling Co Inc 800 289-7978
6 E 43rd St Fl 18 New York (10017) *(G-9447)*
BP Beyond Printing Inc 516 328-2700
117 Fulton Ave Hempstead (11550) *(G-6266)*
BP Digital Imaging LLC 607 753-0022
87 Main St Cortland (13045) *(G-4016)*
Bpe Studio Inc 212 868-9896
270 W 38th St Rm 702 New York (10018) *(G-9448)*
Bqp, Glens Falls *Also called Brennans Quick Print Inc (G-5673)*
Bracci Ironworks Inc 718 629-2374
1440 Utica Ave Brooklyn (11203) *(G-1711)*
Brach Knitting Mills Inc 845 651-4450
12 Roosevelt Ave Florida (10921) *(G-5210)*
Brach Machine Inc 585 343-9134
4814 Ellicott Street Rd Batavia (14020) *(G-626)*
Bradford Publications Inc 716 373-2500
639 W Norton Dr Olean (14760) *(G-13137)*
Bradley Marketing Group Inc 212 967-6100
1431 Broadway Fl 12 New York (10018) *(G-9449)*
Braga Woodworks 845 342-4636
19 Montgomery St Middletown (10940) *(G-8428)*
Bragley Mfg Co Inc 718 622-7469
924 Bergen St Brooklyn (11238) *(G-1712)*
Bragley Shipg Carrying Cases, Brooklyn *Also called Bragley Mfg Co Inc (G-1712)*
Braided Oak Spirits LLC 845 381-1525
12 Roberts St Middletown (10940) *(G-8429)*
Braiform Enterprises Inc (HQ) 800 738-7396
237 W 35th St Ste 504 New York (10001) *(G-9450)*
Brainpop Group, New York *Also called Brainpop LLC (G-9451)*
Brainpop LLC 212 574-6017
71 W 23rd St Fl 17 New York (10010) *(G-9451)*
Brainwave Toys-New York, New York *Also called Vogel Applied Technologies (G-12563)*
Brainworks Software Dev Corp (PA) 631 563-5000
100 S Main St Ste 102 Sayville (11782) *(G-15204)*
Brakewell Stl Fabricators Inc 845 469-9131
55 Leone Ln Chester (10918) *(G-3601)*
Bral Nader Fine Jewelry Inc 800 493-1222
576 5th Ave New York (10036) *(G-9452)*
Bramson House Inc 516 764-5006
151 Albany Ave Freeport (11520) *(G-5390)*
Brands Within Reach LLC 847 720-9090
141 Halstead Ave Ste 201 Mamaroneck (10543) *(G-8025)*
Brandt Equipment LLC 718 994-0800
4461 Bronx Blvd Bronx (10470) *(G-1288)*
Brandt Industries, Bronx *Also called Brandt Equipment LLC (G-1288)*
Brandys Mold and Tool Ctr Ltd (PA) 585 334-8333
10 Riverton Way West Henrietta (14586) *(G-16871)*
Brannkey Inc (PA) 212 371-1515
1385 Broadway Fl 14 New York (10018) *(G-9453)*
Brannock Device Co Inc 315 475-9862
116 Luther Ave Liverpool (13088) *(G-7512)*
Branson Ultrasonics Corp 585 624-8000
475 Quaker Meeting Hse Rd Honeoye Falls (14472) *(G-6525)*
Brant Art Publications Inc 212 941-2800
110 Greene St Ph 2 New York (10012) *(G-9454)*
Brant Publications Inc (PA) 212 941-2800
110 Greene St Ph 2 New York (10012) *(G-9455)*
Brasilans Press Pblcations Inc 212 764-6161
60 W 46th St Rm 302 New York (10036) *(G-9456)*
Brauen Constrution 585 492-0042
1087 Chaffee Rd Arcade (14009) *(G-390)*
Braun Brothers Brushes Inc 631 667-2179
35 4th St Valley Stream (11581) *(G-16402)*
Braun Brush Company, Albertson *Also called Braun Industries Inc (G-152)*
Braun Horticulture Inc 716 282-6101
3302 Highland Ave Niagara Falls (14305) *(G-12798)*
Braun Industries Inc 516 741-6000
43 Albertson Ave Albertson (11507) *(G-152)*
Brave Chefs Incorporated 347 956-5905
4130 249th St Ste 2 Little Neck (11363) *(G-7507)*
Brayley Tool & Machine Inc 585 342-7190
1685 Lyell Ave Rochester (14606) *(G-14244)*
Braze Alloy Inc 718 815-5757
3075 Richmond Ter Staten Island (10303) *(G-15651)*
Brazen Street LLC 516 305-7951
734 Pennsylvania Ave Brooklyn (11207) *(G-1713)*
Bread Factory LLC 914 637-8150
30 Grove Ave New Rochelle (10801) *(G-8889)*
Bread Market Cafe 212 768-9292
16 W 45th St Fl 5 New York (10036) *(G-9457)*
Breed Enterprises Inc 585 388-0126
34 Water St Fairport (14450) *(G-4849)*
Bren-Trnics Batteries Intl Inc 631 499-5155
10 Brayton Ct Commack (11725) *(G-3825)*
Bren-Trnics Batteries Intl LLC 631 499-5155
10 Brayton Ct Commack (11725) *(G-3826)*
Bren-Tronics Inc 631 499-5155
10 Brayton Ct Commack (11725) *(G-3827)*
Brennans Quick Print Inc 518 793-4999
6 Collins Dr Glens Falls (12804) *(G-5673)*
Brenseke George Wldg Ir Works 631 271-4870
915 Long Island Ave Ste A Deer Park (11729) *(G-4111)*
Brenseke's, Deer Park *Also called Brenseke George Wldg Ir Works (G-4111)*
Breton Industries Inc (PA) 518 842-3030
1 Sam Stratton Rd Amsterdam (12010) *(G-336)*
Brewer & Newell Printing, Rochester *Also called Forward Enterprises Inc (G-14379)*
Brewer-Cantelmo Co Inc 212 244-4600
55 W 39th St Rm 205 New York (10018) *(G-9458)*
Brewerton Special Tee's, Brewerton *Also called Irene Cerone (G-1204)*
Brewery Ommegang Ltd 607 286-4144
656 County Highway 33 Cooperstown (13326) *(G-3883)*
Brewster Coachworks, Lagrangeville *Also called Graphics Slution Providers Inc (G-7253)*
Brewster Transit Mix Corp (PA) 845 279-3738
31 Fields Ln Brewster (10509) *(G-1213)*
Brewster Transit Mix Corp 845 279-3738
Fields Ln Brewster (10509) *(G-1214)*
Brick & Ballerstein Inc 718 497-1400
1085 Irving Ave Ridgewood (11385) *(G-14103)*
Brickit 631 727-8977
17 Central Ave Hauppauge (11788) *(G-6037)*
Bridal Guide, New York *Also called Rfp LLC (G-11855)*
Brides Inc 718 435-6092
4817 New Utrecht Ave Brooklyn (11219) *(G-1714)*

Bridge Components Inc 716 731-1184
2122 Cory Dr Sanborn (14132) *(G-15113)*
Bridge Enterprises Inc 718 625-6622
544 Park Ave Brooklyn (11205) *(G-1715)*
Bridge Metal Industries LLC 914 663-9200
717 S 3rd Ave Mount Vernon (10550) *(G-8667)*
Bridge Printing Inc 212 243-5390
4710 32nd Pl Fl 2 Long Island City (11101) *(G-7690)*
Bridge Records Inc 914 654-9270
200 Clinton Ave New Rochelle (10801) *(G-8890)*
Bridgehampton Steel & Wldg Inc 631 537-2486
27 Foster Ave Bridgehampton (11932) *(G-1232)*
Bridgeport Metalcraft Inc 315 623-9597
567 County Route 23 Constantia (13044) *(G-3880)*
Bridgestone APM Company 419 423-9552
6350 Inducon Dr E Sanborn (14132) *(G-15114)*
Bridgewater Mdsg Concepts 718 383-5500
924 Meeker Ave Brooklyn (11222) *(G-1716)*
Brigadoon Software Inc (PA) 845 624-0909
119 Rockland Ctr 250 Nanuet (10954) *(G-8752)*
Brigantine Inc (HQ) 212 354-8550
225 W 37th St New York (10018) *(G-9459)*
Brigden Memorials, Albion *Also called Woodside Granite Industries (G-171)*
Briggs & Stratton Corporation 315 495-0100
4245 Highbridge Rd Sherrill (13461) *(G-15404)*
Briggs & Stratton Corporation 315 495-0100
5375 N Main St Munnsville (13409) *(G-8749)*
Bright Chair Co, Middletown *Also called Princeton Upholstery Co Inc (G-8458)*
Bright Kids Nyc Inc 917 539-4575
225 Broadway Ste 1504 New York (10007) *(G-9460)*
Bright Way Supply Inc 718 833-2882
6302 Fort Hamilton Pkwy Brooklyn (11219) *(G-1717)*
Brightline Ventures I LLC 212 626-6829
1120 Avenue Of The Americ New York (10036) *(G-9461)*
Brighton Bakery 315 475-2948
335 E Brighton Ave Syracuse (13210) *(G-15874)*
Brighton Design, Tonawanda *Also called Brighton Tool & Die Designers (G-16148)*
Brighton Tool & Die Designers (PA) 716 876-0879
463 Brighton Rd Tonawanda (14150) *(G-16148)*
Brijon, Ronkonkoma *Also called Lanco Corporation (G-14929)*
Brilliant Jewelers/Mjj Inc 212 353-2326
902 Broadway Fl 18 New York (10010) *(G-9462)*
Brinkman Intl Group Inc (PA) 585 429-5000
167 Ames St Rochester (14611) *(G-14245)*
Brinkman Precision Inc 585 429-5001
100 Park Centre Dr West Henrietta (14586) *(G-16872)*
Brinkman Products Inc (HQ) 585 235-4545
167 Ames St Rochester (14611) *(G-14246)*
Bristol Boarding Inc 585 271-7860
1336 Culver Rd Rochester (14609) *(G-14247)*
Bristol Core Inc 585 919-0302
5310 North St Canandaigua (14424) *(G-3336)*
Bristol Gift Co Inc 845 496-2821
8 North St Washingtonville (10992) *(G-16598)*
Bristol Instruments Inc 585 924-2620
50 Victor Heights Pkwy Victor (14564) *(G-16464)*
Bristol Metals Inc 585 657-7665
7817 State Route 5 And 20 Bloomfield (14469) *(G-982)*
Bristol Seamless Ring Corp 212 874-2645
209 W 86th St Apt 817 New York (10024) *(G-9463)*
Bristol-Myers Squibb Company (PA) 212 546-4000
345 Park Ave Bsmt Lc3 New York (10154) *(G-9464)*
Bristol-Myers Squibb Company 315 432-2000
6000 Thompson Rd East Syracuse (13057) *(G-4512)*
Bristol-Myers Squibb Company 516 832-2191
1000 Stewart Ave Garden City (11530) *(G-5497)*
Bristol/White Plains 914 681-1800
305 North St White Plains (10605) *(G-17088)*
British American Publishing 518 786-6000
19 British American Blvd Latham (12110) *(G-7356)*
British Science Corporation (PA) 212 980-8700
100 Wheeler Ave Staten Island (10314) *(G-15652)*
Brittish American Envmtl, Clifton Park *Also called Microb Phase Services (G-3702)*
Broadalbin Manufacturing Corp 518 883-5313
8 Pine St Broadalbin (12025) *(G-1240)*
Broadcast Manager Inc 212 509-1200
65 Broadway Ste 602 New York (10006) *(G-9465)*
Broadnet Technologies Inc 315 443-3694
2-212 Center For Science Syracuse (13244) *(G-15875)*
Broadway Knitting Mills Inc 716 692-4421
1333 Strad Ave Ste 216 North Tonawanda (14120) *(G-12961)*
Broadway National, Ronkonkoma *Also called Broadway Neon Sign Corp (G-14881)*
Broadway Neon Sign Corp 908 241-4177
1900 Ocean Ave Ronkonkoma (11779) *(G-14881)*
Broadway Technology LLC (PA) 646 912-6450
140 Broadway Ste 4320 New York (10005) *(G-9466)*
Brocade Cmmnctions Systems Inc 212 497-8500
1 Penn Plz Ste 1820 New York (10119) *(G-9467)*
Brock Awnings Ltd 631 765-5200
211 E Montauk Hwy Ste 1 Hampton Bays (11946) *(G-5960)*
Brockyn Corporation 631 244-2770
606 Johnson Ave Ste 31 Bohemia (11716) *(G-1027)*
Broda Machine Co Inc 716 297-3221
8745 Packard Rd Niagara Falls (14304) *(G-12799)*
Brodco Inc 631 842-4477
67 Woodhail St Lido Beach (11561) *(G-7440)*
Broder Mfg Inc 718 366-1667
566 Johnson Ave Brooklyn (11237) *(G-1718)*
Brodock Press Inc (PA) 315 735-9577
502 Court St Ste G Utica (13502) *(G-16310)*
Broetje Automation-Usa Inc 716 204-8640
165 Lawrence Bell Dr # 116 Williamsville (14221) *(G-17236)*
Broken Threads Inc 212 730-4351
147 W 35th St Ste 501 New York (10001) *(G-9468)*
Bronson Labrotaries, Hauppauge *Also called Bronson Nutritionals LLC (G-6038)*
Bronson Nutritionals LLC (PA) 631 750-0000
70 Commerce Dr Hauppauge (11788) *(G-6038)*
Bronx Design Group, The, Bronx *Also called G&J Graphics Inc (G-1340)*
Bronx New Way Corp 347 431-1385
113 E Kingsbridge Rd Bronx (10468) *(G-1289)*
Bronx Times Reporter, Brooklyn *Also called Community News Group LLC (G-1796)*
Bronx Wstchester Tempering Inc 914 663-9400
160 S Macquesten Pkwy Mount Vernon (10550) *(G-8668)*
Bronxville Review, New Rochelle *Also called Gannett Co Inc (G-8903)*
Brook North Farms Inc 315 834-9390
89 York St Auburn (13021) *(G-487)*
Brook Telephone Mfg & Sup Co 718 449-4222
2338 Mcdonald Ave Brooklyn (11223) *(G-1719)*
Brook-Tel, Brooklyn *Also called Brook Telephone Mfg & Sup Co (G-1719)*
Brooke Leigh Ltd (PA) 212 736-9098
520 8th Ave Fl 20 New York (10018) *(G-9469)*
Brooke Maya Inc 212 279-2340
124 W 36th St Fl 7 New York (10018) *(G-9470)*
Brookhaven Instruments Corp 631 758-3200
750 Blue Point Rd Holtsville (11742) *(G-6501)*
Brooklyn Baby Cakes Inc 917 334-2518
411 Hancock St Brooklyn (11216) *(G-1720)*
Brooklyn Bangers LLC 718 875-3535
111 Atlantic Ave Ste 1r Brooklyn (11201) *(G-1721)*
Brooklyn Brew Shop LLC 718 874-0119
20 Jay St Ste 410 Brooklyn (11201) *(G-1722)*
Brooklyn Btlg Milton NY Inc (PA) 845 795-2171
643 South Rd Milton (12547) *(G-8482)*
Brooklyn Casing Co Inc 718 522-0866
412 3rd St Brooklyn (11215) *(G-1723)*
Brooklyn Cstm Met Fbrction Inc 718 499-1573
48 Prospect Park Sw Brooklyn (11215) *(G-1724)*
Brooklyn Denim Co 718 782-2600
85 N 3rd St Brooklyn (11249) *(G-1725)*
Brooklyn Heights Press, Brooklyn *Also called Brooklyn Journal Publications (G-1729)*
Brooklyn Industries LLC 718 788-5250
328 7th Ave Brooklyn (11215) *(G-1726)*
Brooklyn Industries LLC 718 486-6464
162 Bedford Ave Ste A Brooklyn (11249) *(G-1727)*
Brooklyn Industries LLC 718 789-2764
206 5th Ave Ste 1 Brooklyn (11217) *(G-1728)*
Brooklyn Journal Publications 718 422-7400
16 Court St 30 Brooklyn (11241) *(G-1729)*
Brooklyn Rail Inc 718 349-8427
99 Commercial St Apt 15 Brooklyn (11222) *(G-1730)*
Brooklyn Remembers Inc 718 491-1705
9201 4th Ave Brooklyn (11209) *(G-1731)*
Brooklyn Store Front Co Inc 718 384-4372
62 Throop Ave Brooklyn (11206) *(G-1732)*
Brooklyn Sweet Spot Inc 718 522-2577
366 Myrtle Ave Brooklyn (11205) *(G-1733)*
Brooklyn Winery 347 763-1506
213 N 8th St Brooklyn (11211) *(G-1734)*
Brooks Bottling Co LLC 607 432-1782
5560 State Highway 7 Oneonta (13820) *(G-13174)*
Brooks Litho Digital Group Inc 631 789-4500
35 W Jefryn Blvd Ste A Deer Park (11729) *(G-4112)*
Brooks Woodworking Inc 914 666-2029
15 Kensico Dr Mount Kisco (10549) *(G-8623)*
Brookside Lumber Inc 315 497-0937
4191 Duryea St Moravia (13118) *(G-8616)*
Brookvale Records Inc 631 587-7722
31 Brookvale Ave West Babylon (11704) *(G-16776)*
Broom Tioga Boces, Binghamton *Also called Boces Business Office (G-897)*
Broome County 607 785-9567
2001 E Main St Endicott (13760) *(G-4797)*
Bross Quality Paving 845 532-7116
4 Kossar Pl Ellenville (12428) *(G-4632)*
Brotherhood Amer Oldest Wnery 845 496-3661
100 Brotherhood Plaza Dr Washingtonville (10992) *(G-16599)*
Brothers Roofing Supplies Co 718 779-0280
10514 Astoria Blvd East Elmhurst (11369) *(G-4389)*
Brothers-In-Lawn Property 716 279-6191
176 Vulcan Tonawanda (14150) *(G-16149)*
Brown Printers of Troy Inc 518 235-4080
363 5th Ave Troy (12182) *(G-16228)*
Brown Printing Co, Troy *Also called Brown Printers of Troy Inc (G-16228)*
Brown Printing Company 212 782-7800
1500 Broadway Ste 505 New York (10036) *(G-9471)*

ALPHABETIC

Brown Publishing Network Inc — ALPHABETIC SECTION

Brown Publishing Network Inc 212 682-3330
  122 E 42nd St Rm 2810 New York (10168) *(G-9472)*
Brown Strauss Steel Division, New York Also called Blue Tee Corp *(G-9422)*
Brownstone Capitl Partners LLC 212 889-0069
  251 5th Ave Fl 3 New York (10016) *(G-9473)*
Brownstone Publishers Inc 212 473-8200
  149 5th Ave Fl 10 New York (10010) *(G-9474)*
Brucci Ltd 914 965-0707
  861 Nepperhan Ave Yonkers (10703) *(G-17422)*
Bruce Pierce 716 731-9310
  2386 Lockport Rd Sanborn (14132) *(G-15115)*
Bruce Woehr 585 654-6746
  146 Halstead St Rochester (14610) *(G-14248)*
Brueton Industries Inc (PA) 516 379-3400
  146 Hanse Ave Ste 1 Freeport (11520) *(G-5391)*
Brunner International Inc 585 798-6000
  3959 Bates Rd Medina (14103) *(G-8268)*
Bruno & Canio Ltd 845 624-3060
  130 Blauvelt Rd Nanuet (10954) *(G-8753)*
Bruno Associates, Altamont Also called Rsb Associates Inc *(G-212)*
Bruno Associates, Voorheesville Also called Rfb Associates Inc *(G-16517)*
Bruno Magli, New York Also called Bm America LLC *(G-9427)*
Brunschwig & Fils LLC (HQ) 800 538-1880
  245 Central Ave Bethpage (11714) *(G-865)*
Brushtech (disc) Inc 518 563-8420
  4 Matt Ave Plattsburgh (12901) *(G-13656)*
Bruynswick Sales Inc 845 789-2049
  14 Bruynswick Rd New Paltz (12561) *(G-8873)*
Bryant Machine & Development 716 894-8282
  63 Stanley St Buffalo (14206) *(G-2845)*
Bryant Machine Co Inc 716 894-8282
  63 Stanley St Buffalo (14206) *(G-2846)*
Bryant Manufacturing Wny Inc 716 894-8282
  63 Stanley St Buffalo (14206) *(G-2847)*
Bryit Group LLC 631 563-6603
  1724 Church St Holbrook (11741) *(G-6433)*
Brzozka Industries Inc 631 588-8164
  790 Broadway Ave Holbrook (11741) *(G-6434)*
BSC Associates LLC 607 321-2980
  100 Eldredge St Binghamton (13901) *(G-899)*
BSD Aluminum Foil LLC 347 689-3875
  260 Hewest St Brooklyn (11211) *(G-1735)*
BSD Top Direct Inc 646 468-0156
  68 Route 109 West Babylon (11704) *(G-16777)*
Bsu Inc 607 272-8100
  445 E State St Ithaca (14850) *(G-6829)*
Bsv Enterprises, Spencerport Also called Bsv Metal Finishers Inc *(G-15567)*
Bsv Metal Finishers Inc 585 349-7072
  11 Aristocrat Cir Spencerport (14559) *(G-15567)*
Bucket Links LLC 212 290-2900
  261 W 35th St Ste 1003 New York (10001) *(G-9475)*
Buckeye Corrugated Inc 315 437-1181
  151 Midler Park Dr Syracuse (13206) *(G-15876)*
Buckeye Corrugated Inc 585 924-1600
  797 Old Dutch Rd Victor (14564) *(G-16465)*
Buckle Down, Farmingdale Also called Custom Sitecom LLC *(G-4971)*
Buckley Qc Fasteners Inc 716 662-1490
  3874 California Rd Orchard Park (14127) *(G-13255)*
Bud Barger Assoc Inc 631 696-6703
  3 Mount Mckinley Ave Farmingville (11738) *(G-5159)*
Budd Woodwork Inc 718 389-1110
  54 Franklin St Brooklyn (11222) *(G-1736)*
Buell Fuel LLC 315 841-3000
  2676 State Route 12b Deansboro (13328) *(G-4084)*
Buffallo Sports Inc 716 826-7700
  3840 Mckinley Pkwy Blasdell (14219) *(G-961)*
Buffalo, Plattsburgh Also called Gbg Denim Usa LLC *(G-13663)*
Buffalo Abrasives Inc (PA) 716 693-3856
  960 Erie Ave North Tonawanda (14120) *(G-12962)*
Buffalo Armory LLC 716 935-6346
  1050 Military Rd Buffalo (14217) *(G-2848)*
Buffalo Bioblower Tech LLC 716 625-8618
  6100 Donner Rd Lockport (14094) *(G-7573)*
Buffalo Blends Inc (PA) 716 825-4422
  1400 William St Buffalo (14206) *(G-2849)*
Buffalo Circuits Inc 716 662-2113
  105 Mid County Dr Orchard Park (14127) *(G-13256)*
Buffalo Compressed Air Inc 716 783-8673
  2727 Broadway St Ste 3a Cheektowaga (14227) *(G-3563)*
Buffalo Crushed Stone Inc (HQ) 716 826-7310
  500 Como Park Blvd Buffalo (14227) *(G-2850)*
Buffalo Crushed Stone Inc 716 566-9636
  Rr 16 Franklinville (14737) *(G-5368)*
Buffalo Crushed Stone Inc 607 587-8102
  638 State Route 244 Alfred Station (14803) *(G-196)*
Buffalo Dental Mfg Co Inc 516 496-7200
  159 Lafayette Dr Syosset (11791) *(G-15815)*
Buffalo Envelope, Depew Also called Cenveo Inc *(G-4252)*
Buffalo Envelope Company, Depew Also called Buffalo Envelope Inc *(G-4249)*
Buffalo Envelope Inc 716 686-0100
  2914 Walden Ave Ste 300 Depew (14043) *(G-4249)*

Buffalo Filter LLC 716 835-7000
  5900 Genesee St Lancaster (14086) *(G-7307)*
Buffalo Finishing Company, Ithaca Also called F M Abdulky Inc *(G-6840)*
Buffalo Finishing Works Inc 716 893-5266
  1255 Niagara St Buffalo (14213) *(G-2851)*
Buffalo Games Inc 716 827-8393
  220 James E Casey Dr Buffalo (14206) *(G-2852)*
Buffalo Games & Puzzles, Buffalo Also called Buffalo Games Inc *(G-2852)*
Buffalo Gear Inc 716 731-2100
  3635 Lockport Rd Sanborn (14132) *(G-15116)*
Buffalo Hardwood Floor Center, Buffalo Also called Mm of East Aurora LLC *(G-3069)*
Buffalo Hearg & Speech 716 558-1105
  1026 Union Rd West Seneca (14224) *(G-16940)*
Buffalo Investors Corp (HQ) 212 702-4363
  1 Wall Street Ct Apt 980 New York (10005) *(G-9476)*
Buffalo Law Journal 716 541-1600
  465 Main St Ste 100 Buffalo (14203) *(G-2853)*
Buffalo Lining & Fabricating 716 883-6500
  73 Gillette Ave Buffalo (14214) *(G-2854)*
Buffalo Machine Tls of Niagara 716 201-1310
  4935 Lockport Rd Lockport (14094) *(G-7574)*
Buffalo Metal Casting Co Inc 716 874-6211
  1875 Elmwood Ave Buffalo (14207) *(G-2855)*
Buffalo Metal Finishing Co (PA) 716 883-2751
  135 Dart St Buffalo (14213) *(G-2856)*
Buffalo Metal Forming Inc 716 856-4575
  21 Creekview Dr West Seneca (14224) *(G-16941)*
Buffalo News Inc 716 849-4401
  1 News Plz Buffalo (14203) *(G-2857)*
Buffalo Newspress Inc 716 852-1600
  200 Broadway St Buffalo (14204) *(G-2858)*
Buffalo Polymer Processors Inc 716 537-3153
  42 Edgewood Dr Holland (14080) *(G-6480)*
Buffalo Power Elec Ctr De 716 651-1600
  166 Taylor Dr Ste 1 Depew (14043) *(G-4250)*
Buffalo Provisions Co Inc 718 292-4300
  4009 76th St Elmhurst (11373) *(G-4658)*
Buffalo Pumps Inc (HQ) 716 693-1850
  874 Oliver St North Tonawanda (14120) *(G-12963)*
Buffalo Rocket, Buffalo Also called Rocket Communications Inc *(G-3162)*
Buffalo Snowmelter, North Tonawanda Also called Roemac Industrial Sales Inc *(G-12991)*
Buffalo Spree Publishing Inc 585 413-0040
  100 Allens Creek Rd Ste 8 Rochester (14618) *(G-14249)*
Buffalo Spree Publishing Inc (PA) 716 783-9119
  1738 Elmwood Ave Ste 103 Buffalo (14207) *(G-2859)*
Buffalo Standard Printing Corp 716 835-9454
  3620 Harlem Rd Ste 5 Buffalo (14215) *(G-2860)*
Buffalo Tungsten Inc 716 759-6353
  2 Main St Depew (14043) *(G-4251)*
Buflovak LLC (PA) 716 895-2100
  750 E Ferry St Buffalo (14211) *(G-2861)*
Building Management Assoc Inc 718 542-4779
  998 E 167th St Ofc Bronx (10459) *(G-1290)*
Bulkley Dunton (HQ) 212 863-1800
  1 Penn Plz Ste 2814 New York (10119) *(G-9477)*
Bull Street LLC 212 495-9855
  19 W 69th St Apt 201 New York (10023) *(G-9478)*
Bullet Industries Inc 585 352-0836
  7 Turner Dr Spencerport (14559) *(G-15568)*
Bulletin Boards & Dirctry Pdts 914 248-8008
  2986 Navajo Rd Ste 1 Yorktown Heights (10598) *(G-17507)*
Bullex Inc (HQ) 518 689-2023
  20 Corporate Cir Ste 3 Albany (12203) *(G-58)*
Bullex Inc 518 689-2023
  20 Corporate Cir Ste 3 Albany (12203) *(G-59)*
Bullex Digital Safety, Albany Also called Bullex Inc *(G-58)*
Bullex Digital Safety, Albany Also called Bullex Inc *(G-59)*
Bullitt Group, Bohemia Also called Bullitt Mobile LLC *(G-1028)*
Bullitt Mobile LLC 631 424-1749
  80 Orville Dr Ste 100 Bohemia (11716) *(G-1028)*
Bulow & Associates Inc 716 838-0298
  317 Wheeler St Tonawanda (14150) *(G-16150)*
Buna Besta Tortillas 347 987-3995
  219 Johnson Ave Brooklyn (11206) *(G-1737)*
Buncee LLC 631 591-1390
  4603 Middle Country Rd Calverton (11933) *(G-3287)*
Bunge Limited Finance Corp 914 684-2800
  50 Main St White Plains (10606) *(G-17089)*
Bunger Sayville, Sayville Also called Bungers Surf Shop *(G-15205)*
Bungers Surf Shop 631 244-3646
  247 W Main St Sayville (11782) *(G-15205)*
Burdick Publications Inc 315 685-9500
  2352 E Lake Rd Skaneateles (13152) *(G-15456)*
Bureau of National Affairs Inc 212 687-4530
  25 W 43rd St Ste 1007 New York (10036) *(G-9479)*
Burgess Products Division, New York Mills Also called Fountainhead Group Inc *(G-12722)*
Burgess-Manning Inc (HQ) 716 662-6540
  50 Cobham Dr Orchard Park (14127) *(G-13257)*
Burke & Bannayan 585 723-1010
  2465 W Ridge Rd Ste 2 Rochester (14626) *(G-14250)*
Burke Frging Heat Treating Inc 585 235-6060
  30 Sherer St Rochester (14611) *(G-14251)*

Burlen Corp.....212 684-0052
6 E 32nd St Fl 10 New York (10016) ***(G-9480)***
Burnett Concrete Products Inc.....315 594-2242
5941 Auburn St Wolcott (14590) ***(G-17276)***
Burnett Process Inc (HQ).....585 254-8080
545 Colfax St Rochester (14606) ***(G-14252)***
Burnett Process Inc.....585 277-1623
545 Colfax St Rochester (14606) ***(G-14253)***
Burnham Polymeric Inc.....518 792-3040
1408 Route 9 Fort Edward (12828) ***(G-5340)***
Burnhams, The, Fort Edward *Also called Burnham Polymeric Inc* ***(G-5340)***
Burns Archive Photographic Dis.....212 889-1938
140 E 38th St Frnt 1 New York (10016) ***(G-9481)***
Burnt Hills Fabricators Inc.....518 885-1115
318 Charlton Rd B Ballston Spa (12020) ***(G-592)***
Burnt Mill Smithing.....585 293-2380
127 Burnt Mill Rd Churchville (14428) ***(G-3634)***
Burr & Son Inc.....315 446-1550
119 Seeley Rd Syracuse (13224) ***(G-15877)***
Burrows Paper Corporation.....315 348-8491
Lyonsdale Rd Lyons Falls (13368) ***(G-7977)***
Burrows Paper Corporation.....315 823-2300
730 E Mill St Little Falls (13365) ***(G-7497)***
Burrows Paper Corporation.....315 823-2300
489 W Main St Little Falls (13365) ***(G-7498)***
Burrows Paper Mill, Little Falls *Also called Burrows Paper Corporation* ***(G-7497)***
Burt Millwork Corporation.....718 257-4601
1010 Stanley Ave Brooklyn (11208) ***(G-1738)***
Burt Rigid Box Inc.....607 433-2510
58 Browne St Oneonta (13820) ***(G-13175)***
Burt Rigid Box Inc (PA).....607 433-2510
58 Browne St Oneonta (13820) ***(G-13176)***
Burton Corporation.....802 862-4500
21 Lawrence Paquette Dr Champlain (12919) ***(G-3539)***
Burton Industries Inc.....631 643-6660
243 Wyandanch Ave Ste A West Babylon (11704) ***(G-16778)***
Burton Snowboards, Champlain *Also called Burton Corporation* ***(G-3539)***
Busch Products Inc.....315 474-8422
110 Baker St Syracuse (13206) ***(G-15878)***
Bush Industries Inc (PA).....716 665-2000
1 Mason Dr Jamestown (14701) ***(G-6978)***
Bushwick Kitchen LLC.....917 297-1045
630 Flushing Ave Fl 5 Brooklyn (11206) ***(G-1739)***
Business Advisory Services.....718 337-3740
1104 Bay 25th St Far Rockaway (11691) ***(G-4919)***
Business Card Express Inc.....631 669-3400
300 Farmingdale Rd West Babylon (11704) ***(G-16779)***
Business Directory Inc.....718 486-8099
137 Division Ave Ste A Brooklyn (11211) ***(G-1740)***
Business First of New York (HQ).....716 854-5822
465 Main St Ste 100 Buffalo (14203) ***(G-2862)***
Business First of New York.....518 640-6800
40 British American Blvd Latham (12110) ***(G-7357)***
Business Integrity Inc (HQ).....718 238-2008
79 Madison Ave Fl 2 New York (10016) ***(G-9482)***
Business Journal, Syracuse *Also called CNY Business Review Inc* ***(G-15898)***
Business Journals.....212 790-5100
1166 Ave Of The America New York (10036) ***(G-9483)***
Business Management Systems.....914 245-8558
2404 Loring Pl Yorktown Heights (10598) ***(G-17508)***
Business Review, Latham *Also called Business First of New York* ***(G-7357)***
Business Tech Communications.....516 354-5205
18 Hudson Rd Garden City (11530) ***(G-5498)***
Busse Hospital Disposables, Hauppauge *Also called Robert Busse & Co Inc* ***(G-6178)***
Bust Inc.....212 675-1707
253 36th St Unit 3 Brooklyn (11232) ***(G-1741)***
Bust Magazine, Brooklyn *Also called Bust Inc* ***(G-1741)***
Butter Cooky Bakery.....516 354-3831
217 Jericho Tpke Floral Park (11001) ***(G-5196)***
Butterck McCall Vogue Pattern, New York *Also called McCall Pattern Company* ***(G-11195)***
Butterwood Desserts Inc.....716 652-0131
1863 Davis Rd West Falls (14170) ***(G-16844)***
Buttons & Trimcom Inc.....212 868-1971
519 8th Ave Rm 26 New York (10018) ***(G-9484)***
Buxton Machine and Tool Co Inc.....716 876-2312
2181 Elmwood Ave Buffalo (14216) ***(G-2863)***
Buxton Medical Equipment Corp.....631 957-4500
1178 Route 109 Lindenhurst (11757) ***(G-7457)***
BW Elliott Mfg Co LLC.....607 772-0404
11 Beckwith Ave Binghamton (13901) ***(G-900)***
Bwog, New York *Also called Blue and White Publishing Inc* ***(G-9420)***
Bws Specialty Fabrication, Orchard Park *Also called Quality Industrial Services* ***(G-13294)***
By Robert James.....212 253-2121
74 Orchard St New York (10002) ***(G-9485)***
Bycmac Corp.....845 255-0884
144 Main St Gardiner (12525) ***(G-5548)***
Byelocorp Scientific Inc (PA).....212 785-2580
76 Perry St New York (10014) ***(G-9486)***
Byer California.....212 944-8989
1407 Broadway Rm 807 New York (10018) ***(G-9487)***
Byfusion Inc.....347 563-5286
350 Manhattan Ave Apt 104 Brooklyn (11211) ***(G-1742)***
Byk USA Inc.....845 469-5800
48 Leone Ln Chester (10918) ***(G-3602)***
Bylada Foods LLC.....845 623-1300
250 W Nyack Rd Ste 110 West Nyack (10994) ***(G-16914)***
Byliner Inc.....415 680-3608
27 W 24th St Ste 202 New York (10010) ***(G-9488)***
Byram Concrete & Supply LLC.....914 682-4477
145 Virginia Rd White Plains (10603) ***(G-17090)***
Byrne Dairy Inc (PA).....315 475-2121
2394 Us Route 11 La Fayette (13084) ***(G-7241)***
Byrne Dairy Inc.....315 475-2111
275 Cortland Ave Syracuse (13202) ***(G-15879)***
Byrne Distribution Center, Syracuse *Also called Byrne Dairy Inc* ***(G-15879)***
Bys Publishing LLC.....315 655-9431
118 Albany St Cazenovia (13035) ***(G-3442)***
Byte Consulting Inc.....646 500-8606
295 Madison Ave Fl 35 New York (10017) ***(G-9489)***
Bytheway Publishing Services.....607 334-8365
365 Follett Hill Rd Norwich (13815) ***(G-13020)***
Bz Media LLC.....631 421-4158
225 Broadhollow Rd 211e Melville (11747) ***(G-8299)***
C & A Atelier, Richmond Hill *Also called Carlos & Alex Atelier Inc* ***(G-14070)***
C & A Service Inc (PA).....516 354-1200
65 S Tyson Ave Floral Park (11001) ***(G-5197)***
C & C Athletic Inc.....845 713-4670
11 Myrtle Ave Walden (12586) ***(G-16531)***
C & C Bindery Co Inc.....631 752-7078
25 Central Ave Unit B Farmingdale (11735) ***(G-4954)***
C & C Custom Metal Fabricators.....631 235-9646
2 N Hoffman Ln Hauppauge (11788) ***(G-6039)***
C & C Duplicators Inc.....631 244-0800
220 Knickerbocker Ave # 1 Bohemia (11716) ***(G-1029)***
C & C Metal Fabrications Inc.....315 598-7607
159 Hubbard St Fulton (13069) ***(G-5453)***
C & C Ready-Mix Corporation (PA).....607 797-5108
3112 Vestal Rd Vestal (13850) ***(G-16443)***
C & C Ready-Mix Corporation.....607 687-1690
3818 Rt 17 C Owego (13827) ***(G-13351)***
C & D Assembly Inc.....607 898-4275
107 Corona Ave Groton (13073) ***(G-5897)***
C & F Fabricators & Erectors.....607 432-3520
Rr 7 Colliersville (13747) ***(G-3814)***
C & F Iron Works Inc.....914 592-2450
14 N Payne St Ste 1 Elmsford (10523) ***(G-4738)***
C & F Steel Corp.....914 592-3928
14 N Payne St Ste 2 Elmsford (10523) ***(G-4739)***
C & G of Kingston Inc.....845 331-0148
25 Cornell St Kingston (12401) ***(G-7180)***
C & G Video Systems Inc (PA).....315 452-1490
7778 Tirrell Hill Cir Liverpool (13090) ***(G-7513)***
C & H Cstm Bkbinding Embossing.....800 871-8980
1 Forte Ave Medford (11763) ***(G-8237)***
C & H Machining Inc.....631 582-6737
281 Knickerbocker Ave Bohemia (11716) ***(G-1030)***
C & H Precision Tools Inc.....631 758-3806
194 Morris Ave Ste 20 Holtsville (11742) ***(G-6502)***
C & M Circuits Inc.....631 589-0208
50 Orville Dr Bohemia (11716) ***(G-1031)***
C & M Products Inc.....315 471-3303
1209 N Salina St Ste 1 Syracuse (13208) ***(G-15880)***
C & N Packaging Inc.....631 491-1400
105 Wyandanch Ave Wyandanch (11798) ***(G-17371)***
C & R De Santis Inc.....718 447-5076
2645 Forest Ave Ste 2 Staten Island (10303) ***(G-15653)***
C & T Tool & Instrument Co.....718 429-1253
4125 58th St Woodside (11377) ***(G-17321)***
C A M Graphics Co Inc.....631 842-3400
24 Central Dr Farmingdale (11735) ***(G-4955)***
C B I, Oriskany *Also called Caldwell Bennett Inc* ***(G-13305)***
C B Management Services Inc.....845 735-2300
73 S Pearl St Pearl River (10965) ***(G-13455)***
C B S Food Products Corp.....718 452-2500
770 Chauncey St Brooklyn (11207) ***(G-1743)***
C C Industries Inc.....518 581-7633
344 Burgoyne Rd Saratoga Springs (12866) ***(G-15146)***
C C M, Wolcott *Also called Carballo Contract Machining* ***(G-17278)***
C D A Inc.....631 473-1595
66 Southern Blvd Ste A Nesconset (11767) ***(G-8774)***
C E Chquie Ltd.....212 268-0006
15 W 36th St Ph New York (10018) ***(G-9490)***
C E King & Sons Inc.....631 324-4944
10 Saint Francis Pl East Hampton (11937) ***(G-4406)***
C F Peters Corp.....718 416-7800
7030 80th St Ste 2 Glendale (11385) ***(G-5648)***
C F Print Ltd Inc.....631 567-2110
35 W Jefryn Blvd Ste 2 Deer Park (11729) ***(G-4113)***
C G & Son Machining Inc.....315 964-2430
87 Nichols Rd Williamstown (13493) ***(G-17228)***
C H Thompson Company Inc.....607 724-1094
69-93 Eldredge St Binghamton (13902) ***(G-901)***
C Howard Company Inc.....631 286-7940
1007 Station Rd Bellport (11713) ***(G-827)***
C I G, New York *Also called Cambridge Info Group Inc* ***(G-9506)***

ALPHABETIC

C J & C Sheet Metal Corp 631 376-9425
433 Falmouth Rd West Babylon (11704) ***(G-16780)***
C J Winter Machine Tech (HQ) 585 429-5000
167 Ames St Rochester (14611) ***(G-14254)***
C K Printing 718 965-0388
267 41st St Brooklyn (11232) ***(G-1744)***
C L Precision Machine & Tl Co 718 651-8475
5015 70th St Woodside (11377) ***(G-17322)***
C M, Amherst *Also called Columbus McKinnon Corporation* ***(G-234)***
C M E Corp 315 451-7101
1005 W Fayette St Ste 3c Syracuse (13204) ***(G-15881)***
C P Chemical Co Inc 914 428-2517
25 Home St White Plains (10606) ***(G-17091)***
C Q Communications Inc 516 681-2922
17 W John St Unit 1 Hicksville (11801) ***(G-6328)***
C R Bard Inc 518 793-2531
289 Bay Rd Queensbury (12804) ***(G-13993)***
C R Bard Inc 518 793-2531
289 Bay Rd Glens Falls (12804) ***(G-5674)***
C R C Manufacturing Inc 585 254-8820
37 Curlew St Rochester (14606) ***(G-14255)***
C S I G Inc 845 383-3800
721 Broadway 270 Kingston (12401) ***(G-7181)***
C S L, North Creek *Also called Creative Stage Lighting Co Inc* ***(G-12933)***
C S Welding, Ontario *Also called Cs Automation Inc* ***(G-13198)***
C Speed LLC 315 453-1043
316 Commerce Blvd Liverpool (13088) ***(G-7514)***
C T A Digital Inc 845 513-0433
326 State Route 208 Monroe (10950) ***(G-8551)***
C T Hogan, Copake Falls *Also called Alumiseal Corp* ***(G-3888)***
C T M Industries Ltd (HQ) 718 479-3300
22005 97th Ave Jamaica (11429) ***(G-6899)***
C To C Design & Print Inc 631 885-4020
1850 Pond Rd Unit B Ronkonkoma (11779) ***(G-14882)***
C W Sheet Metal, Maspeth *Also called Nelson Air Device Corporation* ***(G-8155)***
C&A Aromatics, Floral Park *Also called Citrus and Allied Essences Ltd* ***(G-5200)***
C&C Automatics Inc 315 331-1436
127 W Shore Blvd Newark (14513) ***(G-12730)***
C&C Diecuts, Farmingdale *Also called C & C Bindery Co Inc* ***(G-4954)***
C&H Bookbinding & Embossing, Medford *Also called C & H Cstm Bkbinding Embossing* ***(G-8237)***
C&T Tool & Instrmnt, Woodside *Also called C & T Tool & Instrument Co* ***(G-17321)***
C-Air International, Valley Stream *Also called Parnasa International Inc* ***(G-16418)***
C-Flex Bearing Co Inc 315 895-7454
104 Industrial Dr Frankfort (13340) ***(G-5350)***
C.C.I. Industries, Bohemia *Also called Clip Clop International Inc* ***(G-1035)***
C.H.thompson Finishing, Binghamton *Also called Tcmf Inc* ***(G-954)***
C/O Court Sq Capitl Partners, New York *Also called Mdi Holdings LLC* ***(G-11203)***
C/O M&M Fowarding, Tonawanda *Also called Fiber Laminations Limited* ***(G-16161)***
C/O Pdell Ndell Fine Winberger, New York *Also called Mom Dad Publishing Inc* ***(G-11296)***
Ca Inc (PA) 800 225-5224
520 Madison Ave Fl 22 New York (10022) ***(G-9491)***
Ca Inc 800 225-5224
520 Madison Ave Fl 22 New York (10022) ***(G-9492)***
Cab Plastics, Brooklyn *Also called Cab Signs Inc* ***(G-1745)***
Cab Signs Inc 718 479-2424
38 Livonia Ave Brooklyn (11212) ***(G-1745)***
Cab-Network Inc 516 334-8666
1500 Shames Dr Unit B Westbury (11590) ***(G-16972)***
Cabezon Design Group Inc 718 488-9868
197 Waverly Ave Brooklyn (11205) ***(G-1746)***
Cabinet Shapes Corp 718 784-6255
3721 12th St Long Island City (11101) ***(G-7691)***
Cabinetry By Tbr Inc 516 365-8500
1492 Northern Blvd Manhasset (11030) ***(G-8055)***
Cabinets By Stanley Inc 718 222-5861
46 Hall St Brooklyn (11205) ***(G-1747)***
Cable Management Solutions Inc 631 674-0004
291 Skip Ln Bay Shore (11706) ***(G-680)***
Cable Your World Inc 631 509-1180
1075 Route 112 Ste 4 Port Jeff STA (11776) ***(G-13764)***
Cables and Chips Inc (PA) 212 619-3132
121 Fulton St Fl 4 New York (10038) ***(G-9493)***
Cables Unlimited Inc 631 563-6363
3 Old Dock Rd Yaphank (11980) ***(G-17387)***
Caboodle Printing Inc 716 693-6000
1975 Wehrle Dr Ste 120 Williamsville (14221) ***(G-17237)***
Cabriole Designs Inc 212 593-4528
315 E 91st St Ste 3 New York (10128) ***(G-9494)***
Cachet Industries Inc 212 944-2188
1400 Broadway Rm 709 New York (10018) ***(G-9495)***
Caddell Dry Dock & Repr Co Inc 718 442-2112
Foot Of Broadway 1 W Staten Island (10310) ***(G-15654)***
Caddell Ship Yards, Staten Island *Also called Caddell Dry Dock & Repr Co Inc* ***(G-15654)***
Caddy Concepts Inc 516 570-6279
15 Cuttermill Rd Great Neck (11021) ***(G-5795)***
Cadmus Journal Services Inc 212 736-2002
11 Penn Plz Bsmt 100 New York (10001) ***(G-9496)***
Cadmus Journal Services Inc 607 762-5365
136 Carlin Rd Conklin (13748) ***(G-3866)***

CAF Usa Inc 607 737-3004
300 E 18th St Elmira Heights (14903) ***(G-4709)***
Cafe Kubal 315 278-2812
202 Lockwood Rd Syracuse (13214) ***(G-15882)***
Cahoon Farms Inc 315 594-8081
10951 Lummisville Rd Wolcott (14590) ***(G-17277)***
Cai Inc (PA) 212 819-0008
430 E 56th St New York (10022) ***(G-9497)***
Caithness Equities Corporation (PA) 212 599-2112
565 5th Ave Fl 29 New York (10017) ***(G-9498)***
Cal Blen Electronic Industries 631 242-6243
44 W Jefryn Blvd Ste H Deer Park (11729) ***(G-4114)***
Calchem Corporation (PA) 631 423-5696
2001 Ocean Ave Ronkonkoma (11779) ***(G-14883)***
Caldeira USA Inc 212 532-2292
230 5th Ave Ste 300 New York (10001) ***(G-9499)***
Caldwell Bennett Inc 315 337-8540
6152 County Seat Rd Oriskany (13424) ***(G-13305)***
Caldwell Cor, Fairport *Also called Mastercraft Decorators Inc* ***(G-4863)***
Calfonex Company 845 778-2212
121 Orchard St Walden (12586) ***(G-16532)***
Calgon Carbon Corporation 716 531-9113
830 River Rd North Tonawanda (14120) ***(G-12964)***
Calia Consultants, Staten Island *Also called Calia Technical Inc* ***(G-15655)***
Calia Technical Inc 718 447-3928
420 Jefferson Blvd Staten Island (10312) ***(G-15655)***
Calibrated Instruments Inc 914 741-5700
306 Aerie Ct Manhasset (11030) ***(G-8056)***
Calibration Technologies Inc 631 676-6133
30 Woodland Blvd Centereach (11720) ***(G-3470)***
Calico Cottage Inc 631 841-2100
210 New Hwy Amityville (11701) ***(G-278)***
California Fragrance Company 631 424-4023
171 E 2nd St Huntington Station (11746) ***(G-6698)***
California Petro Trnspt Corp 212 302-5151
114 W 47th St New York (10036) ***(G-9500)***
California US Holdings Inc 212 726-6500
417 5th Ave Lbby 7th New York (10016) ***(G-9501)***
Caliper Architecture PC 718 302-2427
67 Metropolitan Ave Ste 2 Brooklyn (11249) ***(G-1748)***
Caliperstudio Co 718 302-3504
75 Scott Ave Brooklyn (11237) ***(G-1749)***
Call Forwarding Technologies 516 621-3600
55 Northern Blvd Ste 3b Greenvale (11548) ***(G-5879)***
Callahan & Nannini Quarry Inc 845 496-4323
276 Clove Rd Salisbury Mills (12577) ***(G-15112)***
Callanan Industries Inc 315 697-9569
6375 Tuttle Rd Canastota (13032) ***(G-3364)***
Callanan Industries Inc (HQ) 518 374-2222
1245 Kings Rd Ste 1 Schenectady (12303) ***(G-15236)***
Callanan Industries Inc 845 457-3158
215 Montgomery Rd Montgomery (12549) ***(G-8592)***
Callanan Industries Inc 845 331-6868
Salem St Kingston (12401) ***(G-7182)***
Callanan Industries Inc 518 382-5354
145 Cordell Rd Schenectady (12303) ***(G-15237)***
Callaway Arts & Entrmt Inc 212 798-3168
41 Union Sq W Ste 1101 New York (10003) ***(G-9502)***
Callaway Digital Arts Inc 212 675-3050
41 Union Sq W Ste 1101 New York (10003) ***(G-9503)***
Callidus Software Inc 212 554-7300
152 W 57th St Fl 8 New York (10019) ***(G-9504)***
Calmetrics Inc 631 580-2522
1340 Lincoln Ave Ste 6 Holbrook (11741) ***(G-6435)***
Calpac Incorporated 631 789-0502
44 Seabro Ave Amityville (11701) ***(G-279)***
Calspan Corporation (PA) 716 631-6955
4455 Genesee St Buffalo (14225) ***(G-2864)***
Calspan Corporation 716 236-1040
2041 Niagara Falls Blvd Niagara Falls (14304) ***(G-12800)***
Calspan Flight Research Center, Niagara Falls *Also called Calspan Corporation* ***(G-12800)***
Caltex International Ltd 315 425-1040
60 Presidential Plz # 1405 Syracuse (13202) ***(G-15883)***
CALVARY AUTOMATION SYSTEMS, Webster *Also called Calvary Design Team Inc* ***(G-16714)***
Calvary Design Team Inc (PA) 585 347-6127
855 Publishers Pkwy Webster (14580) ***(G-16714)***
Calvin Klein Inc 212 292-9000
654 Madison Ave New York (10065) ***(G-9505)***
CAM Fuel Inc 718 246-4306
50 Commerce St Brooklyn (11231) ***(G-1750)***
CAM Machinery Co, Brooklyn *Also called S & S Machinery Corp* ***(G-2520)***
CAM Touchview Products Inc 631 842-3400
24 Central Dr Farmingdale (11735) ***(G-4956)***
Cama Graphics Inc 718 707-9747
3200 Skillman Ave Ste B Long Island City (11101) ***(G-7692)***
Cambridge Info Group Inc (PA) 301 961-6700
888 7th Ave Ste 1701 New York (10106) ***(G-9506)***
Cambridge Kitchens Mfg Inc 516 935-5100
280 Duffy Ave Unit 1 Hicksville (11801) ***(G-6329)***
Cambridge Manufacturing LLC 516 326-1350
1700 Jericho Tpke New Hyde Park (11040) ***(G-8820)***

ALPHABETIC

Cambridge Resources, Brooklyn *Also called Coda Resources Ltd* ***(G-1790)***
Cambridge Security Seals LLC............845 520-4111
1 Cambridge Plz Pomona (10970) ***(G-13729)***
Cambridge University Press............212 337-5000
1 Liberty Plz Fl 20 New York (10006) ***(G-9507)***
Cambridge Whos Who Pubg Inc (PA)............516 833-8440
498 Rxr Plz Fl 4 Uniondale (11556) ***(G-16290)***
Cambridge-Pacific Inc............518 677-5988
891 State Rd 22 Cambridge (12816) ***(G-3305)***
Camco, Ronkonkoma *Also called Gliptone Manufacturing Inc* ***(G-14904)***
Camden House, Rochester *Also called Boydell & Brewer Inc* ***(G-14243)***
Camden News Inc............315 245-1849
39 Main St Camden (13316) ***(G-3312)***
Camden Wire Co Inc............315 245-3800
12 Masonic Ave Camden (13316) ***(G-3313)***
Camellia Foods, Buffalo *Also called Camellia General Provision Co* ***(G-2865)***
Camellia General Provision Co............716 893-5352
1333 Genesee St Buffalo (14211) ***(G-2865)***
Cameo Metal Products Inc............718 788-1106
127 12th St Brooklyn (11215) ***(G-1751)***
Cameo Process Corp............914 948-0082
15 Stewart Pl Apt 7g White Plains (10603) ***(G-17092)***
Cameron Bridge Works LLC............607 734-9456
1051 S Main St Elmira (14904) ***(G-4672)***
Cameron Mfg & Design Inc............607 739-3606
727 Blostein Blvd Horseheads (14845) ***(G-6571)***
Camfil USA Inc............518 456-6085
6600 Deere Rd Syracuse (13206) ***(G-15884)***
Caminus Corporation (HQ)............212 515-3600
340 Madison Ave Fl 8 New York (10173) ***(G-9508)***
Campanellis Poultry Farm Inc............845 482-2222
4 Perry Rd Bethel (12720) ***(G-860)***
Campbell Alliance Group Inc............212 377-2740
335 Madison Ave Fl 17 New York (10017) ***(G-9509)***
Campbell's Print Shop, Bronx *Also called Linda Campbell* ***(G-1382)***
Campus Course Paks Inc............516 877-3967
1 South Ave Fl 1 Garden City (11530) ***(G-5499)***
Campus Crafts Inc............585 328-6780
160 Murray St Rochester (14606) ***(G-14256)***
Camso Manufacturing Usa Ltd (HQ)............518 561-7528
1 Martina Cir Plattsburgh (12901) ***(G-13657)***
Canaan Printing Inc............718 729-3100
20007 46th Ave Bayside (11361) ***(G-768)***
Canada Goose Us Inc............303 832-7097
300 International Dr Williamsville (14221) ***(G-17238)***
Canal Asphalt Inc............914 667-8500
800 Canal St Mount Vernon (10550) ***(G-8669)***
Canali USA Inc (HQ)............212 767-0205
611 Ffth Ave Saks 5th Ave 5 Saks New York (10014) ***(G-9510)***
Canalside Creamery Inc............716 695-2876
985 Ruie Rd North Tonawanda (14120) ***(G-12965)***
Canandaigua Msgnr Incorporated (PA)............585 394-0770
73 Buffalo St Canandaigua (14424) ***(G-3337)***
Canandaigua Quick Print, Canandaigua *Also called Carges Entps of Canandaigua* ***(G-3338)***
Canandaigua Technology Center, Canandaigua *Also called Pactiv LLC* ***(G-3354)***
Canarm Ltd (HQ)............800 267-4427
808 Commerce Park Dr Ogdensburg (13669) ***(G-13113)***
Canarsie Courier Inc............718 257-0600
1142 E 92nd St 44 Brooklyn (11236) ***(G-1752)***
Canastota Publishing Co Inc............315 697-9010
130 E Center St Canastota (13032) ***(G-3365)***
Cancer Targeting Systems............212 965-4534
100 Wall St New York (10005) ***(G-9511)***
Candex Solutions Inc............215 650-3214
410 Park Ave 1878 New York (10022) ***(G-9512)***
Candid Litho Printing Ltd............212 431-3800
2511 Hunters Point Ave Long Island City (11101) ***(G-7693)***
Candid Worldwide LLC (PA)............212 799-5300
2511 Hunters Point Ave # 2 Long Island City (11101) ***(G-7694)***
Candle In The Window Inc............718 852-5743
43 Hall St Ste C10 Brooklyn (11205) ***(G-1753)***
Candlelight Cabinetry Inc............716 434-2114
24 Michigan St Lockport (14094) ***(G-7575)***
Candles By Foster............914 739-9226
810 South St Peekskill (10566) ***(G-13475)***
Candy Kraft, Altamont *Also called Robert Pikcilingis* ***(G-211)***
Candy Land, Rome *Also called Noras Candy Shop* ***(G-14825)***
Candy Man, Wilmington *Also called Adirondack Chocolate Co Ltd* ***(G-17267)***
Candy Planet Division, New York *Also called Toymax Inc* ***(G-12384)***
Cane Simple, New York *Also called Cane Sugar LLC* ***(G-9513)***
Cane Sugar LLC............212 329-2695
950 3rd Ave Ste 2200 New York (10022) ***(G-9513)***
Canfield & Tack Inc............585 235-7710
925 Exchange St Rochester (14608) ***(G-14257)***
Canfield Aerospace & Mar Inc............631 648-1050
90 Remington Blvd Ronkonkoma (11779) ***(G-14884)***
Canfield Electronics Inc (PA)............631 585-4100
6 Burton Pl Lindenhurst (11757) ***(G-7458)***
Canfield Machine & Tool LLC............315 593-8062
121 Howard Rd Fulton (13069) ***(G-5454)***
Cannizzaro Seal & Engraving Co............718 513-6125
435 Avenue U Brooklyn (11223) ***(G-1754)***
Cannoli Factory Inc............631 643-2700
75 Wyandanch Ave Wyandanch (11798) ***(G-17372)***
Cannon Co, Brooklyn *Also called Attias Oven Corp* ***(G-1650)***
Cannon Industries Inc (PA)............585 254-8080
525 Lee Rd Rochester (14606) ***(G-14258)***
Cannonsville Lumber Inc............607 467-3380
199 Old Route 10 Deposit (13754) ***(G-4276)***
Canopy Books LLC (PA)............516 354-4888
50 Carnation Ave Bldg 2-1 Floral Park (11001) ***(G-5198)***
Canova Inc............212 352-3582
511 W 25th St Ste 809 New York (10001) ***(G-9514)***
Cantinafoods Inc............716 602-3536
258 Amherst St Buffalo (14207) ***(G-2866)***
Canton Bio-Medical Inc (PA)............518 283-5963
11 Sicho Rd Poestenkill (12140) ***(G-13722)***
Canton Noodle Corporation............212 226-3276
101 Mott St New York (10013) ***(G-9515)***
Canvas Products Company Inc............516 742-1058
234 Herricks Rd Mineola (11501) ***(G-8500)***
Canyon Publishing Inc............212 334-0227
55 John St Ste 6 New York (10038) ***(G-9516)***
Cap USA Jerseyman Harlem Inc (PA)............212 222-7942
112 W 125th St New York (10027) ***(G-9517)***
Capco Marketing............315 699-1687
8417 Oswego Rd 177 Baldwinsville (13027) ***(G-567)***
Capco Wai Shing LLC............212 268-1976
132 W 36th St Rm 509 New York (10018) ***(G-9518)***
Capital Concrete Inc............716 648-8001
5690 Camp Rd Hamburg (14075) ***(G-5919)***
Capital District Stairs Inc............518 383-2449
45 Dunsbach Rd Halfmoon (12065) ***(G-5909)***
Capital Dst Print & Imaging............518 456-6773
2075 Central Ave Schenectady (12304) ***(G-15238)***
Capital Gold Corporation (PA)............212 668-0842
601 Lexington Ave Fl 36 New York (10022) ***(G-9519)***
Capital Kit Cab & Door Mfrs............718 886-0303
1425 128th St College Point (11356) ***(G-3779)***
Capital Ktchens Cab Doors Mfrs, College Point *Also called Capital Kit Cab & Door Mfrs* ***(G-3779)***
Capital Mercury Shirtmakers Co, New York *Also called Gce International Inc* ***(G-10261)***
Capital Programs Inc............212 842-4640
420 Lexington Ave Lbby 6 New York (10170) ***(G-9520)***
Capital Reg Wkly Newsppr Group............518 674-2841
29 Sheer Rd Averill Park (12018) ***(G-533)***
Capital Region Wkly Newspapers............518 877-7160
645 Albany Shaker Rd Albany (12211) ***(G-60)***
Capital Sawmill Service............518 479-0729
4119 Us Highway 20 Nassau (12123) ***(G-8770)***
Capital Stone LLC............518 382-7588
2241 Central Ave Schenectady (12304) ***(G-15239)***
Capital Stone Saratoga LLC............518 226-8677
4295 Route 50 Saratoga Springs (12866) ***(G-15147)***
Capitol Awning & Shade Co, Jamaica *Also called Capitol Awning Co Inc* ***(G-6900)***
Capitol Awning Co Inc............212 505-1717
10515 180th St Jamaica (11433) ***(G-6900)***
Capitol Cups Inc............518 627-0051
1030 Riverfront Ctr Amsterdam (12010) ***(G-337)***
Capitol Eq 2 LLC............518 886-8341
376 Broadway Ste 27 Saratoga Springs (12866) ***(G-15148)***
Capitol Newspaper, Albany *Also called Newspaper Times Union* ***(G-108)***
Capitol Plastic Products Inc............518 627-0051
1030 Riverfront Ctr Amsterdam (12010) ***(G-338)***
Capitol Plastic Products LLC............518 627-0051
1030 Riverfront Ctr Amsterdam (12010) ***(G-339)***
Capitol Poly Corp............718 855-6000
101 Spencer St Brooklyn (11205) ***(G-1755)***
Capitol Restoration Corp............516 783-1425
2473 Belmond Ave North Bellmore (11710) ***(G-12915)***
Caplugs, Buffalo *Also called Protective Industries Inc* ***(G-3139)***
Caplugs, Buffalo *Also called Protective Industries Inc* ***(G-3140)***
Capstone Printing, New York *Also called Kallen Corp* ***(G-10805)***
Capstream Technologies LLC............716 945-7100
16 Main St Salamanca (14779) ***(G-15100)***
Captech Industries LLC............347 374-1182
6 Revere Park Rome (13440) ***(G-14807)***
Captive Plastics LLC............716 366-2112
3565 Chadwick Dr Dunkirk (14048) ***(G-4333)***
Capture Globa Integ Solut Inc............718 352-0579
21214 48th Ave Bayside Hills (11364) ***(G-779)***
Caputo Bakery Inc............718 875-6871
329 Court St Ste 1 Brooklyn (11231) ***(G-1756)***
Caputo's Bake Shop, Brooklyn *Also called Caputo Bakery Inc* ***(G-1756)***
Capy Machine Shop Inc (PA)............631 694-6916
114 Spagnoli Rd Melville (11747) ***(G-8300)***
Car Doctor Motor Sports LLC............631 537-1548
610 Scuttle Hole Rd Water Mill (11976) ***(G-16603)***
Car Doctor, The, Water Mill *Also called Car Doctor Motor Sports LLC* ***(G-16603)***
Car Engineering and Mfg, Victor *Also called Charles A Rogers Entps Inc* ***(G-16466)***

A L P H A B E T I C

Car Essentials Inc.....518 745-1300
299 Dix Ave Queensbury (12804) *(G-13994)*
Car-Freshner Corporation (HQ).....315 788-6250
21205 Little Tree Dr Watertown (13601) *(G-16641)*
Car-Freshner Corporation.....315 788-6250
22569 Fisher Cir Watertown (13601) *(G-16642)*
Car-Go Industries Inc (PA).....718 472-1443
5007 49th St Woodside (11377) *(G-17323)*
Caranda Emporium LLC.....212 866-7100
2292 Frdrick Douglas Blvd New York (10027) *(G-9521)*
Caraustar Industries Inc.....716 874-0393
25 Dewberry Ln Buffalo (14227) *(G-2867)*
Caravan International Corp.....212 223-7190
641 Lexington Ave Fl 13 New York (10022) *(G-9522)*
Caravella Food Corp.....646 552-0455
16611 Cryders Ln Whitestone (11357) *(G-17204)*
Carballo Contract Machining.....315 594-2511
6205 Lake Ave Wolcott (14590) *(G-17278)*
Carbaugh Tool Company Inc.....607 739-3293
126 Philo Rd W Elmira (14903) *(G-4673)*
Carbert Music Inc.....212 725-9277
126 E 38th St New York (10016) *(G-9523)*
Carbide-Usa LLC.....607 331-9353
100 Home St Elmira (14904) *(G-4674)*
Carbon Activated Corporation.....716 662-2005
336 Stonehenge Dr Orchard Park (14127) *(G-13258)*
Carbon Copies, Cortland *Also called BP Digital Imaging LLC (G-4016)*
Carbon Graphite Materials Inc.....716 792-7979
115 Central Ave Brocton (14716) *(G-1248)*
Card Pak Start Up, East Hampton *Also called Luria Communications Inc (G-4413)*
Card Printing.us, Monsey *Also called Tele-Pak Inc (G-8585)*
Cardiac Life Products Inc.....585 267-7775
349 W Coml St Ste 1400 East Rochester (14445) *(G-4454)*
Cardinal Boiler and Tank, Brooklyn *Also called Cardinal Tank Corp (G-1757)*
Cardinal Tank Corp.....718 625-4350
700 Hicks St Brooklyn (11231) *(G-1757)*
Cardinali Bakery, Carle Place *Also called Gennaris Itln French Bky Inc (G-3389)*
Cardish Machine Works Inc.....518 273-2329
7 Elm St Watervliet (12189) *(G-16681)*
Cardona Industries USA Ltd (PA).....516 466-5200
505 Northern Blvd Ste 213 Great Neck (11021) *(G-5796)*
Cardullo, J Iron Works, Bay Shore *Also called Jerry Cardullo Iron Works Inc (G-709)*
Carduner Sales Company, Farmingville *Also called Bud Barger Assoc Inc (G-5159)*
Care Enterprises Inc.....631 472-8155
435 Renee Dr Bayport (11705) *(G-755)*
Careconnector.....919 360-2987
177 Concord St Apt 2a Brooklyn (11201) *(G-1758)*
Careers and The Disabled, Melville *Also called Equal Opprtnity Pblcations Inc (G-8314)*
Carefree Daily Money Managemen.....631 751-1281
5 Cedarwood Ct Setauket (11733) *(G-15375)*
Carefree Kitchens Inc.....631 567-2120
925 Lincoln Ave Ste 1 Holbrook (11741) *(G-6436)*
Carelli Costumes Inc.....212 765-6166
109 W 26th St Fl 2 New York (10001) *(G-9524)*
Carestream Health Inc.....585 627-1800
1669 Lake Ave Rochester (14652) *(G-14259)*
Carges Entps of Canandaigua.....585 394-2600
330 S Main St Canandaigua (14424) *(G-3338)*
Cargill Incorporated.....607 535-6300
518 E 4th St Watkins Glen (14891) *(G-16694)*
Cargill Incorporated.....716 665-6570
1029 Poland Center Rd Kennedy (14747) *(G-7153)*
Cargill Incorporated.....315 622-3533
7700 Maltage Dr Liverpool (13090) *(G-7515)*
Carib News Inc.....212 944-1991
35 W 35th St Rm 702 New York (10001) *(G-9525)*
Caribbean Communication, New York *Also called Carib News Inc (G-9525)*
Caribbean Foods Delight Inc.....845 398-3000
117 Route 303 Ste B Tappan (10983) *(G-16079)*
Caribe Bakery, Bronx *Also called 527 Franco Bakery Corporation (G-1250)*
Carl Fischer LLC (PA).....212 777-0900
48 Wall St 28 New York (10005) *(G-9526)*
Carl Zeiss Inc (HQ).....914 747-1800
1 Zeiss Dr Thornwood (10594) *(G-16117)*
Carlara Group Ltd.....914 769-2020
467 Bedford Rd Pleasantville (10570) *(G-13712)*
Carleton Technologies Inc (HQ).....716 662-0006
10 Cobham Dr Orchard Park (14127) *(G-13259)*
Carlo Monte Designs Inc.....212 935-5611
17 E 48th St Fl 8 New York (10017) *(G-9527)*
Carlos & Alex Atelier Inc.....718 441-8911
10010 91st Ave Fl 2 Richmond Hill (11418) *(G-14070)*
Carlson Wood Products Inc (PA).....716 287-2923
1705 Bates Rd Sinclairville (14782) *(G-15452)*
Carlson, L A Co, East Greenbush *Also called Leonard Carlson (G-4403)*
Carlton Ice Cream Co, Brooklyn *Also called Macedonia Ltd (G-2250)*
Carmine Street Bagels Inc.....212 691-3041
107 Park Dr N Staten Island (10314) *(G-15656)*
Carmona Nyc LLC.....718 227-6662
9830 67th Ave Apt 1d Rego Park (11374) *(G-14031)*
Carnel Printing and Copying, Port Washington *Also called Carnels Printing Inc (G-13803)*
Carnels Printing Inc.....516 883-3355
22 Main St Frnt A Port Washington (11050) *(G-13803)*
Carnival, New York *Also called Cookies Inc (G-9716)*
Carob Industries Inc.....631 225-0900
215 W Hoffman Ave Lindenhurst (11757) *(G-7459)*
Caroda Inc.....212 630-9986
254 W 35th St New York (10001) *(G-9528)*
Carol Dauplaise Ltd (PA).....212 564-7301
29 W 36th St Fl 12 New York (10018) *(G-9529)*
Carol Dauplaise Ltd.....212 997-5290
134 W 37th St Fl 3 New York (10018) *(G-9530)*
Carol For Eva Graham Inc (PA).....212 889-8686
366 5th Ave Rm 815 New York (10001) *(G-9531)*
Carol Group Ltd.....212 505-2030
150 W 30th St Rm 902 New York (10001) *(G-9532)*
Carol Peretz.....516 248-6300
49 Windsor Ave Ste 103 Mineola (11501) *(G-8501)*
Carol Peretz Workshop, Mineola *Also called Carol Peretz (G-8501)*
Carol Vail, Salem *Also called Carolina Eastern-Vail Inc (G-15111)*
Carole Hchman Design Group Inc (HQ).....918 423-3535
16 E 34th St Fl 10 New York (10016) *(G-9533)*
CAROLE WREN, New York *Also called Rmll Corp (G-11885)*
Carolina Amato Inc.....212 768-9095
270 W 38th St Rm 902 New York (10018) *(G-9534)*
Carolina Eastern-Vail Inc.....518 854-9785
4134 State Route 22 Salem (12865) *(G-15111)*
Carolina Herrera Ltd (HQ).....212 944-5757
501 Fashion Ave Fl 17 New York (10018) *(G-9535)*
Carolina Precision Plas LLC.....631 981-0743
115 Comac St Ronkonkoma (11779) *(G-14885)*
Carolinas Desserts Inc.....914 779-4000
1562 Central Park Ave Yonkers (10710) *(G-17423)*
Carols Polar Parlor.....315 468-3404
3800 W Genesee St Syracuse (13219) *(G-15885)*
Carolyn Ray Inc.....914 476-0619
578 Nepperhan Ave Ste C10 Yonkers (10701) *(G-17424)*
Caron Distribution Center, New York *Also called National Spinning Co Inc (G-11351)*
Carousel ADS, Brooklyn *Also called Drns Corp (G-1881)*
Carpenter Industries Inc.....315 463-4284
1 General Motors Dr # 10 Syracuse (13206) *(G-15886)*
Carpenter Manufacturing Co.....315 682-9176
110 Fairgrounds Dr Manlius (13104) *(G-8068)*
Carpentier Industries LLC.....585 385-5550
119 Despatch Dr East Rochester (14445) *(G-4455)*
Carpet Fabrications Intl.....914 381-6060
628 Waverly Ave Ste 1 Mamaroneck (10543) *(G-8026)*
Carr Communications Group LLC.....607 748-0481
513 Prentice Rd Vestal (13850) *(G-16444)*
Carr Jewelers, Latham *Also called Carr Manufacturing Jewelers (G-7358)*
Carr Manufacturing Jewelers.....518 783-6093
22 West Ln Latham (12110) *(G-7358)*
Carr Printing, Vestal *Also called Carr Communications Group LLC (G-16444)*
Carrera Casting Corp.....212 382-3296
64 W 48th St Fl 2 New York (10036) *(G-9536)*
Carriage House Companies Inc (HQ).....716 672-4321
196 Newton St Fredonia (14063) *(G-5371)*
Carriage House Companies Inc.....716 673-1000
26 E Talcott St Dunkirk (14048) *(G-4334)*
Carrier Corporation.....315 432-6000
Carrier Pkwy Trl 20 Syracuse (13221) *(G-15887)*
Carrier Corporation.....315 463-5744
6390 Fly Rd East Syracuse (13057) *(G-4513)*
Carrier Corporation.....315 432-6000
Carrier Pkwy Tr 20 Syracuse (13221) *(G-15888)*
Carrier Corporation.....315 432-6000
Carrier Global Account Syracuse (13221) *(G-15889)*
Carrier Corporation.....315 432-6000
Kinne St East Syracuse (13057) *(G-4514)*
Carrier Corporation.....315 432-3844
Carrier Pkwy Bldg Tr 20 East Syracuse (13057) *(G-4515)*
Carrier Globl Engrg Conference, Syracuse *Also called Carrier Corporation (G-15887)*
Carrier Hardware Building Pdts, Brooklyn *Also called Link Group Inc (G-2228)*
Carrier News, Hicksville *Also called All Island Media Inc (G-6319)*
Carrmet Industries, Farmingdale *Also called Joe P Industries Inc (G-5018)*
Carry Hot Inc.....212 279-7535
545 W 45th St Rm 501 New York (10036) *(G-9537)*
Carry-All Canvas Bag Co Inc.....718 375-4230
1983 Coney Island Ave Brooklyn (11223) *(G-1759)*
Cars Magazine, Roslyn Heights *Also called National Marketing Services (G-15030)*
Carta Usa LLC.....585 436-3012
1600 Lexington Ave # 116 Rochester (14606) *(G-14260)*
Carter Enterprises LLC (PA).....718 853-5052
4610 12th Ave Brooklyn (11219) *(G-1760)*
Carter Precision Metals LLC.....516 333-1917
99 Urban Ave Westbury (11590) *(G-16973)*
Carter Street Bakery Inc.....585 749-7104
580 Child St Rochester (14606) *(G-14261)*
Carters Inc.....315 637-3128
537 Towne Dr Fayetteville (13066) *(G-5163)*
Carters Inc.....718 980-1759
430 New Dorp Ln Staten Island (10306) *(G-15657)*

ALPHABETIC

Carters Inc.......631 549-6781
350 Walt Whitman Rd Huntington Station (11746) ***(G-6699)***
Carthage Fibre Drum Inc (PA).......315 493-2730
14 Hewitt Dr Carthage (13619) ***(G-3408)***
Carts Mobile Food Eqp Corp.......718 788-5540
113 8th St Brooklyn (11215) ***(G-1761)***
Carvart Glass Inc (PA).......212 675-0030
180 Varick St Rm 1304 New York (10014) ***(G-9538)***
Carver Creek Enterprises Inc.......585 657-7511
2524 Cannan Rd Bloomfield (14469) ***(G-983)***
Carver Sand & Gravel, Schoharie *Also called Masick Soil Conservation Co* ***(G-15317)***
Carvin French Jewelers Inc.......212 755-6474
515 Madison Ave Rm 1605 New York (10022) ***(G-9539)***
Cas, Cheektowaga *Also called Culinary Arts Specialties Inc* ***(G-3566)***
Casa Collection Inc.......718 694-0272
106 Ferris St Brooklyn (11231) ***(G-1762)***
Casa Innovations Inc.......718 965-6600
140 58th St Ste 5h-1 Brooklyn (11220) ***(G-1763)***
Casa Larga Vineyards (PA).......585 223-4210
27 Emerald Hill Cir Fairport (14450) ***(G-4850)***
Casa Larga Vineyards.......585 223-4210
2287 Turk Hill Rd Fairport (14450) ***(G-4851)***
Casa Nueva Custom Furnishing.......914 476-2272
510 Nepperhan Ave Yonkers (10701) ***(G-17425)***
Casa Redimix Concrete Corp.......718 589-1555
886 Edgewater Rd Bronx (10474) ***(G-1291)***
Casablanca Foods LLC.......212 317-1111
135 E 57th St Unit 96 New York (10022) ***(G-9540)***
Casablanca Records, New York *Also called Tm Music Inc* ***(G-12356)***
Cascade Helmets Holdings Inc.......315 453-3073
4697 Crssrads Pk Dr Ste 1 Liverpool (13088) ***(G-7516)***
Cascade Mountain Winery & Rest.......845 373-9021
835 Cascade Rd Amenia (12501) ***(G-215)***
Cascade Technical Services LLC (HQ).......516 596-6300
30 N Prospect Ave Lynbrook (11563) ***(G-7949)***
Cascade Technical Services LLC.......518 355-2201
2846 Curry Rd Ste B Schenectady (12303) ***(G-15240)***
Cascades Cntnerboard Packg Inc.......716 285-3681
4001 Packard Rd Niagara Falls (14303) ***(G-12801)***
Cascades Cntnerboard Packg Inc (HQ).......450 923-3031
4001 Packard Rd Niagara Falls (14303) ***(G-12802)***
Cascades Tissue Group - NY Inc.......518 238-1900
148 Hudson River Rd Wynantskill (12198) ***(G-17379)***
Cascades Tssue Group-Sales Inc.......518 238-1900
148 Hudson River Rd Waterford (12188) ***(G-16608)***
Cascades Tssue Group-Sales Inc (HQ).......819 363-5100
148 Hudson River Rd Waterford (12188) ***(G-16609)***
Cascades USA Inc.......518 880-3632
148 Hudson River Rd Waterford (12188) ***(G-16610)***
Casco Security, Rochester *Also called Custom Sound and Video* ***(G-14296)***
Case Brothers Inc.......716 925-7172
370 Quinn Rd Limestone (14753) ***(G-7450)***
Case Group LLC.......518 720-3100
195 Cohoes Ave Green Island (12183) ***(G-5854)***
Case Window and Door, Green Island *Also called Case Group LLC* ***(G-5854)***
Casey Machine Co Inc.......716 651-0150
74 Ward Rd Lancaster (14086) ***(G-7308)***
Cassadaga Designs Inc.......716 595-3030
309 Maple Ave Cassadaga (14718) ***(G-3414)***
Cassinelli Food Products Inc.......718 274-4881
3112 23rd Ave Long Island City (11105) ***(G-7695)***
Cassini Parfums Ltd.......212 753-7540
3 W 57th St Fl 8 New York (10019) ***(G-9541)***
Cast-All Corporation (PA).......516 741-4025
229 Liberty Ave Mineola (11501) ***(G-8502)***
Cast-All Corporation.......516 741-4025
229 Liberty Ave Mineola (11501) ***(G-8503)***
Castek Inc (HQ).......914 636-1000
20 Jones St New Rochelle (10801) ***(G-8891)***
Castel Grisch Winery, Montour Falls *Also called Malina Management Company Inc* ***(G-8610)***
Castella Imports Inc.......631 231-5500
60 Davids Dr Hauppauge (11788) ***(G-6040)***
Castelli America LLC.......716 782-2101
5151 Fairbanks Rd Ashville (14710) ***(G-426)***
Casters Custom Sawing.......315 387-5104
6323 Us Route 11 Sandy Creek (13145) ***(G-15131)***
Castle Brands Inc (PA).......646 356-0200
122 E 42nd St Rm 5000 New York (10168) ***(G-9542)***
Castle Connolly Medical Ltd.......212 367-8400
42 W 24th St Fl 2 New York (10010) ***(G-9543)***
Castle Fuels Corporation.......914 381-6600
440 Mamaroneck Ave Harrison (10528) ***(G-5977)***
Castle Harvester Co Inc.......585 526-5884
3165 Seneca Castle Rd Seneca Castle (14547) ***(G-15359)***
Castle Harvstr Met Fabricators, Seneca Castle *Also called Castle Harvester Co Inc* ***(G-15359)***
Castle Power Solutions LLC.......518 743-1000
22 Hudson Falls Rd Ste 55 South Glens Falls (12803) ***(G-15523)***
Castle Reagh Print Craft, Freeport *Also called Castlereagh Printcraft Inc* ***(G-5392)***
Castlereagh Printcraft Inc.......516 623-1728
320 Buffalo Ave Freeport (11520) ***(G-5392)***
Castoleum Corporation.......914 664-5877
240 E 7th St Mount Vernon (10550) ***(G-8670)***
Castoleum Corportation, Mount Vernon *Also called Naval Stores Co* ***(G-8709)***
Casttle Harbor, Plainview *Also called Hot Line Industries Inc* ***(G-13605)***
Casual Friday Inc.......585 544-9470
1561 Lyell Ave Rochester (14606) ***(G-14262)***
Casual Home Worldwide Inc.......631 789-2999
38 William St Amityville (11701) ***(G-280)***
Casuals Etc Inc.......212 838-1319
16 E 52nd St Fl 4 New York (10022) ***(G-9544)***
Caswell Inc.......315 946-1213
7696 State Route 31 Lyons (14489) ***(G-7970)***
Catalina Products Corp (PA).......718 336-8288
2455 Mcdonald Ave Brooklyn (11223) ***(G-1764)***
Catalyst Group Design, New York *Also called Catalyst Group Inc* ***(G-9545)***
Catalyst Group Inc.......212 243-7777
345 7th Ave Rm 1100 New York (10001) ***(G-9545)***
Catalyst Systms Div of US Chmc, Round Lake *Also called Alco Industries Inc* ***(G-15036)***
Catame Inc.......213 749-2610
158 W 29th St New York (10001) ***(G-9546)***
Cataract Hose Co.......914 941-9019
6 Waller Ave Ossining (10562) ***(G-13321)***
Cataract Hose Co No 2, Ossining *Also called Cataract Hose Co* ***(G-13321)***
Cataract Steel Industries, Niagara Falls *Also called Costanzos Welding Inc* ***(G-12807)***
Catch Ventures Inc.......347 620-4351
30 W 63rd St Apt 14o New York (10023) ***(G-9547)***
Catchmaster, Brooklyn *Also called AP&g Co Inc* ***(G-1615)***
Cathay Global Co Inc.......718 229-0920
5815 215th St Bayside Hills (11364) ***(G-780)***
Cathay Home Inc (PA).......212 213-0988
261 5th Ave Rm 412 New York (10016) ***(G-9548)***
Cathay Resources Inc.......516 922-2839
38 Cord Pl East Norwich (11732) ***(G-4445)***
Cathedral Candle Co.......315 422-9119
510 Kirkpatrick St Syracuse (13208) ***(G-15890)***
Cathedral Corporation (PA).......315 338-0021
632 Ellsworth Rd Rome (13441) ***(G-14808)***
Catherine Deane, New York *Also called Arcangel Inc* ***(G-9194)***
Catherine Stein Designs Inc.......212 840-1188
411 5th Ave Rm 600 New York (10016) ***(G-9549)***
Catholic Courier, Rochester *Also called Rochester Catholic Press* ***(G-14637)***
Catholic New York, New York *Also called Ecclesiastical Communications* ***(G-9974)***
Catholic News Publishing Co.......914 632-7771
606 Halstead Ave Mamaroneck (10543) ***(G-8027)***
Catholic Sun, The, Syracuse *Also called Syracuse Catholic Press Assn* ***(G-16049)***
Cathy Daniels Ltd (PA).......212 354-8000
1411 Broadway New York (10018) ***(G-9550)***
Catskill Boiler Co., Greenville *Also called Hawkencatskills LLC* ***(G-5885)***
Catskill Castings Co, Bloomville *Also called G Haynes Holdings Inc* ***(G-995)***
Catskill Craftsmen Inc.......607 652-7321
15 W End Ave Stamford (12167) ***(G-15624)***
Catskill Delaware Publications (PA).......845 887-5200
5 Lower Main St Callicoon (12723) ***(G-3284)***
Catskill Mountain News, Arkville *Also called Catskill Mountain Publishing* ***(G-411)***
Catskill Mountain Publishing.......845 586-2601
43414 State Hwy 28 Arkville (12406) ***(G-411)***
Catskill Mtn Brewing Co Inc.......845 256-1700
3 Main St New Paltz (12561) ***(G-8874)***
Catsmo Corp.......845 895-2296
25 Myers Rd Wallkill (12589) ***(G-16542)***
Cattaraugus Containers Inc.......716 676-2000
21 Elm St 23 Franklinville (14737) ***(G-5369)***
Cava Spiliadis USA.......212 247-8214
200 W 57th St Ste 908 New York (10019) ***(G-9551)***
Cavalry Solutions.......315 422-1699
449 E Wshngtn St Ste 100 Syracuse (13202) ***(G-15891)***
Cayuga Crushed Stone Inc.......607 533-4273
87 Portland Point Rd Lansing (14882) ***(G-7348)***
Cayuga Enterprise 21.......607 441-9166
4384 Pompey Center Rd Manlius (13104) ***(G-8069)***
Cayuga Press Cortland Inc.......888 229-8421
5795 Bridge St East Syracuse (13057) ***(G-4516)***
Cayuga Tool and Die Inc.......607 533-7400
182 Newman Rd Groton (13073) ***(G-5898)***
Cayuga Wooden Boatworks Inc.......315 253-7447
381 Enfield Main Rd Ithaca (14850) ***(G-6830)***
Cazar Printing & Advertising.......718 446-4606
4215 102nd St Corona (11368) ***(G-3994)***
Cazenovia Equipment Co Inc.......315 736-0898
8186 Seneca Tpke Clinton (13323) ***(G-3717)***
CB Products, Floral Park *Also called CB Publishing LLC* ***(G-5199)***
CB Publishing LLC.......516 354-4888
50 Carnation Ave Bldg 2-1 Floral Park (11001) ***(G-5199)***
Cbc Custom Millwork Inc.......718 499-6742
232 42nd St Brooklyn (11232) ***(G-1765)***
Cbe/New York, Plainview *Also called Conrad Blasius Equipment Co* ***(G-13590)***
CBM Fabrications Inc.......518 399-8023
15 Westside Dr Ballston Lake (12019) ***(G-581)***
Cbord Group Inc (HQ).......607 257-2410
950 Danby Rd Ste 100c Ithaca (14850) ***(G-6831)***

ALPHABETIC

CBS, White Plains *Also called Connecticut Bus Systems LLC* ***(G-17096)***
CC Family LLC 516 666-8116
146 Spencer St Ste 5015 Brooklyn (11205) ***(G-1766)***
CCA Holding Inc 716 446-8800
300 Corporate Pkwy Amherst (14226) ***(G-230)***
CCC Publications Inc 718 306-1008
12020 Flatlands Ave Brooklyn (11207) ***(G-1767)***
CCL Label Inc 716 852-2155
685 Howard St Buffalo (14206) ***(G-2868)***
Ccmi Inc 315 781-3270
88 Middle St Geneva (14456) ***(G-5571)***
Ccn International Inc 315 789-4400
200 Lehigh St Geneva (14456) ***(G-5572)***
CCS Machinery Inc 631 968-0900
2175 Union Blvd Bay Shore (11706) ***(G-681)***
CCT (us) Inc 716 297-7509
2221 Niagara Falls Blvd # 5 Niagara Falls (14304) ***(G-12803)***
Cct Inc 212 532-3355
60 Madison Ave Ste 1209 New York (10010) ***(G-9552)***
Ccz Ready Mix Concrete Corp 516 579-7352
2 Loring Rd Levittown (11756) ***(G-7426)***
Cda Machine Inc 585 671-5959
514 Vosburg Rd Webster (14580) ***(G-16715)***
Cdc Publishing LLC 215 579-1695
19 North St Morrisville (13408) ***(G-8619)***
Cdj Stamping Inc 585 224-8120
146 Halstead St Ste 123 Rochester (14610) ***(G-14263)***
Cdl Manufacturing Inc 585 589-2533
15661 Telegraph Rd Albion (14411) ***(G-163)***
Cdml Computer Services Ltd 718 428-9063
5343 198th St Fresh Meadows (11365) ***(G-5439)***
Cdnv Wood Carving Frames Inc (PA) 914 375-3447
498 Nepperhan Ave Yonkers (10701) ***(G-17426)***
Cds Productions Inc 518 385-8255
108 Erie Blvd Ste 400 Schenectady (12305) ***(G-15241)***
CEC Elevator Cab Corp 718 328-3632
540 Manida St Bronx (10474) ***(G-1292)***
Cedar West Inc (PA) 631 467-1444
1700 Ocean Ave Ste 1 Ronkonkoma (11779) ***(G-14886)***
Cegid Corporation 212 757-9038
274 Madison Ave Rm 1400 New York (10016) ***(G-9553)***
Cego Custom Shirts, New York *Also called Sifonya Inc* ***(G-12065)***
Ceipal LLC 585 351-2934
722 Weiland Rd Rochester (14626) ***(G-14264)***
Ceipal LLC 585 351-2934
722 Weiland Rd Rochester (14626) ***(G-14265)***
CEIT Corp 518 825-0649
625 State Route 3 Unit 2 Plattsburgh (12901) ***(G-13658)***
Cejon Inc 201 437-8788
390 5th Ave Fl 6 New York (10018) ***(G-9554)***
Cellboat Company, The, Melville *Also called Cellboat Development Corp* ***(G-8301)***
Cellboat Development Corp 800 973-4659
510 Broadhollow Rd Melville (11747) ***(G-8301)***
Cellect LLC 508 744-6906
10 New St Saint Johnsville (13452) ***(G-15092)***
Cellect Plastics LLC 518 568-7036
12 New St Saint Johnsville (13452) ***(G-15093)***
Cellu Tissue - Long Island LLC 631 232-2626
555 N Research Pl Central Islip (11722) ***(G-3489)***
Cellufun Inc 212 385-2255
120 Broadway Ste 3330 New York (10271) ***(G-9555)***
Cellular Empire Inc 347 587-7795
2614 W 13th St Brooklyn (11223) ***(G-1768)***
Cellvation Inc 212 554-4520
2 Gansevoort St Fl 9 New York (10014) ***(G-9556)***
Celonis Inc 941 615-9670
1820 Avenue M Unit 544 Brooklyn (11230) ***(G-1769)***
Celoxica Inc 212 880-2075
1133 Broadway New York (10010) ***(G-9557)***
Cem Machine Inc (PA) 315 493-4258
571 W End Ave Carthage (13619) ***(G-3409)***
Cemac Foods Corp 914 835-0526
8 Cayuga Trl Harrison (10528) ***(G-5978)***
Cementex Latex Corp 212 741-1770
121 Varick St Frnt 2 New York (10013) ***(G-9558)***
Cemex Cement Inc 212 317-6000
590 Madison Ave Fl 41 New York (10022) ***(G-9559)***
Cemoi Inc (PA) 212 583-4920
5 Penn Plz Ste 2325 New York (10001) ***(G-9560)***
Cemtrex Inc (PA) 631 756-9116
19 Engineers Ln Farmingdale (11735) ***(G-4957)***
Cenere, New York *Also called Precision International Co Inc* ***(G-11697)***
Cenibra Inc 212 818-8242
335 Madison Ave Fl 23 New York (10017) ***(G-9561)***
Ceno Technologies Inc 716 885-5050
1234 Delaware Ave Buffalo (14209) ***(G-2869)***
Centar Fuel Co Inc 516 538-2424
700 Nassau Blvd West Hempstead (11552) ***(G-16851)***
Center For Inquiry Inc (PA) 716 636-4869
3965 Rensch Rd Amherst (14228) ***(G-231)***
Center Line Studios Inc (PA) 845 534-7143
112 Forge Hill Rd New Windsor (12553) ***(G-8934)***
Center Sheet Metal Inc 718 378-4476
1371 E Bay Ave Bronx (10474) ***(G-1293)***
Center State Propane LLC (PA) 315 841-4044
1130 Mason Rd Waterville (13480) ***(G-16677)***
Centerra Wine Company, Canandaigua *Also called Constellation Brands US Oprs* ***(G-3341)***
Central Adirondack Textiles, Boonville *Also called S M S C Inc* ***(G-1169)***
Central Apparel Group Ltd 212 868-6505
16 W 36th St Rm 1202 New York (10018) ***(G-9562)***
Central Asphalt, Oriskany *Also called Suit-Kote Corporation* ***(G-13314)***
Central Asphalt, Watkins Glen *Also called Suit-Kote Corporation* ***(G-16697)***
Central Cnfrnce of Amrcn Rbbis 212 972-3636
355 Lexington Ave Fl 18 New York (10017) ***(G-9563)***
Central Dover Development 917 709-3266
247 Dover Furnace Rd Dover Plains (12522) ***(G-4314)***
Central Garden & Pet Company 631 451-8021
1100 Middle Country Rd Selden (11784) ***(G-15349)***
Central Garden & Pet Company 212 877-1270
2475 Broadway New York (10025) ***(G-9564)***
Central Island Juice Corp 516 338-8301
128 Magnolia Ave Westbury (11590) ***(G-16974)***
Central Islip Pharmacy Inc 631 234-6039
1629 Islip Ave Central Islip (11722) ***(G-3490)***
Central Kitchen Corp 631 283-1029
871 County Road 39 Southampton (11968) ***(G-15541)***
Central Marking Equipment, Syracuse *Also called C M E Corp* ***(G-15881)***
Central Mills Inc 212 221-0748
1400 Broadway Rm 1605 New York (10018) ***(G-9565)***
Central Nat Pulp & Ppr Sls Inc 914 696-9000
3 Manhattanville Rd Purchase (10577) ***(G-13955)***
Central New York Golf Center 315 463-1200
310 E 1st St East Syracuse (13057) ***(G-4517)***
Central Park Active Wear, New York *Also called Central Apparel Group Ltd* ***(G-9562)***
Central Rede Sign Co Inc 716 213-0797
317 Wheeler St Tonawanda (14150) ***(G-16151)***
Central Semiconductor Corp 631 435-1110
145 Adams Ave Hauppauge (11788) ***(G-6041)***
Central Textiles Inc 212 213-8740
10 E 40th St Rm 3410 New York (10016) ***(G-9566)***
Central Timber Co Inc 518 638-6338
9088 State Route 22 Granville (12832) ***(G-5773)***
Central Timber Research/Devt, Granville *Also called Central Timber Co Inc* ***(G-5773)***
Central Time Clock Inc 718 784-4900
523 50th Ave Long Island City (11101) ***(G-7696)***
Centre Interiors Wdwkg Co Inc 718 323-1343
10001 103rd Ave Ozone Park (11417) ***(G-13376)***
Centrisource Inc 716 871-1105
777 E Park Dr Tonawanda (14150) ***(G-16152)***
Centro Inc 212 791-9450
841 Broadway Fl 6 New York (10003) ***(G-9567)***
Centroid Inc 516 349-0070
111 E Ames Ct Unit 1 Plainview (11803) ***(G-13586)***
Centurion Diamonds Inc 718 946-6918
580 5th Ave New York (10036) ***(G-9568)***
Century Direct LLC 212 763-0600
15 Enter Ln Islandia (11749) ***(G-6789)***
Century Grand Inc 212 925-3838
302 Grand St New York (10002) ***(G-9569)***
Century Metal Parts Corp 631 667-0800
230 S Fehr Way Bay Shore (11706) ***(G-682)***
Century Mold Company Inc (PA) 585 352-8600
25 Vantage Point Dr Rochester (14624) ***(G-14266)***
Century Mold Mexico LLC (HQ) 585 352-8600
25 Vantage Point Dr Rochester (14624) ***(G-14267)***
Century Pharmacy Three, New York *Also called Century Grand Inc* ***(G-9569)***
Century Ready Mix Inc 631 888-2200
615 Cord Ave West Babylon (11704) ***(G-16781)***
Century Systems Ltd 718 543-5991
485 W 246th St Bronx (10471) ***(G-1294)***
Century Tom Inc 347 654-3179
12214 18th Ave College Point (11356) ***(G-3780)***
Century-Tech Inc 718 326-9400
32 Intersection St Hempstead (11550) ***(G-6267)***
Century-Tech Inc (PA) 718 326-9400
5825 63rd St Hempstead (11550) ***(G-6268)***
Cenveo Inc 716 662-2800
100 Centre Dr Orchard Park (14127) ***(G-13260)***
Cenveo Inc 716 686-0100
2914 Walden Ave Ste 300 Depew (14043) ***(G-4252)***
Ceo Cast Inc 212 732-4300
211 E 43rd St Rm 400 New York (10017) ***(G-9570)***
Ceoentano, Buffalo *Also called Rosina Food Products Inc* ***(G-3165)***
Cep Technologies Corporation (PA) 914 968-4100
763 Saw Mill River Rd Yonkers (10710) ***(G-17427)***
Ceramaterials LLC 518 701-6722
226 Route 209 Port Jervis (12771) ***(G-13781)***
Ceramica V. A. R. M., New Rochelle *Also called Ceramica Varm* ***(G-8892)***
Ceramica Varm (PA) 914 381-6215
479 5th Ave New Rochelle (10801) ***(G-8892)***
Ceres Technologies Inc 845 247-4701
5 Tower Dr Saugerties (12477) ***(G-15181)***
Cerion Energy Inc 585 271-5630
1 Blossom Rd Rochester (14610) ***(G-14268)***

ALPHABETIC

Cerion LLC 585 271-5630
1 Blossom Rd Rochester (14610) *(G-14269)*
Ceros Inc (PA) 347 744-9250
151 W 25th St Rm 200 New York (10001) *(G-9571)*
Cerovene Inc 845 359-1101
10 Corporate Dr Orangeburg (10962) *(G-13221)*
Cerovene Inc (PA) 845 267-2055
612 Corporate Way Ste 10 Valley Cottage (10989) *(G-16377)*
Certainteed Corporation 716 823-3684
231 Ship Canal Pkwy Lackawanna (14218) *(G-7243)*
Certainteed Corporation 716 827-7560
231 Ship Canal Pkwy Buffalo (14218) *(G-2870)*
Certified Fabrications Inc 716 731-8123
2127 Cory Dr Sanborn (14132) *(G-15117)*
Certified Flameproofing Corp 631 265-4824
17 N Ingelore Ct Smithtown (11787) *(G-15484)*
Certified Health Products Inc 718 339-7498
67 35th St Unit 12 Brooklyn (11232) *(G-1770)*
Certified Prcsion McHining Inc 631 244-3671
70 Knickerbocker Ave # 4 Bohemia (11716) *(G-1032)*
Ces Industries Inc 631 782-7088
95 Hoffman Ln Ste S Islandia (11749) *(G-6790)*
Cetek Inc (PA) 845 452-3510
19 Commerce St Poughkeepsie (12603) *(G-13892)*
Cettel Studio of New York Inc 518 494-3622
636 Atateka Dr Chestertown (12817) *(G-3621)*
Cfe, Brooklyn *Also called Carts Mobile Food Eqp Corp* ***(G-1761)***
Cffco USA Inc 718 747-1118
55 Jericho Tpke Ste 302 Jericho (11753) *(G-7061)*
Cfo Publishing LLC (PA) 212 459-3004
45 W 45th St Fl 12 New York (10036) *(G-9572)*
Cfp Purchasing Inc 705 806-0383
4760 197th St Flushing (11358) *(G-5231)*
CFS Enterprises Inc 718 585-0500
650 E 132nd St Bronx (10454) *(G-1295)*
CFS Steel Company, Bronx *Also called CFS Enterprises Inc* ***(G-1295)***
Cgi Technologies Solutions Inc 212 682-7411
655 3rd Ave Ste 700 New York (10017) *(G-9573)*
Cgm, Brocton *Also called Carbon Graphite Materials Inc* ***(G-1248)***
Cgs Fabrication LLC 585 347-6127
855 Publishers Pkwy Ste 3 Webster (14580) *(G-16716)*
Cgsi Group LLC 516 986-5503
3835 Sedgwick Ave Bronx (10463) *(G-1296)*
Cgw Corp (PA) 631 472-6600
102 S Gillette Ave Bayport (11705) *(G-756)*
Chabot Jewelry, Brooklyn *Also called E Chabot Ltd* ***(G-1890)***
Chad Pierson 518 251-0186
Chad Pierson Bakers Mills (12811) *(G-557)*
Chad Pierson Logging & Trckg, Bakers Mills *Also called Chad Pierson* ***(G-557)***
Chadwicks Town Park, New Hartford *Also called Hartford Hwy Dept* ***(G-8806)***
Chain Store Age Magazine 212 756-5000
425 Park Ave New York (10022) *(G-9574)*
Chain Stores Age, New York *Also called Lebhar-Friedman Inc* ***(G-10951)***
Chaindom Enterprises Inc 212 719-4778
48 W 48th St Ste 200 New York (10036) *(G-9575)*
Chair Factory 718 363-2383
1355 Atlantic Ave Brooklyn (11216) *(G-1771)*
Chakra Communications Inc 607 748-7491
32 Washington Ave Endicott (13760) *(G-4798)*
Chakra Communications Inc 716 505-7300
80 W Drullard Ave Lancaster (14086) *(G-7309)*
Challenge Graphics Svcs Inc (PA) 631 586-0171
22 Connor Ln Deer Park (11729) *(G-4115)*
Chamart Exclusives Inc 914 345-3870
68 Williams St Elmsford (10523) *(G-4740)*
Chamberlin Rubber Company Inc 585 427-7780
3333 Brighton Henrietta Rochester (14623) *(G-14270)*
Chambord LLC 718 859-1110
4302 Farragut Rd Brooklyn (11203) *(G-1772)*
Chameleon Color Cards Ltd 716 625-9452
6530 S Transit Rd Lockport (14094) *(G-7576)*
Chameleon Gems Inc 516 829-3333
98 Cuttermill Rd Ste 398n Great Neck (11021) *(G-5797)*
Champion Aluminum Corp 631 656-3424
250 Kennedy Dr Hauppauge (11788) *(G-6042)*
Champion Cutting Tool Corp 516 536-8200
11-15 Saint Marks Ave Rockville Centre (11570) *(G-14789)*
Champion Home Builders Inc 315 841-4122
951 Rte 12 S Sangerfield (13455) *(G-15132)*
Champion Materials Inc (PA) 315 493-2654
502 S Washington St Carthage (13619) *(G-3410)*
Champion Materials Inc 315 493-2654
21721 Cole Rd Carthage (13619) *(G-3411)*
Champion Millwork Inc 315 463-0711
140 Hiawatha Pl Syracuse (13208) *(G-15892)*
Champion Photochemistry Inc 585 760-6444
1669 Lake Ave Rochester (14615) *(G-14271)*
Champion Window and Door, Hauppauge *Also called Champion Aluminum Corp* ***(G-6042)***
Champion Zipper Corp 212 239-0414
447 W 36th St Fl 2 New York (10018) *(G-9576)*
Champlain Hanger, Rouses Point *Also called Champlain Plastics Inc* ***(G-15041)***
Champlain Hudson Power Ex Inc 518 465-0710
600 Broadway Fl 3 Albany (12207) *(G-61)*
Champlain Plastics Inc 518 297-3700
87 Pillsbury Rd Rouses Point (12979) *(G-15041)*
Champlain Valley Milling Corp 518 962-4711
6679 Main St Westport (12993) *(G-17067)*
Champs Sports, Hicksville *Also called Foot Locker Retail Inc* ***(G-6345)***
Chams, New York *Also called North American Mills Inc* ***(G-11456)***
Chamtek Mfg Inc 585 328-4900
123 Louise St Rochester (14606) *(G-14272)*
Chan & Chan (usa) Corp 718 388-9633
2 Rewe St Brooklyn (11211) *(G-1773)*
Chan Kee Dried Bean Curd Inc 718 622-0820
71 Steuben St Brooklyn (11205) *(G-1774)*
Chan Luu LLC 212 398-3163
1441 Broadway New York (10018) *(G-9577)*
Chancelle Fashions/Tango, New York *Also called Chancelle Suits Inc* ***(G-9578)***
Chancelle Suits Inc 212 921-5300
141 W 36th St Rm 900 New York (10018) *(G-9578)*
Changes, Glendale *Also called Bowe Industries Inc* ***(G-5646)***
Channel Manufacturing Inc (PA) 516 944-6271
55 Channel Dr Port Washington (11050) *(G-13804)*
Chanse Petroleum Corporation (PA) 212 682-3789
828 5th Ave Apt 1f New York (10065) *(G-9579)*
Chapin International Inc 585 343-3140
700 Ellicott St Batavia (14020) *(G-627)*
Chapin Manufacturing Inc (PA) 585 343-3140
700 Ellicott St Ste 3 Batavia (14020) *(G-628)*
Chapin Watermatics Inc 315 782-1170
740 Water St Watertown (13601) *(G-16643)*
Chapman Skateboard Co Inc 631 321-4773
87 N Industry Ct Ste A Deer Park (11729) *(G-4116)*
Chapman Stained Glass Studio 518 449-5552
212 Quail St Albany (12203) *(G-62)*
Charing Cross Music Inc 212 541-7571
3 Columbus Cir Ste 1720 New York (10019) *(G-9580)*
Charl Industries Inc 631 234-0100
225 Engineers Rd Hauppauge (11788) *(G-6043)*
Charles A Hones Inc 607 273-5720
222 S Albany St Ste 3 Ithaca (14850) *(G-6832)*
Charles A Rogers Entps Inc 585 924-6400
51 Victor Heights Pkwy Victor (14564) *(G-16466)*
Charles Freihofer Baking Co 518 463-2221
1 Prospect Rd Albany (12206) *(G-63)*
Charles H Beckley Inc (PA) 718 665-2218
749 E 137th St Bronx (10454) *(G-1297)*
Charles Henricks Inc 212 243-5800
121 Varick St Fl 9 New York (10013) *(G-9581)*
Charles Lay (PA) 607 432-4518
138 Roundhouse Rd Oneonta (13820) *(G-13177)*
Charles Lay 607 656-4204
47 Birdsall St Greene (13778) *(G-5862)*
Charles P Rogers Brass Beds (PA) 212 675-4400
26 W 17th St New York (10011) *(G-9582)*
Charles P Rogers Brass Ir Bed, New York *Also called Charles P Rogers Brass Beds* ***(G-9582)***
Charles Perrella Inc 845 348-4777
78 S Broadway Nyack (10960) *(G-13046)*
Charles Richter, Wallkill *Also called Richter Metalcraft Corporation* ***(G-16545)***
Charles Ross & Son Company (PA) 631 234-0500
710 Old Willets Path Hauppauge (11788) *(G-6044)*
Charles V Weber Machine Shop 518 272-8033
2 Campbell Ave Troy (12180) *(G-16229)*
Charles Vaillant Inc 212 752-4832
37 W 57th St Ste 803 New York (10019) *(G-9583)*
Charlotte Neuville Design LLC 646 530-4570
882 3rd Ave Brooklyn (11232) *(G-1775)*
Charlton Precision Pdts Inc 845 338-2351
461 Sawkill Rd Kingston (12401) *(G-7183)*
Charm Mfg Co Inc 607 565-8161
251 State Route 17c Waverly (14892) *(G-16699)*
Charm Pools, Waverly *Also called Charm Mfg Co Inc* ***(G-16699)***
Charming Fashion Inc 212 730-2872
247 W 38th St Rm 1400 New York (10018) *(G-9584)*
Chart Inc 518 272-3565
302 10th St Troy (12180) *(G-16230)*
Chart Industries Inc 716 691-0202
260 Creekside Dr Ste 200 Amherst (14228) *(G-232)*
Chart Industries Inc 716 691-0202
500 Commerce Dr Amherst (14228) *(G-233)*
Charter Ventures LLC 212 868-0222
135 W 36th St Rm 1800 New York (10018) *(G-9585)*
Chartwell Pharma Nda B2 Holdin 845 268-5000
77 Brenner Dr Congers (10920) *(G-3854)*
Chartwell Pharmaceuticals LLC 845 268-5000
77 Brenner Dr Congers (10920) *(G-3855)*
Chase Corporation 212 644-7281
610 Madison Ave New York (10022) *(G-9586)*
Chase Corporation 631 243-6380
1948 Deer Park Ave Deer Park (11729) *(G-4117)*
Chase Corporation 631 827-0476
7 Harbour Point Dr Northport (11768) *(G-13009)*
Chase Instrument Co, West Babylon *Also called Peyser Instrument Corporation* ***(G-16818)***

Chase Media Group ALPHABETIC SECTION

Chase Media Group...914 962-3871
1520 Front St Yorktown Heights (10598) **(G-17509)**
Chase Partners, Northport *Also called Chase Corporation* **(G-13009)**
Chase Press, Yorktown Heights *Also called Shop Smart Central Inc* **(G-17519)**
Chateau La Fayette Reneau, Hector *Also called Lafayette Chateau* **(G-6258)**
Chateau Royal, Lewiston *Also called Alta Group Inc* **(G-7433)**
Chatham Courier, The, Hudson *Also called Johnson Acquisition Corp* **(G-6622)**
Chautauqua Circuits Inc...716 366-5771
855 Main St Dunkirk (14048) **(G-4335)**
Chautauqua Iron Works, Mayville *Also called Kleinfelder John* **(G-8216)**
Chautauqua Machine Spc LLC...716 782-3276
1880 Open Meadows Rd Ashville (14710) **(G-427)**
Chautauqua Sign Co Inc...716 665-2222
2164 Allen Street Ext Falconer (14733) **(G-4893)**
Chautauqua Wine Company Inc...716 934-9463
2627 Chapin Rd Silver Creek (14136) **(G-15447)**
Chautauqua Woods Corp...716 366-3808
134 Franklin Ave Dunkirk (14048) **(G-4336)**
Chautqua Prcsion Machining Inc...716 763-3752
1287 Hunt Rd Ashville (14710) **(G-428)**
Check Group LLC...212 221-4700
1385 Broadway Fl 16 New York (10018) **(G-9587)**
Check-Mate Industries Inc...631 491-1777
370 Wyandanch Ave West Babylon (11704) **(G-16782)**
Check-O-Matic Inc...845 781-7675
13 D A Weider Blvd # 101 Monroe (10950) **(G-8552)**
Checklist Boards Corporation...585 586-0152
763 Linden Ave Ste 2 Rochester (14625) **(G-14273)**
Checkm8 Inc (PA)...212 268-0048
307 W 36th St Fl 13 New York (10018) **(G-9588)**
Cheese Experts USA Ltd Lblty...908 275-3889
14 Notus Ave Staten Island (10312) **(G-15658)**
Chefs Delight Packing Co...718 388-8581
94 N 8th St Brooklyn (11249) **(G-1776)**
Chelsea Plastics Inc...212 924-4530
200 Lexington Ave Rm 914 New York (10016) **(G-9589)**
Chem-Puter Friendly Inc...631 331-2259
1 Sevilla Walk Mount Sinai (11766) **(G-8654)**
Chem-Tainer Industries Inc (PA)...631 422-8300
361 Neptune Ave West Babylon (11704) **(G-16783)**
Chem-Tek Systems Inc...631 253-3010
208 S Fehr Way Bay Shore (11706) **(G-683)**
Chemark International USA Inc...631 593-4566
729 Acorn St Deer Park (11729) **(G-4118)**
Chembio Diagnostic Systems Inc...631 924-1135
3661 Horseblock Rd Ste A Medford (11763) **(G-8238)**
Chembio Diagnostics Inc (PA)...631 924-1135
3661 Horseblock Rd Ste C Medford (11763) **(G-8239)**
Chemclean Corporation...718 525-4500
13045 180th St Jamaica (11434) **(G-6901)**
Chemicolloid Laboratories Inc...516 747-2666
55 Herricks Rd New Hyde Park (11040) **(G-8821)**
Chemistry Department, Oswego *Also called Energy Nuclear Operations* **(G-13331)**
Chemite Inc...607 529-3218
407 County Road 60 Waverly (14892) **(G-16700)**
Chemlube International LLC (PA)...914 381-5800
500 Mmaroneck Ave Ste 306 Harrison (10528) **(G-5979)**
Chemlube Marketing Inc...914 381-5800
500 Mmaroneck Ave Ste 308 Harrison (10528) **(G-5980)**
Chemours Company Fc LLC...716 278-5100
3181 Buffalo Ave Niagara Falls (14303) **(G-12804)**
Chemprene Inc...845 831-2800
483 Fishkill Ave Beacon (12508) **(G-782)**
Chemprene Holding Inc...845 831-2800
483 Fishkill Ave Beacon (12508) **(G-783)**
Chemtrade Chemicals US LLC...315 430-7650
1421 Willis Ave Syracuse (13204) **(G-15893)**
Chemtrade Chemicals US LLC...315 478-2323
344 W Genesee St Ste 100 Syracuse (13202) **(G-15894)**
Chemung Cty Assc Retrd Ctzns (HQ)...607 734-6151
711 Sullivan St Elmira (14901) **(G-4675)**
Chenango Asphalt Products...607 334-3117
23 State St Norwich (13815) **(G-13021)**
Chenango Concrete Corp (PA)...518 294-9964
145 Podpadic Rd Richmondville (12149) **(G-14089)**
Chenango Union Printing Inc...607 334-2112
15 American Ave Norwich (13815) **(G-13022)**
Chenango Valley Tech Inc...607 674-4115
328 Route 12b Sherburne (13460) **(G-15389)**
Chentronics Corporation...607 334-5531
115 County Rd 45 Norwich (13815) **(G-13023)**
Chepaume Industries LLC...315 829-6400
6201 Cooper St Vernon (13476) **(G-16433)**
Chequedcom Inc...888 412-0699
513 Broadway Ste 1 Saratoga Springs (12866) **(G-15149)**
Cheri Mon Baby LLC...212 354-5511
1562 E 4th St Brooklyn (11230) **(G-1777)**
Cheri Pink Inc (PA)...212 869-1948
1430 Broadway Fl 21 New York (10018) **(G-9590)**
Cheribundi Inc (PA)...800 699-0460
500 Technology Farm Dr Geneva (14456) **(G-5573)**
Cherry Creek Woodcraft Inc (PA)...716 988-3211
1 Cherry St South Dayton (14138) **(G-15518)**
Cherry Holding Ltd...516 679-3748
1536 Broad St North Bellmore (11710) **(G-12916)**
Cherry Lane Lithographing Corp...516 293-9294
15 E Bethpage Rd Unit A Plainview (11803) **(G-13587)**
Cherry Lane Magazine LLC...212 561-3000
1745 Broadway 19 New York (10019) **(G-9591)**
Cherry Metal Works, North Bellmore *Also called Cherry Holding Ltd* **(G-12916)**
Cherry Stix, New York *Also called Csco LLC* **(G-9762)**
Chesky Records Inc...212 586-7799
1650 Broadway Ste 900 New York (10019) **(G-9592)**
Chester Printing Service, Middletown *Also called Triad Printing Inc* **(G-8466)**
Chester Shred-It/West...914 347-4460
420 Columbus Ave Ste 202 Valhalla (10595) **(G-16365)**
Chester West County Press...914 684-0006
29 W 4th St Mount Vernon (10550) **(G-8671)**
Chester-Jensen Company...610 876-6276
124 S Main St Cattaraugus (14719) **(G-3437)**
Chesu Inc...239 564-2803
81 Newtown Ln East Hampton (11937) **(G-4407)**
Chet Kruszka's Svce, Orchard Park *Also called Chet Kruszkas Service Inc* **(G-13261)**
Chet Kruszkas Service Inc...716 662-7450
3536 Southwestern Blvd Orchard Park (14127) **(G-13261)**
Chia Company, New York *Also called Chia Usa LLC* **(G-9593)**
Chia Usa LLC...212 226-7512
315 W 36th St Fl 10 New York (10018) **(G-9593)**
Chicago Watermark Company, New York *Also called Donald Bruhnke* **(G-9897)**
Chicone Builders LLC...607 535-6540
302 W South St Montour Falls (14865) **(G-8609)**
Chief, The, New York *Also called New York Cvl Srvc Emplys Pblsh* **(G-11398)**
Child Nutrition Prog Dept Ed...212 371-1000
1011 1st Ave Fl 6 New York (10022) **(G-9594)**
Child's Work-Child's Play, Melville *Also called Guidance Group Inc* **(G-8325)**
Childrens Progress Inc...212 730-0905
108 W 39th St Rm 1305 New York (10018) **(G-9595)**
Chim-Cap Corp...631 454-7576
120 Schmitt Blvd Farmingdale (11735) **(G-4958)**
Chimney Doctors Americas Corp...631 868-3586
738a Montauk Hwy Bayport (11705) **(G-757)**
China Daily Distribution Corp (HQ)...212 537-8888
1500 Broadway Ste 2800 New York (10036) **(G-9596)**
China Huaren Organic Pdts Inc...212 232-0120
100 Wall St Fl 15 New York (10005) **(G-9597)**
China Imprint LLC...585 563-3391
750 Saint Paul St Rochester (14605) **(G-14274)**
China Industrial Steel Inc...646 328-1502
110 Wall St Fl 11 New York (10005) **(G-9598)**
China Lithium Technologies (PA)...212 391-2688
15 W 39th St Fl 14 New York (10018) **(G-9599)**
China N E Petro Holdings Ltd...212 307-3568
445 Park Ave Ste 900 New York (10022) **(G-9600)**
China Newsweek Corporation...212 481-2510
15 E 40th St Fl 11 New York (10016) **(G-9601)**
China Ruitai Intl Holdings Ltd...718 740-2278
8710 Clover Pl Hollis (11423) **(G-6495)**
China Ting Fashion Group (usa)...212 716-1600
525 7th Ave Rm 1606 New York (10018) **(G-9602)**
Chinese Medical Report Inc...718 359-5676
3907 Prince St Ste 5b Flushing (11354) **(G-5232)**
Chip It All Ltd...631 473-2040
366 Sheep Pasture Rd Port Jefferson (11777) **(G-13774)**
Chipita America Inc...845 292-2540
1243 Old Route 17 Ferndale (12734) **(G-5168)**
Chiplogic Inc...631 617-6317
14a Old Dock Rd Yaphank (11980) **(G-17388)**
Chiptek, Arcade *Also called Gowanda - Bti LLC* **(G-394)**
Chivvis Enterprises Inc...631 842-9055
10 Grant St Copiague (11726) **(G-3897)**
Chloe International Inc...212 730-6661
525 Fashion Ave Rm 1601 New York (10018) **(G-9603)**
Chloe's Soft Serve Fruit Co, New York *Also called Soft Serve Fruit Co LLC* **(G-12116)**
Chloe's Soft Serve Fruit Co, New York *Also called Soft Serve Apple LLC* **(G-12115)**
Chlor Alkali Products & Vinyls, Niagara Falls *Also called Olin Chlor Alkali Logistics* **(G-12857)**
Chobani LLC (PA)...607 337-1246
147 State Highway 320 Norwich (13815) **(G-13024)**
Chobani LLC...607 847-6181
669 County Road 25 New Berlin (13411) **(G-8779)**
Chocnyc LLC...917 804-4848
4996 Broadway New York (10034) **(G-9604)**
Choco Peanuts Inc...716 998-2353
2495 Main St Ste 524 Buffalo (14214) **(G-2871)**
Choco-Logo, Buffalo *Also called Dilese International Inc* **(G-2915)**
Chocolat Moderne LLC...212 229-4797
27 W 20th St Ste 904 New York (10011) **(G-9605)**
Chocolate By Design Inc...631 737-0082
700 Union Pkwy Ste 4 Ronkonkoma (11779) **(G-14887)**
Chocolate Delivery Systems, Buffalo *Also called N Make Mold Inc* **(G-3080)**

Chocolate Delivery Systems Inc (PA) ...716 854-6050
85 River Rock Dr Ste 202 Buffalo (14207) ***(G-2872)***

Chocolate Pizza Company Inc ...315 673-4098
3774 Lee Mulroy Rd Marcellus (13108) ***(G-8087)***

Chocolatier Magazine, New York *Also called Haymarket Group Ltd* ***(G-10429)***

Chocolations LLC ...914 777-3600
607 E Boston Post Rd Mamaroneck (10543) ***(G-8028)***

Chocomaker Inc ...716 877-3146
85 River Rock Dr Ste 202 Buffalo (14207) ***(G-2873)***

Chocomize Inc ...718 729-3264
3010 41st Ave Long Island City (11101) ***(G-7697)***

Chocovision Corporation ...845 473-4970
14 Catharine St Poughkeepsie (12601) ***(G-13893)***

Chohehco LLC ...315 420-4624
78 State St Skaneateles (13152) ***(G-15457)***

Choice Magazine Listening Inc ...516 883-8280
85 Channel Dr Ste 3 Port Washington (11050) ***(G-13805)***

Chomerics Div, Fairport *Also called Parker-Hannifin Corporation* ***(G-4867)***

Choppy V M & Sons LLC ...518 266-1444
4 Van Buren St Troy (12180) ***(G-16231)***

Chopt Creative Salad Co LLC (PA) ...646 374-0386
853 Broadway New York (10003) ***(G-9606)***

Christi Plastics Inc ...585 436-8510
215 Tremont St Rochester (14608) ***(G-14275)***

Christian Book Publishing ...646 559-2533
213 Bennett Ave New York (10040) ***(G-9607)***

Christian Bus Endeavors Inc (PA) ...315 788-8560
210 Court St Ste 10 Watertown (13601) ***(G-16644)***

Christian Casey LLC (PA) ...212 500-2200
1440 Broadway Frnt 3 New York (10018) ***(G-9608)***

Christian Casey LLC ...212 500-2200
1440 Broadway Frnt 3 New York (10018) ***(G-9609)***

Christian Dior Perfumes LLC (HQ) ...212 931-2200
19 E 57th St New York (10022) ***(G-9610)***

Christian Fabrication LLC ...315 822-0135
122 South St West Winfield (13491) ***(G-16957)***

Christian Press Inc ...718 886-4400
14317 Franklin Ave Flushing (11355) ***(G-5233)***

Christian Siriano Holdings LLC ...212 695-5494
260 W 35th St Ste 403 New York (10001) ***(G-9611)***

Christiana Millwork Inc (PA) ...315 492-9099
4755 Jamesville Rd Jamesville (13078) ***(G-7046)***

Christina Sales Inc ...212 391-0710
1441 Broadway New York (10018) ***(G-9612)***

Christiny, Wantagh *Also called Christopher Anthony Pubg Co* ***(G-16555)***

Christo-Vac, Cornwall *Also called Costume Armour Inc* ***(G-3987)***

Christophe Danhier, New York *Also called Danhier Co LLC* ***(G-9801)***

Christopher Anthony Pubg Co ...516 826-9205
2225 Wantagh Ave Wantagh (11793) ***(G-16555)***

Christopher Designs Inc ...212 382-1013
50 W 47th St Fl 1507 New York (10036) ***(G-9613)***

Christos Inc ...212 921-0025
318 W 39th St Fl 12 New York (10018) ***(G-9614)***

Chroma Communications Inc ...631 289-8871
2030 Route 112 Medford (11763) ***(G-8240)***

Chroma Logic ...716 736-2458
6651 Wiley Rd Ripley (14775) ***(G-14135)***

Chromagraphics Press Inc ...631 367-6160
3 Martha Dr Melville (11747) ***(G-8302)***

Chromalloy American LLC (HQ) ...845 230-7355
330 Blaisdell Rd Orangeburg (10962) ***(G-13222)***

Chromalloy Gas Turbine LLC ...845 359-2462
330 Blaisdell Rd Orangeburg (10962) ***(G-13223)***

Chromalloy Gas Turbine LLC ...845 692-8912
105 Tower Dr Middletown (10941) ***(G-8430)***

Chromalloy Middletown, Middletown *Also called Chromalloy Gas Turbine LLC* ***(G-8430)***

Chromalloy New York, Orangeburg *Also called Chromalloy Gas Turbine LLC* ***(G-13223)***

Chromananotech LLC ...607 239-9626
85 Murray Hill Rd Vestal (13850) ***(G-16445)***

Chromosense LLC ...347 770-5421
1 Metrotech Ctr Fl 19 Brooklyn (11201) ***(G-1778)***

Chronicle Express ...315 536-4422
138 Main St Penn Yan (14527) ***(G-13508)***

Chronicle, The, Glens Falls *Also called Oak Lone Publishing Co Inc* ***(G-5693)***

Chudnow Manufacturing Co Inc ...516 593-4222
3055 New St Oceanside (11572) ***(G-13074)***

Chula Girls, New York *Also called Detour Apparel Inc* ***(G-9861)***

Church & Dwight Co Inc ...518 887-5109
706 Ennis Rd Schenectady (12306) ***(G-15242)***

Church Bulletin Inc ...631 249-4994
200 Dale St West Babylon (11704) ***(G-16784)***

Church Communities NY Inc ...518 589-5103
2255 Platte Clove Rd Elka Park (12427) ***(G-4629)***

Church Communities NY Inc ...518 589-5103
Platte Clove Rd Elka Park (12427) ***(G-4630)***

Church Publishing Incorporated (HQ) ...212 592-1800
445 5th Ave Frnt 1 New York (10016) ***(G-9615)***

CHv Printed Company ...516 997-1101
1905 Hempstead Tpke B East Meadow (11554) ***(G-4419)***

Chyronhego Corporation (HQ) ...631 845-2000
5 Hub Dr Melville (11747) ***(G-8303)***

Cibao Meat Products Inc ...718 993-5072
630 Saint Anns Ave Bronx (10455) ***(G-1298)***

CIC International Ltd ...212 213-0089
1118 42nd St Brooklyn (11219) ***(G-1779)***

Ciccarelli Custom Taylor, Long Island City *Also called Primo Coat Corp* ***(G-7847)***

Cid Technologies, Liverpool *Also called Thermo Cidtec Inc* ***(G-7553)***

CIDC Corp ...718 342-5820
2015 Pitkin Ave Brooklyn (11207) ***(G-1780)***

Cidega American Trim, Durham *Also called Advanced Yarn Technologies Inc* ***(G-4354)***

Cierra Industries Inc ...315 252-6630
491 Grant Avenue Rd Auburn (13021) ***(G-488)***

Cigar Box Studios Inc ...845 236-9283
24 Riverview Dr Marlboro (12542) ***(G-8105)***

Cigar Oasis Inc ...516 520-5258
79 Heisser Ct Farmingdale (11735) ***(G-4959)***

Cilyox Inc ...716 853-3809
345 Broadway St Buffalo (14204) ***(G-2874)***

Ciment St-Laurent Inc ...518 943-4040
6446 Route 9w Catskill (12414) ***(G-3426)***

Cinderella Press Ltd ...212 431-3130
327 Canal St 3 New York (10013) ***(G-9616)***

Cinderellas Sweets Ltd ...516 374-7976
874 Lakeside Dr Woodmere (11598) ***(G-17312)***

Cine Design Group LLC ...646 747-0734
110 Leroy St Fl 8 New York (10014) ***(G-9617)***

Cinedeck, New York *Also called Cine Design Group LLC* ***(G-9617)***

Cinedigm Software ...212 206-9001
902 Broadway Fl 9 New York (10010) ***(G-9618)***

Ciner Manufacturing Co Inc ...212 947-3770
20 W 37th St Fl 10 New York (10018) ***(G-9619)***

Cintube Ltd ...518 324-3333
139 Distribution Way Plattsburgh (12901) ***(G-13659)***

Circle 5 Deli Corp ...718 525-5687
13440 Guy R Brewer Blvd Jamaica (11434) ***(G-6902)***

Circle Peak Capital MGT LLC (PA) ...646 230-8812
1325 Ave Of The Americas New York (10019) ***(G-9620)***

Circle Press Inc (PA) ...212 924-4277
121 Varick St Fl 7 New York (10013) ***(G-9621)***

Circo File Corp ...516 922-1848
69 Hamilton Ave Ste 1 Oyster Bay (11771) ***(G-13367)***

Circo-O-File, Oyster Bay *Also called Circo File Corp* ***(G-13367)***

Circor Aerospace Inc ...631 737-1900
425 Rabro Dr Ste 1 Hauppauge (11788) ***(G-6045)***

Circuits & Systems Inc ...516 593-4301
59 2nd St East Rockaway (11518) ***(G-4468)***

Circulation Dept, New York *Also called Lebhar-Friedman Inc* ***(G-10952)***

Cirrus Healthcare Products LLC (PA) ...631 692-7600
60 Main St Cold Spring Harbor (11724) ***(G-3768)***

Cisco Systems Inc ...212 714-4000
1 Penn Plz Ste 3306 New York (10119) ***(G-9622)***

Citation Manufacturing Co Inc ...845 425-6868
42 Harmony Rd Spring Valley (10977) ***(G-15579)***

Citiforms Inc ...212 334-9671
134 W 29th St Rm 704 New York (10001) ***(G-9623)***

Citigroup Inc ...212 816-6000
388 Greenwich St New York (10013) ***(G-9624)***

Citisource Industries Inc ...212 683-1033
244 5th Ave Ste 229 New York (10001) ***(G-9625)***

Citixsys Technologies Inc ...212 745-1365
1 Rockefeller Plz Fl 11 New York (10020) ***(G-9626)***

Citizen , The, Auburn *Also called Auburn Publishing Co* ***(G-480)***

Citizen Publishing Corp ...845 627-1414
119 Main St Ste 2 Nanuet (10954) ***(G-8754)***

Citros Building Materials Co ...718 779-0727
10514 Astoria Blvd East Elmhurst (11369) ***(G-4390)***

Citrus and Allied Essences, Floral Park *Also called C & A Service Inc* ***(G-5197)***

Citrus and Allied Essences Ltd (PA) ...516 354-1200
65 S Tyson Ave Floral Park (11001) ***(G-5200)***

City and State Ny LLC ...212 268-0442
61 Broadway Rm 1320 New York (10006) ***(G-9627)***

City Bakery Inc (PA) ...212 366-1414
3 W 18th St Frnt 1 New York (10011) ***(G-9628)***

City Baking LLC ...718 392-8514
1041 45th Ave Long Island City (11101) ***(G-7698)***

City Casting Corp ...212 938-0511
151 W 46th St Fl 5 New York (10036) ***(G-9629)***

City Cooling Enterprises Inc ...718 331-7400
1624 61st St Brooklyn (11204) ***(G-1781)***

City Evolutionary ...718 861-7585
336 Barretto St Bronx (10474) ***(G-1299)***

City Gear Inc ...914 450-4746
213 Taxter Rd Irvington (10533) ***(G-6767)***

City Hats, New York *Also called Beila Group Inc* ***(G-9346)***

City Jeans Inc ...718 239-5353
845 White Plins Rd Frnt 1 Bronx (10473) ***(G-1300)***

City Mason Corp ...718 658-3796
10417 148th St Jamaica (11435) ***(G-6903)***

City Newspaper ...585 244-3329
250 N Goodman St Ste 1 Rochester (14607) ***(G-14276)***

City of Kingston ...845 331-2490
91 E Strand St Kingston (12401) ***(G-7184)***

ALPHABETIC

(PA)=Parent Co (HQ)=Headquarters (DH)=Div Headquarters
2017 Harris
New York Manufacturers Directory
923

City of New York

City of New York	718 965-8787
4014 1st Ave Fl 3 Brooklyn (11232) *(G-1782)*	
City of New York	718 236-2693
5602 19th Ave Brooklyn (11204) *(G-1783)*	
City of Olean	716 376-5694
174 S 19th St Olean (14760) *(G-13138)*	
City of Oneonta	607 433-3470
110 East St Oneonta (13820) *(G-13178)*	
City Pattern Shop Inc	315 463-5239
4052 New Court Ave Syracuse (13206) *(G-15895)*	
City Post Express Inc	718 995-8690
17518 147th Ave Jamaica (11434) *(G-6904)*	
City Real Estate Book Inc	516 593-2949
9831 S Franklin Ave Valley Stream (11580) *(G-16403)*	
City Signs Inc	718 375-5933
1940 Mcdonald Ave Brooklyn (11223) *(G-1784)*	
City Sites Sportswear Inc (PA)	718 375-2990
2421 Mcdonald Ave Brooklyn (11223) *(G-1785)*	
City Sports Inc	212 730-2009
64 W 48th St Frnt B New York (10036) *(G-9630)*	
City Sports Imaging Inc	212 481-3600
20 E 46th St Rm 200 New York (10017) *(G-9631)*	
City Store Gates Mfg Corp	718 939-9700
1520 129th St College Point (11356) *(G-3781)*	
Cityscape Ob/Gyn PLLC	212 683-3595
38 E 32nd St Fl 4 New York (10016) *(G-9632)*	
Cives Corporation	315 287-2200
8 Church St Gouverneur (13642) *(G-5743)*	
Cives Corporation	315 543-2321
14331 Mill St Harrisville (13648) *(G-5995)*	
Cives Steel Company Nthrn Div, Gouverneur Also called Cives Corporation *(G-5743)*	
Civil Svc Rtred Employees Assn	718 937-0290
3427 Steinway St Ste 1 Long Island City (11101) *(G-7699)*	
CJ Component Products LLC	631 567-3733
624 Tower Mews Oakdale (11769) *(G-13057)*	
CJ Indstries A Div Smrset Inds, Gloversville Also called Somerset Industries Inc *(G-5721)*	
CJ Jewelry Inc	212 719-2464
2 W 47th St Ste 1106 New York (10036) *(G-9633)*	
Cjk Manufacturing LLC	585 663-6370
100 Boxart St Rochester (14612) *(G-14277)*	
Cjn Machinery Corp	631 244-8030
917 Lincoln Ave Ste 13 Holbrook (11741) *(G-6437)*	
CK Coatings	585 502-0425
57 North St Ste 150 Le Roy (14482) *(G-7404)*	
Clad Metal Specialties Inc	631 666-7750
1516 5th Industrial Ct Bay Shore (11706) *(G-684)*	
Claddagh Electronics Ltd	718 784-0571
1032 47th Rd Long Island City (11101) *(G-7700)*	
Clapper Hollow Designs Inc	518 234-9561
369 N Grand St Cobleskill (12043) *(G-3734)*	
Clara Papa	315 733-2660
1323 Blandina St 1 Utica (13501) *(G-16311)*	
Clarence Resins and Chemicals	716 406-9804
9585 Keller Rd Clarence Center (14032) *(G-3673)*	
Clarion Publications Inc	585 243-3530
38 Main St Geneseo (14454) *(G-5564)*	
Clarityad Inc	646 397-4198
833 Broadway Apt 2 New York (10003) *(G-9634)*	
Clark Botanicals Inc	914 826-4319
9 Paradise Rd Bronxville (10708) *(G-1499)*	
Clark Concrete Co Inc (PA)	315 478-4101
434 E Brighton Ave Syracuse (13210) *(G-15896)*	
Clark Laboratories Inc (HQ)	716 483-3851
2823 Girts Rd Jamestown (14701) *(G-6979)*	
Clark Rigging & Rental Corp	585 265-2910
680 Basket Rd Webster (14580) *(G-16717)*	
Clark Specialty Co Inc	607 776-3193
323 W Morris St Bath (14810) *(G-655)*	
Clark Trucking Co Div, Syracuse Also called Clark Concrete Co Inc *(G-15896)*	
Clarke Hess Communication RES	631 698-3350
3243 Route 112 Ste 1 Medford (11763) *(G-8241)*	
Clarke-Boxit Corporation	716 487-1950
45 Norwood Ave Jamestown (14701) *(G-6980)*	
Clarkson N Potter Inc	212 782-9000
1745 Broadway New York (10019) *(G-9635)*	
Clarsons Corp	585 235-8775
215 Tremont St Ste 8 Rochester (14608) *(G-14278)*	
Classic & Performance Spc	716 759-1800
80 Rotech Dr Lancaster (14086) *(G-7310)*	
Classic Album	718 388-2818
343 Lorimer St Brooklyn (11206) *(G-1786)*	
Classic Album LLC	718 388-2818
343 Lorimer St Brooklyn (11206) *(G-1787)*	
Classic Auto Crafts Inc	518 966-8003
6501 State Route 32 Greenville (12083) *(G-5884)*	
Classic Automation LLC (PA)	585 241-6010
800 Salt Rd Webster (14580) *(G-16718)*	
Classic Awnings Inc	716 649-0390
1 Elmview Ave Hamburg (14075) *(G-5920)*	
Classic Awnings & Party Tents, Hamburg Also called Classic Awnings Inc *(G-5920)*	
Classic Brass Inc	716 763-1400
2051 Stoneman Cir Lakewood (14750) *(G-7288)*	
Classic Cabinets	845 357-4331
375 Spook Rock Rd Suffern (10901) *(G-15787)*	
Classic Collections Fine Art	914 591-4500
20 Haarlem Ave Ste 408 White Plains (10603) *(G-17093)*	
Classic Color Graphics Inc (PA)	516 822-9090
268 N Broadway Unit 8 Hicksville (11801) *(G-6330)*	
Classic Color Graphics Inc	516 822-9090
87 Broadway Hicksville (11801) *(G-6331)*	
Classic Concrete Corp	516 822-1800
29a Midland Ave Hicksville (11801) *(G-6332)*	
Classic Cooking LLC	718 439-0200
16535 145th Dr Jamaica (11434) *(G-6905)*	
Classic Creations Inc	516 498-1991
1 Linden Pl Ste 409 Great Neck (11021) *(G-5798)*	
Classic Flavors Fragrances Inc	212 777-0004
878 W End Ave Apt 12b New York (10025) *(G-9636)*	
Classic Hosiery Inc	845 342-6661
33 Mulberry St Ste 4 Middletown (10940) *(G-8431)*	
Classic Labels Inc	631 467-2300
217 River Ave Patchogue (11772) *(G-13417)*	
Classic Medallics Inc	718 392-5410
520 S Fulton Ave Mount Vernon (10550) *(G-8672)*	
Classic News	718 698-5256
2655 Richmond Ave Staten Island (10314) *(G-15659)*	
Classic Sofa Ltd	212 620-0485
130 E 63rd St Ph B New York (10065) *(G-9637)*	
Classic Tool Design Inc	845 562-8700
31 Walnut St New Windsor (12553) *(G-8935)*	
Classic Tube, Lancaster Also called Classic & Performance Spc *(G-7310)*	
Classified Advertising, Troy Also called Want-Ad Digest Inc *(G-16262)*	
Classpass Inc (PA)	646 701-2172
275 7th Ave Fl 11 New York (10001) *(G-9638)*	
Classroom Inc	212 545-8400
245 5th Ave Fl 20 New York (10016) *(G-9639)*	
Claude Tribastone Inc	585 265-3776
6367 Dean Pkwy Ontario (14519) *(G-13197)*	
Clayton Dubilier & Rice Fun (PA)	212 407-5200
375 Park Ave Fl 18 New York (10152) *(G-9640)*	
Clayville Ice Co Inc	315 839-5405
2514 Foundry Pl Clayville (13322) *(G-3687)*	
Clean All of Syracuse LLC	315 472-9189
838 Erie Blvd W Syracuse (13204) *(G-15897)*	
Clean Gas Systems Inc	631 467-1600
380 Townline Rd Ste 120 Hauppauge (11788) *(G-6046)*	
Clean Room Depot Inc	631 589-3033
1730 Church St Holbrook (11741) *(G-6438)*	
Cleaning Tech Group LLC	716 665-2340
9 N Main St Jamestown (14701) *(G-6981)*	
Cleanse TEC	718 346-9111
1000 Linwood St Brooklyn (11208) *(G-1788)*	
Clear Cast Technologies Inc (PA)	914 945-0848
99 N Water St Ossining (10562) *(G-13322)*	
Clear Channel Outdoor Inc	212 812-0000
99 Park Ave Fl 2 New York (10016) *(G-9641)*	
Clear Edge Crosible Inc	315 685-3466
4653 Jordan Rd Skaneateles Falls (13153) *(G-15467)*	
Clear Edge Filtration, Skaneateles Falls Also called Clear Edge Crosible Inc *(G-15467)*	
Clear View Bag Company Inc	518 458-7153
5 Burdick Dr Albany (12205) *(G-64)*	
Clearcove Systems Inc	585 734-3012
7910 Rae Blvd Victor (14564) *(G-16467)*	
Clearlake Land Co Inc	315 848-2427
Hanks Rd Star Lake (13690) *(G-15628)*	
Clearstep Technologies LLC	315 952-3628
213 Emann Dr Camillus (13031) *(G-3322)*	
Clearview Shower Doors, Monroe Also called G & M Clearview Inc *(G-8555)*	
Clearview Social Inc	801 414-7675
640 Ellicott St Ste 108 Buffalo (14203) *(G-2875)*	
Clearwater Paper Corporation	315 287-1200
4921 State Highway 58 Gouverneur (13642) *(G-5744)*	
Clearweld, Binghamton Also called Crysta-Lyn Chemical Company *(G-905)*	
Clearwood Custom Carpentry and	315 432-8422
617 W Manlius St Ste 1 East Syracuse (13057) *(G-4518)*	
Cleary Custom Cabinets Inc	516 939-2475
794 S Broadway Hicksville (11801) *(G-6333)*	
Clemente Latham Concrete Corp	518 374-2222
1245 Kings Rd Schenectady (12303) *(G-15243)*	
Clemente Latham North Div, Schenectady Also called Clemente Latham Concrete Corp *(G-15243)*	
Clements Burrville Sawmill	315 782-4549
18181 Van Allen Rd N Watertown (13601) *(G-16645)*	
Clerio Vision Inc	617 216-7881
312 Susquehanna Rd Rochester (14618) *(G-14279)*	
Cleveland Biolabs Inc (PA)	716 849-6810
73 High St Buffalo (14203) *(G-2876)*	
Cleveland Polymer Tech LLC (PA)	518 326-9146
125 Monroe St Bldg 125 Watervliet (12189) *(G-16682)*	
Clever Devices Ltd	845 566-0051
546 Fostertown Rd Newburgh (12550) *(G-12752)*	
Clever Devices Ltd (PA)	516 433-6100
300 Crossways Park Dr Woodbury (11797) *(G-17283)*	
Clever Fellows I, Troy Also called Chart Inc *(G-16230)*	

Clever Goats Media LLC 917 512-0340
40 Exchange Pl Ste 1602 New York (10005) ***(G-9642)***
Click It Inc 631 686-2900
85 Corporate Dr Hauppauge (11788) ***(G-6047)***
Clifford H Jones Inc 716 693-2444
608 Young St Tonawanda (14150) ***(G-16153)***
Cliffstar LLC (HQ) 716 366-6100
1 Cliffstar Dr Dunkirk (14048) ***(G-4337)***
Climatronics Corp (HQ) 541 471-7111
606 Johnson Ave Ste 28 Bohemia (11716) ***(G-1033)***
Climax Manufacturing Company (PA) 315 376-8000
30 Champion St Carthage (13619) ***(G-3412)***
Climax Manufacturing Company 315 376-8000
5204 Climax St Castorland (13620) ***(G-3422)***
Climax Packaging, Carthage *Also called Climax Manufacturing Company* ***(G-3412)***
Climax Packaging Inc 315 376-8000
7840 State Route 26 Lowville (13367) ***(G-7935)***
Clinique Services Inc (HQ) 212 572-4200
767 5th Ave New York (10153) ***(G-9643)***
Clinton Clrs & EMB Shoppe Inc 315 853-8421
43 College St Clinton (13323) ***(G-3718)***
Clinton Creamery Inc 917 324-9699
13221 220th St Laurelton (11413) ***(G-7386)***
Clinton Signs Inc 585 482-1620
1407 Empire Blvd Webster (14580) ***(G-16719)***
Clinton Vineyards Inc 845 266-5372
450 Schultzville Rd Clinton Corners (12514) ***(G-3724)***
Clintons Ditch Coop Co Inc 315 699-2695
8478 Pardee Rd Cicero (13039) ***(G-3643)***
Clintrak Clinical Labeling S (PA) 631 467-3900
2800 Veterans Mem Hwy Bohemia (11716) ***(G-1034)***
Clip Clop International Inc 631 392-1340
271 Knickerbocker Ave Bohemia (11716) ***(G-1035)***
Clique Apparel Inc 516 375-7969
2034 Green Acres Mall Valley Stream (11581) ***(G-16404)***
Cliquer's, New York *Also called Colors Fashion Inc* ***(G-9675)***
Clo-Shure Intl Inc (PA) 212 268-5029
224 W 35th St Ste 1000 New York (10001) ***(G-9644)***
Clopay Ames True Tmper Hldng (HQ) 516 938-5544
100 Jericho Quadrangle # 224 Jericho (11753) ***(G-7062)***
Closet Systems Group, The, Brooklyn *Also called Designs By Robert Scott Inc* ***(G-1857)***
Cloud Rock Group LLC 516 967-6023
525 Bryant Ave Roslyn (11576) ***(G-15017)***
Cloud Toronto Inc 408 569-4542
1967 Wehrle Dr Ste 1 Williamsville (14221) ***(G-17239)***
Cloudsense Inc 917 880-6195
1325 Avenue Of The Flr 28 New York (10019) ***(G-9645)***
Clover Wire Forming Co Inc 914 375-0400
1021 Saw Mill River Rd Yonkers (10710) ***(G-17428)***
Clovis Point, Queens Village *Also called East End Vineyards LLC* ***(G-13976)***
Clp Pb LLC (PA) 212 340-8100
250 W 57th St Fl 15 New York (10107) ***(G-9646)***
Clpa Embroidery 516 409-0002
2635 Pettit Ave Bellmore (11710) ***(G-816)***
Club 1100 ....585 235-3478
1100 Jay St Rochester (14611) ***(G-14280)***
Club Monaco US Inc 212 886-2660
601 W 26th St Rm 800 New York (10001) ***(G-9647)***
Club Protector Inc 716 652-4787
191 Buffalo Creek Rd Elma (14059) ***(G-4645)***
Clues Fashion, New York *Also called Cheri Pink Inc* ***(G-9590)***
Clyde Duneier Inc (PA) 212 398-1122
415 Madison Ave Fl 6 New York (10017) ***(G-9648)***
Cmb Wireless Group LLC (PA) 631 750-4700
116 Wilbur Pl Bohemia (11716) ***(G-1036)***
Cmc-Kuhnke Inc 518 694-3310
1060 Brdwy Albany (12204) ***(G-65)***
Cmp Adaptive Equipment Supply, Deer Park *Also called Crosley Medical Products Inc* ***(G-4122)***
Cmp Advnced Mech Sltons NY LLC 607 352-1712
90 Bevier Ct Binghamton (13901) ***(G-902)***
Cmp Industries LLC (PA) 518 434-3147
413 N Pearl St Albany (12207) ***(G-66)***
Cmp Industries LLC 518 434-3147
413 N Pearl St Albany (12207) ***(G-67)***
Cmp Media, New York *Also called Ubm LLC* ***(G-12442)***
Cmp New York, Binghamton *Also called Cmp Advnced Mech Sltons NY LLC* ***(G-902)***
CMS Heat Transfer Division Inc 631 968-0084
273 Knickerbocker Ave Bohemia (11716) ***(G-1037)***
CMX Media LLC 917 793-5831
1271 Av Of The Americas New York (10020) ***(G-9649)***
CN Group Incorporated 914 358-5690
76 Mamaroneck Ave White Plains (10601) ***(G-17094)***
CNA Specialties Inc 631 567-7929
226 Mcneil St Sayville (11782) ***(G-15206)***
Cnc Manufacturing Corp 718 728-6800
3214 49th St Long Island City (11103) ***(G-7701)***
Cntry Cross Communications LLC 386 758-9696
106 W 3rd St Ste 106 Jamestown (14701) ***(G-6982)***
Cnv Architectural Coatings Inc 718 418-9584
538 Johnson Ave Brooklyn (11237) ***(G-1789)***
CNY Business Review Inc 315 472-3104
269 W Jefferson St Syracuse (13202) ***(G-15898)***
CNy Business Solutions 315 733-5031
502 Court St Ste 206 Utica (13502) ***(G-16312)***
Co-Op City News, New Rochelle *Also called Hagedorn Communications Inc* ***(G-8906)***
Co-Optics America Lab Inc 607 432-0557
297 River Street Svc Rd Service Oneonta (13820) ***(G-13179)***
Co-Optics Groups, The, Oneonta *Also called Co-Optics America Lab Inc* ***(G-13179)***
Co2 Textiles LLC (PA) 212 269-2222
88 Greenwich St Apt 1507 New York (10006) ***(G-9650)***
Coach Inc 212 581-4115
10 Columbus Cir Ste 101a New York (10019) ***(G-9651)***
Coach Inc 718 760-0624
90 Queens Blvd Elmhurst (11373) ***(G-4659)***
Coach Inc 585 425-7720
7979 Pittsford Victor Rd Victor (14564) ***(G-16468)***
Coach Inc 212 245-4148
620 5th Ave Frnt 3 New York (10020) ***(G-9652)***
Coach Inc 212 473-6925
143 Prince St Frnt A New York (10012) ***(G-9653)***
Coach Inc 212 754-0041
595 Madison Ave Frnt 1 New York (10022) ***(G-9654)***
Coach Inc 212 675-6403
79 5th Ave Frnt 3 New York (10003) ***(G-9655)***
Coach Inc (PA) 212 594-1850
10 Hudson Yards New York (10001) ***(G-9656)***
Coach Leatherware Company, New York *Also called Coach Stores Inc* ***(G-9659)***
Coach Leatherware Intl 212 594-1850
516 W 34th St Bsmt 5 New York (10001) ***(G-9657)***
Coach Services Inc 212 594-1850
516 W 34th St Bsmt 5 New York (10001) ***(G-9658)***
Coach Stores Inc 212 643-9727
516 W 34th St Bsmt 5 New York (10001) ***(G-9659)***
Coalition On Positive Health 212 633-2500
1751 Park Ave Fl 4 New York (10035) ***(G-9660)***
Coast To Coast Circuits Inc 585 254-2980
205 Lagrange Ave Rochester (14613) ***(G-14281)***
Coastal Pipeline Products Corp 631 369-4000
55 Twomey Ave Calverton (11933) ***(G-3288)***
Coastal Publications Inc 631 725-1700
22 Division St Sag Harbor (11963) ***(G-15076)***
Coastel Cable Tools Inc 315 471-5361
344 E Brighton Ave Syracuse (13210) ***(G-15899)***
Coastel Cable Tools Intl, Syracuse *Also called Coastel Cable Tools Inc* ***(G-15899)***
Coated Abrasive Division, Watervliet *Also called Saint-Gobain Abrasives Inc* ***(G-16688)***
Coating Technology Inc 585 546-7170
800 Saint Paul St Rochester (14605) ***(G-14282)***
Cobbe Industries Inc 716 287-2661
1397 Harris Hollow Rd Gerry (14740) ***(G-5592)***
Cobblestone Bakery Corp 631 491-3777
39 Wyandanch Ave Wyandanch (11798) ***(G-17373)***
Cobblestone Frm Winery Vinyrd 315 549-1004
5102 State Route 89 Romulus (14541) ***(G-14841)***
Cobey Inc (PA) 716 362-9550
1 Ship Canal Pkwy Buffalo (14218) ***(G-2877)***
Cobham Holdings (us) Inc 716 662-0006
10 Cobham Dr Orchard Park (14127) ***(G-13262)***
Cobham Holdings Inc (HQ) 716 662-0006
10 Orchard Park Dr Orchard Park (14127) ***(G-13263)***
Cobham Management Services Inc 716 662-0006
10 Cobham Dr Orchard Park (14127) ***(G-13264)***
Cobham Mission Systems Div, Orchard Park *Also called Cobham Management Services Inc* ***(G-13264)***
Cobleskill Concrete Ready Mix, Amsterdam *Also called Cobleskill Red E Mix & Supply* ***(G-340)***
Cobleskill Red E Mix & Supply (PA) 518 234-2015
774 State Highway 5s Amsterdam (12010) ***(G-340)***
Cobleskill Stone Products Inc 518 299-3066
395 Falke Rd Prattsville (12468) ***(G-13945)***
Cobleskill Stone Products Inc 518 295-7121
163 Eastern Ave Schoharie (12157) ***(G-15316)***
Cobleskill Stone Products Inc (PA) 518 234-0221
112 Rock Rd Cobleskill (12043) ***(G-3735)***
Cobleskill Stone Products Inc 607 432-8321
57 Ceperley Ave Oneonta (13820) ***(G-13180)***
Cobleskill Stone Products Inc 607 637-4271
1565 Green Flats Rd Hancock (13783) ***(G-5962)***
Cobra Manufacturing Corp 845 514-2505
68 Leggs Mills Rd Lake Katrine (12449) ***(G-7269)***
Cobra Operating Industries LLC 607 639-1700
37 Main St Afton (13730) ***(G-9)***
Cobra Systems Inc 845 338-6675
2669 New York 32 Bloomington (12411) ***(G-993)***
Coca-Cola, Horseheads *Also called Rochester Coca Cola Bottling* ***(G-6591)***
Coca-Cola, Rochester *Also called Rochester Coca Cola Bottling* ***(G-14638)***
Coca-Cola Bottling Co of NY 518 459-2010
38 Warehouse Row Albany (12205) ***(G-68)***
Coca-Cola Bottling Company 518 483-0422
15 Ida Pkwy Malone (12953) ***(G-8008)***
Coca-Cola Btlg Co Buffalo Inc 716 874-4610
200 Milens Rd Tonawanda (14150) ***(G-16154)***

A L P H A B E T I C

Coca-Cola Btlg Co of NY Inc 845 562-3037
10 Heampstead Rd New Windsor (12553) ***(G-8936)***

Coca-Cola Btlg Co of NY Inc 718 326-3334
5902 Borden Ave Maspeth (11378) ***(G-8122)***

Coca-Cola Btlg Co of NY Inc 914 592-4574
111 Fairview Pk Dr Ste 1 Elmsford (10523) ***(G-4741)***

Coca-Cola Btlg Co of NY Inc 315 457-9221
298 Farrell Rd Syracuse (13209) ***(G-15900)***

Coca-Cola Btlg Co of NY Inc 718 416-7575
5840 Borden Ave Maspeth (11378) ***(G-8123)***

Coca-Cola Btlg Co of NY Inc 631 434-3535
375 Wireless Blvd Hauppauge (11788) ***(G-6048)***

Coca-Cola Btlg Co of NY Inc 718 420-6800
400 Western Ave Staten Island (10303) ***(G-15660)***

Coca-Cola Btlg Co of NY Inc 914 789-1580
115 Fairview Pk Dr Ste 1 Elmsford (10523) ***(G-4742)***

Coca-Cola Refreshments USA Inc 718 401-5200
977 E 149th St Bronx (10455) ***(G-1301)***

Coca-Cola Refreshments USA Inc 315 785-8907
22614 County Route 51 Watertown (13601) ***(G-16646)***

Coca-Cola Refreshments USA Inc 914 592-0806
3 Skyline Dr Hawthorne (10532) ***(G-6245)***

Coccadotts Inc 518 438-4937
1179 Central Ave Albany (12205) ***(G-69)***

Cochecton Mills Inc (PA) 845 932-8282
30 Depot Rd Cochecton (12726) ***(G-3740)***

Cockpit Usa Inc 212 575-1616
15 W 39th St Fl 12 New York (10018) ***(G-9661)***

Cockpit Usa Inc (PA) 212 575-1616
15 W 39th St Fl 12 New York (10018) ***(G-9662)***

Cockpit Usa Inc 908 558-9704
15 W 39th St Fl 12 New York (10018) ***(G-9663)***

Cockpit, The, New York *Also called Cockpit Usa Inc* ***(G-9662)***

Coco Rico Southeast, Bronx *Also called Goodo Beverage Company* ***(G-1346)***

Coda Resources Ltd (PA) 718 649-1666
960 Alabama Ave Brooklyn (11207) ***(G-1790)***

Codesters Inc 646 232-1025
900 Broadway Ste 903 New York (10003) ***(G-9664)***

Codinos Limited Inc 518 372-3308
704 Corporation Park # 5 Schenectady (12302) ***(G-15244)***

Cody Printing Corp 718 651-8854
3728 56th St Woodside (11377) ***(G-17324)***

Coe Displays Inc 718 937-5658
4301 22nd St Ste 603 Long Island City (11101) ***(G-7702)***

Coecles Hbr Marina & Boat Yard 631 749-0856
68 Cartwright Rd Shelter Island (11964) ***(G-15386)***

Coffee Holding Co Inc (PA) 718 832-0800
3475 Victory Blvd Ste 4 Staten Island (10314) ***(G-15661)***

Coffing, Getzville *Also called Columbus McKinnon Corporation* ***(G-5597)***

Cofire Paving Corporation 718 463-1403
12030 28th Ave Flushing (11354) ***(G-5234)***

Cognigen Acquisition, Buffalo *Also called Cognigen Corporation* ***(G-2878)***

Cognigen Corporation 716 633-3463
1780 Wehrle Dr Ste 110 Buffalo (14221) ***(G-2878)***

Cognitiveflow Sensor Tech 631 513-9369
9 Melville Ct Stony Brook (11790) ***(G-15768)***

Cognotion Inc 347 692-0640
1407 Broadway Fl 24 New York (10018) ***(G-9665)***

Coham/Rvrdale Dcrative Fabrics, New York *Also called Richloom Home Fashions Corp* ***(G-11871)***

Cohber Press Inc (PA) 585 475-9100
1000 John St West Henrietta (14586) ***(G-16873)***

Cohens Bakery Inc 716 892-8149
1132 Broadway St Buffalo (14212) ***(G-2879)***

Coil Stamping Inc 631 588-3040
1340 Lincoln Ave Ste 1 Holbrook (11741) ***(G-6439)***

Coil-Q Corporation 914 779-7109
340 Bronxville Rd Bronxville (10708) ***(G-1500)***

Coinmach Service Corp 516 349-8555
303 Sunnyside Blvd # 70 Plainview (11803) ***(G-13588)***

Colad Group LLC (HQ) 716 961-1776
693 Seneca St 5 Buffalo (14210) ***(G-2880)***

Colarusso Blacktop Co, Hudson *Also called A Colarusso and Son Inc* ***(G-6603)***

Colburns AC Rfrgn 716 569-3695
17 White Dr Frewsburg (14738) ***(G-5449)***

Cold Mix Manufacturing Corp 718 463-1444
65 Edison Ave Mount Vernon (10550) ***(G-8673)***

Cold Point Corporation 315 339-2331
7500 Cold Point Dr Rome (13440) ***(G-14809)***

Cold Spring Granite Company 518 647-8191
Rr 9 Box S Au Sable Forks (12912) ***(G-475)***

Cold Springs R & D Inc 315 413-1237
1207 Van Vleck Rd Ste A Syracuse (13209) ***(G-15901)***

Colden Closet LLC 716 713-6125
1375 Boies Rd East Aurora (14052) ***(G-4368)***

Coldstream Group Inc (PA) 914 698-5959
420 Railroad Way Mamaroneck (10543) ***(G-8029)***

Colgat-Plmolive Centl Amer Inc (HQ) 212 310-2000
300 Park Ave New York (10022) ***(G-9666)***

Colgate-Palmolive Company (PA) 212 310-2000
300 Park Ave Fl 5 New York (10022) ***(G-9667)***

Colgate-Palmolive Company 718 506-3961
21818 100th Ave Queens Village (11429) ***(G-13975)***

Colgate-Palmolive Globl Trdg 212 310-2000
300 Park Ave Fl 8 New York (10022) ***(G-9668)***

Colgate-Palmolive Nj Inc 212 310-2000
300 Park Ave Fl 8 New York (10022) ***(G-9669)***

Coliseum, New York *Also called Plugg LLC* ***(G-11678)***

Collaborative Laboratories (HQ) 631 689-0200
3 Technology Dr Ste 400 East Setauket (11733) ***(G-4479)***

Collection Xiix Ltd (PA) 212 686-8990
1370 Broadway Fl 17 New York (10018) ***(G-9670)***

College Calendar Company 315 768-8242
148 Clinton St Whitesboro (13492) ***(G-17192)***

College Nnoscale Science Engrg, Albany *Also called University At Albany* ***(G-147)***

Collegebound Teen Magazine, Staten Island *Also called Ramholtz Publishing Inc* ***(G-15727)***

Collegeville Imagineering, Bay Shore *Also called Rubies Costume Company Inc* ***(G-741)***

Collinite Corporation 315 732-2282
1520 Lincoln Ave Utica (13502) ***(G-16313)***

Collins Pet & Garden Center, Malone *Also called Scotts Feed Inc* ***(G-8015)***

Colonial Electric, Farmingdale *Also called Colonial Precision Machinery* ***(G-4960)***

Colonial Group LLC 516 349-8010
150 Express St Ste 2 Plainview (11803) ***(G-13589)***

Colonial Label, Patchogue *Also called Depot Label Company Inc* ***(G-13418)***

Colonial Label Systems Inc 631 254-0111
50 Corbin Ave Ste L Bay Shore (11706) ***(G-685)***

Colonial Precision Machinery 631 249-0738
134 Rome St Farmingdale (11735) ***(G-4960)***

Colonial Rapid, Bay Shore *Also called Colonial Label Systems Inc* ***(G-685)***

Colonial Redi Record Corp 718 972-7433
1225 36th St Brooklyn (11218) ***(G-1791)***

Colonial Tag & Label Co Inc 516 482-0508
425 Northern Blvd Ste 36 Great Neck (11021) ***(G-5799)***

Colonial Tanning Corporation (PA) 518 725-7171
8 Wilson St 810 Gloversville (12078) ***(G-5709)***

Colonial Terrace Hotel, Cortlandt Manor *Also called Terrace Management Inc* ***(G-4054)***

Colonial Wire & Cable Co Inc (PA) 631 234-8500
40 Engineers Rd Hauppauge (11788) ***(G-6049)***

Colonie Block and Supply Co 518 869-8411
124 Lincoln Ave Colonie (12205) ***(G-3819)***

Colonie Plastics Corp 631 434-6969
188 Candlewood Rd Bay Shore (11706) ***(G-686)***

Colony Holdings Intl LLC 212 868-2800
131 W 35th St Fl 6 New York (10001) ***(G-9671)***

Color Card LLC 631 232-1300
1065 Islip Ave Central Islip (11722) ***(G-3491)***

Color Carton Corp 718 665-0840
341 Canal Pl Bronx (10451) ***(G-1302)***

Color Craft Finishing Corp 631 563-3230
30 Floyds Run Ste A Bohemia (11716) ***(G-1038)***

Color Fx, New York *Also called Joseph Industries Inc* ***(G-10765)***

Color Industries LLC 718 392-8301
3002 48th Ave Ste H Long Island City (11101) ***(G-7703)***

Color ME Mine 585 383-8420
3349 Monroe Ave Ste 32 Rochester (14618) ***(G-14283)***

Color Merchants Inc 212 682-4788
6 E 45th St Fl 17 New York (10017) ***(G-9672)***

Color Pro Sign, Schenectady *Also called Ray Sign Inc* ***(G-15289)***

Color Story, New York *Also called Leser Enterprises Ltd* ***(G-10973)***

Color Unlimited Inc 212 802-7547
244 5th Ave Frnt New York (10001) ***(G-9673)***

Color-Aid Corporation 212 673-5500
38 La Fayette St Ste 2 Hudson Falls (12839) ***(G-6639)***

Colorfast 212 929-2440
121 Varick St Fl 9 New York (10013) ***(G-9674)***

Colorfully Yours Inc 631 242-8600
11 Grant Ave Bay Shore (11706) ***(G-687)***

Colorpak, Melville *Also called Poly-Pak Industries Inc* ***(G-8348)***

Colors Fashion Inc 212 629-0401
901 Avenue Of The Ste 153 New York (10001) ***(G-9675)***

Colors In Optics Ltd 718 845-0300
120 Broadway G New Hyde Park (11040) ***(G-8822)***

Colorspec Coatings Intl Inc 631 472-8251
1716 Church St Holbrook (11741) ***(G-6440)***

Colortex Inc 212 564-2000
1202 Lexington Ave 115 New York (10028) ***(G-9676)***

Columbia, Macedon *Also called Water Technologies Inc* ***(G-7992)***

Columbia Button Nailhead Corp 718 386-3414
306 Stagg St 316 Brooklyn (11206) ***(G-1792)***

Columbia Daily Spectator, New York *Also called Spectator Publishing Co Inc* ***(G-12155)***

Columbia Metal Fabricators 631 476-7527
801 Hallock Ave Port Jeff STA (11776) ***(G-13765)***

Columbia Pool Accessories Inc 718 993-0389
111 Bruckner Blvd Bronx (10454) ***(G-1303)***

Columbia Records Inc 212 833-8000
25 Madison Ave Fl 19 New York (10010) ***(G-9677)***

Columbia Seal N Sew, Brooklyn *Also called Dlx Industries Inc* ***(G-1869)***

Columbia Sportswear Company 631 274-6091
152 The Arches Cir Deer Park (11729) ***(G-4119)***

Columbia Univ Publications, New York *Also called Trust of Colum Unive In The Ci* ***(G-12412)***

ALPHABETIC

Columbia University Press Inc (HQ) 212 459-0600
61 W 62nd St Fl 3 New York (10023) *(G-9678)*
Columbia University Press Inc 212 459-0600
61 W 62nd St Fl 3 New York (10023) *(G-9679)*
Columbia University Press Inc 212 459-0600
61 W 62nd St Fl 3 New York (10023) *(G-9680)*
Columbus Accessories, New York *Also called Columbus Trading Corp (G-9681)*
Columbus Baking Co, Syracuse *Also called George Retzos (G-15952)*
Columbus McKinnon Corporation (PA) 716 689-5400
205 Crosspoint Pkwy Getzville (14068) *(G-5595)*
Columbus McKinnon Corporation 716 689-5400
470 John Jmes Adubon Pkwy Amherst (14228) *(G-234)*
Columbus McKinnon Corporation 716 689-5400
205 Crosspoint Pkwy Getzville (14068) *(G-5596)*
Columbus McKinnon Corporation 716 689-5400
205 Crosspoint Pkwy Getzville (14068) *(G-5597)*
Columbus McKinnon Corporation 716 689-5400
205 Crosspoint Pkwy Getzville (14068) *(G-5598)*
Columbus McKnnon- Lift TEC Div, Getzville *Also called Columbus McKinnon Corporation (G-5596)*
Columbus Trading Corp 212 564-1780
120 W 31st St Rm 600 New York (10001) *(G-9681)*
Columbus Woodworking Inc 607 674-4546
164 Casey Cheese Fctry Rd Sherburne (13460) *(G-15390)*
Comairco Equipment Inc (HQ) 716 656-0211
3250 Union Rd Cheektowaga (14227) *(G-3564)*
Comander Terminals LLC 516 922-7600
1 Commander Sq Oyster Bay (11771) *(G-13368)*
Comax Aromatics Corporation 631 249-0505
130 Baylis Rd Melville (11747) *(G-8304)*
Comax Flavors, Melville *Also called Comax Manufacturing Corp (G-8305)*
Comax Manufacturing Corp 631 249-0505
130 Baylis Rd Melville (11747) *(G-8305)*
Combe Incorporated (PA) 914 694-5454
1101 Westchester Ave White Plains (10604) *(G-17095)*
Combine Graphics Corp 212 695-4044
10714 Queens Blvd Forest Hills (11375) *(G-5322)*
Comboland Packing Corp 718 858-4200
2 Cumberland St Brooklyn (11205) *(G-1793)*
Comco Plastics Inc 718 849-9000
9831 Jamaica Ave Woodhaven (11421) *(G-17305)*
Comely International Trdg Inc 212 683-1240
303 5th Ave Rm 1903 New York (10016) *(G-9682)*
Comerford Collection, Bridgehampton *Also called Comerford Hennessy At Home Inc (G-1233)*
Comerford Hennessy At Home Inc 631 537-6200
2442 Main St Bridgehampton (11932) *(G-1233)*
Comet Flasher Inc (PA) 716 821-9595
1 Babcock St Buffalo (14210) *(G-2881)*
Comet Informatics LLC 585 385-2310
642 Kreag Rd Ste 300 Pittsford (14534) *(G-13557)*
Comfort Bedding Inc 718 485-7662
13 Christopher Ave Brooklyn (11212) *(G-1794)*
Comfort Care Textiles Inc (HQ) 631 543-0531
368 Veterans Memorial Hwy # 5 Commack (11725) *(G-3828)*
Comfort Wax Incorporated 718 204-7028
3174 Steinway St Fl 5 Astoria (11103) *(G-434)*
Comfortex Corporation (HQ) 518 273-3333
21 Elm St Watervliet (12189) *(G-16683)*
Comfortex Window Fashions, Watervliet *Also called Comfortex Corporation (G-16683)*
Comgraph Sales Service 716 601-7243
7491 Clinton St Elma (14059) *(G-4646)*
Comint Apparel Group LLC (PA) 212 947-7474
463 7th Ave Fl 4 New York (10018) *(G-9683)*
Command Components Corporation 631 666-4411
6 Cherry St Bay Shore (11706) *(G-688)*
Command Systems Division, Farmingdale *Also called Telephonics Corporation (G-5128)*
Comme-Ci Comme-CA AP Group 631 300-1035
380 Rabo Dr Hauppauge (11788) *(G-6050)*
Commentary Inc 212 891-1400
165 E 56th St Fl 16 New York (10022) *(G-9684)*
Commentary Magazine, New York *Also called American Jewish Committee (G-9122)*
Commerce Offset Ltd 914 769-6671
657 Commerce St Thornwood (10594) *(G-16118)*
Commerce Spring Corp 631 293-4844
143 Allen Blvd Farmingdale (11735) *(G-4961)*
Commercehub Inc (PA) 518 810-0700
201 Fuller Rd Fl 6 Albany (12203) *(G-70)*
Commercial Communications LLC 845 343-9078
14 Montgomery St Middletown (10940) *(G-8432)*
Commercial Concrete, Westbury *Also called New York Ready Mix Inc (G-17014)*
Commercial Display Design LLC 607 336-7353
120 Kemper Ln Norwich (13815) *(G-13025)*
Commercial Draperies Unlimited, Mamaroneck *Also called White Plains Drapery Uphl Inc (G-8050)*
Commercial Fabrics Inc 716 694-0641
908 Niagara Falls Blvd North Tonawanda (14120) *(G-12966)*
Commercial Gaskets New York 212 244-8130
247 W 38th St Rm 409 New York (10018) *(G-9685)*
Commercial Millworks Inc 315 475-7479
221 W Division St Syracuse (13204) *(G-15902)*
Commercial Press Inc 315 274-0028
6589 Us Highway 11 Canton (13617) *(G-3381)*
Commercial Print & Imaging 716 597-0100
4778 Main St Buffalo (14226) *(G-2882)*
Commercial Solutions Inc 716 731-5825
6359 Ward Rd Sanborn (14132) *(G-15118)*
Commify Technology 917 603-1822
228 Park Ave S New York (10003) *(G-9686)*
Commitment 2000 Inc 716 439-1206
105 Msgr Valente Dr Buffalo (14206) *(G-2883)*
Committee For Color & Trends, New York *Also called Cct Inc (G-9552)*
Commodity Resource Corporation 585 538-9500
2773 Caledonia Leroy Rd Caledonia (14423) *(G-3278)*
Commodore Chocolatier USA Inc 845 561-3960
482 Broadway Newburgh (12550) *(G-12753)*
Commodore Machine Co Inc 585 657-6916
26 Maple Ave Bloomfield (14469) *(G-984)*
Commodore Manufacutring Corp 718 788-2600
3913 2nd Ave Brooklyn (11232) *(G-1795)*
Commodore Plastics LLC 585 657-7777
26 Maple Ave Bloomfield (14469) *(G-985)*
Commodore Tool, Brooklyn *Also called Commodore Manufacutring Corp (G-1795)*
Common Sense Natural Soap, Cambridge *Also called Robert Racine (G-3309)*
Common Sense Natural Soap 518 677-0224
7 Pearl St Cambridge (12816) *(G-3306)*
Commonweal Foundation Inc 212 662-4200
475 Riverside Dr Rm 405 New York (10115) *(G-9687)*
Commonweal Magazine, New York *Also called Commonweal Foundation Inc (G-9687)*
Commonwealth Home Fashion Inc 514 384-8290
31 Station Rd Willsboro (12996) *(G-17264)*
Commonwealth Toy Novelty Inc (PA) 212 242-4070
45 W 25th St Fl 7 New York (10010) *(G-9688)*
Commscope Technologies LLC 315 768-3573
5662 Mohawk St Marcy (13403) *(G-8090)*
Communication Power Corp 631 434-7306
80 Davids Dr Ste 3 Hauppauge (11788) *(G-6051)*
Communications & Energy Corp 315 446-5723
204 Ambergate Rd Syracuse (13214) *(G-15903)*
Communications Systems Div, Farmingdale *Also called Telephonics Corporation (G-5126)*
Community Cpons Frnchising Inc 516 277-1968
100 Carney St Ste 2 Glen Cove (11542) *(G-5613)*
Community Directory, Brooklyn *Also called Business Directory Inc (G-1740)*
Community Glass Inc 607 737-8860
139 W 17th St Elmira (14903) *(G-4676)*
Community Magazine, Brooklyn *Also called Bnei Aram Soba Inc (G-1707)*
Community Media Group LLC (PA) 518 439-4949
125 Adams St Delmar (12054) *(G-4244)*
Community Media LLC 212 229-1890
515 Canal St Fl 1 New York (10013) *(G-9689)*
Community News Group LLC (PA) 718 260-2500
1 Metrotech Ctr Fl 10 Brooklyn (11201) *(G-1796)*
Community Newspaper Group LLC 607 432-1000
102 Chestnut St Oneonta (13820) *(G-13181)*
Community Newspaper Group LLC 518 565-4114
170 Margaret St Plattsburgh (12901) *(G-13660)*
Community Newspapers, Moravia *Also called Republican Registrar Inc (G-8617)*
Community Newsppr Holdings Inc 585 798-1400
541-543 Main St Medina (14103) *(G-8269)*
Community Newsppr Holdings Inc 716 693-1000
473 3rd St Ste 201 Niagara Falls (14301) *(G-12805)*
Community Newsppr Holdings Inc 716 282-2311
473 3rd St Ste 201 Niagara Falls (14301) *(G-12806)*
Community Newsppr Holdings Inc 716 439-9222
135 Main St Ste 1 Lockport (14094) *(G-7577)*
Community Playthings, Chester *Also called Community Products LLC (G-3603)*
Community Playthings, Elka Park *Also called Church Communities NY Inc (G-4629)*
Community Playthings, Elka Park *Also called Church Communities NY Inc (G-4630)*
COMMUNITY PLAYTHINGS AND RIFTO, Rifton *Also called Community Products LLC (G-14132)*
Community Products LLC (PA) 845 658-8799
2032 Route 213 St Rifton (12471) *(G-14132)*
Community Products LLC 845 658-7720
359 Gibson Hill Rd Chester (10918) *(G-3603)*
Community Products LLC 845 572-3433
24 Elizabeth Dr Chester (10918) *(G-3604)*
Community Products LLC 845 658-8351
2032 Route 213 St Rifton (12471) *(G-14133)*
Community Products LLC 518 589-5103
2255 Platte Clove Rd Elka Park (12427) *(G-4631)*
Compar Manufacturing Corp 212 304-2777
308 Dyckman St New York (10034) *(G-9690)*
Compass Printing Plus 518 891-7050
42 Main St Saranac Lake (12983) *(G-15135)*
Compass Printing Plus (PA) 518 523-3308
42 Main St Saranac Lake (12983) *(G-15136)*
Competicion Mower Repair 516 280-6584
75 Windsor Ave Mineola (11501) *(G-8504)*
Complemar Print LLC 716 875-7238
3034 Genesee St Buffalo (14225) *(G-2884)*
Complete Orthopedic Svcs Inc 516 357-9113
2094 Front St East Meadow (11554) *(G-4420)*

ALPHABETIC

Complete Publishing Solutions 212 242-7321
350 W 51st St Apt 13b New York (10019) *(G-9691)*
Complete SEC & Contrls Inc 631 421-7200
100 Hillwood Dr Huntington Station (11746) *(G-6700)*
Complex Biosystems Inc 315 464-8007
8266 Warbler Way Apt C6 Liverpool (13090) *(G-7517)*
Complex Magazine, New York *Also called CMX Media LLC (G-9649)*
Complex Media Inc (PA) 917 793-5831
1271 Avenue Of Americas New York (10020) *(G-9692)*
Complystream, New York *Also called Thinktrek Inc (G-12318)*
Composite Forms Inc 914 937-1808
7 Merritt St Port Chester (10573) *(G-13740)*
Composite Systems & Tech LLC 716 491-8490
21 Trade Rd Massena (13662) *(G-8192)*
Compositech Ltd 516 835-1458
4 Fairbanks Blvd Woodbury (11797) *(G-17284)*
Compoz A Puzzle Inc 516 883-2311
2 Secatoag Ave Port Washington (11050) *(G-13806)*
Comprehensive Dental Tech 607 467-4456
Rr 1 Box 69 Hancock (13783) *(G-5963)*
Comps Inc 516 676-0400
3 School St Ste 101b Glen Cove (11542) *(G-5614)*
Compucolor Associates Inc 516 358-0000
2200 Marcus Ave Ste C New Hyde Park (11042) *(G-8823)*
Compumatic Time Recorders Inc 718 531-5749
1518 Bellmore Ave North Bellmore (11710) *(G-12917)*
Computer Conversions Corp 631 261-3300
6 Dunton Ct East Northport (11731) *(G-4434)*
Computer Instruments Corp 516 876-8400
963a Brush Hollow Rd Westbury (11590) *(G-16975)*
Computerized Metal Bending Ser 631 249-1177
91 Cabot St Unit A West Babylon (11704) *(G-16785)*
Comsec Ventures International 518 523-1600
17 Tamarack Ave Lake Placid (12946) *(G-7273)*
Comstock Food, Leicester *Also called Seneca Foods Corporation (G-7422)*
Comstock Foods Division, South Dayton *Also called Birds Eye Foods Inc (G-15517)*
Comtech PST Corp (HQ) 631 777-8900
105 Baylis Rd Melville (11747) *(G-8306)*
Comtech Telecom Corp (PA) 631 962-7000
68 S Service Rd Ste 230 Melville (11747) *(G-8307)*
Con Rel Auto Electric Inc 518 356-1646
3637 Carman Rd Schenectady (12303) *(G-15245)*
Conax Technologies LLC (PA) 716 684-4500
2300 Walden Ave Buffalo (14225) *(G-2885)*
Concept Components, Bohemia *Also called McGuigan Inc (G-1103)*
Concept One Accessories, New York *Also called Uspa Accessories LLC (G-12492)*
Concept Printing and Promotion, Nyack *Also called Concept Printing Inc (G-13047)*
Concept Printing Inc 845 353-4040
40 Lydecker St Nyack (10960) *(G-13047)*
Concepts In Wood of CNY 315 463-8084
4021 New Court Ave Syracuse (13206) *(G-15904)*
Concepts New York, The, Brooklyn *Also called Milla Global Inc (G-2315)*
Concepts Nyc Inc 212 244-1033
20 W 33rd St Fl 9 New York (10001) *(G-9693)*
Concinnity Division, Melville *Also called I W Industries Inc (G-8330)*
Concord Express Cargo Inc 718 276-7200
17214 119th Ave Jamaica (11434) *(G-6906)*
Concord Jewelry Mfg Co LLC 212 719-4030
64 W 48th St Ste 1004 New York (10036) *(G-9694)*
Concord Jwlry Mfrs, New York *Also called Concord Jewelry Mfg Co LLC (G-9694)*
Concord Settings, New York *Also called Kaprielian Enterprises Inc (G-10808)*
Concorde Apparel Company LLC (PA) 212 307-7848
55 W 39th St Fl 11 New York (10018) *(G-9695)*
Concrete Mixer Supplycom Inc (PA) 716 375-5565
1721 Cornell Dr Olean (14760) *(G-13139)*
Cond Nast's, New York *Also called Conde Nast International Inc (G-9697)*
Conde Nast (PA) 212 630-3642
750 3rd Ave Fl 8 New York (10017) *(G-9696)*
Conde Nast International Inc (PA) 212 286-2860
1 World Trade Ctr New York (10007) *(G-9697)*
Conde Nast Publications, New York *Also called Advance Magazine Publs Inc (G-9037)*
Conde Nast Publications Div, New York *Also called Advance Magazine Publs Inc (G-9038)*
Conde Pumps Div, Sherrill *Also called Westmoor Ltd (G-15410)*
Condeco Software Inc (HQ) 917 677-7600
370 Lexington Ave Rm 1409 New York (10017) *(G-9698)*
Condor Electronics Corp 585 235-1500
295 Mount Read Blvd Rochester (14611) *(G-14284)*
Cone Buddy System Inc 585 427-9940
3495 Winton Pl Ste E290 Rochester (14623) *(G-14285)*
Conesus Lake Association Inc 585 346-6864
5828 Big Tree Rd Lakeville (14480) *(G-7283)*
Confer Plastics Inc 800 635-3213
97 Witmer Rd North Tonawanda (14120) *(G-12967)*
Conference Board Inc (PA) 212 759-0900
845 3rd Ave Fl 2 New York (10022) *(G-9699)*
Conformer Products Inc 516 504-6300
60 Cuttermill Rd Ste 411 Great Neck (11021) *(G-5800)*
Confrtrnity of Prescious Blood 718 436-1120
5300 Fort Hamilton Pkwy Brooklyn (11219) *(G-1797)*
Congress For Jewish Culture 212 505-8040
1133 Broadway Ste 1019 New York (10010) *(G-9700)*
Conic Systems Inc 845 856-4053
11 Rebel Ln Port Jervis (12771) *(G-13782)*
Conkur Printing Co Inc 212 541-5980
121 Varick St Rm 400 New York (10013) *(G-9701)*
Conley Caseworks Inc 716 655-5830
580 Conley Rd Elma (14059) *(G-4647)*
Conmed Andover Medical Inc (HQ) 315 797-8375
525 French Rd Ste 3 Utica (13502) *(G-16314)*
Conmed Corporation 315 797-8375
525 French Rd Utica (13502) *(G-16315)*
Conmed Corporation (PA) 315 797-8375
525 French Rd Ste 3 Utica (13502) *(G-16316)*
Connecticut Bus Systems LLC 914 696-1900
108 Corporate Park Dr # 118 White Plains (10604) *(G-17096)*
Connection Mold Inc 585 458-6463
585 Ling Rd Rochester (14612) *(G-14286)*
Connectiva Systems Inc 646 722-8741
19 W 44th St Ste 611 New York (10036) *(G-9702)*
Connex Grinding & Machining 315 946-4340
65 Clyde Rd Lyons (14489) *(G-7971)*
Connie Cleaners, Great Neck *Also called Connie French Cleaners Inc (G-5801)*
Connie French Cleaners Inc 516 487-1343
801 Middle Neck Rd Great Neck (11024) *(G-5801)*
Connie's T Shirt Shop, East Northport *Also called Island Silkscreen Inc (G-4437)*
Connies Laundry 716 822-2800
1494 S Park Ave Buffalo (14220) *(G-2886)*
Connover Packaging Inc 585 377-2510
119 Despatch Dr East Rochester (14445) *(G-4456)*
Conopco Inc 585 647-8322
28 Mansfield St Rochester (14606) *(G-14287)*
Conrad Blasius Equipment Co 516 753-1200
199 Newtown Rd Plainview (11803) *(G-13590)*
Consoldted Precision Pdts Corp 315 687-0014
901 E Genesee St Chittenango (13037) *(G-3630)*
Consolidated Barricades Inc 518 922-7944
179 Dillenbeck Rd Fultonville (12072) *(G-5478)*
Consolidated Childrens AP Inc (HQ) 212 239-8615
100 W 33rd St Ste 1105 New York (10001) *(G-9703)*
Consolidated Color Press Inc 212 929-8197
307 7th Ave Rm 602 New York (10001) *(G-9704)*
Consolidated Container Co LLC 585 262-6470
18 Champeney Ter Rochester (14605) *(G-14288)*
Consolidated Container Co LLC 585 343-9351
14 Hall St Batavia (14020) *(G-629)*
Consolidated Edison Co NY Inc 914 933-2936
511 Theodore Fremd Ave Rye (10580) *(G-15055)*
Consolidated Fashion Corp 212 719-3000
225 W 39th St Fl 12 New York (10018) *(G-9705)*
Consolidated Loose Leaf Inc (PA) 212 924-5800
989 Avnue Of The Americas New York (10018) *(G-9706)*
Constas Printing Corporation 315 474-2176
1120 Burnet Ave Syracuse (13203) *(G-15905)*
Constellation Brands Inc (PA) 585 678-7100
207 High Point Dr # 100 Victor (14564) *(G-16469)*
Constellation Brands Inc 585 393-4880
3325 Marvin Sands Dr Canandaigua (14424) *(G-3339)*
Constellation Brands Smo LLC 585 396-7161
111 8th Ave New York (10011) *(G-9707)*
Constellation Brands US Oprs 585 396-7600
116 Buffalo St Canandaigua (14424) *(G-3340)*
Constellation Brands US Oprs (HQ) 585 396-7600
235 N Bloomfield Rd Canandaigua (14424) *(G-3341)*
Constellium 212 675-5087
830 3rd Ave Rm 901 New York (10022) *(G-9708)*
Construction Parts Whse Inc 315 445-1310
5841 Butternut Dr East Syracuse (13057) *(G-4519)*
Construction Technology Inc (PA) 914 747-8900
400 Columbus Ave Ste 110s Valhalla (10595) *(G-16366)*
Consumer Audio Facility, Woodbury *Also called Harman International Inds Inc (G-17289)*
Consumer Flavoring Extract Co 718 435-0201
921 Mcdonald Ave Brooklyn (11218) *(G-1798)*
Consumer Reports, Yonkers *Also called Consumers Union US Inc (G-17429)*
Consumers Beverages Inc 716 837-3087
3025 Sheridan Dr Buffalo (14226) *(G-2887)*
Consumers Beverages Inc 716 675-4934
1375 Union Rd West Seneca (14224) *(G-16942)*
Consumers Union US Inc (PA) 914 378-2000
101 Truman Ave Yonkers (10703) *(G-17429)*
Contactive Inc 646 476-9059
137 Varick St Ste 605 New York (10013) *(G-9709)*
Container Tstg Solutions LLC 716 487-3300
17 Tiffany Ave Jamestown (14701) *(G-6983)*
Container Tstg Solutions LLC (PA) 716 487-3300
17 Lester St Sinclairville (14782) *(G-15453)*
Contech Engnered Solutions LLC 716 870-9091
34 Birdsong Pkwy Orchard Park (14127) *(G-13265)*
Contempra Design Inc 718 984-8586
20 Grille Ct Staten Island (10309) *(G-15662)*
Conti Auto Body Corp 516 921-6435
44 Jericho Tpke Syosset (11791) *(G-15816)*

ALPHABETIC

Continental Buchanan LLC 703 480-3800
350 Broadway Buchanan (10511) *(G-2785)*
Continental Cordage Corp (HQ) 315 655-9800
75 Burton St Cazenovia (13035) *(G-3443)*
Continental Instruments LLC (HQ) 631 842-9400
355 Bayview Ave Amityville (11701) *(G-281)*
Continental Knitting Mills 631 242-5330
156 Brook Ave Deer Park (11729) *(G-4120)*
Continental Kraft Corp 516 681-9090
100 Jericho Quadrangle # 219 Jericho (11753) *(G-7063)*
Continental Latex Corp 718 783-7883
1489 Shore Pkwy Apt 1g Brooklyn (11214) *(G-1799)*
Continental Lift Truck Inc 718 738-4738
12718 Foch Blvd South Ozone Park (11420) *(G-15532)*
Continental Quilting Co Inc 718 499-9100
72 87th St Brooklyn (11209) *(G-1800)*
Continuity Publishing Inc 212 869-4170
15 W 39th St Fl 9 New York (10018) *(G-9710)*
Continuity Software Inc 646 216-8628
5 Penn Plz Fl 23 New York (10001) *(G-9711)*
Continuum Intl Pubg Group Inc 646 649-4215
15 W 26th St Fl 8 New York (10010) *(G-9712)*
Contract Pharmacal Corp 631 231-4610
110 Plant Ave Hauppauge (11788) *(G-6052)*
Contract Pharmacal Corp 631 231-4610
1324 Motor Pkwy Hauppauge (11749) *(G-6053)*
Contract Pharmacal Corp 631 231-4610
250 Kennedy Dr Hauppauge (11788) *(G-6054)*
Contract Pharmacal Corp 631 231-4610
145 Oser Ave Hauppauge (11788) *(G-6055)*
Contract Pharmacal Corp 631 231-4610
160 Commerce Dr Hauppauge (11788) *(G-6056)*
Contract Pharmacal Corp 631 231-4610
150 Commerce Dr Hauppauge (11788) *(G-6057)*
Contract Phrmctcals Ltd Nagara 716 887-3400
100 Forest Ave Buffalo (14213) *(G-2888)*
Control Elec Div Fil-Coil, Sayville *Also called Esc Control Electronics LLC* *(G-15208)*
Control Electropolishing Corp 718 858-6634
109 Walworth St Brooklyn (11205) *(G-1801)*
Control Global Solutions, Halfmoon *Also called Ebeling Associates Inc* *(G-5910)*
Control Logic Corporation 607 965-6423
2533 State Highway 80 West Burlington (13482) *(G-16841)*
Control Research Inc 631 225-1111
385 Bayview Ave Unit C Amityville (11701) *(G-282)*
Controlled Castings Corp 516 349-1718
31 Commercial Ct Plainview (11803) *(G-13591)*
Convenience Store News 214 217-7800
770 Broadway Fl 5 New York (10003) *(G-9713)*
Convergent Audio Tech Inc 585 359-2700
85 High Tech Dr Rush (14543) *(G-15046)*
Convergent Cnnctivity Tech Inc 845 651-5250
1751 State Route 17a Florida (10921) *(G-5211)*
Convergent Med MGT Svcs LLC 718 921-6159
7513 3rd Ave Brooklyn (11209) *(G-1802)*
Conversant LLC 212 471-9570
150 E 62nd St New York (10065) *(G-9714)*
Converter Design Inc (PA) 518 745-7138
25 Murdock Ave Glens Falls (12801) *(G-5675)*
Coocoo SMS Inc 646 459-4260
356 New York Ave Ste 1 Huntington (11743) *(G-6659)*
Cookie Connection Inc 315 422-2253
705 Park Ave Syracuse (13204) *(G-15906)*
Cookie Factory, Bronx *Also called Golden Glow Cookie Co Inc* *(G-1345)*
Cookie Factory LLC 518 268-1060
520 Congress St Troy (12180) *(G-16232)*
Cookie Pnache By Bet The Bread 212 757-4145
250 W 54th St New York (10019) *(G-9715)*
Cookiebaker LLC 716 878-8000
1 Robert Rich Way Buffalo (14213) *(G-2889)*
Cookies Inc 646 452-5552
1 E 33rd St Fl 6 New York (10016) *(G-9716)*
Cookies United LLC 631 581-4000
141 Freeman Ave Islip (11751) *(G-6807)*
Cooking With Chef Michelle LLC 516 662-2324
4603 Middle Country Rd Calverton (11933) *(G-3289)*
Cooks Intl Ltd Lblty Co 212 741-4407
7 World Trade Ctr Fl 46 New York (10007) *(G-9717)*
Coolit, Scarsdale *Also called Spaghetti Bridge LLC* *(G-15224)*
Coomer McLoud, Queensbury *Also called Car Essentials Inc* *(G-13994)*
Cooper & Clement Inc 315 454-8135
1840 Lemoyne Ave Syracuse (13208) *(G-15907)*
Cooper Crouse Hinds Elec Pdts, Syracuse *Also called Cooper Crouse-Hinds LLC* *(G-15908)*
Cooper Crouse-Hinds LLC (HQ) 315 477-7000
1201 Wolf St Syracuse (13208) *(G-15908)*
Cooper Industries LLC 315 477-7000
Wolf & 7th North St Syracuse (13208) *(G-15909)*
Cooper Lighting LLC 516 470-1000
100 Andrews Rd Ste 1 Hicksville (11801) *(G-6334)*
Cooper Molded Products, Syracuse *Also called Cooper Industries LLC* *(G-15909)*
Cooper Power Systems LLC 716 375-7100
1648 Dugan Rd Olean (14760) *(G-13140)*
Cooper Turbocompressor Inc (HQ) 716 896-6600
3101 Broadway St Buffalo (14227) *(G-2890)*
Cooperfriedman Elc Sup Co Inc 718 269-4906
2219 41st Ave Long Island City (11101) *(G-7704)*
Coopers Cave Ale Co S-Corp 518 792-0007
2 Sagamore St Glens Falls (12801) *(G-5676)*
Cooperstown Bat Co Inc (PA) 607 547-2415
Rr 28 Fly Creek (13337) *(G-5314)*
Cooperstown Bat Co Inc 607 547-2415
118 Main St Cooperstown (13326) *(G-3884)*
Cooperstown Brewing Co LLC 607 286-9330
110 River St Milford (13807) *(G-8473)*
Coopervision Inc 585 385-6810
180 Thruway Park Dr West Henrietta (14586) *(G-16874)*
Coopervision Inc 585 889-3301
711 North Rd Scottsville (14546) *(G-15335)*
Coopervision Inc 585 385-6810
209 High Point Dr Victor (14564) *(G-16470)*
Coopervision Inc (HQ) 585 385-6810
209 High Point Dr Victor (14564) *(G-16471)*
Copeland Coating Company Inc 518 766-2932
3600 Us Highway 20 Nassau (12123) *(G-8771)*
Copen International Limited, New York *Also called Cai Inc* *(G-9497)*
Copen United LLC 212 819-0008
37 W 39th St Rm 603 New York (10018) *(G-9718)*
Copesetic Inc 315 684-7780
62 E Main St Morrisville (13408) *(G-8620)*
Copia Interactive LLC 212 481-0520
105 Madison Ave New York (10016) *(G-9719)*
Copier & Printer Supply LLC 585 329-1077
27 Locke Dr Mendon (14506) *(G-8380)*
Copper John Corporation 315 258-9269
173 State St Auburn (13021) *(G-489)*
Copper Ridge Oil Inc 716 372-4021
111 W 2nd St Ste 404 Jamestown (14701) *(G-6984)*
Copy Color Inc 212 889-6202
307 W 36th St Fl 10 New York (10018) *(G-9720)*
Copy Corner Inc 718 388-4545
200 Division Ave Brooklyn (11211) *(G-1803)*
Copy Room Inc 212 371-8600
885 3rd Ave Lowr 2ll New York (10022) *(G-9721)*
Copy Stop Inc 914 428-5188
50 Main St Ste 32 White Plains (10606) *(G-17097)*
Copy X/Press Ltd 631 585-2200
700 Union Pkwy Ste 5 Ronkonkoma (11779) *(G-14888)*
Copy4les Inc 212 487-9778
146 W 29th St Rm 9w New York (10001) *(G-9722)*
Cora Materials Corp 516 488-6300
30 Nassau Terminal Rd New Hyde Park (11040) *(G-8824)*
Cora Matrls, New Hyde Park *Also called Cora Materials Corp* *(G-8824)*
Coral Blood Service 800 483-4888
525 Executive Blvd # 285 Elmsford (10523) *(G-4743)*
Coral Cast LLC 516 349-1300
31 Commercial Ct Plainview (11803) *(G-13592)*
Coral Color Process Ltd 631 543-5200
50 Mall Dr Commack (11725) *(G-3829)*
Coral Graphic Services Inc (HQ) 516 576-2100
840 S Broadway Hicksville (11801) *(G-6335)*
Coral Graphic Services Inc 516 576-2100
840 S Broadway Hicksville (11801) *(G-6336)*
Coral Graphic Svce, Hicksville *Also called Coral Graphic Services Inc* *(G-6335)*
Coral Management Corp 718 893-9286
923 Bryant Ave Bronx (10474) *(G-1304)*
Corbertex LLC 212 971-0008
1412 Broadway Rm 1100 New York (10018) *(G-9723)*
Corbett Hill Gravel Products, Jamestown *Also called Jamestown Macadam Inc* *(G-7009)*
Corbett Stves Pttern Works Inc 585 546-7109
80 Lowell St Rochester (14605) *(G-14289)*
Core Welding, Sanborn *Also called Bruce Pierce* *(G-15115)*
Coremet Trading Inc 212 964-3600
160 Brdwy Ste 1107 New York (10038) *(G-9724)*
Corey Creek Vineyards, Cutchogue *Also called Vedell North Fork LLC* *(G-4074)*
Corey Rugs, Great Neck *Also called Rosecore Division* *(G-5835)*
Corfu Machine Inc (PA) 585 418-4083
1977 Genesee St Corfu (14036) *(G-3953)*
Corian Design Studio, New York *Also called Evans & Paul Unlimited Corp* *(G-10088)*
Corinne McCormack Inc 212 868-7919
7 W 36th St Fl 9 New York (10018) *(G-9725)*
Corinthian Cast Stone Inc 631 920-2340
115 Wyandanch Ave Wyandanch (11798) *(G-17374)*
Corium Corporation (PA) 914 381-0100
147 Palmer Ave Mamaroneck (10543) *(G-8030)*
Corkhill Grp, Jamaica *Also called Corkhill Manufacturing Co Inc* *(G-6907)*
Corkhill Manufacturing Co Inc 718 528-7413
13121 Merrick Blvd Jamaica (11434) *(G-6907)*
Cornell Beverages Inc 718 381-3000
105 Harrison Pl Brooklyn (11237) *(G-1804)*
Cornell Laboratory Ornithology, Ithaca *Also called Cornell University* *(G-6834)*
Cornell University 607 277-2338
512 E State St Ithaca (14850) *(G-6833)*
Cornell University 607 254-2473
159 Sapsucker Woods Rd Ithaca (14850) *(G-6834)*

ALPHABETIC

Cornell University 607 255-0897
152 Riley Robb Hall Ithaca (14853) *(G-6835)*
Cornell University Press, Ithaca *Also called Cornell University* *(G-6833)*
Corning Cable Systems Cr Un 607 974-9000
1 Riverfront Plz Corning (14831) *(G-3960)*
Corning Consumer Products Co, Corning *Also called Corning Vitro Corporation* *(G-3971)*
Corning Inc 607 974-9000
1 Riverfront Plz Corning (14831) *(G-3961)*
Corning Incorporated (PA) 607 974-9000
1 Riverfront Plz Corning (14831) *(G-3962)*
Corning Incorporated 607 974-9000
Decker Bldg Corning (14831) *(G-3963)*
Corning Incorporated 607 974-1274
905 Addison Rd Painted Post (14870) *(G-13390)*
Corning Incorporated 607 974-9000
1 Riverfront Plz Corning (14831) *(G-3964)*
Corning Incorporated 315 379-3200
334 County Route 16 Canton (13617) *(G-3382)*
Corning Incorporated 607 433-3100
275 River St Oneonta (13820) *(G-13182)*
Corning Incorporated 607 974-0206
271 County Rt 64 Big Flats (14814) *(G-880)*
Corning Incorporated 607 248-1200
Hp-Ab-01-A9b Corning (14831) *(G-3965)*
Corning Incorporated 607 974-0206
271 Rr 64 Big Flats (14814) *(G-881)*
Corning Incorporated 646 521-9600
767 5th Ave Ste 2301 New York (10153) *(G-9726)*
Corning Incorporated 607 974-6729
9261 Addison Rd Painted Post (14870) *(G-13391)*
Corning Incorporated 607 974-4488
1 W Market St Ste 601 Corning (14830) *(G-3966)*
Corning Incorporated 607 974-8496
1 Museum Way Corning (14830) *(G-3967)*
Corning International Corp (HQ) 607 974-9000
1 Riverfront Plz Corning (14831) *(G-3968)*
Corning Optcal Cmmncations LLC 607 974-7543
22 W 3rd St Corning (14830) *(G-3969)*
Corning Rubber Company Inc 631 738-0041
1744 Julia Goldbach Ave Ronkonkoma (11779) *(G-14889)*
Corning Specialty Mtls Inc 607 974-9000
1 Riverfront Plz Corning (14831) *(G-3970)*
Corning Tropel Corporation 585 377-3200
60 Oconnor Rd Fairport (14450) *(G-4852)*
Corning Vitro Corporation 607 974-8605
1 Riverfront Plz Corning (14830) *(G-3971)*
Corning Wax, Ronkonkoma *Also called Corning Rubber Company Inc* *(G-14889)*
Cornwall Local, Cornwall *Also called News of The Highlands Inc* *(G-3990)*
Corona Ready Mix Inc 718 271-5940
5025 97th Pl Corona (11368) *(G-3995)*
Coronet Kitchen & Bath, Ronkonkoma *Also called Dak Mica and Wood Products* *(G-14892)*
Coronet Parts Mfg Co Inc (PA) 718 649-1750
883 Elton St Brooklyn (11208) *(G-1805)*
Coronet Parts Mfg Co Inc 718 649-1750
901 Elton St Fl 1 Brooklyn (11208) *(G-1806)*
Corpkit Legal Supplies, Islip *Also called Rike Enterprises Inc* *(G-6812)*
Corporate News, Pearl River *Also called 21st Century Fox America Inc* *(G-13454)*
Corporate Offices & Plant, Brooklyn *Also called Victoria Fine Foods LLC* *(G-2725)*
Cort Contracting 845 758-1190
188 W Market St Red Hook (12571) *(G-14028)*
Cortice Biosciences Inc 646 747-9090
1345 Avenue Of The Americ New York (10105) *(G-9727)*
Cortland, Cortland *Also called Actuant Corporation* *(G-4011)*
Cortland Company Inc (HQ) 607 753-8276
44 River St Cortland (13045) *(G-4017)*
Cortland Industries Inc 212 575-2710
1400 Broadway New York (10018) *(G-9728)*
Cortland Line Mfg LLC 607 756-2851
3736 Kellogg Rd Cortland (13045) *(G-4018)*
Cortland Machine and Tool Co 607 756-5852
60 Grant St Cortland (13045) *(G-4019)*
Cortland Plastics Intl LLC 607 662-0120
211 S Main St Cortland (13045) *(G-4020)*
Cortland Ready Mix, Cortland *Also called Saunders Concrete Co Inc* *(G-4044)*
Cortland Ready Mix Inc 607 753-3063
6 Locust Ave Ofc Rte 13 Cortland (13045) *(G-4021)*
Cortland Standard Printing Co 607 756-5665
110 Main St Cortland (13045) *(G-4022)*
Cortland-Ithaca Subn Shopper, Freeville *Also called Freeville Publishing Co Inc* *(G-5435)*
Corzane Cabinets, Farmingdale *Also called Kazac Inc* *(G-5024)*
Cos TEC Manufacturing Corp 631 589-7170
390 Knickerbocker Ave # 1 Bohemia (11716) *(G-1039)*
Cosa Xentaur Corporation (PA) 631 345-3434
84 Horseblock Rd Unit G Yaphank (11980) *(G-17389)*
Cosco Enterprises Inc 718 383-4488
1930 Troutman St Ridgewood (11385) *(G-14104)*
Cosco Soap & Detergent, Ridgewood *Also called Cosco Enterprises Inc* *(G-14104)*
Cosense Inc 516 364-9161
125 Coachman Pl W Syosset (11791) *(G-15817)*
Cosmetic World, New York *Also called Ledes Group Inc* *(G-10956)*

Cosmetics Plus Ltd 516 768-7250
23 Deep Wood Ln Amagansett (11930) *(G-213)*
Cosmic Enterprise 718 342-6257
147 Rockaway Ave Ste A Brooklyn (11233) *(G-1807)*
Cosmicoat of Wny Inc 716 772-2644
8419 East Ave Gasport (14067) *(G-5556)*
Cosmo Electronic Machine Corp 631 249-2535
113 Gazza Blvd Farmingdale (11735) *(G-4962)*
Cosmo Optics, Albany *Also called Ion Optics Inc* *(G-90)*
Cosmopolitan Cabinet Company 631 467-4960
40 Fleetwood Ct Ste 1 Ronkonkoma (11779) *(G-14890)*
Cosmos Communications Inc 718 482-1800
1105 44th Dr Long Island City (11101) *(G-7705)*
Cosmos Electronic Machine Corp (PA) 631 249-2535
140 Schmitt Blvd Farmingdale (11735) *(G-4963)*
Cossitt Concrete Products Inc 315 824-2700
6543 Middleport Rd Hamilton (13346) *(G-5947)*
Costanza Ready Mix Inc 516 334-7788
1345 Newbridge Rd North Bellmore (11710) *(G-12918)*
Costanzos Bakery Inc 716 656-9093
30 Innsbruck Dr Buffalo (14227) *(G-2891)*
Costanzos Welding Inc (PA) 716 282-0845
22nd Allen St Niagara Falls (14302) *(G-12807)*
Costello Bros Petroleum Corp (PA) 914 237-3189
990 Mclean Ave Ste 3 Yonkers (10704) *(G-17430)*
Costello Tagliapietra, New York *Also called CTS LLC* *(G-9763)*
Costume Armour Inc 845 534-9120
2 Mill St Stop 4 Cornwall (12518) *(G-3987)*
Costume Culture By Franco LLC 718 821-7100
7030 80th St Glendale (11385) *(G-5649)*
Cote Hardwood Products Inc (PA) 607 898-5737
4725 Cat Path Rd Locke (13092) *(G-7568)*
Cote Wood Products, Locke *Also called Cote Hardwood Products Inc* *(G-7568)*
Coto Technology, New York *Also called Kearney-National Inc* *(G-10828)*
Cotswolt Industries, New York *Also called Central Textiles Inc* *(G-9566)*
Cott Beverages, Dunkirk *Also called Cliffstar LLC* *(G-4337)*
Cotton Emporium Inc (PA) 718 894-3365
8000 Cooper Ave Glendale (11385) *(G-5650)*
Cotton Express Inc 212 921-4588
1407 Broadway Rm 1807 New York (10018) *(G-9729)*
Cotton Tail Shop, Flushing *Also called Steve Zinn* *(G-5298)*
Cotton Well Drilling Co Inc 716 672-2788
Center Rd Sheridan (14135) *(G-15400)*
Cottonwood Metals Inc 646 807-8674
1625 Sycamore Ave Ste A Bohemia (11716) *(G-1040)*
Cottrell Paper Company Inc 518 885-1702
1135 Rock City Rd Rock City Falls (12863) *(G-14777)*
Coty Inc (HQ) 212 389-7300
350 5th Ave Ste 2700 New York (10118) *(G-9730)*
Coty US LLC (HQ) 212 389-7000
350 5th Ave Fl C1700 New York (10118) *(G-9731)*
Coty US LLC 212 389-7000
726 Eab Plz Uniondale (11556) *(G-16291)*
Cougar Sport Inc 212 947-3054
55 W 39th St Rm 305 New York (10018) *(G-9732)*
Coughlin Printing Group, Watertown *Also called Christian Bus Endeavors Inc* *(G-16644)*
Coughlin Printing Group 315 788-8560
210 Court St Ste 10 Watertown (13601) *(G-16647)*
Councel For Sclar Hmnism Cscop, Amherst *Also called Center For Inquiry Inc* *(G-231)*
Counter Evolution 212 647-7505
37 W 17th St New York (10011) *(G-9733)*
Countertop Creations, Rochester *Also called Frank J Martello* *(G-14381)*
Countertops & Cabinets Inc 315 433-1038
4073 New Court Ave Syracuse (13206) *(G-15910)*
Countess Corporation 212 869-7070
225 W 37th St Fl 12 New York (10018) *(G-9734)*
Countess Mara Inc 212 768-7300
120 W 45th St Fl 37 New York (10036) *(G-9735)*
Country Coin-Op, Newport *Also called Reynolds Drapery Service Inc* *(G-12792)*
Country Printer, The, Huntington *Also called Photo Agents Ltd* *(G-6674)*
Country Side Sand & Gravel (HQ) 716 988-3271
Taylor Hollow Rd Collins (14034) *(G-3815)*
Country Side Sand & Gravel 716 988-3271
8458 Route 62 South Dayton (14138) *(G-15519)*
County Draperies Inc 845 342-9009
64 Genung St Middletown (10940) *(G-8433)*
County Energy Corp 718 626-7000
65 S 11th St Apt 1e Brooklyn (11249) *(G-1808)*
County Fabricators 914 741-0219
175 Marble Ave Pleasantville (10570) *(G-13713)*
County Line Stone Co Inc 716 542-5435
4515 Crittenden Rd Akron (14001) *(G-21)*
County Waste Management Inc 914 592-5007
565 Harrison Ave Harrison (10528) *(G-5981)*
County WD ApplInc & TV Srvc of 585 328-7417
95 Mount Read Blvd Ste 14 Rochester (14611) *(G-14290)*
Courage Clothing Co Inc 212 354-5690
1407 Broadway Rm 3604 New York (10018) *(G-9736)*
Courier Life Publications, Brooklyn *Also called Courier-Life Inc* *(G-1810)*
Courier Observer, Ogdensburg *Also called St Lawrence County Newspapers* *(G-13122)*

Courier Packaging Inc.....718 349-2390
220 West St Brooklyn (11222) **(G-1809)**

Courier Printing Corp.....607 467-2191
24 Laurel Bank Ave Ste 2 Deposit (13754) **(G-4277)**

Courier-Life Inc.....718 260-2500
1 Metrotech Ctr Brooklyn (11201) **(G-1810)**

Courser Inc.....607 739-3861
802 County Road 64 # 100 Elmira (14903) **(G-4677)**

Courtaulds Textiles Ltd.....212 946-8000
358 5th Ave Fl 6 New York (10001) **(G-9737)**

Courtlandt Boot Jack Co Inc.....718 445-6200
3334 Prince St Flushing (11354) **(G-5235)**

Cousin's Furniture, Deer Park *Also called Cousins Furniture & Hm Imprvs* **(G-4121)**

Cousins Furniture & Hm Imprvs.....631 254-3752
515 Acorn St Deer Park (11729) **(G-4121)**

Couture Inc.....212 921-1166
16 W 37th St Frnt 1 New York (10018) **(G-9738)**

Couture Logging Inc.....607 753-6445
3060 State Route 13 Cortland (13045) **(G-4023)**

Couture Press.....310 734-4831
200 Park Ave New York (10166) **(G-9739)**

Couture Timber Harvesting.....607 836-4719
2760 Phelps Rd Mc Graw (13101) **(G-8221)**

Cove Point Holdings LLC (PA).....212 599-3388
60 E 42nd St Rm 3210 New York (10165) **(G-9740)**

Coventry Manufacturing Co Inc (PA).....914 668-2212
115 E 3rd St Mount Vernon (10550) **(G-8674)**

Coventya Inc.....315 768-6635
132 Ceral Ln Oriskany (13424) **(G-13306)**

Coverall Manufacturing.....315 652-2731
3653 Hayes Rd Baldwinsville (13027) **(G-568)**

Covergrip Corporation.....855 268-3747
30 Aero Rd Bohemia (11716) **(G-1041)**

Covidien, Hobart *Also called Mallinckrodt LLC* **(G-6426)**

Covington Sound.....646 256-7486
2705 Kingsbridge Ter Bronx (10463) **(G-1305)**

Cowee Forest Products Inc.....518 658-2233
28 Taylor Ave Berlin (12022) **(G-855)**

Cox & Company Inc.....212 366-0200
1664 Old Country Rd Plainview (11803) **(G-13593)**

Coyote Moon LLC (PA).....315 686-5600
17371 County Route 3 Clayton (13624) **(G-3685)**

Coyote Moon Vineyards, Clayton *Also called Coyote Moon LLC* **(G-3685)**

Coyote Motorsports, Spencerport *Also called Bullet Industries Inc* **(G-15568)**

Cpac Inc (HQ).....585 382-3223
2364 State Route 20a Leicester (14481) **(G-7420)**

Cpac Equipment Inc.....585 382-3223
2364 State Route 20a Leicester (14481) **(G-7421)**

CPI, New York *Also called Capital Programs Inc* **(G-9520)**

CPI Aerostructures Inc.....631 586-5200
91 Heartland Blvd Edgewood (11717) **(G-4596)**

CPI Industries Inc.....631 909-3434
275 Dayton Ave Manorville (11949) **(G-8078)**

CPI of Falconer Inc.....716 664-4444
1890 Lyndon Blvd Falconer (14733) **(G-4894)**

Cpp - Guaymas.....315 687-0014
901 E Genesee St Chittenango (13037) **(G-3631)**

Cpp - Steel Treaters.....315 736-3081
100 Furnace St Oriskany (13424) **(G-13307)**

Cpp Global, Ronkonkoma *Also called Carolina Precision Plas LLC* **(G-14885)**

Cpp-Syracuse Inc (HQ).....315 687-0014
901 E Genesee St Chittenango (13037) **(G-3632)**

CPS Creative, New York *Also called Complete Publishing Solutions* **(G-9691)**

CPT Usa LLC (PA).....212 575-1616
15 W 39th St Fl 12 New York (10018) **(G-9741)**

CPW Direct Mail Group LLC.....631 588-6565
110 Schmitt Blvd Farmingdale (11735) **(G-4964)**

Cq Magazine, Hicksville *Also called C Q Communications Inc* **(G-6328)**

Cq Traffic Control Devices LLC.....518 767-0057
1521 Us Rte 9w Selkirk (12158) **(G-15354)**

Cq Traffic Control Products, Selkirk *Also called Cq Traffic Control Devices LLC* **(G-15354)**

Crabtree Publishing Inc.....212 496-5040
350 5th Ave Ste 3304 New York (10118) **(G-9742)**

Craft Atlantic, New York *Also called Craftatlantic LLC* **(G-9744)**

Craft Clerical Clothes Inc (PA).....212 764-6122
247 W 37th St Rm 1700 New York (10018) **(G-9743)**

Craft Custom Woodwork Co Inc.....718 821-2162
5949 56th Ave Maspeth (11378) **(G-8124)**

Craft Packaging Inc.....718 633-4045
1274 49th St Ste 350 Brooklyn (11219) **(G-1811)**

Craft Pak Inc.....718 257-2700
67 Gateway Dr Staten Island (10304) **(G-15663)**

Craft Robe Co., New York *Also called Craft Clerical Clothes Inc* **(G-9743)**

Craft-Pak Inc.....718 763-0700
2771 Strickland Ave Brooklyn (11234) **(G-1812)**

Craft-Tech Mfg Corp.....631 563-4949
1750 Artic Ave Bohemia (11716) **(G-1042)**

Craftatlantic LLC.....646 726-4205
115 Greenwich Ave New York (10014) **(G-9744)**

Craftech.....518 828-5011
5 Dock St Chatham (12037) **(G-3557)**

Craftech Industries Inc.....518 828-5001
8 Dock St Hudson (12534) **(G-6611)**

Crafters Workshop Inc.....914 345-2838
116 S Central Ave Ste 1 Elmsford (10523) **(G-4744)**

Craftmaster Flavor Technology.....631 789-8607
23 Albany Ave Amityville (11701) **(G-283)**

Craftsman Manufacturing Co In.....585 426-5780
1279 Mount Read Blvd Rochester (14606) **(G-14291)**

Craftsmen Woodworkers Ltd.....718 326-3350
5865 Maspeth Ave Maspeth (11378) **(G-8125)**

Craig Envelope Corp.....718 786-4277
1201 44th Ave Long Island City (11101) **(G-7706)**

Crain Communications Inc.....212 210-0100
685 3rd Ave New York (10017) **(G-9745)**

Crain News Service.....212 254-0890
440 E 23rd St New York (10010) **(G-9746)**

Crains New York Business.....212 210-0250
711 3rd Ave New York (10017) **(G-9747)**

Crainville Block Co, Queensbury *Also called Glens Falls Ready Mix Inc* **(G-13997)**

Crandall Filling Machinery Inc.....716 897-3486
80 Gruner Rd Buffalo (14227) **(G-2892)**

Crane Equipment & Service Inc (HQ).....716 689-5400
140 John Jmes Adubon Pkwy Amherst (14228) **(G-235)**

Cranesville Block Co Inc (PA).....518 684-6000
1250 Riverfront Ctr Amsterdam (12010) **(G-341)**

Cranesville Block Co Inc.....315 732-2135
895 Catherine St Utica (13501) **(G-16317)**

Cranesville Block Co Inc.....845 292-1585
1794 State Route 52 Liberty (12754) **(G-7436)**

Cranesville Block Co Inc.....845 896-5687
70 Route 9 Fishkill (12524) **(G-5182)**

Cranesville Block Co Inc.....315 773-2296
23903 Cemetery Rd Felts Mills (13638) **(G-5167)**

Cranesville Block Co Inc.....845 331-1775
637 E Chester St Kingston (12401) **(G-7185)**

Cranesville Block Co Inc.....315 384-4000
8405 State Highway 56 Norfolk (13667) **(G-12898)**

Cranesville Concrete, Norfolk *Also called Cranesville Block Co Inc* **(G-12898)**

Cranesville Concrete Co, Utica *Also called Cranesville Block Co Inc* **(G-16317)**

Cranesville Concrete Co, Liberty *Also called Cranesville Block Co Inc* **(G-7436)**

Cranesville Ready-Mix, Amsterdam *Also called Cranesville Block Co Inc* **(G-341)**

Crawford Furniture Mfg Corp.....716 483-2102
347 Broadhead Ave Jamestown (14701) **(G-6985)**

Crawford Print Shop Inc.....607 359-4970
6120 Herrington Rd Addison (14801) **(G-5)**

Craz Woodworking Assoc Inc.....631 205-1890
24 Sawgrass Dr Bellport (11713) **(G-828)**

Crazy Hatter, Holtsville *Also called Screen The World Inc* **(G-6508)**

Cream Bebe.....917 578-2088
694 Myrtle Ave Ste 220 Brooklyn (11205) **(G-1813)**

Create-A-Card Inc.....631 584-2273
16 Brasswood Rd Saint James (11780) **(G-15087)**

Creation Baumann USA Inc.....516 764-7431
114 N Centre Ave Rockville Centre (11570) **(G-14790)**

Creations In Canvas, Yonkers *Also called Dalee Bookbinding Co Inc* **(G-17434)**

Creations In Lucite Inc.....718 871-2000
165 Franklin Ave Apt 5 Brooklyn (11205) **(G-1814)**

Creative Cabinet Corp America.....631 751-5768
3 Onyx Dr Stony Brook (11790) **(G-15769)**

Creative Cabinetry Corporation.....914 963-6061
42 Morsemere Pl Yonkers (10701) **(G-17431)**

Creative Compositions, Amityville *Also called Jeffrey John* **(G-299)**

Creative Costume Co.....212 564-5552
242 W 36th St Rm 800 New York (10018) **(G-9748)**

Creative Counter Tops Inc.....845 471-6480
17 Van Kleeck Dr Poughkeepsie (12601) **(G-13894)**

Creative Custom Shades, Brooklyn *Also called Custom Lampshades Inc* **(G-1826)**

Creative Design and Mch Inc.....845 778-9001
197 Stone Castle Rd Rock Tavern (12575) **(G-14780)**

Creative Forms Inc.....212 431-7540
80 Varick St Apt 10a New York (10013) **(G-9749)**

Creative Gold LLC.....718 686-2225
1425 37th St Ste 5 Brooklyn (11218) **(G-1815)**

Creative Home Furnishings (PA).....631 582-8000
250 Creative Dr Central Islip (11722) **(G-3492)**

Creative Images & Applique.....718 821-8700
5208 Grand Ave Ste 2 Maspeth (11378) **(G-8126)**

Creative Kids Far East Inc.....845 368-0246
382 Route 59 Airmont (10952) **(G-13)**

Creative Laminates Inc.....315 463-7580
4003 Eastbourne Dr Syracuse (13206) **(G-15911)**

Creative Metal Fabricators.....631 567-2266
360 Knickerbocker Ave # 13 Bohemia (11716) **(G-1043)**

Creative Models & Prototypes.....516 433-6828
160 Lauman Ln Unit A Hicksville (11801) **(G-6337)**

Creative Orthotics Prosthetics, Ithaca *Also called Hanger Prsthetcs & Ortho Inc* **(G-6846)**

Creative Orthotics Prosthetics (PA).....607 734-7215
1300 College Ave Ste 1 Elmira (14901) **(G-4678)**

Creative Orthotics Prosthetics.....607 771-4672
65 Pennsylvania Ave 207 Binghamton (13903) **(G-903)**

Creative Orthotics Prosthetics.....607 431-2526
37 Associate Dr Oneonta (13820) **(G-13183)**

Creative Printing Corp 212 226-3870
121 Varick St Fl 9 New York (10013) ***(G-9750)***
Creative Prntng, New York *Also called Creative Printing Corp* ***(G-9750)***
Creative Relations LLC 212 462-4392
425 W 23rd St Rm 1f New York (10011) ***(G-9751)***
Creative Scents USA Inc 718 522-5901
183 Wilson St Ste 106 Brooklyn (11211) ***(G-1816)***
Creative Solutions Group Inc (PA) 914 771-4200
555 Tuckahoe Rd Yonkers (10710) ***(G-17432)***
Creative Stage Lighting Co Inc 518 251-3302
149 State Route 28n North Creek (12853) ***(G-12933)***
Creative Stone & Cabinets 631 772-6548
448 Middle Country Rd # 1 Selden (11784) ***(G-15350)***
Creative Tools & Supply Inc 212 279-7077
135 W 29th St Rm 205 New York (10001) ***(G-9752)***
Creative Window Fashions Inc 718 746-5817
315 Cresthaven Ln Whitestone (11357) ***(G-17205)***
Creative Yard Designs Inc 315 706-6143
8329 Us Route 20 Manlius (13104) ***(G-8070)***
Creatron Services Inc 516 437-5119
504 Cherry Ln Floral Park (11001) ***(G-5201)***
Credit Union Journal Inc (PA) 212 803-8200
1 State St Fl 26 New York (10004) ***(G-9753)***
Crepe Team, The, Brooklyn *Also called Crepini LLC* ***(G-1817)***
Crepini LLC 347 422-0829
5600 1st Ave Brooklyn (11220) ***(G-1817)***
Crescent Duck Farm Inc 631 722-8700
10 Edgar Ave Aquebogue (11931) ***(G-384)***
Crescent Manufacturing, North Collins *Also called Crescent Marketing Inc* ***(G-12927)***
Crescent Marketing Inc (PA) 716 337-0145
10285 Eagle Dr North Collins (14111) ***(G-12927)***
Crescent Wedding Rings Inc 212 869-8296
36 W 47th St Ste 306 New York (10036) ***(G-9754)***
Crest Haven Precast Inc 518 483-4750
4925 State Route 11 Burke (12917) ***(G-3266)***
Crest Lock Co Inc 718 345-9898
342 Herzl St Brooklyn (11212) ***(G-1818)***
Cri Graphic, Amityville *Also called Control Research Inc* ***(G-282)***
Crisada Inc 718 729-9730
3913 23rd St Long Island City (11101) ***(G-7707)***
Crisray Printing Corp 631 293-3770
50 Executive Blvd Ste A Farmingdale (11735) ***(G-4965)***
Cristina, Hempstead *Also called King Cracker Corp* ***(G-6277)***
Criterion Bell & Specialty 718 788-2600
4312 2nd Ave Brooklyn (11232) ***(G-1819)***
Critical Imaging LLC 315 732-5020
2428 Chenango Rd Utica (13502) ***(G-16318)***
Critical Link LLC 315 425-4045
6712 Brooklawn Pkwy # 203 Syracuse (13211) ***(G-15912)***
Crocs Inc 212 362-1655
270 Columbus Ave New York (10023) ***(G-9755)***
Crocs Inc 845 928-3002
498 Red Apple Ct Central Valley (10917) ***(G-3521)***
Crocs Medical Apparel, New York *Also called Icer Scrubs LLC* ***(G-10551)***
Cromwell Group, Mamaroneck *Also called Corium Corporation* ***(G-8030)***
Cronin Enterprises Inc 914 345-9600
120 E Main St Elmsford (10523) ***(G-4745)***
Crosby Company 716 852-3522
183 Pratt St Buffalo (14204) ***(G-2893)***
Croscill Home Fashions, New York *Also called Mistdoda Inc* ***(G-11284)***
Crosley Medical Products Inc 631 595-2547
60 S 2nd St Ste E Deer Park (11729) ***(G-4122)***
Crosman Corporation (HQ) 585 657-6161
7629 State Route 5 And 20 Bloomfield (14469) ***(G-986)***
Crosman Corporation 585 398-3920
1360 Rural Rte 8 Farmington (14425) ***(G-5148)***
Cross Border Transactions LLC 914 631-0878
4 Emerald Woods Tarrytown (10591) ***(G-16089)***
Cross Border Usa Inc 212 425-9649
25 Broadway Fl 9 New York (10004) ***(G-9756)***
Cross Country Mfg Inc 607 656-4103
2355 Rte 206 Greene (13778) ***(G-5863)***
Cross Country Mfg Inc (PA) 607 656-4103
2355 State Highway 206 Greene (13778) ***(G-5864)***
Crosstex International Inc (HQ) 631 582-6777
10 Ranick Rd Hauppauge (11788) ***(G-6058)***
Crosswinds Farm & Creamery 607 327-0363
6762 Log City Rd Ovid (14521) ***(G-13345)***
Crosswinds Sourcing LLC 646 438-6904
260 W 39th St Fl 10 New York (10018) ***(G-9757)***
Croton Watch Co Inc 800 443-7639
250 W Nyack Rd Ste 114 West Nyack (10994) ***(G-16915)***
Crowley Fabg Machining Co Inc (PA) 607 484-0299
403 N Nanticoke Ave Endicott (13760) ***(G-4799)***
Crowley Foods, Binghamton *Also called HP Hood LLC* ***(G-922)***
Crowley Foods Inc (HQ) 800 637-0019
93 Pennsylvania Ave Binghamton (13903) ***(G-904)***
Crowley Tar Products Co Inc (PA) 212 682-1200
305 Madison Ave Ste 1035 New York (10165) ***(G-9758)***
Crown Aircraft Lighting Inc 718 767-3410
1021 Clintonville St # 4 Whitestone (11357) ***(G-17206)***
Crown Brand Twine, Maspeth *Also called A & A Line & Wire Corp* ***(G-8110)***
Crown Cork & Seal Usa Inc 845 343-9586
21 Industrial Pl Middletown (10940) ***(G-8434)***
Crown Delta Corporation 914 245-8910
1550 Front St Yorktown Heights (10598) ***(G-17510)***
Crown Die Casting Corp 914 667-5400
268 W Lincoln Ave Mount Vernon (10550) ***(G-8675)***
Crown Equipment Corporation 516 822-5100
5 Charlotte Ave Ste 1 Hicksville (11801) ***(G-6338)***
Crown Hill Stone Inc 716 326-4601
59 Franklin St Westfield (14787) ***(G-17047)***
Crown Industrial 607 745-8709
839 State Route 13 Cortland (13045) ***(G-4024)***
Crown Industries Inc 973 672-2277
220 W 98th St Apt 2b New York (10025) ***(G-9759)***
Crown Jewelers Intl Inc 212 420-7800
168 7th Ave S New York (10014) ***(G-9760)***
Crown Lift Trucks, Hicksville *Also called Crown Equipment Corporation* ***(G-6338)***
Crown Medical Products, Suffern *Also called Advanced Medical Mfg Corp* ***(G-15784)***
Crown Mill Work Corp 845 371-2200
12 Melnick Dr Monsey (10952) ***(G-8570)***
Crown Novelty Works Inc 631 253-0949
42 Elkland Rd Melville (11747) ***(G-8308)***
Crown Sign Systems Inc 914 375-2118
7 Odell Plz Ste 140 Yonkers (10701) ***(G-17433)***
Crown Tank Company LLC 855 276-9682
60 Electric Pkwy Horseheads (14845) ***(G-6572)***
Crown Woodworking Corp 718 974-6415
583 Montgomery St Brooklyn (11225) ***(G-1820)***
Crownlite Mfg Corp 631 589-9100
1650 Sycamore Ave Ste 24 Bohemia (11716) ***(G-1044)***
CRS Nuclear Services LLC 716 810-0688
840 Aero Dr Ste 150 Cheektowaga (14225) ***(G-3565)***
CRS Remanufacturing Co Inc 718 739-1720
9440 158th St Jamaica (11433) ***(G-6908)***
Crucible Industries LLC 800 365-1180
575 State Fair Blvd Syracuse (13209) ***(G-15913)***
Cruise Industry News, New York *Also called Mathisen Ventures Inc* ***(G-11179)***
Crumbrubber Technology Inc 718 468-3988
18740 Hollis Ave Hollis (11423) ***(G-6496)***
Crusader Candle Co Inc 718 625-0005
325 Nevins St Ste 327329 Brooklyn (11215) ***(G-1821)***
Cruzin Management Inc (HQ) 212 641-8700
401 Park Ave S Fl 7 New York (10016) ***(G-9761)***
Cryomech Inc 315 455-2555
113 Falso Dr Syracuse (13211) ***(G-15914)***
Crysta-Lyn Chemical Company 607 296-4721
6 Emma St Binghamton (13905) ***(G-905)***
Crystal Ceres Industries Inc 716 283-0445
2250 Liberty Dr Niagara Falls (14304) ***(G-12808)***
Crystal Fusion Tech Inc 631 253-9800
25 Dubon Ct Farmingdale (11735) ***(G-4966)***
Crystal Is Inc 518 271-7375
70 Cohoes Ave Ste 1b Troy (12183) ***(G-16219)***
Crystal Linton Technologies 585 444-8784
2180 Brigh Henri Town Lin Rochester (14623) ***(G-14292)***
Crystal Rock LLC 716 626-7460
100 Stradtman St Ste 1 Buffalo (14206) ***(G-2894)***
Crystalizations Systems Inc 631 467-0090
1401 Lincoln Ave Holbrook (11741) ***(G-6441)***
Crystalonics Inc 631 981-6140
2805 Veterans Mem Hwy 14 Ronkonkoma (11779) ***(G-14891)***
Cs Automation Inc 315 524-5123
518 Berg Rd Ontario (14519) ***(G-13198)***
Cs Manufacturing Limited 607 587-8154
56 S Main St Alfred (14802) ***(G-193)***
CSC Serviceworks Inc (HQ) 516 349-8555
303 Sunnyside Blvd # 70 Plainview (11803) ***(G-13594)***
CSC Serviceworks Holdings (PA) 516 349-8555
303 Sunnyside Blvd # 70 Plainview (11803) ***(G-13595)***
Csco LLC (PA) 212 221-5100
525 7th Ave Rm 1006 New York (10018) ***(G-9762)***
Csi, Falconer *Also called Reynolds Packaging McHy Inc* ***(G-4910)***
Csi International Inc 716 282-5408
1001 Main St Niagara Falls (14301) ***(G-12809)***
CSP Technologies Inc (HQ) 518 627-0051
1031 Riverfront Ctr Amsterdam (12010) ***(G-342)***
Csrea, Long Island City *Also called Civil Svc Rtred Employees Assn* ***(G-7699)***
Csw Inc 585 247-4010
70 Pixley Industrial Pkwy Rochester (14624) ***(G-14293)***
CT Industrial Supply Co Inc 718 417-3226
305 Ten Eyck St Brooklyn (11206) ***(G-1822)***
CT Publications Co 718 592-2196
4808 111th St Corona (11368) ***(G-3996)***
Ctac Holdings LLC 212 924-2280
68 35th Street Brooklyn Brooklyn (11232) ***(G-1823)***
CTB Enterprise LLC 631 563-0088
1170 Lincoln Ave Unit 7 Holbrook (11741) ***(G-6442)***
CTI Software Inc 631 253-3550
44 W Jefryn Blvd Ste P Deer Park (11729) ***(G-4123)***
CTS LLC 212 278-0058
211 E 18th St Apt 4d New York (10003) ***(G-9763)***
CTX Printing, Cambridge *Also called Cambridge-Pacific Inc* ***(G-3305)***

ALPHABETIC

Cuba Specialty Mfg Co Inc ... 585 567-4176
81 S Genesee St Fillmore (14735) *(G-5175)*

Cubbies Unlimited Corporation ... 631 586-8572
74 N Industry Ct Deer Park (11729) *(G-4124)*

Cubic Trnsp Systems Inc ... 212 255-1810
245 W 17th St Fl 8 New York (10011) *(G-9764)*

Cubitek Inc ... 631 665-6900
95 Emjay Blvd Ste 2 Brentwood (11717) *(G-1179)*

Cuccio-Zanetti Inc ... 518 587-1363
455 Middle Grove Rd Middle Grove (12850) *(G-8404)*

Cuddeback Machining Inc ... 585 392-5889
18 Draffin Rd Hilton (14468) *(G-6417)*

Cuffs Planning & Models Ltd ... 914 632-1883
317 Beechmont Dr New Rochelle (10804) *(G-8893)*

Culicover & Shapiro Inc ... 516 597-4888
270 Duffy Ave Ste K Hicksville (11801) *(G-6339)*

Culin/Colella Inc ... 914 698-7727
632 Center Ave Mamaroneck (10543) *(G-8031)*

Culinary Arts Specialties Inc ... 716 656-8943
2268 Union Rd Cheektowaga (14227) *(G-3566)*

Cult Records LLC ... 718 395-2077
263 Bowery Apt 3 New York (10002) *(G-9765)*

Cultureiq Inc (PA) ... 212 755-8633
7 Penn Plz Ste 1112 New York (10001) *(G-9766)*

Cumberland Packing Corp (PA) ... 718 858-4200
2 Cumberland St Brooklyn (11205) *(G-1824)*

Cummins - Allison Corp ... 718 263-2482
8002 Kew Gardens Rd # 402 Kew Gardens (11415) *(G-7159)*

Cummins Eng Company/James Town, Lakewood *Also called Cummins Inc (G-7290)*

Cummins Inc ... 716 456-2676
4720 Baker St Lakewood (14750) *(G-7289)*

Cummins Inc ... 716 456-2111
4720 Baker St Lakewood (14750) *(G-7290)*

Cummins Inc ... 812 377-5000
101-133 Jackson Ave Jamestown (14701) *(G-6986)*

Cummins Inc ... 718 892-2400
890 Zerega Ave Bronx (10473) *(G-1306)*

Cummins Northeast LLC ... 315 437-2296
6193 Eastern Ave Syracuse (13211) *(G-15915)*

Cuore Technology, Cheektowaga *Also called Leo Schultz (G-3577)*

Cupcake Contessas Corporation ... 516 307-1222
1242 Julia Ln North Bellmore (11710) *(G-12919)*

Cupid Foundations Inc (PA) ... 212 686-6224
475 Park Ave S Manhattan New York (10022) *(G-9767)*

Cupid Intimates, New York *Also called Cupid Foundations Inc (G-9767)*

Curaegis Technologies Inc (PA) ... 585 254-1100
1999 Mount Read Blvd # 3 Rochester (14615) *(G-14294)*

Curbell Incorporated ... 315 434-7240
6805 Crossbow Dr East Syracuse (13057) *(G-4520)*

Curbell Medical Products Inc ... 716 667-2520
20 Centre Dr Orchard Park (14127) *(G-13266)*

Curbell Medical Products Inc (HQ) ... 716 667-2520
7 Cobham Dr Orchard Park (14127) *(G-13267)*

Curbell Plastics Inc (PA) ... 585 426-1690
100 Aviation Ave Rochester (14624) *(G-14295)*

Cure MD, New York *Also called Curemdcom Inc (G-9769)*

Cureatr Inc ... 212 203-3927
222 Broadway Fl 19 New York (10038) *(G-9768)*

Curemdcom Inc ... 646 224-2201
120 Broadway Fl 35 New York (10271) *(G-9769)*

Curran Manufacturing Corp (PA) ... 631 273-1010
200 Oser Ave Hauppauge (11788) *(G-6059)*

Curran Manufacturing Corp ... 631 273-1010
210 Oser Ave Hauppauge (11788) *(G-6060)*

Curran Renewable Energy LLC ... 315 769-2000
20 Commerce Dr Massena (13662) *(G-8193)*

Currant Company LLC ... 845 266-8999
59 Walnut Ln Staatsburg (12580) *(G-15617)*

Currantc, Staatsburg *Also called Currant Company LLC (G-15617)*

Current Applications Inc ... 315 788-4689
275 Bellew Ave S Watertown (13601) *(G-16648)*

Current Controls Inc ... 585 593-1544
353 S Brooklyn Ave Wellsville (14895) *(G-16750)*

Currier Plastics Inc ... 315 255-1779
101 Columbus St Auburn (13021) *(G-490)*

Curtin-Hebert Co Inc ... 518 725-7157
11 Forest St Gloversville (12078) *(G-5710)*

Curtin-Hebert Machines, Gloversville *Also called Curtin-Hebert Co Inc (G-5710)*

Curtis Instruments Inc (PA) ... 914 666-2971
200 Kisco Ave Mount Kisco (10549) *(G-8624)*

Curtis L Maclean L C ... 716 898-7800
50 Thielman Dr Buffalo (14206) *(G-2895)*

Curtis PMC Division, Mount Kisco *Also called Curtis Instruments Inc (G-8624)*

Curtis Prtg Co The Del Press ... 518 477-4820
711 Columbia Tpke East Greenbush (12061) *(G-4402)*

Curtis Screw Co Inc ... 716 898-7800
50 Thielman Dr Buffalo (14206) *(G-2896)*

Curtis/Palmer Hydroelectric LP ... 518 654-6297
15 Pine St Corinth (12822) *(G-3957)*

Curtiss-Wrght Intgrted Sensing, Farmingdale *Also called Curtiss-Wright Controls (G-4967)*

Curtiss-Wright Controls ... 631 756-4740
175 Central Ave Ste 100 Farmingdale (11735) *(G-4967)*

Curtiss-Wright Flow Control ... 845 382-6918
731 Grant Ave Lake Katrine (12449) *(G-7270)*

Curtiss-Wright Flow Ctrl Corp (HQ) ... 631 293-3800
1966 Broadhollow Rd Ste E Farmingdale (11735) *(G-4968)*

Curtiss-Wright Flow Ctrl Corp ... 631 293-3800
1966 Broadhollow Rd Ste E Farmingdale (11735) *(G-4969)*

Cusimano, Michael, Rochester *Also called Empire Fabricators Inc (G-14346)*

Custom Bags Unlimited, Hamburg *Also called Kragel Co Inc (G-5932)*

Custom Brewcrafters Inc ... 585 624-4386
300 Village Square Blvd Honeoye Falls (14472) *(G-6526)*

Custom Candy Concepts Inc ... 516 824-3228
50 Inip Dr Inwood (11096) *(G-6754)*

Custom Canvas Manufacturing Co ... 716 852-6372
775 Seneca St Buffalo (14210) *(G-2897)*

Custom CAS Inc ... 718 726-3575
2631 1st St Long Island City (11102) *(G-7708)*

Custom Coatings, Farmingdale *Also called Time-Cap Laboratories Inc (G-5131)*

Custom Controls ... 315 253-4785
2804 Skillett Rd Scipio Center (13147) *(G-15322)*

Custom Cool, Bronx *Also called S & V Restaurant Eqp Mfrs Inc (G-1445)*

Custom Countertops Inc ... 716 646-1579
5260 Armor Duells Rd Orchard Park (14127) *(G-13268)*

Custom Countertops Inc (PA) ... 716 685-2871
3192 Walden Ave Depew (14043) *(G-4253)*

Custom Design Kitchens Inc ... 518 355-4446
1700 Duanesburg Rd Duanesburg (12056) *(G-4325)*

Custom Design Metals Inc ... 631 563-2444
1612 Locust Ave Ste C Bohemia (11716) *(G-1045)*

Custom Display Manufacture ... 516 783-6491
1686 Logan St North Bellmore (11710) *(G-12920)*

Custom Door & Mirror Inc ... 631 414-7725
148 Milbar Blvd Farmingdale (11735) *(G-4970)*

Custom Eco Friendly Bags, Roslyn *Also called Custom Eco Friendly LLC (G-15018)*

Custom Eco Friendly LLC (PA) ... 347 227-0229
50 Spruce Dr Roslyn (11576) *(G-15018)*

Custom Electronics Inc ... 607 432-3880
87 Browne St Oneonta (13820) *(G-13184)*

Custom European Imports Inc ... 845 357-5718
100 Sterling Mine Rd Sloatsburg (10974) *(G-15480)*

Custom Fixtures Inc ... 718 965-1141
129 13th St Brooklyn (11215) *(G-1825)*

Custom Frame & Molding Co ... 631 491-9091
97 Lamar St 101 West Babylon (11704) *(G-16786)*

Custom House Engravers Inc ... 631 567-3004
104 Keyland Ct Bohemia (11716) *(G-1046)*

Custom Klean Corp ... 315 865-8101
8890 Boak Rd E Holland Patent (13354) *(G-6487)*

Custom Lampshades Inc ... 718 254-0500
544 Park Ave Ste 503 Brooklyn (11205) *(G-1826)*

Custom Laser Inc ... 716 434-8600
6747 Akron Rd Lockport (14094) *(G-7578)*

Custom Lucite Creations Inc ... 718 871-2000
165 Franklin Ave Apt 5 Brooklyn (11205) *(G-1827)*

Custom Manufacturing Inc ... 607 569-2738
10034 E Lake Rd Hammondsport (14840) *(G-5954)*

Custom Metal Fabrication, West Babylon *Also called Custom Metal Incorporated (G-16787)*

Custom Metal Incorporated ... 631 643-4075
72 Otis St West Babylon (11704) *(G-16787)*

Custom Mix Concrete Inc ... 607 737-0281
Smith Hill Rd Coopers Plains (14827) *(G-3882)*

Custom Mix Concrete Inc ... 607 737-0281
Chemung Flat Rd Chemung (14825) *(G-3593)*

Custom Mix Inc ... 516 797-7090
31 Clark Blvd Massapequa Park (11762) *(G-8185)*

Custom Molding Solutions Inc ... 585 293-1702
456 Sanford Rd N Churchville (14428) *(G-3635)*

Custom Patches Inc ... 845 679-6320
1760 Glasco Tpke Woodstock (12498) *(G-17362)*

Custom Pins Inc ... 914 690-9378
150 Clearbrook Rd Ste 139 Elmsford (10523) *(G-4746)*

Custom Power System, Sayville *Also called Fil-Coil (fc) Corp (G-15209)*

Custom Power Systems, Central Islip *Also called Berkshire Transformer (G-3487)*

Custom Prtrs Guilderland Inc ... 518 456-2811
2210 Western Ave Guilderland (12084) *(G-5902)*

Custom Publishing Group Ltd ... 212 840-8800
8 W 38th St 204 New York (10018) *(G-9770)*

Custom Service Solutions Inc ... 585 637-3760
1900 Transit Way Brockport (14420) *(G-1243)*

Custom Sheet Metal Contg LLC ... 716 896-2122
303 Central Ave Buffalo (14206) *(G-2898)*

Custom Sheet Metal Corp ... 315 463-9105
1 General Motors Dr Ste 5 Syracuse (13206) *(G-15916)*

Custom Shipping Products Inc ... 716 355-4437
8661 Knowlton Rd Clymer (14724) *(G-3733)*

Custom Sitecom LLC ... 631 420-4238
470 Smith St Farmingdale (11735) *(G-4971)*

Custom Sound and Video ... 585 424-5000
40 Rutter St Rochester (14606) *(G-14296)*

Custom Sports Lab Inc ... 212 832-1648
515 Madison Ave Rm 1204 New York (10022) *(G-9771)*

Custom Sportswear Corp ... 914 666-9200
375 Adams St Bedford Hills (10507) *(G-800)*

Custom Stair & Millwork Co 315 839-5793
6 Gridley Pl Sauquoit (13456) *(G-15199)*
Custom Studio Division, Tappan *Also called Nationwide Custom Services (G-16081)*
Custom Wood Inc 718 927-4700
770 E 94th St Brooklyn (11236) *(G-1828)*
Custom Woodcraft LLC 315 843-4234
2525 Perry Schumaker Rd Munnsville (13409) *(G-8750)*
Custom Woodwork Ltd 631 727-5260
205 Marcy Ave Riverhead (11901) *(G-14140)*
Customize Elite Socks LLC 212 533-8551
156 2nd Ave Apt 2c New York (10003) *(G-9772)*
Customshow Inc 800 255-5303
216 E 45th St Fl 17 New York (10017) *(G-9773)*
Cutco Cutlery Corporation (HQ) 716 372-3111
1116 E State St Olean (14760) *(G-13141)*
Cutting Edge Metal Works 631 981-8333
12 Long Island Ave Holtsville (11742) *(G-6503)*
Cuzins Duzin Corp 347 724-6200
8420 Austin St Apt 3a Kew Gardens (11415) *(G-7160)*
Cvd Equipment Corporation 845 246-3631
1117 Kings Hwy Saugerties (12477) *(G-15182)*
Cvd Equipment Corporation (PA) 631 981-7081
355 S Technology Dr Central Islip (11722) *(G-3493)*
CVI Laser LLC 585 244-7220
55 Science Pkwy Rochester (14620) *(G-14297)*
Cw Fasteners & Zippers Corp 212 594-3203
142 W 36th St Fl 5 New York (10018) *(G-9774)*
Cw Metals Inc 917 416-7906
3421 Greenpoint Ave Long Island City (11101) *(G-7709)*
Cwr Manufacturing Corporation 315 437-1032
7000 Fly Rd East Syracuse (13057) *(G-4521)*
Cws Powder Coatings Company LP 845 398-2911
2234 Bradley Hill Rd # 12 Blauvelt (10913) *(G-970)*
Cy Plastics Works Inc 585 229-2555
8601 Main St Honeoye (14471) *(G-6523)*
Cya Action Funwell, Patchogue *Also called Gem West Inc (G-13420)*
Cyandia Inc 315 679-4268
843 Malden Rd Syracuse (13211) *(G-15917)*
Cyber Knit, New York *Also called Lifestyle Design Usa Ltd (G-10988)*
Cyber Swag Merchandise of NY, Maspeth *Also called Creative Images & Applique (G-8126)*
Cyberlimit Inc 212 840-9597
257 W 38th St Fl 6 New York (10018) *(G-9775)*
Cybersports Inc (PA) 315 737-7150
11 Avery Pl Utica (13502) *(G-16319)*
Cyclone Air Power Inc 718 447-3038
12 Van St Staten Island (10310) *(G-15664)*
Cyclotherm of Watertown Inc 315 782-1100
787 Pearl St Watertown (13601) *(G-16649)*
Cygnet Studio Inc 646 450-4550
251 W 39th St Fl 17 New York (10018) *(G-9776)*
Cygnus Automation Inc 631 981-0909
1605 9th Ave Bohemia (11716) *(G-1047)*
Cyncal Steel Fabricators Inc 631 254-5600
225 Pine Aire Dr Bay Shore (11706) *(G-689)*
Cynosure Inc 516 594-3333
400 Karin Ln Hicksville (11801) *(G-6340)*
Cynthia Rowley Inc (PA) 212 242-3803
376 Bleecker St New York (10014) *(G-9777)*
Cynthia Steffe, New York *Also called Bernard Chaus Inc (G-9365)*
Cypress Bioscience Inc 858 452-2323
110 E 59th St Fl 33 New York (10022) *(G-9778)*
Cypress Semiconductor Corp 631 261-1358
34 Rowley Dr Northport (11768) *(G-13010)*
Cytec Industries Inc 716 372-9650
1405 Buffalo St Olean (14760) *(G-13142)*
Cytec Olean Inc 716 372-9650
1405 Buffalo St Olean (14760) *(G-13143)*
Cytexone Technology LLC 212 792-6700
50 Hudson St Fl 3 New York (10013) *(G-9779)*
Cz USA Dwf Dan Wesson Firearm, Norwich *Also called Dan Wesson Corp (G-13026)*
D & A Offset Services Inc 212 924-0612
185 Varick St Ste 3 New York (10014) *(G-9780)*
D & C Cleaning Inc 631 789-5659
1095 Campagnoli Ave Copiague (11726) *(G-3898)*
D & D Creations Co Inc 212 840-1198
71 W 47th St Ste 606 New York (10036) *(G-9781)*
D & D Motor Systems Inc 315 701-0861
215 Park Ave Syracuse (13204) *(G-15918)*
D & D Printing, Buffalo *Also called Dan Trent Company Inc (G-2901)*
D & D Window Tech Inc (PA) 212 308-2822
979 3rd Ave Lbby 132 New York (10022) *(G-9782)*
D & E Industrial, Akron *Also called Re-Al Industrial Corp (G-28)*
D & F Pallet Inc 716 672-2984
134 Clinton Ave Fredonia (14063) *(G-5372)*
D & G Sheet Metal Co Inc 718 326-9111
5400 Grand Ave Maspeth (11378) *(G-8127)*
D & G Welding Inc 716 873-3088
249 Hertel Ave Buffalo (14207) *(G-2899)*
D & I Finishing Inc 631 471-3034
1560 Ocean Ave Ste 7 Bohemia (11716) *(G-1048)*
D & L Electronic Die, Farmingdale *Also called Cosmo Electronic Machine Corp (G-4962)*
D & L Manufacturing, Bronx *Also called L & D Manufacturing Corp (G-1375)*
D & M Custom Cabinets Inc 516 678-2818
2994 Long Beach Rd Oceanside (11572) *(G-13075)*
D & M Enterprises Incorporated 914 937-6430
1 Mill St Ste 2 Port Chester (10573) *(G-13741)*
D & R Silk Screening Ltd 631 234-7464
201 Creative Dr Central Islip (11722) *(G-3494)*
D & S Supplies Inc 718 721-5256
2067 21st St Astoria (11105) *(G-435)*
D & W Design Inc (PA) 845 343-3366
62 Industrial Pl Middletown (10940) *(G-8435)*
D & W Diesel Inc 518 437-1300
51 Sicker Rd Ste 3 Latham (12110) *(G-7359)*
D & W Enterprises LLC 585 590-6727
10775 W Shelby Rd Medina (14103) *(G-8270)*
D and D Sheet Metal Corp 718 465-7585
9510 218th St Ste 4 Jamaica (11429) *(G-6909)*
D B F Associates 718 328-0005
1150 E 156th St Bronx (10474) *(G-1307)*
D Bag Lady Inc 585 425-8095
183 Perinton Pkwy Fairport (14450) *(G-4853)*
D Best Glass & Mirror, Brooklyn *Also called D Best Service Co Inc (G-1829)*
D Best Service Co Inc 718 972-6133
729 Church Ave Brooklyn (11218) *(G-1829)*
D C C, New York *Also called Digital Color Concepts Inc (G-9875)*
D C I Plasma Center Inc (PA) 914 241-1646
71 S Bedford Rd Mount Kisco (10549) *(G-8625)*
D C I Technical Inc 516 355-0464
475 Franklin Ave Fl 2 Franklin Square (11010) *(G-5362)*
D C M, West Babylon *Also called Display Components Mfg Inc (G-16789)*
D D & L Inc 607 729-9131
3 Alice St Binghamton (13904) *(G-906)*
D D C, Mechanicville *Also called Decrescente Distributing Co (G-8226)*
D F Stauffer Biscuit Co Inc 585 968-2700
8670 Farnsworth Rd Cuba (14727) *(G-4068)*
D G M Graphics Inc 516 223-2220
55 Merrick Ave Merrick (11566) *(G-8383)*
D J Crowell Co Inc 716 684-3343
2815 Town Line Rd Alden (14004) *(G-176)*
D J Night Ltd 212 302-9050
225 W 37th St Fl 6 New York (10018) *(G-9783)*
D K Machine Inc 518 747-0626
48 Sullivan Pkwy Fort Edward (12828) *(G-5341)*
D K P Wood Railings & Stairs 631 665-8656
1971 Union Blvd Bay Shore (11706) *(G-690)*
D M J Casting Inc 212 719-1951
62 W 47th St Ste 508 New York (10036) *(G-9784)*
D Maldari & Sons Inc 718 499-3555
557 3rd Ave Brooklyn (11215) *(G-1830)*
D N Gannon Fabricating Inc 315 463-7466
404 Wavel St Syracuse (13206) *(G-15919)*
D Oro Onofrio Inc 718 491-2961
1051 73rd St Apt 1 Brooklyn (11228) *(G-1831)*
D P Mount Vernon, Mount Vernon *Also called Sentage Corporation (G-8733)*
D R Cornue Woodworks 315 655-9463
3206 Us Route 20 Cazenovia (13035) *(G-3444)*
D R M Management Inc (PA) 716 668-0333
3430 Transit Rd Depew (14043) *(G-4254)*
D R S Watch Materials 212 819-0470
56 W 47th St Fl 2 New York (10036) *(G-9785)*
D S I, Poestenkill *Also called Dynamic Systems Inc (G-13723)*
D S M, Schenectady *Also called DSM Nutritional Products LLC (G-15249)*
D Squared Technologies Inc 516 932-7319
71 Birchwood Park Dr Jericho (11753) *(G-7064)*
D T B, Bohemia *Also called Dayton T Brown Inc (G-1052)*
D T I, Rochester *Also called Dimension Technologies Inc (G-14309)*
D V S Iron & Aluminum Works 718 768-7961
117 14th St Brooklyn (11215) *(G-1832)*
D W Haber & Son Inc 718 993-6405
825 E 140th St Bronx (10454) *(G-1308)*
D W S Associates Inc 631 667-6616
89 N Industry Ct Deer Park (11729) *(G-4125)*
D W S Printing, Deer Park *Also called D W S Associates Inc (G-4125)*
D-Best Equipment Corp 516 358-0965
77 Hempstead Gardens Dr West Hempstead (11552) *(G-16852)*
D-C Theatricks 716 847-0180
747 Main St Buffalo (14203) *(G-2900)*
D-K Manufacturing Corp 315 592-4327
551 W 3rd St S Fulton (13069) *(G-5455)*
D-Lite Donuts 718 626-5953
4519 Broadway Astoria (11103) *(G-436)*
D.A.M. Construction, Company, Arverne *Also called Darrell Mitchell (G-425)*
Da Electric 347 270-3422
6 E Clarke Pl Bronx (10452) *(G-1309)*
Dab-O-Matic Corp (PA) 914 699-7070
896 S Columbus Ave Mount Vernon (10550) *(G-8676)*
Dabby-Reid Ltd 212 356-0040
347 W 36th St Rm 701 New York (10018) *(G-9786)*
DAc Lighting Inc 914 698-5959
420 Railroad Way Mamaroneck (10543) *(G-8032)*
Dacobe Enterprises LLC 315 368-0093
325 Lafayette St Utica (13502) *(G-16320)*

ALPHABETIC

Dada Group US Inc....631 888-0818
22104 67th Ave Apt B Bayside (11364) *(G-769)*
DAddario & Company Inc....631 439-3300
99 Marcus Dr Melville (11747) *(G-8309)*
DAddario & Company Inc (PA)....631 439-3300
595 Smith St Farmingdale (11735) *(G-4972)*
DAF Office Networks Inc....315 699-7070
6121 Jemola Runne Cicero (13039) *(G-3644)*
DAgostino Iron Works Inc....585 235-8850
10 Deep Rock Rd Rochester (14624) *(G-14298)*
Daheshist Publishing Co Ltd....212 581-8360
1775 Broadway 501 New York (10019) *(G-9787)*
Dahill Distributors Inc....347 371-9453
975 Dahill Rd Brooklyn (11204) *(G-1833)*
Dahlstrom Roll Form, Jamestown *Also called Lakeside Capital Corporation (G-7015)*
Dahua Electronics Corporation....718 886-2188
13412 59th Ave Flushing (11355) *(G-5236)*
Daige Products Inc....516 621-2100
1 Albertson Ave Ste 3 Albertson (11507) *(G-153)*
Daikin Applied Americas Inc....315 253-2771
4900 Technology Park Blvd Auburn (13021) *(G-491)*
Dail Cornell Sun, The, Ithaca *Also called Daily Cornell Sun (G-6836)*
Daily Beast Company LLC (HQ)....212 445-4600
7 Hanover Sq New York (10004) *(G-9788)*
Daily Cornell Sun....607 273-0746
139 W State St Ithaca (14850) *(G-6836)*
Daily Freeman....845 331-5000
79 Hurley Ave Kingston (12401) *(G-7186)*
Daily Gazette Company (PA)....518 374-4141
2345 Maxon Rd Ext Schenectady (12308) *(G-15246)*
Daily Gazette Company....518 395-3060
2345 Maxon Rd Ext Schenectady (12308) *(G-15247)*
Daily Mail & Greene Cnty News (HQ)....518 943-2100
414 Main St Catskill (12414) *(G-3427)*
Daily Media, Rochester *Also called Daily Record (G-14299)*
Daily Messenger, Canandaigua *Also called Canandaigua Msgnr Incorporated (G-3337)*
Daily Muse Inc....646 861-0284
1375 Broadway Fl 20 New York (10018) *(G-9789)*
Daily News LP (PA)....212 210-2100
4 New York Plz Fl 6 New York (10004) *(G-9790)*
Daily Newsppr For Torah Jewry, Brooklyn *Also called Hamodia Corp (G-2064)*
Daily Orange Corporation....315 443-2314
744 Ostrom Ave Syracuse (13210) *(G-15920)*
Daily Racing Form....212 514-2180
75 Broad St New York (10004) *(G-9791)*
Daily Racing Form Inc (HQ)....212 366-7600
708 3rd Ave Fl 12 New York (10017) *(G-9792)*
Daily Record (PA)....585 232-2035
16 W Main St Ste G9 Rochester (14614) *(G-14299)*
Daily Sun New York, New York *Also called Daily World Press Inc (G-9793)*
Daily Voice, Armonk *Also called Main Street Connect LLC (G-417)*
Daily Wear Sportswear Corp (PA)....718 972-0533
2308 Mcdonald Ave Brooklyn (11223) *(G-1834)*
Daily World Press Inc....212 922-9201
228 E 45th St Rm 700 New York (10017) *(G-9793)*
Dailycandy Inc....646 230-8719
584 Broadway Rm 510 New York (10012) *(G-9794)*
Daimler Buses North Amer Inc....315 768-8101
165 Base Rd Oriskany (13424) *(G-13308)*
Dainty Home, New York *Also called Baby Signature Inc (G-9298)*
Dairy Conveyor Corp (PA)....845 278-7878
38 Mount Ebo Rd S Brewster (10509) *(G-1215)*
Dairy Delite, Farmingdale *Also called Noga Dairies Inc (G-5066)*
Dairy Farmers America Inc....816 801-6440
5001 Brittonfield Pkwy East Syracuse (13057) *(G-4522)*
Dairy Maid Raviolo Mfg (PA)....718 449-2620
216 Avenue U Fl 1 Brooklyn (11223) *(G-1835)*
Daisy Brand Confectionery, Bronx *Also called Scaccianoce Inc (G-1449)*
Daisy Memory Products, Roslyn *Also called Dynamic Photography Inc (G-15019)*
Dak Mica and Wood Products....631 467-0749
2147 5th Ave Ronkonkoma (11779) *(G-14892)*
Dakota Systems Mfg Corp....631 249-5811
1885 New Hwy Ste 2 Farmingdale (11735) *(G-4973)*
Dakota Wall, Farmingdale *Also called Dakota Systems Mfg Corp (G-4973)*
Dakotah, Central Islip *Also called Creative Home Furnishings (G-3492)*
Dakott LLC....888 805-6795
244 Madison Ave Ste 211 New York (10016) *(G-9795)*
Dal-Tile Corporation....718 894-9574
5840 55th Dr Maspeth (11378) *(G-8128)*
Dal-Tile Corporation....914 835-1801
31 Oakland Ave Harrison (10528) *(G-5982)*
Dalcom USA Ltd....516 466-7733
11 Middle Neck Rd Ste 301 Great Neck (11021) *(G-5802)*
Dale Press Inc....718 543-6200
5676 Riverdale Ave # 311 Bronx (10471) *(G-1310)*
Dalee Bookbinding Co Inc....914 965-1660
129 Clinton Pl Yonkers (10701) *(G-17434)*
Dalfon, Great Neck *Also called Dalcom USA Ltd (G-5802)*
Dalma Dress Mfg Co Inc....212 391-8296
3 Carman Rd Greenvale (11548) *(G-5880)*
Dalrymple Grav & Contg Co Inc (HQ)....607 739-0391
2105 S Broadway Pine City (14871) *(G-13550)*
Dalrymple Grav & Contg Co Inc....607 529-3235
Chemung Flats Rd Chemung (14825) *(G-3594)*
Dalrymple Holding Corp (PA)....607 737-6200
2105 S Broadway Pine City (14871) *(G-13551)*
Daly Meghan....347 699-3259
78 5th Ave Brooklyn (11217) *(G-1836)*
Damascus Bakery Inc....718 855-1456
56 Gold St Brooklyn (11201) *(G-1837)*
Damianou Sportswear Inc....718 204-5600
6001 31st Ave Ste 2 Woodside (11377) *(G-17325)*
Dampits International Inc....212 581-3047
425 W 57th St New York (10019) *(G-9796)*
Dan Ann Associates, Kirkwood *Also called Belden Manufacturing Inc (G-7232)*
Dan Kane Plating Co Inc....212 675-4947
357 W 36th St New York (10018) *(G-9797)*
Dan Trent Company Inc....716 822-1422
1728 Clinton St Buffalo (14206) *(G-2901)*
Dan Wesson Corp....607 336-1174
65 Borden Ave Norwich (13815) *(G-13026)*
Dana Michele LLC....917 757-7777
3 E 84th St New York (10028) *(G-9798)*
Danaher Corporation....516 443-9432
445 E 14th St Apt 3f New York (10009) *(G-9799)*
Danaher Corporation....716 691-9100
45 Hazelwood Dr Amherst (14228) *(G-236)*
Danbury Creek Inc....315 822-5640
67 South St West Winfield (13491) *(G-16958)*
Danbury Pharma LLC....631 393-6333
220 Smith St Farmingdale (11735) *(G-4974)*
Dancker Sellew & Douglas Inc....908 231-1600
6067 Corporate Dr East Syracuse (13057) *(G-4523)*
DAndrea Inc....516 496-2200
115 Eileen Way Ste 106 Syosset (11791) *(G-15818)*
Danet Inc....718 266-4444
8518 17th Ave Fl 2 Brooklyn (11214) *(G-1838)*
DAngelico Guitars of America....732 380-0995
141 W 28th St Fl 4 New York (10001) *(G-9800)*
DAngelo Home Collections Inc....917 267-8920
39 Warwick Tpke Warwick (10990) *(G-16587)*
Danhier Co LLC....212 563-7683
380 Rector Pl Apt 3d New York (10280) *(G-9801)*
Dani II Inc (PA)....212 869-5999
231 W 39th St Rm 1002 New York (10018) *(G-9802)*
Dani Lu Inc....518 782-5411
601 New Loudon Rd Ste 4 Latham (12110) *(G-7360)*
Danice Stores Inc....212 665-0389
305 W 125th St New York (10027) *(G-9803)*
Daniel & Lois Lyndaker Logging....315 346-6527
10460 Monnat School Rd Castorland (13620) *(G-3423)*
Daniel Demarco and Assoc Inc....631 598-7000
25 Greene Ave Amityville (11701) *(G-284)*
Daniel M Friedman & Assoc Inc....212 695-5545
19 W 34th St Fl 4 New York (10001) *(G-9804)*
Daniels Jewels Art, New York *Also called Danwak Jewelry Corp (G-9808)*
Danisco US Inc....585 256-5200
3490 Winton Pl Rochester (14623) *(G-14300)*
Danisco US Inc....585 277-4300
1700 Lexington Ave Rochester (14606) *(G-14301)*
Danner, Eg Mfg, Central Islip *Also called Eugene G Danner Mfg Inc (G-3495)*
Danny & Nicole, New York *Also called Kelly Grace Corp (G-10830)*
Danny Couture, New York *Also called Danny R Couture Corp (G-9806)*
Danny Macaroons Inc....260 622-8463
2191 3rd Ave Ste 3 New York (10035) *(G-9805)*
Danny R Couture Corp (PA)....212 594-1095
261 W 35th St Ground Fl New York (10001) *(G-9806)*
Danone Nutricia Early....914 872-8556
100 Hillside Ave White Plains (10603) *(G-17098)*
Danray Textiles Corp (PA)....212 354-5213
270 W 39th St Fl 5 New York (10018) *(G-9807)*
Dans Paper Inc....631 537-0500
158 County Road 39 Southampton (11968) *(G-15542)*
Dansville Logging & Lumber....585 335-5879
10903 State Route 36 Dansville (14437) *(G-4076)*
Dantex Trimming & Textile Co, New York *Also called Danray Textiles Corp (G-9807)*
Danwak Jewelry Corp....212 730-4541
55 W 47th St Ste 860 New York (10036) *(G-9808)*
Dapper Dads Inc....917 903-8045
45 Rochester Ave Brooklyn (11233) *(G-1839)*
Darby Dental Supply....516 688-6421
105 Executive Ct Jericho (11753) *(G-7065)*
Darco Manufacturing Inc....315 432-8905
6756 Thompson Rd Syracuse (13211) *(G-15921)*
DArcy Printing and Lithog....212 924-1554
121 Varick St Fl 9 New York (10013) *(G-9809)*
Dark Star Lithograph Corp....845 634-3780
9 Perth Ln New City (10956) *(G-8782)*
Darman Manufacturing Coinc....315 724-9632
1410 Lincoln Ave Utica (13502) *(G-16321)*
Darmiyan LLC....917 689-0389
450 E 63rd St Apt 5a New York (10065) *(G-9810)*

ALPHABETIC

Darrell Mitchell 646 659-7075
704 Beach 67th St Arverne (11692) *(G-425)*
Dart Awning Inc 718 945-4224
365 S Main St Freeport (11520) *(G-5393)*
Dart Communications, New Hartford *Also called Dartcom Incorporated (G-8802)*
Dartcom Incorporated 315 790-5456
2 Oxford Xing Ste 1 New Hartford (13413) *(G-8802)*
Das Yidishe Licht Inc 718 387-3166
66 Middleton St Apt 1 Brooklyn (11206) *(G-1840)*
Dasan Inc 212 244-5410
54 W 39th St Fl 8 New York (10018) *(G-9811)*
Dash Printing Inc 212 643-8534
153 W 27th St New York (10001) *(G-9812)*
Data Control Inc 585 265-2980
277 David Pkwy Ontario (14519) *(G-13199)*
Data Device Corporation (HQ) 631 567-5600
105 Wilbur Pl Bohemia (11716) *(G-1049)*
Data Display USA Inc 631 218-2130
1330 Lincoln Ave Ste 2 Holbrook (11741) *(G-6443)*
Data Flow Inc 631 436-9200
6 Balsam Dr Medford (11763) *(G-8242)*
Data Implementation Inc 212 979-2015
5 E 22nd St Apt 14t New York (10010) *(G-9813)*
Data Interchange Systems Inc 914 277-7775
9 Ridge Way Purdys (10578) *(G-13972)*
Data Key Communication LLC 315 445-2347
7573 Hunt Ln Fayetteville (13066) *(G-5164)*
Data Max, New York *Also called Datamax International Inc (G-9815)*
Data Palette Info Svcs LLC 718 433-1060
35 Marino Ave Port Washington (11050) *(G-13807)*
Data Transmission Essentials 516 378-8820
83 Calvert St Ste 3 Harrison (10528) *(G-5983)*
Data-Pac Mailing Systems Corp 585 671-0210
1217 Bay Rd Ste 12 Webster (14580) *(G-16720)*
Datacom Systems Inc 315 463-9541
9 Adler Dr East Syracuse (13057) *(G-4524)*
Datadog Inc (PA) 866 329-4466
286 5th Ave Fl 12 New York (10001) *(G-9814)*
Datagraphic Business Systems 516 485-9069
79 Emjay Blvd Brentwood (11717) *(G-1180)*
Datalink Computer Products 914 666-2358
165 E Main St 175 Mount Kisco (10549) *(G-8626)*
Datamax International Inc 212 693-0933
132 Nassau St Rm 511 New York (10038) *(G-9815)*
Datasonic Inc 516 248-7330
1413 Cleveland Ave East Meadow (11554) *(G-4421)*
Datatran Labs Inc 845 856-4313
11 Rebel Ln Port Jervis (12771) *(G-13783)*
Dates Weiser Furniture Corp (PA) 716 891-1700
1700 Broadway St Buffalo (14212) *(G-2902)*
Datorib Inc 631 698-6222
974 Middle Country Rd Selden (11784) *(G-15351)*
Datum Alloys Inc 607 239-6274
407 Airport Rd Endicott (13760) *(G-4800)*
Dau Thrmal Slutions N Amer Inc 585 678-9025
1657 E Park Dr Macedon (14502) *(G-7985)*
Dave & Johnny Ltd 212 302-9050
225 W 37th St Fl 6 New York (10018) *(G-9816)*
Dave Sandel Cranes Inc 631 325-5588
56 S Country Rd Westhampton (11977) *(G-17056)*
Davel Systems Inc 718 382-6024
1314 Avenue M Brooklyn (11230) *(G-1841)*
Davenport, Rochester *Also called Brinkman Products Inc (G-14246)*
Daves Electric Motors & Pumps 212 982-2930
282 E 7th St Apt 1 New York (10009) *(G-9817)*
Daves Precision Machine Shop 845 626-7263
56 Webster Ave Kerhonkson (12446) *(G-7155)*
David & Young Co Inc 212 594-6034
366 5th Ave Rm 707 New York (10001) *(G-9818)*
David Christy 607 863-4610
2810 Cincinnatus Rd Cincinnatus (13040) *(G-3653)*
David Fehlman 315 455-8888
6729 Pickard Dr Syracuse (13211) *(G-15922)*
David Flatt Furniture Ltd 718 937-7944
3842 Review Ave Ste 2 Long Island City (11101) *(G-7710)*
David Friedman and Sons, New York *Also called David Friedman Chain Co Inc (G-9819)*
David Friedman Chain Co Inc 212 684-1760
10 E 38th St Fl 6 New York (10016) *(G-9819)*
David Helsing 607 796-2681
2077 Grand Central Ave Horseheads (14845) *(G-6573)*
David Howell & Company, Bedford Hills *Also called David Howell Product Design (G-801)*
David Howell Product Design 914 666-4080
405 Adams St Bedford Hills (10507) *(G-801)*
David Isseks & Sons Inc 212 966-8694
298 Broome St New York (10002) *(G-9820)*
David Johnson 315 493-4735
Deer River Rd Carthage (13619) *(G-3413)*
David King Linen Inc 718 241-7298
523 E 82nd St Brooklyn (11236) *(G-1842)*
David Kucera Inc 845 255-1044
42 Steves Ln Gardiner (12525) *(G-5549)*
David Peyser Sportswear Inc (PA) 631 231-7788
88 Spence St Bay Shore (11706) *(G-691)*
David Peyser Sportswear Inc 212 695-7716
1071 Ave Americas Fl 12 New York (10018) *(G-9821)*
David S Diamonds Inc 212 921-8029
546 5th Ave Fl 7 New York (10036) *(G-9822)*
David Sutherland Showrooms - N (PA) 212 871-9717
D&D Building 979 3rd New York (10022) *(G-9823)*
David Weeks Studio 212 966-3433
38 Walker St Frnt 1 New York (10013) *(G-9824)*
David Weisz & Sons Inc 212 840-4747
20 W 47th St Ste 601 New York (10036) *(G-9825)*
David Yurman, New York *Also called Yurman Retail Inc (G-12700)*
David Yurman Enterprises LLC 914 539-4444
125 Westchester Ave # 1060 White Plains (10601) *(G-17099)*
David Yurman Enterprises LLC (PA) 212 896-1550
24 Vestry St New York (10013) *(G-9826)*
David Yurman Enterprises LLC 516 627-1700
2046 Northern Blvd Manhasset (11030) *(G-8057)*
David Yurman Enterprises LLC 845 928-8660
484 Evergreen Ct Central Valley (10917) *(G-3522)*
David Yurman Retail LLC 877 226-1400
712 Madison Ave New York (10065) *(G-9827)*
Davidoff Gneva Madison Ave Inc 212 751-9060
515 Madison Ave New York (10022) *(G-9828)*
Davidoff of Geneva Ny. , Inc, New York *Also called Davidoff Gneva Madison Ave Inc (G-9828)*
Davidson Corporation (HQ) 718 439-6300
5002 2nd Ave Brooklyn (11232) *(G-1843)*
Davidson Publishing, New York *Also called Boardman Simons Publishing (G-9432)*
Davies Office Refurbishing Inc (PA) 518 426-7188
40 Loudonville Rd Albany (12204) *(G-71)*
Davinci Designs Inc 631 595-1095
899 Long Island Ave Deer Park (11729) *(G-4126)*
Davinci Dsgns Distinctive Furn, Deer Park *Also called Davinci Designs Inc (G-4126)*
Davis 716 833-4678
283 Minnesota Ave Buffalo (14215) *(G-2903)*
Davis Aircraft Products Co Inc 631 563-1500
1150 Walnut Ave Ste 1 Bohemia (11716) *(G-1050)*
Davis International Inc 585 421-8175
388 Mason Rd Fairport (14450) *(G-4854)*
Davis Logging & Lumber 315 245-1040
1450 Curtiss Rd Camden (13316) *(G-3314)*
Davis Restraint Systems Inc 631 563-1500
1150 Walnut Ave Bohemia (11716) *(G-1051)*
Davis Trailer World LLC 585 538-6640
1640 Main St York (14592) *(G-17505)*
Davis Trlr World & Cntry Mall, York *Also called Davis Trailer World LLC (G-17505)*
Davis Ziff Publishing Inc (HQ) 212 503-3500
28 E 28th St Fl 10 New York (10016) *(G-9829)*
Davler Media Group LLC 212 315-0800
498 Fashion Ave Fl 10 New York (10018) *(G-9830)*
Dawn Food Products Inc 716 830-8214
160 Lawrence Bell Dr # 120 Williamsville (14221) *(G-17240)*
Dawn Paper Co Inc (PA) 516 596-9110
4 Leonard Dr East Rockaway (11518) *(G-4469)*
Dawn Printing Company, East Rockaway *Also called Dawn Paper Co Inc (G-4469)*
Dawnex Industries Inc 718 384-0199
861 Park Ave Brooklyn (11206) *(G-1844)*
Dawson Doors, Jamestown *Also called Dawson Metal Company Inc (G-6987)*
Dawson Metal Company Inc 716 664-3811
825 Allen St Jamestown (14701) *(G-6987)*
Daxor Corporation (PA) 212 244-0555
350 5th Ave Ste 4740 New York (10118) *(G-9831)*
Day Automation Systems Inc (PA) 585 924-4630
7931 Rae Blvd Victor (14564) *(G-16472)*
Dayleen Intimates Inc 914 969-5900
540 Nepperhan Ave Yonkers (10701) *(G-17435)*
Daylight Technology USA Inc 973 255-8100
5971 59th St Maspeth (11378) *(G-8129)*
Dayton Industries Inc 718 542-8144
1350 Garrison Ave Bronx (10474) *(G-1311)*
Dayton Rogers New York LLC 585 349-4040
150 Fedex Way Rochester (14624) *(G-14302)*
Dayton T Brown Inc (PA) 631 589-6300
1175 Church St Bohemia (11716) *(G-1052)*
Dbase LLC 607 729-0234
31 Front St Binghamton (13905) *(G-907)*
DBC Inc 212 819-1177
35 W 45th St Fl 2 New York (10036) *(G-9832)*
Dbg Media 718 599-6828
358 Classon Ave Brooklyn (11238) *(G-1845)*
Dbs Interiors Corp 631 491-3013
81 Otis St West Babylon (11704) *(G-16788)*
DC Contracting & Building Corp 631 385-1117
136 Railroad St Huntington Station (11746) *(G-6701)*
DC Fabrication & Welding Inc 845 295-0215
17 Radcliff Rd Ferndale (12734) *(G-5169)*
Dcl Furniture Manufacturing 516 248-2683
96 Windsor Ave Mineola (11501) *(G-8505)*
Ddc Technologies Inc 516 594-1533
311 Woods Ave Oceanside (11572) *(G-13076)*
De Ans Pork Products Inc (PA) 718 788-2464
899 4th Ave Brooklyn (11232) *(G-1846)*
De Iorio's Bakery, Utica *Also called Deiorio Foods Inc (G-16322)*

ALPHABETIC

De La Rue North America Inc 518 463-7621
Swan Street Building Albany (12210) *(G-72)*
De Luxe Packaging Corp 416 754-4633
63 North St Saugerties (12477) *(G-15183)*
De Meo Brothers Hair, New York *Also called Demeo Brothers Inc (G-9843)*
De Santis Holster and Lea Gds, Amityville *Also called Helgen Industries Inc (G-293)*
De Witt Plastics Inc 315 255-1209
28 Aurelius Ave Auburn (13021) *(G-492)*
Dead Ringer LLC 585 355-4685
2100 Brghton Hnrtta St375 Ste 375 Rochester (14623) *(G-14303)*
Deakon Homes and Interiors 518 271-0342
16 Industrial Park Rd Troy (12180) *(G-16233)*
Deal, New York *Also called Dnp Electronics America LLC (G-9892)*
Deal International Inc 585 288-4444
110 Halstead St Ste 1 Rochester (14610) *(G-14304)*
Dealer-Presscom Inc 631 589-0434
1595 Smithtown Ave Ste A Bohemia (11716) *(G-1053)*
Dean Foods Company 315 452-5001
6867 Schuyler Rd East Syracuse (13057) *(G-4525)*
Dean Manufacturing Inc 607 770-1300
413 Commerce Rd Vestal (13850) *(G-16446)*
Dean Trading Corp 718 485-0600
200 Junius St Brooklyn (11212) *(G-1847)*
Deanco Digital Printing LLC 212 371-2025
4545 39th St Sunnyside (11104) *(G-15805)*
Deangelis Ltd 212 348-8225
312 E 95th St New York (10128) *(G-9833)*
Deans Paving Inc 315 736-7601
6002 Cavanaugh Rd Marcy (13403) *(G-8091)*
Dearfoams Div, New York *Also called RG Barry Corporation (G-11856)*
Death Wish Coffee Company LLC 518 400-1050
19 Wood Rd Ste 500 Round Lake (12151) *(G-15037)*
Debmar-Mercury 212 669-5025
75 Rockefeller Plz # 1600 New York (10019) *(G-9834)*
Debra Fisher, Valley Stream *Also called Ready To Assemble Company Inc (G-16424)*
Debrucque Cleveland Tramrail S 315 697-5160
3 Technology Blvd Canastota (13032) *(G-3366)*
Debt Resolve Inc 914 949-5500
1133 Westchester Ave S-223 White Plains (10604) *(G-17100)*
Decal Makers Inc 516 221-7200
2477 Merrick Rd Bellmore (11710) *(G-817)*
Decal Techniques Inc 631 491-1800
40 Corbin Ave Ste I Bay Shore (11706) *(G-692)*
Deck Bros Inc 716 852-0262
222 Chicago St Buffalo (14204) *(G-2904)*
Decker Forest Products Inc 607 563-2345
New York State Rte 8 Sidney (13838) *(G-15438)*
Deckers Outdoor Corporation 212 486-2509
600 Madison Ave New York (10022) *(G-9835)*
Deco Division, Elmsford *Also called Amscan Inc (G-4732)*
Decor By Dene Inc 718 376-5566
2569 Mcdonald Ave Brooklyn (11223) *(G-1848)*
Decorated Cookie Company LLC 315 487-2111
314 Lakeside Rd Syracuse (13209) *(G-15923)*
Decorative Hardeware 914 238-5251
180 Hunts Ln Chappaqua (10514) *(G-3551)*
Decorative Novelty Co Inc 718 965-8600
74 20th St Brooklyn (11232) *(G-1849)*
Decree Signs & Graphics Inc 973 278-3603
91 Tulip Ave Apt Kd1 Floral Park (11001) *(G-5202)*
Decrescente Distributing Co 518 664-9866
211 N Main St Mechanicville (12118) *(G-8226)*
Dedeco International Sales Inc (PA) 845 887-4840
11617 State Route 97 Long Eddy (12760) *(G-7642)*
Deedee Desserts LLC 716 627-2330
6969 Southwestern Blvd Lake View (14085) *(G-7279)*
Deejays, Spring Valley *Also called DJS Nyc Inc (G-15581)*
Deelka Vision Corp 718 937-4121
4502 Queens Blvd Sunnyside (11104) *(G-15806)*
Deep Dyeing Inc 718 418-7187
120 Bayview Ave Manhasset (11030) *(G-8058)*
Deer Park Driveshaft & Hose 631 667-4091
85 Brook Ave Ste C Deer Park (11729) *(G-4127)*
Deer Park Drv Shaft & Hose Co, Deer Park *Also called Deer Park Driveshaft & Hose (G-4127)*
Deer Park Macaroni Co Inc (PA) 631 667-4600
1882 Deer Park Ave Deer Park (11729) *(G-4128)*
Deer Park Macaroni Co Inc 631 667-4600
1882 Deer Park Ave Deer Park (11729) *(G-4129)*
Deer Park Ravioli & Macaroni, Deer Park *Also called Deer Park Macaroni Co Inc (G-4129)*
Deer Park Sand & Gravel Corp 631 586-2323
145 S 4th St Bay Shore (11706) *(G-693)*
Deer Pk Stair Bldg Mllwk Inc 631 363-5000
51 Kennedy Ave Blue Point (11715) *(G-998)*
Deer Run Enterprises Inc 585 346-0850
3772 W Lake Rd Geneseo (14454) *(G-5565)*
Deer Run Winery, Geneseo *Also called Deer Run Enterprises Inc (G-5565)*
Deerfield Millwork Inc 631 726-9663
58 Deerfield Rd Unit 2 Water Mill (11976) *(G-16604)*
Dees Audio & Vision 585 719-9256
347 Seneca Pkwy Rochester (14613) *(G-14305)*
Defelsko Corporation 315 393-4450
800 Proctor Ave Ogdensburg (13669) *(G-13114)*
Defense Systems, Amityville *Also called Edo LLC (G-287)*
Definition Press Inc 212 777-4490
141 Greene St New York (10012) *(G-9836)*
Defran Systems Inc 212 727-8342
1 Penn Plz Ste 1700 New York (10119) *(G-9837)*
Degennaro Fuel Service LLC 518 239-6350
242 County Route 357 Medusa (12120) *(G-8285)*
Deiorio Foods Inc (PA) 315 732-7612
2200 Bleecker St Utica (13501) *(G-16322)*
Dejah Associates Inc 631 265-2185
1515 5th Industrial Ct Bay Shore (11706) *(G-694)*
Dejah Enterprises, Bay Shore *Also called Dejah Associates Inc (G-694)*
Dejana Trck Utility Eqp Co LLC (HQ) 631 544-9000
490 Pulaski Rd Kings Park (11754) *(G-7170)*
Dejana Trck Utility Eqp Co LLC 631 549-0944
743 Park Ave Huntington (11743) *(G-6660)*
Dejana Truck & Utility Eqp Co, Huntington *Also called Dejana Trck Utility Eqp Co LLC (G-6660)*
Delaney Books Inc 516 921-8888
212 Michael Dr Syosset (11791) *(G-15819)*
Delaney Machine Products Ltd 631 225-1032
150 S Alleghany Ave Ste A Lindenhurst (11757) *(G-7460)*
Delaval Inc 585 599-4696
850 Main Rd Corfu (14036) *(G-3954)*
Delaware County Times Inc 607 746-2176
56 Main St Delhi (13753) *(G-4237)*
Delaware Graphics LLC 716 627-7582
1934 Crescent Ter Lake View (14085) *(G-7280)*
Delaware Manufacturing Inds, North Tonawanda *Also called Dmic Inc (G-12969)*
Delaware Mfg Inds Corp (PA) 716 743-4360
3776 Commerce Ct North Tonawanda (14120) *(G-12968)*
Delaware Valley Forge Inc 716 447-9140
241 Rano St Buffalo (14207) *(G-2905)*
Delbia Do Company Inc (PA) 718 585-2226
2550 Park Ave Bronx (10451) *(G-1312)*
Delbia Do Company Inc 718 585-2226
11 Canal Pl Bronx (10451) *(G-1313)*
Delcath Systems Inc (PA) 212 489-2100
1301 Ave Of The Amer 43 New York (10019) *(G-9838)*
Delfingen Us-New York Inc 716 215-0300
2221 Niagara Falls Blvd # 12 Niagara Falls (14304) *(G-12810)*
Delford Industries Inc 845 342-3901
82 Washington St 84 Middletown (10940) *(G-8436)*
Delft Blue LLC 315 768-7100
36 Garden St A New York Mills (13417) *(G-12720)*
Delft Printing Inc 716 683-1100
4401 Walden Ave Ste 8 Lancaster (14086) *(G-7311)*
Delicias Andinas Food Corp 718 416-2922
5750 Maspeth Ave Flushing (11378) *(G-5237)*
Delicioso Coco Helado Inc 718 292-1930
849 Saint Anns Ave Bronx (10456) *(G-1314)*
Delicious Foods Inc 718 446-9352
11202 Roosevelt Ave Corona (11368) *(G-3997)*
Delivery Systems Inc 212 221-7007
19 W 44th St New York (10036) *(G-9839)*
Dell Communications Inc 212 989-3434
109 W 27th St Frnt 2 New York (10001) *(G-9840)*
Dell Graphics, New York *Also called Dell Communications Inc (G-9840)*
Dell Tool, Penfield *Also called Jordan Products Inc (G-13500)*
Della Systems Inc 631 580-0010
951 S 2nd St Ronkonkoma (11779) *(G-14893)*
Dellas Graphics, Rochester *Also called Canfield & Tack Inc (G-14257)*
Dellet Industries Inc 718 965-0101
1 43rd St Ste L8 Brooklyn (11232) *(G-1850)*
Dells Maraschino Cherries Inc (PA) 718 624-4380
175 Dikeman St Ste 177 Brooklyn (11231) *(G-1851)*
Delocon Wholesale Inc 716 592-2711
270 W Main St Springville (14141) *(G-15609)*
Deloka LLC 315 946-6910
150 Dunn Rd Lyons (14489) *(G-7972)*
Delphi Amherst Test Operations, Amherst *Also called Delphi Automotive LLP (G-237)*
Delphi Automotive LLP 716 438-4886
4326 Ridge Lea Rd Amherst (14226) *(G-237)*
Delphi Automotive Systems LLC 585 359-6000
5500 W Henrietta Rd West Henrietta (14586) *(G-16875)*
Delphi Automotive Systems LLC 585 359-6000
5500 W Henrietta Rd West Henrietta (14586) *(G-16876)*
Delphi Automotive Systems LLC 585 359-6000
5500 W Henrietta Rd West Henrietta (14586) *(G-16877)*
Delphi Powertrain Systems, West Henrietta *Also called Delphi Automotive Systems LLC (G-16877)*
Delphi Thermal Systems 716 439-2454
350 Upper Mountain Rd Lockport (14094) *(G-7579)*
Delphi Thrmal Lckport Model Sp, Lockport *Also called Mahle Behr USA Inc (G-7598)*
Delphi-T Compressor Engrg Ctr, Amherst *Also called Mahle Indstrbeteiligungen GMBH (G-250)*
Delroyd Worm Gear, Niagara Falls *Also called Nuttall Gear L L C (G-12854)*

ALPHABETIC

Delsur Parts
ALPHABETIC SECTION

Delsur Parts 631 630-1606
112 Pheasant Cir Brentwood (11717) *(G-1181)*

Delta Lock Company LLC 631 238-7035
366 Central Ave Bohemia (11716) *(G-1054)*

Delta Metal Products Co Inc 718 855-4200
476 Flushing Ave Brooklyn (11205) *(G-1852)*

Delta Polymers Inc 631 254-6240
130 S 2nd St Bay Shore (11706) *(G-695)*

Delta Press Inc 212 989-3445
2426 Lucas Tpke High Falls (12440) *(G-6400)*

Delta Sheet Metal Corp 718 429-5805
3935 Skillman Ave Long Island City (11104) *(G-7711)*

Delta Upholsterers, New York *Also called Henry B Urban Inc (G-10457)*

Delta Upholsterers Inc 212 489-3308
619 W 54th St Fl 6 New York (10019) *(G-9841)*

Deltacraft Paper Company, Buffalo *Also called Millcraft Paper Company (G-3066)*

Deltacraft Paper Company LLC 716 856-5135
99 Bud Mil Dr Buffalo (14206) *(G-2906)*

Deluxe Corporation 845 362-4054
9 Lincoln Ave Spring Valley (10977) *(G-15580)*

Deluxe Corporation 212 472-7222
979 Lexington Ave New York (10021) *(G-9842)*

Deluxe Machine & Tool Co, Batavia *Also called Bill Shea Enterprises Inc (G-625)*

Deluxe Packaging Corp 845 246-6090
63 North St Saugerties (12477) *(G-15184)*

Deluxe Paint 718 768-9494
605 4th Ave Brooklyn (11215) *(G-1853)*

Demartini Oil Equipment Svc 518 463-5752
214 River Rd Glenmont (12077) *(G-5667)*

Demeo Brothers Inc 212 268-1400
129 W 29th St Fl 5 New York (10001) *(G-9843)*

Democrat & Chronicle, Rochester *Also called Gannett Co Inc (G-14387)*

Democrat & Chronicle, Farmington *Also called Gannett Co Inc (G-5151)*

Democrat & Chronicle, Lakeville *Also called Gannett Co Inc (G-7284)*

Demos Medical Publishing LLC 516 889-1791
11 W 42nd St Ste 15c New York (10036) *(G-9844)*

Den-Jo Woodworking Corp 718 388-2287
415 Withers St Brooklyn (11222) *(G-1854)*

Deniz Information Systems 212 750-5199
208 E 51st St Ste 129 New York (10022) *(G-9845)*

Denmar Electric 845 624-4430
202 Main St Nanuet (10954) *(G-8755)*

Dennies Manufacturing Inc 585 393-4646
2543 State Route 21 Canandaigua (14424) *(G-3342)*

Dennis Basso Couture Inc 212 794-4500
825 Madison Ave New York (10065) *(G-9846)*

Dennis Basso Furs, New York *Also called Dennis Basso Couture Inc (G-9846)*

Dennis Publishing Inc 646 717-9500
55 W 39th St Fl 5 New York (10018) *(G-9847)*

Denny Machine Co Inc 716 873-6865
20 Norris St Buffalo (14207) *(G-2907)*

Dennys Drive Shaft Service 716 875-6640
1189 Military Rd Kenmore (14217) *(G-7146)*

Dent-X, Mount Kisco *Also called AFP Imaging Corporation (G-8622)*

Dental Tribune America LLC 212 244-7181
116 W 23rd St Ste 500 New York (10011) *(G-9848)*

Denton Advertising Inc 631 586-4333
1650 Sycamore Ave Ste 28 Bohemia (11716) *(G-1055)*

Denton Publications Inc (PA) 518 873-6368
14 Hand Ave Elizabethtown (12932) *(G-4626)*

Denton Publications Inc 518 561-9680
21 Mckinley Ave Ste 3 Plattsburgh (12901) *(G-13661)*

Denton Stoneworks Inc 516 746-1500
94 Denton Ave Garden City Park (11040) *(G-5539)*

Denvin Inc 718 232-3389
6520 New Utrecht Ave Brooklyn (11219) *(G-1855)*

Department of Sanitation, Brooklyn *Also called City of New York (G-1783)*

Departures Magazine 212 382-5600
1120 Ave Of The Amrcs 9 New York (10036) *(G-9849)*

Depco Inc 631 582-1995
20 Newton Pl Hauppauge (11788) *(G-6061)*

Dependable Acme Threaded Pdts 516 338-4700
167 School St Westbury (11590) *(G-16976)*

Dependable Lithographers Inc 718 472-4200
3200 Skillman Ave Long Island City (11101) *(G-7712)*

Dependable Tool & Die Co Inc 315 453-5696
129 Dwight Park Cir # 2 Syracuse (13209) *(G-15924)*

Depot Label Company Inc 631 467-2952
217 River Ave Patchogue (11772) *(G-13418)*

Depp Glass Inc 718 784-8500
4140 38th St Long Island City (11101) *(G-7713)*

Depuy Synthes Inc 607 271-2500
35 Airport Rd Horseheads (14845) *(G-6574)*

Der Blatt Inc 845 783-1148
6 Taitch Ct Unit 112 Monroe (10950) *(G-8553)*

Der Yid Inc 718 797-3900
84 Bay St Brooklyn (11231) *(G-1856)*

DER YID PUBLICATION, Brooklyn *Also called Der Yid Inc (G-1856)*

Deraffele Mfg Co Inc 914 636-6850
2525 Palmer Ave Ste 4 New Rochelle (10801) *(G-8894)*

Derby Fashion Center, Conklin *Also called S & T Knitting Co Inc (G-3874)*

Derecktor Shipyards, Mamaroneck *Also called Robert E Derecktor Inc (G-8045)*

Dereon/24 K Style, New York *Also called Rvc Enterprises LLC (G-11939)*

Derm/Buro Inc (PA) 516 694-8300
229 Newtown Rd Plainview (11803) *(G-13596)*

Dermatech Labs Inc 631 225-1700
165 S 10th St Lindenhurst (11757) *(G-7461)*

Dern Moore Machine Company Inc 716 433-6243
151 S Niagara St Lockport (14094) *(G-7580)*

Deronde Doors and Frames Inc 716 895-8888
330 Greene St Buffalo (14206) *(G-2908)*

Derosa Fabrications Inc 631 563-0640
250 Knickerbocker Ave Bohemia (11716) *(G-1056)*

Derrick Corporation (PA) 716 683-9010
590 Duke Rd Buffalo (14225) *(G-2909)*

Derrick Corporation 716 685-4892
2540 Walden Ave Cheektowaga (14225) *(G-3567)*

Derrick Equipment, Buffalo *Also called Derrick Corporation (G-2909)*

Desi Talk LLC 212 675-7515
115 W 30th St Rm 1206 New York (10001) *(G-9850)*

Design A Sign of Putnam Inc 845 279-5328
1456 Route 22 Ste A102 Brewster (10509) *(G-1216)*

Design Archives Inc 212 768-0617
1460 Broadway New York (10036) *(G-9851)*

Design Craft Division, Jamestown *Also called Larson Metal Manufacturing Co (G-7016)*

Design Distributors Inc 631 242-2000
300 Marcus Blvd Deer Park (11729) *(G-4130)*

Design For All LLC 212 523-0021
240 W 37th St Rm 601 New York (10018) *(G-9852)*

Design Interiors, Brooklyn *Also called Atlantic Stairs Corp (G-1647)*

Design Lithographers Inc 212 645-8900
519 8th Ave Ste 3 New York (10018) *(G-9853)*

Design Printing Corp 631 753-9801
101 Verdi St Ste 3 Farmingdale (11735) *(G-4975)*

Design Prototyping Tech Inc, East Syracuse *Also called Md4 Holdings Inc (G-4549)*

Design Research Ltd 212 228-7675
243 Centre St New York (10013) *(G-9854)*

Design Solutions Ll Inc 631 656-8700
711 Middle Country Rd Saint James (11780) *(G-15088)*

Design Source By Lg Inc 212 274-0022
115 Bowery Frnt 1 New York (10002) *(G-9855)*

Design Works Craft Inc (PA) 631 244-5749
70 Orville Dr Ste 1 Bohemia (11716) *(G-1057)*

Design-A-Sign, Brewster *Also called Design A Sign of Putnam Inc (G-1216)*

Design/Ol Inc 631 474-5536
200 Wilson St Unit D2 Port Jeff STA (11776) *(G-13766)*

Designatronics Incorporated (PA) 516 328-3300
2101 Jericho Tpke Ste 1 New Hyde Park (11040) *(G-8825)*

Designatronics Incorporated 516 328-3300
55 Denton Ave S New Hyde Park (11040) *(G-8826)*

Designer Epoxy Finishes Inc 646 943-6044
445 Broadhollow Rd Ste 25 Melville (11747) *(G-8310)*

Designer Glass, College Point *Also called Gmd Industries Inc (G-3785)*

Designer Hardwood Flrg CNY Inc 315 207-0044
193 E Seneca St Oswego (13126) *(G-13329)*

Designers Folding Box Corp 716 853-5141
84 Tennessee St Buffalo (14204) *(G-2910)*

Designers Touch Inc (PA) 718 641-3718
750 Shore Rd Apt 6b Long Beach (11561) *(G-7639)*

Designlogocom Inc 212 564-0200
200 W 37th St New York (10018) *(G-9856)*

Designplex LLC 845 358-6647
107 Cedar Hill Ave Nyack (10960) *(G-13048)*

Designs By Hc, New York *Also called Horo Creations LLC (G-10508)*

Designs By Lanie Inc 718 945-4221
211 Beach 90th St Rockaway Beach (11693) *(G-14781)*

Designs By Novello Inc 914 934-7711
505 N Main St Port Chester (10573) *(G-13742)*

Designs By Robert Scott Inc 718 609-2535
810 Humboldt St Ste 3 Brooklyn (11222) *(G-1857)*

Designs For Vision Inc 631 585-3300
760 Koehler Ave Ronkonkoma (11779) *(G-14894)*

Designs On Fifth Ltd 212 921-4162
20 W 47th St Ste 701 New York (10036) *(G-9857)*

Designway Ltd 212 254-2220
27 E 21st St Fl 7 New York (10010) *(G-9858)*

Desiron, New York *Also called F&M Ornamental Designs LLC (G-10117)*

Desiron, New York *Also called F&M Ornamental Designs LLC (G-10118)*

Desktop Publishing Concepts 631 752-1934
855 Conklin St Ste T Farmingdale (11735) *(G-4976)*

Desku Group Inc 646 436-1464
7206 7th Ave Brooklyn (11209) *(G-1858)*

Deslauriers, Brooklyn *Also called Interntnal Strpping Diecutting (G-2113)*

Desmi-Afti Inc 716 662-0632
227 Thorn Ave Bldg C Orchard Park (14127) *(G-13269)*

Dessin/Fournir Inc 212 758-0844
232 E 59th St Fl 2 New York (10022) *(G-9859)*

Dessy Group, New York *Also called A & M Rosenthal Entps Inc (G-8981)*

Desu Machinery Corporation 716 681-5798
200 Gould Ave Depew (14043) *(G-4255)*

Detector Pro 845 635-3488
1447 Route 44 Pleasant Valley (12569) *(G-13711)*

ALPHABETIC

ALPHABETIC SECTION Dimar Manufacturing Corp

Detekion Security Systems Inc 607 729-7179
200 Plaza Dr Ste 1 Vestal (13850) ***(G-16447)***
Detny Footwear Inc 212 423-1040
1 River Pl Apt 1224 New York (10036) ***(G-9860)***
Detour Apparel Inc (PA) 212 221-3265
530 7th Ave Rm 608 New York (10018) ***(G-9861)***
Detox Water, Brooklyn *Also called Superleaf LLC* ***(G-2629)***
Deunall Corporation 516 667-8875
147 Blacksmith Rd E Levittown (11756) ***(G-7427)***
Deutsch Corporate Inc 212 710-5870
1633 Broadway Ste 1804 New York (10019) ***(G-9862)***
Deutsch Relays 631 342-1700
55 Engineers Rd Hauppauge (11788) ***(G-6062)***
Deux Lux Inc 212 620-0801
37 W 20th St Ste 1204 New York (10011) ***(G-9863)***
Deva Concepts LLC 212 343-0344
75 Spring St Fl 8 New York (10012) ***(G-9864)***
Devacurl, New York *Also called Deva Concepts LLC* ***(G-9864)***
Devil Dog Manufacturing Co Inc (PA) 845 647-4411
23 Market St Ellenville (12428) ***(G-4633)***
Devin Mfg Inc 585 496-5770
40 Edward St Arcade (14009) ***(G-391)***
Devonian Stone New York Inc 607 655-2600
463 Atwell Hill Rd Windsor (13865) ***(G-17272)***
Dew Graphics, New York *Also called DEW Graphics Inc* ***(G-9865)***
DEW Graphics Inc 212 727-8820
519 8th Ave Fl 18 New York (10018) ***(G-9865)***
Dewes Gumbs Die Co Inc 718 784-9755
3833 24th St Long Island City (11101) ***(G-7714)***
Dewey Machine & Tool Inc 607 749-3930
49 James St Homer (13077) ***(G-6516)***
Dex Media Inc 603 263-2811
6215 Sheridan Dr Ste 200 Buffalo (14221) ***(G-2911)***
Dex Media Inc 315 251-3300
6215 Sheridan Dr Ste 200 Buffalo (14221) ***(G-2912)***
Df Mavens Inc 347 813-4705
2420 49th St Astoria (11103) ***(G-437)***
DFA New York LLC 212 523-0021
240 W 37th St New York (10018) ***(G-9866)***
Dfci Solutions Inc (PA) 631 669-0494
425 Union Blvd West Islip (11795) ***(G-16904)***
Dhs Systems LLC (HQ) 845 359-6066
560 Route 303 Ste 206 Orangeburg (10962) ***(G-13224)***
Di Borghese Castello LLC 631 734-5111
17150 County Road 48 Cutchogue (11935) ***(G-4071)***
Di Domenico Packaging Co Inc 718 727-5454
304 Bertram Ave Staten Island (10312) ***(G-15665)***
Di Fiore and Sons Custom Wdwkg 718 278-1663
4202 Astoria Blvd Long Island City (11103) ***(G-7715)***
Di Highway Sign Structure Corp 315 736-8312
40 Greenman Ave New York Mills (13417) ***(G-12721)***
Di Sanos Creative Canvas Inc 315 894-3137
113 W Main St Frankfort (13340) ***(G-5351)***
Di Vico Craft Products Ltd 845 265-9390
3441 Route 9 Cold Spring (10516) ***(G-3762)***
Di Zukunft, New York *Also called Congress For Jewish Culture* ***(G-9700)***
Dia 212 675-4097
535 W 22nd St Fl 4 New York (10011) ***(G-9867)***
Dia-Nielsen USA Incorporated (HQ) 856 642-9700
400 Exchange St Buffalo (14204) ***(G-2913)***
Dialase Inc 212 575-8833
36 W 47th St Ste 709 New York (10036) ***(G-9868)***
Diam International, Yonkers *Also called Creative Solutions Group Inc* ***(G-17432)***
Diamex Inc 212 575-8145
580 5th Ave Ste 625 New York (10036) ***(G-9869)***
Diamond Boutique 516 444-3373
77 Main St Port Washington (11050) ***(G-13808)***
Diamond Brass Corp 718 418-3871
1231 Flushing Ave Brooklyn (11237) ***(G-1859)***
Diamond Bridal Collection Ltd 212 302-0210
260 W 39th St Fl 17 New York (10018) ***(G-9870)***
Diamond Collection LLC 718 846-1008
1 Rubie Plz Richmond Hill (11418) ***(G-14071)***
Diamond Constellation Corp 212 819-0324
37 W 47th St Ste 506 New York (10036) ***(G-9871)***
Diamond Coring & Cutting Inc 718 381-4545
5919 55th St Maspeth (11378) ***(G-8130)***
Diamond Distributors Inc (PA) 212 921-9188
608 5th Ave Fl 10 New York (10020) ***(G-9872)***
Diamond Inscription Tech 646 366-7944
36 W 47th St Ste 1008 New York (10036) ***(G-9873)***
Diamond Packaging Holdings LLC 585 334-8030
111 Commerce Dr Rochester (14623) ***(G-14306)***
Diamond Precast Products Inc 631 874-3777
170 Railroad Ave Center Moriches (11934) ***(G-3464)***
Diamond Saw Works Inc (PA) 716 496-7417
12290 Olean Rd Chaffee (14030) ***(G-3532)***
Diamond Seafoods LLC 503 351-3240
150 Main St Port Washington (11050) ***(G-13809)***
Diamond Venetian Blind Shade, Long Beach *Also called Designers Touch Inc* ***(G-7639)***
Diana Kane Incorporated 718 638-6520
229 5th Ave Ste B Brooklyn (11215) ***(G-1860)***
Diane Artemis Studios, Brooklyn *Also called Artemis Studios Inc* ***(G-1635)***
Diane Studios Inc (PA) 718 788-6007
34 35th St Ste 2b Brooklyn (11232) ***(G-1861)***
Diane Von Furstenberg The Shop, New York *Also called Dvf Studio LLC* ***(G-9942)***
Dianos Kathryn Designs 212 267-1584
376 Broadway Apt 13b New York (10013) ***(G-9874)***
Dib Managmnt Inc 718 439-8190
251 53rd St Brooklyn (11220) ***(G-1862)***
Dicamillo Marble and Granite 845 878-0078
20 Jon Barrett Rd Patterson (12563) ***(G-13437)***
Dice America Inc 585 869-6200
7676 Netlink Dr Victor (14564) ***(G-16473)***
Dick Bailey Printers, Brooklyn *Also called Dick Bailey Service Inc* ***(G-1863)***
Dick Bailey Service Inc 718 522-4363
25 Chapel St Ste 602 Brooklyn (11201) ***(G-1863)***
Dickard Widder Industries Inc 718 326-3700
5602 Maspeth Ave Maspeth (11378) ***(G-8131)***
Dicks Concrete Co Inc (PA) 845 374-5966
1053 County Route 37 New Hampton (10958) ***(G-8799)***
Dico Products, Utica *Also called Divine Brothers Company* ***(G-16327)***
Dico Products Corporation 315 797-0470
200 Seward Ave Utica (13502) ***(G-16323)***
Didco Inc 212 997-5022
8570 67th Ave Rego Park (11374) ***(G-14032)***
Die-Matic Products LLC 516 433-7900
130 Express St Plainview (11803) ***(G-13597)***
Diegraphics Group, Rochester *Also called Csw Inc* ***(G-14293)***
Diehl Development Inc 585 494-2920
5922 N Lake Rd Bergen (14416) ***(G-845)***
Diehl Sand & Gravel, Bergen *Also called Diehl Development Inc* ***(G-845)***
Diemax of Rochester Inc 585 288-3912
1555 Lyell Ave Ste 141 Rochester (14606) ***(G-14307)***
Diemolding Corporation (PA) 315 697-2221
125 Rasbach St Canastota (13032) ***(G-3367)***
Diemolding Corporation 315 697-2221
7887 Rt 13 N Canastota (13032) ***(G-3368)***
Digicom International Inc 631 249-8999
155 Rome St Farmingdale (11735) ***(G-4977)***
Digiday, New York *Also called Dm2 Media LLC* ***(G-9889)***
Digital Analysis Corporation 315 685-0760
716 Visions Dr Skaneateles (13152) ***(G-15458)***
Digital Associates LLC 631 983-6075
50 Karl Ave Ste 303 Smithtown (11787) ***(G-15485)***
Digital Color Concepts Inc (PA) 212 989-4888
42 W 39th St Fl 6 New York (10018) ***(G-9875)***
Digital Evolution Inc 212 732-2722
123 William St Fl 26 New York (10038) ***(G-9876)***
Digital First Media LLC (PA) 212 257-7212
20 W 33rd St Fl 7 New York (10001) ***(G-9877)***
Digital Home Creations Inc 585 576-7070
350 Shadowbrook Dr Webster (14580) ***(G-16721)***
Digital Imaging Tech LLC 518 885-4400
425 Eastline Rd D Ballston Spa (12020) ***(G-593)***
Digital Imiging Technologies, Ballston Spa *Also called Dit Prints Incorporated* ***(G-594)***
Digital Instruments Inc 716 874-5848
580 Ensminger Rd Tonawanda (14150) ***(G-16155)***
Digital Matrix Corp 516 481-7990
34 Sarah Dr Ste B Farmingdale (11735) ***(G-4978)***
Digital One USA Inc 718 396-4890
7230 Roosevelt Ave Flushing (11372) ***(G-5238)***
Digital Page LLC 518 446-9129
75 Benjamin St Albany (12202) ***(G-73)***
Digital Print Services 877 832-1200
1057 Kensington Ave Buffalo (14215) ***(G-2914)***
Digital Print Svces, Buffalo *Also called Digital Print Services* ***(G-2914)***
Digital Printing, Conklin *Also called Cadmus Journal Services Inc* ***(G-3866)***
Digital United Color Prtg Inc 845 986-9846
33 South St Warwick (10990) ***(G-16588)***
Digitech Printers, New York *Also called Balajee Enterprises Inc* ***(G-9308)***
Digitronik Dev Labs Inc 585 360-0043
181 Saint Paul St Apt 6d Rochester (14604) ***(G-14308)***
Digitronik Labs, Rochester *Also called Digitronik Dev Labs Inc* ***(G-14308)***
Dijifi LLC 646 519-2447
1166 Manhattan Ave # 100 Brooklyn (11222) ***(G-1864)***
Dilese International Inc 716 855-3500
141 Broadway St Buffalo (14203) ***(G-2915)***
Diligent Board Member Svcs LLC 212 741-8181
310 5th Ave Fl 7 New York (10001) ***(G-9878)***
Diligent Corporation (PA) 212 741-8181
1385 Brdwy Fl 19 New York (10018) ***(G-9879)***
Dillner Precast Inc 631 421-9130
200 W 9th St Huntington Station (11746) ***(G-6702)***
Dillner Precast Inc (PA) 631 421-9130
14 Meadow Ln Lloyd Harbor (11743) ***(G-7566)***
Dimaio Millwork Corporation 914 476-1937
12 Bright Pl Yonkers (10705) ***(G-17436)***
Dimanco Inc (PA) 315 797-0470
200 Seward Ave Utica (13502) ***(G-16324)***
Dimar Manufacturing Corp 716 759-0351
10123 Main St Clarence (14031) ***(G-3656)***

ALPHABETIC

(PA)=Parent Co (HQ)=Headquarters (DH)=Div Headquarters
2017 Harris
New York Manufacturers Directory
939

Dimarzio Inc ALPHABETIC SECTION

Dimarzio Inc 718 442-6655
1388 Richmond Ter Staten Island (10310) ***(G-15666)***

Dimension Development Corp 718 361-8825
3630 37th St Fl 1 Long Island City (11101) ***(G-7716)***

Dimension Fabricators Inc 518 374-1936
2000 7th St Schenectady (12302) ***(G-15248)***

Dimension Technologies Inc 585 436-3530
315 Mount Read Blvd Ste 5 Rochester (14611) ***(G-14309)***

Dimensional Mills, Hudson Falls *Also called Dwa Pallet Inc* ***(G-6641)***

Dimensional Mills Inc 518 746-1047
337 Main St Hudson Falls (12839) ***(G-6640)***

Dimoda Designs Inc 212 355-8166
48 W 48th St Ste 403 New York (10036) ***(G-9880)***

Dine Right Seating, Lindenhurst *Also called Excel Commercial Seating* ***(G-7464)***

Dine Rite Seating Products Inc 631 592-8126
165 E Hoffman Ave Unit 3 Lindenhurst (11757) ***(G-7462)***

Dinette Depot Ltd 516 515-9623
350 Dewitt Ave Brooklyn (11207) ***(G-1865)***

Dining Furniture, Brooklyn *Also called Dinette Depot Ltd* ***(G-1865)***

Dinos Sausage & Meat Co Inc 315 732-2661
722 Catherine St Utica (13501) ***(G-16325)***

Dinosaw Inc (PA) 518 828-9942
340 Power Ave Hudson (12534) ***(G-6612)***

Dionics-Usa Inc 516 997-7474
96b Urban Ave Westbury (11590) ***(G-16977)***

Dipaolo Baking Co Inc 585 303-5013
598 Plymouth Ave N Rochester (14608) ***(G-14310)***

Dipexium Pharmaceuticals Inc 212 269-2834
14 Wall St Ste 3d New York (10005) ***(G-9881)***

Direct 2 Market Solutions, Fairport *Also called Selby Marketing Associates Inc* ***(G-4876)***

Direct Alliance, New York *Also called T & R Knitting Mills Inc* ***(G-12265)***

Direct Oil LLC 914 495-3073
10 Saint Charles St Ste 9 Thornwood (10594) ***(G-16119)***

Direct Print Inc (PA) 212 987-6003
77 E 125th St New York (10035) ***(G-9882)***

Directory Major Malls Inc 845 348-7000
20 N Broadway Ste 2 Nyack (10960) ***(G-13049)***

Direkt Force LLC 716 652-3022
455 Olean Rd Ste 3 East Aurora (14052) ***(G-4369)***

Dirt T Shirts Inc 845 336-4230
444 Old Neighborhood Rd Kingston (12401) ***(G-7187)***

Dis, Islandia *Also called Duetto Integrated Systems Inc* ***(G-6792)***

Dis, New York *Also called Deniz Information Systems* ***(G-9845)***

Disc Graphics Inc 631 300-1129
30 Gilpin Ave Hauppauge (11788) ***(G-6063)***

Disc Graphics Inc (PA) 631 234-1400
10 Gilpin Ave Hauppauge (11788) ***(G-6064)***

Discountclocks.com, Long Island City *Also called Central Time Clock Inc* ***(G-7696)***

Discover Magazine, New York *Also called Discover Media LLC* ***(G-9883)***

Discover Media LLC 212 624-4800
90 5th Ave Ste 1100 New York (10011) ***(G-9883)***

Disney Publishing Worldwide (HQ) 212 633-4400
44 Brad Ln White Plains (10605) ***(G-17101)***

Dispatch Graphics Inc 212 307-5943
344 W 38th St Fl 4r New York (10018) ***(G-9884)***

Dispatch Letter Service, New York *Also called Dispatch Graphics Inc* ***(G-9884)***

Dispersion Technology Inc 914 241-4777
364 Adams St Bedford Hills (10507) ***(G-802)***

Display Components Mfg Inc 631 420-0600
267 Edison Ave West Babylon (11704) ***(G-16789)***

Display Fireworks, Canandaigua *Also called Young Explosives Corp* ***(G-3361)***

Display Logic USA Inc (PA) 516 513-1420
315 Roslyn Rd Mineola (11501) ***(G-8506)***

Display Marketing Group Inc 631 348-4450
170 Oval Dr Ste B Islandia (11749) ***(G-6791)***

Display Presentations Ltd 631 951-4050
104 Parkway Dr S Hauppauge (11788) ***(G-6065)***

Display Producers Inc 718 904-1200
40 Winding Brook Rd New Rochelle (10804) ***(G-8895)***

Display Technologies LLC (HQ) 718 321-3100
1111 Marcus Ave New Hyde Park (11042) ***(G-8827)***

Displays & Beyond Inc 718 805-7786
8816 77th Ave Glendale (11385) ***(G-5651)***

Displays By Rioux Inc 315 458-3639
6090 E Taft Rd North Syracuse (13212) ***(G-12941)***

Dissent Magazine 212 316-3120
120 Wall St Fl 31 New York (10005) ***(G-9885)***

Distech Systems Inc (HQ) 585 254-7020
1000 University Ave # 400 Rochester (14607) ***(G-14311)***

Distinction Magazine Inc 631 843-3522
235 Pinelawn Rd Melville (11747) ***(G-8311)***

Distinctive Printing Inc 212 727-3000
225 W 37th St Fl 16 New York (10018) ***(G-9886)***

Distribio USA LLC 212 989-6077
261 5th Ave Rm 1612 New York (10016) ***(G-9887)***

Dit Prints Incorporated 518 885-4400
425 Eastline Rd Ste D Ballston Spa (12020) ***(G-594)***

Diva Farms Ltd 315 735-4397
1301 Broad St Utica (13501) ***(G-16326)***

Diversified Electrical Pdts 631 567-5710
1430 Church St Unit H Bohemia (11716) ***(G-1058)***

Diversified Envelope Ltd 585 615-4697
95 Mount Read Blvd # 103 Rochester (14611) ***(G-14312)***

Diversified Manufacturing Inc 716 681-7670
4401 Walden Ave Lancaster (14086) ***(G-7312)***

Diversify Apparel, New York *Also called Babyfair Inc* ***(G-9299)***

Diversion Magazine, New York *Also called Hearst Business Publishing Inc* ***(G-10436)***

Diversity Best Practices, New York *Also called Working Mother Media Inc* ***(G-12659)***

Divico Products, Cold Spring *Also called Di Vico Craft Products Ltd* ***(G-3762)***

Divine Art Furniture Inc 718 834-0111
43 Hall St Ste C9 Brooklyn (11205) ***(G-1866)***

Divine Bros, Utica *Also called Dimanco Inc* ***(G-16324)***

Divine Brothers Company 315 797-0470
200 Seward Ave Utica (13502) ***(G-16327)***

Divine Phoenix LLC 585 737-1482
2985 Benson Rd Skaneateles (13152) ***(G-15459)***

Divine Phoenix Books, Skaneateles *Also called Divine Phoenix LLC* ***(G-15459)***

Division Den-Bar Enterprises 914 381-2220
745 W Boston Post Rd Mamaroneck (10543) ***(G-8033)***

Division of Emergency Services, Holbrook *Also called M C Products* ***(G-6459)***

Division Street News Corp 518 234-2515
108 Division St Apt 7 Cobleskill (12043) ***(G-3736)***

Dixie Foam Ltd 212 645-8999
1205 Manhattan Ave # 311 Brooklyn (11222) ***(G-1867)***

Dixiefoam Beds, Brooklyn *Also called Dixie Foam Ltd* ***(G-1867)***

Dixon Tool and Manufacturing 585 235-1352
240 Burrows St Rochester (14606) ***(G-14313)***

Diyzeitung, Brooklyn *Also called News Report Inc* ***(G-2370)***

Dj Acquisition Management Corp 585 265-3000
6364 Dean Pkwy Ontario (14519) ***(G-13200)***

Dj Pirrone Industries Inc 518 864-5496
8865 Mariaville Rd Pattersonville (12137) ***(G-13447)***

Dj Publishing Inc 516 767-2500
25 Willowdale Ave Port Washington (11050) ***(G-13810)***

DJS Nyc Inc 845 445-8618
34 Union Rd Spring Valley (10977) ***(G-15581)***

DK, Fulton *Also called D-K Manufacturing Corp* ***(G-5455)***

DK Publishing 212 366-2000
345 Hudson St New York (10014) ***(G-9888)***

Dkm Ad Art, Buffalo *Also called Dkm Sales LLC* ***(G-2916)***

Dkm Sales LLC 716 893-7777
1352 Genesee St Buffalo (14211) ***(G-2916)***

Dkny, New York *Also called Donna Karan Company LLC* ***(G-9901)***

Dkny Jeans, New York *Also called Donna Karan Company LLC* ***(G-9899)***

Dkny Underwear, New York *Also called Wacoal America Inc* ***(G-12575)***

Dl Manufacturing Inc 315 432-8977
340 Gateway Park Dr North Syracuse (13212) ***(G-12942)***

Dlc Comprehensive Medical PC 718 857-1200
979 Fulton St Brooklyn (11238) ***(G-1868)***

Dlh Energy Service LLC 716 410-0028
4422 W Fairmount Ave Lakewood (14750) ***(G-7291)***

Dli, Cazenovia *Also called Knowles Cazenovia Inc* ***(G-3447)***

Dlx Industries Inc 718 272-9420
1970 Pitkin Ave Brooklyn (11207) ***(G-1869)***

Dm2 Media LLC 646 419-4357
26 Mercer St Apt 4 New York (10013) ***(G-9889)***

DMD International Ltd 212 944-7300
99 Park Ave Rm 330 New York (10016) ***(G-9890)***

DMD Machining Technology Inc 585 659-8180
17231 Roosevelt Hwy Kendall (14476) ***(G-7143)***

Dmef/Edge, New York *Also called Marketing Edge* ***(G-11160)***

Dmic Inc 716 743-4360
3776 Commerce Ct North Tonawanda (14120) ***(G-12969)***

Dmx Enteprise 212 481-1010
192 Lexington Ave Rm 901 New York (10016) ***(G-9891)***

Dnano Inc 607 316-3694
Weill Hall 526 Campus 4 Ithaca (14853) ***(G-6837)***

Dnp Electronics America LLC 212 503-1060
335 Madison Ave Fl 3 New York (10017) ***(G-9892)***

Do It Different Inc 917 842-0230
59 W 71st St New York (10023) ***(G-9893)***

Dobrin Industries Inc (PA) 800 353-2229
210 Walnut St Ste 22 Lockport (14094) ***(G-7581)***

Docchat, Rye *Also called Smn Medical PC* ***(G-15068)***

Dock Hardware Incorporated 585 266-7920
24 Seneca Ave Ste 4 Rochester (14621) ***(G-14314)***

Doco Quick Print Inc 315 782-6623
808 Huntington St Watertown (13601) ***(G-16650)***

Doctor Bronze Solar Potions 516 775-4974
104 Hillsboro Ave Elmont (11003) ***(G-4718)***

Doctor Print Inc (PA) 631 873-4560
18 Commerce Dr Ste 1 Hauppauge (11788) ***(G-6066)***

Doctorow Communications Inc 845 708-5166
180 Phillips Hill Rd 1b New City (10956) ***(G-8783)***

Document Journal Inc 917 287-2141
122 W 27th St Fl 8 New York (10001) ***(G-9894)***

Document Strategies LLC 585 506-9000
185 Gibbs St Rochester (14605) ***(G-14315)***

Doery Awning Co, Lawrence *Also called TG Peppe Inc* ***(G-7401)***

Dog Good Products LLC 212 789-7000
1407 Broadway Fl 41 New York (10018) ***(G-9895)***

ALPHABETIC

Dog Guard, Troy *Also called Sunward Electronics Inc* ***(G-16257)***
Doheny Nice and Easy 518 793-1733
150 Broad St Glens Falls (12801) ***(G-5677)***
Doheny's Mobil, Glens Falls *Also called Doheny Nice and Easy* ***(G-5677)***
Dohnsco Inc 516 773-4800
19 Gracewood Dr Manhasset (11030) ***(G-8059)***
Dol Avim, Watertown *Also called United States Dept of Army* ***(G-16674)***
Dolby Laboratories Inc 212 767-1700
1350 6th Ave Fl 28 New York (10019) ***(G-9896)***
Dolce Vite International LLC 713 962-5767
386 12th St Brooklyn (11215) ***(G-1870)***
Dollar Popular Inc 914 375-0361
473 S Broadway Yonkers (10705) ***(G-17437)***
Dolmen 912 596-1537
216 Broome Corporate Pkwy Conklin (13748) ***(G-3867)***
Dolomite Group, Walworth *Also called Rochester Asphalt Materials* ***(G-16551)***
Dolomite Products Company Inc (HQ) 315 524-1998
1150 Penfield Rd Rochester (14625) ***(G-14316)***
Dolomite Products Company Inc 607 324-3636
7610 County Road 65 Hornell (14843) ***(G-6561)***
Dolomite Products Company Inc 585 586-2568
746 Whalen Rd Penfield (14526) ***(G-13498)***
Dolomite Products Company Inc 585 768-7295
8250 Golf Rd Le Roy (14482) ***(G-7405)***
Dolomite Products Company Inc 585 352-0460
2540 S Union St Spencerport (14559) ***(G-15569)***
Doma Marketing Inc 516 684-1111
28 Haven Ave Ste 226 Port Washington (11050) ***(G-13811)***
Domain, Brooklyn *Also called Sweater Brand Inc* ***(G-2635)***
Domani Fashions Corp 718 797-0505
86 S 1st St Brooklyn (11249) ***(G-1871)***
Domenick Denigris Inc (PA) 718 823-2264
1485 Bassett Ave Bronx (10461) ***(G-1315)***
Domestic Casing Co 718 522-1902
410 3rd Ave Brooklyn (11215) ***(G-1872)***
Dominic De Nigris Inc 718 597-4460
3255 E Tremont Ave Frnt Bronx (10461) ***(G-1316)***
Dominion Voting Systems Inc 404 955-9799
221 Hopkins Ave Jamestown (14701) ***(G-6988)***
Dominique Intimate Apparel, Yonkers *Also called Dayleen Intimates Inc* ***(G-17435)***
Domoteck Interiors Inc 718 433-4300
2430 Brooklyn Queens Expy # 1 Woodside (11377) ***(G-17326)***
Don Alleson Athletic, Geneva *Also called Alleson of Rochester Inc* ***(G-5569)***
Don Beck Inc 585 493-3040
5249 State Route 39 Castile (14427) ***(G-3416)***
Donald Bruhnke 212 600-1260
455 W 37th St Apt 1018 New York (10018) ***(G-9897)***
Donald R Husband Inc 607 770-1990
1140 E Maine Rd Johnson City (13790) ***(G-7091)***
Donald Snyder Jr 315 265-4485
528 Allen Falls Rd Potsdam (13676) ***(G-13878)***
Donald Snyder Jr Logging, Potsdam *Also called Donald Snyder Jr* ***(G-13878)***
Donald Stefan 716 492-1110
3428 W Yorkshire Rd Chaffee (14030) ***(G-3533)***
Donmaar Enterprises, Barneveld *Also called Sampo Inc* ***(G-617)***
Donmar Printing Co 516 280-2239
363 Union Ave Westbury (11590) ***(G-16978)***
Donna Degan, New York *Also called Leslie Stuart Co Inc* ***(G-10975)***
Donna Distefano Ltd (PA) 212 594-3757
37 W 20th St Ste 1106 New York (10011) ***(G-9898)***
Donna Karan Company LLC 212 372-6500
240 W 40th St Bsmt 2 New York (10018) ***(G-9899)***
Donna Karan Company LLC 212 789-1500
240 W 40th St Bsmt New York (10018) ***(G-9900)***
Donna Karan Company LLC 716 297-0752
1900 Military Rd Niagara Falls (14304) ***(G-12811)***
Donna Karan Company LLC (HQ) 212 789-1500
240 W 40th St New York (10018) ***(G-9901)***
Donna Karan International Inc (HQ) 212 789-1500
550 Fashion Ave Fl 14 New York (10018) ***(G-9902)***
Donna Karan International Inc 212 768-5800
240 W 40th St Bsmt New York (10018) ***(G-9903)***
Donna Morgan LLC 212 575-2550
132 W 36th St Rm 801 New York (10018) ***(G-9904)***
Donne Dieu 212 226-0573
315 W 36th St Frnt 3 New York (10018) ***(G-9905)***
Donnelley Financial LLC (HQ) 212 425-0298
55 Water St Lowr L1 New York (10041) ***(G-9906)***
Donorwall Inc 212 766-9670
125 Maiden Ln New York (10038) ***(G-9907)***
Dons Collection, New York *Also called Golden Season Fashion USA Inc* ***(G-10335)***
Donver Incorporated 716 945-1910
4185 Killbuck Rd Kill Buck (14748) ***(G-7166)***
Door Dam, Wassaic *Also called Presray Corporation* ***(G-16601)***
Doortec Archtctural Met GL LLC 718 567-2730
234 46th St Brooklyn (11220) ***(G-1873)***
Dor-A-Mar Canvas Products Co 631 750-9202
182 Cherry Ave West Sayville (11796) ***(G-16934)***
Doral Apparel Group Inc 917 208-5652
498 Fashion Ave Fl 10 New York (10018) ***(G-9908)***
Doral Refining Corp 516 223-3684
533 Atlantic Ave Freeport (11520) ***(G-5394)***
Doreen Chrysler 607 257-2241
40 Catherwood Rd Ithaca (14850) ***(G-6838)***
Doreen Interiors Ltd 212 255-9008
76 Nottingham Rd New Hyde Park (11040) ***(G-8828)***
Dorel Hat Co (PA) 845 831-5231
1 Main St Beacon (12508) ***(G-784)***
Doremus FP LLC 212 366-3800
228 E 45th St Fl 10 New York (10017) ***(G-9909)***
Dorgan Welding Service 315 462-9030
1378 White Rd Phelps (14532) ***(G-13531)***
Doric Vault of Wny Inc 716 828-1776
73 Gilbert St Buffalo (14206) ***(G-2917)***
Doris Panos Designs Ltd 631 245-0580
130 Old East Neck Rd Melville (11747) ***(G-8312)***
Dorling Kindersley Publishing (HQ) 212 213-4800
375 Hudson St New York (10014) ***(G-9910)***
Dorm Co., Clarence *Also called Dorm Company Corporation* ***(G-3657)***
Dorm Company Corporation 502 551-6195
9150 Hillview Dr Clarence (14031) ***(G-3657)***
Dormitory Authority - State NY 631 434-1487
998 Crooked Hill Rd # 26 Brentwood (11717) ***(G-1182)***
Dorose Albums, East Elmhurst *Also called Dorose Novelty Co Inc* ***(G-4391)***
Dorose Novelty Co Inc 718 451-3088
3107 103rd St East Elmhurst (11369) ***(G-4391)***
Dorset Farms Inc 631 734-6010
38355 Main Rd Peconic (11958) ***(G-13470)***
Dorsey Metrology Intl Inc 845 229-2929
53 Oakley St Poughkeepsie (12601) ***(G-13895)***
Dortronics Systems Inc 631 725-0505
1668 Bhmpton Sag Hbr Tpke Sag Harbor (11963) ***(G-15077)***
Dory Enterprises Inc 607 565-7079
184 State Route 17c Waverly (14892) ***(G-16701)***
DOT Publishing 315 593-2510
117 Cayuga St Fulton (13069) ***(G-5456)***
DOT Tool Co Inc 607 724-7001
131 Nowlan Rd Binghamton (13901) ***(G-908)***
Dotto Wagner 315 342-8020
185 E Seneca St Oswego (13126) ***(G-13330)***
Double Star USA Inc 212 929-2210
307 Kingsland Ave Brooklyn (11222) ***(G-1874)***
Double Take Fashions Inc 718 832-9000
68 34th St Unit 5 Brooklyn (11232) ***(G-1875)***
Dougs Machine Shop Inc 585 905-0004
5300 North St Canandaigua (14424) ***(G-3343)***
Dovelin Printing Company Inc 718 302-3951
43 Hall St Ste C2 Brooklyn (11205) ***(G-1876)***
Dover Corporation 212 922-1640
500 5th Ave Ste 1828 New York (10110) ***(G-9911)***
Dover Enterprises, Syracuse *Also called Burr & Son Inc* ***(G-15877)***
Dover Global Holdings Inc 212 922-1640
280 Park Ave New York (10017) ***(G-9912)***
Dover Marine Mfg & Sup Co Inc 631 667-4300
98 N Industry Ct Deer Park (11729) ***(G-4131)***
Dow Jones & Company Inc (HQ) 609 627-2999
1211 Avenue Of The Americ New York (10036) ***(G-9913)***
Dow Jones & Company Inc 212 597-5600
1211 Avenue Of The New York (10036) ***(G-9914)***
Dow Jones & Company Inc 212 597-5983
1211 Avenue Of The Americ New York (10036) ***(G-9915)***
Dow Jones Aer Company Inc 212 416-2000
1211 Av Of The Am Lwr C3r New York (10036) ***(G-9916)***
Dowa International Corp 212 697-3217
370 Lexington Ave Rm 1002 New York (10017) ***(G-9917)***
Dowd - Witbeck Printing Corp 518 274-2421
599 Pawling Ave Troy (12180) ***(G-16234)***
Downtown Express Newspaper, New York *Also called Community Media LLC* ***(G-9689)***
Downtown Interiors Inc 212 337-0230
250 Hudson St Lbby 1 New York (10013) ***(G-9918)***
Downtown Media Group LLC 646 723-4510
12 W 27th St Ste 1000 New York (10001) ***(G-9919)***
Downtown Music LLC 212 625-2980
485 Broadway Fl 3 New York (10013) ***(G-9920)***
Doyle & Roth Mfg Co Inc (PA) 212 269-7840
39 Broad St Ste 710 New York (10004) ***(G-9921)***
Doyle Sails, Huntington Station *Also called Melbourne C Fisher Yacht Sails* ***(G-6716)***
Doyle-Hild Sailmakers 718 885-2255
225 Fordham St Bronx (10464) ***(G-1317)***
Dp Accessories, New York *Also called Sarina Accessories LLC* ***(G-11973)***
DP Murphy Co Inc 631 673-9400
945 Grand Blvd Deer Park (11729) ***(G-4132)***
Dpi of Rochester LLC 585 325-3610
1560 Emerson St Rochester (14606) ***(G-14317)***
Dpr Food Service, Deer Park *Also called Deer Park Macaroni Co Inc* ***(G-4128)***
Dr Jayscom 888 437-5297
853 Broadway Ste 1900 New York (10003) ***(G-9922)***
Dr Mineral, Port Washington *Also called Mineralbious Corp* ***(G-13846)***
Dr Miracles Inc 212 481-3584
2900 Westchester Ave Purchase (10577) ***(G-13956)***
Dr Pepper Snapple Group Inc 315 589-4911
4363 State Route 104 Williamson (14589) ***(G-17222)***

ALPHABETIC

Dr Pepper Snapple Group Inc 914 846-2300
55 Hunter Ln Elmsford (10523) *(G-4747)*
Dr Pepper Snapple Group Inc 718 246-6200
212 Wolcott St Brooklyn (11231) *(G-1877)*
Dr Print, Hauppauge *Also called Doctor Print Inc* *(G-6066)*
Dr Reddys Laboratories NY Inc 518 827-7702
1974 State Route 145 Middleburgh (12122) *(G-8418)*
Dr Sofa, Bronx *Also called Sofa Doctor Inc* *(G-1458)*
Dra Imaging PC 845 296-1057
169 Myers Corners Rd # 250 Wappingers Falls (12590) *(G-16566)*
Drag Specialties, Ballston Spa *Also called Parts Unlimited Inc* *(G-606)*
DRAGON STEEL PRODUCTS, New York *Also called Dragon Trading Inc* *(G-9923)*
Dragon Trading Inc 212 717-1496
211 E 70th St Apt 20d New York (10021) *(G-9923)*
Draper Associates Incorporated 212 255-2727
121 Varick St Rm 203 New York (10013) *(G-9924)*
Drapery Industries Inc 585 232-2992
175 Humboldt St Ste 222 Rochester (14610) *(G-14318)*
Drasgow Inc 585 786-3603
4150 Poplar Tree Rd Gainesville (14066) *(G-5483)*
Dray Enterprises Inc 585 768-2201
1 Church St Le Roy (14482) *(G-7406)*
Dream Fabric Printing, Warwick *Also called Dream Green Productions* *(G-16589)*
Dream Green Productions 917 267-8920
39 Warwick Tpke Warwick (10990) *(G-16589)*
Dream Statuary Inc 718 647-2024
251 Cleveland St Brooklyn (11208) *(G-1878)*
Dreams To Print 718 483-8020
10101 Foster Ave Brooklyn (11236) *(G-1879)*
Dreamseats LLC 631 656-1066
60 Austin Blvd Commack (11725) *(G-3830)*
Dreamwave LLC 212 594-4250
34 W 33rd St Fl 2 New York (10001) *(G-9925)*
Drescher Paper Box Inc 716 854-0288
459 Broadway St Buffalo (14204) *(G-2918)*
Dresdiam Inc 212 819-2217
36 W 47th St Ste 1008 New York (10036) *(G-9926)*
Dresser Rand, Si, Wellsville *Also called Siemens Government Tech Inc* *(G-16759)*
Dresser-Argus Inc 718 643-1540
36 Bridge St Brooklyn (11201) *(G-1880)*
Dresser-Rand Group Inc 716 375-3000
500 Paul Clark Dr Olean (14760) *(G-13144)*
Dresser-Rand LLC 585 596-3100
37 Coats St Wellsville (14895) *(G-16751)*
Dressy Tessy Inc (PA) 212 869-0750
1410 Broadway Rm 502 New York (10018) *(G-9927)*
Drew Philips Corp (PA) 212 354-0095
231 W 39th St New York (10018) *(G-9928)*
Dreyfus Ashby Inc (HQ) 212 818-0770
630 3rd Ave Rm 1501 New York (10017) *(G-9929)*
DRG New York Holdings Corp (PA) 914 668-9000
700 S Fulton Ave Mount Vernon (10550) *(G-8677)*
Dri Relays Inc (HQ) 631 342-1700
60 Commerce Dr Hauppauge (11788) *(G-6067)*
Drill America Inc 516 764-5700
3574 Lawson Blvd Oceanside (11572) *(G-13077)*
Drillco Equipment Co Inc 718 777-5986
3452 11th St Long Island City (11106) *(G-7717)*
Drillco National Group Inc (PA) 718 726-9801
2432 44th St Long Island City (11103) *(G-7718)*
Drive Shaft Shop Inc 631 348-1818
210 Blydenburg Rd Unit A Hauppauge (11749) *(G-6068)*
Drns Corp 718 369-4530
140 58th St Ste 3f Brooklyn (11220) *(G-1881)*
Drone Usa Inc (PA) 212 220-8795
285 Fulton St Fl 85 New York (10007) *(G-9930)*
Dropcar Inc 212 464-8860
511 Ave Of The Amricas New York (10011) *(G-9931)*
Drs-Electronic Warfare & Netwo 716 631-6200
485 Cayuga Rd Buffalo (14225) *(G-2919)*
Drt Laboratories LLC 845 547-2034
331 Spook Rock Rd Airmont (10901) *(G-14)*
Drt Power Systems LLC - Lane 585 247-5940
500 Mile Crossing Blvd Rochester (14624) *(G-14319)*
Drum Ready-Mix, Felts Mills *Also called Cranesville Block Co Inc* *(G-5167)*
Drummond Framing Inc 212 647-1701
38 W 21st St Fl 10 New York (10010) *(G-9932)*
Dryden & Palmer Co, Canajoharie *Also called Gravymaster Inc* *(G-3332)*
DSI Group Inc 800 553-2202
5713 49th St Maspeth (11378) *(G-8132)*
DSM Nutritional Products LLC (HQ) 518 372-5155
2105 Technology Dr Schenectady (12308) *(G-15249)*
DSM Nutritional Products LLC 518 372-5155
300 Tech Park Glenville (12302) *(G-5701)*
Dsr International Corp 631 427-2600
107 Northern Blvd Ste 401 Great Neck (11021) *(G-5803)*
Dsti Inc 716 557-2362
301 W Franklin St Olean (14760) *(G-13145)*
Dt Industry, New York *Also called Dressy Tessy Inc* *(G-9927)*
Du Monde Trading Inc 212 944-1306
1407 Brrdwy Rm 1905 New York (10018) *(G-9933)*
Du Serv Development Co, Troy *Also called George M Dujack* *(G-16236)*
Dual Print & Mail LLC (HQ) 716 775-8001
3235 Grand Island Blvd Grand Island (14072) *(G-5754)*
Dual Print & Mail LLC 716 684-3825
340 Nagel Dr Cheektowaga (14225) *(G-3568)*
Duall Finishing Inc 716 827-1707
53 Hopkins St Buffalo (14220) *(G-2920)*
Dualtron Manufacturing, West Babylon *Also called Vandilay Industries Inc* *(G-16838)*
Duane Park Patisserie Inc 212 274-8447
179 Duane St Frnt 1 New York (10013) *(G-9934)*
Ducduc LLC 212 226-1868
524 Broadway Rm 206 New York (10012) *(G-9935)*
Duck Flats Pharma 315 689-3407
245 E Main St Elbridge (13060) *(G-4625)*
Duck River Textiles Inc (PA) 212 679-2980
295 5th Ave New York (10016) *(G-9936)*
Duck Walk Vinyards 631 726-7555
231 Montauk Hwy Water Mill (11976) *(G-16605)*
Ducommun Aerostructures NY Inc 518 731-2791
171 Stacey Rd Coxsackie (12051) *(G-4056)*
Ducon Technologies Inc (PA) 631 694-1700
5 Penn Plz Ste 2403 New York (10001) *(G-9937)*
Ducon Technologies Inc 631 420-4900
19 Engineers Ln Farmingdale (11735) *(G-4979)*
Ducts Webzine Association 718 383-6728
158 Noble St Brooklyn (11222) *(G-1882)*
Dude Publishing, Port Chester *Also called National Prof Resources* *(G-13755)*
Duetto Integrated Systems Inc 631 851-0102
85 Hoffman Ln Ste Q Islandia (11749) *(G-6792)*
Dufour Pastry Kitchens Inc 718 402-8800
251 Locust Ave Bronx (10454) *(G-1318)*
Duke Concrete Products Inc 518 793-7743
50 Duke Dr Queensbury (12804) *(G-13995)*
Duke of Iron Inc 631 543-3600
1039 W Jericho Tpke Smithtown (11787) *(G-15486)*
Dun-Rite Spclized Carriers LLC 718 991-1100
1561 Southern Blvd Bronx (10460) *(G-1319)*
Duncan & Son Carpentry Inc 914 664-4311
1 W Prospect Ave Mount Vernon (10550) *(G-8678)*
Dundas-Jafine Inc 716 681-9690
11099 Broadway St Alden (14004) *(G-177)*
Dundee Foods LLC (PA) 585 377-7700
815 Whitney Rd W Fairport (14450) *(G-4855)*
Dundeespirits, Fairport *Also called Dundee Foods LLC* *(G-4855)*
Dundy Glass & Mirror Corp 718 723-5800
12252 Montauk St Springfield Gardens (11413) *(G-15608)*
Dune Inc 212 925-6171
200 Lexington Ave Rm 200 New York (10016) *(G-9938)*
Dunkirk Construction Products 716 366-5220
852 Main St Dunkirk (14048) *(G-4338)*
Dunkirk Metal Products Wny LLC (PA) 716 366-2555
3575 Chadwick Dr Dunkirk (14048) *(G-4339)*
Dunkirk Specialty Steel LLC 716 366-1000
830 Brigham Rd Dunkirk (14048) *(G-4340)*
Dunlea Whl GL & Mirror Inc 914 664-5277
147 S Macquesten Pkwy Mount Vernon (10550) *(G-8679)*
Dunmore Corporation 845 279-5061
3633 Danbury Rd Brewster (10509) *(G-1217)*
Dunn Paper - Natural Dam Inc 315 287-1200
4921 St Rt 58 Gouverneur (13642) *(G-5745)*
Dupli Envelope & Graphics, Syracuse *Also called Dupli Graphics Corporation* *(G-15925)*
Dupli Graphics Corporation (HQ) 315 234-7286
6761 Thompson Rd Syracuse (13211) *(G-15925)*
Dupli Graphics Corporation 315 422-4732
Dupli Park Dr Syracuse (13218) *(G-15926)*
Dupont, Buffalo *Also called E I Du Pont De Nemours & Co* *(G-2924)*
Dupont, Rochester *Also called E I Du Pont De Nemours & Co* *(G-14323)*
Dura Architectural Signage, Long Island City *Also called Dura Engraving Corporation* *(G-7719)*
Dura Engraving Corporation 718 706-6400
4815 32nd Pl Long Island City (11101) *(G-7719)*
Dura Foam Inc 718 894-2488
6302 59th Ave Maspeth (11378) *(G-8133)*
Dura Spec Inc 718 526-3053
1239 Village Ct North Baldwin (11510) *(G-12904)*
Dura-Mill Inc 518 899-2255
16 Stonebreak Rd Ballston Spa (12020) *(G-595)*
Dural Door Company Inc 718 729-1333
3128 Greenpoint Ave Long Island City (11101) *(G-7720)*
Durall Dolly LLC 802 728-7122
48 Spencer St Brooklyn (11205) *(G-1883)*
Duran Jewelry Inc 212 431-1959
36 W 47th St Ste 1205 New York (10036) *(G-9939)*
Duranm Inc 914 774-3367
101 Dale Ave Cortlandt Manor (10567) *(G-4049)*
Durasol Systems Inc (HQ) 845 610-1100
445 Bellvale Rd Chester (10918) *(G-3605)*
Durata Therapeutics Inc 646 871-6400
7 Times Sq Ste 3502 New York (10036) *(G-9940)*
Durez Corporation 716 286-0100
5000 Packard Rd Niagara Falls (14304) *(G-12812)*
Duro Dyne Corporation (HQ) 631 249-9000
130 Broadhollow Rd Farmingdale (11735) *(G-4980)*

ALPHABETIC

ALPHABETIC SECTION
E J Manufacturing Inc

Duro Dyne Machinery Corp 631 249-9000
81 Spence St Bay Shore (11706) *(G-696)*
Duro Dyne National Corp (PA)....631 249-9000
81 Spence St Bay Shore (11706) *(G-697)*
Duro-Shed Inc (PA)....585 344-0800
721 Center Rd Buffalo (14224) *(G-2921)*
Dutch Spirits LLC 518 398-1022
98 Ryan Rd Pine Plains (12567) *(G-13555)*
Dutch's Spirits, Pine Plains *Also called Dutch Spirits LLC (G-13555)*
Dutchess Plumbing & Heating....845 889-8255
28 Reservoir Rd Staatsburg (12580) *(G-15618)*
Dutchess Wines LLC....845 876-1319
39 Lorraine Dr Rhinebeck (12572) *(G-14056)*
Dutchland Plastics Corp....315 280-0247
102 E Seneca St Sherrill (13461) *(G-15405)*
Dutchtreat, Buffalo *Also called Pdi Cone Co Inc (G-3116)*
Duvel Mortgage USA Inc....607 267-6121
656 County Highway 33 Cooperstown (13326) *(G-3885)*
Duxiana Dux Bed....212 755-2600
235 E 58th St New York (10022) *(G-9941)*
Duzmor Painting Inc....585 768-4760
7959 E Main Rd Le Roy (14482) *(G-7407)*
Dvash Foods Inc....845 578-1959
2 Brewer Rd Monsey (10952) *(G-8571)*
Dvf Studio LLC (PA)....212 741-6607
440 W 14th St New York (10014) *(G-9942)*
Dvmax, New York *Also called Sneakers Software Inc (G-12112)*
Dwa Pallet Inc 518 746-1047
337 Main St Hudson Falls (12839) *(G-6641)*
Dweck Industries Inc (PA)....718 615-1695
2455 Mcdonald Ave Fl 2 Brooklyn (11223) *(G-1884)*
Dweck Industries Inc....718 615-1695
2247 E 16th St Fl 2 Brooklyn (11229) *(G-1885)*
Dwell Life Inc....212 382-2010
192 Lexington Ave Fl 16 New York (10016) *(G-9943)*
Dwell Store The, New York *Also called Dwell Life Inc (G-9943)*
Dwj Books LLC 631 899-4500
21 Division St Sag Harbor (11963) *(G-15078)*
Dwm International Inc 646 290-7448
37-18 Nthrn Blvd Ste 516 Long Island City (11101) *(G-7721)*
Dwnld Inc....484 483-6572
13 Laight St Ste 24 New York (10013) *(G-9944)*
Dwyer Farm LLC....914 456-2742
40 Bowman Ln Walden (12586) *(G-16533)*
Dyco Electronics Inc....607 324-2030
7775 Industrial Park Rd Hornell (14843) *(G-6562)*
Dyenamix Inc 212 941-6642
151 Grand St Fl 2 New York (10013) *(G-9945)*
Dylans Candy Bar Inc....212 620-2700
315 E 62nd St Fl 6 New York (10065) *(G-9946)*
Dylix Corporation 719 773-2985
347 Lang Blvd Grand Island (14072) *(G-5755)*
Dyna-Empire Inc....516 222-2700
1075 Stewart Ave Garden City (11530) *(G-5500)*
Dyna-Tech Quality Inc....585 458-9970
1570 Emerson St Rochester (14606) *(G-14320)*
Dyna-Vac Equipment Inc....315 865-8084
8963 State Route 365 Stittville (13469) *(G-15762)*
Dynabrade Inc (PA)....716 631-0100
8989 Sheridan Dr Clarence (14031) *(G-3658)*
Dynak Inc....585 271-2255
530 Savage Rd Churchville (14428) *(G-3636)*
Dynamasters Inc....585 458-9970
1570 Emerson St Rochester (14606) *(G-14321)*
Dynamic Design Group Inc....212 840-9400
15 W 47th St Ste 801 New York (10036) *(G-9947)*
Dynamic Diamond, New York *Also called White Coat Inc (G-12624)*
Dynamic Dies Inc....585 247-4010
70 Pixley Industrial Pkwy Rochester (14624) *(G-14322)*
Dynamic Health Labs Inc....718 858-0100
110 Bridge St Ste 2 Brooklyn (11201) *(G-1886)*
Dynamic Hybirds Inc 315 426-8110
1201 E Fayette St Ste 11 Syracuse (13210) *(G-15927)*
Dynamic Intl Mfrs & Distrs Inc....347 993-1914
78 Lafayette Ave Ste 201 Suffern (10901) *(G-15788)*
Dynamic Laboratories Inc....631 231-7474
30 Haynes Ct Ronkonkoma (11779) *(G-14895)*
Dynamic Labs, Ronkonkoma *Also called Dynamic Laboratories Inc (G-14895)*
Dynamic Packaging Inc....718 388-0800
1825 65th St Ste 1 Brooklyn (11204) *(G-1887)*
Dynamic Pak, Syracuse *Also called Weather Products Corporation (G-16069)*
Dynamic Photography Inc....516 381-2951
48 Flamingo Rd N Roslyn (11576) *(G-15019)*
Dynamic Printing, Central Islip *Also called Richard Ruffner (G-3509)*
Dynamic Screenprinting....518 487-4256
12 Vatrano Rd Albany (12205) *(G-74)*
Dynamic Sealing Tech Inc 716 376-0708
301 W Franklin St Olean (14760) *(G-13146)*
Dynamic Systems Inc....518 283-5350
323 Rte 355 Poestenkill (12140) *(G-13723)*
Dynamica Inc 212 818-1900
930 5th Ave Apt 3f New York (10021) *(G-9948)*
Dynamo Development Inc....212 385-1552
860 Broadway Fl 5 New York (10003) *(G-9949)*
Dynasty Belts Inc....516 625-6280
161 Railroad Ave New Hyde Park (11040) *(G-8829)*
Dynasty Chemical Corp 518 463-1146
444 N Pearl St Menands (12204) *(G-8370)*
Dynasty Metal Works Inc 631 284-3719
787 Raynor Ave Riverhead (11901) *(G-14141)*
Dynasty Stainless Steel & Meta 718 205-6623
5985 Maurice Ave Maspeth (11378) *(G-8134)*
Dynatabs LLC 718 376-6084
1933 E 12th St Brooklyn (11229) *(G-1888)*
Dynatic Solutions Inc....914 358-9599
1 Water St Ste 225 White Plains (10601) *(G-17102)*
Dynax Corporation 914 764-0202
79 Westchester Ave Pound Ridge (10576) *(G-13943)*
Dyno Nobel Inc....845 338-2144
161 Ulster Ave Ulster Park (12487) *(G-16285)*
Dynocoat Inc....631 244-9344
1738 Church St Holbrook (11741) *(G-6444)*
Dyson-Kissner-Moran Corp (PA)....212 661-4600
2515 South Rd Ste 5 Poughkeepsie (12601) *(G-13896)*
E & D Specialty Stands Inc....716 337-0161
2081 Franklin St North Collins (14111) *(G-12928)*
E & G Bedding Corp....718 369-1092
1901 8th Ave Brooklyn (11215) *(G-1889)*
E & G Press, Catskill *Also called Hill Crest Press (G-3429)*
E & J Iron Works Inc....718 665-6040
801 E 136th St Bronx (10454) *(G-1320)*
E & J Offset Inc....718 663-8850
520 S 4th Ave Mount Vernon (10550) *(G-8680)*
E & O Mari Inc 845 562-4400
256 Broadway Newburgh (12550) *(G-12754)*
E & R Machine Inc 716 434-6639
211 Grand St Lockport (14094) *(G-7582)*
E & T Plastic Mfg Co Inc (PA) 718 729-6226
4545 37th St Long Island City (11101) *(G-7722)*
E & W Manufacturing Co Inc 516 367-8571
15 Pine Dr Woodbury (11797) *(G-17285)*
E & Y General Cnstr Co Inc....718 567-7011
16 Bradley Ave 2 Staten Island (10314) *(G-15667)*
E and E USA, Brooklyn *Also called Emerald Electronics Usa Inc (G-1917)*
E and V Energy Corporation....315 786-2067
22925 State Route 12 Watertown (13601) *(G-16651)*
E B Atlas Steel Corp....716 876-0900
120 Tonawanda St Buffalo (14207) *(G-2922)*
E B B Graphics Inc....516 750-5510
75 State St Westbury (11590) *(G-16979)*
E B Industries LLC (PA) 631 293-8565
90 Carolyn Blvd Farmingdale (11735) *(G-4981)*
E B Industries LLC 631 293-8565
90 Carolyn Blvd Farmingdale (11735) *(G-4982)*
E B Iron Art LLC....716 876-7510
70 Tonawanda St Buffalo (14207) *(G-2923)*
E B Trottnow Machine Spc 716 694-0600
330 E Niagara St Tonawanda (14150) *(G-16156)*
E C C Corp....518 873-6494
7 Church St Elizabethtown (12932) *(G-4627)*
E C Lyons, Bronx *Also called Edward C Lyons Company Inc (G-1323)*
E C S, Brooklyn *Also called Energy Conservation & Sup Inc (G-1924)*
E C Sumereau & Sons, Huntington Station *Also called John Larocca & Son Inc (G-6712)*
E Chabot Ltd 212 575-1026
1544 E 13th St Apt 1a Brooklyn (11230) *(G-1890)*
E D I Window Systems, Binghamton *Also called D D & L Inc (G-906)*
E F Iron Works & Construction....631 242-4766
241 N Fehr Way Ste 3 Bay Shore (11706) *(G-698)*
E F Lippert Co Inc....716 373-1100
4451 S Nine Mile Rd Allegany (14706) *(G-199)*
E F Thresh Inc....315 437-7301
6000 Galster Rd East Syracuse (13057) *(G-4526)*
E G M Restaurant Equipment Mfg....718 782-9800
688 Flushing Ave Brooklyn (11206) *(G-1891)*
E G S, Port Washington *Also called E Global Solutions Inc (G-13812)*
E Global Solutions Inc 516 767-5138
8 Haven Ave Ste 221 Port Washington (11050) *(G-13812)*
E Gluck Corporation (PA) 718 784-0700
6015 Little Neck Pkwy Little Neck (11362) *(G-7508)*
E Graphics Corporation....718 486-9767
160 Havemeyer St Brooklyn (11211) *(G-1892)*
E H Hurwitz & Associates 718 884-3766
3000 Kingsbridge Ave Bronx (10463) *(G-1321)*
E I Du Pont De Nemours & Co....716 876-4420
3115 River Rd Buffalo (14207) *(G-2924)*
E I Du Pont De Nemours & Co....718 761-0043
10 Teleport Dr Staten Island (10311) *(G-15668)*
E I Du Pont De Nemours & Co....716 879-4507
River Rd & Sheridan Dr Tonawanda (14150) *(G-16157)*
E I Du Pont De Nemours & Co....585 339-4200
69 Seneca Ave Rochester (14621) *(G-14323)*
E J Manufacturing Inc 516 313-9380
2935 Charlotte Dr Merrick (11566) *(G-8384)*

ALPHABETIC

E J Willis Company Inc 315 891-7602
37 N Main St Middleville (13406) *(G-8472)*
E L Smith Printing Co Inc 201 373-0111
3 Lisa Ct New City (10956) *(G-8784)*
E M G Creations Inc 212 643-0960
8 W 37th St New York (10018) *(G-9950)*
E M I, Rome *Also called Enviromaster International LLC* *(G-14810)*
E M T Manufacturing Inc 516 333-1917
273 Cherry Pl East Meadow (11554) *(G-4422)*
E P Sewing Pleating Inc 212 967-2575
327 W 36th St Frnt 2 New York (10018) *(G-9951)*
E S P Metal Crafts Inc 718 381-2443
379 Harman St Brooklyn (11237) *(G-1893)*
E Schreiber Inc 212 382-0280
580 5th Ave Fl 32a New York (10036) *(G-9952)*
E T C, New York *Also called Casuals Etc Inc* *(G-9544)*
E Tetz & Sons Inc (PA) 845 692-4486
130 Crotty Rd Middletown (10941) *(G-8437)*
E V G Division, Lynbrook *Also called Russell Industries Inc* *(G-7960)*
E W Smith Publishing Co 845 562-1218
36 Meriline Ave New Windsor (12553) *(G-8937)*
E W Williams Publications 212 661-1516
370 Lexington Ave Rm 1409 New York (10017) *(G-9953)*
E Z Entry Doors Inc 716 434-3440
5299 Enterprise Dr Lockport (14094) *(G-7583)*
E&I Printing 212 206-0506
545 8th Ave Rm 5e New York (10018) *(G-9954)*
E&M Power, Binghamton *Also called Mechanical Pwr Conversion LLC* *(G-934)*
E&T Plastics, Long Island City *Also called E & T Plastic Mfg Co Inc* *(G-7722)*
E-Beam Services Inc (PA) 516 622-1422
270 Duffy Ave Ste H Hicksville (11801) *(G-6341)*
E-One Inc 716 646-6790
4760 Camp Rd Hamburg (14075) *(G-5921)*
E-Play Brands LLC 212 563-2646
25 W 39th St Fl 5 New York (10018) *(G-9955)*
E-Systems Group LLC (HQ) 607 775-1100
100 Progress Pkwy Conklin (13748) *(G-3868)*
E-Won Industrial Co Inc 212 750-9610
625 Main St Apt 1532 New York (10044) *(G-9956)*
E-Z Global Wholesale Inc 888 769-7888
925 E 14th St Brooklyn (11230) *(G-1894)*
E-Z Red Co, Deposit *Also called Walter R Tucker Entps Ltd* *(G-4282)*
E-Z Ware Dishes Inc 718 376-3244
1002 Quentin Rd Brooklyn (11223) *(G-1895)*
E-Z-Em Inc (HQ) 609 524-2864
155 Pinelawn Rd Ste 230n Melville (11747) *(G-8313)*
E-Zoil Products Inc 716 213-0103
234 Fillmore Ave Tonawanda (14150) *(G-16158)*
E.J. McKenica & Sons Inc, Buffalo *Also called Edwin J McKenica & Sons Inc* *(G-2932)*
E/One Utility Systems, Schenectady *Also called Environment-One Corporation* *(G-15252)*
EAC Holdings of NY Corp 716 822-2500
701 Willet Rd Buffalo (14218) *(G-2925)*
Ead Cases 845 343-2111
43 Smith St Middletown (10940) *(G-8438)*
Eag Electric Inc 201 376-5103
496 Mosel Ave Staten Island (10304) *(G-15669)*
Eagle Art Publishing Inc 212 685-7411
475 Park Ave S Rm 2800 New York (10016) *(G-9957)*
Eagle Bridge Machine & Tl Inc 518 686-4541
135 State Route 67 Eagle Bridge (12057) *(G-4356)*
Eagle Business Systems, Bohemia *Also called Clintrak Clinical Labeling S* *(G-1034)*
Eagle Comtronics Inc 315 451-3313
7665 Henry Clay Blvd Liverpool (13088) *(G-7518)*
Eagle Crest Vineyard LLC 585 346-5760
7107 Vineyard Rd Conesus (14435) *(G-3850)*
Eagle Envelope Company Inc 607 387-3195
1891 State Route 96 3 Trumansburg (14886) *(G-16265)*
Eagle Fashions U S A, Brooklyn *Also called Eagle Finishing* *(G-1896)*
Eagle Finishing 718 497-7875
49 Wyckoff Ave Brooklyn (11237) *(G-1896)*
Eagle Graphics Inc 585 244-5006
149 Anderson Ave Rochester (14607) *(G-14324)*
Eagle Harbor Sand & Gravel Inc 585 798-4501
4780 Eagle Harbour Rd Albion (14411) *(G-164)*
Eagle Instruments Inc 914 939-6843
35 Grove St Port Chester (10573) *(G-13743)*
Eagle International LLC 917 282-2536
228 E Route 59 Ste 50 Nanuet (10954) *(G-8756)*
Eagle Lace Dyeing Corp 212 947-2712
335 W 35th St Fl 2 New York (10001) *(G-9958)*
Eagle Media Partners LP (PA) 315 434-8889
2501 James St Ste 100 Syracuse (13206) *(G-15928)*
Eagle Nesher, Brooklyn *Also called Imperial Sweater Mills Inc* *(G-2100)*
Eagle Newspapers, Syracuse *Also called Eagle Media Partners LP* *(G-15928)*
Eagle Regalia Co Inc 845 425-2245
747 Chestnut Ridge Rd # 101 Spring Valley (10977) *(G-15582)*
Eagle Telephonics Inc 631 471-3600
3880 Veterans Mem Hwy Bohemia (11716) *(G-1059)*
Eagle Welding Machine 315 594-1845
13458 Ridge Rd Wolcott (14590) *(G-17279)*
Eagles Nest Holdings LLC (PA) 513 874-5270
455 E 86th St New York (10028) *(G-9959)*
Eaglesome Graphics Inc 716 665-1116
20 W 3rd St Ste 10 Jamestown (14701) *(G-6989)*
Earl G Graves Pubg Co Inc (HQ) 212 242-8000
260 Madison Ave Ste 11 New York (10016) *(G-9960)*
Earlville Paper Box Co Inc 315 691-2131
19 Clyde St Earlville (13332) *(G-4360)*
Earring King Jewelry Mfg Inc 718 544-7947
62 W 47th St Ste 1202 New York (10036) *(G-9961)*
Earth Spectrum, New York *Also called Spectrum Prtg Lithography Inc* *(G-12158)*
Easco Boiler, Bronx *Also called A L Eastmond & Sons Inc* *(G-1254)*
Easco Boiler Corp 718 378-3000
1175 Leggett Ave Bronx (10474) *(G-1322)*
Easel, New York *Also called Ksk International Inc* *(G-10891)*
East Aurora Advertiser, East Aurora *Also called Grant Hamilton* *(G-4371)*
East Branch Winery Inc (PA) 607 292-3999
5503 Dutch St Dundee (14837) *(G-4326)*
East Cast Clor Compounding Inc 631 491-9000
15 Kean St West Babylon (11704) *(G-16790)*
East Cast Envlope Graphics LLC 718 326-2424
5615 55th Dr Maspeth (11378) *(G-8135)*
East Cast Orthtics Prosthetics 716 856-5192
505 Delaware Ave Buffalo (14202) *(G-2926)*
East Coast Cultures LLC 917 261-3010
906 State Route 28 Kingston (12401) *(G-7188)*
East Coast Cycle LLC 631 780-5360
80 Smith St Ste 1 Farmingdale (11735) *(G-4983)*
East Coast Embroidery Ltd 631 254-3878
74 Brook Ave Ste 1 Deer Park (11729) *(G-4133)*
East Coast Envmtl Group Inc 516 352-1946
136 Allen Blvd Farmingdale (11735) *(G-4984)*
East Coast Intl Tire Inc 718 386-9088
5746 Flushing Ave Bldg C Maspeth (11378) *(G-8136)*
East Coast Mines & Material, East Quogue *Also called East Coast Mines Ltd* *(G-4450)*
East Coast Mines Ltd 631 653-5445
2 Lewis Rd East Quogue (11942) *(G-4450)*
East Coast Molders Inc 516 240-6000
3001 New St Ste F Oceanside (11572) *(G-13078)*
East Coast Orthoic & Pros Cor (PA) 516 248-5566
75 Burt Dr Deer Park (11729) *(G-4134)*
East Coast Orthoic & Pros Cor 212 923-2161
3927 Broadway New York (10032) *(G-9962)*
East Coast Spring Mix Inc 845 355-1215
211 Lynch Ave New Hampton (10958) *(G-8800)*
East Coast Thermographers Inc 718 321-3211
1558 127th St Ste 1 College Point (11356) *(G-3782)*
East Coast Tool & Mfg 716 826-5183
1 Alliance Dr Buffalo (14218) *(G-2927)*
East End 716 532-2622
1995 Lenox Rd Collins (14034) *(G-3816)*
East End Country Kitchens Inc 631 727-2258
121 Edwards Ave Calverton (11933) *(G-3290)*
East End Sign Design Inc 631 399-2574
1161 Montauk Hwy Mastic (11950) *(G-8202)*
East End Vineyards LLC 718 468-0500
21548 Jamaica Ave Queens Village (11428) *(G-13976)*
East Hampton Ind News Inc 631 324-2500
74 Montauk Hwy Unit 19 East Hampton (11937) *(G-4408)*
East Hampton Independent The, East Hampton *Also called East Hampton Ind News Inc* *(G-4408)*
East Hampton Star Inc 631 324-0002
153 Main St East Hampton (11937) *(G-4409)*
East Hills Instrument Inc 516 621-8686
60 Shames Dr Unit B Westbury (11590) *(G-16980)*
East Hudson Watershed Corp 845 319-6349
2 Route 164 Patterson (12563) *(G-13438)*
East Main Associates 585 624-1990
7520 E Main St Lima (14485) *(G-7444)*
East Meet East Inc 650 450-4446
347 5th Ave Rm 1402 New York (10016) *(G-9963)*
East Pattern & Model Corp (PA) 585 461-3240
75 N Main St Fairport (14450) *(G-4856)*
East Penn Manufacturing Co 631 321-7161
790 Railroad Ave Babylon (11704) *(G-547)*
East Resources Inc (HQ) 716 373-0944
51 W Main St Allegany (14706) *(G-200)*
East Ridge Quick Print 585 266-4911
1249 Ridgeway Ave Ste Y Rochester (14615) *(G-14325)*
East Side Machine Inc 585 265-4560
625 Phillips Rd Webster (14580) *(G-16722)*
East Side Printers, East Syracuse *Also called Eastside Printers* *(G-4527)*
East To West Architectral Pdts 631 433-9690
103 Tinton Pl Ste 1a East Northport (11731) *(G-4435)*
East West Global Sourcing Inc 917 887-2286
425 Neptune Ave Apt 22a Brooklyn (11224) *(G-1897)*
East/West Industries Inc 631 981-5900
80 13th Ave Ronkonkoma (11779) *(G-14896)*
Eastchester Photo Services 914 961-6596
132 Fisher Ave Eastchester (10709) *(G-4582)*
Eastchester Photo Svce, Eastchester *Also called Eastchester Photo Services* *(G-4582)*

Eastco Manufacturing Corp 914 738-5667
323 Fifth Ave Pelham (10803) ***(G-13490)***

Eastend Enforcement Products 631 878-8424
24 Chichester Ave Center Moriches (11934) ***(G-3465)***

Eastern Air Products LLC 716 391-1866
41 Ward Rd Lancaster (14086) ***(G-7313)***

Eastern Castings Co 518 677-5610
2 Pearl St Cambridge (12816) ***(G-3307)***

Eastern Color Imaging, Bohemia *Also called Eastern Color Stripping Inc* ***(G-1060)***

Eastern Color Stripping Inc 631 563-3700
1566 Ocean Ave Ste 8 Bohemia (11716) ***(G-1060)***

Eastern Company 315 468-6251
3000 Milton Ave Solvay (13209) ***(G-15507)***

Eastern Concepts Ltd 718 472-3377
4125 39th St Sunnyside (11104) ***(G-15807)***

Eastern Enterprise Corp 718 727-8600
465 Bay St Ste 2 Staten Island (10304) ***(G-15670)***

Eastern Exterior Wall 631 589-3880
869 Lincoln Ave Bohemia (11716) ***(G-1061)***

Eastern Feather & Down Corp 718 387-4100
1027 Metropolitan Ave Brooklyn (11211) ***(G-1898)***

Eastern Finding Corp 516 747-6640
116 County Courthouse Rd New Hyde Park (11040) ***(G-8830)***

Eastern Harbor Media 212 725-9260
37 W 17th St Ste 3e New York (10011) ***(G-9964)***

Eastern Hills Printing (PA) 716 741-3300
9195 Main St Clarence (14031) ***(G-3659)***

Eastern Industrial Steel Corp (PA) 845 639-9749
4 Fringe Ct New City (10956) ***(G-8785)***

Eastern Jewelry Mfg Co Inc 212 840-0001
48 W 48th St Ste 707 New York (10036) ***(G-9965)***

Eastern Jungle Gym Inc (PA) 845 878-9800
30 Commerce Dr Carmel (10512) ***(G-3399)***

Eastern Machine and Electric 716 284-8271
1041 Niagara Ave Niagara Falls (14305) ***(G-12813)***

Eastern Manufacturing Inc 716 741-4572
9760 County Rd Clarence Center (14032) ***(G-3674)***

Eastern Metal of Elmira Inc (PA) 607 734-2295
1430 Sullivan St Elmira (14901) ***(G-4679)***

Eastern Niagra Radiology 716 882-6544
899 Main St Buffalo (14203) ***(G-2928)***

Eastern Offset, Albany *Also called Northeast Commercial Prtg Inc* ***(G-109)***

Eastern Precision Machining 631 286-4758
11 Farber Dr Ste I Bellport (11713) ***(G-829)***

Eastern Precision Mfg 845 358-1951
76 S Franklin St 78 Nyack (10960) ***(G-13050)***

Eastern Silk Mills Inc 212 730-1300
148 W 37th St Fl 3 New York (10018) ***(G-9966)***

Eastern Silver of Boro Park 718 854-5600
4901 16th Ave Brooklyn (11204) ***(G-1899)***

Eastern Storefronts & Mtls Inc 631 471-7065
1739 Julia Goldbach Ave Ronkonkoma (11779) ***(G-14897)***

Eastern Strategic Materials 212 332-1619
45 Rockefeller Plz # 2000 New York (10111) ***(G-9967)***

Eastern Unit Exch Rmnfacturing 718 739-7113
186 Beech St Floral Park (11001) ***(G-5203)***

Eastern Welding Inc 631 727-0306
274 Mill Rd Riverhead (11901) ***(G-14142)***

Eastland Electronics Co Inc 631 580-3800
700 Union Pkwy Ste 9 Ronkonkoma (11779) ***(G-14898)***

Eastman Chemical Company 585 722-2905
2255 Mount Read Blvd Rochester (14615) ***(G-14326)***

Eastman Kodak Company 585 722-2187
233 Olde Harbour Trl Rochester (14612) ***(G-14327)***

Eastman Kodak Company (PA) 585 724-4000
343 State St Rochester (14650) ***(G-14328)***

Eastman Kodak Company 585 724-5600
1669 Lake Ave Bldg 31-4 Rochester (14652) ***(G-14329)***

Eastman Kodak Company 585 722-9695
1818 W Jefferson Rd Pittsford (14534) ***(G-13558)***

Eastman Kodak Company 585 726-6261
39 Kaywood Dr Rochester (14626) ***(G-14330)***

Eastman Kodak Company 585 724-4000
2600 Manitou Rd Rochester (14650) ***(G-14331)***

Eastman Kodak Company 800 698-3324
343 State St Rochester (14650) ***(G-14332)***

Eastman Kodak Company 585 722-4385
1999 Lake Ave 6/83/RI Rochester (14650) ***(G-14333)***

Eastman Kodak Company 585 588-5598
300 Weiland Road Rochester (14650) ***(G-14334)***

Eastman Kodak Company 585 726-7000
343 State St Rochester (14650) ***(G-14335)***

Eastman Kodak Company 585 722-4007
2400 Mount Read Blvd Rochester (14615) ***(G-14336)***

Eastman Kodak Company 585 588-3896
100 Latona Rd Gate 340 Rochester (14652) ***(G-14337)***

Eastman Kodak Company 585 724-4000
343 State St Rochester (14650) ***(G-14338)***

Eastman Machine Company 716 856-2200
779 Washington St Buffalo (14203) ***(G-2929)***

Eastman Park Micrographics Inc 866 934-4376
100 Latona Rd Bldg 318 Rochester (14652) ***(G-14339)***

Eastnets Americas Corp 212 631-0666
450 Fashion Ave Ste 1509 New York (10123) ***(G-9968)***

Eastport Management, New York *Also called Eastport Operating Partners LP* ***(G-9969)***

Eastport Operating Partners LP (PA) 212 387-8791
204 E 20th St Fl 3 New York (10003) ***(G-9969)***

Eastside Orthotics Prosthetics, New York *Also called Manhattan Eastside Dev Corp* ***(G-11129)***

Eastside Oxide Co 607 734-1253
211 Judson St Elmira (14901) ***(G-4680)***

Eastside Printers 315 437-6515
6163 E Molloy Rd East Syracuse (13057) ***(G-4527)***

Eastwood Litho Inc 315 437-2626
4020 New Court Ave Syracuse (13206) ***(G-15929)***

Easy Book Publishing Inc 518 459-6281
260 Osborne Rd Ste 3 Albany (12211) ***(G-75)***

Easy H2b, Hudson *Also called Micosta Enterprises Inc* ***(G-6627)***

Eating Evolved Inc 516 510-2601
10 Technology Dr Unit 5 East Setauket (11733) ***(G-4480)***

Eatingevolved LLC 631 675-2440
10 Technology Dr Setauket (11733) ***(G-15376)***

Eaton Brothers Corp 716 649-8250
3530 Lakeview Rd Hamburg (14075) ***(G-5922)***

Eaton Corporation 212 319-2100
830 3rd Ave Fl 7 New York (10022) ***(G-9970)***

Eaton Corporation 585 394-1780
2375 State Route 332 # 250 Canandaigua (14424) ***(G-3344)***

Eaton Corporation 516 353-3017
280 Bellmore Rd East Meadow (11554) ***(G-4423)***

Eaton Corporation 315 579-2872
125 E Jefferson St Syracuse (13202) ***(G-15930)***

Eaton Corporation 716 691-0008
55 Pineview Dr Ste 600 Buffalo (14228) ***(G-2930)***

Eaton Crouse-Hinds 315 477-7000
500 7th North St Syracuse (13208) ***(G-15931)***

Eaton Electric Holdings LLC 607 756-2821
45 Cleveland St Cortland (13045) ***(G-4025)***

Eaton Hydraulics LLC 716 375-7132
1648 Dugan Rd Olean (14760) ***(G-13147)***

Eatons Crouse Hinds Business 315 477-7000
1201 Wolf St Syracuse (13208) ***(G-15932)***

Eaw Electronic Systems Inc 845 471-5290
16 Victory Ln Ste 3 Poughkeepsie (12603) ***(G-13897)***

Eazy Locks LLC 718 327-7770
1914 Mott Ave Far Rockaway (11691) ***(G-4920)***

Eazy Movements 716 837-2083
337 Hoyt St Buffalo (14213) ***(G-2931)***

Eazylift Albany LLC 518 452-6929
836 Troy Schenectady Rd Latham (12110) ***(G-7361)***

EB Acquisitions LLC 212 355-3310
444 Madison Ave Ste 501 New York (10022) ***(G-9971)***

Eb Automation Industries, West Hempstead *Also called Genesis One Unlimeted* ***(G-16854)***

EB&I Marketing, Skaneateles *Also called Burdick Publications Inc* ***(G-15456)***

Ebara Technologies Inc 845 896-1370
20 Corporate Park Rd B Hopewell Junction (12533) ***(G-6548)***

Ebeling Associates Inc (PA) 518 688-8700
9 Corporate Dr Ste 1 Halfmoon (12065) ***(G-5910)***

Ebenezer Railcar Services Inc 716 674-5650
1005 Indian Church Rd West Seneca (14224) ***(G-16943)***

Eberhardt Enterprises Inc 585 458-7681
1325 Mount Read Blvd Rochester (14606) ***(G-14340)***

EBM, Westbury *Also called Executive Business Media Inc* ***(G-16983)***

EBM Care Inc 212 500-5000
317 Madison Ave New York (10017) ***(G-9972)***

Eboost, New York *Also called Vitalize Labs LLC* ***(G-12556)***

Ebsco Industries Inc 585 398-2000
5815 County Road 41 Farmington (14425) ***(G-5149)***

EBY Electro Inc 516 576-7777
210 Express St Plainview (11803) ***(G-13598)***

EC Publications Inc 212 728-1844
1700 Broadway Frnt 5 New York (10019) ***(G-9973)***

EC Wood & Company Inc 718 388-2287
110 E Industry Ct Deer Park (11729) ***(G-4135)***

Ecclesiastical Communications 212 688-2399
1011 1st Ave Fl 6 New York (10022) ***(G-9974)***

Ecclesiastical Press, Edmeston *Also called Bishop Print Shop Inc* ***(G-4622)***

Ecco Bay Sportswear, New York *Also called Cathy Daniels Ltd* ***(G-9550)***

Echo Appellate Press Inc 516 432-3601
30 W Park Ave Ste 200 Long Beach (11561) ***(G-7640)***

Echo Group Inc 917 608-7440
62 W 39th St Ste 1005 New York (10018) ***(G-9975)***

Eci, Norwich *Also called Electron Coil Inc* ***(G-13027)***

Eck Plastic Arts Inc 607 722-3227
87 Prospect Ave Binghamton (13901) ***(G-909)***

Ecker Window Corp 914 776-0000
1 Odell Plz Yonkers (10701) ***(G-17438)***

Eckerson Drugs Inc 845 352-1800
275 N Main St Ste 12 Spring Valley (10977) ***(G-15583)***

Ecko Fin & Tooling Inc 716 487-0200
221 Hopkins Ave Ste 2 Jamestown (14701) ***(G-6990)***

Eclectic Cntract Furn Inds Inc 212 967-5504
450 Fashion Ave Ste 2710 New York (10123) ***(G-9976)***

(PA)=Parent Co (HQ)=Headquarters (DH)=Div Headquarters
2017 Harris
New York Manufacturers Directory
945

Eclipse Collection Jewelers ...212 764-6883
7 W 45th St Ste 1401 New York (10036) ***(G-9977)***
Eco-Bat America LLC ...845 692-4414
65 Ballard Rd Middletown (10941) ***(G-8439)***
Ecolab Inc ...716 683-6298
3719 Union Rd Ste 121 Cheektowaga (14225) ***(G-3569)***
Ecological Laboratories Inc (PA) ...516 823-3441
13 Hendrickson Ave Lynbrook (11563) ***(G-7950)***
Econocraft Worldwide Mfg Inc ...914 966-2280
56 Worth St Frnt Unit Yonkers (10701) ***(G-17439)***
Economist Group, The, New York *Also called Economist Newspaper Group Inc* ***(G-9979)***
Economist Intelligence Unit NA ...212 554-0600
750 3rd Ave Fl 5 New York (10017) ***(G-9978)***
Economist Magazine, The, New York *Also called Economist Newspaper NA Inc* ***(G-9980)***
Economist Newspaper Group Inc (HQ) ...212 541-0500
750 3rd Ave Fl 5 New York (10017) ***(G-9979)***
Economist Newspaper NA Inc (HQ) ...212 554-0676
750 3rd Ave Fl 5 New York (10017) ***(G-9980)***
Economy 24/7 Inc ...917 403-8876
167 6th Ave Brooklyn (11217) ***(G-1900)***
Economy Energy LLC ...845 222-3384
500 Highland Ave Peekskill (10566) ***(G-13476)***
Economy Pump & Motor Repair ...718 433-2600
3652 36th St Astoria (11106) ***(G-438)***
Ecoplast & Packaging LLC ...718 996-0800
4619 Surf Ave Brooklyn (11224) ***(G-1901)***
Ecosmartplastics, Islandia *Also called Repellem Consumer Pdts Corp* ***(G-6802)***
ECR International Inc (PA) ...315 797-1310
2201 Dwyer Ave Utica (13501) ***(G-16328)***
ECR International Inc ...716 366-5500
85 Middle Rd Dunkirk (14048) ***(G-4341)***
Ecto Tech Automation, Buffalo *Also called Multisorb Technologies Inc* ***(G-3079)***
Ecuador News Inc ...718 205-7014
6403 Roosevelt Ave Fl 2 Woodside (11377) ***(G-17327)***
Ed Beach Forest Management ...607 538-1745
2042 Scott Rd Bloomville (13739) ***(G-994)***
Ed Levin Inc ...518 677-8595
52 W Main St Cambridge (12816) ***(G-3308)***
Ed Levin Jewelry, Cambridge *Also called Ed Levin Inc* ***(G-3308)***
Ed Negron Fine Woodworking ...718 246-1016
43 Hall St Fl 5 Brooklyn (11205) ***(G-1902)***
Edco Supply Corporation ...718 788-8108
323 36th St Brooklyn (11232) ***(G-1903)***
Eden Tool & Die Inc ...716 992-4240
2721 Hemlock Rd Eden (14057) ***(G-4586)***
Edge Display Group Entp Inc ...631 498-1373
35 Sawgrass Dr Ste 2 Bellport (11713) ***(G-830)***
Edge-Craft Process Co, West Babylon *Also called Flexene Corp* ***(G-16792)***
Edgeucational Publishing, New York *Also called Hazan Cohen Group LLC* ***(G-10432)***
Edgewood Industries Inc ...516 227-2447
635 Commercial Ave Garden City (11530) ***(G-5501)***
Edgian Press Inc ...516 931-2114
10 Bethpage Rd Hicksville (11801) ***(G-6342)***
Edison Power & Light Co Inc ...718 522-0002
204 Van Dyke St Ste 207 Brooklyn (11231) ***(G-1904)***
Edison Price Lighting Inc (PA) ...718 685-0700
4150 22nd St Long Island City (11101) ***(G-7723)***
Edison Price Lighting Inc ...718 685-0700
4105 21st St Long Island City (11101) ***(G-7724)***
Edith Lances Corp ...212 683-1990
247 W 35th St Fl 2 New York (10001) ***(G-9981)***
Editions Schellmann Inc ...212 219-1821
50 Greene St Fl 2 New York (10013) ***(G-9982)***
Editorial America S A, New York *Also called Et Publishing Intl LLC* ***(G-10075)***
Edlaw Pharmaceuticals Inc ...631 454-6888
195 Central Ave Ste B Farmingdale (11735) ***(G-4985)***
EDM Mfg ...631 669-1966
141 John St Ste 600 Babylon (11702) ***(G-548)***
Edo Corporation, Amityville *Also called Edo LLC* ***(G-285)***
Edo Crprtion-Fiber Science Div, Bohemia *Also called Edo LLC* ***(G-1062)***
Edo LLC (HQ) ...631 630-4000
1500 New Horizons Blvd Amityville (11701) ***(G-285)***
Edo LLC ...631 630-4200
1500 New Horizons Blvd Amityville (11701) ***(G-286)***
Edo LLC ...631 218-1413
5852 Johnson Ave Bohemia (11716) ***(G-1062)***
Edo LLC ...631 630-4000
1500 New Horizons Blvd Amityville (11701) ***(G-287)***
EDP Renewables North Amer LLC ...518 426-1650
1971 Western Ave 230 Albany (12203) ***(G-76)***
Edr Industries Inc ...516 868-1928
100 Commercial St Freeport (11520) ***(G-5395)***
Edrington Group Usa LLC (PA) ...212 352-6000
150 5th Ave Fl 11 New York (10011) ***(G-9983)***
Edroy Products Co Inc ...845 358-6600
245 N Midland Ave Nyack (10960) ***(G-13051)***
Edsal Machine Products Inc (PA) ...718 439-9163
126 56th St Brooklyn (11220) ***(G-1905)***
Edsim Leather Co Inc (PA) ...212 695-8500
131 W 35th St Fl 14 New York (10001) ***(G-9984)***
Educa Publishing Inc ...516 472-0678
391 Great Neck Rd Unit C Great Neck (11021) ***(G-5804)***

ALPHABETIC

Edward C Lyons Company Inc ...718 515-5361
3646 White Plains Rd Frnt Bronx (10467) ***(G-1323)***
Edward C Muller Corp ...718 881-7270
3646 White Plains Rd Frnt Bronx (10467) ***(G-1324)***
Edward C. Lyons, Bronx *Also called Edward C Muller Corp* ***(G-1324)***
Edward Fields Incorporated (PA) ...212 310-0400
150 E 58th St Ste 1101 New York (10155) ***(G-9985)***
Edwards Graphic Co Inc ...718 548-6858
3801 Hudson Manor Ter 4s Bronx (10463) ***(G-1325)***
Edwards Vacuum LLC (HQ) ...800 848-9800
6416 Inducon Dr W Sanborn (14132) ***(G-15119)***
Edwin J McKenica & Sons Inc ...716 823-4646
1200 Clinton St Buffalo (14206) ***(G-2932)***
Edwin Mellen Press Inc ...716 754-2796
442 Center St Lewiston (14092) ***(G-7434)***
Eeg Enterprises Inc ...516 293-7472
586 Main St Farmingdale (11735) ***(G-4986)***
Eele Laboratories LLC ...631 244-0051
50 Orville Dr Bohemia (11716) ***(G-1063)***
Efam Enterprises LLC ...718 204-1760
2919 39th Ave Long Island City (11101) ***(G-7725)***
Effanjay Pens Inc ...212 316-9565
2109 Borden Ave Fl 2 Long Island City (11101) ***(G-7726)***
Efficiency Printing Co Inc ...914 949-8611
126 S Lexington Ave White Plains (10606) ***(G-17103)***
Efficient Automated Mch Corp ...718 937-9393
3913 23rd St Fl 1 Long Island City (11101) ***(G-7727)***
Efficient Mach Shop, Long Island City *Also called Efficient Automated Mch Corp* ***(G-7727)***
Efj Inc ...518 234-4799
128 Macarthur Ave Cobleskill (12043) ***(G-3737)***
Efron Designs Ltd ...718 482-8440
2121 41st Ave Ste 5b Long Island City (11101) ***(G-7728)***
Efront Financial Solutions Inc ...212 220-0660
11 E 44th St Ste 900 New York (10017) ***(G-9986)***
Efs Designs ...718 852-9511
610 Smith St Ste 3 Brooklyn (11231) ***(G-1906)***
Eft Energy Inc ...212 290-2300
251 W 30th St Ste 15e New York (10001) ***(G-9987)***
Eg Indsturies, Rochester *Also called Ernie Green Industries Inc* ***(G-14358)***
Eg Industries, Rochester *Also called Ernie Green Industries Inc* ***(G-14357)***
Egg Low Farms Inc ...607 674-4653
35 W State St Sherburne (13460) ***(G-15391)***
Egli Machine Company Inc ...607 563-3663
240 State Highway 7 Sidney (13838) ***(G-15439)***
Ehrlich Enterprises Inc ...631 956-0690
91 Marcus Blvd Hauppauge (11788) ***(G-6069)***
Ehs Group LLC ...914 937-6162
69 Townsend St Port Chester (10573) ***(G-13744)***
Ei, Endicott *Also called Endicott Interconnect Tech Inc* ***(G-4802)***
Ei Electronics Inc ...516 334-0870
1800 Shames Dr Westbury (11590) ***(G-16981)***
Eidosmedia Inc ...646 795-2100
14 Wall St Ste 6c New York (10005) ***(G-9988)***
Eighteen Liana Trading Inc ...718 369-4247
110 W 40th St Rm 606 New York (10018) ***(G-9989)***
Eileen Fisher Inc (PA) ...914 591-5700
2 Bridge St Ste 230 Irvington (10533) ***(G-6768)***
Eileen Fisher Womens Apparel, Irvington *Also called Eileen Fisher Inc* ***(G-6768)***
Eileens Special Cheesecake ...212 966-5585
17 Cleveland Pl Frnt A New York (10012) ***(G-9990)***
Eis Inc ...585 426-5330
40 Hytec Cir Rochester (14606) ***(G-14341)***
Eiseman-Ludmar Co Inc ...516 932-6990
56 Bethpage Dr Hicksville (11801) ***(G-6343)***
Eisen Bros, Brooklyn *Also called National Die & Button Mould Co* ***(G-2350)***
Ej Group Inc ...315 699-2601
6177 S Bay Rd Cicero (13039) ***(G-3645)***
Eko-Blu, New York *Also called N Y Winstons Inc* ***(G-11337)***
Ekostinger Inc ...585 739-0450
33 Saginaw Dr Rochester (14623) ***(G-14342)***
Eks Manufacturing Inc ...917 217-0784
577 Wortman Ave Brooklyn (11208) ***(G-1907)***
El Aguila ...212 410-2450
137 E 116th St Frnt 1 New York (10029) ***(G-9991)***
El Diario LLC ...212 807-4600
1 Metrotech Ctr Fl 18 Brooklyn (11201) ***(G-1908)***
EL Erman International Ltd ...212 444-9440
1205 E 29th St Brooklyn (11210) ***(G-1909)***
El Greco Woodworking Inc (PA) ...716 483-0315
106 E 1st St Ste 1 Jamestown (14701) ***(G-6991)***
El-Don Battery Post Inc ...716 627-3697
4109 Saint Francis Dr Hamburg (14075) ***(G-5923)***
El-Gen LLC ...631 218-3400
7 Shirley St Unit 1 Bohemia (11716) ***(G-1064)***
El-La Design Inc ...212 382-1080
209 W 38th St Rm 901 New York (10018) ***(G-9992)***
Ela, New York *Also called Electric Lighting Agencies* ***(G-9996)***
Elab Smokers Boutique ...585 865-4513
4373 Lake Ave Rochester (14612) ***(G-14343)***
Elam Sand & Gravel Corp (PA) ...585 657-8000
8222 State Route 5 And 20 Bloomfield (14469) ***(G-987)***

Elan Upholstery Inc ... 631 563-0650
120b Wilbur Pl Ste B Bohemia (11716) *(G-1065)*

Elana Laderos Ltd ... 212 764-0840
230 W 38th St Fl 15 New York (10018) *(G-9993)*

Elanco Animal Health, New Hyde Park *Also called Eli Lilly and Company (G-8832)*

Elara Fdsrvice Disposables LLC ... 516 470-1523
420 Jericho Tpke Ste 320 Jericho (11753) *(G-7066)*

Elastomers Inc ... 716 633-4883
2095 Wehrle Dr Williamsville (14221) *(G-17241)*

Elco Manufacturing Co Inc (PA) ... 516 767-3577
26 Ivy Way Port Washington (11050) *(G-13813)*

Eldeen Clothing Inc ... 212 719-9190
250 W 39th St New York (10018) *(G-9994)*

Elderlee Incorporated (HQ) ... 315 789-6670
729 Cross Rd Oaks Corners (14518) *(G-13069)*

Eldorado Coffee Distributors, Maspeth *Also called Eldorado Coffee Roasters Ltd (G-8137)*

Eldorado Coffee Roasters Ltd ... 718 418-4100
5675 49th St Maspeth (11378) *(G-8137)*

Eleanor Ettinger Inc ... 212 925-7474
24 W 57th St Ste 609 New York (10019) *(G-9995)*

Eleanors Best ... 845 809-5621
15 Peacock Way Garrison (10524) *(G-5554)*

Electomechanical Componets, Auburn *Also called Emcom Inc (G-493)*

Electrcal Instrumentation Ctrl ... 518 861-5789
208 Hillman Rd Delanson (12053) *(G-4232)*

Electric Boat Corporation ... 518 884-1270
350 Atomic Project Rd Ballston Spa (12020) *(G-596)*

Electric Boat Corporation ... 518 884-1596
Atomic Project Rd Rock City Falls (12863) *(G-14778)*

Electric City Concrete Co Inc (HQ) ... 518 887-5560
774 State Highway 5s Amsterdam (12010) *(G-343)*

Electric Lighting Agencies (PA) ... 212 645-4580
36 W 25th St Fl 6 New York (10010) *(G-9996)*

Electric Lighting Agencies ... 212 645-4580
500 N Broadway Jericho (11753) *(G-7067)*

Electric Motor Specialties, Jamestown *Also called Electric Motor Specialty Inc (G-6992)*

Electric Motor Specialty, Jamestown *Also called Sunset Ridge Holdings Inc (G-7034)*

Electric Motor Specialty Inc ... 716 487-1458
490 Crescent St Jamestown (14701) *(G-6992)*

Electric Motors and Pumps Inc ... 718 935-9118
466 Carroll St Brooklyn (11215) *(G-1910)*

Electric Swtchbard Sltions LLC ... 718 643-1105
270 Park Ave New Hyde Park (11040) *(G-8831)*

Electrical Controls Link ... 585 924-7010
100 Rawson Rd Ste 220 Victor (14564) *(G-16474)*

Electro Abrasives LLC ... 716 822-2500
701 Willet Rd Buffalo (14218) *(G-2933)*

Electro Form Corp ... 607 722-6404
128 Bevier St Binghamton (13904) *(G-910)*

Electro Industries, Westbury *Also called El Electronics Inc (G-16981)*

Electro Plating Service Inc ... 914 948-3777
127 Oakley Ave White Plains (10601) *(G-17104)*

Electro-Harmonix, Long Island City *Also called New Sensor Corporation (G-7824)*

Electro-Kinetics Inc ... 845 887-4930
51 Creamery Rd Callicoon (12723) *(G-3285)*

Electro-Metrics Corporation ... 518 762-2600
231 Enterprise Rd Johnstown (12095) *(G-7109)*

Electro-Optical Products Corp ... 718 456-6000
6240 Forest Ave Fl 2 Ridgewood (11385) *(G-14105)*

Electrochem Solutions Inc (HQ) ... 716 759-5800
10000 Wehrle Dr Clarence (14031) *(G-3660)*

Electron Coil Inc ... 607 336-7414
141 Barr Rd Norwich (13815) *(G-13027)*

Electron Top Mfg Co Inc ... 718 846-7400
12615 89th Ave Richmond Hill (11418) *(G-14072)*

Electronic Arts Inc ... 212 672-0722
1515 Broadway Rm 3601 New York (10036) *(G-9997)*

Electronic Business Tech ... 845 353-8549
199 Van Houten Flds West Nyack (10994) *(G-16916)*

Electronic Coating Tech Inc (PA) ... 518 688-2048
1 Mustang Dr Ste 4 Cohoes (12047) *(G-3747)*

Electronic Devices Inc (HQ) ... 914 965-4400
21 Gray Oaks Ave Yonkers (10710) *(G-17440)*

Electronic Devices Inc, Yonkers *Also called Electronic Devices Inc (G-17440)*

Electronic Die Corp ... 718 455-3200
19th St Fl 2 Brooklyn (11232) *(G-1911)*

Electronic Machine Parts LLC ... 631 434-3700
400 Oser Ave Ste 2000 Hauppauge (11788) *(G-6070)*

Electronic Printing Inc ... 631 218-2200
50 Keyland Ct Bohemia (11716) *(G-1066)*

Electronic Systems Inc ... 631 589-4389
1742 Church St Holbrook (11741) *(G-6445)*

Electronic Tech Briefs, New York *Also called Associated Bus Publications Co (G-9239)*

Electronics & Innovation Ltd ... 585 214-0598
150 Research Blvd Rochester (14623) *(G-14344)*

Electronics Systems Division, Hauppauge *Also called Parker-Hannifin Corporation (G-6158)*

Electrotech Service Eqp Corp ... 718 626-7700
2450 46th St Astoria (11103) *(G-439)*

Elegance Coating Ltd ... 386 668-8379
33 W Service Rd 100 Champlain (12919) *(G-3540)*

Elegance Lighting Ltd ... 631 509-0640
326 Mn St Port Jefferson (11777) *(G-13775)*

Elegant Desserts By Metro Inc ... 718 388-1323
868 Kent Ave Brooklyn (11205) *(G-1912)*

Elegant Entries Inc (PA) ... 631 595-1000
235 Robbins Ln Unit F Syosset (11791) *(G-15820)*

Elegant Headwear Co Inc ... 212 695-8520
10 W 33rd St Rm 1122 New York (10001) *(G-9998)*

Elegant Jewelers Mfg Co Inc ... 212 869-4951
31 W 47th St Ste 301 New York (10036) *(G-9999)*

Elegant Linen Inc (PA) ... 718 871-3535
5719 New Utrecht Ave Brooklyn (11219) *(G-1913)*

Elegant Sportswear, Brooklyn *Also called K & S Childrens Wear Inc (G-2162)*

ELEKTRA DESIGNS, Rochester *Also called JK Jewelry Inc (G-14461)*

Eleni's Cookies, Long Island City *Also called Elenis Nyc Inc (G-7729)*

Elenis Nyc Inc (PA) ... 718 361-8136
4725 34th St Ste 305 Long Island City (11101) *(G-7729)*

Elepath Inc ... 347 417-4975
110 Kent Ave 9 Brooklyn (11249) *(G-1914)*

Elephant Talk Cmmncations Corp ... 866 901-3309
100 Park Ave New York (10017) *(G-10000)*

Elevator Accessories Mfg ... 914 739-7004
1035 Howard St 37 Peekskill (10566) *(G-13477)*

Elevator Systems Inc ... 516 239-4044
465 Endo Blvd Unit 1 Garden City (11530) *(G-5502)*

Elevator Ventures Corporation ... 212 375-1900
9720 99th St Ozone Park (11416) *(G-13377)*

Elg Utica Alloys Inc (HQ) ... 315 733-0475
378 Gros Blvd Ste 3 Herkimer (13350) *(G-6299)*

Elg Utica Alloys Holdings Inc ... 315 733-0475
91 Wurz Ave Utica (13502) *(G-16329)*

Eli Lilly and Company ... 516 622-2244
1979 Marcus Ave New Hyde Park (11042) *(G-8832)*

Elias Artmetal Inc ... 516 873-7501
70 E 2nd St Mineola (11501) *(G-8507)*

Elias Fragrances Inc (PA) ... 718 693-6400
3 Hunter Dr Rye Brook (10573) *(G-15070)*

Elie Tahari Ltd ... 212 398-2622
501 5th Ave Fl 2 New York (10017) *(G-10001)*

Elie Tahari Ltd ... 212 398-2622
510 5th Ave Fl 3 New York (10036) *(G-10002)*

Elie Tahari Ltd ... 631 329-8883
1 Main St East Hampton (11937) *(G-4410)*

Elie Tahari Ltd ... 212 763-2000
1114 Ave Of The Americas New York (10036) *(G-10003)*

Elie Tahari Ltd ... 973 671-6300
11 W 42nd St Fl 14 New York (10036) *(G-10004)*

Elis Bread (eli Zabar) Inc (PA) ... 212 772-2011
1064 Madison Ave Apt 5 New York (10028) *(G-10005)*

Elite Cellular Accessories Inc ... 877 390-2502
61 E Industry Ct Deer Park (11729) *(G-4136)*

Elite Group International NY ... 917 334-1919
15 W 37th St New York (10018) *(G-10006)*

Elite Machine Inc ... 585 289-4733
3 Merrick Cir Manchester (14504) *(G-8051)*

Elite Medical Supply of NY ... 716 712-0881
1900 Ridge Rd West Seneca (14224) *(G-16944)*

Elite Parfums Ltd (HQ) ... 212 983-2640
551 5th Ave Rm 1500 New York (10176) *(G-10007)*

Elite Precise Manufacturer LLC ... 518 993-3040
55 Willett St Fort Plain (13339) *(G-5347)*

Elite Semi Conductor Products ... 631 884-8400
860 N Richmond Ave Lindenhurst (11757) *(G-7463)*

Elite Signs Inc ... 718 993-7342
238 Quaker Rd Pomona (10970) *(G-13730)*

Elite Traveler Magazine, New York *Also called Universal Cmmncations of Miami (G-12469)*

Elite Uniforms Ltd ... 516 487-5481
310 Northern Blvd Ste A Great Neck (11021) *(G-5805)*

Elizabeth Eakins Inc (PA) ... 212 628-1950
654 Madison Ave Rm 1409 New York (10065) *(G-10008)*

Elizabeth Fillmore LLC ... 212 647-0863
27 W 20th St Ste 705 New York (10011) *(G-10009)*

Elizabeth Gillett Designs, New York *Also called Elizabeth Gillett Ltd (G-10010)*

Elizabeth Gillett Ltd ... 212 629-7993
260 W 36th St Rm 802 New York (10018) *(G-10010)*

Elizabeth Wilson ... 516 486-2157
579 Edgemere Ave Uniondale (11553) *(G-16292)*

Elizabeth Wood ... 315 492-5470
4900 Broad Rd Syracuse (13215) *(G-15933)*

Elizabeth's, Uniondale *Also called Elizabeth Wilson (G-16292)*

Ella Design, New York *Also called Lai Apparel Design Inc (G-10918)*

Elle Magazine, New York *Also called Hearst Corporation (G-10441)*

Eller, New York *Also called Clear Channel Outdoor Inc (G-9641)*

Ellicottville Kitchen Eqp, Salamanca *Also called Strategies North America Inc (G-15108)*

Elliot Gantz & Company Inc ... 631 249-0680
115 Schmitt Blvd Farmingdale (11735) *(G-4987)*

Elliot Industries Inc ... 716 287-3100
Leach Rd Ellington (14732) *(G-4644)*

Elliot Lauren, New York *Also called I S C A Corp (G-10541)*

Elliot Lucca, New York *Also called Indonesian Imports Inc (G-10590)*

Elliott Associates LP (PA) ... 212 586-9431
712 5th Ave Fl 36 New York (10019) *(G-10011)*

Elliquence LLC 516 277-9000
2455 Grand Ave Baldwin (11510) ***(G-558)***
Ellis Products Corp (PA) 516 791-3732
628 Golf Dr Valley Stream (11581) ***(G-16405)***
Ellison Bronze Inc 716 665-6522
125 W Main St Falconer (14733) ***(G-4895)***
Ellman International, Hicksville *Also called Cynosure Inc* ***(G-6340)***
Elm Graphics Inc 315 737-5984
9694 Mallory Rd New Hartford (13413) ***(G-8803)***
Elma Press, Elma *Also called Frederick Coon Inc* ***(G-4648)***
Elmar Industries Inc 716 681-5650
200 Gould Ave Depew (14043) ***(G-4256)***
Elmat Quality Printing Ltd 516 569-5722
79 Columbia Ave Cedarhurst (11516) ***(G-3456)***
Elmgang Enterprises I Inc 212 868-4142
354 W 38th St Frnt New York (10018) ***(G-10012)***
Elmgrove Technologies Div, Rochester *Also called Photonamics Inc* ***(G-14583)***
Elmhurst Dairy Inc 718 526-3442
15525 Styler Rd Jamaica (11433) ***(G-6910)***
Elmira Country Club Inc 607 734-6251
1538 W Church St Elmira (14905) ***(G-4681)***
Elmira Grinding Works Inc 607 734-1579
311 Main St Wellsburg (14894) ***(G-16747)***
Elmira Heat Treating Inc 607 734-1577
407 S Kinyon St Elmira (14904) ***(G-4682)***
Elmira Metal Works Inc 607 734-9813
1493 Cedar St Elmira (14904) ***(G-4683)***
Elmira Star-Gazette, Elmira *Also called Star-Gazette Fund Inc* ***(G-4702)***
Elmont North Little League 516 775-8210
1532 Clay St Elmont (11003) ***(G-4719)***
Elmsford Sheet Metal Works Inc 914 739-6300
23 Arlo Ln Cortlandt Manor (10567) ***(G-4050)***
Elo Touch Solutions Inc 585 427-2802
2245 Brdgtn Hnrtta Twn Ln Rochester (14623) ***(G-14345)***
Elodina Inc 646 402-5202
222 Broadway Fl 19 New York (10038) ***(G-10013)***
Elramida Holdings Inc 646 280-0503
2555 E 29th St Brooklyn (11235) ***(G-1915)***
Elrene Home Fashions, New York *Also called Josie Accessories Inc* ***(G-10768)***
Elsag North America LLC 877 773-5724
7 Sutton Pl Ste A Brewster (10509) ***(G-1218)***
Elsener Organ Works Inc 631 254-2744
120 E Jefryn Blvd Ste A Deer Park (11729) ***(G-4137)***
Elsevier Engineering Info Inc 201 356-6800
360 Park Ave S New York (10010) ***(G-10014)***
Elsevier Inc (HQ) 212 633-3773
230 Park Ave Fl 7 New York (10169) ***(G-10015)***
Eltee Tool & Die Co 607 748-4301
404 E Franklin St Endicott (13760) ***(G-4801)***
Elton El Mantle Inc 315 432-9067
6072 Court Street Rd Syracuse (13206) ***(G-15934)***
Eluminocity US Inc 651 528-1165
80 Pine St Fl 24 New York (10005) ***(G-10016)***
Elvo, Mount Kisco *Also called Zumbach Electronics Corp* ***(G-8649)***
Elwood International Inc 631 842-6600
89 Hudson St Copiague (11726) ***(G-3899)***
Elwood Specialty Products Inc 716 877-6622
2180 Elmwood Ave Buffalo (14216) ***(G-2934)***
Elwood, William J, Copiague *Also called Elwood International Inc* ***(G-3899)***
Ely Beach Solar LLC 718 796-9400
5030 Broadway Ste 819 New York (10034) ***(G-10017)***
EM Pfaff & Son Inc 607 739-3691
204 E Franklin St Horseheads (14845) ***(G-6575)***
Em-Kay Molds Inc 716 895-6180
398 Ludington St Buffalo (14206) ***(G-2935)***
Ema Jewelry Inc 212 575-8989
246 W 38th St Fl 6 New York (10018) ***(G-10018)***
Emagin Corporation (PA) 845 838-7900
2070 Route 52 Hopewell Junction (12533) ***(G-6549)***
Embassy Apparel Inc 212 768-8330
37 W 37th St Fl 10 New York (10018) ***(G-10019)***
Embassy Dinettes Inc 631 253-2292
70 N Industry Ct Deer Park (11729) ***(G-4138)***
Embassy Industries Inc 631 435-0209
315 Oser Ave Ste 1 Hauppauge (11788) ***(G-6071)***
Embassy Millwork Inc 518 839-0965
3 Sam Stratton Rd Amsterdam (12010) ***(G-344)***
Emblaze Systems Inc (HQ) 212 371-1100
424 Madison Ave Fl 16 New York (10017) ***(G-10020)***
Embroidery Screen Prtg Netwrk, Vestal *Also called Spst Inc* ***(G-16453)***
EMC Corporation 212 899-5500
1180 Ave Of The Americas New York (10036) ***(G-10021)***
EMC Corporation 716 833-5348
500 Corporate Pkwy # 122 Amherst (14226) ***(G-238)***
EMC Corporation 585 387-9505
105 Despatch Dr East Rochester (14445) ***(G-4457)***
EMC Fintech 716 488-9071
1984 Allen Street Ext Falconer (14733) ***(G-4896)***
Emc2, East Rochester *Also called EMC Corporation* ***(G-4457)***
Emco Chemical (usa) Corp 718 797-3652
334 Douglass St Brooklyn (11217) ***(G-1916)***
Emco Electric Services LLC 212 420-9766
526 W 26th St Rm 1012 New York (10001) ***(G-10022)***
Emco Finishing Products Inc 716 483-1176
470 Crescent St Jamestown (14701) ***(G-6993)***
Emcom Inc 315 255-5300
62 Columbus St Ste 4 Auburn (13021) ***(G-493)***
Emcom Industries Inc 716 852-3711
235 Genesee St Buffalo (14204) ***(G-2936)***
Emcs LLC 716 523-2002
4414 Manor Ln Hamburg (14075) ***(G-5924)***
Emda Inc 631 243-6363
250 Executive Dr Ste J Edgewood (11717) ***(G-4597)***
Emerald Electronics Usa Inc 718 872-5544
251 Avenue W Ste 2 Brooklyn (11223) ***(G-1917)***
Emerald Holdings Inc 718 797-4404
63 Flushing Ave Unit 201 Brooklyn (11205) ***(G-1918)***
Emerald Knitting, Brooklyn *Also called Emerald Holdings Inc* ***(G-1918)***
Emerald Models Inc 585 584-3739
10204 Transit Rd East Bethany (14054) ***(G-4382)***
Emergency Beacon Corp 914 576-2700
15 River St New Rochelle (10801) ***(G-8896)***
Emergent Power Inc (HQ) 201 441-3590
968 Albany Shaker Rd Latham (12110) ***(G-7362)***
Emerson Control Techniques, Grand Island *Also called Emerson Indus Automtn USA LLC* ***(G-5756)***
Emerson Electric Co 212 244-2490
1250 Broadway Ste 2300 New York (10001) ***(G-10023)***
Emerson Indus Automtn USA LLC 716 774-1193
359 Lang Blvd Bldg B Grand Island (14072) ***(G-5756)***
Emerson Network Power 516 349-8500
79 Express St Fl 14 Plainview (11803) ***(G-13599)***
Emerson Network Power 607 724-2484
100 Emerson Pkwy Binghamton (13905) ***(G-911)***
Emes Motor Inc 718 387-2445
876 Metropolitan Ave Brooklyn (11211) ***(G-1919)***
Emhart Glass Manufacturing Inc 607 734-3671
74 Kahler Rd Horseheads (14845) ***(G-6576)***
EMI Music Publishing, New York *Also called Screen Gems-EMI Music Inc* ***(G-12007)***
Emilia Interiors Inc (PA) 718 629-4202
867 E 52nd St Brooklyn (11203) ***(G-1920)***
Emily and Ashley, New York *Also called Greenbeads Llc* ***(G-10361)***
Emitled Inc 516 531-3533
2300 Shames Dr Westbury (11590) ***(G-16982)***
Emkay Bordeaux, Arcade *Also called Emkay Trading Corp* ***(G-392)***
Emkay Candle Company, Syracuse *Also called Muench-Kreuzer Candle Company* ***(G-15994)***
Emkay Trading Corp (PA) 914 592-9000
250 Clearbrook Rd Ste 127 Elmsford (10523) ***(G-4748)***
Emkay Trading Corp 585 492-3800
58 Church St Arcade (14009) ***(G-392)***
Emmi USA Inc 845 268-9990
100 Dutch Hill Rd Ste 220 Orangeburg (10962) ***(G-13225)***
Emory Machine & Tool Co Inc 585 436-9610
6176 Hunters Dr Farmington (14425) ***(G-5150)***
Emp, Hauppauge *Also called Electronic Machine Parts LLC* ***(G-6070)***
Empire Air Specialties Inc 518 689-4440
40 Kraft Ave Albany (12205) ***(G-77)***
Empire Archtctural Systems Inc 518 773-5109
125 Belzano Rd Johnstown (12095) ***(G-7110)***
Empire Bias Binding Co Inc 718 545-0300
3439 31st St Long Island City (11106) ***(G-7730)***
Empire Brewing Company Inc 315 925-8308
120 Walton St Syracuse (13202) ***(G-15935)***
Empire Building Products Inc 518 695-6094
12 Spring St Schuylerville (12871) ***(G-15319)***
Empire Central, Deer Park *Also called Empire Scientific* ***(G-4140)***
Empire Cheese Inc 585 968-1552
4520 County Road 6 Cuba (14727) ***(G-4069)***
Empire Coachworks Intl LLC 732 257-7981
475 Haverstraw Rd Suffern (10901) ***(G-15789)***
Empire Coffee Company Inc 914 934-1100
106 Purdy Ave Port Chester (10573) ***(G-13745)***
Empire Devleopment 716 789-2097
5889 Magnolia Stedman Rd Mayville (14757) ***(G-8215)***
Empire Division Inc 315 476-6273
201 Kirkpatrick St # 207 Syracuse (13208) ***(G-15936)***
Empire Exhibits & Displays Inc 518 266-9362
131 Round Lake Ave Mechanicville (12118) ***(G-8227)***
Empire Exhibits and Displays, Mechanicville *Also called Empire Exhibits & Displays Inc* ***(G-8227)***
Empire Fabricators Inc 585 235-3050
95 Saginaw Dr Rochester (14623) ***(G-14346)***
Empire Gypsum Pdts & Sup Corp 914 592-8141
25 Haven St Elmsford (10523) ***(G-4749)***
Empire Industrial Burner Svc 631 242-4619
550 Brook Ave Deer Park (11729) ***(G-4139)***
Empire Industrial Systems Corp (PA) 631 242-4619
40 Corbin Ave Bay Shore (11706) ***(G-699)***
Empire Innovation Group LLC 716 852-5000
410 Main St Ste 5 Buffalo (14202) ***(G-2937)***
Empire Metal Fabricators Inc 585 288-2140
1385 Empire Blvd Ste 3 Rochester (14609) ***(G-14347)***

Empire Metal Finishing Inc 718 545-6700
2469 46th St Astoria (11103) *(G-440)*
Empire National, Brooklyn *Also called A To Z Kosher Meat Products Co (G-1535)*
Empire Open Mri 914 961-1777
1915 Central Park Ave # 25 Yonkers (10710) *(G-17441)*
Empire Optical Inc 585 454-4470
1249 Ridgeway Ave Ste P Rochester (14615) *(G-14348)*
Empire Plastics Inc 607 754-9132
2011 E Main St Endwell (13760) *(G-4835)*
Empire Precision Plastics, Rochester *Also called Epp Team Inc (G-14354)*
Empire Press Co (PA) 718 756-9500
550 Empire Blvd Brooklyn (11225) *(G-1921)*
Empire Publishing Inc 516 829-4000
1525 Central Ave Ste 1 Far Rockaway (11691) *(G-4921)*
Empire Scientific, Deer Park *Also called TAe Trans Atlantic Elec Inc (G-4216)*
Empire Scientific 630 510-8636
151 E Industry Ct Deer Park (11729) *(G-4140)*
Empire Signs, East Elmhurst *Also called Liberty Awnings & Signs Inc (G-4394)*
Empire State Metal Pdts Inc 718 847-1617
10110 Jamaica Ave Richmond Hill (11418) *(G-14073)*
Empire State Weeklies Inc 585 671-1533
46 North Ave Webster (14580) *(G-16723)*
Empire Transit Mix Inc 718 384-3000
430 Maspeth Ave Brooklyn (11211) *(G-1922)*
Empire Ventilation Eqp Co Inc (PA) 718 728-2143
9 Industrial Dr Florida (10921) *(G-5212)*
Empowrx LLC 212 755-3577
249 E 53rd St Apt 2a New York (10022) *(G-10024)*
Empresas De Manufactura Inc (PA) 631 240-9251
7 S Jersey Ave Ste 3 East Setauket (11733) *(G-4481)*
Empro Niagara Inc 716 433-2769
5027 Ridge Rd Lockport (14094) *(G-7584)*
Ems Development Corporation (HQ) 631 924-4736
95 Horseblock Rd Unit 2 Yaphank (11980) *(G-17390)*
Ems Development Corporation 631 345-6200
95 Horseblock Rd Unit 2a Yaphank (11980) *(G-17391)*
Ems Technologies Inc 607 723-3676
71 Frederick St Binghamton (13901) *(G-912)*
Emsaru USA Corp 212 459-9355
608 5th Ave Ste 500 New York (10020) *(G-10025)*
Emsig Manufacturing Corp (PA) 718 784-7717
263 W 38th St Fl 5 New York (10018) *(G-10026)*
Emsig Manufacturing Corp 518 828-7301
160 Fairview Ave Ste 202 Hudson (12534) *(G-6613)*
Emsig Manufacturing Corp 718 784-7717
263 W 38th St Fl 5 New York (10018) *(G-10027)*
Emt, New York *Also called Enterprise Management Tech LLC (G-10042)*
Emt, Albany *Also called Engineered Molding Tech LLC (G-78)*
Emtron Hybrids Inc 631 924-9668
86 Horseblock Rd Unit G Yaphank (11980) *(G-17392)*
Emulso Corp 716 854-2889
2750 Kenmore Ave Tonawanda (14150) *(G-16159)*
Emusiccom Inc (PA) 212 201-9240
215 Lexington Ave Fl 18 New York (10016) *(G-10028)*
Emvi Chocolate, Broadalbin *Also called Emvi Inc (G-1241)*
Emvi Inc 518 883-5111
111 Bellen Rd Ste 2 Broadalbin (12025) *(G-1241)*
En Tech Corp 845 398-0776
375 Western Hwy Tappan (10983) *(G-16080)*
Enable Labs, Troy *Also called Vita Rara Inc (G-16261)*
Enbi Indiana Inc 585 647-1627
1661 Lyell Ave Rochester (14606) *(G-14349)*
Enchante Accessories Inc (PA) 212 689-6008
16 E 34th St Fl 16 New York (10016) *(G-10029)*
Enchante Lites LLC (HQ) 212 602-1818
15 W 34th St Fl 8 New York (10001) *(G-10030)*
Encore Chocolates Inc 585 266-2970
147 Pattonwood Dr Rochester (14617) *(G-14350)*
Encore Electronics Inc 518 584-5354
4400 Route 50 Saratoga Springs (12866) *(G-15150)*
Encore Refining and Recycleing 631 319-1910
1120 Lincoln Ave Holbrook (11741) *(G-6446)*
Encore Retail Systems Inc (PA) 718 385-3443
138 Hinsdale St Brooklyn (11207) *(G-1923)*
Encysive Pharmaceuticals Inc (HQ) 212 733-2323
235 E 42nd St New York (10017) *(G-10031)*
Endava Inc (HQ) 212 920-7240
441 Lexington Ave Rm 702 New York (10017) *(G-10032)*
Endeavor Printing LLC 718 570-2720
3704 29th St Long Island City (11101) *(G-7731)*
Endicott Interconnect Tech Inc 866 820-4820
1701 North St Endicott (13760) *(G-4802)*
Endicott Precision Inc 607 754-7076
1328-30 Campville Rd Endicott (13760) *(G-4803)*
Endicott Research Group Inc 607 754-9187
2601 Wayne St Endicott (13760) *(G-4804)*
Endoscopic Procedure Center, Syracuse *Also called Elizabeth Wood (G-15933)*
Endres Knitwear Co Inc 718 933-8687
3020 Jerome Ave Bronx (10468) *(G-1326)*
Endurance LLC 212 719-2500
530 7th Ave Rm 902 New York (10018) *(G-10033)*
Endurart Inc 212 473-7000
132 Nassau St Rm 1100 New York (10038) *(G-10034)*
Enecon Corporation (PA) 516 349-0022
6 Platinum Ct Medford (11763) *(G-8243)*
Eneflux Armtek Magnetics Inc (HQ) 516 576-3434
6 Platinum Ct Medford (11763) *(G-8244)*
Ener-G Cogen LLC 718 551-7170
1261 Broadway New York (10001) *(G-10035)*
Ener-G-Rotors Inc 518 372-2608
17 Fern Ave Schenectady (12306) *(G-15250)*
Ener1 Inc (HQ) 212 920-3500
1540 Broadway Fl 25c New York (10036) *(G-10036)*
Enerac Inc 516 997-1554
1320 Lincoln Ave Ste 1 Holbrook (11741) *(G-6447)*
Energy Brands Inc (HQ) 212 545-6000
260 Madison Ave Fl 10 New York (10016) *(G-10037)*
Energy Conservation & Sup Inc 718 855-5888
55 Washington St Ste 302a Brooklyn (11201) *(G-1924)*
Energy Intelligence Group Inc (PA) 212 532-1112
270 Madison Ave Fl 19 New York (10016) *(G-10038)*
Energy Nuclear Operations 315 342-0055
268 Lake Rd Oswego (13126) *(G-13331)*
Energy Panel Structures Inc 315 923-7777
10269 Old Route 31 Clyde (14433) *(G-3726)*
Energy Panel Structures Inc 585 343-1777
5773 E Main Street Rd Batavia (14020) *(G-630)*
Energy Panel Structures Inc 518 355-6708
864 Burdeck St Schenectady (12306) *(G-15251)*
Enertech Labs Inc 716 332-9074
714 Northland Ave Buffalo (14211) *(G-2938)*
Enertiv Inc 646 350-3525
555 W 23rd St Ph M New York (10011) *(G-10039)*
Enetics Inc 585 924-5010
830 Canning Pkwy Victor (14564) *(G-16475)*
Engagement Technology LLC 914 591-7600
33 W Main St Ste 303 Elmsford (10523) *(G-4750)*
Engelack Gem Corporation 212 719-3094
36 W 47th St Ste 601 New York (10036) *(G-10040)*
Engineered Air Products, Lancaster *Also called Eastern Air Products LLC (G-7313)*
Engineered Composites Inc 716 362-0295
55 Roberts Ave Buffalo (14206) *(G-2939)*
Engineered Lifting Tech, Orchard Park *Also called Kinedyne Inc (G-13278)*
Engineered Metal Products Inc 631 842-3780
10 Reith St Copiague (11726) *(G-3900)*
Engineered Molding Tech LLC 518 482-2004
59 Exchange St Albany (12205) *(G-78)*
Engineered Plastics Inc 800 682-2525
300 International Dr # 100 Williamsville (14221) *(G-17242)*
Engineered Polymer Systems Div, Marion *Also called Parker-Hannifin Corporation (G-8097)*
Engineered Products Oper Epo, Rochester *Also called Pulsafeeder Inc (G-14609)*
Engineering Educational Eqp Co, New Paltz *Also called Kevco Industries (G-8875)*
Engineering Maint Pdts Inc 516 624-9774
250 Berry Hill Rd Oyster Bay (11771) *(G-13369)*
Engineering Mfg & Tech, East Meadow *Also called E M T Manufacturing Inc (G-4422)*
Engineering Mfg Tech LLC 607 754-7111
101 Delaware Ave Endicott (13760) *(G-4805)*
Engrav-O-Type Press Inc 585 262-7590
30 Bermar Park Ste 2 Rochester (14624) *(G-14351)*
Enhanced Tool Inc 716 691-5200
90 Pineview Dr Amherst (14228) *(G-239)*
Eni Mks Products Group 585 427-8300
100 Highpower Rd Rochester (14623) *(G-14352)*
Eni Technology Inc (HQ) 585 427-8300
100 Highpower Rd Rochester (14623) *(G-14353)*
Enivate - Aerospace Division, Orchard Park *Also called ITT Enidine Inc (G-13275)*
Enjoy, Scarsdale *Also called Japan America Learning Ctr Inc (G-15218)*
Enjoy City North Inc 607 584-5061
31 Front St Binghamton (13905) *(G-913)*
Enlighten Air Inc 917 656-1248
200 E 71st St New York (10021) *(G-10041)*
Enrg Inc 716 873-2939
155 Rano St Ste 300 Buffalo (14207) *(G-2940)*
Ensil Technical Services Inc 716 282-1020
1901 Maryland Ave Niagara Falls (14305) *(G-12814)*
Entermarket 914 437-7268
280 N Bedford Rd Ste 305 Mount Kisco (10549) *(G-8627)*
Enterprise Bagels Inc 845 896-3823
986 Main St Ste 3 Fishkill (12524) *(G-5183)*
Enterprise Container LLC 631 253-4400
44 Island Container Plz Wyandanch (11798) *(G-17375)*
Enterprise Folding Box Co Inc 716 876-6421
75 Isabelle St Buffalo (14207) *(G-2941)*
Enterprise Management Tech LLC 212 835-1557
1 Penn Plz Ste 360025 New York (10119) *(G-10042)*
Enterprise Metalworks Inc 718 328-9331
1162 Southern Blvd Bronx (10459) *(G-1327)*
Enterprise Network of New York 516 263-0641
1407 E 101st St Ste B Brooklyn (11236) *(G-1925)*
Enterprise Press Inc 212 741-2111
627 Greenwich St New York (10014) *(G-10043)*
Enterprise Tech Group Inc 914 588-0327
15 Irving Pl New Rochelle (10801) *(G-8897)*

ALPHABETIC

Enterprise Wood Products Inc — 718 853-9243
4712 18th Ave Brooklyn (11204) *(G-1926)*

Entertainment Weekly Inc (HQ) — 212 522-5600
135 W 50th St Fl 3 New York (10020) *(G-10044)*

Enticing Lingerie Inc — 718 998-8625
166 Gravesend Neck Rd Brooklyn (11223) *(G-1927)*

Entrainant Inc — 212 946-4724
112 W 34th St Fl 18 New York (10120) *(G-10045)*

Enumeral Biomedical Corp (PA) — 347 227-4787
1370 Broadway Fl 5 New York (10018) *(G-10046)*

Envent Systems Inc. — 646 294-6980
62 Harmon Ave Pelham (10803) *(G-13491)*

Enviro Service & Supply Corp — 347 838-6500
45b Marble Loop Staten Island (10309) *(G-15671)*

Enviroform Recycled Pdts Inc — 315 789-1810
287 Gambee Rd Geneva (14456) *(G-5574)*

Enviromaster International LLC — 315 336-3716
5780 Success Dr Rome (13440) *(G-14810)*

Environment-One Corporation — 518 346-6161
2773 Balltown Rd Schenectady (12309) *(G-15252)*

Environmental Closures, Mineola Also called Geotechnical Drilling Inc *(G-8512)*

Environmental Temp Systems LLC — 516 640-5818
111 Roosevelt Ave Ste C Mineola (11501) *(G-8508)*

Envy Publishing Group Inc — 212 253-9874
118 E 25th St Bsmt Ll New York (10010) *(G-10047)*

Enyce, New York Also called 5 Star Apparel LLC *(G-8977)*

Enzo Diagnostics, Farmingdale Also called Enzo Life Sciences Inc *(G-4988)*

Enzo Life Sciences Inc (HQ) — 631 694-7070
10 Executive Blvd Farmingdale (11735) *(G-4988)*

Enzo Life Sciences Intl Inc — 610 941-0430
10 Executive Blvd Farmingdale (11735) *(G-4989)*

Enzo Manzoni LLC — 212 464-7000
2896 W 12th St Brooklyn (11224) *(G-1928)*

Eon Collections — 212 695-1263
247 W 35th St Rm 401 New York (10001) *(G-10048)*

Eon Labs Inc (HQ) — 516 478-9700
1999 Marcus Ave Ste 300 New Hyde Park (11042) *(G-8833)*

Ephesus Lighting, Syracuse Also called Eaton Corporation *(G-15930)*

Ephesus Lighting Inc — 315 579-2873
125 E Jefferson St Lbby 1 Syracuse (13202) *(G-15937)*

Epi Printing & Finishing, Rochester Also called Engrav-O-Type Press Inc *(G-14351)*

Epic Beauty Co LLC — 212 327-3059
929 Park Ave 5 New York (10028) *(G-10049)*

Epic Pharma LLC — 718 276-8600
22715 N Conduit Ave Laurelton (11413) *(G-7387)*

Epl, Long Island City Also called Edison Price Lighting Inc *(G-7723)*

Epner Technology Incorporated (PA) — 718 782-5948
78 Kingsland Ave Brooklyn (11222) *(G-1929)*

Epner Technology Incorporated — 718 782-8722
78 Kingsland Ave Brooklyn (11222) *(G-1930)*

Epoch Microelectronics Inc — 914 332-8570
420 Columbus Ave Ste 204 Valhalla (10595) *(G-16367)*

Epoch Times International Inc — 212 239-2808
229 W 28th St Fl 6 New York (10001) *(G-10050)*

Epost International Inc — 212 352-9390
483 10th Ave New York (10018) *(G-10051)*

Epp Team Inc — 585 454-4995
500 Lee Rd Ste 400 Rochester (14606) *(G-14354)*

Eps Iron Works Inc — 516 294-5840
38 Windsor Ave Ste 101 Mineola (11501) *(G-8509)*

Equal Opprtnity Pblcations Inc — 631 421-9421
445 Broadhollow Rd # 425 Melville (11747) *(G-8314)*

Equicenter Inc — 585 742-2522
3247 Rush Mendon Rd Honeoye Falls (14472) *(G-6527)*

Equicheck LLC — 631 987-6356
20 Medford Ave Ste 7 Patchogue (11772) *(G-13419)*

Equilend Holdings LLC (PA) — 212 901-2200
225 Liberty St Fl 10 New York (10281) *(G-10052)*

Equipment Apparel LLC — 212 502-1890
19 W 34th St Fl 8 New York (10001) *(G-10053)*

Equissentials LLC — 607 432-2856
3200 Chestnut St Ste 5 Oneonta (13820) *(G-13185)*

Equityarcade LLC — 678 232-1301
33 Nassau Ave Brooklyn (11222) *(G-1931)*

Equival Inc — 646 513-4169
19 W 34th St Rm 1018 New York (10001) *(G-10054)*

ER Butler & Co Inc (PA) — 212 925-3565
55 Prince St New York (10012) *(G-10055)*

Era-Contact Usa LLC — 631 524-5530
55 Cabot Ct Ste B Hauppauge (11788) *(G-6072)*

Eraser Company Inc (PA) — 315 454-3237
123 Oliva Dr Mattydale (13211) *(G-8212)*

Erbessd Reliability LLC — 518 874-2700
22 Hudson Falls Rd South Glens Falls (12803) *(G-15524)*

Erbessd Reliability Instrs, South Glens Falls Also called Erbessd Reliability LLC *(G-15524)*

Ercole Nyc Inc (PA) — 212 675-2218
142 26th St Brooklyn (11232) *(G-1932)*

Erdle Perforating Holdings Inc (PA) — 585 247-4700
100 Pixley Indus Pkwy Rochester (14624) *(G-14355)*

Ergotech Group Inc — 914 347-3800
8 Westchester Plz Ste 184 Elmsford (10523) *(G-4751)*

Ergun Inc — 631 721-0049
10 Mineola Ave Unit B Roslyn Heights (11577) *(G-15025)*

Erhard & Gilcher Inc — 315 474-1072
235 Cortland Ave Syracuse (13202) *(G-15938)*

Eric S Hapeman — 716 731-5416
6611 Hunt St Niagara Falls (14304) *(G-12815)*

Eric S Turner & Company Inc — 914 235-7114
3335 Centre Ave New Rochelle (10801) *(G-8898)*

Eric Signature, New York Also called Harrison Sportswear Inc *(G-10418)*

Eric Winterling Inc — 212 629-7686
20 W 20th St Fl 5 New York (10011) *(G-10056)*

Ericeira Inc — 516 294-4034
54 E Jericho Tpke Mineola (11501) *(G-8510)*

Erickson Beamon Ltd — 212 643-4810
498 Fashion Ave Rm 2406 New York (10018) *(G-10057)*

Erie Engineered Products Inc — 716 206-0204
3949 Walden Ave Lancaster (14086) *(G-7314)*

Erika T Schwartz MD PC — 212 873-3420
724 5th Ave Fl 10 New York (10019) *(G-10058)*

Erin Fetherston, New York Also called Fetherston Design Group LLC *(G-10156)*

Erm Thermal Technologies Inc, Ontario Also called Vette Corp New York *(G-13216)*

Ernex Chocolate, Brooklyn Also called Ernex Corporation Inc *(G-1933)*

Ernex Corporation Inc — 718 951-2251
5518 Avenue N Brooklyn (11234) *(G-1933)*

Ernie Green Industries Inc — 585 295-8951
85 Pixley Industrial Pkwy Rochester (14624) *(G-14356)*

Ernie Green Industries Inc — 585 647-2300
1667 Emerson St Rochester (14606) *(G-14357)*

Ernie Green Industries Inc — 585 647-2300
460 Buffalo Rd Ste 220 Rochester (14611) *(G-14358)*

Ernst Publishing Co, Albany Also called Ucc Guide Inc *(G-145)*

Ert Software Inc — 845 358-5721
4 Pine Glen Dr Blauvelt (10913) *(G-971)*

Ertel Alsop, Kingston Also called Stavo Industries Inc *(G-7213)*

Ertel Engineering Co, Kingston Also called Stavo Industries Inc *(G-7214)*

Es Beta Inc — 631 582-6740
110 Nicon Ct Hauppauge (11788) *(G-6073)*

Esc Control Electronics LLC — 631 467-5328
98 Lincoln Ave Sayville (11782) *(G-15207)*

Esc Control Electronics LLC — 631 467-5328
98 Lincoln Ave Sayville (11782) *(G-15208)*

Eschen Prosthetic & Orthotic L — 212 606-1262
510 E 73rd St Ste 201 New York (10021) *(G-10059)*

Escholar LLC — 914 989-2900
222 Bloomingdale Rd # 107 White Plains (10605) *(G-17105)*

Eser Realty Corp (PA) — 718 383-0565
62 Greenpoint Ave 64 Brooklyn (11222) *(G-1934)*

Eshel Jewelry Mfg Co Inc — 212 588-8800
17 E 48th St Fl 9 New York (10017) *(G-10060)*

Esi, Rochester Also called Ftt Medical Inc *(G-14384)*

Esi, Holbrook Also called Electronic Systems Inc *(G-6445)*

ESi Cases & Accessories Inc — 212 883-8838
44 E 32nd St Rm 601 New York (10016) *(G-10061)*

Eskay Metal Fabricating, Buffalo Also called Schuler-Subra Inc *(G-3177)*

Esm Group Inc (HQ) — 716 446-8985
300 Corporate Pkwy 118n Amherst (14226) *(G-240)*

Esm II Inc (HQ) — 716 446-8888
300 Corporate Pkwy 118n Amherst (14226) *(G-241)*

Esm Special Metals & Tech Inc — 716 446-8914
300 Corporate Pkwy 118n Amherst (14226) *(G-242)*

Espey Mfg & Electronics Corp (PA) — 518 245-4400
233 Ballston Ave Saratoga Springs (12866) *(G-15151)*

Espostos Fnest Qlty Ssage Pdts, New York Also called Elmgang Enterprises I Inc *(G-10012)*

Esquire Magazine, New York Also called Hearst Corporation *(G-10444)*

Esquire Mechanical Corp — 718 625-4006
79 Sandford St Brooklyn (11205) *(G-1935)*

Ess Bee Industries Inc — 718 894-5202
95 Evergreen Ave Brooklyn (11206) *(G-1936)*

Essar Americas — 212 292-2600
277 Park Ave 47th New York (10172) *(G-10062)*

Essar Steel Minnesota LLC (PA) — 212 292-2600
277 Park Ave Fl 35 New York (10172) *(G-10063)*

Essence Communications Inc (HQ) — 212 522-1212
225 Liberty St New York (10281) *(G-10064)*

Essence Magazine, New York Also called Essence Communications Inc *(G-10064)*

Essential Ribbons Inc — 212 967-4173
53 W 36th St Rm 405 New York (10018) *(G-10065)*

Essex Box & Pallet Co Inc — 518 834-7279
49 Industrial Park Rd Keeseville (12944) *(G-7137)*

Essex Industries — 518 942-6671
17 Pilfershire Rd Mineville (12956) *(G-8540)*

Essex Manufacturing Inc — 212 239-0080
350 5th Ave Ste 2400 New York (10118) *(G-10066)*

Essex Works Ltd — 718 495-4575
446 Riverdale Ave Brooklyn (11207) *(G-1937)*

Essie Cosmetics Ltd — 212 818-1500
575 5th Ave New York (10017) *(G-10067)*

Essilor Laboratories Amer Inc — 845 365-6700
165 Route 303 Orangeburg (10962) *(G-13226)*

Estebania Enterprises Inc — 585 529-9330
15 Mcardle St Ste A Rochester (14611) *(G-14359)*

Estee Lauder Companies Inc 917 606-3240
9 W 22nd St New York (10010) ***(G-10068)***
Estee Lauder Companies Inc 212 572-4200
767 5th Ave Fl 37 New York (10153) ***(G-10069)***
Estee Lauder Companies Inc (PA) 212 572-4200
767 5th Ave Fl 37 New York (10153) ***(G-10070)***
Estee Lauder Companies Inc 212 572-4015
7 Corporate Center Dr Melville (11747) ***(G-8315)***
Estee Lauder Companies Inc 646 602-7590
65 Bleecker St Frnt 1 New York (10012) ***(G-10071)***
Estee Lauder Inc (HQ) 212 572-4200
767 5th Ave Fl 37 New York (10153) ***(G-10072)***
Estee Lauder Inc 631 531-1000
125 Pinelawn Rd Melville (11747) ***(G-8316)***
Estee Lauder Inc 631 454-7000
350 S Service Rd Melville (11747) ***(G-8317)***
Estee Lauder Inc 212 756-4800
655 Madison Ave Fl 10 New York (10065) ***(G-10073)***
Estee Lauder International Inc (HQ) 212 572-4200
767 5th Ave Bsmt 1 New York (10153) ***(G-10074)***
Estiator, New York *Also called Interhellenic Publishing Inc* ***(G-10628)***
ET Oakes Corporation 631 630-9837
686 Old Willets Path Hauppauge (11788) ***(G-6074)***
ET Precision Optics Inc 585 254-2560
33 Curlew St Rochester (14606) ***(G-14360)***
Et Publishing Intl LLC 212 838-7220
150 E 58th St Ste 2200 New York (10155) ***(G-10075)***
Etc Hosiery & Underwear Ltd 212 947-5151
350 5th Ave Ste 2525 New York (10118) ***(G-10076)***
Etcetera Wallpapers, Glen Cove *Also called Sunnyside Decorative Prints Co* ***(G-5630)***
Eternal Fortune Fashion LLC 212 965-5322
135 W 36th St Fl 5 New York (10018) ***(G-10077)***
Eternal Line 845 856-1999
1237 State Route 42 Sparrow Bush (12780) ***(G-15562)***
Eternal Love Parfums Corp 516 921-6100
485 Underhill Blvd # 207 Syosset (11791) ***(G-15821)***
Eternal Love Perfumes, Syosset *Also called Eternal Love Parfums Corp* ***(G-15821)***
Ethis Communications Inc 212 791-1440
44 Church St Ste 200 White Plains (10601) ***(G-17106)***
Etna Products Co Inc (PA) 212 989-7591
53 W 23rd St Fl 3 New York (10010) ***(G-10078)***
Etna Tool & Die Corporation 212 475-4350
42 Bond St Frnt A New York (10012) ***(G-10079)***
Eton Institute 855 334-3688
1 Rockefeller Plz Fl 11 New York (10020) ***(G-10080)***
Eton International, New York *Also called Basil S Kadhim* ***(G-9330)***
Ets, Mineola *Also called Environmental Temp Systems LLC* ***(G-8508)***
Eu Design LLC 212 420-7788
73 Spring St Rm 506 New York (10012) ***(G-10081)***
Euchner USA Inc 315 701-0315
6723 Lyons St East Syracuse (13057) ***(G-4528)***
Eugene G Danner Mfg Inc 631 234-5261
160 Oval Dr Central Islip (11749) ***(G-3495)***
Eugenia Selective Living Inc 631 277-1461
122 Freeman Ave Islip (11751) ***(G-6808)***
Euphorbia Productions Ltd 212 533-1700
632 Broadway Fl 9 New York (10012) ***(G-10082)***
Euphrates Inc 518 762-3488
230 Enterprise Rd Johnstown (12095) ***(G-7111)***
Euro Bands Inc 212 719-9777
247 W 37th St Rm 700 New York (10018) ***(G-10083)***
Euro Fine Paper Inc 516 238-5253
220 Nassau Blvd Garden City (11530) ***(G-5503)***
Euro Fuel Co 914 424-5052
2499 Route 22 Patterson (12563) ***(G-13439)***
Euro Gear (usa) Inc 518 578-1775
1 Cumberland Ave Plattsburgh (12901) ***(G-13662)***
Euro Pacific Precious Metals 212 481-0310
152 Madison Ave Rm 1003 New York (10016) ***(G-10084)***
Euro Woodworking Inc 718 246-9172
303 Park Ave Fl 8 Brooklyn (11205) ***(G-1938)***
Euroco Costumes Inc 212 629-9665
254 W 35th St Fl 15 New York (10001) ***(G-10085)***
Eurocraft Custom Furniture 718 956-0600
3425 11th St Long Island City (11106) ***(G-7732)***
Euromed Inc 845 359-4039
25 Corporate Dr Orangeburg (10962) ***(G-13227)***
Europadisk LLC 718 407-7300
2402 Queens Plz S Long Island City (11101) ***(G-7733)***
European Craft Inc 516 313-2243
48 Rose Ave Great Neck (11021) ***(G-5806)***
European Marble Works Co Inc 718 387-9778
54 Nassau Blvd Garden City (11530) ***(G-5504)***
Europrojects Intl Inc 917 262-0795
152 W 25th St Fl 8b New York (10001) ***(G-10086)***
Eurotex Inc 716 205-8861
4600 Witmer Rd Niagara Falls (14305) ***(G-12816)***
Eurotex North America, Niagara Falls *Also called Eurotex Inc* ***(G-12816)***
Eva Fehren, New York *Also called Gorga Fehren Fine Jewelry LLC* ***(G-10339)***
Evado Filip 917 774-8666
159 Bleecker St New York (10012) ***(G-10087)***
Evangelist, The, Albany *Also called Albany Catholic Press Assoc* ***(G-38)***
Evans & Paul LLC 516 576-0800
140 Dupont St Plainview (11803) ***(G-13600)***
Evans & Paul Unlimited Corp 212 255-7272
49 W 23rd St Fl 3 New York (10010) ***(G-10088)***
Evans Chemetics LP 315 539-9221
228 E Main St Waterloo (13165) ***(G-16624)***
Evans Manufacturing LLC 631 439-3300
595 Smith St Farmingdale (11735) ***(G-4990)***
Eve Sales Corp 718 589-6800
945 Close Ave Bronx (10473) ***(G-1328)***
Evelo Inc 917 251-8743
327 Beach 101st St Rockaway Park (11694) ***(G-14785)***
Evenhouse Printing 716 649-2666
4783 Southwestern Blvd Hamburg (14075) ***(G-5925)***
Evening Telegram, Herkimer *Also called Gatehouse Media LLC* ***(G-6300)***
Evening Tribune, Hornell *Also called Gatehouse Media LLC* ***(G-6564)***
Event Journal Inc 516 470-1811
700 Hicksville Rd Bethpage (11714) ***(G-866)***
Event Pad, New York *Also called Tep Events International Inc* ***(G-12301)***
Event Services Corporation 315 488-9357
6171 Airport Rd Solvay (13209) ***(G-15508)***
Ever-Nu-Metal Products Inc 646 423-5833
471 20th St Brooklyn (11215) ***(G-1939)***
Everblock Systems LLC 844 422-5625
790 Madison Ave Rm 601 New York (10065) ***(G-10089)***
Evercore Partners Svcs E LLC 212 857-3100
55 E 52nd St New York (10055) ***(G-10090)***
Everest Bbn Inc 212 268-7979
42 Broadway Ste 1736 New York (10004) ***(G-10091)***
Everfab Inc 716 655-1550
12928 Big Tree Rd East Aurora (14052) ***(G-4370)***
Everflow Supplies Inc 908 436-1100
1457 58th St Brooklyn (11219) ***(G-1940)***
Evergreen, New York *Also called Integrated Copyright Group* ***(G-10615)***
Evergreen Bleachers Inc 518 654-9084
122 Maple St Corinth (12822) ***(G-3958)***
Evergreen Corp Central NY 315 454-4175
235 Cortland Ave Syracuse (13202) ***(G-15939)***
Evergreen High Voltage LLC 281 814-9973
140 Peninsula Way Lake Placid (12946) ***(G-7274)***
Evergreen Manufacturing, Syracuse *Also called Evergreen Corp Central NY* ***(G-15939)***
Evergreen Slate Company Inc 518 642-2530
2027 County Route 23 Middle Granville (12849) ***(G-8398)***
Everi Games Inc 518 881-1122
1 Broadway Ctr Fl 7 Schenectady (12305) ***(G-15253)***
Everlast Seals and Supply LLC 718 388-7373
41 Montrose Ave Brooklyn (11206) ***(G-1941)***
Everlast Sports Mfg Corp (HQ) 212 239-0990
42 W 39th St New York (10018) ***(G-10092)***
Everlast Worldwide Inc (HQ) 212 239-0990
42 W 39th St Fl 3 New York (10018) ***(G-10093)***
Everlasting Images 607 785-8743
504 Shady Dr Endicott (13760) ***(G-4806)***
Everlasting Memories 716 833-1111
3701 Mckinley Pkwy # 210 Blasdell (14219) ***(G-962)***
Everplans, New York *Also called Beyondly Inc* ***(G-9384)***
Eversan Inc 315 736-3967
34 Main St Ste 3 Whitesboro (13492) ***(G-17193)***
Every Toe Covered, New York *Also called Etc Hosiery & Underwear Ltd* ***(G-10076)***
Everybodys Carribbean Magazine, Brooklyn *Also called Herman Hall Communications* ***(G-2077)***
Evoke Healthy Foods, Rochester *Also called Muesli Fusion Inc* ***(G-14524)***
Evolution Impressions Inc 585 473-6600
160 Commerce Dr Rochester (14623) ***(G-14361)***
Evolution Spirits Inc 917 543-7880
401 Park Ave S New York (10016) ***(G-10094)***
Evolve Guest Controls LLC (PA) 855 750-9090
16 S Maryland Ave Port Washington (11050) ***(G-13814)***
Evonik Corporation 518 233-7090
7 Schoolhouse Ln Waterford (12188) ***(G-16611)***
Ewatchfactory Corp (PA) 212 564-8318
390 5th Ave Rm 910 New York (10018) ***(G-10095)***
Ewt Holdings III Corp (HQ) 212 644-5900
666 5th Ave Fl 36 New York (10103) ***(G-10096)***
Ex El Enterprises Ltd 212 489-4500
630 Fort Washington Ave New York (10040) ***(G-10097)***
Ex-It Medical Devices Inc 212 653-0637
1330 Ave Of The Americas New York (10019) ***(G-10098)***
Exact Machining & Mfg 585 334-7090
305 Commerce Dr Ste 7 Rochester (14623) ***(G-14362)***
Exact Solutions Inc 212 707-8627
139 Fulton St Rm 511 New York (10038) ***(G-10099)***
Exacta LLC 716 406-2303
8955 Williams Ct Clarence Center (14032) ***(G-3675)***
Exacttarget Inc 646 560-2275
155 Av Of The Americas Fl New York (10013) ***(G-10100)***
Excalbur Brnze Sculpture Fndry 718 366-3444
309 Starr St Brooklyn (11237) ***(G-1942)***
Excel Aluminum Products Inc 315 471-0925
563 N Salina St Syracuse (13208) ***(G-15940)***
Excel Commercial Seating 828 428-8338
165 E Hoffman Ave Unit 2 Lindenhurst (11757) ***(G-7464)***

A L P H A B E T I C

(PA)=Parent Co (HQ)=Headquarters (DH)=Div Headquarters
2017 Harris
New York Manufacturers Directory
951

Excel Graphics Services Inc....212 929-2183
519 8th Ave Fl 18 New York (10018) ***(G-10101)***
Excel Industries Inc....716 542-5468
11737 Main St Clarence (14031) ***(G-3661)***
Excel Paint Applicators Inc....347 221-1968
555 Doughty Blvd Inwood (11096) ***(G-6755)***
Excel Technology Inc....212 355-3400
780 3rd Ave New York (10017) ***(G-10102)***
Excelco Developments Inc....716 934-2651
65 Main St Silver Creek (14136) ***(G-15448)***
Excelco/Newbrook Inc....716 934-2644
16 Mechanic St Silver Creek (14136) ***(G-15449)***
Excell Print & Promotions Inc....914 437-8668
50 Main St Ste 100 White Plains (10606) ***(G-17107)***
Excelled Shpskin Lea Coat Corp (PA)....212 594-5843
1400 Brdwy Fl 31 New York (10018) ***(G-10103)***
Excellent Art Mfg Corp....718 388-7075
531 Bayview Ave Inwood (11096) ***(G-6756)***
Excellent Cabinet Works, Brooklyn *Also called Den-Jo Woodworking Corp* ***(G-1854)***
Excellent Photocopies, Brooklyn *Also called Excellent Printing Inc* ***(G-1944)***
Excellent Poly Inc....718 768-6555
820 4th Ave Brooklyn (11232) ***(G-1943)***
Excellent Printing Inc....718 384-7272
165 Hooper St Brooklyn (11211) ***(G-1944)***
Excelsior Graphics Inc....212 730-6200
485 Madison Ave Fl 13 New York (10022) ***(G-10104)***
Excelsior Mlt-Cltural Inst Inc....706 627-4285
13340 Roosevelt Ave 7g Flushing (11354) ***(G-5239)***
Excelsior Packaging Group Inc....914 968-1300
159 Alexander St Yonkers (10701) ***(G-17442)***
Excelsior Publications....607 746-7600
133 Main St Delhi (13753) ***(G-4238)***
Excelsus Solutions LLC....585 533-0003
300b Commerce Dr Rochester (14623) ***(G-14363)***
Exchange My Mail Inc....516 605-1835
30 Jericho Executive Plz 100c Jericho (11753) ***(G-7068)***
Exclusive Designs....516 378-5258
84 Albany Ave Freeport (11520) ***(G-5396)***
Executive Business Media Inc....516 334-3030
825 Old Country Rd Westbury (11590) ***(G-16983)***
Executive Creations Inc....212 422-2640
44 Wall St Fl 12 New York (10005) ***(G-10105)***
Executive Machines Inc....718 965-6600
882 3rd Ave Fl 10-1 Brooklyn (11232) ***(G-1945)***
Executive Mirror Doors Inc....631 234-1090
1 Comac Loop Unit 7 Ronkonkoma (11779) ***(G-14899)***
Executive Prtg & Direct Mail....914 592-3200
8 Westchester Plz Ste 117 Elmsford (10523) ***(G-4752)***
Executive Sign Corp....212 397-4050
43 Boulevard Cornwall On Hudson (12520) ***(G-3992)***
Executive Sign Corporation....212 397-4050
347 W 36th St Rm 902 New York (10018) ***(G-10106)***
Exelis, Rochester *Also called Harris Corporation* ***(G-14425)***
Exelis, Rome *Also called Harris Corporation* ***(G-14813)***
Exelis Geospatial Systems, Rochester *Also called Harris Corporation* ***(G-14423)***
Exelis Geospatial Systems, Rochester *Also called Harris Corporation* ***(G-14424)***
Exergy LLC....516 832-9300
320 Endo Blvd Unit 1 Garden City (11530) ***(G-5505)***
Exfo Burleigh Pdts Group Inc....585 301-1530
181 S Main St Ste 10 Canandaigua (14424) ***(G-3345)***
Exhibit Corporation America....718 937-2600
4623 Crane St Ste 3 Long Island City (11101) ***(G-7734)***
Exhibit Portables, Long Island City *Also called Exhibit Corporation America* ***(G-7734)***
Exhibits & More....585 924-4040
7615 Omnitech Pl Ste 4a Victor (14564) ***(G-16476)***
Exide Batteries, Batavia *Also called Exide Technologies* ***(G-631)***
Exide Technologies....585 344-0656
4330 Commerce Dr Batavia (14020) ***(G-631)***
Exigo Precision Inc....585 254-5818
190 Murray St Rochester (14606) ***(G-14364)***
Eximus Connections Corporation....631 421-1700
2387 New York Ave Unit 3 Huntington Station (11746) ***(G-6703)***
Exotic Print and Paper Inc....212 807-0465
15 E 13th St New York (10003) ***(G-10107)***
Expedi-Printing Inc....516 513-0919
41 Red Brook Rd Great Neck (11024) ***(G-5807)***
Expedient Heat Treating Corp....716 433-1177
61 Dale Dr North Tonawanda (14120) ***(G-12970)***
Experiment LLC....212 889-1659
260 5th Ave Fl 3 New York (10001) ***(G-10108)***
Experiment Publishing LLC....212 889-1273
220 E 23rd St Ste 301 New York (10010) ***(G-10109)***
Expert Industries Inc....718 434-6060
848 E 43rd St Brooklyn (11210) ***(G-1946)***
Expert Machine Services Inc....718 786-1200
3944a 28th St Long Island City (11101) ***(G-7735)***
Expert Metal Slitters Corp....718 361-2735
3740 12th St Long Island City (11101) ***(G-7736)***
Expo Furniture Designs Inc....516 674-1420
1 Garvies Point Rd Glen Cove (11542) ***(G-5615)***
Expo Lighting Design, Glen Cove *Also called Expo Furniture Designs Inc* ***(G-5615)***

Expositor Newspapers Inc....585 427-2468
2535 Brighton Henrietta Rochester (14623) ***(G-14365)***
Express Building Supply Inc....516 608-0379
3550 Lawson Blvd Oceanside (11572) ***(G-13079)***
Express Checkout LLC....646 512-2068
110 E 1st St Apt 20 New York (10009) ***(G-10110)***
Express Concrete Inc....631 273-4224
1250 Suffolk Ave Brentwood (11717) ***(G-1183)***
Express Mart, Watertown *Also called Petre Alii Petroleum* ***(G-16670)***
Express Press, Rochester *Also called Clarsons Corp* ***(G-14278)***
Express Seal Div, Lancaster *Also called Apple Rubber Products Inc* ***(G-7303)***
Express Tag & Label, Brooklyn *Also called Jerry Tomaselli* ***(G-2137)***
Expresseal, Lancaster *Also called Apple Rubber Products Inc* ***(G-7304)***
Expression Embroidery, Jamaica *Also called Expressions Punching & Digitiz* ***(G-6911)***
Expressions Punching & Digitiz....718 291-1177
9315 179th Pl Jamaica (11433) ***(G-6911)***
Expressive Scent, Brooklyn *Also called Jacmax Industries LLC* ***(G-2130)***
Exquis LLC....845 537-5380
16 Berwynn Rd Harriman (10926) ***(G-5971)***
Exquisite Glass & Stone Inc....718 937-9266
3117 12th St Astoria (11106) ***(G-441)***
Extek Inc....585 533-1672
7500 W Henrietta Rd Rush (14543) ***(G-15047)***
Exten II LLC....716 895-2214
50 Stradtman St Buffalo (14206) ***(G-2942)***
Extreme Auto Accessories Corp (PA)....718 978-6722
12019 Rockaway Blvd South Ozone Park (11420) ***(G-15533)***
Extreme Group Holdings LLC (HQ)....212 833-8000
550 Madison Ave Fl 6 New York (10022) ***(G-10111)***
Extreme Molding LLC....518 326-9319
25 Gibson St Ste 2 Watervliet (12189) ***(G-16684)***
Exxelia-Raf Tabtronics LLC....585 243-4331
2854 Genesee St Piffard (14533) ***(G-13547)***
Exxonmobil Chemical Company....315 966-1000
729 State Route 31 Macedon (14502) ***(G-7986)***
EY Industries Inc....718 624-9122
63 Flushing Ave Unit 331 Brooklyn (11205) ***(G-1947)***
Eye Deal Eyewear Inc....716 297-1500
4611 Military Rd Niagara Falls (14305) ***(G-12817)***
Eye Graphics & Printing Inc....718 488-0606
499 Van Brunt St Ste 3a Brooklyn (11231) ***(G-1948)***
Eye Shadow, New York *Also called Stony Apparel Corp* ***(G-12209)***
Eyeglass Service Industries....914 666-3150
777 Bedford Rd Bedford Hills (10507) ***(G-803)***
Eyelock Corporation....914 619-5570
355 Lexington Ave New York (10017) ***(G-10112)***
Eyelock LLC (HQ)....855 393-5625
355 Lexington Ave Fl 12 New York (10017) ***(G-10113)***
Eyeworks Inc....585 454-4470
1249 Ridgeway Ave Ste M Rochester (14615) ***(G-14366)***
EZ CMS Systems US, Brooklyn *Also called EZ Systems US Inc* ***(G-1950)***
EZ Lift Garage Door Service, Spring Valley *Also called EZ Lift Operator Corp* ***(G-15584)***
EZ Lift Operator Corp....845 356-1676
111 S Main St Spring Valley (10977) ***(G-15584)***
EZ Newsletter LLC....412 943-7777
1449 Bay Ridge Ave 2 Brooklyn (11219) ***(G-1949)***
EZ Systems US Inc....212 634-6899
35 Meadow St 103 Brooklyn (11206) ***(G-1950)***
F & B Photo Offset Co Inc (PA)....516 431-5433
4 California Pl N Island Park (11558) ***(G-6779)***
F & D Printing, Staten Island *Also called F & D Services Inc* ***(G-15672)***
F & D Services Inc....718 984-1635
34 E Augusta Ave Staten Island (10308) ***(G-15672)***
F & H Metal Finishing Co Inc....585 798-2151
700 Genesee St Medina (14103) ***(G-8271)***
F & J Designs Inc....212 302-8755
526 Fashion Ave Fl 8 New York (10018) ***(G-10114)***
F & M Precise Metals Co, Farmingdale *Also called Pirnat Precise Metals Inc* ***(G-5080)***
F & R Enterprises Inc (PA)....315 841-8189
1594 State Route 315 Waterville (13480) ***(G-16678)***
F & T Graphics Inc....631 643-1000
690 Old Willets Path Hauppauge (11788) ***(G-6075)***
F & V Distribution Company LLC....516 812-0393
1 Arizona Plz Woodbury (11797) ***(G-17286)***
F A Alpine Windows Mfg....845 469-5700
1683 State Route 17m Chester (10918) ***(G-3606)***
F A Printing....212 974-5982
690 10th Ave Frnt 1 New York (10019) ***(G-10115)***
F C W Division, Uniondale *Also called Hearst Business Media* ***(G-16296)***
F Cappiello Dairy Pdts Inc....518 374-5064
115 Van Guysling Ave Schenectady (12305) ***(G-15254)***
F E Hale Mfg Co....315 894-5490
120 Benson Pl Frankfort (13340) ***(G-5352)***
F H Stickles & Son Inc....518 851-9048
2590 Rr 9 Livingston (12541) ***(G-7560)***
F I S, Oriskany *Also called Fiber Instrument Sales Inc* ***(G-13309)***
F J Remey Co Inc....516 741-5112
121 Willis Ave Mineola (11501) ***(G-8511)***
F K Williams Division, North Tonawanda *Also called Gardei Industries LLC* ***(G-12973)***

ALPHABETIC

ALPHABETIC SECTION
Faradyne Motors LLC

F L Demeter Inc.....516 487-5187
12 N Gate Rd Great Neck (11023) ***(G-5808)***
F Logic, Hastings On Hudson *Also called Flogic Inc* ***(G-6003)***
F M Abdulky Inc (PA).....607 272-7373
527 W Seneca St Ithaca (14850) ***(G-6839)***
F M Abdulky Inc.....607 272-7373
527 W Seneca St Ithaca (14850) ***(G-6840)***
F M C Aricultural Chem Group, Middleport *Also called FMC Corporation* ***(G-8421)***
F M C Peroxygen Chemicals Div, Tonawanda *Also called FMC Corporation* ***(G-16164)***
F M Group Inc.....845 589-0102
100 Wells Ave Congers (10920) ***(G-3856)***
F M Howell & Company (PA).....607 734-6291
79 Pennsylvania Ave Elmira (14904) ***(G-4684)***
F M L Industries Inc.....607 749-7273
10 Hudson St Homer (13077) ***(G-6517)***
F Olivers LLC.....585 244-2585
747 Park Ave Rochester (14607) ***(G-14367)***
F P H Communications.....212 528-1728
225 Broadway Ste 2008 New York (10007) ***(G-10116)***
F R A M Technologies Inc.....718 338-6230
3048 Bedford Ave Brooklyn (11210) ***(G-1951)***
F W Roberts Mfg Co Inc.....716 434-3555
73 Lock St Lockport (14094) ***(G-7585)***
F X Graphix Inc.....716 871-1511
3043 Delaware Ave Buffalo (14217) ***(G-2943)***
F&M Ornamental Designs LLC.....212 353-2600
151 Wooster St Frnt 2 New York (10012) ***(G-10117)***
F&M Ornamental Designs LLC (PA).....908 241-7776
200 Lexington Ave Rm 702 New York (10016) ***(G-10118)***
F+w Media Inc.....212 447-1400
1140 Broadway Fl 14 New York (10001) ***(G-10119)***
F-O-R Software LLC.....212 231-9506
757 3rd Ave Fl 20 New York (10017) ***(G-10120)***
F-O-R Software LLC (PA).....914 220-8800
10 Bank St Ste 830 White Plains (10606) ***(G-17108)***
F-O-R Software LLC.....212 724-3920
100 Park Ave Rm 1600 New York (10017) ***(G-10121)***
F5 Networks Inc.....888 882-7535
424 W 33rd St Rm 530 New York (10001) ***(G-10122)***
Fab Industries Corp (HQ).....516 498-3200
98 Cuttermill Rd Ste 412 Great Neck (11021) ***(G-5809)***
Fabbian USA Corp.....973 882-3824
307 W 38th St Rm 1103 New York (10018) ***(G-10123)***
Fabric Concepts For Industry.....914 375-2565
354 Ashburton Ave Yonkers (10701) ***(G-17443)***
Fabric Quilters Unlimited Inc.....516 333-2866
1400 Shames Dr Westbury (11590) ***(G-16984)***
Fabric Resources Intl Ltd (PA).....516 829-4550
9 Park Pl Great Neck (11021) ***(G-5810)***
Fabrication Enterprises Inc.....914 591-9300
250 Clearbrook Rd Ste 240 Elmsford (10523) ***(G-4753)***
Fabrication Specialties Corp.....631 242-0326
2 Saxwood St Ste G Deer Park (11729) ***(G-4141)***
Fabritex Inc.....706 376-6584
215 W 40th St Fl 9 New York (10018) ***(G-10124)***
Faces Magazine Inc (PA).....201 843-4004
46 Violet Ave Poughkeepsie (12601) ***(G-13898)***
Faces Magazine Inc.....845 454-7420
40 Violet Ave Poughkeepsie (12601) ***(G-13899)***
Facilamatic Instrument Corp.....516 825-6300
39 Clinton Ave Valley Stream (11580) ***(G-16406)***
Facilities, New York *Also called Bedrock Communications* ***(G-9345)***
Facilities Exchange, Brooklyn *Also called X F Inc* ***(G-2770)***
Facsimile Cmmncations Inds Inc (PA).....212 741-6400
134 W 26th St Fl 3 New York (10001) ***(G-10125)***
Factory East.....718 280-1558
723 Kent Ave Brooklyn (11249) ***(G-1952)***
Factory Nyc, Brooklyn *Also called Factory East* ***(G-1952)***
Factory Wheel Warehouse Inc.....516 605-2131
30 W Ames Ct Plainview (11803) ***(G-13601)***
Facts On File Inc (HQ).....212 967-8800
132 W 31st St Fl 17 New York (10001) ***(G-10126)***
Fad Inc.....631 385-2460
630 New York Ave Ste B Huntington (11743) ***(G-6661)***
FAD TREASURES, Huntington *Also called Fad Inc* ***(G-6661)***
Fage USA Dairy Industry Inc.....518 762-5912
1 Opportunity Dr Johnstown (12095) ***(G-7112)***
Fage USA Holdings (HQ).....518 762-5912
1 Opportunity Dr Johnstown (12095) ***(G-7113)***
Fage USA Yogurt Mfg Plant, Johnstown *Also called Fage USA Dairy Industry Inc* ***(G-7112)***
Fahrenheit NY Inc.....212 354-6554
315 W 39th St Rm 700 New York (10018) ***(G-10127)***
Fahy-Williams Publishing Inc.....315 781-6820
171 Reed St Geneva (14456) ***(G-5575)***
Fair-Rite Products Corp (PA).....845 895-2055
1 Commercial Row Wallkill (12589) ***(G-16543)***
Fairbank Farms, Ashville *Also called Fairbank Reconstruction Corp* ***(G-429)***
Fairbank Reconstruction Corp.....800 628-3276
5151 Fairbanks Rd Ashville (14710) ***(G-429)***
Fairbanks Mfg LLC.....845 341-0002
79 Industrial Pl Middletown (10940) ***(G-8440)***
Fairchild Publications Inc (HQ).....212 630-4000
475 5th Ave New York (10017) ***(G-10128)***
Fairchild Publishing LLC.....212 286-3897
4 Times Sq Fl 17 New York (10036) ***(G-10129)***
Fairmount Press.....212 255-2300
121 Varick St Fl 9 New York (10013) ***(G-10130)***
Fairview Bell and Intercom.....718 627-8621
502 Gravesend Neck Rd B Brooklyn (11223) ***(G-1953)***
Fairview Fitting & Mfg Inc.....716 614-0320
3777 Commerce Ct North Tonawanda (14120) ***(G-12971)***
Fairview Paper Box Corp.....585 786-5230
200 Allen St Warsaw (14569) ***(G-16582)***
Fait Usa Inc.....215 674-5310
350 5th Ave Fl 41 New York (10118) ***(G-10131)***
Fal Coffee Inc.....718 305-4255
240 Kent Ave Ste A8 Brooklyn (11249) ***(G-1954)***
Fala Technologies Inc.....845 336-4000
430 Old Neighborhood Rd Kingston (12401) ***(G-7189)***
Falcon Chair and Table Inc.....716 664-7136
121 S Work St Falconer (14733) ***(G-4897)***
Falcon Perspectives Inc.....718 706-9168
28 Vernon Blvd Ste 45 Long Island City (11101) ***(G-7737)***
Falcone Food Distribution, Brooklyn *Also called Falcones Cookie Land Ltd* ***(G-1955)***
Falconer Electronics Inc (PA).....716 665-4176
421 W Everett St Falconer (14733) ***(G-4898)***
Falconer Printing & Design Inc.....716 665-2121
66 E Main St Falconer (14733) ***(G-4899)***
Falcones Cookie Land Ltd (PA).....718 236-4200
1648 61st St Brooklyn (11204) ***(G-1955)***
Falconstor Software Inc (PA).....631 777-5188
2 Huntington Quadrangle 2s Melville (11747) ***(G-8318)***
Falk Industries Inc.....518 725-2777
179 Corporate Dr Johnstown (12095) ***(G-7114)***
Falke's Quarry, Prattsville *Also called Cobleskill Stone Products Inc* ***(G-13945)***
Fallon Inc.....718 326-7226
5930 56th Rd Maspeth (11378) ***(G-8138)***
Falls Manufacturing Inc (PA).....518 672-7189
95 Main St Philmont (12565) ***(G-13540)***
Falso Industries Inc.....315 463-0266
4100 New Court Ave Syracuse (13206) ***(G-15941)***
Falso Metal Fabricating, Syracuse *Also called Falso Industries Inc* ***(G-15941)***
Falvo Manufacturing Co Inc.....315 738-7682
20 Harbor Point Rd Utica (13502) ***(G-16330)***
Fam Creations.....212 869-4833
46 W 46th St Fl 4 New York (10036) ***(G-10132)***
Fambus Inc.....607 785-3700
2800 Watson Blvd Endicott (13760) ***(G-4807)***
Fame Construction Inc.....718 626-1000
2388 Brklyn Queens Expy W Astoria (11103) ***(G-442)***
Family Fuel Co Inc.....718 232-2009
1571 W 10th St Brooklyn (11204) ***(G-1956)***
Family Hearing Center.....845 897-3059
18 Westage Dr Ste 16 Fishkill (12524) ***(G-5184)***
Family Publications Ltd.....212 947-2177
325 W 38th St Rm 804 New York (10018) ***(G-10133)***
Family Publishing Group Inc.....914 381-7474
141 Halstead Ave Mamaroneck (10543) ***(G-8034)***
Famous Box Scooter Co.....631 943-2013
75 Rogers Ct West Babylon (11704) ***(G-16791)***
Famous Doughnuts Inc.....716 834-6356
3043 Main St Buffalo (14214) ***(G-2944)***
Famous Manhattan Soup Chef, Staten Island *Also called Interntional Gourmet Soups Inc* ***(G-15688)***
Fancy, New York *Also called Thing Daemon Inc* ***(G-12317)***
Fancy Flamingo LLC.....516 209-7306
450 W 17th St Apt 528 New York (10011) ***(G-10134)***
Fancy Window & Door, Brooklyn *Also called Fancy Windows & Doors Mfg Corp* ***(G-1957)***
Fancy Windows & Doors Mfg Corp.....718 366-7800
100 Morgan Ave Brooklyn (11237) ***(G-1957)***
Fanshawe Foods LLC.....212 757-3130
5 Columbus Cir New York (10019) ***(G-10135)***
Fantasia Jewelry Inc.....212 921-9590
42 W 39th St Fl 14 New York (10018) ***(G-10136)***
Fantasy Fireworks Display.....518 664-1809
28 Flike Rd Stillwater (12170) ***(G-15759)***
Fantasy Furniture Inc.....718 386-8078
24a Woodward Ave Ridgewood (11385) ***(G-14106)***
Fantasy Glass Compan.....845 786-5818
61 Beach Rd Stony Point (10980) ***(G-15773)***
Fantasy Home Improvement Corp.....718 277-4021
2731 Atlantic Ave Brooklyn (11207) ***(G-1958)***
Fantasy Sports Media Group Inc.....416 917-6002
27 W 20th St Ste 900 New York (10011) ***(G-10137)***
Fantasy Sports Network, New York *Also called Fantasy Sports Media Group Inc* ***(G-10137)***
Fao Printing.....718 282-3310
5107 Avenue H Brooklyn (11234) ***(G-1959)***
Far Eastern Coconut Company.....631 851-8800
200 Corporate Plz 201a Central Islip (11749) ***(G-3496)***
Far Rockaway Drugs Inc.....718 471-2500
1727 Seagirt Blvd Far Rockaway (11691) ***(G-4922)***
Faradyne Motors LLC.....315 331-5985
2077 Division St Palmyra (14522) ***(G-13405)***

A L P H A B E T I C

Farber Plastics Inc...516 378-4860
162 Hanse Ave Freeport (11520) ***(G-5397)***
Farber Trucking Corp...516 378-4860
162 Hanse Ave Freeport (11520) ***(G-5398)***
Farino & Sons Asphalt, Kings Park *Also called Amfar Asphalt Corp* ***(G-7169)***
Farley Windows Inc...315 764-1111
Trade Dr Massena (13662) ***(G-8194)***
Farmers Hub LLC...646 380-6770
8 Francine Ct White Plains (10607) ***(G-17109)***
Farmingdale Iron Works Inc...631 249-5995
105 Florida St Farmingdale (11735) ***(G-4991)***
Farney Lumber Corporation...315 346-6013
7194 Brewery Rd Lowville (13367) ***(G-7936)***
Farney Tree & Excavation LLC...315 783-1161
7610 Yousey Rd Croghan (13327) ***(G-4058)***
Faro Industries Inc...585 647-6000
340 Lyell Ave Rochester (14606) ***(G-14368)***
Farrand Controls Division, Valhalla *Also called Ruhle Companies Inc* ***(G-16372)***
Farrant Screw Machine Products...585 457-3213
Gulf Rd Java Village (14083) ***(G-7053)***
Farrar Straus and Giroux LLC (HQ)...212 741-6900
18 W 18th St Fl 7 New York (10011) ***(G-10138)***
Farrington Packaging Corp...315 733-4600
2007 Beechgrove Pl Utica (13501) ***(G-16331)***
Farrow and Ball Inc (HQ)...212 752-5544
979 3rd Ave Ste 1519 New York (10022) ***(G-10139)***
Farthing Press Inc...716 852-4674
258 Oak St Ste 260 Buffalo (14203) ***(G-2945)***
Fashion Apparel Industries...212 704-0800
1412 Broadway Ste 1818 New York (10018) ***(G-10140)***
Fashion Ave Sweater Knits LLC...212 302-8282
525 7th Ave Fl 4 New York (10018) ***(G-10141)***
Fashion Avenue Knits Inc...718 456-9000
1400 Broadway Rm 2401 New York (10018) ***(G-10142)***
Fashion Calendar International...212 289-0420
153 E 87th St Apt 6a New York (10128) ***(G-10143)***
Fashion Chef, The, Brooklyn *Also called Charlotte Neuville Design LLC* ***(G-1775)***
Fashion Deli Inc...818 772-5637
2353 Fredrck Douglss Blvd Apt 3 New York (10027) ***(G-10144)***
Fashion Ribbon Co Inc (PA)...718 482-0100
3401 38th Ave Long Island City (11101) ***(G-7738)***
Fashiondex Inc...914 271-6121
153 W 27th St Ste 701 New York (10001) ***(G-10145)***
Fasprint...518 483-4631
20 Finney Blvd Malone (12953) ***(G-8009)***
Fast By Gast Inc...716 773-1536
120 Industrial Dr Grand Island (14072) ***(G-5757)***
Fast Company Magazine, New York *Also called Mansueto Ventures LLC* ***(G-11142)***
Fast-Trac Entertainment Ltd...888 758-8886
7 E 74th St Apt 5 New York (10021) ***(G-10146)***
Fastener Dimensions Inc...718 847-6321
9403 104th St Ozone Park (11416) ***(G-13378)***
Fasteners Depot LLC...718 622-4222
5308 13th Ave Brooklyn (11219) ***(G-1960)***
Faster-Form Corp...800 327-3676
1 Faster Form Cir Ste 1 New Hartford (13413) ***(G-8804)***
Fastsigns, Tonawanda *Also called Fletcher Enterprises Inc* ***(G-16163)***
Fastsigns, Staten Island *Also called Vez Inc* ***(G-15752)***
Fastsigns...518 456-7446
1593 Central Ave Albany (12205) ***(G-79)***
Fat Baby, New York *Also called Nycjbs LLC* ***(G-11481)***
Father Sam's Bakery, Buffalo *Also called Commitment 2000 Inc* ***(G-2883)***
Faulkner Truss Company Inc...315 536-8894
1830 King Hill Rd Dresden (14441) ***(G-4319)***
Faviana International Inc (PA)...212 594-4422
320 W 37th St Rm 100 New York (10018) ***(G-10147)***
Favorite Plastic Corp...718 253-7000
1465 Utica Ave Brooklyn (11234) ***(G-1961)***
Faye Bernard Loungewear...718 951-7245
2604 Avenue M Brooklyn (11210) ***(G-1962)***
Fayette Street Coatings Inc (HQ)...315 488-5401
1970 W Fayette St Syracuse (13204) ***(G-15942)***
Fayette Street Coatings Inc...315 488-5401
1 Burr Dr Liverpool (13088) ***(G-7519)***
FB Laboratories Inc...631 750-0000
70 Commerce Dr Hauppauge (11788) ***(G-6076)***
FB Sale LLC...315 986-9999
1688 Wayneport Rd Macedon (14502) ***(G-7987)***
FBC Chemical Corporation...716 681-1581
4111 Walden Ave Lancaster (14086) ***(G-7315)***
Fca LLC...518 756-9655
149 Coeymans Ind Pk Ln Coeymans (12045) ***(G-3745)***
FCC Acquisition LLC...716 282-1399
4120 Hyde Park Blvd Niagara Falls (14305) ***(G-12818)***
Fcmp Inc...716 692-4623
230 Fire Tower Dr Tonawanda (14150) ***(G-16160)***
Fearby Enterprises, Medina *Also called F & H Metal Finishing Co Inc* ***(G-8271)***
Fedders Islandaire Inc...631 471-2900
22 Research Way East Setauket (11733) ***(G-4482)***
Fedders Islandaire Company, East Setauket *Also called Fedders Islandaire Inc* ***(G-4482)***
Federal Contract MGT Svcs, Brooklyn *Also called It Commodity Sourcing Inc* ***(G-2118)***
Federal Envelope Inc...212 243-8380
22 W 32nd St New York (10001) ***(G-10148)***
Federal Prison Industries...845 386-6819
2 Mile Dr Otisville (10963) ***(G-13344)***
Federal Prison Industries...518 897-4000
Old Ray Brook Rd Ray Brook (12977) ***(G-14024)***
Federal Pump Corporation (PA)...718 451-2000
1144 Utica Ave Brooklyn (11203) ***(G-1963)***
Federal Sample Card Corp...718 458-1344
4520 83rd St Elmhurst (11373) ***(G-4660)***
Federal Sheet Metal Works Inc...315 735-4730
1416 Dudley Ave Utica (13501) ***(G-16332)***
Federal Yellow Book, New York *Also called Leadership Directories Inc* ***(G-10946)***
Federated Media Publishing LLC...917 677-7976
31 W 27th St Fl 8 New York (10001) ***(G-10149)***
Fedex Office & Print Svcs Inc...718 982-5223
2456 Richmond Ave Ste C Staten Island (10314) ***(G-15673)***
Fei Communications Inc...516 794-4500
55 Charles Lindbergh Blvd Uniondale (11553) ***(G-16293)***
Fei Products LLC (PA)...716 693-6230
825 Wurlitzer Dr North Tonawanda (14120) ***(G-12972)***
Fei-Zyfer Inc...714 933-4045
55 Charles Lindbergh Blvd Uniondale (11553) ***(G-16294)***
Feinkind Inc...800 289-6136
17 Algonquin Dr Irvington (10533) ***(G-6769)***
Feinstein Iron Works Inc...516 997-8300
990 Brush Hollow Rd Westbury (11590) ***(G-16985)***
Felber Metal Fabricators, Holbrook *Also called Brzozka Industries Inc* ***(G-6434)***
Felchar Manufacturing Corp (HQ)...607 723-3106
196 Corporate Dr Binghamton (13904) ***(G-914)***
Feldheim Publishers, Nanuet *Also called Philipp Feldheim Inc* ***(G-8760)***
Feldman Company Inc...212 966-1303
7 W 34th St Ste 900 New York (10001) ***(G-10150)***
Feldman Jewelry Creations Inc...718 438-8895
4821 16th Ave Brooklyn (11204) ***(G-1964)***
Feldman Manufacturing Corp...718 433-1700
3010 41st Ave Ste 3fl Long Island City (11101) ***(G-7739)***
Feldmeier Equipment Inc (PA)...315 823-2000
6800 Townline Rd Syracuse (13211) ***(G-15943)***
Feldmeier Equipment Inc...315 823-2000
245 Riverside Ind Park Little Falls (13365) ***(G-7499)***
Feldmeier Equipment Inc...315 823-2000
575 E Mill St Little Falls (13365) ***(G-7500)***
Feldware Inc...718 372-0486
250 Avenue W Brooklyn (11223) ***(G-1965)***
Felicetti Concrete Products...716 284-5740
4129 Hyde Park Blvd Niagara Falls (14305) ***(G-12819)***
Felix Roma & Sons Inc...607 748-3336
2 S Page Ave Endicott (13760) ***(G-4808)***
Felix Schoeller North Amer Inc...315 298-5133
179 County Route 2a Pulaski (13142) ***(G-13946)***
Felix Schoeller Technical Pprs, Pulaski *Also called Felix Schoeller North Amer Inc* ***(G-13946)***
Felix Storch Inc (PA)...718 893-3900
770 Garrison Ave Bronx (10474) ***(G-1329)***
Felluss Recording...212 727-8055
36 E 23rd St Rm 9l New York (10010) ***(G-10151)***
Felton Machine Co Inc...716 215-9001
2221 Niagara Falls Blvd Niagara Falls (14304) ***(G-12820)***
Feminist Press Inc...212 817-7929
365 5th Ave Ste 5406 New York (10016) ***(G-10152)***
Femtech Women Powered Software...516 328-2631
1230 Hempstead Tpke Franklin Square (11010) ***(G-5363)***
Fenbar Prcision Machinists Inc...914 769-5506
633 Commerce St Thornwood (10594) ***(G-16120)***
Fence Plaza Corp...718 469-2200
1020 Rogers Ave Brooklyn (11226) ***(G-1966)***
Fenix Furniture Co...631 273-3500
35 Drexel Dr Bay Shore (11706) ***(G-700)***
Fennell Industries LLC (PA)...607 733-6693
108 Stephens Pl Elmira (14901) ***(G-4685)***
Fennell Spring Company LLC...607 739-3541
295 Hemlock St Horseheads (14845) ***(G-6577)***
Fenway Holdings LLC...212 757-0606
152 W 57th St Fl 59 New York (10019) ***(G-10153)***
Feraco Industries...631 547-8120
3 Plumb Ct Huntington Station (11746) ***(G-6704)***
Ferguson Enterprises Inc...800 437-1146
200 Atlantic Ave New Hyde Park (11040) ***(G-8834)***
Fermer Precision Inc...315 822-6371
114 Johnson Rd Ilion (13357) ***(G-6740)***
Ferrara Bakery & Cafe Inc (PA)...212 226-6150
195 Grand St New York (10013) ***(G-10154)***
Ferrara Bros Bldg Mtls Corp (PA)...718 939-3030
12005 31st Ave Flushing (11354) ***(G-5240)***
Ferrara Manufacturing, New York *Also called Rogers Group Inc* ***(G-11907)***
Ferrara Manufacturing Company, New York *Also called HC Contracting Inc* ***(G-10433)***
Ferraro Manufacturing Company...631 752-1509
150 Central Ave Farmingdale (11735) ***(G-4992)***
Ferris USA LLC...617 895-8102
18 W 108th St New York (10025) ***(G-10155)***
Ferro Corporation...585 586-8770
603 W Commercial St East Rochester (14445) ***(G-4458)***

ALPHABETIC

ALPHABETIC SECTION Fiorentina LLC

Ferro Corporation 315 536-3357
1789 Transelco Dr Penn Yan (14527) ***(G-13509)***

Ferro Electronic Mtl Systems, Penn Yan *Also called Ferro Electronics Materials* ***(G-13510)***

Ferro Electronic Mtl Systems, Penn Yan *Also called Ferro Electronics Materials* ***(G-13511)***

Ferro Electronics Materials 716 278-9400
4511 Hyde Park Blvd Niagara Falls (14305) ***(G-12821)***

Ferro Electronics Materials (HQ) 315 536-3357
1789 Transelco Dr Penn Yan (14527) ***(G-13510)***

Ferro Electronics Materials 315 536-3357
1789 Transelco Dr Penn Yan (14527) ***(G-13511)***

Ferro Fabricators Inc 718 851-4027
1119 38th St Brooklyn (11218) ***(G-1967)***

Ferro Machine Co Inc 845 398-3641
70 S Greenbush Rd Orangeburg (10962) ***(G-13228)***

Festival Bakers, Bronx *Also called Waldorf Bakers Inc* ***(G-1492)***

Fetherston Design Group LLC 212 643-7537
225 W Broadway New York (10013) ***(G-10156)***

Feyem USA Inc 845 363-6253
7 Sutton Pl Brewster (10509) ***(G-1219)***

Ffc Holding Corp Subsidiaries (PA) 716 366-5400
1 Ice Cream Dr Dunkirk (14048) ***(G-4342)***

FG Galassi Moulding Co Inc 845 258-2100
699 Pulaski Hwy Goshen (10924) ***(G-5734)***

Fgi, Amsterdam *Also called Fiber Glass Industries Inc* ***(G-345)***

Fiber Foot Appliances Inc 631 465-9199
34 Sarah Dr Ste A Farmingdale (11735) ***(G-4993)***

Fiber Glass Industries Inc (PA) 518 842-4000
69 Edson St Amsterdam (12010) ***(G-345)***

Fiber Glass Industries Inc 518 843-3533
1 Homestead Pl Amsterdam (12010) ***(G-346)***

Fiber Instrument Sales Inc (PA) 315 736-2206
161 Clear Rd Oriskany (13424) ***(G-13309)***

Fiber Laminations Limited 716 692-1825
600 Main St Tonawanda (14150) ***(G-16161)***

Fiber Optics Schott America, Auburn *Also called Schott Corporation* ***(G-517)***

Fiber USA Corp 718 888-1512
13620 38th Ave Ste 11f Flushing (11354) ***(G-5241)***

Fiber-Seal of New York Inc (PA) 212 888-5580
979 3rd Ave Ste 903 New York (10022) ***(G-10157)***

Fiberall Corp 516 371-5200
449 Sheridan Blvd Inwood (11096) ***(G-6757)***

Fibercel Packaging LLC (HQ) 716 933-8703
46 Brooklyn St Portville (14770) ***(G-13874)***

Fiberdyne Labs Inc 315 895-8470
127 Business Park Dr Frankfort (13340) ***(G-5353)***

Fiberfrax Manufacturing, Tonawanda *Also called American Securities LLC* ***(G-16138)***

Fiberglass Replacement Parts 716 893-6471
200 Colorado Ave Buffalo (14215) ***(G-2946)***

Fibermark North America Inc 315 376-3571
5492 Bostwick St Lowville (13367) ***(G-7937)***

Fibermark North America Inc 315 782-5800
101 Bridge St Brownville (13615) ***(G-2783)***

Fiberone LLC 315 434-8877
5 Technology Pl Ste 4 East Syracuse (13057) ***(G-4529)***

Fiberwave Corporation 718 802-9011
140 58th St Ste 6e Brooklyn (11220) ***(G-1968)***

Fiberwave Technologies, Brooklyn *Also called Fiberwave Corporation* ***(G-1968)***

Fibre Case & Novelty Co Inc (PA) 212 254-6060
270 Lafayette St Ste 1510 New York (10012) ***(G-10158)***

Fibre Materials Corp 516 349-1660
40 Dupont St Plainview (11803) ***(G-13602)***

Fibrix LLC 716 683-4100
3307 Walden Ave Depew (14043) ***(G-4257)***

Fibron Products Inc 716 886-2378
170 Florida St Buffalo (14208) ***(G-2947)***

Fics Inc 607 359-4474
25 Community Dr Addison (14801) ***(G-6)***

Fidazzel Inc 917 557-3860
2280 Olinville Ave # 409 Bronx (10467) ***(G-1330)***

Fidelus Technologies LLC 212 616-7800
240 W 35th St Fl 6 New York (10001) ***(G-10159)***

Fidesa US Corporation 212 269-9000
17 State St Unit 122 New York (10004) ***(G-10160)***

Field Trip Jerky, New York *Also called Provisionaire & Co LLC* ***(G-11741)***

Fieldbrook Foods Corporation (HQ) 716 366-5400
1 Ice Cream Dr Dunkirk (14048) ***(G-4343)***

Fieldston Clothes Inc (HQ) 212 354-8550
500 Fashion Ave Fl 6a New York (10018) ***(G-10161)***

Fieldtex Products Inc 585 427-2940
3055 Brighton Henrietta Rochester (14623) ***(G-14369)***

Fierce Fun Toys LLC 646 322-7172
100 Riverside Dr Ste 2 New York (10024) ***(G-10162)***

Fil Doux Inc 212 202-1459
227 5th Ave Brooklyn (11215) ***(G-1969)***

Fil-Coil (fc) Corp (PA) 631 467-5328
98 Lincoln Ave Sayville (11782) ***(G-15209)***

Filestream Inc 516 759-4100
257 Buckram Rd Locust Valley (11560) ***(G-7629)***

Filling Equipment Co Inc 718 445-2111
1539 130th St College Point (11356) ***(G-3783)***

Fillmore Greenhouses Inc 585 567-2678
11589 State Route 19a Portageville (14536) ***(G-13872)***

Filmpak Extrusion LLC 631 293-6767
125 Spagnoli Rd Melville (11747) ***(G-8319)***

Films Media Group, New York *Also called Infobase Publishing Company* ***(G-10595)***

Filta Clean Co Inc 718 495-3800
107 Georgia Ave Brooklyn (11207) ***(G-1970)***

Filter Tech Inc (PA) 315 682-8815
113 Fairgrounds Dr Manlius (13104) ***(G-8071)***

Filtros Ltd 585 586-8770
603 W Commercial St East Rochester (14445) ***(G-4459)***

Filtros Plant, East Rochester *Also called Filtros Ltd* ***(G-4459)***

Fina Cabinet Corp 718 409-2900
20 N Macquesten Pkwy Mount Vernon (10550) ***(G-8681)***

Final Cut Letterpress Spc, Buffalo *Also called LAM Western New York Inc* ***(G-3045)***

Final Dimension Inc 718 786-0100
57-401 59th St Fl 1 Maspeth (11378) ***(G-8139)***

Final Touch Printing Inc 845 352-2677
29 Decatur Ave Unit 1 Spring Valley (10977) ***(G-15585)***

Finals, The, Port Jervis *Also called Swimwear Anywhere Inc* ***(G-13794)***

Finance Manager, East Setauket *Also called Mml Software Ltd* ***(G-4488)***

Financial Times, New York *Also called FT Publications Inc* ***(G-10218)***

Financial Times Newspaper, New York *Also called FT Publications Inc* ***(G-10219)***

Fine and Raw Chocolate 718 366-3633
288 Seigel St Brooklyn (11206) ***(G-1971)***

Fine Architectural Met Smiths, Florida *Also called New England Tool Co Ltd* ***(G-5214)***

Fine Arts Furniture Inc 212 744-9139
3872 13th St Long Island City (11101) ***(G-7740)***

Fine Cut Diamonds Corporation 212 575-8780
580 5th Ave Ste 901 New York (10036) ***(G-10163)***

Fine Sheer Industries Inc (PA) 212 594-4224
350 5th Ave Ste 5001 New York (10118) ***(G-10164)***

Fine Sounds Group Inc (PA) 212 364-0219
214 Lafayette St New York (10012) ***(G-10165)***

Fineline Thermographers Inc 718 643-1100
544 Park Ave Ste 308 Brooklyn (11205) ***(G-1972)***

Finer Touch Printing Corp 516 944-8000
4 Yennicock Ave Port Washington (11050) ***(G-13815)***

Finesse Accessories, Plainview *Also called Mgd Brands Inc* ***(G-13620)***

Finesse Creations Inc 718 692-2100
3004 Avenue J Brooklyn (11210) ***(G-1973)***

Finesse La Model Handbags, New York *Also called Sibeau Handbags Inc* ***(G-12059)***

Finest Cc Corp 917 574-4525
3111 E Tremont Ave Bronx (10461) ***(G-1331)***

Finestar, Long Island City *Also called Efam Enterprises LLC* ***(G-7725)***

Finger Food Products Inc 716 297-4888
2045 Niagara Falls Blvd # 1 Niagara Falls (14304) ***(G-12822)***

Finger Lakes Cheese Trail 607 857-5726
4970 County Road 14 Odessa (14869) ***(G-13108)***

Finger Lakes Chemicals Inc (PA) 585 454-4760
420 Saint Paul St Rochester (14605) ***(G-14370)***

Finger Lakes Conveyors Inc 315 539-9246
2359 State Route 414 E Waterloo (13165) ***(G-16625)***

Finger Lakes Distilling 607 546-5510
4676 State Route 414 Burdett (14818) ***(G-3265)***

Finger Lakes Extrusion Corp 585 905-0632
2437 State Route 21 Canandaigua (14424) ***(G-3346)***

Finger Lakes Lea Crafters LLC 315 252-4107
42 Washington St Auburn (13021) ***(G-494)***

Finger Lakes Massage Group (PA) 607 272-9024
215 E State St Ste 2 Ithaca (14850) ***(G-6841)***

Finger Lakes Media Inc 607 243-7600
45 Water St Dundee (14837) ***(G-4327)***

Finger Lakes Printing Co Inc (HQ) 315 789-3333
218 Genesee St Geneva (14456) ***(G-5576)***

Finger Lakes Radiology LLC 315 787-5399
196 North St Geneva (14456) ***(G-5577)***

Finger Lakes School of Massage, Ithaca *Also called Finger Lakes Massage Group* ***(G-6841)***

Finger Lakes Stone Co Inc 607 273-4646
33 Quarry Rd Ithaca (14850) ***(G-6842)***

Finger Lakes Timber Co Inc 585 346-2990
6274 Decker Rd Livonia (14487) ***(G-7564)***

Finger Lakes Trellis Supply 315 904-4007
4041a Railroad Ave Williamson (14589) ***(G-17223)***

Finger Lakes/Castle, Rochester *Also called Finger Lakes Chemicals Inc* ***(G-14370)***

Fingerlakes Construction, Clyde *Also called Energy Panel Structures Inc* ***(G-3726)***

Fingerlakes Construction, Batavia *Also called Energy Panel Structures Inc* ***(G-630)***

Fingerlakes Construction, Schenectady *Also called Energy Panel Structures Inc* ***(G-15251)***

Fingerprint America Inc 518 435-1609
1843 Central Ave Albany (12205) ***(G-80)***

Fingertech USA, Brooklyn *Also called BDB Technologies LLC* ***(G-1675)***

Finish Line Technologies Inc (PA) 631 666-7300
50 Wireless Blvd Hauppauge (11788) ***(G-6077)***

Finishing Line, The, Le Roy *Also called Duzmor Painting Inc* ***(G-7407)***

Finzer Holding LLC 315 597-1147
2085 Division St Palmyra (14522) ***(G-13406)***

Finzer Roller New York, Palmyra *Also called Finzer Holding LLC* ***(G-13406)***

Fiora Italy, Bay Shore *Also called Innovative Jewelry Inc* ***(G-705)***

Fiorentina LLC 516 208-5448
1519 Hendrickson Ave Merrick (11566) ***(G-8385)***

ALPHABETIC

Fire Apparatus Service Tech.....716 753-3538
7895 Lyons Rd Sherman (14781) ***(G-15402)***
Fire Fox Security Corp.....917 981-9280
2070 72nd St Apt B1 Brooklyn (11204) ***(G-1974)***
Fire Island Fuel.....631 772-1482
106 Parkwood Dr Shirley (11967) ***(G-15418)***
Fire Island News, Bronx *Also called Five Islands Publishing Inc* ***(G-1332)***
Fire Island Sea Clam Co Inc.....631 589-2199
132 Atlantic Ave West Sayville (11796) ***(G-16935)***
Fire Island Tide Publication.....631 567-7470
40 Main St Sayville (11782) ***(G-15210)***
Fire Island Tide The, Sayville *Also called Fire Island Tide Publication* ***(G-15210)***
Firecom Inc (PA).....718 899-6100
3927 59th St Woodside (11377) ***(G-17328)***
Firefighters Journal.....718 391-0283
2420 Jackson Ave Long Island City (11101) ***(G-7741)***
Firematic Supply Co Inc (PA).....631 924-3181
10 Ramsey Rd East Yaphank (11967) ***(G-4581)***
Firetronics Inc (PA).....516 997-5151
50 Jericho Tpke Jericho (11753) ***(G-7069)***
Fireworks By Grucci Inc.....631 286-0088
20 Pinehurst Dr Bellport (11713) ***(G-831)***
First Displays Inc.....347 642-5972
2415 43rd Ave Fl 2 Long Island City (11101) ***(G-7742)***
First Games Publr Netwrk Inc.....212 983-0501
420 Lexington Ave Rm 412 New York (10170) ***(G-10166)***
First Image Design Corp.....212 221-8282
98 Cuttrmill Rd Ste 231 New York (10036) ***(G-10167)***
First Impressions Finishing.....631 467-2244
132 Remington Blvd Ronkonkoma (11779) ***(G-14900)***
First International USA Ltd.....718 854-0181
768 39th St Brooklyn (11232) ***(G-1975)***
First Light Farm & Creamery, East Bethany *Also called Sandvoss Farms LLC* ***(G-4383)***
First Line Printing Inc.....718 606-0860
3728 56th St Woodside (11377) ***(G-17329)***
First Love Fashions LLC.....212 256-1089
1407 Broadway Rm 2010 New York (10018) ***(G-10168)***
First Presbyterian Church.....315 252-3861
112 South St Auburn (13021) ***(G-495)***
First Qlty Packg Solutions LLC (PA).....516 829-3030
80 Cuttermill Rd Ste 500 Great Neck (11021) ***(G-5811)***
First Quality Products Inc (HQ).....516 829-4949
80 Cuttermill Rd Ste 500 Great Neck (11021) ***(G-5812)***
First Sbf Holding Inc (PA).....845 425-9882
9 Pinecrest Rd Ste 101 Valley Cottage (10989) ***(G-16378)***
First Source LLC.....716 877-0800
100 Pirson Pkwy Tonawanda (14150) ***(G-16162)***
First View, New York *Also called Viewfinder Inc* ***(G-12543)***
First2print Inc.....212 868-6886
494 8th Ave Fl 12 New York (10001) ***(G-10169)***
Firth Rixson Inc (HQ).....585 328-1383
181 Mckee Rd Rochester (14611) ***(G-14371)***
Firth Rixson Monroe, Rochester *Also called Firth Rixson Inc* ***(G-14371)***
Fisau, Yorktown Heights *Also called Business Management Systems* ***(G-17508)***
Fischer Diamonds Inc.....212 869-1990
1212 Avenue Of The Americ New York (10036) ***(G-10170)***
Fischler Diamonds Inc.....212 921-8196
580 5th Ave Ste 3100 New York (10036) ***(G-10171)***
Fischler Hockey Service.....212 749-4152
200 W 109th St Apt C5 New York (10025) ***(G-10172)***
Fish & Crown Ltd (PA).....212 707-9603
42 W 39th St New York (10018) ***(G-10173)***
Fishing Valley LLC.....716 523-6158
7217 N Canal Rd Lockport (14094) ***(G-7586)***
Fisonic Corp.....212 732-3777
4402 23rd St Long Island City (11101) ***(G-7743)***
Fisonic Corp (PA).....716 763-0295
31-00 47th Ave Ste 106 New York (10023) ***(G-10174)***
Fisonic Technology, New York *Also called Fisonic Corp* ***(G-10174)***
Fist Inc.....718 643-3478
20 Jay St Ste 212 Brooklyn (11201) ***(G-1976)***
Fitch Graphics Ltd.....212 619-3800
229 W 28th St Fl 9 New York (10001) ***(G-10175)***
Fitch Group, New York *Also called Francis Emory Fitch Inc* ***(G-10199)***
Fitzgerald Publishing Co Inc.....914 793-5016
1853 Central Park Ave # 8 Yonkers (10710) ***(G-17444)***
Fitzpatrick and Weller Inc.....716 699-2393
12 Mill St Ellicottville (14731) ***(G-4641)***
Fitzsimmons Systems Inc.....315 214-7010
53 Nelson St Cazenovia (13035) ***(G-3445)***
Five Boro Holding LLC.....718 431-9500
1425 37th St Ste 3 Brooklyn (11218) ***(G-1977)***
Five Corners Repair Inc.....585 322-7369
6653 Hardys Rd Bliss (14024) ***(G-980)***
Five Islands Publishing Inc.....631 583-5345
8 Fort Charles Pl Bronx (10463) ***(G-1332)***
Five Star Awnings Inc.....718 860-6070
5923 Decatur St Ridgewood (11385) ***(G-14107)***
Five Star Creations Inc.....845 783-1187
4 Preshburg Blvd Unit 302 Monroe (10950) ***(G-8554)***
Five Star Field Services.....347 446-6816
584 Carroll St Fl 1 Brooklyn (11215) ***(G-1978)***
Five Star Industries Inc.....716 674-2589
114 Willowdale Dr West Seneca (14224) ***(G-16945)***
Five Star Measurement, Brooklyn *Also called Five Star Field Services* ***(G-1978)***
Five Star Millwork LLC.....845 920-0247
6 E Dexter Plz Pearl River (10965) ***(G-13456)***
Five Star Printing, Jamaica *Also called Ssrja LLC* ***(G-6950)***
Five Star Prtg & Mailing Svcs.....212 929-0300
225 W 37th St Fl 16 New York (10018) ***(G-10176)***
Five Star Tool Co Inc.....585 328-9580
125 Elmgrove Park Rochester (14624) ***(G-14372)***
Fiveboro Printing & Supplies.....718 431-9500
1425 37th St Ste 5 Brooklyn (11218) ***(G-1979)***
Fixture Hardware Mfg Corp.....718 499-9422
4116 1st Ave Ste 13 Brooklyn (11232) ***(G-1980)***
Fiz Beverages, Rochester *Also called Load/N/Go Beverage Corp* ***(G-14481)***
Fjs Industries Inc.....917 428-3797
970 E 92nd St Brooklyn (11236) ***(G-1981)***
Flado Enterprises Inc.....716 668-6400
1380 French Rd Ste 6 Depew (14043) ***(G-4258)***
Flagpoles Incorporated.....631 751-5500
95 Gnarled Hollow Rd East Setauket (11733) ***(G-4483)***
Flair Display Inc.....718 324-9330
3920 Merritt Ave Bronx (10466) ***(G-1333)***
Flair Printers, Brooklyn *Also called Printing Sales Group Limited* ***(G-2449)***
Flame Control Coatings, Niagara Falls *Also called FCC Acquisition LLC* ***(G-12818)***
Flanagans Creative Disp Inc.....845 858-2542
55 Jersey Ave Port Jervis (12771) ***(G-13784)***
Flare Multi Copy, Brooklyn *Also called Flare Multicopy Corp* ***(G-1982)***
Flare Multicopy Corp.....718 258-8860
1840 Flatbush Ave Brooklyn (11210) ***(G-1982)***
Flash Ventures Inc.....212 255-7070
853 Broadway Ste 400 New York (10003) ***(G-10177)***
Flashflo Manufacturing Inc.....716 826-9500
88 Hopkins St Buffalo (14220) ***(G-2948)***
Flashflo Manufacturing Inc.....716 840-9594
222 Chicago St Buffalo (14204) ***(G-2949)***
Flatbush Surgical Supply Co.....516 775-0507
174 Meacham Ave Ste C Elmont (11003) ***(G-4720)***
Flatcut LLC.....212 542-5732
68 Jay St Ste 901 Brooklyn (11201) ***(G-1983)***
Flaum Appetizing, Brooklyn *Also called M & M Food Products Inc* ***(G-2244)***
Flaum Appetizing Corp.....718 821-1970
288 Scholes St Brooklyn (11206) ***(G-1984)***
Flavor League, Brooklyn *Also called Flavor Paper Ltd* ***(G-1985)***
Flavor Paper Ltd.....718 422-0230
216 Pacific St Brooklyn (11201) ***(G-1985)***
Flavormatic Industries Inc.....845 297-9100
90 Brentwood Dr Wappingers Falls (12590) ***(G-16567)***
Flavors Holdings Inc (HQ).....212 572-8677
35 E 62nd St New York (10065) ***(G-10178)***
Fleetcom Inc.....914 776-5582
1081 Yonkers Ave Yonkers (10704) ***(G-17445)***
Fleetwood Cabinet Co Inc (PA).....516 379-2139
673 Livonia Ave Brooklyn (11207) ***(G-1986)***
Fleischman Vinegar, North Rose *Also called Fleischmanns Vinegar Co Inc* ***(G-12936)***
Fleischmanns Vinegar Co Inc.....315 587-4414
4754 State Route 414 North Rose (14516) ***(G-12936)***
Fletcher Enterprises Inc.....716 837-7446
2865 Sheridan Dr Tonawanda (14150) ***(G-16163)***
Flex Enterprises Inc.....585 742-1000
820 Canning Pkwy Victor (14564) ***(G-16477)***
Flex Supply, Farmingdale *Also called Custom Door & Mirror Inc* ***(G-4970)***
Flex Tubing, Canandaigua *Also called Finger Lakes Extrusion Corp* ***(G-3346)***
Flex-Hose Company Inc.....315 437-1903
6801 Crossbow Dr East Syracuse (13057) ***(G-4530)***
Flexbar Machine Corporation.....631 582-8440
250 Gibbs Rd Islandia (11749) ***(G-6793)***
Flexene Corp.....631 491-0580
108 Lamar St West Babylon (11704) ***(G-16792)***
Flexfit Llc.....516 932-8800
350 Karin Ln Unit A Hicksville (11801) ***(G-6344)***
Flexim Americas Corporation (HQ).....631 492-2300
250 Executive Dr Ste V Edgewood (11717) ***(G-4598)***
Flexlume Sign Corporation.....716 884-2020
1464 Main St Buffalo (14209) ***(G-2950)***
Flexo Transparent Inc.....716 825-7710
28 Wasson St Buffalo (14210) ***(G-2951)***
Flexographic Printing, Rochester *Also called American Packaging Corporation* ***(G-14198)***
Flexsin.....212 470-9279
1441 Broadway Fl 5 New York (10018) ***(G-10179)***
Flextrade Systems Inc (PA).....516 627-8993
111 Great Neck Rd Ste 314 Great Neck (11021) ***(G-5813)***
Flickinger Glassworks Inc.....718 875-1531
204 Van Dyke St Ste 207 Brooklyn (11231) ***(G-1987)***
Flightline Electronics Inc (HQ).....585 742-5340
7625 Omnitech Pl Victor (14564) ***(G-16478)***
Flint Group Incorporated.....585 458-1223
1128 Lexington Ave Bldg 3 Rochester (14606) ***(G-14373)***
Flint Ink North America Div, Rochester *Also called Flint Group Incorporated* ***(G-14373)***
Flirtatious, New York *Also called Soho Apparel Ltd* ***(G-12118)***

ALPHABETIC

ALPHABETIC SECTION — Fortune Magazine, New York

Flo-Tech Orthotic & Prosthetic 607 387-3070
7325 Hulseyville Rd Trumansburg (14886) *(G-16266)*
Float Tech Inc 518 266-0964
216 River St Ste 1 Troy (12180) *(G-16235)*
Flogic Inc 914 478-1352
25 Chestnut Dr Hastings On Hudson (10706) *(G-6003)*
Flomatic Corporation 518 761-9797
15 Pruyns Island Dr Glens Falls (12801) *(G-5678)*
Flomatic Valves, Glens Falls Also called Flomatic Corporation *(G-5678)*
Floored Inc 908 347-5845
111 8th Ave Fl 16 New York (10011) *(G-10180)*
Florelle Tissue Corporation 647 997-7405
1 Bridge St Brownville (13615) *(G-2784)*
Florida North Inc 518 868-2888
134 Vanderwerken Rd Sloansville (12160) *(G-15479)*
Flour Power Bakery Cafe 917 747-6895
87 Debruce Rd Livingston Manor (12758) *(G-7561)*
Flow Dental, Deer Park Also called Flow X Ray Corporation *(G-4142)*
Flow Society, New York Also called Big Idea Brands LLC *(G-9394)*
Flow X Ray Corporation 631 242-9729
100 W Industry Ct Deer Park (11729) *(G-4142)*
Flow-Safe Inc 716 662-2585
3865 Taylor Rd Orchard Park (14127) *(G-13270)*
Flower City Printing Inc (PA) 585 663-9000
1725 Mount Read Blvd Rochester (14606) *(G-14374)*
Flower City Printing Inc 585 512-1235
1001 Lee Rd Rochester (14606) *(G-14375)*
Flower Cy Tissue Mills Co Inc (PA) 585 458-9200
700 Driving Park Ave Rochester (14613) *(G-14376)*
Flownet LLC 716 685-4036
580 Lake Ave Lancaster (14086) *(G-7316)*
Floymar Manufacturing, Hauppauge Also called Ehrlich Enterprises Inc *(G-6069)*
Flp Group LLC 315 252-7583
301 Clark St Auburn (13021) *(G-496)*
Fluid Handling LLC 716 897-2800
175 Standard Pkwy Cheektowaga (14227) *(G-3570)*
Fluid Handling LLC (HQ) 716 897-2800
175 Standard Pkwy Cheektowaga (14227) *(G-3571)*
Fluid Mechanisms Hauppauge Inc 631 234-0100
225 Engineers Rd Hauppauge (11788) *(G-6078)*
Fluid Metering Inc (HQ) 516 922-6050
5 Aerial Way Ste 500 Syosset (11791) *(G-15822)*
Fluoro Seal, Buffalo Also called Inhance Technologies LLC *(G-3009)*
Fluorologic Inc 585 248-2796
33 Bishops Ct Pittsford (14534) *(G-13559)*
Flushing Boiler & Welding Co 718 463-1266
8720 Ditmas Ave Brooklyn (11236) *(G-1988)*
Flushing Iron Weld Inc 718 359-2208
13125 Maple Ave Flushing (11355) *(G-5242)*
Flushing Pharmacy Inc 718 260-8999
414 Flushing Ave Ste 1 Brooklyn (11205) *(G-1989)*
Flushing Terminal, Flushing Also called Tilcon New York Inc *(G-5301)*
Fluxdata Incorporated 800 425-0176
176 Anderson Ave Ste F304 Rochester (14607) *(G-14377)*
Fly-Tyers Carry-All LLC 607 821-1460
112 Meade Rd Charlotteville (12036) *(G-3555)*
Flycell Inc 212 400-1212
80 Pine St Fl 29 New York (10005) *(G-10181)*
Flynn Burner Corporation 914 636-1320
425 Fifth Ave New Rochelle (10801) *(G-8899)*
Flynn's Xerox, New York Also called Flynns Inc *(G-10182)*
Flynns Inc (PA) 212 339-8700
115 W 30th St New York (10001) *(G-10182)*
FM Brush Co Inc 718 821-5939
7002 72nd Pl Glendale (11385) *(G-5652)*
FMC Corporation 716 735-3761
100 Niagara St Middleport (14105) *(G-8421)*
FMC Corporation 716 879-0400
78 Sawyer Ave Ste 1 Tonawanda (14150) *(G-16164)*
FMC International Ltd 914 935-0918
8 Slater St Ste 2 Port Chester (10573) *(G-13746)*
Foam Products Inc 718 292-4830
360 Southern Blvd Bronx (10454) *(G-1334)*
Focus Camera Inc (PA) 718 437-8800
895 Mcdonald Ave Brooklyn (11218) *(G-1990)*
Focus Point Windows & Doors, Long Beach Also called Air Tite Manufacturing Inc *(G-7637)*
Fodera Guitars Inc 718 832-3455
68 34th St Unit 3 Brooklyn (11232) *(G-1991)*
Fog Creek Software Inc 866 364-2733
1 Exchange Plz Fl 25 New York (10006) *(G-10183)*
Fogel Neckwear Corp 212 686-7673
44 W 28th St Fl 15 New York (10001) *(G-10184)*
Folene Packaging LLC 917 626-6740
2509 Avenue M Brooklyn (11210) *(G-1992)*
Folio Graphics Co Inc 718 763-2076
2759 E 66th St Brooklyn (11234) *(G-1993)*
Folstaf Company, The, Charlotteville Also called Fly-Tyers Carry-All LLC *(G-3555)*
Fonar Corporation (PA) 631 694-2929
110 Marcus Dr Melville (11747) *(G-8320)*
Fontrick Door Inc 585 345-6032
9 Apollo Dr Batavia (14020) *(G-632)*

Foo Yuan Food Products Co Inc 212 925-2840
2301 Borden Ave Long Island City (11101) *(G-7744)*
Food Gems Ltd 718 296-7788
8423 Rockaway Blvd Ozone Park (11416) *(G-13379)*
Food52 Inc 718 596-5560
116 Willow St Apt 2 Brooklyn (11201) *(G-1994)*
Foot Locker Retail Inc 516 827-5306
358 Broadway Mall Hicksville (11801) *(G-6345)*
For A Safer America, Amsterdam Also called Keep America Beautiful Inc *(G-354)*
Forbes Precision Inc 585 865-7069
100 Boxart St Ste 105 Rochester (14612) *(G-14378)*
Forbes Products, Dansville Also called GPM Associates LLC *(G-4077)*
Force Digital Media Inc 631 243-0243
39 W Jefryn Blvd Ste 2 Deer Park (11729) *(G-4143)*
Force Dynamics Inc 607 546-5023
4995 Voorheis Rd Trumansburg (14886) *(G-16267)*
Ford Gum & Machine Company Inc (PA) 716 542-4561
18 Newton Ave Akron (14001) *(G-22)*
Ford Motor Company 716 821-4000
3663 Lake Shore Rd Buffalo (14219) *(G-2952)*
Ford Regulator Valve Corp 718 497-3255
199 Varet St Brooklyn (11206) *(G-1995)*
Fordham Marble Co Inc 914 682-6699
45 Crane Ave White Plains (10603) *(G-17110)*
Fordham University 718 817-4795
2546 Belmont Ave Bronx (10458) *(G-1335)*
Fordham University Press, Bronx Also called Fordham University *(G-1335)*
Forecast Consoles Inc 631 253-9000
681 Old Willets Path Hauppauge (11788) *(G-6079)*
Forerunner Technologies Inc (PA) 631 337-2100
1430 Church St Unit A Bohemia (11716) *(G-1067)*
Forest Hills Courier, Bayside Also called Schneps Publications Inc *(G-775)*
Forest Iron Works Inc 516 671-4229
3 Elm St Ste A Locust Valley (11560) *(G-7630)*
Forest Laboratories LLC (HQ) 212 421-7850
909 3rd Ave Fl 23 New York (10022) *(G-10185)*
Forest Laboratories LLC 212 421-7850
45 Adams Ave Hauppauge (11788) *(G-6080)*
Forest Laboratories LLC 631 858-6010
500 Commack Rd Commack (11725) *(G-3831)*
Forest Medical LLC 315 434-9000
6700 Old Collamer Rd # 114 East Syracuse (13057) *(G-4531)*
Forest Uniforms, New York Also called Urban Textiles Inc *(G-12481)*
Forever Yours Intl Corp 516 443-2743
50 James Nck Saint James (11780) *(G-15089)*
Forkey Construction & Fabg Inc 607 849-4879
3690 Luker Rd Cortland (13045) *(G-4026)*
Form A Rockland Plastics Inc 315 848-3300
7152 Main St Cranberry Lake (12927) *(G-4057)*
Form-Tec Inc 516 867-0200
216 N Main St Ste E Freeport (11520) *(G-5399)*
Formac Welding Inc 631 421-5525
42 W Hills Rd Huntington Station (11746) *(G-6705)*
Formaggio Italian Cheese, Hurleyville Also called Mongiellos Itln Cheese Spc LLC *(G-6732)*
Formart Corp 212 819-1819
312 5th Ave Fl 6 New York (10001) *(G-10186)*
Formatix Corp 631 467-3399
9 Colt Ct Ronkonkoma (11779) *(G-14901)*
Formats Unlimited Inc 631 249-9200
19 W Jefryn Blvd Ste 2 Deer Park (11729) *(G-4144)*
Formcraft Display Products 914 632-1410
42 Beverly Rd New Rochelle (10804) *(G-8900)*
Formed Plastics Inc 516 334-2300
207 Stonehinge Ln Carle Place (11514) *(G-3388)*
Foro Marble Co Inc 718 852-2322
166 2nd Ave Brooklyn (11215) *(G-1996)*
Forrest Engravg, New Rochelle Also called Forrest Engraving Co Inc *(G-8901)*
Forrest Engraving Co Inc 845 228-0200
92 1st St New Rochelle (10801) *(G-8901)*
Forsyth Industries Inc 716 652-1070
1195 Colvin Blvd Buffalo (14223) *(G-2953)*
Forsythe Cosmetic Group Ltd 516 239-4200
10 Niagara Ave Freeport (11520) *(G-5400)*
Forsythe Licensing, Freeport Also called Forsythe Cosmetic Group Ltd *(G-5400)*
Fort Miller Group Inc 518 695-5000
688 Wilbur Ave Greenwich (12834) *(G-5887)*
Fort Miller Service Corp (PA) 518 695-5000
688 Wilbur Ave Greenwich (12834) *(G-5888)*
Fort Orange Press Inc 518 489-3233
11 Sand Creek Rd Albany (12205) *(G-81)*
Forte Network 631 390-9050
75 Lockfield Rd East Northport (11731) *(G-4436)*
Forte Security Group, East Northport Also called Forte Network *(G-4436)*
Forteq North America Inc 585 427-9410
150 Park Centre Dr West Henrietta (14586) *(G-16878)*
Fortitech Inc (HQ) 518 372-5155
2105 Technology Dr Schenectady (12308) *(G-15255)*
Fortitude Industries 607 324-1500
7200 County Route 70a Hornell (14843) *(G-6563)*
Fortress Biotech Inc (PA) 781 652-4500
3 Columbus Cir Fl 15 New York (10019) *(G-10187)*
Fortune Magazine, New York Also called Time Inc *(G-12344)*

Fortune Poly Products Inc...718 361-0767
17910 93rd Ave Jamaica (11433) *(G-6912)*
Fortune Sign...646 383-8682
1334 39th St Brooklyn (11218) *(G-1997)*
Forum Publishing Co...631 754-5000
383 E Main St Centerport (11721) *(G-3476)*
Forum South, The, Howard Beach *Also called Vpj Publication Inc (G-6600)*
Forward Enterprises Inc...585 235-7670
215 Tremont St Ste 8 Rochester (14608) *(G-14379)*
Forwardlane Inc...310 779-8590
120 W 21st St Apt 1014 New York (10011) *(G-10188)*
Forwear, New York *Also called A and J Apparel Corp (G-8983)*
Foscarini Inc...212 247-2218
17 Greene St New York (10013) *(G-10189)*
Foscarini Showroom, New York *Also called Foscarini Inc (G-10189)*
Foseco Inc...914 345-4760
777 Old Saw Mill River Rd Tarrytown (10591) *(G-16090)*
Fossil Industries Inc...631 254-9200
44 W Jefryn Blvd Ste A Deer Park (11729) *(G-4145)*
Foster - Gordon Manufacturing...631 589-6776
55 Knickerbocker Ave G Bohemia (11716) *(G-1068)*
Foster Reeve & Associates Inc (PA)...718 609-0090
1155 Manhattan Ave # 1011 Brooklyn (11222) *(G-1998)*
Foster Refrigerators Entp...518 671-6036
300 Fairview Ave Hudson (12534) *(G-6614)*
Fotis Oneonta Italian Bakery...607 432-3871
42 River St Oneonta (13820) *(G-13186)*
Fotofiles, Vestal *Also called Truebite Inc (G-16455)*
Fougera Pharmaceuticals Inc (HQ)...631 454-7677
60 Baylis Rd Melville (11747) *(G-8321)*
Fougera Pharmaceuticals Inc...631 454-7677
55 Cantiague Rock Rd Hicksville (11801) *(G-6346)*
Foundation Center Inc (PA)...212 620-4230
1 Financial Sq Fl 24 New York (10005) *(G-10190)*
Foundation For Cultural Review...212 247-6980
900 Broadway Ste 602 New York (10003) *(G-10191)*
Fountain Tile Outlet Inc...718 927-4555
609 Fountain Ave Ste A Brooklyn (11208) *(G-1999)*
Fountainhead Group Inc (PA)...315 736-0037
23 Garden St New York Mills (13417) *(G-12722)*
Fountainhead Group Inc...315 736-0037
23 Garden St New York Mills (13417) *(G-12723)*
Fountainhead Group Inc...708 598-7100
3 Graden St New York Mills (13417) *(G-12724)*
Four &TWenty Blackbirds, Brooklyn *Also called Blackbirds Brooklyn LLC (G-1700)*
Four Brothers Italian Bakery...914 741-5434
332 Elwood Ave Hawthorne (10532) *(G-6246)*
Four Dee Inc...718 615-1695
2247 E 16th St Brooklyn (11229) *(G-2000)*
Four Directions Inc...315 829-8388
4677 State Route 5 Vernon (13476) *(G-16434)*
Four Fat Fowl Inc...518 733-5230
324 State Route 43 Stop B Stephentown (12168) *(G-15757)*
Four K Machine Shop Inc...516 997-0752
54 Brooklyn Ave Westbury (11590) *(G-16986)*
Four Paws Products Ltd...631 436-7421
3125 Vtrans Mem Hwy Ste 1 Ronkonkoma (11779) *(G-14902)*
Four Quarter, Westbury *Also called Cab-Network Inc (G-16972)*
Four S Showcase Manufacturing...718 649-4900
1044 Linwood St Brooklyn (11208) *(G-2001)*
Four Sasons Multi-Services Inc...347 843-6262
3525 Decatur Ave Apt 2k Bronx (10467) *(G-1336)*
Four Seasons Fashion Mfg Inc...212 947-6820
270 W 39th St Fl 12 New York (10018) *(G-10192)*
Four Seasons Sunrooms, Holbrook *Also called Latium USA Trading LLC (G-6455)*
Four Square Tool, Conklin *Also called Toolroom Express Inc (G-3876)*
Four Star, New York *Also called Vanity Room Inc (G-12503)*
Four Wheel Drive, Staten Island *Also called Cyclone Air Power Inc (G-15664)*
Four-Way Pallet Corp...631 351-3401
191 E 2nd St Huntington Station (11746) *(G-6706)*
Fourteen Arnold Ave Corp...315 272-1700
14 Arnold Ave Utica (13502) *(G-16333)*
Fourtys Ny Inc...212 382-0301
231 W 39th St Rm 806 New York (10018) *(G-10193)*
Fowler Route Co Inc...917 653-4640
25 Sunnyside Dr Yonkers (10705) *(G-17446)*
Fownes Brothers & Co Inc (PA)...212 683-0150
16 E 34th St Fl 5 New York (10016) *(G-10194)*
Fownes Brothers & Co Inc...518 752-4411
204 County Highway 157 Gloversville (12078) *(G-5711)*
Fox Run Vineyards Inc...315 536-4616
670 State Route 14 Penn Yan (14527) *(G-13512)*
Fox Unlimited Inc...212 736-3071
345 7th Ave Rm 2b New York (10001) *(G-10195)*
Fox's U-Bet Syrups, Brooklyn *Also called H Fox & Co Inc (G-2059)*
Foxhill Press Inc...212 995-9620
37 E 7th St Ste 2 New York (10003) *(G-10196)*
Fpg, Cedarhurst *Also called Franklin Printing Group Ltd (G-3457)*
Fppf Chemical Co Inc (PA)...716 856-9607
117 W Tupper St Ste 1 Buffalo (14201) *(G-2954)*
Fra-Rik Formica Fabg Co Inc...718 597-3335
1464 Blondell Ave Fl 2 Bronx (10461) *(G-1337)*
Fradan Manufacturing Corp...914 632-3653
499 5th Ave New Rochelle (10801) *(G-8902)*
Fragrance Acquisitions LLC...845 534-9172
1900 Corporate Blvd Newburgh (12550) *(G-12755)*
Fragrance Outlet Inc...845 928-1408
404 Evergreen Ct Central Valley (10917) *(G-3523)*
Fralo, Syracuse *Also called Roth Global Plastics Inc (G-16026)*
Frame Shoppe & Art Gallery...516 365-6014
447 Plandome Rd Manhasset (11030) *(G-8060)*
Frame Shoppe & Gallery, Manhasset *Also called Frame Shoppe & Art Gallery (G-8060)*
Frame Works America Inc...631 288-1300
146 Mill Rd Westhampton Beach (11978) *(G-17058)*
Framedcom...212 400-2200
575 Madison Ave Fl 24 New York (10022) *(G-10197)*
Framerica Corporation...631 650-1000
2 Todd Ct Yaphank (11980) *(G-17393)*
Frames Plus Inc...518 462-1842
991 Broadway Ste 208 Menands (12204) *(G-8371)*
Framing Technology Inc...585 464-8470
137 Syke St Rochester (14611) *(G-14380)*
Francepress LLC (PA)...646 202-9828
115 E 57th St Fl 11 New York (10022) *(G-10198)*
Franchet Metal Craft Inc...718 658-6400
17832 93rd Ave Jamaica (11433) *(G-6913)*
Francis Emory Fitch Inc (PA)...212 619-3800
229 W 28th St Fl 9 New York (10001) *(G-10199)*
Franco Apparel Group Inc...212 967-7272
1407 Broadway New York (10018) *(G-10200)*
Franco Apparel Group Team, New York *Also called Franco Apparel Group Inc (G-10200)*
Franetta, New York *Also called Beyond Loom Inc (G-9383)*
Frank Billanti Casting Co Inc...212 221-0440
42 W 38th St Rm 204 New York (10018) *(G-10201)*
Frank Blancato Inc...212 768-1495
64 W 48th St Fl 16 New York (10036) *(G-10202)*
Frank J Martello...585 235-2780
1227 Maple St Rochester (14611) *(G-14381)*
Frank Lowe Rbr & Gasket Co Inc...631 777-2707
44 Ramsey Rd Shirley (11967) *(G-15419)*
Frank Merriwell Inc...516 921-8888
212 Michael Dr Syosset (11791) *(G-15823)*
Frank Murken Products, Schenectady *Also called Tattersall Industries LLC (G-15304)*
Frank Torrone & Sons Inc...718 273-7600
400 Broadway Staten Island (10310) *(G-15674)*
Frank Wardynski & Sons Inc...716 854-6083
336 Peckham St Buffalo (14206) *(G-2955)*
Frank Wines Inc...646 765-6637
345 E 80th St Apt 8b New York (10075) *(G-10203)*
Franklin Electric Co Inc...718 244-7744
17501 Rockaway Blvd # 309 Jamaica (11434) *(G-6914)*
Franklin Manufacturing Div, Hauppauge *Also called Embassy Industries Inc (G-6071)*
Franklin Packaging Inc (PA)...631 582-8900
96 Sea Cove Rd Northport (11768) *(G-13011)*
Franklin Poly Film Inc...718 492-3523
1149 56th St Brooklyn (11219) *(G-2002)*
Franklin Printing Group Ltd...516 569-1248
140 Washington Ave Unit A Cedarhurst (11516) *(G-3457)*
Franklin Report LLC...212 639-9100
201 E 69th St Apt 14j New York (10021) *(G-10204)*
Franklin's Printing, Cheektowaga *Also called Hugh F McPherson Inc (G-3575)*
Franklin-Douglas Inc...516 883-0121
52 Main St Side Port Washington (11050) *(G-13816)*
Franz Fischer Inc...718 821-1300
1267 Flushing Ave Brooklyn (11237) *(G-2003)*
Frasier and Jones, Syracuse *Also called American Foundrymens Society (G-15853)*
Fratellis LLC...607 722-5663
20 Campbell Rd Binghamton (13905) *(G-915)*
Frazer & Jones Division, Solvay *Also called Eastern Company (G-15507)*
Frazer Computing Inc...315 379-3500
6196 Us Highway 11 Canton (13617) *(G-3383)*
Frazier Industrial Company...315 539-9256
1291 Waterloo Geneva Rd Waterloo (13165) *(G-16626)*
Fred A Nudd Corporation (PA)...315 524-2531
1743 State Route 104 Ontario (14519) *(G-13201)*
Fred Lawrence Co, Bay Shore *Also called Lanwood Industries Inc (G-711)*
Fred M Lawrence Co Inc (PA)...718 786-7227
45 Drexel Dr Bay Shore (11706) *(G-701)*
Fred M Velepec Co Inc...718 821-6636
7172 70th St Glendale (11385) *(G-5653)*
Fred Schulz Inc...845 724-3409
4 Jordan Ct Poughquag (12570) *(G-13941)*
Fred Weidner & Son Printers...212 964-8676
15 Maiden Ln Ste 1505 New York (10038) *(G-10205)*
Frederick Coon Inc...716 683-6812
5751 Clinton St Elma (14059) *(G-4648)*
Frederick Cowan & Company Inc...631 369-0360
48 Kroemer Ave Riverhead (11901) *(G-14143)*
Frederick Machine Repair Inc...716 332-0104
405 Ludington St Buffalo (14206) *(G-2956)*
Fredonia Pennysaver Inc (PA)...716 679-1509
276 W Main St Ste 1 Fredonia (14063) *(G-5373)*

ALPHABETIC

Free Trader, Elizabethtown *Also called Denton Publications Inc* ***(G-4626)***
Free Trader, Plattsburgh *Also called Denton Publications Inc* ***(G-13661)***
Freeda Vitamins Inc...718 433-4337
4725 34th St Fl 3 Long Island City (11101) ***(G-7745)***
Freedom Mfg LLC...518 584-0441
3 Duplainville Rd Bldg 4 Saratoga Springs (12866) ***(G-15152)***
Freedom Rains Inc...646 710-4512
230 W 39th St Fl 7 New York (10018) ***(G-10206)***
Freedom Run Winery Inc...716 433-4136
5138 Lower Mountain Rd Lockport (14094) ***(G-7587)***
Freeman Technology Inc...732 829-8345
2355 Bell Blvd Apt 2h Bayside (11360) ***(G-770)***
Freeport Baldwin Leader, Garden City *Also called L & M Publications Inc* ***(G-5513)***
Freeport Paper Industries Inc...631 851-1555
120 Windsor Pl Central Islip (11722) ***(G-3497)***
Freeport Screen & Stamping...516 379-0330
31 Hanse Ave Freeport (11520) ***(G-5401)***
Freescale Semiconductor Inc...585 425-4000
135 Sullys Trl Ste 9 Pittsford (14534) ***(G-13560)***
Freetime Magazine Inc...585 473-2266
1255 University Ave # 270 Rochester (14607) ***(G-14382)***
Freeville Publishing Co Inc...607 844-9119
9 Main St Freeville (13068) ***(G-5435)***
Freeze Clothing, New York *Also called Central Mills Inc* ***(G-9565)***
Freeze-Dry Foods Inc...585 589-6399
111 West Ave Ste 2 Albion (14411) ***(G-165)***
Freirich Julian Co Inc (PA)...718 361-9111
815 Kerr St Long Island City (11101) ***(G-7746)***
French & Itln Furn Craftsmen...718 599-5000
999 Grand St Brooklyn (11211) ***(G-2004)***
French Accnt Rugs & Tapestries...212 686-6097
36 E 31st St Frnt B New York (10016) ***(G-10207)***
French Associates Inc...718 387-9880
7339 172nd St Fresh Meadows (11366) ***(G-5440)***
French Atmosphere Inc (PA)...516 371-9100
421 7th Ave 525 New York (10001) ***(G-10208)***
French Itln Furn Craftsmen Cor, Brooklyn *Also called French & Itln Furn Craftsmen* ***(G-2004)***
French Morning LLC...646 290-7463
27 W 20th St Ste 800 New York (10011) ***(G-10209)***
French Pdts Frnch Pickle Works, Fresh Meadows *Also called French Associates Inc* ***(G-5440)***
French Toast, New York *Also called Lollytogs Ltd* ***(G-11024)***
Frenz Group LLC...212 465-0908
14932 3rd Ave Whitestone (11357) ***(G-17207)***
Frequency Electronics Inc (PA)...516 794-4500
55 Charles Lindbergh Blvd # 2 Uniondale (11553) ***(G-16295)***
Frequency Selective Networks...718 424-7500
5572 61st St Maspeth (11378) ***(G-8140)***
Fresenius Kabi Usa LLC...716 773-0053
3159 Staley Rd Grand Island (14072) ***(G-5758)***
Fresenius Kabi USA LLC...716 773-0800
3159 Staley Rd Grand Island (14072) ***(G-5759)***
Fresh Bake Pizza Co, Depew *Also called D R M Management Inc* ***(G-4254)***
Fresh Fanatic Inc...516 521-6574
88 Washington Ave Brooklyn (11205) ***(G-2005)***
Fresh Harvest Incorporated...845 296-1024
1574 Route 9 Wappingers Falls (12590) ***(G-16568)***
Fresh Ice Cream Company LLC...347 603-6021
630 Flushing Ave 4 Brooklyn (11206) ***(G-2006)***
Fresh Prints LLC...917 826-2752
134 E 70th St New York (10021) ***(G-10210)***
Freshop Inc...585 738-6035
125 Tech Park Dr Rochester (14623) ***(G-14383)***
Freshway Distributors, Hicksville *Also called Kozy Shack Enterprises LLC* ***(G-6360)***
Frew Run Gravel Products Inc...716 569-4712
984 Frew Run Rd Frewsburg (14738) ***(G-5450)***
Frey Concrete Incoprorated, Orchard Park *Also called United Materials LLC* ***(G-13301)***
Fridge Magazine Inc...212 997-7673
108 W 39th St Fl 4 New York (10018) ***(G-10211)***
Friedel Paper Box & Converting...315 437-3325
7596 Rania Rd Baldwinsville (13027) ***(G-569)***
Friendly Fuel Incorporated...518 581-7036
54 Church St Saratoga Springs (12866) ***(G-15153)***
Friendly Star Fuel Inc...718 369-8801
889 3rd Ave Brooklyn (11232) ***(G-2007)***
Friendship Dairies LLC...585 973-3031
6701 County Road 20 Friendship (14739) ***(G-5452)***
Frieslndcmpina Ingrdnts N Amer...607 746-0196
40196 State Hwy 10 Delhi Delhi (13753) ***(G-4239)***
Frigo Design, Brewerton *Also called Ae Fund Inc* ***(G-1202)***
Frisch Plastics Corp...973 685-5936
7 Joyce Rd Hartsdale (10530) ***(G-5998)***
Frito-Lay North America Inc...716 631-2360
25 Curtwright Dr Williamsville (14221) ***(G-17243)***
Frito-Lay North America Inc...585 343-5456
8063 Kelsey Rd Batavia (14020) ***(G-633)***
Frito-Lay North America Inc...607 775-7000
10 Spud Ln Binghamton (13904) ***(G-916)***
Frito-Lay North America Inc...607 397-1008
10 Main St Worcester (12197) ***(G-17368)***

Fritters & Buns Inc...845 227-6609
236 Blue Hill Rd Hopewell Junction (12533) ***(G-6550)***
Froebe Group LLC...646 649-2150
154 W 27th St Rm 4 New York (10001) ***(G-10212)***
Frog International, Hauppauge *Also called Organic Frog Inc* ***(G-6156)***
Fronhofer Tool Company Inc...518 692-2496
4197 County Rd 48 Cossayuna (12823) ***(G-4055)***
Frontier Ht-Dip Glvanizing Inc...716 875-2091
1740 Elmwood Ave Buffalo (14207) ***(G-2957)***
Frontier Hydraulics Corp...716 694-2070
1738 Elmwood Ave Ste 2 Buffalo (14207) ***(G-2958)***
Frontier Plating...716 896-2811
68 Dignity Cir Buffalo (14211) ***(G-2959)***
Frontier Plating Co, Buffalo *Also called Frontier Plating* ***(G-2959)***
Frontiers Unlimited Inc...631 283-4663
52 Jagger Ln Southampton (11968) ***(G-15543)***
Fross Industries Inc...716 297-0652
3315 Haseley Dr Niagara Falls (14304) ***(G-12823)***
Frost Publications Inc...845 726-3232
55 Laurel Hill Dr Westtown (10998) ***(G-17068)***
Frozen Food Digest Inc...212 557-8600
271 Madison Ave Ste 805 New York (10016) ***(G-10213)***
Frozen Food Partners LLC (PA)...203 661-7500
601 Lexington Ave New York (10022) ***(G-10214)***
Frozen Pastry Products Corp...845 364-9833
41 Lincoln Ave Spring Valley (10977) ***(G-15586)***
Frp Apparel Group LLC...212 695-8000
110 W 40th St Fl 26 New York (10018) ***(G-10215)***
Fruitcrown Products Corp (PA)...631 694-5800
250 Adams Blvd Farmingdale (11735) ***(G-4994)***
FSI - New York Inc...212 730-9545
1407 Broadway Rm 3107 New York (10018) ***(G-10216)***
Fsr Beauty Ltd...212 447-0036
411 5th Ave Rm 804 New York (10016) ***(G-10217)***
FT Publications Inc (HQ)...212 641-6500
330 Hudson St New York (10013) ***(G-10218)***
FT Publications Inc...212 641-2420
330 Hudson St New York (10013) ***(G-10219)***
FT Seismic Support Inc...607 527-8595
70 E 1st St Ste 101 Corning (14830) ***(G-3972)***
Fts Systems Inc (HQ)...845 687-5300
3538 Main St Stone Ridge (12484) ***(G-15763)***
Ftt Automation, Geneseo *Also called Ppi Corp* ***(G-5567)***
Ftt Medical Inc (PA)...585 235-1430
37 Centennial St Rochester (14611) ***(G-14384)***
Ftt Mfg, Geneseo *Also called Ppi Corp* ***(G-5568)***
Fuel Data Systems Inc...800 447-7870
772 Greenville Tpke Middletown (10940) ***(G-8441)***
Fuel Efficiency LLC...315 923-2511
101 Davis Pkwy Clyde (14433) ***(G-3727)***
Fuel Energy Services USA Ltd...607 846-2650
250 Industrial Park Rd Horseheads (14845) ***(G-6578)***
Fuel Systems Solutions Inc (HQ)...646 502-7170
780 3rd Ave Fl 25 New York (10017) ***(G-10220)***
Fuel Tank Environmental...631 902-1408
674 Washington Dr Centerport (11721) ***(G-3477)***
Fuel Watchman Sales & Service...718 665-6100
364 Jackson Ave Bronx (10454) ***(G-1338)***
Fujitsu Ntwrk Cmmnications Inc...845 731-2000
2 Blue Hill Plz Ste 1609 Pearl River (10965) ***(G-13457)***
Fulcrum Promos, New York *Also called Fulcrum Promotions & Prtg LLC* ***(G-10221)***
Fulcrum Promotions & Prtg LLC...203 909-6362
1460 Broadway New York New York (10036) ***(G-10221)***
Full Circle Home LLC...212 432-0001
146 W 29th St Rm 9w New York (10001) ***(G-10222)***
Full Circle Studios LLC...716 875-7740
710 Main St Buffalo (14202) ***(G-2960)***
Full Motion Beverage Inc (PA)...631 585-1100
998 Old Country Rd Plainview (11803) ***(G-13603)***
Full Service Auto Body Inc...718 831-9300
25601 Jericho Tpke Floral Park (11001) ***(G-5204)***
Full Timer, Bronx *Also called Fuel Watchman Sales & Service* ***(G-1338)***
Fuller Sportswear Co Inc...516 773-3353
10 Grenfell Dr Great Neck (11020) ***(G-5814)***
Fuller Tool Incorporated...315 891-3183
225 Platform Rd Newport (13416) ***(G-12790)***
Fulmont Ready-Mix Company Inc (PA)...518 887-5560
774 State Highway 5s Amsterdam (12010) ***(G-347)***
Fulton Boiler Works Inc (PA)...315 298-5121
3981 Port St Pulaski (13142) ***(G-13947)***
Fulton Boiler Works Inc...315 298-5121
972 Centerville Rd Pulaski (13142) ***(G-13948)***
Fulton Companies, Pulaski *Also called Fulton Volcanic Inc* ***(G-13950)***
Fulton Daily News, Fulton *Also called DOT Publishing* ***(G-5456)***
Fulton Heating Solutions Inc...315 298-5121
972 Centerville Rd Pulaski (13142) ***(G-13949)***
Fulton Newspapers Inc...315 598-6397
67 S 2nd St Fulton (13069) ***(G-5457)***
Fulton Patriot, Fulton *Also called Fulton Newspapers Inc* ***(G-5457)***
Fulton Tool Co Inc...315 598-2900
802 W Broadway Ste 1 Fulton (13069) ***(G-5458)***

ALPHABETIC

(PA)=Parent Co (HQ)=Headquarters (DH)=Div Headquarters
2017 Harris
New York Manufacturers Directory
959

Fulton Volcanic Inc (PA)....315 298-5121
3981 Port St Pulaski (13142) ***(G-13950)***
Fultonville Machine & Tool Co....518 853-4441
73 Union St Fultonville (12072) ***(G-5479)***
Fun Industries of NY....631 845-3805
111 Milbar Blvd Farmingdale (11735) ***(G-4995)***
Fun Media Inc....646 472-0135
1001 Ave Of The Americas New York (10018) ***(G-10223)***
Funda-Mantels LLC....631 399-3223
659 Mastic Rd Mastic (11950) ***(G-8203)***
Fung Wong Bakery Inc....212 267-4037
30 Mott St Frnt New York (10013) ***(G-10224)***
Fung Wong Bakery Shop, New York *Also called Fung Wong Bakery Inc* ***(G-10224)***
Fungilab Inc....631 750-6361
89 Cabot Ct Ste K Hauppauge (11788) ***(G-6081)***
Furniture By Craftmaster Ltd....631 750-0658
1595 Ocean Ave Ste A9 Bohemia (11716) ***(G-1069)***
Furniture Doctor Inc....585 657-6941
7007 State Route 5 And 20 Bloomfield (14469) ***(G-988)***
Furniture Dsign By Knossos Inc....718 729-0404
2430 Bklyn Qns Expy Ste 3 Woodside (11377) ***(G-17330)***
Furniture World, New Rochelle *Also called Towse Publishing Co* ***(G-8925)***
Fuse Electronics Inc....607 352-3222
1223 Us Route 11 Kirkwood (13795) ***(G-7233)***
Fusion Brands America Inc....212 269-1387
444 Madison Ave Ste 700 New York (10022) ***(G-10225)***
Fusion Pro Performance Ltd....917 833-0761
16 W 36th St Rm 1202 New York (10018) ***(G-10226)***
Fusion Telecom Intl Inc (PA)....212 201-2400
420 Lexington Ave Rm 1718 New York (10170) ***(G-10227)***
Futon City Discounters Inc....315 437-1328
6361 Thompson Rd Syracuse (13206) ***(G-15944)***
Future Mobility Products Inc....716 783-9130
1 Buffalo River Pl Buffalo (14210) ***(G-2961)***
Future Screw Machine Pdts Inc....631 765-1610
41155 County Road 48 Southold (11971) ***(G-15558)***
Future Spray Finishing Co....631 242-6252
78 Brook Ave Ste A Deer Park (11729) ***(G-4146)***
Future Star Digatech....718 666-0350
713 Monroe St Brooklyn (11221) ***(G-2008)***
Future Us Inc....844 779-2822
79 Madison Ave Fl 2 New York (10016) ***(G-10228)***
Futurebiotics, Hauppauge *Also called FB Laboratories Inc* ***(G-6076)***
Futurebiotics LLC....631 273-6300
70 Commerce Dr Hauppauge (11788) ***(G-6082)***
FWC Networks Inc....718 408-1558
1615 Carroll St Brooklyn (11213) ***(G-2009)***
Fx Silk Screen Printing I....585 266-6773
1555 Lyell Ave Rochester (14606) ***(G-14385)***
G & C Welding Co Inc....516 883-3228
39 Annette Dr Port Washington (11050) ***(G-13817)***
G & G C Machine & Tool Co Inc....516 873-0999
18 Sylvester St Westbury (11590) ***(G-16987)***
G & G Window Repair Inc....585 334-3370
6710 W Henrietta Rd Ste 4 Rush (14543) ***(G-15048)***
G & H Wood Products LLC....716 372-5510
2427 N Union Street Ext Olean (14760) ***(G-13148)***
G & J Rdymx & Masnry Sup Inc....718 454-0800
18330 Jamaica Ave Hollis (11423) ***(G-6497)***
G & M Clearview Inc....845 781-4877
118 Mountain Rd Monroe (10950) ***(G-8555)***
G & M Dege Inc....631 475-1450
250 Orchard Rd Bldg 1 East Patchogue (11772) ***(G-4447)***
G & M Roaster....718 984-5235
680 Sharrotts Rd Ste 4 Staten Island (10309) ***(G-15675)***
G & O Equipment Corp....718 218-7844
1211 Oakpoint Ave Bronx (10474) ***(G-1339)***
G & P Printing Inc....212 274-8092
142 Baxter St New York (10013) ***(G-10229)***
G & S Farm & Home Inc....716 542-9922
13550 Bloomingdale Rd Akron (14001) ***(G-23)***
G & W Tool & Die Co, Valley Stream *Also called Precision Tl Die & Stamping Co* ***(G-16420)***
G A Braun Inc (PA)....315 475-3123
79 General Irwin Blvd North Syracuse (13212) ***(G-12943)***
G A Braun Inc....315 475-3123
461 E Brighton Ave Syracuse (13210) ***(G-15945)***
G A Richards & Co Inc....516 334-5412
18 Sylvester St Westbury (11590) ***(G-16988)***
G and G Service....518 785-9247
21 Nelson Ave Latham (12110) ***(G-7363)***
G B International Trdg Co Ltd....607 785-0938
408 Airport Rd Endicott (13760) ***(G-4809)***
G Bopp USA Inc....845 296-1065
4 Bill Horton Way Wappingers Falls (12590) ***(G-16569)***
G C Casting, Oneonta *Also called Charles Lay* ***(G-13177)***
G C Castings Inc....607 432-4518
138 Roundhouse Rd Oneonta (13820) ***(G-13187)***
G C Controls Inc....607 656-4117
1408 County Road 2 Greene (13778) ***(G-5865)***
G C D M Ironworks Inc....914 347-2058
55 N Evarts Ave Elmsford (10523) ***(G-4754)***
G C Hanford Manufacturing Co (PA)....315 476-7418
304 Oneida St Syracuse (13202) ***(G-15946)***
G C Ironworks, Elmsford *Also called G C D M Ironworks Inc* ***(G-4754)***
G C Mobile Svces, Cortlandt Manor *Also called Gc Mobile Services Inc* ***(G-4051)***
G E Inspection Technologies LP....315 554-2000
721 Visions Dr Skaneateles (13152) ***(G-15460)***
G F Labels, Queensbury *Also called Glens Falls Business Forms Inc* ***(G-13996)***
G Fried Carpet Service....516 333-3900
800 Old Country Rd Westbury (11590) ***(G-16989)***
G Fried Carpet and Design Ctr, Westbury *Also called G Fried Carpert Service* ***(G-16989)***
G Haynes Holdings Inc....607 538-1160
51971 State Highway 10 Bloomville (13739) ***(G-995)***
G I Certified Inc....212 397-1945
623 W 51st St New York (10019) ***(G-10230)***
G J C Ltd Inc....607 770-4500
6 Emma St Binghamton (13905) ***(G-917)***
G J Olney Inc....315 827-4208
9057 Dopp Hill Rd Westernville (13486) ***(G-17043)***
G L 7 Sales Plus Ltd....631 696-8290
125 Middle Country Rd F Coram (11727) ***(G-3942)***
G M I, Hornell *Also called Gray Manufacturing Inds LLC* ***(G-6565)***
G Marks Hdwr Liquidating Corp....631 225-5400
333 Bayview Ave Amityville (11701) ***(G-288)***
G N R Co, Smithtown *Also called G N R Plastics Inc* ***(G-15487)***
G N R Plastics Inc....631 724-8758
11 Wandering Way Smithtown (11787) ***(G-15487)***
G Pesso & Sons Inc....718 224-9130
20320 35th Ave Bayside (11361) ***(G-771)***
G R M, Bellmore *Also called Rush Gold Manufacturing Ltd* ***(G-820)***
G S Communications USA Inc....718 389-7371
179 Greenpoint Ave Brooklyn (11222) ***(G-2010)***
G S W Worldwide LLC....646 437-4800
1180 Av Of The Amrcs 10 New York (10036) ***(G-10231)***
G Schirmer Inc (HQ)....212 254-2100
180 Madison Ave Ste 2400 New York (10016) ***(G-10232)***
G Schirmer Inc....845 469-4699
2 Old Rt 17 Chester (10918) ***(G-3607)***
G Sicuranza Ltd....516 759-0259
4 East Ave Glen Cove (11542) ***(G-5616)***
G T Machine & Tool, Long Island City *Also called Theodosiou Inc* ***(G-7900)***
G Tech Natureal Gasses Systems, Buffalo *Also called Gas Tchnlogy Enrgy Cncepts LLC* ***(G-2965)***
G W Canfield & Son Inc....315 735-5522
600 Plant St Utica (13502) ***(G-16334)***
G W Manufacturing, Ridgewood *Also called Fantasy Furniture Inc* ***(G-14106)***
G X Electric Corporation....212 921-0400
8 W 38th St New York (10018) ***(G-10233)***
G Z G Rest & Kit Met Works....718 788-8621
120 13th St Brooklyn (11215) ***(G-2011)***
G&G Sealcoating and Paving Inc....585 787-1500
1449 Ontario Ontario (14519) ***(G-13202)***
G&J Graphics Inc....718 409-9874
2914 Westchester Ave Bronx (10461) ***(G-1340)***
G-III Apparel Group, New York *Also called G-III Leather Fashions Inc* ***(G-10236)***
G-III Apparel Group Ltd (PA)....212 403-0500
512 7th Ave Fl 35 New York (10018) ***(G-10234)***
G-III Apparel Group Ltd....212 403-0500
512 Fashion Ave Fl 35 New York (10018) ***(G-10235)***
G-III Leather Fashions Inc....212 403-0500
512 7th Ave Fl 35 New York (10018) ***(G-10236)***
G-S Plastic Optics, Rochester *Also called Germanow-Simon Corporation* ***(G-14399)***
G. Marks Hardware, Inc., Amityville *Also called G Marks Hdwr Liquidating Corp* ***(G-288)***
G18 Corporation....212 869-0010
215 W 40th St Fl 9 New York (10018) ***(G-10237)***
G4i, Rensselaer *Also called Great 4 Image* ***(G-14047)***
Gabani Inc....631 283-4930
81 Lee Ave Southampton (11968) ***(G-15544)***
Gabbagoods, New York *Also called M&S Accessory Network Corp* ***(G-11078)***
Gabila & Sons Mfg Inc....631 789-2220
100 Wartburg Ave Copiague (11726) ***(G-3901)***
Gabila Food Products Inc....631 789-2220
100 Wartburg Ave Copiague (11726) ***(G-3902)***
Gabila's Knishes, Copiague *Also called Gabila & Sons Mfg Inc* ***(G-3901)***
Gabriela Systems Ltd....631 225-7952
135 Bangor St Lindenhurst (11757) ***(G-7465)***
Gabriella Importers Inc (PA)....212 579-3945
481 Johnson Ave Ste D Bohemia (11716) ***(G-1070)***
Gabriella Importers Inc....212 579-3945
305 W 87th St New York (10024) ***(G-10238)***
Gabrielle Andra....212 366-9624
305 W 21st St New York (10011) ***(G-10239)***
Gac....631 357-8600
1 Ca Plz Ste 100 Islandia (11749) ***(G-6794)***
Gad Systems, Lawrence *Also called John J Richardson* ***(G-7392)***
Gadabout USA Wheelchairs Inc....585 338-2110
892 E Ridge Rd Rochester (14621) ***(G-14386)***
Gaddis Engineering, Locust Valley *Also called Gaddis Industrial Equipment* ***(G-7631)***
Gaddis Industrial Equipment....516 759-3100
168 Forest Ave Locust Valley (11560) ***(G-7631)***
Gaebel Enterprises, East Syracuse *Also called Gei International Inc* ***(G-4533)***
Gaffney Kroese Electrial, Garden City *Also called Gaffney Kroese Supply Corp* ***(G-5506)***

ALPHABETIC

960
2017 Harris
New York Manufacturers Directory
(G-0000) Company's Geographic Section entry number

Gaffney Kroese Supply Corp......516 228-5091
377 Oak St Ste 202 Garden City (11530) ***(G-5506)***
Gagne Associates Inc......800 800-5954
41 Commercial Dr Johnson City (13790) ***(G-7092)***
Galas Framing Services......718 706-0007
4224 Orchard St Fl 4 Long Island City (11101) ***(G-7747)***
Galaxy Knitting Mills, Long Island City *Also called In Toon Amkor Fashions Inc* ***(G-7765)***
Galaxy Software LLC......631 244-8405
154 Middlesex Ave Oakdale (11769) ***(G-13058)***
Galian Handbags, New York *Also called Rodem Incorporated* ***(G-11901)***
Galison Publishing LLC......212 354-8840
25 W 43rd St Ste 1411 New York (10036) ***(G-10240)***
Galison/Mudpuppy, New York *Also called Galison Publishing LLC* ***(G-10240)***
Galiva Inc......903 600-5755
236 Broadway Ste 214 Brooklyn (11211) ***(G-2012)***
Gallagher Printing Inc......716 873-2434
2518 Delaware Ave Buffalo (14216) ***(G-2962)***
Gallant Graphices Ltd Inc......845 868-1166
242 Attlebury Hill Rd Stanfordville (12581) ***(G-15627)***
Galle & Zinter Inc......716 833-4212
3405 Harlem Rd Buffalo (14225) ***(G-2963)***
Galle Mamorial, Buffalo *Also called Galle & Zinter Inc* ***(G-2963)***
Gallery 57 Dental......212 246-8700
24 W 57th St Ste 701 New York (10019) ***(G-10241)***
Gallery 91......212 966-3722
91 Grand St Apt 2 New York (10013) ***(G-10242)***
Gallery of Machines LLC......607 849-6028
20 Front St Marathon (13803) ***(G-8083)***
Galli Shirts and Sports AP......845 226-7305
246 Judith Dr Stormville (12582) ***(G-15779)***
Galmer Ltd......718 392-4609
4301 21st St Ste 130b Long Island City (11101) ***(G-7748)***
Galmer Silversmiths, Long Island City *Also called Galmer Ltd* ***(G-7748)***
Galt Industries Inc......212 758-0770
121 E 71st St New York (10021) ***(G-10243)***
Gamble & Gamble Inc (PA)......716 731-3239
5890 West St Sanborn (14132) ***(G-15120)***
GAME Sportswear Ltd (PA)......914 962-1701
1401 Front St Yorktown Heights (10598) ***(G-17511)***
Game Time LLC......914 557-9662
1407 Broadway Rm 400 New York (10018) ***(G-10244)***
Games For Change Inc......212 242-4922
205 E 42nd St Fl 20 New York (10017) ***(G-10245)***
Gametime Media Inc......212 860-2090
120 E 87th St Apt R8e New York (10128) ***(G-10246)***
Gametime Sportswear Plus LLC......315 724-5893
1206 Belle Ave Utica (13501) ***(G-16335)***
Gamma Enterprises LLC......631 755-1080
113 Alder St West Babylon (11704) ***(G-16793)***
Gamma Instrument Co Inc......516 486-5526
52 Chasner St Hempstead (11550) ***(G-6269)***
Gamma Lab, West Babylon *Also called Gamma Enterprises LLC* ***(G-16793)***
Gamma North Corporation......716 902-5100
13595 Broadway St Alden (14004) ***(G-178)***
Gamma Products Inc......845 562-3332
509 Temple Hill Rd New Windsor (12553) ***(G-8938)***
Gan Kavod Inc......315 797-3114
2050 Tilden Ave New Hartford (13413) ***(G-8805)***
Ganesh Foods, Waterloo *Also called Gharana Industries LLC* ***(G-16627)***
Gangi Distributors Inc......718 442-5745
135 Mcclean Ave Staten Island (10305) ***(G-15676)***
Gannett Co Inc......516 484-7510
99 Seaview Blvd Ste 200 Port Washington (11050) ***(G-13818)***
Gannett Co Inc......585 232-7100
245 E Main St Rochester (14604) ***(G-14387)***
Gannett Co Inc......585 924-3406
6300 Collett Rd Farmington (14425) ***(G-5151)***
Gannett Co Inc......607 798-1234
4421 Vestal Pkwy E Vestal (13850) ***(G-16448)***
Gannett Co Inc......914 278-9315
92 North Ave New Rochelle (10801) ***(G-8903)***
Gannett Co Inc......607 352-2702
10 Gannett Dr Johnson City (13790) ***(G-7093)***
Gannett Co Inc......585 346-4150
3155 Rochester Rd Bldg E Lakeville (14480) ***(G-7284)***
Gannett NY Production Facility, Johnson City *Also called Gannett Co Inc* ***(G-7093)***
Gannett Stllite Info Ntwrk Inc......914 965-5000
1 Odell Plz Yonkers (10701) ***(G-17447)***
Gannett Stllite Info Ntwrk Inc......585 798-1400
413 Main St Medina (14103) ***(G-8272)***
Gannett Stllite Info Ntwrk Inc......914 381-3400
700 Waverly Ave Mamaroneck (10543) ***(G-8035)***
Gannett Stllite Info Ntwrk LLC......845 578-2300
1 Crosfield Ave West Nyack (10994) ***(G-16917)***
Gannett Stllite Info Ntwrk LLC......845 454-2000
85 Civic Center Plz Poughkeepsie (12601) ***(G-13900)***
Gannett Suburban Newspapers, Mamaroneck *Also called Gannett Stllite Info Ntwrk Inc* ***(G-8035)***
Gantz-Newman LLC......631 249-0680
115 Schmitt Blvd Farmingdale (11735) ***(G-4996)***
Gappa Textiles Inc......212 481-7100
295 5th Ave Ste 1021 New York (10016) ***(G-10247)***
Gar Wood Custom Boats......518 494-2966
20 Duell Hill Rd Brant Lake (12815) ***(G-1173)***
Garan Incorporated (HQ)......212 563-1292
200 Madison Ave Fl 4 New York (10016) ***(G-10248)***
Garan Manufacturing Corp (HQ)......212 563-2000
200 Madison Ave Fl 4 New York (10016) ***(G-10249)***
Garb-O-Liner Inc......914 235-1585
64 Drake Ave New Rochelle (10805) ***(G-8904)***
Garco, Penfield *Also called Robinson Tools LLC* ***(G-13503)***
Garco Manufacturing Corp Inc......718 287-3330
4802 Farragut Rd Brooklyn (11203) ***(G-2013)***
Gardall Safe Corporation......315 432-9115
219 Lamson St Ste 1 Syracuse (13206) ***(G-15947)***
Gardei Industries LLC (PA)......716 693-7100
1087 Erie Ave North Tonawanda (14120) ***(G-12973)***
Gardei Manufacturing, North Tonawanda *Also called Pioneer Printers Inc* ***(G-12986)***
Garden City Printers & Mailers......516 485-1600
144 Cherry Valley Ave West Hempstead (11552) ***(G-16853)***
Garden State Shavings Inc......845 544-2835
16 Almond Tree Ln Warwick (10990) ***(G-16590)***
Gardner Dnver Oberdorfer Pumps......315 437-0361
5900 Firestone Dr Syracuse (13206) ***(G-15948)***
Gardner The Train Doctor, North Rose *Also called Gargraves Trackage Corporation* ***(G-12937)***
Garey Mfg & Design Corp......315 463-5306
4411 James St East Syracuse (13057) ***(G-4532)***
Gargraves Trackage Corporation (PA)......315 483-6577
8967 Ridge Rd North Rose (14516) ***(G-12937)***
Garland Technology LLC......716 242-8500
199 Delaware Ave Buffalo (14202) ***(G-2964)***
Garlock Sealing Tech LLC......315 597-4811
1666 Division St Palmyra (14522) ***(G-13407)***
Garment Care Systems LLC......518 674-1826
50 Blue Heron Dr Averill Park (12018) ***(G-534)***
Garrett J Cronin......914 761-9299
1 Stuart Way White Plains (10607) ***(G-17111)***
Garrison Woodworking Inc......845 726-3525
226 Hoslers Rd Westtown (10998) ***(G-17069)***
Gary Gelbfish MD......718 258-3004
2502 Avenue I Brooklyn (11210) ***(G-2014)***
Gary Plastic, Bronx *Also called Viele Manufacturing Corp* ***(G-1490)***
Gary Plastic Packaging Corp (PA)......718 893-2200
1340 Viele Ave Bronx (10474) ***(G-1341)***
Gary Roth & Associates Ltd......516 333-1000
1400 Old Country Rd # 305 Westbury (11590) ***(G-16990)***
Gary Stock Corporation......914 276-2700
597 Rte 22 Croton Falls (10519) ***(G-4061)***
Garyline, Bronx *Also called Gary Plastic Packaging Corp* ***(G-1341)***
Garys Loft......212 244-0970
28 W 36th St New York (10018) ***(G-10250)***
Gas Field Specialists Inc......716 378-6422
224 N Main St Horseheads (14845) ***(G-6579)***
Gas Recovery Systems LLC (HQ)......914 421-4903
1 N Lexington Ave Ste 620 White Plains (10601) ***(G-17112)***
Gas Recovery Systems Illinois, White Plains *Also called Gas Recovery Systems LLC* ***(G-17112)***
Gas Tchnlogy Enrgy Cncepts LLC......716 831-9695
401 William L Gaiter Pkwy Buffalo (14215) ***(G-2965)***
Gas Turbine Controls Corp......914 693-0830
6 Skyline Dr Ste 150 Hawthorne (10532) ***(G-6247)***
Gasoft Equipment Inc......845 863-1010
231 Dubois St Newburgh (12550) ***(G-12756)***
Gasport Welding & Fabg Inc......716 772-7205
8430 Telegraph Rd Gasport (14067) ***(G-5557)***
Gasser & Sons Inc (PA)......631 543-6600
440 Moreland Rd Commack (11725) ***(G-3832)***
Gassho Body & Mind Inc......518 695-9991
76 Broad St Schuylerville (12871) ***(G-15320)***
GATECOMUSA, Flushing *Also called Yellow E House Inc* ***(G-5311)***
Gatehouse Media LLC (HQ)......585 598-0030
175 Sullys Trl Ste 300 Pittsford (14534) ***(G-13561)***
Gatehouse Media LLC......315 792-5000
350 Willowbrook Office Pa Utica (13501) ***(G-16336)***
Gatehouse Media LLC......607 776-2121
10 W Steuben St Bath (14810) ***(G-656)***
Gatehouse Media LLC......315 866-2220
111 Green St Herkimer (13350) ***(G-6300)***
Gatehouse Media LLC......607 936-4651
34 W Pulteney St Corning (14830) ***(G-3973)***
Gatehouse Media LLC......585 394-0770
73 Buffalo St Canandaigua (14424) ***(G-3347)***
Gatehouse Media LLC......607 324-1425
32 Broadway Mall Hornell (14843) ***(G-6564)***
Gatehouse Media MO Holdings......530 846-3661
175 Sullys Trl Ste 300 Pittsford (14534) ***(G-13562)***
Gatehuse Media PA Holdings Inc (HQ)......585 598-0030
175 Sullys Trl Fl 3 Pittsford (14534) ***(G-13563)***
Gateway Newspapers Inc......845 628-8400
928 S Lake Blvd Apt 1e Mahopac (10541) ***(G-7996)***
Gateway Prtg & Graphics Inc......716 823-3873
3970 Big Tree Rd Hamburg (14075) ***(G-5926)***
Gatherer's Gourmet Granola, Delmar *Also called Sanzdranz LLC* ***(G-4246)***

ALPHABETIC

(PA)=Parent Co (HQ)=Headquarters (DH)=Div Headquarters
2017 Harris
New York Manufacturers Directory
961

Gatti Tool & Mold Inc.....585 328-1350
997 Beahan Rd Rochester (14624) *(G-14388)*
Gaughan Construction Corp.....718 850-9577
13034 90th Ave Richmond Hill (11418) *(G-14074)*
Gavin Mfg Corp.....631 467-0040
25 Central Ave Unit A Farmingdale (11735) *(G-4997)*
Gay Sheet Metal Dies Inc.....716 877-0208
301 Hinman Ave Buffalo (14216) *(G-2966)*
Gaylord Archival, North Syracuse *Also called Gaylord Bros Inc (G-12944)*
Gaylord Bros Inc.....315 457-5070
7282 William Barry Blvd North Syracuse (13212) *(G-12944)*
Gaymar Industries Inc.....800 828-7341
10 Centre Dr Orchard Park (14127) *(G-13271)*
Gazette & Press, Rye *Also called Mason & Gore Inc (G-15063)*
Gazette Press Inc.....914 963-8300
2 Clinton Ave Rye (10580) *(G-15056)*
Gb Aero Engine LLC.....914 925-9600
555 Theodore Fremd Ave Rye (10580) *(G-15057)*
Gb Group Inc.....212 594-3748
Umpire State Bldg 1808 New York (10021) *(G-10251)*
Gbf, Tonawanda *Also called Green Buffalo Fuel LLC (G-16168)*
Gbg Denim Usa LLC.....646 839-7000
14 Area Dev Dr Ste 200 Plattsburgh (12901) *(G-13663)*
Gbg National Brands Group LLC.....646 839-7000
350 5th Ave Lbby 9 New York (10118) *(G-10252)*
Gbg Socks LLC.....646 839-7000
350 5th Ave Lbby 9 New York (10118) *(G-10253)*
Gbg USA Inc.....646 839-7083
350 5th Ave Ste 700 New York (10118) *(G-10254)*
Gbg USA Inc.....212 615-3400
261 W 35th St Fl 15 New York (10001) *(G-10255)*
Gbg USA Inc.....212 290-8041
1333 Broadway Fl 9 New York (10018) *(G-10256)*
Gbg West LLC (HQ).....646 839-7000
350 5th Ave Fl 5 New York (10118) *(G-10257)*
Gbt Global.....718 593-9698
175-20 Wexford Ter Ste F1 New York (10001) *(G-10258)*
Gbv Promotions Inc.....631 231-7300
44 Drexel Dr Bay Shore (11706) *(G-702)*
Gc Mobile Services Inc.....914 736-9730
32 William Puckey Dr Cortlandt Manor (10567) *(G-4051)*
Gce International Inc (PA).....212 704-4800
1385 Broadway Fl 21 New York (10018) *(G-10259)*
Gce International Inc.....212 868-0500
350 5th Ave Ste 616 New York (10118) *(G-10260)*
Gce International Inc.....773 263-1210
1359 Broadway Rm 2000 New York (10018) *(G-10261)*
GCM Metal Industries Inc.....718 386-4059
454 Troutman St Brooklyn (11237) *(G-2015)*
Gcm Steel Products Inc.....718 386-3346
454 Troutman St Brooklyn (11237) *(G-2016)*
Gcns Technology Group Inc.....347 713-8160
597 Rutland Rd Brooklyn (11203) *(G-2017)*
Gdi Custom Marble & Granite.....718 996-9100
134 Avenue T Brooklyn (11223) *(G-2018)*
Gds Publishing Inc.....212 796-2000
40 Wall St Ste 500 New York (10005) *(G-10262)*
GE Aviation Systems LLC.....631 467-5500
1000 Macarthur Mem Hwy Bohemia (11716) *(G-1071)*
GE Global Research.....518 387-5000
1 Research Cir Niskayuna (12309) *(G-12894)*
GE Healthcare Fincl Svcs Inc.....212 713-2000
299 Park Ave Fl 3 New York (10171) *(G-10263)*
GE Healthcare Inc.....516 626-2799
80 Seaview Blvd Ste E Port Washington (11050) *(G-13819)*
GE Mds LLC (HQ).....585 242-9600
175 Science Pkwy Rochester (14620) *(G-14389)*
GE Plastics.....518 475-5011
1 Noryl Ave Selkirk (12158) *(G-15355)*
GE Polymershapes.....516 433-4092
120 Andrews Rd Hicksville (11801) *(G-6347)*
GE Transportation Energy, Schenectady *Also called GE Transportation Eng Systems (G-15256)*
GE Transportation Eng Systems.....518 258-9276
1 River Rd Bldg 2-333d Schenectady (12345) *(G-15256)*
Gear, Hicksville *Also called Genetclly Enhnced Athc RES Inc (G-6348)*
Gear Motions Incorporated.....716 885-1080
1120 Niagara St Buffalo (14213) *(G-2967)*
Gear Motions Incorporated (PA).....315 488-0100
1750 Milton Ave Syracuse (13209) *(G-15949)*
Geddes Bakery Co Inc.....315 437-8084
421 S Main St North Syracuse (13212) *(G-12945)*
Gefa Instrument Corp.....516 420-4419
205 Bethpage Sweet Old Bethpage (11804) *(G-13127)*
Gehring Textiles, Garden City *Also called Gehring Tricot Corporation (G-5507)*
Gehring Tricot Corporation (PA).....315 429-8551
1225 Franklin Ave Ste 300 Garden City (11530) *(G-5507)*
Gehring Tricot Corporation.....315 429-8551
68 Ransom St Ste 272 Dolgeville (13329) *(G-4305)*
Gei International Inc (PA).....315 463-9261
100 Ball St East Syracuse (13057) *(G-4533)*
Geier Bindery Co, Farmingdale *Also called Mid Island Group (G-5054)*
Geigtech East Bay LLC.....844 543-4437
150 E 58th St Frnt 3 New York (10155) *(G-10264)*
Geliko LLC.....212 876-5620
1751 2nd Ave Rm 102 New York (10128) *(G-10265)*
Gem Fabrication of NC.....704 278-6713
586 Commercial Ave Garden City (11530) *(G-5508)*
Gem Manufacturing Inc.....585 235-1670
853 West Ave Bldg 17a Rochester (14611) *(G-14390)*
Gem Metal Spinning & Stamping.....718 729-7014
517 47th Rd Long Island City (11101) *(G-7749)*
Gem Mine Corp.....516 367-1075
84 Cypress Dr Woodbury (11797) *(G-17287)*
Gem Reproduction Services Corp.....845 298-0172
1299 Route 9 Ste 105 Wappingers Falls (12590) *(G-16570)*
Gem West Inc.....631 567-4228
433 E Main St Unit 1 Patchogue (11772) *(G-13420)*
Gem-Bar Setting Inc.....212 869-9238
15 W 46th St New York (10036) *(G-10266)*
Gemcor Automation LLC.....716 674-9300
100 Gemcor Dr West Seneca (14224) *(G-16946)*
Gemfields USA Incorporated.....212 398-5400
589 5th Ave Rm 909 New York (10017) *(G-10267)*
Gemini Manufactures.....716 633-0306
160 Holtz Dr Cheektowaga (14225) *(G-3572)*
Gemini Manufacturing LLC.....914 375-0855
56 Lafayette Ave Ste 380 White Plains (10603) *(G-17113)*
Gemini Pharmaceuticals Inc.....631 543-3334
87 Modular Ave Ste 1 Commack (11725) *(G-3833)*
Gemoro Inc.....212 768-8844
48 W 48th St Ste 1102 New York (10036) *(G-10268)*
Gemprint Corporation.....212 997-0007
580 5th Ave Bsmt Ll05 New York (10036) *(G-10269)*
Gemson Graphics Inc.....516 873-8400
820 Willis Ave Ste 2c Albertson (11507) *(G-154)*
Gemtex Inc.....212 302-0102
1410 Broadway Rm 304 New York (10018) *(G-10270)*
Gemtrol Inc.....716 894-0716
1800 Broadway St Bldg 1c Buffalo (14212) *(G-2968)*
Gemveto Jewelry Company Inc.....212 755-2522
18 E 48th St Rm 501 New York (10017) *(G-10271)*
Gen Publishing Inc.....914 834-3880
140 Huguenot St Fl 3 New Rochelle (10801) *(G-8905)*
Gen-West Associates LLC.....315 255-1779
101 Columbus St Auburn (13021) *(G-497)*
Genco John.....716 483-5446
71 River St Jamestown (14701) *(G-6994)*
Genencor Division Danisco US, Rochester *Also called Danisco US Inc (G-14300)*
Genencor International, Rochester *Also called Danisco US Inc (G-14301)*
General Art Company Inc.....212 255-1298
14 E 38th St Fl 6 New York (10016) *(G-10272)*
General Art Framing, New York *Also called General Art Company Inc (G-10272)*
General Bearing Corporation (HQ).....845 358-6000
44 High St West Nyack (10994) *(G-16918)*
General Business Supply Inc.....518 720-3939
2550 9th Ave Watervliet (12189) *(G-16685)*
General Chemical, Syracuse *Also called Chemtrade Chemicals US LLC (G-15893)*
General Cinema Bevs of Ohio.....914 767-6000
1 Pepsi Way Ste 1 Somers (10589) *(G-15509)*
General Coatings Tech Inc (PA).....718 821-1232
24 Woodward Ave Ridgewood (11385) *(G-14108)*
General Composites Inc.....518 963-7333
39 Myers Way Willsboro (12996) *(G-17265)*
General Control Systems Inc.....518 270-8045
60 Cohoes Ave Ste 101 Green Island (12183) *(G-5855)*
General Cryogenic Tech LLC.....516 334-8200
400 Shames Dr Westbury (11590) *(G-16991)*
General Cutting Inc.....631 580-5011
2111 9th Ave Ronkonkoma (11779) *(G-14903)*
General Diaries Corporation.....516 371-2244
56 John St Inwood (11096) *(G-6758)*
General Die and Die Cutng Inc.....516 665-3584
151 Babylon Tpke Roosevelt (11575) *(G-15004)*
General Elc Capitl Svcs Inc.....315 554-2000
721 Visions Dr Skaneateles (13152) *(G-15461)*
General Electric Company.....315 456-3304
5990 E Molloy Rd Syracuse (13211) *(G-15950)*
General Electric Company.....518 385-4022
1 River Rd Bldg 55 Schenectady (12305) *(G-15257)*
General Electric Company.....518 385-2211
1 River Rd Bldg 33 Schenectady (12305) *(G-15258)*
General Electric Company.....518 459-4110
11 Anderson Dr Albany (12205) *(G-82)*
General Electric Company.....518 385-3716
1 River Rd Schenectady (12345) *(G-15259)*
General Electric Company.....203 373-2756
1 River Rd Bldg 43 Schenectady (12345) *(G-15260)*
General Electric Company.....518 385-2211
1 River Rd Bldg 37 Schenectady (12345) *(G-15261)*
General Electric Company.....518 746-5750
446 Lock 8 Way 8th Hudson Falls (12839) *(G-6642)*
General Electric Company.....315 456-7901
443 Electronics Pkwy Liverpool (13088) *(G-7520)*

General Electric Company ... 845 567-7410
169 New York 17k 17 K Newburgh (12550) ***(G-12757)***
General Electric Company ... 518 387-5000
1 Research Cir Schenectady (12309) ***(G-15262)***
General Electric Company ... 518 385-7620
2690 Balltown Rd Bldg 600 Niskayuna (12309) ***(G-12895)***
General Electric Company ... 518 385-3439
705 Corporation Park Schenectady (12302) ***(G-15263)***
General Fibre Products Corp ... 516 358-7500
170 Nassau Terminal Rd New Hyde Park (11040) ***(G-8835)***
General Fire-Proof Door Corp ... 718 893-5500
913 Edgewater Rd Bronx (10474) ***(G-1342)***
General Galvanizing Sup Co Inc (PA) ... 718 589-4300
652 Whittier St Fl Mezz Bronx (10474) ***(G-1343)***
General Media Strategies Inc ... 212 586-4141
483 10th Ave Rm 325 New York (10018) ***(G-10273)***
General Microwave Corporation (HQ) ... 516 802-0900
227a Michael Dr Syosset (11791) ***(G-15824)***
General Mills Inc ... 716 856-6060
54 S Michigan Ave Buffalo (14203) ***(G-2969)***
General Mills Inc ... 716 856-6060
315 Ship Canal Pkwy Buffalo (14218) ***(G-2970)***
General Motors LLC ... 315 764-2000
56 Chevrolet Rd Massena (13662) ***(G-8195)***
General Motors LLC ... 716 879-5000
2995 River Rd 2 Buffalo (14207) ***(G-2971)***
General Oil Equipment Co Inc (PA) ... 716 691-7012
60 John Glenn Dr Amherst (14228) ***(G-243)***
General Plating LLC ... 585 423-0830
850 Saint Paul St Ste 10 Rochester (14605) ***(G-14391)***
General Refining & Smelting ... 516 538-4747
106 Taft Ave Hempstead (11550) ***(G-6270)***
General Refining Corporation ... 516 538-4747
59 Madison Ave Hempstead (11550) ***(G-6271)***
General Semiconductor Inc ... 631 300-3818
150 Motor Pkwy Ste 101 Hauppauge (11788) ***(G-6083)***
General Specialties, Shokan *Also called Mack Wood Working* ***(G-15432)***
General Splice Corporation ... 914 271-5131
Hwy 129 Croton On Hudson (10520) ***(G-4063)***
General Sportwear Company Inc (PA) ... 212 764-5820
230 W 38th St Fl 4 New York (10018) ***(G-10274)***
General Trade Mark La ... 718 979-7261
31 Hylan Blvd Apt 14c Staten Island (10305) ***(G-15677)***
General Traffic Equipment Corp ... 845 569-9000
259 Broadway Newburgh (12550) ***(G-12758)***
General Vy-Coat LLC ... 718 266-6002
1636 Coney Island Ave 2b Brooklyn (11230) ***(G-2019)***
General Welding & Fabg Inc (PA) ... 716 652-0033
991 Maple Rd Elma (14059) ***(G-4649)***
General Welding & Fabg Inc ... 716 568-7958
4545 Transit Rd Williamsville (14221) ***(G-17244)***
General Welding & Fabg Inc ... 716 824-1572
3701 Mckinley Pkwy Blasdell (14219) ***(G-963)***
General Welding & Fabg Inc ... 716 681-8200
1 Walden Galleria Buffalo (14225) ***(G-2972)***
General Welding & Fabg Inc ... 716 304-3622
360 Rainbow Blvd Niagara Falls (14303) ***(G-12824)***
General Welding & Fabg Inc ... 585 697-7660
60 Saginaw Dr Ste 4 Rochester (14623) ***(G-14392)***
Generation Power LLC ... 315 234-2451
238 W Division St Syracuse (13204) ***(G-15951)***
Generic Compositors, Stamford *Also called Stone Crest Industries Inc* ***(G-15626)***
Genesco Inc ... 585 227-3080
271 Greece Rdg 69a Rochester (14626) ***(G-14393)***
Genesee Building Products LLC ... 585 548-2726
7982 Byron Stafford Rd Stafford (14143) ***(G-15620)***
Genesee County Express, Hornell *Also called Seneca Media Inc* ***(G-6566)***
Genesee Manufacturing Co Inc ... 585 266-3201
566 Hollenbeck St Rochester (14621) ***(G-14394)***
Genesee Metal Products Inc ... 585 968-6000
106 Railroad Ave Wellsville (14895) ***(G-16752)***
Genesee Metal Stampings Inc ... 585 475-0450
975 John St West Henrietta (14586) ***(G-16879)***
Genesee Plant, Piffard *Also called Arkema Inc* ***(G-13546)***
Genesee Precision Inc ... 585 344-0385
4300 Commerce Dr Batavia (14020) ***(G-634)***
Genesee Reserve Buffalo LLC ... 716 824-3116
300 Bailey Ave Buffalo (14210) ***(G-2973)***
Genesee Vly Met Finshg Co Inc ... 585 232-4412
244 Verona St Rochester (14608) ***(G-14395)***
Genesis Digital Imaging Inc ... 310 305-7358
150 Verona St Rochester (14608) ***(G-14396)***
Genesis Electl Motor, Woodside *Also called Genesis Electrical Motors* ***(G-17331)***
Genesis Electrical Motors ... 718 274-7030
6010 32nd Ave Woodside (11377) ***(G-17331)***
Genesis Machining Corp ... 516 377-1197
725 Brooklyn Ave North Baldwin (11510) ***(G-12905)***
Genesis Mannequins USA II Inc ... 212 505-6600
151 W 25th St Fl 4 New York (10001) ***(G-10275)***
Genesis One Unlimeted ... 516 208-5863
600 Pinebrook Ave West Hempstead (11552) ***(G-16854)***
Genesis Vision Inc ... 585 254-0193
1260 Lyell Ave Rochester (14606) ***(G-14397)***
Genetclly Enhnced Athc RES Inc ... 631 750-3195
960 S Broadway Ste 120 Hicksville (11801) ***(G-6348)***
Genetic Engineering News, New Rochelle *Also called Gen Publishing Inc* ***(G-8905)***
Geneva Granite Co Inc (PA) ... 315 789-8142
272 Border City Rd Geneva (14456) ***(G-5578)***
Geneva Printing Company Inc ... 315 789-8191
40 Castle St Geneva (14456) ***(G-5579)***
Geneva Watch Company Inc (HQ) ... 212 221-1177
1407 Broadway Rm 400 New York (10018) ***(G-10276)***
Genie Fastener Mfg Co, Bohemia *Also called Treo Industries Inc* ***(G-1145)***
Genie Instant Printing Center, New York *Also called Genie Instant Printing Co Inc* ***(G-10277)***
Genie Instant Printing Co Inc ... 212 575-8258
37 W 43rd St New York (10036) ***(G-10277)***
Genius Media Group Inc ... 509 670-7502
92 3rd St Brooklyn (11231) ***(G-2020)***
Genius Tool Americas, Orchard Park *Also called Genius Tools Americas Corp* ***(G-13272)***
Genius Tools Americas Corp ... 716 662-6872
15 Cobham Dr Orchard Park (14127) ***(G-13272)***
Gennaris Itln French Bky Inc ... 516 997-8968
465 Westbury Ave Carle Place (11514) ***(G-3389)***
Genoa Sand & Gravel Lnsg ... 607 533-4551
390 Peruville Rd Freeville (13068) ***(G-5436)***
Genomeweb LLC ... 212 651-5636
40 Fulton St Rm 1002 New York (10038) ***(G-10278)***
Genpak, Glens Falls *Also called Great Pacific Entps US Inc* ***(G-5682)***
Genpak LLC (HQ) ... 518 798-9511
68 Warren St Glens Falls (12801) ***(G-5679)***
Genpak LLC ... 845 343-7971
Republic Plz Middletown (10940) ***(G-8442)***
Gentner Precision Components ... 315 597-5734
406 Stafford Rd Palmyra (14522) ***(G-13408)***
Geo Publishing, New York *Also called Emblaze Systems Inc* ***(G-10020)***
Geoffrey Beene Inc ... 212 371-5570
37 W 57th St Frnt 2 New York (10019) ***(G-10279)***
Geometric Circuits Inc ... 631 249-0230
920 Lincoln Ave Unit 1 Holbrook (11741) ***(G-6448)***
Geonex International Corp ... 212 473-4555
200 Park Ave S Ste 920 New York (10003) ***(G-10280)***
Geopump Inc ... 585 798-6666
213 State St Medina (14103) ***(G-8273)***
Geordie Magee Uphl & Canvas ... 315 676-7679
Weber Rd Brewerton (13029) ***(G-1203)***
George Basch Co Inc ... 516 378-8100
1554 Peapond Rd North Bellmore (11710) ***(G-12921)***
George Chilson Logging ... 607 732-1558
54 Franklin St Elmira (14904) ***(G-4686)***
George G Sharp Inc (PA) ... 212 732-2800
160 Broadway Fl 8 New York (10038) ***(G-10281)***
George Industries LLC ... 607 748-3371
1 S Page Ave Endicott (13760) ***(G-4810)***
George Knitting Mills Corp ... 212 242-3300
116 W 23rd St Fl 4 New York (10011) ***(G-10282)***
George Lederman Inc ... 212 753-4556
515 Madison Ave Rm 1218 New York (10022) ***(G-10283)***
George M Dujack ... 518 279-1303
80 Town Office Rd Troy (12180) ***(G-16236)***
George Ponte Inc ... 914 243-4202
500 E Main St Jefferson Valley (10535) ***(G-7056)***
George Raum Manufacturing, Central Islip *Also called Gmr Manufacturing Inc* ***(G-3498)***
George Retzos ... 315 422-2913
502 Pearl St Syracuse (13203) ***(G-15952)***
Georgia-Pacific LLC ... 518 561-3500
327 Margaret St Plattsburgh (12901) ***(G-13664)***
Georgia-Pacific LLC ... 518 346-6151
801 Corporation Park Schenectady (12302) ***(G-15264)***
Georgia-Pacific Corrugared LLC ... 585 343-3800
4 Etreadeasy Ave Batavia (14020) ***(G-635)***
Georgie Kaye, New York *Also called Georgy Creative Fashions Inc* ***(G-10284)***
Georgy Creative Fashions Inc ... 212 279-4885
249 W 29th St New York (10001) ***(G-10284)***
Georland Corporation ... 212 730-4730
745 5th Ave Fl 5 New York (10151) ***(G-10285)***
Geospatial Systems Inc (HQ) ... 585 427-8310
150 Lucius Gordon Dr # 211 West Henrietta (14586) ***(G-16880)***
Geosync Microwave Inc ... 631 760-5567
320 Oser Ave Hauppauge (11788) ***(G-6084)***
Geotec, Westbury *Also called Tishcon Corp* ***(G-17033)***
Geotech Associates Ltd ... 631 286-0251
20 Stiriz Rd Brookhaven (11719) ***(G-1507)***
Geotechnical Drilling Inc ... 516 616-6055
75 E 2nd St Mineola (11501) ***(G-8512)***
Geoweb3d Inc ... 607 323-1212
45 Lewis St Binghamton (13901) ***(G-918)***
Gerald Frd Packg Display LLC (PA) ... 716 692-2705
550 Fillmore Ave Tonawanda (14150) ***(G-16165)***
Gerald Frd Packg Display LLC ... 716 692-2705
550 Gilmore Ave North Tonawanda (14120) ***(G-12974)***
Gerald McGlone ... 518 482-2613
17 Zoar Ave Colonie (12205) ***(G-3820)***
Geri-Gentle Corporation (PA) ... 917 804-7807
3841 Ocean View Ave Brooklyn (11224) ***(G-2021)***

ALPHABETIC

(PA)=Parent Co (HQ)=Headquarters (DH)=Div Headquarters
2017 Harris
New York Manufacturers Directory
963

ALPHABETIC SECTION

Geritrex LLC..914 668-4003
  144 E Kingsbridge Rd Mount Vernon (10550) *(G-8682)*
Geritrex Holdings Inc (PA)..........................914 668-4003
  144 E Kingsbridge Rd Mount Vernon (10550) *(G-8683)*
Gerli & Co Inc (PA).......................................212 213-1919
  41 Madison Ave Ste 4101 New York (10010) *(G-10286)*
German Machine & Assembly Inc................585 546-4200
  226 Jay St Rochester (14608) *(G-14398)*
Germanium Corp America Inc......................315 853-4900
  34 Robinson Rd Clinton (13323) *(G-3719)*
Germanow-Simon Corporation....................585 232-1440
  408 Saint Paul St Rochester (14605) *(G-14399)*
Gernatt Asphalt Products Inc (PA)..............716 532-3371
  13870 Taylor Hollow Rd Collins (14034) *(G-3817)*
Gernatt Asphalt Products Inc......................716 496-5111
  Benz Dr Springville (14141) *(G-15610)*
Gernatt Companies, Collins *Also called Gernatt Asphalt Products Inc (G-3817)*
Gerome Technologies Inc............................518 463-1324
  85 Broadway Ste 1 Menands (12204) *(G-8372)*
Gerson & Gerson Inc (PA)...........................212 244-6775
  100 W 33rd St Ste 911 New York (10001) *(G-10287)*
Gertrude Hawk Chocolates Inc....................
  21182 Salmon Run Mall Loo Watertown (13601) *(G-16652)*
Get Real Surfaces Inc (PA)...........................845 337-4483
  121 Washington St Poughkeepsie (12601) *(G-13901)*
Getec Inc..845 292-0800
  624 Harris Rd Ferndale (12734) *(G-5170)*
Getinge Sourcing LLC..................................585 475-1400
  1777 E Henrietta Rd Rochester (14623) *(G-14400)*
Getinge Usa Inc (HQ)...................................585 475-1400
  1777 E Henrietta Rd Rochester (14623) *(G-14401)*
Getting The Word Out Inc............................518 891-9352
  36 Church St Apt 106 Saranac Lake (12983) *(G-15137)*
Gevril, Valley Cottage *Also called First Sbf Holding Inc (G-16378)*
Gfb Fashions Ltd...212 239-9230
  463 Fashion Ave Rm 1502 New York (10018) *(G-10288)*
Gfh Orthotic & Prosthetic Labs....................631 467-3725
  161 Keyland Ct Bohemia (11716) *(G-1072)*
Gfl Amenities, Brooklyn *Also called Gfl USA Inc (G-2022)*
Gfl USA Inc..917 297-8701
  81 Prospect St Brooklyn (11201) *(G-2022)*
Gg Design and Printing................................718 321-3220
  93 Henry St Frnt 1 New York (10002) *(G-10289)*
Ggp Publishing Inc.......................................914 834-8896
  105 Calvert St Ste 201 Harrison (10528) *(G-5984)*
GH Bass & Co (HQ)......................................212 381-3900
  200 Madison Ave New York (10016) *(G-10290)*
Gh Induction Atmospheres LLC...................585 368-2120
  35 Industrial Park Cir Rochester (14624) *(G-14402)*
Ghani Textiles Inc...718 859-4561
  2459 Coyle St Fl 2 Brooklyn (11235) *(G-2023)*
Gharana Industries LLC...............................315 651-4004
  61 Swift St Waterloo (13165) *(G-16627)*
Ghostery Inc (PA)...917 262-2530
  10 E 39th St Fl 8 New York (10016) *(G-10291)*
Gia Lingerie Inc...212 448-0918
  485 Fashion Ave Rm 1200 New York (10018) *(G-10292)*
Giagni Enterprises, Mount Vernon *Also called Promptus Electronic Hdwr Inc (G-8721)*
Giagni Enterprises LLC................................914 699-6500
  550 S Columbus Ave Mount Vernon (10550) *(G-8684)*
Giagni International Corp............................914 699-6500
  548 S Columbus Ave Mount Vernon (10550) *(G-8685)*
Gibar Inc...315 452-5656
  7838 Brewerton Rd Cicero (13039) *(G-3646)*
Gibraltar Industries Inc (PA)........................716 826-6500
  3556 Lake Shore Rd # 100 Buffalo (14219) *(G-2974)*
Gifford Group Inc..212 569-8500
  250 Dyckman St New York (10034) *(G-10293)*
Gift Valleys.com, Ronkonkoma *Also called Bobley-Harmann Corporation (G-14880)*
Gifts Software Inc...904 438-6000
  360 Lexington Ave Rm 601 New York (10017) *(G-10294)*
Gig-It, New York *Also called 212 Db Corp (G-8965)*
Gigi New York, Melville *Also called Graphic Image Incorporated (G-8324)*
Gilber Braid, New York *Also called Tamber Knits Inc (G-12275)*
Gild-Rite Inc..631 752-9000
  51 Carolyn Blvd Farmingdale (11735) *(G-4998)*
Gildan Apparel USA Inc................................716 759-6273
  4055 Casillio Pkwy Clarence (14031) *(G-3662)*
Gildan Apparel USA Inc (HQ).......................212 476-0341
  48 W 38th St Fl 8 New York (10018) *(G-10295)*
Gildan Media Corp.......................................718 459-6299
  6631 Wetherole St Flushing (11374) *(G-5243)*
Gilded Otter Brewing, New Paltz *Also called Catskill Mtn Brewing Co Inc (G-8874)*
Giliberto Designs Inc...................................212 695-0216
  142 W 36th St Fl 8 New York (10018) *(G-10296)*
Gillette Creamery, Albany *Also called Phyljohn Distributors Inc (G-120)*
Gillies Coffee Company................................718 499-7766
  150 19th St Brooklyn (11232) *(G-2024)*
Gillinder Brothers Inc...................................845 856-5375
  39 Erie St 55 Port Jervis (12771) *(G-13785)*
Gillinder Glass, Port Jervis *Also called Gillinder Brothers Inc (G-13785)*

Gilmores Sound Advice Inc..........................212 265-4445
  599 11th Ave Fl 5 New York (10036) *(G-10297)*
Gim Electronics Corp...................................516 942-3382
  270 Duffy Ave Ste H Hicksville (11801) *(G-6349)*
Gina Group LLC...212 947-2445
  10 W 33rd St Ph 3 New York (10001) *(G-10298)*
Gina Hosiery, New York *Also called Gina Group LLC (G-10298)*
Ginny Lee Cafe, Lodi *Also called Wagner Vineyards & Brewing Co (G-7636)*
Giovane Ltd..212 332-7373
  592 5th Ave Ste L New York (10036) *(G-10299)*
Giovane Piranesi, New York *Also called Giovane Ltd (G-10299)*
Giovanni Bakery Corp..................................212 695-4296
  476 9th Ave New York (10018) *(G-10300)*
Giovanni Food Co Inc (PA)...........................315 463-7770
  6050 Court Street Rd Syracuse (13206) *(G-15953)*
Giuliante Machine Tool Inc...........................914 835-0008
  12 John Walsh Blvd Peekskill (10566) *(G-13478)*
Giulietta LLC...212 334-1859
  25 Peck Slip Apt 4 New York (10038) *(G-10301)*
Giumenta Corp (PA).....................................718 832-1200
  42 2nd Ave Brooklyn (11215) *(G-2025)*
Givaudan Fragrances Corp..........................212 649-8800
  40 W 57th St Fl 11 New York (10019) *(G-10302)*
Givi Inc..212 586-5029
  16 W 56th St Fl 4 New York (10019) *(G-10303)*
Gizmo Products Inc......................................585 301-0970
  205 Seneca Pkwy Rochester (14613) *(G-14403)*
GKN Aerospace Monitor Inc........................562 619-8558
  1000 New Horizons Blvd Amityville (11701) *(G-289)*
GL & RL Logging Inc.....................................518 883-3936
  713 Union Mills Rd Broadalbin (12025) *(G-1242)*
GL&v USA Inc...518 747-2444
  27 Allen St Hudson Falls (12839) *(G-6643)*
GL&v USA Inc (HQ)......................................518 747-2444
  27 Allen St Hudson Falls (12839) *(G-6644)*
Glaceau, New York *Also called Energy Brands Inc (G-10037)*
Glacee Skincare LLC....................................212 690-7632
  611 W 136th St Apt 4 New York (10031) *(G-10304)*
Gladding Braided Products LLC..................315 653-7211
  1 Gladding St South Otselic (13155) *(G-15531)*
Glamour Magazine.......................................212 286-2860
  4 Times Sq Fl 16 New York (10036) *(G-10305)*
Glamourpuss Nyc LLC.................................212 722-1370
  1305 Madison Ave New York (10128) *(G-10306)*
Glaro Inc...631 234-1717
  735 Calebs Path Ste 1 Hauppauge (11788) *(G-6085)*
Glasbau Hahn America LLC.........................845 566-3331
  15 Little Brook Ln Ste 2 Newburgh (12550) *(G-12759)*
Glasgow Products Inc...................................516 374-5937
  886 Lakeside Dr Woodmere (11598) *(G-17313)*
Glass Apps LLC (PA)....................................310 987-1536
  25 W 43rd St Ste 902 New York (10036) *(G-10307)*
Glass East America Inc................................631 291-9432
  15 Frowein Rd Bldg E2 Center Moriches (11934) *(G-3466)*
Glassart Inc..607 739-3939
  2011 Maple St Millport (14864) *(G-8481)*
Glassbox US Inc...917 378-2933
  234 5th Ave Ste 207 New York (10001) *(G-10308)*
Glasses USA LLC...212 784-6094
  954 Lexington Ave Ste 537 New York (10021) *(G-10309)*
Glassesusa.com, New York *Also called Glasses USA LLC (G-10309)*
Glassfab Inc..585 262-4000
  257 Ormond St Rochester (14605) *(G-14404)*
Glassteel Parts and Services, Rochester *Also called Pfaudler Inc (G-14578)*
Glasteel Parts & Services Inc (HQ)..............585 235-1010
  1000 West Ave Rochester (14611) *(G-14405)*
Glaxosmithkline LLC....................................845 341-7590
  3 Tyler St Montgomery (12549) *(G-8593)*
Glaxosmithkline LLC....................................845 797-3259
  6 Alpert Dr Wappingers Falls (12590) *(G-16571)*
Glaxosmithkline LLC....................................585 738-9025
  1177 Winton Rd S Rochester (14618) *(G-14406)*
Glaxosmithkline LLC....................................716 913-5679
  17 Mahogany Dr Buffalo (14221) *(G-2975)*
Glaxosmithkline LLC....................................518 239-6901
  3169 Route 145 East Durham (12423) *(G-4387)*
Glaxosmithkline LLC....................................518 852-9637
  108 Woodfield Blvd Mechanicville (12118) *(G-8228)*
Glaxosmthkline Cnsmr Heathcare, East Durham *Also called Glaxosmithkline LLC (G-4387)*
Gleaner Company Ltd..................................718 657-0788
  9205 172nd St Fl 2 Jamaica (11433) *(G-6915)*
Gleason Corporation (PA)...........................585 473-1000
  1000 University Ave Rochester (14607) *(G-14407)*
Gleason Works (HQ)....................................585 473-1000
  1000 University Ave Rochester (14607) *(G-14408)*
Gleason-Avery, Auburn *Also called John G Rubino Inc (G-504)*
Glen Plaza Marble & Gran Inc.....................516 671-1100
  75 Glen Cove Ave Ste A Glen Cove (11542) *(G-5617)*
Glenda Inc..718 442-8981
  1732 Victory Blvd Staten Island (10314) *(G-15678)*
Glendale Architectural WD Pdts..................718 326-2700
  7102 80th St Glendale (11385) *(G-5654)*

Glendale Products, Glendale *Also called Glendale Architectural WD Pdts (G-5654)*
Glenn Foods Inc (PA) 516 377-1400
371 S Main St Ste 119-405 Freeport (11520) ***(G-5402)***
Glenn Wayne Bakery, Bohemia *Also called Glenn Wayne Wholesale Bky Inc (G-1073)*
Glenn Wayne Wholesale Bky Inc 631 289-9200
1800 Artic Ave Bohemia (11716) ***(G-1073)***
Glenny's, Freeport *Also called Glenn Foods Inc (G-5402)*
Glennys Inc 516 377-1400
1960 59th St Brooklyn (11204) ***(G-2026)***
Glenora Wine Cellars Inc 607 243-9500
5435 State Route 14 Dundee (14837) ***(G-4328)***
Glenridge Fabricators Inc 718 456-2297
7945 77th Ave Glendale (11385) ***(G-5655)***
Glens Falls Business Forms Inc 518 798-6643
10 Ferguson Ln Queensbury (12804) ***(G-13996)***
Glens Falls Newspapers Inc 518 792-3131
76 Lawrence St Glens Falls (12801) ***(G-5680)***
Glens Falls Printing LLC 518 793-0555
51 Hudson Ave Glens Falls (12801) ***(G-5681)***
Glens Falls Ready Mix Inc (HQ) 518 793-1695
774 State Highway 5s Amsterdam (12010) ***(G-348)***
Glens Falls Ready Mix Inc 518 793-1695
112 Big Boom Rd Queensbury (12804) ***(G-13997)***
Glenwood Cast Stone Inc 718 859-6500
4106 Glenwood Rd Brooklyn (11210) ***(G-2027)***
Glenwood Mason Supply, Brooklyn *Also called Glenwood Cast Stone Inc (G-2027)*
Glenwood Masonry Products, Brooklyn *Also called Superior Block Corp (G-2626)*
Gli-Dex Sales Corp 716 692-6501
855 Wurlitzer Dr North Tonawanda (14120) ***(G-12975)***
Glidden Machine & Tool, North Tonawanda *Also called Gli-Dex Sales Corp (G-12975)*
Glidden Professional Paint Ctr, Rochester *Also called PPG Architectural Finishes Inc (G-14590)*
Gliptone Manufacturing Inc 631 285-7250
1740 Julia Goldbach Ave Ronkonkoma (11779) ***(G-14904)***
Glissade New York LLC 631 756-4800
399 Smith St Farmingdale (11735) ***(G-4999)***
Glissen Chemical Co Inc (PA) 718 436-4200
1321 58th St Brooklyn (11219) ***(G-2028)***
Glitner Ticketing, Levittown *Also called Glitnir Ticketing Inc (G-7428)*
Glitnir Ticketing Inc 516 390-5168
3 Snapdragon Ln Levittown (11756) ***(G-7428)***
Glitter, New York *Also called Magic Numbers Inc (G-11105)*
Glk Foods LLC 585 289-4414
11 Clark St Shortsville (14548) ***(G-15433)***
Globa Phoni Compu Techn Solut (PA) 607 257-7279
21 Dutch Mill Rd Ithaca (14850) ***(G-6843)***
Global Abrasive Products Inc (PA) 716 438-0047
62 Mill St Lockport (14094) ***(G-7588)***
Global Alliance For Tb 212 227-7540
40 Wall St Fl 24 New York (10005) ***(G-10310)***
Global Alumina Corporation (PA) 212 351-0000
277 Park Ave Fl 40 New York (10172) ***(G-10311)***
Global Alumina Services Co 212 309-8060
277 Park Ave Fl 40 New York (10172) ***(G-10312)***
Global Applctions Solution LLC 212 741-9595
125 Park Ave Fl 25 New York (10017) ***(G-10313)***
Global Brands Inc 845 358-1212
1031 Route 9w S Nyack (10960) ***(G-13052)***
Global Creations, New York *Also called Global Gem Corporation (G-10317)*
Global Earth Energy 716 332-7150
534 Delaware Ave Ste 412 Buffalo (14202) ***(G-2976)***
Global Entity Media Inc 631 580-7772
2090 5th Ave Ste 2 Ronkonkoma (11779) ***(G-14905)***
Global Finance Magazine 212 447-7900
411 5th Ave New York (10016) ***(G-10314)***
Global Finance Magazine., New York *Also called Global Finance Media Inc (G-10315)*
Global Finance Magazine., New York *Also called Global Finance Magazine (G-10314)*
Global Finance Media Inc 212 447-7900
7 E 20th St Fl 2 New York (10003) ***(G-10315)***
Global Fire Corporation 888 320-1799
244 5th Ave Ste 2238 New York (10001) ***(G-10316)***
Global Food Source & Co Inc 914 320-9615
114 Carpenter Ave Tuckahoe (10707) ***(G-16270)***
Global Gem Corporation 212 350-9936
425 Madison Ave Rm 400 New York (10017) ***(G-10317)***
Global Glass Corp 516 681-2309
134 Woodbury Rd Hicksville (11801) ***(G-6350)***
Global Gold Inc 212 239-4657
1410 Broadway Fl 8 New York (10018) ***(G-10318)***
Global Gold Corporation (PA) 914 925-0020
555 Theodore Fremd Ave C208 Rye (10580) ***(G-15058)***
Global Graphics Inc 718 939-4967
3711 Prince St Ste D Flushing (11354) ***(G-5244)***
Global Grind Digital 212 840-9399
512 Fashion Ave Fl 42 New York (10018) ***(G-10319)***
Global Instrumentation LLC 315 682-0272
8104 Cazenovia Rd Ste 2/3 Manlius (13104) ***(G-8072)***
Global Marine Power Inc 631 208-2933
221 Scott Ave Calverton (11933) ***(G-3291)***
Global Market Development Inc 631 667-1002
200 Executive Dr Ste G Edgewood (11717) ***(G-4599)***
Global Natural Foods Inc 845 439-3292
672 Old Route 17 Rear Ofc Livingston Manor (12758) ***(G-7562)***
Global Payment Tech Inc 516 887-0700
20 E Sunrise Hwy Valley Stream (11581) ***(G-16407)***
Global Payment Tech Inc (PA) 631 563-2500
170 Wilbur Pl Ste 600 Bohemia (11716) ***(G-1074)***
Global Precision Inds Inc 585 254-0010
955 Millstead Way Rochester (14624) ***(G-14409)***
Global Precision Products Inc 585 334-4640
90 High Tech Dr Rush (14543) ***(G-15049)***
Global Resources Sg Inc 212 686-1411
267 5th Ave Rm 506 New York (10016) ***(G-10320)***
Global Security Tech LLC 917 838-4507
1407 Broadway Fl 30 New York (10018) ***(G-10321)***
Global Steel Products Corp (HQ) 631 586-3455
95 Marcus Blvd Deer Park (11729) ***(G-4147)***
Global Textile, New York *Also called Himatsingka America Inc (G-10479)*
Global Tissue Group Inc (PA) 631 924-3019
870 Expressway Dr S Medford (11763) ***(G-8245)***
Global Tower LLC 561 995-0320
23696 Bacon Rd La Fargeville (13656) ***(G-7235)***
Global Video LLC (HQ) 516 222-2600
1000 Woodbury Rd Ste 1 Woodbury (11797) ***(G-17288)***
Globalfoundries US Inc 512 457-3900
2070 Route 52 Hopewell Junction (12533) ***(G-6551)***
Globalfoundries US Inc 518 305-9013
400 Stone Break Rd Ext Malta (12020) ***(G-8019)***
Globalfoundries US Inc 408 462-3900
107 Hermes Rd Ballston Spa (12020) ***(G-597)***
Globalquest Solutions Inc 716 601-3524
2805 Wehrle Dr Ste 11 Williamsville (14221) ***(G-17245)***
Globe Electronic Hardware Inc 718 457-0303
3424 56th St Woodside (11377) ***(G-17332)***
Globe Grinding Corp 631 694-1970
1365 Akron St Copiague (11726) ***(G-3903)***
Globe Metallurgical Inc 716 804-0862
3807 Highland Ave Niagara Falls (14305) ***(G-12825)***
Globe Specialty Metals, Niagara Falls *Also called Globe Metallurgical Inc (G-12825)*
Globe-Tex, New Rochelle *Also called HB Athletic Inc (G-8910)*
Globe-Tex Apparal, New York *Also called Tbhl International LLC (G-12282)*
Globecomm Systems Inc (HQ) 631 231-9800
45 Oser Ave Hauppauge (11788) ***(G-6086)***
Globeop Financial Services LLC (HQ) 914 670-3600
1 South Rd Harrison (10528) ***(G-5985)***
Globex Kosher Foods Inc 718 630-5555
5600 1st Ave Ste 19 Brooklyn (11220) ***(G-2029)***
Globmarble LLC 347 717-4088
2201 Neptune Ave Ste 5 Brooklyn (11224) ***(G-2030)***
Globus Cork Inc 347 963-4059
741 E 136th St Bronx (10454) ***(G-1344)***
Gloede Neon Signs Ltd Inc 845 471-4366
97 N Clinton St Poughkeepsie (12601) ***(G-13902)***
Glopak USA Corp (PA) 347 869-9252
1816 127th St 2 College Point (11356) ***(G-3784)***
Glopak USA Corp 516 433-3214
35 Engel St Ste B Hicksville (11801) ***(G-6351)***
Gloria Apparel Inc 212 947-0869
256 W 38th St Fl 700 New York (10018) ***(G-10322)***
Glowa Manufacturing Inc 607 770-0811
6 Emma St Binghamton (13905) ***(G-919)***
Gluck Orgelbau Inc 212 233-2684
170 Park Row Apt 20a New York (10038) ***(G-10323)***
Gluten Free Bake Shop Inc 845 782-5307
19 Industry Dr Mountainville (10953) ***(G-8747)***
GM Components Holdings LLC 716 439-2011
200 Upper Mountain Rd Lockport (14094) ***(G-7589)***
GM Components Holdings LLC 585 647-7000
1000 Lexington Ave Rochester (14606) ***(G-14410)***
GM Components Holdings LLC 716 439-2463
200 Upper Mountain Rd Lockport (14094) ***(G-7590)***
GM Components Holdings LLC 716 439-2402
200 Upper Mountain Rd # 10 Lockport (14094) ***(G-7591)***
GM Ice Cream Inc 646 236-7383
8911 207th St Queens Village (11427) ***(G-13977)***
GM Insulation Corp 516 354-6000
1345 Rosser Ave Elmont (11003) ***(G-4721)***
GM Palmer Inc 585 492-2990
51 Edward St Arcade (14009) ***(G-393)***
GM Pre Cast Products, Jamestown *Also called Suhor Industries Inc (G-7032)*
GM Printing, Long Island City *Also called Grand Meridian Printing Inc (G-7752)*
GM Sheet Metal Inc 718 349-2830
193 Newell St Brooklyn (11222) ***(G-2031)***
GMC Mercantile Corp 212 498-9488
231 W 39th St Rm 612 New York (10018) ***(G-10324)***
Gmch Lockport, Lockport *Also called GM Components Holdings LLC (G-7590)*
Gmch Lockport Ptc, Lockport *Also called GM Components Holdings LLC (G-7589)*
Gmch Rochester, Rochester *Also called GM Components Holdings LLC (G-14410)*
Gmd Industries Inc 718 445-8779
12920 18th Ave College Point (11356) ***(G-3785)***
Gmp LLC 914 939-0571
47 Purdy Ave Ste 2 Port Chester (10573) ***(G-13747)***

ALPHABETIC

(PA)=Parent Co (HQ)=Headquarters (DH)=Div Headquarters
2017 Harris
New York Manufacturers Directory
965

Gmr Manufacturing Inc....631 582-2600
101 Windsor Pl Unit D Central Islip (11722) **(G-3498)**
Gms Drum Co Inc....516 586-8820
330 Conklin St Farmingdale (11735) **(G-5000)**
Gms Hicks Street Corporation....718 858-1010
214 Hicks St Brooklyn (11201) **(G-2032)**
Gn Printing....718 784-1713
4216 34th Ave Long Island City (11101) **(G-7750)**
Gncc Capital Inc (PA)....702 951-9793
244 5th Ave Ste 2525 New York (10001) **(G-10325)**
GNI Commerce Inc....347 275-1155
458 Neptune Ave Apt 11f Brooklyn (11224) **(G-2033)**
Gnosis Chocolate Inc....646 688-5549
4003 27th St Long Island City (11101) **(G-7751)**
Gny Equipment LLC....631 667-1010
20 Drexel Dr Bay Shore (11706) **(G-703)**
Go Blue Technologies Ltd....631 404-6285
325 August Rd North Babylon (11703) **(G-12901)**
Gocare247, Brooklyn *Also called Mdcare911 LLC* **(G-2287)**
Goddard Design Co....718 599-0170
51 Nassau Ave Ste 1b Brooklyn (11222) **(G-2034)**
Godfrey Prpeller Adjusting Svc....718 768-3744
155 25th St Brooklyn (11232) **(G-2035)**
Godiva Chocolatier Inc (HQ)....212 984-5900
333 W 34th St Fl 6 New York (10001) **(G-10326)**
Godiva Chocolatier Inc....718 271-3603
9015 Queens Blvd Ste 2045 Elmhurst (11373) **(G-4661)**
Godiva Chocolatier Inc....718 677-1452
5378 Kings Plz Brooklyn (11234) **(G-2036)**
Godiva Chocolatier Inc....212 809-8990
33 Maiden Ln Frnt 1 New York (10038) **(G-10327)**
Goergen-Mackwirth Co Inc....716 874-4800
765 Hertel Ave Buffalo (14207) **(G-2977)**
Gold & Diamonds Wholesale Outl....718 438-7888
4417 5th Ave Brooklyn (11220) **(G-2037)**
Gold Coast Gazette, Glen Cove *Also called Kch Publications Inc* **(G-5619)**
Gold Mark Mfg Co, Brooklyn *Also called Goldmark Inc* **(G-2039)**
Gold Medal Packing Inc....315 337-1911
8301 Old River Rd Oriskany (13424) **(G-13310)**
Gold Pride Press Inc....585 224-8800
12 Pixley Industrial Pkwy Rochester (14624) **(G-14411)**
Gold Pure Food Products Co Inc....516 483-5600
1 Brooklyn Rd Hempstead (11550) **(G-6272)**
Goldarama Company Inc....212 730-7299
56 W 45th St Ste 1504 New York (10036) **(G-10328)**
Goldberg Prosthetic & Orthotic....631 689-6606
9 Technology Dr East Setauket (11733) **(G-4484)**
Goldberger Company LLC (PA)....212 924-1194
36 W 25th St Fl 14 New York (10010) **(G-10329)**
Goldberger International, New York *Also called Goldberger Company LLC* **(G-10329)**
Golden Artist Colors Inc....607 847-6154
188 Bell Rd New Berlin (13411) **(G-8780)**
Golden Bridge Group Inc....718 335-8882
7416 Grand Ave Elmhurst (11373) **(G-4662)**
Golden Eagle Marketing LLC....212 726-1242
244 5th Ave New York (10001) **(G-10330)**
Golden Egret LLC....516 922-2839
38 Cord Pl East Norwich (11732) **(G-4446)**
Golden Glow Cookie Co Inc....718 379-6223
1844 Givan Ave Bronx (10469) **(G-1345)**
Golden Group International Ltd....845 440-1025
305 Quaker Rd Patterson (12563) **(G-13440)**
Golden Horse Enterprise NY Inc....212 594-3339
70 W 36th St Rm 12e New York (10018) **(G-10331)**
Golden Integrity Inc....212 764-6753
37 W 47th St Ste 1601 New York (10036) **(G-10332)**
Golden Leaves Knitwear Inc....718 875-8235
43 Hall St Ste B3 Brooklyn (11205) **(G-2038)**
Golden Legacy Ilstrd Histry, Yonkers *Also called Fitzgerald Publishing Co Inc* **(G-17444)**
Golden Owl Publishing Company....914 962-6911
29 E 21st St Fl 2 New York (10010) **(G-10333)**
Golden Pacific Lxj Inc....267 975-6537
156 W 56th St Ste 2002 New York (10019) **(G-10334)**
Golden Renewable Energy LLC....914 920-9800
700 Nepperhan Ave Yonkers (10703) **(G-17448)**
Golden Season Fashion USA Inc....212 268-6048
234 W 39th St Fl 7 New York (10018) **(G-10335)**
Golden Taste Inc....845 356-4133
318 Roosevelt Ave Spring Valley (10977) **(G-15587)**
Goldmark Inc....718 438-0295
3611 14th Ave Ste B01 Brooklyn (11218) **(G-2039)**
Goldmark Products Inc....631 777-3343
855 Conklin St Ste D Farmingdale (11735) **(G-5001)**
Goldmont Enterprises Inc....212 947-3633
7603 Caldwell Ave Middle Village (11379) **(G-8411)**
Goldsmith, Binghamton *Also called Mellem Corporation* **(G-935)**
Goldstar Lighting LLC....646 543-6811
1407 Broadway Fl 30 New York (10018) **(G-10336)**
Golf Directories USA Inc....516 365-5351
39 Orchard St Ste 7 Manhasset (11030) **(G-8061)**
Golfing Magazine....516 822-5446
22 W Nicholai St Ste 200 Hicksville (11801) **(G-6352)**
Golos Printing Inc....607 732-1896
110 E 9th St Elmira Heights (14903) **(G-4710)**
Golub Corporation....518 943-3903
320 W Bridge St Catskill (12414) **(G-3428)**
Golub Corporation....518 899-6063
3 Hemphill Pl Ste 116 Malta (12020) **(G-8020)**
Golub Corporation....315 363-0679
142 Genesee St Oneida (13421) **(G-13155)**
Golub Corporation....607 336-2588
5631 State Highway 12 Norwich (13815) **(G-13028)**
Golub Corporation....518 583-3697
3045 Route 50 Saratoga Springs (12866) **(G-15154)**
Golub Corporation....518 822-0076
351 Fairview Ave Ste 3 Hudson (12534) **(G-6615)**
Golub Corporation....607 235-7243
33 Chenango Bridge Rd Binghamton (13901) **(G-920)**
Golub Corporation....845 344-0327
511 Schutt Road Ext Middletown (10940) **(G-8443)**
Gone South Concrete Block Inc....315 598-2141
2809 State Route 3 Fulton (13069) **(G-5459)**
Good Bread Bakery....914 939-3900
33 New Broad St Ste 1 Port Chester (10573) **(G-13748)**
Good Earth Inc....716 684-8111
5960 Broadway St Lancaster (14086) **(G-7317)**
Good Earth Organics Corp (PA)....716 684-8111
5960 Broadway St Lancaster (14086) **(G-7318)**
Good Health Healthcare Newsppr....585 421-8109
106 Cobblestone Court Dr Victor (14564) **(G-16479)**
Good Home Co Inc....212 352-1509
132 W 24th St New York (10011) **(G-10337)**
Good Show Sportswear, New York *Also called Good Show Sportwear Inc* **(G-10338)**
Good Show Sportwear Inc....212 334-8751
132 Mulberry St 3 New York (10013) **(G-10338)**
Good Times Magazine....516 280-2100
346 Westbury Ave Ste Ll Carle Place (11514) **(G-3390)**
Gooding & Associates Inc....631 749-3313
15 Dinah Rock Rd Shelter Island (11964) **(G-15387)**
Gooding Co Inc....716 434-5501
5568 Davison Rd Lockport (14094) **(G-7592)**
Goodlite Products Inc....718 697-7502
2042 Pitkin Ave Brooklyn (11207) **(G-2040)**
Goodnature Products Inc (PA)....716 855-3325
3860 California Rd Orchard Park (14127) **(G-13273)**
Goodo Beverage Company....347 226-9996
1801 Boone Ave Bronx (10460) **(G-1346)**
Goodrich Corporation....315 838-1200
104 Otis St Rome (13441) **(G-14811)**
Goodwill Inds of Greater NY....914 621-0781
80 Route 6 Unit 605 Baldwin Place (10505) **(G-563)**
Goodwill Inds Wstn NY Inc....716 633-3305
4311 Transit Rd Williamsville (14221) **(G-17246)**
Gorbel Inc (PA)....585 924-6262
600 Fishers Run Fishers (14453) **(G-5178)**
Gorbel Inc....585 924-6262
590 Fishers Run Fishers (14453) **(G-5179)**
Gorbel Inc....800 821-0086
600 Fishers Run Victor (14564) **(G-16480)**
Gorden Automotive Equipment....716 674-2700
60 N America Dr West Seneca (14224) **(G-16947)**
Gordon Fire Equipment LLC....845 691-5700
3199 Us Highway 9w Highland (12528) **(G-6404)**
Gordon S Anderson Mfg Co....845 677-3304
215 N Mabbettsville Rd Millbrook (12545) **(G-8475)**
Gorga Fehren Fine Jewelry LLC....646 861-3595
153 E 88th St New York (10128) **(G-10339)**
Gorilla Coffee Inc (PA)....718 230-3244
97 5th Ave Brooklyn (11217) **(G-2041)**
Goshen Quarry, Goshen *Also called Tilcon New York Inc* **(G-5740)**
Got Power Inc....631 767-9493
5 Campus Ln Ronkonkoma (11779) **(G-14906)**
Gotenna Inc....415 894-2616
81 Willoughby St Fl 3 Brooklyn (11201) **(G-2042)**
Gotham City Industries Inc....985 851-5474
372 Fort Hill Rd Scarsdale (10583) **(G-15217)**
Gotham Diamonds, New York *Also called American Originals Corporation* **(G-9126)**
Gotham Energy 360 LLC....917 338-1023
48 Wall St Fl 5 New York (10005) **(G-10340)**
Gotham Ink & Color Co Inc....845 947-4000
19 Holt Dr Stony Point (10980) **(G-15774)**
Gotham Ink Corp....516 677-1969
19 Teibrook Ave Syosset (11791) **(G-15825)**
Gotham Pen and Pencil, Yonkers *Also called Gotham Pen Co Inc* **(G-17449)**
Gotham Pen Co Inc....212 675-7904
1 Roundtop Rd Yonkers (10710) **(G-17449)**
Gotham T-Shirt Corp....516 676-0900
211 Glen Cove Ave Unit 5 Sea Cliff (11579) **(G-15341)**
Gotham Veterinary Center PC....212 222-1900
700 Columbus Ave Frnt 5 New York (10025) **(G-10341)**
Gottlieb & Sons Inc....212 575-1907
21 W 47th St Fl 4 New York (10036) **(G-10342)**
Gottlieb Jewelery Mfg, New York *Also called Gottlieb & Sons Inc* **(G-10342)**
Gottlieb Schwartz Family....718 761-2010
724 Collfield Ave Staten Island (10314) **(G-15679)**

Gould J Perfect Screen Prtrs...607 272-0099
245 Cherry St Ithaca (14850) ***(G-6844)***
Goulds Pumps, Seneca Falls *Also called ITT Water Technology Inc* ***(G-15365)***
Goulds Pumps Incorporated (HQ)...315 568-2811
240 Fall St Seneca Falls (13148) ***(G-15360)***
Goulds Pumps Incorporated...315 258-4949
1 Goulds Dr Auburn (13021) ***(G-498)***
Gourmet Boutique LLC (PA)...718 977-1200
14402 158th St Jamaica (11434) ***(G-6916)***
Gourmet Connection, Baldwinsville *Also called Capco Marketing* ***(G-567)***
Gourmet Crafts Inc...718 372-0505
152 Highlawn Ave Brooklyn (11223) ***(G-2043)***
Gourmet Guru Inc...718 842-2828
1123 Worthen St Bronx (10474) ***(G-1347)***
Gourmet Toast Corp...718 852-4536
345 Park Ave Brooklyn (11205) ***(G-2044)***
Government Data Publication...347 789-8719
1661 Mcdonald Ave Brooklyn (11230) ***(G-2045)***
Gowanda - Bti LLC...716 492-4081
7426a Tanner Pkwy Arcade (14009) ***(G-394)***
Goya Foods Inc...716 549-0076
200 S Main St Angola (14006) ***(G-380)***
Goya Foods Great Lakes, Angola *Also called Goya Foods Inc* ***(G-380)***
Goyard Inc (HQ)...212 813-0005
20 E 63rd St New York (10065) ***(G-10343)***
Goyard US, New York *Also called Goyard Inc* ***(G-10343)***
Gpc International Inc (PA)...631 752-9600
510 Broadhollow Rd # 205 Melville (11747) ***(G-8322)***
Gpi Equipment Company, Jefferson Valley *Also called George Ponte Inc* ***(G-7056)***
GPM Associates LLC...585 335-3940
10 Forbes St Dansville (14437) ***(G-4077)***
GPM Associates LLC...585 359-1770
45 High Tech Dr Ste 100 Rush (14543) ***(G-15050)***
Gpt, Bohemia *Also called Global Payment Tech Inc* ***(G-1074)***
Gq Magazine...212 286-2860
4 Times Sq Fl 9 New York (10036) ***(G-10344)***
Grace Associates Inc...718 767-9000
470 West St Harrison (10528) ***(G-5986)***
Grace Ryan & Magnus Mllwk LLC...914 665-0902
17 N Bleeker St Mount Vernon (10550) ***(G-8686)***
Grace Wheeler...716 664-6501
118 E 1st St Jamestown (14701) ***(G-6995)***
Gradian Health Systems Inc...212 537-0340
915 Broadway Ste 1001 New York (10010) ***(G-10345)***
Gradient Lens Corporation...585 235-2620
207 Tremont St Ste 1 Rochester (14608) ***(G-14412)***
Grado Group Inc...718 556-4200
66 Willow Ave Staten Island (10305) ***(G-15680)***
Grado Laboratories Inc...718 435-5340
4614 7th Ave Ste 1 Brooklyn (11220) ***(G-2046)***
Graham Corporation (PA)...585 343-2216
20 Florence Ave Batavia (14020) ***(G-636)***
Gramco Inc (PA)...716 592-2845
299 Waverly St Springville (14141) ***(G-15611)***
Gramercy Jewelry Mfg Corp...212 268-0461
35 W 45th St Fl 5 New York (10036) ***(G-10346)***
Granada Electronics Inc...718 387-1157
485 Kent Ave Brooklyn (11249) ***(G-2047)***
Grand Central Publishing (HQ)...212 364-1200
1290 Ave Of The Americas New York (10104) ***(G-10347)***
Grand Island Animal Hospital...716 773-7645
2323 Whitehaven Rd Grand Island (14072) ***(G-5760)***
Grand Island Research & Dev, Grand Island *Also called Grand Island Animal Hospital* ***(G-5760)***
Grand Knitting Mills Inc (PA)...631 226-5000
7050 New Horizons Blvd # 1 Amityville (11701) ***(G-290)***
Grand Marnier, New York *Also called Marnier-Lapostolle Inc* ***(G-11164)***
Grand Meridian Printing Inc...718 937-3888
3116 Hunters Point Ave Long Island City (11101) ***(G-7752)***
Grand Prix Litho Inc...631 242-4182
101 Colin Dr Unit 5 Holbrook (11741) ***(G-6449)***
Grand Processing Inc...718 388-0600
1050 Grand St Brooklyn (11211) ***(G-2048)***
Grand Slam Holdings LLC (HQ)...212 583-5000
345 Park Ave Bsmt Lb4 New York (10154) ***(G-10348)***
Grand Slam Safety LLC...315 766-7008
9793 S Bridge St Croghan (13327) ***(G-4059)***
Grandeur Creations Inc...212 643-1277
146 W 29th St Rm 9e New York (10001) ***(G-10349)***
Grandma Browns Beans Inc...315 963-7221
5837 Scenic Ave Mexico (13114) ***(G-8395)***
Grandma Maes Cntry Nturals LLC...212 348-8171
340 E 93rd St Apt 30h New York (10128) ***(G-10350)***
Grandview Block & Supply Co...518 346-7981
1705 Hamburg St Schenectady (12304) ***(G-15265)***
Grandview Concrete Corp...518 346-7981
1705 Hamburg St Schenectady (12304) ***(G-15266)***
Granite & Marble Works Inc...518 584-2800
8 Commerce Park Dr Gansevoort (12831) ***(G-5486)***
Granite Tops Inc...914 699-2909
716 S Columbus Ave Mount Vernon (10550) ***(G-8687)***
Granite Works LLC...607 565-7012
133 William Donnelly Waverly (14892) ***(G-16702)***
Grannys Kitchens LLC...315 735-5000
178 Industrial Park Dr Frankfort (13340) ***(G-5354)***
Grant Hamilton (PA)...716 652-0320
710 Main St East Aurora (14052) ***(G-4371)***
Grant's Interest Rate Observer, New York *Also called Grants Financial Publishing* ***(G-10352)***
Grant-Noren...845 726-4281
83 Ridge Rd Westtown (10998) ***(G-17070)***
Grantoo LLC...646 356-0460
60 Broad St Ste 3502 New York (10004) ***(G-10351)***
Grants Financial Publishing...212 809-7994
2 Wall St Ste 603 New York (10005) ***(G-10352)***
Granville Glass & Granite...518 812-0492
131 Revere Rd Hudson Falls (12839) ***(G-6645)***
Grapes & Grains...518 283-9463
279 Troy Rd Ste 4 Rensselaer (12144) ***(G-14046)***
Graph-Tex Inc...607 756-7791
46 Elm St Cortland (13045) ***(G-4027)***
Graph-Tex Inc (PA)...607 756-1875
24 Court St Cortland (13045) ***(G-4028)***
Graphalloy, Yonkers *Also called Graphite Metallizing Corp* ***(G-17450)***
Graphic Artisan Ltd...845 368-1700
3 Cross St Suffern (10901) ***(G-15790)***
Graphic Cntrls Acqisition Corp (HQ)...716 853-7500
400 Exchange St Buffalo (14204) ***(G-2978)***
Graphic Concepts, Plainview *Also called Steval Graphics Concepts Inc* ***(G-13636)***
Graphic Connections, Geneva *Also called Tramwell Inc* ***(G-5587)***
Graphic Controls Holdings Inc (HQ)...716 853-7500
400 Exchange St Buffalo (14204) ***(G-2979)***
Graphic Design U S A, New York *Also called American Graphic Design Awards* ***(G-9118)***
Graphic Dimensions Press Inc...718 252-4003
3502 Quentin Rd Brooklyn (11234) ***(G-2049)***
Graphic Fabrications Inc...516 763-3222
488a Sunrise Hwy Rockville Centre (11570) ***(G-14791)***
Graphic For Industry, New York *Also called Copy Color Inc* ***(G-9720)***
Graphic Image Associates LLC...631 249-9600
305 Spagnoli Rd Melville (11747) ***(G-8323)***
Graphic Image Incorporated...631 249-9600
305 Spagnoli Rd Melville (11747) ***(G-8324)***
Graphic Lab Inc...212 682-1815
228 E 45th St Fl 4 New York (10017) ***(G-10353)***
Graphic Management Partners, Port Chester *Also called Gmp LLC* ***(G-13747)***
Graphic Printing...718 701-4433
2376 Jerome Ave Bronx (10468) ***(G-1348)***
Graphic Signs & Awnings Ltd...718 227-6000
165 Industrial Loop Ste 1 Staten Island (10309) ***(G-15681)***
Graphicomm Inc...716 283-0830
7703 Niagara Falls Blvd Niagara Falls (14304) ***(G-12826)***
Graphics 247 Corp...718 729-2470
4402 23rd St Ste 113 Long Island City (11101) ***(G-7753)***
Graphics of Utica...315 797-4868
10436 Dustin Rd Remsen (13438) ***(G-14040)***
Graphics Plus Printing Inc...607 299-0500
215 S Main St Cortland (13045) ***(G-4029)***
Graphics Slution Providers Inc (PA)...845 677-5088
115 Barmore Rd Lagrangeville (12540) ***(G-7253)***
Graphis Inc...212 532-9387
389 5th Ave Rm 1105 New York (10016) ***(G-10354)***
Graphite Metallizing Corp (PA)...914 968-8400
1050 Nepperhan Ave Yonkers (10703) ***(G-17450)***
Graphitek Inc...518 686-5966
4883 State Route 67 Hoosick Falls (12090) ***(G-6539)***
Graphtex A Div of Htc, Utica *Also called Human Technologies Corporation* ***(G-16340)***
Grasers Dental Ceramics...716 649-5100
5020 Armor Duells Rd # 2 Orchard Park (14127) ***(G-13274)***
Gratitude & Company Inc...607 277-3188
215 N Cayuga St Ste 71 Ithaca (14850) ***(G-6845)***
Graver Technologies LLC...585 624-1330
300 W Main St Honeoye Falls (14472) ***(G-6528)***
Gravity East Village Inc...212 388-9788
515 E 5th St New York (10009) ***(G-10355)***
Gravymaster Inc...203 453-1893
101 Erie Blvd Canajoharie (13317) ***(G-3332)***
Gray Glass Inc...718 217-2943
21744 98th Ave Ste C Queens Village (11429) ***(G-13978)***
Gray Manufacturing Inds LLC...607 281-1325
6258 Ice House Rd Hornell (14843) ***(G-6565)***
Grayhawk Leasing LLC (HQ)...914 767-6000
1 Pepsi Way Somers (10589) ***(G-15510)***
Graymont Materials (ny) Inc (HQ)...518 561-5321
111 Quarry Rd Plattsburgh (12901) ***(G-13665)***
Graymont Materials (ny) Inc...518 873-2275
Rr 9 Lewis (12950) ***(G-7431)***
Graymont Materials (ny) Inc...518 891-0236
909 State Route 3 Saranac Lake (12983) ***(G-15138)***
Graymont Materials (ny) Inc...518 483-2671
359 Elm St Malone (12953) ***(G-8010)***
Graymont Materials (ny) Inc...315 265-8036
111 Quarry Rd Plattsburgh (12901) ***(G-13666)***
Graymont Materials Inc...518 561-5200
111 Quarry Rd Plattsburgh (12901) ***(G-13667)***

ALPHABETIC

(PA)=Parent Co (HQ)=Headquarters (DH)=Div Headquarters
2017 Harris
New York Manufacturers Directory
967

Graywood Companies Inc (PA) ... 585 254-7000
1390 Mount Read Blvd Rochester (14606) ***(G-14413)***

Grc, Hempstead *Also called General Refining & Smelting* ***(G-6270)***

Great 4 Image ... 518 424-2058
5 Forest Hills Blvd Rensselaer (12144) ***(G-14047)***

Great Adirondack Yarn Company ... 518 843-3381
950 County Highway 126 Amsterdam (12010) ***(G-349)***

Great American Awning & Patio ... 518 899-2300
43 Round Lake Rd Ballston Spa (12020) ***(G-598)***

Great American Bicycle LLC ... 518 584-8100
41 Geyser Rd Saratoga Springs (12866) ***(G-15155)***

Great American Dessert Co LLC ... 718 894-3494
5842 Maurice Ave Maspeth (11378) ***(G-8141)***

Great American Industries Inc (HQ) ... 607 729-9331
300 Plaza Dr Vestal (13850) ***(G-16449)***

Great American Tool Co Inc ... 716 646-5700
7223 Boston State Rd Hamburg (14075) ***(G-5927)***

Great Arrow Graphics, Buffalo *Also called Massimo Friedman Inc* ***(G-3057)***

Great ATL Pr-Cast Con Statuary ... 718 948-5677
225 Ellis St Staten Island (10307) ***(G-15682)***

Great Brands of Europe Inc ... 914 872-8804
100 Hillside Ave Fl 3 White Plains (10603) ***(G-17114)***

Great China Empire, New York *Also called Gce International Inc* ***(G-10259)***

Great Eastern Color Lith (PA) ... 845 454-7420
46 Violet Ave Poughkeepsie (12601) ***(G-13903)***

Great Eastern Pasta Works LLC ... 631 956-0889
385 Sheffield Ave West Babylon (11704) ***(G-16794)***

Great Gates Etc, New York *Also called North Eastern Fabricators Inc* ***(G-11457)***

Great Impressions, South Dayton *Also called Cherry Creek Woodcraft Inc* ***(G-15518)***

Great Impressions Inc ... 212 989-8555
135 W 20th St Rm 600 New York (10011) ***(G-10356)***

Great Jones Lumber Corp ... 212 254-5560
45 Great Jones St New York (10012) ***(G-10357)***

Great Lakes Cheese NY Inc ... 315 232-4511
23 Phelps St Adams (13605) ***(G-3)***

Great Lakes Gear Co Inc ... 716 694-0715
126 E Niagara St Ste 2 Tonawanda (14150) ***(G-16166)***

Great Lakes Metal Treating ... 716 694-1240
300 E Niagara St Tonawanda (14150) ***(G-16167)***

Great Lakes Orthopedic Labs ... 716 878-7307
219 Bryant St Buffalo (14222) ***(G-2980)***

Great Lakes Plastics Co Inc ... 716 896-3100
2371 Broadway St Buffalo (14212) ***(G-2981)***

Great Lakes Pressed Steel Corp ... 716 885-4037
1400 Niagara St Buffalo (14213) ***(G-2982)***

Great Lakes Specialites ... 716 672-4622
9491 Route 60 Fredonia (14063) ***(G-5374)***

Great Lakes Technologies, Liverpool *Also called Scapa North America* ***(G-7546)***

Great North Road Media Inc ... 646 619-1355
3115 Broadway Apt 61 New York (10027) ***(G-10358)***

Great Northern Printing Co, Potsdam *Also called Randy Sixberry* ***(G-13883)***

Great Pacific Entps US Inc (HQ) ... 518 761-2593
68 Warren St Glens Falls (12801) ***(G-5682)***

Great Universal Corp ... 917 302-0065
1441 Broadway Fl 5 New York (10018) ***(G-10359)***

Great Wall Corp ... 212 704-4372
4727 36th St Long Island City (11101) ***(G-7754)***

Great Western Malting Co ... 800 496-7732
16 Beeman Way Champlain (12919) ***(G-3541)***

Greatbatch Inc ... 716 759-5200
4098 Barton Rd Clarence (14031) ***(G-3663)***

Greatbatch Medical, Alden *Also called Integer Holdings Corporation* ***(G-180)***

Greatbatch Medical, Clarence *Also called Precimed Inc* ***(G-3669)***

Greater Niagara Bldg Ctr Inc ... 716 299-0543
9540 Niagara Falls Blvd Niagara Falls (14304) ***(G-12827)***

Greater Niagara Newspaper, Medina *Also called Gannett Stllite Info Ntwrk Inc* ***(G-8272)***

Greater Rchster Advertiser Inc ... 585 385-1974
201 Main St East Rochester (14445) ***(G-4460)***

Greco Bros Rdymx Con Co Inc ... 718 855-6271
381 Hamilton Ave Brooklyn (11231) ***(G-2050)***

Greek Nat Hrald Dily Nwsppr In, Long Island City *Also called National Herald Inc* ***(G-7820)***

Green Buffalo Fuel LLC ... 716 768-0600
720 Riverview Blvd Tonawanda (14150) ***(G-16168)***

Green Energy Concepts Inc ... 845 238-2574
37 Elkay Dr Ste 51 Chester (10918) ***(G-3608)***

Green Girl Prtg & Msgnr Inc ... 212 575-0357
44 W 39th St New York (10018) ***(G-10360)***

Green Global Energy Inc ... 716 501-9770
2526 Niagara Falls Blvd Niagara Falls (14304) ***(G-12828)***

Green Island Power Authority ... 518 273-0661
20 Clinton St Green Island (12183) ***(G-5856)***

Green Mountain Graphics, Sunnyside *Also called Eastern Concepts Ltd* ***(G-15807)***

Green Prosthetics & Orthotics ... 716 484-1088
1290 E 2nd St Jamestown (14701) ***(G-6996)***

Green Renewable Inc ... 518 658-2233
28 Taylor Ave Berlin (12022) ***(G-856)***

Green Valley Foods LLC ... 315 926-4280
3736 S Main St Marion (14505) ***(G-8094)***

Green Wave International Inc ... 718 499-3371
5423 1st Ave Brooklyn (11220) ***(G-2051)***

Greenbeads Llc ... 212 327-2765
220 E 72nd St Apt 17d New York (10021) ***(G-10361)***

Greenbelt Industries Inc ... 800 668-1114
45 Comet Ave Buffalo (14216) ***(G-2983)***

Greenbuds LLC ... 718 483-9212
1434 57th St Brooklyn (11219) ***(G-2052)***

Greenbush Tape & Label Inc ... 518 465-2389
40 Broadway Unit 31 Albany (12202) ***(G-83)***

Greene Brass & Alum Fndry LLC ... 607 656-4204
51971 State Highway 10 Bloomville (13739) ***(G-996)***

Greene Brass & Aluminum Fndry, Greene *Also called Charles Lay* ***(G-5862)***

Greene Lumber Co LP ... 607 278-6101
16991 State Highway 23 Davenport (13750) ***(G-4080)***

Greene Technologies Inc ... 607 656-4166
Grand & Clinton St Greene (13778) ***(G-5866)***

Greenebuild LLC ... 917 562-0556
390a Lafayette Ave Brooklyn (11238) ***(G-2053)***

Greenfiber Albany Inc ... 518 842-1470
210 County Highway 102 Gloversville (12078) ***(G-5712)***

Greenfield Die Casting Corp ... 516 623-9230
99 Doxsee Dr Freeport (11520) ***(G-5403)***

Greenfield Industries Inc ... 516 623-9230
99 Doxsee Dr Freeport (11520) ***(G-5404)***

Greenfield Manufacturing Inc ... 518 581-2368
25 Freedom Way Saratoga Springs (12866) ***(G-15156)***

Greenfield Martin Clothiers, Brooklyn *Also called Martin Greenfield Clothiers* ***(G-2277)***

Greenleaf Cabinet Makers LLC ... 315 432-4600
6691 Pickard Dr Syracuse (13211) ***(G-15954)***

Greenmaker Industries LLC ... 866 684-7800
885 Conklin St Farmingdale (11735) ***(G-5002)***

Greenpac Mill LLC (HQ) ... 716 299-0560
4400 Royal Ave Niagara Falls (14303) ***(G-12829)***

Greentree Pharmacy Inc ... 718 768-2700
291 7th Ave Brooklyn (11215) ***(G-2054)***

Greenvale Bagel Inc ... 516 221-8221
3060 Merrick Rd Wantagh (11793) ***(G-16556)***

Greenville Local, Ravena *Also called Bleezarde Publishing Inc* ***(G-14020)***

Greenway Cabinetry Inc ... 516 877-0009
485 Willis Ave Williston Park (11596) ***(G-17261)***

Greenwood Graphics Inc ... 516 822-4856
960 S Broadway Ste 106 Hicksville (11801) ***(G-6353)***

Greenwood Winery LLC ... 315 432-8132
6475 Collamer Rd East Syracuse (13057) ***(G-4534)***

Gregg Sadwick, Rochester *Also called Jml Optical Industries LLC* ***(G-14462)***

Gregson-Clark, Caledonia *Also called Rhett M Clark Inc* ***(G-3281)***

Greif Inc ... 716 836-4200
2122 Colvin Blvd Tonawanda (14150) ***(G-16169)***

Greno Industries Inc (PA) ... 518 393-4195
2820 Amsterdam Rd Scotia (12302) ***(G-15325)***

Grey House Publishing Inc ... 845 483-3535
84 Patrick Ln Stop 3 Poughkeepsie (12603) ***(G-13904)***

Grey House Publishing Inc (PA) ... 518 789-8700
4919 Route 22 Amenia (12501) ***(G-216)***

Greyhouse Publshng, Poughkeepsie *Also called Grey House Publishing Inc* ***(G-13904)***

Greyline Signs Inc ... 716 947-4526
6681 Schuyler Dr Derby (14047) ***(G-4283)***

Greyston Bakery Inc ... 914 375-1510
104 Alexander St Yonkers (10701) ***(G-17451)***

Grid Typographic Services Inc ... 212 627-0303
27 W 24th St Ste 9c New York (10010) ***(G-10362)***

Grid Typographic Svces, New York *Also called Grid Typographic Services Inc* ***(G-10362)***

Griffin Automation Inc ... 716 674-2300
240 Westminster Rd West Seneca (14224) ***(G-16948)***

Griffin Chemical Company LLC ... 716 693-2465
889 Erie Ave Ste 1 North Tonawanda (14120) ***(G-12976)***

Griffin Manufacturing Company ... 585 265-1991
1656 Ridge Rd Webster (14580) ***(G-16724)***

Griffon Corporation (PA) ... 212 957-5000
712 5th Ave Fl 18 New York (10019) ***(G-10363)***

Grillbot LLC ... 646 258-5639
1562 1st Ave Ste 251 New York (10028) ***(G-10364)***

Grillbot LLC ... 646 369-7242
87 E 116th St Ste 202 New York (10029) ***(G-10365)***

Grillmaster Inc ... 718 272-9191
15314 83rd St Howard Beach (11414) ***(G-6597)***

Grimaldi Bakery, Ridgewood *Also called Grimaldis Home Bread Inc* ***(G-14109)***

Grimaldis Home Bread Inc ... 718 497-1425
2101 Menahan St Ridgewood (11385) ***(G-14109)***

Grimble Bakery, Bronx *Also called Miss Grimble Associates Inc* ***(G-1399)***

Grind ... 646 558-3250
419 Park Ave S Fl 2 New York (10016) ***(G-10366)***

Grinnell Designs Ltd ... 212 391-5277
260 W 39th St Rm 302 New York (10018) ***(G-10367)***

Grolier International Inc (HQ) ... 212 343-6100
557 Broadway New York (10012) ***(G-10368)***

Grom Columbus LLC ... 212 974-3444
1796 Broadway New York (10019) ***(G-10369)***

Grosso Materials Inc ... 845 361-5211
90 Collabar Rd Montgomery (12549) ***(G-8594)***

Group Commerce Inc (PA) ... 646 346-0598
902 Broadway Fl 6 New York (10010) ***(G-10370)***

ALPHABETIC SECTION

Group Enterainment LLC 212 868-5233
115 W 29th St Rm 1102 New York (10001) *(G-10371)*
Group International LLC 718 475-8805
14711 34th Ave Flushing (11354) *(G-5245)*
Groupe 16sur20 LLC (PA) 212 625-1620
56 Greene St New York (10012) *(G-10372)*
Grover Aluminum Products Inc 631 475-3500
577 Medford Ave Patchogue (11772) *(G-13421)*
Grover Cleveland Press Inc 716 564-2222
2676 Sweet Home Rd Amherst (14228) *(G-244)*
Grover Home Headquarters, Patchogue *Also called Grover Aluminum Products Inc (G-13421)*
Growmark Fs LLC 585 538-2186
2936 Telephone Rd Caledonia (14423) *(G-3279)*
Grownbeans Inc 212 989-3486
110 Bank St Apt 2j New York (10014) *(G-10373)*
Growth Products Ltd 914 428-1316
80 Lafayette Ave White Plains (10603) *(G-17115)*
Grphics Grafek, Syracuse *Also called Matt Industries Inc (G-15984)*
Gruber Display Co Inc 718 882-8220
3920g Merritt Ave Bronx (10466) *(G-1349)*
Grumman Field Support Services 516 575-0574
S Oyster Bay Rd Bethpage (11714) *(G-867)*
Gruner & Jahr USA 212 782-7870
375 Lexington Ave New York (10017) *(G-10374)*
Gruner + Jahr Prtg & Pubg Co 212 463-1000
110 5th Ave Fl 7 New York (10011) *(G-10375)*
Gruner + Jahr USA Group Inc (PA) 866 323-9336
1745 Broadway Fl 16 New York (10019) *(G-10376)*
Gruner Jahr USA Publishing Div, New York *Also called Gruner + Jahr USA Group Inc (G-10376)*
Gryphon Sensors LLC 315 452-8810
7351 Round Pond Rd North Syracuse (13212) *(G-12946)*
Gs Communications USA, Brooklyn *Also called G S Communications USA Inc (G-2010)*
Gs Direct LLC 212 902-1000
85 Broad St New York (10004) *(G-10377)*
Gschwind Group, Patchogue *Also called Suffolk McHy & Pwr Tl Corp (G-13435)*
Gscp Emax Acquisition LLC 212 902-1000
85 Broad St New York (10004) *(G-10378)*
GSE Composites Inc 631 389-1300
110 Oser Ave Hauppauge (11788) *(G-6087)*
Gsn Government Security News, Massapequa Park *Also called World Business Media LLC (G-8191)*
Gsp Components Inc 585 436-3377
1190 Brooks Ave Rochester (14624) *(G-14414)*
Gt Innovations LLC 585 739-7659
116 Bridgeman Rd Churchville (14428) *(G-3637)*
Gt Machine & Tool, Long Island City *Also called Cnc Manufacturing Corp (G-7701)*
Gt Parts & Services, Clifton Park *Also called Worldwide Gas Turbine Pdts Inc (G-3711)*
Gti Graphic Technology Inc (PA) 845 562-7066
211 Dupont Ave Newburgh (12550) *(G-12760)*
Guaranteed Printing Svc Co Inc 212 929-2410
4710 33rd St Long Island City (11101) *(G-7755)*
Guardian Booth LLC 844 992-6684
29 Roosevelt Ave Ste 301 Spring Valley (10977) *(G-15588)*
Guardian Concrete Inc 518 372-0080
2140 Maxon Rd Ext Schenectady (12308) *(G-15267)*
Guardian Concrete Steps, Schenectady *Also called Guardian Concrete Inc (G-15267)*
Guardian Industries Corp 315 787-7000
50 Forge Ave Geneva (14456) *(G-5580)*
Guardian Systems Tech Inc 716 481-5597
659 Oakwood Ave East Aurora (14052) *(G-4372)*
Guernica 914 414-7318
63 3rd Pl Apt 4r Brooklyn (11231) *(G-2055)*
Guernica Magazine, Brooklyn *Also called Guernica (G-2055)*
Guess Inc 845 928-3930
498 Red Apple Ct Central Valley (10917) *(G-3524)*
Guess Inc 315 539-5634
655 State Route 318 # 96 Waterloo (13165) *(G-16628)*
Guess Inc 212 286-9856
575 5th Ave Lbby 1 New York (10017) *(G-10379)*
Guess Inc 716 298-3561
1826 Military Rd Spc 113 Niagara Falls (14304) *(G-12830)*
Guest Informat LLC 212 557-3010
110 E 42nd St Rm 1714 New York (10017) *(G-10380)*
Guesthouse Division, Brooklyn *Also called R H Guest Incorporated (G-2471)*
Guidance Channel, Woodbury *Also called Global Video LLC (G-17288)*
Guidance Group Inc 631 756-4618
1 Huntington Quad 1n03 Melville (11747) *(G-8325)*
Guide Group, New York *Also called Soul Journ LLC (G-12142)*
Guild Diamond Products Inc (PA) 212 871-0007
1212 Avenue Of The Americ New York (10036) *(G-10381)*
Guilderland Printing, Guilderland *Also called Custom Prtrs Guilderland Inc (G-5902)*
Guilford Press, New York *Also called Guilford Publications Inc (G-10382)*
Guilford Publications Inc 212 431-9800
7 Penn Plz Ste 1200 New York (10001) *(G-10382)*
Guitar Specialist Inc 914 533-5589
219 Oakridge Cmn South Salem (10590) *(G-15535)*
Guldenschuh Logging & Lbr LLC 585 538-4750
143 Wheatland Center Rd Caledonia (14423) *(G-3280)*

Gullo Machine & Tool Inc 585 657-7318
4 E Main St Bloomfield (14469) *(G-989)*
Gumbusters (PA) 866 846-8486
1424 74th St Brooklyn (11228) *(G-2056)*
Gumuchian Fils Ltd 212 593-3118
16 E 52nd St Ste 701 New York (10022) *(G-10383)*
Gun Week, Buffalo *Also called Second Amendment Foundation (G-3180)*
Gunlocke Company LLC (HQ) 585 728-5111
1 Gunlocke Dr Wayland (14572) *(G-16710)*
Gunther Partners LLC (HQ) 212 521-2930
655 Madison Ave Fl 11 New York (10065) *(G-10384)*
Guosa Life Sciences Inc 516 481-1540
846 Center Dr North Baldwin (11510) *(G-12906)*
Gurley Precision Instrs Inc 518 272-6300
514 Fulton St Troy (12180) *(G-16237)*
Gustbuster Ltd 631 391-9000
855 Conklin St Ste O Farmingdale (11735) *(G-5003)*
Gutchess Freedom Inc 716 492-2824
10699 Maple Grove Rd Freedom (14065) *(G-5378)*
Gutchess Lumber Co Inc (PA) 607 753-3393
890 Mclean Rd Cortland (13045) *(G-4030)*
Guthrie Heli-ARC Inc 585 548-5053
6276 Clinton Street Rd Bergen (14416) *(G-846)*
Gutts Corporation of America, Irvington *Also called Guttz Corporation of America (G-6770)*
Guttz Corporation of America 914 591-9600
50 S Buckhout St Ste 104 Irvington (10533) *(G-6770)*
Guyson Corporation of USa (PA) 518 587-7894
13 Grande Blvd Saratoga Springs (12866) *(G-15157)*
GW Lisk Company Inc 315 548-2165
1369 Phelps Junction Rd Phelps (14532) *(G-13532)*
Gym Store Inc 718 366-7804
5889 57th St Maspeth (11378) *(G-8142)*
Gym Store.com, Maspeth *Also called Gym Store Inc (G-8142)*
H & C Chemists Inc 212 535-1700
1299 1st Ave New York (10021) *(G-10385)*
H & H Furniture Co 718 850-5252
11420 101st Ave Jamaica (11419) *(G-6917)*
H & H Hulls Inc 518 828-1339
35 Industrial Tract Anx Hudson (12534) *(G-6616)*
H & H Laboratories Inc (PA) 718 624-8041
61 4th St Brooklyn (11231) *(G-2057)*
H & H Laboratories Inc 718 624-8041
409 Hoyt St Brooklyn (11231) *(G-2058)*
H & H Metal Specialty Inc 716 665-2110
153 Hopkins Ave Jamestown (14701) *(G-6997)*
H & H Technologies Inc 631 567-3526
10 Colt Ct Ronkonkoma (11779) *(G-14907)*
H & M Leasing Corp 631 225-5246
1245 Marconi Blvd Copiague (11726) *(G-3904)*
H & R Precision, Farmingdale *Also called Precision Envelope Co Inc (G-5086)*
H & S Edible Products Corp 914 413-3489
119 Fulton Ln Mount Vernon (10550) *(G-8688)*
H & T Goldman Corporation 800 822-0272
2 W 46th St Ste 607 New York (10036) *(G-10386)*
H A Guden Company Inc 631 737-2900
99 Raynor Ave Ronkonkoma (11779) *(G-14908)*
H B Millwork Inc (PA) 631 289-8086
500 Long Island Ave Medford (11763) *(G-8246)*
H B Millwork Inc 631 924-4195
9 Old Dock Rd Yaphank (11980) *(G-17394)*
H Best Ltd 212 354-2400
1411 Broadway Fl 8 New York (10018) *(G-10387)*
H C Kionka & Co Inc 212 227-3155
15 Maiden Ln Ste 908 New York (10038) *(G-10388)*
H C Young Tool & Machine Co 315 463-0663
3700 New Court Ave Syracuse (13206) *(G-15955)*
H D M Labs Inc 516 431-8357
153 Kingston Blvd Island Park (11558) *(G-6780)*
H F Brown Machine Co Inc 315 732-6129
708 State St Utica (13502) *(G-16337)*
H F Cary & Sons 607 598-2563
70 Reniff Rd Lockwood (14859) *(G-7627)*
H F W Communications Inc (HQ) 315 703-7979
6437 Collamer Rd Ste 1 East Syracuse (13057) *(G-4535)*
H Fox & Co Inc 718 385-4600
416 Thatford Ave Brooklyn (11212) *(G-2059)*
H Freund Woodworking Co Inc 516 334-3774
589 Main St Westbury (11590) *(G-16992)*
H G Maybeck Co Inc 718 297-4410
17930 93rd Ave Ste 2 Jamaica (11433) *(G-6918)*
H Group 212 719-5500
462 7th Ave Fl 9 New York (10018) *(G-10389)*
H H B Bakery of Little Neck 718 631-7004
24914 Horace Harding Expy Flushing (11362) *(G-5246)*
H K Technologies Inc 212 779-0100
303 5th Ave Rm 1707 New York (10016) *(G-10390)*
H L Robinson Sand & Gravel (PA) 607 659-5153
535 Ithaca Rd Candor (13743) *(G-3377)*
H M W, Brewster *Also called Hudson Machine Works Inc (G-1221)*
H Risch Inc 585 442-0110
44 Saginaw Dr Rochester (14623) *(G-14415)*
H S Assembly Inc 585 266-4287
570 Hollandback Rochester (14605) *(G-14416)*

H T L & S Ltd ... 718 435-4474
5820 Fort Hamilton Pkwy Brooklyn (11219) ***(G-2060)***
H T Specialty Inc ... 585 458-4060
70 Bermar Park Rochester (14624) ***(G-14417)***
H Theophile, New York *Also called Kathmando Valley Preservation* ***(G-10818)***
H W Naylor Co Inc ... 607 263-5145
121 Main St Morris (13808) ***(G-8618)***
H W Wilson Company Inc ... 718 588-8635
950 University Ave Bronx (10452) ***(G-1350)***
H&L Computers Inc ... 516 873-8088
13523 Northern Blvd Flushing (11354) ***(G-5247)***
H2 At Hammerman, New York *Also called Hammerman Bros Inc* ***(G-10401)***
H2o Solutions Inc ... 518 527-0915
61 Major Dickinson Ave Stillwater (12170) ***(G-15760)***
Haanen Packard Machinery Inc (PA) ... 518 747-2330
16 Allen St Hudson Falls (12839) ***(G-6646)***
Haarstick Sailmakers Inc ... 585 342-5200
1461 Hudson Ave Rochester (14621) ***(G-14418)***
Habasit America Inc ... 716 824-8484
1400 Clinton St Buffalo (14206) ***(G-2984)***
Habco Corp ... 631 789-1400
41 Ranick Dr E Amityville (11701) ***(G-291)***
Habco Sales, Amityville *Also called Habco Corp* ***(G-291)***
Habermaass Corporation ... 315 685-8919
4407 Jordan Rd Skaneateles (13152) ***(G-15462)***
Habitat Magazine, New York *Also called Carol Group Ltd* ***(G-9532)***
Hachette Book Group Inc (HQ) ... 212 364-1200
1290 Ave Of The Americas New York (10104) ***(G-10391)***
Hachette Book Group USA Inc ... 212 364-1200
466 Lexington Ave Ste 13l New York (10017) ***(G-10392)***
Hacker Boat Company Inc (PA) ... 518 543-6731
8 Delaware Ave Silver Bay (12874) ***(G-15446)***
Haculla Nyc Inc ... 718 886-3163
6805 Fresh Meadow Ln Fresh Meadows (11365) ***(G-5441)***
Hadco Metal Trading Co LLC ... 631 270-9724
120 Spagnoli Rd Ste 1 Melville (11747) ***(G-8326)***
Haddad Bros Inc (PA) ... 212 563-2117
28 W 36th St Rm 1026 New York (10018) ***(G-10393)***
Haddad Bros Inc ... 718 377-5505
1200 Mcdonald Ave Brooklyn (11230) ***(G-2061)***
Haddad Hosiery LLC ... 212 251-0022
34 W 33rd St Rm 401 New York (10001) ***(G-10394)***
Hadeka Stone Corp (PA) ... 518 282-9605
115 Staso Ln Hampton (12837) ***(G-5959)***
Hades Manufacturing Corp ... 631 249-4244
135 Florida St Farmingdale (11735) ***(G-5004)***
Hadfield Inc ... 631 981-4314
840 S 2nd St Ronkonkoma (11779) ***(G-14909)***
Hadley Exhibits Inc (PA) ... 716 874-3666
1700 Elmwood Ave Buffalo (14207) ***(G-2985)***
Hadleys Fab-Weld Inc ... 315 926-5101
4202 Sunset Dr Marion (14505) ***(G-8095)***
Hagadah Passover Bakery ... 718 638-1589
814 Bergen St Brooklyn (11238) ***(G-2062)***
Hagedorn Communications Inc (PA) ... 914 636-7400
662 Main St Ste 1 New Rochelle (10801) ***(G-8906)***
Hagner Industries Inc ... 716 873-5720
95 Botsford Pl Buffalo (14216) ***(G-2986)***
Hahns Old Fashioned Cake Co ... 631 249-3456
75 Allen Blvd Farmingdale (11735) ***(G-5005)***
Haig Graphic Communications, Hauppauge *Also called Haig Press Inc* ***(G-6088)***
Haig Press Inc ... 631 582-5800
690 Old Willets Path Hauppauge (11788) ***(G-6088)***
Haights Cross Cmmnications Inc (PA) ... 212 209-0500
136 Madison Ave Fl 8 New York (10016) ***(G-10395)***
Haights Cross Operating Co (HQ) ... 914 289-9400
10 New King St Ste 102 White Plains (10604) ***(G-17116)***
Hailo Network Usa Inc ... 646 561-8552
568 Broadway Fl 11 New York (10012) ***(G-10396)***
Hain Blueprint Inc ... 212 414-5741
1111 Marcus Ave Ste 100 New Hyde Park (11042) ***(G-8836)***
Hain Celestial Group Inc (PA) ... 516 587-5000
1111 Marcus Ave Ste 100 New Hyde Park (11042) ***(G-8837)***
Haines and Company, Auburn *Also called Haines Publishing Inc* ***(G-499)***
Haines Equipment Inc ... 607 566-8531
20 Carrington St Avoca (14809) ***(G-537)***
Haines Publishing Inc ... 315 252-2178
144 Genesee St Ste 305 Auburn (13021) ***(G-499)***
Hair Color Research Group Inc ... 718 445-6026
13320 Whitestone Expy Flushing (11354) ***(G-5248)***
Hair Ventures LLC ... 718 664-7689
94 Fargo Ln Irvington (10533) ***(G-6771)***
Hairstory, Irvington *Also called Hair Ventures LLC* ***(G-6771)***
Haitian Times Inc ... 718 230-8700
80 Lakeside Dr New Rochelle (10801) ***(G-8907)***
Hal-Hen Company Inc ... 516 294-3200
180 Atlantic Ave New Hyde Park (11040) ***(G-8838)***
Halcyon Business Publications ... 516 338-0900
400 Post Ave Ste 304 Westbury (11590) ***(G-16993)***
Hale Electrical Dist Svcs Inc ... 716 818-7595
12088 Big Tree Rd Wales Center (14169) ***(G-16540)***
Haley Concrete Inc (PA) ... 716 492-0849
10413 Delevan Elton Rd Delevan (14042) ***(G-4234)***
Haleys Comet Seafood Corp ... 212 571-1828
605 3rd Ave Fl 34 New York (10158) ***(G-10397)***
Half Time, Poughkeepsie *Also called Quench It Inc* ***(G-13927)***
Halfmoon Town Water Department ... 518 233-7489
8 Brookwood Rd Waterford (12188) ***(G-16612)***
Halfway House LLC ... 518 873-2198
7158 Us Route 9 Elizabethtown (12932) ***(G-4628)***
Hall Construction Pdts & Svcs ... 518 747-7047
31 Allen St Hudson Falls (12839) ***(G-6647)***
Hallagan Manufacturing Co Inc ... 315 331-4640
500 Hoffman St Newark (14513) ***(G-12731)***
Hallock Fabricating Corp ... 631 727-2441
324 Doctors Path Riverhead (11901) ***(G-14144)***
Halm Industries Co Inc (PA) ... 516 676-6700
180 Glen Head Rd Glen Head (11545) ***(G-5632)***
Halm Instrument Co Inc ... 516 676-6700
180 Glen Head Rd Glen Head (11545) ***(G-5633)***
Halmark Architectural Finshg ... 718 272-1831
353 Stanley Ave Brooklyn (11207) ***(G-2063)***
Halmode Apparel Inc ... 212 819-9114
1400 Brdwy 11th & Fl 16 New York (10018) ***(G-10398)***
Halmode Petite Div, New York *Also called Halmode Apparel Inc* ***(G-10398)***
Halo Associates ... 212 691-9549
289 Bleecker St Fl 5 New York (10014) ***(G-10399)***
Halo Optical Products Inc ... 518 773-4256
9 Phair St Ste 1 Gloversville (12078) ***(G-5713)***
Halpern Tool Corp (PA) ... 914 633-0038
111 Plain Ave New Rochelle (10801) ***(G-8908)***
Hamil America Inc ... 212 244-2645
42 W 39th St Fl 15 New York (10018) ***(G-10400)***
Hamilton County News, Amsterdam *Also called William J Kline & Son Inc* ***(G-374)***
Hamilton Design Kit Homes, Queensbury *Also called Northern Design & Bldg Assoc* ***(G-14006)***
Hamilton Marketing Corporation ... 585 395-0678
5211 Lake Rd S Brockport (14420) ***(G-1244)***
Hamilton Printing Company Inc ... 518 732-2161
22 Hamilton Ave Troy (12180) ***(G-16238)***
Hamlet Products Inc ... 914 665-0307
221 N Macquesten Pkwy Mount Vernon (10550) ***(G-8689)***
Hammer Communications Inc ... 631 261-5806
28 Sunken Meadow Rd Northport (11768) ***(G-13012)***
Hammer Magazine, Northport *Also called Hammer Communications Inc* ***(G-13012)***
Hammer Packaging Corp (PA) ... 585 424-3880
200 Lucius Gordon Dr West Henrietta (14586) ***(G-16881)***
Hammerman Bros Inc ... 212 956-2800
50 W 57th St Fl 12 New York (10019) ***(G-10401)***
Hammond & Irving Inc (PA) ... 315 253-6265
254 North St Auburn (13021) ***(G-500)***
Hammond Manufacturing Co Inc ... 716 630-7030
475 Cayuga Rd Cheektowaga (14225) ***(G-3573)***
Hamodia Corp ... 718 853-9094
207 Foster Ave Brooklyn (11230) ***(G-2064)***
Hampshire Chemical Corp ... 315 539-9221
228 E Main St Waterloo (13165) ***(G-16629)***
Hampshire Jewels, New York *Also called Emsaru USA Corp* ***(G-10025)***
Hampshire Lithographers, New York *Also called Advantage Quick Print Inc* ***(G-9047)***
Hampton Art LLC ... 631 924-1335
19 Scouting Blvd Medford (11763) ***(G-8247)***
Hampton Press Incorporated ... 646 638-3800
307 7th Ave Rm 506 New York (10001) ***(G-10402)***
Hampton Sand Corp ... 631 325-5533
1 High St Westhampton (11977) ***(G-17057)***
Hampton Shipyards Inc ... 631 653-6777
7 Carter Ln East Quogue (11942) ***(G-4451)***
Hampton Technologies LLC ... 631 924-1335
19 Scouting Blvd Medford (11763) ***(G-8248)***
Hampton Transport Inc ... 631 716-4445
3655 Route 112 Coram (11727) ***(G-3943)***
Hamptons Magazine, Southampton *Also called Hamptons Media LLC* ***(G-15546)***
Hamptons Magazine ... 631 283-7125
67 Hampton Rd Unit 5 Southampton (11968) ***(G-15545)***
Hamptons Media LLC ... 631 283-6900
67 Hampton Rd Unit 5 Southampton (11968) ***(G-15546)***
Hamptons Media LLC ... 646 835-5211
915 Broadway Ste 1204 New York (10010) ***(G-10403)***
Hamtronics Inc ... 585 392-9430
39 Willnick Cir Rochester (14626) ***(G-14419)***
Han-Kraft Uniform Headwear, Buffalo *Also called Hankin Brothers Cap Co* ***(G-2987)***
Hana Pastries Inc ... 718 369-7593
34 35th St Unit 9 Brooklyn (11232) ***(G-2065)***
Hana Sheet Metal Inc ... 914 377-0773
9 Celli Pl 11 Yonkers (10701) ***(G-17452)***
Hana Sportswear Inc ... 315 639-6332
321 Lakeview Dr Dexter (13634) ***(G-4285)***
Hanan Products Company Inc ... 516 938-1000
196 Miller Pl Hicksville (11801) ***(G-6354)***
Hanco Metal Products Inc ... 212 787-5992
25 Jay St Brooklyn (11201) ***(G-2066)***
Hancock Manufacturing Corp ... 315 696-8906
7693 State Route 281 Tully (13159) ***(G-16276)***

Hancock Quarry/Asphalt, Hancock *Also called Cobleskill Stone Products Inc (G-5962)*
Hancor Inc...607 565-3033
1 William Donnly Inds Waverly (14892) **(G-16703)**
Hand Care Inc...516 747-5649
42 Sugar Maple Dr Roslyn (11576) **(G-15020)**
Hand Held Products Inc (HQ)...315 554-6000
700 Visions Dr Skaneateles Falls (13153) **(G-15468)**
Hand Held Products Inc...315 554-6000
700 Visions Dr Skaneateles Falls (13153) **(G-15469)**
Handcraft Cabinetry Inc...914 681-9437
230 Ferris Ave Ste 1 White Plains (10603) **(G-17117)**
Handcraft Manufacturing Corp (PA)...212 251-0022
34 W 33rd St Rm 401 New York (10001) **(G-10404)**
Handmade Frames Inc...718 782-8364
1013 Grand St Ste 2 Brooklyn (11211) **(G-2067)**
Handone Studios Inc...585 421-8175
388 Mason Rd Fairport (14450) **(G-4857)**
Handsome Dans LLC (PA)...917 965-2499
186 1st Ave New York (10009) **(G-10405)**
Handy & Harman (HQ)...914 461-1300
1133 Westchester Ave N-222 White Plains (10604) **(G-17118)**
Handy & Harman Group Ltd (HQ)...914 461-1300
1133 Westchester Ave N-222 White Plains (10604) **(G-17119)**
Handy & Harman Ltd (HQ)...914 461-1300
1133 Westchester Ave N-222 White Plains (10604) **(G-17120)**
Handy Laundry Products Corp (PA)...800 263-5973
382 Route 59 Ste 318 Airmont (10952) **(G-15)**
Handy Tool & Mfg Co Inc...718 478-9203
1205 Rockaway Ave Brooklyn (11236) **(G-2068)**
Hanes Supply Inc...518 438-0139
156 Railroad Ave Ste 3 Albany (12205) **(G-84)**
Hanesbrands Inc...212 576-9300
260 Madison Ave Fl 6 New York (10016) **(G-10406)**
Hanet Plastics Usa Inc...518 324-5850
139 Distribution Way Plattsburgh (12901) **(G-13668)**
Hanford Pharmaceuticals, Syracuse *Also called G C Hanford Manufacturing Co (G-15946)*
Hanger Inc...718 575-5504
11835 Queens Blvd Ste Ll3 Forest Hills (11375) **(G-5323)**
Hanger Inc...516 678-3650
556 Merrick Rd Ste 101 Rockville Centre (11570) **(G-14792)**
Hanger Clinic, Oneonta *Also called Creative Orthotics Prosthetics (G-13183)*
Hanger Headquarters LLC...212 391-8607
32 Broadway Ste 511 New York (10004) **(G-10407)**
Hanger Prosthectics Orthotics, Forest Hills *Also called Hanger Inc (G-5323)*
Hanger Prsthetcs & Ortho Inc...607 277-6620
310 Taughannock Blvd 1a Ithaca (14850) **(G-6846)**
Hanger Prsthetcs & Ortho Inc...607 776-8013
47 W Steuben St Bath (14810) **(G-657)**
Hanger Prsthetcs & Ortho Inc...518 446-1774
1315 Central Ave Albany (12205) **(G-85)**
Hanger Prsthetcs & Ortho Inc...607 771-4672
65 Pennsylvania Ave Binghamton (13903) **(G-921)**
Hanger Prsthetcs & Ortho Inc...315 472-5200
910 Erie Blvd E Ste 3 Syracuse (13210) **(G-15956)**
Hanger Prsthetcs & Ortho Inc...585 292-9510
333 Metro Park Ste F200 Rochester (14623) **(G-14420)**
Hanger Prsthetcs & Ortho Inc...607 795-1220
1300 College Ave Ste 1 Elmira (14901) **(G-4687)**
Hanger Prsthetcs & Ortho Inc...315 789-4810
787 State Route 5 And 20 Geneva (14456) **(G-5581)**
Hania By Anya Cole LLC...212 302-3550
16 W 56th St Fl 4 New York (10019) **(G-10408)**
Hankin Brothers Cap Co...716 892-8840
1910 Genesee St Buffalo (14211) **(G-2987)**
Hanna Altinis Co Inc...718 706-1134
3601 48th Ave Long Island City (11101) **(G-7756)**
Hannay Reels Inc...518 797-3791
553 State Route 143 Westerlo (12193) **(G-17042)**
Hansa Plastics Inc...631 269-9050
8 Meadow Glen Rd Kings Park (11754) **(G-7171)**
Hansa Usa LLC...646 412-6407
18 E 48th St Fl 3 New York (10017) **(G-10409)**
Hansae Co Ltd...212 354-6690
501 Fashion Ave Rm 208 New York (10018) **(G-10410)**
Hansel n Gretel Brand Inc...718 326-0041
7936 Cooper Ave Glendale (11385) **(G-5656)**
Hansen & Hansen Qulty Prtg Div, Syracuse *Also called Syracuse Computer Forms Inc (G-16050)*
Hansen Metal Fabrications, Farmington *Also called Hansen Steel (G-5152)*
Hansen Steel...585 398-2020
6021 County Road 41 Farmington (14425) **(G-5152)**
Hanson Aggregates East LLC...585 344-1810
6895 Ellicott Street Rd Batavia (14020) **(G-637)**
Hanson Aggregates East LLC...716 372-1574
4419 S Nine Mile Rd Allegany (14706) **(G-201)**
Hanson Aggregates East LLC...585 798-0762
Glenwood Ave Medina (14103) **(G-8274)**
Hanson Aggregates East LLC...716 372-1574
4419 S 9 Mile Rd Falconer (14733) **(G-4900)**
Hanson Aggregates East LLC...585 343-1787
5870 Main Rd Stafford (14143) **(G-15621)**
Hanson Aggregates East LLC...315 536-9391
131 Garfield Ave Penn Yan (14527) **(G-13513)**
Hanson Aggregates East LLC...315 548-2911
392 State Route 96 Phelps (14532) **(G-13533)**
Hanson Aggregates East LLC...315 493-3721
County Rt 47 Great Bend (13643) **(G-5783)**
Hanson Aggregates New York LLC...716 665-4620
2237 Allen St Jamesville (13078) **(G-7047)**
Hanson Aggregates New York LLC...716 665-4620
2237 Allen Street Ext Jamestown (14701) **(G-6998)**
Hanson Aggregates New York LLC...585 638-5841
6895 Ellicott Street Rd Pavilion (14525) **(G-13449)**
Hanson Aggregates New York LLC...315 469-5501
4800 Jamesville Rd Jamesville (13078) **(G-7048)**
Hanson Aggregates New York LLC...607 276-5881
546 Clark Rd Almond (14804) **(G-204)**
Hanson Aggregates PA Inc...315 858-1100
237 Kingdom Rd Jordanville (13361) **(G-7132)**
Hanson Aggregates PA Inc...518 568-2444
7904 St Hwy 5 Saint Johnsville (13452) **(G-15094)**
Hanson Aggregates PA LLC...585 624-3800
2049 County Rd 6 Honeoye Falls (14472) **(G-6529)**
Hanson Aggregates PA LLC...585 624-1220
2049 Honeoye Falls 6 Rd Honeoye Falls (14472) **(G-6530)**
Hanson Aggregates PA LLC...315 469-5501
4800 Jamesville Rd Jamesville (13078) **(G-7049)**
Hanson Aggregates PA LLC...315 685-3321
Rr 321 Skaneateles (13152) **(G-15463)**
Hanson Aggregates PA LLC...315 782-2300
25133 Nys Rt 3 Watertown (13601) **(G-16653)**
Hanson Aggregates PA LLC...315 821-7222
1780 State Route 12b Oriskany Falls (13425) **(G-13318)**
Hanson Aggregates PA LLC...315 393-3743
701 Cedar St Ogdensburg (13669) **(G-13115)**
Hanson Aggregates PA LLC...315 789-6202
2026 County Rd Ste 6 Oaks Corners (14518) **(G-13070)**
Hanson Aggregates PA LLC...585 436-3250
1535 Scottsville Rd Rochester (14623) **(G-14421)**
Hanson Ready Mix Concrete, Almond *Also called Hanson Aggregates New York LLC (G-204)*
Hanson Sign & Screen Process...716 484-8564
82 Carter St Falconer (14733) **(G-4901)**
Hanson Sign Companies, Falconer *Also called Hanson Sign & Screen Process (G-4901)*
Hansteel (usa) Inc...212 226-0105
230 Grand St Ste 602 New York (10013) **(G-10411)**
Hanyan & Higgins Company Inc...315 769-8838
9772 State Highway 56 Massena (13662) **(G-8196)**
Hanzlian Sausage Deli, Cheektowaga *Also called Hanzlian Sausage Incorporated (G-3574)*
Hanzlian Sausage Incorporated...716 891-5247
2351 Genesee St Cheektowaga (14225) **(G-3574)**
Hapeman's Seal Coating, Niagara Falls *Also called Eric S Hapeman (G-12815)*
Happy Fella, New York *Also called Hf Mfg Corp (G-10470)*
Happy Printer, The, New York *Also called Litho Partners Inc (G-11009)*
Happy Software Inc...518 584-4668
11 Federal St Saratoga Springs (12866) **(G-15158)**
Har-Son Mfg Inc...716 532-2641
7 Palmer St Gowanda (14070) **(G-5748)**
Harbec Inc...585 265-0010
369 State Route 104 Ontario (14519) **(G-13203)**
Harbor Elc Fabrication Tls Inc...914 636-4400
29 Portman Rd New Rochelle (10801) **(G-8909)**
Harbor Wldg & Fabrication Corp...631 667-1880
208 S Fehr Way Bay Shore (11706) **(G-704)**
Harbors Maine Lobster LLC...516 775-2400
969 Lakeville Rd New Hyde Park (11040) **(G-8839)**
Harbour Roads, Albany *Also called Kal-Harbour Inc (G-93)*
Hard Copy Printing, New York *Also called Top Copi Reproductions Inc (G-12368)*
Hard Manufacturing Co Inc...716 893-1800
230 Grider St Buffalo (14215) **(G-2988)**
Hard Ten, Brooklyn *Also called Dreams To Print (G-1879)*
Hard Ten Clothing Inc...212 302-1321
231 W 39th St Rm 606 New York (10018) **(G-10412)**
Harden Furniture Inc (PA)...315 675-3600
8550 Mill Pond Way Mc Connellsville (13401) **(G-8220)**
Hardinge Inc (PA)...607 734-2281
1 Hardinge Dr Elmira (14902) **(G-4688)**
Hargrave Development...716 877-7880
84 Shepard Ave Kenmore (14217) **(G-7147)**
Hargraves Bus MGT Consulting, Kenmore *Also called Hargrave Development (G-7147)*
Haring, J V & Son, Staten Island *Also called J V Haring & Son (G-15691)*
Harley Robert D Company Ltd...212 947-1872
240 W 35th St Ste 1005 New York (10001) **(G-10413)**
Harmac Medical Products Inc (PA)...716 897-4500
2201 Bailey Ave Buffalo (14211) **(G-2989)**
Harman International Inds Inc...516 496-3400
210 Crossways Park Dr Woodbury (11797) **(G-17289)**
Harmon and Castella Printing...845 471-9163
164 Garden St Poughkeepsie (12601) **(G-13905)**
Harmonic Drive LLC...631 231-6630
89 Cabot Ct Ste A Hauppauge (11788) **(G-6089)**
Harold Wood Co Inc...716 873-1535
329 Hinman Ave Buffalo (14216) **(G-2990)**

ALPHABETIC

Harome Designs LLC 631 864-1900
75 Modular Ave Commack (11725) *(G-3834)*
Harper International Corp 716 276-9900
4455 Genesee St Ste 123 Buffalo (14225) *(G-2991)*
Harper Products Ltd 516 997-2330
117 State St Westbury (11590) *(G-16994)*
Harper's Bazaar, New York *Also called Hearst Corporation (G-10446)*
Harpercollins 212 207-7000
195 Broadway Fl 2 New York (10007) *(G-10414)*
Harpercollins Publishers LLC 212 553-4200
233 Broadway Rm 1001 New York (10279) *(G-10415)*
Harpercollins Publishers LLC 212 207-7000
10 E 53rd St Fl Cellar2 New York (10022) *(G-10416)*
Harpers Magazine Foundation 212 420-5720
666 Broadway Fl 11 New York (10012) *(G-10417)*
Harris Assembly Group, Binghamton *Also called Arnold-Davis LLC (G-889)*
Harris Broadcast, New York *Also called Imagine Communications Corp (G-10568)*
Harris Corporation 585 244-5830
1680 University Ave Rochester (14610) *(G-14422)*
Harris Corporation 585 269-6600
400 Initiative Dr Rochester (14624) *(G-14423)*
Harris Corporation 585 269-5001
800 Lee Rd Bldg 601 Rochester (14606) *(G-14424)*
Harris Corporation 413 263-6200
800 Lee Rd Rochester (14606) *(G-14425)*
Harris Corporation 703 668-6239
474 Phoenix Dr Rome (13441) *(G-14812)*
Harris Corporation 315 838-7000
474 Phoenix Dr Rome (13441) *(G-14813)*
Harris Corporation 585 269-5000
2696 Manitou Rd Bldg 101 Rochester (14624) *(G-14426)*
Harris Corporation 585 244-5830
570 Culver Rd Rochester (14609) *(G-14427)*
Harris Corporation 585 244-5830
50 Carlson Rd Rochester (14610) *(G-14428)*
Harris Corporation 718 767-1100
1902 Whitestone Expy # 204 Whitestone (11357) *(G-17208)*
Harris Corporation 585 244-5830
1350 Jefferson Rd Rochester (14623) *(G-14429)*
Harris Logging Inc 518 792-1083
39 Mud Pond Rd Queensbury (12804) *(G-13998)*
Harris Machine, Newark *Also called Van Laeken Richard (G-12747)*
Harris Rf Communications, Rochester *Also called Harris Corporation (G-14429)*
Harrison Bakery West 315 422-1468
1306 W Genesee St Syracuse (13204) *(G-15957)*
Harrison Sportswear Inc 212 391-1051
260 W 39th St Fl 7 New York (10018) *(G-10418)*
Harry N Abrams Incorporated 212 206-7715
115 W 18th St Fl 6 New York (10011) *(G-10419)*
Harry Winston Inc (HQ) 212 399-1000
718 5th Ave New York (10019) *(G-10420)*
Harry's Razor Company, New York *Also called Harrys Inc (G-10421)*
Harrys Inc (PA) 888 212-6855
161 Ave Of The New York (10013) *(G-10421)*
Hart Energy Publishing Lllp 212 621-4621
110 William St Fl 18 New York (10038) *(G-10422)*
Hart Reproduction Services 212 704-0556
242 W 36th St Rm 801 New York (10018) *(G-10423)*
Hart Rifle Barrel Inc 315 677-9841
1680 Jamesville Ave Syracuse (13210) *(G-15958)*
Hart Specialties Inc 631 226-5600
5000 New Horizons Blvd Amityville (11701) *(G-292)*
Hart Sports Inc 631 385-1805
4 Roxanne Ct Huntington Station (11746) *(G-6707)*
Hart To Hart Industries Inc 716 492-2709
13520 Chaffee Curriers Rd Chaffee (14030) *(G-3534)*
Hartchrom Inc 518 880-0411
25 Gibson St Ste 1 Watervliet (12189) *(G-16686)*
Hartford Hwy Dept 315 724-0654
48 Genesee St New Hartford (13413) *(G-8806)*
Hartman Enterprises Inc 315 363-7300
455 Elizabeth St Oneida (13421) *(G-13156)*
Harvard Maintenance Inc 212 682-2617
245 Park Ave New York (10167) *(G-10424)*
Harvard University Press 212 337-0280
150 5th Ave Ste 632 New York (10011) *(G-10425)*
Harvard Woven Label, New York *Also called Imperial-Harvard Label Co (G-10574)*
Harvest Homes Inc 518 895-2341
1331 Cole Rd Delanson (12053) *(G-4233)*
Harvest Technologies Inc 518 899-7124
36 Featherfoil Way Ballston Spa (12020) *(G-599)*
Harvy Canes, Flushing *Also called Harvy Surgical Supply Corp (G-5249)*
Harvy Surgical Supply Corp 718 939-1122
3435 Collins Pl Flushing (11354) *(G-5249)*
Harwitt Industries Inc 516 623-9787
61 S Main St Unit A Freeport (11520) *(G-5405)*
Hasco Componets 516 328-9292
906 Jericho Tpke New Hyde Park (11040) *(G-8840)*
Haskell Machine & Tool Inc 607 749-2421
5 S Fulton St Homer (13077) *(G-6518)*
Hastings Hide Inc 516 295-2400
335 Central Ave Ste 4 Lawrence (11559) *(G-7391)*
Hastings Tile & Bath Inc (PA) 516 379-3500
711 Koehler Ave Ste 8 Ronkonkoma (11779) *(G-14910)*
Hat Attack I Bujibaja, Bronx *Also called Hat Attack Inc (G-1351)*
Hat Attack Inc (PA) 718 994-1000
4643 Bullard Ave Ste A Bronx (10470) *(G-1351)*
Hat Depot, Brooklyn *Also called Room At The Top Inc (G-2505)*
Hat World & Lids, Rochester *Also called Genesco Inc (G-14393)*
Hatfield Metal Fab Inc 845 454-9078
16 Hatfield Ln Poughkeepsie (12603) *(G-13906)*
Hathaway Prcess Instrmentation, Amherst *Also called Allied Motion Systems Corp (G-220)*
Hatherleigh Company Ltd 607 538-1092
62545 State Highway 10 Hobart (13788) *(G-6425)*
Haun Welding Supply Inc 607 846-2289
1100 Sullivan St Elmira (14901) *(G-4689)*
Haun Welding Supply Inc 315 592-5012
214 N 4th St Fulton (13069) *(G-5460)*
Hauppauge Computer Works Inc (HQ) 631 434-1600
91 Cabot Ct Hauppauge (11788) *(G-6090)*
Hauppauge Digital Inc (PA) 631 434-1600
91 Cabot Ct Hauppauge (11788) *(G-6091)*
Hauppuge Cmpt Dgtal Erope Sarl, Hauppauge *Also called Hauppauge Computer Works Inc (G-6090)*
Haute By Blair Stanley LLC 212 557-7868
330 E 38th St Apt 23e New York (10016) *(G-10426)*
Havaianas, New York *Also called Alpargatas Usa Inc (G-9098)*
Haverstraw Quarry, Haverstraw *Also called Tilcon New York Inc (G-6241)*
Hawk-I Security Inc 631 656-1056
355 Oser Ave Hauppauge (11788) *(G-6092)*
Hawkencatskills LLC 518 966-8900
18 Shultes Rd Greenville (12083) *(G-5885)*
Hawkeye Forest Products, Hamburg *Also called Hawkeye Forest Products LP (G-5928)*
Hawkeye Forest Products LP (PA) 608 534-6156
4002 Legion Dr Hamburg (14075) *(G-5928)*
Hawkins Fabrics Inc (PA) 518 773-9550
111 Woodside Ave Ste 1 Gloversville (12078) *(G-5714)*
Hawver Display Inc (PA) 585 544-2290
140 Carter St Rochester (14621) *(G-14430)*
Hax Pheroceuticals Inc 212 401-8695
228 Park Ave S Ste 35370 New York (10003) *(G-10427)*
Hayman-Chaffey Designs Inc 212 889-7771
137 E 25th St New York (10010) *(G-10428)*
Haymarket Group Ltd 212 239-0855
12 W 37th St 9 New York (10018) *(G-10429)*
Haymarket Media Inc (HQ) 646 638-6000
275 7th Ave Fl 10 New York (10001) *(G-10430)*
Haynes Roberts Inc 212 989-1901
601 W 26th St Rm 1655 New York (10001) *(G-10431)*
Hazan Cohen Group LLC 646 827-0030
1400 Brdwy Rm 700 New York (10018) *(G-10432)*
Hazlitt 1852 Vineyards, Hector *Also called Hazlitts 1852 Vineyards Inc (G-6257)*
Hazlitts 1852 Vineyards Inc 607 546-9463
5712 State Route 414 Hector (14841) *(G-6257)*
Hazlow Electronics Inc 585 325-5323
49 Saint Bridgets Dr Rochester (14605) *(G-14431)*
HB, Hauppauge *Also called Hohmann & Barnard Inc (G-6095)*
HB Architectural Lighting Inc 347 851-4123
862 E 139th St Bronx (10454) *(G-1352)*
HB Athletic Inc (PA) 914 560-8422
56 Harrison St Fl 4 New Rochelle (10801) *(G-8910)*
Hbs, Great Neck *Also called Toni Industries Inc (G-5845)*
Hc Brill Co Inc 716 685-4000
3765 Walden Ave Lancaster (14086) *(G-7319)*
HC Contracting Inc 212 643-9292
318 W 39th St Fl 4 New York (10018) *(G-10433)*
Hci Engineering 315 336-3450
5880 Bartlett Rd Rome (13440) *(G-14814)*
Hdm Hydraulics LLC 716 694-8004
125 Fire Tower Dr Tonawanda (14150) *(G-16170)*
Hdt Group LLC 914 490-2107
225 Rector Pl New York (10280) *(G-10434)*
Heads & Tails Lure Co 607 739-7900
283 Hibbard Rd Horseheads (14845) *(G-6580)*
Healing Garden Calgon, The, Irvington *Also called Ilex Consumer Pdts Group LLC (G-6772)*
Health Care Compliance (HQ) 516 478-4100
30 Jericho Executive Plz 400c Jericho (11753) *(G-7070)*
Health Care Originals Inc 585 967-1398
150 Lucius Gordon Dr West Henrietta (14586) *(G-16882)*
Health Matters America Inc 716 235-8772
2501 Broadway St Unit 2 Buffalo (14227) *(G-2992)*
Healthalliance Hospital 845 338-2500
105 Marys Ave Kingston (12401) *(G-7190)*
Healthee Endeavors Inc 718 653-5499
3565c Boston Rd Bronx (10469) *(G-1353)*
Healthone Pharmacy Inc 718 495-9015
119 Pennsylvania Ave Brooklyn (11207) *(G-2069)*
Healthway Home Products Inc 315 298-2904
3420 Maple Ave Pulaski (13142) *(G-13951)*
Healthway Products Company 315 207-1410
249a Mitchell St Oswego (13126) *(G-13332)*
Healthy Basement Systems LLC 516 650-9046
79 Cedarhurst Ave Medford (11763) *(G-8249)*

Healthy Brand Oil Corp (PA)......718 937-0806
5215 11th St Ste 3 Long Island City (11101) **(G-7757)**
Healthy N Fit Intl Inc......914 271-6040
435 Yorktown Rd Croton On Hudson (10520) **(G-4064)**
Healthy Way of Life Magazine......718 616-1681
1529 Voorhies Ave Brooklyn (11235) **(G-2070)**
Heany Industries Inc......585 889-2700
249 Briarwood Ln Scottsville (14546) **(G-15336)**
Hearing Aid Office, The, Albany *Also called Benway-Haworth-Lwlr-lacosta He* **(G-54)**
Hearst Bus Communications Inc (PA)......212 649-2000
300 W 57th St New York (10019) **(G-10435)**
Hearst Business Media (HQ)......516 227-1300
50 Charles Lindbergh Blvd # 100 Uniondale (11553) **(G-16296)**
Hearst Business Media Corp......631 650-6151
3500 Sunrise Hwy Ste 100 Great River (11739) **(G-5850)**
Hearst Business Media Corp......631 650-4441
3500 Sunrise Hwy Great River (11739) **(G-5851)**
Hearst Business Publishing Inc......212 969-7500
888 7th Ave Fl 2 New York (10106) **(G-10436)**
Hearst Communications Inc (HQ)......212 649-2000
300 W 57th St New York (10019) **(G-10437)**
Hearst Corporation (PA)......212 649-2000
300 W 57th St Fl 42 New York (10019) **(G-10438)**
Hearst Corporation......212 649-3100
300 W 57th St Fl 29 New York (10019) **(G-10439)**
Hearst Corporation......212 903-5366
224 W 57th St Frnt 1 New York (10019) **(G-10440)**
Hearst Corporation......212 767-5800
1633 Broadway Fl 44 New York (10019) **(G-10441)**
Hearst Corporation......516 382-4580
810 7th Ave New York (10019) **(G-10442)**
Hearst Corporation......212 830-2980
1790 Broadway New York (10019) **(G-10443)**
Hearst Corporation......518 454-5694
645 Albany Shaker Rd Albany (12211) **(G-86)**
Hearst Corporation......212 649-4271
300 W 57th St Fl 21 New York (10019) **(G-10444)**
Hearst Corporation......212 204-4300
1440 Broadway Fl 13 New York (10018) **(G-10445)**
Hearst Corporation......212 903-5000
300 W 57th St Fl 42 New York (10019) **(G-10446)**
Hearst Corporation......212 649-2275
300 W 57th St Fl 42 New York (10019) **(G-10447)**
Hearst Digital Studios Inc......212 969-7552
300 W 57th St New York (10019) **(G-10448)**
Hearst Holdings Inc (HQ)......212 649-2000
300 W 57th St New York (10019) **(G-10449)**
Hearst Interactive Media, New York *Also called Hearst Communications Inc* **(G-10437)**
Hearst Magazines, New York *Also called Hearst Corporation* **(G-10438)**
Heart of Tea......917 725-3164
419 Lafayette St Fl 2f New York (10003) **(G-10450)**
Hearth Cabinets and More Ltd......315 641-1197
4483 Buckley Rd Liverpool (13088) **(G-7521)**
Heartland Commerce Inc......845 920-0800
1 Blue Hill Plz Ste 16 Pearl River (10965) **(G-13458)**
Hearts of Palm LLC......212 944-6660
1411 Broadway Fl 23 New York (10018) **(G-10451)**
Hearts of Palm LLC (PA)......212 944-6660
1411 Broadway Fl 25 New York (10018) **(G-10452)**
Heartwood Specialties Inc......607 654-0102
10249 Gibson Rd Hammondsport (14840) **(G-5955)**
Heary Bros Lghtning Protection......716 941-6141
11291 Moore Rd Springville (14141) **(G-15612)**
Heat and Frost Inslatrs & Asbs......718 784-3456
3553 24th St Astoria (11106) **(G-443)**
Heat USA II LLC (PA)......212 254-4328
11902 23rd Ave College Point (11356) **(G-3786)**
Heat USA II LLC......212 564-4328
35 E 21st St New York (10010) **(G-10453)**
Heat-Timer Corporation......212 481-2020
79 Alexander Ave Ste 36a Bronx (10454) **(G-1354)**
Heat-Timer Service, Bronx *Also called Heat-Timer Corporation* **(G-1354)**
Heath Manufacturing Company......800 444-3140
700 Ellicott St Batavia (14020) **(G-638)**
Heath Outdoors Products, Batavia *Also called Heath Manufacturing Company* **(G-638)**
Heatherdell RB Hammers, Blauvelt *Also called Rbhammers Corp* **(G-973)**
Heating & Burner Supply Inc......718 665-0006
479 Walton Ave Bronx (10451) **(G-1355)**
Heaven Fresh USA Inc......800 642-0367
4600 Witmer Industrial Es Niagara Falls (14305) **(G-12831)**
Hebeler Corporation (PA)......716 873-9300
2000 Military Rd Tonawanda (14150) **(G-16171)**
Hecht & Sohn Glass Co Inc......718 782-8295
406 Willoughby Ave Brooklyn (11205) **(G-2071)**
Hedges and Gardens, East Hampton *Also called Irony Limited Inc* **(G-4411)**
Hedonist Artisan Chocolates......585 461-2815
674 South Ave Ste B Rochester (14620) **(G-14432)**
Hefti, New Rochelle *Also called Harbor Elc Fabrication Tls Inc* **(G-8909)**
Heidelberg Group Inc......315 866-0999
3056 State Hwy Rte 28 N Herkimer (13350) **(G-6301)**
Heidenhain International Inc (HQ)......716 661-1700
1 Precision Way Jamestown (14701) **(G-6999)**
Heindl Printers, Rochester *Also called Louis Heindl & Son Inc* **(G-14483)**
Heineck Associates Inc......631 207-2347
28 Curtis Ave Bellport (11713) **(G-832)**
Heintz & Weber Co Inc......716 852-7171
150 Reading St Buffalo (14220) **(G-2993)**
Heleo.com, New York *Also called Helium Media Inc* **(G-10454)**
Helgen Industries Inc......631 841-6300
431 Bayview Ave Amityville (11701) **(G-293)**
Heliojet Cleaning Tech Inc......585 768-8710
57 North St Ste 120 Le Roy (14482) **(G-7408)**
Helium Media Inc......917 596-4081
165 Duane St Apt 7b New York (10013) **(G-10454)**
Hellas Stone Inc......718 545-4716
3344 9th St Astoria (11106) **(G-444)**
Hellenic Corporation......212 986-6881
823 11th Ave Fl 5 New York (10019) **(G-10455)**
Hellenic Times, New York *Also called Hellenic Corporation* **(G-10455)**
Heller Performance Polymers, New York *Also called Atc Plastics LLC* **(G-9245)**
Hello and Hola Media Inc......212 807-4795
1 Metrotech Ctr Fl 18 Brooklyn (11201) **(G-2072)**
Helmel Engineering Pdts Inc......716 297-8644
6520 Lockport Rd Niagara Falls (14305) **(G-12832)**
Helmer Avenue, West Winfield *Also called Precisionmatics Co Inc* **(G-16959)**
Helmont Mills Inc (HQ)......518 568-7913
15 Lion Ave Saint Johnsville (13452) **(G-15095)**
Helvetica Press Incorporated......212 737-1857
244 5th Ave New York (10001) **(G-10456)**
Hemisphere Novelties Inc......914 378-4100
167 Saw Mill River Rd 3c Yonkers (10701) **(G-17453)**
Hempstead Sentinel Inc......516 486-5000
55 Chasner St Hempstead (11550) **(G-6273)**
Hemstrought's Bakeries, New Hartford *Also called B & D Enterprises of Utica* **(G-8801)**
Henderson Hbr Prfrmg Arts Assn......315 938-7333
12459 County Route 123 Henderson Harbor (13651) **(G-6291)**
Henderson Products Inc......315 785-0994
22686 Fisher Rd Ste A Watertown (13601) **(G-16654)**
Henderson Truck Equipment, Watertown *Also called Henderson Products Inc* **(G-16654)**
Hendrickson Custom Cabinetry......718 401-0137
132 Saint Anns Ave Fl 2 Bronx (10454) **(G-1356)**
Hengyuan Copper USA Inc......718 357-6666
14107 20th Ave Ste 506 Whitestone (11357) **(G-17209)**
Henley Brands LLC......516 883-8220
1 Channel Dr Port Washington (11050) **(G-13820)**
Hennig Custom Woodwork Corp......516 536-3460
2497 Long Beach Rd Oceanside (11572) **(G-13080)**
Hennig Custom Woodworking, Oceanside *Also called Hennig Custom Woodwork Corp* **(G-13080)**
Henpecked Husband Farms Corp......631 728-2800
1212 Speonk Riverhead Rd Speonk (11972) **(G-15575)**
Henry B Urban Inc......212 489-3308
619 W 54th St Ste 6l New York (10019) **(G-10457)**
Henry Design Studios Inc......516 801-2760
129 Birch Hill Rd Ste 2 Locust Valley (11560) **(G-7632)**
Henry Dunay Designs Inc......212 768-9700
10 W 46th St Ste 1200 New York (10036) **(G-10458)**
Henry Holt and Company LLC......646 307-5095
175 5th Ave Ste 400 New York (10010) **(G-10459)**
Henry Morgan......718 317-5013
433 Tennyson Dr Staten Island (10312) **(G-15683)**
Henry Newman LLC......607 273-8512
312 4th St Ithaca (14850) **(G-6847)**
Henry Schein Inc......315 431-0340
6057 Corporate Dr Ste 2 East Syracuse (13057) **(G-4536)**
Henry Schein Fincl Svcs LLC (HQ)......631 843-5500
135 Duryea Rd Melville (11747) **(G-8327)**
Henry Schein International Inc, Melville *Also called Henry Schein Fincl Svcs LLC* **(G-8327)**
Henry Segal Co, Hempstead *Also called Shane Tex Inc* **(G-6287)**
Henrys Deals Inc......347 821-4685
1002 Quentin Rd Ste 2009 Brooklyn (11223) **(G-2073)**
Herald Journal, The, Syracuse *Also called Herald Newspapers Company Inc* **(G-15959)**
Herald Newspapers Company Inc (HQ)......315 470-0011
220 S Warren St Syracuse (13202) **(G-15959)**
Herald Press Inc......718 784-5255
3710 30th St Long Island City (11101) **(G-7758)**
Herald Publishing Company LLC......315 470-2022
4 Times Sq Fl 23 New York (10036) **(G-10460)**
Herald Statesman, Yonkers *Also called Gannett Stllite Info Ntwrk Inc* **(G-17447)**
Herbal Destination, Huntington Station *Also called Eximus Connections Corporation* **(G-6703)**
Herbert Jaffe Inc......718 392-1956
4011 Skillman Ave Long Island City (11104) **(G-7759)**
Herbert Wolf Corp......212 242-0300
95 Vandam St Apt C New York (10013) **(G-10461)**
Hercules, Huntington Station *Also called I A S National Inc* **(G-6710)**
Hercules Candy Co......315 463-4339
209 W Heman St East Syracuse (13057) **(G-4537)**
Hercules Gift & Gormet, East Syracuse *Also called Hercules Candy Co* **(G-4537)**
Hercules Group Inc......212 813-8000
27 Seaview Blvd Port Washington (11050) **(G-13821)**

ALPHABETIC

Hercules Heat Treating Corp 718 625-1266
101 Classon Ave 113 Brooklyn (11205) *(G-2074)*
Hercules Incorporated 718 383-1717
761 Humboldt St Brooklyn (11222) *(G-2075)*
Hercules Incorporated 315 461-4730
911 Old Liverpool Rd Liverpool (13088) *(G-7522)*
Hercules International Inc 631 423-6900
95 W Hills Rd Huntington Station (11746) *(G-6708)*
Hergo Ergonomic Support (PA) 718 894-0639
5601 55th Ave Maspeth (11378) *(G-8143)*
Heritage Contract Flooring LLC 716 853-1555
29 Depot St Buffalo (14206) *(G-2994)*
Heritage Packaging, Victor *Also called W Stuart Smith Inc (G-16512)*
Heritage Printing Center 518 563-8240
94 Margaret St Plattsburgh (12901) *(G-13669)*
Heritage Wide Plank Flooring, Riverhead *Also called Custom Woodwork Ltd (G-14140)*
Herkimer Cheese, Ilion *Also called Original Hrkmer Cnty Chese Inc (G-6743)*
Herkimer Diamond Mines Inc 315 891-7355
800 Mohawk St Herkimer (13350) *(G-6302)*
Herkimer Tool & Equipment Co, Herkimer *Also called Herkimer Tool & Machining Corp (G-6303)*
Herkimer Tool & Machining Corp 315 866-2110
125 Marginal Rd Herkimer (13350) *(G-6303)*
Herman H Sticht Company Inc 718 852-7602
45 Main St Ste 401 Brooklyn (11201) *(G-2076)*
Herman Hall Communications 718 941-1879
1630 Nostrand Ave Brooklyn (11226) *(G-2077)*
Herman Kay, New York *Also called Mystic Inc (G-11334)*
Herman Kay Company Ltd 212 239-2025
463 7th Ave Fl 12 New York (10018) *(G-10462)*
Herman Kay Div-Mystic, New York *Also called Herman Kay Company Ltd (G-10462)*
Hermann Gerdens Inc 631 841-3132
1725 N Strongs Rd Copiague (11726) *(G-3905)*
Hermann J Wiemer Vineyard 607 243-7971
3962 Rte 14 Dundee (14837) *(G-4329)*
Hermosa Corp 315 768-4320
102 Main St New York Mills (13417) *(G-12725)*
Heron Hill Vineyards Inc (PA) 607 868-4241
9301 County Route 76 Hammondsport (14840) *(G-5956)*
Heron Hill Winery, Hammondsport *Also called Heron Hill Vineyards Inc (G-5956)*
Herr Manufacturing Co Inc 716 754-4341
17 Pearce Ave Tonawanda (14150) *(G-16172)*
Herris Gourmet Inc 917 578-2308
536 Grand St Brooklyn (11211) *(G-2078)*
Herrmann Group LLC 716 876-9798
2320 Elmwood Ave Kenmore (14217) *(G-7148)*
Hersco-Arch Products, Long Island City *Also called Hersco-Orthotic Labs Corp (G-7760)*
Hersco-Orthotic Labs Corp 718 391-0416
3928 Crescent St Long Island City (11101) *(G-7760)*
Hershel Horowitz Corp 212 719-1710
580 5th Ave Ste 901 New York (10036) *(G-10463)*
Hershey Kiss 203 Inc 516 503-3740
3536 Bunker Ave Wantagh (11793) *(G-16557)*
Hertling Trousers Inc 718 784-6100
236 Greenpoint Ave Brooklyn (11222) *(G-2079)*
Hes Inc 607 359-2974
6303 Symonds Hill Rd Addison (14801) *(G-7)*
Hess Corporation (PA) 212 997-8500
1185 Ave Of The Americas New York (10036) *(G-10464)*
Hess Energy Exploration Ltd (HQ) 732 750-6500
1185 Ave Of The Americas New York (10036) *(G-10465)*
Hess Explrtion Prod Hldngs Ltd (HQ) 732 750-6000
1185 Ave Of The Americas New York (10036) *(G-10466)*
Hess Oil Virgin Island Corp 212 997-8500
1185 Ave Of The Amer 39 New York (10036) *(G-10467)*
Hess Pipeline Corporation 212 997-8500
1185 Ave Of The Amer 39 New York (10036) *(G-10468)*
Hess Tioga Gas Plant LLC 212 997-8500
1185 Ave Of The Americas New York (10036) *(G-10469)*
Heterochemical Corporation 516 561-8225
111 E Hawthorne Ave Valley Stream (11580) *(G-16408)*
Hexion Inc 518 792-8040
64 Fernan Rd South Glens Falls (12803) *(G-15525)*
Hey Doll, New York *Also called Lesilu Productions Inc (G-10974)*
Hf Mfg Corp (PA) 212 594-9142
65 W 36th St Fl 11 New York (10018) *(G-10470)*
Hf Technologies LLC 585 254-5030
810 Martin Rd Hamlin (14464) *(G-5950)*
Hfi, New York *Also called Home Fashions Intl LLC (G-10501)*
Hgi Skydyne, Port Jervis *Also called Sky Dive (G-13792)*
Hh Liquidating Corp 646 282-2500
110 E 59th St Fl 34 New York (10022) *(G-10471)*
Hl Speed Envelope Co Inc 718 617-1600
560 S 3rd Ave Ste 1 Mount Vernon (10550) *(G-8690)*
Hl Tech Signs of NY Inc 516 794-7880
415 E Meadow Ave East Meadow (11554) *(G-4424)*
Hl Wines, New York *Also called Frank Wines Inc (G-10203)*
Hi-Lites, Watkins Glen *Also called Skylark Publications Ltd (G-16696)*
Hi-Med, Old Bethpage *Also called Hitemco Medical Applications (G-13128)*
Hi-Tech Advanced Solutions Inc 718 926-3488
10525 65th Ave Apt 4h Forest Hills (11375) *(G-5324)*
Hi-Tech Cnc Machining Corp 914 668-5090
13 Elm Ave Mount Vernon (10550) *(G-8691)*
Hi-Tech Industries NY Inc 607 217-7361
23 Ozalid Rd Johnson City (13790) *(G-7094)*
Hi-Tech Metals Inc 718 894-1212
5920 56th Ave Maspeth (11378) *(G-8144)*
Hi-Tech Packg World-Wide LLC 845 947-1912
110 Corporate Dr New Windsor (12553) *(G-8939)*
Hi-Tech Pharmacal - An Akorn, Amityville *Also called Hi-Tech Pharmacal Co Inc (G-294)*
Hi-Tech Pharmacal Co Inc (HQ) 631 789-8228
369 Bayview Ave Amityville (11701) *(G-294)*
Hi-Temp Brazing Inc 631 491-4917
539 Acorn St Deer Park (11729) *(G-4148)*
Hi-Temp Fabrication Inc 716 852-5655
79 Perry St Ste 2 Buffalo (14203) *(G-2995)*
Hi-Temp Specialty Metals Inc 631 775-8750
355 Sills Rd Yaphank (11980) *(G-17395)*
Hi-Tron Semiconductor Corp 631 231-1500
85 Engineers Rd Hauppauge (11788) *(G-6093)*
Hibert Publishing LLC 914 381-7474
222 Purchase St Rye (10580) *(G-15059)*
Hibu Inc (HQ) 516 730-1900
90 Merrick Ave Ste 530 East Meadow (11554) *(G-4425)*
Hickey Freeman Tailored CL Inc 585 467-7240
1155 N Clinton Ave Rochester (14621) *(G-14433)*
Hickory Hollow Wind Cellars, Dundee *Also called Hickory Road Land Co LLC (G-4330)*
Hickory Road Land Co LLC 607 243-9114
5289 Route 14 Dundee (14837) *(G-4330)*
Hicksville Machine Works Corp 516 931-1524
761 S Broadway Hicksville (11801) *(G-6355)*
Hickville Illustrated News 516 747-8282
132 E 2nd St Mineola (11501) *(G-8513)*
Hig Capital, Williamsville *Also called Ashton-Potter USA Ltd (G-17233)*
Higgins Supl Co, Mc Graw *Also called Higgins Supply Company Inc (G-8222)*
Higgins Supply Company Inc 607 836-6474
18-23 South St Mc Graw (13101) *(G-8222)*
High Energy U. S. A., New York *Also called Kidz World Inc (G-10843)*
High Falls Brewing Company LLC (HQ) 585 546-1030
445 Saint Paul St Rochester (14605) *(G-14434)*
High Falls Operating Co LLC 585 546-1030
445 Saint Paul St Rochester (14605) *(G-14435)*
High Frequency Tech Co Inc 631 242-3020
172 Brook Ave Ste D Deer Park (11729) *(G-4149)*
High Performance Sftwr USA Inc 866 616-4958
145 Hook Creek Blvd Valley Stream (11581) *(G-16409)*
High Point Design LLC 212 354-2400
1411 Broadway Fl 8 New York (10018) *(G-10472)*
High Prfmce Plymr Cmposits Div, Medford *Also called Enecon Corporation (G-8243)*
High Quality Video Inc (PA) 212 686-9534
12 W 27th St Fl 7 New York (10001) *(G-10473)*
High Ridge News LLC 718 548-7412
5818 Broadway Bronx (10463) *(G-1357)*
High Speed Hammer Company Inc 585 266-4287
313 Norton St Rochester (14621) *(G-14436)*
High Voltage Inc 518 329-3275
31 County Route 7a Copake (12516) *(G-3887)*
Highcrest Investors LLC (HQ) 212 702-4323
Icahn Associates Corp 767 New York (10153) *(G-10474)*
Highland Museum & Lighthouse 508 487-1121
111 M Simons Rd Cairo (12413) *(G-3272)*
Highland Organization Corp 631 991-3240
435 Unit 23 Brook Ave Deer Park (11729) *(G-4150)*
Highland Sand & Gravel Inc 845 928-2221
911 State Route 32 Highland Mills (10930) *(G-6412)*
Highland Stone, Highland Mills *Also called Highland Sand & Gravel Inc (G-6412)*
Highland Valley Supply Inc 845 849-2863
30 Airport Dr Wappingers Falls (12590) *(G-16572)*
Highlander Realty Inc 914 235-8073
70 Church St New Rochelle (10805) *(G-8911)*
Highline Media LLC 859 692-2100
375 Park Ave New York (10152) *(G-10475)*
Highway Bagels Corp 347 350-6493
1921 Kings Hwy 1923 Brooklyn (11229) *(G-2080)*
Highway Garage 518 568-2837
110 State Highway 331 Saint Johnsville (13452) *(G-15096)*
Highway Toll ADM LLC 516 684-9584
66 Powerhouse Rd Ste 402 Roslyn Heights (11577) *(G-15026)*
Hill Crest Press 518 943-0671
138 Grandview Ave Catskill (12414) *(G-3429)*
Hill Knitting Mills Inc 718 846-5000
10005 92nd Ave Ste Mgmt Richmond Hill (11418) *(G-14075)*
Hill, Lois Accessories, New York *Also called Ancient Modern Art LLC (G-9151)*
Hillary Hats & Accessories, Rockaway Beach *Also called Designs By Lanie Inc (G-14781)*
Hillary Merchant Inc 646 575-9242
2 Wall St Ste 807 New York (10005) *(G-10476)*
Hillburn Granite Company Inc 845 357-8900
166 Sixth St Hillburn (10931) *(G-6415)*
Hilliard Corporation (PA) 607 733-7121
100 W 4th St Elmira (14901) *(G-4690)*

ALPHABETIC

ALPHABETIC SECTION Homer Logging Contractor

Hilliard Corporation...607 733-7121
1420 College Ave Elmira (14901) ***(G-4691)***
Hills Pet Products Inc (HQ)...212 310-2000
300 Park Ave New York (10022) ***(G-10477)***
Hillside Iron Works, Waterford *Also called Maximum Security Products Corp* ***(G-16613)***
Hillside Printing Inc...718 658-6719
16013 Hillside Ave Jamaica (11432) ***(G-6919)***
Hilltop Slate Inc...518 642-1453
Rr 22 Box A Middle Granville (12849) ***(G-8399)***
Hilltown Pork Inc (PA)...518 781-4050
12948 State Route 22 Canaan (12029) ***(G-3331)***
Hilord Chemical Corporation...631 234-7373
70 Engineers Rd Hauppauge (11788) ***(G-6094)***
Himatsingka America Inc (HQ)...212 545-8929
261 5th Ave Rm 1400 New York (10016) ***(G-10478)***
Himatsingka America Inc...212 252-0802
261 5th Ave Rm 501 New York (10016) ***(G-10479)***
Himatsingka Holdings NA Inc (HQ)...212 545-8929
261 5th Ave Rm 1400 New York (10016) ***(G-10480)***
Hinge Inc...502 445-3111
137 5th Ave Fl 5 New York (10010) ***(G-10481)***
Hinspergers Poly Industries...585 798-6625
430 W Oak Orchard St Medina (14103) ***(G-8275)***
Hipotronics Inc (HQ)...845 279-8091
1650 Route 22 Brewster (10509) ***(G-1220)***
Hippo Industries, Oyster Bay *Also called Engineering Maint Pdts Inc* ***(G-13369)***
Hippocrene Books Inc (PA)...212 685-4371
171 Madison Ave Rm 1605 New York (10016) ***(G-10482)***
Hipshot Products Inc...607 532-9404
8248 State Route 96 Interlaken (14847) ***(G-6747)***
Hirsch Optical Corp...516 752-2211
91 Carolyn Blvd Farmingdale (11735) ***(G-5006)***
His Productions USA Inc...212 594-3737
139 Fulton St Rm 317 New York (10038) ***(G-10483)***
His Vision Inc...585 254-0022
1260 Lyell Ave Rochester (14606) ***(G-14437)***
Hispanic Com Pub Inc...718 224-5863
3815 Bell Blvd Fl 2 Bayside (11361) ***(G-772)***
Historcal Soc of Mddltown Walk...845 342-0941
25 East Ave Middletown (10940) ***(G-8444)***
Historic TW Inc (HQ)...212 484-8000
75 Rockefeller Plz New York (10019) ***(G-10484)***
History Publishing Company LLC...845 398-8161
173 Route 9w Palisades (10964) ***(G-13401)***
Hisun Led, Flushing *Also called Hisun Optoelectronics Co Ltd* ***(G-5250)***
Hisun Optoelectronics Co Ltd...718 886-6966
4109 College Point Blvd Flushing (11355) ***(G-5250)***
Hitachi Cable America Inc (HQ)...914 694-9200
2 Manhattanville Rd # 301 Purchase (10577) ***(G-13957)***
Hitachi Metals America Ltd...914 694-9200
2 Manhattanville Rd # 301 Purchase (10577) ***(G-13958)***
Hitachi Metals America Ltd (HQ)...914 694-9200
2 Manhattanville Rd # 301 Purchase (10577) ***(G-13959)***
Hitemco, Old Bethpage *Also called Barson Composites Corporation* ***(G-13126)***
Hitemco Medical Applications...516 752-7882
160 Bethpage Sweet Holw Old Bethpage (11804) ***(G-13128)***
Hje Company Inc...518 792-8733
820 Quaker Rd Queensbury (12804) ***(G-13999)***
Hjn Inc (PA)...212 398-9564
16 W 46th St Ste 900 New York (10036) ***(G-10485)***
HK Metal Trading Ltd...212 868-3333
450 Fashion Ave Ste 2300 New York (10123) ***(G-10486)***
Hks Printing Company Inc...212 675-2529
115 E 27th St New York (10016) ***(G-10487)***
Hlp Klearfold Packaging Pdts...718 554-3271
75 Maiden Ln Rm 808 New York (10038) ***(G-10488)***
Hlp Klearfold Visualize, New York *Also called Hlp Klearfold Packaging Pdts* ***(G-10488)***
Hlw Acres LLC...585 591-0795
1727 Exchange Street Rd Attica (14011) ***(G-473)***
Hlw Acres Poultry Processing, Attica *Also called Hlw Acres LLC* ***(G-473)***
Hmi Metal Powders, Clayville *Also called Homogeneous Metals Inc* ***(G-3689)***
Hmi Metal Powders...315 839-5421
2395 Main St Clayville (13322) ***(G-3688)***
Hmo Beverage Corp...917 371-6100
68 33rd St Unit 4 Brooklyn (11232) ***(G-2081)***
HMS Productions Inc (PA)...212 719-9190
250 W 39th St Fl 12 New York (10018) ***(G-10489)***
Hmx LLC (PA)...212 682-9073
125 Park Ave Fl 7 New York (10017) ***(G-10490)***
Hmx Operating Co, New York *Also called Hmx LLC* ***(G-10490)***
Hn Precision-Ny, Rochester *Also called Nationwide Precision Pdts Corp* ***(G-14529)***
Hnh, White Plains *Also called Handy & Harman Ltd* ***(G-17120)***
Hni Corporation...212 683-2232
200 Lexington Ave Rm 1112 New York (10016) ***(G-10491)***
HNST Mold Inspections LLC (PA)...845 215-9258
6 Kevin Ct Nanuet (10954) ***(G-8757)***
Hnw Inc (PA)...212 258-9215
666 3rd Ave Frnt A New York (10017) ***(G-10492)***
Hobart Corporation...631 864-3440
71 Mall Dr Ste 1 Commack (11725) ***(G-3835)***
Hobart Corporation...585 427-9000
3495 Winton Pl Rochester (14623) ***(G-14438)***
Hockey Facility...518 452-7396
830 Albany Shaker Rd Albany (12211) ***(G-87)***
Hodgins Engraving Co Inc...585 343-4444
3817 W Main Street Rd Batavia (14020) ***(G-639)***
Hoehn Inc...518 463-8900
159 Chestnut St Albany (12210) ***(G-88)***
Hoehn.us, Albany *Also called Hoehn Inc* ***(G-88)***
Hoercher Industries Inc...585 398-2982
A1 Country Club Rd Ste 1 East Rochester (14445) ***(G-4461)***
Hoffman & Hoffman...315 536-4773
489 State Route 54 Penn Yan (14527) ***(G-13514)***
Hoffmans Trade Group LLC...518 250-5556
64 2nd St Troy (12180) ***(G-16239)***
Hofset Fabrics Ltd...718 522-6228
445 Park Ave Bsmt Brooklyn (11205) ***(G-2082)***
Hogan Flavors & Fragrances...212 598-4310
130 E 18th St Frnt New York (10003) ***(G-10493)***
Hogan Fragrances International, New York *Also called Hogan Flavors & Fragrances* ***(G-10493)***
Hogil Pharmaceutical Corp...914 681-1800
237 Mmaroneck Ave Ste 207 White Plains (10605) ***(G-17121)***
Hohenforst Splitting Co Inc...518 725-0012
152 W Fulton St Gloversville (12078) ***(G-5715)***
Hohl Machine & Conveyor Co Inc...716 882-7210
1580 Niagara St Buffalo (14213) ***(G-2996)***
Hohlveyor, Buffalo *Also called Hohl Machine & Conveyor Co Inc* ***(G-2996)***
Hohmann & Barnard Inc (HQ)...631 234-0600
30 Rasons Ct Hauppauge (11788) ***(G-6095)***
Hohmann & Barnard Inc...518 357-9757
310 Wayto Rd Schenectady (12303) ***(G-15268)***
Hola Publishing Co...718 424-3129
2932 Northern Blvd Long Island City (11101) ***(G-7761)***
Holbrooke By Sberry, New York *Also called Holbrooke Inc* ***(G-10494)***
Holbrooke Inc...646 397-4674
444 E 20th St Apt 1b New York (10009) ***(G-10494)***
Holdens Screen Supply Corp...212 627-2727
121 Varick St New York (10013) ***(G-10495)***
Holiday House Inc...212 688-0085
425 Madison Ave Fl 12 New York (10017) ***(G-10496)***
Holistic Blends Inc...315 468-4300
6726 Townline Rd Stop 1 Syracuse (13211) ***(G-15960)***
Holland & Sherry Inc (PA)...212 542-8410
330 E 59th St Ph New York (10022) ***(G-10497)***
Holland & Sherry Intr Design, New York *Also called Holland & Sherry Inc* ***(G-10497)***
Holland Manufacturing Inc...716 685-4129
415 Lawrence Bell Dr # 6 Williamsville (14221) ***(G-17247)***
Hollander HM Fshons Hldngs LLC...212 575-0400
440 Park Ave S Fl 10 New York (10016) ***(G-10498)***
Hollander Sleep Products LLC...212 575-0400
440 Park Ave S New York (10016) ***(G-10499)***
Hollingsworth & Vose Company...518 695-8000
3235 County Rte 113 Greenwich (12834) ***(G-5889)***
Hollywood Advertising Banners...631 842-3000
539 Oak St Copiague (11726) ***(G-3906)***
Hollywood Banners, Copiague *Also called Hollywood Advertising Banners* ***(G-3906)***
Hollywood Banners Inc...631 842-3000
539 Oak St Copiague (11726) ***(G-3907)***
Hollywood Cabinets Co...516 354-0857
182 Hendrickson Ave Elmont (11003) ***(G-4722)***
Hollywood Signs Inc...917 577-7333
388 3rd Ave Brooklyn (11215) ***(G-2083)***
Holmes Group The Inc...212 333-2300
271 W 47th St Apt 23a New York (10036) ***(G-10500)***
Holstein World, East Syracuse *Also called H F W Communications Inc* ***(G-4535)***
Holy Cow Kosher LLC...347 788-8620
750 Chestnut Ridge Rd Spring Valley (10977) ***(G-15589)***
Home and Above LLC...914 220-3451
199 Lee Ave Ste 895 Brooklyn (11211) ***(G-2084)***
Home Depot USA Inc...845 561-6540
1220 Route 300 Newburgh (12550) ***(G-12761)***
Home Depot, The, Newburgh *Also called Home Depot USA Inc* ***(G-12761)***
Home Fashions Intl LLC...212 684-0091
295 5th Ave Ste 1520 New York (10016) ***(G-10501)***
Home Ideal Inc...718 762-8998
4528 159th St Flushing (11358) ***(G-5251)***
Home Lighting & Accessories, New City *Also called Doctorow Communications Inc* ***(G-8783)***
Home Maide Inc...845 837-1700
1 Short St Harriman (10926) ***(G-5972)***
Home Reporter & Sunset News, Brooklyn *Also called Home Reporter Inc* ***(G-2085)***
Home Reporter Inc...718 238-6600
8723 3rd Ave Brooklyn (11209) ***(G-2085)***
Home Service Publications (HQ)...914 238-1000
1 Readers Digest Rd Pleasantville (10570) ***(G-13714)***
Home4u Inc...347 262-7214
152 Skillman St Apt 8 Brooklyn (11205) ***(G-2086)***
Homegrown For Good LLC...857 540-6361
29 Beechwood Ave New Rochelle (10801) ***(G-8912)***
Homer Iron Works LLC...607 749-3963
5130 Us Route 11 Homer (13077) ***(G-6519)***
Homer Logging Contractor...607 753-8553
6176 Sunnyside Dr Homer (13077) ***(G-6520)***

ALPHABETIC

Homes Land Eastrn Long Island, Southampton *Also called Frontiers Unlimited Inc* ***(G-15543)***
Homesell Inc 718 514-0346
4010 Hylan Blvd Staten Island (10308) ***(G-15684)***
Homogeneous Metals Inc 315 839-5421
2395 Main St Clayville (13322) ***(G-3689)***
Honeoye Falls Distillery LLC (PA) 201 780-4618
168 W Main St Honeoye Falls (14472) ***(G-6531)***
Honeybee Rbtics Cft Mechanisms, Brooklyn *Also called Honeybee Robotics Ltd* ***(G-2087)***
Honeybee Robotics Ltd (PA) 212 966-0661
Suit Bldg 128 Brooklyn (11205) ***(G-2087)***
Honeywell Imaging and Mobility, Skaneateles Falls *Also called Hand Held Products Inc* ***(G-15468)***
Honeywell International Inc 518 270-0200
3 Tibbits Ave Troy (12183) ***(G-16220)***
Honeywell International Inc 315 554-6643
700 Visions Dr Skaneateles Falls (13153) ***(G-15470)***
Honeywell International Inc 845 342-4400
13 Bedford Ave Middletown (10940) ***(G-8445)***
Honeywell International Inc 212 964-5111
263 Old Country Rd Melville (11747) ***(G-8328)***
Honeywell International Inc 516 577-2000
2 Corporate Center Dr # 100 Melville (11747) ***(G-8329)***
Honeywell Scanning & Mobility, Skaneateles Falls *Also called Hand Held Products Inc* ***(G-15469)***
Hong Hop Co Inc 212 962-1735
10 Bowery New York (10013) ***(G-10502)***
Hong Hop Noodle Company, New York *Also called Hong Hop Co Inc* ***(G-10502)***
Honor Brand Feeds, Narrowsburg *Also called Narrowsburg Feed & Grain Co* ***(G-8768)***
Honora, New York *Also called Brannkey Inc* ***(G-9453)***
Hooek Produktion Inc 212 367-9111
147 W 26th St Fl 6 New York (10001) ***(G-10503)***
Hoosier Magnetics Inc 315 393-1813
110 Denny St Ogdensburg (13669) ***(G-13116)***
Hootz Family Bowling Inc 518 756-4668
100 Main St Ravena (12143) ***(G-14021)***
Hope International Productions 212 247-3188
315 W 57th St Apt 6h New York (10019) ***(G-10504)***
Hopes Windows Inc 716 665-5124
84 Hopkins Ave Jamestown (14701) ***(G-7000)***
Hopewell Precision Inc 845 221-2737
19 Ryan Rd Hopewell Junction (12533) ***(G-6552)***
Hopp Companies Inc 516 358-4170
815 2nd Ave New Hyde Park (11040) ***(G-8841)***
Hoptron Brewtique 631 438-0296
22 W Main St Ste 11 Patchogue (11772) ***(G-13422)***
Horace J Metz 716 873-9103
2385 Elmwood Ave Kenmore (14217) ***(G-7149)***
Horizon Apparel Mfg Inc 516 361-4878
115 Bayside Dr Atlantic Beach (11509) ***(G-469)***
Horizon Floors I LLC 212 509-9686
11 Broadway Lbby 5 New York (10004) ***(G-10505)***
Horizon Hosiery Mills, New York *Also called Horizon Imports Inc* ***(G-10506)***
Horizon Imports Inc 212 239-8660
10 W 33rd St Rm 606 New York (10001) ***(G-10506)***
Horizon Power Source LLC 877 240-0580
50 Glen St Glen Cove (11542) ***(G-5618)***
Horizons Magazine, Brooklyn *Also called Targum Press USA Inc* ***(G-2646)***
Horly Novelty Co Inc 212 226-4800
17 Ludlow St Frnt 2 New York (10002) ***(G-10507)***
Horne Organization Inc (PA) 914 572-1330
15 Arthur Pl Yonkers (10701) ***(G-17454)***
Horne Products Inc 631 293-0773
144 Verdi St Farmingdale (11735) ***(G-5007)***
Hornell Brewing Co Inc 914 597-7911
222 Bloomingdale Rd Ste 4 White Plains (10605) ***(G-17122)***
Horo Creations LLC 212 719-4818
71 W 47th St Ste 404 New York (10036) ***(G-10508)***
Horseheads Brewing Inc 607 734-8055
959 Lattabrook Rd Lowman (14861) ***(G-7934)***
Horseheads Printing, Horseheads *Also called David Helsing* ***(G-6573)***
Hosel & Ackerson Inc (PA) 212 575-1490
570 Fashion Ave Rm 805 New York (10018) ***(G-10509)***
Hoshizaki Nrtheastern Dist Ctr 516 605-1411
150 Dupont St Ste 100 Plainview (11803) ***(G-13604)***
Hoskie Co Inc 718 628-8672
132 Harrison Pl Brooklyn (11237) ***(G-2088)***
Hosmer Inc 888 467-9463
6999 State Route 89 Ovid (14521) ***(G-13346)***
Hosmer's Winery, Ovid *Also called Hosmer Inc* ***(G-13346)***
Hospira Inc 716 684-9400
2501 Walden Ave Buffalo (14225) ***(G-2997)***
Hospitality Graphics Inc 212 643-6700
545 8th Ave Rm 401 New York (10018) ***(G-10510)***
Hospitality Inc 212 268-1930
247 W 35th St 4 New York (10001) ***(G-10511)***
Hot Cashews, New York *Also called Just Bottoms & Tops Inc* ***(G-10791)***
Hot Kiss Inc 212 730-0404
1407 Brdwy Ste 2000 New York (10018) ***(G-10512)***
Hot Line Industries Inc (PA) 516 764-0400
28 South Mall Plainview (11803) ***(G-13605)***
Hot Shot Hk LLC 212 921-1111
1407 Broadway Rm 2018 New York (10018) ***(G-10513)***
Hot Sox Company Incorporated (PA) 212 957-2000
95 Madison Ave Fl 15 New York (10016) ***(G-10514)***
Hotel Business, Islandia *Also called Icd Publications Inc* ***(G-6796)***
Hotelexpert, New York *Also called Tyme Global Technologies LLC* ***(G-12437)***
Hotelinteractive Inc 631 424-7755
155 E Main St Ste 140 Smithtown (11787) ***(G-15488)***
Hotrock Ovens LLC 917 224-4342
886 Gusky Rd Red Hook (12571) ***(G-14029)***
Houghton Mifflin Clarion Books, New York *Also called Houghton Mifflin Harcourt Pubg* ***(G-10515)***
Houghton Mifflin Harcourt Pubg 212 420-5800
3 Park Ave Fl 18 New York (10016) ***(G-10515)***
Houghton Mifflin Harcourt Pubg 914 747-2709
28 Claremont Ave Thornwood (10594) ***(G-16121)***
Houles USA Inc 212 935-3900
979 3rd Ave Ste 1200 New York (10022) ***(G-10516)***
Hound & Gatos Pet Foods Corp 212 618-1917
14 Wall St Fl 20 New York (10005) ***(G-10517)***
House O'Weenies, Bronx *Also called Marathon Enterprises Inc* ***(G-1385)***
House of Heydenryk Jr Inc 212 206-9611
601 W 26th St Rm 305 New York (10001) ***(G-10518)***
House of Heydenryk The, New York *Also called House of Heydenryk Jr Inc* ***(G-10518)***
House of Portfolios Co Inc (PA) 212 206-7323
133 W 25th St Rm 7w New York (10001) ***(G-10519)***
House of Portfolios Co Inc 212 206-7323
48 W 21st St New York (10010) ***(G-10520)***
House of Stone Inc 845 782-7271
1015 State Route 17m Monroe (10950) ***(G-8556)***
House of Tarling, New York *Also called Siegfrieds Basement Inc* ***(G-12061)***
House of The Foaming Case Inc 718 454-0101
110 08 Dunkirk St Saint Albans (11412) ***(G-15083)***
House Pearl Fashions (us) Ltd 212 840-3183
1410 Broadway Rm 1501 New York (10018) ***(G-10521)***
Hovee Inc 646 249-6200
722 Saint Nicholas Ave New York (10031) ***(G-10522)***
Hover-Davis Inc (HQ) 585 352-9590
100 Paragon Dr Rochester (14624) ***(G-14439)***
Howard Charles Inc 917 902-6934
180 Froehlich Farm Blvd Woodbury (11797) ***(G-17290)***
Howard Formed Steel Pdts Div, Bronx *Also called Truxton Corp* ***(G-1480)***
Howard J Moore Company Inc 631 351-8467
210 Terminal Dr Ste B Plainview (11803) ***(G-13606)***
Howden Fan Company, Depew *Also called Howden North America Inc* ***(G-4260)***
Howden North America Inc (HQ) 803 741-2700
2475 George Urban Blvd # 100 Depew (14043) ***(G-4259)***
Howden North America Inc 716 817-6900
2475 George Urban Blvd # 100 Depew (14043) ***(G-4260)***
Howdens, Depew *Also called Howden North America Inc* ***(G-4259)***
Howe Machine & Tool Corp 516 931-5687
236 Park Ave Bethpage (11714) ***(G-868)***
Howell Packaging, Elmira *Also called F M Howell & Company* ***(G-4684)***
Howmedica Osteonics Corp 518 783-1880
2 Northway Ln Latham (12110) ***(G-7364)***
HP Hood LLC 607 295-8134
25 Hurlbut St Arkport (14807) ***(G-410)***
HP Hood LLC 315 363-3870
252 Genesee St Oneida (13421) ***(G-13157)***
HP Hood LLC 315 658-2132
20700 State Route 411 La Fargeville (13656) ***(G-7236)***
HP Hood LLC 518 218-9097
9 Norman Dr Albany (12205) ***(G-89)***
HP Hood LLC 315 829-3339
19 Ward St Vernon (13476) ***(G-16435)***
HP Hood LLC 607 772-6580
93 Pennsylvania Ave Binghamton (13903) ***(G-922)***
HP Inc 212 835-1640
5 Penn Plz Ste 1912 New York (10001) ***(G-10523)***
Hpi Co Inc (PA) 718 851-2753
1656 41st St Brooklyn (11218) ***(G-2089)***
Hpk Industries LLC 315 724-0196
1208 Broad St Utica (13501) ***(G-16338)***
HRA Poster Project, Brooklyn *Also called City of New York* ***(G-1782)***
Hrd Metal Products Inc 631 243-6700
120 E Jefryn Blvd Ste A Deer Park (11729) ***(G-4151)***
Hrg Group Inc (PA) 212 906-8555
450 Park Ave Fl 29 New York (10022) ***(G-10524)***
Hs Associates Corp 516 496-2940
290 Vista Dr Jericho (11753) ***(G-7071)***
HSM Machine Works Inc (PA) 631 924-6600
3671 Horseblock Rd Medford (11763) ***(G-8250)***
HSM Packaging Corporation 315 476-7996
4529 Crown Rd Liverpool (13090) ***(G-7523)***
HSN, New York *Also called Macfadden Cmmnctions Group LLC* ***(G-11083)***
Htf Components Inc 914 703-6795
134 Bowbell Rd White Plains (10607) ***(G-17123)***
Hub Surgical & Orthopedic Sups (PA) 718 585-5415
288 E 149th St Frnt A Bronx (10451) ***(G-1358)***
Hubbard Tool and Die Corp 315 337-7840
Rome Indus Ctr Bldg 5 Rome (13440) ***(G-14815)***

Hubbell Galvanising, Yorkville *Also called O W Hubbell & Sons Inc* ***(G-17523)***
Hubco Inc 716 683-5940
2885 Commerce Dr Alden (14004) ***(G-179)***
Hubray Inc 800 645-2855
2045 Grand Ave North Baldwin (11510) ***(G-12907)***
Huck International Inc 845 331-7300
1 Corporate Dr Kingston (12401) ***(G-7191)***
Huckleberry Inc 631 630-5450
655 Old Willets Path Hauppauge (11788) ***(G-6096)***
Huda Kawshai LLC 929 255-7009
8514 168th St Ste 3 Jamaica (11432) ***(G-6920)***
Hudson Dying & Finishing LLC 518 752-4389
68 Harrison St Gloversville (12078) ***(G-5716)***
Hudson Energy Services LLC (PA) 630 300-0013
4 Executive Blvd Ste 301 Suffern (10901) ***(G-15791)***
Hudson Envelope Corporation (PA) 212 473-6666
135 3rd Ave New York (10003) ***(G-10525)***
Hudson Fabrics LLC 518 671-6100
128 2nd Street Ext Hudson (12534) ***(G-6617)***
Hudson Industries Corporation 518 762-4638
100 Maple Ave Johnstown (12095) ***(G-7115)***
Hudson Machine Works Inc 845 279-1413
30 Branch Rd Brewster (10509) ***(G-1221)***
Hudson Mirror LLC 914 930-8906
710 Washington St Peekskill (10566) ***(G-13479)***
Hudson Park Press Inc 212 929-8898
232 Madison Ave Rm 1400 New York (10016) ***(G-10526)***
Hudson Power Transmission Co 718 622-3869
241 Halsey St Brooklyn (11216) ***(G-2090)***
Hudson Printing Co Inc 718 937-8600
747 3rd Ave Lbby 3 New York (10017) ***(G-10527)***
Hudson River Met Detector Sls, Pleasant Valley *Also called Detector Pro* ***(G-13711)***
Hudson Scenic Studio Inc (PA) 914 375-0900
130 Fernbrook St Yonkers (10705) ***(G-17455)***
Hudson Software Corporation 914 773-0400
3 W Main St Ste 106 Elmsford (10523) ***(G-4755)***
Hudson Steel Fabricators 585 454-3923
444 Hudson Ave Rochester (14605) ***(G-14440)***
Hudson Technologies Company (PA) 845 735-6000
1 Blue Hill Plz Ste 1541 Pearl River (10965) ***(G-13459)***
Hudson Valley Apple Products, Milton *Also called Brooklyn Btlg Milton NY Inc* ***(G-8482)***
Hudson Valley Baking Co, Mamaroneck *Also called Richard Engdal Baking Corp* ***(G-8044)***
Hudson Valley Black Press 845 562-1313
343 Broadway Newburgh (12550) ***(G-12762)***
Hudson Valley Chocolatier Inc (PA) 845 831-8240
269 Main St Beacon (12508) ***(G-785)***
Hudson Valley Coatings LLC 845 398-1778
175 N Route 9w Ste 12 Congers (10920) ***(G-3857)***
Hudson Valley Creamery LLC 518 851-2570
2986 Us Route 9 Hudson (12534) ***(G-6618)***
Hudson Valley Foie Gras LLC 845 292-2500
80 Brooks Rd Ferndale (12734) ***(G-5171)***
Hudson Valley Lighting Inc 845 561-0300
151 Airport Dr Wappingers Falls (12590) ***(G-16573)***
Hudson Valley Magazine, Poughkeepsie *Also called Suburban Publishing Inc* ***(G-13936)***
Hudson Valley Office Furn Inc 845 565-6673
7 Wisner Ave Newburgh (12550) ***(G-12763)***
Hudson Valley Paper Works Inc 845 569-8883
8 Lander St 15 Newburgh (12550) ***(G-12764)***
Huersch Marketing Group LLC 518 874-1045
70 Cohoes Ave Ste 4 Green Island (12183) ***(G-5857)***
Huffington Post, The, New York *Also called Thehuffingtonpostcom Inc* ***(G-12311)***
Hugh F McPherson Inc 716 668-6107
70 Innsbruck Dr Cheektowaga (14227) ***(G-3575)***
Hughes-Treitler, Garden City *Also called Ametek Inc* ***(G-5494)***
Hugo Boss Usa Inc (HQ) 212 940-0600
55 Water St Fl 48 New York (10041) ***(G-10528)***
Huhtamaki Inc 315 593-5311
100 State St Fulton (13069) ***(G-5461)***
Human Electronics Inc 315 724-9850
155 Genesee St Utica (13501) ***(G-16339)***
Human Life Foundation Inc 212 685-5210
353 Lexington Ave Rm 802 New York (10016) ***(G-10529)***
Human Technologies Corporation 315 735-3532
2260 Dwyer Ave Utica (13501) ***(G-16340)***
Humana Press Inc 212 460-1500
233 Spring St Fl 6 New York (10013) ***(G-10530)***
Humanscale Corporation (PA) 212 725-4749
11 E 26th St Fl 8 New York (10010) ***(G-10531)***
Humanware USA Inc (PA) 800 722-3393
1 Ups Way Champlain (12919) ***(G-3542)***
Humor Rainbow Incorporated 646 402-9113
129 W 29th St Fl 10 New York (10001) ***(G-10532)***
Hunt Country Furniture Inc (PA) 845 832-6601
19 Dog Tail Corners Rd Wingdale (12594) ***(G-17274)***
Hunt Country Vineyards 315 595-2812
4021 Italy Hill Rd Branchport (14418) ***(G-1172)***
Hunt Graphics Inc 631 751-5349
43 Pineview Ln Coram (11727) ***(G-3944)***
Hunter Displays, East Patchogue *Also called Hunter Metal Industries Inc* ***(G-4448)***
Hunter Douglas Inc (HQ) 845 664-7000
1 Blue Hill Plz Ste 1569 Pearl River (10965) ***(G-13460)***
Hunter Douglas Inc 212 588-0564
979 3rd Ave New York (10022) ***(G-10533)***
Hunter Machine Inc 585 924-7480
6551 Anthony Dr Victor (14564) ***(G-16481)***
Hunter Metal Industries Inc 631 475-5900
14 Hewlett Ave East Patchogue (11772) ***(G-4448)***
Hunter Panels LLC 386 753-0786
9 Hudson Crossing Dr Montgomery (12549) ***(G-8595)***
Huntington Ice & Cube Corp (PA) 718 456-2013
335 Moffat St Brooklyn (11237) ***(G-2091)***
Huntington Ingalls Inc 518 884-3834
33 Cady Hill Blvd Saratoga Springs (12866) ***(G-15159)***
Huntington Services Inc 516 795-8500
727 N Broadway Ste A4 Massapequa (11758) ***(G-8179)***
Huntington Welding & Iron 631 423-3331
139 W Pulaski Rd Huntington Station (11746) ***(G-6709)***
Huron Tl & Cutter Grinding Co 631 420-7000
2045 Wellwood Ave Farmingdale (11735) ***(G-5008)***
Hurryworks LLC 516 998-4600
990 Seaview Blvd Port Washington (11050) ***(G-13822)***
Hustler Powerboats, Calverton *Also called Global Marine Power Inc* ***(G-3291)***
Hutchinson Industries Inc 716 852-1435
92 Msgr Valente Dr Buffalo (14206) ***(G-2998)***
Hutnick Rehab, Bohemia *Also called Gfh Orthotic & Prosthetic Labs* ***(G-1072)***
Hvr Advnced Pwr Components Inc 716 693-4700
2090 Old Union Rd Cheektowaga (14227) ***(G-3576)***
Hw Holdings Inc (HQ) 212 399-1000
718 5th Ave New York (10019) ***(G-10534)***
Hw Specialties Co Inc 631 589-0745
210 Knickerbocker Ave B Bohemia (11716) ***(G-1075)***
Hy Gold Jewelers Inc 212 744-3202
1070 Madison Ave Frnt 4 New York (10028) ***(G-10535)***
Hy-Grade Metal Products Corp 315 475-4221
906 Burnet Ave Syracuse (13203) ***(G-15961)***
Hy-Tech Mold Inc 585 247-2450
60 Elmgrove Park Rochester (14624) ***(G-14441)***
Hyatt Times Square New York 212 398-2158
135 W 45th St New York (10036) ***(G-10536)***
Hybrid Cases, Holbrook *Also called Roadie Products Inc* ***(G-6468)***
Hyde Park, Poughkeepsie *Also called Architectural Dctg Co LLC* ***(G-13888)***
Hyde Park Brewing Co Inc 845 229-8277
4076 Albany Post Rd Hyde Park (12538) ***(G-6734)***
Hydra Technology Corp 716 896-8316
179 Grider St Buffalo (14215) ***(G-2999)***
Hydramec Inc 585 593-5190
4393 River St Scio (14880) ***(G-15321)***
Hydrive Energy 914 925-9100
350 Theodore Fremd Ave Rye (10580) ***(G-15060)***
Hydro-Air Components Inc 716 827-6510
100 Rittling Blvd Buffalo (14220) ***(G-3000)***
Hydroacoustics Inc 585 359-1000
999 Lehigh Station Rd # 100 Henrietta (14467) ***(G-6294)***
Hygrade Fuel Inc 516 741-0723
260 Columbus Pkwy Mineola (11501) ***(G-8514)***
Hyman Podrusnick Co Inc 718 853-4502
212 Foster Ave Brooklyn (11230) ***(G-2092)***
Hyperbaric Technologies Inc 518 842-3030
1 Sam Stratton Rd Amsterdam (12010) ***(G-350)***
Hyperlaw Inc 212 873-6982
17 W 70th St Apt 4 New York (10023) ***(G-10537)***
Hypoxico Inc 212 972-1009
50 Lexington Ave Ste 249 New York (10010) ***(G-10538)***
Hypres Inc 914 592-1190
175 Clearbrook Rd Elmsford (10523) ***(G-4756)***
Hytech Tool & Die Inc 716 488-2796
2202 Washington St Jamestown (14701) ***(G-7001)***
I & I Systems 845 753-9126
66 Table Rock Rd Tuxedo Park (10987) ***(G-16283)***
I & S of NY Inc 716 373-7001
4174 Route 417 Allegany (14706) ***(G-202)***
I 2 Print Inc 718 937-8800
3819 24th St Long Island City (11101) ***(G-7762)***
I A Construction Corporation 716 933-8787
Rr 305 Box S Portville (14770) ***(G-13875)***
I A S National Inc 631 423-6900
95 W Hills Rd Huntington Station (11746) ***(G-6710)***
I ABC Corporation 315 639-3100
349 Lakeview Dr Dexter (13634) ***(G-4286)***
I C M, Woodside *Also called International Creative Met Inc* ***(G-17333)***
I C S, New York *Also called Integrated Graphics Inc* ***(G-10616)***
I D E Processes Corporation (PA) 718 544-1177
106 81st Ave Kew Gardens (11415) ***(G-7161)***
I D Machine Inc 607 796-2549
1580 Lake St Elmira (14901) ***(G-4692)***
I D Tel Corp 718 876-6000
55 Canal St Staten Island (10304) ***(G-15685)***
I Do Machining, Elmira *Also called I D Machine Inc* ***(G-4692)***
I E D Corp 631 348-0424
88 Bridge Rd Islandia (11749) ***(G-6795)***
I E M, Troy *Also called Interntnal Elctronic Mchs Corp* ***(G-16241)***
I F I, Ronkonkoma *Also called Instruments For Industry Inc* ***(G-14913)***

ALPHABETIC

ALPHABETIC SECTION

I Fix Screen 631 421-1938
  203 Centereach Mall Centereach (11720) *(G-3471)*
I J White Corporation 631 293-3788
  20 Executive Blvd Farmingdale (11735) *(G-5009)*
I L C, Bohemia Also called Ilc Industries LLC *(G-1077)*
I Love Accessories Inc 212 239-1875
  10 W 33rd St Rm 210 New York (10001) *(G-10539)*
I Meglio Corp 631 617-6900
  151 Alkier St Brentwood (11717) *(G-1184)*
I N K T Inc 212 957-2700
  250 W 54th St Fl 9 New York (10019) *(G-10540)*
I On Youth 716 832-6509
  115 Godfrey St Buffalo (14215) *(G-3001)*
I P A, Woodstock Also called Innovative Pdts of Amer Inc *(G-17363)*
I R M, Plainview Also called Aufhauser Corporation *(G-13584)*
I Rauchs Sons Inc 718 507-8844
  3220 112th St East Elmhurst (11369) *(G-4392)*
I S C A Corp (HQ) 212 719-5123
  512 7th Ave Fl 7 New York (10018) *(G-10541)*
I Spiewak & Sons Inc 212 695-1620
  225 W 37th St Fl 15l New York (10018) *(G-10542)*
I Trade Technology Ltd 615 348-7233
  400 Rella Blvd Ste 165 Suffern (10901) *(G-15792)*
I Triple E Spectrum, New York Also called Magazine I Spectrum E *(G-11098)*
I W Industries Inc (PA) 631 293-9494
  35 Melville Park Rd Melville (11747) *(G-8330)*
I W M, Dryden Also called Integrated Water Management *(G-4321)*
I'M Nuts, Hewlett Also called Yes Were Nuts Ltd *(G-6317)*
I-Evolve Techonology Services (PA) 801 566-5268
  501 John James Audubon Pk Amherst (14228) *(G-245)*
I3 Assemblies Inc 607 238-7077
  100 Eldredge St Binghamton (13901) *(G-923)*
I3 Cable & Harness LLC 607 238-7077
  100 Eldredge St Binghamton (13901) *(G-924)*
I3 Electronics Inc (PA) 866 820-4820
  1701 North St Endicott (13760) *(G-4811)*
I3 Electronics Inc 866 820-4820
  Mdc Bldg 48 Odell Ave Endicott (13760) *(G-4812)*
Iaas , The, Flushing Also called Intercultural Alliance Artists *(G-5253)*
IAC Search LLC (HQ) 212 314-7300
  555 W 18th St New York (10011) *(G-10543)*
Iac/Interactivecorp (PA) 212 314-7300
  555 W 18th St New York (10011) *(G-10544)*
Iadc Inc 718 238-0623
  845 Father Capodanno Blvd Staten Island (10305) *(G-15686)*
Iahcp Inc 631 650-2499
  181 Freeman Ave Unit C Islip (11751) *(G-6809)*
IaM Maliamills LLC 805 845-2137
  32 33rd St Unit 13 Brooklyn (11232) *(G-2093)*
Iat Interactive LLC 914 273-2233
  333 N Bedford Rd Ste 110 Mount Kisco (10549) *(G-8628)*
Iba Industrial Inc 631 254-6800
  151 Heartland Blvd Edgewood (11717) *(G-4600)*
IBC/ Worldwide, New Hyde Park Also called Interntnal Bus Cmmncations Inc *(G-8842)*
Iberia Foods Corp (HQ) 718 272-8900
  1900 Linden Blvd Brooklyn (11207) *(G-2094)*
Ibio Inc 302 355-0650
  600 Madison Ave Ste 1601 New York (10022) *(G-10545)*
IBIt Inc 212 768-0292
  257 W 38th St Fl 2 New York (10018) *(G-10546)*
IBM, Endicott Also called International Bus Mchs Corp *(G-4813)*
IBM, New York Also called International Bus Mchs Corp *(G-10631)*
IBM, Armonk Also called International Bus Mchs Corp *(G-414)*
IBM, Poughkeepsie Also called International Bus Mchs Corp *(G-13907)*
IBM, Hopewell Junction Also called International Bus Mchs Corp *(G-6554)*
IBM, Armonk Also called International Bus Mchs Corp *(G-415)*
IBM World Trade Corporation (HQ) 914 765-1900
  1 New Orchard Rd Ste 1 Armonk (10504) *(G-413)*
Ibrands International LLC 212 354-1330
  230 W 39th St New York (10018) *(G-10547)*
Ibt Media Inc (PA) 646 867-7100
  7 Hanover Sq Fl 5 New York (10004) *(G-10548)*
Ic Optics, New Hyde Park Also called Colors In Optics Ltd *(G-8822)*
Ic Technologies LLC 212 966-7895
  475 Greenwich St New York (10013) *(G-10549)*
Icahn, New York Also called Ieh FM Holdings LLC *(G-10559)*
Icarus Enterprises Inc 917 969-4461
  568 Broadway Fl 11 New York (10012) *(G-10550)*
Icd Publications Inc (PA) 631 246-9300
  1377 Motor Pkwy Ste 410 Islandia (11749) *(G-6796)*
Ice Air LLC 914 668-4700
  80 Hartford Ave Mount Vernon (10553) *(G-8692)*
Ice Box Water, Cold Spring Harbor Also called Water Resources Group LLC *(G-3771)*
Ice Cream Man Inc 518 692-8382
  417 State Route 29 Greenwich (12834) *(G-5890)*
Icell Inc 516 590-0007
  133 Fulton Ave Hempstead (11550) *(G-6274)*
Icer Scrubs LLC 212 221-4700
  1385 Broadway Fl 16 New York (10018) *(G-10551)*
Icer Sports LLC 212 221-4700
  1385 Broadway Fl 16 New York (10018) *(G-10552)*
Ices Queen, Brooklyn Also called Primo Frozen Desserts Inc *(G-2442)*
Icestone LLC 718 624-4900
  63 Flushing Ave Unit 283b Brooklyn (11205) *(G-2095)*
ICM, North Syracuse Also called Interntnal Cntrls Msrmnts Corp *(G-12948)*
ICM Controls Corp 315 233-5266
  7313 William Barry Blvd North Syracuse (13212) *(G-12947)*
Icommunicator, Brooklyn Also called Ppr Direct Inc *(G-2432)*
Icon Design LLC 585 768-6040
  9 Lent Ave Le Roy (14482) *(G-7409)*
Icon Enterprises Intl Inc 718 752-9764
  5025 35th St Long Island City (11101) *(G-7763)*
Icon-TV, Long Island City Also called Icon Enterprises Intl Inc *(G-7763)*
Iconix Inc 516 307-1324
  315 Roslyn Rd Mineola (11501) *(G-8515)*
ICP, West Seneca Also called International Control Products *(G-16949)*
ICP, Depew Also called Pcb Group Inc *(G-4268)*
Icpme-Ithaca Center, Ithaca Also called International Center For Postg *(G-6851)*
Ics Penetron International Ltd 631 928-8282
  45 Research Way Ste 203 East Setauket (11733) *(G-4485)*
Icy Hot Lingerie, New York Also called Sensual Inc *(G-12030)*
ID Signsystems Inc 585 266-5750
  410 Atlantic Ave Ste 401 Rochester (14609) *(G-14442)*
Idalia Solar Technologies LLC 212 792-3913
  270 Lafayette St Ste 1402 New York (10012) *(G-10553)*
Idc, West Babylon Also called Isolation Dynamics Corp *(G-16795)*
Idc Printing & Sty Co Inc (PA) 516 599-0400
  536 Merrick Rd Lynbrook (11563) *(G-7951)*
Ideal Brilliant Co Inc 212 840-2044
  580 5th Ave Ste 600 New York (10036) *(G-10554)*
Ideal Burial Vault Company 585 599-2242
  1166 Vision Pkwy Corfu (14036) *(G-3955)*
Ideal Creations Inc 212 563-5928
  10 W 33rd St Rm 708 New York (10001) *(G-10555)*
Ideal Manufacturing Inc 585 872-7190
  80 Bluff Dr East Rochester (14445) *(G-4462)*
Ideal Signs Inc 718 292-9196
  538 Wales Ave Bronx (10455) *(G-1359)*
Ideal Snacks Corporation 845 292-7000
  89 Mill St Liberty (12754) *(G-7437)*
Ideal Stair Parts, Little Falls Also called Ideal Wood Products Inc *(G-7501)*
Ideal Wood Products Inc 315 823-1124
  225 W Main St Little Falls (13365) *(G-7501)*
Ideas International Inc 914 937-4302
  800 Westchester Ave # 337 Rye Brook (10573) *(G-15071)*
Identfication Data Imaging LLC 516 484-6500
  26 Harbor Park Dr Port Washington (11050) *(G-13823)*
Identifycom Inc 212 235-0000
  120 W 45th St Ste 2701 New York (10036) *(G-10556)*
Identity Ink & Custom Tee, Kenmore Also called Herrmann Group LLC *(G-7148)*
Idesco Corp 212 889-2530
  37 W 26th St Fl 10 New York (10010) *(G-10557)*
Idex Corporation 585 292-8121
  2883 Brghtn Hnretta Tl Rd Rochester (14623) *(G-14443)*
Idg, New York Also called International Direct Group Inc *(G-10634)*
Idg LLC 315 797-1000
  31 Faass Ave Utica (13502) *(G-16341)*
Idg Technetwork, New York Also called International Data Group Inc *(G-10632)*
IDI, Port Washington Also called Identfication Data Imaging LLC *(G-13823)*
Idl, Ronkonkoma Also called Ingenious Designs LLC *(G-14912)*
Idonethis, New York Also called West Internet Trading Company *(G-12612)*
Idra Alta Moda LLC 914 644-8202
  200 West St 305 New York (10282) *(G-10558)*
Idt Energy Inc 877 887-6866
  315 N Main St Ste 300 Jamestown (14701) *(G-7002)*
IEC Electronics Corp (PA) 315 331-7742
  105 Norton St Newark (14513) *(G-12732)*
IEC Electronics Corp 585 647-1760
  1365 Emerson St Rochester (14606) *(G-14444)*
IEC Electronics Wire Cable Inc 585 924-9010
  105 Norton St Newark (14513) *(G-12733)*
IEC Holden Corporation 518 213-3991
  51 Distribution Way Plattsburgh (12901) *(G-13670)*
Ieh Corporation 718 492-4440
  140 58th St Ste 8e Brooklyn (11220) *(G-2096)*
Ieh FM Holdings LLC (HQ) 212 702-4300
  767 5th Ave Ste 4700 New York (10153) *(G-10559)*
Iet Labs Inc (PA) 516 334-5959
  1 Expressway Plz Ste 120 Roslyn Heights (11577) *(G-15027)*
Iff, New York Also called Interntnal Flvors Frgrnces Inc *(G-10639)*
Iff International Inc 212 765-5500
  521 W 57th St Fl 9 New York (10019) *(G-10560)*
Ifg Corp 212 629-9600
  1372 Brdwy 12ae 12 Ae New York (10018) *(G-10561)*
Ifg Corp 212 239-8615
  463 7th Ave Fl 4 New York (10018) *(G-10562)*
Igc New York Inc 212 764-0949
  580 5th Ave Ste 708 New York (10036) *(G-10563)*

Ignelzi Interiors Inc....718 464-0279
9805 217th St Queens Village (11429) **(G-13979)**
Igniter Systems Inc....716 542-5511
12600 Clarence Center Rd Akron (14001) **(G-24)**
Igt Global Solutions Corp....518 382-2900
1 Broadway Ctr Fl 2 Schenectady (12305) **(G-15269)**
Ihd Motorsports LLC....979 690-1669
1152 Upper Front St Binghamton (13905) **(G-925)**
Iheartcommunications Inc....585 454-4884
100 Chestnut St Ste 1700 Rochester (14604) **(G-14445)**
Iheartcommunications Inc....212 603-4660
1133 Ave Of Amricas Fl 34 New York (10036) **(G-10564)**
Iimak, Amherst *Also called International Imaging Mtls Inc* **(G-246)**
Ikeddi Enterprises Inc (PA)....212 302-7644
1407 Brdwy Ste 2900 New York (10018) **(G-10565)**
Ikeddi Enterprises Inc....212 302-7644
1407 Broadway Rm 1805 New York (10018) **(G-10566)**
Ilab America Inc....631 615-5053
45 Hemlock St Selden (11784) **(G-15352)**
Ilc Holdings Inc (HQ)....631 567-5600
105 Wilbur Pl Bohemia (11716) **(G-1076)**
Ilc Industries LLC (HQ)....631 567-5600
105 Wilbur Pl Bohemia (11716) **(G-1077)**
Ilex Consumer Pdts Group LLC....410 897-0701
323 W Camden St Ste 700 Irvington (10533) **(G-6772)**
Ilico Jewelry Inc....516 482-0201
98 Cuttermill Rd Ste 396 Great Neck (11021) **(G-5815)**
Ilion Plastics Inc....315 894-4868
27 Pleasant Ave Ilion (13357) **(G-6741)**
Illinois Tool Works Inc....860 435-2574
5979 N Elm Ave Millerton (12546) **(G-8479)**
Illinois Tool Works Inc....716 681-8222
4471 Walden Ave Lancaster (14086) **(G-7320)**
Illinois Tool Works Inc....607 770-4945
33 Lewis Rd Binghamton (13905) **(G-926)**
Illumination Technologies Inc....315 463-4673
5 Adler Dr East Syracuse (13057) **(G-4538)**
Iluv, Port Washington *Also called Jwin Electronics Corp* **(G-13831)**
Ima Life North America Inc....716 695-6354
2175 Military Rd Tonawanda (14150) **(G-16173)**
Imacor Inc....516 393-0970
821 Franklin Ave Ste 301 Garden City (11530) **(G-5509)**
Image Iron Works Inc....718 592-8276
5050 98th St Corona (11368) **(G-3998)**
Image Press, The, Cicero *Also called Add Associates Inc* **(G-3641)**
Image Sales & Marketing Inc....516 238-7023
106 Thornwood Rd Massapequa Park (11762) **(G-8186)**
Image Specialists Inc....631 475-0867
80 Elderwood Dr Saint James (11780) **(G-15090)**
Image Tech....716 635-0167
96 Donna Lea Blvd Buffalo (14221) **(G-3002)**
Image Typography Inc....631 218-6932
751 Coates Ave Ste 31 Holbrook (11741) **(G-6450)**
Image360....585 272-1234
275 Marketplace Dr Rochester (14623) **(G-14446)**
Imaginant Inc....585 264-0480
3800 Monroe Ave Ste 29 Pittsford (14534) **(G-13564)**
Imagination Playground LLC....212 463-0334
5 Union Sq W New York (10003) **(G-10567)**
Imagine Communications Corp....212 303-4200
1 Penn Plz Fl 39 New York (10119) **(G-10568)**
Imaging and Sensing Technology, Horseheads *Also called Mirion Technologies Ist Corp* **(G-6584)**
Imago Recording Company (PA)....212 751-3033
240 E 47th St Apt 20f New York (10017) **(G-10569)**
IMC Teddy Food Service....631 789-8881
50 Ranick Dr E Amityville (11701) **(G-295)**
Imco Inc....585 352-7810
15 Turner Dr Spencerport (14559) **(G-15570)**
Imek Media LLC....212 422-9000
32 Broadway Ste 511 New York (10004) **(G-10570)**
Imena Jewelry Manufacturer Inc....212 827-0073
2 W 45th St Ste 1000 New York (10036) **(G-10571)**
Imerys Fsed Mnrl Ngara FLS Inc....716 286-1234
3455 Hyde Park Blvd Niagara Falls (14305) **(G-12833)**
Imerys Fsed Mnrl Ngara FLS Inc (HQ)....716 286-1250
2000 College Ave Niagara Falls (14305) **(G-12834)**
Imerys Steelcasting Usa Inc (HQ)....716 278-1634
4111 Witmer Rd Niagara Falls (14305) **(G-12835)**
Imerys Usa Inc....315 287-0780
16a Main St Hailesboro Rd Gouverneur (13642) **(G-5746)**
IMG The Daily....212 541-5640
432 W 45th St Fl 5 New York (10036) **(G-10572)**
Immco Diagnostics Inc....716 691-6955
640 Ellicott St Fl 3 Buffalo (14203) **(G-3003)**
Immco Diagnostics Inc (HQ)....716 691-6911
60 Pineview Dr Buffalo (14228) **(G-3004)**
Immudyne Inc....914 244-1777
50 Spring Meadow Rd Mount Kisco (10549) **(G-8629)**
Immune Pharmaceuticals Inc (PA)....646 440-9310
430 E 29th St Ste 940 New York (10016) **(G-10573)**
Impact Tech A Skrsky Innvtions, Rochester *Also called Sikorsky Aircraft Corporation* **(G-14687)**
Impala Press Ltd....631 588-4262
931 S 2nd St Ronkonkoma (11779) **(G-14911)**
Imperia Masonry Supply Corp (PA)....914 738-0900
57 Canal Rd Pelham (10803) **(G-13492)**
Imperial Color, Brentwood *Also called Lauricella Press Inc* **(G-1189)**
Imperial Damper & Louver Co....718 731-3800
907 E 141st St Bronx (10454) **(G-1360)**
Imperial Frames & Albums LLC....718 832-9793
8200 21st Ave Brooklyn (11214) **(G-2097)**
Imperial Instrmnt & Mach, Westbury *Also called Imperial Instrument Corp* **(G-16995)**
Imperial Instrument Corp....516 739-6644
18 Sylvester St Westbury (11590) **(G-16995)**
Imperial Laminators Co Inc....718 272-9500
961 Elton St Brooklyn (11208) **(G-2098)**
Imperial Polymers Inc....718 387-4741
534 Grand St Brooklyn (11211) **(G-2099)**
Imperial Pools Inc (PA)....518 786-1200
33 Wade Rd Latham (12110) **(G-7365)**
Imperial Sweater Mills Inc....718 871-4414
1365 38th St Brooklyn (11218) **(G-2100)**
Imperial-Harvard Label Co....212 736-8420
225 W 35th St Ste 1102 New York (10001) **(G-10574)**
Impladent Ltd (PA)....718 465-1810
19845 Foothill Ave Jamaica (11423) **(G-6921)**
Import-Export Corporation....718 707-0880
3814 30th St Long Island City (11101) **(G-7764)**
Impremedia LLC (HQ)....212 807-4785
1 Metrotech Ctr Fl 18 Brooklyn (11201) **(G-2101)**
Impress Graphic Technologies....516 781-0845
141 Linden Ave Westbury (11590) **(G-16996)**
Impressions Inc....212 594-5954
36 W 37th St Rm 400 New York (10018) **(G-10575)**
Impressions International Inc....585 442-5240
1255 University Ave # 150 Rochester (14607) **(G-14447)**
Impressions Prtg & Graphics, New York *Also called Designlogocom Inc* **(G-9856)**
Impressive Imprints....716 692-0905
601 Division St North Tonawanda (14120) **(G-12977)**
Impressive Imprints Inc....631 293-6161
195 Central Ave Ste N Farmingdale (11735) **(G-5010)**
Imprinted Sportswear, Camillus *Also called Steve Poli Sales* **(G-3324)**
IMR Test Labs, Lansing *Also called Metal Improvement Company LLC* **(G-7349)**
Imrex LLC (PA)....516 479-3675
55 Sandy Hill Rd Oyster Bay (11771) **(G-13370)**
Imtech At Avon, New York *Also called Imtech Graphics Inc* **(G-10576)**
Imtech Graphics Inc....212 282-7010
1251 Avenue Of The Americ New York (10020) **(G-10576)**
In Mocean Group LLC (PA)....732 960-2415
501 Fashion Ave Fl 12 New York (10018) **(G-10577)**
In Moda com Inc....718 788-4466
241 W 37th St Rm 803 New York (10018) **(G-10578)**
In Northeast Precision Welding....518 441-2260
1177 Route 9 Castleton On Hudson (12033) **(G-3418)**
In Room Plus Inc....716 838-9433
2495 Main St Ste 217 Buffalo (14214) **(G-3005)**
In The Crease, Penn Yan *Also called Warrior Sports Inc* **(G-13523)**
In Toon Amkor Fashions Inc....718 937-4546
4809 34th St Long Island City (11101) **(G-7765)**
In-House Inc....718 445-9007
1535 126th St Ste 3 College Point (11356) **(G-3787)**
In-Step Marketing Inc (PA)....212 797-3450
39 Broadway Fl 32 New York (10006) **(G-10579)**
Inboxmind LLC....646 773-7726
1 Penn Plz Fl 36th New York (10119) **(G-10580)**
Incentivate Health LLC....518 469-8491
60 Railroad Pl Ste 101 Saratoga Springs (12866) **(G-15160)**
Incisive Rwg Inc....212 457-9400
55 Broad St Fl 22 New York (10004) **(G-10581)**
Incitec Pivot Limited....212 238-3010
120 Broadway Fl 32 New York (10271) **(G-10582)**
Incodema Inc....607 277-7070
407 Cliff St Ithaca (14850) **(G-6848)**
Incodema3d LLC....607 269-4390
407 Cliff St Ithaca (14850) **(G-6849)**
Incon Gems Inc....212 221-8560
2 W 46th St Ste 603 New York (10036) **(G-10583)**
Incorporated Village Garden Cy....516 465-4020
103 11th St Garden City (11530) **(G-5510)**
Incredible Scents Inc....516 656-3300
1009 Glen Cove Ave Ste 6 Glen Head (11545) **(G-5634)**
Incycle Software Corp (PA)....212 626-2608
1120 Ave Of The Americas New York (10036) **(G-10584)**
Ind Rev LLC....212 221-4700
1385 Broadway Fl 16 New York (10018) **(G-10585)**
Indegy Inc....866 801-5394
154 Grand St New York (10013) **(G-10586)**
Independence Harley-Davidson, Binghamton *Also called Ihd Motorsports LLC* **(G-925)**
Independent Baptist Voice, Conklin *Also called Newspaper Publisher LLC* **(G-3871)**
Independent Field Svc LLC (PA)....315 559-9243
6744 Pickard Dr Syracuse (13211) **(G-15962)**

ALPHABETIC

Independent Home Products LLC

ALPHABETIC SECTION

Independent Home Products LLC 718 541-1256
   59 Hempstead Gardens Dr West Hempstead (11552) *(G-16855)*
Index Magazine 212 243-1428
   526 W 26th St Rm 920 New York (10001) *(G-10587)*
India Abroad Publications Inc 212 929-1727
   102 Madison Ave Frnt B New York (10016) *(G-10588)*
Indian Ladder Farmstead Brewer 518 577-1484
   287 Altamont Rd Altamont (12009) *(G-208)*
Indian Larry Legacy 718 609-9184
   400 Union Ave Brooklyn (11211) *(G-2102)*
Indian Springs Mfg Co Inc 315 635-6101
   2095 W Genesee Rd Baldwinsville (13027) *(G-570)*
Indian Time 518 358-9531
   1 Hilltop Dr Hogansburg (13655) *(G-6427)*
Indian Valley, Binghamton Also called Ivi Services Inc *(G-929)*
Indian Water Treatment Plant, Ossining Also called Ossining Village of Inc *(G-13325)*
Indigo Home Inc 212 684-4146
   230 5th Ave Ste 1916 New York (10001) *(G-10589)*
Indikon Company, New Hartford Also called Riverhawk Company LP *(G-8809)*
Indira Foods Inc 718 343-1500
   25503 Hillside Ave # 255 Floral Park (11004) *(G-5208)*
Indium Corporation of America (PA) 800 446-3486
   34 Robinson Rd Clinton (13323) *(G-3720)*
Indium Corporation of America 315 793-8200
   1676 Lincoln Ave Utica (13502) *(G-16342)*
Indium Corporation of America 315 381-2330
   111 Business Park Dr Utica (13502) *(G-16343)*
Indonesian Imports Inc (PA) 888 800-5899
   339 5th Ave Fl 2 New York (10016) *(G-10590)*
Industrial Cables, Chester Also called Nexans Energy USA Inc *(G-3610)*
Industrial Color Inc (PA) 212 334-4667
   32 Ave Of The Am New York (10013) *(G-10591)*
Industrial Elec & Automtn, Buffalo Also called 4695 Main Street Snyder Inc *(G-2789)*
Industrial Electronic Hardware 718 492-4440
   140 58th St Ste 8e Brooklyn (11220) *(G-2103)*
Industrial Fabricating Corp (PA) 315 437-3353
   6201 E Molloy Rd East Syracuse (13057) *(G-4539)*
Industrial Fabricating Corp. 315 437-8234
   4 Collamer Cir East Syracuse (13057) *(G-4540)*
Industrial Finishing Products 718 342-4871
   820 Remsen Ave Brooklyn (11236) *(G-2104)*
Industrial Handling Svcs Inc 518 399-0488
   209 Alplaus Ave Alplaus (12008) *(G-205)*
Industrial Indxing Systems Inc 585 924-9181
   626 Fishers Run Victor (14564) *(G-16482)*
Industrial Machine & Gear Work 516 569-4820
   9 Neil Ct Oceanside (11572) *(G-13081)*
Industrial Machine Repair 607 272-0717
   1144 Taughannock Blvd Ithaca (14850) *(G-6850)*
Industrial Machs & Gear Wks, Oceanside Also called Industrial Machine & Gear Work *(G-13081)*
Industrial Oil Tank Service 315 736-6080
   120 Dry Rd Oriskany (13424) *(G-13311)*
Industrial Paint Services Corp 607 687-0107
   60 W Main St 62 Owego (13827) *(G-13352)*
Industrial Paper Tube Inc 718 893-5000
   1335 E Bay Ave Bronx (10474) *(G-1361)*
Industrial Precision Pdts Inc 315 343-4421
   350 Mitchell St Oswego (13126) *(G-13333)*
Industrial Raw Materials LLC 212 688-8080
   39 West Mall Plainview (11803) *(G-13607)*
Industrial SEC Systems Contrls, Garden City Also called Issco Corporation *(G-5512)*
Industrial Services of Wny 716 799-7788
   7221 Niagara Falls Blvd Niagara Falls (14304) *(G-12836)*
Industrial Support Inc 716 662-2954
   36 Depot St Buffalo (14206) *(G-3006)*
Industrial Test Eqp Co Inc 516 883-6423
   2 Manhasset Ave Port Washington (11050) *(G-13824)*
Industrial Tool & Die Co Inc 518 273-7383
   14 Industrial Park Rd Troy (12180) *(G-16240)*
Industrial Wax, Plainview Also called Industrial Raw Materials LLC *(G-13607)*
Industrial Welding & Fabg Co, Jamestown Also called Wilston Enterprises Inc *(G-7044)*
Industry Forecast 914 244-8617
   69 S Moger Ave Ste 202 Mount Kisco (10549) *(G-8630)*
Ineedmd Holdings Inc (PA) 212 256-9669
   650 1st Ave Fl 3 New York (10016) *(G-10592)*
Inertia Switch Inc 845 359-8300
   70 S Greenbush Rd Orangeburg (10962) *(G-13229)*
Inex Inc 716 537-2270
   9229 Olean Rd Holland (14080) *(G-6481)*
Infant Formula Laboratory Svc 718 257-3000
   711 Livonia Ave Brooklyn (11207) *(G-2105)*
Inficon Inc (HQ) 315 434-1149
   2 Technology Pl East Syracuse (13057) *(G-4541)*
Inficon Holding AG 315 434-1100
   2 Technology Pl East Syracuse (13057) *(G-4542)*
Infimed Inc (PA) 315 453-4545
   121 Metropolitan Park Dr Liverpool (13088) *(G-7524)*
Infimed Inc. 585 383-1710
   15 Fishers Rd Pittsford (14534) *(G-13565)*
Infinite Software Solutions 718 982-1315
   1110 South Ave Ste 303 Staten Island (10314) *(G-15687)*
Infinity Architectual Systems 716 882-2321
   1555 Niagara St Buffalo (14213) *(G-3007)*
Infinity Augmented Reality Inc 917 677-2084
   228 Park Ave S 61130 New York (10003) *(G-10593)*
Infinity Design LLC 718 416-3853
   5830 Grand Ave Maspeth (11378) *(G-8145)*
Infinity Sourcing Services LLC 212 868-2900
   224 W 35th St Ste 600 New York (10001) *(G-10594)*
Infitec Inc 315 433-1150
   6500 Badgley Rd East Syracuse (13057) *(G-4543)*
Inflation Systems Inc 914 381-8070
   500 Ogden Ave Mamaroneck (10543) *(G-8036)*
Influence Graphics, Long Island City Also called Sizzal LLC *(G-7878)*
Info Label Inc 518 664-0791
   12 Enterprise Ave Halfmoon (12065) *(G-5911)*
Info Quick Solutions 315 463-1400
   7460 Morgan Rd Liverpool (13090) *(G-7525)*
Infobase Learning, New York Also called Facts On File Inc *(G-10126)*
Infobase Publishing Company (PA) 212 967-8800
   132 W 31st St Fl 17 New York (10001) *(G-10595)*
Infor Global Solutions Inc (HQ) 646 336-1700
   641 Ave Of Americas Fl 4 New York (10011) *(G-10596)*
Inform Studio Inc 718 401-6149
   480 Austin Pl Frnt E Bronx (10455) *(G-1362)*
Informa Solutions Inc. 516 543-3733
   237 Ellington Ave W Garden City (11530) *(G-5511)*
Informa Uk Ltd 646 957-8966
   52 Vanderbilt Ave Fl 7 New York (10017) *(G-10597)*
Informatica LLC 212 845-7650
   125 Park Ave Rm 1510 New York (10017) *(G-10598)*
Information Commerce Group, New York Also called Rovi Corporation *(G-11922)*
Informerly Inc 646 238-7137
   35 Essex St New York (10002) *(G-10599)*
Infoservices International 631 549-1805
   1 Saint Marks Pl Cold Spring Harbor (11724) *(G-3769)*
Infrared Components Corp 315 732-1544
   2306 Bleecker St Utica (13501) *(G-16344)*
Ingenious Designs LLC 631 254-3376
   2060 9th Ave Ronkonkoma (11779) *(G-14912)*
Ingersoll-Rand Company 716 896-6600
   3101 Broadway St Buffalo (14227) *(G-3008)*
Ingham Industries Inc 631 242-2493
   1363 Lincoln Ave Ste 1 Holbrook (11741) *(G-6451)*
Ingleside Machine Co Inc 585 924-4363
   1120 Hook Rd Farmington (14425) *(G-5153)*
Inglis Co Inc 315 475-1315
   116 Granger St Syracuse (13202) *(G-15963)*
Ings Mata Stone, New York Also called Mata Ig *(G-11177)*
Inhance Technologies LLC 716 825-9031
   1951 Hamburg Tpke Ste 5 Buffalo (14218) *(G-3009)*
Ink Publishing Corporation 347 294-1220
   68 Jay St Ste 315 Brooklyn (11201) *(G-2106)*
Ink Well 718 253-9736
   1440 Coney Island Ave Brooklyn (11230) *(G-2107)*
Ink-It Printing Inc 718 229-5590
   1535 126th St Ste 1 College Point (11356) *(G-3788)*
Ink-It Prtg Inc/Angle Offset, College Point Also called Ink-It Printing Inc *(G-3788)*
Inkkas LLC 646 845-9803
   38 E 29th St Rm 6r New York (10016) *(G-10600)*
Inland Paper Products Corp 718 827-8150
   444 Liberty Ave Brooklyn (11207) *(G-2108)*
Inland Vacuum Industries Inc (PA) 585 293-3330
   35 Howard Ave Churchville (14428) *(G-3638)*
Inner Workings Inc 646 352-4394
   1440 Broadway Fl 22 New York (10018) *(G-10601)*
Inner-Pak Container Inc 631 289-9700
   116 West Ave Patchogue (11772) *(G-13423)*
Innex Industries Inc 585 247-3575
   6 Marway Dr Rochester (14624) *(G-14448)*
Innotech Graphic Eqp Corp 845 268-6900
   614 Corporate Way Ste 5 Valley Cottage (10989) *(G-16379)*
Innova Interiors Inc 718 401-2122
   780 E 134th St Fl 2 Bronx (10454) *(G-1363)*
Innovant Inc 212 929-4883
   37 W 20th St Ste 209 New York (10011) *(G-10602)*
Innovant Inc 212 929-4883
   37 W 20th St Ste 1101 New York (10011) *(G-10603)*
Innovation Associates Inc 607 798-9376
   530 Columbia Dr Ste 101 Johnson City (13790) *(G-7095)*
Innovation MGT Group Inc 800 889-0987
   999 Montauk Hwy Shirley (11967) *(G-15420)*
Innovative Automation Inc 631 439-3300
   595 Smith St Farmingdale (11735) *(G-5011)*
Innovative Cleaning Solutions 716 731-4408
   2990 Carney Dr Sanborn (14132) *(G-15121)*
Innovative Cosmtc Concepts LLC 212 391-8110
   1430 Broadway Rm 308 New York (10018) *(G-10604)*
Innovative Design, New York Also called Innovative Cosmtc Concepts LLC *(G-10604)*
Innovative Designs LLC 212 695-0892
   141 W 36th St Fl 8 New York (10018) *(G-10605)*
Innovative Industries LLC 718 784-7300
   4322 22nd St Ste 205 Long Island City (11101) *(G-7766)*

Innovative Jewelry Inc (PA) 718 408-8950
5 Inez Dr Bay Shore (11706) **(G-705)**
Innovative Labs LLC 631 231-5522
85 Commerce Dr Hauppauge (11788) **(G-6097)**
Innovative Municipal Pdts US 800 387-5777
454 River Rd Glenmont (12077) **(G-5668)**
Innovative Pdts of Amer Inc 845 679-4500
234 Tinker St Woodstock (12498) **(G-17363)**
Innovative Plastics Corp (PA) 845 359-7500
400 Route 303 Orangeburg (10962) **(G-13230)**
Innovative Power Products Inc 631 563-0088
1170 Lincoln Ave Unit 7 Holbrook (11741) **(G-6452)**
Innovative Surface Solutions, Glenmont *Also called Innovative Municipal Pdts US* **(G-5668)**
Innovative Systems of New York 516 541-7410
201 Rose St Massapequa Park (11762) **(G-8187)**
Innovative Video Tech Inc 516 840-2587
355 Oser Ave Hauppauge (11788) **(G-6098)**
Innowave Rf LLC 914 230-4060
520 White Plains Rd Tarrytown (10591) **(G-16091)**
Ino-Tex LLC 212 400-2205
135 W 36th St Fl 6 New York (10018) **(G-10606)**
Inori Jewels 347 703-5078
580 5th Ave New York (10036) **(G-10607)**
Inova LLC 212 932-0366
685 W End Ave Ste 1b New York (10025) **(G-10608)**
Inova LLC 518 861-3400
6032 Depot Rd Altamont (12009) **(G-209)**
Inpora Technologies LLC 646 838-2474
1501 Broadway New York (10036) **(G-10609)**
Inprotopia Corporation 917 338-7501
401 W 110th St Apt 2001 New York (10025) **(G-10610)**
Inquiring Minds Inc (PA) 845 246-5775
65 S Partition St Saugerties (12477) **(G-15185)**
Inscape (new York) Inc (HQ) 716 665-6210
221 Lister Ave 1 Falconer (14733) **(G-4902)**
Inscape Archtectural Interiors, Falconer *Also called Inscape (new York) Inc* **(G-4902)**
Insert Outsert Experts, The, Lockport *Also called Gooding Co Inc* **(G-7592)**
Insight Unlimited Inc 914 861-2090
660 Quaker Rd Chappaqua (10514) **(G-3552)**
Insomnia Cookies On The Hill, New York *Also called U Serve Brands Inc* **(G-12439)**
Instant Again LLC 585 436-8003
1277 Mount Read Blvd # 2 Rochester (14606) **(G-14449)**
Instant Monogramming Inc 585 654-5550
1150 University Ave Ste 5 Rochester (14607) **(G-14450)**
Instant Printing Service, Ithaca *Also called Madison Printing Corp* **(G-6857)**
Instant Stream Inc 917 438-7182
1271 Ave Of The Americas New York (10020) **(G-10611)**
Instant Verticals Inc 631 501-0001
330 Broadhollow Rd Farmingdale (11735) **(G-5012)**
Instantwhip of Buffalo Inc 716 892-7031
2117 Genesee St Buffalo (14211) **(G-3010)**
Institute of Electrical and El 212 705-8900
3 Park Ave Fl 17 New York (10016) **(G-10612)**
Institutional Invester 212 224-3300
225 Park Ave S Fl 7 New York (10003) **(G-10613)**
Instore Magazine, New York *Also called Retail Management Pubg Inc* **(G-11845)**
Instrumentation Laboratory Co 845 680-0028
526 Route 303 Orangeburg (10962) **(G-13231)**
Instruments For Industry Inc 631 467-8400
903 S 2nd St Ronkonkoma (11779) **(G-14913)**
Insty Trints, Kenmore *Also called Horace J Metz* **(G-7149)**
Insty-Prints, Buffalo *Also called L Loy Press Inc* **(G-3040)**
Insty-Prints, Niagara Falls *Also called Graphicomm Inc* **(G-12826)**
Insulating Coatings Corp 607 723-1727
27 Link Dr Ste D Binghamton (13904) **(G-927)**
Insulators Local 12, Astoria *Also called Heat and Frost Inslatrs & Asbs* **(G-443)**
Insultech, North Tonawanda *Also called Shannon Entps Wstn NY Inc* **(G-12993)**
Int Trading USA LLC 212 760-2338
261 W 35th St Ste 1100 New York (10001) **(G-10614)**
Intech 21 Inc 516 626-7221
21 Harbor Park Dr Port Washington (11050) **(G-13825)**
Inteco Intimates, New York *Also called Intimateco LLC* **(G-10644)**
Integer Holdings Corporation 716 937-5100
11900 Walden Ave Alden (14004) **(G-180)**
Integra Microsystem 1988 Inc 718 609-6099
61 Greenpoint Ave Ste 412 Brooklyn (11222) **(G-2109)**
Integrated Control Corp 631 673-5100
748 Park Ave Huntington (11743) **(G-6662)**
Integrated Copyright Group 615 329-3999
1745 Broadway 19 New York (10019) **(G-10615)**
Integrated Graphics Inc (PA) 212 592-5600
7 W 36th St Fl 12 New York (10018) **(G-10616)**
Integrated Indus Resources, Lockport *Also called GM Components Holdings LLC* **(G-7591)**
Integrated Liner Tech Inc (PA) 518 621-7422
45 Discovery Dr Rensselaer (12144) **(G-14048)**
Integrated Medical Devices 315 457-4200
549 Electronics Pkwy # 200 Liverpool (13088) **(G-7526)**
Integrated Solar Tech LLC 914 249-9364
181 Westchester Ave Port Chester (10573) **(G-13749)**
Integrated Tech Support Svcs 718 454-2497
18616 Jordan Ave Saint Albans (11412) **(G-15084)**
Integrated Water Management 607 844-4276
289 Cortland Rd Dryden (13053) **(G-4321)**
Integrated Wood Components Inc 607 467-1739
791 Airport Rd Deposit (13754) **(G-4278)**
Integrity Tool Incorporated 315 524-4409
6485 Furnace Rd Ontario (14519) **(G-13204)**
Integrted Work Envronments LLC 716 725-5088
6346 Everwood Ct N East Amherst (14051) **(G-4361)**
Integument Technologies Inc 716 873-1199
72 Pearce Ave Tonawanda (14150) **(G-16174)**
Intek Precision 585 293-0853
539 Attridge Rd Churchville (14428) **(G-3639)**
INTEL Corporation 408 765-8080
55 Dodge Rd Getzville (14068) **(G-5599)**
Intellicell Biosciences Inc 646 576-8700
460 Park Ave Fl 17 New York (10022) **(G-10617)**
Intellicheck Mobilisa Inc (PA) 360 344-3233
100 Jericho Quadrangle # 202 Jericho (11753) **(G-7072)**
Intellidyne LLC 516 676-0777
303 Sunnyside Blvd # 75 Plainview (11803) **(G-13608)**
Intelligen Power Systems LLC 212 750-0373
301 Winding Rd Old Bethpage (11804) **(G-13129)**
Intelligence Newsletter, New York *Also called Intellignc The Ftr Cmptng Nwsl* **(G-10619)**
Intelligent Traffic Systems 631 567-5994
140 Keyland Ct Unit 1 Bohemia (11716) **(G-1078)**
Intelligize Incorporated (PA) 571 612-8580
261 5th Ave Rm 1414 New York (10016) **(G-10618)**
Intellignc The Ftr Cmptng Nwsl 212 222-1123
360 Central Park W New York (10025) **(G-10619)**
Intellimetal Inc 585 424-3260
2025 Brighton Henrietta Rochester (14623) **(G-14451)**
Intellitravel Media Inc (HQ) 646 695-6700
530 Fashion Ave Rm 201 New York (10018) **(G-10620)**
Intentions Jewelry LLC 845 226-4650
83 Miller Hill Dr Lagrangeville (12540) **(G-7254)**
Inter Craft Custom Furniture 718 278-2573
1431 Astoria Blvd Astoria (11102) **(G-445)**
Inter Molds Inc 631 667-8580
26 Cleveland Ave Bay Shore (11706) **(G-706)**
Inter Pacific Consulting Corp 718 460-2787
14055 34th Ave Apt 3n Flushing (11354) **(G-5252)**
Inter Parfums Inc (PA) 212 983-2640
551 5th Ave New York (10176) **(G-10621)**
Inter State Laminates Inc 518 283-8355
44 Main St Poestenkill (12140) **(G-13724)**
Inter-Fence Co Inc 718 939-9700
1520 129th St College Point (11356) **(G-3789)**
Interaction Insight Corp 800 285-2950
750 3rd Ave Fl 9 New York (10017) **(G-10622)**
Interactive Instruments Inc 518 347-0955
704 Corporation Park # 1 Scotia (12302) **(G-15326)**
Interaxissourcingcom Inc 212 905-6001
41 E 11th St Fl 11 New York (10003) **(G-10623)**
Interbrand LLC 212 840-9595
1 W 37th St Fl 9 New York (10018) **(G-10624)**
Intercall of New York, Mineola *Also called Intercall Systems Inc* **(G-8516)**
Intercall Systems Inc 516 294-4524
150 Herricks Rd Mineola (11501) **(G-8516)**
Intercept Pharmaceuticals Inc (PA) 646 747-1000
450 W 15th St Ste 505 New York (10011) **(G-10625)**
Intercos America Inc 845 732-3900
11 Centerock Rd West Nyack (10994) **(G-16919)**
Intercotton Company Inc 212 265-3809
888 7th Ave Fl 29 New York (10106) **(G-10626)**
Intercultural Alliance Artists 917 406-1202
4510 165th St Flushing (11358) **(G-5253)**
Interdgital Communications LLC 631 622-4000
2 Huntington Quad Ste 4s Melville (11747) **(G-8331)**
Interdynamics 914 241-1423
100 S Bedford Rd Ste 300 Mount Kisco (10549) **(G-8631)**
Interface Performance Mtls 315 346-3100
9635 Main St Beaver Falls (13305) **(G-794)**
Interface Performance Mtls Inc 315 592-8100
2885 State Route 481 Fulton (13069) **(G-5462)**
Interface Performance Mtls Inc 518 686-3400
12 Davis St Hoosick Falls (12090) **(G-6540)**
Interface Products Co Inc 631 242-4605
215 N Fehr Way Ste C Bay Shore (11706) **(G-707)**
Interfaceflor LLC 212 686-8284
330 5th Ave Fl 12 New York (10001) **(G-10627)**
Interhellenic Publishing Inc 212 967-5016
421 7th Ave Ste 810 New York (10001) **(G-10628)**
Interior Metals 718 439-7324
255 48th St Brooklyn (11220) **(G-2110)**
Interior Solutions of Wny LLC 716 332-0372
472 Franklin St Buffalo (14202) **(G-3011)**
Interiors By Robert, Richmond Hill *Also called Terbo Ltd* **(G-14087)**
Interiors-Pft Inc 212 244-9600
3200 Skillman Ave Fl 3 Long Island City (11101) **(G-7767)**
Intermedia Outdoors Inc (PA) 212 852-6600
1040 Ave Of The Americas New York (10018) **(G-10629)**
International Aids Vaccine Ini (PA) 212 847-1111
125 Broad St Fl 9 New York (10004) **(G-10630)**

ALPHABETIC

International Association, Islip *Also called Iahcp Inc* ***(G-6809)***

International Bronze Manufac 516 248-3080
810 Willis Ave Albertson (11507) ***(G-155)***

International Bus Mchs Corp 845 894-2121
2070 State Rte 52 Hopewell Junction (12533) ***(G-6553)***

International Bus Mchs Corp 607 754-9558
1701 North St Endicott (13760) ***(G-4813)***

International Bus Mchs Corp 212 324-5000
55 Broad St Fl 27 New York (10004) ***(G-10631)***

International Bus Mchs Corp 914 345-5219
1 New Orchard Rd Ste 1 Armonk (10504) ***(G-414)***

International Bus Mchs Corp 845 433-1234
2455 South Rd Poughkeepsie (12601) ***(G-13907)***

International Bus Mchs Corp 800 426-4968
10 North Dr Hopewell Junction (12533) ***(G-6554)***

International Bus Mchs Corp 914 499-2000
20 Old Post Rd Armonk (10504) ***(G-415)***

International Business Times, New York *Also called Ibt Media Inc* ***(G-10548)***

International Casein Corp Cal 516 466-4363
111 Great Neck Rd Ste 218 Great Neck (11021) ***(G-5816)***

International Center For Postg 607 257-5860
179 Graham Rd Ste E Ithaca (14850) ***(G-6851)***

International Climbing Mchs 607 288-4001
630 Elmira Rd Ithaca (14850) ***(G-6852)***

International Control Products 716 558-4400
1700 Union Rd Ste 2 West Seneca (14224) ***(G-16949)***

International Creative Met Inc 718 424-8179
3728 61st St Woodside (11377) ***(G-17333)***

International Data Group Inc 212 331-7883
117 E 55th St Ste 204 New York (10022) ***(G-10632)***

International Design Assoc Ltd 212 687-0333
747 3rd Ave Rm 218 New York (10017) ***(G-10633)***

International Direct Group Inc 212 921-9036
525 7th Ave Rm 208 New York (10018) ***(G-10634)***

International Fire-Shield Inc 315 255-1006
194 Genesee St Auburn (13021) ***(G-501)***

International Imaging Mtls Inc (PA) 716 691-6333
310 Commerce Dr Amherst (14228) ***(G-246)***

International Inspirations Ltd (PA) 212 465-8500
362 5th Ave Ste 601 New York (10001) ***(G-10635)***

International Insurance Soc 212 815-9291
101 Murray St Fl 4 New York (10007) ***(G-10636)***

International Leisure Pdts Inc 631 254-2155
191 Rodeo Dr Edgewood (11717) ***(G-4601)***

International Life Science 631 549-0471
23 Gloria Ln Huntington (11743) ***(G-6663)***

International Mdse Svcs Inc 914 699-4000
336 S Fulton Ave Fl 1 Mount Vernon (10553) ***(G-8693)***

International MGT Netwrk 646 401-0032
445 Park Ave Fl 9 New York (10022) ***(G-10637)***

International Mtls & Sups Inc 518 834-9899
56 Industrial Park Rd Keeseville (12944) ***(G-7138)***

International Newspaper Prntng, Glen Head *Also called International Newsppr Prtg Co* ***(G-5635)***

International Newsppr Prtg Co 516 626-6095
18 Carlisle Dr Glen Head (11545) ***(G-5635)***

International Ord Tech Inc 716 664-1100
101 Harrison St Jamestown (14701) ***(G-7003)***

International Paper Company 518 585-6761
568 Shore Airport Rd Ticonderoga (12883) ***(G-16126)***

International Paper Company 585 663-1000
200 Boxart St Rochester (14612) ***(G-14452)***

International Paper Company 845 986-6409
1422 Long Meadow Rd Tuxedo Park (10987) ***(G-16284)***

International Paper Company 607 775-1550
1240 Conklin Rd Conklin (13748) ***(G-3869)***

International Paper Company 315 797-5120
50 Harbor Point Rd Utica (13502) ***(G-16345)***

International Paper Company 716 852-2144
100 Bud Mil Dr Buffalo (14206) ***(G-3012)***

International Paper Company 518 372-6461
803 Corporation Park Glenville (12302) ***(G-5702)***

International Patterns Inc 631 952-2000
8 Arthur Ct Plainview (11803) ***(G-13609)***

International Robotics Inc 914 630-1060
2001 Palmer Ave Ste Ll1 Larchmont (10538) ***(G-7350)***

International Stone Accessrs 718 522-5399
703 Myrtle Ave Brooklyn (11205) ***(G-2111)***

International Time Products 516 931-0005
410 Jericho Tpke Ste 110 Jericho (11753) ***(G-7073)***

International Tool & Mch Inc 585 654-6955
121 Lincoln Ave Rochester (14611) ***(G-14453)***

International Wire Group, Camden *Also called Camden Wire Co Inc* ***(G-3313)***

International Wire Group (PA) 315 245-3800
12 Masonic Ave Camden (13316) ***(G-3315)***

International Wire Group Inc (HQ) 315 245-2000
12 Masonic Ave Camden (13316) ***(G-3316)***

Internationl Studios Inc 212 819-1616
108 W 39th St Rm 1300 New York (10018) ***(G-10638)***

Internodal International Inc 631 765-0037
54800 Route 25 Southold (11971) ***(G-15559)***

Interntional Fireprof Door Inc 718 783-1310
1005 Greene Ave Brooklyn (11221) ***(G-2112)***

Interntional Gourmet Soups Inc 212 768-7687
1110 South Ave Ste 300 Staten Island (10314) ***(G-15688)***

Interntnal Bus Cmmncations Inc (PA) 516 352-4505
1981 Marcus Ave Ste C105 New Hyde Park (11042) ***(G-8842)***

Interntnal Cntrls Msrmnts Corp (PA) 315 233-5266
7313 William Barry Blvd North Syracuse (13212) ***(G-12948)***

Interntnal Elctronic Mchs Corp 518 268-1636
850 River St Troy (12180) ***(G-16241)***

Interntnal Flvors Frgrnces Inc (PA) 212 765-5500
521 W 57th St New York (10019) ***(G-10639)***

Interntnal Strpping Diecutting 718 383-7720
200 Franklin St Brooklyn (11222) ***(G-2113)***

Interntnl Publcatns Media Grup 917 604-9602
708 3rd Ave Ste 145 New York (10017) ***(G-10640)***

Interntonal Consmr Connections 516 481-3438
5 Terminal Rd Unit A West Hempstead (11552) ***(G-16856)***

Interntonal Glatt Kosher Meats, Brooklyn *Also called Globex Kosher Foods Inc* ***(G-2029)***

Interntonal Telecom Components 631 243-1444
94 E Jefryn Blvd Ste B Deer Park (11729) ***(G-4152)***

Interparts International Inc (PA) 516 576-2000
190 Express St Plainview (11803) ***(G-13610)***

Interplex Industries Inc (HQ) 718 961-6212
1434 110th St Ste 301 College Point (11356) ***(G-3790)***

Interplex Nas Electronics, College Point *Also called Nas CP Corp* ***(G-3799)***

Interstate Chemical Co Inc 585 344-2822
4 Treadeasy Ave Batavia (14020) ***(G-640)***

Interstate Litho Corp 631 232-6025
151 Alkier St Brentwood (11717) ***(G-1185)***

Interstate Thermographers Corp 914 948-1745
70 Westmoreland Ave White Plains (10606) ***(G-17124)***

Interstate Window Corporation 631 231-0800
345 Crooked Hill Rd Ste 1 Brentwood (11717) ***(G-1186)***

Interstate Wood & Vinyl Pdts, Amityville *Also called Interstate Wood Products Inc* ***(G-296)***

Interstate Wood Products Inc 631 842-4488
1084 Sunrise Hwy Amityville (11701) ***(G-296)***

Intersurgical Incorporated (PA) 315 451-2900
6757 Kinne St East Syracuse (13057) ***(G-4544)***

Intertex USA Inc 212 279-3601
131 W 35th St Fl 10 New York (10001) ***(G-10641)***

Interview Inc 212 941-2900
575 Broadway Fl 5 New York (10012) ***(G-10642)***

Interview Magazine, New York *Also called Interview Inc* ***(G-10642)***

Inteva Products LLC 248 655-8886
30 Rockefeller Plz New York (10112) ***(G-10643)***

Intex Company Inc (PA) 718 336-3491
5317 Church Ave Brooklyn (11203) ***(G-2114)***

Intimateco LLC 212 239-4411
149 Madison Ave Rm 300 New York (10016) ***(G-10644)***

Intra-Cellular Therapies Inc 212 923-3344
430 E 29th St New York (10016) ***(G-10645)***

Intralinks Holdings Inc (PA) 212 543-7700
150 E 42nd St Fl 8 New York (10017) ***(G-10646)***

Intrapac International Corp 518 561-2030
4 Plant St Plattsburgh (12901) ***(G-13671)***

Intrepid Control Service Inc 718 886-8771
29 Francis Lewis Blvd Flushing (11351) ***(G-5254)***

Intri-Cut Inc 716 691-5200
90 Pineview Dr Amherst (14228) ***(G-247)***

Intrigue Concepts Inc 800 424-8170
8 Gilbert Pl Ste 8 Roosevelt (11575) ***(G-15005)***

Intriguing Threads Apparel Inc (PA) 212 768-8733
552 Fashion Ave Rm 603 New York (10018) ***(G-10647)***

Intrinsiq Materials Inc 585 301-4432
1200 Ridgeway Ave Ste 110 Rochester (14615) ***(G-14454)***

Intuition Publishing Limited 212 838-7115
40 E 34th St Rm 1101 New York (10016) ***(G-10648)***

Invagen Pharmaceuticals Inc 631 949-6367
550 S Research Pl Central Islip (11722) ***(G-3499)***

Invagen Pharmaceuticals Inc (HQ) 631 231-3233
7 Oser Ave Ste 4 Hauppauge (11788) ***(G-6099)***

Invensys Systems Inc 214 527-3099
7 E 8th St New York (10003) ***(G-10649)***

Investars, New York *Also called Netologic Inc* ***(G-11372)***

Investment News 212 210-0100
711 3rd Ave Fl 3 New York (10017) ***(G-10650)***

Investmentwires Inc 212 331-8995
99 Wall St Ste 1700 New York (10005) ***(G-10651)***

Investors Business Daily Inc 212 626-7676
1501 Broadway Fl 12 New York (10036) ***(G-10652)***

Invid Tech, Hauppauge *Also called Innovative Video Tech Inc* ***(G-6098)***

Invision Inc (HQ) 212 557-5554
25 W 43rd St Ste 609 New York (10036) ***(G-10653)***

Inwood Material 516 371-1842
1 Sheridan Blvd Inwood (11096) ***(G-6759)***

Ion Optics Inc 518 339-6853
75 Benjamin St Albany (12202) ***(G-90)***

Ip Med Inc 516 766-3800
3571 Hargale Rd Oceanside (11572) ***(G-13082)***

IPC/Razor LLC (PA) 212 551-4500
277 Park Ave Fl 39 New York (10172) ***(G-10654)***

Ipcc, Flushing *Also called Inter Pacific Consulting Corp* ***(G-5252)***

Ipe, Orchard Park *Also called Bos-Hatten Inc* ***(G-13253)***

Ipm US Inc 212 481-7967
276 5th Ave Rm 203 New York (10001) *(G-10655)*
Ipp Energy LLC 607 773-3307
22 Charles St Binghamton (13905) *(G-928)*
Iquit Cig LLC 718 475-1422
4014 13th Ave Brooklyn (11218) *(G-2115)*
Ir Magazine, New York *Also called Cross Border Usa Inc (G-9756)*
Iradj Moini Couture Ltd 212 594-9242
403 W 46th St New York (10036) *(G-10656)*
Irene Cerone 315 668-2899
9600 Brewerton Rd Brewerton (13029) *(G-1204)*
Irene Goodman Literary Agency 212 604-0330
27 W 24th St Ste 700b New York (10010) *(G-10657)*
Iridesse Inc 212 230-6000
600 Madison Ave Fl 5 New York (10022) *(G-10658)*
Iridium Industries Inc 516 504-9700
17 Barstow Rd Ste 302 Great Neck (11021) *(G-5817)*
Iriniri Designs Ltd 845 469-7934
1358 Kings Hwy Sugar Loaf (10981) *(G-15804)*
Irish America Inc 212 725-2993
875 Avnue Of Amricas 2100 New York (10001) *(G-10659)*
Irish America Magazine, New York *Also called Irish America Inc (G-10659)*
Irish Echo Newspaper Corp 212 482-4818
165 Madison Ave Rm 302 New York (10016) *(G-10660)*
Irish Tribune Inc 212 684-3366
875 Avenue Of The Amerrm2 Rm 2100 New York (10001) *(G-10661)*
Irish Voice Newspaper, New York *Also called Irish Tribune Inc (G-10661)*
Iron Art Inc 914 592-7977
14 N Payne St Elmsford (10523) *(G-4757)*
Iron Eagle Group Inc (PA) 888 481-4445
160 W 66th St Apt 41g New York (10023) *(G-10662)*
Iron Flamingo Brewery, Corning *Also called Rising Sons 6 Brewing Coinc (G-3979)*
Iron Horse Graphics Ltd 631 537-3400
112 Maple Ln Bridgehampton (11932) *(G-1234)*
Iron Worker 516 338-2756
1039 W Jericho Tpke Smithtown (11787) *(G-15489)*
Ironshore Holdings Inc 315 457-1052
290 Elwood Davis Rd Liverpool (13088) *(G-7527)*
Irony Limited Inc (PA) 631 329-4065
53 Sag Harbor Tpke East Hampton (11937) *(G-4411)*
Irpenscom 585 507-7997
4 Katsura Ct Penfield (14526) *(G-13499)*
Irtronics Instruments Inc 914 693-6291
132 Forest Blvd Ardsley (10502) *(G-405)*
Irv Inc 212 334-4507
540 Broadway Fl 4 New York (10012) *(G-10663)*
Irv & Vic Sportswear Co, Yonkers *Also called Robert Viggiani (G-17481)*
Irv Schroder & Sons Inc 518 828-0194
2906 Atlantic Ave Stottville (12172) *(G-15781)*
Irving Consumer Products Inc (HQ) 518 747-4151
1 Eddy St Fort Edward (12828) *(G-5342)*
Irving Farm Coffee Co Inc (PA) 212 206-0707
151 W 19th St Fl 6 New York (10011) *(G-10664)*
Irving Tissue Div, Fort Edward *Also called Irving Consumer Products Inc (G-5342)*
Irving Woodlands LLC 607 723-4862
53 Shaw Rd Conklin (13748) *(G-3870)*
Isaac Waldman Inc 212 354-8220
36 W 47th St Ste 1002 New York (10036) *(G-10665)*
Isabel and Nina, New York *Also called Travis Ayers Inc (G-12394)*
Isabel Toledo Enterprises Inc 212 685-0948
1181 Broadway Fl 7 New York (10001) *(G-10666)*
Isabella Products Inc 516 699-8404
15 Cuttermill Rd Ste 242 Great Neck (11021) *(G-5818)*
Isco Industries 502 714-5306
50 Electric Pkwy Horseheads (14845) *(G-6581)*
Isfel Co Inc (PA) 212 736-6216
110 W 34th St Rm 1101 New York (10001) *(G-10667)*
Ish Precision Machine Corp (PA) 718 436-8858
786 Mcdonald Ave Brooklyn (11218) *(G-2116)*
Isimulate LLC 877 947-2831
90 State St Ste 700 Albany (12207) *(G-91)*
Isine Inc (PA) 631 913-4400
4155 Veterans Memorial Hw Ronkonkoma (11779) *(G-14914)*
Island Audio Engineering 631 543-2372
7 Glenmere Ct Commack (11725) *(G-3836)*
Island Automated Gate Co LLC 631 425-0196
125 W Hills Rd Huntington Station (11746) *(G-6711)*
Island Chimney Service, Bohemia *Also called Ace Cntracting Consulting Corp (G-1006)*
Island Circuits International 516 625-5555
1318 130th St Fl 2 College Point (11356) *(G-3791)*
Island Components Group Inc 631 563-4224
101 Colin Dr Unit 4 Holbrook (11741) *(G-6453)*
Island Container Corp 631 253-4400
44 Island Container Plz Wyandanch (11798) *(G-17376)*
Island Custom Stairs Inc 631 205-5335
23 Scouting Blvd Unit C Medford (11763) *(G-8251)*
Island Industries Corp 631 451-8825
480 Mill Rd Coram (11727) *(G-3945)*
Island Instrument Corp 631 243-0550
65 Burt Dr Deer Park (11729) *(G-4153)*
Island Interiors, West Babylon *Also called Dbs Interiors Corp (G-16788)*
Island Lite Louvers Inc 631 608-4250
35 Albany Ave Amityville (11701) *(G-297)*
Island Machine Inc 518 562-1232
86 Boynton Ave Plattsburgh (12901) *(G-13672)*
Island Marketing Corp 516 739-0500
95 Searing Ave Ste 2 Mineola (11501) *(G-8517)*
Island Nameplate Inc 845 651-4005
124 S Main St Florida (10921) *(G-5213)*
Island Ordnance Systems LLC 516 746-2100
267 E Jericho Tpke Ste 2 Mineola (11501) *(G-8518)*
Island Precision, Ronkonkoma *Also called Roger Latari (G-14980)*
Island Publications, Melville *Also called Distinction Magazine Inc (G-8311)*
Island Pyrochemical Inds Corp (PA) 516 746-2100
267 E Jericho Tpke Ste 2 Mineola (11501) *(G-8519)*
Island Ready Mix Inc 631 874-3777
170 Railroad Ave Center Moriches (11934) *(G-3467)*
Island Recycling Corp 631 234-6688
228 Blydenburg Rd Central Islip (11749) *(G-3500)*
Island Research and Dev Corp 631 471-7100
200 13th Ave Unit 12 Ronkonkoma (11779) *(G-14915)*
Island Silkscreen Inc 631 757-4567
328 Larkfield Rd East Northport (11731) *(G-4437)*
Island Stairs Corp 347 645-0560
178 Industrial Loop Staten Island (10309) *(G-15689)*
Island Street Lumber Co Inc 716 692-4127
11 Felton St North Tonawanda (14120) *(G-12978)*
Island Technology, Ronkonkoma *Also called Island Research and Dev Corp (G-14915)*
Island Vitamin, Farmingdale *Also called Maxus Pharmaceuticals Inc (G-5045)*
Islandaire, East Setauket *Also called RE Hansen Industries Inc (G-4491)*
Islandia Mri Associates PC 631 234-2828
200 Corporate Plz Ste 203 Central Islip (11749) *(G-3501)*
Islechem LLC 716 773-8618
2801 Long Rd Grand Island (14072) *(G-5761)*
Islip Bulletin, Patchogue *Also called John Lor Publishing Ltd (G-13425)*
Islip Miniture Golf 631 940-8900
500 E Main St Bay Shore (11706) *(G-708)*
ISO Plastics Corp 914 663-8300
160 E 1st St Mount Vernon (10550) *(G-8694)*
Isoflux Hollow Cathodes, Rochester *Also called Isoflux Incorporated (G-14455)*
Isoflux Incorporated 585 349-0640
10 Vantage Point Dr Ste 4 Rochester (14624) *(G-14455)*
Isolation Dynamics Corp 631 491-5670
66 Otis St Unit A West Babylon (11704) *(G-16795)*
Isolation Systems Inc 716 694-6390
889 Erie Ave Ste 1 North Tonawanda (14120) *(G-12979)*
Isolation Technology Inc 631 253-3314
73 Nancy St Unit A West Babylon (11704) *(G-16796)*
Isonics Corporation (PA) 212 356-7400
535 8th Ave Fl 3 New York (10018) *(G-10668)*
Isp Optics Corporation (PA) 914 591-3070
50 S Buckhout St Irvington (10533) *(G-6773)*
Israeli Yellow Pages 718 520-1000
12510 Queens Blvd Ste 14 Kew Gardens (11415) *(G-7162)*
Issacs Yisroel 718 851-7430
4424 18th Ave Brooklyn (11204) *(G-2117)*
Issco Corporation (PA) 212 732-8748
111 Cherry Valley Ave # 410 Garden City (11530) *(G-5512)*
Ist Conax Nuclear, Buffalo *Also called Mirion Tech Conax Nuclear Inc (G-3068)*
It Commodity Sourcing Inc 718 677-1577
1640 E 22nd St Brooklyn (11210) *(G-2118)*
It's About Time, Mount Kisco *Also called Iat Interactive LLC (G-8628)*
It's About Time Publishing, Mount Kisco *Also called Laurtom Inc (G-8634)*
Itac Label & Tag Corp 718 625-2148
179 Lexington Ave Brooklyn (11216) *(G-2119)*
Italian Marble & Granite Inc 716 741-1800
8526 Roll Rd Clarence Center (14032) *(G-3676)*
Italmatch USA Corporation 732 383-8309
660 White Plains Rd # 510 Tarrytown (10591) *(G-16092)*
Itc, Deer Park *Also called Interntonal Telecom Components (G-4152)*
Itc Mfg Group Inc 212 684-3696
109 W 38th St Rm 701 New York (10018) *(G-10669)*
Itelinso, Cold Spring Harbor *Also called Infoservices International (G-3769)*
Item-Eyes Inc (HQ) 631 321-0923
114 W 41st St Fl 5 New York (10036) *(G-10670)*
Ithaca Beer Company Inc 607 272-1305
122 Ithaca Beer Dr Ithaca (14850) *(G-6853)*
Ithaca Ice Company, The, Ithaca *Also called Henry Newman LLC (G-6847)*
Ithaca Journal News Co Inc 607 272-2321
123 W State St Ste 1 Ithaca (14850) *(G-6854)*
Ithaca Peripherals, Ithaca *Also called Transact Technologies Inc (G-6880)*
Ithaca Times, Ithaca *Also called New Ski Inc (G-6867)*
Itin Scale Co Inc 718 336-5900
4802 Glenwood Rd Brooklyn (11234) *(G-2120)*
ITR Industries Inc (PA) 914 964-7063
441 Saw Mill River Rd Yonkers (10701) *(G-17456)*
Its Our Time, New York *Also called Fashion Avenue Knits Inc (G-10142)*
Itss, Saint Albans *Also called Integrated Tech Support Svcs (G-15084)*
Itt LLC (HQ) 914 641-2000
1133 Westchester Ave N-100 White Plains (10604) *(G-17125)*

ALPHABETIC

(PA)=Parent Co (HQ)=Headquarters (DH)=Div Headquarters
2017 Harris
New York Manufacturers Directory
983

ITT Aerospace Controls LLC....914 641-2000
4 W Red Oak Ln White Plains (10604) ***(G-17126)***
ITT Corporation....585 269-7109
4847 Main St Hemlock (14466) ***(G-6263)***
ITT Corporation....315 258-4904
1 Goulds Dr Auburn (13021) ***(G-502)***
ITT Corporation....914 641-2000
2881 E Bayard Street Ext Seneca Falls (13148) ***(G-15361)***
ITT Corporation....315 568-2811
240 Fall St Seneca Falls (13148) ***(G-15362)***
ITT Engineered Valves LLC (HQ)....662 257-6982
240 Fall St Seneca Falls (13148) ***(G-15363)***
ITT Enidine Inc (HQ)....716 662-1900
7 Centre Dr Orchard Park (14127) ***(G-13275)***
ITT Fluid Technology Corp (HQ)....914 641-2000
1133 Westcstr Ave N100 Ste N White Plains (10604) ***(G-17127)***
ITT Goulds Pumps Inc (HQ)....914 641-2129
240 Fall St Seneca Falls (13148) ***(G-15364)***
ITT Inc (PA)....914 641-2000
1133 Westchester Ave N-100 White Plains (10604) ***(G-17128)***
ITT Industries Holdings Inc (HQ)....914 641-2000
1133 Westchester Ave N-100 White Plains (10604) ***(G-17129)***
ITT Water Technology, Auburn *Also called ITT Corporation* ***(G-502)***
ITT Water Technology Inc....315 568-2811
2881 E Bayard Street Ext Seneca Falls (13148) ***(G-15365)***
Itts Industrial Inc....718 605-6934
165 Industrial Loop Ste C Staten Island (10309) ***(G-15690)***
Iver Printing Inc....718 275-2070
6703 Main St Flushing (11367) ***(G-5255)***
Ives Farm Market....315 592-4880
2652 Rr 176 Fulton (13069) ***(G-5463)***
Ives Slaughterhouse, Fulton *Also called Ives Farm Market* ***(G-5463)***
Ivi Services Inc....607 729-5111
5 Pine Camp Dr Binghamton (13904) ***(G-929)***
Ivy Classic Industries Inc....914 632-8200
40 Plain Ave New Rochelle (10801) ***(G-8913)***
Ivy Enterprises Inc (HQ)....516 621-9779
3 Seaview Blvd Port Washington (11050) ***(G-13826)***
Iwci, Deposit *Also called Integrated Wood Components Inc* ***(G-4278)***
Iwe, East Amherst *Also called Integrted Work Envronments LLC* ***(G-4361)***
Izi Creations, New York *Also called Adamor Inc* ***(G-9025)***
Izquierdo Studios Ltd....212 807-9757
34 W 28th St 6 New York (10001) ***(G-10671)***
Izun Pharmaceuticals Corp (PA)....212 618-6357
1 Rockefeller Plz Fl 11 New York (10020) ***(G-10672)***
Izzi Clothes, New York *Also called Fieldston Clothes Inc* ***(G-10161)***
J & A Usa Inc....631 243-3336
335 Crooked Hill Rd Brentwood (11717) ***(G-1187)***
J & C Finishing....718 456-1087
1067 Wyckoff Ave Ridgewood (11385) ***(G-14110)***
J & E Talit Inc....718 850-1333
13011 Atlantic Ave Fl 2 Richmond Hill (11418) ***(G-14076)***
J & F Advertising, Carle Place *Also called Market Place Publications* ***(G-3395)***
J & G Machine & Tool Co Inc....315 310-7130
4510 Smith Rd Marion (14505) ***(G-8096)***
J & H Creations Inc....212 465-0962
19 W 36th St Fl 3 New York (10018) ***(G-10673)***
J & H International, New York *Also called Jay Import Company Inc* ***(G-10704)***
J & J Bronze & Aluminum Cast....718 383-2111
249 Huron St Brooklyn (11222) ***(G-2121)***
J & J Log & Lumber Corp....845 832-6535
528 Old State Route 22 Dover Plains (12522) ***(G-4315)***
J & J Printing Inc (PA)....315 458-7411
500 Cambridge Ave Syracuse (13208) ***(G-15964)***
J & J Swiss Precision Inc....631 243-5584
160 W Industry Ct Ste F Deer Park (11729) ***(G-4154)***
J & J TI Die Mfg & Stampg Corp....845 228-0242
594 Horsepound Rd Carmel (10512) ***(G-3400)***
J & L Precision Co Inc....585 768-6388
9222 Summit Street Rd Le Roy (14482) ***(G-7410)***
J & M Feed Corporation....631 281-2152
675 Montauk Hwy Shirley (11967) ***(G-15421)***
J & M Textile Co Inc....212 268-8000
505 8th Ave Rm 701 New York (10018) ***(G-10674)***
J & N Computer Services Inc....585 388-8780
1387 Fairport Rd Ste 900j Fairport (14450) ***(G-4858)***
J & R Unique Giftware....718 821-0398
5863 56th St Maspeth (11378) ***(G-8146)***
J & S Logging Inc....315 262-2112
3860 State Highway 56 South Colton (13687) ***(G-15515)***
J & T Metal Products Co Inc....631 226-7400
89 Eads St West Babylon (11704) ***(G-16797)***
J & X Production....646 366-8288
247 W 37th St Rm 1501 New York (10018) ***(G-10675)***
J A G Diamond Manufacturers....212 575-0660
580 5th Ave Ste 905b New York (10036) ***(G-10676)***
J A T Printing Inc....631 427-1155
46 Gerard St Unit 2 Huntington (11743) ***(G-6664)***
J A Yansick Lumber Co Inc....585 492-4312
16 Rule Dr Arcade (14009) ***(G-395)***
J and M Schwarz, Albany *Also called Smiths Gas Service Inc* ***(G-134)***
J B S, Scotia *Also called Jbs LLC* ***(G-15327)***
J B Tool & Die Co Inc....516 333-1480
629 Main St Westbury (11590) ***(G-16997)***
J C Industries Inc....631 420-1920
89 Eads St West Babylon (11704) ***(G-16798)***
J D Calato Manufacturing Co (PA)....716 285-3546
4501 Hyde Park Blvd Niagara Falls (14305) ***(G-12837)***
J D Cousins Inc....716 824-1098
667 Tifft St Buffalo (14220) ***(G-3013)***
J D Handling Systems Inc....518 828-9676
1346 State Route 9h Ghent (12075) ***(G-5607)***
J D Steward Inc....718 358-0169
4537 162nd St Flushing (11358) ***(G-5256)***
J Davis Manufacturing Co Inc....315 337-7574
222 Erie Blvd E Rome (13440) ***(G-14816)***
J E T, Ronkonkoma *Also called Jet Redi Mix Concrete Inc* ***(G-14919)***
J Edlin Interiors Ltd....212 243-2111
122 W 27th St Fl 2 New York (10001) ***(G-10677)***
J F B & Sons Lithographers....631 467-1444
1700 Ocean Ave Lake Ronkonkoma (11779) ***(G-7278)***
J F M Sheet Metal Inc....631 737-8494
2090 Pond Rd Ronkonkoma (11779) ***(G-14916)***
J F Machining Company Inc....716 791-3910
2382 Balmer Rd Ransomville (14131) ***(G-14019)***
J Gimbel Inc....718 296-5200
275 Hempstead Tpke Ste A West Hempstead (11552) ***(G-16857)***
J H Buhrmaster Company Inc....518 843-1700
164 W Main St Amsterdam (12010) ***(G-351)***
J H Buscher Inc....716 667-2003
227 Thorn Ave Ste 30 Orchard Park (14127) ***(G-13276)***
J H C Fabrications Inc (PA)....718 649-0065
595 Berriman St Brooklyn (11208) ***(G-2122)***
J H Jewelry Co Inc....212 239-1330
12 W 32nd St Fl 12 New York (10001) ***(G-10678)***
J H M Engineering....718 871-1810
4014 8th Ave Brooklyn (11232) ***(G-2123)***
J H Rhodes Company Inc....315 829-3600
10 Ward St Vernon (13476) ***(G-16436)***
J H Robotics Inc....607 729-3758
109 Main St Johnson City (13790) ***(G-7096)***
J I Intrntnal Contact Lens Lab....718 997-1212
6352 Saunders St Ste A Rego Park (11374) ***(G-14033)***
J Ironwork, Brooklyn *Also called Railings By New Star Brass* ***(G-2474)***
J J Creations Inc....718 392-2828
4742 37th St Long Island City (11101) ***(G-7768)***
J K Fertility, Yonkers *Also called J Kendall LLC* ***(G-17457)***
J Kendall LLC....646 739-4956
71 Belvedere Dr Yonkers (10705) ***(G-17457)***
J Kraft Microscopy Svcs Inc....716 592-4402
243 W Main St Ste 2 Springville (14141) ***(G-15613)***
J L M, New York *Also called Jlm Couture Inc* ***(G-10741)***
J Lowy Co....718 338-7324
940 E 19th St Brooklyn (11230) ***(G-2124)***
J Lowy Lea Skullcaps Mfg Co, Brooklyn *Also called J Lowy Co* ***(G-2124)***
J M B Apparel Designer Group....212 764-8410
214 W 39th St Rm 508 New York (10018) ***(G-10679)***
J M C Bow Co Inc....718 686-8110
1271 39th St Ste 3 Brooklyn (11218) ***(G-2125)***
J M Canty Inc....716 625-4227
6100 Donner Rd Lockport (14094) ***(G-7593)***
J M Haley Corp....631 845-5200
151 Toledo St Ste 1 Farmingdale (11735) ***(G-5013)***
J M L Productions Inc....718 643-1674
162 Spencer St Brooklyn (11205) ***(G-2126)***
J M P Display Fixture Co Inc....718 649-0333
760 E 96th St Brooklyn (11236) ***(G-2127)***
J M R Plastics Corporation....718 898-9825
5847 78th St Middle Village (11379) ***(G-8412)***
J Mackenzie Ltd....585 321-1770
234 Wallace Way Rochester (14624) ***(G-14456)***
J N White Associates Inc....585 237-5191
129 N Center St Perry (14530) ***(G-13524)***
J P Installations Warehouse....914 576-3188
29 Portman Rd New Rochelle (10801) ***(G-8914)***
J P Machine Products Inc....631 249-9229
144 Rome St Farmingdale (11735) ***(G-5014)***
J P Printing Inc (PA)....516 293-6110
331 Main St Farmingdale (11735) ***(G-5015)***
J P R Pharmacy Inc....718 327-0600
529 Beach 20th St Far Rockaway (11691) ***(G-4923)***
J Pahura Contractors....585 589-5793
415 East Ave Albion (14411) ***(G-166)***
J Percoco Industries Inc....631 312-4572
1546 Ocean Ave Ste 4 Bohemia (11716) ***(G-1079)***
J Percy For Mrvin Rchards Ltd (HQ)....212 944-5300
512 Fashion Ave New York (10018) ***(G-10680)***
J Petrocelli Wine Cellars LLC....631 765-1100
39390 Route 25 Peconic (11958) ***(G-13471)***
J R Gold Designs Ltd....212 922-9292
555 5th Ave Fl 19 New York (10017) ***(G-10681)***
J R Nites (PA)....212 354-9670
1400 Broadway 6th Frl New York (10018) ***(G-10682)***
J R Products Inc....716 633-7565
9680 County Rd Clarence Center (14032) ***(G-3677)***

ALPHABETIC

ALPHABETIC SECTION
Jamestown Bronze Works Inc

J R S Precision Machining.....631 737-1330
40 Raynor Ave Ste 2 Ronkonkoma (11779) ***(G-14917)***

J Rivera, Bohemia *Also called Pro Torque* ***(G-1122)***

J Soehner Corporation.....516 599-2534
200 Brower Ave Rockville Centre (11570) ***(G-14793)***

J Sussman Inc.....718 297-0228
10910 180th St Jamaica (11433) ***(G-6922)***

J T D Stamping Co Inc.....631 643-4144
403 Wyandanch Ave West Babylon (11704) ***(G-16799)***

J T Enterprises LLC.....716 433-9368
6602 Mulligan Dr Lockport (14094) ***(G-7594)***

J T Systematic.....607 754-0929
39 Valley St Endwell (13760) ***(G-4836)***

J V Haring & Son.....718 720-1947
1277 Clove Rd Ste 2 Staten Island (10301) ***(G-15691)***

J V Precision Inc.....518 851-3200
3031 Us Route 9 Hudson (12534) ***(G-6619)***

J Valdi, New York *Also called Lgb Inc* ***(G-10982)***

J Vogler Enterprise LLC.....585 247-1625
15 Evelyn St Rochester (14606) ***(G-14457)***

J W Stevens Co Inc.....315 472-6311
6059 Corporate Dr East Syracuse (13057) ***(G-4545)***

J Zeluck Inc (PA).....718 251-8060
5300 Kings Hwy Brooklyn (11234) ***(G-2128)***

J&T Macquesten Realty, Mount Vernon *Also called Dunlea Whl GL & Mirror Inc* ***(G-8679)***

J-K Prosthetics & Orthotics.....914 699-2077
699 N Macquesten Pkwy Mount Vernon (10552) ***(G-8695)***

J-Trend Systems Inc.....646 688-3272
244 5th Ave Ste C294 New York (10001) ***(G-10683)***

J.hoaglund, New York *Also called THE Design Group Inc* ***(G-12309)***

J.N. White Designs, Perry *Also called J N White Associates Inc* ***(G-13524)***

J9 Technologies Inc.....412 586-5038
25 Broadway Fl 9 New York (10004) ***(G-10684)***

Jaab Precision Inc.....631 218-3725
180 Gary Way Ronkonkoma (11779) ***(G-14918)***

Jab Concrete Supply Corp.....718 842-5250
1465 Bronx River Ave Bronx (10472) ***(G-1364)***

Jabil Circuit Inc.....845 471-9237
2455 South Rd Poughkeepsie (12601) ***(G-13908)***

Jabo Agricultural Inc.....631 475-1800
9 Northwood Ln Patchogue (11772) ***(G-13424)***

Jac Usa Inc.....212 841-7430
45 Broadway Fl 18 New York (10006) ***(G-10685)***

Jack J Florio Jr.....716 434-9123
36b Main St Lockport (14094) ***(G-7595)***

Jack L Popkin & Co Inc.....718 361-6700
12510 84th Rd Kew Gardens (11415) ***(G-7163)***

Jack Luckner Steel Shelving Co.....718 363-0500
5454 43rd St Maspeth (11378) ***(G-8147)***

Jack Merkel Inc.....631 234-2600
1720 Express Dr S Hauppauge (11788) ***(G-6100)***

Jack W Miller.....585 538-2399
2339 North Rd Scottsville (14546) ***(G-15337)***

Jackdaw Publications, New York *Also called Golden Owl Publishing Company* ***(G-10333)***

Jackdaw Publications.....914 962-6911
2 Watergate Dr Amawalk (10501) ***(G-214)***

Jackel Inc.....908 359-2039
1359 Broadway Fl 17 New York (10018) ***(G-10686)***

Jackel International, New York *Also called Jackel Inc* ***(G-10686)***

Jackie's Girls, New York *Also called Waterbury Garment LLC* ***(G-12597)***

Jacknob International Ltd.....631 546-6560
290 Oser Ave Hauppauge (11788) ***(G-6101)***

Jacks and Jokers 52 LLC.....917 740-2595
215 E 68th St Apt 5o New York (10065) ***(G-10687)***

Jacks Gourmet LLC.....718 954-4681
1000 Dean St Ste 214 Brooklyn (11238) ***(G-2129)***

Jackson Dakota Inc.....718 786-8600
3010 41st Ave Ste 3 Long Island City (11101) ***(G-7769)***

Jackson Dakota Inc (PA).....212 838-9444
979 3rd Ave Ste 503 New York (10022) ***(G-10688)***

Jackson Woodworks Inc.....518 651-2032
6340 State Route 374 Brainardsville (12915) ***(G-1171)***

Jaclyn Inc.....212 736-5657
330 5th Ave Rm 1305 New York (10001) ***(G-10689)***

Jacmax Industries LLC.....718 439-3743
14a 53rd St Unit 501 Brooklyn (11232) ***(G-2130)***

Jacmel Jewelry Inc (PA).....718 349-4300
1385 Broadway Fl 8 New York (10018) ***(G-10690)***

Jacob Dresdner Co, New York *Also called Dresdiam Inc* ***(G-9926)***

Jacob Hidary Foundation Inc.....212 736-6540
10 W 33rd St Rm 900 New York (10001) ***(G-10691)***

Jacob Inc.....646 450-3067
287 Keap St Brooklyn (11211) ***(G-2131)***

Jacobi Industries, Medford *Also called Jacobi Tool & Die Mfg Inc* ***(G-8252)***

Jacobi Tool & Die Mfg Inc.....631 736-5394
131 Middle Island Rd Medford (11763) ***(G-8252)***

Jacobs Juice Corp.....646 255-2860
388 Avenue X Apt 2h Brooklyn (11223) ***(G-2132)***

Jacobs Manufacturing, Hogansburg *Also called Jacobs Tobacco Company* ***(G-6428)***

Jacobs Press Inc.....315 252-4861
87 Columbus St Auburn (13021) ***(G-503)***

Jacobs Tobacco Company.....518 358-4948
344 Frogtown Rd Hogansburg (13655) ***(G-6428)***

Jacobs Woodworking LLC.....315 427-8999
801 W Fayette St Syracuse (13204) ***(G-15965)***

Jacoby Enterprises LLC.....718 435-0289
1615 54th St Brooklyn (11204) ***(G-2133)***

Jacques Moret Inc (PA).....212 354-2400
1411 Broadway Fl 8 New York (10018) ***(G-10692)***

Jacques Torres Chocolate, Brooklyn *Also called Mrchocolatecom LLC* ***(G-2341)***

Jacques Torres Chocolate LLC.....212 414-2462
350 Hudson St Frnt 1 New York (10014) ***(G-10693)***

Jad Corp of America.....718 762-8900
2048 119th St College Point (11356) ***(G-3792)***

Jadak LLC (HQ).....315 701-0678
7279 William Barry Blvd North Syracuse (13212) ***(G-12949)***

Jadak Technologies Inc (HQ).....315 701-0678
7279 William Barry Blvd North Syracuse (13212) ***(G-12950)***

Jado Sewing Machines Inc.....718 784-2314
4008 22nd St Long Island City (11101) ***(G-7770)***

Jaf Converters Inc.....631 842-3131
60 Marconi Blvd Copiague (11726) ***(G-3908)***

Jag Manufacturing Inc.....518 762-9558
26 Grecco Dr Johnstown (12095) ***(G-7116)***

Jags Manufacturing Network Inc.....631 750-6367
13403 Lincoln Ave Holbrook (11741) ***(G-6454)***

Jaguar Casting Co Inc.....212 869-0197
100 United Nations Plz New York (10017) ***(G-10694)***

Jaguar Industries Inc.....845 947-1800
89 Broadway Haverstraw (10927) ***(G-6237)***

Jaguar Jewelry Casting NY Inc.....212 768-4848
48 W 48th St Ste 500 New York (10036) ***(G-10695)***

Jaidan Industries Inc.....516 944-3650
16 Capi Ln Port Washington (11050) ***(G-13827)***

Jakes Sneakers Inc.....718 233-1132
845 Classon Ave Brooklyn (11238) ***(G-2134)***

Jakob Schlaepfer Inc.....212 221-2323
307 W 38th St Rm 804 New York (10018) ***(G-10696)***

Jal Signs Inc.....516 536-7280
540 Merrick Rd Baldwin (11510) ***(G-559)***

Jalex Industries Ltd.....631 491-5072
86 Nancy St West Babylon (11704) ***(G-16800)***

Jam Industries Inc.....585 458-9830
1580 Emerson St Rochester (14606) ***(G-14458)***

Jam Paper, New York *Also called Hudson Envelope Corporation* ***(G-10525)***

Jam Printing Publishing Inc.....914 345-8400
11 Clearbrook Rd Ste 133 Elmsford (10523) ***(G-4758)***

Jamaica Electroplating, North Baldwin *Also called Dura Spec Inc* ***(G-12904)***

Jamaica Iron Works Inc.....718 657-4849
10847 Merrick Blvd Jamaica (11433) ***(G-6923)***

Jamaica Lamp Corp.....718 776-5039
21220 Jamaica Ave Queens Village (11428) ***(G-13980)***

Jamaican Weekly Gleaner, Jamaica *Also called Gleaner Company Ltd* ***(G-6915)***

Jamar Precision Products Co.....631 254-0234
5 Lucon Dr Deer Park (11729) ***(G-4155)***

Jamco Aerospace Inc.....631 586-7900
121a E Industry Ct Deer Park (11729) ***(G-4156)***

James A Staley Co Inc.....845 878-3344
5 Bowen Ct Carmel (10512) ***(G-3401)***

James B Crowell & Sons Inc.....845 895-3464
242 Lippincott Rd Wallkill (12589) ***(G-16544)***

James Conolly Printing Co.....585 426-4150
72 Marway Cir Rochester (14624) ***(G-14459)***

James D Rubino Inc.....631 244-8730
20 Jules Ct Ste 5 Bohemia (11716) ***(G-1080)***

James King Woodworking Inc.....518 761-6091
656 County Line Rd Queensbury (12804) ***(G-14000)***

James L Taylor Mfg Co (PA).....845 452-3780
130 Salt Point Tpke Poughkeepsie (12603) ***(G-13909)***

James L Taylor Mfg Co.....845 452-3780
130 Salt Point Tpke Poughkeepsie (12603) ***(G-13910)***

James L. Taylor Mfg., Poughkeepsie *Also called James L Taylor Mfg Co* ***(G-13909)***

James Morgan Publishing (PA).....212 655-5470
5 Penn Plz Fl 23 New York (10001) ***(G-10697)***

James Morris.....315 824-8519
6697 Airport Rd Hamilton (13346) ***(G-5948)***

James Richard Specialty Chem.....914 478-7500
24 Ridge St Hastings On Hudson (10706) ***(G-6004)***

James Thompson & Company Inc (PA).....212 686-4242
381 Park Ave S Rm 718 New York (10016) ***(G-10698)***

James Town Macadam Inc.....716 665-4504
1946 New York Ave Falconer (14733) ***(G-4903)***

James Wire Die Co.....315 894-3233
138 West St Ilion (13357) ***(G-6742)***

James Woerner Inc.....631 454-9330
130 Allen Blvd Farmingdale (11735) ***(G-5016)***

Jamesport Vineyards, Jamesport *Also called North House Vineyards Inc* ***(G-6966)***

Jamestown Advanced Pdts Corp.....716 483-3406
2855 Girts Rd Jamestown (14701) ***(G-7004)***

Jamestown Awning Inc.....716 483-1435
313 Steele St Jamestown (14701) ***(G-7005)***

Jamestown Bronze Works Inc.....716 665-2302
174 Hopkins Ave Jamestown (14701) ***(G-7006)***

ALPHABETIC

Jamestown Cont of Rochester....585 254-9190
82 Edwards Deming Dr Rochester (14606) *(G-14460)*
Jamestown Container Corp (PA)....716 665-4623
14 Deming Dr Falconer (14733) *(G-4904)*
Jamestown Engine Plant, Lakewood *Also called Cummins Inc (G-7289)*
Jamestown Envelope, Falconer *Also called Falconer Printing & Design Inc (G-4899)*
Jamestown Fab Stl & Sup Inc....716 665-2227
1034 Allen St Jamestown (14701) *(G-7007)*
Jamestown Industrial Trcks Inc....716 893-6105
999 Harlem Rd Buffalo (14224) *(G-3014)*
Jamestown Iron Works Inc....716 665-2818
2022 Allen Street Ext Falconer (14733) *(G-4905)*
Jamestown Kitchen & Bath Inc....716 665-2299
1085 E 2nd St Jamestown (14701) *(G-7008)*
Jamestown Macadam Inc (PA)....716 664-5108
74 Walden Ave Jamestown (14701) *(G-7009)*
Jamestown Mattress Co....716 665-2247
150 Blackstone Ave Jamestown (14701) *(G-7010)*
Jamestown Metal Products LLC....716 665-5313
178 Blackstone Ave Jamestown (14701) *(G-7011)*
Jamestown Mvp LLC....716 846-1418
2061 Allen Street Ext Falconer (14733) *(G-4906)*
Jamestown Plastics Inc (PA)....716 792-4144
8806 Highland Ave Brocton (14716) *(G-1249)*
Jamestown Royal, Jamestown *Also called Royal Jamestown Furniture Inc (G-7026)*
Jamestown Scientific Inds LLC....716 665-3224
1300 E 2nd St Jamestown (14701) *(G-7012)*
Jana Kos Collection, The, New York *Also called Style Partners Inc (G-12223)*
Janco Press Inc....631 563-3003
20 Floyds Run Bohemia (11716) *(G-1081)*
Jane Bohan Inc....212 529-6090
611 Broadway New York (10012) *(G-10699)*
Jane Lewis....607 722-0584
82 Castle Creek Rd Binghamton (13901) *(G-930)*
Janed Enterprises....631 694-4494
48 Allen Blvd Unit B Farmingdale (11735) *(G-5017)*
Janlynn Corporation, The, Bohemia *Also called Spectrum Crafts Inc (G-1136)*
Janowski Hamburger, Rockville Centre *Also called Bianca Burgers LLC (G-14788)*
Japan America Learning Ctr Inc (PA)....914 723-7600
81 Montgomery Ave Scarsdale (10583) *(G-15218)*
Japan Printing & Graphics Inc....212 406-2905
160 Broadway Lbby D New York (10038) *(G-10700)*
Jaquith Industries Inc....315 478-5700
600 E Brighton Ave Syracuse (13210) *(G-15966)*
Jar Metals Inc....845 425-8901
50 2nd Ave Nanuet (10954) *(G-8758)*
Jarets Stuffed Cupcakes....607 658-9096
116 Oak Hill Ave Endicott (13760) *(G-4814)*
Jarvik Heart Inc....212 397-3911
333 W 52nd St Ste 700 New York (10019) *(G-10701)*
Jasani Designs Usa Inc....212 257-6465
25 W 43rd St Ste 704 New York (10036) *(G-10702)*
Jasco Cutting Tools, Rochester *Also called Graywood Companies Inc (G-14413)*
Jasco Heat Treating Inc....585 388-0071
75 Macedon Center Rd Fairport (14450) *(G-4859)*
Jason & Jean Products Inc....718 271-8300
104 Corona Ave Corona (11368) *(G-3999)*
Jason Ladanye Guitar Piano & H....518 527-3973
605 Park Ave Albany (12208) *(G-92)*
Jason Manufacturing Company, Rochester *Also called Three R Enterprises Inc (G-14725)*
Jasper Transport LLC....315 729-5760
1680 Flat St Penn Yan (14527) *(G-13515)*
Javcon Machine Inc....631 586-1890
255 Skidmores Rd Deer Park (11729) *(G-4157)*
Javin Machine Corp....631 643-3322
31 Otis St West Babylon (11704) *(G-16801)*
Jax Coco USA LLC....347 688-8198
5 Penn Plz Ste 2300 New York (10001) *(G-10703)*
Jax Signs and Neon Inc....607 727-3420
108 Odell Ave Endicott (13760) *(G-4815)*
Jaxi's Sportswear, Brooklyn *Also called Jaxis Inc (G-2135)*
Jaxis Inc (PA)....212 302-7611
1365 38th St Brooklyn (11218) *(G-2135)*
Jaxson Rollforming Inc....631 842-7775
145 Dixon Ave Ste 1 Amityville (11701) *(G-298)*
Jay Bags Inc....845 459-6500
55 Union Rd Ste 107 Spring Valley (10977) *(G-15590)*
Jay Import Company Inc (PA)....212 683-2727
41 Madison Ave Fl 12 New York (10010) *(G-10704)*
Jay Little Oil Well Servi....716 925-8905
5460 Nichols Run Limestone (14753) *(G-7451)*
Jay Moulding Corporation....518 237-4200
7 Bridge Ave Ste 1 Cohoes (12047) *(G-3748)*
Jay Turoff....718 856-7300
681 Coney Island Ave Brooklyn (11218) *(G-2136)*
Jay-Aimee Designs Inc....718 609-0333
99 Railroad Station Plz # 200 Hicksville (11801) *(G-6356)*
Jay-Art Nvelties/Tower Grafics, Brooklyn *Also called Jay Turoff (G-2136)*
Jaya Apparel Group LLC....212 764-4980
1384 Broadway Fl 18 New York (10018) *(G-10705)*
Jayden Star LLC....212 686-0400
385 5th Ave Rm 507 New York (10016) *(G-10706)*
Jayen Chemical Supplies Inc....516 933-3311
1120 Old Country Rd # 311 Plainview (11803) *(G-13611)*
Jaymar Jewelry Co Inc....212 564-4788
357 W 36th St Rm 203 New York (10018) *(G-10707)*
Jays Furniture Products Inc....716 876-8854
321 Ramsdell Ave Buffalo (14216) *(G-3015)*
Jazzles, White Plains *Also called Readent Inc (G-17162)*
Jbf Stainless LLC....315 569-2800
4905 E Lake Rd Cazenovia (13035) *(G-3446)*
Jbs LLC....518 346-0001
6 Maple Ave Scotia (12302) *(G-15327)*
JC Crystal Inc....212 594-0858
260 W 35th St Fl 10 New York (10001) *(G-10708)*
Jcdecaux Mallscape LLC (HQ)....646 834-1200
3 Park Ave Fl 33 New York (10016) *(G-10709)*
JD Class Inc....212 764-6663
463 Fashion Ave Rm 600 New York (10018) *(G-10710)*
JD Tool Inc....607 786-3129
521 E Main St Endicott (13760) *(G-4816)*
Jdlr Enterprises LLC....315 813-2911
104 E Seneca St Sherrill (13461) *(G-15406)*
Jds Graphics, New York *Also called JDS Graphics Inc (G-10711)*
JDS Graphics Inc....973 330-3300
226 W 37th St Fl 10 New York (10018) *(G-10711)*
Jdt International LLC....212 400-7570
276 5th Ave Rm 704 New York (10001) *(G-10712)*
JE Miller Inc....315 437-6811
747 W Manlius St East Syracuse (13057) *(G-4546)*
JE Monahan Fabrications LLC....518 761-0414
559 Queensbury Ave 1/2 Queensbury (12804) *(G-14001)*
Jeam Imports, Brooklyn *Also called Executive Machines Inc (G-1945)*
Jean & Alex Jewelry Mfg & Cons....212 935-7621
587 5th Ave Fl 2 New York (10017) *(G-10713)*
Jean Philippe Fragrances LLC....212 983-2640
551 5th Ave Rm 1500 New York (10176) *(G-10714)*
Jean Pierre Cosmetics, New York *Also called Jean Pierre Inc (G-10715)*
Jean Pierre Inc....718 440-7349
320 5th Ave Fl 3 New York (10001) *(G-10715)*
Jeanjer LLC....212 944-1330
1400 Broadway Fl 15 New York (10018) *(G-10716)*
Jeans Inc....646 223-1122
1357 Broadway Ste 411 New York (10018) *(G-10717)*
Jed Lights Inc....516 812-5001
4 3rd St Garden City Park (11040) *(G-5540)*
Jeff Cooper Inc....516 333-8200
288 Westbury Ave Carle Place (11514) *(G-3391)*
Jefferson Concrete Corp....315 788-4171
22850 County Route 51 Watertown (13601) *(G-16655)*
Jeffersonville Volunteer....845 482-3110
49 Callicoon Center Rd Jeffersonville (12748) *(G-7059)*
Jeffrey D Menoff....716 665-1468
785 Fairmount Ave Jamestown (14701) *(G-7013)*
Jeffrey John....631 842-2850
25 Elm Pl Amityville (11701) *(G-299)*
Jeffrey Spring Modern Art, Astoria *Also called Modern Art Foundry Inc (G-449)*
Jekerda Sales, Jericho *Also called North American Pipe Corp (G-7079)*
Jem Container Corp....516 349-7770
151 Fairchild Ave Ste 1 Plainview (11803) *(G-13612)*
Jem Sign Corp (PA)....516 867-4466
470 S Franklin St Hempstead (11550) *(G-6275)*
Jem Threading Specialties Inc....718 665-3341
1059 Washington Ave Bronx (10456) *(G-1365)*
Jem Tool & Die Corp....631 539-8734
81 Paris Ct West Islip (11795) *(G-16905)*
JEm Wdwkg & Cabinets Inc....518 828-5361
250 Falls Rd Hudson (12534) *(G-6620)*
Jemcap Servicing LLC....212 213-9353
360 Madison Ave Rm 1902 New York (10017) *(G-10718)*
Jenalex Creative Marketing Inc....212 935-2266
116 E 57th St Fl 3 New York (10022) *(G-10719)*
Jenlor Ltd....315 637-9080
523 E Genesee St Fayetteville (13066) *(G-5165)*
Jenmar Door & Glass Inc....718 767-7900
15038 12th Ave Whitestone (11357) *(G-17210)*
Jenna Concrete Corporation....718 842-5250
1465 Bronx River Ave Bronx (10472) *(G-1366)*
Jenna Harlem River Inc....718 842-5997
1465 Bronx River Ave Bronx (10472) *(G-1367)*
Jenray Products Inc....914 375-5596
252 Lake Ave Fl 2a Yonkers (10701) *(G-17458)*
Jentronics, Holbrook *Also called Bryit Group LLC (G-6433)*
Jentsch & Co Inc....716 852-4111
107 Dorothy St Buffalo (14206) *(G-3016)*
JEnvie Sport Inc....212 967-2322
255 W 36th St 6 New York (10018) *(G-10720)*
Jeric Knit Wear....631 979-8827
61 Hofstra Dr Smithtown (11787) *(G-15490)*
Jerome Stvens Phrmcuticals Inc....631 567-1113
60 Davinci Dr Bohemia (11716) *(G-1082)*
Jerry Cardullo Iron Works Inc....631 242-8881
101 Spence St Bay Shore (11706) *(G-709)*
Jerry Miller I.D. Shoes, Buffalo *Also called Jerry Miller Molded Shoes Inc (G-3017)*

A L P H A B E T I C

Jerry Miller Molded Shoes Inc (PA)....716 881-3920
36 Mason St Buffalo (14213) *(G-3017)*
Jerry Sorbara Furs Inc....212 594-3897
39 W 32nd St Rm 1400 New York (10001) *(G-10721)*
Jerry Tomaselli....718 965-1400
141 32nd St Brooklyn (11232) *(G-2137)*
Jerry's Bagels & Bakery, Valley Stream *Also called Jerrys Bagels (G-16410)*
Jerrys Bagels....516 791-0063
951 Rosedale Rd Valley Stream (11581) *(G-16410)*
Jersey Express Inc....716 834-6151
3080 Main St Buffalo (14214) *(G-3018)*
Jesco Lighting Inc (PA)....718 366-3211
15 Harbor Park Dr Port Washington (11050) *(G-13828)*
Jesco Lighting Group LLC (PA)....718 366-3211
15 Harbor Park Dr Port Washington (11050) *(G-13829)*
Jesse Joeckel....631 668-2772
65 Tuthill Rd Montauk (11954) *(G-8588)*
Jessel Marking Equipment, Syracuse *Also called New York Marking Devices Corp (G-15998)*
Jessica Michelle, New York *Also called Orchid Manufacturing Co Inc (G-11524)*
Jet Components Inc....631 436-7300
62 Bridge Rd Islandia (11749) *(G-6797)*
Jet Line, White Plains *Also called Gemini Manufacturing LLC (G-17113)*
Jet Redi Mix Concrete Inc....631 580-3640
2101 Pond Rd Ste 1 Ronkonkoma (11779) *(G-14919)*
Jet Sew Corporation....315 896-2683
8119 State Route 12 Barneveld (13304) *(G-614)*
Jet-Black Sealers Inc....716 891-4197
555 Ludwig Ave Buffalo (14227) *(G-3019)*
Jets Lefrois Corp....585 637-5003
56 High St Brockport (14420) *(G-1245)*
Jets Lefrois Foods, Brockport *Also called Jets Lefrois Corp (G-1245)*
Jetson Electric Bikes LLC....908 309-8880
175 Varick St Fl 5 New York (10014) *(G-10722)*
Jette Group, Bay Shore *Also called Cable Management Solutions Inc (G-680)*
Jewelers Machinist Co Inc....631 661-5020
400 Columbus Ave Babylon (11704) *(G-549)*
Jewelers Solder Supply Inc....718 637-1256
1362 54th St Brooklyn (11219) *(G-2138)*
Jewelmak Inc....212 398-2999
344 E 59th St Fl 1&2 New York (10022) *(G-10723)*
Jewelry Arts Manufacturing....212 382-3583
151 W 46th St Fl 12 New York (10036) *(G-10724)*
Jewels By Star Ltd....212 308-3490
555 5th Ave Fl 7 New York (10017) *(G-10725)*
Jeweltex Mfg Corp....212 921-8188
48 W 48th St Ste 507 New York (10036) *(G-10726)*
Jewish Heritage For Blind....718 338-4999
1655 E 24th St Brooklyn (11229) *(G-2139)*
Jewish Journal....718 630-9350
7014 13th Ave Brooklyn (11228) *(G-2140)*
Jewish Press Inc....718 330-1100
4915 16th Ave Brooklyn (11204) *(G-2141)*
Jewish Week Inc (PA)....212 921-7822
1501 Broadway Ste 505 New York (10036) *(G-10727)*
Jewler's Solder Sheet & Wire, Brooklyn *Also called Jewelers Solder Supply Inc (G-2138)*
Jeypore Group, New York *Also called Incon Gems Inc (G-10583)*
JF Machine Shop Inc....631 491-7273
89 Otis St Unit A West Babylon (11704) *(G-16802)*
Jf Rafter The Lexington Co, Eden *Also called John F Rafter Inc (G-4587)*
Jfb Print Solutions Inc....631 694-8300
21 Park Dr Lido Beach (11561) *(G-7441)*
Jfe Engineering Corporation....212 310-9320
350 Park Ave Fl 27th New York (10022) *(G-10728)*
Jfe Steel America Inc (PA)....212 310-9320
600 3rd Ave Rm 1201 New York (10016) *(G-10729)*
Jfs Inc....646 264-1200
531 W 26th St Unit 531 New York (10001) *(G-10730)*
JG Innovative Industries Inc....718 784-7300
8002 Kew Gardens Rd Kew Gardens (11415) *(G-7164)*
Jgx LLC....212 575-1244
1407 Broadway Rm 1416 New York (10018) *(G-10731)*
Jhc Labresin, Brooklyn *Also called J H C Fabrications Inc (G-2122)*
Jifft Tite, Batavia *Also called Protech Automation LLC (G-646)*
Jill Fagin Enterprises Inc (PA)....212 674-9383
107 Avenue B New York (10009) *(G-10732)*
Jill Fenichell Inc....718 237-2490
169 Prospect Pl Brooklyn (11238) *(G-2142)*
Jillery, New York *Also called Jill Fagin Enterprises Inc (G-10732)*
Jim Henson Company Inc....212 794-2400
117 E 69th St New York (10021) *(G-10733)*
Jim Henson Productions, New York *Also called Jim Henson Company Inc (G-10733)*
Jim Quinn....518 356-0398
12 Morningside Dr Schenectady (12303) *(G-15270)*
Jim Quinn and Associates, Schenectady *Also called Jim Quinn (G-15270)*
Jim Romas Bakery Inc....607 748-7425
202 N Nanticoke Ave Endicott (13760) *(G-4817)*
Jim Wachtler Inc....212 755-4367
1212 Avenue Of The Ste 2200 New York (10036) *(G-10734)*
Jimeale Incorporated....917 686-5383
130 Church St Ste 163 New York (10007) *(G-10735)*
Jimmy Crystal New York Co Ltd....212 594-0858
47 W 37th St Fl 3 New York (10018) *(G-10736)*
Jimmy Sales, Brooklyn *Also called Tie King Inc (G-2659)*
Jinglebell Inc....914 219-5395
190 Byram Lake Rd Armonk (10504) *(G-416)*
JINGLENOG DBA, Armonk *Also called Jinglebell Inc (G-416)*
Jiranimo Industries Ltd....212 921-5106
49a W 37th St New York (10018) *(G-10737)*
Jisan Trading Corporation....212 244-1269
519 8th Ave Rm 810 New York (10018) *(G-10738)*
Jj Basics LLC (PA)....212 768-4779
525 7th Ave Rm 307 New York (10018) *(G-10739)*
JJ Cassone Bakery Inc....914 939-1568
202 S Regent St Port Chester (10573) *(G-13750)*
Jj Fantasia Inc....212 868-1198
38 W 32nd St New York (10001) *(G-10740)*
Jj Marco, New York *Also called Hy Gold Jewelers Inc (G-10535)*
JK Jewelry Inc....585 346-3464
1500 Brighton Henrietta Rochester (14623) *(G-14461)*
JK Manufacturing Inc....212 683-3535
115 Forest Ave Unit 22 Locust Valley (11560) *(G-7633)*
Jlm Couture Inc (PA)....212 921-7058
525 Fashion Ave Rm 1703 New York (10018) *(G-10741)*
Jlnw Inc (PA)....212 719-4666
3030 47th Ave Long Island City (11101) *(G-7771)*
JM Manufacturer Inc....212 869-0626
241 W 37th St Rm 924 New York (10018) *(G-10742)*
JM Murray Center Inc (PA)....607 756-9913
823 State Route 13 Ste 1 Cortland (13045) *(G-4031)*
JM Murray Center Inc....607 756-0246
4057 West Rd Cortland (13045) *(G-4032)*
JM Originals Inc....845 647-3003
70 Berme Rd Ellenville (12428) *(G-4634)*
JM Studio Inc....646 546-5514
247 W 35th St Fl 3 New York (10001) *(G-10743)*
Jma Wireless, Liverpool *Also called John Mezzalingua Assoc LLC (G-7528)*
Jmg Fuel Inc....631 579-4319
3 Fowler Ave Ronkonkoma (11779) *(G-14920)*
Jmk Enterprises LLC....845 634-8100
301 N Main St Ste 1 New City (10956) *(G-8786)*
Jml Optical Industries LLC....585 248-8900
820 Linden Ave Rochester (14625) *(G-14462)*
Jml Quarries Inc....845 932-8206
420 Bernas Rd Cochecton (12726) *(G-3741)*
JMS Ices Inc....718 448-0853
501 Port Richmond Ave Staten Island (10302) *(G-15692)*
Jmt Program Leadership Group....585 217-1134
1305 Emerson St Rochester (14606) *(G-14463)*
Jn Marina, New York *Also called Marina Jewelry Co Inc (G-11152)*
Jnc Repair, Brooklyn *Also called Godfrey Prpeller Adjusting Svc (G-2035)*
Jo Mart Chocolates, Brooklyn *Also called Jo-Mart Candies Corp (G-2143)*
Jo-Mart Candies Corp....718 375-1277
2917 Avenue R Brooklyn (11229) *(G-2143)*
Jo-Vin Decorators Inc....718 441-9350
9423 Jamaica Ave Woodhaven (11421) *(G-17306)*
Joan Boyce Ltd (PA)....212 867-7474
19 W 44th St Ste 417 New York (10036) *(G-10744)*
Joanna Mastroianni, New York *Also called Elana Laderos Ltd (G-9993)*
Jobs Weekly Inc....716 648-5627
31 Buffalo St Ste 2 Hamburg (14075) *(G-5929)*
Jobson Medical Information LLC (PA)....212 274-7000
100 Ave Of Amer Fl 9 New York (10013) *(G-10745)*
Jockey International Inc....212 840-4900
1411 Broadway Rm 1010 New York (10018) *(G-10746)*
Jockey International Inc....518 761-0965
1439 State Route 9 Ste 10 Lake George (12845) *(G-7261)*
Jockey Store, New York *Also called Jockey International Inc (G-10746)*
Joe Benbasset Inc (PA)....212 268-4920
213 W 35th St Fl 11 New York (10001) *(G-10747)*
Joe Fresh, New York *Also called Jfs Inc (G-10730)*
Joe Moro....607 272-0591
214 Fayette St Ithaca (14850) *(G-6855)*
Joe P Industries Inc....631 293-7889
6 Commerce Dr Farmingdale (11735) *(G-5018)*
Joe Pietryka Incorporated (PA)....845 855-1201
85 Charles Colman Blvd Pawling (12564) *(G-13450)*
Joed Press....212 243-3620
242 W 36th St Fl 8 New York (10018) *(G-10748)*
Joel Kiryas Meat Market Corp....845 782-9194
51 Forest Rd Ste 345 Monroe (10950) *(G-8557)*
Joel Zelcer....917 525-6790
102 S 8th St Brooklyn (11249) *(G-2144)*
Joerger Enterprises Inc....631 239-5579
166 Laurel Rd Ste 214 East Northport (11731) *(G-4438)*
Joes Jeans, New York *Also called Gbg West LLC (G-10257)*
John A Eberly Inc....315 449-3034
136 Beattie St Syracuse (13224) *(G-15967)*
John A Vassilaros & Son Inc....718 886-4140
2905 120th St Flushing (11354) *(G-5257)*
John Auguliaro Printing Co....718 382-5283
2533 Mcdonald Ave Brooklyn (11223) *(G-2145)*

ALPHABETIC

John Bossone, Glendale *Also called New Day Woodwork Inc (G-5659)*
John C Dolph Company Inc 732 329-2333
200 Von Roll Dr Schenectady (12306) ***(G-15271)***
John Crane Inc 315 593-6237
2314 County Route 4 Fulton (13069) ***(G-5464)***
John Deere Authorized Dealer, Fulton *Also called Gone South Concrete Block Inc (G-5459)*
John E Potente & Sons Inc 516 935-8585
114 Woodbury Rd Unit 1 Hicksville (11801) ***(G-6357)***
John F Krell Jr 315 492-3201
4046 W Seneca Trpk Syracuse (13215) ***(G-15968)***
John F Rafter Inc 716 992-3425
2746 W Church St Eden (14057) ***(G-4587)***
John G Rubino Inc 315 253-7396
45 Aurelius Ave Auburn (13021) ***(G-504)***
John Gailer Inc 212 243-5662
3718 Northern Blvd Ste 3 Long Island City (11101) ***(G-7772)***
John Hassall LLC (HQ) 516 334-6200
609 Cantiague Rock Rd # 1 Westbury (11590) ***(G-16998)***
John Hassall LLC 323 869-0150
609 Cantiague Rock Rd # 1 Westbury (11590) ***(G-16999)***
John J Mazur Inc 631 242-4554
94 E Jefryn Blvd Ste K Deer Park (11729) ***(G-4158)***
John J Richardson 516 538-6339
12 Bernard St Lawrence (11559) ***(G-7392)***
John Kochis Custom Designs 212 244-6046
237 W 35th St Ste 702 New York (10001) ***(G-10749)***
John Kristiansen New York Inc 212 388-1097
665 Broadway Frnt New York (10012) ***(G-10750)***
John Langenbacher Co Inc 718 328-0141
888 Longfellow Ave Bronx (10474) ***(G-1368)***
John Larocca & Son Inc 631 423-5256
290 Broadway Huntington Station (11746) ***(G-6712)***
John Lor Publishing Ltd 631 475-1000
20 Medford Ave Ste 1 Patchogue (11772) ***(G-13425)***
John Marshall Sound Inc 212 265-6066
630 9th Ave Ste 1108 New York (10036) ***(G-10751)***
John Mezzalingua Assoc LLC (PA) 315 431-7100
7645 Henry Clay Blvd # 678 Liverpool (13088) ***(G-7528)***
John N Fehlinger Co Inc (PA) 212 233-5656
20 Vesey St Rm 1000 New York (10007) ***(G-10752)***
John Patrick, Germantown *Also called On The Double Inc (G-5591)*
John Prior 516 520-9801
2545 Hempstead Tpke # 402 East Meadow (11554) ***(G-4426)***
John R Robinson Inc 718 786-6088
3805 30th St Long Island City (11101) ***(G-7773)***
John Ramsey Elec Svcs LLC 585 298-9596
7940 Rae Blvd Victor (14564) ***(G-16483)***
John Szoke Editions, New York *Also called John Szoke Graphics Inc (G-10753)*
John Szoke Graphics Inc 212 219-8300
24 W 57th St Ste 304 New York (10019) ***(G-10753)***
John T Montecalvo Inc 631 325-1492
1233 Speonk River Head Rd Speonk (11972) ***(G-15576)***
John V Agugliaro Printing, Brooklyn *Also called John Auguliaro Printing Co (G-2145)*
John Varvatos Company 212 812-8000
26 W 17th St Fl 12 New York (10011) ***(G-10754)***
John Vespa Inc (PA) 315 788-6330
19626 Overlook Dr Watertown (13601) ***(G-16656)***
John Wiley & Sons Inc 845 457-6250
46 Wavey Willow Ln Montgomery (12549) ***(G-8596)***
Johnnie Ryan Co Inc 716 282-1606
3084 Niagara St Niagara Falls (14303) ***(G-12838)***
Johnny Bienstock Music 212 779-7977
126 E 38th St New York (10016) ***(G-10755)***
Johnny Mica Inc 631 225-5213
116 E Hoffman Ave Lindenhurst (11757) ***(G-7466)***
Johnny's Ideal Prntng Co, Hudson *Also called Johnnys Ideal Printing Co (G-6621)*
Johnnys Ideal Printing Co 518 828-6666
352 Warren St Hudson (12534) ***(G-6621)***
Johnnys Machine Shop 631 338-9733
81 Mahan St West Babylon (11704) ***(G-16803)***
Johns Manville Corporation 518 565-3000
1 Kaycee Loop Rd Plattsburgh (12901) ***(G-13673)***
Johns Ravioli Company Inc 914 576-7030
15 Drake Ave New Rochelle (10805) ***(G-8915)***
Johnson & Hoffman LLC 516 742-3333
40 Voice Rd Carle Place (11514) ***(G-3392)***
Johnson Acquisition Corp (HQ) 518 828-1616
364 Warren St Hudson (12534) ***(G-6622)***
Johnson Bros Lumber, Cazenovia *Also called PDJ Inc (G-3450)*
Johnson Contrls Authorized Dlr, North Baldwin *Also called Split Systems Corp (G-12909)*
Johnson Controls Inc 585 924-9346
7612 Main Street Fishers Victor (14564) ***(G-16484)***
Johnson Controls Inc 518 884-8313
339 Brownell Rd Ballston Spa (12020) ***(G-600)***
Johnson Controls Inc 585 671-1930
237 Birch Ln Webster (14580) ***(G-16725)***
Johnson Controls Inc 914 593-5200
8 Skyline Dr Ste 115 Hawthorne (10532) ***(G-6248)***
Johnson Controls Inc 716 688-7340
130 John Muir Dr Ste 100 Buffalo (14228) ***(G-3020)***
Johnson Controls Inc 585 724-2232
1669 Lake Ave Bldg 333 Rochester (14652) ***(G-14464)***

Johnson Manufacturing Co 631 472-1184
326 3rd Ave Bayport (11705) ***(G-758)***
Johnson Manufacturing Company 716 881-3030
1489 Niagara St Buffalo (14213) ***(G-3021)***
Johnson Mch & Fibr Pdts Co Inc 716 665-2003
142 Hopkins Ave Jamestown (14701) ***(G-7014)***
Johnson Newspaper Corporation 518 483-4700
469 E Main St Ste 2 Malone (12953) ***(G-8011)***
Johnson Outdoors Inc 607 779-2200
625 Conklin Rd Binghamton (13903) ***(G-931)***
Johnson S Sand Gravel Inc 315 771-1450
23284 County Route 3 La Fargeville (13656) ***(G-7237)***
Johnston Dandy Company 315 455-5773
100 Dippold Ave Syracuse (13208) ***(G-15969)***
Johnston Forest Products Inc 607 363-2947
O And W Rd East Branch (13756) ***(G-4384)***
Johnston Precision Inc 315 253-4181
7 Frank Smith St Auburn (13021) ***(G-505)***
Joka Industries Inc 631 589-0444
65 Knickerbocker Ave A Bohemia (11716) ***(G-1083)***
Joldeson One Aerospace Inds, Ozone Park *Also called Joldeson One Aerospace Inds (G-13380)*
Joldeson One Aerospace Inds 718 848-7396
10002 103rd Ave Ozone Park (11417) ***(G-13380)***
Jolin Machining Corp 631 589-1305
1561 Smithtown Ave Bohemia (11716) ***(G-1084)***
Jomar Industries Inc 845 357-5773
382 Route 59 Ste 352 Airmont (10952) ***(G-16)***
Jomart Associates Inc 212 627-2153
170 Oval Dr Ste A Islandia (11749) ***(G-6798)***
Jomat New York Inc 718 369-7641
4100 1st Ave Ste 3 Brooklyn (11232) ***(G-2146)***
Jon Barry Company Division, Brooklyn *Also called Kwik Ticket Inc (G-2183)*
Jon Lyn Ink Inc 516 546-2312
255 Sunrise Hwy Ste 1 Merrick (11566) ***(G-8386)***
Jon Teri Sports Inc (PA) 212 398-0657
241 W 37th St Frnt 2 New York (10018) ***(G-10756)***
Jonas Louis Paul Studios Inc 518 851-2211
304 Miller Rd Hudson (12534) ***(G-6623)***
Jonathan David Publishers Inc 718 456-8611
6822 Eliot Ave Middle Village (11379) ***(G-8413)***
Jonathan Lord Corp 631 563-4445
87 Carlough Rd Unit A Bohemia (11716) ***(G-1085)***
Jonathan Meizler LLC 212 213-2977
37 W 26th St Ph New York (10010) ***(G-10757)***
Jonathan Metal & Glass Ltd 718 846-8000
17818 107th Ave Jamaica (11433) ***(G-6924)***
Jonathan Michael Coat Corp 212 239-9230
463 Fashion Ave Rm 1502 New York (10018) ***(G-10758)***
Jonathan Michael Coats, New York *Also called Gfb Fashions Ltd (G-10288)*
Jonden Manufacturing Co Inc (PA) 516 442-4895
1410 Broadway Rm 1103 New York (10018) ***(G-10759)***
Jonden Manufacturing Co Inc 718 369-4925
3069 Lawson Blvd Oceanside (11572) ***(G-13083)***
Jones Humdinger 607 771-6501
204 Hayes Rd Binghamton (13905) ***(G-932)***
Jones Jeanswear Group, New York *Also called One Jeanswear Group Inc (G-11506)*
Jones New York, New York *Also called Nine West Holdings Inc (G-11438)*
Jones New York, New York *Also called Nine West Holdings Inc (G-11441)*
Jones New York, New York *Also called Nine West Holdings Inc (G-11439)*
Jonice Industires 516 640-4283
95 Angevine Ave Hempstead (11550) ***(G-6276)***
Jordache Enterprises Inc 212 944-1330
1400 Broadway Rm 1415 New York (10018) ***(G-10760)***
Jordache Enterprises Inc (PA) 212 643-8400
1400 Broadway Rm 1404b New York (10018) ***(G-10761)***
Jordache Woodworking Corp 718 349-3373
276 Greenpoint Ave # 1303 Brooklyn (11222) ***(G-2147)***
Jordan Box Co, Syracuse *Also called Jordon Box Company Inc (G-15970)*
Jordan Panel Systems Corp (PA) 631 754-4900
196 Laurel Rd Unit 2 East Northport (11731) ***(G-4439)***
Jordan Products Inc 585 385-7777
430 Whitney Rd Penfield (14526) ***(G-13500)***
Jordan Scott Designs Ltd 212 947-4250
25 W 36th St Fl 12 New York (10018) ***(G-10762)***
Jordon Box Company Inc 315 422-3419
140 Dickerson St Syracuse (13202) ***(G-15970)***
Jordon Controls, Rochester *Also called Rotork Controls Inc (G-14659)*
Jos H Lowenstein and Sons Inc 718 218-8013
420 Morgan Ave Brooklyn (11222) ***(G-2148)***
Joseph (uk) Inc 212 570-0077
1061 Madison Ave Grnd New York (10028) ***(G-10763)***
Joseph A Filippazzo Software 718 987-1626
106 Lovell Ave Staten Island (10314) ***(G-15693)***
Joseph Abboud Manufacturing 212 586-9140
650 5th Ave Fl 20 New York (10019) ***(G-10764)***
Joseph Corcoran Marble Inc 631 423-8712
50 W Hills Rd Unit B Huntington Station (11746) ***(G-6713)***
Joseph Fedele 718 448-3658
1950b Richmond Ter Staten Island (10302) ***(G-15694)***
Joseph H Navaie 607 936-9030
81 W Market St Corning (14830) ***(G-3974)***

ALPHABETIC

Joseph Industries Inc (PA) 212 764-0010
1410 Broadway Rm 1501 New York (10018) *(G-10765)*
Joseph Paul 718 693-4269
1064 Rogers Ave Apt 5 Brooklyn (11226) *(G-2149)*
Joseph Shalhoub & Son Inc 718 871-6300
1258 Prospect Ave Brooklyn (11218) *(G-2150)*
Joseph Struhl Co Inc 516 741-3660
195 Atlantic Ave New Hyde Park (11040) *(G-8843)*
Joseph Treu Successors Inc 212 691-7026
104 W 27th St Rm 5b New York (10001) *(G-10766)*
Joseph Zakon Winery Ltd 718 604-1430
586 Montgomery St Brooklyn (11225) *(G-2151)*
Joseph's Cloak, New York *Also called Americo Group Inc (G-9131)*
Josh Packaging Inc 631 822-1660
245 Marcus Blvd Ste 1 Hauppauge (11788) *(G-6102)*
Joshua Liner Gallery LLC 212 244-7415
540 W 28th St Frnt New York (10001) *(G-10767)*
Josie Accessories Inc (PA) 212 889-6376
261 5th Ave Fl 10 New York (10016) *(G-10768)*
Jotaly Inc 212 886-6000
1385 Broadway Fl 12 New York (10018) *(G-10769)*
Journal and Republican, Lowville *Also called Lowville Newspaper Corporation (G-7940)*
Journal News 914 694-5000
1133 Westchester Ave N-110 White Plains (10604) *(G-17130)*
Journal News 845 578-2324
200 N Route 303 West Nyack (10994) *(G-16920)*
Journal Register Company 212 257-7212
450 W 33rd St Fl 11 New York (10001) *(G-10770)*
Journal Register Company 518 584-4242
20 Lake Ave Saratoga Springs (12866) *(G-15161)*
Journal Register Company (PA) 212 257-7212
5 Hanover Sq Fl 25 New York (10004) *(G-10771)*
Journal Stationers, Greenwich *Also called Tefft Publishers Inc (G-5894)*
Jovani Fashion Ltd 212 279-0222
1370 Broadway Fl 4 New York (10018) *(G-10772)*
Joy Edward Company 315 474-3360
6747 W Benedict Rd East Syracuse (13057) *(G-4547)*
Joy of Learning 718 443-6463
992 Gates Ave Brooklyn (11221) *(G-2152)*
Joy Process Mechanical, East Syracuse *Also called Joy Edward Company (G-4547)*
Joya LLC 718 852-6979
19 Vanderbilt Ave Brooklyn (11205) *(G-2153)*
Joya Studio, Brooklyn *Also called Joya LLC (G-2153)*
Joyce Center, Manhasset *Also called Advanced Prosthetics Orthotics (G-8054)*
Joyce Trimming Inc 212 719-3110
109 W 38th St New York (10018) *(G-10773)*
Joycharge Inc 646 321-1127
510 Madison Ave New York (10022) *(G-10774)*
Joyva Corp (PA) 718 497-0170
53 Varick Ave Brooklyn (11237) *(G-2154)*
JP Bus & Truck Repair Ltd (PA) 516 767-2700
135 Haven Ave Port Washington (11050) *(G-13830)*
JP Filling Inc 845 534-4793
20 Industry Dr Mountainville (10953) *(G-8748)*
JP Oil Group Inc 607 563-1360
49 Union St Sidney (13838) *(G-15440)*
JP Signs 518 569-3907
9592 State Route 9 Chazy (12921) *(G-3562)*
Jpm and Associates 516 483-4699
639 Nostrand Ave Uniondale (11553) *(G-16297)*
Jpm Fine Woodworking LLC 516 236-7605
103 Estate Dr Jericho (11753) *(G-7074)*
Jpmorgan Chase & Co 845 298-2461
1460 Route 9 Wappingers Falls (12590) *(G-16574)*
Jpmorgan Chase Bank Nat Assn 718 767-3592
13207 14th Ave College Point (11356) *(G-3793)*
Jpmorgan Chase Bank Nat Assn 718 668-0346
1690 Hylan Blvd Staten Island (10305) *(G-15695)*
Jpw Riggers & Erectors, Syracuse *Also called Jpw Structural Contracting Inc (G-15971)*
Jpw Structural Contracting Inc 315 432-1111
6376 Thompson Rd Syracuse (13206) *(G-15971)*
Jre Test, Victor *Also called John Ramsey Elec Svcs LLC (G-16483)*
Jre Test LLC 585 298-9736
7940 Rae Blvd Victor (14564) *(G-16485)*
Jrg Apparel Group Company Ltd 212 997-0900
1407 Broadway Rm 317 New York (10018) *(G-10775)*
Jrlon Inc 315 597-4067
4344 Fox Rd Palmyra (14522) *(G-13409)*
JRs Fuels Inc 518 622-9939
8037 Route 32 Cairo (12413) *(G-3273)*
JRS Pharma LP (HQ) 845 878-8300
2981 Route 22 Ste 1 Patterson (12563) *(G-13441)*
JS Blank & Co Inc 212 689-4835
112 Madison Ave Fl 7 New York (10016) *(G-10776)*
JSA Jewelry Inc 212 764-4504
2 W 46th St Ste 506 New York (10036) *(G-10777)*
Jsc Design, New York *Also called Badgley Mischka Licensing LLC (G-9301)*
Jsc Designs Ltd 212 302-1001
550 Fashion Ave Fl 22 New York (10018) *(G-10778)*
JSM Vinyl Products Inc 516 775-4520
44 Orchid Ln New Hyde Park (11040) *(G-8844)*
Jsp, Bohemia *Also called Jerome Stvens Phrmcuticals Inc (G-1082)*
Jsr Ultrasonics Division, Pittsford *Also called Imaginant Inc (G-13564)*
Jt Precision Inc 716 795-3860
8701 Haight Rd Barker (14012) *(G-613)*
Jt Roselle Lighting & Sup Inc 914 666-3700
333 N Bedford Rd Mount Kisco (10549) *(G-8632)*
JT Systems Inc 315 622-1980
8132 Oswego Rd Liverpool (13090) *(G-7529)*
Jta USA Inc 718 722-0902
63 Flushing Ave Unit 339 Brooklyn (11205) *(G-2155)*
Jtekt Torsen North America 585 464-5000
2 Jetview Dr Rochester (14624) *(G-14465)*
Juan Motors, Palmyra *Also called Faradyne Motors LLC (G-13405)*
Judaica Press Inc 718 972-6202
123 Ditmas Ave Brooklyn (11218) *(G-2156)*
Judgement Clothing, New York *Also called Fashion Apparel Industries (G-10140)*
Judi Boisson American Country, Southampton *Also called American Country Quilts & Lin (G-15538)*
Judis Lampshades Inc 917 561-3921
1495 E 22nd St Brooklyn (11210) *(G-2157)*
Judith Lewis Printer Inc 516 997-7777
1915 Ladenburg Dr Westbury (11590) *(G-17000)*
Judith N Graham Inc 914 921-5446
64 Halls Ln Rye (10580) *(G-15061)*
Judscott Handprints Ltd (PA) 914 347-5515
2269 Saw Mill River Rd 4d Elmsford (10523) *(G-4759)*
Judys Group Inc 212 921-0515
1400 Broadway Rm 919 New York (10018) *(G-10779)*
Juice Press LLC (PA) 212 777-0034
110 E 59th St Fl 28 New York (10022) *(G-10780)*
Juices Enterprises Inc 718 953-1860
1142 Nostrand Ave Brooklyn (11225) *(G-2158)*
Juicy Vapor LLC (PA) 855 525-8429
188 Creekside Dr Amherst (14228) *(G-248)*
Jules Smith Llc 718 783-2495
1369 Broadway Fl 4 New York (10018) *(G-10781)*
Julia Jordan Corporation 646 214-3090
530 Fashion Ave Rm 505 New York (10018) *(G-10782)*
Julia Knit Inc 718 848-1900
8050 Pitkin Ave Ozone Park (11417) *(G-13381)*
Julian A McDermott Corporation 718 456-3606
1639 Stephen St Ridgewood (11385) *(G-14111)*
Julians Recipe LLC 888 640-8880
128 Norman Ave Brooklyn (11222) *(G-2159)*
Julius Cohen Jewelers Inc 212 371-3050
699 Madison Ave Fl 4 New York (10065) *(G-10783)*
Julius Klein Group 212 719-1811
580 5th Ave Ste 500 New York (10036) *(G-10784)*
Julius Lowy Frame Restoring Co 212 861-8585
232 E 59th St 4fn New York (10022) *(G-10785)*
Jump Apparel Group, The, New York *Also called Jump Design Group Inc (G-10786)*
Jump Design Group Inc 212 869-3300
1400 Broadway Fl 2 New York (10018) *(G-10786)*
Jumprope Inc 347 927-5867
121 W 27th St Ste 1204 New York (10001) *(G-10787)*
June Jacobs Labs LLC 212 471-4830
460 Park Ave Fl 16 New York (10022) *(G-10788)*
Junior Achevement of Eastrn NY 518 783-4336
8 Stanley Cir Ste 8 Latham (12110) *(G-7366)*
Juniors Cheesecake Inc 718 852-5257
386 Flatbush Avenue Ext Brooklyn (11201) *(G-2160)*
Juniper Elbow Co Inc (PA) 718 326-2546
7215 Metropolitan Ave Middle Village (11379) *(G-8414)*
Juniper Industries, Middle Village *Also called Juniper Elbow Co Inc (G-8414)*
Juniper Industries Florida Inc 718 326-2546
7215 Metropolitan Ave Middle Village (11379) *(G-8415)*
Juniper Networks Inc 212 520-3300
1 Penn Plz Ste 1901 New York (10119) *(G-10789)*
Junk In My Trunk Inc 631 420-5865
266 Route 109 Farmingdale (11735) *(G-5019)*
Juno Chefs 845 294-5400
1 6 1/2 Station Rd Goshen (10924) *(G-5735)*
Jupiter Creations Inc 917 493-9393
330 7th Ave Ste 901 New York (10001) *(G-10790)*
Juris Publishing Inc 631 351-5430
71 New St Ste 1 Huntington (11743) *(G-6665)*
Jurist Company Inc 212 243-8008
1105 44th Dr Long Island City (11101) *(G-7774)*
Jus-Sar Fuel Inc 845 791-8900
884 Old Route 17 Harris (12742) *(G-5976)*
Just Beverages LLC 480 388-1133
31 Broad St Glens Falls (12801) *(G-5683)*
Just Bottoms & Tops Inc (PA) 212 564-3202
1412 Broadway Rm 1808 New York (10018) *(G-10791)*
Just Brass Inc 212 724-5447
215 W 90th St Apt 9a New York (10024) *(G-10792)*
Just For Men Div, New York *Also called Jeanjer LLC (G-10716)*
Just In Time Cnc Machining 585 335-2010
88 Ossian St Dansville (14437) *(G-4078)*
Just In Time Company, Endwell *Also called J T Systematic (G-4836)*
Just Lamps of New York Inc 716 626-2240
334 Harris Hill Rd Apt 1 Buffalo (14221) *(G-3022)*

ALPHABETIC

Just Perfect MSP Ltd 877 201-0005
48 W 48th St Ste 401 New York (10036) *(G-10793)*
Just Plastics, New York *Also called Gifford Group Inc (G-10293)*
Just Right Carbines LLC 585 261-5331
231 Saltonstall St Canandaigua (14424) *(G-3348)*
Just Wood Pallets Inc 718 644-7013
78 Vails Gate Heights Dr New Windsor (12553) *(G-8940)*
Justa Company 718 932-6139
3464 9th St Long Island City (11106) *(G-7775)*
Justin Ashley Designs Inc 718 707-0200
4301 21st St Ste 212a Long Island City (11101) *(G-7776)*
Justin Gregory Inc 631 249-5187
6 Banfi Plz W Farmingdale (11735) *(G-5020)*
Justyna Kaminska NY Inc 917 423-5527
1270 Broadway Rm 708 New York (10001) *(G-10794)*
JW Burg Machine & Tool Inc 716 434-0015
7430 Rapids Rd Clarence Center (14032) *(G-3678)*
JW Consulting Inc 845 325-7070
20 Chevron Rd Unit 201 Monroe (10950) *(G-8558)*
Jwin Electronics Corp (PA) 516 626-7188
2 Harbor Park Dr Port Washington (11050) *(G-13831)*
K & B Signs, Mount Vernon *Also called K & B Stamping Co Inc (G-8696)*
K & B Stamping Co Inc 914 664-8555
29 Mount Vernon Ave Mount Vernon (10550) *(G-8696)*
K & B Woodworking Inc 518 634-7253
133 Rolling Meadow Rd Cairo (12413) *(G-3274)*
K & E Fabricating Co Inc 716 829-1829
40 Stanley St Buffalo (14206) *(G-3023)*
K & H Industries Inc (PA) 716 312-0088
160 Elmview Ave Hamburg (14075) *(G-5930)*
K & H Industries Inc 716 312-0088
160 Elmview Ave Hamburg (14075) *(G-5931)*
K & H Precision Products Inc 585 624-4894
45 Norton St Honeoye Falls (14472) *(G-6532)*
K & R Allied Inc 718 625-6610
39 Pearl St Fl 2 Brooklyn (11201) *(G-2161)*
K & S & East, Pelham *Also called Eastco Manufacturing Corp (G-13490)*
K & S Childrens Wear Inc 718 624-0006
204 Wallabout St Brooklyn (11206) *(G-2162)*
K Barthelmes Mfg Co Inc 585 328-8140
61 Brooklea Dr Rochester (14624) *(G-14466)*
K C Technical Services, Bohemia *Also called Cos TEC Manufacturing Corp (G-1039)*
K C Technical Services Inc 631 589-7170
390 Knickerbocker Ave # 1 Bohemia (11716) *(G-1086)*
K D Dance, Bronx *Also called KD Dids Inc (G-1369)*
K D M Die Company Inc 716 828-9000
620 Elk St Buffalo (14210) *(G-3024)*
K Displays 718 854-6045
1363 47th St Brooklyn (11219) *(G-2163)*
K F I Inc 516 546-2904
33 Debevoise Ave Roosevelt (11575) *(G-15006)*
K Hein Machines Inc 607 748-1546
341 Vestal Pkwy E Vestal (13850) *(G-16450)*
K Kitchen, Buffalo *Also called Kalnitz Kitchens Inc (G-3026)*
K M Drive Line Inc 718 599-0628
966 Grand St Brooklyn (11211) *(G-2164)*
K P I Plastics, Howes Cave *Also called W Kintz Plastics Inc (G-6601)*
K P Signs, North Bellmore *Also called KP Industries Inc (G-12922)*
K Road Moapa Solar LLC 212 351-0535
295 Madison Ave Fl 37 New York (10017) *(G-10795)*
K Road Power Management LLC (PA) 212 351-0535
767 3rd Ave Fl 37 New York (10017) *(G-10796)*
K Sidrane Inc 631 393-6974
24 Baiting Place Rd Farmingdale (11735) *(G-5021)*
K T A V Publishing House Inc 201 963-9524
527 Empire Blvd Brooklyn (11225) *(G-2165)*
K T P Design Co Inc 212 481-6613
118 E 28th St Rm 707 New York (10016) *(G-10797)*
K Tooling LLC 607 637-3781
396 E Front St Hancock (13783) *(G-5964)*
K Z Precision, Lancaster *Also called Kz Precision Inc (G-7321)*
K&G of Syracuse Inc 315 446-1921
2500 Erie Blvd E Syracuse (13224) *(G-15972)*
K&Ns Foods Usa LLC 315 598-8080
607 Phillips St Fulton (13069) *(G-5465)*
K-Binet Inc 845 348-1149
624 Route 303 Blauvelt (10913) *(G-972)*
K-D Stone Inc 518 642-2082
Rr 22 Middle Granville (12849) *(G-8400)*
K-Technologies Inc 716 828-4444
4090 Jeffrey Blvd Buffalo (14219) *(G-3025)*
K2 International Corp 212 947-1734
22 W 32nd St Fl 9 New York (10001) *(G-10798)*
K2 Plastics Inc 585 494-2727
8210 Buffalo Rd Bergen (14416) *(G-847)*
Kabar Manufacturing Corp (HQ) 631 694-6857
140 Schmitt Blvd Farmingdale (11735) *(G-5022)*
Kabar Manufacturing Corp 631 694-1036
113 Gazza Blvd Farmingdale (11735) *(G-5023)*
Kabbalah Centre, Richmond Hill *Also called Research Centre of Kabbalah (G-14079)*
Kabco Pharmaceuticals Inc 631 842-3600
2000 New Horizons Blvd Amityville (11701) *(G-300)*
Kabrics 607 962-6344
2737 Forest Hill Dr Corning (14830) *(G-3975)*
Kadant Inc 518 793-8801
436 Quaker Rd Glens Falls (12804) *(G-5684)*
Kadco Usa Inc 518 661-6068
17 W Main St Mayfield (12117) *(G-8213)*
Kaddis Manufacturing Corp 585 624-3070
1175 Bragg St Honeoye Falls (14472) *(G-6533)*
Kader Lithograph Company Inc 917 664-4380
3002 48th Ave Ste C Long Island City (11101) *(G-7777)*
Kadmon Corporation LLC (PA) 212 308-6000
450 E 29th St Fl 5 New York (10016) *(G-10799)*
Kadmon Holdings Inc 212 308-6000
450 E 29th St New York (10016) *(G-10800)*
Kafko (us) Corp 877 721-7665
787 Watervliet Shaker Rd Latham (12110) *(G-7367)*
Kahn-Lucas-Lancaster Inc 212 239-2407
112 W 34th St Ste 600 New York (10120) *(G-10801)*
Kaitery Furs Ltd 718 204-1396
2529 49th St Long Island City (11103) *(G-7778)*
Kal Manufacturing Corporation 585 265-4310
657 Basket Rd Webster (14580) *(G-16726)*
Kal Pac Corp 845 457-7013
10 Factory St Montgomery (12549) *(G-8597)*
Kal-Harbour Inc 518 266-0690
11 Villa Rd Albany (12204) *(G-93)*
Kale Factory Inc 917 363-6361
790 Washington Ave Brooklyn (11238) *(G-2166)*
Kaleidoscope Imaging Inc 212 631-9947
307 W 38th St Fl 6 New York (10018) *(G-10802)*
Kaleko Bros 212 819-0100
580 5th Ave Ste 928 New York (10036) *(G-10803)*
Kalel Partners LLC 347 561-7804
7012 170th St Ste 101 Flushing (11365) *(G-5258)*
Kalikow Brothers LP 212 643-0315
34 W 33rd St Fl 4n New York (10001) *(G-10804)*
Kallen Corp 212 242-1470
99 Hudson St Lbby 2 New York (10013) *(G-10805)*
Kalnitz Kitchens Inc 716 684-1700
2620 Walden Ave Buffalo (14225) *(G-3026)*
Kaltec Food Packaging Inc 845 856-9888
36 Center St 40 Port Jervis (12771) *(G-13786)*
Kaltech Food Packaging Inc 845 856-1210
3640 Center St Port Jervis (12771) *(G-13787)*
Kaltex America Inc 212 971-0575
350 5th Ave Ste 7100 New York (10118) *(G-10806)*
Kaltex North America Inc (HQ) 212 894-3200
350 5th Ave Ste 7100 New York (10118) *(G-10807)*
Kamali Group Inc 516 627-4000
17 Barstow Rd Ste 206 Great Neck (11021) *(G-5819)*
Kamali Leather Corp 518 762-2522
204 Harrison St Johnstown (12095) *(G-7117)*
Kaman Automation Inc 585 254-8840
1000 University Ave Rochester (14607) *(G-14467)*
Kamerys Wholesale Meats Inc 716 372-6756
322 E Riverside Dr Olean (14760) *(G-13149)*
Kammetal Inc 718 625-2628
75 Huntington St Brooklyn (11231) *(G-2167)*
Kammetal Inc (PA) 718 722-9991
29 Imlay St Brooklyn (11231) *(G-2168)*
Kangaroo Crossing, Manlius *Also called Mayberry Shoe Company Inc (G-8074)*
Kannalife Sciences Inc 516 669-3219
4 Knoll Ct Lloyd Harbor (11743) *(G-7567)*
Kantek Inc 516 594-4600
3460a Hampton Rd Oceanside (11572) *(G-13084)*
Kantian Skincare LLC 631 780-4711
496 Smithtown Byp Smithtown (11787) *(G-15491)*
Kaprielian Enterprises Inc 212 645-6623
207 W 25th St Fl 8 New York (10001) *(G-10808)*
Kaps-All Packaging Systems 631 574-8778
200 Mill Rd Riverhead (11901) *(G-14145)*
Kapstone Container Corporation 518 842-2450
28 Park Dr Amsterdam (12010) *(G-352)*
Karbra Company 212 736-9300
151 W 46th St Fl 10 New York (10036) *(G-10809)*
Karen Kane Inc 212 827-0980
1441 Broadway Fl 33 New York (10018) *(G-10810)*
Karen Miller Ltd (PA) 212 819-9550
60 W 38th St Rm 200 New York (10018) *(G-10811)*
Karey Kassl Corp 516 349-8484
180 Terminal Dr Plainview (11803) *(G-13613)*
Karey Products, Plainview *Also called Karey Kassl Corp (G-13613)*
Karishma Fashions Inc 718 565-5404
3708 74th St Jackson Heights (11372) *(G-6888)*
Karlyn Industries Inc 845 351-2249
16 Spring St Southfields (10975) *(G-15556)*
Karo Sheet Metal Inc 718 542-8420
229 Russell St Brooklyn (11222) *(G-2169)*
Karosheet Metal, Brooklyn *Also called Karo Sheet Metal Inc (G-2169)*
Karp Associates Inc (PA) 631 768-8300
260 Spagnoli Rd Melville (11747) *(G-8332)*
Karp Overseas Corporation 718 784-2105
5454 43rd St Maspeth (11378) *(G-8148)*

Karr Graphics Corp 718 784-9390
2219 41st Ave Fl 2a Long Island City (11101) *(G-7779)*
Kart, Maspeth *Also called Jack Luckner Steel Shelving Co (G-8147)*
Karter Bias Binding, Long Island City *Also called Empire Bias Binding Co Inc (G-7730)*
Kas Direct LLC 516 934-0541
1600 Stewart Ave Ste 411 Westbury (11590) *(G-17001)*
Kas-Kel, Fonda *Also called Kasson & Keller Inc (G-5315)*
Kas-Ray Industries Inc 212 620-3144
122 W 26th St New York (10001) *(G-10812)*
Kaseya US Sales LLC 415 694-5700
62 W 22nd St Ste 2r New York (10010) *(G-10813)*
Kasper, New York *Also called Nine West Holdings Inc (G-11442)*
Kasper Group LLC (HQ) 212 354-4311
1412 Broadway Fl 5 New York (10018) *(G-10814)*
Kasper Group LLC 212 354-4311
1412 Broadway Fl 5 New York (10018) *(G-10815)*
Kasson & Keller Inc 518 853-3421
60 School St Fonda (12068) *(G-5315)*
Kastor Consulting Inc 718 224-9109
3919 218th St Bayside (11361) *(G-773)*
Kat Nap Products, Brooklyn *Also called Steinbock-Braff Inc (G-2606)*
Kate Spade & Company (PA) 212 354-4900
2 Park Ave Fl 8 New York (10016) *(G-10816)*
Kates Paperie Ltd 212 966-3904
188 Lafayette St Frnt A New York (10013) *(G-10817)*
Katherine Blizniak (PA) 716 674-8545
525 Bullis Rd West Seneca (14224) *(G-16950)*
Kathleen B Mead 585 247-0146
1675 Buffalo Rd Rochester (14624) *(G-14468)*
Kathmando Valley Preservation 212 727-0074
36 W 25th St Fl 17 New York (10010) *(G-10818)*
Katikati Inc 585 678-1764
150 Lucius Gordon Dr West Henrietta (14586) *(G-16883)*
Katz Americas, Sanborn *Also called Katz Group Americas Inc (G-15122)*
Katz Gluten Free, Mountainville *Also called Gluten Free Bake Shop Inc (G-8747)*
Katz Group Americas Inc 716 995-3071
3685 Lockport Rd Sanborn (14132) *(G-15122)*
Katz Martell Fashion Trdg Intl 212 840-0070
1385 Broadway Rm 1401 New York (10018) *(G-10819)*
Kaufman Brothers Printing 212 563-1854
327 W 36th St Rm 403 New York (10018) *(G-10820)*
Kawasaki Rail Car Inc (HQ) 914 376-4700
29 Wells Ave Bldg 4 Yonkers (10701) *(G-17459)*
Kay See Dental Mfg Co 816 842-2817
777 Avenue Of The Apt 32 New York (10001) *(G-10821)*
Kay Unger, New York *Also called Phoebe Company LLC (G-11650)*
Kay-Ray Industries, New York *Also called Kas-Ray Industries Inc (G-10812)*
Kaymil Printing Company Inc 212 594-3718
140 W 30th St Frnt New York (10001) *(G-10822)*
Kaymil Ticket Company, New York *Also called Kaymil Printing Company Inc (G-10822)*
Kayo of California 212 354-6336
525 Fashion Ave Rm 309 New York (10018) *(G-10823)*
Kays Caps Inc (PA) 518 273-6079
65 Arch St Troy (12183) *(G-16221)*
Kazac Inc 631 249-7299
55 Allen Blvd Ste C Farmingdale (11735) *(G-5024)*
KB Millwork Inc 516 280-2183
36 Grey Ln Levittown (11756) *(G-7429)*
Kbc, Bronx *Also called Kirschner Brush LLC (G-1373)*
Kbl Healthcare LP 212 319-5555
757 3rd Ave Fl 20 New York (10017) *(G-10824)*
Kbs Communications LLC 212 765-7124
331 W 57th St Ste 148 New York (10019) *(G-10825)*
Kc Collections LLC 212 302-4412
1407 Broadway Rm 1710 New York (10018) *(G-10826)*
Kc Tag Co 518 842-6666
108 Edson St Amsterdam (12010) *(G-353)*
Kch Publications Inc 516 671-2360
57 Glen St Ste 1 Glen Cove (11542) *(G-5619)*
Kcp Holdco Inc 212 265-1500
603 W 50th St New York (10019) *(G-10827)*
KD Dids Inc (PA) 718 402-2012
140 E 144th St Bronx (10451) *(G-1369)*
KDI Paragon, Lagrangeville *Also called Paragon Aquatics (G-7257)*
KDO Industries Inc 631 608-4612
32 Ranick Dr W Amityville (11701) *(G-301)*
Ke Durasol Awnings Inc 845 610-1100
445 Bellvale Rd Chester (10918) *(G-3609)*
Kearney-National Inc (HQ) 212 661-4600
565 5th Ave Fl 4 New York (10017) *(G-10828)*
Keck Group Inc (PA) 845 988-5757
314 State Route 94 S Warwick (10990) *(G-16591)*
Kedco Inc 516 454-7800
564 Smith St Farmingdale (11735) *(G-5025)*
Kedco Wine Storage Systems, Farmingdale *Also called Kedco Inc (G-5025)*
Keebler Company 585 948-8010
2999 Judge Rd Oakfield (14125) *(G-13065)*
Keebler Company 631 234-3700
55 Gilpin Ave Hauppauge (11788) *(G-6103)*
Keebler Company 518 464-1051
12 Selina Dr Albany (12205) *(G-94)*
Keebler Company 845 365-5200
29 Corporate Dr Orangeburg (10962) *(G-13232)*
Keegan Ales LLC 845 331-2739
20 Saint James St Kingston (12401) *(G-7192)*
Keeler Services 607 776-5757
47 W Steuben St Ste 4 Bath (14810) *(G-658)*
Keeners East End Litho Inc 631 324-8565
10 Prospect Blvd East Hampton (11937) *(G-4412)*
Keep America Beautiful Inc 518 842-4388
1 Prospect St Amsterdam (12010) *(G-354)*
Keep Healthy Inc 631 651-9090
1019 Fort Salonga Rd Northport (11768) *(G-13013)*
Kefa Industries Group Inc 718 568-9297
9219 63rd Dr Rego Park (11374) *(G-14034)*
Kehr-Buffalo Wire Frame Co Inc 716 897-2288
127 Kehr St Buffalo (14211) *(G-3027)*
Keilhauer 646 742-0192
200 Lexington Ave Rm 1101 New York (10016) *(G-10829)*
Keith Lewis Studio Inc 845 339-5629
35 Rifton Ter Rifton (12471) *(G-14134)*
Keller Bros & Miller Inc 716 854-2374
401 Franklin St Buffalo (14202) *(G-3028)*
Keller International Pubg LLC (PA) 516 829-9210
150 Main St Ste 10 Port Washington (11050) *(G-13832)*
Keller Technology Corporation (PA) 716 693-3840
2320 Military Rd Tonawanda (14150) *(G-16175)*
Kelley Bros Llc 315 852-3302
1714 Albany St De Ruyter (13052) *(G-4081)*
Kelley Farm & Garden Inc 518 234-2332
239 W Main St Cobleskill (12043) *(G-3738)*
Kellogg Company 315 452-0310
7350 Round Pond Rd North Syracuse (13212) *(G-12951)*
Kellogg Company 845 365-5284
29 Corporate Dr Orangeburg (10962) *(G-13233)*
Kelly Foundry & Machine Co 315 732-8313
300 Hubbell St Ste 308 Utica (13501) *(G-16346)*
Kelly Grace Corp (PA) 212 704-9603
49 W 37th St Fl 10 New York (10018) *(G-10830)*
Kelly Window Systems Inc 631 420-8500
460 Smith St Farmingdale (11735) *(G-5026)*
Kelmar Systems Inc 631 421-1230
284 Broadway Huntington Station (11746) *(G-6714)*
Kelson Products Inc 716 825-2585
3300 N Benzing Rd Orchard Park (14127) *(G-13277)*
Kelta Inc (PA) 631 789-5000
141 Rodeo Dr Edgewood (11717) *(G-4602)*
Keltron Connector Co., Ronkonkoma *Also called Keltron Electronics (de Corp) (G-14921)*
Keltron Electronics (de Corp) 631 567-6300
3385 Vtrans Mem Hwy Ste E Ronkonkoma (11779) *(G-14921)*
Kem Medical Products Corp (PA) 631 454-6565
400 Broadhollow Rd Ste 2 Farmingdale (11735) *(G-5027)*
Kemco Sales LLC 203 762-1902
119 Despatch Dr East Rochester (14445) *(G-4463)*
Kemet Properties LLC 718 654-8079
1179 E 224th St Bronx (10466) *(G-1370)*
Kemp Metal Products Inc 516 997-8860
2300 Shames Dr Westbury (11590) *(G-17002)*
Kemp Technologies Inc (PA) 917 688-4067
1540 Broadway Fl 23 New York (10036) *(G-10831)*
Kemper System America Inc (HQ) 716 558-2971
1200 N America Dr West Seneca (14224) *(G-16951)*
Ken-Ton Open Mri PC 716 876-7000
2882 Elmwood Ave Kenmore (14217) *(G-7150)*
Kenal Services Corp 315 788-9226
1109 Water St Watertown (13601) *(G-16657)*
Kenan International Trading 718 672-4922
10713 Northern Blvd Corona (11368) *(G-4000)*
Kenbenco Inc 845 246-3066
437 Route 212 Saugerties (12477) *(G-15186)*
Kendall Circuits Inc 631 473-3636
5507-10 Nesconset Hwy 105 Mount Sinai (11766) *(G-8655)*
Kendi Iron Works Inc (PA) 718 821-2722
236 Johnson Ave Brooklyn (11206) *(G-2170)*
Kendor Music Inc 716 492-1254
21 Grove St Delevan (14042) *(G-4235)*
Kenmar Shirts Inc (PA) 718 824-3880
1415 Blondell Ave Bronx (10461) *(G-1371)*
Kennedy Valve Division, Elmira *Also called McWane Inc (G-4694)*
Kennel Klub, Utica *Also called Clara Papa (G-16311)*
Kenneth Cole Productions LP (HQ) 212 265-1500
603 W 50th St New York (10019) *(G-10832)*
Kenneth Cole Productions Inc (PA) 212 265-1500
603 W 50th St New York (10019) *(G-10833)*
Kenneth J Lane Inc 212 868-1780
20 W 37th St Fl 9 New York (10018) *(G-10834)*
Kenney Manufacturing Displays 631 231-5563
12 Grand Blvd Brentwood (11717) *(G-1188)*
Kenny Mfg, Brentwood *Also called Kenney Manufacturing Displays (G-1188)*
Kens Service & Sales Inc 716 683-1155
11500 Clinton St Elma (14059) *(G-4650)*
Kensington & Sons LLC 646 450-5735
270 Lafayette St Ste 200 New York (10012) *(G-10835)*

ALPHABETIC

Kensington Publishing Corp....212 407-1500
119 W 40th St Fl 21 New York (10018) ***(G-10836)***
Kenstan Lock & Hardware Co Inc....631 423-1977
101 Commercial St Ste 100 Plainview (11803) ***(G-13614)***
Kenstan Lock Co., Plainview *Also called Kenstan Lock & Hardware Co Inc* ***(G-13614)***
Kent Associates Inc....212 675-0722
99 Battery Pl Apt 11p New York (10280) ***(G-10837)***
Kent Chemical Corporation....212 521-1700
460 Park Ave Fl 7 New York (10022) ***(G-10838)***
Kent Electro-Plating Corp....718 358-9599
5 Dupont Ct Dix Hills (11746) ***(G-4292)***
Kent Gage & Tool Company, Poughkeepsie *Also called Stanfordville Mch & Mfg Co Inc* ***(G-13934)***
Kent Nutrition Group Inc....315 788-0032
810 Waterman Dr Watertown (13601) ***(G-16658)***
Kent Optronics Inc....845 897-0138
40 Corporate Park Rd Hopewell Junction (12533) ***(G-6555)***
Kentronics Inc....631 567-5994
140 Keyland Ct Unit 1 Bohemia (11716) ***(G-1087)***
Kenwell Corporation....315 592-4263
871 Hannibal St Fulton (13069) ***(G-5466)***
Kenwin Sales Corp....516 933-7553
1100 Shames Dr Westbury (11590) ***(G-17003)***
Kenyon Press Inc....607 674-9066
1 Kenyon Press Dr Sherburne (13460) ***(G-15392)***
Keon Optics Inc....845 429-7103
30 John F Kennedy Dr Stony Point (10980) ***(G-15775)***
Kepco Inc (PA)....718 461-7000
13138 Sanford Ave Flushing (11355) ***(G-5259)***
Kepco Inc....718 461-7000
13140 Maple Ave Flushing (11355) ***(G-5260)***
Kepco Inc....718 461-7000
13138 Sanford Ave Flushing (11355) ***(G-5261)***
Kerner and Merchant....315 463-8023
104 Johnson St East Syracuse (13057) ***(G-4548)***
Kernow North America....585 586-3590
5 Park Forest Dr Pittsford (14534) ***(G-13566)***
Kerns Manufacturing Corp (PA)....718 784-4044
3714 29th St Long Island City (11101) ***(G-7780)***
Kerry Bio-Science, Norwich *Also called Kerry Inc* ***(G-13029)***
Kerry Inc....845 584-3080
225 New York Hwy 303 N St Congers (10920) ***(G-3858)***
Kerry Inc (HQ)....607 334-1700
158 State Highway 320 Norwich (13815) ***(G-13029)***
Keryakos Inc....518 344-7092
1080 Catalyn St Fl 2 Schenectady (12303) ***(G-15272)***
Kesser Wine, Brooklyn *Also called Joseph Zakon Winery Ltd* ***(G-2151)***
Kessler Thermometer Corp....631 841-5500
40 Gleam St West Babylon (11704) ***(G-16804)***
Kesso Foods Inc....718 777-5303
7720 21st Ave East Elmhurst (11370) ***(G-4393)***
Ketcham Medicine Cabinets....631 615-6151
3505 Vtrans Mem Hwy Ste L Ronkonkoma (11779) ***(G-14922)***
Ketcham Pump Co Inc....718 457-0800
3420 64th St Woodside (11377) ***(G-17334)***
Ketchum Manufacturing Co Inc....518 696-3331
11 Town Shed Rd Lake Luzerne (12846) ***(G-7272)***
Keuka Brewing Co LLC....607 868-4648
8572 Briglin Rd Hammondsport (14840) ***(G-5957)***
Keuka Studios Inc....585 624-5960
1011 Rush Henrietta Townl Rush (14543) ***(G-15051)***
Kevco Industries....845 255-7407
6 Millbrook Rd New Paltz (12561) ***(G-8875)***
Kevin Freeman....631 447-5321
414 S Service Rd Ste 119 Patchogue (11772) ***(G-13426)***
Kevin J Kassman....585 529-4245
1408 Buffalo Rd Rochester (14624) ***(G-14469)***
Kevin Regan Logging Ltd....315 245-3890
1011 Hillsboro Rd Camden (13316) ***(G-3317)***
Key Brand Entertainment Inc....212 966-5400
104 Franklin St New York (10013) ***(G-10839)***
Key Cast Stone Company Inc....631 789-2145
113 Albany Ave Amityville (11701) ***(G-302)***
Key Computer Svcs of Chelsea....212 206-8060
227 E 56th St New York (10022) ***(G-10840)***
Key Container Corp....631 582-3847
135 Hollins Ln East Islip (11730) ***(G-4417)***
Key Digital Systems Inc....914 667-9700
521 E 3rd St Mount Vernon (10553) ***(G-8697)***
Key High Vacuum Products Inc....631 584-5959
36 Southern Blvd Nesconset (11767) ***(G-8775)***
Key Signals....631 433-2962
47 Tuthill Point Rd East Moriches (11940) ***(G-4429)***
Key Tech Finishing....716 832-1232
2929 Main St Ste 2 Buffalo (14214) ***(G-3029)***
Keyes Machine Works Inc....585 426-5059
147 Park Ave Gates (14606) ***(G-5561)***
Keymark Corporation....518 853-3421
1188 Cayadutta St Fonda (12068) ***(G-5316)***
Keynote Systems Corporation....716 564-1332
2810 Sweet Home Rd Buffalo (14228) ***(G-3030)***
Keystone Corporation (PA)....716 832-1232
2929 Main St Buffalo (14214) ***(G-3031)***
Keystone Electronics Corp (PA)....718 956-8900
3107 20th Rd Astoria (11105) ***(G-446)***
Keystone Iron & Wire Works Inc....718 392-1616
217 54th Ave Long Island City (11101) ***(G-7781)***
Ki Pro Performance, New York *Also called Fusion Pro Performance Ltd* ***(G-10226)***
Kicks Closet Sportswear Inc....347 577-0857
1031 Southern Blvd Frnt 2 Bronx (10459) ***(G-1372)***
Kids, New York *Also called Bagznyc Corp* ***(G-9305)***
Kids Discover, New York *Also called Mark Levine* ***(G-11155)***
Kids Uv Suncare Products, Brooklyn *Also called Baby Uv/Kids Uv Inc* ***(G-1661)***
Kidtellect Inc....617 803-1456
222 Broadway Level19 New York (10038) ***(G-10841)***
Kidz Concepts LLC....212 398-1110
1412 Brdwy Fl 3 New York (10018) ***(G-10842)***
Kidz World Inc....212 563-4949
226 W 37th St Fl 12 New York (10018) ***(G-10843)***
Kiklord LLC....917 859-1700
10 W Broadway Apt 5l Long Beach (11561) ***(G-7641)***
Kilian Manufacturing Corp (HQ)....315 432-0700
1728 Burnet Ave Syracuse (13206) ***(G-15973)***
Kiltronx Enviro Systems LLC....239 273-8870
845 3rd Ave Fl 11 New York (10022) ***(G-10844)***
Kiltronx Enviro Systems LLC....917 971-7177
330 Motor Pkwy Ste 201 Hauppauge (11788) ***(G-6104)***
Kim Eugenia Inc....212 674-1345
347 W 36th St Rm 502 New York (10018) ***(G-10845)***
Kim Jae Printing Co Inc....212 691-6289
249 Parkside Dr Roslyn Heights (11577) ***(G-15028)***
Kim Seybert Inc (PA)....212 564-7850
37 W 37th St Fl 9 New York (10018) ***(G-10846)***
Kimball Office Inc....212 753-6161
215 Park Ave S Fl 3 New York (10003) ***(G-10847)***
Kimber Mfg Inc....914 965-0753
16 Harrison Ave Yonkers (10705) ***(G-17460)***
Kimber Mfg Inc (PA)....914 964-0771
1 Lawton St Yonkers (10705) ***(G-17461)***
Kimber Mfg Inc....406 758-2222
555 Taxter Rd Ste 235 Elmsford (10523) ***(G-4760)***
Kimberley Diamond, New York *Also called H C Kionka & Co Inc* ***(G-10388)***
Kimbri Liquor, Mohegan Lake *Also called Shopping Center Wine & Liquor* ***(G-8544)***
Kimmeridge Energy MGT Co LLC (PA)....646 517-7252
400 Madison Ave Rm 14c New York (10017) ***(G-10848)***
Kimmiekakes LLC....212 946-0311
270 W 38th St Rm 1704 New York (10018) ***(G-10849)***
Kimsco Business Systems Inc....516 599-5658
424 Scranton Ave Lynbrook (11563) ***(G-7952)***
Kinaneco Inc (PA)....315 468-6201
2925 Milton Ave Syracuse (13209) ***(G-15974)***
Kinaneco Printing Systems, Syracuse *Also called Kinaneco Inc* ***(G-15974)***
Kind Group LLC (PA)....212 645-0800
19 W 44th St Ste 811 New York (10036) ***(G-10850)***
Kindling Inc....212 400-6296
440 Park Ave S Fl 14 New York (10016) ***(G-10851)***
Kinedyne Inc....716 667-6833
3566 S Benzing Rd Orchard Park (14127) ***(G-13278)***
Kinemotive Corporation....631 249-6440
222 Central Ave Ste 1 Farmingdale (11735) ***(G-5028)***
Kinequip Inc....716 694-5000
365 Old Niagara Fls Blvd Buffalo (14228) ***(G-3032)***
Kinetic Fuel Technology Inc....716 745-1461
1205 Balmer Rd Youngstown (14174) ***(G-17531)***
Kinetic Laboratories, Youngstown *Also called Kinetic Fuel Technology Inc* ***(G-17531)***
Kinetic Marketing Inc....212 620-0600
1133 Broadway Ste 221 New York (10010) ***(G-10852)***
Kinfolk Studios Inc....347 799-2946
90 Wythe Ave Brooklyn (11249) ***(G-2171)***
King Album Inc....631 253-9500
20 Kean St West Babylon (11704) ***(G-16805)***
King Cracker Corp....516 539-9251
307 Peninsula Blvd Hempstead (11550) ***(G-6277)***
King Displays Inc....212 629-8455
333 W 52nd St New York (10019) ***(G-10853)***
King Lithographers Inc (PA)....914 667-4200
245 S 4th Ave Mount Vernon (10550) ***(G-8698)***
King Paving, Schenectady *Also called King Road Materials Inc* ***(G-15273)***
King Research Inc....718 788-0122
114 12th St Ste 1 Brooklyn (11215) ***(G-2172)***
King Road Materials Inc (HQ)....518 381-9995
1245 Kings Rd Schenectady (12303) ***(G-15273)***
King Road Materials Inc....518 382-5354
145 Cordell Rd Schenectady (12303) ***(G-15274)***
King Road Materials Inc....518 382-5354
Cordell Rd Albany (12212) ***(G-95)***
King Sales Inc....718 301-9862
284 Wallabout St Brooklyn (11206) ***(G-2173)***
King Steel Iron Work Corp....718 384-7500
2 Seneca Ave Brooklyn (11237) ***(G-2174)***
Kingform Cap Company Inc....516 822-2501
121 New South Rd Hicksville (11801) ***(G-6358)***
Kinglift Elevator Inc....917 923-3517
1 Maiden Ln Fl 5 New York (10038) ***(G-10854)***

Kings Film & Sheet Inc...718 624-7510
482 Baltic St Brooklyn (11217) *(G-2175)*
Kings Material, Brooklyn *Also called US Concrete Inc (G-2712)*
Kings Park Asphalt Corporation...631 269-9774
201 Moreland Rd Ste 2 Hauppauge (11788) *(G-6105)*
Kings Park Ready Mix Corp...631 269-4330
140 Old Northport Rd E Kings Park (11754) *(G-7172)*
Kings Quarry, Adams Center *Also called R G King General Construction (G-4)*
Kings Quartet Corp...845 986-9090
270 Kings Hwy Warwick (10990) *(G-16592)*
Kings Ready Mix, Roslyn Heights *Also called US Concrete Inc (G-15034)*
Kings Specialty Co, Brooklyn *Also called Kings Film & Sheet Inc (G-2175)*
Kingsbury Printing Co Inc...518 747-6606
813 Bay Rd Queensbury (12804) *(G-14002)*
Kingston Hoops Summer...845 401-6830
68 Glen St Kingston (12401) *(G-7193)*
Kingston Pharma LLC...315 705-4019
5 County Route 42 Massena (13662) *(G-8197)*
Kingston Pharmaceuticals, Massena *Also called Kingston Pharma LLC (G-8197)*
Kingston Wste Wtr Trment Plant, Kingston *Also called City of Kingston (G-7184)*
Kingstreet Sounds, New York *Also called His Productions USA Inc (G-10483)*
Kinplex Corp (PA)...631 242-4800
200 Heartland Blvd Edgewood (11717) *(G-4603)*
Kinplex Corp...631 242-4800
200 Heartland Blvd Edgewood (11717) *(G-4604)*
Kinro Manufacturing Inc (HQ)...817 483-7791
200 Mmaroneck Ave Ste 301 White Plains (10601) *(G-17131)*
Kinshofer Usa Inc...716 731-4333
6420 Inducon Dr W Ste G Sanborn (14132) *(G-15123)*
Kintex Inc...716 297-0652
3315 Haseley Dr Niagara Falls (14304) *(G-12839)*
Kionix Inc...607 257-1080
36 Thornwood Dr Ithaca (14850) *(G-6856)*
Kirays & Joel Meat Market, Monroe *Also called Joel Kiryas Meat Market Corp (G-8557)*
Kirschner Brush LLC...718 292-1809
605 E 132nd St Frnt 3 Bronx (10454) *(G-1373)*
Kirtas Inc...585 924-2420
7620 Omnitech Pl Ste 1 Victor (14564) *(G-16486)*
Kirtas Technologies, Inc., Victor *Also called Kirtas Inc (G-16486)*
Kiss My Face, Gardiner *Also called Bycmac Corp (G-5548)*
Kissle, Jamaica *Also called Whitney Foods Inc (G-6964)*
Kitchen Cabinet Co, Poughkeepsie *Also called Modern Cabinet Company Inc (G-13917)*
Kitchen Design Center, Sauquoit *Also called Custom Stair & Millwork Co (G-15199)*
Kitchen Specialty Craftsmen...607 739-0833
2366 Corning Rd Elmira (14903) *(G-4693)*
Kiton Building Corp...212 486-3224
4 E 54th St New York (10022) *(G-10855)*
Kittinger Company Inc...716 876-1000
4675 Transit Rd Buffalo (14221) *(G-3033)*
Kittywalk Systems Inc...516 627-8418
10 Farmview Rd Port Washington (11050) *(G-13833)*
KJ MEAT DIRECT, Monroe *Also called JW Consulting Inc (G-8558)*
KKR Millennium GP LLC...212 750-8300
9 W 57th St Ste 4150 New York (10019) *(G-10856)*
KKR Ntral Rsources Fund I-A LP (HQ)...212 750-8300
9 W 57th St Ste 4200 New York (10019) *(G-10857)*
Kkw Corp...631 589-5454
90 Bourne Blvd Sayville (11782) *(G-15211)*
Klara Technologies Inc...844 215-5272
1 State St Fl 25 New York (10004) *(G-10858)*
Klauber Brothers Inc (PA)...212 686-2531
980 Ave Of The Ave Frnt 2 New York (10018) *(G-10859)*
Kld Labs Inc...631 549-4222
55 Cabot Ct Hauppauge (11788) *(G-6106)*
Klearbar Inc...516 684-9892
8 Graywood Rd Port Washington (11050) *(G-13834)*
Klee Corp...585 272-0320
340 Jefferson Rd Rochester (14623) *(G-14470)*
Kleen Stik Industries Inc...718 984-5031
44 Lenzie St Staten Island (10312) *(G-15696)*
Kleer - View Index Co Inc...718 896-3800
6938 Garfield Ave Woodside (11377) *(G-17335)*
Kleer-Fax Inc...631 225-1100
750 New Horizons Blvd Amityville (11701) *(G-303)*
Klees Car Wash and Detailing, Rochester *Also called Klee Corp (G-14470)*
Klein & Company, Massapequa *Also called R Klein Jewelry Co Inc (G-8181)*
Klein & Sons Logging Inc...845 292-6682
3114 State Route 52 Wht Sphr Spgs (12787) *(G-17221)*
Klein Cutlery LLC...585 928-2500
7971 Refinery Rd Bolivar (14715) *(G-1159)*
Klein Reinforcing Services Inc...585 352-9433
11 Turner Dr Spencerport (14559) *(G-15571)*
Kleinfelder John...716 753-3163
5239 W Lake Rd Mayville (14757) *(G-8216)*
Klemmt Orthopaedic Services, Johnson City *Also called Klemmt Orthotics & Prosthetics (G-7097)*
Klemmt Orthotics & Prosthetics...607 770-4400
130 Oakdale Rd Johnson City (13790) *(G-7097)*
Klg Usa LLC...845 856-5311
20 W King St Port Jervis (12771) *(G-13788)*
Kling Magnetics Inc...518 392-4000
343 State Route 295 Chatham (12037) *(G-3558)*
Klutz (HQ)...650 687-2600
568 Broadway Rm 503 New York (10012) *(G-10860)*
Klutz Store, New York *Also called Klutz (G-10860)*
KMA Corporation...518 743-1330
153 Maple St Ste 5 Glens Falls (12801) *(G-5685)*
Kms Contracting Inc...718 495-6500
86 Georgia Ave Brooklyn (11207) *(G-2176)*
Knf Clean Room Products Corp...631 588-7000
1800 Ocean Ave Ronkonkoma (11779) *(G-14923)*
Kng Construction Co Inc...212 595-1451
19 Silo Ln Warwick (10990) *(G-16593)*
Knickerbocker Graphics Svcs...212 244-7485
256 W 38th St Rm 504 New York (10018) *(G-10861)*
Knickerbocker Partition Corp (PA)...516 546-0550
193 Hanse Ave Freeport (11520) *(G-5406)*
Knight Sttlement Sand Grav LLC...607 776-2048
7291 County Route 15 Bath (14810) *(G-659)*
Knightly Endeavors...845 340-0949
319 Wall St Ste 2 Kingston (12401) *(G-7194)*
Knise & Krick Inc...315 422-3516
324 Pearl St Syracuse (13203) *(G-15975)*
Knit Illustrated Inc...212 268-9054
247 W 37th St Frnt 3 New York (10018) *(G-10862)*
Knit Resource Center Ltd...212 221-1990
250 W 39th St Rm 207 New York (10018) *(G-10863)*
Knitty City, New York *Also called A Thousand Cranes Inc (G-8993)*
Knj Fabricators LLC...347 234-6985
4341 Wickham Ave Bronx (10466) *(G-1374)*
Knogo, Ronkonkoma *Also called Sentry Technology Corporation (G-14982)*
Knoll Inc...917 359-8620
1330 Ave Of The A New York (10019) *(G-10864)*
Knoll Printing & Packaging Inc...516 621-0100
149 Eileen Way Syosset (11791) *(G-15826)*
Knoll Textile, New York *Also called Knoll Inc (G-10864)*
Knoll Worldwide, Syosset *Also called Knoll Printing & Packaging Inc (G-15826)*
Knorr Brake Company LLC...518 561-1387
613 State Route 3 Unit 1 Plattsburgh (12901) *(G-13674)*
Knorr Brake Holding Corp (HQ)...315 786-5356
748 Starbuck Ave Watertown (13601) *(G-16659)*
Knorr Brake Truck Systems Co (HQ)...315 786-5200
748 Starbuck Ave Watertown (13601) *(G-16660)*
Knowles Cazenovia Inc (HQ)...315 655-8710
2777 Us Route 20 Cazenovia (13035) *(G-3447)*
Knowlton Technologies LLC...315 782-0600
213 Factory St Watertown (13601) *(G-16661)*
Knr Fragrances & Cosmetics Inc...631 586-8500
250 Executive Dr Ste M Edgewood (11717) *(G-4605)*
Knucklehead Embroidery Inc...607 797-2725
800 Valley Plz Ste 4 Johnson City (13790) *(G-7098)*
Ko Fro Foods Inc...718 972-6480
4418 18th Ave 4420 Brooklyn (11204) *(G-2177)*
Ko-Sure Food Distributors, Brooklyn *Also called Taam-Tov Foods Inc (G-2641)*
Kobalt Music Pubg Amer Inc (PA)...212 247-6204
220 W 42nd St Fl 11 New York (10036) *(G-10865)*
Kobe Steel USA Holdings Inc (HQ)...212 751-9400
535 Madison Ave Fl 5 New York (10022) *(G-10866)*
Koch Container Div, Victor *Also called Buckeye Corrugated Inc (G-16465)*
Koch Metal Spinning Co Inc...716 835-3631
74 Jewett Ave Buffalo (14214) *(G-3034)*
Kodak Alaris Inc (HQ)...585 290-2891
2400 Mount Read Blvd # 1175 Rochester (14615) *(G-14471)*
Kodak Gallery - Cohber, West Henrietta *Also called Cohber Press Inc (G-16873)*
Kodansha USA Inc...917 322-6200
451 Park Ave S Fl 7 New York (10016) *(G-10867)*
Kodiak Studios Inc...718 769-5399
3030 Emmons Ave Apt 3t Brooklyn (11235) *(G-2178)*
Koehler Instrument Company Inc...631 589-3800
1595 Sycamore Ave Bohemia (11716) *(G-1088)*
Koehler-Gibson Mkg & Graphics, Buffalo *Also called Koehlr-Gibson Mkg Graphics Inc (G-3035)*
Koehlr-Gibson Mkg Graphics Inc...716 838-5960
875 Englewood Ave Buffalo (14223) *(G-3035)*
Koenig Iron Works Inc...718 433-0900
814 37th Ave Long Island City (11101) *(G-7782)*
Koeppels Kustom Kitchens Inc...518 489-0092
16 Van Rensselaer Rd Albany (12205) *(G-96)*
Kogeto Inc (PA)...646 490-8169
51 Wooster St Fl 2 New York (10013) *(G-10868)*
Kohlberg Sports Group Inc (HQ)...914 241-7430
111 Radio Circle Dr Mount Kisco (10549) *(G-8633)*
Kohler Awning Inc...716 685-3333
2600 Walden Ave Buffalo (14225) *(G-3036)*
Kohler Co...212 529-2800
37 E New York (10003) *(G-10869)*
Koke Inc...800 535-5303
582 Queensbury Ave Queensbury (12804) *(G-14003)*
Kokin Inc...212 643-8225
247 W 38th St Rm 701 New York (10018) *(G-10870)*
Kolcorp Industries Ltd (PA)...212 354-0400
10 E 36th St New York (10016) *(G-10871)*

Kollage Work Too Ltd 212 695-1821
261 W 35th St Ste 302 New York (10001) *(G-10872)*
Komar Kids LLC (HQ) 212 725-1500
16 E 34th St Fl 14 New York (10016) *(G-10873)*
Komar Layering LLC (HQ) 212 725-1500
16 E 34th St Fl 10 New York (10016) *(G-10874)*
Komar Luxury Brands 646 472-0060
16 E 34th St Fl 10 New York (10016) *(G-10875)*
Kon Tat Group Corporation 718 207-5022
1491 E 34th St Brooklyn (11234) *(G-2179)*
Konar Precision Mfg Inc 631 242-4466
62 S 2nd St Ste F Deer Park (11729) *(G-4159)*
Kondor Technologies Inc 631 471-8832
206 Christopher St Ronkonkoma (11779) *(G-14924)*
Konecranes Inc 585 359-4450
1020 Lehigh Station Rd # 4 Henrietta (14467) *(G-6295)*
Kong Kee Food Corp 718 937-2746
4831 Van Dam St Long Island City (11101) *(G-7783)*
Konica Mnolta Sups Mfg USA Inc 845 294-8400
51 Hatfield Ln Goshen (10924) *(G-5736)*
Konrad Design, Farmingdale *Also called T A Tool & Molding Inc (G-5123)*
Konrad Prosthetics & Orthotics (PA) 516 485-9164
596 Jennings Ave West Hempstead (11552) *(G-16858)*
Konstantin D FRAnk& Sons Vini 607 868-4884
9749 Middle Rd Hammondsport (14840) *(G-5958)*
Konstantinos Floral Decorators 718 434-3603
1502 Avenue J Brooklyn (11230) *(G-2180)*
Kontrolscan Inc 917 743-0481
22 Murray Hill Rd Scarsdale (10583) *(G-15219)*
Koon Enterprises LLC 718 886-3163
6805 Fresh Madow Ln Ste B Fresh Meadows (11365) *(G-5442)*
Koonichi Inc 718 886-8338
6805 Fresh Madow Ln Ste B Fresh Meadows (11365) *(G-5443)*
Koral Industries 212 719-0392
1384 Broadway Fl 18 New York (10018) *(G-10876)*
Korangy Publishing Inc 212 260-1332
158 W 29th St Fl 4 New York (10001) *(G-10877)*
Kore Infrastructure LLC (PA) 646 532-9060
4 High Pine Glen Cove (11542) *(G-5620)*
Korea Central Daily News Inc (HQ) 718 361-7700
4327 36th St Long Island City (11101) *(G-7784)*
Korea Times New York Inc (HQ) 718 784-4526
3710 Skillman Ave Long Island City (11101) *(G-7785)*
Korea Times New York Inc 718 729-5555
3710 Skillman Ave Long Island City (11101) *(G-7786)*
Korea Times New York Inc 718 961-7979
15408 Nthrn Blvd Ste 2b Flushing (11354) *(G-5262)*
Korean New York Daily, The, Flushing *Also called New York IL Bo Inc (G-5272)*
Korean Yellow Pages 718 461-0073
14809 Northern Blvd Flushing (11354) *(G-5263)*
Koregon Enterprises Inc 450 218-6836
102 W Service Rd Champlain (12919) *(G-3543)*
Korin Japanese Trading Corp 212 587-7021
57 Warren St Frnt A New York (10007) *(G-10878)*
Koring Bros Inc 888 233-1292
30 Pine St New Rochelle (10801) *(G-8916)*
Koshii Maxelum America Inc 845 471-0500
12 Van Kleeck Dr Poughkeepsie (12601) *(G-13911)*
Kossars Bialys LLC 212 473-4810
367 Grand St New York (10002) *(G-10879)*
Kossars On Grand LLC 212 473-4810
367 Grand St New York (10002) *(G-10880)*
Koster Keunen Waxes, Sayville *Also called Kkw Corp (G-15211)*
Koster Keunen Waxes Ltd 631 589-0400
90 Bourne Blvd Sayville (11782) *(G-15212)*
Kotel Importers Inc 212 245-6200
22 W 48th St Ste 607 New York (10036) *(G-10881)*
Kourosh, College Point *Also called Lahoya Enterprise Inc (G-3794)*
Kowa American Corporation (HQ) 212 303-7800
55 E 59th St Fl 19 New York (10022) *(G-10882)*
Kozy Shack Enterprises LLC (HQ) 516 870-3000
83 Ludy St Hicksville (11801) *(G-6359)*
Kozy Shack Enterprises LLC 516 870-3000
50 Ludy St Hicksville (11801) *(G-6360)*
KP Industries Inc 516 679-3161
2481 Charles Ct Ste 1 North Bellmore (11710) *(G-12922)*
KPP Ltd 516 338-5201
81 Urban Ave Westbury (11590) *(G-17004)*
Kps Capital Partners LP (PA) 212 338-5100
485 Lexington Ave Fl 31 New York (10017) *(G-10883)*
Kraft Hat Manufacturers Inc 845 735-6200
7 Veterans Pkwy Pearl River (10965) *(G-13461)*
Kraft Heinz Foods Company 607 865-7131
261 Delaware St Walton (13856) *(G-16548)*
Kraft Heinz Foods Company 315 376-6575
7388 Utica Blvd Lowville (13367) *(G-7938)*
Kraft Heinz Foods Company 914 335-2500
555 S Broadway Tarrytown (10591) *(G-16093)*
Kraft Heinz Foods Company 607 527-4584
8600 Main St Campbell (14821) *(G-3329)*
Kraft Heinz Foods Company 607 527-4584
8596 Main St Campbell (14821) *(G-3330)*
Kraft Heinz Foods Company 585 226-4400
140 Spring St Avon (14414) *(G-540)*
Kragel Co Inc 716 648-1344
23 Lake St Hamburg (14075) *(G-5932)*
Krainz Creations Inc 212 583-1555
589 5th Ave New York (10017) *(G-10884)*
Kraman Iron Works Inc 212 460-8400
410 E 10th St New York (10009) *(G-10885)*
Kramartron Precision Inc 845 368-3668
2 Spook Rock Rd Unit 107 Tallman (10982) *(G-16077)*
Krasner Group Inc (PA) 212 268-4100
40 W 37th St Ph A New York (10018) *(G-10886)*
Kratos General Microwave, Syosset *Also called General Microwave Corporation (G-15824)*
Kraus & Sons Inc 212 620-0408
355 S End Ave Apt 10j New York (10280) *(G-10887)*
Kraus Organization Limited (PA) 212 686-5411
181 Hudson St Ste 2a New York (10013) *(G-10888)*
Kraus USA Inc 516 621-1300
12 Harbor Park Dr Port Washington (11050) *(G-13835)*
Kravet Fabrics Inc (PA) 516 293-2000
225 Central Ave S Bethpage (11714) *(G-869)*
Kravitz Design Inc (PA) 212 625-1644
13 Crosby St Rm 401 New York (10013) *(G-10889)*
Krefab Corporation 631 842-5151
240 N Oak St Copiague (11726) *(G-3909)*
Krengel Manufacturing Co Inc 212 227-1901
121 Fulton Ave Fl 2 Fulton (13069) *(G-5467)*
Kreon Inc 516 470-9522
999 S Oyster Bay Rd # 105 Bethpage (11714) *(G-870)*
Krepe Kraft Inc 716 826-7086
1801 Elmwood Ave Buffalo (14207) *(G-3037)*
Krepe-Kraft, Buffalo *Also called Krepe Kraft Inc (G-3037)*
Kris-Tech Wire Company Inc (PA) 315 339-5268
80 Otis St Rome (13441) *(G-14817)*
Kristen Graphics Inc 212 929-2183
44 W 28th St Fl 3 New York (10001) *(G-10890)*
Kroger Packaging Inc 631 249-6690
215 Central Ave Ste M Farmingdale (11735) *(G-5029)*
Kronenberger Mfg Corp 585 385-2340
115 Despatch Dr East Rochester (14445) *(G-4464)*
Krug Precision Inc 516 944-9350
7 Carey Pl Port Washington (11050) *(G-13836)*
Kryten Iron Works Inc 914 345-0990
3 Browns Ln Ste 201 Hawthorne (10532) *(G-6249)*
KSA Manufacturing LLC 315 488-0809
5050 Smoral Rd Camillus (13031) *(G-3323)*
Ksk International Inc (PA) 212 354-7770
450 Park Ave Ste 2703 New York (10022) *(G-10891)*
Ksm Group Ltd 716 751-6006
2905 Beebe Rd Newfane (14108) *(G-12787)*
Kt Group Inc 212 760-2500
13 W 36th St Fl 3 New York (10018) *(G-10892)*
Ktd Screw Machine Inc 631 243-6861
70 E Jefryn Blvd Ste D Deer Park (11729) *(G-4160)*
Kubota Authorized Dealer, Mendon *Also called Saxby Implement Corp (G-8382)*
Kuno Steel Products Corp 516 938-8500
132 Duffy Ave Hicksville (11801) *(G-6361)*
Kuraray America Inc 212 986-2230
33 Maiden Ln Fl 6 New York (10038) *(G-10893)*
Kureha Advanced Materials Inc 724 295-3352
420 Lexington Ave Rm 2510 New York (10170) *(G-10894)*
Kurrier Inc 718 389-3018
145 Java St Brooklyn (11222) *(G-2181)*
Kurt Gaum Inc 212 719-2836
580 5th Ave Ste 303 New York (10036) *(G-10895)*
Kurtz Truck Equipment Inc 607 849-3468
1085 Mcgraw Marathon Rd Marathon (13803) *(G-8084)*
Kurz and Zobel Inc 585 254-9060
688 Colfax St Rochester (14606) *(G-14472)*
Kush Oasis Enterprises LLC 516 513-1316
228 Martin Dr Syosset (11791) *(G-15827)*
Kussmaul Electronics Co Inc 631 218-0298
170 Cherry Ave West Sayville (11796) *(G-16936)*
Kustom Collabo, Brooklyn *Also called Vsg International LLC (G-2737)*
Kustom Korner 716 646-0173
5140 Camp Rd Hamburg (14075) *(G-5933)*
Kutters Cheese Factory Inc 585 599-3693
857 Main Rd Corfu (14036) *(G-3956)*
Kw Distributors Group Inc 718 843-3500
9018 Liberty Ave Ozone Park (11417) *(G-13382)*
Kwadair LLC 646 824-2511
137 Kent St Brooklyn (11222) *(G-2182)*
Kwik Kopy Printing, Jamestown *Also called Eaglesome Graphics Inc (G-6989)*
Kwik Kut Manufacturing Co, Mohawk *Also called Mary F Morse (G-8542)*
Kwik Ticket Inc (PA) 718 421-3800
4101 Glenwood Rd Brooklyn (11210) *(G-2183)*
Kwong CHI Metal Fabrication 718 369-6429
166 41st St Brooklyn (11232) *(G-2184)*
Kww Productions Corp 212 398-8181
1410 Broadway Fl 24 New York (10018) *(G-10896)*
Kybod Group LLC 408 306-1657
222 E 34th St Apt 1005 New York (10016) *(G-10897)*

ALPHABETIC

ALPHABETIC SECTION

Kyle Editing LLC 212 675-3464
15 W 26th St Fl 8 New York (10010) *(G-10898)*

Kyntec Corporation 716 810-6956
2100 Old Union Rd Buffalo (14227) *(G-3038)*

Kyocera Precision Tools Inc 607 687-0012
1436 Taylor Rd Owego (13827) *(G-13353)*

Kyra Communications Corp 516 783-6244
3864 Bayberry Ln Seaford (11783) *(G-15344)*

Kz Precision Inc 716 683-3202
1 Mason Pl Lancaster (14086) *(G-7321)*

L & D Acquisition LLC 585 531-9000
1 Lake Niagara Ln Naples (14512) *(G-8765)*

L & D Manufacturing Corp 718 665-5226
366 Canal Pl Frnt Bronx (10451) *(G-1375)*

L & J Interiors Inc 631 218-0838
35 Orville Dr Ste 3 Bohemia (11716) *(G-1089)*

L & K Graphics Inc 631 667-2269
1917 Deer Park Ave Deer Park (11729) *(G-4161)*

L & L Overhead Garage Doors (PA) 718 721-2518
3125 45th St Long Island City (11103) *(G-7787)*

L & L Precision Machining 631 462-9587
35 Doyle Ct Ste 3 East Northport (11731) *(G-4440)*

L & L Trucking Inc 315 339-2550
1 Revere Park Rome (13440) *(G-14818)*

L & M Optical Disc LLC 718 649-3500
65 W 36th St Fl 11 New York (10018) *(G-10899)*

L & M Publications Inc 516 378-3133
2 Endo Blvd Garden City (11530) *(G-5513)*

L & M Uniserv Corp 718 854-3700
4416 18th Ave Pmb 133 Brooklyn (11204) *(G-2185)*

L & M Welding LLC 516 220-1722
10 Taylor St Unit A Freeport (11520) *(G-5407)*

L & M West, New York Also called L & M Optical Disc LLC *(G-10899)*

L & S Metals Inc 716 692-6865
111 Witmer Rd North Tonawanda (14120) *(G-12980)*

L A R Electronics Corp 716 285-0555
2733 Niagara St Niagara Falls (14303) *(G-12840)*

L A S Replacement Parts Inc 718 583-4700
1645 Webster Ave Bronx (10457) *(G-1376)*

L Allmeier 212 243-7390
1201 Broadway Ste 705 New York (10001) *(G-10900)*

L American Ltd 716 372-9480
222 Homer St Olean (14760) *(G-13150)*

L and S Packing Co 631 845-1717
101 Central Ave Farmingdale (11735) *(G-5030)*

L Builders Supply Inc 518 355-7190
500 Duanesburg Rd Schenectady (12306) *(G-15275)*

L D Flecken Inc 631 777-4881
11 Old Dock Rd Unit 11 Yaphank (11980) *(G-17396)*

L F Fashion Orient Intl Co Ltd 917 667-3398
32 W 40th St Apt 2l New York (10018) *(G-10901)*

L F International Inc 212 756-5000
425 Park Ave Fl 5 New York (10022) *(G-10902)*

L I C Screen Printing Inc 516 546-7289
2949 Joyce Ln Merrick (11566) *(G-8387)*

L I F Publishing Corp (PA) 631 345-5200
14 Ramsey Rd Shirley (11967) *(G-15422)*

L I Fur Factory & Salon, Westbury Also called Alexis & Gianni Retail Inc *(G-16964)*

L I Stamp, Ridgewood Also called Long Island Stamp & Seal Co *(G-14112)*

L J Valente Inc 518 674-3750
8957 Ny Highway 66 Averill Park (12018) *(G-535)*

L K Manufacturing Corp 631 243-6910
56 Eads St West Babylon (11704) *(G-16806)*

L K Printing, White Plains Also called Copy Stop Inc *(G-17097)*

L K Printing Corp 914 761-1944
50 Main St Ste 32 White Plains (10606) *(G-17132)*

L LLC 716 885-3918
106 Soldiers Pl Buffalo (14222) *(G-3039)*

L Loy Press Inc 716 634-5966
3959 Union Rd Buffalo (14225) *(G-3040)*

L M N Printing Company Inc 516 285-8526
23 W Merrick Rd Ste A Valley Stream (11580) *(G-16411)*

L M R, New York Also called Lefrak Entertainment Co Ltd *(G-10960)*

L Magazine LLC 212 807-1254
45 Main St Ste 806 Brooklyn (11201) *(G-2186)*

L Miller Design Inc 631 242-1163
100 E Jefryn Blvd Ste F Deer Park (11729) *(G-4162)*

L N D Incorporated 516 678-6141
3230 Lawson Blvd Oceanside (11572) *(G-13085)*

L P R Precision Parts & Tls Co 631 293-7334
108 Rome St Ste 1 Farmingdale (11735) *(G-5031)*

L P Transportation, Selkirk Also called Palpross Incorporated *(G-15357)*

L S I, East Aurora Also called Luminescent Systems Inc *(G-4373)*

L S Z Inc 914 948-4040
30 Glenn St Ste 309 White Plains (10603) *(G-17133)*

L T Sales Corp 631 886-1390
Northside Rd Wading River (11792) *(G-16523)*

L V D, Akron Also called Strippit Inc *(G-29)*

L W S Inc 631 580-0472
125 Gary Way Ste 1 Ronkonkoma (11779) *(G-14925)*

L Y Z Creations Ltd Inc 718 768-2977
78 18th St Brooklyn (11232) *(G-2187)*

L& JG Stickley Incorporated (PA) 315 682-5500
1 Stickley Dr Manlius (13104) *(G-8073)*

L'Etoile Jewelers, Lynbrook Also called Master Craft Jewelry Co Inc *(G-7954)*

L'Oreal Paris, New York Also called LOreal Usa Inc *(G-11038)*

L-3 Cmmnctons Fgn Holdings Inc (HQ) 212 697-1111
600 3rd Ave Fl 32 New York (10016) *(G-10903)*

L-3 Cmmnctons Ntronix Holdings 212 697-1111
600 3rd Ave Fl 34 New York (10016) *(G-10904)*

L-3 Cmmunications Corp Gcs Div, Victor Also called L-3 Communications Corporation *(G-16487)*

L-3 Cmmunications Holdings Inc (PA) 212 697-1111
600 3rd Ave New York (10016) *(G-10905)*

L-3 Communications Corporation (HQ) 212 697-1111
600 3rd Ave New York (10016) *(G-10906)*

L-3 Communications Corporation 631 231-1700
435 Moreland Rd Hauppauge (11788) *(G-6107)*

L-3 Communications Corporation 631 436-7400
100 Davids Dr Hauppauge (11788) *(G-6108)*

L-3 Communications Corporation 631 289-0363
49 Rider Ave Patchogue (11772) *(G-13427)*

L-3 Communications Corporation 607 721-5465
265 Industrial Park Dr Kirkwood (13795) *(G-7234)*

L-3 Communications Corporation 631 231-1700
435 Moreland Rd Hauppauge (11788) *(G-6109)*

L-3 Communications Corporation 631 436-7400
330 Oser Ave Hauppauge (11788) *(G-6110)*

L-3 Communications Corporation (HQ) 585 742-9100
7640 Omnitech Pl Victor (14564) *(G-16487)*

L-3 Narda-Miteq, Hauppauge Also called L-3 Communications Corporation *(G-6108)*

L-3 Narda-Miteq, Hauppauge Also called L-3 Communications Corporation *(G-6110)*

L3 Communication, New York Also called L-3 Cmmnctons Fgn Holdings Inc *(G-10903)*

La Bella Strings, Newburgh Also called E & O Mari Inc *(G-12754)*

La Calenita Bakery & Cafeteria 718 205-8273
4008 83rd St Elmhurst (11373) *(G-4663)*

La Cola 1 Inc 917 509-6669
529 W 42nd St Apt 5b New York (10036) *(G-10907)*

La Escondida Inc 845 562-1387
129 Lake St Newburgh (12550) *(G-12765)*

La Fina Design Inc 212 689-6725
42 W 38th St Rm 1200 New York (10018) *(G-10908)*

La Flor Products Company Inc (PA) 631 851-9601
25 Hoffman Ave Hauppauge (11788) *(G-6111)*

La Flor Spices, Hauppauge Also called La Flor Products Company Inc *(G-6111)*

La Lame Inc 212 921-9770
132 W 36th St Rm 1101 New York (10018) *(G-10909)*

La Lame Importers, New York Also called La Lame Inc *(G-10909)*

La Mar Lighting Co Inc 631 777-7700
485 Smith St Farmingdale (11735) *(G-5032)*

La Mart Manufacturing Corp 718 384-6917
248 Flushing Ave Ste 1 Brooklyn (11205) *(G-2188)*

La Nuit Collection, New York Also called Patra Ltd *(G-11581)*

La Prima Bakery Inc (PA) 718 584-4442
765 E 182nd St Bronx (10460) *(G-1377)*

La Raza, Brooklyn Also called Impremedia LLC *(G-2101)*

La Regina Di San Marzano 212 269-4202
17 Battery Pl Ste 610 New York (10004) *(G-10910)*

La Strada Dance Footwear Inc 631 242-1401
770 Grand Blvd Ste 1 Deer Park (11729) *(G-4163)*

La Vita Health Foods Ltd 845 368-4101
257 Route 59 Suffern (10901) *(G-15793)*

La Voz Hispana, New York Also called Nick Lugo Inc *(G-11426)*

La-Mar Fashions, Deer Park Also called Continental Knitting Mills *(G-4120)*

Lab Crafters Inc 631 471-7755
2085 5th Ave Ronkonkoma (11779) *(G-14926)*

Lab-Aids Inc 631 737-1133
17 Colt Ct Ronkonkoma (11779) *(G-14927)*

Labatt USA LLC 716 604-1050
50 Fountain Plz Ste 900 Buffalo (14202) *(G-3041)*

Labco of Palmyra Inc 315 597-5202
904 Canandaigua Rd Palmyra (14522) *(G-13410)*

Label Gallery Inc 607 334-3244
1 Lee Ave 11 Norwich (13815) *(G-13030)*

Label Makers Inc 631 319-6329
170 Wilbur Pl Ste 100 Bohemia (11716) *(G-1090)*

Label Source Inc 212 244-1403
321 W 35th St New York (10001) *(G-10911)*

Labella Pasta Inc 845 331-9130
906 State Route 28 Kingston (12401) *(G-7195)*

Labels I-G, New York Also called Labels Inter-Global Inc *(G-10912)*

Labels Inter-Global Inc 212 398-0006
109 W 38th St Rm 701 New York (10018) *(G-10912)*

Labels X Press, Tonawanda Also called Magazines & Brochures Inc *(G-16178)*

Labels, Stickers & More, Holbrook Also called Stickershopcom Inc *(G-6474)*

Labeltex Mills Inc 212 279-6165
1430 Broadway Rm 1510 New York (10018) *(G-10913)*

Labgrafix Printing Inc 516 280-8300
43 Rocklyn Ave Unit B Lynbrook (11563) *(G-7953)*

Labhar - Freidman, New York Also called L F International Inc *(G-10902)*

Labortory For Laser Energetics, Rochester Also called University of Rochester *(G-14745)*

Lace Marble & Granite Inc 718 854-9028
1465 39th St Brooklyn (11218) ***(G-2189)***
Lackawanna Hot Rolled Plant, Blasdell *Also called Republic Steel Inc* ***(G-965)***
Lactalis American Group Inc 716 827-2622
2375 S Park Ave Buffalo (14220) ***(G-3042)***
Lactalis American Group Inc (HQ) 716 823-6262
2376 S Park Ave Buffalo (14220) ***(G-3043)***
Lady Brass Co Inc 516 887-8040
1717 Broadway Unit 2 Hewlett (11557) ***(G-6308)***
Lady Burd Exclusive Cosmt Inc (PA) 631 454-0444
44 Executive Blvd Ste 1 Farmingdale (11735) ***(G-5033)***
Lady Burd Private Label Cosmt, Farmingdale *Also called Lady Burd Exclusive Cosmt Inc* ***(G-5033)***
Lady Ester Lingerie Corp 212 689-1729
33 E 33rd St Rm 800 New York (10016) ***(G-10914)***
Lady Linda Cakes, Bronx *Also called Operative Cake Corp* ***(G-1417)***
Lady-N-Th-wndow Chocolates Inc 631 549-1059
319 Main St Huntington (11743) ***(G-6666)***
Ladybird Bakery Inc 718 499-8108
1112 8th Ave Brooklyn (11215) ***(G-2190)***
Lafarge Building Materials Inc 518 756-5000
Rr Ravena (12143) ***(G-14022)***
Lafarge North America Inc 716 651-9235
6125 Genesee St Lancaster (14086) ***(G-7322)***
Lafarge North America Inc 716 854-5791
575 Ohio St Buffalo (14203) ***(G-3044)***
Lafarge North America Inc 716 772-2621
400 Hinman Rd Lockport (14094) ***(G-7596)***
Lafarge North America Inc 716 297-3031
8875 Quarry Rd Niagara Falls (14304) ***(G-12841)***
Lafarge North America Inc 914 930-3027
350 Broadway Buchanan (10511) ***(G-2786)***
Lafarge North America Inc 518 756-5000
1916 Route 9 W Ravena (12143) ***(G-14023)***
Lafarge North America Inc 716 876-8788
4001 River Rd Tonawanda (14150) ***(G-16176)***
Lafayette Chateau 607 546-2062
Rr 414 Hector (14841) ***(G-6258)***
Lafayette Mirror & Glass Co 718 768-0660
2300 Marcus Ave New Hyde Park (11042) ***(G-8845)***
Lafayette Pub Inc 212 925-4242
332 Lafayette St New York (10012) ***(G-10915)***
Lagardere North America Inc (HQ) 212 477-7373
60 E 42nd St Ste 1940 New York (10165) ***(G-10916)***
Lagasse Works Inc 315 946-9202
5 Old State Route 31 Lyons (14489) ***(G-7973)***
Lage Industries Corporation 718 342-3400
9814 Ditmas Ave Brooklyn (11236) ***(G-2191)***
Lagoe-Oswego Corp 315 343-3160
429 Antlers Dr Rochester (14618) ***(G-14473)***
Lagoner Farms Inc 315 589-4899
6954 Tuckahoe Rd Williamson (14589) ***(G-17224)***
Lagunatic Music & Filmworks 212 353-9600
636 Broadway Ste 1210 New York (10012) ***(G-10917)***
Lahoya Enterprise Inc 718 886-8799
1842 College Point Blvd College Point (11356) ***(G-3794)***
Lahr Plastics, Fairport *Also called Lahr Recycling & Resins Inc* ***(G-4860)***
Lahr Recycling & Resins Inc 585 425-8608
164 Daley Rd Fairport (14450) ***(G-4860)***
Lai Apparel Design Inc 212 382-1075
209 W 38th St Rm 901 New York (10018) ***(G-10918)***
Lai International Inc 763 780-0060
1 Tibbits Ave Green Island (12183) ***(G-5858)***
Laird Telemedia 845 339-9555
2000 Sterling Rd Mount Marion (12456) ***(G-8650)***
Lake Champlain Weekly, Plattsburgh *Also called Studley Printing & Publishing* ***(G-13701)***
Lake Country Pennysaver, Albion *Also called Albion-Holley Pennysaver Inc* ***(G-161)***
Lake Country Woodworkers Ltd 585 374-6353
12 Clark St Naples (14512) ***(G-8766)***
Lake Image Systems Inc 585 321-3630
205 Summit Point Dr Ste 2 Henrietta (14467) ***(G-6296)***
Lake Immunogenics Inc 585 265-1973
348 Berg Rd Ontario (14519) ***(G-13205)***
Lake Placid Advertisers Wkshp 518 523-3359
Cold Brook Plz Lake Placid (12946) ***(G-7275)***
Lake Region Medical Inc 716 662-5025
3902 California Rd Orchard Park (14127) ***(G-13279)***
Lake View Manufacturing LLC 315 364-7892
1690 State Route 90 N King Ferry (13081) ***(G-7168)***
Lakeland Industries Inc (PA) 631 981-9700
3555 Vtrans Mem Hwy Ste C Ronkonkoma (11779) ***(G-14928)***
Lakelands Concrete, Lima *Also called East Main Associates* ***(G-7444)***
Lakelands Concrete Pdts Inc 585 624-1990
7520 E Main St Lima (14485) ***(G-7445)***
Lakeshore Carbide Inc 716 462-4349
5696 Minerva Dr Lake View (14085) ***(G-7281)***
Lakeshore Pennysaver, Fredonia *Also called Fredonia Pennysaver Inc* ***(G-5373)***
Lakeside Capital Corporation 716 664-2555
402 Chandler St Ste 2 Jamestown (14701) ***(G-7015)***
Lakeside Cider Mill Farm Inc 518 399-8359
336 Schauber Rd Ballston Lake (12019) ***(G-582)***
Lakeside Container Corp (PA) 518 561-6150
299 Arizona Ave Plattsburgh (12903) ***(G-13675)***
Lakeside Industries Inc 716 386-3031
2 Lakeside Dr Bemus Point (14712) ***(G-844)***
Lakeside Precision Inc 716 366-5030
208 Dove St Dunkirk (14048) ***(G-4344)***
Lakestar Semi Inc (PA) 212 974-6254
888 7th Ave Ste 3300 New York (10106) ***(G-10919)***
Lakeview Innovations Inc 212 502-6702
112 W 34th St Ste 18030 New York (10120) ***(G-10920)***
Lakeview Sportswear Corp 347 663-9519
1425 37th St Ste 607 Brooklyn (11218) ***(G-2192)***
Lakeville Service Station, Floral Park *Also called Full Service Auto Body Inc* ***(G-5204)***
Lakewood Vineyards Inc 607 535-9252
4024 State Route 14 Watkins Glen (14891) ***(G-16695)***
Lali Jewelry Inc 212 944-2277
50 W 47th St Ste 1610 New York (10036) ***(G-10921)***
Lali Jewels, New York *Also called Lali Jewelry Inc* ***(G-10921)***
Lalique Boutique, New York *Also called Lalique North America Inc* ***(G-10922)***
Lalique North America Inc 212 355-6550
609 Madison Ave New York (10022) ***(G-10922)***
Lam Research Corporation 845 896-0606
300 Westage Bus Ctr Dr # 190 Fishkill (12524) ***(G-5185)***
Lam Tech, Wading River *Also called L T Sales Corp* ***(G-16523)***
LAM Western New York Inc 716 856-0308
32 Cornelia St Buffalo (14210) ***(G-3045)***
Lamar Plastics Packaging Ltd 516 378-2500
216 N Main St Ste F Freeport (11520) ***(G-5408)***
Lamart Manufacturing Co, Brooklyn *Also called La Mart Manufacturing Corp* ***(G-2188)***
Lambro Industries Inc (PA) 631 842-8088
115 Albany Ave Amityville (11701) ***(G-304)***
Laminated Window Products Inc 631 242-6883
211 N Fehr Way Bay Shore (11706) ***(G-710)***
Lamm Audio Lab, Brooklyn *Also called Lamm Industries Inc* ***(G-2193)***
Lamm Industries Inc 718 368-0181
2621 E 24th St Ste 1 Brooklyn (11235) ***(G-2193)***
Lamontage, New York *Also called Mgk Group Inc* ***(G-11246)***
Lamoreaux Landing WI 607 582-6162
9224 State Route 414 Lodi (14860) ***(G-7635)***
Lamothermic Corp 845 278-6118
391 Route 312 Brewster (10509) ***(G-1222)***
Lamparts Co Inc 914 723-8986
160 E 3rd St Ste 2 Mount Vernon (10550) ***(G-8699)***
Lams Foods Inc 718 217-0476
9723 218th St Queens Village (11429) ***(G-13981)***
Lancaster Knives Inc (PA) 716 683-5050
165 Court St Lancaster (14086) ***(G-7323)***
Lancaster Quality Pork Inc 718 439-8822
5600 1st Ave Ste 6 Brooklyn (11220) ***(G-2194)***
Lance Valves 716 681-5825
15 Enterprise Dr Lancaster (14086) ***(G-7324)***
Lanco Corporation 631 231-2300
2905 Vtrans Mem Hwy Ste 3 Ronkonkoma (11779) ***(G-14929)***
Land and Sea Trailer Shop, Coram *Also called G L 7 Sales Plus Ltd* ***(G-3942)***
Land n Sea Inc (PA) 212 703-2980
1375 Broadway Fl 2 New York (10018) ***(G-10923)***
Land OLakes Inc 516 681-2980
50 Ludy St Hicksville (11801) ***(G-6362)***
Land Packaging Corp 914 472-5976
7 Black Birch Ln Scarsdale (10583) ***(G-15220)***
Land Self Prtction Systems Div, Buffalo *Also called Northrop Grumman Intl Trdg Inc* ***(G-3096)***
Landies Candies Co Inc 716 834-8212
2495 Main St Ste 350 Buffalo (14214) ***(G-3046)***
Landlord Guard Inc 212 695-6505
1 Maiden Ln Fl 7 New York (10038) ***(G-10924)***
Landmark Group Inc 845 358-0350
709 Executive Blvd Ste A Valley Cottage (10989) ***(G-16380)***
Lane Enterprises Inc 607 776-3366
16 May St Bath (14810) ***(G-660)***
Lane Enterprises Inc 518 885-4385
825 State Route 67 Ballston Spa (12020) ***(G-601)***
Lane Metal Products, Bath *Also called Lane Enterprises Inc* ***(G-660)***
Lane Park Graphics Inc 914 273-5898
93 Mcmanus Rd S Patterson (12563) ***(G-13442)***
Lane Park Litho Plate 212 255-9100
155 Ave Of The Amer Fl 8 New York (10013) ***(G-10925)***
Lanel, Floral Park *Also called Creatron Services Inc* ***(G-5201)***
Lanel Inc 516 437-5119
504 Cherry Ln Ste 3 Floral Park (11001) ***(G-5205)***
Lanes Flr Cvrngs Intriors Inc 212 532-5200
30 W 26th St Fl 11r New York (10010) ***(G-10926)***
Langer Biomechanics Inc 800 645-5520
2905 Vtrans Mem Hwy Ste 2 Ronkonkoma (11779) ***(G-14930)***
Language and Graphics Inc 212 315-5266
350 W 57th St Apt 14i New York (10019) ***(G-10927)***
Lanier Clothes, New York *Also called Oxford Industries Inc* ***(G-11540)***
Lanoves Inc 718 384-1880
72 Anthony St Brooklyn (11222) ***(G-2195)***
Lanwood Industries Inc 718 786-3000
45 Drexel Dr Bay Shore (11706) ***(G-711)***

ALPHABETIC

Lanza Corp 914 937-6360
404 Willett Ave Port Chester (10573) *(G-13751)*
Lapp Insulator Company LLC 585 768-6221
130 Gilbert St Le Roy (14482) *(G-7411)*
Lapp Insulators LLC 585 768-6221
130 Gilbert St Le Roy (14482) *(G-7412)*
Lapp Management Corp 607 243-5141
3700 Route 14 Himrod (14842) *(G-6422)*
Larcent Enterprises Inc 845 562-3332
509 Temple Hill Rd New Windsor (12553) *(G-8941)*
Laregence Inc 212 736-2548
34 W 27th St Fl 2 New York (10001) *(G-10928)*
Largo Music Inc 212 756-5080
425 Park Ave Ste 501 New York (10022) *(G-10929)*
Larkin Anya Ltd 718 361-1827
4310 23rd St Ste 2b Long Island City (11101) *(G-7788)*
Larosa Cupcakes 347 866-3920
314 Lake Ave Staten Island (10303) *(G-15697)*
Larry Kings Corporation 718 481-8741
13708 250th St Rosedale (11422) *(G-15013)*
Larson Metal Manufacturing Co 716 665-6807
1831 Mason Dr Jamestown (14701) *(G-7016)*
Larte Del Gelato Inc 212 366-0570
75 9th Ave Frnt 38 New York (10011) *(G-10930)*
Lasalle Brands Inc 718 542-0900
547 Manida St Bronx (10474) *(G-1378)*
Laser and Varicose Vein Trtmnt 718 667-1777
500 Seaview Ave Ste 240 Staten Island (10305) *(G-15698)*
Laser Consultants Inc 631 423-4905
344 W Hills Rd Huntington (11743) *(G-6667)*
Laser Printer Checks Corp 845 782-5837
7 Vayoel Moshe Ct # 101 Monroe (10950) *(G-8559)*
Lasermax Inc 585 272-5420
3495 Winton Pl Ste A37 Rochester (14623) *(G-14474)*
Lasertech Crtridge RE-Builders 518 373-1246
7 Longwood Dr Clifton Park (12065) *(G-3698)*
Lasser Products Incorporated 585 249-5180
63 Winfield Rd Rochester (14622) *(G-14475)*
Last Magazine, The, New York *Also called Berger & Wild LLC (G-9363)*
Last N Last, New Rochelle *Also called Paint Over Rust Products Inc (G-8919)*
Last Resort, The, Rouses Point *Also called Sandys Deli Inc (G-15044)*
Last Straw Inc 516 371-2727
22 Lawrence Ln Unit 1 Lawrence (11559) *(G-7393)*
Lasticks Aerospace Inc 631 242-8484
35 Washington Ave Ste E Bay Shore (11706) *(G-712)*
Latchable Inc 646 833-0604
450 W 33rd St Fl 12 New York (10001) *(G-10931)*
Latham International Inc (PA) 518 783-7776
787 Watervliet Shaker Rd Latham (12110) *(G-7368)*
Latham International Inc 518 346-5292
706 Corporation Park 1 Schenectady (12302) *(G-15276)*
Latham Manufacturing, Schenectady *Also called Latham International Inc (G-15276)*
Latham Manufacturing, Latham *Also called Latham Pool Products Inc (G-7370)*
Latham Pool Products Inc (PA) 518 951-1000
787 Watervliet Shaker Rd Latham (12110) *(G-7369)*
Latham Pool Products Inc 260 432-8731
787 Watervliet Shaker Rd Latham (12110) *(G-7370)*
Latham Seamless Gutters, Altamont *Also called Alfred B Parella (G-206)*
Latham Software Sciences Inc 518 785-1100
678 Troy Schenectady Rd # 104 Latham (12110) *(G-7371)*
Latin Business Chronicle 305 441-0002
72 Madison Ave Fl 11 New York (10016) *(G-10932)*
Latina Media Ventures LLC (PA) 212 642-0200
120 Broadway Fl 34 New York (10271) *(G-10933)*
Latino Show Magazine Inc 718 709-1151
8025 88th Rd Woodhaven (11421) *(G-17307)*
Latique Handbags and ACC LLC 212 564-2914
10 W 33rd St Rm 405 New York (10001) *(G-10934)*
Latium USA Trading LLC (PA) 631 563-4000
5005 Veterans Mem Hwy Holbrook (11741) *(G-6455)*
Latorre Orthopedic Laboratory 518 786-8655
960 Troy Schenectady Rd Latham (12110) *(G-7372)*
Laufer Wind Group LLC 212 792-3912
270 Lafayette St Ste 1402 New York (10012) *(G-10935)*
Laumont Editions, New York *Also called Laumont Labs Inc (G-10936)*
Laumont Labs Inc 212 664-0595
333 W 52nd St Fl 14 New York (10019) *(G-10936)*
Laundress Inc 212 209-0074
247 W 30th St Rm 202 New York (10001) *(G-10937)*
Laura Star Service Center, Averill Park *Also called Garment Care Systems LLC (G-534)*
Lauricella Press Inc 516 931-5906
81 Emjay Blvd Brentwood (11717) *(G-1189)*
Laurtom Inc 914 273-2233
333 N Bedford Rd Ste 100 Mount Kisco (10549) *(G-8634)*
Laurus Development Inc 716 823-1202
3556 Lake Shore Rd # 121 Buffalo (14219) *(G-3047)*
Lavanya, Jackson Heights *Also called Karishma Fashions Inc (G-6888)*
Lavish Layette Inc 516 256-9130
406 Central Ave Cedarhurst (11516) *(G-3458)*
Law360, New York *Also called Portfolio Media Inc (G-11687)*
Lawdy Miss Clawdy, Pound Ridge *Also called Lloyd Price Icon Food Brands (G-13944)*
Lawn Elements Inc 631 656-9711
1150 Lincoln Ave Ste 4 Holbrook (11741) *(G-6456)*
Lawrence Packaging Inc 516 420-1930
43 Sheer Plz Plainview (11803) *(G-13615)*
Lawson M Whiting Inc 315 986-3064
15 State Route 350 Macedon (14502) *(G-7988)*
Lawton Electric Co, Ogdensburg *Also called Lawtons Electric Motor Service (G-13117)*
Lawtons Electric Motor Service 315 393-2728
148 Cemetery Rd Ogdensburg (13669) *(G-13117)*
Layton Manufacturing Corp (PA) 718 498-6000
864 E 52nd St Brooklyn (11203) *(G-2196)*
Lazare Kaplan Intl Inc (PA) 212 972-9700
19 W 44th St Fl 16 New York (10036) *(G-10938)*
Lazarek Inc 315 343-1242
209 Erie St Oswego (13126) *(G-13334)*
Lazer Incorporated (PA) 336 744-8047
1465 Jefferson Rd Ste 110 Rochester (14623) *(G-14476)*
Lazer Marble & Granite Corp 718 859-9644
1053 Dahill Rd Brooklyn (11204) *(G-2197)*
Lazer Photo Engraving, Rochester *Also called Lazer Incorporated (G-14476)*
Lazo Setter Company, New York *Also called Mataci Inc (G-11178)*
Lb Furniture Industries LLC 518 828-1501
99 S 3rd St Hudson (12534) *(G-6624)*
Lb Laundry Inc 347 399-8030
4431 Kissena Blvd Flushing (11355) *(G-5264)*
Lbg Acquisition LLC 212 226-1276
158 Bowery New York (10012) *(G-10939)*
Lcdrives Corp 860 712-8926
65 Main St Pytn Hl 3204 Rm 3204 Peyton Hall Potsdam (13676) *(G-13879)*
Lco Destiny LLC 315 782-3302
22476 Fisher Rd Watertown (13601) *(G-16662)*
LD McCauley LLC 716 662-6744
3875 California Rd Orchard Park (14127) *(G-13280)*
LDB Interior Textiles, New York *Also called E W Williams Publications (G-9953)*
Ldc 516 822-2499
127 Brenner Ave Bethpage (11714) *(G-871)*
LDI Lighting Inc (PA) 718 384-4490
240 Broadway Ste C Brooklyn (11211) *(G-2198)*
LDI Lighting Inc 718 384-4490
193 Williamsburg St W A Brooklyn (11211) *(G-2199)*
Le Book Publishing Inc (HQ) 212 334-5252
552 Broadway Apt 6s New York (10012) *(G-10940)*
Le Chameau USA Inc 646 356-0460
60 Broad St Ste 3502 New York (10004) *(G-10941)*
Le Chocolat LLC 845 352-8301
41 Main St Monsey (10952) *(G-8572)*
Le Chocolate of Rockland LLC 845 533-4125
1 Ramapo Ave Suffern (10901) *(G-15794)*
Le Creuset, Riverhead *Also called Schiller Stores Inc (G-14155)*
Le Hook Rouge LLC 212 947-6272
275 Conover St Ste 3q-3p Brooklyn (11231) *(G-2200)*
Le Lab, Valley Stream *Also called Lelab Dental Laboratory Inc (G-16412)*
Le Labo Fragrances, New York *Also called Le Labo Inc (G-10942)*
Le Labo Inc (PA) 212 532-7206
584 Broadway Rm 1103 New York (10012) *(G-10942)*
Le Labo Inc 646 719-1740
80 39th St Fl Ground Brooklyn (11232) *(G-2201)*
Le Paveh Ltd 212 736-6110
23 W 47th St Ste 501 New York (10036) *(G-10943)*
Le Roi Inc 315 342-3681
21 S 2nd St Fulton (13069) *(G-5468)*
Le Roy Pennysaver, Le Roy *Also called Dray Enterprises Inc (G-7406)*
Le Vian Corp (PA) 516 466-7200
235 Great Neck Rd Great Neck (11021) *(G-5820)*
Le Vian Corp 516 466-7200
10 W 46th St New York (10036) *(G-10944)*
Lea & Viola Inc 646 918-6866
525 Fashion Ave Rm 1401 New York (10018) *(G-10945)*
Lea Apparel Inc 718 418-2800
6126 Cooper Ave Glendale (11385) *(G-5657)*
Leader Herald, The, Gloversville *Also called William B Collins Company (G-5729)*
Leader Printing Inc 516 546-1544
2272 Babylon Tpke Merrick (11566) *(G-8388)*
Leader Sheet Metal Inc 347 271-4961
759 E 133rd St 2 Bronx (10454) *(G-1379)*
Leader, The, Corning *Also called Gatehouse Media LLC (G-3973)*
Leadership Directories Inc (PA) 212 627-4140
1407 Broadway Rm 318 New York (10018) *(G-10946)*
Leadertex Group, New York *Also called Leadertex Intl Inc (G-10947)*
Leadertex Intl Inc 212 563-2242
135 W 36th St Fl 12 New York (10018) *(G-10947)*
Leading Edge Fabrication 631 274-9797
699 Acorn St Ste B Deer Park (11729) *(G-4164)*
Leape Resources,, Alexander *Also called Lenape Energy Inc (G-187)*
Learnimation 917 868-7261
55 Washington St Ste 454 Brooklyn (11201) *(G-2202)*
Learningateway LLC 212 920-7969
106 Saint James Pl Brooklyn (11238) *(G-2203)*
Learningexpress LLC 646 274-6454
80 Broad St Fl 4 New York (10004) *(G-10948)*

ALPHABETIC

(PA)=Parent Co (HQ)=Headquarters (DH)=Div Headquarters

Learnvest Inc 212 675-6711
113 University Pl Fl 2 New York (10003) ***(G-10949)***
Leather Artisan 518 359-3102
Rr 3 Childwold (12922) ***(G-3628)***
Leather Craftsmen Inc (PA) 631 752-9000
160a Marine St Farmingdale (11735) ***(G-5034)***
Leather Impact Inc 212 382-2788
240 W 38th St Frnt 1 New York (10018) ***(G-10950)***
Leather Indexes Corp 516 827-1900
174a Miller Pl Hicksville (11801) ***(G-6363)***
Leather Outlet 518 668-0328
1656 State Route 9 Lake George (12845) ***(G-7262)***
Leatherstocking Mobile Home PA 315 839-5691
2089 Doolittle Rd Sauquoit (13456) ***(G-15200)***
Lebhar-Friedman Inc (PA) 212 756-5000
150 W 30th St Fl 19 New York (10001) ***(G-10951)***
Lebhar-Friedman Inc 212 756-5000
425 Park Ave Fl 6 New York (10022) ***(G-10952)***
Leblon Cachaca, New York *Also called Leblon LLC* ***(G-10954)***
Leblon Holdings LLC 212 741-2675
428 Broadway Fl 4 New York (10013) ***(G-10953)***
Leblon LLC 954 649-0148
428 Broadway Fl 4 New York (10013) ***(G-10954)***
Leblon LLC 786 281-5672
266 W 26th St Ste 801 New York (10001) ***(G-10955)***
Lebron Equipment Supply, New York *Also called 3835 Lebron Rest Eqp & Sup Inc* ***(G-8973)***
Lechler Laboratories Inc 845 426-6800
100 Red Schoolhse Rd C2 Spring Valley (10977) ***(G-15591)***
Lechler Labs, Chestnut Ridge *Also called Mehron Inc* ***(G-3623)***
Lechler Labs, Spring Valley *Also called Lechler Laboratories Inc* ***(G-15591)***
Lecreuset of America, Central Valley *Also called Schiller Stores Inc* ***(G-3527)***
Led Lumina USA LLC 631 750-4433
116 Wilbur Pl Bohemia (11716) ***(G-1091)***
Led Next, Westbury *Also called Emitled Inc* ***(G-16982)***
Led Waves Inc 347 416-6182
4100 1st Ave Ste 3n Brooklyn (11232) ***(G-2204)***
Ledan Inc 631 239-1226
6 Annetta Ave Northport (11768) ***(G-13014)***
Ledan Design Group, Northport *Also called Ledan Inc* ***(G-13014)***
Ledes Group Inc 212 840-8800
85 5th Ave Fl 12 New York (10003) ***(G-10956)***
Lee & Low Books Incorporated 212 779-4400
95 Madison Ave Rm 1205 New York (10016) ***(G-10957)***
Lee Dyeing Company NC Inc 518 736-5232
328 N Perry St Johnstown (12095) ***(G-7118)***
Lee Enterprises Incorporated 518 792-3131
76 Lawrence St Glens Falls (12801) ***(G-5686)***
Lee Newspapers Inc 518 673-3237
6113 State Highway 5 Palatine Bridge (13428) ***(G-13395)***
Lee Philips Packaging Inc 631 580-3306
750 Union Pkwy Ronkonkoma (11779) ***(G-14931)***
Lee Printing Inc 718 237-1651
188 Lee Ave Brooklyn (11211) ***(G-2205)***
Lee Publications Inc (PA) 518 673-3237
6113 State Highway 5 Palatine Bridge (13428) ***(G-13396)***
Lee Spring Company Div, New York *Also called Unimex Corporation* ***(G-12458)***
Lee Spring Company LLC (HQ) 718 362-5183
140 58th St Ste 3c Brooklyn (11220) ***(G-2206)***
Lee Spring LLC (PA) 718 236-2222
140 58th St Ste 3c Brooklyn (11220) ***(G-2207)***
Lee World Industries LLC 212 265-8866
150 Broadway Ste 1608 New York (10038) ***(G-10958)***
Lee Yuen Fung Trading Co Inc (PA) 212 594-9595
125 W 29th St Fl 5 New York (10001) ***(G-10959)***
Leesa Designs Ltd 631 261-3991
31 Glenn Cres Centerport (11721) ***(G-3478)***
Leetech Manufacturing Inc 631 563-1442
105 Carlough Rd Unit C Bohemia (11716) ***(G-1092)***
Lefrak Entertainment Co Ltd 212 586-3600
40 W 57th St Fl 4 New York (10019) ***(G-10960)***
Leg Resource Inc (PA) 212 736-4574
390 5th Ave Rm 405 New York (10018) ***(G-10961)***
Legacy Furniture Inc (PA) 718 527-5331
6 Shinev Ct Unit 201 Monroe (10950) ***(G-8560)***
Legacy Valve LLC 914 403-5075
14 Railroad Ave Valhalla (10595) ***(G-16368)***
Legal Servicing LLC 716 565-9300
2801 Wehrle Dr Ste 5 Williamsville (14221) ***(G-17248)***
Legal Strategies Inc 516 377-3940
1795 Harvard Ave Merrick (11566) ***(G-8389)***
Legendary Auto Interiors Ltd 315 331-1212
121 W Shore Blvd Newark (14513) ***(G-12734)***
Legge System, Peekskill *Also called Walter G Legge Company Inc* ***(G-13485)***
Leggiadro International Inc (PA) 212 997-8766
8 W 36th St Fl 9 New York (10018) ***(G-10962)***
Legion Lighting Co Inc 718 498-1770
221 Glenmore Ave Brooklyn (11207) ***(G-2208)***
Legno Veneto USA 716 651-9169
3283 Walden Ave Depew (14043) ***(G-4261)***
Lehigh Cement Company (HQ) 518 792-1137
313 Warren St Glens Falls (12801) ***(G-5687)***
Lehigh Cement Company 518 943-5940
120 Alpha Rd Catskill (12414) ***(G-3430)***
Lehigh Cement Company LLC 518 792-1137
313 Lower Warren St Glens Falls (12804) ***(G-5688)***
Lehigh Northeast Cement, Glens Falls *Also called Lehigh Cement Company* ***(G-5687)***
Lehmann Printing Company Inc 212 929-2395
247 W 37th St Rm 2a New York (10018) ***(G-10963)***
Lehneis Orthotics Prosthetic 631 360-3859
517 Route 111 Ste 300 Hauppauge (11788) ***(G-6112)***
Lehneis Orthotics Prosthetic 631 369-3115
518 E Main St Riverhead (11901) ***(G-14146)***
Leica Microsystems Inc 716 686-3000
3362 Walden Ave Depew (14043) ***(G-4262)***
Leidel Corporation (PA) 631 244-0900
95 Orville Dr Bohemia (11716) ***(G-1093)***
Leigh Scott Enterprises Inc 718 343-5440
24802 Union Tpke Bellerose (11426) ***(G-810)***
Leiter Sukkahs Inc 718 436-0303
1346 39th St Brooklyn (11218) ***(G-2209)***
Lela Rose, New York *Also called Stitch & Couture Inc* ***(G-12206)***
Lelab Dental Laboratory Inc 516 561-5050
550 W Merrick Rd Ste 8 Valley Stream (11580) ***(G-16412)***
Lemetric Hair Centers Inc 212 986-5620
124 E 40th St Rm 601 New York (10016) ***(G-10964)***
Lemode Concepts Inc 631 841-0796
19 Elm Pl Amityville (11701) ***(G-305)***
Lemode Plumbing & Heating 718 545-3336
3455 11th St Astoria (11106) ***(G-447)***
Lemon Brothers Foundation Inc 347 920-2749
23b Debs Pl Bronx (10475) ***(G-1380)***
Lemoyne Machine Products Corp 315 454-0708
106 Evelyn Ter Syracuse (13208) ***(G-15976)***
Lemral Knitwear Inc 718 210-0175
70 Franklin Ave Brooklyn (11205) ***(G-2210)***
Lenape Energy Inc (PA) 585 344-1200
9489 Alexander Rd Alexander (14005) ***(G-187)***
Lenape Resources Inc 585 344-1200
9489 Alexander Rd Alexander (14005) ***(G-188)***
Lenaro Paper Co Inc 631 439-8800
31 Windsor Pl Central Islip (11722) ***(G-3502)***
Lenco, Amityville *Also called Saraga Industries Corp* ***(G-324)***
Lencore Acoustics Corp (PA) 516 682-9292
1 Crossways Park Dr W Woodbury (11797) ***(G-17291)***
Lencore Acoustics Corp 315 384-9114
1 S Main St Norfolk (13667) ***(G-12899)***
Lending Trimming Co Inc 212 242-7502
179 Christopher St New York (10014) ***(G-10965)***
Lennons Litho Inc 315 866-3156
234 Kast Hill Rd Herkimer (13350) ***(G-6304)***
Lenon Models Inc 212 229-1581
236 W 27th St Rm 900 New York (10001) ***(G-10966)***
Lenore Marshall Inc 212 947-5945
231 W 29th St Frnt 1 New York (10001) ***(G-10967)***
Lens Lab 718 379-2020
2124 Bartow Ave Bronx (10475) ***(G-1381)***
Lens Lab Express 718 921-5488
482 86th St Brooklyn (11209) ***(G-2211)***
Lens Lab Express of Graham Ave 718 486-0117
28 Graham Ave Brooklyn (11206) ***(G-2212)***
Lens Lab Express Southern Blvd 718 626-5184
3073 Steinway St Astoria (11103) ***(G-448)***
Lens Triptar Co Inc 585 473-4470
439 Monroe Ave Ste 1 Rochester (14607) ***(G-14477)***
Lenz, Peconic *Also called Dorset Farms Inc* ***(G-13470)***
Leo D Bernstein & Sons Inc (PA) 212 337-9578
151 W 25th St Frnt 1 New York (10001) ***(G-10968)***
Leo Diamond, The, New York *Also called Leo Schachter Diamonds LLC* ***(G-10972)***
Leo Ingwer Inc 212 719-1342
62 W 47th St Ste 1004 New York (10036) ***(G-10969)***
Leo International Inc 718 290-8005
471 Sutter Ave Brooklyn (11207) ***(G-2213)***
Leo P Callahan Inc 607 797-7314
229 Lwer Stlla Ireland Rd Binghamton (13905) ***(G-933)***
Leo Paper Inc 917 305-0708
27 W 24th St Ste 601 New York (10010) ***(G-10970)***
Leo Schachter & Co Inc 212 688-2000
529 5th Ave New York (10017) ***(G-10971)***
Leo Schachter Diamonds LLC 212 688-2000
50 W 47th St Fl 2100 New York (10036) ***(G-10972)***
Leo Schultz 716 969-0945
1144 Maryvale Dr Cheektowaga (14225) ***(G-3577)***
Leonard Bus Sales Inc 607 467-3100
730 Ellsworth Rd Rome (13441) ***(G-14819)***
Leonard Carlson 518 477-4710
90 Waters Rd East Greenbush (12061) ***(G-4403)***
Leonard Martin Bus Systems 845 638-9350
120 N Main St Ste 202 New City (10956) ***(G-8787)***
Leonardo Printing Corp 914 664-7890
529 E 3rd St Mount Vernon (10553) ***(G-8700)***
Leonardo Prntng, Mount Vernon *Also called Leonardo Printing Corp* ***(G-8700)***
Leonore Doskow Inc 914 737-1335
1 Doskow Rd Montrose (10548) ***(G-8613)***

ALPHABETIC

ALPHABETIC SECTION
Lifetime Brands Inc (PA)

Lep, Hawthorne *Also called Ludl Electronic Products Ltd* ***(G-6250)***
Lepore, Nanette, New York *Also called Nl Shoes and Bags LLC* ***(G-11444)***
Leprino Foods Company 570 888-9658
400 Leprino Ave Waverly (14892) ***(G-16704)***
Leray Homes Inc 315 788-6087
22732 Duffy Rd Watertown (13601) ***(G-16663)***
Leroux Fuels 518 563-3653
994 Military Tpke Plattsburgh (12901) ***(G-13676)***
Leroy Plastics Inc 585 768-8158
20 Lent Ave Le Roy (14482) ***(G-7413)***
Les Chateaux De France Inc 516 239-6795
1 Craft Ave Inwood (11096) ***(G-6760)***
Lesanne Life Sciences LLC 914 234-0860
47 Brook Farm Rd Bedford (10506) ***(G-797)***
Leser Enterprises Ltd 212 644-8921
18 E 48th St Rm 1104 New York (10017) ***(G-10973)***
Lesilu Productions Inc 212 947-6419
60 W 38th St Rm 302 New York (10018) ***(G-10974)***
Leslie Stuart Co Inc 212 629-4551
149 W 36th St Fl 8 New York (10018) ***(G-10975)***
Lesly Enterprise & Associates 631 988-1301
29 Columbo Dr Deer Park (11729) ***(G-4165)***
Lessoilcom 516 319-5052
672 Dogwood Ave Franklin Square (11010) ***(G-5364)***
Let Water Be Water LLC 212 627-2630
40 W 27th St Fl 3 New York (10001) ***(G-10976)***
Letigre, New York *Also called Lt2 LLC* ***(G-11056)***
Letterama Inc (PA) 516 349-0800
111 Cabot St West Babylon (11704) ***(G-16807)***
Lettergraphics, Bridgeport *Also called Syracuse Letter Company Inc* ***(G-1237)***
Levi Strauss & Co 212 944-8555
1501 Broadway New York (10036) ***(G-10977)***
Levi Strauss & Co 917 213-6263
13432 Blossom Ave Flushing (11355) ***(G-5265)***
Levindi (HQ) 212 572-7000
800 3rd Ave New York (10022) ***(G-10978)***
Levition Manufacturing Co 631 812-6000
201 N Service Rd Melville (11747) ***(G-8333)***
Leviton Manufacturing Co Inc (PA) 631 812-6000
201 N Service Rd Melville (11747) ***(G-8334)***
Levitt Industrial Textile, Westbury *Also called Kenwin Sales Corp* ***(G-17003)***
Levolor Window Furnishings Inc (HQ) 845 664-7000
1 Blue Hill Plz Pearl River (10965) ***(G-13462)***
Levon Graphics Corp 631 753-2022
210 Route 109 Farmingdale (11735) ***(G-5035)***
Levy Group Inc (PA) 212 398-0707
1333 Broadway Fl 9 New York (10018) ***(G-10979)***
Lewbro Ready Mix Inc (PA) 315 497-0498
502 Locke Rd Groton (13073) ***(G-5899)***
Lewis & Myers Inc (PA) 585 494-1410
7307 S Lake Rd Bergen (14416) ***(G-848)***
Lewis Machine Co Inc 718 625-0799
209 Congress St Brooklyn (11201) ***(G-2214)***
Lewis Sand & Gravel, Lewis *Also called Graymont Materials (ny) Inc* ***(G-7431)***
Lewis, S J Machine Co, Brooklyn *Also called Lewis Machine Co Inc* ***(G-2214)***
Lexan Industries Inc 631 434-7586
15 Harold Ct Bay Shore (11706) ***(G-713)***
Lexar Global LLC 845 352-9700
711 Executive Blvd Ste K Valley Cottage (10989) ***(G-16381)***
Lexington Machining LLC 585 235-0880
677 Buffalo Rd Rochester (14611) ***(G-14478)***
Lexington Machining LLC (PA) 585 235-0880
677 Buffalo Rd Rochester (14611) ***(G-14479)***
Lexis Nexis Mathew Bender, Menands *Also called Lexis Publishing* ***(G-8373)***
Lexis Publishing 518 487-3000
1275 Broadway Menands (12204) ***(G-8373)***
Lexisnexis, Conklin *Also called Relx Inc* ***(G-3873)***
Lexmark International Inc 212 949-1090
529 5th Ave New York (10017) ***(G-10980)***
Lexstar Inc (PA) 845 947-1415
25 Lincoln St Haverstraw (10927) ***(G-6238)***
Lf Outerwear LLC 212 239-2025
463 7th Ave Fl 12 New York (10018) ***(G-10981)***
Lgb Inc 212 278-8280
1410 Broadway Rm 3205 New York (10018) ***(G-10982)***
Lgn Materials & Solutions 888 414-0005
149 Esplanade Mount Vernon (10553) ***(G-8701)***
Lhv Precast Inc 845 336-8880
540 Ulster Landing Rd Kingston (12401) ***(G-7196)***
Ll Community Newspapers Inc 516 747-8282
132 E 2nd St Mineola (11501) ***(G-8520)***
Ll Fireproof Door, Whitestone *Also called Long Island Fireproof Door* ***(G-17211)***
Ll Pipe Supply, Garden City *Also called Long Island Pipe Supply Inc* ***(G-5515)***
Ll Script LLC 631 321-3850
333 Crossways Park Dr Woodbury (11797) ***(G-17292)***
Liana Uniforms, New York *Also called Eighteen Liana Trading Inc* ***(G-9989)***
Libbys Bakery Cafe LLC 603 918-8825
92 Montcalm St Ticonderoga (12883) ***(G-16127)***
Liberty Apparel Company Inc 212 221-0101
1407 Broadway Rm 214 New York (10018) ***(G-10983)***
Liberty Apparel Company Inc (PA) 718 625-4000
1407 Broadway Rm 1500 New York (10018) ***(G-10984)***
Liberty Awnings & Signs Inc 347 203-1470
7705 21st Ave East Elmhurst (11370) ***(G-4394)***
Liberty Brass Turning Co Inc 718 784-2911
1200 Shames Dr Unit C Westbury (11590) ***(G-17005)***
Liberty Controls Inc 718 461-0600
1505 132nd St Fl 2 College Point (11356) ***(G-3795)***
Liberty Displays Inc 716 743-1757
4230b Ridge Lea Rd # 110 Amherst (14226) ***(G-249)***
Liberty Fabrication Inc 718 495-5735
226 Glenmore Ave Brooklyn (11207) ***(G-2215)***
Liberty Food and Fuel 315 299-4039
1131 N Salina St Syracuse (13208) ***(G-15977)***
Liberty Install Inc 631 651-5655
100 Centershore Rd Centerport (11721) ***(G-3479)***
Liberty Label Mfg Inc 631 737-2365
21 Peachtree Ct Holbrook (11741) ***(G-6457)***
Liberty Machine & Tool 315 699-3242
7908 Ontario Ave Cicero (13039) ***(G-3647)***
Liberty Panel & Home Center, Brooklyn *Also called Liberty Panel Center Inc* ***(G-2216)***
Liberty Panel Center Inc (PA) 718 647-2763
1009 Liberty Ave Brooklyn (11208) ***(G-2216)***
Liberty Pipe Incorporated 516 747-2472
128 Liberty Ave Mineola (11501) ***(G-8521)***
Liberty Pumps Inc 585 494-1817
7000 Appletree Ave Bergen (14416) ***(G-849)***
Liberty Tire Recycling LLC 716 433-7370
490 Ohio St Lockport (14094) ***(G-7597)***
Library of America, New York *Also called Literary Classics of US* ***(G-11008)***
Library Tales Publishing Inc 347 394-2629
244 5th Ave Ste Q222 New York (10001) ***(G-10985)***
Licenders (PA) 212 759-5200
939 8th Ave New York (10019) ***(G-10986)***
Lickity Splits 585 345-6091
238 East Ave Batavia (14020) ***(G-641)***
Liddabit Sweets 917 912-1370
330 Wythe Ave Apt 2g Brooklyn (11249) ***(G-2217)***
Liddell Corporation 716 297-8557
4600 Witmer Ind Est 5 Niagara Falls (14305) ***(G-12842)***
Lidestri Food and Drink, Fairport *Also called Lidestri Foods Inc* ***(G-4861)***
Lidestri Foods Inc 585 458-8335
1000 Lee Rd Rochester (14606) ***(G-14480)***
Lidestri Foods Inc (PA) 585 377-7700
815 Whitney Rd W Fairport (14450) ***(G-4861)***
Lids Corporation 718 338-7790
5385 Kings Plz Brooklyn (11234) ***(G-2218)***
Lids Corporation 518 459-7060
131 Colonie Ctr Spc 429 Albany (12205) ***(G-97)***
Lieb Cellars LLC 631 298-1942
35 Cox Neck Rd Mattituck (11952) ***(G-8207)***
Lieb Cellars Tasting Room, Mattituck *Also called Lieb Cellars LLC* ***(G-8207)***
Liebe NY, Perry *Also called R J Liebe Athletic Company* ***(G-13525)***
Lif Distributing Inc 631 630-6900
155 Oval Dr Islandia (11749) ***(G-6799)***
Lif Industries Inc (PA) 516 390-6800
5 Harbor Park Dr Ste 1 Port Washington (11050) ***(G-13837)***
Lifc Corp 516 426-5737
101 Haven Ave Port Washington (11050) ***(G-13838)***
Life Juice Brands LLC 585 944-7982
115 Brook Rd Pittsford (14534) ***(G-13567)***
Life Medical Technologies LLC 845 894-2121
2070 Rte 52 21a Bldg 320a Hopewell Junction (12533) ***(G-6556)***
Life Plus Style, New York *Also called International Design Assoc Ltd* ***(G-10633)***
Life Style Design Group 212 391-8666
1441 Broadway Fl 7 New York (10018) ***(G-10987)***
Life Technologies Corporation 716 774-6700
3175 Staley Rd Grand Island (14072) ***(G-5762)***
Life Time Fitness Inc 914 290-5100
1 Westchester Park Dr Harrison (10528) ***(G-5987)***
Life Watch Technology Inc (PA) 917 669-2428
42-10 Polen St Ste 412 Flushing (11355) ***(G-5266)***
Lifeforms Printing 716 685-4500
786 Terrace Blvd Ste 2 Depew (14043) ***(G-4263)***
Lifegas, Cohoes *Also called Linde Gas North America LLC* ***(G-3749)***
Lifegas, Cheektowaga *Also called Linde Gas North America LLC* ***(G-3578)***
Lifegas, Syracuse *Also called Linde Gas North America LLC* ***(G-15979)***
Lifelink Monitoring Corp (PA) 845 336-2098
3201 Route 212 Bearsville (12409) ***(G-792)***
Lifesake Division, New Hartford *Also called Faster-Form Corp* ***(G-8804)***
Lifescan Inc 516 557-2693
15 Tardy Ln N Wantagh (11793) ***(G-16558)***
Lifesciences Technology Inc 516 569-0085
906 Wateredge Pl Hewlett (11557) ***(G-6309)***
Lifestyle Design Usa Ltd 212 279-9400
315 W 39th St Rm 709 New York (10018) ***(G-10988)***
Lifestyle-Trimco (PA) 718 257-9101
323 Malta St Brooklyn (11207) ***(G-2219)***
Lifestyle-Trimco Viaggo, Brooklyn *Also called Lifestyle-Trimco* ***(G-2219)***
Lifetime Brands Inc (PA) 516 683-6000
1000 Stewart Ave Garden City (11530) ***(G-5514)***

ALPHABETIC

ALPHABETIC SECTION

Lifetime Chimney Supply LLC..................516 576-8144
171 E Ames Ct Plainview (11803) *(G-13616)*
Lifetime Stainless Steel Corp..................585 924-9393
7387 Ny 96 850 Victor (14564) *(G-16488)*
Lifewatch Inc..................800 716-1433
1344 Broadway Ste 106 Hewlett (11557) *(G-6310)*
Lifewatch Personal Mergency, Hewlett Also called Lifewatch Inc *(G-6310)*
Liffey Sheet Metal Corp..................347 381-1134
117 Hausman St Brooklyn (11222) *(G-2220)*
Lift Safe - Fuel Safe Inc..................315 423-7702
212 W Seneca Tpke Syracuse (13205) *(G-15978)*
Liftforward Inc..................917 693-4993
261 Madison Ave Fl 9 New York (10016) *(G-10989)*
Light Blue USA LLC..................718 475-2515
697 Mcdonald Ave Brooklyn (11218) *(G-2221)*
Light Dental Labs Inc..................516 785-7730
1939 Wantagh Ave Unit A Wantagh (11793) *(G-16559)*
Light Fabrications, Rochester Also called Eis Inc *(G-14341)*
Light House Hill Marketing..................212 354-1338
38 W 39th St Fl 4l New York (10018) *(G-10990)*
Light Inc..................212 629-1095
530 Fashion Ave Rm 1002 New York (10018) *(G-10991)*
Light Waves Concept Inc..................212 677-6400
1 Bond St Apt 2c New York (10012) *(G-10992)*
Lightbulb Press Inc..................212 485-8800
39 W 28th St New York (10001) *(G-10993)*
Lighthouse Components..................917 993-6820
14 Wall St New York (10005) *(G-10994)*
Lighting By Dom Yonkers Inc..................914 968-8700
253 S Broadway Yonkers (10705) *(G-17462)*
Lighting By Gregory, New York Also called Lbg Acquisition LLC *(G-10939)*
Lighting Collaborative Inc..................212 253-7220
124 W 24th St New York (10011) *(G-10995)*
Lighting Holdings Intl LLC (PA)..................845 306-1850
4 Manhattanville Rd Purchase (10577) *(G-13960)*
Lighting Products Division, Skaneateles Falls Also called Welch Allyn Inc *(G-15473)*
Lighting Sculptures Inc..................631 242-3387
66 N Industry Ct Deer Park (11729) *(G-4166)*
Lighting Services (PA)..................845 942-2800
2 Holt Dr Stony Point (10980) *(G-15776)*
Lightron Corporation..................516 938-5544
100 Jericho Quadrangle Jericho (11753) *(G-7075)*
Lightspin Technologies Inc..................301 656-7600
616 Lowell Dr Endwell (13760) *(G-4837)*
Liiiike Shopping Inc..................914 271-2001
37 W 37th St Fl 6 New York (10018) *(G-10996)*
Lik LLC..................516 848-5135
6 Bluff Point Rd Northport (11768) *(G-13015)*
Lilac Quarries LLC..................607 867-4016
1702 State Highway 8 Mount Upton (13809) *(G-8658)*
Lilly Collection, New York Also called Lily & Taylor Inc *(G-10997)*
Lillys Homestyle Bakeshop Inc..................718 491-2904
6210 9th Ave Brooklyn (11220) *(G-2222)*
Lily & Taylor Inc..................212 564-5459
247 W 37th St Frnt 6 New York (10018) *(G-10997)*
Limited Papers, Brooklyn Also called 3 Star Papers Limited *(G-1514)*
Limo-Print.com, Central Islip Also called Color Card LLC *(G-3491)*
Lin Jin Feng..................718 232-3039
7718 18th Ave Brooklyn (11214) *(G-2223)*
Lincdoc LLC..................585 563-1669
401 Main St East Rochester (14445) *(G-4465)*
Linco Printing Inc..................718 937-5141
5022 23rd St Long Island City (11101) *(G-7789)*
Lincware, East Rochester Also called Lincdoc LLC *(G-4465)*
Linda Campbell..................718 994-4026
4420 Richardson Ave Bronx (10470) *(G-1382)*
Linda Richards, New York Also called Linrich Designs Inc *(G-11002)*
Linda Tool & Die Corporation..................718 522-2066
163 Dwight St Brooklyn (11231) *(G-2224)*
Linda Wine & Spirit..................718 703-5707
1219 Flatbush Ave Brooklyn (11226) *(G-2225)*
Linde Gas North America LLC
10 Arrowhead Ln Cohoes (12047) *(G-3749)*
Linde Gas North America LLC..................866 543-3427
45 Boxwood Ln Cheektowaga (14227) *(G-3578)*
Linde Gas North America LLC..................315 431-4081
147 Midler Park Dr Syracuse (13206) *(G-15979)*
Linde LLC..................716 847-0748
101 Katherine St Buffalo (14210) *(G-3048)*
Linde LLC..................518 439-8187
76 W Yard Rd Feura Bush (12067) *(G-5172)*
Linde LLC..................716 773-7552
3279 Grand Island Blvd Grand Island (14072) *(G-5763)*
Linde Merchant Production Inc..................315 593-1360
370 Owen Rd Fulton (13069) *(G-5469)*
Linden Care LLC (PA)..................516 221-7600
130 Crossways Park Dr # 101 Woodbury (11797) *(G-17293)*
Linden Cookies LLC..................845 268-5050
25 Brenner Dr Congers (10920) *(G-3859)*
Linden Forms & Systems Inc..................212 219-1100
40 S 6th St Brooklyn (11249) *(G-2226)*
Linden Pro Care, Woodbury Also called Linden Care LLC *(G-17293)*

Lindenhurst Fabricators Inc..................631 226-3737
117 S 13th St Lindenhurst (11757) *(G-7467)*
Linder New York LLC..................646 678-5819
195 Chrystie St Rm 900 New York (10002) *(G-10998)*
Lindley Wood Works Inc..................607 523-7786
9625 Morgan Creek Rd Lindley (14858) *(G-7496)*
Lindsay & Co, New York Also called Lindsay-Hoenig Ltd *(G-10999)*
Lindsay Lyn Accessories Div, New York Also called Jaclyn Inc *(G-10689)*
Lindsay-Hoenig Ltd..................212 575-9711
64 W 48th St Ste 1306 New York (10036) *(G-10999)*
Lindsey Adelman..................718 623-3013
27 Prospect Park W Brooklyn (11215) *(G-2227)*
Lindt & Sprungli (usa) Inc..................212 582-3047
692 5th Ave New York (10019) *(G-11000)*
Line Ward Corporation..................716 675-7373
157 Seneca Creek Rd Buffalo (14224) *(G-3049)*
Linear Lighting Corporation..................718 361-7552
3130 Hunters Point Ave Long Island City (11101) *(G-7790)*
Linear Signs Inc..................631 532-5330
275 W Hoffman Ave Ste 1 Lindenhurst (11757) *(G-7468)*
Linen Micarta LLC..................212 203-5145
65 Broadway Ste 1101 New York (10006) *(G-11001)*
Linita Design & Mfg Corp..................716 566-7753
1951 Hamburg Tpke Ste 24 Lackawanna (14218) *(G-7244)*
Link Control Systems Inc..................631 471-3950
16 Colt Ct Ronkonkoma (11779) *(G-14932)*
Link Group Inc..................718 567-7082
6204 5th Ave Brooklyn (11220) *(G-2228)*
Linli Color, West Babylon Also called East Cast Clor Compounding Inc *(G-16790)*
Lino International Inc..................516 482-7100
111 Great Neck Rd 300a Great Neck (11021) *(G-5821)*
Lino Metal, Great Neck Also called Lino International Inc *(G-5821)*
Lino Press Inc..................718 665-2625
652 Southern Blvd Bronx (10455) *(G-1383)*
Linrich Designs Inc..................212 382-2257
256 W 38th St Fl 8 New York (10018) *(G-11002)*
Lintex Linens Inc..................212 679-8046
295 5th Ave Ste 1702 New York (10016) *(G-11003)*
Lion & Bear Distributors, Jericho Also called Satnam Distributors LLC *(G-7084)*
Lion Biotechnologies Inc (PA)..................212 946-4856
112 W 34th St Fl 17 New York (10120) *(G-11004)*
Lion Die-Cutting Co Inc..................718 383-8841
95 Dobbin St Ste 1 Brooklyn (11222) *(G-2229)*
Lion In The Sun Park Slope Ltd..................718 369-4006
232 7th Ave Brooklyn (11215) *(G-2230)*
Lionel Habas Associates Inc..................212 860-8454
1601 3rd Ave Apt 22d New York (10128) *(G-11005)*
Lipe Automation, Liverpool Also called Ironshore Holdings Inc *(G-7527)*
Lippincott Massie McQuilkin L..................212 352-2055
27 W 20th St Ste 305 New York (10011) *(G-11006)*
Liptis Pharmaceuticals USA Inc..................845 627-0260
110 Red Schoolhouse Rd Spring Valley (10977) *(G-15592)*
Liquid Industries Inc..................716 628-2999
7219 New Jersey Ave Niagara Falls (14305) *(G-12843)*
Liquid Knits Inc..................718 706-6600
3200 Skillman Ave Fl 2 Long Island City (11101) *(G-7791)*
Liquid Management Partners LLC..................516 775-5050
1983 Marcus Ave Ste E138 New Hyde Park (11042) *(G-8846)*
Liquitane, Rochester Also called Consolidated Container Co LLC *(G-14288)*
Liquitane, Batavia Also called Consolidated Container Co LLC *(G-629)*
Liquor Bottle Packg Intl Inc..................212 922-2813
305 Madison Ave Ste 1357 New York (10165) *(G-11007)*
Lisk Coils, Phelps Also called GW Lisk Company Inc *(G-13532)*
Liston Manufacturing Inc..................716 695-2111
421 Payne Ave North Tonawanda (14120) *(G-12981)*
Litchfield Fabrics of NC (PA)..................518 773-9500
111 Woodside Ave Gloversville (12078) *(G-5717)*
Lite Brite Manufacturing Inc..................718 855-9797
575 President St Brooklyn (11215) *(G-2231)*
Lite FM Radio, New York Also called Iheartcommunications Inc *(G-10564)*
Lite-Makers Inc..................718 739-9300
10715 180th St Jamaica (11433) *(G-6925)*
Litelab Corp..................718 361-6829
540 54th Ave Long Island City (11101) *(G-7792)*
Litelab Corp (PA)..................716 856-4300
251 Elm St Buffalo (14203) *(G-3050)*
Literary Classics of US..................212 308-3360
14 E 60th St Ste 1101 New York (10022) *(G-11008)*
Lites On West Soho, Haverstraw Also called Lexstar Inc *(G-6238)*
Litho Partners Inc..................212 627-9225
175 Varick St Fl 8 New York (10014) *(G-11009)*
Lithomatic Business Forms Inc..................212 255-6700
233 W 18th St Frnt A New York (10011) *(G-11010)*
Litmor Publications, Hicksville Also called Litmor Publishing Corp *(G-6364)*
Litmor Publishing Corp (PA)..................516 931-0012
81 E Barclay St Hicksville (11801) *(G-6364)*
Little Bee Books Inc..................212 321-0237
251 Park Ave S Fl 12 New York (10010) *(G-11011)*
Little Bird Chocolates Inc..................646 620-6395
25 Fairchild Ave Ste 200 Massapequa (11758) *(G-8180)*
Little Curios Confections, Massapequa Also called Little Bird Chocolates Inc *(G-8180)*

Little Eric Shoes On Madison...212 717-1513
1118 Madison Ave New York (10028) ***(G-11012)***
Little Store, The, Roscoe *Also called Roscoe Little Store Inc* ***(G-15012)***
Little Trees, Watertown *Also called Car-Freshner Corporation* ***(G-16641)***
Little Valley Sand & Gravel...716 938-6676
8984 New Albion Rd Little Valley (14755) ***(G-7511)***
Little Wolf Cabinet Shop Inc...212 734-1116
1583 1st Ave Frnt 1 New York (10028) ***(G-11013)***
Littlebits Electronics Inc...917 464-4577
601 W 26th St Ste M274 New York (10001) ***(G-11014)***
Live Oak Media, Pine Plains *Also called ABRA Media Inc* ***(G-13554)***
Liveright Publishing Corp...212 354-5500
500 5th Ave Fl 6 New York (10110) ***(G-11015)***
Livermoore Logging, Cassadaga *Also called Wrights Hardwoods Inc* ***(G-3415)***
Livetiles Corp...917 472-7887
60 Madison Ave Fl 8 New York (10010) ***(G-11016)***
Living Doors Inc...631 924-5393
22 Scouting Blvd Ste 3 Medford (11763) ***(G-8253)***
Living Media, Long Island City *Also called Thomson Press (india) Limited* ***(G-7901)***
Living Well Innovations Inc...646 517-3200
115 Engineers Rd Hauppauge (11788) ***(G-6113)***
Livingston County News...585 243-1234
122 Main St Geneseo (14454) ***(G-5566)***
Livingston Lighting and Power, Scottsville *Also called Power and Cnstr Group Inc* ***(G-15338)***
Liz Claiborne Coats, New York *Also called Levy Group Inc* ***(G-10979)***
Liz Claiborne Swimwear, Farmingdale *Also called Swimwear Anywhere Inc* ***(G-5121)***
Liz Lange, Brooklyn *Also called Zoomers Inc* ***(G-2782)***
Lizotte Logging Inc...518 359-2200
50 Haymeadow Rd Tupper Lake (12986) ***(G-16277)***
Ljmm Inc...845 454-5876
188 Washington St Poughkeepsie (12601) ***(G-13912)***
Lk Industries Inc...716 941-9202
9731 Center St Glenwood (14069) ***(G-5703)***
Llcs Publishing Corp...718 569-2703
2071 Flatbush Ave Ste 189 Brooklyn (11234) ***(G-2232)***
Lloyd Price Icon Food Brands...914 764-8624
95 Horseshoe Hill Rd Pound Ridge (10576) ***(G-13944)***
Lloyds Fashions Inc (PA)...631 435-3353
335 Crooked Hill Rd Brentwood (11717) ***(G-1190)***
Lm Mignon LLC...212 730-9221
499 Fashion Ave Fl 4n New York (10018) ***(G-11017)***
Lmg National Publishing Inc (HQ)...585 598-6874
350 Willowbrook Office Pa Fairport (14450) ***(G-4862)***
Lmgi, Liverpool *Also called Lockheed Martin Global Inc* ***(G-7532)***
LMI, Bergen *Also called Lewis & Myers Inc* ***(G-848)***
Lnd, Oceanside *Also called L N D Incorporated* ***(G-13085)***
LNK International Inc...631 435-3500
22 Arkay Dr Hauppauge (11788) ***(G-6114)***
LNK International Inc...631 435-3500
100 Ricefield Ln Hauppauge (11788) ***(G-6115)***
LNK International Inc...631 435-3500
325 Kennedy Dr Hauppauge (11788) ***(G-6116)***
LNK International Inc...631 543-3787
145 Ricefield Ln Hauppauge (11788) ***(G-6117)***
LNK International Inc...631 435-3500
40 Arkay Dr Hauppauge (11788) ***(G-6118)***
LNK International Inc...631 231-3415
60 Oscer Ave Hauppauge (11788) ***(G-6119)***
LNK International Inc...631 231-4020
55 Arkay Dr Hauppauge (11788) ***(G-6120)***
Lo & Sons Inc...917 775-4025
20 Jay St Ste 840 Brooklyn (11201) ***(G-2233)***
Lo-Co Fuel Corp...631 929-5086
10 Stephen Dr Wading River (11792) ***(G-16524)***
Load/N/Go Beverage Corp (PA)...585 218-4019
355 Portland Ave Rochester (14605) ***(G-14481)***
Loar Group Inc (PA)...212 210-9348
450 Lexington Ave Fl 31 New York (10017) ***(G-11018)***
Local Media Group Inc (HQ)...845 341-1100
40 Mulberry St Middletown (10940) ***(G-8446)***
Local Media Group Inc...845 341-1100
40 Mulberry St Middletown (10940) ***(G-8447)***
Local Media Group Inc...845 341-1100
60 Brookline Ave Middletown (10940) ***(G-8448)***
Local Media Group Inc...845 794-3712
479 Broadway Monticello (12701) ***(G-8605)***
Local Media Group Inc...845 340-4910
34 John St Kingston (12401) ***(G-7197)***
Local News, Oswego *Also called Dotto Wagner* ***(G-13330)***
Locations Magazine...212 288-4745
124 E 79th St New York (10075) ***(G-11019)***
Locker Masters Inc...518 288-3203
10329 State Route 22 Granville (12832) ***(G-5774)***
Lockheed Martin Corporation...716 297-1000
2221 Niagara Falls Blvd Niagara Falls (14304) ***(G-12844)***
Lockheed Martin Corporation...212 953-1510
420 Lexington Ave Rm 2601 New York (10170) ***(G-11020)***
Lockheed Martin Corporation...315 456-1548
497 Electronics Pkwy Liverpool (13088) ***(G-7530)***
Lockheed Martin Corporation...315 793-5800
8373 Seneca Tpke New Hartford (13413) ***(G-8807)***
Lockheed Martin Corporation...516 228-2000
55 Charles Lindbergh Blvd # 1 Uniondale (11553) ***(G-16298)***
Lockheed Martin Corporation...607 751-2000
1801 State Route 17 Owego (13827) ***(G-13354)***
Lockheed Martin Corporation...607 751-7434
1801 State Rd 17c 17 C Owego (13827) ***(G-13355)***
Lockheed Martin Corporation...315 456-0123
497 Electronics Pkwy # 5 Liverpool (13088) ***(G-7531)***
Lockheed Martin Corporation...315 456-6604
6060 Tarbell Rd Syracuse (13206) ***(G-15980)***
Lockheed Martin Corporation...212 697-1105
600 3rd Ave Fl 35 New York (10016) ***(G-11021)***
Lockheed Martin Global Inc (HQ)...315 456-2982
497 Electronics Pkwy # 5 Liverpool (13088) ***(G-7532)***
Lockheed Martin Integrated...315 456-3333
497 Electronics Pkwy Syracuse (13221) ***(G-15981)***
Lockheed Martin Overseas...315 456-0123
497 Electronics Pkwy # 7 Liverpool (13088) ***(G-7533)***
Lockwood Trade Journal Co Inc...212 391-2060
3743 Crescent St Fl 2 Long Island City (11101) ***(G-7793)***
Lodolce Machine Co Inc...845 246-7017
196 Malden Tpke Saugerties (12477) ***(G-15187)***
Loffreno Cstm Interiors Contg...718 981-0319
33 Ada Pl Staten Island (10301) ***(G-15699)***
Logic Controls Inc...516 248-0400
999 S Oyster Bay Rd Bethpage (11714) ***(G-872)***
Logical Control Solutions Inc...585 424-5340
829 Phillips Rd Ste 100 Victor (14564) ***(G-16489)***
Logical Operations Inc...585 350-7000
3535 Winton Pl Rochester (14623) ***(G-14482)***
Logitek Inc...631 567-1100
110 Wilbur Pl Bohemia (11716) ***(G-1094)***
Logo...212 846-2568
1515 Broadway New York (10036) ***(G-11022)***
Logomax Inc...631 420-0484
242 Route 109 Ste B Farmingdale (11735) ***(G-5036)***
Lokai Holdings LLC...646 979-3474
36 E 31st St Rm 602 New York (10016) ***(G-11023)***
Lollipop Tree Inc...845 471-8733
181 York St Auburn (13021) ***(G-506)***
Lollipops Inc...845 352-8642
52 Brewer Rd Monsey (10952) ***(G-8573)***
Lollytogs Ltd (PA)...212 502-6000
100 W 33rd St Ste 1012 New York (10001) ***(G-11024)***
Lomak Petroleum, Mayville *Also called Range Rsurces - Appalachia LLC* ***(G-8218)***
Lombardi Design & Mfg, Freeport *Also called Anna Young Assoc Ltd* ***(G-5388)***
Lomin Construction Company...516 759-5734
328 Glen Cove Rd Glen Head (11545) ***(G-5636)***
Lomir Inc...518 483-7697
213 W Main St Malone (12953) ***(G-8012)***
London Paris Ltd...718 564-4793
4211 13th Ave Brooklyn (11219) ***(G-2234)***
London Theater News Ltd...212 517-8608
12 E 86th St Apt 620 New York (10028) ***(G-11025)***
Long Ireland Brewing LLC...631 403-4303
723 Pulaski St Riverhead (11901) ***(G-14147)***
Long Island Advance, Patchogue *Also called Patchogue Advance Inc* ***(G-13430)***
Long Island Analytical Labs...631 472-3400
110 Colin Dr Holbrook (11741) ***(G-6458)***
Long Island Brand Bevs LLC...855 542-2832
3788 Review Ave Ste 15 Long Island City (11101) ***(G-7794)***
Long Island Business News...631 737-1700
2150 Smithtown Ave Ste 7 Ronkonkoma (11779) ***(G-14933)***
Long Island Catholic Newspaper...516 594-1212
200 W Centennial Ave # 201 Roosevelt (11575) ***(G-15007)***
Long Island Cmnty Nwsppers Inc (PA)...516 482-4490
132 E 2nd St Mineola (11501) ***(G-8522)***
Long Island Cmnty Nwsppers Inc...631 427-7000
322 Main St Huntington (11743) ***(G-6668)***
Long Island Compost Corp...516 334-6600
100 Urban Ave Westbury (11590) ***(G-17006)***
Long Island Fireproof Door, Port Washington *Also called Lif Industries Inc* ***(G-13837)***
Long Island Fireproof Door...718 767-8800
1105 Clintonville St Whitestone (11357) ***(G-17211)***
Long Island Geotech...631 473-1044
6 Berkshire Ct Port Jefferson (11777) ***(G-13776)***
Long Island Golfer Magazine, Hicksville *Also called Golfing Magazine* ***(G-6352)***
Long Island Green Guys...631 664-4306
26 Silverbrook Dr Riverhead (11901) ***(G-14148)***
Long Island Iced Tea Corp (PA)...855 542-2832
116 Charlotte Ave Ste 1 Hicksville (11801) ***(G-6365)***
Long Island Metalform Inc...631 242-9088
12 Lucon Dr Deer Park (11729) ***(G-4167)***
Long Island Pipe Supply Inc (PA)...516 222-8008
586 Commercial Ave Garden City (11530) ***(G-5515)***
Long Island Pipe Supply Inc...718 456-7877
5858 56th St Flushing (11378) ***(G-5267)***
Long Island Pipe Supply Inc...518 270-2159
60 Cohoes Ave Troy (12183) ***(G-16222)***
Long Island Pipe Supply Inc (PA)...516 222-8008
586 Commercial Ave Garden City (11530) ***(G-5516)***

ALPHABETIC

Long Island Precast Inc 631 286-0240
20 Stiriz Rd Brookhaven (11719) *(G-1508)*
Long Island Press, Farmingdale *Also called Morey Publishing (G-5060)*
Long Island Radiant Heat, Mastic Beach *Also called Vincent Genovese (G-8205)*
Long Island Spirits Inc 631 630-9322
2182 Sound Ave Calverton (11933) *(G-3292)*
Long Island Stamp & Seal Co 718 628-8550
5431 Myrtle Ave Ste 2 Ridgewood (11385) *(G-14112)*
Long Island Tool & Die Inc 631 225-0600
1445 S Strong Ave Copiague (11726) *(G-3910)*
Long Islander Newspapers LLC 631 427-7000
14 Wall St Ste A Huntington (11743) *(G-6669)*
Long Islndr Nrth/Sth Pblctns, Huntington *Also called Long Island Cmnty Nwsppers Inc (G-6668)*
Long Lumber and Supply Corp 518 439-1661
2100 New Scotland Rd Slingerlands (12159) *(G-15477)*
Long Paige, New York *Also called Jiranimo Industries Ltd (G-10737)*
Longford's Own, Port Chester *Also called Longfords Ice Cream Ltd (G-13752)*
Longfords Ice Cream Ltd 914 935-9469
151 Wilkins Ave Port Chester (10573) *(G-13752)*
Longo Cabinets, Lindenhurst *Also called Longo Commercial Cabinets Inc (G-7469)*
Longo Commercial Cabinets Inc 631 225-4290
829 N Richmond Ave Lindenhurst (11757) *(G-7469)*
Longo New York Inc 212 929-7128
444 W 17th St New York (10011) *(G-11026)*
Longstem Organizers Inc 914 777-2174
380 E Main St Jefferson Valley (10535) *(G-7057)*
Longtail Studios Inc 646 443-8146
180 Varick St Rm 820 New York (10014) *(G-11027)*
Loobrica International Corp 347 997-0296
41 Darnell Ln Staten Island (10309) *(G-15700)*
Look By M Inc 212 213-4019
838 Ave Of The Americas New York (10001) *(G-11028)*
Lookbooks Media Inc 646 737-3360
208 W 30th St Rm 802 New York (10001) *(G-11029)*
Loom Concepts LLC 212 813-9586
767 Lexington Ave Rm 405 New York (10065) *(G-11030)*
Loominus Handwoven, Woodstock *Also called Marsha Fleisher (G-17364)*
Loomstate LLC 212 219-2300
270 Bowery Fl 3 New York (10012) *(G-11031)*
Looney Tunes CD Store, West Babylon *Also called Brookvale Records Inc (G-16776)*
Looseleaf Law Publications Inc 718 359-5559
4308 162nd St Flushing (11358) *(G-5268)*
Loosesleeve Law Publications, Flushing *Also called Warodean Corporation (G-5307)*
Lopez Restorations Inc (PA) 718 383-1555
394 Mcguinness Blvd Ste 4 Brooklyn (11222) *(G-2235)*
Lopopolo Iron Works Inc 718 339-0572
2495 Mcdonald Ave Brooklyn (11223) *(G-2236)*
Loral Space & Commnctns Holdng 212 697-1105
565 5th Ave Fl 19 New York (10017) *(G-11032)*
Loral Space Communications Inc (PA) 212 697-1105
565 5th Ave New York (10017) *(G-11033)*
Loral Spacecom Corporation (HQ) 212 697-1105
565 5th Ave Fl 19 New York (10017) *(G-11034)*
Lord & Berry North America Ltd 516 745-0088
585 Stewart Ave Fl 5 Garden City (11530) *(G-5517)*
LOreal Usa Inc 212 818-1500
575 5th Ave Bsmt New York (10017) *(G-11035)*
LOreal Usa Inc 917 606-9554
435 Hudson St New York (10014) *(G-11036)*
LOreal Usa Inc 212 389-4201
575 5th Ave Fl 20 New York (10017) *(G-11037)*
LOreal Usa Inc 212 984-4704
575 5th Ave Fl 23 New York (10017) *(G-11038)*
LOreal Usa Inc 646 658-5477
575 5th Ave Fl 25 New York (10017) *(G-11039)*
LOreal USA Products Inc (HQ) 732 873-3520
575 5th Ave Bsmt New York (10017) *(G-11040)*
Lorelei Orthotics Prosthetics 212 727-2011
19 W 21st St Rm 204 New York (10010) *(G-11041)*
Loreman's, Keeseville *Also called Loremanss Embroidery Engrav (G-7139)*
Loremanss Embroidery Engrav 518 834-9205
1599 Route 9 Keeseville (12944) *(G-7139)*
Loremi Jewelry Inc 212 840-3429
17 W 45th St Ste 501 New York (10036) *(G-11042)*
Lorena Canals USA Inc 844 567-3622
104 Burnside Dr Hastings On Hudson (10706) *(G-6005)*
Lori Silverman Shoes, White Plains *Also called Lsil & Co Inc (G-17134)*
Lornamead Inc 716 874-7190
175 Cooper Ave Tonawanda (14150) *(G-16177)*
Lornamead Inc (HQ) 914 630-7733
1359 Broadway Fl 17 New York (10018) *(G-11043)*
Los Angeles Mag Holdg Co Inc (HQ) 212 456-7777
77 W 66th St New York (10023) *(G-11044)*
Los Olivos Ltd 631 773-6439
105 Bi County Blvd Farmingdale (11735) *(G-5037)*
Lost Worlds Inc 212 923-3423
920 Riverside Dr Apt 68 New York (10032) *(G-11045)*
Losurdo Creamery, Heuvelton *Also called Losurdo Foods Inc (G-6305)*
Losurdo Foods Inc 518 842-1500
78 Sam Stratton Rd Amsterdam (12010) *(G-355)*
Losurdo Foods Inc 315 344-2444
34 Union St Heuvelton (13654) *(G-6305)*
Lots O' Luv, Syosset *Also called Bektrom Foods Inc (G-15813)*
Lotta Luv Beauty LLC 646 786-2847
1359 Broadway Fl 17 New York (10018) *(G-11046)*
Lotus Apparel Designs Inc 646 236-9363
661 Oakwood Ct Westbury (11590) *(G-17007)*
Lotus Awnings Enterprises Inc 718 965-4824
157 11th St Brooklyn (11215) *(G-2237)*
Lou Sally Fashions Corp (PA) 212 354-9670
1400 Broadway Rm 601 New York (10018) *(G-11047)*
Lou Sally Fashions Corp 212 354-1283
1400 Broadway Lbby 3 New York (10018) *(G-11048)*
Loudon Ltd 631 757-4447
281 Larkfield Rd East Northport (11731) *(G-4441)*
Loughlin Manufacturing Corp 631 585-4422
1601 9th Ave Bohemia (11716) *(G-1095)*
Louis Heindl & Son Inc 585 454-5080
306 Central Ave Rochester (14605) *(G-14483)*
Louis Hornick & Co Inc 212 679-2448
117 E 38th St New York (10016) *(G-11049)*
Louis Iannettoni 315 454-3231
1841 Lemoyne Ave Syracuse (13208) *(G-15982)*
Louis Schwartz 845 356-6624
28 Lawrence St Spring Valley (10977) *(G-15593)*
Louis Tamis & Sons Inc 212 684-1760
10 E 38th St Fl 6 New York (10016) *(G-11050)*
Louis Vuitton North Amer Inc 212 644-2574
1000 3rd Ave New York (10022) *(G-11051)*
Louise Blouin Media, New York *Also called Ltb Media (usa) Inc (G-11057)*
Loungehouse LLC 646 524-2965
34 W 33rd St Fl 11 New York (10001) *(G-11052)*
Lourdes Industries Inc (PA) 631 234-6600
65 Hoffman Ave Hauppauge (11788) *(G-6121)*
Lourdes Systems Inc 631 234-7077
21 Newton Pl Hauppauge (11788) *(G-6122)*
Love & Quiches Desserts, Freeport *Also called Love & Quiches Ltd (G-5409)*
Love & Quiches Ltd 516 623-8800
178 Hanse Ave Freeport (11520) *(G-5409)*
Love Bright Jewelry Inc 516 620-2509
3446 Frederick St Oceanside (11572) *(G-13086)*
Love Unlimited NY Inc 718 359-8500
762 Summa Ave Westbury (11590) *(G-17008)*
Lovebrightjewelry.com, Oceanside *Also called Love Bright Jewelry Inc (G-13086)*
Lovee Doll & Toy Co Inc 212 242-1545
39 W 38th St Rm 4w New York (10018) *(G-11053)*
Lovejoy Chaplet Corporation 518 686-5232
12 River St Hoosick Falls (12090) *(G-6541)*
Lovely Bride LLC 212 924-2050
182 Duane St Frnt A New York (10013) *(G-11054)*
Low-Cost Mfg Co Inc 516 627-3282
318 Westbury Ave Carle Place (11514) *(G-3393)*
Lowel-Light Manufacturing Inc 718 921-0600
140 58th St Ste 8c Brooklyn (11220) *(G-2238)*
Lowville Farmers Coop Inc 315 376-6587
5500 Shady Ave Lowville (13367) *(G-7939)*
Lowville Newspaper Corporation 315 376-3525
7567 S State St Lowville (13367) *(G-7940)*
Lrc Electronics, Horseheads *Also called Belden Inc (G-6569)*
Ls Power Equity Partners LP (PA) 212 615-3456
1700 Broadway Fl 35 New York (10019) *(G-11055)*
Lsc Peripherals Incorporated 631 244-0707
415 Central Ave Ste F Bohemia (11716) *(G-1096)*
LSI Computer Systems 631 271-0400
1235 Walt Whitman Rd Melville (11747) *(G-8335)*
LSI Lightron Inc 845 562-5500
500 Hudson Valley Ave New Windsor (12553) *(G-8942)*
Lsil & Co Inc 914 761-0998
2 Greene Ln White Plains (10605) *(G-17134)*
Lt2 LLC 212 684-1510
250 Park Ave S Fl 10 New York (10003) *(G-11056)*
Ltb Media (usa) Inc 212 447-9555
88 Laight St New York (10013) *(G-11057)*
LTS (chemical) Inc 845 494-2940
37 Ramland Rd 2 Orangeburg (10962) *(G-13234)*
Lu Biscuits, White Plains *Also called Great Brands of Europe Inc (G-17114)*
Lubow Machine Corp 631 226-1700
1700 N Strongs Rd Copiague (11726) *(G-3911)*
Lucas Dental Equipment Co Inc 631 244-2807
360 Knickerbocker Ave # 4 Bohemia (11716) *(G-1097)*
Lucas Electric 516 809-8619
3524 Merrick Rd Seaford (11783) *(G-15345)*
Lucas Vineyards & Winery 607 532-4825
3862 County Road 150 Interlaken (14847) *(G-6748)*
Lucia Group Inc 631 392-4900
45 W Jefryn Blvd Ste 108 Deer Park (11729) *(G-4168)*
Lucinas Gourmet Food Inc 646 835-9784
825 E 21st St Brooklyn (11210) *(G-2239)*
Lucky Brand, New York *Also called Trebbianno LLC (G-12396)*
Lucky Brand Dungarees LLC 631 350-7358
100 Walt Whitman Rd 1090b Huntington Station (11746) *(G-6715)*

Lucky Magazine ... 212 286-6220
4 Times Sq Fl 22 New York (10036) *(G-11058)*
Lucky Peach LLC ... 212 228-0031
128 Lafayette St New York (10013) *(G-11059)*
Ludl Electronic Products Ltd ... 914 769-6111
171 Brady Ave Hawthorne (10532) *(G-6250)*
Ludlow Music Inc ... 212 594-9795
266 W 37th St Fl 17 New York (10018) *(G-11060)*
Ludwig Holdings Corp ... 845 340-9727
20 Kieffer Ln Kingston (12401) *(G-7198)*
Lufkin Industries LLC ... 585 593-7930
2475 Tarantine Blvd Wellsville (14895) *(G-16753)*
Luitpold Pharmaceuticals Inc (HQ) ... 631 924-4000
5 Ramsey Rd Shirley (11967) *(G-15423)*
Luitpold Pharmaceuticals Inc ... 631 924-4000
5 Ramsey Rd Shirley (11967) *(G-15424)*
Lukas Lighting Inc ... 800 841-4011
4020 22nd St Ste 11 Long Island City (11101) *(G-7795)*
Lukoil Americas Corporation (HQ) ... 212 421-4141
505 5th Ave Fl 9 New York (10017) *(G-11061)*
Lukoil North America LLC (HQ) ... 212 421-4141
505 5th Ave Fl 9 New York (10017) *(G-11062)*
Lulu DK LLC ... 212 223-4234
245 E 60th St Apt 1 New York (10022) *(G-11063)*
Luluvise Inc ... 914 309-7812
229 W 116th St Apt 5a New York (10026) *(G-11064)*
Lumetrics Inc ... 585 214-2455
1565 Jefferson Rd Ste 420 Rochester (14623) *(G-14484)*
Lumia Energy Solutions LLC ... 516 478-5795
48 Jericho Tpke Jericho (11753) *(G-7076)*
Luminary Publishing Inc ... 845 334-8600
314 Wall St Kingston (12401) *(G-7199)*
Luminati Aerospace LLC ... 631 574-2616
400 David Ct Calverton (11933) *(G-3293)*
Luminatta Inc ... 914 664-3600
717 S 3rd Ave Mount Vernon (10550) *(G-8702)*
Luminescent Systems Inc (HQ) ... 716 655-0800
130 Commerce Way East Aurora (14052) *(G-4373)*
Luna Luz, New York *Also called Azibi Ltd (G-9286)*
Luria Communications Inc ... 631 329-4922
31 Shorewood Dr Fl 1 East Hampton (11937) *(G-4413)*
Luthier Musical Corp ... 212 397-6038
49 W 24th St Fl 4 New York (10010) *(G-11065)*
Luvata Heat Transfer Solutions ... 716 879-6700
70 Sayre St Buffalo (14207) *(G-3051)*
Lux Accessories, New York *Also called International Inspirations Ltd (G-10635)*
Lux Mundi Corp ... 631 244-4596
10 Colt Ct Ronkonkoma (11779) *(G-14934)*
Luxe Imagine Consulting LLC ... 212 273-9770
261 W 35th St Ste 404 New York (10001) *(G-11066)*
Luxerdame Co Inc ... 718 752-9800
4315 Queens St Ste A Long Island City (11101) *(G-7796)*
Luxfer Magtech Inc ... 631 727-8600
680 Elton St Riverhead (11901) *(G-14149)*
Luxo Corporation ... 914 345-0067
5 Westchester Plz Ste 110 Elmsford (10523) *(G-4761)*
Lwa Works Inc ... 518 271-8360
2622 7th Ave Ste 50s Watervliet (12189) *(G-16687)*
Lws Precision Deburring Inc ... 631 580-0472
125 Gary Way Ste 1 Ronkonkoma (11779) *(G-14935)*
Lycian Stage Lighting, Chester *Also called Ric-Lo Productions Ltd (G-3613)*
Lydall Performance Mtl Inc ... 518 273-6320
68 George St Green Island (12183) *(G-5859)*
Lydall Performance Mtls Inc ... 518 273-6320
68 George St Green Island (12183) *(G-5860)*
Lydia H Soifer & Assoc Inc ... 914 683-5401
1025 Westchester Ave White Plains (10604) *(G-17135)*
Lyn Jo Enterprises Ltd ... 716 753-2776
Rr 394 Box 147 Mayville (14757) *(G-8217)*
Lyn Jo Kitchens Inc ... 718 336-6060
1679 Mcdonald Ave Brooklyn (11230) *(G-2240)*
Lynch Knitting Mills Inc ... 718 821-3436
538 Johnson Ave Brooklyn (11237) *(G-2241)*
Lyndaker Timber Harvesting LLC ... 315 346-1328
10204 State Route 812 Castorland (13620) *(G-3424)*
Lynmar Printing Corp ... 631 957-8500
8600 New Horizons Blvd Amityville (11701) *(G-306)*
Lyntronics Inc ... 631 205-1061
7 Old Dock Rd Unit 1 Yaphank (11980) *(G-17397)*
Lynx Product Group LLC ... 716 751-3100
650 Lake St Wilson (14172) *(G-17268)*
Lyons & Sullivan Inc ... 518 584-1523
376 Caroline St Saratoga Springs (12866) *(G-15162)*
Lyons Press, New York *Also called Morris Communications Co LLC (G-11307)*
Lyophilization Systems Inc ... 845 338-0456
14 Hickory Hill Rd New Paltz (12561) *(G-8876)*
Lyric Lighting Ltd Inc ... 718 497-0109
4825 Metro Ave Ste 3 Ridgewood (11385) *(G-14113)*
M & C Furniture ... 718 422-2136
375 Park Ave Brooklyn (11205) *(G-2242)*
M & Co Ltd ... 212 414-6400
76 9th Ave Fl 11 New York (10011) *(G-11067)*
M & D Fire Door, Brooklyn *Also called M & D Installers Inc (G-2243)*
M & D Installers Inc (PA) ... 718 782-6978
70 Flushing Ave Brooklyn (11205) *(G-2243)*
M & D Millwork LLC ... 631 789-1439
178 New Hwy Amityville (11701) *(G-307)*
M & E Mfg Co Inc ... 845 331-7890
19 Progress St Kingston (12401) *(G-7200)*
M & H Research and Dev Corp ... 607 734-2346
471 Post Creek Rd Beaver Dams (14812) *(G-793)*
M & J Custom Lampshade Company, Brooklyn *Also called Mjk Enterprises LLC (G-2324)*
M & L Steel & Ornamental Iron ... 718 816-8660
27 Housman Ave Staten Island (10303) *(G-15701)*
M & M Bagel Corp ... 516 295-1222
507 Central Ave Cedarhurst (11516) *(G-3459)*
M & M Canvas & Awnings Inc ... 631 424-5370
180 Oval Dr Islandia (11749) *(G-6800)*
M & M Food Products Inc ... 718 821-1970
286 Scholes St Brooklyn (11206) *(G-2244)*
M & M Molding Corp ... 631 582-1900
250 Creative Dr Central Islip (11722) *(G-3503)*
M & M Signs & Awnings, Islandia *Also called M & M Canvas & Awnings Inc (G-6800)*
M & R Design, New York *Also called Mrinalini Inc (G-11316)*
M & R Woodworking & Finishing ... 718 486-5480
49 Withers St Brooklyn (11211) *(G-2245)*
M & S Precision Machine Co LLC ... 518 747-1193
27 Casey Rd Queensbury (12804) *(G-14004)*
M & S Quality Co Ltd ... 212 302-8757
26 W 47th St Ste 502 New York (10036) *(G-11068)*
M & S Schmalberg Inc ... 212 244-2090
242 W 36th St Rm 700 New York (10018) *(G-11069)*
M & W Aluminum Products Inc ... 315 414-0005
321 Wavel St Syracuse (13206) *(G-15983)*
M &L Industry of NY Inc ... 845 827-6255
583 State Route 32 Ste 1u Highland Mills (10930) *(G-6413)*
M A C, Elmsford *Also called Magnetic Analysis Corporation (G-4762)*
M A M Knitting Mills Corp ... 800 570-0093
43 Hall St Brooklyn (11205) *(G-2246)*
M A Moslow & Bros Inc ... 716 896-2950
375 Norfolk Ave Buffalo (14215) *(G-3052)*
M A R A Metals Ltd ... 718 786-7868
2520 40th Ave Long Island City (11101) *(G-7797)*
M and J Hair Center Inc ... 516 872-1010
1103 Stewart Ave Ste 100 Garden City (11530) *(G-5518)*
M and M Industrial Welding ... 631 451-6044
2890 Route 112 Medford (11763) *(G-8254)*
M B C Metal Inc ... 718 384-6713
68 Lombardy St Brooklyn (11222) *(G-2247)*
M B M Manufacturing Inc ... 718 769-4148
331 Rutledge St Ste 203 Brooklyn (11211) *(G-2248)*
M C Kitchen & Bath, Brooklyn *Also called M & C Furniture (G-2242)*
M C Packaging Corp Plant, Babylon *Also called M C Packaging Corporation (G-550)*
M C Packaging Corporation (PA) ... 631 414-7840
200 Adams Blvd Farmingdale (11735) *(G-5038)*
M C Packaging Corporation ... 631 643-3763
300 Governor Ave Babylon (11704) *(G-550)*
M C Products ... 631 471-4070
1330 Lincoln Ave Ste 2 Holbrook (11741) *(G-6459)*
M D I, Shirley *Also called Modular Devices Inc (G-15426)*
M D I Industries, Deer Park *Also called MD International Industries (G-4173)*
M D L, New York *Also called Meryl Diamond Ltd (G-11236)*
M F L B Inc ... 631 254-8300
7 Grant Ave Bay Shore (11706) *(G-714)*
M F Manufacturing Enterprises ... 516 822-5135
2 Ballad Ln Hicksville (11801) *(G-6366)*
M G New York Inc ... 212 371-5566
14 E 60th St Ste 400 New York (10022) *(G-11070)*
M H Mandelbaum Orthotic ... 631 473-8668
116 Oakland Ave Port Jefferson (11777) *(G-13777)*
M H Manufacturing Incorporated ... 212 461-6900
50 W 47th St New York (10036) *(G-11071)*
M H Stryke Co Inc ... 631 242-2660
181 E Industry Ct Ste A Deer Park (11729) *(G-4169)*
M Heskia Company Inc ... 212 768-1845
98 Cutter Rd Ste 125 New York (10036) *(G-11072)*
M Hidary & Co Inc ... 212 736-6540
10 W 33rd St Rm 900 New York (10001) *(G-11073)*
M I, Hauppauge *Also called Mason Industries Inc (G-6126)*
M I I, Mamaroneck *Also called Marval Industries Inc (G-8038)*
M I T Poly-Cart Corp ... 212 724-7290
211 Central Park W New York (10024) *(G-11074)*
M J K, Brooklyn *Also called Mjk Cutting Inc (G-2323)*
M J M Tooling Corp ... 718 292-3590
1059 Washington Ave Bronx (10456) *(G-1384)*
M K S, Rochester *Also called Mks Medical Electronics (G-14518)*
M K Ulrich Construction Inc ... 716 893-5777
1601 Harlem Rd Buffalo (14206) *(G-3053)*
M L A, New York *Also called Modern Language Assn Amer Inc (G-11288)*
M L Design Inc (PA) ... 212 233-0213
77 Ludlow St Frnt 1 New York (10002) *(G-11075)*
M M Tool and Manufacturing ... 845 691-4140
175 Chapel Hill Rd Highland (12528) *(G-6405)*

ALPHABETIC

M M Welding ALPHABETIC SECTION

M M Welding...315 363-3980
558 Lenox Ave Oneida (13421) *(G-13158)*
M Manastrip-M Corporation...518 664-2089
821 Main St Clifton Park (12065) *(G-3699)*
M O S S Communications, Franklin Square *Also called Movin On Sounds and SEC Inc (G-5365)*
M P I, Tarrytown *Also called Micro Powders Inc (G-16097)*
M R C Industries Inc...516 328-6900
99 Seaview Blvd Ste 210 Port Washington (11050) *(G-13839)*
M S B International Ltd (PA)...212 302-5551
1412 Broadway Rm 1210 New York (10018) *(G-11076)*
M Santoliquido Corp...914 375-6674
925 Saw Mill River Rd Yonkers (10710) *(G-17463)*
M Shanken Communications Inc (PA)...212 684-4224
825 8th Ave Fl 33 New York (10019) *(G-11077)*
M Squared Graphics, Oyster Bay *Also called Miroddi Imaging Inc (G-13372)*
M T D Corporation...631 491-3905
41 Otis St West Babylon (11704) *(G-16808)*
M T M Printing Co Inc...718 353-3297
2321 College Point Blvd College Point (11356) *(G-3796)*
M V Sport, Bay Shore *Also called Mv Corp Inc (G-720)*
M W Microwave Corp...516 295-1814
45 Auerbach Ln Lawrence (11559) *(G-7394)*
M&A Metals, Brooklyn *Also called Interior Metals (G-2110)*
M&C Associates LLC...631 467-8760
3920 Vtrans Mem Hwy Ste 7 Bohemia (11716) *(G-1098)*
M&F Stringing LLC...914 664-1600
2 Cortlandt St Mount Vernon (10550) *(G-8703)*
M&G Duravent Inc...518 463-7284
10 Jupiter Ln Albany (12205) *(G-98)*
M&H Soaring, Beaver Dams *Also called M & H Research and Dev Corp (G-793)*
M&M Printing Inc...516 796-3020
245 Westbury Ave Carle Place (11514) *(G-3394)*
M&S Accessory Network Corp...347 492-7790
10 W 33rd St Rm 718 New York (10001) *(G-11078)*
M. C. Container, Brooklyn *Also called Base Container Inc (G-1669)*
M/B Midtown LLC...212 477-2495
141 5th Ave Fl 2 New York (10010) *(G-11079)*
M/Wbe, Brooklyn *Also called Active World Solutions Inc (G-1559)*
M2 Apparel, New York *Also called M2 Fashion Group Holdings Inc (G-11080)*
M2 Fashion Group Holdings Inc...917 208-2948
153 E 87th St Apt 10d New York (10128) *(G-11080)*
Mac Artspray Finishing Corp...718 649-3800
799 Sheffield Ave Brooklyn (11207) *(G-2249)*
Mac Crete Corporation...718 932-1803
3412 10th St Long Island City (11106) *(G-7798)*
Mac Donuts of New York, Long Island City *Also called Mac Crete Corporation (G-7798)*
Mac Fadden Holdings Inc (PA)...212 614-3980
333 7th Ave Fl 11 New York (10001) *(G-11081)*
Mac Swed Inc (PA)...917 617-3885
20 W 36th St Rm 5r New York (10018) *(G-11082)*
Mac-Artspray Finshg, Brooklyn *Also called Mac Artspray Finishing Corp (G-2249)*
Macadoodles...607 652-9019
26 River St Stamford (12167) *(G-15625)*
Macaran Printed Products, Cohoes *Also called W N Vanalstine & Sons Inc (G-3761)*
Macauto Usa Inc...585 342-2060
80 Excel Dr Rochester (14621) *(G-14485)*
Macedonia Ltd...718 462-3596
34 E 29th St Brooklyn (11226) *(G-2250)*
Macfadden Cmmnctions Group LLC...212 979-4800
333 7th Ave Fl 11 New York (10001) *(G-11083)*
Macgregor Golf North Amer Inc (PA)...646 840-5200
110 W 57th St Fl 4 New York (10019) *(G-11084)*
Machias Furniture Factory Inc (PA)...716 353-8687
3638 Route 242 Machias (14101) *(G-7993)*
Machida Incorporated...845 365-0600
40 Ramland Rd S Ste 1 Orangeburg (10962) *(G-13235)*
Machina Deus Lex Inc...917 577-0972
15921 Grand Central Pkwy Jamaica (11432) *(G-6926)*
Machine Clothing Company, New York *Also called Billion Tower Intl LLC (G-9397)*
Machine Components Corp...516 694-7222
70 Newtown Rd Plainview (11803) *(G-13617)*
Machine Technology Inc...845 454-4030
104 Bushwick Rd Poughkeepsie (12603) *(G-13913)*
Machine Tool Repair & Sales...631 580-2550
1537 Lincoln Ave Holbrook (11741) *(G-6460)*
Machine Tool Specialty...315 699-5287
8125 Thompson Rd Cicero (13039) *(G-3648)*
Machinecraft Inc...585 436-1070
1645 Lyell Ave Ste 125 Rochester (14606) *(G-14486)*
Machinery Mountings Inc...631 851-0480
41 Sarah Dr Hauppauge (11788) *(G-6123)*
Machinit Inc...631 454-9297
400 Smith St Farmingdale (11735) *(G-5039)*
Macinnes Tool Corporation...585 467-1920
1700 Hudson Ave Ste 3 Rochester (14617) *(G-14487)*
Mack Studios Displays Inc...315 252-7542
5500 Technology Park Blvd Auburn (13021) *(G-507)*
Mack Wood Working...845 657-6625
2792 State Route 28 Shokan (12481) *(G-15432)*
Mackenzie-Childs LLC (PA)...315 364-7567
3260 State Route 90 Aurora (13026) *(G-530)*
Maclean Curtis, Buffalo *Also called Curtis L Maclean L C (G-2895)*
Macmillan Academic Pubg Inc (HQ)...212 226-1476
75 Varick St Fl 9 New York (10013) *(G-11085)*
Macmillan College Pubg Co Inc...212 702-2000
866 3rd Ave Frnt 2 New York (10022) *(G-11086)*
Macmillan Holdings LLC...212 576-9428
1 New York Plz Ste 4500 New York (10004) *(G-11087)*
Macmillan Publishers Inc...646 307-5151
175 5th Ave Ste 400 New York (10010) *(G-11088)*
Macmillan Publishing Group LLC (HQ)...212 674-5151
175 5th Ave New York (10010) *(G-11089)*
Macneil Polymers Inc (PA)...716 681-7755
3155 Broadway St Buffalo (14227) *(G-3054)*
Maco Bag Corporation...315 226-1000
412 Van Buren St Newark (14513) *(G-12735)*
Macro Tool & Machine Company...845 223-3824
1397 Route 55 Lagrangeville (12540) *(G-7255)*
Macrochem Corporation (HQ)...212 514-8094
80 Broad St Ste 2210 New York (10004) *(G-11090)*
Macrodyne Inc...518 383-3800
1 Fairchild Sq Ste 5 Clifton Park (12065) *(G-3700)*
Macrolink Inc...631 924-8265
25 Scouting Blvd Ste 1 Medford (11763) *(G-8255)*
Mad Scntsts Brwing Prtners LLC...347 766-2739
40 Van Dyke St Brooklyn (11231) *(G-2251)*
Madame Alexander Doll Co LLC...212 244-4500
112 W 34th St Ste 1207 New York (10120) *(G-11091)*
Madden Zone, New York *Also called Steven Madden Ltd (G-12201)*
Made Close LLC...917 837-1357
141 Meserole Ave Brooklyn (11222) *(G-2252)*
Made Fresh Daily...212 285-2253
226 Front St New York (10038) *(G-11092)*
Madelaine Chocolate Company, Rockaway Beach *Also called Madelaine Chocolate Novlt Inc (G-14782)*
Madelaine Chocolate Novlt Inc (PA)...718 945-1500
9603 Beach Channel Dr Rockaway Beach (11693) *(G-14782)*
Madhat Inc...518 947-0732
108 Charles St Apt 1c New York (10014) *(G-11093)*
Madison & Dunn...585 563-7760
850 Saint Paul St Ste 29 Rochester (14605) *(G-14488)*
Madison County Distillery LLC...315 391-6070
2420 Rte 20 Cazenovia (13035) *(G-3448)*
Madison Electric...718 358-4121
21916 Linden Blvd Cambria Heights (11411) *(G-3303)*
Madison Industries Inc (PA)...212 679-5110
295 5th Ave Ste 512 New York (10016) *(G-11094)*
Madison Manufacturing, Hamilton *Also called James Morris (G-5948)*
Madison Printing Corp...607 273-3535
704 W Buffalo St Ithaca (14850) *(G-6857)*
Madison Square Press, New York *Also called Annuals Publishing Co Inc (G-9165)*
Madisons Delight LLC...718 720-8900
711 Forest Ave Staten Island (10310) *(G-15702)*
Madjek Inc...631 842-4475
185 Dixon Ave Amityville (11701) *(G-308)*
Madoff Energy III LLC...212 744-1918
319 Lafayette St New York (10012) *(G-11095)*
Madonna, New York *Also called Haddad Bros Inc (G-10393)*
Madrid Fire District...315 322-4346
26 10 Church St Madrid (13660) *(G-7995)*
Maehr Industries Inc...631 924-1661
14 Sawgrass Dr Bellport (11713) *(G-833)*
Mafco Consolidated Group Inc (HQ)...212 572-8600
35 E 62nd St New York (10065) *(G-11096)*
Mag Brands LLC...212 629-9600
463 7th Ave Fl 4 New York (10018) *(G-11097)*
Mag Inc...607 257-6970
20 Eastlake Rd Ithaca (14850) *(G-6858)*
Magazine Antiques, The, New York *Also called Brant Publications Inc (G-9455)*
Magazine Group, New York *Also called Thomas Publishing Company LLC (G-12323)*
Magazine I Spectrum E...212 419-7555
3 Park Ave Fl 17 New York (10016) *(G-11098)*
Magazines & Brochures Inc...716 875-9699
245 Cooper Ave Ste 108 Tonawanda (14150) *(G-16178)*
Magcrest Packaging Inc...845 425-0451
5 Highview Rd Monsey (10952) *(G-8574)*
Mageba USA LLC...212 317-1991
575 Lexington Ave Fl 4 New York (10022) *(G-11099)*
Magee Canvas & Trailer Sales, Brewerton *Also called Geordie Magee Uphl & Canvas (G-1203)*
Magellan Aerospace NY Inc (HQ)...718 699-4000
9711 50th Ave Corona (11368) *(G-4001)*
Magellan Aerospace NY Inc...631 589-2440
25 Aero Rd Bohemia (11716) *(G-1099)*
Mager & Gougelman Inc (PA)...212 661-3939
345 E 37th St Rm 316 New York (10016) *(G-11100)*
Mager & Gougelman Inc...212 661-3939
230 Hilton Ave Ste 112 Hempstead (11550) *(G-6278)*
Mager & Gougelman Inc...516 489-0202
230 Hilton Ave Ste 112 Hempstead (11550) *(G-6279)*

Maggio Data Forms Printing Ltd 631 348-0343
1735 Express Dr N Hauppauge (11788) ***(G-6124)***
Maggy Boutique Ltd 212 997-5222
530 Fashion Ave Fl 6 New York (10018) ***(G-11101)***
Maggy London, New York *Also called Maggy Boutique Ltd* ***(G-11101)***
Maggy London Blouse Div, New York *Also called Maggy London International Ltd* ***(G-11102)***
Maggy London International Ltd (PA) 212 944-7199
530 Fashion Ave Fl 16 New York (10018) ***(G-11102)***
Magic Brands International LLC 212 563-4999
31 W 34th St Rm 401 New York (10001) ***(G-11103)***
Magic Maestro Music, New York *Also called Simon & Simon LLC* ***(G-12080)***
Magic Novelty Co Inc (PA) 212 304-2777
308 Dyckman St New York (10034) ***(G-11104)***
Magic Numbers Inc 646 839-8578
29 Little West 12th St New York (10014) ***(G-11105)***
Magic Tank LLC 877 646-2442
80 Maiden Ln Rm 2204 New York (10038) ***(G-11106)***
Magic Tech Co Ltd 516 539-7944
401 Hempstead Tpke West Hempstead (11552) ***(G-16859)***
Magic Touch Icewares Intl 212 794-2852
220 E 72nd St Apt 11g New York (10021) ***(G-11107)***
Magjak Graphic Communications, Port Chester *Also called Magjak Printing Corporation* ***(G-13753)***
Magjak Printing Corporation 914 939-8800
114 Pearl St Port Chester (10573) ***(G-13753)***
Magna Products Corp 585 647-2280
777 Mount Read Blvd Rochester (14606) ***(G-14489)***
Magnaworks Technology Inc 631 218-3431
36 Carlough Rd Unit H Bohemia (11716) ***(G-1100)***
Magnet Wire Division, Edgewood *Also called Weico Wire & Cable Inc* ***(G-4621)***
Magnet-Ndctive Systems Ltd USA 585 924-4000
7625 Omnitech Pl Victor (14564) ***(G-16490)***
Magnetic Aids Inc 845 863-1400
201 Ann St Newburgh (12550) ***(G-12766)***
Magnetic Analysis Corporation (PA) 914 530-2000
103 Fairview Pk Dr Ste 2 Elmsford (10523) ***(G-4762)***
Magnetic Technologies Corp (HQ) 585 385-9010
770 Linden Ave Rochester (14625) ***(G-14490)***
Magnetic Technology, Rochester *Also called Arnold Magnetic Tech Corp* ***(G-14211)***
Magnificat Inc 914 502-1820
86 Main St Ste 303 Yonkers (10701) ***(G-17464)***
Magniflood Inc 631 226-1000
7200 New Horizons Blvd Amityville (11701) ***(G-309)***
Magnolia Bakery, New York *Also called Magnolia Operating LLC* ***(G-11108)***
Magnolia Operating LLC (PA) 212 265-2777
1841 Broadway New York (10023) ***(G-11108)***
Magnum Creation Inc 212 642-0993
23 W 47th St Fl 5 New York (10036) ***(G-11109)***
Magnum Energy Partners, Brooklyn *Also called Mep Alaska LLC* ***(G-2297)***
Magnum Shielding Corporation 585 381-9957
3800 Monroe Ave Ste 14f Pittsford (14534) ***(G-13568)***
Magnus Precision Mfg Inc 315 548-8032
1912 State Route 96 Phelps (14532) ***(G-13534)***
Magnus Sands Point Shop, Port Washington *Also called Robert Bartholomew Ltd* ***(G-13859)***
Magsoft Corporation 518 877-8390
1 Fairchild Sq Ste 108 Clifton Park (12065) ***(G-3701)***
Magtrol Inc 716 668-5555
70 Gardenville Pkwy W Buffalo (14224) ***(G-3055)***
Maharlika Holdings LLC 631 319-6203
111 Trade Zone Ct Unit A Ronkonkoma (11779) ***(G-14936)***
Mahle Behr USA Inc 716 439-2011
350 Upper Mountain Rd Lockport (14094) ***(G-7598)***
Mahle Indstrbeteiligungen GMBH 716 319-6700
4236 Ridge Lea Rd Amherst (14226) ***(G-250)***
Mahle Industries Incorporated 248 735-3623
4236 Ridge Lea Rd Amherst (14226) ***(G-251)***
Maia Systems LLC 718 206-0100
8344 Parsons Blvd Ste 101 Jamaica (11432) ***(G-6927)***
Maidenform LLC 718 494-0268
2655 Richmond Ave Staten Island (10314) ***(G-15703)***
Maidenform LLC 201 436-9200
260 Madison Ave Fl 6 New York (10016) ***(G-11110)***
Maidstone Coffee Co 585 272-1040
60 Mushroom Blvd Rochester (14623) ***(G-14491)***
Mailers-Pblsher Wlfare Tr Fund 212 869-5986
1501 Broadway New York (10036) ***(G-11111)***
Main Street Connect LLC 203 803-4110
200 Business Park Dr # 209 Armonk (10504) ***(G-417)***
Main Street Fashions Inc (PA) 212 764-2613
512 Fashion Ave Rm 3700 New York (10018) ***(G-11112)***
Main Street Sweets 914 332-5757
35 Main St Tarrytown (10591) ***(G-16094)***
Maine Coil & Transformer Co, Johnson City *Also called Donald R Husband Inc* ***(G-7091)***
Maine Power Express LLC 518 465-0710
600 Broadway Fl 3 Albany (12207) ***(G-99)***
Mainly Monograms Inc 845 624-4923
260 W Nyack Rd Ste 1 West Nyack (10994) ***(G-16921)***
Maiyet Inc 646 602-0000
676 Broadway Fl 4 New York (10012) ***(G-11113)***
Maizteca Foods Inc 718 641-3933
13005 Liberty Ave South Richmond Hill (11419) ***(G-15534)***
Majani Tea Company 817 896-5720
1745 Brdwy Fl 17 New York (10019) ***(G-11114)***
Majani Teas, New York *Also called Majani Tea Company* ***(G-11114)***
Majestic Curtains LLC 718 898-0774
4410 Ketcham St Apt 2g Elmhurst (11373) ***(G-4664)***
Majestic Home Imprvs Distr 718 853-5079
5902 Fort Hamilton Pkwy Brooklyn (11219) ***(G-2253)***
Majestic Mold & Tool Inc 315 695-2079
177 Volney St Phoenix (13135) ***(G-13542)***
Majestic Rayon Corporation 212 929-6443
116 W 23rd St Fl 4 New York (10011) ***(G-11115)***
Majic Corrugated Inc, Batavia *Also called Georgia-Pacific Corrugared LLC* ***(G-635)***
Major-IPC Inc 845 292-2200
53 Webster Ave Liberty (12754) ***(G-7438)***
Makarenko Studios Inc 914 968-7673
2984 Saddle Ridge Dr Yorktown Heights (10598) ***(G-17512)***
Makari, New York *Also called Victoria Albi Intl Inc* ***(G-12539)***
Make Holding LLC 646 313-1957
850 3rd Ave New York (10022) ***(G-11116)***
Make My Cake II Inc 212 234-2344
2380 Adam Clytn Powll Jr New York (10030) ***(G-11117)***
Make-Waves Instrument Corp (PA) 716 681-7524
4444 Broadway Depew (14043) ***(G-4264)***
Makerbot Industries LLC (HQ) 347 334-6800
1 Metrotech Ctr Fl 21 Brooklyn (11201) ***(G-2254)***
Makerbot Industries LLC 347 457-5758
298 Mulberry St New York (10012) ***(G-11118)***
Makers Nutrition LLC (PA) 631 456-5397
315 Oser Ave Hauppauge (11788) ***(G-6125)***
Makins Hats Ltd 212 594-6666
212 W 35th St Fl 12 New York (10001) ***(G-11119)***
Makiplastic 716 772-2222
4904 Gasport Rd Gasport (14067) ***(G-5558)***
Makkos of Brooklyn Ltd 718 366-9800
200 Moore St Brooklyn (11206) ***(G-2255)***
Malcon Inc 914 666-7146
405 Adams St Bedford Hills (10507) ***(G-804)***
Male Power Apparel, Hauppauge *Also called Comme-Ci Comme-CA AP Group* ***(G-6050)***
Maler Technologies Inc 212 391-2070
337 E 81st St Bsmt New York (10028) ***(G-11120)***
Malhame Publs & Importers Inc 631 694-8600
180 Orville Dr Unit A Bohemia (11716) ***(G-1101)***
Malia Mills Inc 212 354-4200
32 33rd St Unit 13 Brooklyn (11232) ***(G-2256)***
Malia Mills Studio, Brooklyn *Also called IaM Maliamills LLC* ***(G-2093)***
Malibu Cabinets, Suffern *Also called American Best Cabinets Inc* ***(G-15785)***
Malin + Goetz Inc (PA) 212 244-7771
210 W 29th St Fl 3 New York (10001) ***(G-11121)***
Malina Management Company Inc 607 535-9614
3620 County Road 16 Montour Falls (14865) ***(G-8610)***
Malisa Branko Inc 631 225-9741
95 Garfield Ave Copiague (11726) ***(G-3912)***
Mallery Lumber LLC 607 637-2236
158 Labarre St Hancock (13783) ***(G-5965)***
Mallinckrodt LLC 607 538-9124
172 Railroad Ave Hobart (13788) ***(G-6426)***
Malone Concrete Products Div, Malone *Also called Graymont Materials (ny) Inc* ***(G-8010)***
Malone Industrial Press Inc 518 483-5880
10 Stevens St Malone (12953) ***(G-8013)***
Malone News, Malone *Also called Johnson Newspaper Corporation* ***(G-8011)***
Malone Newspapers Corp 518 483-2000
469 E Main St Ste 2 Malone (12953) ***(G-8014)***
Malone Telegram, Malone *Also called Malone Newspapers Corp* ***(G-8014)***
Malone Welding, Montour Falls *Also called Robert M Brown* ***(G-8611)***
Malouf Colette Inc 212 941-9588
594 Broadway Rm 1216 New York (10012) ***(G-11122)***
Maloya Laser Inc 631 543-2327
65a Mall Dr Ste 1 Commack (11725) ***(G-3837)***
Malyn Industrial Ceramics Inc 716 741-1510
8640 Roll Rd Clarence Center (14032) ***(G-3679)***
Mam Knitg, Brooklyn *Also called M A M Knitting Mills Corp* ***(G-2246)***
Mam USA Corporation 914 269-2500
2700 Westchester Ave # 315 Purchase (10577) ***(G-13961)***
Mama Luca Production Inc 212 582-9700
156 W 56th St Ste 1803 New York (10019) ***(G-11123)***
Mamas 518 399-2828
119 Lake Hill Rd Burnt Hills (12027) ***(G-3267)***
Mamco, Oneonta *Also called Mold-A-Matic Corporation* ***(G-13189)***
Mamitas Ices Ltd 718 738-3238
10411 100th St Ozone Park (11417) ***(G-13383)***
Mamma Says, Ferndale *Also called Chipita America Inc* ***(G-5168)***
Man of World 212 915-0017
25 W 39th St Fl 5 New York (10018) ***(G-11124)***
Man Products Inc 631 789-6500
99 Milbar Blvd Unit 1 Farmingdale (11735) ***(G-5040)***
Mana Products Inc (PA) 718 361-2550
3202 Queens Blvd Fl 6 Long Island City (11101) ***(G-7799)***
Mana Products Inc 718 361-5204
3202 Queens Blvd Fl 6 Long Island City (11101) ***(G-7800)***
Manacraft Precision Inc 914 654-0967
945 Spring Rd Pelham (10803) ***(G-13493)***

ALPHABETIC

Manchester Newspaper Inc (PA).....518 642-1234
14 E Main St Granville (12832) ***(G-5775)***
Manchester Wood Inc.....518 642-9518
1159 County Route 24 Granville (12832) ***(G-5776)***
Manchu New York Inc.....212 921-5050
530 Fashion Ave Rm 1906 New York (10018) ***(G-11125)***
Manchu Times Fashion Inc.....212 921-5050
530 Sventh Ave Ste 1906 New York (10018) ***(G-11126)***
Mancum Graphics, New York *Also called Mc Squared Nyc Inc* ***(G-11193)***
Mandalay Food Products Inc.....718 230-3370
640 Dean St Brooklyn (11238) ***(G-2257)***
Mandarin Soy Sauce Inc.....845 343-1505
4 Sands Station Rd Middletown (10940) ***(G-8449)***
MANE Enterprises Inc.....718 472-4955
3100 47th Ave Unit 5e Long Island City (11101) ***(G-7801)***
Mango Usa Inc.....718 998-6050
5620 1st Ave Ste 1 Brooklyn (11220) ***(G-2258)***
Manhasset Tool & Die Co Inc.....716 684-6066
4270 Walden Ave Lancaster (14086) ***(G-7325)***
Manhattan Cabinets, Island Park *Also called A-1 Manhattan Custom Furn Inc* ***(G-6777)***
Manhattan Cabinets Inc.....212 548-2436
1349 2nd Ave New York (10021) ***(G-11127)***
Manhattan Comfort Inc.....888 230-2225
1784 Atlantic Ave Brooklyn (11213) ***(G-2259)***
Manhattan Cooling Towers Inc.....212 279-1045
540 W 35th St New York (10001) ***(G-11128)***
Manhattan Display Inc.....718 392-1365
1215 Jackson Ave Ste B Long Island City (11101) ***(G-7802)***
Manhattan Eastside Dev Corp.....212 305-3275
622 W 168th St Ste Vc333 New York (10032) ***(G-11129)***
Manhattan Map Co, New York *Also called Yale Robbins Inc* ***(G-12687)***
Manhattan Media LLC (PA).....212 268-8600
72 Madison Ave Fl 11 New York (10016) ***(G-11130)***
Manhattan Milling & Drying Co.....516 496-1041
78 Pond Rd Woodbury (11797) ***(G-17294)***
Manhattan Neon Sign Corp.....212 714-0430
640 W 28th St Fl 2 New York (10001) ***(G-11131)***
Manhattan Poly Bag Corporation.....917 689-7549
1228 47th St Brooklyn (11219) ***(G-2260)***
Manhattan Scientifics Inc (PA).....212 541-2405
405 Lexington Ave Fl 26 New York (10174) ***(G-11132)***
Manhattan Shade & Glass Co Inc (PA).....212 288-5616
1299 3rd Ave Frnt New York (10021) ***(G-11133)***
Manhattan Signs, Floral Park *Also called Decree Signs & Graphics Inc* ***(G-5202)***
Manhattan Special Bottling.....718 388-4144
342 Manhattan Ave Brooklyn (11211) ***(G-2261)***
Manhattan Times Inc.....212 569-5800
5030 Broadway Ste 801 New York (10034) ***(G-11134)***
Manhole Brrier SEC Systems Inc.....516 741-1032
8002 Kew Gardens Rd # 901 Kew Gardens (11415) ***(G-7165)***
Manic Panic, Long Island City *Also called Tish & Snookys NYC Inc* ***(G-7902)***
Manifestation-Glow Press Inc.....718 380-5259
7740 164th St Fresh Meadows (11366) ***(G-5444)***
Manifold Center, The, Medford *Also called B & R Industries Inc* ***(G-8235)***
Manitou Concrete.....585 424-6040
1260 Jefferson Rd Rochester (14623) ***(G-14492)***
Mann Consultants LLC.....914 763-0512
67 Chapel Rd Waccabuc (10597) ***(G-16520)***
Mann Publications Inc.....212 840-6266
450 Fashion Ave Ste 2306 New York (10123) ***(G-11135)***
Mannesmann Corporation.....212 258-4000
601 Lexington Ave Fl 56 New York (10022) ***(G-11136)***
Manning Lewis Div Rubicon Inds.....908 687-2400
848 E 43rd St Brooklyn (11210) ***(G-2262)***
Mannington Mills Inc.....212 251-0290
200 Lexington Ave Rm 430 New York (10016) ***(G-11137)***
Mannix, Brentwood *Also called Interstate Window Corporation* ***(G-1186)***
Manny Grunberg Inc.....212 302-6173
62 W 47th St Ste 703 New York (10036) ***(G-11138)***
Manor Electric Supply Corp.....347 312-2521
2737 Ocean Ave Brooklyn (11229) ***(G-2263)***
Manrico Cashmere, New York *Also called Manrico Usa Inc* ***(G-11139)***
Manrico Usa Inc.....212 794-4200
922 Madison Ave New York (10021) ***(G-11139)***
Manrico Usa Inc (PA).....212 794-4200
922 Madison Ave New York (10021) ***(G-11140)***
Mansfield Press Inc.....212 265-5411
599 11th Ave Fl 3 New York (10036) ***(G-11141)***
Mansueto Ventures LLC.....212 389-5300
7 World Trade Ctr Fl 29 New York (10007) ***(G-11142)***
Mantel & Mantel Stamping Corp.....631 467-1916
802 S 4th St Ronkonkoma (11779) ***(G-14937)***
Manth Mfg Inc.....716 693-6525
131 Fillmore Ave Tonawanda (14150) ***(G-16179)***
Manth-Brownell Inc.....315 687-7263
1120 Fyler Rd Kirkville (13082) ***(G-7227)***
Manuf Appld Renova Sys.....518 654-9084
105 Mill St Corinth (12822) ***(G-3959)***
Manufacturers Indexing Pdts.....631 271-0956
53 Gristmill Ln Halesite (11743) ***(G-5905)***
Manufacturers Tool & Die Co.....585 352-1080
3 Turner Dr Spencerport (14559) ***(G-15572)***
Manufacturing Engineering Svcs, Dobbs Ferry *Also called Akzo Nobel Chemicals LLC* ***(G-4301)***
Manufacturing Facility, Middletown *Also called President Cont Group II LLC* ***(G-8457)***
Manufacturing Resources Inc.....631 481-0041
2392 Innovation Way # 4 Rochester (14624) ***(G-14493)***
Manufacturing Solutions Inc.....585 235-3320
850 Saint Paul St Ste 11 Rochester (14605) ***(G-14494)***
Manzella Knitting.....716 825-0808
3345 N Benzing Rd Orchard Park (14127) ***(G-13281)***
Manzione Enterprises, Brooklyn *Also called Manzione Ready Mix Corp* ***(G-2264)***
Manzione Ready Mix Corp.....718 628-3837
46 Knickerbocker Ave Brooklyn (11237) ***(G-2264)***
Mapeasy Inc.....631 537-6213
54 Industrial Rd Wainscott (11975) ***(G-16529)***
Maple Grove and Enterprises, Arcade *Also called Maple Grove Corp* ***(G-396)***
Maple Grove Corp.....585 492-5286
7075 Route 98 Arcade (14009) ***(G-396)***
Maple Hill Creamery LLC.....518 758-7777
285 Allendale Rd W Stuyvesant (12173) ***(G-15782)***
Maplewood Ice Co Inc.....518 499-2345
9785 State Route 4 Whitehall (12887) ***(G-17190)***
Mar-A-Thon Filters Inc.....631 957-4774
369 41st St Lindenhurst (11757) ***(G-7470)***
Maracle Industrial Finshg Co.....585 387-9077
93 Kilbourn Rd Rochester (14618) ***(G-14495)***
Maramont Corporation (PA).....718 439-8900
5600 1st Ave Brooklyn (11220) ***(G-2265)***
Marathon Boat Group Inc.....607 849-3211
1 Grumman Way Marathon (13803) ***(G-8085)***
Marathon Enterprises Inc.....718 665-2560
787 E 138th St Bronx (10454) ***(G-1385)***
Marathon Heater Co Inc.....607 657-8113
13 Town Barn Rd Richford (13835) ***(G-14063)***
Marathon Roofing Products Inc.....716 685-3340
3310 N Benzing Rd Orchard Park (14127) ***(G-13282)***
Marble Doctors LLC.....203 628-8339
244 5th Ave Ste 2608 New York (10001) ***(G-11143)***
Marble Knits Inc.....718 237-7990
544 Park Ave Ste 3 Brooklyn (11205) ***(G-2266)***
Marble Knitting Mills, Brooklyn *Also called Marble Knits Inc* ***(G-2266)***
Marble Works Inc.....914 376-3653
660 Saw Mill River Rd Yonkers (10710) ***(G-17465)***
Marc New York, Riverhead *Also called Andrew Marc Outlet* ***(G-14138)***
Marcal Printing Inc.....516 942-9500
85 N Broadway Hicksville (11801) ***(G-6367)***
Marcasiano Inc.....212 614-9412
296 Elizabeth St Apt 2f New York (10012) ***(G-11144)***
Marcel Finishing Corp.....718 381-2889
4 David Ct Plainview (11803) ***(G-13618)***
Marcellus Energy Services LLC.....607 236-0038
3 Mill St Ste 6 Candor (13743) ***(G-3378)***
Marchesa Accesories, New York *Also called Akh Group LLC* ***(G-9066)***
Marco Hi-Tech JV LLC (PA).....212 798-8114
475 Park Ave S Fl 10 New York (10016) ***(G-11145)***
Marco Manufacturing Inc.....845 485-1571
55 Page Park Dr Poughkeepsie (12603) ***(G-13914)***
Marco Moore Inc.....212 575-2090
825 Northern Blvd Ste 201 Great Neck (11021) ***(G-5822)***
Marcon Electronic Systems LLC.....516 633-6396
152 Westend Ave Freeport (11520) ***(G-5410)***
Marcon Services.....516 223-8019
152 Westend Ave Freeport (11520) ***(G-5411)***
Marconi Intl USA Co Ltd.....212 391-2626
214 W 39th St Rm 1100 New York (10018) ***(G-11146)***
Marcovicci-Wenz Engineering.....631 467-9040
33 Comac Loop Unit 10 Ronkonkoma (11779) ***(G-14938)***
Marcus Goldman Inc.....212 431-0707
37 W 39th St Rm 1201 New York (10018) ***(G-11147)***
Marcy Business Forms Inc.....718 935-9100
1468 40th St Brooklyn (11218) ***(G-2267)***
Marcy Printing Inc.....718 935-9100
777 Kent Ave Ste A Brooklyn (11205) ***(G-2268)***
Mardek LLC.....585 735-9333
73 N Wilmarth Rd Pittsford (14534) ***(G-13569)***
Mardon Tool & Die Co Inc.....585 254-4545
19 Lois St Rochester (14606) ***(G-14496)***
Marex Aquisition Corp.....585 458-3940
1385 Emerson St Rochester (14606) ***(G-14497)***
Mari Strings Inc.....212 799-6781
14 W 71st St New York (10023) ***(G-11148)***
Mariah Metal Products Inc.....516 938-9783
89 Tec St Hicksville (11801) ***(G-6368)***
Marian Goodman Gallery Inc.....212 977-7160
24 W 57th St Fl 4 New York (10019) ***(G-11149)***
Marie Claire, New York *Also called Hearst Corporation* ***(G-10443)***
Marie Claire USA.....212 841-8493
300 W 57th St Fl 34 New York (10019) ***(G-11150)***
Marietta Corporation (HQ).....607 753-6746
37 Huntington St Cortland (13045) ***(G-4033)***
Marietta Corporation.....607 753-0982
106 Central Ave Cortland (13045) ***(G-4034)***

ALPHABETIC

Marigold Signs Inc 516 433-7446
485 S Broadway Ste 34 Hicksville (11801) *(G-6369)*
Marilyn Model Management Inc 646 556-7587
32 Union Sq E Ph 1 New York (10003) *(G-11151)*
Marina Holding Corp 718 646-9283
3939 Emmons Ave Brooklyn (11235) *(G-2269)*
Marina Ice Cream 718 235-3000
888 Jamaica Ave Brooklyn (11208) *(G-2270)*
Marina Jewelry Co Inc 212 354-5027
42 W 48th St Ste 804 New York (10036) *(G-11152)*
Marine & Indus Hydraulics Inc 914 698-2036
329 Center Ave Mamaroneck (10543) *(G-8037)*
Marine Boiler & Welding Inc 718 378-1900
1428 Sheridan Expy Bronx (10459) *(G-1386)*
Marine Park Appliances LLC 718 513-1808
3412 Avenue N Brooklyn (11234) *(G-2271)*
Marinos Italian Ices, Richmond Hill *Also called Olympic Ice Cream Co Inc (G-14077)*
Marion's Italian Ices, Jamaica *Also called Olympic Ice Cream Co Inc (G-6936)*
Maripharm Laboratories 716 984-6520
2045 Niagara Falls Blvd Niagara Falls (14304) *(G-12845)*
Maritime Activity Reports (PA) 212 477-6700
118 E 25th St Fl 2 New York (10010) *(G-11153)*
Maritime Broadband Inc 347 404-6041
1143 47th Ave Long Island City (11101) *(G-7803)*
Mark - 10 Corporation 631 842-9200
11 Dixon Ave Copiague (11726) *(G-3913)*
Mark Dri Products Inc 516 484-6200
999 S Oyster Bay Rd # 312 Bethpage (11714) *(G-873)*
Mark Ecko Enterprises, New York *Also called Mee Accessories LLC (G-11218)*
Mark F Rosenhaft N A O 516 374-1010
538 Central Ave Cedarhurst (11516) *(G-3460)*
Mark I Publications Inc 718 205-8000
6233 Woodhaven Blvd Rego Park (11374) *(G-14035)*
Mark King Jewelry Inc 212 921-0746
62 W 47th St Ste 310r New York (10036) *(G-11154)*
Mark Levine 212 677-4457
149 5th Ave Fl 10 New York (10010) *(G-11155)*
Mark Nelson Designs LLC 646 422-7020
404 E 55th St Fl 4 New York (10022) *(G-11156)*
Mark Peri International 516 208-6824
3516 Hargale Rd Oceanside (11572) *(G-13087)*
Mark Posner 718 258-6241
1950 52nd St Brooklyn (11204) *(G-2272)*
Mark Robinson Inc 212 223-3515
18 E 48th St Rm 1102 New York (10017) *(G-11157)*
Mark T Westinghouse 518 678-3262
138 Grandview Ave Catskill (12414) *(G-3431)*
Markar Architectural Products 716 685-4104
68 Ward Rd Lancaster (14086) *(G-7326)*
Marken LLP 631 396-7454
123 Smith St Farmingdale (11735) *(G-5041)*
Market Factory Inc 212 625-9988
425 Broadway Fl 3 New York (10013) *(G-11158)*
Market Place Publications 516 997-7909
234 Silverlake Blvd Ste 2 Carle Place (11514) *(G-3395)*
Marketer's Forum Magazine, Centerport *Also called Forum Publishing Co (G-3476)*
Marketfax Information Services, Hastings On Hudson *Also called Alternative Technology Corp (G-6002)*
Marketing Action Xecutives Inc 212 971-9155
50 W 96th St Apt 7b New York (10025) *(G-11159)*
Marketing Edge 212 790-1512
1333 Broadway Rm 301 New York (10018) *(G-11160)*
Marketing Group International 631 754-8095
225 Main St Ste 301 Northport (11768) *(G-13016)*
Marketplace Slutions Group LLC 631 868-0111
48 Nimbus Rd Ste 303 Holbrook (11741) *(G-6461)*
Marketplace, The, Chester *Also called Advertiser Publications Inc (G-3598)*
Marketresearchcom Inc 212 807-2600
641 Ave Of The America New York (10011) *(G-11161)*
Markets Media LLC 646 442-4646
110 Wall St Fl 15 New York (10005) *(G-11162)*
Marketshare LLC 631 273-0598
90 Cain Dr Brentwood (11717) *(G-1191)*
Markin Tubing LP (PA) 585 495-6211
1 Markin Ln Wyoming (14591) *(G-17380)*
Markin Tubing LP 585 495-6211
400 Ingham Ave Buffalo (14218) *(G-3056)*
Markin Tubing Division, Buffalo *Also called Markin Tubing LP (G-3056)*
Markin Tubing Inc 585 495-6211
Pearl Creek Rd Wyoming (14591) *(G-17381)*
Markowitz Jewelry Co Inc 845 774-1175
53 Forest Rd Ste 104 Monroe (10950) *(G-8561)*
Markpericom 516 208-6824
3516 Hargale Rd Oceanside (11572) *(G-13088)*
Marks Corpex Banknote Co (PA) 631 968-0277
1440 5th Ave Bay Shore (11706) *(G-715)*
Marksmen Manufacturing Corp 800 305-6942
355 Marcus Blvd Deer Park (11729) *(G-4170)*
Marktech International Corp (PA) 518 956-2980
3 Northway Ln N Latham (12110) *(G-7373)*
Marktech Optoelectronics, Latham *Also called Marktech International Corp (G-7373)*

Markwik Corp 516 470-1990
309 W John St Hicksville (11801) *(G-6370)*
Marlborough Jewels Inc 718 768-2000
67 35th St Unit 2 Brooklyn (11232) *(G-2273)*
Marley Spoon Inc 646 934-6970
336 W 37th St Rm 1400 New York (10018) *(G-11163)*
Marlou Garments Inc 516 739-7100
2115 Jericho Tpke New Hyde Park (11040) *(G-8847)*
Marlow Printing Co Inc 718 625-4949
667 Kent Ave Brooklyn (11249) *(G-2274)*
Marmach Machine Inc 585 768-8800
11 Lent Ave Le Roy (14482) *(G-7414)*
Marnier-Lapostolle Inc 212 207-4350
183 Madison Ave New York (10016) *(G-11164)*
Marotta Dental Studio Inc 631 249-7520
130 Finn Ct Farmingdale (11735) *(G-5042)*
Marovato Industries Inc 718 389-0800
100 Dobbin St Brooklyn (11222) *(G-2275)*
Marplex Furniture Corporation 914 969-7755
167 Saw Mill Rver Rd Fl 1 Yonkers (10701) *(G-17466)*
Marquardt Switches Inc (HQ) 315 655-8050
2711 Us Route 20 Cazenovia (13035) *(G-3449)*
Marretti USA Inc 212 255-5565
101 Ave Of The Americas New York (10013) *(G-11165)*
Marros Equipment & Trucks 315 539-8702
2354 State Route 414 Waterloo (13165) *(G-16630)*
Mars, Corinth *Also called Manuf Appld Renova Sys (G-3959)*
Mars Fashions Inc 718 402-2200
780 E 134th St Fl 5 Bronx (10454) *(G-1387)*
Marsal & Sons, Lindenhurst *Also called Middleby Corporation (G-7472)*
Marsha Fleisher 845 679-6500
18 Tinker St Woodstock (12498) *(G-17364)*
Marshall Cavendish Corp 914 332-8888
99 White Plains Rd Tarrytown (10591) *(G-16095)*
Marshall Ingredients LLC 800 796-9353
5786 Limekiln Rd Wolcott (14590) *(G-17280)*
Marsid Group Ltd 516 334-1603
245 Westbury Ave Carle Place (11514) *(G-3396)*
Marsid Press, Carle Place *Also called Marsid Group Ltd (G-3396)*
MARsid-M&m Group, The, Carle Place *Also called M&M Printing Inc (G-3394)*
Mart-Tex Athletics Inc 631 454-9583
180 Allen Blvd Farmingdale (11735) *(G-5043)*
Martec Industries 585 458-3940
1385 Emerson St Rochester (14606) *(G-14498)*
Martens Country Kit Pdts LLC 315 776-8821
1323 Towpath Rd Port Byron (13140) *(G-13734)*
Martha Stewart Living (HQ) 212 827-8000
601 W 26th St Rm 900 New York (10001) *(G-11166)*
Martha Stewart Living Omni LLC 212 827-8000
20 W 43rd St New York (10036) *(G-11167)*
Martin Brass Works Inc 718 523-3146
17544 Liberty Ave Jamaica (11433) *(G-6928)*
Martin Chafkin 718 383-1155
1155 Manhattan Ave # 431 Brooklyn (11222) *(G-2276)*
Martin D Whitbeck 607 746-7642
68 Meredith St Delhi (13753) *(G-4240)*
Martin Dental Studio, Watertown *Also called Martins Dental Studio (G-16664)*
Martin Flyer Incorporated 212 840-8899
70 W 36th St Rm 602 New York (10018) *(G-11168)*
Martin Greenfield Clothiers 718 497-5480
239 Varet St Brooklyn (11206) *(G-2277)*
Martin Orna Ir Works II Inc 516 354-3923
266 Elmont Rd Elmont (11003) *(G-4723)*
Martinelli Holdings LLC 302 504-1361
2 Clinton Ave Rye (10580) *(G-15062)*
Martinelli Publications, Yonkers *Also called Yonkers Time Publishing Co (G-17503)*
Martinez Hand Made Cigars 212 239-4049
171 W 29th St Frnt A New York (10001) *(G-11169)*
Martinez Specialties Inc 607 898-3053
205 Bossard Rd Groton (13073) *(G-5900)*
Martins Dental Studio 315 788-0800
162 Sterling St Watertown (13601) *(G-16664)*
Marval Industries Inc 914 381-2400
315 Hoyt Ave Mamaroneck (10543) *(G-8038)*
Marvel Dairy Whip Inc 516 889-4232
258 Lido Blvd Lido Beach (11561) *(G-7442)*
Marvel Entertainment LLC (HQ) 212 576-4000
135 W 50th St Fl 7 New York (10020) *(G-11170)*
Marvel Equipment Corp Inc 718 383-6597
215 Eagle St Brooklyn (11222) *(G-2278)*
Marvellissima Intl Ltd 212 682-7306
333 E 46th St Apt 20a New York (10017) *(G-11171)*
Marx Myles Graphic Services, New York *Also called X Myles Mar Inc (G-12673)*
Mary Ann Liebert Inc 914 740-2100
140 Huguenot St Fl 3 New Rochelle (10801) *(G-8917)*
Mary Bright Inc 212 677-1970
269 E 10th St Apt 7 New York (10009) *(G-11172)*
Mary F Morse 315 866-2741
125 Columbia St Ste 1 Mohawk (13407) *(G-8542)*
Mas Cutting Inc 212 869-0826
257 W 39th St Rm 11e New York (10018) *(G-11173)*

ALPHABETIC

Masick Soil Conservation Co 518 827-5354
  4860 State Route 30 Schoharie (12157) *(G-15317)*
Mason & Gore Inc 914 921-1025
  2 Clinton Ave Rye (10580) *(G-15063)*
Mason Carvings Inc 716 664-9402
  101 Water St Jamestown (14701) *(G-7017)*
Mason Contract Products LLC 516 328-6900
  85 Denton Ave New Hyde Park (11040) *(G-8848)*
Mason Industries Inc (PA) 631 348-0282
  350 Rabro Dr Hauppauge (11788) *(G-6126)*
Mason Industries Inc 631 348-0282
  33 Ranick Rd Ste 1 Hauppauge (11788) *(G-6127)*
Mason Medical Products, Port Washington Also called M R C Industries Inc *(G-13839)*
Mason Scott Industries LLC 516 349-1800
  159 Westwood Cir Roslyn Heights (11577) *(G-15029)*
Mason Transparent Package Inc 718 792-6000
  1180 Commerce Ave Bronx (10462) *(G-1388)*
Masonville Stone Incorporated 607 265-3597
  12999 State Highway 8 Masonville (13804) *(G-8108)*
Maspeth Press Inc 718 429-2363
  6620 Grand Ave Maspeth (11378) *(G-8149)*
Maspeth Steel Fabricators Inc 718 361-9192
  5215 11th St Ste 21 Long Island City (11101) *(G-7804)*
Maspeth Welding Inc 718 497-5430
  5930 54th St Maspeth (11378) *(G-8150)*
Mass Appeal Magazine 718 858-0979
  261 Vandervoort Ave Brooklyn (11211) *(G-2279)*
Mass Mdsg Self Selection Eqp 631 234-3300
  35 Orville Dr Ste 2 Bohemia (11716) *(G-1102)*
Massapequa Post 516 798-5100
  1045b Park Blvd Massapequa Park (11762) *(G-8188)*
Massapqua Prcsion McHining Ltd 631 789-1485
  30 Seabro Ave Amityville (11701) *(G-310)*
Massena Metals Inc 315 769-3846
  86 S Racquette River Rd Massena (13662) *(G-8198)*
Massimo Friedman Inc 716 836-0408
  2495 Main St Ste 457 Buffalo (14214) *(G-3057)*
Mast Brothers Inc 718 388-2625
  105 N 3rd St Apt A Brooklyn (11249) *(G-2280)*
Masten Enterprises LLC (PA) 845 932-8206
  420 Bernas Rd Cochecton (12726) *(G-3742)*
Master & Dynamics, New York Also called New Audio LLC *(G-11379)*
Master Art Corp 845 362-6430
  131 Clinton Ln Ste E Spring Valley (10977) *(G-15594)*
Master Craft Finishers Inc 631 586-0540
  30 W Jefryn Blvd Ste 1 Deer Park (11729) *(G-4171)*
Master Craft Jewelry Co Inc 516 599-1012
  150 Vincent Ave Lynbrook (11563) *(G-7954)*
Master Image Printing Inc 914 347-4400
  75 N Central Ave Ste 202 Elmsford (10523) *(G-4763)*
Master Juvenile Products Inc 845 647-8400
  70 Berme Rd Ellenville (12428) *(G-4635)*
Master Machine Incorporated 716 487-2555
  155 Blackstone Ave Jamestown (14701) *(G-7018)*
Master Molding Inc 631 694-1444
  97 Gazza Blvd Farmingdale (11735) *(G-5044)*
Master Window & Door Corp 718 782-5407
  199 Starr St Brooklyn (11237) *(G-2281)*
Master-Halco Inc 631 585-8150
  25 Mill Rd Unit 1 Ronkonkoma (11779) *(G-14939)*
Mastercraft Decorators Inc 585 223-5150
  320 Macedon Center Rd Fairport (14450) *(G-4863)*
Mastercraft Manufacturing Co 718 729-5620
  3715 11th St Long Island City (11101) *(G-7805)*
Masterdisk Corporation 212 541-5022
  134 S Central Ave Ste C Elmsford (10523) *(G-4764)*
Masterpiece Color LLC 917 279-6056
  240 W 35th St Ste 1200 New York (10001) *(G-11174)*
Masterpiece Diamonds LLC 212 937-0681
  240 W 35th St Ste 1200 New York (10001) *(G-11175)*
Mastro Concrete Inc 718 528-6788
  15433 Brookville Blvd Rosedale (11422) *(G-15014)*
Mastro Graphic Arts Inc 585 436-7570
  67 Deep Rock Rd Rochester (14624) *(G-14499)*
Mastroianni Bros Inc 518 355-5310
  51 Opus Blvd Schenectady (12306) *(G-15277)*
Mastroianni Bros Bakery, Schenectady Also called Mastroianni Bros Inc *(G-15277)*
Mata Fashions LLC 917 716-7894
  214 W 39th St Ste 608 New York (10018) *(G-11176)*
Mata Ig 212 979-7921
  332 Bleecker St New York (10014) *(G-11177)*
Mataci Inc 212 502-1899
  247 W 35th St Fl 15 New York (10001) *(G-11178)*
Match Eyewear LLC 516 877-0170
  1600 Shames Dr Westbury (11590) *(G-17009)*
Matchables Inc 718 389-9318
  106 Green St Ste A Brooklyn (11222) *(G-2282)*
Material Measuring Corporation 516 334-6167
  121 Hopper St Westbury (11590) *(G-17010)*
Material Process Systems Inc 718 302-3081
  87 Richardson St Ste 2 Brooklyn (11211) *(G-2283)*
Materials Design Workshop 718 893-1954
  830 Barry St Bronx (10474) *(G-1389)*
Materials Recovery Company 518 274-3681
  8000 Main St Troy (12180) *(G-16242)*
Materion Advanced Materials (HQ) 800 327-1355
  2978 Main St Buffalo (14214) *(G-3058)*
Materion Brewster LLC 845 279-0900
  42 Mount Ebo Rd S Brewster (10509) *(G-1223)*
Matheson Tri-Gas Inc 518 203-5003
  15 Green Mountain Dr Cohoes (12047) *(G-3750)*
Matheson Tri-Gas Inc 518 439-0362
  1297 Feura Bush Rd Feura Bush (12067) *(G-5173)*
Mathisen Ventures Inc 212 986-1025
  441 Lexington Ave Rm 809 New York (10017) *(G-11179)*
Matic Industries Inc 718 886-5470
  1540 127th St College Point (11356) *(G-3797)*
Matov Industries Inc 718 392-5060
  1011 40th Ave Long Island City (11101) *(G-7806)*
Matrix Machining Corp 631 643-6690
  69 B Nancy St Unitb West Babylon (11704) *(G-16809)*
Matrix Railway Corp 631 643-1483
  69 Nancy St Unit A West Babylon (11704) *(G-16810)*
Matrix Steel Company Inc 718 381-6800
  50 Bogart St Brooklyn (11206) *(G-2284)*
Matrox Graphics Inc 518 561-4417
  625 State Route 3 1/2 Plattsburgh (12901) *(G-13677)*
Matt Industries Inc (PA) 315 472-1316
  6761 Thompson Rd Syracuse (13211) *(G-15984)*
Matt Textile Inc 212 967-6010
  142 W 36th St Fl 3 New York (10018) *(G-11180)*
Mattel Inc 716 714-8514
  609 Girard Ave East Aurora (14052) *(G-4374)*
Matteo & Antonio Bartolotta 315 252-2220
  282 State St Auburn (13021) *(G-508)*
Matteson Logging Inc 585 593-3037
  2808 Beech Hill Rd Wellsville (14895) *(G-16754)*
Mattessich Iron LLC 315 409-8496
  7841 River Rd Baldwinsville (13027) *(G-571)*
Matthew Shively LLC 914 937-3531
  28 Bulkley Ave Port Chester (10573) *(G-13754)*
Matthew-Lee Corporation 631 226-0100
  149 Pennsylvania Ave Lindenhurst (11757) *(G-7471)*
Matthews Hats 718 859-4683
  99 Kenilworth Pl Fl 1 Brooklyn (11210) *(G-2285)*
Mattress Factory 718 760-4202
  5312 104th St Corona (11368) *(G-4002)*
Mauceri Sign & Awning Co, Jamaica Also called Mauceri Sign Inc *(G-6929)*
Mauceri Sign Inc 718 656-7700
  16725 Rockaway Blvd Jamaica (11434) *(G-6929)*
Maurice Max Inc 212 334-6573
  49 W 27th St Fl 5 New York (10001) *(G-11181)*
Maury's Cookie Dough, New York Also called City Bakery Inc *(G-9628)*
Maurybakes LLC 646 722-6570
  18 W 18th St New York (10011) *(G-11182)*
Mausner Equipment Co Inc 631 689-7358
  8 Heritage Ln Setauket (11733) *(G-15377)*
Maven Marketing LLC (PA) 615 510-3248
  349 5th Ave Fl 8 New York (10016) *(G-11183)*
Maverik Lacrosse LLC 516 213-3050
  535 W 24th St Fl 5 New York (10011) *(G-11184)*
Maviano Corp 845 494-2598
  21 Robert Pitt Dr Ste 207 Monsey (10952) *(G-8575)*
Mavito Fine Jewelry Ltd Inc 212 398-9384
  37 W 47th St Ste 500 New York (10036) *(G-11185)*
Max 200 Performance Dog Eqp 315 776-9588
  2113 State Route 31 Port Byron (13140) *(G-13735)*
Max Brenner Union Square LLC 646 467-8803
  841 Broadway New York (10003) *(G-11186)*
Max Kahan Inc 212 575-4646
  20 W 47th St Ste 300 New York (10036) *(G-11187)*
Max Leather, New York Also called Gbg USA Inc *(G-10256)*
Max Leon Inc 845 928-8201
  825 Grapevine Ct Central Valley (10917) *(G-3525)*
Max Thermo Corporation 845 294-3640
  5 Reservoir Rd Goshen (10924) *(G-5737)*
Maxam North America Inc 313 322-8651
  3 Cemetary Dr Ogdensburg (13669) *(G-13118)*
Maxi Companies Inc 315 446-1002
  4317 E Genesee St De Witt (13214) *(G-4083)*
Maxim Hygiene Products Inc (PA) 516 621-3323
  121 E Jericho Tpke Mineola (11501) *(G-8523)*
Maximillion Communications LLC 212 564-3945
  245 W 17th St Fl 2 New York (10011) *(G-11188)*
Maximum Security Products Corp 518 233-1800
  3 Schoolhouse Ln Waterford (12188) *(G-16613)*
Maxine Denker Inc (PA) 212 689-1440
  212 Manhattan St Staten Island (10307) *(G-15704)*
Maxivision, Long Island City Also called Bestec Concept Inc *(G-7683)*
Maxsecure Systems Inc 800 657-4336
  300 International Dr # 100 Buffalo (14221) *(G-3059)*
Maxsun Corporation (PA) 718 418-6800
  5711 49th St Maspeth (11378) *(G-8151)*
Maxsun Furnishings, Maspeth Also called Maxsun Corporation *(G-8151)*
Maxus Pharmaceuticals Inc 631 249-0003
  50 Executive Blvd Ste B Farmingdale (11735) *(G-5045)*

Maxwell Bakery Inc....718 498-2200
2700 Atlantic Ave Brooklyn (11207) ***(G-2286)***
Maxworld Inc....212 242-7588
213 W 14th St New York (10011) ***(G-11189)***
May Ship Repair Contg Corp....718 442-9700
3075 Richmond Ter Ste 3 Staten Island (10303) ***(G-15705)***
May Tool & Die Inc....716 695-1033
9 Hackett Dr Tonawanda (14150) ***(G-16180)***
Maybelline Inc....212 885-1310
575 5th Ave Bsmt Fl New York (10017) ***(G-11190)***
Mayberry Shoe Company Inc....315 692-4086
131 W Seneca St Ste B Manlius (13104) ***(G-8074)***
Maybrook Asphalt, Montgomery *Also called Tilcon New York Inc* ***(G-8603)***
Mayer Bros Apple Products Inc (PA)....716 668-1787
3300 Transit Rd West Seneca (14224) ***(G-16952)***
Mayfair Machine Company Inc....631 981-6644
128 Remington Blvd Ronkonkoma (11779) ***(G-14940)***
Mayfair Sales, Tonawanda *Also called First Source LLC* ***(G-16162)***
Mayflower Splint Co....631 549-5131
16 Arbor Ln Dix Hills (11746) ***(G-4293)***
Mayim Chaim Beverages, Bronx *Also called New York Bottling Co Inc* ***(G-1408)***
Maz Digital Inc (PA)....646 692-9799
135 W 26th St Ste 10a New York (10001) ***(G-11191)***
Mazza Classics Incorporated....631 390-9060
117 Gazza Blvd Farmingdale (11735) ***(G-5046)***
Mazza Co, The, North Baldwin *Also called W & B Mazza & Sons Inc* ***(G-12913)***
Mazzella Blasting Mat Co, Bronx *Also called T M International LLC* ***(G-1471)***
MB Food Processing Inc....845 436-5001
5190 S Fallsburg Main St South Fallsburg (12779) ***(G-15520)***
MB Plastics Inc (PA)....718 523-1180
130 Stony Hollow Rd Greenlawn (11740) ***(G-5874)***
MBA Orthotics Inc....631 392-4755
60 Corbin Ave Unit 60g Bay Shore (11706) ***(G-716)***
Mbh Furniture Innovations Inc....845 354-8202
28 Lincoln Ave Spring Valley (10977) ***(G-15595)***
MBI Firearms, Mineola *Also called Michael Britt Inc* ***(G-8525)***
Mbny LLC (PA)....646 467-8810
260 5th Ave Fl 9 New York (10001) ***(G-11192)***
Mbss, Kew Gardens *Also called Manhole Brrier SEC Systems Inc* ***(G-7165)***
Mc Coy Tops and Covers, Woodside *Also called Mc Coy Tops and Interiors Inc* ***(G-17336)***
Mc Coy Tops and Interiors Inc....718 458-5800
6914 49th Ave Woodside (11377) ***(G-17336)***
Mc Duffies Bakery, Clarence *Also called McDuffies of Scotland Inc* ***(G-3664)***
Mc Gregor Vineyard Winery, Dundee *Also called East Branch Winery Inc* ***(G-4326)***
Mc Ivor Manufacturing Inc....716 825-1808
400 Ingham Ave Buffalo (14218) ***(G-3060)***
Mc Mahon Group, New York *Also called McMahon Publishing Company* ***(G-11202)***
Mc Squared Nyc Inc....212 947-2260
121 Varick St Frnt B New York (10013) ***(G-11193)***
McAfee Inc....646 728-1440
1133 Avenue Of The Americ New York (10036) ***(G-11194)***
McAllisters Precision Wldg Inc....518 221-3455
1076 Broadway Menands (12204) ***(G-8374)***
McAlpin Industries Inc (PA)....585 266-3060
255 Hollenbeck St Rochester (14621) ***(G-14500)***
McAlpin Industries Inc....585 544-5335
265 Hollenbeck St Rochester (14621) ***(G-14501)***
McAuliffe Paper Inc....315 453-2222
100 Commerce Blvd Liverpool (13088) ***(G-7534)***
McBooks Press Inc....607 272-2114
520 N Meadow St 2 Ithaca (14850) ***(G-6859)***
McCall Pattern Company (HQ)....212 465-6800
120 Broadway Fl 34 New York (10271) ***(G-11195)***
McCarroll Uphl Designs LLC....518 828-0500
743 Columbia St Hudson (12534) ***(G-6625)***
McCarthy LLC....646 862-5354
32 Union Sq E New York (10003) ***(G-11196)***
McCarthy Tire and Auto Ctr, Menands *Also called McCarthy Tire Svc Co NY Inc* ***(G-8375)***
McCarthy Tire Svc Co NY Inc....518 449-5185
980 Broadway Menands (12204) ***(G-8375)***
McCullagh Coffee, Buffalo *Also called S J McCullagh Inc* ***(G-3172)***
McD Metals LLC....518 456-9694
20 Corporate Cir Ste 2 Albany (12203) ***(G-100)***
McDermott Light & Signal, Ridgewood *Also called Julian A McDermott Corporation* ***(G-14111)***
McDonough Hardwoods Ltd....315 829-3449
6426 Skinner Rd Vernon Center (13477) ***(G-16437)***
McDowell Research Co Inc (HQ)....315 332-7100
2000 Technology Pkwy Newark (14513) ***(G-12736)***
McDuffies of Scotland Inc....716 759-8510
9920 Main St Clarence (14031) ***(G-3664)***
McEwan Trucking & Grav Produc....716 609-1828
11696 Route 240 East Concord (14055) ***(G-4385)***
McG Electronics Inc....631 586-5125
12 Burt Dr Deer Park (11729) ***(G-4172)***
McG Graphics Inc....631 499-0730
101 Village Hill Dr Dix Hills (11746) ***(G-4294)***
McG Surge Protection, Deer Park *Also called McG Electronics Inc* ***(G-4172)***
McGaw Framed Art, New York *Also called McGaw Group LLC* ***(G-11197)***
McGaw Group LLC....212 876-8822
233 E 93rd St New York (10128) ***(G-11197)***
McGraw Wood Products LLC (PA)....607 836-6465
1 Charles St Mc Graw (13101) ***(G-8223)***
McGraw-Hill Glbl Edctn Hldngs (PA)....646 766-2000
2 Penn Plz Fl 20 New York (10121) ***(G-11198)***
McGraw-Hill School Education H (PA)....646 766-2000
2 Penn Plz Fl 20 New York (10121) ***(G-11199)***
McGraw-Hill School Educatn LLC....646 766-2060
2 Penn Plz Fl 20 New York (10121) ***(G-11200)***
McGuigan Inc....631 750-6222
210 Knickerbocker Ave Bohemia (11716) ***(G-1103)***
McHone Industries Inc....716 945-3380
110 Elm St Salamanca (14779) ***(G-15101)***
McHugh Painting Co Inc....716 741-8077
10335 Clarence Center Rd Clarence (14031) ***(G-3665)***
McIntosh Box & Pallet Co Inc....315 789-8750
40 Doran Ave Geneva (14456) ***(G-5582)***
McIntosh Box & Pallet Co Inc....315 675-8511
741 State Route 49 Bernhards Bay (13028) ***(G-858)***
McIntosh Box & Pallet Co Inc....315 446-9350
200 6th St Rome (13440) ***(G-14820)***
McKee Foods Corporation....631 979-9364
111 Serene Pl Hauppauge (11788) ***(G-6128)***
McKeon Rolling Stl Door Co Inc (PA)....631 803-3000
44 Sawgrass Dr Bellport (11713) ***(G-834)***
MCM Natural Stone Inc....585 586-6510
860 Linden Ave Ste 1 Rochester (14625) ***(G-14502)***
McM Products USA Inc....646 756-4090
712 5th Ave Ste 702 New York (10019) ***(G-11201)***
McMahon Publishing Company (PA)....212 957-5300
545 W 45th St Fl 8 New York (10036) ***(G-11202)***
McQuilling Partners Inc (PA)....516 227-5718
1035 Stewart Ave Ste 100 Garden City (11530) ***(G-5519)***
McWane Inc....607 734-2211
1021 E Water St Elmira (14901) ***(G-4694)***
MD Electronics of Illinois....716 488-0300
33 Precision Way Jamestown (14701) ***(G-7019)***
MD International Industries....631 254-3100
120 E Jefryn Blvd Ste Aa Deer Park (11729) ***(G-4173)***
Md-Reports, Staten Island *Also called Infinite Software Solutions* ***(G-15687)***
Md4 Holdings Inc....315 434-1869
6713 Collamer Rd East Syracuse (13057) ***(G-4549)***
Mdcare911 LLC....917 640-4869
30 Main St Apt 5c Brooklyn (11201) ***(G-2287)***
Mdek Inc....347 569-7318
9728 3rd Ave Brooklyn (11209) ***(G-2288)***
Mdi, Hauppauge *Also called Metal Dynamics Intl Corp* ***(G-6134)***
Mdi East Inc....518 747-8730
22 Hudson Falls Rd Ste 6 South Glens Falls (12803) ***(G-15526)***
Mdi Holdings LLC....212 559-1127
399 Park Ave Fl 14 New York (10022) ***(G-11203)***
Mdj Sales Associates Inc....914 420-5897
27 Doris Rd Mamaroneck (10543) ***(G-8039)***
Mdr Printing Corp....516 627-3221
490 Plandome Rd Manhasset (11030) ***(G-8062)***
Mds Hot Bagels Deli Inc....718 438-5650
127 Church Ave Brooklyn (11218) ***(G-2289)***
Mds USA Inc....718 358-5588
13244 Booth Memorial Ave Flushing (11355) ***(G-5269)***
ME & Ro Inc (PA)....212 431-8744
305 Broadway Ste 1101 New York (10007) ***(G-11204)***
Meade Machine Co Inc....315 923-1703
31 Ford St Clyde (14433) ***(G-3728)***
Meades Welding and Fabricating....631 581-1555
331 Islip Ave Islip (11751) ***(G-6810)***
Meadowbrook Distributing Corp....516 226-9000
95 Jefferson St Garden City (11530) ***(G-5520)***
Mealplan Corp....909 706-8398
203 E 4th St Apt 6 New York (10009) ***(G-11205)***
Measupro Inc (PA)....845 425-8777
1 Alpine Ct Spring Valley (10977) ***(G-15596)***
Measurement Incorporated....914 682-1969
7-11 S Broadway Ste 402 White Plains (10601) ***(G-17136)***
Meat Industry Newsletter, West Islip *Also called Spc Marketing Company* ***(G-16907)***
Mecca Printing, Buffalo *Also called B & P Jays Inc* ***(G-2830)***
Mechanical Displays Inc....718 258-5588
4420 Farragut Rd Brooklyn (11203) ***(G-2290)***
Mechanical Pwr Conversion LLC....607 766-9620
6 Emma St Binghamton (13905) ***(G-934)***
Mechanical Rubber Pdts Co Inc....845 986-2271
77 Forester Ave Ste 1 Warwick (10990) ***(G-16594)***
Mechanical Specialties Co, Binghamton *Also called Ms Machining Inc* ***(G-938)***
Mechanical Technology Inc (PA)....518 218-2550
325 Washington Avenue Ext Albany (12205) ***(G-101)***
Mecho Systems....718 729-8373
3708 34th St Long Island City (11101) ***(G-7807)***
Mechoshade Systems Inc (HQ)....718 729-2020
4203 35th St Long Island City (11101) ***(G-7808)***
Mechtronics Corporation (PA)....845 231-1400
511 Fishkill Ave Beacon (12508) ***(G-786)***
Mechtronics Corporation....845 831-9300
511 Fishkill Ave Beacon (12508) ***(G-787)***
Med Reviews LLC....212 239-5860
247 W 35th St Rm 801 New York (10001) ***(G-11206)***

ALPHABETIC

Med Services Inc 631 218-6450
100 Knickerbocker Ave C Bohemia (11716) ***(G-1104)***
Med-Eng LLC 315 713-0103
103 Tulloch Dr Ogdensburg (13669) ***(G-13119)***
Medallion Associates Inc 212 929-9130
37 W 20th St Fl 4 New York (10011) ***(G-11207)***
Medallion Security Door & Win, New Hyde Park *Also called Texas Home Security Inc* ***(G-8865)***
Medco, Edgewood *Also called Merit Electronic Design Co Inc* ***(G-4606)***
Medco Machine LLC 315 986-2109
2320 Walworth Marion Rd Walworth (14568) ***(G-16550)***
Medek Laboratories Inc 845 943-4988
63 First Ave Monroe (10950) ***(G-8562)***
Meder Textile Co Inc 516 883-0409
20 Lynn Rd Port Washington (11050) ***(G-13840)***
Medi-Physics, Port Washington *Also called GE Healthcare Inc* ***(G-13819)***
Medi-Ray Inc 877 898-3003
150 Marbledale Rd Tuckahoe (10707) ***(G-16271)***
Medi-Tech International Corp (PA) 800 333-0109
26 Court St Ste 1301 Brooklyn (11242) ***(G-2291)***
Media Press Corp 212 791-6347
55 John St 520 New York (10038) ***(G-11208)***
Media Signs LLC 718 252-7575
6404 14th Ave Brooklyn (11219) ***(G-2292)***
Media Technologies Ltd 631 467-7900
220 Sonata Ct Eastport (11941) ***(G-4584)***
Media Transcripts Inc 212 362-1481
41 W 83rd St Apt 1b New York (10024) ***(G-11209)***
Media Trust LLC (PA) 212 802-1162
404 Park Ave S Fl 2 New York (10016) ***(G-11210)***
Mediaplanet Publishing Hse Inc (PA) 646 922-1409
3 E 28th St Fl 10 New York (10016) ***(G-11211)***
Mediapost Communications LLC 212 204-2000
1460 Broadway Fl 12 New York (10036) ***(G-11212)***
Medical Acoustics LLC 716 218-7353
640 Ellicott St Ste 407 Buffalo (14203) ***(G-3061)***
Medical Action Industries Inc 631 231-4600
150 Motor Pkwy Ste 205 Hauppauge (11788) ***(G-6129)***
Medical Coaches Incorporated (PA) 607 432-1333
399 County Highway 58 Oneonta (13820) ***(G-13188)***
Medical Daily Inc 646 867-7100
7 Hanover Sq Fl 6 New York (10004) ***(G-11213)***
Medical Depot Inc (PA) 516 998-4600
99 Seaview Blvd Ste 210 Port Washington (11050) ***(G-13841)***
Medical Information Systems 516 621-7200
2 Seaview Blvd Ste 104 Port Washington (11050) ***(G-13842)***
Medical Technology Products 631 285-6640
33a Smith St Greenlawn (11740) ***(G-5875)***
Medical Transcription Billing 631 863-1198
237 W 35th St Ste 1202 New York (10001) ***(G-11214)***
Medicine Rules Inc 631 334-5395
2 Constance Ct East Setauket (11733) ***(G-4486)***
Medico, New Windsor *Also called S M Frank & Company Inc* ***(G-8951)***
Medidata Solutions Inc (PA) 212 918-1800
350 Hudson St Fl 9 New York (10014) ***(G-11215)***
Mediflex, Islandia *Also called Flexbar Machine Corporation* ***(G-6793)***
Medikidz Usa Inc 646 895-9319
200 Varick St New York (10014) ***(G-11216)***
Medima LLC 716 741-0400
5727 Strickler Rd Clarence (14031) ***(G-3666)***
Medina Journal Register, Medina *Also called Community Newsppr Holdings Inc* ***(G-8269)***
Medina Millworks LLC 585 798-2969
10694 Ridge Rd Medina (14103) ***(G-8276)***
Medipoint Inc 516 294-8822
72 E 2nd St Mineola (11501) ***(G-8524)***
Medipoint International,, Mineola *Also called Medipoint Inc* ***(G-8524)***
Mediterranean Thick Yogurt, East Elmhurst *Also called Kesso Foods Inc* ***(G-4393)***
Mediterrean Dyro Company 718 786-4888
1102 38th Ave Long Island City (11101) ***(G-7809)***
Meditub Incorporated 866 633-4882
11 Wedgewood Ln Lawrence (11559) ***(G-7395)***
Medius North America, New York *Also called Medius Software Inc* ***(G-11217)***
Medius Software Inc 877 295-0058
14 E 44th St Fl 5 New York (10017) ***(G-11217)***
Medline Industries Inc 845 344-3301
3301 Route 6 Middletown (10940) ***(G-8450)***
Medsafe Systems Inc 516 883-8222
46 Orchard Farm Rd Port Washington (11050) ***(G-13843)***
Medsim-Eagle Simulation Inc 607 658-9354
811 North St Endicott (13760) ***(G-4818)***
Medsource Technologies LLC 716 662-5025
3902 California Rd Orchard Park (14127) ***(G-13283)***
Medsurg Direct, Plainview *Also called Peter Digioia* ***(G-13628)***
Medtech Products Inc (HQ) 914 524-6810
660 White Plains Rd Tarrytown (10591) ***(G-16096)***
Medtek Lighting Corporation (PA) 518 745-7264
206 Glen St Ste 5 Glens Falls (12801) ***(G-5689)***
Mee Accessories LLC (PA) 917 262-1000
475 10th Ave Fl 9 New York (10018) ***(G-11218)***
Meeco Sullivan LLC 800 232-3625
3 Chancellor Ln Warwick (10990) ***(G-16595)***
Meegenius Inc 212 283-7285
151 W 25th St Fl 3 New York (10001) ***(G-11219)***
Meeker Sales Corp 718 384-5400
551 Sutter Ave Brooklyn (11207) ***(G-2293)***
Meethappy Inc 917 903-0591
2122 Bit Path Seaford (11783) ***(G-15346)***
Mega Cabinets Inc 631 789-4112
51 Ranick Dr E Amityville (11701) ***(G-311)***
Mega Graphics Inc 914 962-1402
1725 Front St Ste 1 Yorktown Heights (10598) ***(G-17513)***
Mega Power Sports Corporation 212 627-3380
1123 Broadway Ph New York (10010) ***(G-11220)***
Mega Tool & Mfg Corp 607 734-8398
1023 Caton Ave Elmira (14904) ***(G-4695)***
Mega Vations Inc 718 934-2192
3177 Coney Island Ave A Brooklyn (11235) ***(G-2294)***
Mega Vision Inc 718 228-1065
1274 Flushing Ave Brooklyn (11237) ***(G-2295)***
Megamatt Inc 516 536-3541
35 Vassar Pl Rockville Centre (11570) ***(G-14794)***
Megohmer Vbrating Reed Standco, Brooklyn *Also called Herman H Sticht Company Inc* ***(G-2076)***
Mehron Inc 845 426-1700
100 Red Schoolhouse Rd C2 Chestnut Ridge (10977) ***(G-3623)***
Meisel-Peskin Co Inc (PA) 718 497-1840
349 Scholes St 353 Brooklyn (11206) ***(G-2296)***
Mekanism Inc 212 226-2772
80 Broad St Fl 35 New York (10004) ***(G-11221)***
Mekatronics Incorporated 516 883-6805
85 Channel Dr Ste 2 Port Washington (11050) ***(G-13844)***
Melbourne C Fisher Yacht Sails 631 673-5055
1345 New York Ave Ste 2 Huntington Station (11746) ***(G-6716)***
Melcher Media Inc 212 727-2322
124 W 13th St New York (10011) ***(G-11222)***
Meliorum Technologies Inc 585 313-0616
620 Park Ave 145 Rochester (14607) ***(G-14503)***
Melissa, Interlaken *Also called Hipshot Products Inc* ***(G-6747)***
Melita Corp 718 392-7280
828 E 144th St Bronx (10454) ***(G-1390)***
Melland Gear Instr of Huppauge 631 234-0100
225 Engineers Rd Hauppauge (11788) ***(G-6130)***
Mellanox Technologies Inc 408 970-3400
165 Broadway Ste 2301 New York (10006) ***(G-11223)***
Mellem Corporation 607 723-0001
31 Lewis St Ste 1 Binghamton (13901) ***(G-935)***
Mellen Press, The, Lewiston *Also called PSR Press Ltd* ***(G-7435)***
Mellen Pressroom & Bindery, Lewiston *Also called 450 Ridge St Inc* ***(G-7432)***
Melles Griot, Rochester *Also called CVI Laser LLC* ***(G-14297)***
Melmont Fine Pringng/Graphics 516 939-2253
6 Robert Ct Ste 24 Bethpage (11714) ***(G-874)***
Meloon Foundries LLC 315 454-3231
1841 Lemoyne Ave Syracuse (13208) ***(G-15985)***
Melto Metal Products Co Inc 516 546-8866
37 Hanse Ave Freeport (11520) ***(G-5412)***
Meltz Lumber Co of Mellenville 518 672-7021
483 Route 217 Hudson (12534) ***(G-6626)***
Melwood Partners Inc (PA) 516 307-8030
100 Qentin Roosevelt Blvd Garden City (11530) ***(G-5521)***
Memorial Sloan Kttering Cancer, New York *Also called Mskcc Rmipc* ***(G-11319)***
Memory Md Inc 917 318-0215
205 E 42nd St Fl 14 New York (10017) ***(G-11224)***
Memory Protection Devices Inc 631 293-5891
200 Broadhollow Rd Ste 4 Farmingdale (11735) ***(G-5047)***
Men's Health Magazine, New York *Also called Rodale Inc* ***(G-11900)***
Mend All, Deer Park *Also called Alney Group Ltd* ***(G-4094)***
Mendon Hnoye FLS Lima Sentinel 585 624-5470
201 N Main St Honeoye Falls (14472) ***(G-6534)***
Mens Journal, New York *Also called Straight Arrow Publishing Co* ***(G-12210)***
Mens Journal LLC 212 484-1616
1290 Ave Of The Americas New York (10104) ***(G-11225)***
Mentholatum Company (HQ) 716 677-2500
707 Sterling Dr Orchard Park (14127) ***(G-13284)***
Menu Solutions Inc 718 575-5160
4510 White Plains Rd Bronx (10470) ***(G-1391)***
Meopta USA Inc 631 436-5900
50 Davids Dr Hauppauge (11788) ***(G-6131)***
Mep Alaska LLC 646 535-9005
3619 Bedford Ave Apt 4e Brooklyn (11210) ***(G-2297)***
Mer Gems Corp 212 714-9129
62 W 47th St Ste 614 New York (10036) ***(G-11226)***
Merb LLC 631 393-3621
140 Carolyn Blvd Farmingdale (11735) ***(G-5048)***
Mercer Milling Co 315 701-1334
4698 Crossroads Park Dr Liverpool (13088) ***(G-7535)***
Mercer Rubber Co 631 348-0282
350 Rabro Dr Hauppauge (11788) ***(G-6132)***
Mercer's Dairy, Boonville *Also called Quality Dairy Farms Inc* ***(G-1168)***
Merchandiser Inc 315 462-6411
70 Stephens St Clifton Springs (14432) ***(G-3714)***
Merchant Publishing Inc 212 691-6666
34 W 13th St Bsmt New York (10011) ***(G-11227)***

ALPHABETIC SECTION — Metro Millwork, North Salem

Merco Hackensack Inc 845 357-3699
  201 Route 59 Ste D2 Hillburn (10931) *(G-6416)*
MERCO TAPE, Hillburn *Also called Merco Hackensack Inc (G-6416)*
Mercury Apparel, West Nyack *Also called Mainly Monograms Inc (G-16921)*
Mercury Envelope Co Inc 516 678-6744
  100 Merrick Rd Ste 204e Rockville Centre (11570) *(G-14795)*
Mercury Envelope Printing, Rockville Centre *Also called Mercury Envelope Co Inc (G-14795)*
Mercury Lock and Door Service 718 542-7048
  529 C Wortham St Bronx (10474) *(G-1392)*
Mercury Paint Corporation (PA) 718 469-8787
  4808 Farragut Rd Brooklyn (11203) *(G-2298)*
Mercury Pen Company Inc 518 899-9653
  245 Eastline Rd Ballston Lake (12019) *(G-583)*
Mercury Plastics Corp 718 498-5400
  989 Utica Ave 995 Brooklyn (11203) *(G-2299)*
Mercury Print Productions Inc (PA) 585 458-7900
  2332 Innovation Way 4 Rochester (14624) *(G-14504)*
Meredith Corporate Solutions, New York *Also called Meredith Corporation (G-11229)*
Meredith Corporation 212 557-6600
  125 Park Ave Fl 20 New York (10017) *(G-11228)*
Meredith Corporation 212 499-2000
  805 3rd Ave Fl 22 New York (10022) *(G-11229)*
Meredith Corporation 515 284-2157
  805 3rd Ave Fl 29 New York (10022) *(G-11230)*
Meredith Hispanic Ventures, New York *Also called Meredith Corporation (G-11230)*
Mergence Studios Ltd 212 288-5616
  135 Ricefield Ln Hauppauge (11788) *(G-6133)*
Mergent Inc 212 413-7700
  444 Madison Ave Ste 502 New York (10022) *(G-11231)*
Meridian Manufacturing Inc 518 885-0450
  27 Kent St Ste 103a Ballston Spa (12020) *(G-602)*
Meridian Technologies Inc 516 285-1000
  700 Elmont Rd Elmont (11003) *(G-4724)*
Merit Electronic Design Co Inc 631 667-9699
  190 Rodeo Dr Edgewood (11717) *(G-4606)*
Meritool LLC 716 699-6005
  5 Park Ave Ste 1 Ellicottville (14731) *(G-4642)*
Merkos Bookstore, Brooklyn *Also called Merkos LInyonei Chinuch Inc (G-2300)*
Merkos LInyonei Chinuch Inc 718 778-0226
  291 Kingston Ave Brooklyn (11213) *(G-2300)*
Merlin Printing Inc 631 842-6666
  215 Dixon Ave Amityville (11701) *(G-312)*
Merola Sales Company Inc 800 963-7652
  7308 88th St Glendale (11385) *(G-5658)*
Merrill Communications, New York *Also called Merrill New York Company Inc (G-11235)*
Merrill Communications LLC 212 620-5600
  1345 Ave Of The Amrcs 1 New York (10105) *(G-11232)*
Merrill Corporation 917 934-7300
  25 W 45th St Fl 10 New York (10036) *(G-11233)*
Merrill Corporation Inc 212 620-5600
  1345 Ave Of The Ave Fl 17 New York (10105) *(G-11234)*
Merrill New York Company Inc 212 229-6500
  246 W 54th St New York (10019) *(G-11235)*
Merrill Press, Buffalo *Also called Complemar Print LLC (G-2884)*
Merrimac Leasing, Johnstown *Also called Lee Dyeing Company NC Inc (G-7118)*
Merritt Estate Winery Inc 716 965-4800
  2264 King Rd Forestville (14062) *(G-5334)*
Merritt Machinery LLC 716 434-5558
  10 Simonds St Lockport (14094) *(G-7599)*
Meryl Diamond Ltd (PA) 212 730-0333
  1375 Broadway Fl 9 New York (10018) *(G-11236)*
Merz Metal & Machine Corp 716 893-7786
  237 Chelsea Pl Buffalo (14211) *(G-3062)*
Merzon Leather Co Inc 718 782-6260
  810 Humboldt St Ste 2 Brooklyn (11222) *(G-2301)*
Mesh LLC 646 839-7000
  350 5th Ave Lbby 9 New York (10118) *(G-11237)*
Meskita Lifestyle Brands LLC 212 695-5054
  336 W 37th St New York (10018) *(G-11238)*
Mesoblast Inc 212 880-2060
  505 5th Ave Fl 3 New York (10017) *(G-11239)*
Mesorah Publications Ltd 718 921-9000
  4401 2nd Ave Brooklyn (11232) *(G-2302)*
Messenger Post Media, Canandaigua *Also called Wolfe Publications Inc (G-3360)*
Messenger Press 518 885-9231
  1826 Amsterdam Rd Ballston Spa (12020) *(G-603)*
Messex Group Inc 646 229-2582
  244 5th Ave Ste D256 New York (10001) *(G-11240)*
Mestel Brothers Stairs & Rails 516 496-4127
  11 Gary Rd Ste 102 Syosset (11791) *(G-15828)*
Met Weld International LLC 518 765-2318
  5727 Ostrander Rd Altamont (12009) *(G-210)*
Meta Pharmacy Systems Inc 516 488-6189
  401 Franklin Ave Ste 106 Garden City (11530) *(G-5522)*
Meta-Therm Corp 914 697-4840
  70 W Red Oak Ln White Plains (10604) *(G-17137)*
Metadure Defense & SEC LLC 631 249-2141
  165 Gazza Blvd Farmingdale (11735) *(G-5049)*
Metadure Parts & Sales Inc 631 249-2141
  165 Gazza Blvd Farmingdale (11735) *(G-5050)*

Metal Cladding Inc 716 434-5513
  230 S Niagara St Lockport (14094) *(G-7600)*
Metal Coated Fibers Inc 518 280-8514
  679 Mariaville Rd Schenectady (12306) *(G-15278)*
Metal Concepts 845 592-1863
  9 Hanna Ln 12 Beacon (12508) *(G-788)*
Metal Container Corporation 845 567-1500
  1000 Breunig Rd New Windsor (12553) *(G-8943)*
Metal Crafts Inc 718 443-3333
  650 Berriman St Brooklyn (11208) *(G-2303)*
Metal Dynamics Intl Corp 631 231-1153
  25 Corporate Dr Hauppauge (11788) *(G-6134)*
Metal Fab LLC 607 775-3200
  13 Spud Ln Binghamton (13904) *(G-936)*
Metal Finishing Supply Inc 315 655-8068
  6032 Nelson Rd Canastota (13032) *(G-3369)*
Metal Improvement Company LLC 631 567-2610
  210 Candlewood Rd Bay Shore (11706) *(G-717)*
Metal Improvement Company LLC 607 533-7000
  131 Woodsedge Dr Lansing (14882) *(G-7349)*
Metal Man Restoration 914 662-4218
  254 E 3rd St Fl 1 Mount Vernon (10553) *(G-8704)*
Metal Man Services, Watertown *Also called Kenal Services Corp (G-16657)*
Metal Parts Manufacturing Inc 315 831-2530
  9498 State Route 12 Remsen (13438) *(G-14041)*
Metal Products Intl LLC 716 215-1930
  7510 Porter Rd Ste 4 Niagara Falls (14304) *(G-12846)*
Metal Solutions Inc 315 732-6271
  1821 Broad St Ste 5 Utica (13501) *(G-16347)*
Metal Stampings, Honeoye Falls *Also called Stever-Locke Industries Inc (G-6538)*
Metal Works of NY Inc 718 525-9440
  11603 Merrick Blvd Jamaica (11434) *(G-6930)*
Metalcraft By N Barzel, Brooklyn *Also called Metal Crafts Inc (G-2303)*
Metalcraft Marine Us Inc 315 501-4015
  583 E Broadway St Cape Vincent (13618) *(G-3384)*
Metalico Aluminum Recovery Inc 315 463-9292
  6223 Thompson Rd Syracuse (13206) *(G-15986)*
Metallic Ladder Mfg Corp 716 358-6201
  41 S Washington St Randolph (14772) *(G-14016)*
Metalline Fire Door Co Inc (PA) 718 583-2320
  4110 Park Ave Bronx (10457) *(G-1393)*
Metallized Carbon Corporation (PA) 914 941-3738
  19 S Water St Ossining (10562) *(G-13323)*
Metalocke Industries Inc 718 267-9200
  3202 57th St Woodside (11377) *(G-17337)*
Metals Building Products 844 638-2527
  5005 Veterans Mem Hwy Holbrook (11741) *(G-6462)*
Metalsmith Inc 631 467-1500
  1340 Lincoln Ave Ste 13 Holbrook (11741) *(G-6463)*
Metalworks Inc 718 319-0011
  1303 Herschell St Bronx (10461) *(G-1394)*
Metavac LLC 631 207-2344
  4000 Point St Holtsville (11742) *(G-6504)*
Metcar Products, Ossining *Also called Metallized Carbon Corporation (G-13323)*
Meteor Express Inc 718 551-9177
  16801 Rockaway Blvd # 202 Jamaica (11434) *(G-6931)*
Methods Tooling & Mfg Inc 845 246-7100
  635 Glasco Tpke Mount Marion (12456) *(G-8651)*
Methodsourcing Corp 914 217-7276
  9 W Main St Elmsford (10523) *(G-4765)*
Metpak Inc 917 309-0196
  320 Roebling St Ste 601 Brooklyn (11211) *(G-2304)*
Metpar Corp 516 333-2600
  95 State St Westbury (11590) *(G-17011)*
Metro Center Western New York, Buffalo *Also called William S Hein & Co Inc (G-3256)*
Metro City Group Inc 516 781-2500
  2283 Bellmore Ave Bellmore (11710) *(G-818)*
Metro Creative Graphics Inc (PA) 212 947-5100
  519 8th Ave Fl 18 New York (10018) *(G-11241)*
Metro Door Inc (HQ) 631 277-6490
  3500 Sunrise Hwy Great River (11739) *(G-5852)*
Metro Door A Cintas Company, Great River *Also called Metro Door Inc (G-5852)*
Metro Duct Systems Inc 718 278-4294
  1219 Astoria Blvd Apt 2 Long Island City (11102) *(G-7810)*
Metro Dynmc Scntific Instr Lab 631 842-4300
  80 Ralph Ave Copiague (11726) *(G-3914)*
Metro Group Inc (PA) 718 392-3616
  5023 23rd St Long Island City (11101) *(G-7811)*
Metro Group Inc 716 434-4055
  8 South St Lockport (14094) *(G-7601)*
Metro Grouping, Long Island City *Also called Metro Group Inc (G-7811)*
Metro Kitchens Corp 718 434-1166
  1040 E 45th St Brooklyn (11203) *(G-2305)*
Metro Lining Company 718 383-2700
  68 Java St Brooklyn (11222) *(G-2306)*
Metro Lube (PA) 718 947-1167
  9110 Metropolitan Ave Rego Park (11374) *(G-14036)*
Metro Machining & Fabricating 718 545-0104
  3234 61st St Woodside (11377) *(G-17338)*
Metro Mattress Corp 716 205-2300
  2212 Military Rd Niagara Falls (14304) *(G-12847)*
Metro Millwork, North Salem *Also called Metropolitan Fine Mllwk Corp (G-12939)*

(PA)=Parent Co (HQ)=Headquarters (DH)=Div Headquarters

Metro Nespaper, New York *Also called Seabay Media Holdings LLC* ***(G-12009)***
Metro New York, New York *Also called Sb New York Inc* ***(G-11980)***
Metro Service Center, Elmsford *Also called Westinghouse A Brake Tech Corp* ***(G-4793)***
Metro Storage Center, Getzville *Also called William S Hein & Co Inc* ***(G-5606)***
Metro Tel Communications, Staten Island *Also called I D Tel Corp* ***(G-15685)***
Metrofab Pipe Incorporated....516 349-7373
15 Fairchild Ct Plainview (11803) ***(G-13619)***
Metropltan Data Sltons MGT Inc....516 586-5520
279 Conklin St Farmingdale (11735) ***(G-5051)***
Metropolis Magazine, New York *Also called Bellerophon Publications Inc* ***(G-9351)***
Metropolitan Fine Mllwk Corp....914 669-4900
230 Hardscrabble Rd North Salem (10560) ***(G-12939)***
Metropolitan Granite & MBL Inc....585 342-7020
860 Maple St Ste 100 Rochester (14611) ***(G-14505)***
Metropolitan Packaging, Brooklyn *Also called Metro Lining Company* ***(G-2306)***
Metropolitan Packg Mfg Corp....718 383-2700
68 Java St Brooklyn (11222) ***(G-2307)***
Metropolitan Sign & Riggin....718 231-0010
330 Casanova St Bronx (10474) ***(G-1395)***
Metropolitan Signs Inc (PA)....315 638-1448
3760 Patchett Rd Baldwinsville (13027) ***(G-572)***
Metrosource Publishing Inc....212 691-5127
111 W 19th St Fl 6 New York (10011) ***(G-11242)***
Mettle Concept Inc....888 501-0680
545 8th Ave Rm 401 New York (10018) ***(G-11243)***
Mettler-Toledo Inc....607 257-6000
5 Barr Rd Ithaca (14850) ***(G-6860)***
Mettowee Lumber & Plastics Co....518 642-1100
82 Church St Granville (12832) ***(G-5777)***
Metzger Speciality Brands....212 957-0055
161 W 54th St Apt 802 New York (10019) ***(G-11244)***
Mexico Independent Inc (PA)....315 963-3763
80 N Jefferson St Mexico (13114) ***(G-8396)***
Mexicone....315 591-1971
5775 Scenic Ave Mexico (13114) ***(G-8397)***
Mexicone Ice Cream, Mexico *Also called Mexicone* ***(G-8397)***
Meyco Products Inc (PA)....631 421-9800
1225 Walt Whitman Rd Melville (11747) ***(G-8336)***
Mezmeriz Inc....607 216-8140
33 Thornwood Dr Ste 100 Ithaca (14850) ***(G-6861)***
Mf Digital, Deer Park *Also called Formats Unlimited Inc* ***(G-4144)***
Mg Concepts (de) LLC....631 608-8090
185 Dixon Ave Amityville (11701) ***(G-313)***
Mg Imaging....212 704-4073
229 W 28th St Rm 300 New York (10001) ***(G-11245)***
Mgd Brands Inc....516 545-0150
30 Commercial Ct Plainview (11803) ***(G-13620)***
Mgi, Hauppauge *Also called Mini Graphics Inc* ***(G-6139)***
Mgi, Northport *Also called Marketing Group International* ***(G-13016)***
Mgk Group Inc....212 989-2732
979 3rd Ave Ste 1811 New York (10022) ***(G-11246)***
MGM, Buffalo *Also called Tyson Deli Inc* ***(G-3228)***
Mgr Equipment Corp....516 239-3030
22 Gates Ave Inwood (11096) ***(G-6761)***
Mgs Buffalo, Buffalo *Also called Mgs Mfg Group Inc* ***(G-3063)***
Mgs Group, The, Rome *Also called MGS Manufacturing Inc* ***(G-14821)***
MGS Manufacturing Inc (PA)....315 337-3350
122 Otis St Rome (13441) ***(G-14821)***
Mgs Mfg Group Inc....716 684-9400
2400 Walden Ave Buffalo (14225) ***(G-3063)***
Mht Lighting, Staten Island *Also called North American Mfg Entps Inc* ***(G-15712)***
Miami Media LLC (HQ)....212 268-8600
72 Madison Ave Fl 11 New York (10016) ***(G-11247)***
Mib Industries Inc....718 497-2200
4805 Metro Ave Ste 1 Ridgewood (11385) ***(G-14114)***
Mibro Group....716 631-5713
4039 Genesee St Buffalo (14225) ***(G-3064)***
Mica America, Bay Shore *Also called Fenix Furniture Co* ***(G-700)***
Mica International Ltd....516 378-3400
126 Albany Ave Freeport (11520) ***(G-5413)***
Micatu Inc....888 705-8836
315 Daniel Zenker Dr # 202 Horseheads (14845) ***(G-6582)***
Micelli Chocalate Mold Co, West Babylon *Also called Sweet Tooth Enterprises LLC* ***(G-16835)***
Michael Anthony Jewelers LLC (HQ)....914 699-0000
115 S Macquesten Pkwy Mount Vernon (10550) ***(G-8705)***
Michael Benalt Inc....845 628-1008
100 Buckshollow Rd Mahopac (10541) ***(G-7997)***
Michael Bernstein Design Assoc....718 456-9277
361 Stagg St Fl 4 Brooklyn (11206) ***(G-2308)***
Michael Bondanza Inc....212 869-0043
10 E 38th St Fl 6 New York (10016) ***(G-11248)***
Michael Britt Inc....516 248-2010
89 Mineola Blvd Fl 1 Mineola (11501) ***(G-8525)***
Michael Feldman Inc....718 433-1700
3010 41st Ave Ste 3 Long Island City (11101) ***(G-7812)***
Michael Fiore Ltd....516 561-8238
126 E Fairview Ave Valley Stream (11580) ***(G-16413)***
Michael K Lennon Inc....631 288-5200
851 Riverhead Rd Westhampton Beach (11978) ***(G-17059)***
Michael Karp Music Inc....212 840-3285
59 W 71st St Apt 7a New York (10023) ***(G-11249)***
Michael Neuman, Rye *Also called Western Oil and Gas JV Inc* ***(G-15069)***
Michael P Mmarr....315 623-9380
1358 State Route 49 Constantia (13044) ***(G-3881)***
Michael Stuart Inc....718 821-0704
199 Cook St Brooklyn (11206) ***(G-2309)***
Michael Todd Stevens....585 436-9957
95 Mount Read Blvd # 125 Rochester (14611) ***(G-14506)***
Michael Vollbracht LLC....212 753-0123
57 W 57th St Ste 603 New York (10019) ***(G-11250)***
Michaelian & Kohlberg Inc....212 431-9009
225 E 59th St New York (10022) ***(G-11251)***
Michbi Doors Inc....631 231-9050
75 Emjay Blvd Brentwood (11717) ***(G-1192)***
Mick Radio Nuclear Instrument....718 597-3999
521 Homestead Ave Mount Vernon (10550) ***(G-8706)***
Mickelberry Communications Inc (PA)....212 832-0303
405 Park Ave New York (10022) ***(G-11252)***
Micosta Enterprises Inc....518 822-9708
3007 County Route 20 Hudson (12534) ***(G-6627)***
Micro Centric Corporation (PA)....800 573-1139
25 S Terminal Dr Plainview (11803) ***(G-13621)***
Micro Contacts Inc (PA)....516 433-4830
1 Enterprise Pl Unit E Hicksville (11801) ***(G-6371)***
Micro Contract Manufacturing....631 738-7874
119 Comac St Ronkonkoma (11779) ***(G-14941)***
Micro Essential Laboratory....718 338-3618
4224 Avenue H Brooklyn (11210) ***(G-2310)***
Micro Graphics, Lockport *Also called Jack J Florio Jr* ***(G-7595)***
Micro Instrument Corp....585 458-3150
1199 Emerson St Rochester (14606) ***(G-14507)***
Micro Photo Acoustics Inc....631 750-6035
105 Comac St Ronkonkoma (11779) ***(G-14942)***
Micro Powders Inc (PA)....914 332-6400
580 White Plains Rd # 400 Tarrytown (10591) ***(G-16097)***
Micro Publishing Inc....212 533-9180
71 W 23rd St Lbby A New York (10010) ***(G-11253)***
Micro Semicdtr Researches LLC (PA)....646 863-6070
310 W 52nd St Apt 12b New York (10019) ***(G-11254)***
Micro Systems Specialists Inc....845 677-6150
3280 Franklin Ave Fl 2 Millbrook (12545) ***(G-8476)***
Micro Threaded Products Inc....585 288-0080
325 Mount Read Blvd Ste 4 Rochester (14611) ***(G-14508)***
Micro-Tech Machine Inc....315 331-6671
301 W Shore Blvd Newark (14513) ***(G-12737)***
Microb Phase Services....518 877-8948
14 Nottingham Way S Clifton Park (12065) ***(G-3702)***
Microcad Trning Consulting Inc....617 923-0500
1110 Route 55 Ste 209 Lagrangeville (12540) ***(G-7256)***
Microcad Trning Consulting Inc....631 291-9484
77 Arkay Dr Ste C2 Hauppauge (11788) ***(G-6135)***
Microchip Technology Inc....631 233-3280
80 Arkay Dr Hauppauge (11788) ***(G-6136)***
Microchip Technology Inc....607 785-5992
3301 Country Club Rd Endicott (13760) ***(G-4819)***
Microera Printers Inc....585 783-1300
304 Whitney St Rochester (14606) ***(G-14509)***
Microfoam, Utica *Also called Idg LLC* ***(G-16341)***
Microgen Systems Inc....585 214-2426
150 Lucius Gordon Dr # 117 West Henrietta (14586) ***(G-16884)***
Micromem Technologies....212 672-1806
245 Park Ave Fl 24 New York (10167) ***(G-11255)***
Micromod Automation Inc....585 321-9200
3 Townline Cir Ste 4 Rochester (14623) ***(G-14510)***
Micromod Automtn & Contrls Inc....585 321-9209
3 Townline Cir Ste 4 Rochester (14623) ***(G-14511)***
Micromold Products Inc....914 969-2850
7 Odell Plz 133 Yonkers (10701) ***(G-17467)***
Micron Inds Rochester Inc....585 247-6130
31 Industrial Park Cir Rochester (14624) ***(G-14512)***
Micron Powder Industries LLC....718 851-0011
5114 Fort Hamilton Pkwy Brooklyn (11219) ***(G-2311)***
Micropage, New York *Also called Micro Publishing Inc* ***(G-11253)***
Micropen Division, Honeoye Falls *Also called Micropen Technologies Corp* ***(G-6535)***
Micropen Technologies Corp....585 624-2610
93 Papermill St Honeoye Falls (14472) ***(G-6535)***
Microsoft Corporation....585 240-6037
100 Corporate Woods # 240 Rochester (14623) ***(G-14513)***
Microsoft Corporation....914 323-2150
125 Westchester Ave White Plains (10601) ***(G-17138)***
Microsoft Corporation....212 245-2100
11 Times Sq Fl 9 New York (10036) ***(G-11256)***
Microsoft Corporation....516 380-1531
2929 Expressway Dr N # 300 Hauppauge (11749) ***(G-6137)***
Microstrategy Incorporated....888 537-8135
5 Penn Plz Ste 901 New York (10001) ***(G-11257)***
Microwave Circuit Tech Inc....631 845-1041
45 Central Dr Farmingdale (11735) ***(G-5052)***
Microwave Filter Company Inc (PA)....315 438-4700
6743 Kinne St East Syracuse (13057) ***(G-4550)***
Mid Atlantic Graphics Corp....631 345-3800
14 Ramsey Rd Shirley (11967) ***(G-15425)***

Mid Enterprise Inc 631 924-3933
809 Middle Country Rd Middle Island (11953) *(G-8407)*
Mid Hdson Wkshp For The Dsbled 845 471-3820
188 Washington St Poughkeepsie (12601) *(G-13915)*
Mid Hudson Plating Inc 845 849-1277
132 Smith St Poughkeepsie (12601) *(G-13916)*
Mid Island Die Cutting Corp 631 293-0180
77 Schmitt Blvd Farmingdale (11735) *(G-5053)*
Mid Island Group 631 293-0180
77 Schmitt Blvd Farmingdale (11735) *(G-5054)*
Mid-Hudson Concrete Pdts Inc 845 265-3141
3504 Route 9 Cold Spring (10516) *(G-3763)*
Mid-Island Bindery Inc 631 293-0180
77 Schmitt Blvd Farmingdale (11735) *(G-5055)*
Mid-State Ready Mix, Central Square *Also called Torrington Industries Inc (G-3518)*
Mid-York Press Inc 607 674-4491
2808 State Highway 80 Sherburne (13460) *(G-15393)*
Midas Mdici Group Holdings Inc (PA) 212 792-0920
445 Park Ave Frnt 5 New York (10022) *(G-11258)*
Midbury Industries Inc 516 868-0600
86 E Merrick Rd Freeport (11520) *(G-5414)*
Middle Ages Brewing Company 315 476-4250
120 Wilkinson St Ste 3 Syracuse (13204) *(G-15987)*
Middleby Corporation 631 226-6688
175 E Hoffman Ave Lindenhurst (11757) *(G-7472)*
Middletown Press (PA) 845 343-1895
20 W Main St 26 Middletown (10940) *(G-8451)*
Midgley Printing Corp 315 475-1864
433 W Onondaga St Ste B Syracuse (13202) *(G-15988)*
Midland Farms Inc (PA) 518 436-7038
375 Broadway Menands (12204) *(G-8376)*
Midland Machinery Co Inc 716 692-1200
101 Cranbrook Road Ext Exd Tonawanda (14150) *(G-16181)*
Midstate Printing Corp 315 475-4101
230 Ainsley Dr Syracuse (13210) *(G-15989)*
Midstate Spring Inc 315 437-2623
4054 New Court Ave Syracuse (13206) *(G-15990)*
Midura Jewels Inc 213 265-8090
36 W 47th St Ste 809i New York (10036) *(G-11259)*
Midway News Inc 212 628-3009
302 E 86th St New York (10028) *(G-11260)*
Midwood Signs & Design Inc 718 499-9041
202 28th St Brooklyn (11232) *(G-2312)*
Miggins Screw Products Inc 845 279-2307
66 Putnam Ave Brewster (10509) *(G-1224)*
Mighty Quinns Barbeque LLC 973 777-8340
103 2nd Ave Frnt 1 New York (10003) *(G-11261)*
Mignon Group, The, New York *Also called Lm Mignon LLC (G-11017)*
Miguelina Inc 212 925-0320
325 W 37th St Fl 2 New York (10018) *(G-11262)*
Mikael Aghal LLC 212 596-4010
49 W 38th St Fl 4 New York (10018) *(G-11263)*
Mikam Graphics LLC 212 684-9393
1440 Broadway Fl 22 New York (10018) *(G-11264)*
Mike Wilke 585 482-5230
851 Rolins Run Webster (14580) *(G-16727)*
Mike's Custom Cabinets, Constantia *Also called Michael P Mmarr (G-3881)*
Miken Companies Inc 716 668-6311
75 Boxwood Ln Buffalo (14227) *(G-3065)*
Mil & Mir Steel Products Co 718 328-7596
1210 Randall Ave Bronx (10474) *(G-1396)*
Mil-Spec Industries Corp 516 625-5787
42 Herb Hill Rd Glen Cove (11542) *(G-5621)*
Mil-Spec. Enterprises, Brooklyn *Also called Carter Enterprises LLC (G-1760)*
Milaaya Embroideries, New York *Also called Milaaya Inc (G-11265)*
Milaaya Inc 212 764-6386
566 Fashion Ave Rm 805 New York (10018) *(G-11265)*
Milan Accessories, New York *Also called AKOS Group Ltd (G-9067)*
Milan Provision Co Inc 718 899-7678
10815 Roosevelt Ave Corona (11368) *(G-4003)*
Milanese Commercial Door LLC 518 658-0398
28 Taylor Ave Berlin (12022) *(G-857)*
Milano Granite and Marble Corp 718 477-7200
3521 Victory Blvd Staten Island (10314) *(G-15706)*
Milburn Printing, Bohemia *Also called Mpe Graphics Inc (G-1106)*
Miles Alexander LLC 516 937-5262
485 S Broadway Ste 11 Hicksville (11801) *(G-6372)*
Miles Machine Inc 716 484-6026
85 Jones And Gifford Ave Jamestown (14701) *(G-7020)*
Milestone Construction Corp 718 459-8500
9229 Queens Blvd Ste C2 Rego Park (11374) *(G-14037)*
Milex Precision Inc 631 595-2393
66 S 2nd St Ste G Bay Shore (11706) *(G-718)*
Milgo Industrial, Brooklyn *Also called M B C Metal Inc (G-2247)*
Milgo Industrial Inc (PA) 718 388-6476
68 Lombardy St Brooklyn (11222) *(G-2313)*
Milgo Industrial Inc 718 387-0406
514 Varick Ave Brooklyn (11222) *(G-2314)*
Milgo/Bufkin, Brooklyn *Also called Milgo Industrial Inc (G-2313)*
Mill Services, Cobleskill *Also called Efj Inc (G-3737)*
Mill, The, Corning *Also called Ryers Creek Corp (G-3980)*
Mill-Max Mfg Corp 516 922-6000
190 Pine Hollow Rd Oyster Bay (11771) *(G-13371)*
Milla Global Inc 516 488-3601
1301 Metropolitan Ave Brooklyn (11237) *(G-2315)*
Millbrook Family Eyecare 845 677-5012
61 Front St Millbrook (12545) *(G-8477)*
Millbrook Vineyard, Millbrook *Also called Millbrook Winery Inc (G-8478)*
Millbrook Winery Inc 845 677-8383
26 Wing Rd Millbrook (12545) *(G-8478)*
Millco Woodworking LLC 585 526-6844
1710 Railroad Pl Hall (14463) *(G-5917)*
Millcraft Paper Company 716 856-5135
99 Bud Mil Dr Buffalo (14206) *(G-3066)*
Millennium Antenna Corp 315 798-9374
1001 Broad St Ste 401 Utica (13501) *(G-16348)*
Millennium Medical Publishing 212 995-2211
611 Broadway Rm 310 New York (10012) *(G-11266)*
Millennium Productions Inc 212 944-6203
265 W 37th St 11 New York (10018) *(G-11267)*
Millennium Rmnfctred Toner Inc 718 585-9887
7 Bruckner Blvd Bronx (10454) *(G-1397)*
Millennium Signs & Display Inc 516 292-8000
90 W Graham Ave Hempstead (11550) *(G-6280)*
Millennium Stl Rack Rntals Inc (PA) 212 594-2190
253 Bond St Brooklyn (11217) *(G-2316)*
Miller & Berkowitz Ltd 212 244-5459
345 7th Ave Fl 20 New York (10001) *(G-11268)*
Miller & Veit Inc 212 247-2275
22 W 48th St Ste 703 New York (10036) *(G-11269)*
Miller & Weber Inc 718 821-7110
507 Davie St Westbury (11590) *(G-17012)*
Miller Blaker Inc 718 665-3930
620 E 132nd St Bronx (10454) *(G-1398)*
Miller Enterprises CNY Inc 315 682-4999
131 W Seneca St Ste B Manlius (13104) *(G-8075)*
Miller Mechanical Services Inc 518 792-0430
55-57 Walnut St Glens Falls (12801) *(G-5690)*
Miller Metal Fabricating Inc 585 359-3400
315 Commerce Dr Rochester (14623) *(G-14514)*
Miller Mohr Display Inc 631 941-2769
12 Technology Dr Unit 6 East Setauket (11733) *(G-4487)*
Miller Printing & Litho Inc 518 842-0001
97 Guy Park Ave Amsterdam (12010) *(G-356)*
Miller Technology Inc 631 694-2224
61 Gazza Blvd Farmingdale (11735) *(G-5056)*
Miller Truck Rental, Scottsville *Also called Jack W Miller (G-15337)*
Miller's Ready Mix, Gloversville *Also called Stephen Miller Gen Contrs Inc (G-5723)*
Millercoors LLC 585 385-0670
1000 Pittsford Victor Rd Pittsford (14534) *(G-13570)*
Millers Bulk Food and Bakery 585 798-9700
10858 Ridge Rd Medina (14103) *(G-8277)*
Millers Millworks Inc 585 494-1420
29 N Lake Ave Bergen (14416) *(G-850)*
Millers Presentation Furniture, Bergen *Also called Millers Millworks Inc (G-850)*
Millhouse 1889 LLC 631 259-4777
24 Woodbine Ave Ste 8 Northport (11768) *(G-13017)*
Milli Home, New York *Also called Global Resources Sg Inc (G-10320)*
Milligan & Higgins Div, Johnstown *Also called Hudson Industries Corporation (G-7115)*
Milliore Fashion Inc 212 302-0001
250 W 39th St Rm 506 New York (10018) *(G-11270)*
Millivac Instruments Inc 518 355-8300
2818 Curry Rd Schenectady (12303) *(G-15279)*
Millrock Technology Inc 845 339-5700
39 Kieffer Ln Ste 2 Kingston (12401) *(G-7201)*
Mills, William J & Company, Greenport *Also called 125-127 Main Street Corp (G-5876)*
Millwood Inc 518 233-1475
430 Hudson River Rd Waterford (12188) *(G-16614)*
Millwright Wdwrk Installetion 631 587-2635
991 Peconic Ave West Babylon (11704) *(G-16811)*
Milmar Food Group, Goshen *Also called Juno Chefs (G-5735)*
Milmar Food Group II LLC 845 294-5400
1 6 1/2 Station Rd Goshen (10924) *(G-5738)*
Milne Mfg Inc 716 772-2536
8411 State St Gasport (14067) *(G-5559)*
Milnot Holding Corporation 518 839-0300
1 Nutritious Pl Amsterdam (12010) *(G-357)*
Milso Industries Inc 631 234-1133
25 Engineers Rd Hauppauge (11788) *(G-6138)*
Milton Merl & Associates Inc 212 634-9292
647 W 174th St Bsmt B New York (10033) *(G-11271)*
Miltons of New York Inc 212 997-3359
110 W 40th St Rm 1001 New York (10018) *(G-11272)*
Milward Alloys Inc 716 434-5536
500 Mill St Lockport (14094) *(G-7602)*
Mimeocom Inc (PA) 212 847-3000
3 Park Ave Fl 22 New York (10016) *(G-11273)*
Mimi So International LLC 212 300-8600
22 W 48th St Ste 902 New York (10036) *(G-11274)*
Mimi So New York, New York *Also called Mimi So International LLC (G-11274)*
Min Ho Designs Inc 212 838-3667
425 Madison Ave Rm 1703 New York (10017) *(G-11275)*
Min New York, New York *Also called Salonclick LLC (G-11959)*

ALPHABETIC

Min Run (usa) Inc....646 331-1018
14 West Dr Port Washington (11050) ***(G-13845)***
Min-Max Machine Ltd....631 585-4378
1971 Pond Rd Ronkonkoma (11779) ***(G-14943)***
Mind Designs Inc (PA)....631 563-3644
5 Gregory Ct Farmingville (11738) ***(G-5160)***
Mind Music Production, Valley Stream *Also called Musical Links Production LLC* ***(G-16414)***
Mindbodygreen LLC....347 529-6952
45 Main St Ste 422 Brooklyn (11201) ***(G-2317)***
Mineo & Sapio Meats Inc....716 884-2398
410 Connecticut St Buffalo (14213) ***(G-3067)***
Mineralbious Corp....516 498-9715
46 Graywood Rd Port Washington (11050) ***(G-13846)***
Minerals Technologies Inc (PA)....212 878-1800
622 3rd Ave Fl 38 New York (10017) ***(G-11276)***
Minero & Sapio Sausage, Buffalo *Also called Mineo & Sapio Meats Inc* ***(G-3067)***
Mines Press Inc....914 788-1800
231 Croton Ave Cortlandt Manor (10567) ***(G-4052)***
Ming Pao (new York) Inc....212 334-2220
265 Canal St Ste 403 New York (10013) ***(G-11277)***
Ming Pao (new York) Inc (HQ)....718 786-2888
4331 33rd St Long Island City (11101) ***(G-7813)***
Ming Pay N Y, Long Island City *Also called Ming Pao (new York) Inc* ***(G-7813)***
Mini Circuits, Brooklyn *Also called Scientific Components Corp* ***(G-2539)***
Mini Circuits Lab, Deer Park *Also called Scientific Components Corp* ***(G-4207)***
Mini Graphics Inc....516 223-6464
140 Commerce Dr Hauppauge (11788) ***(G-6139)***
Mini-Circuits, Brooklyn *Also called Scientific Components Corp* ***(G-2538)***
Mini-Circuits Fort Wayne LLC....718 934-4500
13 Neptune Ave Brooklyn (11235) ***(G-2318)***
Mini-Max Dntl Repr Eqpmnts Inc....631 242-0322
25 W Jefryn Blvd Ste B Deer Park (11729) ***(G-4174)***
Minico Industries Inc....631 595-1455
66a S 2nd St Ste A Bay Shore (11706) ***(G-719)***
Minimal USA, New York *Also called Canova Inc* ***(G-9514)***
Minimill Technologies Inc....315 692-4557
5792 Widewaters Pkwy # 1 Syracuse (13214) ***(G-15991)***
Minisink Rubber, Warwick *Also called Mechanical Rubber Pdts Co Inc* ***(G-16594)***
Minitec Framing Systems LLC....585 924-4690
100 Rawson Rd Ste 228 Victor (14564) ***(G-16491)***
Mink Mart Inc....212 868-2785
345 7th Ave Fl 9 New York (10001) ***(G-11278)***
Minority Reporter Inc (PA)....585 225-3628
19 Borrowdale Dr Rochester (14626) ***(G-14515)***
Mint-X Products Corporation....877 646-8224
2048 119th St College Point (11356) ***(G-3798)***
Minute Man Printing Company, White Plains *Also called Garrett J Cronin* ***(G-17111)***
Minuteman Press, Manhasset *Also called Mdr Printing Corp* ***(G-8062)***
Minuteman Press, Hewlett *Also called Torsaf Printers Inc* ***(G-6314)***
Minuteman Press, Glen Oaks *Also called Wynco Press One Inc* ***(G-5641)***
Minuteman Press, Huntington *Also called J A T Printing Inc* ***(G-6664)***
Minuteman Press, Deer Park *Also called L & K Graphics Inc* ***(G-4161)***
Minuteman Press, Liverpool *Also called Seaboard Graphic Services LLC* ***(G-7547)***
Minuteman Press, Hauppauge *Also called Huckleberry Inc* ***(G-6096)***
Minuteman Press, Bellerose *Also called Leigh Scott Enterprises Inc* ***(G-810)***
Minuteman Press, Adams *Also called Benjamin Printing Inc* ***(G-2)***
Minuteman Press, Rockville Centre *Also called Graphic Fabrications Inc* ***(G-14791)***
Minuteman Press, Elmsford *Also called Cronin Enterprises Inc* ***(G-4745)***
Minuteman Press, Rochester *Also called Baum Christine and John Corp* ***(G-14224)***
Minuteman Press, Selden *Also called Datorib Inc* ***(G-15351)***
Minuteman Press, Rochester *Also called Multiple Imprssons of Rchester* ***(G-14525)***
Minuteman Press, Fairport *Also called Bernard Hall* ***(G-4848)***
Minuteman Press, Farmingdale *Also called J P Printing Inc* ***(G-5015)***
Minuteman Press, Bayside *Also called Alexander Polakovich* ***(G-766)***
Minuteman Press, Merrick *Also called Jon Lyn Ink Inc* ***(G-8386)***
Minuteman Press, East Northport *Also called Loudon Ltd* ***(G-4441)***
Minuteman Press, Port Washington *Also called Sammba Printing Inc* ***(G-13862)***
Minuteman Press Inc....845 623-2277
121 W Nyack Rd Ste 3 Nanuet (10954) ***(G-8759)***
Minuteman Press Intl Inc....718 343-5440
24814 Union Tpke Jamaica (11426) ***(G-6932)***
Minutemen Precsn McHning Tool....631 467-4900
135 Raynor Ave Ronkonkoma (11779) ***(G-14944)***
Miny Group Inc....212 925-6722
148 Lafayette St Fl 2 New York (10013) ***(G-11279)***
Minyanville Media Inc....212 991-6200
708 3rd Ave Fl 6 New York (10017) ***(G-11280)***
Mip, Halesite *Also called Manufacturers Indexing Pdts* ***(G-5905)***
Mirage Moulding & Supply, Farmingdale *Also called Mirage Moulding Mfg Inc* ***(G-5057)***
Mirage Moulding Mfg Inc....631 843-6168
160 Milbar Blvd Farmingdale (11735) ***(G-5057)***
Mirandy Products Ltd....516 489-6800
1078 Grand Ave South Hempstead (11550) ***(G-15530)***
Mirion Tech Conax Nuclear Inc....716 681-1973
402 Sonwil Dr Buffalo (14225) ***(G-3068)***
Mirion Tech Imaging LLC....607 562-4300
315 Daniel Zenker Dr Horseheads (14845) ***(G-6583)***
Mirion Tech Imging Systems Div, Horseheads *Also called Mirion Tech Imaging LLC* ***(G-6583)***
Mirion Technologies Ist Corp (HQ)....607 562-4300
315 Daniel Zenker Dr # 204 Horseheads (14845) ***(G-6584)***
Miroddi Imaging Inc (PA)....516 624-6898
27 Centre View Dr Oyster Bay (11771) ***(G-13372)***
Mirror-Tech Manufacturing Co....914 965-1232
286 Nepperhan Ave Yonkers (10701) ***(G-17468)***
Mirrorlite Superscript, Peekskill *Also called Hudson Mirror LLC* ***(G-13479)***
Miscellnous Ir Fabricators Inc....518 355-1822
1404 Dunnsville Rd Schenectady (12306) ***(G-15280)***
Mishpacha Magazine Inc....718 686-9339
5809 16th Ave Brooklyn (11204) ***(G-2319)***
Mison Concepts Inc....516 933-8000
485 S Broadway Ste 33 Hicksville (11801) ***(G-6373)***
Misonix Inc (PA)....631 694-9555
1938 New Hwy Farmingdale (11735) ***(G-5058)***
Miss Grimble Associates Inc....718 665-2253
909 E 135th St Bronx (10454) ***(G-1399)***
Miss Group (PA)....212 391-2535
1410 Broadway Rm 703 New York (10018) ***(G-11281)***
Miss Group, The, New York *Also called MISS Sportswear Inc* ***(G-11283)***
Miss Group, The, Brooklyn *Also called MISS Sportswear Inc* ***(G-2321)***
Miss Jessies LLC....718 643-9016
441 Broadway Fl 2 New York (10013) ***(G-11282)***
Miss Jessies Products, New York *Also called Miss Jessies LLC* ***(G-11282)***
MISS Sportswear Inc....212 391-2535
117 9th St Brooklyn (11215) ***(G-2320)***
MISS Sportswear Inc (PA)....212 391-2535
1410 Broadway Rm 703 New York (10018) ***(G-11283)***
MISS Sportswear Inc....718 369-6012
117 9th St Brooklyn (11215) ***(G-2321)***
Mission Crane Service Inc (PA)....718 937-3333
4700 33rd St Long Island City (11101) ***(G-7814)***
Mission Critical Energy Inc....716 276-8465
1801 N French Rd Getzville (14068) ***(G-5600)***
Mission Systems & Training, Owego *Also called Lockheed Martin Corporation* ***(G-13355)***
Missiontex Inc....718 532-9053
236 Greenpoint Ave Ste 12 Brooklyn (11222) ***(G-2322)***
Mistdoda Inc (HQ)....919 735-7111
261 5th Ave Fl 25 New York (10016) ***(G-11284)***
Mitchell Electronics Corp....914 699-3800
85 W Grand St Mount Vernon (10552) ***(G-8707)***
Mitchell Machine Tool LLC....585 254-7520
190 Murray St Rochester (14606) ***(G-14516)***
Mitchell Prtg & Mailing Inc (PA)....315 343-3531
125 E 1st St 129 Oswego (13126) ***(G-13335)***
Mitchell's Speedway Press, Oswego *Also called Speedway Press Inc* ***(G-13341)***
Mitegen LLC....607 266-8877
95 Brown Rd Ste 1034 Ithaca (14850) ***(G-6862)***
Mitsubishi Elc Pwr Pdts Inc....516 962-2813
55 Marcus Dr Melville (11747) ***(G-8337)***
Mitsui Chemicals America Inc (HQ)....914 253-0777
800 Westchester Ave N607 Rye Brook (10573) ***(G-15072)***
Mitten Manufacturing Inc....315 437-7564
5960 Court Street Rd Syracuse (13206) ***(G-15992)***
Mixture Screen Printing....845 561-2857
1607 Route 300 100 Newburgh (12550) ***(G-12767)***
Mizkan America Inc....585 765-9171
247 West Ave Lyndonville (14098) ***(G-7968)***
Mizkan Americas Inc....585 798-5720
711 Park Ave Medina (14103) ***(G-8278)***
Mizkan Americas Inc....315 483-6944
7673 Sodus Center Rd Sodus (14551) ***(G-15503)***
MJB Printing Corp....631 581-0177
280 Islip Ave Islip (11751) ***(G-6811)***
Mjj Brilliant, New York *Also called Brilliant Jewelers/Mjj Inc* ***(G-9462)***
Mjk Cutting Inc....718 384-7613
117 9th St Brooklyn (11215) ***(G-2323)***
Mjk Enterprises LLC....917 653-9042
34 35th St Brooklyn (11232) ***(G-2324)***
MJM Jewelry Corp (PA)....212 354-5014
29 W 38th St Rm 1601 New York (10018) ***(G-11285)***
MJM Jewelry Corp....718 596-1600
400 3rd Ave Brooklyn (11215) ***(G-2325)***
Mjs Woodworking, Bohemia *Also called J Percoco Industries Inc* ***(G-1079)***
Mkj Communications Corp....212 206-0072
174 Hudson St Fl 2 New York (10013) ***(G-11286)***
Mks Instruments Inc....585 292-7472
100 Highpower Rd Rochester (14623) ***(G-14517)***
Mks Medical Electronics....585 292-7400
100 Highpower Rd Rochester (14623) ***(G-14518)***
Mkt329 Inc....631 249-5500
565 Broadhollow Rd Ste 5 Farmingdale (11735) ***(G-5059)***
MLS Sales....516 681-2736
226 10th St Bethpage (11714) ***(G-875)***
Mm of East Aurora LLC....716 651-9663
3801 Harlem Rd Buffalo (14215) ***(G-3069)***
MMC Enterprises Corp....800 435-1088
175 Commerce Dr Ste E Hauppauge (11788) ***(G-6140)***

ALPHABETIC

MMC Magnetics Corp 631 435-9888
175 Commerce Dr Ste E Hauppauge (11788) ***(G-6141)***
Mml Software Ltd 631 941-1313
45 Research Way Ste 207 East Setauket (11733) ***(G-4488)***
Mmo Music Group Inc 914 592-1188
50 Executive Blvd Ste 236 Elmsford (10523) ***(G-4766)***
Mnm Service Distributors Inc 914 337-5268
1 Greystone Cir Bronxville (10708) ***(G-1501)***
Mnn Holding Company LLC 404 558-5251
155 Water St Ste 616 Brooklyn (11201) ***(G-2326)***
MNS Fuel Corp 516 735-3835
2154 Pond Rd Ronkonkoma (11779) ***(G-14945)***
Mobile Data Systems Inc 631 360-3400
110 Lake Ave S Ste 35 Nesconset (11767) ***(G-8776)***
Mobile Fleet Inc (PA) 631 206-2920
10 Commerce Dr Hauppauge (11788) ***(G-6142)***
Mobile Hatch Inc 212 314-7300
555 W 18th St New York (10011) ***(G-11287)***
Mobile Media Inc (PA) 845 744-8080
24 Center St Pine Bush (12566) ***(G-13548)***
Mobile Mini Inc 315 732-4555
2222 Oriskany St W Ste 3 Utica (13502) ***(G-16349)***
Mobile Mini Inc 631 543-4900
1158 Jericho Tpke Commack (11725) ***(G-3838)***
Mobileapp Systems LLC 716 667-2780
4 Grand View Trl Buffalo (14217) ***(G-3070)***
Mod Printing, Islip *Also called MJB Printing Corp* ***(G-6811)***
Mod-A-Can Inc (PA) 516 931-8545
178 Miller Pl Hicksville (11801) ***(G-6374)***
Mod-Pac Corp (PA) 716 873-0640
1801 Elmwood Ave Ste 1 Buffalo (14207) ***(G-3071)***
Mod-Pac Corp 716 447-9013
1801 Elmwood Ave Ste 1 Buffalo (14207) ***(G-3072)***
Model Power, Farmingdale *Also called ATI Model Products Inc* ***(G-4946)***
Modern Art Foundry Inc 718 728-2030
1870 41st St Astoria (11105) ***(G-449)***
Modern Block LLC 315 923-7443
2440 Wyne Zandra Rose Vly Clyde (14433) ***(G-3729)***
Modern Cabinet Company Inc 845 473-4900
17 Van Kleeck Dr Poughkeepsie (12601) ***(G-13917)***
Modern Coating and Research 315 597-3517
400 E Main St Palmyra (14522) ***(G-13411)***
Modern Craft Bar Rest Equip, Lindenhurst *Also called Modern Craft Bar Rest Equip* ***(G-7473)***
Modern Craft Bar Rest Equip 631 226-5647
165 E Hoffman Ave Unit 3 Lindenhurst (11757) ***(G-7473)***
Modern Farmer Media Inc 518 828-7447
403 Warren St Hudson (12534) ***(G-6628)***
Modern Heat Trting Forging Inc (PA) 716 884-2176
1112 Niagara St Buffalo (14213) ***(G-3073)***
Modern Itln Bky of W Babylon 631 589-7300
301 Locust Ave Oakdale (11769) ***(G-13059)***
Modern Language Assn Amer Inc 646 576-5000
85 Broad St Fl 5 New York (10004) ***(G-11288)***
Modern Mechanical Fab Inc 518 298-5177
100 Walnut St Ste 7 Champlain (12919) ***(G-3544)***
Modern Packaging Inc 631 595-2437
505 Acorn St Deer Park (11729) ***(G-4175)***
Modern Plastic Bags Mfg Inc 718 237-2985
63 Flushing Ave Unit 303 Brooklyn (11205) ***(G-2327)***
Modern Publishing, New York *Also called Unisystems Inc* ***(G-12463)***
Modern Settings LLC 631 351-1212
1540 New York Ave Huntington Station (11746) ***(G-6717)***
Modern-TEC Manufacturing Inc 716 625-8700
4935 Lockport Rd Lockport (14094) ***(G-7603)***
Modo Eyeware, New York *Also called Modo Retail LLC* ***(G-11289)***
Modo Retail LLC 212 965-4900
252 Mott St New York (10012) ***(G-11289)***
Modu-Craft Inc (PA) 716 694-0709
276 Creekside Dr Tonawanda (14150) ***(G-16182)***
Modu-Craft Inc 716 694-0709
337 Payne Ave North Tonawanda (14120) ***(G-12982)***
Modular Devices Inc 631 345-3100
1 Roned Rd Shirley (11967) ***(G-15426)***
Modular Medical Corp 718 829-2626
1513 Olmstead Ave Bronx (10462) ***(G-1400)***
Modulex New York Inc 646 742-1320
192 Lexington Ave Rm 1002 New York (10016) ***(G-11290)***
Modulightor Inc 212 371-0336
246 E 58th St New York (10022) ***(G-11291)***
Modutank Inc 718 392-1112
4104 35th Ave Long Island City (11101) ***(G-7815)***
Moes Wear Apparel Inc 718 940-1597
1020 E 48th St Ste 8 Brooklyn (11203) ***(G-2328)***
Moffett Turf Equipment Inc 585 334-0100
33 Thruway Park Dr West Henrietta (14586) ***(G-16885)***
Moffit Fan, Le Roy *Also called Moffitt Corporation Inc* ***(G-7415)***
Moffitt Corporation Inc 585 768-7010
54 Church St Le Roy (14482) ***(G-7415)***
Moffitt Fan Corporation 585 768-7010
54 Church St Le Roy (14482) ***(G-7416)***
Moga Trading Company Inc 718 760-2966
57 Granger St Corona (11368) ***(G-4004)***
Mogen David Winegroup, Westfield *Also called Wine Group Inc* ***(G-17055)***
Mohawk Cabinet Company Inc 518 725-0645
137 E State St Gloversville (12078) ***(G-5718)***
Mohawk Electro Techniques Inc 315 896-2661
8063 State Route 12 Barneveld (13304) ***(G-615)***
Mohawk Fabric Company Inc 518 842-3090
96 Guy Park Ave Amsterdam (12010) ***(G-358)***
Mohawk Fine Papers Inc (PA) 518 237-1740
465 Saratoga St Cohoes (12047) ***(G-3751)***
Mohawk Fine Papers Inc 518 237-1741
465 Saratoga St Cohoes (12047) ***(G-3752)***
Mohawk Metal Mfg & Sls 315 853-7663
4901 State Route 233 Westmoreland (13490) ***(G-17062)***
Mohawk Resources Ltd 518 842-1431
65 Vrooman Ave Amsterdam (12010) ***(G-359)***
Mohawk River Leather Works 518 853-3900
32 Broad St Fultonville (12072) ***(G-5480)***
Mohawk Sign Systems Inc 518 842-5303
5 Dandreano Dr Amsterdam (12010) ***(G-360)***
Mohawk Valley Knt McHy Co Inc 315 736-3038
561 Main St New York Mills (13417) ***(G-12726)***
Mohawk Valley Manufacturing 315 797-0851
2237 Broad St Frankfort (13340) ***(G-5355)***
Mohawk Valley Mill, Little Falls *Also called Burrows Paper Corporation* ***(G-7498)***
Mohawk Valley Printing Co, Herkimer *Also called Lennons Litho Inc* ***(G-6304)***
Moira New Hope Food Pantry 518 529-6524
2341 County Route 5 Moira (12957) ***(G-8546)***
Moishe L Horowitz 212 719-4247
36 W 47th St Ste 303a New York (10036) ***(G-11292)***
Moishe L Horowitz Diamonds, New York *Also called Moishe L Horowitz* ***(G-11292)***
Mokai Manufacturing Inc 845 566-8287
13 Jeanne Dr Newburgh (12550) ***(G-12768)***
Molabs Inc 310 721-6828
32 Little West 12th St New York (10014) ***(G-11293)***
Mold-A-Matic Corporation 607 433-2121
147 River St Oneonta (13820) ***(G-13189)***
Mold-Rite Plastics LLC (HQ) 518 561-1812
1 Plant St Plattsburgh (12901) ***(G-13678)***
Moldcraft Inc 716 684-1126
240 Gould Ave Depew (14043) ***(G-4265)***
Moldedtanks.com, Bay Shore *Also called Chem-Tek Systems Inc* ***(G-683)***
Molding Decor Inc 718 377-2930
1946 50th St Brooklyn (11204) ***(G-2329)***
Moldova Pickles & Salads Inc 718 284-2220
1060 E 46th St Brooklyn (11203) ***(G-2330)***
Moldtech Inc 716 685-3344
1900 Commerce Pkwy Lancaster (14086) ***(G-7327)***
Molecular Glasses Inc 585 210-2861
1667 Lake Ave Ste 278b Rochester (14615) ***(G-14519)***
Moleskine America Inc 646 461-3018
210 11th Ave Rm 1004 New York (10001) ***(G-11294)***
Mollys Cupcakes New York 212 255-5441
228 Bleecker St New York (10014) ***(G-11295)***
Mom Dad Publishing Inc 646 476-9170
59 Maiden Ln Fl 27 New York (10038) ***(G-11296)***
Momentive, Waterford *Also called Mpm Silicones LLC* ***(G-16619)***
Momentive Performance Mtls Inc 614 986-2495
260 Hudson River Rd Waterford (12188) ***(G-16615)***
Momentive Performance Mtls Inc 914 784-4807
769 Old Saw Mill River Rd Tarrytown (10591) ***(G-16098)***
Momentive Performance Mtls Inc (HQ) 518 237-3330
260 Hudson River Rd Waterford (12188) ***(G-16616)***
Momentive Prfmce Mtls Holdings, Albany *Also called Momentive Prfmce Mtls Holdings* ***(G-102)***
Momentive Prfmce Mtls Holdings 518 533-4600
22 Corporate Woods Blvd Albany (12211) ***(G-102)***
Momentummedia Sports Pubg, Ithaca *Also called Mag Inc* ***(G-6858)***
Momn Pops Inc 845 567-0640
13 Orr Hatch Cornwall (12518) ***(G-3988)***
Momofuku 171 First Avenue LLC 212 777-7773
171 1st Ave New York (10003) ***(G-11297)***
Mona Belts, Bronx *Also called Mona Slide Fasteners Inc* ***(G-1401)***
Mona Slide Fasteners Inc (PA) 718 325-7700
4510 White Plains Rd Bronx (10470) ***(G-1401)***
Monacelli Press LLC 212 229-9925
236 W 27th St Rm 4a New York (10001) ***(G-11298)***
Monaghan Medical Corporation (PA) 518 561-7330
5 Latour Ave Ste 1600 Plattsburgh (12901) ***(G-13679)***
Monaghan Medical Corporation 315 472-2136
327 W Fayette St Ste 212 Syracuse (13202) ***(G-15993)***
Monarch Electric Products Inc 718 583-7996
4077 Park Ave Fl 5 Bronx (10457) ***(G-1402)***
Monarch Graphics Inc 631 232-1300
1065 Islip Ave Central Islip (11722) ***(G-3504)***
Monarch Metal Fabrication Inc 631 563-8967
1625 Sycamore Ave Ste A Bohemia (11716) ***(G-1105)***
Monarch Plastics Inc 716 569-2175
225 Falconer St Frewsburg (14738) ***(G-5451)***
Monasani Signs Inc 631 266-2635
22 Compton St East Northport (11731) ***(G-4442)***

ALPHABETIC

Mondelez Global LLC ALPHABETIC SECTION

Mondelez Global LLC 585 345-3300
4303 Federal Dr Batavia (14020) ***(G-642)***
Mondo Publishing Inc (PA) 212 268-3560
980 Avenue Of The America New York (10018) ***(G-11299)***
Moneast Inc 845 298-8898
1708 Route 9 Wappingers Falls (12590) ***(G-16575)***
Monelle Jewelry 212 977-9535
608 5th Ave Ste 504 New York (10020) ***(G-11300)***
Moneypaper Inc 914 925-0022
411 Theodore Fremd Ave # 132 Rye (10580) ***(G-15064)***
Moneysaver Advertising Inc 585 593-1275
218 N Main St Bolivar (14715) ***(G-1160)***
Moneysaver Shopping News, Bolivar *Also called Moneysaver Advertising Inc* ***(G-1160)***
Monfefo LLC 347 779-2600
630 Flushing Ave 5q Brooklyn (11206) ***(G-2331)***
Mongiello Sales Inc 845 436-4200
250 Hilldale Rd Hurleyville (12747) ***(G-6731)***
Mongiellos Itln Cheese Spc LLC 845 436-4200
250 Hilldale Rd Hurleyville (12747) ***(G-6732)***
Mongru Neckwear Inc 718 706-0406
1010 44th Ave Fl 2 Long Island City (11101) ***(G-7816)***
Monitor Controls, Hauppauge *Also called Monitor Elevator Products LLC* ***(G-6143)***
Monitor Elevator Products LLC 631 543-4334
125 Ricefield Ln Hauppauge (11788) ***(G-6143)***
Monkey Joe Roasting Company 845 331-4598
478 Broadway Ste A Kingston (12401) ***(G-7202)***
Monkey Rum, New York *Also called Evolution Spirits Inc* ***(G-10094)***
Mono Plate Inc 631 643-3100
15 Otis St West Babylon (11704) ***(G-16812)***
Mono-Systems Inc 716 821-1344
180 Hopkins St Buffalo (14220) ***(G-3074)***
Monofrax LLC 716 483-7200
1870 New York Ave Falconer (14733) ***(G-4907)***
Monolithic Coatings Inc 914 621-2765
916 Highway Route 20 Sharon Springs (13459) ***(G-15384)***
Monroe Cable Company Inc 845 692-2800
14 Commercial Ave Middletown (10941) ***(G-8452)***
Monroe County Auto Svcs Inc (PA) 585 764-3741
1505 Lyell Ave Rochester (14606) ***(G-14520)***
Monroe Fluid Technology Inc 585 392-3434
36 Draffin Rd Hilton (14468) ***(G-6418)***
Monroe Industries Inc 585 226-8230
5611 Tec Dr Avon (14414) ***(G-541)***
Monroe Plating Div, Rochester *Also called McAlpin Industries Inc* ***(G-14501)***
Monroe Stair Products Inc (PA) 845 783-4245
1 Stair Way Monroe (10950) ***(G-8563)***
Monroe Stair Products Inc 845 791-4016
309 E Broadway Monticello (12701) ***(G-8606)***
Monroe Table Company Inc 716 945-7700
255 Rochester St Ste 15 Salamanca (14779) ***(G-15102)***
Montana Global LLC 212 213-1572
9048 160th St Jamaica (11432) ***(G-6933)***
Montauk Brewing Company Inc 631 668-8471
62 S Erie Ave Montauk (11954) ***(G-8589)***
Montauk Inlet Seafood Inc 631 668-3419
E Lake Dr Ste 540-541 Montauk (11954) ***(G-8590)***
Monte Goldman Embroidery Co 212 874-5397
15 W 72nd St Apt 11n New York (10023) ***(G-11301)***
Monte Press Inc 718 325-4999
4808 White Plains Rd Bronx (10470) ***(G-1403)***
Montero International Inc 212 695-1787
149 Sullivan Ln Unit 1 Westbury (11590) ***(G-17013)***
Montezuma Winery LLC 315 568-8190
2981 Us Route 20 Seneca Falls (13148) ***(G-15366)***
Montfort Brothers Inc 845 896-6694
44 Elm St Fishkill (12524) ***(G-5186)***
Monthly Gift Inc 888 444-9661
401 Park Ave S New York (10016) ***(G-11302)***
Monthly Review Foundation Inc 212 691-2555
146 W 29th St Rm 6fw New York (10001) ***(G-11303)***
Monticello Black Top Corp 845 434-7280
80 Patio Dr Thompsonville (12784) ***(G-16115)***
Montly Gift, New York *Also called Monthly Gift Inc* ***(G-11302)***
Montrose Equipment Sales Inc 718 388-7446
202 N 10th St Brooklyn (11211) ***(G-2332)***
Moo Goong Hwa, Corona *Also called Kenan International Trading* ***(G-4000)***
Moog - Isp, Niagara Falls *Also called Moog Inc* ***(G-12848)***
Moog Inc (PA) 716 652-2000
400 Jamison Rd Plant26 Elma (14059) ***(G-4651)***
Moog Inc 716 655-3000
300 Jamison Rd East Aurora (14052) ***(G-4375)***
Moog Inc 716 805-8100
7021 Sneca St At Jmson Rd East Aurora (14052) ***(G-4376)***
Moog Inc 716 731-6300
6686 Walmore Rd Niagara Falls (14304) ***(G-12848)***
Moog Inc 716 687-4778
160 Jamison Rd Elma (14059) ***(G-4652)***
Moog Inc 716 687-5486
500 Jamison Rd East Aurora (14052) ***(G-4377)***
Moog Space and Defense Group, East Aurora *Also called Moog Inc* ***(G-4377)***
Moon Gates Company 718 426-0023
3243 104th St East Elmhurst (11369) ***(G-4395)***
Moon, Wm, Catskill *Also called William Moon Iron Works Inc* ***(G-3434)***
Mooney-Keehley Inc 585 271-1573
38 Saginaw Dr Rochester (14623) ***(G-14521)***
Moonlight Creamery 585 223-0880
36 West Ave Fairport (14450) ***(G-4864)***
Moor Electronics Inc 716 821-5304
95 Dorothy St Ste 6 Buffalo (14206) ***(G-3075)***
Mooradian Hydraulics & Eqp Co (PA) 518 766-3866
1190 Route 9 Castleton On Hudson (12033) ***(G-3419)***
Moore Business Forms, Lakewood *Also called RR Donnelley & Sons Company* ***(G-7294)***
Moore Business Forms, Grand Island *Also called RR Donnelley & Sons Company* ***(G-5766)***
Moore Printing Company Inc 585 394-1533
9 Coy St Canandaigua (14424) ***(G-3349)***
Moore Research Center, Grand Island *Also called RR Donnelley & Sons Company* ***(G-5767)***
Moran Ship Yard, Staten Island *Also called Moran Towing Corporation* ***(G-15708)***
Moran Shipyard Corporation (HQ) 718 981-5600
2015 Richmond Ter Staten Island (10302) ***(G-15707)***
Moran Towing Corporation 718 981-5600
2015 Richmond Ter Staten Island (10302) ***(G-15708)***
Morania Oil of Long Island, Farmingdale *Also called O C P Inc* ***(G-5069)***
Morco, Plainview *Also called Howard J Moore Company Inc* ***(G-13606)***
Morco Products Corp 718 853-4005
556 39th St Brooklyn (11232) ***(G-2333)***
Morehouse Publishing, New York *Also called Church Publishing Incorporated* ***(G-9615)***
Moreland Hose & Belting Corp 631 563-7071
4118 Sunrise Hwy Oakdale (11769) ***(G-13060)***
Morelle Products Ltd 212 391-8070
211 E 18th St Apt 4d New York (10003) ***(G-11304)***
Moresca Clothing and Costume 845 331-6012
361 Union Center Rd Ulster Park (12487) ***(G-16286)***
Moret Group, The, New York *Also called Jacques Moret Inc* ***(G-10692)***
Morey Publishing 516 284-3300
20 Hempstead Tpke Unit B Farmingdale (11735) ***(G-5060)***
Morgan Fuel & Heating Co Inc 845 856-7831
6 Sleepy Hollow Rd Port Jervis (12771) ***(G-13789)***
Morgan Fuel & Heating Co Inc 845 246-4931
240 Ulster Ave Saugerties (12477) ***(G-15188)***
Morgan Fuel & Heating Co Inc 845 626-7766
5 Webster Ave Kerhonkson (12446) ***(G-7156)***
Morgik Metal Designs 212 463-0304
145 Hudson St Frnt 4 New York (10013) ***(G-11305)***
Morgood Tools Inc 585 436-8828
940 Millstead Way Rochester (14624) ***(G-14522)***
Morlyn Asphalt Corp 845 888-2695
420 Bernas Rd Cochecton (12726) ***(G-3743)***
Morningstar Concrete Products 716 693-4020
528 Young St Tonawanda (14150) ***(G-16183)***
Morningstar Foods, Delhi *Also called Saputo Dairy Foods Usa LLC* ***(G-4242)***
Moro Corporation 607 724-4241
23 Griswold St Binghamton (13904) ***(G-937)***
Moro Design, Ithaca *Also called Joe Moro* ***(G-6855)***
Morris Brothers Sign Svc Inc 212 675-9130
37 W 20th St Ste 708 New York (10011) ***(G-11306)***
Morris Communications Co LLC 212 620-9580
123 W 18th St Fl 6 New York (10011) ***(G-11307)***
Morris Fine Furniture Workshop, Brooklyn *Also called Walter P Sauer LLC* ***(G-2743)***
Morris Golf Ventures 631 283-0559
Sebonac Inlet Rd Southampton (11968) ***(G-15547)***
Morris Kitchen Inc 646 413-5186
30 Chester Ct Brooklyn (11225) ***(G-2334)***
Morris Machining Service Inc 585 527-8100
95 Mount Read Blvd Rochester (14611) ***(G-14523)***
Morris Products Inc 518 743-0523
53 Carey Rd Queensbury (12804) ***(G-14005)***
Morse Systems, Ithaca *Also called Borgwarner Ithaca LLC* ***(G-6825)***
Mortech Industries Inc 845 628-6138
961 Route 6 Mahopac (10541) ***(G-7998)***
Mortgage Press Ltd 516 409-1400
1220 Wantagh Ave Wantagh (11793) ***(G-16560)***
Morton Buildings Inc 585 786-8191
5616 Route 20a E Warsaw (14569) ***(G-16583)***
Morton Salt Inc 585 493-2511
45 Ribaud Ave Silver Springs (14550) ***(G-15451)***
Mosby Holdings Corp (HQ) 212 309-8100
125 Park Ave New York (10017) ***(G-11308)***
Moschos Furs Inc 212 244-0255
345 7th Ave Rm 1501 New York (10001) ***(G-11309)***
Moscot Wholesale Corp 212 647-1550
69 W 14th St Fl 2 New York (10011) ***(G-11310)***
Mother Mousse Ltd (PA) 718 983-8366
3767 Victory Blvd Ste D Staten Island (10314) ***(G-15709)***
Mother Nature & Partners, Brooklyn *Also called Mnn Holding Company LLC* ***(G-2326)***
Moti Ganz (usa) Inc 212 302-0040
1200 Ave Of The Americas New York (10036) ***(G-11311)***
Moti Inc 718 436-4280
4118 13th Ave Brooklyn (11219) ***(G-2335)***
Motiganz Group, New York *Also called Moti Ganz (usa) Inc* ***(G-11311)***
Motion Intelligence Inc 607 227-4400
95 Brown Rd Ste 208 Ithaca (14850) ***(G-6863)***
Motion Message Inc 631 924-9500
20 Frontier Trl Manorville (11949) ***(G-8079)***

ALPHABETIC

Motivair Corporation 716 691-9222
85 Woodridge Dr Amherst (14228) *(G-252)*
Motor Components LLC 607 737-8011
2243 Corning Rd Elmira Heights (14903) *(G-4711)*
Motorad of America, Niagara Falls *Also called Transcedar Industries Ltd (G-12884)*
Motorola Solutions Inc 518 348-0833
7 Deer Run Holw Halfmoon (12065) *(G-5912)*
Motorola Solutions Inc 718 330-2163
335 Adams St Fl 7 Brooklyn (11201) *(G-2336)*
Motorola Solutions Inc 518 869-9517
251 New Karner Rd Albany (12205) *(G-103)*
Mott's, Williamson *Also called Dr Pepper Snapple Group Inc (G-17222)*
Motts, Elmsford *Also called Motts LLP (G-4767)*
Motts LLP (HQ) 972 673-8088
55 Hunter Ln Elmsford (10523) *(G-4767)*
Mount Gay Rum 212 399-4200
1290 Ave Of The Americas New York (10104) *(G-11312)*
Mount Kisco Transfer Stn Inc 914 666-6350
10 Lincoln Pl Mount Kisco (10549) *(G-8635)*
Mount Vernon Iron Works Inc 914 668-7064
130 Miller Pl Mount Vernon (10550) *(G-8708)*
Mount Vernon Machine Inc 845 268-9400
614 Corporate Way Ste 8 Valley Cottage (10989) *(G-16382)*
Mountain Forest Products Inc 518 597-3674
3281 Nys Route 9n Crown Point (12928) *(G-4067)*
Mountain Gift and Powder Co 518 327-3516
1353 Blue Mountain Rd Paul Smiths (12970) *(G-13448)*
Mountain T-Shirts Inc 518 943-4533
8 W Bridge St Catskill (12414) *(G-3432)*
Mountain T-Shirts & Sign Works, Catskill *Also called Mountain T-Shirts Inc (G-3432)*
Movin On Sounds and SEC Inc 516 489-2350
636 Hempstead Tpke Franklin Square (11010) *(G-5365)*
Movinads & Signs LLC 518 378-3000
1771 Route 9 Halfmoon (12065) *(G-5913)*
Moznaim Co, Brooklyn *Also called Moznaim Publishing Co Inc (G-2337)*
Moznaim Publishing Co Inc 718 853-0525
4304 12th Ave Brooklyn (11219) *(G-2337)*
MP Caroll Inc 716 683-8520
4822 Genesee St Cheektowaga (14225) *(G-3579)*
Mp Displays LLC 845 268-4113
704 Executive Blvd Ste 1 Valley Cottage (10989) *(G-16383)*
Mp Holdings Inc (PA) 212 465-6800
11 Penn Plz Fl 19 New York (10001) *(G-11313)*
Mp Studio Inc 212 302-5666
147 W 35th St Ste 1603 New York (10001) *(G-11314)*
Mpdraw LLC 212 228-8383
109 Ludlow St New York (10002) *(G-11315)*
Mpe Graphics Inc 631 582-8900
120 Wilbur Pl Ste A Bohemia (11716) *(G-1106)*
Mpi Consulting Incorporated 631 253-2377
87 Jersey St West Babylon (11704) *(G-16813)*
Mpi Consulting Incorporated 631 253-2377
87 Jersey St West Babylon (11704) *(G-16814)*
Mpi Incorporated 845 471-7630
165 Smith St Stop 5 Poughkeepsie (12601) *(G-13918)*
Mpl Inc 607 266-0480
41 Dutch Mill Rd Ithaca (14850) *(G-6864)*
Mpm Holdings Inc (PA) 518 237-3330
260 Hudson River Rd Waterford (12188) *(G-16617)*
Mpm Intermediate Holdings Inc (HQ) 518 237-3330
260 Hudson River Rd Waterford (12188) *(G-16618)*
Mpm Silicones LLC 518 233-3330
260 Hudson River Rd Waterford (12188) *(G-16619)*
Mpr Magazine App Inc 718 403-0303
2653 E 19th St Fl 2 Brooklyn (11235) *(G-2338)*
Mr Disposable Inc 718 388-8574
101 Richardson St Ste 2 Brooklyn (11211) *(G-2339)*
Mr Sign, East Northport *Also called Monasani Signs Inc (G-4442)*
Mr Sign, Brooklyn *Also called Penn Signs Inc (G-2414)*
Mr Sign Usa Inc 718 218-3321
1920 Atlantic Ave Brooklyn (11233) *(G-2340)*
Mr Smoothie 845 296-1686
207 South Ave Ste F102 Poughkeepsie (12601) *(G-13919)*
Mr Steam, Long Island City *Also called Sussman-Automatic Corporation (G-7898)*
Mr.-Bar-B-q-, Melville *Also called Blue Rhino Global Sourcing Inc (G-8298)*
MRC Global (us) Inc 607 739-8575
224 N Main St Horseheads (14845) *(G-6585)*
Mrchocolatecom LLC 718 875-9772
66 Water St Ste 2 Brooklyn (11201) *(G-2341)*
Mri Northtowns Group PC 716 836-4646
199 Park Club Ln Ste 300 Buffalo (14221) *(G-3076)*
Mrinalini Inc 646 510-2747
469 7th Ave Rm 1254 New York (10018) *(G-11316)*
Mrs John L Strong & Co LLC 212 838-3775
699 Madison Ave Fl 5 New York (10065) *(G-11317)*
Mrt Textile Inc 800 674-1073
350 5th Ave New York (10118) *(G-11318)*
Ms Machining Inc 607 723-1105
2 William St Binghamton (13904) *(G-938)*
Ms Paper Products Co Inc 718 624-0248
930 Bedford Ave Brooklyn (11205) *(G-2342)*
Ms Spares LLC 607 223-3024
8055 Evesborough Dr Clay (13041) *(G-3683)*
Ms. Michelles, Calverton *Also called Cooking With Chef Michelle LLC (G-3289)*
Msdivisions, Middletown *Also called Commercial Communications LLC (G-8432)*
Msi Inc 845 639-6683
329 Strawtown Rd New City (10956) *(G-8788)*
Msi-Molding Solutions Inc 315 736-2412
6247 State Route 233 Rome (13440) *(G-14822)*
Mskcc Rmipc 212 639-6212
1250 1st Ave Ste S-C24 New York (10065) *(G-11319)*
MSP Technologycom LLC 631 424-7542
77 Bankside Dr Centerport (11721) *(G-3480)*
MSQ Corporation 718 465-0900
21504 Hempstead Ave Queens Village (11429) *(G-13982)*
Mssi, Millbrook *Also called Micro Systems Specialists Inc (G-8476)*
Mt Morris Shopper Inc 585 658-3520
85 N Main St Mount Morris (14510) *(G-8653)*
MTI, Albany *Also called Mechanical Technology Inc (G-101)*
MTI, New York *Also called Minerals Technologies Inc (G-11276)*
MTI Instruments Inc 518 218-2550
325 Washington Ave 3 Albany (12206) *(G-104)*
MTK Electronics Inc 631 924-7666
1 National Blvd Medford (11763) *(G-8256)*
Mtm Publishing Inc 212 242-6930
435 W 23rd St Apt 8c New York (10011) *(G-11320)*
MTS Systems Corporation 518 899-2140
30 Gleneagles Blvd Ballston Lake (12019) *(G-584)*
Mualema LLC 609 820-6098
128 W 112th St Apt 1a New York (10026) *(G-11321)*
Mud Puddle Books Inc 212 647-9168
36 W 25th St Fl 5 New York (10010) *(G-11322)*
Muench-Kreuzer Candle Company (PA) 315 471-4515
617 Hiawatha Blvd E Syracuse (13208) *(G-15994)*
Muesli Fusion Inc 716 984-0855
875 Atlantic Ave Ste C Rochester (14609) *(G-14524)*
Mulitex Usa Inc 212 398-0440
215 W 40th St Fl 7 New York (10018) *(G-11323)*
Muller Tool Inc 716 895-3658
74 Anderson Rd Buffalo (14225) *(G-3077)*
Mullican Flooring LP 716 537-2642
209 Vermont St Holland (14080) *(G-6482)*
Multi Packaging Solutions Inc 516 488-2000
325 Duffy Ave Unit 1 Hicksville (11801) *(G-6375)*
Multi Packaging Solutions Inc 812 422-4104
325 Duffy Ave Unit 5 Hicksville (11801) *(G-6376)*
Multi Packaging Solutions Inc (HQ) 646 885-0157
150 E 52nd St Ste 2800 New York (10022) *(G-11324)*
Multi Packg Solutions Intl Ltd (PA) 646 885-0005
150 E 52nd St Fl 28 New York (10022) *(G-11325)*
Multi Tech Electric 718 606-2695
2526 50th St Woodside (11377) *(G-17339)*
Multi-Health Systems Inc 800 456-3003
Indus Pkwy Ste 70660 60 Cheektowaga (14227) *(G-3580)*
Multifold Die Ctng Finshg Corp 631 232-1235
120 Ricefield Ln Ste B Hauppauge (11788) *(G-6144)*
Multiline Technology Inc 631 249-8300
75 Roebling Ct Ronkonkoma (11779) *(G-14946)*
Multimatic Products Inc 800 767-7633
900 Marconi Ave Ronkonkoma (11779) *(G-14947)*
Multimedia Plus Inc 212 982-3229
853 Broadway Ste 1605 New York (10003) *(G-11326)*
Multimedia Services Inc 607 936-3186
11136 River Rd 40 Corning (14830) *(G-3976)*
Multiple Imprssons of Rchester (PA) 585 546-1160
41 Chestnut St Rochester (14604) *(G-14525)*
Multisorb Tech Intl LLC (PA) 716 824-8900
325 Harlem Rd Buffalo (14224) *(G-3078)*
Multisorb Technologies Inc 716 668-4191
20 French Rd Cheektowaga (14227) *(G-3581)*
Multisorb Technologies Inc 716 656-1402
10 French Rd Buffalo (14227) *(G-3079)*
Multitone Finishing Co Inc 516 485-1043
56 Hempstead Gardens Dr West Hempstead (11552) *(G-16860)*
Multiwire Laboratories Ltd 607 257-3378
95 Brown Rd 1018266a Ithaca (14850) *(G-6865)*
Munson Machinery Company Inc 315 797-0090
210 Seward Ave Utica (13502) *(G-16350)*
Murphy Manufacturing Co Inc 585 223-0100
38 West Ave Fairport (14450) *(G-4865)*
Murray Bresky Consultants Ltd (PA) 845 436-5001
5190 Main St South Fallsburg (12779) *(G-15521)*
Murray Logging LLC 518 834-7372
1535 Route 9 Keeseville (12944) *(G-7140)*
Murray's Chicken, South Fallsburg *Also called Murray Bresky Consultants Ltd (G-15521)*
Muscle Sports Products 631 755-1388
80 Orville Dr Ste 112 Bohemia (11716) *(G-1107)*
Muse, The, New York *Also called Daily Muse Inc (G-9789)*
Music & Sound Retailer Inc 516 767-2500
25 Willowdale Ave Port Washington (11050) *(G-13847)*
Music Library, New York *Also called Boosey & Hawkes Inc (G-9439)*
Music Minus One, Elmsford *Also called Mmo Music Group Inc (G-4766)*
Music Sales, New York *Also called G Schirmer Inc (G-10232)*

ALPHABETIC

Music Sales, Chester *Also called G Schirmer Inc* ***(G-3607)***
Music Sales Corporation (PA) 212 254-2100
180 Madison Ave Ste 2400 New York (10016) ***(G-11327)***
Musical Links Production LLC 516 996-1522
91 S Montague St Valley Stream (11580) ***(G-16414)***
Musicskins LLC 646 827-4271
140 58th St Ste 197 Brooklyn (11220) ***(G-2343)***
Must USA Inc 212 391-8288
1400 Broadway Rm 2204 New York (10018) ***(G-11328)***
Mustang-Major Tool & Die Co 716 992-9200
3243 N Boston Rd Eden (14057) ***(G-4588)***
Mutual Engraving Company Inc 516 489-0534
511 Hempstead Ave Ste 13 West Hempstead (11552) ***(G-16861)***
Mutual Harware, Long Island City *Also called Mutual Sales Corp* ***(G-7817)***
Mutual Library Bindery Inc 315 455-6638
6295 E Molloy Rd Ste 3 East Syracuse (13057) ***(G-4551)***
Mutual Sales Corp 718 361-8373
545 49th Ave Long Island City (11101) ***(G-7817)***
Muzet Inc 315 452-0050
104 S Main St Syracuse (13212) ***(G-15995)***
Mv Corp Inc 631 273-8020
88 Spence St Ste 90 Bay Shore (11706) ***(G-720)***
Mvp Plastics, Falconer *Also called Jamestown Mvp LLC* ***(G-4906)***
MW Samara LLC (PA) 212 764-3332
390 5th Ave Fl 2 New York (10018) ***(G-11329)***
Mwi Inc (PA) 585 424-4200
1269 Brighton Henrietta T Rochester (14623) ***(G-14526)***
Mwsi Inc (PA) 914 347-4200
12 Skyline Dr Ste 230 Hawthorne (10532) ***(G-6251)***
Mx Solar USA LLC 732 356-7300
100 Wall St Ste 1000 New York (10005) ***(G-11330)***
My Apparel, New York *Also called El-La Design Inc* ***(G-9992)***
My Hanky Inc 646 321-0869
680 81st St Apt 4d Brooklyn (11228) ***(G-2344)***
My Life My Health, Flushing *Also called Life Watch Technology Inc* ***(G-5266)***
My Most Favorite Food 212 580-5130
247 W 72nd St Frnt 1 New York (10023) ***(G-11331)***
My Publisher Inc 212 935-5215
845 3rd Ave Rm 1410 New York (10022) ***(G-11332)***
Myles Tool Company Inc 716 731-1300
6300 Inducon Corporate Dr Sanborn (14132) ***(G-15124)***
Mynt 1792 LLC 212 249-4562
300 E 71st St Apt 10g New York (10021) ***(G-11333)***
Mypublisher Inc (PA) 914 773-4312
8 Westchester Plz Ste 145 Elmsford (10523) ***(G-4768)***
Myrtle Leola Inc 516 228-2312
73 Sealey Ave Hempstead (11550) ***(G-6281)***
Mystery Scene Magazine, New York *Also called Kbs Communications LLC* ***(G-10825)***
Mystic Display Co Inc 718 485-2651
909 Remsen Ave Brooklyn (11236) ***(G-2345)***
Mystic Inc (PA) 212 239-2025
463 7th Ave Fl 12 New York (10018) ***(G-11334)***
MZB Accessories LLC 718 472-7500
2976 Northern Blvd Fl 4 Long Island City (11101) ***(G-7818)***
N & G of America Inc 516 428-3414
28 W Lane Dr Plainview (11803) ***(G-13622)***
N & L Fuel Corp 718 863-3538
2014 Blackrock Ave Bronx (10472) ***(G-1404)***
N & L Instruments Inc 631 471-4000
90 13th Ave Unit 1 Ronkonkoma (11779) ***(G-14948)***
N A Alumil Corporation 718 355-9393
4401 21st St Ste 203 Long Island City (11101) ***(G-7819)***
N A P, Brooklyn *Also called Nap Industries Inc* ***(G-2348)***
N A R Associates Inc 845 557-8713
128 Rte 55 Barryville (12719) ***(G-620)***
N A S C O, Watertown *Also called Northern Awning & Sign Company* ***(G-16667)***
N C Iron Works Inc 718 633-4660
1117 60th St Brooklyn (11219) ***(G-2346)***
N E Controls LLC 315 626-2480
7048 Interstate Island Rd Syracuse (13209) ***(G-15996)***
N F & M International Inc (PA) 516 997-4212
131 Jericho Tpke Ste 204 Jericho (11753) ***(G-7077)***
N I Boutique, Long Island City *Also called Nazim Izzak Inc* ***(G-7821)***
N Make Mold Inc 716 854-6050
85 River Rock Dr Ste 202 Buffalo (14207) ***(G-3080)***
N Pologeorgis Furs Inc 212 563-2250
143 W 29th St Fl 8 New York (10001) ***(G-11335)***
N R S I, Syosset *Also called National Rding Styles Inst Inc* ***(G-15831)***
N Sketch Build Inc 800 975-0597
982 Main St Ste 4-130 Fishkill (12524) ***(G-5187)***
N V Magazine, New York *Also called Envy Publishing Group Inc* ***(G-10047)***
N Y B P Inc 585 624-2541
1355 Pittsford Mendon Rd Mendon (14506) ***(G-8381)***
N Y Bijoux Corp 212 244-9585
1261 Broadway Rm 606 New York (10001) ***(G-11336)***
N Y Contract Seating Inc 718 417-9298
5560 60th St Maspeth (11378) ***(G-8152)***
N Y Elli Design Corp 718 228-0014
5105 Flushing Ave 2 Maspeth (11378) ***(G-8153)***
N Y Western Concrete Corp 585 343-6850
638 E Main St Batavia (14020) ***(G-643)***
N Y Winstons Inc 212 665-3166
5 W 86th St Apt 9e New York (10024) ***(G-11337)***
N3a Corporation 516 284-6799
345 Doughty Blvd Inwood (11096) ***(G-6762)***
Nabisco, Batavia *Also called Mondelez Global LLC* ***(G-642)***
Nadcor, Plattsburgh *Also called North American Door Corp* ***(G-13680)***
Nae, Central Islip *Also called North American Enclosures Inc* ***(G-3507)***
Nafco, Newark *Also called North American Filter Corp* ***(G-12739)***
Nagad Cabinets Inc 718 382-7200
1039 Mcdonald Ave Brooklyn (11230) ***(G-2347)***
Nakano Foods, Medina *Also called Mizkan Americas Inc* ***(G-8278)***
Nakano Foods, Lyndonville *Also called Mizkan America Inc* ***(G-7968)***
Nalco Company LLC 518 796-1985
6 Butler Pl 2 Saratoga Springs (12866) ***(G-15163)***
Nalge Nunc International Corp (HQ) 585 586-8800
75 Panorama Creek Dr Rochester (14625) ***(G-14527)***
Name Base Inc 212 545-1400
172 Lexington Ave Apt 1 New York (10016) ***(G-11338)***
Nameplate Mfrs of Amer 631 752-0055
65 Toledo St Farmingdale (11735) ***(G-5061)***
Namm Singer Inc 212 947-2566
261 W 35th St Fl 12 New York (10001) ***(G-11339)***
Nanette Lepore, New York *Also called Nlhe LLC* ***(G-11445)***
Nanette Lepore, New York *Also called Robespierre Inc* ***(G-11893)***
Nanette Lepore Showroom, New York *Also called Robespierre Inc* ***(G-11892)***
Nannit, New York *Also called Udisense Inc* ***(G-12443)***
Nano Vibronix Inc 516 374-8330
601 Chestnut St Cedarhurst (11516) ***(G-3461)***
Nanobionovum LLC 518 581-1171
117 Grand Ave Saratoga Springs (12866) ***(G-15164)***
Nanoprobes Inc 631 205-9490
95 Horseblock Rd Unit 1 Yaphank (11980) ***(G-17398)***
Nanopv Corporation 609 851-3666
7526 Morgan Rd Liverpool (13090) ***(G-7536)***
Nanorx Inc 914 671-0224
6 Devoe Pl Chappaqua (10514) ***(G-3553)***
Nanovibronix Inc 914 233-3004
525 Executive Blvd Elmsford (10523) ***(G-4769)***
Nantier Ball Minoustchine Pubg, New York *Also called NBM Publishing Inc* ***(G-11363)***
Nantucket Allserve Inc 914 612-4000
55 Hunter Ln Elmsford (10523) ***(G-4770)***
Nantucket Nectars, Elmsford *Also called Nantucket Allserve Inc* ***(G-4770)***
Nanz Company, The, New York *Also called Nanz Custom Hardware Inc* ***(G-11340)***
Nanz Custom Hardware Inc (PA) 212 367-7000
20 Vandam St Fl 5l New York (10013) ***(G-11340)***
Nanz Custom Hardware Inc 212 367-7000
105 E Jefryn Blvd Deer Park (11729) ***(G-4176)***
Naomi Manufacturing, Island Park *Also called Nathan Berrie & Sons Inc* ***(G-6781)***
Nap Industries, Brooklyn *Also called Marlow Printing Co Inc* ***(G-2274)***
Nap Industries Inc 718 625-4948
667 Kent Ave Brooklyn (11249) ***(G-2348)***
Napco Security Tech Inc (PA) 631 842-9400
333 Bayview Ave Amityville (11701) ***(G-314)***
Naples Vly Mrgers Acqstons LLC 585 490-1339
154 N Main St Naples (14512) ***(G-8767)***
Narda Satellite Networks, Hauppauge *Also called L-3 Communications Corporation* ***(G-6109)***
Narde Paving Company Inc 607 737-7177
400 E 14th St Elmira (14903) ***(G-4696)***
Narratively Inc 203 536-0332
221 Cumberland St Apt 4 Brooklyn (11205) ***(G-2349)***
Narrowsburg Feed & Grain Co 845 252-3936
Fifth And Main St Narrowsburg (12764) ***(G-8768)***
Nas CP Corp (HQ) 718 961-6757
1434 110th St Apt 4a College Point (11356) ***(G-3799)***
Nas Quick Sign Inc 716 876-7599
1628 Elmwood Ave Buffalo (14207) ***(G-3081)***
Nas-Tra Automotive Inds Inc 631 225-1225
3 Sidney Ct Lindenhurst (11757) ***(G-7474)***
Nasco Enterprises Inc 516 921-9696
95 Woodcrest Dr Syosset (11791) ***(G-15829)***
Nasdaq Omx, New York *Also called Omx (us) Inc* ***(G-11504)***
Nash Metalware Co Inc 315 339-5794
200 Railroad St Rome (13440) ***(G-14823)***
Nash Printing Inc 516 935-4567
101 Dupont St Ste 2 Plainview (11803) ***(G-13623)***
Nasiff Associates Inc 315 676-2346
841 County Route 37 Central Square (13036) ***(G-3517)***
Nassau Auto Remanufacturer 516 485-4500
25 Chasner St Hempstead (11550) ***(G-6282)***
Nassau Auto Remanufacturers, Hempstead *Also called Nassau Auto Remanufacturer* ***(G-6282)***
Nassau Chromium Plating Co Inc 516 746-6666
122 2nd St Mineola (11501) ***(G-8526)***
Nassau County Publications 516 481-5400
5 Centre St Hempstead (11550) ***(G-6283)***
Nassau Suffolk Brd of Womens 631 666-8835
145 New York Ave Bay Shore (11706) ***(G-721)***
Nassau Tool Works Inc 631 643-0420
34 Lamar St West Babylon (11704) ***(G-16815)***

Nastel Technologies Inc (PA)....631 761-9100
48 S Service Rd Ste 205 Melville (11747) *(G-8338)*
Nastra Automotive, Lindenhurst *Also called Nas-Tra Automotive Inds Inc (G-7474)*
Nat Nast Company Inc (PA)....212 575-1186
1370 Broadway Rm 900 New York (10018) *(G-11341)*
Natalie Creations, New York *Also called Beverly Creations Inc (G-9381)*
Natech Plastics Inc....631 580-3506
85 Remington Blvd Ronkonkoma (11779) *(G-14949)*
Nathan Berrie & Sons Inc....516 432-8500
3956 Long Beach Rd Island Park (11558) *(G-6781)*
Nathan Boning Co LLC....212 244-4781
302 W 37th St Fl 4 New York (10018) *(G-11342)*
Nathan Love LLC....212 925-7111
407 Broome St Rm 6r New York (10013) *(G-11343)*
Nathan Printing Express Inc....914 472-0914
740 Central Park Ave Scarsdale (10583) *(G-15221)*
Nathan Steel Corp....315 797-1335
36 Wurz Ave Utica (13502) *(G-16351)*
Nation Company LP....212 209-5400
520 8th Ave Rm 2100 New York (10018) *(G-11344)*
Nation Magazine....212 209-5400
33 Irving Pl Fl 8 New York (10003) *(G-11345)*
Nation, The, New York *Also called Nation Company LP (G-11344)*
National Advertising & Prtg....212 629-7650
231 W 29th St Frnt New York (10001) *(G-11346)*
National Catholic Wkly Review, New York *Also called America Press Inc (G-9113)*
National Computer & Electronic....631 242-7222
367 Bay Shore Rd Ste D Deer Park (11729) *(G-4177)*
National Contract Industries....212 249-0045
510 E 86th St Apt 16b New York (10028) *(G-11347)*
National Die & Button Mould Co....201 939-7800
1 Kent Ave Brooklyn (11249) *(G-2350)*
National Elev Cab & Door Corp....718 478-5900
5315 37th Ave Woodside (11377) *(G-17340)*
National Equipment Corporation (PA)....718 585-0200
801 E 141st St 825 Bronx (10454) *(G-1405)*
National Equipment Corporation....718 585-0200
801 E 141st St Bronx (10454) *(G-1406)*
National Flag & Display Co Inc (PA)....212 228-6600
30 E 21st St Apt 2b New York (10010) *(G-11348)*
National Grape Coop Assn Inc (PA)....716 326-5200
2 S Portage St Westfield (14787) *(G-17048)*
National Health Prom Assoc....914 421-2525
711 Westchester Ave # 301 White Plains (10604) *(G-17139)*
National Herald Inc....718 784-5255
3710 30th St Long Island City (11101) *(G-7820)*
National Learning Corp (PA)....516 921-8888
212 Michael Dr Syosset (11791) *(G-15830)*
National Maint Contg Corp....716 285-1583
5600 Niagara Falls Blvd Niagara Falls (14304) *(G-12849)*
National Marketing Services....516 942-9595
200 S Service Rd Ste 100 Roslyn Heights (11577) *(G-15030)*
National Military Industries....908 782-1646
78 White Rd Ext Palenville (12463) *(G-13397)*
National Pad & Paper, Syracuse *Also called Automation Papers Inc (G-15862)*
National Paper Converting Inc....607 687-6049
207 Corporate Dr Owego (13827) *(G-13356)*
National Parachute Industries....908 782-1646
78 White Rd Extensio Palenville (12463) *(G-13398)*
National Parachute Industry, Palenville *Also called National Parachute Industries (G-13398)*
National Parts Peddler Newsppr....315 699-7583
7408 Lakeshore Rd Cicero (13039) *(G-3649)*
National Parts Peddler, The, Cicero *Also called National Parts Peddler Newsppr (G-3649)*
National Pipe & Plastics Inc (PA)....607 729-9381
3421 Vestal Rd Vestal (13850) *(G-16451)*
National Prfmce Solutions Inc....718 833-4767
7106 13th Ave Brooklyn (11228) *(G-2351)*
National Prof Resources....914 937-8879
25 S Regent St Ste 2 Port Chester (10573) *(G-13755)*
National Prosthetic Orthot....718 767-8400
21441 42nd Ave Ste 3a Bayside (11361) *(G-774)*
National Ramp, Valley Cottage *Also called Landmark Group Inc (G-16380)*
National Rding Styles Inst Inc....516 921-5500
179 Lafayette Dr Syosset (11791) *(G-15831)*
National Reproductions Inc....212 619-3800
229 W 28th St Fl 9 New York (10001) *(G-11349)*
National Review Inc (PA)....212 679-7330
215 Lexington Ave Fl 11 New York (10016) *(G-11350)*
National Review Online, New York *Also called National Review Inc (G-11350)*
National Security Systems Inc....516 627-2222
511 Manhasset Woods Rd Manhasset (11030) *(G-8063)*
National Spinning Co Inc....212 382-6400
1212 Ave Of The Americ St New York (10036) *(G-11351)*
National Steel Rule Die Inc....718 402-1396
2407 3rd Ave Bronx (10451) *(G-1407)*
National Time Recording Eqp Co....212 227-3310
64 Reade St Fl 2 New York (10007) *(G-11352)*
National Tobacco Company LP....212 253-8185
257 Park Ave S Fl 7 New York (10010) *(G-11353)*
National Vac Envmtl Svcs Corp....518 743-0563
80 Park Rd Glens Falls (12804) *(G-5691)*
National Wire & Metal Tech Inc....716 661-9180
200 Harrison St Ste 10 Jamestown (14701) *(G-7021)*
Nationwide Circuits Inc....585 328-0791
1444 Emerson St Rochester (14606) *(G-14528)*
Nationwide Coils Inc (PA)....914 277-7396
24 Foxwood Cir Mount Kisco (10549) *(G-8636)*
Nationwide Custom Services....845 365-0414
77 Main St Tappan (10983) *(G-16081)*
Nationwide Dairy Inc....347 689-8148
792 E 93rd St Brooklyn (11236) *(G-2352)*
Nationwide Displays, Central Islip *Also called Nationwide Exhibitor Svcs Inc (G-3505)*
Nationwide Exhibitor Svcs Inc....631 467-2034
110 Windsor Pl Central Islip (11722) *(G-3505)*
Nationwide Lifts, Queensbury *Also called S & H Enterprises Inc (G-14010)*
Nationwide Precision Pdts Corp....585 272-7100
200 Tech Park Dr Rochester (14623) *(G-14529)*
Nationwide Sales and Service....631 491-6625
303 Smith St Ste 4 Farmingdale (11735) *(G-5062)*
Nationwide Tarps Incorporated (PA)....518 843-1545
50 Willow St Amsterdam (12010) *(G-361)*
Native Amercn Enrgy Group Inc (PA)....718 408-2323
7211 Austin St Ste 288 Forest Hills (11375) *(G-5325)*
Native Textiles Inc (PA)....212 951-5100
411 5th Ave Rm 901 New York (10016) *(G-11354)*
Natori Company Incorporated (PA)....212 532-7796
180 Madison Ave Fl 19 New York (10016) *(G-11355)*
Natori Company Incorporated....212 532-7796
180 Madison Ave Fl 19 New York (10016) *(G-11356)*
Natori Company, The, New York *Also called Natori Company Incorporated (G-11356)*
Natural E Creative LLC....516 488-1143
1110 Jericho Tpke New Hyde Park (11040) *(G-8849)*
Natural Image Hair Concepts, Garden City *Also called M and J Hair Center Inc (G-5518)*
Natural Lab Inc....718 321-8848
13538 39th Ave Ste 4 Flushing (11354) *(G-5270)*
Natural Organics Inc (PA)....631 293-0030
548 Broadhollow Rd Melville (11747) *(G-8339)*
Natural Organics Labroratories....631 957-5600
9500 New Horizons Blvd Amityville (11701) *(G-315)*
Natural Stone & Cabinet Inc....718 388-2988
1365 Halsey St Brooklyn (11237) *(G-2353)*
Naturally Free Food Inc....631 361-9710
35 Roundabout Rd Smithtown (11787) *(G-15492)*
Nature America Inc (HQ)....212 726-9200
1 New York Plz Ste 4500 New York (10004) *(G-11357)*
Nature Only Inc....917 922-6539
10420 Queens Blvd Apt 3b Forest Hills (11375) *(G-5326)*
Nature Publishing Group, New York *Also called Nature America Inc (G-11357)*
Nature's Plus, Melville *Also called Natural Organics Inc (G-8339)*
Natures Bounty Inc....631 567-9500
90 Orville Dr Bohemia (11716) *(G-1108)*
Natures Bounty Inc (HQ)....631 580-6137
2100 Smithtown Ave Ronkonkoma (11779) *(G-14950)*
Natures Value Inc (PA)....631 846-2500
468 Mill Rd Coram (11727) *(G-3946)*
Naturpathica Holistic Hlth Inc....631 329-8792
74 Montauk Hwy Unit 23 East Hampton (11937) *(G-4414)*
Natus Medical Incorporated....631 457-4430
150 Motor Pkwy Ste 106 Hauppauge (11788) *(G-6145)*
Nautica International Inc (HQ)....212 541-5757
40 W 57th St Fl 3 New York (10019) *(G-11358)*
Nautical Marine Paint Corp....718 462-7000
4802 Farragut Rd Brooklyn (11203) *(G-2354)*
Nautical Paint, Brooklyn *Also called Nautical Marine Paint Corp (G-2354)*
Naval Stores Co....914 664-5877
240 E 7th St Mount Vernon (10550) *(G-8709)*
Navas Designs Inc....818 988-9050
200 E 58th St Apt 17b New York (10022) *(G-11359)*
Navatar Consulting Group Inc....212 863-9655
90 Brd St New York (10004) *(G-11360)*
Navatar Consulting Group Inc (PA)....212 863-9655
90 Broad St Ste 1703 New York (10004) *(G-11361)*
Navatar Group, New York *Also called Navatar Consulting Group Inc (G-11361)*
Navilyst Medical Inc....800 833-9973
10 Glens Fls Technical Pa Glens Falls (12801) *(G-5692)*
Navitar Inc (PA)....585 359-4000
200 Commerce Dr Rochester (14623) *(G-14530)*
Navy Plum LLC....845 641-7441
47 Plum Rd Monsey (10952) *(G-8576)*
Nazim Izzak Inc....212 920-5546
4402 23rd St Ste 517 Long Island City (11101) *(G-7821)*
NBC Internet Inc....212 315-9016
30 Rockefeller Plz Fl 2 New York (10112) *(G-11362)*
NBC Universal LLC....718 482-8310
210 54th Ave Long Island City (11101) *(G-7822)*
Nbci.com, New York *Also called NBC Internet Inc (G-11362)*
Nbets Corporation....516 785-1259
1901 Wantagh Ave Wantagh (11793) *(G-16561)*
NBM Publishing Inc....212 643-5407
160 Broadway Ste 700e New York (10038) *(G-11363)*
Nbn Technologies LLC....585 355-5556
136 Wilshire Rd Rochester (14618) *(G-14531)*
Nbs, Amityville *Also called New Business Solutions Inc (G-316)*

ALPHABETIC

Nbty Inc 631 200-2000
10 Vitamin Dr Bayport (11705) ***(G-759)***
Nbty Inc 631 244-2065
2100 Smithtown Ave Ronkonkoma (11779) ***(G-14951)***
Nbty Inc 518 452-5813
120 Wash Ave Ext Ste 110 Albany (12203) ***(G-105)***
Nbty Inc 631 244-2021
2100 Smithtown Ave Ronkonkoma (11779) ***(G-14952)***
Nbty Inc (HQ) 631 200-2000
2100 Smithtown Ave Ronkonkoma (11779) ***(G-14953)***
Nbty Inc 631 200-7338
2145 9th Ave Ronkonkoma (11779) ***(G-14954)***
Nbty Inc 631 588-3492
4320 Veterans Mem Hwy Holbrook (11741) ***(G-6464)***
Nbty Manufacturing LLC (HQ) 631 567-9500
2100 Smithtown Ave Ronkonkoma (11779) ***(G-14955)***
NC Industries Inc (PA) 248 528-5200
200 John James Audubon Buffalo (14228) ***(G-3082)***
Ncc Ny LLC 718 943-7000
140 58th St Ste A Brooklyn (11220) ***(G-2355)***
Nceec, Deer Park *Also called National Computer & Electronic* ***(G-4177)***
Nci, New York *Also called National Contract Industries* ***(G-11347)***
Nci Group Inc 315 339-1245
6168 State Route 233 Rome (13440) ***(G-14824)***
Nci Panel Systems, Montgomery *Also called Northeast Cnstr Inds Inc* ***(G-8598)***
NCM Publishers Inc 212 691-9100
200 Varick St Rm 608 New York (10014) ***(G-11364)***
NCR Corporation 607 273-5310
950 Danby Rd Ithaca (14850) ***(G-6866)***
NCR Corporation 516 876-7200
30 Jericho Executive Plz Jericho (11753) ***(G-7078)***
ND Labs Inc 516 612-4900
202 Merrick Rd Lynbrook (11563) ***(G-7955)***
Ne & Ws Inc 718 326-4699
6050 60th St Maspeth (11378) ***(G-8154)***
NEa Manufacturing Corp 516 371-4200
345 Doughty Blvd Inwood (11096) ***(G-6763)***
Necd, Woodside *Also called National Elev Cab & Door Corp* ***(G-17340)***
Necessary Objects Ltd (PA) 212 334-9888
530 7th Ave M1 New York (10018) ***(G-11365)***
Nefab Packaging North East LLC 518 346-9105
203 Glenville Indus Park Scotia (12302) ***(G-15328)***
Nefco, Copiague *Also called North East Finishing Co Inc* ***(G-3917)***
Neff Holding Company 914 595-8200
357 Main St Armonk (10504) ***(G-418)***
Negys New Land Vinyrd Winery 315 585-4432
623 Lerch Rd Ste 1 Geneva (14456) ***(G-5583)***
Neighbor Newspapers 631 226-2636
565 Broadhollow Rd Ste 3 Farmingdale (11735) ***(G-5063)***
Neighbor To Neighbor News Inc 585 492-2525
223 Main St Arcade (14009) ***(G-397)***
Neilson International Inc 631 454-0400
144 Allen Blvd Ste B Farmingdale (11735) ***(G-5064)***
Nelco Laboratories Inc 631 242-0082
154 Brook Ave Deer Park (11729) ***(G-4178)***
Nell-Joy Industries Inc (PA) 631 842-8989
8 Reith St Ste 10 Copiague (11726) ***(G-3915)***
Nelson Air Device Corporation 718 729-3801
4628 54th Ave Maspeth (11378) ***(G-8155)***
Nelson Holdings Ltd (PA) 607 772-1794
71 Frederick St Binghamton (13901) ***(G-939)***
Nelson Prsthtics Orthotics Lab, Cheektowaga *Also called Prosthetics By Nelson Inc* ***(G-3587)***
Nemaris Inc 646 794-8648
306 E 15th St Apt 1r New York (10003) ***(G-11366)***
Neo Cabinetry LLC 718 403-0456
400 Liberty Ave Brooklyn (11207) ***(G-2356)***
Neo Ray Lighting Products, Hicksville *Also called Cooper Lighting LLC* ***(G-6334)***
Neometrics, Hauppauge *Also called Natus Medical Incorporated* ***(G-6145)***
Neon 212 727-5628
1400 Broadway Rm 300 New York (10018) ***(G-11367)***
Neopost USA Inc 631 435-9100
415 Oser Ave Ste K Hauppauge (11788) ***(G-6146)***
Nepco, Warrensburg *Also called Northeastern Products Corp* ***(G-16580)***
Nepenthes America Inc 212 343-4262
307 W 38th St Rm 201 New York (10018) ***(G-11368)***
Neptune Machine Inc 718 852-4100
521 Carroll St Brooklyn (11215) ***(G-2357)***
Neptune Soft Water Inc 315 446-5151
1201 E Fayette St Ste 6 Syracuse (13210) ***(G-15997)***
Nervecom Inc 212 625-9914
199 Lafayette St Apt 3b New York (10012) ***(G-11369)***
Nervve Technologies Inc (PA) 716 800-2250
500 Seneca St Ste 501 Buffalo (14204) ***(G-3083)***
Nes Bearing Company Inc 716 372-6532
1601 Johnson St Olean (14760) ***(G-13151)***
Nes Costume, New York *Also called Nes Jewelry Inc* ***(G-11370)***
Nes Jewelry Inc 212 502-0025
20 W 33rd St Fl 6 New York (10001) ***(G-11370)***
Nesher Printing Inc 212 760-2521
30 E 33rd St Frnt A New York (10016) ***(G-11371)***
Nessen Lighting, The, Mamaroneck *Also called Coldstream Group Inc* ***(G-8029)***
Nestle Purina Factory, Dunkirk *Also called Nestle Purina Petcare Company* ***(G-4345)***
Nestle Purina Petcare Company 716 366-8080
3800 Middle Rd Dunkirk (14048) ***(G-4345)***
Nestle Usa Inc 914 272-4021
1311 Mmroneck Ave Ste 350 White Plains (10605) ***(G-17140)***
NET & Die Inc 315 592-4311
24 Foster St Fulton (13069) ***(G-5470)***
Netech Corporation 631 531-0100
110 Toledo St Farmingdale (11735) ***(G-5065)***
Netegrity Inc (HQ) 631 342-6000
1 Ca Plz Central Islip (11749) ***(G-3506)***
Netologic Inc 212 269-3796
17 State St Fl 38 New York (10004) ***(G-11372)***
Netsuite Inc 646 652-5700
8 W 40th St 5f New York (10018) ***(G-11373)***
Network Components LLC 212 799-5890
52 Vanderbilt Ave Fl 18 New York (10017) ***(G-11374)***
Network Journal Inc 212 962-3791
39 Broadway Rm 2120 New York (10006) ***(G-11375)***
Neumann Jutta New York Inc 212 982-7048
355 E 4th St New York (10009) ***(G-11376)***
Neurotrope Inc 973 242-0005
60 Hampden Ln Irvington (10533) ***(G-6774)***
Neva Slip, Inwood *Also called Excellent Art Mfg Corp* ***(G-6756)***
Nevaeh Jeans Company 845 641-4255
450 W 152nd St Apt 31 New York (10031) ***(G-11377)***
Neverware Inc 516 302-3223
112 W 27th St Ste 201 New York (10001) ***(G-11378)***
Neville Mfg Svc & Dist Inc (PA) 716 834-3038
2320 Clinton St Cheektowaga (14227) ***(G-3582)***
New Age Ironworks Inc 718 277-1895
183 Van Siclen Ave Brooklyn (11207) ***(G-2358)***
New Age Precision Tech Inc 631 588-1692
151 Remington Blvd Ronkonkoma (11779) ***(G-14956)***
New American, Brooklyn *Also called Afro Times Newspaper* ***(G-1568)***
New Art Publications Inc 718 636-9100
80 Hanson Pl Ste 703 Brooklyn (11217) ***(G-2359)***
New Art Signs Co Inc 718 443-0900
78 Plymouth Dr N Glen Head (11545) ***(G-5637)***
New Atlantic Ready Mix Corp 718 812-0739
18330 Jamaica Ave Hollis (11423) ***(G-6498)***
New Audio LLC 212 213-6060
132 W 31st St Rm 701 New York (10001) ***(G-11379)***
New Avon LLC 212 282-8500
777 3rd Ave Fl 8 New York (10017) ***(G-11380)***
New Balance Underwear, New York *Also called Balanced Tech Corp* ***(G-9309)***
New Berlin Gazette 607 847-6131
29 Lackawanna Ave Norwich (13815) ***(G-13031)***
New Bgnnngs Win Door Dstrs LLC 845 214-0698
28 Willowbrook Hts Poughkeepsie (12603) ***(G-13920)***
New Business Solutions Inc 631 789-1500
31 Sprague Ave Amityville (11701) ***(G-316)***
New City Press Inc 845 229-0335
202 Cardinal Rd Hyde Park (12538) ***(G-6735)***
New Classic Inc 718 609-1100
4143 37th St Long Island City (11101) ***(G-7823)***
New Classic Trade Inc 347 822-9052
17211 93rd Ave Jamaica (11433) ***(G-6934)***
New Concepts of New York LLC 212 695-4999
132 W 36th St Rm 4 New York (10018) ***(G-11381)***
New Cov Manufacturing, West Henrietta *Also called Semans Enterprises Inc* ***(G-16894)***
NEW CRITERION MAGAZINE, New York *Also called Foundation For Cultural Review* ***(G-10191)***
New Day Woodwork Inc 718 275-1721
8861 76th Ave Glendale (11385) ***(G-5659)***
New Deal Printing Corp (PA) 718 729-5800
420 E 55th St Apt Grdp New York (10022) ***(G-11382)***
New Dimension Awards Inc (PA) 718 236-8200
6505 11th Ave Brooklyn (11219) ***(G-2360)***
New Dimension Trophies, Brooklyn *Also called New Dimension Awards Inc* ***(G-2360)***
New Dimensions Office Group 718 387-0995
540 Morgan Ave Brooklyn (11222) ***(G-2361)***
New Dimensions Research Corp 631 694-1356
260 Spagnoli Rd Melville (11747) ***(G-8340)***
New Direct Product Corp 212 929-0515
150 W 22nd St Fl 12 New York (10011) ***(G-11383)***
New Directions Publishing 212 255-0230
80 8th Ave Fl 19 New York (10011) ***(G-11384)***
New Dynamics Corporation 845 692-0022
15 Fortune Rd W Middletown (10941) ***(G-8453)***
New Eagle Silo Corp 585 492-1300
7648 Hurdville Rd Arcade (14009) ***(G-398)***
New Energy Systems Group 917 573-0302
116 W 23rd St Fl 5 New York (10011) ***(G-11385)***
New England Barns Inc 631 445-1461
45805 Route 25 Southold (11971) ***(G-15560)***
New England Orthotic & Prost 212 831-3600
235 E 38th St New York (10016) ***(G-11386)***
New England Orthotic & Prost 845 471-7777
2656 South Rd Ste B Poughkeepsie (12601) ***(G-13921)***

ALPHABETIC

New England Reclamation Inc 914 949-2000
20 Haarlem Ave White Plains (10603) *(G-17141)*
New England Tool Co Ltd 845 651-7550
44 Jayne St Florida (10921) *(G-5214)*
New ERA Cap Co Inc 716 604-9000
160 Delaware Ave Buffalo (14202) *(G-3084)*
New ERA Cap Co Inc (PA) 716 604-9000
160 Delaware Ave Buffalo (14202) *(G-3085)*
New ERA Cap Co Inc 716 549-0445
8061 Erie Rd Derby (14047) *(G-4284)*
New Generation Lighting Inc 212 966-0328
144 Bowery Frnt 1 New York (10013) *(G-11387)*
New Goldstar 1 Printing Corp 212 343-3909
63 Orchard St New York (10002) *(G-11388)*
New Hampton Creations Inc 212 244-7474
237 W 35th St Ste 502 New York (10001) *(G-11389)*
New Hope Media LLC 646 366-0830
108 W 39th St Rm 805 New York (10018) *(G-11390)*
New Hope Mills Inc 315 252-2676
181 York St Auburn (13021) *(G-509)*
New Hope Mills Mfg Inc (PA) 315 252-2676
181 York St Auburn (13021) *(G-510)*
New Horizon Graphics Inc 631 231-8055
1200 Prime Pl Hauppauge (11788) *(G-6147)*
New Horizons Bakery, Binghamton *Also called Fratellis LLC (G-915)*
New Jersey Pulverizing Co Inc (PA) 516 921-9595
4 Rita St Syosset (11791) *(G-15832)*
New Kit On The Block 631 757-5655
100 Knickerbocker Ave K Bohemia (11716) *(G-1109)*
New Living Inc 631 751-8819
99 Waverly Ave Apt 6d Patchogue (11772) *(G-13428)*
New Market Products Co Inc 607 292-6226
9671 Back St Wayne (14893) *(G-16712)*
New Media Investment Group Inc (PA) 212 479-3160
1345 Avenue Of The Americ New York (10105) *(G-11391)*
New Mount Pleasant Bakery 518 374-7577
941 Crane St Schenectady (12303) *(G-15281)*
New Paltz Times, New Paltz *Also called Ulster Publishing Co Inc (G-8881)*
New Press 212 629-8802
120 Wall St Fl 31 New York (10005) *(G-11392)*
New Project LLC 718 788-3444
122 18th St Brooklyn (11215) *(G-2362)*
New Rosen Printing, Buffalo *Also called Cilyox Inc (G-2874)*
New Scale Technologies Inc 585 924-4450
121 Victor Heights Pkwy Victor (14564) *(G-16492)*
New Sensor Corporation (PA) 718 937-8300
5501 2nd St Long Island City (11101) *(G-7824)*
New Ski Inc 607 277-7000
109 N Cayuga St Ste A Ithaca (14850) *(G-6867)*
New Skin, Tarrytown *Also called Medtech Products Inc (G-16096)*
New Star Bakery 718 961-8868
4121a Kissena Blvd Flushing (11355) *(G-5271)*
New Style Signs Limited Inc 212 242-7848
149 Madison Ave Rm 606 New York (10016) *(G-11393)*
New Top Sales Company, Baldwinsville *Also called Coverall Manufacturing (G-568)*
New Triad For Collaborative 212 873-9610
205 W 86th St Apt 911 New York (10024) *(G-11394)*
New Vision Industries Inc 607 687-7700
1239 Campville Rd Endicott (13760) *(G-4820)*
New Windsor Waste Water Plant 845 561-2550
145 Caesars Ln New Windsor (12553) *(G-8944)*
New Wop Records 631 617-9732
317 W 14th St Deer Park (11729) *(G-4179)*
New World Records, Brooklyn *Also called Recorded Anthlogy of Amrcn Mus (G-2484)*
New York Accessories Group, New York *Also called New York Accessory Group Inc (G-11395)*
New York Accessory Group Inc (PA) 212 532-7911
411 5th Ave Fl 4 New York (10016) *(G-11395)*
New York Air Brake, Watertown *Also called Knorr Brake Truck Systems Co (G-16660)*
New York Air Brake LLC (HQ) 315 786-5219
748 Starbuck Ave Watertown (13601) *(G-16665)*
New York Binding Co Inc 718 729-2454
2121 41st Ave Ste A Long Island City (11101) *(G-7825)*
New York Blood Pressure, Mendon *Also called N Y B P Inc (G-8381)*
New York Bottling Co Inc 718 963-3232
626 Whittier St Bronx (10474) *(G-1408)*
New York Cartridge Exchange 212 840-2227
225 W 37th St New York (10018) *(G-11396)*
New York Chocolatier Inc 516 561-1570
396 Rockaway Ave Valley Stream (11581) *(G-16415)*
New York Christan Times Inc 718 638-6397
1061 Atlantic Ave Brooklyn (11238) *(G-2363)*
New York CT Loc246 Seiu Wel BF 212 233-0616
217 Broadway New York (10007) *(G-11397)*
New York Cutting & Gumming Co 212 563-4146
265 Ballard Rd Middletown (10941) *(G-8454)*
New York Cvl Srvc Emplys Pblsh 212 962-2690
277 Broadway Ste 1506 New York (10007) *(G-11398)*
New York Daily Challenge Inc (PA) 718 636-9500
1195 Atlantic Ave Fl 2 Brooklyn (11216) *(G-2364)*
New York Daily News, New York *Also called Daily News LP (G-9790)*
New York Daily News 212 248-2100
4 New York Plz Fl 6 New York (10004) *(G-11399)*
New York Digital Corporation 631 630-9798
33 Walt Whitman Rd # 117 Huntington Station (11746) *(G-6718)*
New York Digital Print Center 718 767-1953
15050 14th Rd Ste 1 Whitestone (11357) *(G-17212)*
New York Division, Owego *Also called Kyocera Precision Tools Inc (G-13353)*
New York Elegance Entps Inc 212 685-3088
385 5th Ave Rm 709 New York (10016) *(G-11400)*
New York Embroidery & Monogram, Hicksville *Also called NY Embroidery Inc (G-6378)*
New York Enrgy Synthetics Inc 212 634-4787
375 Park Ave Ste 2607 New York (10152) *(G-11401)*
New York Enterprise Report, New York *Also called Rsl Media LLC (G-11931)*
New York Eye, Amityville *Also called Hart Specialties Inc (G-292)*
New York Familypublications, Mamaroneck *Also called Family Publishing Group Inc (G-8034)*
New York Fan Coil LLC 646 580-1344
7 Chesapeake Bay Rd Coram (11727) *(G-3947)*
New York Findings Corp 212 925-5745
70 Bowery Unit 8 New York (10013) *(G-11402)*
New York Gourmet Coffee Inc 631 254-0076
204 N Fehr Way Ste C Bay Shore (11706) *(G-722)*
New York Health Care Inc (PA) 718 375-6700
20 E Sunrise Hwy Ste 201 Valley Stream (11581) *(G-16416)*
New York Hospital Disposable 718 384-1620
101 Richardson St Ste 1 Brooklyn (11211) *(G-2365)*
New York IL Bo Inc 718 961-1538
4522 162nd St Fl 2 Flushing (11358) *(G-5272)*
New York Imaging Service Inc 716 834-8022
255 Cooper Ave Tonawanda (14150) *(G-16184)*
New York Industrial Works Inc (PA) 718 292-0615
796 E 140th St Bronx (10454) *(G-1409)*
New York Knitting Processor 718 366-3469
5900 Decatur St Ste 3 Ridgewood (11385) *(G-14115)*
New York Laser & Aestheticks 516 627-7777
1025 Nthrn Blvd Ste 206 Roslyn (11576) *(G-15021)*
New York Law Journal, New York *Also called Alm Media LLC (G-9095)*
New York Legal Publishing 518 459-1100
120 Broadway Ste 1a Menands (12204) *(G-8377)*
New York Manufactured Products 585 254-9353
6 Cairn St Rochester (14611) *(G-14532)*
New York Manufacturing Corp 585 254-9353
6 Cairn St Rochester (14611) *(G-14533)*
New York Marble and Stone Corp 718 729-7272
4411 55th Ave Maspeth (11378) *(G-8156)*
New York Marine Elec Inc 631 734-6050
124 Springville Rd Ste 1 Hampton Bays (11946) *(G-5961)*
New York Marking Devices Corp 585 454-5188
700 Clinton Ave S Ste 2 Rochester (14620) *(G-14534)*
New York Marking Devices Corp (PA) 315 463-8641
2207 Teall Ave Syracuse (13206) *(G-15998)*
New York Media LLC 212 508-0700
75 Varick St New York (10013) *(G-11403)*
New York Nautical Inc 212 962-4522
200 Church St Frnt 4 New York (10013) *(G-11404)*
New York Observer Llc 212 887-8460
321 W 44th St 6th New York (10036) *(G-11405)*
New York Packaging Corp 516 746-0600
135 Fulton Ave New Hyde Park (11040) *(G-8850)*
New York Packaging II LLC 516 746-0600
135 Fulton Ave Garden City (11530) *(G-5523)*
New York Poplin LLC 718 768-3296
4611 1st Ave Brooklyn (11232) *(G-2366)*
New York Popular Inc 718 499-2020
168 39th St Unit 3 Brooklyn (11232) *(G-2367)*
New York Post, Brooklyn *Also called Nyp Holdings Inc (G-2385)*
New York Post, New York *Also called Nyp Holdings Inc (G-11485)*
New York Press & Graphics Inc 518 489-7089
12 Interstate Ave Albany (12205) *(G-106)*
New York Press Inc 212 268-8600
72 Madison Ave Fl 11 New York (10016) *(G-11406)*
New York Pretzel, Brooklyn *Also called Makkos of Brooklyn Ltd (G-2255)*
New York Qrtrly Foundation Inc 917 843-8825
322 76th St Brooklyn (11209) *(G-2368)*
New York Quarries Inc 518 756-3138
305 Rte 111 Alcove (12007) *(G-172)*
New York Ravioli Pasta Co Inc 516 270-2852
12 Denton Ave S New Hyde Park (11040) *(G-8851)*
New York Ready Mix Inc 516 338-6969
120 Rushmore St Westbury (11590) *(G-17014)*
NEW YORK REVIEW OF BOOKS, New York *Also called Nyrev Inc (G-11486)*
New York Rhbilitative Svcs LLC 516 239-0990
135 Rockaway Tpke Ste 107 Lawrence (11559) *(G-7396)*
New York Running Co, New York *Also called PRC Liquidating Company (G-11694)*
New York Sample Card Co Inc 212 242-1242
151 W 26th St Fl 12 New York (10001) *(G-11407)*
New York Sand & Stone LLC 718 596-2897
5700 47th St Maspeth (11378) *(G-8157)*
New York Skateboards, Deer Park *Also called Chapman Skateboard Co Inc (G-4116)*
New York Spring Water Inc 212 777-4649
517 W 36th St New York (10018) *(G-11408)*

ALPHABETIC

New York State Foam Enrgy LLC....845 534-4656
2 Commercial Dr Cornwall (12518) ***(G-3989)***

New York State Tool Co Inc....315 737-8985
3343 Oneida St Chadwicks (13319) ***(G-3530)***

New York Steel Services Co....718 291-7770
18009 Liberty Ave Jamaica (11433) ***(G-6935)***

New York Style Eats, Sunnyside *Also called Deelka Vision Corp* ***(G-15806)***

New York Sweater Company Inc....845 629-9533
141 W 36th St Rm 17 New York (10018) ***(G-11409)***

New York Tank Co, Watervliet *Also called Bigbee Steel and Tank Company* ***(G-16679)***

New York Times Co Mag Group, New York *Also called Gruner + Jahr Prtg & Pubg Co* ***(G-10375)***

New York Times Company (PA)....212 556-1234
620 8th Ave New York (10018) ***(G-11410)***

New York Times Company....718 281-7000
1 New York Times Plz Flushing (11354) ***(G-5273)***

New York Times Company....212 556-4300
620 8th Ave Bsmt 1 New York (10018) ***(G-11411)***

New York Trading Co, New York *Also called E-Won Industrial Co Inc* ***(G-9956)***

New York Typing & Printing Co....718 268-7900
10816 72nd Ave Forest Hills (11375) ***(G-5327)***

New York University....212 998-4300
7 E 12th St Ste 800 New York (10003) ***(G-11412)***

New York Vanity and Mfg Co....718 417-1010
10 Henry St Freeport (11520) ***(G-5415)***

New York1 News Operations....212 379-3311
75 9th Ave Frnt 6 New York (10011) ***(G-11413)***

Newbay Media LLC....516 944-5940
6 Manhasset Ave Port Washington (11050) ***(G-13848)***

Newburgh Brewing Company LLC....845 569-2337
88 S Colden St Newburgh (12550) ***(G-12769)***

Newburgh Distribution Corp (PA)....845 561-6330
463 Temple Hill Rd New Windsor (12553) ***(G-8945)***

Newburgh Envelope Corp....845 566-4211
1720 Route 300 Newburgh (12550) ***(G-12770)***

Newcastle Fabrics Corp....718 388-6600
86 Beadel St Brooklyn (11222) ***(G-2369)***

Newchem Inc....315 331-7680
434 E Union St Newark (14513) ***(G-12738)***

Newco, New York *Also called Namm Singer Inc* ***(G-11339)***

Newco Products Division, Ballston Spa *Also called Dura-Mill Inc* ***(G-595)***

Newcut, Newark *Also called Newchem Inc* ***(G-12738)***

Newkirk Products Inc (HQ)....518 862-3200
15 Corporate Cir Albany (12203) ***(G-107)***

Newline Products Inc (PA)....972 881-3318
509 Temple Hill Rd New Windsor (12553) ***(G-8946)***

Newmat Northeast Corp....631 253-9277
81b Mahan St West Babylon (11704) ***(G-16816)***

Newport Business Solutions Inc....631 319-6129
61 Keyland Ct Bohemia (11716) ***(G-1110)***

Newport Corporation....585 248-4246
705 Saint Paul St Rochester (14605) ***(G-14535)***

Newport Graphics Inc....212 924-2600
121 Varick St Rm 302 New York (10013) ***(G-11414)***

Newport Magnetics Inc....315 845-8878
396 Old State Rd Newport (13416) ***(G-12791)***

Newport Rochester Inc....585 262-1325
705 Saint Paul St Rochester (14605) ***(G-14536)***

News Communications Inc (PA)....212 689-2500
501 Madison Ave Fl 23 New York (10022) ***(G-11415)***

News Corporation (PA)....212 416-3400
1211 Ave Of The Americas New York (10036) ***(G-11416)***

News India Times, New York *Also called News India USA Inc* ***(G-11418)***

News India Times, New York *Also called News India Usa LLC* ***(G-11417)***

News India Usa LLC....212 675-7515
37 W 20th St Ste 1109 New York (10011) ***(G-11417)***

News India USA Inc....212 675-7515
37 W 20th St Ste 1109 New York (10011) ***(G-11418)***

News of The Highlands Inc (PA)....845 534-7771
35 Hasbrouck Ave Cornwall (12518) ***(G-3990)***

News Report Inc....718 851-6607
1281 49th St Ste 3 Brooklyn (11219) ***(G-2370)***

News Review, The, Mattituck *Also called Times Review Newspaper Corp* ***(G-8211)***

News/Sprts Microwave Rentl Inc....619 670-0572
415 Madison Ave Fl 11 New York (10017) ***(G-11419)***

Newsday LLC (HQ)....631 843-4050
235 Pinelawn Rd Melville (11747) ***(G-8341)***

Newsday LLC....631 843-3135
25 Deshon Dr Melville (11747) ***(G-8342)***

Newsday Media Group, Melville *Also called Newsday LLC* ***(G-8341)***

Newsgraphics of Delmar Inc....518 439-5363
125 Adams St Delmar (12054) ***(G-4245)***

Newspaper Association Amer Inc....212 856-6300
20 W 33rd St Fl 7 New York (10001) ***(G-11420)***

Newspaper Delivery Solutions....718 370-1111
309 Bradley Ave Staten Island (10314) ***(G-15710)***

Newspaper Publisher LLC....607 775-0472
1035 Conklin Rd Conklin (13748) ***(G-3871)***

Newspaper Times Union....518 454-5676
645 Albany Shaker Rd Albany (12211) ***(G-108)***

Newsweek/Daily Beast Co LLC, New York *Also called Daily Beast Company LLC* ***(G-9788)***

Newtex Industries Inc (PA)....585 924-9135
8050 Victor Mendon Rd Victor (14564) ***(G-16493)***

Newtown Finishing, Brooklyn *Also called Newcastle Fabrics Corp* ***(G-2369)***

Newyork Pedorthic Associates....718 236-7700
2102 63rd St Brooklyn (11204) ***(G-2371)***

Nex-Gen Ready Mix Corp....347 231-0073
334 Faile St Bronx (10474) ***(G-1410)***

Nexans Energy USA Inc....845 469-2141
25 Oakland Ave Chester (10918) ***(G-3610)***

Nexgen Enviro Systems Inc....631 226-2930
190 E Hoffman Ave Ste D Lindenhurst (11757) ***(G-7475)***

Nexstar Holding Corp....716 929-9000
275 Northpointe Pkwy Amherst (14228) ***(G-253)***

Next Advance Inc (PA)....518 674-3510
24 Prospect Ave Averill Park (12018) ***(G-536)***

Next Big Sound Inc....646 657-9837
125 Park Ave Fl 19 New York (10017) ***(G-11421)***

Next Magazine, New York *Also called Rnd Enterprises Inc* ***(G-11886)***

Next Potential LLC....401 742-5190
278 E 10th St Apt 5b New York (10009) ***(G-11422)***

Next Step Magazine, The, Victor *Also called Next Step Publishing Inc* ***(G-16494)***

Next Step Publishing Inc....585 742-1260
2 W Main St Ste 200 Victor (14564) ***(G-16494)***

Nextpotential, New York *Also called Next Potential LLC* ***(G-11422)***

Nfe Management LLC....212 798-6100
1345 Ave Of The Americas New York (10105) ***(G-11423)***

Nfk International, Brooklyn *Also called Slava Industries Incorporated* ***(G-2568)***

Niabraze LLC....716 447-1082
675 Ensminger Rd Tonawanda (14150) ***(G-16185)***

Niagara Blower Company (HQ)....800 426-5169
91 Sawyer Ave Tonawanda (14150) ***(G-16186)***

Niagara Chocolates, Buffalo *Also called Sweetworks Inc* ***(G-3205)***

Niagara Cooler Inc....716 434-1235
6605 Slyton Settlement Rd Lockport (14094) ***(G-7604)***

Niagara Cutter, Buffalo *Also called NC Industries Inc* ***(G-3082)***

Niagara Development & Mfg Div, Niagara Falls *Also called Fross Industries Inc* ***(G-12823)***

Niagara Dispensing Tech Inc....716 636-9827
170 Northpointe Pkwy Buffalo (14228) ***(G-3086)***

Niagara Falls Plant, Niagara Falls *Also called Tulip Molded Plastics Corp* ***(G-12885)***

Niagara Fiberboard Inc....716 434-8881
140 Van Buren St Lockport (14094) ***(G-7605)***

Niagara Fiberglass Inc....716 822-3921
88 Okell St Buffalo (14220) ***(G-3087)***

Niagara Gazette, Niagara Falls *Also called Community Newsppr Holdings Inc* ***(G-12806)***

Niagara Gear Corporation....716 874-3131
941 Military Rd Buffalo (14217) ***(G-3088)***

Niagara Label Company Inc....716 542-3000
12715 Lewis Rd Akron (14001) ***(G-25)***

Niagara Lasalle Corporation....716 827-7010
110 Hopkins St Buffalo (14220) ***(G-3089)***

Niagara Precision Inc....716 439-0956
233 Market St Lockport (14094) ***(G-7606)***

Niagara Printing, Niagara Falls *Also called Quantum Color Inc* ***(G-12865)***

Niagara Punch & Die Corp....716 896-7619
176 Gruner Rd Buffalo (14227) ***(G-3090)***

Niagara Refining LLC....716 706-1400
5661 Transit Rd Depew (14043) ***(G-4266)***

Niagara Sample Book Co Inc....716 284-6151
1717 Mackenna Ave Niagara Falls (14303) ***(G-12850)***

Niagara Scientific Inc....315 437-0821
6743 Kinne St East Syracuse (13057) ***(G-4552)***

Niagara Sheets LLC....716 692-1129
7393 Shawnee Rd North Tonawanda (14120) ***(G-12983)***

Niagara Specialty Metals Inc....716 542-5552
12600 Clarence Center Rd Akron (14001) ***(G-26)***

Niagara Thermo Products, Niagara Falls *Also called Kintex Inc* ***(G-12839)***

Niagara Transformer Corp....716 896-6500
1747 Dale Rd Buffalo (14225) ***(G-3091)***

Niagara Truss & Pallet LLC....716 433-5400
5626 Old Saunders Settle Lockport (14094) ***(G-7607)***

Niagara Tying Service Inc....716 825-0066
176 Dingens St Buffalo (14206) ***(G-3092)***

Nibble Inc Baking Co....518 334-3950
451 Broadway Apt 5 Troy (12180) ***(G-16243)***

Nibmor Project LLC....718 374-5091
11 Middle Neck Rd Great Neck (11021) ***(G-5823)***

Nice-Pak Products Inc (PA)....845 365-2772
2 Nice Pak Park Orangeburg (10962) ***(G-13236)***

Nice-Pak Products Inc....845 353-6090
100 Brookhill Dr West Nyack (10994) ***(G-16922)***

Niche Media Holdings LLc (HQ)....702 990-2500
711 3rd Ave Rm 501 New York (10017) ***(G-11424)***

Nicholas Dfine Furn Decorators....914 245-8982
546 E 170th St 48 Bronx (10456) ***(G-1411)***

Nicholas Kirkwood LLC (PA)....646 559-5239
807 Washington St New York (10014) ***(G-11425)***

Nicholson Steam Trap, Walden *Also called Spence Engineering Company Inc* ***(G-16536)***

Nick Lugo Inc....212 348-2100
159 E 116th St Fl 2 New York (10029) ***(G-11426)***

Nickel Group LLC....212 706-7906
212 Beach 141st St Rockaway Park (11694) ***(G-14786)***

Nickelodeon Magazines Inc (HQ) 212 541-1949
1633 Broadway Fl 7 New York (10019) ***(G-11427)***
Nicoform Inc 585 454-5530
72 Cascade Dr Rochester (14614) ***(G-14537)***
Nicolia Concrete Products Inc 631 669-0700
640 Muncy St Lindenhurst (11757) ***(G-7476)***
Nicolia of Long Island, Lindenhurst *Also called Nicolia Concrete Products Inc* ***(G-7476)***
Nicolia Ready Mix Inc 631 669-7000
615 Cord Ave Lindenhurst (11757) ***(G-7477)***
Nicolo Raineri 212 925-6128
82 Bowery New York (10013) ***(G-11428)***
Nicolo Raineri Jeweler, New York *Also called Nicolo Raineri* ***(G-11428)***
Nicraft, Buffalo *Also called Deltacraft Paper Company LLC* ***(G-2906)***
Nidec Motor Corporation 315 434-9303
6268 E Molloy Rd East Syracuse (13057) ***(G-4553)***
Niebylski Bakery Inc 718 721-5152
2364 Steinway St Astoria (11105) ***(G-450)***
Nielsen Hardware Corporation (PA) 607 821-1475
71 Frederick St Binghamton (13901) ***(G-940)***
Nielsen/Sessions, Binghamton *Also called Nielsen Hardware Corporation* ***(G-940)***
Nifty Bar Grinding & Cutting 585 381-0450
450 Whitney Rd Penfield (14526) ***(G-13501)***
Nightingale Food Entps Inc 347 577-1630
2306 1st Ave New York (10035) ***(G-11429)***
Nihao Media LLC 609 903-4264
1230 Avenue Of The Flr 7 New York (10020) ***(G-11430)***
Nijon Tool Co Inc 631 242-3434
12 Evergreen Pl 12 Deer Park (11729) ***(G-4180)***
Nike Inc 212 226-5433
21 Mercer St Frnt A New York (10013) ***(G-11431)***
Nike Inc 631 242-3014
102 The Arches Cir Deer Park (11729) ***(G-4181)***
Nike Inc 631 960-0184
2675 Sunrise Hwy Islip Terrace (11752) ***(G-6815)***
Nikish Software Corp 631 754-1618
801 Motor Pkwy Hauppauge (11788) ***(G-6148)***
Nikkei America Inc (HQ) 212 261-6200
1325 Avenue Of The Americ New York (10019) ***(G-11432)***
Nikkei Visual Images Amer Inc 212 261-6200
1325 Ave Of The Americas New York (10019) ***(G-11433)***
Nikon Instruments Inc (HQ) 631 547-4200
1300 Walt Whitman Rd Fl 2 Melville (11747) ***(G-8343)***
Nilda Desserts, Poughkeepsie *Also called Ljmm Inc* ***(G-13912)***
Nildas Desserts Limited 845 454-5876
188 Washington St Poughkeepsie (12601) ***(G-13922)***
Nimbletv Inc 646 502-7010
450 Fashion Ave Fl 43 New York (10123) ***(G-11434)***
Ninas Custard 716 636-0345
2577 Millersport Hwy Getzville (14068) ***(G-5601)***
Nine West Footwear Corporation (PA) 800 999-1877
1411 Broadway Fl 20 New York (10018) ***(G-11435)***
Nine West Group Inc (HQ) 800 999-1877
1129 Westchester Ave White Plains (10604) ***(G-17142)***
Nine West Holdings Inc 212 642-3860
1411 Broadway Fl 38 New York (10018) ***(G-11436)***
Nine West Holdings Inc 212 221-6376
1411 Broadway Fl 38 New York (10018) ***(G-11437)***
Nine West Holdings Inc 212 575-2571
1441 Broadway Fl 25 New York (10018) ***(G-11438)***
Nine West Holdings Inc 215 785-4000
1441 Broadway Fl 10 New York (10018) ***(G-11439)***
Nine West Holdings Inc 212 642-3860
1411 Broadway Fl 15 New York (10018) ***(G-11440)***
Nine West Holdings Inc 212 642-3860
575 Fashion Ave Frnt 1 New York (10018) ***(G-11441)***
Nine West Holdings Inc 212 968-1521
2 Broadway Frnt 1 New York (10004) ***(G-11442)***
Nine West Holdings Inc 212 822-1300
1441 Broadway New York (10018) ***(G-11443)***
Nireco America, Port Jervis *Also called Datatran Labs Inc* ***(G-13783)***
Nirvana Inc 315 942-4900
1 Nirvana Plz Forestport (13338) ***(G-5331)***
Nirx Medical Technologies LLC 516 676-6479
15 Cherry Ln Glen Head (11545) ***(G-5638)***
Nis Manufacturing Inc 518 456-2566
1 Mustang Dr Ste 5 Cohoes (12047) ***(G-3753)***
Nisonger Instrument Sls & Svc, Mamaroneck *Also called Secor Marketing Group Inc* ***(G-8046)***
Nite Train R, Champlain *Also called Koregon Enterprises Inc* ***(G-3543)***
Nitel Inc 347 731-1558
199 Lee Ave Ste 119 Brooklyn (11211) ***(G-2372)***
Nitram Energy Inc 716 662-6540
50 Cobham Dr Orchard Park (14127) ***(G-13285)***
Nitro Manufacturing LLC 716 646-9900
440 Shirley Rd North Collins (14111) ***(G-12929)***
Nitro Manufacturing LLC 716 646-9900
106 Evans St Ste E Hamburg (14075) ***(G-5934)***
Nitro Wheels Inc 716 337-0709
4440 Shirley Rd North Collins (14111) ***(G-12930)***
Nixon Gear, Syracuse *Also called Gear Motions Incorporated* ***(G-15949)***
Nixteria Crafted By Juicyvapor, Amherst *Also called Juicy Vapor LLC* ***(G-248)***
Njf Publishing Corp 631 345-5200
14 Ramsey Rd Shirley (11967) ***(G-15427)***
Njr Medical Devices 440 258-8204
390 Oak Ave Cedarhurst (11516) ***(G-3462)***
Nk Electric LLC 914 271-0222
22 Scenic Dr Croton On Hudson (10520) ***(G-4065)***
NK Medical Products Inc (PA) 716 759-7200
80 Creekside Dr Amherst (14228) ***(G-254)***
Nl Shoes and Bags LLC 212 594-0012
225 W 35th St Fl 17 New York (10001) ***(G-11444)***
Nlhe LLC 212 594-0012
225 W 35th St New York (10001) ***(G-11445)***
Nlr Counter Tops LLC 347 295-0410
902 E 92nd St New York (10128) ***(G-11446)***
Nmcc, Niagara Falls *Also called National Maint Contg Corp* ***(G-12849)***
Nmny Group LLC 212 944-6500
1400 Broadway Fl 16 New York (10018) ***(G-11447)***
Noah Enterprises Ltd (PA) 212 736-2888
520 8th Ave Lbby 2 New York (10018) ***(G-11448)***
Nobilium, Albany *Also called Cmp Industries LLC* ***(G-67)***
Noble Checks Inc 212 537-6241
1682 43rd St Apt 2 Brooklyn (11204) ***(G-2373)***
Noble Pine Products Co Inc 914 664-5877
240 E 7th St Mount Vernon (10550) ***(G-8710)***
Noble Vintages, Fredonia *Also called Woodbury Vineyards Inc* ***(G-5377)***
Noble Wood Shavings, Sherrill *Also called Jdlr Enterprises LLC* ***(G-15406)***
Nochairs Inc 917 748-8731
325 W 38th St Rm 310 New York (10018) ***(G-11449)***
Nochem Paint Stripping Inc 631 563-2750
32 Bergen Ln Blue Point (11715) ***(G-999)***
Noco Incorporated (PA) 716 833-6626
2440 Sheridan Dr Ste 202 Tonawanda (14150) ***(G-16187)***
Nodus Noodle Corporation 718 309-3725
4504 Queens Blvd Sunnyside (11104) ***(G-15808)***
Noel Assoc 516 371-5420
114 Henry St Ste A Inwood (11096) ***(G-6764)***
Noga Dairies Inc 516 293-5448
175 Price Pkwy Farmingdale (11735) ***(G-5066)***
Noir Jewelry LLC 212 465-8500
362 5th Ave Fl 6 New York (10001) ***(G-11450)***
Nola Speaker, Holbrook *Also called Accent Speaker Technology Ltd* ***(G-6429)***
Noll Reynolds Met Fabrication 315 422-3333
554 E Brighton Ave Ste 1 Syracuse (13210) ***(G-15999)***
Nomad Editions LLC 212 918-0992
123 Ellison Ave Bronxville (10708) ***(G-1502)***
None, College Point *Also called City Store Gates Mfg Corp* ***(G-3781)***
Noodle Education Inc 646 289-7800
59 Charles St Suite200 New York (10014) ***(G-11451)***
Norampac Industries Inc., Niagara Falls *Also called Cascades Cntnerboard Packg Inc* ***(G-12802)***
Norampac New England Inc 860 923-9563
801 Corporation Park Schenectady (12302) ***(G-15282)***
Norampac New York City Inc 718 340-2100
5515 Grand Ave Maspeth (11378) ***(G-8158)***
Norampac Schenectady Inc 518 346-6151
801 Corporation Park Schenectady (12302) ***(G-15283)***
Norampac Thompson Inc., Schenectady *Also called Norampac New England Inc* ***(G-15282)***
Norandex Inc Vestal 607 786-0778
2300 Vestal Rd Vestal (13850) ***(G-16452)***
Noras Candy Shop 315 337-4530
321 N Doxtator St Rome (13440) ***(G-14825)***
Norazza Inc (PA) 716 706-1160
3938 Broadway St Buffalo (14227) ***(G-3093)***
Norcatec LLC (PA) 516 222-7070
100 Garden Cy Plz Ste 530 Garden City (11530) ***(G-5524)***
Norcorp Inc 914 666-1310
400 E Main St Mount Kisco (10549) ***(G-8637)***
Nordic Interior Inc 718 456-7000
5601 Maspeth Ave Gf Maspeth (11378) ***(G-8159)***
Nordic Press Inc 212 686-3356
243 E 34th St New York (10016) ***(G-11452)***
Nordon Inc (PA) 585 546-6200
691 Exchange St Rochester (14608) ***(G-14538)***
Noresco Industrial Group Inc 516 759-3355
3 School St Ste 103 Glen Cove (11542) ***(G-5622)***
Norjac Boxes Inc 631 842-1300
570 Oak St Copiague (11726) ***(G-3916)***
Norlite Corporation 518 235-0030
628 Saratoga St Cohoes (12047) ***(G-3754)***
Noroc Enterprises Inc (PA) 718 585-3230
415 Concord Ave Bronx (10455) ***(G-1412)***
Norse Energy Corp USA 716 568-2048
3556 Lake Shore Rd # 700 Buffalo (14219) ***(G-3094)***
Norsk Titanium US Inc 646 277-7514
1350 Ave Of The Americas New York (10019) ***(G-11453)***
Nortech Laboratories Inc 631 501-1452
125 Sherwood Ave Farmingdale (11735) ***(G-5067)***
Nortek Powder Coating LLC 315 337-2339
5900 Success Dr Rome (13440) ***(G-14826)***
North America Pastel Artists 718 463-4701
13303 41st Ave Apt 1a Flushing (11355) ***(G-5274)***

ALPHABETIC

North American Bear Co Inc 212 388-0700
1261 Broadway Rm 815 New York (10001) ***(G-11454)***
North American Breweries Inc (HQ) 585 546-1030
445 Saint Paul St Rochester (14605) ***(G-14539)***
North American Carbide, Orchard Park *Also called Transport National Dev Inc* ***(G-13299)***
North American Carbide of NY, Orchard Park *Also called Transport National Dev Inc* ***(G-13300)***
North American DF Inc (PA) 718 698-2500
280 Watchogue Rd Staten Island (10314) ***(G-15711)***
North American Door Corp 518 566-0161
1471 Military Tpke Plattsburgh (12901) ***(G-13680)***
North American Enclosures Inc (PA) 631 234-9500
85 Jetson Ln Ste B Central Islip (11722) ***(G-3507)***
North American Filter Corp (PA) 800 265-8943
200 W Shore Blvd Newark (14513) ***(G-12739)***
North American Graphics Inc 212 725-2200
150 Varick St Rm 303 New York (10013) ***(G-11455)***
North American Hoganas Inc 716 285-3451
5950 Packard Rd Niagara Falls (14304) ***(G-12851)***
North American MBL Systems Inc 718 898-8700
3354 62nd St Woodside (11377) ***(G-17341)***
North American Mfg Entps Inc (PA) 718 524-4370
1961 Richmond Ter Staten Island (10302) ***(G-15712)***
North American Mfg Entps Inc 718 524-4370
1961 Richmond Ter Staten Island (10302) ***(G-15713)***
North American Mills Inc 212 695-6146
1370 Broadway Rm 1101 New York (10018) ***(G-11456)***
North American Mint Inc 585 654-8500
1600 Lexington Ave 240a Rochester (14606) ***(G-14540)***
North American Pipe Corp 516 338-2863
420 Jericho Tpke Ste 222 Jericho (11753) ***(G-7079)***
North American Service Group, Ballston Spa *Also called North American Svcs Group LLC* ***(G-604)***
North American Signs Buffalo, Buffalo *Also called Nas Quick Sign Inc* ***(G-3081)***
North American Slate Inc 518 642-1702
50 Columbus St Granville (12832) ***(G-5778)***
North American Stone Inc 585 266-4020
1358 E Ridge Rd Rochester (14621) ***(G-14541)***
North American Svcs Group LLC (HQ) 518 885-1820
1240 Saratoga Rd Ballston Spa (12020) ***(G-604)***
North Americas Breweries, Rochester *Also called High Falls Brewing Company LLC* ***(G-14434)***
North Amrcn Brwries Hldngs LLC (PA) 585 546-1030
445 Saint Paul St Rochester (14605) ***(G-14542)***
North Atlantic Industries Inc (PA) 631 567-1100
110 Wilbur Pl Bohemia (11716) ***(G-1111)***
North Atlantic Trading Co, New York *Also called National Tobacco Company LP* ***(G-11353)***
North Bronx Retinal & Ophthlmi 347 535-4932
3725 Henry Hudson Pkwy Bronx (10463) ***(G-1413)***
North Coast Outfitters Ltd 631 727-5580
1015 E Main St Ste 1 Riverhead (11901) ***(G-14150)***
North Country Behavioral, Saranac Lake *Also called Northern New York Rural* ***(G-15139)***
North Country Books Inc 315 735-4877
220 Lafayette St Utica (13502) ***(G-16352)***
North Country Dairy, North Lawrence *Also called Upstate Niagara Coop Inc* ***(G-12935)***
North Country Malt Supply LLC 518 298-2300
16 Beeman Way Champlain (12919) ***(G-3545)***
North Country This Week 315 265-1000
19 Depot St Ste 1 Potsdam (13676) ***(G-13880)***
North Country Welding Inc 315 788-9718
904 Leray St Watertown (13601) ***(G-16666)***
North County News, Yorktown Heights *Also called Northern Tier Publishing Corp* ***(G-17514)***
North Delaware Printing Inc 716 692-0576
645 Delaware St Ste 1 Tonawanda (14150) ***(G-16188)***
North E Rggers Erectors NY Inc 518 842-6377
178 Clizbe Ave Amsterdam (12010) ***(G-362)***
North East Finishing Co Inc 631 789-8000
245 Ralph Ave Copiague (11726) ***(G-3917)***
North East Fuel Group Inc 718 984-6774
51 Stuyvesant Ave Staten Island (10312) ***(G-15714)***
North Eastern Fabricators Inc 718 542-0450
910 Park Ave Ph Ph New York (10075) ***(G-11457)***
North End Paper Co Inc 315 593-8100
702 Hannibal St Fulton (13069) ***(G-5471)***
North Face, Central Valley *Also called Vf Outdoor LLC* ***(G-3528)***
NORTH FIELD, Island Park *Also called Northfeld Precision Instr Corp* ***(G-6782)***
North Fork Wood Works Inc 631 255-4028
5175 Route 48 Mattituck (11952) ***(G-8208)***
North Hills Signal Proc Corp (HQ) 516 682-7700
6851 Jericho Tpke Ste 170 Syosset (11791) ***(G-15833)***
North Hills Signal Proc Corp 516 682-7740
6851 Jericho Tpke Ste 170 Syosset (11791) ***(G-15834)***
North House Vineyards Inc 631 779-2817
1216 Main Rd Rr 25 Jamesport (11947) ***(G-6966)***
North Hudson Woodcraft Corp 315 429-3105
152 N Helmer Ave Dolgeville (13329) ***(G-4306)***
North Pk Innovations Group Inc (PA) 716 699-2031
6442 Route 242 E Ellicottville (14731) ***(G-4643)***
North Point Press, New York *Also called Farrar Straus and Giroux LLC* ***(G-10138)***
North Point Technologies 607 238-1114
530 Columbia Dr Johnson City (13790) ***(G-7099)***
North Point Technology LLC 866 885-3377
816 Buffalo St Endicott (13760) ***(G-4821)***
North Salina Cigar Store, Syracuse *Also called Saakshi Inc* ***(G-16028)***
North Shore Home Improver 631 474-2824
200 Wilson St Port Jeff STA (11776) ***(G-13767)***
North Shore Monuments Inc 516 759-2156
667 Cedar Swamp Rd Ste 5 Glen Head (11545) ***(G-5639)***
North Shore Neon Sign Co Inc 718 937-4848
4649 54th Ave Flushing (11378) ***(G-5275)***
North Shore News Group, Smithtown *Also called Smithtown News Inc* ***(G-15498)***
North Shore Orthtics Prsthtics 631 928-3040
591 Bicycle Path Ste D Port Jeff STA (11776) ***(G-13768)***
North Shore Pallet Inc 631 673-4700
191 E 2nd St Huntington Station (11746) ***(G-6719)***
North Six Inc 212 463-7227
176 Grand St Ste 5f New York (10013) ***(G-11458)***
North Star Knitting Mills Inc 718 894-4848
7030 80th St Glendale (11385) ***(G-5660)***
North-East Machine Inc 518 746-1837
4160 State Route 4 Hudson Falls (12839) ***(G-6648)***
North-South Books Inc 212 706-4545
600 3rd Ave Fl 2 New York (10016) ***(G-11459)***
Northamerican Breweries, Rochester *Also called North American Breweries Inc* ***(G-14539)***
Northast Coml Win Trtments Inc 845 331-0148
25 Cornell St Kingston (12401) ***(G-7203)***
Northeast Cnstr Inds Inc 845 565-1000
657 Rte 17 K S St Ste 2 Montgomery (12549) ***(G-8598)***
Northeast Commercial Prtg Inc (PA) 518 459-5047
1237 Central Ave Ste 3 Albany (12205) ***(G-109)***
Northeast Concrete Pdts Inc 518 563-0700
1024 Military Tpke Plattsburgh (12901) ***(G-13681)***
Northeast Conveyors Inc 585 768-8912
7620 Evergreen St Lima (14485) ***(G-7446)***
Northeast Data Destruction & R 845 331-5554
619 State Route 28 Kingston (12401) ***(G-7204)***
Northeast Doulas 845 621-0654
23 Hilltop Dr Mahopac (10541) ***(G-7999)***
Northeast Fabricators LLC 607 865-4031
30-35 William St Walton (13856) ***(G-16549)***
Northeast Group 518 563-8214
12 Nepco Way Plattsburgh (12903) ***(G-13682)***
Northeast Hardware Specialties 516 487-6868
393 Jericho Tpke Ste 103 Mineola (11501) ***(G-8527)***
Northeast Mesa LLC (PA) 845 878-9344
10 Commerce Dr Carmel (10512) ***(G-3402)***
Northeast Metrology Corp 716 827-3770
2601 Genesee St Buffalo (14225) ***(G-3095)***
Northeast Pallet & Cont Co Inc 518 271-0535
1 Mann Ave Bldg 300 Troy (12180) ***(G-16244)***
Northeast Panel & Truss LLC 845 339-3656
2 Kieffer Ln Kingston (12401) ***(G-7205)***
Northeast Paving Concepts LLC 518 477-1338
33 Brookside Dr East Schodack (12063) ***(G-4473)***
Northeast Promotional Group In 518 793-1024
75 Main St South Glens Falls (12803) ***(G-15527)***
Northeast Prtg & Dist Co Inc (PA) 518 563-8214
12 Nepco Way Plattsburgh (12903) ***(G-13683)***
Northeast Solite Corporation (PA) 845 246-2646
1135 Kings Hwy Saugerties (12477) ***(G-15189)***
Northeast Solite Corporation 845 246-2177
962 Kings Hwy Mount Marion (12456) ***(G-8652)***
Northeast Stitches & Ink Inc 518 798-5549
95 Main St South Glens Falls (12803) ***(G-15528)***
Northeast Toner Inc 518 899-5545
26 Walden Gln Fl 2 Ballston Lake (12019) ***(G-585)***
Northeast Treaters Inc 518 945-2660
796 Schoharie Tpke Athens (12015) ***(G-464)***
Northeast Treaters NY LLC 518 945-2660
796 Schoharie Tpke Athens (12015) ***(G-465)***
Northeast Water Systems LLC 585 943-9225
2338 W Kendall Rd Kendall (14476) ***(G-7144)***
Northeast Windows Usa Inc 516 378-6577
1 Kees Pl Merrick (11566) ***(G-8390)***
Northeast Wire and Cable Co 716 297-8483
8635 Packard Rd Niagara Falls (14304) ***(G-12852)***
Northeastern Air Quality Inc 518 857-3641
730 3rd St Albany (12206) ***(G-110)***
Northeastern Electric Motors 518 793-5939
34 Hollow Rd Hadley (12835) ***(G-5903)***
Northeastern Fuel Corp 917 560-6241
51 Stuyvesant Ave Staten Island (10312) ***(G-15715)***
Northeastern Fuel NY Inc 718 761-5360
414 Spencer St Staten Island (10314) ***(G-15716)***
Northeastern Paper Corp 631 659-3634
2 Lilac Ct Huntington (11743) ***(G-6670)***
Northeastern Products Corp (PA) 518 623-3161
115 Sweet Rd Warrensburg (12885) ***(G-16580)***
Northeastern Sign Corp 315 265-6657
102 Cold Brook Dr South Colton (13687) ***(G-15516)***
Northeastern Water Jet Inc 518 843-4988
4 Willow St Amsterdam (12010) ***(G-363)***

Northern Adhesives Inc 718 388-5834
97 Apollo St Brooklyn (11222) *(G-2374)*

Northern Air Systems Inc (PA) 585 594-5050
3605 Buffalo Rd Rochester (14624) *(G-14543)*

Northern Air Technology Inc (PA) 585 594-5050
3605 Buffalo Rd Rochester (14624) *(G-14544)*

Northern Awning & Sign Company 315 782-8515
22891 County Route 51 Watertown (13601) *(G-16667)*

Northern Biodiesel Inc 585 545-4534
317 State Route 104 Ontario (14519) *(G-13206)*

Northern Bituminous Mix Inc 315 598-2141
32 Silk Rd Fulton (13069) *(G-5472)*

Northern Design & Bldg Assoc 518 747-2200
100 Park Rd Queensbury (12804) *(G-14006)*

Northern Design Inc 716 652-7071
12990 Old Big Tree Rd East Aurora (14052) *(G-4378)*

Northern Forest Pdts Co Inc 315 942-6955
9833 Crolius Dr Boonville (13309) *(G-1166)*

Northern Goose Polar Project, New York *Also called Freedom Rains Inc (G-10206)*

Northern Indus Svces Mech Div, Cohoes *Also called Nis Manufacturing Inc (G-3753)*

Northern King Lures Inc (PA) 585 865-3373
167 Armstrong Rd Rochester (14616) *(G-14545)*

Northern Lights Candles, Wellsville *Also called Northern Lights Entps Inc (G-16755)*

Northern Lights Entps Inc 585 593-1200
3474 Andover Rd Wellsville (14895) *(G-16755)*

Northern Machining Inc 315 384-3189
2a N Main St Norfolk (13667) *(G-12900)*

Northern New York Rural 518 891-9460
126 Kiwassa Rd Saranac Lake (12983) *(G-15139)*

Northern NY Newspapers Corp 315 782-1000
260 Washington St Watertown (13601) *(G-16668)*

Northern Ready-Mix Inc (PA) 315 598-2141
32 Silk Rd Fulton (13069) *(G-5473)*

Northern Tier Publishing Corp 914 962-4748
1520 Front St Yorktown Heights (10598) *(G-17514)*

Northern Timber Harvesting LLC 585 233-7330
6042 State Route 21 Alfred Station (14803) *(G-197)*

NORTHERN WESTCHESTER HOSPITAL, Mount Kisco *Also called Norcorp Inc (G-8637)*

Northfeld Precision Instr Corp 516 431-1112
4400 Austin Blvd Island Park (11558) *(G-6782)*

Northknight Logistics Inc 716 283-3090
7724 Buffalo Ave Niagara Falls (14304) *(G-12853)*

Northland Filter Intl LLC 315 207-1410
249a Mitchell St Oswego (13126) *(G-13336)*

Northpoint Trading Inc (PA) 212 481-8001
347 5th Ave New York (10016) *(G-11460)*

Northport Printing, West Babylon *Also called Bartolomeo Publishing Inc (G-16774)*

Northrock Industries Inc 631 924-6130
31 Crossway E Bohemia (11716) *(G-1112)*

Northrop Grumman Corporation 703 280-2900
660 Grumman Rd W Bethpage (11714) *(G-876)*

Northrop Grumman Intl Trdg Inc 716 626-7233
1740 Wehrle Dr Buffalo (14221) *(G-3096)*

Northrop Grumman Systems Corp 516 575-0574
925 S Oyster Bay Rd Bethpage (11714) *(G-877)*

Northrop Grumman Systems Corp 716 626-4600
1740 Wehrle Dr Buffalo (14221) *(G-3097)*

Northrop Grumman Systems Corp 631 423-1014
70 Dewey St Huntington (11743) *(G-6671)*

Northrop Grumman Systems Corp 315 336-0500
Rr 26 Box N Rome (13440) *(G-14827)*

Northside Media Group LLC (HQ) 917 318-6513
1 Metrotech Ctr Ste 1803 Brooklyn (11201) *(G-2375)*

Northside Media Group LLC 917 318-6513
1 Metrotech Ctr Fl 18 Brooklyn (11201) *(G-2376)*

Northtown Imaging, Buffalo *Also called Mri Northtowns Group PC (G-3076)*

Northwell Health Inc 888 387-5811
521 Park Ave New York (10065) *(G-11461)*

Northwest Company LLC (PA) 516 484-6996
49 Bryant Ave Roslyn (11576) *(G-15022)*

Northwind Graphics 518 899-9651
2453 State Route 9 Ballston Spa (12020) *(G-605)*

Norton Performance Plas Corp 518 642-2200
1 Sealants Park Granville (12832) *(G-5779)*

Norton Pulpstones Incorporated 716 433-9400
53 Caledonia St Lockport (14094) *(G-7608)*

Norton, Ww & Company,, New York *Also called Liveright Publishing Corp (G-11015)*

Norton-Smith Hardwoods Inc (PA) 716 945-0346
25 Morningside Ave Salamanca (14779) *(G-15103)*

Norwesco Inc 607 687-8081
263 Corporate Dr Owego (13827) *(G-13357)*

Norwich Aero, Norwich *Also called Sureseal Corporation (G-13038)*

Norwich Aero Products Inc (HQ) 607 336-7636
50 Ohara Dr Norwich (13815) *(G-13032)*

Norwich Manufacturing Division, Binghamton *Also called Felchar Manufacturing Corp (G-914)*

Norwich Pharma Services, Norwich *Also called Norwich Pharmaceuticals Inc (G-13033)*

Norwich Pharmaceuticals Inc 607 335-3000
6826 State Highway 12 Norwich (13815) *(G-13033)*

Norwood Quar Btmnous Con Plnts, Norwood *Also called Barrett Paving Materials Inc (G-13040)*

Norwood Screw Machine Parts 516 481-6644
200 E 2nd St Ste 2 Mineola (11501) *(G-8528)*

Noteworthy Company, The, Amsterdam *Also called Noteworthy Industries Inc (G-364)*

Noteworthy Industries Inc 518 842-2662
336 Forest Ave Amsterdam (12010) *(G-364)*

Noticia Hispanoamericana Inc 516 223-5678
53 E Merrick Rd Ste 353 Baldwin (11510) *(G-560)*

Noto Industrial Corp 631 736-7600
11 Thomas St Coram (11727) *(G-3948)*

Nouveaux Div, New York *Also called Item-Eyes Inc (G-10670)*

Nova Bus Lfs, A Division of PR, Plattsburgh *Also called Prevost Car US Inc (G-13689)*

Nova Health Systems Inc 315 798-9018
1001 Broad St Ste 3 Utica (13501) *(G-16353)*

Nova Metal Inc 718 981-4000
351 Walker St Ste 4 Staten Island (10303) *(G-15717)*

Nova Optical, Orangeburg *Also called Essilor Laboratories Amer Inc (G-13226)*

Nova Pack, Philmont *Also called Pvc Container Corporation (G-13541)*

Nova Packaging Ltd Inc 914 232-8406
7 Sunrise Ave Katonah (10536) *(G-7133)*

Nova Science Publishers Inc 631 231-7269
400 Oser Ave Ste 1600 Hauppauge (11788) *(G-6149)*

Novamed-Usa Inc 914 789-2100
4 Westchester Plz Ste 137 Elmsford (10523) *(G-4771)*

Novanta Inc 818 341-5151
7279 William Barry Blvd Syracuse (13212) *(G-16000)*

Novartis Corporation (HQ) 212 307-1122
608 5th Ave New York (10020) *(G-11462)*

Novartis Corporation 845 368-6000
25 Old Mill Rd Suffern (10901) *(G-15795)*

Novartis Corporation 718 276-8600
22715 N Conduit Ave Laurelton (11413) *(G-7388)*

Novartis Pharmaceuticals Corp 888 669-6682
230 Park Ave New York (10169) *(G-11463)*

Novartis Pharmaceuticals Corp 718 276-8600
22715 N Conduit Ave Laurelton (11413) *(G-7389)*

Novatech Inc 716 892-6682
190 Gruner Rd Cheektowaga (14227) *(G-3583)*

Novel Box Company Ltd 718 965-2222
659 Berriman St Brooklyn (11208) *(G-2377)*

Novelis Corporation 315 342-1036
448 County Route 1a Oswego (13126) *(G-13337)*

Novelis Corporation 315 349-0121
72 Alcan W Entrance Rd Oswego (13126) *(G-13338)*

Novelis Inc 315 349-0121
448 County Route 1a Oswego (13126) *(G-13339)*

Novelty Crystal Corp (PA) 718 458-6700
3015 48th Ave Long Island City (11101) *(G-7826)*

Novelty Scenic Studios Inc, Monroe *Also called Associated Drapery & Equipment (G-8548)*

Noven Pharmaceuticals Inc 212 682-4420
350 5th Ave Ste 3700 New York (10118) *(G-11464)*

Novetree Coffee, Brooklyn *Also called Fal Coffee Inc (G-1954)*

Novita Fabrics Furnishing Corp 516 299-4500
1 Brewster St Glen Cove (11542) *(G-5623)*

Novoye Rsskoye Slovo Pubg Corp 646 460-4566
2614 Voorhies Ave Brooklyn (11235) *(G-2378)*

Novum Medical Products Inc 716 759-7200
80 Creekside Dr Amherst (14228) *(G-255)*

NP Roniet Creations Inc 212 302-1847
10 W 46th St Ste 1708 New York (10036) *(G-11465)*

Nppi, Vestal *Also called National Pipe & Plastics Inc (G-16451)*

Nrd LLC 716 773-7634
2937 Alt Blvd Grand Island (14072) *(G-5764)*

Nsgv Inc 212 367-3167
90 5th Ave New York (10011) *(G-11466)*

Nsgv Inc 212 367-4118
90 5th Ave Frnt 2 New York (10011) *(G-11467)*

Nsgv Inc 212 367-3100
90 5th Ave New York (10011) *(G-11468)*

Nsh, Menands *Also called Simmons Machine Tool Corp (G-8378)*

Nsi Industries LLC 800 841-2505
1 Grove St Mount Vernon (10550) *(G-8711)*

NSM Surveillance, New York *Also called News/Sprts Microwave Rentl Inc (G-11419)*

Nsusa, Deer Park *Also called Nutra Solutions USA Inc (G-4183)*

NTI Global, Amsterdam *Also called Nationwide Tarps Incorporated (G-361)*

Nu - Communitek LLC 516 433-3553
108 New South Rd Ste A Hicksville (11801) *(G-6377)*

Nu Image, Commack *Also called Twins Enterprise Inc (G-3844)*

Nu Life Restorations of L I 516 489-5200
51 Valley Rd Old Westbury (11568) *(G-13133)*

Nu Ways Inc 585 254-7510
655 Pullman Ave Rochester (14615) *(G-14546)*

Nu-Chem Laboratories, Bellport *Also called Optisource International Inc (G-835)*

Nu-Life Long Island, Old Westbury *Also called Nu Life Restorations of L I (G-13133)*

Nu-Tech Lighting Corp (PA) 212 541-7397
608 5th Ave Ste 810 New York (10020) *(G-11469)*

Nubian Heritage 631 265-3551
367 Old Willets Path Hauppauge (11788) *(G-6150)*

Nucare Pharmacy & Surgical, New York *Also called Nucare Pharmacy West LLC (G-11471)*

Nucare Pharmacy & Surgical, New York *Also called Nucare Pharmacy Inc (G-11470)*

Nucare Pharmacy Inc 212 426-9300
1789 1st Ave New York (10128) **(G-11470)**
Nucare Pharmacy West LLC 212 462-2525
250 9th Ave New York (10001) **(G-11471)**
Nuclear Diagnostic Pdts NY Inc 516 575-4201
130 Commercial St Plainview (11803) **(G-13624)**
Nucor Steel Auburn Inc 315 253-4561
25 Quarry Rd Auburn (13021) **(G-511)**
Nugent Printing Company, Oceanside *Also called The Nugent Organization Inc* **(G-13101)**
Nuhart & Co Inc 718 383-8484
49 Dupont St Brooklyn (11222) **(G-2379)**
Nulux Inc 718 383-1112
1717 Troutman St Ridgewood (11385) **(G-14116)**
Numed Pharmaceuticals, Brooklyn *Also called Ys Marketing Inc* **(G-2778)**
Nupro Technologies LLC 412 422-5922
23 Coach St Ste 2a Canandaigua (14424) **(G-3350)**
Nutec Components Inc 631 242-1224
81 E Jefryn Blvd Ste A Deer Park (11729) **(G-4182)**
Nutech, New York *Also called Nu-Tech Lighting Corp* **(G-11469)**
Nutra Solutions USA Inc 631 392-1900
1019 Grand Blvd Deer Park (11729) **(G-4183)**
Nutra-Scientifics LLC 917 238-8510
108 Overlook Rd Pomona (10970) **(G-13731)**
Nutra-Vet Research Corp 845 473-1900
201 Smith St Poughkeepsie (12601) **(G-13923)**
Nutraceutical Wellness LLC 888 454-3320
155 E 37th St Apt 4b New York (10016) **(G-11472)**
Nutrafol, New York *Also called Nutraceutical Wellness LLC* **(G-11472)**
Nutraqueen LLC 347 368-6568
138 E 34th St Apt 2f New York (10016) **(G-11473)**
Nutrascience Labs Inc 631 247-0660
70 Carolyn Blvd Farmingdale (11735) **(G-5068)**
Nutrifast LLC 347 671-3181
244 5th Ave Ste W249 New York (10001) **(G-11474)**
Nutritional Designs, Lynbrook *Also called ND Labs Inc* **(G-7955)**
Nuttall Gear L L C (HQ) 716 298-4100
2221 Niagara Falls Blvd # 17 Niagara Falls (14304) **(G-12854)**
Nuvite Chemical Compounds Corp 718 383-8351
213 Freeman St 215 Brooklyn (11222) **(G-2380)**
NV Prrcone MD Cosmeceuticals 212 734-2537
1745 Broadway New York (10019) **(G-11475)**
Nxxi Inc 914 701-4500
4 Manhattanville Rd # 205 Purchase (10577) **(G-13962)**
NY 1 Art Gallery Inc 917 698-0626
32 3rd St New Hyde Park (11040) **(G-8852)**
NY Accessory Group Ltd Lblty (PA) 212 989-6350
130 Madison Ave New York (10016) **(G-11476)**
NY Cabinet Factory Inc 718 256-6541
6901 14th Ave Brooklyn (11228) **(G-2381)**
NY Cutting Inc 845 368-1459
382 Route 59 Ste 286 Airmont (10952) **(G-17)**
NY Denim Inc 212 764-6668
1407 Broadway Rm 1021 New York (10018) **(G-11477)**
NY Embroidery Inc 516 822-6456
25 Midland Ave Hicksville (11801) **(G-6378)**
NY Froyo LLC 516 312-4588
324 W 19th St Deer Park (11729) **(G-4184)**
NY Iron Inc 718 302-9000
3131 48th Ave Unit C Long Island City (11101) **(G-7827)**
NY Orthopedic Usa Inc 718 852-5330
63 Flushing Ave Unit 333 Brooklyn (11205) **(G-2382)**
NY Phrmacy Compounding Ctr Inc 201 403-5151
3715 23rd Ave Astoria (11105) **(G-451)**
NY Print Partners, Sunnyside *Also called Deanco Digital Printing LLC* **(G-15805)**
NY Tempering LLC 718 326-8989
6021 Flushing Ave Maspeth (11378) **(G-8160)**
NY Tilemakers 989 278-8453
331 Grand St Brooklyn (11211) **(G-2383)**
Nybg 718 817-8700
2900 Southern Blvd Bronx (10458) **(G-1414)**
Nyc Community Media LLC 212 229-1890
1 Metrotech Ctr N Fl 10 Brooklyn (11201) **(G-2384)**
Nyc Design Co, New York *Also called M S B International Ltd* **(G-11076)**
Nyc District Council Ubcja 212 366-7500
395 Hudson St Lbby 3 New York (10014) **(G-11478)**
Nyc Fireplaces & Kitchens 718 326-4328
5830 Maspeth Ave Maspeth (11378) **(G-8161)**
Nyc Idol Apparel Inc 212 997-9797
214 W 39th St Rm 807 New York (10018) **(G-11479)**
Nyc Knitwear Inc 212 840-1313
525 Fashion Ave Rm 701 New York (10018) **(G-11480)**
Nyc Thermography, New York *Also called Hart Reproduction Services* **(G-10423)**
Nyc Trade Printers Corp 718 606-0610
3245 62nd St Woodside (11377) **(G-17342)**
Nycd, New York *Also called Inner Workings Inc* **(G-10601)**
Nycjbs LLC 212 533-1888
112 Rivington St Frnt New York (10002) **(G-11481)**
Nycom Business Solutions Inc 516 345-6000
804 Hempstead Tpke Franklin Square (11010) **(G-5366)**
Nyemac Inc 631 668-1303
Paradise Ln Montauk (11954) **(G-8591)**
Nyg, New York *Also called NY Accessory Group Ltd Lblty* **(G-11476)**
Nykon Inc 315 483-0504
8175 Stell Rd Sodus (14551) **(G-15504)**
Nylon LLc 212 226-6454
110 Greene St Ste 607 New York (10012) **(G-11482)**
Nylon Magazine, New York *Also called Nylon LLc* **(G-11482)**
Nylon Media Inc 212 226-6454
110 Greene St Ste 607 New York (10012) **(G-11483)**
Nylonshop, New York *Also called Nylon Media Inc* **(G-11483)**
Nyman Jewelry Inc (PA) 212 944-1976
66 W 9th St New York (10011) **(G-11484)**
Nyp Holdings Inc 718 260-2500
1 Metrotech Ctr N Fl 10 Brooklyn (11201) **(G-2385)**
Nyp Holdings Inc (HQ) 212 997-9272
1211 Avenue Of The Amer New York (10036) **(G-11485)**
Nyrev Inc 212 757-8070
435 Hudson St Rm 300 New York (10014) **(G-11486)**
Nys Nyu-Cntr Intl Cooperation 212 998-3680
418 Lafayette St New York (10003) **(G-11487)**
Nysco Products LLC 718 792-9000
2350 Lafayette Ave Bronx (10473) **(G-1415)**
Nyt Capital LLC (HQ) 212 556-1234
620 8th Ave New York (10018) **(G-11488)**
O & S Machine & Tool Co Inc 716 941-5542
8143 State Rd Colden (14033) **(G-3772)**
O Brien Gere Mfg Inc 315 437-6100
7600 Morgan Rd Ste 1 Liverpool (13090) **(G-7537)**
O C Choppers, Newburgh *Also called Orange County Choppers Inc* **(G-12771)**
O C P Inc 516 679-2000
500 Bi County Blvd # 209 Farmingdale (11735) **(G-5069)**
O C Tanner Company 914 921-2025
27 Park Dr S Rye (10580) **(G-15065)**
O C Tanner Company 518 348-2035
636 Plank Rd Ste 110 Clifton Park (12065) **(G-3703)**
O P I, Rochester *Also called Ontario Plastics Inc* **(G-14550)**
O P I Industries, Ronkonkoma *Also called Paramount Equipment Inc* **(G-14964)**
O Tex, Rochester *Also called Robert J Faraone* **(G-14630)**
O Val Nick Music Co Inc 212 873-2179
254 W 72nd St Apt 1a New York (10023) **(G-11489)**
O W Hubbell & Sons Inc 315 736-8311
5124 Commercial Dr Yorkville (13495) **(G-17523)**
O'Bryan Bros, New York *Also called Komar Layering LLC* **(G-10874)**
O'Neil Construction, Glen Head *Also called Lomin Construction Company* **(G-5636)**
O-At-Ka Milk Products Coop Inc (PA) 585 343-0536
700 Ellicott St Batavia (14020) **(G-644)**
O-Neh-Da Vineyard, Conesus *Also called Eagle Crest Vineyard LLC* **(G-3850)**
Oak Lone Publishing Co Inc 518 792-1126
15 Ridge St Glens Falls (12801) **(G-5693)**
Oak-Bark Corporation 518 372-5691
37 Maple Ave Scotia (12302) **(G-15329)**
Oak-Mitsui Inc 518 686-8060
1 Mechanic St Bldg 2 Hoosick Falls (12090) **(G-6542)**
Oak-Mitsui Technologies LLC 518 686-4961
80 1st St Hoosick Falls (12090) **(G-6543)**
Oakdale Industrial Elec Corp 631 737-4090
1995 Pond Rd Ronkonkoma (11779) **(G-14957)**
Oakhurst Partners LLC 212 502-3220
148 Madison Ave Fl 13 New York (10016) **(G-11490)**
Oaklee International Inc 631 436-7900
125 Raynor Ave Ronkonkoma (11779) **(G-14958)**
Oakley Inc 212 575-0960
1515 Broadway Frnt 4 New York (10036) **(G-11491)**
Oakwood Publishing Co 516 482-7720
14 Bond St Ste 386 Great Neck (11021) **(G-5824)**
Oasis Cosmetic Labs Inc 631 758-0038
182 Long Island Ave Holtsville (11742) **(G-6505)**
Oberdorfer Pumps Inc 315 437-0361
5900 Firestone Dr Syracuse (13206) **(G-16001)**
Oberon, New York *Also called Tabrisse Collections Inc* **(G-12270)**
Observer Daily Sunday Newsppr 716 366-3000
10 E 2nd St Dunkirk (14048) **(G-4346)**
Observer Dispatch, Utica *Also called Gatehouse Media LLC* **(G-16336)**
Obvious Inc 212 278-0007
214 W 39th St Rm 905a New York (10018) **(G-11492)**
Ocala Group LLC 516 233-2750
1981 Marcus Ave Ste 227 New Hyde Park (11042) **(G-8853)**
Occhioerosso John 718 541-7025
75 Santa Monica Ln Staten Island (10309) **(G-15718)**
Occidental Chemical Corp 716 278-7795
4700 Buffalo Ave Niagara Falls (14304) **(G-12855)**
Occidental Chemical Corp 716 773-8100
2801 Long Rd Grand Island (14072) **(G-5765)**
Occidental Chemical Corp 716 278-7794
56 Street & Energy Blvd Niagara Falls (14302) **(G-12856)**
Occidental Chemical Corp 716 694-3827
3780 Commerce Ct Ste 600 North Tonawanda (14120) **(G-12984)**
Occidental Energy Mktg Inc 212 632-4950
1230 Av Of The Amrcs 80 New York (10020) **(G-11493)**
Occunomix International LLC 631 741-1940
585 Bicycle Path Ste 52 Port Jeff STA (11776) **(G-13769)**
Ocean Cardiac Monitoring 631 777-3700
38 W 17th St Deer Park (11729) **(G-4185)**

Ocean Park Drugs & Surgical, Far Rockaway Also called Far Rockaway Drugs Inc *(G-4922)*
Ocean Printing, Ronkonkoma Also called Copy X/Press Ltd *(G-14888)*
Ocean Waves Swim LLC 212 967-4481
231 W 39th St Rm 500 New York (10018) *(G-11494)*
Oceans Cuisine Ltd 631 209-9200
367 Sheffield Ct Ridge (11961) *(G-14092)*
Oceanside-Island Park Herald, Lawrence Also called Richner Communications Inc *(G-7399)*
Ocip Holding LLC (PA) 646 589-6180
660 Madison Ave Fl 19 New York (10065) *(G-11495)*
Ocs, Brooklyn Also called Original Convector Specialist *(G-2395)*
Ocs Industries, Brooklyn Also called CIDC Corp *(G-1780)*
Octagon Process LLC (HQ) 845 680-8800
30 Ramland Rd S Ste 103 Orangeburg (10962) *(G-13237)*
Octopus Advanced Systems Inc 914 771-6110
27 Covington Rd Yonkers (10710) *(G-17469)*
Octopus City.com, New York Also called Auric Technology LLC *(G-9265)*
Ocular Sciences A Coopervision, Victor Also called Coopervision Inc *(G-16471)*
Odegard Inc 212 545-0069
3030 47th Ave Ste 700 Long Island City (11101) *(G-7828)*
Oden Machinery Inc (PA) 716 874-3000
199 Fire Tower Dr Tonawanda (14150) *(G-16189)*
ODY Accessories Inc 212 239-0580
1239 Broadway New York (10001) *(G-11496)*
Odyssey Controls Inc 585 548-9800
6256 Clinton Street Rd Bergen (14416) *(G-851)*
Odyssey Mag Pubg Group Inc 212 545-4800
4 New York Plz New York (10004) *(G-11497)*
Oehlers Wldg & Fabrication Inc 716 821-1800
242 Elk St Buffalo (14210) *(G-3098)*
OEM Solutions Inc 716 864-9324
4995 Rockhaven Dr Clarence (14031) *(G-3667)*
Oerlikon Balzers Coating USA 716 564-8557
375 N French Rd Ste 104 Buffalo (14228) *(G-3099)*
Oerlikon Metco (us) Inc 716 270-2228
6000 N Bailey Ave Amherst (14226) *(G-256)*
Oestreich Metal Works Inc 315 463-4268
6131 Court Street Rd Syracuse (13206) *(G-16002)*
Off State Water Group, Montgomery Also called On Point Reps Inc *(G-8599)*
Offi & Company 800 958-6334
60 E Market St Ste 101 Corning (14830) *(G-3977)*
Office Grabs NY Inc 212 444-1331
1303 53rd St 105 Brooklyn (11219) *(G-2386)*
Official Offset Corporation 631 957-8500
8600 New Horizons Blvd Amityville (11701) *(G-317)*
Official Press, The, New York Also called Hks Printing Company Inc *(G-10487)*
Ogd V-Hvac Inc 315 858-1002
174 Pumkinhook Rd Van Hornesville (13475) *(G-16432)*
Ogden Newspapers Inc 716 487-1111
15 W 2nd St Jamestown (14701) *(G-7022)*
Ogi Limited, New York Also called Osnat Gad Inc *(G-11532)*
Ogilvie Press, Lancaster Also called Rmf Printing Technologies Inc *(G-7339)*
Ogosport LLC 718 554-0777
63 Flushing Ave Unit 137 Brooklyn (11205) *(G-2387)*
Ogulnick Uniforms, New York Also called Tailored Sportsman LLC *(G-12274)*
OH How Cute Inc 347 838-6031
38 Androvette St Staten Island (10309) *(G-15719)*
Ohio Baking Company Inc 315 724-2033
10585 Cosby Manor Rd Utica (13502) *(G-16354)*
Ohr Pharmaceutical Inc (PA) 212 682-8452
800 3rd Ave Fl 11 New York (10022) *(G-11498)*
Ohserase Manufacturing LLC 518 358-9309
26 Eagle Dr Akwesasne (13655) *(G-32)*
Oil and Lubricant Depot LLC 718 258-9220
61 Ranick Dr S Amityville (11701) *(G-318)*
Oil Depot, The, Amityville Also called Oil and Lubricant Depot LLC *(G-318)*
Olan Laboratories Inc 631 582-2006
20 Newton Pl Hauppauge (11788) *(G-6151)*
Old Castle Precast, Middle Island Also called Afco Precast Sales Corp *(G-8405)*
Old Dutch Mustard Co Inc (PA) 516 466-0522
98 Cuttermill Rd Ste 260s Great Neck (11021) *(G-5825)*
Old Dutchmans Wrough Iron Inc 716 688-2034
2800 Millersport Hwy Getzville (14068) *(G-5602)*
Old Poland Foods LLC 718 486-7700
149 N 8th St Brooklyn (11249) *(G-2388)*
Old Ue LLC 718 707-0700
4511 33rd St Long Island City (11101) *(G-7829)*
Old Williamsburgh Candle Corp 718 566-1500
143 Alabama Ave Brooklyn (11207) *(G-2389)*
Old World Mouldings Inc 631 563-8660
821 Lincoln Ave Bohemia (11716) *(G-1113)*
Old World Provisions Inc (PA) 518 465-7306
12 Industrial Park Rd Troy (12180) *(G-16245)*
Oldcastle Building Envelope 212 957-5400
1350 Ave Of The Americas New York (10019) *(G-11499)*
Oldcastle Buildingenvelope Inc 631 234-2200
895 Motor Pkwy Hauppauge (11788) *(G-6152)*
Oldcastle Precast Inc 518 767-2116
100 S County Rte 101 South Bethlehem (12161) *(G-15514)*
Oldcastle Precast Inc 518 767-2112
123 County Route 101 Selkirk (12158) *(G-15356)*
Oldcastle Precast Bldg Systems, Selkirk Also called Oldcastle Precast Inc *(G-15356)*

Olde Chtqua Vneyards Ltd Lblty 716 792-2749
6654 W Main Rd Portland (14769) *(G-13873)*
Olde Saratoga Brewing 518 581-0492
131 Excelsior Ave Saratoga Springs (12866) *(G-15165)*
Olean Advanced Products, Olean Also called AVX Corporation *(G-13134)*
Olean Waste Water Treatment, Olean Also called City of Olean *(G-13138)*
Oledworks LLC (PA) 585 287-6802
1645 Lyell Ave Ste 140 Rochester (14606) *(G-14547)*
Oligomerix Inc 914 997-8877
3960 Broadway Ste 340d New York (10032) *(G-11500)*
Olin Chlor Alkali Logistics 716 278-6411
2400 Buffalo Ave Niagara Falls (14303) *(G-12857)*
Olive Led Lighting Inc 718 746-0830
2819 119th St Flushing (11354) *(G-5276)*
Olivea Mathews, New York Also called Pride & Joys Inc *(G-11704)*
Oliveplaste LLC 315 356-2670
1 Olive Grove St Rome (13441) *(G-14828)*
Oliver Gear, Buffalo Also called Gear Motions Incorporated *(G-2967)*
Oliver Gear Inc 716 885-1080
1120 Niagara St Buffalo (14213) *(G-3100)*
Olmstead Machine Inc 315 587-9864
10399 Warehouse Ave North Rose (14516) *(G-12938)*
Olmstead Products Corp 516 681-3700
1 Jefry Ln Hicksville (11801) *(G-6379)*
Olollo Inc 877 701-0110
43 Hall St Ste B8 Brooklyn (11205) *(G-2390)*
Olson Sign Company Inc 518 370-2118
1750 Valley Rd Ext Schenectady (12302) *(G-15284)*
Olson Signs & Graphics, Schenectady Also called Olson Sign Company Inc *(G-15284)*
Olympia Company, Elmsford Also called Olympia Sports Company Inc *(G-4772)*
Olympia Sports Company Inc 914 347-4737
500 Executive Blvd # 170 Elmsford (10523) *(G-4772)*
Olympic Ice Cream Co Inc (PA) 718 849-6200
12910 91st Ave Richmond Hill (11418) *(G-14077)*
Olympic Ice Cream Co Inc 718 849-6200
12910 91st Ave Jamaica (11418) *(G-6936)*
Olympic Jewelry Inc 212 768-7004
62 W 47th St Ste 509 New York (10036) *(G-11501)*
Olympic Manufacturing Inc 631 231-8900
195 Marcus Blvd Hauppauge (11788) *(G-6153)*
Olympic Press Inc 212 242-4934
950 3rd Ave Fl 7 New York (10022) *(G-11502)*
Olympic Software & Consulting 631 351-0655
290 Broadhollow Rd 130e Melville (11747) *(G-8344)*
Omc Inc 718 731-5001
4010 Park Ave Bronx (10457) *(G-1416)*
Omega Consolidated Corporation 585 392-9262
101 Heinz St Hilton (14468) *(G-6419)*
Omega Die Casting Co, Hauppauge Also called Jacknob International Ltd *(G-6101)*
Omega Furniture Manufacturing 315 463-7428
102 Wavel St Syracuse (13206) *(G-16003)*
Omega Heater Company Inc 631 588-8820
2059 9th Ave Ronkonkoma (11779) *(G-14959)*
Omega Industries & Development 516 349-8010
150 Express St Ste 2 Plainview (11803) *(G-13625)*
Omega Wire Inc 315 337-4300
900 Railroad St Rome (13440) *(G-14829)*
Omega Wire Inc 315 689-7115
24 N Beaver St Jordan (13080) *(G-7130)*
Omega Wire Inc (HQ) 315 245-3800
12 Masonic Ave Camden (13316) *(G-3318)*
Omg Desserts Inc 585 698-1561
1227 Ridgeway Ave Ste J Rochester (14615) *(G-14548)*
Omicron Technologies Inc 631 434-7697
1736 Church St Holbrook (11741) *(G-6465)*
Omilk LLC 646 530-2908
189 Schermerhorn St 14d Brooklyn (11201) *(G-2391)*
Omni-ID Usa Inc 585 697-9913
1200 Ridgeway Ave Ste 106 Rochester (14615) *(G-14549)*
Omniafiltra LLC 315 346-7300
9567 Main St Beaver Falls (13305) *(G-795)*
Omnicare Anesthesia PC (PA) 718 433-0044
3636 33rd St Ste 211 Astoria (11106) *(G-452)*
Omnimusic, Port Washington Also called Franklin-Douglas Inc *(G-13816)*
Omniumedia LLC 516 593-2735
77 Freeman Ave Elmont (11003) *(G-4725)*
Omntec Mfg Inc 631 981-2001
1993 Pond Rd Ronkonkoma (11779) *(G-14960)*
Omp Printing & Graphics, Clinton Also called Tenney Media Group *(G-3722)*
Omrix Biopharmaceuticals Inc 908 218-0707
1 Rckfller Ctr Ste 2322 New York (10020) *(G-11503)*
Omt, Yorkville Also called Oriskany Mfg Tech LLC *(G-17525)*
Omx (us) Inc 646 428-2800
140 Broadway Fl 25 New York (10005) *(G-11504)*
On Demand Books LLC 212 966-2222
939 Lexington Ave New York (10065) *(G-11505)*
On Line Power Technologies 914 968-4440
113 Sunnyside Dr Yonkers (10705) *(G-17470)*
On Montauk, Montauk Also called Nyemac Inc *(G-8591)*
On Point Reps Inc 518 258-2268
20a Wellroad Ave Montgomery (12549) *(G-8599)*

On The Double Inc 518 431-3571
178 Viewmont Rd Germantown (12526) ***(G-5591)***
On The Job Embroidery & AP 914 381-3556
154 E Boston Post Rd # 1 Mamaroneck (10543) ***(G-8040)***
On The Mark Digital Printing & 716 823-3373
5758 S Park Ave Hamburg (14075) ***(G-5935)***
On The Spot Binding Inc 718 497-2200
4805 Metropolitan Ave Ridgewood (11385) ***(G-14117)***
Once Again Nut Butter Collectv (PA) 585 468-2535
12 S State St Nunda (14517) ***(G-13041)***
Ondrivesus Corp 516 771-6777
216 N Main St Bldg B2 Freeport (11520) ***(G-5416)***
One Girl Cookies Ltd 212 675-4996
68 Dean St Ste A Brooklyn (11201) ***(G-2392)***
One In A Million Inc 516 829-1111
51 Franklin Ave Valley Stream (11580) ***(G-16417)***
One Jeanswear Group Inc (HQ) 212 835-2500
1441 Broadway New York (10018) ***(G-11506)***
One Mountain Imports LLC 212 643-0805
226 W 37th St Fl 16 New York (10018) ***(G-11507)***
One Step Up Kids, New York *Also called Kidz Concepts LLC* ***(G-10842)***
One Step Up Ltd 212 398-1110
1412 Broadway Fl 3 New York (10018) ***(G-11508)***
One Story Inc 917 816-3659
232 3rd St Ste A108 Brooklyn (11215) ***(G-2393)***
One Technologies LLC 718 509-0704
44 Court St Ste 1217 Brooklyn (11201) ***(G-2394)***
One-Blue LLC 212 223-4380
1350 Broadway Rm 1406 New York (10018) ***(G-11509)***
Oneh2 Inc 703 862-9656
3870 Dugue Rd Hector (14841) ***(G-6259)***
Oneida Air Systems Inc 315 476-5151
1001 W Fayette St Ste 2a Syracuse (13204) ***(G-16004)***
Oneida Concrete Products, Buffalo *Also called Oneida Sales & Service Inc* ***(G-3101)***
Oneida Concrete Products, Lackawanna *Also called Oneida Sales & Service Inc* ***(G-7245)***
Oneida Dispatch, Oneida *Also called Oneida Publications Inc* ***(G-13163)***
Oneida Foundries Inc 315 363-4570
559 Fitch St Oneida (13421) ***(G-13159)***
Oneida International Inc 315 361-3000
163-181 Kenwood Ave Oneida (13421) ***(G-13160)***
Oneida Molded Plastics LLC (PA) 315 363-7990
104 S Warner St Oneida (13421) ***(G-13161)***
Oneida Molded Plastics LLC 315 363-7990
104 S Warner St Oneida (13421) ***(G-13162)***
Oneida Publications Inc 315 363-5100
130 Broad St Oneida (13421) ***(G-13163)***
Oneida Sales & Service Inc (PA) 716 822-8205
155 Commerce Dr Buffalo (14218) ***(G-3101)***
Oneida Sales & Service Inc 716 270-0433
155 Commerce Dr Lackawanna (14218) ***(G-7245)***
Oneida Silversmiths Inc 315 361-3000
163 Kenwood Ave 181 Oneida (13421) ***(G-13164)***
Oneonta Asphalt, Oneonta *Also called Cobleskill Stone Products Inc* ***(G-13180)***
Oneonta City Wtr Trtmnt Plant, Oneonta *Also called City of Oneonta* ***(G-13178)***
Oneonta Fence 607 433-6707
2 Washburn St Oneonta (13820) ***(G-13190)***
Online Publishers Association 646 473-1000
1350 Broadway Rm 606 New York (10018) ***(G-11510)***
Only Hearts Ltd (PA) 718 783-3218
134 W 37th St Fl 9 New York (10018) ***(G-11511)***
Only Natural Inc 516 897-7001
31 Saratoga Blvd Island Park (11558) ***(G-6783)***
Ontario Knife Company 716 676-5527
26 Empire St Ste 1 Franklinville (14737) ***(G-5370)***
Ontario Label Graphics Inc 716 434-8505
6444 Ridge Rd Lockport (14094) ***(G-7609)***
Ontario Plastics Inc (PA) 585 663-2644
2503 Dewey Ave Rochester (14616) ***(G-14550)***
Ontra Presentations LLC 212 213-1315
440 Park Ave S Fl 3 New York (10016) ***(G-11512)***
Ony Inc 716 636-9096
1576 Sweet Home Rd # 114 Amherst (14228) ***(G-257)***
Ony Inc Baird Researchpark 716 636-9096
1576 Sweet Home Rd Buffalo (14228) ***(G-3102)***
Onyx Solar Group LLC 917 951-9732
1123 Broadway Ste 908 New York (10010) ***(G-11513)***
Opd, Depew *Also called Leica Microsystems Inc* ***(G-4262)***
Open & Shut Doors, Brentwood *Also called Michbi Doors Inc* ***(G-1192)***
Open-Xchange Inc 914 332-5720
303 S Broadway Ste 224 Tarrytown (10591) ***(G-16099)***
Openfin Inc 917 450-8822
25 Broadway Fl 9 New York (10004) ***(G-11514)***
Openroad Integrated Media Inc 212 691-0900
180 Maiden Ln Ste 2803 New York (10038) ***(G-11515)***
Operative Cake Corp 718 278-5600
711 Brush Ave Bronx (10465) ***(G-1417)***
Operative Media Inc (PA) 212 994-8930
6 E 32nd St Fl 3 New York (10016) ***(G-11516)***
Oprah Magazine, New York *Also called Hearst Corporation* ***(G-10440)***
Opta Minerals 905 689-7361
266 Elmwood Ave Buffalo (14222) ***(G-3103)***
Opthotech Corp 212 845-8200
1 Penn Plz Ste 1924 New York (10119) ***(G-11517)***
Optic Solution LLC 518 293-4321
133 Standish Rd Saranac (12981) ***(G-15133)***
Optical Gaging Products Div, Rochester *Also called Quality Vision Intl Inc* ***(G-14613)***
Opticool Solutions LLC 585 347-6127
855 Publishers Pkwy Webster (14580) ***(G-16728)***
Opticool Technologies, Webster *Also called Opticool Solutions LLC* ***(G-16728)***
Optics Plus Inc 716 744-2636
4291 Delaware Ave Tonawanda (14150) ***(G-16190)***
Optics Technology Inc 585 586-0950
3800 Monroe Ave Ste 3 Pittsford (14534) ***(G-13571)***
Optika Eyes Ltd 631 567-8852
153 Main St Unit 1 Sayville (11782) ***(G-15213)***
Optimax Systems Inc (PA) 585 265-1020
6367 Dean Pkwy Ontario (14519) ***(G-13207)***
Optimized Devices Inc 914 769-6100
220 Marble Ave Pleasantville (10570) ***(G-13715)***
Optimum Applied Systems Inc 845 471-3333
16 Victory Ln Ste 5 Poughkeepsie (12603) ***(G-13924)***
Optimum Window Mfg Corp 845 647-1900
28 Canal St Ellenville (12428) ***(G-4636)***
Options Publishing, New York *Also called Triumph Learning LLC* ***(G-12408)***
Options Publishing LLC 603 429-2698
136 Madison Ave Fl 8 New York (10016) ***(G-11518)***
Optipro Systems LLC 585 265-0160
6368 Dean Pkwy Ontario (14519) ***(G-13208)***
Optisource International Inc 631 924-8360
40 Sawgrass Dr Ste 1 Bellport (11713) ***(G-835)***
Optogenics of Syracuse Inc 315 446-3000
2840 Erie Blvd E Syracuse (13224) ***(G-16005)***
Opus Technology Corporation 631 271-1883
10 Gwynne Rd Melville (11747) ***(G-8345)***
Oracle America Inc 518 427-9353
7 Southwoods Blvd Ste 1 Albany (12211) ***(G-111)***
Oracle America Inc 585 317-4648
345 Woodcliff Dr Ste 1 Fairport (14450) ***(G-4866)***
Oracle Corporation 516 247-4500
330 Old Country Rd Mineola (11501) ***(G-8529)***
Oracle Corporation 585 383-1998
400 Linden Oaks Ste 310 Rochester (14625) ***(G-14551)***
Oracle Corporation 212 508-7700
520 Madison Ave Fl 30 New York (10022) ***(G-11519)***
Oracle Corporation 212 508-7700
120 Park Ave Fl 26 New York (10017) ***(G-11520)***
Orafol Americas Inc 585 272-0290
200 Park Centre Dr West Henrietta (14586) ***(G-16886)***
Orafol Americas Inc 585 272-0309
200 Park Centre Dr Henrietta (14467) ***(G-6297)***
Orafol Display Optics Inc (HQ) 585 647-1140
200 Park Centre Dr West Henrietta (14586) ***(G-16887)***
Oramaax Dental Products Inc 516 771-8514
216 N Main St Ste A Freeport (11520) ***(G-5417)***
Orange County Choppers Inc 845 522-5200
14 Crossroads Ct Newburgh (12550) ***(G-12771)***
Orange County Ironworks LLC 845 769-3000
36 Maybrook Rd Montgomery (12549) ***(G-8600)***
Orange Die Cutting Corp 845 562-0900
1 Favoriti Ave Newburgh (12550) ***(G-12772)***
Orange Packaging, Newburgh *Also called Orange Die Cutting Corp* ***(G-12772)***
Orangenius Inc 631 742-0648
115 W 18th St Fl 2 New York (10011) ***(G-11521)***
Orbcomm Inc 703 433-6396
125 Business Park Dr Utica (13502) ***(G-16355)***
Orbis Brynmore Lithographics 212 987-2100
1735 2nd Ave Frnt 1 New York (10128) ***(G-11522)***
Orbit Industries LLC 914 244-1500
116 Radio Circle Dr # 302 Mount Kisco (10549) ***(G-8638)***
Orbit International Corp (PA) 631 435-8300
80 Cabot Ct Hauppauge (11788) ***(G-6154)***
Orbit International Corp 631 435-8300
80 Cabot Ct Hauppauge (11788) ***(G-6155)***
Orbital Holdings Inc 951 360-7100
2775 Broadway St Ste 200 Buffalo (14227) ***(G-3104)***
Orcam Inc 800 713-3741
99 Jericho Tpke Ste 2013 Jericho (11753) ***(G-7080)***
Orchard Apparel Group Ltd 212 268-8701
212 W 35th St Fl 7 New York (10001) ***(G-11523)***
Orchid Manufacturing Co Inc 212 840-5700
77 W 55th St Apt 4k New York (10019) ***(G-11524)***
Orcon Industries Corp (PA) 585 768-7000
8715 Lake Rd Le Roy (14482) ***(G-7417)***
Ore-Lube Corporation 631 205-0030
20 Sawgrass Dr Bellport (11713) ***(G-836)***
Orege North America Inc (PA) 770 862-9388
575 Madison Ave Fl 25 New York (10022) ***(G-11525)***
Orelube, Bellport *Also called Ore-Lube Corporation* ***(G-836)***
Orens Daily Roast Inc (PA) 212 348-5400
12 E 46th St Fl 6 New York (10017) ***(G-11526)***
Orffeo Printing & Imaging Inc 716 681-5757
99 Cambria St Lancaster (14086) ***(G-7328)***
Orfit Industries America, Jericho *Also called SC Medical Overseas Inc* ***(G-7085)***

ALPHABETIC

Organic Frog Inc ... 516 897-0369
85 Commerce Dr Hauppauge (11788) ***(G-6156)***
Organic Peak, Mineola *Also called Maxim Hygiene Products Inc* ***(G-8523)***
Orics Industries Inc ... 718 461-8613
240 Smith St Farmingdale (11735) ***(G-5070)***
Origin Press Inc ... 516 746-2262
131 Liberty Ave Mineola (11501) ***(G-8530)***
Original Convector Specialist ... 718 342-5820
2015 Pitkin Ave Brooklyn (11207) ***(G-2395)***
Original Dream Statuary, Brooklyn *Also called Dream Statuary Inc* ***(G-1878)***
Original Fowlers Choclat Inc ... 716 668-2113
2563 Union Rd Ste 101 Cheektowaga (14227) ***(G-3584)***
Original Hrkmer Cnty Chese Inc ... 315 895-7428
2745 State Route 51 Ilion (13357) ***(G-6743)***
Oriskany Arms Inc ... 315 737-2196
175 Clear Rd Oriskany (13424) ***(G-13312)***
Oriskany Manufacturing LLC ... 315 732-4962
2 Wurz Ave Yorkville (13495) ***(G-17524)***
Oriskany Mfg Tech LLC ... 315 732-4962
2 Wurz Ave Yorkville (13495) ***(G-17525)***
Orlandi Inc (PA) ... 631 756-0110
131 Executive Blvd Farmingdale (11735) ***(G-5071)***
Orlandi Inc ... 631 756-0110
121 Executive Blvd Farmingdale (11735) ***(G-5072)***
Orlandi Scented Products, Farmingdale *Also called Orlandi Inc* ***(G-5071)***
Orleans Custom Packing Inc ... 585 314-8227
101 Cadbury Way Holley (14470) ***(G-6490)***
Orleans Pallet Company Inc ... 585 589-0781
227 West Ave Albion (14411) ***(G-167)***
Ormec Systems Corp (PA) ... 585 385-3520
19 Linden Park Rochester (14625) ***(G-14552)***
Ornametal Inc ... 845 562-5151
216 S William St Newburgh (12550) ***(G-12773)***
Oro Avanti Inc (PA) ... 516 487-5185
250 Kings Point Rd Great Neck (11024) ***(G-5826)***
Orolia Usa Inc ... 585 321-5800
1565 Jefferson Rd Ste 460 Rochester (14623) ***(G-14553)***
Orpheo USA Corp ... 212 464-8255
315 Madison Ave Rm 2601 New York (10017) ***(G-11527)***
Ortho Dent Laboratory Inc ... 716 839-1900
6325 Sheridan Dr Williamsville (14221) ***(G-17249)***
Ortho Medical Products (PA) ... 212 879-3700
315 E 83rd St New York (10028) ***(G-11528)***
Ortho Rite Inc ... 914 235-9100
65 Plain Ave New Rochelle (10801) ***(G-8918)***
Ortho-Clinical Diagnostics Inc ... 716 631-1281
15 Limestone Dr Williamsville (14221) ***(G-17250)***
Ortho-Clinical Diagnostics Inc ... 585 453-5200
2402 Innovation Way # 3 Rochester (14624) ***(G-14554)***
Ortho-Clinical Diagnostics Inc ... 585 453-4771
100 Latona Rd Bldg 313 Rochester (14626) ***(G-14555)***
Ortho-Clinical Diagnostics Inc ... 585 453-3000
1000 Lee Rd Rochester (14626) ***(G-14556)***
Ortho/Rochester Tech, Rochester *Also called Ortho-Clinical Diagnostics Inc* ***(G-14554)***
Orthocon Inc ... 914 357-2600
1 Bridge St Ste 121 Irvington (10533) ***(G-6775)***
Orthocraft Inc ... 718 692-0113
1477 E 27th St Brooklyn (11210) ***(G-2396)***
Orthogonal ... 585 254-2775
1999 Lake Ave Rochester (14650) ***(G-14557)***
Orthopedic Arts Laboratory Inc ... 718 858-2400
141 Atlantic Ave Apt 1 Brooklyn (11201) ***(G-2397)***
Orthopedic Treatment Facility ... 718 898-7326
4906 Queens Blvd Woodside (11377) ***(G-17343)***
Orthotic & Prosthetic Images ... 516 292-8726
500 Front St Hempstead (11550) ***(G-6284)***
Orthotics & Prosthetics Dept ... 585 341-9299
4901 Lac De Ville Blvd Rochester (14618) ***(G-14558)***
Orthstar Enterprises Inc ... 607 562-2100
119 Sing Sing Rd Horseheads (14845) ***(G-6586)***
Orza Bakery Inc ... 914 965-5736
261 New Main St Ste 263 Yonkers (10701) ***(G-17471)***
Os33 Inc ... 708 336-3466
16 W 22nd St Fl 6 New York (10010) ***(G-11529)***
Osaka Gas Energy America Corp ... 914 253-5500
1 N Lexington Ave Ste 504 White Plains (10601) ***(G-17143)***
Oscar Blandi, New York *Also called Blandi Products LLC* ***(G-9413)***
Oscar Heyman & Bros Inc (PA) ... 212 593-0400
501 Madison Ave Fl 15 New York (10022) ***(G-11530)***
Osf Flavors Inc ... 860 298-8350
259 W 10th St New York (10014) ***(G-11531)***
OSI Pharmaceuticals LLC ... 631 847-0175
500 Bi County Blvd # 118 Farmingdale (11735) ***(G-5073)***
OSI Pharmaceuticals LLC (HQ) ... 631 962-2000
1 Bioscience Way Dr Farmingdale (11735) ***(G-5074)***
OSI Specialties, Tarrytown *Also called Momentive Performance Mtls Inc* ***(G-16098)***
Osmose Holdings Inc ... 716 882-5905
2475 George Urban Blvd Depew (14043) ***(G-4267)***
Osnat Gad Inc ... 212 957-0535
608 5th Ave Ste 609 New York (10020) ***(G-11532)***
Oso Industries Inc ... 917 709-2050
647 Myrtle Ave Ste 1 Brooklyn (11205) ***(G-2398)***
Osprey Boat ... 631 331-4153
96 Mount Sinai Ave Mount Sinai (11766) ***(G-8656)***
Osprey Publishing Inc ... 212 419-5300
1385 Broadway Fl 5 New York (10018) ***(G-11533)***
Ossining Bakery Lmp Inc ... 914 941-2654
50 N Highland Ave Ossining (10562) ***(G-13324)***
Ossining Village of Inc ... 914 202-9668
25 Fowler Ave Ossining (10562) ***(G-13325)***
Osteohealth Company, Shirley *Also called Luitpold Pharmaceuticals Inc* ***(G-15424)***
Oswald Manufacturing Co Inc ... 516 883-8850
65 Channel Dr Port Washington (11050) ***(G-13849)***
Otex Protective Inc ... 585 232-7160
2180 Brighton Henrietta Rochester (14623) ***(G-14559)***
Other Press LLC ... 212 414-0054
267 5th Ave Fl 6 New York (10016) ***(G-11534)***
Otis Bedding Mfg Co Inc (PA) ... 716 825-2599
80 James E Casey Dr Buffalo (14206) ***(G-3105)***
Otis Elevator Company ... 315 736-0167
5172 Commercial Dr Yorkville (13495) ***(G-17526)***
Otis Elevator Company ... 917 339-9600
1 Penn Plz Ste 410 New York (10119) ***(G-11535)***
Otis Elevator Company ... 914 375-7800
1 Odell Plz Ste 120 Yonkers (10701) ***(G-17472)***
Otis Elevator Company ... 518 426-4006
20 Loudonville Rd Ste 1 Albany (12204) ***(G-112)***
Otis Products Inc (PA) ... 315 348-4300
6987 Laura St Lyons Falls (13368) ***(G-7978)***
Otis Technology, Lyons Falls *Also called Otis Products Inc* ***(G-7978)***
Otiwti, Fairport *Also called Qualitrol Company LLC* ***(G-4872)***
Otsego Ready Mix Inc ... 607 432-3400
2 Wells Ave Oneonta (13820) ***(G-13191)***
Ottaway Newspapers Inc ... 845 343-2181
40 Mulberry St Middletown (10940) ***(G-8455)***
Otto-Tech Machine Co Inc ... 845 687-8800
2452b Lucas Tpke High Falls (12440) ***(G-6401)***
Our Daily Eats LLC ... 518 810-8412
10 Burdick Dr Ste 1 Albany (12205) ***(G-113)***
Our Own Candle Company Inc (PA) ... 716 769-5000
10349 Main St Findley Lake (14736) ***(G-5177)***
Our Terms Fabricators Inc ... 631 752-1517
48 Cabot St West Babylon (11704) ***(G-16817)***
Ourem Iron Works Inc ... 914 476-4856
498 Nepperhan Ave Ste 5 Yonkers (10701) ***(G-17473)***
Outdoor Group LLC ... 585 201-5358
1325 John St West Henrietta (14586) ***(G-16888)***
Outdoor Lightning Perspectives ... 631 266-6200
1 Warner Ct Huntington (11743) ***(G-6672)***
Outerstuff LLC (PA) ... 212 594-9700
1412 Broadway Fl 18 New York (10018) ***(G-11536)***
Outlook Newspaper ... 845 356-6261
145 College Rd Suffern (10901) ***(G-15796)***
Outreach Publishing Corp ... 718 773-0525
546 Montgomery St Brooklyn (11225) ***(G-2399)***
Ovation Instore, Maspeth *Also called DSI Group Inc* ***(G-8132)***
Overhead Door Corporation ... 518 828-7652
1 Hudson Ave Hudson (12534) ***(G-6629)***
Overlook Press, The, New York *Also called Peter Mayer Publishers Inc* ***(G-11632)***
Overnight Labels Inc ... 631 242-4240
151 W Industry Ct Ste 15 Deer Park (11729) ***(G-4186)***
Overnight Mountings Inc ... 516 865-3000
1400 Plaza Ave New Hyde Park (11040) ***(G-8854)***
Overture Media Inc ... 917 446-7455
411 Lafayette St Ste 638 New York (10003) ***(G-11537)***
Ovitz Corporation ... 585 474-4695
150 Lucius Gordon Dr # 115 West Henrietta (14586) ***(G-16889)***
Owasco Recycling Center ... 315 252-0332
38a E Lake Rd Auburn (13021) ***(G-512)***
OWayne Enterprises Inc ... 718 326-2200
4901 Maspeth Ave Maspeth (11378) ***(G-8162)***
Owego Pennysaver Press Inc ... 607 687-2434
181 Front St Owego (13827) ***(G-13358)***
Owens Corning Sales LLC ... 518 475-3600
1277 Feura Bush Rd Feura Bush (12067) ***(G-5174)***
Owens-Brockway Glass Cont Inc ... 315 258-3211
7134 County House Rd Auburn (13021) ***(G-513)***
Owi Corporation ... 315 245-4305
12 Masonic Ave Camden (13316) ***(G-3319)***
Owl Books Div, New York *Also called Henry Holt and Company LLC* ***(G-10459)***
Owl Wire & Cable LLC ... 315 697-2011
3127 Seneca Tpke Canastota (13032) ***(G-3370)***
Owletts Saw Mills ... 607 525-6340
4214 Cook Rd Woodhull (14898) ***(G-17309)***
Own Instrument Inc ... 914 668-6546
250 E 7th St Mount Vernon (10550) ***(G-8712)***
Oxair Ltd ... 716 298-8288
8320 Quarry Rd Niagara Falls (14304) ***(G-12858)***
Oxbo International Corporation (HQ) ... 585 548-2665
7275 Batavia Byron Rd Byron (14422) ***(G-3269)***
Oxford Book Company Inc ... 212 227-2120
9 Pine St New York (10005) ***(G-11538)***
Oxford Cleaners ... 212 734-0006
847 Lexington Ave Frnt New York (10065) ***(G-11539)***

ALPHABETIC

Oxford Industries Inc 212 247-7712
600 5th Ave Fl 12 New York (10020) *(G-11540)*
Oxford Industries Inc 212 840-2288
25 W 39th St New York (10018) *(G-11541)*
Oxford University Press LLC (HQ) 212 726-6000
198 Madison Ave Fl 8 New York (10016) *(G-11542)*
Oxford University Press LLC 212 726-6000
198 Madison Ave Fl 8 New York (10016) *(G-11543)*
Oxford University Press, Inc., New York *Also called Oxford University Press LLC (G-11542)*
Oxo International Inc 212 242-3333
601 W 26th St Rm 1050 New York (10001) *(G-11544)*
Oxygen Inc (PA) 516 433-1144
6 Midland Ave Hicksville (11801) *(G-6380)*
Oxygen Generating Systems Intl, North Tonawanda *Also called Audubon Machinery Corporation (G-12957)*
Oyster Bay Pump Works Inc 516 922-3789
78 Midland Ave Unit 1 Hicksville (11801) *(G-6381)*
Oz Baking Company Ltd 516 466-5114
114 Middle Neck Rd Great Neck (11021) *(G-5827)*
Ozipko Enterprises Inc 585 424-6740
125 White Spruce Blvd # 5 Rochester (14623) *(G-14560)*
Ozmodyl Ltd 212 226-0622
233 Broadway Rm 707 New York (10279) *(G-11545)*
Ozteck Industries Inc 516 883-8857
65 Channel Dr Port Washington (11050) *(G-13850)*
P & B Woodworking Inc 845 744-2508
2415 State Route 52 Pine Bush (12566) *(G-13549)*
P & C Gas Measurements Service 716 257-3412
9505 Tannery Rd Cattaraugus (14719) *(G-3438)*
P & C Service, Cattaraugus *Also called P & C Gas Measurements Service (G-3438)*
P & D Equipment Sales LLC 585 343-2394
10171 Brookville Rd Alexander (14005) *(G-189)*
P & F Bakers Inc 516 931-6821
640 S Broadway Hicksville (11801) *(G-6382)*
P & F Industries Inc (PA) 631 694-9800
445 Broadhollow Rd # 100 Melville (11747) *(G-8346)*
P & F Industries of NY Corp 718 894-3501
6006 55th Dr Maspeth (11378) *(G-8163)*
P & H Inc 631 231-7660
15 Oser Ave Hauppauge (11788) *(G-6157)*
P & H Machine Shop Inc 585 247-5500
40 Industrial Park Cir Rochester (14624) *(G-14561)*
P & H Thermotech Inc 585 624-1310
1883 Heath Markham Rd Lima (14485) *(G-7447)*
P & I Sportswear Inc 718 934-4587
384 5th Ave New York (10018) *(G-11546)*
P & L Development LLC 516 986-1700
200 Hicks St Westbury (11590) *(G-17015)*
P & L Development LLC 516 986-1700
275 Grand Blvd Unit 1 Westbury (11590) *(G-17016)*
P & L Development LLC (PA) 516 986-1700
200 Hicks St Westbury (11590) *(G-17017)*
P & M LLC 631 842-2200
50 Ranick Dr E Amityville (11701) *(G-319)*
P & M Safe America LLC 718 292-6363
555 Longfellow Ave Bronx (10474) *(G-1418)*
P & R Industries Inc (PA) 585 266-6725
1524 N Clinton Ave Rochester (14621) *(G-14562)*
P & R Industries Inc 585 544-1811
1524 N Clinton Ave Rochester (14621) *(G-14563)*
P & R Truss Co 716 496-5484
13989 E Schutt Rd Chaffee (14030) *(G-3535)*
P & W Press Inc 646 486-3417
20 W 22nd St Ste 710 New York (10010) *(G-11547)*
P and F Machine Industries, Maspeth *Also called P & F Industries of NY Corp (G-8163)*
P B & H Moulding Corporation 315 455-1756
7121 Woodchuck Hill Rd Fayetteville (13066) *(G-5166)*
P B O E Pwred By Our Envmt Inc 917 803-9474
419 Madison St Apt 2a Brooklyn (11221) *(G-2400)*
P C I Manufacturing Div, Westbury *Also called Procomponents Inc (G-17023)*
P C I Paper Conversions Inc (PA) 315 437-1641
3584 Walters Rd Syracuse (13209) *(G-16006)*
P C I Paper Conversions Inc 315 703-8300
6761 Thompson Rd Syracuse (13211) *(G-16007)*
P C I Paper Conversions Inc 315 634-3317
6761 Thompson Rd Syracuse (13211) *(G-16008)*
P C I Paper Conversions Inc 315 437-1641
6761 Thompson Rd Syracuse (13211) *(G-16009)*
P C Rfrs Radiology 212 586-5700
3630 37th St Frnt Long Island City (11101) *(G-7830)*
P C T, Amsterdam *Also called Power and Composite Tech LLC (G-365)*
P D A Panache, Bohemia *Also called Pda Panache Corp (G-1116)*
P D I, Brooklyn *Also called Promotional Development Inc (G-2455)*
P D R Inc 516 829-5300
101 Dupont St Plainview (11803) *(G-13626)*
P E Guerin (PA) 212 243-5270
23 Jane St New York (10014) *(G-11548)*
P E Machine Works, Plainview *Also called Port Everglades Machine Works (G-13630)*
P G I, Forest Hills *Also called Preston Glass Industries Inc (G-5328)*
P G M, Rochester *Also called Precision Grinding & Mfg Corp (G-14593)*
P G Media, New York *Also called Parents Guide Network Corp (G-11571)*
P H Gucker Inc 518 834-9501
419 Frontage Rd Keeseville (12944) *(G-7141)*
P J D Publications Ltd 516 626-0650
1315 Jericho Tpke New Hyde Park (11040) *(G-8855)*
P J R Industries Inc 716 825-9300
1951 Hamburg Tpke Frnt Buffalo (14218) *(G-3106)*
P K G Equipment Incorporated 585 436-4650
367 Paul Rd Rochester (14624) *(G-14564)*
P L X, Deer Park *Also called Plx Inc (G-4189)*
P M Belts Usa Inc 800 762-3580
131 32nd St Brooklyn (11232) *(G-2401)*
P M Plastics Inc 716 662-1255
1 Bank St Ste 1 Orchard Park (14127) *(G-13286)*
P P I Business Forms Inc 716 825-1241
94 Spaulding St Buffalo (14220) *(G-3107)*
P Pascal Coffee Roasters, Yonkers *Also called P Pascal Inc (G-17474)*
P Pascal Inc 914 969-7933
960 Nepperhan Ave Yonkers (10703) *(G-17474)*
P R B Metal Products Inc 631 467-1800
200 Christopher St Ronkonkoma (11779) *(G-14961)*
P Ryton Corp 718 937-7052
504 50th Ave Long Island City (11101) *(G-7831)*
P S M Group Inc 716 532-6686
17 Main St Forestville (14062) *(G-5335)*
P T E Inc 516 775-3839
36 Ontario Rd Floral Park (11001) *(G-5206)*
P Tool & Die Co Inc 585 889-1340
3535 Union St North Chili (14514) *(G-12925)*
P V C Molding Technologies 315 331-1212
122 W Shore Blvd Newark (14513) *(G-12740)*
P&G Metal Components Corp 716 896-7900
54 Gruner Rd Buffalo (14227) *(G-3108)*
P-Hgh 2 Co Inc 954 534-6058
180 Cambridge Ave Buffalo (14215) *(G-3109)*
P.A.t, Bohemia *Also called Precision Assembly Tech Inc (G-1119)*
P3 Technologies 585 730-7340
383 Buell Rd Rochester (14624) *(G-14565)*
PA Pellets LLC (HQ) 814 848-9970
1 Fischers Rd Ste 160 Pittsford (14534) *(G-13572)*
Paal Technologies Inc 631 319-6262
152 Remington Blvd Ste 1 Ronkonkoma (11779) *(G-14962)*
Pacamor/Kubar Bearings, Troy *Also called S/N Precision Enterprises Inc (G-16252)*
Pace Editions Inc (PA) 212 421-3237
32 E 57th St Fl 3 New York (10022) *(G-11549)*
Pace Editions Inc 212 675-7431
44 W 18th St Fl 5 New York (10011) *(G-11550)*
Pace Manufacturing Company 607 936-0431
894 Addison Rd Painted Post (14870) *(G-13392)*
Pace Polyethylene Mfg Co Inc (PA) 914 381-3000
46 Calvert St Harrison (10528) *(G-5988)*
Pace Prints, New York *Also called Pace Editions Inc (G-11549)*
Pace Technology Inc 631 981-2400
2200 Smithtown Ave Ronkonkoma (11779) *(G-14963)*
Pace Up Pharmaceuticals LLC 631 450-4495
200 Bangor St Lindenhurst (11757) *(G-7478)*
Pace Walkers of America Inc 631 444-2147
105 Washington Ave Port Jefferson (11777) *(G-13778)*
Pace Window & Door, Victor *Also called Pace Window and Door Corp (G-16495)*
Pace Window and Door Corp (PA) 585 924-8350
7224 State Route 96 Victor (14564) *(G-16495)*
Pacemaker Packaging Corp 718 458-1188
7200 51st Rd Woodside (11377) *(G-17344)*
Pacific Alliance Usa Inc 336 500-8184
350 5th Ave Fl 5 New York (10118) *(G-11551)*
Pacific Alliance Usa Inc (HQ) 646 839-7000
1359 Broadway Fl 21 New York (10018) *(G-11552)*
Pacific Concepts, New York *Also called Ewatchfactory Corp (G-10095)*
Pacific Designs Intl Inc 718 364-2867
2743 Webster Ave Bronx (10458) *(G-1419)*
Pacific Die Cast Inc 845 778-6374
827 Route 52 Ste 2 Walden (12586) *(G-16534)*
Pacific Poly Product Corp 718 786-7129
3934 Crescent St Long Island City (11101) *(G-7832)*
Pacific Worldwide Inc 212 502-3360
20 W 33rd St Fl 11 New York (10001) *(G-11553)*
Pack America Corp (HQ) 212 508-6666
108 W 39th St Fl 16 New York (10018) *(G-11554)*
Package One Inc (PA) 518 344-5425
414 Union St Schenectady (12305) *(G-15285)*
Package Pavement Company Inc 845 221-2224
3530 Route 52 Stormville (12582) *(G-15780)*
Package Print Technologies 716 871-9905
1831 Niagara St Buffalo (14207) *(G-3110)*
Packaging Corporation America 315 457-6780
4471 Steelway Blvd S Liverpool (13090) *(G-7538)*
Packaging Corporation America 315 785-9083
20400 Old Rome State Rd Watertown (13601) *(G-16669)*
Packaging Dynamics Ltd 631 563-4499
35 Carlough Rd Ste 2 Bohemia (11716) *(G-1114)*
Packstar Group Inc 716 853-1688
215 John Glenn Dr Buffalo (14228) *(G-3111)*

ALPHABETIC

Pactech Packaging LLC 585 458-8008
2605 Manitou Rd Rochester (14624) *(G-14566)*
Pactiv Corporation 518 743-3100
6 Haskell Ave Glens Falls (12801) *(G-5694)*
Pactiv LLC 518 562-6101
74 Weed St Plattsburgh (12901) *(G-13684)*
Pactiv LLC 585 394-1525
2480 Sommers Dr Canandaigua (14424) *(G-3351)*
Pactiv LLC 315 457-6780
4471 Steelway Blvd S Liverpool (13090) *(G-7539)*
Pactiv LLC 518 793-2524
18 Peck Ave Glens Falls (12801) *(G-5695)*
Pactiv LLC 847 482-2000
5310 North St Canandaigua (14424) *(G-3352)*
Pactiv LLC 518 562-6120
74 Weed St Plattsburgh (12901) *(G-13685)*
Pactiv LLC 585 393-3229
5250 North St Canandaigua (14424) *(G-3353)*
Pactiv LLC 585 393-3149
5250 North St Canandaigua (14424) *(G-3354)*
Pactiv LLC 585 248-1213
1169 Pittsford Victor Rd Pittsford (14534) *(G-13573)*
Paddock Chevrolet Golf Dome 716 504-4059
175 Brompton Rd Tonawanda (14150) *(G-16191)*
Paddy Lee Fashions Inc 718 786-6020
4709 36th St Fl 2nd Long Island City (11101) *(G-7833)*
Paesana, Farmingdale *Also called L and S Packing Co (G-5030)*
Page Devices Inc 516 735-8376
11 Sunny Ln Levittown (11756) *(G-7430)*
Page Front Group Inc 716 823-8222
2703 S Park Ave Lackawanna (14218) *(G-7246)*
Paint Over Rust Products Inc 914 636-0700
38 Portman Rd New Rochelle (10801) *(G-8919)*
Paiping Carpets, New York *Also called Edward Fields Incorporated (G-9985)*
Paklab, Commack *Also called Universal Packg Systems Inc (G-3845)*
Pal Aluminum Inc (PA) 516 937-1990
230 Duffy Ave Unit B Hicksville (11801) *(G-6383)*
Pal Aluminum Inc 718 262-0091
10620 180th St Jamaica (11433) *(G-6937)*
Pal Industries, Hicksville *Also called Pal Aluminum Inc (G-6383)*
Pal Industries, Jamaica *Also called Pal Aluminum Inc (G-6937)*
Pal Manufacturing Corp 516 937-1990
230 Duffy Ave Unit B Hicksville (11801) *(G-6384)*
Paladino Prtg & Graphics Inc 718 279-6000
20009 32nd Ave Flushing (11361) *(G-5277)*
Palagonia Bakery Co Inc 718 272-5400
508 Junius St Brooklyn (11212) *(G-2402)*
Palagonia Italian Bread, Brooklyn *Also called Palagonia Bakery Co Inc (G-2402)*
Palagrave Macmillan, New York *Also called Macmillan Publishing Group LLC (G-11089)*
Paleteria Fernandez Inc 914 315-1598
350 Mamaroneck Ave Mamaroneck (10543) *(G-8041)*
Paletot Ltd 212 268-3774
499 Fashion Ave Rm 25s New York (10018) *(G-11555)*
Paley Studios Ltd 585 232-5260
1677 Lyell Ave A Rochester (14606) *(G-14567)*
Palgrave Macmillan Ltd 646 307-5028
175 5th Ave Frnt 4 New York (10010) *(G-11556)*
Palisades Paper Inc 845 354-0333
13 Jackson Ave Spring Valley (10977) *(G-15597)*
Pall Biomedical Inc 516 484-3600
25 Harbor Park Dr Port Washington (11050) *(G-13851)*
Pall Corporation (HQ) 516 484-5400
25 Harbor Park Dr Port Washington (11050) *(G-13852)*
Pall Corporation 607 753-6041
3643 State Route 281 Cortland (13045) *(G-4035)*
Pall Corporation 607 753-6041
3669 State Route 281 Cortland (13045) *(G-4036)*
Pall Corporation 516 484-2818
25 Harbor Park Dr Port Washington (11050) *(G-13853)*
Pall Corporation 607 753-6041
839 State Route 13 Ste 12 Cortland (13045) *(G-4037)*
Pall International Corporation 516 484-5400
25 Harbor Park Dr Port Washington (11050) *(G-13854)*
Pall Life Sciences, Port Washington *Also called Pall Corporation (G-13853)*
Pall Medical, Port Washington *Also called Pall Biomedical Inc (G-13851)*
Pall Trinity Micro, Cortland *Also called Pall Corporation (G-4035)*
Pall Trinity Micro Corporation 607 753-6041
3643 State Route 281 Cortland (13045) *(G-4038)*
Pall Well Technology Div, Cortland *Also called Pall Trinity Micro Corporation (G-4038)*
Pall's Advnced Sprtons Systems, Cortland *Also called Pall Corporation (G-4037)*
Palladia Inc 212 206-3669
105 W 17th St New York (10011) *(G-11557)*
Palladium Times, Oswego *Also called Sample News Group LLC (G-13340)*
Pallet Division Inc 585 328-3780
40 Silver St Rochester (14611) *(G-14568)*
Pallet Services Inc 585 647-4020
1681 Lyell Ave Rochester (14606) *(G-14569)*
Pallets Inc 518 747-4177
99 1/2 East St Fort Edward (12828) *(G-5343)*
Pallets Plus, Olean *Also called G & H Wood Products LLC (G-13148)*
Pallets R US Inc 631 758-2360
555 Woodside Ave Bellport (11713) *(G-837)*
Pallette Stone Corporation 518 584-2421
269 Ballard Rd Gansevoort (12831) *(G-5487)*
Palma Tool & Die Company Inc 716 681-4685
40 Ward Rd Lancaster (14086) *(G-7329)*
Palmbay Ltd 718 424-3388
3739 58th St Woodside (11377) *(G-17345)*
Palmer Industries Inc 607 754-8741
2320 Lewis St Endicott (13760) *(G-4822)*
Palmer Industries Inc (PA) 607 754-2957
509 Paden St Endicott (13760) *(G-4823)*
Palmer Industries Inc 607 754-1954
1 Heath St Endicott (13760) *(G-4824)*
Palpross Incorporated 845 469-2188
Maple Ave Rr 396 Selkirk (12158) *(G-15357)*
Palumbo Block, Dover Plains *Also called Palumbo Sand & Gravel Company (G-4317)*
Palumbo Block Co Inc 845 832-6100
365 Dover Furnace Rd Dover Plains (12522) *(G-4316)*
Palumbo Sand & Gravel Company 845 832-3356
155 Sherman Hill Rd Dover Plains (12522) *(G-4317)*
Pama Enterprises Inc 516 504-6300
60 Cuttermill Rd Ste 411 Great Neck (11021) *(G-5828)*
Pan American Leathers Inc (PA) 978 741-4150
347 W 36th St Rm 1204 New York (10018) *(G-11558)*
Pan American Roller Inc 914 762-8700
5 Broad Ave Ossining (10562) *(G-13326)*
Panagraphics Inc 716 312-8088
30 Quail Run Orchard Park (14127) *(G-13287)*
Pane DOro 914 964-0043
166 Ludlow St Yonkers (10705) *(G-17475)*
Pane Vita LLC 888 509-3310
10 White St Rochester (14608) *(G-14570)*
Panelogic Inc 607 962-6319
366 Baker Street Ext Corning (14830) *(G-3978)*
Panevita Foods, Rochester *Also called Pane Vita LLC (G-14570)*
Pangea Brands LLC (PA) 617 638-0001
6 W 20th St Fl 3 New York (10011) *(G-11559)*
Pangea Brands LLC 617 638-0001
6 W 20th St Fl 3 New York (10011) *(G-11560)*
Panther Graphics Inc (PA) 585 546-7163
465 Central Ave Rochester (14605) *(G-14571)*
Panvidea Inc 212 967-9613
44 W 28th St Fl 14 New York (10001) *(G-11561)*
Pap Chat Inc 516 350-1888
3105 Quentin Rd Brooklyn (11234) *(G-2403)*
Papa Bubble 212 966-2599
380 Broome St Frnt A New York (10013) *(G-11562)*
Paper Box Corp 212 226-7490
1751 2nd Ave Apt 10a New York (10128) *(G-11563)*
Paper House Productions Inc 845 246-7261
160 Malden Tpke Bldg 2 Saugerties (12477) *(G-15190)*
Paper Magazine, New York *Also called Paper Publishing Company Inc (G-11565)*
Paper Magic Group Inc 631 521-3682
345 7th Ave Fl 6 New York (10001) *(G-11564)*
Paper Publishing Company Inc 212 226-4405
15 E 32nd St New York (10016) *(G-11565)*
Paper Solutions Inc 718 499-4226
342 37th St Brooklyn (11232) *(G-2404)*
Papercutz Inc 646 559-4681
160 Broadway Rm 700e New York (10038) *(G-11566)*
Paperworks, Baldwinsville *Also called Specialized Packg Group Inc (G-575)*
Paperworks Industries Inc 913 621-0922
2900 Mclane Rd Baldwinsville (13027) *(G-573)*
Paperworld Inc 516 221-2702
3054 Lee Pl Bellmore (11710) *(G-819)*
Par Pharmaceutical Inc (HQ) 845 425-7100
1 Ram Ridge Rd Spring Valley (10977) *(G-15598)*
Par Phrmceutical Companies Inc (HQ) 845 573-5500
1 Ram Ridge Rd Chestnut Ridge (10977) *(G-3624)*
Par Sterile Products LLC (HQ) 845 573-5500
1 Ram Ridge Rd Chestnut Ridge (10977) *(G-3625)*
Par Technology Corporation (PA) 315 738-0600
8383 Seneca Tpke Ste 2 New Hartford (13413) *(G-8808)*
Par-Foam Products Inc 716 855-2066
239 Van Rensselaer St Buffalo (14210) *(G-3112)*
Parabit Systems Inc 516 378-4800
35 Debevoise Ave Roosevelt (11575) *(G-15008)*
PARABOLA, New York *Also called Society For The Study (G-12114)*
Parace Bionics LLC 877 727-2231
276 Landmark Ct Yorktown Heights (10598) *(G-17515)*
Parachute Publishing LLC 212 337-6743
322 8th Ave Ste 702 New York (10001) *(G-11567)*
Paraco Gas Corporation 845 279-8414
4 Joes Hill Rd Brewster (10509) *(G-1225)*
Paraco Gas Corporation (PA) 800 647-4427
800 Westchester Ave S604 Rye Brook (10573) *(G-15073)*
Parade Magazine, New York *Also called Parade Publications Inc (G-11568)*
Parade Publications Inc (HQ) 212 450-7000
711 3rd Ave New York (10017) *(G-11568)*
Paradigm Group LLC 718 860-1538
1357 Lafayette Ave Frnt 1 Bronx (10474) *(G-1420)*

ALPHABETIC

Paradigm Mktg Consortium Inc ALPHABETIC SECTION

Paradigm Mktg Consortium Inc 516 677-6012
350 Michael Dr Syosset (11791) ***(G-15835)***

Paradigm Spine LLC 212 367-7274
505 Park Ave Fl 14 New York (10022) ***(G-11569)***

Paradise Plastics LLC 718 788-3733
116 39th St Brooklyn (11232) ***(G-2405)***

Paradox Brewery LLC 518 351-5036
154 Us 9 Schroon Lake (12870) ***(G-15318)***

Paragon Aquatics 845 452-5500
1351 Route 55 Unit 1 Lagrangeville (12540) ***(G-7257)***

Paragon Corporation 516 484-6090
21 Forest Dr Port Washington (11050) ***(G-13855)***

Paragon Publishing Inc 718 302-2093
97 Harrison Ave Brooklyn (11206) ***(G-2406)***

Paragon Steel Rule Dies Inc 585 254-3395
979 Mount Read Blvd Rochester (14606) ***(G-14572)***

Paramount Cord & Brackets 212 325-9100
6 Tournament Dr White Plains (10605) ***(G-17144)***

Paramount Cords, Bronx *Also called Roanwell Corporation* ***(G-1441)***

Paramount Equipment Inc 631 981-4422
201 Christopher St Ronkonkoma (11779) ***(G-14964)***

Paramount Textiles Inc 212 966-1040
34 Walker St New York (10013) ***(G-11570)***

Paratore Signs Inc 315 455-5551
1551 Brewerton Rd Syracuse (13208) ***(G-16010)***

Paratus Industries Inc 716 826-2000
6659 E Quaker St Orchard Park (14127) ***(G-13288)***

Pardazzio Uomo, Westbury *Also called Montero International Inc* ***(G-17013)***

Parents Guide Network Corp 212 213-8840
419 Park Ave S Rm 505 New York (10016) ***(G-11571)***

Parfums Boucheron Jewelry, New York *Also called Boucheron Joaillerie USA Inc* ***(G-9442)***

Parfuse Corp 516 997-1795
62 Kinkel St Westbury (11590) ***(G-17018)***

Parijat Jewels Inc 212 286-2326
12 E 46th St Rm 200 New York (10017) ***(G-11572)***

Parikh Worldwide Media, LLC, New York *Also called Desi Talk LLC* ***(G-9850)***

Paris Art Label Co Inc 631 467-2300
217 River Ave Patchogue (11772) ***(G-13429)***

Paris Baguette 718 961-0404
15624 Northern Blvd Flushing (11354) ***(G-5278)***

Paris Wedding Center Corp (PA) 347 368-4085
42-53 42 55 Main St Flushing (11355) ***(G-5279)***

Paris Wedding Center Corp 212 267-8088
45 E Broadway Fl 2 New York (10002) ***(G-11573)***

Park Ave Bldg & Roofg Sups LLC 718 403-0100
2120 Atlantic Ave Brooklyn (11233) ***(G-2407)***

Park Avenue Imprints LLC (PA) 716 822-5737
2955 S Park Ave Buffalo (14218) ***(G-3113)***

Park Avenue Nutrition, Richmond Hill *Also called Womens Health Care PC* ***(G-14088)***

Park Avenue Sportswear Ltd (PA) 718 369-0520
820 4th Ave Brooklyn (11232) ***(G-2408)***

Park Electrochemical Corp (PA) 631 465-3600
48 S Service Rd Ste 300 Melville (11747) ***(G-8347)***

Park Enterprises Rochester Inc 585 546-4200
226 Jay St Rochester (14608) ***(G-14573)***

Park West Jewelery Inc 646 329-6145
565 W End Ave Apt 8b New York (10024) ***(G-11574)***

Park's Department, Williamsville *Also called Town of Amherst* ***(G-17258)***

Parkchester Dps LLC 718 823-4411
2000 E Tremont Ave Bronx (10462) ***(G-1421)***

Parker Machine Company Inc 518 747-0675
28 Sullivan Pkwy Fort Edward (12828) ***(G-5344)***

Parker Warby Retail Inc (PA) 646 517-5223
161 Ave Of The Ave Rm 201 New York (10013) ***(G-11575)***

Parker-Hannifin Aerospace, Clyde *Also called Parker-Hannifin Corporation* ***(G-3730)***

Parker-Hannifin Corporation 631 231-3737
124 Columbia St Clyde (14433) ***(G-3730)***

Parker-Hannifin Corporation 248 628-6017
4087 Walden Ave Lancaster (14086) ***(G-7330)***

Parker-Hannifin Corporation 631 231-3737
300 Marcus Blvd Hauppauge (11788) ***(G-6158)***

Parker-Hannifin Corporation 585 425-7000
83 Estates Dr W Fairport (14450) ***(G-4867)***

Parker-Hannifin Corporation 315 926-4211
3967 Buffalo St Marion (14505) ***(G-8097)***

Parker-Hannifin Corporation 716 685-4040
4087 Walden Ave Lancaster (14086) ***(G-7331)***

Parks Paving & Sealing Inc 315 737-5761
3220 Valley Pl Sauquoit (13456) ***(G-15201)***

Parks TRUcking&paving, Sauquoit *Also called Parks Paving & Sealing Inc* ***(G-15201)***

Parkside Candy Co Inc (PA) 716 833-7540
3208 Main St Buffalo (14214) ***(G-3114)***

Parkside Printing Co Inc 516 933-5423
4 Tompkins Ave Jericho (11753) ***(G-7081)***

Parkway Bread Distributors Inc 845 362-1221
15 Conklin Rd Pomona (10970) ***(G-13732)***

Parlec Inc (PA) 585 425-4400
101 Perinton Pkwy Fairport (14450) ***(G-4868)***

Parlor City Paper Box Co Inc 607 772-0600
2 Eldredge St Binghamton (13901) ***(G-941)***

Parlor Labs Inc 646 217-0918
515 W 19th St New York (10011) ***(G-11576)***

Parnasa International Inc 516 394-0400
181 S Franklin Ave # 400 Valley Stream (11581) ***(G-16418)***

Parrinello Printing Inc 716 633-7780
84 Aero Dr Buffalo (14225) ***(G-3115)***

Parry Machine Co Inc 315 597-5014
2081a Division St Palmyra (14522) ***(G-13412)***

Parrys 315 824-0002
100 Utica St Hamilton (13346) ***(G-5949)***

Parsley Apparel Corp 631 981-7181
2153 Pond Rd Ronkonkoma (11779) ***(G-14965)***

Parsons & Whittemore Inc (HQ) 914 937-9009
4 International Dr # 300 Port Chester (10573) ***(G-13756)***

Parsons Whittemore Entps Corp (PA) 914 937-9009
4 International Dr # 300 Port Chester (10573) ***(G-13757)***

Parsons-Meares Ltd 212 242-3378
2107 41st Ave Ste 1l Long Island City (11101) ***(G-7834)***

Partlow Corporation 518 922-5315
156 Auriesville Rd Fultonville (12072) ***(G-5481)***

Partlow West, Fultonville *Also called Partlow Corporation* ***(G-5481)***

Parts Unlimited Inc 518 885-7500
10 Mccrea Hill Rd Ballston Spa (12020) ***(G-606)***

Pasabahce USA 212 683-1600
41 Madison Ave Fl 7 New York (10010) ***(G-11577)***

Pascale Madonna, Long Island City *Also called Fashion Ribbon Co Inc* ***(G-7738)***

Pass & Seymour Inc (HQ) 315 468-6211
50 Boyd Ave Syracuse (13209) ***(G-16011)***

Pass Em-Entries Inc (PA) 718 392-0100
3914 Crescent St Long Island City (11101) ***(G-7835)***

Passive-Plus Inc 631 425-0938
48 Elm St Huntington (11743) ***(G-6673)***

Passport Magazine, New York *Also called Q Communications Inc* ***(G-11762)***

Passur Aerospace Inc 631 589-6800
35 Orville Dr Ste 1 Bohemia (11716) ***(G-1115)***

Pasta People, West Babylon *Also called Great Eastern Pasta Works LLC* ***(G-16794)***

Pat & Rose Dress Inc 212 279-1357
327 W 36th St Rm 3a New York (10018) ***(G-11578)***

Patchogue Advance Inc 631 475-1000
20 Medford Ave Ste 1 Patchogue (11772) ***(G-13430)***

Patchogue Electric Motors Inc 631 475-0117
71 Sycamore St Patchogue (11772) ***(G-13431)***

Patco Group, Maspeth *Also called Patco Tapes Inc* ***(G-8164)***

PATCO PACKAGING, Copiague *Also called Norjac Boxes Inc* ***(G-3916)***

Patco Tapes Inc 718 497-1527
5927 56th St Maspeth (11378) ***(G-8164)***

Patdan Fuel Corporation 718 326-3668
7803 68th Rd Middle Village (11379) ***(G-8416)***

Pathfinder 103 Inc 315 363-4260
229 Park Ave Oneida (13421) ***(G-13165)***

Pathfinder Industries Inc 315 593-2483
117 N 3rd St Fulton (13069) ***(G-5474)***

Pati Inc 718 244-6788
Jfk Intl Airprt Hngar 16 Jamaica (11430) ***(G-6938)***

Patience Brewster Inc 315 685-8336
3872 Jordan Rd Skaneateles (13152) ***(G-15464)***

Patient Portal Tech Inc (PA) 315 638-2030
8276 Willett Pkwy Ste 200 Baldwinsville (13027) ***(G-574)***

Patient-Wear LLC 914 740-7770
3940 Merritt Ave Bronx (10466) ***(G-1422)***

Patmian LLC 212 758-0770
655 Madison Ave Fl 24 New York (10065) ***(G-11579)***

Patra Ltd 212 764-6575
318 W 39th St Fl 2 New York (10018) ***(G-11580)***

Patra Ltd 212 764-6575
318 W 39th St New York (10018) ***(G-11581)***

Patra Ltd (PA) 212 764-6575
318 W 39th St New York (10018) ***(G-11582)***

Patricia Underwood, New York *Also called Paletot Ltd* ***(G-11555)***

Patrick Rohan 718 781-2573
9 Green St Monticello (12701) ***(G-8607)***

Patrick Mackin Custom Furn 718 237-2592
612 Degraw St Brooklyn (11217) ***(G-2409)***

Patrick Ryans Modern Press 518 434-2921
1 Colonie St Albany (12207) ***(G-114)***

Patron Technology Inc 212 271-4328
850 7th Ave Ste 704 New York (10019) ***(G-11583)***

Patsy Strocchia & Sons Iron Wo 516 625-8800
175 I U Willets Rd Ste 4 Albertson (11507) ***(G-156)***

Patterson Blacktop Corp 845 628-3425
1181 Route 6 Carmel (10512) ***(G-3403)***

Patterson Blacktop Corp (HQ) 914 949-2000
20 Haarlem Ave White Plains (10603) ***(G-17145)***

Patterson Materials Corp 845 832-6000
322 Walsh Ave New Windsor (12553) ***(G-8947)***

Patterson Materials Corp (HQ) 914 949-2000
20 Haarlem Ave White Plains (10603) ***(G-17146)***

Paul & Franza LLC 718 342-8106
90 Junius St Brooklyn (11212) ***(G-2410)***

Paul Bunyan Products Inc 315 696-6164
890 Mclean Rd Cortland (13045) ***(G-4039)***

Paul David Enterprises Inc 646 667-5530
19 W 34th St Rm 1018 New York (10001) ***(G-11584)***

Paul De Lima Coffee Company, Liverpool *Also called Paul De Lima Company Inc* ***(G-7540)***

ALPHABETIC

Paul De Lima Company Inc (PA) 315 457-3725
7546 Morgan Rd Ste 1 Liverpool (13090) *(G-7540)*
Paul De Lima Company Inc 315 457-3725
8550 Pardee Rd Cicero (13039) *(G-3650)*
Paul Delima Coffee Company 315 457-3725
8550 Pardee Rd Cicero (13039) *(G-3651)*
Paul J Mitchell Logging Inc 518 359-7029
15 Mitchell Ln Tupper Lake (12986) *(G-16278)*
Paul Michael Group Inc 631 585-5700
460 Hawkins Ave Ronkonkoma (11779) *(G-14966)*
Paul T Freund Corporation (PA) 315 597-4873
216 Park Dr Palmyra (14522) *(G-13413)*
Paula Dorf Cosmetics Inc 212 582-0073
850 7th Ave Ste 801 New York (10019) *(G-11585)*
Paula Varsalona Ltd 212 570-9100
552 Fashion Ave Rm 602 New York (10018) *(G-11586)*
Paulin Investment Company 631 957-8500
8600 New Horizons Blvd Amityville (11701) *(G-320)*
Paulpac LLC 631 283-7610
104 Foster Xing Southampton (11968) *(G-15548)*
Pauls Rods & Restos Inc 631 665-7637
131 Brook Ave Ste 13 Deer Park (11729) *(G-4187)*
Paumanok Vineyards Ltd 631 722-8800
1074 Main Rd Rr 25 Aquebogue (11931) *(G-385)*
Pavana USA Inc 646 833-8811
10 W 33rd St Rm 408 New York (10001) *(G-11587)*
Pavco Asphalt Inc 631 289-3223
615 Furrows Rd Holtsville (11742) *(G-6506)*
Pawling Corporation (PA) 845 855-1000
157 Charles Colman Blvd Pawling (12564) *(G-13451)*
Pawling Corporation 845 373-9300
32 Nelson Hill Rd Wassaic (12592) *(G-16600)*
Pawling Engineered Pdts Inc 845 855-1000
157 Charles Colman Blvd Pawling (12564) *(G-13452)*
Pawling Engineered Products, Pawling *Also called Pawling Corporation (G-13451)*
Paxar Corporation (HQ) 845 398-3229
524 Route 303 Orangeburg (10962) *(G-13238)*
Paxton Metal Craft Division, Peekskill *Also called Elevator Accessories Mfg (G-13477)*
Paya Printing of NY Inc 516 625-8346
87 Searingtown Rd Albertson (11507) *(G-157)*
Pb Industries, Homer *Also called Solidus Industries Inc (G-6522)*
Pb Leiner-USA 516 822-4040
143 Orchard St Plainview (11803) *(G-13627)*
Pb Mapinfo Corporation 518 285-6000
1 Global Vw Troy (12180) *(G-16246)*
Pb08 Inc 347 866-7353
40 Bloomingdale Rd Hicksville (11801) *(G-6385)*
Pbi Media Inc., New York *Also called Access Intelligence LLC (G-9009)*
PBL Industries Corp 631 979-4266
49 Dillmont Dr Smithtown (11787) *(G-15493)*
PBR Graphics Inc 518 458-2909
20 Railroad Ave Ste 1 Albany (12205) *(G-115)*
PC Solutions & Consulting 607 735-0466
407 S Walnut St Elmira (14904) *(G-4697)*
Pca/Syracuse, 384, Liverpool *Also called Packaging Corporation America (G-7538)*
Pca/Watertown 393, Watertown *Also called Packaging Corporation America (G-16669)*
Pcamerica, Pearl River *Also called Heartland Commerce Inc (G-13458)*
Pcb Coach Builders Corp 718 897-7606
6334 Austin St Rego Park (11374) *(G-14038)*
Pcb Group Inc (HQ) 716 684-0001
3425 Walden Ave Depew (14043) *(G-4268)*
Pcb Piezotronics Inc 716 684-0001
3425 Walden Ave Depew (14043) *(G-4269)*
Pcb Piezotronics Inc 716 684-0003
3425 Walden Ave Depew (14043) *(G-4270)*
PCI, Bohemia *Also called Precision Charts Inc (G-1120)*
PCI Industries Corp 914 662-2700
550 Franklin Ave Mount Vernon (10550) *(G-8713)*
Pcore Electric Company Inc 585 768-1200
135 Gilbert St Le Roy (14482) *(G-7418)*
Pcx Aerostructures LLC 631 249-7901
70 Raynor Ave Ronkonkoma (11779) *(G-14967)*
Pcx Aerostructures LLC 631 467-2632
60 Milbar Blvd Farmingdale (11735) *(G-5075)*
Pda Panache Corp 631 776-0523
70 Knickerbocker Ave # 7 Bohemia (11716) *(G-1116)*
Pdf Seal Incorporated 631 595-7035
503 Acorn St Deer Park (11729) *(G-4188)*
Pdi, New York *Also called Props Displays & Interiors (G-11737)*
Pdi Cone Co Inc 716 825-8750
69 Leddy St Buffalo (14210) *(G-3116)*
Pdj Components Inc 845 469-9191
35 Brookside Ave Chester (10918) *(G-3611)*
PDJ Inc 315 655-8824
2550 E Ballina Rd Cazenovia (13035) *(G-3450)*
PDM Litho Inc 718 301-1740
2219 41st Ave Fl 3 Long Island City (11101) *(G-7836)*
PDM Studios Inc 716 694-8337
510 Main St Tonawanda (14150) *(G-16192)*
PDQ Manufacturing Co Inc 845 889-3123
29 Hilee Rd Rhinebeck (12572) *(G-14057)*
PDQ Printing, New Paltz *Also called PDQ Shipping Services (G-8877)*
PDQ Shipping Services 845 255-5500
8 New Paltz Plz 299 New Paltz (12561) *(G-8877)*
Peace Times Weekly Inc 718 762-6500
14527 33rd Ave Flushing (11354) *(G-5280)*
Peaceful Valley Maple Farm (PA) 518 762-0491
116 Lagrange Rd Johnstown (12095) *(G-7119)*
Peachtree Enterprises Inc 212 989-3445
2219 41st Ave Ste 4a Long Island City (11101) *(G-7837)*
Peak Holdings LLC 212 583-5000
345 Park Ave Fl 30 New York (10154) *(G-11588)*
Peak Motion Inc 716 534-4925
11190 Main St Clarence (14031) *(G-3668)*
Pearl Erwin Inc (PA) 212 889-7410
389 5th Ave Fl 9 New York (10016) *(G-11589)*
Pearl Erwin Inc 212 883-0650
300 Madison Ave Frnt 1 New York (10017) *(G-11590)*
Pearl Leather Finishers Inc 518 762-4543
11 Industrial Pkwy 21 Johnstown (12095) *(G-7120)*
Pearl Leather Group LLC 516 627-4047
17 Barstow Rd Ste 206 Great Neck (11021) *(G-5829)*
Pearl Meadow Stables Inc 518 762-7733
11 Industrial Pkwy 21 Johnstown (12095) *(G-7121)*
Pearl River Pastries LLC 845 735-5100
389 W Nyack Rd West Nyack (10994) *(G-16923)*
Pearl River Pastry Chocolates, West Nyack *Also called Pearl River Pastries LLC (G-16923)*
Pearl Technologies Inc 315 365-2632
13297 Seneca St Savannah (13146) *(G-15202)*
Pearltek, New York *Also called Robin Stanley Inc (G-11894)*
Pearson Education Inc 845 340-8700
317 Wall St Kingston (12401) *(G-7206)*
Pearson Education Inc 212 782-3337
1185 Avenue Of The Americ New York (10036) *(G-11591)*
Pearson Education Inc 212 366-2000
375 Hudson St New York (10014) *(G-11592)*
Pearson Education Inc 201 236-7000
59 Brookhill Dr West Nyack (10994) *(G-16924)*
Pearson Education Holdings Inc (HQ) 201 236-6716
330 Hudson St Fl 9 New York (10013) *(G-11593)*
Pearson Inc (HQ) 212 641-2400
330 Hudson St Fl 9 New York (10013) *(G-11594)*
Pearson Longman LLC 917 981-2200
51 Madison Ave Fl 27 New York (10010) *(G-11595)*
Pearson Longman LLC (HQ) 212 641-2400
10 Bank St Ste 1030 White Plains (10606) *(G-17147)*
Peck & Hale LLC 631 589-2510
180 Division Ave West Sayville (11796) *(G-16937)*
Pecker Iron Works LLC 914 665-0100
137 Ruxton Rd Mount Kisco (10549) *(G-8639)*
Peckham Industries Inc (PA) 914 949-2000
20 Haarlem Ave Ste 200 White Plains (10603) *(G-17148)*
Peckham Industries Inc 518 943-0155
7065 Us Highway 9w Catskill (12414) *(G-3433)*
Peckham Industries Inc 518 893-2176
430 Coy Rd Greenfield Center (12833) *(G-5871)*
Peckham Industries Inc 518 945-1120
Uninn St Athens (12015) *(G-466)*
Peckham Materials, Carmel *Also called Patterson Blacktop Corp (G-3403)*
Peckham Materials Corp (HQ) 914 686-2045
20 Haarlem Ave Ste 200 White Plains (10603) *(G-17149)*
Peckham Materials Corp 518 747-3353
438 Vaughn Rd Hudson Falls (12839) *(G-6649)*
Peckham Materials Corp 518 945-1120
2 Union St Ext Athens (12015) *(G-467)*
Peckham Materials Corp 518 494-2313
5983 State Route 9 Chestertown (12817) *(G-3622)*
Peco Conduit Fittings, Orangeburg *Also called Producto Electric Corp (G-13243)*
Peco Pallet Inc (HQ) 914 376-5444
2 Bridge St Ste 210 Irvington (10533) *(G-6776)*
Peconic B Shopper, Southold *Also called Academy Printing Services Inc (G-15557)*
Peconic Ironworks Ltd 631 204-0323
33 Flying Point Rd # 108 Southampton (11968) *(G-15549)*
Peconic Plastics Inc 631 653-3676
6062 Old Country Rd Quogue (11959) *(G-14015)*
Pecoraro Dairy Products Inc (PA) 718 388-2379
287 Leonard St Brooklyn (11211) *(G-2411)*
Pedifix Inc 845 277-2850
281 Fields Ln Brewster (10509) *(G-1226)*
Pedre Corp (PA) 212 868-2935
270 Duffy Ave Ste G Hicksville (11801) *(G-6386)*
Pedre Watch, Hicksville *Also called Pedre Corp (G-6386)*
Peeled Inc 212 706-2001
65 15th St Ste 1 Brooklyn (11215) *(G-2412)*
Peeled Snack, Brooklyn *Also called Peeled Inc (G-2412)*
Peelle Company (PA) 631 231-6000
373 Smithtown Byp 311 Hauppauge (11788) *(G-6159)*
Peer International Corp (HQ) 212 265-3910
250 W 57th St Ste 820 New York (10107) *(G-11596)*
Peer Software Incorporated (PA) 631 979-1770
1363 Veterans Hwy Ste 44 Hauppauge (11788) *(G-6160)*
Peer-Southern Productions Inc (HQ) 212 265-3910
250 W 57th St New York (10107) *(G-11597)*
Peerless Envelopes & Prtg Co, Brooklyn *Also called H T L & S Ltd (G-2060)*

ALPHABETIC

Peerless Instrument Co Inc 631 396-6500
1966 Broadhollow Rd Ste D Farmingdale (11735) *(G-5076)*
Peerless Mfg Co 716 539-7400
50 Cobham Dr Orchard Park (14127) *(G-13289)*
Peerless-Winsmith Inc 716 592-9311
172 Eaton St Springville (14141) *(G-15614)*
Peermusic III Ltd (PA) 212 265-3910
250 W 57th St Ste 820 New York (10107) *(G-11598)*
Peermusic Ltd (HQ) 212 265-3910
250 W 57th St Ste 820 New York (10107) *(G-11599)*
Pefin Technologies LLC 917 715-3720
39 W 32nd St Rm 1500 New York (10001) *(G-11600)*
Pegasystems Inc 212 626-6550
1120 Ave Of The Americas New York (10036) *(G-11601)*
Peggy Jennings Designs, New York *Also called PJ Designs Inc (G-11671)*
Pei Liquidation Company 518 489-5101
1240 Central Ave Albany (12205) *(G-116)*
Pei Liquidation Company 315 431-4697
6515 Basile Rowe East Syracuse (13057) *(G-4554)*
Pei/Genesis Inc 631 256-1747
2410 N Ocean Ave Ste 401 Farmingville (11738) *(G-5161)*
Peking Food LLC 718 628-8080
47 Stewart Ave Brooklyn (11237) *(G-2413)*
Peko Precision Products Inc 585 301-1386
70 Holworthy St Rochester (14606) *(G-14574)*
Pelican Bay Ltd 718 729-9300
3901 22nd St Long Island City (11101) *(G-7838)*
Pelican Products Co Inc (PA) 718 860-3220
1049 Lowell St Bronx (10459) *(G-1423)*
Pelkowski Precast Corp 631 269-5727
294a Old Northport Rd Kings Park (11754) *(G-7173)*
Pella Corporation 516 385-3622
77 Albertson Ave Ste 2 Albertson (11507) *(G-158)*
Pella Corporation 516 385-3622
77 Albertson Ave Ste 2 Albertson (11507) *(G-159)*
Pella Corporation 607 223-2023
800 Valley Plz Ste 5 Johnson City (13790) *(G-7100)*
Pella Corporation 607 231-8550
800 Valley Plz Ste 5 Johnson City (13790) *(G-7101)*
Pella Corporation 607 231-8550
800 Valley Plz Ste 5 Johnson City (13790) *(G-7102)*
Pella Corporation 607 238-2812
800 Valley Plz Ste 5 Johnson City (13790) *(G-7103)*
Pella Corporation 607 238-2812
800 Valley Plz Ste 5 Johnson City (13790) *(G-7104)*
Pella Corporation 631 208-0710
901 Burman Blvd Calverton (11933) *(G-3294)*
Pella Window Door, Albertson *Also called Pella Corporation (G-158)*
Pella Window Door, Albertson *Also called Pella Corporation (G-159)*
Pella Window Door, Johnson City *Also called Pella Corporation (G-7100)*
Pella Window Door, Johnson City *Also called Pella Corporation (G-7101)*
Pella Window Door, Johnson City *Also called Pella Corporation (G-7102)*
Pella Window Door, Johnson City *Also called Pella Corporation (G-7103)*
Pella Window Door, Johnson City *Also called Pella Corporation (G-7104)*
Pellegrini Vineyards LLC 631 734-4111
23005 Main Rd Cutchogue (11935) *(G-4072)*
Pellets LLC 716 693-1750
63 Industrial Dr Ste 3 North Tonawanda (14120) *(G-12985)*
Pellicano Specialty Foods Inc 716 822-2366
195 Reading St Buffalo (14220) *(G-3117)*
Peloton Interactive Inc 818 571-7236
158 W 27th St Fl 4 New York (10001) *(G-11602)*
Peltrix, Purdys *Also called Data Interchange Systems Inc (G-13972)*
Pems Tool & Machine Inc 315 823-3595
125 Southern Ave Little Falls (13365) *(G-7502)*
Pemystifying Diital, Woodbury *Also called Photo Industry Inc (G-17295)*
Penasack Machine Company Inc 585 589-7044
49 Sanford St Albion (14411) *(G-168)*
Pencoa, Westbury *Also called Harper Products Ltd (G-16994)*
Penetradar Corporation 716 731-2629
2509 Niagara Falls Blvd Niagara Falls (14304) *(G-12859)*
Penfli Industries Inc 212 947-6080
11 Woodland Pl Great Neck (11021) *(G-5830)*
Penguin Random House LLC 212 782-1000
1540 Broadway New York (10036) *(G-11603)*
Penguin Random House LLC (HQ) 212 782-9000
1745 Broadway New York (10019) *(G-11604)*
Penguin Random House LLC 212 572-6162
1745 Broadway Frnt 3 New York (10019) *(G-11605)*
Penguin Random House LLC 212 782-9000
1745 Broadway Frnt 3 New York (10019) *(G-11606)*
Penguin Random House LLC 212 366-2377
80 State St Albany (12207) *(G-117)*
Penhouse Media Group Inc (PA) 212 702-6000
11 Penn Plz Fl 12 New York (10001) *(G-11607)*
Peninsula Plastics Ltd 716 854-3050
161 Marine Dr Apt 6e Buffalo (14202) *(G-3118)*
Penn & Fletcher Inc 212 239-6868
2107 41st Ave Fl 5 Long Island City (11101) *(G-7839)*
Penn Can Asphalt Materials, Lyons *Also called Penn Can Equipment Corporation (G-7974)*
Penn Can Equipment Corporation 315 378-0337
300 Cole Rd Lyons (14489) *(G-7974)*
Penn Enterprises Inc 845 446-0765
845 Washington Rd West Point (10996) *(G-16930)*
Penn Signs Inc 718 797-1112
1920 Atlantic Ave Brooklyn (11233) *(G-2414)*
Penn State Metal Fabri 718 786-8814
810 Humboldt St Ste 9 Brooklyn (11222) *(G-2415)*
Pennant Foods, Rochester *Also called Aryzta LLC (G-14215)*
Pennant Ingredients Inc 585 235-8160
64 Chester St Rochester (14611) *(G-14575)*
Penner Elbow Company Inc 718 526-9000
4700 76th St Elmhurst (11373) *(G-4665)*
Pennsauken Packing Company LLC 585 377-7700
815 Whitney Rd W Fairport (14450) *(G-4869)*
Penny Express, Avon *Also called Penny Lane Printing Inc (G-542)*
Penny Lane Printing Inc 585 226-8111
1471 Rte 15 Avon (14414) *(G-542)*
Penny Saver News, Edgewood *Also called S G New York LLC (G-4610)*
Pennysaver Group Inc 914 966-1400
80 Alexander St Yonkers (10701) *(G-17476)*
Pennysaver News, Bohemia *Also called S G New York LLC (G-1128)*
Pennysaver/Town Crier, Edgewood *Also called All Island Media Inc (G-4592)*
Pennysavers Rw Publications, Elma *Also called R W Publications Div of Wtrhs (G-4654)*
Pensrus, Staten Island *Also called Henry Morgan (G-15683)*
Penta-Tech Coated Products LLC 315 986-4098
1610 Commons Pkwy Macedon (14502) *(G-7989)*
Pentair Water Pool and Spa Inc 845 452-5500
341 Route 55 Lagrangeville (12540) *(G-7258)*
Pentaplastics, Bohemia *Also called Leidel Corporation (G-1093)*
Penthouse Group, The, Freeport *Also called Penthouse Manufacturing Co Inc (G-5418)*
Penthouse Manufacturing Co Inc 516 379-1300
225 Buffalo Ave Freeport (11520) *(G-5418)*
Penton Business Media Inc 914 949-8500
707 Westchester Ave # 101 White Plains (10604) *(G-17150)*
Penton Media Inc (HQ) 212 204-4200
1166 Avenue Of The Americ New York (10036) *(G-11608)*
Penton Media Inc 212 204-4200
1166 Avenue Of The Americ New York (10036) *(G-11609)*
Penton Media - Aviation Week, New York *Also called Penton Media Inc (G-11608)*
Peoples Choice M R I 716 681-7377
125 Galileo Dr Buffalo (14221) *(G-3119)*
Pep Realty, New York *Also called Atlas Recycling LLC (G-9257)*
Pepe Creations Inc 212 391-1514
2 W 45th St Ste 1003 New York (10036) *(G-11610)*
Peppermints Salon Inc 718 357-6304
15722 Powells Cove Blvd Whitestone (11357) *(G-17213)*
Pepsi Beverages Co 518 782-2150
421 Old Niskayuna Rd Latham (12110) *(G-7374)*
Pepsi Beverages Company, Watertown *Also called Bottling Group LLC (G-16640)*
Pepsi Beverages Company, White Plains *Also called Bottling Group LLC (G-17086)*
Pepsi Beverages Company, White Plains *Also called Bottling Group LLC (G-17087)*
Pepsi Bottle and Group, Somers *Also called General Cinema Bevs of Ohio (G-15509)*
Pepsi Bottling Holdings Inc (PA) 800 433-2652
700 Anderson Hill Rd Purchase (10577) *(G-13963)*
Pepsi Bottling Ventures LLC 631 772-6144
4141 Parklane Ave Ste 600 Patchogue (11772) *(G-13432)*
Pepsi Bottling Ventures LLC 631 226-9000
550 New Horizons Blvd Amityville (11701) *(G-321)*
Pepsi Btlg Group Globl Fin LLC (HQ) 914 767-6000
1 Pepsi Way Ste 1 Somers (10589) *(G-15511)*
Pepsi Cola Buffalo Btlg Corp 716 684-2800
2770 Walden Ave Cheektowaga (14225) *(G-3585)*
Pepsi Lipton Tea Partnership 914 253-2000
700 Anderson Hill Rd Fl 3 Purchase (10577) *(G-13964)*
Pepsi-Cola, Patchogue *Also called Pepsi Bottling Ventures LLC (G-13432)*
Pepsi-Cola Allied Bottlers 518 783-8811
1 Pepsi Cola Dr Latham (12110) *(G-7375)*
Pepsi-Cola Bottling Co NY Inc 718 649-2465
11202 15th Ave College Point (11356) *(G-3800)*
Pepsi-Cola Bottling Co NY Inc 914 699-2600
601 S Fulton Ave Mount Vernon (10550) *(G-8714)*
Pepsi-Cola Bottling Co NY Inc 718 392-1000
1 Pepsi Way New York (10016) *(G-11611)*
Pepsi-Cola Bottling Co NY Inc 718 786-8550
5035 56th Rd Maspeth (11378) *(G-8165)*
Pepsi-Cola Bottling Co NY Inc 718 892-1570
650 Brush Ave Bronx (10465) *(G-1424)*
Pepsi-Cola Bottling Co NY Inc (PA) 718 392-1000
11402 15th Ave Ste 5 College Point (11356) *(G-3801)*
Pepsi-Cola Bottling Group (HQ) 914 767-6000
1111 Westchester Ave White Plains (10604) *(G-17151)*
Pepsi-Cola Metro Btlg Co Inc (HQ) 914 767-6000
1111 Westchester Ave White Plains (10604) *(G-17152)*
Pepsi-Cola Metro Btlg Co Inc 914 253-2000
700 Anderson Hill Rd Purchase (10577) *(G-13965)*
Pepsi-Cola Metro Btlg Co Inc 607 795-1399
140 Wygant Rd Horseheads (14845) *(G-6587)*
Pepsi-Cola Newburgh Btlg Inc 845 562-5400
1 Pepsi Way Newburgh (12550) *(G-12774)*

ALPHABETIC

ALPHABETIC SECTION Petersons Nelnet LLC

Pepsi-Cola Operating Company (HQ).....914 767-6000
1111 Westchester Ave White Plains (10604) **(G-17153)**
Pepsico, White Plains *Also called Pepsi-Cola Metro Btlg Co Inc* **(G-17152)**
Pepsico, Newburgh *Also called Pepsi-Cola Newburgh Btlg Inc* **(G-12774)**
Pepsico, Latham *Also called Pepsi Beverages Co* **(G-7374)**
Pepsico, Horseheads *Also called Pepsi-Cola Metro Btlg Co Inc* **(G-6587)**
Pepsico, White Plains *Also called Pepsi-Cola Bottling Group* **(G-17151)**
Pepsico, Amityville *Also called Pepsi Bottling Ventures LLC* **(G-321)**
Pepsico.....419 252-0247
3 Skyline Dr Hawthorne (10532) **(G-6252)**
Pepsico.....914 801-1500
100 Summit Lake Dr # 103 Valhalla (10595) **(G-16369)**
Pepsico Inc (PA).....914 253-2000
700 Anderson Hill Rd Purchase (10577) **(G-13966)**
Pepsico Inc.....914 253-2000
1111 Westchester Ave White Plains (10604) **(G-17154)**
Pepsico Inc.....914 742-4500
100 E Stevens Ave Valhalla (10595) **(G-16370)**
Pepsico Inc.....914 253-2000
Anderson Hill Rd Purchase (10577) **(G-13967)**
Pepsico Inc.....914 253-3474
150 Airport Rd Hngr V White Plains (10604) **(G-17155)**
Pepsico Inc.....914 253-2713
700 Anderson Hill Rd Purchase (10577) **(G-13968)**
Pepsico Inc.....914 767-6976
1111 Westchester Ave White Plains (10604) **(G-17156)**
Pepsico Capital Resources Inc.....914 253-2000
700 Anderson Hill Rd Purchase (10577) **(G-13969)**
Pepsico World Trading Co Inc.....914 767-6000
1111 Westchester Ave White Plains (10604) **(G-17157)**
Per Annum Inc.....212 647-8700
555 8th Ave Rm 202 New York (10018) **(G-11612)**
Peraflex Hose Inc.....716 876-8806
155 Great Arrow Ave Ste 4 Buffalo (14207) **(G-3120)**
Peralta Metal Works Inc.....718 649-8661
602 Atkins Ave Brooklyn (11208) **(G-2416)**
Perception Imaging Inc.....631 676-5262
90 Colin Dr Unit 11 Holbrook (11741) **(G-6466)**
Perceptive Pixel Inc (HQ).....701 367-5845
641 Avenue Of The Ste 7 New York (10011) **(G-11613)**
Peregrine Industries Inc.....631 838-2870
40 Wall St New York (10005) **(G-11614)**
Perfect Form Manufacturing LLC.....585 500-5923
1325 John St West Henrietta (14586) **(G-16890)**
Perfect Forms and Systems Inc.....631 462-1100
35 Riverview Ter Smithtown (11787) **(G-15494)**
Perfect Gear & Instrument (HQ).....516 328-3330
55 Denton Ave S New Hyde Park (11040) **(G-8856)**
Perfect Gear & Instrument.....516 873-6122
125 Railroad Ave Garden City Park (11040) **(G-5541)**
Perfect Poly Inc.....631 265-0539
1 Gina Ct Nesconset (11767) **(G-8777)**
Perfect Print Inc.....718 832-5280
220 36th St Unit 2a Brooklyn (11232) **(G-2417)**
Perfect Publications, Brooklyn *Also called Joseph Paul* **(G-2149)**
Perfect Shoulder Company Inc.....914 699-8100
2 Cortlandt St Mount Vernon (10550) **(G-8715)**
Perfection Electricks, Brooklyn *Also called Martin Chafkin* **(G-2276)**
Perfection Gear Inc.....716 592-9310
172 Eaton St Springville (14141) **(G-15615)**
Perfex Corporation.....315 826-3600
32 Case St Poland (13431) **(G-13727)**
Perforated Screen Surfaces.....866 866-8690
216 Broome Corporate Pkwy Conklin (13748) **(G-3872)**
Performance Advantage Co Inc.....716 683-7413
6 W Main St Lowr Rear Lancaster (14086) **(G-7332)**
Performance Custom Trailer.....518 504-4021
230 Lockhart Mountain Rd Lake George (12845) **(G-7263)**
Performance Designed By Peters.....585 223-9062
7 Duxbury Hts Fairport (14450) **(G-4870)**
Performance Diesel Service LLC.....315 854-5269
24 Latour Ave Plattsburgh (12901) **(G-13686)**
Performance Lacrosse Group Inc (HQ).....315 453-3073
4697 Crossroads Park Dr Liverpool (13088) **(G-7541)**
Performance Mfg Inc.....716 735-3500
80 Telegraph Rd Middleport (14105) **(G-8422)**
Performance Precision Mfg LLC.....518 993-3033
55 Willett St Fort Plain (13339) **(G-5348)**
Performance Systems Contg Inc.....607 277-6240
124 Brindley St Ithaca (14850) **(G-6868)**
Performance Technologies Inc (HQ).....585 256-0200
3500 Winton Pl Ste 4 Rochester (14623) **(G-14576)**
Performance Wire & Cable Inc.....315 245-2594
9482 State Route 13 Camden (13316) **(G-3320)**
Perfume Americana Inc (PA).....212 683-8029
1216 Broadway New York (10001) **(G-11615)**
Perfume Americana Wholesale, New York *Also called Perfume Americana Inc* **(G-11615)**
Perfume Amrcana Whlesalers Inc.....212 683-8029
11 W 30th St Betwe Broad Between New York (10001) **(G-11616)**
Perfumers Workshop Intl Ltd (PA).....212 644-8950
350 7th Ave Rm 802 New York (10001) **(G-11617)**
Peri, Pearl River *Also called Piezo Electronics Research* **(G-13463)**
Peri-Facts Academy.....585 275-6037
601 Elmwood Ave Rochester (14642) **(G-14577)**
Perimondo LLC.....212 749-0721
331 W 84th St Apt 2 New York (10024) **(G-11618)**
Periodical Services Co Inc.....518 822-9300
351 Fairview Ave Ste 300 Hudson (12534) **(G-6630)**
Perkins International Inc (HQ).....309 675-1000
672 Delaware Ave Buffalo (14209) **(G-3121)**
Perma Glow Ltd Inc.....212 575-9677
48 W 48th St Ste 301 New York (10036) **(G-11619)**
Perma Tech Inc.....716 854-0707
363 Hamburg St Buffalo (14204) **(G-3122)**
Permanent Press, Sag Harbor *Also called Second Chance Press Inc* **(G-15081)**
Permit Fashion Group Inc.....212 912-0988
135 W 36th St Fl 16 New York (10018) **(G-11620)**
Pernod Ricard Usa LLC (HQ).....914 848-4800
250 Park Ave Ste 17a New York (10177) **(G-11621)**
Perretta Graphics Corp.....845 473-0550
46 Violet Ave Poughkeepsie (12601) **(G-13925)**
Perrigo Company.....718 960-9900
1625 Bathgate Ave Bronx (10457) **(G-1425)**
Perrigo New York Inc.....718 901-2800
455 Claremont Pkwy Bronx (10457) **(G-1426)**
Perrigo New York Inc (HQ).....718 960-9900
1700 Bathgate Ave Bronx (10457) **(G-1427)**
Perrone Aerospace, Fultonville *Also called Perrone Leather LLC* **(G-5482)**
Perrone Leather LLC (PA).....518 853-4300
182a Riverside Dr Fultonville (12072) **(G-5482)**
Perrottas Bakery Inc.....518 283-4711
766 Pawling Ave Troy (12180) **(G-16247)**
Perry Ellis America, New York *Also called Perry Ellis Menswear LLC* **(G-11624)**
Perry Ellis International Inc.....212 536-5400
1126 Avenue Of The Americ New York (10036) **(G-11622)**
Perry Ellis International Inc.....212 536-5499
42 W 39th St Fl 4 New York (10018) **(G-11623)**
Perry Ellis Menswear LLC (HQ).....212 221-7500
1120 Ave Of The Americas New York (10036) **(G-11624)**
Perry Plastics Inc.....718 747-5600
3050 Whitestone Expy # 300 Flushing (11354) **(G-5281)**
Perry Street Software Inc.....415 935-1429
489 5th Ave Rm 2900 New York (10017) **(G-11625)**
Perrys Ice Cream Company Inc.....716 542-5492
1 Ice Cream Plz Akron (14001) **(G-27)**
Persch Service Print Inc (PA).....716 366-2677
11 W 3rd St Dunkirk (14048) **(G-4347)**
Perseus Books Group, New York *Also called Clp Pb LLC* **(G-9646)**
Persistent Systems LLC.....212 561-5895
303 5th Ave Rm 306 New York (10016) **(G-11626)**
Personal Alarm SEC Systems.....212 448-1944
379 5th Ave Fl 3 New York (10016) **(G-11627)**
Personal Graphics Corporation.....315 853-3421
5123 State Route 233 Westmoreland (13490) **(G-17063)**
Pervi Precision Company.....631 589-5557
220 Knickerbocker Ave # 1 Bohemia (11716) **(G-1117)**
PES Group, Brooklyn *Also called Project Energy Savers LLC* **(G-2454)**
Pesce Bakery, Saugerties *Also called Pesces Bakery Inc* **(G-15191)**
Pesces Bakery Inc.....845 246-4730
20 Pesce Ct Saugerties (12477) **(G-15191)**
Pesselnik & Cohen Inc.....212 925-0287
82 Bowery Unit 10 New York (10013) **(G-11628)**
Pet Authority, Brooklyn *Also called Dynamic Health Labs Inc* **(G-1886)**
Pet Proteins LLC.....888 293-1029
347 W 36th St Rm 1204 New York (10018) **(G-11629)**
Petcap Press Corporation.....718 609-0910
3200 Skillman Ave Ste F Long Island City (11101) **(G-7840)**
Pete Levin Music Inc.....845 247-9211
598 Schoolhouse Rd Saugerties (12477) **(G-15192)**
Peter Atman Inc.....212 644-8882
6 E 45th St Rm 1100 New York (10017) **(G-11630)**
Peter C Herman Inc.....315 926-4100
5395 Skinner Rd Marion (14505) **(G-8098)**
Peter Digioia.....516 644-5517
7 Sherwood Dr Plainview (11803) **(G-13628)**
Peter Kwasny Inc.....727 641-1462
400 Oser Ave Ste 1650 Hauppauge (11788) **(G-6161)**
Peter Lang Publishing Inc (HQ).....212 647-7700
29 Broadway Rm 1800 New York (10006) **(G-11631)**
Peter Mayer Publishers Inc.....212 673-2210
141 Wooster St Fl 4 New York (10012) **(G-11632)**
Peter Papastrat.....607 723-8112
193 Main St Binghamton (13905) **(G-942)**
Peter Pauper Press Inc.....914 681-0144
202 Mmaroneck Ave Ste 400 White Plains (10601) **(G-17158)**
Peter Productions Devivi Inc.....315 568-8484
2494 Kingdom Rd Waterloo (13165) **(G-16631)**
Peter Thomas Roth Labs LLC (PA).....212 581-5800
460 Park Ave Fl 16 New York (10022) **(G-11633)**
Peters LLC.....607 637-5470
5259 Peas Eddy Rd Hancock (13783) **(G-5966)**
Petersons Nelnet LLC.....609 896-1800
3 Columbia Cir Ste 205 Albany (12203) **(G-118)**

ALPHABETIC

(PA)=Parent Co (HQ)=Headquarters (DH)=Div Headquarters
2017 Harris
New York Manufacturers Directory
1035

Petit Printing Corp ... 716 871-9490
42 Hunters Gln Getzville (14068) *(G-5603)*

Petland Discounts Inc ... 516 821-3194
1340 Peninsula Blvd Hewlett (11557) *(G-6311)*

Petre Alii Petroleum ... 315 785-1037
1268 Arsenal St Watertown (13601) *(G-16670)*

PETRILLO'S BAKERY, Rochester Also called Scaife Enterprises Inc *(G-14672)*

Petro Inc ... 516 686-1717
3 Fairchild Ct Plainview (11803) *(G-13629)*

Petro Inc ... 516 686-1900
477 W John St Hicksville (11801) *(G-6387)*

Petro Metro Mfg, Long Island City Also called Petro Moore Manufacturing Corp *(G-7841)*

Petro Moore Manufacturing Corp ... 718 784-2516
3641 Vernon Blvd Long Island City (11106) *(G-7841)*

Petrune, Ithaca Also called Petrunia LLC *(G-6869)*

Petrunia LLC ... 607 277-1930
126 E State St Ithaca (14850) *(G-6869)*

Pets n People Inc ... 631 232-1200
2100 Pacific St Hauppauge (11788) *(G-6162)*

Petteys Lumber ... 518 792-5943
10247 State Route 149 Fort Ann (12827) *(G-5337)*

Pexco LLC ... 518 792-1199
12 Glens Fls Technical Pa Glens Falls (12801) *(G-5696)*

Pexip Inc (HQ) ... 703 338-3544
240 W 35th St Ste 1002 New York (10001) *(G-11634)*

Peyser Instrument Corporation ... 631 841-3600
40 Gleam St West Babylon (11704) *(G-16818)*

Pezera Associates, Calverton Also called East End Country Kitchens Inc *(G-3290)*

Pfannenberg Inc ... 716 685-6866
68 Ward Rd Lancaster (14086) *(G-7333)*

Pfaudler Inc (HQ) ... 585 464-5663
1000 West Ave Rochester (14611) *(G-14578)*

Pfaudler US Inc ... 585 235-1000
1000 West Ave Rochester (14611) *(G-14579)*

Pfeil & Holing Inc ... 718 545-4600
5815 Northern Blvd Woodside (11377) *(G-17346)*

Pfizer HCP Corporation (HQ) ... 212 733-2323
235 E 42nd St New York (10017) *(G-11635)*

Pfizer Inc (PA) ... 212 733-2323
235 E 42nd St New York (10017) *(G-11636)*

Pfizer Inc ... 518 297-6611
64 Maple St Rouses Point (12979) *(G-15042)*

Pfizer Inc ... 914 437-5868
4 Martine Ave White Plains (10606) *(G-17159)*

Pfizer Inc ... 937 746-3603
150 E 42nd St Bsmt 2 New York (10017) *(G-11637)*

Pfizer Inc ... 212 733-6276
150 E 42nd St Bsmt 2 New York (10017) *(G-11638)*

Pfizer Inc ... 804 257-2000
235 E 42nd St New York (10017) *(G-11639)*

Pfizer Inc ... 212 733-2323
235 E 42nd St New York (10017) *(G-11640)*

Pfizer Overseas LLC ... 212 733-2323
235 E 42nd St New York (10017) *(G-11641)*

Pgm of New England LLC ... 585 458-4300
1305 Emerson St Rochester (14606) *(G-14580)*

Pgs Millwork Inc (PA) ... 212 244-6610
535 8th Ave Rm 20n New York (10018) *(G-11642)*

Phaidon Press Inc ... 212 652-5400
65 Bleecker St Fl 8 New York (10012) *(G-11643)*

Phantom Laboratory Inc ... 518 692-1190
2727 State Route 29 Greenwich (12834) *(G-5891)*

Phantom Laboratory, The, Greenwich Also called Phantom Laboratory Inc *(G-5891)*

Pharbest Pharmaceuticals Inc ... 631 249-5130
14 Engineers Ln Ste 1 Farmingdale (11735) *(G-5077)*

Pharma-Smart International Inc ... 585 427-0730
773 Elmgrove Rd Bldg 2 Rochester (14624) *(G-14581)*

Pharmaceutic Labs LLC ... 518 608-1060
15 Walker Way Albany (12205) *(G-119)*

Pharmaderm, Melville Also called Fougera Pharmaceuticals Inc *(G-8321)*

Pharmadva LLC ... 585 469-1410
150 Lucius Gordon Dr # 209 West Henrietta (14586) *(G-16891)*

Pharmalife Inc ... 631 249-4040
130 Gazza Blvd Farmingdale (11735) *(G-5078)*

Pharmasmart, Rochester Also called Pharma-Smart International Inc *(G-14581)*

Pharmavantage LLC ... 631 321-8171
15 Lakeland Ave Babylon (11702) *(G-551)*

Pharmline, Florida Also called Stauber Prfmce Ingredients Inc *(G-5215)*

PHASE IL MARKETING DBA, Amherst Also called Nexstar Holding Corp *(G-253)*

PHC Restoration Holdings LLC ... 212 643-0517
147 W 29th St Fl 4 New York (10001) *(G-11644)*

Phelinger Tool & Die Corp ... 716 685-1780
1254 Town Line Rd Alden (14004) *(G-181)*

Phelps Cement Products Inc ... 315 548-9415
5 S Newark St Phelps (14532) *(G-13535)*

Pheonix Custom Furniture Ltd ... 212 727-2648
2107 41st Ave Fl 2 Long Island City (11101) *(G-7842)*

Philcom Limited ... 716 875-8005
1144 Military Rd Buffalo (14217) *(G-3123)*

Philip Crangi, New York Also called PHC Restoration Holdings LLC *(G-11644)*

Philip Morris Intl Inc (PA) ... 917 663-2000
120 Park Ave Fl 6 New York (10017) *(G-11645)*

Philipp Feldheim Inc (PA) ... 845 356-2282
208 Airport Executive Par Nanuet (10954) *(G-8760)*

Philipp Plein Madison Ave LLC ... 212 644-3304
625 Madison Ave New York (10022) *(G-11646)*

Philipp Plein North America, New York Also called Philipp Plein Madison Ave LLC *(G-11646)*

Philippe Adec Paris, New York Also called Morelle Products Ltd *(G-11304)*

Philips Elec N Amer Corp ... 607 776-3692
7265 State Route 54 Bath (14810) *(G-661)*

Philips Healthcare, Latham Also called Philips Medical Systems Mr *(G-7376)*

Philips Lighting N Amer Corp ... 646 265-7170
267 5th Ave New York (10016) *(G-11647)*

Philips Medical Systems Mr (HQ) ... 518 782-1122
450 Old Niskayuna Rd Latham (12110) *(G-7376)*

Phillifox Music ... 646 260-9300
239 W 145th St Apt 2g New York (10039) *(G-11648)*

Phillip J Ortiz Manufacturing ... 845 226-7030
44 Railroad Ave Hopewell Junction (12533) *(G-6557)*

Phillip Juan ... 800 834-4543
9 Union Ave Staten Island (10303) *(G-15720)*

Phillips-Van Heusen Europe ... 212 381-3500
200 Madison Ave Bsmt 1 New York (10016) *(G-11649)*

Philpac Corporation (PA) ... 716 875-8005
1144 Military Rd Buffalo (14217) *(G-3124)*

Phoebe Company LLC ... 212 302-5556
230 W 38th St Fl 11 New York (10018) *(G-11650)*

Phoenix Cables Corporation ... 845 691-6253
131 Tillson Avenue Ext Highland (12528) *(G-6406)*

Phoenix Graphics Inc ... 585 232-4040
464 State St 470 Rochester (14608) *(G-14582)*

Phoenix Laboratories Inc ... 516 822-1230
200 Adams Blvd Farmingdale (11735) *(G-5079)*

Phoenix Material Handling, Phoenix Also called Phoenix Welding & Fabg Inc *(G-13543)*

Phoenix Mch Pdts of Hauppauge ... 631 234-0100
225 Engineers Rd Hauppauge (11788) *(G-6163)*

Phoenix Ribbon Co Inc ... 212 239-0155
20 W 36th St Fl 7 New York (10018) *(G-11651)*

Phoenix Services Group LLC ... 518 828-6611
1 Hudson City Ctr Hudson (12534) *(G-6631)*

Phoenix Usa LLC ... 646 351-6598
315 W 33rd St Apt 30h New York (10001) *(G-11652)*

Phoenix Venture Fund LLC ... 212 759-1909
70 E 55th St Fl 10 New York (10022) *(G-11653)*

Phoenix Welding & Fabg Inc ... 315 695-2223
10 County Route 6 Phoenix (13135) *(G-13543)*

Phoenix Wood Wrights Ltd ... 631 727-9691
132 Kroemer Ave 3 Riverhead (11901) *(G-14151)*

Photo Agents Ltd ... 631 421-0258
716 New York Ave Huntington (11743) *(G-6674)*

Photo Industry Inc ... 516 364-0016
7600 Jericho Tpke Ste 301 Woodbury (11797) *(G-17295)*

Photo Medic Equipment Inc ... 631 242-6600
239 S Fehr Way Bay Shore (11706) *(G-723)*

Photo Research, Syracuse Also called Novanta Inc *(G-16000)*

Photon Gear Inc ... 585 265-3360
245 David Pkwy Ontario (14519) *(G-13209)*

Photon Vision Systems Inc (PA) ... 607 749-2689
1 Technology Pl Homer (13077) *(G-6521)*

Photonamics Inc ... 585 426-3774
558 Elmgrove Rd Rochester (14606) *(G-14583)*

Photonic Controls LLC ... 607 562-4585
500 1st Ctr Ste 2 Horseheads (14845) *(G-6588)*

Photonics Industries Intl Inc (PA) ... 631 218-2240
1800 Ocean Ave Unit A Ronkonkoma (11779) *(G-14968)*

Photonix Technologies Inc ... 607 786-4600
48 Washington Ave Endicott (13760) *(G-4825)*

Photoscribe, New York Also called DBC Inc *(G-9832)*

Phototherapeutix, Glens Falls Also called Medtek Lighting Corporation *(G-5689)*

Phreesia New York ... 888 654-7473
432 Park Ave S Fl 12 New York (10016) *(G-11654)*

Phyljohn Distributors Inc ... 518 459-2775
6 Interstate Ave Albany (12205) *(G-120)*

Phymetrix Inc ... 631 627-3950
28 Scouting Blvd Ste C Medford (11763) *(G-8257)*

Physicalmind Institute ... 212 343-2150
84 Wooster St Ste 605 New York (10012) *(G-11655)*

Physiologics LLC ... 800 765-6775
2100 Smithtown Ave Ronkonkoma (11779) *(G-14969)*

Phytofilter Technologies Inc ... 518 507-6399
9 Kirby Rd Apt 19 Saratoga Springs (12866) *(G-15166)*

Piaget ... 212 355-6444
663 5th Ave Fl 7 New York (10022) *(G-11656)*

Piaggio Group Americas Inc ... 212 380-4400
257 Park Ave S Fl 4 New York (10010) *(G-11657)*

Piazzas Ice Cream Ice Hse Inc ... 718 818-8811
41 Housman Ave Staten Island (10303) *(G-15721)*

Pibbs Industries, Flushing Also called PS Pibbs Inc *(G-5284)*

Pic A Poc Enterprises Inc ... 631 981-2094
53 Union Ave Ronkonkoma (11779) *(G-14970)*

Pic Nic LLC ... 914 245-6500
123 Holmes Ct Yorktown Heights (10598) *(G-17516)*

Picador USA ... 646 307-5629
175 5th Ave New York (10010) *(G-11658)*

Picasso Coach Builders, Rego Park *Also called Pcb Coach Builders Corp* ***(G-14038)***
Piccini Industries Ltd 845 365-0614
37 Ramland Rd Orangeburg (10962) ***(G-13239)***
Pickett Building Materials, Oneonta *Also called Arnan Development Corp* ***(G-13171)***
Picone Meat Specialties Ltd 914 381-3002
180 Jefferson Ave Mamaroneck (10543) ***(G-8042)***
Picone's Sausage, Mamaroneck *Also called Picone Meat Specialties Ltd* ***(G-8042)***
Picture Perfect Framing 718 851-1884
1758 50th St Brooklyn (11204) ***(G-2418)***
Pidyon Controls Inc (PA) 212 683-9523
141 W 24th St Apt 4 New York (10011) ***(G-11659)***
Pie, Webster *Also called Practical Instrument Elec Inc* ***(G-16730)***
Piedmont Plastics Inc 518 724-0563
4 Access Rd Albany (12205) ***(G-121)***
Piemonte Company, Woodside *Also called Piemonte Home Made Ravioli Co* ***(G-17347)***
Piemonte Home Made Ravioli Co (PA) 718 429-1972
3436 65th St Woodside (11377) ***(G-17347)***
Piemonte Home Made Ravioli Co 212 226-0475
190 Grand St New York (10013) ***(G-11660)***
Pier-Tech Inc 516 442-5420
7 Hampton Rd Oceanside (11572) ***(G-13089)***
Pierce Arrow Draperies, Buffalo *Also called Pierce Arrow Drapery Mfg* ***(G-3125)***
Pierce Arrow Drapery Mfg 716 876-3023
1685 Elmwood Ave Ste 312 Buffalo (14207) ***(G-3125)***
Pierce Industries LLC 585 458-0888
465 Paul Rd Rochester (14624) ***(G-14584)***
Pierce Steel Fabricators 716 372-7652
430 N 7th St Olean (14760) ***(G-13152)***
Pierrepont Visual Graphics 585 305-9672
15 Elser Ter Rochester (14611) ***(G-14585)***
Pietro Demarco Importers Inc 914 969-3201
1185 Saw Mill River Rd # 4 Yonkers (10710) ***(G-17477)***
Piezo Electronics Research 845 735-9349
30 Walter St Pearl River (10965) ***(G-13463)***
Pii Holdings Inc (HQ) 716 876-9951
2150 Elmwood Ave Buffalo (14207) ***(G-3126)***
Pilgrim Foods Co, Great Neck *Also called Old Dutch Mustard Co Inc* ***(G-5825)***
Pilgrim Surf & Supply 718 218-7456
68 N 3rd St Brooklyn (11249) ***(G-2419)***
Pilkington North America Inc 315 438-3341
6412 Deere Rd Ste 1 Syracuse (13206) ***(G-16012)***
Piller Power Systems, Middletown *Also called Piller Usa Inc* ***(G-8456)***
Piller Usa Inc (HQ) 845 695-6600
45 Wes Warren Dr Middletown (10941) ***(G-8456)***
Pillow Perfections Ltd Inc 718 383-2259
252 Norman Ave Ste 101 Brooklyn (11222) ***(G-2420)***
Pilot Products Inc 718 728-2141
2413 46th St Long Island City (11103) ***(G-7843)***
Pin People LLC 888 309-7467
35 West St Spring Valley (10977) ***(G-15599)***
Pin Pharma Inc 212 543-2583
3960 Broadway Fl 2 New York (10032) ***(G-11661)***
Pin Pretty Inc 718 887-5290
5415 14th Ave Brooklyn (11219) ***(G-2421)***
Pincharming Inc 516 663-5115
215 Brixton Rd Garden City (11530) ***(G-5525)***
Pindar Vineyards LLC 631 734-6200
37645 Route 25 Peconic (11958) ***(G-13472)***
Pinder International Inc (PA) 631 273-0324
1140 Motor Pkwy Ste A Hauppauge (11788) ***(G-6164)***
Pine Barrens Printing, Westhampton Beach *Also called Michael K Lennon Inc* ***(G-17059)***
Pine Bush Printing Co Inc 518 456-2431
2005 Western Ave Albany (12203) ***(G-122)***
Pine Hill Fabricators 716 823-2474
2731 Seneca St Buffalo (14224) ***(G-3127)***
Pine Pharmaceuticals LLC 716 248-1025
100 Colvin Woods Pkwy Tonawanda (14150) ***(G-16193)***
Pine Ridge Log HM Restoration, Lacona *Also called Pine Ridge Log HM Restorations* ***(G-7251)***
Pine Ridge Log HM Restorations 315 387-3360
1866 County Route 48 Lacona (13083) ***(G-7251)***
Pine Tree Farms Inc 607 532-4312
3714 Cayuga St Interlaken (14847) ***(G-6749)***
Pinewood Marketing, Hartsdale *Also called Richard Edelson* ***(G-5999)***
Pingmd Inc 212 632-2665
136 Madison Ave Fl 6 New York (10016) ***(G-11662)***
Pink Inc 212 352-8282
23 E 10th St Apt 1b New York (10003) ***(G-11663)***
Pink and Palmer, Rye *Also called Judith N Graham Inc* ***(G-15061)***
Pink Box Accessories LLC 716 777-4477
1170 72nd St Brooklyn (11228) ***(G-2422)***
Pink Crush LLC 718 788-6978
1410 Broadway Rm 1002 New York (10018) ***(G-11664)***
Pinnacle Manufacturing Co Inc 585 343-5664
56 Harvester Ave Batavia (14020) ***(G-645)***
Pinnacle Wine Vault LLC (PA) 212 736-0040
810 7th Ave Fl 28 New York (10019) ***(G-11665)***
Pinos Press Inc 315 935-0110
201 E Jefferson St Syracuse (13202) ***(G-16013)***
Pinpoint Systems Intl Inc (PA) 631 775-2100
10 Pinehurst Dr Bellport (11713) ***(G-838)***
Pinquist Tool & Die Co Inc 718 389-3900
451 Sunrise Hwy Ste 4 Lynbrook (11563) ***(G-7956)***
Pins and Lanes, Lowville *Also called Qubicaamf Worldwide LLC* ***(G-7941)***
Pins N Needles 212 535-6222
1045 Lexington Ave New York (10021) ***(G-11666)***
Pioneer Printers Inc 716 693-7100
1087 Erie Ave North Tonawanda (14120) ***(G-12986)***
Pioneer Tanning Equipment, Johnstown *Also called Stephen A Manoogian Inc* ***(G-7129)***
Pioneer Window Holdings Inc (PA) 516 822-7000
15 Frederick Pl Hicksville (11801) ***(G-6388)***
Pioneer Window Holdings Inc 518 762-5526
200 Union Ave Ext Johnstown (12095) ***(G-7122)***
Pioneer Windows Manufacturing, Hicksville *Also called Pioneer Window Holdings Inc* ***(G-6388)***
PIP Printing, Oceanside *Also called Ahw Printing Corp* ***(G-13072)***
PIP Printing, Lynbrook *Also called Pro Printing* ***(G-7957)***
PIP Printing, Syosset *Also called Vivona Business Printers Inc* ***(G-15842)***
PIP Printing, White Plains *Also called Alamar Printing Inc* ***(G-17074)***
PIP Printing, Hicksville *Also called Marcal Printing Inc* ***(G-6367)***
Pipe Dream 607 777-2515
4400 Vestal Pkwy Binghamton (13902) ***(G-943)***
Piper Plastics Corp 631 842-6889
102 Ralph Ave Copiague (11726) ***(G-3918)***
Pipkarnia Starodolska, Brooklyn *Also called Old Poland Foods LLC* ***(G-2388)***
Pirnat Precise Metals Inc 631 293-9169
127 Marine St Farmingdale (11735) ***(G-5080)***
Piroke Trade Inc 646 515-1537
1430 35th St Fl 2 Brooklyn (11218) ***(G-2423)***
Pit Stop Motorsports, Forestville *Also called P S M Group Inc* ***(G-5335)***
Pitney Bowes Inc 212 564-7548
637 W 27th St Fl 8 New York (10001) ***(G-11667)***
Pitney Bowes Inc 203 356-5000
90 Park Ave Rm 1110 New York (10016) ***(G-11668)***
Pitney Bowes Inc 516 822-0900
220 Miller Pl Hicksville (11801) ***(G-6389)***
Pitney Bowes Software Inc 518 272-0014
1 Global Vw Troy (12180) ***(G-16248)***
Pituitary Society 212 263-6772
423 E 23rd St Rm 16048 New York (10010) ***(G-11669)***
Pivot Punch Corporation 716 625-8000
6550 Campbell Blvd Lockport (14094) ***(G-7610)***
Pivot Records LLC 718 417-1213
600 Johnson Ave Brooklyn (11237) ***(G-2424)***
Piwik Pro LLC 888 444-0049
222 Broadway Fl 19 New York (10038) ***(G-11670)***
Pixy Dust, Amagansett *Also called Cosmetics Plus Ltd* ***(G-213)***
Pj Decorators Inc 516 735-9693
257 Pontiac Pl East Meadow (11554) ***(G-4427)***
PJ Designs Inc 212 355-3100
100 E 50th St Ste 38a New York (10022) ***(G-11671)***
Pk Metals, Coram *Also called Suffolk Indus Recovery Corp* ***(G-3951)***
Pk30 System LLC 212 473-8050
3607 Atwood Rd Stone Ridge (12484) ***(G-15764)***
Pkg Group 212 965-0112
560 Broadway Rm 406 New York (10012) ***(G-11672)***
Pkk Inc 716 257-3451
261 S Main St Cattaraugus (14719) ***(G-3439)***
Pl Developments, Westbury *Also called P & L Development LLC* ***(G-17017)***
Pl Developments New York, Westbury *Also called P & L Development LLC* ***(G-17016)***
Place Vendome Holding Co Inc (PA) 212 696-0765
4238 Bronx Blvd Frnt 2 Bronx (10466) ***(G-1428)***
Placemeter Inc 917 225-4579
865 President St Brooklyn (11215) ***(G-2425)***
Placid Baker 518 326-2657
250 Broadway Troy (12180) ***(G-16249)***
Planar Optics Inc 585 671-0100
858 Hard Rd Webster (14580) ***(G-16729)***
Planet Embroidery 718 381-4827
6695 Forest Ave Ridgewood (11385) ***(G-14118)***
Planet Going, Riverhead *Also called Precision Consulting* ***(G-14152)***
Plant Office, Wyoming *Also called Texas Brine Company LLC* ***(G-17382)***
Plant-Tech2o Inc 516 483-7845
30 Chasner St Hempstead (11550) ***(G-6285)***
Plascal Corp 516 249-2200
361 Eastern Pkwy Farmingdale (11735) ***(G-5081)***
Plascoline Inc 917 410-5754
275 Madison Ave Fl 14 New York (10016) ***(G-11673)***
Plaslok Corp 716 681-7755
3155 Broadway St Buffalo (14227) ***(G-3128)***
Plasti-Form, New York *Also called Braiform Enterprises Inc* ***(G-9450)***
Plasti-Vue Corp 718 463-2300
4130 Murray St Flushing (11355) ***(G-5282)***
Plastic & Reconstructive Svcs 914 584-5605
333 N Bedford Rd Mount Kisco (10549) ***(G-8640)***
Plastic Solutions Inc 631 234-9013
158 Schenck Ave Bayport (11705) ***(G-760)***
Plastic Sys/Gr Bflo Inc 716 835-7555
465 Cornwall Ave Buffalo (14215) ***(G-3129)***
Plastic Techniques, Binghamton *Also called Binghamton Precision Tool Inc* ***(G-894)***

A L P H A B E T I C

Plastic Works ALPHABETIC SECTION

Plastic Works 914 576-2050
26 Garden St New Rochelle (10801) *(G-8920)*
Plastic-Craft Products Corp 845 358-3010
744 W Nyack Rd West Nyack (10994) *(G-16925)*
Plasticware LLC (PA) 845 267-0790
13 Wilsher Dr Monsey (10952) *(G-8577)*
Plasticweld Systems, Newfane *Also called Vante Inc (G-12789)*
Plasticycle Corporation (PA) 914 997-6882
245 Main St Ste 430 White Plains (10601) *(G-17160)*
Plastifold Industries Division, Brooklyn *Also called Visitainer Corp (G-2731)*
Plastikoil Binding Systems, Rochester *Also called Bruce Woehr (G-14248)*
Plastirun Corporation 631 273-2626
70 Emjay Blvd Bldg A Brentwood (11717) *(G-1193)*
Platform Experts Inc 646 843-7100
2938 Quentin Rd Brooklyn (11229) *(G-2426)*
Platina, New York *Also called Alexander Primak Jewelry Inc (G-9082)*
Platinum Carting Corp 631 649-4322
1806 Carleton Ave Bay Shore (11706) *(G-724)*
Platinum Printing & Graphics 631 249-3325
70 Carolyn Blvd Ste C Farmingdale (11735) *(G-5082)*
Platinum Sales Promotion Inc 718 361-0200
3514a Crescent St Long Island City (11106) *(G-7844)*
Plattco Corporation (PA) 518 563-4640
7 White St Plattsburgh (12901) *(G-13687)*
Platter's Chocolates, North Tonawanda *Also called Roger L Urban Inc (G-12992)*
Plattsburgh Press-Republican, Plattsburgh *Also called Community Newspaper Group LLC (G-13660)*
Plattsburgh Quarry, Plattsburgh *Also called Graymont Materials Inc (G-13667)*
Plattsburgh Sheet Metal Inc 518 561-4930
95 Sailly Ave Plattsburgh (12901) *(G-13688)*
Play-It Productions Inc 212 695-6530
735 Port Washington Blvd Port Washington (11050) *(G-13856)*
Playbill Incorporated (PA) 212 557-5757
729 7th Ave Fl 4 New York (10019) *(G-11674)*
Playbill Incorporated 718 335-4033
3715 61st St Woodside (11377) *(G-17348)*
Playfitness Corp 917 497-5443
27 Palisade St Staten Island (10305) *(G-15722)*
Playlife LLC 646 207-9082
297 Church St Fl 5 New York (10013) *(G-11675)*
Plaza Braceltte Mounting, New Hyde Park *Also called Satco Castings Service Inc (G-8860)*
Plaza Group Creation, New York *Also called Jordan Scott Designs Ltd (G-10762)*
PLC Apparel LLC 212 239-3434
137 Grand St Fl 3 New York (10013) *(G-11676)*
Pleatco LLC 516 609-0200
28 Garvies Point Rd Glen Cove (11542) *(G-5624)*
Pleating Plus Ltd 201 863-2991
34 Route 340 Orangeburg (10962) *(G-13240)*
Plexi Craft Quality Products 212 924-3244
200 Lexington Ave Rm 914 New York (10016) *(G-11677)*
Pliant LLC 315 986-6286
200 Main St Macedon (14502) *(G-7990)*
Pliotron Company America LLC 716 298-4457
4650 Witmer Indus Est Niagara Falls (14305) *(G-12860)*
Plug Power Inc (PA) 518 782-7700
968 Albany Shaker Rd Latham (12110) *(G-7377)*
Plugg LLC 212 840-6655
1410 Broadway Frnt 2 New York (10018) *(G-11678)*
Plures Technologies Inc (PA) 585 905-0554
4070 County Road 16 Canandaigua (14424) *(G-3355)*
Pluribus Products Inc 718 852-1614
77 Washington Ave Brooklyn (11205) *(G-2427)*
Plus Its Cheap LLC (PA) 845 233-2435
873 Route 45 Ste 101 New City (10956) *(G-8789)*
Plx Inc (PA) 631 586-4190
25 W Jefryn Blvd Ste A Deer Park (11729) *(G-4189)*
Pmb Precision Products Inc 631 491-6753
725 Mount Ave North Babylon (11703) *(G-12902)*
Pmd, Victor *Also called Progressive Mch & Design LLC (G-16497)*
PMF, Brooklyn *Also called Precision Mtal Fabricators Inc (G-2435)*
PMG, Ronkonkoma *Also called Paul Michael Group Inc (G-14966)*
PMI Global Services Inc 917 663-2000
120 Park Ave Fl 7 New York (10017) *(G-11679)*
PMI Industries LLC 585 464-8050
350 Buell Rd Rochester (14624) *(G-14586)*
Pmrnyc, Brooklyn *Also called Total Metal Resource (G-2669)*
PNC Sports 516 665-2244
1880 Deer Park Ave Deer Park (11729) *(G-4190)*
Pneumercator Company Inc 631 293-8450
1785 Express Dr N Hauppauge (11788) *(G-6165)*
Pni Capital Partners 516 466-7120
1400 Old Country Rd # 103 Westbury (11590) *(G-17019)*
Pocket Solutions Inc 631 355-1073
3 Andiron Ln Brookhaven (11719) *(G-1509)*
Pocono Pool Products-North 518 283-1023
15 Krey Blvd Rensselaer (12144) *(G-14049)*
Poerformance Design, Fairport *Also called Performance Designed By Peters (G-4870)*
Poetry Mailing List Marsh Hawk 516 766-1891
2823 Rockaway Ave Oceanside (11572) *(G-13090)*
Poets House Inc 212 431-7920
10 River Ter New York (10282) *(G-11680)*
Point Canvas Company Inc 607 692-4381
5952 State Route 26 Whitney Point (13862) *(G-17220)*
Point Electric Div, Blauvelt *Also called Swivelier Company Inc (G-975)*
Point Industrial, Bemus Point *Also called Lakeside Industries Inc (G-844)*
Point of Sale Outfitters, Geneva *Also called R M Reynolds (G-5584)*
Pointwise Information Service 315 457-4111
223 1st St Liverpool (13088) *(G-7542)*
Pol-Tek Industries Ltd 716 823-1502
2300 Clinton St Buffalo (14227) *(G-3130)*
Polanco Mills Woodwork 845 271-3639
132 E Railroad Ave West Haverstraw (10993) *(G-16846)*
Pole Position Raceway 716 683-7223
1 Walden Galleria Cheektowaga (14225) *(G-3586)*
Pole-Tech Co Inc 631 689-5525
97 Gnarled Hollow Rd East Setauket (11733) *(G-4489)*
Poletech Flagpole Manufaturer, East Setauket *Also called Pole-Tech Co Inc (G-4489)*
Policy ADM Solutions Inc 914 332-4320
505 White Plains Rd Tarrytown (10591) *(G-16100)*
Polish American Journal, Orchard Park *Also called Panagraphics Inc (G-13287)*
Political Risk Services, The, East Syracuse *Also called The PRS Group Inc (G-4571)*
POLITICAL SCIENCE QUARTERLY, New York *Also called Academy of Political Science (G-9008)*
Polkadot Usa Inc 914 835-3697
33 Country Rd Mamaroneck (10543) *(G-8043)*
Pollack Graphics Inc 212 727-8400
601 W 26th St Ste M204 New York (10001) *(G-11681)*
Pollardwater, New Hyde Park *Also called Ferguson Enterprises Inc (G-8834)*
Polly Treating, New York *Also called Xinya International Trading Co (G-12679)*
Polo Ralph Lauren Hosiery Div, New York *Also called Hot Sox Company Incorporated (G-10514)*
Polska Gazeta, Brooklyn *Also called Spring Publishing Corporation (G-2592)*
Poly Can, Carthage *Also called David Johnson (G-3413)*
Poly Craft Industries Corp 631 630-6731
40 Ranick Rd Hauppauge (11788) *(G-6166)*
Poly Scientific R&D Corp 631 586-0400
70 Cleveland Ave Bay Shore (11706) *(G-725)*
Poly Software International 845 735-9301
7 Kerry Ct Pearl River (10965) *(G-13464)*
Poly-Flex Corp (PA) 631 586-9500
250 Executive Dr Ste S Edgewood (11717) *(G-4607)*
Poly-Pak Industries Inc (PA) 631 293-6767
125 Spagnoli Rd Melville (11747) *(G-8348)*
Polycast Industries Inc 631 595-2530
130 S 2nd St Bay Shore (11706) *(G-726)*
Polyethylene Foam Div, Schenectady *Also called Sealed Air Corporation (G-15295)*
Polygen Pharmaceuticals Inc 631 392-4044
41 Mercedes Way Unit 17 Edgewood (11717) *(G-4608)*
Polymag Inc 631 286-4111
685 Station Rd Ste 2 Bellport (11713) *(G-839)*
Polymag Tek Inc 585 235-8390
215 Tremont St Ste 2 Rochester (14608) *(G-14587)*
Polymer Conversions Inc 716 662-8550
5732 Big Tree Rd Orchard Park (14127) *(G-13290)*
Polymer Engineered Pdts Inc 585 426-1811
23 Moonlanding Rd Rochester (14624) *(G-14588)*
Polymer Slutions Group Fin LLC (PA) 212 771-1717
100 Park Ave Fl 31 New York (10017) *(G-11682)*
Polyplastic Forms Inc 631 249-5011
49 Gazza Blvd Farmingdale (11735) *(G-5083)*
Polyseal Packaging Corp 718 792-5530
1178 E 180th St Bronx (10460) *(G-1429)*
Polyset Company Inc 518 664-6000
65 Hudson Ave Mechanicville (12118) *(G-8229)*
Polyshot Corporation 585 292-5010
75 Lucius Gordon Dr West Henrietta (14586) *(G-16892)*
Polytech Pool Mfg Inc 718 492-8991
262 48th St 262 Brooklyn (11220) *(G-2428)*
Polytex Inc 716 549-5100
1305 Eden Evans Center Rd Angola (14006) *(G-381)*
Pompian Manufacturing Co Inc 914 476-7076
280 Nepperhan Ave Yonkers (10701) *(G-17478)*
Poncio Signs 718 543-4851
3007 Albany Cres Bronx (10463) *(G-1430)*
Pony Farm Press & Graphics 607 432-9020
330 Pony Farm Rd Oneonta (13820) *(G-13192)*
Pooran Pallet Inc 718 938-7970
319 Barretto St Bronx (10474) *(G-1431)*
Pop A2z, New York *Also called Sky Frame & Art Inc (G-12095)*
Pop Bar LLC 212 255-4874
5 Carmine St Frnt 6 New York (10014) *(G-11683)*
Pop Nyc, New York *Also called Popnyc 1 LLC (G-11684)*
Pop Printing Incorporated 212 808-7800
288 Hamilton Ave Brooklyn (11231) *(G-2429)*
Popnyc 1 LLC 646 684-4600
75 Saint Nicholas Pl 2e New York (10032) *(G-11684)*
Poppin Inc 212 391-7200
1115 Broadway Fl 3 New York (10010) *(G-11685)*
Popular Mechanics, New York *Also called Hearst Corporation (G-10442)*

Popular Pattern, New York *Also called Stephen Singer Pattern Co Inc* ***(G-12196)***
Popularity Products, Brooklyn *Also called New York Popular Inc* ***(G-2367)***
Porcelain Refinishing Corp 516 352-4841
19905 32nd Ave Flushing (11358) ***(G-5283)***
Pork King Sausage Inc 718 542-2810
F22 Hunts Point Co Op Mkt Bronx (10474) ***(G-1432)***
Porous Materials Inc (PA) 607 257-5544
20 Dutch Mill Rd Ithaca (14850) ***(G-6870)***
Port Authority of NY & NJ 718 390-2534
2777 Goethals Rd N Fl 2 Staten Island (10303) ***(G-15723)***
Port Everglades Machine Works 516 367-2280
57 Colgate Dr Plainview (11803) ***(G-13630)***
Port Jervis Machine Corp 845 856-6210
176 1/2 Jersey Ave Port Jervis (12771) ***(G-13790)***
Porta Decor 516 826-6900
290 Duffy Ave Unit 3 Hicksville (11801) ***(G-6390)***
Portable Tech Solutions LLC 631 727-8084
221 David Ct Calverton (11933) ***(G-3295)***
Portequip Work Stations, Niagara Falls *Also called Stephenson Custom Case Company* ***(G-12878)***
Portfab LLC 718 542-3600
45 Ranick Dr E Amityville (11701) ***(G-322)***
Portfolio Decisionware Inc 212 947-1326
250 W 57th St Ste 1032 New York (10107) ***(G-11686)***
Portfolio Media Inc 646 783-7100
111 W 19th St Ste 507 New York (10011) ***(G-11687)***
Portville Sand & Gravel Div, Portville *Also called I A Construction Corporation* ***(G-13875)***
Portware LLC (HQ) 212 425-5233
233 Broadway Fl 24 New York (10279) ***(G-11688)***
Poseidon Systems LLC 585 239-6025
200 Canal View Blvd # 300 Rochester (14623) ***(G-14589)***
Posillico Materials LLC 631 249-1872
1750 New Hwy Farmingdale (11735) ***(G-5084)***
Posimech Inc 631 924-5959
15 Scouting Blvd Unit 3 Medford (11763) ***(G-8258)***
Positive Print Litho Offset 212 431-4850
121 Varick St Rm 204 New York (10013) ***(G-11689)***
Post Community Media LLC 518 374-4141
376 Broadway Saratoga Springs (12866) ***(G-15167)***
Post Journal 716 487-1111
412 Murray Ave Jamestown (14701) ***(G-7023)***
Post Road 203 545-2122
101 E 16th St Apt 4b New York (10003) ***(G-11690)***
Post Star, Glens Falls *Also called Lee Enterprises Incorporated* ***(G-5686)***
Post-Journal, The, Jamestown *Also called Ogden Newspapers Inc* ***(G-7022)***
Potential Poly Bag Inc 718 258-0800
1253 Coney Island Ave Brooklyn (11230) ***(G-2430)***
Potsdam Specialty Paper Inc (HQ) 315 265-4000
547a Sissonville Rd Potsdam (13676) ***(G-13881)***
Potsdam Specialty Paper, Inc., Potsdam *Also called Potsdam Specialty Paper Inc* ***(G-13881)***
Potsdam Stone Concrete, Plattsburgh *Also called Graymont Materials (ny) Inc* ***(G-13666)***
Potter Lumber Co Inc 716 373-1260
3786 Potter Rd Allegany (14706) ***(G-203)***
Potter Lumber Co LLC 814 438-7888
4002 Legion Dr Hamburg (14075) ***(G-5936)***
Potters Industries LLC 315 265-4920
72 Reynolds Rd Potsdam (13676) ***(G-13882)***
Poughkeepsie Journal, Poughkeepsie *Also called Gannett Stllite Info Ntwrk LLC* ***(G-13900)***
Poultry Dist, Brooklyn *Also called Vineland Kosher Poultry Inc* ***(G-2728)***
Powa Technologies Inc 347 344-7848
1 Bryant Park Ste 39 New York (10036) ***(G-11691)***
Power and Cnstr Group Inc 585 889-6020
86 River Rd Scottsville (14546) ***(G-15338)***
Power and Composite Tech LLC 518 843-6825
119 Genessee Ln Amsterdam (12010) ***(G-365)***
Power Connector Inc 631 563-7878
140 Wilbur Pl Ste 4 Bohemia (11716) ***(G-1118)***
Power Gneration Indus Engs Inc 315 633-9389
8927 Tyler Rd Bridgeport (13030) ***(G-1235)***
Power Line Constructors Inc 315 853-6183
24 Robinson Rd Clinton (13323) ***(G-3721)***
Power Scrub It Inc 516 997-2500
75 Urban Ave Westbury (11590) ***(G-17020)***
Power Up Manufacturing Inc 716 876-4890
275 N Pointe Pkwy Ste 100 Buffalo (14228) ***(G-3131)***
Powercomplete LLC 212 228-4129
636 Broadway Rm 1000 New York (10012) ***(G-11692)***
Powerflow Inc 716 892-1014
1714 Broadway St Buffalo (14212) ***(G-3132)***
Powermate Cellular 718 833-9400
140 58th St Ste 1d Brooklyn (11220) ***(G-2431)***
Powers Fasteners, Brewster *Also called Black & Decker (us) Inc* ***(G-1212)***
Powertex Inc (PA) 518 297-4000
1 Lincoln Blvd Ste 101 Rouses Point (12979) ***(G-15043)***
Powr-UPS Corp 631 345-5700
1 Roned Rd Shirley (11967) ***(G-15428)***
Poz Publishing, New York *Also called Smart & Strong LLC* ***(G-12100)***
PPG Architectural Finishes Inc 607 334-9951
158 State Highway 320 Norwich (13815) ***(G-13034)***
PPG Architectural Finishes Inc 585 271-1363
566 Clinton Ave S Rochester (14620) ***(G-14590)***
Ppi Corp 585 880-7277
112 Riverside Dr Geneseo (14454) ***(G-5567)***
Ppi Corp 585 243-0300
112 Riverside Dr Geneseo (14454) ***(G-5568)***
Ppr Direct Inc 718 965-8600
74 20th St Fl 2 Brooklyn (11232) ***(G-2432)***
Ppr Direct Marketing LLC (PA) 718 965-8600
74 20th St Brooklyn (11232) ***(G-2433)***
PR & Stone & Tile Inc 718 383-1115
17 Beadel St Brooklyn (11222) ***(G-2434)***
Practical Instrument Elec Inc 585 872-9350
82 E Main St Ste 3 Webster (14580) ***(G-16730)***
Practicepro Software Systems 516 222-0010
666 Old Country Rd Bsmt Garden City (11530) ***(G-5526)***
Prager Metis Cpas LLC 212 972-7555
675 3rd Ave New York (10017) ***(G-11693)***
Pragmatics Technology Inc 845 795-5071
14 Old Indian Trl Milton (12547) ***(G-8483)***
Pratt With ME Hmi Met Powders, Clayville *Also called Hmi Metal Powders* ***(G-3688)***
Praxair Inc 716 879-2000
175 E Park Dr Tonawanda (14150) ***(G-16194)***
Praxair Inc 845 267-2337
614 Corporate Way Ste 4 Valley Cottage (10989) ***(G-16384)***
Praxair Inc 716 649-1600
5322 Scranton Rd Hamburg (14075) ***(G-5937)***
Praxair Inc 518 482-4360
116 Railroad Ave Albany (12205) ***(G-123)***
Praxair Inc 716 286-4600
4501 Royal Ave Niagara Falls (14303) ***(G-12861)***
Praxair Inc 845 359-4200
542 Route 303 Orangeburg (10962) ***(G-13241)***
Praxair Inc 716 879-4000
135 E Park Dr Tonawanda (14150) ***(G-16195)***
Praxair Distribution Inc 315 457-5821
4560 Morgan Pl Liverpool (13090) ***(G-7543)***
Praxair Distribution Inc 315 735-6153
9432 State Route 49 Marcy (13403) ***(G-8092)***
Praxair Surface Tech Inc 845 398-8322
560 Route 303 Orangeburg (10962) ***(G-13242)***
Praxis Powder Technology Inc 518 812-0112
604 Queensbury Ave Queensbury (12804) ***(G-14007)***
PRC Liquidating Company 212 823-9626
10 Columbus Cir New York (10019) ***(G-11694)***
Pre Cycled Inc 845 278-7611
1689 Route 22 Brewster (10509) ***(G-1227)***
Pre-Tech Plastics Inc 518 942-5950
3085 Plank Rd Mineville (12956) ***(G-8541)***
Precare Corp 631 524-5171
400 Wireless Blvd Hauppauge (11788) ***(G-6167)***
Precare Corp (PA) 631 667-1055
100 Oser Ave Hauppauge (11788) ***(G-6168)***
Precimed Inc 716 759-5600
10000 Wehrle Dr Clarence (14031) ***(G-3669)***
Precious Plate Inc 716 283-0690
2124 Liberty Dr Niagara Falls (14304) ***(G-12862)***
Precipart Corporation 631 777-8727
120 Finn Ct Farmingdale (11735) ***(G-5085)***
Precise Optics, Bay Shore *Also called Photo Medic Equipment Inc* ***(G-723)***
Precise Punch Corporation 716 625-8000
6550 Campbell Blvd Lockport (14094) ***(G-7611)***
Precise Tool & Mfg Inc 585 247-0700
9 Coldwater Cres Rochester (14624) ***(G-14591)***
Preciseled Inc 516 418-5337
52 Railroad Ave Valley Stream (11580) ***(G-16419)***
Precision Abrasives Corp 716 826-5833
3176 Abbott Rd Orchard Park (14127) ***(G-13291)***
Precision Arms Inc 845 225-1130
421 Route 52 Carmel (10512) ***(G-3404)***
Precision Assembly Tech Inc 631 699-9400
160 Wilbur Pl Ste 500 Bohemia (11716) ***(G-1119)***
Precision Biologics Inc 516 482-1200
445 Northern Blvd Ste 24 Great Neck (11021) ***(G-5831)***
Precision Built Tops LLC 607 336-5417
89 Borden Ave Norwich (13815) ***(G-13035)***
Precision Charts Inc 631 244-8295
130 Wilbur Pl Dept Pc Bohemia (11716) ***(G-1120)***
Precision Cnc 631 847-3999
71 E Jefryn Blvd Deer Park (11729) ***(G-4191)***
Precision Co., Menands *Also called McAllisters Precision Wldg Inc* ***(G-8374)***
Precision Consulting 631 727-0847
760 Osborn Ave Riverhead (11901) ***(G-14152)***
Precision Cosmetics Mfg Co 914 667-1200
519 S 5th Ave Ste 6 Mount Vernon (10550) ***(G-8716)***
Precision Cstm Coatings I LLC 212 868-5770
234 W 39th St New York (10018) ***(G-11695)***
Precision Dental Cabinets Inc (PA) 631 543-3870
900 W Jericho Tpke Smithtown (11787) ***(G-15495)***
Precision Dental Ceramics of B 716 681-4133
5204 Genesee St Bowmansville (14026) ***(G-1170)***
Precision Design Systems Inc 585 426-4500
1645 Lyell Ave Ste 136 Rochester (14606) ***(G-14592)***
Precision Diamond Cutters Inc 212 719-4438
2 W 46th St Ste 1007 New York (10036) ***(G-11696)***

ALPHABETIC

(PA)=Parent Co (HQ)=Headquarters (DH)=Div Headquarters

Precision Diecutting Inc......315 776-8465
1381 Spring Lake Rd Port Byron (13140) *(G-13736)*
Precision Disc Grinding Corp......516 747-5450
255 E 2nd St Mineola (11501) *(G-8531)*
Precision Eforming LLC......607 753-7730
839 State Route 13 Ste 1 Cortland (13045) *(G-4040)*
Precision Elctro Mnrl Pmco Inc......716 284-2484
150 Portage Rd Niagara Falls (14303) *(G-12863)*
Precision Electronics Inc......631 842-4900
1 Di Tomas Ct Copiague (11726) *(G-3919)*
Precision Engraving Company, Amityville *Also called Precision Signscom Inc (G-323)*
Precision Envelope Co Inc......631 694-3990
110 Schmitt Blvd 7a Farmingdale (11735) *(G-5086)*
Precision Extrusion, Glens Falls *Also called Pexco LLC (G-5696)*
Precision Fabrication LLC......585 591-3449
40 S Pearl St Attica (14011) *(G-474)*
Precision Filters Inc (PA)......607 277-3550
240 Cherry St Ithaca (14850) *(G-6871)*
Precision Furniture, Bronx *Also called Precision Orna Ir Works Inc (G-1433)*
Precision Gear Incorporated......718 321-7200
11207 14th Ave College Point (11356) *(G-3802)*
Precision Grinding & Mfg Corp (PA)......585 458-4300
1305 Emerson St Rochester (14606) *(G-14593)*
Precision International Co Inc......212 268-9090
201 E 28th St 9n New York (10016) *(G-11697)*
Precision Label Corporation......631 270-4490
175 Marine St Farmingdale (11735) *(G-5087)*
Precision Laser Technology LLC......585 458-6208
1001 Lexington Ave Ste 4 Rochester (14606) *(G-14594)*
Precision Lathe Work Co Inc......845 357-3110
395 Spook Rock Rd Suffern (10901) *(G-15797)*
Precision Locker, Jamestown *Also called Rollform of Jamestown Inc (G-7025)*
Precision Machine Tech LLC......585 467-1840
85 Excel Dr Rochester (14621) *(G-14595)*
Precision Machining and Mfg......845 647-5380
190 Port Ben Rd Wawarsing (12489) *(G-16708)*
Precision Magnetics LLC......585 385-9010
770 Linden Ave Rochester (14625) *(G-14596)*
Precision Mechanisms Corp......516 333-5955
50 Bond St Westbury (11590) *(G-17021)*
Precision Metals Corp......631 586-5032
221 Skip Ln Bay Shore (11706) *(G-727)*
Precision Mtal Fabricators Inc......718 832-9805
236 39th St Brooklyn (11232) *(G-2435)*
Precision Orna Ir Works Inc......718 379-5200
1838 Adee Ave Bronx (10469) *(G-1433)*
Precision Packaging Pdts Inc......585 638-8200
88 Nesbitt Dr Holley (14470) *(G-6491)*
Precision Pharma Services Inc......631 752-7314
155 Duryea Rd Melville (11747) *(G-8349)*
Precision Photo-Fab Inc......716 821-9393
4020 Jeffrey Blvd Buffalo (14219) *(G-3133)*
Precision Plus Vacuum Parts......716 297-2039
6416 Inducon Dr W Sanborn (14132) *(G-15125)*
Precision Polish LLC......315 894-3792
144 Adams St Frankfort (13340) *(G-5356)*
Precision Process Inc (PA)......716 731-1587
2111 Liberty Dr Niagara Falls (14304) *(G-12864)*
Precision Product Inc......718 852-7127
18 Steuben St Brooklyn (11205) *(G-2436)*
Precision Ready Mix Inc......718 658-5600
14707 Liberty Ave Jamaica (11435) *(G-6939)*
Precision Signscom Inc......631 842-5060
243 Dixon Ave Amityville (11701) *(G-323)*
Precision Spclty Fbrctions LLC......716 824-2108
51 N Gates Ave Buffalo (14218) *(G-3134)*
Precision Systems Mfg Inc......315 451-3480
4855 Executive Dr Liverpool (13088) *(G-7544)*
Precision Techniques Inc......718 991-1440
1169 E 156th St Bronx (10474) *(G-1434)*
Precision Tl Die & Stamping Co......516 561-0041
68 Franklin Ave Valley Stream (11580) *(G-16420)*
Precision Tool and Mfg......518 678-3130
314 Pennsylvania Ave Palenville (12463) *(G-13399)*
Precision Valve & Automtn Inc (PA)......518 371-2684
1 Mustang Dr Ste 3 Cohoes (12047) *(G-3755)*
Precisionmatics Co Inc......315 822-6324
1 Helmer Ave West Winfield (13491) *(G-16959)*
Preebro Printing......718 633-7300
5319 Fort Hamilton Pkwy Brooklyn (11219) *(G-2437)*
Prefab Construction Inc......631 821-9613
16 Jackson Ave Sound Beach (11789) *(G-15513)*
Prefered Directors Share, Amityville *Also called Casual Home Worldwide Inc (G-280)*
Preferred Wholesale, New York *Also called R-S Restaurant Eqp Mfg Corp (G-11784)*
Pregis LLC......518 743-3100
18 Peck Ave Glens Falls (12801) *(G-5697)*
Prejean Winery Inc......315 536-7524
2634 State Route 14 Penn Yan (14527) *(G-13516)*
Preload Concrete Structures......631 231-8100
60 Commerce Dr Hauppauge (11788) *(G-6169)*
Premco Inc......914 636-7095
11 Beechwood Ave New Rochelle (10801) *(G-8921)*
Premier, Richmond Hill *Also called 131-11 Atlantic RE Inc (G-14064)*
Premier Brands of America Inc (PA)......914 667-6200
31 South St Ste 2s Mount Vernon (10550) *(G-8717)*
Premier Brands of America Inc......718 325-3000
120 Pearl St Mount Vernon (10550) *(G-8718)*
Premier Cabinet Wholesalers, Rochester *Also called Rochester Countertop Inc (G-14640)*
Premier Care Industries, Hauppauge *Also called Precare Corp (G-6167)*
PREMIER CARE INDUSTRIES, Hauppauge *Also called Precare Corp (G-6168)*
Premier Fixtures LLC (PA)......631 236-4100
400 Oser Ave Ste 350 Hauppauge (11788) *(G-6170)*
Premier Group NY......212 229-1200
18 W 23rd St Fl 3 New York (10010) *(G-11698)*
Premier Hardwood Products Inc......315 492-1786
4800 Solvay Rd Jamesville (13078) *(G-7050)*
Premier Ingridients Inc......516 641-6763
3 Johnstone Rd Great Neck (11021) *(G-5832)*
Premier Ink Systems Inc......845 782-5802
2 Commerce Dr S Harriman (10926) *(G-5973)*
Premier Knits Ltd......718 323-8264
9735 133rd Ave Ozone Park (11417) *(G-13384)*
Premier Machining Tech Inc......716 608-1311
2100 Old Union Rd Buffalo (14227) *(G-3135)*
Premier Metals Group......585 436-4020
11 Cairn St Rochester (14611) *(G-14597)*
Premier Packaging Corporation......585 924-8460
6 Framark Dr Victor (14564) *(G-16496)*
Premier Paint Roller Co LLC......718 441-7700
13111 Atlantic Ave Richmond Hill (11418) *(G-14078)*
Premier Sign Systems LLC......585 235-0390
10 Excel Dr Rochester (14621) *(G-14598)*
Premier Skirting Products Inc......516 239-6581
241 Mill St Lawrence (11559) *(G-7397)*
Premier Skrting Tblecloths Too, Lawrence *Also called Premier Skirting Products Inc (G-7397)*
Premier Store Fixtures, Hauppauge *Also called Premier Fixtures LLC (G-6170)*
Premier Supplies, New York *Also called Print By Premier LLC (G-11716)*
Premier Systems LLC......631 587-9700
41 John St Ste 6 Babylon (11702) *(G-552)*
Premier Woodcraft Ltd......610 383-6624
277 Martine Ave 214 White Plains (10601) *(G-17161)*
Premier Woodworking Inc......631 236-4100
400 Oser Ave Hauppauge (11788) *(G-6171)*
Premiere Living Products LLC......631 873-4337
22 Branwood Dr Dix Hills (11746) *(G-4295)*
Premium Bldg Components Inc......518 885-0194
831 Rt 67 Bldg 46 Ballston Spa (12020) *(G-607)*
Premium Mulch & Materials Inc......631 320-3666
482 Mill Rd Coram (11727) *(G-3949)*
Premium Ocean LLC......917 231-1061
1271 Ryawa Ave Bronx (10474) *(G-1435)*
Premium Shirts Lerma Mexico, New York *Also called American T Shirts Inc (G-9129)*
Premium Sweets USA Inc......718 739-6000
16803 Hillside Ave Jamaica (11432) *(G-6940)*
Premium Valve Services LLC......607 565-7571
685 Broad Street Ext Waverly (14892) *(G-16705)*
Premium Wine Group LLC......631 298-1900
35 Cox Neck Rd Mattituck (11952) *(G-8209)*
Premium Woodworking LLC......718 782-7747
78 Division Pl Fl 1 Brooklyn (11222) *(G-2438)*
Premiumbag LLC......718 657-6219
14550 Liberty Ave Jamaica (11435) *(G-6941)*
Prepac Designs Inc......914 524-7800
25 Abner Pl Yonkers (10704) *(G-17479)*
Preparatory Magazine Group......718 761-4800
1200 South Ave Ste 202 Staten Island (10314) *(G-15724)*
Presbrey- Leland Memorials, Valhalla *Also called Presbrey-Leland Inc (G-16371)*
Presbrey-Leland Inc......914 949-2264
250 Lakeview Ave Valhalla (10595) *(G-16371)*
Prescribing Reference Inc......646 638-6000
275 7th Ave Fl 10 New York (10001) *(G-11699)*
Preserving Chrstn Publications (PA)......315 942-6617
12614 State Route 46 Boonville (13309) *(G-1167)*
President Cont Group II LLC......845 516-1600
290 Ballard Rd Middletown (10941) *(G-8457)*
Presray Corporation......845 373-9300
32 Nelson Hill Rd Wassaic (12592) *(G-16601)*
Press Air, Mamaroneck *Also called Bassin Technical Sales Co (G-8024)*
Press Express......914 592-3790
400 Executive Blvd # 146 Elmsford (10523) *(G-4773)*
Press of Fremont Payne Inc......212 966-6570
55 Broad St Frnt 3 New York (10004) *(G-11700)*
Press of Manorville & Moriches, Southampton *Also called Southampton Town Newspapers (G-15552)*
Press Room New York Division, New York *Also called Circle Press Inc (G-9621)*
Presser Kosher Baking Corp......718 375-5088
1720 Avenue M Brooklyn (11230) *(G-2439)*
Presstek Printing LLC......585 266-2770
20 Balfour Dr Rochester (14621) *(G-14599)*
Pressure Washer Sales, Holland Patent *Also called Custom Klean Corp (G-6487)*
Pressure Washing Services Inc......607 286-7458
26 Maple St Milford (13807) *(G-8474)*

ALPHABETIC

Prestel Publishing Inc ... 212 995-2720
900 Broadway Ste 603 New York (10003) *(G-11701)*

Presti Ready Mix Concrete Inc ... 516 378-6006
210 E Merrick Rd Freeport (11520) *(G-5419)*

Presti Stone and Mason, Freeport *Also called Presti Ready Mix Concrete Inc (G-5419)*

Prestige Box Corporation (PA) ... 516 773-3115
115 Cuttermill Rd Great Neck (11021) *(G-5833)*

Prestige Brands Holdings Inc (PA) ... 914 524-6800
660 White Plains Rd Tarrytown (10591) *(G-16101)*

Prestige Envelope & Lithograph ... 631 521-7043
1745 Merrick Ave Ste 2 Merrick (11566) *(G-8391)*

Prestige Hangers Str Fixs Corp ... 718 522-6777
1026 55th St Brooklyn (11219) *(G-2440)*

Prestige Litho & Graphics, Merrick *Also called Prestige Envelope & Lithograph (G-8391)*

Prestige Printing Company, Brooklyn *Also called 6727 11th Ave Corp (G-1521)*

Prestige Xs, New City *Also called Plus Its Cheap LLC (G-8789)*

Prestigeline Inc ... 631 273-3636
5 Inez Dr Bay Shore (11706) *(G-728)*

Prestolite Electric Inc ... 585 492-2278
400 Main St Arcade (14009) *(G-399)*

Preston Glass Industries Inc ... 718 997-8888
10420 Queens Blvd Apt 17a Forest Hills (11375) *(G-5328)*

Prestone Press LLC ... 347 468-7900
4750 30th St Long Island City (11101) *(G-7845)*

Prestone Printing Company, Long Island City *Also called Prestone Press LLC (G-7845)*

Pretlist ... 646 368-1849
545 W 110th St Apt 2b New York (10025) *(G-11702)*

Prevost Car US Inc ... 518 957-2052
260 Banker Rd Plattsburgh (12901) *(G-13689)*

Prg Integrated Solutions, Armonk *Also called Production Resource Group LLC (G-419)*

Price Chopper Operating Co ... 518 562-3565
19 Centre Dr Plattsburgh (12901) *(G-13690)*

Price Chopper Pharmacy, Catskill *Also called Golub Corporation (G-3428)*

Price Chopper Pharmacy, Oneida *Also called Golub Corporation (G-13155)*

Price Chopper Pharmacy, Norwich *Also called Golub Corporation (G-13028)*

Price Chopper Pharmacy, Hudson *Also called Golub Corporation (G-6615)*

Price Chopper Pharmacy, Middletown *Also called Golub Corporation (G-8443)*

Price Chopper Pharmacy 184, Malta *Also called Golub Corporation (G-8020)*

Price Chopper Pharmacy 234, Binghamton *Also called Golub Corporation (G-920)*

Pricet Printing ... 315 655-0369
3852 Charles Rd Cazenovia (13035) *(G-3451)*

Pricing Engine Inc ... 917 549-3289
175 Varick St Fl 4 New York (10014) *(G-11703)*

Pride & Joys Inc ... 212 594-9820
1400 Broadway Rm 503 New York (10018) *(G-11704)*

Pride Lines Ltd ... 631 225-0033
651 W Hoffman Ave Lindenhurst (11757) *(G-7479)*

Prim Hall Enterprises Inc ... 518 561-7408
11 Spellman Rd Plattsburgh (12901) *(G-13691)*

Prima Asphalt and Concrete ... 631 289-3223
615 Furrows Rd Holtsville (11742) *(G-6507)*

Primary Wave Publishing LLC ... 212 661-6990
116 E 16th St Fl 9 New York (10003) *(G-11705)*

Prime Components, Deer Park *Also called Prime Electronic Components (G-4192)*

Prime Electric Motors Inc ... 718 784-1124
4850 33rd St Long Island City (11101) *(G-7846)*

Prime Electronic Components ... 631 254-0101
150 W Industry Ct Deer Park (11729) *(G-4192)*

Prime Feather Industries Ltd ... 718 326-8701
7-11 Suffern Pl Suffern (10901) *(G-15798)*

Prime Food Processing Corp ... 718 963-2323
300 Vandervoort Ave Brooklyn (11211) *(G-2441)*

Prime Garments Inc ... 212 354-7294
1407 Broadway Rm 1200 New York (10018) *(G-11706)*

Prime Lite Mfg, Freeport *Also called Primelite Manufacturing Corp (G-5420)*

Prime Marketing and Sales LLC ... 888 802-3836
111 W Hmpstead Tpke Fl 3 New York (10001) *(G-11707)*

Prime Materials Recovery Inc ... 315 697-5251
51 Madison Blvd Canastota (13032) *(G-3371)*

Prime Pack LLC ... 732 253-7734
303 5th Ave Rm 1007 New York (10016) *(G-11708)*

Prime Pharmaceutical, New York *Also called Prime Pack LLC (G-11708)*

Prime Time, Garden City *Also called Richner Communications Inc (G-5529)*

Prime Tool & Die LLC ... 607 334-5435
6277 County Road 32 Norwich (13815) *(G-13036)*

Prime Wood Products ... 518 792-1407
1288 Vaughn Rd Queensbury (12804) *(G-14008)*

Primedia Special Interest Publ (HQ) ... 212 726-4300
260 Madison Ave Fl 8 New York (10016) *(G-11709)*

Primelite Manufacturing Corp ... 516 868-4411
407 S Main St Freeport (11520) *(G-5420)*

Primesouth Inc ... 585 567-4191
11537 Route 19 Fillmore (14735) *(G-5176)*

Primo Coat Corp ... 718 349-2070
4315 Queens St Fl 3 Long Island City (11101) *(G-7847)*

Primo Frozen Desserts Inc ... 718 252-2312
1633 Utica Ave Brooklyn (11234) *(G-2442)*

Primo Plastics Inc ... 718 349-1000
162 Russell St Brooklyn (11222) *(G-2443)*

Primoplast Inc ... 631 750-0680
1555 Ocean Ave Ste E Bohemia (11716) *(G-1121)*

Prince Foundry, New York *Also called Prince Minerals LLC (G-11711)*

Prince Mineral Holding Corp (PA) ... 646 747-4222
21 W 46th St Fl 14th New York (10036) *(G-11710)*

Prince Minerals, New York *Also called American Minerals Inc (G-9125)*

Prince Minerals LLC (HQ) ... 646 747-4222
21 W 46th St Fl 14 New York (10036) *(G-11711)*

Prince of The Sea Ltd ... 516 333-6344
28 Urban Ave Westbury (11590) *(G-17022)*

Prince Rubber & Plas Co Inc (PA) ... 225 272-1653
137 Arthur St Buffalo (14207) *(G-3136)*

Prince Seating Corp ... 718 363-2300
1355 Atlantic Ave Brooklyn (11216) *(G-2444)*

Princess Marcella Borghese, New York *Also called Borghese Inc (G-9441)*

Princess Music Publishing Co ... 212 586-0240
1650 Broadway Ste 701 New York (10019) *(G-11712)*

Princeton Label & Packaging ... 609 490-0800
217 River Ave Patchogue (11772) *(G-13433)*

Princeton Sciences ... 845 368-1214
386 Route 59 Ste 402 Airmont (10952) *(G-18)*

Princeton Upholstery Co Inc (PA) ... 845 343-2196
51 Railroad Ave Middletown (10940) *(G-8458)*

Principia Partners LLC ... 212 480-2270
140 Broadway Fl 46 New York (10005) *(G-11713)*

Princton Archtctural Press LLC ... 212 995-9620
37 E 7th St Ste 2 New York (10003) *(G-11714)*

Print & Graphics Group ... 518 371-4649
12 Fire Rd Clifton Park (12065) *(G-3704)*

Print Bear LLC (PA) ... 518 703-6098
411 Lafayette St Fl 6 New York (10003) *(G-11715)*

Print Better Inc ... 347 348-1841
5939 Myrtle Ave Ridgewood (11385) *(G-14119)*

Print By Premier LLC ... 212 947-1365
212 W 35th St Fl 2 New York (10001) *(G-11716)*

Print Center Inc ... 718 643-9559
3 Harbor Rd Ste 21 Cold Spring Harbor (11724) *(G-3770)*

Print City Corp ... 212 487-9778
165 W 29th St New York (10001) *(G-11717)*

Print Cottage LLC ... 516 369-1749
1138 Lakeshore Dr Massapequa Park (11762) *(G-8189)*

Print House Inc ... 718 443-7500
538 Johnson Ave Brooklyn (11237) *(G-2445)*

Print Mall ... 718 437-7700
4122 16th Ave Brooklyn (11204) *(G-2446)*

Print Management Group Corp ... 212 213-1555
33 E 33rd St Fl 3 New York (10016) *(G-11718)*

Print Market Inc ... 631 940-8181
66 E Jefryn Blvd Ste 1 Deer Park (11729) *(G-4193)*

Print Media Inc ... 212 563-4040
350 7th Ave Rm 401 New York (10001) *(G-11719)*

Print On Demand Initiative Inc ... 585 239-6044
1240 Jefferson Rd Rochester (14623) *(G-14600)*

Print Pack Inc (HQ) ... 404 460-7000
70 Schmitt Blvd Farmingdale (11735) *(G-5088)*

Print Shop ... 607 734-4937
3153 Lake Rd Horseheads (14845) *(G-6589)*

Print Shoppe ... 315 792-9585
311 Turner St Ste 310 Utica (13501) *(G-16356)*

Print Solutions Plus Inc ... 315 234-3801
7325 Oswego Rd Liverpool (13090) *(G-7545)*

Print-O-Rama Copy Center, Merrick *Also called Leader Printing Inc (G-8388)*

Printcorp Inc ... 631 696-0641
2050 Ocean Ave Ronkonkoma (11779) *(G-14971)*

Printech Business Systems Inc ... 212 290-2542
519 8th Ave Fl 3 New York (10018) *(G-11720)*

Printed Image ... 716 821-1880
1906 Clinton St Buffalo (14206) *(G-3137)*

Printer Components Inc (HQ) ... 585 924-5190
100 Photikon Dr Ste 2 Fairport (14450) *(G-4871)*

Printers 3, Hauppauge *Also called Avm Printing Inc (G-6030)*

Printers 3 Inc ... 631 351-1331
43 Corporate Dr Ste 2 Hauppauge (11788) *(G-6172)*

Printery ... 516 922-3250
43 W Main St Oyster Bay (11771) *(G-13373)*

Printery ... 315 253-7403
55 Arterial W Auburn (13021) *(G-514)*

Printex Packaging Corporation ... 631 234-4300
555 Raymond Dr Islandia (11749) *(G-6801)*

Printfacility Inc ... 212 349-4009
225 Broadway Fl 3 New York (10007) *(G-11721)*

Printhouse, The, Brooklyn *Also called Print House Inc (G-2445)*

Printing, Brooklyn *Also called Reliable Press II Inc (G-2489)*

Printing Emporium, Merrick *Also called D G M Graphics Inc (G-8383)*

Printing Express, Jamaica *Also called Hillside Printing Inc (G-6919)*

Printing Factory LLC ... 718 451-0500
1940 Utica Ave Brooklyn (11234) *(G-2447)*

Printing House of W S Miller, Oyster Bay *Also called Printery (G-13373)*

Printing Max New York Inc ... 718 692-1400
2282 Flatbush Ave Brooklyn (11234) *(G-2448)*

Printing Plus, Rochester *Also called Ozipko Enterprises Inc (G-14560)*

ALPHABETIC SECTION

Printing Prmtnal Solutions LLC 315 474-1110
2320 Milton Ave Ste 5 Syracuse (13209) *(G-16014)*
Printing Promotional Solutions, Syracuse Also called Printing Prmtnal Solutions LLC *(G-16014)*
Printing Resources Inc 518 482-2470
100 Fuller Rd Ste 1 Albany (12205) *(G-124)*
Printing Sales Group Limited 718 258-8860
1856 Flatbush Ave Brooklyn (11210) *(G-2449)*
Printing Spectrum Inc 631 689-1010
12 Research Way Ste 1 East Setauket (11733) *(G-4490)*
Printing X Press Ions 631 242-1992
5 Dix Cir Dix Hills (11746) *(G-4296)*
Printinghouse Press Ltd 212 719-0990
10 E 39th St Rm 700 New York (10016) *(G-11722)*
Printout Copy Corp 718 855-4040
829 Bedford Ave Brooklyn (11205) *(G-2450)*
Printroc Inc 585 461-2556
620 South Ave Rochester (14620) *(G-14601)*
Printutopia 718 788-1545
393 Prospect Ave Brooklyn (11215) *(G-2451)*
Printworks Printing & Design 315 433-8587
5982 E Molloy Rd Syracuse (13211) *(G-16015)*
Printz and Patternz LLC 518 944-6020
1550 Altamont Ave Ste 1 Schenectady (12303) *(G-15286)*
Printz Pttrnz Scrn-Prnting EMB, Schenectady Also called Printz and Patternz LLC *(G-15286)*
Priority Enterprise, New York Also called Priority Printing Entps Inc *(G-11723)*
Priority Printing Entps Inc 646 285-0684
315 W 36th St New York (10018) *(G-11723)*
Priscilla Quart Co Firts 516 365-2755
160 Plandome Rd Fl 2 Manhasset (11030) *(G-8064)*
Prism Solar Technologies Inc (PA) 845 883-4200
180 South St Highland (12528) *(G-6407)*
Prisma Glass & Mirror Inc 718 366-7191
1815 Decatur St Ridgewood (11385) *(G-14120)*
Prismatic Dyeing & Finshg Inc 845 561-1800
40 Wisner Ave Newburgh (12550) *(G-12775)*
Priva USA Inc 518 963-4074
39 Myers Way Willsboro (12996) *(G-17266)*
Private Lbel Fods Rchester Inc 585 254-9205
1686 Lyell Ave Rochester (14606) *(G-14602)*
Private Portfolio, New York Also called Coty US LLC *(G-9731)*
Prms Inc 631 851-7945
45 Ramsey Rd Unit 26 Shirley (11967) *(G-15429)*
Prms Electronic Components, Shirley Also called Prms Inc *(G-15429)*
Pro Drones Usa LLC 718 530-3558
115 E 57th St Fl 11 New York (10022) *(G-11724)*
Pro Hitter Corp 845 358-8670
170 S Main St New City (10956) *(G-8790)*
Pro Lettering LLC 607 484-0255
127 W Main St Endicott (13760) *(G-4826)*
Pro Metal of NY Corp 516 285-0440
814 W Merrick Rd Valley Stream (11580) *(G-16421)*
Pro Pack, Eagle Bridge Also called Professional Packg Svcs Inc *(G-4357)*
Pro Printers of Greene County, Catskill Also called Mark T Westinghouse *(G-3431)*
Pro Printing 516 561-9700
359 Merrick Rd Lynbrook (11563) *(G-7957)*
Pro Publica Inc 212 514-5250
155 Ave Of The Americas New York (10013) *(G-11725)*
Pro Torque 631 218-8700
1440 Church St Bohemia (11716) *(G-1122)*
Pro-Gear Co Inc 716 684-3811
1120 Niagara St Buffalo (14213) *(G-3138)*
Pro-Line Solutions Inc 914 664-0002
18 Sargent Pl Mount Vernon (10550) *(G-8719)*
Pro-Print, New York Also called Kolcorp Industries Ltd *(G-10871)*
Pro-TEC V I P, Gloversville Also called Protech (llc) *(G-5719)*
Pro-Tech Sno Pusher, Rochester Also called Pro-Tech Wldg Fabrication Inc *(G-14603)*
Pro-Tech Wldg Fabrication Inc 585 436-9855
711 West Ave Rochester (14611) *(G-14603)*
Pro-Teck Coating Inc 716 537-2619
7785 Olean Rd Holland (14080) *(G-6483)*
Pro-Tek Packaging Group, Ronkonkoma Also called Oaklee International Inc *(G-14958)*
Pro-Value Distribution Inc 585 783-1461
1547 Lyell Ave Ste 3 Rochester (14606) *(G-14604)*
Proactive Medical Products LLC 845 205-6004
270 Washington St Mount Vernon (10553) *(G-8720)*
Procab, Woodridge Also called Professional Cab Detailing Co *(G-17315)*
Procomponents Inc (PA) 516 683-0909
900 Merchants Concourse Westbury (11590) *(G-17023)*
Procter & Gamble Company 646 885-4201
120 W 45th St Fl 3 New York (10036) *(G-11726)*
Product Development Intl LLC 212 279-6170
215 W 40th St Fl 8 New York (10018) *(G-11727)*
Product Integration & Mfg Inc 585 436-6260
55 Fessenden St Rochester (14611) *(G-14605)*
Product Station Inc 516 942-4220
366 N Broadway Ste 410 Jericho (11753) *(G-7082)*
Productand Design Inc 718 858-2440
63 Flushing Ave Unit 322 Brooklyn (11205) *(G-2452)*
Production Metal Cutting Inc 585 458-7136
1 Curlew St Rochester (14606) *(G-14606)*
Production Milling Company 914 666-0792
364 Adams St Ste 5 Bedford Hills (10507) *(G-805)*
Production Resource Group LLC (PA) 212 589-5400
200 Business Park Dr # 109 Armonk (10504) *(G-419)*
Production Resource Group LLC 845 567-5700
539 Temple Hill Rd New Windsor (12553) *(G-8948)*
Producto Corporation 716 484-7131
2980 Turner Rd Jamestown (14701) *(G-7024)*
Producto Electric Corp 845 359-4900
11 Kings Hwy Orangeburg (10962) *(G-13243)*
Products Superb Inc 315 923-7057
231 Clyde Marengo Rd Clyde (14433) *(G-3731)*
Professional Access LLC 212 432-2844
88 Old Farm Rd N Chappaqua (10514) *(G-3554)*
Professional Buty Holdings Inc 631 787-8576
150 Motor Pkwy Ste 401 Hauppauge (11788) *(G-6173)*
Professional Cab Detailing Co 845 436-7282
Navograrsky Rd Woodridge (12789) *(G-17315)*
Professional Disposables Inc 845 365-1700
2 Nice Pak Park Orangeburg (10962) *(G-13244)*
Professional Health Imaging, Wantagh Also called R M F Health Management L L C *(G-16562)*
Professional Manufacturers 631 586-2440
475 Brook Ave Deer Park (11729) *(G-4194)*
Professional Medical Devices 914 835-0614
10 Century Trl Harrison (10528) *(G-5989)*
Professional Packg Svcs Inc 518 677-5100
62 Owlkill Rd Eagle Bridge (12057) *(G-4357)*
Professional Pavers Corp 718 784-7853
6605 Woodhaven Blvd Bsmt Rego Park (11374) *(G-14039)*
Professional Remodelers Inc 516 565-9300
340 Hempstead Ave Unit A West Hempstead (11552) *(G-16862)*
Professional Solutions Print 631 231-9300
125 Wireless Blvd Ste E Hauppauge (11788) *(G-6174)*
Professional Tape Corporation 516 656-5519
100 Pratt Oval Glen Cove (11542) *(G-5625)*
Professional Technologies, Rome Also called Professional Technology Inc *(G-14830)*
Professional Technology Inc 315 337-4156
5433 Lowell Rd Rome (13440) *(G-14830)*
Professnal Spt Pblications Inc (PA) 212 697-1460
519 8th Ave New York (10018) *(G-11728)*
Professnal Spt Pblications Inc 516 327-9500
570 Elmont Rd Elmont (11003) *(G-4726)*
Professnal Spt Pblications Inc 516 327-9500
570 Elmont Rd Ste 202 Elmont (11003) *(G-4727)*
Proficient Surgical Eqp Inc 516 487-1175
99 Seaview Blvd Ste 1c Port Washington (11050) *(G-13857)*
Profile, New York Also called Eternal Fortune Fashion LLC *(G-10077)*
Profile Printing & Graphics (PA) 631 273-2727
275 Marcus Blvd Hauppauge (11788) *(G-6175)*
Profoot Inc 718 965-8600
74 20th St Fl 2 Brooklyn (11232) *(G-2453)*
Progenics Pharmaceuticals Inc (PA) 646 975-2500
1 World Trade Ctr Fl 47 New York (10007) *(G-11729)*
Proginet Corporation 516 535-3600
200 Garden Cy Plz Ste 220 Garden City (11530) *(G-5527)*
Programatic Platers Inc 718 721-4330
4925 20th Ave East Elmhurst (11370) *(G-4396)*
Progress Industries Sales, Utica Also called Fourteen Arnold Ave Corp *(G-16333)*
Progressive Accounting, West Nyack Also called Electronic Business Tech *(G-16916)*
Progressive Color Graphics 212 292-8787
122 Station Rd Great Neck (11023) *(G-5834)*
Progressive Fibre Products Co 212 566-2720
160 Broadway Rm 1105 New York (10038) *(G-11730)*
Progressive Graphics & Prtg 315 331-3635
1171 E Union St Newark (14513) *(G-12741)*
Progressive Hardware Co Inc 631 445-1826
63 Brightside Ave East Northport (11731) *(G-4443)*
Progressive Mch & Design LLC (PA) 585 924-5250
727 Rowley Rd Victor (14564) *(G-16497)*
Progressive Orthotics Ltd (PA) 631 732-5556
280 Middle Country Rd G Selden (11784) *(G-15353)*
Progressive Orthotics Ltd 631 447-3860
285 Sills Rd Bldg 8c East Patchogue (11772) *(G-4449)*
Progressive Products LLC 914 417-6022
4 International Dr # 224 Rye Brook (10573) *(G-15074)*
Progressive Tool Company Inc 607 748-8294
3221 Lawndale St Endwell (13760) *(G-4838)*
Progressus Company Inc 516 255-0245
100 Merrick Rd Ste 510w Rockville Centre (11570) *(G-14796)*
Prohibition Distillery LLC 917 685-8989
10 Union St Roscoe (12776) *(G-15011)*
Project Energy Savers LLC 718 596-4231
68 Jay St Ste 516 Brooklyn (11201) *(G-2454)*
Project Visual, Islandia Also called Zahk Sales Inc *(G-6805)*
Projector Lamp Services LLC 631 244-0051
120 Wilbur Pl Ste C Bohemia (11716) *(G-1123)*
Prokosch and Sonn Sheet Metal 845 562-4211
772 South St Newburgh (12550) *(G-12776)*
Prolocksusa, Hauppauge Also called Olan Laboratories Inc *(G-6151)*
Promats Athletics LLC (PA) 607 746-8911
41155 State Highway 10 Delhi (13753) *(G-4241)*

Promed Products Inc 800 993-4010
500 Nepperhan Ave Yonkers (10701) *(G-17480)*
Prometheus Books Inc 716 691-2158
59 John Glenn Dr Amherst (14228) *(G-258)*
Prometheus International Inc 718 472-0700
4502 11th St Long Island City (11101) *(G-7848)*
Promolines, New York *Also called Maxworld Inc (G-11189)*
Promosuite, New York *Also called Broadcast Manager Inc (G-9465)*
Promotional Development Inc 718 485-8550
909 Remsen Ave Brooklyn (11236) *(G-2455)*
Promotional Sales Books LLC 212 675-0364
30 W 26th St Frnt New York (10010) *(G-11731)*
Prompt Bindery Co Inc 212 675-5181
350 W 38th St New York (10018) *(G-11732)*
Prompt Printing Inc 631 454-6524
160 Rome St Farmingdale (11735) *(G-5089)*
Promptus Electronic Hdwr Inc 914 699-4700
520 Homestead Ave Mount Vernon (10550) *(G-8721)*
Pronovias USA Inc 212 897-6393
14 E 52nd St New York (10022) *(G-11733)*
Pronto Jewelry Inc 212 719-9455
23 W 47th St New York (10036) *(G-11734)*
Pronto Printer 914 737-0800
2085 E Main St Ste 3 Cortlandt Manor (10567) *(G-4053)*
Pronto Tool & Die Co Inc 631 981-8920
50 Remington Blvd Ronkonkoma (11779) *(G-14972)*
Proof 7 Ltd 212 680-1843
121 Varick St Rm 301 New York (10013) *(G-11735)*
Proof Industries Inc 631 694-7663
125 Rome St Farmingdale (11735) *(G-5090)*
Proof Magazine, New York *Also called Rough Draft Publishing LLC (G-11920)*
Propak Inc 518 677-5100
70 Owlkill Rd Eagle Bridge (12057) *(G-4358)*
Proper Chemical Ltd 631 420-8000
280 Smith St Farmingdale (11735) *(G-5091)*
Proper Cloth LLC 646 964-4221
450 Broadway Ste 2 New York (10013) *(G-11736)*
Props Displays & Interiors 212 620-3840
132 W 18th St New York (10011) *(G-11737)*
Props For Today, Long Island City *Also called Interiors-Pft Inc (G-7767)*
Prospect News 212 374-2800
6 Maiden Ln Fl 9 New York (10038) *(G-11738)*
Prospector Network 212 601-2781
350 5th Ave Fl 59 New York (10118) *(G-11739)*
Prosthetic Rehabilitation Ctr (PA) 845 565-8255
2 Winding Ln Newburgh (12550) *(G-12777)*
Prosthetics By Nelson Inc (PA) 716 894-6666
2959 Genesee St Cheektowaga (14225) *(G-3587)*
Prosthodontic & Implant Den 212 319-6363
693 5th Ave New York (10022) *(G-11740)*
Protec Friction Supply, Mount Kisco *Also called Rpb Distributors LLC (G-8645)*
Protech (llc) 518 725-7785
11 Cayadutta St Gloversville (12078) *(G-5719)*
Protech Automation LLC 585 344-3201
1 Mill St Ste 205 Batavia (14020) *(G-646)*
Protective Industries Inc (HQ) 716 876-9951
2150 Elmwood Ave Buffalo (14207) *(G-3139)*
Protective Industries Inc 716 876-9855
2150 Elmwood Ave Buffalo (14207) *(G-3140)*
Protective Industries Inc 716 876-9951
2510 Elmwood Ave Buffalo (14217) *(G-3141)*
Protective Lining Corp 718 854-3838
601 39th St Brooklyn (11232) *(G-2456)*
Protective Power Systms & Cntr 845 773-9016
259 N Grand Ave Poughkeepsie (12603) *(G-13926)*
Protege, Brooklyn *Also called Schwartz Textile Converting Co (G-2537)*
Protex International Corp 631 563-4250
366 Central Ave Bohemia (11716) *(G-1124)*
Proto Machine Inc 631 392-1159
60 Corbin Ave Ste D Bay Shore (11706) *(G-729)*
Protofast Holding Corp 631 753-2549
182 N Oak St Copiague (11726) *(G-3920)*
Prototype Manufacturing Corp 716 695-1700
836 Wurlitzer Dr North Tonawanda (14120) *(G-12987)*
Provident Fuel Inc 516 224-4427
4 Stillwell Ln Woodbury (11797) *(G-17296)*
Provisionaire & Co LLC 315 491-8240
155 W 68th St Apt 611 New York (10023) *(G-11741)*
Prsa, New York *Also called Public Relations Soc Amer Inc (G-11746)*
Prweek/Prescribing Reference, New York *Also called Haymarket Media Inc (G-10430)*
Pry Care Products, Mount Vernon *Also called Pro-Line Solutions Inc (G-8719)*
Prz Technologies Inc 716 683-1300
5490 Broadway St Lancaster (14086) *(G-7334)*
PS Pibbs Inc (PA) 718 445-8046
13315 32nd Ave Flushing (11354) *(G-5284)*
Ps38 LLC 212 819-1123
545 8th Ave Rm 350 New York (10018) *(G-11742)*
Psb Ltd 585 654-7078
543 Atlantic Ave Ste 2 Rochester (14609) *(G-14607)*
Psg Innovations Inc 917 299-8986
924 Kilmer Ln Valley Stream (11581) *(G-16422)*
PSI Transit Mix Corp 631 382-7930
34 E Main St Smithtown (11787) *(G-15496)*
Psp Unlimited, Ithaca *Also called Gould J Perfect Screen Prtrs (G-6844)*
Pspi, Elmont *Also called Professnal Spt Pblications Inc (G-4727)*
PSR Press Ltd 716 754-2266
415 Ridge St Lewiston (14092) *(G-7435)*
Psychology Today, New York *Also called Sussex Publishers Inc (G-12247)*
Psychonomic Society Inc 512 381-1494
233 Spring St Fl 7 New York (10013) *(G-11743)*
Pti-Pacific Inc 212 414-8495
166 5th Ave Fl 4t New York (10010) *(G-11744)*
Pts Financial Technology LLC 844 825-7634
1001 Ave Of The Americas New York (10018) *(G-11745)*
Public Relations Soc Amer Inc (PA) 212 460-1400
33 Maiden Ln Fl 11 New York (10038) *(G-11746)*
Public School, New York *Also called Ps38 LLC (G-11742)*
Publimax Printing Corp 718 366-7133
6615 Traffic Ave Ridgewood (11385) *(G-14121)*
Publishers Clearing House LLC 516 249-4063
265 Spagnoli Rd Ste 1 Melville (11747) *(G-8350)*
Publishers Weekly, New York *Also called Pwxyz LLC (G-11761)*
Publishing Group America Inc 646 658-0550
60 E 42nd St Ste 1146 New York (10165) *(G-11747)*
Publishing Synthesis Ltd 212 219-0135
39 Crosby St Apt 2n New York (10013) *(G-11748)*
Puccio Design International 516 248-6426
54 Nassau Blvd Garden City (11530) *(G-5528)*
Puccio European Marble & Onyx, Garden City *Also called Puccio Design International (G-5528)*
Puccio Marble and Onyx, Garden City *Also called European Marble Works Co Inc (G-5504)*
Pugliese Vineyards Inc 631 734-4057
34515 Main Rd Rr 25 Cutchogue (11935) *(G-4073)*
Puglisi & Co 212 300-2285
800 3rd Ave Ste 902 New York (10022) *(G-11749)*
Puig Usa Inc (PA) 212 271-5940
40 E 34th St Fl 19 New York (10016) *(G-11750)*
Pullman Mfg Corporation 585 334-1350
77 Commerce Dr Rochester (14623) *(G-14608)*
Pulmuone Foods Usa Inc 845 365-3300
30 Rockland Park Ave Tappan (10983) *(G-16082)*
Pulsafeeder Inc (HQ) 585 292-8000
2883 Brighton Henrietta T Rochester (14623) *(G-14609)*
Pulsar Technology Systems Inc 718 361-9292
2720 42nd Rd Long Island City (11101) *(G-7849)*
Pulse Plastics Products Inc 718 328-5224
1156 E 165th St Bronx (10459) *(G-1436)*
Pumilia's Pizza Shell, Waterville *Also called F & R Enterprises Inc (G-16678)*
Pupa Tek Inc 631 664-7817
6 Queens St Huntington (11743) *(G-6675)*
Pupellos Organic Chips Inc 718 710-9154
509 Ockers Dr Oakdale (11769) *(G-13061)*
Pura Fruta LLC 415 279-5727
2323 Borden Ave Long Island City (11101) *(G-7850)*
Pure Acoustics Inc 718 788-4411
18 Fuller Pl Brooklyn (11215) *(G-2457)*
Pure Design, Corning *Also called Offi & Company (G-3977)*
Pure Ghee Inc (PA) 718 224-7399
5701 225th St Flushing (11364) *(G-5285)*
Pure Kemika LLC 718 745-2200
6228 136th St Apt 2 Flushing (11367) *(G-5286)*
Pure Planet Waters LLC 718 676-7900
4809 Avenue N Ste 185 Brooklyn (11234) *(G-2458)*
Pure Trade Us Inc 212 256-1600
347 5th Ave Rm 604 New York (10016) *(G-11751)*
Purebase Networks Inc 646 670-8964
37 Wall St Apt 9a New York (10005) *(G-11752)*
Purely Maple LLC 203 997-9309
902 Broadway Fl 6 New York (10010) *(G-11753)*
Pureology Research LLC 212 984-4360
565 5th Ave New York (10017) *(G-11754)*
Purespice LLC 617 549-8400
173 Shagbark Ln Hopewell Junction (12533) *(G-6558)*
Purest of America, Saint Albans *Also called Zzz Mattress Manufacturing (G-15085)*
Purine Pharma LLC 315 705-4030
5 County Route 42 Massena (13662) *(G-8199)*
Purity Ice Cream Co Inc (PA) 607 272-1545
700 Cascadilla St Ste A Ithaca (14850) *(G-6872)*
Purity Products Inc 516 767-1967
200 Terminal Dr Plainview (11803) *(G-13631)*
Purvi Enterprises Incorporated 347 808-9448
5556 44th St Maspeth (11378) *(G-8166)*
Putnam Cnty News Recorder LLC 845 265-2468
144 Main St Ste 1 Cold Spring (10516) *(G-3764)*
Putnam Press, Mahopac *Also called Gateway Newspapers Inc (G-7996)*
Putnam Rolling Ladder Co Inc (PA) 212 226-5147
32 Howard St New York (10013) *(G-11755)*
Putnam Rolling Ladder Co Inc 718 381-8219
444 Jefferson St Brooklyn (11237) *(G-2459)*
PVA, Cohoes *Also called Precision Valve & Automtn Inc (G-3755)*
Pvc Container Corporation 518 672-7721
370 Stevers Crossing Rd Philmont (12565) *(G-13541)*

ALPHABETIC

Pvh Corp (PA)....212 381-3500
200 Madison Ave Bsmt 1 New York (10016) ***(G-11756)***
Pvh Corp....845 561-0233
1073 State Route 94 New Windsor (12553) ***(G-8949)***
Pvh Corp....631 254-8200
1358 The Arches Cir Deer Park (11729) ***(G-4195)***
Pvh Corp....212 381-3800
200 Madison Ave Bsmt 1 New York (10016) ***(G-11757)***
Pvh Corp....212 502-6300
404 5th Ave Fl 4 New York (10018) ***(G-11758)***
Pvh Corp....212 719-2600
205 W 39th St Fl 4 New York (10018) ***(G-11759)***
Pvh Europe, New York *Also called Phillips-Van Heusen Europe* ***(G-11649)***
Pvi Solar Inc....212 280-2100
599 11th Ave Bby New York (10036) ***(G-11760)***
PVS Chemical Solutions, Buffalo *Also called PVS Technologies Inc* ***(G-3143)***
PVS Chemical Solutions Inc....716 825-5762
55 Lee St Buffalo (14210) ***(G-3142)***
PVS Technologies Inc....716 825-5762
55 Lee St Buffalo (14210) ***(G-3143)***
Pwxyz LLC....212 377-5500
71 W 23rd St Ste 1608 New York (10010) ***(G-11761)***
Pylantis New York LLC....310 429-5911
102 E Cortland St Groton (13073) ***(G-5901)***
Pyrotechnique By Grucci Inc (PA)....540 639-8800
20 Pinehurst Dr Bellport (11713) ***(G-840)***
Pyrotek Incorporated....607 756-3050
641 State Route 13 Cortland (13045) ***(G-4041)***
Pyrotek Incorporated....716 731-3221
2040 Cory Dr Sanborn (14132) ***(G-15126)***
Pyx Enterprise, Brooklyn *Also called Pyx Inc* ***(G-2460)***
Pyx Inc....718 469-4253
143 E 29th St Brooklyn (11226) ***(G-2460)***
Q Communications Inc....212 594-6520
247 W 35th St Rm 1200 New York (10001) ***(G-11762)***
Q Omni Inc....914 962-2726
1994 Commerce St Yorktown Heights (10598) ***(G-17517)***
Q Squared Design LLC....212 686-8860
41 Madison Ave Ste 1905 New York (10010) ***(G-11763)***
Q.E.d, Rochester *Also called QED Technologies Intl Inc* ***(G-14610)***
Qca, Rochester *Also called Quality Contract Assemblies* ***(G-14612)***
Qcr Express Corp....888 924-5888
2565 23rd St Apt 3d Astoria (11102) ***(G-453)***
QED Technologies Intl Inc....585 256-6540
1040 University Ave Rochester (14607) ***(G-14610)***
Qes Solutions Inc (PA)....585 254-8693
1547 Lyell Ave Rochester (14606) ***(G-14611)***
Qlc, Long Island City *Also called Quadlogic Controls Corporation* ***(G-7852)***
Qls Solutions Group Inc....716 852-2203
701 Seneca St Ste 600 Buffalo (14210) ***(G-3144)***
Qmc Technologies Inc....716 681-0810
4388 Broadway Depew (14043) ***(G-4271)***
Qmi, Mount Vernon *Also called Giagni Enterprises LLC* ***(G-8684)***
Qna Tech, Ridge *Also called Quality and Asrn Tech Corp* ***(G-14093)***
Qps Die Cutters Finishers Corp....718 966-1811
140 Alverson Ave Staten Island (10309) ***(G-15725)***
Qsf Inc....585 247-6200
140 Cherry Rd Gates (14624) ***(G-5562)***
Qsr Medical Communications, Westhampton Beach *Also called Shugar Publishing* ***(G-17060)***
Qssi, Walden *Also called Pacific Die Cast Inc* ***(G-16534)***
Qta Machining Inc....716 862-8108
876 Bailey Ave Buffalo (14206) ***(G-3145)***
Quad/Graphics Inc....212 672-1300
140 E 42nd St Bsmt 2 New York (10017) ***(G-11764)***
Quad/Graphics Inc....718 706-7600
4402 11th St Fl 1 Long Island City (11101) ***(G-7851)***
Quad/Graphics Inc....518 581-4000
56 Duplainville Rd Saratoga Springs (12866) ***(G-15168)***
Quad/Graphics Inc....212 206-5535
60 5th Ave Lowr Level New York (10011) ***(G-11765)***
Quad/Graphics Inc....212 741-1001
375 Hudson St New York (10014) ***(G-11766)***
Quadlogic Controls Corporation....212 930-9300
3300 Northern Blvd Fl 2 Long Island City (11101) ***(G-7852)***
Quadpharma LLC....877 463-7823
11342 Main St Clarence (14031) ***(G-3670)***
Quadra Flex Corp....607 758-7066
1955 State Route 13 Cortland (13045) ***(G-4042)***
Quadra Flex Quality Labels, Cortland *Also called Quadra Flex Corp* ***(G-4042)***
Quadrangle Quick Print, Melville *Also called Quadrangle Quickprints Ltd* ***(G-8351)***
Quadrangle Quickprints Ltd....631 694-4464
1 Huntington Quad Ll04 Melville (11747) ***(G-8351)***
Quaker Bonnet Inc....716 885-7208
54 Irving Pl Buffalo (14201) ***(G-3146)***
Quaker Boy Inc (PA)....716 662-3979
5455 Webster Rd Orchard Park (14127) ***(G-13292)***
Quaker Boy Turkey Calls, Orchard Park *Also called Quaker Boy Inc* ***(G-13292)***
Quaker Millwork & Lumber Inc....716 662-3388
77 S Davis St Orchard Park (14127) ***(G-13293)***

Qualicoat Inc....585 293-2650
14 Sanford Rd N Churchville (14428) ***(G-3640)***
Qualified Manufacturing Corp....631 249-4440
134 Toledo St Farmingdale (11735) ***(G-5092)***
Qualitrol Company LLC (HQ)....586 643-3717
1385 Fairport Rd Fairport (14450) ***(G-4872)***
Qualitrol Finance Corp....585 586-1515
1385 Fairport Rd Fairport (14450) ***(G-4873)***
Quality and Asrn Tech Corp....646 450-6762
18 Marginwood Dr Ridge (11961) ***(G-14093)***
Quality Bindery Service Inc....716 883-5185
501 Amherst St Buffalo (14207) ***(G-3147)***
Quality Candle Mfg Co Inc....631 842-8475
121 Cedar St Copiague (11726) ***(G-3921)***
Quality Castings Inc....732 409-3203
3100 47th Ave Ste 2120b Long Island City (11101) ***(G-7853)***
Quality Circle Products Inc....914 736-6600
2108 Albany Post Rd Montrose (10548) ***(G-8614)***
Quality Components Framing Sys....315 768-1167
44 Mohawk St Bldg 10 Whitesboro (13492) ***(G-17194)***
Quality Contract Assemblies....585 663-9030
100 Boxart St Ste 251 Rochester (14612) ***(G-14612)***
Quality Dairy Farms Inc....315 942-2611
13584 State Route 12 Boonville (13309) ***(G-1168)***
Quality Embedments Mfg Co, New York *Also called Endurart Inc* ***(G-10034)***
Quality Enclosures Inc (PA)....631 234-0115
101 Windsor Pl Unit H Central Islip (11722) ***(G-3508)***
Quality Fence, Merrick *Also called Quality Lineals Usa Inc* ***(G-8392)***
Quality Foam Inc....718 381-3644
137 Gardner Ave Brooklyn (11237) ***(G-2461)***
Quality Fuel 1 Corporation....631 392-4090
1235 Deer Park Ave North Babylon (11703) ***(G-12903)***
Quality Graphics Tri State....845 735-2523
171 Center St Pearl River (10965) ***(G-13465)***
Quality Graphics West Seneca....716 668-4528
2460 Union Rd Cheektowaga (14227) ***(G-3588)***
Quality Guides....716 326-3163
39 E Main St Westfield (14787) ***(G-17049)***
Quality HM Brands Holdings LLC (PA)....718 292-2024
125 Rose Feiss Blvd Bronx (10454) ***(G-1437)***
Quality Impressions Inc....646 613-0002
163 Varick St Fl 6 New York (10013) ***(G-11767)***
Quality Industrial Services....716 667-7703
75 Bank St Orchard Park (14127) ***(G-13294)***
Quality King Distributors Inc....631 439-2027
201 Comac St Ronkonkoma (11779) ***(G-14973)***
Quality Life Inc....718 939-5787
2047 129th St College Point (11356) ***(G-3803)***
Quality Lineals Usa Inc....516 378-6577
105 Bennington Ave Ste 1 Freeport (11520) ***(G-5421)***
Quality Lineals Usa Inc (PA)....516 378-6577
1 Kees Pl Merrick (11566) ***(G-8392)***
Quality Machining Service Inc....315 736-5774
70 Sauquoit St New York Mills (13417) ***(G-12727)***
Quality Manufacturing Sys LLC....716 763-0988
1995 Stoneman Cir Lakewood (14750) ***(G-7292)***
Quality Metal Stamping LLC (PA)....516 255-9000
100 Merrick Rd Ste 310w Rockville Centre (11570) ***(G-14797)***
Quality Millwork Corp....718 892-2250
425 Devoe Ave Bronx (10460) ***(G-1438)***
Quality Nature Inc....718 484-4666
8225 5th Ave Ste 215 Brooklyn (11209) ***(G-2462)***
Quality Offset LLC....347 342-4660
4750 30th St Long Island City (11101) ***(G-7854)***
Quality One Wireless LLC....631 233-3337
2127 Lakeland Ave Unit 2 Ronkonkoma (11779) ***(G-14974)***
Quality Pattern Corp....212 704-0355
246 W 38th St Fl 9 New York (10018) ***(G-11768)***
Quality Plus, Rochester *Also called Rapid Precision Machining Inc* ***(G-14620)***
Quality Quick Signs, Depew *Also called Flado Enterprises Inc* ***(G-4258)***
Quality Ready Mix Inc....516 437-0100
1824 Gilford Ave New Hyde Park (11040) ***(G-8857)***
Quality Saw & Knife Inc....631 491-4747
115 Otis St West Babylon (11704) ***(G-16819)***
Quality Stainless Fabrication, Gates *Also called Qsf Inc* ***(G-5562)***
Quality Stair Builders Inc....631 694-0711
95 Schmitt Blvd Farmingdale (11735) ***(G-5093)***
Quality Strapping Inc....718 418-1111
55 Meadow St Brooklyn (11206) ***(G-2463)***
Quality Vision International, Rochester *Also called Quality Vision Services Inc* ***(G-14614)***
Quality Vision Intl Inc (PA)....585 544-0400
850 Hudson Ave Rochester (14621) ***(G-14613)***
Quality Vision Services Inc....585 544-0450
1175 North St Rochester (14621) ***(G-14614)***
Quality Woodworking Corp....718 875-3437
260 Butler St Brooklyn (11217) ***(G-2464)***
Qualtech NP, Lake Katrine *Also called Curtiss-Wright Flow Control* ***(G-7270)***
Qualtech Tool & Machine Inc....585 223-9227
1000 Turk Hill Rd Ste 292 Fairport (14450) ***(G-4874)***
Qualtronic Devices Inc....631 360-0859
130 Oakside Dr Smithtown (11787) ***(G-15497)***

ALPHABETIC

Quanta Electronics Inc 631 961-9953
48 Fran Ln Centereach (11720) *(G-3472)*
Quantum Asset Recovery 716 393-2712
482 Niagara Falls Blvd Buffalo (14223) *(G-3148)*
Quantum Color Inc 716 283-8700
8742 Buffalo Ave Niagara Falls (14304) *(G-12865)*
Quantum Knowledge LLC 631 727-6111
356 Reeves Ave Riverhead (11901) *(G-14153)*
Quantum Logic Corp 516 746-1380
91 5th Ave New Hyde Park (11040) *(G-8858)*
Quantum Medical Imaging LLC 631 567-5800
2002 Orville Dr N Ronkonkoma (11779) *(G-14975)*
Quantum Performance Company 518 642-3111
31 County Route 28 Granville (12832) *(G-5780)*
Quantum Sails Rochester LLC 585 342-5200
1461 Hudson Ave Rochester (14621) *(G-14615)*
Quartet Financial Systems Inc (PA) 845 358-6071
1412 Broadway Rm 2300 New York (10018) *(G-11769)*
Quarto Group Inc (HQ) 212 779-0700
276 5th Ave Rm 205 New York (10001) *(G-11770)*
Quattro Frameworks Inc 718 361-2620
4310 23rd St Ste 307 Long Island City (11101) *(G-7855)*
Qub9 Inc 585 484-1808
181 Saint Paul St Apt 3a Rochester (14604) *(G-14616)*
Qubicaamf Worldwide LLC 315 376-6541
7412 Utica Blvd Lowville (13367) *(G-7941)*
Quebracho Inc 718 326-3605
421 Troutman St Brooklyn (11237) *(G-2465)*
Queen Ann Macaroni Mfg Co Inc 718 256-1061
7205 18th Ave Brooklyn (11204) *(G-2466)*
Queen Ann Ravioli, Brooklyn *Also called Queen Ann Macaroni Mfg Co Inc (G-2466)*
Queen City Manufacturing Inc 716 877-1102
333 Henderson Ave Buffalo (14217) *(G-3149)*
Queenaire Technologies Inc 315 393-5454
9483 State Highway 37 Ogdensburg (13669) *(G-13120)*
Queens Central News, Camden *Also called Camden News Inc (G-3312)*
Queens Chronicle, Rego Park *Also called Mark I Publications Inc (G-14035)*
Queens Ready Mix Inc 718 526-4919
14901 95th Ave Jamaica (11435) *(G-6942)*
Queens Times, Corona *Also called CT Publications Co (G-3996)*
Queens Tribune, Whitestone *Also called Tribco LLC (G-17216)*
Quemere International 914 934-8366
330 N Main St Port Chester (10573) *(G-13758)*
Quench It Inc 845 462-5400
2290 South Rd Poughkeepsie (12601) *(G-13927)*
Quest Bead & Cast Inc 212 354-1737
49 W 37th St Fl 16 New York (10018) *(G-11771)*
Quest Beads, New York *Also called Quest Bead & Cast Inc (G-11771)*
Quest Magazine, New York *Also called Quest Media Llc (G-11772)*
Quest Manufacturing Inc 716 312-8000
5600 Camp Rd Hamburg (14075) *(G-5938)*
Quest Media Llc 646 840-3404
920 3rd Ave Fl 6 New York (10022) *(G-11772)*
Queue Solutions LLC 631 750-6440
250 Knickerbocker Ave Bohemia (11716) *(G-1125)*
Quick Cut Gasket & Rubber 716 684-8628
192 Erie St Lancaster (14086) *(G-7335)*
Quick Frzen Foods Annual Prcss, New York *Also called Frozen Food Digest Inc (G-10213)*
Quick Guide, New York *Also called Guest Informat LLC (G-10380)*
Quick Roll Leaf Mfg Co Inc (PA) 845 457-1500
118 Bracken Rd Montgomery (12549) *(G-8601)*
Quick Sign F X 516 249-6531
6 Powell St Farmingdale (11735) *(G-5094)*
Quick Turn Around Machining, Buffalo *Also called Qta Machining Inc (G-3145)*
Quicker Printer Inc 607 734-8622
210 W Gray St Elmira (14901) *(G-4698)*
Quickprint 585 394-2600
330 S Main St Canandaigua (14424) *(G-3356)*
Quikrete Companies Inc 716 213-2027
11 N Steelawanna Ave Lackawanna (14218) *(G-7247)*
Quikrete Companies Inc 315 673-2020
4993 Limeledge Rd Ste 560 Marcellus (13108) *(G-8088)*
Quikrete-Buffalo, Lackawanna *Also called Quikrete Companies Inc (G-7247)*
Quilted Koala Ltd 800 223-5678
1384 Broadway Rm 1501 New York (10018) *(G-11773)*
Quinn and Co of NY Ltd 212 868-1900
520 8th Ave Rm 2101 New York (10018) *(G-11774)*
Quintel Usa Inc 585 420-8364
1200 Ridgeway Ave Ste 132 Rochester (14615) *(G-14617)*
Quip Nyc Inc 703 615-1076
45 Main St Ste 628 Brooklyn (11201) *(G-2467)*
Quist Industries Ltd 718 243-2800
204 Van Dyke St Ste 320a Brooklyn (11231) *(G-2468)*
Quo Vadis Editions Inc 716 648-2602
120 Elmview Ave Hamburg (14075) *(G-5939)*
Quogue Capital LLC 212 554-4475
1285 Ave Of The Ave Fl 35 New York (10019) *(G-11775)*
Quoin LLC 914 967-9400
555 Theodore Fremd Ave B302 Rye (10580) *(G-15066)*
Quoizel Inc 631 436-4402
590 Old Willets Path # 1 Hauppauge (11788) *(G-6176)*
Quorum Group LLC 585 798-8888
11601 Maple Ridge Rd Medina (14103) *(G-8279)*
Quotable Cards Inc 212 420-7552
611 Broadway Rm 810 New York (10012) *(G-11776)*
Quovo Inc 646 216-9437
251 W 30th St Ste 16e New York (10001) *(G-11777)*
Qworldstar Inc 212 768-4500
200 Park Ave S Fl 8 New York (10003) *(G-11778)*
R & A Industrial Products 716 823-4300
30 Cornelia St Buffalo (14210) *(G-3150)*
R & B Machinery Corp 716 894-3332
400 Kennedy Rd Ste 3 Buffalo (14227) *(G-3151)*
R & F Boards & Dividers Inc 718 331-1529
1678 57th St Brooklyn (11204) *(G-2469)*
R & F Handmade Paints Inc 845 331-3112
84 Ten Broeck Ave Kingston (12401) *(G-7207)*
R & F Marketing, Bronx *Also called Place Vendome Holding Co Inc (G-1428)*
R & H Baking Co Inc 718 852-1768
19 5th St Brooklyn (11231) *(G-2470)*
R & J Displays Inc 631 491-3500
96 Otis St West Babylon (11704) *(G-16820)*
R & J Graphics Inc 631 293-6611
45 Central Ave Farmingdale (11735) *(G-5095)*
R & J Sheet Metal Distrs Inc 518 433-1525
119 Sheridan Ave Albany (12210) *(G-125)*
R & L Press Inc 718 447-8557
896 Forest Ave Staten Island (10310) *(G-15726)*
R & M Graphics of New York 212 929-0294
121 Varick St Fl 9 New York (10013) *(G-11779)*
R & M Industries Inc 212 366-6414
111 Broadway Rm 1112 New York (10006) *(G-11780)*
R & M Richards Inc (PA) 212 921-8820
1400 Broadway Fl 9 New York (10018) *(G-11781)*
R & M Thermofoil Doors Inc 718 206-4991
14830 94th Ave Jamaica (11435) *(G-6943)*
R & R Grosbard Inc 212 575-0077
1156 Avenue Of The Americ New York (10036) *(G-11782)*
R & S Machine Center Inc 518 563-4016
44 Academy St West Chazy (12992) *(G-16842)*
R and J Sheet Metal, Albany *Also called R & J Sheet Metal Distrs Inc (G-125)*
R Bruce Mapes 518 761-2020
15 E Washington St Glens Falls (12801) *(G-5698)*
R C Henderson Stair Builders 516 876-9898
100 Summa Ave Westbury (11590) *(G-17024)*
R C Kolstad Water Corp 585 216-2230
73 Lake Rd Ontario (14519) *(G-13210)*
R D A Container Corporation 585 247-2323
70 Cherry Rd Gates (14624) *(G-5563)*
R D Drive and Shop, Little Falls *Also called R D S Mountain View Trucking (G-7503)*
R D Manufacturing Corp 914 238-1000
Readers Digest Rd Pleasantville (10570) *(G-13716)*
R D Printing Associates Inc 631 390-5964
1865 New Hwy Ste 1 Farmingdale (11735) *(G-5096)*
R D S Mountain View Trucking 315 823-4265
1600 State Route 5s Little Falls (13365) *(G-7503)*
R D Specialties Inc 585 265-0220
560 Salt Rd Webster (14580) *(G-16731)*
R E F Precision Products 631 242-4471
517 Acorn St Ste A Deer Park (11729) *(G-4196)*
R E Rich Family Holding Corp 716 878-8000
1 Robert Rich Way Buffalo (14213) *(G-3152)*
R F Giardina Co 516 922-1364
200 Lexington Ave Apt 3a Oyster Bay (11771) *(G-13374)*
R G Flair Co Inc 631 586-7311
199 S Fehr Way Bay Shore (11706) *(G-730)*
R G Glass, New York *Also called RG Glass Creations Inc (G-11857)*
R G King General Construction 315 583-3560
13018 County Route 155 Adams Center (13606) *(G-4)*
R Goldsmith 718 239-1396
1974 Mayflower Ave Bronx (10461) *(G-1439)*
R H Crown Co Inc 518 762-4589
100 N Market St Johnstown (12095) *(G-7123)*
R H Guest Incorporated 718 675-7600
1300 Church Ave Brooklyn (11226) *(G-2471)*
R Hochman Papers Incorporated 516 466-6414
1000 Dean St Ste 315 Brooklyn (11238) *(G-2472)*
R I C, Ontario *Also called Rochester Industrial Ctrl Inc (G-13213)*
R I R Communications Systems (PA) 718 706-9957
20 Nuvern Ave Mount Vernon (10550) *(G-8722)*
R I R Communications Systems 718 706-9957
20 Nuvern Ave Mount Vernon (10550) *(G-8723)*
R J Liebe Athletic Company 585 237-6111
200 Main St N Perry (14530) *(G-13525)*
R J Reynolds Tobacco Company 716 871-1553
275 Cooper Ave Ste 116 Tonawanda (14150) *(G-16196)*
R J S Direct Marketing Inc 631 667-5768
561 Acorn St Ste E Deer Park (11729) *(G-4197)*
R J Valente Gravel Inc 518 279-1001
3349 Rte 2 Cropseyville (12052) *(G-4060)*
R K B Opto-Electronics Inc (PA) 315 455-6636
6677 Moore Rd Syracuse (13211) *(G-16016)*
R Klein Jewelry Co Inc 516 482-3260
39 Brockmeyer Dr Massapequa (11758) *(G-8181)*

ALPHABETIC

R L C Electronics Inc.....914 241-1334
83 Radio Circle Dr Mount Kisco (10549) ***(G-8641)***
R M F Health Management L L C.....718 854-5400
3361 Park Ave Wantagh (11793) ***(G-16562)***
R M Reynolds (PA).....315 789-7365
504 Exchange St Geneva (14456) ***(G-5584)***
R M S Motor Corporation.....607 723-2323
41 Travis Dr Binghamton (13904) ***(G-944)***
R P Fedder Corp (PA).....585 288-1600
740 Driving Park Ave B Rochester (14613) ***(G-14618)***
R P M, Bay Shore *Also called Rinaldi Precision Machine* ***(G-734)***
R P M Industries Inc.....315 255-1105
26 Aurelius Ave Auburn (13021) ***(G-515)***
R P M Machine Co.....585 671-3744
755 Gravel Rd Webster (14580) ***(G-16732)***
R P O, West Henrietta *Also called Rochester Precision Optics LLC* ***(G-16893)***
R S T Cable and Tape Inc.....631 981-0096
2130 Pond Rd Ste B Ronkonkoma (11779) ***(G-14976)***
R Schleider Contracting Corp.....631 269-4249
135 Old Northport Rd Kings Park (11754) ***(G-7174)***
R Spoor Finishing Corp.....607 748-5905
3006 Wayne St Endicott (13760) ***(G-4827)***
R Steiner Technologies Inc.....585 425-5912
180 Perinton Pkwy Fairport (14450) ***(G-4875)***
R T C A, Elmsford *Also called Radon Testing Corp of America* ***(G-4774)***
R T F Manufacturing, Hudson *Also called Atmost Refrigeration Co Inc* ***(G-6608)***
R V Dow Enterprises Inc.....585 454-5862
466 Central Ave Rochester (14605) ***(G-14619)***
R V H Estates Inc.....914 664-9888
138 Mount Vernon Ave Mount Vernon (10550) ***(G-8724)***
R W Publications Div of Wtrhs (PA).....716 714-5620
6091 Seneca St Bldg C Elma (14059) ***(G-4653)***
R W Publications Div of Wtrhs.....716 714-5620
6091 Seneca St Bldg C Elma (14059) ***(G-4654)***
R&A Prods, Buffalo *Also called R & A Industrial Products* ***(G-3150)***
R&S Machine, West Chazy *Also called R & S Machine Center Inc* ***(G-16842)***
R&S Steel LLC.....315 281-0123
412 Canal St Rome (13440) ***(G-14831)***
R-Co Products Corporation.....800 854-7657
1855 Big Tree Rd Lakewood (14750) ***(G-7293)***
R-Pac International Corp (PA).....212 465-1818
132 W 36th St Fl 7 New York (10018) ***(G-11783)***
R-S Restaurant Eqp Mfg Corp (PA).....212 925-0335
272 Bowery New York (10012) ***(G-11784)***
R-Tronics, Rome *Also called J Davis Manufacturing Co Inc* ***(G-14816)***
RA Newhouse Inc (PA).....516 248-6670
110 Liberty Ave Mineola (11501) ***(G-8532)***
Racing Industries Inc.....631 905-0100
901 Scott Ave Calverton (11933) ***(G-3296)***
Radar Sports LLC.....516 678-1919
2660 Washington Ave Oceanside (11572) ***(G-13091)***
Radarsport.com, Oceanside *Also called Radar Sports LLC* ***(G-13091)***
Radax Industries Inc.....585 265-2055
700 Basket Rd Ste A Webster (14580) ***(G-16733)***
Radiant Pro Ltd.....516 763-5678
245 Merrick Rd Oceanside (11572) ***(G-13092)***
Radiation Shielding Systems.....888 631-2278
415 Spook Rock Rd Suffern (10901) ***(G-15799)***
Radio Circle Realty Inc.....914 241-8742
136 Radio Circle Dr Mount Kisco (10549) ***(G-8642)***
Radiology Film Reading Svcs, Long Island City *Also called P C Rfrs Radiology* ***(G-7830)***
Radnor-Wallace (PA).....516 767-2131
921 Port Washington Blvd # 1 Port Washington (11050) ***(G-13858)***
Radon Testing Corp of America (PA).....914 345-3380
2 Hayes St Elmsford (10523) ***(G-4774)***
Raff Enterprises.....518 218-7883
12 Petra Ln Ste 6 Albany (12205) ***(G-126)***
Raffettos Corp.....212 777-1261
144 W Houston St New York (10012) ***(G-11785)***
Rag & Bone Industries LLC.....212 249-3331
416 W 13th St New York (10014) ***(G-11786)***
Rag & Bone Industries LLC (PA).....212 278-8214
425 W 13th St Ofc 2 New York (10014) ***(G-11787)***
Rago Foundations LLC.....718 728-8436
1815 27th Ave Astoria (11102) ***(G-454)***
Rago Shapewear, Astoria *Also called Rago Foundations LLC* ***(G-454)***
Ragozin Data.....212 674-3123
4402 11th St Ste 617 Long Island City (11101) ***(G-7856)***
Rags Knitwear Ltd.....718 782-8417
850 Metropolitan Ave Brooklyn (11211) ***(G-2473)***
Railex Corp.....518 347-6040
105 Rotterdam Indus Park Schenectady (12306) ***(G-15287)***
Railings By New Star Brass.....516 358-1153
26 Cobeck Ct Brooklyn (11223) ***(G-2474)***
Railtech Composites Inc.....518 324-6190
80 Montana Dr Plattsburgh (12903) ***(G-13692)***
Railworks Transit Systems Inc (HQ).....212 502-7900
5 Penn Plz New York (10001) ***(G-11788)***
Rain Catchers Seamless Gutters.....516 520-1956
39 Park Ln Bethpage (11714) ***(G-878)***
Rainbeau Ridge Farm.....914 234-2197
49 Davids Way Bedford Hills (10507) ***(G-806)***
Rainbow Custom Counter Tops, Staten Island *Also called Joseph Fedele* ***(G-15694)***
Rainbow Leather Inc.....718 939-8762
1415 112th St College Point (11356) ***(G-3804)***
Rainbow Lettering.....607 732-5751
1329 College Ave Elmira (14901) ***(G-4699)***
Rainbow Plastics Inc.....718 218-7288
371 Vandervoort Ave Brooklyn (11211) ***(G-2475)***
Rainbow Poly Bag Co Inc.....718 386-3500
179 Morgan Ave Brooklyn (11237) ***(G-2476)***
Rainbow Powder Coating Corp.....631 586-4019
86 E Industry Ct Deer Park (11729) ***(G-4198)***
Rainforest Apothecary, Long Island City *Also called Anima Mundi Herbals LLC* ***(G-7660)***
Rainforest Apparel LLC.....212 840-0880
1385 Broadway Fl 24 New York (10018) ***(G-11789)***
Rainforest Inc.....212 575-7620
420 5th Ave Fl 27 New York (10018) ***(G-11790)***
Raith America Inc.....518 874-3000
300 Jordan Rd Troy (12180) ***(G-16250)***
Rajbhog Foods Inc.....718 358-5105
4123 Murray St Flushing (11355) ***(G-5287)***
RAK Finishing Corp.....718 416-4242
15934 83rd St Howard Beach (11414) ***(G-6598)***
Raleigh and Drake Pbc.....212 625-8212
110 E 25th St Fl 3 New York (10010) ***(G-11791)***
Raloid Tool Co Inc.....518 664-4261
Hc 146 Mechanicville (12118) ***(G-8230)***
Ralph Lauren Corporation (PA).....212 318-7000
650 Madison Ave Fl C1 New York (10022) ***(G-11792)***
Ralph Lauren Corporation.....212 421-1570
979 3rd Ave Ste 404 New York (10022) ***(G-11793)***
Ralph Lauren Corporation.....917 934-4200
205 W 39th St Fl 13 New York (10018) ***(G-11794)***
Ralph Lauren Corporation.....212 221-7751
25 W 39th St Fl 8 New York (10018) ***(G-11795)***
Ralph Martinelli.....914 345-3055
100 Clearbrook Rd Ste 170 Elmsford (10523) ***(G-4775)***
Ralph Payne.....718 222-4200
475 Van Buren St Ste 11c Brooklyn (11221) ***(G-2477)***
Ralph's Ices, Staten Island *Also called JMS Ices Inc* ***(G-15692)***
Ram Fabricating LLC.....315 437-6654
412 Wavel St Syracuse (13206) ***(G-16017)***
Ram Precision Tool Inc.....716 759-8722
139 Gunnville Rd Lancaster (14086) ***(G-7336)***
Ram Transformer Technologies.....914 632-3988
11 Beechwood Ave New Rochelle (10801) ***(G-8922)***
Rambachs International Bakery.....518 563-1721
65 S Peru St Plattsburgh (12901) ***(G-13693)***
Ramco Arts, Sodus *Also called Nykon Inc* ***(G-15504)***
Ramholtz Publishing Inc.....718 761-4800
1200 South Ave Ste 202 Staten Island (10314) ***(G-15727)***
Rami Sheet Metal Inc.....845 426-2948
25 E Hickory St Spring Valley (10977) ***(G-15600)***
Ramick Welding, Farmingdale *Also called W R P Welding Ltd* ***(G-5139)***
Ramler International Ltd.....516 353-3106
485 Underhill Blvd # 100 Syosset (11791) ***(G-15836)***
Ramsbury Property Us Inc (HQ).....212 223-6250
601 5th Ave Fl 4 New York (10017) ***(G-11796)***
Ramsey Charles Company.....845 338-1464
401 Sawkill Rd Kingston (12401) ***(G-7208)***
Ramsey Electronics, Victor *Also called Avcom of Virginia Inc* ***(G-16461)***
Ramsey Electronics LLC.....585 924-4560
590 Fishers Station Dr Victor (14564) ***(G-16498)***
Ramy Brook LLC.....212 744-2789
231 W 39th St Rm 720 New York (10018) ***(G-11797)***
Ran Mar Enterprises Ltd.....631 666-4754
143 Anchor Ln Bay Shore (11706) ***(G-731)***
Rand & Paseka Mfg Co Inc.....516 867-1500
10 Hanse Ave Freeport (11520) ***(G-5422)***
Rand Luxury Inc.....212 655-4505
276 5th Ave Rm 906 New York (10001) ***(G-11798)***
Rand Machine Products Inc (PA).....716 665-5217
2072 Allen Street Ext Falconer (14733) ***(G-4908)***
Rand Machine Products Inc.....716 985-4681
5035 Route 60 Sinclairville (14782) ***(G-15454)***
Rand Mfg, Schenectady *Also called Rand Products Manufacturing Co* ***(G-15288)***
Rand Products Manufacturing Co.....518 374-9871
1602 Van Vranken Ave Schenectady (12308) ***(G-15288)***
Randa Accessories Lea Gds LLC.....212 354-5100
417 5th Ave Fl 11 New York (10016) ***(G-11799)***
Randall Loeffler Inc.....212 226-8787
588 Broadway Rm 1203 New York (10012) ***(G-11800)***
Randgold Resources Ltd.....212 815-2129
101 Barclay St New York (10007) ***(G-11801)***
Randob Labs Ltd.....845 534-2197
45 Quaker Ave Ste 207 Cornwall (12518) ***(G-3991)***
Randolph Dimension Corporation.....716 358-6901
216 Main St Ste 216 Randolph (14772) ***(G-14017)***
Randy Sixberry.....315 265-6211
6 Main St Ste 101 Potsdam (13676) ***(G-13883)***
Range Repair Warehouse.....585 235-0980
421 Penbrooke Dr Ste 2 Penfield (14526) ***(G-13502)***

ALPHABETIC

Range Rsurces - Appalachia LLC 716 753-3385
100 E Chautauqua St Mayville (14757) ***(G-8218)***
Ranger Design Us Inc 800 565-5321
6377 Dean Pkwy Ontario (14519) ***(G-13211)***
Ranney Precision 716 731-6418
6421 Wendt Dr Niagara Falls (14304) ***(G-12866)***
Ranney Precision Machining, Niagara Falls *Also called Ranney Precision* ***(G-12866)***
Rap Genius, Brooklyn *Also called Genius Media Group Inc* ***(G-2020)***
Rapa Independent North America 518 561-0513
124 Connecticut Rd Plattsburgh (12903) ***(G-13694)***
Rapacki & Sons (PA) 516 538-3939
633 N Queens Ave Lindenhurst (11757) ***(G-7480)***
Rapacki & Sons Kielbasa, Lindenhurst *Also called Rapacki & Sons* ***(G-7480)***
Rapha Pharmaceuticals Inc 956 229-0049
616 Corporate Way Valley Cottage (10989) ***(G-16385)***
Raphael, Peconic *Also called J Petrocelli Wine Cellars LLC* ***(G-13471)***
Rapid Fan & Blower Inc 718 786-2060
2314 39th Ave Long Island City (11101) ***(G-7857)***
Rapid Intellect Group Inc 518 929-3210
77b Church St Chatham (12037) ***(G-3559)***
Rapid Precision Machining Inc 585 467-0780
50 Lafayette Rd Rochester (14609) ***(G-14620)***
Rapid Print and Marketing Inc 585 924-1520
8 High St Victor (14564) ***(G-16499)***
Rapid Rays Printing & Copying 716 852-0550
300 Broadway St Buffalo (14204) ***(G-3153)***
Rapid Removal LLC 716 665-4663
1599 Route 394 Falconer (14733) ***(G-4909)***
Rapid Reproductions LLC 607 843-2221
4511 State Hwy 12 Oxford (13830) ***(G-13364)***
Rapid Service Engraving Co 716 896-4555
1593 Genesee St Buffalo (14211) ***(G-3154)***
Rapid-Lite Fixture Corporation 347 599-2600
249 Huron St Brooklyn (11222) ***(G-2478)***
Rapistak Corporation 716 822-2804
2025 Electric Ave Blasdell (14219) ***(G-964)***
Rapp Signs Inc 607 656-8167
3979 State Route 206 Greene (13778) ***(G-5867)***
Rare Editions, New York *Also called Star Childrens Dress Co Inc* ***(G-12184)***
Rasa Services Inc 516 294-4292
3366 Hillside Ave Ste 10 New Hyde Park (11040) ***(G-8859)***
Rasco Graphics Inc 212 206-0447
519 8th Ave Fl 18 New York (10018) ***(G-11802)***
Rasjada Enterprises Ltd 631 242-1055
1337 Richland Blvd Bay Shore (11706) ***(G-732)***
Rason Asphalt Inc (PA) 631 293-6210
Rr 110 Farmingdale (11735) ***(G-5097)***
Rason Asphalt Inc 516 671-1500
44 Morris Ave Glen Cove (11542) ***(G-5626)***
Rason Asphalt Inc 516 239-7880
4 Johnson Rd Lawrence (11559) ***(G-7398)***
Rasp Incorporated 518 747-8020
8 Dukes Way Gansevoort (12831) ***(G-5488)***
Ratan Ronkonkoma 631 588-6800
3055 Veterans Mem Hwy Ronkonkoma (11779) ***(G-14977)***
Rational Enterprises, Albany *Also called Rational Retention LLC* ***(G-127)***
Rational Retention LLC (PA) 518 489-3000
2 Tower Pl Ste 13 Albany (12203) ***(G-127)***
Rauch Industries Inc 704 867-5333
828 S Broadway Tarrytown (10591) ***(G-16102)***
Raulli and Sons Inc (PA) 315 479-6693
213 Teall Ave Syracuse (13210) ***(G-16018)***
Raulli and Sons Inc 315 474-1370
660 Burnet Ave Syracuse (13203) ***(G-16019)***
Raulli and Sons Inc 315 479-2515
920 Canal St Syracuse (13210) ***(G-16020)***
Raulli Iron Works Inc 315 337-8070
133 Mill St Rome (13440) ***(G-14832)***
Raven New York LLC 212 584-9690
450 W 15th St New York (10011) ***(G-11803)***
Ravioli Store Inc 718 729-9300
4344 21st St Long Island City (11101) ***(G-7858)***
Ravioli Store, The, Long Island City *Also called Pelican Bay Ltd* ***(G-7838)***
Raw Indulgence Ltd 866 498-4671
200 Saw Mill River Rd Hawthorne (10532) ***(G-6253)***
Raw Revolution, Hawthorne *Also called Raw Indulgence Ltd* ***(G-6253)***
Rawlings Sporting Goods Co Inc 315 429-8511
52 Mckinley Ave Dolgeville (13329) ***(G-4307)***
Rawpothecary Inc 917 783-7770
630 Flushing Ave Brooklyn (11206) ***(G-2479)***
Raxon Fabrics Corp (HQ) 212 532-6816
261 5th Ave New York (10016) ***(G-11804)***
Ray Gold Shade Inc 718 377-8892
16 Wellington Ct Brooklyn (11230) ***(G-2480)***
Ray Griffiths Inc 212 689-7209
303 5th Ave Rm 1901 New York (10016) ***(G-11805)***
Ray Medica Inc 952 885-0500
505 Park Ave Ste 1400 New York (10022) ***(G-11806)***
Ray Sign Inc 518 377-1371
28 Colonial Ave Schenectady (12304) ***(G-15289)***
Rayana Designs Inc 718 786-2040
2520 40th Ave Long Island City (11101) ***(G-7859)***
Rayco Enterprises Inc 716 685-6860
4087 Walden Ave Lancaster (14086) ***(G-7337)***
Rayco Manufacturing Co Inc 516 431-2006
10715 180th St Jamaica (11433) ***(G-6944)***
Rayco Manufacturing Div, Jamaica *Also called Rayco Manufacturing Co Inc* ***(G-6944)***
Rayco of Schenectady Inc 518 212-5113
4 Sam Stratton Rd Amsterdam (12010) ***(G-366)***
Raydon Precision Bearing Co 516 887-2582
75 Merrick Rd Lynbrook (11563) ***(G-7958)***
Raydoor Inc 212 421-0641
134 W 29th St Rm 909 New York (10001) ***(G-11807)***
Raymond Consolidated Corp (HQ) 800 235-7200
22 S Canal St Greene (13778) ***(G-5868)***
Raymond Corporation (HQ) 607 656-2311
22 S Canal St Greene (13778) ***(G-5869)***
Raymond Corporation 607 656-2311
6650 Kirkville Rd East Syracuse (13057) ***(G-4555)***
Raymond Corporation 315 463-5000
6517 Chrysler Ln East Syracuse (13057) ***(G-4556)***
Raymond Corporation 315 643-5000
6533 Chrysler Ln East Syracuse (13057) ***(G-4557)***
Raymond Leasing, East Syracuse *Also called Raymond Corporation* ***(G-4555)***
Raymond Sales Corporation (HQ) 607 656-2311
22 S Canal St Greene (13778) ***(G-5870)***
Rays Italian Bakery Inc 516 825-9170
45 Railroad Ave Valley Stream (11580) ***(G-16423)***
Rays Restaurant & Bakery Inc 718 441-7707
12325 Jamaica Ave Jamaica (11418) ***(G-6945)***
Raytech Corp Asbestos Personal (PA) 516 747-0300
190 Willis Ave Mineola (11501) ***(G-8533)***
Raytech Corporation (HQ) 718 259-7388
97 Froehlich Farm Blvd Woodbury (11797) ***(G-17297)***
Razorfish LLC 212 798-6600
1440 Broadway Fl 18 New York (10018) ***(G-11808)***
RB Converting Inc 607 777-1325
28 Track Dr Binghamton (13904) ***(G-945)***
RB Diamond Inc 212 398-4560
22 W 48th St Ste 904 New York (10036) ***(G-11809)***
RB Woodcraft Inc 315 474-2429
1860 Erie Blvd E Ste 1 Syracuse (13210) ***(G-16021)***
Rbhammers Corp 845 353-5042
500 Bradley Hill Rd Blauvelt (10913) ***(G-973)***
Rbw Studio LLC 212 388-1621
67 34th St Unit 5 Brooklyn (11232) ***(G-2481)***
RC Entps Bus & Trck Inc 518 568-5753
5895 State Highway 29 Saint Johnsville (13452) ***(G-15097)***
RC Imaging Inc 585 392-4336
50 Old Hojack Ln Hilton (14468) ***(G-6420)***
Rce Manufacturing LLC 631 856-9005
10 Brayton Ct Commack (11725) ***(G-3839)***
RD Intrntnl Style 212 382-2360
275 W 39th St Fl 7 New York (10018) ***(G-11810)***
Rd Publications Inc (HQ) 914 238-1000
1 Readers Digest Rd Pleasantville (10570) ***(G-13717)***
Rd2 Construction & Dem LLC 718 980-1650
63 Trossach Rd Staten Island (10304) ***(G-15728)***
Rdi, Edgewood *Also called Iba Industrial Inc* ***(G-4600)***
Rdi Inc (PA) 914 773-1000
333 N Bedford Rd Ste 135 Mount Kisco (10549) ***(G-8643)***
RDI ELECTRONICS, Mount Kisco *Also called Rdi Inc* ***(G-8643)***
RE 99 Cents Inc 718 639-2325
4905 Roosevelt Ave Woodside (11377) ***(G-17349)***
RE Hansen Industries Inc (PA) 631 471-2900
22 Research Way East Setauket (11733) ***(G-4491)***
Re-Al Industrial Corp 716 542-4556
5391 Crittenden Rd Akron (14001) ***(G-28)***
Read Manufacturing Company Inc 631 567-4487
330 Dante Ct Holbrook (11741) ***(G-6467)***
Readent Inc 212 710-3004
445 Hamilton Ave Ste 1102 White Plains (10601) ***(G-17162)***
Reader's Digest, New York *Also called Trusted Media Brands Inc* ***(G-12413)***
Readers Dgest Latinoamerica SA 914 238-1000
Readers Digest Rd Pleasantville (10570) ***(G-13718)***
Readers Dgest Yung Fmilies Inc 914 238-1000
Readers Digest Rd Pleasantville (10570) ***(G-13719)***
Readers Digest Assn Incthe 414 423-0100
16 E 34th St Fl 14 New York (10016) ***(G-11811)***
Readers Digest Assn Incthe 914 238-1000
100 S Bedford Rd Ste 340 Mount Kisco (10549) ***(G-8644)***
Reading Room Inc (PA) 212 463-1029
48 Wall St Fl 5 New York (10005) ***(G-11812)***
Ready Check Glo Inc 516 547-1849
23 Bruce Ln Ste E East Northport (11731) ***(G-4444)***
Ready Egg Farms Inc 607 674-4653
35 W State St Sherburne (13460) ***(G-15394)***
Ready To Assemble Company Inc 516 825-4397
115 S Corona Ave Valley Stream (11580) ***(G-16424)***
Readyjet Technical Svcs Inc 518 705-4019
1 Warren St Johnstown (12095) ***(G-7124)***
Real Bark Mulch LLC 518 747-3650
1380 Towpath Ln Fort Edward (12828) ***(G-5345)***
Real Co Inc 347 433-8549
616 Corporate Way Valley Cottage (10989) ***(G-16386)***

ALPHABETIC

Real Deal, The, New York *Also called Korangy Publishing Inc* ***(G-10877)***
Real Design Inc....315 429-3071
187 S Main St Dolgeville (13329) ***(G-4308)***
Real Est Book of Long Island....516 364-5000
575 Underhill Blvd # 110 Syosset (11791) ***(G-15837)***
Real Estate Media Inc....212 929-6976
120 Broadway Fl 5 New York (10271) ***(G-11813)***
Real Goods Solar Inc....845 708-0800
22 Third St New City (10956) ***(G-8791)***
Real Wood Tiles, Buffalo *Also called Fibron Products Inc* ***(G-2947)***
Realtimetraderscom....716 632-6600
1325 N Forest Rd Ste 350 Buffalo (14221) ***(G-3155)***
Rear View Safety Inc....855 815-3842
1797 Atlantic Ave Brooklyn (11233) ***(G-2482)***
Recharge Net Inc....585 546-1060
439 Central Ave Ste 108 Rochester (14605) ***(G-14621)***
Recom Power Inc....718 855-9713
18 Bridge St Ste 3g Brooklyn (11201) ***(G-2483)***
Recommunity Recycling....845 926-1071
508 Fishkill Ave Beacon (12508) ***(G-789)***
Recon Construction Corp....718 939-1305
1108 Shore Rd Little Neck (11363) ***(G-7509)***
Record....518 270-1200
20 Lake Ave Saratoga Springs (12866) ***(G-15169)***
Record Advertiser....716 693-1000
435 River Rd North Tonawanda (14120) ***(G-12988)***
Record Press Inc....212 619-4949
157 Chambers St New York (10007) ***(G-11814)***
Record Review LLC....914 244-0533
264 Adams St Fl 2 Bedford Hills (10507) ***(G-807)***
Recorded Anthlogy of Amrcn Mus....212 290-1695
20 Jay St Ste 1001 Brooklyn (11201) ***(G-2484)***
Recorder, The, Amsterdam *Also called Tri-Village Publishers Inc* ***(G-371)***
Recycled Brooklyn Group LLC....917 902-0662
84 Ferris St Brooklyn (11231) ***(G-2485)***
Red Creek Cold Storage LLC (PA)....315 576-2069
14127 Keeley St Red Creek (13143) ***(G-14025)***
Red Line Networx Screen Prtg, Brooklyn *Also called Body Builders Inc* ***(G-1708)***
Red Newt Cellars Inc....607 546-4100
3675 Tichenor Rd Hector (14841) ***(G-6260)***
Red Oak Software Inc....585 454-3170
3349 Monroe Ave Ste 175 Rochester (14618) ***(G-14622)***
Red Tail Moulding & Mllwk LLC....516 852-4613
23 Frowein Rd Ste 1 Center Moriches (11934) ***(G-3468)***
Red Tail Ridge Inc....315 536-4580
846 State Route 14 Penn Yan (14527) ***(G-13517)***
Red Tail Ridge Winery, Penn Yan *Also called Red Tail Ridge Inc* ***(G-13517)***
Red White & Blue Entps Corp....718 565-8080
3443 56th St Woodside (11377) ***(G-17350)***
Redbook Magazine....212 649-3331
224 W 57th St Lbby Fl22 New York (10019) ***(G-11815)***
Redco Foods Inc....315 823-1300
1 Hansen Is Little Falls (13365) ***(G-7504)***
Redcom Laboratories Inc....585 924-6567
1 Redcom Ctr Victor (14564) ***(G-16500)***
Reddi Car Corp....631 589-3141
174 Greeley Ave Sayville (11782) ***(G-15214)***
Redding Reloading Equipment, Cortland *Also called Redding-Hunter Inc* ***(G-4043)***
Redding-Hunter Inc....607 753-3331
1089 Starr Rd Cortland (13045) ***(G-4043)***
Redi Bag Brand, Garden City *Also called New York Packaging II LLC* ***(G-5523)***
Redi Records Payroll....718 854-6990
1225 36th St Brooklyn (11218) ***(G-2486)***
Redi-Bag USA, New Hyde Park *Also called New York Packaging Corp* ***(G-8850)***
Redken 5th Avenue Nyc LLC....212 984-5113
565 5th Ave New York (10017) ***(G-11816)***
Redland Foods Corp....716 288-9061
40 Sonwil Dr Cheektowaga (14225) ***(G-3589)***
Redspring Communications Inc....518 587-0547
125 High Rock Ave Saratoga Springs (12866) ***(G-15170)***
Redwood Cllaborative Media Inc....631 393-6051
105 Maxess Rd Melville (11747) ***(G-8352)***
Reebok International Ltd....914 948-3719
125 Westchester Ave White Plains (10601) ***(G-17163)***
Reebok International Ltd....718 370-0471
2655 Richmond Ave Staten Island (10314) ***(G-15729)***
Reed Business Information, New York *Also called Relx Inc* ***(G-11826)***
Reed Systems Ltd....845 647-3660
17 Edwards Pl Ellenville (12428) ***(G-4637)***
Reefer Tek Llc....347 590-1067
885 E 149th St Fl 2a Bronx (10455) ***(G-1440)***
Reelcology Inc....845 258-1880
39 Transport Ln Pine Island (10969) ***(G-13553)***
Reelex Packaging Solutions Inc....845 878-7878
39 Jon Barrett Rd Patterson (12563) ***(G-13443)***
Reenergy Black River, Fort Drum *Also called Black River Generations LLC* ***(G-5338)***
Reentry Games Inc....646 421-0080
215 E 5th St New York (10003) ***(G-11817)***
Reese Manufacturing Inc....631 842-3780
16 Reith St Copiague (11726) ***(G-3922)***
Refill Services LLC....607 369-5864
16 Winkler Rd Sidney (13838) ***(G-15441)***

A
L
P
H
A
B
E
T
I
C

REFINEDKIND PET PRODUCTS, Irvington *Also called Feinkind Inc* ***(G-6769)***
Reflex Offset Inc....516 746-4142
305 Suburban Ave Deer Park (11729) ***(G-4199)***
Reflexite Display Optics, West Henrietta *Also called Orafol Display Optics Inc* ***(G-16887)***
Reflexite Precision Tech Ctr, Henrietta *Also called Orafol Americas Inc* ***(G-6297)***
Refuel Inc (PA)....917 645-2974
1384 Broadway Rm 407 New York (10018) ***(G-11818)***
Regal Commodities, Purchase *Also called Regal Trading Inc* ***(G-13970)***
Regal Emblem Co Inc....212 925-8833
250 W Broadway Fl 2 New York (10013) ***(G-11819)***
Regal Screen Printing Intl....845 356-8181
42 Grove St Spring Valley (10977) ***(G-15601)***
Regal Tip, Niagara Falls *Also called J D Calato Manufacturing Co* ***(G-12837)***
Regal Trading Inc....914 694-6100
2975 Westchester Ave # 210 Purchase (10577) ***(G-13970)***
Regan Arts LLC....646 488-6613
65 Bleecker St Fl 4 New York (10012) ***(G-11820)***
Rege Inc....845 565-7772
110 Corporate Dr New Windsor (12553) ***(G-8950)***
Regence Picture Frames Inc....718 779-0888
12 Cherry Ln Lynbrook (11563) ***(G-7959)***
Regeneron Pharmaceuticals Inc (PA)....914 847-7000
777 Old Saw Mill River Rd # 10 Tarrytown (10591) ***(G-16103)***
Regeneron Pharmaceuticals Inc....518 488-6000
33 Riverside Ave Rensselaer (12144) ***(G-14050)***
Regeneron Pharmaceuticals Inc....518 488-6000
81 Columbia Tpke Rensselaer (12144) ***(G-14051)***
Regenron Hlthcare Slutions Inc....914 847-7000
745 Old Saw Mill River Rd Tarrytown (10591) ***(G-16104)***
Regina Press, Bohemia *Also called Malhame Publs & Importers Inc* ***(G-1101)***
Regional MGT & Consulting Inc....718 599-3718
79 Bridgewater St Brooklyn (11222) ***(G-2487)***
Register Graphics Inc....716 358-2921
220 Main St Randolph (14772) ***(G-14018)***
Rehab Tech, Syracuse *Also called Rehablitation Tech of Syracuse* ***(G-16022)***
Rehabilitation International....212 420-1500
15350 89th Ave Apt 1101 Jamaica (11432) ***(G-6946)***
Rehablitation Tech of Syracuse....315 426-9920
1101 Erie Blvd E Ste 209 Syracuse (13210) ***(G-16022)***
Reichert Inc....716 686-4500
3362 Walden Ave Depew (14043) ***(G-4272)***
Reichert Technologies, Depew *Also called Reichert Inc* ***(G-4272)***
Reid K Dalland....845 687-8728
5 Silver Fox Rd Stone Ridge (12484) ***(G-15765)***
Reilly Windows & Doors, Calverton *Also called Pella Corporation* ***(G-3294)***
Reimann & Georger Corporation....716 895-1156
1849 Harlem Rd Buffalo (14212) ***(G-3156)***
Reinhold Brothers Inc....212 867-8310
799 Park Ave New York (10021) ***(G-11821)***
Reino Manufacturing Co Inc....914 636-8990
34 Circuit Rd New Rochelle (10805) ***(G-8923)***
Reis D Furniture Mfg....516 248-5676
327 Sagamore Ave Ste 2 Mineola (11501) ***(G-8534)***
Reisman Bros Bakery Inc....718 331-1975
110 Avenue O Brooklyn (11204) ***(G-2488)***
Reismans Bros. Bakery, Brooklyn *Also called Reisman Bros Bakery Inc* ***(G-2488)***
Reiss Ltd (PA)....212 488-2411
309 Bleecker St 313 New York (10014) ***(G-11822)***
Relavis Corporation....212 995-2900
40 Wall St Ste 3300 New York (10005) ***(G-11823)***
Release Coatings New York Inc....585 593-2335
125 S Brooklyn Ave Wellsville (14895) ***(G-16756)***
Reliable Autmtc Sprnklr Co Inc (PA)....914 829-2042
103 Fairview Pk Dr Ste 1 Elmsford (10523) ***(G-4776)***
Reliable Brothers Inc....518 273-6732
185 Cohoes Ave Green Island (12183) ***(G-5861)***
Reliable Elec Mt Vernon Inc....914 668-4440
519 S 5th Ave Mount Vernon (10550) ***(G-8725)***
Reliable Press II Inc....718 840-5812
148 39th St Unit 6 Brooklyn (11232) ***(G-2489)***
Reliable Welding & Fabrication....631 758-2637
214 W Main St Patchogue (11772) ***(G-13434)***
Reliance Fluid Tech LLC....716 332-0988
3943 Buffalo Ave Niagara Falls (14303) ***(G-12867)***
Reliance Gayco, Kingston *Also called Universal Metal Fabricators* ***(G-7221)***
Reliance Machining Inc....718 784-0314
4335 Vernon Blvd Long Island City (11101) ***(G-7860)***
Reliance Mica Co Inc....718 788-0282
336 Beach 149th St Rockaway Park (11694) ***(G-14787)***
Reliant Security....917 338-2200
450 Fashion Ave Ste 503 New York (10123) ***(G-11824)***
Relmada Therapeutics Inc....646 677-3853
275 Madison Ave Ste 702 New York (10016) ***(G-11825)***
Relx Inc (HQ)....212 309-8100
230 Park Ave New York (10169) ***(G-11826)***
Relx Inc....212 463-6644
249 W 17th St New York (10011) ***(G-11827)***
Relx Inc....212 633-3900
655 6th Ave New York (10010) ***(G-11828)***
Relx Inc....607 772-2600
136 Carlin Rd Conklin (13748) ***(G-3873)***

ALPHABETIC SECTION
RG Barry Corporation

REM Printing Inc....518 438-7338
55 Railroad Ave Albany (12205) *(G-128)*
Rem-Tronics Inc....716 934-2697
659 Brigham Rd Dunkirk (14048) *(G-4348)*
Remains Lighting....212 675-8051
130 W 28th St Frnt 1 New York (10001) *(G-11829)*
Rembar Company LLC....914 693-2620
67 Main St Dobbs Ferry (10522) *(G-4302)*
Remedies Surgical Supplies....718 599-5301
331 Rutledge St Ste 204 Brooklyn (11211) *(G-2490)*
Remington Arms Company LLC....315 895-3482
14 Hoefler Ave Ilion (13357) *(G-6744)*
Remsen Fuel Inc....718 984-9551
4668 Amboy Rd Staten Island (10312) *(G-15730)*
Remsen Graphics Corp....718 643-7500
52 Court St 2 Brooklyn (11201) *(G-2491)*
Remus Industries....914 906-1544
11 Oakbrook Rd Ossining (10562) *(G-13327)*
Ren Tool & Manufacturing Co....518 377-2123
1801 Chrisler Ave Schenectady (12303) *(G-15290)*
Renaissance Bijou Ltd....212 869-1969
20 W 47th St Ste 18 New York (10036) *(G-11830)*
Renaissance Import, Lockport *Also called Candlelight Cabinetry Inc (G-7575)*
Renaissnce Crpt Tapestries Inc....212 696-0080
200 Lexington Ave Rm 912 New York (10016) *(G-11831)*
Renaldos Sales and Service Ctr....716 337-3760
1770 Milestrip Rd North Collins (14111) *(G-12931)*
Renanssance The Book, Port Chester *Also called Albumx Corp (G-13738)*
Renco Group Inc (PA)....212 541-6000
1 Rockefeller Plz Fl 29 New York (10020) *(G-11832)*
Renco Manufacturing Inc....718 392-8877
1040 45th Ave Fl 2 Long Island City (11101) *(G-7861)*
Rene Portier Inc....718 853-7896
3611 14th Ave Ste 6 Brooklyn (11218) *(G-2492)*
Renegade Nation Ltd....212 868-9000
434 Av Of The Amercs Fl 6 New York (10011) *(G-11833)*
Renegade Nation Online LLC....212 868-9000
434 Av Of The Americas Fl Flr 6 New York (10011) *(G-11834)*
Renewable Energy Inc....718 690-2691
6 Cornell Ln Little Neck (11363) *(G-7510)*
Renewal By Andersen LLC....631 843-1716
2029 New Hwy Farmingdale (11735) *(G-5098)*
Renewal By Andrsen Long Island, Farmingdale *Also called Renewal By Andersen LLC (G-5098)*
Rennen International, South Ozone Park *Also called Extreme Auto Accessories Corp (G-15533)*
Renold Ajax, Westfield *Also called Renold Holdings Inc (G-17050)*
Renold Holdings Inc (HQ)....716 326-3121
100 Bourne St Westfield (14787) *(G-17050)*
Renold Inc....716 326-3121
100 Bourne St Westfield (14787) *(G-17051)*
Renovatio Med & Surgical Sups, Buffalo *Also called Yr Blanc & Co LLC (G-3261)*
Rent-A-Center Inc....718 322-2400
11211 Liberty Ave Jamaica (11419) *(G-6947)*
Rentschler Biotechnologie GMBH....631 656-7137
400 Oser Ave Ste 1650 Hauppauge (11788) *(G-6177)*
REO Welding Inc....518 238-1022
5 New Cortland St Cohoes (12047) *(G-3756)*
Repellem Consumer Pdts Corp....631 273-3992
10 Oval Dr Islandia (11749) *(G-6802)*
Repertoire International De Ll....212 817-1990
365 5th Ave Fl 3 New York (10016) *(G-11835)*
Repro Med Systems Inc....845 469-2042
24 Carpenter Rd Ste 1 Chester (10918) *(G-3612)*
Republic Clothing Corporation....212 719-3000
1411 Broadway Fl 37 New York (10018) *(G-11836)*
Republic Clothing Group, New York *Also called Republic Clothing Corporation (G-11836)*
Republic Clothing Group Inc....212 719-3000
1411 Broadway Fl 37 New York (10018) *(G-11837)*
Republic Construction Co Inc....914 235-3654
305 North Ave New Rochelle (10801) *(G-8924)*
Republic Steel Inc....716 827-2800
3049 Lake Shore Rd Blasdell (14219) *(G-965)*
Republican Registrar Inc....315 497-1551
6 Central St Moravia (13118) *(G-8617)*
Request Inc....518 899-1254
14 Corporate Dr Ste 6 Halfmoon (12065) *(G-5914)*
Request Jeans, New York *Also called US Design Group Ltd (G-12485)*
Request Multimedia, Halfmoon *Also called Request Inc (G-5914)*
Request Serious Play LLC....518 899-1254
14 Corporate Dr Halfmoon (12065) *(G-5915)*
RES Magazine, New York *Also called Res Media Group Inc (G-11838)*
Res Media Group Inc....212 320-3750
601 W 26th St Fl 11 New York (10001) *(G-11838)*
Rescuestuff Inc....718 318-7570
962 Washington St Peekskill (10566) *(G-13480)*
Research Centre of Kabbalah....718 805-0380
8384 115th St Richmond Hill (11418) *(G-14079)*
Research Frontiers Inc (PA)....516 364-1902
240 Crossways Park Dr Woodbury (11797) *(G-17298)*
Reserve Confections Chocolate, Monsey *Also called Reserve Confections Inc (G-8578)*
Reserve Confections Inc....845 371-7744
9 Butterman Pl Monsey (10952) *(G-8578)*
Reserve Gas Company, Alden *Also called Alden Aurora Gas Company Inc (G-174)*
Reserve Gas Company Inc....716 937-9484
13441 Railroad St Alden (14004) *(G-182)*
Reservoir Media Management Inc (PA)....212 675-0541
225 Varick St Fl 6 New York (10014) *(G-11839)*
Residential Fences Corp....631 205-9758
1760 Middle Country Rd Ridge (11961) *(G-14094)*
Resonance Technologies Inc....631 237-4901
109 Comac St Ronkonkoma (11779) *(G-14978)*
Resonant Legal Media LLC....212 687-7100
1040 Av Of The Amrcs 18 New York (10018) *(G-11840)*
Resonant Legal Media LLC (PA)....800 781-3591
1 Penn Plz Ste 1514 New York (10119) *(G-11841)*
Resource PTRlm&ptrochmcl Intl....212 537-3856
3 Columbus Cir Fl 15 New York (10019) *(G-11842)*
Responcer Inc....917 572-0895
1781 Riverside Dr Apt 3g New York (10034) *(G-11843)*
Response Care Inc....585 671-4144
1450 E Ridge Rd Rochester (14621) *(G-14623)*
Responselink Inc....518 424-7776
31 Dussault Dr Latham (12110) *(G-7378)*
Responselink of Albany, Latham *Also called Responselink Inc (G-7378)*
Restaurant 570 8th Avenue LLC....646 722-8191
213 W 40th St Fl 3 New York (10018) *(G-11844)*
Restonic, Buffalo *Also called Royal Bedding Co Buffalo Inc (G-3168)*
Retail Management Pubg Inc....212 981-0217
12 W 37th St Rm 502 New York (10018) *(G-11845)*
Retailer, Lockport *Also called Metro Group Inc (G-7601)*
Retailer, The, Port Washington *Also called Music & Sound Retailer Inc (G-13847)*
Retirement Insiders....631 751-1329
15 Triangle Dr Setauket (11733) *(G-15378)*
Retracase, Brooklyn *Also called P B O E Pwred By Our Envmt Inc (G-2400)*
Retrophin LLC....212 983-1310
330 Madison Ave Fl 6 New York (10017) *(G-11846)*
Return Textiles LLC....646 408-0108
187 Lafayette St Fl 5 New York (10013) *(G-11847)*
Reuter Pallet Pkg Sys Inc....845 457-9937
272 Neelytown Rd Montgomery (12549) *(G-8602)*
Rev Holdings Inc....212 527-4000
466 Lexington Ave Fl 21 New York (10017) *(G-11848)*
Revana Inc....212 244-6137
350 5th Ave Ste 5912 New York (10118) *(G-11849)*
Revana Digital, New York *Also called Revana Inc (G-11849)*
Revival Industries Inc....315 868-1085
126 Old Forge Rd Ilion (13357) *(G-6745)*
Revlon Inc....212 527-6330
237 Park Ave New York (10017) *(G-11850)*
Revlon Inc (PA)....212 527-4000
1 New York Plz New York (10004) *(G-11851)*
Revlon Co, New York *Also called Revlon Inc (G-11850)*
Revlon Consumer Products Corp (HQ)....212 527-4000
1 New York Plz New York (10004) *(G-11852)*
Revlon Holdings Inc (HQ)....212 527-4000
237 Park Ave New York (10017) *(G-11853)*
Revman International Inc (HQ)....212 894-3100
350 5th Ave Fl 70 New York (10118) *(G-11854)*
Revolution Golf, New York *Also called Maven Marketing LLC (G-11183)*
Revolution Vapor LLC....518 627-4133
4715 State Highway 30 Amsterdam (12010) *(G-367)*
Revonate Manufacturing LLC....315 433-1160
7401 Round Pond Rd Syracuse (13212) *(G-16023)*
Rexford Services Inc....716 366-6671
4849 W Lake Rd Dunkirk (14048) *(G-4349)*
Reynolds Book Bindery LLC....607 772-8937
37 Milford St Binghamton (13904) *(G-946)*
Reynolds Drapery Service Inc....315 845-8632
7440 Main St Newport (13416) *(G-12792)*
Reynolds Manufacturing Inc....607 562-8936
3298 State Rte 352 Big Flats (14814) *(G-882)*
Reynolds Packaging McHy Inc....716 358-6451
2632 S Work St Ste 24 Falconer (14733) *(G-4910)*
Reynolds Shipyard Corporation....718 981-2800
200 Edgewater St Staten Island (10305) *(G-15731)*
Reynolds Tech Fabricators Inc....315 437-0532
6895 Kinne St East Syracuse (13057) *(G-4558)*
Rf Communications, Rochester *Also called Harris Corporation (G-14427)*
Rf Inter Science Co, Patchogue *Also called Kevin Freeman (G-13426)*
Rfb Associates Inc....518 271-0551
11 Drywall Ln Voorheesville (12186) *(G-16517)*
Rfn Inc....516 764-5100
40 Drexel Dr Bay Shore (11706) *(G-733)*
Rfp LLC....212 838-7733
228 E 45th St Fl 11 New York (10017) *(G-11855)*
Rft, New York *Also called Rainforest Inc (G-11790)*
RG, Buffalo *Also called Roberts-Gordon LLC (G-3160)*
RG Apparel Group, New York *Also called Excelled Shpskin Lea Coat Corp (G-10103)*
RG Barry Corporation....212 244-3145
9 E 37th St Fl 11 New York (10016) *(G-11856)*

ALPHABETIC

RG Glass Creations Inc ... 212 675-0030
180 Varick St Rm 1304 New York (10014) *(G-11857)*
RGH Associates Inc ... 631 643-1111
86 Nancy St West Babylon (11704) *(G-16821)*
RGI Group Incorporated (HQ) ... 212 527-4000
625 Madison Ave Frnt 4 New York (10022) *(G-11858)*
Rgm Signs Inc ... 718 442-0598
1234 Castleton Ave Staten Island (10310) *(G-15732)*
Rheinwald Printing Corp ... 585 637-5100
15 Main St Brockport (14420) *(G-1246)*
Rheonix Inc (PA) ... 607 257-1242
10 Brown Rd Ste 103 Ithaca (14850) *(G-6873)*
Rhett M Clark Inc ... 585 538-9570
3213 Lehigh St Caledonia (14423) *(G-3281)*
Rhi US Ltd (HQ) ... 716 483-7200
1870 New York Ave Falconer (14733) *(G-4911)*
Rhino Trunk & Case Inc ... 585 244-4553
565 Blossom Rd Ste J Rochester (14610) *(G-14624)*
Rhoda Lee Inc ... 212 840-5700
77 W 55th St Apt 4k New York (10019) *(G-11859)*
Riazul Imports LLC ... 713 894-9177
310 W 120th St Apt 5d New York (10027) *(G-11860)*
Ribble Lumber Inc ... 315 536-6221
249 1/2 Lake St Penn Yan (14527) *(G-13518)*
Ribz LLC ... 212 764-9595
1407 Broadway Rm 1402 New York (10018) *(G-11861)*
Ric-Lo Productions Ltd ... 845 469-2285
1144 Kings Hwy Chester (10918) *(G-3613)*
Rich Brilliant Willing, Brooklyn Also called Rbw Studio LLC *(G-2481)*
Rich Products Corporation (PA) ... 716 878-8422
1 Robert Rich Way Buffalo (14213) *(G-3157)*
Richard Anthony Corp ... 914 922-7141
1500 Front St Ste 12 Yorktown Heights (10598) *(G-17518)*
Richard Anthony Custom Mllwk, Yorktown Heights Also called Richard Anthony Corp *(G-17518)*
Richard Bauer Logging ... 585 343-4149
3936 Cookson Rd Alexander (14005) *(G-190)*
Richard C Owen Publishers Inc ... 914 232-3903
243 Route 100 Somers (10589) *(G-15512)*
Richard Edelson ... 914 428-7573
80 Pinewood Rd Hartsdale (10530) *(G-5999)*
Richard Engdal Baking Corp ... 914 777-9600
421 Waverly Ave Mamaroneck (10543) *(G-8044)*
Richard H Williams Associates ... 631 751-4156
7 White Pine Ln Setauket (11733) *(G-15379)*
Richard Leeds Intl Inc (PA) ... 212 532-4546
135 Madison Ave Fl 10 New York (10016) *(G-11862)*
Richard Manno & Company Inc ... 631 643-2200
42 Lamar St West Babylon (11704) *(G-16822)*
Richard Manufacturing Co Inc ... 718 254-0958
63 Flushing Ave Unit 327 Brooklyn (11205) *(G-2493)*
Richard R Cain Inc ... 845 229-7410
50 Scenic Dr Hyde Park (12538) *(G-6736)*
Richard Rothbard Inc ... 845 355-2300
1866 Route 284 Slate Hill (10973) *(G-15474)*
Richard Ruffner ... 631 234-4600
69 Carleton Ave Central Islip (11722) *(G-3509)*
Richard Stacey Rs Automation, Albion Also called Rs Automation *(G-169)*
Richard Stewart ... 518 632-5363
4495 State Rte 149 Hartford (12838) *(G-5996)*
Richards & West Inc ... 585 461-4088
501 W Commercial St Ste 1 East Rochester (14445) *(G-4466)*
Richards Logging LLC ... 518 359-2775
201 State Route 3 Tupper Lake (12986) *(G-16279)*
Richards Machine Tool Co Inc ... 716 683-3380
3753 Walden Ave Lancaster (14086) *(G-7338)*
Richards Screw Machine, West Babylon Also called RGH Associates Inc *(G-16821)*
Richardson Brands Company (HQ) ... 518 673-3553
101 Erie Blvd Canajoharie (13317) *(G-3333)*
Richardson Foods, Canajoharie Also called Richardson Brands Company *(G-3333)*
Richemont North America Inc ... 212 891-2440
645 5th Ave Fl 6 New York (10022) *(G-11863)*
Richemont North America Inc ... 212 644-9500
729 Madison Ave New York (10065) *(G-11864)*
Richer's Bakery, Flushing Also called H H B Bakery of Little Neck *(G-5246)*
Richlar Custom Foam Div, East Syracuse Also called Richlar Industries Inc *(G-4559)*
Richlar Industries Inc ... 315 463-5144
6741 Old Collamer Rd East Syracuse (13057) *(G-4559)*
Richline Group Inc ... 212 643-2908
245 W 29th St Rm 900 New York (10001) *(G-11865)*
Richline Group Inc ... 212 764-8454
1385 Broadway Fl 12 New York (10018) *(G-11866)*
Richline Group Inc ... 914 699-0000
1385 Broadway Fl 12 New York (10018) *(G-11867)*
Richloom Corp ... 212 685-5400
261 5th Ave Fl 12 New York (10016) *(G-11868)*
Richloom Fabrics Corp (PA) ... 212 685-5400
261 5th Ave Fl 12 New York (10016) *(G-11869)*
Richloom Fabrics Group Inc ... 212 685-5400
261 5th Ave Fl 12 New York (10016) *(G-11870)*
Richloom Home Fashion, New York Also called Richloom Corp *(G-11868)*
Richloom Home Fashions Corp ... 212 685-5400
261 5th Ave Fl 12 New York (10016) *(G-11871)*
Richmond Ready Mix Corp ... 917 731-8400
328 Park St Staten Island (10306) *(G-15733)*
Richner Communications Inc (PA) ... 516 569-4000
2 Endo Blvd Garden City (11530) *(G-5529)*
Richner Communications Inc ... 516 569-4000
379 Central Ave Lawrence (11559) *(G-7399)*
Richs Sttches EMB Screenprint ... 845 621-2175
407 Route 6 Mahopac (10541) *(G-8000)*
Richter Metalcraft Corporation ... 845 895-2025
80 Cottage St Wallkill (12589) *(G-16545)*
Rick-Mic Industries Inc ... 631 563-8389
1951 Ocean Ave Ste 6 Ronkonkoma (11779) *(G-14979)*
Rico International ... 818 767-7711
8484 San Fernando Rd Farmingdale (11735) *(G-5099)*
Rid Lom Precision Mfg ... 585 594-8600
50 Regency Oaks Blvd Rochester (14624) *(G-14625)*
Ridge Cabinet & Showcase Inc ... 585 663-0560
1545 Mount Read Blvd # 2 Rochester (14606) *(G-14626)*
Ridgewood Times Prtg & Pubg ... 718 821-7500
6071 Woodbine St Fl 1 Ridgewood (11385) *(G-14122)*
Riefler Concrete Products LLC ... 716 649-3260
5690 Camp Rd Hamburg (14075) *(G-5940)*
Right Fit Shoes LLC ... 212 575-9445
1385 Broadway New York (10018) *(G-11872)*
Right World View ... 914 406-2994
2900 Purchase St 528 Purchase (10577) *(G-13971)*
Rigidized Metals Corporation ... 716 849-4703
658 Ohio St Buffalo (14203) *(G-3158)*
Rigidized-Metal, Buffalo Also called Rigidized Metals Corporation *(G-3158)*
Rij Pharmaceutical Corporation ... 845 692-5799
40 Commercial Ave Middletown (10941) *(G-8459)*
Rike Enterprises Inc ... 631 277-8338
46 Taft Ave Islip (11751) *(G-6812)*
Riley Gear Corporation ... 716 694-0900
61 Felton St North Tonawanda (14120) *(G-12989)*
RILM, New York Also called Repertoire International De LI *(G-11835)*
Rimco Plastics Corp ... 607 739-3864
316 Colonial Dr Horseheads (14845) *(G-6590)*
Rimmel Inc ... 212 479-4300
2 Park Ave Rm 1800 New York (10016) *(G-11873)*
Rims Like New Inc ... 845 537-0396
507 Union School Rd Middletown (10941) *(G-8460)*
Rina, Plattsburgh Also called Rapa Independent North America *(G-13694)*
Rinaldi Precision Machine ... 631 242-4141
60 Corbin Ave Ste F Bay Shore (11706) *(G-734)*
Ring Division Producto Machine, Jamestown Also called Producto Corporation *(G-7024)*
Ringhoff Fuel Inc ... 631 878-0663
72 Atlantic Ave East Moriches (11940) *(G-4430)*
Ringlead Inc ... 310 906-0545
205 E Main St Ste 2-3a Huntington (11743) *(G-6676)*
Rings Wire Inc ... 212 741-9779
24 W 25th St Fl 7 New York (10010) *(G-11874)*
Rini Tank & Truck Service ... 718 384-6606
327 Nassau Ave Brooklyn (11222) *(G-2494)*
Rino, Freeport Also called Ondrivesus Corp *(G-5416)*
Rio Apparel USA Inc ... 212 869-9150
237 W 37th St Rm 13l New York (10018) *(G-11875)*
Rio Garment SA ... 212 822-3182
114 W 41st St Fl 4 New York (10036) *(G-11876)*
Riot New Media Group Inc ... 604 700-4896
147 Prince St Ste 1 Brooklyn (11201) *(G-2495)*
Ripi Precision Co Inc (PA) ... 631 694-2453
92 Toledo St Farmingdale (11735) *(G-5100)*
Ripley Machine & Tool Co Inc ... 716 736-3205
9825 E Main Rd Ripley (14775) *(G-14136)*
Riri USA Inc (HQ) ... 212 268-3866
350 5th Ave Ste 6700 New York (10118) *(G-11877)*
Risa Management Corp ... 718 361-2606
5501 43rd St Fl 3 Maspeth (11378) *(G-8167)*
Risa's, Maspeth Also called Risa Management Corp *(G-8167)*
Rising Sons 6 Brewing Coinc ... 607 368-4836
196 Baker St Corning (14830) *(G-3979)*
Rising Stars Soccer Club CNY ... 315 381-3096
4980 State Route 233 Westmoreland (13490) *(G-17064)*
Rision Inc ... 212 987-2628
306 E 78th St Apt 1b New York (10075) *(G-11878)*
Risk Management Magazine, New York Also called Risk Society Management Pubg *(G-11879)*
Risk Society Management Pubg ... 212 286-9364
655 3rd Ave Fl 2 New York (10017) *(G-11879)*
Risk Waters Group, New York Also called Incisive Rwg Inc *(G-10581)*
RIT Printing Corp ... 631 586-6220
250 N Fairway Bay Shore (11706) *(G-735)*
Ritchie Brothers Slate Co, Middle Granville Also called Vermont Natural Stoneworks *(G-8403)*
Ritchie Corp ... 212 768-0083
263 W 38th St Fl 13 New York (10018) *(G-11880)*
Rite Price Printing, Ridgewood Also called Mib Industries Inc *(G-14114)*

Ritnoa Inc 212 660-2148
24019 Jamaica Ave Fl 2 Bellerose (11426) *(G-811)*
Riva Jewelry Manufacturing Inc 718 361-3100
140 58th St Ste 8b Brooklyn (11220) *(G-2496)*
River & Sound Publication LLC 631 225-7100
620 Montauk Hwy Copiague (11726) *(G-3923)*
River Rat Design 315 393-4770
1801 Ford St Ste A Ogdensburg (13669) *(G-13121)*
Rivera 718 458-1488
3330 109th St Flushing (11368) *(G-5288)*
Riverdale Press, The, Bronx *Also called Dale Press Inc (G-1310)*
Riverfront Costume Design 716 693-2501
200 River Rd North Tonawanda (14120) *(G-12990)*
Riverhawk Company LP 315 624-7171
215 Clinton Rd New Hartford (13413) *(G-8809)*
Riverside Automation, Rochester *Also called Riverview Associates Inc (G-14628)*
Riverside Iron LLC 315 535-4864
26 Water St Gouverneur (13642) *(G-5747)*
Riverside Machinery Company (PA) 718 492-7400
140 53rd St Brooklyn (11232) *(G-2497)*
Riverside Machinery Company 718 492-7400
132 54th St Brooklyn (11220) *(G-2498)*
Riverside Mfg Acquisition LLC 585 458-2090
655 Driving Park Ave Rochester (14613) *(G-14627)*
Rivertowns Enterprise, Dobbs Ferry *Also called W H White Publications Inc (G-4304)*
Riverview Associates Inc 585 235-5980
1040 Jay St Rochester (14611) *(G-14628)*
Riverview Industries Inc 845 265-5284
3012 Route 9 Ste 1 Cold Spring (10516) *(G-3765)*
Riverwood Sgns By Dndev Dsigns 845 229-0282
3 Terwilliger Rd Hyde Park (12538) *(G-6737)*
Rize Enterprises LLC 631 249-9000
81 Spence St Bay Shore (11706) *(G-736)*
Rizzoli Intl Publications Inc (HQ) 212 387-3400
300 Park Ave S Fl 4 New York (10010) *(G-11881)*
Rizzoli Intl Publications Inc 212 387-3572
300 Park Ave S Fl 3 New York (10010) *(G-11882)*
Rizzoli Intl Publications Inc 212 308-2000
300 Park Ave Frnt 4 New York (10022) *(G-11883)*
RJ Harvey Instrument Corp 845 359-3943
11 Jane St Tappan (10983) *(G-16083)*
Rj Millworkers Inc 607 433-0525
12 Lewis St Oneonta (13820) *(G-13193)*
RJ Precision LLC 585 768-8030
6662 Main Rd Stafford (14143) *(G-15622)*
Rj Welding & Fabricating Inc 315 523-1288
2300 Wheat Rd Clifton Springs (14432) *(G-3715)*
Rjm2 Ltd 212 944-1660
241 W 37th St Rm 926 New York (10018) *(G-11884)*
Rjs Machine Works Inc 716 826-1778
1611 Electric Ave Lackawanna (14218) *(G-7248)*
RKI Building Spc Co Inc 718 728-7788
1530 131st St College Point (11356) *(G-3805)*
Rlp Holdings Inc 716 852-0832
1049 Military Rd Buffalo (14217) *(G-3159)*
Rls Holdings Inc 716 418-7274
11342 Main St Clarence (14031) *(G-3671)*
Rm Bakery LLC 718 472-3036
4425 54th Dr Maspeth (11378) *(G-8168)*
Rmb Embroidery Service 585 271-5560
176 Anderson Ave Ste F110 Rochester (14607) *(G-14629)*
Rmd Holding Inc 845 628-0030
593 Route 6 Mahopac (10541) *(G-8001)*
Rmf Print Management Group 716 683-4351
786 Terrace Blvd Ste 3 Depew (14043) *(G-4273)*
Rmf Printing Technologies Inc 716 683-7500
50 Pearl St Lancaster (14086) *(G-7339)*
Rmi Printing, New York *Also called Rosen Mandell & Immerman Inc (G-11916)*
Rmll Corp 212 719-4666
1385 Broadway Rm 1100 New York (10018) *(G-11885)*
RMS MEDICAL PRODUCTS, Chester *Also called Repro Med Systems Inc (G-3612)*
RMS Packaging Inc 914 205-2070
1050 Lower South St Peekskill (10566) *(G-13481)*
Rmw Filtration Products Co LLC 631 226-9412
230 Lambert Ave Copiague (11726) *(G-3924)*
Rn Furniture Corp 347 960-9622
11409 Atlantic Ave Richmond Hill (11418) *(G-14080)*
Rnd Enterprises Inc 212 627-0165
121 Varick St New York (10013) *(G-11886)*
Road Cases USA Inc 631 563-0633
1625 Sycamore Ave Ste A Bohemia (11716) *(G-1126)*
Roadie Products Inc 631 567-8588
1121 Lincoln Ave Unit 20 Holbrook (11741) *(G-6468)*
Roadrunner Records Inc (HQ) 212 274-7500
1290 Av Of The Amrcs Fl New York (10104) *(G-11887)*
Roanwell Corporation 718 401-0288
2564 Park Ave Bronx (10451) *(G-1441)*
Roar Biomedical Inc 631 591-2749
4603 Middle Country Rd Calverton (11933) *(G-3297)*
Rob Herschenfeld Design Inc 718 456-6801
304 Boerum St Brooklyn (11206) *(G-2499)*
Rob Salamida Company Inc 607 729-4868
71 Pratt Ave Ste 1 Johnson City (13790) *(G-7105)*
Robat Inc 518 812-6244
1 Fairchild Sq Ste 114 Clifton Park (12065) *(G-3705)*
Robeco/Ascot Products Inc 516 248-1521
100 Ring Rd W Garden City (11530) *(G-5530)*
Robell Research Inc 212 755-6577
635 Madison Ave Fl 13 New York (10022) *(G-11888)*
Robert & William Inc (PA) 631 727-5780
224 Griffing Ave Riverhead (11901) *(G-14154)*
Robert Abady Dog Food Co Ltd 845 473-1900
201 Smith St Poughkeepsie (12601) *(G-13928)*
Robert Bartholomew Ltd 516 767-2970
15 Main St Port Washington (11050) *(G-13859)*
Robert Bosch LLC 315 733-3312
2118 Beechgrove Pl Utica (13501) *(G-16357)*
Robert Busse & Co Inc 631 435-4711
75 Arkay Dr Hauppauge (11788) *(G-6178)*
Robert Cohen 718 789-0996
10540 Rockaway Blvd Ste A Ozone Park (11417) *(G-13385)*
Robert Danes Danes Inc (PA) 212 226-1351
481 Greenwich St Apt 5b New York (10013) *(G-11889)*
Robert E Derecktor Inc 914 698-0962
311 E Boston Post Rd Mamaroneck (10543) *(G-8045)*
Robert Ehrlich 516 353-4617
75 Saint Marks Pl New York (10003) *(G-11890)*
Robert Greenburg (PA) 845 586-2226
Cross Rd Margaretville (12455) *(G-8093)*
Robert J Faraone 585 232-7160
1600 N Clinton Ave Rochester (14621) *(G-14630)*
Robert M Brown 607 426-6250
150 Mill St Montour Falls (14865) *(G-8611)*
Robert M Vault 315 243-1447
1360 Lestina Beach Rd Bridgeport (13030) *(G-1236)*
Robert Miller Associate, Rosedale *Also called Water Cooling Corp (G-15015)*
Robert Miller Associates LLC 718 392-1640
4310 23rd St Long Island City (11101) *(G-7862)*
Robert Pikcilingis 518 355-1860
2575 Western Ave Altamont (12009) *(G-211)*
Robert Portegello Graphics 718 241-8118
2028 Utica Ave Brooklyn (11234) *(G-2500)*
Robert Racine (PA) 518 677-0224
41 N Union St Cambridge (12816) *(G-3309)*
Robert Tabatznik Assoc Inc (PA) 845 336-4555
867 Flatbush Rd Kingston (12401) *(G-7209)*
Robert Viggiani 914 423-4046
37 Vredenburgh Ave Ste B Yonkers (10704) *(G-17481)*
Robert W Butts Logging Co 518 643-2897
420 Mannix Rd Peru (12972) *(G-13527)*
Robert W Still 315 942-5594
11755 State Route 26 Ava (13303) *(G-531)*
Robert-Masters Corp 718 545-1030
3217 61st St Woodside (11377) *(G-17351)*
Roberto Coin Inc (PA) 212 486-4545
579 5th Ave Fl 17 New York (10017) *(G-11891)*
Roberts Nichols Fire Apparatus 518 431-1945
3 Industry Dr Waterford (12188) *(G-16620)*
Roberts-Gordon LLC (HQ) 716 852-4400
1250 William St Buffalo (14206) *(G-3160)*
Robespierre Inc 212 764-8810
214 W 39th St Ph Ste 602 New York (10018) *(G-11892)*
Robespierre Inc (PA) 212 594-0012
225 W 35th St Ste 600 New York (10001) *(G-11893)*
Robin Industries Ltd 718 218-9616
56 N 3rd St Brooklyn (11249) *(G-2501)*
Robin Stanley Inc 212 871-0007
1212 Avenue Of The Americ New York (10036) *(G-11894)*
Robinson Concrete Inc (PA) 315 253-6666
3486 Franklin Street Rd Auburn (13021) *(G-516)*
Robinson Concrete Inc 315 492-6200
3537 Apulia Rd Jamesville (13078) *(G-7051)*
Robinson Concrete Inc 315 676-4662
7020 Corporate Park Dr Brewerton (13029) *(G-1205)*
Robinson Knife 716 685-6300
2615 Walden Ave Buffalo (14225) *(G-3161)*
Robinson Tools LLC 585 586-5432
477 Whitney Rd Penfield (14526) *(G-13503)*
Robly Digital Marketing LLC 917 238-0730
93 Leonard St Apt 6 New York (10013) *(G-11895)*
Robo Self Serve, Williamsville *Also called Schmitt Sales Inc (G-17251)*
Robocom Systems International, Farmingdale *Also called Robocom Us LLC (G-5101)*
Robocom Us LLC (PA) 631 861-2045
1111 Broadhollow Rd # 100 Farmingdale (11735) *(G-5101)*
Roboshop Inc 315 437-6454
226 Midler Park Dr Syracuse (13206) *(G-16024)*
Robot Fruit Inc 631 423-7250
40 Radcliff Dr Huntington (11743) *(G-6677)*
Robotic Directions 585 453-9417
8 Black Spruce Ct Rochester (14616) *(G-14631)*
Robs Cycle Supply 315 292-6878
613 Wolf St Syracuse (13208) *(G-16025)*
Robs Really Good LLC 516 671-4411
100 Roslyn Ave Sea Cliff (11579) *(G-15342)*
Roccera LLC 585 426-0887
771 Elmgrove Rd Bldg No2 Rochester (14624) *(G-14632)*

ALPHABETIC

Rocco Bormioli Glass Co Inc (PA)......212 719-0606
41 Madison Ave Ste 1603 New York (10010) ***(G-11896)***
Rochester 100 Inc......585 475-0200
40 Jefferson Rd Rochester (14623) ***(G-14633)***
Rochester Asphalt Materials (HQ)......585 381-7010
1150 Penfield Rd Rochester (14625) ***(G-14634)***
Rochester Asphalt Materials......315 524-4619
1200 Atlantic Ave Walworth (14568) ***(G-16551)***
Rochester Asphalt Materials......585 924-7360
5929 Loomis Rd Farmington (14425) ***(G-5154)***
Rochester Automated Systems Inc......585 594-3222
40 Regency Oaks Blvd Rochester (14624) ***(G-14635)***
Rochester Business Journal......585 546-8303
45 East Ave Ste 500 Rochester (14604) ***(G-14636)***
Rochester Catholic Press (PA)......585 529-9530
1150 Buffalo Rd Rochester (14624) ***(G-14637)***
Rochester Coca Cola Bottling......607 739-5678
210 Industrial Park Rd Horseheads (14845) ***(G-6591)***
Rochester Coca Cola Bottling......585 546-3900
123 Upper Falls Blvd Rochester (14605) ***(G-14638)***
Rochester Colonial Mfg Corp (PA)......585 254-8191
1794 Lyell Ave Rochester (14606) ***(G-14639)***
Rochester Countertop Inc (PA)......585 338-2260
3300 Monroe Ave Ste 212 Rochester (14618) ***(G-14640)***
Rochester Democrat & Chronicle......585 232-7100
55 Exchange Blvd Rochester (14614) ***(G-14641)***
Rochester Gear Inc......585 254-5442
213 Norman St Rochester (14613) ***(G-14642)***
Rochester Golf Week, Rochester *Also called Expositor Newspapers Inc* ***(G-14365)***
Rochester Industrial Ctrl Inc (PA)......315 524-4555
6400 Furnace Rd Ontario (14519) ***(G-13212)***
Rochester Industrial Ctrl Inc......315 524-4555
6345 Furnace Rd Ontario (14519) ***(G-13213)***
Rochester Insulated Glass Inc......585 289-3611
73 Merrick Cir Manchester (14504) ***(G-8052)***
Rochester Lumber Company......585 924-7171
6080 Collett Rd Farmington (14425) ***(G-5155)***
Rochester Magnet, East Rochester *Also called Carpentier Industries LLC* ***(G-4455)***
Rochester Midland Corporation (PA)......585 336-2200
155 Paragon Dr Rochester (14624) ***(G-14643)***
Rochester Optical, Rochester *Also called Genesis Vision Inc* ***(G-14397)***
Rochester Orthopedic Labs (PA)......585 272-1060
460 White Spruce Blvd Rochester (14623) ***(G-14644)***
Rochester Overnight Pltg LLC......585 328-4590
2 Cairn St Rochester (14611) ***(G-14645)***
Rochester Photonics Corp......585 387-0674
115 Canal Landing Blvd Rochester (14626) ***(G-14646)***
Rochester Precision Optics LLC......585 292-5450
850 John St West Henrietta (14586) ***(G-16893)***
Rochester Screen Printing, Rochester *Also called Michael Todd Stevens* ***(G-14506)***
Rochester Silver Works LLC......585 477-9501
100 Latona Rd Bldg 110 Rochester (14652) ***(G-14647)***
Rochester Silver Works LLC......585 743-1610
240 Aster St Rochester (14615) ***(G-14648)***
Rochester Stampings Inc......585 467-5241
400 Trade Ct Rochester (14624) ***(G-14649)***
Rochester Steel Treating Works......585 546-3348
962 E Main St Rochester (14605) ***(G-14650)***
Rochester Structural LLC......585 436-1250
961 Lyell Ave Bldg 5 Rochester (14606) ***(G-14651)***
Rochester Tool and Mold Inc......585 464-9336
515 Lee Rd Rochester (14606) ***(G-14652)***
Rochester Tube Fabricators......585 254-0290
1128 Lexington Ave 5d Rochester (14606) ***(G-14653)***
Rochling Advent Tool & Mold LP......585 254-2000
999 Ridgeway Ave Rochester (14615) ***(G-14654)***
Rock Hill Bakehouse Ltd......518 743-1627
21 Saratoga Rd Gansevoort (12831) ***(G-5489)***
Rock Iroquois Products Inc (HQ)......585 381-7010
1150 Penfield Rd Rochester (14625) ***(G-14655)***
Rock Iroquois Products Inc......585 637-6834
5251 Sweden Walker Rd Brockport (14420) ***(G-1247)***
Rock Mountain Farms Inc......845 647-9084
11 Spring St Ellenville (12428) ***(G-4638)***
Rock Stream Vineyards......607 243-8322
162 Fir Tree Point Rd Rock Stream (14878) ***(G-14779)***
Rockaloid, Piermont *Also called Rockland Colloid Corp* ***(G-13545)***
Rockaway Stairs Ltd......718 945-0047
1011 Bay 24th St Far Rockaway (11691) ***(G-4924)***
Rockefeller University......212 327-8568
950 3rd Ave Fl 2 New York (10022) ***(G-11897)***
Rocket Communications, Buffalo *Also called Gallagher Printing Inc* ***(G-2962)***
Rocket Communications Inc......716 873-2594
2507 Delaware Ave Buffalo (14216) ***(G-3162)***
Rocket Fuel Inc......212 594-8888
195 Broadway 10 New York (10007) ***(G-11898)***
Rocket Tech Fuel Corp......516 810-8947
20 Corbin Ave Bay Shore (11706) ***(G-737)***
Rocking The Boat Inc......718 466-5799
812 Edgewater Rd Bronx (10474) ***(G-1442)***
Rockland Bakery Inc (PA)......845 623-5800
94 Demarest Mill Rd W Nanuet (10954) ***(G-8761)***
Rockland Colloid Corp (PA)......845 359-5559
44 Franklin St Piermont (10968) ***(G-13545)***
Rockland County Times, Nanuet *Also called Citizen Publishing Corp* ***(G-8754)***
Rockland Insulated Wire Cable......845 429-3103
87 Broadway Haverstraw (10927) ***(G-6239)***
Rockland Review Publishing, West Nyack *Also called Angel Media and Publishing* ***(G-16911)***
Rockmills Steel Products Corp......718 366-8300
5912 54th St Maspeth (11378) ***(G-8169)***
Rockport Company LLC......631 243-0418
1288 The Arches Cir Deer Park (11729) ***(G-4200)***
Rockport Company LLC......718 271-3627
9015 Queens Blvd Ste 1025 Elmhurst (11373) ***(G-4666)***
Rockport Pa LLC......212 482-8580
477 Madison Ave Fl 18 New York (10022) ***(G-11899)***
Rockville Pro, Inwood *Also called Audiosavings Inc* ***(G-6752)***
Rockwell Automation Inc......585 487-2700
300 Red Creek Dr Ste 100 Rochester (14623) ***(G-14656)***
Rockwell Collins Simulation......607 352-1298
31 Lewis Rd Binghamton (13905) ***(G-947)***
Rockwell Video Solutions LLC......631 745-0582
10 Koral Dr Southampton (11968) ***(G-15550)***
Rodac USA Corp......716 741-3931
5605 Kraus Rd Clarence (14031) ***(G-3672)***
Rodale Electronics, Hauppauge *Also called Rodale Wireless Inc* ***(G-6179)***
Rodale Inc......212 697-2040
733 3rd Ave Fl 15 New York (10017) ***(G-11900)***
Rodale Wireless Inc......631 231-0044
20 Oser Ave Ste 2 Hauppauge (11788) ***(G-6179)***
Rodan, Hicksville *Also called Oxygen Inc* ***(G-6380)***
Rodem Incorporated......212 779-7122
120 W 29th St Frnt A New York (10001) ***(G-11901)***
Rodeo of NY Inc......212 730-0744
62 W 47th St Ste 14a2 New York (10036) ***(G-11902)***
Rodgard Corporation......716 852-1435
92 Msgr Valente Dr Buffalo (14206) ***(G-3163)***
Roemac Industrial Sales Inc......716 692-7332
27 Fredericka St North Tonawanda (14120) ***(G-12991)***
Roessel & Co Inc......585 458-5560
199 Lagrange Ave Rochester (14613) ***(G-14657)***
Roethel, Ogdensburg *Also called River Rat Design* ***(G-13121)***
Roffe Accessories Inc (PA)......212 213-1440
833 Broadway Apt 4 New York (10003) ***(G-11903)***
Rogan LLC......212 680-1407
330 Bowery New York (10012) ***(G-11904)***
Rogan LLC (PA)......646 496-9339
270 Bowery 3 New York (10012) ***(G-11905)***
Roger & Sons Inc (PA)......212 226-4734
268 Bowery Frnt 6 New York (10012) ***(G-11906)***
Roger L Urban Inc (PA)......716 693-5391
954 Oliver St North Tonawanda (14120) ***(G-12992)***
Roger Latari......631 580-2422
30 Raynor Ave Ste 1 Ronkonkoma (11779) ***(G-14980)***
Roger Michael Press Inc (PA)......732 752-0800
499 Van Brunt St Ste 6b Brooklyn (11231) ***(G-2502)***
Rogers Enterprises, Rochester *Also called Dock Hardware Incorporated* ***(G-14314)***
Rogers Group Inc......212 643-9292
318 W 39th St Fl 4 New York (10018) ***(G-11907)***
Rogers Industrial Spring, Buffalo *Also called Kehr-Buffalo Wire Frame Co Inc* ***(G-3027)***
Rohlfs Stined Leaded GL Studio......914 699-4848
783 S 3rd Ave Mount Vernon (10550) ***(G-8726)***
Rohto USA Inc (HQ)......716 677-2500
707 Sterling Dr Orchard Park (14127) ***(G-13295)***
Rokon Tech LLC......718 429-0729
5223 74th St Elmhurst (11373) ***(G-4667)***
Roli Retreads Inc......631 694-7670
212 E Carmans Rd Unit A Farmingdale (11735) ***(G-5102)***
Roli Tire and Auto Repair, Farmingdale *Also called Roli Retreads Inc* ***(G-5102)***
Roli USA Inc......412 600-4840
100 5th Ave New York (10011) ***(G-11908)***
Rolite Mfg Inc......716 683-0259
10 Wendling Ct Lancaster (14086) ***(G-7340)***
Roll Lock Truss, Waddington *Also called Structural Wood Corporation* ***(G-16521)***
Rolla Daily News Plus, Pittsford *Also called Gatehouse Media MO Holdings* ***(G-13562)***
Rollers Inc......716 837-0700
2495 Main St Ste 359 Buffalo (14214) ***(G-3164)***
Rollers Unlimited, Syracuse *Also called David Fehlman* ***(G-15922)***
Rollform of Jamestown Inc......716 665-5310
181 Blackstone Ave Jamestown (14701) ***(G-7025)***
Rollhaus Seating Products Inc......718 729-9111
2109 Borden Ave Fl 4 Long Island City (11101) ***(G-7863)***
Rolling Gate Supply Corp......718 366-5258
7919 Cypress Ave Glendale (11385) ***(G-5661)***
Rolling Star Manufacturing Inc......315 896-4767
125 Liberty Ln Barneveld (13304) ***(G-616)***
Rolling Stone, New York *Also called Wenner Media LLC* ***(G-12611)***
Rolling Stone Magazine......212 484-1616
1290 Ave Of The Amer Fl 2 New York (10104) ***(G-11909)***
Rollo Mio Artisan Bakery, Maspeth *Also called Rm Bakery LLC* ***(G-8168)***
Rollson Inc......631 423-9578
10 Smugglers Cv Huntington (11743) ***(G-6678)***

ALPHABETIC

Roly Door Sales Inc............716 877-1515
5659 Herman Hill Rd Hamburg (14075) ***(G-5941)***
Roma Bakery Inc............516 825-9170
45 Railroad Ave Valley Stream (11580) ***(G-16425)***
Roma Industries LLC............212 268-0723
12 W 37th St Fl 10 New York (10018) ***(G-11910)***
Roma Ray Bakery, Valley Stream *Also called Rays Italian Bakery Inc* ***(G-16423)***
Romac Electronics Inc............516 349-7900
155 E Ames Ct Unit 1 Plainview (11803) ***(G-13632)***
Roman Malakov Diamonds Ltd............212 944-8500
1 W 47th St Frnt 5 New York (10036) ***(G-11911)***
Roman Stone Construction Co............631 667-0566
85 S 4th St Bay Shore (11706) ***(G-738)***
Romance & Co Inc............212 382-0337
2 W 47th St Ste 1111 New York (10036) ***(G-11912)***
Romantic Times Inc............718 237-1097
81 Willoughby St Ste 701 Brooklyn (11201) ***(G-2503)***
Romantic Times Magazine, Brooklyn *Also called Romantic Times Inc* ***(G-2503)***
Romar Contracting Inc............845 778-2737
630 State Route 52 Walden (12586) ***(G-16535)***
Romark Diagnostics, Tappan *Also called RJ Harvey Instrument Corp* ***(G-16083)***
Rome Fastener, New York *Also called Rings Wire Inc* ***(G-11874)***
Rome Sign & Display Co............315 336-0550
510 Erie Blvd W Rome (13440) ***(G-14833)***
Rome Specialty Company Inc............315 337-8200
501 W Embargo St Rome (13440) ***(G-14834)***
Romir Enterprises, New York *Also called Mer Gems Corp* ***(G-11226)***
Romold Inc............585 529-4440
5 Moonlanding Rd Rochester (14624) ***(G-14658)***
Rona Precision Inc............631 737-4034
142 Remington Blvd Ste 2 Ronkonkoma (11779) ***(G-14981)***
Rona Precision Mfg, Ronkonkoma *Also called Rona Precision Inc* ***(G-14981)***
Ronan Paints, Bronx *Also called T J Ronan Paint Corp* ***(G-1470)***
Ronbar Laboratories Inc............718 937-6755
5202 Van Dam St Long Island City (11101) ***(G-7864)***
Roner Inc (PA)............718 392-6020
3553 24th St Long Island City (11106) ***(G-7865)***
Roner Inc............718 392-6020
1433 31st Ave Long Island City (11106) ***(G-7866)***
Ronni Nicole Group LLC............212 764-1000
1400 Broadway Rm 2102 New York (10018) ***(G-11913)***
Roode Hoek & Co Inc............718 522-5921
55 Ferris St Brooklyn (11231) ***(G-2504)***
Roofing Consultant, Buffalo *Also called Tiedemann Waldemar Inc* ***(G-3218)***
Room At The Top Inc............718 257-0766
632 Hegeman Ave Brooklyn (11207) ***(G-2505)***
Roomactually LLC............646 388-1922
175 Varick St New York (10014) ***(G-11914)***
Roome Technologies Inc............585 229-4437
4796 Honeoye Business Par Honeoye (14471) ***(G-6524)***
Rooster Hill Vineyards, Penn Yan *Also called Hoffman & Hoffman* ***(G-13514)***
Ropack USA Inc............631 482-7777
49 Mall Dr Commack (11725) ***(G-3840)***
Rosco Inc (PA)............718 526-2601
9021 144th Pl Jamaica (11435) ***(G-6948)***
Rosco Div, Rome *Also called Rome Specialty Company Inc* ***(G-14834)***
Roscoe Brothers Inc............607 844-3750
15 Freeville Rd Dryden (13053) ***(G-4322)***
Roscoe Little Store Inc............607 498-5553
59 Stewart Ave Roscoe (12776) ***(G-15012)***
Rose Cumming, New York *Also called Dessin/Fournir Inc* ***(G-9859)***
Rose Fence Inc (PA)............516 223-0777
345 W Sunrise Hwy Freeport (11520) ***(G-5423)***
Rose Fence Inc............516 790-2308
356 Bay Ave Halesite (11743) ***(G-5906)***
Rose Fence Inc............516 223-0777
345 Sunrise Hwy Baldwin (11510) ***(G-561)***
Rose Graphics LLC............516 547-6142
109 Kean St West Babylon (11704) ***(G-16823)***
Rose Solomon Co............718 855-1788
63 Flushing Ave Unit 330 Brooklyn (11205) ***(G-2506)***
Rose Trunk Mfg Co Inc............516 766-6686
3935 Sally Ln Oceanside (11572) ***(G-13093)***
Rose, Herbert, Long Island City *Also called Rosenwach Tank Co Inc* ***(G-7867)***
Rose-Ann Division, New York *Also called Texport Fabrics Corp* ***(G-12305)***
Rosecore Division............516 504-4530
11 Grace Ave Ste 100 Great Neck (11021) ***(G-5835)***
Rosemont Press Incorporated (PA)............212 239-4770
253 Church St Apt 2 New York (10013) ***(G-11915)***
Rosemont Press Incorporated............212 239-4770
35 W Jefryn Blvd Ste A Deer Park (11729) ***(G-4201)***
Rosen Mandell & Immerman Inc............212 691-2277
121 Varick St Rm 301 New York (10013) ***(G-11916)***
Rosen Publishing Group Inc............212 777-3017
29 E 21st St Fl 2 New York (10010) ***(G-11917)***
Rosenau Beck Inc............212 279-6202
135 W 36th St Rm 10l New York (10018) ***(G-11918)***
Rosenbaum Foot, Brooklyn *Also called Newyork Pedorthic Associates* ***(G-2371)***
Rosendahl Industries Ltd Inc............718 436-2711
1449 37th St Brooklyn (11218) ***(G-2507)***
Rosenwach Group, The, Astoria *Also called Rosenwach Tank Co Inc* ***(G-455)***
Rosenwach Tank Co, Astoria *Also called Sitecraft Inc* ***(G-457)***
Rosenwach Tank Co Inc (PA)............212 972-4411
4302 Ditmars Blvd Astoria (11105) ***(G-455)***
Rosenwach Tank Co Inc............718 274-3250
4302 Ditmars Blvd Long Island City (11105) ***(G-7867)***
Rosetti Handbags and ACC (HQ)............212 273-3765
1333 Broadway Fl 9 New York (10018) ***(G-11919)***
Rosina Food Products Inc (HQ)............716 668-0123
170 French Rd Buffalo (14227) ***(G-3165)***
Rosina Holding Inc (PA)............716 668-0123
170 French Rd Buffalo (14227) ***(G-3166)***
Roslyn Bread Company Inc............516 625-1470
190 Mineola Ave Roslyn Heights (11577) ***(G-15031)***
Ross, Williamsville *Also called Simulated Surgical Systems LLC* ***(G-17253)***
Ross Communications Associates............631 393-5089
200 Broadhollow Rd # 207 Melville (11747) ***(G-8353)***
Ross Electronics Ltd............718 569-6643
12 Maple Ave Haverstraw (10927) ***(G-6240)***
Ross JC Inc............716 439-1161
6722 Lincoln Ave Lockport (14094) ***(G-7612)***
Ross L Sports Screening Inc............716 824-5350
2756 Seneca St Buffalo (14224) ***(G-3167)***
Ross Metal Fabricators Div, Hauppauge *Also called Charles Ross & Son Company* ***(G-6044)***
Ross Metal Fabricators Inc............631 586-7000
225 Marcus Blvd Deer Park (11729) ***(G-4202)***
Ross Microsystems Inc............845 918-1208
1 Tioga Ct New City (10956) ***(G-8792)***
Ross Valve Mfg............518 274-0961
75 102nd St Troy (12180) ***(G-16251)***
Ross-Ellis Ltd............212 260-9200
67 Irving Pl Valley Stream (11580) ***(G-16426)***
Rossi Tool & Dies Inc............845 267-8246
161 Route 303 Valley Cottage (10989) ***(G-16387)***
Rossiter & Schmitt Co Inc............516 937-3610
220 S Fehr Way Bay Shore (11706) ***(G-739)***
Rota File Corporation............516 496-7200
159 Lafayette Dr Syosset (11791) ***(G-15838)***
Rota Pack Inc............631 274-1037
34 Sarah Dr Ste B Farmingdale (11735) ***(G-5103)***
Rota Tool, Syosset *Also called Rota File Corporation* ***(G-15838)***
Rotation Dynamics Corporation............585 352-9023
3581 Big Ridge Rd Spencerport (14559) ***(G-15573)***
Roth Clothing Co Inc (PA)............718 384-4927
300 Penn St Brooklyn (11211) ***(G-2508)***
Roth Design & Consulting Inc............718 209-0193
132 Bogart St Brooklyn (11206) ***(G-2509)***
Roth Global Plastics Inc............315 475-0100
1 General Motors Dr Syracuse (13206) ***(G-16026)***
Roth's Metal Works, Brooklyn *Also called Roth Design & Consulting Inc* ***(G-2509)***
Rothe Welding Inc............845 246-3051
1455 Route 212 Saugerties (12477) ***(G-15193)***
Rothschild Mens Div, New York *Also called S Rothschild & Co Inc* ***(G-11947)***
Roto Salt Company Inc............315 536-3742
118 Monell St Penn Yan (14527) ***(G-13519)***
Rotork Controls Inc............585 328-1550
675 Mile Crossing Blvd Rochester (14624) ***(G-14659)***
Rotork Controls Inc (HQ)............585 328-1550
675 Mile Crossing Blvd Rochester (14624) ***(G-14660)***
Rotron Incorporated (HQ)............845 679-2401
55 Hasbrouck Ln Woodstock (12498) ***(G-17365)***
Rotron Incorporated............845 679-2401
9 Hasbrouck Ln Woodstock (12498) ***(G-17366)***
Rotronic Instrument Corp (HQ)............631 348-6844
135 Engineers Rd Ste 150 Hauppauge (11788) ***(G-6180)***
Rottkamp Tennis Inc............631 421-0040
100 Broadway Huntington Station (11746) ***(G-6720)***
Rough Draft Publishing LLC............212 741-4773
1916 Old Chelsea Sta New York (10113) ***(G-11920)***
Rough Guides US Ltd............212 414-3635
345 Hudson St Fl 4 New York (10014) ***(G-11921)***
Round Top Knit & Screening............518 622-3600
Rr 31 Round Top (12473) ***(G-15040)***
Roust USA, New York *Also called Russian Standard Vodka USA Inc* ***(G-11937)***
Rovel Manufacturing Co Inc............516 365-2752
52 Wimbledon Dr Roslyn (11576) ***(G-15023)***
Rovi Corporation............212 524-7000
18 W 18th St Fl 11 New York (10011) ***(G-11922)***
Rovi Corporation............212 824-0355
1345 Avenue Of The Americ New York (10105) ***(G-11923)***
Row, The, New York *Also called Tr Apparel LLC* ***(G-12386)***
Roxanne Assoulin, New York *Also called Maurice Max Inc* ***(G-11181)***
Roxter Lighting, Long Island City *Also called Matov Industries Inc* ***(G-7806)***
Royal Adhesives & Sealants LLC............315 451-1755
3584 Walters Rd Rsd Syracuse (13209) ***(G-16027)***
Royal Bedding Co Buffalo Inc............716 895-1414
201 James E Casey Dr Buffalo (14206) ***(G-3168)***
Royal Caribbean Bakery, Mount Vernon *Also called Royal Caribbean Jamaican Bky* ***(G-8727)***
Royal Caribbean Jamaican Bky (PA)............914 668-6868
620 S Fulton Ave Mount Vernon (10550) ***(G-8727)***

ALPHABETIC

Royal Clothing Corp...718 436-5841
1316 48th St Apt 1 Brooklyn (11219) ***(G-2510)***
Royal Copenhagen Inc (PA)...845 454-4442
63 Page Park Dr Poughkeepsie (12603) ***(G-13929)***
Royal Custom Cabinets...315 376-6042
6149 Patty St Lowville (13367) ***(G-7942)***
Royal Engraving, Brooklyn *Also called Tripi Engraving Co Inc* ***(G-2682)***
Royal Fireworks Printing Co...845 726-3333
First Ave Unionville (10988) ***(G-16302)***
Royal Home Fashions Inc (HQ)...212 689-7222
261 5th Ave Fl 25 New York (10016) ***(G-11924)***
Royal Industries Inc (PA)...718 369-3046
225 25th St Brooklyn (11232) ***(G-2511)***
Royal Jamestown Furniture Inc...716 664-5260
300 Crescent St Jamestown (14701) ***(G-7026)***
Royal Jewelry Mfg Inc (PA)...212 302-2500
825 Northern Blvd Fl 2 Great Neck (11021) ***(G-5836)***
Royal Kedem Wine, Marlboro *Also called Royal Wine Corporation* ***(G-8106)***
Royal Line LLC...800 516-7450
3351 Park Ave Wantagh (11793) ***(G-16563)***
Royal Line The, Brooklyn *Also called Royal Industries Inc* ***(G-2511)***
Royal Marble & Granite Inc...516 536-5900
3295 Royal Ave Oceanside (11572) ***(G-13094)***
Royal Media Group, New York *Also called Royal News Corp* ***(G-11926)***
Royal Metal Products Inc...518 966-4442
463 West Rd Surprise (12176) ***(G-15811)***
Royal Miracle Corp...212 921-5797
2 W 46th St Rm 9209 New York (10036) ***(G-11925)***
Royal Molds Inc...718 382-7686
1634 Marine Pkwy Brooklyn (11234) ***(G-2512)***
Royal News Corp...212 564-8972
80 Broad St Ste 1701 New York (10004) ***(G-11926)***
Royal Paint Roller Corp...516 367-4370
1 Harvard Dr Woodbury (11797) ***(G-17299)***
Royal Paint Roller Mfg, Woodbury *Also called Royal Paint Roller Corp* ***(G-17299)***
Royal Plastics Corp...718 647-7500
2840 Atlantic Ave Ste 1 Brooklyn (11207) ***(G-2513)***
Royal Press, Staten Island *Also called C & R De Santis Inc* ***(G-15653)***
Royal Press, White Plains *Also called L K Printing Corp* ***(G-17132)***
Royal Prestige Lasting Co...516 280-5148
198 Jerusalem Ave Hempstead (11550) ***(G-6286)***
Royal Products, Hauppauge *Also called Curran Manufacturing Corp* ***(G-6059)***
Royal Products, Hauppauge *Also called Curran Manufacturing Corp* ***(G-6060)***
Royal Promotion Group Inc...212 246-3780
119 W 57th St Ste 906 New York (10019) ***(G-11927)***
Royal Sweet Bakery Inc...718 567-7770
119 49th St Brooklyn (11232) ***(G-2514)***
Royal Tees Inc...845 357-9448
29 Lafayette Ave Suffern (10901) ***(G-15800)***
Royal Windows and Doors, Bay Shore *Also called Royal Windows Mfg Corp* ***(G-740)***
Royal Windows Mfg Corp...631 435-8888
1769 5th Ave Unit A Bay Shore (11706) ***(G-740)***
Royal Wine Corporation...845 236-4000
1519 Route 9w Marlboro (12542) ***(G-8106)***
Royalton Millwork & Design...716 439-4092
7526 Tonawanda Creek Rd Lockport (14094) ***(G-7613)***
Royalty Network Inc (PA)...212 967-4300
224 W 30th St Rm 1007 New York (10001) ***(G-11928)***
Royce Associates A Ltd Partnr...516 367-6298
366 N Broadway Ste 400 Jericho (11753) ***(G-7083)***
Rozal Industries Inc...631 420-4277
151 Marine St Farmingdale (11735) ***(G-5104)***
Rp55 Inc...212 840-4035
230 W 39th St Fl 7 New York (10018) ***(G-11929)***
Rpb Distributors LLC...914 244-3600
45 Kensico Dr Mount Kisco (10549) ***(G-8645)***
Rpc Inc...347 873-3935
165 Emporia Ave Elmont (11003) ***(G-4728)***
RPC Car Service, Elmont *Also called Rpc Inc* ***(G-4728)***
RPC Photonics Inc...585 272-2840
330 Clay Rd Rochester (14623) ***(G-14661)***
Rpf Associates Inc...631 462-7446
2155 Jericho Tpke Ste A Commack (11725) ***(G-3841)***
Rpg, New York *Also called Royal Promotion Group Inc* ***(G-11927)***
RPM Displays, Auburn *Also called R P M Industries Inc* ***(G-515)***
RPS Holdings Inc...607 257-7778
2415 N Triphammer Rd # 2 Ithaca (14850) ***(G-6874)***
RR Donnelley & Sons Company...716 763-2613
112 Winchester Rd Lakewood (14750) ***(G-7294)***
RR Donnelley & Sons Company...716 773-0647
300 Lang Blvd Grand Island (14072) ***(G-5766)***
RR Donnelley & Sons Company...518 438-9722
4 Executive Park Dr Ste 2 Albany (12203) ***(G-129)***
RR Donnelley & Sons Company...646 755-8125
250 W 26th St Rm 402 New York (10001) ***(G-11930)***
RR Donnelley & Sons Company...716 773-0300
300 Lang Blvd Grand Island (14072) ***(G-5767)***
RR Donnelley Financial, Inc., New York *Also called Donnelley Financial LLC* ***(G-9906)***
Rs Automation...585 589-0199
4015 Oak Orchard Rd Albion (14411) ***(G-169)***
RS Precision Industries Inc...631 420-0424
295 Adams Blvd Farmingdale (11735) ***(G-5105)***
Rsb Associates Inc...518 281-5067
488 Picard Rd Altamont (12009) ***(G-212)***
Rsl Media LLC...212 307-6760
1001 Ave Of The Ave Fl 11 New York (10018) ***(G-11931)***
RSM Electron Power Inc (PA)...631 586-7600
221 W Industry Ct Deer Park (11729) ***(G-4203)***
RSM Electron Power Inc...631 586-7600
100 Engineers Rd Hauppauge (11788) ***(G-6181)***
Rsquared Ny Inc...631 521-8700
100 Heartland Blvd Edgewood (11717) ***(G-4609)***
RSR, Middletown *Also called Eco-Bat America LLC* ***(G-8439)***
Rt Machined Specialties...716 731-2055
2221 Niagara Falls Blvd Niagara Falls (14304) ***(G-12868)***
Rt Solutions LLC...585 245-3456
80 Linden Oaks Ste 210 Rochester (14625) ***(G-14662)***
RTD Manufacturing Inc...315 337-3151
6273 State Route 233 Rome (13440) ***(G-14835)***
Rtr Bag & Co Ltd...212 620-0011
27 W 20th St New York (10011) ***(G-11932)***
Rubber Stamp X Press...631 423-1322
7 Bradford Pl Huntington Station (11747) ***(G-6721)***
Rubber Stamps Inc...212 675-1180
174 Herricks Rd Mineola (11501) ***(G-8535)***
Rubberform Recycled Pdts LLC...716 478-0404
75 Michigan St Lockport (14094) ***(G-7614)***
Rubicon Industries Corp (PA)...718 434-4700
848 E 43rd St Brooklyn (11210) ***(G-2515)***
Rubie's Distribution Center, Bay Shore *Also called Rubies Costume Company Inc* ***(G-742)***
Rubies Costume Company Inc (PA)...718 846-1008
12008 Jamaica Ave Richmond Hill (11418) ***(G-14081)***
Rubies Costume Company Inc...631 777-3300
158 Candlewood Rd Bay Shore (11706) ***(G-741)***
Rubies Costume Company Inc...718 441-0834
12017 Jamaica Ave Richmond Hill (11418) ***(G-14082)***
Rubies Costume Company Inc...631 951-3688
1 Holloween Hwy Bay Shore (11706) ***(G-742)***
Rubies Costume Company Inc...516 326-1500
1770 Walt Whitman Rd Melville (11747) ***(G-8354)***
Rubies Costume Company Inc...718 846-1008
1 Rubie Plz Richmond Hill (11418) ***(G-14083)***
Rubies Masquerade Company LLC (PA)...718 846-1008
1 Rubie Plz Richmond Hill (11418) ***(G-14084)***
Rubinstein Jewelry Mfg Co...718 784-8650
3100 47th Ave Long Island City (11101) ***(G-7868)***
Ruby Engineering LLC...646 391-4600
354 Sackett St Brooklyn (11231) ***(G-2516)***
Ruby Newco LLC...212 852-7000
1211 Ave Of The Americas New York (10036) ***(G-11933)***
Ruby Road, New York *Also called Hearts of Palm LLC* ***(G-10451)***
Ruby Road, New York *Also called Hearts of Palm LLC* ***(G-10452)***
Ruckel Manufacturing Co, Brooklyn *Also called EY Industries Inc* ***(G-1947)***
Rudolf Friedman Inc...212 869-5070
42 W 48th St Ste 1102 New York (10036) ***(G-11934)***
Rudy Stempel & Family Sawmill...518 872-0431
73 Stemple Rd East Berne (12059) ***(G-4381)***
Ruga Grinding & Mfg Corp...631 924-5067
84 Horseblock Rd Unit A Yaphank (11980) ***(G-17399)***
Rugby Magazine, White Plains *Also called American Intl Media LLC* ***(G-17077)***
Ruggeri Manufacturing, Rochester *Also called Van Thomas Inc* ***(G-14751)***
Ruhle Companies Inc...914 287-4000
99 Wall St Valhalla (10595) ***(G-16372)***
Rui Xing International Trdg Co...516 298-2667
89 Jerusalem Ave Hicksville (11801) ***(G-6391)***
Ruleville Manufacturing Co Inc (PA)...212 695-1620
469 Fashion Ave Fl 10 New York (10018) ***(G-11935)***
Rumsey Corp...914 751-3640
15 Rumsey Rd Yonkers (10705) ***(G-17482)***
Rumson Acquisition LLC...718 349-4300
1385 Broadway Fl 9 New York (10018) ***(G-11936)***
Run It Systems, New York *Also called Marcus Goldman Inc* ***(G-11147)***
Rural Hill Sand and Grav Corp...315 846-5212
10262 County Route 79 Woodville (13650) ***(G-17367)***
Rus Industries Inc...716 284-7828
3255 Lockport Rd Niagara Falls (14305) ***(G-12869)***
Rush Gold Manufacturing Ltd...516 781-3155
2400 Merrick Rd Bellmore (11710) ***(G-820)***
Rush Gravel Corp...585 533-1740
130 Kavanaugh Rd Honeoye Falls (14472) ***(G-6536)***
Rush Machinery Inc...585 554-3070
4761 State Route 364 Rushville (14544) ***(G-15053)***
Russco Metal Spinning Co Inc...516 872-6055
3064 Lawson Blvd Oceanside (11572) ***(G-13095)***
Russell Bass...607 637-5253
59 Saw Mill Rd Hancock (13783) ***(G-5967)***
Russell Bass & Son Lumber, Hancock *Also called Russell Bass* ***(G-5967)***
Russell Industries Inc...516 536-5000
40 Horton Ave Lynbrook (11563) ***(G-7960)***
Russell Plastics Tech Co Inc...631 963-8602
521 W Hoffman Ave Lindenhurst (11757) ***(G-7481)***
Russian Bazaar, Brooklyn *Also called Danet Inc* ***(G-1838)***

ALPHABETIC

ALPHABETIC SECTION S1 Biopharma Inc

Russian Daily, Brooklyn *Also called Novoye Rsskoye Slovo Pubg Corp* **(G-2378)**
Russian Mix Inc 347 385-7198
2225 Benson Ave Apt 74 Brooklyn (11214) **(G-2517)**
Russian Standard Vodka USA Inc 212 679-1894
232 Madison Ave Fl 16 New York (10016) **(G-11937)**
Russin Lumber Corp 845 457-4000
75 Pierces Rd Newburgh (12550) **(G-12778)**
Russkaya Reklama Inc 718 769-3000
2699 Coney Island Ave Brooklyn (11235) **(G-2518)**
Russo's Gluten Free Gourmet, Shirley *Also called Anthony Gigi Inc* **(G-15412)**
Rutcarele Inc 347 830-5353
3449 110th St Corona (11368) **(G-4005)**
Ruthy's Bakery & Cafe, New York *Also called Ruthys Cheesecake Rugelach Bky* **(G-11938)**
Ruthys Cheesecake Rugelach Bky 212 463-8800
300 E 54th St Apt 31b New York (10022) **(G-11938)**
Rv Printing 631 567-8658
39 Portside Dr Holbrook (11741) **(G-6469)**
Rvc Enterprises LLC (PA) 212 391-4600
1384 Broadway Fl 17 New York (10018) **(G-11939)**
Rw Manufacturing Company, East Rochester *Also called Richards & West Inc* **(G-4466)**
Rwb Controls Inc 716 897-4341
471 Connecticut St Buffalo (14213) **(G-3169)**
RWS Manufacturing Inc 518 361-1657
22 Ferguson Ln Queensbury (12804) **(G-14009)**
Ry-Gan Printing Inc 585 482-7770
111 Humboldt St Rochester (14609) **(G-14663)**
Ry-Lecia Inc 631 244-0011
1535 Locust Ave Bohemia (11716) **(G-1127)**
Ryan Gems Inc 212 697-0149
20 E 46th St Rm 200 New York (10017) **(G-11940)**
Ryan Printing, Hilton *Also called William J Ryan* **(G-6421)**
Ryan Printing Inc 845 535-3235
300 Corporate Dr Ste 6 Blauvelt (10913) **(G-974)**
Ryba General Merchandise Inc 718 522-2028
63 Flushing Ave Unit 332 Brooklyn (11205) **(G-2519)**
Rye Record 914 713-3213
14 Elm Pl Ste 200 Rye (10580) **(G-15067)**
Ryers Creek Corp 607 523-6617
1330 Mill Dr Corning (14830) **(G-3980)**
Ryland Peters & Small Inc 646 791-5410
341 E 116th St New York (10029) **(G-11941)**
Rynone Manufacturing Corp 607 565-8187
229 Howard St Waverly (14892) **(G-16706)**
Rynone Packaging Corp 607 565-8173
184 State Route 17c Waverly (14892) **(G-16707)**
S & B Fashion Inc 718 482-1386
4315 Queens St Ste B Long Island City (11101) **(G-7869)**
S & B Machine Works Inc 516 997-2666
111 New York Ave Westbury (11590) **(G-17025)**
S & C Bridals LLC (PA) 212 789-7000
1407 Broadway Fl 41 New York (10018) **(G-11942)**
S & D Welding Corp 631 454-0383
229 Edison Ave Ste A West Babylon (11704) **(G-16824)**
S & H Enterprises Inc 888 323-8755
10b Holden Ave Queensbury (12804) **(G-14010)**
S & H Machine Company Inc 716 834-1194
83 Clyde Ave Buffalo (14215) **(G-3170)**
S & H Uniform Corp 914 937-6800
1 Aqueduct Rd White Plains (10606) **(G-17164)**
S & J Trading Inc 718 347-1323
8030 263rd St Floral Park (11004) **(G-5209)**
S & K Counter Tops Inc 716 662-7986
4708 Duerr Rd Orchard Park (14127) **(G-13296)**
S & L Aerospace Metals LLC 718 326-1821
12012 28th Ave Flushing (11354) **(G-5289)**
S & M Ring Corp 212 382-0900
1080 Channel Dr Hewlett (11557) **(G-6312)**
S & R Tool Inc 585 346-2029
6066 Stone Hill Rd Lakeville (14480) **(G-7285)**
S & S Enterprises, Jamestown *Also called Genco John* **(G-6994)**
S & S Fashions Inc 718 328-0001
941 Longfellow Ave Bronx (10474) **(G-1443)**
S & S Graphics Inc 914 668-4230
521 E 3rd St Mount Vernon (10553) **(G-8728)**
S & S Machinery Corp (PA) 718 492-7400
140 53rd St Brooklyn (11232) **(G-2520)**
S & S Machinery Corp 718 492-7400
132 54th St Brooklyn (11220) **(G-2521)**
S & S Manufacturing Co Inc (PA) 212 444-6000
1375 Broadway Fl 2 New York (10018) **(G-11943)**
S & S Prtg Die-Cutting Co Inc 718 388-8990
488 Morgan Ave Ste A Brooklyn (11222) **(G-2522)**
S & S Soap Co Inc 718 585-2900
815 E 135th St Bronx (10454) **(G-1444)**
S & T Knitting Co Inc (PA) 607 722-7558
1010 Conklin Rd Conklin (13748) **(G-3874)**
S & T Machine, Brooklyn *Also called Fjs Industries Inc* **(G-1981)**
S & T Machine Inc 718 272-2484
970 E 92nd St Fl 1 Brooklyn (11236) **(G-2523)**
S & V Custom Furniture Mfg 516 746-8299
75 Windsor Ave Unit E Mineola (11501) **(G-8536)**
S & V Knits Inc 631 752-1595
117 Marine St Farmingdale (11735) **(G-5106)**
S & V Restaurant Eqp Mfrs Inc 718 220-1140
4320 Park Ave Bronx (10457) **(G-1445)**
S & W Knitting Mills Inc 718 237-2416
703 Bedford Ave Fl 3 Brooklyn (11206) **(G-2524)**
S & W Metal Trading Corp 212 719-5070
36 W 47th St Ste 1606 New York (10036) **(G-11944)**
S A Baxter LLC (PA) 845 469-7995
37 Elkay Dr Ste 33 Chester (10918) **(G-3614)**
S A S Industries Inc 631 727-1441
939 Wding River Manor Rd Manorville (11949) **(G-8080)**
S A W, Kingston *Also called Spiegel Woodworks Inc* **(G-7211)**
S and G Imaging, Walworth *Also called Software & General Services Co* **(G-16552)**
S B B, East Syracuse *Also called Sullivan Bazinet Bongio Inc* **(G-4568)**
S B Manufacturing LLC 845 352-3700
161 Route 59 Monsey (10952) **(G-8579)**
S B Whistler & Sons Inc 585 798-3000
11023 W Center Street Ext Medina (14103) **(G-8280)**
S Broome and Co Inc 718 663-6800
3300 47th Ave Fl 1 Long Island City (11101) **(G-7870)**
S C T 585 467-7740
3000 E Ridge Rd Rochester (14622) **(G-14664)**
S D C, Armonk *Also called Surgical Design Corp* **(G-421)**
S D I, Binghamton *Also called Sensor & Decontamination Inc* **(G-950)**
S D S of Long Island, Bay Shore *Also called M F L B Inc* **(G-714)**
S D Warren Company 914 696-5544
925 Westchester Ave # 115 White Plains (10604) **(G-17165)**
S D Z Metal Spinning Stamping 718 778-3600
1807 Pacific St Brooklyn (11233) **(G-2525)**
S Donadic Woodworking Inc 718 361-9888
4525 39th St Sunnyside (11104) **(G-15809)**
S E A Supls, Plainview *Also called S E A Supplies Ltd* **(G-13633)**
S E A Supplies Ltd 516 694-6677
1670 Old Country Rd # 104 Plainview (11803) **(G-13633)**
S G I 917 386-0385
40 E 52nd St Frnt A New York (10022) **(G-11945)**
S G New York LLC 631 698-8400
1 Rodeo Dr Edgewood (11717) **(G-4610)**
S G New York LLC (PA) 631 665-4000
2950 Vtrans Mem Hwy Ste 1 Bohemia (11716) **(G-1128)**
S Hellerman Inc (PA) 718 622-2995
242 Green St Brooklyn (11222) **(G-2526)**
S I Communications Inc 914 725-2500
8 Harwood Ct Scarsdale (10583) **(G-15222)**
S J B Fabrication 716 895-0281
430 Kennedy Rd Buffalo (14227) **(G-3171)**
S J McCullagh Inc (PA) 716 856-3473
245 Swan St Buffalo (14204) **(G-3172)**
S K Circuits Inc (PA) 703 376-8718
483 Foxwood Ter Oneida (13421) **(G-13166)**
S Kashi & Sons Inc 212 869-9393
175 Great Neck Rd Ste 204 Great Neck (11021) **(G-5837)**
S L C Industries Incorporated 607 775-2299
63 Barlow Rd Binghamton (13904) **(G-948)**
S L Fashions, New York *Also called Lou Sally Fashions Corp* **(G-11047)**
S M Frank & Company Inc 914 739-3100
1073 State Route 94 Ste 7 New Windsor (12553) **(G-8951)**
S M I, New York *Also called Specialty Minerals Inc* **(G-12152)**
S M P, Pearl River *Also called Strategic Mktg Promotions Inc* **(G-13467)**
S M S C Inc 315 942-4394
101 Water St Boonville (13309) **(G-1169)**
S P Books Inc 212 431-5011
99 Spring St Fl 3 New York (10012) **(G-11946)**
S P Industries Inc 845 255-5000
815 Rte 208 Gardiner (12525) **(G-5550)**
S R & R Industries Inc 845 692-8329
45 Enterprise Pl Middletown (10941) **(G-8461)**
S R Instruments Inc (PA) 716 693-5977
600 Young St Tonawanda (14150) **(G-16197)**
S R S Inc 732 548-6630
5920 56th Ave Maspeth (11378) **(G-8170)**
S R Sloan Inc (PA) 315 736-7730
8111 Halsey Rd Whitesboro (13492) **(G-17195)**
S Rothschild & Co Inc (PA) 212 354-8550
1407 Broadway Fl 10 New York (10018) **(G-11947)**
S S Precision Gear & Instr 718 457-7474
4512 104th St Corona (11368) **(G-4006)**
S Scharf Inc 516 541-9552
278 N Richmond Ave Massapequa (11758) **(G-8182)**
S T J Orthotic Svces, Lindenhurst *Also called Stj Orthotic Services Inc* **(G-7484)**
S Z Design & Prints, Monsey *Also called Sz - Design & Print Inc* **(G-8583)**
S&B Alternative Fuels Inc 631 585-6637
1232 Stony Brook Rd Lake Grove (11755) **(G-7265)**
S&D Welding, West Babylon *Also called S & D Welding Corp* **(G-16824)**
S&G Optical, Long Island City *Also called 21st Century Optics Inc* **(G-7643)**
S/N Precision Enterprises Inc 518 283-8002
145 Jordan Rd Ste 1 Troy (12180) **(G-16252)**
S1 Biopharma Inc 201 839-0941
7 World Trade Ctr 250g New York (10007) **(G-11948)**

ALPHABETIC

S2 Sportswear Inc 347 335-0713
4100 1st Ave Ste 5n Brooklyn (11232) ***(G-2527)***
S3j Electronics LLC 716 206-1309
2000 Commerce Pkwy Lancaster (14086) ***(G-7341)***
SA Day Buffalo Flux Facility, Buffalo *Also called Johnson Manufacturing Company **(G-3021)***
Saab Defense and SEC USA LLC 315 445-5009
5717 Enterprise Pkwy East Syracuse (13057) ***(G-4560)***
Saab Sensis Corporation 315 445-0550
5717 Enterprise Pkwy East Syracuse (13057) ***(G-4561)***
Saad Collection Inc (PA) 212 937-0341
1165 Broadway Ste 305 New York (10001) ***(G-11949)***
Saakshi Inc 315 475-3988
851 N Salina St Syracuse (13208) ***(G-16028)***
Sabbsons International Inc 718 360-1947
474 50th St Brooklyn (11220) ***(G-2528)***
Saber Awards, New York *Also called Holmes Group The Inc **(G-10500)***
Sabic Innovative Plas US LLC 518 475-5011
1 Noryl Ave Selkirk (12158) ***(G-15358)***
Sabic Innovative Plastics 713 448-7474
1 Gail Ct East Greenbush (12061) ***(G-4404)***
Sabin Metal Corporation (PA) 631 329-1695
300 Pantigo Pl Ste 102 East Hampton (11937) ***(G-4415)***
Sabin Metal Corporation 585 538-2194
1647 Wheatland Center Rd Scottsville (14546) ***(G-15339)***
Sabin Robbins, New York *Also called Eagles Nest Holdings LLC **(G-9959)***
Sabin Robbins Paper Company 513 874-5270
455 E 86th St Apt 5e New York (10028) ***(G-11950)***
Sabon Management LLC 212 982-0968
123 Prince St Frnt A New York (10012) ***(G-11951)***
Sabra Dental Products 914 945-0836
24 Quail Hollow Rd Ossining (10562) ***(G-13328)***
Sabra Dipping Company LLC (HQ) 914 372-3900
777 Westchester Ave Fl 3 White Plains (10604) ***(G-17166)***
Sabra Dipping Company LLC 516 249-0151
535 Smith St Farmingdale (11735) ***(G-5107)***
Sabre Energy Services LLC 518 514-1572
1891 New Scotland Rd Slingerlands (12159) ***(G-15478)***
Sabre Enterprises Inc 315 430-3127
1813 Lemoyne Ave Syracuse (13208) ***(G-16029)***
Saccomize Inc 818 287-3000
1554 Stillwell Ave Bronx (10461) ***(G-1446)***
Sacks and Company New York (PA) 212 741-1000
423 W 14th St Ste 429-3f New York (10014) ***(G-11952)***
Sadowsky Guitars Ltd 718 433-1990
2107 41st Ave Fl 4 Long Island City (11101) ***(G-7871)***
Saes Memry, New Hartford *Also called Saes Smart Materials Inc **(G-8810)***
Saes Smart Materials Inc 315 266-2026
4355 Middle Settlement Rd New Hartford (13413) ***(G-8810)***
Safavieh Inc 516 945-1900
40 Harbor Park Dr Port Washington (11050) ***(G-13860)***
Safe Circuits Inc 631 586-3682
15 Shoreham Dr W Dix Hills (11746) ***(G-4297)***
Safe Flight Instrument Corp 914 220-1125
20 New King St White Plains (10604) ***(G-17167)***
Safe Passage International Inc 585 292-4910
333 Metro Park Ste F204 Rochester (14623) ***(G-14665)***
Safe Skies LLC (PA) 888 632-5027
954 3rd Ave Ste 504 New York (10022) ***(G-11953)***
Safe-Dent Enterprises LLC 845 362-0141
4 Orchard Hill Dr Monsey (10952) ***(G-8580)***
Safeguard Inc 631 929-3273
578 Sound Ave Wading River (11792) ***(G-16525)***
Safespan Platform Systems Inc 716 694-1100
237 Fillmore Ave Tonawanda (14150) ***(G-16198)***
Safespan Platform Systems Inc (PA) 716 694-3332
252 Fillmore Ave Tonawanda (14150) ***(G-16199)***
Safetec of America Inc 716 895-1822
887 Kensington Ave Buffalo (14215) ***(G-3173)***
Safety-Kleen Systems Inc 716 855-2212
60 Katherine St Buffalo (14210) ***(G-3174)***
Safeworks LLC 800 696-5577
3030 60th St Ste 1 Woodside (11377) ***(G-17352)***
Safina Center 808 888-9440
118 Administration Stony Brook (11794) ***(G-15770)***
Sag Harbor, New York *Also called Life Style Design Group **(G-10987)***
Sag Harbor Express 631 725-1700
35 Main St Sag Harbor (11963) ***(G-15079)***
Sag Harbor Industries Inc (PA) 631 725-0440
1668 Bhmpton Sag Hbr Tpke Sag Harbor (11963) ***(G-15080)***
Saga International Recycl LLC 718 621-5900
6623 13th Ave Brooklyn (11219) ***(G-2529)***
Sage Knitwear Inc 718 628-7902
103 Jersey St Unit D West Babylon (11704) ***(G-16825)***
Sagelife Parenting LLC 315 299-5713
235 Harrison St Ste 2 Syracuse (13202) ***(G-16030)***
Sagemylife, Syracuse *Also called Sagelife Parenting LLC **(G-16030)***
Sahadi Fine Foods Inc 718 369-0100
4215 1st Ave Brooklyn (11232) ***(G-2530)***
Sahlen Packing Company Inc 716 852-8677
318 Howard St Buffalo (14206) ***(G-3175)***
Saint Gobain Grains & Powders 716 731-8200
6600 Walmore Rd Niagara Falls (14304) ***(G-12870)***
Saint Honore Pastry Shop Inc 516 767-2555
993 Port Washington Blvd Port Washington (11050) ***(G-13861)***
Saint Laurie Ltd 212 643-1916
22 W 32nd St Fl 5 New York (10001) ***(G-11954)***
Saint Martins Press, New York *Also called Bedford Freeman & Worth **(G-9343)***
Saint-Gbain Advnced Crmics LLC 716 691-2000
168 Creekside Dr Amherst (14228) ***(G-259)***
Saint-Gbain Advnced Crmics LLC (HQ) 716 278-6066
23 Acheson Dr Niagara Falls (14303) ***(G-12871)***
Saint-Gobain Abrasives Inc 518 266-2200
2600 10th Ave Watervliet (12189) ***(G-16688)***
Saint-Gobain Adfors Amer Inc (HQ) 716 775-3900
1795 Baseline Rd Grand Island (14072) ***(G-5768)***
Saint-Gobain Adfors Amer Inc 585 589-4401
14770 East Ave Albion (14411) ***(G-170)***
Saint-Gobain Dynamics Inc 716 278-6007
23 Acheson Dr Niagara Falls (14303) ***(G-12872)***
Saint-Gobain Performance Plas, Poestenkill *Also called Canton Bio-Medical Inc **(G-13722)***
Saint-Gobain Prfmce Plas Corp 518 642-2200
1 Sealants Park Granville (12832) ***(G-5781)***
Saint-Gobain Prfmce Plas Corp 518 686-7301
14 Mccaffrey St Hoosick Falls (12090) ***(G-6544)***
Saint-Gobain Prfmce Plas Corp 518 283-5963
11 Sicho Rd Poestenkill (12140) ***(G-13725)***
Saint-Gobain Prfmce Plas Corp 518 686-7301
1 Liberty St Hoosick Falls (12090) ***(G-6545)***
Saint-Gobain Strl Ceramics 716 278-6233
23 Acheson Dr Niagara Falls (14303) ***(G-12873)***
Saint-Gobain-Paris France, Grand Island *Also called Saint-Gobain Adfors Amer Inc **(G-5768)***
Sakonnet Technology LLC 212 849-9267
11 E 44th St Fl 1000 New York (10017) ***(G-11955)***
Sal MA Instrument Corp 631 242-2227
2 Saxwood St Ste F Deer Park (11729) ***(G-4204)***
Salamanca Daily Reporter, Salamanca *Also called Sun-Times Media Group Inc **(G-15110)***
Salamanca Lumber Company Inc 716 945-4810
59 Rochester St Salamanca (14779) ***(G-15104)***
Salamanca Penny Saver, Salamanca *Also called Salamanca Press Penny Saver **(G-15105)***
Salamanca Press Penny Saver 716 945-1500
36 River St Salamanca (14779) ***(G-15105)***
Salarinos Italian Foods Inc 315 697-9766
110 James St Canastota (13032) ***(G-3372)***
Sale 121 Corp 240 855-8988
1324 Lexington Ave # 111 New York (10128) ***(G-11956)***
Salentica Systems Inc 212 672-1777
245 Park Ave Fl 39 New York (10167) ***(G-11957)***
Salerno Plastic Film (HQ) 518 563-3636
14 Gus Lapham Ln Plattsburgh (12901) ***(G-13695)***
Sales & Marketing Office, Syracuse *Also called Monaghan Medical Corporation **(G-15993)***
Sales Department, Floral Park *Also called Allomatic Products Company **(G-5192)***
Sales Office, Northport *Also called Cypress Semiconductor Corp **(G-13010)***
Salisbury Sportswear Inc 516 221-9519
2523 Marine Pl Bellmore (11710) ***(G-821)***
Salko Kitchens Inc 845 565-4420
256 Walsh Ave New Windsor (12553) ***(G-8952)***
Sally Beauty Supply LLC 716 831-3286
310 Main St Amherst (14226) ***(G-260)***
Sally Sherman Foods, Mount Vernon *Also called UFS Industries Inc **(G-8744)***
Salmco Jewelry Corp (PA) 212 695-8792
22 W 32nd St Fl 16 New York (10001) ***(G-11958)***
Salmon Crek Cabinetry Inc 315 589-5419
6687 Salmon Creek Rd Williamson (14589) ***(G-17225)***
Salmon River News, Mexico *Also called Mexico Independent Inc **(G-8396)***
Salonclick LLC 718 643-6793
117 Crosby St New York (10012) ***(G-11959)***
Salsburg Dimensional Stone 631 653-6790
18 Pine St Brookhaven (11719) ***(G-1510)***
Salty Road Inc 347 673-3925
190 Bedford Ave 404 Brooklyn (11249) ***(G-2531)***
Salutem Group LLC 347 620-2640
44 Wall St Fl 12 New York (10005) ***(G-11960)***
Salvador Colletti Blank 718 217-6725
25141 Van Zandt Ave Douglaston (11362) ***(G-4310)***
Salvin Company, Kingston *Also called Vincent Conigliaro **(G-7224)***
Sam A Lupo & Sons Inc (PA) 607 748-1141
1219 Campville Rd Endicott (13760) ***(G-4828)***
Sam Bonk Uniform, Bronx *Also called Bonk Sam Unforms Civilian Cap **(G-1286)***
Sam Hee International Inc 212 594-7815
213 W 35th St Ste 503 New York (10001) ***(G-11961)***
Sam NY, New York *Also called Andrew M Schwartz LLC **(G-9155)***
Samaki Inc 845 858-1012
62 Jersey Ave Port Jervis (12771) ***(G-13791)***
Samco LLC 518 725-4705
308 W Main St Johnstown (12095) ***(G-7125)***
Samco Scientific Corporation 800 522-3359
75 Panorama Creek Dr Rochester (14625) ***(G-14666)***
Sammba Printing Inc 516 944-4449
437 Port Washington Blvd Port Washington (11050) ***(G-13862)***
Sampla Belting North Amer LLC 716 667-7450
61 N Gates Ave Lackawanna (14218) ***(G-7249)***
Sample News Group LLC 315 343-3800
140 W 1st St Oswego (13126) ***(G-13340)***

ALPHABETIC

Sampo Inc 315 896-2606
119 Remsen Rd Barneveld (13304) ***(G-617)***
Sampsons Prsthtic Orthotic Lab, Schenectady *Also called Sampsons Prsthtic Orthotic Lab* ***(G-15291)***
Sampsons Prsthtic Orthotic Lab 518 374-6011
1737 State St Schenectady (12304) ***(G-15291)***
Samscreen Inc 607 722-3979
216 Broome Corporate Pkwy Conklin (13748) ***(G-3875)***
Samson Technologies Corp (HQ) 631 784-2200
45 Gilpin Ave Ste 100 Hauppauge (11788) ***(G-6182)***
Samuel Aaron Inc (HQ) 718 392-5454
115 S Macquesten Pkwy Mount Vernon (10550) ***(G-8729)***
Samuel Aaron International, Mount Vernon *Also called Samuel Aaron Inc* ***(G-8729)***
Samuel B Collection Inc 516 466-1826
98 Cuttermill Rd Great Neck (11021) ***(G-5838)***
Samuel Broome Uniform ACC, Long Island City *Also called S Broome and Co Inc* ***(G-7870)***
Samuel French Inc (PA) 212 206-8990
235 Park Ave S Fl 5 New York (10003) ***(G-11962)***
Samuel Schulman Furs Inc 212 736-5550
150 W 30th St Fl 13 New York (10001) ***(G-11963)***
San Jae Educational Resou 845 364-5458
9 Chamberlain Ct Pomona (10970) ***(G-13733)***
San Signs & Awnings, Yonkers *Also called M Santoliquido Corp* ***(G-17463)***
Sanctuary Brands LLC (PA) 212 704-4014
70 W 40th St Fl 5 New York (10018) ***(G-11964)***
Sand Hill Industries Inc 518 885-7991
12 Grove St Ballston Spa (12020) ***(G-608)***
Sandbox Brands Inc 212 647-8877
26 W 17th St Lbby New York (10011) ***(G-11965)***
Sandford Blvd Donuts Inc 914 663-7708
440 E Sandford Blvd Mount Vernon (10550) ***(G-8730)***
Sandle Custom Bearing Corp 585 593-7000
1110 State Route 19 Wellsville (14895) ***(G-16757)***
Sandow Media LLC 646 805-0200
1271 Ave Of The Ave Fl 17 New York (10020) ***(G-11966)***
Sandstone Technologies Corp (PA) 585 785-5537
2117 Buffalo Rd 245 Rochester (14624) ***(G-14667)***
Sandstone Technologies Corp 585 785-5537
2117 Buffalo Rd Unit 245 Rochester (14624) ***(G-14668)***
Sandvoss Farms LLC 585 297-7044
10198 East Rd East Bethany (14054) ***(G-4383)***
Sandy Dalal Ltd 212 532-5822
220 Central Park S 10f New York (10019) ***(G-11967)***
Sandy Duftler Designs Ltd 516 379-3084
775 Brooklyn Ave Ste 105 North Baldwin (11510) ***(G-12908)***
Sandy Littman Inc 845 562-1112
420 N Montgomery St Newburgh (12550) ***(G-12779)***
Sandys Bumper Mart Inc 315 472-8149
120 Wall St Syracuse (13204) ***(G-16031)***
Sandys Deli Inc 518 297-6951
90 Montgomery St Rouses Point (12979) ***(G-15044)***
Sanford Printing Inc 718 461-1202
13335 41st Rd Flushing (11355) ***(G-5290)***
Sanford Stone LLC 607 467-1313
185 Latham Rd Deposit (13754) ***(G-4279)***
Sangster Foods Inc 212 993-9129
225 Parkside Ave Apt 3p Brooklyn (11226) ***(G-2532)***
Sanjay Pallets Inc 347 590-2485
424 Coster St Bronx (10474) ***(G-1447)***
Sanmina Corporation 607 689-5000
1200 Taylor Rd Owego (13827) ***(G-13359)***
Sanoy Inc 212 695-6384
19 W 36th St Fl 11 New York (10018) ***(G-11968)***
Santa Fe Manufacturing Corp 631 234-0100
225 Engineers Rd Hauppauge (11788) ***(G-6183)***
Santee Print Works (PA) 212 997-1570
58 W 40th St Fl 11 New York (10018) ***(G-11969)***
Santoro Signs Inc 716 895-8875
3180 Genesee St Ste 1 Buffalo (14225) ***(G-3176)***
Sanzdranz LLC (PA) 518 894-8625
83 Dumbarton Dr Delmar (12054) ***(G-4246)***
Sanzdranz LLC 518 894-8625
388 Broadway Schenectady (12305) ***(G-15292)***
Sapienza Bake Shop, Elmont *Also called Sapienza Pastry Inc* ***(G-4729)***
Sapienza Pastry Inc 516 352-5232
1376 Hempstead Tpke Elmont (11003) ***(G-4729)***
Sapphire Systems Inc (PA) 212 905-0100
405 Lexington Ave Fl 49 New York (10174) ***(G-11970)***
Saptalis Pharmaceuticals LLC 631 231-2751
45 Davids Dr Hauppauge (11788) ***(G-6184)***
Saputo Dairy Foods Usa LLC 607 746-2141
40236 State Highway 10 Delhi (13753) ***(G-4242)***
Sara Beth Division, New York *Also called Carole Hchman Design Group Inc* ***(G-9533)***
Sara Lee Courtaulds USA, New York *Also called Courtaulds Textiles Ltd* ***(G-9737)***
Sarabeth's Bakery, Bronx *Also called Sbk Preserves Inc* ***(G-1448)***
Saraga Industries Corp 631 842-4049
690 Albany Ave Unit D Amityville (11701) ***(G-324)***
Sarar Usa Inc 845 928-8874
873 Grapevine Ct Central Valley (10917) ***(G-3526)***
Saratoga Horseworks Ltd 518 843-6756
57 Edson St Amsterdam (12010) ***(G-368)***
Saratoga Lighting Holdings LLC (PA) 212 906-7800
535 Madison Ave Fl 4 New York (10022) ***(G-11971)***
Saratoga Pharmaceuticals Inc 518 894-1875
705 Route 146a Clifton Park (12065) ***(G-3706)***
Saratoga Spring Water Company 518 584-6363
11 Geyser Rd Saratoga Springs (12866) ***(G-15171)***
Saratoga Trunk and Furniture 518 463-3252
5 Macaffer Dr Albany (12204) ***(G-130)***
Saratogian USA Today, Saratoga Springs *Also called Journal Register Company* ***(G-15161)***
Saraval Industries 516 768-9033
348 N Midland Ave Nyack (10960) ***(G-13053)***
Sares International Inc 718 366-8412
95 Evergreen Ave Ste 5 Brooklyn (11206) ***(G-2533)***
Sargent Manufacturing Inc 212 722-7000
120 E 124th St New York (10035) ***(G-11972)***
Sarina Accessories LLC 212 239-8106
445 5th Ave New York (10016) ***(G-11973)***
Sarkisians Jewelry Co 212 869-1060
17 W 45th St Ste 201 New York (10036) ***(G-11974)***
Sartek Industries Inc (PA) 631 473-3555
34 Jamaica Ave Ste 1 Port Jefferson (11777) ***(G-13779)***
Sarug Inc 718 339-2791
2055 Mcdonald Ave Brooklyn (11223) ***(G-2534)***
Sarug Inc 718 381-7300
1616 Summerfield St Ridgewood (11385) ***(G-14123)***
Sarug Knitwear, Ridgewood *Also called Sarug Inc* ***(G-14123)***
Sas Institute Inc 212 757-3826
787 Seventh Ave Fl 47 New York (10019) ***(G-11975)***
Sas Maintenance Services Inc 718 837-2124
8435 Bay 16th St Ste A Brooklyn (11214) ***(G-2535)***
Sassy Sauce Inc 585 621-1050
740 Driving Park Ave F Rochester (14613) ***(G-14669)***
Satco Castings Service Inc 516 354-1500
1400 Plaza Ave New Hyde Park (11040) ***(G-8860)***
Satco Lighting, Edgewood *Also called Satco Products Inc* ***(G-4611)***
Satco Products Inc (PA) 631 243-2022
110 Heartland Blvd Edgewood (11717) ***(G-4611)***
Satellite Incorporated 212 221-6687
43 W 46th St Ste 503 New York (10036) ***(G-11976)***
Satellite Network Inc 718 336-2698
2030 Mcdonald Ave Brooklyn (11223) ***(G-2536)***
Satin Fine Foods Inc 845 469-1034
32 Leone Ln Chester (10918) ***(G-3615)***
Satispie LLC 716 982-4600
155 Balta Dr Rochester (14623) ***(G-14670)***
Satnam Distributors LLC 516 802-0600
200 Robbins Ln Unit B Jericho (11753) ***(G-7084)***
Saturn Industries Inc (PA) 518 828-9956
157 Union Tpke Hudson (12534) ***(G-6632)***
Saturn Sales Inc 519 658-5125
4500 Witmer Indstrl 202 Niagara Falls (14305) ***(G-12874)***
Saunders Concrete Co Inc 607 756-7905
6 Locust Ave Cortland (13045) ***(G-4044)***
Sausbiers Awning Shop Inc 518 828-3748
43 8th St Hudson (12534) ***(G-6633)***
SAV Thermo Inc 631 249-9444
133 Cabot St West Babylon (11704) ***(G-16826)***
Savaco Inc 716 751-9455
2905 Beebe Rd Newfane (14108) ***(G-12788)***
Savage & Son Installations LLC 585 342-7533
676 Pullman Ave Rochester (14615) ***(G-14671)***
Save Around, Binghamton *Also called Enjoy City North Inc* ***(G-913)***
Save More Beverage Corp 518 371-2520
1512 Route 9 Ste 1 Halfmoon (12065) ***(G-5916)***
Save O Seal Corporation Inc 914 592-3031
90 E Main St Elmsford (10523) ***(G-4777)***
Savenergy Inc 516 239-1958
645 South St Unit A Garden City (11530) ***(G-5531)***
Saveur Magazine 212 219-7400
304 Park Ave S Fl 8 New York (10010) ***(G-11977)***
Savwatt Usa Inc (PA) 646 478-2676
475 Park Ave S Fl 30 New York (10016) ***(G-11978)***
Saw Mill Pediatrics Pllc 914 449-6064
95 Locust Rd Pleasantville (10570) ***(G-13720)***
Saw Mill Woodworking Inc 914 963-1841
1900 Central Park Ave Yonkers (10710) ***(G-17483)***
Saxby Implement Corp (PA) 585 624-2938
180 Mendon Victor Rd Mendon (14506) ***(G-8382)***
Saxon Glass Technologies Inc 607 587-9630
200 N Main St Ste 114 Alfred (14802) ***(G-194)***
Saxton Corporation 518 732-7705
1320 Route 9 Castleton On Hudson (12033) ***(G-3420)***
Sayeda Manufacturing Corp 631 345-2525
20 Scouting Blvd Medford (11763) ***(G-8259)***
Sb Corporation 212 822-3166
114 W 41st St Fl 4 New York (10036) ***(G-11979)***
Sb Molds LLC 845 352-3700
161 Route 59 Ste 203a Monsey (10952) ***(G-8581)***
Sb New York Inc (HQ) 212 457-7790
120 Broadway New York (10271) ***(G-11980)***
Sbb Inc 315 422-2376
6500 New Venture Gear Dr # 1000 East Syracuse (13057) ***(G-4562)***
Sbcontract.com, Farmingdale *Also called Metadure Parts & Sales Inc* ***(G-5050)***

A L P H A B E T I C

Sbi Enterprises, Ellenville *Also called Master Juvenile Products Inc* ***(G-4635)***
Sbi Enterprises, Ellenville *Also called JM Originals Inc* ***(G-4634)***
Sbk Preserves Inc....800 773-7378
1161 E 156th St Bronx (10474) ***(G-1448)***
SC Medical Overseas Inc....516 935-8500
350 Jericho Tpke Ste 302 Jericho (11753) ***(G-7085)***
SC Supply Chain Management LLC....212 344-3322
90 Broad St Ste 1504 New York (10004) ***(G-11981)***
SC Textiles Inc....631 944-6262
434 New York Ave Huntington (11743) ***(G-6679)***
Sca Tissue North America LLC....518 692-8434
72 County Route 53 Greenwich (12834) ***(G-5892)***
Sca Tissue North America LLC....518 583-2785
49 Geyser Rd Saratoga Springs (12866) ***(G-15172)***
Scaccianoce Inc....718 991-4462
1165 Burnett Pl Bronx (10474) ***(G-1449)***
Scaife Enterprises Inc....585 454-5231
67 Lyell Ave Rochester (14608) ***(G-14672)***
Scala Furniture Industries NY, Bronx *Also called Bel Art International* ***(G-1282)***
Scalamandre Silks, Hauppauge *Also called Scalamandre Wallpaper Inc* ***(G-6185)***
Scalamandre Silks Inc (PA)....212 980-3888
979 3rd Ave Ste 202 New York (10022) ***(G-11982)***
Scalamandre Silks Inc....212 376-2900
942 3rd Ave New York (10022) ***(G-11983)***
Scalamandre Wallpaper Inc....631 467-8800
350 Wireless Blvd Hauppauge (11788) ***(G-6185)***
Scale-Tronix Inc (PA)....914 948-8117
4341 State Street Rd Skaneateles (13152) ***(G-15465)***
Scan-A-Chrome Color Inc....631 532-6146
555 Oak St Copiague (11726) ***(G-3925)***
Scancorp Inc....315 454-5596
1840 Lemoyne Ave Syracuse (13208) ***(G-16032)***
Scanga Woodworking Corp....845 265-9115
22 Corporate Park W Cold Spring (10516) ***(G-3766)***
Scapa North America....315 413-1111
1111 Vine St Liverpool (13088) ***(G-7546)***
Scara-Mix Inc....718 442-7357
2537 Richmond Ter Staten Island (10303) ***(G-15734)***
Scarano Boat Building Inc....518 463-3401
194 S Port Rd Albany (12202) ***(G-131)***
Scarano Boatbuilding Inc....518 463-3401
194 S Port Rd Albany (12202) ***(G-132)***
Scarguard Labs LLC....516 482-8050
15 Barstow Rd Great Neck (11021) ***(G-5839)***
Scarsdale Inquirer, Scarsdale *Also called S I Communications Inc* ***(G-15222)***
Scehenvus Fire Dist....607 638-9017
40 Main St Schenevus (12155) ***(G-15315)***
Scehenvus Gram Hose Co, Schenevus *Also called Scehenvus Fire Dist* ***(G-15315)***
Scent 2 Market, Yonkers *Also called Belmay Holding Corporation* ***(G-17420)***
Scent-A-Vision Inc....631 424-4905
171 E 2nd St Huntington Station (11746) ***(G-6722)***
Scent-Sation Inc....718 672-4300
9312 Vanderveer St Queens Village (11428) ***(G-13983)***
Scepter Inc....315 568-4225
11 Lamb Rd Seneca Falls (13148) ***(G-15367)***
Scepter New York, Seneca Falls *Also called Scepter Inc* ***(G-15367)***
Scepter Publishers....212 354-0670
10 E 39th St Ste 908 New York (10016) ***(G-11984)***
Scerri Quality Wood Floors, New York *Also called Wood Floor Expo Inc* ***(G-12655)***
Sch Dpx Corporation....917 405-5377
22 W 21st St Ste 700 New York (10010) ***(G-11985)***
Schaap Brothers....518 459-2220
6 Brown Rd Albany (12205) ***(G-133)***
Schaefer Entps of Deposit....607 467-4990
315 Old Route 10 Deposit (13754) ***(G-4280)***
Schaefer Logging Inc....607 467-4990
315 Old Route 10 Deposit (13754) ***(G-4281)***
Schaefer Machine Co Inc....516 248-6880
100 Hudson St Mineola (11501) ***(G-8537)***
Schaller & Weber, New York *Also called Schaller Manufacturing Corp* ***(G-11986)***
Schaller Manufacturing Corp (PA)....718 721-5480
1654 2nd Ave Apt 2n New York (10028) ***(G-11986)***
Scharf and Breit Inc....516 282-0287
2 Hillside Ave Ste F Williston Park (11596) ***(G-17262)***
Schatz Bearing Corporation....845 452-6000
10 Fairview Ave Poughkeepsie (12601) ***(G-13930)***
Schenck Corporation (HQ)....631 242-4010
535 Acorn St Deer Park (11729) ***(G-4205)***
Schenck Trebel Corp (HQ)....631 242-4397
535 Acorn St Deer Park (11729) ***(G-4206)***
SCHENECTADY HERALD PRINTING CO, Troy *Also called Dowd - Witbeck Printing Corp* ***(G-16234)***
Schenectady Steel Co Inc....518 355-3220
18 Mariaville Rd Schenectady (12306) ***(G-15293)***
Schenectady Steel Co Inc....607 275-0086
234 Durfee Hill Rd Ithaca (14850) ***(G-6875)***
Schiller Stores Inc....845 928-4316
869 Grapevine Ct Central Valley (10917) ***(G-3527)***
Schiller Stores Inc (PA)....631 208-9400
509 Tanger Mall Dr Riverhead (11901) ***(G-14155)***
Schilling Forge Inc....315 454-4421
606 Factory Ave Syracuse (13208) ***(G-16033)***
Schindler Elevator Corporation....212 708-1000
620 12th Ave Fl 4 New York (10036) ***(G-11987)***
Schindler Elevator Corporation....718 417-3131
8400 72nd Dr Ste 2 Glendale (11385) ***(G-5662)***
Schindler Elevator Corporation....516 860-1321
7 Midland Ave Hicksville (11801) ***(G-6392)***
Schindler Elevator Corporation....800 225-3123
1211 6th Ave Ste 2950 New York (10036) ***(G-11988)***
Schlegel Electronic Mtls Inc (PA)....585 295-2030
1600 Lexington Ave 236a Rochester (14606) ***(G-14673)***
Schlegel Systems Inc (HQ)....585 427-7200
1555 Jefferson Rd Rochester (14623) ***(G-14674)***
Schlesinger Siemans Elec LLC....718 386-6230
527 Madison Ave Fl 8 New York (10022) ***(G-11989)***
Schlumberger Technology Corp....607 378-0200
224 N Main St Bldg S Horseheads (14845) ***(G-6592)***
Schmersal Inc....914 347-4775
15 Skyline Dr Ste 230 Hawthorne (10532) ***(G-6254)***
Schmitt Sales Inc....716 632-8595
5095 Main St Williamsville (14221) ***(G-17251)***
Schneeman Studio Limited....212 244-3330
330 W 38th St Rm 505 New York (10018) ***(G-11990)***
Schneider Amalco Inc....917 470-9674
600 3rd Ave Fl 2 New York (10016) ***(G-11991)***
Schneider Brothers Corporation....315 458-8369
7371 Eastman Rd Syracuse (13212) ***(G-16034)***
Schneider Electric It Corp....646 335-0216
520 8th Ave Rm 2103 New York (10018) ***(G-11992)***
Schneider Electric Usa Inc....646 335-0220
112 W 34th St Ste 908 New York (10120) ***(G-11993)***
Schneider Electric Usa Inc....585 377-1313
441 Penbrooke Dr Ste 9 Penfield (14526) ***(G-13504)***
Schneider M Soap & Chemical Co....718 389-1000
1930 Troutman St Ridgewood (11385) ***(G-14124)***
Schneider Mills Inc (PA)....212 768-7500
1430 Broadway Rm 1202 New York (10018) ***(G-11994)***
Schnell Publishing Company Inc (HQ)....212 791-4200
360 Park Ave S Fl 10 New York (10010) ***(G-11995)***
Schneps Publications, Bayside *Also called Hispanic Com Pub Inc* ***(G-772)***
Schneps Publications Inc (PA)....718 224-5863
3815 Bell Blvd Ste 38 Bayside (11361) ***(G-775)***
Schoen Trimming & Cord Co Inc....212 255-3949
151 W 25th St Fl 10 New York (10001) ***(G-11996)***
Schoharie Quarry/Asphalt, Schoharie *Also called Cobleskill Stone Products Inc* ***(G-15316)***
Scholastic Copy Center, New York *Also called Scholastic Inc* ***(G-11999)***
Scholastic Corporation (PA)....212 343-6100
557 Broadway Lbby 1 New York (10012) ***(G-11997)***
Scholastic Inc (HQ)....800 724-6527
557 Broadway Lbby 1 New York (10012) ***(G-11998)***
Scholastic Inc....212 343-6100
557 Broadway Lbby 1 New York (10012) ***(G-11999)***
Scholastic Inc....212 343-7100
568 Broadway Rm 809 New York (10012) ***(G-12000)***
Scholium International Inc....516 883-8032
151 Cow Neck Rd Port Washington (11050) ***(G-13863)***
Schonbek, Plattsburgh *Also called Swarovski Lighting Ltd* ***(G-13702)***
Schonbek Shipping Bldg, Plattsburgh *Also called Swarovski Lighting Ltd* ***(G-13703)***
Schonwetter Enterprises Inc....518 237-0171
41 Lark St Cohoes (12047) ***(G-3757)***
School Guide Publications, Mamaroneck *Also called Catholic News Publishing Co* ***(G-8027)***
School of Management, Binghamton *Also called Binghamton University* ***(G-896)***
Schoolnet Inc (HQ)....646 496-9000
525 Fashion Ave Fl 4 New York (10018) ***(G-12001)***
Schott Corporation (HQ)....914 831-2200
555 Taxter Rd Ste 470 Elmsford (10523) ***(G-4778)***
Schott Corporation....315 255-2791
62 Columbus St Auburn (13021) ***(G-517)***
Schott Defense, Elmsford *Also called Schott Government Services LLC* ***(G-4780)***
Schott Gemtron Corporation....423 337-3522
555 Taxter Rd Ste 470 Elmsford (10523) ***(G-4779)***
Schott Government Services LLC....703 418-1409
555 Taxter Rd Ste 470 Elmsford (10523) ***(G-4780)***
Schott Lithotec USA Corp....845 463-5300
555 Taxter Rd Ste 470 Elmsford (10523) ***(G-4781)***
Schott Solar Pv Inc....888 457-6527
555 Taxter Rd Ste 470 Elmsford (10523) ***(G-4782)***
Schrader Meat Market....607 869-6328
1937 Summerville Rd Romulus (14541) ***(G-14842)***
Schroeder Machine Div, East Syracuse *Also called Niagara Scientific Inc* ***(G-4552)***
Schuler-Haas Electric Corp....607 936-3514
598 Ritas Way Painted Post (14870) ***(G-13393)***
Schuler-Subra Inc....716 893-3100
83 Doat St Buffalo (14211) ***(G-3177)***
Schulz Interiors, Poughquag *Also called Fred Schulz Inc* ***(G-13941)***
Schurman Retail Group....212 206-0067
275 7th Ave Frnt 6 New York (10001) ***(G-12002)***
Schuster & Richard Lab, College Point *Also called Schuster & Richard Labortories* ***(G-3806)***
Schuster & Richard Labortories....718 358-8607
1420 130th St College Point (11356) ***(G-3806)***

ALPHABETIC

Schutt Cider Mill 585 872-2924
  1063 Plank Rd Webster (14580) *(G-16734)*
Schutte-Buffalo Hammer Mill, Buffalo *Also called Schutte-Buffalo Hammermill LLC* *(G-3178)*
Schutte-Buffalo Hammermill LLC 716 855-1202
  61 Depot St Buffalo (14206) *(G-3178)*
Schwab Corp (HQ) 585 381-4900
  900 Linden Ave Rochester (14625) *(G-14675)*
Schwab Corp 812 547-2956
  900 Linden Ave Rochester (14625) *(G-14676)*
Schwabel Fabricating Co Inc (PA) 716 876-2086
  349 Sawyer Ave Tonawanda (14150) *(G-16200)*
Schwartz Textile Converting Co 718 499-8243
  160 7th St Brooklyn (11215) *(G-2537)*
Schweitzer-Mauduit Intl Inc 518 329-4222
  2424 Route 82 Ancram (12502) *(G-375)*
SCI Bore Inc 212 674-7128
  70 Irving Pl Apt 5c New York (10003) *(G-12003)*
Sciarra Laboratories Inc 516 933-7853
  48509 S Broadway Hicksville (11801) *(G-6393)*
Sciegen Pharmaceuticals Inc 631 434-2723
  89 Arkay Dr Hauppauge (11788) *(G-6186)*
Sciegen Pharmaceuticals Inc 631 434-2723
  89 Arkay Dr Hauppauge (11788) *(G-6187)*
Scienta Pharmaceuticals LLC 845 589-0774
  612 Corporate Way Ste 9 Valley Cottage (10989) *(G-16388)*
Scientific American Library, New York *Also called Bedford Freeman & Worth* *(G-9342)*
Scientific Components Corp (PA) 718 934-4500
  13 Neptune Ave Brooklyn (11235) *(G-2538)*
Scientific Components Corp 631 243-4901
  161 E Industry Ct Deer Park (11729) *(G-4207)*
Scientific Components Corp 718 368-2060
  2450 Knapp St Brooklyn (11235) *(G-2539)*
Scientific Industries Inc (PA) 631 567-4700
  80 Orville Dr Ste 102 Bohemia (11716) *(G-1129)*
Scientific Plastics Inc 212 967-1199
  243 W 30th St Fl 8 New York (10001) *(G-12004)*
Scientific Polymer Products 585 265-0413
  6265 Dean Pkwy Ontario (14519) *(G-13214)*
Scientific Tool Co Inc (PA) 315 431-4243
  101 Arterial Rd Syracuse (13206) *(G-16035)*
Scientifics Direct Inc 716 773-7500
  532 Main St Tonawanda (14150) *(G-16201)*
Scissor Online, Bolivar *Also called Klein Cutlery LLC* *(G-1159)*
Scj Associates Inc 585 359-0600
  60 Commerce Dr Rochester (14623) *(G-14677)*
SCM, New York *Also called SC Supply Chain Management LLC* *(G-11981)*
SCM, Suffern *Also called Super Conductor Materials Inc* *(G-15801)*
Scomac Inc 585 494-2200
  8629 Buffalo Rd Bergen (14416) *(G-852)*
Scooby Dog Food, Utica *Also called Scooby Rendering & Inc* *(G-16358)*
Scooby Rendering & Inc 315 793-1014
  1930 Oriskany St W Utica (13502) *(G-16358)*
Scoops R US Incorporated 212 730-7959
  1514 Broadway New York (10036) *(G-12005)*
Score International 407 322-3230
  137 Commercial St Ste 300 Plainview (11803) *(G-13634)*
Scorpion Security Products Inc 607 724-9999
  1429 Upper Front St Binghamton (13901) *(G-949)*
Scotsman Press, Syracuse *Also called Badoud Communications Inc* *(G-15866)*
Scott Kay Inc 201 287-0100
  154 W 14th St Fl 6 New York (10011) *(G-12006)*
Scott Rotary Seals, Olean *Also called Dsti Inc* *(G-13145)*
Scott Rotary Seals, Olean *Also called Dynamic Sealing Tech Inc* *(G-13146)*
Scotti Graphics Inc 212 367-9602
  3200 Skillman Ave Fl 1 Long Island City (11101) *(G-7872)*
Scotts Company LLC 631 478-6843
  65 Engineers Rd Hauppauge (11788) *(G-6188)*
Scotts Company LLC 631 289-7444
  445 Horseblock Rd Yaphank (11980) *(G-17400)*
Scotts Feed Inc 518 483-3110
  245 Elm St Malone (12953) *(G-8015)*
Screen Gems Inc 845 561-0036
  41 Windsor Hwy New Windsor (12553) *(G-8953)*
Screen Gems-EMI Music Inc (HQ) 212 786-8000
  150 5th Ave Fl 7 New York (10011) *(G-12007)*
Screen Team Inc 718 786-2424
  3402c Review Ave Long Island City (11101) *(G-7873)*
Screen The World Inc 631 475-0023
  658 Blue Point Rd Holtsville (11742) *(G-6508)*
Screw Compressor Tech Inc 716 827-6600
  158 Ridge Rd Buffalo (14218) *(G-3179)*
Script-Master Div, New York *Also called Brewer-Cantelmo Co Inc* *(G-9458)*
Scriven Duplicating Service 518 233-8180
  100 Eastover Rd Troy (12182) *(G-16253)*
Scriven Press, Troy *Also called Scriven Duplicating Service* *(G-16253)*
Scroll Media Inc 617 395-8904
  235 W 102nd St Apt 14i New York (10025) *(G-12008)*
Scully Sanitation 315 899-8996
  11146 Skaneateles Tpke West Edmeston (13485) *(G-16843)*
Sculptgraphicz Inc 646 837-7302
  67 35th St Unit B520 Brooklyn (11232) *(G-2540)*

SD Christie Associates Inc 914 734-1800
  424 Central Ave Ste 5 Peekskill (10566) *(G-13482)*
SD Eagle Global Inc 516 822-1778
  2 Kay St Jericho (11753) *(G-7086)*
SD Times, Melville *Also called Bz Media LLC* *(G-8299)*
SDC, Saugerties *Also called Stainless Design Concepts Ltd* *(G-15195)*
SDJ Machine Shop Inc 585 458-1236
  1215 Mount Read Blvd # 1 Rochester (14606) *(G-14678)*
Sdp/Si, New Hyde Park *Also called Designatronics Incorporated* *(G-8825)*
Sdr Technology Inc 716 583-1249
  1613 Lindan Dr Alden (14004) *(G-183)*
SDS Business Cards Inc 516 747-3131
  170 The Vale Syosset (11791) *(G-15839)*
Se-Mar Electric Co Inc 716 674-7404
  101 South Ave West Seneca (14224) *(G-16953)*
Sea Isle Custom Rod Builders 516 868-8855
  495 Guy Lombardo Ave Freeport (11520) *(G-5424)*
Sea Mats, Malone *Also called Seaway Mats Inc* *(G-8016)*
Sea Waves Inc (PA) 516 766-4201
  2425 Long Beach Rd Oceanside (11572) *(G-13096)*
Seabay Media Holdings LLC (PA) 212 457-7790
  120 Broadway Fl 6 New York (10271) *(G-12009)*
Seaboard Electronics, New Rochelle *Also called Highlander Realty Inc* *(G-8911)*
Seaboard Graphic Services LLC 315 652-4200
  7570 Oswego Rd Liverpool (13090) *(G-7547)*
Seabreeze Pavement of Ny LLC 585 338-2333
  14 Maryknoll Park Rochester (14622) *(G-14679)*
Seal & Design Inc 315 432-8021
  6741 Thompson Rd Syracuse (13211) *(G-16036)*
Seal Reinforced Fiberglass Inc (PA) 631 842-2230
  19 Bethpage Rd Copiague (11726) *(G-3926)*
Seal Reinforced Fiberglass Inc 631 842-2230
  23 Bethpage Rd Copiague (11726) *(G-3927)*
Sealcraft Industries Inc 718 517-2000
  5308 13th Ave Ste 251 Brooklyn (11219) *(G-2541)*
Sealed Air Corporation 518 370-1693
  201 A St Schenectady (12302) *(G-15294)*
Sealed Air Corporation 518 370-1693
  Scotia Glenvl Ind Pk A St Schenectady (12302) *(G-15295)*
Sealmaster, Buffalo *Also called Jet-Black Sealers Inc* *(G-3019)*
Sealtest Dairy Products, Rochester *Also called Upstate Niagara Coop Inc* *(G-14748)*
Sealy Mattress Co Albany Inc 518 880-1600
  30 Veterans Memorial Dr Troy (12183) *(G-16223)*
Sean John, New York *Also called Christian Casey LLC* *(G-9608)*
Sean John Clothing, New York *Also called Christian Casey LLC* *(G-9609)*
Sean John Clothing Inc 212 500-2200
  1710 Broadway Frnt 1 New York (10019) *(G-12010)*
Sean John Clothing Inc (PA) 212 500-2200
  1440 Broadway Frnt 3 New York (10018) *(G-12011)*
Seanair Machine Co Inc 631 694-2820
  95 Verdi St Farmingdale (11735) *(G-5108)*
Searles Graphics Inc (PA) 631 345-2202
  56 Old Dock Rd Yaphank (11980) *(G-17401)*
Seasons Soyfood Inc 718 797-9896
  605 Degraw St Brooklyn (11217) *(G-2542)*
Seating Inc 800 468-2475
  60 N State St Nunda (14517) *(G-13042)*
Seaward Candies 585 638-6761
  3588 N Main Street Rd Holley (14470) *(G-6492)*
Seaway Mats Inc 518 483-2560
  252 Park St Malone (12953) *(G-8016)*
Seaway Timber Harvesting Inc (PA) 315 769-5970
  15121 State Highway 37 Massena (13662) *(G-8200)*
Second Amendment Foundation 716 885-6408
  267 Linwood Ave Ste A Buffalo (14209) *(G-3180)*
Second Chance Press Inc 631 725-1101
  4170 Noyac Rd Sag Harbor (11963) *(G-15081)*
Secondary Services Inc 716 896-4000
  757 E Ferry St Buffalo (14211) *(G-3181)*
Secor Marketing Group Inc 914 381-3600
  225 Hoyt Ave Mamaroneck (10543) *(G-8046)*
Secret Celebrity Licensing LLC 212 812-9277
  1431 Broadway Fl 10 New York (10018) *(G-12012)*
Secs Inc (PA) 914 667-5600
  550 S Columbus Ave Mount Vernon (10550) *(G-8731)*
Secs Inc 914 667-5600
  550 S Columbus Ave Mount Vernon (10550) *(G-8732)*
Sector Microwave Inds Inc 631 242-2245
  999 Grand Blvd Deer Park (11729) *(G-4208)*
Secuprint Inc 585 341-3100
  1560 Emerson St Rochester (14606) *(G-14680)*
Securax, Bohemia *Also called Protex International Corp* *(G-1124)*
Secured Services Inc (PA) 866 419-3900
  110 William St Fl 14 New York (10038) *(G-12013)*
Securevue Inc 631 587-5850
  28 Trues Dr West Islip (11795) *(G-16906)*
Securities Data Publishing Inc (PA) 212 631-1411
  11 Penn Plz Fl 17 New York (10001) *(G-12014)*
Security Defense System 718 357-6200
  15038 12th Ave Whitestone (11357) *(G-17214)*
Security Dynamics Inc 631 392-1701
  217 Knickerbocker Ave Bohemia (11716) *(G-1130)*

Security Letter 212 348-1553
166 E 96th St Apt 3b New York (10128) ***(G-12015)***
Security Offset Services Inc 631 944-6031
11 Grandview St Huntington (11743) ***(G-6680)***
Security Software & Consulting, New York *Also called SS&c Technologies Inc* ***(G-12177)***
Seed Media Group LLC 646 502-7050
405 Greenwich St Apt 2 New York (10013) ***(G-12016)***
Seedlngs Lf Scnce Ventures LLC 917 913-8511
230 E 15th St Apt 1a New York (10003) ***(G-12017)***
Seeley Machine Inc 518 798-9510
75 Big Boom Rd Queensbury (12804) ***(G-14011)***
Seeley Machine & Fabrication, Queensbury *Also called Seeley Machine Inc* ***(G-14011)***
Sefaira Inc 855 733-2472
115 E 23rd St Fl 11 New York (10010) ***(G-12018)***
Sefi Fabricator, Amityville *Also called IMC Teddy Food Service* ***(G-295)***
Sefi Fabricators, Amityville *Also called P & M LLC* ***(G-319)***
Segovia Technology Co 212 868-4412
115 W 18th St Fl 2 New York (10011) ***(G-12019)***
Seibel Modern Mfg & Wldg Corp 716 683-1536
38 Palmer Pl Lancaster (14086) ***(G-7342)***
Seidlin Consulting 212 496-2043
580 W End Ave New York (10024) ***(G-12020)***
Seifert Graphics Inc 315 736-2744
6133 Judd Rd Oriskany (13424) ***(G-13313)***
Seifert Transit Graphics, Oriskany *Also called Seifert Graphics Inc* ***(G-13313)***
Seize Sur Vingt, New York *Also called Groupe 16sur20 LLC* ***(G-10372)***
Sekas International Ltd 212 629-6095
345 7th Ave Fl 9 New York (10001) ***(G-12021)***
Selby Marketing Associates Inc (PA) 585 377-0750
1387 Fairport Rd Ste 800 Fairport (14450) ***(G-4876)***
Select Controls Inc 631 567-9010
45 Knickerbocker Ave # 3 Bohemia (11716) ***(G-1131)***
Select Door, North Java *Also called Select Interior Door Ltd* ***(G-12934)***
Select Fabricators Inc 585 393-0650
5310 North St Bldg 5 Canandaigua (14424) ***(G-3357)***
Select Industries New York Inc 800 723-5333
450 Fashion Ave Ste 3002 New York (10123) ***(G-12022)***
Select Information Exchange 212 496-6435
175 W 79th St 3a New York (10024) ***(G-12023)***
Select Interior Door Ltd 585 535-9900
2074 Perry Rd North Java (14113) ***(G-12934)***
Select Jewelry Inc 718 784-3626
4728 37th St Fl 3 Long Island City (11101) ***(G-7874)***
Select Products Holdings LLC 855 777-3532
1 Arnold Dr Unit 3 Huntington (11743) ***(G-6681)***
Select-A-Form Inc 631 981-3076
4717 Veterans Mem Hwy Holbrook (11741) ***(G-6470)***
Select-Tech Inc 845 895-8111
3050 State Route 208 Wallkill (12589) ***(G-16546)***
Selective Beauty Corporation 585 336-7600
315 Bleecker St 109 New York (10014) ***(G-12024)***
Selectrode Industries Inc 631 547-5470
230 Broadway Huntington Station (11746) ***(G-6723)***
Selflock Screw Products Co Inc 315 541-4464
461 E Brighton Ave Syracuse (13210) ***(G-16037)***
Selia Yang Bridal, New York *Also called Selia Yang Inc* ***(G-12025)***
Selia Yang Inc 212 480-4252
15 Broad St Apt 714 New York (10005) ***(G-12025)***
Selini Neckwear Inc 212 268-5488
248 W 37th St New York (10018) ***(G-12026)***
Sellco Industries Inc 607 756-7594
58 Grant St Cortland (13045) ***(G-4045)***
Selux Corporation 845 691-7723
5 Lumen Ln Highland (12528) ***(G-6408)***
Semans Enterprises Inc 585 444-0097
25 Hendrix Rd Ste E West Henrietta (14586) ***(G-16894)***
Semco Ceramics Inc (HQ) 315 782-3000
363 Eastern Blvd Watertown (13601) ***(G-16671)***
Semec Corp 518 825-0160
20 Gateway Dr Plattsburgh (12901) ***(G-13696)***
Semi-Linear Inc 212 243-2108
1123 Broadway Ste 718 New York (10010) ***(G-12027)***
Semitronics Corp (HQ) 516 223-0200
80 Commercial St Freeport (11520) ***(G-5425)***
Semrock, Rochester *Also called Semrok Inc* ***(G-14681)***
Semrok Inc (HQ) 585 594-7050
3625 Buffalo Rd Ste 6 Rochester (14624) ***(G-14681)***
Semtex Industrial, Brooklyn *Also called Intex Company Inc* ***(G-2114)***
Sencer Inc 315 536-3474
1 Keuka Business Park Penn Yan (14527) ***(G-13520)***
Sendec Corp (HQ) 585 425-3390
72 Perinton Pkwy Fairport (14450) ***(G-4877)***
Sendyne Corp 212 966-0663
250 W Broadway Fl 6 New York (10013) ***(G-12028)***
Seneca Ceramics Corp 315 781-0100
835 Mcivor Rd Phelps (14532) ***(G-13536)***
Seneca County Area Shopper 607 532-4333
1885 State Route 96a Ovid (14521) ***(G-13347)***
Seneca Falls Capital Inc (PA) 315 568-5804
314 Fall St Seneca Falls (13148) ***(G-15368)***
Seneca Falls Machine, Seneca Falls *Also called Seneca Falls Capital Inc* ***(G-15368)***
Seneca Falls Machine Tool Co 315 568-5804
314 Fall St Seneca Falls (13148) ***(G-15369)***
Seneca Falls Technology Group, Seneca Falls *Also called Seneca Falls Machine Tool Co* ***(G-15369)***
Seneca FLS Spc & Logistics Co (PA) 315 568-4139
50 Johnston St Seneca Falls (13148) ***(G-15370)***
Seneca Foods Corporation (PA) 315 926-8100
3736 S Main St Marion (14505) ***(G-8099)***
Seneca Foods Corporation 315 781-8733
100 Gambee Rd Geneva (14456) ***(G-5585)***
Seneca Foods Corporation 315 926-0531
3709 Mill St Marion (14505) ***(G-8100)***
Seneca Foods Corporation 315 926-4277
3732 S Main St Marion (14505) ***(G-8101)***
Seneca Foods Corporation 585 658-2211
5705 Rte 36 Leicester (14481) ***(G-7422)***
Seneca Manufacturing Company 716 945-4400
175 Rochester St Salamanca (14779) ***(G-15106)***
Seneca Media Inc (PA) 607 324-1425
32 Broadway Mall Hornell (14843) ***(G-6566)***
Seneca Media Inc 585 593-5300
159 N Main St Wellsville (14895) ***(G-16758)***
Seneca Nation Enterprise 716 934-7430
11482 Route 20 Irving (14081) ***(G-6765)***
Seneca Resources Corporation 716 630-6750
165 Lawrence Bell Dr Williamsville (14221) ***(G-17252)***
Seneca Signs LLC 315 446-9420
102 Headson Dr Syracuse (13214) ***(G-16038)***
Seneca Stone Corporation 315 549-8253
Cty Rd 121 Hoster Cors Rd Fayette (13065) ***(G-5162)***
Seneca Stone Corporation (HQ) 607 737-6200
2105 S Broadway Pine City (14871) ***(G-13552)***
Seneca TEC Inc 585 381-2645
73 Country Corner Ln Fairport (14450) ***(G-4878)***
Seneca Truck & Trailer Inc 315 781-1100
2200 State Route 14 Geneva (14456) ***(G-5586)***
Seneca West Printing Inc 716 675-8010
860 Center Rd West Seneca (14224) ***(G-16954)***
Senera Co Inc 516 639-3774
834 Glenridge Ave Valley Stream (11581) ***(G-16427)***
Senneth LLC 347 232-3170
26 Ronald Dr Ste 500 Monsey (10952) ***(G-8582)***
Sensational Collection Inc (PA) 212 840-7388
1410 Broadway Rm 505 New York (10018) ***(G-12029)***
Sensio America 877 501-5337
18 Division St Ste 207a Saratoga Springs (12866) ***(G-15173)***
Sensitron Semiconductor, Deer Park *Also called RSM Electron Power Inc* ***(G-4203)***
Sensitron Semiconductor, Hauppauge *Also called RSM Electron Power Inc* ***(G-6181)***
Sensor & Decontamination Inc 301 526-8389
892 Powderhouse Rd Binghamton (13903) ***(G-950)***
Sensor Films Incorporated 585 738-3500
687 Rowley Rd Victor (14564) ***(G-16501)***
Sensormatic Electronics LLC 718 597-6719
1575 Williamsbridge Rd 3c Bronx (10461) ***(G-1450)***
Sensormatic Electronics LLC 845 365-3125
10 Corporate Dr Orangeburg (10962) ***(G-13245)***
Sensual Inc 212 869-1450
183 Madison Ave Rm 401 New York (10016) ***(G-12030)***
Sentage Corporation 914 664-2200
161 S Macquesten Pkwy 2 Mount Vernon (10550) ***(G-8733)***
Sentinel Printing, Hempstead *Also called Hempstead Sentinel Inc* ***(G-6273)***
Sentinel Printing Inc 516 334-7400
75 State St Westbury (11590) ***(G-17026)***
Sentinel Printing Services Inc 845 562-1218
36 Merline Ave New Windsor (12553) ***(G-8954)***
Sentinel Products Corp 518 568-7036
12 New St Saint Johnsville (13452) ***(G-15098)***
Sentinel Publishing, Honeoye Falls *Also called Mendon Hnoye FLS Lima Sentinel* ***(G-6534)***
Sentinel, The, New Windsor *Also called E W Smith Publishing Co* ***(G-8937)***
Sentry Automatic Sprinkler 631 723-3095
735 Flanders Rd Riverhead (11901) ***(G-14156)***
Sentry Devices Corp 631 491-3191
33 Rustic Gate Ln Dix Hills (11746) ***(G-4298)***
Sentry Funding Partnership, Ronkonkoma *Also called Sentry Technology Corporation* ***(G-14983)***
Sentry Metal Blast Inc 716 285-5241
401 47th St Niagara Falls (14304) ***(G-12875)***
Sentry Metal Services, Niagara Falls *Also called Sentry Metal Blast Inc* ***(G-12875)***
Sentry Technology Corporation 631 739-2000
1881 Lakeland Ave Ronkonkoma (11779) ***(G-14982)***
Sentry Technology Corporation (PA) 800 645-4224
1881 Lakeland Ave Ronkonkoma (11779) ***(G-14983)***
Seo Ryung Inc 718 321-0755
4128 Murray St Flushing (11355) ***(G-5291)***
Sepac Inc 607 732-2030
1580 Lake St Elmira (14901) ***(G-4700)***
Sepco-Sturges Electronics, Dryden *Also called Sturges Elec Pdts Co Inc* ***(G-4323)***
Sephardic Yellow Pages 718 998-0299
2150 E 4th St Brooklyn (11223) ***(G-2543)***
Sepsa North America, Ballston Spa *Also called Albatros North America Inc* ***(G-590)***
September Associates, Oakdale *Also called Steel-Brite Ltd* ***(G-13063)***

ALPHABETIC SECTION

Shenfeld Studio Tile, Syracuse

Sequa Corporation 813 434-4522
300 Blaisdell Rd Orangeburg (10962) ***(G-13246)***
Sequa Corporation 201 343-1122
300 Blaisdell Rd Orangeburg (10962) ***(G-13247)***
Sequential Electronics Systems 914 592-1345
399 Executive Blvd Elmsford (10523) ***(G-4783)***
Serendipity Consulting Corp 914 763-8251
48 Twin Lakes Rd South Salem (10590) ***(G-15536)***
Serengeti Teas and Spices, New York *Also called Caranda Emporium LLC* ***(G-9521)***
Serge Duct Designs Inc 718 783-7799
535 Dean St Apt 124 Brooklyn (11217) ***(G-2544)***
Seri Systems Inc 585 272-5515
172 Metro Park Rochester (14623) ***(G-14682)***
Service Advertising Group Inc 718 361-6161
4216 34th Ave Long Island City (11101) ***(G-7875)***
Service Canvas Co Inc 716 853-0558
149 Swan St Unit 155 Buffalo (14203) ***(G-3182)***
Service Education Incorporated 585 264-9240
790 Canning Pkwy Ste 1 Victor (14564) ***(G-16502)***
Service Filtration Corp 716 877-2608
225 E Park Dr Tonawanda (14150) ***(G-16202)***
Service Machine & Tool Company 607 732-0413
206 E Mccanns Blvd Elmira Heights (14903) ***(G-4712)***
Service Mfg Group Inc (PA) 716 893-1482
400 Scajaquada St Buffalo (14211) ***(G-3183)***
Service Mfg Group Inc 716 893-1482
400 Scajaquada St Buffalo (14211) ***(G-3184)***
Service Specialties Inc 716 822-7706
127 Langner Rd Buffalo (14224) ***(G-3185)***
Servicenow Inc 914 318-1168
60 E 42nd St Ste 1230 New York (10165) ***(G-12031)***
Servo Reeler System, Queens Village *Also called Xedit Corp* ***(G-13985)***
Servotec Usa LLC 518 671-6120
1 Industrial Tract Anx # 3 Hudson (12534) ***(G-6634)***
Servotronics Inc (PA) 716 655-5990
1110 Maple Rd Elma (14059) ***(G-4655)***
Serway Bros Inc (PA) 315 337-0601
Plant 2 Rome Indus Ctr Rome (13440) ***(G-14836)***
Serway Cabinet Trends, Rome *Also called Serway Bros Inc* ***(G-14836)***
Sesco Industries Inc 718 939-5137
11019 15th Ave College Point (11356) ***(G-3807)***
Setauket Manufacturing Co 631 231-7272
202 Christopher St Ronkonkoma (11779) ***(G-14984)***
Settapani Bakery, Brooklyn *Also called Settepani Inc* ***(G-2545)***
Settepani Inc (PA) 718 349-6524
602 Lorimer St Brooklyn (11211) ***(G-2545)***
Setterstix Corporation, Cattaraugus *Also called Pkk Inc* ***(G-3439)***
Setton Farms, Commack *Also called Settons Intl Foods Inc* ***(G-3842)***
Settons Intl Foods Inc (PA) 631 543-8090
85 Austin Blvd Commack (11725) ***(G-3842)***
Seven Springs Gravel Pdts LLC 585 343-4336
8479 Seven Springs Rd Batavia (14020) ***(G-647)***
Seven Stories Press Inc 212 226-8760
140 Watts St New York (10013) ***(G-12032)***
Seventeen Magazine, New York *Also called Hearst Corporation* ***(G-10445)***
Seville Central Mix Corp (PA) 516 868-3000
157 Albany Ave Freeport (11520) ***(G-5426)***
Seville Central Mix Corp 516 293-6190
495 Wining Rd Old Bethpage (11804) ***(G-13130)***
Seville Central Mix Corp 516 239-8333
101 Johnson Rd Lawrence (11559) ***(G-7400)***
Seviroli Foods Inc (PA) 516 222-6220
601 Brook St Garden City (11530) ***(G-5532)***
Sew True, New York *Also called Champion Zipper Corp* ***(G-9576)***
Sextet Fabrics Inc 516 593-0608
21 Ryder Pl Ste 4 East Rockaway (11518) ***(G-4470)***
Seymour Science LLC 516 699-8404
4 Sheffield Rd Great Neck (11021) ***(G-5840)***
Sfoglini LLC 646 872-1035
630 Flushing Ave Fl 2 Brooklyn (11206) ***(G-2546)***
Sg Blocks Inc (PA) 212 520-6218
115 W 18th St Fl 3 New York (10011) ***(G-12033)***
Sg Nyc LLC 310 210-1837
385 5th Ave Rm 809 New York (10016) ***(G-12034)***
SGD North America 212 753-4200
900 3rd Ave Fl 4 New York (10022) ***(G-12035)***
Sgg, Long Island City *Also called Stanley Creations Inc* ***(G-7885)***
Sgl Services Corp 718 630-0392
1221 Ave Of Americas 42 New York (10020) ***(G-12036)***
Sh Ironworks Inc 917 907-0507
15142 17th Ave Flushing (11357) ***(G-5292)***
Sh Leather Novelty Company 718 387-7742
123 Clymer St Bsmt Brooklyn (11249) ***(G-2547)***
Shaant Industries Inc 716 366-3654
134 Franklin Ave Dunkirk (14048) ***(G-4350)***
Shabtai Gourmet, Woodmere *Also called Cinderellas Sweets Ltd* ***(G-17312)***
Shad Industries Inc 631 504-6028
7 Old Dock Rd Unit 1 Yaphank (11980) ***(G-17402)***
Shade & Shutter Systems of NY 631 208-0275
260 Hampton Rd Southampton (11968) ***(G-15551)***
Shadow Lake Golf & Racquet CLB, Rochester *Also called Dolomite Products Company Inc* ***(G-14316)***
Shadowtv Inc 212 445-2540
630 9th Ave Ste 1000 New York (10036) ***(G-12037)***
Shafer & Sons 315 853-5285
4932 State Route 233 Westmoreland (13490) ***(G-17065)***
Shah Diamonds Inc 212 888-9393
22 W 48th St Ste 600 New York (10036) ***(G-12038)***
Shahin Designs Ltd 212 737-7225
766 Madison Ave Fl 3 New York (10065) ***(G-12039)***
Shake Inc 650 544-5479
175 Varick St Fl 4 New York (10014) ***(G-12040)***
Shake-N-Go Fashion Inc (PA) 516 944-7777
85 Harbor Rd Port Washington (11050) ***(G-13864)***
Shako Inc 315 437-1294
6191 E Molloy Rd East Syracuse (13057) ***(G-4563)***
Shalam Imports Inc (PA) 718 686-6271
1552 Dahill Rd Ste B Brooklyn (11204) ***(G-2548)***
Shalamex, Brooklyn *Also called Shalam Imports Inc* ***(G-2548)***
Shalom Toy Co Inc 718 499-3770
128 32nd St Fl 4 Brooklyn (11232) ***(G-2549)***
Shamrock Plastics & Tool Inc 585 328-6040
95 Mount Read Blvd # 149 Rochester (14611) ***(G-14683)***
Shamron Mills Ltd 212 354-0430
242 W 38th St Fl 14 New York (10018) ***(G-12041)***
Shane & Shawn, New York *Also called Detny Footwear Inc* ***(G-9860)***
Shane Tex Inc 516 486-7522
50 Polk Ave Hempstead (11550) ***(G-6287)***
Shanghai Stove Inc 718 599-4583
78 Gerry St 82 Brooklyn (11206) ***(G-2550)***
Shanker Industries Inc (PA) 631 940-9889
301 Suburban Ave Deer Park (11729) ***(G-4209)***
Shannon Entps Wstn NY Inc 716 693-7954
75 Main St North Tonawanda (14120) ***(G-12993)***
Shanu Gems Inc 212 921-4470
1212 Ave Of The Americas New York (10036) ***(G-12042)***
Shapes Etc Inc 585 335-6619
9094 Rte 36 Dansville (14437) ***(G-4079)***
Shapeways Inc (PA) 914 356-5816
419 Park Ave S Fl 9 New York (10016) ***(G-12043)***
Shapiro Bernstein & Co Inc 212 588-0878
488 Madison Ave Fl 1201 New York (10022) ***(G-12044)***
Shapiro William NY Univ Med Ctr, New York *Also called William H Shapiro* ***(G-12635)***
Shar-Mar Machine Company 631 567-8040
1648 Locust Ave Ste F Bohemia (11716) ***(G-1132)***
Sharedbook Inc 646 442-8840
110 William St Fl 30 New York (10038) ***(G-12045)***
Sharenet Inc 315 477-1100
920 Spencer St Syracuse (13204) ***(G-16039)***
Sharmeen Textile Inc 646 298-5757
469 Fashion Ave Fl 4 New York (10018) ***(G-12046)***
Sharodine Inc 516 767-3548
18 Haven Ave Frnt 2 Port Washington (11050) ***(G-13865)***
Sharon Manufacturing Co Inc 631 242-8870
540 Brook Ave Deer Park (11729) ***(G-4210)***
Sharon Metal Stamping Corp 718 828-4510
1457 Bassett Ave Bronx (10461) ***(G-1451)***
Sharonana Enterprises Inc 631 875-5619
52 Sharon Dr Coram (11727) ***(G-3950)***
Sharp Printing Inc 716 731-3994
3477 Lockport Rd Sanborn (14132) ***(G-15127)***
Shaw Contract Flrg Svcs Inc 212 953-7429
521 5th Ave Fl 37 New York (10175) ***(G-12047)***
Shawmut Woodworking & Sup Inc 212 920-8900
3 E 54th St Fl 8 New York (10022) ***(G-12048)***
Shawmutdesign and Construction, New York *Also called Shawmut Woodworking & Sup Inc* ***(G-12048)***
Sheets, The, Long Island City *Also called Ragozin Data* ***(G-7856)***
Shehawken Archery Co Inc 607 967-8333
40 S Main St Bainbridge (13733) ***(G-554)***
Shelby Crushed Stone Inc 585 798-4501
10830 Blair Rd Medina (14103) ***(G-8281)***
Sheldon Slate Products Co Inc 518 642-1280
Fox Rd Middle Granville (12849) ***(G-8401)***
Sheldrake Point Vineyard LLC 607 532-8967
7448 County Road 153 Ovid (14521) ***(G-13348)***
Sheldrake Point Winery, Ovid *Also called Sheldrake Point Vineyard LLC* ***(G-13348)***
Shell Ann Printing, Stony Point *Also called Stony Point Graphics Ltd* ***(G-15777)***
Shell Containers Inc (ny) 516 352-4505
1981 Marcus Ave Ste C105 New Hyde Park (11042) ***(G-8861)***
Shelley Promotions Inc 212 924-4987
87 5th Ave New York (10003) ***(G-12049)***
Shelter Enterprises Inc 518 237-4100
8 Saratoga St Cohoes (12047) ***(G-3758)***
Shelter Island Cmnty Nwspapers, Shelter Island *Also called Shelter Island Reporter Inc* ***(G-15388)***
Shelter Island Reporter Inc 631 749-1000
50 N Ferry Rd Shelter Island (11964) ***(G-15388)***
Sheltred Wkshp For Dsabled Inc 607 722-2364
200 Court St Binghamton (13901) ***(G-951)***
Shenfeld Studio Tile, Syracuse *Also called Shenfield Studio LLC* ***(G-16040)***

ALPHABETIC

(PA)=Parent Co (HQ)=Headquarters (DH)=Div Headquarters

2017 Harris
New York Manufacturers Directory

1061

Shenfield Studio LLC — ALPHABETIC SECTION

Shenfield Studio LLC 315 436-8869
  6361 Thompson Rd Stop 12 Syracuse (13206) *(G-16040)*
Shepards Sawmill 585 638-5664
  15547 Brown Scholhouse Rd Holley (14470) *(G-6493)*
Shepherds Flat, New York Also called Caithness Equities Corporation *(G-9498)*
Sherburne Metal Sales Inc (PA) 607 674-4441
  40 S Main St Sherburne (13460) *(G-15395)*
Sherco Services LLC 516 676-3028
  2 Park Pl Ste A Glen Cove (11542) *(G-5627)*
Sheridan House Inc 914 725-5431
  230 Nelson Rd Scarsdale (10583) *(G-15223)*
Sherrill Manufacturing Inc 315 280-0727
  102 E Seneca St Sherrill (13461) *(G-15407)*
Sherry-Mica Products Inc 631 471-7513
  45 Remington Blvd Ste D Ronkonkoma (11779) *(G-14985)*
Sherwin Commerce, New York Also called AT&T Corp *(G-9244)*
Shield Press Inc 212 431-7489
  9 Lispenard St Fl 1 New York (10013) *(G-12050)*
Shindo Usa Inc 212 868-9311
  162 W 36th St New York (10018) *(G-12051)*
Shining Creations Inc 845 358-4911
  40 S Main St Ste 1 New City (10956) *(G-8793)*
Shinn Vineyard, Mattituck Also called Shinn Winery LLC *(G-8210)*
Shinn Winery LLC 631 804-0367
  2000 Oregon Rd Mattituck (11952) *(G-8210)*
Shipman Print Solutions, Niagara Falls Also called Shipman Printing Inds Inc *(G-12876)*
Shipman Printing Inds Inc 716 504-7700
  2424 Niagara Falls Blvd Niagara Falls (14304) *(G-12876)*
Shipmtes/Printmates Holdg Corp (PA) 518 370-1158
  705 Corporation Park # 2 Scotia (12302) *(G-15330)*
Shiprite Software Inc 315 733-6191
  1312 Genesee St Utica (13502) *(G-16359)*
Shira Accessories Ltd 212 594-4455
  30 W 36th St Rm 504 New York (10018) *(G-12052)*
Shirl-Lynn of New York (PA) 315 363-5898
  266 Wilson St Oneida (13421) *(G-13167)*
Shiro Limited 212 780-0007
  928 Broadway Ste 806 New York (10010) *(G-12053)*
Shirt Shack, Spring Valley Also called Regal Screen Printing Intl *(G-15601)*
Shiseido Americas Corporation (HQ) 212 805-2300
  900 3rd Ave Fl 15 New York (10022) *(G-12054)*
Shiseido Cosmetics, New York Also called Shiseido Americas Corporation *(G-12054)*
Shop Smart Central Inc 914 962-3871
  1520 Front St Yorktown Heights (10598) *(G-17519)*
Shopping Bag, The, East Rochester Also called Greater Rchster Advertiser Inc *(G-4460)*
Shopping Center Wine & Liquor 914 528-1600
  3008 E Main St Mohegan Lake (10547) *(G-8544)*
Shore Line Momogramming & EMB, Mamaroneck Also called Shore Line Monogramming Inc *(G-8047)*
Shore Line Monogramming Inc 914 698-8000
  115 Hoyt Ave Mamaroneck (10543) *(G-8047)*
Shore Products Co, Auburn Also called T Shore Products Ltd *(G-522)*
Shoreline Fruit LLC 585 765-2639
  10190 Route 18 Lyndonville (14098) *(G-7969)*
Shoreline Publishing Inc 914 738-7869
  629 Fifth Ave Ste B01 Pelham (10803) *(G-13494)*
Shoretel Inc 877 654-3573
  300 State St Ste 100 Rochester (14614) *(G-14684)*
Short Jj Associates Inc (PA) 315 986-3511
  1645 Wayneport Rd Macedon (14502) *(G-7991)*
Short Run Forms Inc 631 567-7171
  171 Keyland Ct Bohemia (11716) *(G-1133)*
Showeray Co (PA) 718 965-3633
  225 25th St Brooklyn (11232) *(G-2551)*
Shred Center 716 664-3052
  428 Livingston Ave Jamestown (14701) *(G-7027)*
Shredder Essentials, Brooklyn Also called Casa Innovations Inc *(G-1763)*
Shrineeta Pharmacy 212 234-7959
  1749 Amsterdam Ave Frnt New York (10031) *(G-12055)*
Shrineeta Pharmacy Inc 212 234-7959
  1743 Amsterdam Ave New York (10031) *(G-12056)*
Shritec Consultants Inc 516 621-7072
  91 Searingtown Rd Albertson (11507) *(G-160)*
Shugar Publishing 631 288-4404
  99b Main St Westhampton Beach (11978) *(G-17060)*
Shugaray Division of Zaralo, New York Also called Zaralo LLC *(G-12704)*
Shyam Ahuja Limited 212 644-5910
  201 E 56th St Frnt A New York (10022) *(G-12057)*
Shyk International Corp 212 663-3302
  258 Riverside Dr Apt 7b New York (10025) *(G-12058)*
Shykat Promotions 866 574-2757
  10561 Creek Rd Forestville (14062) *(G-5336)*
Si Funeral Services, Fairport Also called Suhor Industries Inc *(G-4883)*
Si Group Inc (PA) 518 347-4200
  2750 Balltown Rd Schenectady (12309) *(G-15296)*
Si Group Inc 518 347-4200
  Rr 5 Box South Rotterdam Junction (12150) *(G-15035)*
SI Partners Inc 516 433-1415
  15 E Carl St Unit 1 Hicksville (11801) *(G-6394)*
Sibeau Handbags Inc 212 686-0210
  33 E 33rd St Rm 1001 New York (10016) *(G-12059)*

Sick Inc 585 347-2000
  855 Publishers Pkwy Webster (14580) *(G-16735)*
Sidco Filter Corporation 585 289-3100
  58 North Ave Manchester (14504) *(G-8053)*
Sidco Food Distribution Corp 718 733-3939
  2324 Webster Ave Bronx (10458) *(G-1452)*
Side Hill Farmers Coop Inc 315 447-4693
  8275 State Route 13 Canastota (13032) *(G-3373)*
Side Hustle Music Group LLC 800 219-4003
  600 3rd Ave Fl 2 New York (10016) *(G-12060)*
Sidney A Bush Co 718 742-9629
  728 E 136th St Ste 4 Bronx (10454) *(G-1453)*
Sidney Favorite Printing Div, Sidney Also called Tri-Town News Inc *(G-15442)*
Siegfrieds Basement Inc 212 629-3523
  320 W 37th St Ground Fl New York (10018) *(G-12061)*
Siegfrieds Call Inc 845 765-2275
  20 Kent St 109 Beacon (12508) *(G-790)*
Siemens Corporation 905 528-8811
  302 Sonwill Rd Buffalo (14225) *(G-3186)*
Siemens Corporation 202 434-7800
  527 Madison Ave Fl 8 New York (10022) *(G-12062)*
Siemens Electro Industrial Sa 212 258-4000
  527 Madison Ave Fl 8 New York (10022) *(G-12063)*
Siemens Government Tech Inc 585 593-1234
  37 Coats St Wellsville (14895) *(G-16759)*
Siemens Hlthcare Dgnostics Inc 914 631-0475
  511 Benedict Ave Tarrytown (10591) *(G-16105)*
Siemens Industries Inc 607 936-9512
  23 W Market St Ste 3 Corning (14830) *(G-3981)*
Siemens Industry Inc 716 568-0983
  85 Northpointe Pkwy Amherst (14228) *(G-261)*
Siemens Industry Inc 716 568-0983
  85 Northpointe Pkwy Ste 8 Buffalo (14228) *(G-3187)*
Siemens Industry Inc 631 218-1000
  50 Orville Dr Ste 2 Bohemia (11716) *(G-1134)*
Siemens Industry Inc 631 231-3600
  155 Plant Ave Hauppauge (11788) *(G-6189)*
Siemens Product Life Mgmt Sftw 585 389-8699
  345 Woodcliff Dr Fairport (14450) *(G-4879)*
Siemens USA Holdings Inc 212 258-4000
  601 Lexington Ave Fl 56 New York (10022) *(G-12064)*
Sierra Processing LLC 518 433-0020
  2 Moyer Ave Schenectady (12306) *(G-15297)*
Sierson Crane & Welding Inc 315 723-6914
  4822 State Route 233 Westmoreland (13490) *(G-17066)*
Sifonya Inc 212 620-4512
  303 Park Ave S Frnt 2 New York (10010) *(G-12065)*
Siga Technologies Inc (PA) 212 672-9100
  660 Madison Ave Ste 1700 New York (10065) *(G-12066)*
Sigma Intl Gen Med Apprtus LLC 585 798-3901
  711 Park Ave Medina (14103) *(G-8282)*
Sigma Manufacturing Inds Inc 718 842-9180
  1361 E Bay Ave Bronx (10474) *(G-1454)*
Sigma Worldwide LLC 646 217-0629
  65 W 83rd St Apt 5 New York (10024) *(G-12067)*
Sigmamotor Inc 716 735-3115
  3 N Main St Middleport (14105) *(G-8423)*
Sigmund Cohn Corp 914 664-5300
  121 S Columbus Ave Mount Vernon (10553) *(G-8734)*
Sign & Signs 718 941-6200
  785 Coney Island Ave Brooklyn (11218) *(G-2552)*
Sign A Rama Inc 631 952-3324
  663 Old Willets Path C Hauppauge (11788) *(G-6190)*
Sign A Rama of Syracuse 315 446-9420
  3060 Erie Blvd E Ste 1 Syracuse (13224) *(G-16041)*
Sign Center Inc 212 967-2113
  54 W 21st St Rm 201 New York (10010) *(G-12068)*
Sign Company 212 967-2113
  54 W 21st St Rm 201 New York (10010) *(G-12069)*
Sign Company, The, New York Also called Sign Center Inc *(G-12068)*
Sign Design, Port Chester Also called Lanza Corp *(G-13751)*
Sign Design Group New York Inc 718 392-0779
  3326 Northern Blvd Long Island City (11101) *(G-7876)*
Sign Expo Enterprises (PA) 212 925-8585
  127 W 26th St Rm 401 New York (10001) *(G-12070)*
Sign Group Inc 718 438-7103
  5215 New Utrecht Ave Brooklyn (11219) *(G-2553)*
Sign Guys LLC 315 253-4276
  67 Franklin St Auburn (13021) *(G-518)*
Sign Here Enterprises LLC 914 328-3111
  28 N Central Ave Rear Hartsdale (10530) *(G-6000)*
Sign Impressions Inc 585 723-0420
  2590 W Ridge Rd Ste 6 Rochester (14626) *(G-14685)*
Sign Language Custom WD Signs, Perry Also called Sign Language Inc *(G-13526)*
Sign Language Inc 585 237-2620
  6491 State Route 20a Perry (14530) *(G-13526)*
Sign Shop Inc 631 226-4145
  1272 Montauk Hwy Copiague (11726) *(G-3928)*
Sign Studio Inc 518 266-0877
  1 Ingalls Ave Troy (12180) *(G-16254)*
Sign Up Now Inc 516 221-3394
  2541 Merrick Rd Bellmore (11710) *(G-822)*

ALPHABETIC SECTION Sinn- Tech Industries Inc

Sign Works Incorporated 914 592-0700
150 Clearbrook Rd Ste 118 Elmsford (10523) *(G-4784)*
Sign World Inc 212 619-9000
1194 Utica Ave Brooklyn (11203) *(G-2554)*
Sign-A-Rama, Hartsdale *Also called Sign Here Enterprises LLC (G-6000)*
Sign-A-Rama, Baldwin *Also called Jal Signs Inc (G-559)*
Sign-A-Rama, Mount Kisco *Also called Westchester Signs Inc (G-8646)*
Sign-A-Rama, Syracuse *Also called Sign A Rama of Syracuse (G-16041)*
Sign-A-Rama, Huntington Station *Also called Z-Car-D Corp (G-6730)*
Sign-A-Rama, Bellmore *Also called Speedy Sign A Rama USA Inc (G-823)*
Sign-A-Rama, Hicksville *Also called Marigold Signs Inc (G-6369)*
Sign-A-Rama, New Hyde Park *Also called Three Gems Inc (G-8866)*
Sign-A-Rama, Hauppauge *Also called Sign A Rama Inc (G-6190)*
Signa Chemistry Inc (PA) 212 933-4101
400 Madison Ave Fl 21 New York (10017) *(G-12071)*
Signal Graphics Printing, Wappingers Falls *Also called Gem Reproduction Services Corp (G-16570)*
Signal Transformer, Inwood *Also called Bel Transformer Inc (G-6753)*
Signature Diamond Entps LLC 212 869-5115
15 W 47th St Ste 203 New York (10036) *(G-12072)*
Signature Industries Inc 516 679-5177
32 Saint Johns Pl Freeport (11520) *(G-5427)*
Signature Metal MBL Maint LLC 718 292-8280
791 E 132nd St Bronx (10454) *(G-1455)*
Signature Name Plate Co Inc 585 321-9960
292 Commerce Dr Rochester (14623) *(G-14686)*
Signature Systems Group LLC 800 569-2751
38 E 29th St Fl 3l New York (10016) *(G-12073)*
Signatures, New York *Also called Light House Hill Marketing (G-10990)*
Signpost Inc 646 503-4231
127 W 26th St Fl 2 New York (10001) *(G-12074)*
Signs & Decal Corp 718 486-6400
410 Morgan Ave Brooklyn (11211) *(G-2555)*
Signs By Sunrise, Jamaica *Also called Tru-Art Sign Co Inc (G-6959)*
Signs By Tomorrow, Commack *Also called Rpf Associates Inc (G-3841)*
Signs Inc 518 483-4759
2 Boyer Ave Malone (12953) *(G-8017)*
Signs Ink Ltd 914 739-9059
3255 Crompond Rd Yorktown Heights (10598) *(G-17520)*
Signs Now, Rochester *Also called Image360 (G-14446)*
Signs of Success Ltd 516 295-6000
247 Merrick Rd Ste 101 Lynbrook (11563) *(G-7961)*
Sigro Precision, West Babylon *Also called BEAM Manufacturing Corp (G-16775)*
Sihi Pumps Inc (HQ) 716 773-6450
303 Industrial Dr Grand Island (14072) *(G-5769)*
Sikorsky Aircraft Corporation 585 424-1990
300 Canal View Blvd Rochester (14623) *(G-14687)*
Silar Laboratories Division, Scotia *Also called Oak-Bark Corporation (G-15329)*
Silarx Pharmaceuticals Inc 845 352-4020
1033 Stoneleigh Ave Carmel (10512) *(G-3405)*
Silgan Containers Mfg Corp 315 946-4826
8673 Lyons Marengo Rd Lyons (14489) *(G-7975)*
Silgan Plastics LLC 315 536-5690
40 Powell Ln Penn Yan (14527) *(G-13521)*
Silicon Carbide Products Inc 607 562-8599
361 Daniel Zenker Dr Horseheads (14845) *(G-6593)*
Silicon Imaging Inc 518 374-3367
25 Covington Ct Niskayuna (12309) *(G-12896)*
Silicon Pulsed Power LLC 610 407-4700
958 Main St Ste A Clifton Park (12065) *(G-3707)*
Silicone Products & Technology 716 684-1155
4471 Walden Ave Lancaster (14086) *(G-7343)*
Silipos Holding LLC 716 283-0700
7049 Williams Rd Niagara Falls (14304) *(G-12877)*
Silk Screen Art Inc 518 762-8423
1 School St Johnstown (12095) *(G-7126)*
Silly Phillie Creations Inc 718 492-6300
140 58th St Ste 6f Brooklyn (11220) *(G-2556)*
Silva Cabinetry Inc 914 737-7697
12 White St Ste C Buchanan (10511) *(G-2787)*
Silvatrim Corp 212 675-0933
324 W 22nd St New York (10011) *(G-12075)*
Silvatrim Corporation America, New York *Also called Silvatrim Corp (G-12075)*
Silver City Group Inc 315 363-0344
27577 W Seneca St Sherrill (13461) *(G-15408)*
Silver City Metals, Sherrill *Also called Silver City Group Inc (G-15408)*
Silver Creek Carpet, New York *Also called Bloomsburg Carpet Inds Inc (G-9417)*
Silver Creek Enterprises Inc 716 934-2611
25 Howard St Silver Creek (14136) *(G-15450)*
Silver Griffin Inc 518 272-7771
691 Hoosick Rd Troy (12180) *(G-16255)*
Silver Oak Pharmacy Inc 718 922-3400
5105 Church Ave Brooklyn (11203) *(G-2557)*
Silverman & Gorf Inc 718 625-1309
60 Franklin Ave Brooklyn (11205) *(G-2558)*
Silverstone Shtmtl Fbrications 718 422-0380
66 Huntington St Brooklyn (11231) *(G-2559)*
Silvertique Fine Jewelry, New York *Also called Goldarama Company Inc (G-10328)*
Sima Technologies LLC 412 828-9130
125 Commerce Dr Hauppauge (11788) *(G-6191)*
Simcha Candle Co Inc 845 783-0406
244 MacArthur Ave New Windsor (12553) *(G-8955)*
Simco Leather Corporation 518 762-7100
99 Pleasant Ave Johnstown (12095) *(G-7127)*
Simco Manufacturing Jewelers 212 575-8390
62 W 47th St Ste 903 New York (10036) *(G-12076)*
Similarweb Inc 347 685-5422
251 W Nyack Rd West Nyack (10994) *(G-16926)*
Simka Diamond Corp 212 921-4420
580 5th Ave Ste 709 New York (10036) *(G-12077)*
Simmons Machine Tool Corp 518 462-5431
1700 Broadway Menands (12204) *(G-8378)*
Simmons-Boardman Pubg Corp (HQ) 212 620-7200
55 Broad St Fl 26 New York (10004) *(G-12078)*
Simon & Schuster Inc 212 698-7000
1230 Ave Of The Americas New York (10020) *(G-12079)*
Simon & Simon LLC 202 419-0490
1745 Broadway Fl 17 New York (10019) *(G-12080)*
Simon Defense Inc 516 217-6000
1533 Rocky Point Rd Middle Island (11953) *(G-8408)*
Simon Liu Inc 718 567-2011
5113 2nd Ave Brooklyn (11232) *(G-2560)*
Simon S Decorating Inc 718 339-2931
1670 E 19th St Brooklyn (11229) *(G-2561)*
Simon Schuster Digital Sls Inc 212 698-4391
51 W 52d St New York (10019) *(G-12081)*
Simple Elegance New York, Brooklyn *Also called Sabbsons International Inc (G-2528)*
Simple Elegance New York Inc 718 360-1947
474 50th St Brooklyn (11220) *(G-2562)*
Simplex Manufacturing Co Inc 315 252-7524
105 Dunning Ave Auburn (13021) *(G-519)*
Simplexgrinnell LP 585 288-6200
90 Goodway Dr Rochester (14623) *(G-14688)*
Simplexgrinnell LP 518 952-6040
1399 Vischer Ferry Rd Clifton Park (12065) *(G-3708)*
Simplexgrinnell LP 845 774-4120
4 Commerce Dr S Ste 3 Harriman (10926) *(G-5974)*
Simplexgrinnell LP 315 437-4660
6731 Collamer Rd Ste 4 East Syracuse (13057) *(G-4564)*
Simplexgrinnell LP 607 338-5100
6731 Collamer Rd Ste 4 East Syracuse (13057) *(G-4565)*
Simplicity Bandsaw Inc 716 557-8805
3674 Main St Hinsdale (14743) *(G-6424)*
Simplicity Creative Group Inc (HQ) 212 686-7676
261 Madison Ave Fl 4 New York (10016) *(G-12082)*
Simply Amazing Enterprises Inc 631 503-6452
68 S Service Rd Ste 1 Melville (11747) *(G-8355)*
Simply Gum Inc 917 721-8032
270 Lafayette St Ste 1301 New York (10012) *(G-12083)*
Simply Lite Foods, Commack *Also called Simply Natural Foods LLC (G-3843)*
Simply Logic Labs LLC 516 626-6228
200 S Service Rd Ste 211 Roslyn Heights (11577) *(G-15032)*
Simply Natural Foods LLC 631 543-9600
74 Mall Dr Commack (11725) *(G-3843)*
Simplycultivated Group LLC 646 389-0682
110 N Main St Ste 103 Horseheads (14845) *(G-6594)*
Simpore Inc 585 748-5980
150 Lucius Gordon Dr # 121 West Henrietta (14586) *(G-16895)*
Sims Group USA Holdings Corp 718 786-6031
3027 Greenpoint Ave Long Island City (11101) *(G-7877)*
Sims Metal Management, New York *Also called Smm - North America Trade Corp (G-12108)*
Sims Steel Corporation 631 587-8670
650 Muncy St Lindenhurst (11757) *(G-7482)*
Simtec Industries Corporation 631 293-0080
65 Marine St Ste A Farmingdale (11735) *(G-5109)*
Simulaids Inc 845 679-2475
16 Simulaids Dr Saugerties (12477) *(G-15194)*
Simulated Surgical Systems LLC 716 633-7216
5225 Shrdan Dr Tkf Suites Williamsville (14221) *(G-17253)*
Sinapi's Italian Ice, Hawthorne *Also called Four Brothers Italian Bakery (G-6246)*
Sincerus LLC 800 419-2804
2478 Mcdonald Ave Brooklyn (11223) *(G-2563)*
Sinclair International Company (PA) 518 798-2361
85 Boulevard Queensbury (12804) *(G-14012)*
Sinclair Technologies Inc (HQ) 716 874-3682
5811 S Park Ave 3 Hamburg (14075) *(G-5942)*
Sing Ah Poultry 718 625-7253
114 Sackett St Brooklyn (11231) *(G-2564)*
Sing Tao Daily, New York *Also called Sing Tao Newspapers NY Ltd (G-12084)*
Sing Tao Newspapers NY Ltd 212 431-9030
5317 8th Ave Brooklyn (11220) *(G-2565)*
Sing Tao Newspapers NY Ltd 718 821-0123
905 Flushing Ave Fl 2 Brooklyn (11206) *(G-2566)*
Sing Tao Newspapers NY Ltd (PA) 212 699-3800
188 Lafayette St New York (10013) *(G-12084)*
Sing Trix 212 352-1500
118 W 22nd St Fl 3 New York (10011) *(G-12085)*
Singlecut Beersmiths LLC 718 606-0788
1933 37th St Astoria (11105) *(G-456)*
Sinn- Tech Industries Inc 631 643-1171
48 Gleam St West Babylon (11704) *(G-16827)*

ALPHABETIC

Sinn-Tech Industries Inc 631 643-1171
48 Gleam St West Babylon (11704) *(G-16828)*
Sinnara, Maspeth *Also called Purvi Enterprises Incorporated (G-8166)*
Sino Printing Inc 212 334-6896
30 Allen St Frnt A New York (10002) *(G-12086)*
Sir Industries Inc 631 234-2444
208 Blydenburg Rd Unit C Hauppauge (11749) *(G-6192)*
Sir Kensington's, New York *Also called Kensington & Sons LLC (G-10835)*
Sir Speedy, Bay Shore *Also called Bondy Printing Corp (G-679)*
Sir Speedy, Rochester *Also called Beastons Budget Printing (G-14227)*
Sir Speedy, Westbury *Also called E B B Graphics Inc (G-16979)*
Sir Speedy, Plainview *Also called Nash Printing Inc (G-13623)*
Sir Speedy, Wappingers Falls *Also called Moneast Inc (G-16575)*
Sir Speedy, Pleasantville *Also called Carlara Group Ltd (G-13712)*
Sir Speedy, Westbury *Also called Sentinel Printing Inc (G-17026)*
Sir Speedy, Lake Placid *Also called Lake Placid Advertisers Wkshp (G-7275)*
Sir Speedy, Plainview *Also called P D R Inc (G-13626)*
Sirianni Hardwoods Inc 607 962-4688
912 Addison Rd Painted Post (14870) *(G-13394)*
Sister Sister Inc (PA) 212 629-9600
463 7th Ave Fl 4 New York (10018) *(G-12087)*
Sita Finishing Inc 718 417-5295
207 Starr St Ste 1 Brooklyn (11237) *(G-2567)*
Sita Knitting, Brooklyn *Also called Sita Finishing Inc (G-2567)*
Sitecompli LLC 800 564-1152
45 W 25th St Fl 3 New York (10010) *(G-12088)*
Sitecraft Inc 718 729-4900
4302 Ditmars Blvd Astoria (11105) *(G-457)*
Sitewatch Technology LLC 207 778-3246
22 Sunset Ave East Quogue (11942) *(G-4452)*
Sivko Furs Inc 607 698-4827
3089 County Route 119 Canisteo (14823) *(G-3379)*
Siw Inc 631 888-0130
271 Skip Ln Bay Shore (11706) *(G-743)*
Six Boro Publishing 347 589-6756
221 E 122nd St Apt 1703 New York (10035) *(G-12089)*
Sixnet LLC 518 877-5173
331 Ushers Rd Ste 14 Ballston Lake (12019) *(G-586)*
Sixnet Holdings LLC 518 877-5173
331 Ushers Rd Ste 10 Ballston Lake (12019) *(G-587)*
Sixpoint Brewery, Brooklyn *Also called Mad Scntsts Brwing Prtners LLC (G-2251)*
Sizzal LLC 212 354-6123
1105 44th Rd Long Island City (11101) *(G-7878)*
Sj Associates Inc (PA) 516 942-3232
500 N Broadway Ste 159 Jericho (11753) *(G-7087)*
Sjm Interface, New York *Also called Sign Company (G-12069)*
Sk Energy Shots, New York *Also called Street King LLC (G-12212)*
Skae Power Solutions LLC (PA) 845 365-9103
348 Route 9w Palisades (10964) *(G-13402)*
Skd Distribution Corp 718 525-6000
28 Westchester Ave Jericho (11753) *(G-7088)*
Skd Tactical Inc 845 897-2889
291 Main St Highland Falls (10928) *(G-6410)*
Skechers Factory Outlet 315, Bronx *Also called Skechers USA Inc (G-1456)*
Skechers USA Inc 718 585-3024
651 River Ave Bronx (10451) *(G-1456)*
Skelton Screw Products Co, Westbury *Also called All Type Screw Machine Pdts (G-16965)*
Sketch Studio Trading Inc 212 244-2875
221 W 37th St New York (10018) *(G-12090)*
SKF Aeroengine North America, Falconer *Also called SKF USA Inc (G-4912)*
SKF USA Inc 716 661-2869
1 Maroco St Falconer (14733) *(G-4912)*
SKF USA Inc 716 661-2600
402 Chandler St Jamestown (14701) *(G-7028)*
SKF USA Inc 716 661-2600
1 Maroco St Falconer (14733) *(G-4913)*
Skil-Care Corporation 914 963-2040
29 Wells Ave Bldg 4 Yonkers (10701) *(G-17484)*
Skills Alliance Inc 646 492-5300
135 W 29th St Rm 201 New York (10001) *(G-12091)*
Skimovex USA, Orchard Park *Also called Burgess-Manning Inc (G-13257)*
Skin Atelier Inc 845 294-1202
1997 Route 17m Goshen (10924) *(G-5739)*
Skin Nutrition Intl Inc 212 231-8355
410 Park Ave Fl 15 New York (10022) *(G-12092)*
Skin Prints Inc 845 920-8756
63 Walter St Pearl River (10965) *(G-13466)*
Skincare Products Inc 917 837-5255
118 E 57th St New York (10022) *(G-12093)*
Skinprint, Goshen *Also called Skin Atelier Inc (G-5739)*
Skinz Inc 516 593-3139
156 Union Ave Lynbrook (11563) *(G-7962)*
Skinz Mfg, Lynbrook *Also called Skinz Inc (G-7962)*
Skooba Design, Rochester *Also called Three Point Ventures LLC (G-14724)*
Sky Aerospace Products, Westbury *Also called John Hassall LLC (G-16999)*
Sky Art Media Inc 917 355-9022
175 Varick St Fl 8 New York (10014) *(G-12094)*
Sky Bounce Ball Company Inc 516 305-4883
301 Mill Rd Ste U4 Hewlett (11557) *(G-6313)*
Sky Dive 845 858-6400
100 River Rd Port Jervis (12771) *(G-13792)*
Sky Frame & Art Inc (PA) 212 925-7856
141 W 28th St Fl 12 New York (10001) *(G-12095)*
Sky Geek, Lagrangeville *Also called Styles Aviation Inc (G-7259)*
Sky Laundromat Inc 718 639-7070
8615 Ava Pl Apt 4e Jamaica (11432) *(G-6949)*
Skydyne Company 845 858-6400
100 River Rd Port Jervis (12771) *(G-13793)*
Skyguard, Hauppauge *Also called Vehicle Manufacturers Inc (G-6222)*
Skyhorse Publishing Inc 212 643-6816
307 W 36th St Fl 11 New York (10018) *(G-12096)*
Skylark Publications Ltd 607 535-9866
217 N Franklin St Watkins Glen (14891) *(G-16696)*
Skyler Brand Ventures LLC 646 979-5904
590 Madison Ave Fl 19 New York (10022) *(G-12097)*
Skyline LLC 631 403-4131
16 Hulse Rd Ste 1 East Setauket (11733) *(G-4492)*
Skyline New York, Hauppauge *Also called Watson Productions LLC (G-6230)*
Skystem LLC 877 778-3320
100 W 92nd St Apt 20d New York (10025) *(G-12098)*
Skytravel (usa) LLC 518 888-2610
20 Talon Dr Schenectady (12309) *(G-15298)*
Slant/Fin Corporation (PA) 516 484-2600
100 Forest Dr Greenvale (11548) *(G-5881)*
Slantco Manufacturing Inc (HQ) 516 484-2600
100 Forest Dr Greenvale (11548) *(G-5882)*
Slanto Manufacturing Inc 516 759-5721
40 Garvies Point Rd Glen Cove (11542) *(G-5628)*
Slava Industries Incorporated (PA) 718 499-4850
555 16th St Brooklyn (11215) *(G-2568)*
Sleep Care Enterprises Inc 631 246-9000
1212 N Country Rd Ste 3b Stony Brook (11790) *(G-15771)*
Sleep Improvement Center Inc 516 536-5799
178 Sunrise Hwy Fl 2 Rockville Centre (11570) *(G-14798)*
Sleep Master, Syracuse *Also called Futon City Discounters Inc (G-15944)*
Sleeping Partners Home Fashion, Brooklyn *Also called Sleeping Partners Intl Inc (G-2569)*
Sleeping Partners Intl Inc 212 254-1515
140 58th St Ste 11 Brooklyn (11220) *(G-2569)*
Sleepy Head Inc 718 237-9655
230 3rd St Brooklyn (11215) *(G-2570)*
Sleepy Hollow Chimney Sup Ltd 631 231-2333
85 Emjay Blvd Brentwood (11717) *(G-1194)*
Slim Line Case Co Inc 585 546-3639
64 Spencer St Rochester (14608) *(G-14689)*
Slims Bagels Unlimited Inc (PA) 718 229-1140
22118 Horace Harding Expy Oakland Gardens (11364) *(G-13067)*
Sliperfection, New York *Also called Lady Ester Lingerie Corp (G-10914)*
Sln Group Inc 718 677-5969
2172 E 26th St Brooklyn (11229) *(G-2571)*
Sloane Design Inc 212 539-0184
336 W 37th St Rm 204 New York (10018) *(G-12099)*
Slosson Edctl Publications Inc 716 652-0930
538 Buffalo Rd East Aurora (14052) *(G-4379)*
Slyde Inc 917 331-2114
474 48th Ave Apt 18a Long Island City (11109) *(G-7879)*
SM New York 718 446-1800
5216 Barnett Ave Long Island City (11104) *(G-7880)*
Small Business Advisors Inc 516 374-1387
2005 Park St Atlantic Beach (11509) *(G-470)*
Small Packages Inc 845 255-7710
6 Da Vinci Way New Paltz (12561) *(G-8878)*
Smart & Strong LLC 212 938-2051
212 W 35th St Fl 8 New York (10001) *(G-12100)*
Smart High Voltage Solutions 631 563-6724
390 Knickerbocker Ave # 6 Bohemia (11716) *(G-1135)*
Smart Space Products LLC (PA) 877 777-2441
244 5th Ave Ste 2487 New York (10001) *(G-12101)*
Smart Systems Inc 607 776-5380
320 E Washington St Bath (14810) *(G-662)*
Smart USA Inc 718 416-4400
6907 69th Pl Glendale (11385) *(G-5663)*
Smart Weigh, Spring Valley *Also called Measupro Inc (G-15596)*
Smartoners Inc (PA) 718 975-0197
289 Keap St Ste A Brooklyn (11211) *(G-2572)*
Smartpill Corporation 716 882-0701
847 Main St Buffalo (14203) *(G-3188)*
Smartys Corner 607 239-5276
501 W Main St Endicott (13760) *(G-4829)*
SMC, Conklin *Also called E-Systems Group LLC (G-3868)*
Smg Control Systems, Buffalo *Also called Service Mfg Group Inc (G-3184)*
SMI, Salamanca *Also called Snyder Manufacturing Inc (G-15107)*
Smidgens Inc 585 624-1486
7336 Community Dr Lima (14485) *(G-7448)*
Smile Specialists 877 337-6135
236 E 36th St New York (10016) *(G-12102)*
Smith & Johnson Dry Goods (PA) 212 951-7067
295 5th Ave Ste 114 New York (10016) *(G-12103)*
Smith & Sons Fuels Inc 518 661-6112
36 2nd Ave Mayfield (12117) *(G-8214)*

ALPHABETIC

Smith & Watson 212 686-6444
200 Lexington Ave Rm 805 New York (10016) *(G-12104)*
Smith Control Systems Inc 518 828-7646
1839 Route 9h Hudson (12534) *(G-6635)*
Smith Graphics Inc 631 420-4180
40 Florida St Farmingdale (11735) *(G-5110)*
Smith International Inc 585 265-2330
1915 Lake Rd Ontario (14519) *(G-13215)*
Smith International Inc 212 350-9400
601 Lexington Ave Fl 57 New York (10022) *(G-12105)*
Smith Metal Works Newark Inc 315 331-1651
1000 E Union St Newark (14513) *(G-12742)*
Smith Sand & Gravel Inc 315 673-4124
4782 Shepard Rd Marcellus (13108) *(G-8089)*
Smith Service Corps, Ontario *Also called Smith International Inc (G-13215)*
Smith Street Bread Co LLC 718 797-9712
17 5th St Brooklyn (11231) *(G-2573)*
Smith Tool & Die Inc 607 674-4165
714 Pleasant Valley Rd Sherburne (13460) *(G-15396)*
Smith, E W Publishing, New Windsor *Also called Sentinel Printing Services Inc (G-8954)*
Smithers Tools & Mch Pdts Inc 845 876-3063
3718 Route 9g Rhinebeck (12572) *(G-14058)*
Smiths Gas Service Inc 518 438-0400
5 Walker Way Ste 1 Albany (12205) *(G-134)*
Smithtown Concrete Products 631 265-1815
441 Middle Country Rd Saint James (11780) *(G-15091)*
Smithtown News Inc 631 265-2100
1 Brooksite Dr Smithtown (11787) *(G-15498)*
SMK Wines & Liquors LLC 212 685-7651
23 E 28th St New York (10016) *(G-12106)*
Sml Acquisition LLC 914 592-3130
33 W Main St Ste 505 Elmsford (10523) *(G-4785)*
Sml Brothers Holding Corp 718 402-2000
820 E 140th St Bronx (10454) *(G-1457)*
Sml USA Inc (PA) 212 736-8800
5 Penn Plz Ste 1500 New York (10001) *(G-12107)*
Smm - North America Trade Corp 212 604-0710
16 W 22nd St Fl 10 New York (10010) *(G-12108)*
Smn Medical PC 844 362-2428
2 Allendale Dr Rye (10580) *(G-15068)*
Smokey Joes, Oceanside *Also called Yale Trouser Corporation (G-13107)*
Smooth Industries Incorporated 212 869-1080
1411 Broadway Rm 3000 New York (10018) *(G-12109)*
Smooth Magazine 212 925-1150
55 John St Ste 800 New York (10038) *(G-12110)*
Smoothbore International Inc 315 754-8124
13881 Westbury Cutoff Rd Red Creek (13143) *(G-14026)*
Smsc, Hauppauge *Also called Standard Microsystems Corp (G-6199)*
Snack Innovations Inc 718 509-9366
67 35th St Unit 3 Brooklyn (11232) *(G-2574)*
Snacks On 48 Inc 347 663-1100
1960 59th St Brooklyn (11204) *(G-2575)*
Snapp Too Enterprise 718 224-5252
3312 211th St Flushing (11361) *(G-5293)*
Snapple 914 846-2300
55 Hunter Ln Elmsford (10523) *(G-4786)*
Snapple Distributors, Ronkonkoma *Also called American Bottling Company (G-14868)*
Snapple Distributors, Staten Island *Also called Gangi Distributors Inc (G-15676)*
Sneaker News Inc 347 687-1588
41 Elizabeth St Ste 301 New York (10013) *(G-12111)*
Sneakers Software Inc 800 877-9221
519 8th Ave Rm 812 New York (10018) *(G-12112)*
Sneaky Chef Foods LLC 914 301-3277
520 White Plains Rd Tarrytown (10591) *(G-16106)*
Snow Craft Co Inc 516 739-1399
200 Fulton Ave New Hyde Park (11040) *(G-8862)*
Snowman 212 239-8818
1181 Broadway Fl 6 New York (10001) *(G-12113)*
Snr Cctv Systems Division, Port Jefferson *Also called Sartek Industries Inc (G-13779)*
Sns Machinery, Brooklyn *Also called Riverside Machinery Company (G-2497)*
Snyder Industries Inc (PA) 716 694-1240
340 Wales Ave Tonawanda (14150) *(G-16203)*
Snyder Logging 315 265-1462
528 Allen Falls Rd Potsdam (13676) *(G-13884)*
Snyder Manufacturing Inc 716 945-0354
255 Rochester St Unit 1 Salamanca (14779) *(G-15107)*
Snyder Neon & Plastic Signs, Colonie *Also called Snyders Neon Displays Inc (G-3821)*
Snyders Neon Displays Inc 518 857-4100
5 Highland Ave Colonie (12205) *(G-3821)*
Soavedra Masonry Inc 347 695-5254
77 Batavia Pl Harrison (10528) *(G-5990)*
Sobi, Brooklyn *Also called Social Bicycles Inc (G-2576)*
Soc America Inc 631 472-6666
3505 Veterans Memorial Hw Ronkonkoma (11779) *(G-14986)*
Social Bicycles Inc 917 746-7624
47 Hall St Ste 414 Brooklyn (11205) *(G-2576)*
Social Science Electronic Pubg 585 442-8170
2171 Monroe Ave Ste 203 Rochester (14618) *(G-14690)*
Society Awards, Long Island City *Also called Dwm International Inc (G-7721)*
Society For The Study 212 822-8806
20 W 20th St Fl 2 New York (10011) *(G-12114)*
Socket Products Mfg Corp 631 232-9870
175 Bridge Rd Islandia (11749) *(G-6803)*
Socks and More of NY Inc 718 769-1785
1605 Avenue Z Fl 1 Brooklyn (11235) *(G-2577)*
Socks For Everyone Inc 347 754-0210
18415 58th Ave Fresh Meadows (11365) *(G-5445)*
Sofa Doctor Inc 718 292-6300
220 E 134th St Frnt 1b Bronx (10451) *(G-1458)*
Sofanou, Niagara Falls *Also called Delfingen Us-New York Inc (G-12810)*
Soft Serve Apple LLC 646 442-8002
37 W 17th St Ste 4w New York (10011) *(G-12115)*
Soft Serve Fruit Co LLC (PA) 646 442-8002
37 W 17th St Ste 4w New York (10011) *(G-12116)*
Soft Sheen Products Inc (HQ) 212 818-1500
575 5th Ave New York (10017) *(G-12117)*
Soft-Noze Usa Inc 315 732-2726
2216 Broad St Frankfort (13340) *(G-5357)*
Soft-Tex International Inc 518 235-3645
428 Hudson River Rd Waterford (12188) *(G-16621)*
Soft-Tex Manufacturing Co, Waterford *Also called Soft-Tex International Inc (G-16621)*
Softlink International 914 574-8197
297 Knollwood Rd Ste 301 White Plains (10607) *(G-17168)*
Software & General Services Co 315 986-4184
1365 Fairway 5 Cir Walworth (14568) *(G-16552)*
Sohha Savory Yogurt, New York *Also called Mualema LLC (G-11321)*
Soho and Tribeca Map, New York *Also called Ozmodyl Ltd (G-11545)*
Soho Apparel Ltd 212 840-1109
525 Fashion Ave Fl 6 New York (10018) *(G-12118)*
Soho Editions Inc 914 591-5100
2641 Deer St Mohegan Lake (10547) *(G-8545)*
Soho Guilds, Kew Gardens *Also called A & B Color Corp (del) (G-7157)*
Soho Letterpress Inc 718 788-2518
68 35th St Unit 6 Brooklyn (11232) *(G-2578)*
Soho Press Inc 212 260-1900
853 Broadway Ste 1402 New York (10003) *(G-12119)*
Soifer Center, The, White Plains *Also called Lydia H Soifer & Assoc Inc (G-17135)*
Sokolin LLC (PA) 631 537-4434
445 Sills Rd Unit K Yaphank (11980) *(G-17403)*
Sokolin Wine, Yaphank *Also called Sokolin LLC (G-17403)*
Sol Markowitz, Monroe *Also called C T A Digital Inc (G-8551)*
Sola Home Expo Inc 718 646-3383
172 Neptune Ave Brooklyn (11235) *(G-2579)*
Solabia USA Inc 212 847-2397
60 Broad St Lbby A New York (10004) *(G-12120)*
Solar Energy Systems LLC (PA) 718 389-1545
1205 Manhattan Ave # 1210 Brooklyn (11222) *(G-2580)*
Solar Metrology LLC 845 247-4701
1340 Lincoln Ave Ste 6 Holbrook (11741) *(G-6471)*
Solar Screen Co Inc 718 592-8222
5311 105th St Corona (11368) *(G-4007)*
Solar Thin Films Inc (PA) 516 341-7787
1136 Rxr Plz Uniondale (11556) *(G-16299)*
Solarpath Inc 201 490-4499
415 Madison Ave Fl 14 New York (10017) *(G-12121)*
Solarpath Sun Solutions, New York *Also called Solarpath Inc (G-12121)*
Solartech Renewables LLC 646 675-1853
75 Vassar Rd Poughkeepsie (12603) *(G-13931)*
Solarwaterstar, Brooklyn *Also called Solarwaterway (G-2581)*
Solarwaterway 646 387-9346
4703 Bay Pkwy Brooklyn (11230) *(G-2581)*
Solarz Bros Printing Corp 718 383-1330
231 Norman Ave Ste 105 Brooklyn (11222) *(G-2582)*
Soldi, Brooklyn *Also called Mpr Magazine App Inc (G-2338)*
Solenis 212 772-0560
240 E 82nd St New York (10028) *(G-12122)*
Solenis 212 204-6679
108 E 38th St New York (10016) *(G-12123)*
Solenis 212 362-1759
310 W 85th St New York (10024) *(G-12124)*
Solepoxy Inc 716 372-6300
211 W Franklin St Olean (14760) *(G-13153)*
Solex Catsmo Fine Foods, Wallkill *Also called Catsmo Corp (G-16542)*
Solid Bilt Construction 315 893-1738
7561 State Route 20 Madison (13402) *(G-7994)*
Solid Cell Inc 585 426-5000
771 Elmgrove Rd Rochester (14624) *(G-14691)*
Solid Surface Acrylics Inc 716 743-1870
800 Walck Rd Ste 14 North Tonawanda (14120) *(G-12994)*
Solid Surface Acrylics LLC 716 743-1870
800 Walck Rd Ste 14 North Tonawanda (14120) *(G-12995)*
Solid Surfaces Inc 585 292-5340
1 Townline Cir Rochester (14623) *(G-14692)*
Solid-Look Corporation 917 683-1780
4628 243rd St Douglaston (11362) *(G-4311)*
Solidus Industries Inc 607 749-4540
6849 N Glen Haven Rd Homer (13077) *(G-6522)*
Solitec Incorporated 315 298-4213
3981 Port St Pulaski (13142) *(G-13952)*
Solivaira Specialties Inc 716 693-4009
4 Detroit St North Tonawanda (14120) *(G-12996)*

ALPHABETIC

ALPHABETIC SECTION

Solmac Inc 716 630-7061
1975 Wehrle Dr Ste 130 Williamsville (14221) *(G-17254)*
Solo, Brooklyn Also called Air Skate & Air Jump Corp *(G-1572)*
Solo Licensing Corp 212 244-5505
358 5th Ave Rm 1205 New York (10001) *(G-12125)*
Solomon Schwimmer 718 625-5719
65 Heyward St Brooklyn (11249) *(G-2583)*
Solowave Design Corp 716 646-3103
4625 Clark St Hamburg (14075) *(G-5943)*
Solstarny, New York Also called Solstars Inc *(G-12126)*
Solstars Inc 212 605-0430
575 Madison Ave Ste 1006 New York (10022) *(G-12126)*
Solstiss Inc 212 719-9194
561 Fashion Ave Fl 16 New York (10018) *(G-12127)*
Solutia Business Entps Inc 314 674-1000
111 8th Ave New York (10011) *(G-12128)*
Solvaira Specialties Inc (PA) 716 693-4040
50 Bridge St North Tonawanda (14120) *(G-12997)*
Solve Advisors Inc 646 699-5041
265 Sunrise Hwy Ste 22 Rockville Centre (11570) *(G-14799)*
Solvents Company Inc 631 595-9300
9 Cornell St Kingston (12401) *(G-7210)*
Somers Stain Glass Inc 631 586-7772
108 Brook Ave Ste A Deer Park (11729) *(G-4211)*
Somerset Dyeing & Finishing 518 773-7383
68 Harrison St Gloversville (12078) *(G-5720)*
Somerset Industries Inc (PA) 518 773-7383
68 Harrison St Gloversville (12078) *(G-5721)*
Somerset Manufacturers Inc 516 626-3832
36 Glen Cove Rd Roslyn Heights (11577) *(G-15033)*
Somerset Production Co LLC 716 932-6480
338 Harris Hill Rd # 102 Buffalo (14221) *(G-3189)*
Somerville Acquisitions Co Inc 845 856-5261
15 Big Pond Rd Huguenot (12746) *(G-6651)*
Somerville Tech Group Inc 908 782-9500
15 Big Pond Rd Huguenot (12746) *(G-6652)*
Sommer, Amherst Also called Sterling United Inc *(G-262)*
Sommer and Sons Printing Inc 716 822-4311
2222 S Park Ave Buffalo (14220) *(G-3190)*
Somml Health LLC 518 880-2170
43 New Scotland Ave Mc25 Albany (12208) *(G-135)*
Sonaal Industries Inc 718 383-3860
210 Kingsland Ave Brooklyn (11222) *(G-2584)*
Sonaer Inc 631 756-4780
68 Lamar St Unit D West Babylon (11704) *(G-16829)*
Sonic Boom Inc 212 242-2852
259 W 30th St Rm 801 New York (10001) *(G-12129)*
Sonicor Inc 631 920-6555
82 Otis St West Babylon (11704) *(G-16830)*
Sonneman-A Way of Light 845 926-5469
151 Airport Dr Wappingers Falls (12590) *(G-16576)*
Sono-Tek Corporation (PA) 845 795-2020
2012 Route 9w Stop 3 Milton (12547) *(G-8484)*
Sonoco-Crellin Inc (HQ) 518 392-2000
87 Center St Chatham (12037) *(G-3560)*
Sonoco-Crellin Intl Inc (HQ) 518 392-2000
87 Center St Chatham (12037) *(G-3561)*
Sonomed Inc 516 354-0900
1979 Marcus Ave Ste C105 New Hyde Park (11042) *(G-8863)*
Sonomed Escalon, New Hyde Park Also called Sonomed Inc *(G-8863)*
Sonotec US Inc 631 404-7497
15 2nd Ave Central Islip (11722) *(G-3510)*
Sontek Industries Inc (PA) 781 749-3055
36 E 12th St Fl 6 New York (10003) *(G-12130)*
Sony Broadband Entertainment (HQ) 212 833-6800
550 Madison Ave Fl 6 New York (10022) *(G-12131)*
Sony Corporation of America (HQ) 212 833-8000
25 Madison Ave Fl 27 New York (10010) *(G-12132)*
Sony Dadc US Inc 212 833-8800
550 Madison Ave New York (10022) *(G-12133)*
Sony Music Entertainment, New York Also called Sony Corporation of America *(G-12132)*
Sony Music Entertainment Inc 212 833-8000
25 Madison Ave Fl 19 New York (10010) *(G-12134)*
Sony Music Entertainment Inc (HQ) 212 833-8500
25 Madison Ave Fl 19 New York (10010) *(G-12135)*
Sony Music Entertainment Inc 212 833-5057
79 5th Ave Fl 16 New York (10003) *(G-12136)*
Sony Music Holdings, New York Also called Sony Music Entertainment Inc *(G-12134)*
Sony Music Holdings Inc (HQ) 212 833-8000
550 Madison Ave Fl 6 New York (10022) *(G-12137)*
Sony Style, New York Also called Sony Dadc US Inc *(G-12133)*
Sony Wonder, New York Also called Sony Music Entertainment Inc *(G-12135)*
Sony/Atv Music Publishing LLC (HQ) 212 833-7730
25 Madison Ave Fl 24 New York (10010) *(G-12138)*
Sopark Corp (PA) 716 822-0434
3300 S Park Ave Buffalo (14218) *(G-3191)*
Soper Designs, New York Also called Kurt Gaum Inc *(G-10895)*
Sophiexx Corporation 917 963-5339
14715 33rd Ave Flushing (11354) *(G-5294)*
Sorfin Yoshimura Ic Disc Ltd 516 802-4600
100 Crossways Park Dr W # 200 Woodbury (11797) *(G-17300)*

Soroc Technology Corp 716 849-5913
1051 Clinton St Buffalo (14206) *(G-3192)*
Sorrento Lactalis, Buffalo Also called Lactalis American Group Inc *(G-3043)*
Sorrento Lactalis Incorporated 716 823-6262
37 Franklin St Buffalo (14202) *(G-3193)*
SOS Chefs of New York Inc 212 505-5813
104 Avenue B Apt 1 New York (10009) *(G-12139)*
SOS International LLC (HQ) 212 742-2410
40 Fulton St Fl 26 New York (10038) *(G-12140)*
Sosi, New York Also called SOS International LLC *(G-12140)*
Sotek Inc 716 821-5961
3590 Jeffrey Blvd Blasdell (14219) *(G-966)*
Soterix Medical Inc 888 990-8327
237 W 35th St Ste 1401 New York (10001) *(G-12141)*
Soterix Medical Technologies, New York Also called Soterix Medical Inc *(G-12141)*
Soul Full Cup, Corning Also called Joseph H Navaie *(G-3974)*
Soul Journ LLC 646 823-9882
251 W 136th St Apt 2b New York (10030) *(G-12142)*
Sound & Communication, Port Washington Also called Testa Communications Inc *(G-13868)*
Sound Communications Inc 516 767-2500
25 Willowdale Ave Port Washington (11050) *(G-13866)*
Sound Source Inc 585 271-5370
161 Norris Dr Rochester (14610) *(G-14693)*
Sound Video Systems Wny LLC 716 684-8200
1720 Military Rd Buffalo (14217) *(G-3194)*
Soundcoat Company Inc (HQ) 631 242-2200
1 Burt Dr Deer Park (11729) *(G-4212)*
Source Envelope Inc 866 284-0707
104 Allen Blvd Ste I Farmingdale (11735) *(G-5111)*
Source Media, New York Also called Credit Union Journal Inc *(G-9753)*
Source Media Inc (HQ) 212 803-8200
1 State St Fl 26 New York (10004) *(G-12143)*
Source One Promotional Product 516 208-6996
2024 Brian Dr Merrick (11566) *(G-8393)*
Source Technologies 718 708-0305
9728 3rd Ave Brooklyn (11209) *(G-2585)*
South Bridge Press Inc 212 233-4047
122 W 26th St Fl 3 New York (10001) *(G-12144)*
South Brooklyn Book Company, New York Also called Welcome Rain Publishers LLC *(G-12606)*
South Central Boyz 718 496-7270
2568 Bedford Ave Apt 1a Brooklyn (11226) *(G-2586)*
South of The Highway, Southampton Also called Dans Paper Inc *(G-15542)*
South Seneca Vinyl LLC 315 585-6050
1585 Yale Farm Rd Romulus (14541) *(G-14843)*
South Shore Ice Co Inc 516 379-2056
89 E Fulton Ave Roosevelt (11575) *(G-15009)*
South Shore Ready Mix Inc 516 872-3049
116 E Hawthorne Ave Valley Stream (11580) *(G-16428)*
South Shore Tribune Inc 516 431-5628
4 California Pl N Island Park (11558) *(G-6784)*
Southampton Town Newspapers (PA) 631 283-4100
135 Windmill Ln Southampton (11968) *(G-15552)*
Southampton Town Newspapers 631 288-1100
12 Mitchell Rd Westhampton Beach (11978) *(G-17061)*
Southbay Fuel Injectors 516 442-4707
566 Merrick Rd Ste 3 Rockville Centre (11570) *(G-14800)*
Southco Inc 585 624-2545
250 East St Honeoye Falls (14472) *(G-6537)*
Southern Adrndck Fbr Prdcrs CP 518 692-2700
2532 State Route 40 Greenwich (12834) *(G-5893)*
Southern Graphic Systems LLC 315 695-7079
67 County Route 59 Phoenix (13135) *(G-13544)*
Southern Standard Cartons, East Elmhurst Also called Standard Group *(G-4397)*
Southern Standard Cartoons, East Elmhurst Also called Standard Group LLC *(G-4398)*
Southern States Coop Inc 315 438-4500
6701 Manlius Center Rd # 240 East Syracuse (13057) *(G-4566)*
Southern Tier Industries, Elmira Also called Chemung Cty Assc Retrd Ctzns *(G-4675)*
Southern Tier Patterns 607 734-1265
608 Chester St Elmira (14904) *(G-4701)*
Southern Tier Pennysaver, Jamestown Also called Spartan Publishing Inc *(G-7029)*
Southern Tier Plastics Inc 607 723-2601
Kirkwood Industrial Park Binghamton (13902) *(G-952)*
Southside Precast Products, Buffalo Also called P J R Industries Inc *(G-3106)*
Soutine Inc 212 496-1450
104 W 70th St Frnt 1 New York (10023) *(G-12145)*
Sovereign Brands LLC 212 343-8366
81 Greene St Apt 2 New York (10012) *(G-12146)*
Sovereign Servicing System LLC 914 779-1400
1 Stone Pl Ste 200 Bronxville (10708) *(G-1503)*
Sp Scientific, Gardiner Also called S P Industries Inc *(G-5550)*
Spa Sciara, Mount Kisco Also called Plastic & Reconstructive Svcs *(G-8640)*
Space 150 .... 612 332-6458
20 Jay St Ste 928 Brooklyn (11201) *(G-2587)*
Space Age Plstic Fbrcators Inc 718 324-4062
4519 White Plains Rd Bronx (10470) *(G-1459)*
Space Coast Semiconductor Inc 631 414-7131
1111 Broadhollow Rd Fl 3 Farmingdale (11735) *(G-5112)*

ALPHABETIC SECTION

Spinmedia Group Inc

Space Sign....718 961-1112
1525 132nd St College Point (11356) **(G-3808)**
Space-Craft Worldwide Inc....631 603-3000
91 Rodeo Dr Edgewood (11717) **(G-4612)**
Spaceship Company, The, New York *Also called Tsc LLC* **(G-12416)**
Spaeth Design Inc....718 606-9685
6006 37th Ave Woodside (11377) **(G-17353)**
Spaghetti Bridge LLC....646 369-7505
27 Dorchester Rd Scarsdale (10583) **(G-15224)**
Spancraft Ltd....516 295-0055
920 Railroad Ave Woodmere (11598) **(G-17314)**
Spandage, Brooklyn *Also called Medi-Tech International Corp* **(G-2291)**
Spanish Artisan Wine Group LLC....914 414-6982
370 Cushman Rd Patterson (12563) **(G-13444)**
Spanish Artisan Wine Group Ltd, Patterson *Also called Spanish Artisan Wine Group LLC* **(G-13444)**
Spanish Tele Dirctry Hola 912, Long Island City *Also called Hola Publishing Co* **(G-7761)**
Spanjer Corp....347 448-8033
3856 11th St Long Island City (11101) **(G-7881)**
Spanjer Signs, Long Island City *Also called Spanjer Corp* **(G-7881)**
Spano's Bread, Utica *Also called Ohio Baking Company Inc* **(G-16354)**
Spark Creations Inc....212 575-8385
10 W 46th St Fl 9 New York (10036) **(G-12147)**
Sparkle Light Manufacturing, Yonkers *Also called Lighting By Dom Yonkers Inc* **(G-17462)**
Sparkspread, New York *Also called Great North Road Media Inc* **(G-10358)**
Sparrow Mining Co (PA)....718 519-6600
3743 White Plains Rd Bronx (10467) **(G-1460)**
Spartacist Publishing Co....212 732-7860
48 Warren St New York (10007) **(G-12148)**
Spartan Brands Inc (PA)....212 340-0320
451 Park Ave S Fl 5 New York (10016) **(G-12149)**
Spartan Brands Inc....212 340-0320
451 Park Ave S Fl 5 New York (10016) **(G-12150)**
Spartan Instruments, North Babylon *Also called Pmb Precision Products Inc* **(G-12902)**
Spartan Precision Machining....516 546-5171
9 Niagara Ave Freeport (11520) **(G-5428)**
Spartan Publishing Inc....716 664-7373
2 Harding Ave Jamestown (14701) **(G-7029)**
Spatula LLC....917 582-8684
2165 Broadway New York (10024) **(G-12151)**
Spaulding & Rogers Mfg Inc....518 768-2070
3252 New Scotland Rd Voorheesville (12186) **(G-16518)**
Spaulding Law Printing Inc....315 422-4805
231 Walton St Ste 103 Syracuse (13202) **(G-16042)**
Spc Marketing Company....631 661-2727
191 Norma Ave West Islip (11795) **(G-16907)**
Speaqua Corp....516 380-5008
46 W Jefryn Blvd Deer Park (11729) **(G-4213)**
Special Metals Corporation....315 798-2900
4317 Middle Settlement Rd New Hartford (13413) **(G-8811)**
Special Metals Corporation....716 366-5663
100 Willowbrook Ave Dunkirk (14048) **(G-4351)**
Special Tees....718 980-0987
250 Buel Ave Staten Island (10305) **(G-15735)**
Speciality Quality Packaging, Schenectady *Also called Sqp Inc* **(G-15299)**
Specialized Packg Group Inc (HQ)....315 638-4355
2900 Mclane Rd Baldwinsville (13027) **(G-575)**
Specialized Packg Radisson LLC....315 638-4355
8800 Sixty Rd Baldwinsville (13027) **(G-576)**
Specialized Printed Forms Inc....585 538-2381
352 Center St Caledonia (14423) **(G-3282)**
Specialty Bldg Solutions Inc....631 393-6918
Eads St Ste 165a West Babylon (11704) **(G-16831)**
Specialty Fabricators....631 256-6982
4120 Sunrise Hwy Oakdale (11769) **(G-13062)**
Specialty Ink Co Inc (PA)....631 586-3666
40 Harbour Dr Blue Point (11715) **(G-1000)**
Specialty Microwave Corp....631 737-2175
120 Raynor Ave Ronkonkoma (11779) **(G-14987)**
Specialty Minerals Inc....518 585-7982
35 Highland St Ticonderoga (12883) **(G-16128)**
Specialty Minerals Inc (HQ)....212 878-1800
622 3rd Ave Fl 38 New York (10017) **(G-12152)**
Specialty Quality Packg LLC....914 580-3200
602 Potential Pkwy Scotia (12302) **(G-15331)**
Specialty Services....585 728-5650
2631e Naples St Wayland (14572) **(G-16711)**
Specialty Signs Co Inc....212 243-8521
54 W 21st St Rm 201 New York (10010) **(G-12153)**
Specialty Silicone Pdts Inc....518 885-8826
3 Mccrea Hill Rd Ballston Spa (12020) **(G-609)**
Specialty Steel Fabg Corp....718 893-6326
555 Longfellow Ave Bronx (10474) **(G-1461)**
Specialty Wldg & Fabg NY Inc (PA)....315 426-1807
1025 Hiawatha Blvd E Syracuse (13208) **(G-16043)**
Specilty Bus Mchs Holdings LLC....212 587-9600
260 W 35th St Fl 11 New York (10001) **(G-12154)**
Spectaculars, Westhampton Beach *Also called Frame Works America Inc* **(G-17058)**
Spectator Publishing Co Inc....212 854-9550
2875 Broadway Ste 3 New York (10025) **(G-12155)**
Spectra Color Corp....631 563-4828
45 Knickerbocker Ave 4 Holbrook (11741) **(G-6472)**
Spectra Vista Corporation....845 471-7007
29 Firemens Way Poughkeepsie (12603) **(G-13932)**
Spectracom, Rochester *Also called Orolia Usa Inc* **(G-14553)**
Spectral Systems LLC (PA)....845 896-2200
35 Corporate Park Rd Hopewell Junction (12533) **(G-6559)**
Spectralink Corporation....212 372-6997
1 Penn Plz Ste 4800 New York (10119) **(G-12156)**
Spectron Glass & Electronics....631 582-5600
595 Old Willets Path A Hauppauge (11788) **(G-6193)**
Spectron Systems Technology (PA)....631 582-5600
595 Old Willets Path A Hauppauge (11788) **(G-6194)**
Spectronics Corporation....516 333-4840
956 Brush Hollow Rd Westbury (11590) **(G-17027)**
Spectrum, Oceanside *Also called Kantek Inc* **(G-13084)**
Spectrum Apparel Inc....212 239-2025
463 Fashion Ave Fl 12 New York (10018) **(G-12157)**
Spectrum Brands Inc....631 232-1200
2100 Pacific St Hauppauge (11788) **(G-6195)**
Spectrum Cable Corporation....585 235-7714
295 Mount Read Blvd Ste 2 Rochester (14611) **(G-14694)**
Spectrum Catalysts Inc....631 560-3683
69 Windsor Pl Central Islip (11722) **(G-3511)**
Spectrum Crafts Inc....631 244-5749
70 Orville Dr Ste 1 Bohemia (11716) **(G-1136)**
Spectrum Graphics & Print....845 473-4400
306 Main St Poughkeepsie (12601) **(G-13933)**
Spectrum Microwave Inc....315 253-6241
23 N Division St Auburn (13021) **(G-520)**
Spectrum On Broadway....718 932-5388
6106 34th Ave Woodside (11377) **(G-17354)**
Spectrum Prtg Lithography Inc....212 255-3131
505 8th Ave Rm 1802 New York (10018) **(G-12158)**
Spectrum Signs Inc....631 756-1010
6106 34th Ave Woodside (11377) **(G-17355)**
Spectrum Thin Films Inc....631 901-1010
135 Marcus Blvd Hauppauge (11788) **(G-6196)**
Speedcard Inc....631 472-1904
133 Glenmere Way Holbrook (11741) **(G-6473)**
Speedpro Imaging, East Syracuse *Also called Bk Printing Inc* **(G-4511)**
Speedway LLC....631 738-2536
2825 Middle Country Rd Lake Grove (11755) **(G-7266)**
Speedway LLC....718 815-6897
951 Bay St Staten Island (10305) **(G-15736)**
Speedway Press Inc....315 343-3531
1 Burkle St Oswego (13126) **(G-13341)**
Speedways Conveyors Inc....716 893-2222
1210 E Ferry St Buffalo (14211) **(G-3195)**
Speedy Enterprise of USA Corp....718 463-3000
4120 162nd St Flushing (11358) **(G-5295)**
Speedy Sign A Rama USA Inc....516 783-1075
2956 Merrick Rd Bellmore (11710) **(G-823)**
Speer Equipment Inc....585 964-2700
832 Moscow Rd Hamlin (14464) **(G-5951)**
Spektrix Inc....646 741-5110
115 W 30th St Rm 501 New York (10001) **(G-12159)**
Spellman High Vltage Elec Corp (PA)....631 630-3000
475 Wireless Blvd Hauppauge (11788) **(G-6197)**
Spence Engineering Company Inc....845 778-5566
150 Coldenham Rd Walden (12586) **(G-16536)**
Spencer AB Inc....646 831-3728
265 W 37th St Rm 2388 New York (10018) **(G-12160)**
Spencer Jeremy, New York *Also called HMS Productions Inc* **(G-10489)**
Sperry Advertising, South Glens Falls *Also called Northeast Stitches & Ink Inc* **(G-15528)**
Spex, Rochester *Also called Precision Machine Tech LLC* **(G-14595)**
Speyside Holdings LLC....845 928-2221
911 State Route 32 Highland Mills (10930) **(G-6414)**
Spf Holdings II LLC (HQ)....212 750-8300
9 W 57th St Ste 4200 New York (10019) **(G-12161)**
Spfm Corp (PA)....718 788-6800
162 2nd Ave Brooklyn (11215) **(G-2588)**
Spforms, Caledonia *Also called Specialized Printed Forms Inc* **(G-3282)**
Sph Group Holdings LLC (PA)....212 520-2300
590 Madison Ave Fl 32 New York (10022) **(G-12162)**
Spic and Span Company....914 524-6823
660 White Plains Rd Tarrytown (10591) **(G-16107)**
Spider, Woodside *Also called Safeworks LLC* **(G-17352)**
Spiegel Woodworks Inc....845 336-8090
418 Old Neighborhood Rd Kingston (12401) **(G-7211)**
Spin Holdco Inc (HQ)....516 349-8555
303 Sunnyside Blvd # 70 Plainview (11803) **(G-13635)**
Spin Magazine Media....212 231-7400
276 5th Ave Rm 800 New York (10001) **(G-12163)**
Spin-Rite Corporation....585 266-5200
30 Dubelbeiss Ln Rochester (14622) **(G-14695)**
Spinco Metal Products Inc....315 331-6285
1 Country Club Dr Newark (14513) **(G-12743)**
Spinergy, Rochester *Also called BMA Media Services Inc* **(G-14238)**
Spinmedia Group Inc....646 274-9110
276 5th Ave Fl 7 New York (10001) **(G-12164)**

ALPHABETIC

Spirent Inc (HQ)....631 208-0680
303 Griffing Ave Riverhead (11901) ***(G-14157)***
Spirit Music Group Inc (HQ)....212 533-7672
235 W 23rd St Ste 4 New York (10011) ***(G-12165)***
Spirit Pharmaceuticals LLC....215 943-4000
1919 Middle Country Rd Centereach (11720) ***(G-3473)***
Splice Technologies Inc....631 924-8108
625 North St Manorville (11949) ***(G-8081)***
Split Rock Trading Co Inc....631 929-3261
22 Creek Rd Wading River (11792) ***(G-16526)***
Split Systems Corp (PA)....516 223-5511
1593 Grand Ave North Baldwin (11510) ***(G-12909)***
Splp, New York *Also called Steel Partners Holdings LP* ***(G-12189)***
Spongebath LLC....917 475-1347
2334 28th St Apt 2r Astoria (11105) ***(G-458)***
Sport Helmets, Inc., Liverpool *Also called Performance Lacrosse Group Inc* ***(G-7541)***
Sports Illustrated For Kids....212 522-1212
1271 Ave Of The Americas New York (10020) ***(G-12166)***
Sports Pblications Prod NY LLC....212 366-7700
708 3rd Ave Fl 12 New York (10017) ***(G-12167)***
Sports Products America LLC....212 594-5511
34 W 33rd St Fl 2 New York (10001) ***(G-12168)***
Sports Reporter Inc....212 737-2750
527 3rd Ave Ste 327 New York (10016) ***(G-12169)***
Sportsfield Specialties Inc....607 746-8911
41155 State Highway 10 Delhi (13753) ***(G-4243)***
Sportsmaster Apparel, Troy *Also called Standard Manufacturing Co Inc* ***(G-16256)***
Sportswear Unlimited, Bedford Hills *Also called Custom Sportswear Corp* ***(G-800)***
Spot Certified Inc....212 643-6770
278 Van Brunt St Brooklyn (11231) ***(G-2589)***
Spotless Plastics (usa) Inc (HQ)....631 951-9000
100 Motor Pkwy Ste 155 Hauppauge (11788) ***(G-6198)***
Spotlight Newspaper, Delmar *Also called Community Media Group LLC* ***(G-4244)***
Spotlight Publications LLC....914 345-9473
100 Clearbrook Rd Ste 170 Elmsford (10523) ***(G-4787)***
Spray Market, The, Brooklyn *Also called Spfm Corp* ***(G-2588)***
Spray Nine Corporation....800 477-7299
309 W Montgomery St Johnstown (12095) ***(G-7128)***
Spray-Tech Finishing Inc....716 664-6317
443 Buffalo St Jamestown (14701) ***(G-7030)***
Spri Clinical Trials....718 616-2400
3044 Coney Island Ave Brooklyn (11235) ***(G-2590)***
Spring Inc....646 732-0323
41 E 11th St Fl 11 New York (10003) ***(G-12170)***
Spring Printing Inc....718 797-2818
489 Baltic St Brooklyn (11217) ***(G-2591)***
Spring Publishing Corporation....718 782-0881
419 Manhattan Ave Brooklyn (11222) ***(G-2592)***
Spring Street Design Group, New York *Also called Vetta Jewelry Inc* ***(G-12531)***
Springer Adis Us LLC (HQ)....212 460-1500
233 Spring St Fl 6 New York (10013) ***(G-12171)***
Springer Business Media, New York *Also called Springer Scnce + Bus Media LLC* ***(G-12175)***
Springer Customer Svc Ctr LLC....212 460-1500
233 Spring St Fl 6 New York (10013) ***(G-12172)***
Springer Healthcare LLC....212 460-1500
233 Spring St Fl 6 New York (10013) ***(G-12173)***
Springer Publishing Co LLC....212 431-4370
11 W 42nd St Fl 15 New York (10036) ***(G-12174)***
Springer Scnce + Bus Media LLC (HQ)....781 871-6600
233 Spring St Fl 6 New York (10013) ***(G-12175)***
Springfield Control Systems....718 631-0870
4056 Douglaston Pkwy Douglaston (11363) ***(G-4312)***
Springfield LLC (PA)....516 861-6250
100 Jericho Quadrangle # 340 Jericho (11753) ***(G-7089)***
Springfield Oil Services Inc (PA)....914 315-6812
550 Mmaroneck Ave Ste 503 Harrison (10528) ***(G-5991)***
Springfield Oil Services Inc....516 482-5995
40 Cuttermill Rd Ste 201 Great Neck (11021) ***(G-5841)***
Springville Mfg Co Inc....716 592-4957
8798 North St Springville (14141) ***(G-15616)***
SPS Medical Supply Corp (HQ)....585 359-0130
6789 W Henrietta Rd Rush (14543) ***(G-15052)***
SPS Medical Supply Corp....585 968-2377
31 Water St Ste 1 Cuba (14727) ***(G-4070)***
Spst Inc....607 798-6952
119b Rano Blvd Vestal (13850) ***(G-16453)***
SPX Corporation....631 249-7900
70 Raynor Ave Ronkonkoma (11779) ***(G-14988)***
SPX Corporation....585 279-1216
1000 Millstead Way Rochester (14624) ***(G-14696)***
SPX Corporation....585 436-5550
135 Mount Read Blvd Rochester (14611) ***(G-14697)***
SPX Flow Tech Systems Inc (HQ)....716 692-3000
105 Crosspoint Pkwy Getzville (14068) ***(G-5604)***
SPX Flow Technology, Rochester *Also called SPX Flow Us LLC* ***(G-14698)***
SPX Flow Us LLC....585 436-5550
135 Mount Read Blvd Rochester (14611) ***(G-14698)***
SPX Precision Components, Ronkonkoma *Also called SPX Corporation* ***(G-14988)***
Sqp, Scotia *Also called Specialty Quality Packg LLC* ***(G-15331)***
Sqp Inc....518 831-6800
602 Potential Pkwy Schenectady (12302) ***(G-15299)***
Square One Publishers Inc....516 535-2010
115 Herricks Rd Garden City Park (11040) ***(G-5542)***
Square Stamping Mfg Corp....315 896-2641
108 Old Remsen Rd Barneveld (13304) ***(G-618)***
Squeaky Clean, Brooklyn *Also called National Prfmce Solutions Inc* ***(G-2351)***
Squond Inc....718 778-6630
185 Marcy Ave Ste 302 Brooklyn (11211) ***(G-2593)***
SRC Liquidation Company....716 631-3900
435 Lawrence Bell Dr # 4 Williamsville (14221) ***(G-17255)***
SRC Tec, Inc., Syracuse *Also called Srctec LLC* ***(G-16044)***
Srctec LLC....315 452-8700
5801 E Taft Rd Ste 7 Syracuse (13212) ***(G-16044)***
Sriracha2go, New York *Also called Kybod Group LLC* ***(G-10897)***
SRP, New York *Also called Structured Retail Products* ***(G-12216)***
SRP Apparel Group Inc....212 764-4810
530 Fashion Ave Rm 809 New York (10018) ***(G-12176)***
SRS, Maspeth *Also called Stain Rail Systems Inc* ***(G-8171)***
Srtech Industry Corp....718 496-7001
5022 201st St Oakland Gardens (11364) ***(G-13068)***
SS&c Technologies Inc....212 503-6400
675 3rd Ave New York (10017) ***(G-12177)***
Ssa Trading Ltd....646 465-9500
226 W 37th St Fl 6 New York (10018) ***(G-12178)***
Ssac Inc....800 843-8848
8242 Loop Rd Baldwinsville (13027) ***(G-577)***
Ssf Production LLC....518 324-3407
194 Pleasant Ridge Rd Plattsburgh (12901) ***(G-13697)***
SSG Fashions Ltd....212 221-0933
27 E 37th St Frnt 1 New York (10016) ***(G-12179)***
SSP, Syracuse *Also called Selflock Screw Products Co Inc* ***(G-16037)***
SSP, Ballston Spa *Also called Specialty Silicone Pdts Inc* ***(G-609)***
SSP Window Cleaning Corp....917 750-2619
2351 E 26th St Brooklyn (11229) ***(G-2594)***
Ssrja LLC....718 725-7020
10729 180th St Jamaica (11433) ***(G-6950)***
St Gerard Enterprises Inc....631 473-2003
507 Bicycle Path Port Jeff STA (11776) ***(G-13770)***
St Gerard Printing, Port Jeff STA *Also called St Gerard Enterprises Inc* ***(G-13770)***
St James Printing Inc....631 981-2095
656 Rosevale Ave Ronkonkoma (11779) ***(G-14989)***
St John....718 720-8367
229 Morrison Ave Staten Island (10310) ***(G-15737)***
St John....718 771-4541
1700 Saint Johns Pl Brooklyn (11233) ***(G-2595)***
St Lawrence Cement Co, Catskill *Also called Ciment St-Laurent Inc* ***(G-3426)***
St Lawrence County Newspapers (HQ)....315 393-1003
230 Caroline St Ste 1 Ogdensburg (13669) ***(G-13122)***
St Lawrence Lumber Inc....315 649-2990
27140 County Route 57 Three Mile Bay (13693) ***(G-16123)***
St Raymond Monument Co....718 824-3600
2727 Lafayette Ave Bronx (10465) ***(G-1462)***
St Regis Sportswear Ltd....518 725-6767
51 Beaver St Gloversville (12078) ***(G-5722)***
St Remo, New York *Also called C E Chquie Ltd* ***(G-9490)***
St Silicones Corporation....518 406-3208
821 Main St Clifton Park (12065) ***(G-3709)***
St Silicones Inc....518 664-0745
95 N Central Ave Mechanicville (12118) ***(G-8231)***
St Tropez Inc....800 366-6383
530 Broadway Fl 10 New York (10012) ***(G-12180)***
St Vincent Press Inc....585 325-5320
250 Cumberland St Ste 260 Rochester (14605) ***(G-14699)***
Stack Electronics, Deer Park *Also called Veja Electronics Inc* ***(G-4222)***
Stafford Labs Orthotics/Prosth....845 692-5227
189 Monhagen Ave Middletown (10940) ***(G-8462)***
Stag Brothers Cast Stone Co....718 629-0975
909 E 51st St Brooklyn (11203) ***(G-2596)***
Stain Rail Systems Inc....732 548-6630
5920 56th Ave Maspeth (11378) ***(G-8171)***
Staining Plant, Newburgh *Also called Russin Lumber Corp* ***(G-12778)***
Stainless Design Concepts Ltd....845 246-3631
1117 Kings Hwy Saugerties (12477) ***(G-15195)***
Stainless Metals Inc....718 784-1454
6001 31st Ave Ste 1 Woodside (11377) ***(G-17356)***
Stairworld Inc....718 441-9722
10114 Jamaica Ave Richmond Hill (11418) ***(G-14085)***
Stallion Inc (PA)....718 706-0111
3620 34th St Long Island City (11106) ***(G-7882)***
Stallion Technologies Inc....315 622-1176
4324 Loveland Dr Liverpool (13090) ***(G-7548)***
Stamp, Rhinebeck *Also called Smithers Tools & Mch Pdts Inc* ***(G-14058)***
Stamp Rite Tool & Die Inc....718 752-0334
4311 35th St Long Island City (11101) ***(G-7883)***
Stampcrete Decorative Concrete, Liverpool *Also called Stampcrete International Ltd* ***(G-7549)***
Stampcrete International Ltd....315 451-2837
325 Commerce Blvd Liverpool (13088) ***(G-7549)***
Stamped Fittings Inc....607 733-9988
217 Lenox Ave Elmira Heights (14903) ***(G-4713)***

A L P H A B E T I C

Stamper Technology Inc 585 247-8370
232 Wallace Way Rochester (14624) *(G-14700)*
Stand Up Mri of Lynbrook PC 516 256-1558
229 Broadway Lynbrook (11563) *(G-7963)*
Standard Analytics Io Inc 917 882-5422
7 World Trade Ctr 46th New York (10007) *(G-12181)*
Standard Ascnsion Towers Group 716 681-2222
5136 Transit Rd Depew (14043) *(G-4274)*
Standard Group (PA) 718 335-5500
7520 Astoria Blvd Ste 100 East Elmhurst (11370) *(G-4397)*
Standard Group LLC (HQ) 718 507-6430
7520 Astoria Blvd Ste 100 East Elmhurst (11370) *(G-4398)*
Standard Industrial Works Inc 631 888-0130
271 Skip Ln Bay Shore (11706) *(G-744)*
Standard Manufacturing Co Inc (PA) 518 235-2200
750 2nd Ave Troy (12182) *(G-16256)*
Standard Microsystems Corp (HQ) 631 435-6000
80 Arkay Dr Ste 100 Hauppauge (11788) *(G-6199)*
Standard Motor Products Inc (PA) 718 392-0200
3718 Northern Blvd # 600 Long Island City (11101) *(G-7884)*
Standard Paper Box Machine Co 718 328-3300
347 Coster St Fl 2 Bronx (10474) *(G-1463)*
Standard Portable, Mayville *Also called Lyn Jo Enterprises Ltd (G-8217)*
Standard Products Division, Wassaic *Also called Pawling Corporation (G-16600)*
Standard Register Inc 937 221-1303
155 Pinelawn Rd Ste 120s Melville (11747) *(G-8356)*
Standard Screen Supply Corp (PA) 212 627-2727
121 Varick St Rm 200 New York (10013) *(G-12182)*
Standard Steel Fabricators 518 765-4820
Dutch Hill Rd Voorheesville (12186) *(G-16519)*
Standard Wedding Band Co 516 294-0954
951 Franklin Ave Garden City (11530) *(G-5533)*
Standardware Inc 914 738-6382
424 Pelham Manor Rd Pelham (10803) *(G-13495)*
Standex Air Dist Pdts Inc 585 798-0300
214 Commercial St Medina (14103) *(G-8283)*
Standing Stone Vineyards 607 582-6051
9934 State Route 414 Hector (14841) *(G-6261)*
Standwill Packaging Inc 631 752-1236
220 Sherwood Ave Farmingdale (11735) *(G-5113)*
Stanfordville Mch & Mfg Co Inc (PA) 845 868-2266
29 Victory Ln Poughkeepsie (12603) *(G-13934)*
Stanley Creations Inc 718 361-6100
3100 47th Ave Ste 4105 Long Island City (11101) *(G-7885)*
Stanley Home Products, Leicester *Also called Cpac Inc (G-7420)*
Stanley Industrial Eqp LLC 315 656-8733
8094 Saintsville Rd Kirkville (13082) *(G-7228)*
Stanley M Indig 718 692-0648
2173 E 38th St Brooklyn (11234) *(G-2597)*
Stanley Paper Co Inc 518 489-1131
1 Terminal St Albany (12206) *(G-136)*
Stanley Pleating Stitching Co 718 392-2417
2219 41st Ave Fl 3 Long Island City (11101) *(G-7886)*
Stanmark Jewelry Inc 212 730-2557
64 W 48th St Ste 1303 New York (10036) *(G-12183)*
Stanson Automated LLC 866 505-7826
145 Saw Mill River Rd # 2 Yonkers (10701) *(G-17485)*
Staplex Company Inc 718 768-3333
777 5th Ave Brooklyn (11232) *(G-2598)*
Star Childrens Dress Co Inc (PA) 212 244-1390
1250 Broadway Rm 1800 New York (10001) *(G-12184)*
Star Communications, Hauppauge *Also called Star Quality Printing Inc (G-6200)*
Star Community Pubg Group LLC, Melville *Also called Star Community Pubg Group LLC (G-8357)*
Star Community Pubg Group LLC 631 843-4050
235 Pinelawn Rd Melville (11747) *(G-8357)*
Star Corrugated Box Co Inc 718 386-3200
5515 Grand Ave Flushing (11378) *(G-5296)*
Star Desk Pad Co Inc 914 963-9400
60 Mclean Ave Yonkers (10705) *(G-17486)*
Star Draperies Inc 631 756-7121
24 Florida St Farmingdale (11735) *(G-5114)*
Star Headlight Lantern Co Inc (PA) 585 226-9500
455 Rochester St Avon (14414) *(G-543)*
Star Kay White Inc (PA) 845 268-2600
151 Wells Ave Congers (10920) *(G-3860)*
Star Mold Co Inc 631 694-2283
125 Florida St Farmingdale (11735) *(G-5115)*
Star Mountain Coffee, Jamaica *Also called Star Mountain JFK Inc (G-6951)*
Star Mountain JFK Inc 718 553-6787
Federal Cir Bldg 141 Jamaica (11430) *(G-6951)*
Star Poly Bag Inc (PA) 718 384-3130
200 Liberty Ave Brooklyn (11207) *(G-2599)*
Star Press Pearl River Inc 845 268-2294
614 Corporate Way Ste 8 Valley Cottage (10989) *(G-16389)*
Star Quality Printing Inc 631 273-1900
270 Oser Ave Hauppauge (11788) *(G-6200)*
Star Ready Mix East Inc 631 289-8787
225 Springs Fireplace Rd East Hampton (11937) *(G-4416)*
Star Ready Mix Inc 631 289-8787
172 Peconic Ave Medford (11763) *(G-8260)*
Star Seal of New York, Gasport *Also called Cosmicoat of Wny Inc (G-5556)*
Star Sports Corp 516 773-4075
747 Middle Neck Rd # 103 Great Neck (11024) *(G-5842)*
Star Tubing Corp 716 483-1703
53 River St Jamestown (14701) *(G-7031)*
Star Wire Mesh Fabricators 212 831-4133
518 E 119th St New York (10035) *(G-12185)*
Star X-Ray Co Inc 631 842-3010
2 Sheffield Hl Woodbury (11797) *(G-17301)*
Star-Gazette Fund Inc 607 734-5151
310 E Church St Elmira (14901) *(G-4702)*
Starboard Sun, Getzville *Also called Mission Critical Energy Inc (G-5600)*
Starcraft Press Inc 718 383-6700
4402 11th St Ste 311 Long Island City (11101) *(G-7887)*
Starfire Holding Corporation (PA) 914 614-7000
445 Hamilton Ave Ste 1210 White Plains (10601) *(G-17169)*
Starfire Printing, Holbrook *Also called Image Typography Inc (G-6450)*
Starfire Printing Inc 631 736-1495
28 Washington Ave Holtsville (11742) *(G-6509)*
Starfire Swords Ltd Inc 607 589-7244
74 Railroad Ave Spencer (14883) *(G-15564)*
Starfire Systems Inc 518 899-9336
8 Sarnowski Dr Schenectady (12302) *(G-15300)*
Starfuels Inc (HQ) 914 289-4800
50 Main St White Plains (10606) *(G-17170)*
Stargate Computer Corp 516 474-4799
24 Harmony Dr Port Jeff STA (11776) *(G-13771)*
Stark Aquarium Products Co Inc 718 445-5357
2914 122nd St Flushing (11354) *(G-5297)*
Stark Fish, Flushing *Also called Stark Aquarium Products Co Inc (G-5297)*
Starkey & Henricks, New York *Also called Charles Henricks Inc (G-9581)*
Starlight Paint Factory, Bronx *Also called Starlite Pnt & Varnish Co Inc (G-1464)*
Starlight Properties, Bellport *Also called Pyrotechnique By Grucci Inc (G-840)*
Starline Usa Inc 716 773-0100
3036 Alt Blvd Grand Island (14072) *(G-5770)*
Starliner Shipping & Travel 718 385-1515
5305 Church Ave Ste 1 Brooklyn (11203) *(G-2600)*
Starlite Media LLC (PA) 212 909-7700
151 W 19th St Fl 4 New York (10011) *(G-12186)*
Starlite Pnt & Varnish Co Inc 718 292-6420
724 E 140th St Bronx (10454) *(G-1464)*
Starmark Apparel Inc 212 967-6347
255 W 36th St Lbby New York (10018) *(G-12187)*
Staroba Plastics Inc 716 537-3153
42 Edgewood Dr Holland (14080) *(G-6484)*
Starwalk Kids Media, Great Neck *Also called Isabella Products Inc (G-5818)*
State Bags LLC 617 895-8532
495 Broadway Rm 3f New York (10012) *(G-12188)*
Statebook LLC 845 383-1991
185 Fair St Ste 2 Kingston (12401) *(G-7212)*
Stated Island Stair Inc 718 317-9276
439 Sharrotts Rd Staten Island (10309) *(G-15738)*
Staten Island Parent Magazine 718 761-4800
16 Shenandoah Ave Ste 2 Staten Island (10314) *(G-15739)*
Staten Island Stair Inc 718 317-9276
439 Sharrotts Rd Staten Island (10309) *(G-15740)*
Statewide Fireproof Door Co 845 268-6043
178 Charles Blvd Valley Cottage (10989) *(G-16390)*
Station Hill of Barrytown 845 758-5293
120 Station Hill Rd Barrytown (12507) *(G-619)*
Stature Electric, Watertown *Also called Allied Motion Technologies Inc (G-16634)*
Stature Electric Inc 315 782-5910
22543 Fisher Rd Watertown (13601) *(G-16672)*
Staub Machine Company Inc 716 649-4211
206 Lake St Hamburg (14075) *(G-5944)*
Staub Square, Hamburg *Also called Staub Machine Company Inc (G-5944)*
Staub Usa Inc 914 747-0300
270 Marble Ave Pleasantville (10570) *(G-13721)*
Stauber Prfmce Ingredients Inc 845 651-4443
41 Bridge St Florida (10921) *(G-5215)*
Stavo Industries Inc (PA) 845 331-4552
132 Flatbush Ave Kingston (12401) *(G-7213)*
Stavo Industries Inc 845 331-5389
132 Flatbush Ave Kingston (12401) *(G-7214)*
Stealth Archtctral Windows Inc 718 821-6666
232 Varet St Brooklyn (11206) *(G-2601)*
Stealth Inc 718 252-7900
1129 E 27th St Brooklyn (11210) *(G-2602)*
Stealth Window, Brooklyn *Also called Stealth Archtctral Windows Inc (G-2601)*
Steamline Machine, Fairport *Also called Streamline Precision Inc (G-4882)*
Stebe Shcjhjff 839 383-9833
18 Lynbrook Rd Poughkeepsie (12603) *(G-13935)*
Stedman Energy Inc 716 789-3018
4411 Canterbury Dr Mayville (14757) *(G-8219)*
Steel & Obrien Mfg Inc 585 492-5800
274 Rte 98 S Arcade (14009) *(G-400)*
Steel Craft, Brooklyn *Also called Steelcraft Manufacturing Co (G-2603)*
Steel Craft Rolling Door 631 608-8662
5 Di Tomas Ct Copiague (11726) *(G-3929)*
Steel Crazy, Buffalo *Also called E B Iron Art LLC (G-2923)*
Steel Excel Inc (HQ) 914 461-1300
1133 Westchester Ave N-222 White Plains (10604) *(G-17171)*

ALPHABETIC

Steel Partners Holdings LP (PA) 212 520-2300
590 Madison Ave Rm 3202 New York (10022) ***(G-12189)***
Steel Sales Inc 607 674-6363
8085 New York St Hwy 12 Sherburne (13460) ***(G-15397)***
Steel Tech SA LLC 845 786-3691
7 Hillside Dr Thiells (10984) ***(G-16114)***
Steel Work Inc 585 232-1555
340 Oak St Rochester (14608) ***(G-14701)***
Steel-Brite Ltd 631 589-4044
2 Dawn Dr Oakdale (11769) ***(G-13063)***
Steelcraft Manufacturing Co 718 277-2404
352 Pine St Brooklyn (11208) ***(G-2603)***
Steeldeck Ny Inc 718 599-3700
141 Banker St Brooklyn (11222) ***(G-2604)***
Steele Truss Company Inc 518 562-4663
118 Trade Rd Plattsburgh (12901) ***(G-13698)***
Steelflex Electro Corp 516 226-4466
145 S 13th St Lindenhurst (11757) ***(G-7483)***
Steelmasters Inc 718 498-2854
135 Liberty Ave Brooklyn (11212) ***(G-2605)***
Steelways Inc 845 562-0860
401 S Water St Newburgh (12553) ***(G-12780)***
Steelways Shipyard, Newburgh *Also called Steelways Inc* ***(G-12780)***
Steezys LLC 646 276-5333
80 8th Ave 202 New York (10011) ***(G-12190)***
Stefan & Sons Welding, Chaffee *Also called Donald Stefan* ***(G-3533)***
Stefan Furs Inc 212 594-2788
150 W 30th St Fl 15 New York (10001) ***(G-12191)***
Stefan Sydor Optics Inc 585 271-7300
31 Jetview Dr Rochester (14624) ***(G-14702)***
Steffen Publishing Inc 315 865-4100
9584 Main St Holland Patent (13354) ***(G-6488)***
Steigercraft, Bellport *Also called AVS Laminates Inc* ***(G-826)***
Steilmann European Selections 914 997-0015
354 N Main St Port Chester (10573) ***(G-13759)***
Stein Fibers Ltd (PA) 518 489-5700
4 Computer Dr W Ste 200 Albany (12205) ***(G-137)***
Stein Industries Inc 631 789-2222
22 Sprague Ave Amityville (11701) ***(G-325)***
Steinbock-Braff Inc 718 972-6500
3611 14th Ave Brooklyn (11218) ***(G-2606)***
Steindl Cast Stone Co Inc 718 296-8530
9107 76th St Woodhaven (11421) ***(G-17308)***
Steiner Doors, Brooklyn *Also called A G M Deco Inc* ***(G-1534)***
Steiner Technologies Inc 585 425-5910
180 Perinton Pkwy Fairport (14450) ***(G-4880)***
Steinway Inc (HQ) 718 721-2600
1 Steinway Pl Long Island City (11105) ***(G-7888)***
Steinway and Sons (HQ) 718 721-2600
1 Steinway Pl Long Island City (11105) ***(G-7889)***
Steinway Awning II LLC (PA) 718 729-2965
4230 24th St Astoria (11101) ***(G-459)***
Steinway Awnings, Astoria *Also called Steinway Awning II LLC* ***(G-459)***
Steinway Hall, Long Island City *Also called Steinway Inc* ***(G-7888)***
Steinway Musical Instrs Inc (HQ) 781 894-9770
1133 Ave Of The Am Fl 33 New York (10036) ***(G-12192)***
Steinway Pasta & Gelati Inc 718 246-5414
37 Grand Ave Ste 1 Brooklyn (11205) ***(G-2607)***
Stellar Alliance, New York *Also called Alen Sands York Associates Ltd* ***(G-9080)***
Stellar Printing Inc 718 361-1600
3838 9th St Long Island City (11101) ***(G-7890)***
Stemcultures LLC 518 621-0848
1 Discovery Dr Rensselaer (12144) ***(G-14052)***
Stemline Therapeutics Inc 646 502-2311
750 Lexington Ave Fl 11 New York (10022) ***(G-12193)***
Stephan & Company ACC Ltd (PA) 212 481-3888
10 E 38th St Fl 9 New York (10016) ***(G-12194)***
Stephen A Manoogian Inc 518 762-2525
12 Industrial Pkwy Johnstown (12095) ***(G-7129)***
Stephen Bader Company Inc 518 753-4456
10 Charles St Valley Falls (12185) ***(G-16396)***
Stephen Dweck, New York *Also called Rumson Acquisition LLC* ***(G-11936)***
Stephen Dweck Industries, Brooklyn *Also called Dweck Industries Inc* ***(G-1884)***
Stephen Gould Corporation 212 497-8180
450 7th Ave Fl 32 New York (10123) ***(G-12195)***
Stephen Hanley 718 729-3360
2111 44th Ave Long Island City (11101) ***(G-7891)***
Stephen J Lipkins Inc 631 249-8866
855 Conklin St Ste A Farmingdale (11735) ***(G-5116)***
Stephen M Kiernan 716 836-6300
701 Seneca St Ste 300 Buffalo (14210) ***(G-3196)***
Stephen Miller Gen Contrs Inc 518 661-5601
301 Riceville Rd Gloversville (12078) ***(G-5723)***
Stephen Singer Pattern Co Inc 212 947-2902
340 W 39th St Fl 4 New York (10018) ***(G-12196)***
Stephenson Custom Case Company 905 542-8762
1623 Military Rd Niagara Falls (14304) ***(G-12878)***
Stephenson Lumber Company Inc 518 548-7521
Rr 8 Speculator (12164) ***(G-15563)***
Stepping Stones One Day Signs 518 237-5774
105 Broad St Waterford (12188) ***(G-16622)***
Steps Plus Inc 315 432-0885
6375 Thompson Rd Syracuse (13206) ***(G-16045)***
Stereo Advantage Inc 716 656-7161
45 Boxwood Ln Cheektowaga (14227) ***(G-3590)***
Steri-Pharma LLC 315 473-7180
429 S West St Syracuse (13202) ***(G-16046)***
Sterilator Company, Cuba *Also called SPS Medical Supply Corp* ***(G-4070)***
Steriliz LLC 585 415-5411
95 Allens Creek Rd Rochester (14618) ***(G-14703)***
Sterling Building Systems 716 685-0505
2 Main St Depew (14043) ***(G-4275)***
Sterling Industries Inc 631 753-3070
410 Eastern Pkwy Farmingdale (11735) ***(G-5117)***
Sterling McFadden, New York *Also called Mac Fadden Holdings Inc* ***(G-11081)***
Sterling Molded Products Inc 845 344-4546
9-17 Oliver Ave Middletown (10940) ***(G-8463)***
Sterling North America Inc 631 243-6933
270 Oser Ave Hauppauge (11788) ***(G-6201)***
Sterling Pierce Company Inc 516 593-1170
395 Atlantic Ave East Rockaway (11518) ***(G-4471)***
Sterling Possessions Ltd 212 594-0418
251 W 39th St New York (10018) ***(G-12197)***
Sterling Sound Inc 212 604-9433
88 10th Ave Frnt 6 New York (10011) ***(G-12198)***
Sterling Toggle Inc 631 491-0500
99 Mahan St West Babylon (11704) ***(G-16832)***
Sterling United Inc 716 835-9290
6030 N Bailey Ave Ste 1 Amherst (14226) ***(G-262)***
Stern & Stern Industries Inc 607 324-4485
188 Thacher St Hornell (14843) ***(G-6567)***
Sterrx LLC (PA) 518 324-7879
141 Idaho Ave Plattsburgh (12903) ***(G-13699)***
Sterrx LLC 518 324-7879
141 Idaho Ave Ste 1 Plattsburgh (12903) ***(G-13700)***
Sterrx Cmo, Plattsburgh *Also called Sterrx LLC* ***(G-13700)***
Stetron International Inc (PA) 716 854-3443
90 Broadway St Ste 1 Buffalo (14203) ***(G-3197)***
Steuben Courier Advocate, Bath *Also called Gatehouse Media LLC* ***(G-656)***
Steuben Foods Incorporated (PA) 718 291-3333
15504 Liberty Ave Jamaica (11433) ***(G-6952)***
Steuben Foods Incorporated 716 655-4000
1150 Maple Rd Elma (14059) ***(G-4656)***
Steval Graphics Concepts Inc 516 576-0220
7 Fairchild Ct Ste 200 Plainview (11803) ***(G-13636)***
Steve & Andys Organics Inc 718 499-7933
102 E 7th St Apt 6 New York (10009) ***(G-12199)***
STEVE MADDEN, Long Island City *Also called Steven Madden Ltd* ***(G-7892)***
Steve Poli Sales 315 487-0394
102 Farmington Dr Camillus (13031) ***(G-3324)***
Steve Zinn 718 746-8551
16111 29th Ave Flushing (11358) ***(G-5298)***
Steven Coffey Pallet S Inc 585 261-6783
3376 Edgemere Dr Rochester (14612) ***(G-14704)***
Steven John Opticians 718 543-3336
5901 Riverdale Ave Bronx (10471) ***(G-1465)***
Steven Kraus Associates Inc 631 923-2033
9 Private Rd Huntington (11743) ***(G-6682)***
Steven Madden Ltd 845 348-7026
1661 Palisades Center Dr West Nyack (10994) ***(G-16927)***
Steven Madden Ltd 212 736-3283
41 W 34th St New York (10001) ***(G-12200)***
Steven Madden Ltd (PA) 718 446-1800
5216 Barnett Ave Long Island City (11104) ***(G-7892)***
Steven Madden Ltd 718 446-1800
19 W 34th St Fl 4 New York (10001) ***(G-12201)***
Steven Madden Retail Inc 718 446-1800
5216 Barnett Ave Long Island City (11104) ***(G-7893)***
Stevens Bandes Graphics Corp 212 675-1128
333 Hudson St Fl 3 New York (10013) ***(G-12202)***
Stevenson Printing Co Inc 516 676-1233
1 Brewster St Ste 2 Glen Cove (11542) ***(G-5629)***
Stever-Locke Industries Inc 585 624-3450
179 N Main St Honeoye Falls (14472) ***(G-6538)***
Steves Original Furs Inc 212 967-8007
150 W 30th St Rm 700 New York (10001) ***(G-12203)***
Stewart Efi LLC 914 965-0816
630 Central Park Ave Yonkers (10704) ***(G-17487)***
Stewart Tobori & Chang Div, New York *Also called Harry N Abrams Incorporated* ***(G-10419)***
Stewarts Processing Corp (PA) 518 581-1200
2907 State Route 9 Ballston Spa (12020) ***(G-610)***
Stf, Uniondale *Also called Solar Thin Films Inc* ***(G-16299)***
STf Services Inc 315 463-8506
26 Corporate Cir Ste 2 East Syracuse (13057) ***(G-4567)***
STI-Co Industries Inc 716 662-2680
11 Cobham Dr Ste A Orchard Park (14127) ***(G-13297)***
Stickershopcom Inc 631 563-4323
10 Ferraro Dr Holbrook (11741) ***(G-6474)***
Sticky ADS TV Inc 646 668-1346
747 3rd Ave Fl 2 New York (10017) ***(G-12204)***
Sticky Socks LLC 212 541-5927
200 W 60th St Apt 7g New York (10023) ***(G-12205)***

Stidd Systems Inc...631 477-2400
220 Carpenter St Greenport (11944) *(G-5877)*
Stiegelbauer Associates Inc (PA)...718 624-0835
Bldg 280 Brooklyn (11205) *(G-2608)*
Stillwater Wood & Iron...518 664-4501
114 Hudson Ave Stillwater (12170) *(G-15761)*
Stitch & Couture Inc (PA)...212 947-9204
224 W 30th St Fl 14 New York (10001) *(G-12206)*
Stj Enterprises...516 612-0110
540 Willow Ave Cedarhurst (11516) *(G-3463)*
Stj Orthotic Services Inc (PA)...631 956-0181
920 Wellwood Ave Ste B Lindenhurst (11757) *(G-7484)*
Stk Electronics Inc...315 655-8476
2747 Rte 20 Cazenovia (13035) *(G-3452)*
Stock Drive Products Div, New Hyde Park *Also called Designatronics Incorporated* *(G-8826)*
Stoffel Polygon Systems Inc...914 961-2000
199 Marbledale Rd Tuckahoe (10707) *(G-16272)*
Stone and Bath Gallery...718 438-4500
856 39th St Brooklyn (11232) *(G-2609)*
Stone Bridge Iron and Stl Inc...518 695-3752
426 Purinton Rd Gansevoort (12831) *(G-5490)*
Stone Crafters International, Brooklyn *Also called PR & Stone & Tile Inc* *(G-2434)*
Stone Crest Industries Inc...607 652-2665
152 Starheim Rd Stamford (12167) *(G-15626)*
Stone Expo & Cabinetry LLC...516 292-2988
7 Terminal Rd West Hempstead (11552) *(G-16863)*
Stone Glo Products, Bronx *Also called TWI-Laq Industries Inc* *(G-1482)*
Stone House Associates Inc...212 221-7447
37 W 47th St Ste 910 New York (10036) *(G-12207)*
Stone Well Bodies & Mch Inc...315 497-3512
625 Sill Rd Genoa (13071) *(G-5590)*
Stonegate Stables...518 746-7133
106 Reynolds Rd Fort Edward (12828) *(G-5346)*
Stones Homemade Candies Inc...315 343-8401
145 W Bridge St Oswego (13126) *(G-13342)*
Stonesong Press LLC...212 929-4600
270 W 39th St Rm 201 New York (10018) *(G-12208)*
Stoney Croft Converters Inc...718 608-9800
364 Sharrotts Rd Staten Island (10309) *(G-15741)*
Stony Apparel Corp...212 391-0022
1407 Broadway Rm 3300 New York (10018) *(G-12209)*
Stony Brook Mfg Co Inc (PA)...631 369-9530
652 Scott Ave Calverton (11933) *(G-3298)*
Stony Brook University...631 632-6434
310 Administration Bldg Stony Brook (11794) *(G-15772)*
Stony Manufacturing Inc...716 652-6730
591 Pound Rd Elma (14059) *(G-4657)*
Stony Point Graphics Ltd...845 786-3322
1 S Liberty Dr Stony Point (10980) *(G-15777)*
Stop Entertainment Inc...212 242-7867
408 Rye Hill Rd Monroe (10950) *(G-8564)*
Stop N Shop LLC...518 512-9657
911 Central Ave Ste 149 Albany (12206) *(G-138)*
Storage Sheds, Westmoreland *Also called Shafer & Sons* *(G-17065)*
Storflex Fixture, Corning *Also called Storflex Holdings Inc* *(G-3982)*
Storflex Holdings Inc...607 962-2137
392 Pulteney St Corning (14830) *(G-3982)*
Stork H & E Turbo Blading Inc...607 277-4968
334 Comfort Rd Ithaca (14850) *(G-6876)*
Stormberg Brand, Valley Cottage *Also called Stromberg Brand Corporation* *(G-16391)*
Storybooks Forever...716 822-7845
4 Magnolia Ave Buffalo (14220) *(G-3198)*
Strada Soft Inc...718 556-6940
20 Clifton Ave Staten Island (10305) *(G-15742)*
Strahl & Pitsch Inc...631 669-0175
230 Great East Neck Rd West Babylon (11704) *(G-16833)*
Straight Arrow Publishing Co...212 484-1616
1290 Ave Of The Amer Fl 2 New York (10104) *(G-12210)*
Stratconglobal Inc...212 989-2355
685 3rd Ave Fl 4 New York (10017) *(G-12211)*
Strategic Mktg Promotions Inc (PA)...845 623-7777
10 N Main St Pearl River (10965) *(G-13467)*
Strategic Signage Sourcing LLC...518 450-1093
2 Gilbert Rd Saratoga Springs (12866) *(G-15174)*
Strategies North America Inc...716 945-6053
150 Elm St Salamanca (14779) *(G-15108)*
Stratford Oriented, Macedon *Also called Exxonmobil Chemical Company* *(G-7986)*
Strathmore Directories Ltd...516 997-2525
26 Bond St Westbury (11590) *(G-17028)*
Strathmore Products, Inc., Syracuse *Also called Fayette Street Coatings Inc* *(G-15942)*
Strathmore Publications, Westbury *Also called Strathmore Directories Ltd* *(G-17028)*
Strativa Pharmaceuticals...201 802-4000
1 Ram Ridge Rd Spring Valley (10977) *(G-15602)*
Strato Transit Components LLC...518 686-4541
155 State Route 67 Eagle Bridge (12057) *(G-4359)*
Straus Communications...845 782-4000
20 West Ave Ste 201 Chester (10918) *(G-3616)*
Straus Newspaper, Chester *Also called Straus Communications* *(G-3616)*
Straus Newspapers Inc...845 782-4000
20 West Ave Chester (10918) *(G-3617)*
Strauss Eye Prosthetics Inc...585 424-1350
360 White Spruce Blvd Rochester (14623) *(G-14705)*
Strawtown Jewerly, New City *Also called Shining Creations Inc* *(G-8793)*
Stream Police, New York *Also called Instant Stream Inc* *(G-10611)*
Streamline Plastics Co Inc...718 401-4000
2590 Park Ave Bronx (10451) *(G-1466)*
Streamline Precision Inc...585 421-9050
205 Turk Hill Park Fairport (14450) *(G-4881)*
Streamline Precision Inc...585 421-9050
1000 Turk Hill Rd Ste 205 Fairport (14450) *(G-4882)*
Streck's Machinery, Watervliet *Also called Strecks Inc* *(G-16689)*
Strecks Inc...518 273-4410
800 1st St Watervliet (12189) *(G-16689)*
Street Beat Sportswear Inc (PA)...718 302-1500
462 Kent Ave Fl 2 Brooklyn (11249) *(G-2610)*
Street King LLC...212 400-2200
575 Madison Ave Fl 24 New York (10022) *(G-12212)*
Street Smart Designs Inc...646 865-0056
29 W 35th St Fl 6 New York (10001) *(G-12213)*
Streetline, New York *Also called Gemtex Inc* *(G-10270)*
Streit Matzoh Co, New York *Also called Aron Streit Inc* *(G-9205)*
Striano Electric Co Inc...516 408-4969
246 Park Ave Garden City Park (11040) *(G-5543)*
Striata Inc...212 918-4677
48 Wall St Ste 1100 New York (10005) *(G-12214)*
Strictly Business, Plattsburgh *Also called Northeast Group* *(G-13682)*
Strider Global LLC...212 726-1302
261 W 28th St Apt 6a New York (10001) *(G-12215)*
Strippit Inc (HQ)...716 542-5500
12975 Clarence Center Rd Akron (14001) *(G-29)*
Strocchia Iron Works, Albertson *Also called Patsy Strocchia & Sons Iron Wo* *(G-156)*
Stroehmann Bakeries 33, Maspeth *Also called Bimbo Bakeries Usa Inc* *(G-8121)*
Stroehmann Bakeries 56, Olean *Also called Bimbo Bakeries Usa Inc* *(G-13136)*
Stroehmann Bakeries 72, Goshen *Also called Bimbo Bakeries Usa Inc* *(G-5731)*
Stroehmann Bakeries 90, Vestal *Also called Bimbo Bakeries Usa Inc* *(G-16441)*
Stromberg Brand Corporation...914 739-7410
12 Ford Products Rd Valley Cottage (10989) *(G-16391)*
Strong Forge & Fabrication...585 343-5251
20 Liberty St Batavia (14020) *(G-648)*
Strong Group Inc...516 766-6300
222 Atlantic Ave Unit B Oceanside (11572) *(G-13097)*
Strong Hospital, Rochester *Also called Orthotics & Prosthetics Dept* *(G-14558)*
Strong Tempering GL Indust LLC...718 765-0007
530 63rd St Ste B Brooklyn (11220) *(G-2611)*
Strong Ventures, New York *Also called Mrs John L Strong & Co LLC* *(G-11317)*
Structural Ceramics Division, Niagara Falls *Also called Saint-Gbain Advnced Crmics LLC* *(G-12871)*
Structural Ceramics Group, Niagara Falls *Also called Saint-Gobain Dynamics Inc* *(G-12872)*
Structural Industries Inc...631 471-5200
2950 Veterans Memorial Hw Bohemia (11716) *(G-1137)*
Structural Wood Corporation...315 388-4442
243 Lincoln Ave Waddington (13694) *(G-16521)*
Structured 3d Inc...346 704-2614
188 Dixon Ave Amityville (11701) *(G-326)*
Structured Retail Products...212 224-3692
225 Park Ave S Fl 8 New York (10003) *(G-12216)*
Structuredweb Inc...201 325-3110
20 W 20th St Ste 402 New York (10011) *(G-12217)*
Struthers Electronics, Bay Shore *Also called Lexan Industries Inc* *(G-713)*
Strux Corp...516 768-3969
100 Montauk Hwy Lindenhurst (11757) *(G-7485)*
STS Refill America LLC...516 934-8008
399 W John St Unit A Hicksville (11801) *(G-6395)*
STS Steel Inc...518 370-2693
301 Nott St Ste 2 Schenectady (12305) *(G-15301)*
Stu-Art Supplies, North Baldwin *Also called Hubray Inc* *(G-12907)*
Stuart Communications Inc...845 252-7414
93 Erie Ave Narrowsburg (12764) *(G-8769)*
Stuart Mold & Manufacturing...716 488-9765
560 N Work St Falconer (14733) *(G-4914)*
Stuart Spector Designs Ltd...845 246-6124
1450 Route 212 Saugerties (12477) *(G-15196)*
Stuart Tool & Die Inc...716 488-1975
600 N Work St Falconer (14733) *(G-4915)*
Stuart Weitzman LLC...212 823-9560
625 Madison Ave Frnt 3 New York (10022) *(G-12218)*
Stuart-Dean Co Inc...718 472-1326
4350 10th St Long Island City (11101) *(G-7894)*
Stubbs Printing Inc...315 769-8641
271 E Orvis St Ste B Massena (13662) *(G-8201)*
Stucki Embroidery Works Inc (PA)...845 657-2308
Rr 28 Box W Boiceville (12412) *(G-1158)*
Studco Building Systems US LLC...585 545-3000
1700 Boulter Indus Park Webster (14580) *(G-16736)*
Student Association At The, Binghamton *Also called Pipe Dream* *(G-943)*
Student Lifeline Inc...516 327-0800
922 Hempstead Tpke Franklin Square (11010) *(G-5367)*
Student Safety Books, Franklin Square *Also called Student Lifeline Inc* *(G-5367)*
Studio 21 LA Inc...718 965-6579
13 42nd St Fl 5 Brooklyn (11232) *(G-2612)*
Studio 26, New York *Also called RR Donnelley & Sons Company* *(G-11930)*

ALPHABETIC

Studio 40 Inc 212 420-8631
  810 Humboldt St Ste 4 Brooklyn (11222) *(G-2613)*
Studio Associates of New York 212 268-1163
  242 W 30th St Rm 902 New York (10001) *(G-12219)*
Studio Dellarte 718 599-3715
  74 Bayard St Brooklyn (11222) *(G-2614)*
Studio Fun International Inc 914 238-1000
  44 S Broadway Fl 7 White Plains (10601) *(G-17172)*
Studio Krp LLC 310 589-5777
  210 11th Ave Rm 500 New York (10001) *(G-12220)*
Studio One Leather Design Inc 212 760-1701
  270 W 39th St Rm 505 New York (10018) *(G-12221)*
Studio Silversmiths Inc 718 418-6785
  6315 Traffic Ave Ridgewood (11385) *(G-14125)*
Studley Printing & Publishing 518 563-1414
  4701 State Route 9 Plattsburgh (12901) *(G-13701)*
Stuff Magazine 212 302-2626
  1040 Ave Of The Amrcas New York (10018) *(G-12222)*
Stuhrling Original LLC 718 840-5760
  449 20th St Brooklyn (11215) *(G-2615)*
Sturdy Store Displays Inc 718 389-9919
  485 Johnson Ave Brooklyn (11237) *(G-2616)*
Sturges Elec Pdts Co Inc 607 844-8604
  23 North St Dryden (13053) *(G-4323)*
Sturges Manufacturing Co Inc 315 732-6159
  2030 Sunset Ave Utica (13502) *(G-16360)*
Stutzman Management Corp 800 735-2013
  11 Saint Joseph St Lancaster (14086) *(G-7344)*
Style Partners Inc 212 904-1499
  318 W 39th St Fl 7 New York (10018) *(G-12223)*
Style Plus Hosiery Mills, Valley Stream Also called Ellis Products Corp *(G-16405)*
Stylebuilt Accessories Inc (PA) 917 439-0578
  45 Rose Ln East Rockaway (11518) *(G-4472)*
Stylebuilt Acesries, East Rockaway Also called Stylebuilt Accessories Inc *(G-4472)*
Styleclick Inc (HQ) 212 329-0300
  810 7th Ave Fl 18 New York (10019) *(G-12224)*
Stylecraft Interiors Inc 516 487-2133
  22 Watermill Ln Great Neck (11021) *(G-5843)*
Stylemaster, Richmond Hill Also called Belle Maison USA Ltd *(G-14068)*
Styles Aviation Inc (PA) 845 677-8185
  30 Airway Dr Ste 2 Lagrangeville (12540) *(G-7259)*
Styles Manufacturing Corp 516 763-5303
  3571 Hargale Rd Oceanside (11572) *(G-13098)*
Stylesprit, New York Also called Entrainant Inc *(G-10045)*
Stylist Pleating Corp 718 384-8181
  109 S 5th St Brooklyn (11249) *(G-2617)*
Stylistic Press Inc 212 675-0797
  99 Battery Pl Apt 11p New York (10280) *(G-12225)*
Subcon Industries 716 945-4430
  65 South Ave Salamanca (14779) *(G-15109)*
Suburban Marketing Assoc, Elmsford Also called Ralph Martinelli *(G-4775)*
Suburban News, Spencerport Also called Westside News Inc *(G-15574)*
Suburban Publishing Inc (PA) 845 463-0542
  2678 South Rd Ste 202 Poughkeepsie (12601) *(G-13936)*
Successware Inc 716 565-2338
  8860 Main St 102 Williamsville (14221) *(G-17256)*
Successware Remote LLC 716 842-1439
  403 Main St Ste 200 Buffalo (14203) *(G-3199)*
Such Intl Incorporation 212 686-9888
  10 Mill River Rd Setauket (11733) *(G-15380)*
Sue & Sam Co Inc (PA) 718 436-1672
  720 39th St 720 Brooklyn (11232) *(G-2618)*
Suffolk Cement Precast Inc (PA) 631 727-4432
  1813 Middle Rd Calverton (11933) *(G-3299)*
Suffolk Cement Products Inc 631 727-2317
  1843 Middle Rd Calverton (11933) *(G-3300)*
Suffolk Community Council Inc (PA) 631 434-9277
  819 Grand Blvd Ste 1 Deer Park (11729) *(G-4214)*
Suffolk Copy Center Inc 631 665-0570
  26 W Main St Bay Shore (11706) *(G-745)*
Suffolk Granite Manufacturing 631 226-4774
  25 Gear Ave Lindenhurst (11757) *(G-7486)*
Suffolk Indus Recovery Corp 631 732-6403
  3542 Route 112 Coram (11727) *(G-3951)*
Suffolk McHy & Pwr Tl Corp (PA) 631 289-7153
  12 Waverly Ave Patchogue (11772) *(G-13435)*
Suffolk Molds, Wyandanch Also called C & N Packaging Inc *(G-17371)*
Suffolk Monument Mfg, Lindenhurst Also called Suffolk Granite Manufacturing *(G-7486)*
Suffolk Printing, Bay Shore Also called Suffolk Copy Center Inc *(G-745)*
Sugar & Plumm Upper West LLC 201 334-1600
  377 Amsterdam Ave New York (10024) *(G-12226)*
Sugar Foods Corporation (PA) 212 753-6900
  950 3rd Ave Fl 21 New York (10022) *(G-12227)*
Sugar Shack Desert Company Inc 518 523-7540
  2567 Main St Lake Placid (12946) *(G-7276)*
Sugarbear Cupcakes 917 698-9005
  14552 159th St Jamaica (11434) *(G-6953)*
Suhor Industries Inc (PA) 585 377-5100
  72 Oconnor Rd Fairport (14450) *(G-4883)*
Suhor Industries Inc 716 483-6818
  584 Buffalo St Jamestown (14701) *(G-7032)*

Suit-Kote Corporation (PA) 607 753-1100
  1911 Lorings Crossing Rd Cortland (13045) *(G-4046)*
Suit-Kote Corporation 315 735-8501
  191 Dry Rd Oriskany (13424) *(G-13314)*
Suit-Kote Corporation 585 473-6321
  2 Rockwood St Frnt Rochester (14610) *(G-14706)*
Suit-Kote Corporation 607 535-2743
  20 Fairgrounds Ln Watkins Glen (14891) *(G-16697)*
Suit-Kote Corporation 585 268-7127
  5628 Tuckers Corners Rd Belmont (14813) *(G-843)*
Suit-Kote Corporation 716 664-3750
  57 Lister St Jamestown (14701) *(G-7033)*
Suit-Kote Corporation 716 683-8850
  505 Como Park Blvd Buffalo (14227) *(G-3200)*
Suite Solutions Inc 716 929-3050
  100 Corporate Pkwy # 338 Amherst (14226) *(G-263)*
Sukkah Center, Brooklyn Also called Y & A Trading Inc *(G-2772)*
Sullivan Bazinet Bongio Inc 315 437-6500
  6500 New Venture Gear Dr East Syracuse (13057) *(G-4568)*
Sullivan Concrete Inc 845 888-2235
  420 Bernas Rd Cochecton (12726) *(G-3744)*
Sullivan County Democrat, Callicoon Also called Catskill Delaware Publications *(G-3284)*
Sullivan St Bky - Hlls Kit Inc 212 265-5580
  533 W 47th St New York (10036) *(G-12228)*
Sullivan Structures, Cochecton Also called Sullivan Concrete Inc *(G-3744)*
Sulphur Creations Inc 212 719-2223
  71 W 47th St Ste 402 New York (10036) *(G-12229)*
Sum Sum LLC 516 812-3959
  3595 Lawson Blvd Whse D Warehouse D Oceanside (11572) *(G-13099)*
Suma Industries Inc 646 436-5202
  345 E 52nd St Apt 9d New York (10022) *(G-12230)*
Sumax Cycle Products Inc 315 768-1058
  122 Clear Rd Oriskany (13424) *(G-13315)*
Sumer Gold Ltd 212 354-8677
  33 W 46th St Fl 4 New York (10036) *(G-12231)*
Sumitomo Elc USA Holdings Inc (HQ) 212 490-6610
  600 5th Ave Fl 18 New York (10020) *(G-12232)*
Summit Aerospace Inc 718 433-1326
  4301 21st St Ste 203 Long Island City (11101) *(G-7895)*
Summit Apparel Inc (PA) 631 213-8299
  65 Commerce Dr Hauppauge (11788) *(G-6202)*
Summit Appliances, Bronx Also called Felix Storch Inc *(G-1329)*
Summit Communications 914 273-5504
  28 Half Mile Rd Armonk (10504) *(G-420)*
Summit Financial Printing LLC 212 913-0510
  216 E 45th St Fl 15 New York (10017) *(G-12233)*
Summit Graphics 716 433-1014
  6042 Old Beattie Rd Lockport (14094) *(G-7615)*
Summit Instrument Corp 516 433-0140
  99 Engineers Dr Hicksville (11801) *(G-6396)*
Summit Laser Products, Holbrook Also called Summit Technologies LLC *(G-6475)*
Summit Lubricants Inc 585 815-0798
  4d Treadeasy Ave Batavia (14020) *(G-649)*
Summit Manufacturing (PA) 631 952-1570
  100 Spence St Bay Shore (11706) *(G-746)*
Summit Manufacturing 631 952-1570
  59 Spence St Bay Shore (11706) *(G-747)*
Summit Plastics, Bay Shore Also called Summit Manufacturing *(G-746)*
Summit Print & Mail LLC 716 433-1014
  6042 Old Beattie Rd Lockport (14094) *(G-7616)*
Summit Professional Networks 212 557-7480
  469 Fashion Ave Fl 10 New York (10018) *(G-12234)*
Summit Promotions LLC 631 952-1570
  59 Spence St Bay Shore (11706) *(G-748)*
Summit Research Laboratories, Huguenot Also called Somerville Acquisitions Co Inc *(G-6651)*
Summit Research Labs Inc (PA) 845 856-5261
  15 Big Pond Rd Huguenot (12746) *(G-6653)*
Summit Technologies LLC 631 590-1040
  723 Broadway Ave Holbrook (11741) *(G-6475)*
Summitreheis, Huguenot Also called Summit Research Labs Inc *(G-6653)*
Sumner Industries Inc 631 666-7290
  309 Orinoco Dr Bay Shore (11706) *(G-749)*
Sun Circuits International Inc 631 240-9251
  7 S Jersey Ave Ste 3 Setauket (11733) *(G-15381)*
Sun Microsystems, Albany Also called Oracle America Inc *(G-111)*
Sun Ming Jan Inc 718 418-8221
  145 Noll St Brooklyn (11206) *(G-2619)*
Sun Printing Incorporated 607 337-3034
  57 Borden Ave 65 Norwich (13815) *(G-13037)*
Sun Scientific Inc 914 479-5108
  88 Ashford Ave Dobbs Ferry (10522) *(G-4303)*
Sun Valley Printing, Binghamton Also called Jane Lewis *(G-930)*
Sun-Times Media Group Inc 716 945-1644
  36 River St Salamanca (14779) *(G-15110)*
Suna Bros Inc 212 869-5670
  10 W 46th St Fl 5 New York (10036) *(G-12235)*
Sunbelt Industries Inc (PA) 315 823-2947
  540 E Mill St Little Falls (13365) *(G-7505)*
Sunbilt Solar Pdts By Sussman 718 297-0228
  10910 180th St Jamaica (11433) *(G-6954)*

Sunborn Swiss Watches LLC 516 967-8836
55 Dail St New Hyde Park (11040) **(G-8864)**
Sunburst Studios Inc 718 768-6360
584 3rd Ave Brooklyn (11215) **(G-2620)**
Sunbuster, Farmingdale *Also called Gustbuster Ltd* **(G-5003)**
Sundance Enterprises Inc (HQ) 914 946-2942
79 Primrose St White Plains (10606) **(G-17173)**
Sundance Industries Inc 845 795-5809
36 Greentree Ln Milton (12547) **(G-8485)**
Sundance Solutions, White Plains *Also called Sundance Enterprises Inc* **(G-17173)**
Sunday Record, The, Saratoga Springs *Also called Record* **(G-15169)**
Sundial Brands LLC 631 842-8800
11 Ranick Dr S Amityville (11701) **(G-327)**
Sundial Creations, Farmingdale *Also called Sundial Group LLC* **(G-5118)**
Sundial Fragrances & Flavors 631 842-8800
11 Ranick Dr S Amityville (11701) **(G-328)**
Sundial Group LLC 631 842-8800
100 Adams Blvd Farmingdale (11735) **(G-5118)**
Sundown Ski & Sport Shop Inc (PA) 631 737-8600
3060 Middle Country Rd Lake Grove (11755) **(G-7267)**
Sunfeather Herbal Soap, Potsdam *Also called Sunfeather Natural Soap Co Inc* **(G-13885)**
Sunfeather Natural Soap Co Inc 315 265-1776
1551 State Highway 72 Potsdam (13676) **(G-13885)**
Sunham Home Fashions LLC (PA) 212 695-1218
136 Madison Ave Fl 16 New York (10016) **(G-12236)**
Sunlight US Co Inc (HQ) 716 826-6500
3556 Lake Shore Rd # 100 Buffalo (14219) **(G-3201)**
Sunny Names, New York *Also called Sunynams Fashions Ltd* **(G-12240)**
Sunnycrest Inc (PA) 315 252-7214
58 Prospect St Auburn (13021) **(G-521)**
Sunnyside Decorative Prints Co 516 671-1935
67 Robinson Ave Glen Cove (11542) **(G-5630)**
Sunquest Pharmaceuticals Inc 855 478-6779
150 Eileen Way Unit 1 Syosset (11791) **(G-15840)**
Sunrise Baking Co LLC 718 499-0800
4564 2nd Ave Brooklyn (11232) **(G-2621)**
Sunrise Bkg Acquisition Co LLC 718 499-0800
4564 2nd Ave Brooklyn (11232) **(G-2622)**
Sunrise Door Solutions 631 464-4139
1215 Sunrise Hwy Copiague (11726) **(G-3930)**
Sunrise Installation, Copiague *Also called Sunrise Door Solutions* **(G-3930)**
Sunrise Jewelers of NY Inc 516 541-1302
1220 Sunrise Hwy Massapequa (11758) **(G-8183)**
Sunrise Tile Inc 718 939-0538
13309 35th Ave Flushing (11354) **(G-5299)**
Sunset Ridge Holdings Inc 716 487-1458
490-496 Crescent St Jamestown (14701) **(G-7034)**
Sunshine Diamond Cutter Inc 212 221-1028
38 W 48th St Ste 905 New York (10036) **(G-12237)**
Sunshine Distribution Corp 888 506-7051
555 Madison Ave Ste 1800 New York (10022) **(G-12238)**
Sunward Electronics Inc 518 687-0030
258 Broadway Ste 2a Troy (12180) **(G-16257)**
Sunwin Global Industry Inc 646 370-6196
295 5th Ave Ste 515 New York (10016) **(G-12239)**
Sunwire Electric Corp 718 456-7500
70 Wyckoff Ave Apt 4h Brooklyn (11237) **(G-2623)**
Sunynams Fashions Ltd 212 268-5200
270 W 38th St Fl 2 New York (10018) **(G-12240)**
Supdates, New York *Also called Bull Street LLC* **(G-9478)**
Super Conductor Materials Inc 845 368-0240
391 Spook Rock Rd Suffern (10901) **(G-15801)**
Super Express USA Pubg Corp 212 227-5800
8410 101st St Apt 4l Richmond Hill (11418) **(G-14086)**
Super Moderna/Magic Master, New Hyde Park *Also called Joseph Struhl Co Inc* **(G-8843)**
Super Neon Light Co Inc 718 236-5667
7813 16th Ave Brooklyn (11214) **(G-2624)**
Super Price Chopper Inc 716 893-3323
1580 Genesee St Buffalo (14211) **(G-3202)**
Super Software 845 735-0000
151 S Main St Ste 303 New City (10956) **(G-8794)**
Super Steelworks Corporation 718 386-4770
12 Lucon Dr Deer Park (11729) **(G-4215)**
Super Stud Building Products, Long Island City *Also called Superior Metals & Processing* **(G-7896)**
Super Web Inc 631 643-9100
97 Lamar St West Babylon (11704) **(G-16834)**
Super-Tek Products Inc 718 278-7900
2544 Borough Pl Woodside (11377) **(G-17357)**
Super-Trim Inc 212 255-2370
30 W 24th St Fl 4 New York (10010) **(G-12241)**
Superboats Inc 631 226-1761
694 Roosevelt Ave Lindenhurst (11757) **(G-7487)**
Superchat LLC 212 352-8581
310 E 70th St Apt 6lm New York (10021) **(G-12242)**
Superflex Ltd 718 768-1400
152 44th St Brooklyn (11232) **(G-2625)**
Supergen Products LLC 315 573-7887
320 Hoffman St Newark (14513) **(G-12744)**
Superior Aggragates Supply LLC 516 333-2923
612 Muncy St Lindenhurst (11757) **(G-7488)**

Superior Bat Company, Jamestown *Also called Grace Wheeler* **(G-6995)**
Superior Block Corp 718 421-0900
4106 Glenwood Rd Brooklyn (11210) **(G-2626)**
Superior Confections Inc 718 698-3300
1150 South Ave Staten Island (10314) **(G-15743)**
Superior Decorators Inc 718 381-4793
7416 Cypress Hills St Glendale (11385) **(G-5664)**
Superior Elec Enclosure Inc 718 797-9090
16 Spencer St Brooklyn (11205) **(G-2627)**
Superior Energy Services Inc 716 483-0100
1720 Foote Avenue Ext Jamestown (14701) **(G-7035)**
Superior Exteriors of Buffalo 716 873-1000
275 Vulcan St Buffalo (14207) **(G-3203)**
Superior Fiber Mills Inc 718 782-7500
181 Lombardy St Brooklyn (11222) **(G-2628)**
Superior Furs Inc 516 365-4123
1697 Northern Blvd Manhasset (11030) **(G-8065)**
Superior Metal & Woodwork Inc 631 465-9004
70 Central Ave Farmingdale (11735) **(G-5119)**
Superior Metals & Processing 718 545-7500
801 26th Ave Long Island City (11102) **(G-7896)**
Superior Model Form Co, Middle Village *Also called Goldmont Enterprises Inc* **(G-8411)**
Superior Motion Controls Inc 516 420-2921
40 Smith St Farmingdale (11735) **(G-5120)**
Superior Packaging, Farmingdale *Also called Mkt329 Inc* **(G-5059)**
Superior Plastic Slipcovers, Glendale *Also called Superior Decorators Inc* **(G-5664)**
Superior Plus Cnstr Pdts Corp 315 463-5144
6741 Old Collamer Rd East Syracuse (13057) **(G-4569)**
Superior Print On Demand 607 240-5231
165 Charles St Vestal (13850) **(G-16454)**
Superior Stl Door Trim Co Inc 716 665-3256
154 Fairmount Ave Jamestown (14701) **(G-7036)**
Superior Technology Inc 585 352-6556
200 Paragon Dr Rochester (14624) **(G-14707)**
Superior Tool Co Inc 716 692-3900
1020 Oliver St North Tonawanda (14120) **(G-12998)**
Superior Walls of Hudson Vly, Poughkeepsie *Also called Superior Wlls of Hdson Vly Inc* **(G-13937)**
Superior Walls Upstate NY Inc 585 624-9390
7574 E Main St Lima (14485) **(G-7449)**
Superior Washer & Gasket Corp (PA) 631 273-8282
170 Adams Ave Hauppauge (11788) **(G-6203)**
Superior Welding 631 676-2751
331 Dante Ct Ste G Holbrook (11741) **(G-6476)**
Superior Wlls of Hdson Vly Inc 845 485-4033
68 Violet Ave Poughkeepsie (12601) **(G-13937)**
Superior Wood Turnings 716 483-1254
118 E 1st St Jamestown (14701) **(G-7037)**
Superite Gear Instr of Hppauge (PA) 631 234-0100
225 Engineers Rd Hauppauge (11788) **(G-6204)**
Superleaf LLC 607 280-9198
286 Flushing Ave Brooklyn (11205) **(G-2629)**
Supermarket Equipment Depo Inc 718 665-6200
1135 Bronx River Ave Bronx (10472) **(G-1467)**
Supermedia LLC 212 513-9700
2 Penn Plz Fl 22 New York (10121) **(G-12243)**
Superpower Inc 518 346-1414
450 Duane Ave Ste 1 Schenectady (12304) **(G-15302)**
Supersil LLC 347 266-9900
4750 Bedford Ave Apt 6l Brooklyn (11235) **(G-2630)**
Supersmile, New York *Also called Robell Research Inc* **(G-11888)**
Supply & Demand, New York *Also called Drew Philips Corp* **(G-9928)**
Supply Technologies (ny) (HQ) 212 966-3310
80 State St Albany (12207) **(G-139)**
Supplynet Inc (PA) 845 267-2655
706 Executive Blvd Ste B Valley Cottage (10989) **(G-16392)**
Suppositoria Laboratory, Bronx *Also called Perrigo New York Inc* **(G-1427)**
Supreme Boilers Inc 718 342-2220
9221 Ditmas Ave Brooklyn (11236) **(G-2631)**
Supreme Chocolatier LLC 718 761-9600
1150 South Ave Fl 1 Staten Island (10314) **(G-15744)**
Supreme Fire-Proof Door Co Inc 718 665-4224
391 Rider Ave Bronx (10451) **(G-1468)**
Supreme Leather Products, Spring Valley *Also called Louis Schwartz* **(G-15593)**
Supreme Poly Plastics Inc 718 456-9300
299 Meserole St Brooklyn (11206) **(G-2632)**
Supreme Poultry Inc 718 472-0300
3788 Review Ave Long Island City (11101) **(G-7897)**
Supreme Screw Products Inc 718 293-6600
10 Skyline Dr Unit B Plainview (11803) **(G-13637)**
Supreme Steel Inc 631 884-1320
690 N Jefferson Ave Lindenhurst (11757) **(G-7489)**
Supresta US LLC (HQ) 914 674-9434
420 Saw Mill River Rd Ardsley (10502) **(G-406)**
Sure Fit Inc 212 395-9340
58 W 40th St Rm 2a New York (10018) **(G-12244)**
Sure Flow Equipment Inc 800 263-8251
250 Cooper Ave Ste 102 Tonawanda (14150) **(G-16204)**
Sure Iron Works, Brooklyn *Also called Kms Contracting Inc* **(G-2176)**
Sure-Kol Refrigerator Co Inc 718 625-0601
490 Flushing Ave Brooklyn (11205) **(G-2633)**

Sure-Lock Industries LLC ALPHABETIC SECTION

Sure-Lock Industries LLC 315 207-0044
193 E Seneca St Oswego (13126) *(G-13343)*
Surepure Inc 917 368-8480
405 Lexington Ave Fl 25 New York (10174) *(G-12245)*
Surescan Corporation 607 321-0042
100 Eldredge St Binghamton (13901) *(G-953)*
Sureseal Corporation 607 336-6676
50 Ohara Dr Norwich (13815) *(G-13038)*
Surf-Tech Manufacturing Corp 631 589-1194
80 Orville Dr Ste 115 Bohemia (11716) *(G-1138)*
Surface Finish Technology 607 732-2909
215 Judson St Elmira (14901) *(G-4703)*
Surface Magazine 646 805-0200
134 W 26th St Frnt 1 New York (10001) *(G-12246)*
Surface Publishing, New York *Also called Surface Magazine (G-12246)*
Surgical Design Corp 914 273-2445
3 Macdonald Ave Armonk (10504) *(G-421)*
Surmet Ceramics Corporation 716 875-4091
699 Hertel Ave Ste 290 Buffalo (14207) *(G-3204)*
Surmotech LLC 585 742-1220
7676 Netlink Dr Victor (14564) *(G-16503)*
Surprise Plastics Inc 718 492-6355
124 57th St Brooklyn (11220) *(G-2634)*
Surving Studios 845 355-1430
17 Millsburg Rd Middletown (10940) *(G-8464)*
Survival Inc 631 385-5060
90 Washington Dr Ste C Centerport (11721) *(G-3481)*
Sussex Publishers Inc (PA) 212 260-7210
115 E 23rd St Fl 9 New York (10010) *(G-12247)*
Sussman-Automatic Corporation (PA) 718 937-4500
4320 34th St Long Island City (11101) *(G-7898)*
Sutphen Corporation 845 583-4720
30 Sutphen Pl Fl 2 White Lake (12786) *(G-17071)*
Sutter Machine Tool and Die, Bronx *Also called M J M Tooling Corp (G-1384)*
Sutton Place Software Inc 631 421-1737
13 Tappen Dr Melville (11747) *(G-8358)*
Svyz Trading Corp 718 220-1140
4320 Park Ave Bronx (10457) *(G-1469)*
Swagelok Western NY 585 359-8470
10 Thruway Park Dr West Henrietta (14586) *(G-16896)*
Swain Technology Inc 585 889-2786
963 North Rd Scottsville (14546) *(G-15340)*
Swamp Island Dessert Co, West Falls *Also called Butterwood Desserts Inc (G-16844)*
Swank Inc 212 867-2600
90 Park Ave Rm 1302 New York (10016) *(G-12248)*
Swanson Lumber 716 499-1726
5273 N Hill Rd Gerry (14740) *(G-5593)*
Swaps Monitor Publications Inc 212 742-8550
29 Broadway Rm 1315 New York (10006) *(G-12249)*
Swarovski Lighting Ltd (PA) 518 563-7500
61 Industrial Blvd Plattsburgh (12901) *(G-13702)*
Swarovski Lighting Ltd 518 324-6378
1483 Military Tpke Ste B Plattsburgh (12901) *(G-13703)*
Swarovski North America Ltd 914 423-4132
6080 Mall Walk Yonkers (10704) *(G-17488)*
Swarovski North America Ltd 212 695-1502
1 Penn Plz Frnt 4 New York (10119) *(G-12250)*
Swatfame Inc 212 944-8022
530 Fashion Ave Rm 1204 New York (10018) *(G-12251)*
Swatt Baking Co, Olean *Also called L American Ltd (G-13150)*
Sweater Brand Inc 718 797-0505
86 S 1st St Brooklyn (11249) *(G-2635)*
Swed Masters Workshop LLC 212 644-8822
214 E 82nd St Frnt 1 New York (10028) *(G-12252)*
Swedish Hill Vineyard Inc 607 403-0029
4565 State Route 414 Romulus (14541) *(G-14844)*
Swedish Hill Winery, Romulus *Also called Swedish Hill Vineyard Inc (G-14844)*
Sweet Melodys LLC 716 580-3227
8485 Transit Rd East Amherst (14051) *(G-4362)*
Sweet Mouth Inc 800 433-7758
244 5th Ave Ste L243 New York (10001) *(G-12253)*
Sweet Tooth Enterprises LLC 631 752-2888
135 Dale St West Babylon (11704) *(G-16835)*
Sweeteners Plus Inc 585 728-3770
5768 Sweeteners Blvd Lakeville (14480) *(G-7286)*
Sweetriot Inc 212 431-7468
131 Varick St Ste 936 New York (10013) *(G-12254)*
Sweetwater Energy Inc 585 647-5760
500 Lee Rd Ste 200 Rochester (14606) *(G-14708)*
Sweetworks Inc (PA) 716 634-4545
3500 Genesee St Buffalo (14225) *(G-3205)*
Swift Fulfillment Services 516 593-1198
290 Broadway Lynbrook (11563) *(G-7964)*
Swift Glass Co Inc 607 733-7166
131 22nd St Elmira Heights (14903) *(G-4714)*
Swift Multigraphics LLC 585 442-8000
55 Southwood Ln Rochester (14618) *(G-14709)*
Swift River Associates Inc (PA) 716 875-0902
4051 River Rd Tonawanda (14150) *(G-16205)*
Swimline Corp (PA) 631 254-2155
191 Rodeo Dr Edgewood (11717) *(G-4613)*
Swimline International Corp 631 254-2155
191 Rodeo Dr Edgewood (11717) *(G-4614)*
Swimwear Anywhere Inc (PA) 631 420-1400
85 Sherwood Ave Farmingdale (11735) *(G-5121)*
Swimwear Anywhere Inc 845 858-4141
21 Minisink Ave Port Jervis (12771) *(G-13794)*
Swing Frame, Freeport *Also called Access Display Group Inc (G-5380)*
Swirl Bliss LLC 516 867-9475
1777 Grand Ave North Baldwin (11510) *(G-12910)*
Swiss Specialties Inc 631 567-8800
15 Crescent Ct Wading River (11792) *(G-16527)*
Swiss Tool Corporation 631 842-7766
100 Court St Copiague (11726) *(G-3931)*
Swissbit Na Inc 914 935-1400
18 Willett Ave 202 Port Chester (10573) *(G-13760)*
Swisse Cheeks, Brooklyn *Also called Silly Phillie Creations Inc (G-2556)*
Swissmar Inc 905 764-1121
6391 Walmore Rd Niagara Falls (14304) *(G-12879)*
Swissway Inc 631 351-5350
123 W Hills Rd Huntington Station (11746) *(G-6724)*
Switch Beverage Company LLC 203 202-7383
2 Seaview Blvd Fl 3 Port Washington (11050) *(G-13867)*
Switches and Sensors Inc 631 924-2167
86 Horseblock Rd Unit J Yaphank (11980) *(G-17404)*
Switching Power Inc 631 981-7231
3601 Veterans Mem Hwy Ronkonkoma (11779) *(G-14990)*
Switzer, Buffalo *Also called Precision Photo-Fab Inc (G-3133)*
Swivelier Company Inc 845 353-1455
600 Bradley Hill Rd Ste 3 Blauvelt (10913) *(G-975)*
Swremote, Buffalo *Also called Successware Remote LLC (G-3199)*
Sybase Inc 212 596-1100
1114 Avenue Of The Americ New York (10036) *(G-12255)*
Sycamore Hill Designs Inc 585 820-7322
7585 Modock Rd Victor (14564) *(G-16504)*
Sylhan LLC (PA) 631 243-6600
210 Rodeo Dr Edgewood (11717) *(G-4615)*
Symantec Corporation 631 656-0185
98 Sunrise Ln Smithtown (11787) *(G-15499)*
Symantec Corporation 646 487-6000
1 Penn Plz Ste 5420 New York (10119) *(G-12256)*
Symbio Technologies LLC 914 576-1205
333 Mamaroneck Ave White Plains (10605) *(G-17174)*
Symbol Technologies LLC 631 738-2400
110 Orville Dr Bohemia (11716) *(G-1139)*
Symbol Technologies LLC 631 738-3346
1 Zebra Plz Holtsville (11742) *(G-6510)*
Symbol Technologies LLC 631 218-3907
25 Andrea Rd Holbrook (11741) *(G-6477)*
Symphony Talent LLC (PA) 212 999-9000
45 Rockefeller Plz # 659 New York (10111) *(G-12257)*
Symrise Inc 646 459-5000
505 Park Ave Fl 15 New York (10022) *(G-12258)*
Symrise Inc 845 469-7675
45 Leone Ln Chester (10918) *(G-3618)*
Symwave Inc (HQ) 949 542-4400
80 Arkay Dr Hauppauge (11788) *(G-6205)*
Synaptics Incorporated 585 899-4300
90 Linden Oaks Ste 100 Rochester (14625) *(G-14710)*
Synced Inc 917 565-5591
120 Walker St Ste 4 New York (10013) *(G-12259)*
Synco Chemical Corporation 631 567-5300
24 Davinci Dr Bohemia (11716) *(G-1140)*
Synco Technologies Inc 212 255-2031
54 W 21st St Rm 602 New York (10010) *(G-12260)*
Synergx Systems Inc (HQ) 516 433-4700
3927 59th St Woodside (11377) *(G-17358)*
Synergy Digital 718 643-2742
43 Hall St Brooklyn (11205) *(G-2636)*
Synergy Flavors NY Company LLC 585 232-6648
86 White St Rochester (14608) *(G-14711)*
Synergy Intrntnal Optrnics LLC 631 277-0500
101 Comac St Ronkonkoma (11779) *(G-14991)*
Synergy Pharmaceuticals Inc (HQ) 212 227-8611
420 Lexington Ave Rm 2500 New York (10170) *(G-12261)*
Synergy Pharmaceuticals Inc (PA) 212 297-0020
420 Lexington Ave Rm 2012 New York (10170) *(G-12262)*
Synergy Tooling Systems Inc (PA) 716 834-4457
287 Commerce Dr Amherst (14228) *(G-264)*
Syntec Optics, Rochester *Also called Syntec Technologies Inc (G-14712)*
Syntec Optics, Rochester *Also called Syntec Technologies Inc (G-14713)*
Syntec Technologies Inc (PA) 585 768-2513
515 Lee Rd Rochester (14606) *(G-14712)*
Syntec Technologies Inc 585 464-9336
515 Lee Rd Rochester (14606) *(G-14713)*
Syntel Inc 212 785-9810
1 Exchange Plz Ste 2001 New York (10006) *(G-12263)*
Synthes USA, Horseheads *Also called Depuy Synthes Inc (G-6574)*
Synthetic Textiles Inc (PA) 716 842-2598
398 Broadway St Buffalo (14204) *(G-3206)*
Syntho Pharmaceuticals Inc 631 755-9898
230 Sherwood Ave Farmingdale (11735) *(G-5122)*
Syraco Products Inc 800 581-5555
1054 S Clinton St Syracuse (13202) *(G-16047)*

ALPHABETIC

Syracusa Sand and Gravel Inc 585 924-7146
1389 Malone Rd Victor (14564) ***(G-16505)***
Syracuse Casing Co Inc 315 475-0309
528 Erie Blvd W Syracuse (13204) ***(G-16048)***
Syracuse Catholic Press Assn 315 422-8153
421 S Warren St Fl 2 Syracuse (13202) ***(G-16049)***
Syracuse Computer Forms Inc 315 478-0108
216 Burnet Ave Syracuse (13203) ***(G-16050)***
Syracuse Corrugated Box Corp 315 437-9901
302 Stoutenger St East Syracuse (13057) ***(G-4570)***
Syracuse Cultural Workers Prj 315 474-1132
400 Lodi St Syracuse (13203) ***(G-16051)***
Syracuse Heat Treating Corp 315 451-0000
7055 Interstate Island Rd Syracuse (13209) ***(G-16052)***
Syracuse Hvac, Syracuse *Also called John F Krell Jr* ***(G-15968)***
Syracuse Industrial Sls Co Ltd 315 478-5751
1850 Lemoyne Ave Syracuse (13208) ***(G-16053)***
Syracuse Label & Surround Prtg, Liverpool *Also called Syracuse Label Co Inc* ***(G-7550)***
Syracuse Label Co Inc 315 422-1037
110 Luther Ave Liverpool (13088) ***(G-7550)***
Syracuse Letter Company Inc 315 476-8328
1179 Oak Ln Bridgeport (13030) ***(G-1237)***
Syracuse Midstate Spring, Syracuse *Also called Midstate Spring Inc* ***(G-15990)***
Syracuse New Times, Syracuse *Also called All Times Publishing LLC* ***(G-15847)***
Syracuse New Times, Syracuse *Also called A Zimmer Ltd* ***(G-15845)***
Syracuse Plastics LLC 315 637-9881
7400 Morgan Rd Liverpool (13090) ***(G-7551)***
Syracuse Prosthetic Center Inc 315 476-9697
1124 E Fayette St Syracuse (13210) ***(G-16054)***
Syracuse Sand & Gravel LLC 315 548-8207
1902 County Route 57 Fulton (13069) ***(G-5475)***
Syracuse Stamping Company, Syracuse *Also called Syraco Products Inc* ***(G-16047)***
Syracuse Technical Center, Syracuse *Also called Chemtrade Chemicals US LLC* ***(G-15894)***
Syracuse University Press Inc 315 443-5534
621 Skytop Rd Ste 110 Syracuse (13244) ***(G-16055)***
Syrasoft LLC 315 708-0341
6 Canton St Baldwinsville (13027) ***(G-578)***
System of AME Binding 631 390-8560
95 Hoffman Ln Central Islip (11749) ***(G-3512)***
Systems Drs C3 Inc (HQ) 716 631-6200
485 Cayuga Rd Buffalo (14225) ***(G-3207)***
Systems Trading Inc 718 261-8900
48 S Svc Rd Ste Ll90 Melville (11747) ***(G-8359)***
Sz - Design & Print Inc 845 352-0395
33 Rita Ave Monsey (10952) ***(G-8583)***
T & C Power Conversion Inc 585 482-5551
132 Humboldt St Rochester (14610) ***(G-14714)***
T & G Wholesale Electric Corp 585 396-9690
200 Saltonstall St Canandaigua (14424) ***(G-3358)***
T & K Printing, Brooklyn *Also called T&K Printing Inc* ***(G-2640)***
T & L Automatics Inc 585 647-3717
770 Emerson St Rochester (14613) ***(G-14715)***
T & L Trading Co 718 782-5550
17 Meserole St Brooklyn (11206) ***(G-2637)***
T & M Plating Inc 212 967-1110
357 W 36th St Fl 7 New York (10018) ***(G-12264)***
T & R Knitting Mills Inc (PA) 718 497-4017
8000 Cooper Ave Ste 6 Glendale (11385) ***(G-5665)***
T & R Knitting Mills Inc 212 840-8665
214 W 39th St New York (10018) ***(G-12265)***
T & Smoothie Inc 631 804-6653
499 N Service Rd Ste 83 Patchogue (11772) ***(G-13436)***
T A C, New York *Also called Accessory Corporation* ***(G-9010)***
T A S Sales Service LLC 518 234-4919
105 Kenyon Rd Cobleskill (12043) ***(G-3739)***
T A Tool & Molding Inc 631 293-0172
185 Marine St Farmingdale (11735) ***(G-5123)***
T C Dunham Paint Company Inc 914 969-4202
581 Saw Mill River Rd Yonkers (10701) ***(G-17489)***
T C I, Whitesboro *Also called Telecommunication Concepts* ***(G-17196)***
T C Peters Printing Co Inc 315 724-4149
2336 W Whitesboro St Utica (13502) ***(G-16361)***
T C Timber, Skaneateles *Also called Habermaass Corporation* ***(G-15462)***
T E Q, Huntington Station *Also called Tequipment Inc* ***(G-6726)***
T Eason Land Surveyor 631 474-2200
27 Poplar St Port Jeff STA (11776) ***(G-13772)***
T G M Products Inc 631 491-0515
90 Wyandanch Ave Unit E Wyandanch (11798) ***(G-17377)***
T G S Inc 516 629-6905
6 Wildwood Ct Locust Valley (11560) ***(G-7634)***
T J Ronan Paint Corp 718 292-1100
749 E 135th St Bronx (10454) ***(G-1470)***
T J Signs Unlimited LLC (PA) 631 273-4800
171 Freeman Ave Islip (11751) ***(G-6813)***
T Jn Electric 917 560-0981
116 Cortlandt Rd Mahopac (10541) ***(G-8002)***
T Jn Electric Inc 845 628-6970
901 Route 6 Mahopac (10541) ***(G-8003)***
T L F Graphics Inc 585 272-5500
235 Metro Park Rochester (14623) ***(G-14716)***
T L X, Plainview *Also called Xpress Printing Inc* ***(G-13647)***
T Lemme Mechanical Inc 518 436-4136
1074 Broadway Menands (12204) ***(G-8379)***
T M Design Screen Printing, Rochester *Also called Todd Walbridge* ***(G-14727)***
T M I of New York, Brooklyn *Also called Technipoly Manufacturing Inc* ***(G-2650)***
T M I Plastics Industries Inc 718 383-0363
28 Wythe Ave Brooklyn (11249) ***(G-2638)***
T M International LLC 718 842-0949
413 Faile St 15 Bronx (10474) ***(G-1471)***
T M Machine Inc 716 822-0817
176 Reading St Buffalo (14220) ***(G-3208)***
T M W Diamonds Mfg Co (PA) 212 869-8444
15 W 47th St Ste 302 New York (10036) ***(G-12266)***
T Mix Inc 646 379-6814
6217 5th Ave Brooklyn (11220) ***(G-2639)***
T O Dey Service Corp 212 683-6300
151 W 46th St Fl 3 New York (10036) ***(G-12267)***
T O Gronlund Company Inc 212 679-3535
200 Lexington Ave Rm 1515 New York (10016) ***(G-12268)***
T R P Machine Inc 631 567-9620
35 Davinci Dr Ste B Bohemia (11716) ***(G-1141)***
T R W Automotive, Auburn *Also called TRW Automotive US LLC* ***(G-526)***
T Rj Shirts Inc 347 642-3071
3050 90th St East Elmhurst (11369) ***(G-4399)***
T RS Great American Rest 516 294-1680
17 Hillside Ave Williston Park (11596) ***(G-17263)***
T S B A Group Inc (PA) 718 565-6000
3830 Woodside Ave Sunnyside (11104) ***(G-15810)***
T S O General Corp 631 952-5320
81 Emjay Blvd Unit 1 Brentwood (11717) ***(G-1195)***
T S P Corp 585 768-6769
78 One Half Lake St Le Roy (14482) ***(G-7419)***
T S Pink Corp 607 432-1100
139 Pony Farm Rd Oneonta (13820) ***(G-13194)***
T Shore Products Ltd 315 252-9174
5 Eagle Dr Auburn (13021) ***(G-522)***
T T I, Oriskany *Also called Terahertz Technologies Inc* ***(G-13316)***
T V Trade Media Inc 212 288-3933
216 E 75th St Apt 1w New York (10021) ***(G-12269)***
T&B Bakery Corp 646 642-4300
5870 56th St Maspeth (11378) ***(G-8172)***
T&K Printing Inc 718 439-9454
262 44th St Brooklyn (11232) ***(G-2640)***
T-Base Communications USA Inc 315 713-0013
806 Commerce Park Dr Ogdensburg (13669) ***(G-13123)***
T-Company LLC 646 290-6365
16 Monitor Rd Smithtown (11787) ***(G-15500)***
T-S-K Electronics Inc 716 693-3916
908 Niagara Falls Blvd # 122 North Tonawanda (14120) ***(G-12999)***
T-Shirt Graphics, Ballston Spa *Also called Sand Hill Industries Inc* ***(G-608)***
Taam-Tov Foods Inc 718 788-8880
196 28th St Brooklyn (11232) ***(G-2641)***
Taber Acquisition Corp 716 694-4000
455 Bryant St North Tonawanda (14120) ***(G-13000)***
Taber Industries, North Tonawanda *Also called Taber Acquisition Corp* ***(G-13000)***
Table Tops Paper Corp 718 598-7832
43 Hall St Ste C2 Brooklyn (11205) ***(G-2642)***
Tablecloths For Granted Ltd 518 370-5481
510 Union St Schenectady (12305) ***(G-15303)***
Tables Manufacturing, Edgewood *Also called Kinplex Corp* ***(G-4604)***
Tablet Newspaper, The, Brooklyn *Also called Tablet Publishing Company Inc* ***(G-2643)***
Tablet Publishing Company Inc 718 965-7333
1712 10th Ave Brooklyn (11215) ***(G-2643)***
Tabrisse Collections Inc 212 921-1014
1412 Broadway New York (10018) ***(G-12270)***
TAC Screw Products Inc 585 663-5840
170 Bennington Dr Rochester (14616) ***(G-14717)***
Tackle Factory, Fillmore *Also called Cuba Specialty Mfg Co Inc* ***(G-5175)***
Taconic, Petersburg *Also called Tonoga Inc* ***(G-13528)***
Tacr, Middletown *Also called Turbine Arfoil Cating Repr LLC* ***(G-8467)***
Tactair Fluid Controls Inc 315 451-3928
4806 W Taft Rd Liverpool (13088) ***(G-7552)***
Tactica International Inc (PA) 212 575-0500
11 W 42nd St New York (10036) ***(G-12271)***
TAe Trans Atlantic Elec Inc (PA) 631 595-9206
151 E Industry Ct Deer Park (11729) ***(G-4216)***
Tag Dental Implant Solutions, Valley Stream *Also called Total Dntl Implant Sltions LLC* ***(G-16430)***
Tag Envelope Co Inc 718 389-6844
1419 128th St College Point (11356) ***(G-3809)***
Tag Flange & Machining Inc 516 536-1300
3375 Royal Ave Oceanside (11572) ***(G-13100)***
Tahari Arthur S Levine, New York *Also called Tahari ASL LLC* ***(G-12272)***
Tahari ASL LLC 212 763-2800
1114 Ave Of The Americas New York (10036) ***(G-12272)***
Tai Seng 718 399-6311
106 Lexington Ave Brooklyn (11238) ***(G-2644)***
Taikoh USA Inc 646 556-6652
369 Lexington Ave Fl 2 New York (10017) ***(G-12273)***
Tailorbyrd, New York *Also called Sanctuary Brands LLC* ***(G-11964)***

ALPHABETIC

(PA)=Parent Co (HQ)=Headquarters (DH)=Div Headquarters
2017 Harris
New York Manufacturers Directory
1075

Tailored Coatings Inc 716 893-4869
1800 Brdwy St Bldg 2a Buffalo (14212) ***(G-3209)***
Tailored Sportsman LLC 646 366-8733
230 W 38th St Fl 6 New York (10018) ***(G-12274)***
Takasago Intl Corp USA 845 751-0799
114 Commerce Dr S Harriman (10926) ***(G-5975)***
Takeform Architectural Graphics, Medina *Also called Quorum Group LLC* ***(G-8279)***
Talas, Brooklyn *Also called Technical Library Service Inc* ***(G-2649)***
Talbots Inc 914 328-1034
125 Westchester Ave # 2460 White Plains (10601) ***(G-17175)***
Talisman Energy USA Inc 607 562-4000
337 Daniel Zenker Dr Horseheads (14845) ***(G-6595)***
Tallmans Express Lube 315 266-1033
8421 Seneca Tpke New Hartford (13413) ***(G-8812)***
Talyarps Corporation (PA) 914 699-3030
143 Sparks Ave Pelham (10803) ***(G-13496)***
Talyarps Corporation 914 699-3030
716 S Columbus Ave Mount Vernon (10550) ***(G-8735)***
Tam Ceramics Group of Ny LLC 716 278-9400
4511 Hyde Park Blvd Niagara Falls (14305) ***(G-12880)***
Tam Ceramics LLC 716 278-9480
4511 Hyde Park Blvd Niagara Falls (14305) ***(G-12881)***
Tamber Knits Inc 212 730-1121
231 W 39th St Fl 8 New York (10018) ***(G-12275)***
Tambetti Inc 212 751-9584
48 W 48th St Ste 501 New York (10036) ***(G-12276)***
Tami Great Food Corp 845 352-7901
22 Briarcliff Dr Monsey (10952) ***(G-8584)***
Tamka Sport LLC 718 224-7820
225 Beverly Rd Douglaston (11363) ***(G-4313)***
Tamperproof Screw Company Inc 516 931-1616
30 Laurel St Hicksville (11801) ***(G-6397)***
Tamsen Z LLC 212 292-6412
350 Park Ave Fl 4 New York (10022) ***(G-12277)***
Tanagro Jewelry Corp 212 753-2817
36 W 44th St Ste 1101 New York (10036) ***(G-12278)***
Tandus Centiva Inc 212 206-7170
71 5th Ave Fl 2 New York (10003) ***(G-12279)***
Tandy Leather Factory Inc 845 480-3588
298 Main St Nyack (10960) ***(G-13054)***
Tanen & Co, Brooklyn *Also called Tanen Cap Co* ***(G-2645)***
Tanen Cap Co 212 254-7100
397 Bridge St Fl 8 Brooklyn (11201) ***(G-2645)***
Tangent Machine & Tool Corp 631 249-3088
108 Gazza Blvd Farmingdale (11735) ***(G-5124)***
Tangram Company LLC 631 758-0460
125 Corporate Dr Holtsville (11742) ***(G-6511)***
Tape Printers Inc 631 249-5585
155 Allen Blvd Ste A Farmingdale (11735) ***(G-5125)***
Tape Systems Inc 914 668-3700
630 S Columbus Ave Mount Vernon (10550) ***(G-8736)***
Tape-It Inc 631 243-4100
233 N Fehr Way Bay Shore (11706) ***(G-750)***
Tapemaker Sales Co Inc 516 333-0592
48 Urban Ave Westbury (11590) ***(G-17029)***
Tapemaker Supply Company LLC 914 693-3407
22 Sherbrooke Rd Hartsdale (10530) ***(G-6001)***
Tapestries Etc, New York *Also called Vander Heyden Woodworking* ***(G-12500)***
Tappan Wire & Cable Inc (HQ) 845 353-9000
100 Bradley Pkwy Blauvelt (10913) ***(G-976)***
Taqa Entertainment, Valley Stream *Also called Taste and See Entrmt Inc* ***(G-16429)***
Tara Rific Screen Printing Inc 718 583-6864
4197 Park Ave Bronx (10457) ***(G-1472)***
Target Rock, Farmingdale *Also called Curtiss-Wright Flow Ctrl Corp* ***(G-4968)***
Targetprocess Inc (PA) 607 346-0621
1325 Millersport Hwy Amherst (14221) ***(G-265)***
Targum Press USA Inc 248 355-2266
1946 59th St Brooklyn (11204) ***(G-2646)***
Taro Manufacturing Company Inc 315 252-9430
114 Clark St Auburn (13021) ***(G-523)***
Tarrytown Bakery Inc 914 631-0209
150 Wildey St Tarrytown (10591) ***(G-16108)***
Tarsia Technical Industries 631 231-8322
93 Marcus Blvd Hauppauge (11788) ***(G-6206)***
Tarsier Ltd 212 401-6181
488 Madison Ave Fl 23 New York (10022) ***(G-12280)***
Taste and See Entrmt Inc 516 285-3010
255 Dogwood Rd Valley Stream (11580) ***(G-16429)***
Tate's Bake Shop, East Moriches *Also called Tates Wholesale LLC* ***(G-4431)***
Tates Wholesale LLC 631 780-6511
62 Pine St East Moriches (11940) ***(G-4431)***
Tatra Mfg Corporation 631 691-1184
30 Railroad Ave Copiague (11726) ***(G-3932)***
Tattersall Industries LLC 518 381-4270
2125 Technology Dr Schenectady (12308) ***(G-15304)***
Taumel Assembly Systems, Patterson *Also called Taumel Metalforming Corp* ***(G-13445)***
Taumel Metalforming Corp 845 878-3100
25 Jon Barrett Rd Patterson (12563) ***(G-13445)***
Taylor 518 954-2832
166 Wallins Corners Rd Amsterdam (12010) ***(G-369)***
Taylor & Francis Group LLC 212 216-7800
711 3rd Ave Fl 8 New York (10017) ***(G-12281)***
Taylor Concrete Products Inc 315 788-2191
20475 Old Rome Rd Watertown (13601) ***(G-16673)***
Taylor Copy Services, Syracuse *Also called Constas Printing Corporation* ***(G-15905)***
Taylor Devices Inc (PA) 716 694-0800
90 Taylor Dr North Tonawanda (14120) ***(G-13001)***
Taylor Made Group LLC (HQ) 518 725-0681
66 Kingsboro Ave Gloversville (12078) ***(G-5724)***
Taylor Metalworks Inc 716 662-3113
3925 California Rd Orchard Park (14127) ***(G-13298)***
Taylor Precision Machining 607 535-3101
3921 Dug Rd Montour Falls (14865) ***(G-8612)***
Taylor Products Inc (PA) 518 773-9312
66 Kingsboro Ave Gloversville (12078) ***(G-5725)***
Taylor Tank Company Inc 718 434-1300
848 E 43rd St Brooklyn (11210) ***(G-2647)***
Tb, Rochester *Also called Turner Bellows Inc* ***(G-14735)***
Tbhl International LLC 212 799-2007
252 W 38th St Fl 11 New York (10018) ***(G-12282)***
Tbt Group Inc 212 685-1836
267 5th Ave Bsmt B-103 New York (10016) ***(G-12283)***
Tcmf Inc 607 724-1094
85 Eldredge St Binghamton (13901) ***(G-954)***
TCS Electronics Inc 585 337-4301
1124 Corporate Dr Farmington (14425) ***(G-5156)***
TCS Industries Inc 585 426-1160
400 Trabold Rd Rochester (14624) ***(G-14718)***
Tdg Operations LLC 212 779-4300
200 Lexington Ave Rm 1314 New York (10016) ***(G-12284)***
Tdk USA Corporation (HQ) 516 535-2600
455 Rxr Plz Uniondale (11556) ***(G-16300)***
Tdk-Lambda Americas Inc 631 967-3000
145 Marcus Blvd Ste 3 Hauppauge (11788) ***(G-6207)***
Tdl Manufacturing Inc 215 538-8820
80 Cabot Ct Hauppauge (11788) ***(G-6208)***
Tdo Sandblasting, Roosevelt *Also called Tropical Driftwood Originals* ***(G-15010)***
TDS Fitness Equipment 607 733-6789
160 Home St Elmira (14904) ***(G-4704)***
TDS Woodcraft, Staten Island *Also called TDS Woodworking Inc* ***(G-15745)***
TDS Woodworking Inc 718 442-5298
104 Port Richmond Ave Staten Island (10302) ***(G-15745)***
Tdy Industries LLC 716 433-4411
695 Ohio St Lockport (14094) ***(G-7617)***
Te Neues Publishing Company (PA) 212 627-9090
7 W 18th St Fl 9 New York (10011) ***(G-12285)***
Tea & Coffee Trade Journal, Long Island City *Also called Lockwood Trade Journal Co Inc* ***(G-7793)***
Teachergaming LLC 866 644-9323
809 W 181st St 231 New York (10033) ***(G-12286)***
Teachers College Columbia Univ 212 678-3929
1234 Amsterdam Ave New York (10027) ***(G-12287)***
Teachers College Press, New York *Also called Teachers College Columbia Univ* ***(G-12287)***
Teachley LLC 347 552-1272
56 Marx St Staten Island (10301) ***(G-15746)***
Teachspin Inc 716 725-6116
2495 Main St Ste 409 Buffalo (14214) ***(G-3210)***
Teacup Software Inc 212 563-9288
661 Saint Johns Pl Brooklyn (11216) ***(G-2648)***
Teale Machine Company Inc 585 244-6700
1425 University Ave Rochester (14607) ***(G-14719)***
Tealeafs 716 688-8022
5416 Main St Williamsville (14221) ***(G-17257)***
Team Builders Inc 718 979-1005
88 New Dorp Plz S Ste 303 Staten Island (10306) ***(G-15747)***
Team Builders Management, Staten Island *Also called Team Builders Inc* ***(G-15747)***
Team Fabrication Inc 716 655-4038
1055 Davis Rd West Falls (14170) ***(G-16845)***
Teasurebox Publishing LLC 718 506-4354
11730 Sutphin Blvd Jamaica (11434) ***(G-6955)***
Tebbens Steel LLC 631 208-8330
800 Burman Blvd Calverton (11933) ***(G-3301)***
TEC - Crete Transit Mix Corp 718 657-6880
4673 Metropolitan Ave Ridgewood (11385) ***(G-14126)***
TEC Glass & Inst LLC 315 926-7639
4211 Sunset Dr Marion (14505) ***(G-8102)***
Tech Lube, Yaphank *Also called Tribology Inc* ***(G-17405)***
Tech Products Inc 718 442-4900
105 Willow Ave Staten Island (10305) ***(G-15748)***
Tech Valley Printing, Watervliet *Also called General Business Supply Inc* ***(G-16685)***
Tech Valley Technologies Inc 518 584-8899
267 Ballard Rd Ste 2 Wilton (12831) ***(G-17271)***
Techgrass 646 719-2000
77 Water St New York (10005) ***(G-12288)***
Technapulse LLC 631 234-8700
400 Oser Ave Ste 1950 Hauppauge (11788) ***(G-6209)***
Technic Inc 516 349-0700
111 E Ames Ct Unit 2 Plainview (11803) ***(G-13638)***
Technical Library Service Inc 212 219-0770
330 Morgan Ave Brooklyn (11211) ***(G-2649)***
Technical Packaging Inc 516 223-2300
2365 Milburn Ave Baldwin (11510) ***(G-562)***
Technical Service Industries 212 719-9800
17506 Devonshire Rd 5n Jamaica (11432) ***(G-6956)***

ALPHABETIC

ALPHABETIC SECTION
Tesla Motors Inc

Technical Wldg Fabricators LLC......518 463-2229
27 Thatcher St Albany (12207) ***(G-140)***
Techniflo Corporation......716 741-3500
9730 County Rd Clarence Center (14032) ***(G-3680)***
Technimetal Precision Inds......631 231-8900
195 Marcus Blvd Hauppauge (11788) ***(G-6210)***
Technipoly Manufacturing Inc......718 383-0363
20 Wythe Ave Brooklyn (11249) ***(G-2650)***
Technology Crossover MGT VII......212 808-0200
280 Park Ave Fl 26e New York (10017) ***(G-12289)***
Technology Desking Inc......212 257-6998
39 Broadway Rm 1640 New York (10006) ***(G-12290)***
Technomag Inc......631 246-6142
12 Technology Dr Unit 5 East Setauket (11733) ***(G-4493)***
Technopaving New York Inc......631 351-6472
270 Broadway Huntington Station (11746) ***(G-6725)***
Techtrade LLC......212 481-2515
274 Madison Ave Rm 1001 New York (10016) ***(G-12291)***
Techweb LLC......516 562-5000
600 Community Dr Manhasset (11030) ***(G-8066)***
Tecmotiv (usa) Inc......905 669-5911
1500 James Ave Niagara Falls (14305) ***(G-12882)***
Tecnofil Chenango SAC......607 674-4441
40 S Main St Sherburne (13460) ***(G-15398)***
Tecnolux Incorporated......718 369-3900
103 14th St Brooklyn (11215) ***(G-2651)***
Tectonic Flooring USA LLC......212 686-2700
1140 1st Ave Frnt 1 New York (10065) ***(G-12292)***
Tectran Inc......800 776-5549
2345 Walden Ave Ste 1 Cheektowaga (14225) ***(G-3591)***
Tectran Mfg Inc (HQ)......800 776-5549
2345 Walden Ave Ste 1 Buffalo (14225) ***(G-3211)***
Ted Westbrook......716 625-4443
4736 Mapleton Rd Lockport (14094) ***(G-7618)***
Ted-Steel Indstries, New York *Also called Ted-Steel Industries Ltd* ***(G-12293)***
Ted-Steel Industries Ltd......212 279-3878
361 W 36th St Frnt A New York (10018) ***(G-12293)***
Tee Pee Auto Sales Corp......516 338-9333
52 Swan St Westbury (11590) ***(G-17030)***
Tee Pee Fence & Rail, Jamaica *Also called Tee Pee Fence and Railing* ***(G-6957)***
Tee Pee Fence and Railing......718 658-8323
9312 179th Pl Jamaica (11433) ***(G-6957)***
Tee Pee Signs, Hempstead *Also called Jem Sign Corp* ***(G-6275)***
Teen Fire Magazine......646 415-3703
280 1st Ave New York (10009) ***(G-12294)***
Teena Creations Inc......516 867-1500
10 Hanse Ave Freeport (11520) ***(G-5429)***
Tefft Publishers Inc......518 692-9290
35 Salem St Greenwich (12834) ***(G-5894)***
Tegna Inc......716 849-2222
259 Delaware Ave Buffalo (14202) ***(G-3212)***
Tek Precision Co Ltd......631 242-0330
205 W Industry Ct Deer Park (11729) ***(G-4217)***
Tek Weld......631 694-5503
45 Rabro Dr Unit 1 Hauppauge (11788) ***(G-6211)***
Teka Fine Line Brushes Inc......718 692-2928
3691 Bedford Ave Brooklyn (11229) ***(G-2652)***
Teka Precision Inc......845 753-1900
251 Mountainview Ave Nyack (10960) ***(G-13055)***
Teknic Inc......585 784-7454
115 Victor Heights Pkwy Victor (14564) ***(G-16506)***
Tel Tech International......516 393-5174
200 Broadhollow Rd # 207 Melville (11747) ***(G-8360)***
Tel Technology Center Amer LLC (HQ)......512 424-4200
255 Fuller Rd Ste 244 Albany (12203) ***(G-141)***
Tel-Tru Inc (PA)......585 295-0225
408 Saint Paul St Rochester (14605) ***(G-14720)***
Tel-Tru Manufacturing Company, Rochester *Also called Tel-Tru Inc* ***(G-14720)***
Tele-Pak Inc......845 426-2300
421 Route 59 Monsey (10952) ***(G-8585)***
Tele-Vue Optics Inc......845 469-4551
32 Elkay Dr Chester (10918) ***(G-3619)***
Telebyte Inc (PA)......631 423-3232
355 Marcus Blvd Ste 2 Hauppauge (11788) ***(G-6212)***
Telechemische Inc......845 561-3237
222 Dupont Ave Newburgh (12550) ***(G-12781)***
Telecommunication Concepts......315 736-8523
329 Oriskany Blvd Whitesboro (13492) ***(G-17196)***
Teledyne Lecroy Inc (HQ)......845 425-2000
700 Chestnut Ridge Rd Chestnut Ridge (10977) ***(G-3626)***
Teledyne Optech Inc......585 427-8310
150 Lucius Gordon Dr # 215 West Henrietta (14586) ***(G-16897)***
Telemergency Ltd......914 629-4222
3 Quincy Ln White Plains (10605) ***(G-17176)***
Telephone Sales & Service Co (PA)......212 233-8505
132 W Broadway New York (10013) ***(G-12295)***
Telephonics Corporation......631 755-7659
815 Broadhollow Rd Farmingdale (11735) ***(G-5126)***
Telephonics Corporation......631 549-6000
770 Park Ave Huntington (11743) ***(G-6683)***
Telephonics Corporation (HQ)......631 755-7000
815 Broadhollow Rd Farmingdale (11735) ***(G-5127)***
Telephonics Corporation......631 470-8838
7820 Park Ave Huntington (11743) ***(G-6684)***
Telephonics Corporation......631 755-7000
815 Broadhollow Rd Farmingdale (11735) ***(G-5128)***
Telephonics Corporation......631 755-7000
770 Park Ave Huntington (11743) ***(G-6685)***
Telephonics Corporation......631 470-8800
780 Park Ave Huntington (11743) ***(G-6686)***
Telephonics Tlsi Corp......631 470-8854
780 Park Ave Huntington (11743) ***(G-6687)***
Telesca-Heyman Inc......212 534-3442
304 E 94th St 6 New York (10128) ***(G-12296)***
Telesite USA Inc......631 952-2288
89 Arkay Dr Hauppauge (11788) ***(G-6213)***
Teller Printing Corp......718 486-3662
317 Division Ave Brooklyn (11211) ***(G-2653)***
Telmar Information Services (PA)......212 725-3000
711 3rd Ave New York (10017) ***(G-12297)***
Telog Instruments Inc......585 742-3000
830 Canning Pkwy Victor (14564) ***(G-16507)***
Teltech Security Corp......718 871-8800
5014 16th Ave Ste 478 Brooklyn (11204) ***(G-2654)***
Telxon Corporation (HQ)......631 738-2400
1 Zebra Plz Holtsville (11742) ***(G-6512)***
Tempco Glass Fabrication LLC......718 461-6888
13110 Maple Ave Flushing (11355) ***(G-5300)***
Temper Corporation (PA)......518 853-3467
544 Persse Rd Fonda (12068) ***(G-5317)***
Temper Corporation......518 853-3467
544 Persse Rd Fonda (12068) ***(G-5318)***
Temple Bar, New York *Also called Lafayette Pub Inc* ***(G-10915)***
Temple St Clair LLC......212 219-8664
594 Broadway Rm 306 New York (10012) ***(G-12298)***
Tempo Industries Inc......516 334-6900
90 Hopper St Westbury (11590) ***(G-17031)***
Tempo Paris, New York *Also called 6th Avenue Showcase Inc* ***(G-8979)***
Tempt Body Art, New York *Also called Temptu Inc* ***(G-12299)***
Temptu Inc (PA)......212 675-4000
26 W 17th St Rm 302 New York (10011) ***(G-12299)***
Temptu Inc......718 937-9503
522 46th Ave Ste B Long Island City (11101) ***(G-7899)***
Temrex Corporation (PA)......516 868-6221
300 Buffalo Ave Freeport (11520) ***(G-5430)***
Temrick Inc......631 567-8860
1605 Sycamore Ave Unit B Bohemia (11716) ***(G-1142)***
Tenby LLC......646 863-5890
344 W 38th St Fl 3 New York (10018) ***(G-12300)***
Tenney Media Group (PA)......315 853-5569
28 Robinson Rd Clinton (13323) ***(G-3722)***
Tennyson Machine Co Inc......914 668-5468
535 S 5th Ave Mount Vernon (10550) ***(G-8737)***
Tens Machine Company Inc......631 981-0490
800 Grundy Ave Holbrook (11741) ***(G-6478)***
Tensa Software......914 686-5376
66 Greenvale Cir White Plains (10607) ***(G-17177)***
Tensator Group, Bay Shore *Also called Tensator Inc* ***(G-751)***
Tensator Inc......631 666-0300
260 Spur Dr S Bay Shore (11706) ***(G-751)***
Tent and Table Com LLC......716 570-0258
2845 Bailey Ave Buffalo (14215) ***(G-3213)***
Tentina Window Fashions Inc......631 957-9585
1186 Route 109 Lindenhurst (11757) ***(G-7490)***
Tep Events International Inc......646 393-4723
379 W Broadway Lbby 1 New York (10012) ***(G-12301)***
Tequipment Inc......516 922-3508
7 Norden Ln Huntington Station (11746) ***(G-6726)***
Ter-El Engraving Co Inc......315 455-5597
2611 Court St Syracuse (13208) ***(G-16056)***
Terahertz Technologies Inc......315 736-3642
169 Clear Rd Oriskany (13424) ***(G-13316)***
Terani Couture, New York *Also called Countess Corporation* ***(G-9734)***
Terbo Ltd......718 847-2860
8905 130th St Richmond Hill (11418) ***(G-14087)***
Termatec Molding Inc......315 483-4150
28 Foley Dr Sodus (14551) ***(G-15505)***
Terphane Holdings LLC (HQ)......585 657-5800
2754 W Park Dr Bloomfield (14469) ***(G-990)***
Terphane Inc......585 657-5800
2754 W Park Dr Bloomfield (14469) ***(G-991)***
Terra Engry Resource Tech Inc (PA)......212 286-9197
99 Park Ave Ph A New York (10016) ***(G-12302)***
Terrace Management Inc......914 737-0400
119 Oregon Rd Cortlandt Manor (10567) ***(G-4054)***
Terranua US Corp......212 852-9028
535 5th Ave Fl 4 New York (10017) ***(G-12303)***
Terrapin Station Ltd......716 874-6677
1172 Hertel Ave Buffalo (14216) ***(G-3214)***
Terrells Potato Chip Co Inc......315 437-2786
218 Midler Park Dr Syracuse (13206) ***(G-16057)***
Terrys Transmission......315 458-4333
6217 E Taft Rd North Syracuse (13212) ***(G-12952)***
Tesla Motors Inc......212 206-1204
10 Columbus Cir Ste 102d New York (10019) ***(G-12304)***

ALPHABETIC

(PA)=Parent Co (HQ)=Headquarters (DH)=Div Headquarters
2017 Harris
New York Manufacturers Directory
1077

Tessy Plastics Corp (PA) ALPHABETIC SECTION

Tessy Plastics Corp (PA)..........315 689-3924
700 Visions Dr Skaneateles (13152) ***(G-15466)***
Test Cloud, Huntington *Also called Pupa Tek Inc* ***(G-6675)***
Testa Communications Inc..........516 767-2500
25 Willowdale Ave Port Washington (11050) ***(G-13868)***
Testori Interiors Inc..........518 298-4400
107 Lwrnce Paqtte Indstrl Champlain (12919) ***(G-3546)***
Teva Womens Health Inc..........716 693-6230
825 Wurlitzer Dr North Tonawanda (14120) ***(G-13002)***
Texas Brine Company LLC..........585 495-6228
1346 Saltvale Rd Wyoming (14591) ***(G-17382)***
Texas Home Security Inc (PA)..........516 747-2100
50 Rose Pl New Hyde Park (11040) ***(G-8865)***
Texport Fabrics Corp..........212 226-6066
495 Broadway Fl 7 New York (10012) ***(G-12305)***
Texray, New York *Also called Z-Ply Corp* ***(G-12701)***
Texture Plus Inc..........631 218-9200
1611 Lakeland Ave Bohemia (11716) ***(G-1143)***
Texwood Inc (u S A)..........212 262-8383
850 7th Ave Ste 1000 New York (10019) ***(G-12306)***
TG Peppe Inc..........516 239-7852
299 Rockaway Tpke Unit B Lawrence (11559) ***(G-7401)***
Tg Therapeutics Inc..........212 554-4484
3 Columbus Cir Fl 15 New York (10019) ***(G-12307)***
Tgp Flying Cloud Holdings LLC..........646 829-3900
565 5th Ave Fl 27 New York (10017) ***(G-12308)***
Thales Laser SA..........585 223-2370
78 Schuyler Baldwin Dr Fairport (14450) ***(G-4884)***
Thalian, New York *Also called F & J Designs Inc* ***(G-10114)***
Thalle Industries Inc (PA)..........914 762-3415
51 Route 100 Briarcliff Manor (10510) ***(G-1231)***
Thatcher Company New York Inc..........315 589-9330
4135 Rte 104 Williamson (14589) ***(G-17226)***
Thats My Girl Inc (PA)..........212 695-0020
80 39th St Ste 501 Brooklyn (11232) ***(G-2655)***
Thayer Tool & Die Inc..........716 782-4841
1718 Blckvlle Watts Flts Ashville (14710) ***(G-430)***
The Artnewsletter, New York *Also called Artnews Ltd* ***(G-9223)***
The Caldwell Manufacturing Co (PA)..........585 352-3790
2605 Manitou Rd Ste 100 Rochester (14624) ***(G-14721)***
The Caldwell Manufacturing Co..........585 352-2803
Holland Industrial Park Victor (14564) ***(G-16508)***
The Centro Company Inc..........914 533-2200
215 Silver Spring Rd South Salem (10590) ***(G-15537)***
The Chocolate Shop..........716 882-5055
871 Niagara St Buffalo (14213) ***(G-3215)***
The Dannon Company Inc (HQ)..........914 872-8400
100 Hillside Ave Fl 3 White Plains (10603) ***(G-17178)***
THE Design Group Inc..........212 681-1548
240 Madison Ave Fl 8 New York (10016) ***(G-12309)***
The Earth Times Foundation..........718 297-0488
195 Adams St Apt 6j Brooklyn (11201) ***(G-2656)***
The Fisherman, Shirley *Also called L I F Publishing Corp* ***(G-15422)***
The Fisherman, Shirley *Also called Njf Publishing Corp* ***(G-15427)***
The Gramecy Group..........518 348-1325
4 Gramecy Ct Clifton Park (12065) ***(G-3710)***
The Hacker Quarterly, Saint James *Also called 2600 Enterprises Inc* ***(G-15086)***
The Kingsbury Printing Co Inc..........518 747-6606
110 Franklin St Hudson Falls (12839) ***(G-6650)***
The Nugent Organization Inc..........212 645-6600
3433 Ocean Harbor Dr Oceanside (11572) ***(G-13101)***
The Observer, Dundee *Also called Finger Lakes Media Inc* ***(G-4327)***
The Observer, Dunkirk *Also called Observer Daily Sunday Newsppr* ***(G-4346)***
The Printing Company, Albany *Also called Printing Resources Inc* ***(G-124)***
The PRS Group Inc (PA)..........315 431-0511
5800 Hrtge Lndng Dr Ste E East Syracuse (13057) ***(G-4571)***
The River Reporter, Narrowsburg *Also called Stuart Communications Inc* ***(G-8769)***
The Sandhar Corp..........718 523-0819
16427 Highland Ave Jamaica (11432) ***(G-6958)***
The Smoke House of Catskills..........845 246-8767
724 Route 212 Saugerties (12477) ***(G-15197)***
The Spirited Shipper, Long Island City *Also called Platinum Sales Promotion Inc* ***(G-7844)***
The Spotlight, Delmar *Also called Newsgraphics of Delmar Inc* ***(G-4245)***
The Swatch Group U S Inc..........212 297-9192
56 Grand Central Terminal New York (10017) ***(G-12310)***
Thego Corporation..........631 776-2472
2 Mooring Dr Bellport (11713) ***(G-841)***
Thehuffingtonpostcom Inc (HQ)..........212 245-7844
770 Broadway Fl 4 New York (10003) ***(G-12311)***
Theirapp LLC..........212 896-1255
880 3rd Ave New York (10022) ***(G-12312)***
Themis Chimney Inc..........718 937-4716
190 Morgan Ave Brooklyn (11237) ***(G-2657)***
Theodore A Rapp Associates..........845 469-2100
728 Craigville Rd Chester (10918) ***(G-3620)***
Theodosiou Inc..........718 728-6800
3214 49th St Long Island City (11103) ***(G-7900)***
Theory LLC..........212 762-2300
1114 Avenue Of The Americ New York (10036) ***(G-12313)***
Theory LLC..........212 879-0265
1157 Madison Ave New York (10028) ***(G-12314)***
Theory LLC..........631 204-0231
98 Main St Southampton (11968) ***(G-15553)***
Therese The Childrens Collectn..........518 346-2315
301 Nott St Schenectady (12305) ***(G-15305)***
Therm Incorporated..........607 272-8500
1000 Hudson Street Ext Ithaca (14850) ***(G-6877)***
Thermal Foams/Syracuse Inc (PA)..........716 874-6474
2101 Kenmore Ave Buffalo (14207) ***(G-3216)***
Thermal Foams/Syracuse Inc..........315 699-8734
6173 S Bay Rd Cicero (13039) ***(G-3652)***
Thermal Process Cnstr Co..........631 293-6400
19 Engineers Ln Farmingdale (11735) ***(G-5129)***
Thermal Tech Doors Inc (PA)..........516 745-0100
576 Brook St Garden City (11530) ***(G-5534)***
Thermo Cidtec Inc..........315 451-9410
101 Commerce Blvd Liverpool (13088) ***(G-7553)***
Thermo Fisher Scientific Inc..........631 648-4040
2800 Veterans Hwy Wading River (11792) ***(G-16528)***
Thermo Fisher Scientific Inc..........585 458-8008
1999 Mnt Rd Blvd 1-3 Bldg 13 Rochester (14615) ***(G-14722)***
Thermo Fisher Scientific Inc..........585 899-7610
75 Panorama Creek Dr Rochester (14625) ***(G-14723)***
Thermoaura Inc..........518 880-2125
132 Railroad Ave Ste B Albany (12205) ***(G-142)***
Thermold Corporation..........315 697-3924
7059 Harp Rd Canastota (13032) ***(G-3374)***
Thermopatch Corporation (PA)..........315 446-8110
2204 Erie Blvd E Syracuse (13224) ***(G-16058)***
Thermotech Corp..........716 823-3311
3 Bradford St Buffalo (14210) ***(G-3217)***
Theskimm Inc..........212 228-4628
49 W 23rd St Fl 10 New York (10010) ***(G-12315)***
Thestreet Inc (PA)..........212 321-5000
14 Wall St Fl 15 New York (10005) ***(G-12316)***
Theta Industries Inc..........516 883-4088
26 Valley Rd Ste 1 Port Washington (11050) ***(G-13869)***
Thing Daemon Inc..........917 696-5794
96 Spring St Fl 5 New York (10012) ***(G-12317)***
Think Green Junk Removal Inc..........845 297-7771
29 Meadow Wood Ln Wappingers Falls (12590) ***(G-16577)***
Think Tank, New York *Also called City and State Ny LLC* ***(G-9627)***
Thinktrek Inc..........212 884-8399
420 Lexington Ave Rm 300 New York (10170) ***(G-12318)***
Thirsty Owl Wine Company..........607 869-5805
6861 State Route 89 Ovid (14521) ***(G-13349)***
This Business Is Tribaly Owned, Irving *Also called Seneca Nation Enterprise* ***(G-6765)***
Thistle Hill Weavers..........518 284-2729
101 Chestnut Ridge Rd Cherry Valley (13320) ***(G-3597)***
Thom McGinnes Excavating Plbg, Le Roy *Also called T S P Corp* ***(G-7419)***
Thomas C Wilson, Long Island City *Also called Stephen Hanley* ***(G-7891)***
Thomas Electronics Inc (PA)..........315 923-2051
208 Davis Pkwy Clyde (14433) ***(G-3732)***
Thomas Foundry LLC..........315 361-9048
559 Fitch St Oneida (13421) ***(G-13168)***
Thomas Group Inc..........212 947-6400
131 Varick St Rm 1016 New York (10013) ***(G-12319)***
Thomas Group, The, New York *Also called Thomas Group Inc* ***(G-12319)***
Thomas International Pubg Co (HQ)..........212 613-3441
5 Penn Plz Fl 15 New York (10001) ***(G-12320)***
Thomas Jefferson Press, Port Jefferson *Also called Pace Walkers of America Inc* ***(G-13778)***
Thomas Matthews Wdwkg Ltd..........631 287-3657
15 Powell Ave Southampton (11968) ***(G-15554)***
Thomas Matthews Wdwkg Ltd (PA)..........631 287-2023
225 Ocean View Pkwy Southampton (11968) ***(G-15555)***
Thomas Publishing Company LLC (PA)..........212 695-0500
5 Penn Plz Fl 10 New York (10001) ***(G-12321)***
Thomas Publishing Company LLC..........212 629-2127
5 Penn Plz Fl 10 New York (10001) ***(G-12322)***
Thomas Publishing Company LLC..........212 695-0500
5 Penn Plz Fl 8 New York (10001) ***(G-12323)***
Thomas Publishing Company LLC..........212 290-7297
5 Penn Plz Fl 10 New York (10001) ***(G-12324)***
Thomas R Schul TEC GL & Inst, Marion *Also called TEC Glass & Inst LLC* ***(G-8102)***
Thomas Sasson Co Inc..........212 697-4998
555 5th Ave Rm 1900 New York (10017) ***(G-12325)***
Thompson Ferrier LLC..........212 244-2212
230 5th Ave Ste 1004 New York (10001) ***(G-12326)***
Thompson Group, Troy *Also called Pitney Bowes Software Inc* ***(G-16248)***
Thompson Overhead Door Co Inc..........718 788-2470
47 16th St Brooklyn (11215) ***(G-2658)***
Thompson Packaging Novlt Inc (HQ)..........212 686-4242
381 Park Ave S Rm 718 New York (10016) ***(G-12327)***
Thomson Industries Inc..........716 691-9100
45 Hazelwood Dr Amherst (14228) ***(G-266)***
Thomson Press (india) Limited..........646 318-0369
4 Court Sq Fl 3rm2 Long Island City (11101) ***(G-7901)***
Thomson Reuters Corporation..........212 393-9461
500 Pearl St New York (10007) ***(G-12328)***
Thomson Reuters Corporation (HQ)..........646 223-4000
3 Times Sq Lbby Mailroom New York (10036) ***(G-12329)***
Thomson Rters Tax Accnting Inc..........212 367-6300
195 Broadway Fl 2 New York (10007) ***(G-12330)***

Thor Marketing Corp 201 247-7103
616 Corporate Way Ste 2 Valley Cottage (10989) *(G-16393)*
Thornwillow Press Ltd 212 980-0738
57 W 58th St Ste 11e New York (10019) *(G-12331)*
Thornwood Products Ltd 914 769-9161
401 Claremont Ave Ste 7 Thornwood (10594) *(G-16122)*
Thousand Island Ready Mix Con 315 686-3203
38760 State Route 180 La Fargeville (13656) *(G-7238)*
Thousand Islands Printing Co 315 482-2581
45501 St Rt 12 Alexandria Bay (13607) *(G-191)*
Thousand Islands Sun, Alexandria Bay *Also called Thousand Islands Printing Co (G-191)*
Thousand Islands Winery LLC 315 482-9306
43298 Seaway Ave Ste 1 Alexandria Bay (13607) *(G-192)*
Thread Check Inc 631 231-1515
390 Oser Ave Ste 2 Hauppauge (11788) *(G-6214)*
Thread LLC (PA) 212 414-8844
26 W 17th St Rm 301 New York (10011) *(G-12332)*
Three Brothers Winery, Geneva *Also called Negys New Land Vinyrd Winery (G-5583)*
Three Five III-V Materials Inc 212 213-8043
1261 Broadway Rm 401 New York (10001) *(G-12333)*
Three Gems Inc 516 248-0388
2201 Hillside Ave New Hyde Park (11040) *(G-8866)*
Three Point Ventures LLC 585 697-3444
3495 Winton Pl Ste E120 Rochester (14623) *(G-14724)*
Three R Enterprises Inc 585 254-5050
447 Adirondack St Rochester (14606) *(G-14725)*
Three Star Offset Printing 516 867-8223
188 N Main St Freeport (11520) *(G-5431)*
Three Star Supply, Jamaica *Also called City Mason Corp (G-6903)*
Three Tarts, New York *Also called Creative Relations LLC (G-9751)*
Three V, Brooklyn *Also called 3v Company Inc (G-1517)*
Three Village Times, Mineola *Also called Westbury Times (G-8539)*
Thuro Metal Products Inc (PA) 631 435-0444
21-25 Grand Blvd N Brentwood (11717) *(G-1196)*
Thuro Metal Products Inc 631 435-0444
50 Alkier St Brentwood (11717) *(G-1197)*
Thyssenkrupp Elevator Corp 212 268-2020
519 8th Ave Fl 6 New York (10018) *(G-12334)*
Thyssenkrupp Materials NA Inc 212 972-8800
489 5th Ave Fl 20 New York (10017) *(G-12335)*
TI Group Auto Systems LLC 315 568-7042
240 Fall St Seneca Falls (13148) *(G-15371)*
Tia Lattrell 845 373-9494
13 Powder House Rd Amenia (12501) *(G-217)*
Tibana Finishing Inc 718 417-5375
1630 Cody Ave Ridgewood (11385) *(G-14127)*
Tibro Water Technologies Ltd 647 426-3415
106 E Seneca St Unit 25 Sherrill (13461) *(G-15409)*
Tic TAC Toes Mfg Corp 518 773-8187
1 Hamilton St Gloversville (12078) *(G-5726)*
Tickle Hill Winery 607 546-7740
3831 Ball Diamond Rd Hector (14841) *(G-6262)*
Ticonderoga Mch & Wldg Corp 518 585-7444
55 Race Track Rd Ticonderoga (12883) *(G-16129)*
Ticonium Division, Albany *Also called Cmp Industries LLC (G-66)*
Tie King Inc (PA) 718 768-8484
243 44th St Brooklyn (11232) *(G-2659)*
Tie King Inc 212 714-9611
42 W 38th St Rm 1200 New York (10018) *(G-12336)*
Tie View Neckwear Co Inc 718 853-4156
1559 58th St Brooklyn (11219) *(G-2660)*
Tiedemann Waldemar Inc 716 875-5665
1720 Military Rd Ste 2 Buffalo (14217) *(G-3218)*
Tien Wah Press, New York *Also called Twp America Inc (G-12435)*
Tiffen Acquisition LLC 631 273-2500
80 Oser Ave Hauppauge (11788) *(G-6215)*
Tiffen Acquisition LLC (PA) 631 273-2500
90 Oser Ave Hauppauge (11788) *(G-6216)*
Tiffen Co, The, Hauppauge *Also called Tiffen Acquisition LLC (G-6215)*
Tiffen Company LLC 631 273-2500
90 Oser Ave Hauppauge (11788) *(G-6217)*
Tiffen Company, The, Hauppauge *Also called Tiffen Acquisition LLC (G-6216)*
Tiga Holdings Inc 845 838-3000
74 Dennings Ave Beacon (12508) *(G-791)*
Tiger 21 LLC 212 360-1700
6 E 87th St New York (10128) *(G-12337)*
Tiger Fashion Inc 212 244-1175
20 W 36th St Frnt New York (10018) *(G-12338)*
Tiger J LLC (PA) 212 764-5624
1430 Broadway Fl 19 New York (10018) *(G-12339)*
Tiger Supply Inc 631 293-2700
99 Sherwood Ave Farmingdale (11735) *(G-5130)*
Tigerstar Records, New York *Also called Imago Recording Company (G-10569)*
Tii Industries Inc 631 789-5000
1385 Akron St Copiague (11726) *(G-3933)*
Tii Technologies Inc (HQ) 516 364-9300
141 Rodeo Dr Edgewood (11717) *(G-4616)*
Tika Mobile Inc 516 635-1696
112 W 34th St Fl 18 New York (10120) *(G-12340)*
Tilaros Bakery Inc 716 488-3209
32 Willard St Ste 34 Jamestown (14701) *(G-7038)*
Tilcon New York Inc (HQ) 845 358-4500
162 Old Mill Rd West Nyack (10994) *(G-16928)*
Tilcon New York Inc 845 778-5591
272 Berea Rd Walden (12586) *(G-16537)*
Tilcon New York Inc 845 638-3594
66 Scratchup Rd Haverstraw (10927) *(G-6241)*
Tilcon New York Inc 845 480-3249
3466 College Point Blvd Flushing (11354) *(G-5301)*
Tilcon New York Inc 845 615-0216
2 Quarry Rd Goshen (10924) *(G-5740)*
Tilcon New York Inc 845 457-3158
215 Montgomery Rd Montgomery (12549) *(G-8603)*
Tilcon New York Inc 845 358-3100
1 Crusher Rd West Nyack (10994) *(G-16929)*
Tilcon New York Inc 845 942-0602
Fort Of Elm Tomkins Cove (10986) *(G-16131)*
Tile Shop Inc 585 424-2180
420 Jefferson Rd Ste 3 Rochester (14623) *(G-14726)*
Tillsonburg Company USA Inc 267 994-8096
37 W 39th St Rm 1101 New York (10018) *(G-12341)*
Tim Cretin Logging & Sawmill 315 946-4476
3607 Wayne Center Rd Lyons (14489) *(G-7976)*
Timber Frames Inc 585 374-6405
5557 State Route 64 Canandaigua (14424) *(G-3359)*
Time Base Consoles, Edgewood *Also called Time Base Corporation (G-4617)*
Time Base Corporation (PA) 631 293-4068
170 Rodeo Dr Edgewood (11717) *(G-4617)*
Time Home Entertainment Inc 212 522-1212
1271 Ave Of The Americas New York (10020) *(G-12342)*
Time Inc 212 522-1212
1271 Avenue Of The Americ New York (10020) *(G-12343)*
Time Inc 212 522-1633
135 W 50th St New York (10020) *(G-12344)*
Time Inc (PA) 212 522-1212
225 Liberty St New York (10281) *(G-12345)*
Time Inc 212 522-0361
1271 Ave Of The Amer Sb7 New York (10020) *(G-12346)*
Time Inc Affluent Media Group (HQ) 212 382-5600
1120 Ave Of The Americas New York (10036) *(G-12347)*
Time Journal, Cobleskill *Also called Division Street News Corp (G-3736)*
Time Out New York Partners LP 646 432-3000
475 10th Ave Fl 12 New York (10018) *(G-12348)*
Time Precision, Carmel *Also called Precision Arms Inc (G-3404)*
Time Release Sciences Inc 716 823-4580
205 Dingens St Buffalo (14206) *(G-3219)*
Time Square Lighting, Stony Point *Also called Times Square Stage Ltg Co Inc (G-15778)*
Time To Know Inc 212 230-1210
655 3rd Ave Fl 21 New York (10017) *(G-12349)*
Time Warner Companies Inc (HQ) 212 484-8000
1 Time Warner Ctr Bsmt B New York (10019) *(G-12350)*
Time-Cap Laboratories Inc 631 753-9090
7 Michael Ave Farmingdale (11735) *(G-5131)*
Timeless Fashions LLC 212 730-9328
530 Fashion Ave Rm 707 New York (10018) *(G-12351)*
Timeless Frames, Watertown *Also called Lco Destiny LLC (G-16662)*
Timely Signs Inc 516 285-5339
2135 Linden Blvd Elmont (11003) *(G-4730)*
Timely Signs of Kingston Inc 845 331-8710
154 Clinton Ave Fl 1 Kingston (12401) *(G-7215)*
Times Beacon Record Newspapers (PA) 631 331-1154
185 Route 25a Ste 4 East Setauket (11733) *(G-4494)*
Times Center, The, New York *Also called New York Times Company (G-11411)*
Times Herald, The, Olean *Also called Bradford Publications Inc (G-13137)*
Times Herald-Record, Middletown *Also called Local Media Group Inc (G-8448)*
Times Herald-Record, Monticello *Also called Local Media Group Inc (G-8605)*
Times Herald-Record, Kingston *Also called Local Media Group Inc (G-7197)*
Times News Weekly, Ridgewood *Also called Ridgewood Times Prtg & Pubg (G-14122)*
Times Review Newspaper Corp 631 354-8031
7780 Main Rd Mattituck (11952) *(G-8211)*
Times Square Stage Ltg Co Inc 845 947-3034
5 Holt Dr Stony Point (10980) *(G-15778)*
Times Square Studios Ltd 212 930-7720
1500 Broadway Fl 2 New York (10036) *(G-12352)*
Timing Group LLC 646 878-2600
237 W 37th St Ste 1100 New York (10018) *(G-12353)*
Timothy L Simpson 518 234-1401
5819 State Route 145 Sharon Springs (13459) *(G-15385)*
Tin Box Company of America Inc (PA) 631 845-1600
216 Sherwood Ave Farmingdale (11735) *(G-5132)*
Tioga County Courier 607 687-0108
59 Church St Owego (13827) *(G-13360)*
Tioga County Waste Wood Recycl, Owego *Also called Wholesale Mulch & Sawdust Inc (G-13362)*
Tioga Hardwoods Inc (PA) 607 657-8686
12685 State Route 38 Berkshire (13736) *(G-853)*
Tioga Tool Inc (PA) 607 785-6005
160 Glendale Dr Endicott (13760) *(G-4830)*
Tips & Dies Inc 315 337-4161
505 Rome Industrial Park Rome (13440) *(G-14837)*
Tire Conversion Tech Inc 518 372-1600
874 Albany Shaker Rd Latham (12110) *(G-7379)*

ALPHABETIC

ALPHABETIC SECTION

Tish & Snookys NYC Inc 718 937-6055
2107 Borden Ave Fl 4 Long Island City (11101) *(G-7902)*
Tishcon Corp (PA) 516 333-3056
30 New York Ave Westbury (11590) *(G-17032)*
Tishcon Corp 516 333-3056
30 New York Ave Westbury (11590) *(G-17033)*
Tishcon Corp 516 333-3050
41 New York Ave Westbury (11590) *(G-17034)*
Tishcon Corp 516 333-3050
36 New York Ave Westbury (11590) *(G-17035)*
Titan Controls Inc 516 358-2407
122 W 27th St Fl 5 New York (10001) *(G-12354)*
Titan Steel Corp 315 656-7046
6333 N Kirkville Rd Kirkville (13082) *(G-7229)*
Titan Technology Group, New York Also called *Ttg LLC* *(G-12418)*
Titanium Dem Remediation Group 716 433-4100
4907 I D A Park Dr Lockport (14094) *(G-7619)*
Titanx Engine Cooling Inc 716 665-7129
2258 Allen Street Ext Jamestown (14701) *(G-7039)*
Titchener Iron Works Division, Binghamton Also called *Moro Corporation* *(G-937)*
Titherington Design & Mfg 518 324-2205
102 Sharron Ave Unit 1 Plattsburgh (12901) *(G-13704)*
Title of Work, New York Also called *Jonathan Meizler LLC* *(G-10757)*
Tito Moldmaker Co, New York Also called *Vasquez Tito* *(G-12510)*
Titus Mountain Sand & Grav LLC 518 483-3740
17 Junction Rd Malone (12953) *(G-8018)*
Tj Powder Coaters LLC 607 724-4779
24 Broad St Binghamton (13904) *(G-955)*
Tjb Sunshine Enterprises 518 384-6483
6 Redwood Dr Ballston Lake (12019) *(G-588)*
Tkm Technologies Inc 631 474-4700
623 Bicycle Path Ste 5 Port Jeff STA (11776) *(G-13773)*
TLC-Lc Inc (PA) 212 756-8900
115 E 57th St Bsmt New York (10022) *(G-12355)*
TLC-The Light Connection Inc 315 736-7384
132 Base Rd Oriskany (13424) *(G-13317)*
Tlf Graphics, Rochester Also called *T L F Graphics Inc* *(G-14716)*
Tli Import Inc 917 578-4568
151 2nd Ave Brooklyn (11215) *(G-2661)*
Tlsi Incorporated 631 470-8880
780 Park Ave Huntington (11743) *(G-6688)*
Tm Music Inc 212 471-4000
9 E 63rd St Apt 2-3 New York (10065) *(G-12356)*
TMC Usa LLC (PA) 518 587-8920
60 Railroad Pl Ste 501 Saratoga Springs (12866) *(G-15175)*
Tmp Technologies Inc (PA) 716 895-6100
1200 Northland Ave Buffalo (14215) *(G-3220)*
Tmp Technologies Inc 585 495-6231
6110 Lamb Rd Wyoming (14591) *(G-17383)*
Tms Development, Westbury Also called *Vescom Structural Systems Inc* *(G-17041)*
Tntpaving 607 372-4911
1077 Taft Ave Endicott (13760) *(G-4831)*
To Dey, New York Also called *T O Dey Service Corp* *(G-12267)*
Tobay Printing Co Inc 631 842-3300
1361 Marconi Blvd Copiague (11726) *(G-3934)*
Tobeyco Manufacturing Co Inc 607 962-2446
165 Cedar St Corning (14830) *(G-3983)*
Tocare LLC 718 767-0618
15043b 14th Ave Fl 1 Whitestone (11357) *(G-17215)*
Today Media, Rye Also called *Martinelli Holdings LLC* *(G-15062)*
Todaysgentleman.com, Lynbrook Also called *Adf Accessories Inc* *(G-7943)*
Todd Enterprises, West Babylon Also called *Chem-Tainer Industries Inc* *(G-16783)*
Todd Enterprises Inc 516 773-8087
747 Middle Neck Rd # 103 Great Neck (11024) *(G-5844)*
Todd Systems Inc 914 963-3400
50 Ash St Yonkers (10701) *(G-17490)*
Todd Walbridge 585 254-3018
1916 Lyell Ave Rochester (14606) *(G-14727)*
Todt Hill Audiological Svcs 718 816-1952
78 Todt Hill Rd Ste 202 Staten Island (10314) *(G-15749)*
Toga Manufacturing Inc (HQ) 631 242-4800
200 Heartland Blvd Edgewood (11717) *(G-4618)*
Toho Shoji (new York) Inc 212 868-7466
990 Avenue Of The America New York (10018) *(G-12357)*
Token, Brooklyn Also called *3phase Industries LLC* *(G-1515)*
Tokens, Staten Island Also called *Maxine Denker Inc* *(G-15704)*
Tokion Magazine, New York Also called *Downtown Media Group LLC* *(G-9919)*
Tokyo Electron America Inc 518 289-3100
2 Bayberry Dr Malta (12020) *(G-8021)*
Tokyo Electron America Inc 518 292-4200
255 Fuller Rd Ste 214 Albany (12203) *(G-143)*
Toledo Graphics Group, Farmingdale Also called *Desktop Publishing Concepts* *(G-4976)*
Toltec Fabrics Inc 212 706-9310
437 5th Ave Fl 10 New York (10016) *(G-12358)*
Tom & Jerry Printcraft Forms (PA) 914 777-7468
960 Mamaroneck Ave Mamaroneck (10543) *(G-8048)*
Tom & Linda Platt Inc 212 221-7208
29 W 38th St Rm 6l New York (10018) *(G-12359)*
Tom Dixon, New York Also called *Design Research Ltd* *(G-9854)*
Tom Doherty Associates Inc 212 388-0100
175 5th Ave Frnt 1 New York (10010) *(G-12360)*
Tom James Company 212 581-6968
641 Lexington Ave Fl 19 New York (10022) *(G-12361)*
Tom James Company 212 593-0204
717 5th Ave New York (10022) *(G-12362)*
Tom Moriber Furs Inc 212 244-2180
345 7th Ave Fl 19 New York (10001) *(G-12363)*
Tomas Maier 212 988-8686
956 Madison Ave Frnt 1 New York (10021) *(G-12364)*
Tomkins USA, Syracuse Also called *Tompkins Srm LLC* *(G-16059)*
Tommy Boy Entertainment LLC 212 388-8300
220 E 23rd St Ste 400 New York (10010) *(G-12365)*
Tommy John Inc 800 708-3490
100 Broadway Ste 1101 New York (10005) *(G-12366)*
Tomorrow Group, The, Albany Also called *Saratoga Trunk and Furniture* *(G-130)*
Tompkins Metal Finishing Inc 585 344-2600
6 Apollo Dr Batavia (14020) *(G-650)*
Tompkins Srm LLC 315 422-8763
623 Oneida St Syracuse (13202) *(G-16059)*
Tompkins Weekly Inc 607 539-7100
36 Besemer Rd Ithaca (14850) *(G-6878)*
Tomric Plastic, Buffalo Also called *Chocolate Delivery Systems Inc* *(G-2872)*
Tomric Systems Inc 716 854-6050
85 River Rock Dr Buffalo (14207) *(G-3221)*
Tonanwanda News, Niagara Falls Also called *Community Newsppr Holdings Inc* *(G-12805)*
Tonawanda Coke Corporation (PA) 716 876-6222
3875 River Rd Tonawanda (14150) *(G-16206)*
Tonawanda Limb & Brace Inc 716 695-1131
545 Delaware St Tonawanda (14150) *(G-16207)*
Tonche Timber LLC 845 389-3489
3959 State Highway 30 Amsterdam (12010) *(G-370)*
Toner-N-More Inc 718 232-6200
2220 65th St Ste 103 Brooklyn (11204) *(G-2662)*
Tongli Pharmaceuticals USA Inc (PA) 212 842-8837
4260 Main St Apt 6f Flushing (11355) *(G-5302)*
Toni Industries Inc 212 921-0700
111 Great Neck Rd Ste 305 Great Neck (11021) *(G-5845)*
Tonix Phrmceuticals Holdg Corp (PA) 212 980-9155
509 Madison Ave Rm 306 New York (10022) *(G-12367)*
Tonner Doll Company Inc (PA) 845 339-9537
301 Wall St Kingston (12401) *(G-7216)*
Tonoga Inc (PA) 518 658-3202
136 Coon Brook Rd Petersburg (12138) *(G-13528)*
Tony Baird Electronics Inc 315 422-4430
407 S Warren St Ste 200 Syracuse (13202) *(G-16060)*
Tonys Ornamental Ir Works Inc 315 337-3730
6757 Martin St Rome (13440) *(G-14838)*
Tooling Enterprises Inc 716 842-0445
680 New Babcock St Ste 1 Buffalo (14206) *(G-3222)*
Toolroom Express Inc 607 723-5373
1010 Conklin Rd Conklin (13748) *(G-3876)*
Tools & Stamping Corp 718 392-4040
48 Eagle St Brooklyn (11222) *(G-2663)*
Tootter Inc 212 300-7489
1470 Royce St Brooklyn (11234) *(G-2664)*
Top Copi Reproductions Inc 212 571-4141
160 Broadway Fl 3 New York (10038) *(G-12368)*
Top Fortune Usa Ltd 516 608-2694
100 Atlantic Ave Ste 2 Lynbrook (11563) *(G-7965)*
Top Quality Products Inc 212 213-1988
1173 Broadway New York (10001) *(G-12369)*
Top Race Inc 347 424-5795
531 Wortman Ave Brooklyn (11208) *(G-2665)*
Top Shelf Jewelry Inc 845 647-4661
206 Canal St Ellenville (12428) *(G-4639)*
Top Stuff, New York Also called *Isfel Co Inc* *(G-10667)*
Topaz Industries Inc 631 207-0700
130 Corporate Dr Holtsville (11742) *(G-6513)*
Topiderm Inc (PA) 631 226-7979
5200 New Horizons Blvd Amityville (11701) *(G-329)*
Topix Pharmaceuticals Inc 631 225-5757
5200 New Horizons Blvd Amityville (11701) *(G-330)*
Topoo Industries Incorporated 718 331-3755
7815 16th Ave Brooklyn (11214) *(G-2666)*
Toppan Printing Co Amer Inc (HQ) 212 975-9060
747 3rd Ave Rm 1700 New York (10017) *(G-12370)*
Toppan Vite (new York) Inc (PA) 212 596-7747
747 3rd Ave Fl 7 New York (10017) *(G-12371)*
Topps-All Products of Yonkers 914 968-4226
148 Ludlow St Ste 2 Yonkers (10705) *(G-17491)*
Toprint Ltd 718 439-0469
6110 7th Ave Brooklyn (11220) *(G-2667)*
Toptec Products LLC 631 421-9800
1225 Walt Whitman Rd Melville (11747) *(G-8361)*
Tor Books, New York Also called *Tom Doherty Associates Inc* *(G-12360)*
Toray Holding (usa) Inc (HQ) 212 697-8150
461 5th Ave Fl 9 New York (10017) *(G-12372)*
Toray Industries Inc 212 697-8150
600 3rd Ave Fl 5 New York (10016) *(G-12373)*
Torch Graphics Inc 212 679-4334
1001 Ave Of The Americas New York (10018) *(G-12374)*

Torino Industrial Inc 631 509-1640
4 Pinehurst Dr Bellport (11713) ***(G-842)***
Torino Industrial Fabrication, Bellport *Also called Torino Industrial Inc* ***(G-842)***
Tork Inc (PA) 914 664-3542
1 Grove St Mount Vernon (10550) ***(G-8738)***
Toronto Metal Spinning and Ltg 905 793-1174
4500 Witmer Indus Ests Niagara Falls (14305) ***(G-12883)***
Torotron Corporation 718 428-6992
18508 Union Tpke Ste 101 Fresh Meadows (11366) ***(G-5446)***
Torre Products Co Inc 212 925-8989
479 Washington St New York (10013) ***(G-12375)***
Torrent Ems LLC 716 312-4099
190 Walnut St Lockport (14094) ***(G-7620)***
Torrington Industries Inc 315 676-4662
90 Corporate Park Dr Central Square (13036) ***(G-3518)***
Torrone Outdoor Displays, Staten Island *Also called Frank Torrone & Sons Inc* ***(G-15674)***
Torsaf Printers Inc 516 569-5577
1315 Broadway Unit B Hewlett (11557) ***(G-6314)***
Tortilla Heaven Inc 845 339-1550
97 Abeel St Kingston (12401) ***(G-7217)***
Tortilleria Chinantla Inc 718 302-0101
975 Grand St Brooklyn (11211) ***(G-2668)***
Tory Electric 914 292-5036
641 Old Post Rd Bedford (10506) ***(G-798)***
Tosca Brick Oven Pizza Real 718 430-0026
4038 E Tremont Ave Bronx (10465) ***(G-1473)***
Tosch Products Ltd 315 672-3040
25 Main St Camillus (13031) ***(G-3325)***
Toshiba Amer Info Systems Inc (HQ) 949 583-3000
1251 Ave Of The Ste 4110 New York (10020) ***(G-12376)***
Toshiba America Inc (HQ) 212 596-0600
1251 Ave Of Ameri Ste 4100 New York (10020) ***(G-12377)***
Total Concept Graphic Inc 212 229-2626
519 8th Ave Rm 805a New York (10018) ***(G-12378)***
Total Display Solutions Inc 607 724-9999
1429 Upper Front St Binghamton (13901) ***(G-956)***
Total Dntl Implant Sltions LLC 212 877-3777
260 W Sunrise Hwy Valley Stream (11581) ***(G-16430)***
Total Energy Fabrication Corp 580 363-1500
2 Hardscrabble Rd North Salem (10560) ***(G-12940)***
Total Machine and Welding, Bronx *Also called Coral Management Corp* ***(G-1304)***
Total Metal Resource 718 384-7818
175 Bogart St Brooklyn (11206) ***(G-2669)***
Total Offset Graphic, New York *Also called Total Offset Inc* ***(G-12379)***
Total Offset Inc 212 966-4482
200 Hudson St Fl 11 New York (10013) ***(G-12379)***
Total Piping Solutions Inc 716 372-0160
1760 Haskell Rd Olean (14760) ***(G-13154)***
Total Solution Graphics Inc 718 706-1540
2511 49th Ave Long Island City (11101) ***(G-7903)***
Total Webcasting Inc 845 883-0909
8 Bruce St New Paltz (12561) ***(G-8879)***
Toto USA Inc 917 237-0665
20 W 22nd St Ste 1505 New York (10010) ***(G-12380)***
Toto USA Inc 770 282-8686
20 W 22nd St Ste 1505 New York (10010) ***(G-12381)***
Totowa Asphalt, West Nyack *Also called Tilcon New York Inc* ***(G-16928)***
Touch Adjust Clip Co Inc 631 589-3077
1687 Roosevelt Ave Bohemia (11716) ***(G-1144)***
Touch By A Memory, Ellenville *Also called Top Shelf Jewelry Inc* ***(G-4639)***
Touch Tunes, New York *Also called Touchtunes Music Corporation* ***(G-12382)***
Touchdown, New York *Also called Professnal Spt Pblications Inc* ***(G-11728)***
Touchstone Technology Inc 585 458-2690
350 Mile Crossing Blvd Rochester (14624) ***(G-14728)***
Touchtunes Music Corporation (PA) 847 419-3300
850 3rd Ave Ste 15c New York (10022) ***(G-12382)***
Tough Trac Inc 631 504-6700
22 Industrial Blvd Ste 7 Medford (11763) ***(G-8261)***
Toura LLC 646 652-8668
392 2nd St 2 Brooklyn (11215) ***(G-2670)***
Tovie Asarese Royal Prtg Co 716 885-7692
351 Grant St Buffalo (14213) ***(G-3223)***
Tower Computers, Brewster *Also called Base Systems Inc* ***(G-1211)***
Tower Insulating Glass LLC 516 887-3300
2485 Charles Ct North Bellmore (11710) ***(G-12923)***
Tower Isles Frozen Foods Ltd 718 495-2626
2025 Atlantic Ave Brooklyn (11233) ***(G-2671)***
Tower Isles Patties, Brooklyn *Also called Tower Isles Frozen Foods Ltd* ***(G-2671)***
Tower Sales Co, Brooklyn *Also called Turoff Tower Graphics Inc* ***(G-2688)***
Town Food Service Eqp Co Inc (PA) 718 388-5650
72 Beadel St Brooklyn (11222) ***(G-2672)***
Town Line Auto, Greenville *Also called Classic Auto Crafts Inc* ***(G-5884)***
Town of Amherst 716 631-7113
450 Maple Rd Williamsville (14221) ***(G-17258)***
Town of Ohio 315 392-2055
N Lake Rd Forestport (13338) ***(G-5332)***
Town of Ohio Highway Garage, Forestport *Also called Town of Ohio* ***(G-5332)***
Towne House Restorations Inc 718 497-9200
4309 Vernon Blvd Long Island City (11101) ***(G-7904)***
Townley Inc 212 779-0544
10 W 33rd St Rm 418 New York (10001) ***(G-12383)***
Townley Cosmetics, New York *Also called Townley Inc* ***(G-12383)***
Townline Machine Co Inc 315 462-3413
3151 Manchester Clifton Springs (14432) ***(G-3716)***
Towpath Machine Corp 315 252-0112
31 Allen St Auburn (13021) ***(G-524)***
Towse Publishing Co 914 235-3095
1333a North Ave New Rochelle (10804) ***(G-8925)***
Toy Admiration Co Inc 914 963-9400
60 Mclean Ave Yonkers (10705) ***(G-17492)***
Toymax Inc (HQ) 212 633-6611
200 5th Ave New York (10010) ***(G-12384)***
Toyota Industrial Eqp Dlr, Buffalo *Also called Jamestown Industrial Trcks Inc* ***(G-3014)***
Tpa Computer Corp 877 866-6044
531 Route 52 Apt 4 Carmel (10512) ***(G-3406)***
TPC Inc 315 438-8605
6780 Nthrn Blvd Ste 401 East Syracuse (13057) ***(G-4572)***
Tpg Printers Inc 607 273-5310
950 Danby Rd Ithaca (14850) ***(G-6879)***
Tpi Arcade Inc 585 492-0122
7888 Route 98 Arcade (14009) ***(G-401)***
Tpi Industries LLC (HQ) 845 692-2820
265 Ballard Rd Middletown (10941) ***(G-8465)***
Tr Apparel LLC 310 595-4337
609 Greenwich St Fl 3 New York (10014) ***(G-12385)***
Tr Apparel LLC (HQ) 646 358-3888
609 Greenwich St Fl 3 New York (10014) ***(G-12386)***
TR Designs Inc 212 398-9300
260 W 39th St Fl 19 New York (10018) ***(G-12387)***
Trac Medical Solutions Inc 518 346-7799
2165 Technology Dr Schenectady (12308) ***(G-15306)***
Trac Regulators Inc 914 699-9352
160 S Terrace Ave Mount Vernon (10550) ***(G-8739)***
Trac Tech, New York *Also called Color Merchants Inc* ***(G-9672)***
Tracey Welding Co Inc 518 756-6309
29 Riverview Dr Coeymans (12045) ***(G-3746)***
Track 7 Inc 845 544-1810
3 Forester Ave Warwick (10990) ***(G-16596)***
Traco Manufacturing Inc 585 343-2434
4300 Commerce Dr Batavia (14020) ***(G-651)***
Tracy Reese, New York *Also called TR Designs Inc* ***(G-12387)***
Trade Mark Graphics Inc 718 306-0001
2418 Ralph Ave Brooklyn (11234) ***(G-2673)***
Tradepaq Corporation 914 332-9174
220 White Plains Rd # 360 Tarrytown (10591) ***(G-16109)***
Trader Interntnal Publications 914 631-6856
50 Fremont Rd Sleepy Hollow (10591) ***(G-15475)***
Trader Joe's 541, New York *Also called Trader Joes Company* ***(G-12388)***
Trader Joes Company 212 529-6326
138 E 14th St New York (10003) ***(G-12388)***
Tradewins Publishing Corp 631 361-6916
19 Bellemeade Ave Ste B Smithtown (11787) ***(G-15501)***
Trading Edge Ltd 347 699-7079
1923 Bleecker St Apt 1r Ridgewood (11385) ***(G-14128)***
Trading Services International 212 501-0142
133 W 72nd St Rm 601 New York (10023) ***(G-12389)***
Trafalgar Company LLC (HQ) 212 768-8800
417 5th Ave Fl 11 New York (10016) ***(G-12390)***
Traffic Lane Closures LLC 845 228-6100
3620 Danbury Rd Brewster (10509) ***(G-1228)***
Traffic Logix Corporation 866 915-6449
3 Harriet Ln Spring Valley (10977) ***(G-15603)***
Tramwell Inc 315 789-2762
70 State St Geneva (14456) ***(G-5587)***
Trane US Inc 718 721-8844
4518 Court Sq Ste 100 Long Island City (11101) ***(G-7905)***
Trane US Inc 914 593-0303
3 Westchester Plz Ste 198 Elmsford (10523) ***(G-4788)***
Trane US Inc 315 234-1500
15 Technology Pl East Syracuse (13057) ***(G-4573)***
Trane US Inc 518 785-1315
301 Old Niskayuna Rd # 1 Latham (12110) ***(G-7380)***
Trane US Inc 585 256-2500
75 Town Centre Dr Ste I Rochester (14623) ***(G-14729)***
Trane US Inc 716 626-1260
45 Earhart Dr Ste 103 Buffalo (14221) ***(G-3224)***
Trane US Inc 631 952-9477
245 Newtown Rd Ste 500 Plainview (11803) ***(G-13639)***
Trans Tech Bus, Warwick *Also called Transprttion Collaborative Inc* ***(G-16597)***
Trans-High Corporation 212 387-0500
250 W 57th St Ste 920 New York (10107) ***(G-12391)***
Trans-Lux Corporation (PA) 800 243-5544
445 Park Ave Ste 2001 New York (10022) ***(G-12392)***
Transact Technologies Inc 607 257-8901
20 Bomax Dr Ithaca (14850) ***(G-6880)***
Transaction Printer Group 607 274-2500
108 Woodcrest Ter Ithaca (14850) ***(G-6881)***
Transalta, Binghamton *Also called Ipp Energy LLC* ***(G-928)***
Transcedar Industries Ltd 716 731-6442
6292 Walmore Rd Niagara Falls (14304) ***(G-12884)***
Transcntinental Ultra Flex Inc 718 272-9100
975 Essex St Brooklyn (11208) ***(G-2674)***

ALPHABETIC

(PA)=Parent Co (HQ)=Headquarters (DH)=Div Headquarters
2017 Harris
New York Manufacturers Directory
1081

Transco Railway Products Inc..........716 824-1219
Milestrip Rd Blasdell (14219) *(G-967)*
Transcontinental Printing GP..........716 626-3078
300 International Dr # 200 Amherst (14221) *(G-267)*
Transistor Devices Inc..........631 471-7492
125 Comac St Ronkonkoma (11779) *(G-14992)*
Transit Air Inc..........607 324-0216
1 William K Jackson Ln Hornell (14843) *(G-6568)*
Transitair Systems, Hornell *Also called Transit Air Inc (G-6568)*
Transland Sourcing LLC..........718 596-5704
5 Lynch St Brooklyn (11249) *(G-2675)*
Transparency Life Sciences LLC..........862 252-1216
225 W 60th St Apt 15d New York (10023) *(G-12393)*
Transpo Industries Inc (PA)..........914 636-1000
20 Jones St Ste 3 New Rochelle (10801) *(G-8926)*
Transport National Dev Inc (PA)..........716 662-0270
5720 Ellis Rd Orchard Park (14127) *(G-13299)*
Transport National Dev Inc..........716 662-0270
5720 Ellis Rd Orchard Park (14127) *(G-13300)*
Transportgistics Inc..........631 567-4100
28 N Country Rd Ste 103 Mount Sinai (11766) *(G-8657)*
Transprttion Collaborative Inc..........845 988-2333
7 Lake Station Rd Warwick (10990) *(G-16597)*
Transtech Systems Inc (PA)..........518 370-5558
900 Albany Shaker Rd Latham (12110) *(G-7381)*
Travel & Leisure, New York *Also called Departures Magazine (G-9849)*
Travis Ayers Inc..........212 921-5165
1412 Broadway Fl 8 New York (10018) *(G-12394)*
Traxel Labs Inc..........631 590-1095
95 Steuben Blvd Nesconset (11767) *(G-8778)*
Tread Quarters (PA)..........800 876-6676
200 Holleder Pkwy Rochester (14615) *(G-14730)*
Treauu Inc..........703 731-0196
60 E 120th St Fl 2 New York (10035) *(G-12395)*
Trebbianno LLC (PA)..........212 868-2770
19 W 34th St Fl 7 New York (10001) *(G-12396)*
Trebor Instrument Corp..........631 423-7026
39 Balsam Dr Dix Hills (11746) *(G-4299)*
Treehouse Private Brands Inc..........716 693-4715
570 Fillmore Ave Tonawanda (14150) *(G-16208)*
Treiman Publications Corp..........607 657-8473
12724 State Route 38 Berkshire (13736) *(G-854)*
Trek Inc (PA)..........716 438-7555
190 Walnut St Lockport (14094) *(G-7621)*
Tremont Offset Inc..........718 892-7333
1500 Ericson Pl Bronx (10461) *(G-1474)*
Trench & Marine Pump Co Inc..........212 423-9098
3466 Park Ave Bronx (10456) *(G-1475)*
Trend Pot Inc..........212 431-9970
411 Lafayette St Ste 301 New York (10003) *(G-12397)*
Trendlytics Innvation Labs Inc..........415 971-4123
79 Madison Ave Fl 2 New York (10016) *(G-12398)*
Treo Brands LLC..........914 341-1850
106 Calvert St Harrison (10528) *(G-5992)*
Treo Industries Inc..........631 737-4022
35 Carlough Rd Ste 1 Bohemia (11716) *(G-1145)*
Treyco Products Corp..........716 693-6525
131 Fillmore Ave Tonawanda (14150) *(G-16209)*
Tri City Highway Products Inc..........607 722-2967
111 Bevier St Binghamton (13904) *(G-957)*
Tri County Advertiser, Brockport *Also called Rheinwald Printing Co Inc (G-1246)*
Tri County Custom Vacuum..........845 774-7595
653 State Route 17m Monroe (10950) *(G-8565)*
Tri Kolor Printing & Sty..........315 474-6753
1035 Montgomery St Syracuse (13202) *(G-16061)*
Tri Mar Enterprises Inc..........718 418-3644
36 Gardner Ave Brooklyn (11237) *(G-2676)*
Tri Star, Maspeth *Also called Asn Inc (G-8120)*
Tri Star Label Inc..........914 237-4800
630 S Columbus Ave Mount Vernon (10550) *(G-8740)*
Tri State Shearing Bending Inc..........718 485-2200
366 Herzl St Brooklyn (11212) *(G-2677)*
Tri Supreme Optical, Farmingdale *Also called Tri-Supreme Optical LLC (G-5134)*
Tri Valley Iron Inc..........845 365-1013
700 Oak Tree Rd Palisades (10964) *(G-13403)*
Tri-Boro Shlving Prtition Corp..........434 315-5600
1940 Flushing Ave Ridgewood (11385) *(G-14129)*
Tri-Boro Shlving Prtition Corp..........718 782-8527
1940 Flushing Ave Ridgewood (11385) *(G-14130)*
Tri-City Highway Products Inc..........518 294-9964
145 Podpadic Rd Richmondville (12149) *(G-14090)*
Tri-Flex Label Corp..........631 293-0411
48 Allen Blvd Unit A Farmingdale (11735) *(G-5133)*
Tri-Force Sales LLC..........732 261-5507
767 3rd Ave Rm 35b New York (10017) *(G-12399)*
Tri-Lon Clor Lithographers Ltd..........212 255-6140
233 Spring St Frnt 9th New York (10013) *(G-12400)*
Tri-Metal Industries Inc..........716 691-3323
100 Pineview Dr Amherst (14228) *(G-268)*
Tri-Plex Packaging Corporation..........212 481-6070
307 5th Ave Fl 7 New York (10016) *(G-12401)*
Tri-Seal Holdings Inc..........845 353-3300
900 Bradley Hill Rd Blauvelt (10913) *(G-977)*

A
L
P
H
A
B
E
T
I
C

Tri-Seal International Inc (HQ)..........845 353-3300
900 Bradley Hill Rd Blauvelt (10913) *(G-978)*
Tri-Star Offset Corp..........718 894-5555
6020 59th Pl Ste 3 Maspeth (11378) *(G-8173)*
Tri-State Biodiesel LLC..........718 860-6600
531 Barretto St Bronx (10474) *(G-1476)*
Tri-State Brick & Stone NY Inc (PA)..........212 366-0300
333 7th Ave Fl 5 New York (10001) *(G-12402)*
Tri-State Food Jobbers Inc..........718 921-1211
5600 1st Ave Unit A5 Brooklyn (11220) *(G-2678)*
Tri-State Metals LLC..........914 347-8157
41 N Lawn Ave Elmsford (10523) *(G-4789)*
Tri-State Towing Equipment NY, Westbury *Also called Tee Pee Auto Sales Corp (G-17030)*
Tri-State Window Factory Corp..........631 667-8600
360 Marcus Blvd Deer Park (11729) *(G-4218)*
Tri-Supreme Optical LLC..........631 249-2020
91 Carolyn Blvd Farmingdale (11735) *(G-5134)*
Tri-Technologies Inc..........914 699-2001
40 Hartford Ave Mount Vernon (10553) *(G-8741)*
Tri-Town News Inc (PA)..........607 561-3515
74 Main St Sidney (13838) *(G-15442)*
Tri-Town Packing Corp..........315 389-5101
Helena Rd Brasher Falls (13613) *(G-1174)*
Tri-Village Publishers Inc..........518 843-1100
1 Venner Rd Amsterdam (12010) *(G-371)*
Triad Counter Corp..........631 750-0615
1225 Church St Bohemia (11716) *(G-1146)*
Triad Network Technologies..........585 924-8505
75b Victor Heights Pkwy Victor (14564) *(G-16509)*
Triad Printing Inc..........845 343-2722
7 Prospect St Middletown (10940) *(G-8466)*
Trialgraphix, New York *Also called Resonant Legal Media LLC (G-11841)*
Triangle Grinding Machine Corp..........631 643-3636
66 Nancy St Unit A West Babylon (11704) *(G-16836)*
Triangle Label Tag Inc..........718 875-3030
525 Dekalb Ave Brooklyn (11205) *(G-2679)*
Triangle Rubber Co Inc..........631 589-9400
50 Aero Rd Bohemia (11716) *(G-1147)*
Trianon Collection Inc..........212 921-9450
16 W 46th St Fl 10 New York (10036) *(G-12403)*
Tribco LLC..........718 357-7400
15050 14th Rd Ste 2 Whitestone (11357) *(G-17216)*
Tribeca, New York *Also called Flash Ventures Inc (G-10177)*
Tribology Inc..........631 345-3000
35 Old Dock Rd Yaphank (11980) *(G-17405)*
Triboro Bagel Co Inc..........718 359-9245
18312 Horace Harding Expy Flushing (11365) *(G-5303)*
Triboro Iron Works Inc..........718 361-9600
3830 31st St Long Island City (11101) *(G-7906)*
Triborough Electric..........718 321-2144
15044 11th Ave Whitestone (11357) *(G-17217)*
Tribune Entertainment Co Del..........203 866-2204
220 E 42nd St Fl 26 New York (10017) *(G-12404)*
Tribune Media Services Inc (HQ)..........518 792-9914
40 Media Dr Queensbury (12804) *(G-14013)*
Triceutical Inc..........631 249-0003
1652 Hering Ave Bronx (10461) *(G-1477)*
Trico Manufacturing Corp..........718 349-6565
196 Dupont St Brooklyn (11222) *(G-2680)*
Tricon Machine LLC..........585 671-0679
820 Coventry Dr Webster (14580) *(G-16737)*
Tricon Piping Systems Inc..........315 655-4178
2 Technology Blvd Canastota (13032) *(G-3375)*
Tricycle Foundation Inc..........800 873-9871
89 5th Ave Ste 301 New York (10003) *(G-12405)*
Trident Precision Mfg Inc..........585 265-2010
734 Salt Rd Webster (14580) *(G-16738)*
Trident Valve Actuator Co..........914 698-2650
329 Center Ave Mamaroneck (10543) *(G-8049)*
Trihex Manufacturing Inc..........315 589-9331
6708 Pound Rd Williamson (14589) *(G-17227)*
Tril Inc..........631 645-7989
320 Pioxi St Copiague (11726) *(G-3935)*
Trilake Three Press Corp..........518 359-2462
136 Park St Tupper Lake (12986) *(G-16280)*
Trilon Color Lithographers, New York *Also called Tri-Lon Clor Lithographers Ltd (G-12400)*
Trimac Molding Services..........607 967-2900
13 Pruyn St Bainbridge (13733) *(G-555)*
Trimet Coal LLC..........718 951-3654
1615 Avenue I Apt 420 Brooklyn (11230) *(G-2681)*
Trimmer Capacitor Company, The, Cazenovia *Also called Voltronics LLC (G-3454)*
Trimtec Inc..........516 783-5428
4057 Judge Ct Seaford (11783) *(G-15347)*
Trine Rolled Moulding Corp..........718 828-5200
1421 Ferris Pl Bronx (10461) *(G-1478)*
Trinity Biotech Distribution, Jamestown *Also called Biopool Us Inc (G-6974)*
Trinity Biotech USA, Jamestown *Also called Clark Laboratories Inc (G-6979)*
Trinity Packaging Corporation (PA)..........914 273-4111
84 Business Park Dr # 309 Armonk (10504) *(G-422)*
Trinity Tools Inc..........716 694-1111
261 Main St North Tonawanda (14120) *(G-13003)*
Trio French Bakery, New York *Also called Giovanni Bakery Corp (G-10300)*

Tripar Manufacturing Co Inc.....631 563-0855
1620 Ocean Ave Ste 1 Bohemia (11716) ***(G-1148)***
Tripi Engraving Co Inc.....718 383-6500
60 Meserole Ave Brooklyn (11222) ***(G-2682)***
Triple E Manufacturing.....716 761-6996
117 Osborn St Sherman (14781) ***(G-15403)***
Triple H Construction Inc.....516 280-8252
832 Bethlynn Ct East Meadow (11554) ***(G-4428)***
Triple Point Manufacturing.....631 218-4988
1371 Church St Ste 6 Bohemia (11716) ***(G-1149)***
Triplett Machine Inc.....315 548-3198
1374 Phelps Junction Rd Phelps (14532) ***(G-13537)***
Triplex Industries Inc.....585 621-6920
100 Boxart St Ste 27 Rochester (14612) ***(G-14731)***
Tripp Plating Works Inc.....716 894-2424
1491 William St Buffalo (14206) ***(G-3225)***
Triton Builders Inc.....631 841-2534
645 Broadway Ste T Amityville (11701) ***(G-331)***
Triton Infosys Inc.....877 308-2388
1230 Avenue Of The Americ New York (10020) ***(G-12406)***
Trium Strs-Lg Isld LLC.....516 997-5757
717 Main St Westbury (11590) ***(G-17036)***
Triumph Actuation Systems LLC.....516 378-0162
417 S Main St Freeport (11520) ***(G-5432)***
Triumph Apparel Corporation (PA).....212 302-2606
530 Fashion Ave Ste M1 New York (10018) ***(G-12407)***
Triumph Group Inc.....516 997-5757
717 Main St Westbury (11590) ***(G-17037)***
Triumph Learning LLC (HQ).....212 652-0200
136 Madison Ave Fl 7 New York (10016) ***(G-12408)***
Triumph Structures-Long Island, Westbury *Also called Triumph Group Inc* ***(G-17037)***
TRM Linen Inc.....718 686-6075
1546 59th St Brooklyn (11219) ***(G-2683)***
Trojan Metal Fabrication Inc (PA).....631 968-5040
2215 Union Blvd Bay Shore (11706) ***(G-752)***
Trojan Powder Coating, Bay Shore *Also called Trojan Metal Fabrication Inc* ***(G-752)***
Trojan Steel.....518 686-7426
48 Factory Hill Rd Hoosick Falls (12090) ***(G-6546)***
Tronic Plating Co Inc.....516 293-7883
37 Potter St Farmingdale (11735) ***(G-5135)***
Tronser Inc.....315 655-9528
3066 John Trush Jr Blvd Cazenovia (13035) ***(G-3453)***
Tropical Driftwood Originals.....516 623-0980
499 Nassau Rd Roosevelt (11575) ***(G-15010)***
Tropp Printing Corp.....212 233-4519
181 Broadway Fl 3 New York (10007) ***(G-12409)***
Tropp Prntng, New York *Also called Tropp Printing Corp* ***(G-12409)***
Tros Lanscaping Supply Company.....518 783-6954
1266 Loudon Rd Cohoes (12047) ***(G-3759)***
Trove Inc.....212 268-2046
20 Jay St Ste 846 Brooklyn (11201) ***(G-2684)***
Trovvit Inc.....718 908-5376
445 7th St Brooklyn (11215) ***(G-2685)***
Troy Boiler Works Inc.....518 274-2650
2800 7th Ave Troy (12180) ***(G-16258)***
Troy Cabinet Manufacturing Div, Troy *Also called Deakon Homes and Interiors* ***(G-16233)***
Troy Industrial Solutions (PA).....518 272-4920
70 Cohoes Rd Watervliet (12189) ***(G-16690)***
Troy Sand & Gravel Co Inc.....518 674-2854
Rr 43 West Sand Lake (12196) ***(G-16932)***
Troy Sign & Printing.....718 994-4482
4827 White Plains Rd Bronx (10470) ***(G-1479)***
Troy Sign Printing Center, Bronx *Also called Troy Sign & Printing* ***(G-1479)***
Troyer Inc.....585 352-5590
4555 Lyell Rd Rochester (14606) ***(G-14732)***
Trs Packaging, Buffalo *Also called Time Release Sciences Inc* ***(G-3219)***
Tru Mold Shoes Inc.....716 881-4484
42 Breckenridge St Buffalo (14213) ***(G-3226)***
Tru-Art Sign Co Inc.....718 658-5068
10515 180th St Jamaica (11433) ***(G-6959)***
Tru-Tone Metal Products Inc.....718 386-5960
1261 Willoughby Ave Brooklyn (11237) ***(G-2686)***
Truarc Fabrication.....518 691-0430
1 Commerce Park Dr Gansevoort (12831) ***(G-5491)***
Truck-Lite Co LLC.....716 661-1235
2640 1st Ave Falconer (14733) ***(G-4916)***
Truck-Lite Co LLC.....716 665-2614
310 E Elmwood Ave Falconer (14733) ***(G-4917)***
Truck-Lite Co LLC (PA).....716 665-6214
310 E Elmwood Ave Falconer (14733) ***(G-4918)***
True Colors, New York *Also called Richard Leeds Intl Inc* ***(G-11862)***
Truebite Inc.....607 785-7664
2590 Glenwood Rd Vestal (13850) ***(G-16455)***
Truebite Inc.....607 786-3184
129 Squires Ave Endicott (13760) ***(G-4832)***
Trueex LLC.....646 786-8526
162 5th Ave New York (10010) ***(G-12410)***
Trueforge Global McHy Corp.....516 825-7040
100 Merrick Rd Ste 208e Rockville Centre (11570) ***(G-14801)***
Truemade Products Inc.....631 981-4755
910 Marconi Ave Ronkonkoma (11779) ***(G-14993)***
Truesense Imaging Inc.....585 784-5500
1964 Lake Ave Rochester (14615) ***(G-14733)***
Truform Manufacturing Corp.....585 458-1090
1500 N Clinton Ave Rochester (14621) ***(G-14734)***
Trulite Louvre Corp.....516 756-1850
148 Bethpage Sweet Holw Old Bethpage (11804) ***(G-13131)***
Truly Tubular Fitting Corp.....914 664-8686
115 E 3rd St Mount Vernon (10550) ***(G-8742)***
Trunk & Trolley LLC.....212 947-9001
15 W 34th St New York (10001) ***(G-12411)***
Trunk Outlet, Rochester *Also called Rhino Trunk & Case Inc* ***(G-14624)***
Trusses & Trim Division, Farmington *Also called Rochester Lumber Company* ***(G-5155)***
Trust of Colum Unive In The Ci.....212 854-2793
2929 Broadway Fl 3 New York (10025) ***(G-12412)***
Trusted Media Brands Inc (PA).....914 238-1000
750 3rd Ave Fl 3 New York (10017) ***(G-12413)***
Trusted Media Brands Inc.....646 293-6025
750 3rd Ave Fl 4 New York (10017) ***(G-12414)***
Truxton Corp.....718 842-6000
1357 Lafayette Ave Bronx (10474) ***(G-1480)***
TRW Automotive Inc.....315 255-3311
2150 Crane Brook Dr Auburn (13021) ***(G-525)***
TRW Automotive US LLC.....315 255-3311
2150 Crane Brook Dr Auburn (13021) ***(G-526)***
Trylon Wire & Metal Works Inc.....718 542-4472
526 Tiffany St Bronx (10474) ***(G-1481)***
TS Manufactoring, New York *Also called Alpine Creations Ltd* ***(G-9103)***
TS Pink, Oneonta *Also called T S Pink Corp* ***(G-13194)***
TSA Luggage Locks, New York *Also called Safe Skies LLC* ***(G-11953)***
Tsar USA LLC.....646 415-7968
99 Madison Ave Fl 5 New York (10016) ***(G-12415)***
Tsc LLC.....661 824-6609
65 Bleecker St New York (10012) ***(G-12416)***
Tsi Technologies, New York *Also called Trading Services International* ***(G-12389)***
Tsm, Elmsford *Also called Tri-State Metals LLC* ***(G-4789)***
TSS Foam Industries Corp.....585 538-2321
2770 W Main St Caledonia (14423) ***(G-3283)***
Tss-Transport Snltn Sstms.....917 267-8534
20 W 22nd St Ste 612 New York (10010) ***(G-12417)***
Tte Filters LLC (HQ).....716 532-2234
1 Magnetic Pkwy Gowanda (14070) ***(G-5749)***
Ttg LLC.....917 777-0959
115 W 30th St Rm 209 New York (10001) ***(G-12418)***
TTI, Hauppauge *Also called Tarsia Technical Industries* ***(G-6206)***
Tube Fabrication Company Inc.....716 673-1871
183 E Main St Ste 10 Fredonia (14063) ***(G-5375)***
Tucano Usa Inc.....212 966-9211
377 5th Ave Fl 4 New York (10016) ***(G-12419)***
Tucker Jones House Inc.....631 642-9092
1 Enterprise Dr East Setauket (11733) ***(G-4495)***
Tucker Printers Inc.....585 359-3030
270 Middle Rd Henrietta (14467) ***(G-6298)***
Tudor Electrical Supply Co Inc.....212 867-7550
137 W 24th St New York (10011) ***(G-12420)***
Tula Life LLC.....201 895-3309
660 Madison Ave Ste 1600 New York (10065) ***(G-12421)***
Tulip Development Labs, Hauppauge *Also called Tdl Manufacturing Inc* ***(G-6208)***
Tulip Molded Plastics Corp.....716 282-1261
3125 Highland Ave Niagara Falls (14305) ***(G-12885)***
Tully Products Inc.....716 773-3166
2065 Baseline Rd Grand Island (14072) ***(G-5771)***
Tumble Forms Inc (PA).....315 429-3101
1013 Barker Rd Dolgeville (13329) ***(G-4309)***
Tumblehome Boatshop.....518 623-5050
684 State Route 28 Warrensburg (12885) ***(G-16581)***
Tumeric Healing Entps Inc.....508 364-7597
39 Broadway Fl 1110 New York (10006) ***(G-12422)***
Tumericalive, New York *Also called Tumeric Healing Entps Inc* ***(G-12422)***
Tumi Inc.....212 447-8747
261 5th Ave Rm 2010 New York (10016) ***(G-12423)***
Tumi Inc.....212 742-8020
67 Wall St Frnt 3 New York (10005) ***(G-12424)***
Tumi Stores, New York *Also called Tumi Inc* ***(G-12424)***
Tunaverse Media Inc.....631 778-8350
750 Veterans Hwy Ste 200 Hauppauge (11788) ***(G-6218)***
Tunecore Inc (PA).....646 651-1060
45 Main St Ste 705 Brooklyn (11201) ***(G-2687)***
Tupper Lake Free Press Inc.....518 359-2166
136 Park St Tupper Lake (12986) ***(G-16281)***
Tupper Lake Hardwoods Inc.....518 359-8248
167 Pitchfork Pond Rd Tupper Lake (12986) ***(G-16282)***
Turbine Arfoil Cating Repr LLC.....845 692-8912
105 Tower Dr Middletown (10941) ***(G-8467)***
Turbine Engine Comp Utica.....315 768-8070
2 Halsey Rd Whitesboro (13492) ***(G-17197)***
Turbo Dynamics, Plainview *Also called Omega Industries & Development* ***(G-13625)***
Turbo Express Inc.....718 723-3686
16019 Rockaway Blvd Ste D Jamaica (11434) ***(G-6960)***
Turbo Machined Products LLC.....315 895-3010
102 Industrial Dr Frankfort (13340) ***(G-5358)***

ALPHABETIC

(PA)=Parent Co (HQ)=Headquarters (DH)=Div Headquarters
2017 Harris
New York Manufacturers Directory
1083

Turbo Plastics Corp Inc 631 345-9768
18 Old Dock Rd 20 Yaphank (11980) *(G-17406)*
Turbofil Packaging Mchs LLC 914 239-3878
30 Beach St Mount Vernon (10550) *(G-8743)*
Turbopro Inc 716 681-8651
1284 Town Line Rd Alden (14004) *(G-184)*
Turing Pharmaceuticals LLC 646 356-5577
1177 Ave Of The New York (10036) *(G-12425)*
Turn On Products Inc (PA) 212 764-2121
270 W 38th St Rm 1200 New York (10018) *(G-12426)*
Turn On Products Inc 212 764-4545
525 7th Ave Rm 1403 New York (10018) *(G-12427)*
Turner Bellows Inc 585 235-4456
526 Child St Ste 1 Rochester (14606) *(G-14735)*
Turner Plating, New Rochelle *Also called Eric S Turner & Company Inc (G-8898)*
Turning Point Tool LLC 585 288-7380
1197 Mount Read Blvd Rochester (14606) *(G-14736)*
Turnomat Company LLC 585 924-1630
1118 Mertensia Rd Farmington (14425) *(G-5157)*
Turoff Tower Graphics Inc 718 856-7300
681 Coney Island Ave Brooklyn (11218) *(G-2688)*
Turtle Pond Publications LLC 212 579-4393
1 W 72nd St Apt 84 New York (10023) *(G-12428)*
Tusk Manufacturing Inc 631 567-3349
1371 Church St Ste 1 Bohemia (11716) *(G-1150)*
Tuthill Corporation 631 727-1097
75 Kings Dr Riverhead (11901) *(G-14158)*
Tuthilltown Spirits LLC 845 255-1527
14 Gristmill Ln Gardiner (12525) *(G-5551)*
Tutor Perini Corporation 646 473-2924
360 W 31st St Rm 1102 New York (10001) *(G-12429)*
Tuv Taam Corp 718 855-2207
502 Flushing Ave Brooklyn (11205) *(G-2689)*
TV Data, Queensbury *Also called Tribune Media Services Inc (G-14013)*
TV Executive, New York *Also called T V Trade Media Inc (G-12269)*
TV Guide Magazine LLC (HQ) 212 852-7500
50 Rockefeller Plz Fl 14 New York (10020) *(G-12430)*
TV Guide Magazine Group Inc (HQ) 212 852-7500
1211 Ave Of The Americas New York (10036) *(G-12431)*
TV Guilfoil & Associates Inc (PA) 315 453-0920
121 Dwight Park Cir Syracuse (13209) *(G-16062)*
TVI Imports LLC 631 793-3077
178 Abbey St Massapequa Park (11762) *(G-8190)*
Twcc Product and Sales 212 614-9364
122 5th Ave New York (10011) *(G-12432)*
Twenty-First Century Press Inc 716 837-0800
501 Cornwall Ave Buffalo (14215) *(G-3227)*
Twentyone Brix Winery, Portland *Also called Olde Chtqua Vneyards Ltd Lblty (G-13873)*
TWI Watches LLC 718 663-3969
4014 1st Ave Brooklyn (11232) *(G-2690)*
TWI-Laq Industries Inc 718 638-5860
1345 Seneca Ave Bronx (10474) *(G-1482)*
Twin Counties Pro Printers Inc 518 828-3278
59 Fairview Ave Hudson (12534) *(G-6636)*
Twin County Recycling Corp (PA) 516 827-6900
113 Magnolia Ave Westbury (11590) *(G-17038)*
Twin Lake Chemical Inc 716 433-3824
520 Mill St Lockport (14094) *(G-7622)*
Twin Marquis Inc (HQ) 718 386-6868
7 Bushwick Pl Brooklyn (11206) *(G-2691)*
Twin Pane Insulated GL Co Inc 631 924-1060
86 Horseblock Rd Unit D Yaphank (11980) *(G-17407)*
Twinco Mfg Co Inc 631 231-0022
30 Commerce Dr Hauppauge (11788) *(G-6219)*
Twinkle Lighting Inc 718 225-0939
13114 40th Rd Flushing (11354) *(G-5304)*
Twinny Products Inc 718 592-7500
11145 44th Ave Corona (11368) *(G-4008)*
Twins Enterprise Inc 631 368-4702
2171 Jericho Tpke Commack (11725) *(G-3844)*
Twist Intimate Apparel, New York *Also called Twist Intimate Group LLC (G-12433)*
Twist Intimate Group LLC (PA) 212 695-5990
35 W 35th St Rm 903 New York (10001) *(G-12433)*
Twisters 585 346-3730
13 Commercial St Livonia (14487) *(G-7565)*
Two Bills Machine & Tool Co 516 437-2585
17 Concord St Floral Park (11001) *(G-5207)*
Two Palms Press Inc 212 965-8598
476 Broadway Ste 3f New York (10013) *(G-12434)*
Two Rivers Computing Inc 914 968-9239
976 Mclean Ave Yonkers (10704) *(G-17493)*
Two Sisters Kiev Bakery Inc (PA) 718 769-2626
2737 W 15th St Brooklyn (11224) *(G-2692)*
Two Sisters Kiev Bakery Inc 718 627-5438
1627 E 18th St Brooklyn (11229) *(G-2693)*
Two Worlds Arts Ltd 212 929-2210
307 Kingsland Ave Brooklyn (11222) *(G-2694)*
Two-Four Software, New York *Also called F-O-R Software LLC (G-10120)*
Two-Four Software, White Plains *Also called F-O-R Software LLC (G-17108)*
Twp America Inc (HQ) 212 274-8090
299 Broadway Ste 720 New York (10007) *(G-12435)*
TX Rx Systems Inc 716 549-4700
8625 Industrial Pkwy Angola (14006) *(G-382)*
Tyco Electronics Corporation 585 785-2500
2245 Brighton Henrta Twn Rochester (14623) *(G-14737)*
Tyco Simplexgrinnell 315 437-9664
6731 Collamer Rd Ste 4 East Syracuse (13057) *(G-4574)*
Tyco Simplexgrinnell 716 483-0079
527 Foote Ave Jamestown (14701) *(G-7040)*
Tyco Simplexgrinnell 315 337-6333
4057 Wilson Rd E Taberg (13471) *(G-16076)*
Tycoon International Inc 212 563-7107
3436 W 32nd St Fl 4 New York (10001) *(G-12436)*
Tyme Global Technologies LLC 212 796-1950
60 W 66th St Apt 15a New York (10023) *(G-12437)*
Tymetal Corp (HQ) 518 692-9930
678 Wilbur Ave Greenwich (12834) *(G-5895)*
Tymor Park 845 724-5691
249 Duncan Rd Lagrangeville (12540) *(G-7260)*
Tyrolit Company, Hauppauge *Also called Meopta USA Inc (G-6131)*
Tyson Deli Inc (HQ) 716 826-6400
665 Perry St Buffalo (14210) *(G-3228)*
U All Inc 518 438-2558
9 Interstate Ave Albany (12205) *(G-144)*
U B J, New York *Also called United Brothers Jewelry Inc (G-12464)*
U E Systems Incorporated (PA) 914 592-1220
14 Hayes St Elmsford (10523) *(G-4790)*
U K Sailmakers, Bronx *Also called Ulmer Sales LLC (G-1484)*
U S A Today, Port Washington *Also called Gannett Co Inc (G-13818)*
U S Air Tool Co Inc (PA) 631 471-3300
60 Fleetwood Ct Ronkonkoma (11779) *(G-14994)*
U S Air Tool International, Ronkonkoma *Also called U S Air Tool Co Inc (G-14994)*
U S Embroidery Inc 718 585-9662
728 E 136th St Ste 1 Bronx (10454) *(G-1483)*
U S Energy Controls Inc 718 380-1004
270 Park Ave New Hyde Park (11040) *(G-8867)*
U S Energy Development Corp (PA) 716 636-0401
2350 N Forest Rd Getzville (14068) *(G-5605)*
U S Japan Publication NY Inc 212 252-8833
147 W 35th St Ste 1705 New York (10001) *(G-12438)*
U S Orthotic Center, New York *Also called Custom Sports Lab Inc (G-9771)*
U S Plychmical Overseas Corp 845 356-5530
584 Chestnut Ridge Rd # 586 Chestnut Ridge (10977) *(G-3627)*
U S Sugar Co Inc (PA) 716 828-1170
692 Bailey Ave Buffalo (14206) *(G-3229)*
U S TEC, Victor *Also called 331 Holding Inc (G-16458)*
U S Tech Corporation 315 437-7207
6511 Basile Rowe East Syracuse (13057) *(G-4575)*
U Serve Brands Inc 212 286-2403
440 Park Ave S Fl 14 New York (10016) *(G-12439)*
U X World Inc 914 375-6167
245 Saw Mill River Rd # 106 Hawthorne (10532) *(G-6255)*
U-Cut Enterprises Inc 315 492-9316
4800 Solvay Rd Jamesville (13078) *(G-7052)*
U-Lace LLC 716 848-0939
465 Central Ave Rochester (14605) *(G-14738)*
Ubm Inc 212 600-3000
2 Penn Plz New York (10121) *(G-12440)*
Ubm LLC (HQ) 516 562-5085
2 Penn Plz Fl 15 New York (10121) *(G-12441)*
Ubm LLC 516 562-5000
2 Penn Plz Fl 15 New York (10121) *(G-12442)*
Ubm Tech, New York *Also called Ubm LLC (G-12441)*
Uc Coatings Corporation 716 833-9366
2250 Fillmore Ave Buffalo (14214) *(G-3230)*
Ucb Pharma Inc (PA) 919 767-2555
755 Jefferson Rd Rochester (14623) *(G-14739)*
Ucc Guide Inc (PA) 518 434-0909
99 Washington Ave Albany (12210) *(G-145)*
Udisense Inc 858 442-9875
620 8th Ave Fl 38 New York (10018) *(G-12443)*
Ue Music, New York *Also called Universal Edition Inc (G-12470)*
Ufc Biotechnology 716 777-3776
1576 Sweet Home Rd # 225 Amherst (14228) *(G-269)*
Ufn LLC 800 533-1787
1399 Route 52 Ste 100 Fishkill (12524) *(G-5188)*
Ufo Contemporary Inc 212 226-5400
42 W 38th St Rm 1204 New York (10018) *(G-12444)*
Ufp New York LLC 315 381-5093
18 Robinson Rd Clinton (13323) *(G-3723)*
Ufp New York LLC 716 496-5484
13989 E Schutt Rd Chaffee (14030) *(G-3536)*
Ufp New York LLC 518 828-2888
11 Falls Industrial Pk Rd Hudson (12534) *(G-6637)*
Ufp New York LLC (PA) 607 563-1556
13 Winkler Rd Sidney (13838) *(G-15443)*
UFS Industries Inc 718 822-1100
300 N Macquesten Pkwy Mount Vernon (10550) *(G-8744)*
Uft New York, Chaffee *Also called P & R Truss Co (G-3535)*
Ufx Holding I Corporation (HQ) 212 644-5900
55 E 52nd St Fl 35 New York (10055) *(G-12445)*
Ufx Holding II Corporation (HQ) 212 644-5900
55 E 52nd St Fl 35 New York (10055) *(G-12446)*

ALPHABETIC

Uge, New York *Also called Urban Green Energy Inc (G-12479)*
UGI, Brooklyn *Also called United Gemdiam Inc (G-2700)*
Uhmac Inc 716 537-2343
136 N Main St Holland (14080) *(G-6485)*
Ui Acquisition Holding Co (PA) 607 779-7522
33 Broome Corporate Pkwy Conklin (13748) *(G-3877)*
Ui Holding Company (HQ) 607 779-7522
33 Broome Corporate Pkwy Conklin (13748) *(G-3878)*
UI Corp 201 203-4453
3812 Corporal Stone St # 2 Bayside (11361) *(G-776)*
Ulano Product Inc 718 622-5200
110 3rd Ave Brooklyn (11217) *(G-2695)*
Ulmer Sales LLC 718 885-1700
175 City Island Ave Bronx (10464) *(G-1484)*
Ulrich Planfiling Eqp Corp 716 763-1815
2120 4th Ave Lakewood (14750) *(G-7295)*
Ulrich Sign Co Inc 716 434-0167
250 State Rd Lockport (14094) *(G-7623)*
Ulster County Iron Works LLC 845 255-0003
64 N Putt Corners Rd New Paltz (12561) *(G-8880)*
Ulster County Press Office 845 687-4480
1209 State Route 213 High Falls (12440) *(G-6402)*
Ulster Precision Inc 845 338-0995
57 Teller St Kingston (12401) *(G-7218)*
Ulster Publishing, Kingston *Also called Almanac (G-7176)*
Ulster Publishing Co Inc (PA) 845 334-8205
322 Wall St Fl 1 Kingston (12401) *(G-7219)*
Ulster Publishing Co Inc 845 255-7005
29 S Chestnut St Ste 101 New Paltz (12561) *(G-8881)*
Ulster-Greene County A R C 845 331-8451
307 Washington Ave Kingston (12401) *(G-7220)*
Ultimate Pavers Corp 917 417-2652
659 Quincy Ave Staten Island (10305) *(G-15750)*
Ultimate Prcision Met Pdts Inc (PA) 631 249-9441
200 Finn Ct Farmingdale (11735) *(G-5136)*
Ultimate Signs & Designs Inc 516 481-0800
86 Sewell St Hempstead (11550) *(G-6288)*
Ultimate Styles of America 631 254-0219
27 Garfield Ave Unit A Bay Shore (11706) *(G-753)*
Ultra Clarity Corp 719 470-1010
3101 Parkview Dr Spring Valley (10977) *(G-15604)*
Ultra Elec Flightline Systems, Victor *Also called Flightline Electronics Inc (G-16478)*
Ultra Electronics Inc, Victor *Also called Magnet-Ndctive Systems Ltd USA (G-16490)*
Ultra Electronics, Ems, Yaphank *Also called Ems Development Corporation (G-17390)*
Ultra Fine Jewelry Mfg 516 349-2848
180 Dupont St Unit C Plainview (11803) *(G-13640)*
Ultra Thin Pzza Shlls Fltbrads, New Hyde Park *Also called Ultra Thin Ready To Bake Pizza (G-8868)*
Ultra Thin Ready To Bake Pizza 516 679-6655
202 Atlantic Ave New Hyde Park (11040) *(G-8868)*
Ultra Tool and Manufacturing 585 467-3700
129 Seneca Ave Rochester (14621) *(G-14740)*
Ultra-Scan Corporation 716 832-6269
4240 Ridge Lea Rd Ste 10 Amherst (14226) *(G-270)*
Ultradian Diagnostics LLC 518 618-0046
5 University Pl A324 Rensselaer (12144) *(G-14053)*
Ultrafab Inc (PA) 585 924-2186
1050 Hook Rd Farmington (14425) *(G-5158)*
Ultraflex Power Technologies 631 467-6814
158 Remington Blvd Ste 2 Ronkonkoma (11779) *(G-14995)*
Ultralife Corporation (PA) 315 332-7100
2000 Technology Pkwy Newark (14513) *(G-12745)*
Ultrapedics Ltd (PA) 718 748-4806
355 Ovington Ave Ste 104 Brooklyn (11209) *(G-2696)*
Ultravolt Inc 631 471-4444
1800 Ocean Ave Unit A Ronkonkoma (11779) *(G-14996)*
Ultrepet LLC 781 275-6400
136c Fuller Rd Albany (12205) *(G-146)*
Umbro Machine & Tool Co Inc 845 876-4669
3811 Route 9g Rhinebeck (12572) *(G-14059)*
Umi, New York *Also called Urban Mapping Inc (G-12480)*
Umicore Technical Materials 518 792-7700
9 Pruyns Island Dr Glens Falls (12801) *(G-5699)*
Umicore USA Inc 919 874-7171
9 Pruyns Island Dr Glens Falls (12801) *(G-5700)*
Ums Manufacturing LLC 518 562-2410
194 Pleasant Ridge Rd Plattsburgh (12901) *(G-13705)*
Unadilla Laminated Products, Sidney *Also called Unadilla Silo Company Inc (G-15444)*
Unadilla Silo Company Inc 607 369-9341
100 West Rd Sidney (13838) *(G-15444)*
Uncharted Play Inc 646 675-7783
246 Lenox Ave New York (10027) *(G-12447)*
Uncle Wally's, Shirley *Also called United Baking Co Inc (G-15431)*
Uncle Wallys LLC 631 205-0455
41 Natcon Dr Shirley (11967) *(G-15430)*
Unco United Oil Holdings LLC 212 481-1003
100 Park Ave Fl 16 New York (10017) *(G-12448)*
Under Armour Inc 518 761-6787
1444 State Route 9 Lake George (12845) *(G-7264)*
Underline Communications LLC 212 994-4340
12 W 27th St Fl 14 New York (10001) *(G-12449)*
Uneeda Enterprizes Inc 877 863-3321
640 Chestnut Ridge Rd Spring Valley (10977) *(G-15605)*
UNI Jewelry Inc 212 398-1818
48 W 48th St Ste 1401 New York (10036) *(G-12450)*
UNI Source Technology 514 748-8888
1320 Rt 9 Champlain (12919) *(G-3547)*
Unibrands Corporation 212 897-2278
745 5th Ave Ste 500 New York (10151) *(G-12451)*
Unicell Body Company Inc (PA) 716 853-8628
571 Howard St Buffalo (14206) *(G-3231)*
Unicell Body Company Inc 716 853-8628
170 Cordell Rd Schenectady (12303) *(G-15307)*
Unicell Body Company Inc 585 424-2660
1319 Brighton Henrietta Rochester (14623) *(G-14741)*
Unicenter Millwork Inc 716 741-8201
9605 Clarence Center Rd Clarence Center (14032) *(G-3681)*
Unico Inc 845 562-9255
25 Renwick St Newburgh (12550) *(G-12782)*
Unico Special Products Inc 845 562-9255
25 Renwick St Newburgh (12550) *(G-12783)*
Unicom Graphic Communications 212 221-2456
230 Park Ave Rm 1000 New York (10169) *(G-12452)*
Unicor, Otisville *Also called Federal Prison Industries (G-13344)*
Unicor, Ray Brook *Also called Federal Prison Industries (G-14024)*
Unicorn Graphics, Garden City *Also called Won & Lee Inc (G-5538)*
Unidex Corporation Western NY 585 786-3170
2416 State Route 19 N Warsaw (14569) *(G-16584)*
Unifab Inc 585 235-1760
215 Tremont St Ste 31 Rochester (14608) *(G-14742)*
Unified Inc led 646 370-4650
35 W 36th St New York (10018) *(G-12453)*
Unified Media Inc 917 595-2710
180 Madison Ave Lbby L New York (10016) *(G-12454)*
Unified Solutions For Clg Inc 718 782-8800
1829 Pacific St Brooklyn (11233) *(G-2697)*
Unifor Inc 212 673-3434
149 5th Ave Ste 3r New York (10010) *(G-12455)*
Uniform Express, Rochester *Also called Kevin J Kassman (G-14469)*
Uniform Namemakers Inc 716 626-5474
55 Amherst Villa Rd Buffalo (14225) *(G-3232)*
Uniform Professionals, Cincinnatus *Also called David Christy (G-3653)*
Uniforms By Park Coats Inc 718 499-1182
790 3rd Ave Brooklyn (11232) *(G-2698)*
Unifrax Corporation 716 278-3800
2351 Whirlpool St Niagara Falls (14305) *(G-12886)*
Unifrax Holding Co (HQ) 212 644-5900
55 E 52nd St Fl 35 New York (10055) *(G-12456)*
Unifrax I LLC 716 696-3000
360 Fire Tower Dr Tonawanda (14150) *(G-16210)*
Unifrax I LLC (HQ) 716 768-6500
600 Rverwalk Pkwy Ste 120 Tonawanda (14150) *(G-16211)*
Unifuse LLC 845 889-4000
2092 Route 9g Staatsburg (12580) *(G-15619)*
Unify360 LLC 718 213-7687
9914 203rd St Hollis (11423) *(G-6499)*
Unilock Ltd 716 822-6074
510 Smith St Buffalo (14210) *(G-3233)*
Unilock New York Inc (HQ) 845 278-6700
51 International Blvd Brewster (10509) *(G-1229)*
Unilux Advanced Mfg LLC 518 344-7490
30 Commerce Park Rd Schenectady (12309) *(G-15308)*
Unimar Inc 315 699-4400
3195 Vickery Rd Syracuse (13212) *(G-16063)*
Unimax Supply Co Inc (PA) 212 925-1051
269 Canal St New York (10013) *(G-12457)*
Unimex Corporation (PA) 212 755-8800
54 E 64th St New York (10065) *(G-12458)*
Unimex Corporation 718 236-2222
1462 62nd St Brooklyn (11219) *(G-2699)*
Union Standard & Un Conf McHy, Bronx *Also called National Equipment Corporation (G-1406)*
Union Standard Eqp Co Div, Bronx *Also called National Equipment Corporation (G-1405)*
Union Sun & Journal, Lockport *Also called Community Newsppr Holdings Inc (G-7577)*
Unipharm Inc (PA) 212 564-3634
350 5th Ave Ste 6701 New York (10118) *(G-12459)*
Uniqlo USA LLC 877 486-4756
546 Broadway New York (10012) *(G-12460)*
Unique Designs Inc 212 575-7701
521 5th Ave Rm 820 New York (10175) *(G-12461)*
Unique Display Mfg Corp (PA) 516 546-3800
216 N Main St Ste D Freeport (11520) *(G-5433)*
Unique MBL Gran Orgnztion Corp 718 482-0440
3831 9th St Long Island City (11101) *(G-7907)*
Unique Overseas Inc 516 466-9792
425 Northern Blvd Ste 22 Great Neck (11021) *(G-5846)*
Unique Packaging Corporation 514 341-5872
1320 State Route 9 # 3807 Champlain (12919) *(G-3548)*
Unique Petz LLC 212 714-1800
10 W 33rd St Rm 220 New York (10001) *(G-12462)*
Unique Printing Company LLC 718 386-2519
5900 Decatur St Ste 6 Flushing (11385) *(G-5305)*

ALPHABETIC

(PA)=Parent Co (HQ)=Headquarters (DH)=Div Headquarters
2017 Harris
New York Manufacturers Directory
1085

Unique Quality Fabrics Inc ... 845 343-3070
115 Wisner Ave Middletown (10940) *(G-8468)*
Unisend LLC ... 585 414-9575
249 Gallant Fox Ln Webster (14580) *(G-16739)*
Unison Industries LLC ... 607 335-5000
5345 State Highway 12 Norwich (13815) *(G-13039)*
Unisource Food Eqp Systems Inc ... 516 681-0537
1505 Lincoln Ave Holbrook (11741) *(G-6479)*
Unistel LLC ... 585 341-4600
860 Hard Rd Webster (14580) *(G-16740)*
Unisystems Inc (PA) ... 212 826-0850
155 E 55th St Apt 203 New York (10022) *(G-12463)*
Unit Step Company, Sanborn *Also called Gamble & Gamble Inc (G-15120)*
United Baking Co Inc ... 631 413-5116
16 Bronx Ave Central Islip (11722) *(G-3513)*
United Baking Co Inc (PA) ... 631 205-0455
41 Natcon Dr Shirley (11967) *(G-15431)*
United Biochemicals LLC ... 716 731-5161
6351 Inducon Dr E Sanborn (14132) *(G-15128)*
United Brothers Jewelry Inc ... 212 921-2558
48 W 48th St Ste 700 New York (10036) *(G-12464)*
United Business Forms, Long Island City *Also called United Print Group Inc (G-7908)*
United Data Forms Inc ... 631 218-0104
500 Johnson Ave Ste B Bohemia (11716) *(G-1151)*
United Dividers, Elmira *Also called Fennell Industries LLC (G-4685)*
United Farm Processing Corp (PA) ... 718 933-6060
4366 Park Ave Bronx (10457) *(G-1485)*
United Florist Network, Fishkill *Also called Ufn LLC (G-5188)*
United Gemdiam Inc ... 718 851-5083
1537 52nd St Brooklyn (11219) *(G-2700)*
United Graphics Inc ... 716 871-2600
100 River Rock Dr Ste 301 Buffalo (14207) *(G-3234)*
United Iron Inc ... 914 667-5700
6 Roslyn Pl Mount Vernon (10550) *(G-8745)*
United Knitwear International (PA) ... 212 354-2920
1384 Broadway Rm 1210 New York (10018) *(G-12465)*
United Machining Inc ... 631 589-6751
1595 Smithtown Ave Ste D Bohemia (11716) *(G-1152)*
United Materials LLC (PA) ... 716 683-1432
3949 Frest Pk Way Ste 400 North Tonawanda (14120) *(G-13004)*
United Materials LLC ... 716 731-2332
2186 Cory Dr Sanborn (14132) *(G-15129)*
United Materials LLC ... 716 662-0564
75 Bank St Orchard Park (14127) *(G-13301)*
United Metal Industries Inc ... 516 354-6800
1008 3rd Ave New Hyde Park (11040) *(G-8869)*
United Pet Group, Hauppauge *Also called Spectrum Brands Inc (G-6195)*
United Pickle Products Corp ... 718 933-6060
4366 Park Ave Bronx (10457) *(G-1486)*
United Pipe Nipple Co Inc ... 516 295-2468
1602 Lakeview Dr Hewlett (11557) *(G-6315)*
United Plastics Inc ... 718 389-2255
640 Humboldt St Ste 1 Brooklyn (11222) *(G-2701)*
United Print Group Inc ... 718 392-4242
3636 33rd St Ste 303 Long Island City (11106) *(G-7908)*
United Rbotic Integrations LLC ... 716 683-8334
2781 Town Line Rd Alden (14004) *(G-185)*
United Richter Electrical Mtrs ... 716 855-1945
106 Michigan Ave Buffalo (14204) *(G-3235)*
United Rockland Holding Co Inc ... 845 357-1900
9 N Airmont Rd Suffern (10901) *(G-15802)*
United Satcom Inc ... 718 359-4100
4555 Robinson St Flushing (11355) *(G-5306)*
United Sheet Metal Corp ... 718 482-1197
4602 28th St Long Island City (11101) *(G-7909)*
United Ship Repair Inc ... 718 237-2800
54 Richards St Brooklyn (11231) *(G-2702)*
United Silicone Inc ... 716 681-8222
4471 Walden Ave Lancaster (14086) *(G-7345)*
United States Dept of Army ... 315 772-7538
Mnns Crners Rd Bldg P2050 Watertown (13602) *(G-16674)*
United States Gypsum Company ... 585 948-5221
2750 Maple Ave Oakfield (14125) *(G-13066)*
United Steel Products Inc ... 718 478-5330
3340 127th Pl Corona (11368) *(G-4009)*
United Structure Solution Inc ... 347 227-7526
240 W 65th St Apt 26c New York (10023) *(G-12466)*
United Sttes Brnze Sign of Fla ... 516 352-5155
811 2nd Ave New Hyde Park (11040) *(G-8870)*
United Supply Systems, Syosset *Also called Paradigm Mktg Consortium Inc (G-15835)*
United Synggue Cnsrvtive Jdism (PA) ... 212 533-7800
120 Broadway Ste 1540 New York (10271) *(G-12467)*
United Technologies Corp ... 315 432-7849
6304 Carrier Pkwy East Syracuse (13057) *(G-4576)*
United Technologies Corp ... 866 788-5095
1212 Pittsford Victor Rd Pittsford (14534) *(G-13574)*
United Thread Mills Corp (PA) ... 516 536-3900
3530 Lawson Blvd Gf Oceanside (11572) *(G-13102)*
United Transit Mix Inc ... 718 416-3400
318 Boerum St Brooklyn (11206) *(G-2703)*
United Wind Inc ... 800 268-9896
20 Jay St Ste 928 Brooklyn (11201) *(G-2704)*
United Wire Technologies Inc ... 315 675-3558
120 State Route 49 Cleveland (13042) *(G-3692)*
United-Guardian Inc (PA) ... 631 273-0900
230 Marcus Blvd Hauppauge (11788) *(G-6220)*
Unither Manufacturing LLC ... 585 475-9000
755 Jefferson Rd Rochester (14623) *(G-14743)*
Unitone Communication Systems ... 212 777-9090
220 E 23rd St New York (10010) *(G-12468)*
Universal 3d Innovation Inc ... 516 837-9423
1085 Rockaway Ave Valley Stream (11581) *(G-16431)*
Universal Builders Supply Inc ... 845 758-8801
45 Ocallaghan Ln Red Hook (12571) *(G-14030)*
Universal Cmmncations of Miami ... 212 986-5100
801 2nd Ave Lbby New York (10017) *(G-12469)*
Universal Coolers Inc ... 718 788-8621
120 13th St Brooklyn (11215) *(G-2705)*
Universal Custom Millwork Inc ... 518 330-6622
3 Sam Stratton Rd Amsterdam (12010) *(G-372)*
Universal Designs Inc ... 718 721-1111
3517 31st St Long Island City (11106) *(G-7910)*
Universal Edition Inc ... 917 213-2177
331 W 57th St Ste 380 New York (10019) *(G-12470)*
Universal Elliot Corp ... 212 736-8877
327 W 36th St Rm 700 New York (10018) *(G-12471)*
Universal Fire Proof Door ... 718 455-8442
1171 Myrtle Ave Brooklyn (11206) *(G-2706)*
Universal Forest Products, Clinton *Also called Ufp New York LLC (G-3723)*
Universal Forest Products, Chaffee *Also called Ufp New York LLC (G-3536)*
Universal Forest Products, Hudson *Also called Ufp New York LLC (G-6637)*
Universal Forest Products, Sidney *Also called Ufp New York LLC (G-15443)*
Universal Instruments Corp (HQ) ... 800 842-9732
33 Broome Corporate Pkwy Conklin (13748) *(G-3879)*
Universal Jewelry Designs, New York *Also called Zdny & Co Inc (G-12707)*
Universal Metal Fabricators ... 845 331-8248
27 Emerick St Kingston (12401) *(G-7221)*
Universal Metal Works LLC ... 315 598-7607
159 Hubbard St Fulton (13069) *(G-5476)*
Universal Metals Inc ... 516 829-0896
98 Cuttermill Rd Ste 428 Great Neck (11021) *(G-5847)*
Universal Packg Systems Inc (PA) ... 631 543-2277
6080 Jericho Tpke Commack (11725) *(G-3845)*
Universal Parent and Youth ... 917 754-2426
1530 Pa Ave Apt 17e Brooklyn (11239) *(G-2707)*
Universal Precision Corp ... 585 321-9760
40 Commerce Dr Rochester (14623) *(G-14744)*
Universal Proteins, Amityville *Also called Natural Organics Labroratories (G-315)*
Universal Ready Mix Inc ... 516 746-4535
197 Atlantic Ave New Hyde Park (11040) *(G-8871)*
Universal Remote Control Inc (PA) ... 914 630-4343
500 Mmaroneck Ave Ste 502 Harrison (10528) *(G-5993)*
Universal Screening Associates ... 718 232-2744
6509 11th Ave Brooklyn (11219) *(G-2708)*
Universal Shielding Corp ... 631 667-7900
20 W Jefryn Blvd Deer Park (11729) *(G-4219)*
Universal Signs and Svc Inc ... 631 446-1121
435 Brook Ave Unit 2 Deer Park (11729) *(G-4220)*
Universal Stainless & Alloy ... 716 366-1000
830 Brigham Rd Dunkirk (14048) *(G-4352)*
Universal Steel Fabricators ... 718 342-0782
90 Junius St Brooklyn (11212) *(G-2709)*
Universal Step Inc ... 315 437-7611
5970 Butternut Dr East Syracuse (13057) *(G-4577)*
Universal Strapping Inc ... 845 268-2500
630 Corporate Way Valley Cottage (10989) *(G-16394)*
Universal Thin Film Lab Corp ... 845 562-0601
232 N Plank Rd Newburgh (12550) *(G-12784)*
Universal Tooling Corporation ... 716 985-4691
4533 Route 60 Gerry (14740) *(G-5594)*
Universal Water Technology, Far Rockaway *Also called Business Advisory Services (G-4919)*
Universe Publishing, New York *Also called Rizzoli Intl Publications Inc (G-11882)*
University Advertising Agency, Stony Brook *Also called Stony Brook University (G-15772)*
University At Albany ... 518 437-8686
257 Fuller Rd Albany (12203) *(G-147)*
University of Rochester ... 585 275-3483
250 E River Rd Rochester (14623) *(G-14745)*
University Table Cloth Company ... 845 371-3876
10 Centre St Spring Valley (10977) *(G-15606)*
Uniware Houseware Corp ... 631 242-7400
120 Wilshire Blvd Ste B Brentwood (11717) *(G-1198)*
Unlimited Industries Inc ... 631 666-9483
234 Orinoco Dr Brightwaters (11718) *(G-1239)*
Unlimited Ink Inc ... 631 582-0696
595 Old Willets Path B Hauppauge (11788) *(G-6221)*
Unlimited Jeans Co Inc ... 212 661-6355
401 Broadway Frnt A New York (10013) *(G-12472)*
UOP LLC ... 716 879-7600
175 E Park Dr Tonawanda (14150) *(G-16212)*
Up Country, New York *Also called Du Monde Trading Inc (G-9933)*
Upayori, Brooklyn *Also called Universal Parent and Youth (G-2707)*
Upholstery Unlimited, Hudson *Also called McCarroll Uphl Designs LLC (G-6625)*

ALPHABETIC

ALPHABETIC SECTION — Utleys Incorporated

Upper 90 Soccer & Sport 718 643-0167
  359 Atlantic Ave Brooklyn (11217) *(G-2710)*
Upper East Vererinary Center 212 369-8387
  1435 Lexington Ave Frnt 6 New York (10128) *(G-12473)*
Upper Manhattan Arts Project 914 980-9805
  73 Bramblebrook Rd Ardsley (10502) *(G-407)*
Upper Ninty LLC 646 863-3105
  697 Amsterdam Ave New York (10025) *(G-12474)*
Upper Ninty Soccer and Sport, New York Also called Upper Ninty LLC *(G-12474)*
Uppercut, Airmont Also called NY Cutting Inc *(G-17)*
UPS, Manlius Also called Miller Enterprises CNY Inc *(G-8075)*
Upstate Cabinet Co Inc 585 429-5090
  32 Marway Cir Rochester (14624) *(G-14746)*
Upstate Door Inc 585 786-3880
  26 Industrial St Warsaw (14569) *(G-16585)*
Upstate Increte Incorporated 585 254-2010
  49 Adelaide St Rochester (14606) *(G-14747)*
Upstate Insulated Glass Inc 315 475-4960
  47 Weber Rd Central Square (13036) *(G-3519)*
Upstate Medical Solutions Inc 716 799-3782
  25 Minnetonka Rd Buffalo (14220) *(G-3236)*
Upstate Milk Co-Operatives, Buffalo Also called Upstate Niagara Coop Inc *(G-3238)*
Upstate Niagara Coop Inc (PA) 716 892-3156
  25 Anderson Rd Buffalo (14225) *(G-3237)*
Upstate Niagara Coop Inc 716 892-2121
  1730 Dale Rd Buffalo (14225) *(G-3238)*
Upstate Niagara Coop Inc 585 458-1880
  45 Fulton Ave Rochester (14608) *(G-14748)*
Upstate Niagara Coop Inc 716 484-7178
  223 Fluvanna Ave Jamestown (14701) *(G-7041)*
Upstate Niagara Coop Inc 315 389-5111
  22 County Route 52 North Lawrence (12967) *(G-12935)*
Upstate Office Furniture, Johnson City Also called Upstate Office Liquidators Inc *(G-7106)*
Upstate Office Liquidators Inc 607 722-9234
  718 Azon Rd Johnson City (13790) *(G-7106)*
Upstate Printing Inc 315 475-6140
  433 W Onondaga St Syracuse (13202) *(G-16064)*
Upstate Records Management LLC 518 834-1144
  1729 Front St Keeseville (12944) *(G-7142)*
Upstate Refractory Svcs Inc 315 331-2955
  100 Erie Blvd Newark (14513) *(G-12746)*
Upstate Tube Inc 315 488-5636
  5050 Smoral Rd Camillus (13031) *(G-3326)*
Uptek Solutions 631 256-5565
  130 Knickerbocker Ave A Bohemia (11716) *(G-1153)*
Uptown, Halfmoon Also called Save More Beverage Corp *(G-5916)*
Uptown Local 212 988-1704
  1606 1st Ave New York (10028) *(G-12475)*
Uptown Media Group LLC 212 360-5073
  113 E 125th St Frnt 1 New York (10035) *(G-12476)*
Uptown Nails LLC 800 748-1881
  500 5th Ave New York (10110) *(G-12477)*
Upturn Industries Inc 607 967-2923
  2-4 Whitney Way Bainbridge (13733) *(G-556)*
Urban Apparel Group Inc 212 947-7009
  226 W 37th St Fl 17 New York (10018) *(G-12478)*
Urban Green Energy Inc 917 720-5681
  330 W 38th St Rm 1103 New York (10018) *(G-12479)*
Urban Mapping Inc 415 946-8170
  295 Madison Ave Rm 1010 New York (10017) *(G-12480)*
Urban Racercom 718 279-2202
  21333 39th Ave Bayside (11361) *(G-777)*
Urban Rose, New York Also called French Atmosphere Inc *(G-10208)*
Urban Technologies Inc 716 672-2709
  3451 Stone Quarry Rd Fredonia (14063) *(G-5376)*
Urban Textiles Inc 212 777-1900
  49 Elizabeth St Fl 6 New York (10013) *(G-12481)*
Urban Woodworks Ltd 718 827-1570
  18 Crescent St Brooklyn (11208) *(G-2711)*
Urbandaddy Inc 212 929-7905
  900 Broadway Ste 1003 New York (10003) *(G-12482)*
Urdu Times 718 297-8700
  16920 Hillside Ave Jamaica (11432) *(G-6961)*
Urrey Lumber 518 827-4851
  663 Clauverwie Rd Middleburgh (12122) *(G-8419)*
Ursula Company Store, Waterford Also called Ursula of Switzerland Inc *(G-16623)*
Ursula of Switzerland Inc (PA) 518 237-2580
  31 Mohawk Ave Waterford (12188) *(G-16623)*
Urthworx Inc 646 373-7535
  320 W 106th St Apt 2f New York (10025) *(G-12483)*
US Airports Flight Support Svc, Rochester Also called Usairports Services Inc *(G-14749)*
US Allegro Inc 347 408-6601
  5430 44th St Maspeth (11378) *(G-8174)*
US Alliance Paper Inc 631 254-3030
  101 Heartland Blvd Edgewood (11717) *(G-4619)*
US Angels, New York Also called S & C Bridals LLC *(G-11942)*
US Authentic LLC 914 767-0295
  11 Mt Holly Rd E Katonah (10536) *(G-7134)*
US Beverage Net Inc 315 579-2025
  225 W Jefferson St Syracuse (13202) *(G-16065)*
US China Magazine 212 663-4333
  200 W 95th St Apt 21 New York (10025) *(G-12484)*

US Clothing Company, Bronx Also called U S Embroidery Inc *(G-1483)*
US Concrete Inc 718 853-4644
  10 Powerhouse Rd Roslyn Heights (11577) *(G-15034)*
US Concrete Inc 718 438-6800
  692 Mcdonald Ave Brooklyn (11218) *(G-2712)*
US Design Group Ltd 212 354-4070
  1385 Broadway Rm 1905 New York (10018) *(G-12485)*
US Drives Inc 716 731-1606
  2221 Niagara Falls Blvd # 41 Niagara Falls (14304) *(G-12887)*
US Electroplating Corp 631 293-1998
  100 Field St Unit A West Babylon (11704) *(G-16837)*
US Energy Group, New Hyde Park Also called U S Energy Controls Inc *(G-8867)*
US Frontline News Inc 212 922-9090
  228 E 45th St Rm 700 New York (10017) *(G-12486)*
US Greenfiber, Gloversville Also called Greenfiber Albany Inc *(G-5712)*
US Health Equipment Company 845 658-7576
  138 Maple Hill Rd Kingston (12401) *(G-7222)*
US Hispanic Media Inc (HQ) 212 885-8000
  1 Metrotech Ctr Fl 18 Brooklyn (11201) *(G-2713)*
US Hoists Corp 631 472-3030
  800 Burman Blvd Calverton (11933) *(G-3302)*
US Home Textiles Group LLC 212 768-3030
  1400 Broadway Fl 18 New York (10018) *(G-12487)*
US Juice Partners LLC (HQ) 516 621-1122
  2 Seaview Blvd Port Washington (11050) *(G-13870)*
US Milpack & Mfg Corp 718 342-1307
  1567 Bergen St Brooklyn (11213) *(G-2714)*
US News & World Report Inc (PA) 212 716-6800
  4 New York Plz Fl 6 New York (10004) *(G-12488)*
Us Nonwovens Corp (PA) 631 952-0100
  100 Emjay Blvd Brentwood (11717) *(G-1199)*
US Optical LLC 315 463-4800
  6848 Ellicott Dr East Syracuse (13057) *(G-4578)*
US Peroxide 716 775-5585
  1815 Love Rd Ste 1 Grand Island (14072) *(G-5772)*
US Polychemical Holding Corp 845 356-5530
  584 Chestnut Ridge Rd Spring Valley (10977) *(G-15607)*
US Pump Corp 516 303-7799
  707 Woodfield Rd West Hempstead (11552) *(G-16864)*
US Salt LLC 607 535-2721
  Salt Point Rd Watkins Glen (14891) *(G-16698)*
US Sander LLC 518 875-9157
  4131 Rte 20 Esperance (12066) *(G-4839)*
US Weekly LLC 212 484-1616
  1290 Ave Of The Am Fl 2 New York (10104) *(G-12489)*
USA Body Inc 315 852-6123
  994 Middle Lake Rd De Ruyter (13052) *(G-4082)*
USA Custom Pad Corp (PA) 607 563-9550
  16 Winkler Rd Sidney (13838) *(G-15445)*
USA Foil Inc 631 234-5252
  70 Emjay Blvd Bldg C Brentwood (11717) *(G-1200)*
USA Furs By George Inc 212 643-1415
  212 W 30th St New York (10001) *(G-12490)*
USA Illumination Inc 845 565-8500
  1126 River Rd New Windsor (12553) *(G-8956)*
USA Sealing Inc 716 288-9952
  356 Sonwil Dr Cheektowaga (14225) *(G-3592)*
USA Sewing Inc 315 792-8017
  901 Broad St Ste 2 Utica (13501) *(G-16362)*
USA Signs of America Inc 631 254-6900
  172 E Industry Ct Deer Park (11729) *(G-4221)*
USA Tees.com, Brooklyn Also called Universal Screening Associates *(G-2708)*
USA Today International Corp 703 854-3400
  535 Madison Ave Fl 27 New York (10022) *(G-12491)*
Usai, New Windsor Also called USA Illumination Inc *(G-8956)*
Usairports Services Inc 585 527-6835
  1295 Scottsville Rd Rochester (14624) *(G-14749)*
Used Equipment Directory, New York Also called Penton Media Inc *(G-11609)*
Usheco Inc 845 658-9200
  138 Maple Hill Rd Kingston (12401) *(G-7223)*
Ushers Machine and Tool Co Inc 518 877-5501
  180 Ushers Rd Round Lake (12151) *(G-15038)*
Uspa Accessories LLC 212 868-2590
  119 W 40th St Fl 3 New York (10018) *(G-12492)*
Usq Group LLC 212 777-7751
  222 Broadway Fl 19 New York (10038) *(G-12493)*
Utica Boilers, Utica Also called ECR International Inc *(G-16328)*
Utica Cutlery Company 315 733-4663
  820 Noyes St Utica (13502) *(G-16363)*
Utica Metal Products Inc 315 732-6163
  1526 Lincoln Ave Utica (13502) *(G-16364)*
Utility Brass & Bronze Div, Brooklyn Also called Giumenta Corp *(G-2025)*
Utility Canvas Inc (PA) 845 255-9290
  2686 Route 44 55 Gardiner (12525) *(G-5552)*
Utility Engineering Co 845 735-8900
  40 Walter St Pearl River (10965) *(G-13468)*
Utility Manufacturing Co Inc 516 997-6300
  700 Main St Westbury (11590) *(G-17039)*
Utility Systems Tech Inc 518 326-4142
  70 Cohoes Rd Watervliet (12189) *(G-16691)*
Utleys Incorporated 718 956-1661
  3123 61st St Woodside (11377) *(G-17359)*

V & E Kohnstamm & Co Div, Brooklyn *Also called Virginia Dare Extract Co Inc* ***(G-2729)***
V & J Graphics Inc....315 363-1933
153 Phelps St Oneida (13421) ***(G-13169)***
V A I, Ronkonkoma *Also called Vormittag Associates Inc* ***(G-14999)***
V A P Tool & Dye....631 587-5262
436 W 4th St West Islip (11795) ***(G-16908)***
V C N Group Ltd Inc....516 223-4812
1 Clifton St North Baldwin (11510) ***(G-12911)***
V E Power Door Co Inc....631 231-4500
140 Emjay Blvd Brentwood (11717) ***(G-1201)***
V E W, New York *Also called Vera Wang Group LLC* ***(G-12518)***
V Lake Industries Inc....716 885-9141
1555 Niagara St Buffalo (14213) ***(G-3239)***
V M Choppy & Sons, Troy *Also called Choppy V M & Sons LLC* ***(G-16231)***
V Magazine, New York *Also called Visionaire Publishing LLC* ***(G-12553)***
Va Inc....585 385-5930
803 Linden Ave Ste 1 Rochester (14625) ***(G-14750)***
Vaad LHafotzas Sichoes....718 778-5436
788 Eastern Pkwy Brooklyn (11213) ***(G-2715)***
Vac Air Service Inc....716 665-2206
1295 E 2nd St Jamestown (14701) ***(G-7042)***
Vacheron New York Btq, New York *Also called Richemont North America Inc* ***(G-11864)***
Vactronics, Bayside Hills *Also called Cathay Global Co Inc* ***(G-780)***
Vacuum Instrument Corporation (PA)....631 737-0900
2099 9th Ave Ronkonkoma (11779) ***(G-14997)***
Vader Systems LLC....716 636-1742
179 Roxbury Park East Amherst (14051) ***(G-4363)***
Vaire LLC....631 271-4933
200 E 2nd St Ste 34 Huntington Station (11746) ***(G-6727)***
Valad Electric Heating Corp....914 631-4927
160 Wildey St Ste 1 Tarrytown (10591) ***(G-16110)***
Valair Inc....716 751-9480
87 Harbor St Wilson (14172) ***(G-17269)***
Valencia Bakery Inc (PA)....718 991-6400
801 Edgewater Rd Bronx (10474) ***(G-1487)***
Valenti Distributing....716 824-2304
84 Maple Ave Blasdell (14219) ***(G-968)***
Valenti Neckwear Co Inc....914 969-0700
540 Nepperhan Ave Ste 564 Yonkers (10701) ***(G-17494)***
Valentin & Kalich Jwly Mfg Ltd....212 575-9044
42 W 48th St Ste 903 New York (10036) ***(G-12494)***
Valentin Magro, New York *Also called Valentin & Kalich Jwly Mfg Ltd* ***(G-12494)***
Valentine Jewelry Mfg Co Inc....212 382-0606
31 W 47th St Ste 602 New York (10036) ***(G-12495)***
Valentine Packaging Corp....718 418-6000
6020 59th Pl Ste 7 Maspeth (11378) ***(G-8175)***
Valentine Printing Corp....718 444-4400
509 E 79th St Brooklyn (11236) ***(G-2716)***
Valeo....800 634-2704
4 Executive Plz Ste 114 Yonkers (10701) ***(G-17495)***
Valerie Bohigian....914 631-8866
225 Hunter Ave Sleepy Hollow (10591) ***(G-15476)***
Vali Industries Inc....718 821-5555
285 Lombardy St Brooklyn (11222) ***(G-2717)***
Valian Associates, Sleepy Hollow *Also called Valerie Bohigian* ***(G-15476)***
Valid Electric Corp....914 631-9436
160 Wildey St Ste 1 Tarrytown (10591) ***(G-16111)***
Valle Signs and Awnings....516 408-3440
889 Nassau Rd Uniondale (11553) ***(G-16301)***
Valley Creek Side Inc....315 839-5526
1960 State Route 8 Clayville (13322) ***(G-3690)***
Valley Industrial Products Inc....631 385-9300
152 New York Ave Huntington (11743) ***(G-6689)***
Valley Industries, Gerry *Also called Cobbe Industries Inc* ***(G-5592)***
Valley Signs, Clayville *Also called Valley Creek Side Inc* ***(G-3690)***
Valley Stream Sporting Gds Inc....516 593-7800
325 Hendrickson Ave Lynbrook (11563) ***(G-7966)***
Valmont Inc (PA)....212 685-1653
1 W 34th St Rm 303 New York (10001) ***(G-12496)***
Valmont Site Pro 1, Hauppauge *Also called P & H Inc* ***(G-6157)***
Valois of America Inc....845 639-3700
250 N Route 303 Congers (10920) ***(G-3861)***
Valplast International Corp....516 442-3923
200 Shames Dr Westbury (11590) ***(G-17040)***
Value Fragrances & Flavors, Goshen *Also called Value Fragrances Inc* ***(G-5741)***
Value Fragrances Inc....845 294-5726
7 Musket Ct Goshen (10924) ***(G-5741)***
Value Line Inc (HQ)....212 907-1500
485 Lexington Ave Fl 9 New York (10017) ***(G-12497)***
Value Line Publishing LLC....212 907-1500
485 Lexington Ave Fl 9 New York (10017) ***(G-12498)***
Value Spring Technology Inc....917 705-4658
521 Harrison Ave Harrison (10528) ***(G-5994)***
Valvetech Inc....315 548-4551
1391 Phelps Junction Rd Phelps (14532) ***(G-13538)***
Van Alphen & Doran Corp....518 782-9242
1050 Troy Schenectady Rd Latham (12110) ***(G-7382)***
Van Blarcom Closures Inc (PA)....718 855-3810
156 Sanford St Brooklyn (11205) ***(G-2718)***
Van Cpeters Logging Inc....607 637-3574
4480 Peas Eddy Rd Hancock (13783) ***(G-5968)***

Van Heusen, New Windsor *Also called Pvh Corp* ***(G-8949)***
Van Heusen, Deer Park *Also called Pvh Corp* ***(G-4195)***
Van Heusen, New York *Also called Pvh Corp* ***(G-11758)***
Van Heusen, New York *Also called Pvh Corp* ***(G-11759)***
Van Laeken Richard....315 331-0289
2680 Parker Rd Newark (14513) ***(G-12747)***
Van Leeuwen Artisan Ice Cream....718 701-1630
56 Dobbin St Brooklyn (11222) ***(G-2719)***
Van Slyke Belting LLC....518 283-5479
606 Snyders Corners Rd Poestenkill (12140) ***(G-13726)***
Van Thomas Inc....585 426-1414
740 Driving Park Ave G1 Rochester (14613) ***(G-14751)***
Vanberg & Dewulf Co Inc....607 547-8184
52 Pioneer St Ste 4 Cooperstown (13326) ***(G-3886)***
Vance Metal Fabricators Inc....315 789-5626
251 Gambee Rd Geneva (14456) ***(G-5588)***
Vanchlor Company Inc (PA)....716 434-2624
45 Main St Lockport (14094) ***(G-7624)***
Vanchlor Company Inc....716 434-2624
555 W Jackson St Lockport (14094) ***(G-7625)***
Vandam Inc....212 929-0416
121 W 27th St Ste 1102 New York (10001) ***(G-12499)***
Vandemark Chemical Inc (PA)....716 433-6764
1 N Transit Rd Lockport (14094) ***(G-7626)***
Vander Heyden Woodworking....212 242-0525
151 W 25th St Fl 8 New York (10001) ***(G-12500)***
Vandilay Industries Inc....631 226-3064
60 Bell St Unit A West Babylon (11704) ***(G-16838)***
Vanec, Orchard Park *Also called Vibration & Noise Engrg Corp* ***(G-13302)***
Vanguard Graphics LLC....607 272-1212
17 Hallwoods Rd Ithaca (14850) ***(G-6882)***
Vanguard Metals Inc....631 234-6500
135 Brightside Ave Central Islip (11722) ***(G-3514)***
Vanguard Printing, Ithaca *Also called Vanguard Graphics LLC* ***(G-6882)***
Vanhouten Motorsports....315 387-6312
27 Center Rd Lacona (13083) ***(G-7252)***
Vanity Fair....212 286-6052
4 Times Sq Bsmt C1b New York (10036) ***(G-12501)***
Vanity Fair Bathmart Inc....718 584-6700
2971 Webster Ave Bronx (10458) ***(G-1488)***
Vanity Fair Brands LP....212 548-1548
25 W 39th St New York (10018) ***(G-12502)***
Vanity Room Inc....212 921-7154
230 W 39th St Fl 9 New York (10018) ***(G-12503)***
Vanlab, Rochester *Also called Synergy Flavors NY Company LLC* ***(G-14711)***
Vans Inc....631 724-1011
313 Smith Haven Mall Lake Grove (11755) ***(G-7268)***
Vans Inc....718 349-2311
25 Franklin St Brooklyn (11222) ***(G-2720)***
Vansantis Development Inc....315 461-0113
4595 Morgan Pl Liverpool (13090) ***(G-7554)***
Vantage Mfg & Assembly LLC....845 471-5290
900 Dutchess Tpke Poughkeepsie (12603) ***(G-13938)***
Vantage Press Inc....212 736-1767
419 Park Ave S Fl 18 New York (10016) ***(G-12504)***
Vante Inc....716 778-7691
3600 Coomer Rd Newfane (14108) ***(G-12789)***
Varflex Corporation....315 336-4400
512 W Court St Rome (13440) ***(G-14839)***
Variable Graphics LLC....212 691-2323
15 W 36th St Rm 601 New York (10018) ***(G-12505)***
Varian Medical Systems, Liverpool *Also called Infimed Inc* ***(G-7524)***
Varick Street Litho Inc....646 843-0800
121 Varick St New York (10013) ***(G-12506)***
Variety Gem Co Inc (PA)....212 921-1820
295 Northern Blvd Ste 208 Great Neck (11021) ***(G-5848)***
Varnish Software Inc....201 857-2832
85 Broad St Fl 18 New York (10004) ***(G-12507)***
Varonis Systems Inc (PA)....877 292-8767
1250 Broadway Fl 29 New York (10001) ***(G-12508)***
Varsity Monitor LLC....212 691-6292
50 5th Ave Fl 3 New York (10011) ***(G-12509)***
Vasomedical Inc (PA)....516 997-4600
137 Commercial St Ste 200 Plainview (11803) ***(G-13641)***
Vasomedical Solutions Inc....516 997-4600
137 Commercial St Ste 200 Plainview (11803) ***(G-13642)***
Vasquez Tito....212 944-0441
36 W 47th St Ste 206 New York (10036) ***(G-12510)***
Vassilaros Coffee, Flushing *Also called John A Vassilaros & Son Inc* ***(G-5257)***
Vault Wo....212 281-1723
828 E 21st St Brooklyn (11210) ***(G-2721)***
Vault.com, Vault Media, New York *Also called Vaultcom Inc* ***(G-12511)***
Vaultcom Inc (PA)....212 366-4212
132 W 31st St Rm 1501 New York (10001) ***(G-12511)***
Vcp Mobility Inc....718 356-7827
4131 Richmond Ave Staten Island (10312) ***(G-15751)***
Vdc Electronics Inc....631 683-5850
155 W Carver St Ste 2 Huntington (11743) ***(G-6690)***
VDO Lab Inc....914 949-1741
400 Tarrytown Rd White Plains (10607) ***(G-17179)***
Vector Group Ltd....212 409-2800
712 5th Ave New York (10019) ***(G-12512)***

ALPHABETIC

Vector Magnetics LLC 607 273-8351
236 Cherry St Ithaca (14850) *(G-6883)*
Vectra Inc 718 361-1000
3200 Skillman Ave Long Island City (11101) *(G-7911)*
Vedell North Fork LLC 631 323-3526
36225 Main Rd Cutchogue (11935) *(G-4074)*
Veeco Instruments Inc 516 677-0200
100 Sunnyside Blvd Ste B Woodbury (11797) *(G-17302)*
Veeco Instruments Inc 516 349-8300
1 Terminal Dr Plainview (11803) *(G-13643)*
Veeco Instruments Inc (PA) 516 677-0200
1 Terminal Dr Plainview (11803) *(G-13644)*
Veeco Process Equipment, Plainview *Also called Veeco Instruments Inc (G-13643)*
Veeco Process Equipment Inc (HQ) 516 677-0200
1 Terminal Dr Plainview (11803) *(G-13645)*
Veerhouse Voda Haiti LLC 917 353-5944
42 Broadway Fl 12 New York (10004) *(G-12513)*
Veerhouse Voda Haiti SA, New York *Also called Veerhouse Voda Haiti LLC (G-12513)*
Vega Coffee Inc 415 881-7969
300 E 46th St Apt 9h New York (10017) *(G-12514)*
Vegetable Operations, Geneva *Also called Seneca Foods Corporation (G-5585)*
Vegetable Operations, Marion *Also called Seneca Foods Corporation (G-8101)*
Vehicle Manufacturers Inc 631 851-1700
400 Oser Ave Ste 100 Hauppauge (11788) *(G-6222)*
Vehicle Safety Dept 315 458-6683
5801 E Taft Rd Ste 4 Syracuse (13212) *(G-16066)*
Vehicle Tracking Solutions LLC 631 586-7400
152 Veterans Memorial Hwy Commack (11725) *(G-3846)*
Veja Electronics Inc (PA) 631 321-6086
46 W Jefryn Blvd Ste A Deer Park (11729) *(G-4222)*
Velis Associates Inc (PA) 631 225-4220
151 S 14th St Lindenhurst (11757) *(G-7491)*
Vell Company Inc 845 365-1013
700 Oak Tree Rd Palisades (10964) *(G-13404)*
Velmex Inc 585 657-6151
7550 State Route 5 And 20 Bloomfield (14469) *(G-992)*
Velocity Outsourcing LLC 212 891-4043
750 3rd Ave New York (10017) *(G-12515)*
Velocity Pharma LLC 631 393-2905
226 Sherwood Ave Unit B Farmingdale (11735) *(G-5137)*
Velocity Print Solutions, Scotia *Also called Shipmtes/Printmates Holdg Corp (G-15330)*
Velvetop Products, Huntington Station *Also called Walsh & Hughes Inc (G-6728)*
Venco Sales Inc 631 754-0782
755 Park Ave Ste 300 Huntington (11743) *(G-6691)*
Vending Times Inc 516 442-1850
55 Maple Ave Ste 304 Rockville Centre (11570) *(G-14802)*
Vendome Group LLC 646 795-3899
216 E 45th St Fl 6 New York (10017) *(G-12516)*
Vendome Press, New York *Also called Helvetica Press Incorporated (G-10456)*
Veneer One Inc 516 536-6480
3415 Hampton Rd Oceanside (11572) *(G-13103)*
Vengo Inc 866 526-7054
4550 30th St Ste 41 Long Island City (11101) *(G-7912)*
Venice Marina, Brooklyn *Also called Marina Holding Corp (G-2269)*
Vent-A-Fume, Buffalo *Also called Vent-A-Kiln Corporation (G-3240)*
Vent-A-Kiln Corporation 716 876-2023
51 Botsford Pl Buffalo (14216) *(G-3240)*
Ventura Enterprise Co Inc 212 391-0170
512 Fashion Ave Fl 38 New York (10018) *(G-12517)*
Venture Economics, New York *Also called Securities Data Publishing Inc (G-12014)*
Venture Respiratory Inc 718 437-3633
1413 38th St Brooklyn (11218) *(G-2722)*
Venue Graphics Supply Inc 718 361-1690
1120 46th Rd Long Island City (11101) *(G-7913)*
Venus, New York *Also called Shah Diamonds Inc (G-12038)*
Venus Manufacturing Co Inc (PA) 315 639-3100
349 Lakeview Dr Dexter (13634) *(G-4287)*
Venus Pharmaceuticals Intl Inc 631 249-4140
55a Kennedy Dr Hauppauge (11788) *(G-6223)*
Venus Printing Company 212 967-8900
1420 Kew Ave Hewlett (11557) *(G-6316)*
Ver-Tech Elevator, Ozone Park *Also called Elevator Ventures Corporation (G-13377)*
Vera Wang Group LLC (PA) 212 575-6400
15 E 26th St Fl 4 New York (10010) *(G-12518)*
Veranda Magazine, New York *Also called Veranda Publications Inc (G-12519)*
Veranda Publications Inc 212 903-5206
300 W 57th St Fl 28 New York (10019) *(G-12519)*
Veratex Inc (PA) 212 683-9300
254 5th Ave Fl 3 New York (10001) *(G-12520)*
Verdonette Inc 212 719-2003
270 W 39th St Fl 5 New York (10018) *(G-12521)*
Verifyme Inc (PA) 212 994-7002
12 W 21st St Fl 8 New York (10010) *(G-12522)*
Verizon, New York *Also called Supermedia LLC (G-12243)*
Verla International Ltd 845 561-2440
463 Temple Hill Rd New Windsor (12553) *(G-8957)*
Vermed Inc 802 463-9976
400 Exchange St Buffalo (14204) *(G-3241)*
Vermont Multicolor Slate 518 642-2400
146 State Route 22a Middle Granville (12849) *(G-8402)*
Vermont Natural Stoneworks 518 642-2460
146 State Route 22a Middle Granville (12849) *(G-8403)*
Vermont Structural Slate Co 518 499-1912
Buckley Rd Whitehall (12887) *(G-17191)*
Vernon Devices, New Rochelle *Also called Halpern Tool Corp (G-8908)*
Vernon Plating Works Inc 718 639-1124
3318 57th St Woodside (11377) *(G-17360)*
Verns Machine Co Inc 315 926-4223
4929 Steel Point Rd Marion (14505) *(G-8103)*
Verragio Ltd (PA) 212 868-8181
132 W 36th St Bsmt New York (10018) *(G-12523)*
Versailles Drapery Upholstery 212 533-2059
4709 30th St Ste 200 Long Island City (11101) *(G-7914)*
Versailles Industries LLC 212 792-9615
485 Fashion Ave Rm 500 New York (10018) *(G-12524)*
Versaponents, Deer Park *Also called Lighting Sculptures Inc (G-4166)*
Versaponents Inc 631 242-3387
66 N Industry Ct Deer Park (11729) *(G-4223)*
Verse Music Group LLC 212 564-0977
330 W 38th St Rm 405 New York (10018) *(G-12525)*
Verso Inc 718 246-8160
20 Jay St Ste 1010 Brooklyn (11201) *(G-2723)*
Verso Corporation 212 599-2700
370 Lexington Ave Rm 802 New York (10017) *(G-12526)*
Verso Paper Management LP 781 320-8660
370 Lexington Ave Rm 802 New York (10017) *(G-12527)*
Verso Paper Management LP (PA) 212 599-2700
60 W 42nd Ste 1942 New York (10165) *(G-12528)*
Vertana Group LLC (PA) 646 706-7210
35 W 20th St Ste 804 New York (10011) *(G-12529)*
Vertex Innovative Solutions In 315 437-6711
6671 Commerce Blvd Syracuse (13211) *(G-16067)*
Vertical Apparel, New York *Also called American Apparel Trading Corp (G-9114)*
Vertical Lax Inc 518 669-3699
20 Corporate Cir Ste 4 Albany (12203) *(G-148)*
Vertical Research Partners LLC 212 257-6499
52 Vanderbilt Ave Rm 200 New York (10017) *(G-12530)*
Very Best Irtj 914 271-6585
435 Yorktown Rd Croton On Hudson (10520) *(G-4066)*
Vescom Structural Systems Inc 516 876-8100
100 Shames Dr Unit 1 Westbury (11590) *(G-17041)*
Vespa Sand & Stone, Watertown *Also called John Vespa Inc (G-16656)*
Vestal Asphalt Inc (PA) 607 785-3393
201 Stage Rd Vestal (13850) *(G-16456)*
Vestal Electronic Devices LLC 607 773-8461
635 Dickson St Endicott (13760) *(G-4833)*
Veteran Offset Printing, Rochester *Also called Veterans Offset Printing Inc (G-14752)*
Veterans Offset Printing Inc 585 288-2900
500 N Goodman St Rochester (14609) *(G-14752)*
Veterinary Biochemical Ltd 845 473-1900
201 Smith St Poughkeepsie (12601) *(G-13939)*
Vetra Systems Corporation 631 434-3185
275 Marcus Blvd Unit J Hauppauge (11788) *(G-6224)*
Vetta Jewelry Inc (PA) 212 564-8250
70 W 36th St Fl 9 New York (10018) *(G-12531)*
Vette Corp New York 585 265-0330
6377 Dean Pkwy Ontario (14519) *(G-13216)*
Vez Inc 718 273-7002
1209 Forest Ave Staten Island (10310) *(G-15752)*
Vf Imagewear Inc 718 352-2363
333 Pratt Ave Bayside (11359) *(G-778)*
Vf Outdoor Inc 718 698-6215
2655 Richmond Ave # 1570 Staten Island (10314) *(G-15753)*
Vf Outdoor LLC 845 928-4900
461 Evergreen Ct Central Valley (10917) *(G-3528)*
Vf Sportswear Inc 212 541-5757
40 W 57th St Fl 3 New York (10019) *(G-12532)*
Vgg Holding LLC 212 415-6700
590 Madison Ave Fl 41 New York (10022) *(G-12533)*
Vhx Corporation 347 689-1446
555 W 18th St New York (10011) *(G-12534)*
Via America Fine Jewelry Inc 212 302-1218
578 5th Ave Unit 26 New York (10036) *(G-12535)*
Viamedia Corporation 718 485-7792
2610 Atlantic Ave Brooklyn (11207) *(G-2724)*
Viana Signs Corp 516 887-2000
3520 Lawson Blvd Oceanside (11572) *(G-13104)*
Viapack Inc 718 729-5500
3608 Review Ave Long Island City (11101) *(G-7915)*
Viatech Pubg Solutions Inc 631 968-8500
1440 5th Ave Bay Shore (11706) *(G-754)*
Viatran Corporation (HQ) 716 629-3800
3829 Frest Pk Way Ste 500 North Tonawanda (14120) *(G-13005)*
Vibe Magazine, New York *Also called Vibe Media Group LLC (G-12536)*
Vibe Media Group LLC 212 448-7300
120 Wall St Fl 21 New York (10005) *(G-12536)*
Vibra Tech Industries Inc 914 946-1916
126 Oakley Ave White Plains (10601) *(G-17180)*
Vibration & Noise Engrg Corp 716 827-4959
3374 N Benzing Rd Orchard Park (14127) *(G-13302)*
Vibration Eliminator Co Inc (PA) 631 841-4000
15 Dixon Ave Copiague (11726) *(G-3936)*

Vic Demayos Inc.......845 626-4343
4967 Us Highway 209 Accord (12404) **(G-1)**
Vic Leak Detection, Ronkonkoma *Also called Vacuum Instrument Corporation* **(G-14997)**
Vic-Gina Printing Company Inc.......914 636-0200
1299 North Ave New Rochelle (10804) **(G-8927)**
Vicarious Visions Inc.......518 283-4090
350 Jordan Rd Troy (12180) **(G-16259)**
Vickers Stock Research Corp (HQ).......212 425-7500
61 Broadway Rm 1910 New York (10006) **(G-12537)**
Vicks Lithograph & Prtg Corp (PA).......315 272-2401
5166 Commercial Dr Yorkville (13495) **(G-17527)**
Vicks Lithograph & Prtg Corp.......315 736-9344
5210 Commercial Dr Yorkville (13495) **(G-17528)**
Vicon Industries Inc (PA).......631 952-2288
135 Fell Ct Hauppauge (11788) **(G-6225)**
Vicron Electronic Mfg, Bronx *Also called Monarch Electric Products Inc* **(G-1402)**
Victoire Latam Asset MGT LLC.......212 319-6550
598 Madison Ave Fl 9 New York (10022) **(G-12538)**
Victor Insulators Inc.......585 924-2127
280 Maple Ave Victor (14564) **(G-16510)**
Victoria Albi Intl Inc.......212 689-2600
1178 Broadway Fl 5 New York (10001) **(G-12539)**
Victoria Dngelo Intr Cllctions, Warwick *Also called DAngelo Home Collections Inc* **(G-16587)**
Victoria Fine Foods LLC (PA).......718 649-1635
443 E 100th St Brooklyn (11236) **(G-2725)**
Victoria Plating Co Inc.......718 589-1550
650 Tiffany St Bronx (10474) **(G-1489)**
Victoria Precision Inc.......845 473-9309
78 Travis Rd Hyde Park (12538) **(G-6738)**
Victoria Stilwell Positevely, New York *Also called Dog Good Products LLC* **(G-9895)**
Victory Garden.......212 206-7273
31 Carmine St Frnt A New York (10014) **(G-12540)**
Victory Signs Inc.......315 762-0220
8915 Old State Route 13 Canastota (13032) **(G-3376)**
Victory Sports, Staten Island *Also called Glenda Inc* **(G-15678)**
Victory Vision Care Inc.......718 622-2020
565 Atlantic Ave Brooklyn (11217) **(G-2726)**
Vida-Blend LLC.......518 627-4138
1430 State Highway 5s Amsterdam (12010) **(G-373)**
Vidal Candies USA Inc.......609 781-8169
845 3rd Ave Fl 6 New York (10022) **(G-12541)**
Vidbolt Inc.......716 560-8944
4 Elam Pl Buffalo (14214) **(G-3242)**
Videk Inc.......585 377-0377
1387 Fairport Rd 1000c Fairport (14450) **(G-4885)**
Video Technology Services Inc.......516 937-9700
5 Aerial Way Ste 300 Syosset (11791) **(G-15841)**
Videotec Security Incorporated.......518 825-0020
35 Gateway Dr Ste 100 Plattsburgh (12901) **(G-13706)**
Viducci, Great Neck *Also called Classic Creations Inc* **(G-5798)**
Viele Manufacturing Corp.......718 893-2200
1340 Viele Ave Bronx (10474) **(G-1490)**
View Collections Inc.......212 944-4030
265 W 37th St Rm 5w New York (10018) **(G-12542)**
Viewfinder Inc.......212 831-0939
101 W 23rd St Ste 2303 New York (10011) **(G-12543)**
Viewsport Inc.......585 738-6803
11 Feathery Cir Penfield (14526) **(G-13505)**
Vigliotti's Great Garden, Yaphank *Also called Scotts Company LLC* **(G-17400)**
Vigneri Chocolate Inc.......585 254-6160
810 Emerson St Rochester (14613) **(G-14753)**
Viking Athletics Ltd.......631 957-8000
80 Montauk Hwy Ste 1 Lindenhurst (11757) **(G-7492)**
Viking Industries Inc.......845 883-6325
89 S Ohioville Rd New Paltz (12561) **(G-8882)**
Viking Iron Works Inc.......845 471-5010
37 Hatfield Ln Poughkeepsie (12603) **(G-13940)**
Viking Jackets & Athletic Wear, Walden *Also called C & C Athletic Inc* **(G-16531)**
Viking Mar Wldg Ship Repr LLC.......718 758-4116
14 Raleigh Pl Brooklyn (11226) **(G-2727)**
Viking Technologies Ltd.......631 957-8000
80 E Montauk Hwy Lindenhurst (11757) **(G-7493)**
Viking-Cives, Harrisville *Also called Cives Corporation* **(G-5995)**
Viktor Gold Enterprise Corp.......212 768-8885
58 W 47th St Unit 36 New York (10036) **(G-12544)**
Village Decoration Ltd.......315 437-2522
20 Corporate Cir East Syracuse (13057) **(G-4579)**
Village Lantern Baking Corp.......631 225-1690
155 N Wellwood Ave Lindenhurst (11757) **(G-7494)**
Village Metals Inc.......585 271-1250
87 Belmont St Rochester (14620) **(G-14754)**
Village Plaquesmith, Ththe, Bohemia *Also called Custom House Engravers Inc* **(G-1046)**
Village Print Room, Oneonta *Also called Pony Farm Press & Graphics* **(G-13192)**
Village Printing, Endicott *Also called Fambus Inc* **(G-4807)**
Village Times, The, East Setauket *Also called Times Beacon Record Newspapers* **(G-4494)**
Village Video News, West Babylon *Also called Village Video Productions Inc* **(G-16839)**
Village Video Productions Inc.......631 752-9311
107 Alder St West Babylon (11704) **(G-16839)**
Village Wrought Iron Inc.......315 683-5589
7756 Main St Fabius (13063) **(G-4841)**
Villager, The, Brooklyn *Also called Nyc Community Media LLC* **(G-2384)**
Villeroy & Boch Usa Inc.......212 213-8149
41 Madison Ave Ste 1801 New York (10010) **(G-12545)**
Vin Mar Precision Metal Inc.......631 563-6608
1465 S Strong Ave Copiague (11726) **(G-3937)**
Vin-Clair Bindery, West Haverstraw *Also called Vin-Clair Inc* **(G-16847)**
Vin-Clair Inc.......845 429-4998
132 E Railroad Ave West Haverstraw (10993) **(G-16847)**
Vincent Associates, Rochester *Also called Va Inc* **(G-14750)**
Vincent Conigliaro.......845 340-0489
308 State Route 28 Kingston (12401) **(G-7224)**
Vincent Genovese.......631 281-8170
19 Woodmere Dr Mastic Beach (11951) **(G-8205)**
Vincent Manufacturing Co Inc.......315 823-0280
560 E Mill St Little Falls (13365) **(G-7506)**
Vincent Martino Dental Lab.......716 674-7800
74 Ransier Dr Buffalo (14224) **(G-3243)**
Vincents Food Corp.......516 481-3544
179 Old Country Rd Carle Place (11514) **(G-3397)**
Vincys Printing Ltd.......518 355-4363
1832 Curry Rd Schenectady (12306) **(G-15309)**
Vindagra USA Incorporated.......516 605-1960
50 Bethpage Rd Ste 6 Hicksville (11801) **(G-6398)**
Vineland Kosher Poultry Inc.......718 921-1347
5600 1st Ave A7 Brooklyn (11220) **(G-2728)**
Vinevrest Co, Washingtonville *Also called Brotherhood Amer Oldest Wnery* **(G-16599)**
Vinifera Wine Cellard, Hammondsport *Also called Konstantin D FRAnk& Sons Vini* **(G-5958)**
Vinyl Materials Inc.......631 586-9444
365 Bay Shore Rd Deer Park (11729) **(G-4224)**
Vinyl Tech Window, Staten Island *Also called Eastern Enterprise Corp* **(G-15670)**
Vinyl Works Inc.......518 786-1200
33 Wade Rd Latham (12110) **(G-7383)**
Vinyline Window and Door Inc.......914 476-3500
636 Saw Mill River Rd Yonkers (10710) **(G-17496)**
Viola Cabinet Corporation.......716 284-6327
4205 Hyde Park Blvd Niagara Falls (14305) **(G-12888)**
Viola Construction, Niagara Falls *Also called Viola Cabinet Corporation* **(G-12888)**
Violife LLC.......914 207-1820
1 Executive Blvd Ste 4 Yonkers (10701) **(G-17497)**
VIP Foods Inc.......718 821-5330
1080 Wyckoff Ave Ridgewood (11385) **(G-14131)**
VIP Paper Trading Inc.......212 382-4642
1140 Ave Of The New York (10036) **(G-12546)**
VIP Printing.......718 641-9361
16040 95th St Howard Beach (11414) **(G-6599)**
Viraj - USA Inc (HQ).......516 280-8380
100 Quentin Roosevelt Blv Garden City (11530) **(G-5535)**
Virgil Mountain Inc (PA).......212 378-0007
1 E 28th St Fl 4 New York (10016) **(G-12547)**
Virginia Dare Extract Co Inc.......718 788-6320
882 3rd Ave Unit 2 Brooklyn (11232) **(G-2729)**
Viropro Inc.......650 300-5190
49 W 38th St Fl 11 New York (10018) **(G-12548)**
Virtual Frameworks Inc.......646 690-8207
841 Broadway Ste 504 New York (10003) **(G-12549)**
Virtual Super LLC.......212 685-6400
116 E 27th St Fl 3 New York (10016) **(G-12550)**
Virtual Urth.......914 793-1269
80 Barrington Rd Bronxville (10708) **(G-1504)**
Virtualapt Corp.......917 293-3173
45 Main St Ste 408 Brooklyn (11201) **(G-2730)**
Virtue Paintball LLC (PA).......631 617-5560
40 Oser Ave Ste 14 Hauppauge (11788) **(G-6226)**
Virtusphere Inc.......607 760-2207
2 Dewey Ave Binghamton (13903) **(G-958)**
Virtuvent Inc.......646 845-0387
1221 Av Of The Amrcas4200 New York (10020) **(G-12551)**
Visage Swiss Watch LLC.......212 594-7991
29 W 30th St Rm 701 New York (10001) **(G-12552)**
Visage Watches, New York *Also called Visage Swiss Watch LLC* **(G-12552)**
Visant Secondary Holdings Corp (HQ).......914 595-8200
357 Main St Armonk (10504) **(G-423)**
Vishay Americas Inc.......315 938-7575
14992 Snowshoe Rd Henderson (13650) **(G-6290)**
Vishay Thin Film LLC.......716 283-4025
2160 Liberty Dr Niagara Falls (14304) **(G-12889)**
Visible Systems Corporation (PA).......508 628-1510
248 Main St Ste 2 Oneida (13421) **(G-13170)**
Visimetrics Corporation.......716 871-7070
2290 Kenmore Ave Buffalo (14207) **(G-3244)**
Vision Quest, Brooklyn *Also called Lens Lab Express* **(G-2211)**
Vision Quest Lighting Inc.......631 737-4800
90 13th Ave Unit 1 Ronkonkoma (11779) **(G-14998)**
Vision World, Bedford Hills *Also called Eyeglass Service Industries* **(G-803)**
Vision-Sciences, Orangeburg *Also called Machida Incorporated* **(G-13235)**
Visionaire Publishing LLC.......646 434-6091
30 W 24th St New York (10010) **(G-12553)**
Visiontron Corp.......631 582-8600
720 Old Willets Path Hauppauge (11788) **(G-6227)**
Visiplex Instruments Corp.......845 365-0190
250 Clearbrook Rd Elmsford (10523) **(G-4791)**

ALPHABETIC

Visitainer Corp 718 636-0300
148 Classon Ave Brooklyn (11205) *(G-2731)*
Vista Packaging Inc 718 854-9200
1425 37th St Ste 6 Brooklyn (11218) *(G-2732)*
Vista Pharmacy & Surgical, Far Rockaway *Also called J P R Pharmacy Inc (G-4923)*
Vista Visual Group, Lindenhurst *Also called Linear Signs Inc (G-7468)*
Vistalab Technologies Inc 914 244-6226
2 Geneva Rd Brewster (10509) *(G-1230)*
Vistec Lithography, Troy *Also called Raith America Inc (G-16250)*
Vistec Lithography Inc 518 874-3184
300 Jordan Rd Troy (12180) *(G-16260)*
Visual Citi Inc (PA) 631 482-3030
305 Henry St Lindenhurst (11757) *(G-7495)*
Visual Effects Inc 718 324-0011
15929 Jamaica Ave 2 Jamaica (11432) *(G-6962)*
Visual F-X, Brooklyn *Also called Street Beat Sportswear Inc (G-2610)*
Visual ID Source Inc 516 307-9759
65 E 2nd St Mineola (11501) *(G-8538)*
Visual Impact Graphics Inc 585 548-7118
653 Ellicott St Ste 6 Batavia (14020) *(G-652)*
Visual Listing Systems Inc 631 689-7222
19 Technology Dr East Setauket (11733) *(G-4496)*
Visual Millwork & Fixture Mfg 718 267-7800
2515 50th St Woodside (11377) *(G-17361)*
Vita Rara Inc 518 369-7356
415 River St Ste 4 Troy (12180) *(G-16261)*
Vita-Nat Inc 631 293-6000
298 Adams Blvd Farmingdale (11735) *(G-5138)*
Vitafede (PA) 213 488-0136
25 W 26th St Fl 5 New York (10010) *(G-12554)*
Vitakem Nutraceutical Inc 631 956-8343
811 W Jericho Tpke Smithtown (11787) *(G-15502)*
Vital Signs & Graphics Co Inc 518 237-8372
251 Saratoga St Cohoes (12047) *(G-3760)*
Vitale Ready Mix Concrete, Auburn *Also called Robinson Concrete Inc (G-516)*
Vitalis LLC 646 831-7338
902 Broadway Fl 6 New York (10010) *(G-12555)*
Vitalize Labs LLC 212 966-6130
560 Broadway Rm 604 New York (10012) *(G-12556)*
Vitamin Power Incororated 631 676-5790
75 Commerce Dr Hauppauge (11788) *(G-6228)*
Vitamix Laboratories, Farmingdale *Also called Wellmill LLC (G-5142)*
Vitamix Laboratories Inc 631 465-9245
69 Mall Dr Commack (11725) *(G-3847)*
Vitane Pharmaceuticals Inc 845 267-6700
125 Wells Ave Congers (10920) *(G-3862)*
Vitarose Corp of America 718 951-9700
2615 Nostrand Ave Ste 1 Brooklyn (11210) *(G-2733)*
Viterion Corporation 914 333-6033
565 Taxter Rd Ste 175 Elmsford (10523) *(G-4792)*
Vitex Packaging Group Inc (HQ) 212 265-6575
45 Rockefeller Plz New York (10111) *(G-12557)*
Vitobob Furniture Inc 516 676-1696
3879 13th St Long Island City (11101) *(G-7916)*
Vitra Inc (HQ) 212 463-5700
29 9th Ave New York (10014) *(G-12558)*
Vitrix Hot Glass and Crafts, Corning *Also called Vitrix Inc (G-3984)*
Vitrix Inc 607 936-8707
77 W Market St Corning (14830) *(G-3984)*
Vits International Inc 845 353-5000
200 Corporate Dr Blauvelt (10913) *(G-979)*
Vivid Rgb Lighting LLC 718 635-0817
824 Main St Ste 1 Peekskill (10566) *(G-13483)*
Vivona Business Printers Inc 516 496-3453
343 Jackson Ave Syosset (11791) *(G-15842)*
Vivreau Advanced Water Systems 212 502-3749
545 8th Ave Rm 401 New York (10018) *(G-12559)*
Vizbee Inc 650 787-1424
120 E 23rd St Fl 5 New York (10010) *(G-12560)*
Vizio Medical Devices LLC 646 845-7382
200 Chambers St Apt 28a New York (10007) *(G-12561)*
VJ Technologies Inc (PA) 631 589-8800
89 Carlough Rd Bohemia (11716) *(G-1154)*
Vjt, Bohemia *Also called VJ Technologies Inc (G-1154)*
Vma, Poughkeepsie *Also called Vantage Mfg & Assembly LLC (G-13938)*
Vnovom Svete 212 302-9480
55 Broad St Fl 20 New York (10004) *(G-12562)*
Voctoire Finance Capital, New York *Also called Victoire Latam Asset MGT LLC (G-12538)*
Vogel Applied Technologies 212 677-3136
36 E 12th St Fl 7 New York (10003) *(G-12563)*
Vogue China, New York *Also called Advance Magazine Publs Inc (G-9041)*
Vogue Magazine 212 286-2860
4 Times Sq Bsmt C1b New York (10036) *(G-12564)*
Vogue Too Plting Stitching EMB 212 354-1022
265 W 37th St Fl 14 New York (10018) *(G-12565)*
Voice Analysis Clinic 212 245-3803
326 W 55th St Apt 4d New York (10019) *(G-12566)*
Voices For All LLC 518 261-1664
29 Moreland Dr Mechanicville (12118) *(G-8232)*
Voila Sweets LLC 718 366-1100
65 Porter Ave Brooklyn (11237) *(G-2734)*
Volckening Inc (PA) 718 748-0294
6700 3rd Ave Brooklyn (11220) *(G-2735)*
Volkert Precision Tech Inc 718 464-9500
22240 96th Ave Ste 3 Queens Village (11429) *(G-13984)*
Volpi Manufacturing USA Co Inc 315 255-1737
5 Commerce Way Auburn (13021) *(G-527)*
Volt Tek Inc 585 377-2050
111 Parce Ave Fairport (14450) *(G-4886)*
Voltronics LLC 410 749-2424
2777 Us Route 20 Cazenovia (13035) *(G-3454)*
Von Musulin Patricia 212 206-8345
148 W 24th St Fl 10 New York (10011) *(G-12567)*
Von Pok & Chang New York Inc 212 599-0556
4 E 43rd St Fl 7 New York (10017) *(G-12568)*
Von Roll Usa Inc (HQ) 518 344-7100
200 Von Roll Dr Schenectady (12306) *(G-15310)*
Vondom LLC 212 207-3252
979 3rd Ave Ste 1532 New York (10022) *(G-12569)*
Vonn Lighting, Forest Hills *Also called Vonn LLC (G-5329)*
Vonn LLC 917 572-5000
6945 108th St Apt 10b Forest Hills (11375) *(G-5329)*
Voodoo Manufacturing Inc 646 893-8366
361 Stagg St Ste 408 Brooklyn (11206) *(G-2736)*
Vormittag Associates Inc (PA) 800 824-7776
120 Comac St Ste 1 Ronkonkoma (11779) *(G-14999)*
Vortek Tel 87724633365859 585 924-5000
7200 Rawson Rd Victor (14564) *(G-16511)*
Vortex Ventures Inc 516 946-8345
857 Newton Ave North Baldwin (11510) *(G-12912)*
Vosky Precision Machining Corp 631 737-3200
70 Air Park Dr Ronkonkoma (11779) *(G-15000)*
Voss Manufacturing Inc 716 731-5062
2345 Lockport Rd Sanborn (14132) *(G-15130)*
Voss Signs LLC 315 682-6418
112 Fairgrounds Dr Ste 2 Manlius (13104) *(G-8076)*
Voss Usa Inc 212 995-2255
236 W 30th St Rm 900 New York (10001) *(G-12570)*
Vox Systems, Massapequa *Also called Huntington Services Inc (G-8179)*
Voyager Custom Products, Buffalo *Also called Voyager Emblems Inc (G-3245)*
Voyager Emblems Inc 416 255-3421
701 Seneca St Ste D Buffalo (14210) *(G-3245)*
Vpj Publication Inc 718 845-3221
15519 Lahn St Howard Beach (11414) *(G-6600)*
Vr Containment LLC 917 972-3441
17625 Union Tpke Ste 175 Fresh Meadows (11366) *(G-5447)*
Vr Food Equipment Inc 315 531-8133
7 Bush Park Ln Penn Yan (14527) *(G-13522)*
Vsg International LLC 718 300-8171
196 Clinton Ave Apt A2 Brooklyn (11205) *(G-2737)*
Vship Co 718 706-8566
3636 33rd St Ste 207 Astoria (11106) *(G-460)*
VSM Investors LLC (PA) 212 351-1600
245 Park Ave Fl 41 New York (10167) *(G-12571)*
Vtb Holdings Inc (HQ) 914 345-2255
100 Summit Lake Dr Valhalla (10595) *(G-16373)*
Vulcan Iron Works Inc 631 395-6846
190 Weeks Ave Manorville (11949) *(G-8082)*
Vulcan Steam Forging Co 716 875-3680
247 Rano St Buffalo (14207) *(G-3246)*
Vulcraft of New York Inc (HQ) 607 529-9000
621 M St Chemung (14825) *(G-3595)*
Vus Is Neias LLC 347 627-3999
5514 13th Ave Brooklyn (11219) *(G-2738)*
Vuzix Corporation (PA) 585 359-5900
25 Hendrix Rd Ste A West Henrietta (14586) *(G-16898)*
VWR Chemicals LLC (HQ) 518 297-4444
3 Lincoln Blvd Rouses Point (12979) *(G-15045)*
VWR Education LLC 585 359-2502
5100 W Henrietta Rd West Henrietta (14586) *(G-16899)*
Vybion Inc 607 266-0860
33 Thornwood Dr Ste 104 Ithaca (14850) *(G-6884)*
Vytek Inc 631 750-1770
271 Knickerbocker Ave Bohemia (11716) *(G-1155)*
W & B Mazza & Sons Inc 516 379-4130
2145 Marion Pl North Baldwin (11510) *(G-12913)*
W & G Manufacturing, Brooklyn *Also called Sue & Sam Co Inc (G-2618)*
W & H Stampings Inc 631 234-6161
45 Engineers Rd Hauppauge (11788) *(G-6229)*
W & M Headwear Co Inc 718 768-2222
148 39th St Unit 8 Brooklyn (11232) *(G-2739)*
W & W Manufacturing Co 516 942-0011
151 E Industry Ct Deer Park (11729) *(G-4225)*
W A Baum Co Inc 631 226-3940
620 Oak St Copiague (11726) *(G-3938)*
W B Bow Tie Corp 212 683-6130
521 W 26th St Fl 6 New York (10001) *(G-12572)*
W D Technology Inc 914 779-8738
42 Water St Ste B Eastchester (10709) *(G-4583)*
W Designe Inc 914 736-1058
5 John Walsh Blvd Peekskill (10566) *(G-13484)*
W E W Container Corporation 718 827-8150
189 Wyona St Brooklyn (11207) *(G-2740)*

A L P H A B E T I C

(PA)=Parent Co (HQ)=Headquarters (DH)=Div Headquarters
2017 Harris
New York Manufacturers Directory
1091

W F Saunders & Sons Inc (PA) ... 315 469-3217
5126 S Onondaga Rd Nedrow (13120) ***(G-8773)***
W G R Z - T V Channel 2, Buffalo *Also called Tegna Inc* ***(G-3212)***
W H Jones & Son Inc ... 716 875-8233
1208 Military Rd Kenmore (14217) ***(G-7151)***
W H White Publications Inc ... 914 725-2500
95 Main St Dobbs Ferry (10522) ***(G-4304)***
W Hubbell & Sons Inc (PA) ... 315 736-8311
5124 Commercial Dr Yorkville (13495) ***(G-17529)***
W J Albro Machine Works Inc ... 631 345-0657
86 Horseblock Rd Unit L Yaphank (11980) ***(G-17408)***
W K Z A 106.9 K I S S-F M, Jamestown *Also called Cntry Cross Communications LLC* ***(G-6982)***
W Kintz Plastics Inc (PA) ... 518 296-8513
165 Caverns Rd Howes Cave (12092) ***(G-6601)***
W M T Publications Inc ... 585 244-3329
250 N Goodman St Ste 1 Rochester (14607) ***(G-14755)***
W M W, Buffalo *Also called West Metal Works Inc* ***(G-3252)***
W N R Pattern & Tool Inc ... 716 681-9334
21 Pavement Rd Lancaster (14086) ***(G-7346)***
W N Vanalstine & Sons Inc (PA) ... 518 237-1436
18 New Cortland St Cohoes (12047) ***(G-3761)***
W R P Welding Ltd ... 631 249-8859
126 Toledo St Farmingdale (11735) ***(G-5139)***
W Stuart Smith Inc ... 585 742-3310
625 Fishers Run Victor (14564) ***(G-16512)***
W W Custom Clad Inc ... 518 673-3322
75 Creek St Canajoharie (13317) ***(G-3334)***
W W Norton & Company Inc (PA) ... 212 354-5500
500 5th Ave Fl 6 New York (10110) ***(G-12573)***
W W Norton & Company Inc ... 212 354-5500
500 5th Ave Lbby 1 New York (10110) ***(G-12574)***
W&P Design LLC (PA) ... 434 806-1443
86 S 1st St Apt 4b Brooklyn (11249) ***(G-2741)***
W.O.w Brand Products, North Tonawanda *Also called Griffin Chemical Company LLC* ***(G-12976)***
WA Packaging LLC ... 518 724-6466
604 Corporation Park Schenectady (12302) ***(G-15311)***
Wacf Enterprise Inc ... 631 745-5841
275 Asharoken Ave Northport (11768) ***(G-13018)***
Wacoal America Inc ... 718 794-1032
1543 Saint Lawrence Ave Bronx (10460) ***(G-1491)***
Wacoal America Inc ... 212 743-9600
136 Madison Ave Fl 15 New York (10016) ***(G-12575)***
Wacoal International Corp ... 212 532-6100
136 Madison Ave Fl 15 New York (10016) ***(G-12576)***
Wadadda.com, Monticello *Also called Patrick Rohan* ***(G-8607)***
Wadsworth Logging Inc ... 518 863-6870
3095 State Highway 30 Gloversville (12078) ***(G-5727)***
Waffenbauch USA ... 716 326-4508
165 Academy St Westfield (14787) ***(G-17052)***
Wagner Farms, Lodi *Also called Lamoreaux Landing Wl* ***(G-7635)***
Wagner Hardwoods LLC ... 607 594-3321
6307 St Route 224 Cayuta (14824) ***(G-3440)***
Wagner Hardwoods LLC ... 607 594-3321
6307 St Route 224 Cayuta (14824) ***(G-3441)***
Wagner Logging LLC ... 607 467-2347
11188 State Highway 8 Masonville (13804) ***(G-8109)***
Wagner Lumber, Owego *Also called Wagner Millwork Inc* ***(G-13361)***
Wagner Millwork Inc ... 607 687-5362
4060 Gaskill Rd Owego (13827) ***(G-13361)***
Wagner Technical Services Inc ... 845 566-4018
1658 Route 300 Newburgh (12550) ***(G-12785)***
Wagner Vineyards & Brewing Co ... 607 582-6574
9322 State Route 414 Lodi (14860) ***(G-7636)***
Wagners LLC (PA) ... 516 933-6580
366 N Broadway Ste 402 Jericho (11753) ***(G-7090)***
Waguya News, Wolcott *Also called Wayuga Community Newspapers* ***(G-17281)***
Wainland Inc ... 718 626-2233
2460 47th St Astoria (11103) ***(G-461)***
Wal Machine, West Babylon *Also called Mpi Consulting Incorporated* ***(G-16813)***
Wal Machine, West Babylon *Also called Mpi Consulting Incorporated* ***(G-16814)***
Walco Leather Co Inc ... 212 243-2244
22 W 32nd St Fl 8 New York (10001) ***(G-12577)***
Walco Stainless, Utica *Also called Utica Cutlery Company* ***(G-16363)***
Waldman Alexander M Diamond Co ... 212 921-8098
30 W 47th St Ste 805 New York (10036) ***(G-12578)***
Waldman Diamond Company, New York *Also called Waldman Alexander M Diamond Co* ***(G-12578)***
Waldman Publishing Corporation (PA) ... 212 730-9590
570 Fashion Ave Rm 800 New York (10018) ***(G-12579)***
Waldorf Bakers Inc ... 718 665-2253
909 E 135th St Bronx (10454) ***(G-1492)***
Wall Protection Products LLC ... 877 943-6826
32 Nelson Hill Rd Wassaic (12592) ***(G-16602)***
Wall Street Business Pdts Inc ... 212 563-4014
151 W 30th St Fl 8 New York (10001) ***(G-12580)***
Wall Street Reporter Magazine ... 212 363-2600
419 Lafayette St Fl 2 New York (10003) ***(G-12581)***
Wall Tool & Tape Corp ... 718 641-6813
8111 101st Ave Ozone Park (11416) ***(G-13386)***
Wall Tool Manufacturing, Ozone Park *Also called Wall Tool & Tape Corp* ***(G-13386)***
Wallace Home Design Ctr ... 631 765-3890
44500 County Road 48 Southold (11971) ***(G-15561)***
Wallace Refiners Inc ... 212 391-2649
15 W 47th St Ste 808 New York (10036) ***(G-12582)***
Wallguard.com, Wassaic *Also called Wall Protection Products LLC* ***(G-16602)***
Wallico Shoes Corp ... 212 826-7171
417 Park Ave New York (10022) ***(G-12583)***
Wallkill Lodge No 627 F&Am ... 845 778-7148
61 Main St Walden (12586) ***(G-16538)***
Wallkill Valley Publications ... 845 561-0170
300 Stony Brook Ct Ste B Newburgh (12550) ***(G-12786)***
Wallkill Valley Times, Newburgh *Also called Wallkill Valley Publications* ***(G-12786)***
Wally Packaging, Monsey *Also called Magcrest Packaging Inc* ***(G-8574)***
Wally Packaging Inc (HQ) ... 718 377-5323
1168 E 21st St Brooklyn (11210) ***(G-2742)***
Walman, Jerome, New York *Also called Wine On Line International* ***(G-12642)***
Walnut Packaging Inc ... 631 293-3836
450 Smith St Farmingdale (11735) ***(G-5140)***
Walnut Printing Inc ... 718 707-0100
2812 41st Ave Long Island City (11101) ***(G-7917)***
Walpole Woodworkers Inc ... 631 726-2859
779 Montauk Hwy Water Mill (11976) ***(G-16606)***
Walsh & Hughes Inc (PA) ... 631 427-5904
1455 New York Ave Huntington Station (11746) ***(G-6728)***
Walsh & Sons Machine Inc ... 845 526-0301
15 Secor Rd Ste 5 Mahopac (10541) ***(G-8004)***
Walter Edbril Inc ... 212 532-3253
10 E 38th St Fl 6 New York (10016) ***(G-12584)***
Walter G Legge Company Inc ... 914 737-5040
444 Central Ave Peekskill (10566) ***(G-13485)***
Walter P Sauer LLC ... 718 937-0600
276 Greenpoint Ave # 8400 Brooklyn (11222) ***(G-2743)***
Walter R Tucker Entps Ltd ... 607 467-2866
8 Leonard Way Deposit (13754) ***(G-4282)***
Wan Ja Shan, Middletown *Also called Mandarin Soy Sauce Inc* ***(G-8449)***
Wanjashan International LLC ... 845 343-1505
4 Sands Station Rd Middletown (10940) ***(G-8469)***
Want-Ad Digest Inc ... 518 279-1181
870 Hoosick Rd Ste 1 Troy (12180) ***(G-16262)***
Wantagh 5 & 10, Wantagh *Also called Nbets Corporation* ***(G-16561)***
Wantagh Computer Center ... 516 826-2189
10 Stanford Ct Wantagh (11793) ***(G-16564)***
Wappingers Falls Shopper Inc ... 845 297-3723
84 E Main St Wappingers Falls (12590) ***(G-16578)***
Warby Parker Eyewear, New York *Also called Parker Warby Retail Inc* ***(G-11575)***
Ward Diesel Filter Systems, Elmira *Also called Beecher Emssn Sltn Tchnlgs LLC* ***(G-4671)***
Ward Industrial Equipment Inc (PA) ... 716 856-6966
1051 Clinton St Buffalo (14206) ***(G-3247)***
Ward Iron Works Limited, Buffalo *Also called Ward Industrial Equipment Inc* ***(G-3247)***
Ward Lafrance Truck Corp ... 518 893-1865
26 Congress St Ste 259f Saratoga Springs (12866) ***(G-15176)***
Ward Sales Co Inc ... 315 476-5276
1117 W Fayette St Ste 1 Syracuse (13204) ***(G-16068)***
Ward Steel Company Inc ... 315 451-4566
4591 Morgan Pl Liverpool (13090) ***(G-7555)***
Wares of Wood ... 315 964-2983
259 Cc Rd Williamstown (13493) ***(G-17229)***
Warm ... 212 925-1200
181 Mott St Frnt 1 New York (10012) ***(G-12585)***
Warnaco Group Inc (HQ) ... 212 287-8000
501 Fashion Ave New York (10018) ***(G-12586)***
Warnaco Inc (HQ) ... 212 287-8000
501 Fashion Ave Fl 14 New York (10018) ***(G-12587)***
Warnaco Inc ... 718 722-3000
70 Washington St Fl 10 Brooklyn (11201) ***(G-2744)***
Warner ... 716 446-0663
84 Paige Ave Buffalo (14223) ***(G-3248)***
Warner Electric, Amherst *Also called Danaher Corporation* ***(G-236)***
Warner Music Group Corp (HQ) ... 212 275-2000
1633 Broadway New York (10019) ***(G-12588)***
Warner Music Inc (HQ) ... 212 275-2000
75 Rockefeller Plz Bsmt 1 New York (10019) ***(G-12589)***
Warner S, New York *Also called Warnaco Inc* ***(G-12587)***
Warodean Corporation ... 718 359-5559
4308 162nd St Flushing (11358) ***(G-5307)***
Warren Corporation (HQ) ... 860 684-2766
711 5th Ave Fl 11 New York (10022) ***(G-12590)***
Warren Cutlery Corp ... 845 876-3444
3584 Route 9g Rhinebeck (12572) ***(G-14060)***
Warren Energy Services LLC ... 212 697-9660
1114 Ave Of The Americas New York (10036) ***(G-12591)***
Warren Printing Inc ... 212 627-5000
3718 Northern Blvd # 418 Long Island City (11101) ***(G-7918)***
Warrior Sports Inc ... 315 536-0937
26 Powell Ln Penn Yan (14527) ***(G-13523)***
Warshaw Jacobson Group, New York *Also called Irv Inc* ***(G-10663)***
Warwick Press, Warwick *Also called Digital United Color Prtg Inc* ***(G-16588)***

ALPHABETIC

Washburn Litho Envirgo Prtg, Rochester *Also called Presstek Printing LLC* ***(G-14599)***
Washburn Manufacturing Tech.....607 387-3991
9828 State Route 96 Trumansburg (14886) ***(G-16268)***
Washburns Dairy Inc.....518 725-0629
145 N Main St Gloversville (12078) ***(G-5728)***
Washer Solutions Inc.....585 742-6388
760 Canning Pkwy Ste A Victor (14564) ***(G-16513)***
Washingtom Mills Elec Mnrls (HQ).....716 278-6600
1801 Buffalo Ave Niagara Falls (14303) ***(G-12890)***
Washington Mills Tonawanda Inc (HQ).....716 693-4550
1000 E Niagara St Tonawanda (14150) ***(G-16213)***
Washington Square News, New York *Also called New York University* ***(G-11412)***
Waste Management, Palatine Bridge *Also called Lee Publications Inc* ***(G-13396)***
Wastecorp Pumps LLC (PA).....888 829-2783
345 W 85th St Apt 23 New York (10024) ***(G-12592)***
Wataah, New York *Also called Let Water Be Water LLC* ***(G-10976)***
Watch Journal LLC.....212 229-1500
110 E 25th St Fl 4 New York (10010) ***(G-12593)***
Watchanish LLC.....917 558-0404
1 Rockefeller Plz Fl 11 New York (10020) ***(G-12594)***
Watchcraft Inc.....347 531-0382
2214 40th Ave Ste 4 Long Island City (11101) ***(G-7919)***
Watchitoo Inc.....212 354-5888
24 W 40th St Fl 14 New York (10018) ***(G-12595)***
Watec America Corporation.....702 434-6111
720 Route 17m Ste 4 Middletown (10940) ***(G-8470)***
Water Cooling Corp.....718 723-6500
24520 Merrick Blvd Rosedale (11422) ***(G-15015)***
Water Energy Systems LLC.....844 822-7665
1 Maiden Ln New York (10038) ***(G-12596)***
Water Resources Group LLC.....631 824-9088
84 Main St Cold Spring Harbor (11724) ***(G-3771)***
Water Splash Inc.....800 936-3430
25 Locust St Ste 421 Champlain (12919) ***(G-3549)***
Water Street Brass Corporation.....716 763-0059
4515 Gleason Rd Lakewood (14750) ***(G-7296)***
Water Technologies Inc (PA).....315 986-0000
1635 Commons Pkwy Macedon (14502) ***(G-7992)***
Water Treatment Services Inc.....914 241-2261
395 Adams St Bedford Hills (10507) ***(G-808)***
Water Treatment Svce, Bedford Hills *Also called Water Treatment Services Inc* ***(G-808)***
Water Wise of America Inc.....585 232-1210
90 Canal St Rochester (14608) ***(G-14756)***
Water Wise of America Inc (PA).....585 232-1210
75 Bermar Park Ste 5 Rochester (14624) ***(G-14757)***
Waterbury Garment LLC.....212 725-1500
16 E 34th St Fl 10 New York (10016) ***(G-12597)***
Watermark Designs Holdings Ltd.....718 257-2800
350 Dewitt Ave Brooklyn (11207) ***(G-2745)***
Watertown Concrete Inc.....315 788-1040
24471 State Route 12 Watertown (13601) ***(G-16675)***
Watertown Daily Times, Watertown *Also called Northern NY Newspapers Corp* ***(G-16668)***
Watkins Welding and Mch Sp Inc.....914 949-6168
87 Westmoreland Ave White Plains (10606) ***(G-17181)***
Watson Adventures LLC.....212 564-8293
330 W 38th St Rm 407 New York (10018) ***(G-12598)***
Watson Bowman Acme Corp.....716 691-8162
95 Pineview Dr Amherst (14228) ***(G-271)***
Watson Productions LLC.....516 334-9766
740 Old Willets Path # 400 Hauppauge (11788) ***(G-6230)***
Wave of Long Island, The, Rockaway Beach *Also called Wave Publishing Co Inc* ***(G-14783)***
Wave Publishing Co Inc.....718 634-4000
8808 Rockaway Beach Blvd Rockaway Beach (11693) ***(G-14783)***
Waverly Iron Corp.....631 732-2800
25 Commercial Blvd Medford (11763) ***(G-8262)***
Wavodyne Therapeutics Inc.....954 632-6630
150 Lucius Gordon Dr West Henrietta (14586) ***(G-16900)***
Way Out Toys Inc.....212 689-9094
230 5th Ave Ste 800 New York (10001) ***(G-12599)***
Waymor1 Inc (PA).....518 677-8511
879 State Rte 22 Cambridge (12816) ***(G-3310)***
Waymor1 Inc.....518 677-8511
Hc 22 Cambridge (12816) ***(G-3311)***
Wayne County Mail, Webster *Also called Empire State Weeklies Inc* ***(G-16723)***
Wayne Decorators Inc.....718 529-4200
14409 Rockaway Blvd Apt 1 Jamaica (11436) ***(G-6963)***
Wayne Integrated Tech Corp.....631 242-0213
160 Rodeo Dr Edgewood (11717) ***(G-4620)***
Wayne Printing Inc.....914 761-2400
70 W Red Oak Ln Fl 4 White Plains (10604) ***(G-17182)***
Wayne Printing & Lithographic, White Plains *Also called Wayne Printing Inc* ***(G-17182)***
Waynes Welding Inc (PA).....315 768-6146
66 Calder Ave Yorkville (13495) ***(G-17530)***
Wayuga Community Newspapers (PA).....315 754-6229
6784 Main St Red Creek (13143) ***(G-14027)***
Wayuga Community Newspapers.....315 594-2506
12039 E Main St Wolcott (14590) ***(G-17281)***
Wayuga News, Red Creek *Also called Wayuga Community Newspapers* ***(G-14027)***
Wcd Window Coverings Inc.....845 336-4511
1711 Ulster Ave Lake Katrine (12449) ***(G-7271)***
We Work.....877 673-6628
1 Little West 12th St New York (10014) ***(G-12600)***
Wea International Inc (HQ).....212 275-1300
75 Rockefeller Plz New York (10019) ***(G-12601)***
Wear Abouts Apparel Inc.....212 827-0888
260 W 36th St Rm 602 New York (10018) ***(G-12602)***
Weather Products Corporation.....315 474-8593
102 W Division St Fl 1 Syracuse (13204) ***(G-16069)***
Weather Tight Exteriors.....631 375-5108
8 Woodbrook Dr Ridge (11961) ***(G-14095)***
Weatherproof, Bay Shore *Also called David Peyser Sportswear Inc* ***(G-691)***
Weaver Machine & Tool Co Inc.....315 253-4422
44 York St Auburn (13021) ***(G-528)***
Weaver Wind Energy LLC.....607 379-9463
7 Union St Freeville (13068) ***(G-5437)***
Web Associates Inc.....716 883-3377
1255 Niagara St Buffalo (14213) ***(G-3249)***
Web Graphics, Queensbury *Also called Amsterdam Printing & Litho Inc* ***(G-13988)***
Web Seal Inc (PA).....585 546-1320
15 Oregon St Rochester (14605) ***(G-14758)***
Web-Tech Packaging Inc.....716 684-4520
500 Commerce Pkwy Lancaster (14086) ***(G-7347)***
Webb-Mason Inc.....716 276-8792
300 Airborne Pkwy Ste 210 Buffalo (14225) ***(G-3250)***
Weber Intl Packg Co LLC.....518 561-8282
318 Cornelia St Plattsburgh (12901) ***(G-13707)***
Weber's Mach Shop, Troy *Also called Charles V Weber Machine Shop* ***(G-16229)***
Weber-Knapp Company (PA).....716 484-9135
441 Chandler St Jamestown (14701) ***(G-7043)***
Webster Ontrio Wlwrth Pnnysver.....585 265-3620
164 E Main St Webster (14580) ***(G-16741)***
Webster Printing Corporation.....585 671-1533
46 North Ave Webster (14580) ***(G-16742)***
Wecare Organics LLC.....315 689-1937
9293 Bonta Bridge Rd Jordan (13080) ***(G-7131)***
Weco Metal Products, Ontario *Also called Dj Acquisition Management Corp* ***(G-13200)***
Wedco Fabrications Inc.....718 852-6330
2016 130th St College Point (11356) ***(G-3810)***
Wedding Gown Preservation Co.....607 748-7999
707 North St Endicott (13760) ***(G-4834)***
Wedel Sign Company Inc.....631 727-4577
705 W Main St Riverhead (11901) ***(G-14159)***
Week Publications, The, New York *Also called Dennis Publishing Inc* ***(G-9847)***
Weekly Ajkal.....718 565-2100
3707 74th St Ste 8 Jackson Heights (11372) ***(G-6889)***
Weekly Bornomal, Jackson Heights *Also called Bornomala USA Inc* ***(G-6887)***
Weekly Business News Corp.....212 689-5888
274 Madison Ave Rm 1101 New York (10016) ***(G-12603)***
Weeks & Reichel Printing Inc.....631 589-1443
131 Railroad Ave Sayville (11782) ***(G-15215)***
Wego International Floors LLC.....516 487-3510
239 Great Neck Rd Great Neck (11021) ***(G-5849)***
Weico Wire & Cable Inc.....631 254-2970
161 Rodeo Dr Edgewood (11717) ***(G-4621)***
Weicro Graphics Inc.....631 253-3360
95 Mahan St West Babylon (11704) ***(G-16840)***
Weider Publications LLC.....212 545-4800
1 Park Ave Fl 10 New York (10016) ***(G-12604)***
Weighing & Systems Tech Inc.....518 274-2797
274 2nd St Troy (12180) ***(G-16263)***
Weisbeck Publishing Printing.....716 937-9226
13200 Broadway St Alden (14004) ***(G-186)***
Weisco Inc.....212 575-8989
246 W 38th St Fl 6 New York (10018) ***(G-12605)***
Weiss Instruments Inc.....631 207-1200
905 Waverly Ave Holtsville (11742) ***(G-6514)***
Wel Made Enterprises Inc.....631 752-1238
1630 New Hwy Farmingdale (11735) ***(G-5141)***
Welch Allyn Inc.....315 685-4100
4341 State Street Rd Skaneateles Falls (13153) ***(G-15471)***
Welch Allyn Inc (HQ).....315 685-4100
4341 State Street Rd Skaneateles Falls (13153) ***(G-15472)***
Welch Allyn Inc.....315 685-4347
4619 Jordan Rd Skaneateles Falls (13153) ***(G-15473)***
Welch Foods Inc A Cooperative.....716 326-5252
2 S Portage St Westfield (14787) ***(G-17053)***
Welch Foods Inc A Cooperative.....716 326-3131
100 N Portage St Westfield (14787) ***(G-17054)***
Welch Machine Inc.....585 647-3578
961 Lyell Ave Bldg 1-6 Rochester (14606) ***(G-14759)***
Welcome Magazine Inc.....716 839-3121
4511 Harlem Rd Amherst (14226) ***(G-272)***
Welcome Rain Publishers LLC.....212 686-1909
230 5th Ave Ste 1806 New York (10001) ***(G-12606)***
Weld-Built Body Co Inc.....631 643-9700
276 Long Island Ave Wyandanch (11798) ***(G-17378)***
Weldcomputer Corporation.....518 283-2897
105 Jordan Rd Ste 1 Troy (12180) ***(G-16264)***
Welded Tube Usa Inc.....716 828-1111
2537 Hamburg Tpke Lackawanna (14218) ***(G-7250)***
Welding and Brazing Svcs Inc.....607 397-1009
2761 County Highway 26 Richfield Springs (13439) ***(G-14062)***
Welding Chapter of New York.....212 481-1496
44 W 28th St Fl 12 New York (10001) ***(G-12607)***

ALPHABETIC

Welding Metallurgy Inc (HQ)...631 253-0500
110 Plant Ave Hauppauge (11788) *(G-6231)*
Welding Metallurgy Inc...631 253-0500
110 Plant Ave Hauppauge (11788) *(G-6232)*
Weldrite Closures Inc...585 429-8790
2292 Innovation Way Rochester (14624) *(G-14760)*
Well-Made Toy Mfg Corporation...718 381-4225
146 Soundview Dr Port Washington (11050) *(G-13871)*
Wellmill LLC...631 465-9245
141 Central Ave Ste B Farmingdale (11735) *(G-5142)*
Wellquest International Inc (PA)...212 689-9094
230 5th Ave Ste 800 New York (10001) *(G-12608)*
Wells Rugs Inc...516 676-2056
44 Sea Cliff Ave Glen Cove (11542) *(G-5631)*
Wells, George Ruggery, Glen Cove *Also called Wells Rugs Inc (G-5631)*
Wellspring Corp (PA)...212 529-5454
54a Ludlow St New York (10002) *(G-12609)*
Wellspring Omni Holdings Corp...212 318-9800
390 Park Ave Fl 6 New York (10022) *(G-12610)*
Wellsville Daily Reporter, Wellsville *Also called Seneca Media Inc (G-16758)*
Welsh Gold Stampers Inc...718 984-5031
44 Lenzie St Staten Island (10312) *(G-15754)*
Wemco Casting LLC...631 563-8050
20 Jules Ct Ste 2 Bohemia (11716) *(G-1156)*
Wen Hwa Printing, Flushing *Also called Global Graphics Inc (G-5244)*
Wendels Poultry Farm...716 592-2299
12466 Vaughn St East Concord (14055) *(G-4386)*
Wendt Corporation...716 391-1200
2555 Walden Ave Buffalo (14225) *(G-3251)*
Wendys Auto Express Inc...845 624-6100
121 Main St Nanuet (10954) *(G-8762)*
Wenig Company, The, Amityville *Also called Portfab LLC (G-322)*
Wenig Corporation...718 542-3600
230 Manida St Fl 2 Bronx (10474) *(G-1493)*
Wenner Bread Products Inc (PA)...800 869-6262
33 Rajon Rd Bayport (11705) *(G-761)*
Wenner Media LLC (PA)...212 484-1616
1290 Ave Of The Amer Fl 2 New York (10104) *(G-12611)*
Wercs Ltd...518 640-9200
23 British American Blvd # 2 Latham (12110) *(G-7384)*
Were Forms Inc...585 482-4400
500 Helendale Rd Ste 190 Rochester (14609) *(G-14761)*
Werlatone Inc...845 278-2220
17 Jon Barrett Rd Patterson (12563) *(G-13446)*
Werma (usa) Inc...315 414-0200
6731 Collamer Rd Ste 1 East Syracuse (13057) *(G-4580)*
Werner Brothers Electric Inc...518 377-3056
677 Riverview Rd Rexford (12148) *(G-14055)*
Wessie Machine Inc...315 926-4060
5229 Steel Point Rd Marion (14505) *(G-8104)*
West African Movies...718 731-2190
1692 Webster Ave Bronx (10457) *(G-1494)*
West End Iron Works Inc...518 456-1105
4254 Albany St Albany (12205) *(G-149)*
West End Journal, Far Rockaway *Also called Empire Publishing Inc (G-4921)*
West Falls Machine Co Inc...716 655-0440
11692 E Main Rd East Aurora (14052) *(G-4380)*
West Falls Machine Co 1, East Aurora *Also called West Falls Machine Co Inc (G-4380)*
West Gluers...631 232-1235
120 Ricefield Ln Ste 200 Hauppauge (11788) *(G-6233)*
West Herr Automotive Group, Hamburg *Also called Kustom Korner (G-5933)*
West Information Center, New York *Also called West Publishing Corporation (G-12614)*
West Internet Trading Company...415 484-5848
47 Great Jones St Fl 5 New York (10012) *(G-12612)*
West Metal Works Inc...716 895-4900
68 Hayes Pl Buffalo (14210) *(G-3252)*
West Pacific Enterprises Corp...212 564-6800
260 W 39th St Rm 5w New York (10018) *(G-12613)*
West Publishing Corporation...212 922-1920
530 5th Ave Fl 7 New York (10036) *(G-12614)*
West Seneca Bee Inc...716 632-4700
5564 Main St Williamsville (14221) *(G-17259)*
Westbrook Machinery, Lockport *Also called Ted Westbrook (G-7618)*
Westbury Times...516 747-8282
132 E 2nd St Mineola (11501) *(G-8539)*
Westchester County Bus Jurnl, White Plains *Also called Westfair Communications Inc (G-17186)*
Westchester Law Journal Inc...914 948-0715
199 Main St Ste 301 White Plains (10601) *(G-17183)*
Westchester Mailing Service...914 948-1116
39 Westmoreland Ave Fl 2 White Plains (10606) *(G-17184)*
Westchester Modular Homes Inc...845 832-9400
30 Reagans Mill Rd Wingdale (12594) *(G-17275)*
Westchester Signs Inc...914 666-7446
145 Kisco Ave Mount Kisco (10549) *(G-8646)*
Westchester Technologies Inc...914 736-1034
8 John Walsh Blvd Ste 311 Peekskill (10566) *(G-13486)*
Westchester Wine Warehouse LLC...914 824-1400
53 Tarrytown Rd Ste 1 White Plains (10607) *(G-17185)*
Westchster Crankshaft Grinding, East Elmhurst *Also called Westchstr Crnkshft Grndng (G-4400)*
Westchstr Crnkshft Grndng...718 651-3900
3263 110th St East Elmhurst (11369) *(G-4400)*
Westcode Incorporated...607 766-9881
2226 Airport Rd Binghamton (13905) *(G-959)*
Western Bituminous, Rochester *Also called Suit-Kote Corporation (G-14706)*
Western Blending Inc...518 356-6650
1411 Rottrdm Indstl Park Schenectady (12306) *(G-15312)*
Western Edition, Westhampton Beach *Also called Southampton Town Newspapers (G-17061)*
Western New York Energy LLC...585 798-9693
4141 Bates Rd Medina (14103) *(G-8284)*
Western New York Family Mag...716 836-3486
3147 Delaware Ave Ste B Buffalo (14217) *(G-3253)*
Western Oil and Gas JV Inc...914 967-4758
7 Mccullough Pl Rye (10580) *(G-15069)*
Western Queens Gazette, Long Island City *Also called Service Advertising Group Inc (G-7875)*
Western Synthetic Felt, Jericho *Also called Lightron Corporation (G-7075)*
Westfair Communications Inc...914 694-3600
3 Westchester Park Dr G7 White Plains (10604) *(G-17186)*
Westfield Publication, Westfield *Also called Quality Guides (G-17049)*
Westinghouse A Brake Tech Corp...518 561-0044
72 Arizona Ave Plattsburgh (12903) *(G-13708)*
Westinghouse A Brake Tech Corp...914 347-8650
4 Warehouse Ln Ste 144 Elmsford (10523) *(G-4793)*
Westmail Press, White Plains *Also called Westchester Mailing Service (G-17184)*
Westmoor Ltd...315 363-1500
906 W Hamilton Ave Sherrill (13461) *(G-15410)*
Westmore Litho Corp...718 361-9403
4017 22nd St Long Island City (11101) *(G-7920)*
Westmore Litho Printing Co, Long Island City *Also called Westmore Litho Corp (G-7920)*
Westmore News Inc...914 939-6864
38 Broad St Ste 1 Port Chester (10573) *(G-13761)*
Westpoint Home LLC (HQ)...212 930-2074
28 E 28th St Rm 8 New York (10016) *(G-12615)*
Westpoint International Inc (HQ)...212 930-2044
28 E 28th St Bsmt 2 New York (10016) *(G-12616)*
Westprint Inc...212 989-3805
873 Washington St New York (10014) *(G-12617)*
Westrock - Solvay Llc (HQ)...315 484-9050
53 Indl Dr Syracuse (13204) *(G-16070)*
Westrock - Southern Cont LLC...315 487-6111
100 Southern Dr Camillus (13031) *(G-3327)*
Westrock Cp LLC...770 448-2193
45 Campion Rd New Hartford (13413) *(G-8813)*
Westrock CP LLC...315 484-9050
53 Industrial Dr Syracuse (13204) *(G-16071)*
Westrock CP LLC...716 694-1000
51 Robinson St North Tonawanda (14120) *(G-13006)*
Westrock CP LLC...716 692-6510
51 Robinson St North Tonawanda (14120) *(G-13007)*
Westrock Mwv LLC...212 688-5000
299 Park Ave Fl 13 New York (10171) *(G-12618)*
Westrock Rkt Company...330 296-5155
140 W Industry Ct Deer Park (11729) *(G-4226)*
Westrock Rkt Company...770 448-2193
53 Indl Dr Syracuse (13204) *(G-16072)*
Westrock Rkt Company...770 448-2193
4914 W Genesee St Camillus (13031) *(G-3328)*
Westron Corporation...516 678-2300
18 Neil Ct Oceanside (11572) *(G-13105)*
Westron Lighting, Oceanside *Also called Westron Corporation (G-13105)*
Westsea Publishing Co Inc...631 420-1110
149d Allen Blvd Ste D Farmingdale (11735) *(G-5143)*
Westside Clothing Co Inc...212 273-9898
240 W 35th St Ste 1000 New York (10001) *(G-12619)*
Westside News Inc...585 352-3411
1835 N Union St Spencerport (14559) *(G-15574)*
Westypo Printers Inc...914 737-7394
540 Harrison Ave Peekskill (10566) *(G-13487)*
Wet & Wild Pools & Spas, Brooklyn *Also called Polytech Pool Mfg Inc (G-2428)*
Wet Paint, New York *Also called Wetpaintcom Inc (G-12620)*
Wetherall Contracting NY Inc...718 894-7011
8312 Penelope Ave Ste 101 Middle Village (11379) *(G-8417)*
Wetpaintcom Inc...206 859-6300
902 Broadway Fl 11 New York (10010) *(G-12620)*
Wew Container, Brooklyn *Also called Inland Paper Products Corp (G-2108)*
Wey Inc...212 532-3299
21 W 39th St Fl 6 New York (10018) *(G-12621)*
WF Lake Corp...518 798-9934
65 Park Rd Queensbury (12804) *(G-14014)*
Wg Sheet Metal Corp...718 235-3093
341 Amber St Brooklyn (11208) *(G-2746)*
WGB Industries Inc...716 693-5527
233 Fillmore Ave Ste 23 Tonawanda (14150) *(G-16214)*
Whalebone Creative, Montauk *Also called Jesse Joeckel (G-8588)*
Whalens Horseradish Products...518 587-6404
1710 Route 29 Galway (12074) *(G-5484)*
Wham 1180 AM, Rochester *Also called Iheartcommunications Inc (G-14445)*

ALPHABETIC

ALPHABETIC SECTION
Win Set Technologies LLC

Whats Next Manufacturing Inc 585 492-1014
4 Rule Dr Arcade (14009) *(G-402)*
Whats The Big Idea, Huntington Station *Also called Wtbi Inc (G-6729)*
Wheel & Tire Depot Ex Corp 914 375-2100
584 Yonkers Ave Yonkers (10704) *(G-17498)*
Wheeler/Rinstar Ltd 212 244-1130
242 W 30th St New York (10001) *(G-12622)*
Whentech LLC (HQ) 212 571-0042
55 E 52nd St Fl 40 New York (10055) *(G-12623)*
Whirlwind Music Distrs Inc 585 663-8820
99 Ling Rd Rochester (14612) *(G-14762)*
Whispr Group Inc 212 924-3979
45 Main St Ste 1036 Brooklyn (11201) *(G-2747)*
Whistle Stop Bakery, Rockville Centre *Also called Megamatt Inc (G-14794)*
Whitacre Engineering Company 315 622-1075
4522 Wetzel Rd Liverpool (13090) *(G-7556)*
White Coat Inc 212 575-8880
580 5th Ave Ste 501 New York (10036) *(G-12624)*
White Coffee Corp 718 204-7900
1835 38th St Astoria (11105) *(G-462)*
White Eagle Packing Co Inc 518 374-4366
922 Congress St Schenectady (12303) *(G-15313)*
White Gate Holdings Inc (PA) 212 564-3266
22 W 38th St Fl 6 New York (10018) *(G-12625)*
White House Cabinet Shop LLC 607 674-9358
11 Knapp St Sherburne (13460) *(G-15399)*
White Label Partners LLC 917 445-6650
250 Mercer St Apt B1205 New York (10012) *(G-12626)*
White Plains Drapery Uphl Inc 914 381-0908
801 E Boston Post Rd Mamaroneck (10543) *(G-8050)*
White Plains Marble Inc 914 347-6000
186 E Main St Elmsford (10523) *(G-4794)*
White Plains Rubber Stamp Name 914 949-1900
39 Westmrland Ave Ste 105 White Plains (10606) *(G-17187)*
White Workroom Inc 212 941-5910
40 W 27th St Fl 11 New York (10001) *(G-12627)*
Whiteboard Ventures Inc 855 972-6346
31 W 34th St Ste 7020 New York (10001) *(G-12628)*
Whitehall Times, Granville *Also called Manchester Newspaper Inc (G-5775)*
Whitesboro Spring & Alignment (PA) 315 736-4441
247 Oriskany Blvd Whitesboro (13492) *(G-17198)*
Whitesboro Spring Svce, Whitesboro *Also called Whitesboro Spring & Alignment (G-17198)*
Whitestone Pharmacy, Whitestone *Also called Tocare LLC (G-17215)*
Whitewall Magazine, New York *Also called Sky Art Media Inc (G-12094)*
Whitford Development Inc 631 471-7711
646 Main St Ste 301 Port Jefferson (11777) *(G-13780)*
Whiting Door Mfg Corp (PA) 716 542-5427
113 Cedar St Akron (14001) *(G-30)*
Whiting Door Mfg Corp 716 542-3070
13550 Bloomingdale Rd Akron (14001) *(G-31)*
Whitley East LLC 718 403-0050
Brooklyn Navy Yd Bg 2 Fl Brooklyn (11205) *(G-2748)*
Whitney Boin Studio Inc 914 377-4385
42 Warburton Ave Ste 1 Yonkers (10701) *(G-17499)*
Whitney Foods Inc 718 291-3333
15504 Liberty Ave Jamaica (11433) *(G-6964)*
Whitsons Food Svc Bronx Corp 631 424-2700
1800 Motor Pkwy Islandia (11749) *(G-6804)*
Whittall & Shon (PA) 212 594-2626
1201 Broadway Ste 904a New York (10001) *(G-12629)*
Whittier Publications Inc 516 432-8120
3115 Long Beach Rd # 301 Oceanside (11572) *(G-13106)*
Wholesale Mulch & Sawdust Inc 607 687-2637
3711 Waverly Rd Owego (13827) *(G-13362)*
Wholesale Window Warehouse, Oceanside *Also called Express Building Supply Inc (G-13079)*
Wicked Smart LLC 518 459-2855
700 5th Ave Watervliet (12189) *(G-16692)*
Wicked Spoon Inc 646 335-2890
127 W 24th St Fl 6 New York (10011) *(G-12630)*
Wickers Performance Wear, Commack *Also called Wickers Sportswear Inc (G-3848)*
Wickers Sportswear Inc (PA) 631 543-1700
340 Veterans Memorial Hwy # 1 Commack (11725) *(G-3848)*
Wide Flange Inc 718 492-8705
176 27th St Brooklyn (11232) *(G-2749)*
Widetronix Inc 607 330-4752
950 Danby Rd Ste 139 Ithaca (14850) *(G-6885)*
Widex International, Hauppauge *Also called Widex Usa Inc (G-6234)*
Widex Usa Inc (HQ) 718 360-1000
185 Commerce Dr Hauppauge (11788) *(G-6234)*
Widmer Time Recorder Company 212 227-0405
27 Park Pl Rm 219 New York (10007) *(G-12631)*
Wiggby Precision Machine Corp 718 439-6900
140 58th St Ste 56 Brooklyn (11220) *(G-2750)*
Wikoff Color Corporation 585 458-0653
686 Pullman Ave Rochester (14615) *(G-14763)*
Wil-Nic, Freeport *Also called Edr Industries Inc (G-5395)*
Wilbar International Inc 631 951-9800
50 Cabot Ct Hauppauge (11788) *(G-6235)*
Wilbedone Inc 607 756-8813
1133 State Route 222 Cortland (13045) *(G-4047)*
Wilco Finishing Corp 718 417-6405
1288 Willoughby Ave Brooklyn (11237) *(G-2751)*
Wilco Industries Inc 631 676-2593
788 Marconi Ave Ronkonkoma (11779) *(G-15001)*
Wilcro Inc 716 632-4204
90 Earhart Dr Ste 19 Buffalo (14221) *(G-3254)*
Wild Works Incorporated 716 891-4197
30 Railroad Ave Albany (12205) *(G-150)*
Wilda, Long Island City *Also called Import-Export Corporation (G-7764)*
Wildcat Territory Inc 718 361-6726
4401 21st St Ste 202 Long Island City (11101) *(G-7921)*
Wilder Manufacturing Co Inc 516 222-0433
439 Oak St Garden City (11530) *(G-5536)*
Willard Machine 716 885-1630
73 Forest Ave Buffalo (14213) *(G-3255)*
Willco Fine Art Ltd 718 935-9567
145 Nassau St Apt 9c New York (10038) *(G-12632)*
Willemin Macodel Incorporated 914 345-3504
10 Skyline Dr Ste 132 Hawthorne (10532) *(G-6256)*
William B Collins Company (HQ) 518 773-8272
8 E Fulton St Gloversville (12078) *(G-5729)*
William Boyd Printing Co Inc 518 339-5832
4 Weed Rd Ste 1 Latham (12110) *(G-7385)*
William Brooks Woodworking 718 495-9767
856 Saratoga Ave Brooklyn (11212) *(G-2752)*
William Byrd Press, New York *Also called Cadmus Journal Services Inc (G-9496)*
William Charles Prtg Co Inc 516 349-0900
7 Fairchild Ct Ste 100 Plainview (11803) *(G-13646)*
William E Williams Valve Corp 718 392-1660
3850 Review Ave Long Island City (11101) *(G-7922)*
William Goldberg Diamond Corp 212 980-4343
589 5th Ave Fl 14 New York (10017) *(G-12633)*
William H Jackson Company 718 784-4482
3629 23rd St Long Island City (11106) *(G-7923)*
William H Sadlier Inc (PA) 212 233-3646
9 Pine St New York (10005) *(G-12634)*
William H Shapiro 212 263-7037
530 1st Ave Ste 3e New York (10016) *(G-12635)*
William Harvey Studio Inc 718 599-4343
214 N 8th St Brooklyn (11211) *(G-2753)*
William J Blume Worldwide Svcs 914 723-6185
732 Route 9p Saratoga Springs (12866) *(G-15177)*
William J Kline & Son Inc (PA) 518 843-1100
1 Venner Rd Amsterdam (12010) *(G-374)*
William J Ryan 585 392-6200
1365 Hamlin Parma Townlne Hilton (14468) *(G-6421)*
William Kanes Mfg Corp 718 346-1515
23 Alabama Ave Brooklyn (11207) *(G-2754)*
William Moon Iron Works Inc 518 943-3861
80 Main St Catskill (12414) *(G-3434)*
William R Shoemaker Inc 716 649-0511
399 Pleasant Ave Hamburg (14075) *(G-5945)*
William S Hein & Co Inc (PA) 716 882-2600
2350 N Forest Rd Ste 14a Getzville (14068) *(G-5606)*
William S Hein & Co Inc 716 882-2600
1575 Main St Buffalo (14209) *(G-3256)*
William Somerville Maintenance 212 534-4600
166 E 124th St New York (10035) *(G-12636)*
William Ward Logging 518 946-7826
Valley Rd Jay (12941) *(G-7055)*
Williams Tool Inc 315 737-7226
9372 Elm St Chadwicks (13319) *(G-3531)*
Williams-Sonoma Store 154, New York *Also called Williams-Sonoma Stores Inc (G-12637)*
Williams-Sonoma Stores Inc 212 633-2203
110 7th Ave New York (10011) *(G-12637)*
Williamsburg Bulletin 718 387-0123
136 Ross St Brooklyn (11211) *(G-2755)*
Williamson Law Book Co 585 924-3400
790 Canning Pkwy Ste 2 Victor (14564) *(G-16514)*
Willis Mc Donald Co Inc 212 366-1526
44 W 62nd St Ph A New York (10023) *(G-12638)*
Willow Creek Winery, Silver Creek *Also called Chautauqua Wine Company Inc (G-15447)*
Wilmax Usa LLC 917 388-2790
315 5th Ave Rm 505 New York (10016) *(G-12639)*
Wilmington Products USA, Roslyn *Also called Northwest Company LLC (G-15022)*
Wilson & Wilson Group 212 729-4736
6514 110th St Forest Hills (11375) *(G-5330)*
Wilson Electroplating, Binghamton *Also called G J C Ltd Inc (G-917)*
Wilson N Wilson Group & RES, Forest Hills *Also called Wilson & Wilson Group (G-5330)*
Wilson Picture Frames, West Hempstead *Also called Interntonal Consmr Connections (G-16856)*
Wilson Press LLC 315 568-9693
56 Miller St Seneca Falls (13148) *(G-15372)*
Wilsonart Intl Holdings LLC 516 935-6980
999 S Oyster Bay Rd # 3305 Bethpage (11714) *(G-879)*
Wilston Enterprises Inc 716 483-1411
121 Jackson Ave Jamestown (14701) *(G-7044)*
Wilt Industries Inc 518 548-4961
2452 State Route 8 Lake Pleasant (12108) *(G-7277)*
Win Set Technologies LLC 631 234-7077
2364 Middle Country Rd Centereach (11720) *(G-3474)*

ALPHABETIC

(PA)=Parent Co (HQ)=Headquarters (DH)=Div Headquarters
2017 Harris
New York Manufacturers Directory
1095

Win Wood Cabinetry Inc ALPHABETIC SECTION

Win Wood Cabinetry Inc 516 304-2216
200 Forest Dr Ste 7 Greenvale (11548) ***(G-5883)***

Win-Holt Equipment Corp (PA) 516 222-0335
20 Crossways Park Dr N # 205 Woodbury (11797) ***(G-17303)***

Win-Holt Equipment Corp 516 222-0433
439 Oak St Ste 1 Garden City (11530) ***(G-5537)***

Win-Holt Equipment Group, Woodbury *Also called Win-Holt Equipment Corp* ***(G-17303)***

Winchester Optical Company (HQ) 607 734-4251
1935 Lake St Elmira (14901) ***(G-4705)***

Wind Products Inc 212 292-3135
20 Jay St Ste 936 Brooklyn (11201) ***(G-2756)***

Wind Solutions LLC 518 813-8029
251 County Road 156 Esperance (12066) ***(G-4840)***

Window Rama Enterprises Inc 631 462-9054
6333 Jericho Tpke Ste 11 Commack (11725) ***(G-3849)***

Window Tech Systems Inc 518 899-9000
15 Old Stonebreak Rd Ballston Spa (12020) ***(G-611)***

Window Technologies LLC 402 464-0202
555 5th Ave Fl 14 New York (10017) ***(G-12640)***

Window Workshops Inc 716 876-9981
6040 N Bailey Ave Ste 1 Buffalo (14226) ***(G-3257)***

Window-Fix Inc 718 854-3475
331 37th St Fl 1 Brooklyn (11232) ***(G-2757)***

Windowcraft Inc 516 294-3580
77 2nd Ave Garden City Park (11040) ***(G-5544)***

Windowman Inc (usa) 718 246-2626
460 Kingsland Ave Brooklyn (11222) ***(G-2758)***

Windows Media Publishing LLC 917 732-7892
369 Remsen Ave Brooklyn (11212) ***(G-2759)***

Windowtex Inc 877 294-3580
77 2nd Ave Garden City Park (11040) ***(G-5545)***

Windsor Technology LLC 585 461-2500
1527 Lyell Ave Rochester (14606) ***(G-14764)***

Windsor United Industries LLC 607 655-3300
10 Park St Windsor (13865) ***(G-17273)***

Wine & Spirits Magazine Inc (PA) 212 695-4660
2 W 32nd St Ste 601 New York (10001) ***(G-12641)***

Wine Group Inc 716 326-3151
85 Bourne St Westfield (14787) ***(G-17055)***

Wine Market 516 328-8800
2337 New Hyde Park Rd New Hyde Park (11042) ***(G-8872)***

Wine On Line International 212 755-4363
400 E 59th St Apt 9f New York (10022) ***(G-12642)***

Wine Services Inc 631 722-3800
1129 Cross River Dr Ste A Riverhead (11901) ***(G-14160)***

Wineracksccom Inc 845 658-7181
819 Route 32 Tillson (12486) ***(G-16130)***

Winesoft International Corp 914 400-6247
503 S Broadway Ste 220 Yonkers (10705) ***(G-17500)***

Wing Heung Noodle Inc 212 966-7496
144 Baxter St New York (10013) ***(G-12643)***

Wing Kei Noodle Inc 212 226-1644
102 Canal St New York (10002) ***(G-12644)***

Wing Tel Inc 347 508-5802
79 Madison Ave Fl 3 New York (10016) ***(G-12645)***

Winghing 8 Ltd 718 439-0021
6215 6th Ave Brooklyn (11220) ***(G-2760)***

Wink Acquisition Corp., New York *Also called Wink Labs Inc* ***(G-12647)***

Wink Inc 212 389-1382
606 W 28th St Fl 6 New York (10001) ***(G-12646)***

Wink Labs Inc (HQ) 916 717-0437
606 W 28th St Fl 7 New York (10001) ***(G-12647)***

Winn Manufacturing Inc 518 642-3515
12 Burtis Ave Granville (12832) ***(G-5782)***

Winner Press Inc 718 937-7715
4331 33rd St 1 Long Island City (11101) ***(G-7924)***

Winsight LLC 646 708-7309
90 Broad St Ste 402 New York (10004) ***(G-12648)***

Winson Surnamer Inc 718 729-8787
4402 11th St Ste 601 Long Island City (11101) ***(G-7925)***

Winter Water Factory 646 387-3247
191 33rd St Brooklyn (11232) ***(G-2761)***

Winterling, Eric Costumes, New York *Also called Eric Winterling Inc* ***(G-10056)***

Winters Instruments, Tonawanda *Also called Winters Instruments Inc* ***(G-16215)***

Winters Instruments Inc (HQ) 281 880-8607
600 Ensminger Rd Tonawanda (14150) ***(G-16215)***

Winters Railroad Service Inc 716 337-2668
11309 Sisson Hwy North Collins (14111) ***(G-12932)***

Winton Paving, Webster *Also called Mike Wilke* ***(G-16727)***

Wipesplus, Rye Brook *Also called Progressive Products LLC* ***(G-15074)***

Wired Coffee and Bagel Inc 518 506-3194
Rr 9 Malta (12020) ***(G-8022)***

Wired Up Electric Inc 845 878-3122
90 Harmony Rd Pawling (12564) ***(G-13453)***

Wireless Communications Inc 845 353-5921
4 Chemong Ct Nyack (10960) ***(G-13056)***

Wireless Generation Inc 212 213-8177
55 Washington St Ste 900 Brooklyn (11201) ***(G-2762)***

Wizard Equipment Inc 315 414-9999
10 Dwight Park Dr Ste 3 Syracuse (13209) ***(G-16073)***

Wizer Equipment, Rochester *Also called Woerner Industries Inc* ***(G-14765)***

Wizq Inc 586 381-9048
307 5th Ave Fl 8 New York (10016) ***(G-12649)***

Wl Concepts & Production Inc 516 538-5300
1 Bennington Ave Freeport (11520) ***(G-5434)***

Wlj Printers, White Plains *Also called Westchester Law Journal Inc* ***(G-17183)***

Wm E Martin and Sons Co Inc 516 605-2444
55 Bryant Ave Ste 300 Roslyn (11576) ***(G-15024)***

Wmg Acquisition Corp (HQ) 212 275-2000
75 Rockefeller Plz New York (10019) ***(G-12650)***

Wmw Machinery Company, Deer Park *Also called World LLC* ***(G-4229)***

Wny Jobs.com, Hamburg *Also called Jobs Weekly Inc* ***(G-5929)***

Wobbleworks Inc (PA) 415 987-1534
316 E 11th St Apt 3c New York (10003) ***(G-12651)***

Woerner Industries Inc 585 436-1934
485 Hague St Rochester (14606) ***(G-14765)***

Wok To Walk, New York *Also called Restaurant 570 8th Avenue LLC* ***(G-11844)***

Wolak Inc 315 839-5366
2360 King Rd Clayville (13322) ***(G-3691)***

Wolf X-Ray Corporation 631 242-9729
100 W Industry Ct Deer Park (11729) ***(G-4227)***

Wolf-TEC, Kingston *Also called Ludwig Holdings Corp* ***(G-7198)***

Wolfe Lumber Mill Inc 716 772-7750
8416 Ridge Rd Gasport (14067) ***(G-5560)***

Wolfe Publications Inc (PA) 585 394-0770
73 Buffalo St Canandaigua (14424) ***(G-3360)***

Wolff & Dungey Inc 315 475-2105
325 Temple St Syracuse (13202) ***(G-16074)***

Wolffer Estate Vineyard Inc 631 537-5106
139 Sagg Rd Sagaponack (11962) ***(G-15082)***

Wolffer Estate Winery, Sagaponack *Also called Wolffer Estate Vineyard Inc* ***(G-15082)***

Wolfgang B Gourmet Foods Inc 518 719-1727
117 Cauterskill Ave Catskill (12414) ***(G-3435)***

Wolo Mfg Corp 631 242-0333
1 Saxwood St Ste 1 Deer Park (11729) ***(G-4228)***

Wolski Wood Works Inc 718 577-9816
14134 78th Rd Apt 3c Flushing (11367) ***(G-5308)***

Wolters Kluwer US Inc 212 894-8920
111 8th Ave Fl 13 New York (10011) ***(G-12652)***

Wolters Kluwer US Inc 631 517-8060
400 W Main St Ste 244 Babylon (11702) ***(G-553)***

Womens E News Inc 212 244-1720
6 Barclay St Fl 6 New York (10007) ***(G-12653)***

Womens Health Care PC (PA) 718 850-0009
11311 Jamaica Ave Ste C Richmond Hill (11418) ***(G-14088)***

Womens Wear Daily, New York *Also called Fairchild Publications Inc* ***(G-10128)***

Won & Lee Inc 516 222-0712
971 Stewart Ave Garden City (11530) ***(G-5538)***

Wonder Natural Foods Corp (PA) 631 726-4433
30 Blank Ln Water Mill (11976) ***(G-16607)***

Wonder Products, Middletown *Also called Advanced Enterprises Inc* ***(G-8425)***

Wonderly Company, The, Kingston *Also called Northast Coml Win Trtments Inc* ***(G-7203)***

Wonton Food Inc 718 784-8178
5210 37th St Long Island City (11101) ***(G-7926)***

Wonton Food Inc (PA) 718 628-6868
220 Moore St 222 Brooklyn (11206) ***(G-2763)***

Wonton Food Inc 212 677-8865
183 E Broadway New York (10002) ***(G-12654)***

Wood & Hyde Leather Co Inc 518 725-7105
68 Wood St Gloversville (12078) ***(G-5730)***

Wood Design, Peekskill *Also called W Designe Inc* ***(G-13484)***

Wood Etc Inc 315 484-9663
1175 State Fair Blvd # 3 Syracuse (13209) ***(G-16075)***

Wood Floor Expo Inc 212 472-0671
426 E 73rd St Frnt 1 New York (10021) ***(G-12655)***

Wood Innovations of Suffolk 631 698-2345
266 Middle Island Rd # 8 Medford (11763) ***(G-8263)***

Wood Tex Products LLC 607 243-5141
3700 Route 14 Himrod (14842) ***(G-6423)***

Wood-Tex Products, Himrod *Also called Lapp Management Corp* ***(G-6422)***

Woodards Concrete Products Inc 845 361-3471
629 Lybolt Rd Bullville (10915) ***(G-3263)***

Woodbine Products Inc 631 586-3770
110 Plant Ave Hauppauge (11788) ***(G-6236)***

Woodbury Cmmon Premium Outlets, Central Valley *Also called Sarar Usa Inc* ***(G-3526)***

Woodbury Printing Plus + Inc 845 928-6610
96 Turner Rd Central Valley (10917) ***(G-3529)***

Woodbury Systems Group Inc 516 364-2653
30 Glenn Dr Woodbury (11797) ***(G-17304)***

Woodbury Vineyards Inc 716 679-9463
3215 S Roberts Rd Fredonia (14063) ***(G-5377)***

Woodcock Brothers Brewing Comp 716 333-4000
638 Lake St Wilson (14172) ***(G-17270)***

Woodcraft, Rochester *Also called Aces Over Eights Inc* ***(G-14169)***

Wooden Boatworks 631 477-6507
190 Sterling St Unit 2 Greenport (11944) ***(G-5878)***

Woodfalls Industries 518 236-7201
434 Burke Rd Plattsburgh (12901) ***(G-13709)***

Woodmaster Industries, Jamaica *Also called Abbott Industries Inc* ***(G-6891)***

Woodmere Fabrics Inc 212 695-0144
35 W 35th St New York (10001) ***(G-12656)***

ALPHABETIC

ALPHABETIC SECTION Xerox Corporation

Woodmotif Inc...516 564-8325
42 Chasner St Hempstead (11550) *(G-6289)*
Woodmotif Cabinetry, Hempstead *Also called Woodmotif Inc (G-6289)*
Woods Knife Corporation...516 798-4972
19 Brooklyn Ave Massapequa (11758) *(G-8184)*
Woods Machine and Tool LLC...607 699-3253
150 Howell St Nichols (13812) *(G-12892)*
Woodside Decorator, Staten Island *Also called All Signs (G-15635)*
Woodside Granite Industries (PA)...585 589-6500
13890 Ridge Rd W Albion (14411) *(G-171)*
Woodstock Times, Kingston *Also called Ulster Publishing Co Inc (G-7219)*
Woodtronics Inc...914 962-5205
1661 Front St Ste 3 Yorktown Heights (10598) *(G-17521)*
Woodward/White Inc...718 509-6082
45 Main St Ste 820 Brooklyn (11201) *(G-2764)*
Woolmark Americas Inc...347 767-3160
110 E 25th St Fl 3 New York (10010) *(G-12657)*
WOOLMARK COMPANY, THE, New York *Also called Woolmark Americas Inc (G-12657)*
Wordingham Machine Co Inc...585 924-2294
515 Lee Rd Rochester (14606) *(G-14766)*
Wordingham Technologies, Rochester *Also called Wordingham Machine Co Inc (G-14766)*
Wordwise Inc...914 232-5366
1 Brady Ln Katonah (10536) *(G-7135)*
Workers Vanguard...212 732-7862
299 Broadway Ste 318 New York (10007) *(G-12658)*
Working Family Solutions Inc...845 802-6182
359 Washington Avenue Ext Saugerties (12477) *(G-15198)*
Working Mother Media Inc...212 351-6400
2 Park Ave Fl 10 New York (10016) *(G-12659)*
Workman Publishing Co Inc (PA)...212 254-5900
225 Varick St Fl 9 New York (10014) *(G-12660)*
Workman Publishing Co Inc...212 254-5900
708 Broadway Fl 6 New York (10003) *(G-12661)*
Workplace Interiors LLC...585 425-7420
400 Packetts Lndg Fairport (14450) *(G-4887)*
Workshop Art Fabrication...845 331-0385
117 Tremper Ave Kingston (12401) *(G-7225)*
Worksman Cycles, Ozone Park *Also called Worksman Trading Corp (G-13387)*
Worksman Trading Corp...718 322-2000
9415 100th St Ozone Park (11416) *(G-13387)*
World Business Media LLC...212 344-0759
4770 Sunrise Hwy Ste 105 Massapequa Park (11762) *(G-8191)*
World Cheese Co Inc...718 965-1700
178 28th St Brooklyn (11232) *(G-2765)*
World Company...718 551-8282
3533 149th St 119 Flushing (11354) *(G-5309)*
World Guide Publishing...800 331-7840
1271 Ave Of The Americas New York (10020) *(G-12662)*
World Journal Book Store, Flushing *Also called World Journal LLC (G-5310)*
World Journal LLC (HQ)...718 746-8889
14107 20th Ave Fl 2 Whitestone (11357) *(G-17218)*
World Journal LLC...718 445-2277
13619 39th Ave Flushing (11354) *(G-5310)*
World Journal LLC...718 871-5000
6007 8th Ave Brooklyn (11220) *(G-2766)*
World LLC...631 940-9121
513 Acorn St Ste B Deer Park (11729) *(G-4229)*
World of McIntosh, New York *Also called Fine Sounds Group Inc (G-10165)*
World Screen News, New York *Also called Wsn Inc (G-12670)*
World Waters LLC...212 905-2393
191 7th Ave Apt 2r New York (10011) *(G-12663)*
Worlds Finest Chocolate Inc...718 332-2442
73 Exeter St Brooklyn (11235) *(G-2767)*
Worldscale Association NYC...212 422-2786
132 Nassau St Rm 619 New York (10038) *(G-12664)*
Worldwide Arntcal Cmpnents Inc (PA)...631 842-3780
10 Reith St Copiague (11726) *(G-3939)*
Worldwide Arntcal Cmpnents Inc...631 842-3780
10 Reith St Copiague (11726) *(G-3940)*
Worldwide Gas Turbine Pdts Inc...518 877-7200
300 Commerce Dr Clifton Park (12065) *(G-3711)*
Worldwide Protective Pdts LLC...877 678-4568
4255 Mckinley Pkwy Hamburg (14075) *(G-5946)*
Worldwide Resources Inc...718 760-5000
1908 Avenue O Brooklyn (11230) *(G-2768)*
Worldwide Ticket Craft...516 538-6200
1390 Jerusalem Ave Merrick (11566) *(G-8394)*
Worm Power, Rochester *Also called Rt Solutions LLC (G-14662)*
Worth Collection Ltd (PA)...212 268-0312
520 8th Ave Rm 2301 New York (10018) *(G-12665)*
Worth Publishers Inc...212 475-6000
1 New York Plz Ste 4500 New York (10004) *(G-12666)*
Worthington Industries Inc...315 336-5500
530 Henry St Rome (13440) *(G-14840)*
Worzalla Publishing Company...212 967-7909
222 W 37th St Fl 10 New York (10018) *(G-12667)*
Wp Lavori USA Inc...718 855-4295
225 Smith St Brooklyn (11231) *(G-2769)*
Wp Lavori USA Inc (HQ)...212 244-6074
597 Broadway Fl 2 New York (10012) *(G-12668)*
WR Design Corp...212 354-9000
1407 Broadway Rm 448 New York (10018) *(G-12669)*
WR Smith & Sons Inc...845 620-9400
121 W Nyack Rd Nanuet (10954) *(G-8763)*
Wr9000, New York *Also called WR Design Corp (G-12669)*
Wrightcut EDM & Machine Inc...607 733-5018
951 Carl St Elmira (14904) *(G-4706)*
Wrights Hardwoods Inc...716 595-2345
6868 Route 60 Cassadaga (14718) *(G-3415)*
Writing Sculptures, Deer Park *Also called Versaponents Inc (G-4223)*
Wsf Industries Inc...716 692-4930
7 Hackett Dr Tonawanda (14150) *(G-16216)*
Wsn Inc...212 924-7620
1123 Broadway Ste 1207 New York (10010) *(G-12670)*
Wt Motto Building Products...315 457-2211
4591 Morgan Pl Liverpool (13090) *(G-7557)*
Wtbi Inc...631 547-1993
200 E 2nd St Ste 12 Huntington Station (11746) *(G-6729)*
Wtrmln Wtr, New York *Also called World Waters LLC (G-12663)*
Www.dynatabs.com, Brooklyn *Also called Dynatabs LLC (G-1888)*
Www.poppin.com, New York *Also called Poppin Inc (G-11685)*
Wyde Lumber...845 513-5571
419 State Route 17b Monticello (12701) *(G-8608)*
Wyeth, Rouses Point *Also called Pfizer Inc (G-15042)*
Wyeth Holdings LLC...845 602-5000
401 N Middletown Rd Pearl River (10965) *(G-13469)*
Wyeth LLC (HQ)...973 660-5000
235 E 42nd St New York (10017) *(G-12671)*
Wyeth Pharmaceutical, Pearl River *Also called Wyeth Holdings LLC (G-13469)*
Wynco Press One Inc...516 354-6145
7839 268th St Glen Oaks (11004) *(G-5641)*
Wynn Starr Flavors Inc (PA)...845 584-3080
225 N Route 303 Ste 109 Congers (10920) *(G-3863)*
Wyrestorm Technologies LLC...518 289-1293
23 Wood Rd Round Lake (12151) *(G-15039)*
X Brand Editions...718 482-7646
4020 22nd St Ste 1 Long Island City (11101) *(G-7927)*
X F Inc...212 244-2240
349 Arlington Ave Brooklyn (11208) *(G-2770)*
X Function Inc (PA)...212 231-0092
902 Broadway Fl 11 New York (10010) *(G-12672)*
X Myles Mar Inc...212 683-2015
875 Av Of The Americas New York (10001) *(G-12673)*
X Press Screen Printing...716 679-7788
4867 W Lake Rd Dunkirk (14048) *(G-4353)*
X-Gen Pharmaceuticals Inc (PA)...607 562-2700
300 Daniel Zenker Dr Big Flats (14814) *(G-883)*
X-Gen Pharmaceuticals Inc...631 261-8188
744 Baldwin St Elmira (14901) *(G-4707)*
X-Gen Pharmaceuticals Inc...607 562-2700
300 Daniel Zenker Dr Horseheads (14845) *(G-6596)*
X-L Envelope and Printing Inc...716 852-2135
701 Seneca St Ste 100 Buffalo (14210) *(G-3258)*
X-Press Printing & Office Sup, Mahopac *Also called Rmd Holding Inc (G-8001)*
X-Press Signs Inc...716 677-0880
1780 Union Rd Ste 1 West Seneca (14224) *(G-16955)*
X-Treme Ready Mix Inc...718 739-3384
17801 Liberty Ave Jamaica (11433) *(G-6965)*
X1000, Binghamton *Also called Surescan Corporation (G-953)*
Xactra Technologies Inc...585 426-2030
9 Marway Cir Rochester (14624) *(G-14767)*
Xanadu...212 465-0580
150 W 30th St Rm 702 New York (10001) *(G-12674)*
Xania Labs Inc...718 361-2550
3202 Queens Blvd Fl 6 Long Island City (11101) *(G-7928)*
Xborder Entertainment LLC...518 726-7036
568 State Route 3 Plattsburgh (12901) *(G-13710)*
Xedit Corp...718 380-1592
21831 97th Ave Queens Village (11429) *(G-13985)*
Xeku Corporation...607 761-1447
2520 Vestal Pkwy E222 Vestal (13850) *(G-16457)*
Xeleum Lighting LLC...954 617-8170
333 N Bedford Rd Ste 135 Mount Kisco (10549) *(G-8647)*
Xelic Incorporated...585 415-2764
1250 Pittsford Victor Rd # 370 Pittsford (14534) *(G-13575)*
Xentaur Corporation...631 345-3434
84 Horseblock Rd Unit G Yaphank (11980) *(G-17409)*
Xerox Corporation...585 423-4711
100 S Clinton Ave Fl 4 Rochester (14604) *(G-14768)*
Xerox Corporation...585 422-4564
800 Phillips Rd Ste 20599 Webster (14580) *(G-16743)*
Xerox Corporation...212 716-4000
245 Park Ave Fl 21 New York (10167) *(G-12675)*
Xerox Corporation...914 397-1319
8 Hangar Rd White Plains (10604) *(G-17188)*
Xerox Corporation...585 425-6100
1387 Fairport Rd Ste 200 Fairport (14450) *(G-4888)*
Xerox Corporation...516 677-1500
155 Pinelawn Rd Ste 200n Melville (11747) *(G-8362)*
Xerox Corporation...212 633-8190
115 Barrow St New York (10014) *(G-12676)*
Xerox Corporation...212 330-1386
485 Lexington Ave Fl 10 New York (10017) *(G-12677)*

ALPHABETIC

(PA)=Parent Co (HQ)=Headquarters (DH)=Div Headquarters
2017 Harris
New York Manufacturers Directory 1097

Xerox Corporation..........845 918-3147
30 Dunnigan Dr Ste 3 Suffern (10901) **(G-15803)**
Xerox Corporation..........585 423-3538
100 S Clinton Ave Rochester (14604) **(G-14769)**
Xerox Corporation..........585 423-5090
800 Phillips Rd Webster (14580) **(G-16744)**
Xerox Corporation..........585 264-5584
80 Linden Oaks Rochester (14625) **(G-14770)**
Xerox Corporation..........716 831-3300
450 Corporate Pkwy # 100 Buffalo (14226) **(G-3259)**
Xing Lin USA Intl Corp..........212 947-4846
1410 Broadway Fl 34 New York (10018) **(G-12678)**
Xinya International Trading Co..........212 216-9681
115 W 30th St Rm 1109 New York (10001) **(G-12679)**
Xl Graphics Inc..........212 929-8700
121 Varick St Rm 300 New York (10013) **(G-12680)**
Xli Corporation..........585 436-2250
55 Vanguard Pkwy Rochester (14606) **(G-14771)**
Xmh-Hfi Inc (HQ)..........585 467-7240
1155 N Clinton Ave Rochester (14621) **(G-14772)**
Xomox Jewelry Inc..........212 944-8428
151 W 46th St Fl 15 New York (10036) **(G-12681)**
Xpand, New York *Also called Whiteboard Ventures Inc* **(G-12628)**
Xpogo LLC..........717 650-5232
440 9th Ave Fl 17 New York (10001) **(G-12682)**
Xpress Printing Inc..........516 605-1000
7 Fairchild Ct Ste 100 Plainview (11803) **(G-13647)**
Xpresspa Holdings LLC (PA)..........212 750-9595
3 E 54th St Fl 9 New York (10022) **(G-12683)**
Xstatic Pro Inc..........718 237-2299
901 Essex St Brooklyn (11208) **(G-2771)**
Xstelos Holdings Inc..........212 729-4962
630 5th Ave Ste 2600 New York (10111) **(G-12684)**
Xto Incorporated (PA)..........315 451-7807
110 Wrentham Dr Liverpool (13088) **(G-7558)**
Xylem, Cheektowaga *Also called Fluid Handling LLC* **(G-3571)**
Xylem Inc..........716 862-4123
2881 E Bayard Street Ext Seneca Falls (13148) **(G-15373)**
Xylem Inc..........315 258-4949
1 Goulds Dr Auburn (13021) **(G-529)**
Xylem Inc (PA)..........914 323-5700
1 International Dr Rye Brook (10573) **(G-15075)**
Xylon Industries Inc..........631 293-4717
79 Florida St Farmingdale (11735) **(G-5144)**
Y & A Trading Inc..........718 436-6333
1365 38th St Brooklyn (11218) **(G-2772)**
Y & Z Precision Inc..........516 349-8243
155 E Ames Ct Unit 4 Plainview (11803) **(G-13648)**
Y & Z Precision Machine Shop, Plainview *Also called Y & Z Precision Inc* **(G-13648)**
Y Lift New York LLC..........212 861-7787
61 E 66th St New York (10065) **(G-12685)**
Yacoubian Jewelers Inc..........212 302-6729
2 W 45th St Ste 1104 New York (10036) **(G-12686)**
Yale, Getzville *Also called Columbus McKinnon Corporation* **(G-5598)**
Yale Robbins Inc..........212 683-5700
205 Lexington Ave Fl 12 New York (10016) **(G-12687)**
Yale Trouser Corporation..........516 255-0700
3670 Oceanside Rd W Ste 6 Oceanside (11572) **(G-13107)**
Yaloz Mold & Die, Brooklyn *Also called Yaloz Mould & Die Co Inc* **(G-2773)**
Yaloz Mould & Die Co Inc..........718 389-1131
239 Java St Fl 2 Brooklyn (11222) **(G-2773)**
Yam TV LLC..........917 932-5418
144 W 23rd St Apt 8e New York (10011) **(G-12688)**
Yankee Corp..........718 589-1377
1180 Randall Ave Bronx (10474) **(G-1495)**
Yankee Wiping Cloth, Bronx *Also called Yankee Corp* **(G-1495)**
Yarnz International Inc..........212 868-5883
260 W 36th St Rm 201 New York (10018) **(G-12689)**
Yated Neeman Inc..........845 369-1600
53 Olympia Ln Monsey (10952) **(G-8586)**
Yellow E House Inc..........718 888-2000
18812 Northern Blvd Flushing (11358) **(G-5311)**
Yellow Pages Inc (PA)..........845 639-6060
222 N Main St New City (10956) **(G-8795)**
Yellowpagecitycom..........585 410-6688
280 Kenneth Dr Ste 300 Rochester (14623) **(G-14773)**
Yeohlee Inc..........212 631-8099
12 W 29th St New York (10001) **(G-12690)**
Yepes Fine Furniture..........718 383-0221
72 Van Dam St Brooklyn (11222) **(G-2774)**
Yes Dental Laboratory Inc..........914 333-7550
155 White Plains Rd # 223 Tarrytown (10591) **(G-16112)**
Yes Were Nuts Ltd..........516 374-1940
1215 Broadway Hewlett (11557) **(G-6317)**
Yesteryears Vintage Doors LLC..........315 324-5250
66 S Main St Hammond (13646) **(G-5952)**
Yewtree Millworks Corp..........914 320-5851
372 Ashburton Ave Yonkers (10701) **(G-17501)**
Yfd Cabinetry, West Haverstraw *Also called Your Furniture Designers Inc* **(G-16848)**
Yigal-Azrouel Inc..........212 302-1194
225 W 39th St Fl 5 New York (10018) **(G-12691)**
Yingli Green Enrgy Amricas Inc (HQ)..........888 686-8820
33 Irving Pl Fl 3 New York (10003) **(G-12692)**
Yingli Solar, New York *Also called Yingli Green Enrgy Amricas Inc* **(G-12692)**
Yiwen Usa Inc..........212 370-0828
60 E 42nd St Ste 2107 New York (10165) **(G-12693)**
Ymobiz Inc..........917 470-9280
40 Wall St Ste 1700 New York (10005) **(G-12694)**
Yo Fresh Inc..........845 634-1616
170 S Main St New City (10956) **(G-8796)**
Yo Fresh Inc..........518 982-0659
5 Southside Dr Clifton Park (12065) **(G-3712)**
Yofah Religious Articles Inc..........718 435-3288
2001 57th St Ste 1 Brooklyn (11204) **(G-2775)**
Yoga In Daily Life - NY Inc..........718 539-8548
1438 132nd St College Point (11356) **(G-3811)**
Yohay Baking Company, Lindenhurst *Also called Alrajs Inc* **(G-7452)**
Yoland Corporation..........718 499-4803
253 36th St Unit 2 Brooklyn (11232) **(G-2776)**
Yomiuri International Inc..........212 752-2196
747 3rd Ave Fl 28 New York (10017) **(G-12695)**
Yong Ji Productions Inc..........917 559-4616
10219 44th Ave Corona (11368) **(G-4010)**
Yong Xin Kitchen Supplies Inc..........212 995-8908
50 Delancey St Frnt A New York (10002) **(G-12696)**
Yonkers Cabinets Inc..........914 668-2133
1179 Yonkers Ave Yonkers (10704) **(G-17502)**
Yonkers Time Publishing Co..........914 965-4000
40 Larkin Plz Yonkers (10701) **(G-17503)**
Yonkers Whl Beer Distrs Inc..........914 963-8600
424 Riverdale Ave Yonkers (10705) **(G-17504)**
Yooconnect1 LLC..........212 726-2062
244 5th Ave Ste G-269 New York (10001) **(G-12697)**
Yorganic, New York *Also called Bliss Foods Inc* **(G-9414)**
Yorganic, New York *Also called Bliss Foods Inc* **(G-9415)**
York Fuel Incorporated..........718 951-0202
1760 Flatbush Ave Brooklyn (11210) **(G-2777)**
York Industries Inc..........516 746-3736
303 Nassau Blvd Garden City Park (11040) **(G-5546)**
York International Corporation..........718 389-4152
1130 45th Rd Long Island City (11101) **(G-7929)**
York Ladder Inc..........718 784-6666
3720 12th St Long Island City (11101) **(G-7930)**
York Ladders, Long Island City *Also called AAAA York Inc* **(G-7645)**
Yorktown Printing Corp..........914 962-2526
1520 Front St Yorktown Heights (10598) **(G-17522)**
Yorkville Sound Inc..........716 297-2920
4625 Witmer Indus Est Niagara Falls (14305) **(G-12891)**
Yost Neon Displays Inc..........716 674-6780
20 Ransier Dr West Seneca (14224) **(G-16956)**
You and ME Legwear LLC..........212 279-9292
10 W 33rd St Rm 300 New York (10001) **(G-12698)**
Young & Franklin Inc (HQ)..........315 457-3110
942 Old Liverpool Rd Liverpool (13088) **(G-7559)**
Young & Swartz Inc..........716 852-2171
39 Cherry St Buffalo (14204) **(G-3260)**
Young Explosives Corp..........585 394-1783
2165 New Michigan Rd Canandaigua (14424) **(G-3361)**
Younique Clothing, New York *Also called Turn On Products Inc* **(G-12427)**
Your Furniture Designers Inc..........845 947-3046
118 E Railroad Ave West Haverstraw (10993) **(G-16848)**
Your Name Professional Brand, Long Island City *Also called Mana Products Inc* **(G-7799)**
Your Way Custom Cabinets Inc..........914 371-1870
20 N Macquesten Pkwy Mount Vernon (10550) **(G-8746)**
Yourhealth911.com, Brooklyn *Also called GNI Commerce Inc* **(G-2033)**
Yours Trading Inc..........718 539-0088
1521 132nd St College Point (11356) **(G-3812)**
Yoyo Lip Gloss Inc..........718 357-6304
2438 47th St Astoria (11103) **(G-463)**
Ypis of Staten Island Inc..........718 815-4557
130 Stuyvesant Pl Ste 5 Staten Island (10301) **(G-15755)**
Yr Blanc & Co LLC..........716 800-3999
1275 Main St Ste 120 Buffalo (14209) **(G-3261)**
Ys Marketing Inc..........718 778-6080
2004 Mcdonald Ave Brooklyn (11223) **(G-2778)**
YS Publishing Co Inc..........212 682-9360
228 E 45th St Rm 700 New York (10017) **(G-12699)**
Yugo Landau, Brooklyn *Also called Eastern Feather & Down Corp* **(G-1898)**
Yula Corporation..........718 991-0900
330 Bryant Ave Bronx (10474) **(G-1496)**
Yum Yum Noodle Bar..........845 679-7992
275 Fair St Ste 17 Kingston (12401) **(G-7226)**
Yurman Retail Inc..........888 398-7626
712 Madison Ave New York (10065) **(G-12700)**
Z Best Printing Inc..........631 595-1400
699 Acorn St Ste B Deer Park (11729) **(G-4230)**
Z Card North America, New York *Also called In-Step Marketing Inc* **(G-10579)**
Z Works Inc..........631 750-0612
1395 Lakeland Ave Ste 10 Bohemia (11716) **(G-1157)**
Z-Axis Inc..........315 548-5000
1916 State Route 96 Phelps (14532) **(G-13539)**
Z-Car-D Corp..........631 424-2077
403 Oakwood Rd Huntington Station (11746) **(G-6730)**

ALPHABETIC SECTION

Z-Ply Corp 212 398-7011
   213 W 35th St Ste 5w New York (10001) *(G-12701)*
Z-Studios Dsign Fbrication LLC 347 512-4210
   124 Noll St Brooklyn (11206) *(G-2779)*
Zacks Enterprises Inc 800 366-4924
   33 Corporate Dr Orangeburg (10962) *(G-13248)*
Zacmel Graphics LLC 631 944-6031
   11 Grandview St Huntington (11743) *(G-6692)*
Zadig and Voltaire, New York Also called Arteast LLC *(G-9216)*
Zagwear, Orangeburg Also called Zacks Enterprises Inc *(G-13248)*
Zahk Sales Inc 631 348-9300
   75 Hoffman Ln Ste A Islandia (11749) *(G-6805)*
Zahm & Nagel Co Inc 716 833-1532
   210 Vermont St Holland (14080) *(G-6486)*
Zak Jewelry Tools Inc 212 768-8122
   55 W 47th St Fl 2 New York (10036) *(G-12702)*
Zam Barrett Dialogue Inc 646 649-0140
   220 36th St Unit 62 Brooklyn (11232) *(G-2780)*
Zan Optics Products Inc 718 435-0533
   982 39th St Brooklyn (11219) *(G-2781)*
Zanetti Millwork, Middle Grove Also called Cuccio-Zanetti Inc *(G-8404)*
Zanzano Woodworking Inc 914 725-6025
   91 Locust Ave Scarsdale (10583) *(G-15225)*
Zappala Farms AG Systems Inc 315 626-6293
   11404 Schuler Rd Cato (13033) *(G-3425)*
Zar Apparel Group, New York Also called Zar Group LLC *(G-12703)*
Zar Group LLC 212 944-2510
   1375 Broadway Fl 12 New York (10018) *(G-12703)*
Zaralo LLC 212 764-4590
   500 7th Ave Fl 18 New York (10018) *(G-12704)*
Zaro Bake Shop Inc (PA) 718 993-7327
   138 Bruckner Blvd Bronx (10454) *(G-1497)*
Zaro Bake Shop Inc 212 292-0175
   370 Lexington Ave New York (10017) *(G-12705)*
Zaro's Bread Basket, Bronx Also called Zaro Bake Shop Inc *(G-1497)*
Zaro's Bread Basket, New York Also called Zaro Bake Shop Inc *(G-12705)*
Zastech Inc 516 496-4777
   15 Ryan St Syosset (11791) *(G-15843)*
Zazoom LLC (PA) 212 321-2100
   1 Exchange Plz Ste 801 New York (10006) *(G-12706)*
Zazoom Media Group, New York Also called Zazoom LLC *(G-12706)*
Zdny & Co Inc (PA) 212 354-1233
   31 W 47th St Ste 403 New York (10036) *(G-12707)*
Zebra Books, New York Also called Kensington Publishing Corp *(G-10836)*
Zebra Environmental Corp (PA) 516 596-6300
   30 N Prospect Ave Lynbrook (11563) *(G-7967)*
Zebra Technical Services LLC, Lynbrook Also called Cascade Technical Services LLC *(G-7949)*
Zebrowski Industries Inc 716 532-3911
   4345 Route 39 Collins (14034) *(G-3818)*
Zedge Inc 330 577-3424
   22 Cortlandt St Fl 14 New York (10007) *(G-12708)*
Zeeba Jewelry Manufacturing, New York Also called Zeeba Jewelry Mfg Inc *(G-12709)*
Zeeba Jewelry Mfg Inc 212 997-1009
   36 W 47th St Ste 902 New York (10036) *(G-12709)*
Zehnder Rittling, Buffalo Also called Hydro-Air Components Inc *(G-3000)*
Zela International Co 518 436-1833
   13 Manor St Albany (12207) *(G-151)*
Zelman & Friedman Jwly Mfg Co 718 349-3400
   4722 37th St Long Island City (11101) *(G-7931)*
Zenger Group Inc 716 871-1058
   777 E Park Dr Tonawanda (14150) *(G-16217)*
Zenger Partners LLC 716 876-2284
   1881 Kenmore Ave Kenmore (14217) *(G-7152)*
Zenith Autoparts Corp 845 344-1382
   20 Industrial Pl Middletown (10940) *(G-8471)*
Zenith Color Comm Group Inc (PA) 212 989-4400
   4710 33rd St Long Island City (11101) *(G-7932)*
Zenith Promotions, Lawrence Also called Last Straw Inc *(G-7393)*
Zenith Solutions 718 575-8570
   6922 Manse St Flushing (11375) *(G-5312)*
Zeo Health Ltd 845 353-5185
   159 Route 303 Valley Cottage (10989) *(G-16395)*
Zeppelin Electric Company Inc 631 928-9467
   26 Deer Ln East Setauket (11733) *(G-4497)*
Zeptometrix Corporation (PA) 716 882-0920
   872 Main St Buffalo (14202) *(G-3262)*
Zered Inc (PA) 718 353-7464
   12717 20th Ave College Point (11356) *(G-3813)*
Zerovalent Nanometals Inc 585 298-8592
   693 East Ave Ste 103 Rochester (14607) *(G-14774)*
Zeta Machine Corp 631 471-8832
   206 Christopher St Ronkonkoma (11779) *(G-15002)*
Zeteck, New York Also called Zetek Corporation *(G-12710)*
Zetek Corporation 212 668-1485
   13 E 37th St Ste 701 New York (10016) *(G-12710)*

Zg Apparel Group LLC 646 930-1113
   1450 Broadway Fl 7 New York (10018) *(G-12711)*
Zia Power Inc 845 661-8388
   116 E 27th St New York (10016) *(G-12712)*
ZIC Sportswear Inc (PA) 718 361-9022
   2107 41st Ave Fl 3 Long Island City (11101) *(G-7933)*
Ziebart, Rochester Also called Monroe County Auto Svcs Inc *(G-14520)*
Ziegler Truck & Diesl Repr Inc 315 782-7278
   22249 Fabco Rd Watertown (13601) *(G-16676)*
Zielinskis Asphalt Inc 315 306-4057
   4989 State Route 12b Oriskany Falls (13425) *(G-13319)*
Zierick Manufacturing Corp (PA) 800 882-8020
   131 Radio Circle Dr Mount Kisco (10549) *(G-8648)*
Ziff-Davis Publishing, New York Also called Davis Ziff Publishing Inc *(G-9829)*
Zinc Corporation America Div, New York Also called Hh Liquidating Corp *(G-10471)*
Zinepak LLC 212 706-8621
   349 5th Ave New York (10016) *(G-12713)*
Zinerva Pharmaceuticals LLC 630 729-4184
   6017 Corinne Ln Clarence Center (14032) *(G-3682)*
Zings Company LLC 631 454-0339
   250 Adams Blvd Farmingdale (11735) *(G-5145)*
Zinnias Inc 718 746-8551
   24520 Grand Central Pkwy 4l Bellerose (11426) *(G-812)*
Zip Jack Custom Umbrellas, Tarrytown Also called Zip-Jack Industries Ltd *(G-16113)*
Zip Products Inc 585 482-0044
   565 Blossom Rd Ste E Rochester (14610) *(G-14775)*
Zip-Jack Industries Ltd 914 592-2000
   73 Carrollwood Dr Tarrytown (10591) *(G-16113)*
Ziptswitch, Bay Shore Also called Adeptronics Incorporated *(G-665)*
Zircar Ceramics Inc (PA) 845 651-6600
   100 N Main St Ste 2 Florida (10921) *(G-5216)*
Zircar Refr Composites Inc 845 651-2200
   14 Golden Hill Ter Florida (10921) *(G-5217)*
Zircar Refr Composites Inc (PA) 845 651-4481
   46 Jayne St Florida (10921) *(G-5218)*
Zircar Zirconia Inc 845 651-3040
   87 Meadow Rd Florida (10921) *(G-5219)*
Zirconia Creations Intl 212 239-3730
   134 W 29th St Rm 801 New York (10001) *(G-12714)*
Zitomer LLC 212 737-5560
   969 Madison Ave Fl 1 New York (10021) *(G-12715)*
Ziva Gem LLC (PA) 646 416-5828
   200 Madison Ave Ste 2225 New York (10016) *(G-12716)*
Zmz Mfg Inc 518 234-4336
   300 Mickle Hollow Rd Warnerville (12187) *(G-16579)*
Zoe, Long Island City Also called ZIC Sportswear Inc *(G-7933)*
Zoe Sakoutis LLC 212 414-5741
   135 W 29th St Rm 704 New York (10001) *(G-12717)*
Zola Books Inc 917 822-4950
   242 W 38th St Fl 2 New York (10018) *(G-12718)*
Zomega Terahertz Corporation 585 347-4337
   806 Admiralty Way Webster (14580) *(G-16745)*
Zone Fabricators Inc 718 272-0200
   10780 101st St Ozone Park (11417) *(G-13388)*
Zoomers Inc (PA) 718 369-2656
   32 33rd St Brooklyn (11232) *(G-2782)*
Zorlu USA Inc (PA) 212 689-4622
   295 5th Ave Ste 503 New York (10016) *(G-12719)*
Zotos International Inc 315 781-3207
   300 Forge Ave Geneva (14456) *(G-5589)*
Zuant, Valley Stream Also called High Performance Sftwr USA Inc *(G-16409)*
Zuckerbakers Inc 516 785-6900
   2845 Jerusalem Ave Wantagh (11793) *(G-16565)*
Zumbach Electronics Corp 914 241-7080
   140 Kisco Ave Mount Kisco (10549) *(G-8649)*
Zumiez Inc 585 425-8720
   769 Eastview Mall Victor (14564) *(G-16515)*
Zumtobel Lighting Inc (HQ) 845 691-6262
   3300 Us Highway 9w Highland (12528) *(G-6409)*
Zwack Incorporated 518 733-5135
   15875 Ny 22 Stephentown (12168) *(G-15758)*
Zweigles Inc 585 546-1740
   651 Plymouth Ave N Rochester (14608) *(G-14776)*
Zylon Corporation 845 425-9469
   23 Mountain Ave Monsey (10952) *(G-8587)*
Zylon Polymers, Monsey Also called Zylon Corporation *(G-8587)*
Zyloware Corporation (PA) 914 708-1200
   8 Slater St Ste 1 Port Chester (10573) *(G-13762)*
Zyloware Eyewear, Port Chester Also called Zyloware Corporation *(G-13762)*
Zymtrnix Catalytic Systems Inc 918 694-8206
   405 Will Hall Crnell Univ Ithaca (14853) *(G-6886)*
Zyp Precision LLC 315 539-3667
   1098 Birdsey Rd Waterloo (13165) *(G-16632)*
Zzz Mattress Manufacturing 718 454-1468
   11080 Dunkirk St Saint Albans (11412) *(G-15085)*

PRODUCT INDEX

• Product categories are listed in alphabetical order.

A

ABRASIVES
ABRASIVES: Coated
ABRASIVES: Grains
ACADEMIC TUTORING SVCS
ACCELERATION INDICATORS & SYSTEM COMPONENTS: Aerospace
ACCELERATORS: Electron Linear
ACCELERATORS: Particle, High Voltage
ACCOUNTING MACHINES & CASH REGISTERS
ACID RESIST: Etching
ACIDS
ACIDS: Battery
ACOUSTICAL BOARD & TILE
ACRYLIC RESINS
ACTUATORS: Indl, NEC
ADDITIVE BASED PLASTIC MATERIALS: Plasticizers
ADHESIVES
ADHESIVES & SEALANTS
ADVERTISING AGENCIES
ADVERTISING AGENCIES: Consultants
ADVERTISING DISPLAY PRDTS
ADVERTISING MATERIAL DISTRIBUTION
ADVERTISING REPRESENTATIVES: Electronic Media
ADVERTISING REPRESENTATIVES: Magazine
ADVERTISING REPRESENTATIVES: Media
ADVERTISING REPRESENTATIVES: Newspaper
ADVERTISING REPRESENTATIVES: Printed Media
ADVERTISING SPECIALTIES, WHOLESALE
ADVERTISING SVCS: Direct Mail
ADVERTISING SVCS: Display
ADVERTISING SVCS: Outdoor
ADVERTISING SVCS: Sample Distribution
ADVERTISING SVCS: Transit
AERIAL WORK PLATFORMS
AEROSOLS
AGENTS & MANAGERS: Entertainers
AGENTS, BROKERS & BUREAUS: Personal Service
AGRICULTURAL EQPT: BARN, SILO, POULTRY, DAIRY/LIVESTOCK MACH
AGRICULTURAL EQPT: Fertilizng, Sprayng, Dustng/Irrigatn Mach
AGRICULTURAL EQPT: Milking Machines
AGRICULTURAL EQPT: Planting Machines
AGRICULTURAL EQPT: Spreaders, Fertilizer
AGRICULTURAL EQPT: Trailers & Wagons, Farm
AGRICULTURAL EQPT: Turf & Grounds Eqpt
AGRICULTURAL EQPT: Turf Eqpt, Commercial
AIR CLEANING SYSTEMS
AIR CONDITIONERS, AUTOMOTIVE: Wholesalers
AIR CONDITIONING & VENTILATION EQPT & SPLYS: Wholesales
AIR CONDITIONING EQPT
AIR CONDITIONING UNITS: Complete, Domestic Or Indl
AIR COOLERS: Metal Plate
AIR DUCT CLEANING SVCS
AIR MATTRESSES: Plastic
AIR POLLUTION MEASURING SVCS
AIR PURIFICATION EQPT
AIR TRAFFIC CONTROL SYSTEMS & EQPT
AIRCRAFT & AEROSPACE FLIGHT INSTRUMENTS & GUIDANCE SYSTEMS
AIRCRAFT & HEAVY EQPT REPAIR SVCS
AIRCRAFT ASSEMBLY PLANTS
AIRCRAFT CONTROL SYSTEMS: Electronic Totalizing Counters
AIRCRAFT ENGINES & PARTS
AIRCRAFT EQPT & SPLYS WHOLESALERS
AIRCRAFT FLIGHT INSTRUMENT REPAIR SVCS
AIRCRAFT FLIGHT INSTRUMENTS
AIRCRAFT LIGHTING
AIRCRAFT PARTS & AUXILIARY EQPT: Accumulators, Propeller
AIRCRAFT PARTS & AUXILIARY EQPT: Assys, Subassemblies/Parts
AIRCRAFT PARTS & AUXILIARY EQPT: Body Assemblies & Parts
AIRCRAFT PARTS & AUXILIARY EQPT: Gears, Power Transmission
AIRCRAFT PARTS & AUXILIARY EQPT: Landing Assemblies & Brakes
AIRCRAFT PARTS & AUXILIARY EQPT: Military Eqpt & Armament
AIRCRAFT PARTS & AUXILIARY EQPT: Refueling Eqpt, In Flight
AIRCRAFT PARTS & AUXILIARY EQPT: Seat Ejector Devices
AIRCRAFT PARTS & EQPT, NEC
AIRCRAFT SEATS
AIRCRAFT: Airplanes, Fixed Or Rotary Wing
AIRCRAFT: Gliders
AIRCRAFT: Motorized
AIRCRAFT: Research & Development, Manufacturer
ALARM SYSTEMS WHOLESALERS
ALARMS: Burglar
ALARMS: Fire
ALKALIES & CHLORINE
ALKALOIDS & OTHER BOTANICAL BASED PRDTS
ALLERGENS & ALLERGENIC EXTRACTS
ALTERNATORS & GENERATORS: Battery Charging
ALTERNATORS: Automotive
ALUMINUM
ALUMINUM ORE MINING
ALUMINUM PRDTS
ALUMINUM: Rolling & Drawing
AMMONIUM NITRATE OR AMMONIUM SULFATE
AMMUNITION
AMMUNITION: Components
AMMUNITION: Pellets & BB's, Pistol & Air Rifle
AMMUNITION: Small Arms
AMPLIFIERS
AMPLIFIERS: Parametric
AMPLIFIERS: Pulse Amplifiers
AMPLIFIERS: RF & IF Power
AMUSEMENT & RECREATION SVCS: Amusement Ride
AMUSEMENT & RECREATION SVCS: Art Gallery, Commercial
AMUSEMENT & RECREATION SVCS: Arts & Crafts Instruction
AMUSEMENT & RECREATION SVCS: Exposition Operation
AMUSEMENT & RECREATION SVCS: Game Machines
AMUSEMENT & RECREATION SVCS: Golf Club, Membership
AMUSEMENT & RECREATION SVCS: Gun Club, Membership
AMUSEMENT & RECREATION SVCS: Physical Fitness Instruction
AMUSEMENT & RECREATION SVCS: Tennis & Professionals
AMUSEMENT MACHINES: Coin Operated
AMUSEMENT PARK DEVICES & RIDES
ANALGESICS
ANALYZERS: Moisture
ANALYZERS: Network
ANESTHESIA EQPT
ANESTHETICS: Bulk Form
ANIMAL FEED & SUPPLEMENTS: Livestock & Poultry
ANIMAL FEED: Wholesalers
ANIMAL FOOD & SUPPLEMENTS: Bird Food, Prepared
ANIMAL FOOD & SUPPLEMENTS: Dog
ANIMAL FOOD & SUPPLEMENTS: Dog & Cat
ANIMAL FOOD & SUPPLEMENTS: Feed Concentrates
ANIMAL FOOD & SUPPLEMENTS: Feed Premixes
ANIMAL FOOD & SUPPLEMENTS: Feed Supplements
ANIMAL FOOD & SUPPLEMENTS: Mineral feed supplements
ANIMAL FOOD & SUPPLEMENTS: Pet, Exc Dog & Cat, Canned
ANIMAL FOOD & SUPPLEMENTS: Poultry
ANODIZING SVC
ANTENNAS: Radar Or Communications
ANTENNAS: Receiving
ANTIBIOTICS
ANTIBIOTICS, PACKAGED
ANTIFREEZE
ANTIQUE FURNITURE RESTORATION & REPAIR
ANTIQUE REPAIR & RESTORATION SVCS, EXC FURNITURE & AUTOS
ANTIQUE SHOPS
APPAREL ACCESS STORES
APPAREL DESIGNERS: Commercial
APPAREL FILLING MATERIALS: Cotton Waste, Kapok/Related Matl
APPAREL: Hand Woven
APPLIANCE CORDS: Household Electrical Eqpt
APPLIANCES, HOUSEHOLD: Kitchen, Major, Exc Refrigs & Stoves
APPLIANCES, HOUSEHOLD: Refrigerator Cabinets, Metal Or Wood
APPLIANCES, HOUSEHOLD: Refrigs, Mechanical & Absorption
APPLIANCES, HOUSEHOLD: Sewing Machines & Attchmnts, Domestic
APPLIANCES: Household, Refrigerators & Freezers
APPLIANCES: Major, Cooking
APPLIANCES: Small, Electric
APPLICATIONS SOFTWARE PROGRAMMING
AQUARIUM ACCESS, METAL
AQUARIUM DESIGN & MAINTENANCE SVCS
AQUARIUMS & ACCESS: Glass
AQUARIUMS & ACCESS: Plastic
ARCHITECTURAL SVCS
ARMATURE REPAIRING & REWINDING SVC
AROMATIC CHEMICAL PRDTS
ART & ORNAMENTAL WARE: Pottery
ART DEALERS & GALLERIES
ART DESIGN SVCS
ART GOODS & SPLYS WHOLESALERS
ART MARBLE: Concrete
ART NEEDLEWORK, MADE FROM PURCHASED MATERIALS
ART RELATED SVCS
ART RESTORATION SVC
ART SPLY STORES
ARTISTS' EQPT
ARTISTS' MATERIALS, WHOLESALE
ARTISTS' MATERIALS: Canvas Board
ARTISTS' MATERIALS: Frames, Artists' Canvases
ARTISTS' MATERIALS: Ink, Drawing, Black & Colored
ARTISTS' MATERIALS: Paints, Exc Gold & Bronze
ARTISTS' MATERIALS: Pastels
ARTISTS' MATERIALS: Pencils & Leads
ARTISTS' MATERIALS: Wax
ARTWORK: Framed
ASBESTOS PRODUCTS
ASPHALT & ASPHALT PRDTS
ASPHALT COATINGS & SEALERS
ASPHALT MIXTURES WHOLESALERS
ASPHALT PLANTS INCLUDING GRAVEL MIX TYPE
ASSEMBLING SVC: Clocks
ASSEMBLING SVC: Plumbing Fixture Fittings, Plastic
ASSOCIATIONS: Engineering
ASSOCIATIONS: Scientists'
ATOMIZERS
ATTENUATORS
AUDIO & VIDEO EQPT, EXC COMMERCIAL
AUDIO COMPONENTS
AUDIO ELECTRONIC SYSTEMS
AUDIO-VISUAL PROGRAM PRODUCTION SVCS
AUDIOLOGISTS' OFFICES
AUDITING SVCS
AUTO & HOME SUPPLY STORES: Auto & Truck Eqpt & Parts
AUTO & HOME SUPPLY STORES: Automotive Access
AUTO & HOME SUPPLY STORES: Speed Shops, Incl Race Car Splys
AUTO & HOME SUPPLY STORES: Trailer Hitches, Automotive
AUTO & HOME SUPPLY STORES: Truck Eqpt & Parts
AUTOCLAVES: Indl
AUTOCLAVES: Laboratory
AUTOMATIC REGULATING CONTROL: Building Svcs Monitoring, Auto
AUTOMATIC REGULATING CONTROLS: AC & Refrigeration

PRODUCT INDEX

AUTOMATIC REGULATING CONTROLS: Elect Air Cleaner, Automatic
AUTOMATIC REGULATING CONTROLS: Energy Cutoff, Residtl/Comm
AUTOMATIC REGULATING CONTROLS: Ice Maker
AUTOMATIC REGULATING CONTROLS: Pneumatic Relays, Air-Cond
AUTOMATIC REGULATING CONTROLS: Refrig/Air-Cond Defrost
AUTOMATIC REGULATING CTRLS: Damper, Pneumatic Or Electric
AUTOMATIC TELLER MACHINES
AUTOMATIC VENDING MACHINES: Mechanisms & Parts
AUTOMOBILES: Off-Highway, Electric
AUTOMOBILES: Wholesalers
AUTOMOTIVE & TRUCK GENERAL REPAIR SVC
AUTOMOTIVE BODY SHOP
AUTOMOTIVE BODY, PAINT & INTERIOR REPAIR & MAINTENANCE SVC
AUTOMOTIVE CUSTOMIZING SVCS, NONFACTORY BASIS
AUTOMOTIVE PARTS, ACCESS & SPLYS
AUTOMOTIVE PARTS: Plastic
AUTOMOTIVE PRDTS: Rubber
AUTOMOTIVE REPAIR SHOPS: Brake Repair
AUTOMOTIVE REPAIR SHOPS: Diesel Engine Repair
AUTOMOTIVE REPAIR SHOPS: Electrical Svcs
AUTOMOTIVE REPAIR SHOPS: Engine Repair
AUTOMOTIVE REPAIR SHOPS: Machine Shop
AUTOMOTIVE REPAIR SHOPS: Trailer Repair
AUTOMOTIVE REPAIR SVC
AUTOMOTIVE SPLYS & PARTS, NEW, WHOL: Testing Eqpt, Electric
AUTOMOTIVE SPLYS & PARTS, NEW, WHOLESALE: Brakes
AUTOMOTIVE SPLYS & PARTS, NEW, WHOLESALE: Clutches
AUTOMOTIVE SPLYS & PARTS, NEW, WHOLESALE: Engines/Eng Parts
AUTOMOTIVE SPLYS & PARTS, NEW, WHOLESALE: Splys
AUTOMOTIVE SPLYS & PARTS, NEW, WHOLESALE: Trim
AUTOMOTIVE SPLYS & PARTS, NEW, WHOLESALE: Wheels
AUTOMOTIVE SPLYS & PARTS, USED, WHOLESALE: Wheels
AUTOMOTIVE SPLYS & PARTS, WHOLESALE, NEC
AUTOMOTIVE SPLYS/PARTS, NEW, WHOL: Body Rpr/Paint Shop Splys
AUTOMOTIVE SVCS, EXC REPAIR & CARWASHES: Maintenance
AUTOMOTIVE SVCS, EXC REPAIR: Washing & Polishing
AUTOMOTIVE SVCS, EXC RPR/CARWASHES: High Perf Auto Rpr/Svc
AUTOMOTIVE TOWING & WRECKING SVC
AUTOMOTIVE UPHOLSTERY SHOPS
AUTOMOTIVE WELDING SVCS
AUTOMOTIVE: Bodies
AUTOMOTIVE: Seating
AUTOTRANSFORMERS: Electric
AWNING REPAIR SHOP
AWNINGS & CANOPIES
AWNINGS & CANOPIES: Awnings, Fabric, From Purchased Matls
AWNINGS & CANOPIES: Fabric
AWNINGS: Fiberglass
AWNINGS: Metal
AWNINGS: Wood
AXLES

B

BABY FORMULA
BABY PACIFIERS: Rubber
BADGES, WHOLESALE
BADGES: Identification & Insignia
BAGS & BAGGING: Knit
BAGS & CONTAINERS: Textile, Exc Sleeping
BAGS & SACKS: Shipping & Shopping
BAGS: Canvas
BAGS: Cellophane
BAGS: Duffle, Canvas, Made From Purchased Materials
BAGS: Food Storage & Frozen Food, Plastic
BAGS: Food Storage & Trash, Plastic
BAGS: Garment & Wardrobe, Plastic Film
BAGS: Grocers', Made From Purchased Materials
BAGS: Knapsacks, Canvas, Made From Purchased Materials
BAGS: Laundry, Garment & Storage

BAGS: Paper
BAGS: Paper, Made From Purchased Materials
BAGS: Plastic
BAGS: Plastic & Pliofilm
BAGS: Plastic, Made From Purchased Materials
BAGS: Rubber Or Rubberized Fabric
BAGS: Shipping
BAGS: Shoe, From Purchased Materials
BAGS: Shopping, Made From Purchased Materials
BAGS: Tea, Fabric, Made From Purchased Materials
BAGS: Textile
BAGS: Trash, Plastic Film, Made From Purchased Materials
BAGS: Wardrobe, Closet Access, Made From Purchased Materials
BAKERIES, COMMERCIAL: On Premises Baking Only
BAKERIES: On Premises Baking & Consumption
BAKERY FOR HOME SVC DELIVERY
BAKERY MACHINERY
BAKERY PRDTS, FROZEN: Wholesalers
BAKERY PRDTS: Bagels, Fresh Or Frozen
BAKERY PRDTS: Bakery Prdts, Partially Cooked, Exc frozen
BAKERY PRDTS: Biscuits, Dry
BAKERY PRDTS: Bread, All Types, Fresh Or Frozen
BAKERY PRDTS: Buns, Sweet, Frozen
BAKERY PRDTS: Cakes, Bakery, Exc Frozen
BAKERY PRDTS: Cakes, Bakery, Frozen
BAKERY PRDTS: Cones, Ice Cream
BAKERY PRDTS: Cookies
BAKERY PRDTS: Cookies & crackers
BAKERY PRDTS: Cracker Meal & Crumbs
BAKERY PRDTS: Doughnuts, Exc Frozen
BAKERY PRDTS: Doughnuts, Frozen
BAKERY PRDTS: Dry
BAKERY PRDTS: Frozen
BAKERY PRDTS: Matzoth
BAKERY PRDTS: Pastries, Danish, Frozen
BAKERY PRDTS: Pastries, Exc Frozen
BAKERY PRDTS: Pies, Bakery, Frozen
BAKERY PRDTS: Pretzels
BAKERY PRDTS: Rolls, Bread Type, Fresh Or Frozen
BAKERY PRDTS: Wholesalers
BAKERY: Wholesale Or Wholesale & Retail Combined
BANDAGES
BANDS: Copper & Copper Alloy
BANDS: Plastic
BANNERS: Fabric
BANQUET HALL FACILITIES
BAR FIXTURES: Wood
BARBECUE EQPT
BARRICADES: Metal
BARS & BAR SHAPES: Steel, Hot-Rolled
BARS, COLD FINISHED: Steel, From Purchased Hot-Rolled
BARS: Concrete Reinforcing, Fabricated Steel
BARS: Iron, Made In Steel Mills
BASEBOARDS: Metal
BASEMENT WINDOW AREAWAYS: Concrete
BASES, BEVERAGE
BASKETS: Steel Wire
BATCHING PLANTS: Cement Silos
BATH SALTS
BATHING SUIT STORES
BATHMATS, COTTON
BATHROOM ACCESS & FITTINGS: Vitreous China & Earthenware
BATHTUBS: Concrete
BATTERIES, EXC AUTOMOTIVE: Wholesalers
BATTERIES: Alkaline, Cell Storage
BATTERIES: Lead Acid, Storage
BATTERIES: Rechargeable
BATTERIES: Storage
BATTERIES: Wet
BATTERY CASES: Plastic Or Plastics Combination
BATTERY CHARGERS
BATTERY CHARGERS: Storage, Motor & Engine Generator Type
BATTERY CHARGING GENERATORS
BATTS & BATTING: Cotton
BAUXITE MINING
BEARINGS
BEARINGS & PARTS Ball
BEARINGS: Ball & Roller
BEAUTY & BARBER SHOP EQPT
BEAUTY SALONS
BED & BREAKFAST INNS
BEDDING, BEDSPREADS, BLANKETS & SHEETS

BEDDING, BEDSPREADS, BLANKETS & SHEETS: Comforters & Quilts
BEDDING, FROM SILK OR MANMADE FIBER
BEDS & ACCESS STORES
BEDS: Hospital
BEDSPREADS & BED SETS, FROM PURCHASED MATERIALS
BEDSPREADS, COTTON
BEER & ALE WHOLESALERS
BEER & ALE, WHOLESALE: Beer & Other Fermented Malt Liquors
BEER, WINE & LIQUOR STORES
BEER, WINE & LIQUOR STORES: Beer, Packaged
BEER, WINE & LIQUOR STORES: Wine
BELLOWS
BELTING: Rubber
BELTING: Transmission, Rubber
BELTS: Conveyor, Made From Purchased Wire
BELTS: Indl
BELTS: Seat, Automotive & Aircraft
BENCHES: Seating
BEVERAGE BASES & SYRUPS
BEVERAGE, NONALCOHOLIC: Iced Tea/Fruit Drink, Bottled/Canned
BEVERAGES, ALCOHOLIC: Ale
BEVERAGES, ALCOHOLIC: Applejack
BEVERAGES, ALCOHOLIC: Beer
BEVERAGES, ALCOHOLIC: Beer & Ale
BEVERAGES, ALCOHOLIC: Brandy
BEVERAGES, ALCOHOLIC: Cocktails
BEVERAGES, ALCOHOLIC: Distilled Liquors
BEVERAGES, ALCOHOLIC: Gin
BEVERAGES, ALCOHOLIC: Liquors, Malt
BEVERAGES, ALCOHOLIC: Neutral Spirits, Fruit
BEVERAGES, ALCOHOLIC: Rum
BEVERAGES, ALCOHOLIC: Vodka
BEVERAGES, ALCOHOLIC: Wines
BEVERAGES, MALT
BEVERAGES, NONALCOHOLIC: Bottled & canned soft drinks
BEVERAGES, NONALCOHOLIC: Carbonated
BEVERAGES, NONALCOHOLIC: Carbonated, Canned & Bottled, Etc
BEVERAGES, NONALCOHOLIC: Cider
BEVERAGES, NONALCOHOLIC: Flavoring extracts & syrups, nec
BEVERAGES, NONALCOHOLIC: Fruit Drnks, Under 100% Juice, Can
BEVERAGES, NONALCOHOLIC: Soft Drinks, Canned & Bottled, Etc
BEVERAGES, NONALCOHOLIC: Tea, Iced, Bottled & Canned, Etc
BEVERAGES, WINE & DISTILLED ALCOHOLIC, WHOLESALE: Liquor
BEVERAGES, WINE & DISTILLED ALCOHOLIC, WHOLESALE: Neutral Sp
BEVERAGES, WINE & DISTILLED ALCOHOLIC, WHOLESALE: Wine
BEVERAGES, WINE WHOLESALE : Wine Coolers
BICYCLES WHOLESALERS
BICYCLES, PARTS & ACCESS
BILLETS: Steel
BILLFOLD INSERTS: Plastic
BILLIARD & POOL TABLES & SPLYS
BINDING SVC: Books & Manuals
BINDING SVC: Magazines
BINDING SVC: Pamphlets
BINDING SVC: Trade
BINDINGS: Bias, Made From Purchased Materials
BINS: Prefabricated, Sheet Metal
BIOLOGICAL PRDTS: Bacterial Vaccines
BIOLOGICAL PRDTS: Blood Derivatives
BIOLOGICAL PRDTS: Exc Diagnostic
BIOLOGICAL PRDTS: Extracts
BIOLOGICAL PRDTS: Vaccines
BIOLOGICAL PRDTS: Vaccines & Immunizing
BLADES: Saw, Chain Type
BLADES: Saw, Hand Or Power
BLANKBOOKS
BLANKBOOKS & LOOSELEAF BINDERS
BLANKBOOKS: Albums
BLANKBOOKS: Albums, Record
BLANKBOOKS: Checkbooks & Passbooks, Bank
BLANKBOOKS: Diaries
BLANKBOOKS: Memorandum, Printed

PRODUCT INDEX

BLANKETS & BLANKETING, COTTON
BLASTING SVC: Sand, Metal Parts
BLINDS & SHADES: Vertical
BLINDS : Window
BLOCK & BRICK: Sand Lime
BLOCKS & BRICKS: Concrete
BLOCKS: Chimney Or Fireplace, Concrete
BLOCKS: Landscape Or Retaining Wall, Concrete
BLOCKS: Paving, Concrete
BLOCKS: Paving, Cut Stone
BLOCKS: Radiation-Proof, Concrete
BLOCKS: Standard, Concrete Or Cinder
BLOWERS & FANS
BLOWERS & FANS
BLUEPRINTING SVCS
BOAT BUILDING & REPAIR
BOAT BUILDING & REPAIRING: Fiberglass
BOAT BUILDING & REPAIRING: Motorized
BOAT BUILDING & REPAIRING: Non-Motorized
BOAT BUILDING & RPRG: Fishing, Small, Lobster, Crab, Oyster
BOAT DEALERS
BOAT DEALERS: Canoe & Kayak
BOAT LIFTS
BOAT REPAIR SVCS
BOAT YARD: Boat yards, storage & incidental repair
BOATS & OTHER MARINE EQPT: Plastic
BODIES: Truck & Bus
BODY PARTS: Automobile, Stamped Metal
BOILER REPAIR SHOP
BOILERS & BOILER SHOP WORK
BOILERS: Low-Pressure Heating, Steam Or Hot Water
BOLTS: Metal
BONDERIZING: Bonderizing, Metal Or Metal Prdts
BOOK STORES
BOOK STORES: Children's
BOOKS, WHOLESALE
BOOTHS: Spray, Sheet Metal, Prefabricated
BOOTS: Women's
BOTTLE CAPS & RESEALERS: Plastic
BOTTLED GAS DEALERS: Propane
BOTTLED WATER DELIVERY
BOTTLES: Plastic
BOUTIQUE STORES
BOWLING EQPT & SPLYS
BOX & CARTON MANUFACTURING EQPT
BOXES & CRATES: Rectangular, Wood
BOXES & SHOOK: Nailed Wood
BOXES: Corrugated
BOXES: Filing, Paperboard Made From Purchased Materials
BOXES: Mail Or Post Office, Collection/Storage, Sheet Metal
BOXES: Packing & Shipping, Metal
BOXES: Paperboard, Folding
BOXES: Paperboard, Set-Up
BOXES: Plastic
BOXES: Solid Fiber
BOXES: Stamped Metal
BOXES: Switch, Electric
BOXES: Wooden
BRAKES & BRAKE PARTS
BRAKES: Electromagnetic
BRASS FOUNDRY, NEC
BRAZING SVCS
BRAZING: Metal
BRIC-A-BRAC
BRICK, STONE & RELATED PRDTS WHOLESALERS
BRICKS & BLOCKS: Structural
BRICKS: Concrete
BRIDAL SHOPS
BRIDGE COMPONENTS: Bridge sections, prefabricated, highway
BRIEFCASES
BROADCASTING & COMMS EQPT: Antennas, Transmitting/Comms
BROADCASTING & COMMS EQPT: Rcvr-Transmitter Unt, Transceiver
BROADCASTING & COMMUNICATIONS EQPT: Cellular Radio Telephone
BROADCASTING & COMMUNICATIONS EQPT: Studio Eqpt, Radio & TV
BROADCASTING & COMMUNICATIONS EQPT: Transmitting, Radio/TV
BROKERS' SVCS
BROKERS: Automotive
BROKERS: Business
BROKERS: Food
BROKERS: Loan
BROKERS: Printing
BRONZE FOUNDRY, NEC
BROOMS & BRUSHES
BROOMS & BRUSHES: Hair Pencils Or Artists' Brushes
BROOMS & BRUSHES: Household Or Indl
BROOMS & BRUSHES: Paint Rollers
BROOMS & BRUSHES: Paintbrushes
BRUSHES
BUCKLES & PARTS
BUILDING & OFFICE CLEANING SVCS
BUILDING & STRUCTURAL WOOD MBRS: Timbers, Struct, Lam Lumber
BUILDING & STRUCTURAL WOOD MEMBERS
BUILDING & STRUCTURAL WOOD MEMBERS: Arches, Laminated Lumber
BUILDING BOARD & WALLBOARD, EXC GYPSUM
BUILDING BOARD: Gypsum
BUILDING CLEANING & MAINTENANCE SVCS
BUILDING COMPONENTS: Structural Steel
BUILDING ITEM REPAIR SVCS, MISCELLANEOUS
BUILDING PRDTS & MATERIALS DEALERS
BUILDING PRDTS: Concrete
BUILDING PRDTS: Stone
BUILDING STONE, ARTIFICIAL: Concrete
BUILDINGS & COMPONENTS: Prefabricated Metal
BUILDINGS, PREFABRICATED: Wholesalers
BUILDINGS: Portable
BUILDINGS: Prefabricated, Metal
BUILDINGS: Prefabricated, Plastic
BUILDINGS: Prefabricated, Wood
BUILDINGS: Prefabricated, Wood
BULLETIN BOARDS: Wood
BUMPERS: Motor Vehicle
BURIAL VAULTS: Concrete Or Precast Terrazzo
BURLAP & BURLAP PRDTS
BURNERS: Gas, Indl
BUSES: Wholesalers
BUSHINGS & BEARINGS: Copper, Exc Machined
BUSHINGS: Cast Steel, Exc Investment
BUSINESS ACTIVITIES: Non-Commercial Site
BUSINESS FORMS WHOLESALERS
BUSINESS FORMS: Printed, Continuous
BUSINESS FORMS: Printed, Manifold
BUSINESS MACHINE REPAIR, ELECTRIC
BUSINESS SUPPORT SVCS
BUTADIENE: Indl, Organic, Chemical
BUTTONS

C

CABINETS & CASES: Show, Display & Storage, Exc Wood
CABINETS: Bathroom Vanities, Wood
CABINETS: Entertainment
CABINETS: Entertainment Units, Household, Wood
CABINETS: Factory
CABINETS: Filing, Metal
CABINETS: Filing, Wood
CABINETS: Kitchen, Metal
CABINETS: Kitchen, Wood
CABINETS: Office, Metal
CABINETS: Office, Wood
CABINETS: Radio & Television, Metal
CABINETS: Show, Display, Etc, Wood, Exc Refrigerated
CABLE TELEVISION
CABLE TELEVISION PRDTS
CABLE: Fiber
CABLE: Fiber Optic
CABLE: Nonferrous, Shipboard
CABLE: Noninsulated
CABLE: Ropes & Fiber
CABLE: Steel, Insulated Or Armored
CAGES: Wire
CALCULATING & ACCOUNTING EQPT
CALIBRATING SVCS, NEC
CAMERA & PHOTOGRAPHIC SPLYS STORES
CAMERAS & RELATED EQPT: Photographic
CANDLE SHOPS
CANDLES
CANDLES: Wholesalers
CANDY & CONFECTIONS: Cake Ornaments
CANDY & CONFECTIONS: Candy Bars, Including Chocolate Covered
CANDY & CONFECTIONS: Chocolate Candy, Exc Solid Chocolate
CANDY & CONFECTIONS: Fudge
CANDY, NUT & CONFECTIONERY STORES: Candy
CANDY: Chocolate From Cacao Beans
CANNED SPECIALTIES
CANOPIES: Sheet Metal
CANS: Aluminum
CANS: Metal
CANVAS PRDTS
CANVAS PRDTS, WHOLESALE
CANVAS PRDTS: Convertible Tops, Car/Boat, Fm Purchased Mtrl
CANVAS PRDTS: Shades, Made From Purchased Materials
CAPACITORS: Fixed Or Variable
CAPACITORS: NEC
CAPS & PLUGS: Electric, Attachment
CAR WASH EQPT
CARBIDES
CARBON & GRAPHITE PRDTS, NEC
CARBONS: Electric
CARBURETORS
CARDBOARD PRDTS, EXC DIE-CUT
CARDBOARD: Waterproof, Made From Purchased Materials
CARDIOVASCULAR SYSTEM DRUGS, EXC DIAGNOSTIC
CARDS: Color
CARDS: Greeting
CARDS: Identification
CARDS: Playing
CARPETS & RUGS: Tufted
CARPETS, RUGS & FLOOR COVERING
CARPETS: Hand & Machine Made
CARPETS: Textile Fiber
CARRIAGES: Horse Drawn
CARRYING CASES, WHOLESALE
CARTONS: Egg, Molded Pulp, Made From Purchased Materials
CASEMENTS: Aluminum
CASES, WOOD
CASES: Attache'
CASES: Carrying
CASES: Carrying, Clothing & Apparel
CASES: Jewelry
CASES: Nonrefrigerated, Exc Wood
CASES: Packing, Nailed Or Lock Corner, Wood
CASES: Plastic
CASES: Sample Cases
CASES: Shipping, Nailed Or Lock Corner, Wood
CASH REGISTER REPAIR SVCS
CASING-HEAD BUTANE & PROPANE PRODUCTION
CASINGS: Sheet Metal
CASKETS & ACCESS
CASKETS WHOLESALERS
CAST STONE: Concrete
CASTERS
CASTINGS GRINDING: For The Trade
CASTINGS: Aerospace Investment, Ferrous
CASTINGS: Aerospace, Aluminum
CASTINGS: Aerospace, Nonferrous, Exc Aluminum
CASTINGS: Aluminum
CASTINGS: Brass, Bronze & Copper
CASTINGS: Bronze, NEC, Exc Die
CASTINGS: Commercial Investment, Ferrous
CASTINGS: Die, Aluminum
CASTINGS: Die, Lead
CASTINGS: Die, Nonferrous
CASTINGS: Die, Zinc
CASTINGS: Ductile
CASTINGS: Gray Iron
CASTINGS: Machinery, Aluminum
CASTINGS: Machinery, Nonferrous, Exc Die or Aluminum Copper
CASTINGS: Precision
CASTINGS: Steel
CATALOG & MAIL-ORDER HOUSES
CATALOG SALES
CATALOG SHOWROOMS
CATALYSTS: Chemical
CATERERS
CEMENT & CONCRETE RELATED PRDTS & EQPT: Bituminous
CEMENT ROCK: Crushed & Broken
CEMENT: Heat Resistant
CEMENT: Hydraulic
CEMENT: Masonry
CEMENT: Natural
CEMENT: Portland

PRODUCT INDEX

CEMETERY MEMORIAL DEALERS
CERAMIC FIBER
CERAMIC FLOOR & WALL TILE WHOLESALERS
CHAIN: Welded, Made From Purchased Wire
CHAMBERS & CAISSONS
CHANDELIERS: Residential
CHARCOAL: Activated
CHART & GRAPH DESIGN SVCS
CHASSIS: Motor Vehicle
CHEESE WHOLESALERS
CHEMICAL INDICATORS
CHEMICAL PROCESSING MACHINERY & EQPT
CHEMICAL: Sodm Compnds/Salts, Inorg, Exc Rfnd Sodm Chloride
CHEMICALS & ALLIED PRDTS WHOLESALERS, NEC
CHEMICALS & ALLIED PRDTS, WHOLESALE: Alkalines & Chlorine
CHEMICALS & ALLIED PRDTS, WHOLESALE: Anti-Corrosion Prdts
CHEMICALS & ALLIED PRDTS, WHOLESALE: Aromatic
CHEMICALS & ALLIED PRDTS, WHOLESALE: Chemical Additives
CHEMICALS & ALLIED PRDTS, WHOLESALE: Chemicals, Indl
CHEMICALS & ALLIED PRDTS, WHOLESALE: Dry Ice
CHEMICALS & ALLIED PRDTS, WHOLESALE: Essential Oils
CHEMICALS & ALLIED PRDTS, WHOLESALE: Oxygen
CHEMICALS & ALLIED PRDTS, WHOLESALE: Plastics Materials, NEC
CHEMICALS & ALLIED PRDTS, WHOLESALE: Plastics Prdts, NEC
CHEMICALS & ALLIED PRDTS, WHOLESALE: Plastics Sheets & Rods
CHEMICALS & ALLIED PRDTS, WHOLESALE: Polyurethane Prdts
CHEMICALS & ALLIED PRDTS, WHOLESALE: Salts & Polishes, Indl
CHEMICALS & ALLIED PRDTS, WHOLESALE: Syn Resin, Rub/Plastic
CHEMICALS & ALLIED PRDTS, WHOLESALE: Waxes, Exc Petroleum
CHEMICALS/ALLIED PRDTS, WHOL: Coal Tar Prdts, Prim/Intermdt
CHEMICALS: Agricultural
CHEMICALS: Alcohols
CHEMICALS: Aluminum Chloride
CHEMICALS: Aluminum Compounds
CHEMICALS: Aluminum Oxide
CHEMICALS: Brine
CHEMICALS: Calcium & Calcium Compounds
CHEMICALS: Compounds Or Salts, Iron, Ferric Or Ferrous
CHEMICALS: Fire Retardant
CHEMICALS: Formaldehyde
CHEMICALS: High Purity Grade, Organic
CHEMICALS: High Purity, Refined From Technical Grade
CHEMICALS: Hydrogen Peroxide
CHEMICALS: Inorganic, NEC
CHEMICALS: Isotopes, Radioactive
CHEMICALS: Lithium Compounds, Inorganic
CHEMICALS: Medicinal
CHEMICALS: Medicinal, Organic, Uncompounded, Bulk
CHEMICALS: Metal Salts/Compounds, Exc Sodium, Potassium/Alum
CHEMICALS: NEC
CHEMICALS: Organic, NEC
CHEMICALS: Phenol
CHEMICALS: Silica Compounds
CHEMICALS: Sodium Bicarbonate
CHEMICALS: Sodium/Potassium Cmpnds,Exc Bleach,Alkalies/Alum
CHEMICALS: Sulfur Chloride
CHEMICALS: Water Treatment
CHEWING GUM
CHILD DAY CARE SVCS
CHILDREN'S & INFANTS' CLOTHING STORES
CHILDREN'S WEAR STORES
CHIMES: Electric
CHIMNEY CAPS: Concrete
CHIMNEYS & FITTINGS
CHINA COOKWARE
CHLORINE
CHOCOLATE, EXC CANDY FROM BEANS: Chips, Powder, Block, Syrup
CHOCOLATE, EXC CANDY FROM PURCH CHOC: Chips, Powder, Block
CHRISTMAS TREE LIGHTING SETS: Electric
CHUCKS
CHURCHES
CHUTES & TROUGHS
CIGAR LIGHTERS EXC PRECIOUS METAL
CIGARETTE & CIGAR PRDTS & ACCESS
CIRCUIT BOARDS, PRINTED: Television & Radio
CIRCUIT BOARDS: Wiring
CIRCUITS, INTEGRATED: Hybrid
CIRCUITS: Electronic
CIRCULAR KNIT FABRICS DYEING & FINISHING
CLAMPS & COUPLINGS: Hose
CLAY PRDTS: Architectural
CLAYS, EXC KAOLIN & BALL
CLEANING EQPT: Blast, Dustless
CLEANING EQPT: Carpet Sweepers, Exc Household Elec Vacuum
CLEANING EQPT: Commercial
CLEANING EQPT: High Pressure
CLEANING OR POLISHING PREPARATIONS, NEC
CLEANING PRDTS: Degreasing Solvent
CLEANING PRDTS: Deodorants, Nonpersonal
CLEANING PRDTS: Disinfectants, Household Or Indl Plant
CLEANING PRDTS: Drycleaning Preparations
CLEANING PRDTS: Indl Plant Disinfectants Or Deodorants
CLEANING PRDTS: Laundry Preparations
CLEANING PRDTS: Metal Polish
CLEANING PRDTS: Polishing Preparations & Related Prdts
CLEANING PRDTS: Rug, Upholstery/Dry Clng Detergents/Spotters
CLEANING PRDTS: Sanitation Preparations
CLEANING PRDTS: Sanitation Preps, Disinfectants/Deodorants
CLEANING PRDTS: Shoe Polish Or Cleaner
CLEANING PRDTS: Specialty
CLEANING PRDTS: Window Cleaning Preparations
CLEANING SVCS: Industrial Or Commercial
CLIPPERS: Fingernail & Toenail
CLIPS & FASTENERS, MADE FROM PURCHASED WIRE
CLOCKS
CLOSURES: Closures, Stamped Metal
CLOSURES: Plastic
CLOTHES HANGERS, WHOLESALE
CLOTHING & ACCESS, WOMEN, CHILD & INFANT, WHOL: Scarves
CLOTHING & ACCESS, WOMEN, CHILD & INFANT, WHOLESALE: Under
CLOTHING & ACCESS, WOMEN, CHILD & INFANT, WHSLE: Sportswear
CLOTHING & ACCESS, WOMEN, CHILDREN & INFANT, WHOL: Access
CLOTHING & ACCESS, WOMEN, CHILDREN & INFANT, WHOL: Gloves
CLOTHING & ACCESS, WOMEN, CHILDREN & INFANT, WHOL: Handbags
CLOTHING & ACCESS, WOMEN, CHILDREN & INFANT, WHOL: Sweaters
CLOTHING & ACCESS, WOMEN, CHILDREN & INFANTS, WHOL: Purses
CLOTHING & ACCESS, WOMEN, CHILDREN/INFANT, WHOL: Baby Goods
CLOTHING & ACCESS, WOMEN, CHILDREN/INFANT, WHOL: Nightwear
CLOTHING & ACCESS, WOMEN, CHILDREN/INFANT, WHOL: Outerwear
CLOTHING & ACCESS, WOMEN, CHILDREN/INFANT, WHOL: Swimsuits
CLOTHING & ACCESS, WOMENS, CHILDRE'S & INFANTS, WHOL: Suits
CLOTHING & ACCESS, WOMENS, CHILDREN & INFANTS, WHOL: Hats
CLOTHING & ACCESS: Costumes, Masquerade
CLOTHING & ACCESS: Costumes, Theatrical
CLOTHING & ACCESS: Cummerbunds
CLOTHING & ACCESS: Footlets
CLOTHING & ACCESS: Handicapped
CLOTHING & ACCESS: Handkerchiefs, Exc Paper
CLOTHING & ACCESS: Hospital Gowns
CLOTHING & ACCESS: Men's Miscellaneous Access
CLOTHING & ACCESS: Suspenders
CLOTHING & APPAREL STORES: Custom
CLOTHING & FURNISHINGS, MEN & BOY, WHOLESALE: Suits/Trousers
CLOTHING & FURNISHINGS, MEN'S & BOYS', WHOLESALE: Fur
CLOTHING & FURNISHINGS, MEN'S & BOYS', WHOLESALE: Gloves
CLOTHING & FURNISHINGS, MEN'S & BOYS', WHOLESALE: Hats
CLOTHING & FURNISHINGS, MEN'S & BOYS', WHOLESALE: Neckwear
CLOTHING & FURNISHINGS, MEN'S & BOYS', WHOLESALE: Scarves
CLOTHING & FURNISHINGS, MEN'S & BOYS', WHOLESALE: Shirts
CLOTHING & FURNISHINGS, MEN'S & BOYS', WHOLESALE: Trousers
CLOTHING & FURNISHINGS, MEN'S & BOYS', WHOLESALE: Umbrellas
CLOTHING & FURNISHINGS, MEN'S & BOYS', WHOLESALE: Uniforms
CLOTHING & FURNISHINGS, MENS & BOYS, WHOL: Sportswear/Work
CLOTHING & FURNISHINGS, MENS & BOYS, WHOLESALE: Apprl Belts
CLOTHING ACCESS STORES: Umbrellas
CLOTHING STORES, NEC
CLOTHING STORES: Dancewear
CLOTHING STORES: Jeans
CLOTHING STORES: Leather
CLOTHING STORES: Shirts, Custom Made
CLOTHING STORES: T-Shirts, Printed, Custom
CLOTHING STORES: Uniforms & Work
CLOTHING STORES: Unisex
CLOTHING STORES: Work
CLOTHING, WOMEN & CHILD, WHLSE: Dress, Suit, Skirt & Blouse
CLOTHING/ACCESS, WOMEN, CHILDREN/INFANT, WHOL: Apparel Belt
CLOTHING/FURNISHINGS, MEN/BOY, WHOL: Furnishings, Exc Shoes
CLOTHING: Academic Vestments
CLOTHING: Access
CLOTHING: Access, Women's & Misses'
CLOTHING: Aprons, Exc Rubber/Plastic, Women, Misses, Junior
CLOTHING: Aprons, Harness
CLOTHING: Aprons, Work, Exc Rubberized & Plastic, Men's
CLOTHING: Athletic & Sportswear, Men's & Boys'
CLOTHING: Athletic & Sportswear, Women's & Girls'
CLOTHING: Baker, Barber, Lab/Svc Ind Apparel, Washable, Men
CLOTHING: Bathing Suits & Beachwear, Children's
CLOTHING: Bathing Suits & Swimwear, Girls, Children & Infant
CLOTHING: Bathing Suits & Swimwear, Knit
CLOTHING: Bathrobes, Mens & Womens, From Purchased Materials
CLOTHING: Beachwear, Knit
CLOTHING: Belts
CLOTHING: Bibs, Waterproof, From Purchased Materials
CLOTHING: Blouses, Boys', From Purchased Materials
CLOTHING: Blouses, Women's & Girls'
CLOTHING: Blouses, Womens & Juniors, From Purchased Mtrls
CLOTHING: Brassieres
CLOTHING: Bridal Gowns
CLOTHING: Burial
CLOTHING: Capes & Jackets, Women's & Misses'
CLOTHING: Capes, Exc Fur/Rubber, Womens, Misses & Juniors
CLOTHING: Caps, Baseball
CLOTHING: Chemises, Camisoles/Teddies, Women, Misses/Junior
CLOTHING: Children & Infants'
CLOTHING: Children's, Girls'
CLOTHING: Clergy Vestments
CLOTHING: Coats & Jackets, Leather & Sheep-Lined
CLOTHING: Coats & Suits, Men's & Boys'
CLOTHING: Coats, Leatherette, Oiled Fabric, Etc, Mens & Boys
CLOTHING: Coats, Overcoats & Vests
CLOTHING: Coats, Tailored, Mens/Boys, From Purchased Mtls
CLOTHING: Cold Weather Knit Outerwear, Including Ski Wear
CLOTHING: Corset Access, Clasps & Stays
CLOTHING: Costumes
CLOTHING: Diaper Covers, Waterproof, From Purchased Material
CLOTHING: Disposable

PRODUCT INDEX

CLOTHING: Down-Filled, Men's & Boys'
CLOTHING: Dresses
CLOTHING: Dresses & Skirts
CLOTHING: Dresses, Knit
CLOTHING: Dressing Gowns, Mens/Womens, From Purchased Matls
CLOTHING: Foundation Garments, Women's
CLOTHING: Furs
CLOTHING: Garments, Indl, Men's & Boys
CLOTHING: Girdles & Other Foundation Garments, Knit
CLOTHING: Girdles & Panty Girdles
CLOTHING: Gloves, Knit, Exc Dress & Semidress
CLOTHING: Gowns & Dresses, Wedding
CLOTHING: Gowns, Formal
CLOTHING: Hats & Caps, Leather
CLOTHING: Hats & Caps, NEC
CLOTHING: Hats & Caps, Uniform
CLOTHING: Hats & Headwear, Knit
CLOTHING: Hosiery, Men's & Boys'
CLOTHING: Hosiery, Pantyhose & Knee Length, Sheer
CLOTHING: Hospital, Men's
CLOTHING: Housedresses
CLOTHING: Jackets & Vests, Exc Fur & Leather, Women's
CLOTHING: Jackets, Knit
CLOTHING: Jeans, Men's & Boys'
CLOTHING: Knit Underwear & Nightwear
CLOTHING: Leather
CLOTHING: Leather & sheep-lined clothing
CLOTHING: Leg Warmers
CLOTHING: Maternity
CLOTHING: Men's & boy's clothing, nec
CLOTHING: Men's & boy's underwear & nightwear
CLOTHING: Mens & Boys Jackets, Sport, Suede, Leatherette
CLOTHING: Millinery
CLOTHING: Neckties, Knit
CLOTHING: Neckwear
CLOTHING: Outerwear, Knit
CLOTHING: Outerwear, Lthr, Wool/Down-Filled, Men, Youth/Boy
CLOTHING: Outerwear, Women's & Misses' NEC
CLOTHING: Overcoats & Topcoats, Men/Boy, Purchased Materials
CLOTHING: Pants, Work, Men's, Youths' & Boys'
CLOTHING: Panty Hose
CLOTHING: Raincoats, Exc Vulcanized Rubber, Purchased Matls
CLOTHING: Robes & Dressing Gowns
CLOTHING: Robes & Housecoats, Children's
CLOTHING: Scarves & Mufflers, Knit
CLOTHING: Service Apparel, Women's
CLOTHING: Shawls, Knit
CLOTHING: Sheep-Lined
CLOTHING: Shirts
CLOTHING: Shirts, Dress, Men's & Boys'
CLOTHING: Shirts, Knit
CLOTHING: Shirts, Sports & Polo, Men & Boy, Purchased Mtrl
CLOTHING: Shirts, Women's & Juniors', From Purchased Mtrls
CLOTHING: Skirts
CLOTHING: Slacks & Shorts, Dress, Men's, Youths' & Boys'
CLOTHING: Slacks, Girls' & Children's
CLOTHING: Sleeping Garments, Women's & Children's
CLOTHING: Slipper Socks
CLOTHING: Socks
CLOTHING: Sportswear, Women's
CLOTHING: Suits & Skirts, Women's & Misses'
CLOTHING: Suits, Men's & Boys', From Purchased Materials
CLOTHING: Sweaters & Sweater Coats, Knit
CLOTHING: Sweaters, Men's & Boys'
CLOTHING: Sweatshirts & T-Shirts, Men's & Boys'
CLOTHING: Swimwear, Men's & Boys'
CLOTHING: Swimwear, Women's & Misses'
CLOTHING: T-Shirts & Tops, Knit
CLOTHING: T-Shirts & Tops, Women's & Girls'
CLOTHING: Tailored Suits & Formal Jackets
CLOTHING: Ties, Bow, Men's & Boys', From Purchased Materials
CLOTHING: Ties, Handsewn, From Purchased Materials
CLOTHING: Ties, Neck & Bow, Men's & Boys'
CLOTHING: Ties, Neck, Men's & Boys', From Purchased Material
CLOTHING: Tights & Leg Warmers
CLOTHING: Tights, Women's
CLOTHING: Trousers & Slacks, Men's & Boys'
CLOTHING: Underwear, Knit
CLOTHING: Underwear, Men's & Boys'
CLOTHING: Underwear, Women's & Children's
CLOTHING: Uniforms & Vestments
CLOTHING: Uniforms, Ex Athletic, Women's, Misses' & Juniors'
CLOTHING: Uniforms, Men's & Boys'
CLOTHING: Uniforms, Military, Men/Youth, Purchased Materials
CLOTHING: Uniforms, Policemen's, From Purchased Materials
CLOTHING: Uniforms, Team Athletic
CLOTHING: Uniforms, Work
CLOTHING: Warm Weather Knit Outerwear, Including Beachwear
CLOTHING: Waterproof Outerwear
CLOTHING: Work Apparel, Exc Uniforms
CLOTHING: Work, Men's
CLUTCHES OR BRAKES: Electromagnetic
CLUTCHES, EXC VEHICULAR
COAL MINING SERVICES
COAL MINING SVCS: Bituminous, Contract Basis
COAL MINING: Anthracite
COATING COMPOUNDS: Tar
COATING OR WRAPPING SVC: Steel Pipe
COATING SVC
COATING SVC: Electrodes
COATING SVC: Hot Dip, Metals Or Formed Prdts
COATING SVC: Metals & Formed Prdts
COATING SVC: Metals, With Plastic Or Resins
COATING SVC: Rust Preventative
COATING SVC: Silicon
COATINGS: Air Curing
COATINGS: Epoxy
COATINGS: Polyurethane
COFFEE SVCS
COILS & TRANSFORMERS
COILS: Electric Motors Or Generators
COILS: Pipe
COIN OPERATED LAUNDRIES & DRYCLEANERS
COIN-OPERATED LAUNDRY
COKE: Calcined Petroleum, Made From Purchased Materials
COKE: Produced In Chemical Recovery Coke Ovens
COLLECTION AGENCY, EXC REAL ESTATE
COLLEGES, UNIVERSITIES & PROFESSIONAL SCHOOLS
COLLETS
COLOR SEPARATION: Photographic & Movie Film
COLORS: Pigments, Inorganic
COLORS: Pigments, Organic
COMFORTERS & QUILTS, FROM MANMADE FIBER OR SILK
COMMERCIAL & INDL SHELVING WHOLESALERS
COMMERCIAL & LITERARY WRITINGS
COMMERCIAL & OFFICE BUILDINGS RENOVATION & REPAIR
COMMERCIAL ART & GRAPHIC DESIGN SVCS
COMMERCIAL EQPT WHOLESALERS, NEC
COMMERCIAL EQPT, WHOLESALE: Bakery Eqpt & Splys
COMMERCIAL EQPT, WHOLESALE: Comm Cooking & Food Svc Eqpt
COMMERCIAL EQPT, WHOLESALE: Display Eqpt, Exc Refrigerated
COMMERCIAL EQPT, WHOLESALE: Mannequins
COMMERCIAL EQPT, WHOLESALE: Restaurant, NEC
COMMERCIAL EQPT, WHOLESALE: Scales, Exc Laboratory
COMMERCIAL EQPT, WHOLESALE: Store Fixtures & Display Eqpt
COMMERCIAL LAUNDRY EQPT
COMMERCIAL PHOTOGRAPHIC STUDIO
COMMERCIAL PRINTING & NEWSPAPER PUBLISHING COMBINED
COMMON SAND MINING
COMMUNICATION HEADGEAR: Telephone
COMMUNICATIONS CARRIER: Wired
COMMUNICATIONS EQPT & SYSTEMS, NEC
COMMUNICATIONS EQPT REPAIR & MAINTENANCE
COMMUNICATIONS EQPT WHOLESALERS
COMMUNICATIONS EQPT: Microwave
COMMUNICATIONS EQPT: Radio, Marine
COMMUNICATIONS SVCS
COMMUNICATIONS SVCS: Cellular
COMMUNICATIONS SVCS: Data
COMMUNICATIONS SVCS: Facsimile Transmission
COMMUNICATIONS SVCS: Internet Host Svcs
COMMUNICATIONS SVCS: Online Svc Providers
COMMUNICATIONS SVCS: Proprietary Online Svcs Networks
COMMUNICATIONS SVCS: Satellite Earth Stations
COMMUNICATIONS SVCS: Signal Enhancement Network Svcs
COMMUNICATIONS SVCS: Telephone, Local
COMMUNICATIONS SVCS: Telephone, Voice
COMMUNITY CHESTS
COMMUTATORS: Electronic
COMPACT DISCS OR CD'S, WHOLESALE
COMPACT LASER DISCS: Prerecorded
COMPACTORS: Trash & Garbage, Residential
COMPARATORS: Optical
COMPOSITION STONE: Plastic
COMPOST
COMPRESSORS, AIR CONDITIONING: Wholesalers
COMPRESSORS: Air & Gas
COMPRESSORS: Air & Gas, Including Vacuum Pumps
COMPRESSORS: Refrigeration & Air Conditioning Eqpt
COMPUTER & COMPUTER SOFTWARE STORES
COMPUTER & COMPUTER SOFTWARE STORES: Peripheral Eqpt
COMPUTER & COMPUTER SOFTWARE STORES: Software, Bus/Non-Game
COMPUTER & COMPUTER SOFTWARE STORES: Software, Computer Game
COMPUTER & OFFICE MACHINE MAINTENANCE & REPAIR
COMPUTER DISKETTES WHOLESALERS
COMPUTER FORMS
COMPUTER GRAPHICS SVCS
COMPUTER HARDWARE REQUIREMENTS ANALYSIS
COMPUTER INTERFACE EQPT: Indl Process
COMPUTER PERIPHERAL EQPT, NEC
COMPUTER PERIPHERAL EQPT, WHOLESALE
COMPUTER PERIPHERAL EQPT: Encoders
COMPUTER PERIPHERAL EQPT: Film Reader Devices
COMPUTER PERIPHERAL EQPT: Graphic Displays, Exc Terminals
COMPUTER PERIPHERAL EQPT: Input Or Output
COMPUTER PROGRAMMING SVCS
COMPUTER PROGRAMMING SVCS: Custom
COMPUTER RELATED MAINTENANCE SVCS
COMPUTER SERVICE BUREAU
COMPUTER SOFTWARE DEVELOPMENT
COMPUTER SOFTWARE DEVELOPMENT & APPLICATIONS
COMPUTER SOFTWARE SYSTEMS ANALYSIS & DESIGN: Custom
COMPUTER STORAGE DEVICES, NEC
COMPUTER TERMINALS
COMPUTER TERMINALS: CRT
COMPUTER-AIDED DESIGN SYSTEMS SVCS
COMPUTER-AIDED ENGINEERING SYSTEMS SVCS
COMPUTERS, NEC
COMPUTERS, NEC, WHOLESALE
COMPUTERS, PERIPHERALS & SOFTWARE, WHOLESALE: Disk Drives
COMPUTERS, PERIPHERALS & SOFTWARE, WHOLESALE: Printers
COMPUTERS, PERIPHERALS & SOFTWARE, WHOLESALE: Software
COMPUTERS: Indl, Process, Gas Flow
COMPUTERS: Mainframe
COMPUTERS: Mini
COMPUTERS: Personal
CONCENTRATES, DRINK
CONCENTRATES, FLAVORING, EXC DRINK
CONCRETE CURING & HARDENING COMPOUNDS
CONCRETE MIXERS
CONCRETE PLANTS
CONCRETE PRDTS
CONCRETE PRDTS, PRECAST, NEC
CONCRETE: Asphaltic, Not From Refineries
CONCRETE: Bituminous
CONCRETE: Ready-Mixed
CONDENSERS & CONDENSING UNITS: Air Conditioner
CONDENSERS: Fixed Or Variable
CONDENSERS: Heat Transfer Eqpt, Evaporative
CONDENSERS: Motors Or Generators
CONDUITS & FITTINGS: Electric
CONDUITS: Pressed Pulp Fiber, Made From Purchased Materials
CONFECTIONERY PRDTS WHOLESALERS
CONFECTIONS & CANDY

2017 Harris
New York Manufacturers Directory

1105

PRODUCT INDEX

CONNECTORS & TERMINALS: Electrical Device Uses
CONNECTORS: Cord, Electric
CONNECTORS: Electrical
CONNECTORS: Electronic
CONNECTORS: Solderless, Electric-Wiring Devices
CONSTRUCTION & MINING MACHINERY WHOLESALERS
CONSTRUCTION & ROAD MAINTENANCE EQPT: Drags, Road
CONSTRUCTION EQPT: Attachments
CONSTRUCTION EQPT: Attachments, Snow Plow
CONSTRUCTION EQPT: Crane Carriers
CONSTRUCTION EQPT: Cranes
CONSTRUCTION EQPT: Dozers, Tractor Mounted, Material Moving
CONSTRUCTION EQPT: Hammer Mills, Port, Incl Rock/Ore Crush
CONSTRUCTION EQPT: Rollers, Sheepsfoot & Vibratory
CONSTRUCTION EQPT: SCRAPERS, GRADERS, ROLLERS & SIMILAR EQPT
CONSTRUCTION EQPT: Wrecker Hoists, Automobile
CONSTRUCTION MATERIALS, WHOLESALE: Aggregate
CONSTRUCTION MATERIALS, WHOLESALE: Awnings
CONSTRUCTION MATERIALS, WHOLESALE: Block, Concrete & Cinder
CONSTRUCTION MATERIALS, WHOLESALE: Blocks, Building, NEC
CONSTRUCTION MATERIALS, WHOLESALE: Building Stone, Granite
CONSTRUCTION MATERIALS, WHOLESALE: Building, Exterior
CONSTRUCTION MATERIALS, WHOLESALE: Building, Interior
CONSTRUCTION MATERIALS, WHOLESALE: Cement
CONSTRUCTION MATERIALS, WHOLESALE: Clay, Exc Refractory
CONSTRUCTION MATERIALS, WHOLESALE: Concrete Mixtures
CONSTRUCTION MATERIALS, WHOLESALE: Door Frames
CONSTRUCTION MATERIALS, WHOLESALE: Glass
CONSTRUCTION MATERIALS, WHOLESALE: Gravel
CONSTRUCTION MATERIALS, WHOLESALE: Lime Building Prdts
CONSTRUCTION MATERIALS, WHOLESALE: Limestone
CONSTRUCTION MATERIALS, WHOLESALE: Masons' Materials
CONSTRUCTION MATERIALS, WHOLESALE: Millwork
CONSTRUCTION MATERIALS, WHOLESALE: Molding, All Materials
CONSTRUCTION MATERIALS, WHOLESALE: Paving Materials
CONSTRUCTION MATERIALS, WHOLESALE: Paving Mixtures
CONSTRUCTION MATERIALS, WHOLESALE: Prefabricated Structures
CONSTRUCTION MATERIALS, WHOLESALE: Roof, Asphalt/Sheet Metal
CONSTRUCTION MATERIALS, WHOLESALE: Roofing & Siding Material
CONSTRUCTION MATERIALS, WHOLESALE: Sand
CONSTRUCTION MATERIALS, WHOLESALE: Septic Tanks
CONSTRUCTION MATERIALS, WHOLESALE: Siding, Exc Wood
CONSTRUCTION MATERIALS, WHOLESALE: Stone, Crushed Or Broken
CONSTRUCTION MATERIALS, WHOLESALE: Tile, Clay/Other Ceramic
CONSTRUCTION MATERIALS, WHOLESALE: Windows
CONSTRUCTION MATLS, WHOL: Lumber, Rough, Dressed/Finished
CONSTRUCTION SAND MINING
CONSTRUCTION SITE PREPARATION SVCS
CONSTRUCTION: Bridge
CONSTRUCTION: Commercial & Institutional Building
CONSTRUCTION: Dry Cleaning Plant
CONSTRUCTION: Food Prdts Manufacturing or Packing Plant
CONSTRUCTION: Greenhouse
CONSTRUCTION: Guardrails, Highway
CONSTRUCTION: Heavy Highway & Street
CONSTRUCTION: Indl Building & Warehouse
CONSTRUCTION: Indl Buildings, New, NEC
CONSTRUCTION: Pharmaceutical Manufacturing Plant
CONSTRUCTION: Power & Communication Transmission Tower
CONSTRUCTION: Religious Building
CONSTRUCTION: Single-Family Housing
CONSTRUCTION: Single-family Housing, New
CONSTRUCTION: Street Surfacing & Paving
CONSTRUCTION: Tennis Court
CONSTRUCTION: Waste Water & Sewage Treatment Plant
CONSULTING SVC: Business, NEC
CONSULTING SVC: Computer
CONSULTING SVC: Educational
CONSULTING SVC: Engineering
CONSULTING SVC: Financial Management
CONSULTING SVC: Human Resource
CONSULTING SVC: Management
CONSULTING SVC: Marketing Management
CONSULTING SVC: Online Technology
CONSULTING SVC: Sales Management
CONSULTING SVCS, BUSINESS: Communications
CONSULTING SVCS, BUSINESS: Energy Conservation
CONSULTING SVCS, BUSINESS: Publishing
CONSULTING SVCS, BUSINESS: Safety Training Svcs
CONSULTING SVCS, BUSINESS: Sys Engnrg, Exc Computer/Prof
CONSULTING SVCS, BUSINESS: Systems Analysis & Engineering
CONSULTING SVCS, BUSINESS: Systems Analysis Or Design
CONSULTING SVCS, BUSINESS: Test Development & Evaluation
CONSULTING SVCS, BUSINESS: Testing, Educational Or Personnel
CONSULTING SVCS: Oil
CONSULTING SVCS: Scientific
CONTACT LENSES
CONTACTS: Electrical
CONTAINERS, GLASS: Cosmetic Jars
CONTAINERS, GLASS: Food
CONTAINERS: Cargo, Wood & Metal Combination
CONTAINERS: Cargo, Wood & Wood With Metal
CONTAINERS: Corrugated
CONTAINERS: Foil, Bakery Goods & Frozen Foods
CONTAINERS: Food & Beverage
CONTAINERS: Food, Folding, Made From Purchased Materials
CONTAINERS: Food, Liquid Tight, Including Milk
CONTAINERS: Glass
CONTAINERS: Laminated Phenolic & Vulcanized Fiber
CONTAINERS: Liquid Tight Fiber, From Purchased Materials
CONTAINERS: Metal
CONTAINERS: Plastic
CONTAINERS: Sanitary, Food
CONTAINERS: Shipping & Mailing, Fiber
CONTAINERS: Shipping, Bombs, Metal Plate
CONTAINERS: Wood
CONTRACT FOOD SVCS
CONTRACTOR: Framing
CONTRACTOR: Rigging & Scaffolding
CONTRACTORS: Acoustical & Ceiling Work
CONTRACTORS: Acoustical & Insulation Work
CONTRACTORS: Antenna Installation
CONTRACTORS: Awning Installation
CONTRACTORS: Boiler & Furnace
CONTRACTORS: Boiler Maintenance Contractor
CONTRACTORS: Building Eqpt & Machinery Installation
CONTRACTORS: Building Sign Installation & Mntnce
CONTRACTORS: Carpentry Work
CONTRACTORS: Carpentry, Cabinet & Finish Work
CONTRACTORS: Carpentry, Cabinet Building & Installation
CONTRACTORS: Carpentry, Finish & Trim Work
CONTRACTORS: Ceramic Floor Tile Installation
CONTRACTORS: Closed Circuit Television Installation
CONTRACTORS: Commercial & Office Building
CONTRACTORS: Communications Svcs
CONTRACTORS: Concrete
CONTRACTORS: Concrete Repair
CONTRACTORS: Construction Site Cleanup
CONTRACTORS: Countertop Installation
CONTRACTORS: Demountable Partition Installation
CONTRACTORS: Drywall
CONTRACTORS: Electrical
CONTRACTORS: Electronic Controls Installation
CONTRACTORS: Energy Management Control
CONTRACTORS: Excavating
CONTRACTORS: Excavating Slush Pits & Cellars Svcs
CONTRACTORS: Exterior Wall System Installation
CONTRACTORS: Fence Construction
CONTRACTORS: Fire Detection & Burglar Alarm Systems
CONTRACTORS: Fire Escape Installation
CONTRACTORS: Fire Sprinkler System Installation Svcs
CONTRACTORS: Floor Laying & Other Floor Work
CONTRACTORS: Garage Doors
CONTRACTORS: Gas Field Svcs, NEC
CONTRACTORS: Gasoline Condensation Removal Svcs
CONTRACTORS: Glass, Glazing & Tinting
CONTRACTORS: Heating & Air Conditioning
CONTRACTORS: Highway & Street Paving
CONTRACTORS: Home & Office Intrs Finish, Furnish/Remodel
CONTRACTORS: Hydraulic Eqpt Installation & Svcs
CONTRACTORS: Insulation Installation, Building
CONTRACTORS: Kitchen & Bathroom Remodeling
CONTRACTORS: Lighting Syst
CONTRACTORS: Machinery Installation
CONTRACTORS: Marble Installation, Interior
CONTRACTORS: Masonry & Stonework
CONTRACTORS: Mechanical
CONTRACTORS: Multi-Family Home Remodeling
CONTRACTORS: Office Furniture Installation
CONTRACTORS: Oil & Gas Building, Repairing & Dismantling Svc
CONTRACTORS: Oil & Gas Field Geological Exploration Svcs
CONTRACTORS: Oil & Gas Field Geophysical Exploration Svcs
CONTRACTORS: Oil & Gas Well Casing Cement Svcs
CONTRACTORS: Oil & Gas Well Drilling Svc
CONTRACTORS: Oil & Gas Well Flow Rate Measurement Svcs
CONTRACTORS: Oil & Gas Wells Svcs
CONTRACTORS: Oil Field Haulage Svcs
CONTRACTORS: Oil Field Lease Tanks: Erectg, Clng/Rprg Svcs
CONTRACTORS: Oil Sampling Svcs
CONTRACTORS: Oil/Gas Well Construction, Rpr/Dismantling Svcs
CONTRACTORS: On-Site Welding
CONTRACTORS: Ornamental Metal Work
CONTRACTORS: Paint & Wallpaper Stripping
CONTRACTORS: Painting & Wall Covering
CONTRACTORS: Patio & Deck Construction & Repair
CONTRACTORS: Pipe Laying
CONTRACTORS: Plastering, Plain or Ornamental
CONTRACTORS: Plumbing
CONTRACTORS: Power Generating Eqpt Installation
CONTRACTORS: Prefabricated Fireplace Installation
CONTRACTORS: Prefabricated Window & Door Installation
CONTRACTORS: Refrigeration
CONTRACTORS: Roofing
CONTRACTORS: Roustabout Svcs
CONTRACTORS: Safety & Security Eqpt
CONTRACTORS: Sandblasting Svc, Building Exteriors
CONTRACTORS: Seismograph Survey Svcs
CONTRACTORS: Sheet Metal Work, NEC
CONTRACTORS: Sheet metal Work, Architectural
CONTRACTORS: Siding
CONTRACTORS: Single-family Home General Remodeling
CONTRACTORS: Solar Energy Eqpt
CONTRACTORS: Sound Eqpt Installation
CONTRACTORS: Stone Masonry
CONTRACTORS: Store Fixture Installation
CONTRACTORS: Store Front Construction
CONTRACTORS: Structural Iron Work, Structural
CONTRACTORS: Structural Steel Erection
CONTRACTORS: Svc Station Eqpt Installation, Maint & Repair
CONTRACTORS: Textile Warping
CONTRACTORS: Tile Installation, Ceramic
CONTRACTORS: Ventilation & Duct Work
CONTRACTORS: Water Intake Well Drilling Svc
CONTRACTORS: Water Well Drilling
CONTRACTORS: Water Well Servicing
CONTRACTORS: Well Chemical Treating Svcs
CONTRACTORS: Well Logging Svcs
CONTRACTORS: Window Treatment Installation
CONTRACTORS: Windows & Doors
CONTRACTORS: Wood Floor Installation & Refinishing
CONTROL CIRCUIT DEVICES
CONTROL EQPT: Electric
CONTROL EQPT: Noise
CONTROL PANELS: Electrical
CONTROLS & ACCESS: Indl, Electric
CONTROLS & ACCESS: Motor
CONTROLS: Access, Motor

PRODUCT INDEX

CONTROLS: Automatic Temperature
CONTROLS: Electric Motor
CONTROLS: Environmental
CONTROLS: Marine & Navy, Auxiliary
CONTROLS: Numerical
CONTROLS: Positioning, Electric
CONTROLS: Relay & Ind
CONTROLS: Thermostats, Exc Built-in
CONTROLS: Voice
CONVENIENCE STORES
CONVENTION & TRADE SHOW SVCS
CONVERTERS: Data
CONVERTERS: Frequency
CONVERTERS: Phase Or Rotary, Electrical
CONVERTERS: Power, AC to DC
CONVERTERS: Torque, Exc Auto
CONVEYOR SYSTEMS: Belt, General Indl Use
CONVEYOR SYSTEMS: Bulk Handling
CONVEYOR SYSTEMS: Pneumatic Tube
CONVEYOR SYSTEMS: Robotic
CONVEYORS & CONVEYING EQPT
COOKING & FOOD WARMING EQPT: Commercial
COOKING & FOODWARMING EQPT: Commercial
COOKING WARE, EXC PORCELAIN ENAMELED
COOKING WARE: Cooking Ware, Porcelain Enameled
COOKWARE, STONEWARE: Coarse Earthenware & Pottery
COOKWARE: Fine Earthenware
COOLING TOWERS: Metal
COPPER ORES
COPPER PRDTS: Refined, Primary
COPPER: Rolling & Drawing
COPYRIGHT BUYING & LICENSING
CORD & TWINE
CORE WASH OR WAX
CORES: Magnetic
CORK & CORK PRDTS: Tiles
CORRESPONDENCE SCHOOLS
CORRUGATED PRDTS: Boxes, Partition, Display Items, Sheet/Pad
COSMETIC PREPARATIONS
COSMETICS & TOILETRIES
COSMETICS WHOLESALERS
COSTUME JEWELRY & NOVELTIES: Apparel, Exc Precious Metals
COSTUME JEWELRY & NOVELTIES: Bracelets, Exc Precious Metals
COSTUME JEWELRY & NOVELTIES: Costume Novelties
COSTUME JEWELRY & NOVELTIES: Exc Semi & Precious
COSTUME JEWELRY & NOVELTIES: Necklaces, Exc Precious Metals
COSTUME JEWELRY & NOVELTIES: Pins, Exc Precious Metals
COUGH MEDICINES
COUNTER & SINK TOPS
COUNTERS & COUNTING DEVICES
COUNTERS OR COUNTER DISPLAY CASES, EXC WOOD
COUNTERS OR COUNTER DISPLAY CASES, WOOD
COUNTERS: Mechanical
COUNTING DEVICES: Controls, Revolution & Timing
COUNTING DEVICES: Electromechanical
COUNTING DEVICES: Speed Indicators & Recorders, Vehicle
COUPLINGS: Shaft
COUPON REDEMPTION SVCS
COURIER SVCS, AIR: Package Delivery, Private
COURIER SVCS: Ground
COVERS: Automobile Seat
COVERS: Automotive, Exc Seat & Tire
COVERS: Canvas
COVERS: Hot Tub & Spa
COVERS: Slip Made Of Fabric, Plastic, Etc.
CRANE & AERIAL LIFT SVCS
CRANES & MONORAIL SYSTEMS
CRANES: Indl Plant
CRANKSHAFTS & CAMSHAFTS: Machining
CRATES: Fruit, Wood Wirebound
CREDIT BUREAUS
CROWNS & CLOSURES
CRUDE PETROLEUM & NATURAL GAS PRODUCTION
CRUDE PETROLEUM & NATURAL GAS PRODUCTION
CRUDE PETROLEUM PRODUCTION
CRUDES: Cyclic, Organic
CRYOGENIC COOLING DEVICES: Infrared Detectors, Masers
CRYSTALS
CULTURE MEDIA

CULVERTS: Metal Plate
CUPS: Paper, Made From Purchased Materials
CUPS: Plastic Exc Polystyrene Foam
CURBING: Granite Or Stone
CURTAIN & DRAPERY FIXTURES: Poles, Rods & Rollers
CURTAIN WALLS: Building, Steel
CURTAINS & BEDDING: Knit
CURTAINS & CURTAIN FABRICS: Lace
CURTAINS: Cottage Sets, From Purchased Materials
CURTAINS: Shower
CURTAINS: Window, From Purchased Materials
CUSHIONS & PILLOWS
CUSHIONS & PILLOWS: Bed, From Purchased Materials
CUSHIONS: Textile, Exc Spring & Carpet
CUSTOM COMPOUNDING OF RUBBER MATERIALS
CUT STONE & STONE PRODUCTS
CUTLERY
CUTLERY WHOLESALERS
CUTOUTS: Cardboard, Die-Cut, Made From Purchased Materials
CUTOUTS: Distribution
CUTTING SVC: Paper, Exc Die-Cut
CYCLIC CRUDES & INTERMEDIATES
CYLINDER & ACTUATORS: Fluid Power
CYLINDERS: Pressure

D

DAIRY EQPT
DAIRY PRDTS STORE: Cheese
DAIRY PRDTS STORE: Ice Cream, Packaged
DAIRY PRDTS STORES
DAIRY PRDTS WHOLESALERS: Fresh
DAIRY PRDTS: Bakers' Cheese
DAIRY PRDTS: Bottled Baby Formula
DAIRY PRDTS: Butter
DAIRY PRDTS: Canned Baby Formula
DAIRY PRDTS: Cheese
DAIRY PRDTS: Cheese, Cottage
DAIRY PRDTS: Concentrated Skim Milk
DAIRY PRDTS: Cream Substitutes
DAIRY PRDTS: Cream, Sweet
DAIRY PRDTS: Dairy Based Desserts, Frozen
DAIRY PRDTS: Dietary Supplements, Dairy & Non-Dairy Based
DAIRY PRDTS: Dips & Spreads, Cheese Based
DAIRY PRDTS: Dried & Powdered Milk & Milk Prdts
DAIRY PRDTS: Evaporated Milk
DAIRY PRDTS: Farmers' Cheese
DAIRY PRDTS: Fermented & Cultured Milk Prdts
DAIRY PRDTS: Frozen Desserts & Novelties
DAIRY PRDTS: Ice Cream & Ice Milk
DAIRY PRDTS: Ice Cream, Bulk
DAIRY PRDTS: Ice Cream, Packaged, Molded, On Sticks, Etc.
DAIRY PRDTS: Milk, Condensed & Evaporated
DAIRY PRDTS: Milk, Fluid
DAIRY PRDTS: Milk, Processed, Pasteurized, Homogenized/Btld
DAIRY PRDTS: Natural Cheese
DAIRY PRDTS: Processed Cheese
DAIRY PRDTS: Pudding Pops, Frozen
DAIRY PRDTS: Spreads, Cheese
DAIRY PRDTS: Whipped Topping, Exc Frozen Or Dry Mix
DAIRY PRDTS: Yogurt, Exc Frozen
DAIRY PRDTS: Yogurt, Frozen
DATA PROCESSING & PREPARATION SVCS
DATA PROCESSING SYSTEMS
DECORATIVE WOOD & WOODWORK
DEFENSE SYSTEMS & EQPT
DEGREASING MACHINES
DEHYDRATION EQPT
DELAY LINES
DENTAL EQPT
DENTAL EQPT & SPLYS
DENTAL EQPT & SPLYS WHOLESALERS
DENTAL EQPT & SPLYS: Cabinets
DENTAL EQPT & SPLYS: Compounds
DENTAL EQPT & SPLYS: Cutting Instruments
DENTAL EQPT & SPLYS: Dental Materials
DENTAL EQPT & SPLYS: Enamels
DENTAL EQPT & SPLYS: Laboratory
DENTAL EQPT & SPLYS: Orthodontic Appliances
DENTAL EQPT & SPLYS: Sterilizers
DENTAL EQPT & SPLYS: Teeth, Artificial, Exc In Dental Labs
DENTAL EQPT & SPLYS: Tools, NEC

DENTAL EQPT & SPLYS: Wax
DENTAL INSTRUMENT REPAIR SVCS
DENTISTS' OFFICES & CLINICS
DEPILATORIES, COSMETIC
DERMATOLOGICALS
DERRICKS: Oil & Gas Field
DESALTER KITS: Sea Water
DESIGN SVCS, NEC
DESIGN SVCS: Commercial & Indl
DESIGN SVCS: Computer Integrated Systems
DETECTION APPARATUS: Electronic/Magnetic Field, Light/Heat
DIAGNOSTIC SUBSTANCES
DIAGNOSTIC SUBSTANCES OR AGENTS: Blood Derivative
DIAGNOSTIC SUBSTANCES OR AGENTS: In Vivo
DIAGNOSTIC SUBSTANCES OR AGENTS: Microbiology & Virology
DIAGNOSTIC SUBSTANCES OR AGENTS: Veterinary
DIAMOND MINING SVCS: Indl
DIAMOND SETTER SVCS
DIAMONDS, GEMS, WHOLESALE
DIAMONDS: Cutting & Polishing
DIAPERS: Cloth
DIAPERS: Disposable
DIE CUTTING SVC: Paper
DIE SETS: Presses, Metal Stamping
DIES & TOOLS: Special
DIES: Cutting, Exc Metal
DIES: Diamond, Metalworking
DIES: Extrusion
DIES: Paper Cutting
DIES: Plastic Forming
DIES: Steel Rule
DIODES: Light Emitting
DIODES: Solid State, Germanium, Silicon, Etc
DIRECT SELLING ESTABLISHMENTS: Encyclopedias & Publications
DIRECT SELLING ESTABLISHMENTS: Food Svcs
DIRECT SELLING ESTABLISHMENTS: Home Related Prdts
DISCS & TAPE: Optical, Blank
DISHWASHING EQPT: Commercial
DISK & DRUM DRIVES & COMPONENTS: Computers
DISK DRIVES: Computer
DISPENSING EQPT & PARTS, BEVERAGE: Beer
DISPENSING EQPT & PARTS, BEVERAGE: Cold, Exc Coin-Operated
DISPENSING EQPT & PARTS, BEVERAGE: Fountain/Other Beverage
DISPENSING EQPT & SYSTEMS, BEVERAGE: Liquor
DISPLAY CASES: Refrigerated
DISPLAY FIXTURES: Showcases, Wood, Exc Refrigerated
DISPLAY FIXTURES: Wood
DISPLAY ITEMS: Corrugated, Made From Purchased Materials
DISPLAY STANDS: Merchandise, Exc Wood
DISTILLATES: Hardwood
DOCK OPERATION SVCS, INCL BLDGS, FACILITIES, OPERS & MAINT
DOCKS: Floating, Wood
DOCKS: Prefabricated Metal
DOCUMENT EMBOSSING SVCS
DOLLIES: Mechanics'
DOLOMITE: Crushed & Broken
DOLOMITIC MARBLE: Crushed & Broken
DOMESTIC HELP SVCS
DOOR & WINDOW REPAIR SVCS
DOOR OPERATING SYSTEMS: Electric
DOORS & WINDOWS WHOLESALERS: All Materials
DOORS & WINDOWS: Screen & Storm
DOORS & WINDOWS: Storm, Metal
DOORS: Dormers, Wood
DOORS: Fiberglass
DOORS: Fire, Metal
DOORS: Folding, Plastic Or Plastic Coated Fabric
DOORS: Garage, Overhead, Metal
DOORS: Garage, Overhead, Wood
DOORS: Glass
DOORS: Rolling, Indl Building Or Warehouse, Metal
DOORS: Wooden
DOWN FEATHERS
DRAPERIES & CURTAINS
DRAPERIES & DRAPERY FABRICS, COTTON
DRAPERIES: Plastic & Textile, From Purchased Materials
DRAPERY & UPHOLSTERY STORES: Draperies
DRAPERY & UPHOLSTERY STORES: Slip Covers

PRODUCT INDEX

DRAPES & DRAPERY FABRICS, FROM MANMADE FIBER
DRIED FRUITS WHOLESALERS
DRILL BITS
DRILLING MACHINERY & EQPT: Water Well
DRINK MIXES, NONALCOHOLIC: Cocktail
DRINKING PLACES: Alcoholic Beverages
DRINKING PLACES: Night Clubs
DRINKING PLACES: Tavern
DRINKING PLACES: Wine Bar
DRINKING WATER COOLERS WHOLESALERS: Mechanical
DRIVE SHAFTS
DRIVES: High Speed Indl, Exc Hydrostatic
DROP CLOTHS: Fabric
DRUG STORES
DRUG TESTING KITS: Blood & Urine
DRUGS & DRUG PROPRIETARIES, WHOL: Biologicals/Allied Prdts
DRUGS & DRUG PROPRIETARIES, WHOLESALE
DRUGS & DRUG PROPRIETARIES, WHOLESALE: Blood Plasma
DRUGS & DRUG PROPRIETARIES, WHOLESALE: Pharmaceuticals
DRUGS & DRUG PROPRIETARIES, WHOLESALE: Vitamins & Minerals
DRUGS ACTING ON THE CENTRAL NERVOUS SYSTEM & SENSE ORGANS
DRUGS AFFECTING NEOPLASMS & ENDOCRINE SYSTEMS
DRUGS/DRUG PROPRIETARIES, WHOL: Proprietary/Patent Medicines
DRUGS: Parasitic & Infective Disease Affecting
DRUMS: Fiber
DRYCLEANING EQPT & SPLYS: Commercial
DRYCLEANING SVC: Drapery & Curtain
DUCTS: Sheet Metal
DUMPSTERS: Garbage
DYES & PIGMENTS: Organic
DYES & TINTS: Household
DYES: Synthetic Organic

E

EATING PLACES
EDUCATIONAL PROGRAM ADMINISTRATION, GOVERNMENT: State
EDUCATIONAL PROGRAMS ADMINISTRATION SVCS
EDUCATIONAL SVCS
EDUCATIONAL SVCS, NONDEGREE GRANTING: Continuing Education
ELASTOMERS
ELECTRIC MOTOR & GENERATOR AUXILIARY PARTS
ELECTRIC MOTOR REPAIR SVCS
ELECTRIC SERVICES
ELECTRIC SVCS, NEC Power Transmission
ELECTRIC SVCS, NEC: Power Generation
ELECTRICAL APPARATUS & EQPT WHOLESALERS
ELECTRICAL APPLIANCES, TELEVISIONS & RADIOS WHOLESALERS
ELECTRICAL CONSTRUCTION MATERIALS WHOLESALERS
ELECTRICAL CURRENT CARRYING WIRING DEVICES
ELECTRICAL DISCHARGE MACHINING, EDM
ELECTRICAL EQPT & SPLYS
ELECTRICAL EQPT FOR ENGINES
ELECTRICAL EQPT REPAIR & MAINTENANCE
ELECTRICAL EQPT REPAIR SVCS
ELECTRICAL EQPT REPAIR SVCS: High Voltage
ELECTRICAL EQPT: Automotive, NEC
ELECTRICAL EQPT: Household
ELECTRICAL GOODS, WHOLESALE: Batteries, Dry Cell
ELECTRICAL GOODS, WHOLESALE: Burglar Alarm Systems
ELECTRICAL GOODS, WHOLESALE: Capacitors
ELECTRICAL GOODS, WHOLESALE: Connectors
ELECTRICAL GOODS, WHOLESALE: Electronic Parts
ELECTRICAL GOODS, WHOLESALE: Facsimile Or Fax Eqpt
ELECTRICAL GOODS, WHOLESALE: Fans, Household
ELECTRICAL GOODS, WHOLESALE: Fittings & Construction Mat
ELECTRICAL GOODS, WHOLESALE: Intercommunication Eqpt
ELECTRICAL GOODS, WHOLESALE: Light Bulbs & Related Splys
ELECTRICAL GOODS, WHOLESALE: Lighting Fittings & Access
ELECTRICAL GOODS, WHOLESALE: Lighting Fixtures, Comm & Indl
ELECTRICAL GOODS, WHOLESALE: Lighting Fixtures, Residential
ELECTRICAL GOODS, WHOLESALE: Motors
ELECTRICAL GOODS, WHOLESALE: Semiconductor Devices
ELECTRICAL GOODS, WHOLESALE: Signaling, Eqpt
ELECTRICAL GOODS, WHOLESALE: Sound Eqpt
ELECTRICAL GOODS, WHOLESALE: Telephone & Telegraphic Eqpt
ELECTRICAL GOODS, WHOLESALE: Telephone Eqpt
ELECTRICAL GOODS, WHOLESALE: Transformers
ELECTRICAL GOODS, WHOLESALE: VCR & Access
ELECTRICAL GOODS, WHOLESALE: Vacuum Cleaners, Household
ELECTRICAL GOODS, WHOLESALE: Video Eqpt
ELECTRICAL GOODS, WHOLESALE: Wire & Cable
ELECTRICAL GOODS, WHOLESALE: Wire & Cable, Electronic
ELECTRICAL INDL APPARATUS, NEC
ELECTRICAL SPLYS
ELECTRICAL SUPPLIES: Porcelain
ELECTROCARS: Golfer Transportation
ELECTRODES: Fluorescent Lamps
ELECTRODES: Thermal & Electrolytic
ELECTROMEDICAL EQPT
ELECTRON TUBES
ELECTRON TUBES: Cathode Ray
ELECTRONIC COMPONENTS
ELECTRONIC DETECTION SYSTEMS: Aeronautical
ELECTRONIC DEVICES: Solid State, NEC
ELECTRONIC EQPT REPAIR SVCS
ELECTRONIC LOADS & POWER SPLYS
ELECTRONIC PARTS & EQPT WHOLESALERS
ELECTRONIC TRAINING DEVICES
ELECTROPLATING & PLATING SVC
ELEVATORS & EQPT
ELEVATORS WHOLESALERS
ELEVATORS: Installation & Conversion
ELEVATORS: Stair, Motor Powered
EMBLEMS: Embroidered
EMBOSSING SVC: Paper
EMBROIDERING & ART NEEDLEWORK FOR THE TRADE
EMBROIDERING SVC
EMBROIDERING SVC: Schiffli Machine
EMBROIDERING: Swiss Loom
EMBROIDERY ADVERTISING SVCS
EMERGENCY ALARMS
EMPLOYMENT AGENCY SVCS
ENAMELING SVC: Metal Prdts, Including Porcelain
ENAMELS
ENCLOSURES: Electronic
ENERGY MEASUREMENT EQPT
ENGINE REBUILDING: Diesel
ENGINE REBUILDING: Gas
ENGINEERING HELP SVCS
ENGINEERING SVCS
ENGINEERING SVCS: Building Construction
ENGINEERING SVCS: Electrical Or Electronic
ENGINEERING SVCS: Heating & Ventilation
ENGINEERING SVCS: Industrial
ENGINEERING SVCS: Marine
ENGINEERING SVCS: Mechanical
ENGINEERING SVCS: Petroleum
ENGINEERING SVCS: Pollution Control
ENGINEERING SVCS: Professional
ENGINEERING SVCS: Sanitary
ENGINEERING SVCS: Structural
ENGINES: Internal Combustion, NEC
ENGINES: Jet Propulsion
ENGRAVING SVC, NEC
ENGRAVING SVC: Jewelry & Personal Goods
ENGRAVING SVCS
ENGRAVING: Steel line, For The Printing Trade
ENGRAVINGS: Plastic
ENTERTAINERS & ENTERTAINMENT GROUPS
ENTERTAINMENT SVCS
ENVELOPES
ENVELOPES WHOLESALERS
ENVIRONMENTAL QUALITY PROGS ADMIN, GOVT: Waste Management
ENZYMES
EPOXY RESINS
EQUIPMENT: Pedestrian Traffic Control
EQUIPMENT: Rental & Leasing, NEC
ERASERS: Rubber Or Rubber & Abrasive Combined
ESCALATORS: Passenger & Freight
ETCHING & ENGRAVING SVC
ETCHING SVC: Metal
ETCHING SVC: Photochemical
ETHANOLAMINES
ETHYLENE-PROPYLENE RUBBERS: EPDM Polymers
EXCAVATING EQPT
EXPANSION JOINTS: Rubber
EXPLORATION, METAL MINING
EXPLOSIVES
EXPLOSIVES, EXC AMMO & FIREWORKS WHOLESALERS
EXTENSION CORDS
EXTRACTS, FLAVORING
EXTRACTS: Dying Or Tanning, Natural
EYEGLASS CASES
EYEGLASSES
EYEGLASSES: Sunglasses
EYES: Artificial

F

FABRIC FINISHING: Mending, Wool
FABRIC STORES
FABRICATED METAL PRODUCTS, NEC
FABRICS & CLOTH: Quilted
FABRICS: Apparel & Outerwear, Broadwoven
FABRICS: Apparel & Outerwear, Cotton
FABRICS: Apparel & Outerwear, From Manmade Fiber Or Silk
FABRICS: Bags & Bagging, Cotton
FABRICS: Bonded-Fiber, Exc Felt
FABRICS: Broad Woven, Goods, Cotton
FABRICS: Broadwoven, Cotton
FABRICS: Broadwoven, Synthetic Manmade Fiber & Silk
FABRICS: Broadwoven, Wool
FABRICS: Brocade, Cotton
FABRICS: Canvas
FABRICS: Card Roll, Cotton
FABRICS: Chemically Coated & Treated
FABRICS: Coated Or Treated
FABRICS: Corduroys, Cotton
FABRICS: Denims
FABRICS: Elastic, From Manmade Fiber Or Silk
FABRICS: Fiberglass, Broadwoven
FABRICS: Glass, Narrow
FABRICS: Glove, Lining
FABRICS: Hand Woven
FABRICS: Handkerchief, Cotton
FABRICS: Jacquard Woven, From Manmade Fiber Or Silk
FABRICS: Jean
FABRICS: Jersey Cloth
FABRICS: Lace & Decorative Trim, Narrow
FABRICS: Lace & Lace Prdts
FABRICS: Lace, Knit, NEC
FABRICS: Laminated
FABRICS: Linings & Interlinings, Cotton
FABRICS: Long Cloth, Cotton
FABRICS: Nonwoven
FABRICS: Nylon, Broadwoven
FABRICS: Paper, Broadwoven
FABRICS: Pile Warp or Flat Knit
FABRICS: Pile, Circular Knit
FABRICS: Pocketing Twill, Cotton
FABRICS: Print, Cotton
FABRICS: Resin Or Plastic Coated
FABRICS: Rubberized
FABRICS: Satin
FABRICS: Shirting, Cotton
FABRICS: Shoe
FABRICS: Silk, Broadwoven
FABRICS: Silk, Narrow
FABRICS: Spandex, Broadwoven
FABRICS: Specialty Including Twisted Weaves, Broadwoven
FABRICS: Stretch, Cotton
FABRICS: Surgical Fabrics, Cotton
FABRICS: Tapestry, Cotton
FABRICS: Tricot
FABRICS: Trimmings
FABRICS: Trimmings, Textile
FABRICS: Upholstery, Cotton
FABRICS: Varnished Glass & Coated Fiberglass
FABRICS: Wall Covering, From Manmade Fiber Or Silk
FABRICS: Warp & Flat Knit Prdts
FABRICS: Warp Knit, Lace & Netting
FABRICS: Weft Or Circular Knit
FABRICS: Woven Wire, Made From Purchased Wire
FABRICS: Woven, Narrow Cotton, Wool, Silk

PRODUCT INDEX

FACILITIES SUPPORT SVCS
FACSIMILE COMMUNICATION EQPT
FAMILY CLOTHING STORES
FANS, BLOWING: Indl Or Commercial
FANS, EXHAUST: Indl Or Commercial
FANS, VENTILATING: Indl Or Commercial
FARM & GARDEN MACHINERY WHOLESALERS
FARM PRDTS, RAW MATERIALS, WHOLESALE: Bristles
FARM PRDTS, RAW MATERIALS, WHOLESALE: Hides
FARM SPLY STORES
FASTENERS: Metal
FASTENERS: Metal
FASTENERS: Notions, NEC
FASTENERS: Notions, Snaps
FASTENERS: Notions, Zippers
FAUCETS & SPIGOTS: Metal & Plastic
FEATHERS: Renovating
FELT: Acoustic
FENCE POSTS: Iron & Steel
FENCES & FENCING MATERIALS
FENCES OR POSTS: Ornamental Iron Or Steel
FENCING DEALERS
FENCING MATERIALS: Docks & Other Outdoor Prdts, Wood
FENCING MATERIALS: Plastic
FENCING MATERIALS: Wood
FENCING: Chain Link
FERRITES
FERROALLOYS
FERROMANGANESE, NOT MADE IN BLAST FURNACES
FERTILIZERS: NEC
FERTILIZERS: Nitrogenous
FERTILIZERS: Phosphatic
FIBER & FIBER PRDTS: Acrylic
FIBER & FIBER PRDTS: Fluorocarbon
FIBER & FIBER PRDTS: Organic, Noncellulose
FIBER & FIBER PRDTS: Polyester
FIBER & FIBER PRDTS: Protein
FIBER & FIBER PRDTS: Synthetic Cellulosic
FIBER OPTICS
FIBERS: Carbon & Graphite
FILLERS & SEALERS: Wood
FILM & SHEET: Unsuppported Plastic
FILM BASE: Cellulose Acetate Or Nitrocellulose Plastics
FILM PROCESSING & FINISHING LABORATORY
FILM: Motion Picture
FILTERS
FILTERS & SOFTENERS: Water, Household
FILTERS: Air
FILTERS: Air Intake, Internal Combustion Engine, Exc Auto
FILTERS: General Line, Indl
FILTERS: Motor Vehicle
FILTRATION DEVICES: Electronic
FINANCIAL INVESTMENT ACTIVITIES, NEC: Financial Reporting
FINANCIAL INVESTMENT ADVICE
FINANCIAL SVCS
FINDINGS & TRIMMINGS Fabric, NEC
FINDINGS & TRIMMINGS Waistbands, Trouser
FINDINGS & TRIMMINGS: Apparel
FINDINGS & TRIMMINGS: Fabric
FINGERNAILS, ARTIFICIAL
FINGERPRINT EQPT
FINISHING AGENTS: Leather
FIRE ARMS, SMALL: Guns Or Gun Parts, 30 mm & Below
FIRE ARMS, SMALL: Pellet & BB guns
FIRE ARMS, SMALL: Rifles Or Rifle Parts, 30 mm & below
FIRE CONTROL OR BOMBING EQPT: Electronic
FIRE DETECTION SYSTEMS
FIRE ESCAPES
FIRE EXTINGUISHERS: Portable
FIRE OR BURGLARY RESISTIVE PRDTS
FIRE PROTECTION EQPT
FIREARMS & AMMUNITION, EXC SPORTING, WHOLESALE
FIREARMS: Small, 30mm or Less
FIREFIGHTING APPARATUS
FIREPLACE & CHIMNEY MATERIAL: Concrete
FIREPLACE EQPT & ACCESS
FIREWORKS
FIREWORKS DISPLAY SVCS
FISH & SEAFOOD PROCESSORS: Canned Or Cured
FISH & SEAFOOD PROCESSORS: Fresh Or Frozen
FISHING EQPT: Lures
FITTINGS & ASSEMBLIES: Hose & Tube, Hydraulic Or Pneumatic
FITTINGS & SPECIALTIES: Steam
FITTINGS: Pipe
FITTINGS: Pipe, Fabricated
FIXTURES & EQPT: Kitchen, Metal, Exc Cast Aluminum
FIXTURES: Bank, Metal, Ornamental
FIXTURES: Cut Stone
FLAGPOLES
FLAGS: Fabric
FLAT GLASS: Building
FLAT GLASS: Construction
FLAT GLASS: Laminated
FLAT GLASS: Plate, Polished & Rough
FLAT GLASS: Strengthened Or Reinforced
FLAT GLASS: Tempered
FLAT GLASS: Window, Clear & Colored
FLATWARE, STAINLESS STEEL
FLAVORS OR FLAVORING MATERIALS: Synthetic
FLOOR CLEANING & MAINTENANCE EQPT: Household
FLOOR COMPOSITION: Magnesite
FLOOR COVERING STORES: Carpets
FLOOR COVERING: Plastic
FLOOR COVERINGS WHOLESALERS
FLOOR COVERINGS: Textile Fiber
FLOOR COVERINGS: Tile, Support Plastic
FLOORING & GRATINGS: Open, Construction Applications
FLOORING: Hard Surface
FLOORING: Hardwood
FLOORING: Tile
FLORISTS
FLOWER POTS Plastic
FLOWERS: Artificial & Preserved
FLUID METERS & COUNTING DEVICES
FLUID POWER PUMPS & MOTORS
FLUID POWER VALVES & HOSE FITTINGS
FLUORO RUBBERS
FLUXES
FOAM CHARGE MIXTURES
FOAM RUBBER
FOIL & LEAF: Metal
FOIL OR LEAF: Gold
FOIL: Aluminum
FOIL: Copper
FOIL: Laminated To Paper Or Other Materials
FOOD PRDTS, BREAKFAST: Cereal, Granola & Muesli
FOOD PRDTS, BREAKFAST: Cereal, Infants' Food
FOOD PRDTS, BREAKFAST: Cereal, Wheat Flakes
FOOD PRDTS, CANNED OR FRESH PACK: Fruit Juices
FOOD PRDTS, CANNED OR FRESH PACK: Vegetable Juices
FOOD PRDTS, CANNED, NEC
FOOD PRDTS, CANNED: Applesauce
FOOD PRDTS, CANNED: Baby Food
FOOD PRDTS, CANNED: Barbecue Sauce
FOOD PRDTS, CANNED: Beans & Bean Sprouts
FOOD PRDTS, CANNED: Catsup
FOOD PRDTS, CANNED: Ethnic
FOOD PRDTS, CANNED: Fruit Juices, Concentrated
FOOD PRDTS, CANNED: Fruit Juices, Fresh
FOOD PRDTS, CANNED: Fruit Purees
FOOD PRDTS, CANNED: Fruits
FOOD PRDTS, CANNED: Fruits
FOOD PRDTS, CANNED: Fruits & Fruit Prdts
FOOD PRDTS, CANNED: Italian
FOOD PRDTS, CANNED: Jams, Including Imitation
FOOD PRDTS, CANNED: Jams, Jellies & Preserves
FOOD PRDTS, CANNED: Maraschino Cherries
FOOD PRDTS, CANNED: Mexican, NEC
FOOD PRDTS, CANNED: Olives
FOOD PRDTS, CANNED: Puddings, Exc Meat
FOOD PRDTS, CANNED: Ravioli
FOOD PRDTS, CANNED: Sauerkraut
FOOD PRDTS, CANNED: Soup, Chicken
FOOD PRDTS, CANNED: Spaghetti & Other Pasta Sauce
FOOD PRDTS, CANNED: Tomato Sauce.
FOOD PRDTS, CANNED: Tomatoes
FOOD PRDTS, CANNED: Vegetables
FOOD PRDTS, CONFECTIONERY, WHOLESALE: Candy
FOOD PRDTS, CONFECTIONERY, WHOLESALE: Nuts, Salted/Roasted
FOOD PRDTS, CONFECTIONERY, WHOLESALE: Snack Foods
FOOD PRDTS, DAIRY, WHOLESALE: Frozen Dairy Desserts
FOOD PRDTS, DAIRY, WHOLESALE: Milk & Cream, Fluid
FOOD PRDTS, FISH & SEAFOOD, WHOLESALE: Fresh
FOOD PRDTS, FISH & SEAFOOD: Cakes, Canned, Jarred, Etc
FOOD PRDTS, FISH & SEAFOOD: Canned & Jarred, Etc
FOOD PRDTS, FISH & SEAFOOD: Fish, Fresh, Prepared
FOOD PRDTS, FISH & SEAFOOD: Fish, Smoked
FOOD PRDTS, FISH & SEAFOOD: Prepared Cakes & Sticks
FOOD PRDTS, FISH & SEAFOOD: Salmon, Smoked
FOOD PRDTS, FISH & SEAFOOD: Seafood, Frozen, Prepared
FOOD PRDTS, FROZEN: Breakfasts, Packaged
FOOD PRDTS, FROZEN: Dinners, Packaged
FOOD PRDTS, FROZEN: Ethnic Foods, NEC
FOOD PRDTS, FROZEN: Fruit Juice, Concentrates
FOOD PRDTS, FROZEN: Fruits & Vegetables
FOOD PRDTS, FROZEN: Fruits, Juices & Vegetables
FOOD PRDTS, FROZEN: NEC
FOOD PRDTS, FROZEN: Pizza
FOOD PRDTS, FROZEN: Snack Items
FOOD PRDTS, FROZEN: Soups
FOOD PRDTS, FROZEN: Vegetables, Exc Potato Prdts
FOOD PRDTS, FROZEN: Whipped Topping
FOOD PRDTS, MEAT & MEAT PRDTS, WHOLESALE: Fresh
FOOD PRDTS, WHOL: Canned Goods, Fruit, Veg, Seafood/Meats
FOOD PRDTS, WHOLESALE: Beverage Concentrates
FOOD PRDTS, WHOLESALE: Beverages, Exc Coffee & Tea
FOOD PRDTS, WHOLESALE: Chocolate
FOOD PRDTS, WHOLESALE: Coffee & Tea
FOOD PRDTS, WHOLESALE: Coffee, Green Or Roasted
FOOD PRDTS, WHOLESALE: Condiments
FOOD PRDTS, WHOLESALE: Cookies
FOOD PRDTS, WHOLESALE: Diet
FOOD PRDTS, WHOLESALE: Flour
FOOD PRDTS, WHOLESALE: Grains
FOOD PRDTS, WHOLESALE: Health
FOOD PRDTS, WHOLESALE: Juices
FOOD PRDTS, WHOLESALE: Organic & Diet
FOOD PRDTS, WHOLESALE: Pasta & Rice
FOOD PRDTS, WHOLESALE: Sandwiches
FOOD PRDTS, WHOLESALE: Sausage Casings
FOOD PRDTS, WHOLESALE: Specialty
FOOD PRDTS, WHOLESALE: Tea
FOOD PRDTS: Almond Pastes
FOOD PRDTS: Bran, Rice
FOOD PRDTS: Bread Crumbs, Exc Made In Bakeries
FOOD PRDTS: Breakfast Bars
FOOD PRDTS: Cane Syrup, From Purchased Raw Sugar
FOOD PRDTS: Cereals
FOOD PRDTS: Cheese Curls & Puffs
FOOD PRDTS: Chicken, Processed, Frozen
FOOD PRDTS: Chocolate Bars, Solid
FOOD PRDTS: Chocolate Coatings & Syrup
FOOD PRDTS: Cocoa & Cocoa Prdts
FOOD PRDTS: Coconut Oil
FOOD PRDTS: Coconut, Desiccated & Shredded
FOOD PRDTS: Coffee
FOOD PRDTS: Coffee Extracts
FOOD PRDTS: Coffee Roasting, Exc Wholesale Grocers
FOOD PRDTS: Cooking Oils, Refined Vegetable, Exc Corn
FOOD PRDTS: Corn Chips & Other Corn-Based Snacks
FOOD PRDTS: Corn Sugars & Syrups
FOOD PRDTS: Cottonseed Lecithin
FOOD PRDTS: Dessert Mixes & Fillings
FOOD PRDTS: Desserts, Ready-To-Mix
FOOD PRDTS: Dough, Pizza, Prepared
FOOD PRDTS: Doughs & Batters
FOOD PRDTS: Doughs & Batters From Purchased Flour
FOOD PRDTS: Dressings, Salad, Raw & Cooked Exc Dry Mixes
FOOD PRDTS: Dried & Dehydrated Fruits, Vegetables & Soup Mix
FOOD PRDTS: Ducks, Processed, Fresh
FOOD PRDTS: Ducks, Processed, NEC
FOOD PRDTS: Edible Oil Prdts, Exc Corn Oil
FOOD PRDTS: Edible fats & oils
FOOD PRDTS: Egg Substitutes, Made From Eggs
FOOD PRDTS: Eggs, Processed
FOOD PRDTS: Emulsifiers
FOOD PRDTS: Flavored Ices, Frozen
FOOD PRDTS: Flour & Other Grain Mill Products
FOOD PRDTS: Flour Mixes & Doughs
FOOD PRDTS: Flour, Cake From Purchased Flour
FOOD PRDTS: Fruit Juices
FOOD PRDTS: Fruit Pops, Frozen
FOOD PRDTS: Fruits & Vegetables, Pickled
FOOD PRDTS: Fruits, Dehydrated Or Dried

PRODUCT INDEX

FOOD PRDTS: Fruits, Dried Or Dehydrated, Exc Freeze-Dried
FOOD PRDTS: Gelatin Dessert Preparations
FOOD PRDTS: Gluten Meal
FOOD PRDTS: Horseradish, Exc Sauce
FOOD PRDTS: Ice, Blocks
FOOD PRDTS: Ice, Cubes
FOOD PRDTS: Instant Coffee
FOOD PRDTS: Jelly, Corncob
FOOD PRDTS: Juice Pops, Frozen
FOOD PRDTS: Macaroni Prdts, Dry, Alphabet, Rings Or Shells
FOOD PRDTS: Macaroni, Noodles, Spaghetti, Pasta, Etc
FOOD PRDTS: Malt
FOOD PRDTS: Mayonnaise & Dressings, Exc Tomato Based
FOOD PRDTS: Mixes, Bread & Bread-Type Roll
FOOD PRDTS: Mixes, Bread & Roll From Purchased Flour
FOOD PRDTS: Mixes, Doughnut From Purchased Flour
FOOD PRDTS: Mixes, Pancake From Purchased Flour
FOOD PRDTS: Molasses, Mixed/Blended, Purchased Ingredients
FOOD PRDTS: Mustard, Prepared
FOOD PRDTS: Nuts & Seeds
FOOD PRDTS: Olive Oil
FOOD PRDTS: Oriental Noodles
FOOD PRDTS: Pasta, Rice/Potatoes, Uncooked, Pkgd
FOOD PRDTS: Pasta, Uncooked, Packaged With Other Ingredients
FOOD PRDTS: Peanut Butter
FOOD PRDTS: Pickles, Vinegar
FOOD PRDTS: Pizza Doughs From Purchased Flour
FOOD PRDTS: Pizza, Refrigerated
FOOD PRDTS: Potato & Corn Chips & Similar Prdts
FOOD PRDTS: Potato Chips & Other Potato-Based Snacks
FOOD PRDTS: Potato Sticks
FOOD PRDTS: Potatoes, Dried, Packaged With Other Ingredients
FOOD PRDTS: Poultry Sausage, Lunch Meats/Other Poultry Prdts
FOOD PRDTS: Poultry, Processed, NEC
FOOD PRDTS: Poultry, Slaughtered & Dressed
FOOD PRDTS: Preparations
FOOD PRDTS: Prepared Meat Sauces Exc Tomato & Dry
FOOD PRDTS: Prepared Sauces, Exc Tomato Based
FOOD PRDTS: Raw cane sugar
FOOD PRDTS: Relishes, Vinegar
FOOD PRDTS: Rice, Milled
FOOD PRDTS: Salads
FOOD PRDTS: Sauerkraut, Bulk
FOOD PRDTS: Seasonings & Spices
FOOD PRDTS: Soup Mixes, Dried
FOOD PRDTS: Soy Sauce
FOOD PRDTS: Spices, Including Ground
FOOD PRDTS: Spreads, Sandwich, Salad Dressing Base
FOOD PRDTS: Sugar
FOOD PRDTS: Sugar, Beet
FOOD PRDTS: Sugar, Cane
FOOD PRDTS: Sugar, Corn
FOOD PRDTS: Syrup, Maple
FOOD PRDTS: Syrup, Pancake, Blended & Mixed
FOOD PRDTS: Syrups
FOOD PRDTS: Tea
FOOD PRDTS: Tofu Desserts, Frozen
FOOD PRDTS: Tofu, Exc Frozen Desserts
FOOD PRDTS: Tortilla Chips
FOOD PRDTS: Tortillas
FOOD PRDTS: Vegetables, Dried or Dehydrated Exc Freeze-Dried
FOOD PRDTS: Vegetables, Pickled
FOOD PRDTS: Vinegar
FOOD PRODUCTS MACHINERY
FOOD STORES: Delicatessen
FOOD STORES: Grocery, Independent
FOOD STORES: Supermarkets
FOOTWEAR, WHOLESALE: Athletic
FOOTWEAR, WHOLESALE: Shoe Access
FOOTWEAR, WHOLESALE: Shoes
FOOTWEAR: Cut Stock
FORGINGS
FORGINGS: Armor Plate, Iron Or Steel
FORGINGS: Automotive & Internal Combustion Engine
FORGINGS: Gear & Chain
FORGINGS: Machinery, Ferrous
FORGINGS: Metal , Ornamental, Ferrous
FORGINGS: Nonferrous
FORGINGS: Pump & compressor, Nonferrous
FORMS: Concrete, Sheet Metal
FOUNDRIES: Aluminum
FOUNDRIES: Brass, Bronze & Copper
FOUNDRIES: Gray & Ductile Iron
FOUNDRIES: Iron
FOUNDRIES: Nonferrous
FOUNDRIES: Steel
FOUNDRIES: Steel Investment
FRAMES & FRAMING WHOLESALE
FRANCHISES, SELLING OR LICENSING
FREIGHT CONSOLIDATION SVCS
FREIGHT FORWARDING ARRANGEMENTS
FRICTION MATERIAL, MADE FROM POWDERED METAL
FRUITS & VEGETABLES WHOLESALERS: Fresh
FUEL ADDITIVES
FUEL BRIQUETTES & WAXES
FUEL BRIQUETTES OR BOULETS, MADE WITH PETROLEUM BINDER
FUEL CELL FORMS: Cardboard, Made From Purchased Materials
FUEL CELLS: Solid State
FUEL DEALERS: Wood
FUEL OIL DEALERS
FUELS: Diesel
FUELS: Ethanol
FUELS: Oil
FUNDRAISING SVCS
FUNERAL HOMES & SVCS
FUNGICIDES OR HERBICIDES
FUR APPAREL STORES
FUR CLOTHING WHOLESALERS
FUR FINISHING & LINING: For The Fur Goods Trade
FUR: Apparel
FUR: Coats
FUR: Coats & Other Apparel
FUR: Hats
FUR: Jackets
FURNACES & OVENS: Indl
FURNACES: Indl, Electric
FURNACES: Warm Air, Electric
FURNISHINGS: Bridge Sets, Cloth/Napkin, From Purchased Matls
FURNITURE & CABINET STORES: Cabinets, Custom Work
FURNITURE & CABINET STORES: Custom
FURNITURE & FIXTURES Factory
FURNITURE PARTS: Metal
FURNITURE REFINISHING SVCS
FURNITURE STOCK & PARTS: Carvings, Wood
FURNITURE STOCK & PARTS: Dimension Stock, Hardwood
FURNITURE STOCK & PARTS: Frames, Upholstered Furniture, Wood
FURNITURE STOCK & PARTS: Hardwood
FURNITURE STORES
FURNITURE STORES: Cabinets, Kitchen, Exc Custom Made
FURNITURE STORES: Custom Made, Exc Cabinets
FURNITURE STORES: Juvenile
FURNITURE STORES: Office
FURNITURE STORES: Outdoor & Garden
FURNITURE STORES: Unfinished
FURNITURE UPHOLSTERY REPAIR SVCS
FURNITURE WHOLESALERS
FURNITURE, HOUSEHOLD: Wholesalers
FURNITURE, OFFICE: Wholesalers
FURNITURE, WHOLESALE: Beds & Bedding
FURNITURE, WHOLESALE: Racks
FURNITURE: Bar furniture
FURNITURE: Bed Frames & Headboards, Wood
FURNITURE: Bedroom, Wood
FURNITURE: Beds, Household, Incl Folding & Cabinet, Metal
FURNITURE: Bookcases, Office, Wood
FURNITURE: Box Springs, Assembled
FURNITURE: Cabinets & Filing Drawers, Office, Exc Wood
FURNITURE: Cabinets & Vanities, Medicine, Metal
FURNITURE: Chairs & Couches, Wood, Upholstered
FURNITURE: Chairs, Household Upholstered
FURNITURE: Chairs, Household Wood
FURNITURE: Chairs, Office Exc Wood
FURNITURE: Chairs, Office Wood
FURNITURE: China Closets
FURNITURE: Church
FURNITURE: Console Tables, Wood
FURNITURE: Couches, Sofa/Davenport, Upholstered Wood Frames
FURNITURE: Cribs, Metal
FURNITURE: Cut Stone
FURNITURE: Desks & Tables, Office, Exc Wood
FURNITURE: Desks & Tables, Office, Wood
FURNITURE: Desks, Wood
FURNITURE: Dinette Sets, Metal
FURNITURE: Dining Room, Wood
FURNITURE: Foundations & Platforms
FURNITURE: Garden, Exc Wood, Metal, Stone Or Concrete
FURNITURE: Hospital
FURNITURE: Hotel
FURNITURE: Household, Metal
FURNITURE: Household, NEC
FURNITURE: Household, Upholstered On Metal Frames
FURNITURE: Household, Upholstered, Exc Wood Or Metal
FURNITURE: Household, Wood
FURNITURE: Hydraulic Barber & Beauty Shop Chairs
FURNITURE: Institutional, Exc Wood
FURNITURE: Juvenile, Wood
FURNITURE: Kitchen & Dining Room
FURNITURE: Kitchen & Dining Room, Metal
FURNITURE: Laboratory
FURNITURE: Living Room, Upholstered On Wood Frames
FURNITURE: Mattresses & Foundations
FURNITURE: Mattresses, Box & Bedsprings
FURNITURE: Mattresses, Innerspring Or Box Spring
FURNITURE: NEC
FURNITURE: Novelty, Wood
FURNITURE: Office Panel Systems, Exc Wood
FURNITURE: Office, Exc Wood
FURNITURE: Office, Wood
FURNITURE: Outdoor, Wood
FURNITURE: Pews, Church
FURNITURE: Picnic Tables Or Benches, Park
FURNITURE: Rattan
FURNITURE: Restaurant
FURNITURE: Ship
FURNITURE: Silverware Chests, Wood
FURNITURE: Sleep
FURNITURE: Storage Chests, Household, Wood
FURNITURE: Tables & Table Tops, Wood
FURNITURE: Tables, Office, Exc Wood
FURNITURE: Tables, Office, Wood
FURNITURE: Theater
FURNITURE: Upholstered
FURRIERS
FUSES: Electric

G

GAMES & TOYS: Baby Carriages & Restraint Seats
GAMES & TOYS: Banks
GAMES & TOYS: Child Restraint Seats, Automotive
GAMES & TOYS: Craft & Hobby Kits & Sets
GAMES & TOYS: Doll Hats
GAMES & TOYS: Dolls & Doll Clothing
GAMES & TOYS: Dolls, Exc Stuffed Toy Animals
GAMES & TOYS: Electronic
GAMES & TOYS: Game Machines, Exc Coin-Operated
GAMES & TOYS: Miniature Dolls, Collectors'
GAMES & TOYS: Models, Airplane, Toy & Hobby
GAMES & TOYS: Puzzles
GAMES & TOYS: Scooters, Children's
GAMES & TOYS: Structural Toy Sets
GAMES & TOYS: Trains & Eqpt, Electric & Mechanical
GARBAGE CONTAINERS: Plastic
GARBAGE DISPOSALS: Household
GARBAGE DISPOSERS & COMPACTORS: Commercial
GARNET MINING SVCS
GAS & OIL FIELD EXPLORATION SVCS
GAS & OIL FIELD SVCS, NEC
GAS STATIONS
GASES & LIQUIFIED PETROLEUM GASES
GASES: Carbon Dioxide
GASES: Flourinated Hydrocarbon
GASES: Indl
GASES: Neon
GASES: Nitrogen
GASES: Oxygen
GASKET MATERIALS
GASKETS
GASKETS & SEALING DEVICES
GASOLINE FILLING STATIONS
GASOLINE WHOLESALERS
GASTROINTESTINAL OR GENITOURINARY SYSTEM DRUGS
GATES: Dam, Metal Plate

PRODUCT INDEX

GATES: Ornamental Metal
GAUGES
GEARS
GEARS & GEAR UNITS: Reduction, Exc Auto
GEARS: Power Transmission, Exc Auto
GELATIN
GEM STONES MINING, NEC: Natural
GEMSTONE & INDL DIAMOND MINING SVCS
GENERAL & INDUSTRIAL LOAN INSTITUTIONS
GENERAL MERCHANDISE, NONDURABLE, WHOLESALE
GENERATING APPARATUS & PARTS: Electrical
GENERATION EQPT: Electronic
GENERATORS: Electric
GENERATORS: Electrochemical, Fuel Cell
GENERATORS: Ultrasonic
GIFT SHOP
GIFT, NOVELTY & SOUVENIR STORES: Artcraft & carvings
GIFT, NOVELTY & SOUVENIR STORES: Gifts & Novelties
GIFT, NOVELTY & SOUVENIR STORES: Party Favors
GIFTS & NOVELTIES: Wholesalers
GLASS FABRICATORS
GLASS PRDTS, FROM PURCHASED GLASS: Art
GLASS PRDTS, FROM PURCHASED GLASS: Glass Beads, Reflecting
GLASS PRDTS, FROM PURCHASED GLASS: Glassware
GLASS PRDTS, FROM PURCHASED GLASS: Insulating
GLASS PRDTS, FROM PURCHASED GLASS: Mirrored
GLASS PRDTS, FROM PURCHASED GLASS: Mirrors, Framed
GLASS PRDTS, FROM PURCHASED GLASS: Ornaments, Christmas Tree
GLASS PRDTS, FROM PURCHASED GLASS: Sheet, Bent
GLASS PRDTS, FROM PURCHASED GLASS: Watch Crystals
GLASS PRDTS, FROM PURCHASED GLASS: Windshields
GLASS PRDTS, FROM PURCHD GLASS: Strengthened Or Reinforced
GLASS PRDTS, PRESSED OR BLOWN: Bulbs, Electric Lights
GLASS PRDTS, PRESSED OR BLOWN: Chimneys, Lamp
GLASS PRDTS, PRESSED OR BLOWN: Glassware, Art Or Decorative
GLASS PRDTS, PRESSED OR BLOWN: Lens Blanks, Optical
GLASS PRDTS, PRESSED OR BLOWN: Optical
GLASS PRDTS, PRESSED OR BLOWN: Ornaments, Christmas Tree
GLASS PRDTS, PRESSED OR BLOWN: Scientific Glassware
GLASS PRDTS, PRESSED/BLOWN: Glassware, Art, Decor/Novelty
GLASS PRDTS, PURCHASED GLASS: Glassware, Scientific/Tech
GLASS PRDTS, PURCHASED GLASS: Insulating, Multiple-Glazed
GLASS PRDTS, PURCHD GLASS: Furniture Top, Cut, Beveld/Polshd
GLASS PRDTS, PURCHSD GLASS: Ornamental, Cut, Engraved/Décor
GLASS STORE: Leaded Or Stained
GLASS STORES
GLASS: Fiber
GLASS: Flat
GLASS: Insulating
GLASS: Leaded
GLASS: Pressed & Blown, NEC
GLASS: Stained
GLASS: Structural
GLASS: Tempered
GLASSWARE STORES
GLASSWARE WHOLESALERS
GLASSWARE: Laboratory
GLASSWARE: Laboratory & Medical
GLOBAL POSITIONING SYSTEMS & EQPT
GLOVE MENDING, FACTORY BASIS
GLOVES: Fabric
GLOVES: Leather
GLOVES: Leather, Dress Or Semidress
GLOVES: Leather, Work
GLOVES: Plastic
GLOVES: Safety
GLOVES: Work
GLOVES: Woven Or Knit, From Purchased Materials
GLUE
GOLD ORE MINING
GOLD ORES

GOLD STAMPING, EXC BOOKS
GOLF CARTS: Powered
GOLF DRIVING RANGES
GOLF EQPT
GOURMET FOOD STORES
GOVERNMENT, EXECUTIVE OFFICES: Mayors'
GOVERNMENT, GENERAL: Administration
GRANITE: Crushed & Broken
GRANITE: Cut & Shaped
GRANITE: Dimension
GRANITE: Dimension
GRAPHIC ARTS & RELATED DESIGN SVCS
GRAPHIC LAYOUT SVCS: Printed Circuitry
GRASSES: Artificial & Preserved
GRATINGS: Tread, Fabricated Metal
GRAVE MARKERS: Concrete
GRAVEL MINING
GREASE CUPS: Metal
GREASE TRAPS: Concrete
GREASES: Lubricating
GREENHOUSES: Prefabricated Metal
GREETING CARDS WHOLESALERS
GRILLS & GRILLWORK: Woven Wire, Made From Purchased Wire
GRINDING BALLS: Ceramic
GRINDING SVC: Precision, Commercial Or Indl
GRINDING SVCS: Ophthalmic Lens, Exc Prescription
GRIT: Steel
GRITS: Crushed & Broken
GROCERIES WHOLESALERS, NEC
GROCERIES, GENERAL LINE WHOLESALERS
GUARDRAILS
GUIDANCE SYSTEMS & EQPT: Space Vehicle
GUIDED MISSILES & SPACE VEHICLES
GUM & WOOD CHEMICALS
GUN STOCKS: Wood
GUNSMITHS
GUTTERS: Sheet Metal
GYPSUM PRDTS

H

HAIR & HAIR BASED PRDTS
HAIR ACCESS WHOLESALERS
HAIR CARE PRDTS
HAIR CARE PRDTS: Hair Coloring Preparations
HAIRPIN MOUNTINGS
HANDBAG STORES
HANDBAGS
HANDBAGS: Women's
HANDCUFFS & LEG IRONS
HANDLES: Brush Or Tool, Plastic
HANDLES: Wood
HANGERS: Garment, Plastic
HANGERS: Garment, Wire
HANGERS: Garment, Wire
HARDBOARD & FIBERBOARD PRDTS
HARDWARE
HARDWARE & BUILDING PRDTS: Plastic
HARDWARE & EQPT: Stage, Exc Lighting
HARDWARE CLOTH: Woven Wire, Made From Purchased Wire
HARDWARE STORES
HARDWARE STORES: Builders'
HARDWARE STORES: Pumps & Pumping Eqpt
HARDWARE STORES: Tools
HARDWARE WHOLESALERS
HARDWARE, WHOLESALE: Bolts
HARDWARE, WHOLESALE: Builders', NEC
HARDWARE: Aircraft
HARDWARE: Builders'
HARDWARE: Cabinet
HARDWARE: Door Opening & Closing Devices, Exc Electrical
HARDWARE: Furniture
HARDWARE: Furniture, Builders' & Other Household
HARDWARE: Locking Systems, Security Cable
HARDWARE: Luggage
HARDWARE: Piano
HARNESS ASSEMBLIES: Cable & Wire
HARNESSES, HALTERS, SADDLERY & STRAPS
HAT BOXES
HEADPHONES: Radio
HEALTH AIDS: Exercise Eqpt
HEALTH SCREENING SVCS
HEARING AIDS
HEAT EXCHANGERS

HEAT EXCHANGERS: After Or Inter Coolers Or Condensers, Etc
HEAT TREATING: Metal
HEATERS: Space, Exc Electric
HEATERS: Swimming Pool, Oil Or Gas
HEATERS: Unit, Domestic
HEATING & AIR CONDITIONING EQPT & SPLYS WHOLESALERS
HEATING & AIR CONDITIONING UNITS, COMBINATION
HEATING EQPT & SPLYS
HEATING EQPT: Complete
HEATING EQPT: Induction
HEATING SYSTEMS: Radiant, Indl Process
HEATING UNITS & DEVICES: Indl, Electric
HELICOPTERS
HELMETS: Athletic
HIDES & SKINS
HIGH ENERGY PARTICLE PHYSICS EQPT
HIGHWAY SIGNALS: Electric
HOBBY & CRAFT SPLY STORES
HOBBY, TOY & GAME STORES: Ceramics Splys
HOISTS
HOLDING COMPANIES: Banks
HOLDING COMPANIES: Investment, Exc Banks
HOLDING COMPANIES: Personal, Exc Banks
HOME DELIVERY NEWSPAPER ROUTES
HOME ENTERTAINMENT EQPT: Electronic, NEC
HOME FOR THE MENTALLY RETARDED
HOME FURNISHINGS WHOLESALERS
HOME HEALTH CARE SVCS
HOMEBUILDERS & OTHER OPERATIVE BUILDERS
HOMEFURNISHING STORES: Beddings & Linens
HOMEFURNISHING STORES: Lighting Fixtures
HOMEFURNISHING STORES: Mirrors
HOMEFURNISHING STORES: Vertical Blinds
HOMEFURNISHING STORES: Wicker, Rattan, Or Reed
HOMEFURNISHING STORES: Window Furnishings
HOMEFURNISHINGS & SPLYS, WHOLESALE: Decorative
HOMEFURNISHINGS, WHOLESALE: Bedspreads
HOMEFURNISHINGS, WHOLESALE: Blinds, Venetian
HOMEFURNISHINGS, WHOLESALE: Blinds, Vertical
HOMEFURNISHINGS, WHOLESALE: Carpets
HOMEFURNISHINGS, WHOLESALE: Curtains
HOMEFURNISHINGS, WHOLESALE: Draperies
HOMEFURNISHINGS, WHOLESALE: Kitchenware
HOMEFURNISHINGS, WHOLESALE: Linens, Table
HOMEFURNISHINGS, WHOLESALE: Mirrors/Pictures, Framed/Unframd
HOMEFURNISHINGS, WHOLESALE: Pillowcases
HOMEFURNISHINGS, WHOLESALE: Rugs
HOMEFURNISHINGS, WHOLESALE: Sheets, Textile
HOMEFURNISHINGS, WHOLESALE: Stainless Steel Flatware
HOMEFURNISHINGS, WHOLESALE: Window Covering Parts & Access
HOMEFURNISHINGS, WHOLESALE: Wood Flooring
HOMES, MODULAR: Wooden
HOMES: Log Cabins
HONES
HORMONE PREPARATIONS
HORSE & PET ACCESSORIES: Textile
HORSE ACCESS: Harnesses & Riding Crops, Etc, Exc Leather
HOSE: Air Line Or Air Brake, Rubber Or Rubberized Fabric
HOSE: Automobile, Plastic
HOSE: Cotton Fabric, Rubber Lined
HOSE: Fire, Rubber
HOSE: Flexible Metal
HOSE: Plastic
HOSE: Pneumatic, Rubber Or Rubberized Fabric, NEC
HOSE: Rubber
HOSE: Vacuum Cleaner, Rubber
HOSES & BELTING: Rubber & Plastic
HOSPITALS: Cancer
HOSPITALS: Medical & Surgical
HOT TUBS
HOT TUBS: Plastic & Fiberglass
HOUSEHOLD APPLIANCE STORES: Air Cond Rm Units, Self-Contnd
HOUSEHOLD APPLIANCE STORES: Electric Household Appliance, Sm
HOUSEHOLD APPLIANCE STORES: Fans, Electric
HOUSEHOLD APPLIANCE STORES: Garbage Disposals
HOUSEHOLD ARTICLES: Metal
HOUSEHOLD FURNISHINGS, NEC

2017 Harris
New York Manufacturers Directory

PRODUCT INDEX

HOUSEWARE STORES
HOUSEWARES, ELECTRIC: Air Purifiers, Portable
HOUSEWARES, ELECTRIC: Cooking Appliances
HOUSEWARES, ELECTRIC: Extractors, Juice
HOUSEWARES, ELECTRIC: Fryers
HOUSEWARES, ELECTRIC: Heaters, Sauna
HOUSEWARES, ELECTRIC: Heaters, Space
HOUSEWARES, ELECTRIC: Heating, Bsbrd/Wall, Radiant Heat
HOUSEWARES, ELECTRIC: Humidifiers, Household
HOUSEWARES, ELECTRIC: Massage Machines, Exc Beauty/Barber
HOUSEWARES: Dishes, China
HOUSEWARES: Dishes, Earthenware
HOUSEWARES: Dishes, Plastic
HOUSEWARES: Kettles & Skillets, Cast Iron
HOUSEWARES: Pots & Pans, Glass
HUMIDIFIERS & DEHUMIDIFIERS
HYDRAULIC EQPT REPAIR SVC
Hard Rubber & Molded Rubber Prdts

I

ICE
ICE CREAM & ICES WHOLESALERS
IDENTIFICATION TAGS, EXC PAPER
IGNEOUS ROCK: Crushed & Broken
IGNITION APPARATUS & DISTRIBUTORS
IGNITION SYSTEMS: High Frequency
IGNITION SYSTEMS: Internal Combustion Engine
INCINERATORS
INDICATORS: Cabin Environment
INDL & PERSONAL SVC PAPER WHOLESALERS
INDL & PERSONAL SVC PAPER, WHOL: Bags, Paper/Disp Plastic
INDL & PERSONAL SVC PAPER, WHOL: Boxes, Corrugtd/Solid Fiber
INDL & PERSONAL SVC PAPER, WHOL: Cups, Disp, Plastic/Paper
INDL & PERSONAL SVC PAPER, WHOLESALE: Boxes & Containers
INDL & PERSONAL SVC PAPER, WHOLESALE: Press Sensitive Tape
INDL & PERSONAL SVC PAPER, WHOLESALE: Sanitary Food
INDL EQPT SVCS
INDL GASES WHOLESALERS
INDL MACHINERY & EQPT WHOLESALERS
INDL MACHINERY REPAIR & MAINTENANCE
INDL PATTERNS: Foundry Patternmaking
INDL PROCESS INSTRUMENTS: Analyzers
INDL PROCESS INSTRUMENTS: Control
INDL PROCESS INSTRUMENTS: Controllers, Process Variables
INDL PROCESS INSTRUMENTS: Digital Display, Process Variables
INDL PROCESS INSTRUMENTS: Elements, Primary
INDL PROCESS INSTRUMENTS: Fluidic Devices, Circuit & Systems
INDL PROCESS INSTRUMENTS: Indl Flow & Measuring
INDL PROCESS INSTRUMENTS: Level & Bulk Measuring
INDL PROCESS INSTRUMENTS: On-Stream Gas Or Liquid Analysis
INDL PROCESS INSTRUMENTS: Temperature
INDL PROCESS INSTRUMENTS: Water Quality Monitoring/Cntrl Sys
INDL SALTS WHOLESALERS
INDL SPLYS WHOLESALERS
INDL SPLYS, WHOL: Fasteners, Incl Nuts, Bolts, Screws, Etc
INDL SPLYS, WHOLESALE: Abrasives
INDL SPLYS, WHOLESALE: Adhesives, Tape & Plasters
INDL SPLYS, WHOLESALE: Bearings
INDL SPLYS, WHOLESALE: Bins & Containers, Storage
INDL SPLYS, WHOLESALE: Brushes, Indl
INDL SPLYS, WHOLESALE: Clean Room Splys
INDL SPLYS, WHOLESALE: Fasteners & Fastening Eqpt
INDL SPLYS, WHOLESALE: Knives, Indl
INDL SPLYS, WHOLESALE: Power Transmission, Eqpt & Apparatus
INDL SPLYS, WHOLESALE: Rubber Goods, Mechanical
INDL SPLYS, WHOLESALE: Seals
INDL SPLYS, WHOLESALE: Springs
INDL SPLYS, WHOLESALE: Tools
INDL SPLYS, WHOLESALE: Valves & Fittings
INDUCTORS

INFORMATION RETRIEVAL SERVICES
INFRARED OBJECT DETECTION EQPT
INK OR WRITING FLUIDS
INK: Letterpress Or Offset
INK: Printing
INK: Screen process
INSECTICIDES
INSPECTION & TESTING SVCS
INSTR, MEASURE & CONTROL: Gauge, Oil Pressure & Water Temp
INSTRUMENTS & METERS: Measuring, Electric
INSTRUMENTS, LABORATORY: Differential Thermal Analysis
INSTRUMENTS, LABORATORY: Magnetic/Elec Properties Measuring
INSTRUMENTS, LABORATORY: Spectrometers
INSTRUMENTS, MEASURING & CNTRL: Gauges, Auto, Computer
INSTRUMENTS, MEASURING & CNTRL: Radiation & Testing, Nuclear
INSTRUMENTS, MEASURING & CNTRL: Testing, Abrasion, Etc
INSTRUMENTS, MEASURING & CNTRLG: Aircraft & Motor Vehicle
INSTRUMENTS, MEASURING & CNTRLG: Stress, Strain & Measure
INSTRUMENTS, MEASURING & CNTRLG: Tensile Strength Testing
INSTRUMENTS, MEASURING & CONTROLLING: Gas Detectors
INSTRUMENTS, MEASURING & CONTROLLING: Magnetometers
INSTRUMENTS, MEASURING & CONTROLLING: Photogrammetrical
INSTRUMENTS, MEASURING & CONTROLLING: Toll Booths, Automatic
INSTRUMENTS, MEASURING & CONTROLLING: Ultrasonic Testing
INSTRUMENTS, MEASURING/CNTRL: Hydrometers, Exc Indl Process
INSTRUMENTS, MEASURING/CNTRLG: Fare Registers, St Cars/Buses
INSTRUMENTS, MEASURING/CNTRLNG: Med Diagnostic Sys, Nuclear
INSTRUMENTS, OPTICAL: Alignment & Display
INSTRUMENTS, OPTICAL: Borescopes
INSTRUMENTS, OPTICAL: Elements & Assemblies, Exc Ophthalmic
INSTRUMENTS, OPTICAL: Gratings, Diffraction
INSTRUMENTS, OPTICAL: Lenses, All Types Exc Ophthalmic
INSTRUMENTS, OPTICAL: Mirrors
INSTRUMENTS, OPTICAL: Prisms
INSTRUMENTS, OPTICAL: Sights, Telescopic
INSTRUMENTS, OPTICAL: Test & Inspection
INSTRUMENTS, SURGICAL & MEDICAL: Blood & Bone Work
INSTRUMENTS, SURGICAL & MEDICAL: Blood Pressure
INSTRUMENTS, SURGICAL & MEDICAL: Catheters
INSTRUMENTS, SURGICAL & MEDICAL: IV Transfusion
INSTRUMENTS, SURGICAL & MEDICAL: Inhalation Therapy
INSTRUMENTS, SURGICAL & MEDICAL: Inhalators
INSTRUMENTS, SURGICAL & MEDICAL: Knives
INSTRUMENTS, SURGICAL & MEDICAL: Lasers, Surgical
INSTRUMENTS, SURGICAL & MEDICAL: Muscle Exercise, Ophthalmic
INSTRUMENTS, SURGICAL & MEDICAL: Ophthalmic
INSTRUMENTS, SURGICAL & MEDICAL: Physiotherapy, Electrical
INSTRUMENTS, SURGICAL & MEDICAL: Skin Grafting
INSTRUMENTS, SURGICAL & MEDICAL: Suction Therapy
INSTRUMENTS: Analytical
INSTRUMENTS: Colonoscopes, Electromedical
INSTRUMENTS: Combustion Control, Indl
INSTRUMENTS: Electrocardiographs
INSTRUMENTS: Electrolytic Conductivity, Indl
INSTRUMENTS: Electrolytic Conductivity, Laboratory
INSTRUMENTS: Endoscopic Eqpt, Electromedical
INSTRUMENTS: Function Generators
INSTRUMENTS: Generators Tachometer
INSTRUMENTS: Indl Process Control
INSTRUMENTS: Laser, Scientific & Engineering
INSTRUMENTS: Measurement, Indl Process
INSTRUMENTS: Measuring & Controlling
INSTRUMENTS: Measuring Electricity
INSTRUMENTS: Measuring, Electrical Energy
INSTRUMENTS: Measuring, Electrical Power

INSTRUMENTS: Measuring, Electrical Quantities
INSTRUMENTS: Medical & Surgical
INSTRUMENTS: Meteorological
INSTRUMENTS: Microwave Test
INSTRUMENTS: Nautical
INSTRUMENTS: Optical, Analytical
INSTRUMENTS: Oscillographs & Oscilloscopes
INSTRUMENTS: Pressure Measurement, Indl
INSTRUMENTS: Radar Testing, Electric
INSTRUMENTS: Radio Frequency Measuring
INSTRUMENTS: Refractometers, Indl Process
INSTRUMENTS: Signal Generators & Averagers
INSTRUMENTS: Standards & Calibration, Electrical Measuring
INSTRUMENTS: Telemetering, Indl Process
INSTRUMENTS: Temperature Measurement, Indl
INSTRUMENTS: Test, Electronic & Electric Measurement
INSTRUMENTS: Test, Electronic & Electrical Circuits
INSTRUMENTS: Testing, Semiconductor
INSTRUMENTS: Thermal Conductive, Indl
INSTRUMENTS: Vibration
INSTRUMENTS: Viscometer, Indl Process
INSULATING COMPOUNDS
INSULATION & CUSHIONING FOAM: Polystyrene
INSULATION MATERIALS WHOLESALERS
INSULATION: Felt
INSULATION: Fiberglass
INSULATORS & INSULATION MATERIALS: Electrical
INSULATORS, PORCELAIN: Electrical
INSULIN PREPARATIONS
INSURANCE CARRIERS: Life
INTEGRATED CIRCUITS, SEMICONDUCTOR NETWORKS, ETC
INTERCOMMUNICATIONS SYSTEMS: Electric
INTERIOR DECORATING SVCS
INTERIOR DESIGN SVCS, NEC
INTERIOR DESIGNING SVCS
INTERIOR REPAIR SVCS
INTRAVENOUS SOLUTIONS
INVERTERS: Nonrotating Electrical
INVERTERS: Rotating Electrical
INVESTMENT ADVISORY SVCS
INVESTMENT FUNDS: Open-Ended
INVESTORS, NEC
INVESTORS: Real Estate, Exc Property Operators
INVESTORS: Security Speculators For Own Account
IRON & STEEL PRDTS: Hot-Rolled
IRON & STEEL: Corrugating, Cold-Rolled
IRON ORE MINING
IRON OXIDES
IRONING BOARDS

J

JANITORIAL & CUSTODIAL SVCS
JANITORIAL EQPT & SPLYS WHOLESALERS
JEWELERS' FINDINGS & MATERIALS
JEWELERS' FINDINGS & MATERIALS: Castings
JEWELERS' FINDINGS & MATERIALS: Parts, Unassembled
JEWELERS' FINDINGS & MTLS: Jewel Prep, Instr, Tools, Watches
JEWELERS' FINDINGS/MTRLS: Gem Prep, Settings, Real/Imitation
JEWELRY & PRECIOUS STONES WHOLESALERS
JEWELRY APPAREL
JEWELRY FINDINGS & LAPIDARY WORK
JEWELRY FINDINGS WHOLESALERS
JEWELRY REPAIR SVCS
JEWELRY STORES
JEWELRY STORES: Precious Stones & Precious Metals
JEWELRY STORES: Silverware
JEWELRY, PREC METAL: Mountings, Pens, Lthr, Etc, Gold/Silver
JEWELRY, PRECIOUS METAL: Bracelets
JEWELRY, PRECIOUS METAL: Cases
JEWELRY, PRECIOUS METAL: Cigar & Cigarette Access
JEWELRY, PRECIOUS METAL: Earrings
JEWELRY, PRECIOUS METAL: Medals, Precious Or Semiprecious
JEWELRY, PRECIOUS METAL: Mountings & Trimmings
JEWELRY, PRECIOUS METAL: Necklaces
JEWELRY, PRECIOUS METAL: Pearl, Natural Or Cultured
JEWELRY, PRECIOUS METAL: Pins
JEWELRY, PRECIOUS METAL: Rings, Finger
JEWELRY, PRECIOUS METAL: Rosaries/Other Sm Religious Article

PRODUCT INDEX

JEWELRY, PRECIOUS METAL: Settings & Mountings
JEWELRY, PRECIOUS METAL: Trimmings, Canes, Umbrellas, Etc
JEWELRY, WHOLESALE
JEWELRY: Decorative, Fashion & Costume
JEWELRY: Precious Metal
JIGS & FIXTURES
JOB PRINTING & NEWSPAPER PUBLISHING COMBINED
JOB TRAINING & VOCATIONAL REHABILITATION SVCS
JOINTS: Ball Except aircraft & Auto
JOINTS: Expansion
JOINTS: Expansion, Pipe

K

KEYBOARDS: Computer Or Office Machine
KILNS
KITCHEN CABINET STORES, EXC CUSTOM
KITCHEN CABINETS WHOLESALERS
KITCHEN UTENSILS: Bakers' Eqpt, Wood
KITCHEN UTENSILS: Food Handling & Processing Prdts, Wood
KITCHEN UTENSILS: Wooden
KITCHENWARE STORES
KITCHENWARE: Plastic
KNIT GOODS, WHOLESALE
KNIT OUTERWEAR DYEING & FINISHING, EXC HOSIERY & GLOVE
KNIVES: Agricultural Or indl

L

LABELS: Cotton, Printed
LABELS: Paper, Made From Purchased Materials
LABELS: Woven
LABORATORIES, TESTING: Forensic
LABORATORIES, TESTING: Pollution
LABORATORIES, TESTING: Product Testing, Safety/Performance
LABORATORIES: Biological Research
LABORATORIES: Biotechnology
LABORATORIES: Commercial Nonphysical Research
LABORATORIES: Dental
LABORATORIES: Dental Orthodontic Appliance Production
LABORATORIES: Electronic Research
LABORATORIES: Medical
LABORATORIES: Noncommercial Research
LABORATORIES: Physical Research, Commercial
LABORATORIES: Testing
LABORATORIES: Testing
LABORATORY APPARATUS & FURNITURE
LABORATORY APPARATUS: Furnaces
LABORATORY APPARATUS: Pipettes, Hemocytometer
LABORATORY APPARATUS: Shakers & Stirrers
LABORATORY EQPT, EXC MEDICAL: Wholesalers
LABORATORY EQPT: Chemical
LABORATORY EQPT: Clinical Instruments Exc Medical
LABORATORY EQPT: Measuring
LABORATORY EQPT: Sterilizers
LABORATORY INSTRUMENT REPAIR SVCS
LACE GOODS & WARP KNIT FABRIC DYEING & FINISHING
LACQUERING SVC: Metal Prdts
LADDERS: Metal
LADDERS: Portable, Metal
LADDERS: Wood
LAMINATED PLASTICS: Plate, Sheet, Rod & Tubes
LAMINATING SVCS
LAMP & LIGHT BULBS & TUBES
LAMP BULBS & TUBES, ELECTRIC: For Specialized Applications
LAMP BULBS & TUBES, ELECTRIC: Light, Complete
LAMP BULBS & TUBES/PARTS, ELECTRIC: Generalized Applications
LAMP FRAMES: Wire
LAMP SHADES: Glass
LAMP SHADES: Metal
LAMP STORES
LAMPS: Floor, Residential
LAMPS: Fluorescent
LAMPS: Ultraviolet
LAND SUBDIVIDERS & DEVELOPERS: Commercial
LAND SUBDIVISION & DEVELOPMENT
LANGUAGE SCHOOLS
LANTERNS
LAPIDARY WORK & DIAMOND CUTTING & POLISHING
LAPIDARY WORK: Contract Or Other
LAPIDARY WORK: Jewel Cut, Drill, Polish, Recut/Setting

LARD: From Slaughtering Plants
LASER SYSTEMS & EQPT
LASERS: Welding, Drilling & Cutting Eqpt
LAUNDRY & DRYCLEANER AGENTS
LAUNDRY & GARMENT SVCS, NEC: Fur Cleaning, Repairing/Storage
LAUNDRY & GARMENT SVCS, NEC: Garment Alteration & Repair
LAUNDRY & GARMENT SVCS, NEC: Garment Making, Alter & Repair
LAUNDRY & GARMENT SVCS, NEC: Reweaving, Textiles
LAUNDRY & GARMENT SVCS: Dressmaking, Matl Owned By Customer
LAUNDRY EQPT: Commercial
LAUNDRY EQPT: Household
LAUNDRY SVC: Wiping Towel Sply
LAWN & GARDEN EQPT
LAWN & GARDEN EQPT STORES
LAWN & GARDEN EQPT: Carts Or Wagons
LAWN & GARDEN EQPT: Tractors & Eqpt
LAWN & GARDEN EQPT: Trimmers
LAWN MOWER REPAIR SHOP
LEAD & ZINC
LEAD PENCILS & ART GOODS
LEASING & RENTAL SVCS: Oil Field Eqpt
LEASING & RENTAL: Computers & Eqpt
LEASING & RENTAL: Construction & Mining Eqpt
LEASING & RENTAL: Other Real Estate Property
LEASING: Laundry Eqpt
LEASING: Shipping Container
LEATHER GOODS, EXC FOOTWEAR, GLOVES, LUGGAGE/BELTING, WHOL
LEATHER GOODS: Belt Laces
LEATHER GOODS: Belting & Strapping
LEATHER GOODS: Boxes
LEATHER GOODS: Cases
LEATHER GOODS: Cosmetic Bags
LEATHER GOODS: Desk Sets
LEATHER GOODS: Garments
LEATHER GOODS: Holsters
LEATHER GOODS: Key Cases
LEATHER GOODS: NEC
LEATHER GOODS: Personal
LEATHER GOODS: Transmission Belting
LEATHER GOODS: Wallets
LEATHER TANNING & FINISHING
LEATHER, LEATHER GOODS & FURS, WHOLESALE
LEATHER: Accessory Prdts
LEATHER: Artificial
LEATHER: Bag
LEATHER: Bookbinders'
LEATHER: Case
LEATHER: Colored
LEATHER: Cut
LEATHER: Die-cut
LEATHER: Embossed
LEATHER: Finished
LEATHER: Handbag
LEATHER: Processed
LEATHER: Specialty, NEC
LEGAL & TAX SVCS
LEGAL OFFICES & SVCS
LEGITIMATE LIVE THEATER PRODUCERS
LENS COATING: Ophthalmic
LESSORS: Landholding Office
LIFESAVING & SURVIVAL EQPT, EXC MEDICAL, WHOLESALE
LIGHT SENSITIVE DEVICES
LIGHTING EQPT: Flashlights
LIGHTING EQPT: Motor Vehicle, Headlights
LIGHTING EQPT: Motor Vehicle, NEC
LIGHTING EQPT: Outdoor
LIGHTING EQPT: Reflectors, Metal, For Lighting Eqpt
LIGHTING EQPT: Streetcar Fixtures
LIGHTING EQPT: Strobe Lighting Systems
LIGHTING FIXTURES WHOLESALERS
LIGHTING FIXTURES, NEC
LIGHTING FIXTURES: Decorative Area
LIGHTING FIXTURES: Fluorescent, Commercial
LIGHTING FIXTURES: Fluorescent, Residential
LIGHTING FIXTURES: Indl & Commercial
LIGHTING FIXTURES: Motor Vehicle
LIGHTING FIXTURES: Ornamental, Commercial
LIGHTING FIXTURES: Public
LIGHTING FIXTURES: Residential

LIGHTING FIXTURES: Residential, Electric
LIGHTING FIXTURES: Street
LIGHTS: Trouble lights
LIME: Agricultural
LIMESTONE & MARBLE: Dimension
LIMESTONE: Crushed & Broken
LIMESTONE: Cut & Shaped
LIMESTONE: Dimension
LIMESTONE: Ground
LINEN SPLY SVC: Coat
LINENS & TOWELS WHOLESALERS
LINENS: Napkins, Fabric & Nonwoven, From Purchased Materials
LINENS: Tablecloths, From Purchased Materials
LINERS & COVERS: Fabric
LINERS & LINING
LINERS: Indl, Metal Plate
LININGS: Apparel, Made From Purchased Materials
LININGS: Fabric, Apparel & Other, Exc Millinery
LIP BALMS
LIPSTICK
LIQUEFIED PETROLEUM GAS DEALERS
LIQUID CRYSTAL DISPLAYS
LITHOGRAPHIC PLATES
LOCKERS
LOCKERS: Refrigerated
LOCKS
LOCKS: Coin-Operated
LOCKSMITHS
LOG LOADING & UNLOADING SVCS
LOGGING
LOGGING CAMPS & CONTRACTORS
LOGGING: Timber, Cut At Logging Camp
LOGGING: Wood Chips, Produced In The Field
LOGGING: Wooden Logs
LOOSELEAF BINDERS
LOTIONS OR CREAMS: Face
LOTIONS: SHAVING
LOUDSPEAKERS
LOUVERS: Ventilating
LUBRICANTS: Corrosion Preventive
LUBRICATING EQPT: Indl
LUBRICATING OIL & GREASE WHOLESALERS
LUBRICATION SYSTEMS & EQPT
LUGGAGE & BRIEFCASES
LUGGAGE & LEATHER GOODS STORES
LUGGAGE & LEATHER GOODS STORES: Leather, Exc Luggage & Shoes
LUGGAGE: Traveling Bags
LUGGAGE: Wardrobe Bags
LUMBER & BLDG MATLS DEALER, RET: Garage Doors, Sell/Install
LUMBER & BLDG MATRLS DEALERS, RET: Bath Fixtures, Eqpt/Sply
LUMBER & BLDG MTRLS DEALERS, RET: Closets, Interiors/Access
LUMBER & BLDG MTRLS DEALERS, RET: Doors, Storm, Wood/Metal
LUMBER & BLDG MTRLS DEALERS, RET: Windows, Storm, Wood/Metal
LUMBER & BUILDING MATERIALS DEALER, RET: Door & Window Prdts
LUMBER & BUILDING MATERIALS DEALER, RET: Masonry Matls/Splys
LUMBER & BUILDING MATERIALS DEALERS, RETAIL: Brick
LUMBER & BUILDING MATERIALS DEALERS, RETAIL: Countertops
LUMBER & BUILDING MATERIALS DEALERS, RETAIL: Paving Stones
LUMBER & BUILDING MATERIALS DEALERS, RETAIL: Sand & Gravel
LUMBER & BUILDING MATERIALS DEALERS, RETAIL: Tile, Ceramic
LUMBER & BUILDING MATERIALS RET DEALERS: Millwork & Lumber
LUMBER & BUILDING MATLS DEALERS, RET: Concrete/Cinder Block
LUMBER: Dimension, Hardwood
LUMBER: Fiberboard
LUMBER: Fuelwood, From Mill Waste
LUMBER: Furniture Dimension Stock, Softwood
LUMBER: Hardwood Dimension
LUMBER: Hardwood Dimension & Flooring Mills
LUMBER: Kiln Dried
LUMBER: Plywood, Hardwood

PRODUCT INDEX

LUMBER: Plywood, Hardwood or Hardwood Faced
LUMBER: Plywood, Prefinished, Hardwood
LUMBER: Plywood, Softwood
LUMBER: Poles, Wood, Untreated
LUMBER: Siding, Dressed
LUMBER: Silo Stock, Sawn
LUMBER: Treated
LUNCHROOMS & CAFETERIAS

M

MACHINE PARTS: Stamped Or Pressed Metal
MACHINE SHOPS
MACHINE TOOL ACCESS: Balancing Machines
MACHINE TOOL ACCESS: Cams
MACHINE TOOL ACCESS: Cutting
MACHINE TOOL ACCESS: Diamond Cutting, For Turning, Etc
MACHINE TOOL ACCESS: Dies, Thread Cutting
MACHINE TOOL ACCESS: Dressing/Wheel Crushing Attach, Diamond
MACHINE TOOL ACCESS: Drills
MACHINE TOOL ACCESS: Knives, Shear
MACHINE TOOL ACCESS: Milling Machine Attachments
MACHINE TOOL ACCESS: Sockets
MACHINE TOOL ACCESS: Tool Holders
MACHINE TOOL ACCESS: Tools & Access
MACHINE TOOL ATTACHMENTS & ACCESS
MACHINE TOOLS & ACCESS
MACHINE TOOLS, METAL CUTTING: Centering
MACHINE TOOLS, METAL CUTTING: Exotic, Including Explosive
MACHINE TOOLS, METAL CUTTING: Grind, Polish, Buff, Lapp
MACHINE TOOLS, METAL CUTTING: Home Workshop
MACHINE TOOLS, METAL CUTTING: Lathes
MACHINE TOOLS, METAL CUTTING: Numerically Controlled
MACHINE TOOLS, METAL CUTTING: Tool Replacement & Rpr Parts
MACHINE TOOLS, METAL FORMING: Die Casting & Extruding
MACHINE TOOLS, METAL FORMING: Electroforming
MACHINE TOOLS, METAL FORMING: Forging Machinery & Hammers
MACHINE TOOLS, METAL FORMING: Forming, Metal Deposit
MACHINE TOOLS, METAL FORMING: Headers
MACHINE TOOLS, METAL FORMING: High Energy Rate
MACHINE TOOLS, METAL FORMING: Presses, Hyd & Pneumatic
MACHINE TOOLS, METAL FORMING: Pressing
MACHINE TOOLS, METAL FORMING: Punching & Shearing
MACHINE TOOLS, METAL FORMING: Rebuilt
MACHINE TOOLS, METAL FORMING: Spinning, Spline Rollg/Windg
MACHINE TOOLS: Metal Cutting
MACHINE TOOLS: Metal Forming
MACHINERY & EQPT, AGRICULTURAL, WHOLESALE: Dairy
MACHINERY & EQPT, AGRICULTURAL, WHOLESALE: Landscaping Eqpt
MACHINERY & EQPT, AGRICULTURAL, WHOLESALE: Lawn & Garden
MACHINERY & EQPT, INDL, WHOL: Controlling Instruments/Access
MACHINERY & EQPT, INDL, WHOL: Recording Instruments/Access
MACHINERY & EQPT, INDL, WHOLESALE: Conveyor Systems
MACHINERY & EQPT, INDL, WHOLESALE: Countersinks
MACHINERY & EQPT, INDL, WHOLESALE: Fans
MACHINERY & EQPT, INDL, WHOLESALE: Food Manufacturing
MACHINERY & EQPT, INDL, WHOLESALE: Food Product Manufacturng
MACHINERY & EQPT, INDL, WHOLESALE: Heat Exchange
MACHINERY & EQPT, INDL, WHOLESALE: Hoists
MACHINERY & EQPT, INDL, WHOLESALE: Hydraulic Systems
MACHINERY & EQPT, INDL, WHOLESALE: Indl Machine Parts
MACHINERY & EQPT, INDL, WHOLESALE: Instruments & Cntrl Eqpt
MACHINERY & EQPT, INDL, WHOLESALE: Machine Tools & Access
MACHINERY & EQPT, INDL, WHOLESALE: Measure/Test, Electric
MACHINERY & EQPT, INDL, WHOLESALE: Metal Refining
MACHINERY & EQPT, INDL, WHOLESALE: Packaging
MACHINERY & EQPT, INDL, WHOLESALE: Paint Spray
MACHINERY & EQPT, INDL, WHOLESALE: Pneumatic Tools
MACHINERY & EQPT, INDL, WHOLESALE: Power Plant Machinery
MACHINERY & EQPT, INDL, WHOLESALE: Processing & Packaging
MACHINERY & EQPT, INDL, WHOLESALE: Robots
MACHINERY & EQPT, INDL, WHOLESALE: Safety Eqpt
MACHINERY & EQPT, INDL, WHOLESALE: Textile
MACHINERY & EQPT, INDL, WHOLESALE: Water Pumps
MACHINERY & EQPT, INDL, WHOLESALE: Woodworking
MACHINERY & EQPT, WHOLESALE: Construction, General
MACHINERY & EQPT, WHOLESALE: Contractors Materials
MACHINERY & EQPT, WHOLESALE: Crushing, Pulverizng & Screeng
MACHINERY & EQPT, WHOLESALE: Masonry
MACHINERY & EQPT: Electroplating
MACHINERY & EQPT: Farm
MACHINERY & EQPT: Gas Producers, Generators/Other Rltd Eqpt
MACHINERY & EQPT: Liquid Automation
MACHINERY & EQPT: Metal Finishing, Plating Etc
MACHINERY BASES
MACHINERY, COMMERCIAL LAUNDRY: Dryers, Incl Coin-Operated
MACHINERY, COMMERCIAL LAUNDRY: Washing, Incl Coin-Operated
MACHINERY, EQPT & SUPPLIES: Parking Facility
MACHINERY, FOOD PRDTS: Beverage
MACHINERY, FOOD PRDTS: Choppers, Commercial
MACHINERY, FOOD PRDTS: Cutting, Chopping, Grinding, Mixing
MACHINERY, FOOD PRDTS: Dairy & Milk
MACHINERY, FOOD PRDTS: Dairy, Pasteurizing
MACHINERY, FOOD PRDTS: Food Processing, Smokers
MACHINERY, FOOD PRDTS: Juice Extractors, Fruit & Veg, Comm
MACHINERY, FOOD PRDTS: Milk Processing, NEC
MACHINERY, FOOD PRDTS: Mixers, Commercial
MACHINERY, FOOD PRDTS: Oilseed Crushing & Extracting
MACHINERY, FOOD PRDTS: Ovens, Bakery
MACHINERY, FOOD PRDTS: Packing House
MACHINERY, FOOD PRDTS: Presses, Cheese, Beet, Cider & Sugar
MACHINERY, FOOD PRDTS: Roasting, Coffee, Peanut, Etc.
MACHINERY, MAILING: Canceling
MACHINERY, MAILING: Postage Meters
MACHINERY, METALWORKING: Assembly, Including Robotic
MACHINERY, METALWORKING: Cutting & Slitting
MACHINERY, OFFICE: Perforators
MACHINERY, OFFICE: Stapling, Hand Or Power
MACHINERY, OFFICE: Time Clocks &Time Recording Devices
MACHINERY, OFFICE: Typing & Word Processing
MACHINERY, PACKAGING: Canning, Food
MACHINERY, PACKAGING: Carton Packing
MACHINERY, PACKAGING: Packing & Wrapping
MACHINERY, PAPER INDUSTRY: Converting, Die Cutting & Stampng
MACHINERY, PAPER INDUSTRY: Paper Mill, Plating, Etc
MACHINERY, PRINTING TRADES: Copy Holders
MACHINERY, PRINTING TRADES: Plates
MACHINERY, PRINTING TRADES: Plates, Offset
MACHINERY, PRINTING TRADES: Presses, Envelope
MACHINERY, PRINTING TRADES: Printing Trade Parts & Attchts
MACHINERY, PRINTING TRADES: Sticks
MACHINERY, SEWING: Sewing & Hat & Zipper Making
MACHINERY, TEXTILE: Beaming
MACHINERY, TEXTILE: Card Cutting, Jacquard
MACHINERY, TEXTILE: Embroidery
MACHINERY, TEXTILE: Silk Screens
MACHINERY, TEXTILE: Thread Making Or Spinning
MACHINERY, WOODWORKING: Bandsaws
MACHINERY, WOODWORKING: Furniture Makers
MACHINERY, WOODWORKING: Lathes, Wood Turning Includes Access
MACHINERY, WOODWORKING: Pattern Makers'
MACHINERY, WOODWORKING: Sanding, Exc Portable Floor Sanders
MACHINERY: Ammunition & Explosives Loading
MACHINERY: Assembly, Exc Metalworking
MACHINERY: Automotive Maintenance
MACHINERY: Automotive Related
MACHINERY: Billing
MACHINERY: Bottling & Canning
MACHINERY: Brewery & Malting
MACHINERY: Bridge Or Gate, Hydraulic
MACHINERY: Concrete Prdts
MACHINERY: Construction
MACHINERY: Cryogenic, Industrial
MACHINERY: Custom
MACHINERY: Drill Presses
MACHINERY: Electronic Component Making
MACHINERY: Extruding
MACHINERY: Fiber Optics Strand Coating
MACHINERY: Gear Cutting & Finishing
MACHINERY: General, Industrial, NEC
MACHINERY: Glassmaking
MACHINERY: Grinding
MACHINERY: Ice Cream
MACHINERY: Ice Crushers
MACHINERY: Ice Making
MACHINERY: Industrial, NEC
MACHINERY: Jewelers
MACHINERY: Leather Working
MACHINERY: Marking, Metalworking
MACHINERY: Metalworking
MACHINERY: Milling
MACHINERY: Mining
MACHINERY: Optical Lens
MACHINERY: Ozone
MACHINERY: Packaging
MACHINERY: Paper Industry Miscellaneous
MACHINERY: Pharmacuitical
MACHINERY: Photographic Reproduction
MACHINERY: Plastic Working
MACHINERY: Printing Presses
MACHINERY: Recycling
MACHINERY: Riveting
MACHINERY: Road Construction & Maintenance
MACHINERY: Rubber Working
MACHINERY: Semiconductor Manufacturing
MACHINERY: Separation Eqpt, Magnetic
MACHINERY: Sheet Metal Working
MACHINERY: Specialty
MACHINERY: Textile
MACHINERY: Tire Shredding
MACHINERY: Voting
MACHINERY: Wire Drawing
MACHINERY: Woodworking
MACHINES: Forming, Sheet Metal
MACHINISTS' TOOLS: Measuring, Precision
MACHINISTS' TOOLS: Precision
MACHINISTS' TOOLS: Scales, Measuring, Precision
MAGAZINES, WHOLESALE
MAGNETIC INK & OPTICAL SCANNING EQPT
MAGNETIC RESONANCE IMAGING DEVICES: Nonmedical
MAGNETIC TAPE, AUDIO: Prerecorded
MAGNETOHYDRODYNAMIC DEVICES OR MHD
MAGNETS: Ceramic
MAGNETS: Permanent
MAGNIFIERS
MAIL-ORDER BOOK CLUBS
MAIL-ORDER HOUSE, NEC
MAIL-ORDER HOUSES: Book & Record Clubs
MAIL-ORDER HOUSES: Books, Exc Book Clubs
MAIL-ORDER HOUSES: Cards
MAIL-ORDER HOUSES: Clothing, Exc Women's
MAIL-ORDER HOUSES: Computer Eqpt & Electronics
MAIL-ORDER HOUSES: Cosmetics & Perfumes
MAIL-ORDER HOUSES: Fitness & Sporting Goods
MAIL-ORDER HOUSES: Food
MAIL-ORDER HOUSES: Furniture & Furnishings
MAIL-ORDER HOUSES: Gift Items
MAIL-ORDER HOUSES: Jewelry
MAIL-ORDER HOUSES: Magazines
MAILING LIST: Brokers
MAILING LIST: Compilers
MAILING SVCS, NEC
MANAGEMENT CONSULTING SVCS: Automation & Robotics
MANAGEMENT CONSULTING SVCS: Business
MANAGEMENT CONSULTING SVCS: Construction Project
MANAGEMENT CONSULTING SVCS: Distribution Channels
MANAGEMENT CONSULTING SVCS: Food & Beverage
MANAGEMENT CONSULTING SVCS: Foreign Trade
MANAGEMENT CONSULTING SVCS: Industrial
MANAGEMENT CONSULTING SVCS: Industrial & Labor
MANAGEMENT CONSULTING SVCS: Industry Specialist

PRODUCT INDEX

MANAGEMENT CONSULTING SVCS: Real Estate
MANAGEMENT CONSULTING SVCS: Training & Development
MANAGEMENT SERVICES
MANAGEMENT SVCS: Administrative
MANAGEMENT SVCS: Circuit, Motion Picture Theaters
MANAGEMENT SVCS: Construction
MANAGEMENT SVCS: Restaurant
MANDRELS
MANHOLES COVERS: Concrete
MANICURE PREPARATIONS
MANIFOLDS: Pipe, Fabricated From Purchased Pipe
MANNEQUINS
MANUFACTURING INDUSTRIES, NEC
MAPS
MARBLE BOARD
MARBLE, BUILDING: Cut & Shaped
MARINAS
MARINE HARDWARE
MARINE RELATED EQPT
MARINE SVC STATIONS
MARKERS
MARKETS: Meat & fish
MARKING DEVICES
MARKING DEVICES: Date Stamps, Hand, Rubber Or Metal
MARKING DEVICES: Embossing Seals & Hand Stamps
MARKING DEVICES: Figures, Metal
MARKING DEVICES: Irons, Marking Or Branding
MARKING DEVICES: Letters, Metal
MARKING DEVICES: Numbering Machines
MARKING DEVICES: Pads, Inking & Stamping
MARKING DEVICES: Postmark Stamps, Hand, Rubber Or Metal
MARKING DEVICES: Screens, Textile Printing
MASKS: Gas
MASQUERADE OR THEATRICAL COSTUMES STORES
MASTIC ROOFING COMPOSITION
MATERIALS HANDLING EQPT WHOLESALERS
MATS & MATTING, MADE FROM PURCHASED WIRE
MATS OR MATTING, NEC: Rubber
MATS, MATTING & PADS: Auto, Floor, Exc Rubber Or Plastic
MATS: Blasting, Rope
MATTRESS RENOVATING & REPAIR SHOP
MATTRESS STORES
MEAT & MEAT PRDTS WHOLESALERS
MEAT CUTTING & PACKING
MEAT MARKETS
MEAT PRDTS: Bologna, From Purchased Meat
MEAT PRDTS: Boneless Meat, From Purchased Meat
MEAT PRDTS: Canned
MEAT PRDTS: Frankfurters, From Purchased Meat
MEAT PRDTS: Frozen
MEAT PRDTS: Meat By-Prdts, From Slaughtered Meat
MEAT PRDTS: Meat Extracts, From Purchased Meat
MEAT PRDTS: Pork, From Slaughtered Meat
MEAT PRDTS: Prepared Beef Prdts From Purchased Beef
MEAT PRDTS: Prepared Pork Prdts, From Purchased Meat
MEAT PRDTS: Sausage Casings, Natural
MEAT PRDTS: Sausages & Related Prdts, From Purchased Meat
MEAT PRDTS: Sausages, From Purchased Meat
MEAT PRDTS: Sausages, From Slaughtered Meat
MEAT PRDTS: Snack Sticks, Incl Jerky, From Purchased Meat
MEAT PRDTS: Variety, Fresh Edible Organs
MEAT PRDTS: Veal, From Slaughtered Meat
MEAT PROCESSED FROM PURCHASED CARCASSES
MEAT PROCESSING MACHINERY
MED, DENTAL & HOSPITAL EQPT, WHOL: Incontinent Prdts/Splys
MEDIA BUYING AGENCIES
MEDIA: Magnetic & Optical Recording
MEDICAL & HOSPITAL EQPT WHOLESALERS
MEDICAL & HOSPITAL SPLYS: Radiation Shielding Garments
MEDICAL & SURGICAL SPLYS: Bandages & Dressings
MEDICAL & SURGICAL SPLYS: Braces, Orthopedic
MEDICAL & SURGICAL SPLYS: Clothing, Fire Resistant & Protect
MEDICAL & SURGICAL SPLYS: Cosmetic Restorations
MEDICAL & SURGICAL SPLYS: Cotton & Cotton Applicators
MEDICAL & SURGICAL SPLYS: Ear Plugs
MEDICAL & SURGICAL SPLYS: Foot Appliances, Orthopedic
MEDICAL & SURGICAL SPLYS: Gynecological Splys & Appliances
MEDICAL & SURGICAL SPLYS: Limbs, Artificial
MEDICAL & SURGICAL SPLYS: Orthopedic Appliances
MEDICAL & SURGICAL SPLYS: Personal Safety Eqpt
MEDICAL & SURGICAL SPLYS: Prosthetic Appliances
MEDICAL & SURGICAL SPLYS: Respiratory Protect Eqpt, Personal
MEDICAL & SURGICAL SPLYS: Sponges
MEDICAL & SURGICAL SPLYS: Supports, Abdominal, Ankle, Etc
MEDICAL & SURGICAL SPLYS: Suspensories
MEDICAL & SURGICAL SPLYS: Technical Aids, Handicapped
MEDICAL EQPT REPAIR SVCS, NON-ELECTRIC
MEDICAL EQPT: Diagnostic
MEDICAL EQPT: Electromedical Apparatus
MEDICAL EQPT: Electrotherapeutic Apparatus
MEDICAL EQPT: Heart-Lung Machines, Exc Iron Lungs
MEDICAL EQPT: Laser Systems
MEDICAL EQPT: MRI/Magnetic Resonance Imaging Devs, Nuclear
MEDICAL EQPT: PET Or Position Emission Tomography Scanners
MEDICAL EQPT: Patient Monitoring
MEDICAL EQPT: Sterilizers
MEDICAL EQPT: Ultrasonic Scanning Devices
MEDICAL EQPT: Ultrasonic, Exc Cleaning
MEDICAL EQPT: X-Ray Apparatus & Tubes, Radiographic
MEDICAL EQPT: X-Ray Apparatus & Tubes, Therapeutic
MEDICAL PHOTOGRAPHY & ART SVCS
MEDICAL, DENTAL & HOSPITAL EQPT, WHOL: Dentists' Prof Splys
MEDICAL, DENTAL & HOSPITAL EQPT, WHOL: Hosptl Eqpt/Furniture
MEDICAL, DENTAL & HOSPITAL EQPT, WHOL: Surgical Eqpt & Splys
MEDICAL, DENTAL & HOSPITAL EQPT, WHOLESALE: Diagnostic, Med
MEDICAL, DENTAL & HOSPITAL EQPT, WHOLESALE: Med Eqpt & Splys
MEDICAL, DENTAL & HOSPITAL EQPT, WHOLESALE: Medical Lab
MELAMINE RESINS: Melamine-Formaldehyde
MEMBERSHIP ORGANIZATIONS, PROFESSIONAL: Health Association
MEMBERSHIP ORGS, BUSINESS: Growers' Marketing Advisory Svc
MEMBERSHIP ORGS, CIVIC, SOCIAL/FRAT: Educator's Assoc
MEMORIALS, MONUMENTS & MARKERS
MEMORIES: Solid State
MEMORY DEVICES: Magnetic Bubble
MEN'S & BOYS' CLOTHING ACCESS STORES
MEN'S & BOYS' CLOTHING STORES
MEN'S & BOYS' CLOTHING WHOLESALERS, NEC
MEN'S & BOYS' SPORTSWEAR CLOTHING STORES
MEN'S & BOYS' SPORTSWEAR WHOLESALERS
MEN'S & BOYS' UNDERWEAR WHOLESALERS
MEN'S SUITS STORES
MERCHANDISING MACHINE OPERATORS: Vending
METAL & STEEL PRDTS: Abrasive
METAL COMPONENTS: Prefabricated
METAL CUTTING SVCS
METAL DETECTORS
METAL FABRICATORS: Architechtural
METAL FABRICATORS: Plate
METAL FABRICATORS: Sheet
METAL FABRICATORS: Structural, Ship
METAL FABRICATORS: Structural, Ship
METAL FINISHING SVCS
METAL RESHAPING & REPLATING SVCS
METAL SERVICE CENTERS & OFFICES
METAL SPINNING FOR THE TRADE
METAL STAMPING, FOR THE TRADE
METAL STAMPINGS: Patterned
METAL STAMPINGS: Perforated
METAL STAMPINGS: Rigidized
METAL TREATING COMPOUNDS
METAL, TITANIUM: Sponge & Granules
METAL: Heavy, Perforated
METALLIC ORES WHOLESALERS
METALS SVC CENTERS & WHOL: Structural Shapes, Iron Or Steel
METALS SVC CENTERS & WHOLESALERS: Cable, Wire
METALS SVC CENTERS & WHOLESALERS: Iron & Steel Prdt, Ferrous
METALS SVC CENTERS & WHOLESALERS: Misc Nonferrous Prdts
METALS SVC CENTERS & WHOLESALERS: Nonferrous Sheets, Etc
METALS SVC CENTERS & WHOLESALERS: Pipe & Tubing, Steel
METALS SVC CENTERS & WHOLESALERS: Sheets, Metal
METALS SVC CENTERS & WHOLESALERS: Steel
METALS SVC CENTERS & WHOLESALERS: Tin & Tin Base Metals
METALS SVC CENTERS & WHOLESALERS: Tubing, Metal
METALS: Precious NEC
METALS: Precious, Secondary
METALS: Primary Nonferrous, NEC
METALWORK: Miscellaneous
METALWORK: Ornamental
METALWORKING MACHINERY WHOLESALERS
METER READERS: Remote
METERING DEVICES: Flow Meters, Impeller & Counter Driven
METERING DEVICES: Totalizing, Consumption
METERING DEVICES: Water Quality Monitoring & Control Systems
METERS: Elasped Time
METERS: Liquid
METHANOL: Natural
MGMT CONSULTING SVCS: Matls, Incl Purch, Handle & Invntry
MICA PRDTS
MICROCIRCUITS, INTEGRATED: Semiconductor
MICROFILM EQPT
MICROMANIPULATOR
MICROPHONES
MICROPROCESSORS
MICROWAVE COMPONENTS
MICROWAVE OVENS: Household
MILITARY INSIGNIA
MILITARY INSIGNIA, TEXTILE
MILL PRDTS: Structural & Rail
MILLINERY SUPPLIES: Veils & Veiling, Bridal, Funeral, Etc
MILLING: Grain Cereals, Cracked
MILLWORK
MINERAL ABRASIVES MINING SVCS
MINERAL MINING: Nonmetallic
MINERAL PRODUCTS
MINERAL WOOL
MINERAL WOOL INSULATION PRDTS
MINERALS: Ground or Treated
MINIATURES
MINING EXPLORATION & DEVELOPMENT SVCS
MINING SVCS, NEC: Lignite
MINING: Sand & Shale Oil
MIRROR REPAIR SHOP
MIRRORS: Motor Vehicle
MIXING EQPT
MIXTURES & BLOCKS: Asphalt Paving
MOBILE COMMUNICATIONS EQPT
MOBILE HOMES
MOBILE HOMES WHOLESALERS
MODELS
MODELS: General, Exc Toy
MODULES: Computer Logic
MODULES: Solid State
MOLDED RUBBER PRDTS
MOLDING COMPOUNDS
MOLDINGS, ARCHITECTURAL: Plaster Of Paris
MOLDINGS: Picture Frame
MOLDS: Indl
MOLDS: Plastic Working & Foundry
MONUMENTS & GRAVE MARKERS, EXC TERRAZZO
MONUMENTS: Concrete
MONUMENTS: Cut Stone, Exc Finishing Or Lettering Only
MOPS: Floor & Dust
MORTGAGE BANKERS
MOTION PICTURE & VIDEO PRODUCTION SVCS
MOTION PICTURE & VIDEO PRODUCTION SVCS: Non-Theatrical, TV
MOTION PICTURE PRODUCTION & DISTRIBUTION
MOTION PICTURE PRODUCTION & DISTRIBUTION: Television
MOTION PICTURE PRODUCTION ALLIED SVCS
MOTION PICTURE PRODUCTION SVCS
MOTOR & GENERATOR PARTS: Electric
MOTOR HOMES
MOTOR REPAIR SVCS

PRODUCT INDEX

MOTOR SCOOTERS & PARTS
MOTOR VEHICLE ASSEMBLY, COMPLETE: Autos, Incl Specialty
MOTOR VEHICLE ASSEMBLY, COMPLETE: Buses, All Types
MOTOR VEHICLE ASSEMBLY, COMPLETE: Cars, Armored
MOTOR VEHICLE ASSEMBLY, COMPLETE: Fire Department Vehicles
MOTOR VEHICLE ASSEMBLY, COMPLETE: Military Motor Vehicle
MOTOR VEHICLE ASSEMBLY, COMPLETE: Motor Buses
MOTOR VEHICLE ASSEMBLY, COMPLETE: Snow Plows
MOTOR VEHICLE ASSEMBLY, COMPLETE: Truck & Tractor Trucks
MOTOR VEHICLE ASSEMBLY, COMPLETE: Trucks, Pickup
MOTOR VEHICLE DEALERS: Automobiles, New & Used
MOTOR VEHICLE DEALERS: Cars, Used Only
MOTOR VEHICLE PARTS & ACCESS: Acceleration Eqpt
MOTOR VEHICLE PARTS & ACCESS: Air Conditioner Parts
MOTOR VEHICLE PARTS & ACCESS: Bearings
MOTOR VEHICLE PARTS & ACCESS: Body Components & Frames
MOTOR VEHICLE PARTS & ACCESS: Electrical Eqpt
MOTOR VEHICLE PARTS & ACCESS: Engines & Parts
MOTOR VEHICLE PARTS & ACCESS: Fuel Systems & Parts
MOTOR VEHICLE PARTS & ACCESS: Gears
MOTOR VEHICLE PARTS & ACCESS: Power Steering Eqpt
MOTOR VEHICLE PARTS & ACCESS: Propane Conversion Eqpt
MOTOR VEHICLE PARTS & ACCESS: Sanders, Safety
MOTOR VEHICLE PARTS & ACCESS: Tops
MOTOR VEHICLE PARTS & ACCESS: Transmissions
MOTOR VEHICLE PARTS & ACCESS: Wheel rims
MOTOR VEHICLE PARTS & ACCESS: Wiring Harness Sets
MOTOR VEHICLE SPLYS & PARTS WHOLESALERS: New
MOTOR VEHICLE: Hardware
MOTOR VEHICLE: Steering Mechanisms
MOTOR VEHICLES & CAR BODIES
MOTOR VEHICLES, WHOLESALE: Recreational, All-Terrain
MOTOR VEHICLES, WHOLESALE: Truck bodies
MOTORCYCLE & BICYCLE PARTS: Gears
MOTORCYCLE DEALERS
MOTORCYCLES & RELATED PARTS
MOTORS: Electric
MOTORS: Generators
MOTORS: Torque
MOUNTING SVC: Display
MOVIE THEATERS, EXC DRIVE-IN
MOWERS & ACCESSORIES
MULTIPLEXERS: Telephone & Telegraph
MUSEUMS
MUSEUMS & ART GALLERIES
MUSIC BROADCASTING SVCS
MUSIC COPYING SVCS
MUSIC DISTRIBUTION APPARATUS
MUSIC LICENSING & ROYALTIES
MUSIC LICENSING TO RADIO STATIONS
MUSIC RECORDING PRODUCER
MUSICAL ENTERTAINERS
MUSICAL INSTRUMENT PARTS & ACCESS, WHOLESALE
MUSICAL INSTRUMENT REPAIR
MUSICAL INSTRUMENTS & ACCESS: Carrying Cases
MUSICAL INSTRUMENTS & ACCESS: NEC
MUSICAL INSTRUMENTS & ACCESS: Pianos
MUSICAL INSTRUMENTS & ACCESS: Pipe Organs
MUSICAL INSTRUMENTS & PARTS: Brass
MUSICAL INSTRUMENTS & PARTS: String
MUSICAL INSTRUMENTS & SPLYS STORES
MUSICAL INSTRUMENTS & SPLYS STORES: Pianos
MUSICAL INSTRUMENTS WHOLESALERS
MUSICAL INSTRUMENTS: Blowers, Pipe Organ
MUSICAL INSTRUMENTS: Electric & Electronic
MUSICAL INSTRUMENTS: Guitars & Parts, Electric & Acoustic
MUSICAL INSTRUMENTS: Harmonicas
MUSICAL INSTRUMENTS: Organs
MUSICAL INSTRUMENTS: Reeds
MUSICAL INSTRUMENTS: Strings, Instrument

N

NAME PLATES: Engraved Or Etched
NAMEPLATES
NATIONAL SECURITY FORCES
NATIONAL SECURITY, GOVERNMENT: Army
NATURAL BUTANE PRODUCTION
NATURAL GAS DISTRIBUTION TO CONSUMERS
NATURAL GAS LIQUIDS PRODUCTION
NATURAL GAS PRODUCTION
NATURAL GAS TRANSMISSION & DISTRIBUTION
NATURAL GASOLINE PRODUCTION
NATURAL PROPANE PRODUCTION
NAUTICAL & NAVIGATIONAL INSTRUMENT REPAIR SVCS
NAVIGATIONAL SYSTEMS & INSTRUMENTS
NET & NETTING PRDTS
NETS: Laundry
NEW & USED CAR DEALERS
NEWS DEALERS & NEWSSTANDS
NEWS FEATURE SYNDICATES
NEWS PICTURES GATHERING & DISTRIBUTING SVCS
NEWS SYNDICATES
NEWSPAPERS & PERIODICALS NEWS REPORTING SVCS
NEWSPAPERS, WHOLESALE
NEWSSTAND
NICKEL ALLOY
NONCURRENT CARRYING WIRING DEVICES
NONFERROUS: Rolling & Drawing, NEC
NONMETALLIC MINERALS: Support Activities, Exc Fuels
NOTARIES PUBLIC
NOTEBOOKS, MADE FROM PURCHASED MATERIALS
NOTIONS: Button Blanks & Molds
NOTIONS: Pins, Straight, Steel Or Brass
NOTIONS: Studs, Shirt, Exc Precious/Semi Metal/Stone
NOVELTIES
NOVELTIES & SPECIALTIES: Metal
NOVELTIES: Paper, Made From Purchased Materials
NOVELTIES: Plastic
NOVELTY SHOPS
NOZZLES & SPRINKLERS Lawn Hose
NOZZLES: Spray, Aerosol, Paint Or Insecticide
NUCLEAR REACTORS: Military Or Indl
NURSERIES & LAWN & GARDEN SPLY STORES, RETAIL: Fertilizer
NURSERIES & LAWN & GARDEN SPLY STORES, RETAIL: Sod
NURSERIES & LAWN & GARDEN SPLY STORES, RETAIL: Top Soil
NURSERIES & LAWN/GARDEN SPLY STORE, RET: Lawnmowers/Tractors
NURSERY & GARDEN CENTERS
NUTS: Metal

O

OFFICE EQPT WHOLESALERS
OFFICE EQPT, WHOLESALE: Duplicating Machines
OFFICE FIXTURES: Exc Wood
OFFICE FIXTURES: Wood
OFFICE FURNITURE REPAIR & MAINTENANCE SVCS
OFFICE SPLY & STATIONERY STORES
OFFICE SPLY & STATIONERY STORES: Office Forms & Splys
OFFICE SPLY & STATIONERY STORES: Writing Splys
OFFICE SPLYS, NEC, WHOLESALE
OFFICES & CLINICS OF DENTISTS: Prosthodontist
OFFICES & CLINICS OF DRS, MED: Specialized Practitioners
OFFICES & CLINICS OF HEALTH PRACTITIONERS: Nutritionist
OIL & GAS FIELD MACHINERY
OIL FIELD MACHINERY & EQPT
OIL FIELD SVCS, NEC
OIL ROYALTY TRADERS
OILS & GREASES: Blended & Compounded
OILS & GREASES: Lubricating
OILS: Essential
OILS: Lubricating
OILS: Lubricating
OILS: Orange
OILS: Still
OINTMENTS
ON-LINE DATABASE INFORMATION RETRIEVAL SVCS
OPERATOR: Apartment Buildings
OPERATOR: Nonresidential Buildings
OPHTHALMIC GOODS
OPHTHALMIC GOODS WHOLESALERS
OPHTHALMIC GOODS: Frames & Parts, Eyeglass & Spectacle
OPHTHALMIC GOODS: Frames, Lenses & Parts, Eyeglasses
OPHTHALMIC GOODS: Lenses, Ophthalmic
OPHTHALMIC GOODS: Spectacles
OPHTHALMIC GOODS: Temples & Fronts, Ophthalmic
OPTICAL GOODS STORES
OPTICAL GOODS STORES: Opticians
OPTICAL INSTRUMENTS & APPARATUS
OPTICAL INSTRUMENTS & LENSES
OPTICAL SCANNING SVCS
OPTOMETRIC EQPT & SPLYS WHOLESALERS
ORAL PREPARATIONS
ORDNANCE
ORGAN TUNING & REPAIR SVCS
ORGANIZATIONS: Medical Research
ORGANIZATIONS: Noncommercial Biological Research
ORGANIZATIONS: Professional
ORGANIZATIONS: Religious
ORGANIZATIONS: Research Institute
ORGANIZATIONS: Scientific Research Agency
ORGANIZERS, CLOSET & DRAWER Plastic
ORNAMENTS: Christmas Tree, Exc Electrical & Glass
ORTHOPEDIC SUNDRIES: Molded Rubber
OSCILLATORS
OUTLETS: Electric, Convenience

P

PACKAGE DESIGN SVCS
PACKAGED FROZEN FOODS WHOLESALERS, NEC
PACKAGING & LABELING SVCS
PACKAGING MATERIALS, INDL: Wholesalers
PACKAGING MATERIALS, WHOLESALE
PACKAGING MATERIALS: Paper
PACKAGING MATERIALS: Paper, Coated Or Laminated
PACKAGING MATERIALS: Paper, Thermoplastic Coated
PACKAGING MATERIALS: Plastic Film, Coated Or Laminated
PACKAGING MATERIALS: Polystyrene Foam
PACKAGING MATERIALS: Resinous Impregnated Paper
PACKAGING: Blister Or Bubble Formed, Plastic
PACKING & CRATING SVC
PACKING MATERIALS: Mechanical
PACKING SVCS: Shipping
PACKING: Metallic
PADDING: Foamed Plastics
PADS: Desk, Exc Paper
PADS: Desk, Paper, Made From Purchased Materials
PADS: Mattress
PAGERS: One-way
PAINT STORE
PAINTING SVC: Metal Prdts
PAINTS & ADDITIVES
PAINTS & ALLIED PRODUCTS
PAINTS & VARNISHES: Plastics Based
PAINTS, VARNISHES & SPLYS, WHOLESALE: Paints
PALLET REPAIR SVCS
PALLETIZERS & DEPALLETIZERS
PALLETS
PALLETS & SKIDS: Wood
PALLETS: Wood & Metal Combination
PALLETS: Wooden
PANEL & DISTRIBUTION BOARDS: Electric
PANELS: Building, Wood
PANELS: Cardboard, Die-Cut, Made From Purchased Materials
PANELS: Wood
PAPER & BOARD: Die-cut
PAPER CONVERTING
PAPER MANUFACTURERS: Exc Newsprint
PAPER PRDTS: Feminine Hygiene Prdts
PAPER PRDTS: Infant & Baby Prdts
PAPER PRDTS: Molded Pulp Prdts
PAPER PRDTS: Napkins, Sanitary, Made From Purchased Material
PAPER PRDTS: Pattern Tissue
PAPER PRDTS: Pressed & Molded Pulp & Fiber Prdts
PAPER PRDTS: Pressed Pulp Prdts
PAPER PRDTS: Sanitary
PAPER PRDTS: Toilet Paper, Made From Purchased Materials
PAPER PRDTS: Toweling Tissue
PAPER PRDTS: Towels, Napkins/Tissue Paper, From Purchd Mtrls
PAPER, WHOLESALE: Fine
PAPER, WHOLESALE: Printing
PAPER: Absorbent
PAPER: Adding Machine Rolls, Made From Purchased Materials
PAPER: Adhesive
PAPER: Art
PAPER: Bristols
PAPER: Building, Insulating & Packaging

PRODUCT INDEX

PAPER: Business Form
PAPER: Card
PAPER: Chemically Treated, Made From Purchased Materials
PAPER: Cigarette
PAPER: Cloth, Lined, Made From Purchased Materials
PAPER: Coated & Laminated, NEC
PAPER: Corrugated
PAPER: Envelope
PAPER: Filter
PAPER: Insulation Siding
PAPER: Kraft
PAPER: Parchment
PAPER: Printer
PAPER: Specialty
PAPER: Tissue
PAPER: Wrapping
PAPER: Writing
PAPERBOARD
PAPERBOARD CONVERTING
PAPERBOARD PRDTS: Building Insulating & Packaging
PAPERBOARD PRDTS: Container Board
PAPERBOARD PRDTS: Folding Boxboard
PAPERBOARD PRDTS: Kraft Linerboard
PAPERBOARD PRDTS: Packaging Board
PAPERBOARD PRDTS: Pressboard
PAPERBOARD: Boxboard
PAPERBOARD: Liner Board
PAPIER-MACHE PRDTS, EXC STATUARY & ART GOODS
PARACHUTES
PARKING LOTS
PARTITIONS & FIXTURES: Except Wood
PARTITIONS WHOLESALERS
PARTITIONS: Nonwood, Floor Attached
PARTITIONS: Solid Fiber, Made From Purchased Materials
PARTITIONS: Wood & Fixtures
PARTITIONS: Wood, Floor Attached
PARTS: Metal
PARTY & SPECIAL EVENT PLANNING SVCS
PASTES, FLAVORING
PATENT OWNERS & LESSORS
PATTERNS: Indl
PAVERS
PAVING BREAKERS
PAVING MATERIALS: Prefabricated, Concrete
PAVING MIXTURES
PENCILS & PENS WHOLESALERS
PENS & PARTS: Ball Point
PENS & PARTS: Cartridges, Refill, Ball Point
PENS & PENCILS: Mechanical, NEC
PERFUME: Concentrated
PERFUME: Perfumes, Natural Or Synthetic
PERFUMES
PERLITE: Processed
PERSONAL APPEARANCE SVCS
PERSONAL CREDIT INSTITUTIONS: Consumer Finance Companies
PESTICIDES
PET ACCESS: Collars, Leashes, Etc, Exc Leather
PET COLLARS, LEASHES, MUZZLES & HARNESSES: Leather
PET SPLYS
PET SPLYS WHOLESALERS
PETROLEUM & PETROLEUM PRDTS, WHOLESALE Engine Fuels & Oils
PETROLEUM & PETROLEUM PRDTS, WHOLESALE: Bulk Stations
PETROLEUM PRDTS WHOLESALERS
PEWTER WARE
PHARMACEUTICAL PREPARATIONS: Adrenal
PHARMACEUTICAL PREPARATIONS: Barbituric Acid
PHARMACEUTICAL PREPARATIONS: Druggists' Preparations
PHARMACEUTICAL PREPARATIONS: Medicines, Capsule Or Ampule
PHARMACEUTICAL PREPARATIONS: Penicillin
PHARMACEUTICAL PREPARATIONS: Pills
PHARMACEUTICAL PREPARATIONS: Pituitary Gland
PHARMACEUTICAL PREPARATIONS: Proprietary Drug PRDTS
PHARMACEUTICAL PREPARATIONS: Solutions
PHARMACEUTICAL PREPARATIONS: Tablets
PHARMACEUTICAL PREPARATIONS: Water, Sterile, For Injections
PHARMACEUTICALS
PHARMACEUTICALS: Mail-Order Svc
PHARMACEUTICALS: Medicinal & Botanical Prdts
PHARMACIES & DRUG STORES
PHONOGRAPH NEEDLES
PHONOGRAPH RECORDS WHOLESALERS
PHONOGRAPH RECORDS: Prerecorded
PHOSPHATES
PHOTOCOPY MACHINES
PHOTOCOPYING & DUPLICATING SVCS
PHOTOELECTRIC DEVICES: Magnetic
PHOTOENGRAVING SVC
PHOTOFINISHING LABORATORIES
PHOTOGRAPH DEVELOPING & RETOUCHING SVCS
PHOTOGRAPHIC EQPT & SPLY: Sound Recordg/Reprod Eqpt, Motion
PHOTOGRAPHIC EQPT & SPLYS
PHOTOGRAPHIC EQPT & SPLYS WHOLESALERS
PHOTOGRAPHIC EQPT & SPLYS: Cameras, Aerial
PHOTOGRAPHIC EQPT & SPLYS: Cameras, Still & Motion Pictures
PHOTOGRAPHIC EQPT & SPLYS: Developers, Not Chemical Plants
PHOTOGRAPHIC EQPT & SPLYS: Editing Eqpt, Motion Picture
PHOTOGRAPHIC EQPT & SPLYS: Film, Sensitized
PHOTOGRAPHIC EQPT & SPLYS: Graphic Arts Plates, Sensitized
PHOTOGRAPHIC EQPT & SPLYS: Plates, Sensitized
PHOTOGRAPHIC EQPT & SPLYS: Printing Eqpt
PHOTOGRAPHIC EQPT & SPLYS: Processing Eqpt
PHOTOGRAPHIC EQPT & SPLYS: Shutters, Camera
PHOTOGRAPHIC EQPT & SPLYS: Toners, Prprd, Not Chem Pints
PHOTOGRAPHIC EQPT/SPLYS, WHOL: Cameras/Projectors/Eqpt/Splys
PHOTOGRAPHIC LIBRARY SVCS
PHOTOGRAPHIC PEOCESSING CHEMICALS
PHOTOGRAPHIC PROCESSING EQPT & CHEMICALS
PHOTOGRAPHIC SENSITIZED GOODS, NEC
PHOTOGRAPHIC SVCS
PHOTOGRAPHY SVCS: Commercial
PHOTOGRAPHY SVCS: Portrait Studios
PHOTOGRAPHY SVCS: Still Or Video
PHOTOTYPESETTING SVC
PHOTOVOLTAIC Solid State
PHYSICAL FITNESS CENTERS
PHYSICIANS' OFFICES & CLINICS: Medical doctors
PICTURE FRAMES: Metal
PICTURE FRAMES: Wood
PICTURE FRAMING SVCS, CUSTOM
PICTURE PROJECTION EQPT
PIECE GOODS & NOTIONS WHOLESALERS
PIECE GOODS, NOTIONS & DRY GOODS, WHOL: Textile Converters
PIECE GOODS, NOTIONS & DRY GOODS, WHOL: Textiles, Woven
PIECE GOODS, NOTIONS & DRY GOODS, WHOLESALE: Fabrics, Knit
PIECE GOODS, NOTIONS & DRY GOODS, WHOLESALE: Fabrics, Lace
PIECE GOODS, NOTIONS & DRY GOODS, WHOLESALE: Sewing Access
PIECE GOODS, NOTIONS & OTHER DRY GOODS, WHOLESALE: Bridal
PIECE GOODS, NOTIONS & OTHER DRY GOODS, WHOLESALE: Buttons
PIECE GOODS, NOTIONS & OTHER DRY GOODS, WHOLESALE: Fabrics
PIECE GOODS, NOTIONS & OTHER DRY GOODS, WHOLESALE: Woven
PIECE GOODS, NOTIONS/DRY GOODS, WHOL: Drapery Mtrl, Woven
PIECE GOODS, NOTIONS/DRY GOODS, WHOL: Linen Piece, Woven
PIECE GOODS, NOTIONS/DRY GOODS, WHOL: Sewing Splys/Notions
PILLOWS: Sponge Rubber
PINS
PIPE & FITTING: Fabrication
PIPE & FITTINGS: Cast Iron
PIPE & FITTINGS: Pressure, Cast Iron
PIPE CLEANERS
PIPE JOINT COMPOUNDS
PIPE: Concrete
PIPE: Extruded, Aluminum
PIPE: Plastic
PIPE: Seamless Steel
PIPE: Sheet Metal
PIPES & TUBES: Steel
PIPES & TUBES: Welded
PIPES: Steel & Iron
PIPES: Tobacco
PISTONS & PISTON RINGS
PLACEMATS: Plastic Or Textile
PLANING MILLS: Independent, Exc Millwork
PLANING MILLS: Millwork
PLANT CARE SVCS
PLAQUES: Clay, Plaster/Papier-Mache, Factory Production
PLAQUES: Picture, Laminated
PLASMAS
PLASTER WORK: Ornamental & Architectural
PLASTIC COLORING & FINISHING
PLASTIC PRDTS
PLASTIC PRDTS REPAIR SVCS
PLASTICIZERS, ORGANIC: Cyclic & Acyclic
PLASTICS FILM & SHEET
PLASTICS FILM & SHEET: Polyethylene
PLASTICS FILM & SHEET: Polyvinyl
PLASTICS FILM & SHEET: Vinyl
PLASTICS FINISHED PRDTS: Laminated
PLASTICS MATERIAL & RESINS
PLASTICS MATERIALS, BASIC FORMS & SHAPES WHOLESALERS
PLASTICS PROCESSING
PLASTICS SHEET: Packing Materials
PLASTICS: Blow Molded
PLASTICS: Cast
PLASTICS: Extruded
PLASTICS: Finished Injection Molded
PLASTICS: Injection Molded
PLASTICS: Molded
PLASTICS: Polystyrene Foam
PLASTICS: Thermoformed
PLATEMAKING SVC: Color Separations, For The Printing Trade
PLATEMAKING SVC: Embossing, For The Printing Trade
PLATEMAKING SVC: Gravure, Plates Or Cylinders
PLATES
PLATES: Paper, Made From Purchased Materials
PLATES: Plastic Exc Polystyrene Foam
PLATING & FINISHING SVC: Decorative, Formed Prdts
PLATING & POLISHING SVC
PLATING COMPOUNDS
PLATING SVC: Chromium, Metals Or Formed Prdts
PLATING SVC: Electro
PLATING SVC: Gold
PLATING SVC: NEC
PLAYGROUND EQPT
PLEATING & STITCHING FOR THE TRADE: Decorative & Novelty
PLEATING & STITCHING FOR TRADE: Permanent Pleating/Pressing
PLEATING & STITCHING SVC
PLEATING & TUCKING FOR THE TRADE
PLUGS: Electric
PLUMBING & HEATING EQPT & SPLY, WHOL: Htg Eqpt/Panels, Solar
PLUMBING & HEATING EQPT & SPLY, WHOLESALE: Hydronic Htg Eqpt
PLUMBING & HEATING EQPT & SPLYS WHOLESALERS
PLUMBING & HEATING EQPT & SPLYS, WHOL: Plumbing Fitting/Sply
PLUMBING & HEATING EQPT & SPLYS, WHOL: Plumbng/Heatng Valves
PLUMBING & HEATING EQPT & SPLYS, WHOL: Water Purif Eqpt
PLUMBING & HEATING EQPT & SPLYS, WHOLESALE: Brass/Fittings
PLUMBING & HEATING EQPT & SPLYS, WHOLESALE: Sanitary Ware
PLUMBING FIXTURES
PLUMBING FIXTURES: Brass, Incl Drain Cocks, Faucets/Spigots
PLUMBING FIXTURES: Plastic
POINT OF SALE DEVICES
POLISHING SVC: Metals Or Formed Prdts
POLYESTERS
POLYPROPYLENE RESINS
POLYTETRAFLUOROETHYLENE RESINS
POLYVINYL CHLORIDE RESINS
POPCORN & SUPPLIES WHOLESALERS

PRODUCT INDEX

PORCELAIN ENAMELED PRDTS & UTENSILS
POSTERS
POTTERY
POTTERY: Laboratory & Indl
POULTRY & POULTRY PRDTS WHOLESALERS
POULTRY & SMALL GAME SLAUGHTERING & PROCESSING
POULTRY SLAUGHTERING & PROCESSING
POWDER PUFFS & MITTS
POWDER: Metal
POWDER: Silver
POWER GENERATORS
POWER SPLY CONVERTERS: Static, Electronic Applications
POWER SUPPLIES: All Types, Static
POWER SUPPLIES: Transformer, Electronic Type
POWER SWITCHING EQPT
POWER TOOLS, HAND: Grinders, Portable, Electric Or Pneumatic
POWER TOOLS, HAND: Hammers, Portable, Elec/Pneumatic, Chip
POWER TRANSMISSION EQPT WHOLESALERS
POWER TRANSMISSION EQPT: Aircraft
POWER TRANSMISSION EQPT: Mechanical
PRECAST TERRAZZO OR CONCRETE PRDTS
PRECIOUS METALS
PRECIOUS METALS WHOLESALERS
PRECIOUS STONES & METALS, WHOLESALE
PRECIOUS STONES WHOLESALERS
PRERECORDED TAPE, CD & RECORD STORES: Video Discs/Tapes
PRERECORDED TAPE, CD/RECORD STORES: Video Tapes, Prerecorded
PRERECORDED TAPE, COMPACT DISC & RECORD STORES
PRESSED FIBER & MOLDED PULP PRDTS, EXC FOOD PRDTS
PRESSES
PRIMARY METAL PRODUCTS
PRINT CARTRIDGES: Laser & Other Computer Printers
PRINTED CIRCUIT BOARDS
PRINTERS & PLOTTERS
PRINTERS' SVCS: Folding, Collating, Etc
PRINTERS: Computer
PRINTERS: Magnetic Ink, Bar Code
PRINTING & BINDING: Book Music
PRINTING & BINDING: Books
PRINTING & BINDING: Pamphlets
PRINTING & EMBOSSING: Plastic Fabric Articles
PRINTING & ENGRAVING: Card, Exc Greeting
PRINTING & ENGRAVING: Financial Notes & Certificates
PRINTING & ENGRAVING: Invitation & Stationery
PRINTING & ENGRAVING: Plateless
PRINTING & ENGRAVING: Poster & Decal
PRINTING & STAMPING: Fabric Articles
PRINTING & WRITING PAPER WHOLESALERS
PRINTING EQPT & SUPPLIES: Illustration & Poster Woodcuts
PRINTING INKS WHOLESALERS
PRINTING MACHINERY
PRINTING MACHINERY, EQPT & SPLYS: Wholesalers
PRINTING TRADES MACHINERY & EQPT REPAIR SVCS
PRINTING, COMMERCIAL Newspapers, NEC
PRINTING, COMMERCIAL: Announcements, NEC
PRINTING, COMMERCIAL: Bags, Plastic, NEC
PRINTING, COMMERCIAL: Business Forms, NEC
PRINTING, COMMERCIAL: Calendars, NEC
PRINTING, COMMERCIAL: Cards, Visiting, Incl Business, NEC
PRINTING, COMMERCIAL: Certificates, Security, NEC
PRINTING, COMMERCIAL: Circulars, NEC
PRINTING, COMMERCIAL: Decals, NEC
PRINTING, COMMERCIAL: Envelopes, NEC
PRINTING, COMMERCIAL: Imprinting
PRINTING, COMMERCIAL: Invitations, NEC
PRINTING, COMMERCIAL: Labels & Seals, NEC
PRINTING, COMMERCIAL: Letterpress & Screen
PRINTING, COMMERCIAL: Literature, Advertising, NEC
PRINTING, COMMERCIAL: Magazines, NEC
PRINTING, COMMERCIAL: Periodicals, NEC
PRINTING, COMMERCIAL: Post Cards, Picture, NEC
PRINTING, COMMERCIAL: Promotional
PRINTING, COMMERCIAL: Publications
PRINTING, COMMERCIAL: Screen
PRINTING, COMMERCIAL: Stamps, Trading, NEC
PRINTING, COMMERCIAL: Stationery, NEC
PRINTING, COMMERCIAL: Tags, NEC
PRINTING, LITHOGRAPHIC: Advertising Posters
PRINTING, LITHOGRAPHIC: Calendars
PRINTING, LITHOGRAPHIC: Color
PRINTING, LITHOGRAPHIC: Decals
PRINTING, LITHOGRAPHIC: Fashion Plates
PRINTING, LITHOGRAPHIC: Forms & Cards, Business
PRINTING, LITHOGRAPHIC: Forms, Business
PRINTING, LITHOGRAPHIC: Letters, Circular Or Form
PRINTING, LITHOGRAPHIC: Menus
PRINTING, LITHOGRAPHIC: Offset & photolithographic printing
PRINTING, LITHOGRAPHIC: On Metal
PRINTING, LITHOGRAPHIC: Periodicals
PRINTING, LITHOGRAPHIC: Post Cards, Picture
PRINTING, LITHOGRAPHIC: Promotional
PRINTING, LITHOGRAPHIC: Publications
PRINTING, LITHOGRAPHIC: Tags
PRINTING, LITHOGRAPHIC: Tickets
PRINTING, LITHOGRAPHIC: Transfers, Decalcomania Or Dry
PRINTING: Books
PRINTING: Books
PRINTING: Broadwoven Fabrics. Cotton
PRINTING: Checkbooks
PRINTING: Commercial, NEC
PRINTING: Engraving & Plate
PRINTING: Flexographic
PRINTING: Gravure, Business Form & Card
PRINTING: Gravure, Color
PRINTING: Gravure, Forms, Business
PRINTING: Gravure, Imprinting
PRINTING: Gravure, Job
PRINTING: Gravure, Labels
PRINTING: Gravure, Promotional
PRINTING: Gravure, Rotogravure
PRINTING: Gravure, Stamps, Trading
PRINTING: Gravure, Stationery
PRINTING: Gravure, Wrappers
PRINTING: Laser
PRINTING: Letterpress
PRINTING: Lithographic
PRINTING: Offset
PRINTING: Pamphlets
PRINTING: Photo-Offset
PRINTING: Photogravure
PRINTING: Photolithographic
PRINTING: Rotary Photogravure
PRINTING: Rotogravure
PRINTING: Screen, Broadwoven Fabrics, Cotton
PRINTING: Screen, Fabric
PRINTING: Screen, Manmade Fiber & Silk, Broadwoven Fabric
PRINTING: Thermography
PROFESSIONAL EQPT & SPLYS, WHOLESALE: Analytical Instruments
PROFESSIONAL EQPT & SPLYS, WHOLESALE: Engineers', NEC
PROFESSIONAL EQPT & SPLYS, WHOLESALE: Optical Goods
PROFESSIONAL EQPT & SPLYS, WHOLESALE: Scientific & Engineerg
PROFESSIONAL EQPT & SPLYS, WHOLESALE: Theatrical
PROFILE SHAPES: Unsupported Plastics
PROGRAM ADMIN, GOVT: Air, Water & Solid Waste Mgmt, Local
PROMOTION SVCS
PROTECTION EQPT: Lightning
PUBLIC RELATIONS & PUBLICITY SVCS
PUBLISHERS: Art Copy
PUBLISHERS: Art Copy & Poster
PUBLISHERS: Atlases
PUBLISHERS: Book
PUBLISHERS: Book Clubs, No Printing
PUBLISHERS: Books, No Printing
PUBLISHERS: Catalogs
PUBLISHERS: Comic Books, No Printing
PUBLISHERS: Directories, NEC
PUBLISHERS: Directories, Telephone
PUBLISHERS: Guides
PUBLISHERS: Magazines, No Printing
PUBLISHERS: Maps
PUBLISHERS: Miscellaneous
PUBLISHERS: Music Book
PUBLISHERS: Music Book & Sheet Music
PUBLISHERS: Music, Book
PUBLISHERS: Music, Sheet
PUBLISHERS: Newsletter
PUBLISHERS: Newspaper
PUBLISHERS: Newspapers, No Printing
PUBLISHERS: Pamphlets, No Printing
PUBLISHERS: Patterns, Paper
PUBLISHERS: Periodical, With Printing
PUBLISHERS: Periodicals, Magazines
PUBLISHERS: Periodicals, No Printing
PUBLISHERS: Posters
PUBLISHERS: Racing Forms & Programs
PUBLISHERS: Sheet Music
PUBLISHERS: Shopping News
PUBLISHERS: Technical Manuals
PUBLISHERS: Technical Manuals & Papers
PUBLISHERS: Technical Papers
PUBLISHERS: Telephone & Other Directory
PUBLISHERS: Textbooks, No Printing
PUBLISHERS: Trade journals, No Printing
PUBLISHING & BROADCASTING: Internet Only
PUBLISHING & PRINTING: Art Copy
PUBLISHING & PRINTING: Book Clubs
PUBLISHING & PRINTING: Book Music
PUBLISHING & PRINTING: Books
PUBLISHING & PRINTING: Catalogs
PUBLISHING & PRINTING: Comic Books
PUBLISHING & PRINTING: Directories, NEC
PUBLISHING & PRINTING: Guides
PUBLISHING & PRINTING: Magazines: publishing & printing
PUBLISHING & PRINTING: Music, Book
PUBLISHING & PRINTING: Newsletters, Business Svc
PUBLISHING & PRINTING: Newspapers
PUBLISHING & PRINTING: Pamphlets
PUBLISHING & PRINTING: Patterns, Paper
PUBLISHING & PRINTING: Shopping News
PUBLISHING & PRINTING: Technical Manuals
PUBLISHING & PRINTING: Textbooks
PUBLISHING & PRINTING: Trade Journals
PUBLISHING & PRINTING: Yearbooks
PULP MILLS
PULP MILLS: Mech Pulp, Incl Groundwood & Thermomechanical
PULP MILLS: Mechanical & Recycling Processing
PULP MILLS: Soda Pulp
PUMICE
PUMP GOVERNORS: Gas Machines
PUMPS
PUMPS & PARTS: Indl
PUMPS & PUMPING EQPT REPAIR SVCS
PUMPS & PUMPING EQPT WHOLESALERS
PUMPS, HEAT: Electric
PUMPS: Domestic, Water Or Sump
PUMPS: Measuring & Dispensing
PUMPS: Vacuum, Exc Laboratory
PUNCHES: Forming & Stamping
PURIFICATION & DUST COLLECTION EQPT
PURSES: Women's
PUSHCARTS & WHEELBARROWS

Q

QUICKLIME

R

RACE TRACK OPERATION
RACEWAYS
RACKS & SHELVING: Household, Wood
RACKS: Display
RACKS: Garment, Exc Wood
RACKS: Garment, Wood
RACKS: Pallet, Exc Wood
RADAR SYSTEMS & EQPT
RADIATORS, EXC ELECTRIC
RADIO & TELEVISION COMMUNICATIONS EQUIPMENT
RADIO & TELEVISION REPAIR
RADIO BROADCASTING & COMMUNICATIONS EQPT
RADIO BROADCASTING STATIONS
RADIO COMMUNICATIONS: Airborne Eqpt
RADIO RECEIVER NETWORKS
RADIO, TELEVISION & CONSUMER ELECTRONICS STORES: Eqpt, NEC
RADIO, TV & CONSUMER ELECTRONICS: VCR & Access
RADIO, TV/CONSUMER ELEC STORES: Antennas, Satellite Dish
RAILINGS: Prefabricated, Metal
RAILINGS: Wood

PRODUCT INDEX

RAILROAD CAR RENTING & LEASING SVCS
RAILROAD CAR REPAIR SVCS
RAILROAD CARGO LOADING & UNLOADING SVCS
RAILROAD EQPT
RAILROAD EQPT & SPLYS WHOLESALERS
RAILROAD EQPT, EXC LOCOMOTIVES
RAILROAD EQPT: Brakes, Air & Vacuum
RAILROAD EQPT: Cars & Eqpt, Dining
RAILROAD EQPT: Cars & Eqpt, Rapid Transit
RAILROAD EQPT: Cars & Eqpt, Train, Freight Or Passenger
RAILROAD EQPT: Cars, Maintenance
RAILROAD EQPT: Locomotives & Parts, Indl
RAILROAD EQPT: Lubrication Systems, Locomotive
RAILROAD RELATED EQPT: Railway Track
RAILS: Steel Or Iron
RAMPS: Prefabricated Metal
RAZORS: Electric
REAL ESTATE AGENCIES & BROKERS
REAL ESTATE AGENTS & MANAGERS
REAL ESTATE OPERATORS, EXC DEVELOPERS: Apartment Hotel
REAL ESTATE OPERATORS, EXC DEVELOPERS: Commercial/Indl Bldg
RECLAIMED RUBBER: Reworked By Manufacturing Process
RECORD BLANKS: Phonographic
RECORDERS: Sound
RECORDING HEADS: Speech & Musical Eqpt
RECORDING TAPE: Video, Blank
RECORDS & TAPES: Prerecorded
RECORDS OR TAPES: Masters
RECOVERY SVCS: Metal
RECREATIONAL & SPORTING CAMPS
RECTIFIERS: Electrical Apparatus
RECTIFIERS: Solid State
RECYCLABLE SCRAP & WASTE MATERIALS WHOLESALERS
RECYCLING: Paper
REELS: Cable, Metal
REFINERS & SMELTERS: Aluminum
REFINERS & SMELTERS: Antimony, Primary
REFINERS & SMELTERS: Cobalt, Primary
REFINERS & SMELTERS: Copper
REFINERS & SMELTERS: Copper, Secondary
REFINERS & SMELTERS: Gold
REFINERS & SMELTERS: Lead, Secondary
REFINERS & SMELTERS: Nonferrous Metal
REFINERS & SMELTERS: Platinum Group Metal Refining, Primary
REFINERS & SMELTERS: Silicon, Primary, Over 99% Pure
REFINERS & SMELTERS: Silver
REFINERS & SMELTERS: Zinc, Primary, Including Slabs & Dust
REFINING LUBRICATING OILS & GREASES, NEC
REFINING: Petroleum
REFRACTORIES: Alumina Fused
REFRACTORIES: Brick
REFRACTORIES: Brick
REFRACTORIES: Clay
REFRACTORIES: Graphite, Carbon Or Ceramic Bond
REFRACTORIES: Nonclay
REFRACTORIES: Plastic
REFRACTORY CASTABLES
REFRACTORY MATERIALS WHOLESALERS
REFRIGERATION & HEATING EQUIPMENT
REFRIGERATION EQPT & SPLYS WHOLESALERS
REFRIGERATION EQPT: Complete
REFRIGERATION REPAIR SVCS
REFRIGERATION SVC & REPAIR
REFRIGERATORS & FREEZERS WHOLESALERS
REFUSE SYSTEMS
REGULATORS: Generator Voltage
REGULATORS: Power
REGULATORS: Transmission & Distribution Voltage
REGULATORS: Transmission & Distribution Voltage
RELAYS & SWITCHES: Indl, Electric
RELAYS: Electronic Usage
RELIGIOUS SPLYS WHOLESALERS
REMOVERS & CLEANERS
REMOVERS: Paint
RENTAL CENTERS: General
RENTAL SVCS: Business Machine & Electronic Eqpt
RENTAL SVCS: Costume
RENTAL SVCS: Electronic Eqpt, Exc Computers
RENTAL SVCS: Eqpt, Theatrical
RENTAL SVCS: Invalid Splys
RENTAL SVCS: Live Plant
RENTAL SVCS: Pallet
RENTAL SVCS: Tent & Tarpaulin
RENTAL: Video Tape & Disc
REPEATERS: Passive
REPRODUCTION SVCS: Video Tape Or Disk
RESEARCH, DEV & TESTING SVCS, COMM: Chem Lab, Exc Testing
RESEARCH, DEVELOPMENT & TEST SVCS, COMM: Business Analysis
RESEARCH, DEVELOPMENT & TEST SVCS, COMM: Cmptr Hardware Dev
RESEARCH, DEVELOPMENT & TEST SVCS, COMM: Research, Exc Lab
RESEARCH, DEVELOPMENT & TESTING SVCS, COMM: Research Lab
RESEARCH, DEVELOPMENT & TESTING SVCS, COMMERCIAL: Medical
RESEARCH, DEVELOPMENT & TESTING SVCS, COMMERCIAL: Opinion
RESEARCH, DVLPMT & TESTING SVCS, COMM: Merger, Acq & Reorg
RESEARCH, DVLPT & TEST SVCS, COMM: Mkt Analysis or Research
RESIDENTIAL REMODELERS
RESINS: Custom Compound Purchased
RESISTORS
RESISTORS & RESISTOR UNITS
RESORT HOTELS
RESPIRATORS
RESTAURANT EQPT REPAIR SVCS
RESTAURANT EQPT: Carts
RESTAURANT EQPT: Food Wagons
RESTAURANT EQPT: Sheet Metal
RESTAURANTS:Full Svc, American
RESTAURANTS:Full Svc, Seafood
RESTAURANTS:Limited Svc, Coffee Shop
RESTAURANTS:Limited Svc, Ice Cream Stands Or Dairy Bars
RESTAURANTS:Limited Svc, Lunch Counter
RESUME WRITING SVCS
RETAIL BAKERY: Bagels
RETAIL BAKERY: Bread
RETAIL LUMBER YARDS
RETAIL STORES, NEC
RETAIL STORES: Alarm Signal Systems
RETAIL STORES: Alcoholic Beverage Making Eqpt & Splys
RETAIL STORES: Aquarium Splys
RETAIL STORES: Artificial Limbs
RETAIL STORES: Audio-Visual Eqpt & Splys
RETAIL STORES: Awnings
RETAIL STORES: Cake Decorating Splys
RETAIL STORES: Canvas Prdts
RETAIL STORES: Cleaning Eqpt & Splys
RETAIL STORES: Concrete Prdts, Precast
RETAIL STORES: Cosmetics
RETAIL STORES: Electronic Parts & Eqpt
RETAIL STORES: Engine & Motor Eqpt & Splys
RETAIL STORES: Farm Eqpt & Splys
RETAIL STORES: Fiberglass Materials, Exc Insulation
RETAIL STORES: Fire Extinguishers
RETAIL STORES: Gravestones, Finished
RETAIL STORES: Hearing Aids
RETAIL STORES: Ice
RETAIL STORES: Infant Furnishings & Eqpt
RETAIL STORES: Medical Apparatus & Splys
RETAIL STORES: Mobile Telephones & Eqpt
RETAIL STORES: Monuments, Finished To Custom Order
RETAIL STORES: Motors, Electric
RETAIL STORES: Orthopedic & Prosthesis Applications
RETAIL STORES: Pet Food
RETAIL STORES: Photocopy Machines
RETAIL STORES: Religious Goods
RETAIL STORES: Stones, Crystalline, Rough
RETAIL STORES: Telephone Eqpt & Systems
RETAIL STORES: Tents
RETAIL STORES: Water Purification Eqpt
RETAIL STORES: Welding Splys
REUPHOLSTERY & FURNITURE REPAIR
REUPHOLSTERY SVCS
RIBBONS & BOWS
RIBBONS, NEC
RIBBONS: Machine, Inked Or Carbon
RIDING APPAREL STORES
RIVETS: Metal
ROAD MATERIALS: Bituminous, Not From Refineries
ROBOTS: Assembly Line
ROCK SALT MINING
ROCKET LAUNCHERS
ROCKETS: Space & Military
RODS: Extruded, Aluminum
RODS: Plastic
RODS: Steel & Iron, Made In Steel Mills
RODS: Welding
ROLL COVERINGS: Rubber
ROLL FORMED SHAPES: Custom
ROLLED OR DRAWN SHAPES, NEC: Copper & Copper Alloy
ROLLERS & FITTINGS: Window Shade
ROLLING MILL EQPT: Galvanizing Lines
ROLLING MILL MACHINERY
ROLLS & BLANKETS, PRINTERS': Rubber Or Rubberized Fabric
ROLLS: Rubber, Solid Or Covered
ROOFING MATERIALS: Asphalt
ROOFING MATERIALS: Sheet Metal
ROOFING MEMBRANE: Rubber
ROPE
ROTORS: Motor
RUBBER
RUBBER PRDTS: Automotive, Mechanical
RUBBER PRDTS: Mechanical
RUBBER PRDTS: Medical & Surgical Tubing, Extrudd & Lathe-Cut
RUBBER PRDTS: Oil & Gas Field Machinery, Mechanical
RUBBER PRDTS: Reclaimed
RUBBER PRDTS: Silicone
RUBBER PRDTS: Sponge
RUBBER PRDTS: Wet Suits
RUBBER STRUCTURES: Air-Supported
RUGS : Hand & Machine Made
RULERS: Metal

S

SAFES & VAULTS: Metal
SAFETY EQPT & SPLYS WHOLESALERS
SAILBOAT BUILDING & REPAIR
SAILS
SALES PROMOTION SVCS
SALT
SALT & SULFUR MINING
SAMPLE BOOKS
SAND & GRAVEL
SAND MINING
SAND: Hygrade
SANDSTONE: Crushed & Broken
SANITARY SVCS: Waste Materials, Recycling
SANITARY WARE: Metal
SANITATION CHEMICALS & CLEANING AGENTS
SASHES: Door Or Window, Metal
SATCHELS
SATELLITES: Communications
SAW BLADES
SAWDUST & SHAVINGS
SAWDUST, WHOLESALE
SAWING & PLANING MILLS
SAWING & PLANING MILLS: Custom
SAWMILL MACHINES
SAWS & SAWING EQPT
SCAFFOLDS: Mobile Or Stationary, Metal
SCALES & BALANCES, EXC LABORATORY
SCALES: Baby
SCALP TREATMENT SVCS
SCANNING DEVICES: Optical
SCISSORS: Hand
SCRAP & WASTE MATERIALS, WHOLESALE: Ferrous Metal
SCRAP & WASTE MATERIALS, WHOLESALE: Metal
SCRAP & WASTE MATERIALS, WHOLESALE: Plastics Scrap
SCRAP & WASTE MATERIALS, WHOLESALE: Rags
SCREENS: Projection
SCREENS: Window, Metal
SCREENS: Woven Wire
SCREW MACHINE PRDTS
SCREW MACHINES
SCREWS: Metal
SEALANTS
SEARCH & DETECTION SYSTEMS, EXC RADAR
SEARCH & NAVIGATION SYSTEMS
SEAT BELTS: Automobile & Aircraft
SEATING: Bleacher, Portable

PRODUCT INDEX

SEATING: Chairs, Table & Arm
SECRETARIAL SVCS
SECURITY CONTROL EQPT & SYSTEMS
SECURITY DEVICES
SECURITY PROTECTIVE DEVICES MAINTENANCE & MONITORING SVC
SECURITY SYSTEMS SERVICES
SEMICONDUCTOR & RELATED DEVICES: Read-Only Memory Or ROM
SEMICONDUCTOR CIRCUIT NETWORKS
SEMICONDUCTOR DEVICES: Wafers
SEMICONDUCTORS & RELATED DEVICES
SENSORS: Temperature For Motor Windings
SENSORS: Temperature, Exc Indl Process
SEPARATORS: Metal Plate
SEPTIC TANKS: Concrete
SEPTIC TANKS: Plastic
SERVICES, NEC
SERVOMOTORS: Electric
SEWAGE & WATER TREATMENT EQPT
SEWAGE TREATMENT SYSTEMS & EQPT
SEWER CLEANING EQPT: Power
SEWING CONTRACTORS
SEWING MACHINES & PARTS: Indl
SEWING, NEEDLEWORK & PIECE GOODS STORE: Needlework Gds/Sply
SEWING, NEEDLEWORK & PIECE GOODS STORES: Sewing & Needlework
SHADES: Lamp & Light, Residential
SHADES: Lamp Or Candle
SHADES: Window
SHALE MINING, COMMON
SHALE: Expanded
SHAPES & PILINGS, STRUCTURAL: Steel
SHEATHING: Paper
SHEET METAL SPECIALTIES, EXC STAMPED
SHEET MUSIC STORES
SHEET MUSIC, WHOLESALE
SHEETING: Laminated Plastic
SHEETS & STRIPS: Aluminum
SHEETS: Fabric, From Purchased Materials
SHELVES & SHELVING: Wood
SHELVING: Office & Store, Exc Wood
SHERARDIZING SVC: Metals Or Metal Prdts
SHIELDS OR ENCLOSURES: Radiator, Sheet Metal
SHIMS: Metal
SHIP BLDG & RPRG: Drilling & Production Platforms, Oil/Gas
SHIP BUILDING & REPAIRING: Cargo Vessels
SHIP BUILDING & REPAIRING: Cargo, Commercial
SHIP BUILDING & REPAIRING: Ferryboats
SHIP BUILDING & REPAIRING: Lighthouse Tenders
SHIP BUILDING & REPAIRING: Offshore Sply Boats
SHIP BUILDING & REPAIRING: Radar Towers, Floating
SHIP BUILDING & REPAIRING: Rigging, Marine
SHIP BUILDING & REPAIRING: Tankers
SHIPBUILDING & REPAIR
SHIPPING AGENTS
SHOCK ABSORBERS: Indl
SHOE & BOOT ACCESS
SHOE & BOOT MATERIALS: Laces, Leather
SHOE MATERIALS: Body Parts, Outers
SHOE MATERIALS: Counters
SHOE MATERIALS: Quarters
SHOE MATERIALS: Rands
SHOE MATERIALS: Rubber
SHOE MATERIALS: Sole Parts
SHOE MATERIALS: Uppers
SHOE REPAIR SHOP
SHOE STORES
SHOE STORES: Children's
SHOE STORES: Custom
SHOE STORES: Orthopedic
SHOE STORES: Women's
SHOES & BOOTS WHOLESALERS
SHOES: Athletic, Exc Rubber Or Plastic
SHOES: Ballet Slippers
SHOES: Canvas, Rubber Soled
SHOES: Infants' & Children's
SHOES: Men's
SHOES: Men's, Dress
SHOES: Men's, Sandals
SHOES: Orthopedic, Men's
SHOES: Orthopedic, Women's
SHOES: Plastic Or Rubber
SHOES: Plastic Soles Molded To Fabric Uppers
SHOES: Rubber Or Rubber Soled Fabric Uppers
SHOES: Women's
SHOES: Women's, Dress
SHOES: Women's, Sandals
SHOPPING CENTERS & MALLS
SHOT PEENING SVC
SHOWCASES & DISPLAY FIXTURES: Office & Store
SHOWER STALLS: Metal
SHOWER STALLS: Plastic & Fiberglass
SHREDDERS: Indl & Commercial
SIDING & STRUCTURAL MATERIALS: Wood
SIDING MATERIALS
SIGN LETTERING & PAINTING SVCS
SIGN PAINTING & LETTERING SHOP
SIGNALING APPARATUS: Electric
SIGNALING DEVICES: Sound, Electrical
SIGNALS: Railroad, Electric
SIGNALS: Traffic Control, Electric
SIGNALS: Transportation
SIGNS & ADVERTISING SPECIALTIES
SIGNS & ADVERTISING SPECIALTIES: Artwork, Advertising
SIGNS & ADVERTISING SPECIALTIES: Displays, Paint Process
SIGNS & ADVERTISING SPECIALTIES: Novelties
SIGNS & ADVERTISING SPECIALTIES: Scoreboards, Electric
SIGNS & ADVERTISING SPECIALTIES: Signs
SIGNS & ADVERTSG SPECIALTIES: Displays/Cutouts Window/Lobby
SIGNS, EXC ELECTRIC, WHOLESALE
SIGNS: Electrical
SIGNS: Neon
SILICA MINING
SILICON & CHROMIUM
SILICON WAFERS: Chemically Doped
SILICONE RESINS
SILICONES
SILK SCREEN DESIGN SVCS
SILVER ORES
SILVER ORES PROCESSING
SILVERSMITHS
SILVERWARE
SILVERWARE & PLATED WARE
SILVERWARE, SILVER PLATED
SIMULATORS: Flight
SKIN CARE PRDTS: Suntan Lotions & Oils
SKYLIGHTS
SLAB & TILE: Precast Concrete, Floor
SLABS: Steel
SLATE PRDTS
SLATE: Dimension
SLINGS: Rope
SLIPPERS: House
SMOKE DETECTORS
SOAPS & DETERGENTS
SOAPS & DETERGENTS: Textile
SOCIAL SERVICES INFORMATION EXCHANGE
SOCIAL SVCS, HANDICAPPED
SOCIAL SVCS: Individual & Family
SOFT DRINKS WHOLESALERS
SOFTWARE PUBLISHERS: Application
SOFTWARE PUBLISHERS: Business & Professional
SOFTWARE PUBLISHERS: Computer Utilities
SOFTWARE PUBLISHERS: Education
SOFTWARE PUBLISHERS: Home Entertainment
SOFTWARE PUBLISHERS: NEC
SOFTWARE PUBLISHERS: Operating Systems
SOFTWARE PUBLISHERS: Publisher's
SOFTWARE PUBLISHERS: Word Processing
SOFTWARE TRAINING, COMPUTER
SOLAR CELLS
SOLAR HEATING EQPT
SOLDERS
SOLID CONTAINING UNITS: Concrete
SOLVENTS
SONAR SYSTEMS & EQPT
SOUND EQPT: Electric
SOUND EQPT: Underwater
SOUND REPRODUCING EQPT
SOYBEAN PRDTS
SPACE VEHICLE EQPT
SPARK PLUGS: Internal Combustion Engines
SPAS
SPEAKER SYSTEMS
SPECIAL EVENTS DECORATION SVCS
SPECIALTY FOOD STORES: Coffee
SPECIALTY FOOD STORES: Health & Dietetic Food
SPECIALTY FOOD STORES: Juices, Fruit Or Vegetable
SPERM BANK
SPONGES: Plastic
SPOOLS: Fiber, Made From Purchased Materials
SPOOLS: Indl
SPORTING & ATHLETIC GOODS: Bags, Golf
SPORTING & ATHLETIC GOODS: Balls, Baseball, Football, Etc
SPORTING & ATHLETIC GOODS: Bowling Alleys & Access
SPORTING & ATHLETIC GOODS: Bowling Pins
SPORTING & ATHLETIC GOODS: Bows, Archery
SPORTING & ATHLETIC GOODS: Boxing Eqpt & Splys, NEC
SPORTING & ATHLETIC GOODS: Camping Eqpt & Splys
SPORTING & ATHLETIC GOODS: Cartridge Belts
SPORTING & ATHLETIC GOODS: Driving Ranges, Golf, Electronic
SPORTING & ATHLETIC GOODS: Dumbbells & Other Weight Eqpt
SPORTING & ATHLETIC GOODS: Fishing Bait, Artificial
SPORTING & ATHLETIC GOODS: Fishing Eqpt
SPORTING & ATHLETIC GOODS: Fishing Tackle, General
SPORTING & ATHLETIC GOODS: Game Calls
SPORTING & ATHLETIC GOODS: Gymnasium Eqpt
SPORTING & ATHLETIC GOODS: Hockey Eqpt & Splys, NEC
SPORTING & ATHLETIC GOODS: Lacrosse Eqpt & Splys, NEC
SPORTING & ATHLETIC GOODS: Pools, Swimming, Exc Plastic
SPORTING & ATHLETIC GOODS: Pools, Swimming, Plastic
SPORTING & ATHLETIC GOODS: Protective Sporting Eqpt
SPORTING & ATHLETIC GOODS: Shafts, Golf Club
SPORTING & ATHLETIC GOODS: Shooting Eqpt & Splys, General
SPORTING & ATHLETIC GOODS: Skateboards
SPORTING & ATHLETIC GOODS: Skates & Parts, Roller
SPORTING & ATHLETIC GOODS: Target Shooting Eqpt
SPORTING & ATHLETIC GOODS: Team Sports Eqpt
SPORTING & ATHLETIC GOODS: Tennis Eqpt & Splys
SPORTING & REC GOODS, WHOLESALE: Camping Eqpt & Splys
SPORTING & RECREATIONAL GOODS & SPLYS WHOLESALERS
SPORTING & RECREATIONAL GOODS, WHOL: Sharpeners, Sporting
SPORTING & RECREATIONAL GOODS, WHOLESALE: Boat Access & Part
SPORTING & RECREATIONAL GOODS, WHOLESALE: Fishing
SPORTING & RECREATIONAL GOODS, WHOLESALE: Fishing Tackle
SPORTING & RECREATIONAL GOODS, WHOLESALE: Fitness
SPORTING & RECREATIONAL GOODS, WHOLESALE: Hot Tubs
SPORTING & RECREATIONAL GOODS, WHOLESALE: Skiing
SPORTING & RECREATIONAL GOODS, WHOLESALE: Watersports
SPORTING GOODS
SPORTING GOODS STORES, NEC
SPORTING GOODS STORES: Camping Eqpt
SPORTING GOODS STORES: Fishing Eqpt
SPORTING GOODS STORES: Playground Eqpt
SPORTING GOODS STORES: Skateboarding Eqpt
SPORTING GOODS STORES: Specialty Sport Splys, NEC
SPORTING GOODS STORES: Tennis Goods & Eqpt
SPORTING GOODS: Archery
SPORTING GOODS: Fishing Nets
SPORTING GOODS: Sailboards
SPORTING GOODS: Surfboards
SPORTING/ATHLETIC GOODS: Gloves, Boxing, Handball, Etc
SPORTS APPAREL STORES
SPORTS PROMOTION SVCS
SPOUTING: Plastic & Fiberglass Reinforced
SPRAYING & DUSTING EQPT
SPRAYING EQPT: Agricultural
SPRAYS: Artificial & Preserved
SPRINGS: Coiled Flat
SPRINGS: Leaf, Automobile, Locomotive, Etc
SPRINGS: Mechanical, Precision
SPRINGS: Precision
SPRINGS: Sash Balances

PRODUCT INDEX

SPRINGS: Steel
SPRINGS: Wire
SPRINKLING SYSTEMS: Fire Control
STAGE LIGHTING SYSTEMS
STAINLESS STEEL
STAIRCASES & STAIRS, WOOD
STAMPED ART GOODS FOR EMBROIDERING
STAMPING SVC: Book, Gold
STAMPINGS: Automotive
STAMPINGS: Metal
STANDS & RACKS: Engine, Metal
STARTERS: Motor
STATIC ELIMINATORS: Ind
STATIONARY & OFFICE SPLYS, WHOLESALE: Laser Printer Splys
STATIONARY & OFFICE SPLYS, WHOLESALE: Stationery
STATIONER'S SUNDRIES: Rubber
STATIONERY & OFFICE SPLYS WHOLESALERS
STATIONERY PRDTS
STATIONERY: Made From Purchased Materials
STATUARY & OTHER DECORATIVE PRDTS: Nonmetallic
STATUES: Nonmetal
STEAM SPLY SYSTEMS SVCS INCLUDING GEOTHERMAL
STEEL & ALLOYS: Tool & Die
STEEL FABRICATORS
STEEL MILLS
STEEL, COLD-ROLLED: Sheet Or Strip, From Own Hot-Rolled
STEEL, COLD-ROLLED: Strip NEC, From Purchased Hot-Rolled
STEEL, HOT-ROLLED: Sheet Or Strip
STEEL: Cold-Rolled
STEEL: Galvanized
STEEL: Laminated
STENCILS
STONE: Cast Concrete
STONE: Dimension, NEC
STONE: Quarrying & Processing, Own Stone Prdts
STONEWARE CLAY MINING
STORE FIXTURES, EXC REFRIGERATED: Wholesalers
STORE FIXTURES: Exc Wood
STORE FIXTURES: Wood
STORE FRONTS: Prefabricated, Metal
STORE FRONTS: Prefabricated, Wood
STRAPPING
STRAPS: Apparel Webbing
STRAPS: Bindings, Textile
STRAPS: Braids, Textile
STRAPS: Cotton Webbing
STRAWS: Drinking, Made From Purchased Materials
STRUCTURAL SUPPORT & BUILDING MATERIAL: Concrete
STUDIOS: Artist's
STUDIOS: Sculptor's
STUDS & JOISTS: Sheet Metal
SUBMARINE BUILDING & REPAIR
SUBSCRIPTION FULFILLMENT SVCS: Magazine, Newspaper, Etc
SUGAR SUBSTITUTES: Organic
SUNDRIES & RELATED PRDTS: Medical & Laboratory, Rubber
SUNROOMS: Prefabricated Metal
SUPERMARKETS & OTHER GROCERY STORES
SURFACE ACTIVE AGENTS
SURFACE ACTIVE AGENTS: Oils & Greases
SURGICAL & MEDICAL INSTRUMENTS WHOLESALERS
SURGICAL APPLIANCES & SPLYS
SURGICAL APPLIANCES & SPLYS
SURGICAL EQPT: See Also Instruments
SURGICAL IMPLANTS
SURVEYING SVCS: Aerial Digital Imaging
SVC ESTABLISHMENT EQPT & SPLYS WHOLESALERS
SVC ESTABLISHMENT EQPT, WHOL: Cleaning & Maint Eqpt & Splys
SVC ESTABLISHMENT EQPT, WHOLESALE: Beauty Parlor Eqpt & Sply
SVC ESTABLISHMENT EQPT, WHOLESALE: Firefighting Eqpt
SVC ESTABLISHMENT EQPT, WHOLESALE: Laundry Eqpt & Splys
SWEEPING COMPOUNDS
SWIMMING POOL ACCESS: Leaf Skimmers Or Pool Rakes
SWIMMING POOL EQPT: Filters & Water Conditioning Systems
SWIMMING POOL SPLY STORES
SWIMMING POOLS, EQPT & SPLYS: Wholesalers
SWITCHBOARDS & PARTS: Power
SWITCHES
SWITCHES: Electric Power
SWITCHES: Electric Power, Exc Snap, Push Button, Etc
SWITCHES: Electronic
SWITCHES: Electronic Applications
SWITCHES: Silicon Control
SWITCHES: Starting, Fluorescent
SWITCHES: Time, Electrical Switchgear Apparatus
SWITCHGEAR & SWITCHBOARD APPARATUS
SWITCHGEAR & SWITCHGEAR ACCESS, NEC
SWORDS
SYNTHETIC RESIN FINISHED PRDTS, NEC
SYRUPS, DRINK
SYRUPS, FLAVORING, EXC DRINK
SYSTEMS INTEGRATION SVCS
SYSTEMS INTEGRATION SVCS: Local Area Network
SYSTEMS SOFTWARE DEVELOPMENT SVCS

T

TABLE OR COUNTERTOPS, PLASTIC LAMINATED
TABLECLOTHS & SETTINGS
TABLES: Lift, Hydraulic
TABLETS & PADS: Book & Writing, Made From Purchased Material
TABLEWARE OR KITCHEN ARTICLES: Commercial, Fine Earthenware
TABLEWARE: Household & Commercial, Semivitreous
TABLEWARE: Plastic
TABLEWARE: Vitreous China
TAGS & LABELS: Paper
TAGS: Paper, Blank, Made From Purchased Paper
TAILORS: Custom
TALLOW: Animal
TANK REPAIR SVCS
TANKS & OTHER TRACKED VEHICLE CMPNTS
TANKS: Concrete
TANKS: Cryogenic, Metal
TANKS: Fuel, Including Oil & Gas, Metal Plate
TANKS: Lined, Metal
TANKS: Military, Including Factory Rebuilding
TANKS: Plastic & Fiberglass
TANKS: Standard Or Custom Fabricated, Metal Plate
TANKS: Storage, Farm, Metal Plate
TANKS: Water, Metal Plate
TANKS: Wood
TANNERIES: Leather
TAPE DRIVES
TAPES, ADHESIVE: Medical
TAPES: Audio Range, Blank
TAPES: Coated Fiberglass, Pipe Sealing Or Insulating
TAPES: Gummed, Cloth Or Paper Based, From Purchased Matls
TAPES: Magnetic
TAPES: Pressure Sensitive
TARGET DRONES
TELECOMMUNICATION SYSTEMS & EQPT
TELECOMMUNICATIONS CARRIERS & SVCS: Wired
TELEMARKETING BUREAUS
TELEMETERING EQPT
TELEPHONE ANSWERING SVCS
TELEPHONE BOOTHS, EXC WOOD
TELEPHONE EQPT INSTALLATION
TELEPHONE EQPT: NEC
TELEPHONE SVCS
TELEPHONE SWITCHING EQPT
TELEPHONE: Fiber Optic Systems
TELEPHONE: Headsets
TELEPHONE: Sets, Exc Cellular Radio
TELEVISION BROADCASTING & COMMUNICATIONS EQPT
TELEVISION BROADCASTING STATIONS
TELEVISION SETS
TELEVISION: Cameras
TELEVISION: Closed Circuit Eqpt
TEMPERING: Metal
TENT REPAIR SHOP
TENTS: All Materials
TERMINAL BOARDS
TERRA COTTA: Architectural
TEST KITS: Pregnancy
TESTERS: Battery
TESTERS: Environmental
TESTERS: Integrated Circuit
TESTERS: Physical Property
TESTERS: Water, Exc Indl Process
TEXTILE & APPAREL SVCS
TEXTILE BAGS WHOLESALERS
TEXTILE CONVERTERS: Knit Goods
TEXTILE FABRICATORS
TEXTILE FINISH: Chem Coat/Treat, Fire Resist, Manmade
TEXTILE FINISHING: Chemical Coating Or Treating
TEXTILE FINISHING: Dyeing, Broadwoven, Cotton
TEXTILE FINISHING: Dyeing, Finishing & Printng, Linen Fabric
TEXTILE FINISHING: Dyeing, Manmade Fiber & Silk, Broadwoven
TEXTILE FINISHING: Embossing, Cotton, Broadwoven
TEXTILE FINISHING: Embossing, Man Fiber & Silk, Broadwoven
TEXTILE FINISHING: Silk, Broadwoven
TEXTILE FINISHING: Sponging, Cotton, Broadwoven, Trade
TEXTILE PRDTS: Hand Woven & Crocheted
TEXTILE: Finishing, Cotton Broadwoven
TEXTILE: Finishing, Raw Stock NEC
TEXTILE: Goods, NEC
TEXTILES
TEXTILES: Bagging, Jute
TEXTILES: Fibers, Textile, Rcvrd From Mill Waste/Rags
TEXTILES: Flock
TEXTILES: Linen Fabrics
TEXTILES: Linings, Carpet, Exc Felt
TEXTILES: Mill Waste & Remnant
TEXTILES: Tops & Top Processing, Manmade Or Other Fiber
THEATRICAL LIGHTING SVCS
THEATRICAL PRODUCERS & SVCS
THEATRICAL SCENERY
THERMOMETERS: Indl
THERMOMETERS: Liquid-In-Glass & Bimetal
THERMOMETERS: Medical, Digital
THERMOPLASTIC MATERIALS
THERMOPLASTICS
THERMOSETTING MATERIALS
THREAD: All Fibers
THREAD: Embroidery
TICKET OFFICES & AGENCIES: Theatrical
TIES, FORM: Metal
TILE: Asphalt, Floor
TILE: Brick & Structural, Clay
TILE: Drain, Clay
TILE: Fireproofing, Clay
TILE: Mosaic, Ceramic
TILE: Stamped Metal, Floor Or Wall
TILE: Terrazzo Or Concrete, Precast
TILE: Vinyl, Asbestos
TILE: Wall & Floor, Ceramic
TILE: Wall & Floor, clay
TILE: Wall, Enameled Masonite, Made From Purchased Materials
TIMBER PRDTS WHOLESALERS
TIMING DEVICES: Electronic
TIRE & INNER TUBE MATERIALS & RELATED PRDTS
TIRE CORD & FABRIC
TIRE INFLATORS: Hand Or Compressor Operated
TIRES & INNER TUBES
TIRES: Auto
TITANIUM MILL PRDTS
TOBACCO LEAF PROCESSING
TOBACCO: Chewing
TOBACCO: Chewing & Snuff
TOBACCO: Cigarettes
TOBACCO: Cigars
TOBACCO: Smoking
TOILET FIXTURES: Plastic
TOILET PREPARATIONS
TOILETRIES, COSMETICS & PERFUME STORES
TOILETRIES, WHOLESALE: Hair Preparations
TOILETRIES, WHOLESALE: Perfumes
TOILETRIES, WHOLESALE: Toilet Preparations
TOILETRIES, WHOLESALE: Toiletries
TOMBSTONES: Terrazzo Or Concrete, Precast
TOOL & DIE STEEL
TOOLS: Carpenters', Including Levels & Chisels, Exc Saws
TOOLS: Hand
TOOLS: Hand, Engravers'
TOOLS: Hand, Jewelers'
TOOLS: Hand, Mechanics
TOOLS: Hand, Plumbers'
TOOLS: Hand, Power
TOOTHBRUSHES: Electric
TOOTHBRUSHES: Exc Electric

PRODUCT INDEX

TOOTHPASTES, GELS & TOOTHPOWDERS
TOWELS: Indl
TOWELS: Linen & Linen & Cotton Mixtures
TOWERS, SECTIONS: Transmission, Radio & Television
TOYS
TOYS & HOBBY GOODS & SPLYS, WHOLESALE: Arts/Crafts Eqpt/Sply
TOYS & HOBBY GOODS & SPLYS, WHOLESALE: Balloons, Novelty
TOYS & HOBBY GOODS & SPLYS, WHOLESALE: Educational Toys
TOYS & HOBBY GOODS & SPLYS, WHOLESALE: Toys & Games
TOYS & HOBBY GOODS & SPLYS, WHOLESALE: Toys, NEC
TOYS & HOBBY GOODS & SPLYS, WHOLESALE: Video Games
TOYS, HOBBY GOODS & SPLYS WHOLESALERS
TOYS: Dolls, Stuffed Animals & Parts
TOYS: Electronic
TOYS: Video Game Machines
TRADE SHOW ARRANGEMENT SVCS
TRADERS: Commodity, Contracts
TRAILERS & PARTS: Boat
TRAILERS & PARTS: Truck & Semi's
TRAILERS & TRAILER EQPT
TRAILERS: Bus, Tractor Type
TRAILERS: Semitrailers, Truck Tractors
TRANSDUCERS: Electrical Properties
TRANSDUCERS: Pressure
TRANSFORMERS: Control
TRANSFORMERS: Distribution
TRANSFORMERS: Distribution, Electric
TRANSFORMERS: Electric
TRANSFORMERS: Electronic
TRANSFORMERS: Ignition, Domestic Fuel Burners
TRANSFORMERS: Power Related
TRANSFORMERS: Specialty
TRANSLATION & INTERPRETATION SVCS
TRANSMISSIONS: Motor Vehicle
TRANSPORTATION EPQT & SPLYS, WHOLESALE: Acft/Space Vehicle
TRANSPORTATION EPQT/SPLYS, WHOL: Marine Propulsn Mach/Eqpt
TRANSPORTATION EQPT & SPLYS WHOLESALERS, NEC
TRANSPORTATION: Local Passenger, NEC
TRAP ROCK: Crushed & Broken
TRAPS: Animal & Fish, Wire
TRAPS: Stem
TRAVEL AGENCIES
TRAVEL TRAILERS & CAMPERS
TRAYS: Cable, Metal Plate
TRAYS: Plastic
TROPHIES, NEC
TROPHIES, PEWTER
TROPHIES, PLATED, ALL METALS
TROPHIES, SILVER
TROPHIES, WHOLESALE
TROPHIES: Metal, Exc Silver
TROPHY & PLAQUE STORES
TRUCK & BUS BODIES: Ambulance
TRUCK & BUS BODIES: Motor Vehicle, Specialty
TRUCK & BUS BODIES: Truck, Motor Vehicle
TRUCK BODIES: Body Parts
TRUCK GENERAL REPAIR SVC
TRUCK PAINTING & LETTERING SVCS
TRUCK PARTS & ACCESSORIES: Wholesalers
TRUCKING & HAULING SVCS: Garbage, Collect/Transport Only
TRUCKING, DUMP
TRUCKING: Except Local
TRUCKING: Local, Without Storage
TRUCKS & TRACTORS: Industrial
TRUCKS: Forklift
TRUCKS: Indl
TRUNKS
TRUSSES: Wood, Floor
TRUSSES: Wood, Roof
TUBE & TUBING FABRICATORS
TUBES: Finned, For Heat Transfer
TUBES: Generator, Electron Beam, Beta Ray
TUBES: Paper
TUBES: Paper Or Fiber, Chemical Or Electrical Uses
TUBES: Steel & Iron
TUBES: Vacuum

TUBES: Wrought, Welded Or Lock Joint
TUBING: Flexible, Metallic
TUBING: Glass
TUBING: Plastic
TUBING: Seamless
TUNGSTEN CARBIDE
TUNGSTEN CARBIDE POWDER
TURBINE GENERATOR SET UNITS: Hydraulic, Complete
TURBINES & TURBINE GENERATOR SET UNITS, COMPLETE
TURBINES & TURBINE GENERATOR SET UNITS: Gas, Complete
TURBINES & TURBINE GENERATOR SETS
TURBINES & TURBINE GENERATOR SETS & PARTS
TURBINES: Gas, Mechanical Drive
TURBINES: Hydraulic, Complete
TURBINES: Steam
TURBO-GENERATORS
TURKEY PROCESSING & SLAUGHTERING
TURPENTINE
TWINE PRDTS
TYPESETTING SVC
TYPESETTING SVC: Computer
TYPOGRAPHY

U

ULTRASONIC EQPT: Cleaning, Exc Med & Dental
UMBRELLAS & CANES
UMBRELLAS: Garden Or Wagon
UNIFORM STORES
UNIVERSITY
UNSUPPORTED PLASTICS: Floor Or Wall Covering
UPHOLSTERY FILLING MATERIALS
UPHOLSTERY MATERIALS, BROADWOVEN
UPHOLSTERY WORK SVCS
URANIUM ORE MINING, NEC
USED CAR DEALERS
USED MERCHANDISE STORES: Building Materials
UTENSILS: Cast Aluminum, Cooking Or Kitchen
UTENSILS: Household, Cooking & Kitchen, Metal
UTENSILS: Household, Cooking & Kitchen, Porcelain Enameled
UTENSILS: Household, Metal, Exc Cast
UTENSILS: Household, Porcelain Enameled
UTILITY TRAILER DEALERS

V

VACUUM CLEANER STORES
VACUUM CLEANERS: Household
VACUUM CLEANERS: Indl Type
VACUUM SYSTEMS: Air Extraction, Indl
VALUE-ADDED RESELLERS: Computer Systems
VALVES
VALVES & PIPE FITTINGS
VALVES & REGULATORS: Pressure, Indl
VALVES: Aerosol, Metal
VALVES: Aircraft
VALVES: Aircraft, Control, Hydraulic & Pneumatic
VALVES: Aircraft, Fluid Power
VALVES: Control, Automatic
VALVES: Fluid Power, Control, Hydraulic & pneumatic
VALVES: Gas Cylinder, Compressed
VALVES: Hard Rubber
VALVES: Indl
VALVES: Plumbing & Heating
VALVES: Regulating & Control, Automatic
VALVES: Water Works
VARNISHES, NEC
VEGETABLE STANDS OR MARKETS
VEHICLES: All Terrain
VEHICLES: Recreational
VENDING MACHINES & PARTS
VENTILATING EQPT: Metal
VENTILATING EQPT: Sheet Metal
VENTURE CAPITAL COMPANIES
VETERINARY PHARMACEUTICAL PREPARATIONS
VIBRATORS: Concrete Construction
VIDEO & AUDIO EQPT, WHOLESALE
VIDEO EQPT
VIDEO PRODUCTION SVCS
VIDEO REPAIR SVCS
VIDEO TAPE PRODUCTION SVCS
VINYL RESINS, NEC
VISUAL COMMUNICATIONS SYSTEMS
VITAMINS: Natural Or Synthetic, Uncompounded, Bulk

VITAMINS: Pharmaceutical Preparations

W

WALL COVERINGS WHOLESALERS
WALLPAPER & WALL COVERINGS
WALLPAPER: Made From Purchased Paper
WALLS: Curtain, Metal
WAREHOUSE CLUBS STORES
WAREHOUSING & STORAGE FACILITIES, NEC
WAREHOUSING & STORAGE, REFRIGERATED: Frozen Or Refrig Goods
WAREHOUSING & STORAGE: General
WAREHOUSING & STORAGE: General
WAREHOUSING & STORAGE: Refrigerated
WARM AIR HEATING & AC EQPT & SPLYS, WHOLESALE Air Filters
WARM AIR HEATING/AC EQPT/SPLYS, WHOL Dehumidifiers, Exc Port
WASHCLOTHS
WASHERS: Metal
WASHERS: Plastic
WASHERS: Spring, Metal
WATCH STRAPS, EXC METAL
WATCHCASES
WATCHES
WATCHES & PARTS, WHOLESALE
WATER PURIFICATION EQPT: Household
WATER SUPPLY
WATER TREATMENT EQPT: Indl
WATER: Mineral, Carbonated, Canned & Bottled, Etc
WATER: Pasteurized & Mineral, Bottled & Canned
WATER: Pasteurized, Canned & Bottled, Etc
WATERPROOFING COMPOUNDS
WAVEGUIDES & FITTINGS
WAX REMOVERS
WAXES: Mineral, Natural
WAXES: Paraffin
WAXES: Petroleum, Not Produced In Petroleum Refineries
WEATHER STRIPS: Metal
WEAVING MILL, BROADWOVEN FABRICS: Wool Or Similar Fabric
WEDDING CHAPEL: Privately Operated
WEIGHING MACHINERY & APPARATUS
WELDING & CUTTING APPARATUS & ACCESS, NEC
WELDING EQPT
WELDING EQPT & SPLYS WHOLESALERS
WELDING EQPT: Electrical
WELDING MACHINES & EQPT: Ultrasonic
WELDING REPAIR SVC
WELDING SPLYS, EXC GASES: Wholesalers
WELDING TIPS: Heat Resistant, Metal
WELDMENTS
WHEELBARROWS
WHEELCHAIR LIFTS
WHEELCHAIRS
WHEELS
WHEELS & PARTS
WHEELS: Abrasive
WHEELS: Buffing & Polishing
WHEELS: Iron & Steel, Locomotive & Car
WIGS & HAIRPIECES
WIGS, WHOLESALE
WIND TUNNELS
WINDINGS: Coil, Electronic
WINDMILLS: Electric Power Generation
WINDOW & DOOR FRAMES
WINDOW BLIND REPAIR SVCS
WINDOW FRAMES & SASHES: Plastic
WINDOW FRAMES, MOLDING & TRIM: Vinyl
WINDOW TRIMMING SVCS
WINDOWS, LOUVER: Metal
WINDOWS: Frames, Wood
WINDOWS: Storm, Wood
WINDOWS: Wood
WINE & DISTILLED ALCOHOLIC BEVERAGES WHOLESALERS
WINE CELLARS, BONDED: Wine, Blended
WIRE
WIRE & CABLE: Aluminum
WIRE & CABLE: Nonferrous, Aircraft
WIRE & WIRE PRDTS
WIRE CLOTH & WOVEN WIRE PRDTS, MADE FROM PURCHASED WIRE
WIRE FABRIC: Welded Steel
WIRE FENCING & ACCESS WHOLESALERS

PRODUCT INDEX

WIRE MATERIALS: Copper
WIRE MATERIALS: Steel
WIRE PRDTS: Ferrous Or Iron, Made In Wiredrawing Plants
WIRE PRDTS: Steel & Iron
WIRE WHOLESALERS
WIRE: Barbed
WIRE: Barbed & Twisted
WIRE: Communication
WIRE: Mesh
WIRE: Nonferrous
WIRE: Nonferrous, Appliance Fixture
WIRE: Steel, Insulated Or Armored
WOMEN'S & CHILDREN'S CLOTHING WHOLESALERS, NEC
WOMEN'S & GIRLS' SPORTSWEAR WHOLESALERS
WOMEN'S CLOTHING STORES
WOMEN'S CLOTHING STORES: Ready-To-Wear
WOMEN'S SPECIALTY CLOTHING STORES
WOMEN'S SPORTSWEAR STORES
WOOD FENCING WHOLESALERS
WOOD PRDTS
WOOD PRDTS: Clothespins
WOOD PRDTS: Display Forms, Boot & Shoe
WOOD PRDTS: Engraved
WOOD PRDTS: Furniture Inlays, Veneers
WOOD PRDTS: Jalousies, Glass, Wood Framed
WOOD PRDTS: Ladders & Stepladders
WOOD PRDTS: Mantels
WOOD PRDTS: Moldings, Unfinished & Prefinished
WOOD PRDTS: Mulch Or Sawdust
WOOD PRDTS: Novelties, Fiber
WOOD PRDTS: Outdoor, Structural
WOOD PRDTS: Panel Work
WOOD PRDTS: Rulers & Rules
WOOD PRDTS: Shavings & Packaging, Excelsior
WOOD PRDTS: Shoe Trees
WOOD PRDTS: Silo Staves
WOOD PRDTS: Survey Stakes
WOOD PRDTS: Trellises
WOOD PRDTS: Trophy Bases
WOOD PRDTS: Window Backs, Store Or Lunchroom, Prefabricated
WOOD PRDTS: Yard Sticks
WOOD PRODUCTS: Reconstituted
WOOD TREATING: Creosoting
WOOD TREATING: Flooring, Block
WOOD TREATING: Structural Lumber & Timber
WOODWORK & TRIM: Interior & Ornamental
WOODWORK: Carved & Turned
WOODWORK: Interior & Ornamental, NEC
WOOL: Grease
WOVEN WIRE PRDTS, NEC
WRITING FOR PUBLICATION SVCS

X

X-RAY EQPT & TUBES
X-RAY EQPT REPAIR SVCS

Y

YARN & YARN SPINNING
YARN MILLS: Twisting
YARN WHOLESALERS
YARN: Embroidery, Spun
YARN: Manmade & Synthetic Fiber, Spun
YARN: Natural & Animal Fiber, Spun
YARN: Specialty & Novelty
YARN: Weaving, Twisting, Winding Or Spooling
YOGURT WHOLESALERS

Z

ZIRCONIUM

PRODUCT SECTION

Product category — **BOXES:** Folding
Edgar & Son Paperboard ....G...... 999 999-9999
　Yourtown *(G-11480)*
Ready Box Co..................................E...... 999 999-9999
City — 　Anytown *(G-7097)*

Indicates approximate employment figure
A = Over 500 employees, B = 251-500
C = 101-250, D = 51-100, E = 20-50
F = 10-19, G = 5-9
Business phone
Geographic Section entry number where full company information appears.

See footnotes for symbols and codes identification.
• Refer to the Industrial Product Index preceding this section to locate product headings.

ABRASIVES

American Douglas Metals Inc ....F...... 716 856-3170
　Buffalo *(G-2807)*
Buffalo Abrasives Inc ....E...... 716 693-3856
　North Tonawanda *(G-12962)*
Dedeco International Sales Inc..........E...... 845 887-4840
　Long Eddy *(G-7642)*
Dico Products Corporation ....F...... 315 797-0470
　Utica *(G-16323)*
Electro Abrasives LLC ....E...... 716 822-2500
　Buffalo *(G-2933)*
Imerys Fsed Mnrl Ngara FLS Inc ....G...... 716 286-1234
　Niagara Falls *(G-12833)*
Imerys Fsed Mnrl Ngara FLS Inc ....E...... 716 286-1250
　Niagara Falls *(G-12834)*
Meloon Foundries LLC ....E...... 315 454-3231
　Syracuse *(G-15985)*
Precision Elctro Mnrl Pmco Inc ....E...... 716 284-2484
　Niagara Falls *(G-12863)*
Saint-Gbain Advnced Crmics LLC ......E...... 716 691-2000
　Amherst *(G-259)*
Saint-Gobain Abrasives Inc ....B...... 518 266-2200
　Watervliet *(G-16688)*
Select-Tech Inc ....G...... 845 895-8111
　Wallkill *(G-16546)*
Uneeda Enterprizes Inc ....C...... 877 863-3321
　Spring Valley *(G-15605)*
Warren Cutlery Corp ....F...... 845 876-3444
　Rhinebeck *(G-14060)*
Washington Mills Tonawanda Inc ....E...... 716 693-4550
　Tonawanda *(G-16213)*

ABRASIVES: Coated

Barton Mines Company LLC ....C...... 518 798-5462
　Glens Falls *(G-5672)*
Conrad Blasius Equipment Co ....G...... 516 753-1200
　Plainview *(G-13590)*
Global Abrasive Products Inc ....E...... 716 438-0047
　Lockport *(G-7588)*
Precision Abrasives Corp ....E...... 716 826-5833
　Orchard Park *(G-13291)*

ABRASIVES: Grains

EAC Holdings of NY Corp ....E...... 716 822-2500
　Buffalo *(G-2925)*
Sunbelt Industries Inc ....F...... 315 823-2947
　Little Falls *(G-7505)*
Washingtom Mills Elec Mnrls ....D...... 716 278-6600
　Niagara Falls *(G-12890)*

ACADEMIC TUTORING SVCS

Bright Kids Nyc Inc ....E...... 917 539-4575
　New York *(G-9460)*

ACCELERATION INDICATORS & SYSTEM COMPONENTS: Aerospace

Aeroflex Incorporated ....B...... 516 694-6700
　Plainview *(G-13578)*
Cobham Holdings (us) Inc ....A...... 716 662-0006
　Orchard Park *(G-13262)*
Cobham Holdings Inc ....F...... 716 662-0006
　Orchard Park *(G-13263)*
Ieh FM Holdings LLC ....E...... 212 702-4300
　New York *(G-10559)*
Inertia Switch Inc ....E...... 845 359-8300
　Orangeburg *(G-13229)*
Woodbine Products Inc ....E...... 631 586-3770
　Hauppauge *(G-6236)*

ACCELERATORS: Electron Linear

Iba Industrial Inc ....E...... 631 254-6800
　Edgewood *(G-4600)*

ACCELERATORS: Particle, High Voltage

Evergreen High Voltage LLC ....G...... 281 814-9973
　Lake Placid *(G-7274)*

ACCOUNTING MACHINES & CASH REGISTERS

Logic Controls Inc ....E...... 516 248-0400
　Bethpage *(G-872)*

ACID RESIST: Etching

Greenfield Manufacturing Inc ....F...... 518 581-2368
　Saratoga Springs *(G-15156)*

ACIDS

Evans Chemetics LP ....D...... 315 539-9221
　Waterloo *(G-16624)*

ACIDS: Battery

Horizon Power Source LLC ....E...... 877 240-0580
　Glen Cove *(G-5618)*

ACOUSTICAL BOARD & TILE

Lencore Acoustics Corp ....F...... 315 384-9114
　Norfolk *(G-12899)*
Mecho Systems ....F...... 718 729-8373
　Long Island City *(G-7807)*
Ssf Production LLC ....F...... 518 324-3407
　Plattsburgh *(G-13697)*

ACRYLIC RESINS

Creations In Lucite Inc ....G...... 718 871-2000
　Brooklyn *(G-1814)*
PPG Architectural Finishes Inc ....C...... 607 334-9951
　Norwich *(G-13034)*

ACTUATORS: Indl, NEC

Makerbot Industries LLC ....B...... 347 334-6800
　Brooklyn *(G-2254)*
Marine & Indus Hydraulics Inc ....F...... 914 698-2036
　Mamaroneck *(G-8037)*
Rotork Controls Inc ....F...... 585 328-1550
　Rochester *(G-14659)*
Rotork Controls Inc ....C...... 585 328-1550
　Rochester *(G-14660)*
Trident Valve Actuator Co ....F...... 914 698-2650
　Mamaroneck *(G-8049)*
Young & Franklin Inc ....D...... 315 457-3110
　Liverpool *(G-7559)*

ADDITIVE BASED PLASTIC MATERIALS: Plasticizers

Bamberger Polymers Intl Corp ....F...... 516 622-3600
　Jericho *(G-7060)*
De Witt Plastics Inc ....F...... 315 255-1209
　Auburn *(G-492)*
Fougera Pharmaceuticals Inc ....C...... 631 454-7677
　Melville *(G-8321)*

ADHESIVES

Adirondack Spclty Adhsives Inc ....F...... 518 869-5736
　Albany *(G-35)*
Aremco Products Inc ....F...... 845 268-0039
　Valley Cottage *(G-16376)*
Beacon Adhesives Inc ....E...... 914 699-3400
　Mount Vernon *(G-8666)*
Best Adhesives Company Inc ....G...... 718 417-3800
　Ridgewood *(G-14102)*
Hercules Incorporated ....G...... 718 383-1717
　Brooklyn *(G-2075)*
Hercules Incorporated ....G...... 315 461-4730
　Liverpool *(G-7522)*
Northern Adhesives Inc ....E...... 718 388-5834
　Brooklyn *(G-2374)*
PPG Architectural Finishes Inc ....G...... 585 271-1363
　Rochester *(G-14590)*
Ran Mar Enterprises Ltd ....F...... 631 666-4754
　Bay Shore *(G-731)*
Saint Gobain Grains & Powders ....A...... 716 731-8200
　Niagara Falls *(G-12870)*
Solenis ....G...... 212 772-0560
　New York *(G-12122)*
Solenis ....G...... 212 204-6679
　New York *(G-12123)*
Solenis ....G...... 212 362-1759
　New York *(G-12124)*

ADHESIVES & SEALANTS

Able National Corp ....E...... 718 386-8801
　Brooklyn *(G-1549)*
Advanced Polymer Solutions LLC ......G...... 516 621-5800
　Port Washington *(G-13796)*
All Out Die Cutting Inc ....E...... 718 346-6666
　Brooklyn *(G-1587)*
Angiotech Biocoatings Corp ....E...... 585 321-1130
　Henrietta *(G-6292)*
Classic Labels Inc ....E...... 631 467-2300
　Patchogue *(G-13417)*
Divine Brothers Company ....C...... 315 797-0470
　Utica *(G-16327)*
Hexion Inc ....E...... 518 792-8040
　South Glens Falls *(G-15525)*
P C I Paper Conversions Inc ....D...... 315 703-8300
　Syracuse *(G-16007)*
P C I Paper Conversions Inc ....E...... 315 634-3317
　Syracuse *(G-16008)*
Polycast Industries Inc ....G...... 631 595-2530
　Bay Shore *(G-726)*
Polyset Company Inc ....E...... 518 664-6000
　Mechanicville *(G-8229)*
Royal Adhesives & Sealants LLC ......F...... 315 451-1755
　Syracuse *(G-16027)*
Super-Tek Products Inc ....E...... 718 278-7900
　Woodside *(G-17357)*
Utility Manufacturing Co Inc ....E...... 516 997-6300
　Westbury *(G-17039)*
Vitex Packaging Group Inc ....F...... 212 265-6575
　New York *(G-12557)*
Wild Works Incorporated ....G...... 716 891-4197
　Albany *(G-150)*

ADVERTISING AGENCIES

Act Communications Group Inc ....F...... 631 669-2403
　West Islip *(G-16902)*
Ad Makers Long Island Inc ....F...... 631 595-9100
　Deer Park *(G-4087)*
AR Media Inc ....E...... 212 352-0731
　New York *(G-9187)*
Drns Corp ....F...... 718 369-4530
　Brooklyn *(G-1881)*
Gatehouse Media LLC ....D...... 585 598-0030
　Pittsford *(G-13561)*

ADVERTISING AGENCIES

Gruner + Jahr Prtg & Pubg Co ....C 212 463-1000
  New York (G-10375)
Kinaneco Inc ....E 315 468-6201
  Syracuse (G-15974)
Luria Communications Inc ....G 631 329-4922
  East Hampton (G-4413)
Media Trust LLC ....G 212 802-1162
  New York (G-11210)
Mickelberry Communications Inc ....G 212 832-0303
  New York (G-11252)
Middletown Press ....G 845 343-1895
  Middletown (G-8451)
Perception Imaging Inc ....F 631 676-5262
  Holbrook (G-6466)
Scholastic Corporation ....G 212 343-6100
  New York (G-11997)
Service Advertising Group Inc ....F 718 361-6161
  Long Island City (G-7875)
Stop Entertainment Inc ....F 212 242-7867
  Monroe (G-8564)

ADVERTISING AGENCIES: Consultants

Eye Graphics & Printing Inc ....F 718 488-0606
  Brooklyn (G-1948)
Galli Shirts and Sports AP ....G 845 226-7305
  Stormville (G-15779)
Mason & Gore Inc ....E 914 921-1025
  Rye (G-15063)
Whispr Group Inc ....F 212 924-3979
  Brooklyn (G-2747)

ADVERTISING DISPLAY PRDTS

Accenta Incorporated ....G 716 565-6262
  Buffalo (G-2794)
Arnprior Rpid Mfg Slutions Inc ....C 585 617-6301
  Rochester (G-14212)
Federal Sample Card Corp ....D 718 458-1344
  Elmhurst (G-4660)
JG Innovative Industries Inc ....G 718 784-7300
  Kew Gardens (G-7164)
Mack Studios Displays Inc ....E 315 252-7542
  Auburn (G-507)
Nationwide Exhibitor Svcs Inc ....F 631 467-2034
  Central Islip (G-3505)
Promotional Development Inc ....C 718 485-8550
  Brooklyn (G-2455)
Qps Die Cutters Finishers Corp ....E 718 966-1811
  Staten Island (G-15725)
Strategic Mktg Promotions Inc ....F 845 623-7777
  Pearl River (G-13467)
Swift Multigraphics LLC ....G 585 442-8000
  Rochester (G-14709)
Tri-Plex Packaging Corporation ....E 212 481-6070
  New York (G-12401)

ADVERTISING MATERIAL DISTRIBUTION

Penny Lane Printing Inc ....D 585 226-8111
  Avon (G-542)
Real Est Book of Long Island ....F 516 364-5000
  Syosset (G-15837)
Shipmtes/Printmates Holdg Corp ....D 518 370-1158
  Scotia (G-15330)
Technomag Inc ....G 631 246-6142
  East Setauket (G-4493)

ADVERTISING REPRESENTATIVES: Electronic Media

Retail Management Pubg Inc ....F 212 981-0217
  New York (G-11845)
World Business Media LLC ....F 212 344-0759
  Massapequa Park (G-8191)

ADVERTISING REPRESENTATIVES: Magazine

Icd Publications Inc ....E 631 246-9300
  Islandia (G-6796)

ADVERTISING REPRESENTATIVES: Media

Redbook Magazine ....F 212 649-3331
  New York (G-11815)

ADVERTISING REPRESENTATIVES: Newspaper

Advertiser Publications Inc ....F 845 783-1111
  Chester (G-3598)

Bradford Publications Inc ....C 716 373-2500
  Olean (G-13137)
Community Cpons Frnchising Inc ....E 516 277-1968
  Glen Cove (G-5613)
Fire Island Tide Publication ....F 631 567-7470
  Sayville (G-15210)
L & M Publications Inc ....E 516 378-3133
  Garden City (G-5513)
Local Media Group Inc ....E 845 341-1100
  Middletown (G-8446)
Long Island Cmnty Nwsppers Inc ....D 516 482-4490
  Mineola (G-8522)
Market Place Publications ....E 516 997-7909
  Carle Place (G-3395)
Service Advertising Group Inc ....F 718 361-6161
  Long Island City (G-7875)

ADVERTISING REPRESENTATIVES: Printed Media

Economist Newspaper Group Inc ....C 212 541-0500
  New York (G-9979)
Penton Media Inc ....B 212 204-4200
  New York (G-11608)
Press Express ....G 914 592-3790
  Elmsford (G-4773)

ADVERTISING SPECIALTIES, WHOLESALE

A Trusted Name Inc ....F 716 326-7400
  Westfield (G-17045)
Advantage Printing Inc ....F 718 820-0688
  Kew Gardens (G-7158)
All American Awards Inc ....F 631 567-2025
  Bohemia (G-1011)
Concept Printing Inc ....G 845 353-4040
  Nyack (G-13047)
Elco Manufacturing Co Inc ....F 516 767-3577
  Port Washington (G-13813)
In-Step Marketing Inc ....F 212 797-3450
  New York (G-10579)
Leonard Martin Bus Systems ....G 845 638-9350
  New City (G-8787)
Middletown Press ....G 845 343-1895
  Middletown (G-8451)
U All Inc ....E 518 438-2558
  Albany (G-144)
Ward Sales Co Inc ....G 315 476-5276
  Syracuse (G-16068)
Whispr Group Inc ....F 212 924-3979
  Brooklyn (G-2747)

ADVERTISING SVCS: Direct Mail

Advertiser Publications Inc ....F 845 783-1111
  Chester (G-3598)
Century Direct LLC ....C 212 763-0600
  Islandia (G-6789)
Design Distributors Inc ....D 631 242-2000
  Deer Park (G-4130)
Gotham Ink Corp ....G 516 677-1969
  Syosset (G-15825)
Orffeo Printing & Imaging Inc ....G 716 681-5757
  Lancaster (G-7328)
Perception Imaging Inc ....F 631 676-5262
  Holbrook (G-6466)
Shipmtes/Printmates Holdg Corp ....D 518 370-1158
  Scotia (G-15330)
Syracuse Letter Company Inc ....F 315 476-8328
  Bridgeport (G-1237)
Thomas Publishing Company LLC ....B 212 695-0500
  New York (G-12321)

ADVERTISING SVCS: Display

Apple Imprints Apparel Inc ....E 716 893-1130
  Buffalo (G-2817)
Exhibits & More ....G 585 924-4040
  Victor (G-16476)
Greenwood Graphics Inc ....F 516 822-4856
  Hicksville (G-6353)
L Miller Design Inc ....G 631 242-1163
  Deer Park (G-4162)
Mystic Display Co Inc ....G 718 485-2651
  Brooklyn (G-2345)

ADVERTISING SVCS: Outdoor

Artkraft Strauss LLC ....E 212 265-5155
  New York (G-9222)

ADVERTISING SVCS: Sample Distribution

Instantwhip of Buffalo Inc ....E 716 892-7031
  Buffalo (G-3010)

ADVERTISING SVCS: Transit

Danet Inc ....F 718 266-4444
  Brooklyn (G-1838)
Fun Media Inc ....E 646 472-0135
  New York (G-10223)

AERIAL WORK PLATFORMS

Park Ave Bldg & Roofg Sups LLC ....E 718 403-0100
  Brooklyn (G-2407)

AEROSOLS

Fountainhead Group Inc ....C 708 598-7100
  New York Mills (G-12724)

AGENTS & MANAGERS: Entertainers

Fast-Trac Entertainment Ltd ....G 888 758-8886
  New York (G-10146)

AGENTS, BROKERS & BUREAUS: Personal Service

Superior Print On Demand ....G 607 240-5231
  Vestal (G-16454)
T J Signs Unlimited LLC ....E 631 273-4800
  Islip (G-6813)

AGRICULTURAL EQPT: BARN, SILO, POULTRY, DAIRY/LIVESTOCK MACH

P & D Equipment Sales LLC ....G 585 343-2394
  Alexander (G-189)

AGRICULTURAL EQPT: Fertilizng, Sprayng, Dustng/Irrigatn Mach

Chapin Watermatics Inc ....D 315 782-1170
  Watertown (G-16643)

AGRICULTURAL EQPT: Milking Machines

Westmoor Ltd ....F 315 363-1500
  Sherrill (G-15410)

AGRICULTURAL EQPT: Planting Machines

Good Earth Organics Corp ....E 716 684-8111
  Lancaster (G-7318)

AGRICULTURAL EQPT: Spreaders, Fertilizer

Chapin Manufacturing Inc ....C 585 343-3140
  Batavia (G-628)

AGRICULTURAL EQPT: Trailers & Wagons, Farm

Renaldos Sales and Service Ctr ....G 716 337-3760
  North Collins (G-12931)

AGRICULTURAL EQPT: Turf & Grounds Eqpt

Bdp Industries Inc ....E 518 695-6851
  Greenwich (G-5886)

AGRICULTURAL EQPT: Turf Eqpt, Commercial

Moffett Turf Equipment Inc ....E 585 334-0100
  West Henrietta (G-16885)

AIR CLEANING SYSTEMS

Acme Engineering Products Inc ....E 518 236-5659
  Mooers (G-8615)

AIR CONDITIONERS, AUTOMOTIVE: Wholesalers

American Comfort Direct LLC ....E 201 364-8309
  New York (G-9116)

PRODUCT SECTION

AIRCRAFT PARTS & AUXILIARY EQPT: Assys, Subassemblies/Parts

AIR CONDITIONING & VENTILATION EQPT & SPLYS: Wholesales

Layton Manufacturing Corp .... E 718 498-6000
   Brooklyn *(G-2196)*

AIR CONDITIONING EQPT

Carrier Corporation .... E 315 432-6000
   Syracuse *(G-15887)*
Carrier Corporation .... B 315 463-5744
   East Syracuse *(G-4513)*
Carrier Corporation .... B 315 432-6000
   East Syracuse *(G-4514)*
Duro Dyne Corporation .... C 631 249-9000
   Farmingdale *(G-4980)*
Duro Dyne Machinery Corp .... C 631 249-9000
   Bay Shore *(G-696)*
Duro Dyne National Corp .... C 631 249-9000
   Bay Shore *(G-697)*
EMC Fintech .... F 716 488-9071
   Falconer *(G-4896)*
Fedders Islandaire Inc .... D 631 471-2900
   East Setauket *(G-4482)*
Layton Manufacturing Corp .... E 718 498-6000
   Brooklyn *(G-2196)*
M M Tool and Manufacturing .... G 845 691-4140
   Highland *(G-6405)*
RE Hansen Industries Inc .... C 631 471-2900
   East Setauket *(G-4491)*
Split Systems Corp .... G 516 223-5511
   North Baldwin *(G-12909)*
Transit Air Inc .... E 607 324-0216
   Hornell *(G-6568)*

AIR CONDITIONING UNITS: Complete, Domestic Or Indl

AC Air Cooling Co Inc .... F 718 933-1011
   Bronx *(G-1258)*
Balticare Inc .... G 646 380-9470
   New York *(G-9310)*
Ice Air LLC .... E 914 668-4700
   Mount Vernon *(G-8692)*
JE Miller Inc .... F 315 437-6811
   East Syracuse *(G-4546)*
Pfannenberg Inc .... E 716 685-6866
   Lancaster *(G-7333)*

AIR COOLERS: Metal Plate

Thermotech Corp .... G 716 823-3311
   Buffalo *(G-3217)*

AIR DUCT CLEANING SVCS

Filta Clean Co Inc .... E 718 495-3800
   Brooklyn *(G-1970)*

AIR MATTRESSES: Plastic

Berry Plastics Group Inc .... F 716 366-2112
   Dunkirk *(G-4332)*
Diamond Packaging Holdings LLC .... G 585 334-8030
   Rochester *(G-14306)*

AIR POLLUTION MEASURING SVCS

Cemtrex Inc .... E 631 756-9116
   Farmingdale *(G-4957)*
Clean Gas Systems Inc .... E 631 467-1600
   Hauppauge *(G-6046)*

AIR PURIFICATION EQPT

Aeromed Inc .... G 518 843-9144
   Utica *(G-16306)*
Austin Air Systems Limited .... D 716 856-3700
   Buffalo *(G-2824)*
Beecher Emssn Sltn Tchnlgs LLC .... F 607 796-0149
   Elmira *(G-4671)*
Beltran Associates Inc .... E 718 252-2996
   Brooklyn *(G-1680)*
Clean Gas Systems Inc .... E 631 467-1600
   Hauppauge *(G-6046)*
JT Systems Inc .... F 315 622-1980
   Liverpool *(G-7529)*
Phytofilter Technologies Inc .... G 518 507-6399
   Saratoga Springs *(G-15166)*
Sbb Inc .... G 315 422-2376
   East Syracuse *(G-4562)*
Sullivan Bazinet Bongio Inc .... E 315 437-6500
   East Syracuse *(G-4568)*

AIR TRAFFIC CONTROL SYSTEMS & EQPT

Placemeter Inc .... G 917 225-4579
   Brooklyn *(G-2425)*

AIRCRAFT & AEROSPACE FLIGHT INSTRUMENTS & GUIDANCE SYSTEMS

Atair Aerospace Inc .... F 718 923-1709
   Brooklyn *(G-1642)*
Bae Systems Controls Inc .... A 607 770-2000
   Endicott *(G-4796)*
CIC International Ltd .... D 212 213-0089
   Brooklyn *(G-1779)*
Facilamatic Instrument Corp .... F 516 825-6300
   Valley Stream *(G-16406)*
Kwadair LLC .... G 646 824-2511
   Brooklyn *(G-2182)*
Select Fabricators Inc .... F 585 393-0650
   Canandaigua *(G-3357)*

AIRCRAFT & HEAVY EQPT REPAIR SVCS

Binghamton Simulator Co Inc .... E 607 321-2980
   Binghamton *(G-895)*
James A Staley Co Inc .... F 845 878-3344
   Carmel *(G-3401)*

AIRCRAFT ASSEMBLY PLANTS

Aip/Aerospace Holdings LLC .... G 212 916-8142
   New York *(G-9065)*
Altius Aviation LLC .... G 315 455-7555
   Syracuse *(G-15852)*
Barclay Tagg Racing .... E 631 404-8269
   Floral Park *(G-5195)*
Grumman Field Support Services .... D 516 575-0574
   Bethpage *(G-867)*
Joka Industries Inc .... E 631 589-0444
   Bohemia *(G-1083)*
Lesly Enterprise & Associates .... G 631 988-1301
   Deer Park *(G-4165)*
Lockheed Martin Corporation .... G 212 953-1510
   New York *(G-11020)*
Lockheed Martin Corporation .... E 315 456-1548
   Liverpool *(G-7530)*
Lockheed Martin Corporation .... D 315 793-5800
   New Hartford *(G-8807)*
Moog Inc .... B 716 655-3000
   East Aurora *(G-4375)*
Northrop Grumman Systems Corp .... A 516 575-0574
   Bethpage *(G-877)*
Northrop Grumman Systems Corp .... F 716 626-4600
   Buffalo *(G-3097)*
Northrop Grumman Systems Corp .... G 631 423-1014
   Huntington *(G-6671)*
Pro Drones Usa LLC .... F 718 530-3558
   New York *(G-11724)*
Sikorsky Aircraft Corporation .... D 585 424-1990
   Rochester *(G-14687)*
Trium Strs-Lg Isld LLC .... D 516 997-5757
   Westbury *(G-17036)*
Tsc LLC .... G 661 824-6609
   New York *(G-12416)*

AIRCRAFT CONTROL SYSTEMS: Electronic Totalizing Counters

Moog Inc .... A 716 652-2000
   Elma *(G-4651)*
Moog Inc .... E 716 687-4778
   Elma *(G-4652)*
Moog Inc .... B 716 687-5486
   East Aurora *(G-4377)*

AIRCRAFT ENGINES & PARTS

Advanced Atomization Tech LLC .... B 315 923-2341
   Clyde *(G-3725)*
ARC Systems Inc .... E 631 582-8020
   Hauppauge *(G-6023)*
B H Aircraft Company Inc .... D 631 580-9747
   Ronkonkoma *(G-14877)*
Chromalloy American LLC .... E 845 230-7355
   Orangeburg *(G-13222)*
Chromalloy Gas Turbine LLC .... C 845 359-2462
   Orangeburg *(G-13223)*
Chromalloy Gas Turbine LLC .... E 845 692-8912
   Middletown *(G-8430)*
Colonial Group LLC .... E 516 349-8010
   Plainview *(G-13589)*
Davis Aircraft Products Co Inc .... C 631 563-1500
   Bohemia *(G-1050)*
Dyna-Empire Inc .... C 516 222-2700
   Garden City *(G-5500)*
Gb Aero Engine LLC .... B 914 925-9600
   Rye *(G-15057)*
General Electric Company .... A 518 385-4022
   Schenectady *(G-15257)*
General Electric Company .... E 518 385-7620
   Niskayuna *(G-12895)*
Honeywell International Inc .... A 315 554-6643
   Skaneateles Falls *(G-15470)*
Honeywell International Inc .... A 845 342-4400
   Middletown *(G-8445)*
Honeywell International Inc .... A 212 964-5111
   Melville *(G-8328)*
Howe Machine & Tool Corp .... F 516 931-5687
   Bethpage *(G-868)*
ITT Enidine Inc .... B 716 662-1900
   Orchard Park *(G-13275)*
Kerns Manufacturing Corp .... C 718 784-4044
   Long Island City *(G-7780)*
Lourdes Industries Inc .... D 631 234-6600
   Hauppauge *(G-6121)*
McGuigan Inc .... E 631 750-6222
   Bohemia *(G-1103)*
Nell-Joy Industries Inc .... E 631 842-8989
   Copiague *(G-3915)*
Omega Industries & Development .... E 516 349-8010
   Plainview *(G-13625)*
Sequa Corporation .... E 813 434-4522
   Orangeburg *(G-13246)*
SOS International LLC .... E 212 742-2410
   New York *(G-12140)*
Therm Incorporated .... C 607 272-8500
   Ithaca *(G-6877)*
Triumph Actuation Systems LLC .... D 516 378-0162
   Freeport *(G-5432)*
Triumph Group Inc .... D 516 997-5757
   Westbury *(G-17037)*
Turbine Engine Comp Utica .... A 315 768-8070
   Whitesboro *(G-17197)*
United Technologies Corp .... G 315 432-7849
   East Syracuse *(G-4576)*

AIRCRAFT EQPT & SPLYS WHOLESALERS

Fastener Dimensions Inc .... E 718 847-6321
   Ozone Park *(G-13378)*
Magellan Aerospace NY Inc .... C 631 589-2440
   Bohemia *(G-1099)*
Styles Aviation Inc .... G 845 677-8185
   Lagrangeville *(G-7259)*
Worldwide Arntcal Cmpnents Inc .... F 631 842-3780
   Copiague *(G-3939)*

AIRCRAFT FLIGHT INSTRUMENT REPAIR SVCS

Safe Flight Instrument Corp .... C 914 220-1125
   White Plains *(G-17167)*

AIRCRAFT FLIGHT INSTRUMENTS

Mod-A-Can Inc .... E 516 931-8545
   Hicksville *(G-6374)*
Safe Flight Instrument Corp .... C 914 220-1125
   White Plains *(G-17167)*

AIRCRAFT LIGHTING

Aerospace Lighting Corporation .... D 631 563-6400
   Bohemia *(G-1008)*
Astronics Corporation .... C 716 805-1599
   East Aurora *(G-4366)*
B/E Aerospace Inc .... E 631 563-6400
   Bohemia *(G-1022)*
Luminescent Systems Inc .... B 716 655-0800
   East Aurora *(G-4373)*

AIRCRAFT PARTS & AUXILIARY EQPT: Accumulators, Propeller

Honeywell International Inc .... B 516 577-2000
   Melville *(G-8329)*

AIRCRAFT PARTS & AUXILIARY EQPT: Assys, Subassemblies/Parts

Aero Trades Mfg Corp .... E 516 746-3360
   Mineola *(G-8489)*

Employee Codes: A=Over 500 employees, B=251-500
C=101-250, D=51-100, E=20-50, F=10-19, G=5-9

AIRCRAFT PARTS & AUXILIARY EQPT: Assys, Subassemblies/Parts

Company	Code	Phone
Alro Machine Tool & Die Co Inc	F	631 226-5020
Lindenhurst (G-7453)		
Design/OI Inc	F	631 474-5536
Port Jeff STA (G-13766)		
Excelco Developments Inc	E	716 934-2651
Silver Creek (G-15448)		
Excelco/Newbrook Inc	D	716 934-2644
Silver Creek (G-15449)		
GKN Aerospace Monitor Inc	B	562 619-8558
Amityville (G-289)		
Handy Tool & Mfg Co Inc	E	718 478-9203
Brooklyn (G-2068)		
Lai International Inc	D	763 780-0060
Green Island (G-5858)		
Norsk Titanium US Inc	G	646 277-7514
New York (G-11453)		
Posimech Inc	E	631 924-5959
Medford (G-8258)		
Superior Motion Controls Inc	E	516 420-2921
Farmingdale (G-5120)		
Tek Precision Co Ltd	E	631 242-0330
Deer Park (G-4217)		
Wilco Industries Inc	G	631 676-2593
Ronkonkoma (G-15001)		

AIRCRAFT PARTS & AUXILIARY EQPT: Body Assemblies & Parts

Company	Code	Phone
Air Industries Group	D	631 881-4920
Hauppauge (G-6013)		
Reese Manufacturing Inc	G	631 842-3780
Copiague (G-3922)		

AIRCRAFT PARTS & AUXILIARY EQPT: Gears, Power Transmission

Company	Code	Phone
Gleason Works	A	585 473-1000
Rochester (G-14408)		
W J Albro Machine Works Inc	G	631 345-0657
Yaphank (G-17408)		

AIRCRAFT PARTS & AUXILIARY EQPT: Landing Assemblies & Brakes

Company	Code	Phone
Dyna-Empire Inc	C	516 222-2700
Garden City (G-5500)		

AIRCRAFT PARTS & AUXILIARY EQPT: Military Eqpt & Armament

Company	Code	Phone
Armacel Armor Corporation	E	805 384-1144
New York (G-9204)		
Dresser-Argus Inc	G	718 643-1540
Brooklyn (G-1880)		
Edo LLC	G	631 630-4000
Amityville (G-285)		
Metadure Parts & Sales Inc	F	631 249-2141
Farmingdale (G-5050)		
US Milpack & Mfg Corp	G	718 342-1307
Brooklyn (G-2714)		

AIRCRAFT PARTS & AUXILIARY EQPT: Refueling Eqpt, In Flight

Company	Code	Phone
Gny Equipment LLC	F	631 667-1010
Bay Shore (G-703)		
Usairports Services Inc		585 527-6835
Rochester (G-14749)		

AIRCRAFT PARTS & AUXILIARY EQPT: Seat Ejector Devices

Company	Code	Phone
East/West Industries Inc	E	631 981-5900
Ronkonkoma (G-14896)		

AIRCRAFT PARTS & EQPT, NEC

Company	Code	Phone
Air Industries Machining Corp	C	631 968-5000
Bay Shore (G-667)		
Alcoa Fastening Systems	C	845 334-7203
Kingston (G-7175)		
Alken Industries Inc	D	631 467-2000
Ronkonkoma (G-14859)		
Arkwin Industries Inc	B	516 333-2640
Westbury (G-16969)		
Astronics Corporation	C	716 805-1599
East Aurora (G-4366)		
Ausco Inc	D	516 944-9882
Farmingdale (G-4947)		
B & B Precision Components Inc	G	631 273-3321
Ronkonkoma (G-14876)		
B/E Aerospace Inc	E	631 563-6400
Bohemia (G-1022)		
Bar Fields Inc	F	347 587-7795
Brooklyn (G-1667)		
Blair Industries Inc	E	631 924-6600
Medford (G-8236)		
Canfield Aerospace & Mar Inc	E	631 648-1050
Ronkonkoma (G-14884)		
Caravan International Corp	G	212 223-7190
New York (G-9522)		
Carleton Technologies Inc	B	716 662-0006
Orchard Park (G-13259)		
Cellular Empire Inc	F	347 587-7795
Brooklyn (G-1768)		
Circor Aerospace Inc	E	631 737-1900
Hauppauge (G-6045)		
Cox & Company Inc	C	212 366-0200
Plainview (G-13593)		
CPI Aerostructures Inc	B	631 586-5200
Edgewood (G-4596)		
Crown Aircraft Lighting Inc	G	718 767-3410
Whitestone (G-17206)		
Davis Aircraft Products Co Inc	C	631 563-1500
Bohemia (G-1050)		
Drt Power Systems LLC - Lane	D	585 247-5940
Rochester (G-14319)		
Ducommun Aerostructures NY Inc	B	518 731-2791
Coxsackie (G-4056)		
Eastern Precision Machining	G	631 286-4758
Bellport (G-829)		
Engineered Metal Products Inc	G	631 842-3780
Copiague (G-3900)		
Ensil Technical Services Inc	E	716 282-1020
Niagara Falls (G-12814)		
Fluid Mechanisms Hauppauge Inc	E	631 234-0100
Hauppauge (G-6078)		
GE Aviation Systems LLC	C	631 467-5500
Bohemia (G-1071)		
Goodrich Corporation	C	315 838-1200
Rome (G-14811)		
Hicksville Machine Works Corp	F	516 931-1524
Hicksville (G-6355)		
HSM Machine Works Inc	E	631 924-6600
Medford (G-8250)		
Jac Usa Inc	G	212 841-7430
New York (G-10685)		
Jamco Aerospace Inc	E	631 586-7900
Deer Park (G-4156)		
Jaquith Industries Inc	E	315 478-5700
Syracuse (G-15966)		
Joldeson One Aerospace Inds	D	718 848-7396
Ozone Park (G-13380)		
Loar Group Inc	C	212 210-9348
New York (G-11018)		
Magellan Aerospace NY Inc	C	718 699-4000
Corona (G-4001)		
Magellan Aerospace NY Inc	C	631 589-2440
Bohemia (G-1099)		
MD International Industries	E	631 254-3100
Deer Park (G-4173)		
Metal Dynamics Intl Corp	G	631 231-1153
Hauppauge (G-6134)		
Milex Precision Inc	F	631 595-2393
Bay Shore (G-718)		
Min-Max Machine Ltd	F	631 585-4378
Ronkonkoma (G-14943)		
Minutemen Precsn McHning Tool	E	631 467-4900
Ronkonkoma (G-14944)		
Moog Inc	A	716 652-2000
Elma (G-4651)		
Nassau Tool Works Inc	E	631 643-0420
West Babylon (G-16815)		
Omega Industries & Development	F	516 349-8010
Plainview (G-13625)		
Parker-Hannifin Corporation	C	631 231-3737
Clyde (G-3730)		
Precision Cnc	G	631 847-3999
Deer Park (G-4191)		
Ripi Corp Co Inc	F	631 694-2453
Farmingdale (G-5100)		
S & L Aerospace Metals LLC	D	718 326-1821
Flushing (G-5289)		
Santa Fe Manufacturing Corp	G	631 234-0100
Hauppauge (G-6183)		
Servotronics Inc	C	716 655-5990
Elma (G-4655)		
Styles Aviation Inc	E	845 677-8185
Lagrangeville (G-7259)		
Sumner Industries Inc	F	631 666-7290
Bay Shore (G-749)		
Tangent Machine & Tool Corp	E	631 249-3088
Farmingdale (G-5124)		
Tdl Manufacturing Inc	F	215 538-8820
Hauppauge (G-6208)		
Tens Machine Company Inc	E	631 981-0490
Holbrook (G-6478)		
TPC Inc	G	315 438-8605
East Syracuse (G-4572)		
Triumph Actuation Systems LLC	D	516 378-0162
Freeport (G-5432)		
Vosky Precision Machining Corp	F	631 737-3200
Ronkonkoma (G-15000)		
Young & Franklin Inc	D	315 457-3110
Liverpool (G-7559)		

AIRCRAFT SEATS

Company	Code	Phone
B/E Aerospace Inc	E	631 563-6400
Bohemia (G-1022)		
B/E Aerospace Inc	C	631 589-0877
Bohemia (G-1023)		
East/West Industries Inc	E	631 981-5900
Ronkonkoma (G-14896)		
Readyjet Technical Svcs Inc	F	518 705-4019
Johnstown (G-7124)		

AIRCRAFT: Airplanes, Fixed Or Rotary Wing

Company	Code	Phone
Boeing Company	A	201 259-9400
New York (G-9434)		

AIRCRAFT: Gliders

Company	Code	Phone
M & H Research and Dev Corp	G	607 734-2346
Beaver Dams (G-793)		

AIRCRAFT: Motorized

Company	Code	Phone
Drone Usa Inc	G	212 220-8795
New York (G-9930)		
Lockheed Martin Corporation	E	716 297-1000
Niagara Falls (G-12844)		

AIRCRAFT: Research & Development, Manufacturer

Company	Code	Phone
Alliant Tchsystems Oprtons LLC	E	631 737-6100
Ronkonkoma (G-14863)		
Atk Gasl Inc	F	631 737-6100
Ronkonkoma (G-14874)		
Calspan Corporation	C	716 631-6955
Buffalo (G-2864)		
Calspan Corporation	E	716 236-1040
Niagara Falls (G-12800)		
Luminati Aerospace LLC	F	631 574-2616
Calverton (G-3293)		

ALARM SYSTEMS WHOLESALERS

Company	Code	Phone
Lifewatch Inc	F	800 716-1433
Hewlett (G-6310)		

ALARMS: Burglar

Company	Code	Phone
Alarm Controls Corporation	E	631 586-4220
Deer Park (G-4090)		
Datasonic Inc	G	516 248-7330
East Meadow (G-4421)		
Harris Corporation	A	413 263-6200
Rochester (G-14425)		
Sentry Devices Corp	G	631 491-3191
Dix Hills (G-4298)		
Unitone Communication Systems	G	212 777-9090
New York (G-12468)		

ALARMS: Fire

Company	Code	Phone
Fire Apparatus Service Tech	G	716 753-3538
Sherman (G-15402)		

ALKALIES & CHLORINE

Company	Code	Phone
Chemours Company Fc LLC	E	716 278-5100
Niagara Falls (G-12804)		
Occidental Chemical Corp	E	716 278-7795
Niagara Falls (G-12855)		
Occidental Chemical Corp	E	716 773-8100
Grand Island (G-5765)		
Occidental Chemical Corp	C	716 278-7794
Niagara Falls (G-12856)		
Olin Chlor Alkali Logistics	C	716 278-6411
Niagara Falls (G-12857)		

PRODUCT SECTION

ALKALOIDS & OTHER BOTANICAL BASED PRDTS
Bio-Botanica Inc .... D 631 231-0987
  Hauppauge *(G-6034)*

ALLERGENS & ALLERGENIC EXTRACTS
Nelco Laboratories Inc .... E 631 242-0082
  Deer Park *(G-4178)*

ALTERNATORS & GENERATORS: Battery Charging
ARC Systems Inc .... E 631 582-8020
  Hauppauge *(G-6023)*

ALTERNATORS: Automotive
Con Rel Auto Electric Inc .... E 518 356-1646
  Schenectady *(G-15245)*
Eastern Unit Exch Rmnfacturing .... F 718 739-7113
  Floral Park *(G-5203)*
Prestolite Electric Inc .... C 585 492-2278
  Arcade *(G-399)*

ALUMINUM
Alcoa Inc .... D 212 836-2674
  New York *(G-9077)*
Greene Brass & Alum Fndry LLC ...... G 607 656-4204
  Bloomville *(G-996)*

ALUMINUM ORE MINING
American Douglas Metals Inc .... F 716 856-3170
  Buffalo *(G-2807)*

ALUMINUM PRDTS
A-Fab Initiatives Inc .... G 716 877-5257
  Buffalo *(G-2793)*
Alumi-Tech LLC .... G 585 663-7010
  Penfield *(G-13497)*
Amt Incorporated .... E 518 284-2910
  Sharon Springs *(G-15383)*
Constellium .... E 212 675-5087
  New York *(G-9708)*
Flagpoles Incorporated .... D 631 751-5500
  East Setauket *(G-4483)*
Itts Industrial Inc .... G 718 605-6934
  Staten Island *(G-15690)*
J Sussman Inc .... E 718 297-0228
  Jamaica *(G-6922)*
Keymark Corporation .... A 518 853-3421
  Fonda *(G-5316)*
Minitec Framing Systems LLC .... F 585 924-4690
  Victor *(G-16491)*
North Coast Outfitters Ltd .... E 631 727-5580
  Riverhead *(G-14150)*
Pioneer Window Holdings Inc .... E 518 762-5526
  Johnstown *(G-7122)*
Swiss Tool Corporation .... E 631 842-7766
  Copiague *(G-3931)*

ALUMINUM: Rolling & Drawing
N A Alumil Corporation .... G 718 355-9393
  Long Island City *(G-7819)*
Novelis Inc .... F 315 349-0121
  Oswego *(G-13339)*

AMMONIUM NITRATE OR AMMONIUM SULFATE
Ocip Holding LLC .... G 646 589-6180
  New York *(G-11495)*

AMMUNITION
Circor Aerospace Inc .... D 631 737-1900
  Hauppauge *(G-6045)*

AMMUNITION: Components
CIC International Ltd .... D 212 213-0089
  Brooklyn *(G-1779)*

AMMUNITION: Pellets & BB's, Pistol & Air Rifle
Benjamin Sheridan Corporation .... G 585 657-6161
  Bloomfield *(G-981)*

Crosman Corporation .... E 585 657-6161
  Bloomfield *(G-986)*
Crosman Corporation .... E 585 398-3920
  Farmington *(G-5148)*

AMMUNITION: Small Arms
CIC International Ltd .... D 212 213-0089
  Brooklyn *(G-1779)*

AMPLIFIERS
Aguilar Amplification LLC .... F 212 431-9109
  New York *(G-9060)*
Amplitech Group Inc .... G 631 521-7831
  Bohemia *(G-1015)*
Broadcast Manager Inc .... G 212 509-1200
  New York *(G-9465)*
Ilab America Inc .... G 631 615-5053
  Selden *(G-15352)*

AMPLIFIERS: Parametric
Electronics & Innovation Ltd .... F 585 214-0598
  Rochester *(G-14344)*

AMPLIFIERS: Pulse Amplifiers
AMP-Line Corp .... F 845 623-3288
  West Nyack *(G-16910)*

AMPLIFIERS: RF & IF Power
B & H Electronics Corp .... E 845 782-5000
  Monroe *(G-8549)*
Communication Power Corp .... E 631 434-7306
  Hauppauge *(G-6051)*
Instruments For Industry Inc .... E 631 467-8400
  Ronkonkoma *(G-14913)*
Mks Medical Electronics .... C 585 292-7400
  Rochester *(G-14518)*
Srtech Industry Corp .... E 718 496-7001
  Oakland Gardens *(G-13068)*

AMUSEMENT & RECREATION SVCS: Amusement Ride
Billy Beez Usa LLC .... F 315 741-5099
  Syracuse *(G-15869)*
Billy Beez Usa LLC .... F 646 606-2249
  New York *(G-9399)*
Billy Beez Usa LLC .... F 845 915-4709
  West Nyack *(G-16913)*

AMUSEMENT & RECREATION SVCS: Art Gallery, Commercial
Pace Editions Inc .... E 212 421-3237
  New York *(G-11549)*

AMUSEMENT & RECREATION SVCS: Arts & Crafts Instruction
Donne Dieu .... G 212 226-0573
  New York *(G-9905)*

AMUSEMENT & RECREATION SVCS: Exposition Operation
Family Publications Ltd .... F 212 947-2177
  New York *(G-10133)*

AMUSEMENT & RECREATION SVCS: Game Machines
Mission Crane Service Inc .... D 718 937-3333
  Long Island City *(G-7814)*

AMUSEMENT & RECREATION SVCS: Golf Club, Membership
Dolomite Products Company Inc .... E 315 524-1998
  Rochester *(G-14316)*

AMUSEMENT & RECREATION SVCS: Gun Club, Membership
Michael Britt Inc .... G 516 248-2010
  Mineola *(G-8525)*

AMUSEMENT & RECREATION SVCS: Physical Fitness Instruction
Playfitness Corp .... G 917 497-5443
  Staten Island *(G-15722)*

AMUSEMENT & RECREATION SVCS: Tennis & Professionals
Paddock Chevrolet Golf Dome .... E 716 504-4059
  Tonawanda *(G-16191)*

AMUSEMENT MACHINES: Coin Operated
Mission Crane Service Inc .... D 718 937-3333
  Long Island City *(G-7814)*

AMUSEMENT PARK DEVICES & RIDES
Lakeside Industries Inc .... F 716 386-3031
  Bemus Point *(G-844)*
Macro Tool & Machine Company .... G 845 223-3824
  Lagrangeville *(G-7255)*

ANALGESICS
Spirit Pharmaceuticals LLC .... G 215 943-4000
  Centereach *(G-3473)*
Wyeth LLC .... A 973 660-5000
  New York *(G-12671)*

ANALYZERS: Moisture
Phymetrix Inc .... G 631 627-3950
  Medford *(G-8257)*

ANALYZERS: Network
Cgw Corp .... G 631 472-6600
  Bayport *(G-756)*
Everest Bbn Inc .... F 212 268-7979
  New York *(G-10091)*
Gcns Technology Group Inc .... F 347 713-8160
  Brooklyn *(G-2017)*
International Insurance Soc .... G 212 815-9291
  New York *(G-10636)*

ANESTHESIA EQPT
Gradian Health Systems Inc .... G 212 537-0340
  New York *(G-10345)*
Omnicare Anesthesia PC .... E 718 433-0044
  Astoria *(G-452)*

ANESTHETICS: Bulk Form
Ucb Pharma Inc .... B 919 767-2555
  Rochester *(G-14739)*

ANIMAL FEED & SUPPLEMENTS: Livestock & Poultry
Archer-Daniels-Midland Company ..... D 716 849-7333
  Buffalo *(G-2819)*
Bailey Boonville Mills Inc .... G 315 942-2131
  Boonville *(G-1162)*
Baker Commodities Inc .... E 585 482-1880
  Rochester *(G-14222)*
Cargill Incorporated .... E 315 622-3533
  Liverpool *(G-7515)*
Central Garden & Pet Company .... G 631 451-8021
  Selden *(G-15349)*
Central Garden & Pet Company .... G 212 877-1270
  New York *(G-9564)*
J & M Feed Corporation .... G 631 281-2152
  Shirley *(G-15421)*
Kent Nutrition Group Inc .... F 315 788-0032
  Watertown *(G-16658)*
Lowville Farmers Coop Inc .... E 315 376-6587
  Lowville *(G-7939)*
Narrowsburg Feed & Grain Co .... F 845 252-3936
  Narrowsburg *(G-8768)*
Pace Manufacturing Company .... G 607 936-0431
  Painted Post *(G-13392)*
Scotts Feed Inc .... E 518 483-3110
  Malone *(G-8015)*
Southern States Coop Inc .... F 315 438-4500
  East Syracuse *(G-4566)*

ANIMAL FEED: Wholesalers
Kelley Farm & Garden Inc .... E 518 234-2332
  Cobleskill *(G-3738)*

ANIMAL FEED: Wholesalers

Pace Manufacturing Company ....G....... 607 936-0431
  Painted Post *(G-13392)*
Scotts Feed Inc ....E....... 518 483-3110
  Malone *(G-8015)*

ANIMAL FOOD & SUPPLEMENTS: Bird Food, Prepared

Heath Manufacturing Company ....G....... 800 444-3140
  Batavia *(G-638)*
Pine Tree Farms Inc ....E....... 607 532-4312
  Interlaken *(G-6749)*
Wagners LLC ....G....... 516 933-6580
  Jericho *(G-7090)*

ANIMAL FOOD & SUPPLEMENTS: Dog

Dog Good Products LLC ....G....... 212 789-7000
  New York *(G-9895)*
Robert Abady Dog Food Co Ltd ....F....... 845 473-1900
  Poughkeepsie *(G-13928)*
Scooby Rendering & Inc ....G....... 315 793-1014
  Utica *(G-16358)*

ANIMAL FOOD & SUPPLEMENTS: Dog & Cat

Colgate-Palmolive Company ....A....... 212 310-2000
  New York *(G-9667)*
Hills Pet Products Inc ....G....... 212 310-2000
  New York *(G-10477)*
Hound & Gatos Pet Foods Corp ....G....... 212 618-1917
  New York *(G-10517)*
Nestle Purina Petcare Company ....B....... 716 366-8080
  Dunkirk *(G-4345)*
Pet Proteins LLC ....G....... 888 293-1029
  New York *(G-11629)*

ANIMAL FOOD & SUPPLEMENTS: Feed Concentrates

Gramco Inc ....G....... 716 592-2845
  Springville *(G-15611)*

ANIMAL FOOD & SUPPLEMENTS: Feed Premixes

Commodity Resource Corporation ....F....... 585 538-9500
  Caledonia *(G-3278)*

ANIMAL FOOD & SUPPLEMENTS: Feed Supplements

Veterinary Biochemical Ltd ....G....... 845 473-1900
  Poughkeepsie *(G-13939)*

ANIMAL FOOD & SUPPLEMENTS: Mineral feed supplements

Nutra-Vet Research Corp ....F....... 845 473-1900
  Poughkeepsie *(G-13923)*

ANIMAL FOOD & SUPPLEMENTS: Pet, Exc Dog & Cat, Canned

Grandma Maes Cntry Nturals LLC ....G....... 212 348-8171
  New York *(G-10350)*

ANIMAL FOOD & SUPPLEMENTS: Poultry

Cochecton Mills Inc ....E....... 845 932-8282
  Cochecton *(G-3740)*

ANODIZING SVC

Able Anodizing Corp ....F....... 718 252-0660
  Brooklyn *(G-1548)*
C H Thompson Company Inc ....D....... 607 724-1094
  Binghamton *(G-901)*
Fallon Inc ....E....... 718 326-7226
  Maspeth *(G-8138)*
Keymark Corporation ....A....... 518 853-3421
  Fonda *(G-5316)*
P3 Technologies ....G....... 585 730-7340
  Rochester *(G-14565)*
Tru-Tone Metal Products Inc ....E....... 718 386-5960
  Brooklyn *(G-2686)*
Utica Metal Products Inc ....D....... 315 732-6163
  Utica *(G-16364)*

ANTENNAS: Radar Or Communications

B & Z Technologies LLC ....G....... 631 675-9666
  East Setauket *(G-4477)*
Gryphon Sensors LLC ....F....... 315 452-8810
  North Syracuse *(G-12946)*
Srctec LLC ....C....... 315 452-8700
  Syracuse *(G-16044)*

ANTENNAS: Receiving

901 D LLC ....E....... 845 369-1111
  Airmont *(G-11)*
Ampro International Inc ....G....... 845 278-4910
  Brewster *(G-1210)*
Russell Industries Inc ....F....... 516 536-5000
  Lynbrook *(G-7960)*

ANTIBIOTICS

G C Hanford Manufacturing Co ....C....... 315 476-7418
  Syracuse *(G-15946)*
Pfizer Inc ....A....... 212 733-2323
  New York *(G-11636)*
Pfizer Overseas LLC ....G....... 212 733-2323
  New York *(G-11641)*

ANTIBIOTICS, PACKAGED

Durata Therapeutics Inc ....G....... 646 871-6400
  New York *(G-9940)*

ANTIFREEZE

BASF Corporation ....B....... 914 785-2000
  Tarrytown *(G-16087)*
Bass Oil Company Inc ....E....... 718 628-4444
  Brooklyn *(G-1672)*
Fppf Chemical Co Inc ....G....... 716 856-9607
  Buffalo *(G-2954)*

ANTIQUE FURNITURE RESTORATION & REPAIR

Irony Limited Inc ....G....... 631 329-4065
  East Hampton *(G-4411)*
Nicholas Dfine Furn Decorators ....F....... 914 245-8982
  Bronx *(G-1411)*

ANTIQUE REPAIR & RESTORATION SVCS, EXC FURNITURE & AUTOS

A W R Group Inc ....F....... 718 729-0412
  Long Island City *(G-7644)*

ANTIQUE SHOPS

American Country Quilts & Lin ....G....... 631 283-5466
  Southampton *(G-15538)*
Blanche P Field LLC ....E....... 212 355-6616
  New York *(G-9412)*

APPAREL ACCESS STORES

Nazim Izzak Inc ....G....... 212 920-5546
  Long Island City *(G-7821)*
Nine West Footwear Corporation ....B....... 800 999-1877
  New York *(G-11435)*

APPAREL DESIGNERS: Commercial

Arteast LLC ....G....... 212 965-8787
  New York *(G-9216)*
Dianos Kathryn Designs ....G....... 212 267-1584
  New York *(G-9874)*
Fashion Deli Inc ....F....... 818 772-5637
  New York *(G-10144)*

APPAREL FILLING MATERIALS: Cotton Waste, Kapok/Related Matl

Return Textiles LLC ....G....... 646 408-0108
  New York *(G-11847)*

APPAREL: Hand Woven

Jeans Inc ....G....... 646 223-1122
  New York *(G-10717)*

APPLIANCE CORDS: Household Electrical Eqpt

All Shore Industries Inc ....F....... 718 720-0018
  Staten Island *(G-15634)*

APPLIANCES, HOUSEHOLD: Kitchen, Major, Exc Refrigs & Stoves

Ajmadison Corp ....D....... 718 532-1800
  Brooklyn *(G-1573)*
Barrage ....E....... 212 586-9390
  New York *(G-9324)*
Design Solutions LI Inc ....G....... 631 656-8700
  Saint James *(G-15088)*
Hobart Corporation ....E....... 631 864-3440
  Commack *(G-3835)*
Marine Park Appliances LLC ....G....... 718 513-1808
  Brooklyn *(G-2271)*

APPLIANCES, HOUSEHOLD: Refrigerator Cabinets, Metal Or Wood

Ae Fund Inc ....E....... 315 698-7650
  Brewerton *(G-1202)*

APPLIANCES, HOUSEHOLD: Refrigs, Mechanical & Absorption

General Electric Company ....A....... 518 385-4022
  Schenectady *(G-15257)*

APPLIANCES, HOUSEHOLD: Sewing Machines & Attchmnts, Domestic

Jado Sewing Machines Inc ....E....... 718 784-2314
  Long Island City *(G-7770)*

APPLIANCES: Household, Refrigerators & Freezers

Acme Kitchenettes Corp ....E....... 518 828-4191
  Hudson *(G-6604)*
Dover Corporation ....G....... 212 922-1640
  New York *(G-9911)*
Felix Storch Inc ....C....... 718 893-3900
  Bronx *(G-1329)*
Robin Industries Ltd ....F....... 718 218-9616
  Brooklyn *(G-2501)*
Sure-Kol Refrigerator Co Inc ....F....... 718 625-0601
  Brooklyn *(G-2633)*

APPLIANCES: Major, Cooking

Applince Installation Svc Corp ....E....... 716 884-7425
  Buffalo *(G-2818)*
Bakers Pride Oven Co Inc ....C....... 914 576-0200
  New Rochelle *(G-8887)*
Oxo International Inc ....C....... 212 242-3333
  New York *(G-11544)*

APPLIANCES: Small, Electric

Algonquin Power ....G....... 315 393-5595
  Ogdensburg *(G-13110)*
Fulton Volcanic Inc ....D....... 315 298-5121
  Pulaski *(G-13950)*
General Elc Capitl Svcs Inc ....G....... 315 554-2000
  Skaneateles *(G-15461)*
Royal Line LLC ....F....... 800 516-7450
  Wantagh *(G-16563)*
Schlesinger Siemans Elec LLC ....F....... 718 386-6230
  New York *(G-11989)*
Tactica International Inc ....F....... 212 575-0500
  New York *(G-12271)*
Uniware Houseware Corp ....F....... 631 242-7400
  Brentwood *(G-1198)*

APPLICATIONS SOFTWARE PROGRAMMING

Galaxy Software LLC ....G....... 631 244-8405
  Oakdale *(G-13058)*
Maven Marketing LLC ....G....... 615 510-3248
  New York *(G-11183)*

AQUARIUM ACCESS, METAL

Aquarium Pump & Piping Systems ....F....... 631 567-5555
  Sayville *(G-15203)*

AQUARIUM DESIGN & MAINTENANCE SVCS

C B Management Services Inc ....F....... 845 735-2300
  Pearl River *(G-13455)*

PRODUCT SECTION

AQUARIUMS & ACCESS: Glass
C B Management Services Inc............F...... 845 735-2300
Pearl River *(G-13455)*

AQUARIUMS & ACCESS: Plastic
Aquarium Pump & Piping Systems......F...... 631 567-5555
Sayville *(G-15203)*
Eugene G Danner Mfg Inc................E...... 631 234-5261
Central Islip *(G-3495)*

ARCHITECTURAL SVCS
B & F Architectural Support Gr............E...... 212 279-6488
New York *(G-9287)*
Deerfield Millwork Inc.........................F...... 631 726-9663
Water Mill *(G-16604)*
George G Sharp Inc.............................E...... 212 732-2800
New York *(G-10281)*
Productand Design Inc........................F...... 718 858-2440
Brooklyn *(G-2452)*

ARMATURE REPAIRING & REWINDING SVC
Auburn Armature Inc..........................E...... 585 426-4607
Rochester *(G-14218)*
Ener-G-Rotors Inc................................G...... 518 372-2608
Schenectady *(G-15250)*
Sunset Ridge Holdings Inc.................G...... 716 487-1458
Jamestown *(G-7034)*

AROMATIC CHEMICAL PRDTS
C & A Service Inc.................................G...... 516 354-1200
Floral Park *(G-5197)*
Citrus and Allied Essences Ltd...........E...... 516 354-1200
Floral Park *(G-5200)*

ART & ORNAMENTAL WARE: Pottery
American Country Quilts & Lin...........G...... 631 283-5466
Southampton *(G-15538)*

ART DEALERS & GALLERIES
Frame Shoppe & Art Gallery................G...... 516 365-6014
Manhasset *(G-8060)*
Marian Goodman Gallery Inc.............E...... 212 977-7160
New York *(G-11149)*
Penhouse Media Group Inc................C...... 212 702-6000
New York *(G-11607)*

ART DESIGN SVCS
Adflex Corporation...............................E...... 585 454-2950
Rochester *(G-14173)*
Dwm International Inc........................F...... 646 290-7448
Long Island City *(G-7721)*
Graphics Plus Printing Inc..................E...... 607 299-0500
Cortland *(G-4029)*

ART GOODS & SPLYS WHOLESALERS
Gei International Inc............................E...... 315 463-9261
East Syracuse *(G-4533)*
Golden Group International Ltd.........G...... 845 440-1025
Patterson *(G-13440)*

ART MARBLE: Concrete
Fordham Marble Co Inc.......................F...... 914 682-6699
White Plains *(G-17110)*
Milano Granite and Marble Corp........F...... 718 477-7200
Staten Island *(G-15706)*
Royal Marble & Granite Inc................G...... 516 536-5900
Oceanside *(G-13094)*

ART NEEDLEWORK, MADE FROM PURCHASED MATERIALS
Clpa Embroidery...................................G...... 516 409-0002
Bellmore *(G-816)*
Jomar Industries Inc............................E...... 845 357-5773
Airmont *(G-16)*
Knucklehead Embroidery Inc..............G...... 607 797-2725
Johnson City *(G-7098)*
Screen The World Inc..........................F...... 631 475-0023
Holtsville *(G-6508)*
Verdonette Inc.......................................G...... 212 719-2003
New York *(G-12521)*

ART RELATED SVCS
Halo Associates.....................................G...... 212 691-9549
New York *(G-10399)*

ART RESTORATION SVC
Julius Lowy Frame Restoring Co.........E...... 212 861-8585
New York *(G-10785)*
Sunburst Studios Inc............................G...... 718 768-6360
Brooklyn *(G-2620)*

ART SPLY STORES
Simon Liu Inc..F...... 718 567-2011
Brooklyn *(G-2560)*

ARTISTS' EQPT
Simon Liu Inc..F...... 718 567-2011
Brooklyn *(G-2560)*
Spaulding & Rogers Mfg Inc...............D...... 518 768-2070
Voorheesville *(G-16518)*

ARTISTS' MATERIALS, WHOLESALE
R & F Handmade Paints Inc................F...... 845 331-3112
Kingston *(G-7207)*

ARTISTS' MATERIALS: Canvas Board
Tri Mar Enterprises Inc........................G...... 718 418-3644
Brooklyn *(G-2676)*

ARTISTS' MATERIALS: Frames, Artists' Canvases
Clapper Hollow Designs Inc................E...... 518 234-9561
Cobleskill *(G-3734)*
Frames Plus Inc....................................F...... 518 462-1842
Menands *(G-8371)*
Handmade Frames Inc.........................F...... 718 782-8364
Brooklyn *(G-2067)*
Lopez Restorations Inc........................F...... 718 383-1555
Brooklyn *(G-2235)*

ARTISTS' MATERIALS: Ink, Drawing, Black & Colored
Sml Brothers Holding Corp..................D...... 718 402-2000
Bronx *(G-1457)*

ARTISTS' MATERIALS: Paints, Exc Gold & Bronze
Golden Artist Colors Inc......................C...... 607 847-6154
New Berlin *(G-8780)*

ARTISTS' MATERIALS: Pastels
North America Pastel Artists...............G...... 718 463-4701
Flushing *(G-5274)*

ARTISTS' MATERIALS: Pencils & Leads
Gotham Pen Co Inc...............................E...... 212 675-7904
Yonkers *(G-17449)*

ARTISTS' MATERIALS: Wax
Micro Powders Inc................................E...... 914 332-6400
Tarrytown *(G-16097)*

ARTWORK: Framed
Handmade Frames Inc.........................F...... 718 782-8364
Brooklyn *(G-2067)*
McGaw Group LLC.................................F...... 212 876-8822
New York *(G-11197)*

ASBESTOS PRODUCTS
Regional MGT & Consulting Inc..........F...... 718 599-3718
Brooklyn *(G-2487)*

ASPHALT & ASPHALT PRDTS
A Colarusso and Son Inc.....................E...... 518 828-3218
Hudson *(G-6603)*
Amfar Asphalt Corp..............................G...... 631 269-9660
Kings Park *(G-7169)*
Atlas Bituminous Co Inc......................F...... 315 457-2394
Syracuse *(G-15860)*
Barrett Paving Materials Inc................ 315 737-9471
Clayville *(G-3686)*
C & C Ready-Mix Corporation.............E...... 607 797-5108
Vestal *(G-16443)*
Callanan Industries Inc.......................E...... 845 457-3158
Montgomery *(G-8592)*
Cobleskill Stone Products Inc.............F...... 607 432-8321
Oneonta *(G-13180)*
Cobleskill Stone Products Inc.............F...... 607 637-4271
Hancock *(G-5962)*
Cosmicoat of Wny Inc..........................G...... 716 772-2644
Gasport *(G-5556)*
Graymont Materials (ny) Inc...............D...... 518 561-5321
Plattsburgh *(G-13665)*
Hanson Aggregates PA LLC.................E...... 585 624-3800
Honeoye Falls *(G-6529)*
King Road Materials Inc......................E...... 518 381-9995
Schenectady *(G-15273)*
King Road Materials Inc......................F...... 518 382-5354
Schenectady *(G-15274)*
Northern Bituminous Mix Inc............G...... 315 598-2141
Fulton *(G-5472)*
Parks Paving & Sealing Inc.................F...... 315 737-5761
Sauquoit *(G-15201)*
Peckham Materials Corp.....................D...... 914 686-2045
White Plains *(G-17149)*
Posillico Materials LLC........................F...... 631 249-1872
Farmingdale *(G-5084)*
Rason Asphalt Inc.................................G...... 516 239-7880
Lawrence *(G-7398)*
Suit-Kote Corporation..........................C...... 607 753-1100
Cortland *(G-4046)*
Suit-Kote Corporation..........................E...... 585 473-6321
Rochester *(G-14706)*
Suit-Kote Corporation..........................E...... 716 664-3750
Jamestown *(G-7033)*
Vestal Asphalt Inc.................................F...... 607 785-3393
Vestal *(G-16456)*

ASPHALT COATINGS & SEALERS
Barrett Paving Materials Inc...............E...... 315 353-6611
Norwood *(G-13040)*
Callanan Industries Inc.......................E...... 845 457-3158
Montgomery *(G-8592)*
Peckham Materials Corp.....................E...... 518 747-3353
Hudson Falls *(G-6649)*
Sheldon Slate Products Co Inc...........E...... 518 642-1280
Middle Granville *(G-8401)*
Suit-Kote Corporation..........................E...... 607 535-2743
Watkins Glen *(G-16697)*
Tntpaving..G...... 607 372-4911
Endicott *(G-4831)*

ASPHALT MIXTURES WHOLESALERS
A Colarusso and Son Inc.....................E...... 518 828-3218
Hudson *(G-6603)*
County Line Stone Co Inc....................E...... 716 542-5435
Akron *(G-21)*
Hanson Aggregates PA LLC.................E...... 585 624-1220
Honeoye Falls *(G-6530)*
Suit-Kote Corporation..........................E...... 585 473-6321
Rochester *(G-14706)*

ASPHALT PLANTS INCLUDING GRAVEL MIX TYPE
Midland Machinery Co Inc..................D...... 716 692-1200
Tonawanda *(G-16181)*
Patterson Blacktop Corp......................G...... 845 628-3425
Carmel *(G-3403)*
Peckham Materials Corp.....................E...... 518 747-3353
Hudson Falls *(G-6649)*
Penn Can Equipment Corporation.....G...... 315 378-0337
Lyons *(G-7974)*
Rochester Asphalt Materials............... 315 524-4619
Walworth *(G-16551)*

ASSEMBLING SVC: Clocks
M & Co Ltd..G...... 212 414-6400
New York *(G-11067)*

ASSEMBLING SVC: Plumbing Fixture Fittings, Plastic
Mark Posner..G...... 718 258-6241
Brooklyn *(G-2272)*

ASSOCIATIONS: Engineering
American Inst Chem Engineers...........D...... 646 495-1355
New York *(G-9121)*

Employee Codes: A=Over 500 employees, B=251-500
C=101-250, D=51-100, E=20-50, F=10-19, G=5-9

ASSOCIATIONS: Scientists'

Association For Cmpt McHy Inc ....D 212 869-7440
New York *(G-9240)*

ATOMIZERS

Aloi Solutions LLC 585 292-0920
Rochester *(G-14192)*
Ascribe Inc ....E 585 413-0298
Rochester *(G-14216)*
Avanti Advanced Mfg Corp ....G 716 541-8945
Buffalo *(G-2826)*
Boom LLC ....E 646 218-0752
New York *(G-9438)*
Chan & Chan (usa) Corp ....G 718 388-9633
Brooklyn *(G-1773)*
Christian Dior Perfumes LLC ....E 212 931-2200
New York *(G-9610)*
Deva Concepts LLC ....E 212 343-0344
New York *(G-9864)*
Givi Inc ....E 212 586-5029
New York *(G-10303)*
Hoskie Co Inc ....D 718 628-8672
Brooklyn *(G-2088)*
Mitten Manufacturing Inc ....E 315 437-7564
Syracuse *(G-15992)*
Shyam Ahuja Limited 212 644-5910
New York *(G-12057)*

ATTENUATORS

Mini-Circuits Fort Wayne LLC ....B 718 934-4500
Brooklyn *(G-2318)*

AUDIO & VIDEO EQPT, EXC COMMERCIAL

Accent Speaker Technology Ltd ....G 631 738-2540
Holbrook *(G-6429)*
All In Audio Inc ....F 718 506-0948
Brooklyn *(G-1586)*
Audio Video Invasion Inc ....F 516 345-2636
Plainview *(G-13583)*
Audiosavings Inc ....F 888 445-1555
Inwood *(G-6752)*
Avcom of Virginia Inc ....D 585 924-4560
Victor *(G-16461)*
AVI-Spl Employee ....B 212 840-4801
New York *(G-9277)*
B & H Electronics Corp ....E 845 782-5000
Monroe *(G-8549)*
Communication Power Corp ....E 631 434-7306
Hauppauge *(G-6051)*
Digital Home Creations Inc ....G 585 576-7070
Webster *(G-16721)*
G E Inspection Technologies LP ....C 315 554-2000
Skaneateles *(G-15460)*
General Elc Capitl Svcs Inc ....G 315 554-2000
Skaneateles *(G-15461)*
Harman International Inds Inc ....C 516 496-3400
Woodbury *(G-17289)*
Key Digital Systems Inc ....E 914 667-9700
Mount Vernon *(G-8697)*
L-3 Communications Corporation .....A 631 436-7400
Hauppauge *(G-6108)*
Laird Telemedia ....C 845 339-9555
Mount Marion *(G-8650)*
Masterdisk Corporation ....F 212 541-5022
Elmsford *(G-4764)*
Navitar Inc ....D 585 359-4000
Rochester *(G-14530)*
NEa Manufacturing Corp ....E 516 371-4200
Inwood *(G-6763)*
New Audio LLC ....E 212 213-6060
New York *(G-11379)*
New Wop Records ....G 631 617-9732
Deer Park *(G-4179)*
Sima Technologies LLC ....G 412 828-9130
Hauppauge *(G-6191)*
Sony Corporation of America ....C 212 833-8000
New York *(G-12132)*
Sound Video Systems Wny LLC ....F 716 684-8200
Buffalo *(G-3194)*
Tkm Technologies Inc ....G 631 474-4700
Port Jeff STA *(G-13773)*
Touchtunes Music Corporation ....G 847 419-3300
New York *(G-12382)*
Wyrestorm Technologies LLC ....F 518 289-1293
Round Lake *(G-15039)*

AUDIO COMPONENTS

Ashly Audio Inc ....E 585 872-0010
Webster *(G-16713)*
Convergent Audio Tech Inc ....G 585 359-2700
Rush *(G-15046)*

AUDIO ELECTRONIC SYSTEMS

Audio Technology New York Inc ....F 718 369-7528
Brooklyn *(G-1653)*
B & K Components Ltd ....D 323 776-4277
Buffalo *(G-2829)*
Data Interchange Systems Inc ....G 914 277-7775
Purdys *(G-13972)*
Gilmores Sound Advice Inc ....F 212 265-4445
New York *(G-10297)*
Granada Electronics Inc ....G 718 387-1157
Brooklyn *(G-2047)*
Lamm Industries Inc ....G 718 368-0181
Brooklyn *(G-2193)*
Vincent Conigliaro ....F 845 340-0489
Kingston *(G-7224)*
Whirlwind Music Distrs Inc ....D 585 663-8820
Rochester *(G-14762)*
Yorkville Sound Inc ....G 716 297-2920
Niagara Falls *(G-12891)*

AUDIO-VISUAL PROGRAM PRODUCTION SVCS

ABRA Media Inc ....G 518 398-1010
Pine Plains *(G-13554)*
Guilford Publications Inc ....D 212 431-9800
New York *(G-10382)*
Hatherleigh Company Ltd ....G 607 538-1092
Hobart *(G-6425)*
Play-It Productions Inc ....F 212 695-6530
Port Washington *(G-13856)*

AUDIOLOGISTS' OFFICES

Family Hearing Center ....G 845 897-3059
Fishkill *(G-5184)*
Todt Hill Audiological Svcs ....G 718 816-1952
Staten Island *(G-15749)*

AUDITING SVCS

Advance Finance Group LLC ....D 212 630-5900
New York *(G-9035)*

AUTO & HOME SUPPLY STORES: Auto & Truck Eqpt & Parts

K M Drive Line Inc ....G 718 599-0628
Brooklyn *(G-2164)*

AUTO & HOME SUPPLY STORES: Automotive Access

Legendary Auto Interiors Ltd ....E 315 331-1212
Newark *(G-12734)*
Split Rock Trading Co Inc ....G 631 929-3261
Wading River *(G-16526)*
Zappala Farms AG Systems Inc ....E 315 626-6293
Cato *(G-3425)*

AUTO & HOME SUPPLY STORES: Speed Shops, Incl Race Car Splys

Auto Sport Designs Inc ....F 631 425-1555
Huntington Station *(G-6697)*
Marcovicci-Wenz Engineering ....G 631 467-9040
Ronkonkoma *(G-14938)*
Troyer Inc ....F 585 352-5590
Rochester *(G-14732)*

AUTO & HOME SUPPLY STORES: Trailer Hitches, Automotive

General Welding & Fabg Inc ....G 585 697-7660
Rochester *(G-14392)*

AUTO & HOME SUPPLY STORES: Truck Eqpt & Parts

Agri Services Co ....G 716 937-6618
Alden *(G-173)*
Chet Kruszkas Service Inc ....F 716 662-7450
Orchard Park *(G-13261)*
Dejana Trck Utility Eqp Co LLC ....C 631 544-9000
Kings Park *(G-7170)*
General Welding & Fabg Inc ....G 716 652-0033
Elma *(G-4649)*

AUTOCLAVES: Indl

Wsf Industries Inc ....E 716 692-4930
Tonawanda *(G-16216)*

AUTOCLAVES: Laboratory

SPS Medical Supply Corp ....F 585 968-2377
Cuba *(G-4070)*

AUTOMATIC REGULATING CONTROL: Building Svcs Monitoring, Auto

Building Management Assoc Inc 718 542-4779
Bronx *(G-1290)*
Johnson Controls Inc ....C 585 724-2232
Rochester *(G-14464)*
Unisend LLC ....G 585 414-9575
Webster *(G-16739)*
Virtual Super LLC 212 685-6400
New York *(G-12550)*

AUTOMATIC REGULATING CONTROLS: AC & Refrigeration

Bitzer Scroll Inc ....D 315 463-2101
Syracuse *(G-15870)*
Care Enterprises Inc 631 472-8155
Bayport *(G-755)*
Siemens Industry Inc ....D 716 568-0983
Amherst *(G-261)*

AUTOMATIC REGULATING CONTROLS: Elect Air Cleaner, Automatic

Biorem Environmental Inc ....E 585 924-2220
Victor *(G-16462)*

AUTOMATIC REGULATING CONTROLS: Energy Cutoff, Residtl/Comm

Black River Generations LLC ....E 315 773-2314
Fort Drum *(G-5338)*
Eastern Strategic Materials ....E 212 332-1619
New York *(G-9967)*
Johnson Controls Inc ....E 914 593-5200
Hawthorne *(G-6248)*

AUTOMATIC REGULATING CONTROLS: Ice Maker

Henderson Products Inc ....E 315 785-0994
Watertown *(G-16654)*

AUTOMATIC REGULATING CONTROLS: Pneumatic Relays, Air-Cond

A K Allen Co Inc ....C 516 747-5450
Mineola *(G-8488)*

AUTOMATIC REGULATING CONTROLS: Refrig/Air-Cond Defrost

Carrier Corporation ....B 315 432-6000
Syracuse *(G-15888)*
Svyz Trading Corp ....G 718 220-1140
Bronx *(G-1469)*

AUTOMATIC REGULATING CTRLS: Damper, Pneumatic Or Electric

Air Louver & Damper Inc ....E 718 392-3232
Maspeth *(G-8112)*
Air Louver & Damper Inc ....F 718 392-3232
Long Island City *(G-7649)*
Airflex Industrial Inc ....E 631 752-1234
Farmingdale *(G-4933)*

AUTOMATIC TELLER MACHINES

International Mdse Svcs Inc ....G 914 699-4000
Mount Vernon *(G-8693)*
Jpmorgan Chase Bank Nat Assn ......E 718 767-3592
College Point *(G-3793)*
Jpmorgan Chase Bank Nat Assn ......G 718 668-0346
Staten Island *(G-15695)*

PRODUCT SECTION

AUTOMOTIVE SPLYS & PARTS, NEW, WHOLESALE: Clutches

K&G of Syracuse Inc ....G........ 315 446-1921
   Syracuse *(G-15972)*
Mid Enterprise Inc ....G........ 631 924-3933
   Middle Island *(G-8407)*
Parabit Systems Inc ....E........ 516 378-4800
   Roosevelt *(G-15008)*
Sharenet Inc ....G........ 315 477-1100
   Syracuse *(G-16039)*
Stanson Automated LLC ....F........ 866 505-7826
   Yonkers *(G-17485)*

AUTOMATIC VENDING MACHINES: Mechanisms & Parts

Global Payment Tech Inc ....F........ 516 887-0700
   Valley Stream *(G-16407)*
Global Payment Tech Inc ....E........ 631 563-2500
   Bohemia *(G-1074)*
L & L Precision Machining ....F........ 631 462-9587
   East Northport *(G-4440)*

AUTOMOBILES: Off-Highway, Electric

Bombardier Trnsp Holdings USA ....D....... 607 776-4791
   Bath *(G-654)*

AUTOMOBILES: Wholesalers

Split Rock Trading Co Inc ....G........ 631 929-3261
   Wading River *(G-16526)*

AUTOMOTIVE & TRUCK GENERAL REPAIR SVC

Automotive Filters Mfg Inc ....F........ 631 435-1010
   Bohemia *(G-1020)*
Dennys Drive Shaft Service ....G........ 716 875-6640
   Kenmore *(G-7146)*
Homer Iron Works LLC ....G........ 607 749-3963
   Homer *(G-6519)*
James Woerner Inc ....G........ 631 454-9330
   Farmingdale *(G-5016)*
Whitesboro Spring & Alignment ....F........ 315 736-4441
   Whitesboro *(G-17198)*

AUTOMOTIVE BODY SHOP

Chet Kruszkas Service Inc ....F........ 716 662-7450
   Orchard Park *(G-13261)*
Nochem Paint Stripping Inc ....G........ 631 563-2750
   Blue Point *(G-999)*

AUTOMOTIVE BODY, PAINT & INTERIOR REPAIR & MAINTENANCE SVC

Conti Auto Body Corp ....G........ 516 921-6435
   Syosset *(G-15816)*

AUTOMOTIVE CUSTOMIZING SVCS, NONFACTORY BASIS

Apsis USA Inc ....F........ 631 421-6800
   Farmingdale *(G-4944)*

AUTOMOTIVE PARTS, ACCESS & SPLYS

Abasco Inc ....E........ 716 649-4790
   Hamburg *(G-5918)*
Allomatic Products Company ....G........ 516 775-0330
   Floral Park *(G-5192)*
Alloy Metal Products LLC ....F........ 315 676-2405
   Central Square *(G-3515)*
American Auto ACC Incrporation ....E........ 718 886-6600
   Flushing *(G-5226)*
American Engnred Cmponents Inc ....D....... 516 742-8386
   Carle Place *(G-3385)*
American Refuse Supply Inc ....G........ 718 893-8157
   Bronx *(G-1273)*
Anchor Commerce Trading Corp ....G........ 516 881-3485
   Atlantic Beach *(G-468)*
Apsis USA Inc ....F........ 631 421-6800
   Farmingdale *(G-4944)*
Automotive Accessories Group ....B........ 212 736-8100
   New York *(G-9268)*
Axle Express ....E........ 518 347-2220
   Schenectady *(G-15233)*
Bigbee Steel and Tank Company ....E........ 518 273-0501
   Watervliet *(G-16679)*
Borgwarner Inc ....E........ 607 257-1800
   Ithaca *(G-6824)*
Borgwarner Morse TEC Inc ....B........ 607 257-6700
   Ithaca *(G-6826)*
Borgwarner Morse TEC Inc ....D....... 607 266-5111
   Ithaca *(G-6827)*
Borgwarner Morse TEC Inc ....D....... 607 257-6700
   Cortland *(G-4015)*
Borgwarner Morse TEC Inc ....D....... 607 257-6700
   Ithaca *(G-6828)*
Car-Go Industries Inc ....G........ 718 472-1443
   Woodside *(G-17323)*
Classic & Performance Spc ....E........ 716 759-1800
   Lancaster *(G-7310)*
Cubic Trnsp Systems Inc ....F........ 212 255-1810
   New York *(G-9764)*
Cummins Inc ....A........ 716 456-2111
   Lakewood *(G-7290)*
Cummins Inc ....B........ 812 377-5000
   Jamestown *(G-6986)*
Custom Sitecom LLC ....F........ 631 420-4238
   Farmingdale *(G-4971)*
Delphi Automotive LLP ....G........ 716 438-4886
   Amherst *(G-237)*
Delphi Automotive Systems LLC ....C........ 585 359-6000
   West Henrietta *(G-16875)*
Delphi Automotive Systems LLC ....A........ 585 359-6000
   West Henrietta *(G-16876)*
Delphi Automotive Systems LLC ....E........ 585 359-6000
   West Henrietta *(G-16877)*
Delphi Thermal Systems ....F........ 716 439-2454
   Lockport *(G-7579)*
Dmic Inc ....F........ 716 743-4360
   North Tonawanda *(G-12969)*
Electronic Machine Parts LLC ....F........ 631 434-3700
   Hauppauge *(G-6070)*
Exten II LLC ....F........ 716 895-2214
   Buffalo *(G-2942)*
Fast By Gast Inc ....G........ 716 773-1536
   Grand Island *(G-5757)*
General Motors LLC ....B........ 315 764-2000
   Massena *(G-8195)*
GM Components Holdings LLC ....B........ 585 647-7000
   Rochester *(G-14410)*
GM Components Holdings LLC ....B........ 716 439-2463
   Lockport *(G-7590)*
ITT Enidine Inc ....B........ 716 662-1900
   Orchard Park *(G-13275)*
Jtekt Torsen North America ....F........ 585 464-5000
   Rochester *(G-14465)*
Karlyn Industries Inc ....F........ 845 351-2249
   Southfields *(G-15556)*
Kerns Manufacturing Corp ....C........ 718 784-4044
   Long Island City *(G-7780)*
Lee World Industries LLC ....C........ 212 265-8866
   New York *(G-10958)*
Magtrol Inc ....E........ 716 668-5555
   Buffalo *(G-3055)*
Mahle Behr USA Inc ....B........ 716 439-2011
   Lockport *(G-7598)*
Mahle Industries Incorporated ....F........ 248 735-3623
   Amherst *(G-251)*
Nas-Tra Automotive Inds Inc ....C........ 631 225-1225
   Lindenhurst *(G-7474)*
Norcatec LLC ....E........ 516 222-7070
   Garden City *(G-5524)*
Omega Industries & Development ....E........ 516 349-8010
   Plainview *(G-13625)*
Par-Foam Products Inc ....C........ 716 855-2066
   Buffalo *(G-3112)*
Parker-Hannifin Corporation ....D....... 248 628-6017
   Lancaster *(G-7330)*
Performance Designed By Peters ....F........ 585 223-9062
   Fairport *(G-4870)*
Phillip J Ortiz Manufacturing ....G........ 845 226-7030
   Hopewell Junction *(G-6557)*
Powerflow Inc ....D....... 716 892-1014
   Buffalo *(G-3132)*
Pro-Value Distribution Inc ....G........ 585 783-1461
   Rochester *(G-14604)*
Rosco Inc ....C........ 718 526-2601
   Jamaica *(G-6948)*
Secor Marketing Group Inc ....G........ 914 381-3600
   Mamaroneck *(G-8046)*
Specialty Silicone Pdts Inc ....E........ 518 885-8826
   Ballston Spa *(G-609)*
Tesla Motors Inc ....A........ 212 206-1204
   New York *(G-12304)*
Troyer Inc ....F........ 585 352-5590
   Rochester *(G-14732)*
TRW Automotive Inc ....B........ 315 255-3311
   Auburn *(G-525)*
Whiting Door Mfg Corp ....B........ 716 542-5427
   Akron *(G-30)*
Wolo Mfg Corp ....E........ 631 242-0333
   Deer Park *(G-4228)*
Yomiuri International Inc ....G........ 212 752-2196
   New York *(G-12695)*

AUTOMOTIVE PARTS: Plastic

CN Group Incorporated ....A........ 914 358-5690
   White Plains *(G-17094)*
Fiber Laminations Limited ....F........ 716 692-1825
   Tonawanda *(G-16161)*
Koonichi Inc ....G........ 718 886-8338
   Fresh Meadows *(G-5443)*
Macauto Usa Inc ....E........ 585 342-2060
   Rochester *(G-14485)*
P & M Safe America LLC ....F........ 718 292-6363
   Bronx *(G-1418)*

AUTOMOTIVE PRDTS: Rubber

Chamberlin Rubber Company Inc ....E........ 585 427-7780
   Rochester *(G-14270)*
Vehicle Manufacturers Inc ....E........ 631 851-1700
   Hauppauge *(G-6222)*

AUTOMOTIVE REPAIR SHOPS: Brake Repair

Whitesboro Spring & Alignment ....F........ 315 736-4441
   Whitesboro *(G-17198)*

AUTOMOTIVE REPAIR SHOPS: Diesel Engine Repair

Jack W Miller ....G........ 585 538-2399
   Scottsville *(G-15337)*

AUTOMOTIVE REPAIR SHOPS: Electrical Svcs

Gerome Technologies Inc ....D....... 518 463-1324
   Menands *(G-8372)*

AUTOMOTIVE REPAIR SHOPS: Engine Repair

Jack Merkel Inc ....G........ 631 234-2600
   Hauppauge *(G-6100)*

AUTOMOTIVE REPAIR SHOPS: Machine Shop

Bullet Industries Inc ....G........ 585 352-0836
   Spencerport *(G-15568)*
Meade Machine Co Inc ....G........ 315 923-1703
   Clyde *(G-3728)*
Vytek Inc ....F........ 631 750-1770
   Bohemia *(G-1155)*

AUTOMOTIVE REPAIR SHOPS: Trailer Repair

General Welding & Fabg Inc ....G........ 585 697-7660
   Rochester *(G-14392)*

AUTOMOTIVE REPAIR SVC

Banner Transmission & Eng Co ....F........ 516 221-9459
   Bellmore *(G-814)*
Cyclone Air Power Inc ....G........ 718 447-3038
   Staten Island *(G-15664)*

AUTOMOTIVE SPLYS & PARTS, NEW, WHOL: Testing Eqpt, Electric

Katikati Inc ....G........ 585 678-1764
   West Henrietta *(G-16883)*

AUTOMOTIVE SPLYS & PARTS, NEW, WHOLESALE: Brakes

Interparts International Inc ....E........ 516 576-2000
   Plainview *(G-13610)*

AUTOMOTIVE SPLYS & PARTS, NEW, WHOLESALE: Clutches

Rpb Distributors LLC ....G........ 914 244-3600
   Mount Kisco *(G-8645)*

Employee Codes: A=Over 500 employees, B=251-500 C=101-250, D=51-100, E=20-50, F=10-19, G=5-9

AUTOMOTIVE SPLYS & PARTS, NEW, WHOLESALE: Engines/Eng Parts — PRODUCT SECTION

AUTOMOTIVE SPLYS & PARTS, NEW, WHOLESALE: Engines/Eng Parts
Cummins Northeast LLC ....E 315 437-2296
  Syracuse (G-15915)

AUTOMOTIVE SPLYS & PARTS, NEW, WHOLESALE: Splys
Extreme Auto Accessories Corp ....F 718 978-6722
  South Ozone Park (G-15533)

AUTOMOTIVE SPLYS & PARTS, NEW, WHOLESALE: Trim
Legendary Auto Interiors Ltd ....E 315 331-1212
  Newark (G-12734)

AUTOMOTIVE SPLYS & PARTS, NEW, WHOLESALE: Wheels
Factory Wheel Warehouse Inc ....G 516 605-2131
  Plainview (G-13601)

AUTOMOTIVE SPLYS & PARTS, USED, WHOLESALE: Wheels
Factory Wheel Warehouse Inc ....G 516 605-2131
  Plainview (G-13601)

AUTOMOTIVE SPLYS & PARTS, WHOLESALE, NEC
Auto-Mat Company Inc ....E 516 938-7373
  Hicksville (G-6325)
Automotive Filters Mfg Inc ....F 631 435-1010
  Bohemia (G-1020)
Axle Teknology LLC ....G 631 423-3044
  Huntington (G-6655)
Deer Park Driveshaft & Hose ....G 631 667-4091
  Deer Park (G-4127)
Depot Label Company Inc ....G 631 467-2952
  Patchogue (G-13418)
Noresco Industrial Group Inc ....E 516 759-3355
  Glen Cove (G-5622)
Split Rock Trading Co Inc ....G 631 929-3261
  Wading River (G-16526)

AUTOMOTIVE SPLYS/PARTS, NEW, WHOL: Body Rpr/Paint Shop Splys
Auto Body Services LLC ....F 631 431-4640
  Lindenhurst (G-7455)

AUTOMOTIVE SVCS, EXC REPAIR & CARWASHES: Maintenance
Roli Retreads Inc ....E 631 694-7670
  Farmingdale (G-5102)

AUTOMOTIVE SVCS, EXC REPAIR: Washing & Polishing
Saccomize Inc ....G 818 287-3000
  Bronx (G-1446)

AUTOMOTIVE SVCS, EXC RPR/CARWASHES: High Perf Auto Rpr/Svc
Riverview Industries Inc ....G 845 265-5284
  Cold Spring (G-3765)

AUTOMOTIVE TOWING & WRECKING SVC
American Towman Network Inc ....F 845 986-4546
  Warwick (G-16586)

AUTOMOTIVE UPHOLSTERY SHOPS
Sausbiers Awning Shop Inc ....G 518 828-3748
  Hudson (G-6633)

AUTOMOTIVE WELDING SVCS
Big Apple Welding Supply ....G 718 439-3959
  Brooklyn (G-1694)
Chautauqua Machine Spc LLC ....F 716 782-3276
  Ashville (G-427)
In Northeast Precision Welding ....G 518 441-2260
  Castleton On Hudson (G-3418)

AUTOMOTIVE: Bodies
Antiques & Collectible Autos ....G 716 825-3990
  Buffalo (G-2813)
Conti Auto Body Corp ....G 516 921-6435
  Syosset (G-15816)
Empire Coachworks Intl LLC ....D 732 257-7981
  Suffern (G-15789)

AUTOMOTIVE: Seating
Johnson Controls Inc ....D 518 884-8313
  Ballston Spa (G-600)
Johnson Controls Inc ....E 585 671-1930
  Webster (G-16725)
Johnson Controls Inc ....C 585 724-2232
  Rochester (G-14464)

AUTOTRANSFORMERS: Electric
General Electric Company ....A 518 385-4022
  Schenectady (G-15257)
General Electric Company ....E 518 385-7620
  Niskayuna (G-12895)

AWNING REPAIR SHOP
Kohler Awning Inc ....E 716 685-3333
  Buffalo (G-3036)
TG Peppe Inc ....G 516 239-7852
  Lawrence (G-7401)

AWNINGS & CANOPIES
Five Star Awnings Inc ....F 718 860-6070
  Ridgewood (G-14107)
Hart To Hart Industries Inc ....G 716 492-2709
  Chaffee (G-3534)
Ke Durasol Awnings Inc ....G 845 610-1100
  Chester (G-3609)
Lotus Awnings Enterprises Inc ....F 718 965-4824
  Brooklyn (G-2237)
Superior Exteriors of Buffalo ....F 716 873-1000
  Buffalo (G-3203)
Vitarose Corp of America ....G 718 951-9700
  Brooklyn (G-2733)

AWNINGS & CANOPIES: Awnings, Fabric, From Purchased Matls
125-127 Main Street Corp ....F 631 477-1500
  Greenport (G-5876)
Abble Awning Co Inc ....G 516 822-1200
  Bethpage (G-862)
Acme Awning Co Inc ....F 718 409-1881
  Bronx (G-1262)
Awning Mart Inc ....G 315 699-5928
  Cicero (G-3642)
Awnings Plus Inc ....F 716 693-3690
  Tonawanda (G-16142)
C E King & Sons Inc ....G 631 324-4944
  East Hampton (G-4406)
Canvas Products Company Inc ....F 516 742-1058
  Mineola (G-8500)
Capitol Awning Co Inc ....F 212 505-1717
  Jamaica (G-6900)
Classic Awnings Inc ....F 716 649-0390
  Hamburg (G-5920)
Di Sanos Creative Canvas Inc ....G 315 894-3137
  Frankfort (G-5351)
Durasol Systems Inc ....D 845 610-1100
  Chester (G-3605)
Fabric Concepts For Industry ....F 914 375-2565
  Yonkers (G-17443)
Jamestown Awning Inc ....G 716 483-1435
  Jamestown (G-7005)
Kohler Awning Inc ....E 716 685-3333
  Buffalo (G-3036)
Mauceri Sign Inc ....F 718 656-7700
  Jamaica (G-6929)
Perma Tech Inc ....E 716 854-0707
  Buffalo (G-3122)
Sausbiers Awning Shop Inc ....G 518 828-3748
  Hudson (G-6633)
Steinway Awning II LLC ....G 718 729-2965
  Astoria (G-459)
TG Peppe Inc ....G 516 239-7852
  Lawrence (G-7401)

AWNINGS & CANOPIES: Fabric
Lanza Corp ....G 914 937-6360
  Port Chester (G-13751)

AWNINGS: Fiberglass
Acme Awning Co Inc ....F 718 409-1881
  Bronx (G-1262)
Space Sign ....F 718 961-1112
  College Point (G-3808)
Vitarose Corp of America ....G 718 951-9700
  Brooklyn (G-2733)

AWNINGS: Metal
Dart Awning Inc ....F 718 945-4224
  Freeport (G-5393)
Kenan International Trading ....G 718 672-4922
  Corona (G-4000)
Space Sign ....F 718 961-1112
  College Point (G-3808)

AWNINGS: Wood
Midwood Signs & Design Inc ....G 718 499-9041
  Brooklyn (G-2312)

AXLES
Axle Teknology LLC ....G 631 423-3044
  Huntington (G-6655)
Temper Corporation ....G 518 853-3467
  Fonda (G-5318)

BABY FORMULA
Baby Central LLC ....G 718 372-2229
  Brooklyn (G-1660)
Nutra Solutions USA Inc ....E 631 392-1900
  Deer Park (G-4183)

BABY PACIFIERS: Rubber
Mam USA Corporation ....F 914 269-2500
  Purchase (G-13961)

BADGES, WHOLESALE
Paragon Corporation ....F 516 484-6090
  Port Washington (G-13855)

BADGES: Identification & Insignia
Identfication Data Imaging LLC ....G 516 484-6500
  Port Washington (G-13823)

BAGS & BAGGING: Knit
Nochairs Inc ....G 917 748-8731
  New York (G-11449)

BAGS & CONTAINERS: Textile, Exc Sleeping
Carry Hot Inc ....F 212 279-7535
  New York (G-9537)

BAGS & SACKS: Shipping & Shopping
Kapstone Container Corporation ....D 518 842-2450
  Amsterdam (G-352)

BAGS: Canvas
Aka Sport Inc ....F 631 858-9888
  Dix Hills (G-4289)
H G Maybeck Co Inc ....E 718 297-4410
  Jamaica (G-6918)

BAGS: Cellophane
Aladdin Packaging LLC ....D 631 273-4747
  Hauppauge (G-6014)
Excelsior Packaging Group Inc ....C 914 968-1300
  Yonkers (G-17442)

BAGS: Duffle, Canvas, Made From Purchased Materials
Select Fabricators Inc ....F 585 393-0650
  Canandaigua (G-3357)

BAGS: Food Storage & Frozen Food, Plastic
Summit Promotions LLC ....F 631 952-1570
  Bay Shore (G-748)

BAGS: Food Storage & Trash, Plastic
Bag Arts The Art Packaging LLC ....G 212 684-7020
  New York (G-9303)

PRODUCT SECTION

BAKERIES, COMMERCIAL: On Premises Baking Only

Mint-X Products Corporation ....F 877 646-8224
  College Point *(G-3798)*
Pactiv LLC ....C 518 793-2524
  Glens Falls *(G-5695)*

BAGS: Garment & Wardrobe, Plastic Film

Basic Ltd ....E 718 438-5576
  Brooklyn *(G-1670)*

BAGS: Grocers', Made From Purchased Materials

333 J & M Food Corp ....F 718 381-1493
  Ridgewood *(G-14096)*
Bag Arts The Art Packaging LLC ....G 212 684-7020
  New York *(G-9303)*
Lin Jin Feng ....G 718 232-3039
  Brooklyn *(G-2223)*

BAGS: Knapsacks, Canvas, Made From Purchased Materials

Johnson Outdoors Inc ....C 607 779-2200
  Binghamton *(G-931)*

BAGS: Laundry, Garment & Storage

Handy Laundry Products Corp ....G 800 263-5973
  Airmont *(G-15)*

BAGS: Paper

American Packaging Corporation ....C 585 254-9500
  Rochester *(G-14198)*
APC Paper Company Inc ....D 315 384-4225
  Norfolk *(G-12897)*
R P Fedder Corp ....E 585 288-1600
  Rochester *(G-14618)*

BAGS: Paper, Made From Purchased Materials

Polyseal Packaging Corp ....E 718 792-5530
  Bronx *(G-1429)*

BAGS: Plastic

Adart Polyethylene Bag Mfg ....G 516 932-1001
  Plainview *(G-13576)*
American Packaging Corporation ....C 585 254-9500
  Rochester *(G-14198)*
Capitol Poly Corp ....E 718 855-6000
  Brooklyn *(G-1755)*
Clear View Bag Company Inc ....C 518 458-7153
  Albany *(G-64)*
Craft Pak Inc ....G 718 257-2700
  Staten Island *(G-15663)*
Ecoplast & Packaging LLC ....E 718 996-0800
  Brooklyn *(G-1901)*
Edco Supply Corporation ....D 718 788-8108
  Brooklyn *(G-1903)*
Filmpak Extrusion LLC ....D 631 293-6767
  Melville *(G-8319)*
H G Maybeck Co Inc ....E 718 297-4410
  Jamaica *(G-6918)*
Ivi Services Inc ....D 607 729-5111
  Binghamton *(G-929)*
Jay Bags Inc ....G 845 459-6500
  Spring Valley *(G-15590)*
JM Murray Center Inc ....C 607 756-9913
  Cortland *(G-4031)*
JM Murray Center Inc ....C 607 756-0246
  Cortland *(G-4032)*
Kemco Sales LLC ....F 203 762-1902
  East Rochester *(G-4463)*
Magcrest Packaging Inc ....G 845 425-0451
  Monsey *(G-8574)*
Metpak Inc ....G 917 309-0196
  Brooklyn *(G-2304)*
Milla Global Inc ....G 516 488-3601
  Brooklyn *(G-2315)*
Noteworthy Industries Inc ....C 518 842-2662
  Amsterdam *(G-364)*
Nova Packaging Ltd Inc ....E 914 232-8406
  Katonah *(G-7133)*
Select Fabricators Inc ....F 585 393-0650
  Canandaigua *(G-3357)*
Tai Seng ....G 718 399-6311
  Brooklyn *(G-2644)*
Thompson Packaging Novlt Inc ....G 212 686-4242
  New York *(G-12327)*

Vitex Packaging Group Inc ....F 212 265-6575
  New York *(G-12557)*
W E W Container Corporation ....E 718 827-8150
  Brooklyn *(G-2740)*
Wally Packaging Inc ....G 718 377-5323
  Brooklyn *(G-2742)*

BAGS: Plastic & Pliofilm

Maco Bag Corporation ....C 315 226-1000
  Newark *(G-12735)*
Modern Plastic Bags Mfg Inc ....G 718 237-2985
  Brooklyn *(G-2327)*
Primo Plastics Inc ....E 718 349-1000
  Brooklyn *(G-2443)*

BAGS: Plastic, Made From Purchased Materials

Alco Plastics Inc ....E 716 683-3020
  Lancaster *(G-7301)*
Allied Converters Inc ....E 914 235-1585
  New Rochelle *(G-8886)*
Amby International Inc ....E 718 645-0964
  Brooklyn *(G-1597)*
API Industries Inc ....B 845 365-2200
  Orangeburg *(G-13218)*
API Industries Inc ....C 845 365-2200
  Orangeburg *(G-13219)*
Baggu ....G 347 457-5266
  Brooklyn *(G-1664)*
Bags Unlimited Inc ....E 585 436-6282
  Rochester *(G-14221)*
Bison Bag Co Inc ....D 716 434-4380
  Lockport *(G-7572)*
Connover Packaging Inc ....G 585 377-2510
  East Rochester *(G-4456)*
Courier Packaging Inc ....G 718 349-2390
  Brooklyn *(G-1809)*
Craft-Pak Inc ....F 718 763-0700
  Brooklyn *(G-1812)*
Excellent Poly Inc ....F 718 768-6555
  Brooklyn *(G-1943)*
Fortune Poly Products Inc ....F 718 361-0767
  Jamaica *(G-6912)*
Franklin Poly Film Inc ....E 718 492-3523
  Brooklyn *(G-2002)*
Josh Packaging Inc ....E 631 822-1660
  Hauppauge *(G-6102)*
Manhattan Poly Bag Corporation ....E 917 689-7549
  Brooklyn *(G-2260)*
Mason Transparent Package Inc ....E 718 792-6000
  Bronx *(G-1388)*
Metro Lining Company ....G 718 383-2700
  Brooklyn *(G-2306)*
Metropolitan Packg Mfg Corp ....E 718 383-2700
  Brooklyn *(G-2307)*
Nap Industries Inc ....D 718 625-4948
  Brooklyn *(G-2348)*
New York Packaging Corp ....D 516 746-0600
  New Hyde Park *(G-8850)*
New York Packaging II LLC ....C 516 746-0600
  Garden City *(G-5523)*
Pacific Poly Product Corp ....F 718 786-7129
  Long Island City *(G-7832)*
Pack America Corp ....G 212 508-6666
  New York *(G-11554)*
Paradise Plastics LLC ....E 718 788-3733
  Brooklyn *(G-2405)*
Paramount Equipment Inc ....E 631 981-4422
  Ronkonkoma *(G-14964)*
Poly Craft Industries Corp ....E 631 630-6731
  Hauppauge *(G-6166)*
Poly-Pak Industries Inc ....B 631 293-6767
  Melville *(G-8348)*
Polyseal Packaging Corp ....E 718 792-5530
  Bronx *(G-1429)*
Protective Lining Corp ....D 718 854-3838
  Brooklyn *(G-2456)*
Rainbow Poly Bag Co Inc ....E 718 386-3500
  Brooklyn *(G-2476)*
Rege Inc ....F 845 565-7772
  New Windsor *(G-8950)*
Rtr Bag & Co Ltd ....G 212 620-0011
  New York *(G-11932)*
Salerno Plastic Film ....G 518 563-3636
  Plattsburgh *(G-13695)*
Star Poly Bag Inc ....F 718 384-3130
  Brooklyn *(G-2599)*
Supreme Poly Plastics Inc ....E 718 456-9300
  Brooklyn *(G-2632)*

T M I Plastics Industries Inc ....F 718 383-0363
  Brooklyn *(G-2638)*
Technipoly Manufacturing Inc ....E 718 383-0363
  Brooklyn *(G-2650)*
Trinity Packaging Corporation ....E 914 273-4111
  Armonk *(G-422)*
United Plastics Inc ....G 718 389-2255
  Brooklyn *(G-2701)*

BAGS: Rubber Or Rubberized Fabric

Adam Scott Designs Inc ....E 212 420-8866
  New York *(G-9024)*

BAGS: Shipping

Shalam Imports Inc ....F 718 686-6271
  Brooklyn *(G-2548)*

BAGS: Shoe, From Purchased Materials

NI Shoes and Bags LLC ....G 212 594-0012
  New York *(G-11444)*
Stuart Weitzman LLC ....E 212 823-9560
  New York *(G-12218)*

BAGS: Shopping, Made From Purchased Materials

Ampac Paper LLC ....A 845 778-5511
  Walden *(G-16530)*
Custom Eco Friendly LLC ....G 347 227-0229
  Roslyn *(G-15018)*
Rtr Bag & Co Ltd ....G 212 620-0011
  New York *(G-11932)*

BAGS: Tea, Fabric, Made From Purchased Materials

Health Matters America Inc ....F 716 235-8772
  Buffalo *(G-2992)*

BAGS: Textile

Ace Drop Cloth Canvas Pdts Inc ....E 718 731-1550
  Bronx *(G-1260)*
Clear Edge Crosible Inc ....D 315 685-3466
  Skaneateles Falls *(G-15467)*
GPM Associates LLC ....G 585 359-1770
  Rush *(G-15050)*
GPM Associates LLC ....E 585 335-3940
  Dansville *(G-4077)*
Ivi Services Inc ....D 607 729-5111
  Binghamton *(G-929)*
Jag Manufacturing Inc ....E 518 762-9558
  Johnstown *(G-7116)*
Kragel Co Inc ....G 716 648-1344
  Hamburg *(G-5932)*
Kush Oasis Enterprises LLC ....G 516 513-1316
  Syosset *(G-15827)*
Mgk Group Inc ....E 212 989-2732
  New York *(G-11246)*
Paulpac LLC ....G 631 283-7610
  Southampton *(G-15548)*
Redco Foods Inc ....D 315 823-1300
  Little Falls *(G-7504)*

BAGS: Trash, Plastic Film, Made From Purchased Materials

Garb-O-Liner Inc ....G 914 235-1585
  New Rochelle *(G-8904)*
Golden Group International Ltd ....G 845 440-1025
  Patterson *(G-13440)*
Jad Corp of America ....E 718 762-8900
  College Point *(G-3792)*
Repellem Consumer Pdts Corp ....F 631 273-3992
  Islandia *(G-6802)*

BAGS: Wardrobe, Closet Access, Made From Purchased Materials

Colden Closet LLC ....G 716 713-6125
  East Aurora *(G-4368)*

BAKERIES, COMMERCIAL: On Premises Baking Only

40 Street Baking Inc ....G 212 683-4700
  Brooklyn *(G-1518)*
527 Franco Bakery Corporation ....G 718 993-4200
  Bronx *(G-1250)*

Employee Codes: A=Over 500 employees, B=251-500
C=101-250, D=51-100, E=20-50, F=10-19, G=5-9

BAKERIES, COMMERCIAL: On Premises Baking Only

A & M Appel Distributing Inc .... G 516 735-1172
   Massapequa *(G-8176)*
A Angonoa Inc .... D 718 762-4466
   College Point *(G-3773)*
American Vintage Wine Biscuit .... G 718 361-1003
   Long Island City *(G-7657)*
Amincor Inc .... C 347 821-3452
   New York *(G-9136)*
Amy Scherber Inc .... F 212 462-4338
   New York *(G-9142)*
Andrew Sapienza Bakery Inc .... E 516 437-1715
   Elmont *(G-4715)*
Aphrodities .... G 718 224-1774
   Whitestone *(G-17200)*
Aryzta LLC .... C 585 235-8160
   Rochester *(G-14215)*
Aryzta LLC .... D 585 235-8160
   Rochester *(G-14214)*
B & D Enterprises of Utica .... D 315 735-3311
   New Hartford *(G-8801)*
Baked Cupcakery .... G 716 773-2050
   Grand Island *(G-5752)*
Better Baked Foods Inc .... D 716 326-4651
   Westfield *(G-17046)*
Bimbo Bakeries .... G 631 274-4906
   Deer Park *(G-4108)*
Bimbo Bakeries .... G 800 289-7876
   Olean *(G-13135)*
Bimbo Bakeries .... F 518 463-2221
   Albany *(G-56)*
Bimbo Bakeries Usa Inc .... G 716 692-9140
   Tonawanda *(G-16145)*
Bimbo Bakeries Usa Inc .... G 718 601-1561
   Bronx *(G-1284)*
Bimbo Bakeries Usa Inc .... F 516 887-1024
   Lynbrook *(G-7947)*
Bimbo Bakeries Usa Inc .... F 315 379-9069
   Canton *(G-3380)*
Bimbo Bakeries Usa Inc .... G 631 274-4906
   Bay Shore *(G-676)*
Bimbo Bakeries Usa Inc .... F 518 489-4053
   Albany *(G-57)*
Bimbo Bakeries Usa Inc .... F 716 706-0450
   Lancaster *(G-7306)*
Bimbo Bakeries Usa Inc .... F 315 785-7060
   Watertown *(G-16637)*
Bimbo Bakeries Usa Inc .... D 845 568-0943
   Newburgh *(G-12751)*
Bimbo Bakeries Usa Inc .... C 315 782-4189
   Watertown *(G-16638)*
Bimbo Foods Bakeries Inc .... C 631 273-6000
   Bay Shore *(G-678)*
Bread Factory LLC .... E 914 637-8150
   New Rochelle *(G-8889)*
Bread Market Cafe .... G 212 768-9292
   New York *(G-9457)*
Chambord LLC .... E 718 859-1110
   Brooklyn *(G-1772)*
Cohens Bakery Inc .... E 716 892-8149
   Buffalo *(G-2879)*
Costanzos Bakery Inc .... C 716 656-9093
   Buffalo *(G-2891)*
Damascus Bakery Inc .... C 718 855-1456
   Brooklyn *(G-1837)*
Delicias Andinas Food Corp .... E 718 416-2922
   Flushing *(G-5237)*
Felix Roma & Sons Inc .... D 607 748-3336
   Endicott *(G-4808)*
Food Gems Ltd .... E 718 296-7788
   Ozone Park *(G-13379)*
Fratellis LLC .... E 607 722-5663
   Binghamton *(G-915)*
Gabila & Sons Mfg Inc .... E 631 789-2220
   Copiague *(G-3901)*
Gennaris Itln French Bky Inc .... G 516 997-8968
   Carle Place *(G-3389)*
Glenn Wayne Wholesale Bky Inc .... D 631 289-9200
   Bohemia *(G-1073)*
Golden Glow Cookie Co Inc .... E 718 379-6223
   Bronx *(G-1345)*
Gourmet Toast Corp .... G 718 852-4536
   Brooklyn *(G-2044)*
Grannys Kitchens LLC .... B 315 735-5000
   Frankfort *(G-5354)*
Grimaldis Home Bread Inc .... D 718 497-1425
   Ridgewood *(G-14109)*
H & S Edible Products Corp .... E 914 413-3489
   Mount Vernon *(G-8688)*
Hagadah Passover Bakery .... G 718 638-1589
   Brooklyn *(G-2062)*

Hana Pastries Inc .... G 718 369-7593
   Brooklyn *(G-2065)*
Heidelberg Group Inc .... E 315 866-0999
   Herkimer *(G-6301)*
Herris Gourmet Inc .... G 917 578-2308
   Brooklyn *(G-2078)*
Jarets Stuffed Cupcakes .... G 607 658-9096
   Endicott *(G-4814)*
JJ Cassone Bakery Inc .... B 914 939-1568
   Port Chester *(G-13750)*
Jonathan Lord Corp .... F 631 563-4445
   Bohemia *(G-1085)*
King Cracker Corp .... F 516 539-9251
   Hempstead *(G-6277)*
La Calenita Bakery & Cafeteria .... G 718 205-8273
   Elmhurst *(G-4663)*
Larosa Cupcakes .... G 347 866-3920
   Staten Island *(G-15697)*
Make My Cake II Inc .... G 212 234-2344
   New York *(G-11117)*
Megamatt Inc .... F 516 536-3541
   Rockville Centre *(G-14794)*
Melita Corp .... C 718 392-7280
   Bronx *(G-1390)*
New Mount Pleasant Bakery .... E 518 374-7577
   Schenectady *(G-15281)*
New Star Bakery .... G 718 961-8868
   Flushing *(G-5271)*
Nibble Inc Baking Co .... G 518 334-3950
   Troy *(G-16243)*
Nightingale Food Entps Inc .... G 347 577-1630
   New York *(G-11429)*
Operative Cake Corp .... E 718 278-5600
   Bronx *(G-1417)*
Ossining Bakery Lmp Inc .... G 914 941-2654
   Ossining *(G-13324)*
Oz Baking Company Ltd .... G 516 466-5114
   Great Neck *(G-5827)*
Palagonia Bakery Co Inc .... D 718 272-5400
   Brooklyn *(G-2402)*
Parkway Bread Distributors Inc .... G 845 362-1221
   Pomona *(G-13732)*
Peking Food LLC .... E 718 628-8080
   Brooklyn *(G-2413)*
R & H Baking Co Inc .... E 718 852-1768
   Brooklyn *(G-2470)*
Rapacki & Sons .... F 516 538-3939
   Lindenhurst *(G-7480)*
Rays Italian Bakery Inc .... F 516 825-9170
   Valley Stream *(G-16423)*
Reisman Bros Bakery Inc .... F 718 331-1975
   Brooklyn *(G-2488)*
Rm Bakery LLC .... E 718 472-3036
   Maspeth *(G-8168)*
Rockland Bakery Inc .... D 845 623-5800
   Nanuet *(G-8761)*
Roma Bakery Inc .... F 516 825-9170
   Valley Stream *(G-16425)*
Royal Caribbean Jamaican Bky .... E 914 668-6868
   Mount Vernon *(G-8727)*
Royal Sweet Bakery Inc .... F 718 567-7770
   Brooklyn *(G-2514)*
Ruthys Cheesecake Rugelach Bky .... F 212 463-8800
   New York *(G-11938)*
Saint Honore Pastry Shop Inc .... G 516 767-2555
   Port Washington *(G-13861)*
Smith Street Bread Co LLC .... F 718 797-9712
   Brooklyn *(G-2573)*
Sugarbear Cupcakes .... G 917 698-9005
   Jamaica *(G-6953)*
Sullivan St Bky - Hlls Kit Inc .... F 212 265-5580
   New York *(G-12228)*
Sunrise Bkg Acquisition Co LLC .... D 718 499-0800
   Brooklyn *(G-2622)*
Uncle Wallys LLC .... E 631 205-0455
   Shirley *(G-15430)*
Valencia Bakery Inc .... E 718 991-6400
   Bronx *(G-1487)*
Village Lantern Baking Corp .... G 631 225-1690
   Lindenhurst *(G-7494)*
Waldorf Bakers Inc .... F 718 665-2253
   Bronx *(G-1492)*
Zaro Bake Shop Inc .... C 718 993-7327
   Bronx *(G-1497)*
Zuckerbakers Inc .... G 516 785-6900
   Wantagh *(G-16565)*

BAKERIES: On Premises Baking & Consumption

B & D Enterprises of Utica .... D 315 735-3311
   New Hartford *(G-8801)*
Bagel Land .... E 585 442-3080
   Rochester *(G-14220)*
Brighton Bakery .... G 315 475-2948
   Syracuse *(G-15874)*
Caputo Bakery Inc .... G 718 875-6871
   Brooklyn *(G-1756)*
Costanzos Bakery Inc .... C 716 656-9093
   Buffalo *(G-2891)*
Dipaolo Baking Co Inc .... D 585 303-5013
   Rochester *(G-14310)*
Ferrara Bakery & Cafe Inc .... D 212 226-6150
   New York *(G-10154)*
Geddes Bakery Co Inc .... E 315 437-8084
   North Syracuse *(G-12945)*
Gennaris Itln French Bky Inc .... G 516 997-8968
   Carle Place *(G-3389)*
Highway Bagels Corp .... G 347 350-6493
   Brooklyn *(G-2080)*
JJ Cassone Bakery Inc .... B 914 939-1568
   Port Chester *(G-13750)*
L American Ltd .... F 716 372-9480
   Olean *(G-13150)*
Megamatt Inc .... F 516 536-3541
   Rockville Centre *(G-14794)*
New Hope Mills Mfg Inc .... E 315 252-2676
   Auburn *(G-510)*
New Mount Pleasant Bakery .... E 518 374-7577
   Schenectady *(G-15281)*
Niebylski Bakery Inc .... G 718 721-5152
   Astoria *(G-450)*
Ohio Baking Company Inc .... E 315 724-2033
   Utica *(G-16354)*
Perrottas Bakery Inc .... G 518 283-4711
   Troy *(G-16247)*
Pesces Bakery Inc .... G 845 246-4730
   Saugerties *(G-15191)*
Presser Kosher Baking Corp .... E 718 375-5088
   Brooklyn *(G-2439)*
Ruthys Cheesecake Rugelach Bky .... F 212 463-8800
   New York *(G-11938)*
Saint Honore Pastry Shop Inc .... G 516 767-2555
   Port Washington *(G-13861)*
Sapienza Pastry Inc .... E 516 352-5232
   Elmont *(G-4729)*
Settepani Inc .... G 718 349-6524
   Brooklyn *(G-2545)*
T Shore Products Ltd .... G 315 252-9174
   Auburn *(G-522)*
Tarrytown Bakery Inc .... F 914 631-0209
   Tarrytown *(G-16108)*
Wenner Bread Products Inc .... B 800 869-6262
   Bayport *(G-761)*

BAKERY FOR HOME SVC DELIVERY

Circle 5 Deli Corp .... G 718 525-5687
   Jamaica *(G-6902)*

BAKERY MACHINERY

Fresh Harvest Incorporated .... F 845 296-1024
   Wappingers Falls *(G-16568)*
Unisource Food Eqp Systems Inc .... G 516 681-0537
   Holbrook *(G-6479)*

BAKERY PRDTS, FROZEN: Wholesalers

Fratellis LLC .... E 607 722-5663
   Binghamton *(G-915)*
Modern Itln Bky of W Babylon .... C 631 589-7300
   Oakdale *(G-13059)*

BAKERY PRDTS: Bagels, Fresh Or Frozen

999 Bagels Inc .... G 718 915-0742
   Brooklyn *(G-1524)*
A T A Bagel Shoppe Inc .... G 718 352-4948
   Bayside *(G-764)*
Bagel Club Inc .... F 718 423-6106
   Bayside *(G-767)*
Bagel Grove Inc .... G 315 724-8015
   Utica *(G-16309)*
Bagel Land .... E 585 442-3080
   Rochester *(G-14220)*
Bagel Lites LLC .... G 855 813-7888
   Long Island City *(G-7680)*

PRODUCT SECTION

BAKERY PRDTS: Bagels

Company	Code	Phone
Bagelovers Inc — Dryden (G-4320)	F	607 844-3683
Bagels By Bell Ltd — Brooklyn (G-1663)	E	718 272-2780
Enterprise Bagels Inc — Fishkill (G-5183)	F	845 896-3823
FB Sale LLC — Macedon (G-7987)	G	315 986-9999
Greenvale Bagel Inc — Wantagh (G-16556)	E	516 221-8221
Highway Bagels Corp — Brooklyn (G-2080)	G	347 350-6493
M & M Bagel Corp — Cedarhurst (G-3459)	F	516 295-1222
Mds Hot Bagels Deli Inc — Brooklyn (G-2289)	G	718 438-5650

BAKERY PRDTS: Bakery Prdts, Partially Cooked, Exc frozen

Company	Code	Phone
New Hope Mills Mfg Inc — Auburn (G-510)	E	315 252-2676
T&B Bakery Corp — Maspeth (G-8172)	G	646 642-4300

BAKERY PRDTS: Biscuits, Dry

Company	Code	Phone
Biscuits & Bath Companies LLC — New York (G-9404)	E	212 401-3022

BAKERY PRDTS: Bread, All Types, Fresh Or Frozen

Company	Code	Phone
Addeo Bakers Inc — Bronx (G-1263)	F	718 367-8316
Aladdin Bakers Inc — Brooklyn (G-1574)	C	718 499-1818
Bimbo Bakeries Usa Inc — Maspeth (G-8121)	C	718 463-6300
Brighton Bakery — Syracuse (G-15874)	G	315 475-2948
Commitment 2000 Inc — Buffalo (G-2883)	E	716 439-1206
Dipaolo Baking Co Inc — Rochester (G-14310)	D	585 303-5013
George Retzos — Syracuse (G-15952)	G	315 422-2913
Giovanni Bakery Corp — New York (G-10300)	F	212 695-4296
Harrison Bakery West — Syracuse (G-15957)	E	315 422-1468
L American Ltd — Olean (G-13150)	F	716 372-9480
La Prima Bakery Inc — Bronx (G-1377)	F	718 584-4442
Mastroianni Bros Inc — Schenectady (G-15277)	E	518 355-5310
Modern Itln Bky of W Babylon — Oakdale (G-13059)	C	631 589-7300
Ohio Baking Company Inc — Utica (G-16354)	E	315 724-2033
Rock Hill Bakehouse Ltd — Gansevoort (G-5489)	E	518 743-1627
Roslyn Bread Company Inc — Roslyn Heights (G-15031)	E	516 625-1470
Tarrytown Bakery Inc — Tarrytown (G-16108)	F	914 631-0209
Wenner Bread Products Inc — Bayport (G-761)	B	800 869-6262

BAKERY PRDTS: Buns, Sweet, Frozen

Company	Code	Phone
Liddabit Sweets — Brooklyn (G-2217)	G	917 912-1370

BAKERY PRDTS: Cakes, Bakery, Exc Frozen

Company	Code	Phone
Always Baked Fresh — Holbrook (G-6431)	G	631 648-0511
Butter Cooky Bakery — Floral Park (G-5196)	G	516 354-3831
Charlotte Neuville Design LLC — Brooklyn (G-1775)	G	646 530-4570
Chocnyc LLC — New York (G-9604)	G	917 804-4848
Coccadotts — Albany (G-69)	F	518 438-4937
Cupcake Contessas Corporation — North Bellmore (G-12919)	G	516 307-1222
Ferrara Bakery & Cafe Inc — New York (G-10154)	D	212 226-6150
Great American Dessert Co LLC — Maspeth (G-8141)	D	718 894-3494
Hahns Old Fashioned Cake Co — Farmingdale (G-5005)	F	631 249-3456
McKee Foods Corporation — Hauppauge (G-6128)	A	631 979-9364
Pane DOro — Yonkers (G-17475)	F	914 964-0043
Paris Baguette — Flushing (G-5278)	G	718 961-0404
Placid Baker — Troy (G-16249)	G	518 326-2657
Scaife Enterprises Inc — Rochester (G-14672)	F	585 454-5231

BAKERY PRDTS: Cakes, Bakery, Frozen

Company	Code	Phone
Culinary Arts Specialties Inc — Cheektowaga (G-3566)	D	716 656-8943
Sugar & Plumm Upper West LLC — New York (G-12226)	D	201 334-1600

BAKERY PRDTS: Cones, Ice Cream

Company	Code	Phone
Alrajs Inc — Lindenhurst (G-7452)	E	631 225-0300
Cone Buddy System Inc — Rochester (G-14285)	F	585 427-9940
Larte Del Gelato Inc — New York (G-10930)	G	212 366-0570
Pdi Cone Co Inc — Buffalo (G-3116)	D	716 825-8750

BAKERY PRDTS: Cookies

Company	Code	Phone
212kiddish Inc — Brooklyn (G-1512)	G	718 705-7227
AAA Noodle Products Mfg — New York (G-8999)	G	212 431-4090
Chipita America Inc — Ferndale (G-5168)	E	845 292-2540
Cookie Factory LLC — Troy (G-16232)	E	518 268-1060
Cookie Pnache By Bet The Bread — New York (G-9715)	G	212 757-4145
Cooking With Chef Michelle LLC — Calverton (G-3289)	G	516 662-2324
D F Stauffer Biscuit Co Inc — Cuba (G-4068)	E	585 968-2700
Decorated Cookie Company LLC — Syracuse (G-15923)	E	315 487-2111
Elenis Nyc Inc — Long Island City (G-7729)	E	718 361-8136
Falcones Cookie Land Ltd — Brooklyn (G-1955)	G	718 236-4200
Golden Glow Cookie Co Inc — Bronx (G-1345)	E	718 379-6223
Keebler Company — Oakfield (G-13065)	F	585 948-8010
Keebler Company — Hauppauge (G-6103)	E	631 234-3700
Keebler Company — Albany (G-94)	E	518 464-1051
Keebler Company — Orangeburg (G-13232)	E	845 365-5200
La Vita Health Foods Ltd — Suffern (G-15793)	G	845 368-4101
Linden Cookies Inc — Congers (G-3859)	E	845 268-5050
Lloyd Price Icon Food Brands — Pound Ridge (G-13944)	F	914 764-8624
McDuffies of Scotland Inc — Clarence (G-3664)	E	716 759-8510
One Girl Cookies Ltd — Brooklyn (G-2392)	F	212 675-4996
Quaker Bonnet Inc — Buffalo (G-3146)	G	716 885-7208
Treehouse Private Brands Inc — Tonawanda (G-16208)	G	716 693-4715
Wonton Food Inc — Brooklyn (G-2763)	C	718 628-6868

BAKERY PRDTS: Cookies & crackers

Company	Code	Phone
Butterwood Desserts Inc — West Falls (G-16844)	E	716 652-0131
Cookies United LLC — Islip (G-6807)	C	631 581-4000
Danny Macaroons Inc — New York (G-9805)	G	260 622-8463
Great Brands of Europe Inc — White Plains (G-17114)	G	914 872-8804

BAKERY PRDTS: Pastries, Danish, Frozen

Company	Code	Phone
Jonathan Lord Corp — Bohemia (G-1085)	F	631 563-4445
Kaltec Food Packaging Inc — Port Jervis (G-13786)	E	845 856-9888
Ladybird Bakery Inc — Brooklyn (G-2190)	G	718 499-8108
New Mount Pleasant Bakery — Schenectady (G-15281)	E	518 374-7577
Pepsico Inc — Purchase (G-13966)	A	914 253-2000
Sapienza Pastry Inc — Elmont (G-4729)	E	516 352-5232
U Serve Brands Inc — New York (G-12439)	G	212 286-2403
United Baking Co Inc — Central Islip (G-3513)	F	631 413-5116
United Baking Co Inc — Shirley (G-15431)	G	631 205-0455
Zaro Bake Shop Inc — Bronx (G-1497)	C	718 993-7327

BAKERY PRDTS: Cracker Meal & Crumbs

Company	Code	Phone
Wonton Food Inc — Long Island City (G-7926)	E	718 784-8178

BAKERY PRDTS: Doughnuts, Exc Frozen

Company	Code	Phone
3rd Avenue Doughnut Inc — Brooklyn (G-1516)	F	718 748-3294
Alicias Bakery Inc — New Rochelle (G-8885)	G	914 235-4689
Bimbo Bakeries Usa Inc — Bay Shore (G-677)	E	203 531-2311
Cuzins Duzin Corp — Kew Gardens (G-7160)	G	347 724-6200
D-Lite Donuts — Astoria (G-436)	G	718 626-5953
Famous Doughnuts Inc — Buffalo (G-2944)	G	716 834-6356
Sandford Blvd Donuts Inc — Mount Vernon (G-8730)	G	914 663-7708

BAKERY PRDTS: Doughnuts, Frozen

Company	Code	Phone
Grannys Kitchens LLC — Frankfort (G-5354)	B	315 735-5000

BAKERY PRDTS: Dry

Company	Code	Phone
17 Bakers LLC — Williamsville (G-17230)	F	844 687-6836
Aryzta LLC — Rochester (G-14215)	C	585 235-8160
City Baking LLC — Long Island City (G-7698)	G	718 392-8514
Maurybakes LLC — New York (G-11182)	E	646 722-6570
My Most Favorite Food — New York (G-11331)	G	212 580-5130

BAKERY PRDTS: Frozen

Company	Code	Phone
Brooklyn Baby Cakes Inc — Brooklyn (G-1720)	G	917 334-2518
Butterwood Desserts Inc — West Falls (G-16844)	E	716 652-0131
Deiorio Foods Inc — Utica (G-16322)	E	315 732-7612
Dufour Pastry Kitchens Inc — Bronx (G-1318)	E	718 402-8800
Fratellis LLC — Binghamton (G-915)	E	607 722-5663
Ko Fro Foods Inc — Brooklyn (G-2177)	E	718 972-6480
Love & Quiches Ltd — Freeport (G-5409)	C	516 623-8800
R E Rich Family Holding Corp — Buffalo (G-3152)	D	716 878-8000
Rich Products Corporation — Buffalo (G-3157)	A	716 878-8422
Wenner Bread Products Inc — Bayport (G-761)	B	800 869-6262

BAKERY PRDTS: Matzoth

Company	Code	Phone
Aron Streit Inc — New York (G-9205)	E	212 475-7000

BAKERY PRDTS: Pastries, Danish, Frozen

Company	Code	Phone
Pearl River Pastries LLC — West Nyack (G-16923)	E	845 735-5100

Employee Codes: A=Over 500 employees, B=251-500
C=101-250, D=51-100, E=20-50, F=10-19, G=5-9

BAKERY PRDTS: Pastries, Exc Frozen

BAKERY PRDTS: Pastries, Exc Frozen

Alrajs Inc .... E 631 225-0300
  Lindenhurst (G-7452)
Cannoli Factory Inc .... E 631 643-2700
  Wyandanch (G-17372)
Old Poland Foods LLC .... F 718 486-7700
  Brooklyn (G-2388)
Voila Sweets LLC .... B 718 366-1100
  Brooklyn (G-2734)

BAKERY PRDTS: Pies, Bakery, Frozen

Circle Peak Capital MGT LLC .... E 646 230-8812
  New York (G-9620)
Cobblestone Bakery Corp .... E 631 491-3777
  Wyandanch (G-17373)
Micosta Enterprises Inc .... G 518 822-9708
  Hudson (G-6627)

BAKERY PRDTS: Pretzels

Doreen Chrysler .... F 607 257-2241
  Ithaca (G-6838)
Makkos of Brooklyn Ltd .... D 718 366-9800
  Brooklyn (G-2255)

BAKERY PRDTS: Rolls, Bread Type, Fresh Or Frozen

Kossars On Grand LLC .... F 212 473-4810
  New York (G-10880)

BAKERY PRDTS: Wholesalers

A & M Appel Distributing Inc .... G 516 735-1172
  Massapequa (G-8176)
Aron Streit Inc .... E 212 475-7000
  New York (G-9205)
B & D Enterprises of Utica .... D 315 735-3311
  New Hartford (G-8801)
Cannoli Factory Inc .... E 631 643-2700
  Wyandanch (G-17372)
Costanzos Bakery Inc .... C 716 656-9093
  Buffalo (G-2891)
Damascus Bakery Inc .... C 718 855-1456
  Brooklyn (G-1837)
Fratellis LLC .... E 607 722-5663
  Binghamton (G-915)
Hahns Old Fashioned Cake Co .... F 631 249-3456
  Farmingdale (G-5005)
King Cracker Corp .... F 516 539-9251
  Hempstead (G-6277)
Mac Crete Corporation .... F 718 932-1803
  Long Island City (G-7798)
Modern Itln Bky of W Babylon .... C 631 589-7300
  Oakdale (G-13059)
Ohio Baking Company Inc .... G 315 724-2033
  Utica (G-16354)
Operative Cake Corp .... E 718 278-5600
  Bronx (G-1417)
Roslyn Bread Company Inc .... E 516 625-1470
  Roslyn Heights (G-15031)
Royal Caribbean Jamaican Bky .... E 914 668-6868
  Mount Vernon (G-8727)

BAKERY: Wholesale Or Wholesale & Retail Combined

3 Bears Gluten Free Bakery .... F 315 323-0277
  Potsdam (G-13876)
Allies GF Goodies LLC .... F 516 216-1719
  Hicksville (G-6321)
Amiram Dror Inc .... F 212 979-9505
  Brooklyn (G-1611)
Bakerly LLC .... G 212 220-3901
  Brooklyn (G-1665)
Bakery & Coffee Shop .... G 315 287-1829
  Gouverneur (G-5742)
Berardi Bakery Inc .... G 718 746-9529
  Whitestone (G-17203)
Bien Cuit LLC .... G 718 852-0200
  Brooklyn (G-1693)
Bimbo Bakeries Usa Inc .... C 716 372-8444
  Olean (G-13136)
Bimbo Bakeries Usa Inc .... E 516 877-2850
  Mineola (G-8498)
Blackbirds Brooklyn LLC .... G 917 362-4080
  Brooklyn (G-1700)
Blondie S Bakeshop Inc .... G 631 424-4545
  Centerport (G-3475)
Caputo Bakery Inc .... G 718 875-6871
  Brooklyn (G-1756)
Carmine Street Bagels Inc .... F 212 691-3041
  Staten Island (G-15656)
Carolinas Desserts Inc .... G 914 779-4000
  Yonkers (G-17423)
Carter Street Bakery Inc .... G 585 749-7104
  Rochester (G-14261)
Cinderellas Sweets Ltd .... E 516 374-7976
  Woodmere (G-17312)
City Bakery Inc .... G 212 366-1414
  New York (G-9628)
Cookie Connection Inc .... G 315 422-2253
  Syracuse (G-15906)
Creative Relations LLC .... G 212 462-4392
  New York (G-9751)
Daly Meghan .... F 347 699-3259
  Brooklyn (G-1836)
Duane Park Patisserie Inc .... F 212 274-8447
  New York (G-9934)
Eileens Special Cheesecake .... F 212 966-5585
  New York (G-9990)
Ericeira Inc .... G 516 294-4034
  Mineola (G-8510)
Flour Power Bakery Cafe .... G 917 747-6895
  Livingston Manor (G-7561)
Fotis Oneonta Italian Bakery .... G 607 432-3871
  Oneonta (G-13186)
Fung Wong Bakery Inc .... E 212 267-4037
  New York (G-10224)
Geddes Bakery Co Inc .... E 315 437-8084
  North Syracuse (G-12945)
Gluten Free Bake Shop Inc .... E 845 782-5307
  Mountainville (G-8747)
Good Bread Bakery .... F 914 939-3900
  Port Chester (G-13748)
H H B Bakery of Little Neck .... G 718 631-7004
  Flushing (G-5246)
Jerrys Bagels .... G 516 791-0063
  Valley Stream (G-16410)
Jim Romas Bakery Inc .... F 607 748-7425
  Endicott (G-4817)
Kossars Bialys LLC .... G 212 473-4810
  New York (G-10879)
Ladybird Bakery Inc .... G 718 499-8108
  Brooklyn (G-2190)
Lillys Homestyle Bakeshop Inc .... D 718 491-2904
  Brooklyn (G-2222)
Ljmm Inc .... E 845 454-5876
  Poughkeepsie (G-13912)
Made Close LLC .... G 917 837-1357
  Brooklyn (G-2252)
Magnolia Operating LLC .... E 212 265-2777
  New York (G-11108)
Maxwell Bakery Inc .... E 718 498-2200
  Brooklyn (G-2286)
Millers Bulk Food and Bakery .... G 585 798-9700
  Medina (G-8277)
Miss Grimble Associates Inc .... F 718 665-2253
  Bronx (G-1399)
Mollys Cupcakes New York .... G 212 255-5441
  New York (G-11295)
Mother Mousse Ltd .... G 718 983-8366
  Staten Island (G-15709)
Niebylski Bakery Inc .... F 718 721-5152
  Astoria (G-450)
Nildas Desserts Limited .... F 845 454-5876
  Poughkeepsie (G-13922)
Perrottas Bakery Inc .... G 518 283-4711
  Troy (G-16247)
Pesces Bakery Inc .... G 845 246-4730
  Saugerties (G-15191)
Presser Kosher Baking Corp .... E 718 375-5088
  Brooklyn (G-2439)
Quaker Bonnet Inc .... G 716 885-7208
  Buffalo (G-3146)
Rambachs International Bakery .... F 518 563-1721
  Plattsburgh (G-13693)
Rays Restaurant & Bakery Inc .... G 718 441-7707
  Jamaica (G-6945)
Richard Engdal Baking Corp .... F 914 777-9600
  Mamaroneck (G-8044)
Sapienza Pastry Inc .... E 516 352-5232
  Elmont (G-4729)
Settepani Inc .... E 718 349-6524
  Brooklyn (G-2545)
Slims Bagels Unlimited Inc .... E 718 229-1140
  Oakland Gardens (G-13067)
Soutine Inc .... G 212 496-1450
  New York (G-12145)
Stebe Shcjhjff .... F 839 383-9833
  Poughkeepsie (G-13935)
Sunrise Baking Co LLC .... C 718 499-0800
  Brooklyn (G-2621)
Sunshine Distribution Corp .... G 888 506-7051
  New York (G-12238)
Tates Wholesale LLC .... C 631 780-6511
  East Moriches (G-4431)
Tilaros Bakery Inc .... G 716 488-3209
  Jamestown (G-7038)
Triboro Bagel Co Inc .... E 718 359-9245
  Flushing (G-5303)
Two Sisters Kiev Bakery Inc .... G 718 769-2626
  Brooklyn (G-2692)
Two Sisters Kiev Bakery Inc .... E 718 627-5438
  Brooklyn (G-2693)

BANDAGES

Medi-Tech International Corp .... G 800 333-0109
  Brooklyn (G-2291)

BANDS: Copper & Copper Alloy

Milward Alloys Inc .... E 716 434-5536
  Lockport (G-7602)

BANDS: Plastic

Universal Strapping Inc .... E 845 268-2500
  Valley Cottage (G-16394)

BANNERS: Fabric

Ace Banner & Flag Company .... F 212 620-9111
  New York (G-9014)
Arista Flag Corporation .... F 845 246-7700
  Saugerties (G-15180)
Big Apple Sign Corp .... E 212 629-3650
  New York (G-9392)
Big Apple Sign Corp .... E 631 342-0303
  Islandia (G-6788)
Dkm Sales LLC .... E 716 893-7777
  Buffalo (G-2916)
Hollywood Banners Inc .... E 631 842-3000
  Copiague (G-3907)
Kraus & Sons Inc .... F 212 620-0408
  New York (G-10887)
Sellco Industries Inc .... E 607 756-7594
  Cortland (G-4045)

BANQUET HALL FACILITIES

Casa Larga Vineyards .... G 585 223-4210
  Fairport (G-4850)

BAR FIXTURES: Wood

Modern Craft Bar Rest Equip .... G 631 226-5647
  Lindenhurst (G-7473)

BARBECUE EQPT

Korin Japanese Trading Corp .... E 212 587-7021
  New York (G-10878)
Unibrands Corporation .... F 212 897-2278
  New York (G-12451)

BARRICADES: Metal

Backyard Fence Inc .... F 518 452-9496
  Albany (G-51)
Consolidated Barricades Inc .... G 518 922-7944
  Fultonville (G-5478)
Crown Industries Inc .... F 973 672-2277
  New York (G-9759)

BARS & BAR SHAPES: Steel, Hot-Rolled

Vell Company Inc .... G 845 365-1013
  Palisades (G-13404)

BARS, COLD FINISHED: Steel, From Purchased Hot-Rolled

Niagara Lasalle Corporation .... D 716 827-7010
  Buffalo (G-3089)

BARS: Concrete Reinforcing, Fabricated Steel

Agl Industries Inc .... E 718 326-7597
  Maspeth (G-8111)

PRODUCT SECTION

BEAUTY & BARBER SHOP EQPT

Arista Steel Designs Corp..............G..... 718 965-7077
  Brooklyn (G-1627)
Baco Enterprises Inc......................D..... 718 589-6225
  Bronx (G-1279)
Barker Steel LLC...........................E..... 518 465-6221
  Albany (G-52)
City Evolutionary..........................G..... 718 861-7585
  Bronx (G-1299)
Dimension Fabricators Inc..............E..... 518 374-1936
  Schenectady (G-15248)
Ferro Fabricators Inc.....................F..... 718 851-4027
  Brooklyn (G-1967)
GCM Metal Industries Inc..............F..... 718 386-4059
  Brooklyn (G-2015)
Harbor Wldg & Fabrication Corp.....F..... 631 667-1880
  Bay Shore (G-704)
Klein Reinforcing Services Inc........F..... 585 352-9433
  Spencerport (G-15571)
New York Steel Services Co...........G..... 718 291-7770
  Jamaica (G-6935)
Siw Inc...F..... 631 888-0130
  Bay Shore (G-743)
Steel Sales Inc..............................E..... 607 674-6363
  Sherburne (G-15397)
Torino Industrial Inc......................F..... 631 509-1640
  Bellport (G-842)
Wide Flange Inc............................F..... 718 492-8705
  Brooklyn (G-2749)

BARS: Iron, Made In Steel Mills

Crucible Industries LLC.................B..... 800 365-1180
  Syracuse (G-15913)
Tri Valley Iron Inc.........................F..... 845 365-1013
  Palisades (G-13403)

BASEBOARDS: Metal

Slanto Manufacturing Inc...............E..... 516 759-5721
  Glen Cove (G-5628)

BASEMENT WINDOW AREAWAYS: Concrete

Healthy Basement Systems LLC....F..... 516 650-9046
  Medford (G-8249)

BASES, BEVERAGE

Better Fresh Corp.........................G..... 718 628-3682
  Brooklyn (G-1690)
Tealeafs.......................................G..... 716 688-8022
  Williamsville (G-17257)

BASKETS: Steel Wire

Braun Horticulture Inc...................G..... 716 282-6101
  Niagara Falls (G-12798)

BATCHING PLANTS: Cement Silos

New Eagle Silo Corp.....................G..... 585 492-1300
  Arcade (G-398)

BATH SALTS

Aromasong Usa Inc......................F..... 718 838-9669
  Brooklyn (G-1630)

BATHING SUIT STORES

Malia Mills Inc..............................F..... 212 354-4200
  Brooklyn (G-2256)
Shirl-Lynn of New York..................F..... 315 363-5898
  Oneida (G-13167)

BATHMATS, COTTON

Michael Stuart Inc........................E..... 718 821-0704
  Brooklyn (G-2309)

BATHROOM ACCESS & FITTINGS: Vitreous China & Earthenware

AMG Global LLC..........................G..... 212 689-6008
  New York (G-9134)
Gamma Products Inc....................D..... 845 562-3332
  New Windsor (G-8938)
Larcent Enterprises Inc.................E..... 845 562-3332
  New Windsor (G-8941)
Stone and Bath Gallery..................G..... 718 438-4500
  Brooklyn (G-2609)

BATHTUBS: Concrete

Meditub Incorporated....................F..... 866 633-4882
  Lawrence (G-7395)

BATTERIES, EXC AUTOMOTIVE: Wholesalers

El-Don Battery Post Inc................G..... 716 627-3697
  Hamburg (G-5923)
TAe Trans Atlantic Elec Inc...........E..... 631 595-9206
  Deer Park (G-4216)

BATTERIES: Alkaline, Cell Storage

Bren-Trnics Batteries Intl LLC........E..... 631 499-5155
  Commack (G-3826)

BATTERIES: Lead Acid, Storage

Exide Technologies.......................G..... 585 344-0656
  Batavia (G-631)
Johnson Controls Inc....................C..... 585 724-2232
  Rochester (G-14464)

BATTERIES: Rechargeable

Bren-Trnics Batteries Intl Inc.........G..... 631 499-5155
  Commack (G-3825)
Synergy Digital.............................F..... 718 643-2742
  Brooklyn (G-2636)

BATTERIES: Storage

Amco Intl Mfg & Design Inc..........E..... 718 388-8668
  Brooklyn (G-1598)
Battery Energy Storage Systems...G..... 518 256-7029
  Troy (G-16227)
Battsco LLC.................................G..... 516 586-6544
  Hicksville (G-6327)
Bren-Tronics Inc...........................C..... 631 499-5155
  Commack (G-3827)
China Lithium Technologies...........G..... 212 391-2688
  New York (G-9599)
El-Don Battery Post Inc................G..... 716 627-3697
  Hamburg (G-5923)
Ener1 Inc.....................................E..... 212 920-3500
  New York (G-10036)
Hrg Group Inc..............................E..... 212 906-8555
  New York (G-10524)
New Energy Systems Group..........C..... 917 573-0302
  New York (G-11385)
Ultralife Corporation......................B..... 315 332-7100
  Newark (G-12745)
W & W Manufacturing Co..............F..... 516 942-0011
  Deer Park (G-4225)

BATTERIES: Wet

Bren-Tronics Inc...........................C..... 631 499-5155
  Commack (G-3827)
Electrochem Solutions Inc.............E..... 716 759-5800
  Clarence (G-3660)
Empire Scientific...........................G..... 630 510-8636
  Deer Park (G-4140)
Shad Industries Inc.......................G..... 631 504-6028
  Yaphank (G-17402)
TAe Trans Atlantic Elec Inc...........E..... 631 595-9206
  Deer Park (G-4216)

BATTERY CASES: Plastic Or Plastics Combination

Memory Protection Devices Inc.....F..... 631 293-5891
  Farmingdale (G-5047)

BATTERY CHARGERS

Applied Energy Solutions LLC.......E..... 585 538-3270
  Caledonia (G-3277)
China Lithium Technologies...........G..... 212 391-2688
  New York (G-9599)
Eluminocity US Inc.......................G..... 651 528-1165
  New York (G-10016)
Kussmaul Electronics Co Inc.........E..... 631 218-0298
  West Sayville (G-16936)
Walter R Tucker Entps Ltd............E..... 607 467-2866
  Deposit (G-4282)

BATTERY CHARGERS: Storage, Motor & Engine Generator Type

Apogee Power Usa Inc.................F..... 202 746-2890
  Hartsdale (G-5997)
Vdc Electronics Inc......................F..... 631 683-5850
  Huntington (G-6690)

BATTERY CHARGING GENERATORS

Eluminocity US Inc.......................G..... 651 528-1165
  New York (G-10016)

BATTS & BATTING: Cotton

Ino-Tex LLC.................................G..... 212 400-2205
  New York (G-10606)
Rovel Manufacturing Co Inc..........G..... 516 365-2752
  Roslyn (G-15023)
Superior Fiber Mills Inc.................E..... 718 782-7500
  Brooklyn (G-2628)
Vincent Manufacturing Co Inc.......F..... 315 823-0280
  Little Falls (G-7506)

BAUXITE MINING

Alcoa Inc......................................D..... 212 836-2674
  New York (G-9077)

BEARINGS

Turnomat Company LLC................G..... 585 924-1630
  Farmington (G-5157)

BEARINGS & PARTS Ball

A Hyatt Ball Co Ltd.......................G..... 518 747-0272
  Fort Edward (G-5339)
Kilian Manufacturing Corp.............D..... 315 432-0700
  Syracuse (G-15973)
Mageba USA LLC.........................E..... 212 317-1991
  New York (G-11099)
Nes Bearing Company Inc.............E..... 716 372-6532
  Olean (G-13151)
S/N Precision Enterprises Inc........E..... 518 283-8002
  Troy (G-16252)
Schatz Bearing Corporation...........D..... 845 452-6000
  Poughkeepsie (G-13930)
SKF USA Inc................................D..... 716 661-2869
  Falconer (G-4912)
SKF USA Inc................................D..... 716 661-2600
  Falconer (G-4913)

BEARINGS: Ball & Roller

American Refuse Supply Inc.........G..... 718 893-8157
  Bronx (G-1273)
David Fehlman.............................G..... 315 455-8888
  Syracuse (G-15922)
General Bearing Corporation..........C..... 845 358-6000
  West Nyack (G-16918)
Lemoyne Machine Products Corp..G..... 315 454-0708
  Syracuse (G-15976)
Raydon Precision Bearing Co........G..... 516 887-2582
  Lynbrook (G-7958)
Sandle Custom Bearing Corp........G..... 585 593-7000
  Wellsville (G-16757)
SKF USA Inc................................D..... 716 661-2600
  Jamestown (G-7028)

BEAUTY & BARBER SHOP EQPT

Accurate Pnt Powdr Coating Inc....F..... 585 235-1650
  Rochester (G-14167)
Adults and Children With Learn.....E..... 516 593-8230
  East Rockaway (G-4467)
Blackbox Biometrics Inc................E..... 585 329-3399
  Rochester (G-14234)
Brooklyn Industries LLC................F..... 718 788-5250
  Brooklyn (G-1726)
Brooklyn Industries LLC................F..... 718 486-6464
  Brooklyn (G-1727)
Brooklyn Industries LLC................F..... 718 789-2764
  Brooklyn (G-1728)
Callanan Industries Inc..................G..... 518 382-5354
  Schenectady (G-15237)
East Penn Manufacturing Co.........G..... 631 321-7161
  Babylon (G-547)
Global Precision Inds Inc...............F..... 585 254-0010
  Rochester (G-14409)
Goodwill Inds of Greater NY..........C..... 914 621-0781
  Baldwin Place (G-563)

Employee Codes: A=Over 500 employees, B=251-500
C=101-250, D=51-100, E=20-50, F=10-19, G=5-9

BEAUTY & BARBER SHOP EQPT   PRODUCT SECTION

Goodwill Inds Wstn NY Inc ....F 716 633-3305
  Williamsville (G-17246)
Innovative Industries LLC 718 784-7300
  Long Island City (G-7766)
J & A Usa Inc ....G 631 243-3336
  Brentwood (G-1187)
Jags Manufacturing Network Inc ....G 631 750-6367
  Holbrook (G-6454)
Nitro Manufacturing LLC ....F 716 646-9900
  Hamburg (G-5934)
Ohserase Manufacturing LLC ....E 518 358-9309
  Akwesasne (G-32)
Oledworks LLC ....E 585 287-6802
  Rochester (G-14547)
Paperworks Industries Inc ....F 913 621-0922
  Baldwinsville (G-573)
PCI Industries Corp 914 662-2700
  Mount Vernon (G-8713)
PS Pibbs Inc ....E 718 445-8046
  Flushing (G-5284)
S B Manufacturing LLC ....F 845 352-3700
  Monsey (G-8579)

BEAUTY SALONS

Lemetric Hair Centers Inc ....F 212 986-5620
  New York (G-10964)

BED & BREAKFAST INNS

Malina Management Company Inc .....E 607 535-9614
  Montour Falls (G-8610)
Newspaper Publisher LLC ....F 607 775-0472
  Conklin (G-3871)

BEDDING, BEDSPREADS, BLANKETS & SHEETS

Cathay Home Inc ....E 212 213-0988
  New York (G-9548)
Indigo Home Inc ....G 212 684-4146
  New York (G-10589)
Jdt International LLC ....G 212 400-7570
  New York (G-10712)
Northpoint Trading Inc ....F 212 481-8001
  New York (G-11460)
Richloom Fabrics Group Inc ....F 212 685-5400
  New York (G-11870)
Sunham Home Fashions LLC ....D 212 695-1218
  New York (G-12236)
Thor Marketing Corp ....G 201 247-7103
  Valley Cottage (G-16393)

BEDDING, BEDSPREADS, BLANKETS & SHEETS: Comforters & Quilts

Alen Sands York Associates Ltd ....F 212 563-6305
  New York (G-9080)
EY Industries Inc 718 624-9122
  Brooklyn (G-1947)
Kaltex North America Inc ....F 212 894-3200
  New York (G-10807)
Revman International Inc 212 894-3100
  New York (G-11854)
Royal Home Fashions Inc 212 689-7222
  New York (G-11924)

BEDDING, FROM SILK OR MANMADE FIBER

Greenbuds LLC ....G 718 483-9212
  Brooklyn (G-2052)
Westpoint Home LLC ....A 212 930-2074
  New York (G-12615)

BEDS & ACCESS STORES

Charles P Rogers Brass Beds ....F 212 675-4400
  New York (G-9582)
Duxiana Dux Bed ....G 212 755-2600
  New York (G-9941)
Metro Mattress Corp ....E 716 205-2300
  Niagara Falls (G-12847)

BEDS: Hospital

Hard Manufacturing Co Inc ....D 716 893-1800
  Buffalo (G-2988)
NK Medical Products Inc ....G 716 759-7200
  Amherst (G-254)
Novum Medical Products Inc ....F 716 759-7200
  Amherst (G-255)

VSM Investors LLC ....G 212 351-1600
  New York (G-12571)

BEDSPREADS & BED SETS, FROM PURCHASED MATERIALS

Belle Maison USA Ltd ....E 718 805-0200
  Richmond Hill (G-14068)
Bramson House Inc ....C 516 764-5006
  Freeport (G-5390)
C & G of Kingston Inc ....D 845 331-0148
  Kingston (G-7180)
County Draperies Inc ....E 845 342-9009
  Middletown (G-8433)
Fabric Quilters Unlimited Inc ....E 516 333-2866
  Westbury (G-16984)
Himatsingka America Inc ....E 212 545-8929
  New York (G-10478)
Jo-Vin Decorators Inc ....E 718 441-9350
  Woodhaven (G-17306)
Richloom Corp ....F 212 685-5400
  New York (G-11868)
Wayne Decorators Inc ....G 718 529-4200
  Jamaica (G-6963)

BEDSPREADS, COTTON

Mason Contract Products LLC ....D 516 328-6900
  New Hyde Park (G-8848)

BEER & ALE WHOLESALERS

Olde Saratoga Brewing ....F 518 581-0492
  Saratoga Springs (G-15165)

BEER & ALE, WHOLESALE: Beer & Other Fermented Malt Liquors

Constellation Brands Inc ....D 585 678-7100
  Victor (G-16469)
Load/N/Go Beverage Corp ....F 585 218-4019
  Rochester (G-14481)
Save More Beverage Corp ....G 518 371-2520
  Halfmoon (G-5916)

BEER, WINE & LIQUOR STORES

Lucas Vineyards & Winery ....F 607 532-4825
  Interlaken (G-6748)
Mount Gay Rum 212 399-4200
  New York (G-11312)

BEER, WINE & LIQUOR STORES: Beer, Packaged

Load/N/Go Beverage Corp ....F 585 218-4019
  Rochester (G-14481)
Save More Beverage Corp ....G 518 371-2520
  Halfmoon (G-5916)

BEER, WINE & LIQUOR STORES: Wine

Casa Larga Vineyards ....G 585 223-4210
  Fairport (G-4850)
Coyote Moon LLC ....F 315 686-5600
  Clayton (G-3685)
J Petrocelli Wine Cellars LLC ....E 631 765-1100
  Peconic (G-13471)
Negys New Land Vinyrd Winery 315 585-4432
  Geneva (G-5583)
Olde Chtqua Vneyards Ltd Lblty ....F 716 792-2749
  Portland (G-13873)
Standing Stone Vineyards ....G 607 582-6051
  Hector (G-6261)

BELLOWS

Kinemotive Corporation ....E 631 249-6440
  Farmingdale (G-5028)
Nicoform Inc ....F 585 454-5530
  Rochester (G-14537)

BELTING: Rubber

Van Slyke Belting LLC ....G 518 283-5479
  Poestenkill (G-13726)

BELTING: Transmission, Rubber

Sampla Belting North Amer LLC ....F 716 667-7450
  Lackawanna (G-7249)

BELTS: Conveyor, Made From Purchased Wire

Chemprene Inc ....C 845 831-2800
  Beacon (G-782)
Chemprene Holding Inc ....C 845 831-2800
  Beacon (G-783)
Habasit America Inc ....D 716 824-8484
  Buffalo (G-2984)

BELTS: Indl

DC Fabrication & Welding Inc 845 295-0215
  Ferndale (G-5169)

BELTS: Seat, Automotive & Aircraft

Davis Restraint Systems Inc ....F 631 563-1500
  Bohemia (G-1051)

BENCHES: Seating

Jays Furniture Products Inc ....E 716 876-8854
  Buffalo (G-3015)
Jcdecaux Mallscape LLC ....G 646 834-1200
  New York (G-10709)

BEVERAGE BASES & SYRUPS

Agua Enerviva LLC ....F 516 597-5440
  Bethpage (G-864)
Boylan Bottling Co Inc ....E 800 289-7978
  New York (G-9447)
Buffalo Blends Inc ....E 716 825-4422
  Buffalo (G-2849)
Flavormatic Industries Inc ....E 845 297-9100
  Wappingers Falls (G-16567)

BEVERAGE, NONALCOHOLIC: Iced Tea/Fruit Drink, Bottled/Canned

Arizona Beverage Company LLC ......G 516 812-0300
  Woodbury (G-17282)
F & V Distribution Company LLC ......G 516 812-0393
  Woodbury (G-17286)
Hain Celestial Group Inc ....C 516 587-5000
  New Hyde Park (G-8837)
Heart of Tea ....F 917 725-3164
  New York (G-10450)
Long Island Brand Bevs LLC ....G 855 542-2832
  Long Island City (G-7794)
Long Island Iced Tea Corp ....E 855 542-2832
  Hicksville (G-6365)

BEVERAGES, ALCOHOLIC: Ale

Empire Brewing Company Inc ....D 315 925-8308
  Syracuse (G-15935)

BEVERAGES, ALCOHOLIC: Applejack

Honeoye Falls Distillery LLC ....F 201 780-4618
  Honeoye Falls (G-6531)

BEVERAGES, ALCOHOLIC: Beer

Anheuser-Busch LLC ....C 315 638-0365
  Baldwinsville (G-566)
Anheuser-Busch LLC 212 573-8800
  New York (G-9159)
Anheuser-Busch Companies LLC .....G 718 589-2610
  Bronx (G-1276)
Anheuser-Busch Inbev Fin Inc 212 573-8800
  New York (G-9160)
Brazen Street LLC ....E 516 305-7951
  Brooklyn (G-1713)
Catskill Mtn Brewing Co Inc ....D 845 256-1700
  New Paltz (G-8874)
Constellation Brands Inc ....D 585 678-7100
  Victor (G-16469)
Decrescente Distributing Co ....D 518 664-9866
  Mechanicville (G-8226)
High Falls Brewing Company LLC ....C 585 546-1030
  Rochester (G-14434)
Hoptron Brewtique 631 438-0296
  Patchogue (G-13422)
Indian Ladder Farmstead Brewer .....G 518 577-1484
  Altamont (G-208)
Ithaca Beer Company Inc ....E 607 272-1305
  Ithaca (G-6853)
Keegan Ales LLC ....F 845 331-2739
  Kingston (G-7192)

2017 Harris
New York Manufacturers Directory

(G-0000) Company's Geographic Section entry number

PRODUCT SECTION

BEVERAGES, ALCOHOLIC: Wines

Labatt USA LLC .... D 716 604-1050
  Buffalo *(G-3041)*
Middle Ages Brewing Company .... G 315 476-4250
  Syracuse *(G-15987)*
Montauk Brewing Company Inc .... F 631 668-8471
  Montauk *(G-8589)*
Newburgh Brewing Company LLC .... F 845 569-2337
  Newburgh *(G-12769)*
North American Breweries Inc .... F 585 546-1030
  Rochester *(G-14539)*
North Amrcn Brwries Hldngs LLC .... E 585 546-1030
  Rochester *(G-14542)*
Uptown Local .... F 212 988-1704
  New York *(G-12475)*
Vanberg & Dewulf Co Inc .... G 607 547-8184
  Cooperstown *(G-3886)*
Yonkers Whl Beer Distrs Inc .... G 914 963-8600
  Yonkers *(G-17504)*

BEVERAGES, ALCOHOLIC: Beer & Ale

Barrier Brewing Company LLC .... G 516 316-4429
  Long Beach *(G-7638)*
Black River Brewing Co Inc .... G 315 755-2739
  Watertown *(G-16639)*
Brewery Ommegang Ltd .... E 607 286-4144
  Cooperstown *(G-3883)*
Castle Brands Inc .... D 646 356-0200
  New York *(G-9542)*
Coopers Cave Ale Co S-Corp .... F 518 792-0007
  Glens Falls *(G-5676)*
Cooperstown Brewing Co LLC .... G 607 286-9330
  Milford *(G-8473)*
Custom Brewcrafters Inc .... F 585 624-4386
  Honeoye Falls *(G-6526)*
Duvel Mortgage USA Inc .... G 607 267-6121
  Cooperstown *(G-3885)*
Hornell Brewing Co Inc .... G 914 597-7911
  White Plains *(G-17122)*
Horseheads Brewing Inc .... G 607 734-8055
  Lowman *(G-7934)*
Hyde Park Brewing Co Inc .... E 845 229-8277
  Hyde Park *(G-6734)*
Keuka Brewing Co LLC .... G 607 868-4648
  Hammondsport *(G-5957)*
Long Ireland Brewing LLC .... G 631 403-4303
  Riverhead *(G-14147)*
Mad Scntsts Brwing Prtners LLC .... E 347 766-2739
  Brooklyn *(G-2251)*
Millercoors LLC .... E 585 385-0670
  Pittsford *(G-13570)*
Olde Saratoga Brewing .... F 518 581-0492
  Saratoga Springs *(G-15165)*
Paradox Brewery LLC .... G 518 351-5036
  Schroon Lake *(G-15318)*
Rising Sons 6 Brewing Coinc .... G 607 368-4836
  Corning *(G-3979)*
Wagner Vineyards & Brewing Co .... E 607 582-6574
  Lodi *(G-7636)*
Woodcock Brothers Brewing Comp .... G 716 333-4000
  Wilson *(G-17270)*

BEVERAGES, ALCOHOLIC: Brandy

Cruzin Management Inc .... E 212 641-8700
  New York *(G-9761)*
Levindi .... F 212 572-7000
  New York *(G-10978)*
Mount Gay Rum .... G 212 399-4200
  New York *(G-11312)*

BEVERAGES, ALCOHOLIC: Cocktails

Dutch Spirits LLC .... F 518 398-1022
  Pine Plains *(G-13555)*

BEVERAGES, ALCOHOLIC: Distilled Liquors

Braided Oak Spirits LLC .... F 845 381-1525
  Middletown *(G-8429)*
Constellation Brands Inc .... D 585 678-7100
  Victor *(G-16469)*
Finger Lakes Distilling .... F 607 546-5510
  Burdett *(G-3265)*
Leblon LLC .... F 954 649-0148
  New York *(G-10954)*
Leblon LLC .... E 786 281-5672
  New York *(G-10955)*
Levindi .... F 212 572-7000
  New York *(G-10978)*
Long Island Spirits Inc .... F 631 630-9322
  Calverton *(G-3292)*

Marnier-Lapostolle Inc .... D 212 207-4350
  New York *(G-11164)*
Pernod Ricard Usa LLC .... D 914 848-4800
  New York *(G-11621)*
Prohibition Distillery LLC .... G 917 685-8989
  Roscoe *(G-15011)*
Riazul Imports LLC .... F 713 894-9177
  New York *(G-11860)*
Sovereign Brands LLC .... G 212 343-8366
  New York *(G-12146)*
Tuthilltown Spirits LLC .... F 845 255-1527
  Gardiner *(G-5551)*

BEVERAGES, ALCOHOLIC: Gin

Madison County Distillery LLC .... G 315 391-6070
  Cazenovia *(G-3448)*

BEVERAGES, ALCOHOLIC: Liquors, Malt

Marnier-Lapostolle Inc .... D 212 207-4350
  New York *(G-11164)*

BEVERAGES, ALCOHOLIC: Neutral Spirits, Fruit

Dutch Spirits LLC .... F 518 398-1022
  Pine Plains *(G-13555)*

BEVERAGES, ALCOHOLIC: Rum

Castle Brands Inc .... D 646 356-0200
  New York *(G-9542)*
Cruzin Management Inc .... E 212 641-8700
  New York *(G-9761)*
Evolution Spirits Inc .... G 917 543-7880
  New York *(G-10094)*
Leblon Holdings LLC .... E 212 741-2675
  New York *(G-10953)*
Mount Gay Rum .... G 212 399-4200
  New York *(G-11312)*

BEVERAGES, ALCOHOLIC: Vodka

Russian Standard Vodka USA Inc .... G 212 679-1894
  New York *(G-11937)*

BEVERAGES, ALCOHOLIC: Wines

Americana Vineyards & Winery .... F 607 387-6801
  Interlaken *(G-6746)*
Anyelas Vineyards LLC .... F 315 685-3797
  Skaneateles *(G-15455)*
Arrowhead Spring Vineyards LLC .... G 716 434-8030
  Lockport *(G-7570)*
Atwater Estate Vineyards LLC .... G 607 546-8463
  Burdett *(G-3264)*
Billsboro Winery .... G 315 789-9538
  Geneva *(G-5570)*
Brotherhood Amer Oldest Wnery .... E 845 496-3661
  Washingtonville *(G-16599)*
Casa Larga Vineyards .... G 585 223-4210
  Fairport *(G-4850)*
Casa Larga Vineyards .... G 585 223-4210
  Fairport *(G-4851)*
Cascade Mountain Winery & Rest .... F 845 373-9021
  Amenia *(G-215)*
Cava Spiliadis USA .... E 212 247-8214
  New York *(G-9551)*
Chautauqua Wine Company Inc .... G 716 934-9463
  Silver Creek *(G-15447)*
Clinton Vineyards Inc .... G 845 266-5372
  Clinton Corners *(G-3724)*
Constellation Brands US Oprs .... A 585 396-7600
  Canandaigua *(G-3340)*
Constellation Brands US Oprs .... B 585 396-7600
  Canandaigua *(G-3341)*
Coyote Moon LLC .... F 315 686-5600
  Clayton *(G-3685)*
Deer Run Enterprises Inc .... G 585 346-0850
  Geneseo *(G-5565)*
Dorset Farms Inc .... F 631 734-6010
  Peconic *(G-13470)*
Duck Walk Vinyards .... E 631 726-7555
  Water Mill *(G-16605)*
Eagle Crest Vineyard LLC .... G 585 346-5760
  Conesus *(G-3850)*
East End Vineyards LLC .... G 718 468-0500
  Queens Village *(G-13976)*
Fox Run Vineyards Inc .... G 315 536-4616
  Penn Yan *(G-13512)*
Frank Wines Inc .... G 646 765-6637
  New York *(G-10203)*

Freedom Run Winery Inc .... G 716 433-4136
  Lockport *(G-7587)*
Gabriella Importers Inc .... G 212 579-3945
  Bohemia *(G-1070)*
Gabriella Importers Inc .... F 212 579-3945
  New York *(G-10238)*
Glenora Wine Cellars Inc .... E 607 243-9500
  Dundee *(G-4328)*
Grapes & Grains .... G 518 283-9463
  Rensselaer *(G-14046)*
Greenwood Winery LLC .... E 315 432-8132
  East Syracuse *(G-4534)*
Hermann J Wiemer Vineyard .... G 607 243-7971
  Dundee *(G-4329)*
Heron Hill Vineyards Inc .... E 607 868-4241
  Hammondsport *(G-5956)*
Hosmer Inc .... F 888 467-9463
  Ovid *(G-13346)*
J Petrocelli Wine Cellars LLC .... E 631 765-1100
  Peconic *(G-13471)*
Joseph Zakon Winery Ltd .... G 718 604-1430
  Brooklyn *(G-2151)*
Konstantin D FRAnk& Sons Vini .... E 607 868-4884
  Hammondsport *(G-5958)*
Lafayette Chateau .... G 607 546-2062
  Hector *(G-6258)*
Lakewood Vineyards Inc .... F 607 535-9252
  Watkins Glen *(G-16695)*
Lamoreaux Landing WI .... D 607 582-6162
  Lodi *(G-7635)*
Lieb Cellars LLC .... G 631 298-1942
  Mattituck *(G-8207)*
Lucas Vineyards & Winery .... G 607 532-4825
  Interlaken *(G-6748)*
Merritt Estate Winery Inc .... F 716 965-4800
  Forestville *(G-5334)*
Millbrook Winery Inc .... F 845 677-8383
  Millbrook *(G-8478)*
Montezuma Winery LLC .... G 315 568-8190
  Seneca Falls *(G-15366)*
Negys New Land Vinyrd Winery .... G 315 585-4432
  Geneva *(G-5583)*
North House Vineyards Inc .... G 631 779-2817
  Jamestown *(G-6966)*
Olde Chtqua Vneyards Ltd Lblty .... F 716 792-2749
  Portland *(G-13873)*
Paumanok Vineyards Ltd .... E 631 722-8800
  Aquebogue *(G-385)*
Pellegrini Vineyards LLC .... G 631 734-4111
  Cutchogue *(G-4072)*
Pindar Vineyards LLC .... G 631 734-6200
  Peconic *(G-13472)*
Pinnacle Wine Vault LLC .... F 212 736-0040
  New York *(G-11665)*
Prejean Winery Inc .... F 315 536-7524
  Penn Yan *(G-13516)*
Premium Wine Group LLC .... G 631 298-1900
  Mattituck *(G-8209)*
Pugliese Vineyards Inc .... G 631 734-4057
  Cutchogue *(G-4073)*
Red Newt Cellars Inc .... G 607 546-4100
  Hector *(G-6260)*
Red Tail Ridge Inc .... G 315 536-4580
  Penn Yan *(G-13517)*
Rock Stream Vineyards .... G 607 243-8322
  Rock Stream *(G-14779)*
Royal Wine Corporation .... F 845 236-4000
  Marlboro *(G-8106)*
Sheldrake Point Vineyard LLC .... F 607 532-8967
  Ovid *(G-13348)*
Sokolin LLC .... E 631 537-4434
  Yaphank *(G-17403)*
Spanish Artisan Wine Group LLC .... G 914 414-6982
  Patterson *(G-13444)*
Standing Stone Vineyards .... G 607 582-6051
  Hector *(G-6261)*
Swedish Hill Vineyard Inc .... D 607 403-0029
  Romulus *(G-14844)*
Thirsty Owl Wine Company .... G 607 869-5805
  Ovid *(G-13349)*
Thousand Islands Winery LLC .... E 315 482-9306
  Alexandria Bay *(G-192)*
Trader Joes Company .... E 212 529-6326
  New York *(G-12388)*
Vedell North Fork LLC .... G 631 323-3526
  Cutchogue *(G-4074)*
Wagner Vineyards & Brewing Co .... E 607 582-6574
  Lodi *(G-7636)*
Westchester Wine Warehouse LLC .... F 914 824-1400
  White Plains *(G-17185)*

Employee Codes: A=Over 500 employees, B=251-500
C=101-250, D=51-100, E=20-50, F=10-19, G=5-9

Wine Group Inc ..... D 716 326-3151
Westfield *(G-17055)*
Wine Market ..... G 516 328-8800
New Hyde Park *(G-8872)*
Woodbury Vineyards Inc ..... G 716 679-9463
Fredonia *(G-5377)*

BEVERAGES, MALT

High Falls Operating Co LLC ..... A 585 546-1030
Rochester *(G-14435)*
North Country Malt Supply LLC ..... G 518 298-2300
Champlain *(G-3545)*

BEVERAGES, NONALCOHOLIC: Bottled & canned soft drinks

3v Company Inc ..... E 718 858-7333
Brooklyn *(G-1517)*
American Bottling Company ..... F 516 714-0002
Ronkonkoma *(G-14868)*
Beverage Works Nj Inc ..... E 631 293-3501
Farmingdale *(G-4953)*
Beverage Works Ny Inc ..... E 718 812-2034
Brooklyn *(G-1692)*
Big Geyser Inc ..... G 631 549-4940
Melville *(G-8297)*
Borabora Fruit Juices Inc ..... G 845 795-1027
Highland *(G-6403)*
Bottling Group LLC ..... G 914 767-6000
White Plains *(G-17087)*
Brands Within Reach LLC ..... E 847 720-9090
Mamaroneck *(G-8025)*
Brooklyn Btlg Milton NY Inc ..... C 845 795-2171
Milton *(G-8482)*
Cliffstar LLC ..... A 716 366-6100
Dunkirk *(G-4337)*
Coca-Cola Bottling Co of NY ..... F 518 459-2010
Albany *(G-68)*
Coca-Cola Bottling Company ..... E 518 483-0422
Malone *(G-8008)*
Coca-Cola Btlg Co Buffalo Inc ..... C 716 874-4610
Tonawanda *(G-16154)*
Coca-Cola Btlg Co of NY Inc ..... F 845 562-3037
New Windsor *(G-8936)*
Coca-Cola Btlg Co of NY Inc ..... C 718 326-3334
Maspeth *(G-8122)*
Coca-Cola Btlg Co of NY Inc ..... F 914 592-4574
Elmsford *(G-4741)*
Coca-Cola Btlg Co of NY Inc ..... F 315 457-9221
Syracuse *(G-15900)*
Coca-Cola Btlg Co of NY Inc ..... E 718 416-7575
Maspeth *(G-8123)*
Coca-Cola Btlg Co of NY Inc ..... E 631 434-3535
Hauppauge *(G-6048)*
Coca-Cola Btlg Co of NY Inc ..... F 718 420-6800
Staten Island *(G-15660)*
Coca-Cola Btlg Co of NY Inc ..... F 914 789-1580
Elmsford *(G-4742)*
Coca-Cola Refreshments USA Inc ..... E 718 401-5200
Bronx *(G-1301)*
Coca-Cola Refreshments USA Inc ..... E 315 785-8907
Watertown *(G-16646)*
Coca-Cola Refreshments USA Inc ..... G 914 592-0806
Hawthorne *(G-6245)*
Consumers Beverages Inc ..... E 716 837-3087
Buffalo *(G-2887)*
Consumers Beverages Inc ..... G 716 675-4934
West Seneca *(G-16942)*
Doheny Nice and Easy ..... G 518 793-1733
Glens Falls *(G-5677)*
Dr Pepper Snapple Group Inc ..... D 914 846-2300
Elmsford *(G-4747)*
Dr Pepper Snapple Group Inc ..... G 718 246-6200
Brooklyn *(G-1877)*
Fancy Flamingo LLC ..... G 516 209-7306
New York *(G-10134)*
Framedcom ..... E 212 400-2200
New York *(G-10197)*
Gangi Distributors Inc ..... F 718 442-5745
Staten Island *(G-15676)*
Grayhawk Leasing LLC ..... G 914 767-6000
Somers *(G-15510)*
Kraft Heinz Foods Company ..... A 914 335-2500
Tarrytown *(G-16093)*
Linda Wine & Spirit ..... G 718 703-5707
Brooklyn *(G-2225)*
N Y Winstons Inc ..... G 212 665-3166
New York *(G-11337)*
Pepsi Bottling Ventures LLC ..... D 631 772-6144
Patchogue *(G-13432)*
Pepsi-Cola Operating Company ..... E 914 767-6000
White Plains *(G-17153)*
Pepsico Inc ..... A 914 253-2000
Purchase *(G-13966)*
Pepsico Capital Resources Inc ..... G 914 253-2000
Purchase *(G-13969)*
Quench It Inc ..... E 845 462-5400
Poughkeepsie *(G-13927)*
Rochester Coca Cola Bottling ..... E 607 739-5678
Horseheads *(G-6591)*
Rochester Coca Cola Bottling ..... D 585 546-3900
Rochester *(G-14638)*
Shopping Center Wine & Liquor ..... G 914 528-1600
Mohegan Lake *(G-8544)*
Snapp Too Enterprise ..... G 718 224-5252
Flushing *(G-5293)*
Snapple ..... G 914 846-2300
Elmsford *(G-4786)*
Street King LLC ..... G 212 400-2200
New York *(G-12212)*
Tumeric Healing Entps Inc ..... F 508 364-7597
New York *(G-12422)*

BEVERAGES, NONALCOHOLIC: Carbonated

Bottling Group LLC ..... E 315 788-6751
Watertown *(G-16640)*
Clintons Ditch Coop Co Inc ..... C 315 699-2695
Cicero *(G-3643)*
Goodo Beverage Company ..... F 347 226-9996
Bronx *(G-1346)*
Meadowbrook Distributing Corp ..... D 516 226-9000
Garden City *(G-5520)*
Pepsi Beverages Co ..... G 518 782-2150
Latham *(G-7374)*
Pepsi Bottling Ventures LLC ..... E 631 226-9000
Amityville *(G-321)*
Pepsi Btlg Group Globl Fin LLC ..... G 914 767-6000
Somers *(G-15511)*
Pepsi Lipton Tea Partnership ..... E 914 253-2000
Purchase *(G-13964)*
Pepsi-Cola Bottling Group ..... G 914 767-6000
White Plains *(G-17151)*
Pepsi-Cola Metro Btlg Co Inc ..... G 914 767-6000
White Plains *(G-17152)*
Pepsi-Cola Metro Btlg Co Inc ..... E 914 253-2000
Purchase *(G-13965)*
Pepsi-Cola Metro Btlg Co Inc ..... D 607 795-1399
Horseheads *(G-6587)*
Pepsi-Cola Newburgh Btlg Inc ..... C 845 562-5400
Newburgh *(G-12774)*
Pepsico ..... F 419 252-0247
Hawthorne *(G-6252)*
Pepsico ..... E 914 801-1500
Valhalla *(G-16369)*
Pepsico Inc ..... B 914 742-4500
Valhalla *(G-16370)*
Pepsico Inc ..... A 914 253-2000
Purchase *(G-13967)*
Pepsico Inc ..... F 914 253-2713
Purchase *(G-13968)*
Pepsico World Trading Co Inc ..... G 914 767-6000
White Plains *(G-17157)*

BEVERAGES, NONALCOHOLIC: Carbonated, Canned & Bottled, Etc

Beverage Works Incorporated ..... G 718 834-0500
Brooklyn *(G-1691)*
Blue Star Beverages Corp ..... G 718 381-3535
Brooklyn *(G-1704)*
Bottling Group LLC ..... B 800 789-2626
White Plains *(G-17086)*
Brave Chefs Incorporated ..... G 347 956-5905
Little Neck *(G-7507)*
Chohehco LLC ..... G 315 420-4624
Skaneateles *(G-15457)*
Hmo Beverage Corp ..... G 917 371-6100
Brooklyn *(G-2081)*
Hydrive Energy ..... G 914 925-9100
Rye *(G-15060)*
Juices Enterprises Inc ..... G 718 953-1860
Brooklyn *(G-2158)*
Liquid Management Partners LLC ..... F 516 775-5050
New Hyde Park *(G-8846)*
Pepsi Bottling Holdings Inc ..... F 800 433-2652
Purchase *(G-13963)*
Save More Beverage Corp ..... G 518 371-2520
Halfmoon *(G-5916)*
Switch Beverage Company LLC ..... F 203 202-7383
Port Washington *(G-13867)*
Treo Brands LLC ..... G 914 341-1850
Harrison *(G-5992)*

BEVERAGES, NONALCOHOLIC: Cider

Beak & Skiff Cider Mill Inc ..... G 315 677-5105
La Fayette *(G-7239)*
Lakeside Cider Mill Farm Inc ..... G 518 399-8359
Ballston Lake *(G-582)*
Schutt Cider Mill ..... F 585 872-2924
Webster *(G-16734)*

BEVERAGES, NONALCOHOLIC: Flavoring extracts & syrups, nec

Baldwin Richardson Foods Co ..... C 315 986-2727
Macedon *(G-7983)*
Citrus and Allied Essences Ltd ..... E 516 354-1200
Floral Park *(G-5200)*
Danisco US Inc ..... D 585 277-4300
Rochester *(G-14301)*
Delbia Do Company Inc ..... G 718 585-2226
Bronx *(G-1312)*
Delbia Do Company Inc ..... F 718 585-2226
Bronx *(G-1313)*
Dr Pepper Snapple Group Inc ..... C 315 589-4911
Williamson *(G-17222)*
DSM Nutritional Products LLC ..... C 518 372-5155
Glenville *(G-5701)*
Fortitech Inc ..... C 518 372-5155
Schenectady *(G-15255)*
Iff International Inc ..... E 212 765-5500
New York *(G-10560)*
Interntnal Flvors Frgrnces Inc ..... C 212 765-5500
New York *(G-10639)*
Natural Organics Laboratories ..... B 631 957-5600
Amityville *(G-315)*
Pepsi-Cola Bottling Co NY Inc ..... F 718 392-1000
New York *(G-11611)*
Pepsico Inc ..... A 914 253-2000
Purchase *(G-13966)*
Star Kay White Inc ..... D 845 268-2600
Congers *(G-3860)*
Synergy Flavors NY Company LLC ..... G 585 232-6648
Rochester *(G-14711)*
Torre Products Co Inc ..... G 212 925-8989
New York *(G-12375)*
Virginia Dare Extract Co Inc ..... C 718 788-6320
Brooklyn *(G-2729)*
Wynn Starr Flavors Inc ..... E 845 584-3080
Congers *(G-3863)*

BEVERAGES, NONALCOHOLIC: Fruit Drnks, Under 100% Juice, Can

Ba Sports Nutrition LLC ..... B 310 424-5077
Whitestone *(G-17202)*
Cheribundi Inc ..... E 800 699-0460
Geneva *(G-5573)*
Levindi ..... F 212 572-7000
New York *(G-10978)*
Mnm Service Distributors Inc ..... G 914 337-5268
Bronxville *(G-1501)*
Nantucket Allserve Inc ..... B 914 612-4000
Elmsford *(G-4770)*
Purely Maple LLC ..... F 203 997-9309
New York *(G-11753)*

BEVERAGES, NONALCOHOLIC: Soft Drinks, Canned & Bottled, Etc

Adirondack Beverage Co Inc ..... A 518 370-3621
Schenectady *(G-15227)*
Boylan Bottling Co Inc ..... E 800 289-7978
New York *(G-9447)*
Cornell Beverages Inc ..... F 718 381-3000
Brooklyn *(G-1804)*
Dr Pepper Snapple Group Inc ..... C 315 589-4911
Williamson *(G-17222)*
Energy Brands Inc ..... D 212 545-6000
New York *(G-10037)*
General Cinema Bevs of Ohio ..... A 914 767-6000
Somers *(G-15509)*
Johnnie Ryan Co Inc ..... F 716 282-1606
Niagara Falls *(G-12838)*
La Cola 1 Inc ..... G 917 509-6669
New York *(G-10907)*
Load/N/Go Beverage Corp ..... F 585 218-4019
Rochester *(G-14481)*
Manhattan Special Bottling ..... F 718 388-4144
Brooklyn *(G-2261)*

Monfefo LLC ....G....... 347 779-2600
Brooklyn (G-2331)
New York Bottling Co Inc ....F....... 718 963-3232
Bronx (G-1408)
Pepsi Cola Buffalo Btlg Corp............B....... 716 684-2800
Cheektowaga (G-3585)
Pepsi-Cola Allied Bottlers ....A....... 518 783-8811
Latham (G-7375)
Pepsi-Cola Bottling Co NY Inc............B....... 718 649-2465
College Point (G-3800)
Pepsi-Cola Bottling Co NY Inc............E....... 914 699-2600
Mount Vernon (G-8714)
Pepsi-Cola Bottling Co NY Inc............G....... 718 786-8550
Maspeth (G-8165)
Pepsi-Cola Bottling Co NY Inc............D....... 718 892-1570
Bronx (G-1424)
Pepsi-Cola Bottling Co NY Inc............B....... 718 392-1000
College Point (G-3801)
Stewarts Processing Corp ....D....... 518 581-1200
Ballston Spa (G-610)

BEVERAGES, NONALCOHOLIC: Tea, Iced, Bottled & Canned, Etc

East Coast Cultures LLC............F....... 917 261-3010
Kingston (G-7188)

BEVERAGES, WINE & DISTILLED ALCOHOLIC, WHOLESALE: Liquor

Cruzin Management Inc............E....... 212 641-8700
New York (G-9761)
Marnier-Lapostolle Inc............D....... 212 207-4350
New York (G-11164)

BEVERAGES, WINE & DISTILLED ALCOHOLIC, WHOLESALE: Neutral Sp

Spanish Artisan Wine Group LLC ....G....... 914 414-6982
Patterson (G-13444)

BEVERAGES, WINE & DISTILLED ALCOHOLIC, WHOLESALE: Wine

Coyote Moon LLC ....F....... 315 686-5600
Clayton (G-3685)
Royal Wine Corporation............F....... 845 236-4000
Marlboro (G-8106)

BEVERAGES, WINE WHOLESALE : Wine Coolers

Hoptron Brewtique............G....... 631 438-0296
Patchogue (G-13422)

BICYCLES WHOLESALERS

East Coast Cycle LLC............G....... 631 780-5360
Farmingdale (G-4983)

BICYCLES, PARTS & ACCESS

East Coast Cycle LLC............G....... 631 780-5360
Farmingdale (G-4983)
Evelo Inc ....G....... 917 251-8743
Rockaway Park (G-14785)
Great American Bicycle LLC............E....... 518 584-8100
Saratoga Springs (G-15155)
Jetson Electric Bikes LLC............G....... 908 309-8880
New York (G-10722)
Social Bicycles Inc............E....... 917 746-7624
Brooklyn (G-2576)
Worksman Trading Corp ....E....... 718 322-2000
Ozone Park (G-13387)

BILLETS: Steel

Homogeneous Metals Inc............D....... 315 839-5421
Clayville (G-3689)

BILLFOLD INSERTS: Plastic

Quality Lineals Usa Inc............G....... 516 378-6577
Merrick (G-8392)

BILLIARD & POOL TABLES & SPLYS

A Hyatt Ball Co Ltd ....G....... 518 747-0272
Fort Edward (G-5339)
International Leisure Pdts Inc............E....... 631 254-2155
Edgewood (G-4601)

BINDING SVC: Books & Manuals

514 Adams Corporation ....G....... 516 352-6948
Franklin Square (G-5359)
A-Quick Bindery LLC............G....... 631 491-1110
West Babylon (G-16763)
Agrecolor Inc............F....... 516 741-8700
Mineola (G-8491)
Argo Lithographers Inc ....E....... 718 729-2700
Long Island City (G-7669)
Arista Innovations Inc ....E....... 516 746-2262
Mineola (G-8496)
Baum Christine and John Corp............G....... 585 621-8910
Rochester (G-14224)
Beastons Budget Printing............G....... 585 244-2721
Rochester (G-14227)
Benchemark Printing Inc............D....... 518 393-1361
Schenectady (G-15234)
Bernard Hall............G....... 585 425-3340
Fairport (G-4848)
Beyer Graphics Inc ....D....... 631 543-3900
Commack (G-3824)
Bg Bindery Inc............G....... 631 767-4242
Long Island City (G-7684)
Boncraft Inc............D....... 716 662-9720
Tonawanda (G-16146)
Bondy Printing Corp............G....... 631 242-1510
Bay Shore (G-679)
Brodock Press Inc ....D....... 315 735-9577
Utica (G-16310)
Brooks Litho Digital Group Inc............G....... 631 789-4500
Deer Park (G-4112)
Bruce Woehr............F....... 585 654-6746
Rochester (G-14248)
C & C Bindery Co Inc............E....... 631 752-7078
Farmingdale (G-4954)
Carlara Group Ltd ....G....... 914 769-2020
Pleasantville (G-13712)
Carnels Printing Inc............G....... 516 883-3355
Port Washington (G-13803)
Castlereagh Printcraft Inc ....D....... 516 623-1728
Freeport (G-5392)
Chakra Communications Inc ....E....... 607 748-7491
Endicott (G-4798)
Challenge Graphics Svcs Inc............E....... 631 586-0171
Deer Park (G-4115)
Classic Album ....E....... 718 388-2818
Brooklyn (G-1786)
Cohber Press Inc ....D....... 585 475-9100
West Henrietta (G-16873)
Copy Corner Inc............G....... 718 388-4545
Brooklyn (G-1803)
Cosmos Communications Inc ....C....... 718 482-1800
Long Island City (G-7705)
D G M Graphics Inc............F....... 516 223-2220
Merrick (G-8383)
Dalee Bookbinding Co Inc ....F....... 914 965-1660
Yonkers (G-17434)
David Helsing ....G....... 607 796-2681
Horseheads (G-6573)
Dependable Lithographers Inc............F....... 718 472-4200
Long Island City (G-7712)
Dispatch Graphics Inc ....F....... 212 307-5943
New York (G-9884)
Division Den-Bar Enterprises ....G....... 914 381-2220
Mamaroneck (G-8033)
Dowd - Witbeck Printing Corp ....F....... 518 274-2421
Troy (G-16234)
DP Murphy Co Inc ....D....... 631 673-9400
Deer Park (G-4132)
E B B Graphics Inc............F....... 516 750-5510
Westbury (G-16979)
E L Smith Printing Co Inc............E....... 201 373-0111
New City (G-8784)
Eastside Printers............F....... 315 437-6515
East Syracuse (G-4527)
Eastwood Litho Inc ....E....... 315 437-2626
Syracuse (G-15929)
Erhard & Gilcher Inc ....E....... 315 474-1072
Syracuse (G-15938)
Flare Multicopy Corp ....E....... 718 258-8860
Brooklyn (G-1982)
Flp Group LLC............F....... 315 252-7583
Auburn (G-496)
Foster - Gordon Manufacturing............G....... 631 589-6776
Bohemia (G-1068)
Fulton Newspapers Inc............E....... 315 598-6397
Fulton (G-5457)
Gateway Prtg & Graphics Inc............E....... 716 823-3873
Hamburg (G-5926)
Gazette Press Inc ....E....... 914 963-8300
Rye (G-15056)
Graphicomm Inc............G....... 716 283-0830
Niagara Falls (G-12826)
Haig Press Inc ....E....... 631 582-5800
Hauppauge (G-6088)
Hudson Printing Co Inc ....E....... 718 937-8600
New York (G-10527)
In-House Inc ....F....... 718 445-9007
College Point (G-3787)
Interstate Litho Corp............D....... 631 232-6025
Brentwood (G-1185)
Jack J Florio Jr............G....... 716 434-9123
Lockport (G-7595)
James Conolly Printing Co ....E....... 585 426-4150
Rochester (G-14459)
Jane Lewis............G....... 607 722-0584
Binghamton (G-930)
Johnnys Ideal Printing Co............G....... 518 828-6666
Hudson (G-6621)
Jon Lyn Ink Inc............G....... 516 546-2312
Merrick (G-8386)
Kader Lithograph Company Inc ....C....... 917 664-4380
Long Island City (G-7777)
Kaufman Brothers Printing............G....... 212 563-1854
New York (G-10820)
King Lithographers Inc............E....... 914 667-4200
Mount Vernon (G-8698)
L Loy Press Inc ....G....... 716 634-5966
Buffalo (G-3040)
Louis Heindl & Son Inc............G....... 585 454-5080
Rochester (G-14483)
Melcher Media Inc ....F....... 212 727-2322
New York (G-11222)
Mercury Print Productions Inc............C....... 585 458-7900
Rochester (G-14504)
Midgley Printing Corp............G....... 315 475-1864
Syracuse (G-15988)
Moneast Inc ....G....... 845 298-8898
Wappingers Falls (G-16575)
Multiple Imprssons of Rchester ....G....... 585 546-1160
Rochester (G-14525)
Newport Graphics Inc............E....... 212 924-2600
New York (G-11414)
Ozipko Enterprises Inc ....G....... 585 424-6740
Rochester (G-14560)
Prestige Envelope & Lithograph ....F....... 631 521-7043
Merrick (G-8391)
Printing Resources Inc............E....... 518 482-2470
Albany (G-124)
Pro Printing ....G....... 516 561-9700
Lynbrook (G-7957)
Progressive Graphics & Prtg............G....... 315 331-3635
Newark (G-12741)
Prompt Bindery Co Inc ....F....... 212 675-5181
New York (G-11732)
Psychonomic Society Inc............E....... 512 381-1494
New York (G-11743)
Quad/Graphics Inc ....A....... 518 581-4000
Saratoga Springs (G-15168)
Reynolds Book Bindery LLC ....F....... 607 772-8937
Binghamton (G-946)
Richard Ruffner............F....... 631 234-4600
Central Islip (G-3509)
Riverside Mfg Acquisition LLC............C....... 585 458-2090
Rochester (G-14627)
Rmd Holding Inc ....G....... 845 628-0030
Mahopac (G-8001)
Roger Michael Press Inc ....F....... 732 752-0800
Brooklyn (G-2502)
Rosemont Press Incorporated............E....... 212 239-4770
New York (G-11915)
Rosen Mandell & Immerman Inc............E....... 212 691-2277
New York (G-11916)
Sentinel Printing Inc ....G....... 516 334-7400
Westbury (G-17026)
Shipman Printing Inds Inc............E....... 716 504-7700
Niagara Falls (G-12876)
Spectrum Prtg Lithography Inc ....F....... 212 255-3131
New York (G-12158)
Thomas Group Inc ....F....... 212 947-6400
New York (G-12319)
Tobay Printing Co Inc ....E....... 631 842-3300
Copiague (G-3934)
Tom & Jerry Printcraft Forms ....E....... 914 777-7468
Mamaroneck (G-8048)
Tri-Lon Clor Lithographers Ltd............E....... 212 255-6140
New York (G-12400)
Vicks Lithograph & Prtg Corp............C....... 315 272-2401
Yorkville (G-17527)

PRODUCT

Employee Codes: A=Over 500 employees, B=251-500
C=101-250, D=51-100, E=20-50, F=10-19, G=5-9
2017 Harris
New York Manufacturers Directory
1143

BINDING SVC: Books & Manuals

Vin-Clair Inc .... F 845 429-4998
  West Haverstraw (G-16847)
Webster Printing Corporation .... F 585 671-1533
  Webster (G-16742)
Welsh Gold Stampers Inc .... E 718 984-5031
  Staten Island (G-15754)
Westchester Mailing Service .... E 914 948-1116
  White Plains (G-17184)
William Charles Prtg Co Inc .... E 516 349-0900
  Plainview (G-13646)
Wilson Press LLC .... E 315 568-9693
  Seneca Falls (G-15372)
Won & Lee Inc .... E 516 222-0712
  Garden City (G-5538)
Wynco Press One Inc .... G 516 354-6145
  Glen Oaks (G-5641)
X Myles Mar Inc .... E 212 683-2015
  New York (G-12673)
Zan Optics Products Inc .... E 718 435-0533
  Brooklyn (G-2781)
Zenger Partners LLC .... E 716 876-2284
  Kenmore (G-7152)

BINDING SVC: Magazines

Copy Room Inc .... F 212 371-8600
  New York (G-9721)

BINDING SVC: Pamphlets

Mid-Island Bindery Inc .... E 631 293-0180
  Farmingdale (G-5055)

BINDING SVC: Trade

Gold Pride Press Inc .... E 585 224-8800
  Rochester (G-14411)
Piroke Trade Inc .... G 646 515-1537
  Brooklyn (G-2423)
Quality Bindery Service Inc .... E 716 883-5185
  Buffalo (G-3147)
Whitford Development Inc .... F 631 471-7711
  Port Jefferson (G-13780)

BINDINGS: Bias, Made From Purchased Materials

Empire Bias Binding Co Inc .... F 718 545-0300
  Long Island City (G-7730)

BINS: Prefabricated, Sheet Metal

Golden Group International Ltd ...... G 845 440-1025
  Patterson (G-13440)
H & M Leasing Corp .... G 631 225-5246
  Copiague (G-3904)

BIOLOGICAL PRDTS: Bacterial Vaccines

Ip Med Inc .... G 516 766-3800
  Oceanside (G-13082)

BIOLOGICAL PRDTS: Blood Derivatives

Instrumentation Laboratory Co ...... C 845 680-0028
  Orangeburg (G-13231)

BIOLOGICAL PRDTS: Exc Diagnostic

Acorda Therapeutics Inc .... B 914 347-4300
  Ardsley (G-403)
Advance Biofactures Corp .... E 516 593-7000
  Lynbrook (G-7944)
AG Biotech Inc .... E 585 346-0020
  Livonia (G-7563)
Albany Molecular Research Inc ...... E 518 512-2234
  Albany (G-40)
Albany Molecular Research Inc ...... C 518 512-2000
  Albany (G-41)
Cypress Bioscience Inc .... F 858 452-2323
  New York (G-9778)
DSM Nutritional Products LLC .... B 518 372-5155
  Schenectady (G-15249)
Ecological Laboratories Inc .... F 516 823-3441
  Lynbrook (G-7950)
Kadmon Holdings Inc .... C 212 308-6000
  New York (G-10800)
Life Technologies Corporation .... D 716 774-6700
  Grand Island (G-5762)
Nanoprobes Inc .... F 631 205-9490
  Yaphank (G-17398)
Nxxi Inc 914 701-4500
  Purchase (G-13962)

Oligomerix Inc .... G 914 997-8877
  New York (G-11500)
Omrix Biopharmaceuticals Inc .... C 908 218-0707
  New York (G-11503)
Rentschler Biotechnologie GMBH ... G 631 656-7137
  Hauppauge (G-6177)
Roar Biomedical Inc .... G 631 591-2749
  Calverton (G-3297)
Stemcultures LLC .... G 518 621-0848
  Rensselaer (G-14052)
Synergy Pharmaceuticals Inc .... G 212 227-8611
  New York (G-12261)
Turing Pharmaceuticals LLC .... E 646 356-5577
  New York (G-12425)
Wyeth Holdings LLC .... D 845 602-5000
  Pearl River (G-13469)
Wyeth LLC .... A 973 660-5000
  New York (G-12671)
Zeptometrix Corporation .... E 716 882-0920
  Buffalo (G-3262)

BIOLOGICAL PRDTS: Extracts

Akshar Extracts Inc .... G 631 588-9727
  Ronkonkoma (G-14858)

BIOLOGICAL PRDTS: Vaccines

AV Therapeutics Inc .... E 917 497-5523
  New York (G-9271)
International Aids Vaccine Ini .... C 212 847-1111
  New York (G-10630)

BIOLOGICAL PRDTS: Vaccines & Immunizing

Siga Technologies Inc .... E 212 672-9100
  New York (G-12066)

BLADES: Saw, Chain Type

Quality Saw & Knife Inc .... F 631 491-4747
  West Babylon (G-16819)

BLADES: Saw, Hand Or Power

Niabraze LLC .... F 716 447-1082
  Tonawanda (G-16185)

BLANKBOOKS

Dalee Bookbinding Co Inc .... F 914 965-1660
  Yonkers (G-17434)

BLANKBOOKS & LOOSELEAF BINDERS

Acco Brands .... E 607 561-5515
  Sidney (G-15434)
Classic Album .... E 718 388-2818
  Brooklyn (G-1786)
Colad Group LLC .... D 716 961-1776
  Buffalo (G-2880)
Datamax International Inc .... E 212 693-0933
  New York (G-9815)
Foster - Gordon Manufacturing ..... G 631 589-6776
  Bohemia (G-1068)
GPM Associates LLC .... E 585 335-3940
  Dansville (G-4077)
Graphic Image Incorporated .... G 631 249-9600
  Melville (G-8324)
Leather Indexes Corp .... D 516 827-1900
  Hicksville (G-6363)
Roger Michael Press Inc .... F 732 752-0800
  Brooklyn (G-2502)

BLANKBOOKS: Albums

Albumx Corp .... D 914 939-6878
  Port Chester (G-13738)
Classic Album LLC .... D 718 388-2818
  Brooklyn (G-1787)
Dorose Novelty Co Inc .... F 718 451-3088
  East Elmhurst (G-4391)
King Album Inc .... E 631 253-9500
  West Babylon (G-16805)
Lanwood Industries Inc .... E 718 786-3000
  Bay Shore (G-711)
Leather Craftsmen Inc .... D 631 752-9000
  Farmingdale (G-5034)
Mypublisher Inc .... F 914 773-4312
  Elmsford (G-4768)

BLANKBOOKS: Albums, Record

Brookvale Records Inc .... F 631 587-7722
  West Babylon (G-16776)
Renegade Nation Ltd .... F 212 868-9000
  New York (G-11833)
Simon & Simon LLC .... G 202 419-0490
  New York (G-12080)
Tm Music Inc 212 471-4000
  New York (G-12356)
Tommy Boy Entertainment LLC ..... F 212 388-8300
  New York (G-12365)
Wmg Acquisition Corp .... F 212 275-2000
  New York (G-12650)

BLANKBOOKS: Checkbooks & Passbooks, Bank

ABC Check Printing Corp 718 855-4702
  Brooklyn (G-1546)

BLANKBOOKS: Diaries

Quo Vadis Editions Inc .... E 716 648-2602
  Hamburg (G-5939)

BLANKBOOKS: Memorandum, Printed

General Diaries Corporation 516 371-2244
  Inwood (G-6758)
Quotable Cards Inc .... G 212 420-7552
  New York (G-11776)

BLANKETS & BLANKETING, COTTON

Northwest Company LLC .... D 516 484-6996
  Roslyn (G-15022)

BLASTING SVC: Sand, Metal Parts

Carpenter Industries Inc .... F 315 463-4284
  Syracuse (G-15886)
Thomas Foundry LLC 315 361-9048
  Oneida (G-13168)
Tropical Driftwood Originals .... G 516 623-0980
  Roosevelt (G-15010)

BLINDS & SHADES: Vertical

Blindtek Designer Systems Inc .... F 914 347-7100
  Elmsford (G-4737)
Designers Touch Inc 718 641-3718
  Long Beach (G-7639)
J Gimbel Inc .... E 718 296-5200
  West Hempstead (G-16857)
KPP Ltd .... G 516 338-5201
  Westbury (G-17004)
Vertical Research Partners LLC ...... F 212 257-6499
  New York (G-12530)

BLINDS : Window

Comfortex Corporation .... C 518 273-3333
  Watervliet (G-16683)
D & D Window Tech Inc .... G 212 308-2822
  New York (G-9782)
Drapery Industries Inc .... F 585 232-2992
  Rochester (G-14318)
Fabric Quilters Unlimited Inc .... E 516 333-2866
  Westbury (G-16984)
Hunter Douglas Inc .... D 845 664-7000
  Pearl River (G-13460)
Hunter Douglas Inc .... C 212 588-0564
  New York (G-10533)
Instant Verticals Inc .... F 631 501-0001
  Farmingdale (G-5012)
Levolor Window Furnishings Inc .... B 845 664-7000
  Pearl River (G-13462)
Nu Ways Inc .... G 585 254-7510
  Rochester (G-14546)
Tentina Window Fashions Inc .... C 631 957-9585
  Lindenhurst (G-7490)

BLOCK & BRICK: Sand Lime

Everblock Systems LLC .... G 844 422-5625
  New York (G-10089)

BLOCKS & BRICKS: Concrete

All American Concrete Corp .... G 718 497-3301
  Brooklyn (G-1584)
All County Block & Supply Corp ..... G 631 589-3675
  Bohemia (G-1012)

PRODUCT SECTION

Barrasso & Sons Trucking Inc .... E 631 581-0360
  Islip Terrace *(G-6814)*
Cossitt Concrete Products Inc .... F 315 824-2700
  Hamilton *(G-5947)*
Crest Haven Precast Inc .... G 518 483-4750
  Burke *(G-3266)*
Dicks Concrete Co Inc .... E 845 374-5966
  New Hampton *(G-8799)*
Edgewood Industries Inc .... G 516 227-2447
  Garden City *(G-5501)*
Fort Miller Service Corp .... F 518 695-5000
  Greenwich *(G-5888)*
Grace Associates Inc .... G 718 767-9000
  Harrison *(G-5986)*
Hanson Aggregates New York LLC .... G 607 276-5881
  Almond *(G-204)*
Imperia Masonry Supply Corp .... E 914 738-0900
  Pelham *(G-13492)*
Jenna Concrete Corporation .... E 718 842-5250
  Bronx *(G-1366)*
Jenna Harlem River Inc .... G 718 842-5997
  Bronx *(G-1367)*
Modern Block LLC .... G 315 923-7443
  Clyde *(G-3729)*
Palumbo Block Co Inc .... E 845 832-6100
  Dover Plains *(G-4316)*
Phelps Cement Products Inc .... E 315 548-9415
  Phelps *(G-13535)*
Smithtown Concrete Products .... F 631 265-1815
  Saint James *(G-15091)*
Superior Block Corp .... F 718 421-0900
  Brooklyn *(G-2626)*
Unilock New York Inc .... G 845 278-6700
  Brewster *(G-1229)*

BLOCKS: Chimney Or Fireplace, Concrete

Ace Cntracting Consulting Corp .... G 631 567-4752
  Bohemia *(G-1006)*
Chimney Doctors Americas Corp .... G 631 868-3586
  Bayport *(G-757)*
Great American Awning & Patio .... F 518 899-2300
  Ballston Spa *(G-598)*

BLOCKS: Landscape Or Retaining Wall, Concrete

Creative Yard Designs Inc .... G 315 706-6143
  Manlius *(G-8070)*
Everblock Systems LLC .... G 844 422-5625
  New York *(G-10089)*
Northeast Mesa LLC .... G 845 878-9344
  Carmel *(G-3402)*
Tros Lanscaping Supply Company .... F 518 783-6954
  Cohoes *(G-3759)*

BLOCKS: Paving, Concrete

Belden Brick Sales & Svc Inc .... F 212 686-3939
  New York *(G-9348)*
Nicolia Concrete Products Inc .... D 631 669-0700
  Lindenhurst *(G-7476)*
Unilock Ltd .... E 716 822-6074
  Buffalo *(G-3233)*

BLOCKS: Paving, Cut Stone

Unilock New York Inc .... G 845 278-6700
  Brewster *(G-1229)*

BLOCKS: Radiation-Proof, Concrete

Radiation Shielding Systems .... F 888 631-2278
  Suffern *(G-15799)*

BLOCKS: Standard, Concrete Or Cinder

Colonie Block and Supply Co .... G 518 869-8411
  Colonie *(G-3819)*
Cranesville Block Co Inc .... E 518 684-6000
  Amsterdam *(G-341)*
Cranesville Block Co Inc .... E 315 773-2296
  Felts Mills *(G-5167)*
Duke Concrete Products Inc .... E 518 793-7743
  Queensbury *(G-13995)*
Felicetti Concrete Products .... G 716 284-5740
  Niagara Falls *(G-12819)*
Gone South Concrete Block Inc .... E 315 598-2141
  Fulton *(G-5459)*
Grandview Block & Supply Co .... E 518 346-7981
  Schenectady *(G-15265)*
Lafarge North America Inc .... E 518 756-5000
  Ravena *(G-14023)*

Lage Industries Corporation .... F 718 342-3400
  Brooklyn *(G-2191)*
Montfort Brothers Inc .... E 845 896-6694
  Fishkill *(G-5186)*
Morningstar Concrete Products .... F 716 693-4020
  Tonawanda *(G-16183)*
New York Ready Mix Inc .... G 516 338-6969
  Westbury *(G-17014)*
Riefler Concrete Products LLC .... C 716 649-3260
  Hamburg *(G-5940)*
Suffolk Cement Products Inc .... E 631 727-2317
  Calverton *(G-3300)*
Taylor Concrete Products Inc .... E 315 788-2191
  Watertown *(G-16673)*

BLOWERS & FANS

Air Crafters Inc .... C 631 471-7788
  Ronkonkoma *(G-14857)*
American Filtration Tech Inc .... F 585 359-4130
  West Henrietta *(G-16867)*
Applied Safety Inc .... G 718 608-6292
  Long Island City *(G-7664)*
Buffalo Filter LLC .... D 716 835-7000
  Lancaster *(G-7307)*
Camfil USA Inc .... G 518 456-6085
  Syracuse *(G-15884)*
Daikin Applied Americas Inc .... D 315 253-2771
  Auburn *(G-491)*
Delphi Automotive Systems LLC .... A 585 359-6000
  West Henrietta *(G-16876)*
Ducon Technologies Inc .... E 631 420-4900
  Farmingdale *(G-4979)*
Ducon Technologies Inc .... F 631 694-1700
  New York *(G-9937)*
Dundas-Jafine Inc .... E 716 681-9690
  Alden *(G-177)*
Filtros Ltd .... E 585 586-8770
  East Rochester *(G-4459)*
Healthway Products Company .... E 315 207-1410
  Oswego *(G-13332)*
Moffitt Corporation Inc .... E 585 768-7010
  Le Roy *(G-7415)*
Moffitt Fan Corporation .... E 585 768-7010
  Le Roy *(G-7416)*
North American Filter Corp .... D 800 265-8943
  Newark *(G-12739)*
Parker-Hannifin Corporation .... D 248 628-6017
  Lancaster *(G-7330)*
Standard Motor Products Inc .... B 718 392-0200
  Long Island City *(G-7884)*

BLOWERS & FANS

Ametek Tchnical Indus Pdts Inc .... E 845 246-3401
  Saugerties *(G-15179)*
Rotron Incorporated .... B 845 679-2401
  Woodstock *(G-17365)*
Rotron Incorporated .... E 845 679-2401
  Woodstock *(G-17366)*

BLUEPRINTING SVCS

A Esteban & Company Inc .... E 212 989-7000
  New York *(G-8984)*

BOAT BUILDING & REPAIR

American Metalcraft Marine .... G 315 686-9891
  Clayton *(G-3684)*
Cayuga Wooden Boatworks Inc .... E 315 253-7447
  Ithaca *(G-6830)*
Coecles Hbr Marina & Boat Yard .... F 631 749-0856
  Shelter Island *(G-15386)*
Eastern Welding Inc .... G 631 727-0306
  Riverhead *(G-14142)*
Gar Wood Custom Boats .... G 518 494-2966
  Brant Lake *(G-1173)*
Global Marine Power Inc .... E 631 208-2933
  Calverton *(G-3291)*
Hacker Boat Company Inc .... E 518 543-6731
  Silver Bay *(G-15446)*
Hampton Shipyards Inc .... F 631 653-6777
  East Quogue *(G-4451)*
Jag Manufacturing Inc .... E 518 762-9558
  Johnstown *(G-7116)*
Katherine Blizniak .... G 716 674-8545
  West Seneca *(G-16950)*
May Ship Repair Contg Corp .... E 718 442-9700
  Staten Island *(G-15705)*
Metalcraft Marine Us Inc .... F 315 501-4015
  Cape Vincent *(G-3384)*

Mokai Manufacturing Inc .... G 845 566-8287
  Newburgh *(G-12768)*
Robert E Derecktor Inc .... D 914 698-0962
  Mamaroneck *(G-8045)*
Scarano Boatbuilding Inc .... E 518 463-3401
  Albany *(G-132)*
Tumblehome Boatshop .... G 518 623-5050
  Warrensburg *(G-16581)*
Wooden Boatworks .... G 631 477-6507
  Greenport *(G-5878)*

BOAT BUILDING & REPAIRING: Fiberglass

Fantasy Glass Compan .... G 845 786-5818
  Stony Point *(G-15773)*
Stidd Systems Inc .... E 631 477-2400
  Greenport *(G-5877)*
Superboats Inc .... G 631 226-1761
  Lindenhurst *(G-7487)*

BOAT BUILDING & REPAIRING: Motorized

Marathon Boat Group Inc .... F 607 849-3211
  Marathon *(G-8085)*

BOAT BUILDING & REPAIRING: Non-Motorized

Rocking The Boat Inc .... F 718 466-5799
  Bronx *(G-1442)*

BOAT BUILDING & RPRG: Fishing, Small, Lobster, Crab, Oyster

AVS Laminates Inc .... E 631 286-2136
  Bellport *(G-826)*

BOAT DEALERS

Global Marine Power Inc .... E 631 208-2933
  Calverton *(G-3291)*
Marathon Boat Group Inc .... F 607 849-3211
  Marathon *(G-8085)*
Marina Holding Corp .... F 718 646-9283
  Brooklyn *(G-2269)*
Superboats Inc .... G 631 226-1761
  Lindenhurst *(G-7487)*

BOAT DEALERS: Canoe & Kayak

Johnson Outdoors Inc .... C 607 779-2200
  Binghamton *(G-931)*

BOAT LIFTS

Kleinfelder John .... G 716 753-3163
  Mayville *(G-8216)*

BOAT REPAIR SVCS

Cayuga Wooden Boatworks Inc .... E 315 253-7447
  Ithaca *(G-6830)*
Nochem Paint Stripping Inc .... G 631 563-2750
  Blue Point *(G-999)*
Robert E Derecktor Inc .... D 914 698-0962
  Mamaroneck *(G-8045)*
Superboats Inc .... G 631 226-1761
  Lindenhurst *(G-7487)*

BOAT YARD: Boat yards, storage & incidental repair

Robert E Derecktor Inc .... D 914 698-0962
  Mamaroneck *(G-8045)*

BOATS & OTHER MARINE EQPT: Plastic

Global Marine Power Inc .... E 631 208-2933
  Calverton *(G-3291)*

BODIES: Truck & Bus

Able Weldbuilt Industries Inc .... F 631 643-9700
  Deer Park *(G-4085)*
Conti Auto Body Corp .... G 516 921-6435
  Syosset *(G-15816)*
Daimler Buses North Amer Inc .... A 315 768-8101
  Oriskany *(G-13308)*
Donver Incorporated .... F 716 945-1910
  Kill Buck *(G-7166)*
Premium Bldg Components Inc .... E 518 885-0194
  Ballston Spa *(G-607)*

BODIES: Truck & Bus

Unicell Body Company Inc..............F......585 424-2660
  Rochester (G-14741)

BODY PARTS: Automobile, Stamped Metal

Albert Kemperle Inc..........................E......718 629-1084
  Brooklyn (G-1575)
American Blvd Auto Sups Inc............G......718 328-1984
  Bronx (G-1272)
Automotive LLC.................................F......248 728-8642
  Batavia (G-623)
Ford Motor Company.........................B......716 821-4000
  Buffalo (G-2952)
Kustom Korner...................................F......716 646-0173
  Hamburg (G-5933)
M & W Aluminum Products Inc.........F......315 414-0005
  Syracuse (G-15983)
Racing Industries Inc........................E......631 905-0100
  Calverton (G-3296)

BOILER REPAIR SHOP

A L Eastmond & Sons Inc.................D......718 378-3000
  Bronx (G-1254)
Empire Industrial Systems Corp........F......631 242-4619
  Bay Shore (G-699)
Flushing Boiler & Welding Co............G......718 463-1266
  Brooklyn (G-1988)
Troy Boiler Works Inc.......................E......518 274-2650
  Troy (G-16258)

BOILERS & BOILER SHOP WORK

Marine Boiler & Welding Inc..............F......718 378-1900
  Bronx (G-1386)
Supreme Boilers Inc.........................G......718 342-2220
  Brooklyn (G-2631)

BOILERS: Low-Pressure Heating, Steam Or Hot Water

Best Boilers Inc..................................F......718 372-4210
  Brooklyn (G-1687)
ECR International Inc.......................D......315 797-1310
  Utica (G-16328)
ECR International Inc.......................C......716 366-5500
  Dunkirk (G-4341)
Rockmills Steel Products Corp.........F......718 366-8300
  Maspeth (G-8169)

BOLTS: Metal

Baco Enterprises Inc........................D......718 589-6225
  Bronx (G-1279)
Cwr Manufacturing Corporation.......D......315 437-1032
  East Syracuse (G-4521)
Jem Threading Specialties Inc........G......718 665-3341
  Bronx (G-1365)
Simon Defense Inc...........................G......516 217-6000
  Middle Island (G-8408)
Supply Technologies (ny)..................F......212 966-3310
  Albany (G-139)

BONDERIZING: Bonderizing, Metal Or Metal Prdts

Clad Metal Specialties Inc................F......631 666-7750
  Bay Shore (G-684)

BOOK STORES

Barrons Educational Series Inc........D......631 434-3311
  Hauppauge (G-6032)
Penguin Random House LLC............A......212 572-6162
  New York (G-11605)
Penguin Random House LLC............C......212 366-2377
  Albany (G-117)
Rizzoli Intl Publications Inc..............E......212 387-3400
  New York (G-11881)
Romantic Times Inc..........................F......718 237-1097
  Brooklyn (G-2503)
Royal Fireworks Printing Co.............F......845 726-3333
  Unionville (G-16302)
Samuel French Inc............................E......212 206-8990
  New York (G-11962)
Second Chance Press Inc................G......631 725-1101
  Sag Harbor (G-15081)
Sharedbook Inc..................................E......646 442-8840
  New York (G-12045)
Society For The Study......................G......212 822-8806
  New York (G-12114)
Soho Press Inc..................................G......212 260-1900
  New York (G-12119)
Thornwillow Press Ltd......................G......212 980-0738
  New York (G-12331)
W&P Design LLC................................G......434 806-1443
  Brooklyn (G-2741)
William S Hein & Co Inc...................D......716 882-2600
  Getzville (G-5606)

BOOK STORES: Children's

Turtle Pond Publications LLC..........G......212 579-4393
  New York (G-12428)

BOOKS, WHOLESALE

Anthroposophic Press Inc................G......518 851-2054
  Clifton Park (G-3695)
Columbia University Press Inc.........E......212 459-0600
  New York (G-9680)
Kensington Publishing Corp............D......212 407-1500
  New York (G-10836)
Kodansha USA Inc............................G......917 322-6200
  New York (G-10867)
Living Well Innovations Inc.............G......646 517-3200
  Hauppauge (G-6113)
Macmillan Publishers Inc................A......646 307-5151
  New York (G-11088)
Macmillan Publishing Group LLC....E......212 674-5151
  New York (G-11089)
Moznaim Publishing Co Inc.............G......718 853-0525
  Brooklyn (G-2337)
North Country Books Inc.................E......315 735-4877
  Utica (G-16352)
North-South Books Inc.....................G......212 706-4545
  New York (G-11459)
Rizzoli Intl Publications Inc.............E......212 387-3400
  New York (G-11881)
S P Books Inc...................................G......212 431-5011
  New York (G-11946)
Samuel French Inc...........................E......212 206-8990
  New York (G-11962)
Scholium International Inc..............G......516 883-8032
  Port Washington (G-13863)
Swift Fulfillment Services................G......516 593-1198
  Lynbrook (G-7964)
Te Neues Publishing Company.......F......212 627-9090
  New York (G-12285)
W W Norton & Company Inc...........G......212 354-5500
  New York (G-12573)
W&P Design LLC...............................G......434 806-1443
  Brooklyn (G-2741)

BOOTHS: Spray, Sheet Metal, Prefabricated

Auto Body Services LLC...................F......631 431-4640
  Lindenhurst (G-7455)

BOOTS: Women's

Lsil & Co Inc.....................................G......914 761-0998
  White Plains (G-17134)
Nine West Group Inc.......................G......800 999-1877
  White Plains (G-17142)

BOTTLE CAPS & RESEALERS: Plastic

Captive Plastics LLC.........................D......716 366-2112
  Dunkirk (G-4333)

BOTTLED GAS DEALERS: Propane

Blue Rhino Global Sourcing Inc........E......516 752-0670
  Melville (G-8298)

BOTTLED WATER DELIVERY

Mayer Bros Apple Products Inc........D......716 668-1787
  West Seneca (G-16952)
Vivreau Advanced Water Systems....F......212 502-3749
  New York (G-12559)

BOTTLES: Plastic

Alphamed Bottles Inc.......................F......631 275-5042
  Hauppauge (G-6017)
Capitol Plastic Products Inc............C......518 627-0051
  Amsterdam (G-338)
Capitol Plastic Products LLC...........C......518 627-0051
  Amsterdam (G-339)
Chapin International Inc...................C......585 343-3140
  Batavia (G-627)
Chapin Manufacturing Inc...............C......585 343-3140
  Batavia (G-628)
Cortland Plastics Intl LLC.................E......607 662-0120
  Cortland (G-4020)
David Johnson..................................F......315 493-4735
  Carthage (G-3413)
Intrapac International Corp..............E......518 561-2030
  Plattsburgh (G-13671)
Kybod Group LLC.............................G......408 306-1657
  New York (G-10897)
Nalge Nunc International Corp........A......585 586-8800
  Rochester (G-14527)
Pvc Container Corporation...............C......518 672-7721
  Philmont (G-13541)
Samco Scientific Corporation...........C......800 522-3359
  Rochester (G-14666)
Vista Packaging Inc...........................E......718 854-9200
  Brooklyn (G-2732)
Weber Intl Packg Co LLC..................E......518 561-8282
  Plattsburgh (G-13707)
World Company..................................E......718 551-8282
  Flushing (G-5309)

BOUTIQUE STORES

Elab Smokers Boutique.....................G......585 865-4513
  Rochester (G-14343)

BOWLING EQPT & SPLYS

Joe Moro..G......607 272-0591
  Ithaca (G-6855)

BOX & CARTON MANUFACTURING EQPT

Standard Paper Box Machine Co......E......718 328-3300
  Bronx (G-1463)

BOXES & CRATES: Rectangular, Wood

Northeast Pallet & Cont Co Inc........F......518 271-0535
  Troy (G-16244)
R D A Container Corporation............E......585 247-2323
  Gates (G-5563)

BOXES & SHOOK: Nailed Wood

Great Lakes Specialties....................E......716 672-4622
  Fredonia (G-5374)
McGraw Wood Products LLC............E......607 836-6465
  Mc Graw (G-8223)
McIntosh Box & Pallet Co Inc..........D......315 675-8511
  Bernhards Bay (G-858)
McIntosh Box & Pallet Co Inc..........E......315 446-9350
  Rome (G-14820)
Philpac Corporation..........................E......716 875-8005
  Buffalo (G-3124)
Quality Woodworking Corp...............F......718 875-3437
  Brooklyn (G-2464)
Reuter Pallet Pkg Sys Inc.................G......845 457-9937
  Montgomery (G-8602)

BOXES: Corrugated

Arma Container Corp........................E......631 254-1200
  Deer Park (G-4101)
Buckeye Corrugated Inc...................G......315 437-1181
  Syracuse (G-15876)
Buckeye Corrugated Inc...................D......585 924-1600
  Victor (G-16465)
Cattaraugus Containers Inc.............E......716 676-2000
  Franklinville (G-5369)
Georgia-Pacific LLC..........................C......518 346-6151
  Schenectady (G-15264)
Inner-Pak Container Inc..................F......631 289-9700
  Patchogue (G-13423)
International Paper Company............C......585 663-1000
  Rochester (G-14452)
International Paper Company............C......607 775-1550
  Conklin (G-3869)
Island Container Corp......................D......631 253-4400
  Wyandanch (G-17376)
Kapstone Container Corporation.....D......518 842-2450
  Amsterdam (G-352)
Lakeside Container Corp..................F......518 561-6150
  Plattsburgh (G-13675)
Norampac New England Inc.............C......860 923-9563
  Schenectady (G-15282)
Norampac New York City Inc...........C......718 340-2100
  Maspeth (G-8158)
Packaging Corporation America......F......315 785-9083
  Watertown (G-16669)
Pactiv LLC..C......315 457-6780
  Liverpool (G-7539)

PRODUCT SECTION

BRIDGE COMPONENTS: Bridge sections, prefabricated, highway

Philpac Corporation .... E 716 875-8005
  Buffalo (G-3124)
Prestige Box Corporation .... E 516 773-3115
  Great Neck (G-5833)
Professional Packg Svcs Inc .... E 518 677-5100
  Eagle Bridge (G-4357)
R D A Container Corporation .... E 585 247-2323
  Gates (G-5563)
Seneca FLS Spc & Logistics Co .... D 315 568-4139
  Seneca Falls (G-15370)
Star Corrugated Box Co Inc .... G 718 386-3200
  Flushing (G-5296)
Syracuse Corrugated Box Corp .... F 315 437-9901
  East Syracuse (G-4570)
WA Packaging LLC .... E 518 724-6466
  Schenectady (G-15311)
Westrock - Southern Cont LLC .... C 315 487-6111
  Camillus (G-3327)
Westrock CP LLC .... C 716 694-1000
  North Tonawanda (G-13006)
Westrock Rkt Company .... C 330 296-5155
  Deer Park (G-4226)

BOXES: Filing, Paperboard Made From Purchased Materials

Paul T Freund Corporation .... D 315 597-4873
  Palmyra (G-13413)

BOXES: Mail Or Post Office, Collection/Storage, Sheet Metal

Maloya Laser Inc .... E 631 543-2327
  Commack (G-3837)

BOXES: Packing & Shipping, Metal

Alpine Paper Box Co Inc .... E 718 345-4040
  Brooklyn (G-1595)

BOXES: Paperboard, Folding

Abbot & Abbot Box Corp .... F 888 930-5972
  Long Island City (G-7646)
Alpha Packaging Industries Inc .... E 718 267-4115
  Long Island City (G-7654)
Arkay Packaging Corporation .... E 631 273-2000
  Hauppauge (G-6024)
Burt Rigid Box Inc .... D 607 433-2510
  Oneonta (G-13175)
Cattaraugus Containers Inc .... E 716 676-2000
  Franklinville (G-5369)
Climax Manufacturing Company .... C 315 376-8000
  Carthage (G-3412)
Climax Manufacturing Company .... C 315 376-8000
  Castorland (G-3422)
Climax Packaging Inc .... C 315 376-8000
  Lowville (G-7935)
Color Carton Corp .... D 718 665-0840
  Bronx (G-1302)
Designers Folding Box Corp .... E 716 853-5141
  Buffalo (G-2910)
Disc Graphics Inc .... C 631 300-1129
  Hauppauge (G-6063)
Disc Graphics Inc .... B 631 234-1400
  Hauppauge (G-6064)
F M Howell & Company .... D 607 734-6291
  Elmira (G-4684)
Flower City Printing Inc .... C 585 663-9000
  Rochester (G-14374)
Gavin Mfg Corp .... E 631 467-0040
  Farmingdale (G-4997)
Gaylord Bros Inc .... D 315 457-5070
  North Syracuse (G-12944)
HSM Packaging Corporation .... D 315 476-7996
  Liverpool (G-7523)
Knoll Printing & Packaging Inc .... E 516 621-0100
  Syosset (G-15826)
M C Packaging Corporation .... E 631 643-3763
  Babylon (G-550)
Mod-Pac Corp .... C 716 873-0640
  Buffalo (G-3071)
Multi Packg Solutions Intl Ltd .... G 646 885-0005
  New York (G-11325)
Novel Box Company Ltd .... E 718 965-2222
  Brooklyn (G-2377)
Paper Box Corp .... D 212 226-7490
  New York (G-11563)
Premier Packaging Corporation .... E 585 924-8460
  Victor (G-16496)

Prestige Box Corporation .... E 516 773-3115
  Great Neck (G-5833)
Specialized Packg Group Inc .... G 315 638-4355
  Baldwinsville (G-575)
Specialized Packg Radisson LLC .... C 315 638-4355
  Baldwinsville (G-576)
Standard Group .... E 718 335-5500
  East Elmhurst (G-4397)
Standard Group LLC .... C 718 507-6430
  East Elmhurst (G-4398)
Viking Industries Inc .... D 845 883-6325
  New Paltz (G-8882)
Visitainer Corp .... E 718 636-0300
  Brooklyn (G-2731)

BOXES: Paperboard, Set-Up

A Fleisig Paper Box Corp .... F 212 226-7490
  New York (G-8986)
American Package Company Inc .... E 718 389-4444
  Brooklyn (G-1605)
Brick & Ballerstein Inc .... D 718 497-1400
  Ridgewood (G-14103)
Burt Rigid Box Inc .... D 607 433-2510
  Oneonta (G-13175)
Clarke-Boxit Corporation .... G 716 487-1950
  Jamestown (G-6980)
Drescher Paper Box Inc .... F 716 854-0288
  Buffalo (G-2918)
Earlville Paper Box Co Inc .... E 315 691-2131
  Earlville (G-4360)
F M Howell & Company .... D 607 734-6291
  Elmira (G-4684)
Fairview Paper Box Corp .... E 585 786-5230
  Warsaw (G-16582)
Friedel Paper Box & Converting .... G 315 437-3325
  Baldwinsville (G-569)
Jordon Box Company Inc .... E 315 422-3419
  Syracuse (G-15970)
Ketchum Manufacturing Co Inc .... F 518 696-3331
  Lake Luzerne (G-7272)
Lionel Habas Associates Inc .... F 212 860-8454
  New York (G-11005)
Parlor City Paper Box Co Inc .... D 607 772-0600
  Binghamton (G-941)
Prestige Box Corporation .... E 516 773-3115
  Great Neck (G-5833)
Propak Inc .... G 518 677-5100
  Eagle Bridge (G-4358)
Pure Trade Us Inc .... E 212 256-1600
  New York (G-11751)
Seneca FLS Spc & Logistics Co .... D 315 568-4139
  Seneca Falls (G-15370)
West Gluers .... G 631 232-1235
  Hauppauge (G-6233)

BOXES: Plastic

American Package Company Inc .... E 718 389-4444
  Brooklyn (G-1605)
Novel Box Company Ltd .... E 718 965-2222
  Brooklyn (G-2377)
Philcom Limited .... D 716 875-8005
  Buffalo (G-3123)
Printex Packaging Corporation .... D 631 234-4300
  Islandia (G-6801)
R P M Industries Inc .... E 315 255-1105
  Auburn (G-515)
Rui Xing International Trdg Co .... G 516 298-2667
  Hicksville (G-6391)
Sky Dive .... D 845 858-6400
  Port Jervis (G-13792)

BOXES: Solid Fiber

Burt Rigid Box Inc .... D 607 433-2510
  Oneonta (G-13175)
Specialized Packg Radisson LLC .... C 315 638-4355
  Baldwinsville (G-576)

BOXES: Stamped Metal

Novel Box Company Ltd .... E 718 965-2222
  Brooklyn (G-2377)

BOXES: Switch, Electric

Cables and Chips Inc .... E 212 619-3132
  New York (G-9493)

BOXES: Wooden

Abbot & Abbot Box Corp .... F 888 930-5972
  Long Island City (G-7646)
M &L Industry of NY Inc .... G 845 827-6255
  Highland Mills (G-6413)
Norjac Boxes Inc .... E 631 842-1300
  Copiague (G-3916)

BRAKES & BRAKE PARTS

Interparts International Inc .... E 516 576-2000
  Plainview (G-13610)
Rpb Distributors LLC .... G 914 244-3600
  Mount Kisco (G-8645)

BRAKES: Electromagnetic

Magtrol Inc .... E 716 668-5555
  Buffalo (G-3055)

BRASS FOUNDRY, NEC

Eastern Finding Corp .... F 516 747-6640
  New Hyde Park (G-8830)

BRAZING SVCS

Parfuse Corp .... E 516 997-1795
  Westbury (G-17018)
W R P Welding Ltd .... G 631 249-8859
  Farmingdale (G-5139)

BRAZING: Metal

Captech Industries LLC .... G 347 374-1182
  Rome (G-14807)
Hi-Temp Brazing Inc .... E 631 491-4917
  Deer Park (G-4148)
Milgo Industrial Inc .... D 718 388-6476
  Brooklyn (G-2313)
Milgo Industrial Inc .... G 718 387-0406
  Brooklyn (G-2314)

BRIC-A-BRAC

Five Star Creations Inc .... E 845 783-1187
  Monroe (G-8554)

BRICK, STONE & RELATED PRDTS WHOLESALERS

Barrasso & Sons Trucking Inc .... E 631 581-0360
  Islip Terrace (G-6814)
Clemente Latham Concrete Corp .... D 518 374-2222
  Schenectady (G-15243)
East Coast Mines Ltd .... E 631 653-5445
  East Quogue (G-4450)
Hampton Sand Corp .... G 631 325-5533
  Westhampton (G-17057)
Hanson Aggregates PA LLC .... E 585 624-3800
  Honeoye Falls (G-6529)
Imperia Masonry Supply Corp .... E 914 738-0900
  Pelham (G-13492)
Peckham Materials Corp .... F 518 494-2313
  Chestertown (G-3622)
Phelps Cement Products Inc .... E 315 548-9415
  Phelps (G-13535)

BRICKS & BLOCKS: Structural

Everblock Systems LLC .... G 844 422-5625
  New York (G-10089)
Semco Ceramics Inc .... G 315 782-3000
  Watertown (G-16671)

BRICKS: Concrete

Brickit .... E 631 727-8977
  Hauppauge (G-6037)

BRIDAL SHOPS

Vera Wang Group LLC .... C 212 575-6400
  New York (G-12518)

BRIDGE COMPONENTS: Bridge sections, prefabricated, highway

Apollo Steel Corporation .... F 716 283-8758
  Niagara Falls (G-12797)
Port Authority of NY & NJ .... D 718 390-2534
  Staten Island (G-15723)

BRIEFCASES

Coach Stores Inc...................................A....... 212 643-9727
New York *(G-9659)*

BROADCASTING & COMMS EQPT: Antennas, Transmitting/Comms

Century Metal Parts Corp..................E....... 631 667-0800
Bay Shore *(G-682)*
Edo LLC..G....... 631 630-4000
Amityville *(G-285)*
Fei-Zyfer Inc.....................................G....... 714 933-4045
Uniondale *(G-16294)*
John Mezzalingua Assoc LLC ....C....... 315 431-7100
Liverpool *(G-7528)*
Millennium Antenna Corp ....F....... 315 798-9374
Utica *(G-16348)*
Sinclair Technologies Inc.................E....... 716 874-3682
Hamburg *(G-5942)*

BROADCASTING & COMMS EQPT: Rcvr-Transmitter Unt, Transceiver

Magnet-Ndctive Systems Ltd USA........E....... 585 924-4000
Victor *(G-16490)*

BROADCASTING & COMMUNICATIONS EQPT: Cellular Radio Telephone

Advanced Comm Solutions ....G....... 914 693-5076
Ardsley *(G-404)*
Bullitt Mobile LLC ....D....... 631 424-1749
Bohemia *(G-1028)*
Linen Micarta LLC...............................F....... 212 203-5145
New York *(G-11001)*
Nycom Business Solutions Inc ....G....... 516 345-6000
Franklin Square *(G-5366)*
Parrys..F....... 315 824-0002
Hamilton *(G-5949)*

BROADCASTING & COMMUNICATIONS EQPT: Studio Eqpt, Radio & TV

Bet Networks Incorporated ....E....... 212 846-8111
New York *(G-9375)*
Hopewell Precision Inc.......................E....... 845 221-2737
Hopewell Junction *(G-6552)*
Times Square Studios Ltd..................C....... 212 930-7720
New York *(G-12352)*

BROADCASTING & COMMUNICATIONS EQPT: Transmitting, Radio/TV

Armstrong Transmitter Corp................F....... 315 673-1269
Marcellus *(G-8086)*

BROKERS' SVCS

Remsen Graphics Corp ....G....... 718 643-7500
Brooklyn *(G-2491)*

BROKERS: Automotive

Monroe County Auto Svcs Inc.............E....... 585 764-3741
Rochester *(G-14520)*

BROKERS: Business

Spanish Artisan Wine Group LLC .....G....... 914 414-6982
Patterson *(G-13444)*

BROKERS: Food

Frozen Food Partners LLC..................G....... 203 661-7500
New York *(G-10214)*
Quinn and Co of NY Ltd ....E....... 212 868-1900
New York *(G-11774)*

BROKERS: Loan

Mml Software Ltd................................E....... 631 941-1313
East Setauket *(G-4488)*

BROKERS: Printing

Alabaster Group Inc............................G....... 516 867-8223
Freeport *(G-5382)*
C & C Duplicators Inc..........................E....... 631 244-0800
Bohemia *(G-1029)*
Melmont Fine Pringng/Graphics..........G....... 516 939-2253
Bethpage *(G-874)*

Prestige Envelope & Lithograph...........F....... 631 521-7043
Merrick *(G-8391)*

BRONZE FOUNDRY, NEC

Argos Inc...E....... 845 528-0576
Putnam Valley *(G-13973)*
Charles Lay...F....... 607 432-4518
Oneonta *(G-13177)*
Charles Lay...G....... 607 656-4204
Greene *(G-5862)*
Excalibur Brnze Sculpture Fndry ....E....... 718 366-3444
Brooklyn *(G-1942)*

BROOMS & BRUSHES

Braun Industries Inc ....E....... 516 741-6000
Albertson *(G-152)*
Cpac Inc..E....... 585 382-3223
Leicester *(G-7420)*
Eraser Company Inc ....C....... 315 454-3237
Mattydale *(G-8212)*
Full Circle Home LLC..........................G....... 212 432-0001
New York *(G-10222)*
K & R Allied Inc....................................F....... 718 625-6610
Brooklyn *(G-2161)*
Perfex Corporation..............................F....... 315 826-3600
Poland *(G-13727)*

BROOMS & BRUSHES: Hair Pencils Or Artists' Brushes

Teka Fine Line Brushes Inc.................G....... 718 692-2928
Brooklyn *(G-2652)*

BROOMS & BRUSHES: Household Or Indl

Abtex Corporation ....E....... 315 536-7403
Dresden *(G-4318)*
Braun Brothers Brushes Inc................G....... 631 667-2179
Valley Stream *(G-16402)*
Brushtech (disc) Inc ....F....... 518 563-8420
Plattsburgh *(G-13656)*
Culicover & Shapiro Inc ....G....... 516 597-4888
Hicksville *(G-6339)*
FM Brush Co Inc.................................F....... 718 821-5939
Glendale *(G-5652)*
Rossiter & Schmitt Co Inc...................E....... 516 937-3610
Bay Shore *(G-739)*
Volckening Inc.....................................E....... 718 748-0294
Brooklyn *(G-2735)*
Young & Swartz Inc.............................F....... 716 852-2171
Buffalo *(G-3260)*

BROOMS & BRUSHES: Paint Rollers

131-11 Atlantic RE Inc.........................D....... 718 441-7700
Richmond Hill *(G-14064)*
Pan American Roller Inc.....................F....... 914 762-8700
Ossining *(G-13326)*
Premier Paint Roller Co LLC ....F....... 718 441-7700
Richmond Hill *(G-14078)*
Royal Paint Roller Corp ....E....... 516 367-4370
Woodbury *(G-17299)*

BROOMS & BRUSHES: Paintbrushes

E & W Manufacturing Co Inc...............E....... 516 367-8571
Woodbury *(G-17285)*
Kirschner Brush LLC...........................F....... 718 292-1809
Bronx *(G-1373)*

BRUSHES

Walter R Tucker Entps Ltd ....E....... 607 467-2866
Deposit *(G-4282)*

BUCKLES & PARTS

Maxine Denker Inc ....G....... 212 689-1440
Staten Island *(G-15704)*

BUILDING & OFFICE CLEANING SVCS

Rumsey Corp.......................................G....... 914 751-3640
Yonkers *(G-17482)*

BUILDING & STRUCTURAL WOOD MBRS: Timbers, Struct, Lam Lumber

Empire Building Products Inc..............G....... 518 695-6094
Schuylerville *(G-15319)*
New England Barns Inc ....E....... 631 445-1461
Southold *(G-15560)*

BUILDING & STRUCTURAL WOOD MEMBERS

Architctral Mllwk Installation ....E....... 631 499-0755
East Northport *(G-4433)*
Faulkner Truss Company Inc.............G....... 315 536-8894
Dresden *(G-4319)*
Harvest Homes Inc..............................E....... 518 895-2341
Delanson *(G-4233)*
Railtech Composites Inc.....................F....... 518 324-6190
Plattsburgh *(G-13692)*
Structural Wood Corporation ....E....... 315 388-4442
Waddington *(G-16521)*
Timber Frames Inc..............................G....... 585 374-6405
Canandaigua *(G-3359)*
Unadilla Silo Company Inc.................D....... 607 369-9341
Sidney *(G-15444)*
Wt Motto Building Products.................F....... 315 457-2211
Liverpool *(G-7557)*

BUILDING & STRUCTURAL WOOD MEMBERS: Arches, Laminated Lumber

Stephenson Lumber Company Inc........G....... 518 548-7521
Speculator *(G-15563)*

BUILDING BOARD & WALLBOARD, EXC GYPSUM

Continental Buchanan LLC..................D....... 703 480-3800
Buchanan *(G-2785)*

BUILDING BOARD: Gypsum

Continental Buchanan LLC..................D....... 703 480-3800
Buchanan *(G-2785)*

BUILDING CLEANING & MAINTENANCE SVCS

JM Murray Center Inc ....C....... 607 756-9913
Cortland *(G-4031)*
JM Murray Center Inc ....C....... 607 756-0246
Cortland *(G-4032)*
Richard Ruffner..................................F....... 631 234-4600
Central Islip *(G-3509)*

BUILDING COMPONENTS: Structural Steel

Kuno Steel Products Corp ....F....... 516 938-8500
Hicksville *(G-6361)*
Leray Homes Inc.................................G....... 315 788-6087
Watertown *(G-16663)*
Marovato Industries Inc.......................F....... 718 389-0800
Brooklyn *(G-2275)*
Stone Bridge Iron and Stl Inc..............D....... 518 695-3752
Gansevoort *(G-5490)*
Wilston Enterprises Inc.......................F....... 716 483-1411
Jamestown *(G-7044)*

BUILDING ITEM REPAIR SVCS, MISCELLANEOUS

Aireactor Inc..F....... 718 326-2433
Maspeth *(G-8113)*
ER Butler & Co Inc..............................E....... 212 925-3565
New York *(G-10055)*
Manuf Appld Renova Sys ....G....... 518 654-9084
Corinth *(G-3959)*
Otis Elevator Company ....E....... 917 339-9600
New York *(G-11535)*

BUILDING PRDTS & MATERIALS DEALERS

Arnan Development Corp....................D....... 607 432-6641
Oneonta *(G-13171)*
Cossitt Concrete Products Inc ....F....... 315 824-2700
Hamilton *(G-5947)*
Delocon Wholesale Inc.......................F....... 716 592-2711
Springville *(G-15609)*
Gone South Concrete Block Inc.........E....... 315 598-2141
Fulton *(G-5459)*
Imperia Masonry Supply Corp............E....... 914 738-0900
Pelham *(G-13492)*
Norandex Inc Vestal............................G....... 607 786-0778
Vestal *(G-16452)*
Phelps Cement Products Inc ....E....... 315 548-9415
Phelps *(G-13535)*
Structural Wood Corporation ....E....... 315 388-4442
Waddington *(G-16521)*

PRODUCT SECTION

BUILDING PRDTS: Concrete

Access Products Inc .... G 800 679-4022
  Buffalo *(G-2795)*
Hanson Aggregates East LLC .... G 716 372-1574
  Allegany *(G-201)*
Oneida Sales & Service Inc .... F 716 270-0433
  Lackawanna *(G-7245)*

BUILDING PRDTS: Stone

Icestone LLC .... E 718 624-4900
  Brooklyn *(G-2095)*
Roto Salt Company Inc .... E 315 536-3742
  Penn Yan *(G-13519)*

BUILDING STONE, ARTIFICIAL: Concrete

Crown Hill Stone Inc .... E 716 326-4601
  Westfield *(G-17047)*

BUILDINGS & COMPONENTS: Prefabricated Metal

All American Building .... G 607 797-7123
  Binghamton *(G-885)*
Austin Mohawk and Company LLC .... E 315 793-3000
  Utica *(G-16308)*
Birdair Inc .... D 716 633-9500
  Amherst *(G-229)*
Deraffele Mfg Co Inc .... E 914 636-6850
  New Rochelle *(G-8894)*
Framing Technology Inc .... E 585 464-8470
  Rochester *(G-14380)*
Man Products Inc .... E 631 789-6500
  Farmingdale *(G-5040)*
Metals Building Products .... E 844 638-2527
  Holbrook *(G-6462)*
Mobile Mini Inc .... F 315 732-4555
  Utica *(G-16349)*
Morton Buildings Inc .... E 585 786-8191
  Warsaw *(G-16583)*
Overhead Door Corporation .... D 518 828-7652
  Hudson *(G-6629)*
Walpole Woodworkers Inc .... G 631 726-2859
  Water Mill *(G-16606)*

BUILDINGS, PREFABRICATED: Wholesalers

Shafer & Sons .... G 315 853-5285
  Westmoreland *(G-17065)*

BUILDINGS: Portable

Mobile Mini Inc .... E 631 543-4900
  Commack *(G-3838)*
Qub9 Inc .... G 585 484-1808
  Rochester *(G-14616)*
Universal Shielding Corp .... E 631 667-7900
  Deer Park *(G-4219)*
Veerhouse Voda Haiti LLC .... E 917 353-5944
  New York *(G-12513)*

BUILDINGS: Prefabricated, Metal

Energy Panel Structures Inc .... G 315 923-7777
  Clyde *(G-3726)*
Energy Panel Structures Inc .... G 585 343-1777
  Batavia *(G-630)*
Energy Panel Structures Inc .... G 518 355-6708
  Schenectady *(G-15251)*
Metadure Defense & SEC LLC .... F 631 249-2141
  Farmingdale *(G-5049)*
Nci Group Inc .... D 315 339-1245
  Rome *(G-14824)*
Pei Liquidation Company .... F 518 489-5101
  Albany *(G-116)*

BUILDINGS: Prefabricated, Plastic

Euro Woodworking Inc .... G 718 246-9172
  Brooklyn *(G-1938)*

BUILDINGS: Prefabricated, Wood

Cort Contracting .... F 845 758-1190
  Red Hook *(G-14028)*
Duro-Shed Inc .... E 585 344-0800
  Buffalo *(G-2921)*
Eastern Exterior Wall .... E 631 589-3880
  Bohemia *(G-1061)*
Energy Panel Structures Inc .... G 315 923-7777
  Clyde *(G-3726)*
Energy Panel Structures Inc .... G 585 343-1777
  Batavia *(G-630)*
Energy Panel Structures Inc .... G 518 355-6708
  Schenectady *(G-15251)*
Historcal Soc of Mddltown Walk .... G 845 342-0941
  Middletown *(G-8444)*
Northern Design & Bldg Assoc .... E 518 747-2200
  Queensbury *(G-14006)*
Solid Bilt Construction .... G 315 893-1738
  Madison *(G-7994)*
Walpole Woodworkers Inc .... G 631 726-2859
  Water Mill *(G-16606)*
Wood Tex Products LLC .... D 607 243-5141
  Himrod *(G-6423)*

BUILDINGS: Prefabricated, Wood

Lapp Management Corp .... G 607 243-5141
  Himrod *(G-6422)*
Roscoe Brothers Inc .... F 607 844-3750
  Dryden *(G-4322)*
Shafer & Sons .... G 315 853-5285
  Westmoreland *(G-17065)*
Shelter Enterprises Inc .... D 518 237-4100
  Cohoes *(G-3758)*

BULLETIN BOARDS: Wood

Aarco Products Inc .... F 631 924-5461
  Yaphank *(G-17384)*
Bulletin Boards & Dirctry Pdts .... F 914 248-8008
  Yorktown Heights *(G-17507)*

BUMPERS: Motor Vehicle

4bumpers Llc .... F 212 721-9600
  New York *(G-8976)*

BURIAL VAULTS: Concrete Or Precast Terrazzo

Beck Vault Company .... G 315 337-7590
  Rome *(G-14806)*
Doric Vault of Wny Inc .... F 716 828-1776
  Buffalo *(G-2917)*
Ideal Burial Vault Company .... G 585 599-2242
  Corfu *(G-3955)*
Robert M Vault .... G 315 243-1447
  Bridgeport *(G-1236)*
Suhor Industries Inc .... F 585 377-5100
  Fairport *(G-4883)*
Vault Wo .... G 212 281-1723
  Brooklyn *(G-2721)*

BURLAP & BURLAP PRDTS

James Thompson & Company Inc .... G 212 686-4242
  New York *(G-10698)*

BURNERS: Gas, Indl

Dyson-Kissner-Moran Corp .... E 212 661-4600
  Poughkeepsie *(G-13896)*
Flynn Burner Corporation .... E 914 636-1320
  New Rochelle *(G-8899)*
Frederick Cowan & Company Inc .... F 631 369-0360
  Riverhead *(G-14143)*

BUSES: Wholesalers

Leonard Bus Sales Inc .... G 607 467-3100
  Rome *(G-14819)*

BUSHINGS & BEARINGS: Copper, Exc Machined

Amt Incorporated .... E 518 284-2910
  Sharon Springs *(G-15383)*

BUSHINGS: Cast Steel, Exc Investment

Pcore Electric Company Inc .... D 585 768-1200
  Le Roy *(G-7418)*

BUSINESS ACTIVITIES: Non-Commercial Site

Adirondack Leather Pdts Inc .... F 607 547-5798
  Fly Creek *(G-5313)*
Ajmadison Corp .... D 718 532-1800
  Brooklyn *(G-1573)*
Aka Sport Inc .... F 631 858-9888
  Dix Hills *(G-4289)*
American Comfort Direct LLC .... E 201 364-8309
  New York *(G-9116)*
Anne Taintor Inc .... G 718 483-9312
  Brooklyn *(G-1613)*
Arm Construction Company Inc .... G 646 235-6520
  East Elmhurst *(G-4388)*
Aureonic .... G 518 791-9331
  Gansevoort *(G-5485)*
Catch Ventures Inc .... F 347 620-4351
  New York *(G-9547)*
Cfp Purchasing Inc .... G 705 806-0383
  Flushing *(G-5231)*
Cloud Rock Group LLC .... G 516 967-6023
  Roslyn *(G-15017)*
Dapper Dads Inc .... G 917 903-8045
  Brooklyn *(G-1839)*
Darmiyan LLC .... G 917 689-0389
  New York *(G-9810)*
Do It Different Inc .... G 917 842-0230
  New York *(G-9893)*
Envent Systems Inc .... G 646 294-6980
  Pelham *(G-13491)*
Excell Print & Promotions Inc .... G 914 437-8668
  White Plains *(G-17107)*
Exquis LLC .... F 845 537-5380
  Harriman *(G-5971)*
Fresh Prints LLC .... E 917 826-2752
  New York *(G-10210)*
Garrett J Cronin .... G 914 761-9299
  White Plains *(G-17111)*
Gorga Fehren Fine Jewelry LLC .... G 646 861-3595
  New York *(G-10339)*
Greene Brass & Alum Fndry LLC .... G 607 656-4204
  Bloomville *(G-996)*
Hair Ventures LLC .... F 718 664-7689
  Irvington *(G-6771)*
Hovee Inc .... F 646 249-6200
  New York *(G-10522)*
Inscape (new York) Inc .... D 716 665-6210
  Falconer *(G-4902)*
Isabella Products Inc .... F 516 699-8404
  Great Neck *(G-5818)*
Joel Zelcer .... F 917 525-6790
  Brooklyn *(G-2144)*
Joycharge Inc .... D 646 321-1127
  New York *(G-10774)*
Latchable Inc .... E 646 833-0604
  New York *(G-10931)*
Liiiike Shopping Inc .... F 914 271-2001
  New York *(G-10996)*
Lotus Apparel Designs Inc .... G 646 236-9363
  Westbury *(G-17007)*
Magcrest Packaging Inc .... G 845 425-0451
  Monsey *(G-8574)*
Mynt 1792 LLC .... G 212 249-4562
  New York *(G-11333)*
New York Qrtrly Foundation Inc .... F 917 843-8825
  Brooklyn *(G-2368)*
On Line Power Technologies .... G 914 968-4440
  Yonkers *(G-17470)*
Oneh2 Inc .... G 703 862-9656
  Hector *(G-6259)*
Pap Chat Inc .... G 516 350-1888
  Brooklyn *(G-2403)*
Patrick Rohan .... G 718 781-2573
  Monticello *(G-8607)*
Phoenix Usa LLC .... G 646 351-6598
  New York *(G-11652)*
Pink Box Accessories LLC .... G 716 777-4477
  Brooklyn *(G-2422)*
Playfitness Corp .... G 917 497-5443
  Staten Island *(G-15722)*
Playlife LLC .... G 646 207-9082
  New York *(G-11675)*
Qub9 Inc .... G 585 484-1808
  Rochester *(G-14616)*
Ready Check Glo Inc .... G 516 547-1849
  East Northport *(G-4444)*
Ready To Assemble Company Inc .... E 516 825-4397
  Valley Stream *(G-16424)*
Rision Inc .... G 212 987-2628
  New York *(G-11878)*
Roscoe Brothers Inc .... F 607 844-3750
  Dryden *(G-4322)*
Scan-A-Chrome Color Inc .... G 631 532-6146
  Copiague *(G-3925)*
Sensor & Decontamination Inc .... F 301 526-8389
  Binghamton *(G-950)*
Seymour Science LLC .... G 516 699-8404
  Great Neck *(G-5840)*

Slyde Inc ....F.... 917 331-2114
Long Island City *(G-7879)*
Smn Medical PC ....F.... 844 362-2428
Rye *(G-15068)*
South Central Boyz ....G.... 718 496-7270
Brooklyn *(G-2586)*
Treauu Inc ....G.... 703 731-0196
New York *(G-12395)*
Trovvit Inc ....G.... 718 908-5376
Brooklyn *(G-2685)*
Urthworx Inc ....G.... 646 373-7535
New York *(G-12483)*
Vader Systems LLC ....G.... 716 636-1742
East Amherst *(G-4363)*
Vertical Lax Inc ....G.... 518 669-3699
Albany *(G-148)*
Virtuvent Inc ....G.... 646 845-0387
New York *(G-12551)*
Vortex Ventures Inc ....G.... 516 946-8345
North Baldwin *(G-12912)*
Zinerva Pharmaceuticals LLC ....G.... 630 729-4184
Clarence Center *(G-3682)*

BUSINESS FORMS WHOLESALERS

American Print Solutions Inc ....G.... 718 208-2309
Brooklyn *(G-1607)*
Chem-Puter Friendly Inc ....E.... 631 331-2259
Mount Sinai *(G-8654)*
Composite Forms Inc ....F.... 914 937-1808
Port Chester *(G-13740)*

BUSINESS FORMS: Printed, Continuous

Five Boro Holding LLC ....F.... 718 431-9500
Brooklyn *(G-1977)*
Idc Printing & Sty Co Inc ....G.... 516 599-0400
Lynbrook *(G-7951)*
Linden Forms & Systems Inc ....E.... 212 219-1100
Brooklyn *(G-2226)*
Syracuse Computer Forms Inc ....E.... 315 478-0108
Syracuse *(G-16050)*

BUSINESS FORMS: Printed, Manifold

Abra-Ka-Data Systems Ltd ....E.... 631 667-5550
Deer Park *(G-4086)*
Amsterdam Printing & Litho Inc ....F.... 518 842-6000
Amsterdam *(G-332)*
Amsterdam Printing & Litho Inc ....E.... 518 842-6000
Amsterdam *(G-333)*
Bmg Printing and Promotion LLC ....G.... 631 231-9200
Bohemia *(G-1026)*
Gateway Prtg & Graphics Inc ....E.... 716 823-3873
Hamburg *(G-5926)*
Maggio Data Forms Printing Ltd ....C.... 631 348-0343
Hauppauge *(G-6124)*
Marcy Business Forms Inc ....G.... 718 935-9100
Brooklyn *(G-2267)*
P P I Business Forms Inc ....G.... 716 825-1241
Buffalo *(G-3107)*
Resonant Legal Media LLC ....D.... 800 781-3591
New York *(G-11841)*
Richard Ruffner ....F.... 631 234-4600
Central Islip *(G-3509)*
Rmf Printing Technologies Inc ....E.... 716 683-7500
Lancaster *(G-7339)*
RR Donnelley & Sons Company ....D.... 716 773-0647
Grand Island *(G-5766)*
RR Donnelley & Sons Company ....D.... 716 773-0300
Grand Island *(G-5767)*
Select-A-Form Inc ....D.... 631 981-3076
Holbrook *(G-6470)*
Standard Register Inc ....F.... 937 221-1303
Melville *(G-8356)*
Williamson Law Book Co ....F.... 585 924-3400
Victor *(G-16514)*

BUSINESS MACHINE REPAIR, ELECTRIC

National Time Recording Eqp Co ....F.... 212 227-3310
New York *(G-11352)*
Neopost USA Inc ....E.... 631 435-9100
Hauppauge *(G-6146)*
Yellow E House Inc ....G.... 718 888-2000
Flushing *(G-5311)*

BUSINESS SUPPORT SVCS

Cabezon Design Group Inc ....G.... 718 488-9868
Brooklyn *(G-1746)*
Diamond Inscription Tech ....F.... 646 366-7944
New York *(G-9873)*

BUTADIENE: Indl, Organic, Chemical

Unified Solutions For Clg Inc ....F.... 718 782-8800
Brooklyn *(G-2697)*

BUTTONS

Buttons & Trimcom Inc ....F.... 212 868-1971
New York *(G-9484)*
E-Won Industrial Co Inc ....E.... 212 750-9610
New York *(G-9956)*
Empire State Metal Pdts Inc ....E.... 718 847-1617
Richmond Hill *(G-14073)*
Emsig Manufacturing Corp ....F.... 718 784-7717
New York *(G-10026)*
Emsig Manufacturing Corp ....F.... 518 828-7301
Hudson *(G-6613)*
Emsig Manufacturing Corp ....E.... 718 784-7717
New York *(G-10027)*
Eu Design LLC ....G.... 212 420-7788
New York *(G-10081)*
Joyce Trimming Inc ....G.... 212 719-3110
New York *(G-10773)*
Kraus & Sons Inc ....F.... 212 620-0408
New York *(G-10887)*
Mona Slide Fasteners Inc ....E.... 718 325-7700
Bronx *(G-1401)*
Namm Singer Inc ....F.... 212 947-2566
New York *(G-11339)*
National Die & Button Mould Co ....E.... 201 939-7800
Brooklyn *(G-2350)*

CABINETS & CASES: Show, Display & Storage, Exc Wood

260 Oak Street Inc ....G.... 877 852-4676
Buffalo *(G-2788)*
Able Steel Equipment Co Inc ....F.... 718 361-9240
Long Island City *(G-7647)*
S & K Counter Tops Inc ....G.... 716 662-7986
Orchard Park *(G-13296)*

CABINETS: Bathroom Vanities, Wood

Nagad Cabinets Inc ....G.... 718 382-7200
Brooklyn *(G-2347)*
New York Vanity and Mfg Co ....E.... 718 417-1010
Freeport *(G-5415)*

CABINETS: Entertainment

Dbs Interiors Corp ....F.... 631 491-3013
West Babylon *(G-16788)*
Loffreno Cstm Interiors Contg ....E.... 718 981-0319
Staten Island *(G-15699)*
Time Base Corporation ....E.... 631 293-4068
Edgewood *(G-4617)*
W Designe Inc ....E.... 914 736-1058
Peekskill *(G-13484)*

CABINETS: Entertainment Units, Household, Wood

Cleary Custom Cabinets Inc ....F.... 516 939-2475
Hicksville *(G-6333)*
Handcraft Cabinetry Inc ....G.... 914 681-9437
White Plains *(G-17117)*

CABINETS: Factory

Creative Stone & Cabinets ....G.... 631 772-6548
Selden *(G-15350)*
T O Gronlund Company Inc ....F.... 212 679-3535
New York *(G-12268)*
Thornwood Products Ltd ....E.... 914 769-9161
Thornwood *(G-16122)*
Wood Etc Inc ....F.... 315 484-9663
Syracuse *(G-16075)*

CABINETS: Filing, Metal

Schwab Corp ....E.... 585 381-4900
Rochester *(G-14675)*

CABINETS: Filing, Wood

Red White & Blue Entps Corp ....G.... 718 565-8080
Woodside *(G-17350)*

CABINETS: Kitchen, Metal

American Best Cabinets Inc ....E.... 845 369-6666
Suffern *(G-15785)*

Hellas Stone Inc ....G.... 718 545-4716
Astoria *(G-444)*
Majestic Home Imprvs Distr ....G.... 718 853-5079
Brooklyn *(G-2253)*
Manhattan Cabinets Inc ....G.... 212 548-2436
New York *(G-11127)*
Methods Tooling & Mfg Inc ....E.... 845 246-7100
Mount Marion *(G-8651)*

CABINETS: Kitchen, Wood

Able Kitchen ....F.... 877 268-1264
Cedarhurst *(G-3455)*
Acme Kitchenettes Corp ....E.... 518 828-4191
Hudson *(G-6604)*
Aki Cabinets Inc ....F.... 718 721-2541
Astoria *(G-432)*
Amoroso Wood Products Co Inc ....G.... 631 249-4998
Melville *(G-8294)*
Andike Millwork Inc ....G.... 718 894-1796
Maspeth *(G-8118)*
Artone LLC ....D.... 716 664-2232
Jamestown *(G-6972)*
Atlantic States Distributing ....G.... 518 427-6364
Menands *(G-8368)*
Auburn-Watson Corp ....F.... 716 876-8000
Depew *(G-4247)*
Bauerschmidt & Sons Inc ....D.... 718 528-3500
Jamaica *(G-6898)*
Bloch Industries LLC ....D.... 585 334-9600
Rochester *(G-14235)*
Cabinet Shapes Corp ....F.... 718 784-6255
Long Island City *(G-7691)*
Cabinetry By Tbr Inc ....G.... 516 365-8500
Manhasset *(G-8055)*
Cabinets By Stanley Inc ....G.... 718 222-5861
Brooklyn *(G-1747)*
Cambridge Kitchens Mfg Inc ....F.... 516 935-5100
Hicksville *(G-6329)*
Candlelight Cabinetry Inc ....C.... 716 434-2114
Lockport *(G-7575)*
Capital Kit Cab & Door Mfrs ....G.... 718 886-0303
College Point *(G-3779)*
Carefree Kitchens Inc ....G.... 631 567-2120
Holbrook *(G-6436)*
Carlos & Alex Atelier Inc ....E.... 718 441-8911
Richmond Hill *(G-14070)*
Casa Collection Inc ....G.... 718 694-0272
Brooklyn *(G-1762)*
Catskill Craftsmen Inc ....D.... 607 652-7321
Stamford *(G-15624)*
Cbc Custom Millwork Inc ....F.... 718 499-6742
Brooklyn *(G-1765)*
Central Kitchen Corp ....F.... 631 283-1029
Southampton *(G-15541)*
Chicone Builders LLC ....G.... 607 535-6540
Montour Falls *(G-8609)*
Classic Cabinets ....F.... 845 357-4331
Suffern *(G-15787)*
Clearwood Custom Carpentry and ....E.... 315 432-8422
East Syracuse *(G-4518)*
Commercial Millworks Inc ....G.... 315 475-7479
Syracuse *(G-15902)*
Cosmopolitan Cabinet Company ....G.... 631 467-4960
Ronkonkoma *(G-14890)*
Craft Custom Woodwork Co Inc ....F.... 718 821-2162
Maspeth *(G-8124)*
Creative Cabinet Corp America ....E.... 631 751-5768
Stony Brook *(G-15769)*
Custom CAS Inc ....E.... 718 726-3575
Long Island City *(G-7708)*
Custom Woodcraft LLC ....F.... 315 843-4234
Munnsville *(G-8750)*
D & M Custom Cabinets Inc ....F.... 516 678-2818
Oceanside *(G-13075)*
Dak Mica and Wood Products ....G.... 631 467-0749
Ronkonkoma *(G-14892)*
Dbs Interiors Corp ....F.... 631 491-3013
West Babylon *(G-16788)*
Deakon Homes and Interiors ....F.... 518 271-0342
Troy *(G-16233)*
Di Fiore and Sons Custom Wdwkg ....G.... 718 278-1663
Long Island City *(G-7715)*
EC Wood & Company Inc ....F.... 718 388-2287
Deer Park *(G-4135)*
EM Pfaff & Son Inc ....F.... 607 739-3691
Horseheads *(G-6575)*
Enterprise Wood Products Inc ....F.... 718 853-9243
Brooklyn *(G-1926)*
European Craft Inc ....G.... 516 313-2243
Great Neck *(G-5806)*

Fantasy Home Improvement Corp ....G....... 718 277-4021
Brooklyn (G-1958)
Fina Cabinet Corp ....G....... 718 409-2900
Mount Vernon (G-8681)
Fra-Rik Formica Fabg Co Inc ....G....... 718 597-3335
Bronx (G-1337)
Garrison Woodworking Inc ....F....... 845 726-3525
Westtown (G-17069)
Glissade New York LLC ....E....... 631 756-4800
Farmingdale (G-4999)
Greenway Cabinetry Inc ....F....... 516 877-0009
Williston Park (G-17261)
Hearth Cabinets and More Ltd ....G....... 315 641-1197
Liverpool (G-7521)
Hendrickson Custom Cabinetry ....F....... 718 401-0137
Bronx (G-1356)
Hollywood Cabinets Co ....G....... 516 354-0857
Elmont (G-4722)
Home Ideal Inc ....G....... 718 762-8998
Flushing (G-5251)
Ignelzi Interiors Inc ....E....... 718 464-0279
Queens Village (G-13979)
Infinity Design LLC ....F....... 718 416-3853
Maspeth (G-8145)
J Percoco Industries Inc ....G....... 631 312-4572
Bohemia (G-1079)
Jordache Woodworking Corp ....F....... 718 349-3373
Brooklyn (G-2147)
K-Binet Inc ....G....... 845 348-1149
Blauvelt (G-972)
Kalnitz Kitchens Inc ....F....... 716 684-1700
Buffalo (G-3026)
Kw Distributors Group Inc ....F....... 718 843-3500
Ozone Park (G-13382)
Legacy Furniture Inc ....F....... 718 527-5331
Monroe (G-8560)
Little Wolf Cabinet Shop Inc ....E....... 212 734-1116
New York (G-11013)
Longo Commercial Cabinets Inc ....E....... 631 225-4290
Lindenhurst (G-7469)
Lyn Jo Kitchens Inc ....G....... 718 336-6060
Brooklyn (G-2240)
Material Process Systems Inc ....F....... 718 302-3081
Brooklyn (G-2283)
Matteo & Antonio Bartolotta ....F....... 315 252-2220
Auburn (G-508)
McGraw Wood Products LLC ....E....... 607 836-6465
Mc Graw (G-8223)
Mega Cabinets Inc ....E....... 631 789-4112
Amityville (G-311)
Methods Tooling & Mfg Inc ....E....... 845 246-7100
Mount Marion (G-8651)
Metro Kitchens Corp ....F....... 718 434-1166
Brooklyn (G-2305)
Michael Bernstein Design Assoc ....E....... 718 456-9277
Brooklyn (G-2308)
Michael P Mmarr ....G....... 315 623-9380
Constantia (G-3881)
Millco Woodworking LLC ....F....... 585 526-6844
Hall (G-5917)
Modern Cabinet Company Inc ....E....... 845 473-4900
Poughkeepsie (G-13917)
N Y Elli Design Corp ....F....... 718 228-0014
Maspeth (G-8153)
Neo Cabinetry LLC ....F....... 718 403-0456
Brooklyn (G-2356)
NY Cabinet Factory Inc ....F....... 718 256-6541
Brooklyn (G-2381)
Pgs Millwork Inc ....D....... 212 244-6610
New York (G-11642)
Piccini Industries Ltd ....E....... 845 365-0614
Orangeburg (G-13239)
Precision Dental Cabinets Inc ....F....... 631 543-3870
Smithtown (G-15495)
Premier Woodcraft Ltd ....E....... 610 383-6624
White Plains (G-17161)
Premium Woodworking LLC ....G....... 718 782-7747
Brooklyn (G-2438)
R & M Thermofoil Doors Inc ....G....... 718 206-4991
Jamaica (G-6943)
Ralph Payne ....G....... 718 222-4200
Brooklyn (G-2477)
Red White & Blue Entps Corp ....G....... 718 565-8080
Woodside (G-17350)
Ribble Lumber Inc ....G....... 315 536-6221
Penn Yan (G-13518)
Royal Custom Cabinets ....G....... 315 376-6042
Lowville (G-7942)
S & V Custom Furniture Mfg ....F....... 516 746-8299
Mineola (G-8536)
S Donadic Woodworking Inc ....D....... 718 361-9888
Sunnyside (G-15809)
Salko Kitchens Inc ....F....... 845 565-4420
New Windsor (G-8952)
Salmon Crek Cabinetry Inc ....E....... 315 589-5419
Williamson (G-17225)
Serway Bros Inc ....E....... 315 337-0601
Rome (G-14836)
Sherry-Mica Products Inc ....G....... 631 471-7513
Ronkonkoma (G-14985)
Silva Cabinetry Inc ....E....... 914 737-7697
Buchanan (G-2787)
Stone Expo & Cabinetry LLC ....F....... 516 292-2988
West Hempstead (G-16863)
Upstate Cabinet Co Inc ....F....... 585 429-5090
Rochester (G-14746)
Viola Cabinet Corporation ....G....... 716 284-6327
Niagara Falls (G-12888)
W Designe Inc ....E....... 914 736-1058
Peekskill (G-13484)
White House Cabinet Shop LLC ....G....... 607 674-9358
Sherburne (G-15399)
William Brooks Woodworking ....F....... 718 495-9767
Brooklyn (G-2752)
Win Wood Cabinetry Inc ....G....... 516 304-2216
Greenvale (G-5883)
Wood Etc Inc ....F....... 315 484-9663
Syracuse (G-16075)
Yonkers Cabinets Inc ....G....... 914 668-2133
Yonkers (G-17502)
Your Furniture Designers Inc ....G....... 845 947-3046
West Haverstraw (G-16848)
Your Way Custom Cabinets Inc ....G....... 914 371-1870
Mount Vernon (G-8746)

CABINETS: Office, Metal

Creative Cabinetry Corporation ....G....... 914 963-6061
Yonkers (G-17431)
Natural Stone & Cabinet Inc ....G....... 718 388-2988
Brooklyn (G-2353)
Riverfront Costume Design ....G....... 716 693-2501
North Tonawanda (G-12990)

CABINETS: Office, Wood

Chicone Builders LLC ....G....... 607 535-6540
Montour Falls (G-8609)
Commercial Display Design LLC ....F....... 607 336-7353
Norwich (G-13025)
Concepts In Wood of CNY ....E....... 315 463-8084
Syracuse (G-15904)
Craft Custom Woodwork Co Inc ....F....... 718 821-2162
Maspeth (G-8124)
Creative Cabinetry Corporation ....G....... 914 963-6061
Yonkers (G-17431)
Fina Cabinet Corp ....G....... 718 409-2900
Mount Vernon (G-8681)
Loffreno Cstm Interiors Contg ....E....... 718 981-0319
Staten Island (G-15699)
N Y Elli Design Corp ....F....... 718 228-0014
Maspeth (G-8153)
Poppin Inc ....D....... 212 391-7200
New York (G-11685)
Riverfront Costume Design ....G....... 716 693-2501
North Tonawanda (G-12990)
Stylecraft Interiors Inc ....F....... 516 487-2133
Great Neck (G-5843)
Three R Enterprises Inc ....E....... 585 254-5050
Rochester (G-14725)
Wares of Wood ....E....... 315 964-2983
Williamstown (G-17229)
Wood Etc Inc ....F....... 315 484-9663
Syracuse (G-16075)

CABINETS: Radio & Television, Metal

CIDC Corp ....F....... 718 342-5820
Brooklyn (G-1780)

CABINETS: Show, Display, Etc, Wood, Exc Refrigerated

Custom Design Kitchens Inc ....F....... 518 355-4446
Duanesburg (G-4325)
E F Thresh Inc ....G....... 315 437-7301
East Syracuse (G-4526)
Fleetwood Cabinet Co Inc ....G....... 516 379-2139
Brooklyn (G-1986)
Johnny Mica Inc ....G....... 631 225-5213
Lindenhurst (G-7466)
Rasjada Enterprises Ltd ....F....... 631 242-1055
Bay Shore (G-732)
Saw Mill Woodworking Inc ....G....... 914 963-1841
Yonkers (G-17483)
Telesca-Heyman Inc ....F....... 212 534-3442
New York (G-12296)

CABLE TELEVISION

Hearst Holdings Inc ....F....... 212 649-2000
New York (G-10449)
Historic TW Inc ....D....... 212 484-8000
New York (G-10484)
Time Warner Companies Inc ....D....... 212 484-8000
New York (G-12350)

CABLE TELEVISION PRDTS

Arcom Automatics LLC ....G....... 315 422-1230
Syracuse (G-15856)
Arrow-Communication Labs Inc ....B....... 315 422-1230
Syracuse (G-15859)
Belden Inc ....B....... 607 796-5600
Horseheads (G-6569)
Eagle Comtronics Inc ....C....... 315 451-3313
Liverpool (G-7518)
Eeg Enterprises Inc ....F....... 516 293-7472
Farmingdale (G-4986)

CABLE: Fiber

Cables and Chips Inc ....E....... 212 619-3132
New York (G-9493)
Fiber Instrument Sales Inc ....C....... 315 736-2206
Oriskany (G-13309)
Fiberone LLC ....F....... 315 434-8877
East Syracuse (G-4529)
Triad Network Technologies ....E....... 585 924-8505
Victor (G-16509)

CABLE: Fiber Optic

Cable Your World Inc ....G....... 631 509-1180
Port Jeff STA (G-13764)
Corning Inc ....E....... 607 974-9000
Corning (G-3961)
Corning Incorporated ....G....... 607 974-6729
Painted Post (G-13391)
Corning Incorporated ....A....... 607 974-9000
Corning (G-3962)
Corning Incorporated ....E....... 607 248-1200
Corning (G-3965)
Corning Specialty Mtls Inc ....G....... 607 974-9000
Corning (G-3970)
Fiberdyne Labs Inc ....D....... 315 895-8470
Frankfort (G-5353)
TLC-The Light Connection Inc ....D....... 315 736-7384
Oriskany (G-13317)

CABLE: Nonferrous, Shipboard

Monroe Cable Company Inc ....C....... 845 692-2800
Middletown (G-8452)

CABLE: Noninsulated

J Davis Manufacturing Co Inc ....E....... 315 337-7574
Rome (G-14816)
Nexans Energy USA Inc ....C....... 845 469-2141
Chester (G-3610)
Reelcology Inc ....F....... 845 258-1880
Pine Island (G-13553)
Ultra Clarity Corp ....G....... 719 470-1010
Spring Valley (G-15604)
Weico Wire & Cable Inc ....E....... 631 254-2970
Edgewood (G-4621)

CABLE: Ropes & Fiber

Cortland Company Inc ....C....... 607 753-8276
Cortland (G-4017)

CABLE: Steel, Insulated Or Armored

Dragon Trading Inc ....G....... 212 717-1496
New York (G-9923)
Dsr International Corp ....G....... 631 427-2600
Great Neck (G-5803)
Northeast Wire and Cable Co ....G....... 716 297-8483
Niagara Falls (G-12852)

CAGES: Wire

Renco Group Inc .... G 212 541-6000
New York (G-11832)

CALCULATING & ACCOUNTING EQPT

Hand Held Products Inc .... B 315 554-6000
Skaneateles Falls (G-15468)
Rasa Services Inc .... G 516 294-4292
New Hyde Park (G-8859)

CALIBRATING SVCS, NEC

Phymetrix Inc .... G 631 627-3950
Medford (G-8257)
Quality Vision Services Inc .... D 585 544-0450
Rochester (G-14614)

CAMERA & PHOTOGRAPHIC SPLYS STORES

Eastchester Photo Services .... G 914 961-6596
Eastchester (G-4582)

CAMERAS & RELATED EQPT: Photographic

Bescor Video Accessories Ltd .... F 631 420-1717
Farmingdale (G-4952)
Focus Camera Inc .... C 718 437-8800
Brooklyn (G-1990)
Lake Image Systems Inc .... F 585 321-3630
Henrietta (G-6296)
Rear View Safety Inc .... E 855 815-3842
Brooklyn (G-2482)
Watec America Corporation .... E 702 434-6111
Middletown (G-8470)

CANDLE SHOPS

Candles By Foster .... G 914 739-9226
Peekskill (G-13475)
Northern Lights Entps Inc .... C 585 593-1200
Wellsville (G-16755)

CANDLES

A & L Asset Management Ltd .... C 718 566-1500
Brooklyn (G-1526)
Astron Candle Manufacturing Co .... G 718 728-3330
Long Island City (G-7673)
Candle In The Window Inc .... F 718 852-5743
Brooklyn (G-1753)
Candles By Foster .... G 914 739-9226
Peekskill (G-13475)
Cathedral Candle Co .... D 315 422-9119
Syracuse (G-15890)
Crusader Candle Co Inc .... E 718 625-0005
Brooklyn (G-1821)
International Design Assoc Ltd .... G 212 687-0333
New York (G-10633)
Joya LLC .... F 718 852-6979
Brooklyn (G-2153)
Kkw Corp .... E 631 589-5454
Sayville (G-15211)
Lux Mundi Corp .... G 631 244-4596
Ronkonkoma (G-14934)
Muench-Kreuzer Candle Company .... D 315 471-4515
Syracuse (G-15994)
Northern Lights Entps Inc .... C 585 593-1200
Wellsville (G-16755)
Old Williamsburgh Candle Corp .... C 718 566-1500
Brooklyn (G-2389)
Quality Candle Mfg Co Inc .... F 631 842-8475
Copiague (G-3921)
Simcha Candle Co Inc .... G 845 783-0406
New Windsor (G-8955)
Thompson Ferrier LLC .... G 212 244-2212
New York (G-12326)
TV Guilfoil & Associates Inc .... G 315 453-0920
Syracuse (G-16062)

CANDLES: Wholesalers

Candle In The Window Inc .... F 718 852-5743
Brooklyn (G-1753)

CANDY & CONFECTIONS: Cake Ornaments

Naples Vly Mrgers Acqstons LLC .... G 585 490-1339
Naples (G-8767)
OH How Cute Inc .... G 347 838-6031
Staten Island (G-15719)

Pfeil & Holing Inc .... D 718 545-4600
Woodside (G-17346)

CANDY & CONFECTIONS: Candy Bars, Including Chocolate Covered

Chocomaker Inc .... G 716 877-3146
Buffalo (G-2873)
Eatingevolved LLC .... F 631 675-2440
Setauket (G-15376)
Fine and Raw Chocolate .... G 718 366-3633
Brooklyn (G-1971)
N Make Mold Inc .... E 716 854-6050
Buffalo (G-3080)
Nycjbs LLC .... F 212 533-1888
New York (G-11481)
Vigneri Chocolate Inc .... G 585 254-6160
Rochester (G-14753)

CANDY & CONFECTIONS: Chocolate Candy, Exc Solid Chocolate

Aigner Chocolates Inc .... G 718 544-1850
Forest Hills (G-5320)
Amiram Dror Inc .... F 212 979-9505
Brooklyn (G-1611)
Chocolate Pizza Company Inc .... F 315 673-4098
Marcellus (G-8087)
Robert Pikcilingis .... F 518 355-1860
Altamont (G-211)

CANDY & CONFECTIONS: Fudge

Alrajs Inc .... E 631 225-0300
Lindenhurst (G-7452)

CANDY, NUT & CONFECTIONERY STORES: Candy

5th Avenue Chocolatiere Ltd .... F 516 561-1570
Valley Stream (G-16397)
5th Avenue Chocolatiere Ltd .... G 212 935-5454
Freeport (G-5379)
Adirondack Chocolate Co Ltd .... G 518 946-7270
Wilmington (G-17267)
Amiram Dror Inc .... F 212 979-9505
Brooklyn (G-1611)
Commodore Chocolatier USA Inc .... F 845 561-3960
Newburgh (G-12753)
Ford Gum & Machine Company Inc ..... D 716 542-4561
Akron (G-22)
Godiva Chocolatier Inc .... E 212 984-5900
New York (G-10326)
Hercules Candy Co .... F 315 463-4339
East Syracuse (G-4537)
Hudson Valley Chocolatier Inc .... F 845 831-8240
Beacon (G-785)
Jo-Mart Candies Corp .... F 718 375-1277
Brooklyn (G-2143)
Lady-N-Th-wndow Chocolates Inc .... F 631 549-1059
Huntington (G-6666)
Noras Candy Shop .... F 315 337-4530
Rome (G-14825)
Parkside Candy Co Inc .... F 716 833-7540
Buffalo (G-3114)
Roger L Urban Inc .... E 716 693-5391
North Tonawanda (G-12992)
Seaward Candies .... G 585 638-6761
Holley (G-6492)
The Chocolate Shop .... G 716 882-5055
Buffalo (G-3215)

CANDY: Chocolate From Cacao Beans

Adirondack Chocolate Co Ltd .... G 518 946-7270
Wilmington (G-17267)
Aigner Chocolates Inc .... G 718 544-1850
Forest Hills (G-5320)
Chocolate Pizza Company Inc .... F 315 673-4098
Marcellus (G-8087)
Encore Chocolates Inc .... G 585 266-2970
Rochester (G-14350)
Godiva Chocolatier Inc .... E 212 984-5900
New York (G-10326)
Godiva Chocolatier Inc .... F 718 271-3603
Elmhurst (G-4661)
Landies Candies Co Inc .... F 716 834-8212
Buffalo (G-3046)
Madelaine Chocolate Novlt Inc .... D 718 945-1500
Rockaway Beach (G-14782)

Roger L Urban Inc .... E 716 693-5391
North Tonawanda (G-12992)
Superior Confections Inc .... D 718 698-3300
Staten Island (G-15743)

CANNED SPECIALTIES

Global Food Source & Co Inc .... G 914 320-9615
Tuckahoe (G-16270)
Goya Foods Inc .... D 716 549-0076
Angola (G-380)
Grandma Browns Beans Inc .... F 315 963-7221
Mexico (G-8395)

CANOPIES: Sheet Metal

Austin Mohawk and Company LLC ...... E 315 793-3000
Utica (G-16308)

CANS: Aluminum

Anheuser-Busch Companies LLC .... G 718 589-2610
Bronx (G-1276)
Ball Metal Beverage Cont Corp .... C 845 692-3800
Middletown (G-8427)

CANS: Metal

Ardagh Metal Packaging USA Inc .... C 607 584-3300
Conklin (G-3865)
Ball Metal Beverage Cont Corp .... C 518 587-6030
Saratoga Springs (G-15144)
Brakewell Stl Fabricators Inc .... E 845 469-9131
Chester (G-3601)
Crown Cork & Seal Usa Inc .... C 845 343-9586
Middletown (G-8434)
Erie Engineered Products Inc .... E 716 206-0204
Lancaster (G-7314)
J C Industries Inc .... E 631 420-1920
West Babylon (G-16798)
Metal Container Corporation .... C 845 567-1500
New Windsor (G-8943)
Seneca Foods Corporation .... D 315 926-0531
Marion (G-8100)
Silgan Containers Mfg Corp .... C 315 946-4826
Lyons (G-7975)
Sky Dive .... D 845 858-6400
Port Jervis (G-13792)

CANVAS PRDTS

Ace Canvas & Tent Corp .... F 631 648-0614
Ronkonkoma (G-14848)
Anchor Canvas LLC .... G 631 265-5602
Smithtown (G-15483)
Breton Industries Inc .... D 518 842-3030
Amsterdam (G-336)
Broadway Neon Sign Corp .... F 908 241-4177
Ronkonkoma (G-14881)
Brock Awnings Ltd .... F 631 765-5200
Hampton Bays (G-5960)
Coverall Manufacturing .... G 315 652-2731
Baldwinsville (G-568)
Custom European Imports Inc .... E 845 357-5718
Sloatsburg (G-15480)
Dor-A-Mar Canvas Products Co .... F 631 750-9202
West Sayville (G-16934)
Jag Manufacturing Inc .... E 518 762-9558
Johnstown (G-7116)
Kragel Co Inc .... E 716 648-1344
Hamburg (G-5932)
M & M Canvas & Awnings Inc .... G 631 424-5370
Islandia (G-6800)
Nationwide Tarps Incorporated .... D 518 843-1545
Amsterdam (G-361)
Northern Awning & Sign Company ...... G 315 782-8515
Watertown (G-16667)
Point Canvas Company Inc .... G 607 692-4381
Whitney Point (G-17220)
Service Canvas Co Inc .... F 716 853-0558
Buffalo (G-3182)
Utility Canvas Inc .... G 845 255-9290
Gardiner (G-5552)
Y & A Trading Inc .... F 718 436-6333
Brooklyn (G-2772)

CANVAS PRDTS, WHOLESALE

Awning Mart Inc .... G 315 699-5928
Cicero (G-3642)
Brock Awnings Ltd .... F 631 765-5200
Hampton Bays (G-5960)

PRODUCT SECTION

CASEMENTS: Aluminum

Point Canvas Company Inc..................G...... 607 692-4381
  Whitney Point *(G-17220)*

CANVAS PRDTS: Convertible Tops, Car/Boat, Fm Purchased Mtrl

Automtive Uphl Cnvertible Tops ....G...... 914 961-4242
  Tuckahoe *(G-16269)*
Mc Coy Tops and Interiors Inc..............G...... 718 458-5800
  Woodside *(G-17336)*
Quantum Sails Rochester LLC..............G...... 585 342-5200
  Rochester *(G-14615)*

CANVAS PRDTS: Shades, Made From Purchased Materials

Jo-Vin Decorators Inc..........................E...... 718 441-9350
  Woodhaven *(G-17306)*
Laminated Window Products Inc ....F...... 631 242-6883
  Bay Shore *(G-710)*

CAPACITORS: Fixed Or Variable

General Electric Company ....B...... 518 746-5750
  Hudson Falls *(G-6642)*

CAPACITORS: NEC

American Technical Ceramics ....B...... 631 622-4700
  Huntington Station *(G-6696)*
American Technical Ceramics ....B...... 631 622-4700
  Huntington Station *(G-6695)*
AVX Corporation ....D...... 716 372-6611
  Olean *(G-13134)*
Custom Electronics Inc ....D...... 607 432-3880
  Oneonta *(G-13184)*
Electron Coil Inc..................................D...... 607 336-7414
  Norwich *(G-13027)*
Ems Development Corporation ....D...... 631 345-6200
  Yaphank *(G-17391)*
Hipotronics Inc.....................................C...... 845 279-8091
  Brewster *(G-1220)*
Integer Holdings Corporation ....E...... 716 937-5100
  Alden *(G-180)*
Kemet Properties LLC..........................G...... 718 654-8079
  Bronx *(G-1370)*
Knowles Cazenovia Inc ....C...... 315 655-8710
  Cazenovia *(G-3447)*
MTK Electronics Inc..............................E...... 631 924-7666
  Medford *(G-8256)*
Passive-Plus Inc...................................F...... 631 425-0938
  Huntington *(G-6673)*
Stk Electronics Inc ....E...... 315 655-8476
  Cazenovia *(G-3452)*
Strux Corp ....E...... 516 768-3969
  Lindenhurst *(G-7485)*
Tbt Group Inc ....F...... 212 685-1836
  New York *(G-12283)*
Traxel Labs Inc ....G...... 631 590-1095
  Nesconset *(G-8778)*
Tronser Inc...G...... 315 655-9528
  Cazenovia *(G-3453)*
Viking Technologies Ltd ....E...... 631 957-8000
  Lindenhurst *(G-7493)*
Virtue Paintball LLC..............................G...... 631 617-5560
  Hauppauge *(G-6226)*
Voltronics LLC......................................E...... 410 749-2424
  Cazenovia *(G-3454)*

CAPS & PLUGS: Electric, Attachment

Delfingen Us-New York Inc ....E...... 716 215-0300
  Niagara Falls *(G-12810)*

CAR WASH EQPT

Econocraft Worldwide Mfg Inc ....G...... 914 966-2280
  Yonkers *(G-17439)*
Hercules International Inc ....E...... 631 423-6900
  Huntington Station *(G-6708)*
I A S National Inc ....E...... 631 423-6900
  Huntington Station *(G-6710)*
Klee Corp ....G...... 585 272-0320
  Rochester *(G-14470)*
Liquid Industries Inc.............................G...... 716 628-2999
  Niagara Falls *(G-12843)*
Metro Lube...G...... 718 947-1167
  Rego Park *(G-14036)*

CARBIDES

Carbide-Usa LLC..................................G...... 607 331-9353
  Elmira *(G-4674)*
Lakeshore Carbide Inc ....G...... 716 462-4349
  Lake View *(G-7281)*
Transport National Dev Inc ....E...... 716 662-0270
  Orchard Park *(G-13300)*

CARBON & GRAPHITE PRDTS, NEC

Carbon Graphite Materials Inc.............G...... 716 792-7979
  Brocton *(G-1248)*
Ceramaterials LLC ....G...... 518 701-6722
  Port Jervis *(G-13781)*
Go Blue Technologies Ltd ....G...... 631 404-6285
  North Babylon *(G-12901)*
Graphite Metallizing Corp ....D...... 914 968-8400
  Yonkers *(G-17450)*
Hh Liquidating Corp ....A...... 646 282-2500
  New York *(G-10471)*
Kureha Advanced Materials Inc...........F...... 724 295-3352
  New York *(G-10894)*
Mwi Inc ....D...... 585 424-4200
  Rochester *(G-14526)*
Pyrotek Incorporated ....E...... 716 731-3221
  Sanborn *(G-15126)*

CARBONS: Electric

Metallized Carbon Corporation.............C...... 914 941-3738
  Ossining *(G-13323)*

CARBURETORS

Fuel Systems Solutions Inc ....E...... 646 502-7170
  New York *(G-10220)*

CARDBOARD PRDTS, EXC DIE-CUT

M C Packaging Corporation..................E...... 631 414-7840
  Farmingdale *(G-5038)*
M C Packaging Corporation..................E...... 631 643-3763
  Babylon *(G-550)*

CARDBOARD: Waterproof, Made From Purchased Materials

Ums Manufacturing LLC ....F...... 518 562-2410
  Plattsburgh *(G-13705)*

CARDIOVASCULAR SYSTEM DRUGS, EXC DIAGNOSTIC

Mesoblast Inc ....G...... 212 880-2060
  New York *(G-11239)*

CARDS: Color

Mooney-Keeheley Inc..........................G...... 585 271-1573
  Rochester *(G-14521)*
Tele-Pak Inc ....E...... 845 426-2300
  Monsey *(G-8585)*

CARDS: Greeting

1/2 Off Cards Wantagh Inc ....G...... 516 809-9832
  Wantagh *(G-16553)*
Anne Taintor Inc..................................G...... 718 483-9312
  Brooklyn *(G-1613)*
Avanti Press Inc ....E...... 212 414-1025
  New York *(G-9274)*
Massimo Friedman Inc ....E...... 716 836-0408
  Buffalo *(G-3591)*
Paper House Productions Inc..............E...... 845 246-7261
  Saugerties *(G-15190)*
Paper Magic Group Inc ....B...... 631 521-3682
  New York *(G-11564)*
Quotable Cards Inc..............................G...... 212 420-7552
  New York *(G-11776)*
Schurman Retail Group ....C...... 212 206-0067
  New York *(G-12002)*

CARDS: Identification

Allsafe Technologies Inc......................D...... 716 691-0400
  Amherst *(G-222)*
Alpha Incorporated..............................G...... 718 765-1614
  Brooklyn *(G-1593)*
Global Security Tech LLC ....F...... 917 838-4507
  New York *(G-10321)*
Iadc Inc..F...... 718 238-0623
  Staten Island *(G-15686)*

CARDS: Playing

Metropltan Data Sltons MGT Inc..........F...... 516 586-5520
  Farmingdale *(G-5051)*
Multi Packaging Solutions Inc ....E...... 646 885-0157
  New York *(G-11324)*

Marketshare LLC..................................G...... 631 273-0598
  Brentwood *(G-1191)*

CARPETS & RUGS: Tufted

Interfaceflor LLC ....E...... 212 686-8284
  New York *(G-10627)*

CARPETS, RUGS & FLOOR COVERING

Aladdin Manufacturing Corp................C...... 212 561-8715
  New York *(G-9069)*
Bloomsburg Carpet Inds Inc................G...... 212 688-7447
  New York *(G-9417)*
Carpet Fabrications Intl ....E...... 914 381-6060
  Mamaroneck *(G-8026)*
Edward Fields Incorporated ....F...... 212 310-0400
  New York *(G-9985)*
Excellent Art Mfg Corp ....F...... 718 388-7075
  Inwood *(G-6756)*
Lanes Flr Cvrngs Intriors Inc................E...... 212 532-5200
  New York *(G-10926)*
Loom Concepts LLC ....G...... 212 813-9586
  New York *(G-11030)*
Lorena Canals USA Inc ....G...... 844 567-3622
  Hastings On Hudson *(G-6005)*
Michaelian & Kohlberg Inc ....G...... 212 431-9009
  New York *(G-11251)*
Northpoint Trading Inc ....F...... 212 481-8001
  New York *(G-11460)*
Odegard Inc ....F...... 212 545-0069
  Long Island City *(G-7828)*
Pawling Corporation............................D...... 845 373-9300
  Wassaic *(G-16600)*
Rosecore Division ....F...... 516 504-4530
  Great Neck *(G-5835)*
Shaw Contract Flrg Svcs Inc ....G...... 212 953-7429
  New York *(G-12047)*
Shyam Ahuja Limited ....E...... 212 644-5910
  New York *(G-12057)*
Sunrise Tile Inc ....G...... 718 939-0538
  Flushing *(G-5299)*
Tandus Centiva Inc ....C...... 212 206-7170
  New York *(G-12279)*
Tdg Operations LLC ....G...... 212 779-4300
  New York *(G-12284)*
Tiger 21 LLC ....G...... 212 360-1700
  New York *(G-12337)*
Wells Rugs Inc ....G...... 516 676-2056
  Glen Cove *(G-5631)*

CARPETS: Hand & Machine Made

Elizabeth Eakins Inc ....F...... 212 628-1950
  New York *(G-10008)*
Tsar USA LLC ....F...... 646 415-7968
  New York *(G-12415)*

CARPETS: Textile Fiber

Scalamandre Silks Inc ....D...... 212 980-3888
  New York *(G-11982)*

CARRIAGES: Horse Drawn

Tectran Inc...G...... 800 776-5549
  Cheektowaga *(G-3591)*

CARRYING CASES, WHOLESALE

Bristol Boarding Inc.............................G...... 585 271-7860
  Rochester *(G-14247)*
Coach Stores Inc ....A...... 212 643-9727
  New York *(G-9659)*
Sigma Worldwide LLC ....E...... 646 217-0629
  New York *(G-12067)*

CARTONS: Egg, Molded Pulp, Made From Purchased Materials

Tri-Seal International Inc ....G...... 845 353-3300
  Blauvelt *(G-978)*

CASEMENTS: Aluminum

Rohlfs Stined Leaded GL Studio ....E...... 914 699-4848
  Mount Vernon *(G-8726)*

Employee Codes: A=Over 500 employees, B=251-500
C=101-250, D=51-100, E=20-50, F=10-19, G=5-9

CASES, WOOD

CASES, WOOD
Bragley Mfg Co Inc ....E 718 622-7469
  Brooklyn *(G-1712)*
Fca LLC ....F 518 756-9655
  Coeymans *(G-3745)*

CASES: Attache'
Dlx Industries Inc ....D 718 272-9420
  Brooklyn *(G-1869)*
Randa Accessories Lea Gds LLC ....D 212 354-5100
  New York *(G-11799)*
Trafalgar Company LLC ....G 212 768-8800
  New York *(G-12390)*

CASES: Carrying
Ead Cases ....F 845 343-2111
  Middletown *(G-8438)*
Fieldtex Products Inc ....C 585 427-2940
  Rochester *(G-14369)*
Merzon Leather Co Inc ....C 718 782-6260
  Brooklyn *(G-2301)*
Sigma Worldwide LLC ....E 646 217-0629
  New York *(G-12067)*
Three Point Ventures LLC ....F 585 697-3444
  Rochester *(G-14724)*

CASES: Carrying, Clothing & Apparel
212 Biz LLC ....G 212 391-4444
  New York *(G-8964)*
Calvin Klein Inc ....E 212 292-9000
  New York *(G-9505)*
Donna Morgan LLC ....E 212 575-2550
  New York *(G-9904)*

CASES: Jewelry
Astucci US Ltd ....G 212 725-3171
  New York *(G-9243)*
Baublebar Inc ....D 646 664-4803
  New York *(G-9333)*
K Displays ....F 718 854-6045
  Brooklyn *(G-2163)*
Unique Packaging Corporation ....G 514 341-5872
  Champlain *(G-3548)*

CASES: Nonrefrigerated, Exc Wood
R H Guest Incorporated ....G 718 675-7600
  Brooklyn *(G-2471)*

CASES: Packing, Nailed Or Lock Corner, Wood
Falvo Manufacturing Co Inc .....F 315 738-7682
  Utica *(G-16330)*
Technical Packaging Inc ....F 516 223-2300
  Baldwin *(G-562)*

CASES: Plastic
Bragley Mfg Co Inc ....E 718 622-7469
  Brooklyn *(G-1712)*
Displays By Rioux Inc ....G 315 458-3639
  North Syracuse *(G-12941)*
Hamlet Products Inc ....F 914 665-0307
  Mount Vernon *(G-8689)*
Sigma Worldwide LLC ....E 646 217-0629
  New York *(G-12067)*

CASES: Sample Cases
Fibre Case & Novelty Co Inc ....G 212 254-6060
  New York *(G-10158)*
Progressive Fibre Products Co ...E 212 566-2720
  New York *(G-11730)*

CASES: Shipping, Nailed Or Lock Corner, Wood
Bristol Boarding Inc ....G 585 271-7860
  Rochester *(G-14247)*
McIntosh Box & Pallet Co Inc ....F 315 789-8750
  Geneva *(G-5582)*

CASH REGISTER REPAIR SVCS
SPX Flow Us LLC ....G 585 436-5550
  Rochester *(G-14698)*

CASING-HEAD BUTANE & PROPANE PRODUCTION
Blue Rhino Global Sourcing Inc ....E 516 752-0670
  Melville *(G-8298)*

CASINGS: Sheet Metal
Craft-Tech Mfg Corp ....G 631 563-4949
  Bohemia *(G-1042)*

CASKETS & ACCESS
Milso Industries Inc ....F 631 234-1133
  Hauppauge *(G-6138)*
North Hudson Woodcraft Corp ....E 315 429-3105
  Dolgeville *(G-4306)*

CASKETS WHOLESALERS
Milso Industries Inc ....E 631 234-1133
  Hauppauge *(G-6138)*

CAST STONE: Concrete
Steindl Cast Stone Co Inc ....G 718 296-8530
  Woodhaven *(G-17308)*

CASTERS
Dimanco Inc ....G 315 797-0470
  Utica *(G-16324)*
Workshop Art Fabrication ....F 845 331-0385
  Kingston *(G-7225)*

CASTINGS GRINDING: For The Trade
Grind ....G 646 558-3250
  New York *(G-10366)*
Herbert Wolf Corp ....G 212 242-0300
  New York *(G-10461)*
Precision Disc Grinding Corp ....F 516 747-5450
  Mineola *(G-8531)*

CASTINGS: Aerospace Investment, Ferrous
Brinkman Precision Inc ....D 585 429-5001
  West Henrietta *(G-16872)*
Cpp-Syracuse Inc ....E 315 687-0014
  Chittenango *(G-3632)*
Worldwide Resources Inc ....F 718 760-5000
  Brooklyn *(G-2768)*

CASTINGS: Aerospace, Aluminum
Broetje Automation-Usa Inc .....C 716 204-8640
  Williamsville *(G-17236)*
E M T Manufacturing Inc ....F 516 333-1917
  East Meadow *(G-4422)*
Eastern Strategic Materials ....E 212 332-1619
  New York *(G-9967)*
Mpi Consulting Incorporated ....G 631 253-2377
  West Babylon *(G-16814)*
Townline Machine Co Inc ....F 315 462-3413
  Clifton Springs *(G-3716)*

CASTINGS: Aerospace, Nonferrous, Exc Aluminum
Summit Aerospace Inc ....G 718 433-1326
  Long Island City *(G-7895)*

CASTINGS: Aluminum
Airflex Industrial Inc ....E 631 752-1234
  Farmingdale *(G-4933)*
Armstrong Mold Corporation ....E 315 437-1517
  East Syracuse *(G-4504)*
Armstrong Mold Corporation ....D 315 437-1517
  East Syracuse *(G-4505)*
Eastern Castings Co ....F 518 677-5610
  Cambridge *(G-3307)*
Hitachi Metals America Ltd ....E 914 694-9200
  Purchase *(G-13959)*
J & J Bronze & Aluminum Cast ....E 718 383-2111
  Brooklyn *(G-2121)*
Milward Alloys Inc ....E 716 434-5536
  Lockport *(G-7602)*
Taylor Metalworks Inc ....C 716 662-3113
  Orchard Park *(G-13298)*

CASTINGS: Brass, Bronze & Copper
Rodeo of NY Inc ....E 212 730-0744
  New York *(G-11902)*

CASTINGS: Bronze, NEC, Exc Die
Art Bedi-Makky Foundry Corp ......G 718 383-4191
  Brooklyn *(G-1632)*
J & J Bronze & Aluminum Cast ....E 718 383-2111
  Brooklyn *(G-2121)*
Modern Art Foundry Inc ....E 718 728-2030
  Astoria *(G-449)*

CASTINGS: Commercial Investment, Ferrous
Cs Manufacturing Limited ....E 607 587-8154
  Alfred *(G-193)*

CASTINGS: Die, Aluminum
Albest Metal Stamping Corp .....D 718 388-6000
  Brooklyn *(G-1576)*
Crown Die Casting Corp ....E 914 667-5400
  Mount Vernon *(G-8675)*
Greene Brass & Alum Fndry LLC ......G 607 656-4204
  Bloomville *(G-996)*
Greenfield Industries Inc ....D 516 623-9230
  Freeport *(G-5404)*
ITT Corporation ....D 914 641-2000
  Seneca Falls *(G-15361)*
ITT Corporation ....D 315 568-2811
  Seneca Falls *(G-15362)*
Jamestown Bronze Works Inc ....G 716 665-2302
  Jamestown *(G-7006)*
Louis Iannettoni ....D 315 454-3231
  Syracuse *(G-15982)*
Pinnacle Manufacturing Co Inc ....E 585 343-5664
  Batavia *(G-645)*
Tpi Arcade Inc ....D 585 492-0122
  Arcade *(G-401)*
WGB Industries Inc ....F 716 693-5527
  Tonawanda *(G-16214)*

CASTINGS: Die, Lead
American Casting and Mfg Corp ......D 800 342-0333
  Plainview *(G-13581)*
American Casting and Mfg Corp ......G 516 349-7010
  Plainview *(G-13582)*

CASTINGS: Die, Nonferrous
Albest Metal Stamping Corp .....D 718 388-6000
  Brooklyn *(G-1576)*
Crown Die Casting Corp ....E 914 667-5400
  Mount Vernon *(G-8675)*
Crown Novelty Works Inc ....G 631 253-0949
  Melville *(G-8308)*
Mar-A-Thon Filters Inc ....G 631 957-4774
  Lindenhurst *(G-7470)*
Thomas Foundry LLC ....G 315 361-9048
  Oneida *(G-13168)*

CASTINGS: Die, Zinc
Cast-All Corporation ....E 516 741-4025
  Mineola *(G-8503)*
Cast-All Corporation ....E 516 741-4025
  Mineola *(G-8502)*
Greenfield Die Casting Corp .....E 516 623-9230
  Freeport *(G-5403)*
Pinnacle Manufacturing Co Inc ....E 585 343-5664
  Batavia *(G-645)*

CASTINGS: Ductile
Hitachi Metals America Ltd ....E 914 694-9200
  Purchase *(G-13959)*
Jamestown Iron Works Inc ....F 716 665-2818
  Falconer *(G-4905)*
Noresco Industrial Group Inc ....E 516 759-3355
  Glen Cove *(G-5622)*

CASTINGS: Gray Iron
Oneida Foundries Inc ....E 315 363-4570
  Oneida *(G-13159)*

CASTINGS: Machinery, Aluminum
Auto-Mate Technologies LLC ...F 631 727-8886
  Riverhead *(G-14139)*

PRODUCT SECTION

CHEMICALS & ALLIED PRDTS WHOLESALERS, NEC

Corbett Stves Pttern Works Inc ....E 585 546-7109
  Rochester *(G-14289)*

CASTINGS: Machinery, Nonferrous, Exc Die or Aluminum Copper

Plattco Corporation ....E 518 563-4640
  Plattsburgh *(G-13687)*
Zierick Manufacturing Corp ....D 800 882-8020
  Mount Kisco *(G-8648)*

CASTINGS: Precision

Buffalo Metal Casting Co Inc ....E 716 874-6211
  Buffalo *(G-2855)*
Controlled Castings Corp ....E 516 349-1718
  Plainview *(G-13591)*
General Motors LLC ....B 315 764-2000
  Massena *(G-8195)*
Lamothermic Corp ....D 845 278-6118
  Brewster *(G-1222)*
Miller Technology Inc ....G 631 694-2224
  Farmingdale *(G-5056)*
Quality Castings Inc ....E 732 409-3203
  Long Island City *(G-7853)*

CASTINGS: Steel

A & V Castings Inc ....G 212 997-0042
  New York *(G-8982)*

CATALOG & MAIL-ORDER HOUSES

Avcom of Virginia Inc ....D 585 924-4560
  Victor *(G-16461)*
Iac/Interactivecorp ....C 212 314-7300
  New York *(G-10544)*
Kate Spade & Company ....B 212 354-4900
  New York *(G-10816)*
Lechler Laboratories Inc ....E 845 426-6800
  Spring Valley *(G-15591)*
Valmont Inc ....F 212 685-1653
  New York *(G-12496)*

CATALOG SALES

Avon Products Inc ....C 212 282-5000
  New York *(G-9281)*

CATALOG SHOWROOMS

Studio 21 LA Inc ....E 718 965-6579
  Brooklyn *(G-2612)*

CATALYSTS: Chemical

Ames Goldsmith Corp ....E 518 792-7435
  Glens Falls *(G-5669)*
Next Potential LLC ....G 401 742-5190
  New York *(G-11422)*
Signa Chemistry Inc ....F 212 933-4101
  New York *(G-12071)*
UOP LLC ....E 716 879-7600
  Tonawanda *(G-16212)*

CATERERS

Delicious Foods Inc ....F 718 446-9352
  Corona *(G-3997)*
Lifc Corp ....G 516 426-5737
  Port Washington *(G-13838)*
Soutine Inc. ....G 212 496-1450
  New York *(G-12145)*

CEMENT & CONCRETE RELATED PRDTS & EQPT: Bituminous

Presti Ready Mix Concrete Inc ....G 516 378-6006
  Freeport *(G-5419)*

CEMENT ROCK: Crushed & Broken

Schaefer Entps of Deposit ....E 607 467-4990
  Deposit *(G-4280)*

CEMENT: Heat Resistant

Roccera LLC ....F 585 426-0887
  Rochester *(G-14632)*

CEMENT: Hydraulic

Graymont Materials (ny) Inc ....G 518 873-2275
  Lewis *(G-7431)*

Lafarge North America Inc ....E 716 651-9235
  Lancaster *(G-7322)*
Lafarge North America Inc ....G 716 854-5791
  Buffalo *(G-3044)*
Lafarge North America Inc ....E 716 772-2621
  Lockport *(G-7596)*
Lafarge North America Inc ....E 716 297-3031
  Niagara Falls *(G-12841)*
Lafarge North America Inc ....D 914 930-3027
  Buchanan *(G-2786)*
Lafarge North America Inc ....E 518 756-5000
  Ravena *(G-14023)*

CEMENT: Masonry

Ciment St-Laurent Inc ....C 518 943-4040
  Catskill *(G-3426)*
Lafarge Building Materials Inc ....F 518 756-5000
  Ravena *(G-14022)*

CEMENT: Natural

Euro Gear (usa) Inc ....G 518 578-1775
  Plattsburgh *(G-13662)*
Hanson Aggregates New York LLC ..F 716 665-4620
  Jamesville *(G-7047)*

CEMENT: Portland

Lehigh Cement Company ....C 518 792-1137
  Glens Falls *(G-5687)*
Lehigh Cement Company LLC ....E 518 792-1137
  Glens Falls *(G-5688)*
Pallette Stone Corporation ....E 518 584-2421
  Gansevoort *(G-5487)*

CEMETERY MEMORIAL DEALERS

Glen Plaza Marble & Gran Inc ....G 516 671-1100
  Glen Cove *(G-5617)*
North Shore Monuments Inc ....G 516 759-2156
  Glen Head *(G-5639)*

CERAMIC FIBER

American Securities LLC ....E 716 696-3012
  Tonawanda *(G-16138)*
Argosy Ceramic Arospc Mtls LLC .....F 212 268-0003
  New York *(G-9200)*
Cetek Inc ....E 845 452-3510
  Poughkeepsie *(G-13892)*
Enrg Inc ....F 716 873-2939
  Buffalo *(G-2940)*
Heany Industries Inc ....D 585 889-2700
  Scottsville *(G-15336)*
Starfire Systems Inc ....F 518 899-9336
  Schenectady *(G-15300)*
Ufx Holding I Corporation ....G 212 644-5900
  New York *(G-12445)*
Ufx Holding II Corporation ....G 212 644-5900
  New York *(G-12446)*
Unifrax Holding Co ....G 212 644-5900
  New York *(G-12456)*
Unifrax I LLC ....C 716 768-6500
  Tonawanda *(G-16211)*
Unifrax I LLC ....C 716 696-3000
  Tonawanda *(G-16210)*

CERAMIC FLOOR & WALL TILE WHOLESALERS

Dal-Tile Corporation ....G 718 894-9574
  Maspeth *(G-8128)*
Dal-Tile Corporation ....G 914 835-1801
  Harrison *(G-5982)*

CHAIN: Welded, Made From Purchased Wire

Columbus McKinnon Corporation .....C 716 689-5400
  Getzville *(G-5595)*
Columbus McKinnon Corporation .....C 716 689-5400
  Getzville *(G-5597)*
Columbus McKinnon Corporation .....C 716 689-5400
  Getzville *(G-5598)*

CHAMBERS & CAISSONS

Hyperbaric Technologies Inc ....G 518 842-3030
  Amsterdam *(G-350)*

CHANDELIERS: Residential

Swarovski Lighting Ltd ....B 518 324-6378
  Plattsburgh *(G-13703)*

CHARCOAL: Activated

Calgon Carbon Corporation ....G 716 531-9113
  North Tonawanda *(G-12964)*
Carbon Activated Corporation ....G 716 662-2005
  Orchard Park *(G-13258)*

CHART & GRAPH DESIGN SVCS

Orcon Industries Corp ....D 585 768-7000
  Le Roy *(G-7417)*

CHASSIS: Motor Vehicle

Wendys Auto Express Inc ....G 845 624-6100
  Nanuet *(G-8762)*

CHEESE WHOLESALERS

Alps Provision Co Inc ....E 718 721-4477
  Astoria *(G-433)*

CHEMICAL INDICATORS

LTS (chemical) Inc ....F 845 494-2940
  Orangeburg *(G-13234)*

CHEMICAL PROCESSING MACHINERY & EQPT

Charles Ross & Son Company ....D 631 234-0500
  Hauppauge *(G-6044)*
Maharlika Holdings LLC ....F 631 319-6203
  Ronkonkoma *(G-14936)*
National Equipment Corporation ......F 718 585-0200
  Bronx *(G-1405)*
National Equipment Corporation ......F 718 585-0200
  Bronx *(G-1406)*
Silver Creek Enterprises Inc ....G 716 934-2611
  Silver Creek *(G-15450)*
Spectrum Catalysts Inc ....G 631 560-3683
  Central Islip *(G-3511)*
Stainless Design Concepts Ltd ....E 845 246-3631
  Saugerties *(G-15195)*
Surepure Inc ....F 917 368-8480
  New York *(G-12245)*
West Metal Works Inc ....E 716 895-4900
  Buffalo *(G-3252)*

CHEMICAL: Sodm Compnds/Salts, Inorg, Exc Rfnd Sodm Chloride

Chemtrade Chemicals US LLC ....G 315 478-2323
  Syracuse *(G-15894)*

CHEMICALS & ALLIED PRDTS WHOLESALERS, NEC

Aithaca Chemical Corp ....F 516 229-2330
  Uniondale *(G-16288)*
Alumiseal Corp ....E 518 329-2820
  Copake Falls *(G-3888)*
Caswell Inc ....F 315 946-1213
  Lyons *(G-7970)*
Chemlube International LLC ....F 914 381-5800
  Harrison *(G-5979)*
Chemlube Marketing Inc ....F 914 381-5800
  Harrison *(G-5980)*
Cytec Olean Inc ....D 716 372-9650
  Olean *(G-13143)*
Ecological Laboratories Inc ....F 516 823-3441
  Lynbrook *(G-7950)*
FBC Chemical Corporation ....G 716 681-1581
  Lancaster *(G-7315)*
Finger Lakes Chemicals Inc ....E 585 454-4760
  Rochester *(G-14370)*
Island Pyrochemical Inds Corp ....F 516 746-2100
  Mineola *(G-8519)*
Jad Corp of America ....E 718 762-8900
  College Point *(G-3792)*
Nalco Company LLC ....E 518 796-1985
  Saratoga Springs *(G-15163)*
Poly Scientific R&D Corp ....E 631 586-0400
  Bay Shore *(G-725)*
Tattersall Industries LLC ....E 518 381-4270
  Schenectady *(G-15304)*
Thatcher Company New York Inc ....E 315 589-9330
  Williamson *(G-17226)*
Water Wise of America Inc ....G 585 232-1210
  Rochester *(G-14757)*

Employee Codes: A=Over 500 employees, B=251-500
C=101-250, D=51-100, E=20-50, F=10-19, G=5-9

CHEMICALS & ALLIED PRDTS, WHOLESALE: Alkalines & Chlorine

CHEMICALS & ALLIED PRDTS, WHOLESALE: Alkalines & Chlorine
Arcadia Chem Preservative LLC ....G....... 516 466-5258
  Great Neck *(G-5791)*

CHEMICALS & ALLIED PRDTS, WHOLESALE: Anti-Corrosion Prdts
Engineering Maint Pdts Inc...................F....... 516 624-9774
  Oyster Bay *(G-13369)*

CHEMICALS & ALLIED PRDTS, WHOLESALE: Aromatic
Classic Flavors Fragrances Inc ....G....... 212 777-0004
  New York *(G-9636)*

CHEMICALS & ALLIED PRDTS, WHOLESALE: Chemical Additives
Mitsui Chemicals America Inc ....E....... 914 253-0777
  Rye Brook *(G-15072)*
Specialty Minerals Inc ....E....... 212 878-1800
  New York *(G-12152)*

CHEMICALS & ALLIED PRDTS, WHOLESALE: Chemicals, Indl
Dynasty Chemical Corp..........................E....... 518 463-1146
  Menands *(G-8370)*
Umicore USA Inc....................................E....... 919 874-7171
  Glens Falls *(G-5700)*

CHEMICALS & ALLIED PRDTS, WHOLESALE: Dry Ice
South Shore Ice Co Inc ....F....... 516 379-2056
  Roosevelt *(G-15009)*

CHEMICALS & ALLIED PRDTS, WHOLESALE: Essential Oils
Flavormatic Industries Inc ....E....... 845 297-9100
  Wappingers Falls *(G-16567)*

CHEMICALS & ALLIED PRDTS, WHOLESALE: Oxygen
Praxair Distribution Inc ....G....... 315 457-5821
  Liverpool *(G-7543)*

CHEMICALS & ALLIED PRDTS, WHOLESALE: Plastics Materials, NEC
Ampac Paper LLC ....A....... 845 778-5511
  Walden *(G-16530)*
Josh Packaging Inc ....E....... 631 822-1660
  Hauppauge *(G-6102)*
Marval Industries Inc ....D....... 914 381-2400
  Mamaroneck *(G-8038)*

CHEMICALS & ALLIED PRDTS, WHOLESALE: Plastics Prdts, NEC
Albea Cosmetics America Inc................E....... 212 371-5100
  New York *(G-9073)*
Autronic Plastics Inc ....D....... 516 333-7577
  Central Islip *(G-3485)*
Broder Mfg Inc...G....... 718 366-1667
  Brooklyn *(G-1718)*
Vinyl Materials Inc....................................E....... 631 586-9444
  Deer Park *(G-4224)*

CHEMICALS & ALLIED PRDTS, WHOLESALE: Plastics Sheets & Rods
Astra Products Inc ....G....... 631 464-4747
  Copiague *(G-3895)*

CHEMICALS & ALLIED PRDTS, WHOLESALE: Polyurethane Prdts
Vincent Manufacturing Co Inc ....F....... 315 823-0280
  Little Falls *(G-7506)*

CHEMICALS & ALLIED PRDTS, WHOLESALE: Salts & Polishes, Indl
R Schleider Contracting Corp.................G....... 631 269-4249
  Kings Park *(G-7174)*

CHEMICALS & ALLIED PRDTS, WHOLESALE: Syn Resin, Rub/Plastic
Clarence Resins and Chemicals..............G....... 716 406-9804
  Clarence Center *(G-3673)*

CHEMICALS & ALLIED PRDTS, WHOLESALE: Waxes, Exc Petroleum
Collinite Corporation ....G....... 315 732-2282
  Utica *(G-16313)*

CHEMICALS/ALLIED PRDTS, WHOL: Coal Tar Prdts, Prim/Intermdt
Castoleum Corporation ....F....... 914 664-5877
  Mount Vernon *(G-8670)*
Naval Stores Co ....F....... 914 664-5877
  Mount Vernon *(G-8709)*

CHEMICALS: Agricultural
Agrochem Inc..E....... 518 226-4850
  Saratoga Springs *(G-15143)*
BASF Corporation.....................................B....... 914 785-2000
  Tarrytown *(G-16087)*
E I Du Pont De Nemours & Co ....C....... 718 761-0043
  Staten Island *(G-15668)*
E I Du Pont De Nemours & Co ....C....... 716 879-4507
  Tonawanda *(G-16157)*
FMC Corporation......................................E....... 716 735-3761
  Middleport *(G-8421)*
G & S Farm & Home Inc..........................G....... 716 542-9922
  Akron *(G-23)*
Novartis Corporation................................E....... 212 307-1122
  New York *(G-11462)*

CHEMICALS: Alcohols
Full Motion Beverage Inc ....G....... 631 585-1100
  Plainview *(G-13603)*

CHEMICALS: Aluminum Chloride
Vanchlor Company Inc.............................F....... 716 434-2624
  Lockport *(G-7624)*
Vanchlor Company Inc.............................F....... 716 434-2624
  Lockport *(G-7625)*

CHEMICALS: Aluminum Compounds
Benzsay & Harrison Inc..........................G....... 518 895-2311
  Delanson *(G-4231)*
Somerville Acquisitions Co Inc ....F....... 845 856-5261
  Huguenot *(G-6651)*
Somerville Tech Group Inc......................D....... 908 782-9500
  Huguenot *(G-6652)*

CHEMICALS: Aluminum Oxide
Meliorum Technologies Inc....................G....... 585 313-0616
  Rochester *(G-14503)*

CHEMICALS: Brine
Texas Brine Company LLC ....G....... 585 495-6228
  Wyoming *(G-17382)*

CHEMICALS: Calcium & Calcium Compounds
Minerals Technologies Inc ....E....... 212 878-1800
  New York *(G-11276)*

CHEMICALS: Compounds Or Salts, Iron, Ferric Or Ferrous
North American Hoganas Inc..................E....... 716 285-3451
  Niagara Falls *(G-12851)*

CHEMICALS: Fire Retardant
FCC Acquisition LLC ....E....... 716 282-1399
  Niagara Falls *(G-12818)*
Gordon Fire Equipment LLC ....G....... 845 691-5700
  Highland *(G-6404)*
International Fire-Shield Inc....................F....... 315 255-1006
  Auburn *(G-501)*
Kent Chemical Corporation ....E....... 212 521-1700
  New York *(G-10838)*
Safeguard Inc..F....... 631 929-3273
  Wading River *(G-16525)*
Supresta US LLC......................................E....... 914 674-9434
  Ardsley *(G-406)*

CHEMICALS: Formaldehyde
Hexion Inc..E....... 518 792-8040
  South Glens Falls *(G-15525)*

CHEMICALS: High Purity Grade, Organic
Molecular Glasses Inc.............................G....... 585 210-2861
  Rochester *(G-14519)*

CHEMICALS: High Purity, Refined From Technical Grade
Aithaca Chemical Corp.............................F....... 516 229-2330
  Uniondale *(G-16288)*
Germanium Corp America Inc ....F....... 315 853-4900
  Clinton *(G-3719)*
Incitec Pivot Limited ....G....... 212 238-3010
  New York *(G-10582)*

CHEMICALS: Hydrogen Peroxide
US Peroxide..G....... 716 775-5585
  Grand Island *(G-5772)*

CHEMICALS: Inorganic, NEC
Akzo Nobel Chemicals LLC ....C....... 914 674-5008
  Dobbs Ferry *(G-4300)*
Anchor Commerce Trading Corp ....G....... 516 881-3485
  Atlantic Beach *(G-468)*
Arkema Inc..C....... 585 243-6359
  Piffard *(G-13546)*
Auterra Inc..G....... 518 382-9600
  Schenectady *(G-15232)*
BASF Corporation.....................................G....... 973 245-6000
  Tarrytown *(G-16088)*
BASF Corporation.....................................B....... 914 788-1627
  Peekskill *(G-13474)*
BASF Corporation.....................................B....... 212 450-8280
  New York *(G-9329)*
BASF Corporation.....................................C....... 631 689-0200
  East Setauket *(G-4478)*
BASF Corporation.....................................B....... 914 785-2000
  Tarrytown *(G-16087)*
Byk USA Inc..E....... 845 469-5800
  Chester *(G-3602)*
Cerion Energy Inc ....E....... 585 271-5630
  Rochester *(G-14268)*
Cerion LLC..F....... 585 271-5630
  Rochester *(G-14269)*
Chemours Company Fc LLC ....E....... 716 278-5100
  Niagara Falls *(G-12804)*
Chemtrade Chemicals US LLC ....E....... 315 430-7650
  Syracuse *(G-15893)*
Danisco US Inc...D....... 585 277-4300
  Rochester *(G-14301)*
Divine Brothers Company ....C....... 315 797-0470
  Utica *(G-16327)*
Dynasty Chemical Corp...........................E....... 518 463-1146
  Menands *(G-8370)*
E I Du Pont De Nemours & Co ....E....... 585 339-4200
  Rochester *(G-14323)*
Emco Chemical (usa) Corp ....E....... 718 797-3652
  Brooklyn *(G-1916)*
Esm Group Inc..F....... 716 446-8985
  Amherst *(G-240)*
Esm Special Metals & Tech Inc..............E....... 716 446-8914
  Amherst *(G-242)*
Ferro Corporation.....................................E....... 585 586-8770
  East Rochester *(G-4458)*
Ferro Corporation.....................................C....... 315 536-3357
  Penn Yan *(G-13509)*
Ferro Electronics Materials ....C....... 716 278-9400
  Niagara Falls *(G-12821)*
FMC Corporation......................................E....... 716 735-3761
  Middleport *(G-8421)*
Hampshire Chemical Corp ....D....... 315 539-9221
  Waterloo *(G-16629)*
Innovative Municipal Pdts US ....E....... 800 387-5777
  Glenmont *(G-5668)*
Interstate Chemical Co Inc......................F....... 585 344-2822
  Batavia *(G-640)*

PRODUCT SECTION

CHEMICALS: Water Treatment

Kowa American Corporation .... E 212 303-7800
  New York *(G-10882)*
Lawn Elements Inc .... G 631 656-9711
  Holbrook *(G-6456)*
Moog Inc .... D 716 731-6300
  Niagara Falls *(G-12848)*
Multisorb Tech Intl LLC .... G 716 824-8900
  Buffalo *(G-3078)*
Multisorb Technologies Inc .... G 716 668-4191
  Cheektowaga *(G-3581)*
Multisorb Technologies Inc .... E 716 656-1402
  Buffalo *(G-3079)*
Oneh2 Inc .... G 703 862-9656
  Hector *(G-6259)*
Poly Scientific R&D Corp .... E 631 586-0400
  Bay Shore *(G-725)*
Polyset Company Inc .... E 518 664-6000
  Mechanicville *(G-8229)*
Praxair Inc .... F 716 879-2000
  Tonawanda *(G-16194)*
Prince Mineral Holding Corp .... G 646 747-4222
  New York *(G-11710)*
S E A Supplies Ltd .... F 516 694-6677
  Plainview *(G-13633)*
Scientific Polymer Products .... G 585 265-0413
  Ontario *(G-13214)*
Specialty Minerals Inc .... G 518 585-7982
  Ticonderoga *(G-16128)*
Specialty Minerals Inc .... E 212 878-1800
  New York *(G-12152)*
Summit Research Labs Inc .... C 845 856-5261
  Huguenot *(G-6653)*
Tangram Company LLC .... E 631 758-0460
  Holtsville *(G-6511)*
Thatcher Company New York Inc .... E 315 589-9330
  Williamson *(G-17226)*
Vandemark Chemical Inc .... D 716 433-6764
  Lockport *(G-7626)*
VWR Chemicals LLC .... E 518 297-4444
  Rouses Point *(G-15045)*
Washingtom Mills Elec Mnrls .... D 716 278-6600
  Niagara Falls *(G-12890)*

CHEMICALS: Isotopes, Radioactive

Isonics Corporation .... G 212 356-7400
  New York *(G-10668)*

CHEMICALS: Lithium Compounds, Inorganic

Alpha-En Corporation .... F 914 418-2000
  Tarrytown *(G-16085)*

CHEMICALS: Medicinal

Biotemper .... G 516 302-7985
  Carle Place *(G-3387)*
Proper Chemical Ltd .... G 631 420-8000
  Farmingdale *(G-5091)*

CHEMICALS: Medicinal, Organic, Uncompounded, Bulk

Asept Pak Inc .... E 518 651-2026
  Malone *(G-8007)*
Good Earth Inc .... G 716 684-8111
  Lancaster *(G-7317)*

CHEMICALS: Metal Salts/Compounds, Exc Sodium, Potassium/Alum

PVS Technologies Inc .... E 716 825-5762
  Buffalo *(G-3143)*

CHEMICALS: NEC

Akzo Nobel Chemicals LLC .... G 716 778-8554
  Burt *(G-3268)*
Akzo Nobel Chemicals LLC .... C 914 674-5008
  Dobbs Ferry *(G-4300)*
Alco Industries Inc .... E 740 254-4311
  Round Lake *(G-15036)*
Anabec Inc .... G 716 759-1674
  Clarence *(G-3655)*
Balchem Corporation .... B 845 326-5600
  New Hampton *(G-8797)*
Barson Composites Corporation .... E 516 752-7882
  Old Bethpage *(G-13126)*
Bcp Ingredients Inc .... D 845 326-5600
  New Hampton *(G-8798)*
Bonide Products Inc .... C 315 736-8231
  Oriskany *(G-13304)*
C & A Service Inc .... G 516 354-1200
  Floral Park *(G-5197)*
Calfonex Company .... F 845 778-2212
  Walden *(G-16532)*
Citrus and Allied Essences Ltd .... E 516 354-1200
  Floral Park *(G-5200)*
Classic Flavors Fragrances Inc .... G 212 777-0004
  New York *(G-9636)*
Danisco US Inc .... D 585 256-5200
  Rochester *(G-14300)*
Divine Brothers Company .... C 315 797-0470
  Utica *(G-16327)*
E I Du Pont De Nemours & Co .... E 585 339-4200
  Rochester *(G-14323)*
Fitzsimmons Systems Inc .... F 315 214-7010
  Cazenovia *(G-3445)*
Hampshire Chemical Corp .... D 315 539-9221
  Waterloo *(G-16629)*
Heterochemical Corporation .... F 516 561-8225
  Valley Stream *(G-16408)*
I A S National Inc .... E 631 423-6900
  Huntington Station *(G-6710)*
Indium Corporation of America .... E 315 793-8200
  Utica *(G-16342)*
Instrumentation Laboratory Co .... C 845 680-0028
  Orangeburg *(G-13231)*
Italmatch USA Corporation .... F 732 383-8309
  Tarrytown *(G-16092)*
Kemper System America Inc .... E 716 558-2971
  West Seneca *(G-16951)*
Mdi Holdings LLC .... A 212 559-1127
  New York *(G-11203)*
Micro Powders Inc .... E 914 332-6400
  Tarrytown *(G-16097)*
Momentive Performance Mtls Inc .... D 914 784-4807
  Tarrytown *(G-16098)*
Monroe Fluid Technology Inc .... E 585 392-3434
  Hilton *(G-6418)*
Nalco Company LLC .... E 518 796-1985
  Saratoga Springs *(G-15163)*
Octagon Process LLC .... G 845 680-8800
  Orangeburg *(G-13237)*
Pure Kemika LLC .... G 718 745-2200
  Flushing *(G-5286)*
PVS Chemical Solutions Inc .... D 716 825-5762
  Buffalo *(G-3142)*
Reddi Car Corp .... G 631 589-3141
  Sayville *(G-15214)*
Rochester Midland Corporation .... C 585 336-2200
  Rochester *(G-14643)*
Royce Associates A Ltd Partnr .... G 516 367-6298
  Jericho *(G-7083)*
Specialty Minerals Inc .... E 212 878-1800
  New York *(G-12152)*
Tam Ceramics LLC .... D 716 278-9480
  Niagara Falls *(G-12881)*
Tangram Company LLC .... E 631 758-0460
  Holtsville *(G-6511)*
Utility Manufacturing Co Inc .... E 516 997-6300
  Westbury *(G-17039)*
Venue Graphics Supply Inc .... F 718 361-1690
  Long Island City *(G-7913)*
Wyeth Holdings LLC .... D 845 602-5000
  Pearl River *(G-13469)*
Yiwen Usa Inc .... F 212 370-0828
  New York *(G-12693)*

CHEMICALS: Organic, NEC

Akzo Nobel Chemicals LLC .... G 716 778-8554
  Burt *(G-3268)*
Akzo Nobel Chemicals LLC .... F 914 674-5432
  Dobbs Ferry *(G-4301)*
Akzo Nobel Functional Chem LLC .... D 845 276-8200
  Brewster *(G-1208)*
Ames Goldsmith Corp .... E 518 792-7435
  Glens Falls *(G-5669)*
Arcadia Chem Preservative LLC .... G 516 466-5258
  Great Neck *(G-5791)*
Arkema Inc .... C 585 243-6359
  Piffard *(G-13546)*
Balchem Corporation .... B 845 326-5600
  New Hampton *(G-8797)*
Bamboo Global Industries .... G 973 943-1878
  New York *(G-9312)*
BASF Corporation .... C 631 380-2490
  Stony Brook *(G-15767)*
BASF Corporation .... B 518 465-6534
  Rensselaer *(G-14045)*
BASF Corporation .... B 914 785-2000
  Tarrytown *(G-16087)*
Brockyn Corporation .... F 631 244-2770
  Bohemia *(G-1027)*
Caltex International Ltd .... E 315 425-1040
  Syracuse *(G-15883)*
China Ruitai Intl Holdings Ltd .... G 718 740-2278
  Hollis *(G-6495)*
Collaborative Laboratories .... D 631 689-0200
  East Setauket *(G-4479)*
Dancker Sellew & Douglas Inc .... G 908 231-1600
  East Syracuse *(G-4523)*
Danisco US Inc .... D 585 256-5200
  Rochester *(G-14300)*
Eastman Chemical Company .... G 585 722-2905
  Rochester *(G-14326)*
Enviro Service & Supply Corp .... F 347 838-6500
  Staten Island *(G-15671)*
Evonik Corporation .... G 518 233-7090
  Waterford *(G-16611)*
FMC Corporation .... C 716 879-0400
  Tonawanda *(G-16164)*
Hampshire Chemical Corp .... D 315 539-9221
  Waterloo *(G-16629)*
Henpecked Husband Farms Corp .... E 631 728-2800
  Speonk *(G-15575)*
International Mtls & Sups Inc .... G 518 834-9899
  Keeseville *(G-7138)*
Islechem LLC .... E 716 773-8618
  Grand Island *(G-5761)*
Jos H Lowenstein and Sons Inc .... D 718 218-8013
  Brooklyn *(G-2148)*
Marval Industries Inc .... D 914 381-2400
  Mamaroneck *(G-8038)*
Oak-Bark Corporation .... G 518 372-5691
  Scotia *(G-15329)*
Poly Scientific R&D Corp .... E 631 586-0400
  Bay Shore *(G-725)*
Polymer Slutions Group Fin LLC .... G 212 771-1717
  New York *(G-11682)*
Rose Solomon Co .... E 718 855-1788
  Brooklyn *(G-2506)*
Royce Associates A Ltd Partnr .... G 516 367-6298
  Jericho *(G-7083)*
Solvents Company Inc .... F 631 595-9300
  Kingston *(G-7210)*
Telechemische Inc .... G 845 561-3237
  Newburgh *(G-12781)*
Twin Lake Chemical Inc .... F 716 433-3824
  Lockport *(G-7622)*
United Biochemicals LLC .... D 716 731-5161
  Sanborn *(G-15128)*

CHEMICALS: Phenol

Si Group Inc .... C 518 347-4200
  Schenectady *(G-15296)*

CHEMICALS: Silica Compounds

Precision Elctro Mnrl Pmco Inc .... E 716 284-2484
  Niagara Falls *(G-12863)*

CHEMICALS: Sodium Bicarbonate

Church & Dwight Co Inc .... F 518 887-5109
  Schenectady *(G-15242)*

CHEMICALS: Sodium/Potassium Cmpnds,Exc Bleach,Alkalies/Alum

Tibro Water Technologies Ltd .... F 647 426-3415
  Sherrill *(G-15409)*

CHEMICALS: Sulfur Chloride

PVS Chemical Solutions Inc .... D 716 825-5762
  Buffalo *(G-3142)*
Sabre Energy Services LLC .... F 518 514-1572
  Slingerlands *(G-15478)*

CHEMICALS: Water Treatment

Crystal Fusion Tech Inc .... F 631 253-9800
  Farmingdale *(G-4966)*
Cytec Industries Inc .... D 716 372-9650
  Olean *(G-13142)*
Ecological Laboratories Inc .... F 516 823-3441
  Lynbrook *(G-7950)*
Halfmoon Town Water Department .... G 518 233-7489
  Waterford *(G-16612)*
Water Wise of America Inc .... G 585 232-1210
  Rochester *(G-14756)*
Water Wise of America Inc .... G 585 232-1210
  Rochester *(G-14757)*

Employee Codes: A=Over 500 employees, B=251-500
C=101-250, D=51-100, E=20-50, F=10-19, G=5-9

CHEWING GUM

CHEWING GUM
- Ford Gum & Machine Company Inc ......D...... 716 542-4561
  Akron *(G-22)*
- Simply Gum Inc ......F...... 917 721-8032
  New York *(G-12083)*
- Sweetworks Inc ......C...... 716 634-4545
  Buffalo *(G-3205)*

CHILD DAY CARE SVCS
- Parents Guide Network Corp ......E...... 212 213-8840
  New York *(G-11571)*

CHILDREN'S & INFANTS' CLOTHING STORES
- Slims Bagels Unlimited Inc ......E...... 718 229-1140
  Oakland Gardens *(G-13067)*

CHILDREN'S WEAR STORES
- JM Originals Inc ......C...... 845 647-3003
  Ellenville *(G-4634)*
- Lollipops Inc ......E...... 845 352-8642
  Monsey *(G-8573)*
- S & C Bridals LLC ......G...... 212 789-7000
  New York *(G-11942)*

CHIMES: Electric
- Aeb Sapphire Corp ......G...... 516 586-8232
  Massapequa *(G-8178)*
- Analog Digital Technology LLC ......G...... 585 698-1845
  Rochester *(G-14203)*
- Ingham Industries Inc ......G...... 631 242-2493
  Holbrook *(G-6451)*

CHIMNEY CAPS: Concrete
- American Chimney Supplies Inc ......G...... 631 434-2020
  Hauppauge *(G-6020)*

CHIMNEYS & FITTINGS
- American Chimney Supplies Inc ......G...... 631 434-2020
  Hauppauge *(G-6020)*
- Chimney Doctors Americas Corp ......G...... 631 868-3586
  Bayport *(G-757)*

CHINA COOKWARE
- Swissmar Inc ......G...... 905 764-1421
  Niagara Falls *(G-12879)*

CHLORINE
- Indian Springs Mfg Co Inc ......F...... 315 635-6101
  Baldwinsville *(G-570)*

CHOCOLATE, EXC CANDY FROM BEANS: Chips, Powder, Block, Syrup
- 5th Avenue Chocolatiere Ltd ......G...... 212 935-5454
  Freeport *(G-5379)*
- 5th Avenue Chocolatiere Ltd ......F...... 516 561-1570
  Valley Stream *(G-16397)*
- Associated Brands Inc ......G...... 585 798-3475
  New York *(G-9238)*
- Big Heart Pet Brands ......E...... 716 891-6566
  Buffalo *(G-2842)*
- Chocolate By Design Inc ......G...... 631 737-0082
  Ronkonkoma *(G-14887)*
- Chocomize Inc ......F...... 718 729-3264
  Long Island City *(G-7697)*
- Eating Evolved Inc ......G...... 516 510-2601
  East Setauket *(G-4480)*
- Gnosis Chocolate Inc ......G...... 646 688-5549
  Long Island City *(G-7751)*
- Hershey Kiss 203 Inc ......G...... 516 503-3740
  Wantagh *(G-16557)*
- Jo-Mart Candies Corp ......F...... 718 375-1277
  Brooklyn *(G-2143)*
- Joyva Corp ......D...... 718 497-0170
  Brooklyn *(G-2154)*
- Lanco Corporation ......C...... 631 231-2300
  Ronkonkoma *(G-14929)*
- Le Chocolat LLC ......G...... 845 352-8301
  Monsey *(G-8572)*
- Mast Brothers Inc ......E...... 718 388-2625
  Brooklyn *(G-2280)*
- Momn Pops Inc ......G...... 845 567-0640
  Cornwall *(G-3988)*
- New York Chocolatier Inc ......G...... 516 561-1570
  Valley Stream *(G-16415)*
- Noras Candy Shop ......F...... 315 337-4530
  Rome *(G-14825)*
- Robert Pikcilingis ......F...... 518 355-1860
  Altamont *(G-211)*
- Settons Intl Foods Inc ......G...... 631 543-8090
  Commack *(G-3842)*
- Simply Natural Foods LLC ......G...... 631 543-9600
  Commack *(G-3843)*
- Sweetriot Inc ......G...... 212 431-7468
  New York *(G-12254)*
- The Chocolate Shop ......G...... 716 882-5055
  Buffalo *(G-3215)*

CHOCOLATE, EXC CANDY FROM PURCH CHOC: Chips, Powder, Block
- Aletheas Chocolates Inc ......E...... 716 633-8620
  Williamsville *(G-17231)*
- Commodore Chocolatier USA Inc ......F...... 845 561-3960
  Newburgh *(G-12753)*
- Ctac Holdings LLC ......E...... 212 924-2280
  Brooklyn *(G-1823)*
- Dilese International Inc ......F...... 716 855-3500
  Buffalo *(G-2915)*
- Dolce Vite International LLC ......G...... 713 962-5767
  Brooklyn *(G-1870)*
- Doma Marketing Inc ......G...... 516 684-1111
  Port Washington *(G-13811)*
- Emvi Inc ......G...... 518 883-5111
  Broadalbin *(G-1241)*
- Ernex Corporation Inc ......E...... 718 951-2251
  Brooklyn *(G-1933)*
- Godiva Chocolatier Inc ......E...... 718 677-1452
  Brooklyn *(G-2036)*
- Godiva Chocolatier Inc ......G...... 212 809-8990
  New York *(G-10327)*
- Greenwood Winery LLC ......E...... 315 432-8132
  East Syracuse *(G-4534)*
- Jacques Torres Chocolate LLC ......E...... 212 414-2462
  New York *(G-10693)*
- Lady-N-Th-wndow Chocolates Inc ......F...... 631 549-1059
  Huntington *(G-6666)*
- Le Chocolate of Rockland LLC ......E...... 845 533-4125
  Suffern *(G-15794)*
- Lindt & Sprungli (usa) Inc ......E...... 212 582-3047
  New York *(G-11000)*
- Madisons Delight LLC ......F...... 718 720-8900
  Staten Island *(G-15702)*
- Nibmor Project LLC ......F...... 718 374-5091
  Great Neck *(G-5823)*
- Prime Marketing and Sales LLC ......G...... 888 802-3836
  New York *(G-11707)*
- Reserve Confections Inc ......F...... 845 371-7744
  Monsey *(G-8578)*
- Sweetworks Inc ......C...... 716 634-4545
  Buffalo *(G-3205)*
- Yes Were Nuts Ltd ......G...... 516 374-1940
  Hewlett *(G-6317)*

CHRISTMAS TREE LIGHTING SETS: Electric
- Rbw Studio LLC ......E...... 212 388-1621
  Brooklyn *(G-2481)*

CHUCKS
- Northfeld Precision Instr Corp ......E...... 516 431-1112
  Island Park *(G-6782)*

CHURCHES
- Christian Press Inc ......G...... 718 886-4400
  Flushing *(G-5233)*

CHUTES & TROUGHS
- Sargent Manufacturing Inc ......G...... 212 722-7000
  New York *(G-11972)*

CIGAR LIGHTERS EXC PRECIOUS METAL
- Arcadia Mfg Group Inc ......E...... 518 434-6213
  Green Island *(G-5853)*
- Arcadia Mfg Group Inc ......E...... 518 434-6213
  Menands *(G-8367)*

CIGARETTE & CIGAR PRDTS & ACCESS
- Iquit Cig LLC ......G...... 718 475-1422
  Brooklyn *(G-2115)*
- Saakshi Inc ......G...... 315 475-3988
  Syracuse *(G-16028)*

CIRCUIT BOARDS, PRINTED: Television & Radio
- Kendall Circuits Inc ......E...... 631 473-3636
  Mount Sinai *(G-8655)*
- TCS Electronics Inc ......E...... 585 337-4301
  Farmington *(G-5156)*

CIRCUIT BOARDS: Wiring
- Coast To Coast Circuits Inc ......E...... 585 254-2980
  Rochester *(G-14281)*
- Nationwide Circuits Inc ......E...... 585 328-0791
  Rochester *(G-14528)*
- Stever-Locke Industries Inc ......G...... 585 624-3450
  Honeoye Falls *(G-6538)*

CIRCUITS, INTEGRATED: Hybrid
- Emtron Hybrids Inc ......E...... 631 924-9668
  Yaphank *(G-17392)*
- General Microwave Corporation ......F...... 516 802-0900
  Syosset *(G-15824)*

CIRCUITS: Electronic
- A K Allen Co Inc ......C...... 516 747-5450
  Mineola *(G-8488)*
- A R V Precision Mfg Inc ......E...... 631 293-9643
  Farmingdale *(G-4927)*
- AAR Allen Services Inc ......E...... 516 222-9000
  Garden City *(G-5493)*
- Accessories For Electronics ......E...... 631 847-0158
  South Hempstead *(G-15529)*
- Ace Electronics Inc ......F...... 914 773-2000
  Hawthorne *(G-6242)*
- Advance Circuit Technology Inc ......E...... 585 328-2000
  Rochester *(G-14175)*
- Aeroflex Plainview Inc ......B...... 516 694-6700
  Plainview *(G-13579)*
- Aeroflex Plainview Inc ......C...... 631 231-9100
  Hauppauge *(G-6011)*
- All Shore Industries Inc ......F...... 718 720-0018
  Staten Island *(G-15634)*
- Alloy Machine & Tool Co Inc ......G...... 516 593-3445
  Lynbrook *(G-7946)*
- American Quality Technology ......F...... 607 777-9488
  Binghamton *(G-887)*
- Anaren Inc ......B...... 315 432-8909
  East Syracuse *(G-4502)*
- B H M Metal Products Co ......G...... 845 292-5297
  Kauneonga Lake *(G-7136)*
- Canfield Electronics Inc ......F...... 631 585-4100
  Lindenhurst *(G-7458)*
- Chiplogic Inc ......F...... 631 617-6317
  Yaphank *(G-17388)*
- Cloud Toronto Inc ......F...... 408 569-4542
  Williamsville *(G-17239)*
- Communications & Energy Corp ......F...... 315 446-5723
  Syracuse *(G-15903)*
- Dynamic Hybrids Inc ......G...... 315 426-8110
  Syracuse *(G-16297)*
- Eastland Electronics Co Inc ......G...... 631 580-3800
  Ronkonkoma *(G-14898)*
- Empresas De Manufactura Inc ......C...... 631 240-9251
  East Setauket *(G-4481)*
- Fei Communications Inc ......C...... 516 794-4500
  Uniondale *(G-16293)*
- Hs Associates Corp ......G...... 516 496-2940
  Jericho *(G-7071)*
- Hypres Inc ......E...... 914 592-1190
  Elmsford *(G-4756)*
- IEC Electronics Corp ......B...... 315 331-7742
  Newark *(G-12732)*
- Imrex LLC ......B...... 516 479-3675
  Oyster Bay *(G-13370)*
- Island Circuits International ......G...... 516 625-5555
  College Point *(G-3791)*
- Island Research and Dev Corp ......D...... 631 471-7100
  Ronkonkoma *(G-14915)*
- Jaguar Industries Inc ......F...... 845 947-1800
  Haverstraw *(G-6237)*
- Jenlor Ltd ......F...... 315 637-9080
  Fayetteville *(G-5165)*
- Jet Components Inc ......G...... 631 436-7300
  Islandia *(G-6797)*
- Keltron Electronics (de Corp) ......F...... 631 567-6300
  Ronkonkoma *(G-14921)*

PRODUCT SECTION

CLEANING PRDTS: Specialty

Logitek Inc .... D 631 567-1100
  Bohemia *(G-1094)*
Mekatronics Incorporated .... E 516 883-6805
  Port Washington *(G-13844)*
Meridian Technologies Inc .... E 516 285-1000
  Elmont *(G-4724)*
Merit Electronic Design Co Inc .... C 631 667-9699
  Edgewood *(G-4606)*
Mid Hdson Wkshp For The Dsbled .... E 845 471-3820
  Poughkeepsie *(G-13915)*
Mirion Technologies Ist Corp .... D 607 562-4300
  Horseheads *(G-6584)*
Nelson Holdings Ltd .... G 607 772-1794
  Binghamton *(G-939)*
Oakdale Industrial Elec Corp .... F 631 737-4090
  Ronkonkoma *(G-14957)*
Opus Technology Corporation .... F 631 271-1883
  Melville *(G-8345)*
Pcb Piezotronics Inc .... B 716 684-0003
  Depew *(G-4270)*
Photonamics Inc .... F 585 426-3774
  Rochester *(G-14583)*
Polycast Industries Inc .... G 631 595-2530
  Bay Shore *(G-726)*
Precision Assembly Tech Inc .... E 631 699-9400
  Bohemia *(G-1119)*
Premier Systems LLC .... G 631 587-9700
  Babylon *(G-552)*
Quality Contract Assemblies .... F 585 663-9030
  Rochester *(G-14612)*
R L C Electronics Inc .... D 914 241-1334
  Mount Kisco *(G-8641)*
Rdi Inc .... F 914 773-1000
  Mount Kisco *(G-8643)*
Rem-Tronics Inc .... D 716 934-2697
  Dunkirk *(G-4348)*
Rochester Industrial Ctrl Inc .... D 315 524-4555
  Ontario *(G-13213)*
Rochester Industrial Ctrl Inc .... D 315 524-4555
  Ontario *(G-13212)*
Safe Circuits Inc .... G 631 586-3682
  Dix Hills *(G-4297)*
Scientific Components Corp .... B 718 368-2060
  Brooklyn *(G-2539)*
Sendec Corp .... C 585 425-3390
  Fairport *(G-4877)*
Sonaer Inc .... G 631 756-4780
  West Babylon *(G-16829)*
Sopark Corp .... C 716 822-0434
  Buffalo *(G-3191)*
Stetron International Inc .... F 716 854-3443
  Buffalo *(G-3197)*
Sun Circuits International Inc .... B 631 240-9251
  Setauket *(G-15381)*
Surmotech LLC .... D 585 742-1220
  Victor *(G-16503)*
T-S-K Electronics Inc .... G 716 693-3916
  North Tonawanda *(G-12999)*
Telephonics Corporation .... E 631 549-6000
  Huntington *(G-6683)*
Telephonics Corporation .... A 631 755-7000
  Farmingdale *(G-5127)*
Tlsi Incorporated .... D 631 470-8880
  Huntington *(G-6688)*
Torotron Corporation .... G 718 428-6992
  Fresh Meadows *(G-5446)*
Trading Services International .... F 212 501-0142
  New York *(G-12389)*
Tyco Electronics Corporation .... E 585 785-2500
  Rochester *(G-14737)*
Unison Industries LLC .... B 607 335-5000
  Norwich *(G-13039)*
Vestal Electronic Devices LLC .... F 607 773-8461
  Endicott *(G-4833)*
Werlatone Inc .... E 845 278-2220
  Patterson *(G-13446)*
Xedit Corp .... G 718 380-1592
  Queens Village *(G-13985)*

CIRCULAR KNIT FABRICS DYEING & FINISHING

A-One Moving & Storage Inc .... E 718 266-6002
  Brooklyn *(G-1541)*
Gehring Tricot Corporation .... C 315 429-8511
  Dolgeville *(G-4305)*

CLAMPS & COUPLINGS: Hose

United Metal Industries Inc .... G 516 354-6800
  New Hyde Park *(G-8869)*

CLAY PRDTS: Architectural

Lenon Models Inc .... G 212 229-1581
  New York *(G-10966)*

CLAYS, EXC KAOLIN & BALL

Applied Minerals Inc .... E 212 226-4265
  New York *(G-9184)*

CLEANING EQPT: Blast, Dustless

Cleaning Tech Group LLC .... E 716 665-2340
  Jamestown *(G-6981)*
Guyson Corporation of USa .... E 518 587-7894
  Saratoga Springs *(G-15157)*

CLEANING EQPT: Carpet Sweepers, Exc Household Elec Vacuum

American Comfort Direct LLC .... E 201 364-8309
  New York *(G-9116)*

CLEANING EQPT: Commercial

Commercial Solutions Inc .... F 716 731-5825
  Sanborn *(G-15118)*
Oxford Cleaners .... G 212 734-0006
  New York *(G-11539)*

CLEANING EQPT: High Pressure

Arpa USA .... G 212 965-4099
  New York *(G-9206)*
Custom Klean Corp .... F 315 865-8101
  Holland Patent *(G-6487)*
Heliojet Cleaning Tech Inc .... F 585 768-8710
  Le Roy *(G-7408)*
Power Scrub It Inc .... F 516 997-2500
  Westbury *(G-17020)*

CLEANING OR POLISHING PREPARATIONS, NEC

Arrow Chemical Corp .... F 516 377-7770
  Freeport *(G-5389)*
Clean All of Syracuse LLC .... G 315 472-9189
  Syracuse *(G-15897)*
Collinite Corporation .... G 315 732-2282
  Utica *(G-16313)*
FBC Chemical Corporation .... F 716 681-1581
  Lancaster *(G-7315)*
George Basch Co Inc .... F 516 378-8100
  North Bellmore *(G-12921)*
Grillbot LLC .... G 646 258-5639
  New York *(G-10364)*
Mdi Holdings LLC .... A 212 559-1127
  New York *(G-11203)*
Progressive Products LLC .... G 914 417-6022
  Rye Brook *(G-15074)*
Spic and Span Company .... F 914 524-6823
  Tarrytown *(G-16107)*
Topps-All Products of Yonkers .... F 914 968-4226
  Yonkers *(G-17491)*
U S Plychmical Overseas Corp .... E 845 356-5530
  Chestnut Ridge *(G-3627)*
US Polychemical Holding Corp .... E 845 356-5530
  Spring Valley *(G-15607)*

CLEANING PRDTS: Degreasing Solvent

Solvents Company Inc .... F 631 595-9300
  Kingston *(G-7210)*

CLEANING PRDTS: Deodorants, Nonpersonal

Car-Freshner Corporation .... C 315 788-6250
  Watertown *(G-16641)*

CLEANING PRDTS: Disinfectants, Household Or Indl Plant

Castoleum Corporation .... F 914 664-5877
  Mount Vernon *(G-8670)*
King Research Inc .... E 718 788-0122
  Brooklyn *(G-2172)*
Noble Pine Products Co Inc .... F 914 664-5877
  Mount Vernon *(G-8710)*
Spongebath LLC .... G 917 475-1347
  Astoria *(G-458)*

CLEANING PRDTS: Drycleaning Preparations

Connie French Cleaners Inc .... G 516 487-1343
  Great Neck *(G-5801)*
Wedding Gown Preservation Co .... D 607 748-7999
  Endicott *(G-4834)*

CLEANING PRDTS: Indl Plant Disinfectants Or Deodorants

Mirandy Products Ltd .... E 516 489-6800
  South Hempstead *(G-15530)*

CLEANING PRDTS: Laundry Preparations

Connies Laundry .... G 716 822-2800
  Buffalo *(G-2886)*
Laundress Inc .... F 212 209-0074
  New York *(G-10937)*
Lb Laundry Inc .... G 347 399-8030
  Flushing *(G-5264)*

CLEANING PRDTS: Metal Polish

Conrad Blasius Equipment Co .... G 516 753-1200
  Plainview *(G-13590)*

CLEANING PRDTS: Polishing Preparations & Related Prdts

Royce Associates A Ltd Partnr .... G 516 367-6298
  Jericho *(G-7083)*

CLEANING PRDTS: Rug, Upholstery/Dry Clng Detergents/Spotters

Greenmaker Industries LLC .... F 866 684-7800
  Farmingdale *(G-5002)*

CLEANING PRDTS: Sanitation Preparations

Adirondack Waste MGT Inc .... G 518 585-2224
  Ticonderoga *(G-16125)*
City of New York .... C 718 236-2693
  Brooklyn *(G-1783)*
County Waste Management Inc .... G 914 592-5007
  Harrison *(G-5981)*
Simply Amazing Enterprises Inc .... G 631 503-6452
  Melville *(G-8355)*
TWI-Laq Industries Inc .... E 718 638-5860
  Bronx *(G-1482)*

CLEANING PRDTS: Sanitation Preps, Disinfectants/Deodorants

Scully Sanitation .... G 315 899-8996
  West Edmeston *(G-16843)*
Walter G Legge Company Inc .... G 914 737-5040
  Peekskill *(G-13485)*

CLEANING PRDTS: Shoe Polish Or Cleaner

Premier Brands of America Inc .... E 718 325-3000
  Mount Vernon *(G-8718)*
Premier Brands of America Inc .... C 914 667-6200
  Mount Vernon *(G-8717)*

CLEANING PRDTS: Specialty

ATW Resources LLC .... G 212 994-0600
  New York *(G-9261)*
Caltex International Ltd .... E 315 425-1040
  Syracuse *(G-15883)*
Chem-Puter Friendly Inc .... E 631 331-2259
  Mount Sinai *(G-8654)*
Chemclean Corporation .... E 718 525-4500
  Jamaica *(G-6901)*
Enviro Service & Supply Corp .... F 347 838-6500
  Staten Island *(G-15671)*
Finger Lakes Chemicals Inc .... E 585 454-4760
  Rochester *(G-14370)*
Four Sasons Multi-Services Inc .... G 347 843-6262
  Bronx *(G-1336)*
Gliptone Manufacturing Inc .... F 631 285-7250
  Ronkonkoma *(G-14904)*
Griffin Chemical Company LLC .... G 716 693-2465
  North Tonawanda *(G-12976)*
Nuvite Chemical Compounds Corp ..... F 718 383-8351
  Brooklyn *(G-2380)*
Sensor & Decontamination Inc .... F 301 526-8389
  Binghamton *(G-950)*

Employee Codes: A=Over 500 employees, B=251-500
C=101-250, D=51-100, E=20-50, F=10-19, G=5-9

CLEANING PRDTS: Specialty

Spray Nine Corporation.................D........800 477-7299
  Johnstown (G-7128)

CLEANING PRDTS: Window Cleaning Preparations

Tjb Sunshine Enterprises................F........518 384-6483
  Ballston Lake (G-588)

CLEANING SVCS: Industrial Or Commercial

Wellspring Omni Holdings Corp.........A........212 318-9800
  New York (G-12610)

CLIPPERS: Fingernail & Toenail

Rev Holdings Inc...........................A........212 527-4000
  New York (G-11848)
Revlon Consumer Products Corp.......B........212 527-4000
  New York (G-11852)
Revlon Holdings Inc.......................D........212 527-4000
  New York (G-11853)
RGI Group Incorporated.................E........212 527-4000
  New York (G-11858)

CLIPS & FASTENERS, MADE FROM PURCHASED WIRE

Hohmann & Barnard Inc.................E........631 234-0600
  Hauppauge (G-6095)
Hohmann & Barnard Inc.................E........518 357-9757
  Schenectady (G-15268)

CLOCKS

Compumatic Time Recorders Inc......G........718 531-5749
  North Bellmore (G-12917)

CLOSURES: Closures, Stamped Metal

Van Blarcom Closures Inc...............C........718 855-3810
  Brooklyn (G-2718)

CLOSURES: Plastic

C & N Packaging Inc.....................D........631 491-1400
  Wyandanch (G-17371)
Hlp Klearfold Packaging Pdts...........F........718 554-3271
  New York (G-10488)
Industrial Paper Tube Inc................F........718 893-5000
  Bronx (G-1361)
Kleer - View Index Co Inc................F........718 896-3800
  Woodside (G-17335)
Mold-Rite Plastics LLC....................C........518 561-1812
  Plattsburgh (G-13678)
Van Blarcom Closures Inc...............C........718 855-3810
  Brooklyn (G-2718)

CLOTHES HANGERS, WHOLESALE

Accessory Corporation....................A........212 391-8607
  New York (G-9010)

CLOTHING & ACCESS, WOMEN, CHILD & INFANT, WHOL: Scarves

Gce International Inc......................D........212 704-4800
  New York (G-10259)

CLOTHING & ACCESS, WOMEN, CHILD & INFANT, WHOLESALE: Under

Apparel Partnership Group LLC........G........212 302-7722
  New York (G-9178)
Mrt Textile Inc..............................G........800 674-1073
  New York (G-11318)

CLOTHING & ACCESS, WOMEN, CHILD & INFANT, WHSLE: Sportswear

Bandit International Ltd..................F........718 402-2100
  Bronx (G-1280)
Kidz Concepts LLC........................D........212 398-1110
  New York (G-10842)
Sensational Collection Inc...............G........212 840-7388
  New York (G-12029)

CLOTHING & ACCESS, WOMEN, CHILDREN & INFANT, WHOL: Access

Embassy Apparel Inc.....................F........212 768-8330
  New York (G-10019)

Fad Inc..E........631 385-2460
  Huntington (G-6661)

CLOTHING & ACCESS, WOMEN, CHILDREN & INFANT, WHOL: Gloves

Fownes Brothers & Co Inc..............E........212 683-0150
  New York (G-10194)
Fownes Brothers & Co Inc..............E........518 752-4411
  Gloversville (G-5711)

CLOTHING & ACCESS, WOMEN, CHILDREN & INFANT, WHOL: Handbags

Coach Stores Inc..........................A........212 643-9727
  New York (G-9659)
Goyard Inc..................................G........212 813-0005
  New York (G-10343)
Graphic Image Incorporated............C........631 249-9600
  Melville (G-8324)
Quilted Koala Ltd.........................F........800 223-5678
  New York (G-11773)
Street Smart Designs Inc................G........646 865-0056
  New York (G-12213)

CLOTHING & ACCESS, WOMEN, CHILDREN & INFANT, WHOL: Sweaters

B & B Sweater Mills Inc.................F........718 456-8693
  Brooklyn (G-1655)
Keryakos Inc................................F........518 344-7092
  Schenectady (G-15272)

CLOTHING & ACCESS, WOMEN, CHILDREN & INFANTS, WHOL: Purses

Formart Corp...............................F........212 819-1819
  New York (G-10186)

CLOTHING & ACCESS, WOMEN, CHILDREN/INFANT, WHOL: Baby Goods

Sunwin Global Industry Inc..............G........646 370-6196
  New York (G-12239)

CLOTHING & ACCESS, WOMEN, CHILDREN/INFANT, WHOL: Nightwear

Komar Luxury Brands....................G........646 472-0060
  New York (G-10875)

CLOTHING & ACCESS, WOMEN, CHILDREN/INFANT, WHOL: Outerwear

Outerstuff LLC.............................E........212 594-9700
  New York (G-11536)

CLOTHING & ACCESS, WOMEN, CHILDREN/INFANT, WHOL: Swimsuits

Christina Sales Inc........................F........212 391-0710
  New York (G-9612)

CLOTHING & ACCESS, WOMENS, CHILDRE'S & INFANTS, WHOL: Suits

Chancelle Suits Inc.......................F........212 921-5300
  New York (G-9578)
Tiger Fashion Inc..........................E........212 244-1175
  New York (G-12338)
Travis Ayers Inc............................E........212 921-5165
  New York (G-12394)

CLOTHING & ACCESS, WOMENS, CHILDREN & INFANTS, WHOL: Hats

Mega Power Sports Corporation.......G........212 627-3380
  New York (G-11220)

CLOTHING & ACCESS: Costumes, Masquerade

Rubies Masquerade Company LLC....G........718 846-1008
  Richmond Hill (G-14084)

CLOTHING & ACCESS: Costumes, Theatrical

Barbara Matera Ltd.......................D........212 475-5006
  New York (G-9315)

Carelli Costumes Inc.....................E........212 765-6166
  New York (G-9524)
Costume Armour Inc.....................F........845 534-9120
  Cornwall (G-3987)
D-C Theatricks............................G........716 847-0180
  Buffalo (G-2900)
Euroco Costumes Inc....................G........212 629-9665
  New York (G-10085)
Izquierdo Studios Ltd....................G........212 807-9757
  New York (G-10671)
Parsons-Meares Ltd......................D........212 242-3378
  Long Island City (G-7834)
Schneeman Studio Limited............G........212 244-3330
  New York (G-11990)

CLOTHING & ACCESS: Cummerbunds

J M C Bow Co Inc........................F........718 686-8110
  Brooklyn (G-2125)
Lakeview Innovations Inc...............F........212 502-6702
  New York (G-10920)
Westchester Wine Warehouse LLC...F........914 824-1400
  White Plains (G-17185)

CLOTHING & ACCESS: Footlets

Jersey Express Inc.......................F........716 834-6151
  Buffalo (G-3018)

CLOTHING & ACCESS: Handicapped

Brooklyn Denim Co.......................F........718 782-2600
  Brooklyn (G-1725)
Crosswinds Sourcing LLC...............G........646 438-6904
  New York (G-9757)
Danny R Couture Corp..................G........212 594-1095
  New York (G-9806)
Kww Productions Corp..................F........212 398-8181
  New York (G-10896)
M2 Fashion Group Holdings Inc......G........917 208-2948
  New York (G-11080)
Ribz LLC....................................G........212 764-9595
  New York (G-11861)
Timeless Fashions LLC..................G........212 730-9328
  New York (G-12351)

CLOTHING & ACCESS: Handkerchiefs, Exc Paper

Gce International Inc....................D........212 704-4800
  New York (G-10259)
My Hanky Inc..............................F........646 321-0869
  Brooklyn (G-2344)

CLOTHING & ACCESS: Hospital Gowns

New York Hospital Disposable.........E........718 384-1620
  Brooklyn (G-2365)
Shamron Mills Ltd........................G........212 354-0430
  New York (G-12041)

CLOTHING & ACCESS: Men's Miscellaneous Access

Adf Accessories Inc......................G........516 450-5755
  Lynbrook (G-7943)
Apollo Apparel Group LLC..............F........212 398-6585
  New York (G-9175)
Bh Brand Inc...............................E........212 239-1635
  New York (G-9386)
Carter Enterprises LLC..................E........718 853-5052
  Brooklyn (G-1760)
Club Monaco US Inc....................G........212 886-2660
  New York (G-9647)
Dreamwave LLC...........................E........212 594-4250
  New York (G-9925)
Fetherston Design Group LLC.........E........212 643-7537
  New York (G-10156)
Foot Locker Retail Inc...................G........516 827-5306
  Hicksville (G-6345)
Hoehn Inc...................................F........518 463-8900
  Albany (G-88)
Hudson Dying & Finishing LLC.......F........518 752-4389
  Gloversville (G-5716)
Intercotton Company Inc................G........212 265-3809
  New York (G-10626)
J M B Apparel Designer Group........G........212 764-8410
  New York (G-10679)
Jimeale Incorporated.....................G........917 686-5383
  New York (G-10735)
Jonathan Meizler LLC....................G........212 213-2977
  New York (G-10757)

Joseph Industries Inc .... G 212 764-0010
  New York (G-10765)
Linder New York LLC .... F 646 678-5819
  New York (G-10998)
Miles Alexander LLC .... F 516 937-5262
  Hicksville (G-6372)
New York Accessory Group Inc .... E 212 532-7911
  New York (G-11395)
New York Popular Inc .... D 718 499-2020
  Brooklyn (G-2367)
Nmny Group LLC .... E 212 944-6500
  New York (G-11447)
NY 1 Art Gallery Inc .... G 917 698-0626
  New Hyde Park (G-8852)
Ppr Direct Marketing LLC .... G 718 965-8600
  Brooklyn (G-2433)
Rjm2 Ltd .... G 212 944-1660
  New York (G-11884)
Robert Miller Associates LLC .... F 718 392-1640
  Long Island City (G-7862)
Rosetti Handbags and ACC .... E 212 273-3765
  New York (G-11919)
Swank Inc .... B 212 867-2600
  New York (G-12248)
Ufo Contemporary Inc .... F 212 226-5400
  New York (G-12444)
Unified Inc led .... F 646 370-4650
  New York (G-12453)
Zam Barrett Dialogue Inc .... G 646 649-0140
  Brooklyn (G-2780)

CLOTHING & ACCESS: Suspenders

Perry Ellis Menswear LLC .... C 212 221-7500
  New York (G-11624)
Randa Accessories Lea Gds LLC .... D 212 354-5100
  New York (G-11799)
Trafalgar Company LLC .... G 212 768-8800
  New York (G-12390)

CLOTHING & APPAREL STORES: Custom

Knucklehead Embroidery Inc .... G 607 797-2725
  Johnson City (G-7098)
Peter Papastrat .... G 607 723-8112
  Binghamton (G-942)

CLOTHING & FURNISHINGS, MEN & BOY, WHOLESALE: Suits/Trousers

Hugo Boss Usa Inc .... D 212 940-0600
  New York (G-10528)

CLOTHING & FURNISHINGS, MEN'S & BOYS', WHOLESALE: Fur

Georgy Creative Fashions Inc .... G 212 279-4885
  New York (G-10284)

CLOTHING & FURNISHINGS, MEN'S & BOYS', WHOLESALE: Gloves

Fownes Brothers & Co Inc .... E 212 683-0150
  New York (G-10194)
Fownes Brothers & Co Inc .... E 518 752-4411
  Gloversville (G-5711)

CLOTHING & FURNISHINGS, MEN'S & BOYS', WHOLESALE: Hats

Ideal Creations Inc .... E 212 563-5928
  New York (G-10555)
Mega Power Sports Corporation .... G 212 627-3380
  New York (G-11220)
W & M Headwear Co Inc .... F 718 768-2222
  Brooklyn (G-2739)

CLOTHING & FURNISHINGS, MEN'S & BOYS', WHOLESALE: Neckwear

Mongru Neckwear Inc .... E 718 706-0406
  Long Island City (G-7816)
Roffe Accessories Inc .... F 212 213-1440
  New York (G-11903)

CLOTHING & FURNISHINGS, MEN'S & BOYS', WHOLESALE: Scarves

Gce International Inc .... D 212 704-4800
  New York (G-10259)

CLOTHING & FURNISHINGS, MEN'S & BOYS', WHOLESALE: Shirts

Hard Ten Clothing Inc .... G 212 302-1321
  New York (G-10412)
Just Brass Inc .... G 212 724-5447
  New York (G-10792)

CLOTHING & FURNISHINGS, MEN'S & BOYS', WHOLESALE: Trousers

Texwood Inc (u S A) .... G 212 262-8383
  New York (G-12306)

CLOTHING & FURNISHINGS, MEN'S & BOYS', WHOLESALE: Umbrellas

Adam Scott Designs Inc .... E 212 420-8866
  New York (G-9024)

CLOTHING & FURNISHINGS, MEN'S & BOYS', WHOLESALE: Uniforms

Custom Sportswear Corp .... G 914 666-9200
  Bedford Hills (G-800)

CLOTHING & FURNISHINGS, MENS & BOYS, WHOL: Sportswear/Work

John Varvatos Company .... E 212 812-8000
  New York (G-10754)

CLOTHING & FURNISHINGS, MENS & BOYS, WHOLESALE: Apprl Belts

Dynasty Belts Inc .... E 516 625-6280
  New Hyde Park (G-8829)
New Classic Inc .... F 718 609-1100
  Long Island City (G-7823)

CLOTHING ACCESS STORES: Umbrellas

Zip-Jack Industries Ltd .... E 914 592-2000
  Tarrytown (G-16113)

CLOTHING STORES, NEC

Fad Inc .... E 631 385-2460
  Huntington (G-6661)
Kcp Holdco Inc .... A 212 265-1500
  New York (G-10827)
Kenneth Cole Productions Inc .... B 212 265-1500
  New York (G-10833)
Marsha Fleisher .... F 845 679-6500
  Woodstock (G-17364)

CLOTHING STORES: Dancewear

Shirl-Lynn of New York .... F 315 363-5898
  Oneida (G-13167)

CLOTHING STORES: Jeans

Brooklyn Denim Co .... F 718 782-2600
  Brooklyn (G-1725)
Gbg Denim Usa LLC .... G 646 839-7000
  Plattsburgh (G-13663)
Joseph (uk) Inc .... G 212 570-0077
  New York (G-10763)

CLOTHING STORES: Leather

Leather Artisan .... G 518 359-3102
  Childwold (G-3628)
Lost Worlds Inc .... G 212 923-3423
  New York (G-11045)

CLOTHING STORES: Shirts, Custom Made

L Allmeier .... G 212 243-7390
  New York (G-10900)

CLOTHING STORES: T-Shirts, Printed, Custom

JP Signs .... G 518 569-3907
  Chazy (G-3562)
Randy Sixberry .... G 315 265-6211
  Potsdam (G-13883)

CLOTHING STORES: Uniforms & Work

All American Awards Inc .... F 631 567-2025
  Bohemia (G-1011)

CLOTHING STORES: Unisex

David Peyser Sportswear Inc .... E 212 695-7716
  New York (G-9821)

CLOTHING STORES: Work

Protech (llc) .... E 518 725-7785
  Gloversville (G-5719)

CLOTHING, WOMEN & CHILD, WHLSE: Dress, Suit, Skirt & Blouse

Billy Beez Usa LLC .... F 315 741-5099
  Syracuse (G-15869)
Billy Beez Usa LLC .... F 646 606-2249
  New York (G-9399)
Billy Beez Usa LLC .... F 845 915-4709
  West Nyack (G-16913)

CLOTHING/ACCESS, WOMEN, CHILDREN/INFANT, WHOL: Apparel Belt

New Classic Inc .... F 718 609-1100
  Long Island City (G-7823)

CLOTHING/FURNISHINGS, MEN/BOY, WHOL: Furnishings, Exc Shoes

Embassy Apparel Inc .... F 212 768-8330
  New York (G-10019)

CLOTHING: Academic Vestments

Tr Apparel LLC .... E 310 595-4337
  New York (G-12385)
Tr Apparel LLC .... G 646 358-3888
  New York (G-12386)

CLOTHING: Access

David & Young Co Inc .... G 212 594-6034
  New York (G-9818)
J & C Finishing .... E 718 456-1087
  Ridgewood (G-14110)
Jmk Enterprises LLC .... G 845 634-8100
  New City (G-8786)
P B O E Pwred By Our Envmt Inc .... G 917 803-9474
  Brooklyn (G-2400)
Patient-Wear LLC .... G 914 740-7770
  Bronx (G-1422)
Reiss Ltd .... G 212 488-2411
  New York (G-11822)
S & B Fashion Inc .... G 718 482-1386
  Long Island City (G-7869)
Twcc Product and Sales .... E 212 614-9364
  New York (G-12432)

CLOTHING: Access, Women's & Misses'

Bag Bazaar Ltd .... E 212 689-3508
  New York (G-9304)
Bh Brand Inc .... E 212 239-1635
  New York (G-9386)
Carolina Amato Inc .... G 212 768-9095
  New York (G-9534)
Collection Xiix Ltd .... F 212 686-8990
  New York (G-9670)
DFA New York LLC .... E 212 523-0021
  New York (G-9866)
Fad Inc .... E 631 385-2460
  Huntington (G-6661)
Four Dee Inc .... D 718 615-1695
  Brooklyn (G-2000)
Giulietta LLC .... G 212 334-1859
  New York (G-10301)
Hoehn Inc .... F 518 463-8900
  Albany (G-88)
Krasner Group Inc .... G 212 268-4100
  New York (G-10886)
Ksk International Inc .... E 212 354-7770
  New York (G-10891)
New Concepts of New York LLC .... E 212 695-4999
  New York (G-11381)
New York Accessory Group Inc .... E 212 532-7911
  New York (G-11395)
ODY Accessories Inc .... E 212 239-0580
  New York (G-11496)

CLOTHING: Access, Women's & Misses'

One Mountain Imports LLC ....G...... 212 643-0805
  New York (G-11507)
Popnyc 1 LLC ....G...... 646 684-4600
  New York (G-11684)
Uspa Accessories LLC ....C...... 212 868-2590
  New York (G-12492)
White Gate Holdings Inc ....E...... 212 564-3266
  New York (G-12625)

CLOTHING: Aprons, Exc Rubber/Plastic, Women, Misses, Junior

Elizabeth Wilson ....G...... 516 486-2157
  Uniondale (G-16292)
Republic Clothing Group Inc ....C...... 212 719-3000
  New York (G-11837)
Richard Manufacturing Co Inc ....G...... 718 254-0958
  Brooklyn (G-2493)

CLOTHING: Aprons, Harness

Breton Industries Inc ....D...... 518 842-3030
  Amsterdam (G-336)
Mama Luca Production Inc ....G...... 212 582-9700
  New York (G-11123)

CLOTHING: Aprons, Work, Exc Rubberized & Plastic, Men's

Richard Manufacturing Co Inc ....G...... 718 254-0958
  Brooklyn (G-2493)

CLOTHING: Athletic & Sportswear, Men's & Boys'

Adpro Sports Inc ....D...... 716 854-5116
  Buffalo (G-2798)
Bandit International Ltd ....F...... 718 402-2100
  Bronx (G-1280)
Beluga Inc ....E...... 212 594-5511
  New York (G-9353)
Benetton Trading Usa Inc ....G...... 212 593-0290
  New York (G-9359)
Billion Tower USA LLC ....G...... 212 220-0608
  New York (G-9398)
Broken Threads Inc ....G...... 212 730-4351
  New York (G-9468)
C E Chquie Ltd ....G...... 212 268-0006
  New York (G-9490)
Central Mills Inc ....C...... 212 221-0748
  New York (G-9565)
City Jeans Inc ....G...... 718 239-5353
  Bronx (G-1300)
Columbia Sportswear Company ....C...... 631 274-6091
  Deer Park (G-4119)
Continental Knitting Mills ....G...... 631 242-5330
  Deer Park (G-4120)
Cotton Express Inc ....E...... 212 921-4588
  New York (G-9729)
Cougar Sport Inc ....F...... 212 947-3054
  New York (G-9732)
David Peyser Sportswear Inc ....C...... 631 231-7788
  Bay Shore (G-691)
David Peyser Sportswear Inc ....E...... 212 695-7716
  New York (G-9821)
Endurance LLC ....E...... 212 719-2500
  New York (G-10033)
Eternal Fortune Fashion LLC ....F...... 212 965-5322
  New York (G-10077)
Ferris USA LLC ....G...... 617 895-8102
  New York (G-10155)
Feyem USA Inc ....G...... 845 363-6253
  Brewster (G-1219)
Fieldston Clothes Inc ....G...... 212 354-8550
  New York (G-10161)
Gametime Sportswear Plus LLC ....G...... 315 724-5893
  Utica (G-16335)
Gemtex Inc ....G...... 212 302-0102
  New York (G-10270)
General Sportwear Company Inc ....G...... 212 764-5820
  New York (G-10274)
Groupe 16sur20 LLC ....F...... 212 625-1620
  New York (G-10372)
Haculla Nyc Inc ....F...... 718 886-3163
  Fresh Meadows (G-5441)
Hansae Co Ltd ....G...... 212 354-6690
  New York (G-10410)
Hf Mfg Corp ....G...... 212 594-9142
  New York (G-10470)
Icer Sports LLC ....F...... 212 221-4700
  New York (G-10552)

Jacob Hidary Foundation Inc ....F...... 212 736-6540
  New York (G-10691)
John Varvatos Company ....E...... 212 812-8000
  New York (G-10754)
Joseph (uk) Inc ....G...... 212 570-0077
  New York (G-10763)
Kicks Closet Sportswear Inc ....G...... 347 577-0857
  Bronx (G-1372)
Kidz World Inc ....F...... 212 563-4949
  New York (G-10843)
Lakeview Sportswear Corp ....G...... 347 663-9519
  Brooklyn (G-2192)
London Paris Ltd ....G...... 718 564-4793
  Brooklyn (G-2234)
Luxe Imagine Consulting LLC ....G...... 212 273-9770
  New York (G-11066)
M Hidary & Co Inc ....D...... 212 736-6540
  New York (G-11073)
Mann Consultants LLC ....E...... 914 763-0512
  Waccabuc (G-16520)
Mee Accessories LLC ....C...... 917 262-1000
  New York (G-11218)
Miss Group ....G...... 212 391-2535
  New York (G-11281)
Nautica International Inc ....D...... 212 541-5757
  New York (G-11358)
Nine West Holdings Inc ....G...... 212 575-2571
  New York (G-11438)
North American Mills Inc ....F...... 212 695-6146
  New York (G-11456)
On The Double Inc ....G...... 518 431-3571
  Germantown (G-5591)
One Step Up Ltd ....D...... 212 398-1110
  New York (G-11508)
P & I Sportswear Inc ....G...... 718 934-4587
  New York (G-11546)
Ps38 LLC ....F...... 212 819-1123
  New York (G-11742)
Pvh Corp ....G...... 212 381-3800
  New York (G-11757)
Ralph Lauren Corporation ....B...... 212 318-7000
  New York (G-11792)
Ramsbury Property Us Inc ....F...... 212 223-6250
  New York (G-11796)
Rp55 Inc ....G...... 212 840-4035
  New York (G-11929)
Ruleville Manufacturing Co Inc ....G...... 212 695-1620
  New York (G-11935)
S & S Fashions Inc ....G...... 718 328-0001
  Bronx (G-1443)
Sandy Dalal Ltd ....G...... 212 532-5822
  New York (G-11967)
Sb Corporation ....G...... 212 822-3166
  New York (G-11979)
Sister Sister Inc ....G...... 212 629-9600
  New York (G-12087)
Sterling Possessions Ltd ....G...... 212 594-0418
  New York (G-12197)
Tbhl International LLC ....F...... 212 799-2007
  New York (G-12282)
Tibana Finishing Inc ....E...... 718 417-5375
  Ridgewood (G-14127)
Tillsonburg Company USA Inc ....E...... 267 994-8096
  New York (G-12341)
Under Armour Inc ....E...... 518 761-6787
  Lake George (G-7264)
Viewsport Inc ....G...... 585 738-6803
  Penfield (G-13505)
Warnaco Group Inc ....D...... 212 287-8000
  New York (G-12586)
Warnaco Inc ....B...... 212 287-8000
  New York (G-12587)

CLOTHING: Athletic & Sportswear, Women's & Girls'

Adpro Sports Inc ....D...... 716 854-5116
  Buffalo (G-2798)
Alpha 6 Distributions LLC ....F...... 516 801-8290
  Locust Valley (G-7628)
Amber Bever Inc ....G...... 212 391-4911
  New York (G-9109)
Anna Sui Corp ....E...... 212 768-1951
  New York (G-9164)
Avalin LLC ....G...... 212 842-2286
  New York (G-9273)
B Tween LLC ....F...... 212 819-9040
  New York (G-9294)
Bam Sales LLC ....G...... 212 781-3000
  New York (G-9311)

Casuals Etc Inc ....D...... 212 838-1319
  New York (G-9544)
Continental Knitting Mills ....G...... 631 242-5330
  Deer Park (G-4120)
Dianos Kathryn Designs ....G...... 212 267-1584
  New York (G-9874)
Doral Apparel Group Inc ....G...... 917 208-5652
  New York (G-9908)
Dr Jayscom ....F...... 888 437-5297
  New York (G-9922)
First Love Fashions LLC ....F...... 212 256-1089
  New York (G-10168)
Hearts of Palm LLC ....E...... 212 944-6660
  New York (G-10451)
Hearts of Palm LLC ....D...... 212 944-6660
  New York (G-10452)
Hot Shot Hk LLC ....E...... 212 921-1111
  New York (G-10513)
Jacques Moret Inc ....C...... 212 354-2400
  New York (G-10692)
Jaya Apparel Group LLC ....F...... 212 764-4980
  New York (G-10705)
Joseph Abboud Manufacturing ....G...... 212 586-9140
  New York (G-10764)
Katz Martell Fashion Trdg Intl ....G...... 212 840-0070
  New York (G-10819)
Kicks Closet Sportswear Inc ....G...... 347 577-0857
  Bronx (G-1372)
Koral Industries ....F...... 212 719-0392
  New York (G-10876)
Lai Apparel Design Inc ....E...... 212 382-1075
  New York (G-10918)
Lavish Layette Inc ....G...... 516 256-9130
  Cedarhurst (G-3458)
Leslie Stuart Co Inc ....E...... 212 629-4551
  New York (G-10975)
Liquid Knits Inc ....F...... 718 706-6600
  Long Island City (G-7791)
Mango Usa Inc ....G...... 718 998-6050
  Brooklyn (G-2258)
Mars Fashions Inc ....E...... 718 402-2200
  Bronx (G-1387)
MISS Sportswear Inc ....G...... 212 391-2535
  Brooklyn (G-2320)
MISS Sportswear Inc ....G...... 212 391-2535
  New York (G-11283)
MISS Sportswear Inc ....E...... 718 369-6012
  Brooklyn (G-2321)
Mynt 1792 LLC ....G...... 212 249-4562
  New York (G-11333)
Nine West Holdings Inc ....G...... 212 221-6376
  New York (G-11437)
Nine West Holdings Inc ....E...... 215 785-4000
  New York (G-11439)
Nine West Holdings Inc ....G...... 212 575-2571
  New York (G-11438)
On The Double Inc ....G...... 518 431-3571
  Germantown (G-5591)
One Step Up Ltd ....D...... 212 398-1110
  New York (G-11508)
P & I Sportswear Inc ....G...... 718 934-4587
  New York (G-11546)
Penfli Industries Inc ....F...... 212 947-6080
  Great Neck (G-5830)
Richard Leeds Intl Inc ....D...... 212 532-4546
  New York (G-11862)
Robespierre Inc ....G...... 212 764-8810
  New York (G-11892)
Senneth LLC ....G...... 347 232-3170
  Monsey (G-8582)
Sensational Collection Inc ....G...... 212 840-7388
  New York (G-12029)
Shirl-Lynn of New York ....F...... 315 363-5898
  Oneida (G-13167)
SRP Apparel Group Inc ....G...... 212 764-4810
  New York (G-12176)
Stony Apparel Corp ....G...... 212 391-0022
  New York (G-12209)
Swatfame Inc ....G...... 212 944-8022
  New York (G-12251)
Tillsonburg Company USA Inc ....E...... 267 994-8096
  New York (G-12341)
Z-Ply Corp ....E...... 212 398-7011
  New York (G-12701)
Zg Apparel Group LLC ....E...... 646 930-1113
  New York (G-12711)

(G-0000) Company's Geographic Section entry number

PRODUCT SECTION

CLOTHING: Blouses, Womens & Juniors, From Purchased Mtrls

CLOTHING: Baker, Barber, Lab/Svc Ind Apparel, Washable, Men

Bespoke Apparel Inc .... G 212 382-0330
  New York *(G-9372)*
HC Contracting Inc .... D 212 643-9292
  New York *(G-10433)*

CLOTHING: Bathing Suits & Beachwear, Children's

Warnaco Group Inc .... D 212 287-8000
  New York *(G-12586)*

CLOTHING: Bathing Suits & Swimwear, Girls, Children & Infant

Baby Uv/Kids Uv Inc .... F 917 301-9020
  Brooklyn *(G-1661)*
In Mocean Group LLC .... D 732 960-2415
  New York *(G-10577)*
Oxygen Inc .... G 516 433-1144
  Hicksville *(G-6380)*

CLOTHING: Bathing Suits & Swimwear, Knit

IaM Maliamills LLC .... G 805 845-2137
  Brooklyn *(G-2093)*
Tomas Maier .... G 212 988-8686
  New York *(G-12364)*

CLOTHING: Bathrobes, Mens & Womens, From Purchased Materials

Carole Hchman Design Group Inc ... C 918 423-3535
  New York *(G-9533)*
Natori Company Incorporated ...... D 212 532-7796
  New York *(G-11355)*
Richard Leeds Intl Inc .... D 212 532-4546
  New York *(G-11862)*

CLOTHING: Beachwear, Knit

Beachbuttons LLC .... G 917 306-9369
  New York *(G-9338)*

CLOTHING: Belts

Barrera Jose & Maria Co Ltd .... E 212 239-1994
  New York *(G-9325)*
Coach Inc .... B 212 594-1850
  New York *(G-9656)*
Coach Stores Inc .... A 212 643-9727
  New York *(G-9659)*
Courtlandt Boot Jack Co Inc .... E 718 445-6200
  Flushing *(G-5235)*
Daniel M Friedman & Assoc Inc .... E 212 695-5545
  New York *(G-9804)*
Dynasty Belts Inc .... E 516 625-6280
  New Hyde Park *(G-8829)*
Gbg USA Inc .... D 646 839-7083
  New York *(G-10254)*
Gbg USA Inc .... E 212 615-3400
  New York *(G-10255)*
Gbg USA Inc .... E 212 290-8041
  New York *(G-10256)*
Nassau Suffolk Brd of Womens ..... E 631 666-8835
  Bay Shore *(G-721)*
New Classic Inc .... F 718 609-1100
  Long Island City *(G-7823)*
P M Belts Usa Inc .... E 800 762-3580
  Brooklyn *(G-2401)*
Perry Ellis Menswear LLC .... C 212 221-7500
  New York *(G-11624)*
Queue Solutions LLC .... F 631 750-6440
  Bohemia *(G-1125)*
Randa Accessories Lea Gds LLC ... D 212 354-5100
  New York *(G-11799)*
Sandy Duftler Designs Ltd .... F 516 379-3084
  North Baldwin *(G-12908)*
Sh Leather Novelty Company .... G 718 387-7742
  Brooklyn *(G-2547)*
Sibeau Handbags Inc .... E 212 686-0210
  New York *(G-12059)*
Trafalgar Company LLC .... G 212 768-8500
  New York *(G-12390)*
Universal Elliot Corp .... G 212 736-8877
  New York *(G-12471)*
Walco Leather Co Inc .... E 212 243-2444
  New York *(G-12577)*

Xinya International Trading Co ..... G 212 216-9681
  New York *(G-12679)*

CLOTHING: Bibs, Waterproof, From Purchased Materials

Cheri Mon Baby LLC .... G 212 354-5511
  Brooklyn *(G-1777)*

CLOTHING: Blouses, Boys', From Purchased Materials

Jacks and Jokers 52 LLC .... G 917 740-2595
  New York *(G-10687)*
Nat Nast Company Inc .... G 212 575-1186
  New York *(G-11341)*

CLOTHING: Blouses, Women's & Girls'

18 Rocks LLC .... E 631 465-9990
  Melville *(G-8287)*
Apparel Group Ltd .... E 212 328-1200
  New York *(G-9177)*
Ben Wachter Associates Inc .... G 212 736-4064
  New York *(G-9354)*
Bernard Chaus Inc .... D 212 354-1280
  New York *(G-9364)*
Bernard Chaus Inc .... C 646 562-4700
  New York *(G-9365)*
Cyberlimit Inc .... F 212 840-9597
  New York *(G-9775)*
Cynthia Rowley Inc .... F 212 242-3803
  New York *(G-9777)*
Embassy Apparel Inc .... F 212 768-8330
  New York *(G-10019)*
Feyem USA Inc .... G 845 363-6253
  Brewster *(G-1219)*
Fourtys Ny Inc .... F 212 382-0301
  New York *(G-10193)*
FSI - New York Inc .... G 212 730-9545
  New York *(G-10216)*
Gildan Apparel USA Inc .... D 212 476-0341
  New York *(G-10295)*
Glamourpuss Nyc LLC .... G 212 722-1370
  New York *(G-10306)*
Hansae Co Ltd .... G 212 354-6690
  New York *(G-10410)*
Icer Sports LLC .... F 212 221-4700
  New York *(G-10552)*
Ind Rev LLC .... F 212 221-4700
  New York *(G-10585)*
Kate Spade & Company .... B 212 354-4900
  New York *(G-10816)*
Krasner Group Inc .... G 212 268-4100
  New York *(G-10886)*
Ksk International Inc .... E 212 354-7770
  New York *(G-10891)*
Lea & Viola Inc .... G 646 918-6866
  New York *(G-10945)*
Liberty Apparel Company Inc .... E 718 625-4000
  New York *(G-10984)*
Lt2 LLC .... B 212 684-1510
  New York *(G-11056)*
M S B International Ltd .... F 212 302-5551
  New York *(G-11076)*
Maggy London International Ltd ... D 212 944-7199
  New York *(G-11102)*
Melwood Partners Inc .... G 516 307-8030
  Garden City *(G-5521)*
Mulitex Usa Inc .... G 212 398-0440
  New York *(G-11323)*
Nyc Knitwear Inc .... E 212 840-1313
  New York *(G-11480)*
Orchid Manufacturing Co Inc .... F 212 840-5700
  New York *(G-11524)*
Plugg LLC .... F 212 840-6655
  New York *(G-11678)*
Ramy Brook LLC .... E 212 744-2789
  New York *(G-11797)*
Raven New York LLC .... G 212 584-9690
  New York *(G-11803)*
Rio Apparel USA Inc .... G 212 869-9150
  New York *(G-11875)*
Rio Garment SA .... A 212 822-3182
  New York *(G-11876)*
Robert Danes Danes Inc .... G 212 226-1951
  New York *(G-11949)*
Saad Collection Inc .... F 212 937-0341
  New York *(G-11949)*
Soho Apparel Ltd .... G 212 840-1109
  New York *(G-12118)*

Spencer AB Inc .... G 646 831-3728
  New York *(G-12160)*
Style Partners Inc .... F 212 904-1499
  New York *(G-12223)*
Tibana Finishing Inc .... E 718 417-5375
  Ridgewood *(G-14127)*
Triumph Apparel Corporation .... E 212 302-2606
  New York *(G-12407)*
Turn On Products Inc .... D 212 764-2121
  New York *(G-12426)*
Ursula of Switzerland Inc .... E 518 237-2580
  Waterford *(G-16623)*
Vanity Room Inc .... F 212 921-7154
  New York *(G-12503)*
Ventura Enterprise Co Inc .... E 212 391-0170
  New York *(G-12517)*
Westside Clothing Co Inc .... G 212 273-9898
  New York *(G-12619)*
Yeohlee Inc .... F 212 631-8099
  New York *(G-12690)*

CLOTHING: Blouses, Womens & Juniors, From Purchased Mtrls

79 Metro Ltd .... G 212 944-4030
  New York *(G-8980)*
Agi Brooks Production Co Inc ...... F 212 268-1533
  New York *(G-9056)*
Alexander Wang Incorporated ..... D 212 532-3103
  New York *(G-9083)*
Alvin Valley Direct LLC .... F 212 392-4725
  New York *(G-9106)*
Amerex Corporation .... G 212 221-3151
  New York *(G-9111)*
Anna Sui Corp .... E 212 768-1951
  New York *(G-9164)*
Brooke Leigh Ltd .... G 212 736-9098
  New York *(G-9469)*
Donna Karan Company LLC .... C 212 789-1500
  New York *(G-9900)*
Donna Karan Company LLC .... B 212 789-1500
  New York *(G-9901)*
Donna Karan International Inc .... A 212 789-1500
  New York *(G-9902)*
Donna Karan International Inc .... G 212 768-5800
  New York *(G-9903)*
Elie Tahari Ltd .... F 212 398-2622
  New York *(G-10001)*
Elie Tahari Ltd .... D 212 763-2000
  New York *(G-10003)*
Fuller Sportswear Co Inc .... G 516 773-3353
  Great Neck *(G-5814)*
Gabrielle Andra .... G 212 366-9624
  New York *(G-10239)*
Geoffrey Beene Inc .... E 212 371-5570
  New York *(G-10279)*
International Direct Group Inc ..... G 212 921-9036
  New York *(G-10634)*
Jeanjer LLC .... A 212 944-1330
  New York *(G-10716)*
Land n Sea Inc .... D 212 703-2980
  New York *(G-10923)*
Necessary Objects Ltd .... E 212 334-9888
  New York *(G-11365)*
Orchard Apparel Group Ltd .... G 212 268-8701
  New York *(G-11523)*
Paddy Lee Fashions Inc .... F 718 786-6020
  Long Island City *(G-7833)*
Pat & Rose Dress Inc .... D 212 279-1357
  New York *(G-11578)*
Permit Fashion Group Inc .... G 212 912-0988
  New York *(G-11620)*
Phillips-Van Heusen Europe .... F 212 381-3500
  New York *(G-11649)*
Pvh Corp .... D 212 381-3500
  New York *(G-11756)*
Pvh Corp .... G 212 719-2600
  New York *(G-11759)*
Rhoda Lee Inc .... D 212 840-5700
  New York *(G-11859)*
S & S Manufacturing Co Inc .... D 212 444-6000
  New York *(G-11943)*
Stitch & Couture Inc .... E 212 947-9204
  New York *(G-12206)*
Tahari ASL LLC .... B 212 763-2800
  New York *(G-12272)*
Turn On Products Inc .... E 212 764-4545
  New York *(G-12427)*

Employee Codes: A=Over 500 employees, B=251-500
C=101-250, D=51-100, E=20-50, F=10-19, G=5-9

CLOTHING: Brassieres

Cupid Foundations Inc .... D 212 686-6224
  New York (G-9767)
East Coast Molders Inc .... C 516 240-6000
  Oceanside (G-13078)
Edith Lances Corp .... E 212 683-1990
  New York (G-9981)
New York Elegance Entps Inc .... F 212 685-3088
  New York (G-11400)
Valmont Inc .... F 212 685-1653
  New York (G-12496)
Wacoal America Inc .... C 718 794-1032
  Bronx (G-1491)

CLOTHING: Bridal Gowns

B S J Limited .... E 212 764-4600
  New York (G-9291)
B S J Limited .... G 212 221-8403
  New York (G-9292)
Bms Designs Inc .... E 718 828-5792
  Bronx (G-1285)
Brides Inc .... G 718 435-6092
  Brooklyn (G-1714)
Forever Yours Intl Corp .... E 516 443-2743
  Saint James (G-15089)
Lovely Bride LLC .... G 212 924-2050
  New York (G-11054)
Selia Yang Inc .... G 212 480-4252
  New York (G-12025)
Shane Tex Inc .... F 516 486-7522
  Hempstead (G-6287)
Stitch & Couture Inc .... E 212 947-9204
  New York (G-12206)
Thread LLC .... G 212 414-8844
  New York (G-12332)
Vera Wang Group LLC .... G 212 575-6400
  New York (G-12518)

CLOTHING: Burial

Rose Solomon Co .... E 718 855-1788
  Brooklyn (G-2506)

CLOTHING: Capes & Jackets, Women's & Misses'

Uniqlo USA LLC .... F 877 486-4756
  New York (G-12460)

CLOTHING: Capes, Exc Fur/Rubber, Womens, Misses & Juniors

Adrienne Landau Designs Inc .... F 212 695-8362
  New York (G-9031)

CLOTHING: Caps, Baseball

Twins Enterprise Inc .... G 631 368-4702
  Commack (G-3844)

CLOTHING: Chemises, Camisoles/Teddies, Women, Misses/Junior

Mrt Textile Inc .... G 800 674-1073
  New York (G-11318)

CLOTHING: Children & Infants'

Carters Inc .... G 315 637-3128
  Fayetteville (G-5163)
Carters Inc .... G 631 549-6781
  Huntington Station (G-6699)
Consolidated Childrens AP Inc .... G 212 239-8615
  New York (G-9703)
Gce International Inc .... F 212 868-0500
  New York (G-10260)
Grand Knitting Mills Inc .... E 631 226-5000
  Amityville (G-290)
Great Universal Corp .... F 917 302-0065
  New York (G-10359)
Haddad Bros Inc .... E 718 377-5505
  Brooklyn (G-2061)
Haddad Bros Inc .... F 212 563-2117
  New York (G-10393)
JM Originals Inc .... C 845 647-3003
  Ellenville (G-4634)
Manchu New York Inc .... G 212 921-5050
  New York (G-11125)
Michael Stuart Inc .... E 718 821-0704
  Brooklyn (G-2309)
S & C Bridals LLC .... G 212 789-7000
  New York (G-11942)
Silly Phillie Creations Inc .... E 718 492-6300
  Brooklyn (G-2556)
Sports Products America LLC ..... E 212 594-5511
  New York (G-12168)
Steve Zinn .... F 718 746-8551
  Flushing (G-5298)
Thats My Girl Inc .... G 212 695-0020
  Brooklyn (G-2655)

CLOTHING: Children's, Girls'

Aerobic Wear Inc .... G 631 673-1830
  Huntington Station (G-6693)
Amerimade Coat Inc .... G 212 216-0925
  New York (G-9133)
Devil Dog Manufacturing Co Inc .. G 845 647-4411
  Ellenville (G-4633)
Domani Fashions Corp .... G 718 797-0505
  Brooklyn (G-1871)
Franco Apparel Group Inc .... D 212 967-7272
  New York (G-10200)
Gerson & Gerson Inc .... D 212 244-6775
  New York (G-10287)
Haddad Bros Inc .... E 718 377-5505
  Brooklyn (G-2061)
Isfel Co Inc .... G 212 736-6216
  New York (G-10667)
Jeanjer LLC .... A 212 944-1330
  New York (G-10716)
Jj Basics LLC .... E 212 768-4779
  New York (G-10739)
JM Originals Inc .... C 845 647-3003
  Ellenville (G-4634)
Jomat New York Inc .... E 718 369-7641
  Brooklyn (G-2146)
Kahn-Lucas-Lancaster Inc .... D 212 239-2407
  New York (G-10801)
Land n Sea Inc .... D 212 703-2980
  New York (G-10923)
Liberty Apparel Company Inc .... E 718 625-4000
  New York (G-10984)
Lollytogs Ltd .... D 212 502-6000
  New York (G-11024)
M Hidary & Co Inc .... D 212 736-6540
  New York (G-11073)
Michael Stuart Inc .... E 718 821-0704
  Brooklyn (G-2309)
Miltons of New York Inc .... G 212 997-3359
  New York (G-11272)
Outerstuff LLC .... E 212 594-9700
  New York (G-11536)
Pink Crush LLC .... G 718 788-6978
  New York (G-11664)
Pti-Pacific Inc .... G 212 414-8495
  New York (G-11744)
Rogers Group Inc .... G 212 643-9292
  New York (G-11907)
S Rothschild & Co Inc .... C 212 354-8550
  New York (G-11947)
Sch Dpx Corporation .... G 917 405-5377
  New York (G-11985)
Silly Phillie Creations Inc .... E 718 492-6300
  Brooklyn (G-2556)
Swatfame Inc .... G 212 944-8022
  New York (G-12251)
Therese The Childrens Collectn .. G 518 346-2315
  Schenectady (G-15305)
Yigal-Azrouel Inc .... E 212 302-1194
  New York (G-12691)
Z-Ply Corp .... E 212 398-7011
  New York (G-12701)
ZIC Sportswear Inc .... E 718 361-9022
  Long Island City (G-7933)

CLOTHING: Clergy Vestments

Davis .... G 716 833-4678
  Buffalo (G-2903)
Roth Clothing Co Inc .... G 718 384-4927
  Brooklyn (G-2508)
Warner .... G 716 446-0663
  Buffalo (G-3248)

CLOTHING: Coats & Jackets, Leather & Sheep-Lined

Andrew M Schwartz LLC .... G 212 391-7070
  New York (G-9155)
Cockpit Usa Inc .... F 212 575-1616
  New York (G-9661)
Cockpit Usa Inc .... F 212 575-1616
  New York (G-9662)
Excelled Shpskin Lea Coat Corp . F 212 594-5843
  New York (G-10103)
Gloria Apparel Inc .... F 212 947-0869
  New York (G-10322)
J Percy For Mrvin Rchards Ltd .... E 212 944-5300
  New York (G-10680)
Lost Worlds Inc .... G 212 923-3423
  New York (G-11045)

CLOTHING: Coats & Suits, Men's & Boys'

Adrian Jules Ltd .... D 585 342-5886
  Rochester (G-14174)
Advance Apparel Intl Inc .... G 212 944-0984
  New York (G-9034)
Allytex LLC .... G 518 376-7539
  Ballston Spa (G-591)
Amerimade Coat Inc .... G 212 216-0925
  New York (G-9133)
Check Group LLC .... D 212 221-4700
  New York (G-9587)
Christian Casey LLC .... E 212 500-2200
  New York (G-9608)
Christian Casey LLC .... E 212 500-2200
  New York (G-9609)
Concorde Apparel Company LLC . G 212 307-7848
  New York (G-9695)
Excelled Shpskin Lea Coat Corp . F 212 594-5843
  New York (G-10103)
G-III Apparel Group Ltd .... C 212 403-0500
  New York (G-10234)
Giliberto Designs Inc .... E 212 695-0216
  New York (G-10296)
Great 4 Image .... E 518 424-2058
  Rensselaer (G-14047)
Hana Sportswear Inc .... E 315 639-6332
  Dexter (G-4285)
Hickey Freeman Tailored CL Inc .. E 585 467-7240
  Rochester (G-14433)
Hugo Boss Usa Inc .... D 212 940-0600
  New York (G-10528)
J & X Production .... F 646 366-8288
  New York (G-10675)
L Allmeier .... G 212 243-7390
  New York (G-10900)
L F Fashion Orient Intl Co Ltd ...... G 917 667-3398
  New York (G-10901)
M Hidary & Co Inc .... D 212 736-6540
  New York (G-11073)
Manchu New York Inc .... G 212 921-5050
  New York (G-11125)
Mv Corp Inc .... C 631 273-8020
  Bay Shore (G-720)
Pat & Rose Dress Inc .... D 212 279-1357
  New York (G-11578)
Proper Cloth LLC .... G 646 964-4221
  New York (G-11736)
Therese The Childrens Collectn .. G 518 346-2315
  Schenectady (G-15305)
Woodmere Fabrics Inc .... G 212 695-0144
  New York (G-12656)
Wp Lavori USA Inc .... G 718 855-4295
  Brooklyn (G-2769)
Wp Lavori USA Inc .... G 212 244-6074
  New York (G-12668)
Yong Ji Productions Inc .... E 917 559-4616
  Corona (G-4010)

CLOTHING: Coats, Leatherette, Oiled Fabric, Etc, Mens & Boys

House Pearl Fashions (us) Ltd .... F 212 840-3183
  New York (G-10521)

CLOTHING: Coats, Overcoats & Vests

Philipp Plein Madison Ave LLC ... F 212 644-3304
  New York (G-11646)

CLOTHING: Coats, Tailored, Mens/Boys, From Purchased Mtls

Blueduck Trading Ltd .... G 212 268-3122
  New York (G-9424)

PRODUCT SECTION

CLOTHING: Furs

CLOTHING: Cold Weather Knit Outerwear, Including Ski Wear

Kc Collections LLC ....G...... 212 302-4412
 New York *(G-10826)*

CLOTHING: Corset Access, Clasps & Stays

Higgins Supply Company Inc ....D...... 607 836-6474
 Mc Graw *(G-8222)*

CLOTHING: Costumes

Costume Culture By Franco LLC ....F...... 718 821-7100
 Glendale *(G-5649)*
Creative Costume Co ....G...... 212 564-5552
 New York *(G-9748)*
Cygnet Studio Inc ....F...... 646 450-4550
 New York *(G-9776)*
Diamond Collection LLC ....E...... 718 846-1008
 Richmond Hill *(G-14071)*
Eric Winterling Inc ....E...... 212 629-7686
 New York *(G-10056)*
John Kristiansen New York Inc ....F...... 212 388-1097
 New York *(G-10750)*
Kidz Concepts LLC ....D...... 212 398-1110
 New York *(G-10842)*
Kiton Building Corp ....E...... 212 486-3224
 New York *(G-10855)*
Koon Enterprises LLC ....G...... 718 886-3163
 Fresh Meadows *(G-5442)*
Moresca Clothing and Costume ....F...... 845 331-6012
 Ulster Park *(G-16286)*
Rubies Costume Company Inc ....B...... 718 846-1008
 Richmond Hill *(G-14081)*
Rubies Costume Company Inc ....D...... 631 777-3300
 Bay Shore *(G-741)*
Rubies Costume Company Inc ....C...... 718 441-0834
 Richmond Hill *(G-14082)*
Rubies Costume Company Inc ....C...... 631 951-3688
 Bay Shore *(G-742)*
Rubies Costume Company Inc ....E...... 516 326-1500
 Melville *(G-8354)*
Rubies Costume Company Inc ....C...... 718 846-1008
 Richmond Hill *(G-14083)*
South Central Boyz ....G...... 718 496-7270
 Brooklyn *(G-2586)*

CLOTHING: Diaper Covers, Waterproof, From Purchased Material

Hercules Group Inc ....E...... 212 813-8000
 Port Washington *(G-13821)*

CLOTHING: Disposable

A Lunt Design Inc ....F...... 716 662-0781
 Orchard Park *(G-13250)*
Cortland Industries Inc ....F...... 212 575-2710
 New York *(G-9728)*
Dvf Studio LLC ....D...... 212 741-6607
 New York *(G-9942)*
HB Athletic Inc ....F...... 914 560-8422
 New Rochelle *(G-8910)*
Hpk Industries LLC ....F...... 315 724-0196
 Utica *(G-16338)*
Lakeland Industries Inc ....C...... 631 981-9700
 Ronkonkoma *(G-14928)*
Rainforest Apparel LLC ....G...... 212 840-0880
 New York *(G-11789)*

CLOTHING: Down-Filled, Men's & Boys'

Nyc Idol Apparel Inc ....G...... 212 997-9797
 New York *(G-11479)*

CLOTHING: Dresses

18 Rocks LLC ....E...... 631 465-9990
 Melville *(G-8287)*
A & M Rosenthal Entps Inc ....F...... 646 638-9600
 New York *(G-8981)*
Agi Brooks Production Co Inc ....F...... 212 268-1533
 New York *(G-9056)*
Allison Che Fashion Inc ....F...... 212 391-1433
 New York *(G-9091)*
Anna Sui Corp ....E...... 212 768-1951
 New York *(G-9164)*
Arteast LLC ....G...... 212 965-8787
 New York *(G-9216)*
Bangla Clothing USA Inc ....G...... 201 679-2615
 New York *(G-9314)*

Cachet Industries Inc ....E...... 212 944-2188
 New York *(G-9495)*
Cheri Pink Inc ....E...... 212 869-1948
 New York *(G-9590)*
Christian Siriano Holdings LLC ....G...... 212 695-5494
 New York *(G-9611)*
Csco LLC ....E...... 212 221-5100
 New York *(G-9762)*
CTS LLC ....G...... 212 278-0058
 New York *(G-9763)*
Cynthia Rowley Inc ....F...... 212 242-3803
 New York *(G-9777)*
Dalma Dress Mfg Co Inc ....E...... 212 391-8296
 Greenvale *(G-5880)*
Damianou Sportswear Inc ....D...... 718 204-5600
 Woodside *(G-17325)*
Dave & Johnny Ltd ....E...... 212 302-9050
 New York *(G-9816)*
Donna Karan Company LLC ....C...... 212 789-1500
 New York *(G-9900)*
Donna Karan Company LLC ....C...... 716 297-0752
 Niagara Falls *(G-12811)*
Donna Karan Company LLC ....B...... 212 789-1500
 New York *(G-9901)*
Donna Karan International Inc ....A...... 212 789-1500
 New York *(G-9902)*
Donna Karan International Inc ....G...... 212 768-5800
 New York *(G-9903)*
Elana Laderos Ltd ....F...... 212 764-0840
 New York *(G-9993)*
Faviana International Inc ....E...... 212 594-4422
 New York *(G-10147)*
Four Seasons Fashion Mfg Inc ....E...... 212 947-6820
 New York *(G-10192)*
G-III Apparel Group Ltd ....E...... 212 403-0500
 New York *(G-10235)*
Geoffrey Beene Inc ....E...... 212 371-5570
 New York *(G-10279)*
Haddad Bros Inc ....E...... 718 377-5505
 Brooklyn *(G-2061)*
Halmode Apparel Inc ....A...... 212 819-9114
 New York *(G-10398)*
Haute By Blair Stanley LLC ....E...... 212 557-7868
 New York *(G-10426)*
I S C A Corp ....F...... 212 719-5123
 New York *(G-10541)*
Icer Scrubs LLC ....F...... 212 221-4700
 New York *(G-10551)*
Infinity Sourcing Services LLC ....G...... 212 868-2900
 New York *(G-10594)*
J R Nites ....G...... 212 354-9670
 New York *(G-10682)*
Jiranimo Industries Ltd ....F...... 212 921-5106
 New York *(G-10737)*
Jlnw Inc ....D...... 212 719-4666
 Long Island City *(G-7771)*
Jon Teri Sports Inc ....E...... 212 398-0657
 New York *(G-10756)*
Jovani Fashion Ltd ....E...... 212 279-0222
 New York *(G-10772)*
Judys Group Inc ....E...... 212 921-0515
 New York *(G-10779)*
Jump Design Group Inc ....C...... 212 869-3300
 New York *(G-10786)*
Kasper Group LLC ....C...... 212 354-4311
 New York *(G-10815)*
Kelly Grace Corp ....D...... 212 704-9603
 New York *(G-10830)*
Krasner Group Inc ....G...... 212 268-4100
 New York *(G-10886)*
L F Fashion Orient Intl Co Ltd ....G...... 917 667-3398
 New York *(G-10901)*
Lavish Layette Inc ....G...... 516 256-9130
 Cedarhurst *(G-3458)*
Lm Mignon LLC ....F...... 212 730-9221
 New York *(G-11017)*
Lou Sally Fashions Corp ....E...... 212 354-9670
 New York *(G-11047)*
Lou Sally Fashions Corp ....E...... 212 354-1283
 New York *(G-11048)*
Melwood Partners Inc ....G...... 516 307-8030
 Garden City *(G-5521)*
Michael Vollbracht LLC ....F...... 212 753-0123
 New York *(G-11250)*
Milliore Fashion Inc ....G...... 212 302-0001
 New York *(G-11270)*
Necessary Objects Ltd ....E...... 212 334-9888
 New York *(G-11365)*
Pat & Rose Dress Inc ....D...... 212 279-1357
 New York *(G-11578)*

Patra Ltd ....F...... 212 764-6575
 New York *(G-11581)*
Phoebe Company LLC ....D...... 212 302-5556
 New York *(G-11650)*
Plugg LLC ....F...... 212 840-6655
 New York *(G-11678)*
Product Development Intl LLC ....G...... 212 279-6170
 New York *(G-11727)*
Quality Pattern Corp ....D...... 212 704-0355
 New York *(G-11768)*
R & M Richards Inc ....D...... 212 921-8820
 New York *(G-11781)*
Ralph Lauren Corporation ....F...... 212 221-7751
 New York *(G-11795)*
Raven New York LLC ....G...... 212 584-9690
 New York *(G-11803)*
Rogan LLC ....G...... 212 680-1407
 New York *(G-11904)*
Rogan LLC ....E...... 646 496-9339
 New York *(G-11905)*
Ronni Nicole Group LLC ....E...... 212 764-1000
 New York *(G-11913)*
Sg Nyc LLC ....E...... 310 210-1837
 New York *(G-12034)*
Skinz Inc ....E...... 516 593-3139
 Lynbrook *(G-7962)*
Spencer AB Inc ....G...... 646 831-3728
 New York *(G-12160)*
SSG Fashions Ltd ....G...... 212 221-0933
 New York *(G-12179)*
Studio Krp LLC ....G...... 310 589-5777
 New York *(G-12220)*
Style Partners Inc ....F...... 212 904-1499
 New York *(G-12223)*
Tabrisse Collections Inc ....F...... 212 921-1014
 New York *(G-12270)*
Tahari ASL LLC ....B...... 212 763-2800
 New York *(G-12272)*
Texport Fabrics Corp ....F...... 212 226-6066
 New York *(G-12305)*
Therese The Childrens Collectn ....G...... 518 346-2315
 Schenectady *(G-15305)*
Tom & Linda Platt Inc ....F...... 212 221-7208
 New York *(G-12359)*
Turn On Products Inc ....F...... 212 764-4545
 New York *(G-12427)*
Vanity Room Inc ....F...... 212 921-7154
 New York *(G-12503)*
Wear Abouts Apparel Inc ....F...... 212 827-0888
 New York *(G-12602)*
Worth Collection Ltd ....E...... 212 268-0312
 New York *(G-12665)*
Yeohlee Inc ....F...... 212 631-8099
 New York *(G-12690)*

CLOTHING: Dresses & Skirts

Betsy & Adam Ltd ....E...... 212 302-3750
 New York *(G-9378)*

CLOTHING: Dresses, Knit

Summit Apparel Inc ....F...... 631 213-8299
 Hauppauge *(G-6202)*
Winter Water Factory ....G...... 646 387-3247
 Brooklyn *(G-2761)*

CLOTHING: Dressing Gowns, Mens/Womens, From Purchased Matls

Jisan Trading Corporation ....E...... 212 244-1269
 New York *(G-10738)*
Mata Fashions LLC ....G...... 917 716-7894
 New York *(G-11176)*
Sketch Studio Trading Inc ....G...... 212 244-2875
 New York *(G-12090)*

CLOTHING: Foundation Garments, Women's

Deunall Corporation ....C...... 516 667-8875
 Levittown *(G-7427)*
E P Sewing Pleating Inc ....E...... 212 967-2575
 New York *(G-9951)*
Rago Foundations LLC ....D...... 718 728-8436
 Astoria *(G-454)*

CLOTHING: Furs

Alexis & Gianni Retail Inc ....F...... 516 334-3877
 Westbury *(G-16964)*
Anastasia Furs International 212 868-9241
 New York *(G-9150)*

Employee Codes: A=Over 500 employees, B=251-500
C=101-250, D=51-100, E=20-50, F=10-19, G=5-9

CLOTHING: Furs

Avante	G	516	782-4888
Great Neck *(G-5793)*			
B Smith Furs Inc	F	212	967-5290
New York *(G-9293)*			
Dennis Basso Couture Inc	F	212	794-4500
New York *(G-9846)*			
Georgy Creative Fashions Inc	G	212	279-4885
New York *(G-10284)*			
Miller & Berkowitz Ltd	F	212	244-5459
New York *(G-11268)*			
Sekas International Ltd	F	212	629-6095
New York *(G-12021)*			
Stefan Furs Inc	G	212	594-2788
New York *(G-12191)*			
Tom Moriber Furs Inc	F	212	244-2180
New York *(G-12363)*			

CLOTHING: Garments, Indl, Men's & Boys

Beardslee Realty	G	516 747-5557
Mineola *(G-8497)*		
Intermedia Outdoors Inc	D	212 852-6600
New York *(G-10629)*		
Starmark Apparel Inc	E	212 967-6347
New York *(G-12187)*		
Stealth Inc	F	718 252-7900
Brooklyn *(G-2602)*		

CLOTHING: Girdles & Other Foundation Garments, Knit

Maidenform LLC	F	201 436-9200
New York *(G-11110)*		

CLOTHING: Girdles & Panty Girdles

Burlen Corp	F	212 684-0052
New York *(G-9480)*		

CLOTHING: Gloves, Knit, Exc Dress & Semidress

Hawkins Fabrics Inc	E	518 773-9550
Gloversville *(G-5714)*		

CLOTHING: Gowns & Dresses, Wedding

Alvina Vlenta Couture Collectn	F	212 921-7058
New York *(G-9107)*		
Alvina Vlenta Couture Collectn	E	212 921-7058
New York *(G-9108)*		
Arcangel Inc	G	347 771-0789
New York *(G-9194)*		
Bernard Chaus Inc	D	212 354-1280
New York *(G-9364)*		
Birnbaum & Bullock Inc	G	212 242-2914
New York *(G-9403)*		
Christos Inc	E	212 921-0025
New York *(G-9614)*		
Couture Inc	G	212 921-1166
New York *(G-9738)*		
Diamond Bridal Collection Ltd	E	212 302-0210
New York *(G-9870)*		
Everlasting Memories	G	716 833-1111
Blasdell *(G-962)*		
Jlm Couture Inc	D	212 921-7058
New York *(G-10741)*		
Paris Wedding Center Corp	G	347 368-4085
Flushing *(G-5279)*		
Paris Wedding Center Corp	E	212 267-8088
New York *(G-11573)*		
Parsley Apparel Corp	E	631 981-7181
Ronkonkoma *(G-14965)*		
Paula Varsalona Ltd	F	212 570-9100
New York *(G-11586)*		

CLOTHING: Gowns, Formal

Amsale Aberra LLC	E	212 695-5936
New York *(G-9140)*		
Bari-Jay Fashions Inc	E	212 921-1551
New York *(G-9321)*		
Crisada Inc	G	718 729-9730
Long Island City *(G-7707)*		
D J Night Ltd	E	212 302-9050
New York *(G-9783)*		
Elizabeth Fillmore LLC	G	212 647-0863
New York *(G-10009)*		
Lily & Taylor Inc	F	212 564-5459
New York *(G-10997)*		
Patra Ltd	F	212 764-6575
New York *(G-11580)*		
Patra Ltd	E	212 764-6575
New York *(G-11582)*		
Pronovias USA Inc	E	212 897-6393
New York *(G-11733)*		
Ursula of Switzerland Inc	E	518 237-2580
Waterford *(G-16623)*		

CLOTHING: Hats & Caps, Leather

J Lowy Co	G	718 338-7324
Brooklyn *(G-2124)*		

CLOTHING: Hats & Caps, NEC

A-1 Skull Cap Corp	E	718 633-9333
Brooklyn *(G-1539)*		
Athletic Cap Co Inc	E	718 398-1300
Staten Island *(G-15641)*		
Genesco Inc	G	585 227-3080
Rochester *(G-14393)*		
Lids Corporation	E	718 338-7790
Brooklyn *(G-2218)*		
Paletot Ltd	F	212 268-3774
New York *(G-11555)*		
W & M Headwear Co Inc	E	718 768-2222
Brooklyn *(G-2739)*		

CLOTHING: Hats & Caps, Uniform

Bonk Sam Uniforms Civilian Cap	E	718 585-0665
Bronx *(G-1286)*		
Hankin Brothers Cap Co	F	716 892-8840
Buffalo *(G-2987)*		
Kays Caps Inc	G	518 273-6079
Troy *(G-16221)*		
Kingform Cap Company Inc	D	516 822-2501
Hicksville *(G-6358)*		
New ERA Cap Co Inc	B	716 604-9000
Buffalo *(G-3084)*		
New ERA Cap Co Inc	C	716 604-9000
Buffalo *(G-3085)*		
New ERA Cap Co Inc	E	716 549-0445
Derby *(G-4284)*		
Tanen Cap Co	F	212 254-7100
Brooklyn *(G-2645)*		

CLOTHING: Hats & Headwear, Knit

Gce International Inc	D	212 704-4800
New York *(G-10259)*		
Lids Corporation	G	518 459-7060
Albany *(G-97)*		

CLOTHING: Hosiery, Men's & Boys'

Etc Hosiery & Underwear Ltd	G	212 947-5151
New York *(G-10076)*		
Gina Group LLC	E	212 947-2445
New York *(G-10298)*		
Haddad Hosiery LLC	G	212 251-0022
New York *(G-10394)*		
High Point Design LLC	F	212 354-2400
New York *(G-10472)*		
Leg Resource Inc	E	212 736-4574
New York *(G-10961)*		
New Hampton Creations Inc	G	212 244-7474
New York *(G-11389)*		
Richard Edelson	G	914 428-7573
Hartsdale *(G-5999)*		
Spartan Brands Inc	F	212 340-0320
New York *(G-12150)*		
You and ME Legwear LLC	F	212 279-9292
New York *(G-12698)*		

CLOTHING: Hosiery, Pantyhose & Knee Length, Sheer

Classic Hosiery Inc	E	845 342-6661
Middletown *(G-8431)*		
Ellis Products Corp	G	516 791-3732
Valley Stream *(G-16405)*		
Gina Group LLC	E	212 947-2445
New York *(G-10298)*		
Horizon Imports Inc	D	212 239-8660
New York *(G-10506)*		
Hot Sox Company Incorporated	E	212 957-2000
New York *(G-10514)*		

CLOTHING: Hospital, Men's

Adar Medical Uniform LLC	G	718 935-1197
Brooklyn *(G-1560)*		

Eighteen Liana Trading Inc	E	718 369-4247
New York *(G-9989)*		
Norcorp Inc	E	914 666-1310
Mount Kisco *(G-8637)*		

CLOTHING: Housedresses

Fashion Deli Inc	F	818 772-5637
New York *(G-10144)*		
Millennium Productions Inc	F	212 944-6203
New York *(G-11267)*		

CLOTHING: Jackets & Vests, Exc Fur & Leather, Women's

Amerimade Coat Inc	G	212 216-0925
New York *(G-9133)*		
Donna Karan International Inc	A	212 789-1500
New York *(G-9902)*		
Donna Karan International Inc	E	212 768-5800
New York *(G-9903)*		
Standard Manufacturing Co Inc	D	518 235-2200
Troy *(G-16256)*		
Tiger J LLC	E	212 764-5624
New York *(G-12339)*		

CLOTHING: Jackets, Knit

Freedom Rains Inc	G	646 710-4512
New York *(G-10206)*		

CLOTHING: Jeans, Men's & Boys'

Guess Inc	E	845 928-3930
Central Valley *(G-3524)*		
Guess Inc	E	315 539-5634
Waterloo *(G-16628)*		
Guess Inc	E	212 286-9856
New York *(G-10379)*		
Guess Inc	E	716 298-3561
Niagara Falls *(G-12830)*		
Messex Group Inc	G	646 229-2582
New York *(G-11240)*		
One Jeanswear Group Inc	E	212 835-2500
New York *(G-11506)*		

CLOTHING: Knit Underwear & Nightwear

In Toon Amkor Fashions Inc	E	718 937-4546
Long Island City *(G-7765)*		
Jockey International Inc	E	212 840-4900
New York *(G-10746)*		
Maidenform LLC	F	201 436-9200
New York *(G-11110)*		
Native Textiles Inc	E	212 951-5100
New York *(G-11354)*		
Spartan Brands Inc	F	212 340-0320
New York *(G-12150)*		

CLOTHING: Leather

Avanti U S A Ltd	F	716 695-5800
Tonawanda *(G-16141)*		
Dada Group US Inc	G	631 888-0818
Bayside *(G-769)*		
G-III Apparel Group Ltd	C	212 403-0500
New York *(G-10234)*		
Georgy Creative Fashions Inc	G	212 279-4885
New York *(G-10284)*		
Louis Schwartz	G	845 356-6624
Spring Valley *(G-15593)*		
Studio One Leather Design Inc	F	212 760-1701
New York *(G-12221)*		

CLOTHING: Leather & sheep-lined clothing

Cockpit Usa Inc	F	908 558-9704
New York *(G-9663)*		
G-III Leather Fashions Inc	E	212 403-0500
New York *(G-10236)*		

CLOTHING: Leg Warmers

Z Best Printing Inc	F	631 595-1400
Deer Park *(G-4230)*		

CLOTHING: Maternity

Medi-Tech International Corp	G	800 333-0109
Brooklyn *(G-2291)*		
Zoomers Inc	E	718 369-2656
Brooklyn *(G-2782)*		

PRODUCT SECTION

CLOTHING: Outerwear, Women's & Misses' NEC

CLOTHING: Men's & boy's clothing, nec

Company	Code	Phone
Apogee Retail NY, Levittown (G-7423)	G	516 731-1727
By Robert James, New York (G-9485)	G	212 253-2121
Eon Collections, New York (G-10048)	E	212 695-1263
Must USA Inc, New York (G-11328)	G	212 391-8288
Nevaeh Jeans Company, New York (G-11377)	G	845 641-4255
Piaget, New York (G-11656)	F	212 355-6444

CLOTHING: Men's & boy's underwear & nightwear

Company	Code	Phone
Apparel Partnership Group LLC, New York (G-9178)	G	212 302-7722
Christian Casey LLC, New York (G-9608)	E	212 500-2200
Christian Casey LLC, New York (G-9609)	E	212 500-2200
Solo Licensing Corp, New York (G-12125)	G	212 244-5505
Tommy John Inc, New York (G-12366)	E	800 708-3490
Waterbury Garment LLC, New York (G-12597)	E	212 725-1500

CLOTHING: Mens & Boys Jackets, Sport, Suede, Leatherette

Company	Code	Phone
Broadway Knitting Mills Inc, North Tonawanda (G-12961)	G	716 692-4421
G-III Apparel Group Ltd, New York (G-10234)	C	212 403-0500
Standard Manufacturing Co Inc, Troy (G-16256)	D	518 235-2200

CLOTHING: Millinery

Company	Code	Phone
Albrizio Inc, Brooklyn (G-1577)	G	212 719-5290
Lenore Marshall Inc, New York (G-10967)	G	212 947-5945
Lloyds Fashions Inc, Brentwood (G-1190)	D	631 435-3353

CLOTHING: Neckties, Knit

Company	Code	Phone
Mongru Neckwear Inc, Long Island City (G-7816)	E	718 706-0406

CLOTHING: Neckwear

Company	Code	Phone
Fogel Neckwear Corp, New York (G-10184)	D	212 686-7673
JS Blank & Co Inc, New York (G-10776)	E	212 689-4835
MANE Enterprises Inc, Long Island City (G-7801)	D	718 472-4955
Mongru Neckwear Inc, Long Island City (G-7816)	E	718 706-0406
Roffe Accessories Inc, New York (G-11903)	F	212 213-1440
S Broome and Co Inc, Long Island City (G-7870)	D	718 663-6800
Selini Neckwear Inc, New York (G-12026)	G	212 268-5488
Tie View Neckwear Co Inc, Brooklyn (G-2660)	G	718 853-4156
Valenti Neckwear Co Inc, Yonkers (G-17494)	G	914 969-0700
W B Bow Tie Corp, New York (G-12572)	F	212 683-6130
Warnaco Inc, New York (G-12587)	B	212 287-8000
Wetherall Contracting NY Inc, Middle Village (G-8417)	G	718 894-7011

CLOTHING: Outerwear, Knit

Company	Code	Phone
Alpha Knitting Mills Inc, Brooklyn (G-1594)	F	718 628-6300
Andrea Strongwater, New York (G-9154)	G	212 873-0905
Asian Global Trading Corp, Long Island City (G-7672)	F	718 786-0998
Binghamton Knitting Co Inc, Binghamton (G-892)	E	607 722-6941

CLOTHING: Outerwear, Lthr, Wool/Down-Filled, Men, Youth/Boy

Company	Code	Phone
Brigantine Inc, New York (G-9459)	G	212 354-8550
Herman Kay Company Ltd, New York (G-10462)	C	212 239-2025
I Spiewak & Sons Inc, New York (G-10542)	E	212 695-1620
Maiyet Inc, New York (G-11113)	G	646 602-0000
Rainforest Inc, New York (G-11790)	F	212 575-7620
Vf Outdoor Inc, Staten Island (G-15753)	E	718 698-6215
Vf Outdoor LLC, Central Valley (G-3528)	E	845 928-4900

CLOTHING: Outerwear, Women's & Misses' NEC

Company	Code	Phone
525 America LLC, New York (G-8978)	G	212 840-1313
5th & Ocean Clothing Inc, Buffalo (G-2790)	C	716 604-9000
6th Avenue Showcase Inc, New York (G-8979)	G	212 382-0400
A & B Finishing Inc, Brooklyn (G-1525)	E	718 522-4702
Accessory Street LLC, New York (G-9012)	F	212 686-8990
Alleson of Rochester Inc, Rochester (G-14187)	D	585 272-0630
Angel-Made In Heaven Inc, Brooklyn (G-1612)	G	718 832-4778
Aura International Mfg Inc, New York (G-9262)	G	212 719-1418
Bagznyc Corp, New York (G-9305)	F	212 643-8202
Bank-Miller Co Inc, Pelham (G-13489)	E	914 227-9357
Big Bang Clothing Inc, New York (G-9393)	G	212 221-0379
Canada Goose Us Inc, Williamsville (G-17238)	G	303 832-7097
Carolina Herrera Ltd, New York (G-9535)	E	212 944-5757
Central Mills Inc, New York (G-9565)	C	212 221-0748
Cheri Pink Inc, New York (G-9590)	E	212 869-1948
China Ting Fashion Group (usa), New York (G-9602)	G	212 716-1600
Dressy Tessy Inc, New York (G-9927)	G	212 869-0750
E I Du Pont De Nemours & Co, Buffalo (G-2924)	E	716 876-4420
Elegant Headwear Co Inc, New York (G-9998)	G	212 695-8520
Emerald Holdings Inc, Brooklyn (G-1918)	F	718 797-4404
Fashion Avenue Knits Inc, New York (G-10142)	F	718 456-9000
Fast-Trac Entertainment Ltd, New York (G-10146)	G	888 758-8886
Gabani Inc, Southampton (G-15544)	G	631 283-4930
GAME Sportswear Ltd, Yorktown Heights (G-17511)	E	914 962-1701
Gildan Apparel USA Inc, New York (G-10295)	D	212 476-0341
Hamil America Inc, New York (G-10400)	F	212 244-2645
Hania By Anya Cole LLC, New York (G-10408)	E	212 302-3550
Lynch Knitting Mills Inc, Brooklyn (G-2241)	E	718 821-3436
Mars Fashions Inc, Bronx (G-1387)	E	718 402-2200
Mdj Sales Associates Inc, Mamaroneck (G-8039)	G	914 420-5897
Native Textiles Inc, New York (G-11354)	E	212 951-5100
North Star Knitting Mills Inc, Glendale (G-5660)	G	718 894-4848
S & V Knits Inc, Farmingdale (G-5106)	E	631 752-1595
T & R Knitting Mills Inc, New York (G-12265)	F	212 840-8665
Comint Apparel Group LLC, New York (G-9683)	F	212 947-7474
Consolidated Fashion Corp, New York (G-9705)	G	212 719-3000
Cynthia Rowley Inc, New York (G-9777)	F	212 242-3803
Dalma Dress Mfg Co Inc, Greenvale (G-5880)	E	212 391-8296
Dana Michele LLC, New York (G-9798)	G	917 757-7777
Dani II Inc, New York (G-9802)	F	212 869-5999
Design For All LLC, New York (G-9852)	E	212 523-0021
Donna Karan International Inc, New York (G-9902)	A	212 789-1500
Donna Karan International Inc, New York (G-9903)	E	212 768-5800
Elie Tahari Ltd, New York (G-10002)	D	212 398-2622
Emerald Holdings Inc, Brooklyn (G-1918)	E	718 797-4404
Falls Manufacturing Inc, Philmont (G-13540)	G	518 672-7189
Fieldston Clothes Inc, New York (G-10161)	E	212 354-8550
Four Seasons Fashion Mfg Inc, New York (G-10192)	E	212 947-6820
G-III Apparel Group Ltd, New York (G-10234)	C	212 403-0500
G-III Leather Fashions Inc, New York (G-10236)	E	212 403-0500
GAME Sportswear Ltd, Yorktown Heights (G-17511)	E	914 962-1701
Golden Leaves Knitwear Inc, Brooklyn (G-2038)	E	718 875-8235
Golden Season Fashion USA Inc, New York (G-10335)	F	212 268-6048
Hana Sportswear Inc, Dexter (G-4285)	E	315 639-6332
Herman Kay Company Ltd, New York (G-10462)	C	212 239-2025
Hot Line Industries Inc, Plainview (G-13605)	F	516 764-0400
House Pearl Fashions (us) Ltd, New York (G-10521)	F	212 840-3183
Idra Alta Moda LLC, New York (G-10558)	E	914 644-8202
Int Trading USA LLC, New York (G-10614)	C	212 760-2338
Isabel Toledo Enterprises Inc, New York (G-10666)	G	212 685-0948
J Percy For Mrvin Rchards Ltd, New York (G-10680)	E	212 944-5300
Jesse Joeckel, Montauk (G-8588)	G	631 668-2772
Jomat New York Inc, Brooklyn (G-2146)	E	718 369-7641
Just Bottoms & Tops Inc, New York (G-10791)	F	212 564-3202
Karen Kane Inc, New York (G-10810)	F	212 827-0980
Kasper Group LLC, New York (G-10814)	F	212 354-4311
Lahoya Enterprise Inc, College Point (G-3794)	E	718 886-8799
Land n Sea Inc, New York (G-10923)	D	212 703-2980
Lemral Knitwear Inc, Brooklyn (G-2210)	D	718 210-0175
Lgb Inc, New York (G-10982)	E	212 278-8280
Liberty Apparel Company Inc, New York (G-10983)	F	212 221-0101
Liberty Apparel Company Inc, New York (G-10984)	E	718 625-4000
Light Inc, New York (G-10991)	G	212 629-1095
Lily & Taylor Inc, New York (G-10997)	F	212 564-5459
Luxe Imagine Consulting LLC, New York (G-11066)	G	212 273-9770
M A M Knitting Mills Corp, Brooklyn (G-2246)	E	800 570-0093
Machinit Inc, Farmingdale (G-5039)	G	631 454-9297
Maggy Boutique Ltd, New York (G-11101)	E	212 997-5222
Maiyet Inc, New York (G-11113)	G	646 602-0000

Employee Codes: A=Over 500 employees, B=251-500
C=101-250, D=51-100, E=20-50, F=10-19, G=5-9

2017 Harris
New York Manufacturers Directory

CLOTHING: Outerwear, Women's & Misses' NEC

Manchu New York Inc ....G 212 921-5050
  New York (G-11125)
Manchu Times Fashion Inc ....G 212 921-5050
  New York (G-11126)
Marconi Intl USA Co Ltd ....G 212 391-2626
  New York (G-11146)
Marina Holding Corp ....F 718 646-9283
  Brooklyn (G-2269)
Meskita Lifestyle Brands LLC ....E 212 695-5054
  New York (G-11238)
Miguelina Inc ....G 212 925-0320
  New York (G-11262)
Miltons of New York Inc ....G 212 997-3359
  New York (G-11272)
Moes Wear Apparel Inc ....F 718 940-1597
  Brooklyn (G-2328)
Mv Corp Inc ....C 631 273-8020
  Bay Shore (G-720)
Mystic Inc ....D 212 239-2025
  New York (G-11334)
New York Knitting Processor ....G 718 366-3469
  Ridgewood (G-14115)
Only Hearts Ltd ....E 718 783-3218
  New York (G-11511)
Outerstuff LLC ....E 212 594-9700
  New York (G-11536)
Pacific Alliance Usa Inc ....G 336 500-8184
  New York (G-11551)
Pacific Alliance Usa Inc ....E 646 839-7000
  New York (G-11552)
Pat & Rose Dress Inc ....D 212 279-1357
  New York (G-11578)
Perry Ellis International Inc ....G 212 536-5499
  New York (G-11623)
Petrunia LLC ....G 607 277-1930
  Ithaca (G-6869)
Pleating Plus Ltd ....F 201 863-2991
  Orangeburg (G-13240)
Primo Coat Corp ....E 718 349-2070
  Long Island City (G-7847)
Pti-Pacific Inc ....G 212 414-8495
  New York (G-11744)
Pvh Corp ....D 212 502-6300
  New York (G-11758)
Ralph Lauren Corporation ....G 917 934-4200
  New York (G-11794)
RD Intrntnl Style ....G 212 382-2360
  New York (G-11810)
Republic Clothing Corporation ....E 212 719-3000
  New York (G-11836)
Rogers Group Inc ....E 212 643-9292
  New York (G-11907)
Rvc Enterprises LLC ....E 212 391-4600
  New York (G-11939)
S & V Knits Inc ....E 631 752-1595
  Farmingdale (G-5106)
S & W Knitting Mills Inc ....F 718 237-2416
  Brooklyn (G-2524)
Smooth Industries Incorporated ....E 212 869-1080
  New York (G-12109)
Standard Manufacturing Co Inc ....D 518 235-2200
  Troy (G-16256)
Sunynams Fashions Ltd ....G 212 268-5200
  New York (G-12240)
Survival Inc ....G 631 385-5060
  Centerport (G-3481)
Tbhl International LLC ....F 212 799-2007
  New York (G-12282)
THE Design Group Inc ....F 212 681-1548
  New York (G-12309)
Tiger J LLC ....E 212 764-5624
  New York (G-12339)
Vf Imagewear Inc ....E 718 352-2363
  Bayside (G-778)
Vf Outdoor LLC ....E 845 928-4900
  Central Valley (G-3528)
Warnaco Group Inc ....D 212 287-8000
  New York (G-12586)
Yigal-Azrouel Inc ....E 212 302-1194
  New York (G-12691)
Zar Group LLC ....C 212 944-2510
  New York (G-12703)
Zia Power Inc ....E 845 661-8388
  New York (G-12712)

CLOTHING: Overcoats & Topcoats, Men/Boy, Purchased Materials

Ralph Lauren Corporation ....B 212 318-7000
  New York (G-11792)

CLOTHING: Pants, Work, Men's, Youths' & Boys'

Ace Drop Cloth Canvas Pdts Inc ....E 718 731-1550
  Bronx (G-1260)

CLOTHING: Panty Hose

Brach Knitting Mills Inc ....F 845 651-4450
  Florida (G-5210)
Fine Sheer Industries Inc ....F 212 594-4224
  New York (G-10164)

CLOTHING: Raincoats, Exc Vulcanized Rubber, Purchased Matls

Levy Group Inc ....C 212 398-0707
  New York (G-10979)

CLOTHING: Robes & Dressing Gowns

Komar Luxury Brands ....G 646 472-0060
  New York (G-10875)
Lady Ester Lingerie Corp ....E 212 689-1729
  New York (G-10914)
Palmbay Ltd ....G 718 424-3388
  Woodside (G-17345)

CLOTHING: Robes & Housecoats, Children's

Waterbury Garment LLC ....E 212 725-1500
  New York (G-12597)

CLOTHING: Scarves & Mufflers, Knit

180s LLC ....E 410 534-6320
  New York (G-8961)

CLOTHING: Service Apparel, Women's

Bestec Concept Inc ....G 718 937-5848
  Long Island City (G-7683)
Chloe International Inc ....F 212 730-6661
  New York (G-9603)
Fashion Ave Sweater Knits LLC ....D 212 302-8282
  New York (G-10141)
GMC Mercantile Corp ....F 212 498-9488
  New York (G-10324)
HC Contracting Inc ....D 212 643-9292
  New York (G-10433)
Jsc Designs Ltd ....E 212 302-1001
  New York (G-10778)
Lotus Apparel Designs Inc ....G 646 236-9363
  Westbury (G-17007)
Mag Brands LLC ....D 212 629-9600
  New York (G-11097)
PLC Apparel LLC ....G 212 239-3434
  New York (G-11676)
RAK Finishing Corp ....E 718 416-4242
  Howard Beach (G-6598)

CLOTHING: Shawls, Knit

Lloyds Fashions Inc ....D 631 435-3353
  Brentwood (G-1190)

CLOTHING: Sheep-Lined

US Authentic LLC ....G 914 767-0295
  Katonah (G-7134)

CLOTHING: Shirts

Ben Wachter Associates Inc ....G 212 736-4064
  New York (G-9354)
Bowe Industries Inc ....D 718 441-6464
  Glendale (G-5646)
Bowe Industries Inc ....D 718 441-6464
  Glendale (G-5647)
Check Group LLC ....D 212 221-4700
  New York (G-9587)
Christian Casey LLC ....E 212 500-2200
  New York (G-9608)
Christian Casey LLC ....E 212 500-2200
  New York (G-9609)
Colony Holdings Intl LLC ....F 212 868-2800
  New York (G-9671)
Cyberlimit Inc ....F 212 840-9597
  New York (G-9775)
Donna Karan International Inc ....A 212 789-5500
  New York (G-9902)
Donna Karan International Inc ....G 212 768-5800
  New York (G-9903)
Garan Incorporated ....C 212 563-1292
  New York (G-10248)
Garan Manufacturing Corp ....G 212 563-2000
  New York (G-10249)
Gbg National Brands Group LLC ....G 646 839-7000
  New York (G-10252)
Groupe 16sur20 LLC ....F 212 625-1620
  New York (G-10372)
Haddad Bros Inc ....F 212 563-2117
  New York (G-10393)
Interbrand LLC ....E 212 840-9595
  New York (G-10624)
Jordache Enterprises Inc ....D 212 944-1330
  New York (G-10760)
Jordache Enterprises Inc ....C 212 643-8400
  New York (G-10761)
Just Brass Inc ....E 212 724-5447
  New York (G-10792)
Lt2 LLC ....E 212 684-1510
  New York (G-11056)
M S B International Ltd ....F 212 302-5551
  New York (G-11076)
Miltons of New York Inc ....G 212 997-3359
  New York (G-11272)
Mulitex Usa Inc ....F 212 398-0440
  New York (G-11323)
Oxford Industries Inc ....F 212 840-2288
  New York (G-11541)
Perry Ellis International Inc ....F 212 536-5400
  New York (G-11622)
Perry Ellis Menswear LLC ....F 212 221-7500
  New York (G-11624)
Ralph Lauren Corporation ....F 212 421-1570
  New York (G-11793)
Roffe Accessories Inc ....F 212 213-1440
  New York (G-11903)
Saad Collection Inc ....F 212 937-0341
  New York (G-11949)
Schwartz Textile Converting Co ....E 718 499-8243
  Brooklyn (G-2537)
Sifonya Inc ....F 212 620-4512
  New York (G-12065)
Whittall & Shon ....G 212 594-2626
  New York (G-12629)
Yale Trouser Corporation ....F 516 255-0700
  Oceanside (G-13107)

CLOTHING: Shirts, Dress, Men's & Boys'

Americo Group Inc ....F 212 563-2700
  New York (G-9130)
Americo Group Inc ....D 212 563-2700
  New York (G-9131)
Arthur Gluck Shirtmakers Inc ....F 212 755-8165
  Brooklyn (G-1636)
Ferris USA LLC ....G 617 895-8102
  New York (G-10155)
Gce International Inc ....D 773 263-1210
  New York (G-10261)
Great Universal Corp ....F 917 302-0065
  New York (G-10359)
Phillips-Van Heusen Europe ....F 212 381-3500
  New York (G-11649)
Pvh Corp ....D 212 381-3500
  New York (G-11756)
Pvh Corp ....G 845 561-0233
  New Windsor (G-8949)
Pvh Corp ....G 631 254-8200
  Deer Park (G-4195)
Pvh Corp ....G 212 719-2600
  New York (G-11759)
Ralph Lauren Corporation ....B 212 318-7000
  New York (G-11792)
Warnaco Inc ....B 212 287-8000
  New York (G-12587)
Warnaco Inc ....F 718 722-3000
  Brooklyn (G-2744)

CLOTHING: Shirts, Knit

KD Dids Inc ....G 718 402-2012
  Bronx (G-1369)
Ralph Lauren Corporation ....B 212 318-7000
  New York (G-11792)
Warnaco Inc ....F 718 722-3000
  Brooklyn (G-2744)

CLOTHING: Shirts, Sports & Polo, Men & Boy, Purchased Mtrl

Ibrands International LLC ....F 212 354-1330
  New York (G-10547)

Sue & Sam Co Inc ... E ... 718 436-1672
Brooklyn *(G-2618)*

CLOTHING: Shirts, Women's & Juniors', From Purchased Mtrls

Brach Knitting Mills Inc ... F ... 845 651-4450
Florida *(G-5210)*
Jordache Enterprises Inc ... D ... 212 944-1330
New York *(G-10760)*
Jordache Enterprises Inc ... C ... 212 643-8400
New York *(G-10761)*

CLOTHING: Skirts

Alfred Dunner Inc ... D ... 212 478-4300
New York *(G-9084)*
Anna Sui Corp ... E ... 212 768-1951
New York *(G-9164)*
Brooke Leigh Ltd ... F ... 212 736-9098
New York *(G-9469)*
Bruno & Canio Ltd ... E ... 845 624-3060
Nanuet *(G-8753)*
Carolina Herrera Ltd ... E ... 212 944-5757
New York *(G-9535)*
Geoffrey Beene Inc ... E ... 212 371-5570
New York *(G-10279)*
Item-Eyes Inc ... D ... 631 321-0923
New York *(G-10670)*
Kayo of California ... G ... 212 354-6336
New York *(G-10823)*
Nyc Idol Apparel Inc ... G ... 212 997-9797
New York *(G-11479)*
Pat & Rose Dress Inc ... D ... 212 279-1357
New York *(G-11578)*
Permit Fashion Group Inc ... G ... 212 912-0988
New York *(G-11620)*
Rhoda Lee Inc ... D ... 212 840-5700
New York *(G-11859)*
Tenby LLC ... C ... 646 863-5890
New York *(G-12300)*
Turn On Products Inc ... F ... 212 764-4545
New York *(G-12427)*

CLOTHING: Slacks & Shorts, Dress, Men's, Youths' & Boys'

Montero International Inc ... G ... 212 695-1787
Westbury *(G-17013)*

CLOTHING: Slacks, Girls' & Children's

Garan Incorporated ... C ... 212 563-1292
New York *(G-10248)*
Garan Manufacturing Corp ... G ... 212 563-2000
New York *(G-10249)*
Jordache Enterprises Inc ... D ... 212 944-1330
New York *(G-10760)*
Jordache Enterprises Inc ... C ... 212 643-8400
New York *(G-10761)*

CLOTHING: Sleeping Garments, Women's & Children's

Allure Fashions Inc ... G ... 516 829-2470
Great Neck *(G-5789)*
Kokin Inc ... E ... 212 643-8225
New York *(G-10870)*
Komar Luxury Brands ... G ... 646 472-0060
New York *(G-10875)*
Natori Company Incorporated ... D ... 212 532-7796
New York *(G-11355)*
Richard Leeds Intl Inc ... D ... 212 532-4546
New York *(G-11862)*
Waterbury Garment LLC ... E ... 212 725-1500
New York *(G-12597)*

CLOTHING: Slipper Socks

Palmbay Ltd ... G ... 718 424-3388
Woodside *(G-17345)*

CLOTHING: Socks

Ace Drop Cloth Canvas Pdts Inc ... E ... 718 731-1550
Bronx *(G-1260)*
Ashko Group LLC ... F ... 212 594-6050
New York *(G-9229)*
Customize Elite Socks LLC ... G ... 212 533-8551
New York *(G-9772)*
Fine Sheer Industries Inc ... F ... 212 594-4224
New York *(G-10164)*
Galiva Inc ... G ... 903 600-5755
Brooklyn *(G-2012)*
Gbg Socks LLC ... E ... 646 839-7000
New York *(G-10253)*
J T Enterprises LLC ... G ... 716 433-9368
Lockport *(G-7594)*
La Strada Dance Footwear Inc ... G ... 631 242-1401
Deer Park *(G-4163)*
Socks and More of NY Inc ... G ... 718 769-1785
Brooklyn *(G-2577)*
Socks For Everyone Inc ... G ... 347 754-0210
Fresh Meadows *(G-5445)*
Sticky Socks LLC ... G ... 212 541-5927
New York *(G-12205)*

CLOTHING: Sportswear, Women's

31 Phillip Lim LLC ... E ... 212 354-6540
New York *(G-8972)*
American Apparel Trading Corp ... G ... 212 764-5990
New York *(G-9114)*
Angel-Made In Heaven Inc ... G ... 212 869-5678
New York *(G-9157)*
Argee America Inc ... G ... 212 768-9840
New York *(G-9199)*
AZ Yashir Bapaz Inc ... G ... 212 947-7357
New York *(G-9285)*
Bandit International Ltd ... F ... 718 402-2100
Bronx *(G-1280)*
Bernard Chaus Inc ... D ... 212 354-1280
New York *(G-9364)*
Bernard Chaus Inc ... C ... 646 562-4700
New York *(G-9365)*
Cathy Daniels Ltd ... E ... 212 354-8000
New York *(G-9550)*
Central Apparel Group Ltd ... F ... 212 868-6505
New York *(G-9562)*
City Sites Sportswear Inc ... E ... 718 375-2990
Brooklyn *(G-1785)*
Daily Wear Sportswear Corp ... G ... 718 972-0533
Brooklyn *(G-1834)*
Danice Stores Inc ... F ... 212 665-0389
New York *(G-9803)*
Designs By Lanie Inc ... G ... 718 945-4221
Rockaway Beach *(G-14781)*
DMD International Ltd ... D ... 212 944-7300
New York *(G-9890)*
Double Take Fashions Inc ... G ... 718 832-9000
Brooklyn *(G-1875)*
Drew Philips Corp ... G ... 212 354-0095
New York *(G-9928)*
Eileen Fisher Inc ... C ... 914 591-5700
Irvington *(G-6768)*
El-La Design Inc ... G ... 212 382-1080
New York *(G-9992)*
F & J Designs Inc ... G ... 212 302-8755
New York *(G-10114)*
French Atmosphere Inc ... G ... 516 371-9100
New York *(G-10208)*
Halmode Apparel Inc ... A ... 212 819-9114
New York *(G-10398)*
Ikeddi Enterprises Inc ... F ... 212 302-7644
New York *(G-10565)*
Ikeddi Enterprises Inc ... G ... 212 302-7644
New York *(G-10566)*
In Moda com Inc ... E ... 718 788-4466
New York *(G-10578)*
Intriguing Threads Apparel Inc ... F ... 212 768-8733
New York *(G-10647)*
J & E Talit Inc ... G ... 718 850-1333
Richmond Hill *(G-14076)*
Jaxis Inc ... G ... 212 302-7611
Brooklyn *(G-2135)*
JEnvie Sport Inc ... G ... 212 967-2322
New York *(G-10720)*
Jlnw Inc ... D ... 212 719-4666
Long Island City *(G-7771)*
Joe Benbasset Inc ... E ... 212 268-4920
New York *(G-10747)*
Jonden Manufacturing Co Inc ... G ... 516 442-4895
New York *(G-10759)*
Kayo of California ... G ... 212 354-6336
New York *(G-10823)*
Lea Apparel Inc ... G ... 718 418-2800
Glendale *(G-5657)*
Leggiadro International Inc ... E ... 212 997-8766
New York *(G-10962)*
Life Style Design Group ... E ... 212 391-8666
New York *(G-10987)*
Main Street Fashions Inc ... F ... 212 764-2613
New York *(G-11112)*
Marcasiano Inc ... G ... 212 614-9412
New York *(G-11144)*
Max Leon Inc ... F ... 845 928-8201
Central Valley *(G-3525)*
Meryl Diamond Ltd ... E ... 212 730-0333
New York *(G-11236)*
Millennium Productions Inc ... F ... 212 944-6203
New York *(G-11267)*
Morelle Products Ltd ... F ... 212 391-8070
New York *(G-11304)*
Nine West Holdings Inc ... G ... 212 642-3860
New York *(G-11436)*
Nine West Holdings Inc ... E ... 212 642-3860
New York *(G-11441)*
Nlhe LLC ... E ... 212 594-0012
New York *(G-11445)*
Noah Enterprises Ltd ... G ... 212 736-2888
New York *(G-11448)*
Park Avenue Sportswear Ltd ... F ... 718 369-0520
Brooklyn *(G-2408)*
Pride & Joys Inc ... F ... 212 594-9820
New York *(G-11704)*
Pvh Corp ... G ... 212 381-3800
New York *(G-11757)*
Ramsbury Property Us Inc ... F ... 212 223-6250
New York *(G-11796)*
Rene Portier Inc ... G ... 718 853-7896
Brooklyn *(G-2492)*
Ritchie Corp ... F ... 212 768-0083
New York *(G-11880)*
Rmll Corp ... E ... 212 719-4666
New York *(G-11885)*
Robespierre Inc ... C ... 212 594-0012
New York *(G-11893)*
S & S Manufacturing Co Inc ... D ... 212 444-6000
New York *(G-11943)*
S2 Sportswear Inc ... F ... 347 335-0713
Brooklyn *(G-2527)*
Salisbury Sportswear Inc ... E ... 516 221-9519
Bellmore *(G-821)*
Snowman ... G ... 212 239-8818
New York *(G-12113)*
Ssa Trading Ltd ... F ... 646 465-9500
New York *(G-12178)*
SSG Fashions Ltd ... G ... 212 221-0933
New York *(G-12179)*
St John ... G ... 718 720-8367
Staten Island *(G-15737)*
St John ... G ... 718 771-4541
Brooklyn *(G-2595)*
Steilmann European Selections ... D ... 914 997-0015
Port Chester *(G-13759)*
Sterling Possessions Ltd ... G ... 212 594-0418
New York *(G-12197)*
Street Beat Sportswear Inc ... F ... 718 302-1500
Brooklyn *(G-2610)*
TR Designs Inc ... E ... 212 398-9300
New York *(G-12387)*
Turn On Products Inc ... D ... 212 764-2121
New York *(G-12426)*
Urban Apparel Group Inc ... E ... 212 947-7009
New York *(G-12478)*
Warrior Sports Inc ... G ... 315 536-0937
Penn Yan *(G-13523)*
West Pacific Enterprises Corp ... G ... 212 564-6800
New York *(G-12613)*

CLOTHING: Suits & Skirts, Women's & Misses'

Bindle and Keep ... G ... 917 740-5002
Brooklyn *(G-1699)*
R & M Richards Inc ... D ... 212 921-8820
New York *(G-11781)*
Tiger Fashion Inc ... E ... 212 244-1175
New York *(G-12338)*
Zaralo LLC ... G ... 212 764-4590
New York *(G-12704)*

CLOTHING: Suits, Men's & Boys', From Purchased Materials

Bindle and Keep ... G ... 917 740-5002
Brooklyn *(G-1699)*
Canali USA Inc ... G ... 212 767-0205
New York *(G-9510)*
Donna Karan Company LLC ... C ... 212 789-1500
New York *(G-9900)*
Donna Karan Company LLC ... B ... 212 789-1500
New York *(G-9901)*

Employee Codes: A=Over 500 employees, B=251-500
C=101-250, D=51-100, E=20-50, F=10-19, G=5-9
2017 Harris
New York Manufacturers Directory
1169

CLOTHING: Suits, Men's & Boys', From Purchased Materials

Martin Greenfield Clothiers .... C 718 497-5480
 Brooklyn *(G-2277)*
Primo Coat Corp .... E 718 349-2070
 Long Island City *(G-7847)*
Roth Clothing Co Inc .... G 718 384-4927
 Brooklyn *(G-2508)*
Royal Clothing Corp .... G 718 436-5841
 Brooklyn *(G-2510)*
Saint Laurie Ltd .... E 212 643-1916
 New York *(G-11954)*
Tom James Company .... F 212 581-6968
 New York *(G-12361)*
Tom James Company .... F 212 593-0204
 New York *(G-12362)*
Xmh-Hfi Inc .... A 585 467-7240
 Rochester *(G-14772)*

CLOTHING: Sweaters & Sweater Coats, Knit

79 Metro Ltd .... G 212 944-4030
 New York *(G-8980)*
A & B Finishing Inc .... E 718 522-4702
 Brooklyn *(G-1525)*
Accurate Knitting Corp .... G 646 552-2216
 Brooklyn *(G-1551)*
B & B Sweater Mills Inc .... F 718 456-8693
 Brooklyn *(G-1655)*
Blueberry Knitting Inc .... G 718 599-6520
 Brooklyn *(G-1705)*
Charter Ventures LLC .... G 212 868-0222
 New York *(G-9585)*
Domani Fashions Corp .... G 718 797-0505
 Brooklyn *(G-1871)*
Endres Knitwear Co Inc .... G 718 933-8687
 Bronx *(G-1326)*
Golden Leaves Knitwear Inc .... E 718 875-8235
 Brooklyn *(G-2038)*
Great Adirondack Yarn Company ... F 518 843-3381
 Amsterdam *(G-349)*
Imperial Sweater Mills Inc .... G 718 871-4414
 Brooklyn *(G-2100)*
Jeric Knit Wear .... G 631 979-8827
 Smithtown *(G-15490)*
Julia Knit Inc .... G 718 848-1900
 Ozone Park *(G-13381)*
K & S Childrens Wear Inc .... E 718 624-0006
 Brooklyn *(G-2162)*
Keryakos Inc .... F 518 344-7092
 Schenectady *(G-15272)*
Knit Illustrated Inc .... E 212 268-9054
 New York *(G-10862)*
Knit Resource Center Ltd .... G 212 221-1990
 New York *(G-10863)*
M A M Knitting Mills Corp .... E 800 570-0093
 Brooklyn *(G-2246)*
M B M Manufacturing Inc .... F 718 769-4148
 Brooklyn *(G-2248)*
Machinit Inc .... G 631 454-9297
 Farmingdale *(G-5039)*
Manrico Usa Inc .... G 212 794-4200
 New York *(G-11139)*
Marble Knits Inc .... G 718 237-7990
 Brooklyn *(G-2266)*
Matchables Inc .... F 718 389-9318
 Brooklyn *(G-2282)*
New York Knitting Processor .... G 718 366-3469
 Ridgewood *(G-14115)*
New York Sweater Company Inc ... E 845 629-9533
 New York *(G-11409)*
Phillips-Van Heusen Europe .... F 212 381-3500
 New York *(G-11649)*
Premier Knits Ltd .... F 718 323-8264
 Ozone Park *(G-13384)*
Pvh Corp .... D 212 381-3500
 New York *(G-11756)*
Rags Knitwear Ltd .... G 718 782-8417
 Brooklyn *(G-2473)*
S & T Knitting Co Inc .... E 607 722-7558
 Conklin *(G-3874)*
S & W Knitting Mills Inc .... E 718 237-2416
 Brooklyn *(G-2524)*
Sage Knitwear Inc .... G 718 628-7902
 West Babylon *(G-16825)*
Sares International Inc .... E 718 366-8412
 Brooklyn *(G-2533)*
Sarug Inc .... G 718 339-2791
 Brooklyn *(G-2534)*
Sarug Inc .... G 718 381-7300
 Ridgewood *(G-14123)*
Sweater Brand Inc .... G 718 797-0505
 Brooklyn *(G-2635)*

T & R Knitting Mills Inc .... E 718 497-4017
 Glendale *(G-5665)*
United Knitwear International .... G 212 354-2920
 New York *(G-12465)*
WR Design Corp .... E 212 354-9000
 New York *(G-12669)*

CLOTHING: Sweaters, Men's & Boys'

Bernette Apparel LLC .... F 212 279-5526
 New York *(G-9366)*
Cotton Emporium Inc .... G 718 894-3365
 Glendale *(G-5650)*
Just Bottoms & Tops Inc .... F 212 564-3202
 New York *(G-10791)*
Komar Luxury Brands .... G 646 472-0060
 New York *(G-10875)*
M A M Knitting Mills Corp .... E 800 570-0093
 Brooklyn *(G-2246)*
S & W Knitting Mills Inc .... E 718 237-2416
 Brooklyn *(G-2524)*
Scharf and Breit Inc .... E 516 282-0287
 Williston Park *(G-17262)*
Schwartz Textile Converting Co .... E 718 499-8243
 Brooklyn *(G-2537)*
Uniqlo USA LLC .... F 877 486-4756
 New York *(G-12460)*

CLOTHING: Sweatshirts & T-Shirts, Men's & Boys'

Kt Group Inc .... G 212 760-2500
 New York *(G-10892)*

CLOTHING: Swimwear, Men's & Boys'

Comme-Ci Comme-CA AP Group .. E 631 300-1035
 Hauppauge *(G-6050)*
Swimwear Anywhere Inc .... E 845 858-4141
 Port Jervis *(G-13794)*

CLOTHING: Swimwear, Women's & Misses'

A H Schreiber Co Inc .... D 212 594-7234
 New York *(G-8989)*
Christina Sales Inc .... F 212 391-0710
 New York *(G-9612)*
Comme-Ci Comme-CA AP Group .. E 631 300-1035
 Hauppauge *(G-6050)*
Feldman Manufacturing Corp .... D 718 433-1700
 Long Island City *(G-7739)*
I ABC Corporation .... E 315 639-3100
 Dexter *(G-4286)*
Malia Mills Inc .... F 212 354-4200
 Brooklyn *(G-2256)*
Michael Feldman Inc .... D 718 433-1700
 Long Island City *(G-7812)*
Ocean Waves Swim LLC .... G 212 967-4481
 New York *(G-11494)*
Sea Waves Inc .... G 516 766-4201
 Oceanside *(G-13096)*
Swimwear Anywhere Inc .... D 631 420-1400
 Farmingdale *(G-5121)*
Swimwear Anywhere Inc .... E 845 858-4141
 Port Jervis *(G-13794)*
Venus Manufacturing Co Inc .... D 315 639-3100
 Dexter *(G-4287)*

CLOTHING: T-Shirts & Tops, Knit

American T Shirts Inc .... G 212 563-7125
 New York *(G-9129)*
Central Mills Inc .... C 212 221-0748
 New York *(G-9565)*
J & E Talit Inc .... G 718 850-1333
 Richmond Hill *(G-14076)*
Jfs Inc .... F 646 264-1200
 New York *(G-10730)*
Mann Consultants LLC .... E 914 763-0512
 Waccabuc *(G-16520)*

CLOTHING: T-Shirts & Tops, Women's & Girls'

Alfred Dunner Inc .... D 212 478-4300
 New York *(G-9084)*
Bowe Industries Inc .... D 718 441-6864
 Glendale *(G-5646)*
Courage Clothing Co Inc .... F 212 354-5690
 New York *(G-9736)*
Garan Incorporated .... C 212 563-1292
 New York *(G-10248)*

Garan Manufacturing Corp .... G 212 563-2000
 New York *(G-10249)*
Gce International Inc .... D 212 704-4800
 New York *(G-10259)*
Golden Horse Enterprise NY Inc ... G 212 594-3339
 New York *(G-10331)*
T Rj Shirts Inc 347 642-3071
 East Elmhurst *(G-4399)*

CLOTHING: Tailored Suits & Formal Jackets

Crisada Inc .... G 718 729-9730
 Long Island City *(G-7707)*
John Kochis Custom Designs .... G 212 244-6046
 New York *(G-10749)*
Shane Tex Inc .... F 516 486-7522
 Hempstead *(G-6287)*

CLOTHING: Ties, Bow, Men's & Boys', From Purchased Materials

J M C Bow Co Inc .... F 718 686-8110
 Brooklyn *(G-2125)*

CLOTHING: Ties, Handsewn, From Purchased Materials

Ralph Lauren Corporation .... B 212 318-7000
 New York *(G-11792)*
Tie King Inc .... G 212 714-9611
 New York *(G-12336)*

CLOTHING: Ties, Neck & Bow, Men's & Boys'

Tie King Inc .... E 718 768-8484
 Brooklyn *(G-2659)*

CLOTHING: Ties, Neck, Men's & Boys', From Purchased Material

Countess Mara Inc .... G 212 768-7300
 New York *(G-9735)*
Perry Ellis Menswear LLC .... C 212 221-7500
 New York *(G-11624)*
Randa Accessories Lea Gds LLC .. D 212 354-5100
 New York *(G-11799)*

CLOTHING: Tights & Leg Warmers

Look By M Inc .... G 212 213-4019
 New York *(G-11028)*

CLOTHING: Tights, Women's

Leg Resource Inc .... E 212 736-4574
 New York *(G-10961)*

CLOTHING: Trousers & Slacks, Men's & Boys'

Adrian Jules Ltd .... D 585 342-5886
 Rochester *(G-14174)*
C E Chquie Ltd .... G 212 268-0006
 New York *(G-9490)*
Check Group LLC .... D 212 221-4700
 New York *(G-9587)*
Christian Casey LLC .... E 212 500-2200
 New York *(G-9608)*
Christian Casey LLC .... E 212 500-2200
 New York *(G-9609)*
Groupe 16sur20 LLC .... F 212 625-1620
 New York *(G-10372)*
Hertling Trousers Inc .... E 718 784-6100
 Brooklyn *(G-2079)*
Hugo Boss Usa Inc .... D 212 940-0600
 New York *(G-10528)*
Int Trading USA LLC .... C 212 760-2338
 New York *(G-10614)*
Jordache Enterprises Inc .... D 212 944-1330
 New York *(G-10760)*
Jordache Enterprises Inc .... C 212 643-8400
 New York *(G-10761)*
Lucky Brand Dungarees LLC .... E 631 350-7358
 Huntington Station *(G-6715)*
M Hidary & Co Inc .... D 212 736-6540
 New York *(G-11073)*
M S B International Ltd .... F 212 302-5551
 New York *(G-11076)*
Miltons of New York Inc .... G 212 997-3359
 New York *(G-11272)*
Mulitex Usa Inc .... G 212 398-0440
 New York *(G-11323)*

Pat & Rose Dress Inc ....D 212 279-1357
  New York (G-11578)
Perry Ellis International Inc ....F 212 536-5400
  New York (G-11622)
Primo Coat Corp ....E 718 349-2070
  Long Island City (G-7847)
Ralph Lauren Corporation ....B 212 318-7000
  New York (G-11792)
Sean John Clothing Inc ....E 212 500-2200
  New York (G-12010)
Sean John Clothing Inc ....E 212 500-2200
  New York (G-12011)

CLOTHING: Underwear, Knit

Balanced Tech Corp ....E 212 768-8330
  New York (G-9309)
Jockey International Inc ....E 518 761-0965
  Lake George (G-7261)

CLOTHING: Underwear, Men's & Boys'

Becks Classic Mfg Inc ....D 631 435-3800
  Brentwood (G-1178)
Check Group LLC ....D 212 221-4700
  New York (G-9587)
Comme-Ci Comme-CA AP Group ....E 631 300-1035
  Hauppauge (G-6050)
Twist Intimate Group LLC ....G 212 695-5990
  New York (G-12433)
Warnaco Group Inc ....D 212 287-8000
  New York (G-12586)
Warnaco Inc ....B 212 287-8000
  New York (G-12587)
Warnaco Inc ....F 718 722-3000
  Brooklyn (G-2744)
Wickers Sportswear Inc ....G 631 543-1700
  Commack (G-3848)

CLOTHING: Underwear, Women's & Children's

Carole Hchman Design Group Inc ....C 918 423-3535
  New York (G-9533)
Enticing Lingerie Inc ....E 718 998-8625
  Brooklyn (G-1927)
Intimateco LLC ....G 212 239-4411
  New York (G-10644)
Lady Ester Lingerie Corp ....E 212 689-1729
  New York (G-10914)
Luxerdame Co Inc ....E 718 752-9800
  Long Island City (G-7796)
Maidenform LLC ....C 718 494-0268
  Staten Island (G-15703)
Natori Company Incorporated ....E 212 532-7796
  New York (G-11356)
Only Hearts Ltd ....E 718 783-3218
  New York (G-11511)
Solo Licensing Corp ....G 212 244-5505
  New York (G-12125)
Wickers Sportswear Inc ....G 631 543-1700
  Commack (G-3848)

CLOTHING: Uniforms & Vestments

Craft Clerical Clothes Inc ....G 212 764-6122
  New York (G-9743)
JM Studio Inc ....F 646 546-5514
  New York (G-10743)
NY Orthopedic Usa Inc ....D 718 852-5330
  Brooklyn (G-2382)
RA Newhouse Inc ....D 516 248-6670
  Mineola (G-8532)

CLOTHING: Uniforms, Ex Athletic, Women's, Misses' & Juniors'

Adar Medical Uniform LLC ....G 718 935-1197
  Brooklyn (G-1560)
Bestec Concept Inc ....G 718 937-5848
  Long Island City (G-7683)
Elie Tahari Ltd ....D 212 763-2000
  New York (G-10003)
Lady Brass Co Inc ....G 516 887-8040
  Hewlett (G-6308)
Marlou Garments Inc ....F 516 739-7100
  New Hyde Park (G-8847)
Shane Tex Inc ....F 516 486-7522
  Hempstead (G-6287)
Uniforms By Park Coats Inc ....E 718 499-1182
  Brooklyn (G-2698)

CLOTHING: Uniforms, Men's & Boys'

Bestec Concept Inc ....G 718 937-5848
  Long Island City (G-7683)
Elite Uniforms Ltd ....G 516 487-5481
  Great Neck (G-5805)
Occunomix International LLC ....E 631 741-1940
  Port Jeff STA (G-13769)
Otex Protective Inc ....G 585 232-7160
  Rochester (G-14559)
Uniforms By Park Coats Inc ....E 718 499-1182
  Brooklyn (G-2698)
Urban Textiles Inc ....F 212 777-1900
  New York (G-12481)
Vf Imagewear Inc ....E 718 352-2363
  Bayside (G-778)

CLOTHING: Uniforms, Military, Men/Youth, Purchased Materials

Med-Eng LLC ....E 315 713-0103
  Ogdensburg (G-13119)

CLOTHING: Uniforms, Policemen's, From Purchased Materials

Strong Group Inc ....G 516 766-6300
  Oceanside (G-13097)

CLOTHING: Uniforms, Team Athletic

American Challenge Enterprises ....G 631 595-7171
  New Hyde Park (G-8815)
Mayberry Shoe Company Inc ....G 315 692-4086
  Manlius (G-8074)
Nepenthes America Inc ....G 212 343-4262
  New York (G-11368)
Pti-Pacific Inc ....G 212 414-8495
  New York (G-11744)
R J Liebe Athletic Company ....D 585 237-6111
  Perry (G-13525)
Tamka Sport LLC ....G 718 224-7820
  Douglaston (G-4213)
Warrior Sports Inc ....G 315 536-0937
  Penn Yan (G-13523)

CLOTHING: Uniforms, Work

Best Medical Wear Ltd ....G 718 858-5544
  Brooklyn (G-1688)
Bestec Concept Inc ....G 718 937-5848
  Long Island City (G-7683)
David Christy ....G 607 863-4610
  Cincinnatus (G-3653)
Lady Brass Co Inc ....G 516 887-8040
  Hewlett (G-6308)
Vf Imagewear Inc ....E 718 352-2363
  Bayside (G-778)

CLOTHING: Warm Weather Knit Outerwear, Including Beachwear

Warm ....G 212 925-1200
  New York (G-12585)

CLOTHING: Waterproof Outerwear

A W R Group Inc ....F 718 729-0412
  Long Island City (G-7644)
Alpha 6 Distributions LLC ....F 516 801-8290
  Locust Valley (G-7628)
Essex Manufacturing Inc ....D 212 239-0080
  New York (G-10066)
Float Tech Inc ....G 518 266-0964
  Troy (G-16235)
Top Fortune Usa Ltd ....G 516 608-2694
  Lynbrook (G-7965)

CLOTHING: Work Apparel, Exc Uniforms

Enzo Manzoni LLC ....G 212 464-7000
  Brooklyn (G-1928)
Ferris USA LLC ....G 617 895-8102
  New York (G-10155)
Kimmiekakes LLC ....F 212 946-0311
  New York (G-10849)

CLOTHING: Work, Men's

5 Star Apparel LLC ....G 212 563-1233
  New York (G-8977)
AKOS Group Ltd ....E 212 683-4747
  New York (G-9067)
American Apparel Ltd ....G 516 504-4559
  Great Neck (G-5790)
Badgley Mischka Licensing LLC ....E 212 921-1585
  New York (G-9301)
Bangla Clothing USA Inc ....G 201 679-2615
  New York (G-9314)
Billion Tower Intl LLC ....F 212 220-0608
  New York (G-9397)
Broadway Knitting Mills Inc ....G 716 692-4421
  North Tonawanda (G-12961)
Courage Clothing Co Inc ....F 212 354-5690
  New York (G-9736)
Dalcom USA Ltd ....F 516 466-7733
  Great Neck (G-5802)
Doral Apparel Group Inc ....E 917 208-5652
  New York (G-9908)
Du Monde Trading Inc ....E 212 944-1306
  New York (G-9933)
E J Manufacturing Inc ....G 516 313-9380
  Merrick (G-8384)
Hillary Merchant Inc ....G 646 575-9242
  New York (G-10476)
Joseph Abboud Manufacturing ....G 212 586-9140
  New York (G-10764)
Kollage Work Too Ltd ....G 212 695-1821
  New York (G-10872)
Medline Industries Inc ....B 845 344-3301
  Middletown (G-8450)
Mesh LLC ....E 646 839-7000
  New York (G-11237)
New York Hospital Disposable ....E 718 384-1620
  Brooklyn (G-2365)
Occunomix International LLC ....E 631 741-1940
  Port Jeff STA (G-13769)
Penfli Industries Inc ....F 212 947-6080
  Great Neck (G-5830)
Rag & Bone Industries LLC ....E 212 249-3331
  New York (G-11786)
Rag & Bone Industries LLC ....D 212 278-8214
  New York (G-11787)
Ruleville Manufacturing Co Inc ....G 212 695-1620
  New York (G-11935)
S & H Uniform Corp ....D 914 937-6800
  White Plains (G-17164)
Sarar Usa Inc ....G 845 928-8874
  Central Valley (G-3526)
Ventura Enterprise Co Inc ....E 212 391-0170
  New York (G-12517)

CLUTCHES OR BRAKES: Electromagnetic

American Precision Inds Inc ....C 716 691-9100
  Amherst (G-224)
API Deltran Inc ....C 716 691-9100
  Amherst (G-226)
Fortitude Industries ....D 607 324-1500
  Hornell (G-6563)

CLUTCHES, EXC VEHICULAR

Machine Components Corp ....E 516 694-7222
  Plainview (G-13617)
Magtrol Inc ....E 716 668-5555
  Buffalo (G-3055)

COAL MINING SERVICES

Desku Group Inc ....G 646 436-1464
  Brooklyn (G-1858)
Dowa International Corp ....F 212 697-3217
  New York (G-9917)
Randgold Resources Ltd ....G 212 815-2129
  New York (G-11801)
Starfuels Inc ....G 914 289-4800
  White Plains (G-17170)
Trimet Coal LLC ....E 718 951-3654
  Brooklyn (G-2681)

COAL MINING SVCS: Bituminous, Contract Basis

Lessoilcom ....G 516 319-5052
  Franklin Square (G-5364)

COAL MINING: Anthracite

Acrs Inc ....F 914 288-8100
  White Plains (G-17073)
Puglisi & Co ....G 212 300-2285
  New York (G-11749)

COATING COMPOUNDS: Tar

Aremco Products Inc ....F 845 268-0039
Valley Cottage *(G-16376)*
Polyset Company Inc ....E 518 664-6000
Mechanicville *(G-8229)*
Spray-Tech Finishing Inc ....F 716 664-6317
Jamestown *(G-7030)*

COATING OR WRAPPING SVC: Steel Pipe

Advanced Lamp Coatings Corp ....E 631 585-5505
Ronkonkoma *(G-14853)*
Specialty Bldg Solutions Inc ....G 631 393-6918
West Babylon *(G-16831)*

COATING SVC

Cnv Architectural Coatings Inc ....G 718 418-9584
Brooklyn *(G-1789)*
Kwong CHI Metal Fabrication ....E 718 369-6429
Brooklyn *(G-2184)*
Tcmf Inc ....D 607 724-1094
Binghamton *(G-954)*

COATING SVC: Electrodes

Chepaume Industries LLC ....G 315 829-6400
Vernon *(G-16433)*
Hilord Chemical Corporation ....E 631 234-7373
Hauppauge *(G-6094)*

COATING SVC: Hot Dip, Metals Or Formed Prdts

Paradigm Group LLC ....G 718 860-1538
Bronx *(G-1420)*

COATING SVC: Metals & Formed Prdts

Applause Coating LLC ....F 631 231-5223
Brentwood *(G-1176)*
Deloka LLC ....G 315 946-6910
Lyons *(G-7972)*
Dynocoat Inc ....F 631 244-9344
Holbrook *(G-6444)*
Electronic Coating Tech Inc ....F 518 688-2048
Cohoes *(G-3747)*
Future Spray Finishing Co ....G 631 242-6252
Deer Park *(G-4146)*
Greene Technologies Inc ....D 607 656-4166
Greene *(G-5866)*
Isoflux Incorporated ....G 585 349-0640
Rochester *(G-14455)*
Master Craft Finishers Inc ....E 631 586-0540
Deer Park *(G-4171)*
Modern Coating and Research ....F 315 597-3517
Palmyra *(G-13411)*
NC Industries Inc ....F 248 528-5200
Buffalo *(G-3082)*
Oerlikon Balzers Coating USA ....E 716 564-8557
Buffalo *(G-3099)*
Qualicoat Inc ....D 585 293-2650
Churchville *(G-3640)*
R Spoor Finishing Corp ....F 607 748-5905
Endicott *(G-4827)*
Sentry Metal Blast Inc ....E 716 285-5241
Niagara Falls *(G-12875)*
Sequa Corporation ....E 201 343-1122
Orangeburg *(G-13247)*
Solidus Industries Inc ....D 607 749-4540
Homer *(G-6522)*
Swain Technology Inc ....F 585 889-2786
Scottsville *(G-15340)*
Trojan Metal Fabrication Inc ....E 631 968-5040
Bay Shore *(G-752)*
W W Custom Clad Inc ....D 518 673-3322
Canajoharie *(G-3334)*

COATING SVC: Metals, With Plastic Or Resins

Heany Industries Inc ....D 585 889-2700
Scottsville *(G-15336)*
Hudson Valley Coatings LLC ....G 845 398-1778
Congers *(G-3857)*
Metal Cladding Inc ....D 716 434-5513
Lockport *(G-7600)*
Metal Finishing Supply Inc ....G 315 655-8068
Canastota *(G-3369)*
Piper Plastics Corp ....E 631 842-6889
Copiague *(G-3918)*

Pro-Teck Coating Inc ....F 716 537-2619
Holland *(G-6483)*
Tj Powder Coaters LLC ....G 607 724-4779
Binghamton *(G-955)*

COATING SVC: Rust Preventative

Monroe County Auto Svcs Inc ....E 585 764-3741
Rochester *(G-14520)*

COATING SVC: Silicon

Momentive Performance Mtls Inc ....E 518 237-3330
Waterford *(G-16616)*
Momentive Prfmce Mtls Holdings ....A 518 533-4600
Albany *(G-102)*
Mpm Holdings Inc ....G 518 237-3330
Waterford *(G-16617)*
Mpm Intermediate Holdings Inc ....G 518 237-3330
Waterford *(G-16618)*

COATINGS: Air Curing

Enecon Corporation ....D 516 349-0022
Medford *(G-8243)*

COATINGS: Epoxy

Delta Polymers Inc ....G 631 254-6240
Bay Shore *(G-695)*
Designer Epoxy Finishes Inc ....G 646 943-6044
Melville *(G-8310)*
Robert Greenburg ....G 845 586-2226
Margaretville *(G-8093)*

COATINGS: Polyurethane

Absolute Coatings Inc ....E 914 636-0700
New Rochelle *(G-8884)*
Gabriela Systems Ltd ....G 631 225-7952
Lindenhurst *(G-7465)*
Paint Over Rust Products Inc ....E 914 636-0700
New Rochelle *(G-8919)*

COFFEE SVCS

Adirondack Ice & Air Inc ....F 518 483-4340
Malone *(G-8005)*

COILS & TRANSFORMERS

Aeroflex Incorporated ....B 516 694-6700
Plainview *(G-13578)*
All Shore Industries Inc ....F 718 720-0018
Staten Island *(G-15634)*
American Trans-Coil Corp ....F 516 922-9640
Oyster Bay *(G-13365)*
Bel Transformer Inc ....D 516 239-5777
Inwood *(G-6753)*
Coil-Q Corporation ....G 914 779-7109
Bronxville *(G-1500)*
Electron Coil Inc ....D 607 336-7414
Norwich *(G-13027)*
Ems Development Corporation ....D 631 345-6200
Yaphank *(G-17391)*
Ems Development Corporation ....D 631 924-4736
Yaphank *(G-17390)*
Eni Technology Inc ....B 585 427-8300
Rochester *(G-14353)*
Es Beta Inc ....E 631 582-6740
Hauppauge *(G-6073)*
Frequency Selective Networks ....F 718 424-7500
Maspeth *(G-8140)*
Fuse Electronics Inc ....G 607 352-3222
Kirkwood *(G-7233)*
Gowanda - Bti LLC ....D 716 492-4081
Arcade *(G-394)*
Hipotronics Inc ....C 845 279-8091
Brewster *(G-1220)*
M F L B Inc ....F 631 254-8300
Bay Shore *(G-714)*
Mini-Circuits Fort Wayne LLC ....B 718 934-4500
Brooklyn *(G-2318)*
Misonix Inc ....D 631 694-9555
Farmingdale *(G-5058)*
Mitchell Electronics Corp ....E 914 699-3800
Mount Vernon *(G-8707)*
New York Fan Coil LLC ....D 646 580-1344
Coram *(G-3947)*
Rdi Inc ....F 914 773-1000
Mount Kisco *(G-8643)*
Sag Harbor Industries Inc ....E 631 725-0440
Sag Harbor *(G-15080)*

COILS: Electric Motors Or Generators

Electron Coil Inc ....D 607 336-7414
Norwich *(G-13027)*
Sag Harbor Industries Inc ....E 631 725-0440
Sag Harbor *(G-15080)*

COILS: Pipe

Falcon Perspectives Inc ....G 718 706-9168
Long Island City *(G-7737)*

COIN OPERATED LAUNDRIES & DRYCLEANERS

Oxford Cleaners ....G 212 734-0006
New York *(G-11539)*

COIN-OPERATED LAUNDRY

Reynolds Drapery Service Inc ....F 315 845-8632
Newport *(G-12792)*
Sky Laundromat Inc ....F 718 639-7070
Jamaica *(G-6949)*

COKE: Calcined Petroleum, Made From Purchased Materials

Hh Liquidating Corp ....A 646 282-2500
New York *(G-10471)*

COKE: Produced In Chemical Recovery Coke Ovens

Tonawanda Coke Corporation ....D 716 876-6222
Tonawanda *(G-16206)*

COLLECTION AGENCY, EXC REAL ESTATE

Debt Resolve Inc ....G 914 949-5500
White Plains *(G-17100)*
Nyt Capital LLC ....F 212 556-1234
New York *(G-11488)*

COLLEGES, UNIVERSITIES & PROFESSIONAL SCHOOLS

Stony Brook University ....E 631 632-6434
Stony Brook *(G-15772)*

COLLETS

Hardinge Inc ....C 607 734-2281
Elmira *(G-4688)*

COLOR SEPARATION: Photographic & Movie Film

Applied Image Inc ....E 585 482-0300
Rochester *(G-14209)*
Eastern Color Stripping Inc ....F 631 563-3700
Bohemia *(G-1060)*

COLORS: Pigments, Inorganic

BASF Beauty Care Solutions LLC ....F 631 689-0200
Stony Brook *(G-15766)*
BASF Corporation ....B 914 737-2554
Peekskill *(G-13473)*
Deluxe Paint ....F 718 768-9494
Brooklyn *(G-1853)*
Heany Industries Inc ....D 585 889-2700
Scottsville *(G-15336)*

COLORS: Pigments, Organic

Sml Brothers Holding Corp ....D 718 402-2000
Bronx *(G-1457)*

COMFORTERS & QUILTS, FROM MANMADE FIBER OR SILK

Ess Bee Industries Inc ....E 718 894-5202
Brooklyn *(G-1936)*

COMMERCIAL & INDL SHELVING WHOLESALERS

Tri-Boro Shlving Prtition Corp ....F 718 782-8527
Ridgewood *(G-14130)*

PRODUCT SECTION

COMMERCIAL & LITERARY WRITINGS
Newbay Media LLC .... F 516 944-5940
  Port Washington *(G-13848)*

COMMERCIAL & OFFICE BUILDINGS RENOVATION & REPAIR
Kng Construction Co Inc .... F 212 595-1451
  Warwick *(G-16593)*

COMMERCIAL ART & GRAPHIC DESIGN SVCS
Art Digital Technologies LLC .... F 646 649-4820
  Brooklyn *(G-1634)*
Artscroll Printing Corp .... E 212 929-2413
  New York *(G-9224)*
Avalon Copy Centers Amer Inc .... D 315 471-3333
  Syracuse *(G-15863)*
Avalon Copy Centers Amer Inc .... E 716 995-7777
  Buffalo *(G-2825)*
Clinton Signs Inc .... G 585 482-1620
  Webster *(G-16719)*
David Helsing .... G 607 796-2681
  Horseheads *(G-6573)*
Dowd - Witbeck Printing Corp .... F 518 274-2421
  Troy *(G-16234)*
Dynamic Photography Inc .... G 516 381-2951
  Roslyn *(G-15019)*
Eye Graphics & Printing Inc .... F 718 488-0606
  Brooklyn *(G-1948)*
F X Graphix Inc .... G 716 871-1511
  Buffalo *(G-2943)*
Fred Weidner & Son Printers .... G 212 964-8676
  New York *(G-10205)*
Hunt Graphics Inc .... G 631 751-5349
  Coram *(G-3944)*
Jay Turoff .... F 718 856-7300
  Brooklyn *(G-2136)*
Kader Lithograph Company Inc .... C 917 664-4380
  Long Island City *(G-7777)*
Lane Park Graphics Inc .... G 914 273-5898
  Patterson *(G-13442)*
Messenger Press .... G 518 885-9231
  Ballston Spa *(G-603)*
Patrick Rohan .... G 718 781-2573
  Monticello *(G-8607)*
Resonant Legal Media LLC .... E 212 687-7100
  New York *(G-11840)*
Riverwood Sgns By Dndev Dsigns .... G 845 229-0282
  Hyde Park *(G-6737)*
Scan-A-Chrome Color Inc .... G 631 532-6146
  Copiague *(G-3925)*
Spectrum Graphics & Print .... F 845 473-4400
  Poughkeepsie *(G-13933)*
Zacmel Graphics LLC .... G 631 944-6031
  Huntington *(G-6692)*

COMMERCIAL EQPT WHOLESALERS, NEC
Hamlet Products Inc .... F 914 665-0307
  Mount Vernon *(G-8689)*
Sleep Care Enterprises Inc .... G 631 246-9000
  Stony Brook *(G-15771)*

COMMERCIAL EQPT, WHOLESALE: Bakery Eqpt & Splys
Pfeil & Holing Inc .... D 718 545-4600
  Woodside *(G-17346)*

COMMERCIAL EQPT, WHOLESALE: Comm Cooking & Food Svc Eqpt
A and K Machine and Welding .... G 631 231-2552
  Bay Shore *(G-663)*
Genpak LLC .... C 845 343-7971
  Middletown *(G-8442)*
Mar-A-Thon Filters Inc .... G 631 957-4774
  Lindenhurst *(G-7470)*
Meades Welding and Fabricating .... G 631 581-1555
  Islip *(G-6810)*
Modern Craft Bar Rest Equip .... G 631 226-5647
  Lindenhurst *(G-7473)*
S & D Welding Corp .... G 631 454-0383
  West Babylon *(G-16824)*

COMMERCIAL EQPT, WHOLESALE: Display Eqpt, Exc Refrigerated
Bfma Holding Corporation .... G 607 753-6746
  Cortland *(G-4014)*

COMMERCIAL EQPT, WHOLESALE: Mannequins
Lifestyle-Trimco .... E 718 257-9101
  Brooklyn *(G-2219)*
R P M Industries Inc .... E 315 255-1105
  Auburn *(G-515)*

COMMERCIAL EQPT, WHOLESALE: Restaurant, NEC
Bari Engineering Corp .... E 212 966-2080
  New York *(G-9320)*
R-S Restaurant Eqp Mfg Corp .... F 212 925-0335
  New York *(G-11784)*
Roger & Sons Inc .... G 212 226-4734
  New York *(G-11906)*

COMMERCIAL EQPT, WHOLESALE: Scales, Exc Laboratory
A & K Equipment Incorporated .... G 705 428-3573
  Watertown *(G-16633)*
Itin Scale Co Inc .... E 718 336-5900
  Brooklyn *(G-2120)*

COMMERCIAL EQPT, WHOLESALE: Store Fixtures & Display Eqpt
Manhattan Display Inc .... G 718 392-1365
  Long Island City *(G-7802)*

COMMERCIAL LAUNDRY EQPT
Fowler Route Co Inc .... F 917 653-4640
  Yonkers *(G-17446)*

COMMERCIAL PHOTOGRAPHIC STUDIO
Falconer Printing & Design Inc .... F 716 665-2121
  Falconer *(G-4899)*

COMMERCIAL PRINTING & NEWSPAPER PUBLISHING COMBINED
Aspect Printing Inc .... E 347 789-4284
  Brooklyn *(G-1640)*
Bleezarde Publishing Inc .... G 518 756-2030
  Ravena *(G-14020)*
Buffalo Standard Printing Corp .... F 716 835-9454
  Buffalo *(G-2860)*
Catskill Delaware Publications .... F 845 887-5200
  Callicoon *(G-3284)*
Community News Group LLC .... C 718 260-2500
  Brooklyn *(G-1796)*
Daily News LP .... A 212 210-2100
  New York *(G-9790)*
Denton Publications Inc .... D 518 873-6368
  Elizabethtown *(G-4626)*
Denton Publications Inc .... E 518 561-9680
  Plattsburgh *(G-13661)*
Digital First Media LLC .... E 212 257-7212
  New York *(G-9877)*
E W Smith Publishing Co .... F 845 562-1218
  New Windsor *(G-8937)*
Eagle Media Partners LP .... E 315 434-8889
  Syracuse *(G-15928)*
Gatehuse Media PA Holdings Inc .... D 585 598-0030
  Pittsford *(G-13563)*
Holdens Screen Supply Corp .... G 212 627-2727
  New York *(G-10495)*
Huersch Marketing Group LLC .... G 518 874-1045
  Green Island *(G-5857)*
Ithaca Journal News Co Inc .... E 607 272-2321
  Ithaca *(G-6854)*
Local Media Group Inc .... D 845 341-1100
  Middletown *(G-8448)*
New Berlin Gazette .... E 607 847-6131
  Norwich *(G-13031)*
Nyc Trade Printers Corp .... F 718 606-0610
  Woodside *(G-17342)*
Nyp Holdings Inc .... A 212 997-9272
  New York *(G-11485)*
Ogden Newspapers Inc .... C 716 487-1111
  Jamestown *(G-7022)*

COMMUNICATIONS EQPT: Radio, Marine

Prometheus International Inc .... F 718 472-0700
  Long Island City *(G-7848)*
Richner Communications Inc .... C 516 569-4000
  Garden City *(G-5529)*
Ubm LLC .... F 516 562-5000
  New York *(G-12442)*
William Boyd Printing Co Inc .... C 518 339-5832
  Latham *(G-7385)*
Wolfe Publications Inc .... C 585 394-0770
  Canandaigua *(G-3360)*
Zenith Color Comm Group Inc .... E 212 989-4400
  Long Island City *(G-7932)*

COMMON SAND MINING
E F Lippert Co Inc .... F 716 373-1100
  Allegany *(G-199)*
Hanson Aggregates East LLC .... G 315 536-9391
  Penn Yan *(G-13513)*
Hanson Aggregates PA Inc .... E 315 858-1100
  Jordanville *(G-7132)*
Hanson Aggregates PA Inc .... F 518 568-2444
  Saint Johnsville *(G-15094)*
Hanson Aggregates PA LLC .... E 315 469-5501
  Jamesville *(G-7049)*
Hanson Aggregates PA LLC .... E 315 685-3321
  Skaneateles *(G-15463)*
Hanson Aggregates PA LLC .... E 315 821-7222
  Oriskany Falls *(G-13318)*

COMMUNICATION HEADGEAR: Telephone
Astrocom Electronics Inc .... D 607 432-1930
  Oneonta *(G-13172)*
Prager Metis Cpas LLC .... F 212 972-7555
  New York *(G-11693)*
Rus Industries Inc .... E 716 284-7828
  Niagara Falls *(G-12869)*

COMMUNICATIONS CARRIER: Wired
Comsec Ventures International .... G 518 523-1600
  Lake Placid *(G-7273)*
Fiberdyne Labs Inc .... D 315 895-8470
  Frankfort *(G-5353)*

COMMUNICATIONS EQPT & SYSTEMS, NEC
All Products Designs .... G 631 748-6901
  Smithtown *(G-15482)*
Lik LLC .... F 516 848-5135
  Northport *(G-13015)*

COMMUNICATIONS EQPT REPAIR & MAINTENANCE
Unitone Communication Systems .... G 212 777-9090
  New York *(G-12468)*
Zetek Corporation .... F 212 668-1485
  New York *(G-12710)*

COMMUNICATIONS EQPT WHOLESALERS
AES Electronics Inc .... G 212 371-8120
  New York *(G-9052)*
Caravan International Corp .... G 212 223-7190
  New York *(G-9522)*
Communication Power Corp .... E 631 434-7306
  Hauppauge *(G-6051)*
Sinclair Technologies Inc .... E 716 874-3682
  Hamburg *(G-5942)*

COMMUNICATIONS EQPT: Microwave
Amplitech Inc .... G 631 521-7738
  Bohemia *(G-1014)*
Amplitech Group Inc .... G 631 521-7831
  Bohemia *(G-1015)*
Comtech PST Corp .... C 631 777-8900
  Melville *(G-8306)*
Comtech Telecom Corp .... E 631 962-7000
  Melville *(G-8307)*
Specialty Microwave Corp .... F 631 737-2175
  Ronkonkoma *(G-14987)*
United Satcom Inc .... G 718 359-4100
  Flushing *(G-5306)*

COMMUNICATIONS EQPT: Radio, Marine
Maritime Broadband Inc .... E 347 404-6041
  Long Island City *(G-7803)*

Employee Codes: A=Over 500 employees, B=251-500
C=101-250, D=51-100, E=20-50, F=10-19, G=5-9

2017 Harris
New York Manufacturers Directory

COMMUNICATIONS SVCS

COMMUNICATIONS SVCS
Aspire One Communications LLC......F...... 201 281-2998
  Cornwall *(G-3986)*
Forerunner Technologies Inc............E...... 631 337-2100
  Bohemia *(G-1067)*

COMMUNICATIONS SVCS: Cellular
2p Agency Usa Inc..............................G...... 212 203-5586
  Brooklyn *(G-1513)*
Bayside Beepers & Cellular.................G...... 718 343-3888
  Glen Oaks *(G-5640)*
Squond Inc..E...... 718 778-6630
  Brooklyn *(G-2593)*

COMMUNICATIONS SVCS: Data
Forerunner Technologies Inc............E...... 631 337-2100
  Bohemia *(G-1067)*

COMMUNICATIONS SVCS: Facsimile Transmission
Alternative Technology Corp...............G...... 914 478-5900
  Hastings On Hudson *(G-6002)*
Key Computer Svcs of Chelsea..........D...... 212 206-8060
  New York *(G-10840)*

COMMUNICATIONS SVCS: Internet Host Svcs
Nyemac Inc......................................G...... 631 668-1303
  Montauk *(G-8591)*

COMMUNICATIONS SVCS: Online Svc Providers
Beauty America LLC..........................E...... 917 744-1430
  Great Neck *(G-5794)*
Martha Stewart Living.........................B...... 212 827-8000
  New York *(G-11166)*

COMMUNICATIONS SVCS: Proprietary Online Svcs Networks
Working Mother Media Inc.................D...... 212 351-6400
  New York *(G-12659)*

COMMUNICATIONS SVCS: Satellite Earth Stations
L-3 Communications Corporation........C...... 585 742-9100
  Victor *(G-16487)*
Loral Space Communications Inc.......E...... 212 697-1105
  New York *(G-11033)*

COMMUNICATIONS SVCS: Signal Enhancement Network Svcs
Fiberdyne Labs Inc...........................D...... 315 895-8470
  Frankfort *(G-5353)*

COMMUNICATIONS SVCS: Telephone, Local
Highcrest Investors LLC....................D...... 212 702-4323
  New York *(G-10474)*

COMMUNICATIONS SVCS: Telephone, Voice
ABS Talkx Inc....................................G...... 631 254-9100
  Bay Shore *(G-664)*

COMMUNITY CHESTS
Heat and Frost Inslatrs & Asbs...........G...... 718 784-3456
  Astoria *(G-443)*

COMMUTATORS: Electronic
Amron Electronics Inc.......................E...... 631 737-1234
  Ronkonkoma *(G-14870)*

COMPACT DISCS OR CD'S, WHOLESALE
Imago Recording Company................G...... 212 751-3033
  New York *(G-10569)*

COMPACT LASER DISCS: Prerecorded
A To Z Media Inc...............................F...... 212 260-0237
  New York *(G-8994)*

Atlantic Recording Corp.....................B...... 212 707-2000
  New York *(G-9252)*
Bertelsmann Inc................................E...... 212 782-1000
  New York *(G-9370)*
Historic TW Inc.................................D...... 212 484-8000
  New York *(G-10484)*
Media Technologies Ltd....................F...... 631 467-7900
  Eastport *(G-4584)*
Mmo Music Group Inc.......................G...... 914 592-1188
  Elmsford *(G-4766)*
Optic Solution LLC............................F...... 518 293-4321
  Saranac *(G-15133)*
Sony Corporation of America.............C...... 212 833-8000
  New York *(G-12132)*
Time Warner Companies Inc.............D...... 212 484-8000
  New York *(G-12350)*
Vaire LLC...G...... 631 271-4933
  Huntington Station *(G-6727)*

COMPACTORS: Trash & Garbage, Residential
A Gatty Products Inc.........................G...... 914 592-3903
  Elmsford *(G-4731)*

COMPARATORS: Optical
Quality Vision Services Inc...............D...... 585 544-0450
  Rochester *(G-14614)*

COMPOSITION STONE: Plastic
Seaway Mats Inc..............................G...... 518 483-2560
  Malone *(G-8016)*

COMPOST
Long Island Compost Corp................C...... 516 334-6600
  Westbury *(G-17006)*
Scotts Company LLC........................E...... 631 289-7444
  Yaphank *(G-17400)*

COMPRESSORS, AIR CONDITIONING: Wholesalers
Toshiba America Inc.........................E...... 212 596-0600
  New York *(G-12377)*

COMPRESSORS: Air & Gas
Buffalo Compressed Air Inc...............G...... 716 783-8673
  Cheektowaga *(G-3563)*
Chapin International Inc....................C...... 585 343-3140
  Batavia *(G-627)*
Chapin Manufacturing Inc..................C...... 585 343-3140
  Batavia *(G-628)*
Comairco Equipment Inc...................G...... 716 656-0211
  Cheektowaga *(G-3564)*
Cooper Turbocompressor Inc............B...... 716 896-6600
  Buffalo *(G-2890)*
Crosman Corporation........................E...... 585 657-6161
  Bloomfield *(G-986)*
Crosman Corporation........................E...... 585 398-3920
  Farmington *(G-5148)*
Cyclone Air Power Inc......................G...... 718 447-3038
  Staten Island *(G-15664)*
Dresser-Rand Group Inc...................D...... 716 375-3000
  Olean *(G-13144)*
Gas Tchnlgy Enrgy Cncepts LLC......G...... 716 831-9695
  Buffalo *(G-2965)*
GM Components Holdings LLC........B...... 716 439-2463
  Lockport *(G-7590)*
Idex Corporation...............................G...... 585 292-8121
  Rochester *(G-14443)*
Mahle Indstrbeteiligungen GMBH.....D...... 716 319-6700
  Amherst *(G-250)*
Screw Compressor Tech Inc.............F...... 716 827-6600
  Buffalo *(G-3179)*
Turbopro Inc.....................................G...... 716 681-8651
  Alden *(G-184)*

COMPRESSORS: Air & Gas, Including Vacuum Pumps
Air Techniques Inc...........................B...... 516 433-7676
  Melville *(G-8291)*
Atlas Copco Comptec LLC................B...... 518 765-3344
  Voorheesville *(G-16516)*
Eastern Air Products LLC..................F...... 716 391-1866
  Lancaster *(G-7313)*

COMPRESSORS: Refrigeration & Air Conditioning Eqpt
Graham Corporation..........................B...... 585 343-2216
  Batavia *(G-636)*
Standard Motor Products Inc.............B...... 718 392-0200
  Long Island City *(G-7884)*

COMPUTER & COMPUTER SOFTWARE STORES
A I T Computers Inc.........................G...... 518 266-9010
  Troy *(G-16224)*
Astrodyne Inc...................................G...... 516 536-5755
  Oceanside *(G-13073)*
Biofeedback Instrument Corp............F...... 212 222-5665
  New York *(G-9401)*
G S Communications USA Inc..........E...... 718 389-7371
  Brooklyn *(G-2010)*
J & N Computer Services Inc...........F...... 585 388-8780
  Fairport *(G-4858)*
Lasertech Crtridge RE-Builders........G...... 518 373-1246
  Clifton Park *(G-3698)*
Maia Systems LLC...........................G...... 718 206-0100
  Jamaica *(G-6927)*
Taste and See Entrmt Inc.................G...... 516 285-3010
  Valley Stream *(G-16429)*
Tpa Computer Corp..........................F...... 877 866-6044
  Carmel *(G-3406)*

COMPUTER & COMPUTER SOFTWARE STORES: Peripheral Eqpt
Cables and Chips Inc........................E...... 212 619-3132
  New York *(G-9493)*

COMPUTER & COMPUTER SOFTWARE STORES: Software, Bus/Non-Game
Successware Remote LLC................G...... 716 842-1439
  Buffalo *(G-3199)*

COMPUTER & COMPUTER SOFTWARE STORES: Software, Computer Game
Sony Broadband Entertainment.........F...... 212 833-6800
  New York *(G-12131)*

COMPUTER & OFFICE MACHINE MAINTENANCE & REPAIR
Chem-Puter Friendly Inc...................E...... 631 331-2259
  Mount Sinai *(G-8654)*
Innovative Systems of New York.......G...... 516 541-7410
  Massapequa Park *(G-8187)*
Parrys..F...... 315 824-0002
  Hamilton *(G-5949)*

COMPUTER DISKETTES WHOLESALERS
Formats Unlimited Inc......................F...... 631 249-9200
  Deer Park *(G-4144)*
Recharge Net Inc.............................G...... 585 546-1060
  Rochester *(G-14621)*

COMPUTER FORMS
Boces Business Office.....................E...... 607 763-3300
  Binghamton *(G-897)*
Multi Packaging Solutions Inc...........E...... 646 885-0157
  New York *(G-11324)*
Specialized Printed Forms Inc..........E...... 585 538-2381
  Caledonia *(G-3282)*

COMPUTER GRAPHICS SVCS
Affluent Design Inc...........................F...... 631 655-2556
  Mastic Beach *(G-8204)*
Alpina Copyworld Inc........................F...... 212 683-3511
  New York *(G-9101)*
Belsito Communications Inc.............F...... 845 534-9700
  New Windsor *(G-8932)*
Beyer Graphics Inc...........................D...... 631 543-3900
  Commack *(G-3824)*
Christian Bus Endeavors Inc............F...... 315 788-8560
  Watertown *(G-16644)*

PRODUCT SECTION

COMPUTER PROGRAMMING SVCS

COMPUTER HARDWARE REQUIREMENTS ANALYSIS

Quality and Asrn Tech Corp .... G 646 450-6762
  Ridge *(G-14093)*

COMPUTER INTERFACE EQPT: Indl Process

Anchor Commerce Trading Corp .... G 516 881-3485
  Atlantic Beach *(G-468)*
Aspex Incorporated .... E 212 966-0410
  New York *(G-9237)*
ATI Trading Inc .... F 718 888-7918
  Flushing *(G-5228)*
Cal Blen Electronic Industries .... F 631 242-6243
  Deer Park *(G-4114)*
Cosa Xentaur Corporation .... F 631 345-3434
  Yaphank *(G-17389)*
Cytexone Technology LLC .... G 212 792-6700
  New York *(G-9779)*
Industrial Machine Repair .... G 607 272-0717
  Ithaca *(G-6850)*
Macrolink Inc .... E 631 924-8265
  Medford *(G-8255)*
Sixnet LLC .... D 518 877-5173
  Ballston Lake *(G-586)*
Vetra Systems Corporation .... G 631 434-3185
  Hauppauge *(G-6224)*

COMPUTER PERIPHERAL EQPT, NEC

A I T Computers Inc .... G 518 266-9010
  Troy *(G-16224)*
Aalborg Instrs & Contrls Inc .... D 845 398-3160
  Orangeburg *(G-13217)*
Aero-Vision Technologies Inc .... G 631 643-8349
  Melville *(G-8289)*
Aeroflex Plainview Inc .... C 631 231-9100
  Hauppauge *(G-6011)*
Andrea Electronics Corporation .... F 631 719-1800
  Bohemia *(G-1016)*
Anorad Corporation .... C 631 380-2100
  East Setauket *(G-4476)*
Atlaz International Ltd .... F 516 239-1854
  Lawrence *(G-7390)*
Aventura Technologies Inc .... E 631 300-4000
  Commack *(G-3822)*
B V M Associates .... G 631 254-6220
  Shirley *(G-15415)*
Brocade Cmmnctions Systems Inc .... G 212 497-8500
  New York *(G-9467)*
Chem-Puter Friendly Inc .... E 631 331-2259
  Mount Sinai *(G-8654)*
Chemung Cty Assc Retrd Ctzns .... C 607 734-6151
  Elmira *(G-4675)*
Clayton Dubilier & Rice Fun .... E 212 407-5200
  New York *(G-9640)*
Datatran Labs Inc .... G 845 856-4313
  Port Jervis *(G-13783)*
Eastman Kodak Company .... B 585 724-4000
  Rochester *(G-14328)*
Ems Development Corporation .... D 631 345-6200
  Yaphank *(G-17391)*
Gasoft Equipment Inc .... F 845 863-1010
  Newburgh *(G-12756)*
Glowa Manufacturing Inc .... E 607 770-0811
  Binghamton *(G-919)*
Hauppauge Computer Works Inc .... E 631 434-1600
  Hauppauge *(G-6090)*
Hauppauge Digital Inc .... E 631 434-1600
  Hauppauge *(G-6091)*
Hergo Ergonomic Support .... E 718 894-0639
  Maspeth *(G-8143)*
Hitachi Metals America Ltd .... E 914 694-9200
  Purchase *(G-13959)*
HP Inc .... D 212 835-1640
  New York *(G-10523)*
Humanscale Corporation .... E 212 725-4749
  New York *(G-10531)*
IBM World Trade Corporation .... G 914 765-1900
  Armonk *(G-413)*
Innovative Systems of New York .... G 516 541-7410
  Massapequa Park *(G-8187)*
Inpora Technologies LLC .... D 646 838-2474
  New York *(G-10609)*
Juniper Networks Inc .... A 212 520-3300
  New York *(G-10789)*
Kantek Inc .... E 516 594-4600
  Oceanside *(G-13084)*
Lsc Peripherals Incorporated .... G 631 244-0707
  Bohemia *(G-1096)*
Lumiliscent Systems Inc .... B 716 655-0800
  East Aurora *(G-4373)*
Macrolink Inc .... E 631 924-8265
  Medford *(G-8255)*
Maia Systems LLC .... G 718 206-0100
  Jamaica *(G-6927)*
Marco Manufacturing Inc .... E 845 485-1571
  Poughkeepsie *(G-13914)*
Mirion Technologies Ist Corp .... D 607 562-4300
  Horseheads *(G-6584)*
NCR Corporation .... C 607 273-5310
  Ithaca *(G-6866)*
Norazza Inc .... G 716 706-1160
  Buffalo *(G-3093)*
Orbit International Corp .... E 631 435-8300
  Hauppauge *(G-6154)*
Perceptive Pixel Inc .... E 701 367-5845
  New York *(G-11613)*
Performance Technologies Inc .... D 585 256-0200
  Rochester *(G-14576)*
Phoenix Venture Fund LLC .... E 212 759-1909
  New York *(G-11653)*
QED Technologies Intl Inc .... E 585 256-6540
  Rochester *(G-14610)*
Rdi Inc .... F 914 773-1000
  Mount Kisco *(G-8643)*
Reliable Elec Mt Vernon Inc .... E 914 668-4440
  Mount Vernon *(G-8725)*
Rodale Wireless Inc .... E 631 231-0044
  Hauppauge *(G-6179)*
Ruhle Companies Inc .... E 914 287-4000
  Valhalla *(G-16372)*
S G I .... G 917 386-0385
  New York *(G-11945)*
Saab Sensis Corporation .... C 315 445-0550
  East Syracuse *(G-4561)*
Sima Technologies LLC .... G 412 828-9130
  Hauppauge *(G-6191)*
Sony Corporation of America .... C 212 833-8000
  New York *(G-12132)*
Symbol Technologies LLC .... F 631 738-2400
  Bohemia *(G-1139)*
Synaptics Incorporated .... F 585 899-4300
  Rochester *(G-14710)*
Technomag Inc .... G 631 246-6142
  East Setauket *(G-4493)*
Todd Enterprises Inc .... D 516 773-8087
  Great Neck *(G-5844)*
Torrent Ems LLC .... F 716 312-4099
  Lockport *(G-7620)*
Toshiba Amer Info Systems Inc .... B 949 583-3000
  New York *(G-12376)*
Vader Systems LLC .... G 716 636-1742
  East Amherst *(G-4363)*
Vishay Thin Film LLC .... C 716 283-4025
  Niagara Falls *(G-12889)*
Vuzix Corporation .... E 585 359-5900
  West Henrietta *(G-16898)*
Wantagh Computer Center .... F 516 826-2189
  Wantagh *(G-16564)*
Welch Allyn Inc .... A 315 685-4100
  Skaneateles Falls *(G-15471)*
Wilson & Wilson Group .... G 212 729-4736
  Forest Hills *(G-5330)*
Xerox Corporation .... D 516 677-1500
  Melville *(G-8362)*
Xerox Corporation .... E 585 423-3538
  Rochester *(G-14769)*
Z-Axis Inc .... D 315 548-5000
  Phelps *(G-13539)*

COMPUTER PERIPHERAL EQPT, WHOLESALE

Atlaz International Ltd .... F 516 239-1854
  Lawrence *(G-7390)*
Cbord Group Inc .... C 607 257-2410
  Ithaca *(G-6831)*
Chem-Puter Friendly Inc .... E 631 331-2259
  Mount Sinai *(G-8654)*
Digicom International Inc .... F 631 249-8999
  Farmingdale *(G-4977)*

COMPUTER PERIPHERAL EQPT: Encoders

Sequential Electronics Systems .... E 914 592-1345
  Elmsford *(G-4783)*

COMPUTER PERIPHERAL EQPT: Film Reader Devices

P C Rfrs Radiology .... G 212 586-5700
  Long Island City *(G-7830)*

COMPUTER PERIPHERAL EQPT: Graphic Displays, Exc Terminals

Binghamton Simulator Co Inc .... E 607 321-2980
  Binghamton *(G-895)*
Dia-Nielsen USA Incorporated .... G 856 642-9700
  Buffalo *(G-2913)*
Medsim-Eagle Simulation Inc .... E 607 658-9354
  Endicott *(G-4818)*
Mp Displays LLC .... G 845 268-4113
  Valley Cottage *(G-16383)*
Watson Productions LLC .... E 516 334-9766
  Hauppauge *(G-6230)*

COMPUTER PERIPHERAL EQPT: Input Or Output

Gunther Partners LLC .... G 212 521-2930
  New York *(G-10384)*
Pda Panache Corp .... G 631 776-0523
  Bohemia *(G-1116)*

COMPUTER PROGRAMMING SVCS

6n Systems Inc .... E 518 583-6400
  Halfmoon *(G-5907)*
Actv Inc (del Corp) .... D 212 995-9500
  New York *(G-9022)*
Anbeck Inc .... G 518 907-0308
  White Plains *(G-17078)*
Autodesk Inc .... E 607 257-4280
  Ithaca *(G-6820)*
Billing Blocks Inc .... F 718 442-5006
  Staten Island *(G-15647)*
BMC Software Inc .... E 212 730-1389
  New York *(G-9429)*
Cdml Computer Services Ltd .... G 718 428-9063
  Fresh Meadows *(G-5439)*
Data Key Communication LLC .... F 315 445-2347
  Fayetteville *(G-5164)*
Davis Ziff Publishing Inc .... D 212 503-3500
  New York *(G-9829)*
Defran Systems Inc .... E 212 727-8342
  New York *(G-9837)*
Digitronik Dev Labs Inc .... G 585 360-0043
  Rochester *(G-14308)*
Fidesa US Corporation .... B 212 269-9000
  New York *(G-10160)*
Fog Creek Software Inc .... G 866 364-2733
  New York *(G-10183)*
Fuel Data Systems Inc .... G 800 447-7870
  Middletown *(G-8441)*
Hauppauge Computer Works Inc .... E 631 434-1600
  Hauppauge *(G-6090)*
Hnw Inc .... F 212 258-9215
  New York *(G-10492)*
Hudson Software Corporation .... E 914 773-0400
  Elmsford *(G-4755)*
Infinity Augmented Reality Inc .... G 917 677-2084
  New York *(G-10593)*
Irv Inc .... E 212 334-4507
  New York *(G-10663)*
L-3 Communications Corporation .... D 607 721-5465
  Kirkwood *(G-7234)*
Lockheed Martin Corporation .... D 315 793-5800
  New Hartford *(G-8807)*
Openfin Inc .... G 917 450-8822
  New York *(G-11514)*
Panvidea Inc .... F 212 967-9613
  New York *(G-11561)*
PC Solutions & Consulting .... G 607 735-0466
  Elmira *(G-4697)*
Safe Passage International Inc .... F 585 292-4910
  Rochester *(G-14665)*
Standardware Inc .... G 914 738-6382
  Pelham *(G-13495)*
Suite Solutions Inc .... E 716 929-3050
  Amherst *(G-263)*
Syrasoft LLC .... F 315 708-0341
  Baldwinsville *(G-578)*
Wetpaintcom Inc .... E 206 859-6300
  New York *(G-12620)*
X Function Inc .... E 212 231-0092
  New York *(G-12672)*

COMPUTER PROGRAMMING SVCS: Custom

Endava Inc ....G...... 212 920-7240
New York *(G-10032)*
Modern Farmer Media Inc ....F...... 518 828-7447
Hudson *(G-6628)*
US Beverage Net Inc ....F...... 315 579-2025
Syracuse *(G-16065)*

COMPUTER RELATED MAINTENANCE SVCS

Century Direct LLC ....C...... 212 763-0600
Islandia *(G-6789)*
Global Applctions Solution LLC .....G...... 212 741-9595
New York *(G-10313)*
IBM World Trade Corporation ......G...... 914 765-1900
Armonk *(G-413)*
Laurus Development Inc ....F...... 716 823-1202
Buffalo *(G-3047)*

COMPUTER SERVICE BUREAU

Datalink Computer Products ....F...... 914 666-2358
Mount Kisco *(G-8626)*
Hudson Software Corporation ....E...... 914 773-0400
Elmsford *(G-4755)*

COMPUTER SOFTWARE DEVELOPMENT

Advanced Barcode Technology ....F...... 516 570-8100
Great Neck *(G-5784)*
Evolve Guest Controls LLC ....F...... 855 750-9090
Port Washington *(G-13814)*
Falconstor Software Inc ....F...... 631 777-5188
Melville *(G-8318)*
Lake Image Systems Inc ....F...... 585 321-3630
Henrietta *(G-6296)*
Ontra Presentations LLC ....G...... 212 213-1315
New York *(G-11512)*
Os33 Inc ....G...... 708 336-3466
New York *(G-11529)*
Roomactually LLC ....G...... 646 388-1922
New York *(G-11914)*
Sale 121 Corp ....D...... 240 855-8988
New York *(G-11956)*
Standard Analytics Io Inc ....G...... 917 882-5422
New York *(G-12181)*
Structuredweb Inc ....E...... 201 325-3110
New York *(G-12217)*
Thomson Rters Tax Accnting Inc ...D...... 212 367-6300
New York *(G-12330)*
Williamson Law Book Co ....F...... 585 924-3400
Victor *(G-16514)*

COMPUTER SOFTWARE DEVELOPMENT & APPLICATIONS

Amcom Software Inc ....F...... 212 951-7600
New York *(G-9110)*
Forerunner Technologies Inc ....E...... 631 337-2100
Bohemia *(G-1067)*
Hearst Digital Studios Inc ....E...... 212 969-7552
New York *(G-10448)*
Inboxmind LLC ....G...... 646 773-7726
New York *(G-10580)*
Magsoft Corporation ....G...... 518 877-8390
Clifton Park *(G-3701)*
Orpheo USA Corp ....G...... 212 464-8255
New York *(G-11527)*
Pitney Bowes Software Inc ....F...... 518 272-0014
Troy *(G-16248)*
Post Road ....F...... 203 545-2122
New York *(G-11690)*

COMPUTER SOFTWARE SYSTEMS ANALYSIS & DESIGN: Custom

Complex Biosystems Inc ....G...... 315 464-8007
Liverpool *(G-7517)*
Inprotopia Corporation ....F...... 917 338-7501
New York *(G-10610)*
Laurus Development Inc ....F...... 716 823-1202
Buffalo *(G-3047)*
Vizbee Inc ....G...... 650 787-1424
New York *(G-12560)*
Vormittag Associates Inc ....C...... 800 824-7776
Ronkonkoma *(G-14999)*

COMPUTER STORAGE DEVICES, NEC

Datalink Computer Products ....F...... 914 666-2358
Mount Kisco *(G-8626)*

EMC Corporation ....E...... 716 833-5348
Amherst *(G-238)*
EMC Corporation ....E...... 585 387-9505
East Rochester *(G-4457)*
Emcs LLC ....G...... 716 523-2002
Hamburg *(G-5924)*
Garland Technology LLC ....E...... 716 242-8500
Buffalo *(G-2964)*
Gim Electronics Corp ....F...... 516 942-3382
Hicksville *(G-6349)*
Quantum Asset Recovery ....G...... 716 393-2712
Buffalo *(G-3148)*
Quantum Knowledge LLC ....G...... 631 727-6111
Riverhead *(G-14153)*
Quantum Logic Corp ....G...... 516 746-1380
New Hyde Park *(G-8858)*
Quantum Performance Company ...G...... 518 642-3111
Granville *(G-5780)*
Sony Corporation of America ....C...... 212 833-8000
New York *(G-12132)*
Todd Enterprises Inc ....G...... 516 773-8087
Great Neck *(G-5844)*
William S Hein & Co Inc ....D...... 716 882-2600
Getzville *(G-5606)*

COMPUTER TERMINALS

AG Neovo Professional Inc ....F...... 212 647-9080
New York *(G-9055)*
Clayton Dubilier & Rice Fun ....E...... 212 407-5200
New York *(G-9640)*
Igt Global Solutions Corp ....D...... 518 382-2900
Schenectady *(G-15269)*
International Bus Mchs Corp ....A...... 845 433-1234
Poughkeepsie *(G-13907)*
Nu - Communitek LLC ....F...... 516 433-3553
Hicksville *(G-6377)*
Orbit International Corp ....C...... 631 435-8300
Hauppauge *(G-6154)*
Symbio Technologies LLC ....G...... 914 576-1205
White Plains *(G-17174)*

COMPUTER TERMINALS: CRT

Cine Design Group LLC ....G...... 646 747-0734
New York *(G-9617)*

COMPUTER-AIDED DESIGN SYSTEMS SVCS

Circuits & Systems Inc ....E...... 516 593-4301
East Rockaway *(G-4468)*
Trident Precision Mfg Inc ....D...... 585 265-2010
Webster *(G-16738)*

COMPUTER-AIDED ENGINEERING SYSTEMS SVCS

Complex Biosystems Inc ....G...... 315 464-8007
Liverpool *(G-7517)*

COMPUTERS, NEC

Alliance Magnetic LLC ....G...... 914 944-1690
Ossining *(G-13320)*
Argon Corp ....F...... 516 487-5314
Great Neck *(G-5792)*
Arnouse Digital Devices Corp ....F...... 516 673-4444
New Hyde Park *(G-8817)*
Binghamton Simulator Co Inc ....E...... 607 321-2980
Binghamton *(G-895)*
Computer Conversions Corp ....E...... 631 261-3300
East Northport *(G-4434)*
Critical Link LLC ....E...... 315 425-4045
Syracuse *(G-15912)*
Data-Pac Mailing Systems Corp ....F...... 585 671-0210
Webster *(G-16720)*
Datacom Systems Inc ....E...... 315 463-9541
East Syracuse *(G-4524)*
Dees Audio & Vision ....G...... 585 719-9256
Rochester *(G-14305)*
Digicom International Inc ....F...... 631 249-8999
Farmingdale *(G-4977)*
E-Systems Group LLC ....E...... 607 775-1100
Conklin *(G-3868)*
Electronic Systems Inc ....G...... 631 589-4389
Holbrook *(G-6445)*
Envent Systems Inc ....G...... 646 294-6980
Pelham *(G-13491)*
Flash Ventures Inc ....F...... 212 255-7070
New York *(G-10177)*
H&L Computers Inc ....E...... 516 873-8088
Flushing *(G-5247)*

Hand Held Products Inc ....B...... 315 554-6000
Skaneateles Falls *(G-15468)*
Hi-Tech Advanced Solutions Inc ....F...... 718 926-3488
Forest Hills *(G-5324)*
Human Electronics Inc ....G...... 315 724-9850
Utica *(G-16339)*
IBM World Trade Corporation ......G...... 914 765-1900
Armonk *(G-413)*
International Bus Mchs Corp ....A...... 607 754-9558
Endicott *(G-4813)*
Irpenscom ....G...... 585 507-7997
Penfield *(G-13499)*
J & N Computer Services Inc ....F...... 585 388-8780
Fairport *(G-4858)*
Kemp Technologies Inc ....D...... 917 688-4067
New York *(G-10831)*
Lockheed Martin Corporation ....C...... 516 228-2000
Uniondale *(G-16298)*
M&C Associates LLC ....G...... 631 467-8760
Bohemia *(G-1098)*
Medsim-Eagle Simulation Inc ....F...... 607 658-9354
Endicott *(G-4818)*
N & G of America Inc ....G...... 516 428-3414
Plainview *(G-13622)*
N & L Instruments Inc ....F...... 631 471-4000
Ronkonkoma *(G-14948)*
NCR Corporation ....E...... 516 876-7200
Jericho *(G-7078)*
One Technologies LLC ....G...... 718 509-0704
Brooklyn *(G-2394)*
Pace Technology Inc ....E...... 631 981-2400
Ronkonkoma *(G-14963)*
Photon Vision Systems Inc ....F...... 607 749-2689
Homer *(G-6521)*
Qualtronic Devices Inc ....F...... 631 360-0859
Smithtown *(G-15497)*
Revonate Manufacturing LLC ....E...... 315 433-1160
Syracuse *(G-16023)*
Todd Enterprises Inc ....D...... 516 773-8087
Great Neck *(G-5844)*
Toshiba Amer Info Systems Inc ....B...... 949 583-3000
New York *(G-12376)*
Transland Sourcing LLC ....G...... 718 596-5704
Brooklyn *(G-2675)*
Wantagh Computer Center ....F...... 516 826-2189
Wantagh *(G-16564)*
Yellow E House Inc ....G...... 718 888-2000
Flushing *(G-5311)*

COMPUTERS, NEC, WHOLESALE

Todd Enterprises Inc ....D...... 516 773-8087
Great Neck *(G-5844)*

COMPUTERS, PERIPHERALS & SOFTWARE, WHOLESALE: Disk Drives

Formats Unlimited Inc ....F...... 631 249-9200
Deer Park *(G-4144)*

COMPUTERS, PERIPHERALS & SOFTWARE, WHOLESALE: Printers

Newport Business Solutions Inc ....F...... 631 319-6129
Bohemia *(G-1110)*
Printer Components Inc ....F...... 585 924-5190
Fairport *(G-4871)*

COMPUTERS, PERIPHERALS & SOFTWARE, WHOLESALE: Software

Base Systems Inc ....G...... 845 278-1991
Brewster *(G-1211)*
Cgi Technologies Solutions Inc ......F...... 212 682-7411
New York *(G-9573)*
Escholar LLC ....F...... 914 989-2900
White Plains *(G-17105)*
Infinite Software Solutions ....F...... 718 982-1315
Staten Island *(G-15687)*
Intermedia Outdoors Inc ....D...... 212 852-6600
New York *(G-10629)*
Interntnl Publcatns Media Grup ....G...... 917 604-9602
New York *(G-10640)*
Successware Remote LLC ....G...... 716 842-1439
Buffalo *(G-3199)*
Visible Systems Corporation ....E...... 508 628-1510
Oneida *(G-13170)*

PRODUCT SECTION

COMPUTERS: Indl, Process, Gas Flow
Pneumercator Company Inc .... E 631 293-8450
  Hauppauge *(G-6165)*

COMPUTERS: Mainframe
Policy ADM Solutions Inc .... E 914 332-4320
  Tarrytown *(G-16100)*

COMPUTERS: Mini
Oracle America Inc .... D 518 427-9353
  Albany *(G-111)*
Oracle America Inc .... D 585 317-4648
  Fairport *(G-4866)*

COMPUTERS: Personal
Apple Commuter Inc .... G 917 299-0066
  New Hyde Park *(G-8816)*
Apple Healing & Relaxation .... G 718 278-1089
  Long Island City *(G-7663)*
G S Communications USA Inc .... E 718 389-7371
  Brooklyn *(G-2010)*
Stargate Computer Corp .... G 516 474-4799
  Port Jeff STA *(G-13771)*
Telxon Corporation .... E 631 738-2400
  Holtsville *(G-6512)*
Toshiba America Inc .... E 212 596-0500
  New York *(G-12377)*
Wilcro Inc .... G 716 632-4204
  Buffalo *(G-3254)*

CONCENTRATES, DRINK
Carriage House Companies Inc .... A 716 672-4321
  Fredonia *(G-5371)*
Constellation Brands Inc .... D 585 678-7100
  Victor *(G-16469)*
Mr Smoothie .... G 845 296-1686
  Poughkeepsie *(G-13919)*

CONCENTRATES, FLAVORING, EXC DRINK
Consumer Flavoring Extract Co .... F 718 435-0201
  Brooklyn *(G-1798)*

CONCRETE CURING & HARDENING COMPOUNDS
Hanson Aggregates PA LLC .... F 585 436-3250
  Rochester *(G-14421)*
Watson Bowman Acme Corp .... D 716 691-8162
  Amherst *(G-271)*

CONCRETE MIXERS
X-Treme Ready Mix Inc .... G 718 739-3384
  Jamaica *(G-6965)*

CONCRETE PLANTS
Oneida Sales & Service Inc .... E 716 822-8205
  Buffalo *(G-3101)*
Oneida Sales & Service Inc .... F 716 270-0433
  Lackawanna *(G-7245)*
Seville Central Mix Corp .... D 516 293-6190
  Old Bethpage *(G-13130)*

CONCRETE PRDTS
A & R Concrete Products LLC .... E 845 562-0640
  New Windsor *(G-8929)*
Arnan Development Corp .... D 607 432-6641
  Oneonta *(G-13171)*
Baliva Concrete Products Inc .... G 585 328-8442
  Rochester *(G-14223)*
Barrett Paving Materials Inc .... F 315 737-9471
  Clayville *(G-3686)*
Buffalo Crushed Stone Inc .... E 716 826-7310
  Buffalo *(G-2850)*
Burnett Concrete Products Inc .... G 315 594-2242
  Wolcott *(G-17276)*
City Mason Corp .... F 718 658-3796
  Jamaica *(G-6903)*
Diamond Precast Products Inc .... F 631 874-3777
  Center Moriches *(G-3464)*
East Main Associates .... D 585 624-1990
  Lima *(G-7444)*
Elderlee Incorporated .... C 315 789-6670
  Oaks Corners *(G-13069)*
Express Concrete Inc .... G 631 273-4224
  Brentwood *(G-1183)*

Get Real Surfaces Inc .... F 845 337-4483
  Poughkeepsie *(G-13901)*
Grace Associates Inc .... G 718 767-9000
  Harrison *(G-5986)*
Graymont Materials (ny) Inc .... G 518 483-2671
  Malone *(G-8010)*
Graymont Materials (ny) Inc .... G 518 873-2275
  Lewis *(G-7431)*
Great ATL Pr-Cast Con Statuary .... G 718 948-5677
  Staten Island *(G-15682)*
Jab Concrete Supply Corp .... E 718 842-5250
  Bronx *(G-1364)*
Jenna Concrete Corporation .... E 718 842-5250
  Bronx *(G-1366)*
Jenna Harlem River Inc .... G 718 842-5997
  Bronx *(G-1367)*
John E Potente & Sons Inc .... E 516 935-8585
  Hicksville *(G-6357)*
Lafarge North America Inc .... E 518 756-5000
  Ravena *(G-14023)*
Long Island Geotech .... G 631 473-1044
  Port Jefferson *(G-13776)*
M K Ulrich Construction Inc .... F 716 893-5777
  Buffalo *(G-3053)*
Mid-Hudson Concrete Pdts Inc .... G 845 265-3141
  Cold Spring *(G-3763)*
Nicolia Concrete Products Inc .... D 631 669-0700
  Lindenhurst *(G-7476)*
NY Tempering LLC .... G 718 326-8989
  Maspeth *(G-8160)*
Quikrete Companies Inc .... E 716 213-2027
  Lackawanna *(G-7247)*
Riefler Concrete Products LLC .... C 716 649-3260
  Hamburg *(G-5940)*
Stag Brothers Cast Stone Co .... G 718 629-0975
  Brooklyn *(G-2596)*
Suhor Industries Inc .... G 716 483-6818
  Jamestown *(G-7032)*
Taylor Concrete Products Inc .... E 315 788-2191
  Watertown *(G-16673)*
Towne House Restorations Inc .... G 718 497-9200
  Long Island City *(G-7904)*
Unilock New York Inc .... G 845 278-6700
  Brewster *(G-1229)*
Woodards Concrete Products Inc .... E 845 361-3471
  Bullville *(G-3263)*

CONCRETE PRDTS, PRECAST, NEC
Afco Precast Sales Corp .... D 631 924-7114
  Middle Island *(G-8405)*
Callanan Industries Inc .... E 315 697-9569
  Canastota *(G-3364)*
Callanan Industries Inc .... C 518 374-2222
  Schenectady *(G-15236)*
Callanan Industries Inc .... E 845 331-6868
  Kingston *(G-7182)*
Castek Inc .... G 914 636-1000
  New Rochelle *(G-8891)*
David Kucera Inc .... E 845 255-1044
  Gardiner *(G-5549)*
Dillner Precast Inc .... G 631 421-9130
  Huntington Station *(G-6702)*
Dillner Precast Inc .... G 631 421-9130
  Lloyd Harbor *(G-7566)*
Dynasty Metal Works Inc .... E 631 284-3719
  Riverhead *(G-14141)*
Fort Miller Group Inc .... B 518 695-5000
  Greenwich *(G-5887)*
Fort Miller Service Corp .... F 518 695-5000
  Greenwich *(G-5888)*
Gamble & Gamble Inc .... G 716 731-3239
  Sanborn *(G-15120)*
Glens Falls Ready Mix Inc .... F 518 793-1695
  Queensbury *(G-13997)*
Glenwood Cast Stone Inc .... G 718 859-6500
  Brooklyn *(G-2027)*
Guardian Concrete Inc .... F 518 372-0080
  Schenectady *(G-15267)*
Island Ready Mix Inc .... G 631 874-3777
  Center Moriches *(G-3467)*
Lakelands Concrete Pdts Inc .... E 585 624-1990
  Lima *(G-7445)*
Lhv Precast Inc .... G 845 336-8880
  Kingston *(G-7196)*
Long Island Precast Inc .... E 631 286-0240
  Brookhaven *(G-1508)*
Oldcastle Precast Inc .... F 518 767-2116
  South Bethlehem *(G-15514)*
Oldcastle Precast Inc .... E 518 767-2112
  Selkirk *(G-15356)*

CONCRETE: Ready-Mixed

P J R Industries Inc .... E 716 825-9300
  Buffalo *(G-3106)*
Pelkowski Precast Corp .... F 631 269-5727
  Kings Park *(G-7173)*
Robinson Concrete Inc .... E 315 253-6666
  Auburn *(G-516)*
Sunnycrest Inc .... E 315 252-7214
  Auburn *(G-521)*
Transpo Industries Inc .... E 914 636-1000
  New Rochelle *(G-8926)*
Wel Made Enterprises Inc .... F 631 752-1238
  Farmingdale *(G-5141)*

CONCRETE: Asphaltic, Not From Refineries
Monticello Black Top Corp .... G 845 434-7280
  Thompsonville *(G-16115)*
Peckham Industries Inc .... E 914 949-2000
  White Plains *(G-17148)*
Peckham Industries Inc .... F 518 943-0155
  Catskill *(G-3433)*
Peckham Industries Inc .... F 518 893-2176
  Greenfield Center *(G-5871)*
PSI Transit Mix Corp .... G 631 382-7930
  Smithtown *(G-15496)*
Seabreeze Pavement of Ny LLC .... G 585 338-2333
  Rochester *(G-14679)*
Swift River Associates Inc .... F 716 875-0902
  Tonawanda *(G-16205)*

CONCRETE: Bituminous
Barrett Paving Materials Inc .... E 315 353-6611
  Norwood *(G-13040)*
Pallette Stone Corporation .... E 518 584-2421
  Gansevoort *(G-5487)*

CONCRETE: Ready-Mixed
A-1 Transitmix Inc .... F 718 292-3200
  Bronx *(G-1256)*
Advanced Ready Mix Corp .... F 718 497-5020
  Brooklyn *(G-1566)*
All American Transit Mix Corp .... G 718 417-3654
  Brooklyn *(G-1585)*
Atlas Concrete Batching Corp .... D 718 523-3000
  Jamaica *(G-6896)*
Atlas Transit Mix Corp .... C 718 523-3000
  Jamaica *(G-6897)*
Barney & Dickenson Inc .... E 607 729-1536
  Vestal *(G-16440)*
Barrett Paving Materials Inc .... F 315 788-2037
  Watertown *(G-16636)*
Best Concrete Mix Corp .... E 718 463-5500
  Flushing *(G-5230)*
Bonded Concrete Inc .... E 518 273-5800
  Watervliet *(G-16680)*
Bonded Concrete Inc .... F 518 674-2854
  West Sand Lake *(G-16931)*
Brewster Transit Mix Corp .... E 845 279-3738
  Brewster *(G-1213)*
Brewster Transit Mix Corp .... E 845 279-3738
  Brewster *(G-1214)*
Byram Concrete & Supply LLC .... F 914 682-4477
  White Plains *(G-17090)*
C & C Ready-Mix Corporation .... E 607 797-5108
  Vestal *(G-16443)*
C & C Ready-Mix Corporation .... E 607 687-1690
  Owego *(G-13351)*
Capital Concrete Inc .... G 716 648-8001
  Hamburg *(G-5919)*
Casa Redimix Concrete Corp .... F 718 589-1555
  Bronx *(G-1291)*
Ccz Ready Mix Concrete Corp .... G 516 579-7352
  Levittown *(G-7426)*
Cemex Cement Inc .... D 212 317-6000
  New York *(G-9559)*
Century Ready Mix Inc .... G 631 888-2200
  West Babylon *(G-16781)*
Champion Materials Inc .... G 315 493-2654
  Carthage *(G-3410)*
Champion Materials Inc .... E 315 493-2654
  Carthage *(G-3411)*
Chenango Concrete Corp .... F 518 294-9964
  Richmondville *(G-14089)*
Clark Concrete Co Inc .... G 315 478-4101
  Syracuse *(G-15896)*
Classic Concrete Corp .... F 516 822-1800
  Hicksville *(G-6332)*
Clemente Latham Concrete Corp .... D 518 374-2222
  Schenectady *(G-15243)*

Employee Codes: A=Over 500 employees, B=251-500
C=101-250, D=51-100, E=20-50, F=10-19, G=5-9

CONCRETE: Ready-Mixed

Cobleskill Red E Mix & Supply ....F 518 234-2015
  Amsterdam (G-340)
Corona Ready Mix Inc ....F 718 271-5940
  Corona (G-3995)
Cortland Ready Mix Inc ....F 607 753-3063
  Cortland (G-4021)
Cossitt Concrete Products Inc ....G 315 824-2700
  Hamilton (G-5947)
Costanza Ready Mix Inc ....F 516 334-7788
  North Bellmore (G-12918)
Cranesville Block Co Inc ....E 315 732-2135
  Utica (G-16317)
Cranesville Block Co Inc ....F 845 292-1585
  Liberty (G-7436)
Cranesville Block Co Inc ....E 845 896-5687
  Fishkill (G-5182)
Cranesville Block Co Inc ....E 845 331-1775
  Kingston (G-7185)
Cranesville Block Co Inc ....G 315 384-4000
  Norfolk (G-12898)
Cranesville Block Co Inc ....E 518 684-6000
  Amsterdam (G-341)
Cranesville Block Co Inc ....E 315 773-2296
  Felts Mills (G-5167)
Custom Mix Concrete Inc ....G 607 737-0281
  Coopers Plains (G-3882)
Custom Mix Concrete Inc ....G 607 737-0281
  Chemung (G-3593)
Custom Mix Inc ....F 516 797-7090
  Massapequa Park (G-8185)
Dalrymple Grav & Contg Co Inc ....F 607 739-0391
  Pine City (G-13550)
Dalrymple Holding Corp ....E 607 737-6200
  Pine City (G-13551)
Deer Park Sand & Gravel Corp ....F 631 586-2323
  Bay Shore (G-693)
Dicks Concrete Co Inc ....E 845 374-5966
  New Hampton (G-8799)
Dunkirk Construction Products ....G 716 366-5220
  Dunkirk (G-4338)
E Tetz & Sons Inc ....D 845 692-4486
  Middletown (G-8437)
East Coast Spring Mix Inc ....G 845 355-1215
  New Hampton (G-8800)
Electric City Concrete Co Inc ....E 518 887-5560
  Amsterdam (G-343)
Empire Transit Mix Inc ....E 718 384-3000
  Brooklyn (G-1922)
F H Stickles & Son Inc ....F 518 851-9048
  Livingston (G-7560)
Ferrara Bros Bldg Mtls Corp ....F 718 939-3030
  Flushing (G-5240)
Fulmont Ready-Mix Company Inc ....F 518 887-5560
  Amsterdam (G-347)
G & J Rdymx & Masnry Sup Inc ....F 718 454-0800
  Hollis (G-6497)
Glens Falls Ready Mix Inc ....G 518 793-1695
  Amsterdam (G-348)
Glens Falls Ready Mix Inc ....F 518 793-1695
  Queensbury (G-13997)
Grandview Concrete Corp ....E 518 346-7981
  Schenectady (G-15266)
Graymont Materials (ny) Inc ....F 315 265-8036
  Plattsburgh (G-13666)
Graymont Materials (ny) Inc ....D 518 561-5321
  Plattsburgh (G-13665)
Graymont Materials (ny) Inc ....F 518 873-2275
  Lewis (G-7431)
Greco Bros Rdymx Con Co Inc ....G 718 855-6271
  Brooklyn (G-2050)
Haley Concrete Inc ....F 716 492-0849
  Delevan (G-4234)
Hanson Aggregates East LLC ....F 585 344-1810
  Batavia (G-637)
Hanson Aggregates East LLC ....F 585 798-0762
  Medina (G-8274)
Hanson Aggregates East LLC ....F 716 372-1574
  Falconer (G-4900)
Hanson Aggregates East LLC ....F 315 548-2911
  Phelps (G-13533)
Hanson Aggregates New York LLC ....F 716 665-4620
  Jamestown (G-6998)
Hanson Aggregates New York LLC ....F 585 638-5841
  Pavilion (G-13449)
Hanson Aggregates New York LLC ....C 315 469-5501
  Jamesville (G-7048)
Inwood Material ....F 516 371-1842
  Inwood (G-6759)
Island Ready Mix Inc ....E 631 874-3777
  Center Moriches (G-3467)

James Town Macadam Inc ....D 716 665-4504
  Falconer (G-4903)
Jenna Concrete Corporation ....E 718 842-5250
  Bronx (G-1366)
Jenna Harlem River Inc ....G 718 842-5997
  Bronx (G-1367)
Jet Redi Mix Concrete Inc ....F 631 580-3640
  Ronkonkoma (G-14919)
King Road Materials Inc ....F 518 382-5354
  Albany (G-95)
Kings Park Ready Mix Corp ....F 631 269-4330
  Kings Park (G-7172)
Lafarge North America Inc ....F 518 756-5000
  Ravena (G-14023)
Lazarek Inc ....G 315 343-1242
  Oswego (G-13334)
Lehigh Cement Company ....E 518 943-5940
  Catskill (G-3430)
Lewbro Ready Mix Inc ....G 315 497-0498
  Groton (G-5899)
Manitou Concrete ....D 585 424-6040
  Rochester (G-14492)
Manzione Ready Mix Corp ....G 718 628-3837
  Brooklyn (G-2264)
Mastro Concrete Inc ....G 718 528-6788
  Rosedale (G-15014)
N Y Western Concrete Corp ....G 585 343-6850
  Batavia (G-643)
New Atlantic Ready Mix Corp ....G 718 812-0739
  Hollis (G-6498)
Nex-Gen Ready Mix Corp ....G 347 231-0073
  Bronx (G-1410)
Nicolia Ready Mix Inc ....E 631 669-7000
  Lindenhurst (G-7477)
Northern Ready-Mix Inc ....G 315 598-2141
  Fulton (G-5473)
Oldcastle Precast Inc ....F 518 767-2116
  South Bethlehem (G-15514)
Oneida Sales & Service Inc ....G 716 270-0433
  Lackawanna (G-7245)
Otsego Ready Mix Inc ....F 607 432-3400
  Oneonta (G-13191)
Precision Ready Mix Inc ....G 718 658-5600
  Jamaica (G-6939)
Presti Ready Mix Concrete Inc ....G 516 378-6006
  Freeport (G-5419)
Quality Ready Mix Inc ....F 516 437-0100
  New Hyde Park (G-8857)
Queens Ready Mix Inc ....G 718 526-4919
  Jamaica (G-6942)
Quikrete Companies Inc ....E 315 673-2020
  Marcellus (G-8088)
Residential Fences Corp ....F 631 205-9758
  Ridge (G-14094)
Richmond Ready Mix Corp ....G 917 731-8400
  Staten Island (G-15733)
Riefler Concrete Products LLC ....C 716 649-3260
  Hamburg (G-5940)
Robinson Concrete Inc ....E 315 253-6666
  Auburn (G-516)
Robinson Concrete Inc ....F 315 492-6200
  Jamesville (G-7051)
Robinson Concrete Inc ....F 315 676-4662
  Brewerton (G-1205)
Rochester Asphalt Materials ....D 585 924-7360
  Farmington (G-5154)
Rochester Asphalt Materials ....G 585 381-7010
  Rochester (G-14634)
Rock Iroquois Products Inc ....F 585 381-7010
  Rochester (G-14655)
Rural Hill Sand and Grav Corp ....F 315 846-5212
  Woodville (G-17367)
Russian Mix Inc ....G 347 385-7198
  Brooklyn (G-2517)
Saunders Concrete Co Inc ....F 607 756-7905
  Cortland (G-4044)
Scara-Mix Inc ....E 718 442-7357
  Staten Island (G-15734)
Seville Central Mix Corp ....F 516 868-3000
  Freeport (G-5426)
Seville Central Mix Corp ....D 516 293-6190
  Old Bethpage (G-13130)
Seville Central Mix Corp ....G 516 239-8333
  Lawrence (G-7400)
South Shore Ready Mix Inc ....G 516 872-3049
  Valley Stream (G-16428)
Star Ready Mix East Inc ....F 631 289-8787
  East Hampton (G-4416)
Star Ready Mix Inc ....F 631 289-8787
  Medford (G-8260)

Stephen Miller Gen Contrs Inc ....E 518 661-5601
  Gloversville (G-5723)
Suffolk Cement Products Inc ....E 631 727-2317
  Calverton (G-3300)
Sullivan Concrete Inc ....F 845 888-2235
  Cochecton (G-3744)
T Mix Inc ....G 646 379-6814
  Brooklyn (G-2639)
TEC - Crete Transit Mix Corp ....E 718 657-6880
  Ridgewood (G-14126)
Thousand Island Ready Mix Con ....G 315 686-3203
  La Fargeville (G-7238)
Torrington Industries Inc ....G 315 676-4662
  Central Square (G-3518)
United Materials LLC ....D 716 683-1432
  North Tonawanda (G-13004)
United Materials LLC ....E 716 731-2332
  Sanborn (G-15129)
United Materials LLC ....E 716 662-0564
  Orchard Park (G-13301)
United Transit Mix Inc ....E 718 416-3400
  Brooklyn (G-2703)
US Concrete Inc ....E 718 853-4644
  Roslyn Heights (G-15034)
US Concrete Inc ....E 718 438-6800
  Brooklyn (G-2712)
W F Saunders & Sons Inc ....F 315 469-3217
  Nedrow (G-8773)
Watertown Concrete Inc ....F 315 788-1040
  Watertown (G-16675)

CONDENSERS & CONDENSING UNITS: Air Conditioner

Cold Point Corporation ....E 315 339-2331
  Rome (G-14809)
Motivair Corporation ....E 716 691-9222
  Amherst (G-252)

CONDENSERS: Fixed Or Variable

Viking Technologies Ltd ....E 631 957-8000
  Lindenhurst (G-7493)

CONDENSERS: Heat Transfer Eqpt, Evaporative

Alstrom Corporation ....E 718 824-4901
  Bronx (G-1270)
Roemac Industrial Sales Inc ....E 716 692-7332
  North Tonawanda (G-12991)
Rubicon Industries Corp ....E 718 434-4700
  Brooklyn (G-2515)

CONDENSERS: Motors Or Generators

GM Components Holdings LLC ....B 716 439-2463
  Lockport (G-7590)

CONDUITS & FITTINGS: Electric

Highland Valley Supply Inc ....F 845 849-2863
  Wappingers Falls (G-16572)
Producto Electric Corp ....E 845 359-4900
  Orangeburg (G-13243)
Superflex Ltd ....E 718 768-1400
  Brooklyn (G-2625)

CONDUITS: Pressed Pulp Fiber, Made From Purchased Materials

Stanley Paper Co Inc ....F 518 489-1131
  Albany (G-136)

CONFECTIONERY PRDTS WHOLESALERS

Mrchocolatecom LLC ....F 718 875-9772
  Brooklyn (G-2341)
Roger L Urban Inc ....E 716 693-5391
  North Tonawanda (G-12992)

CONFECTIONS & CANDY

5th Avenue Chocolatiere Ltd ....F 516 561-1570
  Valley Stream (G-16397)
5th Avenue Chocolatiere Ltd ....G 212 935-5454
  Freeport (G-5379)
C Howard Company Inc ....G 631 286-7940
  Bellport (G-827)
Calico Cottage Inc ....E 631 841-2100
  Amityville (G-278)

Chocolat Moderne LLC............................G..... 212 229-4797
  New York (G-9605)
Chocolations LLC..................................G..... 914 777-3600
  Mamaroneck (G-8028)
Custom Candy Concepts Inc.................G..... 516 824-3228
  Inwood (G-6754)
Dilese International Inc..........................F..... 716 855-3500
  Buffalo (G-2915)
Dylans Candy Bar Inc............................F..... 212 620-2700
  New York (G-9946)
Fairbanks Mfg LLC.................................C..... 845 341-0002
  Middletown (G-8440)
First Source LLC....................................D..... 716 877-0800
  Tonawanda (G-16162)
Gertrude Hawk Chocolates Inc...............E.....
  Watertown (G-16652)
Godiva Chocolatier Inc..........................E..... 212 984-5900
  New York (G-10326)
Gravymaster Inc....................................E..... 203 453-1893
  Canajoharie (G-3332)
Handsome Dans LLC.............................G..... 917 965-2499
  New York (G-10405)
Hedonist Artisan Chocolates..................F..... 585 461-2815
  Rochester (G-14432)
Hercules Candy Co.................................F..... 315 463-4339
  East Syracuse (G-4537)
Hudson Valley Chocolatier Inc................F..... 845 831-8240
  Beacon (G-785)
In Room Plus Inc....................................E..... 716 838-9433
  Buffalo (G-3005)
Jo-Mart Candies Corp............................F..... 718 375-1277
  Brooklyn (G-2143)
Joyva Corp...D..... 718 497-0170
  Brooklyn (G-2154)
Lady-N-Th-wndow Chocolates Inc..........F..... 631 549-1059
  Huntington (G-6666)
Lanco Corporation.................................C..... 631 231-2300
  Ronkonkoma (G-14929)
Little Bird Chocolates Inc.......................G..... 646 620-6395
  Massapequa (G-8180)
Momn Pops Inc......................................E..... 845 567-0640
  Cornwall (G-3988)
Mrchocolatecom LLC..............................F..... 718 875-9772
  Brooklyn (G-2341)
Noras Candy Shop..................................F..... 315 337-4530
  Rome (G-14825)
Papa Bubble..G..... 212 966-2599
  New York (G-11562)
Premium Sweets USA Inc......................G..... 718 739-6000
  Jamaica (G-6940)
Rajbhog Foods Inc.................................E..... 718 358-5105
  Flushing (G-5287)
Richardson Brands Company.................C..... 518 673-3553
  Canajoharie (G-3333)
Roger L Urban Inc..................................E..... 716 693-5391
  North Tonawanda (G-12992)
Salty Road Inc.......................................G..... 347 673-3925
  Brooklyn (G-2531)
Satin Fine Foods Inc..............................F..... 845 469-1034
  Chester (G-3615)
Scaccianoce Inc....................................F..... 718 991-4462
  Bronx (G-1449)
Seaward Candies...................................G..... 585 638-6761
  Holley (G-6492)
Settons Intl Foods Inc............................E..... 631 543-8090
  Commack (G-3842)
Simply Natural Foods LLC......................E..... 631 543-9600
  Commack (G-3843)
Steve & Andys Organics Inc...................G..... 718 499-7933
  New York (G-12199)
Stones Homemade Candies Inc.............G..... 315 343-8401
  Oswego (G-13342)
Sweetworks Inc.....................................C..... 716 634-4545
  Buffalo (G-3205)
Tomric Systems Inc...............................G..... 716 854-6050
  Buffalo (G-3221)
Valenti Distributing................................G..... 716 824-2304
  Blasdell (G-968)
Vidal Candies USA Inc............................F..... 609 781-8169
  New York (G-12541)
Wellspring Corp.....................................G..... 212 529-5454
  New York (G-12609)
Worlds Finest Chocolate Inc..................C..... 718 332-2442
  Brooklyn (G-2767)

CONNECTORS & TERMINALS: Electrical Device Uses

Fiber Instrument Sales Inc....................C..... 315 736-2206
  Oriskany (G-13309)

Zierick Manufacturing Corp....................D..... 800 882-8020
  Mount Kisco (G-8648)

CONNECTORS: Cord, Electric

Crown Die Casting Corp.........................E..... 914 667-5400
  Mount Vernon (G-8675)
EB Acquisitions LLC...............................D..... 212 355-3310
  New York (G-9971)

CONNECTORS: Electrical

Automatic Connector Inc.......................F..... 631 543-5000
  Hauppauge (G-6029)
Command Components Corporation......G..... 631 666-4411
  Bay Shore (G-688)
Pei/Genesis Inc.....................................G..... 631 256-1747
  Farmingville (G-5161)

CONNECTORS: Electronic

Accessories For Electronics...................E..... 631 847-0158
  South Hempstead (G-15529)
Amphenol Corporation...........................B..... 607 563-5364
  Sidney (G-15436)
Amphenol Corporation...........................A..... 607 563-5011
  Sidney (G-15437)
Automatic Connector Inc.......................F..... 631 543-5000
  Hauppauge (G-6029)
Belden Inc...B..... 607 796-5600
  Horseheads (G-6569)
Casa Innovations Inc............................G..... 718 965-6600
  Brooklyn (G-1763)
Deutsch Corporate Inc..........................F..... 212 710-5870
  New York (G-9862)
EBY Electro Inc......................................E..... 516 576-7777
  Plainview (G-13598)
Executive Machines Inc.........................E..... 718 965-6600
  Brooklyn (G-1945)
Felchar Manufacturing Corp..................A..... 607 723-3106
  Binghamton (G-914)
I Trade Technology Ltd........................G..... 615 348-7233
  Suffern (G-15792)
Ieh Corporation....................................C..... 718 492-4440
  Brooklyn (G-2096)
Keystone Electronics Corp....................C..... 718 956-8900
  Astoria (G-446)
Kirtas Inc..E..... 585 924-2420
  Victor (G-16486)
Leviton Manufacturing Co Inc...............B..... 631 812-6000
  Melville (G-8334)
Mason Industries Inc............................C..... 631 348-0282
  Hauppauge (G-6126)
Mill-Max Mfg Corp.................................C..... 516 922-6000
  Oyster Bay (G-13371)
Mini-Circuits Fort Wayne LLC................B..... 718 934-4500
  Brooklyn (G-2318)
NEa Manufacturing Corp.......................E..... 516 371-4200
  Inwood (G-6763)
Power Connector Inc............................E..... 631 563-7878
  Bohemia (G-1118)
Rdi Inc..F..... 914 773-1000
  Mount Kisco (G-8643)
Resonance Technologies Inc.................E..... 631 237-4901
  Ronkonkoma (G-14978)
Sitewatch Technology LLC....................G..... 207 778-3246
  East Quogue (G-4452)
Supplynet Inc.......................................G..... 845 267-2655
  Valley Cottage (G-16392)
Sureseal Corporation............................G..... 607 336-6676
  Norwich (G-13038)
Taro Manufacturing Company Inc.........F..... 315 252-9430
  Auburn (G-523)
Universal Remote Control Inc................D..... 914 630-4343
  Harrison (G-5993)
Virtue Paintball LLC..............................G..... 631 617-5560
  Hauppauge (G-6226)
Whirlwind Music Distrs Inc....................D..... 585 663-8820
  Rochester (G-14762)

CONNECTORS: Solderless, Electric-Wiring Devices

Andros Manufacturing Corp..................F..... 585 663-5700
  Rochester (G-14205)

CONSTRUCTION & MINING MACHINERY WHOLESALERS

Gone South Concrete Block Inc............E..... 315 598-2141
  Fulton (G-5459)

CONSTRUCTION & ROAD MAINTENANCE EQPT: Drags, Road

Drillco National Group Inc.....................E..... 718 726-9801
  Long Island City (G-7718)
Highway Garage....................................G..... 518 568-2837
  Saint Johnsville (G-15096)

CONSTRUCTION EQPT: Attachments

Hansteel (usa) Inc.................................G..... 212 226-0105
  New York (G-10411)
Primoplast Inc.......................................F..... 631 750-0680
  Bohemia (G-1121)

CONSTRUCTION EQPT: Attachments, Snow Plow

Cives Corporation..................................D..... 315 543-2321
  Harrisville (G-5995)
Eric S Hapeman....................................G..... 716 731-5416
  Niagara Falls (G-12815)
G C Castings Inc...................................F..... 607 432-4518
  Oneonta (G-13187)
Pro-Tech Wldg Fabrication Inc..............E..... 585 436-9855
  Rochester (G-14603)
Town of Ohio..E..... 315 392-2055
  Forestport (G-5332)

CONSTRUCTION EQPT: Crane Carriers

Crane Equipment & Service Inc.............G..... 716 689-5400
  Amherst (G-235)

CONSTRUCTION EQPT: Cranes

Dave Sandel Cranes Inc........................G..... 631 325-5588
  Westhampton (G-17056)
Industrial Handling Svcs Inc..................G..... 518 399-0488
  Alplaus (G-205)
Kinedyne Inc...F..... 716 667-6833
  Orchard Park (G-13278)
Sierson Crane & Welding Inc................G..... 315 723-6914
  Westmoreland (G-17066)

CONSTRUCTION EQPT: Dozers, Tractor Mounted, Material Moving

Rapistak Corporation............................G..... 716 822-2804
  Blasdell (G-964)

CONSTRUCTION EQPT: Hammer Mills, Port, Incl Rock/Ore Crush

Schutte-Buffalo Hammermill LLC..........E..... 716 855-1202
  Buffalo (G-3178)

CONSTRUCTION EQPT: Rollers, Sheepsfoot & Vibratory

S R & R Industries Inc..........................G..... 845 692-8329
  Middletown (G-8461)

CONSTRUCTION EQPT: SCRAPERS, GRADERS, ROLLERS & SIMILAR EQPT

Gei International Inc.............................E..... 315 463-9261
  East Syracuse (G-4533)

CONSTRUCTION EQPT: Wrecker Hoists, Automobile

Pauls Rods & Restos Inc......................G..... 631 665-7637
  Deer Park (G-4187)
Vanhouten Motorsports.........................G..... 315 387-6312
  Lacona (G-7252)

CONSTRUCTION MATERIALS, WHOLESALE: Aggregate

Twin County Recycling Corp..................F..... 516 827-6900
  Westbury (G-17038)

CONSTRUCTION MATERIALS, WHOLESALE: Awnings

Acme Awning Co Inc.............................F..... 718 409-1881
  Bronx (G-1262)

CONSTRUCTION MATERIALS, WHOLESALE: Block, Concrete & Cinder

Lazarek Inc	G	315 343-1242
Oswego *(G-13334)*		
Taylor Concrete Products Inc	E	315 788-2191
Watertown *(G-16673)*		

CONSTRUCTION MATERIALS, WHOLESALE: Blocks, Building, NEC

Sg Blocks Inc	G	212 520-6218
New York *(G-12033)*		

CONSTRUCTION MATERIALS, WHOLESALE: Building Stone, Granite

Glen Plaza Marble & Gran Inc	G	516 671-1100
Glen Cove *(G-5617)*		
MCM Natural Stone Inc	F	585 586-6510
Rochester *(G-14502)*		

CONSTRUCTION MATERIALS, WHOLESALE: Building, Exterior

Bestway Enterprises Inc	E	607 753-8261
Cortland *(G-4012)*		
Bob Murphy Inc	F	607 729-3553
Vestal *(G-16442)*		
Brodco Inc	E	631 842-4477
Lido Beach *(G-7440)*		
Dolomite Products Company Inc	E	315 524-1998
Rochester *(G-14316)*		
Tri-State Brick & Stone NY Inc	D	212 366-0300
New York *(G-12402)*		

CONSTRUCTION MATERIALS, WHOLESALE: Building, Interior

Great American Industries Inc	G	607 729-9331
Vestal *(G-16449)*		
Nanz Custom Hardware Inc	D	212 367-7000
New York *(G-11340)*		
Nanz Custom Hardware Inc	D	212 367-7000
Deer Park *(G-4176)*		

CONSTRUCTION MATERIALS, WHOLESALE: Cement

Dicks Concrete Co Inc	E	845 374-5966
New Hampton *(G-8799)*		
Lehigh Cement Company	E	518 943-5940
Catskill *(G-3430)*		

CONSTRUCTION MATERIALS, WHOLESALE: Clay, Exc Refractory

Walsh & Hughes Inc	G	631 427-5904
Huntington Station *(G-6728)*		

CONSTRUCTION MATERIALS, WHOLESALE: Concrete Mixtures

Barney & Dickenson Inc	E	607 729-1536
Vestal *(G-16440)*		

CONSTRUCTION MATERIALS, WHOLESALE: Door Frames

Lif Industries Inc	D	516 390-6800
Port Washington *(G-13837)*		
Long Island Fireproof Door	E	718 767-8800
Whitestone *(G-17211)*		
Milanese Commercial Door LLC	F	518 658-0398
Berlin *(G-857)*		

CONSTRUCTION MATERIALS, WHOLESALE: Glass

Twin Pane Insulated GL Co Inc	F	631 924-1060
Yaphank *(G-17407)*		

CONSTRUCTION MATERIALS, WHOLESALE: Gravel

Brewster Transit Mix Corp	E	845 279-3738
Brewster *(G-1213)*		
Deer Park Sand & Gravel Corp	E	631 586-2423
Bay Shore *(G-693)*		

Jamestown Macadam Inc	F	716 664-5108
Jamestown *(G-7009)*		

CONSTRUCTION MATERIALS, WHOLESALE: Lime Building Prdts

Specialty Minerals Inc	E	212 878-1800
New York *(G-12152)*		

CONSTRUCTION MATERIALS, WHOLESALE: Limestone

Minerals Technologies Inc	E	212 878-1800
New York *(G-11276)*		

CONSTRUCTION MATERIALS, WHOLESALE: Masons' Materials

Colonie Block and Supply Co	G	518 869-8411
Colonie *(G-3819)*		
Grandview Block & Supply Co	E	518 346-7981
Schenectady *(G-15265)*		

CONSTRUCTION MATERIALS, WHOLESALE: Millwork

I Meglio Corp	E	631 617-6900
Brentwood *(G-1184)*		

CONSTRUCTION MATERIALS, WHOLESALE: Molding, All Materials

Globmarble LLC	G	347 717-4088
Brooklyn *(G-2030)*		
Jaxson Rollforming Inc	E	631 842-7775
Amityville *(G-298)*		

CONSTRUCTION MATERIALS, WHOLESALE: Paving Materials

Barrett Paving Materials Inc	E	315 353-6611
Norwood *(G-13040)*		
Classic Concrete Corp	F	516 822-1800
Hicksville *(G-6332)*		

CONSTRUCTION MATERIALS, WHOLESALE: Paving Mixtures

Peckham Materials Corp	D	914 686-2045
White Plains *(G-17149)*		

CONSTRUCTION MATERIALS, WHOLESALE: Prefabricated Structures

Morton Buildings Inc	E	585 786-8191
Warsaw *(G-16583)*		

CONSTRUCTION MATERIALS, WHOLESALE: Roof, Asphalt/Sheet Metal

Jordan Panel Systems Corp	E	631 754-4900
East Northport *(G-4439)*		

CONSTRUCTION MATERIALS, WHOLESALE: Roofing & Siding Material

Marathon Roofing Products Inc	F	716 685-3340
Orchard Park *(G-13282)*		
Park Ave Bldg & Roofg Sups LLC	E	718 403-0100
Brooklyn *(G-2407)*		

CONSTRUCTION MATERIALS, WHOLESALE: Sand

F H Stickles & Son Inc	F	518 851-9048
Livingston *(G-7560)*		
Monticello Black Top Corp	G	845 434-7280
Thompsonville *(G-16115)*		

CONSTRUCTION MATERIALS, WHOLESALE: Septic Tanks

Guardian Concrete Inc	F	518 372-0080
Schenectady *(G-15267)*		

CONSTRUCTION MATERIALS, WHOLESALE: Siding, Exc Wood

Pal Aluminum Inc	G	516 937-1990
Hicksville *(G-6383)*		

CONSTRUCTION MATERIALS, WHOLESALE: Stone, Crushed Or Broken

Buffalo Crushed Stone Inc	F	716 566-9636
Franklinville *(G-5368)*		
Callahan & Nannini Quarry Inc	G	845 496-4323
Salisbury Mills *(G-15112)*		
Callanan Industries Inc	E	845 457-3158
Montgomery *(G-8592)*		
Dalrymple Grav & Contg Co Inc	E	607 529-3235
Chemung *(G-3594)*		
Grosso Materials Inc	F	845 361-5211
Montgomery *(G-8594)*		
Hanson Aggregates PA LLC	E	315 782-2300
Watertown *(G-16653)*		
Pallette Stone Corporation	E	518 584-2421
Gansevoort *(G-5487)*		
Seneca Stone Corporation	F	315 549-8253
Fayette *(G-5162)*		
Troy Sand & Gravel Co Inc	F	518 674-2854
West Sand Lake *(G-16932)*		

CONSTRUCTION MATERIALS, WHOLESALE: Tile, Clay/Other Ceramic

Foro Marble Co Inc	E	718 852-2322
Brooklyn *(G-1996)*		
Kowa American Corporation	E	212 303-7800
New York *(G-10882)*		

CONSTRUCTION MATERIALS, WHOLESALE: Windows

Excel Aluminum Products Inc	G	315 471-0925
Syracuse *(G-15940)*		
Express Building Supply Inc	E	516 608-0379
Oceanside *(G-13079)*		
New Bgnnngs Win Door Dstrs LLC	F	845 214-0698
Poughkeepsie *(G-13920)*		
Norandex Inc Vestal	G	607 786-0778
Vestal *(G-16452)*		

CONSTRUCTION MATLS, WHOL: Lumber, Rough, Dressed/Finished

Berry Industrial Group Inc	G	845 353-8338
Nyack *(G-13045)*		

CONSTRUCTION SAND MINING

Buffalo Crushed Stone Inc	G	607 587-8102
Alfred Station *(G-196)*		
Country Side Sand & Gravel	F	716 988-3271
South Dayton *(G-15519)*		
Eagle Harbor Sand & Gravel Inc	E	585 798-4501
Albion *(G-164)*		
Elam Sand & Gravel Corp	E	585 657-8000
Bloomfield *(G-987)*		
John Vespa Inc	F	315 788-6330
Watertown *(G-16656)*		
Lazarek Inc	G	315 343-1242
Oswego *(G-13334)*		
Little Valley Sand & Gravel	G	716 938-6676
Little Valley *(G-7511)*		
Palumbo Sand & Gravel Company	E	845 832-3356
Dover Plains *(G-4317)*		
Ruby Engineering LLC	G	646 391-4600
Brooklyn *(G-2516)*		
Rural Hill Sand and Grav Corp	F	315 846-5212
Woodville *(G-17367)*		
Syracusa Sand and Gravel Inc	F	585 924-7146
Victor *(G-16505)*		

CONSTRUCTION SITE PREPARATION SVCS

Kevin Regan Logging Ltd	G	315 245-3890
Camden *(G-3317)*		

CONSTRUCTION: Bridge

Dalrymple Holding Corp	E	607 737-6200
Pine City *(G-13551)*		

CONSTRUCTION: Commercial & Institutional Building

Dynasty Stainless Steel & Meta	E	718 205-6623
Maspeth *(G-8134)*		
Stephen Miller Gen Contrs Inc	E	518 661-5601
Gloversville *(G-5723)*		

(G-0000) Company's Geographic Section entry number

PRODUCT SECTION

CONSULTING SVCS, BUSINESS: Systems Analysis Or Design

CONSTRUCTION: Dry Cleaning Plant
Genco John .... G 716 483-5446
Jamestown *(G-6994)*

CONSTRUCTION: Food Prdts Manufacturing or Packing Plant
Sidco Food Distribution Corp .... F 718 733-3939
Bronx *(G-1452)*

CONSTRUCTION: Greenhouse
Pei Liquidation Company .... F 315 431-4697
East Syracuse *(G-4554)*

CONSTRUCTION: Guardrails, Highway
Elderlee Incorporated .... C 315 789-6670
Oaks Corners *(G-13069)*

CONSTRUCTION: Heavy Highway & Street
A Colarusso and Son Inc .... E 518 828-3218
Hudson *(G-6603)*
Barrett Paving Materials Inc .... F 315 788-2037
Watertown *(G-16636)*
Dalrymple Holding Corp .... E 607 737-6200
Pine City *(G-13551)*
Peckham Materials Corp .... E 518 747-3353
Hudson Falls *(G-6649)*
Suit-Kote Corporation .... E 607 535-2743
Watkins Glen *(G-16697)*

CONSTRUCTION: Indl Building & Warehouse
Siemens Industry Inc .... E 716 568-0983
Buffalo *(G-3187)*

CONSTRUCTION: Indl Buildings, New, NEC
Orange County Ironworks LLC .... E 845 769-3000
Montgomery *(G-8600)*
Stephen Miller Gen Contrs Inc .... E 518 661-5601
Gloversville *(G-5723)*

CONSTRUCTION: Pharmaceutical Manufacturing Plant
Knf Clean Room Products Corp .... E 631 588-7000
Ronkonkoma *(G-14923)*

CONSTRUCTION: Power & Communication Transmission Tower
Standard Ascnsion Towers Group .... D 716 681-2222
Depew *(G-4274)*

CONSTRUCTION: Religious Building
Makarenko Studios Inc .... G 914 968-7673
Yorktown Heights *(G-17512)*

CONSTRUCTION: Single-Family Housing
Fantasy Home Improvement Corp .... G 718 277-4021
Brooklyn *(G-1958)*
Frost Publications Inc .... G 845 726-3232
Westtown *(G-17068)*
Kasson & Keller Inc .... A 518 853-3421
Fonda *(G-5315)*

CONSTRUCTION: Single-family Housing, New
Capitol Restoration Corp .... G 516 783-1425
North Bellmore *(G-12915)*

CONSTRUCTION: Street Surfacing & Paving
Barrett Paving Materials Inc .... E 315 353-6511
Norwood *(G-13040)*
Cofire Paving Corporation .... E 718 463-1403
Flushing *(G-5234)*
John T Montecalvo Inc .... G 631 325-1492
Speonk *(G-15576)*
Lomin Construction Company .... G 516 759-5734
Glen Head *(G-5636)*

CONSTRUCTION: Tennis Court
Lomin Construction Company .... G 516 759-5734
Glen Head *(G-5636)*

CONSTRUCTION: Waste Water & Sewage Treatment Plant
Richard R Cain Inc .... F 845 229-7410
Hyde Park *(G-6736)*

CONSULTING SVC: Business, NEC
Batavia Precision Glass LLC .... G 585 343-6050
Buffalo *(G-2833)*
Cambridge Whos Who Pubg Inc .... E 516 833-8440
Uniondale *(G-16290)*
Ceramaterials LLC .... E 518 701-6722
Port Jervis *(G-13781)*
Chromagraphics Press Inc .... G 631 367-6160
Melville *(G-8302)*
Integrated Graphics Inc .... G 212 592-5600
New York *(G-10616)*
Marketplace Slutions Group LLC .... E 631 868-0111
Holbrook *(G-6461)*
Milmar Food Group II LLC .... C 845 294-5400
Goshen *(G-5738)*
Next Step Publishing Inc .... F 585 742-1260
Victor *(G-16494)*
Resonant Legal Media LLC .... E 212 687-7100
New York *(G-11840)*
Seed Media Group LLC .... E 646 502-7050
New York *(G-12016)*
Slosson Edctl Publications Inc .... F 716 652-0930
East Aurora *(G-4379)*
Wercs Ltd .... E 518 640-9200
Latham *(G-7384)*

CONSULTING SVC: Computer
Caminus Corporation .... D 212 515-3600
New York *(G-9508)*
Cgi Technologies Solutions Inc .... F 212 682-7411
New York *(G-9573)*
Classroom Inc .... E 212 545-8400
New York *(G-9639)*
Dohnsco Inc .... G 516 773-4800
Manhasset *(G-8059)*
Pegasystems Inc .... E 212 626-6550
New York *(G-11601)*
Teacup Software Inc .... G 212 563-9288
Brooklyn *(G-2648)*

CONSULTING SVC: Educational
National Prof Resources .... E 914 937-8879
Port Chester *(G-13755)*
National Rding Styles Inst Inc .... F 516 921-5500
Syosset *(G-15831)*

CONSULTING SVC: Engineering
Complex Biosystems Inc .... G 315 464-8007
Liverpool *(G-7517)*
Exergy LLC .... E 516 832-9300
Garden City *(G-5505)*
General Composites Inc .... E 518 963-7333
Willsboro *(G-17265)*
Glasgow Products Inc .... E 516 374-5937
Woodmere *(G-17313)*
Innovation Associates Inc .... C 607 798-9376
Johnson City *(G-7095)*
Mdek Inc .... G 347 569-7318
Brooklyn *(G-2288)*
Procomponents Inc .... E 516 683-0909
Westbury *(G-17023)*
Select Controls Inc .... E 631 567-9010
Bohemia *(G-1131)*
Skae Power Solutions LLC .... E 845 365-9103
Palisades *(G-13402)*

CONSULTING SVC: Financial Management
Principia Partners LLC .... D 212 480-2270
New York *(G-11713)*

CONSULTING SVC: Human Resource
Chequedcom Inc .... E 888 412-0699
Saratoga Springs *(G-15149)*

CONSULTING SVC: Management
Aj Greentech Holdings Ltd .... G 718 395-8706
Flushing *(G-5223)*
Altius Aviation LLC .... G 315 455-7555
Syracuse *(G-15852)*

Barker Steel LLC .... E 518 465-6221
Albany *(G-52)*
Beer Marketers Insights Inc .... G 845 507-0040
Suffern *(G-15786)*
Ca Inc .... A 800 225-5224
New York *(G-9491)*
Gary Roth & Associates Ltd .... E 516 333-1000
Westbury *(G-16990)*
Marketplace Slutions Group LLC .... E 631 868-0111
Holbrook *(G-6461)*
Res Media Group Inc .... F 212 320-3750
New York *(G-11838)*

CONSULTING SVC: Marketing Management
In-Step Marketing Inc .... F 212 797-3450
New York *(G-10579)*
Maven Marketing LLC .... G 615 510-3248
New York *(G-11183)*
Rainforest Inc .... F 212 575-7620
New York *(G-11790)*
Ramsbury Property Us Inc .... F 212 223-6250
New York *(G-11796)*
Rfn Inc .... F 516 764-5100
Bay Shore *(G-733)*
Tri-Force Sales LLC .... E 732 261-5507
New York *(G-12399)*
Zacks Enterprises Inc .... E 800 366-4924
Orangeburg *(G-13248)*

CONSULTING SVC: Online Technology
Orthstar Enterprises Inc .... D 607 562-2100
Horseheads *(G-6586)*

CONSULTING SVC: Sales Management
Island Marketing Corp .... G 516 739-0500
Mineola *(G-8517)*
Karp Overseas Corporation .... E 718 784-2105
Maspeth *(G-8148)*

CONSULTING SVCS, BUSINESS: Communications
L-3 Communications Corporation .... D 631 231-1700
Hauppauge *(G-6109)*
Redcom Laboratories Inc .... C 585 924-6567
Victor *(G-16500)*

CONSULTING SVCS, BUSINESS: Energy Conservation
Gotham Energy 360 LLC .... F 917 338-1023
New York *(G-10340)*
Project Energy Savers LLC .... F 718 596-4231
Brooklyn *(G-2454)*
Western Oil and Gas JV Inc .... G 914 967-4758
Rye *(G-15069)*

CONSULTING SVCS, BUSINESS: Publishing
Mnn Holding Company LLC .... F 404 558-5251
Brooklyn *(G-2326)*

CONSULTING SVCS, BUSINESS: Safety Training Svcs
Bullex Inc .... F 518 689-2023
Albany *(G-58)*

CONSULTING SVCS, BUSINESS: Sys Engnrg, Exc Computer/Prof
Laurus Development Inc .... F 716 823-1202
Buffalo *(G-3047)*
Sale 121 Corp .... D 240 855-8988
New York *(G-11956)*

CONSULTING SVCS, BUSINESS: Systems Analysis & Engineering
Syntel Inc .... F 212 785-9810
New York *(G-12263)*

CONSULTING SVCS, BUSINESS: Systems Analysis Or Design
Relx Inc .... E 212 309-8100
New York *(G-11826)*
Visible Systems Corporation .... E 508 628-1510
Oneida *(G-13170)*

CONSULTING SVCS, BUSINESS: Test Development & Evaluation

Micro Semicdtr Researches LLC.........G....... 646 863-6070
New York *(G-11254)*

CONSULTING SVCS, BUSINESS: Testing, Educational Or Personnel

Bright Kids Nyc Inc.....................................E....... 917 539-4575
New York *(G-9460)*

CONSULTING SVCS: Oil

Gotham Energy 360 LLC......................F....... 917 338-1023
New York *(G-10340)*

CONSULTING SVCS: Scientific

Cognigen Corporation............................D....... 716 633-3463
Buffalo *(G-2878)*
Guosa Life Sciences Inc.......................F....... 516 481-1540
North Baldwin *(G-12906)*

CONTACT LENSES

Alden Optical Laboratory Inc...............F....... 716 937-9181
Lancaster *(G-7302)*
Coopervision Inc......................................A....... 585 385-6810
West Henrietta *(G-16874)*
Coopervision Inc......................................A....... 585 889-3301
Scottsville *(G-15335)*
Coopervision Inc......................................C....... 585 385-6810
Victor *(G-16470)*
Coopervision Inc......................................D....... 585 385-6810
Victor *(G-16471)*
J I Intrntnal Contact Lens Lab.............G....... 718 997-1212
Rego Park *(G-14033)*
Millbrook Family Eyecare....................G....... 845 677-5012
Millbrook *(G-8477)*

CONTACTS: Electrical

Micro Contacts Inc.................................E....... 516 433-4830
Hicksville *(G-6371)*

CONTAINERS, GLASS: Cosmetic Jars

Baralan Usa Inc.......................................E....... 718 849-5768
Richmond Hill *(G-14067)*

CONTAINERS, GLASS: Food

Pennsauken Packing Company LLC....F....... 585 377-7700
Fairport *(G-4869)*

CONTAINERS: Cargo, Wood & Metal Combination

219 South West..G....... 315 474-2065
Syracuse *(G-15844)*
Sg Blocks Inc...G....... 212 520-6218
New York *(G-12033)*

CONTAINERS: Cargo, Wood & Wood With Metal

Air Goal Intl USA Inc.............................F....... 718 656-5880
Valley Stream *(G-16399)*
Airline Container Services...................G....... 516 371-4125
Lido Beach *(G-7439)*
Concord Express Cargo Inc.................G....... 718 276-7200
Jamaica *(G-6906)*

CONTAINERS: Corrugated

Action Rack Display Mfg......................E....... 718 257-7111
Brooklyn *(G-1558)*
Ares Printing and Packg Corp.............C....... 718 858-8760
Brooklyn *(G-1625)*
Bellotti Packaging Inc............................F....... 315 433-0131
East Syracuse *(G-4510)*
Cascades Cntnerboard Packg Inc......C....... 450 923-3031
Niagara Falls *(G-12802)*
Cascades USA Inc.................................E....... 518 880-3632
Waterford *(G-16610)*
Color Carton Corp...................................D....... 718 665-0840
Bronx *(G-1302)*
Fennell Industries LLC........................E....... 607 733-6693
Elmira *(G-4685)*
Fiber USA Corp.......................................E....... 718 888-1512
Flushing *(G-5241)*

Gavin Mfg Corp.......................................E....... 631 467-0040
Farmingdale *(G-4997)*
International Paper Company.............F....... 716 852-2144
Buffalo *(G-3012)*
International Paper Company.............D....... 518 372-6461
Glenville *(G-5702)*
Jamestown Cont of Rochester............D....... 585 254-9190
Rochester *(G-14460)*
Jamestown Container Corp..................D....... 716 665-4623
Falconer *(G-4904)*
Key Container Corp...............................E....... 631 582-3847
East Islip *(G-4417)*
Lee Philips Packaging Inc....................F....... 631 580-3306
Ronkonkoma *(G-14931)*
M C Packaging Corporation.................E....... 631 643-3763
Babylon *(G-550)*
Mkt329 Inc..F....... 631 249-5500
Farmingdale *(G-5059)*
Norampac Schenectady Inc..................C....... 518 346-6151
Schenectady *(G-15283)*
Orcon Industries Corp...........................D....... 585 768-7000
Le Roy *(G-7417)*
Packaging Corporation America.........C....... 315 457-6780
Liverpool *(G-7538)*
Pactiv LLC...E....... 585 248-1213
Pittsford *(G-13573)*
Parlor City Paper Box Co Inc...............D....... 607 772-0600
Binghamton *(G-941)*
Specialized Packg Group Inc...............G....... 315 638-4355
Baldwinsville *(G-575)*
Technical Packaging Inc.......................F....... 516 223-2300
Baldwin *(G-562)*
Track 7 Inc..G....... 845 544-1810
Warwick *(G-16596)*

CONTAINERS: Foil, Bakery Goods & Frozen Foods

De Luxe Packaging Corp.......................E....... 416 754-4633
Saugerties *(G-15183)*
Tri-State Food Jobbers Inc...................G....... 718 921-1211
Brooklyn *(G-2678)*

CONTAINERS: Food & Beverage

Cmc-Kuhnke Inc......................................F....... 518 694-3310
Albany *(G-65)*
Genpak LLC..E....... 518 798-9511
Glens Falls *(G-5679)*
Marley Spoon Inc....................................G....... 646 934-6970
New York *(G-11163)*

CONTAINERS: Food, Folding, Made From Purchased Materials

Diamond Packaging Holdings LLC......G....... 585 334-8030
Rochester *(G-14306)*
Pactiv LLC...C....... 518 562-6101
Plattsburgh *(G-13684)*

CONTAINERS: Food, Liquid Tight, Including Milk

International Paper Company.............C....... 607 775-1550
Conklin *(G-3869)*

CONTAINERS: Glass

Anchor Glass Container Corp..............B....... 607 737-1933
Elmira Heights *(G-4708)*
Certainteed Corporation........................C....... 716 823-3684
Lackawanna *(G-7243)*
Intrapac International Corp..................C....... 518 561-2030
Plattsburgh *(G-13671)*
Owens-Brockway Glass Cont Inc........C....... 315 258-3211
Auburn *(G-513)*
Rocco Bormioli Glass Co Inc...............E....... 212 719-0606
New York *(G-11896)*
Saint Gobain Grains & Powders..........A....... 716 731-8200
Niagara Falls *(G-12870)*
Schott Corporation..................................D....... 914 831-2200
Elmsford *(G-4778)*
SGD North America................................E....... 212 753-4200
New York *(G-12035)*

CONTAINERS: Laminated Phenolic & Vulcanized Fiber

Diemolding Corporation........................G....... 315 697-2221
Canastota *(G-3367)*

Diemolding Corporation........................G....... 315 697-2221
Canastota *(G-3368)*
Skydyne Company..................................D....... 845 858-6400
Port Jervis *(G-13793)*

CONTAINERS: Liquid Tight Fiber, From Purchased Materials

Acran Spill Containment Inc................G....... 631 841-2300
Amityville *(G-274)*
Custom Manufacturing Inc....................G....... 607 569-2738
Hammondsport *(G-5954)*

CONTAINERS: Metal

Abbot & Abbot Box Corp.......................F....... 888 930-5972
Long Island City *(G-7646)*
Erie Engineered Products Inc..............E....... 716 206-0204
Lancaster *(G-7314)*
Medi-Ray Inc..G....... 877 898-3003
Tuckahoe *(G-16271)*
Mobile Mini Inc.......................................G....... 315 732-4555
Utica *(G-16349)*
Sky Dive..D....... 845 858-6400
Port Jervis *(G-13792)*
Westrock - Southern Cont LLC...........C....... 315 487-6111
Camillus *(G-3327)*
Westrock CP LLC....................................C....... 716 694-1000
North Tonawanda *(G-13006)*

CONTAINERS: Plastic

A R Arena Products Inc........................E....... 585 277-1680
Rochester *(G-14162)*
Albea Cosmetics America Inc.............E....... 212 371-5100
New York *(G-9073)*
Amcor Rigid Plastics Usa LLC............E....... 716 366-2440
Dunkirk *(G-4331)*
Baralan Usa Inc.......................................E....... 718 849-5768
Richmond Hill *(G-14067)*
Berry Plastics Corporation...................C....... 315 484-0397
Solvay *(G-15506)*
Billie-Ann Plastics Pkg Corp................E....... 718 497-3409
Brooklyn *(G-1696)*
Chem-Tainer Industries Inc..................E....... 631 422-8300
West Babylon *(G-16783)*
Consolidated Container Co LLC..........F....... 585 343-9351
Batavia *(G-629)*
Form A Rockland Plastics Inc.............G....... 315 848-3300
Cranberry Lake *(G-4057)*
Forteq North America Inc.....................D....... 585 427-9410
West Henrietta *(G-16878)*
Gary Plastic Packaging Corp...............B....... 718 893-2200
Bronx *(G-1341)*
Great Pacific Entps US Inc...................E....... 518 761-2593
Glens Falls *(G-5682)*
GSE Composites Inc...............................F....... 631 389-1300
Hauppauge *(G-6087)*
Ingenious Designs LLC.........................C....... 631 254-3376
Ronkonkoma *(G-14912)*
Iridium Industries Inc............................E....... 516 504-9700
Great Neck *(G-5817)*
J-Trend Systems Inc..............................G....... 646 688-3272
New York *(G-10683)*
Jamestown Plastics Inc........................E....... 716 792-4144
Brocton *(G-1249)*
Kenney Manufacturing Displays.........F....... 631 231-5563
Brentwood *(G-1188)*
Kernow North America..........................F....... 585 586-3590
Pittsford *(G-13566)*
M I T Poly-Cart Corp..............................G....... 212 724-7290
New York *(G-11074)*
Mgs Mfg Group Inc................................D....... 716 684-9400
Buffalo *(G-3063)*
Micromold Products Inc.......................E....... 914 969-2850
Yonkers *(G-17467)*
Oneida Molded Plastics LLC................D....... 315 363-7990
Oneida *(G-13162)*
Ontario Plastics Inc...............................E....... 585 663-2644
Rochester *(G-14550)*
Pactiv LLC...G....... 847 482-2000
Canandaigua *(G-3352)*
Pactiv LLC...C....... 518 562-6120
Plattsburgh *(G-13685)*
Pactiv LLC...C....... 518 793-2524
Glens Falls *(G-5695)*
Plastic Solutions Inc..............................E....... 631 234-9013
Bayport *(G-760)*
Plastic Sys/Gr Bflo Inc..........................G....... 716 835-7555
Buffalo *(G-3129)*
Plasticware LLC......................................F....... 845 267-0790
Monsey *(G-8577)*

PRODUCT SECTION

CONTRACTORS: Electrical

Powertex Inc .... E 518 297-4000
  Rouses Point *(G-15043)*
Quoin LLC .... A 914 967-9400
  Rye *(G-15066)*
Rynone Manufacturing Corp .... F 607 565-8187
  Waverly *(G-16706)*
Silgan Plastics LLC .... C 315 536-5690
  Penn Yan *(G-13521)*
Summit Manufacturing .... G 631 952-1570
  Bay Shore *(G-746)*
Summit Manufacturing .... E 631 952-1570
  Bay Shore *(G-747)*
Visitainer Corp .... E 718 636-0300
  Brooklyn *(G-2731)*

CONTAINERS: Sanitary, Food

Consolidated Container Co LLC .... C 585 262-6470
  Rochester *(G-14288)*

CONTAINERS: Shipping & Mailing, Fiber

American Intrmdal Cont Mfg LLC .... G 631 774-6790
  Hauppauge *(G-6022)*

CONTAINERS: Shipping, Bombs, Metal Plate

828 Express Inc .... G 917 577-9019
  Staten Island *(G-15629)*
Erie Engineered Products Inc .... E 716 206-0204
  Lancaster *(G-7314)*
Vship Co .... F 718 706-8566
  Astoria *(G-460)*
Wayne Integrated Tech Corp .... E 631 242-0213
  Edgewood *(G-4620)*

CONTAINERS: Wood

Abbot & Abbot Box Corp .... F 888 930-5972
  Long Island City *(G-7646)*
David Isseks & Sons Inc .... E 212 966-8694
  New York *(G-9820)*
Essex Box & Pallet Co Inc .... E 518 834-7279
  Keeseville *(G-7137)*
Great Lakes Specialites .... E 716 672-4622
  Fredonia *(G-5374)*
Pluribus Products Inc .... E 718 852-1614
  Brooklyn *(G-2427)*

CONTRACT FOOD SVCS

Herris Gourmet Inc .... G 917 578-2308
  Brooklyn *(G-2078)*

CONTRACTOR: Framing

Timber Frames Inc .... G 585 374-6405
  Canandaigua *(G-3359)*

CONTRACTOR: Rigging & Scaffolding

Safespan Platform Systems Inc .... D 716 694-3332
  Tonawanda *(G-16199)*

CONTRACTORS: Acoustical & Ceiling Work

Newmat Northeast Corp .... F 631 253-9277
  West Babylon *(G-16816)*

CONTRACTORS: Acoustical & Insulation Work

New York State Foam Enrgy LLC .... G 845 534-4656
  Cornwall *(G-3989)*

CONTRACTORS: Antenna Installation

Fred A Nudd Corporation .... E 315 524-2531
  Ontario *(G-13201)*

CONTRACTORS: Awning Installation

Awning Mart Inc .... G 315 699-5928
  Cicero *(G-3642)*
Awnings Plus Inc .... F 716 693-3690
  Tonawanda *(G-16142)*
Space Sign .... F 718 961-1112
  College Point *(G-3808)*

CONTRACTORS: Boiler & Furnace

Empire Industrial Systems Corp .... F 631 242-4619
  Bay Shore *(G-699)*

CONTRACTORS: Boiler Maintenance Contractor

Empire Industrial Burner Svc .... F 631 242-4619
  Deer Park *(G-4139)*

CONTRACTORS: Building Eqpt & Machinery Installation

Assa Abloy Entrance Systems US .... E 315 492-6600
  East Syracuse *(G-4507)*
Bargold Storage Systems LLC .... E 718 247-7000
  Long Island City *(G-7682)*
Otis Elevator Company .... E 917 339-9600
  New York *(G-11535)*
Schindler Elevator Corporation .... C 212 708-1000
  New York *(G-11987)*
Windowman Inc (usa) .... G 718 246-2626
  Brooklyn *(G-2758)*

CONTRACTORS: Building Sign Installation & Mntnce

Alley Cat Signs Inc .... F 631 924-7446
  Middle Island *(G-8406)*
Clinton Signs Inc .... G 585 482-1620
  Webster *(G-16719)*
Flexlume Sign Corporation .... G 716 884-2020
  Buffalo *(G-2950)*
Gloede Neon Signs Ltd Inc .... F 845 471-4366
  Poughkeepsie *(G-13902)*
Jem Sign Corp .... G 516 867-4466
  Hempstead *(G-6275)*
Lanza Corp .... G 914 937-6360
  Port Chester *(G-13751)*
North Shore Neon Sign Co Inc .... E 718 937-4848
  Flushing *(G-5275)*
Rapp Signs Inc .... F 607 656-8167
  Greene *(G-5867)*
Ray Sign Inc .... F 518 377-1371
  Schenectady *(G-15289)*
Rgm Signs Inc .... G 718 442-0598
  Staten Island *(G-15732)*
Sign Works Incorporated .... E 914 592-0700
  Elmsford *(G-4784)*
T J Signs Unlimited LLC .... E 631 273-4800
  Islip *(G-6813)*

CONTRACTORS: Carpentry Work

EZ Lift Operator Corp .... F 845 356-1676
  Spring Valley *(G-15584)*
Innova Interiors Inc .... E 718 401-2122
  Bronx *(G-1363)*
Mestel Brothers Stairs & Rails .... C 516 496-4127
  Syosset *(G-15828)*

CONTRACTORS: Carpentry, Cabinet & Finish Work

Cabinet Shapes Corp .... F 718 784-6255
  Long Island City *(G-7691)*
Capital Kit Cab & Door Mfrs .... G 718 886-0303
  College Point *(G-3779)*
Central Kitchen Corp .... F 718 283-1029
  Southampton *(G-15541)*
Dak Mica and Wood Products .... G 631 467-0749
  Ronkonkoma *(G-14892)*
Eugenia Selective Living Inc .... F 631 277-1461
  Islip *(G-6808)*
Hennig Custom Woodwork Corp .... G 516 536-3460
  Oceanside *(G-13080)*
Johnny Mica Inc .... G 631 225-5213
  Lindenhurst *(G-7466)*
M & C Furniture .... G 718 422-2136
  Brooklyn *(G-2242)*
Metro Kitchens Corp .... F 718 434-1166
  Brooklyn *(G-2305)*
Ralph Payne .... G 718 222-4200
  Brooklyn *(G-2477)*

CONTRACTORS: Carpentry, Cabinet Building & Installation

Auburn-Watson Corp .... F 716 876-8000
  Depew *(G-4247)*
Daniel Demarco and Assoc Inc .... E 631 598-7000
  Amityville *(G-284)*
Fontrick Door Inc .... E 585 345-6032
  Batavia *(G-632)*
Home Ideal Inc .... G 718 762-8998
  Flushing *(G-5251)*
Koeppels Kustom Kitchens Inc .... G 518 489-0092
  Albany *(G-96)*
Manhattan Cabinets Inc .... G 212 548-2436
  New York *(G-11127)*
Precision Dental Cabinets Inc .... F 631 543-3870
  Smithtown *(G-15495)*
Yost Neon Displays Inc .... G 716 674-6780
  West Seneca *(G-16956)*

CONTRACTORS: Carpentry, Finish & Trim Work

Millwright Wdwrk Installation .... E 631 587-2635
  West Babylon *(G-16811)*

CONTRACTORS: Ceramic Floor Tile Installation

Icestone LLC .... E 718 624-4900
  Brooklyn *(G-2095)*

CONTRACTORS: Closed Circuit Television Installation

Sartek Industries Inc .... G 631 473-3555
  Port Jefferson *(G-13779)*

CONTRACTORS: Commercial & Office Building

United Steel Products Inc .... D 718 478-5330
  Corona *(G-4009)*

CONTRACTORS: Communications Svcs

Professional Technology Inc .... G 315 337-4156
  Rome *(G-14830)*

CONTRACTORS: Concrete

A Colarusso and Son Inc .... E 518 828-3218
  Hudson *(G-6603)*
Geneva Granite Co Inc .... F 315 789-8142
  Geneva *(G-5578)*
Seneca Stone Corporation .... E 607 737-6200
  Pine City *(G-13552)*

CONTRACTORS: Concrete Repair

Capitol Restoration Corp .... G 516 783-1425
  North Bellmore *(G-12915)*

CONTRACTORS: Construction Site Cleanup

Darrell Mitchell .... G 646 659-7075
  Arverne *(G-425)*

CONTRACTORS: Countertop Installation

Contempra Design Inc .... F 718 984-8586
  Staten Island *(G-15662)*
Countertops & Cabinets Inc .... G 315 433-1038
  Syracuse *(G-15910)*
Johnny Mica Inc .... G 631 225-5213
  Lindenhurst *(G-7466)*
Joseph Fedele .... G 718 448-3658
  Staten Island *(G-15694)*
Rochester Countertop Inc .... F 585 338-2260
  Rochester *(G-14640)*
Thornwood Products Ltd .... E 914 769-9161
  Thornwood *(G-16122)*
X F Inc .... F 212 244-2240
  Brooklyn *(G-2770)*

CONTRACTORS: Demountable Partition Installation

Able Steel Equipment Co Inc .... F 718 361-9240
  Long Island City *(G-7647)*

CONTRACTORS: Drywall

L & J Interiors Inc .... G 631 218-0838
  Bohemia *(G-1089)*
Nordic Interior Inc .... C 718 456-7000
  Maspeth *(G-8159)*

CONTRACTORS: Electrical

331 Holding Inc .... E 585 924-1740
  Victor *(G-16458)*

Employee Codes: A=Over 500 employees, B=251-500
C=101-250, D=51-100, E=20-50, F=10-19, G=5-9

CONTRACTORS: Electrical

Company	Code	Phone
A & S Electric	G	212 228-2030
Brooklyn (G-1529)		
B J S Electric	G	845 774-8166
Chester (G-3600)		
C & G Video Systems Inc	G	315 452-1490
Liverpool (G-7513)		
Cooperfriedman Elc Sup Co Inc	G	718 269-4906
Long Island City (G-7704)		
Mitsubishi Elc Pwr Pdts Inc	G	516 962-2813
Melville (G-8337)		
Schuler-Haas Electric Corp	E	607 936-3514
Painted Post (G-13393)		
Spectrum Cable Corporation	G	585 235-7714
Rochester (G-14694)		

CONTRACTORS: Electronic Controls Installation

Company	Code	Phone
Emco Electric Services LLC	G	212 420-9766
New York (G-10022)		
Evolve Guest Controls LLC	F	855 750-9090
Port Washington (G-13814)		
Qsf Inc	G	585 247-6200
Gates (G-5562)		
Zeppelin Electric Company Inc	G	631 928-9467
East Setauket (G-4497)		

CONTRACTORS: Energy Management Control

Company	Code	Phone
T S B A Group Inc	E	718 565-6000
Sunnyside (G-15810)		

CONTRACTORS: Excavating

Company	Code	Phone
Ribble Lumber Inc	G	315 536-6221
Penn Yan (G-13518)		

CONTRACTORS: Excavating Slush Pits & Cellars Svcs

Company	Code	Phone
Alice Perkins	G	716 378-5100
Salamanca (G-15099)		

CONTRACTORS: Exterior Wall System Installation

Company	Code	Phone
Plant-Tech2o Inc	G	516 483-7845
Hempstead (G-6285)		

CONTRACTORS: Fence Construction

Company	Code	Phone
City Store Gates Mfg Corp	E	718 939-9700
College Point (G-3781)		
Dart Awning Inc	F	718 945-4224
Freeport (G-5393)		
Fence Plaza Corp	G	718 469-2200
Brooklyn (G-1966)		
Fort Miller Service Corp	F	518 695-5000
Greenwich (G-5888)		
Interstate Wood Products Inc	E	631 842-4488
Amityville (G-296)		
Master-Halco Inc	F	631 585-8150
Ronkonkoma (G-14939)		
Metro Door Inc	D	631 277-6490
Great River (G-5852)		
Oneida Sales & Service Inc	E	716 822-8205
Buffalo (G-3101)		
Ourem Iron Works Inc	F	914 476-4856
Yonkers (G-17473)		
Universal Steel Fabricators	E	718 342-0782
Brooklyn (G-2709)		
Wood Innovations of Suffolk	G	631 698-2345
Medford (G-8263)		

CONTRACTORS: Fire Detection & Burglar Alarm Systems

Company	Code	Phone
Detekion Security Systems Inc	F	607 729-7179
Vestal (G-16447)		
Sentry Devices Corp	G	631 491-3191
Dix Hills (G-4298)		
Simplexgrinnell LP	G	845 774-4120
Harriman (G-5974)		

CONTRACTORS: Fire Escape Installation

Company	Code	Phone
Firecom Inc	C	718 899-6100
Woodside (G-17328)		
Triboro Iron Works Inc	G	718 361-9600
Long Island City (G-7906)		

CONTRACTORS: Fire Sprinkler System Installation Svcs

Company	Code	Phone
Simplexgrinnell LP	G	845 774-4120
Harriman (G-5974)		

CONTRACTORS: Floor Laying & Other Floor Work

Company	Code	Phone
Delta Polymers Inc	G	631 254-6240
Bay Shore (G-695)		
Designer Epoxy Finishes Inc	G	646 943-6044
Melville (G-8310)		

CONTRACTORS: Garage Doors

Company	Code	Phone
Griffon Corporation	E	212 957-5000
New York (G-10363)		

CONTRACTORS: Gas Field Svcs, NEC

Company	Code	Phone
Petro Inc	G	516 686-1717
Plainview (G-13629)		
Schmitt Sales Inc	G	716 632-8595
Williamsville (G-17251)		
Speedway LLC	F	718 815-6897
Staten Island (G-15736)		
T A S Sales Service LLC	G	518 234-4919
Cobleskill (G-3739)		

CONTRACTORS: Gasoline Condensation Removal Svcs

Company	Code	Phone
Gas Recovery Systems LLC	F	914 421-4903
White Plains (G-17112)		

CONTRACTORS: Glass, Glazing & Tinting

Company	Code	Phone
A&B McKeon Glass Inc	G	718 525-2152
Staten Island (G-15631)		
Benson Industries Inc	F	212 779-3230
New York (G-9360)		
Chapman Stained Glass Studio	G	518 449-5552
Albany (G-62)		
Global Glass Corp	G	516 681-2309
Hicksville (G-6350)		
Jordan Panel Systems Corp	E	631 754-4900
East Northport (G-4439)		
Lafayette Mirror & Glass Co	G	718 768-0660
New Hyde Park (G-8845)		
Upstate Insulated Glass Inc	G	315 475-4960
Central Square (G-3519)		

CONTRACTORS: Heating & Air Conditioning

Company	Code	Phone
Automated Control Logic Inc	F	914 769-8880
Thornwood (G-16116)		
City Cooling Enterprises Inc	G	718 331-7400
Brooklyn (G-1781)		
Fedders Islandaire Inc	D	631 471-2900
East Setauket (G-4482)		
Heat-Timer Corporation	E	212 481-2020
Bronx (G-1354)		
Layton Manufacturing Corp	E	718 498-6000
Brooklyn (G-2196)		
Nelson Air Device Corporation	C	718 729-3801
Maspeth (G-8155)		
Prokosch and Sonn Sheet Metal	E	845 562-4211
Newburgh (G-12776)		
Robin Industries Ltd	F	718 218-9616
Brooklyn (G-2501)		
Vincent Genovese	G	631 281-8170
Mastic Beach (G-8205)		

CONTRACTORS: Highway & Street Paving

Company	Code	Phone
Pavco Asphalt Inc	E	631 289-3223
Holtsville (G-6506)		
Peckham Materials Corp	D	914 686-2045
White Plains (G-17149)		
Suit-Kote Corporation	C	607 753-1100
Cortland (G-4046)		
Suit-Kote Corporation	E	716 664-3750
Jamestown (G-7033)		

CONTRACTORS: Home & Office Intrs Finish, Furnish/Remodel

Company	Code	Phone
Drapery Industries Inc	F	585 232-2992
Rochester (G-14318)		
Griffon Corporation	E	212 957-5000
New York (G-10363)		

CONTRACTORS: Hydraulic Eqpt Installation & Svcs

Company	Code	Phone
A Gatty Products Inc	G	914 592-3903
Elmsford (G-4731)		

CONTRACTORS: Insulation Installation, Building

Company	Code	Phone
Advanced Comfort Systems Inc	F	518 884-8444
Ballston Spa (G-589)		

CONTRACTORS: Kitchen & Bathroom Remodeling

Company	Code	Phone
Di Fiore and Sons Custom Wdwkg	G	718 278-1663
Long Island City (G-7715)		
Triad Counter Corp	E	631 750-0615
Bohemia (G-1146)		

CONTRACTORS: Lighting Syst

Company	Code	Phone
Light Blue USA LLC	F	718 475-2515
Brooklyn (G-2221)		
Vincent Conigliaro	F	845 340-0489
Kingston (G-7224)		

CONTRACTORS: Machinery Installation

Company	Code	Phone
Finger Lakes Conveyors Inc	G	315 539-9246
Waterloo (G-16625)		
Re-Al Industrial Corp	G	716 542-4556
Akron (G-28)		

CONTRACTORS: Marble Installation, Interior

Company	Code	Phone
Aurora Stone Group LLC	F	315 471-6869
East Syracuse (G-4508)		
Marble Doctors LLC	E	203 628-8339
New York (G-11143)		

CONTRACTORS: Masonry & Stonework

Company	Code	Phone
Premier Group NY	F	212 229-1200
New York (G-11698)		

CONTRACTORS: Mechanical

Company	Code	Phone
All-City Metal Inc	E	718 937-3975
Maspeth (G-8114)		
Joy Edward Company	E	315 474-3360
East Syracuse (G-4547)		
Metro Duct Systems Inc	F	718 278-4294
Long Island City (G-7810)		

CONTRACTORS: Multi-Family Home Remodeling

Company	Code	Phone
Rob Herschenfeld Design Inc	F	718 456-6801
Brooklyn (G-2499)		

CONTRACTORS: Office Furniture Installation

Company	Code	Phone
Evans & Paul LLC	E	516 576-0800
Plainview (G-13600)		

CONTRACTORS: Oil & Gas Building, Repairing & Dismantling Svc

Company	Code	Phone
Cotton Well Drilling Co Inc	G	716 672-2788
Sheridan (G-15400)		
Schaap Brothers	G	518 459-2220
Albany (G-133)		
Steel Excel Inc	D	914 461-1300
White Plains (G-17171)		

CONTRACTORS: Oil & Gas Field Geological Exploration Svcs

Company	Code	Phone
Aquifer Drilling & Testing Inc	D	516 616-6026
Mineola (G-8495)		

CONTRACTORS: Oil & Gas Field Geophysical Exploration Svcs

Company	Code	Phone
Schlumberger Technology Corp	C	607 378-0200
Horseheads (G-6592)		
Smith International Inc	D	212 350-9400
New York (G-12105)		

PRODUCT SECTION

CONTRACTORS: Oil & Gas Well Casing Cement Svcs

Sabre Energy Services LLC.................F....... 518 514-1572
 Slingerlands *(G-15478)*

CONTRACTORS: Oil & Gas Well Drilling Svc

Alden Aurora Gas Company Inc............G....... 716 937-9484
 Alden *(G-174)*
Barber & Deline Enrgy Svcs LLC ....F 315 696-8961
 Tully *(G-16274)*
Barber & Deline LLC..............................F 607 749-2619
 Tully *(G-16275)*
Copper Ridge Oil Inc.............................G....... 716 372-4021
 Jamestown *(G-6984)*
Geotechnical Drilling Inc ....D 516 616-6055
 Mineola *(G-8512)*
Joycharge Inc...D 646 321-1127
 New York *(G-10774)*
Lenape Energy Inc................................G....... 585 344-1200
 Alexander *(G-187)*
Lukoil North America LLC ....E 212 421-4141
 New York *(G-11062)*
Schneider Amalco Inc ....F 917 470-9674
 New York *(G-11991)*
Steel Partners Holdings LP...................E 212 520-2300
 New York *(G-12189)*
U S Energy Development Corp.............D 716 636-0401
 Getzville *(G-5605)*
Western Oil and Gas JV Inc..................G....... 914 967-4758
 Rye *(G-15069)*

CONTRACTORS: Oil & Gas Well Flow Rate Measurement Svcs

Five Star Field Services........................G....... 347 446-6816
 Brooklyn *(G-1978)*

CONTRACTORS: Oil & Gas Wells Svcs

I & S of NY Inc ....F 716 373-7001
 Allegany *(G-202)*
Superior Energy Services Inc...............G....... 716 483-0100
 Jamestown *(G-7035)*

CONTRACTORS: Oil Field Haulage Svcs

Lenape Energy Inc................................G....... 585 344-1200
 Alexander *(G-187)*

CONTRACTORS: Oil Field Lease Tanks: Erectg, Clng/Rprg Svcs

Wellspring Omni Holdings Corp............A 212 318-9800
 New York *(G-12610)*

CONTRACTORS: Oil Sampling Svcs

P & C Gas Measurements Service........F 716 257-3412
 Cattaraugus *(G-3438)*

CONTRACTORS: Oil/Gas Well Construction, Rpr/Dismantling Svcs

A & Mt Realty Group LLC ....F 718 974-5871
 Brooklyn *(G-1528)*
Arm Construction Company Inc...........G....... 646 235-6520
 East Elmhurst *(G-4388)*
Babula Construction Inc ....G....... 716 681-0886
 Lancaster *(G-7305)*
Barber & Deline Enrgy Svcs LLC ....F 315 696-8961
 Tully *(G-16274)*
Darrell Mitchell ....G....... 646 659-7075
 Arverne *(G-425)*
Fame Construction Inc ....E 718 626-1000
 Astoria *(G-442)*
Iron Eagle Group Inc............................E 888 481-4445
 New York *(G-10662)*
Mep Alaska LLC ....G....... 646 535-9005
 Brooklyn *(G-2297)*
Occhioerosso John ....F 718 541-7025
 Staten Island *(G-15718)*
Prefab Construction Inc ....F 631 821-9613
 Sound Beach *(G-15513)*
Professional Remodelers Inc...............G....... 516 565-9300
 West Hempstead *(G-16862)*
Tutor Perini Corporation ....B 646 473-2924
 New York *(G-12429)*

CONTRACTORS: On-Site Welding

303 Contracting Inc..............................E 716 896-2122
 Orchard Park *(G-13249)*
A and K Machine and Welding..............G....... 631 231-2552
 Bay Shore *(G-663)*
Abdo Shtmtl & Fabrication Inc ....G....... 315 894-4664
 Frankfort *(G-5349)*
AG Tech Welding Corp..........................G....... 845 398-0005
 Tappan *(G-16078)*
Bridgehampton Steel & Wldg Inc.........F 631 537-2486
 Bridgehampton *(G-1232)*
Dorgan Welding Service.......................G....... 315 462-9030
 Phelps *(G-13531)*
Flushing Boiler & Welding Co...............G....... 718 463-1266
 Brooklyn *(G-1988)*
G & C Welding Co Inc...........................G....... 516 883-3228
 Port Washington *(G-13817)*
Glenridge Fabricators Inc ....F 718 456-2297
 Glendale *(G-5655)*
Hadfield Inc...F 631 981-4314
 Ronkonkoma *(G-14909)*
Hagner Industries Inc ....G....... 716 873-5720
 Buffalo *(G-2986)*
Hallock Fabricating Corp......................G....... 631 727-2441
 Riverhead *(G-14144)*
Kleinfelder John ....G....... 716 753-3163
 Mayville *(G-8216)*
Marine Boiler & Welding Inc ....G....... 718 378-1900
 Bronx *(G-1386)*
Reliable Welding & Fabrication............G....... 631 758-2637
 Patchogue *(G-13434)*
S & D Welding Corp..............................G....... 631 454-0383
 West Babylon *(G-16824)*
Tioga Tool Inc.......................................F 607 785-6005
 Endicott *(G-4830)*

CONTRACTORS: Ornamental Metal Work

Athens Iron Fabrication Inc ....F 718 424-7799
 Woodside *(G-17317)*
Bonura and Sons Iron Works...............F 718 381-4100
 Franklin Square *(G-5361)*
E F Iron Works & Construction.............G....... 631 242-4766
 Bay Shore *(G-698)*
GCM Metal Industries Inc ....F 718 386-4059
 Brooklyn *(G-2015)*
Irony Limited Inc..................................G....... 631 329-4065
 East Hampton *(G-4411)*
M K Ulrich Construction Inc.................F 716 893-5777
 Buffalo *(G-3053)*

CONTRACTORS: Paint & Wallpaper Stripping

Nochem Paint Stripping Inc.................G....... 631 563-2750
 Blue Point *(G-999)*

CONTRACTORS: Painting & Wall Covering

Abdo Shtmtl & Fabrication Inc ....G....... 315 894-4664
 Frankfort *(G-5349)*
D & I Finishing Inc................................G....... 631 471-3043
 Bohemia *(G-1048)*

CONTRACTORS: Patio & Deck Construction & Repair

Pei Liquidation Company......................F 518 489-5101
 Albany *(G-116)*
Pei Liquidation Company......................F 315 431-4697
 East Syracuse *(G-4554)*

CONTRACTORS: Pipe Laying

AAA Welding and Fabrication of ....G....... 585 254-2830
 Rochester *(G-14163)*

CONTRACTORS: Plastering, Plain or Ornamental

Foster Reeve & Associates Inc.............G....... 718 609-0090
 Brooklyn *(G-1998)*

CONTRACTORS: Plumbing

Aquifer Drilling & Testing Inc...............D 516 616-6026
 Mineola *(G-8495)*
Metro City Group Inc............................G....... 516 781-2500
 Bellmore *(G-818)*

CONTRACTORS: Power Generating Eqpt Installation

Ls Power Equity Partners LP................G....... 212 615-3456
 New York *(G-11055)*

CONTRACTORS: Prefabricated Fireplace Installation

Chimney Doctors Americas Corp.........G....... 631 868-3586
 Bayport *(G-757)*

CONTRACTORS: Prefabricated Window & Door Installation

Europrojects Intl Inc.............................G....... 917 262-0795
 New York *(G-10086)*
Pace Window and Door Corp...............E 585 924-8350
 Victor *(G-16495)*
Pella Corporation..................................C 631 208-0710
 Calverton *(G-3294)*
Proof Industries Inc.............................G....... 631 694-7663
 Farmingdale *(G-5090)*
Royal Windows Mfg Corp.....................E 631 435-8888
 Bay Shore *(G-740)*
Tri-State Window Factory Corp ....F 631 667-8600
 Deer Park *(G-4218)*

CONTRACTORS: Refrigeration

Alumiseal Corp......................................E 518 329-2820
 Copake Falls *(G-3888)*

CONTRACTORS: Roofing

Tiedemann Waldemar Inc....................F 716 875-5665
 Buffalo *(G-3218)*

CONTRACTORS: Roustabout Svcs

Jemcap Servicing LLC..........................G....... 212 213-9353
 New York *(G-10718)*
Legal Servicing LLC..............................G....... 716 565-9300
 Williamsville *(G-17248)*
Sovereign Servicing System LLC.........F 914 779-1400
 Bronxville *(G-1503)*

CONTRACTORS: Safety & Security Eqpt

Napco Security Tech Inc ....B 631 842-9400
 Amityville *(G-314)*
Windowman Inc (usa)............................G....... 718 246-2626
 Brooklyn *(G-2758)*

CONTRACTORS: Sandblasting Svc, Building Exteriors

Bruce Pierce...G....... 716 731-9310
 Sanborn *(G-15115)*
Miller Metal Fabricating Inc..................G....... 585 359-3400
 Rochester *(G-14514)*
North Shore Monuments Inc................G....... 516 759-2156
 Glen Head *(G-5639)*

CONTRACTORS: Seismograph Survey Svcs

Elliott Associates LP ....E 212 586-9431
 New York *(G-10011)*
Wellspring Omni Holdings Corp............A 212 318-9800
 New York *(G-12610)*

CONTRACTORS: Sheet Metal Work, NEC

Aabco Sheet Metal Co Inc....................D 718 821-1166
 Ridgewood *(G-14097)*
Berjen Metal Industries Ltd..................G....... 631 673-7979
 Huntington *(G-6656)*
Broadalbin Manufacturing Corp ....E 518 883-5313
 Broadalbin *(G-1240)*
Goergen-Mackwirth Co Inc ....E 716 874-4800
 Buffalo *(G-2977)*
Lodolce Machine Co Inc......................E 845 246-7017
 Saugerties *(G-15187)*
Pro Metal of NY Corp............................G....... 516 285-0440
 Valley Stream *(G-16421)*

CONTRACTORS: Sheet metal Work, Architectural

A&B McKeon Glass Inc.........................G....... 718 525-2152
 Staten Island *(G-15631)*

CONTRACTORS: Sheet metal Work, Architectural — PRODUCT SECTION

Morgik Metal Designs .... F 212 463-0304
  New York *(G-11305)*

CONTRACTORS: Siding

Tri-State Window Factory Corp .... D 631 667-8600
  Deer Park *(G-4218)*

CONTRACTORS: Single-family Home General Remodeling

Bator Bintor Inc .... F 347 546-6503
  Brooklyn *(G-1674)*
Deakon Homes and Interiors .... F 518 271-0342
  Troy *(G-16233)*
Kng Construction Co Inc .... F 212 595-1451
  Warwick *(G-16593)*
Texas Home Security Inc .... E 516 747-2100
  New Hyde Park *(G-8865)*

CONTRACTORS: Solar Energy Eqpt

Aj Greentech Holdings Ltd .... G 718 395-8706
  Flushing *(G-5223)*
Solar Energy Systems LLC .... F 718 389-1545
  Brooklyn *(G-2580)*

CONTRACTORS: Sound Eqpt Installation

L A R Electronics Corp .... G 716 285-0555
  Niagara Falls *(G-12840)*
Telephone Sales & Service Co .... E 212 233-8505
  New York *(G-12295)*

CONTRACTORS: Stone Masonry

Stuart-Dean Co Inc .... F 718 472-1326
  Long Island City *(G-7894)*

CONTRACTORS: Store Fixture Installation

Mass Mdsg Self Selection Eqp .... E 631 234-3300
  Bohemia *(G-1102)*

CONTRACTORS: Store Front Construction

A&B McKeon Glass Inc .... G 718 525-2152
  Staten Island *(G-15631)*
Brooklyn Store Front Co Inc .... G 718 384-4372
  Brooklyn *(G-1732)*

CONTRACTORS: Structural Iron Work, Structural

M & L Steel & Ornamental Iron .... F 718 816-8660
  Staten Island *(G-15701)*
Miscellnous Ir Fabricators Inc .... E 518 355-1822
  Schenectady *(G-15280)*
Moon Gates Company .... G 718 426-0023
  East Elmhurst *(G-4395)*
Triboro Iron Works Inc .... F 718 361-9600
  Long Island City *(G-7906)*

CONTRACTORS: Structural Steel Erection

Barry Steel Fabrication Inc .... F 716 433-2144
  Lockport *(G-7571)*
Cives Corporation .... C 315 287-2200
  Gouverneur *(G-5743)*
GCM Metal Industries Inc .... F 718 386-4059
  Brooklyn *(G-2015)*
Irv Schroder & Sons Inc .... E 518 828-0194
  Stottville *(G-15781)*
Rochester Structural LLC .... E 585 436-1250
  Rochester *(G-14651)*
Roth Design & Consulting Inc .... E 718 209-0193
  Brooklyn *(G-2509)*

CONTRACTORS: Svc Station Eqpt Installation, Maint & Repair

North American Svcs Group LLC .... F 518 885-1820
  Ballston Spa *(G-604)*

CONTRACTORS: Textile Warping

Tli Import Inc .... G 917 578-4568
  Brooklyn *(G-2661)*

CONTRACTORS: Tile Installation, Ceramic

Alp Stone Inc .... F 718 706-6166
  Long Island City *(G-7653)*

Gdi Custom Marble & Granite .... F 718 996-9100
  Brooklyn *(G-2018)*

CONTRACTORS: Ventilation & Duct Work

Aabco Sheet Metal Co Inc .... D 718 821-1166
  Ridgewood *(G-14097)*
Aeroduct Inc .... E 516 248-9550
  Mineola *(G-8490)*
Liffey Sheet Metal Corp .... F 347 381-1134
  Brooklyn *(G-2220)*
Merz Metal & Machine Corp .... E 716 893-7786
  Buffalo *(G-3062)*

CONTRACTORS: Water Intake Well Drilling Svc

US Pump Corp .... G 516 303-7799
  West Hempstead *(G-16864)*

CONTRACTORS: Water Well Drilling

Barber & Deline LLC .... F 607 749-2619
  Tully *(G-16275)*

CONTRACTORS: Water Well Servicing

Yr Blanc & Co LLC .... G 716 800-3999
  Buffalo *(G-3261)*

CONTRACTORS: Well Chemical Treating Svcs

Metro Group Inc .... D 718 392-3616
  Long Island City *(G-7811)*

CONTRACTORS: Well Logging Svcs

Jay Little Oil Well Servi .... G 716 925-8905
  Limestone *(G-7451)*
Schlumberger Technology Corp .... C 607 378-0200
  Horseheads *(G-6592)*
Smith International Inc .... D 212 350-9400
  New York *(G-12105)*

CONTRACTORS: Window Treatment Installation

Instant Verticals Inc .... F 631 501-0001
  Farmingdale *(G-5012)*
Majestic Curtains LLC .... G 718 898-0774
  Elmhurst *(G-4664)*

CONTRACTORS: Windows & Doors

D Best Service Co Inc .... G 718 972-6133
  Brooklyn *(G-1829)*
Ecker Window Corp .... D 914 776-0000
  Yonkers *(G-17438)*
Triple H Construction Inc .... E 516 280-8252
  East Meadow *(G-4428)*
Window-Fix Inc .... F 718 854-3475
  Brooklyn *(G-2757)*
Windowman Inc (usa) .... G 718 246-2626
  Brooklyn *(G-2758)*

CONTRACTORS: Wood Floor Installation & Refinishing

Stuart-Dean Co Inc .... F 718 472-1326
  Long Island City *(G-7894)*
Sunrise Tile Inc .... G 718 939-0538
  Flushing *(G-5299)*
Zahk Sales Inc .... G 631 348-9300
  Islandia *(G-6805)*

CONTROL CIRCUIT DEVICES

Inertia Switch Inc .... E 845 359-8300
  Orangeburg *(G-13229)*

CONTROL EQPT: Electric

Addex Inc .... G 315 331-7700
  Newark *(G-12728)*
Altronix Corp .... D 718 567-8181
  Brooklyn *(G-1596)*
Calia Technical Inc .... G 718 447-3928
  Staten Island *(G-15655)*
Conic Systems Inc .... F 845 856-4053
  Port Jervis *(G-13782)*
Continental Instruments LLC .... E 631 842-9400
  Amityville *(G-281)*

Edo LLC .... C 631 630-4000
  Amityville *(G-287)*
Electronic Machine Parts LLC .... F 631 434-3700
  Hauppauge *(G-6070)*
Goddard Design Co .... G 718 599-0170
  Brooklyn *(G-2034)*
Harris Corporation .... E 315 838-7000
  Rome *(G-14813)*
Itt LLC .... B 914 641-2000
  White Plains *(G-17125)*
ITT Corporation .... E 585 269-7109
  Hemlock *(G-6263)*
ITT Corporation .... D 315 258-4904
  Auburn *(G-502)*
ITT Corporation .... D 914 641-2000
  Seneca Falls *(G-15361)*
ITT Corporation .... D 315 568-2811
  Seneca Falls *(G-15362)*
ITT Inc .... G 914 641-2000
  White Plains *(G-17128)*
Kussmaul Electronics Co Inc .... E 631 218-0298
  West Sayville *(G-16936)*
N E Controls LLC .... F 315 626-2480
  Syracuse *(G-15996)*
Nitram Energy Inc .... E 716 662-6540
  Orchard Park *(G-13285)*
Ruhle Companies Inc .... E 914 287-4000
  Valhalla *(G-16372)*
Weldcomputer Corporation .... F 518 283-2897
  Troy *(G-16264)*

CONTROL EQPT: Noise

Burgess-Manning Inc .... D 716 662-6540
  Orchard Park *(G-13257)*
I D E Processes Corporation .... F 718 544-1177
  Kew Gardens *(G-7161)*
Mason Industries Inc .... C 631 348-0282
  Hauppauge *(G-6126)*
Mason Industries Inc .... C 631 348-0282
  Hauppauge *(G-6127)*
Soundcoat Company Inc .... D 631 242-2200
  Deer Park *(G-4212)*
Vibration & Noise Engrg Corp .... F 716 827-4959
  Orchard Park *(G-13302)*
Vibration Eliminator Co Inc .... F 631 841-4000
  Copiague *(G-3936)*

CONTROL PANELS: Electrical

Abasco Inc .... E 716 649-4790
  Hamburg *(G-5918)*
Avanti Control Systems Inc .... G 518 921-4368
  Gloversville *(G-5707)*
Benfield Control Systems Inc .... F 914 948-6660
  White Plains *(G-17085)*
Boulay Fabrication Inc .... F 315 677-5247
  La Fayette *(G-7240)*
Custom Controls .... G 315 253-4785
  Scipio Center *(G-15322)*
Link Control Systems Inc .... F 631 471-3950
  Ronkonkoma *(G-14932)*
Micro Instrument Corp .... D 585 458-3150
  Rochester *(G-14507)*
Odyssey Controls Inc .... G 585 548-9800
  Bergen *(G-851)*
Se-Mar Electric Co Inc .... E 716 674-7404
  West Seneca *(G-16953)*
Smith Control Systems Inc .... F 518 828-7646
  Hudson *(G-6635)*
Transit Air Inc .... E 607 324-0216
  Hornell *(G-6568)*

CONTROLS & ACCESS: Indl, Electric

Bomac Inc .... F 315 433-9181
  Syracuse *(G-15872)*
Fics Inc .... E 607 359-4474
  Addison *(G-6)*
Gemtrol Inc .... G 716 894-0716
  Buffalo *(G-2968)*
General Oil Equipment Co Inc .... E 716 691-7012
  Amherst *(G-243)*
ICM Controls Corp .... D 315 233-5266
  North Syracuse *(G-12947)*
Interntnl Cntrls Msrmnts Corp .... C 315 233-5266
  North Syracuse *(G-12948)*
Morris Products Inc .... F 518 743-0523
  Queensbury *(G-14005)*
Soft-Noze Usa Inc .... C 315 732-2726
  Frankfort *(G-5357)*

(G-0000) Company's Geographic Section entry number

PRODUCT SECTION

CONVERTERS: Power, AC to DC

Speer Equipment Inc .... G 585 964-2700
   Hamlin *(G-5951)*

CONTROLS & ACCESS: Motor

Designatronics Incorporated .... B 516 328-3300
   New Hyde Park *(G-8826)*
Eaton Corporation .... C 212 319-2100
   New York *(G-9970)*
Eaton Corporation .... C 585 394-1780
   Canandaigua *(G-3344)*
Eaton Corporation .... C 516 353-3017
   East Meadow *(G-4423)*
Eaton Hydraulics LLC .... G 716 375-7132
   Olean *(G-13147)*
Eatons Crouse Hinds Business .... F 315 477-7000
   Syracuse *(G-15932)*
Electro-Kinetics Inc .... F 845 887-4930
   Callicoon *(G-3285)*
ITT Aerospace Controls LLC .... G 914 641-2000
   White Plains *(G-17126)*
Powr-UPS Corp .... E 631 345-5700
   Shirley *(G-15428)*
Teknic Inc .... E 585 784-7454
   Victor *(G-16506)*

CONTROLS: Access, Motor

Bakery Innovative Tech Corp .... F 631 758-3081
   Patchogue *(G-13415)*
Bemco of Western Ny Inc .... G 716 823-8400
   Buffalo *(G-2838)*
Schmersal Inc .... E 914 347-4775
   Hawthorne *(G-6254)*

CONTROLS: Automatic Temperature

Advantex Solutions Inc .... G 718 278-2290
   Bellerose *(G-809)*
Automated Bldg MGT Systems Inc ...... E 516 216-5603
   Floral Park *(G-5194)*
Day Automation Systems Inc .... D 585 924-4630
   Victor *(G-16472)*
Intellidyne LLC .... F 516 676-0777
   Plainview *(G-13608)*
Intrepid Control Service Inc .... G 718 886-8771
   Flushing *(G-5254)*
Johnson Controls Inc .... C 585 924-9346
   Victor *(G-16484)*
Logical Control Solutions Inc .... F 585 424-5340
   Victor *(G-16489)*
Pii Holdings Inc .... G 716 876-9951
   Buffalo *(G-3126)*
Protective Industries Inc .... D 716 876-9951
   Buffalo *(G-3141)*
Protective Industries Inc .... C 716 876-9951
   Buffalo *(G-3139)*
T S B A Group Inc .... E 718 565-6000
   Sunnyside *(G-15810)*
U S Energy Controls Inc .... F 718 380-1004
   New Hyde Park *(G-8867)*

CONTROLS: Electric Motor

Dyson-Kissner-Moran Corp .... E 212 661-4600
   Poughkeepsie *(G-13896)*
US Drives Inc .... D 716 731-1606
   Niagara Falls *(G-12887)*

CONTROLS: Environmental

Anderson Instrument Co Inc .... D 518 922-5315
   Fultonville *(G-5477)*
Automated Building Controls .... G 914 381-2860
   Mamaroneck *(G-8023)*
Cascade Technical Services LLC .... F 516 596-6300
   Lynbrook *(G-7949)*
Cascade Technical Services LLC .... G 518 355-2201
   Schenectady *(G-15240)*
Clean Room Depot Inc .... F 631 589-3033
   Holbrook *(G-6438)*
Cox & Company Inc .... C 212 366-0200
   Plainview *(G-13593)*
Daikin Applied Americas Inc .... D 315 253-2771
   Auburn *(G-491)*
E Global Solutions Inc .... G 516 767-5138
   Port Washington *(G-13812)*
East Hudson Watershed Corp .... G 845 319-6349
   Patterson *(G-13438)*
Evolve Guest Controls LLC .... F 855 750-9090
   Port Washington *(G-13814)*
Fedders Islandaire Inc .... D 631 471-2900
   East Setauket *(G-4482)*
Fuel Watchman Sales & Service .... F 718 665-6100
   Bronx *(G-1338)*
Grillmaster Inc .... E 718 272-9191
   Howard Beach *(G-6597)*
Heating & Burner Supply Inc .... G 718 665-0006
   Bronx *(G-1355)*
Infitec Inc .... D 315 433-1150
   East Syracuse *(G-4543)*
Johnson Controls Inc .... E 716 688-7340
   Buffalo *(G-3020)*
Leo Schultz .... G 716 969-0945
   Cheektowaga *(G-3577)*
Long Island Analytical Labs .... F 631 472-3400
   Holbrook *(G-6458)*
Microb Phase Services .... F 518 877-8948
   Clifton Park *(G-3702)*
Pulsafeeder Inc .... C 585 292-8000
   Rochester *(G-14609)*
RE Hansen Industries Inc .... C 631 471-2900
   East Setauket *(G-4491)*
Solarwaterway .... E 646 387-9346
   Brooklyn *(G-2581)*
Spence Engineering Company Inc ..... C 845 778-5566
   Walden *(G-16536)*
Transit Air Inc .... E 607 324-0216
   Hornell *(G-6568)*
Zebra Environmental Corp .... F 516 596-6300
   Lynbrook *(G-7967)*

CONTROLS: Marine & Navy, Auxiliary

L-3 Cmmnctons Ntronix Holdings .... D 212 697-1111
   New York *(G-10904)*

CONTROLS: Numerical

Teale Machine Company Inc .... D 585 244-6700
   Rochester *(G-14719)*

CONTROLS: Positioning, Electric

Sequential Electronics Systems .... E 914 592-1345
   Elmsford *(G-4783)*

CONTROLS: Relay & Ind

Afi Cybernetics Corporation .... E 607 732-3244
   Elmira *(G-4668)*
Air Crafters Inc .... C 631 471-7788
   Ronkonkoma *(G-14857)*
Alarm Controls Corporation .... E 631 586-4220
   Deer Park *(G-4090)*
Anderson Instrument Co Inc .... D 518 922-5315
   Fultonville *(G-5477)*
Con Rel Auto Electric Inc .... E 518 356-1646
   Schenectady *(G-15245)*
Cox & Company Inc .... C 212 366-0200
   Plainview *(G-13593)*
Designatronics Incorporated .... G 516 328-3300
   New Hyde Park *(G-8825)*
Deutsch Relays .... F 631 342-1700
   Hauppauge *(G-6062)*
Digital Instruments Inc .... F 716 874-5848
   Tonawanda *(G-16155)*
Eaton Corporation .... G 716 691-0008
   Buffalo *(G-2930)*
Elevator Systems Inc .... E 516 239-4044
   Garden City *(G-5502)*
Enetics Inc .... G 585 924-5010
   Victor *(G-16475)*
Exfo Burleigh Pdts Group Inc .... D 585 301-1530
   Canandaigua *(G-3345)*
G C Controls Inc .... E 607 656-4117
   Greene *(G-5865)*
I E D Corp .... F 631 348-0424
   Islandia *(G-6795)*
Industrial Indxing Systems Inc .... E 585 924-9181
   Victor *(G-16482)*
JE Miller Inc .... F 315 437-6811
   East Syracuse *(G-4546)*
Kaman Automation Inc .... G 585 254-8840
   Rochester *(G-14467)*
Kearney-National Inc .... F 212 661-4600
   New York *(G-10828)*
Linde LLC .... D 716 773-7552
   Grand Island *(G-5763)*
Logitek Inc .... D 631 567-1100
   Bohemia *(G-1094)*
Magnus Precision Mfg Inc .... D 315 548-8032
   Phelps *(G-13534)*
Moog Inc .... C 716 805-8100
   East Aurora *(G-4376)*
Moog Inc .... A 716 652-2000
   Elma *(G-4651)*
Nas-Tra Automotive Inds Inc .... C 631 225-1225
   Lindenhurst *(G-7474)*
National Time Recording Eqp Co .... F 212 227-3310
   New York *(G-11352)*
North Point Technology LLC .... F 866 885-3377
   Endicott *(G-4821)*
Nsi Industries LLC .... C 800 841-2505
   Mount Vernon *(G-8711)*
Omntec Mfg Inc .... E 631 981-2001
   Ronkonkoma *(G-14960)*
Panelogic Inc .... E 607 962-6319
   Corning *(G-3978)*
Peerless Instrument Co Inc .... C 631 396-6500
   Farmingdale *(G-5076)*
Precision Mechanisms Corp .... C 516 333-5955
   Westbury *(G-17021)*
Pulsafeeder Inc .... C 585 292-8000
   Rochester *(G-14609)*
Rochester Industrial Ctrl Inc .... D 315 524-4555
   Ontario *(G-13212)*
Rockwell Automation Inc .... E 585 487-2700
   Rochester *(G-14656)*
Service Mfg Group Inc .... F 716 893-1482
   Buffalo *(G-3183)*
Ssac Inc .... E 800 843-8848
   Baldwinsville *(G-577)*
Stetron International Inc .... F 716 854-3443
   Buffalo *(G-3197)*
Techniflo Corporation .... G 716 741-3500
   Clarence Center *(G-3680)*
Tork Inc .... D 914 664-3542
   Mount Vernon *(G-8738)*
Unimar Inc .... F 315 699-4400
   Syracuse *(G-16063)*
Zeppelin Electric Company Inc .... G 631 928-9467
   East Setauket *(G-4497)*

CONTROLS: Thermostats, Exc Built-in

Bilbee Controls Inc .... F 518 622-3033
   Cairo *(G-3271)*

CONTROLS: Voice

Voices For All LLC .... G 518 261-1664
   Mechanicville *(G-8232)*

CONVENIENCE STORES

Schaefer Logging Inc .... F 607 467-4990
   Deposit *(G-4281)*

CONVENTION & TRADE SHOW SVCS

Mechanical Displays Inc .... G 718 258-5588
   Brooklyn *(G-2290)*

CONVERTERS: Data

Annese & Associates Inc .... G 716 972-0076
   Buffalo *(G-2812)*
Cisco Systems Inc .... C 212 714-4000
   New York *(G-9622)*
Data Device Corporation .... B 631 567-5600
   Bohemia *(G-1049)*
Lockheed Martin Integrated .... E 315 456-3333
   Syracuse *(G-15981)*
Redwood Cllaborative Media Inc .... F 631 393-6051
   Melville *(G-8352)*
Scroll Media Inc .... G 617 395-8904
   New York *(G-12008)*

CONVERTERS: Frequency

Applied Power Systems Inc .... E 516 935-2230
   Hicksville *(G-6322)*

CONVERTERS: Phase Or Rotary, Electrical

Automation Source Technologies .... G 631 643-1678
   West Babylon *(G-16772)*

CONVERTERS: Power, AC to DC

Curtis/Palmer Hydroelectric LP .... G 518 654-6297
   Corinth *(G-3957)*
Endicott Research Group Inc .... D 607 754-9187
   Endicott *(G-4804)*
G B International Trdg Co Ltd .... C 607 785-0938
   Endicott *(G-4809)*

Employee Codes: A=Over 500 employees, B=251-500
C=101-250, D=51-100, E=20-50, F=10-19, G=5-9

2017 Harris
New York Manufacturers Directory

CONVERTERS: Torque, Exc Auto

American Torque Inc ....F....... 718 526-2433
  Jamaica *(G-6894)*

CONVEYOR SYSTEMS: Belt, General Indl Use

American Material Processing ....G....... 315 318-0017
  Clifton Springs *(G-3713)*
Desmi-Afti Inc ....E....... 716 662-0632
  Orchard Park *(G-13269)*
Greenbelt Industries Inc ....E....... 800 668-1114
  Buffalo *(G-2983)*

CONVEYOR SYSTEMS: Bulk Handling

Ward Industrial Equipment Inc ....G....... 716 856-6966
  Buffalo *(G-3247)*

CONVEYOR SYSTEMS: Pneumatic Tube

Shako Inc ....G....... 315 437-1294
  East Syracuse *(G-4563)*

CONVEYOR SYSTEMS: Robotic

International Robotics Inc ....F....... 914 630-1060
  Larchmont *(G-7350)*
United Rbotic Integrations LLC ....G....... 716 683-8334
  Alden *(G-185)*

CONVEYORS & CONVEYING EQPT

4695 Main Street Snyder Inc ....G....... 716 833-3270
  Buffalo *(G-2789)*
Chemprene Inc ....E....... 845 831-2800
  Beacon *(G-782)*
Chemprene Holding Inc ....C....... 845 831-2800
  Beacon *(G-783)*
Columbus McKinnon Corporation ....E....... 716 689-5400
  Getzville *(G-5595)*
Columbus McKinnon Corporation ....C....... 716 689-5400
  Getzville *(G-5597)*
Columbus McKinnon Corporation ....C....... 716 689-5400
  Getzville *(G-5598)*
Dairy Conveyor Corp ....D....... 845 278-7878
  Brewster *(G-1215)*
General Splice Corporation ....G....... 914 271-5131
  Croton On Hudson *(G-4063)*
Glasgow Products Inc ....E....... 516 374-5937
  Woodmere *(G-17313)*
Haines Equipment Inc ....E....... 607 566-8531
  Avoca *(G-537)*
Hohl Machine & Conveyor Co Inc ......E....... 716 882-7210
  Buffalo *(G-2996)*
I J White Corporation ....D....... 631 293-3788
  Farmingdale *(G-5009)*
J D Handling Systems Inc ....F....... 518 828-9676
  Ghent *(G-5607)*
Joldeson One Aerospace Inds ....D....... 718 848-7396
  Ozone Park *(G-13380)*
Northeast Conveyors Inc ....F....... 585 768-8912
  Lima *(G-7446)*
Noto Industrial Corp ....G....... 631 736-7600
  Coram *(G-3948)*
Raymond Corporation ....E....... 315 643-5000
  East Syracuse *(G-4557)*
Raymond Corporation ....A....... 607 656-2311
  Greene *(G-5869)*
Re-Al Industrial Corp ....G....... 716 542-4556
  Akron *(G-28)*
Renold Inc ....D....... 716 326-3121
  Westfield *(G-17051)*
Rlp Holdings Inc ....G....... 716 852-0832
  Buffalo *(G-3159)*
Rota Pack Inc ....F....... 631 274-1037
  Farmingdale *(G-5103)*
Service Specialties Inc ....G....... 716 822-7706
  Buffalo *(G-3185)*
Speedways Conveyors Inc ....E....... 716 893-2222
  Buffalo *(G-3195)*
Troy Industrial Solutions ....D....... 518 272-4920
  Watervliet *(G-16690)*

COOKING & FOOD WARMING EQPT: Commercial

Advance Tabco Inc ....D....... 631 242-8270
  Edgewood *(G-4591)*
Attias Oven Corp ....G....... 718 499-0145
  Brooklyn *(G-1650)*

Bakers Pride Oven Co Inc ....C....... 914 576-0200
  New Rochelle *(G-8887)*
Carts Mobile Food Eqp Corp ....E....... 718 788-5540
  Brooklyn *(G-1761)*
IMC Teddy Food Service ....E....... 631 789-8881
  Amityville *(G-295)*
Kinplex Corp ....E....... 631 242-4800
  Edgewood *(G-4603)*
Kinplex Corp ....E....... 631 242-4800
  Edgewood *(G-4604)*
Korin Japanese Trading Corp ....E....... 212 587-7021
  New York *(G-10878)*
R-S Restaurant Eqp Mfg Corp ....F....... 212 925-0335
  New York *(G-11784)*
Roger & Sons Inc ....G....... 212 226-4734
  New York *(G-11906)*
Toga Manufacturing Inc ....E....... 631 242-4800
  Edgewood *(G-4618)*
Wilder Manufacturing Co Inc ....D....... 516 222-0433
  Garden City *(G-5536)*

COOKING & FOODWARMING EQPT: Commercial

Advance Food Service Co Inc ....C....... 631 242-4800
  Edgewood *(G-4590)*

COOKING WARE, EXC PORCELAIN ENAMELED

Allied Metal Spinning Corp ....D....... 718 893-3300
  Bronx *(G-1268)*

COOKING WARE: Cooking Ware, Porcelain Enameled

Schiller Stores Inc ....G....... 631 208-9400
  Riverhead *(G-14155)*
Wilmax Usa LLC ....F....... 917 388-2790
  New York *(G-12639)*

COOKWARE, STONEWARE: Coarse Earthenware & Pottery

Make Holding LLC ....E....... 646 313-1957
  New York *(G-11116)*
Schiller Stores Inc ....G....... 845 928-4316
  Central Valley *(G-3527)*

COOKWARE: Fine Earthenware

Lifetime Stainless Steel Corp ....G....... 585 924-9393
  Victor *(G-16488)*
Mackenzie-Childs LLC ....C....... 315 364-7567
  Aurora *(G-530)*
Williams-Sonoma Stores Inc ....F....... 212 633-2203
  New York *(G-12637)*

COOLING TOWERS: Metal

Manhattan Cooling Towers Inc ....F....... 212 279-1045
  New York *(G-11128)*
SPX Corporation ....E....... 631 249-7900
  Ronkonkoma *(G-14988)*
SPX Corporation ....B....... 585 436-5550
  Rochester *(G-14697)*

COPPER ORES

Global Gold Corporation ....F....... 914 925-0020
  Rye *(G-15058)*

COPPER PRDTS: Refined, Primary

Hengyuan Copper USA Inc ....G....... 718 357-6666
  Whitestone *(G-17209)*

COPPER: Rolling & Drawing

Aurubis Buffalo Inc ....F....... 716 879-6700
  Buffalo *(G-2822)*
Aurubis Buffalo Inc ....B....... 716 879-6700
  Buffalo *(G-2823)*
Continental Cordage Corp ....D....... 315 655-9800
  Cazenovia *(G-3443)*
Luvata Heat Transfer Solutions ....G....... 716 879-6700
  Buffalo *(G-3051)*

COPYRIGHT BUYING & LICENSING

Abkco Music & Records Inc ....E....... 212 399-0300
  New York *(G-9004)*

Acolyte Industries Inc ....F....... 212 629-6830
  New York *(G-11607)*
Penhouse Media Group Inc ....C....... 212 702-6000
  New York *(G-11607)*
Scholastic Corporation ....G....... 212 343-6100
  New York *(G-11997)*

CORD & TWINE

Albany International Corp ....C....... 607 749-7226
  Homer *(G-6515)*
Sampo Inc ....E....... 315 896-2606
  Barneveld *(G-617)*
Schoen Trimming & Cord Co Inc ....F....... 212 255-3949
  New York *(G-11996)*
Simplicity Creative Group Inc ....A....... 212 686-7676
  New York *(G-12082)*

CORE WASH OR WAX

Beyond Beauty Basics LLC ....F....... 516 731-7100
  Levittown *(G-7425)*

CORES: Magnetic

Fair-Rite Products Corp ....C....... 845 895-2055
  Wallkill *(G-16543)*

CORK & CORK PRDTS: Tiles

Globus Cork Inc ....F....... 347 963-4059
  Bronx *(G-1344)*

CORRESPONDENCE SCHOOLS

Boardman Simons Publishing ....E....... 212 620-7200
  New York *(G-9432)*
Simmons-Boardman Pubg Corp ....G....... 212 620-7200
  New York *(G-12078)*

CORRUGATED PRDTS: Boxes, Partition, Display Items, Sheet/Pad

Dory Enterprises Inc ....F....... 607 565-7079
  Waverly *(G-16701)*
Enterprise Container LLC ....E....... 631 253-4400
  Wyandanch *(G-17375)*
General Fibre Products Corp ....D....... 516 358-7500
  New Hyde Park *(G-8835)*
Land Packaging Corp ....F....... 914 472-5976
  Scarsdale *(G-15220)*
Mechtronics Corporation ....G....... 845 831-9300
  Beacon *(G-787)*
Niagara Sheets LLC ....D....... 716 692-1129
  North Tonawanda *(G-12983)*
President Cont Group II LLC ....D....... 845 516-1600
  Middletown *(G-8457)*
Technical Library Service Inc ....F....... 212 219-0770
  Brooklyn *(G-2649)*
Westrock Cp LLC ....C....... 770 448-2193
  New Hartford *(G-8813)*
Westrock CP LLC ....C....... 716 692-6510
  North Tonawanda *(G-13007)*

COSMETIC PREPARATIONS

Abbe Laboratories Inc ....F....... 631 756-2223
  Farmingdale *(G-4929)*
Albion Cosmetics Inc ....G....... 212 869-1052
  New York *(G-9075)*
Ardex Cosmetics of America ....E....... 518 283-6700
  Troy *(G-16226)*
Becca Inc ....F....... 646 568-6250
  New York *(G-9341)*
Brucci Ltd ....E....... 914 965-0707
  Yonkers *(G-17422)*
Bycmac Corp ....E....... 845 255-0884
  Gardiner *(G-5548)*
Clark Botanicals Inc ....F....... 914 826-4319
  Bronxville *(G-1499)*
Dermatech Labs Inc ....F....... 631 225-1700
  Lindenhurst *(G-7461)*
Drt Laboratories LLC ....G....... 845 547-2034
  Airmont *(G-14)*
Epic Beauty Co LLC ....G....... 212 327-3059
  New York *(G-10049)*
Estee Lauder Inc ....C....... 631 454-7000
  Melville *(G-8317)*
Estee Lauder Inc ....D....... 212 756-4800
  New York *(G-10073)*
Ex-It Medical Devices Inc ....F....... 212 653-0637
  New York *(G-10098)*

COSTUME JEWELRY & NOVELTIES: Costume Novelties

Company	Code	Phone
Forsythe Cosmetic Group Ltd Freeport (G-5400)	D	516 239-4200
Fusion Brands America Inc New York (G-10225)	E	212 269-1387
Innovative Cosmtc Concepts LLC New York (G-10604)	G	212 391-8110
Intercos America Inc West Nyack (G-16919)	G	845 732-3900
Jackel Inc New York (G-10686)	D	908 359-2039
Jean Pierre Inc New York (G-10715)	F	718 440-7349
June Jacobs Labs LLC New York (G-10788)	D	212 471-4830
Kantian Skincare LLC Smithtown (G-15491)	G	631 780-4711
Lady Burd Exclusive Cosmt Inc Farmingdale (G-5033)	C	631 454-0444
Lechler Laboratories Inc Spring Valley (G-15591)	E	845 426-6800
Liddell Corporation Niagara Falls (G-12842)	F	716 297-8557
Lord & Berry North America Ltd Garden City (G-5517)	G	516 745-0088
Malin + Goetz Inc New York (G-11121)	F	212 244-7771
Mana Products Inc Long Island City (G-7799)	B	718 361-2550
Marietta Corporation Cortland (G-4033)	B	607 753-6746
Mehron Inc Chestnut Ridge (G-3623)	E	845 426-1700
Nature Only Inc Forest Hills (G-5326)	G	917 922-6539
Naturpathica Holistic Hlth Inc East Hampton (G-4414)	D	631 329-8792
Newburgh Distribution Corp New Windsor (G-8945)	G	845 561-6330
Oasis Cosmetic Labs Inc Holtsville (G-6505)	F	631 758-0038
Olan Laboratories Inc Hauppauge (G-6151)	G	631 582-2006
Peppermints Salon Inc Whitestone (G-17213)	F	718 357-6304
Peter Thomas Roth Labs LLC New York (G-11633)	E	212 581-5800
Plastic & Reconstructive Svcs Mount Kisco (G-8640)	G	914 584-5605
Redken 5th Avenue Nyc LLC New York (G-11816)	G	212 984-5113
Shiseido Americas Corporation New York (G-12054)	G	212 805-2300
Skin Nutrition Intl Inc New York (G-12092)	E	212 231-8555
Solabia USA Inc New York (G-12120)	D	212 847-2397
Temptu Inc Long Island City (G-7899)	G	718 937-9503
Tish & Snookys NYC Inc Long Island City (G-7902)	F	718 937-6055
Topiderm Inc Amityville (G-329)	C	631 226-7979
Universal Packg Systems Inc Commack (G-3845)	A	631 543-2277
Victoria Albi Intl Inc New York (G-12539)	F	212 689-2600
Xania Labs Inc Long Island City (G-7928)	G	718 361-2550
Yoyo Lip Gloss Inc Astoria (G-463)	F	718 357-6304

COSMETICS & TOILETRIES

Company	Code	Phone
AEP Environmental LLC Buffalo (G-2801)	F	716 446-0739
Alexandria Professional LLC Williamsville (G-17232)	G	800 957-8427
Allan John Company New York (G-9086)	F	212 940-2210
Apple Beauty Inc New York (G-9182)	G	646 832-3051
Avon Products Inc New York (G-9281)	C	212 282-5000
Avon Products Inc Buffalo (G-2828)	F	716 572-4842
Bare Escentuals Inc New York (G-9319)	G	646 537-0070
Bellarno International Ltd New York (G-9349)	G	212 302-4107
Bio-Botanica Inc Hauppauge (G-6034)	D	631 231-0987
Bobbi Brown Prof Cosmt Inc New York (G-9433)	E	646 613-6500
Borghese Inc New York (G-9441)	E	212 659-5318
California Fragrance Company Huntington Station (G-6698)	E	631 424-4023
China Huaren Organic Pdts Inc New York (G-9597)	G	212 232-0120
Clinique Services Inc New York (G-9643)	G	212 572-4200
Collaborative Laboratories East Setauket (G-4479)	D	631 689-0200
Common Sense Natural Soap Cambridge (G-3306)	E	518 677-0224
Conopco Inc Rochester (G-14287)	E	585 647-8322
Coty Inc New York (G-9730)	D	212 389-7300
Delbia Do Company Inc Bronx (G-1313)	F	718 585-2226
Elite Parfums Ltd New York (G-10007)	D	212 983-2640
Estee Lauder Companies Inc New York (G-10068)	A	917 606-3240
Estee Lauder Companies Inc New York (G-10069)	A	212 572-4200
Estee Lauder Companies Inc New York (G-10070)	A	212 572-4200
Estee Lauder Companies Inc Melville (G-8315)	A	212 572-4015
Estee Lauder Companies Inc New York (G-10071)	A	646 602-7590
Estee Lauder Inc New York (G-10072)	A	212 572-4200
Estee Lauder International Inc New York (G-10074)	G	212 572-4200
Eternal Love Parfums Corp Syosset (G-15821)	G	516 921-6100
Exquis LLC Harriman (G-5971)	F	845 537-5380
FMC International Ltd Port Chester (G-13746)	G	914 935-0918
Four Paws Products Ltd Ronkonkoma (G-14902)	D	631 436-7421
Good Home Co Inc New York (G-10337)	G	212 352-1509
Hain Celestial Group Inc New Hyde Park (G-8837)	C	516 587-5000
Hax Pherocecuticals Inc New York (G-10427)	G	212 401-8695
Iff International Inc New York (G-10560)	E	212 765-5500
Inter Parfums Inc New York (G-10621)	D	212 983-2640
Interntnal Flvors Frgrnces Inc New York (G-10639)	C	212 765-5500
Jean Philippe Fragrances LLC New York (G-10714)	D	212 983-2640
Judith N Graham Inc Rye (G-15061)	G	914 921-5446
Kind Group LLC New York (G-10850)	G	212 645-0800
Klg Usa LLC Port Jervis (G-13788)	A	845 856-5311
LOreal Usa Inc New York (G-11036)	B	917 606-9554
Lornamead Inc New York (G-11043)	D	914 630-7733
Mana Products Inc Long Island City (G-7800)	B	718 361-5204
Marvellissima Intl Ltd New York (G-11171)	G	212 682-7306
Maybelline Inc New York (G-11190)	A	212 885-1310
Mentholatum Company Orchard Park (G-13284)	E	716 677-2500
New Avon LLC New York (G-11380)	A	212 282-8500
Paula Dorf Cosmetics Inc New York (G-11585)	E	212 582-0073
Procter & Gamble Company New York (G-11726)	C	646 885-4201
Professional Buty Holdings Inc Hauppauge (G-6173)	F	631 787-8576
Puig Usa Inc New York (G-11750)	F	212 271-5940
Quality King Distributors Inc Ronkonkoma (G-14973)	C	631 439-2027
Rev Holdings Inc New York (G-11848)	A	212 527-4000
Revlon Inc New York (G-11850)	E	212 527-6330
Revlon Inc New York (G-11851)	B	212 527-4000
Revlon Consumer Products Corp New York (G-11852)	B	212 527-4000
Revlon Holdings Inc New York (G-11853)	D	212 527-4000
RGI Group Incorporated New York (G-11858)	G	212 527-4000
Rimmel Inc New York (G-11873)	G	212 479-4300
Robert Racine Cambridge (G-3309)	F	518 677-0224
Sally Beauty Supply LLC Amherst (G-260)	G	716 831-3286
Scent-A-Vision Inc Huntington Station (G-6722)	E	631 424-4905
Skin Atelier Inc Goshen (G-5739)	F	845 294-1202
Sml Acquisition LLC Elmsford (G-4785)	C	914 592-3130
Sundial Brands LLC Amityville (G-327)	C	631 842-8800
Sundial Group LLC Farmingdale (G-5118)	E	631 842-8800
Symrise Inc Chester (G-3618)	E	845 469-7675
Temptu Inc New York (G-12299)	G	212 675-4000
Tula Life LLC New York (G-12421)	E	201 895-3309
United-Guardian Inc Hauppauge (G-6220)	E	631 273-0900
Verla International Ltd New Windsor (G-8957)	B	845 561-2440
Zela International Co Albany (G-151)	E	518 436-1833

COSMETICS WHOLESALERS

Company	Code	Phone
Abbe Laboratories Inc Farmingdale (G-4929)	F	631 756-2223
Borghese Inc New York (G-9441)	E	212 659-5318
Dermatech Labs Inc Lindenhurst (G-7461)	F	631 225-1700
Essie Cosmetics Ltd New York (G-10067)	D	212 818-1500
Exquis LLC Harriman (G-5971)	F	845 537-5380
Fusion Brands America Inc New York (G-10225)	E	212 269-1387
Lord & Berry North America Ltd Garden City (G-5517)	G	516 745-0088
Lotta Luv Beauty LLC New York (G-11046)	F	646 786-2847
Mana Products Inc Long Island City (G-7799)	B	718 361-2550
Marvellissima Intl Ltd New York (G-11171)	G	212 682-7306
New Avon LLC New York (G-11380)	A	212 282-8500
Shiseido Americas Corporation New York (G-12054)	G	212 805-2300
Xania Labs Inc Long Island City (G-7928)	G	718 361-2550
Zela International Co Albany (G-151)	E	518 436-1833

COSTUME JEWELRY & NOVELTIES: Apparel, Exc Precious Metals

Company	Code	Phone
Jj Fantasia Inc New York (G-10740)	G	212 868-1198
Kenneth J Lane Inc New York (G-10834)	F	212 868-1780
Von Musulin Patricia New York (G-12567)	G	212 206-8345

COSTUME JEWELRY & NOVELTIES: Bracelets, Exc Precious Metals

Company	Code	Phone
Vitafede New York (G-12554)	F	213 488-0136

COSTUME JEWELRY & NOVELTIES: Costume Novelties

Company	Code	Phone
Jay Turoff Brooklyn (G-2136)	F	718 856-7300

Employee Codes: A=Over 500 employees, B=251-500
C=101-250, D=51-100, E=20-50, F=10-19, G=5-9

COSTUME JEWELRY & NOVELTIES: Exc Semi & Precious

COSTUME JEWELRY & NOVELTIES: Exc Semi & Precious

Accessory Plays LLC .... E 212 564-7301
  New York (G-9011)
Barrera Jose & Maria Co Ltd .... E 212 239-1994
  New York (G-9325)
Ben-Amun Co Inc .... E 212 944-6480
  New York (G-9355)
Carol For Eva Graham Inc .... G 212 889-8686
  New York (G-9531)
Catherine Stein Designs Inc .... E 212 840-1188
  New York (G-9549)
Ciner Manufacturing Co Inc .... E 212 947-3770
  New York (G-9619)
Dabby-Reid Ltd .... F 212 356-0040
  New York (G-9786)
Erickson Beamon Ltd .... F 212 643-4810
  New York (G-10057)
Fantasia Jewelry Inc .... E 212 921-9590
  New York (G-10136)
Horly Novelty Co Inc .... G 212 226-4800
  New York (G-10507)
J & H Creations Inc .... E 212 465-0962
  New York (G-10673)
Jaymar Jewelry Co Inc .... E 212 564-4788
  New York (G-10707)
Lesilu Productions Inc .... E 212 947-6419
  New York (G-10974)
Magic Novelty Co Inc .... E 212 304-2777
  New York (G-11104)
Marlborough Jewels Inc .... G 718 768-2000
  Brooklyn (G-2273)
Mwsi Inc .... D 914 347-4200
  Hawthorne (G-6251)
Salmco Jewelry Corp .... F 212 695-8792
  New York (G-11958)
Steezys LLC .... G 646 276-5333
  New York (G-12190)
Stephan & Company ACC Ltd .... E 212 481-3888
  New York (G-12194)
Top Shelf Jewelry Inc .... F 845 647-4661
  Ellenville (G-4639)

COSTUME JEWELRY & NOVELTIES: Necklaces, Exc Precious Metals

Avon Products Inc .... C 212 282-5000
  New York (G-9281)

COSTUME JEWELRY & NOVELTIES: Pins, Exc Precious Metals

Custom Pins Inc .... G 914 690-9378
  Elmsford (G-4746)

COUGH MEDICINES

Purine Pharma LLC .... E 315 705-4030
  Massena (G-8199)

COUNTER & SINK TOPS

Arcy Plastic Laminates Inc .... E 518 235-0753
  Albany (G-48)
Auratic Inc .... G 914 413-8154
  New York (G-9263)
Countertops & Cabinets Inc .... G 315 433-1038
  Syracuse (G-15910)
Delocon Wholesale Inc .... F 716 592-2711
  Springville (G-15609)
Empire Fabricators Inc .... G 585 235-3050
  Rochester (G-14346)
Frank J Martello .... G 585 235-2780
  Rochester (G-14381)
Icestone LLC .... E 718 624-4900
  Brooklyn (G-2095)
Joseph Fedele .... G 718 448-3658
  Staten Island (G-15694)
Koeppels Kustom Kitchens Inc .... E 518 489-0092
  Albany (G-96)
Metropolitan Granite & MBL Inc .... G 585 342-7020
  Rochester (G-14505)
Nlr Counter Tops LLC .... G 347 295-0410
  New York (G-11446)
Pine Hill Fabricators .... G 716 823-2474
  Buffalo (G-3127)
Precision Built Tops LLC .... G 607 336-5417
  Norwich (G-13035)
Ridge Cabinet & Showcase Inc .... E 585 663-0560
  Rochester (G-14626)
Rochester Countertop Inc .... F 585 338-2260
  Rochester (G-14640)
Solid Surfaces Inc .... E 585 292-5340
  Rochester (G-14692)
Triad Counter Corp .... E 631 750-0615
  Bohemia (G-1146)
Wilbedone Inc .... E 607 756-8813
  Cortland (G-4047)
Wolak Inc .... G 315 839-5366
  Clayville (G-3691)

COUNTERS & COUNTING DEVICES

Cmp Advnced Mech Sltons NY LLC ..... G 607 352-1712
  Binghamton (G-902)
Designatronics Incorporated .... G 516 328-3300
  New Hyde Park (G-8825)
Empresas De Manufactura Inc .... C 631 240-9251
  East Setauket (G-4481)
Encore Electronics Inc .... E 518 584-5354
  Saratoga Springs (G-15150)
Environment-One Corporation .... C 518 346-6161
  Schenectady (G-15252)
Sun Circuits International Inc .... B 631 240-9251
  Setauket (G-15381)

COUNTERS OR COUNTER DISPLAY CASES, EXC WOOD

Gerald Frd Packg Display LLC .... F 716 692-2705
  Tonawanda (G-16165)
Glasbau Hahn America LLC .... G 845 566-3331
  Newburgh (G-12759)
Stone Expo & Cabinetry LLC .... F 516 292-2988
  West Hempstead (G-16863)

COUNTERS OR COUNTER DISPLAY CASES, WOOD

Bloch Industries LLC .... D 585 334-9600
  Rochester (G-14235)
Creative Counter Tops Inc .... F 845 471-6480
  Poughkeepsie (G-13894)
Serway Bros Inc 315 337-0601
  Rome (G-14836)

COUNTERS: Mechanical

Melland Gear Instr of Huppauge .... E 631 234-0100
  Hauppauge (G-6130)

COUNTING DEVICES: Controls, Revolution & Timing

Heat-Timer Corporation .... E 212 481-2020
  Bronx (G-1354)
Schlumberger Technology Corp .... C 607 378-0200
  Horseheads (G-6592)

COUNTING DEVICES: Electromechanical

K-Technologies Inc .... E 716 828-4444
  Buffalo (G-3025)
Vantage Mfg & Assembly LLC .... E 845 471-5290
  Poughkeepsie (G-13938)

COUNTING DEVICES: Speed Indicators & Recorders, Vehicle

Curtis Instruments Inc .... C 914 666-2971
  Mount Kisco (G-8624)

COUPLINGS: Shaft

Cobham Management Services Inc .... A 716 662-0006
  Orchard Park (G-13264)
Howden North America Inc .... D 803 741-2700
  Depew (G-4259)
Kinemotive Corporation .... E 631 249-6440
  Farmingdale (G-5028)

COUPON REDEMPTION SVCS

Syracuse Letter Company Inc .... F 315 476-8328
  Bridgeport (G-1237)

COURIER SVCS, AIR: Package Delivery, Private

Miller Enterprises CNY Inc .... G 315 682-4999
  Manlius (G-8075)

COURIER SVCS: Ground

Comsec Ventures International .... G 518 523-1600
  Lake Placid (G-7273)

COVERS: Automobile Seat

Mc Coy Tops and Interiors Inc .... G 718 458-5800
  Woodside (G-17336)
Stidd Systems Inc .... E 631 477-2400
  Greenport (G-5877)

COVERS: Automotive, Exc Seat & Tire

Automtive Uphl Cnvertible Tops .... G 914 961-4242
  Tuckahoe (G-16269)
Kamali Group Inc .... G 516 627-4000
  Great Neck (G-5819)

COVERS: Canvas

Covergrip Corporation .... G 855 268-3747
  Bohemia (G-1041)
Custom Canvas Manufacturing Co ..... E 716 852-6372
  Buffalo (G-2897)

COVERS: Hot Tub & Spa

Commercial Fabrics Inc .... F 716 694-0641
  North Tonawanda (G-12966)

COVERS: Slip Made Of Fabric, Plastic, Etc.

Superior Decorators Inc .... F 718 381-4793
  Glendale (G-5664)

CRANE & AERIAL LIFT SVCS

Snyders Neon Displays Inc .... G 518 857-4100
  Colonie (G-3821)

CRANES & MONORAIL SYSTEMS

Debrucque Cleveland Tramrail S .... G 315 697-5160
  Canastota (G-3366)

CRANES: Indl Plant

Konecranes Inc .... F 585 359-4450
  Henrietta (G-6295)

CRANKSHAFTS & CAMSHAFTS: Machining

Clip Clop International Inc .... F 631 392-1340
  Bohemia (G-1035)
Peko Precision Products Inc .... F 585 301-1386
  Rochester (G-14574)
Westchstr Crnkshft Grndng .... G 718 651-3900
  East Elmhurst (G-4400)

CRATES: Fruit, Wood Wirebound

Wolfe Lumber Mill Inc .... G 716 772-7750
  Gasport (G-5560)

CREDIT BUREAUS

Nyt Capital LLC .... F 212 556-1234
  New York (G-11488)

CROWNS & CLOSURES

Reynolds Packaging McHy Inc .... D 716 358-6451
  Falconer (G-4910)

CRUDE PETROLEUM & NATURAL GAS PRODUCTION

Hess Energy Exploration Ltd .... G 732 750-6500
  New York (G-10465)
Hess Explrtion Prod Hldngs Ltd .... G 732 750-6000
  New York (G-10466)

CRUDE PETROLEUM & NATURAL GAS PRODUCTION

Dlh Energy Service LLC .... G 716 410-0028
  Lakewood (G-7291)
Lukoil Americas Corporation .... C 212 421-4141
  New York (G-11061)
MRC Global (us) Inc .... F 607 739-8575
  Horseheads (G-6585)
Rocket Tech Fuel Corp .... F 516 810-8947
  Bay Shore (G-737)

PRODUCT SECTION

CUTOUTS: Cardboard, Die-Cut, Made From Purchased Materials

CRUDE PETROLEUM PRODUCTION
Chanse Petroleum Corporation............G....... 212 682-3789
  New York *(G-9579)*
China N E Petro Holdings Ltd................A....... 212 307-3568
  New York *(G-9600)*
Hess Corporation..................................B....... 212 997-8500
  New York *(G-10464)*
Hess Pipeline Corporation ....B....... 212 997-8500
  New York *(G-10468)*
Hess Tioga Gas Plant LLC ....C....... 212 997-8500
  New York *(G-10469)*
Resource PTRlm&ptrochmcl Intl...........E....... 212 537-3856
  New York *(G-11842)*
Speedway LLC ....F....... 631 738-2536
  Lake Grove *(G-7266)*
Stedman Energy Inc ....G....... 716 789-3018
  Mayville *(G-8219)*

CRUDES: Cyclic, Organic
Magic Tank LLC...................................G....... 877 646-2442
  New York *(G-11106)*

CRYOGENIC COOLING DEVICES: Infrared Detectors, Masers
Philips Medical Systems Mr..................B....... 518 782-1122
  Latham *(G-7376)*

CRYSTALS
Crystal Is Inc..E....... 518 271-7375
  Troy *(G-16219)*
Edo LLC..G....... 631 630-4000
  Amityville *(G-285)*
Momentive Performance Mtls Inc........E....... 518 237-3330
  Waterford *(G-16616)*
Mpm Holdings Inc ....G....... 518 237-3330
  Waterford *(G-16617)*
Mpm Intermediate Holdings Inc...........G....... 518 237-3330
  Waterford *(G-16618)*

CULTURE MEDIA
Angus Chemical Company ....E....... 716 283-1434
  Niagara Falls *(G-12796)*
Debmar-Mercury ....G....... 212 669-5025
  New York *(G-9834)*
HP Hood LLC ....D....... 315 829-3339
  Vernon *(G-16435)*
Man of World ....G....... 212 915-0017
  New York *(G-11124)*

CULVERTS: Metal Plate
Lane Enterprises Inc............................F....... 607 776-3366
  Bath *(G-660)*

CUPS: Paper, Made From Purchased Materials
Amscan Inc...C....... 914 345-2020
  Elmsford *(G-4732)*

CUPS: Plastic Exc Polystyrene Foam
Amscan Inc...C....... 914 345-2020
  Elmsford *(G-4732)*
Capitol Cups Inc...................................E....... 518 627-0051
  Amsterdam *(G-337)*

CURBING: Granite Or Stone
Granite Works LLC ....E....... 607 565-7012
  Waverly *(G-16702)*

CURTAIN & DRAPERY FIXTURES: Poles, Rods & Rollers
Abalene Decorating Services ....E....... 718 782-2000
  New York *(G-9000)*
Blinds To Go (us) Inc...........................E....... 718 477-9523
  Staten Island *(G-15648)*
McCarroll Uphl Designs LLC.................G....... 518 828-0500
  Hudson *(G-6625)*
P E Guerin..D....... 212 243-5270
  New York *(G-11548)*
Pj Decorators Inc ....E....... 516 735-9693
  East Meadow *(G-4427)*
Wcd Window Coverings Inc.................E....... 845 336-4511
  Lake Katrine *(G-7271)*

Window Workshops Inc ....F....... 716 876-9981
  Buffalo *(G-3257)*

CURTAIN WALLS: Building, Steel
AM Architectural Metal & Glass...........E....... 845 942-8848
  Garnerville *(G-5553)*

CURTAINS & BEDDING: Knit
Commonwealth Home Fashion Inc ....D....... 514 384-8290
  Willsboro *(G-17264)*

CURTAINS & CURTAIN FABRICS: Lace
Creative Window Fashions Inc..............D....... 718 746-5817
  Whitestone *(G-17205)*
Mary Bright Inc....................................G....... 212 677-1970
  New York *(G-11172)*

CURTAINS: Cottage Sets, From Purchased Materials
Northast Coml Win Trtments Inc..........D....... 845 331-0148
  Kingston *(G-7203)*

CURTAINS: Shower
Catalina Products Corp ....E....... 718 336-8288
  Brooklyn *(G-1764)*
Showeray Co ....D....... 718 965-3633
  Brooklyn *(G-2551)*

CURTAINS: Window, From Purchased Materials
Belle Maison USA Ltd ....E....... 718 805-0200
  Richmond Hill *(G-14068)*
Drapery Industries Inc ....F....... 585 232-2992
  Rochester *(G-14318)*

CUSHIONS & PILLOWS
Alexandra Ferguson LLC ....G....... 718 788-7768
  Brooklyn *(G-1581)*
Allied Down Products Inc ....G....... 718 389-5454
  Brooklyn *(G-1589)*
Anhui Skyworth LLC.............................D....... 917 940-6903
  Hempstead *(G-6264)*
Hollander Sleep Products LLC ....D....... 212 575-0400
  New York *(G-10499)*
Prime Feather Industries Ltd ....F....... 718 326-8701
  Suffern *(G-15798)*
Soft-Tex International Inc ....D....... 518 235-3645
  Waterford *(G-16621)*
Xpresspa Holdings LLC ....F....... 212 750-9595
  New York *(G-12683)*

CUSHIONS & PILLOWS: Bed, From Purchased Materials
Arlee Home Fashions Inc ....D....... 212 213-0425
  New York *(G-9203)*
Hollander HM Fshons Hldngs LLC........F....... 212 575-0400
  New York *(G-10498)*
Home Fashions Intl LLC.......................F....... 212 684-0091
  New York *(G-10501)*
R & M Industries Inc...........................F....... 212 366-6414
  New York *(G-11780)*
Twinny Products Inc ....F....... 718 592-7500
  Corona *(G-4008)*

CUSHIONS: Textile, Exc Spring & Carpet
Advanced Medical Mfg Corp.................E....... 845 369-7535
  Suffern *(G-15784)*
Jakes Sneakers Inc..............................G....... 718 233-1132
  Brooklyn *(G-2134)*
Twinny Products Inc ....F....... 718 592-7500
  Corona *(G-4008)*
Wayne Decorators Inc ....G....... 718 529-4200
  Jamaica *(G-6963)*

CUSTOM COMPOUNDING OF RUBBER MATERIALS
Pawling Corporation.............................C....... 845 855-1000
  Pawling *(G-13451)*
Tire Conversion Tech Inc ....E....... 518 372-1600
  Latham *(G-7379)*

CUT STONE & STONE PRODUCTS
Adirondack Precision Cut Stone...........F....... 518 681-3060
  Queensbury *(G-13986)*
Alart Inc...G....... 212 840-1508
  New York *(G-9071)*
American Bluestone LLC ....F....... 607 369-2235
  Sidney *(G-15435)*
Barra & Trumbore Inc ....G....... 845 626-5442
  Kerhonkson *(G-7154)*
Busch Products Inc..............................E....... 315 474-8422
  Syracuse *(G-15878)*
Crown Hill Stone Inc ....E....... 716 326-4601
  Westfield *(G-17047)*
Denton Stoneworks Inc ....F....... 516 746-1500
  Garden City Park *(G-5539)*
Devonian Stone New York Inc ....E....... 607 655-2600
  Windsor *(G-17272)*
European Marble Works Co Inc...........F....... 718 387-9778
  Garden City *(G-5504)*
First Presbyterian Church....................G....... 315 252-3861
  Auburn *(G-495)*
Fordham Marble Co Inc.......................F....... 914 682-6699
  White Plains *(G-17110)*
Granite Tops Inc ....G....... 914 699-2909
  Mount Vernon *(G-8687)*
Masonville Stone Incorporated............G....... 607 265-3597
  Masonville *(G-8108)*
New York Quarries Inc ....F....... 518 756-3138
  Alcove *(G-172)*
North American Stone Inc ....G....... 585 266-4020
  Rochester *(G-14541)*
North Shore Monuments Inc ....G....... 516 759-2156
  Glen Head *(G-5639)*
Pallette Stone Corporation..................E....... 518 584-2421
  Gansevoort *(G-5487)*
Rivera ....F....... 718 458-1488
  Flushing *(G-5288)*
Sanford Stone LLC...............................F....... 607 467-1313
  Deposit *(G-4279)*
Seneca Stone Corporation ....F....... 315 549-8253
  Fayette *(G-5162)*
Seneca Stone Corporation ....G....... 607 737-6200
  Pine City *(G-13552)*
Vermont Structural Slate Co ....F....... 518 499-1912
  Whitehall *(G-17191)*
W F Saunders & Sons Inc ....F....... 315 469-3217
  Nedrow *(G-8773)*

CUTLERY
Advanced Machine Design Co Inc ....E....... 716 826-2000
  Buffalo *(G-2800)*
Cutco Cutlery Corporation...................B....... 716 372-3111
  Olean *(G-13141)*
Korin Japanese Trading Corp..............E....... 212 587-7021
  New York *(G-10878)*
Lifetime Brands Inc..............................B....... 516 683-6000
  Garden City *(G-5514)*
Niabraze LLC..F....... 716 447-1082
  Tonawanda *(G-16185)*
Novelty Crystal Corp ....E....... 718 458-6700
  Long Island City *(G-7826)*
Oneida International Inc ....G....... 315 361-3000
  Oneida *(G-13160)*
Oneida Silversmiths Inc ....G....... 315 361-3000
  Oneida *(G-13164)*
Ontario Knife Company ....D....... 716 676-5527
  Franklinville *(G-5370)*
Schilling Forge Inc ....G....... 315 454-4421
  Syracuse *(G-16033)*
Servotronics Inc...................................C....... 716 655-5990
  Elma *(G-4655)*
Sherrill Manufacturing Inc...................C....... 315 280-0727
  Sherrill *(G-15407)*
Warren Cutlery Corp ....F....... 845 876-3444
  Rhinebeck *(G-14060)*
Woods Knife Corporation ....E....... 516 798-4972
  Massapequa *(G-8184)*

CUTLERY WHOLESALERS
Utica Cutlery Company ....D....... 315 733-4663
  Utica *(G-16363)*
Warren Cutlery Corp ....F....... 845 876-3444
  Rhinebeck *(G-14060)*

CUTOUTS: Cardboard, Die-Cut, Made From Purchased Materials
Lion Die-Cutting Co Inc.......................E....... 718 383-8841
  Brooklyn *(G-2229)*

Employee Codes: A=Over 500 employees, B=251-500
C=101-250, D=51-100, E=20-50, F=10-19, G=5-9

CUTOUTS: Distribution

CUTOUTS: Distribution
Junior Achevement of Eastrn NY ....G....... 518 783-4336
 Latham *(G-7366)*
Product Station Inc ....F....... 516 942-4220
 Jericho *(G-7082)*

CUTTING SVC: Paper, Exc Die-Cut
A-1 Products Inc ....G....... 718 789-1818
 Brooklyn *(G-1538)*
J Mackenzie Ltd ....E....... 585 321-1770
 Rochester *(G-14456)*

CYCLIC CRUDES & INTERMEDIATES
Chemours Company Fc LLC ....E....... 716 278-5100
 Niagara Falls *(G-12804)*
Durez Corporation ....F....... 716 286-0100
 Niagara Falls *(G-12812)*
Micro Powders Inc ....E....... 914 332-6400
 Tarrytown *(G-16097)*
Mitsui Chemicals America Inc ....E....... 914 253-0777
 Rye Brook *(G-15072)*
Premier Brands of America Inc ....E....... 718 325-3000
 Mount Vernon *(G-8718)*

CYLINDER & ACTUATORS: Fluid Power
A K Allen Co Inc ....C....... 516 747-5450
 Mineola *(G-8488)*
Ameritool Mfg Inc ....E....... 315 668-2172
 Central Square *(G-3516)*
ITT Enidine Inc ....B....... 716 662-1900
 Orchard Park *(G-13275)*
Precision Mechanisms Corp ....E....... 516 333-5955
 Westbury *(G-17021)*
Superior Motion Controls Inc ....E....... 516 420-2921
 Farmingdale *(G-5120)*
Triumph Actuation Systems LLC ....D....... 516 378-0162
 Freeport *(G-5432)*
Young & Franklin Inc ....D....... 315 457-3110
 Liverpool *(G-7559)*

CYLINDERS: Pressure
A K Allen Co Inc ....C....... 516 747-5450
 Mineola *(G-8488)*

DAIRY EQPT
Richard Stewart ....G....... 518 632-5363
 Hartford *(G-5996)*

DAIRY PRDTS STORE: Cheese
Artisanal Brands Inc ....E....... 914 441-3591
 Bronxville *(G-1498)*

DAIRY PRDTS STORE: Ice Cream, Packaged
Bleecker Pastry Tartufo Inc ....G....... 718 937-9830
 Long Island City *(G-7689)*
Clinton Creamery Inc ....F....... 917 324-9699
 Laurelton *(G-7386)*
Delicioso Coco Helado Inc ....F....... 718 292-1930
 Bronx *(G-1314)*
Marvel Dairy Whip Inc ....G....... 516 889-4232
 Lido Beach *(G-7442)*

DAIRY PRDTS STORES
Crosswinds Farm & Creamery ....G....... 607 327-0363
 Ovid *(G-13345)*

DAIRY PRDTS WHOLESALERS: Fresh
HP Hood LLC ....C....... 315 363-3870
 Oneida *(G-13157)*
Longfords Ice Cream Ltd ....F....... 914 935-9469
 Port Chester *(G-13752)*
Upstate Niagara Coop Inc ....E....... 716 484-7178
 Jamestown *(G-7041)*

DAIRY PRDTS: Bakers' Cheese
P & F Bakers Inc ....G....... 516 931-6821
 Hicksville *(G-6382)*

DAIRY PRDTS: Bottled Baby Formula
Infant Formula Laboratory Svc ....F....... 718 257-3000
 Brooklyn *(G-2105)*

DAIRY PRDTS: Butter
Canalside Creamery Inc ....G....... 716 695-2876
 North Tonawanda *(G-12965)*
O-At-Ka Milk Products Coop Inc ....B....... 585 343-0536
 Batavia *(G-644)*
Pure Ghee Inc ....G....... 718 224-7399
 Flushing *(G-5285)*

DAIRY PRDTS: Canned Baby Formula
Danone Nutricia Early ....E....... 914 872-8556
 White Plains *(G-17098)*

DAIRY PRDTS: Cheese
Agri-Mark Inc ....D....... 518 497-6644
 Chateaugay *(G-3556)*
Artisanal Brands Inc ....E....... 914 441-3591
 Bronxville *(G-1498)*
Castelli America LLC ....D....... 716 782-2101
 Ashville *(G-426)*
Emkay Trading Corp ....G....... 914 592-9000
 Elmsford *(G-4748)*
Emkay Trading Corp ....E....... 585 492-3800
 Arcade *(G-392)*
Empire Cheese Inc ....C....... 585 968-1552
 Cuba *(G-4069)*
Euphrates Inc ....D....... 518 762-3488
 Johnstown *(G-7111)*
F Cappiello Dairy Pdts Inc ....E....... 518 374-5064
 Schenectady *(G-15254)*
Friendship Dairies LLC ....C....... 585 973-3031
 Friendship *(G-5452)*
Gharana Industries LLC ....G....... 315 651-4004
 Waterloo *(G-16627)*
Great Lakes Cheese NY Inc ....D....... 315 232-4511
 Adams *(G-3)*
HP Hood LLC ....D....... 607 295-8134
 Arkport *(G-410)*
Hudson Valley Creamery Inc ....F....... 518 851-2570
 Hudson *(G-6618)*
Instantwhip of Buffalo Inc ....E....... 716 892-7031
 Buffalo *(G-3010)*
Kraft Heinz Foods Company ....B....... 315 376-6575
 Lowville *(G-7938)*
Kraft Heinz Foods Company ....B....... 607 527-4584
 Campbell *(G-3330)*
Kraft Heinz Foods Company ....C....... 607 865-7131
 Walton *(G-16548)*
Lactalis American Group Inc ....D....... 716 827-2622
 Buffalo *(G-3042)*
Lactalis American Group Inc ....B....... 716 823-6262
 Buffalo *(G-3043)*
Leprino Foods Company ....C....... 570 888-9658
 Waverly *(G-16704)*
Original Hrkmer Cnty Chese Inc ....D....... 315 895-7428
 Ilion *(G-6743)*
Rainbeau Ridge Farm ....G....... 914 234-2197
 Bedford Hills *(G-806)*
Sorrento Lactalis Incorporated ....C....... 716 823-6262
 Buffalo *(G-3193)*
Taam-Tov Foods Inc ....G....... 718 788-8880
 Brooklyn *(G-2641)*
World Cheese Co Inc ....F....... 718 965-1700
 Brooklyn *(G-2765)*

DAIRY PRDTS: Cheese, Cottage
HP Hood LLC ....D....... 607 295-8134
 Arkport *(G-410)*

DAIRY PRDTS: Concentrated Skim Milk
O-At-Ka Milk Products Coop Inc ....B....... 585 343-0536
 Batavia *(G-644)*

DAIRY PRDTS: Cream Substitutes
Sugar Foods Corporation ....E....... 212 753-6900
 New York *(G-12227)*

DAIRY PRDTS: Cream, Sweet
Emkay Trading Corp ....E....... 585 492-3800
 Arcade *(G-392)*

DAIRY PRDTS: Dairy Based Desserts, Frozen
Sweet Melodys LLC ....E....... 716 580-3227
 East Amherst *(G-4362)*

DAIRY PRDTS: Dietary Supplements, Dairy & Non-Dairy Based
Century Tom Inc ....G....... 347 654-3179
 College Point *(G-3780)*
Dynatabs LLC ....F....... 718 376-6084
 Brooklyn *(G-1888)*
El-Gen LLC ....G....... 631 218-3400
 Bohemia *(G-1064)*
Eximus Connections Corporation ....G....... 631 421-1700
 Huntington Station *(G-6703)*
GNI Commerce Inc ....G....... 347 275-1155
 Brooklyn *(G-2033)*
Makers Nutrition LLC ....E....... 631 456-5397
 Hauppauge *(G-6125)*
Physiologics LLC ....F....... 800 765-6775
 Ronkonkoma *(G-14969)*
Vitakem Nutraceutical Inc ....E....... 631 956-8343
 Smithtown *(G-15502)*
Vitamin Power Incorporated ....G....... 631 676-5790
 Hauppauge *(G-6228)*

DAIRY PRDTS: Dips & Spreads, Cheese Based
Cheese Experts USA Ltd Lblty ....G....... 908 275-3889
 Staten Island *(G-15658)*

DAIRY PRDTS: Dried & Powdered Milk & Milk Prdts
Hain Celestial Group Inc ....G....... 516 587-5000
 New Hyde Park *(G-8837)*
Omilk LLC ....G....... 646 530-2908
 Brooklyn *(G-2391)*

DAIRY PRDTS: Evaporated Milk
Nestle Usa Inc ....C....... 914 272-4021
 White Plains *(G-17140)*

DAIRY PRDTS: Farmers' Cheese
Dwyer Farm LLC ....G....... 914 456-2742
 Walden *(G-16533)*

DAIRY PRDTS: Fermented & Cultured Milk Prdts
Kong Kee Food Corp ....E....... 718 937-2746
 Long Island City *(G-7783)*
Kraft Heinz Foods Company ....C....... 607 865-7131
 Walton *(G-16548)*
Upstate Niagara Coop Inc ....D....... 716 892-3156
 Buffalo *(G-3237)*

DAIRY PRDTS: Frozen Desserts & Novelties
Blue Pig Ice Cream Factory ....G....... 914 271-3850
 Croton On Hudson *(G-4062)*
Carols Polar Parlor ....G....... 315 468-3404
 Syracuse *(G-15885)*
Clinton Creamery Inc ....F....... 917 324-9699
 Laurelton *(G-7386)*
Crepini LLC ....E....... 347 422-0829
 Brooklyn *(G-1817)*
Crowley Foods Inc ....E....... 800 637-0019
 Binghamton *(G-904)*
Df Mavens Inc ....E....... 347 813-4705
 Astoria *(G-437)*
Ffc Holding Corp Subsidiaries ....F....... 716 366-5400
 Dunkirk *(G-4342)*
Fieldbrook Foods Corporation ....C....... 716 366-5400
 Dunkirk *(G-4343)*
Fresh Ice Cream Company LLC ....F....... 347 603-6021
 Brooklyn *(G-2006)*
G Pesso & Sons Inc ....G....... 718 224-9130
 Bayside *(G-771)*
GM Ice Cream Inc ....G....... 646 236-7383
 Queens Village *(G-13977)*
HP Hood LLC ....A....... 607 772-6580
 Binghamton *(G-922)*
Jones Humdinger ....F....... 607 771-6501
 Binghamton *(G-932)*
Kozy Shack Enterprises LLC ....C....... 516 870-3000
 Hicksville *(G-6360)*
Lasalle Brands Inc ....F....... 718 542-0900
 Bronx *(G-1378)*
Lickity Splits ....G....... 585 345-6091
 Batavia *(G-641)*

PRODUCT SECTION

Longfords Ice Cream Ltd .... F 914 935-9469
  Port Chester *(G-13752)*
Macadoodles .... G 607 652-9019
  Stamford *(G-15625)*
Macedonia Ltd .... F 718 462-3596
  Brooklyn *(G-2250)*
Main Street Sweets .... F 914 332-5757
  Tarrytown *(G-16094)*
Marina Ice Cream .... G 718 235-3000
  Brooklyn *(G-2270)*
Mexicone .... G 315 591-1971
  Mexico *(G-8397)*
Moonlight Creamery .... G 585 223-0880
  Fairport *(G-4864)*
MSQ Corporation .... G 718 465-0900
  Queens Village *(G-13982)*
Ninas Custard .... E 716 636-0345
  Getzville *(G-5601)*
Nutrifast LLC .... F 347 671-3181
  New York *(G-11474)*
Olympic Ice Cream Co Inc .... E 718 849-6200
  Richmond Hill *(G-14077)*
Original Fowlers Choclat Inc .... G 716 668-2113
  Cheektowaga *(G-3584)*
Perrys Ice Cream Company Inc .... B 716 542-5492
  Akron *(G-27)*
Phyljohn Distributors Inc .... F 518 459-2775
  Albany *(G-120)*
Piazzas Ice Cream Ice Hse Inc .... F 718 818-8811
  Staten Island *(G-15721)*
Pop Bar LLC .... G 212 255-4874
  New York *(G-11683)*
Quaker Bonnet Inc .... G 716 885-7208
  Buffalo *(G-3146)*
Quality Dairy Farms Inc .... E 315 942-2611
  Boonville *(G-1168)*
Spatula LLC .... F 917 582-8684
  New York *(G-12151)*
Tia Lattrell .... G 845 373-9494
  Amenia *(G-217)*
Twisters .... G 585 346-3730
  Livonia *(G-7565)*
Van Alphen & Doran Corp .... G 518 782-9242
  Latham *(G-7382)*
Van Leeuwen Artisan Ice Cream .... G 718 701-1630
  Brooklyn *(G-2719)*
Wicked Spoon Inc .... F 646 335-2890
  New York *(G-12630)*

DAIRY PRDTS: Ice Cream & Ice Milk

Purity Ice Cream Co Inc .... F 607 272-1545
  Ithaca *(G-6872)*
Stewarts Processing Corp .... D 518 581-1200
  Ballston Spa *(G-610)*
TLC-Lc Inc .... E 212 756-8900
  New York *(G-12355)*
Washburns Dairy Inc .... E 518 725-0629
  Gloversville *(G-5728)*

DAIRY PRDTS: Ice Cream, Bulk

Bleecker Pastry Tartufo Inc .... G 718 937-9830
  Long Island City *(G-7689)*
Blue Marble Ice Cream .... F 718 858-5551
  Brooklyn *(G-1701)*
Byrne Dairy Inc .... E 315 475-2111
  Syracuse *(G-15879)*
Delicioso Coco Helado Inc .... F 718 292-1930
  Bronx *(G-1314)*
Grom Columbus LLC .... G 212 974-3444
  New York *(G-10369)*
Ice Cream Man Inc .... E 518 692-8382
  Greenwich *(G-5890)*
Mamas .... G 518 399-2828
  Burnt Hills *(G-3267)*
Marvel Dairy Whip Inc .... G 516 889-4232
  Lido Beach *(G-7442)*
Paleteria Fernandez Inc .... E 914 315-1598
  Mamaroneck *(G-8041)*
Scoops R US Incorporated .... G 212 730-7959
  New York *(G-12005)*
Smartys Corner .... G 607 239-5276
  Endicott *(G-4829)*
Victory Garden .... G 212 206-7273
  New York *(G-12540)*

DAIRY PRDTS: Ice Cream, Packaged, Molded, On Sticks, Etc.

Byrne Dairy Inc .... B 315 475-2121
  La Fayette *(G-7241)*

DAIRY PRDTS: Milk, Condensed & Evaporated

Alpina Foods Inc .... F 855 886-1914
  Batavia *(G-621)*
Friendship Dairies LLC .... C 585 973-3031
  Friendship *(G-5452)*
FriesIndcmpina Ingrdnts N Amer .... E 607 746-0196
  Delhi *(G-4239)*
Kerry Inc .... D 607 334-1700
  Norwich *(G-13029)*
Nationwide Dairy Inc .... G 347 689-8148
  Brooklyn *(G-2352)*
Rich Products Corporation .... A 716 878-8422
  Buffalo *(G-3157)*
Solivaira Specialties Inc .... D 716 693-4009
  North Tonawanda *(G-12996)*

DAIRY PRDTS: Milk, Fluid

Crowley Foods Inc .... E 800 637-0019
  Binghamton *(G-904)*
Dairy Farmers America Inc .... E 816 801-6440
  East Syracuse *(G-4522)*
Dean Foods Company .... D 315 452-5001
  East Syracuse *(G-4525)*
Finger Lakes Cheese Trail .... F 607 857-5726
  Odessa *(G-13108)*
HP Hood LLC .... C 315 363-3870
  Oneida *(G-13157)*
HP Hood LLC .... B 315 658-2132
  La Fargeville *(G-7236)*
HP Hood LLC .... B 518 218-9097
  Albany *(G-89)*
HP Hood LLC .... A 607 772-6580
  Binghamton *(G-922)*
HP Hood LLC .... D 315 829-3339
  Vernon *(G-16435)*
Instantwhip of Buffalo Inc .... E 716 892-7031
  Buffalo *(G-3010)*
Kesso Foods Inc .... G 718 777-5303
  East Elmhurst *(G-4393)*
Kraft Heinz Foods Company .... B 607 527-4584
  Campbell *(G-3330)*
O-At-Ka Milk Products Coop Inc .... B 585 343-0536
  Batavia *(G-644)*
Purity Ice Cream Co Inc .... F 607 272-1545
  Ithaca *(G-6872)*
Saputo Dairy Foods Usa LLC .... D 607 746-2141
  Delhi *(G-4242)*
Stewarts Processing Corp .... D 518 581-1200
  Ballston Spa *(G-610)*
Upstate Niagara Coop Inc .... D 315 389-5111
  North Lawrence *(G-12935)*
Upstate Niagara Coop Inc .... C 716 892-2121
  Buffalo *(G-3238)*

DAIRY PRDTS: Milk, Processed, Pasteurized, Homogenized/Btld

Byrne Dairy Inc .... B 315 475-2121
  La Fayette *(G-7241)*
Elmhurst Dairy Inc .... C 718 526-3442
  Jamaica *(G-6910)*
Midland Farms Inc .... E 518 436-7038
  Menands *(G-8376)*
Steuben Foods Incorporated .... C 716 655-4000
  Elma *(G-4656)*
Upstate Niagara Coop Inc .... C 585 458-1880
  Rochester *(G-14748)*
Upstate Niagara Coop Inc .... E 716 484-7178
  Jamestown *(G-7041)*

DAIRY PRDTS: Natural Cheese

Cemac Foods Corp .... F 914 835-0526
  Harrison *(G-5978)*
Crosswinds Farm & Creamery .... G 607 327-0363
  Ovid *(G-13345)*
Four Fat Fowl Inc .... G 518 733-5230
  Stephentown *(G-15757)*
Kutters Cheese Factory Inc .... E 585 599-3693
  Corfu *(G-3956)*
Losurdo Foods Inc .... C 315 344-2444
  Heuvelton *(G-6305)*
Mongiello Sales Inc .... E 845 436-4200
  Hurleyville *(G-6731)*
Mongiellos Itln Cheese Spc LLC .... C 845 436-4200
  Hurleyville *(G-6732)*
Pecoraro Dairy Products Inc .... G 718 388-2379
  Brooklyn *(G-2411)*

Red Creek Cold Storage LLC .... G 315 576-2069
  Red Creek *(G-14025)*
Sandvoss Farms LLC .... G 585 297-7044
  East Bethany *(G-4383)*

DAIRY PRDTS: Processed Cheese

Habco Corp .... E 631 789-1400
  Amityville *(G-291)*
J Kraft Microscopy Svcs Inc .... G 716 592-4402
  Springville *(G-15613)*
Kraft Heinz Foods Company .... C 607 527-4584
  Campbell *(G-3329)*

DAIRY PRDTS: Pudding Pops, Frozen

Allied Food Products Inc .... F 718 230-4227
  Brooklyn *(G-1590)*

DAIRY PRDTS: Spreads, Cheese

Noga Dairies Inc .... F 516 293-5448
  Farmingdale *(G-5066)*

DAIRY PRDTS: Whipped Topping, Exc Frozen Or Dry Mix

Hanan Products Company Inc .... E 516 938-1000
  Hicksville *(G-6354)*

DAIRY PRDTS: Yogurt, Exc Frozen

Bliss Foods Inc .... G 212 732-8888
  New York *(G-9414)*
Bliss Foods Inc .... F 212 732-8888
  New York *(G-9415)*
Chobani LLC .... C 607 337-1246
  Norwich *(G-13024)*
Chobani LLC .... A 607 847-6181
  New Berlin *(G-8779)*
Currant Company LLC .... G 845 266-8999
  Staatsburg *(G-15617)*
Fage USA Dairy Industry Inc .... B 518 762-5912
  Johnstown *(G-7112)*
Fage USA Holdings .... B 518 762-5912
  Johnstown *(G-7113)*
Maple Hill Creamery LLC .... E 518 758-7777
  Stuyvesant *(G-15782)*
Mualema LLC .... G 609 820-6098
  New York *(G-11321)*
Noga Dairies Inc .... F 516 293-5448
  Farmingdale *(G-5066)*
Steuben Foods Incorporated .... F 718 291-3333
  Jamaica *(G-6952)*
The Dannon Company Inc .... G 914 872-8400
  White Plains *(G-17178)*
Whitney Foods Inc .... F 718 291-3333
  Jamaica *(G-6964)*
Yo Fresh Inc .... E 845 634-1616
  New City *(G-8796)*
Yo Fresh Inc .... E 518 982-0659
  Clifton Park *(G-3712)*

DAIRY PRDTS: Yogurt, Frozen

Berrywild .... G 212 686-5848
  New York *(G-9368)*
NY Froyo LLC .... G 516 312-4588
  Deer Park *(G-4184)*
Soft Serve Apple LLC .... E 646 442-8002
  New York *(G-12115)*
Swirl Bliss LLC .... G 516 867-9475
  North Baldwin *(G-12910)*

DATA PROCESSING & PREPARATION SVCS

Data Palette Info Svcs LLC .... D 718 433-1060
  Port Washington *(G-13807)*
Informa Solutions Inc .... E 516 543-3733
  Garden City *(G-5511)*
Rational Retention LLC .... E 518 489-3000
  Albany *(G-127)*
Relx Inc .... E 212 309-8100
  New York *(G-11826)*
Standard Analytics Io Inc .... G 917 882-5422
  New York *(G-12181)*

DATA PROCESSING SVCS

DP Murphy Co Inc .... D 631 673-9400
  Deer Park *(G-4132)*
Thomas Publishing Company LLC .... B 212 695-0500
  New York *(G-12321)*

Employee Codes: A=Over 500 employees, B=251-500
C=101-250, D=51-100, E=20-50, F=10-19, G=5-9

DECORATIVE WOOD & WOODWORK

DECORATIVE WOOD & WOODWORK

A Van Hoek Woodworking Limited	G	718 599-4388
Brooklyn *(G-1536)*		
Aces Over Eights Inc	G	585 292-9690
Rochester *(G-14169)*		
Adams Interior Fabrications	F	631 249-8282
Massapequa *(G-8177)*		
Air Chex Equipment Corp	G	845 358-8179
Nyack *(G-13043)*		
Andike Millwork Inc	G	718 894-1796
Maspeth *(G-8118)*		
Architectural Enhancements Inc	F	845 343-9663
Middletown *(G-8426)*		
Art Essentials of New York	G	845 368-1100
Airmont *(G-12)*		
Atelier Viollet Corp	G	718 782-1727
Brooklyn *(G-1644)*		
Brooks Woodworking Inc	F	914 666-2029
Mount Kisco *(G-8623)*		
Budd Woodwork Inc	F	718 389-1110
Brooklyn *(G-1736)*		
Cabinet Shapes Corp	F	718 784-6255
Long Island City *(G-7691)*		
Craz Woodworking Assoc Inc	F	631 205-1890
Bellport *(G-828)*		
Daniel Demarco and Assoc Inc	E	631 598-7000
Amityville *(G-284)*		
Di Fiore and Sons Custom Wdwkg	G	718 278-1663
Long Island City *(G-7715)*		
Ed Negron Fine Woodworking	G	718 246-1016
Brooklyn *(G-1902)*		
Furniture Dsgn By Knossos Inc	E	718 729-0404
Woodside *(G-17330)*		
Hennig Custom Woodwork Corp	G	516 536-3460
Oceanside *(G-13080)*		
Innova Interiors Inc	E	718 401-2122
Bronx *(G-1363)*		
James King Woodworking Inc	G	518 761-6091
Queensbury *(G-14000)*		
Jeffrey John	G	631 842-2850
Amityville *(G-299)*		
Jordache Woodworking Corp	F	718 349-3373
Brooklyn *(G-2147)*		
K & B Woodworking Inc	G	518 634-7253
Cairo *(G-3274)*		
M & R Woodworking & Finishing	G	718 486-5480
Brooklyn *(G-2245)*		
McGraw Wood Products LLC	E	607 836-6465
Mc Graw *(G-8223)*		
N Sketch Build Inc		800 975-0597
Fishkill *(G-5187)*		
Northern Forest Pdts Co Inc	G	315 942-6955
Boonville *(G-1166)*		
Pdj Components Inc	E	845 469-9191
Chester *(G-3611)*		
Pella Corporation	C	631 208-0710
Calverton *(G-3294)*		
Pgs Millwork Inc	D	212 244-6610
New York *(G-11642)*		
Prime Wood Products	G	518 792-1407
Queensbury *(G-14008)*		
Richard Rothbard Inc	G	845 355-2300
Slate Hill *(G-15474)*		
Windsor United Industries LLC	E	607 655-3300
Windsor *(G-17273)*		
Wood Innovations of Suffolk	G	631 698-2345
Medford *(G-8263)*		
Woodmotif Inc	F	516 564-8325
Hempstead *(G-6289)*		
Woodtronics Inc	G	914 962-5205
Yorktown Heights *(G-17521)*		

DEFENSE SYSTEMS & EQPT

Eastern Strategic Materials	E	212 332-1619
New York *(G-9967)*		
Tech Valley Technologies Inc	F	518 584-8899
Wilton *(G-17271)*		
UNI Source Technology	F	514 748-8888
Champlain *(G-3547)*		

DEGREASING MACHINES

Cleaning Tech Group LLC	E	716 665-2340
Jamestown *(G-6981)*		
Ieh FM Holdings LLC	E	212 702-4300
New York *(G-10559)*		

DEHYDRATION EQPT

Purvi Enterprises Incorporated	G	347 808-9448
Maspeth *(G-8166)*		

DELAY LINES

Allen Avionics Inc	E	516 248-8080
Mineola *(G-8493)*		
Esc Control Electronics LLC	E	631 467-5328
Sayville *(G-15208)*		

DENTAL EQPT

Boehm Surgical Instrument	F	585 436-6584
Rochester *(G-14241)*		
Brandt Equipment LLC	G	718 994-0800
Bronx *(G-1288)*		
J H M Engineering	E	718 871-1810
Brooklyn *(G-2123)*		
Kay See Dental Mfg Co	F	816 842-2817
New York *(G-10821)*		
Lucas Dental Equipment Co Inc	F	631 244-2807
Bohemia *(G-1097)*		

DENTAL EQPT & SPLYS

Air Techniques Inc	B	516 433-7676
Melville *(G-8291)*		
American Medical & Dental Sups	F	845 517-5876
Spring Valley *(G-15578)*		
Art Dental Laboratory Inc	G	516 437-1882
Floral Park *(G-5193)*		
Avalonbay Communities Inc	E	516 484-7766
Glen Cove *(G-5612)*		
Buffalo Dental Mfg Co Inc	E	516 496-7200
Syosset *(G-15815)*		
Cmp Industries LLC	E	518 434-3147
Albany *(G-66)*		
Crosstex International Inc	D	631 582-6777
Hauppauge *(G-6058)*		
Cynosure Inc	G	516 594-3333
Hicksville *(G-6340)*		
Darby Dental Supply	G	516 688-6421
Jericho *(G-7065)*		
Dedeco International Sales Inc	E	845 887-4840
Long Eddy *(G-7642)*		
Dmx Enteprise	F	212 481-1010
New York *(G-9891)*		
Gac	G	631 357-8600
Islandia *(G-6794)*		
Glaxosmithkline LLC	D	518 239-6901
East Durham *(G-4387)*		
Henry Schein Inc	E	315 431-0340
East Syracuse *(G-4536)*		
Henry Schein Fincl Svcs LLC	F	631 843-5500
Melville *(G-8327)*		
Impladent Ltd	G	718 465-1810
Jamaica *(G-6921)*		
JM Murray Center Inc	C	607 756-9913
Cortland *(G-4031)*		
JM Murray Center Inc	C	607 756-0246
Cortland *(G-4032)*		
Lelab Dental Laboratory Inc	G	516 561-5050
Valley Stream *(G-16412)*		
Light Dental Labs Inc	G	516 785-7730
Wantagh *(G-16559)*		
Luitpold Pharmaceuticals Inc	E	631 924-4000
Shirley *(G-15424)*		
Mini-Max Dntl Repr Eqpmnts Inc	G	631 242-0322
Deer Park *(G-4174)*		
Oramaax Dental Products Inc	F	516 771-8514
Freeport *(G-5417)*		
Precision Dental Ceramics of B	F	716 681-4133
Bowmansville *(G-1170)*		
Professional Manufacturers	F	631 586-2440
Deer Park *(G-4194)*		
Sabra Dental Products	G	914 945-0836
Ossining *(G-13328)*		
Schilling Forge Inc	E	315 454-4421
Syracuse *(G-16033)*		
Temrex Corporation	E	516 868-6221
Freeport *(G-5430)*		
Tiger Supply Inc	G	631 293-2700
Farmingdale *(G-5130)*		
Total Dntl Implant Sltions LLC	E	212 877-3777
Valley Stream *(G-16430)*		
Valplast International Corp	F	516 442-3923
Westbury *(G-17040)*		

DENTAL EQPT & SPLYS WHOLESALERS

Impladent Ltd	G	718 465-1810
Jamaica *(G-6921)*		
Oramaax Dental Products Inc	F	516 771-8514
Freeport *(G-5417)*		

DENTAL EQPT & SPLYS: Cabinets

Precision Dental Cabinets Inc	F	631 543-3870
Smithtown *(G-15495)*		
Stylecraft Interiors Inc	F	516 487-2133
Great Neck *(G-5843)*		

DENTAL EQPT & SPLYS: Compounds

Lornamead Inc	D	914 630-7733
New York *(G-11043)*		

DENTAL EQPT & SPLYS: Cutting Instruments

Smile Specialists	F	877 337-6135
New York *(G-12102)*		

DENTAL EQPT & SPLYS: Dental Materials

Grasers Dental Ceramics	G	716 649-5100
Orchard Park *(G-13274)*		
Marotta Dental Studio Inc	E	631 249-7520
Farmingdale *(G-5042)*		
Safe-Dent Enterprises LLC	G	845 362-0141
Monsey *(G-8580)*		

DENTAL EQPT & SPLYS: Enamels

Gallery 57 Dental	E	212 246-8700
New York *(G-10241)*		
Gan Kavod Inc	G	315 797-3114
New Hartford *(G-8805)*		
Jeffrey D Menoff	G	716 665-1468
Jamestown *(G-7013)*		

DENTAL EQPT & SPLYS: Laboratory

A D K Dental Lab	G	518 563-6093
Plattsburgh *(G-13649)*		
Cmp Industries LLC	E	518 434-3147
Albany *(G-67)*		
Nu Life Restorations of L I	D	516 489-5200
Old Westbury *(G-13133)*		
Sentage Corporation	E	914 664-2200
Mount Vernon *(G-8733)*		

DENTAL EQPT & SPLYS: Orthodontic Appliances

Cettel Studio of New York Inc	G	518 494-3622
Chestertown *(G-3621)*		
Ortho Dent Laboratory Inc	F	716 839-1900
Williamsville *(G-17249)*		
Vincent Martino Dental Lab	F	716 674-7800
Buffalo *(G-3243)*		

DENTAL EQPT & SPLYS: Sterilizers

Cpac Equipment Inc	F	585 382-3223
Leicester *(G-7421)*		

DENTAL EQPT & SPLYS: Teeth, Artificial, Exc In Dental Labs

A-Implant Dental Lab Corp	G	212 582-4720
New York *(G-8995)*		
Martins Dental Studio	G	315 788-0800
Watertown *(G-16664)*		
Yes Dental Laboratory Inc	E	914 333-7550
Tarrytown *(G-16112)*		

DENTAL EQPT & SPLYS: Tools, NEC

Score International	E	407 322-3230
Plainview *(G-13634)*		

DENTAL EQPT & SPLYS: Wax

Corning Rubber Company Inc	F	631 738-0041
Ronkonkoma *(G-14889)*		

DENTAL INSTRUMENT REPAIR SVCS

Score International	E	407 322-3230
Plainview *(G-13634)*		

PRODUCT SECTION

DENTISTS' OFFICES & CLINICS

Comprehensive Dental Tech ....G....... 607 467-4456
  Hancock *(G-5963)*
Marotta Dental Studio Inc.......................E....... 631 249-7520
  Farmingdale *(G-5042)*

DEPILATORIES, COSMETIC

LOreal Usa Inc ....E....... 212 389-4201
  New York *(G-11037)*

DERMATOLOGICALS

Intellicell Biosciences Inc ....G....... 646 576-8700
  New York *(G-10617)*
Skincare Products Inc ....G....... 917 837-5255
  New York *(G-12093)*

DERRICKS: Oil & Gas Field

Derrick Corporation ....C....... 716 685-4892
  Cheektowaga *(G-3567)*

DESALTER KITS: Sea Water

Luxfer Magtech Inc ....D....... 631 727-8600
  Riverhead *(G-14149)*

DESIGN SVCS, NEC

A To Z Media Inc......................................F....... 212 260-0237
  New York *(G-8994)*
Holland & Sherry Inc..............................E....... 212 542-8410
  New York *(G-10497)*
International Direct Group Inc ....E....... 212 921-9036
  New York *(G-10634)*
Internodal International Inc ....E....... 631 765-0037
  Southold *(G-15559)*
Jinglebell Inc ....G....... 914 219-5395
  Armonk *(G-416)*
Leo D Bernstein & Sons Inc..................E....... 212 337-9578
  New York *(G-10968)*
Linita Design & Mfg Corp ....E....... 716 566-7753
  Lackawanna *(G-7244)*
Northern Design & Bldg Assoc ....E....... 518 747-2200
  Queensbury *(G-14006)*
Peerless Instrument Co Inc..................C....... 631 396-6500
  Farmingdale *(G-5076)*
Polymag Tek Inc ....F....... 585 235-8390
  Rochester *(G-14587)*
Premier Fixtures LLC.............................D....... 631 236-4100
  Hauppauge *(G-6170)*
Skincare Products Inc ....G....... 917 837-5255
  New York *(G-12093)*
Twcc Product and Sales ....E....... 212 614-9364
  New York *(G-12432)*

DESIGN SVCS: Commercial & Indl

New Dimensions Research Corp...........C....... 631 694-1356
  Melville *(G-8340)*
Precision Systems Mfg Inc ....E....... 315 451-3480
  Liverpool *(G-7544)*
Prim Hall Enterprises Inc ....F....... 518 561-7408
  Plattsburgh *(G-13691)*
Riverwood Sgns By Dndev Dsgns ....G....... 845 229-0282
  Hyde Park *(G-6737)*
Voss Manufacturing Inc........................D....... 716 731-5062
  Sanborn *(G-15130)*

DESIGN SVCS: Computer Integrated Systems

331 Holding Inc ....E....... 585 924-1740
  Victor *(G-16458)*
Cisco Systems Inc ....C....... 212 714-4000
  New York *(G-9622)*
Informa Solutions Inc............................E....... 516 543-3733
  Garden City *(G-5511)*
Innovative Systems of New York ....G....... 516 541-7410
  Massapequa Park *(G-8187)*
Kid Labs Inc..E....... 631 549-4222
  Hauppauge *(G-6106)*
Performance Technologies Inc..............D....... 585 256-0200
  Rochester *(G-14576)*
Siemens Industry Inc ....E....... 716 568-0983
  Buffalo *(G-3187)*

DETECTION APPARATUS: Electronic/Magnetic Field, Light/Heat

Sensormatic Electronics LLC................F....... 718 597-6719
  Bronx *(G-1450)*
Sensormatic Electronics LLC................F....... 845 365-3125
  Orangeburg *(G-13245)*
Sentry Technology Corporation ....E....... 631 739-2000
  Ronkonkoma *(G-14982)*
Sentry Technology Corporation ....F....... 800 645-4224
  Ronkonkoma *(G-14983)*

DIAGNOSTIC SUBSTANCES

Alere Inc..B....... 516 767-1112
  Port Washington *(G-13798)*
Bella International Inc............................G....... 716 484-0102
  Jamestown *(G-6973)*
Biochemical Diagnostics Inc ....E....... 631 595-9200
  Edgewood *(G-4595)*
Biopool Us Inc..E....... 716 483-3851
  Jamestown *(G-6974)*
Chembio Diagnostic Systems Inc ....C....... 631 924-1135
  Medford *(G-8238)*
Chembio Diagnostics Inc......................E....... 631 924-1135
  Medford *(G-8239)*
Clark Laboratories Inc...........................E....... 716 483-3851
  Jamestown *(G-6979)*
Danisco US Inc...D....... 585 256-5200
  Rochester *(G-14300)*
Dnano Inc...G....... 607 316-3694
  Ithaca *(G-6837)*
E-Z-Em Inc..E....... 609 524-2864
  Melville *(G-8313)*
Eagle International LLC..........................G....... 917 282-2536
  Nanuet *(G-8756)*
Enzo Life Sciences Inc..........................E....... 631 694-7070
  Farmingdale *(G-4988)*
Immco Diagnostics Inc..........................F....... 716 691-6955
  Buffalo *(G-3003)*
Immco Diagnostics Inc.........................D....... 716 691-6911
  Buffalo *(G-3004)*
Kannalife Sciences Inc..........................F....... 516 669-3219
  Lloyd Harbor *(G-7567)*
Lesanne Life Sciences LLC..................G....... 914 234-0860
  Bedford *(G-797)*
Lifelink Monitoring Corp ....F....... 845 336-2098
  Bearsville *(G-792)*
Siemens Hlthcare Dgnostics Inc ....E....... 914 631-0475
  Tarrytown *(G-16105)*
Welch Allyn Inc..A....... 315 685-4100
  Skaneateles Falls *(G-15472)*

DIAGNOSTIC SUBSTANCES OR AGENTS: Blood Derivative

Lifescan Inc ....B....... 516 557-2693
  Wantagh *(G-16558)*
Ortho-Clinical Diagnostics Inc................E....... 716 631-1281
  Williamsville *(G-17250)*
Ortho-Clinical Diagnostics Inc................E....... 585 453-3000
  Rochester *(G-14556)*

DIAGNOSTIC SUBSTANCES OR AGENTS: In Vivo

Darmiyan LLC..G....... 917 689-0389
  New York *(G-9810)*
Ken-Ton Open Mri PC ....G....... 716 876-7000
  Kenmore *(G-7150)*

DIAGNOSTIC SUBSTANCES OR AGENTS: Microbiology & Virology

Ufc Biotechnology ....F....... 716 777-3776
  Amherst *(G-269)*

DIAGNOSTIC SUBSTANCES OR AGENTS: Veterinary

Gotham Veterinary Center PC...............E....... 212 222-1900
  New York *(G-10341)*

DIAMOND MINING SVCS: Indl

Romance & Co Inc ....G....... 212 382-0337
  New York *(G-11912)*
Signature Diamond Entps LLC..............E....... 212 869-5115
  New York *(G-12072)*

DIAMOND SETTER SVCS

Crystal Ceres Industries Inc ....D....... 716 283-0445
  Niagara Falls *(G-12808)*

DIAMONDS, GEMS, WHOLESALE

Antwerp Diamond Distributors ....F....... 212 319-3300
  New York *(G-9169)*
David Weisz & Sons Inc ....G....... 212 840-4747
  New York *(G-9825)*
Diamex Inc ....E....... 212 575-8145
  New York *(G-9869)*
Diamond Constellation Corp ....G....... 212 819-0324
  New York *(G-9871)*
E Schreiber Inc..E....... 212 382-0280
  New York *(G-9952)*
Fine Cut Diamonds Corporation ....G....... 212 575-8780
  New York *(G-10163)*
Fischler Diamonds Inc...........................E....... 212 921-8196
  New York *(G-10171)*
Global Gem Corporation ....E....... 212 350-9936
  New York *(G-10317)*
Gold & Diamonds Wholesale Outl.........G....... 718 438-7888
  Brooklyn *(G-2037)*
Herkimer Diamond Mines Inc................E....... 315 891-7355
  Herkimer *(G-6302)*
Leo Schachter & Co Inc........................D....... 212 688-2000
  New York *(G-10971)*
Miller & Veit Inc.......................................F....... 212 247-2275
  New York *(G-11269)*
Romance & Co Inc ....G....... 212 382-0337
  New York *(G-11912)*
T M W Diamonds Mfg Co ....G....... 212 869-8444
  New York *(G-12266)*
United Gemdiam Inc ....E....... 718 851-5083
  Brooklyn *(G-2700)*
Waldman Alexander M Diamond Co......E....... 212 921-8098
  New York *(G-12578)*

DIAMONDS: Cutting & Polishing

Ace Diamond Corp...................................G....... 212 730-8231
  New York *(G-9015)*
Antwerp Diamond Distributors ....F....... 212 319-3300
  New York *(G-9169)*
Antwerp Sales Intl Inc.............................F....... 212 354-6515
  New York *(G-9170)*
Baroka Creations Inc.............................E....... 212 768-0527
  New York *(G-9323)*
Centurion Diamonds Inc........................G....... 718 946-6918
  New York *(G-9568)*
Dialase Inc ....E....... 212 575-8833
  New York *(G-9868)*
Diamex Inc ....E....... 212 575-8145
  New York *(G-9869)*
Diamond Constellation Corp ....G....... 212 819-0324
  New York *(G-9871)*
Dresdiam Inc ....E....... 212 819-2217
  New York *(G-9926)*
E Schreiber Inc..E....... 212 382-0280
  New York *(G-9952)*
Fine Cut Diamonds Corporation ....G....... 212 575-8780
  New York *(G-10163)*
Fischler Diamonds Inc...........................E....... 212 921-8196
  New York *(G-10171)*
Guild Diamond Products Inc...................F....... 212 871-0007
  New York *(G-10381)*
Hershel Horowitz Corp ....G....... 212 719-1710
  New York *(G-10463)*
Ideal Brilliant Co Inc................................F....... 212 840-2044
  New York *(G-10554)*
Isaac Waldman Inc ....G....... 212 354-8220
  New York *(G-10665)*
J A G Diamond Manufacturers...............G....... 212 575-0660
  New York *(G-10676)*
Julius Klein Group ....E....... 212 719-1811
  New York *(G-10784)*
Kaleko Bros ....G....... 212 819-0100
  New York *(G-10803)*
Lazare Kaplan Intl Inc.............................D....... 212 972-9700
  New York *(G-10938)*
Miller & Veit Inc.......................................F....... 212 247-2275
  New York *(G-11269)*
Moishe L Horowitz ....F....... 212 719-4247
  New York *(G-11292)*
Precision Diamond Cutters Inc...............G....... 212 719-4438
  New York *(G-11696)*
Shah Diamonds Inc.................................F....... 212 888-9393
  New York *(G-12038)*
T M W Diamonds Mfg Co ....G....... 212 869-8444
  New York *(G-12266)*

Employee Codes: A=Over 500 employees, B=251-500
C=101-250, D=51-100, E=20-50, F=10-19, G=5-9

DIAMONDS: Cutting & Polishing

United Gemdiam Inc .... E 718 851-5083
  Brooklyn *(G-2700)*
Waldman Alexander M Diamond Co ...... E 212 921-8098
  New York *(G-12578)*
White Coat Inc .... E 212 575-8880
  New York *(G-12624)*
William Goldberg Diamond Corp .... E 212 980-4343
  New York *(G-12633)*

DIAPERS: Cloth

Becks Classic Mfg Inc .... D 631 435-3800
  Brentwood *(G-1178)*

DIAPERS: Disposable

Bentley Manufacturing Inc .... G 212 714-1800
  New York *(G-9361)*
Mr Disposable Inc .... F 718 388-8574
  Brooklyn *(G-2339)*

DIE CUTTING SVC: Paper

Able National Corp .... E 718 386-8801
  Brooklyn *(G-1549)*
Baseline Graphics Inc .... F 585 223-0153
  Fairport *(G-4847)*

DIE SETS: Presses, Metal Stamping

Gay Sheet Metal Dies Inc .... G 716 877-0208
  Buffalo *(G-2966)*

DIES & TOOLS: Special

Ace Specialty Co Inc .... G 716 874-3670
  Tonawanda *(G-16134)*
All Out Die Cutting Inc .... E 718 346-6666
  Brooklyn *(G-1587)*
Amada Tool America Inc .... D 585 344-3900
  Batavia *(G-622)*
Anka Tool & Die Inc .... E 845 268-4116
  Congers *(G-3851)*
Arro Tool & Die Inc .... F 716 763-6203
  Lakewood *(G-7287)*
Art Precision Metal Products .... F 631 842-8889
  Copiague *(G-3894)*
Bennett Die & Tool Inc .... F 607 739-5629
  Horseheads *(G-6570)*
Bennett Die & Tool Inc .... F 607 273-2836
  Ithaca *(G-6821)*
Brighton Tool & Die Designers .... F 716 876-0879
  Tonawanda *(G-16148)*
Carbaugh Tool Company Inc .... G 607 739-3293
  Elmira *(G-4673)*
Charles A Rogers Entps Inc .... E 585 924-6400
  Victor *(G-16466)*
Coil Stamping Inc .... F 631 588-3040
  Holbrook *(G-6439)*
Cuddeback Machining Inc .... E 585 392-5889
  Hilton *(G-6417)*
Diemax of Rochester Inc .... G 585 288-3912
  Rochester *(G-14307)*
Dixon Tool and Manufacturing .... F 585 235-1352
  Rochester *(G-14313)*
Eden Tool & Die Inc .... G 716 992-4240
  Eden *(G-4586)*
Electro Form Corp .... F 607 722-6404
  Binghamton *(G-910)*
Enhanced Tool Inc .... E 716 691-5200
  Amherst *(G-239)*
Etna Tool & Die Corporation .... F 212 475-4350
  New York *(G-10079)*
Hytech Tool & Die Inc .... G 716 488-2796
  Jamestown *(G-7001)*
Intri-Cut Inc .... E 716 691-5200
  Amherst *(G-247)*
James Wire Die Co .... G 315 894-3233
  Ilion *(G-6742)*
Jmt Program Leadership Group .... G 585 217-1134
  Rochester *(G-14463)*
K D M Die Company Inc .... F 716 828-9000
  Buffalo *(G-3024)*
Keyes Machine Works Inc .... G 585 426-5059
  Gates *(G-5561)*
Long Island Tool & Die Inc .... G 631 225-0600
  Copiague *(G-3910)*
M J M Tooling Corp .... G 718 292-3590
  Bronx *(G-1384)*
Machine Tool Specialty .... G 315 699-5287
  Cicero *(G-3648)*
Machinecraft Inc .... E 585 436-1070
  Rochester *(G-14486)*
Magnus Precision Mfg Inc .... D 315 548-8032
  Phelps *(G-13534)*
Mantel & Mantel Stamping Corp .... G 631 467-1916
  Ronkonkoma *(G-14937)*
May Tool & Die Inc .... G 716 695-1033
  Tonawanda *(G-16180)*
Micron Inds Rochester Inc .... F 585 247-6130
  Rochester *(G-14512)*
Ms Machining Inc .... G 607 723-1105
  Binghamton *(G-938)*
Multifold Die Ctng Finshg Corp .... G 631 232-1235
  Hauppauge *(G-6144)*
Mustang-Major Tool & Die Co .... G 716 992-9200
  Eden *(G-4588)*
Niagara Punch & Die Corp .... G 716 896-7619
  Buffalo *(G-3090)*
Nijon Tool Co Inc .... F 631 242-3434
  Deer Park *(G-4180)*
P & R Industries Inc .... F 585 544-1811
  Rochester *(G-14563)*
Pacific Die Cast Inc .... F 845 778-6374
  Walden *(G-16534)*
Palma Tool & Die Company Inc .... E 716 681-4685
  Lancaster *(G-7329)*
Phelinger Tool & Die Corp .... G 716 685-1780
  Alden *(G-181)*
Precision Grinding & Mfg Corp .... C 585 458-4300
  Rochester *(G-14593)*
Precision Machining and Mfg .... P 845 647-5380
  Wawarsing *(G-16708)*
Precision TI Die & Stamping Co .... F 516 561-0041
  Valley Stream *(G-16420)*
Pronto Tool & Die Co Inc .... E 631 981-8920
  Ronkonkoma *(G-14972)*
Prototype Manufacturing Corp .... F 716 695-1700
  North Tonawanda *(G-12987)*
Raloid Tool Co Inc .... F 518 664-4261
  Mechanicville *(G-8230)*
Ram Precision Tool Inc .... G 716 759-8722
  Lancaster *(G-7336)*
Rid Lom Precision Mfg .... E 585 594-8600
  Rochester *(G-14625)*
Rochester Stampings Inc .... F 585 467-5241
  Rochester *(G-14649)*
S B Whistler & Sons Inc .... E 585 798-3000
  Medina *(G-8280)*
Sharon Metal Stamping Corp .... G 718 828-4510
  Bronx *(G-1451)*
Stamp Rite Tool & Die Inc .... G 718 752-0334
  Long Island City *(G-7883)*
Thayer Tool & Die Inc .... F 716 782-4841
  Ashville *(G-430)*
Tips & Dies Inc .... F 315 337-4161
  Rome *(G-14837)*
Tools & Stamping Corp .... G 718 392-4040
  Brooklyn *(G-2663)*
Trinity Tools Inc .... E 716 694-1111
  North Tonawanda *(G-13003)*
Ultimate Prcision Met Pdts Inc .... D 631 249-9441
  Farmingdale *(G-5136)*

DIES: Cutting, Exc Metal

Royal Molds Inc .... F 718 382-7686
  Brooklyn *(G-2512)*

DIES: Diamond, Metalworking

Roman Malakov Diamonds Ltd .... G 212 944-8500
  New York *(G-11911)*

DIES: Extrusion

D Maldari & Sons Inc .... E 718 499-3555
  Brooklyn *(G-1830)*

DIES: Paper Cutting

Evergreen Corp Central NY .... F 315 454-4175
  Syracuse *(G-15939)*

DIES: Plastic Forming

Alliance Precision Plas Corp .... C 585 426-5210
  Rochester *(G-14189)*
Alliance Precision Plas Corp .... E 585 426-5210
  Rochester *(G-14190)*
Quality Lineals Usa Inc .... F 516 378-6577
  Freeport *(G-5421)*

DIES: Steel Rule

Dynamic Dies Inc .... F 585 247-4010
  Rochester *(G-14322)*
Great Lakes Pressed Steel Corp .... E 716 885-4037
  Buffalo *(G-2982)*
National Steel Rule Die Inc .... F 718 402-1396
  Bronx *(G-1407)*
Paragon Steel Rule Dies Inc .... F 585 254-3395
  Rochester *(G-14572)*

DIODES: Light Emitting

Acolyte Technologies Corp .... F 212 629-3239
  New York *(G-9020)*
Data Display USA Inc .... C 631 218-2130
  Holbrook *(G-6443)*
Emagin Corporation .... D 845 838-7900
  Hopewell Junction *(G-6549)*
Hisun Optoelectronics Co Ltd .... F 718 886-6966
  Flushing *(G-5250)*
Ic Technologies LLC .... G 212 966-7895
  New York *(G-10549)*
Light Blue USA LLC .... G 718 475-2515
  Brooklyn *(G-2221)*
Oledworks LLC .... E 585 287-6802
  Rochester *(G-14547)*
S3j Electronics LLC .... E 716 206-1309
  Lancaster *(G-7341)*
Tarsier Ltd .... C 212 401-6181
  New York *(G-12280)*

DIODES: Solid State, Germanium, Silicon, Etc

Leviton Manufacturing Co Inc .... B 631 812-6000
  Melville *(G-8334)*

DIRECT SELLING ESTABLISHMENTS: Encyclopedias & Publications

Economist Newspaper Group Inc .... C 212 541-0500
  New York *(G-9979)*

DIRECT SELLING ESTABLISHMENTS: Food Svcs

New Dynamics Corporation .... E 845 692-0022
  Middletown *(G-8453)*

DIRECT SELLING ESTABLISHMENTS: Home Related Prdts

Link Group Inc .... F 718 567-7082
  Brooklyn *(G-2228)*

DISCS & TAPE: Optical, Blank

L & M Optical Disc LLC .... D 718 649-3500
  New York *(G-10899)*
Sony Corporation of America .... C 212 833-8000
  New York *(G-12132)*
Sony Dadc US Inc .... B 212 833-8800
  New York *(G-12133)*

DISHWASHING EQPT: Commercial

Hobart Corporation .... E 585 427-9000
  Rochester *(G-14438)*
Strategies North America Inc .... G 716 945-6053
  Salamanca *(G-15108)*

DISK & DRUM DRIVES & COMPONENTS: Computers

Globalfoundries US Inc .... C 518 305-9013
  Malta *(G-8019)*

DISK DRIVES: Computer

Formats Unlimited Inc .... F 631 249-9200
  Deer Park *(G-4144)*
Sale 121 Corp .... D 240 855-8988
  New York *(G-11956)*
Toshiba Amer Info Systems Inc .... B 949 583-3000
  New York *(G-12376)*

DISPENSING EQPT & PARTS, BEVERAGE: Beer

Niagara Dispensing Tech Inc .... F 716 636-9827
  Buffalo *(G-3086)*

PRODUCT SECTION

DOORS: Rolling, Indl Building Or Warehouse, Metal

DISPENSING EQPT & PARTS, BEVERAGE: Cold, Exc Coin-Operated
Lightron Corporation ....G...... 516 938-5544
  Jericho *(G-7075)*

DISPENSING EQPT & PARTS, BEVERAGE: Fountain/Other Beverage
Chudnow Manufacturing Co Inc............E...... 516 593-4222
  Oceanside *(G-13074)*
Klearbar Inc ....G...... 516 684-9892
  Port Washington *(G-13834)*

DISPENSING EQPT & SYSTEMS, BEVERAGE: Liquor
Oyster Bay Pump Works Inc...................F...... 516 922-3789
  Hicksville *(G-6381)*

DISPLAY CASES: Refrigerated
Mohawk Cabinet Company Inc ....F....... 518 725-0645
  Gloversville *(G-5718)*

DISPLAY FIXTURES: Showcases, Wood, Exc Refrigerated
R H Guest Incorporated..........................G...... 718 675-7600
  Brooklyn *(G-2471)*

DISPLAY FIXTURES: Wood
16 Tons Inc ....E...... 718 418-8446
  Brooklyn *(G-1511)*
All Merchandise Display Corp ....G...... 718 257-2221
  Highland Mills *(G-6411)*
David Flatt Furniture Ltd ....F...... 718 937-7944
  Long Island City *(G-7710)*
Hunter Metal Industries Inc.....................D...... 631 475-5900
  East Patchogue *(G-4448)*
J M P Display Fixture Co Inc...................E...... 718 649-0333
  Brooklyn *(G-2127)*
Marplex Furniture Corporation................G...... 914 969-7755
  Yonkers *(G-17466)*
Specialty Services ....G...... 585 728-5650
  Wayland *(G-16711)*

DISPLAY ITEMS: Corrugated, Made From Purchased Materials
Calpac Incorporated ....F...... 631 789-0502
  Amityville *(G-279)*
Displays & Beyond Inc ....F...... 718 805-7786
  Glendale *(G-5651)*
General Die and Die Cutng Inc ....D...... 516 665-3584
  Roosevelt *(G-15004)*
Mp Displays LLC ....G...... 845 268-4113
  Valley Cottage *(G-16383)*
Spaeth Design Inc..................................E...... 718 606-9685
  Woodside *(G-17353)*

DISPLAY STANDS: Merchandise, Exc Wood
Exclusive Designs ....F...... 516 378-5258
  Freeport *(G-5396)*
Trylon Wire & Metal Works Inc ....E...... 718 542-4472
  Bronx *(G-1481)*

DISTILLATES: Hardwood
Tioga Hardwoods Inc..............................G...... 607 657-8686
  Berkshire *(G-853)*

DOCK OPERATION SVCS, INCL BLDGS, FACILITIES, OPERS & MAINT
Kleinfelder John......................................G...... 716 753-3163
  Mayville *(G-8216)*

DOCKS: Floating, Wood
Meeco Sullivan LLC................................C...... 800 232-3625
  Warwick *(G-16595)*

DOCKS: Prefabricated Metal
Guardian Booth LLC................................F...... 844 992-6684
  Spring Valley *(G-15588)*
Metallic Ladder Mfg Corp ....F...... 716 358-6201
  Randolph *(G-14016)*

T Shore Products Ltd ....G...... 315 252-9174
  Auburn *(G-522)*

DOCUMENT EMBOSSING SVCS
Batavia Press LLC ....E...... 585 343-4429
  Batavia *(G-624)*

DOLLIES: Mechanics'
Durall Dolly LLC......................................F...... 802 728-7122
  Brooklyn *(G-1883)*

DOLOMITE: Crushed & Broken
Dolomite Products Company Inc ....E...... 315 524-1998
  Rochester *(G-14316)*

DOLOMITIC MARBLE: Crushed & Broken
Rock Iroquois Products Inc ....E...... 585 637-6834
  Brockport *(G-1247)*
Tilcon New York Inc ....D...... 845 638-3594
  Haverstraw *(G-6241)*
Tilcon New York Inc ....D...... 845 480-3249
  Flushing *(G-5301)*
Tilcon New York Inc ....D...... 845 615-0216
  Goshen *(G-5740)*
Tilcon New York Inc ....D...... 845 457-3158
  Montgomery *(G-8603)*

DOMESTIC HELP SVCS
Custom Klean Corp.................................F...... 315 865-8101
  Holland Patent *(G-6487)*

DOOR & WINDOW REPAIR SVCS
Long Island Fireproof Door.....................E...... 718 767-8800
  Whitestone *(G-17211)*
United Steel Products Inc ....D...... 718 478-5330
  Corona *(G-4009)*

DOOR OPERATING SYSTEMS: Electric
Assa Abloy Entrance Systems US ....E...... 315 492-6600
  East Syracuse *(G-4507)*
EZ Lift Operator Corp ....F...... 845 356-1676
  Spring Valley *(G-15584)*
V E Power Door Co Inc ....E...... 631 231-4500
  Brentwood *(G-1201)*
Windowman Inc (usa)..............................G...... 718 246-2626
  Brooklyn *(G-2758)*

DOORS & WINDOWS WHOLESALERS: All Materials
Pella Corporation ....C...... 631 208-0710
  Calverton *(G-3294)*
Royal Windows Mfg Corp ....E...... 631 435-8888
  Bay Shore *(G-740)*
Structural Wood Corporation ....E...... 315 388-4442
  Waddington *(G-16521)*
Trulite Louvre Corp.................................E...... 516 756-1850
  Old Bethpage *(G-13131)*

DOORS & WINDOWS: Screen & Storm
I Fix Screen...G...... 631 421-1938
  Centereach *(G-3471)*
Optimum Window Mfg Corp....................E...... 845 647-1900
  Ellenville *(G-4636)*
Pal Manufacturing Corp ....E...... 516 937-1990
  Hicksville *(G-6384)*

DOORS & WINDOWS: Storm, Metal
A & S Window Associates Inc................E...... 718 275-7900
  Glendale *(G-5642)*
Air Tite Manufacturing Inc......................C...... 516 897-0295
  Long Beach *(G-7637)*
All United Window Corp ....E...... 718 624-0490
  Brooklyn *(G-1588)*
Corkhill Manufacturing Co Inc................G...... 718 528-7413
  Jamaica *(G-6907)*
Excel Aluminum Products Inc ....G...... 315 471-0925
  Syracuse *(G-15940)*
Karey Kassl Corp ....E...... 516 349-8484
  Plainview *(G-13613)*
Pioneer Window Holdings Inc ....F...... 516 822-7000
  Hicksville *(G-6388)*
Pioneer Window Holdings Inc ....E...... 518 762-5526
  Johnstown *(G-7122)*

Texas Home Security Inc.......................E...... 516 747-2100
  New Hyde Park *(G-8865)*

DOORS: Dormers, Wood
Dorm Company Corporation ....G...... 502 551-6195
  Clarence *(G-3657)*

DOORS: Fiberglass
Europrojects Intl Inc ....G...... 917 262-0795
  New York *(G-10086)*

DOORS: Fire, Metal
Ace Fire Door Corp................................E...... 718 901-0001
  Bronx *(G-1261)*
Altype Fire Door Corp.............................G...... 718 292-3500
  Bronx *(G-1271)*
General Fire-Proof Door Corp.................E...... 718 893-5500
  Bronx *(G-1342)*
Interntional Fireprof Door Inc ....E...... 718 783-1310
  Brooklyn *(G-2112)*
Long Island Fireproof Door ....E...... 718 767-8800
  Whitestone *(G-17211)*
M & D Installers Inc................................E...... 718 782-6978
  Brooklyn *(G-2243)*
Mercury Lock and Door Service ....E...... 718 542-7048
  Bronx *(G-1392)*
Metalline Fire Door Co Inc......................E...... 718 583-2320
  Bronx *(G-1393)*
Schwab Corp...E...... 585 381-4900
  Rochester *(G-14675)*
Statewide Fireproof Door Co ....F...... 845 268-6043
  Valley Cottage *(G-16390)*
Supreme Fire-Proof Door Co Inc............F...... 718 665-4224
  Bronx *(G-1468)*
Universal Fire Proof Door ....E...... 718 455-8442
  Brooklyn *(G-2706)*

DOORS: Folding, Plastic Or Plastic Coated Fabric
Custom Door & Mirror Inc......................E...... 631 414-7725
  Farmingdale *(G-4970)*
Perma Tech Inc.......................................E...... 716 854-0707
  Buffalo *(G-3122)*

DOORS: Garage, Overhead, Metal
Amarr Company ....F...... 585 426-8290
  Rochester *(G-14195)*
American Rolling Door Ltd ....G...... 718 273-0485
  Staten Island *(G-15637)*
Griffon Corporation ....E...... 212 957-5000
  New York *(G-10363)*
L & L Overhead Garage Doors...............G...... 718 721-2518
  Long Island City *(G-7787)*
Overhead Door Corporation ....D...... 518 828-7652
  Hudson *(G-6629)*
Roly Door Sales Inc ....G...... 716 877-1515
  Hamburg *(G-5941)*

DOORS: Garage, Overhead, Wood
Griffon Corporation ....E...... 212 957-5000
  New York *(G-10363)*

DOORS: Glass
Executive Mirror Doors Inc ....G...... 631 234-1090
  Ronkonkoma *(G-14899)*
Farley Windows Inc ....G...... 315 764-1111
  Massena *(G-8194)*
Hecht & Sohn Glass Co Inc...................G...... 718 782-8295
  Brooklyn *(G-2071)*
Unico Inc...F...... 845 562-9255
  Newburgh *(G-12782)*

DOORS: Rolling, Indl Building Or Warehouse, Metal
American Steel Gate Corp......................G...... 718 291-4050
  Jamaica *(G-6893)*
Robert-Masters Corp..............................G...... 718 545-1030
  Woodside *(G-17351)*
Steelmasters Inc.....................................E...... 718 498-2854
  Brooklyn *(G-2605)*
Thompson Overhead Door Co Inc..........F...... 718 788-2470
  Brooklyn *(G-2658)*

Employee Codes: A=Over 500 employees, B=251-500
C=101-250, D=51-100, E=20-50, F=10-19, G=5-9

2017 Harris
New York Manufacturers Directory

DOORS: Wooden

DOORS: Wooden

Ace Fire Door Corp	E	718 901-0001
Bronx *(G-1261)*		
Burt Millwork Corporation	E	718 257-4601
Brooklyn *(G-1738)*		
Capital Kit Cab & Door Mfrs	E	718 886-0303
College Point *(G-3779)*		
Chautauqua Woods Corp	E	716 366-3808
Dunkirk *(G-4336)*		
D R Cornue Woodworks	G	315 655-9463
Cazenovia *(G-3444)*		
Living Doors Inc	F	631 924-5393
Medford *(G-8253)*		
Overhead Door Corporation	D	518 828-7652
Hudson *(G-6629)*		
Quality Millwork Corp	E	718 892-2250
Bronx *(G-1438)*		
Rochester Lumber Company	E	585 924-7171
Farmington *(G-5155)*		
Select Interior Door Ltd	E	585 535-9900
North Java *(G-12934)*		
Yesteryears Vintage Doors LLC	G	315 324-5250
Hammond *(G-5952)*		

DOWN FEATHERS

Eastern Feather & Down Corp	G	718 387-4100
Brooklyn *(G-1898)*		

DRAPERIES & CURTAINS

Abalene Decorating Services	E	718 782-2000
New York *(G-9000)*		
Associated Drapery & Equipment	F	516 671-5245
Monroe *(G-8548)*		
Baby Signature Inc	G	212 686-1700
New York *(G-9298)*		
Bettertex Inc	F	212 431-3373
New York *(G-9379)*		
Bramson House Inc	C	516 764-5006
Freeport *(G-5390)*		
C & G of Kingston Inc	D	845 331-0148
Kingston *(G-7180)*		
Cabriole Designs Inc	G	212 593-4528
New York *(G-9494)*		
Decorative Novelty Co Inc	F	718 965-8600
Brooklyn *(G-1849)*		
J Edlin Interiors Ltd	F	212 243-2111
New York *(G-10677)*		
Jo-Vin Decorators Inc	E	718 441-9350
Woodhaven *(G-17306)*		
Laregence Inc	E	212 736-2548
New York *(G-10928)*		
Louis Hornick & Co Inc	G	212 679-2448
New York *(G-11049)*		
Majestic Curtains LLC	G	718 898-0774
Elmhurst *(G-4664)*		
Mason Contract Products LLC	D	516 328-6900
New Hyde Park *(G-8848)*		
McCarroll Uphl Designs LLC	G	518 828-0500
Hudson *(G-6625)*		
Mistdoda Inc	E	919 735-7111
New York *(G-11284)*		
Mutual Sales Corp	E	718 361-8373
Long Island City *(G-7817)*		
Richloom Fabrics Corp	F	212 685-5400
New York *(G-11869)*		
Richloom Fabrics Group Inc	G	212 685-5400
New York *(G-11870)*		
Richloom Home Fashions Corp	F	212 685-5400
New York *(G-11871)*		
Royal Home Fashions Inc	G	212 689-7222
New York *(G-11924)*		
Seaway Mats Inc	G	518 483-2560
Malone *(G-8016)*		
Showeray Co	D	718 965-3633
Brooklyn *(G-2551)*		
Shyam Ahuja Limited	G	212 644-5910
New York *(G-12057)*		
Terbo Ltd	G	718 847-2860
Richmond Hill *(G-14267)*		
White Plains Drapery Uphl Inc	E	914 381-0908
Mamaroneck *(G-8050)*		
White Workroom Inc	G	212 941-5910
New York *(G-12627)*		
Wildcat Territory Inc	F	718 361-6726
Long Island City *(G-7921)*		

DRAPERIES & DRAPERY FABRICS, COTTON

Designway Ltd	G	212 254-2220
New York *(G-9858)*		
Richloom Home Fashions Corp	F	212 685-5400
New York *(G-11871)*		
Star Draperies Inc	F	631 756-7121
Farmingdale *(G-5114)*		
Versailles Drapery Upholstery	F	212 533-2059
Long Island City *(G-7914)*		
Wallace Home Design Ctr	E	631 765-3890
Southold *(G-15561)*		

DRAPERIES: Plastic & Textile, From Purchased Materials

A Schneller Sons Inc	F	212 695-9440
New York *(G-8992)*		
Anthony Lawrence of New York	E	212 206-8820
Long Island City *(G-7661)*		
County Draperies Inc	E	845 342-9009
Middletown *(G-8433)*		
Deangelis Ltd	E	212 348-8225
New York *(G-9833)*		
Delta Upholsterers Inc	E	212 489-3308
New York *(G-9841)*		
Fabric Quilters Unlimited Inc	E	516 333-2866
Westbury *(G-16984)*		
Henry B Urban Inc	E	212 489-3308
New York *(G-10457)*		
Laminated Window Products Inc	F	631 242-6883
Bay Shore *(G-710)*		
Revman International Inc	E	212 894-3100
New York *(G-11854)*		
Reynolds Drapery Service Inc	F	315 845-8632
Newport *(G-12792)*		
Wayne Decorators Inc	G	718 529-4200
Jamaica *(G-6963)*		
Wcd Window Coverings Inc	E	845 336-4511
Lake Katrine *(G-7271)*		

DRAPERY & UPHOLSTERY STORES: Draperies

Albert Menin Interiors Ltd	F	212 876-3041
Bronx *(G-1267)*		
Reynolds Drapery Service Inc	F	315 845-8632
Newport *(G-12792)*		
Versailles Drapery Upholstery	F	212 533-2059
Long Island City *(G-7914)*		
White Plains Drapery Uphl Inc	E	914 381-0908
Mamaroneck *(G-8050)*		

DRAPERY & UPHOLSTERY STORES: Slip Covers

McCarroll Uphl Designs LLC	G	518 828-0500
Hudson *(G-6625)*		

DRAPES & DRAPERY FABRICS, FROM MANMADE FIBER

Pierce Arrow Drapery Mfg	G	716 876-3023
Buffalo *(G-3125)*		
Richloom Home Fashions Corp	F	212 685-5400
New York *(G-11871)*		
Unique Quality Fabrics Inc	G	845 343-3070
Middletown *(G-8468)*		

DRIED FRUITS WHOLESALERS

Sahadi Fine Foods Inc	E	718 369-0100
Brooklyn *(G-2530)*		

DRILL BITS

Mibro Group	D	716 631-5713
Buffalo *(G-3064)*		

DRILLING MACHINERY & EQPT: Water Well

Blue Tee Corp	G	212 598-0880
New York *(G-9422)*		

DRINK MIXES, NONALCOHOLIC: Cocktail

Motts LLP	C	972 673-8088
Elmsford *(G-4767)*		

DRINKING PLACES: Alcoholic Beverages

Kurrier Inc	G	718 389-3018
Brooklyn *(G-2181)*		
Lafayette Pub Inc	E	212 925-4242
New York *(G-10915)*		

DRINKING PLACES: Night Clubs

Flushing Pharmacy Inc	C	718 260-8999
Brooklyn *(G-1989)*		

DRINKING PLACES: Tavern

Club 1100	G	585 235-3478
Rochester *(G-14280)*		

DRINKING PLACES: Wine Bar

Wolffer Estate Vineyard Inc	E	631 537-5106
Sagaponack *(G-15082)*		

DRINKING WATER COOLERS WHOLESALERS: Mechanical

Yr Blanc & Co LLC	G	716 800-3999
Buffalo *(G-3261)*		

DRIVE SHAFTS

Deer Park Driveshaft & Hose	G	631 667-4091
Deer Park *(G-4127)*		
Dennys Drive Shaft Service	G	716 875-6640
Kenmore *(G-7146)*		
Drive Shaft Shop Inc	F	631 348-1818
Hauppauge *(G-6068)*		
K M Drive Line Inc	G	718 599-0628
Brooklyn *(G-2164)*		

DRIVES: High Speed Indl, Exc Hydrostatic

Emerson Indus Automtn USA LLC	E	716 774-1193
Grand Island *(G-5756)*		
Magna Products Corp	E	585 647-2280
Rochester *(G-14489)*		

DROP CLOTHS: Fabric

Ace Drop Cloth Canvas Pdts Inc	E	718 731-1550
Bronx *(G-1260)*		

DRUG STORES

GE Healthcare Inc	F	516 626-2799
Port Washington *(G-13819)*		

DRUG TESTING KITS: Blood & Urine

Yr Blanc & Co LLC	G	716 800-3999
Buffalo *(G-3261)*		

DRUGS & DRUG PROPRIETARIES, WHOL: Biologicals/Allied Prdts

Roar Biomedical Inc	G	631 591-2749
Calverton *(G-3297)*		

DRUGS & DRUG PROPRIETARIES, WHOLESALE

Alo Acquisition LLC	G	518 464-0279
Albany *(G-45)*		
Ip Med Inc	G	516 766-3800
Oceanside *(G-13082)*		

DRUGS & DRUG PROPRIETARIES, WHOLESALE: Blood Plasma

C T M Industries Ltd	E	718 479-3300
Jamaica *(G-6899)*		

DRUGS & DRUG PROPRIETARIES, WHOLESALE: Pharmaceuticals

Amneal Pharmaceuticals NY LLC	E	631 952-0214
Brookhaven *(G-1506)*		
Derm/Buro Inc	G	516 694-8300
Plainview *(G-13596)*		
Forest Laboratories LLC	C	212 421-7850
New York *(G-10185)*		
G C Hanford Manufacturing Co	C	315 476-7418
Syracuse *(G-15946)*		

Invagen Pharmaceuticals Inc..............B...... 631 231-3233
  Hauppauge *(G-6099)*
Nutra-Scientifics LLC........................G...... 917 238-8510
  Pomona *(G-13731)*
Polygen Pharmaceuticals Inc ....E...... 631 392-4044
  Edgewood *(G-4608)*
Tocare LLC ....G...... 718 767-0618
  Whitestone *(G-17215)*
Turing Pharmaceuticals LLC ....E...... 646 356-5577
  New York *(G-12425)*
Ucb Pharma Inc...................................B...... 919 767-2555
  Rochester *(G-14739)*

DRUGS & DRUG PROPRIETARIES, WHOLESALE: Vitamins & Minerals

Alphabet Holding Company Inc ....E...... 631 200-2000
  Ronkonkoma *(G-14865)*
Healthy N Fit Intl Inc ....F...... 914 271-6040
  Croton On Hudson *(G-4064)*
Nbty Inc ....D...... 631 244-2021
  Ronkonkoma *(G-14952)*
Nbty Inc ....A...... 631 200-2000
  Ronkonkoma *(G-14953)*
Nbty Manufacturing LLC ....E...... 631 567-9500
  Ronkonkoma *(G-14955)*
Unipharm Inc ....E...... 212 564-3634
  New York *(G-12459)*
Wellquest International Inc ....G...... 212 689-9094
  New York *(G-12608)*

DRUGS ACTING ON THE CENTRAL NERVOUS SYSTEM & SENSE ORGANS

Acorda Therapeutics Inc ....B...... 914 347-4300
  Ardsley *(G-403)*

DRUGS AFFECTING NEOPLASMS & ENDOCRINE SYSTEMS

OSI Pharmaceuticals LLC ....D...... 631 847-0175
  Farmingdale *(G-5073)*
OSI Pharmaceuticals LLC ....G...... 631 962-2000
  Farmingdale *(G-5074)*

DRUGS/DRUG PROPRIETARIES, WHOL: Proprietary/Patent Medicines

Apothecus Pharmaceutical Corp ....F...... 516 624-8200
  Oyster Bay *(G-13366)*

DRUGS: Parasitic & Infective Disease Affecting

Safetec of America Inc ....D...... 716 895-1822
  Buffalo *(G-3173)*

DRUMS: Fiber

Greif Inc ....D...... 716 836-4200
  Tonawanda *(G-16169)*

DRYCLEANING EQPT & SPLYS: Commercial

Q Omni Inc ....G...... 914 962-2726
  Yorktown Heights *(G-17517)*
Thermopatch Corporation....................D...... 315 446-8110
  Syracuse *(G-16058)*

DRYCLEANING SVC: Drapery & Curtain

Abalene Decorating Services ....E...... 718 782-2000
  New York *(G-9000)*
Reynolds Drapery Service Inc ....F...... 315 845-8632
  Newport *(G-12792)*

DUCTS: Sheet Metal

Aabco Sheet Metal Co Inc ....D...... 718 821-1166
  Ridgewood *(G-14097)*
Accurate Specialty Metal Fabri ....E...... 718 418-6895
  Middle Village *(G-8409)*
D and D Sheet Metal Corp ....F...... 718 465-7585
  Jamaica *(G-6909)*
Delta Sheet Metal Corp ....C...... 718 429-5805
  Long Island City *(G-7711)*
Karo Sheet Metal Inc ....E...... 718 542-8420
  Brooklyn *(G-2169)*
Liffey Sheet Metal Corp ....F...... 347 381-1134
  Brooklyn *(G-2220)*
Nelson Air Device Corporation ....C...... 718 729-3801
  Maspeth *(G-8155)*

United Sheet Metal Corp ....E...... 718 482-1197
  Long Island City *(G-7909)*

DUMPSTERS: Garbage

Mount Kisco Transfer Stn Inc ....G...... 914 666-6350
  Mount Kisco *(G-8635)*

DYES & PIGMENTS: Organic

Deep Dyeing Inc ....F...... 718 418-7187
  Manhasset *(G-8058)*
East Cast Clor Compounding Inc.........G...... 631 491-9000
  West Babylon *(G-16790)*
F M Group Inc......................................F...... 845 589-0102
  Congers *(G-3856)*
Novartis Corporation ....E...... 212 307-1122
  New York *(G-11462)*
Rand Machine Products Inc ....F...... 716 985-4681
  Sinclairville *(G-15454)*

DYES & TINTS: Household

Chromananotech LLC ....G...... 607 239-9626
  Vestal *(G-16445)*

DYES: Synthetic Organic

Jos H Lowenstein and Sons Inc ....D...... 718 218-8013
  Brooklyn *(G-2148)*

EATING PLACES

A T A Bagel Shoppe Inc ....G...... 718 352-4948
  Bayside *(G-764)*
Capco Marketing ....F...... 315 699-1687
  Baldwinsville *(G-567)*
Cascade Mountain Winery & Rest......F...... 845 373-9021
  Amenia *(G-215)*
Catskill Mtn Brewing Co Inc ....D...... 845 256-1700
  New Paltz *(G-8874)*
Food Gems Ltd....................................E...... 718 296-7788
  Ozone Park *(G-13379)*
Heron Hill Vineyards Inc.....................E...... 607 868-4241
  Hammondsport *(G-5956)*
Hyde Park Brewing Co Inc ....E...... 845 229-8277
  Hyde Park *(G-6734)*
Lakeside Cider Mill Farm Inc ....G...... 518 399-8359
  Ballston Lake *(G-582)*
Malina Management Company Inc .....E...... 607 535-9614
  Montour Falls *(G-8610)*
Piemonte Home Made Ravioli Co ....F...... 718 429-1972
  Woodside *(G-17347)*
Rawpothecary Inc ....G...... 917 783-7770
  Brooklyn *(G-2479)*
Rosina Food Products Inc ....C...... 716 668-0123
  Buffalo *(G-3165)*
Sign Company ....G...... 212 967-2113
  New York *(G-12069)*
Tortilla Heaven Inc ....E...... 845 339-1550
  Kingston *(G-7217)*

EDUCATIONAL PROGRAM ADMINISTRATION, GOVERNMENT: State

University At Albany ....E...... 518 437-8686
  Albany *(G-147)*

EDUCATIONAL PROGRAMS ADMINISTRATION SVCS

Binghamton University........................D...... 607 777-2316
  Binghamton *(G-896)*
Stony Brook University ....E...... 631 632-6434
  Stony Brook *(G-15772)*

EDUCATIONAL SVCS

Rainbeau Ridge Farm ....G...... 914 234-2197
  Bedford Hills *(G-806)*
Social Science Electronic Pubg ....F...... 585 442-8170
  Rochester *(G-14690)*

EDUCATIONAL SVCS, NONDEGREE GRANTING: Continuing Education

Conference Board Inc.........................C...... 212 759-0900
  New York *(G-9699)*

ELASTOMERS

Elastomers Inc ....G...... 716 633-4883
  Williamsville *(G-17241)*

Everfab Inc..D...... 716 655-1550
  East Aurora *(G-4370)*
Hutchinson Industries Inc ....E...... 716 852-1435
  Buffalo *(G-2998)*
Rodgard Corporation...........................E...... 716 852-1435
  Buffalo *(G-3163)*

ELECTRIC MOTOR & GENERATOR AUXILIARY PARTS

International Control Products ....F...... 716 558-4400
  West Seneca *(G-16949)*

ELECTRIC MOTOR REPAIR SVCS

A & C/Furia Electric Motors ....F...... 914 949-0585
  White Plains *(G-17072)*
Alpha DC Motors Inc...........................F...... 315 432-9039
  Syracuse *(G-15850)*
Auburn Armature Inc ....D...... 315 253-9721
  Auburn *(G-477)*
B & R Electric Motor Inc ....G...... 631 752-7533
  Farmingdale *(G-4950)*
B J S Electric ....G...... 845 774-8166
  Chester *(G-3600)*
Bailey Electric Motor Repair ....G...... 585 542-5902
  Corfu *(G-3952)*
Bayshore Electric Motors ....G...... 631 475-1397
  Patchogue *(G-13416)*
Daves Electric Motors & Pumps.........G...... 212 982-2930
  New York *(G-9817)*
Electric Motor Specialty Inc ....G...... 716 487-1458
  Jamestown *(G-6992)*
General Electric Company ....E...... 315 456-3304
  Syracuse *(G-15950)*
General Electric Company ....E...... 518 459-4110
  Albany *(G-82)*
Genesis Electrical Motors ....G...... 718 274-7030
  Woodside *(G-17331)*
Lawtons Electric Motor Service..........G...... 315 393-2728
  Ogdensburg *(G-13117)*
Longo New York Inc............................F...... 212 929-7128
  New York *(G-11026)*
Northeastern Electric Motors ....G...... 518 793-5939
  Hadley *(G-5903)*
Patchogue Electric Motors Inc ....G...... 631 475-0117
  Patchogue *(G-13431)*
Prime Electric Motors Inc...................G...... 718 784-1124
  Long Island City *(G-7846)*
Troy Industrial Solutions....................D...... 518 272-4920
  Watervliet *(G-16690)*
United Richter Electrical Mtrs ....F...... 716 855-1945
  Buffalo *(G-3235)*

ELECTRIC SERVICES

Besicorp Ltd ....F...... 845 336-7700
  Kingston *(G-7179)*
County Energy Corp ....G...... 718 626-7000
  Brooklyn *(G-1808)*

ELECTRIC SVCS, NEC Power Transmission

Hess Corporation................................B...... 212 997-8500
  New York *(G-10464)*

ELECTRIC SVCS, NEC: Power Generation

Caithness Equities Corporation ....E...... 212 599-2112
  New York *(G-9498)*

ELECTRICAL APPARATUS & EQPT WHOLESALERS

Aerospace Lighting Corporation..........D...... 631 563-6400
  Bohemia *(G-1008)*
Amertac Holdings Inc ....G...... 610 336-1330
  Monsey *(G-8567)*
Bombardier Trnsp Holdings USA ....D...... 607 776-4791
  Bath *(G-654)*
Edison Price Lighting Inc...................D...... 718 685-0700
  Long Island City *(G-7724)*
Ener-G-Rotors Inc ....G...... 518 372-2608
  Schenectady *(G-15250)*
Hammond Manufacturing Co Inc........F...... 716 630-7030
  Cheektowaga *(G-3573)*
Linear Lighting Corporation ....C...... 718 361-7552
  Long Island City *(G-7790)*
LSI Lightron Inc...................................A...... 845 562-5500
  New Windsor *(G-8942)*
Medi-Ray Inc ....D...... 877 898-3003
  Tuckahoe *(G-16271)*

ELECTRICAL APPARATUS & EQPT WHOLESALERS

On Line Power Technologies .... G 914 968-4440
  Yonkers *(G-17470)*
Pcb Piezotronics Inc .... B 716 684-0003
  Depew *(G-4270)*
Pompian Manufacturing Co Inc .... G 914 476-7076
  Yonkers *(G-17478)*
Powr-UPS Corp .... E 631 345-5700
  Shirley *(G-15428)*
S & J Trading Inc .... E 718 347-1323
  Floral Park *(G-5209)*
Stk Electronics Inc .... E 315 655-8476
  Cazenovia *(G-3452)*

ELECTRICAL APPLIANCES, TELEVISIONS & RADIOS WHOLESALERS

AVI-Spl Employee .... B 212 840-4801
  New York *(G-9277)*
Sony Music Entertainment Inc .... A 212 833-8500
  New York *(G-12135)*

ELECTRICAL CONSTRUCTION MATERIALS WHOLESALERS

All-Lifts Incorporated .... E 518 465-3461
  Albany *(G-44)*
Morris Products Inc .... F 518 743-0523
  Queensbury *(G-14005)*

ELECTRICAL CURRENT CARRYING WIRING DEVICES

Alstom Signaling Inc .... E 585 274-8700
  Schenectady *(G-15229)*
Atc Plastics LLC .... E 212 375-2515
  New York *(G-9245)*
Belden Inc .... B 607 796-5600
  Horseheads *(G-6569)*
C A M Graphics Co Inc .... E 631 842-3400
  Farmingdale *(G-4955)*
Charlton Precision Pdts Inc .... G 845 338-2351
  Kingston *(G-7183)*
Cooper Power Systems LLC .... B 716 375-7100
  Olean *(G-13140)*
Cox & Company Inc .... C 212 366-0200
  Plainview *(G-13593)*
Diversified Electrical Pdts .... F 631 567-5710
  Bohemia *(G-1058)*
Exxelia-Raf Tabtronics LLC .... E 585 243-4331
  Piffard *(G-13547)*
Inertia Switch Inc .... E 845 359-8300
  Orangeburg *(G-13229)*
Jaguar Industries Inc .... F 845 947-1800
  Haverstraw *(G-6237)*
Joldeson One Aerospace Inds .... D 718 848-7396
  Ozone Park *(G-13380)*
Kelta Inc .... E 631 789-5000
  Edgewood *(G-4602)*
L-3 Communications Corporation ..... A 631 436-7400
  Hauppauge *(G-6108)*
Leviton Manufacturing Co Inc .... B 631 812-6000
  Melville *(G-8334)*
Lighting Holdings Intl LLC .... F 845 306-1850
  Purchase *(G-13960)*
Lite Brite Manufacturing Inc .... F 718 855-9797
  Brooklyn *(G-2231)*
Lourdes Industries Inc .... D 631 234-6600
  Hauppauge *(G-6121)*
MD Electronics of Illinois .... D 716 488-0300
  Jamestown *(G-7019)*
Mini-Circuits Fort Wayne LLC .... B 718 934-4500
  Brooklyn *(G-2318)*
Mono-Systems Inc .... E 716 821-1344
  Buffalo *(G-3074)*
NEa Manufacturing Corp .... E 516 371-4200
  Inwood *(G-6763)*
Orbit International Corp .... C 631 435-8300
  Hauppauge *(G-6154)*
Pass & Seymour Inc .... B 315 468-6211
  Syracuse *(G-16011)*
Reynolds Packaging McHy Inc .... D 716 358-6451
  Falconer *(G-4910)*
Rodale Wireless Inc .... E 631 231-0044
  Hauppauge *(G-6179)*
Russell Industries Inc .... F 516 536-5000
  Lynbrook *(G-7960)*
Saturn Industries Inc .... E 518 828-9956
  Hudson *(G-6632)*
Sinclair Technologies Inc .... E 716 874-3682
  Hamburg *(G-5942)*
Stever-Locke Industries Inc .... G 585 624-3450
  Honeoye Falls *(G-6538)*
Superpower Inc .... D 518 346-1414
  Schenectady *(G-15302)*
Switching Power Inc .... D 631 981-7231
  Ronkonkoma *(G-14990)*
Swivelier Company Inc .... D 845 353-1455
  Blauvelt *(G-975)*
Tappan Wire & Cable Inc .... C 845 353-9000
  Blauvelt *(G-976)*
Utility Systems Tech Inc .... F 518 326-4142
  Watervliet *(G-16691)*
Whirlwind Music Distrs Inc .... D 585 663-8820
  Rochester *(G-14762)*

ELECTRICAL DISCHARGE MACHINING, EDM

Fermer Precision Inc .... D 315 822-6371
  Ilion *(G-6740)*
Hoercher Industries Inc .... G 585 398-2982
  East Rochester *(G-4461)*
K & H Industries Inc .... F 716 312-0088
  Hamburg *(G-5930)*

ELECTRICAL EQPT & SPLYS

303 Contracting Inc .... E 716 896-2122
  Orchard Park *(G-13249)*
331 Holding Inc .... E 585 924-1740
  Victor *(G-16458)*
A & S Electric .... G 212 228-2030
  Brooklyn *(G-1529)*
Advanced Mfg Techniques .... G 518 877-8560
  Clifton Park *(G-3694)*
Allcom Electric Corp .... G 914 803-0433
  Yonkers *(G-17411)*
Altaquip LLC .... G 631 580-4740
  Ronkonkoma *(G-14867)*
American Avionic Tech Corp .... D 631 924-8200
  Medford *(G-8234)*
Amertac Holdings Inc .... G 610 336-1330
  Monsey *(G-8567)*
Ametek Inc .... D 585 263-7700
  Rochester *(G-14202)*
Atlas Switch Co Inc .... E 516 222-6280
  Garden City *(G-5495)*
B & H Electronics Corp .... E 845 782-5000
  Monroe *(G-8549)*
Binghamton Simulator Co Inc .... E 607 321-2980
  Binghamton *(G-895)*
Bombardier Trnsp Holdings USA .... D 607 776-4791
  Bath *(G-654)*
Bren-Tronics Inc .... C 631 499-5155
  Commack *(G-3827)*
Buffalo Filter LLC .... D 716 835-7000
  Lancaster *(G-7307)*
Castle Power Solutions LLC .... G 518 743-1000
  South Glens Falls *(G-15523)*
Cathay Global Co Inc .... G 718 229-0920
  Bayside Hills *(G-780)*
Cooper Industries LLC .... E 315 477-7000
  Syracuse *(G-15909)*
Cooper Power Systems LLC .... B 716 375-7100
  Olean *(G-13140)*
Cooperfriedman Elc Sup Co Inc .... G 718 269-4906
  Long Island City *(G-7704)*
Da Electric .... E 347 270-3422
  Bronx *(G-1309)*
Dahill Distributors Inc .... G 347 371-9453
  Brooklyn *(G-1833)*
Denmar Electric .... F 845 624-4430
  Nanuet *(G-8755)*
Dorsey Metrology Intl Inc .... E 845 229-2929
  Poughkeepsie *(G-13895)*
Eastco Manufacturing Corp .... F 914 738-5667
  Pelham *(G-13490)*
Eaton Crouse-Hinds .... C 315 477-7000
  Syracuse *(G-15931)*
Edo LLC .... A 631 630-4200
  Amityville *(G-286)*
Emco Electric Services LLC .... C 212 420-9766
  New York *(G-10022)*
Emcom Inc .... D 315 255-5300
  Auburn *(G-493)*
Euchner USA Inc .... F 315 701-0315
  East Syracuse *(G-4528)*
G X Electric Corporation .... E 212 921-0400
  New York *(G-10233)*
General Elc Capitl Svcs Inc .... G 315 554-2000
  Skaneateles *(G-15461)*
Gerome Technologies Inc .... D 518 463-1324
  Menands *(G-8372)*
Green Island Power Authority .... F 518 273-0661
  Green Island *(G-5856)*
Guardian Systems Tech Inc .... F 716 481-5597
  East Aurora *(G-4372)*
Hergo Ergonomic Support .... E 718 894-0639
  Maspeth *(G-8143)*
Home Depot USA Inc .... C 845 561-6540
  Newburgh *(G-12761)*
Htf Components Inc .... G 914 703-6795
  White Plains *(G-17123)*
Iconix Inc .... F 516 307-1324
  Mineola *(G-8515)*
Itin Scale Co Inc .... E 718 336-5900
  Brooklyn *(G-2120)*
J H M Engineering .... E 718 871-1810
  Brooklyn *(G-2123)*
Knf Clean Room Products Corp .... E 631 588-7000
  Ronkonkoma *(G-14923)*
Koregon Enterprises Inc .... E 450 218-6836
  Champlain *(G-3543)*
L-3 Communications Corporation ..... D 607 721-5465
  Kirkwood *(G-7234)*
Levition Manufacturing Co .... E 631 812-6000
  Melville *(G-8333)*
Lucas Electric .... G 516 809-8619
  Seaford *(G-15345)*
Madison Electric .... E 718 358-4121
  Cambria Heights *(G-3303)*
Manhattan Scientifics Inc .... E 212 541-2405
  New York *(G-11132)*
Manor Electric Supply Corp .... F 347 312-2521
  Brooklyn *(G-2263)*
Manufacturing Solutions Inc .... E 585 235-3320
  Rochester *(G-14494)*
Mitsubishi Elc Pwr Pdts Inc .... E 516 962-2813
  Melville *(G-8337)*
Multi Tech Electric .... F 718 606-2695
  Woodside *(G-17339)*
Nbn Technologies LLC .... G 585 355-5556
  Rochester *(G-14531)*
Nk Electric LLC .... G 914 271-0222
  Croton On Hudson *(G-4065)*
OEM Solutions Inc .... G 716 864-9324
  Clarence *(G-3667)*
Optimum Applied Systems Inc .... F 845 471-3333
  Poughkeepsie *(G-13924)*
Piller Usa Inc .... E 845 695-6600
  Middletown *(G-8456)*
Pinpoint Systems Intl Inc .... D 631 775-2100
  Bellport *(G-838)*
Promptus Electronic Hdwr Inc .... E 914 699-4700
  Mount Vernon *(G-8721)*
Robotic Directions .... G 585 453-9417
  Rochester *(G-14631)*
Rodale Wireless Inc .... E 631 231-0044
  Hauppauge *(G-6179)*
Ross Electronics Ltd .... E 718 569-6643
  Haverstraw *(G-6240)*
Schuler-Haas Electric Corp .... E 607 936-3514
  Painted Post *(G-13393)*
Sima Technologies LLC .... G 412 828-9130
  Hauppauge *(G-6191)*
Simulaids Inc .... D 845 679-2475
  Saugerties *(G-15194)*
Skae Power Solutions LLC .... E 845 365-9103
  Palisades *(G-13402)*
Smithers Tools & Mch Pdts Inc .... D 845 876-3063
  Rhinebeck *(G-14058)*
Striano Electric Co Inc .... E 516 408-4969
  Garden City Park *(G-5543)*
Sunwire Electric Corp .... G 718 456-7500
  Brooklyn *(G-2623)*
T & G Wholesale Electric Corp .... G 585 396-9690
  Canandaigua *(G-3358)*
T Jn Electric .... F 917 560-0981
  Mahopac *(G-8002)*
T Jn Electric Inc .... G 845 628-6970
  Mahopac *(G-8003)*
Tory Electric .... G 914 292-5036
  Bedford *(G-798)*
Triborough Electric .... E 718 321-2144
  Whitestone *(G-17217)*
U E Systems Incorporated .... E 914 592-1220
  Elmsford *(G-4790)*
United Technologies Corp .... B 866 788-5095
  Pittsford *(G-13574)*
Werner Brothers Electric Inc .... G 518 377-3056
  Rexford *(G-14055)*
Wired Up Electric Inc .... G 845 878-3122
  Pawling *(G-13453)*

Z-Axis Inc..D........ 315 548-5000
  Phelps (G-13539)

ELECTRICAL EQPT FOR ENGINES

Cummins Inc ....B........ 812 377-5000
  Jamestown (G-6986)
Delphi Automotive Systems LLC ....A........ 585 359-6000
  West Henrietta (G-16876)
Eraser Company Inc ....C........ 315 454-3237
  Mattydale (G-8212)
Kearney-National Inc ....F........ 212 661-4600
  New York (G-10828)
Leviton Manufacturing Co Inc ....B........ 631 812-6000
  Melville (G-8334)
Nas-Tra Automotive Inds Inc ....C........ 631 225-1225
  Lindenhurst (G-7474)
Sopark Corp ....C........ 716 822-0434
  Buffalo (G-3191)

ELECTRICAL EQPT REPAIR & MAINTENANCE

A L Eastmond & Sons Inc ....D........ 718 378-3000
  Bronx (G-1254)
Alstom Transportation Inc ....E........ 212 692-5353
  New York (G-9104)
Hobart Corporation ....E........ 631 864-3440
  Commack (G-3835)
Strecks Inc ....E........ 518 273-4410
  Watervliet (G-16689)

ELECTRICAL EQPT REPAIR SVCS

B & R Electric Motor Inc ....G........ 631 752-7533
  Farmingdale (G-4950)
Zetek Corporation ....F........ 212 668-1485
  New York (G-12710)

ELECTRICAL EQPT REPAIR SVCS: High Voltage

Evergreen High Voltage LLC ....G........ 281 814-9973
  Lake Placid (G-7274)
Safeworks LLC ....F........ 800 696-5577
  Woodside (G-17352)

ELECTRICAL EQPT: Automotive, NEC

Autel US Inc ....G........ 631 923-2620
  Farmingdale (G-4948)
Ieh FM Holdings LLC ....E........ 212 702-4300
  New York (G-10559)

ELECTRICAL EQPT: Household

Kinetic Marketing Inc ....G........ 212 620-0600
  New York (G-10852)

ELECTRICAL GOODS, WHOLESALE: Batteries, Dry Cell

Lyntronics Inc ....E........ 631 205-1061
  Yaphank (G-17397)

ELECTRICAL GOODS, WHOLESALE: Burglar Alarm Systems

Altronix Corp ....D........ 718 567-8181
  Brooklyn (G-1596)
Detekion Security Systems Inc ....F........ 607 729-7179
  Vestal (G-16447)

ELECTRICAL GOODS, WHOLESALE: Capacitors

AVX Corporation ....D........ 716 372-6511
  Olean (G-13134)

ELECTRICAL GOODS, WHOLESALE: Connectors

Cables and Chips Inc ....E........ 212 619-3132
  New York (G-9493)
I Trade Technology Ltd ....G........ 615 348-7233
  Suffern (G-15792)

ELECTRICAL GOODS, WHOLESALE: Electronic Parts

Falconer Electronics Inc ....D........ 716 665-4176
  Falconer (G-4898)

Intex Company Inc ....D........ 718 336-3491
  Brooklyn (G-2114)
Oakdale Industrial Elec Corp ....F........ 631 737-4090
  Ronkonkoma (G-14957)
Sj Associates Inc ....E........ 516 942-3232
  Jericho (G-7087)
Veja Electronics Inc ....D........ 631 321-6086
  Deer Park (G-4222)

ELECTRICAL GOODS, WHOLESALE: Facsimile Or Fax Eqpt

Alternative Technology Corp ....G........ 914 478-5900
  Hastings On Hudson (G-6002)

ELECTRICAL GOODS, WHOLESALE: Fans, Household

Canarm Ltd ....G........ 800 267-4427
  Ogdensburg (G-13113)

ELECTRICAL GOODS, WHOLESALE: Fittings & Construction Mat

Veja Electronics Inc ....D........ 631 321-6086
  Deer Park (G-4222)

ELECTRICAL GOODS, WHOLESALE: Intercommunication Eqpt

Apple Core Electronics Inc ....F........ 718 628-4068
  Brooklyn (G-1618)
Elite Cellular Accessories Inc ....E........ 877 390-2502
  Deer Park (G-4136)
Ingham Industries Inc ....G........ 631 242-2493
  Holbrook (G-6451)

ELECTRICAL GOODS, WHOLESALE: Light Bulbs & Related Splys

Led Waves Inc ....F........ 347 416-6182
  Brooklyn (G-2204)
Olive Led Lighting Inc ....G........ 718 746-0830
  Flushing (G-5276)
Sir Industries Inc ....G........ 631 234-2444
  Hauppauge (G-6192)

ELECTRICAL GOODS, WHOLESALE: Lighting Fittings & Access

Gagne Associates Inc ....E........ 800 800-5954
  Johnson City (G-7092)
Jed Lights Inc ....G........ 516 812-5001
  Garden City Park (G-5540)

ELECTRICAL GOODS, WHOLESALE: Lighting Fixtures, Comm & Indl

Canarm Ltd ....G........ 800 267-4427
  Ogdensburg (G-13113)
Creative Stage Lighting Co Inc ....E........ 518 251-3302
  North Creek (G-12933)
Unimar Inc ....F........ 315 699-4400
  Syracuse (G-16063)

ELECTRICAL GOODS, WHOLESALE: Lighting Fixtures, Residential

Prestigeline Inc ....D........ 631 273-3636
  Bay Shore (G-728)
Rapid-Lite Fixture Corporation ....F........ 347 599-2600
  Brooklyn (G-2478)

ELECTRICAL GOODS, WHOLESALE: Motors

Auburn Armature Inc ....D........ 315 253-9721
  Auburn (G-477)
Electric Motor Specialty Inc ....G........ 716 487-1458
  Jamestown (G-6992)
Empire Division Inc ....D........ 315 476-6273
  Syracuse (G-15936)
Heating & Burner Supply Inc ....G........ 718 665-0006
  Bronx (G-1355)
Northeastern Electric Motors ....G........ 518 793-5939
  Hadley (G-5903)
Patchogue Electric Motors Inc ....G........ 631 475-0117
  Patchogue (G-13431)

ELECTRICAL GOODS, WHOLESALE: Semiconductor Devices

Lakestar Semi Inc ....F........ 212 974-6254
  New York (G-10919)

ELECTRICAL GOODS, WHOLESALE: Signaling, Eqpt

BNo Intl Trdg Co Inc ....G........ 716 487-1900
  Jamestown (G-6977)

ELECTRICAL GOODS, WHOLESALE: Sound Eqpt

L A R Electronics Corp ....G........ 716 285-0555
  Niagara Falls (G-12840)
Magic Tech Co Ltd ....G........ 516 539-7944
  West Hempstead (G-16859)
Samson Technologies Corp ....D........ 631 784-2200
  Hauppauge (G-6182)

ELECTRICAL GOODS, WHOLESALE: Telephone & Telegraphic Eqpt

Data Transmission Essentials ....F........ 516 378-8820
  Harrison (G-5983)

ELECTRICAL GOODS, WHOLESALE: Telephone Eqpt

Harris Corporation ....F........ 718 767-1100
  Whitestone (G-17208)

ELECTRICAL GOODS, WHOLESALE: Transformers

Buffalo Power Elec Ctr De ....E........ 716 651-1600
  Depew (G-4250)

ELECTRICAL GOODS, WHOLESALE: VCR & Access

Toshiba America Inc ....E........ 212 596-0600
  New York (G-12377)

ELECTRICAL GOODS, WHOLESALE: Vacuum Cleaners, Household

Empire Division Inc ....D........ 315 476-6273
  Syracuse (G-15936)

ELECTRICAL GOODS, WHOLESALE: Video Eqpt

Bescor Video Accessories Ltd ....F........ 631 420-1717
  Farmingdale (G-4952)
Russell Industries Inc ....F........ 516 536-5000
  Lynbrook (G-7960)

ELECTRICAL GOODS, WHOLESALE: Wire & Cable

Cortland Company Inc ....C........ 607 753-8276
  Cortland (G-4017)
Cygnus Automation Inc ....E........ 631 981-0909
  Bohemia (G-1047)

ELECTRICAL GOODS, WHOLESALE: Wire & Cable, Electronic

Cables and Chips Inc ....E........ 212 619-3132
  New York (G-9493)
Cables Unlimited Inc ....E........ 631 563-6363
  Yaphank (G-17387)
Dsr International Corp ....G........ 631 427-2600
  Great Neck (G-5803)

ELECTRICAL INDL APPARATUS, NEC

Calibration Technologies Inc ....G........ 631 676-6133
  Centereach (G-3470)
Key Signals ....G........ 631 433-2962
  East Moriches (G-4429)

ELECTRICAL SPLYS

Cooper Industries LLC ....E........ 315 477-7000
  Syracuse (G-15909)

ELECTRICAL SPLYS

Rwb Controls Inc ....G....... 716 897-4341
 Buffalo *(G-3169)*
Tudor Electrical Supply Co Inc ....G....... 212 867-7550
 New York *(G-12420)*

ELECTRICAL SUPPLIES: Porcelain

Cetek Inc ....E....... 845 452-3510
 Poughkeepsie *(G-13892)*
Corning Incorporated ....E....... 607 974-1274
 Painted Post *(G-13390)*
Ferro Electronics Materials ....C....... 716 278-9400
 Niagara Falls *(G-12821)*
Ferro Electronics Materials ....G....... 315 536-3357
 Penn Yan *(G-13510)*
Ferro Electronics Materials ....G....... 315 536-3357
 Penn Yan *(G-13511)*
Filtros Ltd ....E....... 585 586-8770
 East Rochester *(G-4459)*

ELECTROCARS: Golfer Transportation

Mdek Inc...G....... 347 569-7318
 Brooklyn *(G-2288)*

ELECTRODES: Fluorescent Lamps

Preston Glass Industries Inc ....E....... 718 997-8888
 Forest Hills *(G-5328)*

ELECTRODES: Thermal & Electrolytic

J V Precision Inc ....G....... 518 851-3200
 Hudson *(G-6619)*
Saturn Industries Inc ....E....... 518 828-9956
 Hudson *(G-6632)*

ELECTROMEDICAL EQPT

Argon Medical Devices Inc ....G....... 585 321-1130
 Henrietta *(G-6293)*
C R Bard Inc ....A....... 518 793-2531
 Glens Falls *(G-5674)*
Cardiac Life Products Inc.......................G....... 585 267-7775
 East Rochester *(G-4454)*
Conmed Corporation ....D....... 315 797-8375
 Utica *(G-16315)*
Excel Technology Inc ....F....... 212 355-3400
 New York *(G-10102)*
Fonar Corporation ....C....... 631 694-2929
 Melville *(G-8320)*
Forest Medical LLC ....G....... 315 434-9000
 East Syracuse *(G-4531)*
Infimed Inc ....G....... 315 453-4545
 Liverpool *(G-7524)*
Infimed Inc ....G....... 585 383-1710
 Pittsford *(G-13565)*
J H M Engineering ....E....... 718 871-1810
 Brooklyn *(G-2123)*
Kal Manufacturing Corporation ....E....... 585 265-4310
 Webster *(G-16726)*
Med Services Inc ....D....... 631 218-6450
 Bohemia *(G-1104)*
Misonix Inc ....D....... 631 694-9555
 Farmingdale *(G-5058)*
Natus Medical Incorporated ....G....... 631 457-4430
 Hauppauge *(G-6145)*
Netech Corporation ....F....... 631 531-0100
 Farmingdale *(G-5065)*
New York Marine Elec Inc ....G....... 631 734-6050
 Hampton Bays *(G-5961)*
Pharmadva LLC.....................................E....... 585 469-1410
 West Henrietta *(G-16891)*
Philips Medical Systems Mr ....B....... 518 782-1122
 Latham *(G-7376)*
Ray Medica Inc ....E....... 952 885-0500
 New York *(G-11806)*
Sonomed Inc ....E....... 516 354-0900
 New Hyde Park *(G-8863)*
Soterix Medical Inc ....F....... 888 990-8327
 New York *(G-12141)*
Stand Up Mri of Lynbrook PC ....F....... 516 256-1558
 Lynbrook *(G-7963)*
Sun Scientific Inc..................................G....... 914 479-5108
 Dobbs Ferry *(G-4303)*
Ultradian Diagnostics LLC ....G....... 518 618-0046
 Rensselaer *(G-14053)*
Vasomedical Inc ....E....... 516 997-4600
 Plainview *(G-13641)*
Vermed Inc ....D....... 802 463-9976
 Buffalo *(G-3241)*
Visiplex Instruments Corp ....D....... 845 365-0190
 Elmsford *(G-4791)*

Z-Axis Inc..D....... 315 548-5000
 Phelps *(G-13539)*

ELECTRON TUBES

Harris Corporation ....E....... 585 244-5830
 Rochester *(G-14427)*
Y & Z Precision Inc ....F....... 516 349-8243
 Plainview *(G-13648)*

ELECTRON TUBES: Cathode Ray

Passur Aerospace Inc ....G....... 631 589-6800
 Bohemia *(G-1115)*
Thomas Electronics Inc.........................C....... 315 923-2051
 Clyde *(G-3732)*

ELECTRONIC COMPONENTS

Bud Barger Assoc Inc ....G....... 631 696-6703
 Farmingville *(G-5159)*
Haynes Roberts Inc ....F....... 212 989-1901
 New York *(G-10431)*
Lighthouse Components ....E....... 917 993-6820
 New York *(G-10994)*
Marcon Electronic Systems LLC ....G....... 516 633-6396
 Freeport *(G-5410)*
Mezmeriz Inc...G....... 607 216-8140
 Ithaca *(G-6861)*
MLS Sales ....G....... 516 681-2736
 Bethpage *(G-875)*
Sln Group Inc ....G....... 718 677-5969
 Brooklyn *(G-2571)*
Space Coast Semiconductor Inc ....F....... 631 414-7131
 Farmingdale *(G-5112)*

ELECTRONIC DETECTION SYSTEMS: Aeronautical

Accutrak Inc ....F....... 212 925-5330
 New York *(G-9013)*

ELECTRONIC DEVICES: Solid State, NEC

Autodyne Manufacturing Co Inc.............F....... 631 957-5858
 Lindenhurst *(G-7456)*
Automated Control Logic Inc ....F....... 914 769-8880
 Thornwood *(G-16116)*
Bharat Electronics Limited ....G....... 516 248-4021
 Garden City *(G-5496)*
DJS Nyc Inc..G....... 845 445-8618
 Spring Valley *(G-15581)*
Enrg Inc ....F....... 716 873-2939
 Buffalo *(G-2940)*
Orbit International Corp ....C....... 631 435-8300
 Hauppauge *(G-6154)*
Piezo Electronics Research ....F....... 845 735-9349
 Pearl River *(G-13463)*
Sonotec US Inc.......................................C....... 631 404-7497
 Central Islip *(G-3510)*
Thermo Cidtec Inc..................................E....... 315 451-9410
 Liverpool *(G-7553)*

ELECTRONIC EQPT REPAIR SVCS

Ah Elctronic Test Eqp Repr Ctr ....F....... 631 234-8979
 Central Islip *(G-3484)*
Alexy Associates Inc ....E....... 845 482-3000
 Bethel *(G-859)*
Custom Sound and Video ....E....... 585 424-5000
 Rochester *(G-14296)*

ELECTRONIC LOADS & POWER SPLYS

Berkshire Transformer ....G....... 631 467-5328
 Central Islip *(G-3487)*
D & S Supplies Inc ....F....... 718 721-5256
 Astoria *(G-435)*
Engagement Technology LLC ....F....... 914 591-7600
 Elmsford *(G-4750)*
Eni Technology Inc ....B....... 585 427-8300
 Rochester *(G-14353)*
Mechanical Pwr Conversion LLC ....G....... 607 766-9620
 Binghamton *(G-934)*
New York Digital Corporation ....F....... 631 630-9798
 Huntington Station *(G-6718)*
Prime Electronic Components ....F....... 631 254-0101
 Deer Park *(G-4192)*
Pvi Solar Inc ....F....... 212 280-2100
 New York *(G-11760)*
SC Textiles Inc.......................................G....... 631 944-6362
 Huntington *(G-6679)*

Superior Motion Controls Inc ....E....... 516 420-2921
 Farmingdale *(G-5120)*
Three Five III-V Materials Inc ....F....... 212 213-8043
 New York *(G-12333)*
Ultralife Corporation ....B....... 315 332-7100
 Newark *(G-12745)*

ELECTRONIC PARTS & EQPT WHOLESALERS

Aj Greentech Holdings Ltd....................G....... 718 395-8706
 Flushing *(G-5223)*
Apex Signal Corporation ....D....... 631 567-1100
 Bohemia *(G-1017)*
Apollo Display Tech Corp ....E....... 631 580-4360
 Ronkonkoma *(G-14871)*
Auburn Armature Inc ....G....... 315 253-9721
 Auburn *(G-477)*
Becker Electronics Inc ....D....... 631 619-9100
 Ronkonkoma *(G-14879)*
Canfield Electronics Inc ....E....... 631 585-4100
 Lindenhurst *(G-7458)*
Claddagh Electronics Ltd......................E....... 718 784-0571
 Long Island City *(G-7700)*
Cypress Semiconductor Corp ....F....... 631 261-1358
 Northport *(G-13010)*
Electronic Devices Inc ....E....... 914 965-4400
 Yonkers *(G-17440)*
Forerunner Technologies Inc................E....... 631 337-2100
 Bohemia *(G-1067)*
G B International Trdg Co Ltd ....C....... 607 785-0938
 Endicott *(G-4809)*
General Microwave Corporation............F....... 516 802-0900
 Syosset *(G-15824)*
High Frequency Tech Co Inc ....F....... 631 242-3020
 Deer Park *(G-4149)*
Htf Components Inc..............................G....... 914 703-6795
 White Plains *(G-17123)*
Iba Industrial Inc ....E....... 631 254-6800
 Edgewood *(G-4600)*
Iconix Inc ....F....... 516 307-1324
 Mineola *(G-8515)*
Interntonal Telecom Components ....F....... 631 243-1444
 Deer Park *(G-4152)*
Jaguar Industries Inc ....F....... 845 947-1800
 Haverstraw *(G-6237)*
Kinetic Marketing Inc..............................G....... 212 620-0600
 New York *(G-10852)*
L K Manufacturing Corp ....E....... 631 243-6910
 West Babylon *(G-16806)*
Mill-Max Mfg Corp ....C....... 516 922-6000
 Oyster Bay *(G-13371)*
New Sensor Corporation ....D....... 718 937-8300
 Long Island City *(G-7824)*
Omntec Mfg Inc ....F....... 631 981-2001
 Ronkonkoma *(G-14960)*
Sag Harbor Industries Inc ....E....... 631 725-0440
 Sag Harbor *(G-15080)*
Semitronics Corp ....E....... 516 223-0200
 Freeport *(G-5425)*
Switching Power Inc ....D....... 631 981-7231
 Ronkonkoma *(G-14990)*
Ultravolt Inc ....D....... 631 471-4444
 Ronkonkoma *(G-14996)*

ELECTRONIC TRAINING DEVICES

Car Essentials Inc ....G....... 518 745-1300
 Queensbury *(G-13994)*
Ces Industries Inc ....E....... 631 782-7088
 Islandia *(G-6790)*
Full Circle Studios LLC ....C....... 716 875-7740
 Buffalo *(G-2960)*
Rockwell Collins Simulation ....D....... 607 352-1298
 Binghamton *(G-947)*
Telephonics Corporation ....G....... 631 470-8838
 Huntington *(G-6684)*
Telephonics Corporation ....D....... 631 755-7000
 Farmingdale *(G-5128)*
Telephonics Corporation ....D....... 631 470-8800
 Huntington *(G-6686)*

ELECTROPLATING & PLATING SVC

G J C Ltd Inc ....E....... 607 770-4500
 Binghamton *(G-917)*
General Galvanizing Sup Co Inc............E....... 718 589-4300
 Bronx *(G-1343)*
Metal Man Restoration...........................F....... 914 662-4218
 Mount Vernon *(G-8704)*
Psb Ltd ....F....... 585 654-7078
 Rochester *(G-14607)*

ELEVATORS & EQPT

Company	Code	Phone
A & D Entrances LLC	F	718 989-2441
Jamaica *(G-6890)*		
An Excelsior Elevator Corp	F	516 408-3070
Westbury *(G-16968)*		
Bhi Elevator Cabs Inc	F	516 431-5665
Island Park *(G-6778)*		
CEC Elevator Cab Corp	D	718 328-3632
Bronx *(G-1292)*		
Dural Door Company Inc	F	718 729-1333
Long Island City *(G-7720)*		
E Z Entry Doors Inc	F	716 434-3440
Lockport *(G-7583)*		
Elevator Accessories Mfg	F	914 739-7004
Peekskill *(G-13477)*		
Herbert Wolf Corp	G	212 242-0300
New York *(G-10461)*		
Interface Products Co Inc	G	631 242-4605
Bay Shore *(G-707)*		
Keystone Iron & Wire Works Inc	E	718 392-1616
Long Island City *(G-7781)*		
Monitor Elevator Products LLC	D	631 543-4334
Hauppauge *(G-6143)*		
National Elev Cab & Door Corp	E	718 478-5900
Woodside *(G-17340)*		
Otis Elevator Company	F	315 736-0167
Yorkville *(G-17526)*		
Otis Elevator Company	E	917 339-9600
New York *(G-11535)*		
Otis Elevator Company	E	914 375-7800
Yonkers *(G-17472)*		
Otis Elevator Company	E	518 426-4006
Albany *(G-112)*		
Schindler Elevator Corporation	C	718 417-3131
Glendale *(G-5662)*		
Schindler Elevator Corporation	D	516 860-1321
Hicksville *(G-6392)*		
Schindler Elevator Corporation	E	800 225-3123
New York *(G-11988)*		

ELEVATORS WHOLESALERS

Company	Code	Phone
An Excelsior Elevator Corp	F	516 408-3070
Westbury *(G-16968)*		
EZ Lift Operator Corp	F	845 356-1676
Spring Valley *(G-15584)*		

ELEVATORS: Installation & Conversion

Company	Code	Phone
Schindler Elevator Corporation	E	800 225-3123
New York *(G-11988)*		

ELEVATORS: Stair, Motor Powered

Company	Code	Phone
S & H Enterprises Inc	G	888 323-8755
Queensbury *(G-14010)*		

EMBLEMS: Embroidered

Company	Code	Phone
A Garys Treasures	F	518 383-1171
Clifton Park *(G-3693)*		
Eagle Regalia Co Inc	F	845 425-2245
Spring Valley *(G-15582)*		
Glenda Inc	G	718 442-8981
Staten Island *(G-15678)*		
Quist Industries Ltd	F	718 243-2800
Brooklyn *(G-2468)*		
Voyager Emblems Inc	C	416 255-3421
Buffalo *(G-3245)*		

EMBOSSING SVC: Paper

Company	Code	Phone
Welsh Gold Stampers Inc	E	718 984-5031
Staten Island *(G-15754)*		

EMBROIDERING & ART NEEDLEWORK FOR THE TRADE

Company	Code	Phone
Active World Solutions Inc	G	718 922-9404
Brooklyn *(G-1559)*		
Aditiany Inc	G	212 997-8440
New York *(G-9028)*		
All American Awards Inc	F	631 567-2025
Bohemia *(G-1011)*		
Atlantic Coast Embroidery Inc	G	631 283-2175
Southampton *(G-15539)*		
Clinton Clrs & EMB Shoppe Inc	G	315 853-8421
Clinton *(G-3718)*		
Control Research Inc	G	631 225-1111
Amityville *(G-282)*		
Design Archives Inc	G	212 768-0617
New York *(G-9851)*		
Eiseman-Ludmar Co Inc	F	516 932-6990
Hicksville *(G-6343)*		
Expressions Punching & Digitiz	G	718 291-1177
Jamaica *(G-6911)*		
Gildan Apparel USA Inc	G	716 759-6273
Clarence *(G-3662)*		
Holland & Sherry Inc	E	212 542-8410
New York *(G-10497)*		
Instant Monogramming Inc	G	585 654-5550
Rochester *(G-14450)*		
Kabrics	G	607 962-6344
Corning *(G-3975)*		
Karishma Fashions Inc	G	718 565-5404
Jackson Heights *(G-6888)*		
Kevin J Kassman	G	585 529-4245
Rochester *(G-14469)*		
Loremanss Embroidery Engrav	F	518 834-9205
Keeseville *(G-7139)*		
Mrinalini Inc	G	646 510-2747
New York *(G-11316)*		
Northeast Stitches & Ink Inc	E	518 798-5549
South Glens Falls *(G-15528)*		
Planet Embroidery	F	718 381-4827
Ridgewood *(G-14118)*		
Point Canvas Company Inc	G	607 692-4381
Whitney Point *(G-17220)*		
Pro Lettering LLC	G	607 484-0255
Endicott *(G-4826)*		
River Rat Design	F	315 393-4770
Ogdensburg *(G-13121)*		
Ross L Sports Screening Inc	F	716 824-5350
Buffalo *(G-3167)*		
Round Top Knit & Screening	G	518 622-3600
Round Top *(G-15040)*		
Royal Tees Inc	G	845 357-9448
Suffern *(G-15800)*		
Sand Hill Industries Inc	G	518 885-7991
Ballston Spa *(G-608)*		
Screen Gems Inc	G	845 561-0036
New Windsor *(G-8953)*		
Seo Ryung Inc	F	718 321-0755
Flushing *(G-5291)*		
Shykat Promotions	G	866 574-2757
Forestville *(G-5336)*		
Stephen M Kiernan	E	716 836-6300
Buffalo *(G-3196)*		
U All Inc	E	518 438-2558
Albany *(G-144)*		
U S Embroidery Inc	F	718 585-9662
Bronx *(G-1483)*		
Uniform Namemakers Inc	F	716 626-5474
Buffalo *(G-3232)*		
Wicked Smart LLC	F	518 459-2855
Watervliet *(G-16692)*		

EMBROIDERING SVC

Company	Code	Phone
All About Art Inc	F	718 321-0755
Flushing *(G-5225)*		
American Quality Embroidery	G	631 467-3200
Ronkonkoma *(G-14869)*		
Arena Graphics Inc	G	516 767-5108
Port Washington *(G-13801)*		
East Coast Embroidery Ltd	G	631 254-3878
Deer Park *(G-4133)*		
F X Graphix Inc	G	716 871-1511
Buffalo *(G-2943)*		
Hosel & Ackerson Inc	E	212 575-1490
New York *(G-10509)*		
Human Technologies Corporation	F	315 735-3532
Utica *(G-16340)*		
Mainly Monograms Inc	E	845 624-4923
West Nyack *(G-16921)*		
Monte Goldman Embroidery Co	F	212 874-5397
New York *(G-11301)*		
NY Embroidery Inc	E	516 822-6456
Hicksville *(G-6378)*		
On The Job Embroidery & AP	G	914 381-3556
Mamaroneck *(G-8040)*		
Penn & Fletcher Inc	F	212 239-6868
Long Island City *(G-7839)*		
Rescuestuff Inc	G	718 318-7570
Peekskill *(G-13480)*		

EMBROIDERING SVC: Schiffli Machine

Company	Code	Phone
American Images Inc	F	716 825-8888
Buffalo *(G-2808)*		
Rmb Embroidery Service	G	585 271-5560
Rochester *(G-14629)*		

EMBROIDERING: Swiss Loom

Company	Code	Phone
Stucki Embroidery Works Inc	F	845 657-2308
Boiceville *(G-1158)*		

EMBROIDERY ADVERTISING SVCS

Company	Code	Phone
Dray Enterprises Inc	F	585 768-2201
Le Roy *(G-7406)*		
Northeast Promotional Group In	G	518 793-1024
South Glens Falls *(G-15527)*		

EMERGENCY ALARMS

Company	Code	Phone
All Metro Emrgncy Response Sys	G	516 750-9100
Lynbrook *(G-7945)*		
Lifewatch Inc	F	800 716-1433
Hewlett *(G-6310)*		
Napco Security Tech Inc	B	631 842-9400
Amityville *(G-314)*		
Octopus Advanced Systems Inc	G	914 771-6110
Yonkers *(G-17469)*		
Personal Alarm SEC Systems	F	212 448-1944
New York *(G-11627)*		
Simplexgrinnell LP	D	585 288-6200
Rochester *(G-14688)*		
Simplexgrinnell LP	E	518 952-6040
Clifton Park *(G-3708)*		
Simplexgrinnell LP	G	845 774-4120
Harriman *(G-5974)*		
Simplexgrinnell LP	E	315 437-4660
East Syracuse *(G-4564)*		
Simplexgrinnell LP	F	607 338-5100
East Syracuse *(G-4565)*		
Synergx Systems Inc	D	516 433-4700
Woodside *(G-17358)*		
Telemergency Ltd	G	914 629-4222
White Plains *(G-17176)*		
Telephonics Corporation	F	631 755-7000
Huntington *(G-6685)*		
Unibrands Corporation	F	212 897-2278
New York *(G-12451)*		

EMPLOYMENT AGENCY SVCS

Company	Code	Phone
Equal Opprtnity Pblcations Inc	F	631 421-9421
Melville *(G-8314)*		
Symphony Talent LLC	D	212 999-9000
New York *(G-12257)*		
Vaultcom Inc	E	212 366-4212
New York *(G-12511)*		

ENAMELING SVC: Metal Prdts, Including Porcelain

Company	Code	Phone
F & H Metal Finishing Co Inc	F	585 798-2151
Medina *(G-8271)*		

ENAMELS

Company	Code	Phone
Si Group Inc	C	518 347-4200
Schenectady *(G-15296)*		

ENCLOSURES: Electronic

Company	Code	Phone
Fabrication Specialties Corp	G	631 242-0326
Deer Park *(G-4141)*		
Kerns Manufacturing Corp	C	718 784-4044
Long Island City *(G-7780)*		
National Computer & Electronic	G	631 242-7222
Deer Park *(G-4177)*		
Welding Metallurgy Inc	D	631 253-0500
Hauppauge *(G-6232)*		

ENERGY MEASUREMENT EQPT

Company	Code	Phone
New York Enrgy Synthetics Inc	G	212 634-4787
New York *(G-11401)*		
Performance Systems Contg Inc	E	607 277-6240
Ithaca *(G-6868)*		
Urban Green Energy Inc	E	917 720-5681
New York *(G-12479)*		

ENGINE REBUILDING: Diesel

Company	Code	Phone
D & W Diesel Inc	F	518 437-1300
Latham *(G-7359)*		
Jack W Miller	G	585 538-2399
Scottsville *(G-15337)*		

ENGINE REBUILDING: Gas

Company	Code	Phone
Washer Solutions Inc	F	585 742-6388
Victor *(G-16513)*		

ENGINEERING HELP SVCS

Fuel Systems Solutions Inc ....E...... 646 502-7170
New York *(G-10220)*

ENGINEERING SVCS

901 D LLC ....E...... 845 369-1111
Airmont *(G-11)*
Acme Engineering Products Inc ....E...... 518 236-5659
Mooers *(G-8615)*
Alstom Transportation Inc ....E...... 212 692-5353
New York *(G-9104)*
American Avionic Tech Corp ....D...... 631 924-8200
Medford *(G-8234)*
American Engnred Cmponents Inc ....D...... 516 742-8386
Carle Place *(G-3385)*
Atlantic Industrial Tech Inc ....E...... 631 234-3131
Shirley *(G-15414)*
Avanti Control Systems Inc ....G...... 518 921-4368
Gloversville *(G-5707)*
Benfield Control Systems Inc ....F...... 914 948-6660
White Plains *(G-17085)*
Bombardier Trnsp Holdings USA ....D...... 607 776-4791
Bath *(G-654)*
Bsu Inc ....E...... 607 272-8100
Ithaca *(G-6829)*
Critical Link LLC ....E...... 315 425-4045
Syracuse *(G-15912)*
Dayton T Brown Inc ....B...... 631 589-6300
Bohemia *(G-1052)*
Della Systems Inc ....F...... 631 580-0010
Ronkonkoma *(G-14893)*
Digitronik Dev Labs Inc ....G...... 585 360-0043
Rochester *(G-14308)*
Electric Boat Corporation ....C...... 518 884-1596
Rock City Falls *(G-14778)*
Excalibur Brnze Sculpture Fndry ....F...... 718 366-3444
Brooklyn *(G-1942)*
H S Assembly Inc ....G...... 585 266-4287
Rochester *(G-14416)*
Howden North America Inc ....D...... 716 817-6900
Depew *(G-4260)*
Interntnal Elctronic Mchs Corp ....E...... 518 268-1636
Troy *(G-16241)*
Linita Design & Mfg Corp ....E...... 716 566-7753
Lackawanna *(G-7244)*
Lourdes Industries Inc ....D...... 631 234-6600
Hauppauge *(G-6121)*
Millennium Antenna Corp ....F...... 315 798-9374
Utica *(G-16348)*
Optics Technology Inc ....G...... 585 586-0950
Pittsford *(G-13571)*
Photon Gear Inc ....F...... 585 265-3360
Ontario *(G-13209)*
Remington Arms Company LLC ....A...... 315 895-3482
Ilion *(G-6744)*
Rt Solutions LLC ....G...... 585 245-3456
Rochester *(G-14662)*
Sg Blocks Inc ....G...... 212 520-6218
New York *(G-12033)*
SOS International LLC ....E...... 212 742-2410
New York *(G-12140)*
Stone Well Bodies & Mch Inc ....F...... 315 497-3512
Genoa *(G-5590)*
Tbt Group Inc ....F...... 212 685-1836
New York *(G-12283)*

ENGINEERING SVCS: Building Construction

Roth Design & Consulting Inc ....E...... 718 209-0193
Brooklyn *(G-2509)*

ENGINEERING SVCS: Electrical Or Electronic

C Speed LLC ....E...... 315 453-1043
Liverpool *(G-7514)*
Nervve Technologies Inc ....E...... 716 800-2250
Buffalo *(G-3083)*
Tkm Technologies Inc ....G...... 631 474-4700
Port Jeff STA *(G-13773)*

ENGINEERING SVCS: Heating & Ventilation

Vincent Genovese ....G...... 631 281-8170
Mastic Beach *(G-8205)*

ENGINEERING SVCS: Industrial

Advanced Machine Design Co Inc ......E...... 716 826-2000
Buffalo *(G-2800)*

ENGINEERING SVCS: Marine

L-3 Cmmnctns Ntronix Holdings ....D...... 212 697-1111
New York *(G-10904)*

ENGINEERING SVCS: Mechanical

Calvary Design Team Inc ....C...... 585 347-6127
Webster *(G-16714)*

ENGINEERING SVCS: Petroleum

Amincor Inc ....C...... 347 821-3452
New York *(G-9136)*

ENGINEERING SVCS: Pollution Control

Clean Gas Systems Inc ....E...... 631 467-1600
Hauppauge *(G-6046)*

ENGINEERING SVCS: Professional

Nasiff Associates Inc ....G...... 315 676-2346
Central Square *(G-3517)*

ENGINEERING SVCS: Sanitary

Nes Bearing Company Inc ....E...... 716 372-6532
Olean *(G-13151)*

ENGINEERING SVCS: Structural

Marovato Industries Inc ....F...... 718 389-0800
Brooklyn *(G-2275)*
Tebbens Steel LLC ....F...... 631 208-8330
Calverton *(G-3301)*

ENGINES: Internal Combustion, NEC

AB Engine ....G...... 518 557-3510
Latham *(G-7351)*
Briggs & Stratton Corporation ....F...... 315 495-0100
Sherrill *(G-15404)*
Briggs & Stratton Corporation ....C...... 315 495-0100
Munnsville *(G-8749)*
Cummins - Allison Corp ....D...... 718 263-2482
Kew Gardens *(G-7159)*
Cummins Inc ....D...... 716 456-2676
Lakewood *(G-7289)*
Cummins Inc ....A...... 716 456-2111
Lakewood *(G-7290)*
Cummins Inc ....B...... 812 377-5000
Jamestown *(G-6986)*
Cummins Inc ....B...... 718 892-2400
Bronx *(G-1306)*
Cummins Northeast LLC ....E...... 315 437-2296
Syracuse *(G-15915)*
Mannesmann Corporation ....D...... 212 258-4000
New York *(G-11136)*
Perkins International Inc ....G...... 309 675-1000
Buffalo *(G-3121)*

ENGINES: Jet Propulsion

Omega Industries & Development ......E...... 516 349-8010
Plainview *(G-13625)*

ENGRAVING SVC, NEC

Aldine Inc (ny) ....D...... 212 226-2870
New York *(G-9079)*
Bates Jackson Engraving Co Inc ....E...... 716 854-3000
Buffalo *(G-2834)*
Tripi Engraving Co Inc ....E...... 718 383-6500
Brooklyn *(G-2682)*
Zan Optics Products Inc ....E...... 718 435-0533
Brooklyn *(G-2781)*

ENGRAVING SVC: Jewelry & Personal Goods

Ashburns Inc ....G...... 212 227-5692
New York *(G-9227)*
Eastern Silver of Boro Park ....G...... 718 854-5600
Brooklyn *(G-1899)*
Rayana Designs Inc ....E...... 718 786-2040
Long Island City *(G-7859)*
Ter-El Engraving Co Inc ....G...... 315 455-5597
Syracuse *(G-16056)*

ENGRAVING SVCS

C & H Cstm Bkbinding Embossing .....G...... 800 871-8980
Medford *(G-8237)*
Loremanss Embroidery Engrav ....F...... 518 834-9205
Keeseville *(G-7139)*
Mooney-Keehley Inc ....G...... 585 271-1573
Rochester *(G-14521)*

ENGRAVING: Steel line, For The Printing Trade

Lgn Materials & Solutions ....F...... 888 414-0005
Mount Vernon *(G-8701)*

ENGRAVINGS: Plastic

Custom House Engravers Inc ....G...... 631 567-3004
Bohemia *(G-1046)*

ENTERTAINERS & ENTERTAINMENT GROUPS

Comsec Ventures International ....G...... 518 523-1600
Lake Placid *(G-7273)*
G Schirmer Inc ....G...... 212 254-2100
New York *(G-10232)*
Tele-Pak Inc ....E...... 845 426-2300
Monsey *(G-8585)*

ENTERTAINMENT SVCS

Marvel Entertainment LLC ....C...... 212 576-4000
New York *(G-11170)*
Musical Links Production LLC ....E...... 516 996-1522
Valley Stream *(G-16414)*

ENVELOPES

Apec Paper Industries Ltd ....G...... 212 730-0088
New York *(G-9172)*
Buffalo Envelope Inc ....F...... 716 686-0100
Depew *(G-4249)*
Cambridge-Pacific Inc ....E...... 518 677-5988
Cambridge *(G-3305)*
Cenveo Inc ....D...... 716 662-2800
Orchard Park *(G-13260)*
Cenveo Inc ....F...... 716 686-0100
Depew *(G-4252)*
Conformer Products Inc ....F...... 516 504-6300
Great Neck *(G-5800)*
CPW Direct Mail Group LLC ....E...... 631 588-6565
Farmingdale *(G-4964)*
East Cast Envlope Graphics LLC ....E...... 718 326-2424
Maspeth *(G-8135)*
Jacmax Industries LLC ....E...... 718 439-3743
Brooklyn *(G-2130)*
Kleer-Fax Inc ....D...... 631 225-1100
Amityville *(G-303)*
Mercury Envelope Co Inc ....D...... 516 678-6744
Rockville Centre *(G-14795)*
Old Ue LLC ....E...... 718 707-0700
Long Island City *(G-7829)*
Poly-Pak Industries Inc ....B...... 631 293-6767
Melville *(G-8348)*
Premier Packaging Corporation ....E...... 585 924-8460
Victor *(G-16496)*
Rochester 100 Inc ....C...... 585 475-0200
Rochester *(G-14633)*
Westrock Mwv LLC ....C...... 212 688-5000
New York *(G-12618)*
X-L Envelope and Printing Inc ....F...... 716 852-2135
Buffalo *(G-3258)*

ENVELOPES WHOLESALERS

A C Envelope Inc ....G...... 516 420-0646
Farmingdale *(G-4926)*
Apec Paper Industries Ltd ....G...... 212 730-0088
New York *(G-9172)*
Buffalo Envelope Inc ....F...... 716 686-0100
Depew *(G-4249)*
Diversified Envelope Ltd ....F...... 585 615-4697
Rochester *(G-14312)*
Matt Industries Inc ....C...... 315 472-1316
Syracuse *(G-15984)*
Prestige Envelope & Lithograph ....F...... 631 521-7043
Merrick *(G-8391)*

ENVIRONMENTAL QUALITY PROGS ADMIN, GOVT: Waste Management

City of New York ....C...... 718 236-2693
Brooklyn *(G-1783)*

PRODUCT SECTION

FABRICS: Apparel & Outerwear, Cotton

ENZYMES
D-Best Equipment Corp .... E 516 358-0965
  West Hempstead (G-16852)
Zymtrnix Catalytic Systems Inc .... G 918 694-8206
  Ithaca (G-6886)

EPOXY RESINS
American Epoxy and Metal Inc .... G 718 828-7828
  Scarsdale (G-15216)
Astro Chemical Company Inc .... E 518 399-5338
  Ballston Lake (G-579)
John C Dolph Company Inc .... E 732 329-2333
  Schenectady (G-15271)

EQUIPMENT: Pedestrian Traffic Control
Cq Traffic Control Devices LLC .... G 518 767-0057
  Selkirk (G-15354)

EQUIPMENT: Rental & Leasing, NEC
Beck Vault Company .... G 315 337-7590
  Rome (G-14806)
G E Inspection Technologies LP .... C 315 554-2000
  Skaneateles (G-15460)
Millennium Stl Rack Rntals Inc .... G 212 594-2190
  Brooklyn (G-2316)
Mobile Mini Inc .... F 315 732-4555
  Utica (G-16349)
Raymond Corporation .... A 607 656-2311
  Greene (G-5869)
Raymond Corporation .... E 315 643-5000
  East Syracuse (G-4557)

ERASERS: Rubber Or Rubber & Abrasive Combined
Eraser Company Inc .... C 315 454-3237
  Mattydale (G-8212)

ESCALATORS: Passenger & Freight
Allround Logistics Inc .... G 718 544-8945
  Forest Hills (G-5321)

ETCHING & ENGRAVING SVC
Accurate Pnt Powdr Coating Inc .... F 585 235-1650
  Rochester (G-14167)
Advanced Coating Service LLC .... G 585 247-3970
  Rochester (G-14176)
Ascribe Inc .... E 585 413-0298
  Rochester (G-14216)
Custom House Engravers Inc .... G 631 567-3004
  Bohemia (G-1046)
Custom Laser Inc .... E 716 434-8600
  Lockport (G-7578)
Everlasting Images .... G 607 785-8743
  Endicott (G-4806)
Precision Laser Technology LLC .... F 585 458-6208
  Rochester (G-14594)
Steel Partners Holdings LP .... E 212 520-2300
  New York (G-12189)
Stuart-Dean Co Inc .... F 718 472-1326
  Long Island City (G-7894)

ETCHING SVC: Metal
Jamestown Bronze Works Inc .... G 716 665-2302
  Jamestown (G-7006)

ETCHING SVC: Photochemical
Newchem Inc .... E 315 331-7680
  Newark (G-12738)

ETHANOLAMINES
Western New York Energy LLC .... E 585 798-9693
  Medina (G-8284)

ETHYLENE-PROPYLENE RUBBERS: EPDM Polymers
Hilord Chemical Corporation .... E 631 234-7373
  Hauppauge (G-6094)

EXCAVATING EQPT
Kinshofer Usa Inc .... F 716 731-4333
  Sanborn (G-15123)

EXPANSION JOINTS: Rubber
Mercer Rubber Co .... C 631 348-0282
  Hauppauge (G-6132)

EXPLORATION, METAL MINING
Hi-Temp Specialty Metals Inc .... F 631 775-8750
  Yaphank (G-17395)

EXPLOSIVES
Dyno Nobel Inc .... D 845 338-2144
  Ulster Park (G-16285)
Maxam North America Inc .... G 313 322-8651
  Ogdensburg (G-13118)

EXPLOSIVES, EXC AMMO & FIREWORKS WHOLESALERS
Island Ordnance Systems LLC .... F 516 746-2100
  Mineola (G-8518)
Maxam North America Inc .... G 313 322-8651
  Ogdensburg (G-13118)

EXTENSION CORDS
Ncc Ny LLC .... E 718 943-7000
  Brooklyn (G-2355)

EXTRACTS, FLAVORING
Craftmaster Flavor Technology .... F 631 789-8607
  Amityville (G-283)
Osf Flavors Inc .... F 860 298-8350
  New York (G-11531)

EXTRACTS: Dying Or Tanning, Natural
Prismatic Dyeing & Finshg Inc .... D 845 561-1800
  Newburgh (G-12775)

EYEGLASS CASES
Montana Global LLC .... G 212 213-1572
  Jamaica (G-6933)

EYEGLASSES
Colors In Optics Ltd .... D 718 845-0300
  New Hyde Park (G-8822)
Corinne McCormack Inc .... F 212 868-7919
  New York (G-9725)
Essilor Laboratories Amer Inc .... E 845 365-6700
  Orangeburg (G-13226)
Frame Works America Inc .... E 631 288-1300
  Westhampton Beach (G-17058)
Hirsch Optical Corp .... D 516 752-2211
  Farmingdale (G-5006)
Humanware USA Inc .... E 800 722-3393
  Champlain (G-3542)
Optogenics of Syracuse Inc .... D 315 446-3000
  Syracuse (G-16005)
Parker Warby Retail Inc .... E 646 517-5223
  New York (G-11575)

EYEGLASSES: Sunglasses
Xinya International Trading Co .... G 212 216-9681
  New York (G-12679)

EYES: Artificial
Mager & Gougelman Inc .... G 212 661-3939
  New York (G-11100)
Mager & Gougelman Inc .... G 212 661-3939
  Hempstead (G-6278)
Mager & Gougelman Inc .... G 516 489-0202
  Hempstead (G-6279)
Mark F Rosenhaft N A O .... G 516 374-1010
  Cedarhurst (G-3460)
Strauss Eye Prosthetics Inc .... G 585 424-1350
  Rochester (G-14705)

FABRIC FINISHING: Mending, Wool
Woolmark Americas Inc .... G 347 767-3160
  New York (G-12657)

FABRIC STORES
Creation Baumann USA Inc .... E 516 764-7431
  Rockville Centre (G-14790)
Missiontex Inc .... G 718 532-9053
  Brooklyn (G-2322)

FABRICATED METAL PRODUCTS, NEC
Albany Mtal Fbrcation Holdings .... G 518 463-5161
  Albany (G-42)
Atech-Seh Metal Fabricator .... E 716 895-8888
  Buffalo (G-2821)
Brooklyn Cstm Met Fbrction Inc .... G 718 499-1573
  Brooklyn (G-1724)
Factory East .... E 718 280-1558
  Brooklyn (G-1952)
James D Rubino Inc .... E 631 244-8730
  Bohemia (G-1080)
Kwong CHI Metal Fabrication .... G 718 369-6429
  Brooklyn (G-2184)
PBL Industries Corp .... F 631 979-4266
  Smithtown (G-15493)
Range Repair Warehouse .... G 585 235-0980
  Penfield (G-13502)
Total Metal Resource .... F 718 384-7818
  Brooklyn (G-2669)

FABRICS & CLOTH: Quilted
American Country Quilts & Lin .... G 631 283-5466
  Southampton (G-15538)
Pink Inc .... E 212 352-8282
  New York (G-11663)

FABRICS: Apparel & Outerwear, Broadwoven
Eldeen Clothing Inc .... F 212 719-9190
  New York (G-9994)
Equissentials LLC .... G 607 432-2856
  Oneonta (G-13185)
Interaxissourcingcom Inc .... E 212 905-6001
  New York (G-10623)
Light House Hill Marketing .... G 212 354-1338
  New York (G-10990)
Nazim Izzak Inc .... G 212 920-5546
  Long Island City (G-7821)
Oakhurst Partners LLC .... G 212 502-3220
  New York (G-11490)
Pinder International Inc .... G 631 273-0324
  Hauppauge (G-6164)
Yarnz International Inc .... G 212 868-5883
  New York (G-12689)

FABRICS: Apparel & Outerwear, Cotton
A and J Apparel Corp .... G 212 398-8899
  New York (G-8983)
A3 Apparel LLC .... G 888 403-9669
  New York (G-8997)
Advanced Fashions Technology .... G 212 221-0606
  New York (G-9044)
Bandier Corp .... F 212 242-5400
  New York (G-9313)
Basileus Company LLC .... F 315 963-3516
  Manlius (G-8067)
Benartex Inc .... E 212 840-3250
  New York (G-9357)
Bill Blass Group LLC .... F 212 689-8957
  New York (G-9396)
Charming Fashion Inc .... G 212 730-2872
  New York (G-9584)
Creation Baumann USA Inc .... E 516 764-7431
  Rockville Centre (G-14790)
Equipment Apparel LLC .... D 212 502-1890
  New York (G-10053)
Hanesbrands Inc .... G 212 576-9300
  New York (G-10406)
Harley Robert D Company Ltd .... G 212 947-1872
  New York (G-10413)
Hmx LLC .... D 212 682-9073
  New York (G-10490)
Horizon Apparel Mfg Inc .... G 516 361-4878
  Atlantic Beach (G-469)
Internationl Studios Inc .... G 212 819-1616
  New York (G-10638)
Knightly Endeavors .... F 845 340-0949
  Kingston (G-7194)
Magic Brands International LLC .... F 212 563-4999
  New York (G-11103)
Min Run (usa) Inc .... G 646 331-1018
  Port Washington (G-13845)
Obvious Inc .... E 212 278-0007
  New York (G-11492)
Phoenix Usa LLC .... G 646 351-6598
  New York (G-11652)
Refuel Inc .... G 917 645-2974
  New York (G-11818)

Employee Codes: A=Over 500 employees, B=251-500
C=101-250, D=51-100, E=20-50, F=10-19, G=5-9

FABRICS: Apparel & Outerwear, Cotton

Shahin Designs Ltd .... G 212 737-7225
  New York *(G-12039)*
US Design Group Ltd .... F 212 354-4070
  New York *(G-12485)*

FABRICS: Apparel & Outerwear, From Manmade Fiber Or Silk

Concepts Nyc Inc .... E 212 244-1033
  New York *(G-9693)*
JM Manufacturer Inc .... G 212 869-0626
  New York *(G-10742)*
New York Poplin LLC .... G 718 768-3296
  Brooklyn *(G-2366)*

FABRICS: Bags & Bagging, Cotton

Nochairs Inc .... G 917 748-8731
  New York *(G-11449)*

FABRICS: Bonded-Fiber, Exc Felt

Imperial Laminators Co Inc .... F 718 272-9500
  Brooklyn *(G-2098)*

FABRICS: Broad Woven, Goods, Cotton

Beyond Loom Inc .... G 212 575-3100
  New York *(G-9383)*
Gerli & Co Inc .... E 212 213-1919
  New York *(G-10286)*
Lydall Performance Mtl Inc .... C 518 273-6320
  Green Island *(G-5859)*

FABRICS: Broadwoven, Cotton

Ann Gish Inc .... G 212 969-9200
  New York *(G-9163)*
Joy of Learning .... G 718 443-6463
  Brooklyn *(G-2152)*
Marsha Fleisher .... F 845 679-6500
  Woodstock *(G-17364)*
Meder Textile Co Inc .... G 516 883-0409
  Port Washington *(G-13840)*
Scalamandre Wallpaper Inc .... B 631 467-8800
  Hauppauge *(G-6185)*
Westpoint Home LLC .... A 212 930-2074
  New York *(G-12615)*
Westpoint International Inc .... F 212 930-2044
  New York *(G-12616)*

FABRICS: Broadwoven, Synthetic Manmade Fiber & Silk

Ann Gish Inc .... G 212 969-9200
  New York *(G-9163)*
Apex Texicon Inc .... E 516 239-4400
  New York *(G-9173)*
Creation Baumann USA Inc .... E 516 764-7431
  Rockville Centre *(G-14790)*
Eastern Silk Mills Inc .... G 212 730-1300
  New York *(G-9966)*
Fabric Resources Intl Ltd .... F 516 829-4550
  Great Neck *(G-5810)*
Fibrix LLC .... E 716 683-4100
  Depew *(G-4257)*
Gerli & Co Inc .... E 212 213-1919
  New York *(G-10286)*
Ivi Services Inc .... D 607 729-5111
  Binghamton *(G-929)*
Jag Manufacturing Inc .... E 518 762-9558
  Johnstown *(G-7116)*
Jakob Schlaepfer Inc .... G 212 221-2323
  New York *(G-10696)*
Scalamandre Wallpaper Inc .... B 631 467-8800
  Hauppauge *(G-6185)*
Springfield LLC .... E 516 861-6250
  Jericho *(G-7089)*
Superior Fiber Mills Inc .... E 718 782-7500
  Brooklyn *(G-2628)*
Toltec Fabrics Inc .... C 212 706-9310
  New York *(G-12358)*
Toray Industries Inc .... G 212 697-8150
  New York *(G-12373)*

FABRICS: Broadwoven, Wool

Acker & LI Mills Corporation .... G 212 307-7247
  New York *(G-9017)*
Citisource Industries Inc .... E 212 683-1033
  New York *(G-9625)*

Fabric Resources Intl Ltd .... F 516 829-4550
  Great Neck *(G-5810)*
Hawkins Fabrics Inc .... E 518 773-9550
  Gloversville *(G-5714)*
Scalamandre Wallpaper Inc .... B 631 467-8800
  Hauppauge *(G-6185)*

FABRICS: Brocade, Cotton

La Lame Inc .... G 212 921-9770
  New York *(G-10909)*

FABRICS: Canvas

Geordie Magee Uphl & Canvas .... G 315 676-7679
  Brewerton *(G-1203)*
Sita Finishing Inc .... F 718 417-5295
  Brooklyn *(G-2567)*
Taikoh USA Inc .... F 646 556-6652
  New York *(G-12273)*

FABRICS: Card Roll, Cotton

Alessi International Limited .... F 516 676-8841
  Glen Cove *(G-5609)*

FABRICS: Chemically Coated & Treated

Kiltronx Enviro Systems LLC .... E 239 273-8870
  New York *(G-10844)*
Perry Plastics Inc .... F 718 747-5600
  Flushing *(G-5281)*

FABRICS: Coated Or Treated

Breton Industries Inc .... D 518 842-3030
  Amsterdam *(G-336)*
Chemprene Inc .... C 845 831-2800
  Beacon *(G-782)*
Chemprene Holding Inc .... C 845 831-2800
  Beacon *(G-783)*
Comfort Care Textiles Inc .... G 631 543-0531
  Commack *(G-3828)*
Eurotex Inc .... F 716 205-8861
  Niagara Falls *(G-12816)*
Fabric Resources Intl Ltd .... F 516 829-4550
  Great Neck *(G-5810)*
Newtex Industries Inc .... E 585 924-9135
  Victor *(G-16493)*
Precision Cstm Coatings I LLC .... C 212 868-5770
  New York *(G-11695)*

FABRICS: Corduroys, Cotton

Paramount Cord & Brackets .... G 212 325-9100
  White Plains *(G-17144)*

FABRICS: Denims

AV Denim Inc .... E 212 764-6668
  New York *(G-9270)*
Axis Na LLC .... F 212 840-4005
  New York *(G-9284)*
Brooklyn Denim Co .... F 718 782-2600
  Brooklyn *(G-1725)*
Jrg Apparel Group Company Ltd .... G 212 997-0900
  New York *(G-10775)*
SD Eagle Global Inc .... G 516 822-1778
  Jericho *(G-7086)*
Xing Lin USA Intl Corp .... G 212 947-4846
  New York *(G-12678)*

FABRICS: Elastic, From Manmade Fiber Or Silk

A B C Elastic Corp .... G 718 388-2953
  Brooklyn *(G-1531)*

FABRICS: Fiberglass, Broadwoven

Fiber Glass Industries Inc .... D 518 842-4000
  Amsterdam *(G-345)*
Fiber Glass Industries Inc .... D 518 843-3533
  Amsterdam *(G-346)*
Newtex Industries Inc .... E 585 924-9135
  Victor *(G-16493)*
Polytex Inc .... D 716 549-5100
  Angola *(G-381)*

FABRICS: Glass, Narrow

Mergence Studios Ltd .... F 212 288-5616
  Hauppauge *(G-6133)*

FABRICS: Glove, Lining

J & M Textile Co Inc .... F 212 268-8000
  New York *(G-10674)*

FABRICS: Hand Woven

Thistle Hill Weavers .... G 518 284-2729
  Cherry Valley *(G-3597)*

FABRICS: Handkerchief, Cotton

Northpoint Trading Inc .... F 212 481-8001
  New York *(G-11460)*

FABRICS: Jacquard Woven, From Manmade Fiber Or Silk

Simplicity Creative Group Inc .... A 212 686-7676
  New York *(G-12082)*

FABRICS: Jean

Apollo Apparel Group LLC .... F 212 398-6585
  New York *(G-9175)*

FABRICS: Jersey Cloth

Cap USA Jerseyman Harlem Inc .... G 212 222-7942
  New York *(G-9517)*

FABRICS: Lace & Decorative Trim, Narrow

Eiseman-Ludmar Co Inc .... F 516 932-6990
  Hicksville *(G-6343)*

FABRICS: Lace & Lace Prdts

Orbit Industries LLC .... F 914 244-1500
  Mount Kisco *(G-8638)*
Solstiss Inc .... G 212 719-9194
  New York *(G-12127)*
Super-Trim Inc .... E 212 255-2370
  New York *(G-12241)*

FABRICS: Lace, Knit, NEC

Hosel & Ackerson Inc .... G 212 575-1490
  New York *(G-10509)*
Klauber Brothers Inc .... E 212 686-2531
  New York *(G-10859)*

FABRICS: Laminated

A-One Laminating Corp .... G 718 266-6002
  Brooklyn *(G-1540)*
A-One Moving & Storage Inc .... E 718 266-6002
  Brooklyn *(G-1541)*
Co2 Textiles LLC .... G 212 269-2222
  New York *(G-9650)*
Imperial Laminators Co Inc .... F 718 272-9500
  Brooklyn *(G-2098)*
New York Cutting & Gumming Co .... E 212 563-4146
  Middletown *(G-8454)*
Tpi Industries LLC .... E 845 692-2820
  Middletown *(G-8465)*

FABRICS: Linings & Interlinings, Cotton

Navas Designs Inc .... E 818 988-9050
  New York *(G-11359)*

FABRICS: Long Cloth, Cotton

Haleys Comet Seafood Corp .... E 212 571-1828
  New York *(G-10397)*

FABRICS: Nonwoven

Albany International Corp .... C 518 445-2200
  Rensselaer *(G-14042)*
Fabrication Enterprises Inc .... E 914 591-9300
  Elmsford *(G-4753)*
Legendary Auto Interiors Ltd .... E 315 331-1212
  Newark *(G-12734)*
Mgk Group Inc .... E 212 989-2732
  New York *(G-11246)*
Saint-Gobain Adfors Amer Inc .... D 716 775-3900
  Grand Island *(G-5768)*
Saint-Gobain Adfors Amer Inc .... D 585 589-4401
  Albion *(G-170)*

PRODUCT SECTION

FABRICS: Woven, Narrow Cotton, Wool, Silk

FABRICS: Nylon, Broadwoven
Kragel Co Inc .... G 716 648-1344
  Hamburg *(G-5932)*

FABRICS: Paper, Broadwoven
Albany International Corp .... C 518 445-2200
  Rensselaer *(G-14042)*

FABRICS: Pile Warp or Flat Knit
George Knitting Mills Corp .... G 212 242-3300
  New York *(G-10282)*

FABRICS: Pile, Circular Knit
Hill Knitting Mills Inc .... E 718 846-5000
  Richmond Hill *(G-14075)*

FABRICS: Pocketing Twill, Cotton
Cai Inc .... G 212 819-0008
  New York *(G-9497)*

FABRICS: Print, Cotton
Neilson International Inc .... G 631 454-0400
  Farmingdale *(G-5064)*
Perfect Print Inc .... E 718 832-5280
  Brooklyn *(G-2417)*

FABRICS: Resin Or Plastic Coated
GE Polymershapes .... F 516 433-4092
  Hicksville *(G-6347)*
Piedmont Plastics Inc .... G 518 724-0563
  Albany *(G-121)*
Tonoga Inc .... C 518 658-3202
  Petersburg *(G-13528)*

FABRICS: Rubberized
Chemprene Inc .... C 845 831-2800
  Beacon *(G-782)*
Chemprene Holding Inc .... C 845 831-2800
  Beacon *(G-783)*
Kelson Products Inc .... G 716 825-2585
  Orchard Park *(G-13277)*

FABRICS: Satin
Scent-Sation Inc .... D 718 672-4300
  Queens Village *(G-13983)*

FABRICS: Shirting, Cotton
Gotham T-Shirt Corp .... G 516 676-0900
  Sea Cliff *(G-15341)*
L Allmeier .... G 212 243-7390
  New York *(G-10900)*

FABRICS: Shoe
Avitto Leather Goods Inc .... G 212 219-7501
  New York *(G-9279)*

FABRICS: Silk, Broadwoven
Beyond Loom Inc .... G 212 575-3100
  New York *(G-9383)*
Himatsingka America Inc .... E 212 252-0802
  New York *(G-10479)*
Himatsingka Holdings NA Inc .... G 212 545-8929
  New York *(G-10480)*

FABRICS: Silk, Narrow
Solstiss Inc .... G 212 719-9194
  New York *(G-12127)*

FABRICS: Spandex, Broadwoven
La Lame Inc .... G 212 921-9770
  New York *(G-10909)*

FABRICS: Specialty Including Twisted Weaves, Broadwoven
Intertex USA Inc .... F 212 279-3601
  New York *(G-10641)*

FABRICS: Stretch, Cotton
Shindo Usa Inc .... G 212 868-9311
  New York *(G-12051)*

FABRICS: Surgical Fabrics, Cotton
Medline Industries Inc .... B 845 344-3301
  Middletown *(G-8450)*

FABRICS: Tapestry, Cotton
Renaissnce Crpt Tapestries Inc .... F 212 696-0080
  New York *(G-11831)*

FABRICS: Tricot
Hudson Fabrics LLC .... F 518 671-6100
  Hudson *(G-6617)*
Litchfield Fabrics of NC .... G 518 773-9500
  Gloversville *(G-5717)*
Veratex Inc .... F 212 683-9300
  New York *(G-12520)*

FABRICS: Trimmings
Albert Siy .... G 718 359-0389
  Flushing *(G-5224)*
American Spray-On Corp .... E 212 929-2100
  New York *(G-9128)*
Angel Textiles Inc .... G 212 532-0900
  New York *(G-9156)*
Athletic Cap Co Inc .... E 718 398-1300
  Staten Island *(G-15641)*
Barnaby Prints Inc .... F 845 477-2501
  Greenwood Lake *(G-5896)*
Bondy Printing Corp .... G 631 242-1510
  Bay Shore *(G-679)*
C H Thompson Company Inc .... D 607 724-1094
  Binghamton *(G-901)*
Coe Displays Inc .... G 718 937-5658
  Long Island City *(G-7702)*
Cooper & Clement Inc .... E 315 454-8135
  Syracuse *(G-15907)*
D & R Silk Screening Ltd .... F 631 234-7464
  Central Islip *(G-3494)*
Decal Makers Inc .... E 516 221-7200
  Bellmore *(G-817)*
Eagle Lace Dyeing Corp .... F 212 947-2712
  New York *(G-9958)*
Emtron Hybrids Inc .... E 631 924-9668
  Yaphank *(G-17392)*
Flp Group LLC .... F 315 252-7583
  Auburn *(G-496)*
Freeport Screen & Stamping .... E 516 379-0330
  Freeport *(G-5401)*
Ihd Motorsports LLC .... F 979 690-1669
  Binghamton *(G-925)*
Jack J Florio Jr .... G 716 434-9123
  Lockport *(G-7595)*
Kenmar Shirts Inc .... E 718 824-3880
  Bronx *(G-1371)*
L I C Screen Printing Inc .... E 516 546-7289
  Merrick *(G-8387)*
Loremanss Embroidery Engrav .... F 518 834-9205
  Keeseville *(G-7139)*
Master Craft Finishers Inc .... E 631 586-0540
  Deer Park *(G-4171)*
Master Image Printing Inc .... G 914 347-4400
  Elmsford *(G-4763)*
New York Binding Co Inc .... E 718 729-2454
  Long Island City *(G-7825)*
Northeast Stitches & Ink Inc .... E 518 798-5549
  South Glens Falls *(G-15528)*
Round Top Knit & Screening .... G 518 622-3600
  Round Top *(G-15040)*
Sellco Industries Inc .... E 607 756-7594
  Cortland *(G-4045)*
Simplicity Creative Group Inc .... A 212 686-7676
  New York *(G-12082)*
Solidus Industries Inc .... D 607 749-4540
  Homer *(G-6522)*
Todd Walbridge .... G 585 254-3018
  Rochester *(G-14727)*
U All Inc .... E 518 438-2558
  Albany *(G-144)*
Zan Optics Products Inc .... E 718 435-0533
  Brooklyn *(G-2781)*

FABRICS: Trimmings, Textile
American Trim Mfg Inc .... E 518 239-8951
  Durham *(G-4355)*
Bardwil Industries Inc .... G 212 944-1870
  New York *(G-9317)*
Champion Zipper Corp .... G 212 239-0414
  New York *(G-9576)*
Danray Textiles Corp .... F 212 354-5213
  New York *(G-9807)*
Jakob Schlaepfer Inc .... G 212 221-2323
  New York *(G-10696)*
Marketing Action Xecutives Inc .... G 212 971-9155
  New York *(G-11159)*
New Classic Trade Inc .... G 347 822-9052
  Jamaica *(G-6934)*
Scalamandre Silks Inc .... D 212 980-3888
  New York *(G-11982)*
Tamber Knits Inc .... E 212 730-1121
  New York *(G-12275)*

FABRICS: Upholstery, Cotton
Mgk Group Inc .... E 212 989-2732
  New York *(G-11246)*
N Y Contract Seating Inc .... G 718 417-9298
  Maspeth *(G-8152)*

FABRICS: Varnished Glass & Coated Fiberglass
Architectural Fiberglass Corp .... E 631 842-4772
  Copiague *(G-3892)*

FABRICS: Wall Covering, From Manmade Fiber Or Silk
Art People Inc .... G 212 431-4865
  New York *(G-9212)*
Judscott Handprints Ltd .... F 914 347-5515
  Elmsford *(G-4759)*
Mgk Group Inc .... E 212 989-2732
  New York *(G-11246)*
National Contract Industries .... G 212 249-0045
  New York *(G-11347)*

FABRICS: Warp & Flat Knit Prdts
Fab Industries Corp .... E 516 498-3200
  Great Neck *(G-5809)*
Gehring Tricot Corporation .... C 315 429-8551
  Dolgeville *(G-4305)*

FABRICS: Warp Knit, Lace & Netting
Apex Aridyne Corp .... G 516 239-4400
  Inwood *(G-6750)*
Binghamton Knitting Co Inc .... E 607 722-6941
  Binghamton *(G-892)*
Helmont Mills Inc .... G 518 568-7913
  Saint Johnsville *(G-15095)*
Ipm US Inc .... G 212 481-7967
  New York *(G-10655)*
Mohawk Fabric Company Inc .... F 518 842-3090
  Amsterdam *(G-358)*
Somerset Industries Inc .... E 518 773-7383
  Gloversville *(G-5721)*
Sunwin Global Industry Inc .... G 646 370-6196
  New York *(G-12239)*
Thompson Packaging Novlt Inc .... G 212 686-4242
  New York *(G-12327)*

FABRICS: Weft Or Circular Knit
Apex Aridyne Corp .... G 516 239-4400
  Inwood *(G-6750)*
Apex Texicon Inc .... G 516 239-4400
  New York *(G-9173)*
Lemral Knitwear Inc .... D 718 210-0175
  Brooklyn *(G-2210)*
Lifestyle Design Usa Ltd .... G 212 279-9400
  New York *(G-10988)*
S & W Knitting Mills Inc .... E 718 237-2416
  Brooklyn *(G-2524)*

FABRICS: Woven Wire, Made From Purchased Wire
Trimtec Inc .... G 516 783-5428
  Seaford *(G-15347)*

FABRICS: Woven, Narrow Cotton, Wool, Silk
Albany International Corp .... C 518 445-2200
  Rensselaer *(G-14042)*
American Canvas Binders Corp .... G 914 969-0300
  Yonkers *(G-17413)*
Breton Industries Inc .... D 518 842-3030
  Amsterdam *(G-336)*

FABRICS: Woven, Narrow Cotton, Wool, Silk — PRODUCT SECTION

Depot Label Company Inc ....G 631 467-2952
  Patchogue *(G-13418)*
Labeltex Mills Inc ....G 212 279-6165
  New York *(G-10913)*
Newtex Industries Inc ....E 585 924-9135
  Victor *(G-16493)*
Schoen Trimming & Cord Co Inc ....F 212 255-3949
  New York *(G-11996)*
Simplicity Creative Group Inc ....A 212 686-7676
  New York *(G-12082)*
Skil-Care Corporation ....C 914 963-2040
  Yonkers *(G-17484)*
Valley Industrial Products Inc ....E 631 385-9300
  Huntington *(G-6689)*

FACILITIES SUPPORT SVCS

Johnson Controls Inc ....C 585 724-2232
  Rochester *(G-14464)*

FACSIMILE COMMUNICATION EQPT

Alternative Technology Corp ....G 914 478-5900
  Hastings On Hudson *(G-6002)*

FAMILY CLOTHING STORES

Kate Spade & Company ....B 212 354-4900
  New York *(G-10816)*
Land n Sea Inc ....D 212 703-2980
  New York *(G-10923)*
Missiontex Inc ....G 718 532-9053
  Brooklyn *(G-2322)*
Ramsbury Property Us Inc ....F 212 223-6250
  New York *(G-11796)*
Round Top Knit & Screening ....G 518 622-3600
  Round Top *(G-15040)*
S & T Knitting Co Inc ....E 607 722-7558
  Conklin *(G-3874)*

FANS, BLOWING: Indl Or Commercial

Apgn Inc ....F 518 324-4150
  Plattsburgh *(G-13651)*
Canarm Ltd ....G 800 267-4427
  Ogdensburg *(G-13113)*
Oestreich Metal Works Inc ....G 315 463-4268
  Syracuse *(G-16002)*
Rapid Fan & Blower Inc ....F 718 786-2060
  Long Island City *(G-7857)*

FANS, EXHAUST: Indl Or Commercial

Howden North America Inc ....D 803 741-2700
  Depew *(G-4259)*

FANS, VENTILATING: Indl Or Commercial

Brodco Inc ....E 631 842-4477
  Lido Beach *(G-7440)*
Howden North America Inc ....D 716 817-6900
  Depew *(G-4260)*

FARM & GARDEN MACHINERY WHOLESALERS

Oxbo International Corporation ....D 585 548-2665
  Byron *(G-3269)*
Saxby Implement Corp ....F 585 624-2938
  Mendon *(G-8382)*

FARM PRDTS, RAW MATERIALS, WHOLESALE: Bristles

Cenibra Inc ....G 212 818-8242
  New York *(G-9561)*

FARM PRDTS, RAW MATERIALS, WHOLESALE: Hides

Hastings Hide Inc ....G 516 295-2400
  Lawrence *(G-7391)*

FARM SPLY STORES

Bailey Boonville Mills Inc ....G 315 942-2131
  Boonville *(G-1162)*
Gramco Inc ....G 716 592-2845
  Springville *(G-15611)*
Lowville Farmers Coop Inc ....E 315 376-6587
  Lowville *(G-7939)*

FASTENERS: Metal

John Hassall LLC ....D 516 334-6200
  Westbury *(G-16998)*
Pmb Precision Products Inc ....F 631 491-6753
  North Babylon *(G-12902)*
Universal Metals Inc ....G 516 829-0896
  Great Neck *(G-5847)*

FASTENERS: Metal

D Best Service Co Inc ....G 718 972-6133
  Brooklyn *(G-1829)*
Dfci Solutions Inc ....E 631 669-0494
  West Islip *(G-16904)*
Southco Inc ....B 585 624-2545
  Honeoye Falls *(G-6537)*

FASTENERS: Notions, NEC

American Pride Fasteners LLC ....E 631 940-8292
  Bay Shore *(G-670)*
CPI of Falconer Inc ....G 716 664-4444
  Falconer *(G-4894)*
Cw Fasteners & Zippers Corp ....F 212 594-3203
  New York *(G-9774)*
Fasteners Depot LLC ....F 718 622-4222
  Brooklyn *(G-1960)*
Jem Threading Specialties Inc ....G 718 665-3341
  Bronx *(G-1365)*
Kenwin Sales Corp ....G 516 933-7553
  Westbury *(G-17003)*

FASTENERS: Notions, Snaps

M H Stryke Co Inc ....F 631 242-2660
  Deer Park *(G-4169)*
Rings Wire Inc ....G 212 741-9779
  New York *(G-11874)*

FASTENERS: Notions, Zippers

Catame Inc ....F 213 749-2610
  New York *(G-9546)*
Champion Zipper Corp ....G 212 239-0414
  New York *(G-9576)*
Riri USA Inc ....G 212 268-3866
  New York *(G-11877)*

FAUCETS & SPIGOTS: Metal & Plastic

Giagni Enterprises LLC ....G 914 699-6500
  Mount Vernon *(G-8684)*
Giagni International Corp ....G 914 699-6500
  Mount Vernon *(G-8685)*
Hanco Metal Products Inc ....F 212 787-5992
  Brooklyn *(G-2066)*
I W Industries Inc ....C 631 293-9494
  Melville *(G-8330)*

FEATHERS: Renovating

Eser Realty Corp ....E 718 383-0565
  Brooklyn *(G-1934)*

FELT: Acoustic

Ghani Textiles Inc ....G 718 859-4561
  Brooklyn *(G-2023)*
Soundcoat Company Inc ....D 631 242-2200
  Deer Park *(G-4212)*

FENCE POSTS: Iron & Steel

Bonura and Sons Iron Works ....F 718 381-4100
  Franklin Square *(G-5361)*

FENCES & FENCING MATERIALS

Rose Fence Inc ....E 516 223-0777
  Freeport *(G-5423)*
Rose Fence Inc ....D 516 790-2308
  Halesite *(G-5906)*
Sunward Electronics Inc ....F 518 687-0030
  Troy *(G-16257)*

FENCES OR POSTS: Ornamental Iron Or Steel

786 Iron Works Corp ....G 718 418-4808
  Brooklyn *(G-1522)*
Fence Plaza Corp ....G 718 469-2200
  Brooklyn *(G-1966)*
Jamaica Iron Works Inc ....F 718 657-4849
  Jamaica *(G-6923)*
McAllisters Precision Wldg Inc ....F 518 221-3455
  Menands *(G-8374)*
Ourem Iron Works Inc ....F 914 476-4856
  Yonkers *(G-17473)*
Tee Pee Fence and Railing ....F 718 658-8323
  Jamaica *(G-6957)*
Triple H Construction Inc ....E 516 280-8252
  East Meadow *(G-4428)*

FENCING DEALERS

A & T Iron Works Inc ....E 914 632-8992
  New Rochelle *(G-8883)*
Fence Plaza Corp ....G 718 469-2200
  Brooklyn *(G-1966)*
Long Lumber and Supply Corp ....F 518 439-1661
  Slingerlands *(G-15477)*
Rose Fence Inc ....F 516 223-0777
  Baldwin *(G-561)*
Walpole Woodworkers Inc ....G 631 726-2859
  Water Mill *(G-16606)*

FENCING MATERIALS: Docks & Other Outdoor Prdts, Wood

Atlas Fence & Railing Co Inc ....E 718 767-2200
  Whitestone *(G-17201)*
Cffco USA Inc ....G 718 747-1118
  Jericho *(G-7061)*
Di Vico Craft Products Ltd ....G 845 265-9390
  Cold Spring *(G-3762)*

FENCING MATERIALS: Plastic

Amadeo Serrano ....G 516 608-8359
  Freeport *(G-5386)*
Atlas Fence & Railing Co Inc ....E 718 767-2200
  Whitestone *(G-17201)*
Benners Gardens LLC ....F 518 828-1055
  Hudson *(G-6609)*
Oneonta Fence ....G 607 433-6707
  Oneonta *(G-13190)*

FENCING MATERIALS: Wood

Interstate Wood Products Inc ....E 631 842-4488
  Amityville *(G-296)*
Long Lumber and Supply Corp ....F 518 439-1661
  Slingerlands *(G-15477)*
Rose Fence Inc ....F 516 223-0777
  Baldwin *(G-561)*
Walpole Woodworkers Inc ....G 631 726-2859
  Water Mill *(G-16606)*

FENCING: Chain Link

Master-Halco Inc ....F 631 585-8150
  Ronkonkoma *(G-14939)*

FERRITES

Hoosier Magnetics Inc ....D 315 393-1813
  Ogdensburg *(G-13116)*

FERROALLOYS

CCA Holding Inc ....C 716 446-8800
  Amherst *(G-230)*
Medima LLC ....C 716 741-0400
  Clarence *(G-3666)*
Thyssenkrupp Materials NA Inc ....G 212 972-8800
  New York *(G-12335)*

FERROMANGANESE, NOT MADE IN BLAST FURNACES

Globe Metallurgical Inc ....D 716 804-0862
  Niagara Falls *(G-12825)*

FERTILIZERS: NEC

Carolina Eastern-Vail Inc ....E 518 854-9785
  Salem *(G-15111)*
Commodity Resource Corporation ....F 585 538-9500
  Caledonia *(G-3278)*
Growmark Fs LLC ....F 585 538-2186
  Caledonia *(G-3279)*
Lowville Farmers Coop Inc ....E 315 376-6587
  Lowville *(G-7939)*

PRODUCT SECTION

FERTILIZERS: Nitrogenous

Agrium Advanced Tech US Inc .... F 631 286-0598
  Bohemia *(G-1009)*
Growth Products Ltd .... E 914 428-1316
  White Plains *(G-17115)*
Rt Solutions LLC .... G 585 245-3456
  Rochester *(G-14662)*

FERTILIZERS: Phosphatic

Occidental Chemical Corp .... G 716 694-3827
  North Tonawanda *(G-12984)*
Occidental Chemical Corp .... C 716 278-7794
  Niagara Falls *(G-12856)*

FIBER & FIBER PRDTS: Acrylic

Solid Surface Acrylics LLC .... F 716 743-1870
  North Tonawanda *(G-12995)*

FIBER & FIBER PRDTS: Fluorocarbon

Dynax Corporation .... G 914 764-0202
  Pound Ridge *(G-13943)*

FIBER & FIBER PRDTS: Organic, Noncellulose

Dal-Tile Corporation .... G 718 894-9574
  Maspeth *(G-8128)*
Fibrix LLC .... E 716 683-4100
  Depew *(G-4257)*
Solutia Business Entps Inc .... F 314 674-1000
  New York *(G-12128)*

FIBER & FIBER PRDTS: Polyester

Stein Fibers Ltd .... F 518 489-5700
  Albany *(G-137)*

FIBER & FIBER PRDTS: Protein

Vybion Inc .... F 607 266-0860
  Ithaca *(G-6884)*

FIBER & FIBER PRDTS: Synthetic Cellulosic

3M Company .... B 716 876-1596
  Tonawanda *(G-16132)*
Cytec Industries Inc .... D 716 372-9650
  Olean *(G-13142)*
E I Du Pont De Nemours & Co .... E 716 876-4420
  Buffalo *(G-2924)*
Solivaira Specialties Inc .... D 716 693-4009
  North Tonawanda *(G-12996)*
Solvaira Specialties Inc .... C 716 693-4040
  North Tonawanda *(G-12997)*

FIBER OPTICS

Anritsu Instruments Company .... E 315 797-4449
  Utica *(G-16307)*
Biolitec Inc .... E 413 525-0600
  New York *(G-9402)*
Photonic Controls LLC .... F 607 562-4585
  Horseheads *(G-6588)*

FIBERS: Carbon & Graphite

Metal Coated Fibers Inc .... E 518 280-8514
  Schenectady *(G-15278)*

FILLERS & SEALERS: Wood

Uc Coatings Corporation .... E 716 833-9366
  Buffalo *(G-3230)*

FILM & SHEET: Unsuppported Plastic

American Acrylic Corporation .... E 631 422-2200
  West Babylon *(G-16770)*
API Industries Inc .... B 845 365-2200
  Orangeburg *(G-13218)*
API Industries Inc .... C 845 365-2200
  Orangeburg *(G-13219)*
Berry Plastics Corporation .... B 315 986-6270
  Macedon *(G-7984)*
Comco Plastics Inc .... E 718 849-9000
  Woodhaven *(G-17305)*
D Bag Lady Inc .... E 585 425-8095
  Fairport *(G-4853)*
Ecoplast & Packaging LLC .... G 718 996-0800
  Brooklyn *(G-1901)*
Excellent Poly Inc .... F 718 768-6555
  Brooklyn *(G-1943)*
Franklin Poly Film Inc .... E 718 492-3523
  Brooklyn *(G-2002)*
Great Lakes Plastics Co Inc .... E 716 896-3100
  Buffalo *(G-2981)*
Integument Technologies Inc .... F 716 873-1199
  Tonawanda *(G-16174)*
Kent Chemical Corporation .... E 212 521-1700
  New York *(G-10838)*
Knf Clean Room Products Corp ...... E 631 588-7000
  Ronkonkoma *(G-14923)*
Msi Inc .... F 845 639-6683
  New City *(G-8788)*
Nova Packaging Ltd Inc .... E 914 232-8406
  Katonah *(G-7133)*
Oaklee International Inc .... D 631 436-7900
  Ronkonkoma *(G-14958)*
Pace Polyethylene Mfg Co Inc .... E 914 381-3000
  Harrison *(G-5988)*
Pliant LLC .... B 315 986-6286
  Macedon *(G-7990)*
R & F Boards & Dividers Inc .... G 718 331-1529
  Brooklyn *(G-2469)*
Rainbow Poly Bag Co Inc .... E 718 386-3500
  Brooklyn *(G-2476)*
Sand Hill Industries Inc .... G 518 885-7991
  Ballston Spa *(G-608)*
Scapa North America .... E 315 413-1111
  Liverpool *(G-7546)*
Swimline Corp .... E 631 254-2155
  Edgewood *(G-4613)*
Top Quality Products Inc .... G 212 213-1988
  New York *(G-12369)*
Toray Industries Inc .... G 212 697-8150
  New York *(G-12373)*
Turner Bellows Inc .... E 585 235-4456
  Rochester *(G-14735)*

FILM BASE: Cellulose Acetate Or Nitrocellulose Plastics

Bfgg Investors Group LLC .... G 585 424-3456
  Rochester *(G-14230)*
Island Pyrochemical Inds Corp .... F 516 746-2100
  Mineola *(G-8519)*

FILM PROCESSING & FINISHING LABORATORY

Toppan Printing Co Amer Inc .... E 212 975-9060
  New York *(G-12370)*

FILM: Motion Picture

Dolby Laboratories Inc .... F 212 767-1700
  New York *(G-9896)*

FILTERS

American Filtration Tech Inc .... F 585 359-4130
  West Henrietta *(G-16867)*
Burnett Process Inc .... E 585 277-1623
  Rochester *(G-14253)*
Drasgow Inc .... E 585 786-3603
  Gainesville *(G-5483)*
Foseco Inc .... F 914 345-4760
  Tarrytown *(G-16090)*
Hilliard Corporation .... B 607 733-7121
  Elmira *(G-4690)*
Hilliard Corporation .... F 607 733-7121
  Elmira *(G-4691)*
Lydall Performance Mtls Inc .... F 518 273-6320
  Green Island *(G-5860)*
Pall Corporation .... A 516 484-5400
  Port Washington *(G-13852)*
Pall Corporation .... A 607 753-6041
  Cortland *(G-4035)*
Parker-Hannifin Corporation .... D 248 628-6017
  Lancaster *(G-7330)*
Peregrine Industries Inc .... G 631 838-2870
  New York *(G-11614)*
Pyrotek Incorporated .... E 716 731-3221
  Sanborn *(G-15126)*
SC Supply Chain Management LLC ...... G 212 344-3322
  New York *(G-11981)*
Sidco Filter Corporation .... E 585 289-3100
  Manchester *(G-8053)*
Sinclair International Company .... E 518 798-2361
  Queensbury *(G-14012)*
Stavo Industries Inc .... E 845 331-5389
  Kingston *(G-7214)*

FILTERS & SOFTENERS: Water, Household

H2o Solutions Inc .... F 518 527-0915
  Stillwater *(G-15760)*
Pure Planet Waters LLC .... F 718 676-7900
  Brooklyn *(G-2458)*
Royal Prestige Lasting Co .... F 516 280-5148
  Hempstead *(G-6286)*
Water Technologies Inc .... G 315 986-0000
  Macedon *(G-7992)*

FILTERS: Air

Air Engineering Filters Inc .... G 914 238-5945
  Chappaqua *(G-3550)*
Air Export Mechanical .... G 917 709-5310
  Flushing *(G-5222)*
Air Wave Air Conditioning Co .... E 212 545-1122
  Bronx *(G-1265)*
Automotive Filters Mfg Inc .... F 631 435-1010
  Bohemia *(G-1020)*
Filta Clean Co Inc .... E 718 495-3800
  Brooklyn *(G-1970)*
Healthway Home Products Inc .... E 315 298-2904
  Pulaski *(G-13951)*
Isolation Systems Inc .... F 716 694-6390
  North Tonawanda *(G-12979)*
Nexstar Holding Corp .... G 716 929-9000
  Amherst *(G-253)*
Northland Filter Intl LLC .... E 315 207-1410
  Oswego *(G-13336)*
Pliotron Company America LLC ...... G 716 298-4457
  Niagara Falls *(G-12860)*
R P Fedder Corp .... E 585 288-1600
  Rochester *(G-14618)*
Roome Technologies Inc .... G 585 229-4437
  Honeoye *(G-6524)*

FILTERS: Air Intake, Internal Combustion Engine, Exc Auto

Modern-TEC Manufacturing Inc ...... G 716 625-8700
  Lockport *(G-7603)*
Pall Corporation .... A 516 484-5400
  Port Washington *(G-13852)*
Pall Corporation .... A 607 753-6041
  Cortland *(G-4035)*

FILTERS: General Line, Indl

Adams Sfc Inc .... E 716 877-2608
  Tonawanda *(G-16135)*
American Felt & Filter Co Inc .... D 845 561-3560
  New Windsor *(G-8931)*
Filter Tech Inc .... D 315 682-8815
  Manlius *(G-8071)*
Graver Technologies LLC .... E 585 624-1330
  Honeoye Falls *(G-6528)*
North American Filter Corp .... D 800 265-8943
  Newark *(G-12739)*
Service Filtration Corp .... E 716 877-2608
  Tonawanda *(G-16202)*
Stavo Industries Inc .... F 845 331-4552
  Kingston *(G-7213)*

FILTERS: Motor Vehicle

Automotive Filters Mfg Inc .... F 631 435-1010
  Bohemia *(G-1020)*
P & F Industries Inc .... C 631 694-9800
  Melville *(G-8346)*
Pall Corporation .... A 516 484-5400
  Port Washington *(G-13852)*
Pall Corporation .... A 607 753-6041
  Cortland *(G-4035)*

FILTRATION DEVICES: Electronic

Airsys Technologies LLC .... G 716 694-6390
  Tonawanda *(G-16136)*
Allen Avionics Inc .... E 516 248-8080
  Mineola *(G-8493)*
Fil-Coil (fc) Corp .... E 631 467-5328
  Sayville *(G-15209)*
Microwave Filter Company Inc .... E 315 438-4700
  East Syracuse *(G-4550)*
MTK Electronics Inc .... E 631 924-7666
  Medford *(G-8256)*
Pall International Corporation .... B 516 484-5400
  Port Washington *(G-13854)*

Employee Codes: A=Over 500 employees, B=251-500
C=101-250, D=51-100, E=20-50, F=10-19, G=5-9

FILTRATION DEVICES: Electronic

Pall Trinity Micro Corporation .... A 607 753-6041
  Cortland (G-4038)
Prms Inc .... G 631 851-7945
  Shirley (G-15429)
Service Filtration Corp .... E 716 877-2608
  Tonawanda (G-16202)
Tte Filters LLC .... G 716 532-2234
  Gowanda (G-5749)

FINANCIAL INVESTMENT ACTIVITIES, NEC: Financial Reporting

Dow Jones & Company Inc .... E 212 597-5983
  New York (G-9915)
Ruby Newco LLC .... G 212 852-7000
  New York (G-11933)

FINANCIAL INVESTMENT ADVICE

Bernhard Arnold & Company Inc .... G 212 907-1500
  New York (G-9367)
Envy Publishing Group Inc .... G 212 253-9874
  New York (G-10047)
Investmentwires Inc .... G 212 331-8995
  New York (G-10651)
Investors Business Daily Inc .... F 212 626-7676
  New York (G-10652)
Learnvest Inc .... E 212 675-6711
  New York (G-10949)
Moneypaper Inc .... F 914 925-0022
  Rye (G-15064)
Swaps Monitor Publications Inc .... F 212 742-8550
  New York (G-12249)

FINANCIAL SVCS

Retirement Insiders .... G 631 751-1329
  Setauket (G-15378)

FINDINGS & TRIMMINGS Fabric, NEC

Lending Trimming Co Inc .... D 212 242-7502
  New York (G-10965)

FINDINGS & TRIMMINGS Waistbands, Trouser

Cai Inc .... G 212 819-0008
  New York (G-9497)

FINDINGS & TRIMMINGS: Apparel

Eagle Finishing .... E 718 497-7875
  Brooklyn (G-1896)
Mas Cutting Inc .... G 212 869-0826
  New York (G-11173)

FINDINGS & TRIMMINGS: Fabric

Legendary Auto Interiors Ltd .... E 315 331-1212
  Newark (G-12734)

FINGERNAILS, ARTIFICIAL

Ivy Enterprises Inc .... C 516 621-9779
  Port Washington (G-13825)
Uptown Nails LLC .... C 800 748-1881
  New York (G-12477)

FINGERPRINT EQPT

Fingerprint America Inc .... G 518 435-1609
  Albany (G-80)

FINISHING AGENTS: Leather

Androme Leather Inc .... F 518 773-7945
  Gloversville (G-5706)

FIRE ARMS, SMALL: Guns Or Gun Parts, 30 mm & Below

Oriskany Arms Inc .... G 315 737-2196
  Oriskany (G-13312)

FIRE ARMS, SMALL: Pellet & BB guns

Crosman Corporation .... E 585 657-6161
  Bloomfield (G-986)
Crosman Corporation .... E 585 398-3920
  Farmington (G-5148)

FIRE ARMS, SMALL: Rifles Or Rifle Parts, 30 mm & below

Hart Rifle Barrel Inc .... G 315 677-9841
  Syracuse (G-15958)
Kyntec Corporation .... G 716 810-6956
  Buffalo (G-3038)

FIRE CONTROL OR BOMBING EQPT: Electronic

Cooper Crouse-Hinds LLC .... B 315 477-7000
  Syracuse (G-15908)

FIRE DETECTION SYSTEMS

Firecom Inc .... C 718 899-6100
  Woodside (G-17328)
Firetronics Inc .... G 516 997-5151
  Jericho (G-7069)
Zetek Corporation .... F 212 668-1485
  New York (G-12710)

FIRE ESCAPES

Jamestown Fab Stl & Sup Inc .... G 716 665-2227
  Jamestown (G-7007)

FIRE EXTINGUISHERS: Portable

Bullex Inc .... E 518 689-2023
  Albany (G-59)
Nubian Heritage .... G 631 265-3551
  Hauppauge (G-6150)
Trove Inc .... F 212 268-2046
  Brooklyn (G-2684)

FIRE OR BURGLARY RESISTIVE PRDTS

Crystalizations Systems Inc .... F 631 467-0090
  Holbrook (G-6441)
Empire Metal Finishing Inc .... E 718 545-6700
  Astoria (G-440)
Finger Lakes Conveyors Inc .... G 315 539-9246
  Waterloo (G-16625)
Maximum Security Products Corp .... E 518 233-1800
  Waterford (G-16613)
Nrd LLC .... E 716 773-7634
  Grand Island (G-5764)
Thyssenkrupp Materials NA Inc .... G 212 972-8800
  New York (G-12335)

FIRE PROTECTION EQPT

Lifc Corp .... G 516 426-5737
  Port Washington (G-13838)

FIREARMS & AMMUNITION, EXC SPORTING, WHOLESALE

Island Ordnance Systems LLC .... F 516 746-2100
  Mineola (G-8518)

FIREARMS: Small, 30mm or Less

Benjamin Sheridan Corporation .... G 585 657-6161
  Bloomfield (G-981)
Dan Wesson Corp .... F 607 336-1174
  Norwich (G-13026)
Redding-Hunter Inc .... E 607 753-3331
  Cortland (G-4043)
Remington Arms Company LLC .... A 315 895-3482
  Ilion (G-6744)
Sycamore Hill Designs Inc .... G 585 820-7322
  Victor (G-16504)
Tri-Technologies Inc .... E 914 699-2001
  Mount Vernon (G-8741)

FIREFIGHTING APPARATUS

Bullex Inc .... F 518 689-2023
  Albany (G-58)
Eastern Precision Mfg .... G 845 358-1951
  Nyack (G-13050)
Firematic Supply Co Inc .... E 631 924-3181
  East Yaphank (G-4581)
Fountainhead Group Inc .... C 315 736-0037
  New York Mills (G-12722)
William R Shoemaker Inc .... G 716 649-0511
  Hamburg (G-5945)

FIREPLACE & CHIMNEY MATERIAL: Concrete

Chim-Cap Corp .... E 631 454-7576
  Farmingdale (G-4958)
Chimney Doctors Americas Corp .... G 631 868-3586
  Bayport (G-757)

FIREPLACE EQPT & ACCESS

William H Jackson Company .... G 718 784-4482
  Long Island City (G-7923)

FIREWORKS

Alonzo Fire Works Display Inc .... G 518 664-9994
  Mechanicville (G-8225)
Fantasy Fireworks Display .... G 518 664-1809
  Stillwater (G-15759)
Young Explosives Corp .... D 585 394-1783
  Canandaigua (G-3361)

FIREWORKS DISPLAY SVCS

Alonzo Fire Works Display Inc .... G 518 664-9994
  Mechanicville (G-8225)
Young Explosives Corp .... D 585 394-1783
  Canandaigua (G-3361)

FISH & SEAFOOD PROCESSORS: Canned Or Cured

AA USA Trading Inc .... G 917 586-2573
  Brooklyn (G-1544)
Blue Ocean Food Trading Inc .... G 718 689-4290
  Brooklyn (G-1702)
Deelka Vision Corp .... E 718 937-4121
  Sunnyside (G-15806)
Sangster Foods Inc .... F 212 993-9129
  Brooklyn (G-2532)

FISH & SEAFOOD PROCESSORS: Fresh Or Frozen

6th Ave Gourmet Inc .... G 845 782-9067
  Monroe (G-8547)
Foo Yuan Food Products Co Inc .... G 212 925-2840
  Long Island City (G-7744)
Rich Products Corporation .... A 716 878-8422
  Buffalo (G-3157)

FISHING EQPT: Lures

Bruynswick Sales Inc .... F 845 789-2049
  New Paltz (G-8873)
Heads & Tails Lure Co .... G 607 739-7900
  Horseheads (G-6580)
Northern King Lures Inc .... G 585 865-3373
  Rochester (G-14545)

FITTINGS & ASSEMBLIES: Hose & Tube, Hydraulic Or Pneumatic

KSA Manufacturing LLC .... F 315 488-0809
  Camillus (G-3323)

FITTINGS & SPECIALTIES: Steam

Arvos Holding LLC .... G 585 596-2501
  Wellsville (G-16748)

FITTINGS: Pipe

Legacy Valve LLC .... F 914 403-5075
  Valhalla (G-16368)
Martin Brass Works Inc .... G 718 523-3146
  Jamaica (G-6928)
Total Piping Solutions Inc .... F 716 372-0160
  Olean (G-13154)
United Pipe Nipple Co Inc .... F 516 295-2468
  Hewlett (G-6315)

FITTINGS: Pipe, Fabricated

D & G Welding Inc .... G 716 873-3088
  Buffalo (G-2899)

FIXTURES & EQPT: Kitchen, Metal, Exc Cast Aluminum

Acme Kitchenettes Corp .... E 518 828-4191
  Hudson (G-6604)

PRODUCT SECTION

FLUXES

Vanity Fair Bathmart Inc..................F...... 718 584-6700
  Bronx (G-1488)

FIXTURES: Bank, Metal, Ornamental

Jonathan Metal & Glass Ltd................D...... 718 846-8000
  Jamaica (G-6924)

FIXTURES: Cut Stone

Jamestown Kitchen & Bath Inc ....G...... 716 665-2299
  Jamestown (G-7008)

FLAGPOLES

Flagpoles Incorporated ....D...... 631 751-5500
  East Setauket (G-4483)
Pole-Tech Co Inc ....F...... 631 689-5525
  East Setauket (G-4489)

FLAGS: Fabric

AAa Amercn Flag Dctg Co Inc ....G...... 212 279-4644
  New York (G-8998)
Art Flag Company Inc ....F...... 212 334-1890
  New York (G-9210)
City Signs Inc ....G...... 718 375-5933
  Brooklyn (G-1784)
Eagle Regalia Co Inc ....F...... 845 425-2245
  Spring Valley (G-15582)
National Flag & Display Co Inc ....E...... 212 228-6500
  New York (G-11348)

FLAT GLASS: Building

Lazer Marble & Granite Corp ....G...... 718 859-9644
  Brooklyn (G-2197)
Tempco Glass Fabrication LLC ....G...... 718 461-6888
  Flushing (G-5300)

FLAT GLASS: Construction

RG Glass Creations Inc ....E...... 212 675-0030
  New York (G-11857)
Twin Pane Insulated GL Co Inc ....F...... 631 924-1060
  Yaphank (G-17407)

FLAT GLASS: Laminated

Glass Apps LLC ....F...... 310 987-1536
  New York (G-10307)

FLAT GLASS: Plate, Polished & Rough

Lafayette Mirror & Glass Co ....G...... 718 768-0660
  New Hyde Park (G-8845)
Zered Inc ....F...... 718 353-7464
  College Point (G-3813)

FLAT GLASS: Strengthened Or Reinforced

Saxon Glass Technologies Inc ....F...... 607 587-9630
  Alfred (G-194)

FLAT GLASS: Tempered

Strong Tempering GL Indust LLC ....F...... 718 765-0007
  Brooklyn (G-2611)

FLAT GLASS: Window, Clear & Colored

Express Building Supply Inc ....E...... 516 608-0379
  Oceanside (G-13079)
Farley Windows Inc ....G...... 315 764-1111
  Massena (G-8194)
Manhattan Shade & Glass Co Inc ......D...... 212 288-5616
  New York (G-11133)
South Seneca Vinyl LLC ....G...... 315 585-6050
  Romulus (G-14843)
Window-Fix Inc ....E...... 718 854-3475
  Brooklyn (G-2757)

FLATWARE, STAINLESS STEEL

Utica Cutlery Company ....D...... 315 733-4663
  Utica (G-16363)

FLAVORS OR FLAVORING MATERIALS: Synthetic

Classic Flavors Fragrances Inc ....G...... 212 777-0004
  New York (G-9636)
Comax Aromatics Corporation ....E...... 631 249-0505
  Melville (G-8304)

Comax Manufacturing Corp ....D...... 631 249-0505
  Melville (G-8305)
Craftmaster Flavor Technology ....F...... 631 789-8607
  Amityville (G-283)
Interntnal Flvors Frgrnces Inc ....C...... 212 765-5500
  New York (G-10639)
Kent Chemical Corporation ....E...... 212 521-1700
  New York (G-10838)
Mafco Consolidated Group Inc ....F...... 212 572-8600
  New York (G-11096)

FLOOR CLEANING & MAINTENANCE EQPT: Household

Grillbot LLC ....G...... 646 369-7242
  New York (G-10365)

FLOOR COMPOSITION: Magnesite

Vescom Structural Systems Inc ....F...... 516 876-8100
  Westbury (G-17041)

FLOOR COVERING STORES: Carpets

Albert Menin Interiors Ltd ....F...... 212 876-3041
  Bronx (G-1267)
Elizabeth Eakins Inc ....F...... 212 628-1950
  New York (G-10008)
Wallace Home Design Ctr ....G...... 631 765-3890
  Southold (G-15561)

FLOOR COVERING: Plastic

Crown Industries Inc ....F...... 973 672-2277
  New York (G-9759)
Engineered Composites Inc ....E...... 716 362-0295
  Buffalo (G-2939)
H Risch Inc ....D...... 585 442-0110
  Rochester (G-14415)

FLOOR COVERINGS WHOLESALERS

Carpet Fabrications Intl ....E...... 914 381-6060
  Mamaroneck (G-8026)

FLOOR COVERINGS: Textile Fiber

Mannington Mills Inc ....G...... 212 251-0290
  New York (G-11137)

FLOOR COVERINGS: Tile, Support Plastic

Engineered Plastics Inc ....E...... 800 682-2525
  Williamsville (G-17242)

FLOORING & GRATINGS: Open, Construction Applications

Oldcastle Precast Inc ....F...... 518 767-2116
  South Bethlehem (G-15514)

FLOORING: Hard Surface

East To West Architectral Pdts ....G...... 631 433-9690
  East Northport (G-4435)
Heritage Contract Flooring LLC ....E...... 716 853-1555
  Buffalo (G-2994)
Signature Systems Group LLC ....G...... 800 569-2751
  New York (G-12073)

FLOORING: Hardwood

Custom Woodwork Ltd ....F...... 631 727-5260
  Riverhead (G-14140)
Designer Hardwood Flrg CNY Inc ......F...... 315 207-0044
  Oswego (G-13329)
Fountain Tile Outlet Inc ....G...... 718 927-4555
  Brooklyn (G-1999)
Legno Veneto USA ....G...... 716 651-9169
  Depew (G-4261)
Madison & Dunn ....G...... 585 563-7760
  Rochester (G-14488)
MP Caroll Inc ....F...... 716 683-8520
  Cheektowaga (G-3579)
Mullican Flooring LP ....E...... 716 537-2640
  Holland (G-6482)
Tectonic Flooring USA LLC ....G...... 212 686-2700
  New York (G-12292)
Wood Floor Expo Inc ....G...... 212 472-0671
  New York (G-12655)

FLOORING: Tile

Tile Shop Inc ....G...... 585 424-2180
  Rochester (G-14726)

FLORISTS

M & S Schmalberg Inc ....F...... 212 244-2090
  New York (G-11069)

FLOWER POTS Plastic

TVI Imports LLC ....G...... 631 793-3077
  Massapequa Park (G-8190)

FLOWERS: Artificial & Preserved

Faster-Form Corp ....D...... 800 327-3676
  New Hartford (G-8804)
M & S Schmalberg Inc ....F...... 212 244-2090
  New York (G-11069)

FLUID METERS & COUNTING DEVICES

Aalborg Instrs & Contrls Inc ....D...... 845 398-3160
  Orangeburg (G-13217)
Computer Instruments Corp ....E...... 516 876-8400
  Westbury (G-16975)
East Hills Instrument Inc ....F...... 516 621-8686
  Westbury (G-16980)
G & O Equipment Corp ....G...... 718 218-7844
  Bronx (G-1339)

FLUID POWER PUMPS & MOTORS

Atlantic Industrial Tech Inc ....E...... 631 234-3131
  Shirley (G-15414)
Huck International Inc ....C...... 845 331-7300
  Kingston (G-7191)
Hydroacoustics Inc ....F...... 585 359-1000
  Henrietta (G-6294)
Itt LLC ....B...... 914 641-2000
  White Plains (G-17125)
ITT Corporation ....D...... 315 568-2811
  Seneca Falls (G-15362)
ITT Fluid Technology Corp ....B...... 914 641-2000
  White Plains (G-17127)
ITT Inc ....G...... 914 641-2000
  White Plains (G-17128)
Parker-Hannifin Corporation ....C...... 585 425-7000
  Fairport (G-4867)
Trench & Marine Pump Co Inc ....E...... 212 423-9098
  Bronx (G-1475)
Triumph Actuation Systems LLC ....D...... 516 378-0162
  Freeport (G-5432)

FLUID POWER VALVES & HOSE FITTINGS

A K Allen Co Inc ....C...... 516 747-5450
  Mineola (G-8488)
Aalborg Instrs & Contrls Inc ....D...... 845 398-3160
  Orangeburg (G-13217)
Eastport Operating Partners LP ....G...... 212 387-8791
  New York (G-9969)
Key High Vacuum Products Inc ....E...... 631 584-5959
  Nesconset (G-8775)
Kinemotive Corporation ....E...... 631 249-6440
  Farmingdale (G-5028)
Lourdes Industries Inc ....D...... 631 234-6600
  Hauppauge (G-6121)
Moog Inc ....B...... 716 655-3000
  East Aurora (G-4375)
Own Instrument Inc ....F...... 914 668-6546
  Mount Vernon (G-8712)
Servotronics Inc ....C...... 716 655-5990
  Elma (G-4655)
Steel & Obrien Mfg Inc ....D...... 585 492-5800
  Arcade (G-400)
Upstate Tube Inc ....G...... 315 488-5636
  Camillus (G-3326)

FLUORO RUBBERS

Dynax Corporation ....G...... 914 764-0202
  Pound Ridge (G-13943)

FLUXES

Aufhauser Corporation ....F...... 516 694-8696
  Plainview (G-13584)
Johnson Manufacturing Company ......F...... 716 881-3030
  Buffalo (G-3021)

FOAM CHARGE MIXTURES

C P Chemical Co Inc .... G 914 428-2517
White Plains *(G-17091)*

FOAM RUBBER

Foam Products Inc .... E 718 292-4830
Bronx *(G-1334)*
Par-Foam Products Inc .... C 716 855-2066
Buffalo *(G-3112)*
Turner Bellows Inc .... E 585 235-4456
Rochester *(G-14735)*

FOIL & LEAF: Metal

American Packaging Corporation .... C 585 254-9500
Rochester *(G-14198)*
Pactiv LLC .... C 518 793-2524
Glens Falls *(G-5695)*
Quick Roll Leaf Mfg Co Inc .... E 845 457-1500
Montgomery *(G-8601)*
Thermal Process Cnstr Co .... E 631 293-6400
Farmingdale *(G-5129)*
Vitex Packaging Group Inc .... F 212 265-6575
New York *(G-12557)*

FOIL OR LEAF: Gold

Genesis One Unlimited .... G 516 208-5863
West Hempstead *(G-16854)*

FOIL: Aluminum

Alufoil Products Co Inc .... F 631 231-4141
Hauppauge *(G-6018)*

FOIL: Copper

Oak-Mitsui Inc .... D 518 686-8060
Hoosick Falls *(G-6542)*
Oak-Mitsui Technologies LLC .... E 518 686-4961
Hoosick Falls *(G-6543)*
Steel Partners Holdings LP .... E 212 520-2300
New York *(G-12189)*

FOIL: Laminated To Paper Or Other Materials

Alufoil Products Co Inc .... F 631 231-4141
Hauppauge *(G-6018)*

FOOD PRDTS, BREAKFAST: Cereal, Granola & Muesli

Muesli Fusion Inc .... F 716 984-0855
Rochester *(G-14524)*

FOOD PRDTS, BREAKFAST: Cereal, Infants' Food

Group International LLC .... G 718 475-8805
Flushing *(G-5245)*
Sangster Foods Inc .... F 212 993-2532
Brooklyn *(G-2532)*

FOOD PRDTS, BREAKFAST: Cereal, Wheat Flakes

General Mills Inc .... D 716 856-6060
Buffalo *(G-2970)*

FOOD PRDTS, CANNED OR FRESH PACK: Fruit Juices

Apple & Eve LLC .... D 516 621-1122
Port Washington *(G-13800)*
Levindi .... F 212 572-7000
New York *(G-10978)*
Mizkan America Inc .... D 585 765-9171
Lyndonville *(G-7968)*
Motts LLP .... C 972 673-8088
Elmsford *(G-4767)*
National Grape Coop Assn Inc .... E 716 326-5200
Westfield *(G-17048)*
US Juice Partners LLC .... G 516 621-1122
Port Washington *(G-13870)*
Welch Foods Inc A Cooperative .... C 716 326-5252
Westfield *(G-17053)*

FOOD PRDTS, CANNED OR FRESH PACK: Vegetable Juices

Life Juice Brands LLC .... G 585 944-7982
Pittsford *(G-13567)*

FOOD PRDTS, CANNED, NEC

Phillip Juan .... G 800 834-4543
Staten Island *(G-15720)*

FOOD PRDTS, CANNED: Applesauce

Lidestri Foods Inc .... E 585 458-8335
Rochester *(G-14480)*

FOOD PRDTS, CANNED: Baby Food

Beech-Nut Nutrition Company .... B 518 839-0300
Amsterdam *(G-335)*
Novartis Corporation .... E 212 307-1122
New York *(G-11462)*

FOOD PRDTS, CANNED: Barbecue Sauce

Jets Lefrois Corp .... G 585 637-5003
Brockport *(G-1245)*

FOOD PRDTS, CANNED: Beans & Bean Sprouts

Sahadi Fine Foods Inc .... E 718 369-0100
Brooklyn *(G-2530)*

FOOD PRDTS, CANNED: Catsup

Kensington & Sons LLC .... E 646 450-5735
New York *(G-10835)*

FOOD PRDTS, CANNED: Ethnic

Delicious Foods Inc .... F 718 446-9352
Corona *(G-3997)*
Iberia Foods Corp .... D 718 272-8900
Brooklyn *(G-2094)*
Sangster Foods Inc .... F 212 993-9129
Brooklyn *(G-2532)*

FOOD PRDTS, CANNED: Fruit Juices, Concentrated

Old Dutch Mustard Co Inc .... G 516 466-0522
Great Neck *(G-5825)*

FOOD PRDTS, CANNED: Fruit Juices, Fresh

Cahoon Farms Inc .... E 315 594-8081
Wolcott *(G-17277)*
Central Island Juice Corp .... F 516 338-8301
Westbury *(G-16974)*
Cheribundi Inc .... E 800 699-0460
Geneva *(G-5573)*
Cliffstar LLC .... A 716 366-6100
Dunkirk *(G-4337)*
Club 1100 .... G 585 235-3478
Rochester *(G-14280)*
Fresh Fanatic Inc .... G 516 521-6574
Brooklyn *(G-2005)*
Mayer Bros Apple Products Inc .... D 716 668-1787
West Seneca *(G-16952)*

FOOD PRDTS, CANNED: Fruit Purees

Global Natural Foods Inc .... E 845 439-3292
Livingston Manor *(G-7562)*

FOOD PRDTS, CANNED: Fruits

Fruitcrown Products Corp .... E 631 694-5800
Farmingdale *(G-4994)*
Lagoner Farms Inc .... D 315 589-4899
Williamson *(G-17224)*

FOOD PRDTS, CANNED: Fruits

Brooklyn Btlg Milton NY Inc .... C 845 795-2171
Milton *(G-8482)*
Carriage House Companies Inc .... A 716 672-4321
Fredonia *(G-5371)*
Goya Foods Inc .... D 716 549-0076
Angola *(G-380)*
Hc Brill Co Inc .... G 716 685-4000
Lancaster *(G-7319)*

Victoria Fine Foods LLC .... D 718 649-1635
Brooklyn *(G-2725)*
Welch Foods Inc A Cooperative .... E 716 326-3131
Westfield *(G-17054)*

FOOD PRDTS, CANNED: Fruits & Fruit Prdts

Amiram Dror Inc .... F 212 979-9505
Brooklyn *(G-1611)*
Birds Eye Holdings Inc .... A 585 383-1850
Rochester *(G-14232)*
Spf Holdings II LLC .... F 212 750-8300
New York *(G-12161)*

FOOD PRDTS, CANNED: Italian

A & G Food Distributors LLC .... G 917 939-3457
Bayside *(G-762)*
Antico Casale Usa LLC .... C 914 760-1100
Whitestone *(G-17199)*
Indira Foods Inc .... F 718 343-1500
Floral Park *(G-5208)*
Marketplace Slutions Group LLC .... E 631 868-0111
Holbrook *(G-6461)*

FOOD PRDTS, CANNED: Jams, Including Imitation

Sbk Preserves Inc .... E 800 773-7378
Bronx *(G-1448)*

FOOD PRDTS, CANNED: Jams, Jellies & Preserves

Beths Farm Kitchen .... G 518 799-3414
Stuyvesant Falls *(G-15783)*
Eleanors Best .... F 845 809-5621
Garrison *(G-5554)*

FOOD PRDTS, CANNED: Maraschino Cherries

Dells Maraschino Cherries Inc .... E 718 624-4380
Brooklyn *(G-1851)*

FOOD PRDTS, CANNED: Mexican, NEC

Eve Sales Corp .... F 718 589-6800
Bronx *(G-1328)*

FOOD PRDTS, CANNED: Olives

L and S Packing Co .... D 631 845-1717
Farmingdale *(G-5030)*

FOOD PRDTS, CANNED: Puddings, Exc Meat

Steuben Foods Incorporated .... F 718 291-3333
Jamaica *(G-6952)*

FOOD PRDTS, CANNED: Ravioli

Borgattis Ravioli Egg Noodles .... G 718 367-3799
Bronx *(G-1287)*

FOOD PRDTS, CANNED: Sauerkraut

Glk Foods LLC .... E 585 289-4414
Shortsville *(G-15433)*
Seneca Foods Corporation .... C 315 781-8733
Geneva *(G-5585)*

FOOD PRDTS, CANNED: Soup, Chicken

Morris Kitchen Inc .... F 646 413-5186
Brooklyn *(G-2334)*

FOOD PRDTS, CANNED: Spaghetti & Other Pasta Sauce

Kaltech Food Packaging Inc .... E 845 856-1210
Port Jervis *(G-13787)*
Lidestri Foods Inc .... B 585 377-7700
Fairport *(G-4861)*
Sneaky Chef Foods LLC .... F 914 301-3277
Tarrytown *(G-16106)*
Wolfgang B Gourmet Foods Inc .... F 518 719-1727
Catskill *(G-3435)*

FOOD PRDTS, CANNED: Tomato Sauce.

Vincents Food Corp .... F 516 481-3544
Carle Place *(G-3397)*

PRODUCT SECTION

FOOD PRDTS, CANNED: Tomatoes
Giovanni Food Co Inc .... D 315 463-7770
  Syracuse *(G-15953)*
Morris Kitchen Inc .... F 646 413-5186
  Brooklyn *(G-2334)*
Private Lbel Fods Rchester Inc .... E 585 254-9205
  Rochester *(G-14602)*

FOOD PRDTS, CANNED: Vegetables
Green Valley Foods LLC .... G 315 926-4280
  Marion *(G-8094)*
Seneca Foods Corporation .... E 315 926-8100
  Marion *(G-8099)*
Seneca Foods Corporation .... F 315 926-4277
  Marion *(G-8101)*
Seneca Foods Corporation .... E 585 658-2211
  Leicester *(G-7422)*

FOOD PRDTS, CONFECTIONERY, WHOLESALE: Candy
Chocolat Moderne LLC .... G 212 229-4797
  New York *(G-9605)*
Chocolate Delivery Systems Inc .... D 716 854-6050
  Buffalo *(G-2872)*
OH How Cute Inc .... G 347 838-6031
  Staten Island *(G-15719)*
Premium Sweets USA Inc .... G 718 739-6000
  Jamaica *(G-6940)*

FOOD PRDTS, CONFECTIONERY, WHOLESALE: Nuts, Salted/Roasted
Sahadi Fine Foods Inc .... E 718 369-0100
  Brooklyn *(G-2530)*

FOOD PRDTS, CONFECTIONERY, WHOLESALE: Snack Foods
Flaum Appetizing Corp .... E 718 821-1970
  Brooklyn *(G-1984)*
Perrys Ice Cream Company Inc .... B 716 542-5492
  Akron *(G-27)*

FOOD PRDTS, DAIRY, WHOLESALE: Frozen Dairy Desserts
Soft Serve Apple LLC .... E 646 442-8002
  New York *(G-12115)*
Soft Serve Fruit Co LLC .... E 646 442-8002
  New York *(G-12116)*

FOOD PRDTS, DAIRY, WHOLESALE: Milk & Cream, Fluid
Elmhurst Dairy Inc .... C 718 526-3442
  Jamaica *(G-6910)*

FOOD PRDTS, FISH & SEAFOOD, WHOLESALE: Fresh
Fresh Fanatic Inc .... G 516 521-6574
  Brooklyn *(G-2005)*
Montauk Inlet Seafood Inc .... G 631 668-3419
  Montauk *(G-8590)*

FOOD PRDTS, FISH & SEAFOOD: Cakes, Canned, Jarred, Etc
BNC Commodities Inc .... F 631 872-8041
  Wantagh *(G-16554)*

FOOD PRDTS, FISH & SEAFOOD: Canned & Jarred, Etc
Diamond Seafoods LLC .... G 503 351-3240
  Port Washington *(G-13809)*
Harbors Maine Lobster LLC .... E 516 775-2400
  New Hyde Park *(G-8839)*
Premium Ocean LLC .... F 917 231-1061
  Bronx *(G-1435)*

FOOD PRDTS, FISH & SEAFOOD: Fish, Fresh, Prepared
Montauk Inlet Seafood Inc .... G 631 668-3419
  Montauk *(G-8590)*
Prince of The Sea Ltd .... E 516 333-6344
  Westbury *(G-17022)*

FOOD PRDTS, FISH & SEAFOOD: Fish, Smoked
Acme Smoked Fish Corp .... D 954 942-5598
  Brooklyn *(G-1557)*
Banner Smoked Fish Inc .... E 718 449-1992
  Brooklyn *(G-1666)*
Samaki Inc .... G 845 858-1012
  Port Jervis *(G-13791)*

FOOD PRDTS, FISH & SEAFOOD: Prepared Cakes & Sticks
Peak Holdings LLC .... A 212 583-5000
  New York *(G-11588)*

FOOD PRDTS, FISH & SEAFOOD: Salmon, Smoked
Catsmo Corp .... F 845 895-2296
  Wallkill *(G-16542)*

FOOD PRDTS, FISH & SEAFOOD: Seafood, Frozen, Prepared
Oceans Cuisine Ltd .... F 631 209-9200
  Ridge *(G-14092)*

FOOD PRDTS, FROZEN: Breakfasts, Packaged
Juno Chefs .... D 845 294-5400
  Goshen *(G-5735)*

FOOD PRDTS, FROZEN: Dinners, Packaged
Alle Processing Corp .... C 718 894-2000
  Maspeth *(G-8115)*

FOOD PRDTS, FROZEN: Ethnic Foods, NEC
America NY RI Wang Fd Group Co .... E 718 628-8999
  Maspeth *(G-8117)*
Delicious Foods Inc .... F 718 446-9352
  Corona *(G-3997)*

FOOD PRDTS, FROZEN: Fruit Juice, Concentrates
Levindi .... F 212 572-7000
  New York *(G-10978)*

FOOD PRDTS, FROZEN: Fruits & Vegetables
Atlantic Farm & Food Inc .... F 718 441-3152
  Richmond Hill *(G-14066)*
Metzger Speciality Brands .... G 212 957-0055
  New York *(G-11244)*

FOOD PRDTS, FROZEN: Fruits, Juices & Vegetables
Blend Smoothie Bar .... G 845 568-7366
  New Windsor *(G-8933)*
Cahoon Farms Inc .... E 315 594-8081
  Wolcott *(G-17277)*
National Grape Coop Assn Inc .... E 716 326-5200
  Westfield *(G-17048)*
T & Smoothie Inc .... G 631 804-6653
  Patchogue *(G-13436)*

FOOD PRDTS, FROZEN: NEC
Codinos Limited Inc .... E 518 372-3308
  Schenectady *(G-15244)*
Dufour Pastry Kitchens Inc .... E 718 402-8800
  Bronx *(G-1318)*
Dvash Foods Inc .... F 845 578-1959
  Monsey *(G-8571)*
Finger Food Products Inc .... E 716 297-4888
  Niagara Falls *(G-12822)*
Freeze-Dry Foods Inc .... E 585 589-6399
  Albion *(G-165)*
Julians Recipe LLC .... G 888 640-8880
  Brooklyn *(G-2159)*
Milmar Food Group II LLC .... C 845 294-5400
  Goshen *(G-5738)*
Peak Holdings LLC .... A 212 583-5000
  New York *(G-11588)*
Seviroli Foods Inc .... C 516 222-6220
  Garden City *(G-5532)*

FOOD PRDTS, WHOLESALE: Chocolate

Tami Great Food Corp .... G 845 352-7901
  Monsey *(G-8584)*
Tuv Taam Corp .... E 718 855-2207
  Brooklyn *(G-2689)*

FOOD PRDTS, FROZEN: Pizza
D R M Management Inc .... E 716 668-0333
  Depew *(G-4254)*
F & R Enterprises Inc .... G 315 841-8189
  Waterville *(G-16678)*
Salarinos Italian Foods Inc .... F 315 697-9766
  Canastota *(G-3372)*

FOOD PRDTS, FROZEN: Snack Items
Hong Hop Co Inc .... E 212 962-1735
  New York *(G-10502)*
Les Chateaux De France Inc .... E 516 239-6795
  Inwood *(G-6760)*

FOOD PRDTS, FROZEN: Soups
Classic Cooking LLC .... D 718 439-0200
  Jamaica *(G-6905)*

FOOD PRDTS, FROZEN: Vegetables, Exc Potato Prdts
Birds Eye Foods Inc .... G 716 988-3218
  South Dayton *(G-15517)*
Classic Cooking LLC .... D 718 439-0200
  Jamaica *(G-6905)*
Prime Food Processing Corp .... D 718 963-2323
  Brooklyn *(G-2441)*
Seneca Foods Corporation .... E 315 926-8100
  Marion *(G-8099)*
Tami Great Food Corp .... G 845 352-7901
  Monsey *(G-8584)*

FOOD PRDTS, FROZEN: Whipped Topping
Kraft Heinz Foods Company .... B 585 226-4400
  Avon *(G-540)*

FOOD PRDTS, MEAT & MEAT PRDTS, WHOLESALE: Fresh
Alps Provision Co Inc .... E 718 721-4477
  Astoria *(G-433)*
Camellia General Provision Co .... E 716 893-5352
  Buffalo *(G-2865)*
Kamerys Wholesale Meats Inc .... G 716 372-6756
  Olean *(G-13149)*
Reliable Brothers Inc .... E 518 273-6732
  Green Island *(G-5861)*

FOOD PRDTS, WHOL: Canned Goods, Fruit, Veg, Seafood/Meats
Frank Wardynski & Sons Inc .... E 716 854-6083
  Buffalo *(G-2955)*
Spf Holdings II LLC .... F 212 750-8300
  New York *(G-12161)*
Wonton Food Inc .... C 718 628-6868
  Brooklyn *(G-2763)*

FOOD PRDTS, WHOLESALE: Beverage Concentrates
Motts LLP .... C 972 673-8088
  Elmsford *(G-4767)*

FOOD PRDTS, WHOLESALE: Beverages, Exc Coffee & Tea
TLC-Lc Inc .... E 212 756-8900
  New York *(G-12355)*

FOOD PRDTS, WHOLESALE: Chocolate
Amiram Dror Inc .... F 212 979-9505
  Brooklyn *(G-1611)*
Chocolate Pizza Company Inc .... F 315 673-4098
  Marcellus *(G-8087)*
Commodore Chocolatier USA Inc .... F 845 561-3960
  Newburgh *(G-12753)*
Godiva Chocolatier Inc .... E 212 984-5900
  New York *(G-10326)*
Lanco Corporation .... C 631 231-2300
  Ronkonkoma *(G-14929)*

FOOD PRDTS, WHOLESALE: Coffee & Tea

PRODUCT SECTION

FOOD PRDTS, WHOLESALE: Coffee & Tea
Simplycultivated Group LLC .... G 646 389-0682
  Horseheads *(G-6594)*

FOOD PRDTS, WHOLESALE: Coffee, Green Or Roasted
Coffee Holding Co Inc .... D 718 832-0800
  Staten Island *(G-15661)*
Orens Daily Roast Inc .... G 212 348-5400
  New York *(G-11526)*
Paul De Lima Company Inc .... D 315 457-3725
  Liverpool *(G-7540)*

FOOD PRDTS, WHOLESALE: Condiments
Kensington & Sons LLC .... E 646 450-5735
  New York *(G-10835)*

FOOD PRDTS, WHOLESALE: Cookies
212kiddish Inc .... G 718 705-7227
  Brooklyn *(G-1512)*

FOOD PRDTS, WHOLESALE: Diet
Eximus Connections Corporation .... G 631 421-1700
  Huntington Station *(G-6703)*

FOOD PRDTS, WHOLESALE: Flour
Archer-Daniels-Midland Company .... D 518 828-4691
  Hudson *(G-6606)*

FOOD PRDTS, WHOLESALE: Grains
Chia Usa LLC .... F 212 226-7512
  New York *(G-9593)*

FOOD PRDTS, WHOLESALE: Health
Sangster Foods Inc .... F 212 993-9129
  Brooklyn *(G-2532)*

FOOD PRDTS, WHOLESALE: Juices
Brooklyn Btlg Milton NY Inc .... C 845 795-2171
  Milton *(G-8482)*
Schutt Cider Mill .... F 585 872-2924
  Webster *(G-16734)*

FOOD PRDTS, WHOLESALE: Organic & Diet
Natural Lab Inc .... G 718 321-8848
  Flushing *(G-5270)*

FOOD PRDTS, WHOLESALE: Pasta & Rice
Deer Park Macaroni Co Inc .... F 631 667-4600
  Deer Park *(G-4129)*
Great Eastern Pasta Works LLC .... E 631 956-0889
  West Babylon *(G-16794)*
New York Ravioli Pasta Co Inc .... E 516 270-2852
  New Hyde Park *(G-8851)*
Steinway Pasta & Gelati Inc .... F 718 246-5414
  Brooklyn *(G-2607)*
Victoria Fine Foods LLC .... D 718 649-1635
  Brooklyn *(G-2725)*

FOOD PRDTS, WHOLESALE: Sandwiches
Fresh Fanatic Inc .... G 516 521-6574
  Brooklyn *(G-2005)*
Uptown Local .... F 212 988-1704
  New York *(G-12475)*

FOOD PRDTS, WHOLESALE: Sausage Casings
DRG New York Holdings Corp .... D 914 668-9000
  Mount Vernon *(G-8677)*

FOOD PRDTS, WHOLESALE: Specialty
Castella Imports Inc .... C 631 231-5500
  Hauppauge *(G-6040)*
Fanshawe Foods LLC .... F 212 757-3130
  New York *(G-10135)*

FOOD PRDTS, WHOLESALE: Tea
White Coffee Corp .... D 718 204-7900
  Astoria *(G-462)*

FOOD PRDTS: Almond Pastes
American Almond Pdts Co Inc .... E 718 875-8310
  Brooklyn *(G-1599)*

FOOD PRDTS: Bran, Rice
Gassho Body & Mind Inc .... G 518 695-9991
  Schuylerville *(G-15320)*

FOOD PRDTS: Bread Crumbs, Exc Made In Bakeries
Gourmet Toast Corp .... G 718 852-4536
  Brooklyn *(G-2044)*
H & S Edible Products Corp .... E 914 413-3489
  Mount Vernon *(G-8688)*

FOOD PRDTS: Breakfast Bars
Glennys Inc .... G 516 377-1400
  Brooklyn *(G-2026)*
Keep Healthy Inc .... F 631 651-9090
  Northport *(G-13013)*

FOOD PRDTS: Cane Syrup, From Purchased Raw Sugar
Cane Sugar LLC .... G 212 329-2695
  New York *(G-9513)*

FOOD PRDTS: Cereals
Associated Brands Inc .... B 585 798-3475
  New York *(G-9238)*
Avas Corporation .... G 203 470-3587
  New York *(G-9275)*
Chia Usa LLC .... F 212 226-7512
  New York *(G-9593)*
Gabila Food Products Inc .... E 631 789-2220
  Copiague *(G-3902)*
Kellogg Company .... E 315 452-0310
  North Syracuse *(G-12951)*
Kellogg Company .... A 845 365-5284
  Orangeburg *(G-13233)*
Kraft Heinz Foods Company .... A 914 335-2500
  Tarrytown *(G-16093)*
Pepsico Inc .... A 914 253-2000
  Purchase *(G-13966)*
Sanzdranz LLC .... G 518 894-8625
  Delmar *(G-4246)*
Sanzdranz LLC .... E 518 894-8625
  Schenectady *(G-15292)*

FOOD PRDTS: Cheese Curls & Puffs
Emmi USA Inc .... F 845 268-9990
  Orangeburg *(G-13225)*
Pepsico Inc .... E 914 253-3474
  White Plains *(G-17155)*

FOOD PRDTS: Chicken, Processed, Frozen
K&Ns Foods Usa LLC .... E 315 598-8080
  Fulton *(G-5465)*

FOOD PRDTS: Chocolate Bars, Solid
Amiram Dror Inc .... F 212 979-9505
  Brooklyn *(G-1611)*
Cemoi Inc .... G 212 583-4920
  New York *(G-9560)*
Max Brenner Union Square LLC .... G 646 467-8803
  New York *(G-11186)*
Mbny LLC .... F 646 467-8810
  New York *(G-11192)*
Micosta Enterprises Inc .... G 518 822-9708
  Hudson *(G-6627)*
Parkside Candy Co Inc .... F 716 833-7540
  Buffalo *(G-3114)*

FOOD PRDTS: Chocolate Coatings & Syrup
Choco Peanuts Inc .... G 716 998-2353
  Buffalo *(G-2871)*
H Fox & Co Inc .... E 718 385-4600
  Brooklyn *(G-2059)*

FOOD PRDTS: Cocoa & Cocoa Prdts
Simplycultivated Group LLC .... G 646 389-0682
  Horseheads *(G-6594)*

FOOD PRDTS: Coconut Oil
Jax Coco USA LLC .... G 347 688-8198
  New York *(G-10703)*

FOOD PRDTS: Coconut, Desiccated & Shredded
Far Eastern Coconut Company .... F 631 851-8800
  Central Islip *(G-3496)*

FOOD PRDTS: Coffee
Birch Guys LLC .... G 917 763-0751
  Long Island City *(G-7686)*
Cafe Kubal .... F 315 278-2812
  Syracuse *(G-15882)*
Caranda Emporium LLC .... F 212 866-7100
  New York *(G-9521)*
Coffee Holding Co Inc .... D 718 832-0800
  Staten Island *(G-15661)*
Fal Coffee Inc .... F 718 305-4255
  Brooklyn *(G-1954)*
G & M Roaster .... G 718 984-5235
  Staten Island *(G-15675)*
Irving Farm Coffee Co Inc .... G 212 206-0707
  New York *(G-10664)*
Joseph H Navaie .... F 607 936-9030
  Corning *(G-3974)*
Kraft Heinz Foods Company .... A 914 335-2500
  Tarrytown *(G-16093)*
Maidstone Coffee Co .... E 585 272-1040
  Rochester *(G-14491)*
New York Gourmet Coffee Inc .... G 631 254-0076
  Bay Shore *(G-722)*
P Pascal Inc .... E 914 969-7933
  Yonkers *(G-17474)*
Paul De Lima Company Inc .... D 315 457-3725
  Liverpool *(G-7540)*
Paul De Lima Company Inc .... G 315 457-3725
  Cicero *(G-3650)*
Paul Delima Coffee Company .... G 315 457-3725
  Cicero *(G-3651)*
S J McCullagh Inc .... E 716 856-3473
  Buffalo *(G-3172)*
Star Mountain JFK Inc .... G 718 553-6787
  Jamaica *(G-6951)*
Vega Coffee Inc .... G 415 881-7969
  New York *(G-12514)*

FOOD PRDTS: Coffee Extracts
Death Wish Coffee Company LLC .... F 518 400-1050
  Round Lake *(G-15037)*
Eldorado Coffee Roasters Ltd .... D 718 418-4100
  Maspeth *(G-8137)*

FOOD PRDTS: Coffee Roasting, Exc Wholesale Grocers
Bh Coffee Company LLC .... D 914 377-2500
  Elmsford *(G-4736)*
BK Associates Intl Inc .... F 607 432-1499
  Oneonta *(G-13173)*
Empire Coffee Company Inc .... E 914 934-1100
  Port Chester *(G-13745)*
Gillies Coffee Company .... E 718 499-7766
  Brooklyn *(G-2024)*
Gorilla Coffee Inc .... G 718 230-3244
  Brooklyn *(G-2041)*
John A Vassilaros & Son Inc .... E 718 886-4140
  Flushing *(G-5257)*
Monkey Joe Roasting Company .... G 845 331-4598
  Kingston *(G-7202)*
Regal Trading Inc .... E 914 694-6100
  Purchase *(G-13970)*
White Coffee Corp .... D 718 204-7900
  Astoria *(G-462)*

FOOD PRDTS: Cooking Oils, Refined Vegetable, Exc Corn
C B S Food Products Corp .... F 718 452-2500
  Brooklyn *(G-1743)*
Healthy Brand Oil Corp .... E 718 937-0806
  Long Island City *(G-7757)*

PRODUCT SECTION

FOOD PRDTS: Macaroni, Noodles, Spaghetti, Pasta, Etc

FOOD PRDTS: Corn Chips & Other Corn-Based Snacks

Frito-Lay North America Inc .... D 716 631-2360
  Williamsville *(G-17243)*
Glennys Inc .... G 516 377-1400
  Brooklyn *(G-2026)*

FOOD PRDTS: Corn Sugars & Syrups

Archer-Daniels-Midland Company .... G 585 346-2311
  Lakeville *(G-7282)*

FOOD PRDTS: Cottonseed Lecithin

Perimondo LLC .... G 212 749-0721
  New York *(G-11618)*

FOOD PRDTS: Dessert Mixes & Fillings

Deedee Desserts LLC .... G 716 627-2330
  Lake View *(G-7279)*
Rich Products Corporation .... A 716 878-8422
  Buffalo *(G-3157)*
VIP Foods Inc .... E 718 821-5330
  Ridgewood *(G-14131)*

FOOD PRDTS: Desserts, Ready-To-Mix

Butterwood Desserts Inc .... E 716 652-0131
  West Falls *(G-16844)*
Kozy Shack Enterprises LLC .... C 516 870-3000
  Hicksville *(G-6359)*
Kozy Shack Enterprises LLC .... C 516 870-3000
  Hicksville *(G-6360)*
Omg Desserts Inc .... F 585 698-1561
  Rochester *(G-14548)*

FOOD PRDTS: Dough, Pizza, Prepared

Ohio Baking Company Inc .... E 315 724-2033
  Utica *(G-16354)*
Western Blending Inc .... G 518 356-6650
  Schenectady *(G-15312)*

FOOD PRDTS: Doughs & Batters

Losurdo Foods Inc .... E 518 842-1500
  Amsterdam *(G-355)*

FOOD PRDTS: Doughs & Batters From Purchased Flour

Cohens Bakery Inc .... E 716 892-8149
  Buffalo *(G-2879)*

FOOD PRDTS: Dressings, Salad, Raw & Cooked Exc Dry Mixes

Carriage House Companies Inc .... A 716 672-4321
  Fredonia *(G-5371)*
Mizkan Americas Inc .... F 585 798-5720
  Medina *(G-8278)*
Sum Sum LLC .... G 516 812-3959
  Oceanside *(G-13099)*

FOOD PRDTS: Dried & Dehydrated Fruits, Vegetables & Soup Mix

Goya Foods Inc .... D 716 549-0076
  Angola *(G-380)*
Shoreline Fruit LLC .... D 585 765-2639
  Lyndonville *(G-7969)*

FOOD PRDTS: Ducks, Processed, Fresh

Crescent Duck Farm Inc .... E 631 722-8700
  Aquebogue *(G-384)*

FOOD PRDTS: Ducks, Processed, NEC

Hudson Valley Foie Gras LLC .... F 845 292-2500
  Ferndale *(G-5171)*

FOOD PRDTS: Edible Oil Prdts, Exc Corn Oil

Consumer Flavoring Extract Co .... F 718 435-0201
  Brooklyn *(G-1798)*

FOOD PRDTS: Edible fats & oils

Bunge Limited Finance Corp .... C 914 684-2800
  White Plains *(G-17089)*

Kerry Inc .... D 607 334-1700
  Norwich *(G-13029)*

FOOD PRDTS: Egg Substitutes, Made From Eggs

Egg Low Farms Inc .... F 607 674-4653
  Sherburne *(G-15391)*

FOOD PRDTS: Eggs, Processed

Ready Egg Farms Inc .... G 607 674-4653
  Sherburne *(G-15394)*

FOOD PRDTS: Emulsifiers

Broome County .... E 607 785-9567
  Endicott *(G-4797)*
Chemicolloid Laboratories Inc .... F 516 747-2666
  New Hyde Park *(G-8821)*
Momentive Performance Mtls Inc .... D 914 784-4807
  Tarrytown *(G-16098)*
Redland Foods Corp .... F 716 288-9061
  Cheektowaga *(G-3589)*

FOOD PRDTS: Flavored Ices, Frozen

Elegant Desserts By Metro Inc .... F 718 388-1323
  Brooklyn *(G-1912)*
Four Brothers Italian Bakery .... G 914 741-5434
  Hawthorne *(G-6246)*
JMS Ices Inc .... F 718 448-0853
  Staten Island *(G-15692)*
My Most Favorite Food .... G 212 580-5130
  New York *(G-11331)*
Olympic Ice Cream Co Inc .... E 718 849-6200
  Jamaica *(G-6936)*
Primo Frozen Desserts Inc .... G 718 252-2312
  Brooklyn *(G-2442)*

FOOD PRDTS: Flour & Other Grain Mill Products

ADM Milling Co .... D 716 849-7333
  Buffalo *(G-2797)*
Ardent Mills LLC .... D 518 447-1700
  Albany *(G-49)*
Birkett Mills .... G 315 536-3311
  Penn Yan *(G-13506)*
Birkett Mills .... E 315 536-4112
  Penn Yan *(G-13507)*
Champlain Valley Milling Corp .... G 518 962-4711
  Westport *(G-17067)*
Cochecton Mills Inc .... E 845 932-8282
  Cochecton *(G-3740)*

FOOD PRDTS: Flour Mixes & Doughs

Aryzta LLC .... D 585 235-8160
  Rochester *(G-14214)*
Bektrom Foods Inc .... E 516 802-3800
  Syosset *(G-15813)*
Lollipop Tree Inc .... E 845 471-8733
  Auburn *(G-506)*
Western Blending Inc .... G 518 356-6650
  Schenectady *(G-15312)*

FOOD PRDTS: Flour, Cake From Purchased Flour

Peak Holdings LLC .... A 212 583-5000
  New York *(G-11588)*

FOOD PRDTS: Fruit Juices

Cheribundi Inc .... E 800 699-0460
  Geneva *(G-5573)*
Dynamic Health Labs Inc .... E 718 858-0100
  Brooklyn *(G-1886)*
Global Natural Foods Inc .... E 845 439-3292
  Livingston Manor *(G-7562)*
Hain Blueprint Inc .... E 212 414-5741
  New Hyde Park *(G-8836)*
Pepsico Inc .... A 914 253-2000
  Purchase *(G-13966)*
Pura Fruta LLC .... F 415 279-5727
  Long Island City *(G-7850)*
World Waters LLC .... E 212 905-2393
  New York *(G-12663)*
Zoe Sakoutis LLC .... F 212 414-5741
  New York *(G-12717)*

FOOD PRDTS: Fruit Pops, Frozen

Soft Serve Fruit Co LLC .... E 646 442-8002
  New York *(G-12116)*

FOOD PRDTS: Fruits & Vegetables, Pickled

United Farm Processing Corp .... C 718 933-6060
  Bronx *(G-1485)*

FOOD PRDTS: Fruits, Dehydrated Or Dried

Peeled Inc .... G 212 706-2001
  Brooklyn *(G-2412)*
Settons Intl Foods Inc .... E 631 543-8090
  Commack *(G-3842)*

FOOD PRDTS: Fruits, Dried Or Dehydrated, Exc Freeze-Dried

Associated Brands Inc .... B 585 798-3475
  New York *(G-9238)*
Marshall Ingredients LLC .... G 800 796-9353
  Wolcott *(G-17280)*

FOOD PRDTS: Gelatin Dessert Preparations

Original Hrkmer Cnty Chese Inc .... D 315 895-7428
  Ilion *(G-6743)*

FOOD PRDTS: Gluten Meal

Anthony Gigi Inc .... G 860 984-1943
  Shirley *(G-15412)*

FOOD PRDTS: Horseradish, Exc Sauce

Whalens Horseradish Products .... G 518 587-6404
  Galway *(G-5484)*

FOOD PRDTS: Ice, Blocks

Arctic Glacier Texas Inc .... E 215 283-0326
  Fairport *(G-4844)*
Clayville Ice Co Inc .... G 315 839-5405
  Clayville *(G-3687)*
Huntington Ice & Cube Corp .... F 718 456-2013
  Brooklyn *(G-2091)*

FOOD PRDTS: Ice, Cubes

Arctic Glacier USA .... E 215 283-0326
  Fairport *(G-4845)*
Henry Newman LLC .... F 607 273-8512
  Ithaca *(G-6847)*

FOOD PRDTS: Instant Coffee

Orens Daily Roast Inc .... G 212 348-5400
  New York *(G-11526)*
Sangster Foods Inc .... F 212 993-9129
  Brooklyn *(G-2532)*

FOOD PRDTS: Jelly, Corncob

Larte Del Gelato Inc .... G 212 366-0570
  New York *(G-10930)*

FOOD PRDTS: Juice Pops, Frozen

Zings Company LLC .... G 631 454-0339
  Farmingdale *(G-5145)*

FOOD PRDTS: Macaroni Prdts, Dry, Alphabet, Rings Or Shells

Piemonte Home Made Ravioli Co .... F 718 429-1972
  Woodside *(G-17347)*
Queen Ann Macaroni Mfg Co Inc .... G 718 256-1061
  Brooklyn *(G-2466)*
Wing Kei Noodle Inc .... F 212 226-1644
  New York *(G-12644)*

FOOD PRDTS: Macaroni, Noodles, Spaghetti, Pasta, Etc

Cassinelli Food Products Inc .... G 718 274-4881
  Long Island City *(G-7695)*
Dairy Maid Raviolo Mfg .... F 718 449-2620
  Brooklyn *(G-1835)*
Deer Park Macaroni Co Inc .... G 631 667-4600
  Deer Park *(G-4128)*
Deer Park Macaroni Co Inc .... F 631 667-4600
  Deer Park *(G-4129)*

FOOD PRDTS: Macaroni, Noodles, Spaghetti, Pasta, Etc

Piemonte Home Made Ravioli Co .... G 212 226-0475
   New York *(G-11660)*
Raffettos Corp .... E 212 777-1261
   New York *(G-11785)*
Ravioli Store Inc .... G 718 729-9300
   Long Island City *(G-7858)*
Twin Marquis Inc .... D 718 386-6868
   Brooklyn *(G-2691)*

FOOD PRDTS: Malt

Great Western Malting Co .... G 800 496-7732
   Champlain *(G-3541)*

FOOD PRDTS: Mayonnaise & Dressings, Exc Tomato Based

Kensington & Sons LLC .... E 646 450-5735
   New York *(G-10835)*

FOOD PRDTS: Mixes, Bread & Bread-Type Roll

Archer-Daniels-Midland Company .... E 518 828-4691
   Hudson *(G-6605)*

FOOD PRDTS: Mixes, Bread & Roll From Purchased Flour

Elis Bread (eli Zabar) Inc .... F 212 772-2011
   New York *(G-10005)*

FOOD PRDTS: Mixes, Doughnut From Purchased Flour

Dawn Food Products Inc .... C 716 830-8214
   Williamsville *(G-17240)*

FOOD PRDTS: Mixes, Pancake From Purchased Flour

New Hope Mills Inc .... F 315 252-2676
   Auburn *(G-509)*

FOOD PRDTS: Molasses, Mixed/Blended, Purchased Ingredients

Amalfi Ingredients LLC .... G 631 392-1526
   Deer Park *(G-4095)*

FOOD PRDTS: Mustard, Prepared

Old Dutch Mustard Co Inc .... G 516 466-0522
   Great Neck *(G-5825)*

FOOD PRDTS: Nuts & Seeds

American Almond Pdts Co Inc .... E 718 875-8310
   Brooklyn *(G-1599)*
Our Daily Eats LLC .... F 518 810-8412
   Albany *(G-113)*
Scaccianoce Inc .... F 718 991-4462
   Bronx *(G-1449)*
Sugar Foods Corporation .... E 212 753-6900
   New York *(G-12227)*
Whitsons Food Svc Bronx Corp .... B 631 424-2700
   Islandia *(G-6804)*

FOOD PRDTS: Olive Oil

Bonelli Foods LLC .... G 212 346-0942
   New York *(G-9436)*
F Olivers LLC .... G 585 244-2585
   Rochester *(G-14367)*
L LLC .... E 716 885-3918
   Buffalo *(G-3039)*
Pietro Demarco Importers Inc .... F 914 969-3201
   Yonkers *(G-17477)*
Pinos Press Inc .... G 315 935-0110
   Syracuse *(G-16013)*

FOOD PRDTS: Oriental Noodles

Lams Foods Inc .... F 718 217-0476
   Queens Village *(G-13981)*
Twin Marquis Inc .... D 718 386-6868
   Brooklyn *(G-2691)*
Wonton Food Inc .... E 718 784-8178
   Long Island City *(G-7926)*
Wonton Food Inc .... C 718 628-6868
   Brooklyn *(G-2763)*

Wonton Food Inc .... F 212 677-8865
   New York *(G-12654)*

FOOD PRDTS: Pasta, Rice/Potatoes, Uncooked, Pkgd

Barilla America Ny Inc .... C 585 226-5600
   Avon *(G-539)*
Bektrom Foods Inc .... E 516 802-3800
   Syosset *(G-15813)*
New York Ravioli Pasta Co Inc .... E 516 270-2852
   New Hyde Park *(G-8851)*
Steinway Pasta & Gelati Inc .... F 718 246-5414
   Brooklyn *(G-2607)*

FOOD PRDTS: Pasta, Uncooked, Packaged With Other Ingredients

Great Eastern Pasta Works LLC .... E 631 956-0889
   West Babylon *(G-16794)*
Hong Hop Co Inc .... E 212 962-1735
   New York *(G-10502)*
Johns Ravioli Company Inc .... F 914 576-7030
   New Rochelle *(G-8915)*
Labella Pasta Inc .... G 845 331-9130
   Kingston *(G-7195)*
Sfoglini LLC .... F 646 872-1035
   Brooklyn *(G-2546)*

FOOD PRDTS: Peanut Butter

ABC Peanut Butter LLC .... B 212 661-6886
   New York *(G-9002)*
Once Again Nut Butter Collectv .... D 585 468-2535
   Nunda *(G-13041)*
Sneaky Chef Foods LLC .... F 914 301-3277
   Tarrytown *(G-16106)*
Wonder Natural Foods Corp .... G 631 726-4433
   Water Mill *(G-16607)*

FOOD PRDTS: Pickles, Vinegar

Allen Pickle Works Inc .... F 516 676-0640
   Glen Cove *(G-5610)*
Batampte Pickle Products Inc .... D 718 251-2100
   Brooklyn *(G-1673)*
Birds Eye Holdings Inc .... A 585 383-1850
   Rochester *(G-14232)*
French Associates Inc .... F 718 387-9880
   Fresh Meadows *(G-5440)*
Heintz & Weber Co Inc .... F 716 852-7171
   Buffalo *(G-2993)*
Moldova Pickles & Salads Inc .... C 718 284-2220
   Brooklyn *(G-2330)*

FOOD PRDTS: Pizza Doughs From Purchased Flour

Mastroianni Bros Inc .... E 518 355-5310
   Schenectady *(G-15277)*
Tosca Brick Oven Pizza Real .... G 718 430-0026
   Bronx *(G-1473)*

FOOD PRDTS: Pizza, Refrigerated

Ultra Thin Ready To Bake Pizza .... E 516 679-6655
   New Hyde Park *(G-8868)*

FOOD PRDTS: Potato & Corn Chips & Similar Prdts

BSD Top Direct Inc .... G 646 468-0156
   West Babylon *(G-16777)*
Frito-Lay North America Inc .... E 585 343-5456
   Batavia *(G-633)*
Hain Celestial Group Inc .... C 516 587-5000
   New Hyde Park *(G-8837)*
Ideal Snacks Corporation .... C 845 292-7000
   Liberty *(G-7437)*
Pepsico Inc .... A 914 253-2000
   Purchase *(G-13966)*
Pepsico Inc .... B 914 253-2000
   White Plains *(G-17154)*
Pepsico Inc .... C 914 767-6976
   White Plains *(G-17156)*
Robs Really Good LLC .... F 516 671-4411
   Sea Cliff *(G-15342)*
Simplycultivated Group LLC .... G 646 389-0682
   Horseheads *(G-6594)*
Snack Innovations Inc .... E 718 509-9366
   Brooklyn *(G-2574)*

Snacks On 48 Inc .... G 347 663-1100
   Brooklyn *(G-2575)*
Switch Beverage Company LLC .... F 203 202-7383
   Port Washington *(G-13867)*
TLC-Lc Inc .... E 212 756-8900
   New York *(G-12355)*

FOOD PRDTS: Potato Chips & Other Potato-Based Snacks

Birds Eye Holdings Inc .... A 585 383-1850
   Rochester *(G-14232)*
Frito-Lay North America Inc .... D 607 775-7000
   Binghamton *(G-916)*
Terrells Potato Chip Co Inc .... D 315 437-2786
   Syracuse *(G-16057)*

FOOD PRDTS: Potato Sticks

Pupellos Organic Chips Inc .... F 718 710-9154
   Oakdale *(G-13061)*

FOOD PRDTS: Potatoes, Dried, Packaged With Other Ingredients

Martens Country Kit Pdts LLC .... F 315 776-8821
   Port Byron *(G-13734)*

FOOD PRDTS: Poultry Sausage, Lunch Meats/Other Poultry Prdts

Alta Group Inc .... F 905 262-5707
   Lewiston *(G-7433)*

FOOD PRDTS: Poultry, Processed, NEC

Wendels Poultry Farm .... G 716 592-2299
   East Concord *(G-4386)*

FOOD PRDTS: Poultry, Slaughtered & Dressed

Sing Ah Poultry .... G 718 625-7253
   Brooklyn *(G-2564)*

FOOD PRDTS: Preparations

212kiddish Inc .... G 718 705-7227
   Brooklyn *(G-1512)*
3v Company Inc .... E 718 858-7333
   Brooklyn *(G-1517)*
Ahhmigo LLC .... F 212 315-1818
   New York *(G-9061)*
Armour Bearer Group Inc .... G 646 812-4487
   Arverne *(G-424)*
Aryzta LLC .... D 585 235-8160
   Rochester *(G-14214)*
Associated Brands Inc .... B 585 798-3475
   New York *(G-9238)*
Bainbridge & Knight LLC .... E 212 986-5100
   New York *(G-9307)*
Baldwin Richardson Foods Co .... C 315 986-2727
   Macedon *(G-7983)*
Bombay Kitchen Foods Inc .... F 516 767-7401
   Port Washington *(G-13802)*
Brightline Ventures I LLC .... E 212 626-6829
   New York *(G-9461)*
Bylada Foods LLC .... D 845 623-1300
   West Nyack *(G-16914)*
Castella Imports Inc .... C 631 231-5500
   Hauppauge *(G-6040)*
Chan & Chan (usa) Corp .... F 718 388-9633
   Brooklyn *(G-1773)*
Child Nutrition Prog Dept Ed .... D 212 371-1000
   New York *(G-9594)*
China Huaren Organic Pdts Inc .... G 212 232-0120
   New York *(G-9597)*
Cookiebaker LLC .... G 716 878-8000
   Buffalo *(G-2889)*
D R M Management Inc .... E 716 668-0333
   Depew *(G-4254)*
Dundee Foods LLC .... F 585 377-7700
   Fairport *(G-4855)*
Event Services Corporation .... G 315 488-9357
   Solvay *(G-15508)*
Fanshawe Foods LLC .... E 212 757-3130
   New York *(G-10135)*
Flaum Appetizing Corp .... E 718 821-1970
   Brooklyn *(G-1984)*
Frito-Lay North America Inc .... D 607 397-1008
   Worcester *(G-17368)*

PRODUCT SECTION

FOOD PRDTS: Tortillas

Frito-Lay North America Inc ....D....... 607 775-7000
  Binghamton *(G-916)*
Glenn Foods Inc ....F....... 516 377-1400
  Freeport *(G-5402)*
Gold Pure Food Products Co Inc ....D....... 516 483-5600
  Hempstead *(G-6272)*
Gourmet Boutique LLC ....C....... 718 977-1200
  Jamaica *(G-6916)*
Gourmet Crafts Inc ....F....... 718 372-0505
  Brooklyn *(G-2043)*
Gourmet Guru Inc ....E....... 718 842-2828
  Bronx *(G-1347)*
Gravymaster Inc ....E....... 203 453-1893
  Canajoharie *(G-3332)*
HP Hood LLC ....D....... 607 295-8134
  Arkport *(G-410)*
Instantwhip of Buffalo Inc ....E....... 716 892-7031
  Buffalo *(G-3010)*
Joyva Corp ....D....... 718 497-0170
  Brooklyn *(G-2154)*
Kale Factory Inc ....G....... 917 363-6361
  Brooklyn *(G-2166)*
Kerry Inc ....E....... 845 584-3080
  Congers *(G-3858)*
Kerry Inc ....D....... 607 334-1700
  Norwich *(G-13029)*
Kraft Heinz Foods Company ....A....... 914 335-2500
  Tarrytown *(G-16093)*
Kraft Heinz Foods Company ....B....... 585 226-4400
  Avon *(G-540)*
La Regina Di San Marzano ....G....... 212 269-4202
  New York *(G-10910)*
Land OLakes Inc ....G....... 516 681-2980
  Hicksville *(G-6362)*
Lollipop Tree Inc ....E....... 845 471-8733
  Auburn *(G-506)*
Mandalay Food Products Inc ....G....... 718 230-3370
  Brooklyn *(G-2257)*
Mediterrean Dyro Company ....E....... 718 786-4888
  Long Island City *(G-7809)*
Merb LLC ....G....... 631 393-3621
  Farmingdale *(G-5048)*
Meta-Therm Corp ....F....... 914 697-4840
  White Plains *(G-17137)*
Mighty Quinns Barbeque LLC ....E....... 973 777-8340
  New York *(G-11261)*
Milnot Holding Corporation ....G....... 518 839-0300
  Amsterdam *(G-357)*
Mizkan America Inc ....D....... 585 765-9171
  Lyndonville *(G-7968)*
Moira New Hope Food Pantry ....E....... 518 529-6524
  Moira *(G-8546)*
Mondelez Global LLC ....F....... 585 345-3300
  Batavia *(G-642)*
Morris Kitchen Inc ....F....... 646 413-5186
  Brooklyn *(G-2334)*
Natural Lab Inc ....G....... 718 321-8848
  Flushing *(G-5270)*
Naturally Free Food Inc ....G....... 631 361-9710
  Smithtown *(G-15492)*
P-Hgh 2 Co Inc ....G....... 954 534-6058
  Buffalo *(G-3109)*
Pane Vita LLC ....F....... 888 509-3310
  Rochester *(G-14570)*
Parnasa International Inc ....G....... 516 394-0400
  Valley Stream *(G-16418)*
Pelican Bay Ltd ....F....... 718 729-9300
  Long Island City *(G-7838)*
Pellicano Specialty Foods Inc ....F....... 716 822-2366
  Buffalo *(G-3117)*
Pennant Ingredients Inc ....D....... 585 235-8160
  Rochester *(G-14575)*
Raw Indulgence Ltd ....F....... 866 498-4671
  Hawthorne *(G-6253)*
Rob Salamida Company Inc ....F....... 607 729-4868
  Johnson City *(G-7105)*
Sabra Dipping Company LLC ....F....... 516 249-0151
  Farmingdale *(G-5107)*
Salvador Colletti Blank ....G....... 718 217-6725
  Douglaston *(G-4310)*
Sapienza Pastry Inc ....E....... 516 352-5232
  Elmont *(G-4729)*
Settons Intl Foods Inc ....E....... 631 543-8090
  Commack *(G-3842)*
Terrace Management Inc ....F....... 914 737-0400
  Cortlandt Manor *(G-4054)*
Tuv Taam Corp ....E....... 718 855-2207
  Brooklyn *(G-2689)*
UFS Industries Inc ....D....... 718 822-1100
  Mount Vernon *(G-8744)*
Whitsons Food Svc Bronx Corp ....B....... 631 424-2700
  Islandia *(G-6804)*
Win-Holt Equipment Corp ....E....... 516 222-0335
  Woodbury *(G-17303)*

FOOD PRDTS: Prepared Meat Sauces Exc Tomato & Dry

American Specialty Mfg Co ....F....... 585 544-5600
  Rochester *(G-14199)*

FOOD PRDTS: Prepared Sauces, Exc Tomato Based

Bushwick Kitchen LLC ....G....... 917 297-1045
  Brooklyn *(G-1739)*
Elwood International Inc ....F....... 631 842-6600
  Copiague *(G-3899)*
Gold Pure Food Products Co Inc ....D....... 516 483-5600
  Hempstead *(G-6272)*
Gravymaster Inc ....E....... 203 453-1893
  Canajoharie *(G-3332)*
Mandarin Soy Sauce Inc ....E....... 845 343-1505
  Middletown *(G-8449)*
Rob Salamida Company Inc ....F....... 607 729-4868
  Johnson City *(G-7105)*
Sassy Sauce Inc ....G....... 585 621-1050
  Rochester *(G-14669)*
T RS Great American Rest ....F....... 516 294-1680
  Williston Park *(G-17263)*

FOOD PRDTS: Raw cane sugar

Supreme Chocolatier LLC ....E....... 718 761-9600
  Staten Island *(G-15744)*

FOOD PRDTS: Relishes, Vinegar

Jets Lefrois Corp ....G....... 585 637-5003
  Brockport *(G-1245)*

FOOD PRDTS: Rice, Milled

Real Co Inc ....G....... 347 433-8549
  Valley Cottage *(G-16386)*

FOOD PRDTS: Salads

Golden Taste Inc ....E....... 845 356-4133
  Spring Valley *(G-15587)*
M & M Food Products Inc ....F....... 718 821-1970
  Brooklyn *(G-2244)*

FOOD PRDTS: Sauerkraut, Bulk

Glk Foods LLC ....E....... 585 289-4414
  Shortsville *(G-15433)*

FOOD PRDTS: Seasonings & Spices

Aromasong Usa Inc ....F....... 718 838-9669
  Brooklyn *(G-1630)*
Diva Farms Ltd ....G....... 315 735-4397
  Utica *(G-16326)*
La Flor Products Company Inc ....E....... 631 851-9601
  Hauppauge *(G-6111)*
Purespice LLC ....G....... 617 549-8400
  Hopewell Junction *(G-6558)*
SOS Chefs of New York Inc ....G....... 212 505-5813
  New York *(G-12139)*

FOOD PRDTS: Soup Mixes, Dried

Allied Food Products Inc ....F....... 718 230-4227
  Brooklyn *(G-1590)*
Interntional Gourmet Soups Inc ....E....... 212 768-7687
  Staten Island *(G-15688)*

FOOD PRDTS: Soy Sauce

Wanjashan International LLC ....F....... 845 343-1505
  Middletown *(G-8469)*

FOOD PRDTS: Spices, Including Ground

Bektrom Foods Inc ....E....... 516 802-3800
  Syosset *(G-15814)*
Manhattan Milling & Drying Co ....F....... 516 496-1041
  Woodbury *(G-17294)*
Victoria Fine Foods LLC ....D....... 718 649-1635
  Brooklyn *(G-2725)*
Wm E Martin and Sons Co Inc ....E....... 516 605-2444
  Roslyn *(G-15024)*

FOOD PRDTS: Spreads, Sandwich, Salad Dressing Base

Carriage House Companies Inc ....C....... 716 673-1000
  Dunkirk *(G-4334)*
Sabra Dipping Company LLC ....D....... 914 372-3900
  White Plains *(G-17166)*

FOOD PRDTS: Sugar

Real Co Inc ....G....... 347 433-8549
  Valley Cottage *(G-16386)*
Sugar Foods Corporation ....E....... 212 753-6900
  New York *(G-12227)*
Sugar Shack Desert Company Inc ....G....... 518 523-7540
  Lake Placid *(G-7276)*
U S Sugar Co Inc ....E....... 716 828-1170
  Buffalo *(G-3229)*

FOOD PRDTS: Sugar, Beet

Beets Love Production LLC ....E....... 585 270-2471
  Rochester *(G-14228)*

FOOD PRDTS: Sugar, Cane

Asr Group International Inc ....C....... 914 963-2400
  Yonkers *(G-17417)*
Sweeteners Plus Inc ....D....... 585 728-3770
  Lakeville *(G-7286)*

FOOD PRDTS: Sugar, Corn

Sweetwater Energy Inc ....G....... 585 647-5760
  Rochester *(G-14708)*

FOOD PRDTS: Syrup, Maple

Peaceful Valley Maple Farm ....G....... 518 762-0491
  Johnstown *(G-7119)*

FOOD PRDTS: Syrup, Pancake, Blended & Mixed

Peak Holdings LLC ....A....... 212 583-5000
  New York *(G-11588)*

FOOD PRDTS: Syrups

Carriage House Companies Inc ....A....... 716 672-4321
  Fredonia *(G-5371)*
Casablanca Foods LLC ....G....... 212 317-1111
  New York *(G-9540)*
Spf Holdings II LLC ....F....... 212 750-8300
  New York *(G-12161)*

FOOD PRDTS: Tea

Bel Americas Inc ....G....... 646 454-8220
  New York *(G-9347)*
Farmers Hub LLC ....G....... 646 380-6770
  White Plains *(G-17109)*
Gillies Coffee Company ....E....... 718 499-7766
  Brooklyn *(G-2024)*
Majani Tea Company ....F....... 817 896-5720
  New York *(G-11114)*

FOOD PRDTS: Tofu Desserts, Frozen

Pulmuone Foods Usa Inc ....E....... 845 365-3300
  Tappan *(G-16082)*

FOOD PRDTS: Tofu, Exc Frozen Desserts

Chan Kee Dried Bean Curd Inc ....G....... 718 622-0820
  Brooklyn *(G-1774)*
Seasons Soyfood Inc ....G....... 718 797-9896
  Brooklyn *(G-2542)*

FOOD PRDTS: Tortilla Chips

Tortilleria Chinantla Inc ....G....... 718 302-0101
  Brooklyn *(G-2668)*

FOOD PRDTS: Tortillas

Blue Tortilla LLC ....G....... 631 451-0100
  Selden *(G-15348)*
Buna Besta Tortillas ....G....... 347 987-3995
  Brooklyn *(G-1737)*
La Escondida Inc ....G....... 845 562-1387
  Newburgh *(G-12765)*
Maizteca Foods Inc ....E....... 718 641-3933
  South Richmond Hill *(G-15534)*

Employee Codes: A=Over 500 employees, B=251-500
C=101-250, D=51-100, E=20-50, F=10-19, G=5-9

FOOD PRDTS: Tortillas

Tortilla Heaven Inc .... E 845 339-1550
Kingston *(G-7217)*

FOOD PRDTS: Vegetables, Dried or Dehydrated Exc Freeze-Dried

Wm E Martin and Sons Co Inc .... E 516 605-2444
Roslyn *(G-15024)*

FOOD PRDTS: Vegetables, Pickled

United Pickle Products Corp .... E 718 933-6060
Bronx *(G-1486)*

FOOD PRDTS: Vinegar

Fleischmanns Vinegar Co Inc .... E 315 587-4414
North Rose *(G-12936)*
Mizkan Americas Inc .... F 585 798-5720
Medina *(G-8278)*
Mizkan Americas Inc .... F 315 483-6944
Sodus *(G-15503)*
Old Dutch Mustard Co Inc .... G 516 466-0522
Great Neck *(G-5825)*

FOOD PRODUCTS MACHINERY

Ag-Pak Inc .... F 716 772-2651
Gasport *(G-5555)*
Bakers Pride Oven Co Inc .... C 914 576-0200
New Rochelle *(G-8887)*
Bari Engineering Corp .... E 212 966-2080
New York *(G-9320)*
Buflovak LLC .... E 716 895-2100
Buffalo *(G-2861)*
C-Flex Bearing Co Inc .... F 315 895-7454
Frankfort *(G-5350)*
Carts Mobile Food Eqp Corp .... E 718 788-5540
Brooklyn *(G-1761)*
Chester-Jensen Company .... E 610 876-6276
Cattaraugus *(G-3437)*
Delsur Parts .... G 631 630-1606
Brentwood *(G-1181)*
Elmar Industries Inc .... D 716 681-5650
Depew *(G-4256)*
Esquire Mechanical Corp .... E 718 625-4006
Brooklyn *(G-1935)*
Feldmeier Equipment Inc .... C 315 823-2000
Little Falls *(G-7500)*
G J Olney Inc .... E 315 827-4208
Westernville *(G-17043)*
Haines Equipment Inc .... E 607 566-8531
Avoca *(G-537)*
I J White Corporation .... D 631 293-3788
Farmingdale *(G-5009)*
Kinplex Corp .... E 631 242-4800
Edgewood *(G-4604)*
Ludwig Holdings Corp .... D 845 340-9727
Kingston *(G-7198)*
Lyophilization Systems Inc .... E 845 338-0456
New Paltz *(G-8876)*
M & E Mfg Co Inc .... D 845 331-7890
Kingston *(G-7200)*
National Equipment Corporation .... F 718 585-0200
Bronx *(G-1405)*
National Equipment Corporation .... E 718 585-0200
Bronx *(G-1406)*
Olmstead Products Corp .... F 516 681-3700
Hicksville *(G-6379)*
P & M LLC .... E 631 842-2200
Amityville *(G-319)*
Sidco Food Distribution Corp .... F 718 733-3939
Bronx *(G-1452)*
Simply Natural Foods LLC .... E 631 543-9600
Commack *(G-3843)*
SPX Flow Tech Systems Inc .... D 716 692-3000
Getzville *(G-5604)*
Vr Food Equipment Inc .... F 315 531-8133
Penn Yan *(G-13522)*
Wilder Manufacturing Co Inc .... D 516 222-0433
Garden City *(G-5536)*
Win-Holt Equipment Corp .... C 516 222-0433
Garden City *(G-5537)*

FOOD STORES: Delicatessen

Cassinelli Food Products Inc .... G 718 274-4881
Long Island City *(G-7695)*
Jim Romas Bakery Inc .... E 607 748-7425
Endicott *(G-4817)*
Mds Hot Bagels Deli Inc .... G 718 438-5650
Brooklyn *(G-2289)*

Sam A Lupo & Sons Inc .... G 607 748-1141
Endicott *(G-4828)*

FOOD STORES: Grocery, Independent

Mandalay Food Products Inc .... G 718 230-3370
Brooklyn *(G-2257)*

FOOD STORES: Supermarkets

Hana Pastries Inc .... G 718 369-7593
Brooklyn *(G-2065)*
Reisman Bros Bakery Inc .... F 718 331-1975
Brooklyn *(G-2488)*

FOOTWEAR, WHOLESALE: Athletic

Air Skate & Air Jump Corp .... F 212 967-1201
Brooklyn *(G-1572)*

FOOTWEAR, WHOLESALE: Shoe Access

Bfma Holding Corporation .... G 607 753-6746
Cortland *(G-4014)*

FOOTWEAR, WHOLESALE: Shoes

Anthony L & S LLC .... G 212 386-7245
New York *(G-9168)*

FOOTWEAR: Cut Stock

Age Manufacturers Inc .... D 718 927-0048
Brooklyn *(G-1569)*
Golden Pacific Lxj Inc .... G 267 975-6537
New York *(G-10334)*
Premier Brands of America Inc .... C 914 667-6200
Mount Vernon *(G-8717)*

FORGINGS

Biltron Automotive Products .... E 631 928-8613
Port Jeff STA *(G-13763)*
Borgwarner Ithaca LLC .... B 607 257-6700
Ithaca *(G-6825)*
Borgwarner Morse TEC Inc .... B 607 257-6700
Ithaca *(G-6826)*
Borgwarner Morse TEC Inc .... D 607 257-6700
Ithaca *(G-6828)*
Burke Frging Heat Treating Inc .... E 585 235-6060
Rochester *(G-14251)*
Columbus McKinnon Corporation .... D 716 689-5400
Getzville *(G-5596)*
Delaware Valley Forge Inc .... E 716 447-9140
Buffalo *(G-2905)*
Designatronics Incorporated .... E 516 328-3300
New Hyde Park *(G-8825)*
Dragon Trading Inc .... G 212 717-1496
New York *(G-9923)*
Eaton Electric Holdings LLC .... C 607 756-2821
Cortland *(G-4025)*
Firth Rixson Inc .... D 585 328-1383
Rochester *(G-14371)*
Hohmann & Barnard Inc .... E 631 234-0600
Hauppauge *(G-6095)*
Hohmann & Barnard Inc .... E 518 357-9757
Schenectady *(G-15268)*
Jrlon Inc .... D 315 597-4067
Palmyra *(G-13409)*
Mattessich Iron LLC .... G 315 409-8496
Baldwinsville *(G-571)*
Peck & Hale LLC .... E 631 589-2510
West Sayville *(G-16937)*
Schilling Forge Inc .... E 315 454-4421
Syracuse *(G-16033)*
Special Metals Corporation .... D 716 366-5663
Dunkirk *(G-4351)*
Stoffel Polygon Systems Inc .... F 914 961-2000
Tuckahoe *(G-16272)*
Superior Motion Controls Inc .... E 516 420-2921
Farmingdale *(G-5120)*
Viking Iron Works Inc .... F 845 471-5010
Poughkeepsie *(G-13940)*
Vulcan Steam Forging Co .... E 716 875-3680
Buffalo *(G-3246)*
W J Albro Machine Works Inc .... G 631 345-0657
Yaphank *(G-17408)*
York Industries Inc .... E 516 746-3736
Garden City Park *(G-5546)*

FORGINGS: Armor Plate, Iron Or Steel

Trojan Steel .... G 518 686-7426
Hoosick Falls *(G-6546)*

FORGINGS: Automotive & Internal Combustion Engine

General Motors LLC .... A 716 879-5000
Buffalo *(G-2971)*
Ieh FM Holdings LLC .... E 212 702-4300
New York *(G-10559)*

FORGINGS: Gear & Chain

Ball Chain Mfg Co Inc .... D 914 664-7500
Mount Vernon *(G-8664)*
Crown Industrial .... G 607 745-8709
Cortland *(G-4024)*
Kurz and Zobel Inc .... G 585 254-9060
Rochester *(G-14472)*

FORGINGS: Machinery, Ferrous

Alry Tool and Die Co Inc .... E 716 693-2419
Tonawanda *(G-16137)*

FORGINGS: Metal, Ornamental, Ferrous

Paul & Franza LLC .... F 718 342-8106
Brooklyn *(G-2410)*

FORGINGS: Nonferrous

Hammond & Irving Inc .... D 315 253-6265
Auburn *(G-500)*
N F & M International Inc .... D 516 997-4212
Jericho *(G-7077)*
Special Metals Corporation .... D 716 366-5663
Dunkirk *(G-4351)*

FORGINGS: Pump & compressor, Nonferrous

Penn State Metal Fabri .... G 718 786-8814
Brooklyn *(G-2415)*

FORMS: Concrete, Sheet Metal

Gt Innovations LLC .... G 585 739-7659
Churchville *(G-3637)*

FOUNDRIES: Aluminum

Amt Incorporated .... E 518 284-2910
Sharon Springs *(G-15383)*
Carter Precision Metals LLC .... E 516 333-1917
Westbury *(G-16973)*
Charles Lay .... F 607 432-4518
Oneonta *(G-13177)*
Charles Lay .... G 607 656-4204
Greene *(G-5862)*
Consoldted Precision Pdts Corp .... B 315 687-0014
Chittenango *(G-3630)*
Crown Die Casting Corp .... E 914 667-5400
Mount Vernon *(G-8675)*
East Pattern & Model Corp .... E 585 461-3240
Fairport *(G-4856)*
Har-Son Mfg Inc .... F 716 532-2641
Gowanda *(G-5748)*
Massena Metals Inc .... F 315 769-3846
Massena *(G-8198)*
Meloon Foundries LLC .... E 315 454-3231
Syracuse *(G-15985)*
Micro Instrument Corp .... D 585 458-3150
Rochester *(G-14507)*
Pyrotek Incorporated .... D 607 756-3050
Cortland *(G-4041)*
Wolff & Dungey Inc .... E 315 475-2105
Syracuse *(G-16074)*

FOUNDRIES: Brass, Bronze & Copper

David Fehlman .... G 315 455-8888
Syracuse *(G-15922)*
Meloon Foundries LLC .... E 315 454-3231
Syracuse *(G-15985)*
Omega Wire Inc .... E 315 337-4300
Rome *(G-14829)*
Omega Wire Inc .... D 315 689-7115
Jordan *(G-7130)*

FOUNDRIES: Gray & Ductile Iron

Auburn Foundry Inc .... F 315 253-4441
Auburn *(G-479)*
En Tech Corp .... F 845 398-0776
Tappan *(G-16080)*

PRODUCT SECTION

Matrix Steel Company Inc ....G...... 718 381-6800
Brooklyn *(G-2284)*
McWane Inc ....B...... 607 734-2211
Elmira *(G-4694)*

FOUNDRIES: Iron

Eastern Company ....D...... 315 468-6251
Solvay *(G-15507)*
Emcom Industries Inc ....G...... 716 852-3711
Buffalo *(G-2936)*
Noresco Industrial Group Inc ....E...... 516 759-3355
Glen Cove *(G-5622)*
Plattco Corporation ....E...... 518 563-4640
Plattsburgh *(G-13687)*

FOUNDRIES: Nonferrous

Allstar Casting Corporation ....E...... 212 563-0909
New York *(G-9092)*
Argos Inc ....E...... 845 528-0576
Putnam Valley *(G-13973)*
Carrera Casting Corp ....C...... 212 382-3296
New York *(G-9536)*
Cast-All Corporation ....E...... 516 741-4025
Mineola *(G-8502)*
Cpp-Syracuse Inc ....E...... 315 687-0014
Chittenango *(G-3632)*
Crown Die Casting Corp ....E...... 914 667-5400
Mount Vernon *(G-8675)*
Globalfoundries US Inc ....C...... 518 305-9013
Malta *(G-8019)*
Globalfoundries US Inc ....F...... 408 462-3900
Ballston Spa *(G-597)*
Greenfield Die Casting Corp ....E...... 516 623-9230
Freeport *(G-5403)*
J & J Bronze & Aluminum Cast .....E...... 718 383-2111
Brooklyn *(G-2121)*
Jamestown Bronze Works Inc ....G...... 716 665-2302
Jamestown *(G-7006)*
K & H Precision Products Inc ....E...... 585 624-4894
Honeoye Falls *(G-6532)*
Karbra Company ....C...... 212 736-9300
New York *(G-10809)*
Kelly Foundry & Machine Co ....E...... 315 732-8313
Utica *(G-16346)*
Medi-Ray Inc ....D...... 877 898-3003
Tuckahoe *(G-16271)*
Wemco Casting LLC ....D...... 631 563-8050
Bohemia *(G-1156)*

FOUNDRIES: Steel

American Foundrymens Society ....D...... 315 468-6251
Syracuse *(G-15853)*
Amt Incorporated ....E...... 518 284-2910
Sharon Springs *(G-15383)*
Brinkman Intl Group Inc ....G...... 585 429-5000
Rochester *(G-14245)*
C J Winter Machine Tech ....F...... 585 429-5000
Rochester *(G-14254)*
Eastern Industrial Steel Corp ....G...... 845 639-9749
New City *(G-8785)*
Steel Craft Rolling Door ....F...... 631 608-8662
Copiague *(G-3929)*

FOUNDRIES: Steel Investment

Consoldted Precision Pdts Corp .....B...... 315 687-0014
Chittenango *(G-3630)*
Jbf Stainless LLC ....E...... 315 569-2800
Cazenovia *(G-3446)*
Quality Castings Inc ....E...... 732 409-3203
Long Island City *(G-7853)*

FRAMES & FRAMING WHOLESALE

AC Moore Incorporated ....G...... 516 796-5831
Bethpage *(G-863)*
Framerica Corporation ....D...... 631 650-1000
Yaphank *(G-17393)*
Galas Framing Services ....F...... 718 706-0007
Long Island City *(G-7747)*
General Art Company Inc ....F...... 212 255-1298
New York *(G-10272)*
Inter Pacific Consulting Corp ....G...... 718 460-2787
Flushing *(G-5252)*

FRANCHISES, SELLING OR LICENSING

Hugo Boss Usa Inc ....D...... 212 940-0600
New York *(G-10528)*

John Varvatos Company ....E...... 212 812-8000
New York *(G-10754)*
Perry Ellis International Inc ....F...... 212 536-5400
New York *(G-11622)*

FREIGHT CONSOLIDATION SVCS

ITT Industries Holdings Inc ....G...... 914 641-2000
White Plains *(G-17129)*

FREIGHT FORWARDING ARRANGEMENTS

Marken LLP ....G...... 631 396-7454
Farmingdale *(G-5041)*

FRICTION MATERIAL, MADE FROM POWDERED METAL

Materion Brewster LLC ....D...... 845 279-0900
Brewster *(G-1223)*
Raytech Corp Asbestos Personal ..G...... 516 747-0300
Mineola *(G-8533)*
Raytech Corporation ....G...... 718 259-7388
Woodbury *(G-17297)*

FRUITS & VEGETABLES WHOLESALERS: Fresh

Sabra Dipping Company LLC ....F...... 516 249-0151
Farmingdale *(G-5107)*

FUEL ADDITIVES

E-Zoil Products Inc ....E...... 716 213-0103
Tonawanda *(G-16158)*
Enertech Labs Inc ....G...... 716 332-9074
Buffalo *(G-2938)*
Fppf Chemical Co Inc ....G...... 716 856-9607
Buffalo *(G-2954)*
Green Global Energy Inc ....G...... 716 501-9770
Niagara Falls *(G-12828)*
Kinetic Fuel Technology Inc ....G...... 716 745-1461
Youngstown *(G-17531)*

FUEL BRIQUETTES & WAXES

Costello Bros Petroleum Corp ....G...... 914 237-3189
Yonkers *(G-17430)*

FUEL BRIQUETTES OR BOULETS, MADE WITH PETROLEUM BINDER

Cooks Intl Ltd Lblty Co ....G...... 212 741-4407
New York *(G-9717)*

FUEL CELL FORMS: Cardboard, Made From Purchased Materials

Emergent Power Inc ....G...... 201 441-3590
Latham *(G-7362)*
Plug Power Inc ....B...... 518 782-7700
Latham *(G-7377)*

FUEL CELLS: Solid State

American Fuel Cell LLC ....G...... 585 474-3993
Rochester *(G-14197)*
Solid Cell Inc ....G...... 585 426-5000
Rochester *(G-14691)*

FUEL DEALERS: Wood

B & J Lumber Co Inc ....G...... 518 677-3845
Cambridge *(G-3304)*

FUEL OIL DEALERS

Bluebar Oil Co Inc ....F...... 315 245-4328
Blossvale *(G-997)*
Costello Bros Petroleum Corp ....G...... 914 237-3189
Yonkers *(G-17430)*
Montauk Inlet Seafood Inc ....G...... 631 668-3419
Montauk *(G-8590)*

FUELS: Diesel

Algafuel America ....G...... 516 295-2257
Hewlett *(G-6307)*
Northern Biodiesel Inc ....G...... 585 545-4534
Ontario *(G-13206)*
Performance Diesel Service LLC ...F...... 315 854-5269
Plattsburgh *(G-13686)*

Tri-State Biodiesel LLC ....D...... 718 860-6600
Bronx *(G-1476)*

FUELS: Ethanol

A and L Home Fuel LLC ....F...... 607 638-1994
Schenevus *(G-15314)*
Agrasun Inc ....F...... 305 377-3337
New York *(G-9059)*
Aj Greentech Holdings Ltd ....G...... 718 395-8706
Flushing *(G-5223)*
Avstar Fuel Systems Inc ....G...... 315 255-1955
Auburn *(G-483)*
Buell Fuel LLC ....F...... 315 841-3000
Deansboro *(G-4084)*
CAM Fuel Inc ....G...... 718 246-4306
Brooklyn *(G-1750)*
Castle Fuels Corporation ....E...... 914 381-6600
Harrison *(G-5977)*
Centar Fuel Co Inc ....G...... 516 538-2424
West Hempstead *(G-16851)*
Consolidated Edison Co NY Inc ....C...... 914 933-2936
Rye *(G-15055)*
Degennaro Fuel Service LLC ....G...... 518 239-6350
Medusa *(G-8285)*
Dib Managmnt Inc ....F...... 718 439-8190
Brooklyn *(G-1862)*
Economy Energy LLC ....G...... 845 222-3384
Peekskill *(G-13476)*
Euro Fuel Co ....G...... 914 424-5052
Patterson *(G-13439)*
Family Fuel Co Inc ....G...... 718 232-2009
Brooklyn *(G-1956)*
Fire Island Fuel ....G...... 631 772-1482
Shirley *(G-15418)*
Friendly Fuel Incorporated ....G...... 518 581-7036
Saratoga Springs *(G-15153)*
Friendly Star Fuel Inc ....G...... 718 369-8801
Brooklyn *(G-2007)*
Fuel Energy Services USA Ltd ......E...... 607 846-2650
Horseheads *(G-6578)*
Fuel Tank Environmental ....G...... 631 902-1408
Centerport *(G-3477)*
Golden Renewable Energy LLC ....G...... 914 920-9800
Yonkers *(G-17448)*
Jmg Fuel Inc ....G...... 631 579-4319
Ronkonkoma *(G-14920)*
JRs Fuels Inc ....G...... 518 622-9939
Cairo *(G-3273)*
Kore Infrastructure LLC ....G...... 646 532-9060
Glen Cove *(G-5620)*
Leroux Fuels ....G...... 518 563-3653
Plattsburgh *(G-13676)*
Liberty Food and Fuel ....G...... 315 299-4039
Syracuse *(G-15977)*
Lift Safe - Fuel Safe Inc ....F...... 315 423-7702
Syracuse *(G-15978)*
Lo-Co Fuel Corp ....G...... 631 929-5086
Wading River *(G-16524)*
Logo ....G...... 212 846-2568
New York *(G-11022)*
MNS Fuel Corp ....F...... 516 735-3835
Ronkonkoma *(G-14945)*
Morgan Fuel & Heating Co Inc ......E...... 845 856-7831
Port Jervis *(G-13789)*
Morgan Fuel & Heating Co Inc ......E...... 845 246-4931
Saugerties *(G-15188)*
Morgan Fuel & Heating Co Inc ......E...... 845 626-7766
Kerhonkson *(G-7156)*
N & L Fuel Corp ....G...... 718 863-3538
Bronx *(G-1404)*
North East Fuel Group Inc ....G...... 718 984-6774
Staten Island *(G-15714)*
Northeastern Fuel Corp ....G...... 917 560-6241
Staten Island *(G-15715)*
Northeastern Fuel NY Inc ....G...... 718 761-5360
Staten Island *(G-15716)*
Patdan Fuel Corporation ....G...... 718 326-3668
Middle Village *(G-8416)*
Provident Fuel Inc ....G...... 516 224-4427
Woodbury *(G-17296)*
Quality Fuel 1 Corporation ....G...... 631 392-4090
North Babylon *(G-12903)*
Remsen Fuel Inc ....G...... 718 984-9551
Staten Island *(G-15730)*
S&B Alternative Fuels Inc ....G...... 631 585-6637
Lake Grove *(G-7265)*
Smith & Sons Fuels Inc ....G...... 518 661-6112
Mayfield *(G-8214)*
Southbay Fuel Injectors ....G...... 516 442-4707
Rockville Centre *(G-14800)*

FUELS: Ethanol

York Fuel Incorporated ....G....... 718 951-0202
  Brooklyn *(G-2777)*

FUELS: Oil

209 Discount Oil ....E....... 845 386-2090
  Middletown *(G-8424)*
Ergun Inc ....G....... 631 721-0049
  Roslyn Heights *(G-15025)*
Heat USA II LLC ....F....... 212 254-4328
  College Point *(G-3786)*
Heat USA II LLC ....E....... 212 564-4328
  New York *(G-10453)*
Hygrade Fuel Inc ....G....... 516 741-0723
  Mineola *(G-8514)*
Ringhoff Fuel Inc ....G....... 631 878-0663
  East Moriches *(G-4430)*
Starfuels Inc ....G....... 914 289-4800
  White Plains *(G-17170)*

FUNDRAISING SVCS

Consumers Union US Inc ....B....... 914 378-2000
  Yonkers *(G-17429)*

FUNERAL HOMES & SVCS

Sunnycrest Inc ....E....... 315 252-7214
  Auburn *(G-521)*

FUNGICIDES OR HERBICIDES

Bioworks Inc ....G....... 585 924-4362
  Victor *(G-16463)*

FUR APPAREL STORES

Missiontex Inc ....G....... 718 532-9053
  Brooklyn *(G-2322)*

FUR CLOTHING WHOLESALERS

Blum & Fink Inc ....F....... 212 695-2606
  New York *(G-9426)*
Georgy Creative Fashions Inc ....G....... 212 279-4885
  New York *(G-10284)*

FUR FINISHING & LINING: For The Fur Goods Trade

Steves Original Furs Inc ....E....... 212 967-8007
  New York *(G-12203)*

FUR: Apparel

Arbeit Bros Inc ....G....... 212 736-9761
  New York *(G-9190)*
CPT Usa LLC ....E....... 212 575-1616
  New York *(G-9741)*
Fox Unlimited Inc ....G....... 212 736-3071
  New York *(G-10195)*
Jerry Sorbara Furs Inc ....F....... 212 594-3897
  New York *(G-10721)*
Mink Mart Inc ....G....... 212 868-2785
  New York *(G-11278)*
Superior Furs Inc ....F....... 516 365-4123
  Manhasset *(G-8065)*
Xanadu ....G....... 212 465-0580
  New York *(G-12674)*

FUR: Coats

Anastasia First International ....F....... 212 868-9241
  New York *(G-9149)*
Stallion Inc ....E....... 718 706-0111
  Long Island City *(G-7882)*

FUR: Coats & Other Apparel

Blum & Fink Inc ....F....... 212 695-2606
  New York *(G-9426)*
J Percy For Mrvin Rchards Ltd ....E....... 212 944-5300
  New York *(G-10680)*
Moschos Furs Inc ....G....... 212 244-0255
  New York *(G-11309)*
N Pologeorgis Furs Inc ....G....... 212 563-2250
  New York *(G-11335)*
Samuel Schulman Furs Inc ....G....... 212 736-5550
  New York *(G-11963)*
USA Furs By George Inc ....G....... 212 643-1415
  New York *(G-12490)*

FUR: Hats

Best Brands Consumer Pdts Inc ....G....... 212 684-7456
  New York *(G-9373)*
Kaitery Furs Ltd ....G....... 718 204-1396
  Long Island City *(G-7778)*

FUR: Jackets

Anage Inc ....F....... 212 944-6533
  New York *(G-9144)*

FURNACES & OVENS: Indl

Buflovak LLC ....E....... 716 895-2100
  Buffalo *(G-2861)*
Cosmos Electronic Machine Corp ....E....... 631 249-2535
  Farmingdale *(G-4963)*
Embassy Industries Inc ....C....... 631 435-0209
  Hauppauge *(G-6071)*
Harper International Corp ....D....... 716 276-9900
  Buffalo *(G-2991)*
Hpi Co Inc ....G....... 718 851-2753
  Brooklyn *(G-2089)*
J H Buhrmaster Company Inc ....G....... 518 843-1700
  Amsterdam *(G-351)*
Linde LLC ....G....... 716 773-7552
  Grand Island *(G-5763)*
Parker-Hannifin Corporation ....D....... 716 685-4040
  Lancaster *(G-7331)*
Rayco Enterprises Inc ....D....... 716 685-6860
  Lancaster *(G-7337)*
Vincent Genoveso ....G....... 631 281-8170
  Mastic Beach *(G-8205)*

FURNACES: Indl, Electric

Cooks Intl Ltd Lblty Co ....G....... 212 741-4407
  New York *(G-9717)*

FURNACES: Warm Air, Electric

Marathon Heater Co Inc ....G....... 607 657-8113
  Richford *(G-14063)*

FURNISHINGS: Bridge Sets, Cloth/Napkin, From Purchased Matls

State Bags LLC ....F....... 617 895-8532
  New York *(G-12188)*

FURNITURE & CABINET STORES: Cabinets, Custom Work

A Van Hoek Woodworking Limited ....G....... 718 599-4388
  Brooklyn *(G-1536)*
Central Kitchen Corp ....F....... 631 283-1029
  Southampton *(G-15541)*
Custom Woodcraft LLC ....F....... 315 843-4234
  Munnsville *(G-8750)*
Di Fiore and Sons Custom Wdwkg ....G....... 718 278-1663
  Long Island City *(G-7715)*
Jamestown Kitchen & Bath Inc ....G....... 716 665-2299
  Jamestown *(G-7008)*
Time Base Corporation ....E....... 631 293-4068
  Edgewood *(G-4617)*
Ultimate Styles of America ....F....... 631 254-0219
  Bay Shore *(G-753)*

FURNITURE & CABINET STORES: Custom

Red White & Blue Entps Corp ....G....... 718 565-8080
  Woodside *(G-17350)*

FURNITURE & FIXTURES Factory

Adirondack Scenic Inc ....D....... 518 638-8000
  Argyle *(G-409)*
Arper USA Inc ....G....... 212 647-8900
  New York *(G-9207)*
Artistry In Wood of Syracuse ....F....... 315 431-4022
  East Syracuse *(G-4506)*
Futon City Discounters Inc ....F....... 315 437-1328
  Syracuse *(G-15944)*
Interiors-Pft Inc ....E....... 212 244-9600
  Long Island City *(G-7767)*
J P Installations Warehouse ....F....... 914 576-3188
  New Rochelle *(G-8914)*
Modu-Craft Inc ....G....... 716 694-0709
  North Tonawanda *(G-12982)*
Modu-Craft Inc ....G....... 716 694-0709
  Tonawanda *(G-16182)*

T-Company LLC ....G....... 646 290-6365
  Smithtown *(G-15500)*

FURNITURE PARTS: Metal

Dimar Manufacturing Corp ....C....... 716 759-0351
  Clarence *(G-3656)*
Icestone LLC ....E....... 718 624-4900
  Brooklyn *(G-2095)*
Noll Reynolds Met Fabrication ....G....... 315 422-3333
  Syracuse *(G-15999)*
Petro Moore Manufacturing Corp ....G....... 718 784-2516
  Long Island City *(G-7841)*

FURNITURE REFINISHING SVCS

Telesca-Heyman Inc ....F....... 212 534-3442
  New York *(G-12296)*
X F Inc ....F....... 212 244-2240
  Brooklyn *(G-2770)*

FURNITURE STOCK & PARTS: Carvings, Wood

Jim Quinn ....F....... 518 356-0398
  Schenectady *(G-15270)*
Mason Carvings Inc ....G....... 716 664-9402
  Jamestown *(G-7017)*

FURNITURE STOCK & PARTS: Dimension Stock, Hardwood

North Hudson Woodcraft Corp ....E....... 315 429-3105
  Dolgeville *(G-4306)*
Randolph Dimension Corporation ....F....... 716 358-6901
  Randolph *(G-14017)*

FURNITURE STOCK & PARTS: Frames, Upholstered Furniture, Wood

Artistic Frame Corp ....C....... 212 289-2100
  New York *(G-9219)*
Cassadaga Designs Inc ....G....... 716 595-3030
  Cassadaga *(G-3414)*
Empire Exhibits & Displays Inc ....F....... 518 266-9362
  Mechanicville *(G-8227)*
Vitobob Furniture Inc ....G....... 516 676-1696
  Long Island City *(G-7916)*

FURNITURE STOCK & PARTS: Hardwood

Guldenschuh Logging & Lbr LLC ....G....... 585 538-4750
  Caledonia *(G-3280)*

FURNITURE STORES

Chair Factory ....E....... 718 363-2383
  Brooklyn *(G-1771)*
Classic Sofa Ltd ....D....... 212 620-0485
  New York *(G-9637)*
D & W Design Inc ....E....... 845 343-3366
  Middletown *(G-8435)*
French & Itln Furn Craftsmen ....G....... 718 599-5000
  Brooklyn *(G-2004)*
Furniture Doctor Inc ....G....... 585 657-6941
  Bloomfield *(G-988)*
Futon City Discounters Inc ....F....... 315 437-1328
  Syracuse *(G-15944)*
Legacy Furniture Inc ....F....... 718 527-5331
  Monroe *(G-8560)*
Little Wolf Cabinet Shop Inc ....E....... 212 734-1116
  New York *(G-11013)*
Long Lumber and Supply Corp ....F....... 518 439-1661
  Slingerlands *(G-15477)*
Manhattan Comfort Inc ....E....... 888 230-2225
  Brooklyn *(G-2259)*
Omega Furniture Manufacturing ....F....... 315 463-7428
  Syracuse *(G-16003)*
Pillow Perfections Ltd Inc ....G....... 718 383-2259
  Brooklyn *(G-2420)*
Recycled Brooklyn Group LLC ....F....... 917 902-0662
  Brooklyn *(G-2485)*
Royal Jamestown Furniture Inc ....E....... 716 664-5260
  Jamestown *(G-7026)*
Safavieh Inc ....B....... 516 945-1900
  Port Washington *(G-13860)*
Smart Space Products LLC ....G....... 877 777-2441
  New York *(G-12101)*
Studio 21 LA Inc ....E....... 718 965-6579
  Brooklyn *(G-2612)*
Yepes Fine Furniture ....E....... 718 383-0221
  Brooklyn *(G-2774)*

PRODUCT SECTION

FURNITURE: Household, Metal

FURNITURE STORES: Cabinets, Kitchen, Exc Custom Made
- Home Ideal Inc .... G 718 762-8998
  Flushing *(G-5251)*

FURNITURE STORES: Custom Made, Exc Cabinets
- Atelier Viollet Corp .... G 718 782-1727
  Brooklyn *(G-1644)*
- Designway Ltd .... G 212 254-2220
  New York *(G-9858)*
- John Langenbacher Co Inc .... E 718 328-0141
  Bronx *(G-1368)*

FURNITURE STORES: Juvenile
- Casa Collection Inc .... G 718 694-0272
  Brooklyn *(G-1762)*

FURNITURE STORES: Office
- X F Inc .... F 212 244-2240
  Brooklyn *(G-2770)*

FURNITURE STORES: Outdoor & Garden
- Pei Liquidation Company .... F 315 431-4697
  East Syracuse *(G-4554)*
- Walpole Woodworkers Inc .... G 631 726-2859
  Water Mill *(G-16606)*
- Wood Innovations of Suffolk .... G 631 698-2345
  Medford *(G-8263)*

FURNITURE STORES: Unfinished
- Universal Designs Inc .... G 718 721-1111
  Long Island City *(G-7910)*

FURNITURE UPHOLSTERY REPAIR SVCS
- Sofa Doctor Inc .... G 718 292-6300
  Bronx *(G-1458)*

FURNITURE WHOLESALERS
- Etna Products Co Inc .... F 212 989-7591
  New York *(G-10078)*
- Furniture Doctor Inc .... G 585 657-6941
  Bloomfield *(G-988)*
- Harden Furniture Inc .... C 315 675-3600
  Mc Connellsville *(G-8220)*
- Holland & Sherry Inc .... E 212 542-8410
  New York *(G-10497)*

FURNITURE, HOUSEHOLD: Wholesalers
- Legacy Furniture Inc .... F 718 527-5331
  Monroe *(G-8560)*
- Steinbock-Braff Inc .... E 718 972-6500
  Brooklyn *(G-2606)*

FURNITURE, OFFICE: Wholesalers
- Artistic Frame Corp .... C 212 289-2100
  New York *(G-9219)*
- Kas-Ray Industries Inc .... F 212 620-3144
  New York *(G-10812)*
- Workplace Interiors LLC .... F 585 425-7420
  Fairport *(G-4887)*

FURNITURE, WHOLESALE: Beds & Bedding
- Jdt International LLC .... G 212 400-7570
  New York *(G-10712)*
- Wcd Window Coverings Inc .... E 845 336-4511
  Lake Katrine *(G-7271)*

FURNITURE, WHOLESALE: Racks
- ASAP Rack Rental Inc .... G 718 499-4495
  Brooklyn *(G-1638)*
- Reliable Welding & Fabrication .... G 631 758-2637
  Patchogue *(G-13284)*

FURNITURE: Bar furniture
- W&P Design LLC .... G 434 806-1443
  Brooklyn *(G-2741)*

FURNITURE: Bed Frames & Headboards, Wood
- Inova LLC .... E 212 932-0366
  New York *(G-10608)*
- Sleep Care Enterprises Inc .... G 631 246-9000
  Stony Brook *(G-15771)*

FURNITURE: Bedroom, Wood
- Fiber-Seal of New York Inc .... G 212 888-5580
  New York *(G-10157)*

FURNITURE: Beds, Household, Incl Folding & Cabinet, Metal
- Charles P Rogers Brass Beds .... F 212 675-4400
  New York *(G-9582)*

FURNITURE: Bookcases, Office, Wood
- F E Hale Mfg Co .... D 315 894-5490
  Frankfort *(G-5352)*

FURNITURE: Box Springs, Assembled
- Charles H Beckley Inc .... F 718 665-2218
  Bronx *(G-1297)*

FURNITURE: Cabinets & Filing Drawers, Office, Exc Wood
- Falvo Manufacturing Co Inc .... F 315 738-7682
  Utica *(G-16330)*
- Ulrich Planfiling Eqp Corp .... E 716 763-1815
  Lakewood *(G-7295)*

FURNITURE: Cabinets & Vanities, Medicine, Metal
- Glissade New York LLC .... E 631 756-4800
  Farmingdale *(G-4999)*

FURNITURE: Chairs & Couches, Wood, Upholstered
- Jackson Dakota Inc .... F 718 786-8600
  Long Island City *(G-7769)*

FURNITURE: Chairs, Household Upholstered
- Avanti Furniture Corp .... F 516 293-8220
  Farmingdale *(G-4949)*

FURNITURE: Chairs, Household Wood
- Cassadaga Designs Inc .... G 716 595-3030
  Cassadaga *(G-3414)*
- Custom Display Manufacture .... G 516 783-6491
  North Bellmore *(G-12920)*
- Hunt Country Furniture Inc .... D 845 832-6601
  Wingdale *(G-17274)*

FURNITURE: Chairs, Office Exc Wood
- Keilhauer .... F 646 742-0192
  New York *(G-10829)*
- Poppin Inc .... D 212 391-7200
  New York *(G-11685)*
- Vitra Inc .... F 212 463-5700
  New York *(G-12558)*

FURNITURE: Chairs, Office Wood
- Interior Solutions of Wny LLC .... G 716 332-0372
  Buffalo *(G-3011)*

FURNITURE: China Closets
- Raff Enterprises .... G 518 218-7883
  Albany *(G-126)*

FURNITURE: Church
- American Bptst Chrches Mtro NY .... G 212 870-3195
  New York *(G-9115)*

FURNITURE: Console Tables, Wood
- Forecast Consoles Inc .... E 631 253-9000
  Hauppauge *(G-6079)*

FURNITURE: Couches, Sofa/Davenport, Upholstered Wood Frames
- Classic Sofa Ltd .... D 212 620-0485
  New York *(G-9637)*

FURNITURE: Cribs, Metal
- Hard Manufacturing Co Inc .... D 716 893-1800
  Buffalo *(G-2988)*
- NK Medical Products Inc .... G 716 759-7200
  Amherst *(G-254)*
- Novum Medical Products Inc .... F 716 759-7200
  Amherst *(G-255)*

FURNITURE: Cut Stone
- Puccio Design International .... F 516 248-6426
  Garden City *(G-5528)*

FURNITURE: Desks & Tables, Office, Exc Wood
- Kimball Office Inc .... E 212 753-6161
  New York *(G-10847)*

FURNITURE: Desks & Tables, Office, Wood
- Centre Interiors Wdwkg Co Inc .... E 718 323-1343
  Ozone Park *(G-13376)*

FURNITURE: Desks, Wood
- Bush Industries Inc .... C 716 665-2000
  Jamestown *(G-6978)*

FURNITURE: Dinette Sets, Metal
- Embassy Dinettes Inc .... G 631 253-2292
  Deer Park *(G-4138)*

FURNITURE: Dining Room, Wood
- Falcon Chair and Table Inc .... E 716 664-7136
  Falconer *(G-4897)*

FURNITURE: Foundations & Platforms
- Ideal Manufacturing Inc .... E 585 872-7190
  East Rochester *(G-4462)*

FURNITURE: Garden, Exc Wood, Metal, Stone Or Concrete
- Anandamali Inc .... F 212 343-8964
  New York *(G-9147)*
- Holland & Sherry Inc .... E 212 542-8410
  New York *(G-10497)*

FURNITURE: Hospital
- AFC Industries Inc .... D 347 532-1200
  College Point *(G-3777)*
- Brandt Equipment LLC .... G 718 994-0800
  Bronx *(G-1288)*
- Evans & Paul LLC .... E 516 576-0800
  Plainview *(G-13600)*

FURNITURE: Hotel
- N3a Corporation .... D 516 284-6799
  Inwood *(G-6762)*
- Ramler International Ltd .... E 516 353-3106
  Syosset *(G-15836)*
- Smart Space Products LLC .... G 877 777-2441
  New York *(G-12101)*

FURNITURE: Household, Metal
- Brueton Industries Inc .... D 516 379-3400
  Freeport *(G-5391)*
- D & W Design Inc .... E 845 343-3366
  Middletown *(G-8435)*
- F&M Ornamental Designs LLC .... G 212 353-2600
  New York *(G-10117)*
- F&M Ornamental Designs LLC .... F 908 241-7776
  New York *(G-10118)*
- Furniture Doctor Inc .... G 585 657-6941
  Bloomfield *(G-988)*
- Meeker Sales Corp .... G 718 384-5400
  Brooklyn *(G-2293)*
- Royal Metal Products Inc .... E 518 966-4442
  Surprise *(G-15811)*

FURNITURE: Household, Metal

Slava Industries Incorporated ....G....... 718 499-4850
  Brooklyn (G-2568)
Steelcraft Manufacturing Co ....F....... 718 277-2404
  Brooklyn (G-2603)

FURNITURE: Household, NEC

Matthew Shively LLC ....G....... 914 937-3531
  Port Chester (G-13754)

FURNITURE: Household, Upholstered On Metal Frames

Precision Orna Ir Works Inc ....G....... 718 379-5200
  Bronx (G-1433)

FURNITURE: Household, Upholstered, Exc Wood Or Metal

3phase Industries LLC ....G....... 347 763-2942
  Brooklyn (G-1515)
Albert Menin Interiors Ltd ....F....... 212 876-3041
  Bronx (G-1267)
Culin/Colella Inc ....G....... 914 698-7727
  Mamaroneck (G-8031)
Harome Designs LLC ....E....... 631 864-1900
  Commack (G-3834)
L& JG Stickley Incorporated ....A....... 315 682-5500
  Manlius (G-8073)
Mbh Furniture Innovations Inc ....G....... 845 354-8202
  Spring Valley (G-15595)
Olollo Inc 877 701-0110
  Brooklyn (G-2390)
Ready To Assemble Company Inc ....F....... 516 825-4397
  Valley Stream (G-16424)
Spancraft Ltd ....F....... 516 295-0055
  Woodmere (G-17314)

FURNITURE: Household, Wood

A & S Woodworking Inc ....G....... 518 821-0832
  Hudson (G-6602)
A-1 Manhattan Custom Furn Inc ....G....... 212 750-9800
  Island Park (G-6777)
Anthony Lawrence of New York ....E....... 212 206-8820
  Long Island City (G-7661)
Arthur Brown W Mfg Co ....F....... 631 243-5594
  Deer Park (G-4102)
Arthur Lauer Inc ....E....... 845 255-7871
  Gardiner (G-5547)
Artisan Woodworking Ltd ....G....... 516 486-0818
  West Hempstead (G-16849)
Atelier Viollet Corp ....G....... 718 782-1727
  Brooklyn (G-1644)
Bel Art International ....E....... 718 402-2100
  Bronx (G-1282)
Benchmark Furniture Mfg ....D....... 718 257-4707
  Brooklyn (G-1681)
Black River Valley Wdwkg LLC ....G....... 315 376-8405
  Castorland (G-3421)
Brueton Industries Inc ....D....... 516 379-3400
  Freeport (G-5391)
Bush Industries Inc ....C....... 716 665-2000
  Jamestown (G-6978)
Carlos & Alex Atelier Inc ....E....... 718 441-8911
  Richmond Hill (G-14070)
Carver Creek Enterprises Inc ....G....... 585 657-7511
  Bloomfield (G-983)
Charles H Beckley Inc ....F....... 718 665-2218
  Bronx (G-1297)
Comerford Hennessy At Home Inc ....G....... 631 537-6200
  Bridgehampton (G-1233)
Concepts In Wood of CNY ....E....... 315 463-8084
  Syracuse (G-15904)
Conesus Lake Association Inc ....E....... 585 346-6864
  Lakeville (G-7283)
Cousins Furniture & Hm Imprvs ....E....... 631 254-3752
  Deer Park (G-4121)
Crawford Furniture Mfg Corp ....C....... 716 483-2102
  Jamestown (G-6985)
Custom Woodcraft LLC ....F....... 315 843-4234
  Munnsville (G-8750)
D & W Design Inc ....G....... 845 343-3366
  Middletown (G-8435)
David Sutherland Showrooms - N ....G....... 212 871-9717
  New York (G-9823)
Dbs Interiors Corp ....F....... 631 491-3013
  West Babylon (G-16788)
Dcl Furniture Manufacturing 516 248-2683
  Mineola (G-8505)
Deakon Homes and Interiors ....F....... 518 271-0342
  Troy (G-16233)
Designs By Robert Scott Inc ....E....... 718 609-2535
  Brooklyn (G-1857)
Dessin/Fournir Inc ....F....... 212 758-0844
  New York (G-9859)
Dune Inc 212 925-6171
  New York (G-9938)
E-One Inc ....D....... 716 646-6790
  Hamburg (G-5921)
Eclectic Cntract Furn Inds Inc ....F....... 212 967-5504
  New York (G-9976)
El Greco Woodworking Inc ....E....... 716 483-0315
  Jamestown (G-6991)
Emilia Interiors Inc ....F....... 718 629-4202
  Brooklyn (G-1920)
Eugenia Selective Living Inc ....F....... 631 277-1461
  Islip (G-6808)
Eurocraft Custom Furniture 718 956-0600
  Long Island City (G-7732)
Fenix Furniture Co 631 273-3500
  Bay Shore (G-700)
Final Dimension Inc 718 786-0100
  Maspeth (G-8139)
Fine Arts Furniture Inc ....E....... 212 744-9139
  Long Island City (G-7740)
Franz Fischer Inc ....F....... 718 821-1300
  Brooklyn (G-2003)
Fred Schulz Inc ....G....... 845 724-3409
  Poughquag (G-13941)
French & Itln Furn Craftsmen ....G....... 718 599-5000
  Brooklyn (G-2004)
Furniture Doctor Inc ....G....... 585 657-6941
  Bloomfield (G-988)
Glendale Architectural WD Pdts ....E....... 718 326-2700
  Glendale (G-5654)
Hard Manufacturing Co Inc ....D....... 716 893-1800
  Buffalo (G-2988)
Harden Furniture Inc ....C....... 315 675-3600
  Mc Connellsville (G-8220)
Hayman-Chaffey Designs Inc ....F....... 212 889-7771
  New York (G-10428)
Henry B Urban Inc ....E....... 212 489-3308
  New York (G-10457)
Icon Design LLC ....E....... 585 768-6040
  Le Roy (G-7409)
Inter Craft Custom Furniture ....G....... 718 278-2573
  Astoria (G-445)
J Percoco Industries Inc ....G....... 631 312-4572
  Bohemia (G-1079)
K & B Woodworking Inc ....G....... 518 634-7253
  Cairo (G-3274)
Kazac Inc ....G....... 631 249-7299
  Farmingdale (G-5024)
Kittinger Company Inc ....E....... 716 876-1000
  Buffalo (G-3033)
Knoll Inc ....D....... 917 359-8620
  New York (G-10864)
L& JG Stickley Incorporated ....A....... 315 682-5500
  Manlius (G-8073)
Lanoves Inc ....G....... 718 384-1880
  Brooklyn (G-2195)
Little Wolf Cabinet Shop Inc ....E....... 212 734-1116
  New York (G-11013)
M & C Furniture ....G....... 718 422-2136
  Brooklyn (G-2242)
M T D Corporation ....F....... 631 491-3905
  West Babylon (G-16808)
Mackenzie-Childs LLC ....C....... 315 364-7567
  Aurora (G-530)
Manchester Wood Inc ....C....... 518 642-9518
  Granville (G-5776)
Mica International Ltd ....F....... 516 378-3400
  Freeport (G-5413)
New Day Woodwork Inc ....E....... 718 275-1721
  Glendale (G-5659)
Nicholas Dfine Furn Decorators ....F....... 914 245-8982
  Bronx (G-1411)
Patrick Mackin Custom Furn ....G....... 718 237-2592
  Brooklyn (G-2409)
Piccini Industries Ltd ....E....... 845 365-0614
  Orangeburg (G-13239)
Pillow Perfections Ltd Inc ....G....... 718 383-2259
  Brooklyn (G-2420)
Premier Woodcraft Ltd 610 383-6624
  White Plains (G-17161)
Recycled Brooklyn Group LLC ....F....... 917 902-0662
  Brooklyn (G-2485)
Reis D Furniture Mfg ....E....... 516 248-5676
  Mineola (G-8534)
Renco Group Inc ....G....... 212 541-6000
  New York (G-11832)
Royal Jamestown Furniture Inc ....E....... 716 664-5260
  Jamestown (G-7026)
Stillwater Wood & Iron ....G....... 518 664-4501
  Stillwater (G-15761)
Universal Designs Inc ....G....... 718 721-1111
  Long Island City (G-7910)
Wallace Home Design Ctr ....G....... 631 765-3890
  Southold (G-15561)
Walpole Woodworkers Inc ....G....... 631 726-2859
  Water Mill (G-16606)
Walter P Sauer LLC ....E....... 718 937-0600
  Brooklyn (G-2743)
William Somerville Maintenance ....D....... 212 534-4600
  New York (G-12636)
Woodmotif Inc ....F....... 516 564-8325
  Hempstead (G-6289)
Your Furniture Designers Inc ....G....... 845 947-3046
  West Haverstraw (G-16848)

FURNITURE: Hydraulic Barber & Beauty Shop Chairs

Pyrotek Incorporated ....E....... 716 731-3221
  Sanborn (G-15126)
Zebrowski Industries Inc ....G....... 716 532-3911
  Collins (G-3818)

FURNITURE: Institutional, Exc Wood

Able Steel Equipment Co Inc ....F....... 718 361-9240
  Long Island City (G-7647)
Artistry In Wood of Syracuse ....F....... 315 431-4022
  East Syracuse (G-4506)
Artone LLC ....D....... 716 664-2232
  Jamestown (G-6972)
Forecast Consoles Inc ....E....... 631 253-9000
  Hauppauge (G-6079)
Maximum Security Products Corp ....E....... 518 233-1800
  Waterford (G-16613)
Maxsecure Systems Inc ....G....... 800 657-4336
  Buffalo (G-3059)
N Y Elli Design Corp ....F....... 718 228-0014
  Maspeth (G-8153)
Pluribus Products Inc ....E....... 718 852-1614
  Brooklyn (G-2427)
Rosenwach Tank Co Inc ....E....... 212 972-4411
  Astoria (G-455)
Seating Inc ....E....... 800 468-2475
  Nunda (G-13042)
Testori Interiors Inc ....E....... 518 298-4400
  Champlain (G-3546)
Unifor Inc ....F....... 212 673-3434
  New York (G-12455)

FURNITURE: Juvenile, Wood

Community Products LLC ....C....... 845 658-8799
  Rifton (G-14132)
Ducduc LLC ....F....... 212 226-1868
  New York (G-9935)
Offi & Company ....G....... 800 958-6334
  Corning (G-3977)

FURNITURE: Kitchen & Dining Room

Auratic USA Incorporated ....G....... 212 684-8888
  New York (G-9264)
Cab-Network Inc ....G....... 516 334-8666
  Westbury (G-16972)
Catskill Craftsmen Inc ....D....... 607 652-7321
  Stamford (G-15624)
Dinette Depot Ltd ....D....... 516 515-9623
  Brooklyn (G-1865)
East End Country Kitchens Inc ....F....... 631 727-2258
  Calverton (G-3290)
Innovant Inc ....G....... 212 929-4883
  New York (G-10603)
Lemode Concepts Inc ....G....... 631 841-0796
  Amityville (G-305)
Professional Cab Detailing Co ....F....... 845 436-7282
  Woodridge (G-17315)

FURNITURE: Kitchen & Dining Room, Metal

Renco Group Inc ....G....... 212 541-6000
  New York (G-11832)

FURNITURE: Laboratory

J H C Fabrications Inc ....E....... 718 649-0065
  Brooklyn (G-2122)

PRODUCT SECTION

Modu-Craft Inc .... G 716 694-0709
  Tonawanda (G-16182)
Modu-Craft Inc .... G 716 694-0709
  North Tonawanda (G-12982)

FURNITURE: Living Room, Upholstered On Wood Frames

Hallagan Manufacturing Co Inc .... D 315 331-4640
  Newark (G-12731)
Royal Jamestown Furniture Inc .... E 716 664-5260
  Jamestown (G-7026)

FURNITURE: Mattresses & Foundations

E & G Bedding Corp .... E 718 369-1092
  Brooklyn (G-1889)
M R C Industries Inc .... C 516 328-6900
  Port Washington (G-13839)
Steinbock-Braff Inc .... E 718 972-6500
  Brooklyn (G-2606)
VSM Investors LLC .... G 212 351-1600
  New York (G-12571)

FURNITURE: Mattresses, Box & Bedsprings

Brook North Farms Inc .... F 315 834-9390
  Auburn (G-487)
Comfort Bedding Inc .... E 718 485-7662
  Brooklyn (G-1794)
Duxiana Dux Bed .... G 212 755-2600
  New York (G-9941)
Hard Manufacturing Co Inc .... D 716 893-1800
  Buffalo (G-2988)
Jamestown Mattress Co .... E 716 665-2247
  Jamestown (G-7010)
Mattress Factory .... F 718 760-4202
  Corona (G-4002)
Metro Mattress Corp .... E 716 205-2300
  Niagara Falls (G-12847)
Otis Bedding Mfg Co Inc .... E 716 825-2599
  Buffalo (G-3105)
Zzz Mattress Manufacturing .... E 718 454-1468
  Saint Albans (G-15085)

FURNITURE: Mattresses, Innerspring Or Box Spring

KKR Millennium GP LLC .... A 212 750-8300
  New York (G-10856)
Royal Bedding Co Buffalo Inc .... E 716 895-1414
  Buffalo (G-3168)
Sealy Mattress Co Albany Inc .... B 518 880-1600
  Troy (G-16223)

FURNITURE: NEC

Dellet Industries Inc .... F 718 965-0101
  Brooklyn (G-1850)
Inova LLC .... F 518 861-3400
  Altamont (G-209)
Porta Decor .... G 516 826-6900
  Hicksville (G-6390)

FURNITURE: Novelty, Wood

Feinkind Inc .... G 800 289-6136
  Irvington (G-6769)

FURNITURE: Office Panel Systems, Exc Wood

Afco Systems Inc .... C 631 424-3935
  Farmingdale (G-4931)
Aztec Industries Inc .... G 631 585-1331
  Ronkonkoma (G-14875)
Knoll Inc .... D 917 359-8620
  New York (G-10864)

FURNITURE: Office, Exc Wood

3phase Industries LLC .... G 347 763-2942
  Brooklyn (G-1515)
Able Steel Equipment Co Inc .... F 718 361-9240
  Long Island City (G-7647)
Allcraft Fabricators Inc .... D 631 951-4100
  Hauppauge (G-6015)
Aronowitz Metal Works .... G 845 356-1660
  Monsey (G-8568)
Artone LLC .... D 716 664-2232
  Jamestown (G-6972)
Brueton Industries Inc .... D 516 379-3400
  Freeport (G-5391)
Davies Office Refurbishing Inc .... C 518 426-7188
  Albany (G-71)
Davinci Designs Inc .... F 631 595-1095
  Deer Park (G-4126)
Dcl Furniture Manufacturing .... E 516 248-2683
  Mineola (G-8505)
Deakon Homes and Interiors .... F 518 271-0342
  Troy (G-16233)
E-Systems Group LLC .... E 607 775-1100
  Conklin (G-3868)
Eugenia Selective Living Inc .... F 631 277-1461
  Islip (G-6808)
Exhibit Corporation America .... E 718 937-2600
  Long Island City (G-7734)
Forecast Consoles Inc .... E 631 253-9000
  Hauppauge (G-6079)
Hergo Ergonomic Support .... E 718 894-0639
  Maspeth (G-8143)
Hudson Valley Office Furn Inc .... G 845 565-6673
  Newburgh (G-12763)
Integrated Tech Support Svcs .... G 718 454-2497
  Saint Albans (G-15084)
Larson Metal Manufacturing Co .... G 716 665-6807
  Jamestown (G-7016)
Lucia Group Inc .... G 631 392-4900
  Deer Park (G-4168)
New Dimensions Office Group .... D 718 387-0995
  Brooklyn (G-2361)
Nova Metal Inc .... E 718 981-4000
  Staten Island (G-15717)
Piccini Industries Ltd .... E 845 365-0614
  Orangeburg (G-13239)
Premier Woodcraft Ltd .... E 610 383-6624
  White Plains (G-17161)
Royal Metal Products Inc .... E 518 966-4442
  Surprise (G-15811)
Saturn Sales Inc .... E 519 658-5125
  Niagara Falls (G-12874)
Schwab Corp .... C 812 547-2956
  Rochester (G-14676)
Workplace Interiors LLC .... F 585 425-7420
  Fairport (G-4887)
X F Inc .... F 212 244-2240
  Brooklyn (G-2770)

FURNITURE: Office, Wood

A G Master Crafts Ltd .... F 516 745-6262
  Garden City (G-5492)
A Schneller Sons Inc .... F 212 695-9440
  New York (G-8992)
Artistic Products LLC .... E 631 435-0200
  Hauppauge (G-6026)
Artone LLC .... D 716 664-2232
  Jamestown (G-6972)
B D B Typewriter Supply Works .... E 718 232-4800
  Brooklyn (G-1659)
Bauerschmidt & Sons Inc .... D 718 528-3500
  Jamaica (G-6898)
Bloch Industries LLC .... D 585 334-9600
  Rochester (G-14235)
Brueton Industries Inc .... D 516 379-3400
  Freeport (G-5391)
Ccn International Inc .... D 315 789-4400
  Geneva (G-5572)
Culin/Colella Inc .... G 914 698-7727
  Mamaroneck (G-8031)
DAF Office Networks Inc .... F 315 699-7070
  Cicero (G-3644)
Dates Weiser Furniture Corp .... D 716 891-1700
  Buffalo (G-2902)
Davinci Designs Inc .... F 631 595-1095
  Deer Park (G-4126)
Dcl Furniture Manufacturing .... E 516 248-2683
  Mineola (G-8505)
Deakon Homes and Interiors .... F 518 271-0342
  Troy (G-16233)
Den-Jo Woodworking Corp .... F 718 388-2287
  Brooklyn (G-1854)
Designs By Robert Scott Inc .... E 718 609-2535
  Brooklyn (G-1857)
Dimaio Millwork Corporation .... E 914 476-1937
  Yonkers (G-17436)
Divine Art Furniture Inc .... G 718 834-0911
  Brooklyn (G-1866)
E-Systems Group LLC .... E 607 775-1100
  Conklin (G-3868)
Eugenia Selective Living Inc .... F 631 277-1461
  Islip (G-6808)
Exhibit Corporation America .... E 718 937-2600
  Long Island City (G-7734)
Forecast Consoles Inc .... E 631 253-9000
  Hauppauge (G-6079)
Furniture By Craftmaster Ltd .... G 631 750-0658
  Bohemia (G-1069)
Glendale Architectural WD Pdts .... E 718 326-2700
  Glendale (G-5654)
Gunlocke Company LLC .... C 585 728-5111
  Wayland (G-16710)
H Freund Woodworking Co Inc .... F 516 334-3774
  Westbury (G-16992)
Harden Furniture Inc .... C 315 675-3600
  Mc Connellsville (G-8220)
Heartwood Specialties Inc .... G 607 654-0102
  Hammondsport (G-5955)
Hni Corporation .... C 212 683-2232
  New York (G-10491)
Humanscale Corporation .... E 212 725-4749
  New York (G-10531)
Innovant Inc .... D 212 929-4883
  New York (G-10602)
Kazac Inc .... G 631 249-7299
  Farmingdale (G-5024)
Kittinger Company Inc .... E 716 876-1000
  Buffalo (G-3033)
Knoll Inc .... D 917 359-8620
  New York (G-10864)
Krefab Corporation .... F 631 842-5151
  Copiague (G-3909)
Lake Country Woodworkers Ltd .... E 585 374-6353
  Naples (G-8766)
Little Wolf Cabinet Shop Inc .... E 212 734-1116
  New York (G-11013)
Longo Commercial Cabinets Inc .... E 631 225-4290
  Lindenhurst (G-7469)
M T D Corporation .... F 631 491-3905
  West Babylon (G-16808)
Manhattan Comfort Inc .... E 888 230-2225
  Brooklyn (G-2259)
Materials Design Workshop .... F 718 893-1954
  Bronx (G-1389)
Matteo & Antonio Bartolotta .... F 315 252-2220
  Auburn (G-508)
Miller Blaker Inc .... D 718 665-3930
  Bronx (G-1398)
Millers Millworks Inc .... E 585 494-1420
  Bergen (G-850)
New Dimensions Office Group .... D 718 387-0995
  Brooklyn (G-2361)
Nicholas Dfine Furn Decorators .... F 914 245-8982
  Bronx (G-1411)
Omega Furniture Manufacturing .... F 315 463-7428
  Syracuse (G-16003)
Pheonix Custom Furniture Ltd .... E 212 727-2648
  Long Island City (G-7842)
Piccini Industries Ltd .... E 845 365-0614
  Orangeburg (G-13239)
Premier Woodcraft Ltd .... E 610 383-6624
  White Plains (G-17161)
Princeton Upholstery Co Inc .... D 845 343-2196
  Middletown (G-8458)
Saraval Industries .... G 516 768-9033
  Nyack (G-13053)
Technology Desking Inc .... E 212 257-6998
  New York (G-12290)
Universal Designs Inc .... G 718 721-1111
  Long Island City (G-7910)
Upstate Office Liquidators Inc .... F 607 722-9234
  Johnson City (G-7106)
Woodmotif Inc .... F 516 564-8325
  Hempstead (G-6289)
Your Furniture Designers Inc .... G 845 947-3046
  West Haverstraw (G-16848)

FURNITURE: Outdoor, Wood

Long Lumber and Supply Corp .... F 518 439-1661
  Slingerlands (G-15477)
Sitecraft Inc .... G 718 729-4900
  Astoria (G-457)
Sundown Ski & Sport Shop Inc .... E 631 737-8600
  Lake Grove (G-7267)

FURNITURE: Pews, Church

Keck Group Inc .... F 845 988-5757
  Warwick (G-16591)

FURNITURE: Picnic Tables Or Benches, Park

Hartford Hwy Dept .... G 315 724-0654
  New Hartford *(G-8806)*
Ry-Lecia Inc .... G 631 244-0011
  Bohemia *(G-1127)*
Studio 21 LA Inc .... E 718 965-6579
  Brooklyn *(G-2612)*
Town of Amherst .... E 716 631-7113
  Williamsville *(G-17258)*
Tymor Park .... G 845 724-5691
  Lagrangeville *(G-7260)*

FURNITURE: Rattan

Bielecky Bros Inc .... E 718 424-4764
  Woodside *(G-17320)*

FURNITURE: Restaurant

Dine Rite Seating Products Inc .... E 631 592-8126
  Lindenhurst *(G-7462)*
Excel Commercial Seating .... E 828 428-8338
  Lindenhurst *(G-7464)*
Hunt Country Furniture Inc .... D 845 832-6601
  Wingdale *(G-17274)*
L & D Manufacturing Corp .... G 718 665-5226
  Bronx *(G-1375)*
Lb Furniture Industries LLC .... E 518 828-1501
  Hudson *(G-6624)*
Maxsun Corporation .... F 718 418-6800
  Maspeth *(G-8151)*
Rollhaus Seating Products Inc .... F 718 729-9111
  Long Island City *(G-7863)*

FURNITURE: Ship

Starliner Shipping & Travel .... G 718 385-1515
  Brooklyn *(G-2600)*

FURNITURE: Silverware Chests, Wood

McGraw Wood Products LLC .... E 607 836-6465
  Mc Graw *(G-8223)*

FURNITURE: Sleep

Sleep Improvement Center Inc .... F 516 536-5799
  Rockville Centre *(G-14798)*

FURNITURE: Storage Chests, Household, Wood

Premiere Living Products LLC .... F 631 873-4337
  Dix Hills *(G-4295)*

FURNITURE: Tables & Table Tops, Wood

Ercole Nyc Inc .... F 212 675-2218
  Brooklyn *(G-1932)*
Petro Moore Manufacturing Corp ..... G 718 784-2516
  Long Island City *(G-7841)*

FURNITURE: Tables, Office, Exc Wood

Prince Seating Corp .... E 718 363-2300
  Brooklyn *(G-2444)*

FURNITURE: Tables, Office, Wood

Prince Seating Corp .... E 718 363-2300
  Brooklyn *(G-2444)*

FURNITURE: Theater

Steeldeck Ny Inc .... F 718 599-3700
  Brooklyn *(G-2604)*

FURNITURE: Upholstered

A Schneller Sons Inc .... F 212 695-9440
  New York *(G-8992)*
Arthur Lauer Inc .... G 845 255-7871
  Gardiner *(G-5547)*
Artone LLC .... D 716 664-2232
  Jamestown *(G-6972)*
August Studios .... G 718 706-6487
  Long Island City *(G-7678)*
Deangelis Ltd .... G 212 348-8225
  New York *(G-9833)*
Delta Upholsterers Inc .... E 212 489-3308
  New York *(G-9841)*
Doreen Interiors Ltd .... E 212 255-9008
  New Hyde Park *(G-8828)*
Elan Upholstery Inc .... F 631 563-0650
  Bohemia *(G-1065)*
Falvo Manufacturing Co Inc .... F 315 738-7682
  Utica *(G-16330)*
Fiber-Seal of New York Inc .... G 212 888-5580
  New York *(G-10157)*
Furniture By Craftmaster Ltd .... G 631 750-0658
  Bohemia *(G-1069)*
H & H Furniture Co .... G 718 850-5252
  Jamaica *(G-6917)*
Harden Furniture Inc .... C 315 675-3600
  Mc Connellsville *(G-8220)*
Henry B Urban Inc .... E 212 489-3308
  New York *(G-10457)*
Jackson Dakota Inc .... G 212 838-9444
  New York *(G-10688)*
Jays Furniture Products Inc .... E 716 876-8854
  Buffalo *(G-3015)*
Kittinger Company Inc .... E 716 876-1000
  Buffalo *(G-3033)*
Mackenzie-Childs LLC .... C 315 364-7567
  Aurora *(G-530)*
Matteo & Antonio Bartolotta .... F 315 252-2220
  Auburn *(G-508)*
Mazza Classics Incorporated .... G 631 390-9060
  Farmingdale *(G-5046)*
McCarroll Uphl Designs LLC .... G 518 828-0500
  Hudson *(G-6625)*
Nicholas Dfine Furn Decorators ...... F 914 245-8982
  Bronx *(G-1411)*
Pheonix Custom Furniture Ltd .... E 212 727-2648
  Long Island City *(G-7842)*
Princeton Upholstery Co Inc .... D 845 343-2196
  Middletown *(G-8458)*
Rob Herschenfeld Design Inc .... F 718 456-6801
  Brooklyn *(G-2499)*
Simon S Decorating Inc .... G 718 339-2931
  Brooklyn *(G-2561)*
Slava Industries Incorporated .... G 718 499-4850
  Brooklyn *(G-2568)*
Smith & Watson .... E 212 686-6444
  New York *(G-12104)*
Sofa Doctor Inc .... G 718 292-6300
  Bronx *(G-1458)*
Two Worlds Arts Ltd .... G 212 929-2210
  Brooklyn *(G-2694)*
Versailles Drapery Upholstery .... F 212 533-2059
  Long Island City *(G-7914)*
Walco Leather Co Inc .... E 212 243-2244
  New York *(G-12577)*
Wallace Home Design Ctr .... G 631 765-3890
  Southold *(G-15561)*
Yepes Fine Furniture .... E 718 383-0221
  Brooklyn *(G-2774)*

FURRIERS

Alexis & Gianni Retail Inc .... F 516 334-3877
  Westbury *(G-16964)*
Anastasia Furs International .... G 212 868-9241
  New York *(G-9150)*
Superior Furs Inc .... F 516 365-4123
  Manhasset *(G-8065)*

FUSES: Electric

Leviton Manufacturing Co Inc .... B 631 812-6000
  Melville *(G-8334)*
Soc America Inc .... F 631 472-6666
  Ronkonkoma *(G-14986)*

GAMES & TOYS: Baby Carriages & Restraint Seats

Babysafe Usa LLC .... G 877 367-4141
  Afton *(G-8)*

GAMES & TOYS: Banks

E C C Corp .... G 518 873-6494
  Elizabethtown *(G-4627)*

GAMES & TOYS: Child Restraint Seats, Automotive

Pidyon Controls Inc .... G 212 683-9523
  New York *(G-11659)*

GAMES & TOYS: Craft & Hobby Kits & Sets

Design Works Craft Inc .... G 631 244-5749
  Bohemia *(G-1057)*
Master Art Corp .... G 845 362-6430
  Spring Valley *(G-15594)*
R F Giardina Co .... F 516 922-1364
  Oyster Bay *(G-13374)*
Spectrum Crafts Inc .... E 631 244-5749
  Bohemia *(G-1136)*

GAMES & TOYS: Doll Hats

Beila Group Inc .... F 212 260-1948
  New York *(G-9346)*

GAMES & TOYS: Dolls & Doll Clothing

Goldberger Company LLC .... F 212 924-1194
  New York *(G-10329)*

GAMES & TOYS: Dolls, Exc Stuffed Toy Animals

ADC Dolls Inc .... C 212 244-4500
  New York *(G-9026)*
Lovee Doll & Toy Co Inc .... G 212 242-1545
  New York *(G-11053)*
Mattel Inc .... F 716 714-8514
  East Aurora *(G-4374)*
Toy Admiration Co Inc .... E 914 963-9400
  Yonkers *(G-17492)*

GAMES & TOYS: Electronic

212 Db Corp .... E 212 652-5600
  New York *(G-8965)*
Alleghany Capital Corporation .... F 212 752-1356
  New York *(G-9087)*
Barron Games Intl Co LLC .... F 716 630-0054
  Buffalo *(G-2832)*
Everi Games Inc .... G 518 881-1122
  Schenectady *(G-15253)*
Marvel Entertainment LLC .... C 212 576-4000
  New York *(G-11170)*

GAMES & TOYS: Game Machines, Exc Coin-Operated

Ellis Products Corp .... G 516 791-3732
  Valley Stream *(G-16405)*

GAMES & TOYS: Miniature Dolls, Collectors'

Tonner Doll Company Inc .... E 845 339-9537
  Kingston *(G-7216)*

GAMES & TOYS: Models, Airplane, Toy & Hobby

Top Race Inc .... G 347 424-5795
  Brooklyn *(G-2665)*

GAMES & TOYS: Puzzles

Buffalo Games Inc .... D 716 827-8393
  Buffalo *(G-2852)*
Compoz A Puzzle Inc .... G 516 883-2311
  Port Washington *(G-13806)*
Tucker Jones House Inc .... E 631 642-9092
  East Setauket *(G-4495)*

GAMES & TOYS: Scooters, Children's

Dakott LLC .... G 888 805-6795
  New York *(G-9795)*
Famous Box Scooter Co .... G 631 943-2013
  West Babylon *(G-16791)*

GAMES & TOYS: Structural Toy Sets

Solowave Design Corp .... G 716 646-3103
  Hamburg *(G-5943)*

GAMES & TOYS: Trains & Eqpt, Electric & Mechanical

ATI Model Products Inc .... E 631 694-7022
  Farmingdale *(G-4946)*
Gargraves Trackage Corporation .... G 315 483-6577
  North Rose *(G-12937)*
Mechanical Displays Inc .... G 718 258-5588
  Brooklyn *(G-2290)*
Pride Lines Ltd .... G 631 225-0033
  Lindenhurst *(G-7479)*

PRODUCT SECTION

GEARS

GARBAGE CONTAINERS: Plastic

CT Industrial Supply Co Inc .... F 718 417-3226
  Brooklyn *(G-1822)*
Rainbow Plastics Inc .... F 718 218-7288
  Brooklyn *(G-2475)*
Think Green Junk Removal Inc .... G 845 297-7771
  Wappingers Falls *(G-16577)*

GARBAGE DISPOSALS: Household

Platinum Carting Corp .... F 631 649-4322
  Bay Shore *(G-724)*

GARBAGE DISPOSERS & COMPACTORS: Commercial

Blue Tee Corp .... G 212 598-0880
  New York *(G-9422)*

GARNET MINING SVCS

Barton Mines Company LLC .... C 518 798-5462
  Glens Falls *(G-5672)*

GAS & OIL FIELD EXPLORATION SVCS

Able Environmental Services .... G 631 567-6585
  Bohemia *(G-1003)*
Aegis Oil Limited Ventures LLC .... F 646 233-4900
  New York *(G-9051)*
America Capital Energy Corp .... G 212 983-8316
  New York *(G-9112)*
Aterra Exploration LLC .... E 212 315-0030
  New York *(G-9248)*
Bistate Oil Management Corp .... F 212 935-4110
  New York *(G-9405)*
East Resources Inc .... G 716 373-0944
  Allegany *(G-200)*
FT Seismic Support Inc .... C 607 527-8595
  Corning *(G-3972)*
Hess Energy Exploration Ltd .... G 732 750-6500
  New York *(G-10465)*
Hess Explrtion Prod Hldngs Ltd .... G 732 750-6000
  New York *(G-10466)*
JP Oil Group Inc .... G 607 563-1360
  Sidney *(G-15440)*
KKR Ntral Rsources Fund I-A LP .... F 212 750-8300
  New York *(G-10857)*
Lenape Energy Inc .... G 585 344-1200
  Alexander *(G-187)*
Lenape Resources Inc .... F 585 344-1200
  Alexander *(G-188)*
Mac Fadden Holdings Inc .... E 212 614-3980
  New York *(G-11081)*
Madoff Energy III LLC .... G 212 744-1918
  New York *(G-11095)*
Mep Alaska LLC .... G 646 535-9005
  Brooklyn *(G-2297)*
Native Amercn Enrgy Group Inc .... G 718 408-2323
  Forest Hills *(G-5325)*
Norse Energy Corp USA .... G 716 568-2048
  Buffalo *(G-3094)*
Occidental Energy Mktg Inc .... G 212 632-4950
  New York *(G-11493)*
Range Rsurces - Appalachia LLC .... E 716 753-3385
  Mayville *(G-8218)*
Seneca Resources Corporation .... F 716 630-6750
  Williamsville *(G-17252)*
Somerset Production Co LLC .... G 716 932-6480
  Buffalo *(G-3189)*
Springfield Oil Services Inc .... F 914 315-6812
  Harrison *(G-5991)*
Springfield Oil Services Inc .... G 516 482-5995
  Great Neck *(G-5841)*
U S Energy Development Corp .... D 716 636-0401
  Getzville *(G-5605)*
Unco United Oil Holdings LLC .... F 212 481-1003
  New York *(G-12448)*
Waffenbauch USA .... E 716 326-4508
  Westfield *(G-17052)*
Warren Energy Services LLC .... F 212 697-9660
  New York *(G-12591)*

GAS & OIL FIELD SVCS, NEC

Bass Oil & Chemical Llc .... F 718 628-4444
  Brooklyn *(G-1671)*
Case Brothers Inc .... G 716 925-7172
  Limestone *(G-7450)*
Essar Americas .... G 212 292-2600
  New York *(G-10062)*

GAS STATIONS

Marina Holding Corp .... F 718 646-9283
  Brooklyn *(G-2269)*

GASES & LIQUIFIED PETROLEUM GASES

Hudson Energy Services LLC .... G 630 300-0013
  Suffern *(G-15791)*
Osaka Gas Energy America Corp .... E 914 253-5500
  White Plains *(G-17143)*

GASES: Carbon Dioxide

Linde Merchant Production Inc .... G 315 593-1360
  Fulton *(G-5469)*

GASES: Flourinated Hydrocarbon

Hudson Technologies Company .... E 845 735-6000
  Pearl River *(G-13459)*
Spot Certified Inc .... E 212 643-6770
  Brooklyn *(G-2589)*

GASES: Indl

Airgas Inc .... E 585 436-7780
  Rochester *(G-14182)*
Airgas USA LLC .... E 315 433-1295
  Syracuse *(G-15846)*
Airgas USA LLC .... E 585 436-7781
  Rochester *(G-14183)*
Matheson Tri-Gas Inc .... G 518 203-5003
  Cohoes *(G-3750)*
Matheson Tri-Gas Inc .... F 518 439-0362
  Feura Bush *(G-5173)*
Praxair Inc .... E 845 267-2337
  Valley Cottage *(G-16384)*
Praxair Inc .... F 716 649-1600
  Hamburg *(G-5937)*
Praxair Inc .... E 518 482-4360
  Albany *(G-123)*
Praxair Inc .... E 716 286-4600
  Niagara Falls *(G-12861)*
Praxair Inc .... C 845 359-4200
  Orangeburg *(G-13241)*
Praxair Inc .... E 716 879-4000
  Tonawanda *(G-16195)*

GASES: Neon

Neon .... F 212 727-5628
  New York *(G-11367)*

GASES: Nitrogen

Linde Gas North America LLC .... E
  Cohoes *(G-3749)*
Linde Gas North America LLC .... F 866 543-3427
  Cheektowaga *(G-3578)*
Linde Gas North America LLC .... F 315 431-4081
  Syracuse *(G-15979)*
Linde LLC .... E 716 847-0748
  Buffalo *(G-3048)*
Linde LLC .... D 518 439-8187
  Feura Bush *(G-5172)*

GASES: Oxygen

Air Products and Chemicals Inc .... D 518 463-4273
  Glenmont *(G-5666)*
Air Products and Chemicals Inc .... E 585 798-2324
  Medina *(G-8264)*
Airgas Inc .... F 518 690-0068
  Albany *(G-36)*
Oxair Ltd .... G 716 298-8288
  Niagara Falls *(G-12858)*
Praxair Distribution Inc .... E 315 457-5821
  Liverpool *(G-7543)*
Praxair Distribution Inc .... E 315 735-6153
  Marcy *(G-8092)*

GASKET MATERIALS

Hollingsworth & Vose Company .... C 518 695-8000
  Greenwich *(G-5889)*
Noroc Enterprises Inc .... E 718 585-3230
  Bronx *(G-1412)*

GASKETS

Allstate Gasket & Packing Inc .... F 631 254-4050
  Deer Park *(G-4092)*

Frank Lowe Rbr & Gasket Co Inc .... E 631 777-2707
  Shirley *(G-15419)*
Quick Cut Gasket & Rubber .... F 716 684-8628
  Lancaster *(G-7335)*
S A S Industries Inc .... F 631 727-1441
  Manorville *(G-8080)*

GASKETS & SEALING DEVICES

A L Sealing .... G 315 699-6900
  Chittenango *(G-3629)*
Apex Packing & Rubber Co Inc .... F 631 420-8150
  Farmingdale *(G-4943)*
Boonville Manufacturing Corp .... G 315 942-4368
  Boonville *(G-1165)*
Everlast Seals and Supply LLC .... F 718 388-7373
  Brooklyn *(G-1941)*
GM Components Holdings LLC .... D 716 439-2402
  Lockport *(G-7591)*
John Crane Inc .... D 315 593-6237
  Fulton *(G-5464)*
Schlegel Electronic Mtls Inc .... E 585 295-2030
  Rochester *(G-14673)*
Seal & Design Inc .... E 315 432-8021
  Syracuse *(G-16036)*
SKF USA Inc .... D 716 661-2600
  Jamestown *(G-7028)*
Temper Corporation .... E 518 853-3467
  Fonda *(G-5317)*
USA Sealing Inc .... E 716 288-9952
  Cheektowaga *(G-3592)*
Web Seal Inc .... E 585 546-1320
  Rochester *(G-14758)*
Xto Incorporated .... D 315 451-7807
  Liverpool *(G-7558)*

GASOLINE FILLING STATIONS

Hess Corporation .... B 212 997-8500
  New York *(G-10464)*
Lukoil North America LLC .... E 212 421-4141
  New York *(G-11062)*

GASOLINE WHOLESALERS

Bluebar Oil Co Inc .... E 315 245-4328
  Blossvale *(G-997)*
Seneca Nation Enterprise .... F 716 934-7430
  Irving *(G-6765)*

GASTROINTESTINAL OR GENITOURINARY SYSTEM DRUGS

New York Health Care Inc .... G 718 375-6700
  Valley Stream *(G-16416)*

GATES: Dam, Metal Plate

Linita Design & Mfg Corp .... E 716 566-7753
  Lackawanna *(G-7244)*
Riverside Iron LLC .... F 315 535-4864
  Gouverneur *(G-5747)*

GATES: Ornamental Metal

City Store Gates Mfg Corp .... E 718 939-9700
  College Point *(G-3781)*
Inter-Fence Co Inc .... E 718 939-9700
  College Point *(G-3789)*
Moon Gates Company .... G 718 426-0023
  East Elmhurst *(G-4395)*
Vr Containment LLC .... G 917 972-3441
  Fresh Meadows *(G-5447)*

GAUGES

Dorsey Metrology Intl Inc .... E 845 229-2929
  Poughkeepsie *(G-13895)*
Trinity Tools Inc .... E 716 694-1111
  North Tonawanda *(G-13003)*

GEARS

Gear Motions Incorporated .... E 716 885-1080
  Buffalo *(G-2967)*
Gear Motions Incorporated .... E 315 488-0100
  Syracuse *(G-15949)*
Great Lakes Gear Co Inc .... G 716 694-0715
  Tonawanda *(G-16166)*
Perfect Gear & Instrument .... F 516 328-3330
  New Hyde Park *(G-8856)*
Perfect Gear & Instrument .... E 516 873-6122
  Garden City Park *(G-5541)*

Employee Codes: A=Over 500 employees, B=251-500
C=101-250, D=51-100, E=20-50, F=10-19, G=5-9

2017 Harris
New York Manufacturers Directory

1225

GEARS

PRODUCT SECTION

Pro-Gear Co Inc .... G 716 684-3811
   Buffalo *(G-3138)*
Riley Gear Corporation .... E 716 694-0900
   North Tonawanda *(G-12989)*
S R & R Industries Inc 845 692-8329
   Middletown *(G-8461)*
Secs Inc .... E 914 667-5600
   Mount Vernon *(G-8731)*
Secs Inc .... E 914 667-5600
   Mount Vernon *(G-8732)*
Superite Gear Instr of Hppauge .... G 631 234-0100
   Hauppauge *(G-6204)*

GEARS & GEAR UNITS: Reduction, Exc Auto

Perfection Gear Inc .... C 716 592-9310
   Springville *(G-15615)*

GEARS: Power Transmission, Exc Auto

Gleason Works .... A 585 473-1000
   Rochester *(G-14408)*
Jrlon Inc .... D 315 597-4067
   Palmyra *(G-13409)*
McGuigan Inc .... E 631 750-6222
   Bohemia *(G-1103)*
Niagara Gear Corporation .... E 716 874-3131
   Buffalo *(G-3088)*

GELATIN

Geliko LLC .... E 212 876-5620
   New York *(G-10265)*

GEM STONES MINING, NEC: Natural

Gemfields USA Incorporated .... G 212 398-5400
   New York *(G-10267)*
Ray Griffiths Inc .... G 212 689-7209
   New York *(G-11805)*

GEMSTONE & INDL DIAMOND MINING SVCS

Avs Gem Stone Corp .... G 212 944-6380
   New York *(G-9282)*
Didco Inc .... F 212 997-5022
   Rego Park *(G-14032)*
Double Star USA Inc .... G 212 929-2210
   Brooklyn *(G-1874)*
Herkimer Diamond Mines Inc .... E 315 891-7355
   Herkimer *(G-6302)*
Kotel Importers Inc .... F 212 245-6200
   New York *(G-10881)*

GENERAL & INDUSTRIAL LOAN INSTITUTIONS

Mitsui Chemicals America Inc .... E 914 253-0777
   Rye Brook *(G-15072)*

GENERAL MERCHANDISE, NONDURABLE, WHOLESALE

Benson Sales Co Inc .... F 718 236-6743
   Brooklyn *(G-1685)*
Dahill Distributors Inc .... G 347 371-9453
   Brooklyn *(G-1833)*
French Associates Inc .... F 718 387-9880
   Fresh Meadows *(G-5440)*
Lokai Holdings LLC .... F 646 979-3474
   New York *(G-11023)*

GENERATING APPARATUS & PARTS: Electrical

Industrial Test Eqp Co Inc .... E 516 883-6423
   Port Washington *(G-13824)*
Mks Medical Electronics .... C 585 292-7400
   Rochester *(G-14518)*

GENERATION EQPT: Electronic

Alliance Control Systems Inc .... G 845 279-4430
   Brewster *(G-1209)*
C & M Circuits Inc .... E 631 589-0208
   Bohemia *(G-1031)*
Curtis Instruments Inc .... C 914 666-2971
   Mount Kisco *(G-8624)*
Cygnus Automation Inc .... E 631 981-0909
   Bohemia *(G-1047)*
Donald R Husband Inc .... G 607 770-1990
   Johnson City *(G-7091)*

Ems Technologies Inc .... E 607 723-3676
   Binghamton *(G-912)*
General Electric Company .... E 518 459-4110
   Albany *(G-82)*
GW Lisk Company Inc .... E 315 548-2165
   Phelps *(G-13532)*
Tonoga Inc .... C 518 658-3202
   Petersburg *(G-13528)*

GENERATORS: Electric

Getec Inc .... F 845 292-0800
   Ferndale *(G-5170)*

GENERATORS: Electrochemical, Fuel Cell

American Fuel Cell LLC .... G 585 474-3993
   Rochester *(G-14197)*

GENERATORS: Ultrasonic

Uncharted Play Inc .... E 646 675-7783
   New York *(G-12447)*

GIFT SHOP

Exotic Print and Paper Inc .... F 212 807-0465
   New York *(G-10107)*
Frame Shoppe & Art Gallery 516 365-6014
   Manhasset *(G-8060)*

GIFT, NOVELTY & SOUVENIR STORES: Artcraft & carvings

Kleinfelder John 716 753-3163
   Mayville *(G-8216)*

GIFT, NOVELTY & SOUVENIR STORES: Gifts & Novelties

Issacs Yisroel .... G 718 851-7430
   Brooklyn *(G-2117)*
Mainly Monograms Inc .... E 845 624-4923
   West Nyack *(G-16921)*

GIFT, NOVELTY & SOUVENIR STORES: Party Favors

Decorative Novelty Co Inc .... F 718 965-8600
   Brooklyn *(G-1849)*

GIFTS & NOVELTIES: Wholesalers

Cannizzaro Seal & Engraving Co .... G 718 513-6125
   Brooklyn *(G-1754)*
Full Circle Home LLC .... G 212 432-0001
   New York *(G-10222)*
Justa Company .... G 718 932-6139
   Long Island City *(G-7775)*
Mountain T-Shirts Inc .... E 518 943-4533
   Catskill *(G-3432)*
Nubian Heritage .... G 631 265-3551
   Hauppauge *(G-6150)*
OH How Cute Inc .... G 347 838-6031
   Staten Island *(G-15719)*
Studio Silversmiths Inc .... E 718 418-6785
   Ridgewood *(G-14125)*
Trove Inc .... F 212 268-2046
   Brooklyn *(G-2684)*

GLASS FABRICATORS

Benson Industries Inc .... F 212 779-3230
   New York *(G-9360)*
Glassfab Inc .... E 585 262-4000
   Rochester *(G-14404)*
Global Glass Corp .... G 516 681-2309
   Hicksville *(G-6350)*
Granville Glass & Granite .... G 518 812-0492
   Hudson Falls *(G-6645)*
Gray Glass Inc .... E 718 217-2943
   Queens Village *(G-13978)*
Kasson & Keller Inc .... A 518 853-3421
   Fonda *(G-5315)*
Michbi Doors Inc .... D 631 231-9050
   Brentwood *(G-1192)*
Oldcastle Building Envelope .... G 212 957-5400
   New York *(G-11499)*
Pal Manufacturing Corp .... E 516 937-1990
   Hicksville *(G-6384)*
Quality Enclosures Inc .... E 631 234-0115
   Central Islip *(G-3508)*

Royal Metal Products Inc .... E 518 966-4442
   Surprise *(G-15811)*
Select Interior Door Ltd .... E 585 535-9900
   North Java *(G-12934)*
Stark Aquarium Products Co Inc .... E 718 445-5357
   Flushing *(G-5297)*
Swift Glass Co Inc .... D 607 733-7166
   Elmira Heights *(G-4714)*
Vitarose Corp of America .... E 718 951-9700
   Brooklyn *(G-2733)*
Vitrix Inc .... E 607 936-8707
   Corning *(G-3984)*

GLASS PRDTS, FROM PURCHASED GLASS: Art

Carvart Glass Inc .... F 212 675-0030
   New York *(G-9538)*

GLASS PRDTS, FROM PURCHASED GLASS: Glass Beads, Reflecting

Potters Industries LLC .... E 315 265-4920
   Potsdam *(G-13882)*

GLASS PRDTS, FROM PURCHASED GLASS: Glassware

Exquisite Glass & Stone Inc .... G 718 937-9266
   Astoria *(G-441)*
Gmd Industries Inc .... G 718 445-8779
   College Point *(G-3785)*

GLASS PRDTS, FROM PURCHASED GLASS: Insulating

Dunlea Whl GL & Mirror Inc .... G 914 664-5277
   Mount Vernon *(G-8679)*
Rochester Insulated Glass Inc .... D 585 289-3611
   Manchester *(G-8052)*

GLASS PRDTS, FROM PURCHASED GLASS: Mirrored

Ad Notam LLC .... F 631 951-2020
   Hauppauge *(G-6008)*
Depp Glass Inc .... F 718 784-8500
   Long Island City *(G-7713)*
Dundy Glass & Mirror Corp .... E 718 723-5800
   Springfield Gardens *(G-15608)*
G & M Clearview Inc .... G 845 781-4877
   Monroe *(G-8555)*
Lafayette Mirror & Glass Co .... G 718 768-0660
   New Hyde Park *(G-8845)*
Mirror-Tech Manufacturing Co .... F 914 965-1232
   Yonkers *(G-17468)*

GLASS PRDTS, FROM PURCHASED GLASS: Mirrors, Framed

Apf Management Company LLC .... C 914 665-5400
   Yonkers *(G-17414)*
Apf Manufacturing Company LLC .... E 914 963-6300
   Yonkers *(G-17415)*

GLASS PRDTS, FROM PURCHASED GLASS: Ornaments, Christmas Tree

Jinglebell Inc .... G 914 219-5395
   Armonk *(G-416)*
Rauch Industries Inc .... E 704 867-5333
   Tarrytown *(G-16102)*

GLASS PRDTS, FROM PURCHASED GLASS: Sheet, Bent

Flickinger Glassworks Inc .... G 718 875-1531
   Brooklyn *(G-1987)*

GLASS PRDTS, FROM PURCHASED GLASS: Watch Crystals

Jimmy Crystal New York Co Ltd .... E 212 594-0858
   New York *(G-10736)*
Lalique North America Inc .... E 212 355-6550
   New York *(G-10922)*
Sunborn Swiss Watches LLC .... G 516 967-8836
   New Hyde Park *(G-8864)*

PRODUCT SECTION — GLASSWARE WHOLESALERS

GLASS PRDTS, FROM PURCHASED GLASS: Windshields

Taylor Made Group LLC ....D...... 518 725-0681
  Gloversville *(G-5724)*

GLASS PRDTS, FROM PURCHD GLASS: Strengthened Or Reinforced

Campus Crafts Inc ....G...... 585 328-6780
  Rochester *(G-14256)*
Rochester Colonial Mfg Corp ....D...... 585 254-8191
  Rochester *(G-14639)*

GLASS PRDTS, PRESSED OR BLOWN: Bulbs, Electric Lights

Daylight Technology USA Inc ....G...... 973 255-8100
  Maspeth *(G-8129)*
Goodlite Products Inc ....F....... 718 697-7502
  Brooklyn *(G-2040)*
Led Lumina USA LLC ....G...... 631 750-4433
  Bohemia *(G-1091)*

GLASS PRDTS, PRESSED OR BLOWN: Chimneys, Lamp

Sleepy Hollow Chimney Sup Ltd ....F....... 631 231-2333
  Brentwood *(G-1194)*

GLASS PRDTS, PRESSED OR BLOWN: Glassware, Art Or Decorative

Architectural Glass Inc ....F....... 845 831-3116
  Beacon *(G-781)*
Bedford Downing Glass ....G...... 718 418-6409
  Brooklyn *(G-1677)*
King Research Inc ....E....... 718 788-0122
  Brooklyn *(G-2172)*

GLASS PRDTS, PRESSED OR BLOWN: Lens Blanks, Optical

Ion Optics Inc ....F....... 518 339-6853
  Albany *(G-90)*

GLASS PRDTS, PRESSED OR BLOWN: Optical

Match Eyewear LLC ....E....... 516 877-0170
  Westbury *(G-17009)*
R Bruce Mapes ....F....... 518 761-2020
  Glens Falls *(G-5698)*
Semrok Inc ....D...... 585 594-7050
  Rochester *(G-14681)*

GLASS PRDTS, PRESSED OR BLOWN: Ornaments, Christmas Tree

Formcraft Display Products ....G...... 914 632-1410
  New Rochelle *(G-8900)*
Jinglebell Inc ....G...... 914 219-5395
  Armonk *(G-416)*

GLASS PRDTS, PRESSED OR BLOWN: Scientific Glassware

Scientifics Direct Inc ....F....... 716 773-7500
  Tonawanda *(G-16201)*

GLASS PRDTS, PRESSED/BLOWN: Glassware, Art, Decor/Novelty

Bronx Wstchester Tempering Inc ..E....... 914 663-9400
  Mount Vernon *(G-8668)*
Mata Ig ....G...... 212 979-7921
  New York *(G-11177)*
Pasabahce USA ....G...... 212 683-1600
  New York *(G-11577)*

GLASS PRDTS, PURCHASED GLASS: Glassware, Scientific/Tech

Community Glass Inc ....G...... 607 737-8860
  Elmira *(G-4676)*

GLASS PRDTS, PURCHASED GLASS: Insulating, Multiple-Glazed

Upstate Insulated Glass Inc ....G...... 315 475-4960
  Central Square *(G-3519)*

GLASS PRDTS, PURCHD GLASS: Furniture Top, Cut, Beveld/Polshd

Our Terms Fabricators Inc ....E....... 631 752-1517
  West Babylon *(G-16817)*
Rn Furniture Corp ....G...... 347 960-9622
  Richmond Hill *(G-14080)*

GLASS PRDTS, PURCHSD GLASS: Ornamental, Cut, Engraved/DE cor

Oneida International Inc ....G...... 315 361-3000
  Oneida *(G-13160)*
Oneida Silversmiths Inc ....G...... 315 361-3000
  Oneida *(G-13164)*

GLASS STORE: Leaded Or Stained

Flickinger Glassworks Inc ....G...... 718 875-1531
  Brooklyn *(G-1987)*

GLASS STORES

Global Glass Corp ....G...... 516 681-2309
  Hicksville *(G-6350)*
Oldcastle Buildingenvelope Inc .....C....... 631 234-2200
  Hauppauge *(G-6152)*
Upstate Insulated Glass Inc ....G...... 315 475-4960
  Central Square *(G-3519)*

GLASS: Fiber

Corning Incorporated ....A...... 607 974-9000
  Corning *(G-3962)*
Corning Incorporated ....E....... 607 974-0206
  Big Flats *(G-880)*
Corning Incorporated ....E....... 607 248-1200
  Corning *(G-3965)*
Corning Incorporated ....B...... 607 974-0206
  Big Flats *(G-881)*
Corning Specialty Mtls Inc ....G...... 607 974-9000
  Corning *(G-3970)*
New York Energy Synthetics Inc ...G...... 212 634-4787
  New York *(G-11401)*
Schott Corporation ....D...... 914 831-2200
  Elmsford *(G-4778)*
Volpi Manufacturing USA Co Inc ..E....... 315 255-1737
  Auburn *(G-527)*

GLASS: Flat

A Sunshine Glass & Aluminum .....E....... 718 932-8080
  Woodside *(G-17316)*
Corning Incorporated ....E....... 607 974-8496
  Corning *(G-3967)*
Corning Incorporated ....D...... 315 379-3200
  Canton *(G-3382)*
Corning Incorporated ....G...... 607 974-6729
  Painted Post *(G-13391)*
Global Glass Corp ....G...... 516 681-2309
  Hicksville *(G-6350)*
Guardian Industries Corp ....B...... 315 787-7000
  Geneva *(G-5580)*
Hecht & Sohn Glass Co Inc ....G...... 718 782-8295
  Brooklyn *(G-2071)*
Pilkington North America Inc ....C....... 315 438-3341
  Syracuse *(G-16012)*
Schott Corporation ....D...... 914 831-2200
  Elmsford *(G-4778)*
Schott Gemtron Corporation ....C....... 423 337-3522
  Elmsford *(G-4779)*
Schott Government Services LLC .G...... 703 418-1409
  Elmsford *(G-4780)*
Schott Solar Pv Inc ....G...... 888 457-6527
  Elmsford *(G-4782)*
Stefan Sydor Optics Inc ....E....... 585 271-7300
  Rochester *(G-14702)*

GLASS: Insulating

Tower Insulating Glass LLC ....E....... 516 887-3300
  North Bellmore *(G-12923)*

GLASS: Leaded

Batavia Precision Glass LLC ....G...... 585 343-6050
  Buffalo *(G-2833)*

GLASS: Pressed & Blown, NEC

Co-Optics America Lab Inc ....E....... 607 432-0557
  Oneonta *(G-13179)*
Corning Incorporated ....D...... 607 974-9000
  Corning *(G-3963)*
Corning Incorporated ....E....... 607 974-1274
  Painted Post *(G-13390)*
Corning Incorporated ....E....... 607 974-9000
  Corning *(G-3964)*
Corning Incorporated ....D...... 315 379-3200
  Canton *(G-3382)*
Corning Incorporated ....E....... 607 433-3100
  Oneonta *(G-13182)*
Corning Incorporated ....G...... 607 974-4488
  Corning *(G-3966)*
Corning Incorporated ....G...... 607 974-6729
  Painted Post *(G-13391)*
Corning International Corp ....G...... 607 974-9000
  Corning *(G-3968)*
Corning Tropel Corporation ....C....... 585 377-3200
  Fairport *(G-4852)*
Corning Vitro Corporation ....A...... 607 974-8605
  Corning *(G-3971)*
Eye Deal Eyewear Inc ....G...... 716 297-1500
  Niagara Falls *(G-12817)*
Germanow-Simon Corporation ......E....... 585 232-1440
  Rochester *(G-14399)*
Gillinder Brothers Inc ....D...... 845 856-5375
  Port Jervis *(G-13785)*
Glassart Inc ....G...... 607 739-3939
  Millport *(G-8481)*
Glasteel Parts & Services Inc ....E....... 585 235-1010
  Rochester *(G-14405)*
Lighting Holdings Intl LLC ....F....... 845 306-1850
  Purchase *(G-13960)*
Navitar Inc ....D...... 585 359-4000
  Rochester *(G-14530)*
Orafol Display Optics Inc ....E....... 585 647-1140
  West Henrietta *(G-16887)*
Owens Corning Sales LLC ....B...... 518 475-3600
  Feura Bush *(G-5174)*
Saint-Gobain Prfmce Plas Corp ....C....... 518 686-7301
  Hoosick Falls *(G-6544)*
Schott Corporation ....D...... 315 255-2791
  Auburn *(G-517)*
Stefan Sydor Optics Inc ....E....... 585 271-7300
  Rochester *(G-14702)*

GLASS: Stained

Adirondack Stained Glass Works ..G...... 518 725-0387
  Gloversville *(G-5704)*
Chapman Stained Glass Studio .....G...... 518 449-5552
  Albany *(G-62)*
Makarenko Studios Inc ....G...... 914 968-7673
  Yorktown Heights *(G-17512)*
Rohlfs Stined Leaded GL Studio ...E....... 914 699-4848
  Mount Vernon *(G-8726)*
Somers Stain Glass Inc ....F....... 631 586-7772
  Deer Park *(G-4211)*
Sunburst Studios Inc ....G...... 718 768-6360
  Brooklyn *(G-2620)*

GLASS: Structural

Europrojects Intl Inc ....G...... 917 262-0795
  New York *(G-10086)*

GLASS: Tempered

Oldcastle Buildingenvelope Inc .....C....... 631 234-2200
  Hauppauge *(G-6152)*
Taylor Products Inc ....G...... 518 773-9312
  Gloversville *(G-5725)*

GLASSWARE STORES

Benton Announcements Inc ....F....... 716 836-4100
  Buffalo *(G-2839)*
Vitrix Inc ....G...... 607 936-8707
  Corning *(G-3984)*

GLASSWARE WHOLESALERS

A Sunshine Glass & Aluminum .....E....... 718 932-8080
  Woodside *(G-17316)*
Avon Products Inc ....C....... 212 282-5000
  New York *(G-9281)*

Employee Codes: A=Over 500 employees, B=251-500
C=101-250, D=51-100, E=20-50, F=10-19, G=5-9

GLASSWARE: Laboratory

TEC Glass & Inst LLC .... G 315 926-7639
Marion *(G-8102)*

GLASSWARE: Laboratory & Medical

Immco Diagnostics Inc .... G 716 691-6955
Buffalo *(G-3003)*
Immco Diagnostics Inc .... D 716 691-6911
Buffalo *(G-3004)*
Mri Northtowns Group PC .... F 716 836-4646
Buffalo *(G-3076)*

GLOBAL POSITIONING SYSTEMS & EQPT

Evado Filip .... F 917 774-8666
New York *(G-10087)*
Rehabilitation International .... G 212 420-1500
Jamaica *(G-6946)*

GLOVE MENDING, FACTORY BASIS

Radio Circle Realty Inc .... E 914 241-8742
Mount Kisco *(G-8642)*
Valeo .... G 800 634-2704
Yonkers *(G-17495)*

GLOVES: Fabric

Falls Manufacturing Inc .... G 518 672-7189
Philmont *(G-13540)*
Gce International Inc .... F 212 868-0500
New York *(G-10260)*

GLOVES: Leather

American Target Marketing Inc .... E 518 725-4369
Gloversville *(G-5705)*
Fieldtex Products Inc .... C 585 427-2940
Rochester *(G-14369)*
Samco LLC .... E 518 725-4705
Johnstown *(G-7125)*
USA Sewing Inc .... E 315 792-8017
Utica *(G-16203)*

GLOVES: Leather, Dress Or Semidress

Fownes Brothers & Co Inc .... E 212 683-0150
New York *(G-10194)*
Fownes Brothers & Co Inc .... E 518 752-4411
Gloversville *(G-5711)*

GLOVES: Leather, Work

Protech (llc) .... E 518 725-7785
Gloversville *(G-5719)*
Worldwide Protective Pdts LLC .... C 877 678-4568
Hamburg *(G-5946)*

GLOVES: Plastic

Elara Fdsrvice Disposables LLC .... G 516 470-1523
Jericho *(G-7066)*

GLOVES: Safety

Hand Care Inc .... G 516 747-5649
Roslyn *(G-15020)*

GLOVES: Work

Manzella Knitting .... G 716 825-0808
Orchard Park *(G-13281)*

GLOVES: Woven Or Knit, From Purchased Materials

Fownes Brothers & Co Inc .... E 212 683-0150
New York *(G-10194)*
Fownes Brothers & Co Inc .... E 518 752-4411
Gloversville *(G-5711)*

GLUE

Alney Group Ltd .... G 631 242-9100
Deer Park *(G-4094)*
Hudson Industries Corporation .... E 518 762-4638
Johnstown *(G-7215)*

GOLD ORE MINING

Andes Gold Corporation .... D 212 541-2495
New York *(G-9152)*

Capital Gold Corporation .... G 212 668-0842
New York *(G-9519)*

GOLD ORES

Global Gold Corporation .... F 914 925-0020
Rye *(G-15058)*
Gncc Capital Inc .... G 702 951-9793
New York *(G-10325)*

GOLD STAMPING, EXC BOOKS

John Gailer Inc .... E 212 243-5662
Long Island City *(G-7772)*
Welsh Gold Stampers Inc .... E 718 984-5031
Staten Island *(G-15754)*

GOLF CARTS: Powered

Club Protector Inc .... G 716 652-4787
Elma *(G-4645)*

GOLF DRIVING RANGES

Central New York Golf Center .... G 315 463-1200
East Syracuse *(G-4517)*

GOLF EQPT

Central New York Golf Center .... G 315 463-1200
East Syracuse *(G-4517)*
Morris Golf Ventures .... E 631 283-0559
Southampton *(G-15547)*

GOURMET FOOD STORES

Dairy Maid Raviolo Mfg .... F 718 449-2620
Brooklyn *(G-1835)*
Herris Gourmet Inc .... G 917 578-2308
Brooklyn *(G-2078)*
Interntional Gourmet Soups Inc .... E 212 768-7687
Staten Island *(G-15688)*
Johns Ravioli Company Inc .... F 914 576-7030
New Rochelle *(G-8915)*
New York Ravioli Pasta Co Inc .... E 516 270-2852
New Hyde Park *(G-8851)*
Queen Ann Macaroni Mfg Co Inc .... E 718 256-1061
Brooklyn *(G-2466)*
Raffettos Corp .... E 212 777-1261
New York *(G-11785)*

GOVERNMENT, EXECUTIVE OFFICES: Mayors'

City of Olean .... G 716 376-5694
Olean *(G-13138)*
City of Oneonta .... G 607 433-3470
Oneonta *(G-13178)*
Hartford Hwy Dept .... G 315 724-0654
New Hartford *(G-8806)*
Town of Amherst .... E 716 631-7113
Williamsville *(G-17258)*

GOVERNMENT, GENERAL: Administration

City of New York .... E 718 965-8787
Brooklyn *(G-1782)*

GRANITE: Crushed & Broken

Suffolk Granite Manufacturing .... E 631 226-4774
Lindenhurst *(G-7486)*
Tilcon New York Inc .... D 845 358-3100
West Nyack *(G-16929)*

GRANITE: Cut & Shaped

Amendola MBL & Stone Ctr Inc .... D 914 997-7968
White Plains *(G-17076)*
Aurora Stone Group LLC .... F 315 471-6869
East Syracuse *(G-4508)*
Capital Stone LLC .... G 518 382-7588
Schenectady *(G-15239)*
Capital Stone Saratoga LLC .... G 518 226-8677
Saratoga Springs *(G-15147)*
Glen Plaza Marble & Gran Inc .... G 516 671-1100
Glen Cove *(G-5617)*
Granite & Marble Works Inc .... E 518 584-2800
Gansevoort *(G-5486)*
House of Stone Inc .... G 845 782-7271
Monroe *(G-8556)*
Marble Works Inc .... E 914 376-3653
Yonkers *(G-17465)*

MCM Natural Stone Inc .... F 585 586-6510
Rochester *(G-15102)*
PR & Stone & Tile Inc .... G 718 383-1115
Brooklyn *(G-2434)*
Royal Marble & Granite Inc .... G 516 536-5900
Oceanside *(G-13094)*

GRANITE: Dimension

Adirondack Natural Stone LLC .... E 518 499-0602
Whitehall *(G-17189)*
Cold Spring Granite Company .... E 518 647-8191
Au Sable Forks *(G-475)*
Imerys Usa Inc .... F 315 287-0780
Gouverneur *(G-5746)*

GRANITE: Dimension

Alice Perkins .... G 716 378-5100
Salamanca *(G-15099)*

GRAPHIC ARTS & RELATED DESIGN SVCS

Accent Label & Tag Co Inc .... G 631 244-7066
Ronkonkoma *(G-14847)*
Adcomm Graphics Inc .... E 212 645-1298
West Babylon *(G-16765)*
Advantage Printing Inc .... F 718 820-0688
Kew Gardens *(G-7158)*
Alabaster Group Inc .... G 516 867-8223
Freeport *(G-5382)*
Beebie Printing & Art Agcy Inc .... E 518 725-4528
Gloversville *(G-5708)*
Desktop Publishing Concepts .... F 631 752-1934
Farmingdale *(G-4976)*
Digital Evolution Inc .... E 212 732-2722
New York *(G-9876)*
Eastern Metal of Elmira Inc .... D 607 734-2295
Elmira *(G-4679)*
Gg Design and Printing .... G 718 321-3220
New York *(G-10289)*
Greenwood Graphics Inc .... F 516 822-4856
Hicksville *(G-6353)*
Horne Organization Inc .... F 914 572-1330
Yonkers *(G-17454)*
Merlin Printing Inc .... E 631 842-6666
Amityville *(G-312)*
Middletown Press .... G 845 343-1895
Middletown *(G-8451)*
North American Graphics Inc .... F 212 725-2200
New York *(G-11455)*
Pic A Poc Enterprises Inc .... G 631 981-2094
Ronkonkoma *(G-14970)*
Play-It Productions Inc .... F 212 695-6530
Port Washington *(G-13856)*
Proof 7 Ltd .... F 212 680-1843
New York *(G-11735)*
Resonant Legal Media LLC .... D 800 781-3591
New York *(G-11841)*
Tri Kolor Printing & Sty .... F 315 474-6753
Syracuse *(G-16061)*
Vital Signs & Graphics Co Inc .... G 518 237-8372
Cohoes *(G-3760)*

GRAPHIC LAYOUT SVCS: Printed Circuitry

J N White Associates Inc .... D 585 237-5191
Perry *(G-13524)*

GRASSES: Artificial & Preserved

Techgrass .... F 646 719-2000
New York *(G-12288)*

GRATINGS: Tread, Fabricated Metal

Fjs Industries Inc .... F 917 428-3797
Brooklyn *(G-1981)*

GRAVE MARKERS: Concrete

Woodside Granite Industries .... G 585 589-6500
Albion *(G-171)*

GRAVEL MINING

Buffalo Crushed Stone Inc .... F 716 566-9636
Franklinville *(G-5368)*
Central Dover Development .... G 917 709-3266
Dover Plains *(G-4314)*
Dalrymple Grav & Contg Co Inc .... E 607 529-3235
Chemung *(G-3594)*
Diehl Development Inc .... G 585 494-2920
Bergen *(G-845)*

PRODUCT SECTION

Hanson Aggregates PA LLC .... E 585 624-1220
  Honeoye Falls *(G-6530)*
Hanson Aggregates PA LLC .... F 315 782-2300
  Watertown *(G-16653)*
Hanson Aggregates PA LLC .... E 315 789-6202
  Oaks Corners *(G-13070)*
Hanson Aggregates PA LLC .... E 585 624-3800
  Honeoye Falls *(G-6529)*
Hanson Aggregates PA LLC .... F 585 436-3250
  Rochester *(G-14421)*
I A Construction Corporation .... G 716 933-8787
  Portville *(G-13875)*
Knight Sttlement Sand Grav LLC .... E 607 776-2048
  Bath *(G-659)*
Rock Mountain Farms Inc .... G 845 647-9084
  Ellenville *(G-4638)*
Seven Springs Gravel Pdts LLC .... G 585 343-4336
  Batavia *(G-647)*
Shelby Crushed Stone Inc .... F 585 798-4501
  Medina *(G-8281)*

GREASE CUPS: Metal

Blue Manufacturing Co Inc .... G 607 796-2463
  Millport *(G-8480)*

GREASE TRAPS: Concrete

Long Island Green Guys .... G 631 664-4306
  Riverhead *(G-14148)*

GREASES: Lubricating

Summit Lubricants Inc .... E 585 815-0798
  Batavia *(G-649)*

GREENHOUSES: Prefabricated Metal

Fillmore Greenhouses Inc .... E 585 567-2678
  Portageville *(G-13872)*

GREETING CARDS WHOLESALERS

Paper House Productions Inc .... E 845 246-7261
  Saugerties *(G-15190)*

GRILLS & GRILLWORK: Woven Wire, Made From Purchased Wire

Nyc Fireplaces & Kitchens .... G 718 326-4328
  Maspeth *(G-8161)*

GRINDING BALLS: Ceramic

Malyn Industrial Ceramics Inc .... G 716 741-1510
  Clarence Center *(G-3679)*

GRINDING SVC: Precision, Commercial Or Indl

Acme Industries of W Babylon .... F 631 737-5231
  Ronkonkoma *(G-14849)*
Ascribe Inc .... E 585 413-0298
  Rochester *(G-14216)*
Dean Manufacturing Inc .... F 607 770-1300
  Vestal *(G-16446)*
Industrial Machine & Gear Work .... G 516 569-4820
  Oceanside *(G-13081)*
Micro Instrument Corp .... D 585 458-3150
  Rochester *(G-14507)*
Temrick Inc .... G 631 567-8860
  Bohemia *(G-1142)*

GRINDING SVCS: Ophthalmic Lens, Exc Prescription

Empire Optical Inc .... F 585 454-4470
  Rochester *(G-14348)*

GRIT: Steel

Smm - North America Trade Corp ...... G 212 604-0710
  New York *(G-12108)*

GRITS: Crushed & Broken

Graymont Materials (ny) Inc .... D 518 561-2531
  Plattsburgh *(G-13665)*
Hanson Aggregates PA LLC .... F 315 393-3743
  Ogdensburg *(G-13115)*
Hanson Aggregates PA LLC .... F 315 821-7222
  Oriskany Falls *(G-13318)*

Masten Enterprises LLC .... D 845 932-8206
  Cochecton *(G-3742)*

GROCERIES WHOLESALERS, NEC

Bimbo Bakeries Usa Inc .... C 718 463-6300
  Maspeth *(G-8121)*
Bimbo Bakeries Usa Inc .... E 800 856-8544
  Vestal *(G-16441)*
Bimbo Bakeries Usa Inc .... F 845 294-5282
  Goshen *(G-5731)*
Coca-Cola Bottling Co of NY .... F 518 459-2010
  Albany *(G-68)*
Coca-Cola Refreshments USA Inc ...... E 718 401-5200
  Bronx *(G-1301)*
Cohens Bakery Inc .... E 716 892-8149
  Buffalo *(G-2879)*
French Associates Inc .... F 718 387-9880
  Fresh Meadows *(G-5440)*
Infant Formula Laboratory Svc .... F 718 257-3000
  Brooklyn *(G-2105)*
Kozy Shack Enterprises LLC .... C 516 870-3000
  Hicksville *(G-6359)*
Kozy Shack Enterprises LLC .... C 516 870-3000
  Hicksville *(G-6360)*
Luxfer Magtech Inc .... D 631 727-8600
  Riverhead *(G-14149)*
Mandarin Soy Sauce Inc .... E 845 343-1505
  Middletown *(G-8449)*
Rochester Coca Cola Bottling .... D 585 546-3900
  Rochester *(G-14638)*
S J McCullagh Inc .... E 716 856-3473
  Buffalo *(G-3172)*
Wellspring Corp .... G 212 529-5454
  New York *(G-12609)*

GROCERIES, GENERAL LINE WHOLESALERS

Frito-Lay North America Inc .... D 607 397-1008
  Worcester *(G-17368)*
Kong Kee Food Corp .... E 718 937-2746
  Long Island City *(G-7783)*
Mondelez Global LLC .... F 585 345-3300
  Batavia *(G-642)*

GUARDRAILS

Elderlee Incorporated .... C 315 789-6670
  Oaks Corners *(G-13069)*

GUIDANCE SYSTEMS & EQPT: Space Vehicle

Harris Corporation .... A 585 269-6600
  Rochester *(G-14423)*
Harris Corporation .... B 585 269-5001
  Rochester *(G-14424)*
Harris Corporation .... C 585 269-5000
  Rochester *(G-14426)*

GUIDED MISSILES & SPACE VEHICLES

Drt Power Systems LLC - Lane .... D 585 247-5940
  Rochester *(G-14319)*
Edo LLC .... A 631 630-4200
  Amityville *(G-286)*
Lockheed Martin Corporation .... A 607 751-2000
  Owego *(G-13354)*
Lockheed Martin Corporation .... D 607 751-7434
  Owego *(G-13355)*

GUM & WOOD CHEMICALS

Gumbusters .... G 866 846-8486
  Brooklyn *(G-2056)*
Westrock Mwv LLC .... C 212 688-5000
  New York *(G-12618)*

GUN STOCKS: Wood

Revival Industries Inc .... F 315 868-1085
  Ilion *(G-6745)*

GUNSMITHS

Michael Britt Inc .... G 516 248-2010
  Mineola *(G-8525)*
Precision Arms Inc .... G 845 225-1130
  Carmel *(G-3404)*

GUTTERS: Sheet Metal

Alfred B Parella .... G 518 872-1238
  Altamont *(G-206)*

HANDBAG STORES

Genesee Building Products LLC .... G 585 548-2726
  Stafford *(G-15620)*

GYPSUM PRDTS

East Pattern & Model Corp .... E 585 461-3240
  Fairport *(G-4856)*
Empire Gypsum Pdts & Sup Corp .... G 914 592-8141
  Elmsford *(G-4749)*
Henderson Hbr Prfrmg Arts Assn .... F 315 938-7333
  Henderson Harbor *(G-6291)*
Lafarge North America Inc .... G 914 930-3027
  Buchanan *(G-2786)*
United States Gypsum Company .... C 585 948-5221
  Oakfield *(G-13066)*

HAIR & HAIR BASED PRDTS

Age Manufacturers Inc .... D 718 927-0048
  Brooklyn *(G-1569)*
American Culture Hair Inc .... E 631 242-3142
  Huntington Station *(G-6694)*
Blandi Products LLC .... F 908 377-2885
  New York *(G-9413)*
Demeo Brothers Inc .... F 212 268-1400
  New York *(G-9843)*
Hair Color Research Group Inc .... E 718 445-6026
  Flushing *(G-5248)*
Jason & Jean Products Inc .... F 718 271-8300
  Corona *(G-3999)*
Malouf Colette Inc .... F 212 941-9588
  New York *(G-11122)*
Mgd Brands Inc .... D 516 545-0150
  Plainview *(G-13620)*
Miss Jessies LLC .... G 718 643-9016
  New York *(G-11282)*
Spartan Brands Inc .... F 212 340-0320
  New York *(G-12149)*
Tactica International Inc .... F 212 575-0500
  New York *(G-12271)*

HAIR ACCESS WHOLESALERS

Mgd Brands Inc .... D 516 545-0150
  Plainview *(G-13620)*
Yours Trading Inc .... G 718 539-0088
  College Point *(G-3812)*

HAIR CARE PRDTS

All Cultures Inc .... E 631 293-3143
  Greenlawn *(G-5872)*
Belmay Holding Corporation .... E 914 376-1515
  Yonkers *(G-17420)*
Dr Miracles Inc .... F 212 481-3584
  Purchase *(G-13956)*
Hair Ventures LLC .... F 718 664-7689
  Irvington *(G-6771)*
LOreal Usa Inc .... B 212 818-1500
  New York *(G-11035)*
LOreal Usa Inc .... G 212 984-4704
  New York *(G-11038)*
LOreal Usa Inc .... B 646 658-5477
  New York *(G-11039)*
Lornamead Inc .... D 716 874-7190
  Tonawanda *(G-16177)*
Pureology Research LLC .... F 212 984-4360
  New York *(G-11754)*
Yours Trading Inc .... G 718 539-0088
  College Point *(G-3812)*
Zotos International Inc .... B 315 781-3207
  Geneva *(G-5589)*

HAIR CARE PRDTS: Hair Coloring Preparations

LOreal USA Products Inc .... G 732 873-3520
  New York *(G-11040)*
Salonclick LLC .... F 718 643-6793
  New York *(G-11959)*

HAIRPIN MOUNTINGS

Lemetric Hair Centers Inc .... F 212 986-5620
  New York *(G-10964)*
Shake-N-Go Fashion Inc .... D 516 944-7777
  Port Washington *(G-13864)*

HANDBAG STORES

Graphic Image Incorporated .... C 631 249-9600
  Melville *(G-8324)*

Employee Codes: A=Over 500 employees, B=251-500
C=101-250, D=51-100, E=10-50, F=10-19, G=5-9

Quilted Koala Ltd F 800 223-5678
New York (G-11773)
Steven Madden Ltd B 718 446-1800
Long Island City (G-7892)

HANDBAGS

Ahq LLC E 212 328-1560
New York (G-9062)
Akh Group LLC G 646 320-8720
New York (G-9066)
Bagznyc Corp F 212 643-8202
New York (G-9305)
Coach Inc B 212 594-1850
New York (G-9656)
Essex Manufacturing Inc D 212 239-0080
New York (G-10066)
Latique Handbags and ACC LLC F 212 564-2914
New York (G-10934)
McM Products USA Inc E 646 756-4090
New York (G-11201)
Nine West Footwear Corporation B 800 999-1877
New York (G-11435)
Pure Trade Us Inc E 212 256-1600
New York (G-11751)
Quilted Koala Ltd F 800 223-5678
New York (G-11773)
Rodem Incorporated F 212 779-7122
New York (G-11901)
Sibeau Handbags Inc E 212 686-0210
New York (G-12059)

HANDBAGS: Women's

Atalla Handbags Inc G 718 965-5500
Brooklyn (G-1643)
Baikal Inc D 212 239-4650
New York (G-9306)
Coach Inc F 212 581-4115
New York (G-9651)
Coach Inc F 718 760-0624
Elmhurst (G-4659)
Coach Inc F 585 425-7720
Victor (G-16468)
Coach Inc F 212 245-4148
New York (G-9652)
Coach Inc E 212 473-6925
New York (G-9653)
Coach Inc F 212 754-0041
New York (G-9654)
Coach Inc F 212 675-6403
New York (G-9655)
Coach Leatherware Intl G 212 594-1850
New York (G-9657)
Coach Services Inc G 212 594-1850
New York (G-9658)
Coach Stores Inc A 212 643-9727
New York (G-9659)
Deux Lux Inc G 212 620-0801
New York (G-9863)
Frenz Group LLC G 212 465-0908
Whitestone (G-17207)
Kcp Holdco Inc A 212 265-1500
New York (G-10827)
Kenneth Cole Productions Inc B 212 265-1500
New York (G-10833)
Renco Group Inc G 212 541-6000
New York (G-11832)
Roadie Products Inc E 631 567-8588
Holbrook (G-6468)
Stuart Weitzman LLC E 212 823-9560
New York (G-12218)

HANDCUFFS & LEG IRONS

Boa Security Technologies Corp G 516 576-0295
Huntington (G-6658)

HANDLES: Brush Or Tool, Plastic

Allen Field Co Inc F 631 665-2782
Brightwaters (G-1238)

HANDLES: Wood

Fibron Products Inc E 716 886-2378
Buffalo (G-2947)

HANGERS: Garment, Plastic

Accessory Corporation A 212 391-8607
New York (G-9010)
American Intl Trimming G 718 369-9643
Brooklyn (G-1602)
Braiform Enterprises Inc E 800 738-7396
New York (G-9450)
Capco Wai Shing LLC G 212 268-1976
New York (G-9518)
Hanger Headquarters LLC G 212 391-8607
New York (G-10407)
Prestige Hangers Str Fixs Corp G 718 522-6777
Brooklyn (G-2440)
Spotless Plastics (usa) Inc E 631 951-9000
Hauppauge (G-6198)

HANGERS: Garment, Wire

Styles Manufacturing Corp G 516 763-5303
Oceanside (G-13098)

HANGERS: Garment, Wire

American Intl Trimming G 718 369-9643
Brooklyn (G-1602)

HARDBOARD & FIBERBOARD PRDTS

Hi-Temp Fabrication Inc F 716 852-5655
Buffalo (G-2995)

HARDWARE

Advantage Wholesale Supply LLC D 718 839-3499
Brooklyn (G-1567)
American Casting and Mfg Corp G 516 349-7010
Plainview (G-13582)
Amertac Holdings Inc G 610 336-1330
Monsey (G-8567)
Barry Industries Inc F 212 242-5200
New York (G-9326)
Cast-All Corporation E 516 741-4025
Mineola (G-8502)
City Store Gates Mfg Corp E 718 939-9700
College Point (G-3781)
Designatronics Incorporated B 516 328-3300
New Hyde Park (G-8826)
Dico Products Corporation F 315 797-0470
Utica (G-16323)
Eaton Electric Holdings LLC C 607 756-2821
Cortland (G-4025)
ER Butler & Co Inc E 212 925-3565
New York (G-10055)
Excelco Developments Inc E 716 934-2651
Silver Creek (G-15448)
Fixture Hardware Mfg Corp E 718 499-9422
Brooklyn (G-1980)
H A Guden Company Inc E 631 737-2900
Ronkonkoma (G-14908)
Industrial Electronic Hardware D 718 492-4440
Brooklyn (G-2103)
Ingham Industries Inc G 631 242-2493
Holbrook (G-6451)
ITR Industries Inc E 914 964-7063
Yonkers (G-17456)
Jaquith Industries Inc E 315 478-5700
Syracuse (G-15966)
Key High Vacuum Products Inc E 631 584-5959
Nesconset (G-8775)
Kilian Manufacturing Corp D 315 432-0700
Syracuse (G-15973)
Legendary Auto Interiors Ltd E 315 331-1212
Newark (G-12734)
Liberty Brass Turning Co Inc E 718 784-2911
Westbury (G-17005)
Lightron Corporation G 516 938-5544
Jericho (G-7075)
Long Island Fireproof Door E 718 767-8800
Whitestone (G-17211)
Magnetic Aids Inc G 845 863-1400
Newburgh (G-12766)
Nielsen Hardware Corporation E 607 821-1475
Binghamton (G-940)
Orbital Holdings Inc E 951 360-7100
Buffalo (G-3104)
P & F Industries Inc C 631 694-9800
Melville (G-8346)
Pinquist Tool & Die Co Inc E 718 389-3900
Lynbrook (G-7956)
Rosco Inc C 718 526-2601
Jamaica (G-6948)
Stidd Systems Inc E 631 477-2400
Greenport (G-5877)
Syraco Products Inc E 800 581-5555
Syracuse (G-16047)
Tattersall Industries LLC E 518 381-4270
Schenectady (G-15304)
Yaloz Mould & Die Co Inc E 718 389-1131
Brooklyn (G-2773)
York Industries Inc E 516 746-3736
Garden City Park (G-5546)

HARDWARE & BUILDING PRDTS: Plastic

Abbott Industries Inc E 718 291-0800
Jamaica (G-6891)
Associated Materials LLC F 631 467-4535
Ronkonkoma (G-14873)
Cementex Latex Corp F 212 741-1770
New York (G-9558)
Dortronics Systems Inc E 631 725-0505
Sag Harbor (G-15077)
Gagne Associates Inc E 800 800-5954
Johnson City (G-7092)
Hall Construction Pdts & Svcs G 518 747-7047
Hudson Falls (G-6647)
Kelta Inc E 631 789-5000
Edgewood (G-4602)
Markwik Corp F 516 470-1990
Hicksville (G-6370)
Metal Cladding Inc D 716 434-5513
Lockport (G-7600)
Pace Window and Door Corp E 585 924-8350
Victor (G-16495)
Performance Advantage Co Inc F 716 683-7413
Lancaster (G-7332)
Schlegel Systems Inc C 585 427-7200
Rochester (G-14674)
Space Age Plstic Fbrcators Inc F 718 324-4062
Bronx (G-1459)
Tii Technologies Inc E 516 364-9300
Edgewood (G-4616)
Transpo Industries Inc E 914 636-1000
New Rochelle (G-8926)
Ultrafab Inc C 585 924-2186
Farmington (G-5158)

HARDWARE & EQPT: Stage, Exc Lighting

Martin Chafkin G 718 383-1155
Brooklyn (G-2276)
Props Displays & Interiors F 212 620-3840
New York (G-11737)
Steeldeck Ny Inc F 718 599-3700
Brooklyn (G-2604)

HARDWARE CLOTH: Woven Wire, Made From Purchased Wire

Dico Products Corporation F 315 797-0470
Utica (G-16323)

HARDWARE STORES

Lowville Farmers Coop Inc E 315 376-6587
Lowville (G-7939)
New Kit On The Block G 631 757-5655
Bohemia (G-1109)
Syracuse Industrial Sls Co Ltd F 315 478-5751
Syracuse (G-16053)

HARDWARE STORES: Builders'

Ingham Industries Inc G 631 242-2493
Holbrook (G-6451)

HARDWARE STORES: Pumps & Pumping Eqpt

A & C/Furia Electric Motors F 914 949-0585
White Plains (G-17072)

HARDWARE STORES: Tools

Boro Park Cutting Tool Corp E 718 720-0610
Staten Island (G-15650)
Parker Machine Company Inc F 518 747-0675
Fort Edward (G-5344)
Zak Jewelry Tools Inc F 212 768-8122
New York (G-12702)

HARDWARE WHOLESALERS

Amertac Holdings Inc G 610 336-1330
Monsey (G-8567)
Barry Industries Inc F 212 242-5200
New York (G-9326)

PRODUCT

PRODUCT SECTION

HEAT TREATING: Metal

Best Way Tools By Anderson Inc ....G...... 631 586-4702
 Deer Park *(G-4106)*
Brodco Inc ....E...... 631 842-4477
 Lido Beach *(G-7440)*
Expo Furniture Designs Inc ....F...... 516 674-1420
 Glen Cove *(G-5615)*
Globe Electronic Hardware Inc ....F...... 718 457-0303
 Woodside *(G-17332)*
H A Guden Company Inc ....E...... 631 737-2900
 Ronkonkoma *(G-14908)*
Metalline Fire Door Co Inc....................E...... 718 583-2320
 Bronx *(G-1393)*
Steel-Brite Ltd ....F...... 631 589-4044
 Oakdale *(G-13063)*
Sure Flow Equipment Inc ....E...... 800 263-8251
 Tonawanda *(G-16204)*

HARDWARE, WHOLESALE: Bolts

Supply Technologies (ny) ....F...... 212 966-3310
 Albany *(G-139)*

HARDWARE, WHOLESALE: Builders', NEC

ER Butler & Co Inc ....E...... 212 925-3565
 New York *(G-10055)*
P E Guerin ....D...... 212 243-5270
 New York *(G-11548)*
S A Baxter LLC ....G...... 845 469-7995
 Chester *(G-3614)*

HARDWARE: Aircraft

Fastener Dimensions Inc ....E...... 718 847-6321
 Ozone Park *(G-13378)*
Kyntec Corporation ....G...... 716 810-6956
 Buffalo *(G-3038)*
Mpi Consulting Incorporated ....E...... 631 253-2377
 West Babylon *(G-16813)*

HARDWARE: Builders'

Kelley Bros Llc ....G...... 315 852-3302
 De Ruyter *(G-4081)*
Northknight Logistics Inc ....F...... 716 283-3090
 Niagara Falls *(G-12853)*
Pk30 System LLC ....F...... 212 473-8050
 Stone Ridge *(G-15764)*
Progressive Hardware Co Inc ....G...... 631 445-1826
 East Northport *(G-4443)*
RKI Building Spc Co Inc ....G...... 718 728-7788
 College Point *(G-3805)*

HARDWARE: Cabinet

Daniel Demarco and Assoc Inc ....E...... 631 598-7000
 Amityville *(G-284)*
Kenstan Lock & Hardware Co Inc ....E...... 631 423-1977
 Plainview *(G-13614)*

HARDWARE: Door Opening & Closing Devices, Exc Electrical

Nanz Custom Hardware Inc ....D...... 212 367-7000
 New York *(G-11340)*
Nanz Custom Hardware Inc ....D...... 212 367-7000
 Deer Park *(G-4176)*

HARDWARE: Furniture

Dreamseats LLC ....E...... 631 656-1066
 Commack *(G-3830)*
Real Design Inc ....F...... 315 429-3071
 Dolgeville *(G-4308)*
Water Street Brass Corporation ....E...... 716 763-0059
 Lakewood *(G-7296)*
Weber-Knapp Company ....C...... 716 484-9135
 Jamestown *(G-7043)*

HARDWARE: Furniture, Builders' & Other Household

Classic Brass Inc ....D...... 716 763-1400
 Lakewood *(G-7288)*
Decorative Hardeware ....F...... 914 238-5251
 Chappaqua *(G-3551)*
Morgik Metal Designs ....F...... 212 463-0304
 New York *(G-11305)*

HARDWARE: Locking Systems, Security Cable

Rize Enterprises LLC ....G...... 631 249-9000
 Bay Shore *(G-736)*

HARDWARE: Luggage

Crest Lock Co Inc ....F...... 718 345-9898
 Brooklyn *(G-1818)*
Tools & Stamping Corp ....G...... 718 392-4040
 Brooklyn *(G-2663)*

HARDWARE: Piano

Samscreen Inc. ....E...... 607 722-3979
 Conklin *(G-3875)*

HARNESS ASSEMBLIES: Cable & Wire

Advanced Interconnect Mfg Inc ....D...... 585 742-2220
 Victor *(G-16459)*
Altec Datacom LLC ....G...... 631 242-2417
 Bay Shore *(G-669)*
Amphenol Intrconnect Pdts Corp ....G...... 607 754-4444
 Endicott *(G-4795)*
Apx Technologies Inc ....E...... 516 433-1313
 Hicksville *(G-6323)*
Arnold-Davis LLC..................................C...... 607 772-1201
 Binghamton *(G-889)*
B3cg Interconnect Usa Inc ....F...... 450 491-4040
 Plattsburgh *(G-13653)*
Badger Technologies Inc ....E...... 585 869-7101
 Farmington *(G-5146)*
Badger Technologies Inc ....D...... 585 869-7101
 Farmington *(G-5147)*
Becker Electronics Inc ....D...... 631 619-9100
 Ronkonkoma *(G-14879)*
Bryit Group LLC ....F...... 631 563-6603
 Holbrook *(G-6433)*
Cables Unlimited Inc. ....E...... 631 563-6363
 Yaphank *(G-17387)*
Condor Electronics Corp ....E...... 585 235-1500
 Rochester *(G-14284)*
Hazlow Electronics Inc ....E...... 585 325-5323
 Rochester *(G-14431)*
I3 Cable & Harness LLC ....D...... 607 238-7077
 Binghamton *(G-924)*
Lyntronics Inc ....E...... 631 205-1061
 Yaphank *(G-17397)*
North Hills Signal Proc Corp ....G...... 516 682-7700
 Syosset *(G-15833)*
Paal Technologies Inc ....G...... 631 319-6262
 Ronkonkoma *(G-14962)*
Phoenix Cables Corporation ....C...... 845 691-6253
 Highland *(G-6406)*
Sayeda Manufacturing Corp ....F...... 631 345-2525
 Medford *(G-8259)*
Sturges Elec Pdts Co Inc ....E...... 607 844-8604
 Dryden *(G-4323)*
TCS Electronics Inc ....E...... 585 337-4301
 Farmington *(G-5156)*
Tony Baird Electronics Inc ....G...... 315 422-4430
 Syracuse *(G-16060)*

HARNESSES, HALTERS, SADDLERY & STRAPS

Equicenter Inc ....E...... 585 742-2522
 Honeoye Falls *(G-6527)*
Fiorentina LLC ....G...... 516 208-5448
 Merrick *(G-8385)*
Import-Export Corporation ....F...... 718 707-0880
 Long Island City *(G-7764)*
Unique Overseas Inc ....G...... 516 466-9792
 Great Neck *(G-5846)*

HAT BOXES

Tumi Inc ....C...... 212 447-8747
 New York *(G-12423)*

HEADPHONES: Radio

Gotenna Inc ....F...... 415 894-2616
 Brooklyn *(G-2042)*

HEALTH AIDS: Exercise Eqpt

D Squared Technologies Inc ....G...... 516 932-7319
 Jericho *(G-7064)*
Gym Store Inc.......................................G...... 718 366-7804
 Maspeth *(G-8142)*
Hypoxico Inc ....G...... 212 972-1009
 New York *(G-10538)*
Physicalmind Institute ....F...... 212 343-2150
 New York *(G-11655)*

HEALTH SCREENING SVCS

Pharma-Smart International Inc ....E...... 585 427-0730
 Rochester *(G-14581)*

HEARING AIDS

Benway-Haworth-Lwlr-Iacosta He ....F...... 518 432-4070
 Albany *(G-54)*
Buffalo Hearg & Speech ....E...... 716 558-1105
 West Seneca *(G-16940)*
Family Hearing Center ....G...... 845 897-3059
 Fishkill *(G-5184)*
Hal-Hen Company Inc ....E...... 516 294-3200
 New Hyde Park *(G-8838)*
Roner Inc ....G...... 718 392-6020
 Long Island City *(G-7865)*
Roner Inc ....C...... 718 392-6020
 Long Island City *(G-7866)*
Todt Hill Audiological Svcs ....G...... 718 816-1952
 Staten Island *(G-15749)*
Widex Usa Inc. ....D...... 718 360-1000
 Hauppauge *(G-6234)*
William H Shapiro ....G...... 212 263-7037
 New York *(G-12635)*

HEAT EXCHANGERS

Aerco International Inc ....C...... 845 580-8000
 Blauvelt *(G-969)*
Costanzos Welding Inc. ....E...... 716 282-0845
 Niagara Falls *(G-12807)*
Fross Industries Inc. ....C...... 716 297-0652
 Niagara Falls *(G-12823)*
Inex Inc. ....G...... 716 537-2270
 Holland *(G-6481)*
Schwabel Fabricating Co Inc ....E...... 716 876-2086
 Tonawanda *(G-16200)*
Vette Corp New York ....D...... 585 265-0330
 Ontario *(G-13216)*
Yula Corporation ....E...... 718 991-0900
 Bronx *(G-1496)*

HEAT EXCHANGERS: After Or Inter Coolers Or Condensers, Etc

American Precision Inds Inc ....C...... 716 691-9100
 Amherst *(G-224)*
API Heat Transfer Company ....G...... 716 684-6700
 Buffalo *(G-2816)*
API Heat Transfer Inc. ....E...... 585 496-5755
 Arcade *(G-387)*
Nitram Energy Inc ....E...... 716 662-6540
 Orchard Park *(G-13285)*
Slantco Manufacturing Inc ....G...... 516 484-2600
 Greenvale *(G-5882)*

HEAT TREATING: Metal

A1 International Heat Treating ....G...... 718 863-5552
 Bronx *(G-1257)*
Aterian Investment Partners LP ....F...... 212 547-2806
 New York *(G-9247)*
B & W Heat Treating Company ....G...... 716 876-8184
 Tonawanda *(G-16143)*
Bodycote Thermal Proc Inc ....E...... 585 436-7876
 Rochester *(G-14240)*
Bsv Metal Finishers Inc ....E...... 585 349-7072
 Spencerport *(G-15567)*
Buffalo Armory LLC ....G...... 716 935-6346
 Buffalo *(G-2848)*
Burke Frging Heat Treating Inc ....E...... 585 235-6060
 Rochester *(G-14251)*
Burton Industries Inc ....E...... 631 643-6660
 West Babylon *(G-16778)*
Cpp - Steel Treaters ....E...... 315 736-3081
 Oriskany *(G-13307)*
Expedient Heat Treating Corp ....G...... 716 433-1177
 North Tonawanda *(G-12970)*
Gibraltar Industries Inc. ....D...... 716 826-6500
 Buffalo *(G-2974)*
Graywood Companies Inc ....E...... 585 254-7000
 Rochester *(G-14413)*
Great Lakes Metal Treating ....F...... 716 694-1240
 Tonawanda *(G-16167)*
Hercules Heat Treating Corp ....E...... 718 625-1266
 Brooklyn *(G-2074)*

HEAT TREATING: Metal

International Ord Tech Inc .... D 716 664-1100
   Jamestown *(G-7003)*
Jasco Heat Treating Inc .... E 585 388-0071
   Fairport *(G-4859)*
Metal Improvement Company LLC .... F 631 567-2610
   Bay Shore *(G-717)*
Modern Heat Trting Forging Inc .... F 716 884-2176
   Buffalo *(G-3073)*
Parfuse Corp 516 997-1795
   Westbury *(G-17018)*
Rochester Steel Treating Works .... F 585 546-3348
   Rochester *(G-14650)*
Sunlight US Co Inc .... G 716 826-6500
   Buffalo *(G-3201)*
Syracuse Heat Treating Corp .... E 315 451-0000
   Syracuse *(G-16052)*

HEATERS: Space, Exc Electric

American Comfort Direct LLC .... E 201 364-8309
   New York *(G-9116)*

HEATERS: Swimming Pool, Oil Or Gas

Jus-Sar Fuel Inc .... G 845 791-8900
   Harris *(G-5976)*
O C P Inc .... E 516 679-2000
   Farmingdale *(G-5069)*

HEATERS: Unit, Domestic

Roberts-Gordon LLC .... D 716 852-4400
   Buffalo *(G-3160)*

HEATING & AIR CONDITIONING EQPT & SPLYS WHOLESALERS

Split Systems Corp .... G 516 223-5511
   North Baldwin *(G-12909)*

HEATING & AIR CONDITIONING UNITS, COMBINATION

Airsys Technologies LLC .... G 716 694-6390
   Tonawanda *(G-16136)*
Colburns AC Rfrgn .... F 716 569-3695
   Frewsburg *(G-5449)*
Daikin Applied Americas Inc .... D 315 253-2771
   Auburn *(G-491)*
Enviromaster International LLC .... D 315 336-3716
   Rome *(G-14810)*
John F Krell Jr 315 492-3201
   Syracuse *(G-15968)*
Keeler Services .... G 607 776-5757
   Bath *(G-658)*
Northern Air Systems Inc 585 594-5050
   Rochester *(G-14543)*
Pro Metal of NY Corp 516 285-0440
   Valley Stream *(G-16421)*

HEATING EQPT & SPLYS

A Nuclimate Qulty Systems Inc .... F 315 431-0226
   East Syracuse *(G-4498)*
Carrier Corporation .... B 315 432-6000
   Syracuse *(G-15888)*
Chentronics Corporation .... E 607 334-5531
   Norwich *(G-13023)*
CIDC Corp .... F 718 342-5820
   Brooklyn *(G-1780)*
Economy Pump & Motor Repair .... G 718 433-2600
   Astoria *(G-438)*
Embassy Industries Inc .... C 631 435-0209
   Hauppauge *(G-6071)*
Fedders Islandaire Inc .... D 631 471-2900
   East Setauket *(G-4482)*
Fisonic Corp .... G 212 732-3777
   Long Island City *(G-7743)*
Fisonic Corp .... F 716 763-0295
   New York *(G-10174)*
Fulton Volcanic Inc .... D 315 298-5121
   Pulaski *(G-13950)*
Juniper Elbow Co Inc .... C 718 326-2546
   Middle Village *(G-8414)*
Omega Heater Company Inc .... D 631 588-8820
   Ronkonkoma *(G-14959)*
RE Hansen Industries Inc 631 471-2900
   East Setauket *(G-4491)*
Real Goods Solar Inc .... C 845 708-0800
   New City *(G-8791)*
Slant/Fin Corporation .... B 516 484-2600
   Greenvale *(G-5881)*

Stephen Hanley .... D 718 729-3360
   Long Island City *(G-7891)*
Unilux Advanced Mfg LLC .... E 518 344-7490
   Schenectady *(G-15308)*
Vincent Genovese .... G 631 281-8170
   Mastic Beach *(G-8205)*

HEATING EQPT: Complete

A Nuclimate Qulty Systems Inc .... F 315 431-0226
   East Syracuse *(G-4498)*
Dundas-Jafine Inc 716 681-9690
   Alden *(G-177)*
Max Thermo Corporation .... F 845 294-3640
   Goshen *(G-5737)*
Siemens Industry Inc 716 568-0983
   Buffalo *(G-3187)*
Thomson Industries Inc .... F 716 691-9100
   Amherst *(G-266)*

HEATING EQPT: Induction

Ambrell Inc .... G 585 889-9000
   Scottsville *(G-15333)*
Ameritherm Inc .... F 585 889-0236
   Scottsville *(G-15334)*
Ultraflex Power Technologies .... G 631 467-6814
   Ronkonkoma *(G-14995)*

HEATING SYSTEMS: Radiant, Indl Process

Radiant Pro Ltd .... G 516 763-5678
   Oceanside *(G-13092)*

HEATING UNITS & DEVICES: Indl, Electric

API Heat Transf Thermasys Corp .... E 716 901-8504
   Buffalo *(G-2815)*
Easco Boiler Corp .... E 718 378-3000
   Bronx *(G-1322)*
Fulton Volcanic Inc .... D 315 298-5121
   Pulaski *(G-13950)*
Igniter Systems Inc .... E 716 542-5511
   Akron *(G-24)*

HELICOPTERS

CIC International Ltd .... D 212 213-0089
   Brooklyn *(G-1779)*

HELMETS: Athletic

Cascade Helmets Holdings Inc .... E 315 453-3073
   Liverpool *(G-7516)*
Performance Lacrosse Group Inc .... G 315 453-3073
   Liverpool *(G-7541)*

HIDES & SKINS

Adirondack Meat Company Inc .... F 518 585-2333
   Ticonderoga *(G-16124)*

HIGH ENERGY PARTICLE PHYSICS EQPT

Advance Energy Systems NY LLC .... G 315 735-5125
   Utica *(G-16305)*
Spirent Inc .... G 631 208-0680
   Riverhead *(G-14157)*

HIGHWAY SIGNALS: Electric

BNo Intl Trdg Co Inc .... G 716 487-1900
   Jamestown *(G-6977)*
Kentronics Inc .... G 631 567-5994
   Bohemia *(G-1087)*
Traffic Lane Closures LLC .... G 845 228-6100
   Brewster *(G-1228)*

HOBBY & CRAFT SPLY STORES

Paper House Productions Inc .... E 845 246-7261
   Saugerties *(G-15190)*

HOBBY, TOY & GAME STORES: Ceramics Splys

Ceramaterials LLC .... G 518 701-6722
   Port Jervis *(G-13781)*

HOISTS

Columbus McKinnon Corporation .... C 716 689-5400
   Getzville *(G-5595)*
Columbus McKinnon Corporation .... E 716 689-5400
   Getzville *(G-5597)*

Columbus McKinnon Corporation .... C 716 689-5400
   Getzville *(G-5598)*
Mannesmann Corporation .... D 212 258-4000
   New York *(G-11136)*
Marros Equipment & Trucks .... F 315 539-8702
   Waterloo *(G-16630)*
Mohawk Resources Ltd .... D 518 842-1431
   Amsterdam *(G-359)*
Reimann & Georger Corporation .... E 716 895-1156
   Buffalo *(G-3156)*
T Shore Products Ltd 315 252-9174
   Auburn *(G-522)*
Thego Corporation .... G 631 776-2472
   Bellport *(G-841)*
Vortek Tel 87724633365859 .... E 585 924-5000
   Victor *(G-16511)*

HOLDING COMPANIES: Banks

Flavors Holdings Inc .... G 212 572-8677
   New York *(G-10178)*

HOLDING COMPANIES: Investment, Exc Banks

Asp Blade Intrmdate Hldngs Inc .... G 212 476-8000
   New York *(G-9234)*
Chemprene Inc .... C 845 831-2800
   Beacon *(G-782)*
Geritrex Holdings Inc .... G 914 668-4003
   Mount Vernon *(G-8683)*
Global Video LLC .... D 516 222-2600
   Woodbury *(G-17288)*
Graphic Controls Holdings Inc .... F 716 853-7500
   Buffalo *(G-2979)*
Hw Holdings Inc .... G 212 399-1000
   New York *(G-10534)*
Noco Incorporated .... G 716 833-6626
   Tonawanda *(G-16187)*
Pii Holdings Inc .... G 716 876-9951
   Buffalo *(G-3126)*

HOLDING COMPANIES: Personal, Exc Banks

Spf Holdings II LLC .... F 212 750-8300
   New York *(G-12161)*

HOME DELIVERY NEWSPAPER ROUTES

Nyt Capital LLC .... F 212 556-1234
   New York *(G-11488)*

HOME ENTERTAINMENT EQPT: Electronic, NEC

A and K Global Inc .... D 718 412-1876
   Bayside *(G-763)*
Globa Phoni Compu Techn Solut .... E 607 257-7279
   Ithaca *(G-6843)*
Henley Brands LLC .... F 516 883-8220
   Port Washington *(G-13820)*
Request Inc 518 899-1254
   Halfmoon *(G-5914)*
Request Serious Play LLC 518 899-1254
   Halfmoon *(G-5915)*
Shyk International Corp .... G 212 663-3302
   New York *(G-12058)*
Sing Trix 212 352-1500
   New York *(G-12085)*

HOME FOR THE MENTALLY RETARDED

Chemung Cty Assc Retrd Ctzns .... C 607 734-6151
   Elmira *(G-4675)*

HOME FURNISHINGS WHOLESALERS

Feldman Company Inc .... F 212 966-1303
   New York *(G-10150)*
Jay Import Company Inc .... E 212 683-2727
   New York *(G-10704)*
Lifetime Brands Inc .... B 516 683-6000
   Garden City *(G-5514)*
Madison Industries Inc .... F 212 679-5110
   New York *(G-11094)*

HOME HEALTH CARE SVCS

Curemdcom Inc .... B 646 224-2201
   New York *(G-9769)*
New York Health Care Inc .... G 718 375-6700
   Valley Stream *(G-16416)*

PRODUCT SECTION

HOSE: Rubber

HOMEBUILDERS & OTHER OPERATIVE BUILDERS
Hope International Productions .... F 212 247-3188
  New York *(G-10504)*

HOMEFURNISHING STORES: Beddings & Linens
Duxiana Dux Bed .... G 212 755-2600
  New York *(G-9941)*
Metro Mattress Corp .... E 716 205-2300
  Niagara Falls *(G-12847)*
Zzz Mattress Manufacturing .... E 718 454-1468
  Saint Albans *(G-15085)*

HOMEFURNISHING STORES: Lighting Fixtures
David Weeks Studio .... F 212 966-3433
  New York *(G-9824)*
Edison Power & Light Co Inc .... F 718 522-0002
  Brooklyn *(G-1904)*
Maxsun Corporation .... F 718 418-6800
  Maspeth *(G-8151)*
Rapid-Lite Fixture Corporation .... F 347 599-2600
  Brooklyn *(G-2478)*
Serway Bros Inc .... E 315 337-0601
  Rome *(G-14836)*
Sir Industries Inc .... G 631 234-2444
  Hauppauge *(G-6192)*

HOMEFURNISHING STORES: Mirrors
Global Glass Corp .... G 516 681-2309
  Hicksville *(G-6350)*

HOMEFURNISHING STORES: Vertical Blinds
Designers Touch Inc .... G 718 641-3718
  Long Beach *(G-7639)*
Pj Decorators Inc .... E 516 735-9693
  East Meadow *(G-4427)*

HOMEFURNISHING STORES: Wicker, Rattan, Or Reed
Pei Liquidation Company .... F 315 431-4697
  East Syracuse *(G-4554)*

HOMEFURNISHING STORES: Window Furnishings
Blinds To Go (us) Inc .... E 718 477-9523
  Staten Island *(G-15648)*
Wallace Home Design Ctr .... G 631 765-3890
  Southold *(G-15561)*
White Plains Drapery Uphl Inc .... E 914 381-0908
  Mamaroneck *(G-8050)*

HOMEFURNISHINGS & SPLYS, WHOLESALE: Decorative
Gallery 91 .... G 212 966-3722
  New York *(G-10242)*
Mistdoda Inc .... E 919 735-7111
  New York *(G-11284)*
Secret Celebrity Licensing LLC .... G 212 812-9277
  New York *(G-12012)*

HOMEFURNISHINGS, WHOLESALE: Bedspreads
Ess Bee Industries Inc .... E 718 894-5202
  Brooklyn *(G-1936)*

HOMEFURNISHINGS, WHOLESALE: Blinds, Venetian
D & D Window Tech Inc .... G 212 308-2822
  New York *(G-9782)*

HOMEFURNISHINGS, WHOLESALE: Blinds, Vertical
Pj Decorators Inc .... E 516 735-9693
  East Meadow *(G-4427)*

HOMEFURNISHINGS, WHOLESALE: Carpets
Albert Menin Interiors Ltd .... F 212 876-3041
  Bronx *(G-1267)*
Elizabeth Eakins Inc .... F 212 628-1950
  New York *(G-10008)*

HOMEFURNISHINGS, WHOLESALE: Curtains
Baby Signature Inc .... G 212 686-1700
  New York *(G-9298)*
Louis Hornick & Co Inc .... G 212 679-2448
  New York *(G-11049)*

HOMEFURNISHINGS, WHOLESALE: Draperies
Reynolds Drapery Service Inc .... F 315 845-8632
  Newport *(G-12792)*
Star Draperies Inc .... F 631 756-7121
  Farmingdale *(G-5114)*
White Plains Drapery Uphl Inc .... E 914 381-0908
  Mamaroneck *(G-8050)*

HOMEFURNISHINGS, WHOLESALE: Kitchenware
Lifetime Chimney Supply LLC .... G 516 576-8144
  Plainview *(G-13616)*
Methodsourcing Corp .... F 914 217-7276
  Elmsford *(G-4765)*
Vanity Fair Bathmart Inc .... F 718 584-6700
  Bronx *(G-1488)*

HOMEFURNISHINGS, WHOLESALE: Linens, Table
Benson Sales Co Inc .... F 718 236-6743
  Brooklyn *(G-1685)*
Lintex Linens Inc .... B 212 679-8046
  New York *(G-11003)*

HOMEFURNISHINGS, WHOLESALE: Mirrors/Pictures, Framed/Unframd
Ad Notam LLC .... F 631 951-2020
  Hauppauge *(G-6008)*

HOMEFURNISHINGS, WHOLESALE: Pillowcases
Anhui Skyworth LLC .... D 917 940-6903
  Hempstead *(G-6264)*

HOMEFURNISHINGS, WHOLESALE: Rugs
Lorena Canals USA Inc .... G 844 567-3622
  Hastings On Hudson *(G-6005)*

HOMEFURNISHINGS, WHOLESALE: Sheets, Textile
Alok Inc .... G 212 643-4360
  New York *(G-9097)*

HOMEFURNISHINGS, WHOLESALE: Stainless Steel Flatware
Utica Cutlery Company .... D 315 733-4663
  Utica *(G-16363)*

HOMEFURNISHINGS, WHOLESALE: Window Covering Parts & Access
McCarroll Uphl Designs LLC .... G 518 828-0500
  Hudson *(G-6625)*
P E Guerin .... D 212 243-5270
  New York *(G-11548)*

HOMEFURNISHINGS, WHOLESALE: Wood Flooring
Wego International Floors LLC .... F 516 487-3510
  Great Neck *(G-5849)*

HOMES, MODULAR: Wooden
Best Mdlr HMS Afrbe P Q & S In .... F 631 204-0049
  Southampton *(G-15540)*
Bill Lake Homes Construction .... D 518 673-2424
  Sprakers *(G-15577)*
Westchester Modular Homes Inc .... C 845 832-9400
  Wingdale *(G-17275)*
Whitley East LLC .... D 718 403-0050
  Brooklyn *(G-2748)*

HOMES: Log Cabins
Alta Industries Ltd .... F 845 586-3336
  Halcottsville *(G-5904)*
Pine Ridge Log HM Restorations .... F 315 387-3360
  Lacona *(G-7251)*

HONES
09 Flshy Bll/Dsert Sunrise LLC .... G 518 583-6638
  Saratoga Springs *(G-15140)*
Charles A Hones Inc .... G 607 273-5720
  Ithaca *(G-6832)*

HORMONE PREPARATIONS
American Hormones Inc .... F 845 471-7272
  Poughkeepsie *(G-13886)*
Erika T Schwartz MD PC .... F 212 873-3420
  New York *(G-10058)*

HORSE & PET ACCESSORIES: Textile
Saratoga Horseworks Ltd .... E 518 843-6756
  Amsterdam *(G-368)*
Triple E Manufacturing .... F 716 761-6996
  Sherman *(G-15403)*

HORSE ACCESS: Harnesses & Riding Crops, Etc, Exc Leather
Hampton Transport Inc .... F 631 716-4445
  Coram *(G-3943)*
Stonegate Stabless .... G 518 746-7133
  Fort Edward *(G-5346)*

HOSE: Air Line Or Air Brake, Rubber Or Rubberized Fabric
Honeywell International Inc .... D 518 270-0200
  Troy *(G-16220)*

HOSE: Automobile, Plastic
Deer Park Driveshaft & Hose .... G 631 667-4091
  Deer Park *(G-4127)*

HOSE: Cotton Fabric, Rubber Lined
Bedgevant Inc .... G 718 492-0297
  Brooklyn *(G-1678)*

HOSE: Fire, Rubber
Cataract Hose Co .... E 914 941-9019
  Ossining *(G-13321)*

HOSE: Flexible Metal
Flex-Hose Company Inc .... E 315 437-1903
  East Syracuse *(G-4530)*
TI Group Auto Systems LLC .... G 315 568-7042
  Seneca Falls *(G-15371)*

HOSE: Plastic
Chapin Watermatics Inc .... D 315 782-1170
  Watertown *(G-16643)*
Superflex Ltd .... E 718 768-1400
  Brooklyn *(G-2625)*
TI Group Auto Systems LLC .... G 315 568-7042
  Seneca Falls *(G-15371)*

HOSE: Pneumatic, Rubber Or Rubberized Fabric, NEC
Moreland Hose & Belting Corp .... G 631 563-7071
  Oakdale *(G-13060)*

HOSE: Rubber
Mason Industries Inc .... C 631 348-0282
  Hauppauge *(G-6126)*
Mercer Rubber Co .... C 631 348-0282
  Hauppauge *(G-6132)*

HOSE: Vacuum Cleaner, Rubber

Anchor Tech Products Corp ....E 914 592-0240
  Elmsford (G-4733)

HOSES & BELTING: Rubber & Plastic

Flex Enterprises Inc ....E 585 742-1000
  Victor (G-16477)
Habasit America Inc ....D 716 824-8484
  Buffalo (G-2984)
Hitachi Cable America Inc ....F 914 694-9200
  Purchase (G-13957)
Peraflex Hose Inc ....F 716 876-8806
  Buffalo (G-3120)
Standard Motor Products Inc ....B 718 392-0200
  Long Island City (G-7884)
Troy Industrial Solutions ....D 518 272-4920
  Watervliet (G-16690)
WF Lake Corp ....E 518 798-9934
  Queensbury (G-14014)

HOSPITALS: Cancer

Actinium Pharmaceuticals Inc ....F 732 243-9495
  New York (G-9021)

HOSPITALS: Medical & Surgical

Norcorp Inc ....E 914 666-1310
  Mount Kisco (G-8637)

HOT TUBS

D & M Enterprises Incorporated ....G 914 937-6430
  Port Chester (G-13741)

HOT TUBS: Plastic & Fiberglass

D & M Enterprises Incorporated ....G 914 937-6430
  Port Chester (G-13741)
Independent Home Products LLC ..E 718 541-1256
  West Hempstead (G-16855)

HOUSEHOLD APPLIANCE STORES: Air Cond Rm Units, Self-Contnd

Fedders Islandaire Inc ....D 631 471-2900
  East Setauket (G-4482)
RE Hansen Industries Inc ....C 631 471-2900
  East Setauket (G-4491)

HOUSEHOLD APPLIANCE STORES: Electric Household Appliance, Sm

Heaven Fresh USA Inc ....G 800 642-0367
  Niagara Falls (G-12831)

HOUSEHOLD APPLIANCE STORES: Fans, Electric

A & C/Furia Electric Motors ....F 914 949-0585
  White Plains (G-17072)

HOUSEHOLD APPLIANCE STORES: Garbage Disposals

Mount Kisco Transfer Stn Inc ....G 914 666-6350
  Mount Kisco (G-8635)

HOUSEHOLD ARTICLES: Metal

Di Highway Sign Structure Corp ....E 315 736-8312
  New York Mills (G-12721)
Gcm Steel Products Inc ....F 718 386-3346
  Brooklyn (G-2016)
Hatfield Metal Fab Inc ....E 845 454-9078
  Poughkeepsie (G-13906)
L D Flecken Inc ....F 631 777-4881
  Yaphank (G-17396)
New York Manufactured Products ..F 585 254-9353
  Rochester (G-14532)
Ulster County Iron Works LLC ......G 845 255-0003
  New Paltz (G-8880)

HOUSEHOLD FURNISHINGS, NEC

AEP Environmental LLC ....F 716 446-0739
  Buffalo (G-2801)
Ann Gish Inc ....G 212 969-9200
  New York (G-9163)
Area Inc ....G 212 924-7084
  New York (G-9198)

Caddy Concepts Inc ....F 516 570-6279
  Great Neck (G-5795)
Creative Home Furnishings ....G 631 582-8000
  Central Islip (G-3492)
Creative Scents USA Inc ....G 718 522-5901
  Brooklyn (G-1816)
Dico Products Corporation ....F 315 797-0470
  Utica (G-16323)
Ess Bee Industries Inc ....E 718 894-5202
  Brooklyn (G-1936)
Excellent Art Mfg Corp ....F 718 388-7075
  Inwood (G-6756)
Henry B Urban Inc ....E 212 489-3308
  New York (G-10457)
Jay Import Company Inc ....E 212 683-2727
  New York (G-10704)
Kim Seybert Inc ....E 212 564-7850
  New York (G-10846)
Madison Industries Inc ....F 212 679-5110
  New York (G-11094)
McCarroll Uphl Designs LLC ....G 518 828-0500
  Hudson (G-6625)
Medline Industries Inc ....B 845 344-3301
  Middletown (G-8450)
Mgk Group Inc ....E 212 989-2732
  New York (G-11246)
Moga Trading Company Inc ....G 718 760-2966
  Corona (G-4004)
Nationwide Tarps Incorporated ....D 518 843-1545
  Amsterdam (G-361)
Nbets Corporation ....G 516 785-1259
  Wantagh (G-16561)
Paramount Textiles Inc ....F 212 966-1040
  New York (G-11570)
Place Vendome Holding Co Inc ....G 212 696-0765
  Bronx (G-1428)
Q Squared Design LLC ....E 212 686-8860
  New York (G-11763)
Richloom Fabrics Corp ....F 212 685-5400
  New York (G-11869)
Scent-Sation Inc ....D 718 672-4300
  Queens Village (G-13983)
Silly Phillie Creations Inc ....E 718 492-6300
  Brooklyn (G-2556)
Skil-Care Corporation ....C 914 963-2040
  Yonkers (G-17484)
Sleeping Partners Intl Inc ....E 212 254-1515
  Brooklyn (G-2569)
Smith & Johnson Dry Goods ....G 212 951-7067
  New York (G-12103)
Such Intl Incorporation ....G 212 686-9888
  Setauket (G-15380)
Sure Fit Inc ....E 212 395-9340
  New York (G-12244)
Terbo Ltd ....G 718 847-2860
  Richmond Hill (G-14087)
Thompson Packaging Novlt Inc ....G 212 686-4242
  New York (G-12327)
Wildcat Territory Inc ....F 718 361-6726
  Long Island City (G-7921)
William Harvey Studio Inc ....G 718 599-4343
  Brooklyn (G-2753)

HOUSEWARE STORES

Swissmar Inc ....G 905 764-1121
  Niagara Falls (G-12879)

HOUSEWARES, ELECTRIC: Air Purifiers, Portable

Heaven Fresh USA Inc ....G 800 642-0367
  Niagara Falls (G-12831)

HOUSEWARES, ELECTRIC: Cooking Appliances

Emerald Electronics Usa Inc ....G 718 872-5544
  Brooklyn (G-1917)
Hrg Group Inc ....E 212 906-8555
  New York (G-10524)
Plus Its Cheap LLC ....E 845 233-2435
  New City (G-8789)

HOUSEWARES, ELECTRIC: Extractors, Juice

Goodnature Products Inc ....F 716 855-3325
  Orchard Park (G-13273)
Sundance Industries Inc ....G 845 795-5809
  Milton (G-8485)

HOUSEWARES, ELECTRIC: Fryers

Abbott Industries Inc ....E 718 291-0800
  Jamaica (G-6891)

HOUSEWARES, ELECTRIC: Heaters, Sauna

US Health Equipment Company ...E 845 658-7576
  Kingston (G-7222)

HOUSEWARES, ELECTRIC: Heaters, Space

Valad Electric Heating Corp ....F 914 631-4927
  Tarrytown (G-16110)
Valid Electric Corp ....E 914 631-9436
  Tarrytown (G-16111)

HOUSEWARES, ELECTRIC: Heating, Bsbrd/Wall, Radiant Heat

Vincent Genovese ....G 631 281-8170
  Mastic Beach (G-8205)

HOUSEWARES, ELECTRIC: Humidifiers, Household

Dampits International Inc ....G 212 581-3047
  New York (G-9796)
Remedies Surgical Supplies ....G 718 599-5301
  Brooklyn (G-2490)

HOUSEWARES, ELECTRIC: Massage Machines, Exc Beauty/Barber

Advanced Response Corporation ..G 212 459-0887
  New York (G-9046)
Quality Life Inc ....F 718 939-5787
  College Point (G-3803)

HOUSEWARES: Dishes, China

Jill Fagin Enterprises Inc ....G 212 674-9383
  New York (G-10732)
Korin Japanese Trading Corp ....E 212 587-7021
  New York (G-10878)
Oneida International Inc ....G 315 361-3000
  Oneida (G-13160)
Oneida Silversmiths Inc ....G 315 361-3000
  Oneida (G-13164)

HOUSEWARES: Dishes, Earthenware

Ceramica Varm ....G 914 381-6215
  New Rochelle (G-8892)

HOUSEWARES: Dishes, Plastic

E-Z Ware Dishes Inc ....G 718 376-3244
  Brooklyn (G-1895)
Etna Products Co Inc ....F 212 989-7591
  New York (G-10078)
Howard Charles Inc ....G 917 902-6934
  Woodbury (G-17290)
J M R Plastics Corporation ....G 718 898-9825
  Middle Village (G-8412)
Methodsourcing Corp ....F 914 217-7276
  Elmsford (G-4765)
Novelty Crystal Corp ....E 718 458-6700
  Long Island City (G-7826)
Ocala Group LLC ....F 516 233-2750
  New Hyde Park (G-8853)
Prime Marketing and Sales LLC ...G 888 802-3836
  New York (G-11707)
Robinson Knife ....F 716 685-6300
  Buffalo (G-3161)
Villeroy & Boch Usa Inc ....G 212 213-8149
  New York (G-12545)

HOUSEWARES: Kettles & Skillets, Cast Iron

S M S C Inc ....G 315 942-4394
  Boonville (G-1169)
Staub Usa Inc ....G 914 747-0300
  Pleasantville (G-13721)

HOUSEWARES: Pots & Pans, Glass

Art and Cook Inc ....F 718 567-7778
  Brooklyn (G-1631)

HUMIDIFIERS & DEHUMIDIFIERS

Heaven Fresh USA Inc ....G 800 642-0367
  Niagara Falls (G-12831)

PRODUCT SECTION

INDL MACHINERY & EQPT WHOLESALERS

MSP Technologycom LLC .... G 631 424-7542
   Centerport *(G-3480)*

HYDRAULIC EQPT REPAIR SVC

Mooradian Hydraulics & Eqp Co .... F 518 766-3866
   Castleton On Hudson *(G-3419)*

Hard Rubber & Molded Rubber Prdts

Apple Rubber Products Inc .... E 716 684-6560
   Lancaster *(G-7303)*
Apple Rubber Products Inc .... C 716 684-7649
   Lancaster *(G-7304)*
Mason Industries Inc .... C 631 348-0282
   Hauppauge *(G-6126)*
Prince Rubber & Plas Co Inc .... E 225 272-1653
   Buffalo *(G-3136)*
Triangle Rubber Co Inc .... E 631 589-9400
   Bohemia *(G-1147)*

ICE

Adirondack Ice & Air Inc .... F 518 483-4340
   Malone *(G-8005)*
Arctic Glacier Minnesota Inc .... E 585 388-0080
   Fairport *(G-4842)*
Arctic Glacier Newburgh Inc .... G 718 456-2013
   Brooklyn *(G-1623)*
Arctic Glacier Newburgh Inc .... G 845 561-0549
   Newburgh *(G-12750)*
Arctic Glacier PA Inc .... E 610 494-8200
   Fairport *(G-4843)*
Mamitas Ices Ltd .... F 718 738-3238
   Ozone Park *(G-13383)*
Maplewood Ice Co Inc .... E 518 499-2345
   Whitehall *(G-17190)*
South Shore Ice Co Inc .... F 516 379-2056
   Roosevelt *(G-15009)*

ICE CREAM & ICES WHOLESALERS

Four Brothers Italian Bakery .... G 914 741-5434
   Hawthorne *(G-6246)*
Fresh Ice Cream Company LLC .... F 347 603-6021
   Brooklyn *(G-2006)*
Macedonia Ltd .... F 718 462-3596
   Brooklyn *(G-2250)*
Marina Ice Cream .... G 718 235-3000
   Brooklyn *(G-2270)*
Purity Ice Cream Co Inc .... F 607 272-1545
   Ithaca *(G-6872)*
Washburns Dairy Inc .... E 518 725-0629
   Gloversville *(G-5728)*

IDENTIFICATION TAGS, EXC PAPER

Ketchum Manufacturing Co Inc .... F 518 696-3331
   Lake Luzerne *(G-7272)*

IGNEOUS ROCK: Crushed & Broken

Barrett Paving Materials Inc .... F 315 737-9471
   Clayville *(G-3686)*
Cayuga Crushed Stone Inc .... E 607 533-4273
   Lansing *(G-7348)*
Highland Sand & Gravel Inc .... F 845 928-2221
   Highland Mills *(G-6412)*
Peckham Materials Corp .... E 518 747-3353
   Hudson Falls *(G-6649)*

IGNITION APPARATUS & DISTRIBUTORS

Magnum Shielding Corporation .... E 585 381-9957
   Pittsford *(G-13568)*
Martinez Specialties Inc .... G 607 898-3053
   Groton *(G-5900)*
Taro Manufacturing Company Inc .... F 315 252-9430
   Auburn *(G-523)*

IGNITION SYSTEMS: High Frequency

Standard Motor Products Inc .... B 718 392-0200
   Long Island City *(G-7884)*
Zenith Autoparts Corp .... E 845 344-1382
   Middletown *(G-8471)*

IGNITION SYSTEMS: Internal Combustion Engine

Zierick Manufacturing Corp .... D 800 882-8020
   Mount Kisco *(G-8648)*

INCINERATORS

Thermal Process Cnstr Co .... E 631 293-6400
   Farmingdale *(G-5129)*

INDICATORS: Cabin Environment

Excelsior Mlt-Cltural Inst Inc .... F 706 627-4285
   Flushing *(G-5239)*

INDL & PERSONAL SVC PAPER WHOLESALERS

Josh Packaging Inc .... E 631 822-1660
   Hauppauge *(G-6102)*
Stanley Paper Co Inc .... F 518 489-1131
   Albany *(G-136)*

INDL & PERSONAL SVC PAPER, WHOL: Bags, Paper/Disp Plastic

Dawn Paper Co Inc .... F 516 596-9110
   East Rockaway *(G-4469)*
Dory Enterprises Inc .... F 607 565-7079
   Waverly *(G-16701)*
Dynamic Packaging Inc .... F 718 388-0800
   Brooklyn *(G-2861)*
Elara Fdsrvice Disposables LLC .... G 516 470-1523
   Jericho *(G-7066)*
Garb-O-Liner Inc .... G 914 235-1585
   New Rochelle *(G-8904)*
Golden Group International Ltd .... G 845 440-1025
   Patterson *(G-13440)*
M C Packaging Corporation .... E 631 643-3763
   Babylon *(G-550)*
Paramount Equipment Inc .... E 631 981-4422
   Ronkonkoma *(G-14964)*
Poly Craft Industries Corp .... E 631 630-6731
   Hauppauge *(G-6166)*
Primo Plastics Inc .... E 718 349-1000
   Brooklyn *(G-2443)*
Westrock Rkt Company .... C 330 296-5155
   Deer Park *(G-4226)*

INDL & PERSONAL SVC PAPER, WHOL: Boxes, Corrugtd/Solid Fiber

Cattaraugus Containers Inc .... E 716 676-2000
   Franklinville *(G-5369)*
Inner-Pak Container Inc .... F 631 289-9700
   Patchogue *(G-13423)*
Technical Packaging Inc .... F 516 223-2300
   Baldwin *(G-562)*

INDL & PERSONAL SVC PAPER, WHOL: Cups, Disp, Plastic/Paper

Amscan Inc .... C 914 345-2020
   Elmsford *(G-4732)*
S J McCullagh Inc .... E 716 856-3473
   Buffalo *(G-3172)*

INDL & PERSONAL SVC PAPER, WHOLESALE: Boxes & Containers

Base Container Inc .... F 718 636-2004
   Brooklyn *(G-1669)*

INDL & PERSONAL SVC PAPER, WHOLESALE: Press Sensitive Tape

Edco Supply Corporation .... D 718 788-8108
   Brooklyn *(G-1903)*
Tape-It Inc .... E 631 243-4100
   Bay Shore *(G-750)*

INDL & PERSONAL SVC PAPER, WHOLESALE: Sanitary Food

Genpak LLC .... E 518 798-9511
   Glens Falls *(G-5679)*

INDL EQPT SVCS

Burnett Process Inc .... G 585 254-8080
   Rochester *(G-14252)*
Eis Inc .... D 585 426-5330
   Rochester *(G-14341)*
Keyes Machine Works Inc .... G 585 426-5059
   Gates *(G-5561)*

Oliver Gear Inc .... E 716 885-1080
   Buffalo *(G-3100)*

INDL GASES WHOLESALERS

Haun Welding Supply Inc .... F 607 846-2289
   Elmira *(G-4689)*

INDL MACHINERY & EQPT WHOLESALERS

Accurate Industrial Machining .... E 631 242-0566
   Holbrook *(G-6430)*
Advanced Photonics Inc .... F 631 471-3693
   Ronkonkoma *(G-14855)*
Analog Digital Technology LLC .... G 585 698-1845
   Rochester *(G-14203)*
Anderson Instrument Co Inc .... D 518 922-5315
   Fultonville *(G-5477)*
Anthony Manufacturing Inc .... G 631 957-9424
   Lindenhurst *(G-7454)*
Arbe Machinery Inc .... F 631 756-2477
   Farmingdale *(G-4945)*
Brinkman Products Inc .... B 585 235-4545
   Rochester *(G-14246)*
Brooklyn Brew Shop LLC .... F 718 874-0119
   Brooklyn *(G-1722)*
Buflovak LLC .... E 716 895-2100
   Buffalo *(G-2861)*
Charles Ross & Son Company .... D 631 234-0500
   Hauppauge *(G-6044)*
Conrad Blasius Equipment Co .... G 516 753-1200
   Plainview *(G-13590)*
DI Manufacturing Inc .... E 315 432-8977
   North Syracuse *(G-12942)*
Dorsey Metrology Intl Inc .... E 845 229-2929
   Poughkeepsie *(G-13895)*
Filling Equipment Co Inc .... F 718 445-2111
   College Point *(G-3783)*
Genesee Manufacturing Co Inc .... E 585 266-3201
   Rochester *(G-14394)*
Goulds Pumps Incorporated .... A 315 568-2811
   Seneca Falls *(G-15360)*
Goulds Pumps Incorporated .... B 315 258-4949
   Auburn *(G-498)*
Hades Manufacturing Corp .... F 631 249-4244
   Farmingdale *(G-5004)*
Halpern Tool Corp .... G 914 633-0038
   New Rochelle *(G-8908)*
Hunter Douglas Inc .... D 845 664-7000
   Pearl River *(G-13460)*
Innotech Graphic Eqp Corp .... G 845 268-6900
   Valley Cottage *(G-16379)*
ITT Goulds Pumps Inc .... A 914 641-2129
   Seneca Falls *(G-15364)*
John N Fehlinger Co Inc .... F 212 233-5656
   New York *(G-10752)*
Kinequip Inc .... F 716 694-5000
   Buffalo *(G-3032)*
Kps Capital Partners LP .... E 212 338-5100
   New York *(G-10883)*
Lubow Machine Corp .... F 631 226-1700
   Copiague *(G-3911)*
Makerbot Industries LLC .... B 347 334-6800
   Brooklyn *(G-2254)*
Mark - 10 Corporation .... E 631 842-9200
   Copiague *(G-3913)*
Micro Centric Corporation .... E 800 573-1139
   Plainview *(G-13621)*
N E Controls LLC .... F 315 626-2480
   Syracuse *(G-15996)*
Noresco Industrial Group Inc .... E 516 759-3355
   Glen Cove *(G-5622)*
Rapid Fan & Blower Inc .... F 718 786-2060
   Long Island City *(G-7857)*
Riverside Machinery Company .... E 718 492-7400
   Brooklyn *(G-2498)*
Rs Automation .... E 585 589-0199
   Albion *(G-169)*
Simmons Machine Tool Corp .... C 518 462-5431
   Menands *(G-8378)*
Specialty Steel Fabg Corp .... F 718 893-6326
   Bronx *(G-1461)*
Speedways Conveyors Inc .... E 716 893-2222
   Buffalo *(G-3195)*
Thread Check Inc .... D 631 231-1515
   Hauppauge *(G-6214)*
Troy Industrial Solutions .... D 518 272-4920
   Watervliet *(G-16690)*
Uneeda Enterprizes Inc .... C 877 863-3321
   Spring Valley *(G-15605)*
Unicell Body Company Inc .... F 716 853-8628
   Schenectady *(G-15307)*

INDL MACHINERY & EQPT WHOLESALERS — PRODUCT SECTION

Viatran Corporation .... E 716 629-3800
North Tonawanda (G-13005)
Vibration & Noise Engrg Corp .... G 716 827-4959
Orchard Park (G-13302)
Ward Industrial Equipment Inc .... G 716 856-6966
Buffalo (G-3247)

INDL MACHINERY REPAIR & MAINTENANCE

4695 Main Street Snyder Inc .... G 716 833-3270
Buffalo (G-2789)
Alternative Service Inc .... F 631 345-9500
Yaphank (G-17385)
Atlantic Industrial Tech Inc .... E 631 234-3131
Shirley (G-15414)
Dairy Conveyor Corp .... D 845 278-7878
Brewster (G-1215)
Demartini Oil Equipment Svc .... G 518 463-5752
Glenmont (G-5667)
General Oil Equipment Co Inc .... E 716 691-7012
Amherst (G-243)
Konecranes Inc .... F 585 359-4450
Henrietta (G-6295)
Locker Masters Inc .... F 518 288-3203
Granville (G-5774)
Prim Hall Enterprises Inc .... F 518 561-7408
Plattsburgh (G-13691)

INDL PATTERNS: Foundry Patternmaking

G Haynes Holdings Inc .... G 607 538-1160
Bloomville (G-995)
Southern Tier Patterns .... G 607 734-1265
Elmira (G-4701)

INDL PROCESS INSTRUMENTS: Analyzers

Enerac Inc .... F 516 997-1554
Holbrook (G-6447)

INDL PROCESS INSTRUMENTS: Control

Conax Technologies LLC .... C 716 684-4500
Buffalo (G-2885)
Electrcal Instrumentation Ctrl .... F 518 861-5789
Delanson (G-4232)
Emerson Indus Automtn USA LLC .... E 716 774-1193
Grand Island (G-5756)
Inficon Inc .... C 315 434-1149
East Syracuse (G-4541)
Micromod Automtn & Contrls Inc .... F 585 321-9209
Rochester (G-14511)
Partlow Corporation .... C 518 922-5315
Fultonville (G-5481)
Rwb Controls Inc .... G 716 897-4341
Buffalo (G-3169)

INDL PROCESS INSTRUMENTS: Controllers, Process Variables

Anderson Instrument Co Inc .... D 518 922-5315
Fultonville (G-5477)
Applied Power Systems Inc .... E 516 935-2230
Hicksville (G-6322)
Classic Automation LLC .... E 585 241-6010
Webster (G-16718)
Digitronik Dev Labs Inc .... G 585 360-0043
Rochester (G-14308)
Ormec Systems Corp .... E 585 385-3520
Rochester (G-14552)

INDL PROCESS INSTRUMENTS: Digital Display, Process Variables

B Live LLC .... G 212 489-0721
New York (G-9290)
Bae Systems Info & Elec Sys .... F 631 912-1525
Greenlawn (G-5873)
Display Logic USA Inc .... G 516 513-1420
Mineola (G-8506)

INDL PROCESS INSTRUMENTS: Elements, Primary

Aalborg Instrs & Contrls Inc .... D 845 398-3160
Orangeburg (G-13217)

INDL PROCESS INSTRUMENTS: Fluidic Devices, Circuit & Systems

Itt LLC .... B 914 641-2000
White Plains (G-17125)

ITT Corporation .... D 914 641-2000
Seneca Falls (G-15361)
ITT Corporation .... D 315 568-2811
Seneca Falls (G-15362)
ITT Inc .... G 914 641-2000
White Plains (G-17128)
Swagelok Western NY .... G 585 359-8470
West Henrietta (G-16896)

INDL PROCESS INSTRUMENTS: Indl Flow & Measuring

Computer Instruments Corp .... E 516 876-8400
Westbury (G-16975)
Select Controls Inc .... E 631 567-9010
Bohemia (G-1131)

INDL PROCESS INSTRUMENTS: Level & Bulk Measuring

Gizmo Products Inc .... G 585 301-0970
Rochester (G-14403)

INDL PROCESS INSTRUMENTS: On-Stream Gas Or Liquid Analysis

Calibrated Instruments Inc .... F 914 741-5700
Manhasset (G-8056)

INDL PROCESS INSTRUMENTS: Temperature

Norwich Aero Products Inc .... D 607 336-7636
Norwich (G-13032)
Weiss Instruments Inc .... D 631 207-1200
Holtsville (G-6514)

INDL PROCESS INSTRUMENTS: Water Quality Monitoring/Cntrl Sys

A C T Associates .... F 716 759-8348
Clarence (G-3654)
Analytical Technology Inc .... F 646 208-4643
New York (G-9146)
Blue Tee Corp .... G 212 598-0880
New York (G-9422)
Danaher Corporation .... C 516 443-9432
New York (G-9799)
Ewt Holdings III Corp .... E 212 644-5900
New York (G-10096)
Roessel & Co Inc .... G 585 458-5560
Rochester (G-14657)

INDL SALTS WHOLESALERS

American Rock Salt Company LLC .... E 585 991-6878
Retsof (G-14054)

INDL SPLYS WHOLESALERS

Allstate Gasket & Packing Inc .... F 631 254-4050
Deer Park (G-4092)
Applince Installation Svc Corp .... E 716 884-7425
Buffalo (G-2818)
Bfg Marine Inc .... G 631 586-5500
Bay Shore (G-675)
D K Machine Inc .... F 518 747-0626
Fort Edward (G-5341)
Dura-Mill Inc .... E 518 899-2255
Ballston Spa (G-595)
Executive Mirror Doors Inc .... E 631 234-1090
Ronkonkoma (G-14899)
Flex Enterprises Inc .... E 585 742-1000
Victor (G-16477)
Ford Regulator Valve Corp .... G 718 497-3255
Brooklyn (G-1995)
Jar Metals Inc .... F 845 425-8901
Nanuet (G-8758)
Macinnes Tool Corporation .... E 585 467-1920
Rochester (G-14487)
Marks Corpex Banknote Co .... G 631 968-0277
Bay Shore (G-715)
Peraflex Hose Inc .... E 716 876-8806
Buffalo (G-3120)
Rollers Inc .... G 716 837-0700
Buffalo (G-3164)
S A S Industries Inc .... F 631 727-1441
Manorville (G-8080)
Troy Industrial Solutions .... D 518 272-4920
Watervliet (G-16690)

INDL SPLYS, WHOL: Fasteners, Incl Nuts, Bolts, Screws, Etc

Fastener Dimensions Inc .... E 718 847-6321
Ozone Park (G-13378)
Reddi Car Corp .... G 631 589-3141
Sayville (G-15214)
SD Christie Associates Inc .... G 914 734-1800
Peekskill (G-13482)

INDL SPLYS, WHOLESALE: Abrasives

Barton Mines Company LLC .... C 518 798-5462
Glens Falls (G-5672)
Sunbelt Industries Inc .... F 315 823-2947
Little Falls (G-7505)
Uneeda Enterprizes Inc 877 863-3321
Spring Valley (G-15605)
Warren Cutlery Corp .... F 845 876-3444
Rhinebeck (G-14060)

INDL SPLYS, WHOLESALE: Adhesives, Tape & Plasters

Xto Incorporated .... D 315 451-7807
Liverpool (G-7558)

INDL SPLYS, WHOLESALE: Bearings

Raydon Precision Bearing Co .... G 516 887-2582
Lynbrook (G-7958)

INDL SPLYS, WHOLESALE: Bins & Containers, Storage

McIntosh Box & Pallet Co Inc .... E 315 446-9350
Rome (G-14820)

INDL SPLYS, WHOLESALE: Brushes, Indl

Braun Brothers Brushes Inc .... G 631 667-2179
Valley Stream (G-16402)

INDL SPLYS, WHOLESALE: Clean Room Splys

Air Crafters Inc .... C 631 471-7788
Ronkonkoma (G-14857)
Knf Clean Room Products Corp .... E 631 588-7000
Ronkonkoma (G-14923)

INDL SPLYS, WHOLESALE: Fasteners & Fastening Eqpt

American Pride Fasteners LLC .... E 631 940-8292
Bay Shore (G-670)
General Galvanizing Sup Co Inc .... E 718 589-4300
Bronx (G-1343)

INDL SPLYS, WHOLESALE: Knives, Indl

Save O Seal Corporation Inc .... G 914 592-3031
Elmsford (G-4777)

INDL SPLYS, WHOLESALE: Power Transmission, Eqpt & Apparatus

Renold Holdings Inc .... G 716 326-3121
Westfield (G-17050)

INDL SPLYS, WHOLESALE: Rubber Goods, Mechanical

Tattersall Industries LLC .... E 518 381-4270
Schenectady (G-15304)
Triangle Rubber Co Inc .... E 631 589-9400
Bohemia (G-1147)

INDL SPLYS, WHOLESALE: Seals

American Casting and Mfg Corp .... D 800 342-0333
Plainview (G-13581)
Web Seal Inc .... E 585 546-1320
Rochester (G-14758)

INDL SPLYS, WHOLESALE: Springs

Lee Spring Company LLC .... C 718 362-5183
Brooklyn (G-2206)

PRODUCT SECTION

INDL SPLYS, WHOLESALE: Tools
Dinosaw Inc .... E 518 828-9942
  Hudson *(G-6612)*

INDL SPLYS, WHOLESALE: Valves & Fittings
Davidson Corporation .... G 718 439-6300
  Brooklyn *(G-1843)*
John N Fehlinger Co Inc .... F 212 233-5656
  New York *(G-10752)*
McWane Inc .... B 607 734-2211
  Elmira *(G-4694)*
Trident Valve Actuator Co .... F 914 698-2650
  Mamaroneck *(G-8049)*

INDUCTORS
Island Audio Engineering .... G 631 543-2372
  Commack *(G-3836)*

INFORMATION RETRIEVAL SERVICES
Alternative Technology Corp .... G 914 478-5900
  Hastings On Hudson *(G-6002)*
Aquifer Drilling & Testing Inc .... D 516 616-6026
  Mineola *(G-8495)*
Avalon Copy Centers Amer Inc .... D 315 471-3333
  Syracuse *(G-15863)*
Avalon Copy Centers Amer Inc .... E 716 995-7777
  Buffalo *(G-2825)*
Chakra Communications Inc .... E 716 505-7300
  Lancaster *(G-7309)*
Data Key Communication LLC .... F 315 445-2347
  Fayetteville *(G-5164)*
IAC Search LLC .... E 212 314-7300
  New York *(G-10543)*
Iac/Interactivecorp .... C 212 314-7300
  New York *(G-10544)*
Meethappy Inc .... F 917 903-0591
  Seaford *(G-15346)*
NBC Internet Inc .... B 212 315-9016
  New York *(G-11362)*
New York Times Company .... B 212 556-1234
  New York *(G-11410)*
Realtimetraderscom .... E 716 632-6600
  Buffalo *(G-3155)*

INFRARED OBJECT DETECTION EQPT
Infrared Components Corp .... E 315 732-1544
  Utica *(G-16344)*

INK OR WRITING FLUIDS
American Electronic Products .... F 631 924-1299
  Yaphank *(G-17386)*
F M Group Inc .... F 845 589-0102
  Congers *(G-3856)*
Specialty Ink Co Inc .... F 631 586-3666
  Blue Point *(G-1000)*
Spectra Color Corp .... F 631 563-4828
  Holbrook *(G-6472)*

INK: Letterpress Or Offset
Bishop Print Shop Inc .... G 607 965-8155
  Edmeston *(G-4622)*

INK: Printing
Atlas Coatings Corp .... D 718 402-2000
  Bronx *(G-1277)*
Calchem Corporation .... G 631 423-5696
  Ronkonkoma *(G-14883)*
Flint Group Incorporated .... E 585 458-1223
  Rochester *(G-14373)*
Gotham Ink & Color Co Inc .... E 845 947-4000
  Stony Point *(G-15774)*
Image Specialists Inc .... F 631 475-0867
  Saint James *(G-15090)*
Inglis Co Inc .... G 315 475-1315
  Syracuse *(G-15963)*
Intrinsiq Materials Inc .... G 585 301-4432
  Rochester *(G-14454)*
Micro Powders Inc .... E 914 332-6400
  Tarrytown *(G-16097)*
Millennium Rmnfctred Toner Inc .... F 718 585-9887
  Bronx *(G-1397)*
Specialty Ink Co Inc .... F 631 586-3666
  Blue Point *(G-1000)*
Wikoff Color Corporation .... F 585 458-0653
  Rochester *(G-14763)*

INK: Screen process
Standard Screen Supply Corp .... F 212 627-2727
  New York *(G-12182)*

INSECTICIDES
Island Marketing Corp .... G 516 739-0500
  Mineola *(G-8517)*
Noble Pine Products Co Inc .... F 914 664-5877
  Mount Vernon *(G-8710)*

INSPECTION & TESTING SVCS
Cs Automation Inc .... F 315 524-5123
  Ontario *(G-13198)*

INSTR, MEASURE & CONTROL: Gauge, Oil Pressure & Water Temp
Make-Waves Instrument Corp .... E 716 681-7524
  Depew *(G-4264)*

INSTRUMENTS & METERS: Measuring, Electric
Herman H Sticht Company Inc .... G 718 852-7602
  Brooklyn *(G-2076)*
Pulsafeeder Inc .... C 585 292-8000
  Rochester *(G-14609)*
S R Instruments Inc .... E 716 693-5977
  Tonawanda *(G-16197)*
Schlumberger Technology Corp .... C 607 378-0200
  Horseheads *(G-6592)*

INSTRUMENTS, LABORATORY: Differential Thermal Analysis
East Coast Envmtl Group Inc .... G 516 352-1946
  Farmingdale *(G-4984)*

INSTRUMENTS, LABORATORY: Magnetic/Elec Properties Measuring
CTB Enterprise LLC .... F 631 563-0088
  Holbrook *(G-6442)*
MMC Enterprises Corp .... G 800 435-1088
  Hauppauge *(G-6140)*

INSTRUMENTS, LABORATORY: Spectrometers
Spectra Vista Corporation .... G 845 471-7007
  Poughkeepsie *(G-13932)*

INSTRUMENTS, MEASURING & CNTRL: Gauges, Auto, Computer
Parker-Hannifin Corporation .... B 631 231-3737
  Hauppauge *(G-6158)*

INSTRUMENTS, MEASURING & CNTRL: Radiation & Testing, Nuclear
Joerger Enterprises Inc .... G 631 239-5579
  East Northport *(G-4438)*
L N D Incorporated .... E 516 678-6141
  Oceanside *(G-13085)*
Mirion Tech Conax Nuclear Inc .... E 716 681-1973
  Buffalo *(G-3068)*
Mirion Technologies Ist Corp .... D 607 562-4300
  Horseheads *(G-6584)*
VJ Technologies Inc .... E 631 589-8800
  Bohemia *(G-1154)*

INSTRUMENTS, MEASURING & CNTRL: Testing, Abrasion, Etc
Magnetic Analysis Corporation .... D 914 530-2000
  Elmsford *(G-4762)*
Nis Manufacturing Inc .... G 518 456-2566
  Cohoes *(G-3753)*

INSTRUMENTS, MEASURING & CNTRLG: Aircraft & Motor Vehicle
James A Staley Co Inc .... F 845 878-3344
  Carmel *(G-3401)*

INSTRUMENTS, MEASURING & CNTRLG: Stress, Strain & Measure
Mechanical Technology Inc .... E 518 218-2550
  Albany *(G-101)*
MTI Instruments Inc .... F 518 218-2550
  Albany *(G-104)*

INSTRUMENTS, MEASURING & CNTRLG: Tensile Strength Testing
Andor Design Corp .... G 516 364-1619
  Syosset *(G-15812)*

INSTRUMENTS, MEASURING & CONTROLLING: Gas Detectors
Analytical Technology Inc .... F 646 208-4643
  New York *(G-9146)*
Industrial Test Eqp Co Inc .... E 516 883-6423
  Port Washington *(G-13824)*

INSTRUMENTS, MEASURING & CONTROLLING: Magnetometers
Vector Magnetics LLC .... E 607 273-8351
  Ithaca *(G-6883)*

INSTRUMENTS, MEASURING & CONTROLLING: Photogrammetrical
Elsag North America LLC .... G 877 773-5724
  Brewster *(G-1218)*

INSTRUMENTS, MEASURING & CONTROLLING: Toll Booths, Automatic
Highway Toll ADM LLC .... F 516 684-9584
  Roslyn Heights *(G-15026)*

INSTRUMENTS, MEASURING & CONTROLLING: Ultrasonic Testing
Aurora Technical Services Ltd .... G 716 652-1463
  East Aurora *(G-4367)*
U E Systems Incorporated .... E 914 592-1220
  Elmsford *(G-4790)*

INSTRUMENTS, MEASURING/CNTRL: Hydrometers, Exc Indl Process
Peyser Instrument Corporation .... E 631 841-3600
  West Babylon *(G-16818)*

INSTRUMENTS, MEASURING/CNTRLG: Fare Registers, St Cars/Buses
Cubic Trnsp Systems Inc .... F 212 255-1810
  New York *(G-9764)*

INSTRUMENTS, MEASURING/CNTRLNG: Med Diagnostic Sys, Nuclear
Eastern Niagra Radiology .... E 716 882-6544
  Buffalo *(G-2928)*
H D M Labs Inc .... G 516 431-8357
  Island Park *(G-6780)*
Nuclear Diagnostic Pdts NY Inc .... G 516 575-4201
  Plainview *(G-13624)*
Oyster Bay Pump Works Inc .... F 516 922-3789
  Hicksville *(G-6381)*
Precision Biologics Inc .... G 516 482-1200
  Great Neck *(G-5831)*

INSTRUMENTS, OPTICAL: Alignment & Display
New Scale Technologies Inc .... E 585 924-4450
  Victor *(G-16492)*

INSTRUMENTS, OPTICAL: Borescopes
Machida Incorporated .... G 845 365-0600
  Orangeburg *(G-13235)*

INSTRUMENTS, OPTICAL: Elements & Assemblies, Exc Ophthalmic
Applied Coatings Holding Corp .... G 585 482-0300
  Rochester *(G-14208)*

INSTRUMENTS, OPTICAL: Elements & Assemblies, Exc Ophthalmic

Metavac LLC .... E 631 207-2344
  Holtsville *(G-6504)*
Photon Gear Inc .... F 585 265-3360
  Ontario *(G-13209)*

INSTRUMENTS, OPTICAL: Gratings, Diffraction

Newport Rochester Inc .... D 585 262-1325
  Rochester *(G-14536)*

INSTRUMENTS, OPTICAL: Lenses, All Types Exc Ophthalmic

Advanced Glass Industries Inc .... D 585 458-8040
  Rochester *(G-14177)*
Claude Tribastone Inc .... G 585 265-3776
  Ontario *(G-13197)*
Jml Optical Industries LLC .... G 585 248-8900
  Rochester *(G-14462)*
Lens Triptar Co Inc .... G 585 473-4470
  Rochester *(G-14477)*
Meopta USA Inc .... C 631 436-5900
  Hauppauge *(G-6131)*
Optics Technology Inc .... G 585 586-0950
  Pittsford *(G-13571)*
Optimax Systems Inc .... C 585 265-1020
  Ontario *(G-13207)*
Orafol Display Optics Inc .... E 585 647-1140
  West Henrietta *(G-16887)*
Rochester Precision Optics LLC .... C 585 292-5450
  West Henrietta *(G-16893)*
Spectrum Thin Films Inc .... E 631 901-1010
  Hauppauge *(G-6196)*

INSTRUMENTS, OPTICAL: Mirrors

Hudson Mirror LLC .... E 914 930-8906
  Peekskill *(G-13479)*
North American Enclosures Inc .... E 631 234-9500
  Central Islip *(G-3507)*

INSTRUMENTS, OPTICAL: Prisms

Ariel Optics Inc .... G 585 265-4820
  Ontario *(G-13195)*

INSTRUMENTS, OPTICAL: Sights, Telescopic

Evergreen Bleachers Inc .... G 518 654-9084
  Corinth *(G-3958)*

INSTRUMENTS, OPTICAL: Test & Inspection

Quality Vision Intl Inc .... G 585 544-0400
  Rochester *(G-14613)*
Videk Inc .... E 585 377-0377
  Fairport *(G-4885)*

INSTRUMENTS, SURGICAL & MEDICAL: Blood & Bone Work

East Coast Orthoic & Pros Cor .... D 516 248-5566
  Deer Park *(G-4134)*
Elite Medical Supply of NY .... G 716 712-0881
  West Seneca *(G-16964)*
Manhattan Eastside Dev Corp .... F 212 305-3275
  New York *(G-11129)*

INSTRUMENTS, SURGICAL & MEDICAL: Blood Pressure

American Diagnostic Corp .... D 631 273-6155
  Hauppauge *(G-6021)*
N Y B P Inc .... G 585 624-2541
  Mendon *(G-8381)*
W A Baum Co Inc .... D 631 226-3940
  Copiague *(G-3938)*

INSTRUMENTS, SURGICAL & MEDICAL: Catheters

Nasco Enterprises Inc .... G 516 921-9696
  Syosset *(G-15829)*
Novamed-Usa Inc .... E 914 789-2100
  Elmsford *(G-4771)*
Vante Inc .... F 716 778-7691
  Newfane *(G-12789)*

INSTRUMENTS, SURGICAL & MEDICAL: IV Transfusion

Sigma Intl Gen Med Apprtus LLC .... B 585 798-3901
  Medina *(G-8282)*

INSTRUMENTS, SURGICAL & MEDICAL: Inhalation Therapy

Beacon Spch Lnge Pthlgy Phys .... F 516 626-1635
  Roslyn *(G-15016)*

INSTRUMENTS, SURGICAL & MEDICAL: Inhalators

Ip Med Inc .... G 516 766-3800
  Oceanside *(G-13082)*

INSTRUMENTS, SURGICAL & MEDICAL: Knives

Huron Tl & Cutter Grinding Co .... E 631 420-7000
  Farmingdale *(G-5008)*

INSTRUMENTS, SURGICAL & MEDICAL: Lasers, Surgical

Aerolase Corporation .... D 914 345-8300
  Tarrytown *(G-16084)*
Clerio Vision Inc .... F 617 216-7881
  Rochester *(G-14279)*

INSTRUMENTS, SURGICAL & MEDICAL: Muscle Exercise, Ophthalmic

Biodex Medical Systems Inc .... C 631 924-9000
  Shirley *(G-15416)*
Biodex Medical Systems Inc .... E 631 924-3146
  Shirley *(G-15417)*

INSTRUMENTS, SURGICAL & MEDICAL: Ophthalmic

Bausch & Lomb Incorporated .... B 585 338-6000
  Rochester *(G-14225)*
Corning Tropel Corporation .... C 585 377-3200
  Fairport *(G-4852)*
Sonomed Inc .... E 516 354-0900
  New Hyde Park *(G-8863)*

INSTRUMENTS, SURGICAL & MEDICAL: Physiotherapy, Electrical

Fabrication Enterprises Inc .... E 914 591-9300
  Elmsford *(G-4753)*

INSTRUMENTS, SURGICAL & MEDICAL: Skin Grafting

Skyler Brand Ventures LLC .... G 646 979-5904
  New York *(G-12097)*

INSTRUMENTS, SURGICAL & MEDICAL: Suction Therapy

Njr Medical Devices .... E 440 258-8204
  Cedarhurst *(G-3462)*

INSTRUMENTS: Analytical

A S A Precision Co Inc .... G 845 482-4870
  Jeffersonville *(G-7058)*
Advanced Mtl Analytics LLC .... G 321 684-0528
  Vestal *(G-16439)*
Advion Inc .... E 607 266-9162
  Ithaca *(G-6817)*
Bristol Instruments Inc .... G 585 924-2620
  Victor *(G-16464)*
Brookhaven Instruments Corp .... E 631 758-3200
  Holtsville *(G-6501)*
Carl Zeiss Inc .... C 914 747-1800
  Thornwood *(G-16117)*
Ceres Technologies Inc .... D 845 247-4701
  Saugerties *(G-15181)*
Chromosense LLC .... G 347 770-5421
  Brooklyn *(G-1778)*
Corning Incorporated .... G 607 974-6729
  Painted Post *(G-13391)*
East Hills Instrument Inc .... F 516 621-8686
  Westbury *(G-16980)*
General Microwave Corporation .... F 516 802-0900
  Syosset *(G-15824)*
High Voltage Inc .... E 518 329-3275
  Copake *(G-3887)*
Multiwire Laboratories Ltd .... G 607 257-3378
  Ithaca *(G-6865)*
Novartis Pharmaceuticals Corp .... G 888 669-6682
  New York *(G-11463)*
Rheonix Inc .... D 607 257-1242
  Ithaca *(G-6873)*
Smartpill Corporation .... E 716 882-0701
  Buffalo *(G-3188)*
Thermo Fisher Scientific Inc .... B 631 648-4040
  Wading River *(G-16528)*
Thermo Fisher Scientific Inc .... B 585 458-8008
  Rochester *(G-14722)*
Thermo Fisher Scientific Inc .... A 585 899-7610
  Rochester *(G-14723)*
Veeco Instruments Inc .... C 516 677-0200
  Woodbury *(G-17302)*

INSTRUMENTS: Colonoscopes, Electromedical

Gravity East Village Inc .... G 212 388-9788
  New York *(G-10355)*

INSTRUMENTS: Combustion Control, Indl

Aureonic .... G 518 791-9331
  Gansevoort *(G-5485)*

INSTRUMENTS: Electrocardiographs

Integrated Medical Devices .... G 315 457-4200
  Liverpool *(G-7526)*

INSTRUMENTS: Electrolytic Conductivity, Indl

Mark - 10 Corporation .... E 631 842-9200
  Copiague *(G-3913)*

INSTRUMENTS: Electrolytic Conductivity, Laboratory

Tokyo Electron America Inc .... F 518 292-4200
  Albany *(G-143)*

INSTRUMENTS: Endoscopic Eqpt, Electromedical

Elizabeth Wood .... G 315 492-5470
  Syracuse *(G-15933)*

INSTRUMENTS: Function Generators

Allied Motion Technologies Inc .... C 716 242-8634
  Amherst *(G-221)*

INSTRUMENTS: Generators Tachometer

Make-Waves Instrument Corp .... E 716 681-7524
  Depew *(G-4264)*

INSTRUMENTS: Indl Process Control

Ametek Inc .... D 585 263-7700
  Rochester *(G-14202)*
Cemtrex Inc .... E 631 756-9116
  Farmingdale *(G-4957)*
Ceres Technologies Inc .... D 845 247-4701
  Saugerties *(G-15181)*
Defelsko Corporation .... D 315 393-4450
  Ogdensburg *(G-13114)*
Digital Analysis Corporation .... F 315 685-0760
  Skaneateles *(G-15458)*
Diversified Electrical Pdts .... F 631 567-5710
  Bohemia *(G-1058)*
Dyna-Empire Inc .... C 516 222-2700
  Garden City *(G-5500)*
East Hills Instrument Inc .... F 516 621-8686
  Westbury *(G-16980)*
Electronic Machine Parts LLC .... F 631 434-3700
  Hauppauge *(G-6070)*
Emerson Electric Co .... F 212 244-2490
  New York *(G-10023)*
Emerson Network Power .... G 516 349-8500
  Plainview *(G-13599)*
Fts Systems Inc .... D 845 687-5300
  Stone Ridge *(G-15763)*

PRODUCT SECTION

INSTRUMENTS: Measuring, Electrical Energy

Gurley Precision Instrs Inc ....C....... 518 272-6300
   Troy *(G-16237)*
Hades Manufacturing Corp ....F....... 631 249-4244
   Farmingdale *(G-5004)*
Harris Corporation ....C....... 703 668-6239
   Rome *(G-14812)*
Heidenhain International Inc ....C....... 716 661-1700
   Jamestown *(G-6999)*
Herman H Sticht Company Inc ....G....... 718 852-7602
   Brooklyn *(G-2076)*
Hilliard Corporation ....B....... 607 733-7121
   Elmira *(G-4690)*
Hilliard Corporation ....F....... 607 733-7121
   Elmira *(G-4691)*
Inficon Holding AG ....G....... 315 434-1100
   East Syracuse *(G-4542)*
Integrated Control Corp ....E....... 631 673-5100
   Huntington *(G-6662)*
Invensys Systems Inc ....F....... 214 527-3099
   New York *(G-10649)*
Koehler Instrument Company Inc ....D....... 631 589-3800
   Bohemia *(G-1088)*
Magtrol Inc ....E....... 716 668-5555
   Buffalo *(G-3055)*
Mausner Equipment Co Inc ....C....... 631 689-7358
   Setauket *(G-15377)*
Miller & Weber Inc ....E....... 718 821-7110
   Westbury *(G-17012)*
Mks Instruments Inc ....E....... 585 292-7472
   Rochester *(G-14517)*
Nutec Components Inc ....F....... 631 242-1224
   Deer Park *(G-4182)*
Orthstar Enterprises Inc ....D....... 607 562-2100
   Horseheads *(G-6586)*
Pcb Group Inc ....E....... 716 684-0001
   Depew *(G-4268)*
Poseidon Systems LLC ....F....... 585 239-6025
   Rochester *(G-14589)*
Pulsafeeder Inc ....C....... 585 292-8000
   Rochester *(G-14609)*
R K B Opto-Electronics Inc ....F....... 315 455-6636
   Syracuse *(G-16016)*
Sequential Electronics Systems ....E....... 914 592-1345
   Elmsford *(G-4783)*
Sixnet Holdings LLC ....E....... 518 877-5173
   Ballston Lake *(G-587)*
Solar Metrology LLC ....G....... 845 247-4701
   Holbrook *(G-6471)*
Telog Instruments Inc ....E....... 585 742-3000
   Victor *(G-16507)*
Thread Check Inc ....D....... 631 231-1515
   Hauppauge *(G-6214)*
Transtech Systems Inc ....E....... 518 370-5558
   Latham *(G-7381)*
Vacuum Instrument Corporation ....D....... 631 737-0900
   Ronkonkoma *(G-14997)*
Veeco Instruments Inc ....C....... 516 677-0200
   Woodbury *(G-17302)*
Winters Instruments Inc ....E....... 281 880-8607
   Tonawanda *(G-16215)*
Xentaur Corporation ....E....... 631 345-3434
   Yaphank *(G-17409)*

INSTRUMENTS: Laser, Scientific & Engineering

Cambridge Manufacturing LLC ....G....... 516 326-1350
   New Hyde Park *(G-8820)*
Gemprint Corporation ....E....... 212 997-0007
   New York *(G-10269)*
Micro Photo Acoustics Inc ....G....... 631 750-6035
   Ronkonkoma *(G-14942)*
Porous Materials Inc ....E....... 607 257-5544
   Ithaca *(G-6870)*
Uptek Solutions ....F....... 631 256-5565
   Bohemia *(G-1153)*

INSTRUMENTS: Measurement, Indl Process

Riverhawk Company LP ....E....... 315 624-7171
   New Hartford *(G-8809)*
Robat Inc ....G....... 518 812-6244
   Clifton Park *(G-3705)*

INSTRUMENTS: Measuring & Controlling

Aspex Incorporated ....E....... 212 966-0410
   New York *(G-9237)*
Biodesign Inc of New York ....F....... 845 454-6610
   Carmel *(G-3398)*
Carl Zeiss Inc ....C....... 914 747-1800
   Thornwood *(G-16117)*
Circor Aerospace Inc ....D....... 631 737-1900
   Hauppauge *(G-6045)*
Computer Instruments Corp ....E....... 516 876-8400
   Westbury *(G-16975)*
Cosense Inc ....E....... 516 364-9161
   Syosset *(G-15817)*
Dayton T Brown Inc ....B....... 631 589-6300
   Bohemia *(G-1052)*
Defelsko Corporation ....D....... 315 393-4450
   Ogdensburg *(G-13114)*
Dispersion Technology Inc ....G....... 914 241-4777
   Bedford Hills *(G-802)*
Dyna-Empire Inc ....C....... 516 222-2700
   Garden City *(G-5500)*
Dynamic Systems Inc ....E....... 518 283-5350
   Poestenkill *(G-13723)*
East Hills Instrument Inc ....F....... 516 621-8686
   Westbury *(G-16980)*
Electrical Controls Link ....E....... 585 924-7010
   Victor *(G-16474)*
Electro-Optical Products Corp ....G....... 718 456-6000
   Ridgewood *(G-14105)*
Enerac Inc ....F....... 516 997-1554
   Holbrook *(G-6447)*
Erbessd Reliability LLC ....E....... 518 874-2700
   South Glens Falls *(G-15524)*
Fougera Pharmaceuticals Inc ....C....... 631 454-7677
   Melville *(G-8321)*
Freeman Technology Inc ....E....... 732 829-8345
   Bayside *(G-770)*
Gei International Inc ....E....... 315 463-9261
   East Syracuse *(G-4533)*
Hci Engineering ....G....... 315 336-3450
   Rome *(G-14814)*
Helmel Engineering Pdts Inc ....F....... 716 297-8644
   Niagara Falls *(G-12832)*
Herman H Sticht Company Inc ....G....... 718 852-7602
   Brooklyn *(G-2076)*
Hipotronics Inc ....C....... 845 279-8091
   Brewster *(G-1220)*
Imaginant Inc ....E....... 585 264-0480
   Pittsford *(G-13564)*
Itin Scale Co Inc ....E....... 718 336-5900
   Brooklyn *(G-2120)*
Kem Medical Products Corp ....G....... 631 454-6565
   Farmingdale *(G-5027)*
Kld Labs Inc ....E....... 631 549-4222
   Hauppauge *(G-6106)*
Liberty Controls Inc ....G....... 718 461-0600
   College Point *(G-3795)*
Machine Technology Inc ....G....... 845 454-4030
   Poughkeepsie *(G-13913)*
Magtrol Inc ....E....... 716 668-5555
   Buffalo *(G-3055)*
Mason Industries Inc ....C....... 631 348-0282
   Hauppauge *(G-6126)*
Miller & Weber Inc ....E....... 718 821-7110
   Westbury *(G-17012)*
MTS Systems Corporation ....C....... 518 899-2140
   Ballston Lake *(G-584)*
Norwich Aero Products Inc ....D....... 607 336-7636
   Norwich *(G-13032)*
Orolia Usa Inc ....D....... 585 321-5800
   Rochester *(G-14553)*
Pcb Piezotronics Inc ....G....... 716 684-0001
   Depew *(G-4269)*
Peerless Instrument Co Inc ....C....... 631 396-6500
   Farmingdale *(G-5076)*
Poseidon Systems LLC ....F....... 585 239-6025
   Rochester *(G-14589)*
Precision Design Systems Inc ....E....... 585 426-4500
   Rochester *(G-14592)*
Research Frontiers Inc ....F....... 516 364-1902
   Woodbury *(G-17298)*
Riverhawk Company LP ....E....... 315 624-7171
   New Hartford *(G-8809)*
RJ Harvey Instrument Corp ....F....... 845 359-3943
   Tappan *(G-16083)*
S P Industries Inc ....D....... 845 255-5000
   Gardiner *(G-5550)*
Schenck Corporation ....D....... 631 242-4010
   Deer Park *(G-4205)*
Schenck Trebel Corp ....D....... 631 242-4397
   Deer Park *(G-4206)*
Schott Corporation ....D....... 914 831-2200
   Elmsford *(G-4778)*
Teledyne Lecroy Inc ....C....... 845 425-2000
   Chestnut Ridge *(G-3626)*
Telog Instruments Inc ....E....... 585 742-3000
   Victor *(G-16507)*
Vacuum Instrument Corporation ....D....... 631 737-0900
   Ronkonkoma *(G-14997)*
Videk Inc ....E....... 585 377-0377
   Fairport *(G-4885)*
Weiss Instruments Inc ....D....... 631 207-1200
   Holtsville *(G-6514)*
Xeku Corporation ....F....... 607 761-1447
   Vestal *(G-16457)*
York Industries Inc ....E....... 516 746-3736
   Garden City Park *(G-5546)*
Zomega Terahertz Corporation ....F....... 585 347-4337
   Webster *(G-16745)*

INSTRUMENTS: Measuring Electricity

Agilent Technologies Inc ....A....... 877 424-4536
   New York *(G-9057)*
American Quality Technology ....F....... 607 777-9488
   Binghamton *(G-887)*
Ametek Inc ....D....... 585 263-7700
   Rochester *(G-14202)*
C Speed LLC ....E....... 315 453-1043
   Liverpool *(G-7514)*
C-Flex Bearing Co Inc ....C....... 315 895-7454
   Frankfort *(G-5350)*
Cetek Inc ....C....... 845 452-3510
   Poughkeepsie *(G-13892)*
East Hills Instrument Inc ....F....... 516 621-8686
   Westbury *(G-16980)*
Edo LLC ....A....... 631 630-4200
   Amityville *(G-286)*
Edo LLC ....E....... 631 218-1413
   Bohemia *(G-1062)*
Ems Development Corporation ....D....... 631 924-4736
   Yaphank *(G-17390)*
Enertiv Inc ....G....... 646 350-3525
   New York *(G-10039)*
Hipotronics Inc ....C....... 845 279-8091
   Brewster *(G-1220)*
Interntnl Elctronic Mchs Corp ....E....... 518 268-1636
   Troy *(G-16241)*
Interplex Industries Inc ....F....... 718 961-6212
   College Point *(G-3790)*
John Ramsey Elec Svcs LLC ....G....... 585 298-9596
   Victor *(G-16483)*
Larry Kings Corporation ....G....... 718 481-8741
   Rosedale *(G-15013)*
Linde LLC ....D....... 716 773-7552
   Grand Island *(G-5763)*
Logitek Inc ....D....... 631 567-1100
   Bohemia *(G-1094)*
Ludl Electronic Products Ltd ....E....... 914 769-6111
   Hawthorne *(G-6250)*
Magnetic Analysis Corporation ....D....... 914 530-2000
   Elmsford *(G-4762)*
Magtrol Inc ....E....... 716 668-5555
   Buffalo *(G-3055)*
North Atlantic Industries Inc ....C....... 631 567-1100
   Bohemia *(G-1111)*
Optimized Devices Inc ....F....... 914 769-6100
   Pleasantville *(G-13715)*
Peerless Instrument Co Inc ....C....... 631 396-6500
   Farmingdale *(G-5076)*
Practical Instrument Elec Inc ....F....... 585 872-9350
   Webster *(G-16730)*
Qualitrol Finance Corp ....G....... 585 586-1515
   Fairport *(G-4873)*
R K B Opto-Electronics Inc ....F....... 315 455-6636
   Syracuse *(G-16016)*
Rodale Wireless Inc ....E....... 631 231-0044
   Hauppauge *(G-6179)*
Scientific Components Corp ....E....... 631 243-4901
   Deer Park *(G-4207)*
Trek Inc ....F....... 716 438-7555
   Lockport *(G-7621)*
Viatran Corporation ....E....... 716 629-3800
   North Tonawanda *(G-13005)*
W & W Manufacturing Co ....F....... 516 942-0011
   Deer Park *(G-4225)*
Zumbach Electronics Corp ....D....... 914 241-7080
   Mount Kisco *(G-8649)*

INSTRUMENTS: Measuring, Electrical Energy

Apogee Power Usa Inc ....F....... 202 746-2890
   Hartsdale *(G-5997)*
Quadlogic Controls Corporation ....D....... 212 930-9300
   Long Island City *(G-7852)*

Employee Codes: A=Over 500 employees, B=251-500
C=101-250, D=51-100, E=20-50, F=10-19, G=5-9

INSTRUMENTS: Measuring, Electrical Power

INSTRUMENTS: Measuring, Electrical Power

Allied Motion Systems Corp ....F 716 691-5868
  Amherst *(G-220)*
Primesouth Inc ....F 585 567-4191
  Fillmore *(G-5176)*

INSTRUMENTS: Measuring, Electrical Quantities

Qualitrol Company LLC ....C 586 643-3717
  Fairport *(G-4872)*

INSTRUMENTS: Medical & Surgical

Ala Scientific Instruments Inc ....F 631 393-6401
  Farmingdale *(G-4935)*
AM Bickford Inc ....F 716 652-1590
  Wales Center *(G-16539)*
American Healthcare Supply Inc ....F 212 674-3636
  New York *(G-9119)*
Angiodynamics Inc ....B 518 792-4112
  Glens Falls *(G-5671)*
Angiodynamics Inc ....B 518 742-4430
  Queensbury *(G-13989)*
Angiodynamics Inc ....B 518 975-1400
  Queensbury *(G-13990)*
Angiodynamics Inc ....B 518 795-1400
  Latham *(G-7354)*
Argon Medical Devices Inc ....C 585 321-1130
  Henrietta *(G-6293)*
Astra Tool & Instr Mfg Corp ....E 914 747-3863
  Hawthorne *(G-6244)*
Baxter Healthcare Corporation ....B 800 356-3454
  Medina *(G-8266)*
Becton Dickinson and Company ......P 845 353-3371
  Nyack *(G-13044)*
Bioresearch Inc ....G 212 734-5315
  Pound Ridge *(G-13942)*
Boehm Surgical Instrument ....F 585 436-6584
  Rochester *(G-14241)*
Bovie Medical Corporation ....G 727 384-2323
  Purchase *(G-13953)*
Bovie Medical Corporation ....C 914 468-4009
  Purchase *(G-13954)*
Buffalo Filter LLC ....D 716 835-7000
  Lancaster *(G-7307)*
Buxton Medical Equipment Corp ....E 631 957-4500
  Lindenhurst *(G-7457)*
C R Bard Inc ....B 518 793-2531
  Queensbury *(G-13993)*
C R Bard Inc ....A 518 793-2531
  Glens Falls *(G-5674)*
CN Group Incorporated ....C 914 358-5690
  White Plains *(G-17094)*
Cognitiveflow Sensor Tech ....G 631 513-9369
  Stony Brook *(G-15768)*
Conmed Corporation ....D 315 797-8375
  Utica *(G-16315)*
Cynosure Inc ....G 516 594-3333
  Hicksville *(G-6340)*
Daxor Corporation ....E 212 244-0555
  New York *(G-9831)*
Delcath Systems Inc ....E 212 489-2100
  New York *(G-9838)*
Derm/Buro Inc ....G 516 694-8300
  Plainview *(G-13596)*
Designs For Vision Inc ....C 631 585-3300
  Ronkonkoma *(G-14894)*
Elliquence LLC ....F 516 277-9000
  Baldwin *(G-558)*
Esc Control Electronics LLC ....E 631 467-5328
  Sayville *(G-15208)*
Extek Inc ....E 585 533-1672
  Rush *(G-15047)*
Eyeglass Service Industries ....G 914 666-3150
  Bedford Hills *(G-803)*
Flatbush Surgical Supply Co ....G 516 775-0507
  Elmont *(G-4720)*
Flexbar Machine Corporation ....E 631 582-8440
  Islandia *(G-6793)*
Fluorologic Inc ....G 585 248-2796
  Pittsford *(G-13559)*
Ftt Medical Inc ....G 585 235-1430
  Rochester *(G-14384)*
Gaymar Industries Inc ....B 800 828-7341
  Orchard Park *(G-13271)*
Getinge Usa Inc ....C 585 475-1400
  Rochester *(G-14401)*
Greatbatch Inc ....D 716 759-5200
  Clarence *(G-3663)*

Hanger Inc ....F 516 678-3650
  Rockville Centre *(G-14792)*
Harmac Medical Products Inc ....C 716 897-4500
  Buffalo *(G-2989)*
Hogil Pharmaceutical Corp ....F 914 681-1800
  White Plains *(G-17121)*
Hurryworks LLC ....D 516 998-4600
  Port Washington *(G-13822)*
Incredible Scents Inc ....G 516 656-3300
  Glen Head *(G-5634)*
Intersurgical Incorporated ....F 315 451-2900
  East Syracuse *(G-4544)*
J H M Engineering ....E 718 871-1810
  Brooklyn *(G-2123)*
Liberty Install Inc ....F 631 651-5655
  Centerport *(G-3479)*
Mdi East Inc ....E 518 747-8730
  South Glens Falls *(G-15526)*
Medical Depot Inc ....B 516 998-4600
  Port Washington *(G-13841)*
Medical Technology Products ....G 631 285-6640
  Greenlawn *(G-5875)*
Medipoint Inc ....F 516 294-8822
  Mineola *(G-8524)*
Medline Industries Inc ....B 845 344-3301
  Middletown *(G-8450)*
Medsource Technologies LLC ....D 716 662-5025
  Orchard Park *(G-13283)*
Mick Radio Nuclear Instrument ....F 718 597-3999
  Mount Vernon *(G-8706)*
Misonix Inc ....G 631 694-9555
  Farmingdale *(G-5058)*
Modular Medical Corp ....E 718 829-2626
  Bronx *(G-1400)*
Monaghan Medical Corporation ....D 518 561-7330
  Plattsburgh *(G-13679)*
Moog Inc ....A 716 652-2000
  Elma *(G-4651)*
Nano Vibronix Inc ....F 516 374-8330
  Cedarhurst *(G-3461)*
Nasiff Associates Inc ....G 315 676-2346
  Central Square *(G-3517)*
Navilyst Medical Inc ....A 800 833-9973
  Glens Falls *(G-5692)*
Ocala Group LLC ....F 516 233-2750
  New Hyde Park *(G-8853)*
Orics Industries Inc ....E 718 461-8613
  Farmingdale *(G-5070)*
Ortho Medical Products ....F 212 879-3700
  New York *(G-11528)*
Orthocon Inc ....E 914 357-2600
  Irvington *(G-6775)*
P Ryton Corp ....F 718 937-7052
  Long Island City *(G-7831)*
Pall Corporation ....A 607 753-6041
  Cortland *(G-4035)*
Pall Corporation ....A 516 484-5400
  Port Washington *(G-13852)*
Parace Bionics LLC ....G 877 727-2231
  Yorktown Heights *(G-17515)*
Parkchester Dps LLC ....E 718 823-4411
  Bronx *(G-1421)*
Peter Digioia ....G 516 644-5517
  Plainview *(G-13628)*
Praxis Powder Technology Inc ....E 518 812-0112
  Queensbury *(G-14007)*
Precimed Inc ....E 716 759-5600
  Clarence *(G-3669)*
Professional Medical Devices ....F 914 835-0614
  Harrison *(G-5989)*
Progressive Orthotics Ltd ....G 631 732-5556
  Selden *(G-15353)*
Reichert Inc ....C 716 686-4500
  Depew *(G-4272)*
Repro Med Systems Inc ....D 845 469-2042
  Chester *(G-3612)*
Responselink Inc ....G 518 424-7776
  Latham *(G-7378)*
Robert Bosch LLC ....E 315 733-3312
  Utica *(G-16357)*
Seedings Lf Scnce Ventures LLC ....G 917 913-8511
  New York *(G-12017)*
Seneca TEC Inc ....G 585 381-2645
  Fairport *(G-4878)*
Simulaids Inc ....D 845 679-2875
  Saugerties *(G-15194)*
Simulated Surgical Systems LLC .....C 716 633-7216
  Williamsville *(G-17253)*
Solid-Look Corporation ....G 917 683-1780
  Douglaston *(G-4311)*

St Silicones Corporation ....F 518 406-3208
  Clifton Park *(G-3709)*
Stj Enterprises ....D 516 612-0110
  Cedarhurst *(G-3463)*
Tril Inc ....G 631 645-7989
  Copiague *(G-3935)*
Vasomedical Inc ....E 516 997-4600
  Plainview *(G-13641)*
Viterion Corporation ....F 914 333-6033
  Elmsford *(G-4792)*
Vizio Medical Devices LLC ....F 646 845-7382
  New York *(G-12561)*
Wyeth Holdings LLC ....D 845 602-5000
  Pearl River *(G-13469)*

INSTRUMENTS: Meteorological

Climatronics Corp ....F 541 471-7111
  Bohemia *(G-1033)*

INSTRUMENTS: Microwave Test

Hamilton Marketing Corporation ....G 585 395-0678
  Brockport *(G-1244)*

INSTRUMENTS: Nautical

Moor Electronics Inc ....G 716 821-5304
  Buffalo *(G-3075)*
New York Nautical Inc ....G 212 962-4522
  New York *(G-11404)*

INSTRUMENTS: Optical, Analytical

Applied Image Inc ....E 585 482-0300
  Rochester *(G-14209)*
Exfo Burleigh Pdts Group Inc ....D 585 301-1530
  Canandaigua *(G-3345)*

INSTRUMENTS: Oscillographs & Oscilloscopes

Teledyne Lecroy Inc ....C 845 425-2000
  Chestnut Ridge *(G-3626)*

INSTRUMENTS: Pressure Measurement, Indl

Taber Acquisition Corp ....D 716 694-4000
  North Tonawanda *(G-13000)*
Viatran Corporation ....E 716 629-3800
  North Tonawanda *(G-13005)*

INSTRUMENTS: Radar Testing, Electric

Anmar Acquisition LLC ....G 585 352-7777
  Rochester *(G-14206)*

INSTRUMENTS: Radio Frequency Measuring

Omni-ID Usa Inc ....E 585 697-9913
  Rochester *(G-14549)*
T & C Power Conversion Inc ....F 585 482-5551
  Rochester *(G-14714)*
W D Technology Inc ....G 914 779-8738
  Eastchester *(G-4583)*

INSTRUMENTS: Refractometers, Indl Process

Rhi US Ltd ....E 716 483-7200
  Falconer *(G-4911)*

INSTRUMENTS: Signal Generators & Averagers

Macrodyne Inc ....F 518 383-3800
  Clifton Park *(G-3700)*

INSTRUMENTS: Standards & Calibration, Electrical Measuring

Ah Elctronic Test Eqp Repr Ctr ....F 631 234-8979
  Central Islip *(G-3484)*

INSTRUMENTS: Telemetering, Indl Process

Medsafe Systems Inc ....G 516 883-8222
  Port Washington *(G-13843)*

PRODUCT SECTION

INSTRUMENTS: Temperature Measurement, Indl

Rotronic Instrument Corp .... F 631 348-6844
  Hauppauge *(G-6180)*
Siemens Industry Inc .... C 631 218-1000
  Bohemia *(G-1134)*
Springfield Control Systems .... G 718 631-0870
  Douglaston *(G-4312)*
Tel-Tru Inc .... D 585 295-0225
  Rochester *(G-14720)*

INSTRUMENTS: Test, Electronic & Electric Measurement

Avanel Industries Inc .... F 516 333-0990
  Westbury *(G-16971)*
Clayton Dubilier & Rice Fun .... E 212 407-5200
  New York *(G-9640)*
Comtech PST Corp .... C 631 777-8900
  Melville *(G-8306)*
Dynatic Solutions Inc .... G 914 358-9599
  White Plains *(G-17102)*
Evergreen High Voltage LLC .... G 281 814-9973
  Lake Placid *(G-7274)*
Jre Test LLC .... G 585 298-9736
  Victor *(G-16485)*
Millivac Instruments Inc .... G 518 355-8300
  Schenectady *(G-15279)*
Nas CP Corp .... D 718 961-6757
  College Point *(G-3799)*
Northeast Metrology Corp .... F 716 827-3770
  Buffalo *(G-3095)*
Photonix Technologies Inc .... F 607 786-4600
  Endicott *(G-4825)*
Precision Filters Inc .... E 607 277-3550
  Ithaca *(G-6871)*
Ramsey Electronics LLC .... E 585 924-4560
  Victor *(G-16498)*
Scj Associates Inc .... E 585 359-0600
  Rochester *(G-14677)*

INSTRUMENTS: Test, Electronic & Electrical Circuits

Automated Control Logic Inc .... F 914 769-8880
  Thornwood *(G-16116)*
Automation Correct LLC .... G 315 299-3589
  Syracuse *(G-15861)*
Avcom of Virginia Inc .... D 585 924-4560
  Victor *(G-16461)*
Clarke Hess Communication RES ..... G 631 698-3350
  Medford *(G-8241)*
General Microwave Corporation .... F 516 802-0900
  Syosset *(G-15824)*
Iet Labs Inc .... F 516 334-5959
  Roslyn Heights *(G-15027)*
Lexan Industries Inc .... F 631 434-7586
  Bay Shore *(G-713)*
Pulsar Technology Systems Inc .... G 718 361-9292
  Long Island City *(G-7849)*

INSTRUMENTS: Testing, Semiconductor

Pragmatics Technology Inc .... G 845 795-5071
  Milton *(G-8483)*

INSTRUMENTS: Thermal Conductive, Indl

Dau Thrmal Slutions N Amer Inc ...... E 585 678-9025
  Macedon *(G-7985)*

INSTRUMENTS: Vibration

SKF USA Inc .... D 716 661-2600
  Jamestown *(G-7028)*
Voice Analysis Clinic .... G 212 245-3803
  New York *(G-12566)*

INSTRUMENTS: Viscometer, Indl Process

Beauty America LLC .... E 917 744-1430
  Great Neck *(G-5794)*

INSULATING COMPOUNDS

Zircar Ceramics Inc .... E 845 651-6600
  Florida *(G-5216)*

INSULATION & CUSHIONING FOAM: Polystyrene

C P Chemical Co Inc .... G 914 428-2517
  White Plains *(G-17091)*
Foam Products Inc .... E 718 292-4830
  Bronx *(G-1334)*
Hunter Panels LLC .... D 386 753-0786
  Montgomery *(G-8595)*
New York State Foam Enrgy LLC ..... G 845 534-4656
  Cornwall *(G-3989)*
Shelter Enterprises Inc .... D 518 237-4100
  Cohoes *(G-3758)*
Soundcoat Company Inc .... D 631 242-2200
  Deer Park *(G-4212)*
Thermal Foams/Syracuse Inc .... G 716 874-6474
  Buffalo *(G-3216)*

INSULATION MATERIALS WHOLESALERS

Regional MGT & Consulting Inc .... F 718 599-3718
  Brooklyn *(G-2487)*

INSULATION: Felt

Shannon Entps Wstn NY Inc .... D 716 693-7954
  North Tonawanda *(G-12993)*

INSULATION: Fiberglass

Burnett Process Inc .... G 585 254-8080
  Rochester *(G-14252)*
Elliot Industries Inc .... G 716 287-3100
  Ellington *(G-4644)*
Richlar Industries Inc .... F 315 463-5144
  East Syracuse *(G-4559)*
Superior Plus Cnstr Pdts Corp .... F 315 463-5144
  East Syracuse *(G-4569)*

INSULATORS & INSULATION MATERIALS: Electrical

Alumiseal Corp .... E 518 329-2820
  Copake Falls *(G-3888)*
Gerome Technologies Inc .... D 518 463-1324
  Menands *(G-8372)*
Heat and Frost Inslatrs & Asbs .... G 718 784-3456
  Astoria *(G-443)*
J H C Fabrications Inc .... E 718 649-0065
  Brooklyn *(G-2122)*
Jpmorgan Chase & Co .... F 845 298-2461
  Wappingers Falls *(G-16574)*
Varflex Corporation .... C 315 336-4400
  Rome *(G-14839)*
Volt Tek Inc .... F 585 377-2050
  Fairport *(G-4886)*
Von Roll Usa Inc .... C 518 344-7100
  Schenectady *(G-15310)*

INSULATORS, PORCELAIN: Electrical

Lapp Insulator Company LLC .... F 585 768-6221
  Le Roy *(G-7411)*
Lapp Insulators LLC .... C 585 768-6221
  Le Roy *(G-7412)*
Victor Insulators Inc .... C 585 924-2127
  Victor *(G-16510)*

INSULIN PREPARATIONS

Zinerva Pharmaceuticals LLC .... G 630 729-4184
  Clarence Center *(G-3682)*

INSURANCE CARRIERS: Life

Hrg Group Inc .... E 212 906-8555
  New York *(G-10524)*

INTEGRATED CIRCUITS, SEMICONDUCTOR NETWORKS, ETC

Aljo-Gefa Precision Mfg LLC .... E 516 420-4419
  Old Bethpage *(G-13125)*
Artemis Inc .... G 631 232-2424
  Hauppauge *(G-6025)*
Globalfoundries US Inc .... F 408 462-3900
  Ballston Spa *(G-597)*
LSI Computer Systems .... E 631 271-0400
  Melville *(G-8335)*
Philips Medical Systems Mr .... B 518 782-1122
  Latham *(G-7376)*
Plures Technologies Inc .... G 585 905-0554
  Canandaigua *(G-3355)*
Pvi Solar Inc .... G 212 280-2100
  New York *(G-11760)*
Standard Microsystems Corp .... C 631 435-6000
  Hauppauge *(G-6199)*

INTERCOMMUNICATIONS SYSTEMS: Electric

Andrea Systems LLC .... E 631 390-3140
  Farmingdale *(G-4942)*
Apple Core Electronics Inc .... F 718 628-4068
  Brooklyn *(G-1618)*
AVI-Spl Employee .... B 212 840-4801
  New York *(G-9277)*
Capstream Technologies LLC .... G 716 945-7100
  Salamanca *(G-15100)*
Curbell Medical Products Inc .... F 716 667-2520
  Orchard Park *(G-13266)*
Curbell Medical Products Inc .... C 716 667-2520
  Orchard Park *(G-13267)*
Frequency Electronics Inc .... B 516 794-4500
  Uniondale *(G-16295)*
Goddard Design Co .... G 718 599-0170
  Brooklyn *(G-2034)*
Intercall Systems Inc .... E 516 294-4524
  Mineola *(G-8516)*
McDowell Research Co Inc .... D 315 332-7100
  Newark *(G-12736)*
Response Care Inc .... G 585 671-4144
  Rochester *(G-14623)*
Roanwell Corporation .... E 718 401-0288
  Bronx *(G-1441)*
Telebyte Inc .... E 631 423-3232
  Hauppauge *(G-6212)*
Telephonics Corporation .... A 631 755-7000
  Farmingdale *(G-5127)*
Telesite USA Inc .... F 631 952-2288
  Hauppauge *(G-6213)*
TX Rx Systems Inc .... C 716 549-4700
  Angola *(G-382)*
Visiontron Corp .... E 631 582-8600
  Hauppauge *(G-6227)*

INTERIOR DECORATING SVCS

Furniture Doctor Inc .... G 585 657-6941
  Bloomfield *(G-988)*

INTERIOR DESIGN SVCS, NEC

Ann Gish Inc .... G 212 969-9200
  New York *(G-9163)*
Lulu DK LLC .... G 212 223-4234
  New York *(G-11063)*

INTERIOR DESIGNING SVCS

Carole Hchman Design Group Inc ..... C 918 423-3535
  New York *(G-9533)*
Exhibit Corporation America .... E 718 937-2600
  Long Island City *(G-7734)*

INTERIOR REPAIR SVCS

Auto-Mat Company Inc .... E 516 938-7373
  Hicksville *(G-6325)*

INTRAVENOUS SOLUTIONS

Mercer Milling Co .... E 315 701-1334
  Liverpool *(G-7535)*
Zenith Solutions .... G 718 575-8570
  Flushing *(G-5312)*

INVERTERS: Nonrotating Electrical

Applied Power Systems Inc .... E 516 935-2230
  Hicksville *(G-6322)*

INVERTERS: Rotating Electrical

IEC Holden Corporation .... F 518 213-3991
  Plattsburgh *(G-13670)*

INVESTMENT ADVISORY SVCS

Elliott Associates LP .... E 212 586-9431
  New York *(G-10011)*
Nsgv Inc .... E 212 367-3167
  New York *(G-11466)*
Value Line Inc .... D 212 907-1500
  New York *(G-12497)*

Employee Codes: A=Over 500 employees, B=251-500
C=101-250, D=51-100, E=20-50, F=10-19, G=5-9

INVESTMENT FUNDS: Open-Ended

Altius Aviation LLC	G	315 455-7555
Syracuse (G-15852)

Kps Capital Partners LP ....E...... 212 338-5100
New York (G-10883)

INVESTORS, NEC

Aip/Aerospace Holdings LLC ....G...... 212 916-8142
New York (G-9065)

INVESTORS: Real Estate, Exc Property Operators

Radio Circle Realty Inc ....E...... 914 241-8742
Mount Kisco (G-8642)

INVESTORS: Security Speculators For Own Account

Acf Industries Holding Corp ....G...... 212 702-4363
New York (G-9016)

IRON & STEEL PRDTS: Hot-Rolled

A-1 Iron Works Inc ....G...... 718 927-4766
Brooklyn (G-1537)
Image Iron Works Inc ....G...... 718 592-8276
Corona (G-3998)
N C Iron Works Inc ....G...... 718 633-4660
Brooklyn (G-2346)
Niagara Specialty Metals Inc ....E...... 716 542-5552
Akron (G-26)

IRON & STEEL: Corrugating, Cold-Rolled

Renco Group Inc ....G...... 212 541-6000
New York (G-11832)

IRON ORE MINING

Essar Steel Minnesota LLC ....G...... 212 292-2600
New York (G-10063)

IRON OXIDES

Applied Minerals Inc ....E...... 212 226-4265
New York (G-9184)

IRONING BOARDS

Garment Care Systems LLC ....G...... 518 674-1826
Averill Park (G-534)

JANITORIAL & CUSTODIAL SVCS

New Dynamics Corporation ....E...... 845 692-0022
Middletown (G-8453)
R H Crown Co Inc ....E...... 518 762-4589
Johnstown (G-7123)

JANITORIAL EQPT & SPLYS WHOLESALERS

Collinite Corporation ....G...... 315 732-2282
Utica (G-16313)
Emulso Corp ....G...... 716 854-2889
Tonawanda (G-16159)
Nationwide Sales and Service ....F...... 631 491-6625
Farmingdale (G-5062)

JEWELERS' FINDINGS & MATERIALS

Goldmark Inc ....E...... 718 438-0295
Brooklyn (G-2039)
Modern Settings LLC ....E...... 631 351-1212
Huntington Station (G-6717)
Nathan Berrie & Sons Inc ....G...... 516 432-8500
Island Park (G-6781)
New York Findings Corp ....F...... 212 925-5745
New York (G-11402)
Renco Manufacturing Inc ....E...... 718 392-8877
Long Island City (G-7861)

JEWELERS' FINDINGS & MATERIALS: Castings

A J M Enterprises ....F...... 716 626-7294
Buffalo (G-2792)
Allstar Casting Corporation ....E...... 212 563-0909
New York (G-9092)
Ampex Casting Corporation ....F...... 212 719-1318
New York (G-9139)
Asco Castings Inc ....G...... 212 719-9800
Long Island City (G-7671)
Asur Jewelry Inc ....G...... 718 472-1687
Long Island City (G-7675)
Carrera Casting Corp ....C...... 212 382-3296
New York (G-9536)
D M J Casting Inc ....G...... 212 719-1951
New York (G-9784)
Frank Billanti Casting Co Inc ....F...... 212 221-0440
New York (G-10201)
Jaguar Casting Co Inc ....E...... 212 869-0197
New York (G-10694)
Jewelry Arts Manufacturing ....E...... 212 382-3583
New York (G-10724)
Karbra Company ....C...... 212 736-9300
New York (G-10809)
Satco Castings Service Inc ....E...... 516 354-1500
New Hyde Park (G-8860)

JEWELERS' FINDINGS & MATERIALS: Parts, Unassembled

Asa Manufacturing Inc ....E...... 718 853-3033
Brooklyn (G-1637)
Kemp Metal Products Inc ....E...... 516 997-8860
Westbury (G-17002)

JEWELERS' FINDINGS & MTLS: Jewel Prep, Instr, Tools, Watches

A J C Jewelry Contracting Inc ....G...... 212 594-3703
New York (G-8990)
D R S Watch Materials ....E...... 212 819-0470
New York (G-9785)
Zak Jewelry Tools Inc ....F...... 212 768-8122
New York (G-12702)

JEWELERS' FINDINGS/MTRLS: Gem Prep, Settings, Real/Imitation

Jim Wachtler Inc ....G...... 212 755-4367
New York (G-10734)
Nyman Jewelry Inc ....E...... 212 944-1976
New York (G-11484)

JEWELRY & PRECIOUS STONES WHOLESALERS

Ace Diamond Corp ....G...... 212 730-8231
New York (G-9015)
Carol Dauplaise Ltd ....E...... 212 564-7301
New York (G-9529)
Carol Dauplaise Ltd ....E...... 212 997-5290
New York (G-9530)
Clyde Duneier Inc ....D...... 212 398-1122
New York (G-9648)
Dabby-Reid Ltd ....F...... 212 356-0040
New York (G-9786)
Danwak Jewelry Corp ....G...... 212 730-4541
New York (G-9808)
Gemoro Inc ....G...... 212 768-8844
New York (G-10268)
Just Perfect MSP Ltd ....E...... 877 201-0005
New York (G-10793)
Leo Schachter Diamonds LLC ....D...... 212 688-2000
New York (G-10972)
Mark King Jewelry Inc ....G...... 212 921-0746
New York (G-11154)
Michael Anthony Jewelers LLC ....C...... 914 699-0000
Mount Vernon (G-8705)
Midura Jewels Inc ....G...... 213 265-8090
New York (G-11259)
Precision International Co Inc ....G...... 212 268-9090
New York (G-11697)
William Goldberg Diamond Corp ....E...... 212 980-4343
New York (G-12633)

JEWELRY APPAREL

All The Rage Inc ....G...... 516 605-2001
Hicksville (G-6320)
Asher Jewelry Company Inc ....D...... 212 302-6233
New York (G-9228)
CJ Jewelry Inc ....F...... 212 719-2464
New York (G-9633)
E Chabot Ltd ....E...... 212 575-1026
Brooklyn (G-1890)
Eastern Jewelry Mfg Co Inc ....E...... 212 840-0001
New York (G-9965)
Efron Designs Ltd ....G...... 718 482-8440
Long Island City (G-7728)
Fam Creations ....E...... 212 869-4833
New York (G-10132)
First Image Design Corp ....E...... 212 221-8282
New York (G-10167)
H C Kionka & Co Inc ....F...... 212 227-3155
New York (G-10388)
Jaguar Jewelry Casting NY Inc ....G...... 212 768-4848
New York (G-10695)
Jayden Star LLC ....E...... 212 686-0400
New York (G-10706)
JC Crystal Inc ....E...... 212 594-0858
New York (G-10708)
Jean & Alex Jewelry Mfg & Cons ....F...... 212 935-7621
New York (G-10713)
Le Hook Rouge LLC ....E...... 212 947-6272
Brooklyn (G-2200)
Leo Schachter & Co Inc ....D...... 212 688-2000
New York (G-10971)
Love Bright Jewelry Inc ....E...... 516 620-2509
Oceanside (G-13086)
MB Plastics Inc ....F...... 718 523-1180
Greenlawn (G-5874)
Park West Jewelry Inc ....G...... 646 329-6145
New York (G-11574)
R & R Grosbard Inc ....E...... 212 575-0077
New York (G-11782)
Riva Jewelry Manufacturing Inc ....C...... 718 361-3100
Brooklyn (G-2496)
Sterling Possessions Ltd ....E...... 212 594-0418
New York (G-12197)
Thomas Sasson Co Inc ....G...... 212 697-4998
New York (G-12325)
Verragio Ltd ....E...... 212 868-8181
New York (G-12523)
Whitney Boin Studio Inc ....G...... 914 377-4385
Yonkers (G-17499)

JEWELRY FINDINGS & LAPIDARY WORK

Boucheron Joaillerie USA Inc ....G...... 212 715-7330
New York (G-9442)
Christopher Designs Inc ....E...... 212 382-1013
New York (G-9613)
Creative Tools & Supply Inc ....G...... 212 279-7077
New York (G-9752)
Danhier Co LLC ....F...... 212 563-7683
New York (G-9801)
Gemini Manufactures ....F...... 716 633-0306
Cheektowaga (G-3572)
Kaprielian Enterprises Inc ....D...... 212 645-6623
New York (G-10808)
Leo Schachter Diamonds LLC ....D...... 212 688-2000
New York (G-10972)
Loremi Jewelry Inc ....E...... 212 840-3429
New York (G-11042)
Magic Novelty Co Inc ....E...... 212 304-2777
New York (G-11104)
Mavito Fine Jewelry Ltd Inc ....F...... 212 398-9384
New York (G-11185)
Max Kahan Inc ....F...... 212 575-4646
New York (G-11187)
ME & Ro Inc ....G...... 212 431-8744
New York (G-11204)
R G Flair Co Inc ....E...... 631 586-7311
Bay Shore (G-730)
Touch Adjust Clip Co Inc ....F...... 631 589-3077
Bohemia (G-1144)
Townley Inc ....E...... 212 779-0544
New York (G-12383)
Via America Fine Jewelry Inc ....G...... 212 302-1218
New York (G-12535)
Zirconia Creations Intl ....E...... 212 239-3730
New York (G-12714)

JEWELRY FINDINGS WHOLESALERS

Cardona Industries USA Ltd ....G...... 516 466-5200
Great Neck (G-5796)
New York Findings Corp ....F...... 212 925-5745
New York (G-11402)

JEWELRY REPAIR SVCS

Burke & Bannayan ....G...... 585 723-1010
Rochester (G-14250)
Carr Manufacturing Jewelers ....G...... 518 783-6093
Latham (G-7358)
Richards & West Inc ....D...... 585 461-4088
East Rochester (G-4466)

PRODUCT SECTION

JEWELRY: Decorative, Fashion & Costume

JEWELRY STORES

Company	Code	Phone
Burke & Bannayan	G	585 723-1010
Rochester (G-14250)		
Carr Manufacturing Jewelers	G	518 783-6093
Latham (G-7358)		
Charles Perrella Inc	E	845 348-4777
Nyack (G-13046)		
DBC Inc	D	212 819-1177
New York (G-9832)		
Diamond Boutique	G	516 444-3373
Port Washington (G-13808)		
Golden Integrity Inc	E	212 764-6753
New York (G-10332)		
Henry Dunay Designs Inc	E	212 768-9700
New York (G-10458)		
Iriniri Designs Ltd	F	845 469-7934
Sugar Loaf (G-15804)		
Joan Boyce Ltd	G	212 867-7474
New York (G-10744)		
Julius Cohen Jewelers Inc	G	212 371-3050
New York (G-10783)		
Leonore Doskow Inc	E	914 737-1335
Montrose (G-8613)		
Love Bright Jewelry Inc	E	516 620-2509
Oceanside (G-13086)		
Michael Anthony Jewelers LLC	C	914 699-0000
Mount Vernon (G-8705)		
Mimi So International LLC	E	212 300-8600
New York (G-11274)		
Nyman Jewelry Inc	G	212 944-1976
New York (G-11484)		
Royal Jewelry Mfg Inc	E	212 302-2500
Great Neck (G-5836)		
Scott Kay Inc	C	201 287-0100
New York (G-12006)		
Stanmark Jewelry Inc	G	212 730-2557
New York (G-12183)		
Suna Bros Inc	E	212 869-5670
New York (G-12235)		
Zdny & Co Inc	F	212 354-1233
New York (G-12707)		

JEWELRY STORES: Precious Stones & Precious Metals

Company	Code	Phone
Atr Jewelry Inc	F	212 819-0075
New York (G-9258)		
Bourghol Brothers Inc	G	845 268-9752
Congers (G-3853)		
David S Diamonds Inc	F	212 921-8029
New York (G-9822)		
Harry Winston Inc	C	212 399-1000
New York (G-10420)		
Hw Holdings Inc	G	212 399-1000
New York (G-10534)		
Jim Wachtler Inc	G	212 755-4367
New York (G-10734)		
Mellem Corporation	F	607 723-0001
Binghamton (G-935)		
Midura Jewels Inc	G	213 265-8090
New York (G-11259)		
Nicolo Raineri	G	212 925-6128
New York (G-11428)		
O C Tanner Company	G	914 921-2025
Rye (G-15065)		
Peter Atman Inc	F	212 644-8882
New York (G-11630)		
Reinhold Brothers Inc	E	212 867-8310
New York (G-11821)		
Richards & West Inc	D	585 461-4088
East Rochester (G-4466)		
Shining Creations Inc	G	845 358-4911
New City (G-8793)		

JEWELRY STORES: Silverware

Company	Code	Phone
Benton Announcements Inc	F	716 836-4100
Buffalo (G-2839)		

JEWELRY, PREC METAL: Mountings, Pens, Lthr, Etc, Gold/Silver

Company	Code	Phone
Leo Ingwer Inc	E	212 719-1342
New York (G-10969)		

JEWELRY, PRECIOUS METAL: Bracelets

Company	Code	Phone
Hammerman Bros Inc	G	212 956-2800
New York (G-10401)		
Innovative Jewelry Inc	G	718 408-8950
Bay Shore (G-705)		
Jacoby Enterprises LLC	G	718 435-0289
Brooklyn (G-2133)		
Julius Cohen Jewelers Inc	G	212 371-3050
New York (G-10783)		
Lokai Holdings LLC	F	646 979-3474
New York (G-11023)		

JEWELRY, PRECIOUS METAL: Cases

Company	Code	Phone
Albea Cosmetics America Inc	E	212 371-5100
New York (G-9073)		

JEWELRY, PRECIOUS METAL: Cigar & Cigarette Access

Company	Code	Phone
Cigar Oasis Inc	G	516 520-5258
Farmingdale (G-4959)		

JEWELRY, PRECIOUS METAL: Earrings

Company	Code	Phone
Indonesian Imports Inc	E	888 800-5899
New York (G-10590)		
Richline Group Inc	E	212 643-2908
New York (G-11865)		
Unimax Supply Co Inc	E	212 925-1051
New York (G-12457)		

JEWELRY, PRECIOUS METAL: Medals, Precious Or Semiprecious

Company	Code	Phone
Eagle Regalia Co Inc	F	845 425-2245
Spring Valley (G-15582)		
Jacmel Jewelry Inc	C	718 349-4300
New York (G-10690)		
North American Mint Inc	G	585 654-8500
Rochester (G-14540)		
Sarkisians Jewelry Co	G	212 869-1060
New York (G-11974)		

JEWELRY, PRECIOUS METAL: Mountings & Trimmings

Company	Code	Phone
Shining Creations Inc	G	845 358-4911
New City (G-8793)		

JEWELRY, PRECIOUS METAL: Necklaces

Company	Code	Phone
Feldman Jewelry Creations Inc	G	718 438-8895
Brooklyn (G-1964)		
Iridesse Inc	F	212 230-6000
New York (G-10658)		

JEWELRY, PRECIOUS METAL: Pearl, Natural Or Cultured

Company	Code	Phone
Clyde Duneier Inc	D	212 398-1122
New York (G-9648)		
Dweck Industries Inc	G	718 615-1695
Brooklyn (G-1884)		
Robin Stanley Inc	G	212 871-0007
New York (G-11894)		

JEWELRY, PRECIOUS METAL: Pins

Company	Code	Phone
M H Manufacturing Incorporated	G	212 461-6900
New York (G-11071)		
O C Tanner Company	G	914 921-2025
Rye (G-15065)		
O C Tanner Company	G	518 348-2035
Clifton Park (G-3703)		
Pin People LLC	F	888 309-7467
Spring Valley (G-15599)		

JEWELRY, PRECIOUS METAL: Rings, Finger

Company	Code	Phone
Alfred Butler Inc	F	516 829-7460
Great Neck (G-5786)		
Grandeur Creations Inc	G	212 643-1277
New York (G-10349)		
Hjn Inc	F	212 398-9564
New York (G-10485)		
Standard Wedding Band Co	G	516 294-0954
Garden City (G-5533)		

JEWELRY, PRECIOUS METAL: Rosaries/Other Sm Religious Article

Company	Code	Phone
Rand & Paseka Mfg Co Inc	E	516 867-1500
Freeport (G-5422)		
Yofah Religious Articles Inc	F	718 435-3288
Brooklyn (G-2775)		

JEWELRY, PRECIOUS METAL: Settings & Mountings

Company	Code	Phone
AF Design Inc	G	347 548-5273
New York (G-9053)		
Gold & Diamonds Wholesale Outl	G	718 438-7888
Brooklyn (G-2037)		
Golden Integrity Inc	E	212 764-6753
New York (G-10332)		
Kaprielian Enterprises Inc	D	212 645-6623
New York (G-10808)		
Kurt Gaum Inc	F	212 719-2836
New York (G-10895)		
Mavito Fine Jewelry Ltd Inc	F	212 398-9384
New York (G-11185)		
Reinhold Brothers Inc	E	212 867-8310
New York (G-11821)		

JEWELRY, PRECIOUS METAL: Trimmings, Canes, Umbrellas, Etc

Company	Code	Phone
Houles USA Inc	G	212 935-3900
New York (G-10516)		

JEWELRY, WHOLESALE

Company	Code	Phone
AF Design Inc	G	347 548-5273
New York (G-9053)		
American Originals Corporation	G	212 836-4155
New York (G-9126)		
Anatoli Inc	F	845 334-9000
West Hurley (G-16901)		
Classic Medallics Inc	E	718 392-5410
Mount Vernon (G-8672)		
Crown Jewelers Intl Inc	G	212 420-7800
New York (G-9760)		
Dasan Inc	E	212 244-5410
New York (G-9811)		
Diana Kane Incorporated	G	718 638-6520
Brooklyn (G-1860)		
E Chabot Ltd	E	212 575-1026
Brooklyn (G-1890)		
Formart Corp	F	212 819-1819
New York (G-10186)		
J & H Creations Inc	E	212 465-0962
New York (G-10673)		
J R Gold Designs Ltd	F	212 922-9292
New York (G-10681)		
Keith Lewis Studio Inc	G	845 339-5629
Rifton (G-14134)		
Love Bright Jewelry Inc	E	516 620-2509
Oceanside (G-13086)		
Mac Swed Inc	G	917 617-3885
New York (G-11082)		
Magic Novelty Co Inc	E	212 304-2777
New York (G-11104)		
Marlborough Jewels Inc	G	718 768-2000
Brooklyn (G-2273)		
Mgd Brands Inc	D	516 545-0150
Plainview (G-13620)		
Michael Bondanza Inc	E	212 869-0043
New York (G-11248)		
Mimi So International LLC	E	212 300-8600
New York (G-11274)		
Mwsi Inc	D	914 347-4200
Hawthorne (G-6251)		
Pesselnik & Cohen Inc	G	212 925-0287
New York (G-11628)		
R M Reynolds	G	315 789-7365
Geneva (G-5584)		
Richline Group Inc	C	212 764-8454
New York (G-11866)		
Royal Jewelry Mfg Inc	E	212 302-2500
Great Neck (G-5836)		
Select Jewelry Inc	D	718 784-3626
Long Island City (G-7874)		
Shah Diamonds Inc	F	212 888-9393
New York (G-12038)		
Shanu Gems Inc	F	212 921-4470
New York (G-12042)		
Sterling Possessions Ltd	G	212 594-0418
New York (G-12197)		
UNI Jewelry Inc	G	212 398-1818
New York (G-12450)		

JEWELRY: Decorative, Fashion & Costume

Company	Code	Phone
Alexis Bittar LLC	C	718 422-7580
Brooklyn (G-1582)		
Allure Jewelry and ACC LLC	E	646 226-8057
New York (G-9093)		

Employee Codes: A=Over 500 employees, B=251-500
C=101-250, D=51-100, E=20-50, F=10-19, G=5-9

Anatoli Inc ... F ... 845 334-9000
West Hurley *(G-16901)*

Beth Ward Studios LLC ... F ... 646 922-7575
New York *(G-9377)*

Bnns Co Inc ... G ... 212 302-1844
New York *(G-9431)*

Carvin French Jewelers Inc ... E ... 212 755-6474
New York *(G-9539)*

Columbus Trading Corp ... F ... 212 564-1780
New York *(G-9681)*

Designs On Fifth Ltd ... G ... 212 921-4162
New York *(G-9857)*

Ema Jewelry Inc ... D ... 212 575-8989
New York *(G-10018)*

Eu Design LLC ... G ... 212 420-7788
New York *(G-10081)*

First International USA Ltd ... E ... 718 854-0181
Brooklyn *(G-1975)*

Five Star Creations Inc ... E ... 845 783-1187
Monroe *(G-8554)*

Formart Corp ... F ... 212 819-1819
New York *(G-10186)*

Greenbeads Llc ... G ... 212 327-2765
New York *(G-10361)*

Grinnell Designs Ltd ... E ... 212 391-5277
New York *(G-10367)*

Holbrooke Inc ... G ... 646 397-4674
New York *(G-10494)*

I Love Accessories Inc ... G ... 212 239-1875
New York *(G-10539)*

International Inspirations Ltd ... E ... 212 465-8500
New York *(G-10635)*

J J Creations Inc ... E ... 718 392-2828
Long Island City *(G-7768)*

Jewelry Arts Manufacturing ... E ... 212 382-3583
New York *(G-10724)*

Jill Fagin Enterprises Inc ... G ... 212 674-9383
New York *(G-10732)*

Jules Smith Llc ... G ... 718 783-2495
New York *(G-10781)*

K2 International Corp ... G ... 212 947-1734
New York *(G-10798)*

Krainz Creations Inc ... E ... 212 583-1555
New York *(G-10884)*

Leonore Doskow Inc ... E ... 914 737-1335
Montrose *(G-8613)*

Mac Swed Inc ... G ... 917 617-3885
New York *(G-11082)*

Masterpiece Diamonds LLC ... F ... 212 937-0681
New York *(G-11175)*

Mataci Inc ... D ... 212 502-1899
New York *(G-11178)*

Maurice Max Inc ... E ... 212 334-6573
New York *(G-11181)*

Nes Jewelry Inc ... C ... 212 502-0025
New York *(G-11370)*

Noir Jewelry LLC ... G ... 212 465-8500
New York *(G-11450)*

Pearl Erwin Inc ... E ... 212 889-7410
New York *(G-11589)*

Pearl Erwin Inc ... E ... 212 883-0650
New York *(G-11590)*

Pepe Creations Inc ... F ... 212 391-1514
New York *(G-11610)*

Pincharming Inc ... F ... 516 663-5115
Garden City *(G-5525)*

Reino Manufacturing Co Inc ... F ... 914 636-8990
New Rochelle *(G-8923)*

Rush Gold Manufacturing Ltd ... D ... 516 781-3155
Bellmore *(G-820)*

Sanoy Inc ... E ... 212 695-6384
New York *(G-11968)*

Sarina Accessories LLC ... E ... 212 239-8106
New York *(G-11973)*

Shira Accessories Ltd ... F ... 212 594-4455
New York *(G-12052)*

Swarovski North America Ltd ... G ... 914 423-4132
Yonkers *(G-17488)*

Swarovski North America Ltd ... G ... 212 695-1502
New York *(G-12250)*

Talbots Inc ... G ... 914 328-1034
White Plains *(G-17175)*

Toho Shoji (new York) Inc ... F ... 212 868-7466
New York *(G-12357)*

Tycoon International Inc ... G ... 212 563-7107
New York *(G-12436)*

Vetta Jewelry Inc ... E ... 212 564-8250
New York *(G-12531)*

Yacoubian Jewelers Inc ... E ... 212 302-6729
New York *(G-12686)*

Ziva Gem LLC ... F ... 646 416-5828
New York *(G-12716)*

JEWELRY: Precious Metal

A & S Fine Jewelry Corp ... G ... 718 243-2201
Brooklyn *(G-1530)*

A & V Castings Inc ... G ... 212 997-0042
New York *(G-8982)*

A Jaffe Inc ... C ... 212 843-7464
New York *(G-8991)*

Abraham Jwly Designers & Mfrs ... F ... 212 944-1149
New York *(G-9005)*

Abrimian Bros Corp ... F ... 212 382-1106
New York *(G-9006)*

Adamor Inc ... G ... 212 688-8885
New York *(G-9025)*

Alart Inc ... G ... 212 840-1508
New York *(G-9071)*

Alchemy Simya Inc ... E ... 646 230-1122
New York *(G-9076)*

Alex Sepkus Inc ... F ... 212 391-8466
New York *(G-9081)*

Alexander Primak Jewelry Inc ... D ... 212 398-0287
New York *(G-9082)*

Almond Jewelers Inc ... F ... 516 933-6000
Port Washington *(G-13799)*

Alpine Creations Ltd ... G ... 212 308-9353
New York *(G-9103)*

Ambras Fine Jewelry Inc ... E ... 718 784-5252
Long Island City *(G-7655)*

American Craft Jewelers Inc ... G ... 718 972-0945
Brooklyn *(G-1600)*

American Originals Corporation ... G ... 212 836-4155
New York *(G-9126)*

Anatoli Inc ... F ... 845 334-9000
West Hurley *(G-16901)*

Ancient Modern Art LLC ... F ... 212 302-0080
New York *(G-9151)*

Anima Group LLC ... G ... 917 913-2053
New York *(G-9161)*

Apicella Jewelers Inc ... E ... 212 840-2024
New York *(G-9174)*

AR & AR Jewelry Inc ... E ... 212 764-7916
New York *(G-9186)*

Arringement International Inc ... G ... 347 323-7974
Flushing *(G-5227)*

Art-TEC Jewelry Designs Ltd ... F ... 212 719-2941
New York *(G-9215)*

Ateret LLC ... G ... 212 819-0777
New York *(G-9246)*

Atlantic Precious Metal Cast ... G ... 718 937-7100
Long Island City *(G-7676)*

Atr Jewelry Inc ... F ... 212 819-0075
New York *(G-9258)*

B K Jewelry Contractor Inc ... E ... 212 398-9093
New York *(G-9289)*

Barber Brothers Jewelry Mfg ... F ... 212 819-0666
New York *(G-9316)*

Baroka Creations Inc ... G ... 212 768-0527
New York *(G-9323)*

Bartholomew Mazza Ltd Inc ... E ... 212 935-4530
New York *(G-9328)*

Bellataire Diamonds Inc ... F ... 212 687-8881
New York *(G-9350)*

BH Multi Com Corp ... E ... 212 944-0020
New York *(G-9387)*

Bielka Inc ... G ... 212 980-6841
New York *(G-9390)*

Billanti Casting Co Inc ... E ... 516 775-4800
New Hyde Park *(G-8819)*

BJG Services LLC ... E ... 516 592-5692
New York *(G-9408)*

Bourghol Brothers Inc ... G ... 845 268-9752
Congers *(G-3853)*

Bral Nader Fine Jewelry Inc ... G ... 800 493-1222
New York *(G-9452)*

Brannkey Inc ... D ... 212 371-1515
New York *(G-9453)*

Brilliant Jewelers/Mjj Inc ... C ... 212 353-2326
New York *(G-9462)*

Bristol Seamless Ring Corp ... F ... 212 874-2645
New York *(G-9463)*

Burke & Bannayan ... G ... 585 723-1010
Rochester *(G-14250)*

Carlo Monte Designs Inc ... G ... 212 935-5611
New York *(G-9527)*

Carol Dauplaise Ltd ... E ... 212 564-7301
New York *(G-9529)*

Carol Dauplaise Ltd ... E ... 212 997-5290
New York *(G-9530)*

Carr Manufacturing Jewelers ... G ... 518 783-6093
Latham *(G-7358)*

Carvin French Jewelers Inc ... E ... 212 755-6474
New York *(G-9539)*

Chaindom Enterprises Inc ... G ... 212 719-4778
New York *(G-9575)*

Chameleon Gems Inc ... F ... 516 829-3333
Great Neck *(G-5797)*

Charles Perrella Inc ... E ... 845 348-4777
Nyack *(G-13046)*

Charles Vaillant Inc ... G ... 212 752-4832
New York *(G-9583)*

Christopher Designs Inc ... E ... 212 382-1013
New York *(G-9613)*

Color Merchants Inc ... E ... 212 682-4788
New York *(G-9672)*

Concord Jewelry Mfg Co LLC ... E ... 212 719-4030
New York *(G-9694)*

Creative Gold LLC ... E ... 718 686-2225
Brooklyn *(G-1815)*

Crescent Wedding Rings Inc ... G ... 212 869-8296
New York *(G-9754)*

Crown Jewelers Intl Inc ... G ... 212 420-7800
New York *(G-9760)*

Csi International Inc ... E ... 716 282-5408
Niagara Falls *(G-12809)*

D & D Creations Co Inc ... G ... 212 840-1198
New York *(G-9781)*

D Oro Onofrio Inc ... G ... 718 491-2961
Brooklyn *(G-1831)*

Danwak Jewelry Corp ... G ... 212 730-4541
New York *(G-9808)*

Dasan Inc ... E ... 212 244-5410
New York *(G-9811)*

David Friedman Chain Co Inc ... F ... 212 684-1760
New York *(G-9819)*

David Howell Product Design ... E ... 914 666-4080
Bedford Hills *(G-801)*

David S Diamonds Inc ... F ... 212 921-8029
New York *(G-9822)*

David Weisz & Sons Inc ... G ... 212 840-4747
New York *(G-9825)*

David Yurman Enterprises LLC ... G ... 914 539-4444
White Plains *(G-17099)*

David Yurman Enterprises LLC ... B ... 212 896-1550
New York *(G-9826)*

David Yurman Enterprises LLC ... G ... 516 627-1700
Manhasset *(G-8057)*

David Yurman Enterprises LLC ... G ... 845 928-8660
Central Valley *(G-3522)*

David Yurman Retail LLC ... G ... 877 226-1400
New York *(G-9827)*

DBC Inc ... D ... 212 819-1177
New York *(G-9832)*

Diamond Distributors Inc ... G ... 212 921-9188
New York *(G-9872)*

Diana Kane Incorporated ... G ... 718 638-6520
Brooklyn *(G-1860)*

Dimoda Designs Inc ... E ... 212 355-8166
New York *(G-9880)*

Donna Distefano Ltd ... G ... 212 594-3757
New York *(G-9898)*

Doris Panos Designs Ltd ... G ... 631 245-0580
Melville *(G-8312)*

Duran Jewelry Inc ... G ... 212 431-1959
New York *(G-9939)*

Dynamic Design Group Inc ... F ... 212 840-9400
New York *(G-9947)*

E M G Creations Inc ... F ... 212 643-0960
New York *(G-9950)*

Earring King Jewelry Mfg Inc ... G ... 718 544-7947
New York *(G-9961)*

Echo Group Inc ... F ... 917 608-7440
New York *(G-9975)*

Eclipse Collection Jewelers ... F ... 212 764-6883
New York *(G-9977)*

Ed Levin Inc ... E ... 518 677-8595
Cambridge *(G-3308)*

Elegant Jewelers Mfg Co Inc ... F ... 212 869-4951
New York *(G-9999)*

Ema Jewelry Inc ... D ... 212 575-8989
New York *(G-10018)*

Emsaru USA Corp ... G ... 212 459-9355
New York *(G-10025)*

Eshel Jewelry Mfg Co Inc ... F ... 212 588-8800
New York *(G-10060)*

Eternal Line ... G ... 845 856-1999
Sparrow Bush *(G-15562)*

Euro Bands Inc ... F ... 212 719-9777
New York *(G-10083)*

PRODUCT

F M Abdulky Inc .... F 607 272-7373
Ithaca *(G-6839)*
F M Abdulky Inc .... G 607 272-7373
Ithaca *(G-6840)*
Fantasia Jewelry Inc .... E 212 921-9590
New York *(G-10136)*
Five Star Creations Inc .... E 845 783-1187
Monroe *(G-8554)*
Frank Blancato Inc .... F 212 768-1495
New York *(G-10202)*
Gem Mine Corp .... G 516 367-1075
Woodbury *(G-17287)*
Gem-Bar Setting Inc .... G 212 869-9238
New York *(G-10266)*
Gemoro Inc .... G 212 768-8844
New York *(G-10268)*
Gemveto Jewelry Company Inc .... E 212 755-2522
New York *(G-10271)*
George Lederman Inc .... G 212 753-4556
New York *(G-10283)*
Georland Corporation .... G 212 730-4730
New York *(G-10285)*
Giovane Ltd .... E 212 332-7373
New York *(G-10299)*
Global Gem Corporation .... G 212 350-9936
New York *(G-10317)*
Goldarama Company Inc .... G 212 730-7299
New York *(G-10328)*
Goldmark Products Inc .... E 631 777-3343
Farmingdale *(G-5001)*
Gorga Fehren Fine Jewelry LLC .... G 646 861-3595
New York *(G-10339)*
Gottlieb & Sons Inc .... E 212 575-1907
New York *(G-10342)*
Gramercy Jewelry Mfg Corp .... E 212 268-0461
New York *(G-10346)*
Guild Diamond Products Inc .... F 212 871-0007
New York *(G-10381)*
Gumuchian Fils Ltd .... F 212 593-3118
New York *(G-10383)*
H & T Goldman Corporation .... G 800 822-0272
New York *(G-10386)*
Hanna Altinis Co Inc .... E 718 706-1134
Long Island City *(G-7756)*
Hansa Usa LLC .... E 646 412-6407
New York *(G-10409)*
Harry Winston Inc .... C 212 399-1000
New York *(G-10420)*
Henry Design Studios Inc .... G 516 801-2760
Locust Valley *(G-7632)*
Henry Dunay Designs Inc .... E 212 768-9700
New York *(G-10458)*
Horo Creations LLC .... G 212 719-4818
New York *(G-10508)*
Hw Holdings Inc .... G 212 399-1000
New York *(G-10534)*
Hy Gold Jewelers Inc .... G 212 744-3202
New York *(G-10535)*
Ilico Jewelry Inc .... G 516 482-0201
Great Neck *(G-5815)*
Imena Jewelry Manufacturer Inc .... F 212 827-0073
New York *(G-10571)*
Incon Gems Inc .... F 212 221-8560
New York *(G-10583)*
Inori Jewels .... F 347 703-5078
New York *(G-10607)*
Intentions Jewelry LLC .... G 845 226-4650
Lagrangeville *(G-7254)*
Iradj Moini Couture Ltd .... F 212 594-9242
New York *(G-10656)*
Iriniri Designs Ltd .... F 845 469-7934
Sugar Loaf *(G-15804)*
J H Jewelry Co Inc .... F 212 239-1330
New York *(G-10678)*
J J Creations Inc .... E 718 392-2828
Long Island City *(G-7768)*
J R Gold Designs Ltd .... F 212 922-9292
New York *(G-10681)*
Jaguar Casting Co Inc .... E 212 869-0197
New York *(G-10694)*
Jane Bohan Inc .... G 212 529-6090
New York *(G-10699)*
Jasani Designs Usa Inc .... G 212 257-6465
New York *(G-10702)*
Jay-Aimee Designs Inc .... C 718 609-0333
Hicksville *(G-6356)*
Jeff Cooper Inc .... F 516 333-8200
Carle Place *(G-3391)*
Jewelmak Inc .... E 212 398-2999
New York *(G-10723)*
Jewelry Arts Manufacturing .... E 212 382-3583
New York *(G-10724)*
Jewels By Star Ltd .... E 212 308-3490
New York *(G-10725)*
Jeweltex Mfg Corp .... F 212 921-8188
New York *(G-10726)*
Jimmy Crystal New York Co Ltd .... E 212 594-0858
New York *(G-10736)*
JK Jewelry Inc .... D 585 346-3464
Rochester *(G-14461)*
JK Manufacturing Inc .... G 212 683-3535
Locust Valley *(G-7633)*
Joan Boyce Ltd .... G 212 867-7474
New York *(G-10744)*
Jordan Scott Designs Ltd .... E 212 947-4250
New York *(G-10762)*
Jotaly Inc .... A 212 886-6000
New York *(G-10769)*
JSA Jewelry Inc .... F 212 764-4504
New York *(G-10777)*
Just Perfect MSP Ltd .... E 877 201-0005
New York *(G-10793)*
Justin Ashley Designs Inc .... G 718 707-0200
Long Island City *(G-7776)*
Justyna Kaminska NY Inc .... G 917 423-5527
New York *(G-10794)*
Karbra Company .... C 212 736-9300
New York *(G-10809)*
Keith Lewis Studio Inc .... G 845 339-5629
Rifton *(G-14134)*
Krasner Group Inc .... G 212 268-4100
New York *(G-10886)*
La Fina Design Inc .... G 212 689-6725
New York *(G-10908)*
Lali Jewelry Inc .... G 212 944-2277
New York *(G-10921)*
Le Paveh Ltd .... F 212 736-6110
New York *(G-10943)*
Le Roi Inc .... F 315 342-3681
Fulton *(G-5468)*
Le Vian Corp .... D 516 466-7200
Great Neck *(G-5820)*
Le Vian Corp .... E 516 466-7200
New York *(G-10944)*
Leser Enterprises Ltd .... F 212 644-8921
New York *(G-10973)*
Lindsay-Hoenig Ltd .... G 212 575-9711
New York *(G-10999)*
Loremi Jewelry Inc .... E 212 840-3429
New York *(G-11042)*
Louis Tamis & Sons Inc .... E 212 684-1760
New York *(G-11050)*
M & S Quality Co Ltd .... F 212 302-8757
New York *(G-11068)*
M A R A Metals Ltd .... G 718 786-7868
Long Island City *(G-7797)*
M Heskia Company Inc .... G 212 768-1845
New York *(G-11072)*
Magnum Creation Inc .... F 212 642-0993
New York *(G-11109)*
Manny Grunberg Inc .... E 212 302-6173
New York *(G-11138)*
Marco Moore Inc .... D 212 575-2090
Great Neck *(G-5822)*
Marina Jewelry Co Inc .... G 212 354-5027
New York *(G-11152)*
Mark King Jewelry Inc .... G 212 921-0746
New York *(G-11154)*
Mark Robinson Inc .... G 212 223-3515
New York *(G-11157)*
Markowitz Jewelry Co Inc .... E 845 774-1175
Monroe *(G-8561)*
Marlborough Jewels Inc .... G 718 768-2000
Brooklyn *(G-2273)*
Martin Flyer Incorporated .... E 212 840-8899
New York *(G-11168)*
Master Craft Jewelry Co Inc .... D 516 599-1012
Lynbrook *(G-7954)*
Masterpiece Color LLC .... G 917 279-6056
New York *(G-11174)*
Maxine Denker Inc .... G 212 689-1440
Staten Island *(G-15704)*
ME & Ro Inc .... G 212 431-8744
New York *(G-11204)*
Mellem Corporation .... F 607 723-0001
Binghamton *(G-935)*
Mer Gems Corp .... G 212 714-9129
New York *(G-11226)*
Mgd Brands Inc .... D 516 545-0150
Plainview *(G-13620)*
Michael Anthony Jewelers LLC .... C 914 699-0000
Mount Vernon *(G-8705)*
Michael Bondanza Inc .... E 212 869-0043
New York *(G-11248)*
Midura Jewels Inc .... G 213 265-8090
New York *(G-11259)*
Milla Global Inc .... G 516 488-3601
Brooklyn *(G-2315)*
Mimi So International LLC .... E 212 300-8600
New York *(G-11274)*
Min Ho Designs Inc .... G 212 838-3667
New York *(G-11275)*
MJM Jewelry Corp .... E 212 354-5014
New York *(G-11285)*
MJM Jewelry Corp .... D 718 596-1600
Brooklyn *(G-2325)*
Monelle Jewelry .... G 212 977-9535
New York *(G-11300)*
Moti Ganz (usa) Inc .... G 212 302-0040
New York *(G-11311)*
MW Samara LLC .... E 212 764-3332
New York *(G-11329)*
Mwsi Inc .... D 914 347-4200
Hawthorne *(G-6251)*
N Y Bijoux Corp .... G 212 244-9585
New York *(G-11336)*
Nicolo Raineri .... G 212 925-6128
New York *(G-11428)*
NP Roniet Creations Inc .... G 212 302-1847
New York *(G-11465)*
Oscar Heyman & Bros Inc .... E 212 593-0400
New York *(G-11530)*
Osnat Gad Inc .... G 212 957-0535
New York *(G-11532)*
Overnight Mountings Inc .... D 516 865-3000
New Hyde Park *(G-8854)*
Paragon Corporation .... F 516 484-6090
Port Washington *(G-13855)*
Parijat Jewels Inc .... G 212 286-2326
New York *(G-11572)*
Pearl Erwin Inc .... E 212 889-7410
New York *(G-11589)*
Pesselnik & Cohen Inc .... G 212 925-0287
New York *(G-11628)*
Peter Atman Inc .... F 212 644-8882
New York *(G-11630)*
PHC Restoration Holdings LLC .... F 212 643-0517
New York *(G-11644)*
Pink Box Accessories LLC .... G 716 777-4477
Brooklyn *(G-2422)*
Pronto Jewelry Inc .... E 212 719-9455
New York *(G-11734)*
R Klein Jewelry Co Inc .... D 516 482-3260
Massapequa *(G-8181)*
R M Reynolds .... G 315 789-7365
Geneva *(G-5584)*
Renaissance Bijou Ltd .... G 212 869-1969
New York *(G-11830)*
Richards & West Inc .... D 585 461-4088
East Rochester *(G-4466)*
Richline Group Inc .... C 212 764-8454
New York *(G-11866)*
Richline Group Inc .... C 914 699-0000
New York *(G-11867)*
Robert Bartholomew Ltd .... E 516 767-2970
Port Washington *(G-13859)*
Roberto Coin Inc .... F 212 486-4545
New York *(G-11891)*
Roman Malakov Diamonds Ltd .... G 212 944-8500
New York *(G-11911)*
Royal Jewelry Mfg Inc .... E 212 302-2500
Great Neck *(G-5836)*
Royal Miracle Corp .... E 212 921-5797
New York *(G-11925)*
Rubinstein Jewelry Mfg Co .... F 718 784-8650
Long Island City *(G-7868)*
Rudolf Friedman Inc .... F 212 869-5070
New York *(G-11934)*
Rumson Acquisition LLC .... F 718 349-4300
New York *(G-11936)*
Ryan Gems Inc .... E 212 697-0149
New York *(G-11940)*
S & M Ring Corp .... F 212 382-0900
Hewlett *(G-6312)*
S Kashi & Sons Inc .... F 212 869-9393
Great Neck *(G-5837)*
S Scharf Inc .... F 516 541-9552
Massapequa *(G-8182)*
Samuel Aaron Inc .... D 718 392-5454
Mount Vernon *(G-8729)*

Employee Codes: A=Over 500 employees, B=251-500
C=101-250, D=51-100, E=20-50, F=10-19, G=5-9
2017 Harris
New York Manufacturers Directory
1245

JEWELRY: Precious Metal

Samuel B Collection Inc ....G....... 516 466-1826
  Great Neck *(G-5838)*
Sanoy Inc ....E....... 212 695-6384
  New York *(G-11968)*
Satco Castings Service Inc ....E....... 516 354-1500
  New Hyde Park *(G-8860)*
Satellite Incorporated ....G....... 212 221-6687
  New York *(G-11976)*
Scott Kay Inc ....C....... 201 287-0100
  New York *(G-12006)*
Select Jewelry Inc ....D....... 718 784-3626
  Long Island City *(G-7874)*
Shah Diamonds Inc ....F....... 212 888-9393
  New York *(G-12038)*
Shanu Gems Inc ....F....... 212 921-4470
  New York *(G-12042)*
Sharodine Inc ....G....... 516 767-3548
  Port Washington *(G-13865)*
Shiro Limited ....G....... 212 780-0007
  New York *(G-12053)*
Simco Manufacturing Jewelers ....F....... 212 575-8390
  New York *(G-12076)*
Simka Diamond Corp ....F....... 212 921-4420
  New York *(G-12077)*
Somerset Manufacturers Inc ....E....... 516 626-3832
  Roslyn Heights *(G-15033)*
Spark Creations Inc ....F....... 212 575-8385
  New York *(G-12147)*
Stanley Creations Inc ....C....... 718 361-6100
  Long Island City *(G-7885)*
Stanmark Jewelry Inc ....G....... 212 730-2557
  New York *(G-12183)*
Stone House Associates Inc ....G....... 212 221-7447
  New York *(G-12207)*
Sulphur Creations Inc ....G....... 212 719-2223
  New York *(G-12229)*
Sumer Gold Ltd ....G....... 212 354-8677
  New York *(G-12231)*
Suna Bros Inc ....E....... 212 869-5670
  New York *(G-12235)*
Sunrise Jewelers of NY Inc ....G....... 516 541-1302
  Massapequa *(G-8183)*
Tambetti Inc ....G....... 212 751-9584
  New York *(G-12276)*
Tamsen Z LLC ....G....... 212 292-6412
  New York *(G-12277)*
Tanagro Jewelry Corp ....E....... 212 753-2817
  New York *(G-12278)*
Technical Service Industries ....E....... 212 719-9800
  Jamaica *(G-6956)*
Teena Creations Inc ....G....... 516 867-1500
  Freeport *(G-5429)*
Temple St Clair LLC ....E....... 212 219-8664
  New York *(G-12298)*
Tiga Holdings Inc ....E....... 845 838-3000
  Beacon *(G-791)*
Trianon Collection Inc ....G....... 212 921-9450
  New York *(G-12403)*
Ultra Fine Jewelry Mfg ....E....... 516 349-2848
  Plainview *(G-13640)*
UNI Jewelry Inc ....G....... 212 398-1818
  New York *(G-12450)*
Unique Designs Inc ....F....... 212 575-7701
  New York *(G-12461)*
United Brothers Jewelry Inc ....E....... 212 921-2558
  New York *(G-12464)*
Valentin & Kalich Jwly Mfg Ltd ....E....... 212 575-9044
  New York *(G-12494)*
Valentine Jewelry Mfg Co Inc ....E....... 212 382-0606
  New York *(G-12495)*
Variety Gem Co Inc ....F....... 212 921-1820
  Great Neck *(G-5848)*
Viktor Gold Enterprise Corp ....G....... 212 768-8885
  New York *(G-12544)*
Von Musulin Patricia ....G....... 212 206-8345
  New York *(G-12567)*
W & B Mazza & Sons Inc ....E....... 516 379-4130
  North Baldwin *(G-12913)*
Walter Edbril Inc ....E....... 212 532-3253
  New York *(G-12584)*
Weisco Inc ....F....... 212 575-8989
  New York *(G-12605)*
William Goldberg Diamond Corp ....G....... 212 980-4343
  New York *(G-12633)*
Xomox Jewelry Inc ....E....... 212 944-8428
  New York *(G-12681)*
Yurman Retail Inc ....G....... 888 398-7626
  New York *(G-12700)*
Zdny & Co Inc ....F....... 212 354-1233
  New York *(G-12707)*

Zeeba Jewelry Mfg Inc ....G....... 212 997-1009
  New York *(G-12709)*
Zelman & Friedman Jwly Mfg Co ....E....... 718 349-3400
  Long Island City *(G-7931)*

JIGS & FIXTURES

Amsco Inc ....F....... 716 823-4213
  Buffalo *(G-2811)*
Knise & Krick Inc ....E....... 315 422-3516
  Syracuse *(G-15975)*
Manhasset Tool & Die Co Inc ....F....... 716 684-6066
  Lancaster *(G-7325)*
Prime Tool & Die LLC ....G....... 607 334-5435
  Norwich *(G-13036)*

JOB PRINTING & NEWSPAPER PUBLISHING COMBINED

Adirondack Publishing Co Inc ....E....... 518 891-2600
  Saranac Lake *(G-15134)*
Albion-Holley Pennysaver Inc ....D....... 585 589-5641
  Albion *(G-161)*
Empire State Weeklies Inc ....E....... 585 671-1533
  Webster *(G-16723)*
Mexico Independent Inc ....E....... 315 963-3763
  Mexico *(G-8396)*
Thousand Islands Printing Co ....G....... 315 482-2581
  Alexandria Bay *(G-191)*

JOB TRAINING & VOCATIONAL REHABILITATION SVCS

Avcom of Virginia Inc ....D....... 585 924-4560
  Victor *(G-16461)*
Chemung Cty Assc Retrd Ctzns ....C....... 607 734-6151
  Elmira *(G-4675)*

JOINTS: Ball Except aircraft & Auto

Advanced Thermal Systems Inc ....E....... 716 681-1800
  Lancaster *(G-7298)*
York Industries Inc ....E....... 516 746-3736
  Garden City Park *(G-5546)*

JOINTS: Expansion

Adsco Manufacturing Corp ....D....... 716 827-5450
  Buffalo *(G-2799)*
Mageba USA LLC ....E....... 212 317-1991
  New York *(G-11099)*
Mount Vernon Iron Works Inc ....G....... 914 668-7064
  Mount Vernon *(G-8708)*
Vulcraft of New York Inc ....C....... 607 529-9000
  Chemung *(G-3595)*
Watson Bowman Acme Corp ....D....... 716 691-8162
  Amherst *(G-271)*

JOINTS: Expansion, Pipe

Advanced Thermal Systems Inc ....E....... 716 681-1800
  Lancaster *(G-7298)*

KEYBOARDS: Computer Or Office Machine

Wey Inc ....G....... 212 532-3299
  New York *(G-12621)*

KILNS

Vent-A-Kiln Corporation ....G....... 716 876-2023
  Buffalo *(G-3240)*

KITCHEN CABINET STORES, EXC CUSTOM

Carefree Kitchens Inc ....G....... 631 567-2120
  Holbrook *(G-6436)*
Creative Cabinet Corp America ....E....... 631 751-5768
  Stony Brook *(G-15769)*
Custom Design Kitchens Inc ....F....... 518 355-4446
  Duanesburg *(G-4325)*
Joseph Fedele ....G....... 718 448-3658
  Staten Island *(G-15694)*
Kalnitz Kitchens Inc ....F....... 716 684-1700
  Buffalo *(G-3026)*
Michael P Mmarr ....G....... 315 623-9380
  Constantia *(G-3881)*
Mind Designs Inc ....G....... 631 563-3644
  Farmingdale *(G-5160)*
S & K Counter Tops Inc ....G....... 716 662-7986
  Orchard Park *(G-13296)*
Serway Bros Inc ....G....... 315 337-0601
  Rome *(G-14836)*

KITCHEN CABINETS WHOLESALERS

Capital Kit Cab & Door Mfrs ....G....... 718 886-0303
  College Point *(G-3779)*
Carefree Kitchens Inc ....G....... 631 567-2120
  Holbrook *(G-6436)*
Central Kitchen Corp ....F....... 631 283-1029
  Southampton *(G-15541)*
Creative Cabinet Corp America ....E....... 631 751-5768
  Stony Brook *(G-15769)*
Custom Design Kitchens Inc ....F....... 518 355-4446
  Duanesburg *(G-4325)*
Dak Mica and Wood Products ....G....... 631 467-0749
  Ronkonkoma *(G-14892)*
Deer Pk Stair Bldg Mllwk Inc ....E....... 631 363-5000
  Blue Point *(G-998)*
Di Fiore and Sons Custom Wdwkg .....G....... 718 278-1663
  Long Island City *(G-7715)*
Eurocraft Custom Furniture ....G....... 718 956-0600
  Long Island City *(G-7732)*
Hennig Custom Woodwork Corp ....G....... 516 536-3460
  Oceanside *(G-13080)*
Johnny Mica Inc ....G....... 631 225-5213
  Lindenhurst *(G-7466)*
Joseph Fedele ....G....... 718 448-3658
  Staten Island *(G-15694)*
Kalnitz Kitchens Inc ....F....... 716 684-1700
  Buffalo *(G-3026)*
M & C Furniture ....G....... 718 422-2136
  Brooklyn *(G-2242)*
Mega Cabinets Inc ....E....... 631 789-4112
  Amityville *(G-311)*
Metro Kitchens Corp ....F....... 718 434-1166
  Brooklyn *(G-2305)*
Sherry-Mica Products Inc ....G....... 631 471-7513
  Ronkonkoma *(G-14985)*
Triad Counter Corp ....G....... 631 750-0615
  Bohemia *(G-1146)*

KITCHEN UTENSILS: Bakers' Eqpt, Wood

Charles Freihofer Baking Co ....G....... 518 463-2221
  Albany *(G-63)*
Unisource Food Eqp Systems Inc ....G....... 516 681-0537
  Holbrook *(G-6479)*

KITCHEN UTENSILS: Food Handling & Processing Prdts, Wood

Channel Manufacturing Inc ....E....... 516 944-6271
  Port Washington *(G-13804)*

KITCHEN UTENSILS: Wooden

Abbott Industries Inc ....E....... 718 291-0800
  Jamaica *(G-6891)*
Catskill Craftsmen Inc ....D....... 607 652-7321
  Stamford *(G-15624)*
Imperial Frames & Albums LLC ....G....... 718 832-9793
  Brooklyn *(G-2097)*
Thomas Matthews Wdwkg Ltd ....F....... 631 287-3657
  Southampton *(G-15554)*
Thomas Matthews Wdwkg Ltd ....G....... 631 287-2023
  Southampton *(G-15555)*

KITCHENWARE STORES

Lalique North America Inc ....E....... 212 355-6550
  New York *(G-10922)*
Lifetime Brands Inc ....B....... 516 683-6000
  Garden City *(G-5514)*
Nash Metalware Co Inc ....F....... 315 339-5794
  Rome *(G-14823)*
Roger & Sons Inc ....G....... 212 226-4734
  New York *(G-11906)*

KITCHENWARE: Plastic

Home and Above LLC ....F....... 914 220-3451
  Brooklyn *(G-2084)*
L K Manufacturing Corp ....E....... 631 243-6910
  West Babylon *(G-16806)*

KNIT GOODS, WHOLESALE

A & B Finishing Inc ....G....... 718 522-4702
  Brooklyn *(G-1525)*
North Star Knitting Mills Inc ....G....... 718 894-4848
  Glendale *(G-5660)*
Premier Knits Ltd ....G....... 718 323-8264
  Ozone Park *(G-13384)*

PRODUCT SECTION

LABORATORY APPARATUS: Shakers & Stirrers

KNIT OUTERWEAR DYEING & FINISHING, EXC HOSIERY & GLOVE

Grand Processing Inc ....E 718 388-0600
  Brooklyn *(G-2048)*

KNIVES: Agricultural Or indl

Lancaster Knives Inc ....E 716 683-5050
  Lancaster *(G-7323)*
Woods Knife Corporation ....E 516 798-4972
  Massapequa *(G-8184)*

LABELS: Cotton, Printed

Paxar Corporation ....E 845 398-3229
  Orangeburg *(G-13238)*
Sml USA Inc ....E 212 736-8800
  New York *(G-12107)*

LABELS: Paper, Made From Purchased Materials

Accent Label & Tag Co Inc ....G 631 244-7066
  Ronkonkoma *(G-14847)*
Apexx Omni-Graphics Inc ....D 718 326-3330
  Maspeth *(G-8119)*
Master Image Printing Inc ....G 914 347-4400
  Elmsford *(G-4763)*
Precision Label Corporation ....F 631 270-4490
  Farmingdale *(G-5087)*
Quadra Flex Corp ....G 607 758-7066
  Cortland *(G-4042)*
Quality Circle Products Inc ....D 914 736-6600
  Montrose *(G-8614)*
Stoney Croft Converters Inc ....F 718 608-9800
  Staten Island *(G-15741)*
Tri-Flex Label Corp ....E 631 293-0411
  Farmingdale *(G-5133)*

LABELS: Woven

Colonial Tag & Label Co Inc ....F 516 482-0508
  Great Neck *(G-5799)*
Imperial-Harvard Label Co ....F 212 736-8420
  New York *(G-10574)*
Itc Mfg Group Inc ....F 212 684-3696
  New York *(G-10669)*
Label Source Inc ....G 212 244-1403
  New York *(G-10911)*
Labels Inter-Global Inc ....F 212 398-0006
  New York *(G-10912)*
R-Pac International Corp ....E 212 465-1818
  New York *(G-11783)*
Sml USA Inc ....E 212 736-8800
  New York *(G-12107)*
Triangle Label Tag Inc ....G 718 875-3030
  Brooklyn *(G-2679)*

LABORATORIES, TESTING: Forensic

Siemens Hlthcare Dgnostics Inc ....E 914 631-0475
  Tarrytown *(G-16105)*

LABORATORIES, TESTING: Pollution

Amincor Inc ....C 347 821-3452
  New York *(G-9136)*

LABORATORIES, TESTING: Product Testing, Safety/Performance

Custom Sports Lab Inc ....G 212 832-1648
  New York *(G-9771)*

LABORATORIES: Biological Research

Advance Biofactures Corp ....E 516 593-7000
  Lynbrook *(G-7944)*
Neurotrope Inc ....G 973 242-0005
  Irvington *(G-6774)*
Synergy Pharmaceuticals Inc ....G 212 227-8611
  New York *(G-12261)*

LABORATORIES: Biotechnology

Acorda Therapeutics Inc ....B 914 347-4300
  Ardsley *(G-403)*
Albany Molecular Research Inc ....C 518 512-2000
  Albany *(G-41)*
Collaborative Laboratories ....D 631 689-0200
  East Setauket *(G-4479)*

Dnano Inc ....G 607 316-3694
  Ithaca *(G-6837)*

LABORATORIES: Commercial Nonphysical Research

Ubm Inc ....A 212 600-3000
  New York *(G-12440)*

LABORATORIES: Dental

Marotta Dental Studio Inc ....E 631 249-7520
  Farmingdale *(G-5042)*
Martins Dental Studio ....G 315 788-0800
  Watertown *(G-16664)*

LABORATORIES: Dental Orthodontic Appliance Production

Vincent Martino Dental Lab ....F 716 674-7800
  Buffalo *(G-3243)*

LABORATORIES: Electronic Research

C & D Assembly Inc ....E 607 898-4275
  Groton *(G-5897)*
Intrinsiq Materials Inc ....G 585 301-4432
  Rochester *(G-14454)*
Mark - 10 Corporation ....E 631 842-9200
  Copiague *(G-3913)*
Millennium Antenna Corp ....F 315 798-9374
  Utica *(G-16348)*
Terahertz Technologies Inc ....G 315 736-3642
  Oriskany *(G-13316)*

LABORATORIES: Medical

Immco Diagnostics Inc ....D 716 691-6911
  Buffalo *(G-3004)*
Immco Diagnostics Inc ....G 716 691-6955
  Buffalo *(G-3003)*

LABORATORIES: Noncommercial Research

American Institute Physics Inc ....C 516 576-2410
  Melville *(G-8293)*
Human Life Foundation Inc ....G 212 685-5210
  New York *(G-10529)*

LABORATORIES: Physical Research, Commercial

Akzo Nobel Chemicals LLC ....C 914 674-5008
  Dobbs Ferry *(G-4300)*
Albany Molecular Research Inc ....E 518 512-2234
  Albany *(G-40)*
Amherst Systems Inc ....C 716 631-0610
  Buffalo *(G-2810)*
Conmed Corporation ....D 315 797-8375
  Utica *(G-16315)*
Danisco US Inc ....D 585 256-5200
  Rochester *(G-14300)*
Delphi Automotive Systems LLC ......A 585 359-6000
  West Henrietta *(G-16876)*
Durata Therapeutics Inc ....G 646 871-6400
  New York *(G-9940)*
Fujitsu Ntwrk Cmmnications Inc ......F 845 731-2000
  Pearl River *(G-13457)*
Grumman Field Support Services .....D 516 575-0574
  Bethpage *(G-867)*
Interdgital Communications LLC ......C 631 622-4000
  Melville *(G-8331)*
International Aids Vaccine Ini ....C 212 847-1111
  New York *(G-10630)*
International Paper Company ....C 845 986-6409
  Tuxedo Park *(G-16284)*
Islechem LLC ....E 716 773-8618
  Grand Island *(G-5761)*
Macrochem Corporation ....G 212 514-8094
  New York *(G-11090)*
Momentive Performance Mtls Inc .....D 914 784-4807
  Tarrytown *(G-16098)*
Northrop Grumman Systems Corp ...A 516 575-0574
  Bethpage *(G-877)*
OSI Pharmaceuticals LLC ....G 631 962-2000
  Farmingdale *(G-5074)*
Starfire Systems Inc ....F 518 899-9336
  Schenectady *(G-15300)*
Transtech Systems Inc ....E 518 370-5558
  Latham *(G-7381)*

LABORATORIES: Testing

Ken-Ton Open Mri PC ....G 716 876-7000
  Kenmore *(G-7150)*

LABORATORIES: Testing

A & Z Pharmaceutical Inc ....D 631 952-3802
  Hauppauge *(G-6006)*
B & H Electronics Corp ....E 845 782-5000
  Monroe *(G-8549)*
Bga Technology LLC ....F 631 750-4600
  Bohemia *(G-1025)*
Curtiss-Wright Flow Control ....G 845 382-6918
  Lake Katrine *(G-7270)*
Dayton T Brown Inc ....B 631 589-6300
  Bohemia *(G-1052)*
G E Inspection Technologies LP ....C 315 554-2000
  Skaneateles *(G-15460)*
Kyra Communications Corp ....F 516 783-6244
  Seaford *(G-15344)*
Miller & Weber Inc ....E 718 821-7110
  Westbury *(G-17012)*
Northeast Metrology Corp ....F 716 827-3770
  Buffalo *(G-3095)*
Stetron International Inc ....F 716 854-3443
  Buffalo *(G-3197)*

LABORATORY APPARATUS & FURNITURE

Adirondack Machine Corporation ......G 518 792-2258
  Hudson Falls *(G-6638)*
Biodesign Inc of New York ....F 845 454-6610
  Carmel *(G-3398)*
Bioins Inc ....G 646 457-8117
  Yonkers *(G-17421)*
Dynamica Inc ....E 212 818-1900
  New York *(G-9948)*
Fungilab Inc ....G 631 750-6361
  Hauppauge *(G-6081)*
Healthalliance Hospital ....E 845 338-2500
  Kingston *(G-7190)*
Hyman Podrusnick Co Inc ....G 718 853-4502
  Brooklyn *(G-2092)*
Instrumentation Laboratory Co ....C 845 680-0028
  Orangeburg *(G-13231)*
Integrted Work Envronments LLC ....G 716 725-5088
  East Amherst *(G-4361)*
Itin Scale Co Inc ....E 718 336-5900
  Brooklyn *(G-2120)*
Jamestown Metal Products LLC ....C 716 665-5313
  Jamestown *(G-7011)*
Lab Crafters Inc ....E 631 471-7755
  Ronkonkoma *(G-14926)*
Maripharm Laboratories ....F 716 984-6520
  Niagara Falls *(G-12845)*
Nalge Nunc International Corp ....A 585 586-8800
  Rochester *(G-14527)*
Newport Corporation ....F 585 248-4246
  Rochester *(G-14535)*
Radon Testing Corp of America ....F 914 345-3380
  Elmsford *(G-4774)*
S P Industries Inc ....D 845 255-5000
  Gardiner *(G-5550)*
Staplex Company Inc ....E 718 768-3333
  Brooklyn *(G-2598)*
Theta Industries Inc ....F 516 883-4088
  Port Washington *(G-13869)*
VWR Education LLC ....C 585 359-2502
  West Henrietta *(G-16899)*

LABORATORY APPARATUS: Furnaces

Crystal Linton Technologies ....F 585 444-8784
  Rochester *(G-14292)*

LABORATORY APPARATUS: Pipettes, Hemocytometer

Vistalab Technologies Inc ....E 914 244-6226
  Brewster *(G-1230)*

LABORATORY APPARATUS: Shakers & Stirrers

Scientific Industries Inc ....E 631 567-4700
  Bohemia *(G-1129)*

Employee Codes: A=Over 500 employees, B=251-500
C=101-250, D=51-100, E=20-50, F=10-19, G=5-9

LABORATORY EQPT, EXC MEDICAL: Wholesalers

Ankom Technology Corp	E	315 986-8090
Macedon (G-7981)		
Enzo Life Sciences Inc	E	631 694-7070
Farmingdale (G-4988)		
Eugenia Selective Living Inc	F	631 277-1461
Islip (G-6808)		
Integrted Work Envronments LLC	G	716 725-5088
East Amherst (G-4361)		
Lab Crafters Inc	E	631 471-7755
Ronkonkoma (G-14926)		
Magic Touch Icewares Intl	E	212 794-2852
New York (G-11107)		
TEC Glass & Inst LLC	G	315 926-7639
Marion (G-8102)		

LABORATORY EQPT: Chemical

Integrated Liner Tech Inc .....E..... 518 621-7422
Rensselaer (G-14048)

LABORATORY EQPT: Clinical Instruments Exc Medical

Next Advance Inc .....F..... 518 674-3510
Averill Park (G-536)
Techtrade LLC .....G..... 212 481-2515
New York (G-12291)

LABORATORY EQPT: Measuring

East Hills Instrument Inc .....F..... 516 621-8686
Westbury (G-16980)

LABORATORY EQPT: Sterilizers

Steriliz LLC .....G..... 585 415-5411
Rochester (G-14703)

LABORATORY INSTRUMENT REPAIR SVCS

Theta Industries Inc .....F..... 516 883-4088
Port Washington (G-13869)

LACE GOODS & WARP KNIT FABRIC DYEING & FINISHING

Eagle Lace Dyeing Corp .....F..... 212 947-2712
New York (G-9958)
Gehring Tricot Corporation .....D..... 315 429-8551
Garden City (G-5507)
Somerset Dyeing & Finishing .....E..... 518 773-7383
Gloversville (G-5720)

LACQUERING SVC: Metal Prdts

Berkman Bros Inc .....E..... 718 782-1827
Brooklyn (G-1686)

LADDERS: Metal

Brakewell Stl Fabricators Inc .....E..... 845 469-9131
Chester (G-3601)
Trine Rolled Moulding Corp .....E..... 718 828-5200
Bronx (G-1478)

LADDERS: Portable, Metal

Metallic Ladder Mfg Corp .....F..... 716 358-6201
Randolph (G-14016)

LADDERS: Wood

Babcock Co Inc .....E..... 607 776-3341
Bath (G-653)
Putnam Rolling Ladder Co Inc .....F..... 212 226-5147
New York (G-11755)
Putnam Rolling Ladder Co Inc .....E..... 718 381-8219
Brooklyn (G-2459)

LAMINATED PLASTICS: Plate, Sheet, Rod & Tubes

Allred & Associates Inc .....E..... 315 252-2559
Elbridge (G-4624)
American Acrylic Corporation .....E..... 631 422-2200
West Babylon (G-16770)
Architctral Dsign Elements LLC .....G..... 718 218-7800
Brooklyn (G-1621)
Clear Cast Technologies Inc .....E..... 914 945-0848
Ossining (G-13322)
Composite Systems & Tech LLC .....G..... 716 491-8490
Massena (G-8192)
Displays By Rioux Inc .....G..... 315 458-3639
North Syracuse (G-12941)
Favorite Plastic Corp .....C..... 718 253-7000
Brooklyn (G-1961)
Griffon Corporation .....E..... 212 957-5000
New York (G-10363)
Inland Paper Products Corp .....E..... 718 827-8150
Brooklyn (G-2108)
Iridium Industries Inc .....E..... 516 504-9700
Great Neck (G-5817)
Jaguar Industries Inc .....F..... 845 947-1800
Haverstraw (G-6237)
Lawrence Packaging Inc .....G..... 516 420-1930
Plainview (G-13615)
Nalge Nunc International Corp .....A..... 585 586-8800
Rochester (G-14527)
Norton Performance Plas Corp .....G..... 518 642-2200
Granville (G-5779)
Strux Corp .....E..... 516 768-3969
Lindenhurst (G-7485)

LAMINATING SVCS

A & D Offset Printers Ltd .....G..... 516 746-2476
Mineola (G-8486)
Copy Room Inc .....F..... 212 371-8600
New York (G-9721)
Hennig Custom Woodwork Corp .....G..... 516 536-3460
Oceanside (G-13080)

LAMP & LIGHT BULBS & TUBES

Foscarini Inc .....G..... 212 247-2218
New York (G-10189)
Kreon Inc .....G..... 516 470-9522
Bethpage (G-870)
La Mar Lighting Co Inc .....D..... 631 777-7700
Farmingdale (G-5032)
Led Waves Inc .....F..... 347 416-6182
Brooklyn (G-2204)
Lowel-Light Manufacturing Inc .....E..... 718 921-0600
Brooklyn (G-2238)
Lumia Energy Solutions LLC .....G..... 516 478-5795
Jericho (G-7076)
Make-Waves Instrument Corp .....E..... 716 681-7524
Depew (G-4264)
Oledworks LLC .....E..... 585 287-6802
Rochester (G-14547)
Philips Elec N Amer Corp .....C..... 607 776-3692
Bath (G-661)
Ric-Lo Productions Ltd .....E..... 845 469-2285
Chester (G-3613)
Satco Products Inc .....D..... 631 243-2022
Edgewood (G-4611)
Siemens Corporation .....F..... 202 434-7800
New York (G-12062)
Siemens USA Holdings Inc .....B..... 212 258-4000
New York (G-12064)
Welch Allyn Inc .....A..... 315 685-4347
Skaneateles Falls (G-15473)
Westron Corporation .....E..... 516 678-2300
Oceanside (G-13105)

LAMP BULBS & TUBES, ELECTRIC: For Specialized Applications

Boehm Surgical Instrument .....F..... 585 436-6584
Rochester (G-14241)

LAMP BULBS & TUBES, ELECTRIC: Light, Complete

Emitled Inc .....G..... 516 531-3533
Westbury (G-16982)
Goldstar Lighting LLC .....F..... 646 543-6811
New York (G-10336)

LAMP BULBS & TUBES/PARTS, ELECTRIC: Generalized Applications

General Electric Company .....A..... 518 385-4022
Schenectady (G-15257)
Lighting Holdings Intl LLC .....F..... 845 306-1850
Purchase (G-13960)
Saratoga Lighting Holdings LLC .....G..... 212 906-7800
New York (G-11971)

LAMP FRAMES: Wire

Lyn Jo Enterprises Ltd .....G..... 716 753-2776
Mayville (G-8217)

LAMP SHADES: Glass

Depp Glass Inc .....F..... 718 784-8500
Long Island City (G-7713)
Somers Stain Glass Inc .....F..... 631 586-7772
Deer Park (G-4211)

LAMP SHADES: Metal

Judis Lampshades Inc .....F..... 917 561-3921
Brooklyn (G-2157)

LAMP STORES

Lighting Holdings Intl LLC .....F..... 845 306-1850
Purchase (G-13960)

LAMPS: Floor, Residential

Adesso Inc .....E..... 212 736-4440
New York (G-9027)

LAMPS: Fluorescent

K & H Industries Inc .....G..... 716 312-0088
Hamburg (G-5930)
K & H Industries Inc .....E..... 716 312-0088
Hamburg (G-5931)

LAMPS: Ultraviolet

Atlantic Ultraviolet Corp .....E..... 631 234-3275
Hauppauge (G-6028)

LAND SUBDIVIDERS & DEVELOPERS: Commercial

Micro Instrument Corp .....D..... 585 458-3150
Rochester (G-14507)

LAND SUBDIVISION & DEVELOPMENT

Nsgv Inc .....E..... 212 367-3167
New York (G-11466)

LANGUAGE SCHOOLS

Japan America Learning Ctr Inc .....F..... 914 723-7600
Scarsdale (G-15218)

LANTERNS

Mjk Enterprises LLC .....G..... 917 653-9042
Brooklyn (G-2324)
Unibrands Corporation .....F..... 212 897-2278
New York (G-12451)

LAPIDARY WORK & DIAMOND CUTTING & POLISHING

Engelack Gem Corporation .....G..... 212 719-3094
New York (G-10040)
Fischer Diamonds Inc .....F..... 212 869-1990
New York (G-10170)
Igc New York Inc .....G..... 212 764-0949
New York (G-10563)
Sunshine Diamond Cutter Inc .....G..... 212 221-1028
New York (G-12237)

LAPIDARY WORK: Contract Or Other

Dweck Industries Inc .....E..... 718 615-1695
Brooklyn (G-1885)
Elite Group International NY .....F..... 917 334-1919
New York (G-10006)

LAPIDARY WORK: Jewel Cut, Drill, Polish, Recut/Setting

Classic Creations Inc .....G..... 516 498-1991
Great Neck (G-5798)
Diamond Boutique .....G..... 516 444-3373
Port Washington (G-13808)
Moti Ganz (usa) Inc .....G..... 212 302-0040
New York (G-11311)
Perma Glow Ltd Inc .....F..... 212 575-9677
New York (G-11619)
Stephen J Lipkins Inc .....G..... 631 249-8866
Farmingdale (G-5116)

PRODUCT SECTION

LEATHER GOODS: NEC

LARD: From Slaughtering Plants
Bliss-Poston The Second Wind............G...... 212 481-1055
  New York *(G-9416)*

LASER SYSTEMS & EQPT
Advanced Photonics Inc ....F...... 631 471-3693
  Ronkonkoma *(G-14855)*
Bare Beauty Laser Hair Removal ....G...... 718 278-2273
  New York *(G-9318)*
CVI Laser LLC ....D...... 585 244-7220
  Rochester *(G-14297)*
Exfo Burleigh Pdts Group Inc ....D...... 585 301-1530
  Canandaigua *(G-3345)*
Gb Group Inc ....G...... 212 594-3748
  New York *(G-10251)*
Laser Consultants Inc ....G...... 631 423-4905
  Huntington *(G-6667)*
Lasermax Inc ....D...... 585 272-5420
  Rochester *(G-14474)*
Navitar Inc..D...... 585 359-4000
  Rochester *(G-14530)*
Teledyne Optech Inc ....F...... 585 427-8310
  West Henrietta *(G-16897)*
Uptek Solutions....................................F...... 631 256-5565
  Bohemia *(G-1153)*

LASERS: Welding, Drilling & Cutting Eqpt
Crysta-Lyn Chemical Company ....G...... 607 296-4721
  Binghamton *(G-905)*
Empire Plastics Inc ....E...... 607 754-9132
  Endwell *(G-4835)*
Trident Precision Mfg Inc ....D...... 585 265-2010
  Webster *(G-16738)*

LAUNDRY & DRYCLEANER AGENTS
Clinton Clrs & EMB Shoppe Inc............G...... 315 853-8421
  Clinton *(G-3718)*

LAUNDRY & GARMENT SVCS, NEC: Fur Cleaning, Repairing/Storage
Alexis & Gianni Retail Inc....................F...... 516 334-3877
  Westbury *(G-16964)*
Anastasia Furs International.................G...... 212 868-9241
  New York *(G-9150)*

LAUNDRY & GARMENT SVCS, NEC: Garment Alteration & Repair
Connie French Cleaners Inc ....G...... 516 487-1543
  Great Neck *(G-5801)*

LAUNDRY & GARMENT SVCS, NEC: Garment Making, Alter & Repair
Pleating Plus Ltd ....F...... 201 863-2991
  Orangeburg *(G-13240)*

LAUNDRY & GARMENT SVCS, NEC: Reweaving, Textiles
Thistle Hill Weavers ....G...... 518 284-2729
  Cherry Valley *(G-3597)*

LAUNDRY & GARMENT SVCS: Dressmaking, Matl Owned By Customer
IBlt Inc ....E...... 212 768-0292
  New York *(G-10546)*

LAUNDRY EQPT: Commercial
G A Braun Inc ....E...... 315 475-3123
  Syracuse *(G-15945)*
Lb Laundry Inc ....G...... 347 399-8030
  Flushing *(G-5264)*

LAUNDRY EQPT: Household
AES Electronics Inc ....G...... 212 371-8120
  New York *(G-9052)*
Coinmach Service Corp ....A...... 516 349-8555
  Plainview *(G-13588)*
CSC Serviceworks Inc ....E...... 516 349-8555
  Plainview *(G-13594)*
CSC Serviceworks Holdings................E...... 516 349-8555
  Plainview *(G-13595)*

Penn Enterprises Inc ....F...... 845 446-0765
  West Point *(G-16930)*
Spin Holdco Inc ....G...... 516 349-8555
  Plainview *(G-13635)*

LAUNDRY SVC: Wiping Towel Sply
Yankee Corp ....F...... 718 589-1377
  Bronx *(G-1495)*

LAWN & GARDEN EQPT
Briggs & Stratton Corporation..............C...... 315 495-0100
  Munnsville *(G-8749)*
Cazenovia Equipment Co Inc..............G...... 315 736-0898
  Clinton *(G-3717)*
Chapin International Inc ....C...... 585 343-3140
  Batavia *(G-627)*
Chapin Manufacturing Inc ....C...... 585 343-3140
  Batavia *(G-628)*
Clopay Ames True Tmper Hldng ....F...... 516 938-5544
  Jericho *(G-7062)*
Fradan Manufacturing Corp................F...... 914 632-3653
  New Rochelle *(G-8902)*
Real Bark Mulch LLC ....G...... 518 747-3650
  Fort Edward *(G-5345)*
Rhett M Clark Inc................................G...... 585 538-9570
  Caledonia *(G-3281)*

LAWN & GARDEN EQPT STORES
Nelson Holdings Ltd ....G...... 607 772-1794
  Binghamton *(G-939)*

LAWN & GARDEN EQPT: Carts Or Wagons
Kadco Usa Inc ....G...... 518 661-6068
  Mayfield *(G-8213)*

LAWN & GARDEN EQPT: Tractors & Eqpt
Eaton Brothers Corp ....G...... 716 649-8250
  Hamburg *(G-5922)*
Saxby Implement Corp ....F...... 585 624-2938
  Mendon *(G-8382)*

LAWN & GARDEN EQPT: Trimmers
Victoire Latam Asset MGT LLC...........F...... 212 319-6550
  New York *(G-12538)*

LAWN MOWER REPAIR SHOP
Nelson Holdings Ltd ....G...... 607 772-1794
  Binghamton *(G-939)*

LEAD & ZINC
Hh Liquidating Corp ....A...... 646 282-2500
  New York *(G-10471)*

LEAD PENCILS & ART GOODS
Aakron Rule Corp ....C...... 716 542-5483
  Akron *(G-19)*
Effanjay Pens Inc ....E...... 212 316-9565
  Long Island City *(G-7726)*
R & F Handmade Paints Inc ....F...... 845 331-3112
  Kingston *(G-7207)*
Rosendahl Industries Ltd Inc...............E...... 718 436-2711
  Brooklyn *(G-2507)*

LEASING & RENTAL SVCS: Oil Field Eqpt
Steel Excel Inc ....D...... 914 461-1300
  White Plains *(G-17171)*

LEASING & RENTAL: Computers & Eqpt
IBM World Trade Corporation ....G...... 914 765-1900
  Armonk *(G-413)*
Key Computer Svcs of Chelsea...........D...... 212 206-8060
  New York *(G-10840)*
Systems Trading Inc ....G...... 718 261-8900
  Melville *(G-8359)*

LEASING & RENTAL: Construction & Mining Eqpt
Christian Fabrication LLC ....G...... 315 822-0135
  West Winfield *(G-16957)*
Safeworks LLC ....F...... 800 696-5577
  Woodside *(G-17352)*

LEASING & RENTAL: Other Real Estate Property
Beardslee Realty ....G...... 516 747-5557
  Mineola *(G-8497)*

LEASING: Laundry Eqpt
Thermopatch Corporation....................D...... 315 446-8110
  Syracuse *(G-16058)*

LEASING: Shipping Container
A R Arena Products Inc ....E...... 585 277-1680
  Rochester *(G-14162)*
Shiprite Software Inc ....G...... 315 733-6191
  Utica *(G-16359)*

LEATHER GOODS, EXC FOOTWEAR, GLOVES, LUGGAGE/BELTING, WHOL
Pan American Leathers Inc.................G...... 978 741-4150
  New York *(G-11558)*

LEATHER GOODS: Belt Laces
McM Products USA Inc........................E...... 646 756-4090
  New York *(G-11201)*

LEATHER GOODS: Belting & Strapping
Fahrenheit NY Inc ....G...... 212 354-6554
  New York *(G-10127)*
Walco Leather Co Inc ....E...... 212 243-2244
  New York *(G-12577)*

LEATHER GOODS: Boxes
Kamali Leather Corp............................G...... 518 762-2522
  Johnstown *(G-7117)*

LEATHER GOODS: Cases
Sibeau Handbags Inc...........................E...... 212 686-0210
  New York *(G-12059)*
Slim Line Case Co Inc ....F...... 585 546-3639
  Rochester *(G-14689)*

LEATHER GOODS: Cosmetic Bags
Baker Products Inc ....G...... 212 459-2323
  White Plains *(G-17082)*
M G New York Inc ....F...... 212 371-5566
  New York *(G-11070)*
Penthouse Manufacturing Co Inc........B...... 516 379-1300
  Freeport *(G-5418)*

LEATHER GOODS: Desk Sets
Star Desk Pad Co Inc ....E...... 914 963-9400
  Yonkers *(G-17486)*

LEATHER GOODS: Garments
Art Craft Leather Goods Inc................F...... 718 257-7401
  Brooklyn *(G-1633)*
Dvf Studio LLC ....D...... 212 741-6607
  New York *(G-9942)*
East West Global Sourcing Inc............G...... 917 887-2286
  Brooklyn *(G-1897)*
Leather Outlet ....G...... 518 668-0328
  Lake George *(G-7262)*
Perrone Leather LLC ....D...... 518 853-4300
  Fultonville *(G-5482)*
Tucano Usa Inc....................................G...... 212 966-9211
  New York *(G-12419)*

LEATHER GOODS: Holsters
Adirondack Leather Pdts Inc ....F...... 607 547-5798
  Fly Creek *(G-5313)*
Courtlandt Boot Jack Co Inc...............E...... 718 445-6200
  Flushing *(G-5235)*
Helgen Industries Inc..........................C...... 631 841-6300
  Amityville *(G-293)*

LEATHER GOODS: Key Cases
Form A Rockland Plastics Inc.............G...... 315 848-3300
  Cranberry Lake *(G-4057)*

LEATHER GOODS: NEC
112 Jerome Dreyfuss LLC ....G...... 212 334-6920
  New York *(G-8958)*

Employee Codes: A=Over 500 employees, B=251-500
C=101-250, D=51-100, E=20-50, F=10-19, G=5-9

2017 Harris
New York Manufacturers Directory

1249

LEATHER GOODS: Personal

LEATHER GOODS: Personal

American Puff Corp .... D 516 379-1300
  Freeport *(G-5387)*
Astucci US Ltd .... F 718 752-9700
  Long Island City *(G-7674)*
Atlantic Specialty Co Inc .... E 845 356-2502
  Monsey *(G-8569)*
Coach Inc .... B 212 594-1850
  New York *(G-9656)*
Coach Stores Inc .... A 212 643-9727
  New York *(G-9659)*
Datamax International Inc .... E 212 693-0933
  New York *(G-9815)*
Elco Manufacturing Co Inc .... F 516 767-3577
  Port Washington *(G-13813)*
Excelled Shpskin Lea Coat Corp .... F 212 594-5843
  New York *(G-10103)*
Fahrenheit NY Inc .... E 212 354-6554
  New York *(G-10127)*
Grownbeans Inc .... G 212 989-3486
  New York *(G-10373)*
Helgen Industries Inc .... C 631 841-6300
  Amityville *(G-293)*
Hemisphere Novelties Inc .... E 914 378-4100
  Yonkers *(G-17453)*
House of Portfolios Co Inc .... G 212 206-7323
  New York *(G-10519)*
House of Portfolios Co Inc .... F 212 206-7323
  New York *(G-10520)*
Just Brass Inc .... G 212 724-5447
  New York *(G-10792)*
Leather Artisan .... G 518 359-3102
  Childwold *(G-3628)*
Leather Impact Inc .... G 212 382-2788
  New York *(G-10950)*
Merzon Leather Co Inc .... C 718 782-6260
  Brooklyn *(G-2301)*
Neumann Jutta New York Inc .... F 212 982-7048
  New York *(G-11376)*
Walco Leather Co Inc .... E 212 243-2244
  New York *(G-12577)*

LEATHER GOODS: Transmission Belting

Sampla Belting North Amer LLC .... E 716 667-7450
  Lackawanna *(G-7249)*

LEATHER GOODS: Wallets

L Y Z Creations Ltd Inc .... E 718 768-2977
  Brooklyn *(G-2187)*
Randa Accessories Lea Gds LLC .... D 212 354-5100
  New York *(G-11799)*
Trafalgar Company LLC .... G 212 768-8800
  New York *(G-12390)*

LEATHER TANNING & FINISHING

Aston Leather Inc .... G 212 481-2760
  New York *(G-9242)*
Corium Corporation .... F 914 381-0100
  Mamaroneck *(G-8030)*
Edsim Leather Co Inc .... F 212 695-8500
  New York *(G-9984)*
Hastings Hide Inc .... G 516 295-2400
  Lawrence *(G-7391)*
Legendary Auto Interiors Ltd .... E 315 331-1212
  Newark *(G-12734)*
Pearl Leather Finishers Inc .... D 518 762-4543
  Johnstown *(G-7120)*

LEATHER, LEATHER GOODS & FURS, WHOLESALE

C & H Cstm Bkbinding Embossing .... G 800 871-8980
  Medford *(G-8237)*
Leather Artisan .... G 518 359-3102
  Childwold *(G-3628)*
Leather Impact Inc .... G 212 382-2788
  New York *(G-10950)*
Tandy Leather Factory Inc .... G 845 480-3588
  Nyack *(G-13054)*

LEATHER: Accessory Prdts

Adam Scott Designs Inc .... E 212 420-8866
  New York *(G-9024)*
Cejon Inc .... E 201 437-8788
  New York *(G-9554)*
Justin Gregory Inc .... G 631 249-5187
  Farmingdale *(G-5020)*
Kamali Group Inc .... G 516 627-4000
  Great Neck *(G-5819)*
Pacific Worldwide Inc .... F 212 502-3360
  New York *(G-11553)*
Tandy Leather Factory Inc .... G 845 480-3588
  Nyack *(G-13054)*
Vic Demayos Inc .... G 845 626-4343
  Accord *(G-1)*

LEATHER: Artificial

Beckmann Converting Inc .... E 518 842-0073
  Amsterdam *(G-334)*

LEATHER: Bag

Givi Inc .... G 212 586-5029
  New York *(G-10303)*
Hat Attack Inc .... E 718 994-1000
  Bronx *(G-1351)*

LEATHER: Bookbinders'

Graphic Image Associates LLC .... D 631 249-9600
  Melville *(G-8323)*
System of AME Binding .... F 631 390-8560
  Central Islip *(G-3512)*

LEATHER: Case

Baker Products Inc .... G 212 459-2323
  White Plains *(G-17082)*

LEATHER: Colored

Mohawk River Leather Works .... F 518 853-3900
  Fultonville *(G-5480)*

LEATHER: Cut

A-1 Products Inc .... G 718 789-1818
  Brooklyn *(G-1538)*
Hohenforst Splitting Co Inc .... E 518 725-0012
  Gloversville *(G-5715)*

LEATHER: Die-cut

John Gailer Inc .... E 212 243-5662
  Long Island City *(G-7772)*

LEATHER: Embossed

C & H Cstm Bkbinding Embossing .... G 800 871-8980
  Medford *(G-8237)*
Rainbow Leather Inc .... F 718 939-8762
  College Point *(G-3804)*

LEATHER: Finished

Androme Leather Inc .... F 518 773-7945
  Gloversville *(G-5706)*
Arrow Leather Finishing Inc .... E 518 762-3121
  Johnstown *(G-7107)*
Pan American Leathers Inc .... G 978 741-4150
  New York *(G-11558)*
Pearl Meadow Stables Inc .... C 518 762-7733
  Johnstown *(G-7121)*

LEATHER: Handbag

Graphic Image Incorporated .... C 631 249-9600
  Melville *(G-8324)*
Street Smart Designs Inc .... G 646 865-0056
  New York *(G-12213)*
Trebbianno LLC .... D 212 868-2770
  New York *(G-12396)*

LEATHER: Processed

Pearl Leather Group LLC .... E 516 627-4047
  Great Neck *(G-5829)*

LEATHER: Specialty, NEC

Walco Leather Co Inc .... E 212 243-2244
  New York *(G-12577)*

LEGAL & TAX SVCS

Westchester Law Journal Inc .... G 914 948-0715
  White Plains *(G-17183)*

LEGAL OFFICES & SVCS

Dick Bailey Service Inc .... F 718 522-4363
  Brooklyn *(G-1863)*
Thomson Reuters Corporation .... A 646 223-4000
  New York *(G-12329)*
Wave Publishing Co Inc .... F 718 634-4000
  Rockaway Beach *(G-14783)*

LEGITIMATE LIVE THEATER PRODUCERS

Abkco Music & Records Inc .... E 212 399-0300
  New York *(G-9004)*

LENS COATING: Ophthalmic

Equicheck LLC .... G 631 987-6356
  Patchogue *(G-13419)*
Optisource International Inc .... E 631 924-8360
  Bellport *(G-835)*

LESSORS: Landholding Office

Rock Mountain Farms Inc .... G 845 647-9084
  Ellenville *(G-4638)*

LIFESAVING & SURVIVAL EQPT, EXC MEDICAL, WHOLESALE

Aero Healthcare (us) LLC .... G 855 225-2376
  Valley Cottage *(G-16375)*

LIGHT SENSITIVE DEVICES

Nsi Industries LLC .... C 800 841-2505
  Mount Vernon *(G-8711)*
Tork Inc .... D 914 664-3542
  Mount Vernon *(G-8738)*

LIGHTING EQPT: Flashlights

Psg Innovations Inc .... F 917 299-8986
  Valley Stream *(G-16422)*

LIGHTING EQPT: Motor Vehicle, Headlights

Licenders .... G 212 759-5200
  New York *(G-10986)*

LIGHTING EQPT: Motor Vehicle, NEC

Mobile Fleet Inc .... G 631 206-2920
  Hauppauge *(G-6142)*

LIGHTING EQPT: Outdoor

Al Energy Solutions Led Llc .... E 646 380-6670
  New York *(G-9068)*
Northern Air Technology Inc .... G 585 594-5050
  Rochester *(G-14544)*
Outdoor Lightning Perspectives .... G 631 266-6200
  Huntington *(G-6672)*

LIGHTING EQPT: Reflectors, Metal, For Lighting Eqpt

Island Lite Louvers Inc .... E 631 608-4250
  Amityville *(G-297)*
Projector Lamp Services LLC .... F 631 244-0051
  Bohemia *(G-1123)*

LIGHTING EQPT: Streetcar Fixtures

Power and Cnstr Group Inc .... E 585 889-6020
  Scottsville *(G-15338)*

LIGHTING EQPT: Strobe Lighting Systems

Star Headlight Lantern Co Inc .... C 585 226-9500
  Avon *(G-543)*

LIGHTING FIXTURES WHOLESALERS

Expo Furniture Designs Inc .... F 516 674-1420
  Glen Cove *(G-5615)*
Lighting Holdings Intl LLC .... F 845 306-1850
  Purchase *(G-13960)*
Matov Industries Inc .... E 718 392-5060
  Long Island City *(G-7806)*
Quality HM Brands Holdings LLC .... G 718 292-2024
  Bronx *(G-1437)*
Quoizel Inc .... E 631 436-4402
  Hauppauge *(G-6176)*
Satco Products Inc .... D 631 243-2022
  Edgewood *(G-4611)*
Visual Effects Inc .... F 718 324-0011
  Jamaica *(G-6962)*

PRODUCT SECTION

LIGHTING FIXTURES: Public

LIGHTING FIXTURES, NEC

Company	Code	Phone
Acolyte Industries Inc — New York (G-9019)	F	212 629-6830
Coldstream Group Inc — Mamaroneck (G-8029)	F	914 698-5959
Cooper Industries LLC — Syracuse (G-15909)	E	315 477-7000
Creative Stage Lighting Co Inc — North Creek (G-12933)	E	518 251-3302
Edison Power & Light Co Inc — Brooklyn (G-1904)	F	718 522-0002
Fabbian USA Corp — New York (G-10123)	G	973 882-3824
Goddard Design Co — Brooklyn (G-2034)	G	718 599-0170
Gordon S Anderson Mfg Co — Millbrook (G-8475)	G	845 677-3304
Gti Graphic Technology Inc — Newburgh (G-12760)	E	845 562-7066
HB Architectural Lighting Inc — Bronx (G-1352)	E	347 851-4123
Illumination Technologies Inc — East Syracuse (G-4538)	F	315 463-4673
J M Canty Inc — Lockport (G-7593)	E	716 625-4227
Jaquith Industries Inc — Syracuse (G-15966)	E	315 478-5700
Jed Lights Inc — Garden City Park (G-5540)	G	516 812-5001
Jt Roselle Lighting & Sup Inc — Mount Kisco (G-8632)	F	914 666-3700
Julian A McDermott Corporation — Ridgewood (G-14111)	E	718 456-3606
La Mar Lighting Co Inc — Farmingdale (G-5032)	D	631 777-7700
Lamparts Co Inc — Mount Vernon (G-8699)	F	914 723-8986
Lbg Acquisition LLC — New York (G-10939)	E	212 226-1276
Light Blue USA LLC — Brooklyn (G-2221)	G	718 475-2515
Lighting Sculptures Inc — Deer Park (G-4166)	F	631 242-3387
Luminescent Systems Inc — East Aurora (G-4373)	B	716 655-0800
Nu-Tech Lighting Corp — New York (G-11469)	G	212 541-7397
Olive Led Lighting Inc — Flushing (G-5276)	G	718 746-0830
Rodac USA Corp — Clarence (G-3672)	E	716 741-3931
Saratoga Lighting Holdings LLC — New York (G-11971)	G	212 906-7800
Sensio America — Saratoga Springs (G-15173)	F	877 501-5337
Siemens Electro Industrial Sa — New York (G-12063)	A	212 258-4000
Strider Global LLC — New York (G-12215)	G	212 726-1302
Tarsier Ltd — New York (G-12280)	C	212 401-6181
Tecnolux Incorporated — Brooklyn (G-2651)	G	718 369-3900
Times Square Stage Ltg Co Inc — Stony Point (G-15778)	E	845 947-3034
Truck-Lite Co LLC — Falconer (G-4916)	D	716 661-1235
Truck-Lite Co LLC — Falconer (G-4917)	E	716 665-2614
Vertex Innovative Solutions In — Syracuse (G-16067)	E	315 437-6711
Vincent Coniglaro — Kingston (G-7224)	F	845 340-0489
Visual Effects Inc — Jamaica (G-6962)	F	718 324-0011
Vivid Rgb Lighting LLC — Peekskill (G-13483)	G	718 635-0817
William J Blume Worldwide Svcs — Saratoga Springs (G-15177)	G	914 723-6185

LIGHTING FIXTURES: Decorative Area

Company	Code	Phone
Enchante Lites LLC — New York (G-10030)	E	212 602-1818
Lindsey Adelman — Brooklyn (G-2227)	E	718 623-3013
Secret Celebrity Licensing LLC — New York (G-12012)	G	212 812-9277

LIGHTING FIXTURES: Fluorescent, Commercial

Company	Code	Phone
A & L Lighting Ltd — Medford (G-8233)	F	718 821-1188
La Mar Lighting Co Inc — Farmingdale (G-5032)	D	631 777-7700
Legion Lighting Co Inc — Brooklyn (G-2208)	E	718 498-1770
Lite Brite Manufacturing Inc — Brooklyn (G-2231)	F	718 855-9797
Spectronics Corporation — Westbury (G-17027)	C	516 333-4840

LIGHTING FIXTURES: Fluorescent, Residential

Company	Code	Phone
Eaton Corporation — Syracuse (G-15930)	E	315 579-2872
Ephesus Lighting Inc — Syracuse (G-15937)	E	315 579-2873

LIGHTING FIXTURES: Indl & Commercial

Company	Code	Phone
A-1 Stamping & Spinning Corp — Rockaway Park (G-14784)	F	718 388-2626
AEP Environmental LLC — Buffalo (G-2801)	F	716 446-0739
Al Energy Solutions Led Llc — New York (G-9068)	E	646 380-6670
Altman Stage Lighting Co Inc — Yonkers (G-17412)	C	914 476-7987
American Scientific Ltg Corp — Brooklyn (G-1608)	E	718 369-1100
Apogee Translite Inc — Deer Park (G-4100)	E	631 254-6975
Aquarii Inc — Camillus (G-3321)	G	315 672-8807
Aristocrat Lighting Inc — Brooklyn (G-1628)	F	718 522-0003
Arlee Lighting Corp — Inwood (G-6751)	G	516 595-8558
Awaken Led Company — Champlain (G-3537)	F	802 338-5971
Canarm Ltd — Ogdensburg (G-13113)	G	800 267-4427
Cooper Industries LLC — Syracuse (G-15909)	E	315 477-7000
Cooper Lighting LLC — Hicksville (G-6334)	C	516 470-1000
Crownlite Mfg Corp — Bohemia (G-1044)	E	631 589-9100
DAc Lighting Inc — Mamaroneck (G-8032)	E	914 698-5959
Dreyfus Ashby Inc — New York (G-9929)	E	212 818-0770
Edison Price Lighting Inc — Long Island City (G-7723)	C	718 685-0700
Edison Price Lighting Inc — Long Island City (G-7724)	D	718 685-0700
Electric Lighting Agencies — New York (G-9996)	E	212 645-4580
Electric Lighting Agencies — Jericho (G-7067)	E	212 645-4580
Elegance Lighting Ltd — Port Jefferson (G-13775)	F	631 509-0640
Energy Conservation & Sup Inc — Brooklyn (G-1924)	F	718 855-5888
Green Energy Concepts Inc — Chester (G-3608)	G	845 238-2574
Hudson Valley Lighting Inc — Wappingers Falls (G-16573)	D	845 561-0300
Jesco Lighting Inc — Port Washington (G-13828)	E	718 366-3211
Jesco Lighting Group LLC — Port Washington (G-13829)	E	718 366-3211
LDI Lighting Inc — Brooklyn (G-2199)	G	718 384-4490
Light Waves Concept Inc — New York (G-10992)	F	212 677-6400
Lighting By Dom Yonkers Inc — Yonkers (G-17462)	G	914 968-8700
Lighting Services — Stony Point (G-15776)	D	845 942-2800
Linear Lighting Corporation — Long Island City (G-7790)	C	718 361-7552
Lite-Makers Inc — Jamaica (G-6925)	E	718 739-9300
Litelab Corp — Long Island City (G-7792)	G	718 361-6826
Litelab Corp — Buffalo (G-3050)	C	716 856-4300
LSI Lightron Inc — New Windsor (G-8942)	A	845 562-5500
Lukas Lighting Inc — Long Island City (G-7795)	E	800 841-4011
Luminatta Inc — Mount Vernon (G-8702)	G	914 664-3600
Luminescent Systems Inc — East Aurora (G-4373)	B	716 655-0800
Luxo Corporation — Elmsford (G-4761)	F	914 345-0067
Magniflood Inc — Amityville (G-309)	E	631 226-1000
Matov Industries Inc — Long Island City (G-7806)	E	718 392-5060
Modulightor Inc — New York (G-11291)	F	212 371-0336
North American Mfg Entps Inc — Staten Island (G-15712)	E	718 524-4370
North American Mfg Entps Inc — Staten Island (G-15713)	F	718 524-4370
Nulux Inc — Ridgewood (G-14116)	F	718 383-1112
Oledworks LLC — Rochester (G-14547)	E	585 287-6802
Philips Lighting N Amer Corp — New York (G-11647)	C	646 265-7170
Preciseled Inc — Valley Stream (G-16419)	G	516 418-5337
Primelite Manufacturing Corp — Freeport (G-5420)	G	516 868-4411
Rapid-Lite Fixture Corporation — Brooklyn (G-2478)	F	347 599-2600
Remains Lighting — New York (G-11829)	E	212 675-8051
S E A Supplies Ltd — Plainview (G-13633)	F	516 694-6677
Sandy Littman Inc — Newburgh (G-12779)	G	845 562-1112
Saratoga Lighting Holdings LLC — New York (G-11971)	G	212 906-7800
Savenergy Inc — Garden City (G-5531)	G	516 239-1958
Savwatt Usa Inc — New York (G-11978)	F	646 478-2676
Selux Corporation — Highland (G-6408)	C	845 691-7723
Solarpath Inc — New York (G-12121)	G	201 490-4499
Sonneman-A Way of Light — Wappingers Falls (G-16576)	G	845 926-5469
Swivelier Company Inc — Blauvelt (G-975)	D	845 353-1455
Trulite Louvre Corp — Old Bethpage (G-13131)	E	516 756-1850
Twinkle Lighting Inc — Flushing (G-5304)	G	718 225-0939
Versaponents Inc — Deer Park (G-4223)	F	631 242-3387
Vision Quest Lighting Inc — Ronkonkoma (G-14998)	E	631 737-4800
Vonn LLC — Forest Hills (G-5329)	F	917 572-5000
Xeleum Lighting LLC — Mount Kisco (G-8647)	F	954 617-8170
Zumtobel Lighting Inc — Highland (G-6409)	C	845 691-6262

LIGHTING FIXTURES: Motor Vehicle

Company	Code	Phone
Mega Vations Inc — Brooklyn (G-2294)	G	718 934-2192
Truck-Lite Co LLC — Falconer (G-4916)	D	716 661-1235
Truck-Lite Co LLC — Falconer (G-4917)	E	716 665-2614
Truck-Lite Co LLC — Falconer (G-4918)	B	716 665-6214
Wolo Mfg Corp — Deer Park (G-4228)	E	631 242-0333

LIGHTING FIXTURES: Ornamental, Commercial

Company	Code	Phone
LDI Lighting Inc — Brooklyn (G-2198)	G	718 384-4490

LIGHTING FIXTURES: Public

Company	Code	Phone
CEIT Corp — Plattsburgh (G-13658)	F	518 825-0649

Employee Codes: A=Over 500 employees, B=251-500
C=101-250, D=51-100, E=20-50, F=10-19, G=5-9

LIGHTING FIXTURES: Public

USA Illumination Inc ....E 845 565-8500
New Windsor *(G-8956)*

LIGHTING FIXTURES: Residential

A-1 Stamping & Spinning Corp ....F 718 388-2626
Rockaway Park *(G-14784)*
Artemis Studios Inc ....D 718 788-6022
Brooklyn *(G-1635)*
Canarm Ltd ....G 800 267-4427
Ogdensburg *(G-13113)*
Cooper Lighting LLC 516 470-1000
Hicksville *(G-6334)*
Crownlite Mfg Corp ....E 631 589-9100
Bohemia *(G-1044)*
David Weeks Studio ....F 212 966-3433
New York *(G-9824)*
Decor By Dene Inc ....F 718 376-5566
Brooklyn *(G-1848)*
Dreyfus Ashby Inc 212 818-0770
New York *(G-9929)*
ER Butler & Co Inc ....F 212 925-3565
New York *(G-10055)*
Excalbur Brnze Sculpture Fndry ....F 718 366-3444
Brooklyn *(G-1942)*
Hudson Valley Lighting Inc ....D 845 561-0300
Wappingers Falls *(G-16573)*
Jamaica Lamp Corp ....E 718 776-5039
Queens Village *(G-13980)*
Lexstar Inc ....F 845 947-1415
Haverstraw *(G-6238)*
Litelab Corp ....C 716 856-4300
Buffalo *(G-3050)*
Lyric Lighting Ltd Inc ....G 718 497-0109
Ridgewood *(G-14113)*
Matov Industries Inc ....E 718 392-5060
Long Island City *(G-7806)*
Modulightor Inc ....F 212 371-0336
New York *(G-11291)*
New Generation Lighting Inc ....F 212 966-0328
New York *(G-11387)*
Nulux Inc ....E 718 383-1112
Ridgewood *(G-14116)*
Philips Elec N Amer Corp ....C 607 776-3692
Bath *(G-661)*
Pompian Manufacturing Co Inc 914 476-7076
Yonkers *(G-17478)*
Preciseled Inc 516 418-5337
Valley Stream *(G-16419)*
Prestigeline Inc ....D 631 273-3636
Bay Shore *(G-728)*
Quality HM Brands Holdings LLC ....G 718 292-2024
Bronx *(G-1437)*
Quoizel Inc ....E 631 436-4402
Hauppauge *(G-6176)*
Rapid-Lite Fixture Corporation ....F 347 599-2600
Brooklyn *(G-2478)*
Remains Lighting ....E 212 675-8051
New York *(G-11829)*
Sandy Littman Inc ....G 845 562-1112
Newburgh *(G-12779)*
Saratoga Lighting Holdings LLC ....G 212 906-7800
New York *(G-11971)*
Satco Products Inc ....D 631 243-2022
Edgewood *(G-4611)*
Savwatt Usa Inc ....F 646 478-2676
New York *(G-11978)*
Swarovski Lighting Ltd ....B 518 563-7500
Plattsburgh *(G-13702)*
Swivelier Company Inc ....D 845 353-1455
Blauvelt *(G-975)*
Tarsier Ltd ....C 212 401-6181
New York *(G-12280)*
Tudor Electrical Supply Co Inc 212 867-7550
New York *(G-12420)*
Ulster Precision Inc ....E 845 338-0995
Kingston *(G-7218)*
Vision Quest Lighting Inc ....E 631 737-4800
Ronkonkoma *(G-14998)*
Vonn LLC ....F 917 572-5000
Forest Hills *(G-5329)*
Wainland Inc ....E 718 626-2233
Astoria *(G-461)*

LIGHTING FIXTURES: Residential, Electric

Expo Furniture Designs Inc ....F 516 674-1420
Glen Cove *(G-5615)*
Lighting Collaborative Inc ....G 212 253-7220
New York *(G-10995)*
Serway Bros Inc ....E 315 337-0601
Rome *(G-14836)*

LIGHTING FIXTURES: Street

Eluminocity US Inc ....G 651 528-1165
New York *(G-10016)*
Power and Cnstr Group Inc ....E 585 889-6020
Scottsville *(G-15338)*

LIGHTS: Trouble lights

Lyn Jo Enterprises Ltd ....G 716 753-2776
Mayville *(G-8217)*

LIME: Agricultural

Masick Soil Conservation Co ....F 518 827-5354
Schoharie *(G-15317)*

LIMESTONE & MARBLE: Dimension

Domoteck Interiors Inc ....G 718 433-4300
Woodside *(G-17326)*
Minerals Technologies Inc 212 878-1800
New York *(G-11276)*

LIMESTONE: Crushed & Broken

Barrett Paving Materials Inc ....F 315 737-9471
Clayville *(G-3686)*
Cobleskill Stone Products Inc 518 299-3066
Prattsville *(G-13945)*
Cobleskill Stone Products Inc 518 295-7121
Schoharie *(G-15316)*
Cobleskill Stone Products Inc 518 234-0221
Cobleskill *(G-3735)*
Cobleskill Stone Products Inc 607 637-4271
Hancock *(G-5962)*
Graymont Materials (ny) Inc ....E 518 891-0236
Saranac Lake *(G-15138)*
Hanson Aggregates PA Inc ....E 315 858-1100
Jordanville *(G-7132)*
Hanson Aggregates PA LLC ....E 315 469-5501
Jamesville *(G-7049)*
Hanson Aggregates PA LLC ....E 315 685-3321
Skaneateles *(G-15463)*
Hanson Aggregates PA LLC ....E 585 624-1220
Honeoye Falls *(G-6530)*
Hanson Aggregates PA LLC ....E 315 821-7222
Oriskany Falls *(G-13318)*
Hanson Aggregates PA LLC ....E 315 789-6202
Oaks Corners *(G-13070)*
Infinity Architectual Systems ....F 716 882-2321
Buffalo *(G-3007)*
Jml Quarries Inc 845 932-8206
Cochecton *(G-3741)*
John Vespa Inc ....E 315 788-6330
Watertown *(G-16656)*
Lafarge North America Inc ....E 716 876-8788
Tonawanda *(G-16176)*
Lilac Quarries LLC ....G 607 867-4016
Mount Upton *(G-8658)*
Patterson Materials Corp ....E 845 832-6000
New Windsor *(G-8947)*
Shelby Crushed Stone Inc 585 798-4501
Medina *(G-8281)*
Specialty Minerals Inc ....E 212 878-1800
New York *(G-12152)*

LIMESTONE: Cut & Shaped

Hanson Aggregates East LLC ....F 315 493-3721
Great Bend *(G-5783)*
Minerals Technologies Inc 212 878-1800
New York *(G-11276)*

LIMESTONE: Dimension

New York Quarries Inc ....F 518 756-3138
Alcove *(G-172)*

LIMESTONE: Ground

Hanson Aggregates PA Inc ....F 518 568-2444
Saint Johnsville *(G-15094)*
Hanson Aggregates PA LLC ....F 315 393-3743
Ogdensburg *(G-13115)*

LINEN SPLY SVC: Coat

Maple Grove Corp ....E 585 492-5286
Arcade *(G-396)*

LINENS & TOWELS WHOLESALERS

American Country Quilts & Lin ....G 631 283-5466
Southampton *(G-15538)*
David King Linen Inc ....F 718 241-7298
Brooklyn *(G-1842)*
Paramount Textiles Inc ....F 212 966-1040
New York *(G-11570)*

LINENS: Napkins, Fabric & Nonwoven, From Purchased Materials

Bardwil Industries Inc ....G 212 944-1870
New York *(G-9317)*

LINENS: Tablecloths, From Purchased Materials

Benson Sales Co Inc ....F 718 236-6743
Brooklyn *(G-1685)*
Josie Accessories Inc ....D 212 889-6376
New York *(G-10768)*
Michael Stuart Inc ....F 718 821-0704
Brooklyn *(G-2309)*
Premier Skirting Products Inc ....F 516 239-6581
Lawrence *(G-7397)*
Repellem Consumer Pdts Corp ....F 631 273-3992
Islandia *(G-6802)*
Tablecloths For Granted Ltd ....F 518 370-5481
Schenectady *(G-15303)*
University Table Cloth Company ....F 845 371-3876
Spring Valley *(G-15606)*

LINERS & COVERS: Fabric

Meyco Products Inc ....E 631 421-9800
Melville *(G-8336)*
Reid K Dalland ....G 845 687-8728
Stone Ridge *(G-15765)*
Vinyl Works Inc ....E 518 786-1200
Latham *(G-7383)*

LINERS & LINING

Joshua Liner Gallery LLC ....F 212 244-7415
New York *(G-10767)*
Themis Chimney Inc ....F 718 937-4716
Brooklyn *(G-2657)*

LINERS: Indl, Metal Plate

Lifetime Chimney Supply LLC ....G 516 576-8144
Plainview *(G-13616)*

LININGS: Apparel, Made From Purchased Materials

Bpe Studio Inc ....G 212 868-9896
New York *(G-9448)*

LININGS: Fabric, Apparel & Other, Exc Millinery

Amoseastern Apparel Inc ....F 212 921-1859
New York *(G-9138)*
Pangea Brands LLC ....G 617 638-0001
New York *(G-11559)*
Pangea Brands LLC ....G 617 638-0001
New York *(G-11560)*
Polkadot Usa Inc ....G 914 835-3697
Mamaroneck *(G-8043)*

LIP BALMS

Lotta Luv Beauty LLC ....F 646 786-2847
New York *(G-11046)*

LIPSTICK

Precision Cosmetics Mfg Co ....G 914 667-1200
Mount Vernon *(G-8716)*

LIQUEFIED PETROLEUM GAS DEALERS

Praxair Distribution Inc ....G 315 457-5821
Liverpool *(G-7543)*

LIQUID CRYSTAL DISPLAYS

Apollo Display Tech Corp ....E 631 580-4360
Ronkonkoma *(G-14871)*
Dimension Technologies Inc ....G 585 436-3530
Rochester *(G-14309)*

PRODUCT SECTION

LUGGAGE & LEATHER GOODS STORES: Leather, Exc Luggage & Shoes

Ergotech Group Inc .... E 914 347-3800
  Elmsford (G-4751)
Orthogonal .... G 585 254-2775
  Rochester (G-14557)
W D Technology Inc .... G 914 779-8738
  Eastchester (G-4583)

LITHOGRAPHIC PLATES

Chakra Communications Inc .... E 716 505-7300
  Lancaster (G-7309)

LOCKERS

Locker Masters Inc .... F 518 288-3203
  Granville (G-5774)

LOCKERS: Refrigerated

Carrier Corporation .... B 315 432-3844
  East Syracuse (G-4515)
Storflex Holdings Inc .... C 607 962-2137
  Corning (G-3982)

LOCKS

A & L Doors & Hardware LLC .... F 718 585-8400
  Bronx (G-1252)
Delta Lock Company LLC .... F 631 238-7035
  Bohemia (G-1054)
Dortronics Systems Inc .... E 631 725-0505
  Sag Harbor (G-15077)
Eazy Locks LLC .... G 718 327-7770
  Far Rockaway (G-4920)
G Marks Hdwr Liquidating Corp .... D 631 225-5400
  Amityville (G-288)
Safe Skies LLC .... G 888 632-5027
  New York (G-11953)

LOCKS: Coin-Operated

American Lckr SEC Systems Inc .... E 716 699-2773
  Ellicottville (G-4640)

LOCKSMITHS

A & L Doors & Hardware LLC .... F 718 585-8400
  Bronx (G-1252)

LOG LOADING & UNLOADING SVCS

Seaway Timber Harvesting Inc .... D 315 769-5970
  Massena (G-8200)

LOGGING

Attica Package Company Inc .... F 585 591-0510
  Attica (G-472)
B & B Forest Products Ltd .... F 518 622-0811
  Cairo (G-3270)
Central Timber Co Inc .... G 518 638-6338
  Granville (G-5773)
Chad Pierson .... G 518 251-0186
  Bakers Mills (G-557)
Clearlake Land Co Inc .... F 315 848-2427
  Star Lake (G-15628)
Daniel & Lois Lyndaker Logging .... G 315 346-6527
  Castorland (G-3423)
Davis Logging & Lumber .... G 315 245-1040
  Camden (G-3314)
Donald Snyder Jr .... F 315 265-4485
  Potsdam (G-13878)
Ed Beach Forest Management .... G 607 538-1745
  Bloomville (G-994)
Farney Tree & Excavation LLC .... G 315 783-1161
  Croghan (G-4058)
Finger Lakes Timber Co Inc .... G 585 346-2990
  Livonia (G-7564)
George Chilson Logging .... G 607 732-1558
  Elmira (G-4686)
GL & RL Logging Inc .... F 518 883-3936
  Broadalbin (G-1242)
Guldenschuh Logging & Lbr LLC .... G 585 538-4750
  Caledonia (G-3280)
Harris Logging Inc .... E 518 792-1083
  Queensbury (G-13998)
Kevin Regan Logging Ltd .... G 315 245-3890
  Camden (G-3317)
Mountain Forest Products Inc .... G 518 597-3674
  Crown Point (G-4067)
Murray Logging LLC .... G 518 834-7372
  Keeseville (G-7140)
Northern Timber Harvesting LLC .... F 585 233-7330
  Alfred Station (G-197)

Peters LLC .... G 607 637-5470
  Hancock (G-5966)
Robert W Still .... F 315 942-5594
  Ava (G-531)
Russell Bass .... F 607 637-5253
  Hancock (G-5967)
Schaefer Logging Inc .... F 607 467-4990
  Deposit (G-4281)
Seaway Timber Harvesting Inc .... D 315 769-5970
  Massena (G-8200)
Tim Cretin Logging & Sawmill .... F 315 946-4476
  Lyons (G-7976)
Timothy L Simpson .... G 518 234-1401
  Sharon Springs (G-15385)
Van Cpeters Logging Inc .... G 607 637-3574
  Hancock (G-5968)
Wagner Logging LLC .... G 607 467-2347
  Masonville (G-8109)
William Ward Logging .... F 518 946-7826
  Jay (G-7055)

LOGGING CAMPS & CONTRACTORS

Baker Logging & Firewood .... G 585 374-5733
  Naples (G-8764)
Couture Logging Inc .... G 607 753-6445
  Cortland (G-4023)
Couture Timber Harvesting .... G 607 836-4719
  Mc Graw (G-8221)
Decker Forest Products Inc .... G 607 563-2345
  Sidney (G-15438)
Homer Logging Contractor .... G 607 753-8553
  Homer (G-6520)
J & S Logging Inc .... E 315 262-2112
  South Colton (G-15515)
Klein & Sons Logging Inc .... F 845 292-6682
  Wht Sphr Spgs (G-17221)
Lizotte Logging Inc .... F 518 359-2200
  Tupper Lake (G-16277)
Matteson Logging Inc .... G 585 593-3037
  Wellsville (G-16754)
P H Gucker Inc .... G 518 834-9501
  Keeseville (G-7141)
Paul J Mitchell Logging Inc .... E 518 359-7029
  Tupper Lake (G-16278)
Richard Bauer Logging .... G 585 343-4149
  Alexander (G-190)
Richards Logging LLC .... F 518 359-2775
  Tupper Lake (G-16279)
Robert W Butts Logging Co .... G 518 643-2897
  Peru (G-13527)
Smoothbore International Inc .... G 315 754-8124
  Red Creek (G-14026)
Snyder Logging .... F 315 265-1462
  Potsdam (G-13884)
Wadsworth Logging Inc .... F 518 863-6970
  Gloversville (G-5727)

LOGGING: Timber, Cut At Logging Camp

Lyndaker Timber Harvesting LLC .... F 315 346-1328
  Castorland (G-3424)
Tonche Timber LLC .... G 845 389-3489
  Amsterdam (G-370)

LOGGING: Wood Chips, Produced In The Field

Chip It All Ltd .... G 631 473-2040
  Port Jefferson (G-13774)

LOGGING: Wooden Logs

Kapstone Container Corporation .... D 518 842-2450
  Amsterdam (G-352)

LOOSELEAF BINDERS

Acco Brands USA LLC .... C 847 541-9500
  Ogdensburg (G-13109)
Brewer-Cantelmo Co Inc .... E 212 244-4600
  New York (G-9458)
Consolidated Loose Leaf Inc .... G 212 924-5800
  New York (G-9706)
Sellco Industries Inc .... E 607 756-7594
  Cortland (G-4045)

LOTIONS OR CREAMS: Face

3lab Inc .... F 201 567-9100
  New York (G-8974)
Distribio USA LLC .... G 212 989-6077
  New York (G-9887)

EL Erman International Ltd .... G 212 444-9440
  Brooklyn (G-1909)
Fsr Beauty Ltd .... G 212 447-0036
  New York (G-10217)
Gassho Body & Mind Inc .... G 518 695-9991
  Schuylerville (G-15320)

LOTIONS: SHAVING

Glacee Skincare LLC .... G 212 690-7632
  New York (G-10304)

LOUDSPEAKERS

Global Market Development Inc .... E 631 667-1002
  Edgewood (G-4599)
Speaqua Corp .... E 516 380-5008
  Deer Park (G-4213)

LOUVERS: Ventilating

Airflex Industrial Inc .... E 631 752-1234
  Farmingdale (G-4933)
Airflex Industrial Inc .... D 631 752-1234
  Farmingdale (G-4934)
Imperial Damper & Louver Co .... E 718 731-3800
  Bronx (G-1360)

LUBRICANTS: Corrosion Preventive

Engineering Maint Pdts Inc .... F 516 624-9774
  Oyster Bay (G-13369)
Reliance Fluid Tech LLC .... E 716 332-0988
  Niagara Falls (G-12867)

LUBRICATING EQPT: Indl

Advanced Tchncal Solutions Inc .... F 914 214-8230
  Yorktown Heights (G-17506)
Innovative Pdts of Amer Inc .... E 845 679-4500
  Woodstock (G-17363)

LUBRICATING OIL & GREASE WHOLESALERS

Chemlube International LLC .... F 914 381-5800
  Harrison (G-5979)
Chemlube Marketing Inc .... F 914 381-5800
  Harrison (G-5980)

LUBRICATION SYSTEMS & EQPT

Bowen Products Corporation .... G 315 498-4481
  Nedrow (G-8772)

LUGGAGE & BRIEFCASES

Adam Scott Designs Inc .... E 212 420-8866
  New York (G-9024)
Atlantic Specialty Co Inc .... E 845 356-2502
  Monsey (G-8569)
Bragley Mfg Co Inc .... E 718 622-7469
  Brooklyn (G-1712)
Fish & Crown Ltd .... D 212 707-9603
  New York (G-10173)
Golden Bridge Group Inc .... G 718 335-8882
  Elmhurst (G-4662)
Prepac Designs Inc .... G 914 524-7800
  Yonkers (G-17479)
Rhino Trunk & Case Inc .... F 585 244-4553
  Rochester (G-14624)
Rose Trunk Mfg Co Inc .... F 516 766-6686
  Oceanside (G-13093)
Royal Industries Inc .... E 718 369-3046
  Brooklyn (G-2511)
Sky Dive .... D 845 858-6400
  Port Jervis (G-13792)
Trunk & Trolley LLC .... G 212 947-9001
  New York (G-12411)

LUGGAGE & LEATHER GOODS STORES

C & H Cstm Bkbinding Embossing ...... G 800 871-8980
  Medford (G-8237)

LUGGAGE & LEATHER GOODS STORES: Leather, Exc Luggage & Shoes

House of Portfolios Co Inc .... G 212 206-7323
  New York (G-10519)
Tandy Leather Factory Inc .... G 845 480-3588
  Nyack (G-13054)

LUGGAGE: Traveling Bags

Aka Sport Inc	F	631 858-9888	
Dix Hills (G-4289)			
Ameribag Outdoors	E	845 339-4082	
Kingston (G-7177)			
Carry-All Canvas Bag Co Inc	G	718 375-4230	
Brooklyn (G-1759)			
Lo & Sons Inc	F	917 775-4025	
Brooklyn (G-2233)			
Tumi Inc	C	212 742-8020	
New York (G-12424)			

LUGGAGE: Wardrobe Bags

Goyard Inc .... G 212 813-0005
New York (G-10343)

LUMBER & BLDG MATLS DEALER, RET: Garage Doors, Sell/Install

Amarr Company .... F 585 426-8290
Rochester (G-14195)
EZ Lift Operator Corp .... F 845 356-1676
Spring Valley (G-15584)
L & L Overhead Garage Doors .... G 718 721-2518
Long Island City (G-7787)

LUMBER & BLDG MATRLS DEALERS, RET: Bath Fixtures, Eqpt/Sply

Vaire LLC .... G 631 271-4933
Huntington Station (G-6727)

LUMBER & BLDG MTRLS DEALERS, RET: Closets, Interiors/Access

Cubbies Unlimited Corporation .... F 631 586-8572
Deer Park (G-4124)

LUMBER & BLDG MTRLS DEALERS, RET: Doors, Storm, Wood/Metal

Finger Lakes Trellis Supply .... G 315 904-4007
Williamson (G-17223)

LUMBER & BLDG MTRLS DEALERS, RET: Windows, Storm, Wood/Metal

All United Window Corp .... E 718 624-0490
Brooklyn (G-1588)
Express Building Supply Inc .... E 516 608-0379
Oceanside (G-13079)

LUMBER & BUILDING MATERIALS DEALER, RET: Door & Window Prdts

City Store Gates Mfg Corp .... E 718 939-9700
College Point (G-3781)
D D & L Inc .... F 607 729-9131
Binghamton (G-906)
Executive Mirror Doors Inc .... E 631 234-1090
Ronkonkoma (G-14899)
Long Island Fireproof Door .... E 718 767-8800
Whitestone (G-17211)
M & D Installers Inc .... E 718 782-6978
Brooklyn (G-2243)
Thompson Overhead Door Co Inc .... F 718 788-2470
Brooklyn (G-2658)

LUMBER & BUILDING MATERIALS DEALER, RET: Masonry Matls/Splys

Afco Precast Sales Corp .... D 631 924-7114
Middle Island (G-8405)
Cranesville Block Co Inc .... G 315 384-4000
Norfolk (G-12898)
Ferrara Bros Bldg Mtls Corp .... E 718 939-3030
Flushing (G-5240)
Guardian Concrete Inc .... F 518 372-0080
Schenectady (G-15267)
Nicolia Concrete Products Inc .... D 631 669-0700
Lindenhurst (G-7476)
Palumbo Block Co Inc .... E 845 832-6100
Dover Plains (G-4316)

LUMBER & BUILDING MATERIALS DEALERS, RETAIL: Brick

Barrasso & Sons Trucking Inc .... E 631 581-0360
Islip Terrace (G-6814)

LUMBER & BUILDING MATERIALS DEALERS, RETAIL: Countertops

Nlr Counter Tops LLC .... G 347 295-0410
New York (G-11446)

LUMBER & BUILDING MATERIALS DEALERS, RETAIL: Paving Stones

Pallette Stone Corporation .... E 518 584-2421
Gansevoort (G-5487)
Unilock New York Inc .... G 845 278-6700
Brewster (G-1229)

LUMBER & BUILDING MATERIALS DEALERS, RETAIL: Sand & Gravel

Champion Materials Inc .... G 315 493-2654
Carthage (G-3410)
Champion Materials Inc .... E 315 493-2654
Carthage (G-3411)

LUMBER & BUILDING MATERIALS DEALERS, RETAIL: Tile, Ceramic

Amendola MBL & Stone Ctr Inc .... D 914 997-7968
White Plains (G-17076)
Glen Plaza Marble & Gran Inc .... G 516 671-1100
Glen Cove (G-5617)

LUMBER & BUILDING MATERIALS RET DEALERS: Millwork & Lumber

Andike Millwork Inc .... G 718 894-1796
Maspeth (G-8118)
Attica Package Company Inc .... F 585 591-0510
Attica (G-472)
Island Street Lumber Co Inc .... G 716 692-4127
North Tonawanda (G-12978)
L Builders Supply Inc .... B 518 355-7190
Schenectady (G-15275)
Meltz Lumber Co of Mellenville .... E 518 672-7021
Hudson (G-6626)
Pella Corporation .... C 631 208-0710
Calverton (G-3294)
Pgs Millwork Inc .... D 212 244-6610
New York (G-11642)
Stephenson Lumber Company Inc .... G 518 548-7521
Speculator (G-15563)

LUMBER & BUILDING MATLS DEALERS, RET: Concrete/Cinder Block

Cranesville Block Co Inc .... E 518 684-6000
Amsterdam (G-341)
Duke Concrete Products Inc .... E 518 793-7743
Queensbury (G-13995)
Fort Miller Service Corp .... F 518 695-5000
Greenwich (G-5888)
Taylor Concrete Products Inc .... E 315 788-2191
Watertown (G-16673)

LUMBER: Dimension, Hardwood

Norton-Smith Hardwoods Inc .... G 716 945-0346
Salamanca (G-15103)
Wrights Hardwoods Inc .... E 716 595-2345
Cassadaga (G-3415)

LUMBER: Fiberboard

Niagara Fiberboard Inc .... E 716 434-8881
Lockport (G-7605)

LUMBER: Fuelwood, From Mill Waste

GM Palmer Inc .... F 585 492-2990
Arcade (G-393)
PA Pellets LLC .... F 814 848-9970
Pittsford (G-13572)

LUMBER: Furniture Dimension Stock, Softwood

Hennig Custom Woodwork Corp .... G 516 536-3460
Oceanside (G-13080)

LUMBER: Hardwood Dimension

A D Bowman & Son Lumber Co .... E 607 692-2595
Castle Creek (G-3417)
Carlson Wood Products Inc .... G 716 287-2923
Sinclairville (G-15452)
Gutchess Lumber Co Inc .... C 607 753-3393
Cortland (G-4030)
Potter Lumber Co LLC .... D 814 438-7888
Hamburg (G-5936)
Sirianni Hardwoods Inc .... E 607 962-4688
Painted Post (G-13394)

LUMBER: Hardwood Dimension & Flooring Mills

B & B Lumber Company Inc .... D 315 492-1786
Jamesville (G-7045)
Clements Burrville Sawmill .... G 315 782-4549
Watertown (G-16645)
Donver Incorporated .... F 716 945-1910
Kill Buck (G-7166)
Fibron Products Inc .... E 716 886-2378
Buffalo (G-2947)
Fitzpatrick and Weller Inc .... D 716 699-2393
Ellicottville (G-4641)
H B Millwork Inc .... F 631 289-8086
Medford (G-8246)
Horizon Floors I LLC .... E 212 509-9686
New York (G-10505)
J & J Log & Lumber Corp .... D 845 832-6535
Dover Plains (G-4315)
J A Yansick Lumber Co Inc .... E 585 492-4312
Arcade (G-395)
Mm of East Aurora LLC .... F 716 651-9663
Buffalo (G-3069)
Petteys Lumber .... E 518 792-5943
Fort Ann (G-5337)
Potter Lumber Co Inc .... E 716 373-1260
Allegany (G-203)
Premier Hardwood Products Inc .... E 315 492-1786
Jamesville (G-7050)
S Donadic Woodworking Inc .... D 718 361-9888
Sunnyside (G-15809)
Tupper Lake Hardwoods Inc .... E 518 359-8248
Tupper Lake (G-16282)
Wagner Hardwoods LLC .... E 607 594-3321
Cayuta (G-3440)
Wagner Hardwoods LLC .... C 607 594-3321
Cayuta (G-3441)
Wagner Millwork Inc .... D 716 687-5362
Owego (G-13361)

LUMBER: Kiln Dried

Carlson Wood Products Inc .... G 716 287-2923
Sinclairville (G-15452)
Mallery Lumber LLC .... G 607 637-2236
Hancock (G-5965)
Salamanca Lumber Company Inc .... E 716 945-4810
Salamanca (G-15104)

LUMBER: Plywood, Hardwood

Shepards Sawmill .... G 585 638-5664
Holley (G-6493)
Sure-Lock Industries LLC .... F 315 207-0044
Oswego (G-13343)
Veneer One Inc .... E 516 536-6480
Oceanside (G-13103)

LUMBER: Plywood, Hardwood or Hardwood Faced

Kings Quartet Corp .... G 845 986-9090
Warwick (G-16592)

LUMBER: Plywood, Prefinished, Hardwood

Geonex International Corp .... G 212 473-4555
New York (G-10280)

LUMBER: Plywood, Softwood

H B Millwork Inc .... F 631 289-8086
Medford (G-8246)

LUMBER: Poles, Wood, Untreated

3b Timber Company Inc .... F 315 942-6580
Boonville (G-1161)

LUMBER: Siding, Dressed

Weather Tight Exteriors .... G 631 375-5108
Ridge (G-14095)

PRODUCT SECTION

LUMBER: Silo Stock, Sawn

Machina Deus Lex Inc ....G...... 917 577-0972
  Jamaica *(G-6926)*

LUMBER: Treated

Donver Incorporated ....F 716 945-1910
  Kill Buck *(G-7166)*
Northeast Treaters Inc ....E 518 945-2660
  Athens *(G-464)*
Northeast Treaters NY LLC ....E 518 945-2660
  Athens *(G-465)*

LUNCHROOMS & CAFETERIAS

Wired Coffee and Bagel Inc ....F 518 506-3194
  Malta *(G-8022)*

MACHINE PARTS: Stamped Or Pressed Metal

Action Machined Products Inc ....F 631 842-2333
  Copiague *(G-3890)*
Allen Machine Products Inc ....E 631 630-8800
  Hauppauge *(G-6016)*
Belrix Industries Inc ....G...... 716 821-5964
  Buffalo *(G-2837)*
Brach Machine Inc ....F 585 343-9134
  Batavia *(G-626)*
Bryant Machine Co Inc ....F 716 894-8282
  Buffalo *(G-2846)*
Cgs Fabrication LLC ....F 585 347-6127
  Webster *(G-16716)*
Cnc Manufacturing Corp ....E 718 728-6800
  Long Island City *(G-7701)*
Colonial Precision Machinery ....G...... 631 249-0738
  Farmingdale *(G-4960)*
Creative Design and Mch Inc ....E 845 778-9001
  Rock Tavern *(G-14780)*
Custom Metal Incorporated ....F 631 643-4075
  West Babylon *(G-16787)*
Electric Motors and Pumps Inc ....G...... 718 935-9118
  Brooklyn *(G-1910)*
Forkey Construction & Fabg Inc ....E 607 849-4879
  Cortland *(G-4026)*
G A Richards & Co Inc ....F 516 334-5412
  Westbury *(G-16988)*
German Machine & Assembly Inc ....E 585 546-4200
  Rochester *(G-14398)*
J P Machine Products Inc ....F 631 249-9229
  Farmingdale *(G-5014)*
K Tooling LLC ....F 607 637-3781
  Hancock *(G-5964)*
Lancaster Knives Inc ....E 716 683-5050
  Lancaster *(G-7323)*
M F Manufacturing Enterprises ....G...... 516 822-5135
  Hicksville *(G-6366)*
Maehr Industries Inc ....G...... 631 924-1661
  Bellport *(G-833)*
Mega Tool & Mfg Corp ....E 607 734-8398
  Elmira *(G-4695)*
Pervi Precision Company ....G...... 631 589-5557
  Bohemia *(G-1117)*
Rayco Manufacturing Co Inc ....F 516 431-2006
  Jamaica *(G-6944)*
Reynolds Manufacturing Inc ....F 607 562-8936
  Big Flats *(G-882)*
Sharon Manufacturing Co Inc ....G...... 631 242-8870
  Deer Park *(G-4210)*
Solidus Industries Inc ....D 607 749-4540
  Homer *(G-6522)*
Twinco Mfg Co Inc ....E 631 231-0022
  Hauppauge *(G-6219)*
Vosky Precision Machining Corp ....F 631 737-3200
  Ronkonkoma *(G-15000)*
Wessie Machine Inc ....G...... 315 926-4060
  Marion *(G-8104)*
Zeta Machine Corp ....F 631 471-8532
  Ronkonkoma *(G-15002)*

MACHINE SHOPS

A and K Machine and Welding ....G...... 631 231-2552
  Bay Shore *(G-663)*
Addison Precision Mfg Corp ....D...... 585 254-1386
  Rochester *(G-14172)*
Allied Industrial Products Co ....G...... 716 664-3893
  Jamestown *(G-6970)*
Applied Technology Mfg Corp ....E 607 687-6200
  Owego *(G-13350)*
Architectural Coatings Inc ....F 718 418-9584
  Brooklyn *(G-1622)*
B & R Industries Inc ....F 631 736-2275
  Medford *(G-8235)*
Birch Machine & Tool Inc ....G...... 716 735-9802
  Middleport *(G-8420)*
Bms Manufacturing Co Inc ....E 607 535-2426
  Watkins Glen *(G-16693)*
Carballo Contract Machining ....G...... 315 594-2511
  Wolcott *(G-17278)*
Carbaugh Tool Company Inc ....E 607 739-3293
  Elmira *(G-4673)*
Carter Precision Metals LLC ....F 516 333-1917
  Westbury *(G-16973)*
Conesus Lake Association Inc ....E 585 346-6864
  Lakeville *(G-7283)*
Courser Inc ....E 607 739-3861
  Elmira *(G-4677)*
David Fehlman ....G...... 315 455-8888
  Syracuse *(G-15922)*
DMD Machining Technology Inc ....G...... 585 659-8180
  Kendall *(G-7143)*
Elite Precise Manufacturer LLC ....E 518 993-3040
  Fort Plain *(G-5347)*
Engineering Mfg Tech LLC ....D 607 754-7111
  Endicott *(G-4805)*
Euro Gear (usa) Inc ....E 518 578-1775
  Plattsburgh *(G-13662)*
Everfab Inc ....D 716 655-1550
  East Aurora *(G-4370)*
G & G C Machine & Tool Co Inc ....G...... 516 873-0999
  Westbury *(G-16987)*
Genesis Machining Corp ....F 516 377-1197
  North Baldwin *(G-12905)*
Gentner Precision Components ....G...... 315 597-5734
  Palmyra *(G-13408)*
Global Precision Products Inc ....E 585 334-4640
  Rush *(G-15049)*
Harwitt Industries Inc ....F 516 623-9787
  Freeport *(G-5405)*
Hohl Machine & Conveyor Co Inc ....E 716 882-7210
  Buffalo *(G-2996)*
Hunter Machine Inc ....E 585 924-7480
  Victor *(G-16481)*
Indian Springs Mfg Co Inc ....F 315 635-6101
  Baldwinsville *(G-570)*
Industrial Precision Pdts Inc ....E 315 343-4421
  Oswego *(G-13333)*
Industrial Services of Wny ....G...... 716 799-7788
  Niagara Falls *(G-12836)*
Island Machine Inc ....G...... 518 562-1232
  Plattsburgh *(G-13672)*
ISO Plastics Corp ....D 914 663-8300
  Mount Vernon *(G-8694)*
J & J TI Die Mfg & Stampg Corp ....G...... 845 228-0242
  Carmel *(G-3400)*
Jam Industries Inc ....E 585 458-9830
  Rochester *(G-14458)*
Johnnys Machine Shop ....G...... 631 338-9733
  West Babylon *(G-16803)*
Johnston Precision Inc ....G...... 315 253-4181
  Auburn *(G-505)*
Kal Manufacturing Corporation ....E 585 265-4310
  Webster *(G-16726)*
KMA Corporation ....G...... 518 743-1330
  Glens Falls *(G-5685)*
L & L Precision Machining ....F 631 462-9587
  East Northport *(G-4440)*
M & S Precision Machine Co LLC ....F 518 747-1193
  Queensbury *(G-14004)*
Mar-A-Thon Filters Inc ....G...... 631 957-4774
  Lindenhurst *(G-7470)*
Micro Instrument Corp ....D 585 458-3150
  Rochester *(G-14507)*
Mitchell Machine Tool LLC ....G...... 585 254-7520
  Rochester *(G-14516)*
Mount Vernon Machine Inc ....E 845 268-9400
  Valley Cottage *(G-16382)*
Ms Spares LLC ....G...... 607 223-3024
  Clay *(G-3683)*
Neptune Machine Inc ....E 718 852-4100
  Brooklyn *(G-2357)*
New Age Precision Tech Inc ....E 631 588-1692
  Ronkonkoma *(G-14956)*
Nitro Manufacturing LLC ....G...... 716 646-9900
  North Collins *(G-12929)*
Optics Technology Inc ....G...... 585 586-0950
  Pittsford *(G-13571)*
Pgm of New England LLC ....D 585 458-4300
  Rochester *(G-14580)*
Precision Metals Corp ....E 631 586-5032
  Bay Shore *(G-727)*
Precision Systems Mfg Inc ....E 315 451-3480
  Liverpool *(G-7544)*
Progressive Mch & Design LLC ....C 585 924-5250
  Victor *(G-16497)*
Pronto Tool & Die Co Inc ....E 631 981-8920
  Ronkonkoma *(G-14972)*
Prz Technologies Inc ....F 716 683-1300
  Lancaster *(G-7334)*
Roccera LLC ....F 585 426-0887
  Rochester *(G-14632)*
Rochester Atomated Systems Inc ....E 585 594-3222
  Rochester *(G-14635)*
Saturn Industries Inc ....E 518 828-9956
  Hudson *(G-6632)*
Sick Inc ....E 585 347-2000
  Webster *(G-16735)*
Source Technologies ....F 718 708-0305
  Brooklyn *(G-2585)*
T R P Machine Inc ....E 631 567-9620
  Bohemia *(G-1141)*
Tioga Tool Inc ....E 607 785-6005
  Endicott *(G-4830)*
Tobeyco Manufacturing Co Inc ....F 607 962-2446
  Corning *(G-3983)*
Triple Point Manufacturing ....E 631 218-4988
  Bohemia *(G-1149)*
Triplett Machine Inc ....D 315 548-3198
  Phelps *(G-13537)*
Twinco Mfg Co Inc ....E 631 231-0022
  Hauppauge *(G-6219)*
Ultra Tool and Manufacturing ....F 585 467-3700
  Rochester *(G-14740)*
V Lake Industries Inc ....G...... 716 885-9141
  Buffalo *(G-3239)*
Vader Systems LLC ....G...... 716 636-1742
  East Amherst *(G-4363)*
Van Thomas Inc ....F 585 426-1414
  Rochester *(G-14751)*
Verns Machine Co Inc ....E 315 926-4223
  Marion *(G-8103)*
Village Decoration Ltd ....E 315 437-2522
  East Syracuse *(G-4579)*
Wordingham Machine Co Inc ....E 585 924-2294
  Rochester *(G-14766)*
Zip Products Inc ....F 585 482-0044
  Rochester *(G-14775)*

MACHINE TOOL ACCESS: Balancing Machines

Schenck Corporation ....D 631 242-4010
  Deer Park *(G-4205)*
Schenck Trebel Corp ....D 631 242-4397
  Deer Park *(G-4206)*

MACHINE TOOL ACCESS: Cams

Designatronics Incorporated ....G...... 516 328-3300
  New Hyde Park *(G-8825)*

MACHINE TOOL ACCESS: Cutting

Boro Park Cutting Tool Corp ....E 718 720-0610
  Staten Island *(G-15650)*
Champion Cutting Tool Corp ....E 516 536-8200
  Rockville Centre *(G-14789)*
Drill America Inc ....G...... 516 764-5700
  Oceanside *(G-13077)*
Dura-Mill Inc ....E 518 899-2255
  Ballston Spa *(G-595)*
Genesee Manufacturing Co Inc ....G...... 585 266-3201
  Rochester *(G-14394)*
Macinnes Tool Corporation ....E 585 467-1920
  Rochester *(G-14487)*
Morgood Tools Inc ....D 585 436-8828
  Rochester *(G-14522)*
NC Industries Inc ....F 248 528-5200
  Buffalo *(G-3082)*
Northeastern Water Jet Inc ....F 518 843-4988
  Amsterdam *(G-363)*
Rota File Corporation ....E 516 496-7200
  Syosset *(G-15838)*
Steiner Technologies Inc ....F 585 425-5910
  Fairport *(G-4880)*
Superior Tool Co Inc ....F 716 692-3900
  North Tonawanda *(G-12998)*

Employee Codes: A=Over 500 employees, B=251-500
C=101-250, D=51-100, E=20-50, F=10-19, G=5-9

MACHINE TOOL ACCESS: Diamond Cutting, For Turning, Etc

Advance D Tech Inc ....F 845 534-8248
  Cornwall *(G-3985)*

MACHINE TOOL ACCESS: Dies, Thread Cutting

Brinkman Intl Group Inc ....G 585 429-5000
  Rochester *(G-14245)*
C J Winter Machine Tech ....F 585 429-5000
  Rochester *(G-14254)*

MACHINE TOOL ACCESS: Dressing/Wheel Crushing Attach, Diamond

Scomac Inc ....F 585 494-2200
  Bergen *(G-852)*

MACHINE TOOL ACCESS: Drills

Truebite Inc ....F 607 786-3184
  Endicott *(G-4832)*

MACHINE TOOL ACCESS: Knives, Shear

Lancaster Knives Inc ....E 716 683-5050
  Lancaster *(G-7323)*

MACHINE TOOL ACCESS: Milling Machine Attachments

Innex Industries Inc ....E 585 247-3575
  Rochester *(G-14448)*

MACHINE TOOL ACCESS: Sockets

Socket Products Mfg Corp ....G 631 232-9870
  Islandia *(G-6803)*

MACHINE TOOL ACCESS: Tool Holders

New Market Products Co Inc ....F 607 292-6226
  Wayne *(G-16712)*
Robert J Faraone ....G 585 232-7160
  Rochester *(G-14630)*

MACHINE TOOL ACCESS: Tools & Access

Atwood Tool & Machine Inc ....E 607 648-6543
  Chenango Bridge *(G-3596)*
Fred M Velepec Co Inc ....E 718 821-6636
  Glendale *(G-5653)*
Fronhofer Tool Company Inc ....E 518 692-2496
  Cossayuna *(G-4055)*
Genius Tools Americas Corp ....F 716 662-6872
  Orchard Park *(G-13272)*
Huron TI & Cutter Grinding Co ....E 631 420-7000
  Farmingdale *(G-5008)*
JD Tool Inc ....G 607 786-3129
  Endicott *(G-4816)*
Methods Tooling & Mfg Inc ....E 845 246-7100
  Mount Marion *(G-8651)*
Rochling Advent Tool & Mold LP ....E 585 254-2000
  Rochester *(G-14654)*

MACHINE TOOL ATTACHMENTS & ACCESS

Curran Manufacturing Corp ....E 631 273-1010
  Hauppauge *(G-6059)*
Curran Manufacturing Corp ....E 631 273-1010
  Hauppauge *(G-6060)*
Flexbar Machine Corporation ....E 631 582-8440
  Islandia *(G-6793)*
Innovative Automation Inc ....F 631 439-3300
  Farmingdale *(G-5011)*
Jem Tool & Die Corp ....E 631 539-8734
  West Islip *(G-16905)*
Thuro Metal Products Inc ....E 631 435-0444
  Brentwood *(G-1196)*
Velmex Inc ....E 585 657-6151
  Bloomfield *(G-992)*
Willemin Macodel Incorporated ....F 914 345-3504
  Hawthorne *(G-6256)*

MACHINE TOOLS & ACCESS

Ale-Techniques Inc ....F 845 687-7200
  High Falls *(G-6399)*
American Linear Manufacturers ....E 516 333-1351
  Westbury *(G-16966)*

Baldwin Machine Works Inc ....G 631 842-9110
  Copiague *(G-3896)*
Bdp Industries Inc ....E 518 695-6851
  Greenwich *(G-5886)*
Bnm Product Service ....G 631 750-1586
  Holbrook *(G-6432)*
Circo File Corp ....E 516 922-1848
  Oyster Bay *(G-13367)*
Custom Service Solutions Inc ....G 585 637-3760
  Brockport *(G-1243)*
Dinosaw Inc ....E 518 828-9942
  Hudson *(G-6612)*
Dock Hardware Incorporated ....F 585 266-7920
  Rochester *(G-14314)*
Everfab Inc ....D 716 655-1550
  East Aurora *(G-4370)*
F W Roberts Mfg Co Inc ....F 716 434-3555
  Lockport *(G-7585)*
Flashflo Manufacturing Inc ....F 716 826-9500
  Buffalo *(G-2948)*
Flashflo Manufacturing Inc ....G 716 840-9594
  Buffalo *(G-2949)*
Gardei Industries LLC ....F 716 693-7100
  North Tonawanda *(G-12973)*
Germanow-Simon Corporation ....E 585 232-1440
  Rochester *(G-14399)*
Graywood Companies Inc ....E 585 254-7000
  Rochester *(G-14413)*
Griffin Manufacturing Company ....E 585 265-1991
  Webster *(G-16724)*
Heidenhain International Inc ....C 716 661-1700
  Jamestown *(G-6999)*
J H Robotics Inc ....E 607 729-3758
  Johnson City *(G-7096)*
JW Burg Machine & Tool Inc ....G 716 434-0015
  Clarence Center *(G-3678)*
Kps Capital Partners LP ....E 212 338-5100
  New York *(G-10883)*
Linde LLC ....D 716 773-7552
  Grand Island *(G-5763)*
M & S Precision Machine Co LLC ....F 518 747-1193
  Queensbury *(G-14004)*
Make-Waves Instrument Corp ....E 716 681-7524
  Depew *(G-4264)*
Michael Fiore Ltd ....G 516 561-8238
  Valley Stream *(G-16413)*
Micro Centric Corporation ....E 800 573-1139
  Plainview *(G-13621)*
Myles Tool Company Inc ....E 716 731-1300
  Sanborn *(G-15124)*
Parlec Inc ....C 585 425-4400
  Fairport *(G-4868)*
Precision Mechanisms Corp ....E 516 333-5955
  Westbury *(G-17021)*
Production Metal Cutting Inc ....F 585 458-7136
  Rochester *(G-14606)*
Ross JC Inc ....E 716 439-1161
  Lockport *(G-7612)*
S & S Machinery Corp ....E 718 492-7400
  Brooklyn *(G-2520)*
S S Precision Gear & Instr ....E 718 457-7474
  Corona *(G-4006)*
Seneca Falls Machine Tool Co ....D 315 568-5804
  Seneca Falls *(G-15369)*
Sinn- Tech Industries Inc ....F 631 643-1171
  West Babylon *(G-16827)*
Streamline Precision Inc ....G 585 421-9050
  Fairport *(G-4882)*
Strippit Inc ....C 716 542-5500
  Akron *(G-29)*
Transport National Dev Inc ....E 716 662-0270
  Orchard Park *(G-13300)*
Trident Precision Mfg Inc ....D 585 265-2010
  Webster *(G-16738)*
Universal Tooling Corporation ....F 716 985-4691
  Gerry *(G-5594)*
Vandilay Industries Inc ....E 631 226-3064
  West Babylon *(G-16838)*

MACHINE TOOLS, METAL CUTTING: Centering

Rush Machinery Inc ....G 585 554-3070
  Rushville *(G-15053)*

MACHINE TOOLS, METAL CUTTING: Exotic, Including Explosive

High Speed Hammer Company Inc ....F 585 266-4287
  Rochester *(G-14436)*

MACHINE TOOLS, METAL CUTTING: Grind, Polish, Buff, Lapp

Elmira Grinding Works Inc ....F 607 734-1579
  Wellsburg *(G-16747)*
Hartchrom Inc ....F 518 880-0411
  Watervliet *(G-16686)*
Mortech Industries Inc ....G 845 628-6138
  Mahopac *(G-7998)*

MACHINE TOOLS, METAL CUTTING: Home Workshop

Link Group Inc ....F 718 567-7082
  Brooklyn *(G-2228)*

MACHINE TOOLS, METAL CUTTING: Lathes

Zyp Precision LLC ....G 315 539-3667
  Waterloo *(G-16632)*

MACHINE TOOLS, METAL CUTTING: Numerically Controlled

Parlec Inc ....C 585 425-4400
  Fairport *(G-4868)*
Ppi Corp ....E 585 880-7277
  Geneseo *(G-5567)*
Precise Tool & Mfg Inc ....D 585 247-0700
  Rochester *(G-14591)*

MACHINE TOOLS, METAL CUTTING: Tool Replacement & Rpr Parts

Adria Machine & Tool Inc ....G 585 889-3360
  Scottsville *(G-15332)*
Welch Machine Inc ....G 585 647-3578
  Rochester *(G-14759)*

MACHINE TOOLS, METAL FORMING: Die Casting & Extruding

Raloid Tool Co Inc ....F 518 664-4261
  Mechanicville *(G-8230)*

MACHINE TOOLS, METAL FORMING: Electroforming

Precision Eforming LLC ....F 607 753-7730
  Cortland *(G-4040)*

MACHINE TOOLS, METAL FORMING: Forging Machinery & Hammers

Special Metals Corporation ....D 716 366-5663
  Dunkirk *(G-4351)*
Trueforge Global McHy Corp ....G 516 825-7040
  Rockville Centre *(G-14801)*

MACHINE TOOLS, METAL FORMING: Forming, Metal Deposit

Vader Systems LLC ....G 716 636-1742
  East Amherst *(G-4363)*

MACHINE TOOLS, METAL FORMING: Headers

American Racing Headers Inc ....E 631 608-1427
  Deer Park *(G-4096)*

MACHINE TOOLS, METAL FORMING: High Energy Rate

Alcoa Inc ....F 716 358-6451
  Falconer *(G-4890)*
Smart High Voltage Solutions ....F 631 563-6724
  Bohemia *(G-1135)*

MACHINE TOOLS, METAL FORMING: Presses, Hyd & Pneumatic

Servotec Usa LLC ....G 518 671-6120
  Hudson *(G-6634)*

MACHINE TOOLS, METAL FORMING: Pressing

Mpi Incorporated ....D 845 471-7630
  Poughkeepsie *(G-13918)*

MACHINE TOOLS, METAL FORMING: Punching & Shearing

Manhasset Tool & Die Co Inc..............F........716 684-6066
  Lancaster *(G-7325)*

MACHINE TOOLS, METAL FORMING: Rebuilt

Uhmac Inc..F........716 537-2343
  Holland *(G-6485)*

MACHINE TOOLS, METAL FORMING: Spinning, Spline Rollg/Windg

Gemcor Automation LLC................D........716 674-9300
  West Seneca *(G-16946)*

MACHINE TOOLS: Metal Cutting

Abtex Corporation.............................E........315 536-7403
  Dresden *(G-4318)*
Advanced Machine Design Co Inc....E........716 826-2000
  Buffalo *(G-2800)*
Alpine Machine Inc............................F........607 272-1344
  Ithaca *(G-6818)*
Alternative Service Inc......................F........631 345-9500
  Yaphank *(G-17385)*
Alton Manufacturing Inc...................D........585 458-2600
  Rochester *(G-14194)*
Ascension Industries Inc...................D........716 693-9381
  North Tonawanda *(G-12956)*
Aztec Mfg of Rochester....................G........585 352-8152
  Spencerport *(G-15565)*
Brinkman Products Inc.....................B........585 235-4545
  Rochester *(G-14246)*
Coastel Cable Tools Inc....................E........315 471-5361
  Syracuse *(G-15899)*
Crowley Fabg Machining Co Inc......G........607 484-0299
  Endicott *(G-4799)*
Dinosaw Inc.......................................E........518 828-9942
  Hudson *(G-6612)*
East Coast Tool & Mfg......................G........716 826-5183
  Buffalo *(G-2927)*
Gallery of Machines LLC..................G........607 849-6028
  Marathon *(G-8083)*
Gb Aero Engine LLC..........................B........914 925-9600
  Rye *(G-15057)*
Genco John..G........716 483-5446
  Jamestown *(G-6994)*
Gleason Corporation........................A........585 473-1000
  Rochester *(G-14407)*
Graywood Companies Inc................E........585 254-7000
  Rochester *(G-14413)*
H S Assembly Inc..............................G........585 266-4287
  Rochester *(G-14416)*
Halpern Tool Corp.............................G........914 633-0038
  New Rochelle *(G-8908)*
Hardinge Inc......................................C........607 734-2281
  Elmira *(G-4688)*
IPC/Razor LLC...................................D........212 551-4500
  New York *(G-10654)*
Ish Precision Machine Corp.............F........718 436-8858
  Brooklyn *(G-2116)*
J Vogler Enterprise LLC....................F........585 247-1625
  Rochester *(G-14457)*
Jalex Industries Ltd..........................F........631 491-5072
  West Babylon *(G-16800)*
Kps Capital Partners LP...................E........212 338-5100
  New York *(G-10883)*
Kyocera Precision Tools Inc............F........607 687-0012
  Owego *(G-13353)*
Lancaster Knives Inc........................E........716 683-5050
  Lancaster *(G-7323)*
Lk Industries Inc...............................G........716 941-9202
  Glenwood *(G-5703)*
Lubow Machine Corp........................F........631 226-1700
  Copiague *(G-3911)*
Montrose Equipment Sales Inc........F........718 388-7446
  Brooklyn *(G-2332)*
Multimatic Products Inc..................D........800 767-7633
  Ronkonkoma *(G-14947)*
Munson Machinery Company Inc...E........315 797-0090
  Utica *(G-16350)*
Myles Tool Company Inc..................F........716 731-1300
  Sanborn *(G-15124)*
Nifty Bar Grinding & Cutting...........E........585 381-0450
  Penfield *(G-13501)*
Omega Consolidated Corporation..E........585 392-9262
  Hilton *(G-6419)*
P & R Industries Inc.........................E........585 266-6725
  Rochester *(G-14562)*
Producto Corporation.......................C........716 484-7131
  Jamestown *(G-7024)*
R Steiner Technologies Inc..............E........585 425-5912
  Fairport *(G-4875)*
Rapid Precision Machining Inc........D........585 467-0780
  Rochester *(G-14620)*
S & S Machinery Corp.......................E........718 492-7400
  Brooklyn *(G-2520)*
S & S Machinery Corp.......................E........718 492-7400
  Brooklyn *(G-2521)*
Selflock Screw Products Co Inc......E........315 541-1464
  Syracuse *(G-16037)*
Seneca Falls Capital Inc..................G........315 568-5804
  Seneca Falls *(G-15368)*
Seneca Falls Machine Tool Co.........D........315 568-5804
  Seneca Falls *(G-15369)*
Simmons Machine Tool Corp...........C........518 462-5431
  Menands *(G-8378)*
Superior Motion Controls Inc..........E........516 420-2921
  Farmingdale *(G-5120)*
Teka Precision Inc............................G........845 753-1900
  Nyack *(G-13055)*
Transport National Dev Inc.............E........716 662-0270
  Orchard Park *(G-13299)*
Truemade Products Inc....................G........631 981-4755
  Ronkonkoma *(G-14993)*
Verns Machine Co Inc......................E........315 926-4223
  Marion *(G-8103)*
World LLC...F........631 940-9121
  Deer Park *(G-4229)*
Zwack Incorporated.........................E........518 733-5135
  Stephentown *(G-15758)*

MACHINE TOOLS: Metal Forming

Adaptive Mfg Tech Inc......................E........631 580-5400
  Ronkonkoma *(G-14850)*
Advanced Engineered Products.......F........631 435-3535
  Bay Shore *(G-666)*
Advanced Machine Design Co Inc....E........716 826-2000
  Buffalo *(G-2800)*
Advantage Metalwork Finshg LLC..D........585 454-0160
  Rochester *(G-14180)*
Austin Industries Inc........................G........585 589-1353
  Albion *(G-162)*
Bdp Industries Inc.............................E........518 695-6851
  Greenwich *(G-5886)*
Brinkman Intl Group Inc...................G........585 429-5000
  Rochester *(G-14245)*
Buffalo Machine Tls of Niagara........F........716 201-1310
  Lockport *(G-7574)*
C & T Tool & Instrument Co.............E........718 429-1253
  Woodside *(G-17321)*
C J Winter Machine Tech.................F........585 429-5000
  Rochester *(G-14254)*
Commodore Manufacutring Corp....E........718 788-2600
  Brooklyn *(G-1795)*
Dover Global Holdings Inc...............E........212 922-1640
  New York *(G-9912)*
Ecko Fin & Tooling Inc.....................F........716 487-0200
  Jamestown *(G-6990)*
Gh Induction Atmospheres LLC......E........585 368-2120
  Rochester *(G-14402)*
Hydramec Inc....................................E........585 593-5190
  Scio *(G-15321)*
Lourdes Systems Inc........................E........631 234-7077
  Hauppauge *(G-6122)*
Lubow Machine Corp........................F........631 226-1700
  Copiague *(G-3911)*
Miller Mechanical Services Inc.......E........518 792-0430
  Glens Falls *(G-5690)*
Prim Hall Enterprises Inc.................F........518 561-7408
  Plattsburgh *(G-13691)*
Producto Corporation.......................C........716 484-7131
  Jamestown *(G-7024)*
Schaefer Machine Co Inc.................E........516 248-6880
  Mineola *(G-8537)*
Standard Paper Box Machine Co.....E........718 328-3300
  Bronx *(G-1463)*
Strippit Inc..C........716 542-5500
  Akron *(G-29)*
Taumel Metalforming Corp..............E........845 878-3100
  Patterson *(G-13445)*

MACHINERY & EQPT, AGRICULTURAL, WHOLESALE: Dairy

Brook North Farms Inc.....................F........315 834-9390
  Auburn *(G-487)*

MACHINERY & EQPT, AGRICULTURAL, WHOLESALE: Landscaping Eqpt

Graymont Materials (ny) Inc............F........315 265-8036
  Plattsburgh *(G-13666)*
Scotts Company LLC........................E........631 289-7444
  Yaphank *(G-17400)*

MACHINERY & EQPT, AGRICULTURAL, WHOLESALE: Lawn & Garden

Rhett M Clark Inc.............................G........585 538-9570
  Caledonia *(G-3281)*

MACHINERY & EQPT, INDL, WHOL: Controlling Instruments/Access

Unimar Inc..F........315 699-4400
  Syracuse *(G-16063)*

MACHINERY & EQPT, INDL, WHOL: Recording Instruments/Access

His Productions USA Inc.................G........212 594-3737
  New York *(G-10483)*

MACHINERY & EQPT, INDL, WHOLESALE: Conveyor Systems

Vetra Systems Corporation.............G........631 434-3185
  Hauppauge *(G-6224)*

MACHINERY & EQPT, INDL, WHOLESALE: Countersinks

Empire Fabricators Inc....................G........585 235-3050
  Rochester *(G-14346)*
Nlr Counter Tops LLC.......................G........347 295-0410
  New York *(G-11446)*

MACHINERY & EQPT, INDL, WHOLESALE: Fans

Canarm Ltd.......................................G........800 267-4427
  Ogdensburg *(G-13113)*

MACHINERY & EQPT, INDL, WHOLESALE: Food Manufacturing

Vr Food Equipment Inc....................F........315 531-8133
  Penn Yan *(G-13522)*

MACHINERY & EQPT, INDL, WHOLESALE: Food Product Manufacturng

Crepini LLC.......................................E........347 422-0829
  Brooklyn *(G-1817)*
ET Oakes Corporation......................E........631 630-9837
  Hauppauge *(G-6074)*
Hobart Corporation...........................E........631 864-3440
  Commack *(G-3835)*

MACHINERY & EQPT, INDL, WHOLESALE: Heat Exchange

Aavid Niagara LLC...........................F........716 297-0652
  Niagara Falls *(G-12794)*

MACHINERY & EQPT, INDL, WHOLESALE: Hoists

Vortek Tel 87724633365859............E........585 924-5000
  Victor *(G-16511)*

MACHINERY & EQPT, INDL, WHOLESALE: Hydraulic Systems

Ener-G-Rotors Inc.............................G........518 372-2608
  Schenectady *(G-15250)*
Triumph Actuation Systems LLC...D........516 378-0162
  Freeport *(G-5432)*

MACHINERY & EQPT, INDL, WHOLESALE: Indl Machine Parts

Alternative Service Inc....................F........631 345-9500
  Yaphank *(G-17385)*
Rpb Distributors LLC........................G........914 244-3600
  Mount Kisco *(G-8645)*

MACHINERY & EQPT, INDL, WHOLESALE: Instruments & Cntrl Eqpt

Carl Zeiss Inc .... C 914 747-1800
 Thornwood (G-16117)
Winters Instruments Inc .... E 281 880-8607
 Tonawanda (G-16215)

MACHINERY & EQPT, INDL, WHOLESALE: Machine Tools & Access

Cementex Latex Corp .... F 212 741-1770
 New York (G-9558)
Curran Manufacturing Corp .... E 631 273-1010
 Hauppauge (G-6059)
NC Industries Inc .... F 248 528-5200
 Buffalo (G-3082)
S & S Machinery Corp .... E 718 492-7400
 Brooklyn (G-2521)

MACHINERY & EQPT, INDL, WHOLESALE: Measure/Test, Electric

Mausner Equipment Co Inc .... C 631 689-7358
 Setauket (G-15377)

MACHINERY & EQPT, INDL, WHOLESALE: Metal Refining

Metal Finishing Supply Inc .... G 315 655-8068
 Canastota (G-3369)

MACHINERY & EQPT, INDL, WHOLESALE: Packaging

Millwood Inc .... F 518 233-1475
 Waterford (G-16614)
Modern Packaging Inc .... D 631 595-2437
 Deer Park (G-4175)

MACHINERY & EQPT, INDL, WHOLESALE: Paint Spray

Inglis Co Inc .... G 315 475-1315
 Syracuse (G-15963)

MACHINERY & EQPT, INDL, WHOLESALE: Pneumatic Tools

U S Air Tool Co Inc .... E 631 471-3300
 Ronkonkoma (G-14994)

MACHINERY & EQPT, INDL, WHOLESALE: Power Plant Machinery

Ultravolt Inc .... D 631 471-4444
 Ronkonkoma (G-14996)

MACHINERY & EQPT, INDL, WHOLESALE: Processing & Packaging

National Equipment Corporation .... F 718 585-0200
 Bronx (G-1405)
National Equipment Corporation .... E 718 585-0200
 Bronx (G-1406)

MACHINERY & EQPT, INDL, WHOLESALE: Robots

Automated Cells & Eqp Inc .... D 607 936-1431
 Painted Post (G-13389)

MACHINERY & EQPT, INDL, WHOLESALE: Safety Eqpt

Traffic Logix Corporation .... G 866 915-6449
 Spring Valley (G-15603)

MACHINERY & EQPT, INDL, WHOLESALE: Textile

John A Eberly Inc .... G 315 449-3034
 Syracuse (G-15967)
Sml USA Inc .... E 212 736-8800
 New York (G-12107)

MACHINERY & EQPT, INDL, WHOLESALE: Water Pumps

Air Flow Pump Corp .... G 718 241-2800
 Brooklyn (G-1571)

MACHINERY & EQPT, INDL, WHOLESALE: Woodworking

Putnam Rolling Ladder Co Inc .... F 212 226-5147
 New York (G-11755)

MACHINERY & EQPT, WHOLESALE: Construction, General

Zwack Incorporated .... E 518 733-5135
 Stephentown (G-15758)

MACHINERY & EQPT, WHOLESALE: Contractors Materials

Gny Equipment LLC .... F 631 667-1010
 Bay Shore (G-703)

MACHINERY & EQPT, WHOLESALE: Crushing, Pulverizng & Screeng

American Material Processing .... G 315 318-0017
 Clifton Springs (G-3713)

MACHINERY & EQPT, WHOLESALE: Masonry

Arnan Development Corp .... D 607 432-6641
 Oneonta (G-13171)
Duke Concrete Products Inc .... E 518 793-7743
 Queensbury (G-13995)
Inwood Material .... F 516 371-1842
 Inwood (G-6759)
Palumbo Block Co Inc .... E 845 832-6100
 Dover Plains (G-4316)

MACHINERY & EQPT: Electroplating

Caswell Inc .... F 315 946-1213
 Lyons (G-7970)
Digital Matrix Corp .... E 516 481-7990
 Farmingdale (G-4978)
Precision Process Inc .... D 716 731-1587
 Niagara Falls (G-12864)
Sonicor Inc .... F 631 920-6555
 West Babylon (G-16830)
Technic Inc .... F 516 349-0700
 Plainview (G-13638)

MACHINERY & EQPT: Farm

Asp Blade Intrmdate Hldngs Inc .... G 212 476-8000
 New York (G-9234)
Don Beck Inc .... G 585 493-3040
 Castile (G-3416)
Eastern Welding Inc .... G 631 727-0306
 Riverhead (G-14142)
Haines Equipment Inc .... E 607 566-8531
 Avoca (G-537)
House of The Foaming Case Inc .... G 718 454-0101
 Saint Albans (G-15083)
Oxbo International Corporation .... D 585 548-2665
 Byron (G-3269)
Plant-Tech2o Inc .... G 516 483-7845
 Hempstead (G-6285)
Road Cases USA Inc .... E 631 563-0633
 Bohemia (G-1126)
Zappala Farms AG Systems Inc .... E 315 626-6293
 Cato (G-3425)

MACHINERY & EQPT: Gas Producers, Generators/Other Rltd Eqpt

Audubon Machinery Corporation .... D 716 564-5165
 North Tonawanda (G-12957)
Mep Alaska LLC .... G 646 535-9005
 Brooklyn (G-2297)

MACHINERY & EQPT: Liquid Automation

Crandall Filling Machinery Inc .... G 716 897-3486
 Buffalo (G-2892)

MACHINERY & EQPT: Metal Finishing, Plating Etc

Cameo Metal Products Inc .... E 718 788-1106
 Brooklyn (G-1751)
P K G Equipment Incorporated .... E 585 436-4650
 Rochester (G-14564)
Qes Solutions Inc .... D 585 254-8693
 Rochester (G-14611)
R & B Machinery Corp .... G 716 894-3332
 Buffalo (G-3151)
Tompkins Metal Finishing Inc .... D 585 344-2600
 Batavia (G-650)

MACHINERY BASES

American Standard Mfg Inc .... E 518 868-2512
 Central Bridge (G-3482)
Brzozka Industries Inc .... F 631 588-8164
 Holbrook (G-6434)
Cleveland Polymer Tech LLC .... G 518 326-9146
 Watervliet (G-16682)
Kefa Industries Group Inc .... G 718 568-9297
 Rego Park (G-14034)
Machinery Mountings Inc .... F 631 851-0480
 Hauppauge (G-6123)
Win-Holt Equipment Corp .... C 516 222-0433
 Garden City (G-5537)

MACHINERY, COMMERCIAL LAUNDRY: Dryers, Incl Coin-Operated

Maxi Companies Inc .... G 315 446-1002
 De Witt (G-4083)

MACHINERY, COMMERCIAL LAUNDRY: Washing, Incl Coin-Operated

G A Braun Inc .... D 315 475-3123
 North Syracuse (G-12943)
Lynx Product Group LLC .... E 716 751-3100
 Wilson (G-17268)
Pressure Washing Services Inc .... G 607 286-7458
 Milford (G-8474)

MACHINERY, EQPT & SUPPLIES: Parking Facility

Automotion Parking Systems LLC ...... G 516 565-5600
 West Hempstead (G-16850)

MACHINERY, FOOD PRDTS: Beverage

Brooklyn Brew Shop LLC .... F 718 874-0119
 Brooklyn (G-1722)
Kedco .... F 516 454-7800
 Farmingdale (G-5025)
US Beverage Net Inc .... F 315 579-2025
 Syracuse (G-16065)

MACHINERY, FOOD PRDTS: Choppers, Commercial

Mary F Morse .... G 315 866-2741
 Mohawk (G-8542)

MACHINERY, FOOD PRDTS: Cutting, Chopping, Grinding, Mixing

ET Oakes Corporation .... E 631 630-9837
 Hauppauge (G-6074)

MACHINERY, FOOD PRDTS: Dairy & Milk

Chemicolloid Laboratories Inc .... F 516 747-2666
 New Hyde Park (G-8821)

MACHINERY, FOOD PRDTS: Dairy, Pasteurizing

Goodnature Products Inc .... F 716 855-3325
 Orchard Park (G-13273)

MACHINERY, FOOD PRDTS: Food Processing, Smokers

Bonduelle USA Inc .... E 585 948-5252
 Oakfield (G-13064)
Los Olivos Ltd .... F 631 773-6439
 Farmingdale (G-5037)

PRODUCT SECTION

MACHINERY, WOODWORKING: Pattern Makers'

Precision Consulting ....G....... 631 727-0847
  Riverhead *(G-14152)*

MACHINERY, FOOD PRDTS: Juice Extractors, Fruit & Veg, Comm
Juice Press LLC ....G....... 212 777-0034
  New York *(G-10780)*

MACHINERY, FOOD PRDTS: Milk Processing, NEC
Delaval Inc ....F....... 585 599-4696
  Corfu *(G-3954)*

MACHINERY, FOOD PRDTS: Mixers, Commercial
Expert Industries Inc ....E....... 718 434-6060
  Brooklyn *(G-1946)*

MACHINERY, FOOD PRDTS: Oilseed Crushing & Extracting
Caravella Food Corp ....F....... 646 552-0455
  Whitestone *(G-17204)*

MACHINERY, FOOD PRDTS: Ovens, Bakery
Home Maide Inc ....F....... 845 837-1700
  Harriman *(G-5972)*
Hotrock Ovens LLC ....F....... 917 224-4342
  Red Hook *(G-14029)*
Mohawk Valley Manufacturing ...G....... 315 797-0851
  Frankfort *(G-5355)*
Richard H Williams Associates ...G....... 631 751-4156
  Setauket *(G-15379)*
Zaro Bake Shop Inc ....D....... 212 292-0175
  New York *(G-12705)*

MACHINERY, FOOD PRDTS: Packing House
Desu Machinery Corporation .....D....... 716 681-5798
  Depew *(G-4255)*

MACHINERY, FOOD PRDTS: Presses, Cheese, Beet, Cider & Sugar
Blue Toad Hard Cider ....E....... 585 424-5508
  Rochester *(G-14237)*

MACHINERY, FOOD PRDTS: Roasting, Coffee, Peanut, Etc.
Wired Coffee and Bagel Inc ......F....... 518 506-3194
  Malta *(G-8022)*

MACHINERY, MAILING: Canceling
Action Technologies Inc ....G....... 718 278-1000
  Long Island City *(G-7648)*

MACHINERY, MAILING: Postage Meters
Neopost USA Inc ....E....... 631 435-9100
  Hauppauge *(G-6146)*
Pitney Bowes Inc ....E....... 212 564-7548
  New York *(G-11667)*
Pitney Bowes Inc ....E....... 203 356-5000
  New York *(G-11668)*
Pitney Bowes Inc ....E....... 516 822-0900
  Hicksville *(G-6389)*

MACHINERY, METALWORKING: Assembly, Including Robotic
Alliance Automation Systems ....C....... 585 426-2700
  Rochester *(G-14188)*
Hover-Davis Inc ....C....... 585 352-9590
  Rochester *(G-14439)*
Manufacturing Resources Inc ...E....... 631 481-0041
  Rochester *(G-14493)*
Mold-A-Matic Corporation ....E....... 607 433-2121
  Oneonta *(G-13189)*
Pace Technology Inc ....E....... 631 981-2400
  Ronkonkoma *(G-14963)*
Tessy Plastics Corp ....B....... 315 689-3924
  Skaneateles *(G-15466)*
Unidex Corporation Western NY ...F....... 585 786-3170
  Warsaw *(G-16584)*
Van Blarcom Closures Inc ....C....... 718 855-3810
  Brooklyn *(G-2718)*

MACHINERY, METALWORKING: Cutting & Slitting
Expert Metal Slitters Corp ....G....... 718 361-2735
  Long Island City *(G-7736)*

MACHINERY, OFFICE: Perforators
Cummins - Allison Corp ....D....... 718 263-2482
  Kew Gardens *(G-7159)*

MACHINERY, OFFICE: Stapling, Hand Or Power
Staplex Company Inc ....E....... 718 768-3333
  Brooklyn *(G-2598)*

MACHINERY, OFFICE: Time Clocks & Time Recording Devices
Central Time Clock Inc ....F....... 718 784-4900
  Long Island City *(G-7696)*
Widmer Time Recorder Company ...F....... 212 227-0405
  New York *(G-12631)*

MACHINERY, OFFICE: Typing & Word Processing
Magnetic Technologies Corp ......D....... 585 385-9010
  Rochester *(G-14490)*

MACHINERY, PACKAGING: Canning, Food
Reynolds Packaging McHy Inc ....D....... 716 358-6451
  Falconer *(G-4910)*

MACHINERY, PACKAGING: Carton Packing
Niagara Scientific Inc ....D....... 315 437-0821
  East Syracuse *(G-4552)*

MACHINERY, PACKAGING: Packing & Wrapping
Fourteen Arnold Ave Corp ....F....... 315 272-1700
  Utica *(G-16333)*
Turbofil Packaging Mchs LLC .....F....... 914 239-3878
  Mount Vernon *(G-8743)*

MACHINERY, PAPER INDUSTRY: Converting, Die Cutting & Stampng
Friedel Paper Box & Converting ...G....... 315 437-3325
  Baldwinsville *(G-569)*
Richlar Industries Inc ....F....... 315 463-5144
  East Syracuse *(G-4559)*
Rsb Associates Inc ....F....... 518 281-5067
  Altamont *(G-212)*
Superior Plus Cnstr Pdts Corp ...F....... 315 463-5144
  East Syracuse *(G-4569)*

MACHINERY, PAPER INDUSTRY: Paper Mill, Plating, Etc
F W Roberts Mfg Co Inc ....F....... 716 434-3555
  Lockport *(G-7585)*
Sonicor Inc ....F....... 631 920-6555
  West Babylon *(G-16830)*

MACHINERY, PRINTING TRADES: Copy Holders
Copy4les Inc ....F....... 212 487-9778
  New York *(G-9722)*
Exacta LLC ....G....... 716 406-2303
  Clarence Center *(G-3675)*

MACHINERY, PRINTING TRADES: Plates
C M E Corp ....F....... 315 451-7101
  Syracuse *(G-15881)*
Csw Inc ....F....... 585 247-4010
  Rochester *(G-14293)*
Impressions International Inc ....G....... 585 442-5240
  Rochester *(G-14447)*
Rubber Stamps Inc ....E....... 212 675-1180
  Mineola *(G-8535)*

MACHINERY, PRINTING TRADES: Plates, Offset
Apexx Omni-Graphics Inc ....D....... 718 326-3330
  Maspeth *(G-8119)*
Total Offset Inc ....F....... 212 966-4482
  New York *(G-12379)*

MACHINERY, PRINTING TRADES: Presses, Envelope
A C Envelope Inc ....G....... 516 420-0646
  Farmingdale *(G-4926)*

MACHINERY, PRINTING TRADES: Printing Trade Parts & Attchts
Lexar Global LLC ....G....... 845 352-9700
  Valley Cottage *(G-16381)*
Rollers Inc ....G....... 716 837-0700
  Buffalo *(G-3164)*

MACHINERY, PRINTING TRADES: Sticks
Bmp America Inc ....C....... 585 798-0950
  Medina *(G-8267)*

MACHINERY, SEWING: Sewing & Hat & Zipper Making
Cvd Equipment Corporation ....E....... 845 246-3631
  Saugerties *(G-15182)*

MACHINERY, TEXTILE: Beaming
Sharmeen Textile Inc ....G....... 646 298-5757
  New York *(G-12046)*

MACHINERY, TEXTILE: Card Cutting, Jacquard
Mjk Cutting Inc ....F....... 718 384-7613
  Brooklyn *(G-2323)*

MACHINERY, TEXTILE: Embroidery
Herrmann Group LLC ....G....... 716 876-9798
  Kenmore *(G-7148)*

MACHINERY, TEXTILE: Silk Screens
Angel Textiles Inc ....G....... 212 532-0900
  New York *(G-9156)*
Big Apple Sign Corp ....E....... 631 342-0303
  Islandia *(G-6788)*
Screen Team Inc ....F....... 718 786-2424
  Long Island City *(G-7873)*
Viewsport Inc ....G....... 585 738-6803
  Penfield *(G-13505)*

MACHINERY, TEXTILE: Thread Making Or Spinning
Thread Check Inc ....D....... 631 231-1515
  Hauppauge *(G-6214)*

MACHINERY, WOODWORKING: Bandsaws
Phoenix Wood Wrights Ltd ....F....... 631 727-9691
  Riverhead *(G-14151)*

MACHINERY, WOODWORKING: Furniture Makers
Casa Nueva Custom Furnishing ...G....... 914 476-2272
  Yonkers *(G-17425)*
Downtown Interiors Inc ....F....... 212 337-0230
  New York *(G-9918)*

MACHINERY, WOODWORKING: Lathes, Wood Turning Includes Access
Hardinge Inc ....C....... 607 734-2281
  Elmira *(G-4688)*

MACHINERY, WOODWORKING: Pattern Makers'
Corbett Stves Pttern Works Inc ...E....... 585 546-7109
  Rochester *(G-14289)*

MACHINERY, WOODWORKING: Sanding, Exc Portable Floor Sanders

MACHINERY, WOODWORKING: Sanding, Exc Portable Floor Sanders

US Sander LLC .... G 518 875-9157
  Esperance *(G-4839)*

MACHINERY: Ammunition & Explosives Loading

Eastend Enforcement Products .... G 631 878-8424
  Center Moriches *(G-3465)*

MACHINERY: Assembly, Exc Metalworking

Alliance Automation Systems .... C 585 426-2700
  Rochester *(G-14188)*
Distech Systems Inc .... G 585 254-7020
  Rochester *(G-14311)*
Dynamasters Inc .... G 585 458-9970
  Rochester *(G-14321)*
Griffin Automation Inc .... E 716 674-2300
  West Seneca *(G-16948)*
Hubco Inc .... G 716 683-5940
  Alden *(G-179)*
Lubow Machine Corp .... F 631 226-1700
  Copiague *(G-3911)*
Machine Tool Repair & Sales .... G 631 580-2550
  Holbrook *(G-6460)*
New Vision Industries Inc .... F 607 687-7700
  Endicott *(G-4820)*
Quality Manufacturing Sys LLC .... G 716 763-0988
  Lakewood *(G-7292)*
Rfb Associates Inc .... G 518 271-0551
  Voorheesville *(G-16517)*
Trident Precision Mfg Inc .... D 585 265-2010
  Webster *(G-16738)*
Veeco Process Equipment Inc .... G 516 677-0200
  Plainview *(G-13645)*

MACHINERY: Automotive Maintenance

Blue Star Products Inc .... F 631 952-3204
  Hauppauge *(G-6036)*
Glass Star America Inc .... F 631 291-9432
  Center Moriches *(G-3466)*

MACHINERY: Automotive Related

B&K Precision Corporation .... G 631 369-2665
  Manorville *(G-8077)*
Eltee Tool & Die Co .... F 607 748-4301
  Endicott *(G-4801)*
Hitachi Metals America Ltd .... E 914 694-9200
  Purchase *(G-13959)*
Reefer Tek Llc .... F 347 590-1067
  Bronx *(G-1440)*
Rfb Associates Inc .... G 518 271-0551
  Voorheesville *(G-16517)*
Riverview Associates Inc .... G 585 235-5980
  Rochester *(G-14628)*

MACHINERY: Billing

Gary Roth & Associates Ltd .... E 516 333-1000
  Westbury *(G-16990)*

MACHINERY: Bottling & Canning

Pb Leiner-USA .... G 516 822-4040
  Plainview *(G-13627)*

MACHINERY: Brewery & Malting

Singlecut Beersmiths LLC .... F 718 606-0788
  Astoria *(G-456)*
Zahm & Nagel Co Inc .... G 716 833-1532
  Holland *(G-6486)*

MACHINERY: Bridge Or Gate, Hydraulic

Island Automated Gate Co LLC .... G 631 425-0196
  Huntington Station *(G-6711)*

MACHINERY: Concrete Prdts

Northrock Industries Inc .... E 631 924-6130
  Bohemia *(G-1112)*

MACHINERY: Construction

AAAA York Inc .... F 718 784-6666
  Long Island City *(G-7645)*
Air-Flo Mfg Co Inc .... D 607 733-8284
  Elmira *(G-4670)*

Anderson Equipment Company .... D 716 877-1992
  Tonawanda *(G-16139)*
Asp Blade Intrmdate Hldngs Inc .... G 212 476-8000
  New York *(G-9234)*
BW Elliott Mfg Co LLC .... B 607 772-0404
  Binghamton *(G-900)*
Capitol Eq 2 LLC .... G 518 886-8341
  Saratoga Springs *(G-15148)*
CCS Machinery Inc .... F 631 968-0900
  Bay Shore *(G-681)*
Ceno Technologies Inc .... G 716 885-5050
  Buffalo *(G-2869)*
Cooper Industries LLC .... G 315 477-7000
  Syracuse *(G-15909)*
Diamond Coring & Cutting Inc .... G 718 381-4545
  Maspeth *(G-9911)*
Dover Global Holdings Inc .... E 212 922-1640
  New York *(G-9912)*
ET Oakes Corporation .... E 631 630-9837
  Hauppauge *(G-6074)*
Line Ward Corporation .... G 716 675-7373
  Buffalo *(G-3049)*
Mettle Concept Inc .... G 888 501-0680
  New York *(G-11243)*
Oswald Manufacturing Co Inc .... E 516 883-8850
  Port Washington *(G-13849)*
Penn State Metal Fabri .... G 718 786-8814
  Brooklyn *(G-2415)*
Pier-Tech Inc .... E 516 442-5420
  Oceanside *(G-13089)*
Precision Product Inc .... G 718 852-7127
  Brooklyn *(G-2436)*
Ziegler Truck & Diesl Repr Inc .... G 315 782-7278
  Watertown *(G-16676)*

MACHINERY: Cryogenic, Industrial

Cryomech Inc .... D 315 455-2555
  Syracuse *(G-15914)*
General Cryogenic Tech LLC .... F 516 334-8200
  Westbury *(G-16991)*

MACHINERY: Custom

Accede Mold & Tool Co Inc .... D 585 254-6490
  Rochester *(G-14165)*
Acro Industries Inc .... C 585 254-3661
  Rochester *(G-14171)*
Adaptive Mfg Tech Inc .... E 631 580-5400
  Ronkonkoma *(G-14850)*
Advanced Aerospace Machining .... G 631 694-7745
  Farmingdale *(G-4930)*
Aloi Solutions LLC .... E 585 292-0920
  Rochester *(G-14192)*
American Linear Manufacturers .... F 516 333-1351
  Westbury *(G-16966)*
Armstrong Mold Corporation .... D 315 437-1517
  East Syracuse *(G-4505)*
Auburn Bearing & Mfg Inc .... G 315 986-7600
  Macedon *(G-7982)*
Calvary Design Team Inc .... C 585 347-6127
  Webster *(G-16714)*
Chart Inc .... F 518 272-3565
  Troy *(G-16230)*
Chocovision Corporation .... F 845 473-4970
  Poughkeepsie *(G-13893)*
Converter Design Inc .... G 518 745-7138
  Glens Falls *(G-5675)*
Duetto Integrated Systems Inc .... F 631 851-0102
  Islandia *(G-6792)*
Dynak Inc .... F 585 271-2255
  Churchville *(G-3636)*
Endicott Precision Inc .... C 607 754-7076
  Endicott *(G-4803)*
Finesse Creations Inc .... F 718 692-2100
  Brooklyn *(G-1973)*
Hebeler Corporation .... C 716 873-9300
  Tonawanda *(G-16171)*
Interactive Instruments Inc .... G 518 347-0955
  Scotia *(G-15326)*
International Climbing Mchs .... G 607 288-4001
  Ithaca *(G-6852)*
J Soehner Corporation .... F 516 599-2534
  Rockville Centre *(G-14793)*
Jet Sew Corporation .... F 315 896-2683
  Barneveld *(G-614)*
Keller Technology Corporation .... C 716 693-3840
  Tonawanda *(G-16175)*
Keyes Machine Works Inc .... G 585 426-5059
  Gates *(G-5561)*
McGuigan Inc .... E 631 750-6222
  Bohemia *(G-1103)*

Modern Packaging Inc .... D 631 595-2437
  Deer Park *(G-4175)*
Ms Machining Inc .... G 607 723-1105
  Binghamton *(G-938)*
R E F Precision Products .... F 631 242-4471
  Deer Park *(G-4196)*
Rand Machine Products Inc .... D 716 665-5217
  Falconer *(G-4908)*
Roboshop Inc .... G 315 437-6454
  Syracuse *(G-16024)*
Tricon Machine LLC .... G 585 671-0679
  Webster *(G-16737)*
Voss Manufacturing Inc .... D 716 731-5062
  Sanborn *(G-15130)*
W H Jones & Son Inc .... F 716 875-8233
  Kenmore *(G-7151)*
W J Albro Machine Works Inc .... G 631 345-0657
  Yaphank *(G-17408)*
Washburn Manufacturing Tech .... G 607 387-3991
  Trumansburg *(G-16268)*
Wendt Corporation .... D 716 391-1200
  Buffalo *(G-3251)*

MACHINERY: Drill Presses

Baldwin Machine Works Inc .... G 631 842-9110
  Copiague *(G-3896)*

MACHINERY: Electronic Component Making

Designatronics Incorporated .... G 516 328-3300
  New Hyde Park *(G-8825)*
Esc Control Electronics LLC .... G 631 467-5328
  Sayville *(G-15207)*
James Morris .... E 315 824-8519
  Hamilton *(G-5948)*
Multiline Technology Inc .... C 631 249-8300
  Ronkonkoma *(G-14946)*
Sj Associates Inc .... E 516 942-3232
  Jericho *(G-7087)*
Ui Acquisition Holding Co .... G 607 779-7522
  Conklin *(G-3877)*
Ui Holding Company .... G 607 779-7522
  Conklin *(G-3878)*
Universal Instruments Corp .... C 800 842-9732
  Conklin *(G-3879)*

MACHINERY: Extruding

Kobe Steel USA Holdings Inc .... G 212 751-9400
  New York *(G-10866)*

MACHINERY: Fiber Optics Strand Coating

Accurate McHning Incorporation .... F 315 689-1428
  Elbridge *(G-4623)*

MACHINERY: Gear Cutting & Finishing

Gleason Works .... A 585 473-1000
  Rochester *(G-14408)*

MACHINERY: General, Industrial, NEC

Markpericom .... G 516 208-6824
  Oceanside *(G-13088)*

MACHINERY: Glassmaking

Emhart Glass Manufacturing Inc .... C 607 734-3671
  Horseheads *(G-6576)*
Wilt Industries Inc .... G 518 548-4961
  Lake Pleasant *(G-7277)*

MACHINERY: Grinding

Connex Grinding & Machining .... G 315 946-4340
  Lyons *(G-7971)*
Stephen Bader Company Inc .... F 518 753-4456
  Valley Falls *(G-16396)*

MACHINERY: Ice Cream

Pic Nic LLC .... G 914 245-6500
  Yorktown Heights *(G-17516)*

MACHINERY: Ice Crushers

American Material Processing .... G 315 318-0017
  Clifton Springs *(G-3713)*

MACHINERY: Ice Making

Hoshizaki Nrtheastern Dist Ctr .... G 516 605-1411
  Plainview *(G-13604)*

PRODUCT SECTION

MACHINERY: Industrial, NEC

A P Manufacturing ....G....... 909 228-3049
  Bohemia *(G-1001)*
Elg Utica Alloys Holdings Inc ....G....... 315 733-0475
  Utica *(G-16329)*
Exigo Precision Inc ....G....... 585 254-5818
  Rochester *(G-14364)*
Northeast Hardware Specialties ....F....... 516 487-6868
  Mineola *(G-8527)*
Parry Machine Co Inc ....G....... 315 597-5014
  Palmyra *(G-13412)*
Semi-Linear Inc ....G....... 212 243-2108
  New York *(G-12027)*

MACHINERY: Jewelers

Arbe Machinery Inc ....F....... 631 756-2477
  Farmingdale *(G-4945)*

MACHINERY: Leather Working

Stephen A Manoogian Inc ....G....... 518 762-2525
  Johnstown *(G-7129)*

MACHINERY: Marking, Metalworking

Autostat Corporation ....F....... 516 379-9447
  Roosevelt *(G-15003)*

MACHINERY: Metalworking

Advanced Machine Design Co Inc ....E....... 716 826-2000
  Buffalo *(G-2800)*
Bartell Machinery Systems LLC ....C....... 315 336-7600
  Rome *(G-14804)*
Charles A Rogers Entps Inc ....E....... 585 924-6400
  Victor *(G-16466)*
Duall Finishing Inc ....G....... 716 827-1707
  Buffalo *(G-2920)*
Esm II Inc ....E....... 716 446-8888
  Amherst *(G-241)*
Hardinge Inc ....C....... 607 734-2281
  Elmira *(G-4688)*
Hje Company Inc ....G....... 518 792-8733
  Queensbury *(G-13999)*
Mono-Systems Inc ....E....... 716 821-1344
  Buffalo *(G-3074)*
Munson Machinery Company Inc ....E....... 315 797-0090
  Utica *(G-16350)*
Pems Tool & Machine Inc ....E....... 315 823-3595
  Little Falls *(G-7502)*
Precision Systems Mfg Inc ....E....... 315 451-3480
  Liverpool *(G-7544)*
Reelex Packaging Solutions Inc ....E....... 845 878-7878
  Patterson *(G-13443)*
Riverside Machinery Company ....E....... 718 492-7400
  Brooklyn *(G-2498)*
S & S Machinery Corp ....E....... 718 492-7400
  Brooklyn *(G-2520)*
S & S Machinery Corp ....E....... 718 492-7400
  Brooklyn *(G-2521)*
Serge Duct Designs Inc ....E....... 718 783-7799
  Brooklyn *(G-2544)*
Strippit Inc ....C....... 716 542-5500
  Akron *(G-29)*
Vader Systems LLC ....G....... 716 636-1742
  East Amherst *(G-4363)*
Voss Manufacturing Inc ....D....... 716 731-5062
  Sanborn *(G-15130)*
Xto Incorporated ....D....... 315 451-7807
  Liverpool *(G-7558)*

MACHINERY: Milling

Five Star Tool Co Inc ....E....... 585 328-9580
  Rochester *(G-14372)*

MACHINERY: Mining

Flatcut LLC ....G....... 212 542-5732
  Brooklyn *(G-1983)*
Gbt Global ....E....... 718 593-9698
  New York *(G-10258)*
Lawson M Whiting Inc ....G....... 315 986-3064
  Macedon *(G-7988)*
Universal Metal Fabricators ....F....... 845 331-8248
  Kingston *(G-7221)*

MACHINERY: Optical Lens

Optipro Systems LLC ....D....... 585 265-0160
  Ontario *(G-13208)*

Universal Thin Film Lab Corp ....G....... 845 562-0601
  Newburgh *(G-12784)*

MACHINERY: Ozone

Queenaire Technologies Inc ....G....... 315 393-5454
  Ogdensburg *(G-13120)*

MACHINERY: Packaging

A & G Heat Sealing ....G....... 631 724-7764
  Smithtown *(G-15481)*
All Packaging McHy & Sups Corp ....F....... 631 588-7310
  Ronkonkoma *(G-14861)*
Automecha International Ltd ....E....... 607 843-2235
  Oxford *(G-13363)*
Dover Global Holdings Inc ....E....... 212 922-1640
  New York *(G-9912)*
Feldmeier Equipment Inc ....C....... 315 823-2000
  Little Falls *(G-7500)*
Haines Equipment Inc ....E....... 607 566-8531
  Avoca *(G-537)*
Hypres Inc ....E....... 914 592-1190
  Elmsford *(G-4756)*
K C Technical Services Inc ....G....... 631 589-7170
  Bohemia *(G-1086)*
Kabar Manufacturing Corp ....E....... 631 694-6857
  Farmingdale *(G-5022)*
Millwood Inc ....F....... 518 233-1475
  Waterford *(G-16614)*
Modern Packaging Inc ....D....... 631 595-2437
  Deer Park *(G-4175)*
National Equipment Corporation ....F....... 718 585-0200
  Bronx *(G-1405)*
National Equipment Corporation ....E....... 718 585-0200
  Bronx *(G-1406)*
Orics Industries Inc ....E....... 718 461-8613
  Farmingdale *(G-5070)*
Overhead Door Corporation ....D....... 518 828-7652
  Hudson *(G-6629)*
Pacemaker Packaging Corp ....F....... 718 458-1188
  Woodside *(G-17344)*
Packaging Dynamics Ltd ....F....... 631 563-4499
  Bohemia *(G-1114)*
Rfb Associates Inc ....G....... 518 271-0551
  Voorheesville *(G-16517)*
Rota Pack Inc ....F....... 631 274-1037
  Farmingdale *(G-5103)*
Save O Seal Corporation Inc ....G....... 914 592-3031
  Elmsford *(G-4777)*
Sharon Manufacturing Co Inc ....E....... 631 242-8870
  Deer Park *(G-4210)*
Silver Creek Enterprises Inc ....G....... 716 934-2611
  Silver Creek *(G-15450)*
Utleys Incorporated ....E....... 718 956-1661
  Woodside *(G-17359)*
Volckening Inc ....E....... 718 748-0294
  Brooklyn *(G-2735)*

MACHINERY: Paper Industry Miscellaneous

Automecha International Ltd ....E....... 607 843-2235
  Oxford *(G-13363)*
Cyclotherm of Watertown Inc ....E....... 315 782-1100
  Watertown *(G-16649)*
GL&v USA Inc ....D....... 518 747-2444
  Hudson Falls *(G-6643)*
GL&v USA Inc ....D....... 518 747-2444
  Hudson Falls *(G-6644)*
Haanen Packard Machinery Inc ....G....... 518 747-2330
  Hudson Falls *(G-6646)*
Interntnal Strpping Diecutting ....G....... 718 383-7720
  Brooklyn *(G-2113)*
Jacob Inc ....E....... 646 450-3067
  Brooklyn *(G-2131)*
Johnston Dandy Company ....G....... 315 455-5773
  Syracuse *(G-15969)*
Kadant Inc ....F....... 518 793-8801
  Glens Falls *(G-5684)*
Lake Image Systems Inc ....F....... 585 321-3630
  Henrietta *(G-6296)*
Sinclair International Company ....E....... 518 798-2361
  Queensbury *(G-14012)*
Verso Corporation ....B....... 212 599-2700
  New York *(G-12526)*

MACHINERY: Pharmaciutical

George Ponte Inc ....G....... 914 243-4202
  Jefferson Valley *(G-7056)*
Gordon S Anderson Mfg Co ....G....... 845 677-3304
  Millbrook *(G-8475)*

MACHINERY: Semiconductor Manufacturing

Innovation Associates Inc ....C....... 607 798-9376
  Johnson City *(G-7095)*
Michael Benalt Inc ....E....... 845 628-1008
  Mahopac *(G-7997)*
Ross Microsystems Inc ....G....... 845 918-1208
  New City *(G-8792)*

MACHINERY: Photographic Reproduction

Qls Solutions Group Inc ....E....... 716 852-2203
  Buffalo *(G-3144)*
Xerox Corporation ....A....... 585 422-4564
  Webster *(G-16743)*

MACHINERY: Plastic Working

Addex Inc ....G....... 781 344-5800
  Newark *(G-12729)*
Byfusion Inc ....G....... 347 563-5286
  Brooklyn *(G-1742)*
Century-Tech Inc ....G....... 718 326-9400
  Hempstead *(G-6268)*
Germanow-Simon Corporation ....E....... 585 232-1440
  Rochester *(G-14399)*
Haanen Packard Machinery Inc ....G....... 518 747-2330
  Hudson Falls *(G-6646)*
High Frequency Tech Co Inc ....F....... 631 242-3020
  Deer Park *(G-4149)*
Illinois Tool Works Inc ....C....... 716 681-8222
  Lancaster *(G-7320)*
Kabar Manufacturing Corp ....E....... 631 694-1036
  Farmingdale *(G-5023)*
Kabar Manufacturing Corp ....E....... 631 694-6857
  Farmingdale *(G-5022)*
Pearl Technologies Inc ....E....... 315 365-2632
  Savannah *(G-15202)*
Quality Strapping Inc ....D....... 718 418-1111
  Brooklyn *(G-2463)*
Ultrepet LLC ....D....... 781 275-6400
  Albany *(G-146)*
Valplast International Corp ....F....... 516 442-3923
  Westbury *(G-17040)*

MACHINERY: Printing Presses

Advance Grafix Equipment Inc ....G....... 917 202-4593
  Wyandanch *(G-17370)*

MACHINERY: Recycling

Adirondack Plas & Recycl Inc ....E....... 518 746-9212
  Argyle *(G-408)*
Andela Tool & Machine Inc ....G....... 315 858-0055
  Richfield Springs *(G-14061)*
Ben Weitsman of Albany LLC ....E....... 518 462-4444
  Albany *(G-53)*
Crumbrubber Technology Inc ....F....... 718 468-3988
  Hollis *(G-6496)*
Materials Recovery Company ....F....... 518 274-3681
  Troy *(G-16242)*

MACHINERY: Riveting

High Speed Hammer Company Inc .....F....... 585 266-4287
  Rochester *(G-14436)*

MACHINERY: Road Construction & Maintenance

Professional Pavers Corp ....E....... 718 784-7853
  Rego Park *(G-14039)*

MACHINERY: Rubber Working

Curtin-Hebert Co Inc ....F....... 518 725-7157
  Gloversville *(G-5710)*
Mono Plate Inc ....G....... 631 643-3100
  West Babylon *(G-16812)*

MACHINERY: Semiconductor Manufacturing

Cvd Equipment Corporation ....C....... 631 981-7081
  Central Islip *(G-3493)*
Globalfoundries US Inc ....F....... 512 457-3900
  Hopewell Junction *(G-6551)*
Lam Research Corporation ....E....... 845 896-0606
  Fishkill *(G-5185)*
SPX Corporation ....E....... 585 279-1216
  Rochester *(G-14696)*
Standard Ascnsion Towers Group ......D....... 716 681-2222
  Depew *(G-4274)*
Tokyo Electron America Inc ....G....... 518 289-3100
  Malta *(G-8021)*

Employee Codes: A=Over 500 employees, B=251-500
C=101-250, D=51-100, E=20-50, F=10-19, G=5-9

MACHINERY: Semiconductor Manufacturing

Veeco Instruments Inc..................B....... 516 677-0200
  Plainview *(G-13644)*

MACHINERY: Separation Eqpt, Magnetic

Innovative Cleaning Solutions...............G....... 716 731-4408
  Sanborn *(G-15121)*

MACHINERY: Sheet Metal Working

U S Air Tool Co Inc...............F....... 631 471-3300
  Ronkonkoma *(G-14994)*

MACHINERY: Specialty

Force Dynamics Inc...............F....... 607 546-5023
  Trumansburg *(G-16267)*

MACHINERY: Textile

Aglika Trade LLC...............F....... 727 424-1944
  Middle Village *(G-8410)*
Corbertex LLC...............G....... 212 971-0008
  New York *(G-9723)*
Eastman Machine Company...............C....... 716 856-2200
  Buffalo *(G-2929)*
Herr Manufacturing Co Inc...............E....... 716 754-4341
  Tonawanda *(G-16172)*
Mohawk Valley Knt McHy Co Inc...............F....... 315 736-3038
  New York Mills *(G-12726)*
Rfb Associates Inc............... 518 271-0551
  Voorheesville *(G-16517)*
Schwabel Fabricating Co Inc............... 716 876-2086
  Tonawanda *(G-16200)*
Simtec Industries Corporation............... 631 293-0080
  Farmingdale *(G-5109)*

MACHINERY: Tire Shredding

Northeast Data Destruction & R............... 845 331-5554
  Kingston *(G-7204)*
Shred Center...............G....... 716 664-3052
  Jamestown *(G-7027)*

MACHINERY: Voting

Dominion Voting Systems Inc...............F....... 404 955-9799
  Jamestown *(G-6988)*

MACHINERY: Wire Drawing

Carpenter Manufacturing Co...............E....... 315 682-9176
  Manlius *(G-8068)*
Eraser Company Inc...............C....... 315 454-3237
  Mattydale *(G-8212)*
MGS Manufacturing Inc............... 315 337-3350
  Rome *(G-14821)*

MACHINERY: Woodworking

Cem Machine Inc...............E....... 315 493-4258
  Carthage *(G-3409)*
James L Taylor Mfg Co...............E....... 845 452-3780
  Poughkeepsie *(G-13909)*
James L Taylor Mfg Co...............G....... 845 452-3780
  Poughkeepsie *(G-13910)*
Merritt Machinery LLC............... 716 434-5558
  Lockport *(G-7599)*
Oneida Air Systems Inc...............E....... 315 476-5151
  Syracuse *(G-16004)*
Paratus Industries Inc...............E....... 716 826-2000
  Orchard Park *(G-13288)*

MACHINES: Forming, Sheet Metal

Cetek Inc...............E....... 845 452-3510
  Poughkeepsie *(G-13892)*

MACHINISTS' TOOLS: Measuring, Precision

B & B Precision Mfg Inc...............E....... 585 226-6226
  Avon *(G-538)*
Mausner Equipment Co Inc...............C....... 631 689-7358
  Setauket *(G-15377)*

MACHINISTS' TOOLS: Precision

Drt Power Systems LLC - Lane...............D....... 585 247-5940
  Rochester *(G-14319)*
East Side Machine Inc...............E....... 585 265-4560
  Webster *(G-16722)*
Egli Machine Company Inc............... 607 563-3663
  Sidney *(G-15439)*
Garey Mfg & Design Corp............... 315 463-5306
  East Syracuse *(G-4532)*

Hubbard Tool and Die Corp...............E....... 315 337-7840
  Rome *(G-14815)*
Lovejoy Chaplet Corporation...............E....... 518 686-5232
  Hoosick Falls *(G-6541)*
Melland Gear Instr of Huppauge...............E....... 631 234-0100
  Hauppauge *(G-6130)*
Miller Metal Fabricating Inc...............G....... 585 359-3400
  Rochester *(G-14514)*
Novatech Inc...............E....... 716 892-6682
  Cheektowaga *(G-3583)*
Park Enterprises Rochester Inc...............E....... 585 546-4200
  Rochester *(G-14573)*
Ppi Corp...............D....... 585 243-0300
  Geneseo *(G-5568)*
Precision Grinding & Mfg Corp...............C....... 585 458-4300
  Rochester *(G-14593)*
S & R Tool Inc............... 585 346-2029
  Lakeville *(G-7285)*
Streamline Precision Inc...............G....... 585 421-9050
  Fairport *(G-4881)*
Xactra Technologies Inc............... 585 426-2030
  Rochester *(G-14767)*

MACHINISTS' TOOLS: Scales, Measuring, Precision

Atlantic Scale Company Inc...............G....... 914 664-4403
  Yonkers *(G-17418)*

MAGAZINES, WHOLESALE

Economist Newspaper NA Inc...............F....... 212 554-0676
  New York *(G-9980)*
Global Finance Media Inc...............F....... 212 447-7900
  New York *(G-10315)*

MAGNETIC INK & OPTICAL SCANNING EQPT

Capture Globa Integ Solut Inc...............G....... 718 352-0579
  Bayside Hills *(G-779)*
Hand Held Products Inc...............B....... 315 554-6000
  Skaneateles Falls *(G-15468)*
Hand Held Products Inc...............F....... 315 554-6000
  Skaneateles Falls *(G-15469)*
Peoples Choice M R I...............F....... 716 681-7377
  Buffalo *(G-3119)*
Symbol Technologies LLC...............G....... 631 738-3346
  Holtsville *(G-6510)*
Symbol Technologies LLC...............F....... 631 218-3907
  Holbrook *(G-6477)*

MAGNETIC RESONANCE IMAGING DEVICES: Nonmedical

Finger Lakes Radiology LLC...............G....... 315 787-5399
  Geneva *(G-5577)*
Islandia Mri Associates PC...............F....... 631 234-2828
  Central Islip *(G-3501)*

MAGNETIC TAPE, AUDIO: Prerecorded

C & C Duplicators Inc...............E....... 631 244-0800
  Bohemia *(G-1029)*

MAGNETOHYDRODYNAMIC DEVICES OR MHD

Passive-Plus Inc...............F....... 631 425-0938
  Huntington *(G-6673)*

MAGNETS: Ceramic

Arnold Magnetic Tech Corp...............C....... 585 385-9010
  Rochester *(G-14211)*
Eneflux Armtek Magnetics Inc...............G....... 516 576-3434
  Medford *(G-8244)*
Hitachi Metals America Ltd...............E....... 914 694-9200
  Purchase *(G-13959)*

MAGNETS: Permanent

Arnold Magnetic Tech Corp...............C....... 585 385-9010
  Rochester *(G-14211)*
Carpentier Industries LLC...............F....... 585 385-5550
  East Rochester *(G-4455)*
Magnaworks Technology Inc...............G....... 631 218-3431
  Bohemia *(G-1100)*
Magnetic Aids Inc...............G....... 845 863-1400
  Newburgh *(G-12766)*
MMC Magnetics Corp...............F....... 631 435-9888
  Hauppauge *(G-6141)*

Polymag Inc...............E....... 631 286-4111
  Bellport *(G-839)*
Precision Magnetics LLC...............E....... 585 385-9010
  Rochester *(G-14596)*
Technomag Inc...............G....... 631 246-6142
  East Setauket *(G-4493)*
Truebite Inc...............E....... 607 785-7664
  Vestal *(G-16455)*
Wtbi Inc...............G....... 631 547-1993
  Huntington Station *(G-6729)*

MAGNIFIERS

Edroy Products Co Inc...............G....... 845 358-6600
  Nyack *(G-13051)*

MAIL-ORDER BOOK CLUBS

Global Video LLC...............D....... 516 222-2600
  Woodbury *(G-17288)*
Station Hill of Barrytown...............G....... 845 758-5293
  Barrytown *(G-619)*

MAIL-ORDER HOUSE, NEC

American Country Quilts & Lin...............G....... 631 283-5466
  Southampton *(G-15538)*
Chocolat Moderne LLC...............G....... 212 229-4797
  New York *(G-9605)*
Collinite Corporation...............G....... 315 732-2282
  Utica *(G-16313)*
Hamtronics Inc...............G....... 585 392-9430
  Rochester *(G-14419)*
Hubray Inc...............F....... 800 645-2855
  North Baldwin *(G-12907)*
Quaker Boy Inc...............E....... 716 662-3979
  Orchard Park *(G-13292)*
TRM Linen Inc...............G....... 718 686-6075
  Brooklyn *(G-2683)*

MAIL-ORDER HOUSES: Book & Record Clubs

Oxford University Press LLC...............B....... 212 726-6000
  New York *(G-11542)*
Oxford University Press LLC...............G....... 212 726-6000
  New York *(G-11543)*

MAIL-ORDER HOUSES: Books, Exc Book Clubs

Anthroposophic Press Inc...............G....... 518 851-2054
  Clifton Park *(G-3695)*
Looseleaf Law Publications Inc...............F....... 718 359-5559
  Flushing *(G-5268)*
Rizzoli Intl Publications Inc...............E....... 212 387-3400
  New York *(G-11881)*
Syracuse Cultural Workers Prj...............F....... 315 474-1132
  Syracuse *(G-16051)*
Trusted Media Brands Inc...............A....... 914 238-1000
  New York *(G-12413)*

MAIL-ORDER HOUSES: Cards

Color Card LLC...............F....... 631 232-1300
  Central Islip *(G-3491)*

MAIL-ORDER HOUSES: Clothing, Exc Women's

Cockpit Usa Inc...............F....... 212 575-1616
  New York *(G-9661)*
Cockpit Usa Inc...............F....... 212 575-1616
  New York *(G-9662)*

MAIL-ORDER HOUSES: Computer Eqpt & Electronics

Gim Electronics Corp...............F....... 516 942-3382
  Hicksville *(G-6349)*

MAIL-ORDER HOUSES: Cosmetics & Perfumes

Borghese Inc...............E....... 212 659-5318
  New York *(G-9441)*

MAIL-ORDER HOUSES: Fitness & Sporting Goods

KD Dids Inc...............G....... 718 402-2012
  Bronx *(G-1369)*

PRODUCT SECTION

MAIL-ORDER HOUSES: Food

Sbk Preserves Inc .... E 800 773-7378
  Bronx *(G-1448)*

MAIL-ORDER HOUSES: Furniture & Furnishings

Charles P Rogers Brass Beds .... F 212 675-4400
  New York *(G-9582)*
Wink Inc .... E 212 389-1382
  New York *(G-12646)*

MAIL-ORDER HOUSES: Gift Items

Jomar Industries Inc .... E 845 357-5773
  Airmont *(G-16)*

MAIL-ORDER HOUSES: Jewelry

Indonesian Imports Inc .... E 888 800-5899
  New York *(G-10590)*

MAIL-ORDER HOUSES: Magazines

Dlc Comprehensive Medical PC .... F 718 857-1200
  Brooklyn *(G-1868)*

MAILING LIST: Brokers

Luria Communications Inc .... G 631 329-4922
  East Hampton *(G-4413)*

MAILING LIST: Compilers

Select Information Exchange .... F 212 496-6435
  New York *(G-12023)*

MAILING SVCS, NEC

Data Palette Info Svcs LLC .... D 718 433-1060
  Port Washington *(G-13807)*
Dispatch Graphics Inc .... F 212 307-5943
  New York *(G-9884)*
DP Murphy Co Inc .... D 631 673-9400
  Deer Park *(G-4132)*
Five Star Prtg & Mailing Svcs .... F 212 929-0300
  New York *(G-10176)*
Garden City Printers & Mailers .... F 516 485-1600
  West Hempstead *(G-16853)*
Hart Reproduction Services .... G 212 704-0556
  New York *(G-10423)*
Mason & Gore Inc .... E 914 921-1025
  Rye *(G-15063)*
PDQ Shipping Services .... G 845 255-5500
  New Paltz *(G-8877)*
The Nugent Organization Inc .... F 212 645-6600
  Oceanside *(G-13101)*
Westchester Mailing Service .... E 914 948-1116
  White Plains *(G-17184)*

MANAGEMENT CONSULTING SVCS: Automation & Robotics

Cs Automation Inc .... F 315 524-5123
  Ontario *(G-13198)*

MANAGEMENT CONSULTING SVCS: Business

Hargrave Development .... F 716 877-7880
  Kenmore *(G-7147)*
Security Letter .... G 212 348-1553
  New York *(G-12015)*
Yale Robbins Inc .... D 212 683-5700
  New York *(G-12687)*

MANAGEMENT CONSULTING SVCS: Construction Project

Darrell Mitchell .... G 646 659-7075
  Arverne *(G-425)*

MANAGEMENT CONSULTING SVCS: Distribution Channels

Standard Analytics Io Inc .... G 917 882-5422
  New York *(G-12181)*

MANAGEMENT CONSULTING SVCS: Food & Beverage

Marley Spoon Inc .... G 646 934-6970
  New York *(G-11163)*
SPX Flow Tech Systems Inc .... D 716 692-3000
  Getzville *(G-5604)*

MANAGEMENT CONSULTING SVCS: Foreign Trade

Communications & Energy Corp .... F 315 446-5723
  Syracuse *(G-15903)*

MANAGEMENT CONSULTING SVCS: Industrial

GE Global Research .... G 518 387-5000
  Niskayuna *(G-12894)*

MANAGEMENT CONSULTING SVCS: Industrial & Labor

Terahertz Technologies Inc .... G 315 736-3642
  Oriskany *(G-13316)*

MANAGEMENT CONSULTING SVCS: Industry Specialist

ER Butler & Co Inc .... E 212 925-3565
  New York *(G-10055)*
Ludwig Holdings Corp .... D 845 340-9727
  Kingston *(G-7198)*

MANAGEMENT CONSULTING SVCS: Real Estate

Visual Listing Systems Inc .... G 631 689-7222
  East Setauket *(G-4496)*

MANAGEMENT CONSULTING SVCS: Training & Development

Calia Technical Inc .... G 718 447-3928
  Staten Island *(G-15655)*
Ideas International Inc .... E 914 937-4302
  Rye Brook *(G-15071)*
Serendipity Consulting Corp .... F 914 763-8251
  South Salem *(G-15536)*

MANAGEMENT SERVICES

A & Mt Realty Group LLC .... F 718 974-5871
  Brooklyn *(G-1528)*
Arnan Development Corp .... D 607 432-6641
  Oneonta *(G-13171)*
Elie Tahari Ltd .... D 212 398-2622
  New York *(G-10002)*
Fonar Corporation .... C 631 694-2929
  Melville *(G-8320)*
International Center For Postg .... G 607 257-5860
  Ithaca *(G-6851)*
Precision Disc Grinding Corp .... F 516 747-5450
  Mineola *(G-8531)*
Quoizel Inc .... E 631 436-4402
  Hauppauge *(G-6176)*
Retail Management Pubg Inc .... F 212 981-0217
  New York *(G-11845)*

MANAGEMENT SVCS: Administrative

Supermedia LLC .... D 212 513-9700
  New York *(G-12243)*
Tdk USA Corporation .... D 516 535-2600
  Uniondale *(G-16300)*

MANAGEMENT SVCS: Circuit, Motion Picture Theaters

Dolomite Products Company Inc .... E 315 524-1998
  Rochester *(G-14316)*

MANAGEMENT SVCS: Construction

Darrell Mitchell .... G 646 659-7075
  Arverne *(G-425)*
Sg Blocks Inc .... F 212 520-6218
  New York *(G-12033)*

MANAGEMENT SVCS: Restaurant

D R M Management Inc .... E 716 668-0333
  Depew *(G-4254)*

MANDRELS

Safina Center .... G 808 888-9440
  Stony Brook *(G-15770)*

MANHOLES COVERS: Concrete

Jefferson Concrete Corp .... D 315 788-4171
  Watertown *(G-16655)*

MANICURE PREPARATIONS

Essie Cosmetics Ltd .... D 212 818-1500
  New York *(G-10067)*

MANIFOLDS: Pipe, Fabricated From Purchased Pipe

M Manastrip-M Corporation .... G 518 664-2089
  Clifton Park *(G-3699)*

MANNEQUINS

Adel Rootstein (usa) Inc .... E 718 499-5650
  Brooklyn *(G-1561)*
Alvanon Inc .... E 212 868-4314
  New York *(G-9105)*
B Barine Inc .... E 718 499-5650
  Brooklyn *(G-1657)*
Genesis Mannequins USA II Inc .... G 212 505-6600
  New York *(G-10275)*
Lifestyle-Trimco .... E 718 257-9101
  Brooklyn *(G-2219)*

MANUFACTURING INDUSTRIES, NEC

141 Industries LLC .... F 978 273-8831
  New York *(G-8959)*
40 North Industries .... E 212 821-1600
  New York *(G-8975)*
A&M Model Makers LLC .... G 626 813-9661
  Macedon *(G-7979)*
Accessible Bath Tech LLC .... F 518 937-1518
  Albany *(G-33)*
AFP Manufacturing Corp .... F 516 466-6464
  Great Neck *(G-5785)*
Air Flow Manufacturing .... F 607 733-8284
  Elmira *(G-4669)*
Ameritool Mfg LLC .... G 315 668-2172
  West Monroe *(G-16909)*
Atlas Metal Industries Inc .... G 607 776-2048
  Hammondsport *(G-5953)*
B F G Elcpltg and Mfg Co .... E 716 362-0888
  Blasdell *(G-960)*
Bee Green Industries Inc .... G 516 334-3525
  Carle Place *(G-3386)*
Dj Pirrone Industries Inc .... G 518 864-5496
  Pattersonville *(G-13447)*
Dolmen .... F 912 596-1537
  Conklin *(G-3867)*
E-Z Global Wholesale Inc .... G 888 769-7888
  Brooklyn *(G-1894)*
EDM Mfg .... G 631 669-1966
  Babylon *(G-548)*
Essex Industries .... G 518 942-6671
  Mineville *(G-8540)*
Falk Industries Inc .... F 518 725-2777
  Johnstown *(G-7114)*
Feraco Industries .... G 631 547-8120
  Huntington Station *(G-6704)*
Freedom Mfg LLC .... F 518 584-0441
  Saratoga Springs *(G-15152)*
Fun Industries of NY .... F 631 845-3805
  Farmingdale *(G-4995)*
Holland Manufacturing Inc .... G 716 685-4129
  Williamsville *(G-17247)*
Isco Industries .... F 502 714-5306
  Horseheads *(G-6581)*
J & R Unique Giftware .... E 718 821-0398
  Maspeth *(G-8146)*
John Prior .... G 516 520-9801
  East Meadow *(G-4426)*
Just Right Carbines LLC .... G 585 261-5331
  Canandaigua *(G-3348)*
Kafko (us) Corp .... G 877 721-7665
  Latham *(G-7367)*
Martec Industries .... F 585 458-3940
  Rochester *(G-14498)*

MANUFACTURING INDUSTRIES, NEC

O Brien Gere Mfg Inc .... G 315 437-6100
  Liverpool *(G-7537)*
Ogd V-Hvac Inc .... E 315 858-1002
  Van Hornesville *(G-16432)*
Omicron Technologies Inc .... E 631 434-7697
  Holbrook *(G-6465)*
Oriskany Manufacturing LLC .... F 315 732-4962
  Yorkville *(G-17524)*
Oso Industries Inc .... G 917 709-2050
  Brooklyn *(G-2398)*
Performance Precision Mfg LLC .... G 518 993-3033
  Fort Plain *(G-5348)*
Quest Manufacturing Inc .... E 716 312-8000
  Hamburg *(G-5938)*
Remus Industries .... G 914 906-1544
  Ossining *(G-13327)*
Rockwell Video Solutions LLC .... F 631 745-0582
  Southampton *(G-15550)*
Rutcarele Inc .... G 347 830-5353
  Corona *(G-4005)*
Select Industries New York Inc .... F 800 723-5333
  New York *(G-12022)*
Sonaal Industries Inc .... G 718 383-3860
  Brooklyn *(G-2584)*
Subcon Industries .... G 716 945-4430
  Salamanca *(G-15109)*
Supersil LLC .... D 347 266-9900
  Brooklyn *(G-2630)*
Tii Industries Inc .... F 631 789-5000
  Copiague *(G-3933)*
Topoo Industries Incorporated .... G 718 331-3755
  Brooklyn *(G-2666)*
Unistel LLC .... D 585 341-4600
  Webster *(G-16740)*
Unlimited Industries Inc .... G 631 666-9483
  Brightwaters *(G-1239)*
Vali Industries Inc .... G 718 821-5555
  Brooklyn *(G-2717)*
Water Splash Inc .... G 800 936-3430
  Champlain *(G-3549)*
Woodfalls Industries .... F 518 236-7201
  Plattsburgh *(G-13709)*
Zmz Mfg Inc .... G 518 234-4336
  Warnerville *(G-16579)*

MAPS

Mapeasy Inc .... F 631 537-6213
  Wainscott *(G-16529)*

MARBLE BOARD

Amendola MBL & Stone Ctr Inc .... D 914 997-7968
  White Plains *(G-17076)*

MARBLE, BUILDING: Cut & Shaped

Dicamillo Marble and Granite .... E 845 878-0078
  Patterson *(G-13437)*
Gdi Custom Marble & Granite .... F 718 996-9100
  Brooklyn *(G-2018)*
International Stone Accessrs .... G 718 522-5399
  Brooklyn *(G-2111)*
Italian Marble & Granite Inc .... F 716 741-1800
  Clarence Center *(G-3676)*
Joseph Corcoran Marble Inc .... G 631 423-8712
  Huntington Station *(G-6713)*
Lace Marble & Granite Inc .... G 718 854-9028
  Brooklyn *(G-2189)*
Marble Doctors LLC .... E 203 628-8339
  New York *(G-11143)*
Monroe Industries Inc .... G 585 226-8230
  Avon *(G-541)*
Premier Group NY .... F 212 229-1200
  New York *(G-11698)*
Salsburg Dimensional Stone .... F 631 653-6790
  Brookhaven *(G-1510)*
Unique MBL Gran Orgnztion Corp .... G 718 482-0440
  Long Island City *(G-7907)*
White Plains Marble Inc .... G 914 347-6000
  Elmsford *(G-4794)*

MARINAS

Advanced Plstic Fbrctions Corp .... G 631 231-4466
  Hauppauge *(G-6010)*
Meeco Sullivan LLC .... C 800 232-3625
  Warwick *(G-16595)*

MARINE HARDWARE

Bfg Marine Inc .... F 631 586-5500
  Bay Shore *(G-675)*

Dover Marine Mfg & Sup Co Inc .... G 631 667-4300
  Deer Park *(G-4131)*
Rollson Inc .... E 631 423-9578
  Huntington *(G-6678)*
Taylor Made Group LLC .... D 518 725-0681
  Gloversville *(G-5724)*

MARINE RELATED EQPT

Kyntec Corporation .... G 716 810-6956
  Buffalo *(G-3038)*

MARINE SVC STATIONS

Accurate Marine Specialties .... G 631 589-5502
  Bohemia *(G-1005)*

MARKERS

Mark Dri Products Inc .... C 516 484-6200
  Bethpage *(G-873)*

MARKETS: Meat & fish

Schaller Manufacturing Corp .... G 718 721-5480
  New York *(G-11986)*

MARKING DEVICES

Bianca Group Ltd .... G 212 768-3011
  New York *(G-9388)*
C M E Corp .... F 315 451-7101
  Syracuse *(G-15881)*
East Coast Thermographers Inc .... E 718 321-3211
  College Point *(G-3782)*
Effanjay Pens Inc .... E 212 316-9565
  Long Island City *(G-7726)*
Hampton Art LLC .... E 631 924-1335
  Medford *(G-8247)*
Heidenhain International Inc .... G 716 661-1700
  Jamestown *(G-6999)*
Hodgins Engraving Co Inc .... D 585 343-4444
  Batavia *(G-639)*
Joseph Treu Successors Inc .... G 212 691-7026
  New York *(G-10766)*
Kelly Foundry & Machine Co .... E 315 732-8313
  Utica *(G-16346)*
Krengel Manufacturing Co Inc .... G 212 227-1901
  Fulton *(G-5467)*
New York Marking Devices Corp .... G 585 454-5188
  Rochester *(G-14534)*
New York Marking Devices Corp .... G 315 463-8641
  Syracuse *(G-15998)*
Tech Products Inc .... E 718 442-4900
  Staten Island *(G-15748)*
UI Corp .... G 201 203-4453
  Bayside *(G-776)*
United Sttes Brnze Sign of Fla .... E 516 352-5155
  New Hyde Park *(G-8870)*
White Plains Rubber Stamp Name .... G 914 949-1900
  White Plains *(G-17187)*

MARKING DEVICES: Date Stamps, Hand, Rubber Or Metal

Koehlr-Gibson Mkg Graphics Inc .... E 716 838-5960
  Buffalo *(G-3035)*
Long Island Stamp & Seal Co .... F 718 628-8550
  Ridgewood *(G-14112)*

MARKING DEVICES: Embossing Seals & Hand Stamps

A & M Steel Stamps Inc .... G 516 741-6223
  Mineola *(G-8487)*
Cannizzaro Seal & Engraving Co .... G 718 513-6125
  Brooklyn *(G-1754)*
Rubber Stamp X Press .... G 631 423-1322
  Huntington Station *(G-6721)*

MARKING DEVICES: Figures, Metal

Thermopatch Corporation .... D 315 446-8110
  Syracuse *(G-16058)*

MARKING DEVICES: Irons, Marking Or Branding

Name Base Inc .... G 212 545-1400
  New York *(G-11338)*

MARKING DEVICES: Letters, Metal

I & I Systems .... G 845 753-9126
  Tuxedo Park *(G-16283)*

MARKING DEVICES: Numbering Machines

National Time Recording Eqp Co .... F 212 227-3310
  New York *(G-11352)*

MARKING DEVICES: Pads, Inking & Stamping

Dab-O-Matic Corp .... D 914 699-7070
  Mount Vernon *(G-8676)*
Specialty Ink Co Inc .... F 631 586-3666
  Blue Point *(G-1000)*
United Silicone Inc .... D 716 681-8222
  Lancaster *(G-7345)*

MARKING DEVICES: Postmark Stamps, Hand, Rubber Or Metal

Rubber Stamps Inc .... E 212 675-1180
  Mineola *(G-8535)*

MARKING DEVICES: Screens, Textile Printing

Michael Todd Stevens .... G 585 436-9957
  Rochester *(G-14506)*
Ulano Product Inc .... C 718 622-5200
  Brooklyn *(G-2695)*
Ward Sales Co Inc .... G 315 476-5276
  Syracuse *(G-16068)*

MASKS: Gas

Go Blue Technologies Ltd .... G 631 404-6285
  North Babylon *(G-12901)*

MASQUERADE OR THEATRICAL COSTUMES STORES

D-C Theatricks .... G 716 847-0180
  Buffalo *(G-2900)*
Moresca Clothing and Costume .... F 845 331-6012
  Ulster Park *(G-16286)*

MASTIC ROOFING COMPOSITION

Savage & Son Installations LLC .... E 585 342-7533
  Rochester *(G-14671)*

MATERIALS HANDLING EQPT WHOLESALERS

Four-Way Pallet Corp .... E 631 351-3401
  Huntington Station *(G-6706)*
George Ponte Inc .... G 914 243-4202
  Jefferson Valley *(G-7056)*
High Frequency Tech Co Inc .... F 631 242-3020
  Deer Park *(G-4149)*
Koke Inc .... E 800 535-5303
  Queensbury *(G-14003)*
Overhead Door Corporation .... D 518 828-7652
  Hudson *(G-6629)*
Raymond Sales Corporation .... G 607 656-2311
  Greene *(G-5870)*
Tri-Boro Shlving Prtition Corp .... F 718 782-8527
  Ridgewood *(G-14130)*

MATS & MATTING, MADE FROM PURCHASED WIRE

Brook North Farms Inc .... F 315 834-9390
  Auburn *(G-487)*

MATS OR MATTING, NEC: Rubber

Seaway Mats Inc .... G 518 483-2560
  Malone *(G-8016)*

MATS, MATTING & PADS: Auto, Floor, Exc Rubber Or Plastic

Auto-Mat Company Inc .... E 516 938-7373
  Hicksville *(G-6325)*

PRODUCT SECTION

MATS: Blasting, Rope
T M International LLC .... G 718 842-0949
Bronx *(G-1471)*

MATTRESS RENOVATING & REPAIR SHOP
E & G Bedding Corp .... E 718 369-1092
Brooklyn *(G-1889)*

MATTRESS STORES
Otis Bedding Mfg Co Inc .... E 716 825-2599
Buffalo *(G-3105)*
Sleep Care Enterprises Inc .... G 631 246-9000
Stony Brook *(G-15771)*

MEAT & MEAT PRDTS WHOLESALERS
Brooklyn Bangers LLC .... F 718 875-3535
Brooklyn *(G-1721)*
Elmgang Enterprises I Inc .... F 212 868-4142
New York *(G-10012)*
Tri-Town Packing Corp .... F 315 389-5101
Brasher Falls *(G-1174)*

MEAT CUTTING & PACKING
A To Z Kosher Meat Products Co .... E 718 384-7400
Brooklyn *(G-1535)*
Caribbean Foods Delight Inc .... D 845 398-3000
Tappan *(G-16079)*
Chefs Delight Packing Co .... F 718 388-8581
Brooklyn *(G-1776)*
Crescent Duck Farm Inc .... E 631 722-8700
Aquebogue *(G-384)*
Domestic Casing Co .... G 718 522-1902
Brooklyn *(G-1872)*
DRG New York Holdings Corp .... D 914 668-9000
Mount Vernon *(G-8677)*
Fairbank Reconstruction Corp .... D 800 628-3276
Ashville *(G-429)*
Frank Wardynski & Sons Inc .... E 716 854-6083
Buffalo *(G-2955)*
Globex Kosher Foods Inc .... E 718 630-5555
Brooklyn *(G-2029)*
Gold Medal Packing Inc .... D 315 337-1911
Oriskany *(G-13310)*
Ives Farm Market .... G 315 592-4880
Fulton *(G-5463)*
Kamerys Wholesale Meats Inc .... G 716 372-6756
Olean *(G-13149)*
Old World Provisions Inc .... E 518 465-7306
Troy *(G-16245)*
Orleans Custom Packing Inc .... G 585 314-8227
Holley *(G-6490)*
Side Hill Farmers Coop Inc .... G 315 447-4693
Canastota *(G-3373)*
The Smoke House of Catskills .... G 845 246-8767
Saugerties *(G-15197)*
Tri-Town Packing Corp .... F 315 389-5101
Brasher Falls *(G-1174)*
We Work .... G 877 673-6628
New York *(G-12600)*

MEAT MARKETS
Ives Farm Market .... G 315 592-4880
Fulton *(G-5463)*
Mineo & Sapio Meats Inc .... G 716 884-2398
Buffalo *(G-3067)*
The Smoke House of Catskills .... G 845 246-8767
Saugerties *(G-15197)*

MEAT PRDTS: Bologna, From Purchased Meat
Atlantic Pork & Provisions Inc .... E 718 272-9550
Jamaica *(G-6895)*

MEAT PRDTS: Boneless Meat, From Purchased Meat
Tower Isles Frozen Foods Ltd .... D 718 495-2626
Brooklyn *(G-2671)*

MEAT PRDTS: Canned
Birds Eye Holdings Inc .... A 585 383-1850
Rochester *(G-14232)*

MEAT PRDTS: Frankfurters, From Purchased Meat
Marathon Enterprises Inc .... D 718 665-2560
Bronx *(G-1385)*

MEAT PRDTS: Frozen
Caribbean Foods Delight Inc .... D 845 398-3000
Tappan *(G-16079)*
Prime Food Processing Corp .... D 718 963-2323
Brooklyn *(G-2441)*

MEAT PRDTS: Meat By-Prdts, From Slaughtered Meat
Huda Kawshai LLC .... G 929 255-7009
Jamaica *(G-6920)*
Joel Kiryas Meat Market Corp .... F 845 782-9194
Monroe *(G-8557)*
Robert & William Inc .... G 631 727-5780
Riverhead *(G-14154)*
Sam A Lupo & Sons Inc .... G 607 748-1141
Endicott *(G-4828)*

MEAT PRDTS: Meat Extracts, From Purchased Meat
Reliable Brothers Inc .... E 518 273-6732
Green Island *(G-5861)*

MEAT PRDTS: Pork, From Slaughtered Meat
Hilltown Pork Inc .... F 518 781-4050
Canaan *(G-3331)*

MEAT PRDTS: Prepared Beef Prdts From Purchased Beef
Bianca Burgers LLC .... F 516 764-9591
Rockville Centre *(G-14788)*
Freirich Julian Co Inc .... E 718 361-9111
Long Island City *(G-7746)*

MEAT PRDTS: Prepared Pork Prdts, From Purchased Meat
Hansel n Gretel Brand Inc .... C 718 326-0041
Glendale *(G-5656)*
Lancaster Quality Pork Inc .... F 718 439-8822
Brooklyn *(G-2194)*
Schaller Manufacturing Corp .... D 718 721-5480
New York *(G-11986)*

MEAT PRDTS: Sausage Casings, Natural
Brooklyn Casing Co Inc .... G 718 522-0866
Brooklyn *(G-1723)*
Camellia General Provision Co .... E 716 893-5352
Buffalo *(G-2865)*
Domestic Casing Co .... G 718 522-1902
Brooklyn *(G-1872)*
Frank Wardynski & Sons Inc .... E 716 854-6083
Buffalo *(G-2955)*
Niagara Tying Service Inc .... E 716 825-0066
Buffalo *(G-3092)*
Rapa Independent North America ..... G 518 561-0513
Plattsburgh *(G-13694)*

MEAT PRDTS: Sausages & Related Prdts, From Purchased Meat
Elmgang Enterprises I Inc .... F 212 868-4142
New York *(G-10012)*
Schonwetter Enterprises Inc .... E 518 237-0171
Cohoes *(G-3757)*

MEAT PRDTS: Sausages, From Purchased Meat
Arnolds Meat Food Products .... E 718 384-8071
Brooklyn *(G-1629)*
Buffalo Provisions Co Inc .... F 718 292-4300
Elmhurst *(G-4658)*
Cibao Meat Products Inc .... D 718 993-5072
Bronx *(G-1298)*
De Ans Pork Products Inc .... E 718 788-2464
Brooklyn *(G-1846)*
Hanzlian Sausage Incorporated .... G 716 891-5247
Cheektowaga *(G-3574)*
Salarinos Italian Foods Inc .... F 315 697-9766
Canastota *(G-3372)*

MEAT PRDTS: Sausages, From Slaughtered Meat
Sahlen Packing Company Inc .... D 716 852-8677
Buffalo *(G-3175)*

MEAT PRDTS: Snack Sticks, Incl Jerky, From Purchased Meat
Big Johns Adirondack Inc .... G 518 587-3680
Saratoga Springs *(G-15145)*
Holy Cow Kosher LLC .... G 347 788-8620
Spring Valley *(G-15589)*
Provisionaire & Co LLC .... E 315 491-8240
New York *(G-11741)*

MEAT PRDTS: Variety, Fresh Edible Organs
Martin D Whitbeck .... G 607 746-7642
Delhi *(G-4240)*

MEAT PRDTS: Veal, From Slaughtered Meat
Delft Blue LLC .... C 315 768-7100
New York Mills *(G-12720)*

MEAT PROCESSED FROM PURCHASED CARCASSES
Adirondack Meat Company Inc .... F 518 585-2333
Ticonderoga *(G-16124)*
Alle Processing Corp .... C 718 894-2000
Maspeth *(G-8115)*
Alps Provision Co Inc .... E 718 721-4477
Astoria *(G-433)*
Brooklyn Bangers LLC .... F 718 875-3535
Brooklyn *(G-1721)*
Dinos Sausage & Meat Co Inc .... F 315 732-2661
Utica *(G-16325)*
Fairbank Reconstruction Corp .... D 800 628-3276
Ashville *(G-429)*
Hilltown Pork Inc .... F 518 781-4050
Canaan *(G-3331)*
Jacks Gourmet LLC .... E 718 954-4681
Brooklyn *(G-2129)*
Milan Provision Co Inc .... E 718 899-7678
Corona *(G-4003)*
Mineo & Sapio Meats Inc .... G 716 884-2398
Buffalo *(G-3067)*
Picone Meat Specialties Ltd .... G 914 381-3002
Mamaroneck *(G-8042)*
Pork King Sausage Inc .... E 718 542-2810
Bronx *(G-1432)*
Rapacki & Sons .... F 516 538-3939
Lindenhurst *(G-7480)*
Rosina Food Products Inc .... C 716 668-0123
Buffalo *(G-3165)*
Rosina Holding Inc .... G 716 668-0123
Buffalo *(G-3166)*
Schrader Meat Market .... F 607 869-6328
Romulus *(G-14842)*
Sun Ming Jan Inc .... F 718 418-8221
Brooklyn *(G-2619)*
Syracuse Casing Co Inc .... F 315 475-0309
Syracuse *(G-16048)*
Tyson Deli Inc .... B 716 826-6400
Buffalo *(G-3228)*
White Eagle Packing Co Inc .... F 518 374-4366
Schenectady *(G-15313)*
Zweigles Inc .... D 585 546-1740
Rochester *(G-14776)*

MEAT PROCESSING MACHINERY
Cantinafoods Inc .... G 716 602-3536
Buffalo *(G-2866)*

MED, DENTAL & HOSPITAL EQPT, WHOL: Incontinent Prdts/Splys
Koregon Enterprises Inc .... G 450 218-6836
Champlain *(G-3543)*

MEDIA BUYING AGENCIES
Selby Marketing Associates Inc .... F 585 377-0750
Fairport *(G-4876)*
Ubm LLC .... A 516 562-5085
New York *(G-12441)*

Employee Codes: A=Over 500 employees, B=251-500
C=101-250, D=51-100, E=20-50, F=10-19, G=5-9

MEDIA: Magnetic & Optical Recording

Aarfid LLC	G	716 992-3999
Eden (G-4585)		
BMA Media Services Inc	E	585 385-2060
Rochester (G-14238)		
Dm2 Media LLC	E	646 419-4357
New York (G-9889)		
Next Big Sound Inc	G	646 657-9837
New York (G-11421)		
Stamper Technology Inc	G	585 247-8370
Rochester (G-14700)		

MEDICAL & HOSPITAL EQPT WHOLESALERS

AEP Environmental LLC	F	716 446-0739
Buffalo (G-2801)		
Allied Pharmacy Products Inc	G	516 374-8862
Woodmere (G-17310)		
Hogil Pharmaceutical Corp	F	914 681-1800
White Plains (G-17121)		
Nova Health Systems Inc	G	315 798-9018
Utica (G-16353)		
Occunomix International LLC	E	631 741-1940
Port Jeff STA (G-13769)		
Precimed Inc	E	716 759-5600
Clarence (G-3669)		
Progressive Orthotics Ltd	G	631 732-5556
Selden (G-15353)		
Roner Inc	G	718 392-6020
Long Island City (G-7865)		
Sleep Care Enterprises Inc	G	631 246-9000
Stony Brook (G-15771)		
TSS Foam Industries Corp	F	585 538-2321
Caledonia (G-3283)		

MEDICAL & HOSPITAL SPLYS: Radiation Shielding Garments

Biodex Medical Systems Inc	C	631 924-9000
Shirley (G-15416)		
Biodex Medical Systems Inc	E	631 924-3146
Shirley (G-15417)		
Xylon Industries Inc	G	631 293-4717
Farmingdale (G-5144)		

MEDICAL & SURGICAL SPLYS: Bandages & Dressings

Aero Healthcare (us) LLC	G	855 225-2376
Valley Cottage (G-16375)		
Euromed Inc	D	845 359-4039
Orangeburg (G-13227)		

MEDICAL & SURGICAL SPLYS: Braces, Orthopedic

Arimed Orthotics Prosthetics P	F	718 979-6155
Staten Island (G-15640)		
Complete Orthopedic Svcs Inc	E	516 357-9113
East Meadow (G-4420)		
Eschen Prosthetic & Orthotic L	E	212 606-1262
New York (G-10059)		
Hanger Prsthetcs & Ortho Inc	D	607 795-1220
Elmira (G-4687)		
Lorelei Orthotics Prosthetics	G	212 727-2011
New York (G-11041)		

MEDICAL & SURGICAL SPLYS: Clothing, Fire Resistant & Protect

Elwood Specialty Products Inc	F	716 877-6622
Buffalo (G-2934)		

MEDICAL & SURGICAL SPLYS: Cosmetic Restorations

Northwell Health Inc	A	888 387-5811
New York (G-11461)		
Y Lift New York LLC	F	212 861-7787
New York (G-12685)		

MEDICAL & SURGICAL SPLYS: Cotton & Cotton Applicators

Advanced Enterprises Inc	F	845 342-1009
Middletown (G-8425)		

MEDICAL & SURGICAL SPLYS: Ear Plugs

Cirrus Healthcare Products LLC	E	631 692-7600
Cold Spring Harbor (G-3768)		
New Dynamics Corporation	E	845 692-0022
Middletown (G-8453)		

MEDICAL & SURGICAL SPLYS: Foot Appliances, Orthopedic

Brannock Device Co Inc	E	315 475-9862
Liverpool (G-7512)		
Fiber Foot Appliances Inc	F	631 465-9199
Farmingdale (G-4993)		
Schuster & Richard Labortories	G	718 358-8607
College Point (G-3806)		

MEDICAL & SURGICAL SPLYS: Gynecological Splys & Appliances

Cityscape Ob/Gyn PLLC	F	212 683-3595
New York (G-9632)		
Womens Health Care PC	G	718 850-0009
Richmond Hill (G-14088)		

MEDICAL & SURGICAL SPLYS: Limbs, Artificial

Aaaaar Orthopedics Inc	G	845 278-4938
Brewster (G-1206)		
Creative Orthotics Prosthetics	F	607 734-7215
Elmira (G-4678)		
Creative Orthotics Prosthetics	G	607 771-4672
Binghamton (G-903)		
Gfh Orthotic & Prosthetic Labs	G	631 467-3725
Bohemia (G-1072)		
Goldberg Prosthetic & Orthotic	F	631 689-6606
East Setauket (G-4484)		
Green Prosthetics & Orthotics	G	716 484-1088
Jamestown (G-6996)		
Hanger Prsthetcs & Ortho Inc	G	607 771-4672
Binghamton (G-921)		
Hanger Prsthetcs & Ortho Inc	G	315 472-5200
Syracuse (G-15956)		
Hanger Prsthetcs & Ortho Inc	G	315 789-4810
Geneva (G-5581)		
Lehneis Orthotics Prosthetic	G	631 360-3859
Hauppauge (G-6112)		
Lehneis Orthotics Prosthetic	G	631 369-3115
Riverhead (G-14146)		
National Prosthetic Orthot	G	718 767-8400
Bayside (G-774)		
North Shore Orthtics Prsthtics	G	631 928-3040
Port Jeff STA (G-13768)		
Orthopedic Treatment Facility	G	718 898-7326
Woodside (G-17343)		
Progressive Orthotics Ltd	G	631 732-5556
Selden (G-15353)		
Prosthetic Rehabilitation Ctr	G	845 565-8255
Newburgh (G-12777)		
Robert Cohen	G	718 789-0996
Ozone Park (G-13385)		
Rochester Orthopedic Labs	G	585 272-1060
Rochester (G-14644)		

MEDICAL & SURGICAL SPLYS: Orthopedic Appliances

Advantage Orthotics Inc	G	631 368-1754
East Northport (G-4432)		
Church Communities NY Inc	E	518 589-5103
Elka Park (G-4629)		
Church Communities NY Inc	E	518 589-5103
Elka Park (G-4630)		
Community Products LLC	C	845 658-8799
Rifton (G-14132)		
Community Products LLC	F	845 572-3433
Chester (G-3604)		
Custom Sports Lab Inc	G	212 832-1648
New York (G-9771)		
East Cast Orthtics Prosthetics	F	716 856-5192
Buffalo (G-2926)		
East Coast Orthoic & Pros Cor	G	212 923-2161
New York (G-9962)		
Hanger Prsthetcs & Ortho Inc	G	607 776-8013
Bath (G-657)		
Higgins Supply Company Inc	D	607 836-6474
Mc Graw (G-8222)		
Klemmt Orthotics & Prosthetics	G	607 770-4400
Johnson City (G-7097)		
Langer Biomechanics Inc	D	800 645-5520
Ronkonkoma (G-14930)		
Latorre Orthopedic Laboratory	F	518 786-8655
Latham (G-7372)		
M H Mandelbaum Orthotic	F	631 473-8668
Port Jefferson (G-13777)		
Medi-Ray Inc	D	877 898-3003
Tuckahoe (G-16271)		
Ortho Medical Products	E	212 879-3700
New York (G-11528)		
Orthotics & Prosthetics Dept	F	585 341-9299
Rochester (G-14558)		
Profoot Inc	E	718 965-8600
Brooklyn (G-2453)		
Progressive Orthotics Ltd	F	631 447-3860
East Patchogue (G-4449)		
Rehablitation Tech of Syracuse	G	315 426-9920
Syracuse (G-16022)		
Stj Orthotic Services Inc	F	631 956-0181
Lindenhurst (G-7484)		

MEDICAL & SURGICAL SPLYS: Personal Safety Eqpt

Aramsco Inc	F	718 361-7540
Ridgewood (G-14099)		
Bio-Chem Barrier Systems LLC	G	631 261-2682
Northport (G-13008)		
Fist Inc	G	718 643-3478
Brooklyn (G-1976)		
Kem Medical Products Corp	G	631 454-6565
Farmingdale (G-5027)		
Lakeland Industries Inc	C	631 981-9700
Ronkonkoma (G-14928)		
NY Orthopedic Usa Inc	D	718 852-5330
Brooklyn (G-2382)		
Occunomix International LLC	E	631 741-1940
Port Jeff STA (G-13769)		

MEDICAL & SURGICAL SPLYS: Prosthetic Appliances

Advanced Prosthetics Orthotics	F	516 365-7225
Manhasset (G-8054)		
Flo-Tech Orthotic & Prosthetic	G	607 387-3070
Trumansburg (G-16266)		
Great Lakes Orthopedic Labs	G	716 878-7307
Buffalo (G-2980)		
J-K Prosthetics & Orthotics	E	914 699-2077
Mount Vernon (G-8695)		
New England Orthotic & Prost	G	212 831-3600
New York (G-11386)		
New York Rhbilitative Svcs LLC	F	516 239-0990
Lawrence (G-7396)		
Orthocraft Inc	G	718 692-0113
Brooklyn (G-2396)		
Orthopedic Arts Laboratory Inc	G	718 858-2400
Brooklyn (G-2397)		
Orthotic & Prosthetic Images	G	516 292-8726
Hempstead (G-6284)		
Prosthetics By Nelson Inc	F	716 894-6666
Cheektowaga (G-3587)		
Sampsons Prsthtic Orthotic Lab	E	518 374-6011
Schenectady (G-15291)		
Stafford Labs Orthotics/Prosth	F	845 692-5227
Middletown (G-8462)		
Tonawanda Limb & Brace Inc	G	716 695-1131
Tonawanda (G-16207)		

MEDICAL & SURGICAL SPLYS: Respiratory Protect Eqpt, Personal

Monaghan Medical Corporation	G	315 472-2136
Syracuse (G-15993)		
Sontek Industries Inc	G	781 749-3055
New York (G-12130)		
Venture Respiratory Inc	F	718 437-3633
Brooklyn (G-2722)		

MEDICAL & SURGICAL SPLYS: Sponges

54321 Us Inc	F	716 695-0258
Tonawanda (G-16133)		
Medical Action Industries Inc	C	631 231-4600
Hauppauge (G-6129)		

MEDICAL & SURGICAL SPLYS: Supports, Abdominal, Ankle, Etc

Promed Products Inc	G	800 993-4010
Yonkers (G-17480)		

(G-0000) Company's Geographic Section entry number

PRODUCT SECTION

MEDICAL & SURGICAL SPLYS: Suspensories

Ortho Rite Inc ....E....... 914 235-9100
New Rochelle *(G-8918)*

MEDICAL & SURGICAL SPLYS: Technical Aids, Handicapped

Orcam Inc ....F....... 800 713-3741
Jericho *(G-7080)*

MEDICAL EQPT REPAIR SVCS, NON-ELECTRIC

Med Services Inc ....D....... 631 218-6450
Bohemia *(G-1104)*

MEDICAL EQPT: Diagnostic

Advantage Plus Diagnostics Inc ....G....... 631 393-5044
Melville *(G-8288)*
American Bio Medica Corp ....D....... 518 758-8158
Kinderhook *(G-7167)*
Biochemical Diagnostics Inc ....E....... 631 595-9200
Edgewood *(G-4595)*
E-Z-Em Inc ....E....... 609 524-2864
Melville *(G-8313)*
Ineedmd Holdings Inc ....G....... 212 256-9669
New York *(G-10592)*
Ken-Ton Open Mri PC ....G....... 716 876-7000
Kenmore *(G-7150)*
Lydia H Soifer & Assoc Inc ....F....... 914 683-5401
White Plains *(G-17135)*
Memory Md Inc ....G....... 917 318-0215
New York *(G-11224)*
Nanobionovum LLC ....F....... 518 581-1171
Saratoga Springs *(G-15164)*
Ortho-Clinical Diagnostics Inc ....F....... 585 453-5200
Rochester *(G-14554)*
Ortho-Clinical Diagnostics Inc ....B....... 585 453-4771
Rochester *(G-14555)*
Ovitz Corporation ....G....... 585 474-4695
West Henrietta *(G-16889)*
Pharma-Smart International Inc ....E....... 585 427-0730
Rochester *(G-14581)*
Precision Biologics Inc ....G....... 516 482-1200
Great Neck *(G-5831)*
Proactive Medical Products LLC ....G....... 845 205-6004
Mount Vernon *(G-8720)*
RJ Harvey Instrument Corp ....F....... 845 359-3943
Tappan *(G-16083)*
Sundance Enterprises Inc ....G....... 914 946-2942
White Plains *(G-17173)*
Vasomedical Solutions Inc ....D....... 516 997-4600
Plainview *(G-13642)*
Welch Allyn Inc ....A....... 315 685-4100
Skaneateles Falls *(G-15471)*
Welch Allyn Inc ....A....... 315 685-4100
Skaneateles Falls *(G-15472)*
Welch Allyn Inc ....A....... 315 685-4347
Skaneateles Falls *(G-15473)*

MEDICAL EQPT: Electromedical Apparatus

Biofeedback Instrument Corp ....G....... 212 222-5665
New York *(G-9401)*
Conmed Andover Medical Inc ....F....... 315 797-8375
Utica *(G-16314)*
Conmed Corporation ....B....... 315 797-8375
Utica *(G-16316)*
Health Care Originals Inc ....G....... 585 967-1398
West Henrietta *(G-16882)*

MEDICAL EQPT: Electrotherapeutic Apparatus

Complex Biosystems Inc ....G....... 315 464-8007
Liverpool *(G-7517)*

MEDICAL EQPT: Heart-Lung Machines, Exc Iron Lungs

Advd Heart Phys & Surgs ....F....... 212 434-3000
New York *(G-9048)*
Gary Gelbfish MD ....G....... 718 258-3004
Brooklyn *(G-2014)*
Jarvik Heart Inc ....E....... 212 397-3911
New York *(G-10701)*

MEDICAL EQPT: Laser Systems

Buffalo Filter LLC ....D....... 716 835-7000
Lancaster *(G-7307)*
Ddc Technologies Inc ....G....... 516 594-1533
Oceanside *(G-13076)*
Laser and Varicose Vein Trtmnt ....G....... 718 667-1777
Staten Island *(G-15698)*
New York Laser & Aestheticks ....G....... 516 627-7777
Roslyn *(G-15021)*
Photonics Industries Intl Inc ....D....... 631 218-2240
Ronkonkoma *(G-14968)*
Teledyne Optech Inc ....F....... 585 427-8310
West Henrietta *(G-16897)*
University of Rochester ....B....... 585 275-3483
Rochester *(G-14745)*

MEDICAL EQPT: MRI/Magnetic Resonance Imaging Devs, Nuclear

City Sports Imaging Inc ....E....... 212 481-3600
New York *(G-9631)*

MEDICAL EQPT: PET Or Position Emission Tomography Scanners

Nirx Medical Technologies LLC ....F....... 516 676-6479
Glen Head *(G-5638)*

MEDICAL EQPT: Patient Monitoring

Equivital Inc ....E....... 646 513-4169
New York *(G-10054)*
Motion Intelligence Inc ....G....... 607 227-4400
Ithaca *(G-6863)*
Novamed-Usa Inc ....E....... 914 789-2100
Elmsford *(G-4771)*
Ocean Cardiac Monitoring ....G....... 631 777-3700
Deer Park *(G-4185)*

MEDICAL EQPT: Sterilizers

Getinge Sourcing LLC ....C....... 585 475-1400
Rochester *(G-14400)*
Getinge Usa Inc ....C....... 585 475-1400
Rochester *(G-14401)*
Robert Busse & Co Inc ....B....... 631 435-4711
Hauppauge *(G-6178)*
SPS Medical Supply Corp ....F....... 585 968-2377
Cuba *(G-4070)*
Steriliz LLC ....G....... 585 415-5411
Rochester *(G-14703)*

MEDICAL EQPT: Ultrasonic Scanning Devices

Empire Open Mri ....G....... 914 961-1777
Yonkers *(G-17441)*
Global Instrumentation LLC ....F....... 315 682-0272
Manlius *(G-8072)*
Imacor Inc ....E....... 516 393-0970
Garden City *(G-5509)*
Jadak LLC ....F....... 315 701-0678
North Syracuse *(G-12949)*
Lifesciences Technology Inc ....G....... 516 569-0085
Hewlett *(G-6309)*

MEDICAL EQPT: Ultrasonic, Exc Cleaning

Nanovibronix Inc ....F....... 914 233-3004
Elmsford *(G-4769)*
Stj Enterprises ....D....... 516 612-0110
Cedarhurst *(G-3463)*

MEDICAL EQPT: X-Ray Apparatus & Tubes, Radiographic

Genesis Digital Imaging Inc ....F....... 310 305-7358
Rochester *(G-14396)*
Quantum Medical Imaging LLC ....D....... 631 567-5800
Ronkonkoma *(G-14975)*
Siemens Corporation ....F....... 202 434-7800
New York *(G-12062)*
Siemens USA Holdings Inc ....B....... 212 258-4000
New York *(G-12064)*

MEDICAL EQPT: X-Ray Apparatus & Tubes, Therapeutic

Community Products LLC ....C....... 845 658-8799
Rifton *(G-14132)*

MEDICAL PHOTOGRAPHY & ART SVCS

Burns Archive Photographic Dis ....G....... 212 889-1938
New York *(G-9481)*

MEDICAL, DENTAL & HOSPITAL EQPT, WHOL: Dentists' Prof Splys

Crosstex International Inc ....D....... 631 582-6777
Hauppauge *(G-6058)*

MEDICAL, DENTAL & HOSPITAL EQPT, WHOL: Hosptl Eqpt/Furniture

Creative Orthotics Prosthetics ....F....... 607 734-7215
Elmira *(G-4678)*
Medical Action Industries Inc ....C....... 631 231-4600
Hauppauge *(G-6129)*
Star X-Ray Co Inc ....E....... 631 842-3010
Woodbury *(G-17301)*

MEDICAL, DENTAL & HOSPITAL EQPT, WHOL: Surgical Eqpt & Splys

Medline Industries Inc ....B....... 845 344-3301
Middletown *(G-8450)*
Paramount Textiles Inc ....F....... 212 966-1040
New York *(G-11570)*

MEDICAL, DENTAL & HOSPITAL EQPT, WHOLESALE: Diagnostic, Med

Memory Md Inc ....G....... 917 318-0215
New York *(G-11224)*
Pharma-Smart International Inc ....E....... 585 427-0730
Rochester *(G-14581)*

MEDICAL, DENTAL & HOSPITAL EQPT, WHOLESALE: Med Eqpt & Splys

Ala Scientific Instruments Inc ....F....... 631 393-6401
Farmingdale *(G-4935)*
American Healthcare Supply Inc ....F....... 212 674-3636
New York *(G-9119)*
Basil S Kadhim ....G....... 888 520-5192
New York *(G-9330)*
Brinkman Precision Inc ....D....... 585 429-5001
West Henrietta *(G-16872)*
Hub Surgical & Orthopedic Sups ....G....... 718 585-5415
Bronx *(G-1358)*
Lehneis Orthotics Prosthetic ....G....... 631 360-3859
Hauppauge *(G-6112)*
Lehneis Orthotics Prosthetic ....G....... 631 369-3115
Riverhead *(G-14146)*
Peter Digioia ....G....... 516 644-5517
Plainview *(G-13628)*
Quantum Medical Imaging LLC ....D....... 631 567-5800
Ronkonkoma *(G-14975)*
Sontek Industries Inc ....G....... 781 749-3055
New York *(G-12130)*

MEDICAL, DENTAL & HOSPITAL EQPT, WHOLESALE: Medical Lab

Integrted Work Envronments LLC ....G....... 716 725-5088
East Amherst *(G-4361)*

MELAMINE RESINS: Melamine-Formaldehyde

Hexion Inc ....E....... 518 792-8040
South Glens Falls *(G-15525)*
Queen City Manufacturing Inc ....G....... 716 877-1102
Buffalo *(G-3149)*

MEMBERSHIP ORGANIZATIONS, PROFESSIONAL: Health Association

Curemdcom Inc ....B....... 646 224-2201
New York *(G-9769)*

MEMBERSHIP ORGS, BUSINESS: Growers' Marketing Advisory Svc

Atlantic Farm & Food Inc ....F....... 718 441-3152
Richmond Hill *(G-14066)*

MEMBERSHIP ORGS, CIVIC, SOCIAL/FRAT: Educator's Assoc

Modern Language Assn Amer Inc ....C...... 646 576-5000
New York *(G-11288)*

MEMORIALS, MONUMENTS & MARKERS

Domenick Denigris Inc ....E...... 718 823-2264
Bronx *(G-1315)*

MEMORIES: Solid State

Addmm LLC ....F...... 631 913-4400
Ronkonkoma *(G-14851)*

MEMORY DEVICES: Magnetic Bubble

Dynamic Photography Inc ....G...... 516 381-2951
Roslyn *(G-15019)*

MEN'S & BOYS' CLOTHING ACCESS STORES

Broadway Knitting Mills Inc ....G...... 716 692-4421
North Tonawanda *(G-12961)*
Giliberto Designs Inc ....E...... 212 695-0216
New York *(G-10296)*
Swank Inc ....B...... 212 867-2600
New York *(G-12248)*

MEN'S & BOYS' CLOTHING STORES

By Robert James....................................G...... 212 253-2121
New York *(G-9485)*
Elie Tahari Ltd ....F...... 212 398-2622
New York *(G-10001)*
Hugo Boss Usa Inc ....D...... 212 940-0600
New York *(G-10528)*
Kcp Holdco Inc ....A...... 212 265-1500
New York *(G-10827)*
Kenneth Cole Productions Inc ....B...... 212 265-1500
New York *(G-10833)*
Mee Accessories LLC ....C...... 917 262-1000
New York *(G-11218)*
Perrone Leather LLC ....F...... 518 853-4300
Fultonville *(G-5482)*
Perry Ellis Menswear LLC ....C...... 212 221-7500
New York *(G-11624)*
Phillips-Van Heusen Europe ....F...... 212 381-3500
New York *(G-11649)*
Pvh Corp ....D...... 212 381-3500
New York *(G-11756)*
Sanctuary Brands LLC ....G...... 212 704-4014
New York *(G-11964)*

MEN'S & BOYS' CLOTHING WHOLESALERS, NEC

All Net Ltd ....F...... 516 504-4559
Great Neck *(G-5788)*
Alpha 6 Distributions LLC ....F...... 516 801-8290
Locust Valley *(G-7628)*
Billion Tower Intl LLC ....F...... 212 220-0608
New York *(G-9397)*
D-C Theatricks ....G...... 716 847-0180
Buffalo *(G-2900)*
Enzo Manzoni LLC ....F...... 212 464-7000
Brooklyn *(G-1928)*
G-III Apparel Group Ltd ....C...... 212 403-0500
New York *(G-10234)*
Herrmann Group LLC ....G...... 716 876-9798
Kenmore *(G-7148)*
Jeans Inc..G...... 646 223-1122
New York *(G-10717)*
Kate Spade & Company ....B...... 212 354-4900
New York *(G-10816)*
Kenmar Shirts Inc ....E...... 718 824-3880
Bronx *(G-1371)*
M Hidary & Co Inc ....D...... 212 736-6540
New York *(G-11073)*
Moresca Clothing and Costume ....F...... 845 331-6012
Ulster Park *(G-16286)*
Mountain T-Shirts Inc ....E...... 518 943-4533
Catskill *(G-3432)*
Must USA Inc ....G...... 212 391-8288
New York *(G-11328)*
New York Popular Inc ....D...... 718 499-2020
Brooklyn *(G-2367)*
Penfli Industries Inc ....F...... 212 947-6080
Great Neck *(G-5830)*

Ryba General Merchandise Inc............G...... 718 522-2028
Brooklyn *(G-2519)*
Sanctuary Brands LLC ....G...... 212 704-4014
New York *(G-11964)*
United Knitwear International ....G...... 212 354-2920
New York *(G-12465)*
Wp Lavori USA Inc ....G...... 718 855-4295
Brooklyn *(G-2769)*
Wp Lavori USA Inc ....G...... 212 244-6074
New York *(G-12668)*

MEN'S & BOYS' SPORTSWEAR CLOTHING STORES

Cockpit Usa Inc ....F...... 212 575-1616
New York *(G-9661)*
Cockpit Usa Inc ....F...... 212 575-1616
New York *(G-9662)*
Foot Locker Retail Inc ....G...... 516 827-5306
Hicksville *(G-6345)*
Herrmann Group LLC ....G...... 716 876-9798
Kenmore *(G-7148)*
John Varvatos Company ....E...... 212 812-8000
New York *(G-10754)*
Mainly Monograms Inc ....E...... 845 624-4923
West Nyack *(G-16921)*
Royal Tees Inc ....E...... 845 357-9448
Suffern *(G-15800)*

MEN'S & BOYS' SPORTSWEAR WHOLESALERS

Bandit International Ltd.......................F...... 718 402-2100
Bronx *(G-1280)*
Cockpit Usa Inc ....F...... 212 575-1616
New York *(G-9661)*
Cockpit Usa Inc ....F...... 212 575-1616
New York *(G-9662)*
Mee Accessories LLC ....C...... 917 262-1000
New York *(G-11218)*
Sterling Possessions Ltd ....E...... 212 594-0418
New York *(G-12197)*

MEN'S & BOYS' UNDERWEAR WHOLESALERS

Apparel Partnership Group LLC..........E...... 212 302-7722
New York *(G-9178)*

MEN'S SUITS STORES

Royal Clothing Corp ....G...... 718 436-5841
Brooklyn *(G-2510)*
Saint Laurie Ltd ....E...... 212 643-1916
New York *(G-11954)*

MERCHANDISING MACHINE OPERATORS: Vending

Premier Fixtures LLC ....D...... 631 236-4100
Hauppauge *(G-6170)*

METAL & STEEL PRDTS: Abrasive

Datum Alloys Inc ....G...... 607 239-6274
Endicott *(G-4800)*
Pellets LLC ....G...... 716 693-1750
North Tonawanda *(G-12985)*
Raulli and Sons Inc ....E...... 315 479-2515
Syracuse *(G-16020)*

METAL COMPONENTS: Prefabricated

Precision Fabrication LLC ....G...... 585 591-3449
Attica *(G-474)*

METAL CUTTING SVCS

S & S Prtg Die-Cutting Co Inc ....F...... 718 388-8990
Brooklyn *(G-2522)*

METAL DETECTORS

Detector Pro ....G...... 845 635-3488
Pleasant Valley *(G-13711)*

METAL FABRICATORS: Architechtural

A & T Iron Works Inc ....E...... 914 632-8992
New Rochelle *(G-8883)*
A1 Ornamental Iron Works Inc ....G...... 718 265-3055
Brooklyn *(G-1543)*

PRODUCT SECTION

Accurate Welding Service Inc..............G...... 516 333-1730
Westbury *(G-16960)*
Aero-Data Metal Crafters Inc...............C...... 631 471-7733
Ronkonkoma *(G-14856)*
Aldo Frustacci Iron Works Inc ....F...... 718 768-0707
Brooklyn *(G-1578)*
Aldos Iron Works Inc ....G...... 718 834-0408
Brooklyn *(G-1579)*
All American Metal Corporation ....E...... 516 623-0222
Freeport *(G-5384)*
All Metal Specialties Inc ....E...... 716 664-6009
Jamestown *(G-6969)*
Allied Bronze Corp (del Corp)..............G...... 646 421-6400
New York *(G-9089)*
Alpha Iron Works LLC ....F...... 585 424-7260
Rochester *(G-14193)*
Armento Incorporated ....G...... 716 875-2423
Kenmore *(G-7145)*
Babylon Iron Works Inc ....F...... 631 643-3311
West Babylon *(G-16773)*
Bobrick Washroom Equipment Inc ....D...... 518 877-7444
Clifton Park *(G-3697)*
Cabezon Design Group Inc ....G...... 718 488-9868
Brooklyn *(G-1746)*
Caliper Architecture PC ....G...... 718 302-2427
Brooklyn *(G-1748)*
Caliperstudio Co ....G...... 718 302-3504
Brooklyn *(G-1749)*
Creative Metal Fabricators ....G...... 631 567-2266
Bohemia *(G-1043)*
D V S Iron & Aluminum Works ....G...... 718 768-7961
Brooklyn *(G-1832)*
E & J Iron Works Inc ....E...... 718 665-6040
Bronx *(G-1320)*
E F Iron Works & Construction ....G...... 631 242-4766
Bay Shore *(G-698)*
Ej Group Inc..G...... 315 699-2601
Cicero *(G-3645)*
Elevator Accessories Mfg ....F...... 914 739-7004
Peekskill *(G-13477)*
Enterprise Metalworks Inc ....G...... 718 328-9331
Bronx *(G-1327)*
Fixture Hardware Mfg Corp ....E...... 718 499-9422
Brooklyn *(G-1980)*
Flushing Iron Weld Inc ....E...... 718 359-2208
Flushing *(G-5242)*
Forest Iron Works Inc ....G...... 516 671-4229
Locust Valley *(G-7630)*
Giumenta Corp ....F...... 718 832-1200
Brooklyn *(G-2025)*
Global Steel Products Corp ....C...... 631 586-3455
Deer Park *(G-4147)*
Grillmaster Inc ....E...... 718 272-9191
Howard Beach *(G-6597)*
Hi-Tech Metals Inc ....E...... 718 894-1212
Maspeth *(G-8144)*
International Creative Met Inc ....F...... 718 424-8179
Woodside *(G-17333)*
ITR Industries Inc.................................E...... 914 964-7063
Yonkers *(G-17456)*
Jerry Cardullo Iron Works Inc ....F...... 631 242-8881
Bay Shore *(G-709)*
Kammetal Inc ....E...... 718 625-2628
Brooklyn *(G-2167)*
Kammetal Inc ....E...... 718 722-9991
Brooklyn *(G-2168)*
Kenal Services Corp ....G...... 315 788-9226
Watertown *(G-16657)*
Keuka Studios Inc................................G...... 585 624-5960
Rush *(G-15051)*
Kms Contracting Inc ....F...... 718 495-6500
Brooklyn *(G-2176)*
Lopopolo Iron Works Inc ....G...... 718 339-0572
Brooklyn *(G-2236)*
M B C Metal Inc ....F...... 718 384-6713
Brooklyn *(G-2247)*
Martin Chafkin ....G...... 718 383-1155
Brooklyn *(G-2276)*
Martin Orna Ir Works II Inc ....G...... 516 354-3923
Elmont *(G-4723)*
Material Process Systems Inc ....F...... 718 302-3081
Brooklyn *(G-2283)*
Maximum Security Products Corp .....E...... 518 233-1800
Waterford *(G-16613)*
Melto Metal Products Co Inc ....G...... 516 546-8866
Freeport *(G-5412)*
Mestel Brothers Stairs & Rails ....C...... 516 496-4127
Syosset *(G-15828)*
Metalworks Inc ....E...... 718 319-0011
Bronx *(G-1394)*

Milgo Industrial Inc ....D 718 388-6476
Brooklyn *(G-2313)*
Milgo Industrial Inc ....G 718 387-0406
Brooklyn *(G-2314)*
Mison Concepts Inc ....G 516 933-8000
Hicksville *(G-6373)*
Modern Art Foundry Inc ....E 718 728-2030
Astoria *(G-449)*
Morgik Metal Designs ....F 212 463-0304
New York *(G-11305)*
Moro Corporation ....E 607 724-4241
Binghamton *(G-937)*
New Dimensions Office Group ....D 718 387-0995
Brooklyn *(G-2361)*
New England Tool Co Ltd ....G 845 651-7550
Florida *(G-5214)*
Old Dutchmans Wrough Iron Inc ....G 716 688-2034
Getzville *(G-5602)*
Paley Studios Ltd ....F 585 232-5260
Rochester *(G-14567)*
Pawling Corporation ....D 845 373-9300
Wassaic *(G-16600)*
Peconic Ironworks Ltd ....F 631 204-0323
Southampton *(G-15549)*
Pk30 System LLC ....F 212 473-8050
Stone Ridge *(G-15764)*
Railings By New Star Brass ....E 516 358-1153
Brooklyn *(G-2474)*
Raulli and Sons Inc ....D 315 479-6693
Syracuse *(G-16018)*
Raulli Iron Works Inc ....F 315 337-8070
Rome *(G-14832)*
Riverside Iron LLC ....F 315 535-4864
Gouverneur *(G-5747)*
Rollson Inc ....E 631 423-9578
Huntington *(G-6678)*
Royal Metal Products Inc ....E 518 966-4442
Surprise *(G-15811)*
S A Baxter LLC ....G 845 469-7995
Chester *(G-3614)*
Safespan Platform Systems Inc ....D 716 694-3332
Tonawanda *(G-16199)*
Sh Ironworks Inc ....G 917 907-0507
Flushing *(G-5292)*
Steel Sales Inc ....E 607 674-6363
Sherburne *(G-15397)*
Steel Work Inc ....G 585 232-1555
Rochester *(G-14701)*
Steps Plus Inc ....D 315 432-0885
Syracuse *(G-16045)*
Studio 40 Inc ....G 212 420-8631
Brooklyn *(G-2613)*
Studio Dellarte ....G 718 599-3715
Brooklyn *(G-2614)*
Superior Metal & Woodwork Inc ....E 631 465-9004
Farmingdale *(G-5119)*
Tonys Ornamental Ir Works Inc ....E 315 337-3730
Rome *(G-14838)*
Tropical Driftwood Originals ....G 516 623-0980
Roosevelt *(G-15010)*
United Iron Inc ....E 914 667-5700
Mount Vernon *(G-8745)*
Universal Steel Fabricators ....F 718 342-0782
Brooklyn *(G-2709)*
Village Wrought Iron Inc ....F 315 683-5589
Fabius *(G-4841)*
Waverly Iron Corp ....E 631 732-2800
Medford *(G-8262)*
West End Iron Works Inc ....G 518 456-1105
Albany *(G-149)*
Z-Studios Dsign Fbrication LLC ....G 347 512-4210
Brooklyn *(G-2779)*

METAL FABRICATORS: Plate

Acro Industries Inc ....C 585 254-3661
Rochester *(G-14171)*
Aero-Data Metal Crafters Inc ....C 631 471-7733
Ronkonkoma *(G-14856)*
Allstate Gasket & Packing Inc ....F 631 254-4050
Deer Park *(G-4092)*
American Boiler Tank Wldg Inc ....E 518 463-5012
Albany *(G-46)*
Ametek Inc ....C 516 832-7710
Garden City *(G-5494)*
Arvos Inc ....B 585 593-2700
Wellsville *(G-16749)*
Atlantic Industrial Tech Inc ....E 631 234-3131
Shirley *(G-15414)*
Bellmore Steel Products Corp ....F 516 785-9667
Bellmore *(G-815)*
Blackstone Advanced Tech LLC ....C 716 665-5410
Jamestown *(G-6975)*
Breton Industries Inc ....D 518 842-3030
Amsterdam *(G-336)*
Bridgehampton Steel & Wldg Inc ....F 631 537-2486
Bridgehampton *(G-1232)*
Bruce Pierce ....G 716 731-9310
Sanborn *(G-15115)*
Buflovak LLC ....E 716 895-2100
Buffalo *(G-2861)*
C & F Fabricators & Erectors ....G 607 432-3520
Colliersville *(G-3814)*
Charles Ross & Son Company ....D 631 234-0500
Hauppauge *(G-6044)*
Cigar Box Studios Inc ....F 845 236-9283
Marlboro *(G-8105)*
Contech Engnered Solutions LLC ....F 716 870-9091
Orchard Park *(G-13265)*
Curtiss-Wright Flow Control ....G 845 382-6918
Lake Katrine *(G-7270)*
Direkt Force LLC ....E 716 652-3022
East Aurora *(G-4369)*
ECR International Inc ....C 716 366-5500
Dunkirk *(G-4341)*
ECR International Inc ....D 315 797-1310
Utica *(G-16328)*
Endicott Precision Inc ....C 607 754-7076
Endicott *(G-4803)*
Expert Industries Inc ....E 718 434-6060
Brooklyn *(G-1946)*
Feldmeier Equipment Inc ....D 315 823-2000
Syracuse *(G-15943)*
Feldmeier Equipment Inc ....D 315 823-2000
Little Falls *(G-7499)*
Feldmeier Equipment Inc ....C 315 823-2000
Little Falls *(G-7500)*
Fulton Boiler Works Inc ....C 315 298-5121
Pulaski *(G-13948)*
Global Steel Products Corp ....C 631 586-3455
Deer Park *(G-4147)*
Jaquith Industries Inc ....E 315 478-5700
Syracuse *(G-15966)*
Marex Aquisition Corp ....C 585 458-3940
Rochester *(G-14497)*
Methods Tooling & Mfg Inc ....E 845 246-7100
Mount Marion *(G-8651)*
Pfaudler US Inc ....C 585 235-1000
Rochester *(G-14579)*
Roemac Industrial Sales Inc ....G 716 692-7332
North Tonawanda *(G-12991)*
Rosenwach Tank Co Inc ....E 212 972-4411
Astoria *(G-455)*
Seibel Modern Mfg & Wldg Corp ....D 716 683-1536
Lancaster *(G-7342)*
Slant/Fin Corporation ....B 516 484-2600
Greenvale *(G-5881)*
Trulite Louvre Corp ....E 516 756-1850
Old Bethpage *(G-13131)*

METAL FABRICATORS: Sheet

303 Contracting Inc ....E 716 896-2122
Orchard Park *(G-13249)*
A & L Shtmtl Fabrications Corp ....E 718 842-1600
Bronx *(G-1253)*
Abdo Shtmtl & Fabrication Inc ....G 315 894-4664
Frankfort *(G-5349)*
Aberdeen Blower & Shtmtl Works ....G 631 661-6100
West Babylon *(G-16764)*
Accra Sheetmetal LLC ....G 631 920-2087
Wyandanch *(G-17369)*
Acme Architectural Pdts Inc ....D 718 384-7800
Brooklyn *(G-1555)*
Acro Industries Inc ....C 585 254-3661
Rochester *(G-14171)*
Acro-Fab Ltd ....E 315 564-6688
Hannibal *(G-5969)*
Advanced Precision Technology ....F 845 279-3540
Brewster *(G-1207)*
Advantech Industries Inc ....C 585 247-0701
Rochester *(G-14181)*
Aero Trades Mfg Corp ....E 516 746-3360
Mineola *(G-8489)*
Aeroduct Inc ....E 516 248-9550
Mineola *(G-8490)*
Afco Systems Inc ....C 631 424-3935
Farmingdale *(G-4931)*
Aj Genco Mch Sp McHy Rdout Svc ....F 716 664-4925
Falconer *(G-4889)*
Aldo Frustacci Iron Works Inc ....F 718 768-0707
Brooklyn *(G-1578)*
Aleta Industries Inc ....F 718 349-0040
Brooklyn *(G-1580)*
Alkemy Machine LLC ....G 585 436-8730
Rochester *(G-14186)*
All Around Spiral Inc ....G 631 588-0220
Ronkonkoma *(G-14860)*
All Island Blower & Shtmtl ....F 631 567-7070
Bohemia *(G-1013)*
All Star Carts & Vehicles Inc ....D 631 666-5581
Bay Shore *(G-668)*
Allen Machine Products Inc ....E 631 630-8800
Hauppauge *(G-6016)*
Alliance Welding & Steel Fabg ....F 516 775-7600
Floral Park *(G-5191)*
Allure Metal Works Inc ....F 631 588-0220
Ronkonkoma *(G-14864)*
Alnik Service Corporation ....G 516 873-7300
New Hyde Park *(G-8814)*
Alpine Machine Inc ....F 607 272-1344
Ithaca *(G-6818)*
Alternative Service Inc ....F 631 345-9500
Yaphank *(G-17385)*
Amsco Inc ....F 716 823-4213
Buffalo *(G-2811)*
Apparatus Mfg Inc ....G 845 471-5116
Poughkeepsie *(G-13887)*
Arcadia Mfg Group Inc ....E 518 434-6213
Green Island *(G-5853)*
Arcadia Mfg Group Inc ....G 518 434-6213
Menands *(G-8367)*
Architctral Shetmetal Pdts Inc ....G 518 381-6144
Scotia *(G-15323)*
Arlan Damper Corporation ....E 631 589-7431
Bohemia *(G-1019)*
Art Form Sheet Metal Fabricato ....G 718 728-0111
Long Island City *(G-7670)*
Art Precision Metal Products ....F 631 842-8889
Copiague *(G-3894)*
Ascension Industries Inc ....D 716 693-9381
North Tonawanda *(G-12956)*
Asp Industries Inc ....E 585 254-9130
Rochester *(G-14217)*
Atlantis Equipment Corporation ....F 518 733-5910
Stephentown *(G-15756)*
Atlas Sign ....G 718 604-7446
Brooklyn *(G-1649)*
Auburn Tank & Manufacturing Co ....F 315 255-2788
Auburn *(G-481)*
Avalanche Fabrication Inc ....F 585 545-4000
Ontario *(G-13196)*
B & B Sheet Metal Inc ....E 718 433-2501
Long Island City *(G-7679)*
B & H Precision Fabricators ....F 631 563-9620
Bohemia *(G-1021)*
Banner Metalcraft Inc ....D 631 563-7303
Ronkonkoma *(G-14878)*
Bargold Storage Systems LLC ....E 718 247-7000
Long Island City *(G-7682)*
Batavia Enclosures Inc ....G 585 344-1797
Arcade *(G-388)*
Berjen Metal Industries Ltd ....G 631 673-7979
Huntington *(G-6656)*
Best Tinsmith Supply Inc ....G 518 863-2541
Northville *(G-13019)*
Blackstone Advanced Tech LLC ....C 716 665-5410
Jamestown *(G-6975)*
Blackstone Business Entps Inc ....C 716 665-5410
Jamestown *(G-6976)*
Boss Precision Ltd ....D 585 352-7070
Spencerport *(G-15566)*
Broadway Neon Sign Corp ....F 908 241-4177
Ronkonkoma *(G-14881)*
Buffalo Metal Forming Inc ....G 716 856-4575
West Seneca *(G-16941)*
C & T Tool & Instrument Co ....E 718 429-1253
Woodside *(G-17321)*
C J & C Sheet Metal Corp ....F 631 376-9425
West Babylon *(G-16780)*
Cannon Industries Inc ....D 585 254-8080
Rochester *(G-14258)*
CBM Fabrications Inc ....E 518 399-8023
Ballston Lake *(G-581)*
Center Sheet Metal Inc ....C 718 378-4476
Bronx *(G-1293)*
Chamtek Mfg Inc ....E 585 328-4900
Rochester *(G-14272)*
Cherry Holding Ltd ....G 516 679-3748
North Bellmore *(G-12916)*
City Cooling Enterprises Inc ....G 718 331-7400
Brooklyn *(G-1781)*

Employee Codes: A=Over 500 employees, B=251-500
C=101-250, D=51-100, E=20-50, F=10-19, G=5-9
2017 Harris
New York Manufacturers Directory
1269
PRODUCT

METAL FABRICATORS: Sheet

Clark Specialty Co Inc .... E 607 776-3193
  Bath *(G-655)*
CPI Industries Inc .... D 631 909-3434
  Manorville *(G-8078)*
Crown Die Casting Corp. .... E 914 667-5400
  Mount Vernon *(G-8675)*
Custom Sheet Metal Contg LLC ...... F 716 896-2122
  Buffalo *(G-2898)*
Cutting Edge Metal Works .... E 631 981-8333
  Holtsville *(G-6503)*
Cw Metals Inc .... E 917 416-7906
  Long Island City *(G-7709)*
D & G Sheet Metal Co Inc .... F 718 326-9111
  Maspeth *(G-8127)*
Dawson Metal Company Inc .... C 716 664-3811
  Jamestown *(G-6987)*
Dimar Manufacturing Corp. .... C 716 759-0351
  Clarence *(G-3656)*
Dj Acquisition Management Corp .... D 585 265-3000
  Ontario *(G-13200)*
Doortec Archtctural Met GL LLC ..... E 718 567-2730
  Brooklyn *(G-1873)*
DOT Tool Co Inc .... G 607 724-7001
  Binghamton *(G-908)*
Dundas-Jafine Inc .... E 716 681-9690
  Alden *(G-177)*
Dynasty Stainless Steel & Meta ...... E 718 205-6623
  Maspeth *(G-8134)*
ECR International Inc. .... D 315 797-1310
  Utica *(G-16328)*
Elevator Accessories Mfg .... F 914 739-7004
  Peekskill *(G-13477)*
Elmsford Sheet Metal Works Inc ..... D 914 739-6300
  Cortlandt Manor *(G-4050)*
Empire Air Specialties Inc .... E 518 689-4440
  Albany *(G-77)*
Endicott Precision Inc .... C 607 754-7076
  Endicott *(G-4803)*
Engineering Mfg Tech LLC .... D 607 754-7111
  Endicott *(G-4805)*
Expert Industries Inc .... E 718 434-6060
  Brooklyn *(G-1946)*
F M L Industries Inc .... G 607 749-7273
  Homer *(G-6517)*
Federal Sheet Metal Works Inc .... F 315 735-4730
  Utica *(G-16332)*
Five Star Industries Inc .... E 716 674-2589
  West Seneca *(G-16945)*
Fred A Nudd Corporation .... E 315 524-2531
  Ontario *(G-13201)*
Goergen-Mackwirth Co Inc .... E 716 874-4800
  Buffalo *(G-2977)*
Greene Technologies Inc .... D 607 656-4166
  Greene *(G-5866)*
Hana Sheet Metal Inc .... G 914 377-0773
  Yonkers *(G-17452)*
Hansen Steel .... E 585 398-2020
  Farmington *(G-5152)*
Hatfield Metal Fab Inc. .... E 845 454-9078
  Poughkeepsie *(G-13906)*
Hergo Ergonomic Support .... E 718 894-0639
  Maspeth *(G-8143)*
Hermann Gerdens Inc .... G 631 841-3132
  Copiague *(G-3905)*
Hi-Tech Industries NY Inc. .... E 607 217-7361
  Johnson City *(G-7094)*
Hrd Metal Products Inc .... E 631 243-6700
  Deer Park *(G-4151)*
Hunter Douglas Inc .... D 845 664-7000
  Pearl River *(G-13460)*
I Rauchs Sons Inc .... E 718 507-8844
  East Elmhurst *(G-4392)*
IEC Electronics Corp .... B 585 647-1760
  Rochester *(G-14444)*
Incodema Inc .... E 607 277-7070
  Ithaca *(G-6848)*
Industrial Fabricating Corp .... E 315 437-3353
  East Syracuse *(G-4539)*
Intellimetal Inc .... D 585 424-3260
  Rochester *(G-14451)*
Jamestown Advanced Pdts Corp .... E 716 483-3406
  Jamestown *(G-7004)*
Jaquith Industries Inc. .... E 315 478-5700
  Syracuse *(G-15966)*
Jar Metals Inc .... F 845 425-8901
  Nanuet *(G-8758)*
Joe P Industries Inc .... F 631 293-7889
  Farmingdale *(G-5018)*
K Barthelmes Mfg Co Inc .... F 585 328-8140
  Rochester *(G-14466)*

Kal Manufacturing Corporation .... E 585 265-4310
  Webster *(G-16726)*
Ksm Group Ltd .... G 716 751-6006
  Newfane *(G-12787)*
Leader Sheet Metal Inc .... F 347 271-4961
  Bronx *(G-1379)*
Manufacturing Resources Inc .... E 631 481-0041
  Rochester *(G-14493)*
Marex Aquisition Corp. .... C 585 458-3940
  Rochester *(G-14497)*
Mariah Metal Products Inc .... G 516 938-9783
  Hicksville *(G-6368)*
Mason Scott Industries LLC .... F 516 349-1800
  Roslyn Heights *(G-15029)*
McAlpin Industries Inc. .... C 585 266-3060
  Rochester *(G-14500)*
McHone Industries Inc .... D 716 945-3380
  Salamanca *(G-15101)*
MD International Industries .... E 631 254-3100
  Deer Park *(G-4173)*
Mega Vision Inc .... E 718 228-1065
  Brooklyn *(G-2295)*
Merz Metal & Machine Corp .... E 716 893-7786
  Buffalo *(G-3062)*
Metal Solutions Inc .... E 315 732-6271
  Utica *(G-16347)*
Metalsmith Inc .... E 631 467-1500
  Holbrook *(G-6463)*
Methods Tooling & Mfg Inc .... E 845 246-7100
  Mount Marion *(G-8651)*
Metro Duct Systems Inc .... E 718 278-4294
  Long Island City *(G-7810)*
Middleby Corporation .... E 631 226-6688
  Lindenhurst *(G-7472)*
Monarch Metal Fabrication Inc .... E 631 563-8967
  Bohemia *(G-1105)*
Ms Spares LLC .... G 607 223-3024
  Clay *(G-3683)*
N & L Instruments Inc .... F 631 471-4000
  Ronkonkoma *(G-14948)*
Nci Group Inc .... D 315 339-1245
  Rome *(G-14824)*
North Coast Outfitters Ltd. .... E 631 727-5580
  Riverhead *(G-14150)*
Northeast Industries LLC. .... D 607 865-4031
  Walton *(G-16549)*
Northern Awning & Sign Company .. G 315 782-8515
  Watertown *(G-16667)*
Olympic Manufacturing Inc .... E 631 231-8900
  Hauppauge *(G-6153)*
Omc Inc. .... C 718 731-5001
  Bronx *(G-1416)*
Pathfinder Industries Inc .... E 315 593-2483
  Fulton *(G-5474)*
PDQ Manufacturing Co Inc .... E 845 889-3123
  Rhinebeck *(G-14057)*
Pirnat Precise Metals Inc .... G 631 293-9169
  Farmingdale *(G-5080)*
Plattsburgh Sheet Metal Inc .... G 518 561-4930
  Plattsburgh *(G-13688)*
Precision Fabrication LLC .... E 585 591-3449
  Attica *(G-474)*
Precision Metals Corp .... E 631 586-5032
  Bay Shore *(G-727)*
Precision Mtal Fabricators Inc .... F 718 832-9805
  Brooklyn *(G-2435)*
Precision Systems Mfg Inc .... E 315 451-3480
  Liverpool *(G-7544)*
Product Integration & Mfg Inc .... E 585 436-6260
  Rochester *(G-14605)*
Prokosch and Sonn Sheet Metal .... E 845 562-4211
  Newburgh *(G-12776)*
Protofast Holding Corp .... G 631 753-2549
  Copiague *(G-3920)*
Rami Sheet Metal Inc .... G 845 426-2948
  Spring Valley *(G-15600)*
Rayco Manufacturing Co Inc .... F 516 431-2006
  Jamaica *(G-6944)*
Read Manufacturing Company Inc .. E 631 567-4487
  Holbrook *(G-6467)*
Reynolds Manufacturing Inc .... F 607 562-8936
  Big Flats *(G-882)*
Rigidized Metals Corporation .... E 716 849-4703
  Buffalo *(G-3158)*
Robert E Derecktor Inc .... D 914 698-0962
  Mamaroneck *(G-8045)*
Rochester Colonial Mfg Corp .... D 585 254-8191
  Rochester *(G-14639)*
Rollson Inc. .... E 631 423-9578
  Huntington *(G-6678)*

Royal Metal Products Inc .... E 518 966-4442
  Surprise *(G-15811)*
S & B Machine Works Inc .... E 516 997-2666
  Westbury *(G-17025)*
S & T Machine Inc .... F 718 272-2484
  Brooklyn *(G-2523)*
Savaco Inc .... G 716 751-9455
  Newfane *(G-12788)*
Service Mfg Group Inc .... E 716 893-1482
  Buffalo *(G-3184)*
Solidus Industries Inc. .... D 607 749-4540
  Homer *(G-6522)*
Standard Industrial Works Inc .... F 631 888-0130
  Bay Shore *(G-744)*
Steel Sales Inc. .... E 607 674-6363
  Sherburne *(G-15397)*
Steel Work Inc .... G 585 232-1555
  Rochester *(G-14701)*
Sterling Industries Inc .... E 631 753-3070
  Farmingdale *(G-5117)*
T Lemme Mechanical Inc. .... E 518 436-4136
  Menands *(G-8379)*
Tatra Mfg Corporation .... E 631 691-1184
  Copiague *(G-3932)*
TCS Industries Inc .... D 585 426-1160
  Rochester *(G-14718)*
Technimetal Precision Inds .... E 631 231-8900
  Hauppauge *(G-6210)*
Themis Chimney Inc .... F 718 937-4716
  Brooklyn *(G-2657)*
Tri-Metal Industries Inc .... E 716 691-3323
  Amherst *(G-268)*
Tri-Technologies Inc .... E 914 699-2001
  Mount Vernon *(G-8741)*
Trident Precision Mfg Inc .... E 585 265-2010
  Webster *(G-16738)*
Tripar Manufacturing Co Inc .... E 631 563-0855
  Bohemia *(G-1148)*
Truform Manufacturing Corp .... E 585 458-1090
  Rochester *(G-14734)*
Trylon Wire & Metal Works Inc .... E 718 542-4472
  Bronx *(G-1481)*
Ulster Precision Inc .... E 845 338-0995
  Kingston *(G-7218)*
Ultimate Prcision Met Pdts Inc .... D 631 249-9441
  Farmingdale *(G-5136)*
Unadilla Silo Company Inc .... D 607 369-9341
  Sidney *(G-15444)*
Universal Precision Corp .... E 585 321-9760
  Rochester *(G-14744)*
Universal Shielding Corp .... E 631 667-7900
  Deer Park *(G-4219)*
Vance Metal Fabricators Inc. .... D 315 789-5626
  Geneva *(G-5588)*
Vin Mar Precision Metal Inc .... F 631 563-6608
  Copiague *(G-3937)*
Voss Manufacturing Inc. .... D 716 731-5062
  Sanborn *(G-15130)*
Wainland Inc. .... E 718 626-2233
  Astoria *(G-461)*
Wenig Corporation .... E 718 542-3600
  Bronx *(G-1493)*
Wg Sheet Metal Corp .... G 718 235-3093
  Brooklyn *(G-2746)*
William Kanes Mfg Corp .... E 718 346-1515
  Brooklyn *(G-2754)*
Worksman Trading Corp .... E 718 322-2000
  Ozone Park *(G-13387)*
Zahk Sales Inc. .... G 631 348-9300
  Islandia *(G-6805)*

METAL FABRICATORS: Structural, Ship

Standard Ascnsion Towers Group .. D 716 681-2222
  Depew *(G-4274)*

METAL FABRICATORS: Structural, Ship

Cameron Bridge Works LLC .... E 607 734-9456
  Elmira *(G-4672)*
Miller Metal Fabricating Inc .... G 585 359-3400
  Rochester *(G-14514)*

METAL FINISHING SVCS

21st Century Finishes Inc .... F 516 221-7000
  North Bellmore *(G-12914)*
ABS Metal Corp. .... G 646 302-9018
  Hewlett *(G-6306)*
Anthony River Inc .... F 315 475-1315
  Syracuse *(G-15855)*

PRODUCT SECTION

METALS: Precious, Secondary

D & I Finishing Inc ....G....... 631 471-3034
  Bohemia *(G-1048)*
D & W Enterprises LLC ....F....... 585 590-6727
  Medina *(G-8270)*
Eastside Oxide Co ....E....... 607 734-1253
  Elmira *(G-4680)*
Ever-Nu-Metal Products Inc ....F....... 646 423-5833
  Brooklyn *(G-1939)*
First Impressions Finishing ....G....... 631 467-2244
  Ronkonkoma *(G-14900)*
General Plating LLC ....E....... 585 423-0830
  Rochester *(G-14391)*
Halmark Architectural Finshg ....E....... 718 272-1831
  Brooklyn *(G-2063)*
I W Industries Inc ....C....... 631 293-9494
  Melville *(G-8330)*
L W S Inc ....F....... 631 580-0472
  Ronkonkoma *(G-14925)*
Maracle Industrial Finshg Co ....E....... 585 387-9077
  Rochester *(G-14495)*
Master Craft Finishers Inc ....E....... 631 586-0540
  Deer Park *(G-4171)*
Multitone Finishing Co Inc ....G....... 516 485-1043
  West Hempstead *(G-16860)*
Oerlikon Balzers Coating USA ....E....... 716 564-8557
  Buffalo *(G-3099)*
Paradigm Group LLC ....G....... 718 860-1538
  Bronx *(G-1420)*
Products Superb Inc ....G....... 315 923-7057
  Clyde *(G-3731)*
Rainbow Powder Coating Corp ....G....... 631 586-4019
  Deer Park *(G-4198)*
Saccomize Inc ....G....... 818 287-3000
  Bronx *(G-1446)*
Surface Finish Technology ....E....... 607 732-2909
  Elmira *(G-4703)*
Vibra Tech Industries Inc ....F....... 914 946-1916
  White Plains *(G-17180)*

METAL RESHAPING & REPLATING SVCS

Miscellnous Ir Fabricators Inc ....E....... 518 355-1822
  Schenectady *(G-15280)*

METAL SERVICE CENTERS & OFFICES

Albea Cosmetics America Inc ....E....... 212 371-5100
  New York *(G-9073)*
Aufhauser Corporation ....F....... 516 694-8696
  Plainview *(G-13584)*
Cannon Industries Inc ....D....... 585 254-8080
  Rochester *(G-14258)*
Specialty Steel Fabg Corp ....F....... 718 893-6326
  Bronx *(G-1461)*
Steel Sales Inc ....E....... 607 674-6363
  Sherburne *(G-15397)*

METAL SPINNING FOR THE TRADE

Acme Architectural Products ....B....... 718 360-0700
  Brooklyn *(G-1554)*
American Metal Spinning Pdts ....G....... 631 454-6276
  West Babylon *(G-16771)*
Art Precision Metal Products ....F....... 631 842-8889
  Copiague *(G-3894)*
Bridgeport Metalcraft Inc ....G....... 315 623-9597
  Constantia *(G-3880)*
Gem Metal Spinning & Stamping ....G....... 718 729-7014
  Long Island City *(G-7749)*
Hy-Grade Metal Products Corp ....G....... 315 475-4221
  Syracuse *(G-15961)*
Koch Metal Spinning Co Inc ....D....... 716 835-3631
  Buffalo *(G-3034)*
Long Island Metalform Inc ....F....... 631 242-9088
  Deer Park *(G-4167)*
Russco Metal Spinning Co Inc ....F....... 516 872-6055
  Oceanside *(G-13095)*
S D Z Metal Spinning Stamping ....F....... 718 778-3600
  Brooklyn *(G-2525)*
Toronto Metal Spinning and Ltg ....E....... 905 793-1174
  Niagara Falls *(G-12883)*

METAL STAMPING, FOR THE TRADE

A-1 Stamping & Spinning Corp ....F....... 718 388-2626
  Rockaway Park *(G-14784)*
Ajl Manufacturing Inc ....C....... 585 254-1128
  Rochester *(G-14184)*
Albest Metal Stamping Corp ....D....... 718 388-6000
  Brooklyn *(G-1576)*
Alton Manufacturing Inc ....D....... 585 458-2600
  Rochester *(G-14194)*
American Mtal Stmping Spinning ....F....... 718 384-1500
  Brooklyn *(G-1604)*
Belmet Products Inc ....E....... 718 542-8220
  Bronx *(G-1283)*
Charles A Rogers Entps Inc ....E....... 585 924-6400
  Victor *(G-16466)*
D-K Manufacturing Corp ....E....... 315 592-4327
  Fulton *(G-5455)*
Dayton Industries Inc ....E....... 718 542-8144
  Bronx *(G-1311)*
Die-Matic Products LLC ....E....... 516 433-7900
  Plainview *(G-13597)*
Feldware Inc ....E....... 718 372-0486
  Brooklyn *(G-1965)*
Gay Sheet Metal Dies Inc ....G....... 716 877-0208
  Buffalo *(G-2966)*
Genesee Metal Stampings Inc ....G....... 585 475-0450
  West Henrietta *(G-16879)*
Interplex Industries Inc ....F....... 718 961-6212
  College Point *(G-3790)*
Rolite Mfg Inc ....E....... 716 683-0259
  Lancaster *(G-7340)*
S & S Prtg Die-Cutting Co Inc ....F....... 718 388-8990
  Brooklyn *(G-2522)*
Smithers Tools & Mch Pdts Inc ....D....... 845 876-3063
  Rhinebeck *(G-14058)*
Square Stamping Mfg Corp ....E....... 315 896-2641
  Barneveld *(G-618)*
Tools & Stamping Corp ....G....... 718 392-4040
  Brooklyn *(G-2663)*
Trident Precision Mfg Inc ....G....... 585 265-2010
  Webster *(G-16738)*
Ultimate Prcision Met Pdts Inc ....D....... 631 249-9441
  Farmingdale *(G-5136)*
Volkert Precision Tech Inc ....E....... 718 464-9500
  Queens Village *(G-13984)*

METAL STAMPINGS: Patterned

Corbett Stves Pttern Works Inc ....E....... 585 546-7109
  Rochester *(G-14289)*

METAL STAMPINGS: Perforated

Erdle Perforating Holdings Inc ....D....... 585 247-4700
  Rochester *(G-14355)*
National Wire & Metal Tech Inc ....E....... 716 661-9180
  Jamestown *(G-7021)*
Pall Corporation ....A....... 607 753-6041
  Cortland *(G-4035)*

METAL STAMPINGS: Rigidized

Rigidized Metals Corporation ....E....... 716 849-4703
  Buffalo *(G-3158)*

METAL TREATING COMPOUNDS

Foseco Inc ....F....... 914 345-4760
  Tarrytown *(G-16090)*
Technic Inc ....F....... 516 349-0700
  Plainview *(G-13638)*

METAL, TITANIUM: Sponge & Granules

Saes Smart Materials Inc ....E....... 315 266-2026
  New Hartford *(G-8810)*

METAL: Heavy, Perforated

Perforated Screen Surfaces ....E....... 866 866-8690
  Conklin *(G-3872)*

METALLIC ORES WHOLESALERS

Umicore USA Inc ....E....... 919 874-7171
  Glens Falls *(G-5700)*

METALS SVC CENTERS & WHOL: Structural Shapes, Iron Or Steel

Alp Steel Corp ....E....... 716 854-3030
  Buffalo *(G-2804)*
Blue Tee Corp ....G....... 212 598-0880
  New York *(G-9422)*
GCM Metal Industries Inc ....F....... 718 386-4059
  Brooklyn *(G-2015)*
Reliable Welding & Fabrication ....G....... 631 758-2637
  Patchogue *(G-13434)*
Supreme Steel Inc ....F....... 631 884-1320
  Lindenhurst *(G-7489)*
Universal Steel Fabricators ....F....... 718 342-0782
  Brooklyn *(G-2709)*

METALS SVC CENTERS & WHOLESALERS: Cable, Wire

Ultra Clarity Corp ....G....... 719 470-1010
  Spring Valley *(G-15604)*

METALS SVC CENTERS & WHOLESALERS: Iron & Steel Prdt, Ferrous

Ewt Holdings III Corp ....G....... 212 644-5900
  New York *(G-10096)*

METALS SVC CENTERS & WHOLESALERS: Misc Nonferrous Prdts

Amt Incorporated ....E....... 518 284-2910
  Sharon Springs *(G-15383)*

METALS SVC CENTERS & WHOLESALERS: Nonferrous Sheets, Etc

Umicore USA Inc ....E....... 919 874-7171
  Glens Falls *(G-5700)*

METALS SVC CENTERS & WHOLESALERS: Pipe & Tubing, Steel

Accord Pipe Fabricators Inc ....E....... 718 657-3900
  Jamaica *(G-6892)*
ASAP Rack Rental Inc ....G....... 718 499-4495
  Brooklyn *(G-1638)*
Davidson Corporation ....G....... 718 439-6300
  Brooklyn *(G-1843)*

METALS SVC CENTERS & WHOLESALERS: Sheets, Metal

Hatfield Metal Fab Inc ....E....... 845 454-9078
  Poughkeepsie *(G-13906)*

METALS SVC CENTERS & WHOLESALERS: Steel

Asm USA Inc ....G....... 212 925-2906
  New York *(G-9233)*
Hitachi Metals America Ltd ....E....... 914 694-9200
  Purchase *(G-13959)*
Massena Metals Inc ....F....... 315 769-3846
  Massena *(G-8198)*
Nathan Steel Corp ....F....... 315 797-1335
  Utica *(G-16351)*
R & S Machine Center Inc ....F....... 518 563-4016
  West Chazy *(G-16842)*

METALS SVC CENTERS & WHOLESALERS: Tin & Tin Base Metals

Tin Box Company of America Inc ....E....... 631 845-1600
  Farmingdale *(G-5132)*

METALS SVC CENTERS & WHOLESALERS: Tubing, Metal

Advanced Engineered Products ....F....... 631 435-3535
  Bay Shore *(G-666)*
Tube Fabrication Company Inc ....F....... 716 673-1871
  Fredonia *(G-5375)*

METALS: Precious NEC

Doral Refining Corp ....E....... 516 223-3684
  Freeport *(G-5394)*
Eco-Bat America LLC ....C....... 845 692-4414
  Middletown *(G-8439)*
Euro Pacific Precious Metals ....G....... 212 481-0310
  New York *(G-10084)*
Handy & Harman Ltd ....A....... 914 461-1300
  White Plains *(G-17120)*
Sph Group Holdings LLC ....G....... 212 520-2300
  New York *(G-12162)*
Starfuels Inc ....G....... 914 289-4800
  White Plains *(G-17170)*
Wallace Refiners Inc ....G....... 212 391-2649
  New York *(G-12582)*

METALS: Precious, Secondary

Encore Refining and Recycling ....G....... 631 319-1910
  Holbrook *(G-6446)*
Handy & Harman ....E....... 914 461-1300
  White Plains *(G-17118)*

METALS: Precious, Secondary

Sabin Metal Corporation .... F 631 329-1695
  East Hampton *(G-4415)*
Sabin Metal Corporation .... C 585 538-2194
  Scottsville *(G-15339)*

METALS: Primary Nonferrous, NEC

Ames Goldsmith Corp .... E 518 792-7435
  Glens Falls *(G-5669)*
Billanti Casting Co Inc .... E 516 775-4800
  New Hyde Park *(G-8819)*
Goldmark Products Inc .... E 631 777-3343
  Farmingdale *(G-5001)*
Marina Jewelry Co Inc .... G 212 354-5027
  New York *(G-11152)*
Materion Advanced Materials .... C 800 327-1355
  Buffalo *(G-3058)*
RS Precision Industries Inc .... E 631 420-0424
  Farmingdale *(G-5105)*
S & W Metal Trading Corp .... G 212 719-5070
  New York *(G-11944)*
Sabin Metal Corporation .... C 585 538-2194
  Scottsville *(G-15339)*
Sigmund Cohn Corp .... D 914 664-5300
  Mount Vernon *(G-8734)*
Tdy Industries LLC .... E 716 433-4411
  Lockport *(G-7617)*

METALWORK: Miscellaneous

Abasco Inc .... E 716 649-4790
  Hamburg *(G-5918)*
Accurate Metal Weather Strip .... G 914 668-6042
  Mount Vernon *(G-8661)*
Coral Management Corp .... G 718 893-9286
  Bronx *(G-1304)*
Designs By Novello Inc .... G 914 934-7711
  Port Chester *(G-13742)*
Empire Metal Finishing Inc .... E 718 545-6700
  Astoria *(G-440)*
Fala Technologies Inc .... E 845 336-4000
  Kingston *(G-7189)*
Genesee Metal Products Inc .... E 585 968-6000
  Wellsville *(G-16752)*
Halmark Architectural Finshg .... E 718 272-1831
  Brooklyn *(G-2063)*
Integrity Tool Incorporated .... F 315 524-4409
  Ontario *(G-13204)*
Janed Enterprises .... F 631 694-4494
  Farmingdale *(G-5017)*
Kraman Iron Works Inc .... F 212 460-8400
  New York *(G-10885)*
Lane Enterprises Inc .... E 518 885-4385
  Ballston Spa *(G-601)*
Longstem Organizers Inc .... G 914 777-2174
  Jefferson Valley *(G-7057)*
Metal Products Intl LLC .... G 716 215-1930
  Niagara Falls *(G-12846)*
Orange County Ironworks LLC .... E 845 769-3000
  Montgomery *(G-8600)*
Orbital Holdings Inc .... E 951 360-7100
  Buffalo *(G-3104)*
Paragon Aquatics .... E 845 452-5500
  Lagrangeville *(G-7257)*
Ppi Corp .... E 585 880-7277
  Geneseo *(G-5567)*
Risa Management Corp .... E 718 361-2606
  Maspeth *(G-8167)*
Riverside Iron LLC .... F 315 535-4864
  Gouverneur *(G-5747)*
Rollform of Jamestown Inc .... F 716 665-5310
  Jamestown *(G-7025)*
Semans Enterprises Inc .... F 585 444-0097
  West Henrietta *(G-16894)*
Signature Metal MBL Maint LLC ...... D 718 292-8280
  Bronx *(G-1455)*
Sims Steel Corporation .... E 631 587-8670
  Lindenhurst *(G-7482)*
Sinn-Tech Industries Inc .... G 631 643-1171
  West Babylon *(G-16828)*
Sky Dive .... D 845 858-6400
  Port Jervis *(G-13792)*
Tebbens Steel LLC .... F 631 208-8330
  Calverton *(G-3301)*
Tonys Ornamental Ir Works Inc .... E 315 337-3730
  Rome *(G-14838)*
Tough Trac Inc .... G 631 504-6700
  Medford *(G-8261)*
United Iron Inc .... E 914 667-5700
  Mount Vernon *(G-8745)*

METALWORK: Ornamental

Arcadia Mfg Group Inc .... E 518 434-6213
  Green Island *(G-5853)*
Arcadia Mfg Group Inc .... G 518 434-6213
  Menands *(G-8367)*
Duke of Iron Inc .... G 631 543-3600
  Smithtown *(G-15486)*
Iron Art Inc .... G 914 592-7977
  Elmsford *(G-4757)*
Kendi Iron Works Inc .... G 718 821-2722
  Brooklyn *(G-2170)*
Kleinfelder John .... G 716 753-3163
  Mayville *(G-8216)*
Koenig Iron Works Inc .... E 718 433-0900
  Long Island City *(G-7782)*
Kryten Iron Works Inc .... G 914 345-0990
  Hawthorne *(G-6249)*
Shanker Industries Inc .... G 631 940-9889
  Deer Park *(G-4209)*
Tensator Inc .... D 631 666-0300
  Bay Shore *(G-751)*

METALWORKING MACHINERY WHOLESALERS

S & S Machinery Corp .... E 718 492-7400
  Brooklyn *(G-2520)*

METER READERS: Remote

Quadlogic Controls Corporation ...... D 212 930-9300
  Long Island City *(G-7852)*

METERING DEVICES: Flow Meters, Impeller & Counter Driven

Flexim Americas Corporation .... F 631 492-2300
  Edgewood *(G-4598)*
SPX Flow Us LLC .... G 585 436-5550
  Rochester *(G-14698)*
Turbo Machined Products LLC .... E 315 895-3010
  Frankfort *(G-5358)*

METERING DEVICES: Totalizing, Consumption

Siemens Industry Inc .... C 631 231-3600
  Hauppauge *(G-6189)*

METERING DEVICES: Water Quality Monitoring & Control Systems

Gurley Precision Instrs Inc .... C 518 272-6300
  Troy *(G-16237)*

METERS: Elasped Time

Curtis Instruments Inc .... C 914 666-2971
  Mount Kisco *(G-8624)*
Frequency Electronics Inc .... B 516 794-4500
  Uniondale *(G-16295)*

METERS: Liquid

Walter R Tucker Entps Ltd .... E 607 467-2866
  Deposit *(G-4282)*

METHANOL: Natural

Ocip Holding LLC .... G 646 589-6180
  New York *(G-11495)*

MGMT CONSULTING SVCS: Matls, Incl Purch, Handle & Invntry

Color Merchants Inc .... E 212 682-4788
  New York *(G-9672)*

MICA PRDTS

Fra-Rik Formica Fabg Co Inc .... G 718 597-3335
  Bronx *(G-1337)*
Reliance Mica Co Inc .... G 718 788-0282
  Rockaway Park *(G-14787)*
S & J Trading Inc .... G 718 347-1323
  Floral Park *(G-5209)*

MICROCIRCUITS, INTEGRATED: Semiconductor

Aeroflex Incorporated .... B 516 694-6700
  Plainview *(G-13578)*
Aeroflex Plainview Inc .... B 516 694-6700
  Plainview *(G-13579)*
Microchip Technology Inc .... G 631 233-3280
  Hauppauge *(G-6136)*
Park Electrochemical Corp .... C 631 465-3600
  Melville *(G-8347)*
Telephonics Tlsi Corp .... C 631 470-8854
  Huntington *(G-6687)*

MICROFILM EQPT

Mekatronics Incorporated .... E 516 883-6805
  Port Washington *(G-13844)*

MICROMANIPULATOR

Anaren Microwave Inc .... C 315 432-8909
  East Syracuse *(G-4503)*

MICROPHONES

Andrea Electronics Corporation .... F 631 719-1800
  Bohemia *(G-1016)*
Theodore A Rapp Associates .... G 845 469-2100
  Chester *(G-3620)*

MICROPROCESSORS

Eversan Inc .... F 315 736-3967
  Whitesboro *(G-17193)*
I E D Corp .... F 631 348-0424
  Islandia *(G-6795)*
INTEL Corporation .... D 408 765-8080
  Getzville *(G-5599)*

MICROWAVE COMPONENTS

Antenna & Radome Res Assoc .... E 631 231-8400
  Bay Shore *(G-671)*
Cobham Holdings (us) Inc .... A 716 662-0006
  Orchard Park *(G-13262)*
Cobham Holdings Inc .... F 716 662-0006
  Orchard Park *(G-13263)*
Frequency Electronics Inc .... B 516 794-4500
  Uniondale *(G-16295)*
General Microwave Corporation ...... F 516 802-0900
  Syosset *(G-15824)*
Innowave Rf LLC .... G 914 230-4060
  Tarrytown *(G-16091)*
Interntonal Telecom Components ... F 631 243-1444
  Deer Park *(G-4152)*
L-3 Cmmnctons Fgn Holdings Inc ... E 212 697-1111
  New York *(G-10903)*
L-3 Cmmunications Holdings Inc .... D 212 697-1111
  New York *(G-10905)*
L-3 Communications Corporation ... E 631 289-0363
  Patchogue *(G-13427)*
L-3 Communications Corporation ... B 212 697-1111
  New York *(G-10906)*
Lexan Industries Inc .... F 631 434-7586
  Bay Shore *(G-713)*
Microwave Circuit Tech Inc .... E 631 845-1041
  Farmingdale *(G-5052)*
Microwave Filter Company Inc .... E 315 438-4700
  East Syracuse *(G-4550)*
Passive-Plus Inc .... F 631 425-0938
  Huntington *(G-6673)*
Spectrum Microwave Inc .... E 315 253-6241
  Auburn *(G-520)*

MICROWAVE OVENS: Household

Toshiba America Inc .... E 212 596-0600
  New York *(G-12377)*

MILITARY INSIGNIA

Baldwin Ribbon & Stamping Corp ... F 718 335-6700
  Woodside *(G-17319)*

MILITARY INSIGNIA, TEXTILE

Skd Tactical Inc .... G 845 897-2889
  Highland Falls *(G-6410)*

MILL PRDTS: Structural & Rail

Matrix Steel Company Inc .... G 718 381-6800
  Brooklyn *(G-2284)*

PRODUCT SECTION

MIXTURES & BLOCKS: Asphalt Paving

MILLINERY SUPPLIES: Veils & Veiling, Bridal, Funeral, Etc

Paula Varsalona Ltd ....F 212 570-9100
   New York *(G-11586)*

MILLING: Grain Cereals, Cracked

Cargill Incorporated ....G 716 665-6570
   Kennedy *(G-7153)*

MILLWORK

Adams Interior Fabrications ....F 631 249-8282
   Massapequa *(G-8177)*
Amity Woodworking Inc ....G 631 598-7000
   Amityville *(G-275)*
Amstutze Woodworking ....G 518 946-8206
   Upper Jay *(G-16303)*
Architctral Mllwk Installation ....E 631 499-0755
   East Northport *(G-4433)*
Auburn Custom Millwork Inc ....G 315 253-3843
   Auburn *(G-478)*
Bloch Industries LLC ....D 585 334-9600
   Rochester *(G-14235)*
BNC Innovative Woodworking ....F 718 277-2800
   Brooklyn *(G-1706)*
Braga Woodworks ....G 845 342-4636
   Middletown *(G-8428)*
Broadway Neon Sign Corp ....F 908 241-4177
   Ronkonkoma *(G-14881)*
Carob Industries Inc ....F 631 225-0900
   Lindenhurst *(G-7459)*
Christiana Millwork Inc ....E 315 492-9099
   Jamesville *(G-7046)*
City Store Gates Mfg Corp ....E 718 939-9700
   College Point *(G-3781)*
Clearwood Custom Carpentry and ....E 315 432-8422
   East Syracuse *(G-4518)*
Columbus Woodworking Inc ....G 607 674-4546
   Sherburne *(G-15390)*
Concepts In Wood of CNY ....E 315 463-8084
   Syracuse *(G-15904)*
Conley Caseworks Inc ....G 716 655-5830
   Elma *(G-4647)*
Cousins Furniture & Hm Imprvs ....E 631 254-3752
   Deer Park *(G-4121)*
Craftsmen Woodworkers Ltd ....E 718 326-3350
   Maspeth *(G-8125)*
Creative Laminates Inc ....F 315 463-7580
   Syracuse *(G-15911)*
Crown Mill Work Corp ....G 845 371-2200
   Monsey *(G-8570)*
Crown Woodworking Corp ....G 718 974-6415
   Brooklyn *(G-1820)*
Cuccio-Zanetti Inc ....G 518 587-1363
   Middle Grove *(G-8404)*
Custom Door & Mirror Inc ....E 631 414-7725
   Farmingdale *(G-4970)*
Custom Stair & Millwork Co ....G 315 839-5793
   Sauquoit *(G-15199)*
Dbs Interiors Corp ....F 631 491-3013
   West Babylon *(G-16788)*
Deerfield Millwork Inc ....F 631 726-9663
   Water Mill *(G-16604)*
Duncan & Son Carpentry Inc ....E 914 664-4311
   Mount Vernon *(G-8678)*
Ed Negron Fine Woodworking ....G 718 246-1016
   Brooklyn *(G-1902)*
Efj Inc ....D 518 234-4799
   Cobleskill *(G-3737)*
EM Pfaff & Son Inc ....F 607 739-3691
   Horseheads *(G-6575)*
Fantasy Furniture Inc ....E 718 386-8078
   Ridgewood *(G-14106)*
Five Star Millwork LLC ....F 845 920-0247
   Pearl River *(G-13456)*
Garrison Woodworking Inc ....F 845 726-3525
   Westtown *(G-17069)*
Grace Ryan & Magnus Mllwk LLC ....D 914 665-0902
   Mount Vernon *(G-8686)*
H B Millwork Inc ....F 631 289-8086
   Medford *(G-8246)*
H B Millwork Inc ....G 631 924-4195
   Yaphank *(G-17394)*
Highland Organization Corp ....E 631 991-3240
   Deer Park *(G-4150)*
I Meglio Corp ....E 631 617-6900
   Brentwood *(G-1184)*
Island Street Lumber Co Inc ....G 716 692-4127
   North Tonawanda *(G-12978)*

J Percoco Industries Inc ....G 631 312-4572
   Bohemia *(G-1079)*
Jackson Woodworks Inc ....G 518 651-2032
   Brainardsville *(G-1171)*
Jacobs Woodworking LLC ....G 315 427-8999
   Syracuse *(G-15965)*
Jays Furniture Products Inc ....E 716 876-8854
   Buffalo *(G-3015)*
JEm Wdwkg & Cabinets Inc ....F 518 828-5361
   Hudson *(G-6620)*
John Langenbacher Co Inc ....E 718 328-0141
   Bronx *(G-1368)*
KB Millwork Inc ....G 516 280-2183
   Levittown *(G-7429)*
Krefab Corporation ....F 631 842-5151
   Copiague *(G-3909)*
L Builders Supply Inc ....B 518 355-7190
   Schenectady *(G-15275)*
M & D Millwork LLC ....G 631 789-1439
   Amityville *(G-307)*
Mack Wood Working ....G 845 657-6625
   Shokan *(G-15432)*
Medina Millworks LLC ....E 585 798-2969
   Medina *(G-8276)*
Metropolitan Fine Mllwk Corp ....F 914 669-4900
   North Salem *(G-12939)*
Michbi Doors Inc ....D 631 231-9050
   Brentwood *(G-1192)*
Millco Woodworking LLC ....F 585 526-6844
   Hall *(G-5917)*
Millwright Wdwrk Installetion ....E 631 587-2635
   West Babylon *(G-16811)*
North Fork Wood Works Inc ....E 631 255-4028
   Mattituck *(G-8208)*
Northern Forest Pdts Co Inc ....G 315 942-6955
   Boonville *(G-1166)*
Pella Corporation ....C 631 208-0710
   Calverton *(G-3294)*
Peter Productions Devivi Inc ....F 315 568-8484
   Waterloo *(G-16631)*
Pgs Millwork Inc ....D 212 244-6610
   New York *(G-11642)*
Piccini Industries Ltd ....E 845 365-0614
   Orangeburg *(G-13239)*
Professional Cab Detailing Co ....F 845 436-7282
   Woodridge *(G-17315)*
Quaker Millwork & Lumber Inc ....E 716 662-3388
   Orchard Park *(G-13293)*
Randolph Dimension Corporation .....F 716 358-6901
   Randolph *(G-14017)*
RB Woodcraft Inc ....E 315 474-2429
   Syracuse *(G-16021)*
Richard Anthony Corp ....E 914 922-7141
   Yorktown Heights *(G-17518)*
Rj Millworkers Inc ....E 607 433-0525
   Oneonta *(G-13193)*
Roode Hoek & Co Inc ....F 718 522-5921
   Brooklyn *(G-2504)*
Russin Lumber Corp ....F 845 457-4000
   Newburgh *(G-12778)*
S Donadic Woodworking Inc ....D 718 361-9888
   Sunnyside *(G-15809)*
Shawmut Woodworking & Sup Inc ....G 212 920-8900
   New York *(G-12048)*
Specialty Services ....G 585 728-5650
   Wayland *(G-16711)*
Syracuse Industrial Sls Co Ltd ....F 315 478-5751
   Syracuse *(G-16053)*
TDS Woodworking Inc ....F 718 442-5298
   Staten Island *(G-15745)*
Three R Enterprises Inc ....E 585 254-5050
   Rochester *(G-14725)*
Tiedemann Waldemar Inc ....F 716 875-5665
   Buffalo *(G-3218)*
Unicenter Millwork Inc ....G 716 741-8201
   Clarence Center *(G-3681)*
Universal Custom Millwork Inc ....D 518 330-6622
   Amsterdam *(G-372)*
Urban Woodworks Ltd ....G 718 827-1570
   Brooklyn *(G-2711)*
Wagner Millwork Inc ....D 607 687-5362
   Owego *(G-13361)*
Wolfe Lumber Mill Inc ....G 716 772-7950
   Gasport *(G-5560)*
Xylon Industries Inc ....G 631 293-4717
   Farmingdale *(G-5144)*
Zanzano Woodworking Inc ....F 914 725-6025
   Scarsdale *(G-15225)*

MINERAL ABRASIVES MINING SVCS

Capital Gold Corporation ....G 212 668-0842
   New York *(G-9519)*

MINERAL MINING: Nonmetallic

Hargrave Development ....F 716 877-7880
   Kenmore *(G-7147)*

MINERAL PRODUCTS

American Crmic Process RES LLC ...G 315 828-6268
   Phelps *(G-13529)*

MINERAL WOOL

American Securities LLC ....E 716 696-3012
   Tonawanda *(G-16138)*
Owens Corning Sales LLC ....B 518 475-3600
   Feura Bush *(G-5174)*
Soundcoat Company Inc ....D 631 242-2200
   Deer Park *(G-4212)*
Unifrax I LLC ....C 716 696-3000
   Tonawanda *(G-16210)*

MINERAL WOOL INSULATION PRDTS

Unifrax Corporation ....E 716 278-3800
   Niagara Falls *(G-12886)*

MINERALS: Ground or Treated

Allied Aero Services Inc ....G 631 277-9368
   Brentwood *(G-1175)*
DSM Nutritional Products LLC ....C 518 372-5155
   Glenville *(G-5701)*
Fortitech Inc ....C 518 372-5155
   Schenectady *(G-15255)*
Mineralbious Corp ....F 516 498-9715
   Port Washington *(G-13846)*
Minerals Technologies Inc ....E 212 878-1800
   New York *(G-11276)*
Northeast Solite Corporation ....E 845 246-2646
   Saugerties *(G-15189)*
Northeast Solite Corporation ....E 845 246-2177
   Mount Marion *(G-8652)*
Oro Avanti Inc ....G 516 487-5185
   Great Neck *(G-5826)*
Prince Minerals LLC ....D 646 747-4222
   New York *(G-11711)*

MINIATURES

Islip Miniture Golf ....G 631 940-8900
   Bay Shore *(G-708)*

MINING EXPLORATION & DEVELOPMENT SVCS

Coremet Trading Inc ....G 212 964-3600
   New York *(G-9724)*

MINING SVCS, NEC: Lignite

US Pump Corp ....G 516 303-7799
   West Hempstead *(G-16864)*

MINING: Sand & Shale Oil

Kimmeridge Energy MGT Co LLC ....G 646 517-7252
   New York *(G-10848)*

MIRROR REPAIR SHOP

D Best Service Co Inc ....G 718 972-6133
   Brooklyn *(G-1829)*

MIRRORS: Motor Vehicle

Prisma Glass & Mirror Inc ....G 718 366-7191
   Ridgewood *(G-14120)*
Rosco Inc ....C 718 526-2601
   Jamaica *(G-6948)*

MIXING EQPT

Munson Machinery Company Inc .....E 315 797-0090
   Utica *(G-16350)*

MIXTURES & BLOCKS: Asphalt Paving

Albany Asp & Aggregates Corp ....E 518 436-8916
   Albany *(G-37)*

MIXTURES & BLOCKS: Asphalt Paving

All Phases Asp & Ldscpg Dsgn ....F 631 588-1372
  Ronkonkoma *(G-14862)*
Barrett Paving Materials Inc ....G 607 723-5367
  Binghamton *(G-890)*
Barrett Paving Materials Inc ....F 315 788-2037
  Watertown *(G-16636)*
Bross Quality Paving ....G 845 532-7116
  Ellenville *(G-4632)*
C & C Ready-Mix Corporation ....F 607 687-1690
  Owego *(G-13351)*
Callanan Industries Inc ....C 518 374-2222
  Schenectady *(G-15236)*
Callanan Industries Inc ....E 845 331-6868
  Kingston *(G-7182)*
Canal Asphalt Inc ....F 914 667-8500
  Mount Vernon *(G-8669)*
Cofire Paving Corporation ....E 718 463-1403
  Flushing *(G-5234)*
Cold Mix Manufacturing Corp ....F 718 463-1444
  Mount Vernon *(G-8673)*
Deans Paving Inc ....F 315 736-7601
  Marcy *(G-8091)*
Dolomite Products Company Inc ....F 585 352-0460
  Spencerport *(G-13202)*
G&G Sealcoating and Paving Inc ....E 585 787-1500
  Ontario *(G-13202)*
Gernatt Asphalt Products Inc ....E 716 532-3371
  Collins *(G-3817)*
Gernatt Asphalt Products Inc ....G 716 496-5111
  Springville *(G-15610)*
Grace Associates Inc ....G 718 767-9000
  Harrison *(G-5986)*
Graymont Materials (ny) Inc ....G 518 873-2275
  Lewis *(G-7431)*
Graymont Materials Inc ....E 518 561-5200
  Plattsburgh *(G-13667)*
Hanson Aggregates East LLC ....E 585 343-1787
  Stafford *(G-15621)*
J Pahura Contractors ....G 585 589-5793
  Albion *(G-166)*
Jamestown Macadam Inc ....F 716 664-5108
  Jamestown *(G-7009)*
Jet-Black Sealers Inc ....G 716 891-4197
  Buffalo *(G-3019)*
John T Montecalvo Inc ....G 631 325-1492
  Speonk *(G-15576)*
Kal-Harbour Inc ....F 518 266-0690
  Albany *(G-93)*
Kings Park Asphalt Corporation ....G 631 269-9774
  Hauppauge *(G-6105)*
Lafarge North America Inc ....E 518 756-5000
  Ravena *(G-14023)*
Morlyn Asphalt Corp ....G 845 888-2695
  Cochecton *(G-3743)*
Narde Paving Company Inc ....E 607 737-7177
  Elmira *(G-4696)*
Nicolia Concrete Products Inc ....D 631 669-0700
  Lindenhurst *(G-7476)*
Package Pavement Company Inc ....D 845 221-2224
  Stormville *(G-15780)*
Patterson Blacktop Corp ....E 914 949-2000
  White Plains *(G-17145)*
Patterson Materials Corp ....F 914 949-2000
  White Plains *(G-17146)*
Pavco Asphalt Inc ....E 631 289-3223
  Holtsville *(G-6506)*
Peckham Industries Inc ....E 518 945-1120
  Athens *(G-466)*
Peckham Materials Corp ....E 518 945-1120
  Athens *(G-467)*
Peckham Materials Corp ....F 518 494-2313
  Chestertown *(G-3622)*
Peckham Materials Corp ....E 518 747-3353
  Hudson Falls *(G-6649)*
Prima Asphalt and Concrete ....F 631 289-3223
  Holtsville *(G-6507)*
Rason Asphalt Inc ....G 631 293-6210
  Farmingdale *(G-5097)*
Rason Asphalt Inc ....G 516 671-1500
  Glen Cove *(G-5626)*
Sheldon Slate Products Co Inc ....E 518 642-1280
  Middle Granville *(G-8401)*
Suit-Kote Corporation ....F 315 735-8501
  Oriskany *(G-13314)*
Suit-Kote Corporation ....E 607 535-2743
  Watkins Glen *(G-16697)*
Thalle Industries Inc ....E 914 762-3415
  Briarcliff Manor *(G-1231)*
Tri City Highway Products Inc ....E 607 722-2967
  Binghamton *(G-957)*
Tri-City Highway Products Inc ....E 518 294-9964
  Richmondville *(G-14090)*
Twin County Recycling Corp ....F 516 827-6900
  Westbury *(G-17038)*
Ultimate Pavers Corp ....E 917 417-2652
  Staten Island *(G-15750)*
Unilock New York Inc ....G 845 278-6700
  Brewster *(G-1229)*
Universal Ready Mix Inc ....G 516 746-4535
  New Hyde Park *(G-8871)*
Zielinskis Asphalt Inc ....F 315 306-4057
  Oriskany Falls *(G-13319)*

MOBILE COMMUNICATIONS EQPT

2p Agency Usa Inc ....G 212 203-5586
  Brooklyn *(G-1513)*
Andrea Electronics Corporation ....F 631 719-1800
  Bohemia *(G-1016)*
AT&T Corp 716 639-0673
  Williamsville *(G-17234)*
Cmb Wireless Group LLC ....C 631 750-4700
  Bohemia *(G-1036)*
Elite Cellular Accessories Inc ....E 877 390-2502
  Deer Park *(G-4136)*
Flycell Inc ....E 212 400-1212
  New York *(G-10181)*
Icell Inc ....C 516 590-0007
  Hempstead *(G-6274)*
M&S Accessory Network Corp ....F 347 492-7790
  New York *(G-11078)*
Toura LLC ....F 646 652-8668
  Brooklyn *(G-2670)*

MOBILE HOMES

All Star Carts & Vehicles Inc ....D 631 666-5581
  Bay Shore *(G-668)*
American Home Mfg LLC ....D 718 855-0617
  New York *(G-9120)*
Champion Home Builders Inc ....C 315 841-4122
  Sangerfield *(G-15132)*
Leatherstocking Mobile Home PA 315 839-5691
  Sauquoit *(G-15200)*
Sonic Boom Inc ....F 212 242-2852
  New York *(G-12129)*
Sterling Building Systems 716 685-0505
  Depew *(G-4275)*

MOBILE HOMES WHOLESALERS

Century Ready Mix Inc ....G 631 888-2200
  West Babylon *(G-16781)*

MODELS

Copesetic Inc ....F 315 684-7780
  Morrisville *(G-8620)*
Creative Models & Prototypes 516 433-6828
  Hicksville *(G-6337)*
Marilyn Model Management Inc ....F 646 556-7587
  New York *(G-11151)*
Tri-Force Sales LLC 732 261-5507
  New York *(G-12399)*

MODELS: General, Exc Toy

Active Manufacturing Inc ....F 607 775-3162
  Kirkwood *(G-7230)*
Emerald Models Inc ....G 585 584-3739
  East Bethany *(G-4382)*
J T Systematic ....G 607 754-0929
  Endwell *(G-4836)*

MODULES: Computer Logic

Ieh FM Holdings LLC ....E 212 702-4300
  New York *(G-10559)*
Intech 21 Inc ....F 516 626-7221
  Port Washington *(G-13825)*
International Bus Mchs Corp ....E 212 324-5000
  New York *(G-10631)*

MODULES: Solid State

Data Device Corporation ....B 631 567-5600
  Bohemia *(G-1049)*

MOLDED RUBBER PRDTS

Buffalo Lining & Fabricating 716 883-6500
  Buffalo *(G-2854)*
Enviroform Recycled Pdts Inc ....G 315 789-1810
  Geneva *(G-5574)*

Moldtech Inc ....E 716 685-3344
  Lancaster *(G-7327)*
SD Christie Associates Inc ....G 914 734-1800
  Peekskill *(G-13482)*
Short Jj Associates Inc ....F 315 986-3511
  Macedon *(G-7991)*
Traffic Logix Corporation 866 915-6449
  Spring Valley *(G-15603)*

MOLDING COMPOUNDS

Coda Resources Ltd ....D 718 649-1666
  Brooklyn *(G-1790)*
Craftech ....D 518 828-5011
  Chatham *(G-3557)*
Hanet Plastics Usa Inc ....G 518 324-5850
  Plattsburgh *(G-13668)*
Imperial Polymers Inc ....G 718 387-4741
  Brooklyn *(G-2099)*
Jrlon Inc 315 597-4067
  Palmyra *(G-13409)*
Majestic Mold & Tool Inc ....F 315 695-2079
  Phoenix *(G-13542)*
Plaslok Corp ....E 716 681-7755
  Buffalo *(G-3128)*

MOLDINGS, ARCHITECTURAL: Plaster Of Paris

Foster Reeve & Associates Inc ....G 718 609-0090
  Brooklyn *(G-1998)*

MOLDINGS: Picture Frame

AC Moore Incorporated ....G 516 796-5831
  Bethpage *(G-863)*
Frame Shoppe & Art Gallery ....G 516 365-6014
  Manhasset *(G-8060)*
Framerica Corporation ....D 631 650-1000
  Yaphank *(G-17393)*
General Art Company Inc ....F 212 255-1298
  New York *(G-10272)*
Julius Lowy Frame Restoring Co ....E 212 861-8585
  New York *(G-10785)*
P B & H Moulding Corporation ....E 315 455-1756
  Fayetteville *(G-5166)*
Quattro Frameworks Inc ....F 718 361-2620
  Long Island City *(G-7855)*
Quebracho Inc ....G 718 326-3605
  Brooklyn *(G-2465)*
Sky Frame & Art Inc ....E 212 925-7856
  New York *(G-12095)*

MOLDS: Indl

Aaron Tool & Mold Inc ....G 585 426-5100
  Rochester *(G-14164)*
Advanced Mold & Tooling Inc ....E 585 426-2110
  Rochester *(G-14179)*
All American Precision TI Mold ....F 585 436-3080
  West Henrietta *(G-16865)*
Allmetal Chocolate Mold Co Inc ....F 631 752-2888
  West Babylon *(G-16768)*
American Orthotic Lab Co Inc ....G 718 961-6487
  College Point *(G-3778)*
Blue Chip Mold Inc ....F 585 647-1790
  Rochester *(G-14236)*
Century Mold Company Inc ....D 585 352-8600
  Rochester *(G-14266)*
Chenango Valley Tech Inc ....E 607 674-4115
  Sherburne *(G-15389)*
Custom Molding Solutions Inc ....E 585 293-1702
  Churchville *(G-3635)*
East Pattern & Model Corp ....E 585 461-3240
  Fairport *(G-4856)*
G N R Plastics Inc ....F 631 724-8758
  Smithtown *(G-15487)*
Gatti Tool & Mold Inc ....F 585 328-1350
  Rochester *(G-14388)*
Globmarble LLC ....G 347 717-4088
  Brooklyn *(G-2030)*
HNST Mold Inspections LLC ....G 845 215-9258
  Nanuet *(G-8757)*
Hy-Tech Mold Inc ....F 585 247-2450
  Rochester *(G-14441)*
J T Systematic ....G 607 754-0929
  Endwell *(G-4836)*
James B Crowell & Sons Inc ....G 845 895-3464
  Wallkill *(G-16544)*
Nicoform Inc ....F 585 454-5530
  Rochester *(G-14537)*

PRODUCT SECTION

MOTOR VEHICLE PARTS & ACCESS: Air Conditioner Parts

Nordon Inc .... D 585 546-6200
  Rochester *(G-14538)*
PMI Industries LLC .... E 585 464-8050
  Rochester *(G-14586)*
Rochester Tool and Mold Inc .... F 585 464-9336
  Rochester *(G-14652)*
Rochling Advent Tool & Mold LP .... E 585 254-2000
  Rochester *(G-14654)*
Romold Inc .... F 585 529-4440
  Rochester *(G-14658)*
Royal Molds Inc .... F 718 382-7686
  Brooklyn *(G-2512)*
Sb Molds LLC .... D 845 352-3700
  Monsey *(G-8581)*
Star Mold Co Inc .... G 631 694-2283
  Farmingdale *(G-5115)*
Stuart Tool & Die Inc .... E 716 488-1975
  Falconer *(G-4915)*
Syntec Technologies Inc .... F 585 464-9336
  Rochester *(G-14713)*
T A Tool & Molding Inc .... F 631 293-0172
  Farmingdale *(G-5123)*
W N R Pattern & Tool Inc .... G 716 681-9334
  Lancaster *(G-7346)*

MOLDS: Plastic Working & Foundry

A & D Tool Inc .... G 631 243-4339
  Dix Hills *(G-4288)*
Accede Mold & Tool Co Inc .... D 585 254-6490
  Rochester *(G-14165)*
Clifford H Jones Inc .... F 716 693-2444
  Tonawanda *(G-16153)*
Inter Molds Inc .... G 631 667-8580
  Bay Shore *(G-706)*
Moldcraft Inc .... E 716 684-1126
  Depew *(G-4265)*
Northern Design Inc .... F 716 652-7071
  East Aurora *(G-4378)*
Universal Tooling Corporation .... F 716 985-4691
  Gerry *(G-5594)*

MONUMENTS & GRAVE MARKERS, EXC TERRAZZO

Galle & Zinter Inc .... G 716 833-4212
  Buffalo *(G-2963)*

MONUMENTS: Concrete

Presbrey-Leland Inc .... G 914 949-2264
  Valhalla *(G-16371)*
St Raymond Monument Co .... G 718 824-3600
  Bronx *(G-1462)*

MONUMENTS: Cut Stone, Exc Finishing Or Lettering Only

Dominic De Nigris Inc .... E 718 597-4460
  Bronx *(G-1316)*
Suffolk Granite Manufacturing .... E 631 226-4774
  Lindenhurst *(G-7486)*

MOPS: Floor & Dust

Cpac Inc .... E 585 382-3223
  Leicester *(G-7420)*
Ingenious Designs LLC .... C 631 254-3376
  Ronkonkoma *(G-14912)*
National Wire & Metal Tech Inc .... E 716 661-9180
  Jamestown *(G-7021)*
Perfex Corporation .... F 315 826-3600
  Poland *(G-13727)*

MORTGAGE BANKERS

Caithness Equities Corporation .... E 212 599-2112
  New York *(G-9498)*

MOTION PICTURE & VIDEO PRODUCTION SVCS

Chakra Communications Inc .... E 716 505-7300
  Lancaster *(G-7309)*
Crain Communications Inc .... C 212 210-0100
  New York *(G-9745)*
Entertainment Weekly Inc .... C 212 522-5600
  New York *(G-10044)*
Laird Telemedia .... C 845 339-9555
  Mount Marion *(G-8650)*
North Six Inc .... F 212 463-7227
  New York *(G-11458)*
Taste and See Entrmt Inc .... G 516 285-3010
  Valley Stream *(G-16429)*

MOTION PICTURE & VIDEO PRODUCTION SVCS: Non-Theatrical, TV

Scholastic Corporation .... G 212 343-6100
  New York *(G-11997)*

MOTION PICTURE PRODUCTION & DISTRIBUTION

21st Century Fox America Inc .... D 212 852-7000
  New York *(G-8967)*
Historic TW Inc .... D 212 484-8000
  New York *(G-10484)*
Sony Broadband Entertainment .... F 212 833-6800
  New York *(G-12131)*
Time Warner Companies Inc .... D 212 484-8000
  New York *(G-12350)*

MOTION PICTURE PRODUCTION & DISTRIBUTION: Television

Martha Stewart Living .... B 212 827-8000
  New York *(G-11166)*

MOTION PICTURE PRODUCTION ALLIED SVCS

Yam TV LLC .... G 917 932-5418
  New York *(G-12688)*

MOTION PICTURE PRODUCTION SVCS

Abkco Music & Records Inc .... E 212 399-0300
  New York *(G-9004)*

MOTOR & GENERATOR PARTS: Electric

Allied Motion Technologies Inc .... C 315 782-5910
  Watertown *(G-16634)*
Chart Inc .... F 518 272-3565
  Troy *(G-16230)*
Chemark International USA Inc .... G 631 593-4566
  Deer Park *(G-4118)*
Ems Development Corporation .... D 631 924-4736
  Yaphank *(G-17390)*
Hes Inc .... G 607 359-2974
  Addison *(G-7)*
Power and Composite Tech LLC .... D 518 843-6825
  Amsterdam *(G-365)*
Stature Electric Inc .... B 315 782-5910
  Watertown *(G-16672)*

MOTOR HOMES

Authority Transportation Inc .... F 888 933-1268
  Dix Hills *(G-4291)*

MOTOR REPAIR SVCS

Accurate Marine Specialties .... G 631 589-5502
  Bohemia *(G-1005)*
Premco Inc .... F 914 636-7095
  New Rochelle *(G-8921)*
RC Entps Bus & Trck Inc .... G 518 568-5753
  Saint Johnsville *(G-15097)*

MOTOR SCOOTERS & PARTS

Piaggio Group Americas Inc .... E 212 380-4400
  New York *(G-11657)*

MOTOR VEHICLE ASSEMBLY, COMPLETE: Autos, Incl Specialty

Auto Sport Designs Inc .... F 631 425-1555
  Huntington Station *(G-6697)*
Marcovicci-Wenz Engineering .... G 631 467-9040
  Ronkonkoma *(G-14938)*
Medical Coaches Incorporated .... E 607 432-1333
  Oneonta *(G-13188)*
Pcb Coach Builders Corp .... G 718 897-7606
  Rego Park *(G-14038)*

MOTOR VEHICLE ASSEMBLY, COMPLETE: Buses, All Types

JP Bus & Truck Repair Ltd .... F 516 767-2700
  Port Washington *(G-13830)*
Leonard Bus Sales Inc .... G 607 467-3100
  Rome *(G-14819)*
Prevost Car US Inc .... C 518 957-2052
  Plattsburgh *(G-13689)*

MOTOR VEHICLE ASSEMBLY, COMPLETE: Cars, Armored

Armor Dynamics Inc .... F 845 658-9200
  Kingston *(G-7178)*

MOTOR VEHICLE ASSEMBLY, COMPLETE: Fire Department Vehicles

AB Fire Inc .... G 917 416-6444
  Brooklyn *(G-1545)*
Global Fire Corporation .... E 888 320-1799
  New York *(G-10316)*
Madrid Fire District .... G 315 322-4346
  Madrid *(G-7995)*
Scehenvus Fire Dist .... D 607 638-9017
  Schenevus *(G-15315)*
Sutphen Corporation .... E 845 583-4720
  White Lake *(G-17071)*

MOTOR VEHICLE ASSEMBLY, COMPLETE: Military Motor Vehicle

CIC International Ltd .... D 212 213-0089
  Brooklyn *(G-1779)*

MOTOR VEHICLE ASSEMBLY, COMPLETE: Motor Buses

Daimler Buses North Amer Inc .... A 315 768-8101
  Oriskany *(G-13308)*

MOTOR VEHICLE ASSEMBLY, COMPLETE: Snow Plows

Brothers-In-Lawn Property .... G 716 279-6191
  Tonawanda *(G-16149)*
Sabre Enterprises Inc .... G 315 430-3127
  Syracuse *(G-16029)*
Smart Systems Inc .... E 607 776-5380
  Bath *(G-662)*

MOTOR VEHICLE ASSEMBLY, COMPLETE: Truck & Tractor Trucks

Air Flow Manufacturing .... F 607 733-8284
  Elmira *(G-4669)*
Dejana Trck Utility Eqp Co LLC .... C 631 544-9000
  Kings Park *(G-7170)*
Tee Pee Auto Sales Corp .... F 516 338-9333
  Westbury *(G-17030)*

MOTOR VEHICLE ASSEMBLY, COMPLETE: Trucks, Pickup

Dejana Trck Utility Eqp Co LLC .... E 631 549-0944
  Huntington *(G-6660)*

MOTOR VEHICLE DEALERS: Automobiles, New & Used

Split Rock Trading Co Inc .... G 631 929-3261
  Wading River *(G-16526)*

MOTOR VEHICLE DEALERS: Cars, Used Only

Secor Marketing Group Inc .... G 914 381-3600
  Mamaroneck *(G-8046)*

MOTOR VEHICLE PARTS & ACCESS: Acceleration Eqpt

Parts Unlimited Inc .... D 518 885-7500
  Ballston Spa *(G-606)*

MOTOR VEHICLE PARTS & ACCESS: Air Conditioner Parts

GM Components Holdings LLC .... C 716 439-2011
  Lockport *(G-7589)*
Titanx Engine Cooling Inc .... B 716 665-7129
  Jamestown *(G-7039)*
Transcedar Industries Ltd .... G 716 731-6442
  Niagara Falls *(G-12884)*

MOTOR VEHICLE PARTS & ACCESS: Bearings

MOTOR VEHICLE PARTS & ACCESS: Bearings

Fcmp Inc .... F 716 692-4623
   Tonawanda *(G-16160)*

MOTOR VEHICLE PARTS & ACCESS: Body Components & Frames

Johnson Controls Inc .... C 585 724-2232
   Rochester *(G-14464)*
Protech Automation LLC .... G 585 344-3201
   Batavia *(G-646)*

MOTOR VEHICLE PARTS & ACCESS: Electrical Eqpt

Katikati Inc .... G 585 678-1764
   West Henrietta *(G-16883)*
Nassau Auto Remanufacturer .... G 516 485-4500
   Hempstead *(G-6282)*

MOTOR VEHICLE PARTS & ACCESS: Engines & Parts

ARC Remanufacturing Inc .... D 718 728-0701
   Long Island City *(G-7665)*
Curtis L Maclean L C .... B 716 898-7800
   Buffalo *(G-2895)*
Jt Precision Inc .... E 716 795-3860
   Barker *(G-613)*
Marcovicci-Wenz Engineering .... G 631 467-9040
   Ronkonkoma *(G-14938)*
Standard Motor Products Inc .... B 718 392-0200
   Long Island City *(G-7884)*

MOTOR VEHICLE PARTS & ACCESS: Fuel Systems & Parts

Fuel Systems Solutions Inc .... E 646 502-7170
   New York *(G-10220)*
Kearney-National Inc .... F 212 661-4600
   New York *(G-10828)*
TI Group Auto Systems LLC .... G 315 568-7042
   Seneca Falls *(G-15371)*

MOTOR VEHICLE PARTS & ACCESS: Gears

Gleason Works .... A 585 473-1000
   Rochester *(G-14408)*

MOTOR VEHICLE PARTS & ACCESS: Power Steering Eqpt

CRS Remanufacturing Co Inc .... F 718 739-1720
   Jamaica *(G-6908)*

MOTOR VEHICLE PARTS & ACCESS: Propane Conversion Eqpt

Kurtz Truck Equipment Inc .... F 607 849-3468
   Marathon *(G-8084)*

MOTOR VEHICLE PARTS & ACCESS: Sanders, Safety

Smith Metal Works Newark Inc .... E 315 331-1651
   Newark *(G-12742)*
Vehicle Safety Dept .... F 315 458-6683
   Syracuse *(G-16066)*
Zwack Incorporated .... E 518 733-5135
   Stephentown *(G-15758)*

MOTOR VEHICLE PARTS & ACCESS: Tops

Electron Top Mfg Co Inc .... F 718 846-7400
   Richmond Hill *(G-14072)*

MOTOR VEHICLE PARTS & ACCESS: Transmissions

Banner Transmission & Eng Co .... F 516 221-9459
   Bellmore *(G-814)*

MOTOR VEHICLE PARTS & ACCESS: Wheel rims

Extreme Auto Accessories Corp .... F 718 978-6722
   South Ozone Park *(G-15533)*

MOTOR VEHICLE PARTS & ACCESS: Wiring Harness Sets

Agri Services Co .... G 716 937-6618
   Alden *(G-173)*

MOTOR VEHICLE SPLYS & PARTS WHOLESALERS: New

American Auto ACC Incrporation .... E 718 886-6600
   Flushing *(G-5226)*
K M Drive Line Inc .... G 718 599-0628
   Brooklyn *(G-2164)*
Knorr Brake Holding Corp .... G 315 786-5356
   Watertown *(G-16659)*
Trading Services International .... F 212 501-0142
   New York *(G-12389)*
Walter R Tucker Entps Ltd .... E 607 467-2866
   Deposit *(G-4282)*

MOTOR VEHICLE: Hardware

Wolo Mfg Corp .... E 631 242-0333
   Deer Park *(G-4228)*

MOTOR VEHICLE: Steering Mechanisms

Biltron Automotive Products .... E 631 928-8613
   Port Jeff STA *(G-13763)*

MOTOR VEHICLES & CAR BODIES

Antonicelli Vito Race Car .... G 716 684-2205
   Buffalo *(G-2814)*
Fiberglass Replacement Parts .... F 716 893-6471
   Buffalo *(G-2946)*
Jtekt Torsen North America .... F 585 464-5000
   Rochester *(G-14465)*
Ranger Design Us Inc .... E 800 565-5321
   Ontario *(G-13211)*
Roberts Nichols Fire Apparatus .... G 518 431-1945
   Waterford *(G-16620)*
Tesla Motors Inc .... A 212 206-1204
   New York *(G-12304)*
Transprttion Collaborative Inc .... E 845 988-2333
   Warwick *(G-16597)*
Troyer Inc .... F 585 352-5590
   Rochester *(G-14732)*

MOTOR VEHICLES, WHOLESALE: Recreational, All-Terrain

Adirondack Power Sports .... G 518 481-6269
   Malone *(G-8006)*

MOTOR VEHICLES, WHOLESALE: Truck bodies

Smart Systems Inc .... E 607 776-5380
   Bath *(G-662)*

MOTORCYCLE & BICYCLE PARTS: Gears

Pidyon Controls Inc .... G 212 683-9523
   New York *(G-11659)*

MOTORCYCLE DEALERS

Se-Mar Electric Co Inc .... E 716 674-7404
   West Seneca *(G-16953)*
Split Rock Trading Co Inc .... G 631 929-3261
   Wading River *(G-16526)*

MOTORCYCLES & RELATED PARTS

Golub Corporation .... D 518 943-3903
   Catskill *(G-3428)*
Golub Corporation .... D 518 899-6063
   Malta *(G-8020)*
Golub Corporation .... D 315 363-0679
   Oneida *(G-13155)*
Golub Corporation .... D 607 336-2588
   Norwich *(G-13028)*
Golub Corporation .... D 518 583-3697
   Saratoga Springs *(G-15154)*
Golub Corporation .... D 518 822-0076
   Hudson *(G-6615)*
Golub Corporation .... D 607 235-7243
   Binghamton *(G-920)*
Golub Corporation .... C 845 344-0327
   Middletown *(G-8443)*

Ihd Motorsports LLC .... F 979 690-1669
   Binghamton *(G-925)*
Indian Larry Legacy .... G 718 609-9184
   Brooklyn *(G-2102)*
Orange County Choppers Inc .... G 845 522-5200
   Newburgh *(G-12771)*
Price Chopper Operating Co .... F 518 562-3565
   Plattsburgh *(G-13690)*
Robs Cycle Supply .... G 315 292-6878
   Syracuse *(G-16025)*
Sumax Cycle Products Inc .... F 315 768-1058
   Oriskany *(G-13315)*
Super Price Chopper Inc .... G 716 893-3323
   Buffalo *(G-3202)*

MOTORS: Electric

Aeroflex Plainview Inc .... B 516 694-6700
   Plainview *(G-13579)*
Current Applications Inc .... E 315 788-4689
   Watertown *(G-16648)*
Elton El Mantle Inc .... G 315 432-9067
   Syracuse *(G-15934)*
Empire Division Inc .... D 315 476-6273
   Syracuse *(G-15936)*
Franklin Electric Co Inc .... A 718 244-7744
   Jamaica *(G-6914)*
John G Rubino Inc .... E 315 253-7396
   Auburn *(G-504)*
R M S Motor Corporation .... F 607 723-2323
   Binghamton *(G-944)*
Sopark Corp .... C 716 822-0434
   Buffalo *(G-3191)*

MOTORS: Generators

Aeroflex Plainview Inc .... C 631 231-9100
   Hauppauge *(G-6011)*
Allied Motion Technologies Inc .... C 716 242-8634
   Amherst *(G-221)*
American Precision Inds Inc .... C 716 691-9100
   Amherst *(G-224)*
Ametek Inc .... D 607 763-4700
   Binghamton *(G-888)*
Ametek Inc .... D 585 263-7700
   Rochester *(G-14202)*
ARC Systems Inc .... E 631 582-8020
   Hauppauge *(G-6023)*
Auburn Armature Inc .... D 315 253-9721
   Auburn *(G-477)*
D & D Motor Systems Inc .... E 315 701-0861
   Syracuse *(G-15918)*
Designatronics Incorporated .... B 516 328-3300
   New Hyde Park *(G-8826)*
Emes Motor Inc .... G 718 387-2445
   Brooklyn *(G-1919)*
Ener-G-Rotors Inc .... G 518 372-2608
   Schenectady *(G-15250)*
Eni Technology Inc .... B 585 427-8300
   Rochester *(G-14353)*
Faradyne Motors LLC .... F 315 331-5985
   Palmyra *(G-13405)*
Felchar Manufacturing Corp .... A 607 723-3106
   Binghamton *(G-914)*
Gaffney Kroese Supply Corp .... F 516 228-5091
   Garden City *(G-5506)*
General Electric Company .... B 518 385-2211
   Schenectady *(G-15261)*
Generation Power LLC .... G 315 234-2451
   Syracuse *(G-15951)*
Got Power Inc .... G 631 767-9493
   Ronkonkoma *(G-14906)*
Island Components Group Inc .... F 631 563-4224
   Holbrook *(G-6453)*
Kaddis Manufacturing Corp .... G 585 624-3070
   Honeoye Falls *(G-6533)*
Lcdrives Corp .... F 860 712-8926
   Potsdam *(G-13879)*
Makerbot Industries LLC .... B 347 334-6800
   Brooklyn *(G-2254)*
Modular Devices Inc .... G 631 345-3100
   Shirley *(G-15426)*
Nidec Motor Corporation .... F 315 434-9303
   East Syracuse *(G-4553)*
Powercomplete LLC .... G 212 228-4129
   New York *(G-11692)*
Premco Inc .... F 914 636-7095
   New Rochelle *(G-8921)*
Protective Power Systms & Cntr .... F 845 773-9016
   Poughkeepsie *(G-13926)*
Ruhle Companies Inc .... E 914 287-4000
   Valhalla *(G-16372)*

PRODUCT SECTION — NAMEPLATES

Sima Technologies LLC ....G..... 412 828-9130
 Hauppauge *(G-6191)*
Supergen Products LLC.................G..... 315 573-7887
 Newark *(G-12744)*
Troy Industrial Solutions.................D..... 518 272-4920
 Watervliet *(G-16690)*
W J Albro Machine Works Inc.................G..... 631 345-0657
 Yaphank *(G-17408)*

MOTORS: Torque

Aeroflex Incorporated.................B..... 516 694-6700
 Plainview *(G-13578)*

MOUNTING SVC: Display

Gerald Frd Packg Display LLC.................F..... 716 692-2705
 North Tonawanda *(G-12974)*

MOVIE THEATERS, EXC DRIVE-IN

Par Technology Corporation.................D..... 315 738-0600
 New Hartford *(G-8808)*
Sony Broadband Entertainment.................F..... 212 833-6800
 New York *(G-12131)*
Taste and See Entrmt Inc.................G..... 516 285-3010
 Valley Stream *(G-16429)*

MOWERS & ACCESSORIES

Benishty Brothers Corp.................G..... 646 339-9991
 Woodmere *(G-17311)*

MULTIPLEXERS: Telephone & Telegraph

Fiberall Corp.................E..... 516 371-5200
 Inwood *(G-6757)*
Toshiba America Inc.................E..... 212 596-0600
 New York *(G-12377)*

MUSEUMS

Historcal Soc of Mddltown Walk.................G..... 845 342-0941
 Middletown *(G-8444)*

MUSEUMS & ART GALLERIES

Njf Publishing Corp.................G..... 631 345-5200
 Shirley *(G-15427)*
Paley Studios Ltd.................F..... 585 232-5260
 Rochester *(G-14567)*

MUSIC BROADCASTING SVCS

Michael Karp Music Inc.................G..... 212 840-3285
 New York *(G-11249)*

MUSIC COPYING SVCS

Boosey & Hawkes Inc.................E..... 212 358-5300
 New York *(G-9439)*

MUSIC DISTRIBUTION APPARATUS

Nykon Inc.................G..... 315 483-0504
 Sodus *(G-15504)*
Sunshine Distribution Corp.................G..... 888 506-7051
 New York *(G-12238)*
Tunecore Inc.................E..... 646 651-1060
 Brooklyn *(G-2687)*

MUSIC LICENSING & ROYALTIES

Warner Music Group Corp.................B..... 212 275-2000
 New York *(G-12588)*

MUSIC LICENSING TO RADIO STATIONS

Historic TW Inc.................D..... 212 484-8000
 New York *(G-10484)*
Time Warner Companies Inc.................D..... 212 484-8000
 New York *(G-12350)*

MUSIC RECORDING PRODUCER

Euphorbia Productions Ltd.................G..... 212 533-1700
 New York *(G-10082)*
Musical Links Production LLC.................G..... 516 996-1522
 Valley Stream *(G-16414)*

MUSICAL ENTERTAINERS

Wmg Acquisition Corp.................F..... 212 275-2000
 New York *(G-12650)*

MUSICAL INSTRUMENT PARTS & ACCESS, WHOLESALE

Carl Fischer LLC.................E..... 212 777-0900
 New York *(G-9526)*
Musicskins LLC.................F..... 646 827-4271
 Brooklyn *(G-2343)*

MUSICAL INSTRUMENT REPAIR

Fodera Guitars Inc.................F..... 718 832-3455
 Brooklyn *(G-1991)*
Guitar Specialist Inc.................G..... 914 533-5589
 South Salem *(G-15535)*
Sadowsky Guitars Ltd.................F..... 718 433-1990
 Long Island City *(G-7871)*

MUSICAL INSTRUMENTS & ACCESS: Carrying Cases

Roadie Products Inc.................E..... 631 567-8588
 Holbrook *(G-6468)*
Xstatic Pro Inc.................F..... 718 237-2299
 Brooklyn *(G-2771)*

MUSICAL INSTRUMENTS & ACCESS: NEC

DAndrea Inc.................E..... 516 496-2200
 Syosset *(G-15818)*
Evans Manufacturing LLC.................D..... 631 439-3300
 Farmingdale *(G-4990)*
Fodera Guitars Inc.................F..... 718 832-3455
 Brooklyn *(G-1991)*
J D Calato Manufacturing Co.................E..... 716 285-3546
 Niagara Falls *(G-12837)*
Muzet Inc.................F..... 315 452-0050
 Syracuse *(G-15995)*
Nathan Love LLC.................F..... 212 925-7111
 New York *(G-11343)*
Roli USA Inc.................F..... 412 600-4840
 New York *(G-11908)*
Samson Technologies Corp.................D..... 631 784-2200
 Hauppauge *(G-6182)*
Sound Source Inc.................G..... 585 271-5370
 Rochester *(G-14693)*
Steinway Musical Instrs Inc.................E..... 781 894-9770
 New York *(G-12192)*

MUSICAL INSTRUMENTS & ACCESS: Pianos

Steinway Inc.................A..... 718 721-2600
 Long Island City *(G-7888)*
Steinway and Sons.................C..... 718 721-2600
 Long Island City *(G-7889)*

MUSICAL INSTRUMENTS & ACCESS: Pipe Organs

Kerner and Merchant.................G..... 315 463-8023
 East Syracuse *(G-4548)*

MUSICAL INSTRUMENTS & PARTS: Brass

Siegfrieds Call Inc.................G..... 845 765-2275
 Beacon *(G-790)*

MUSICAL INSTRUMENTS & PARTS: String

Barbera Transduser Systems.................F..... 718 816-3025
 Staten Island *(G-15644)*
DAddario & Company Inc.................D..... 631 439-3300
 Melville *(G-8309)*
DAddario & Company Inc.................A..... 631 439-3300
 Farmingdale *(G-4972)*
Sadowsky Guitars Ltd.................F..... 718 433-1990
 Long Island City *(G-7871)*

MUSICAL INSTRUMENTS & SPLYS STORES

Albert Augustine Ltd.................D..... 917 661-0220
 New York *(G-9074)*
Barbera Transduser Systems.................F..... 718 816-3025
 Staten Island *(G-15644)*
Carl Fischer LLC.................E..... 212 777-0900
 New York *(G-9526)*
DAndrea Inc.................E..... 516 496-2200
 Syosset *(G-15818)*
Fodera Guitars Inc.................F..... 718 832-3455
 Brooklyn *(G-1991)*
Hipshot Products Inc.................F..... 607 532-9404
 Interlaken *(G-6747)*

MUSICAL INSTRUMENTS & SPLYS STORES: Pianos

Steinway Inc.................A..... 718 721-2600
 Long Island City *(G-7888)*
Steinway and Sons.................C..... 718 721-2600
 Long Island City *(G-7889)*

MUSICAL INSTRUMENTS WHOLESALERS

Samson Technologies Corp.................D..... 631 784-2200
 Hauppauge *(G-6182)*

MUSICAL INSTRUMENTS: Blowers, Pipe Organ

Elsener Organ Works Inc.................G..... 631 254-2744
 Deer Park *(G-4137)*

MUSICAL INSTRUMENTS: Electric & Electronic

New Sensor Corporation.................D..... 718 937-8300
 Long Island City *(G-7824)*

MUSICAL INSTRUMENTS: Guitars & Parts, Electric & Acoustic

DAngelico Guitars of America.................G..... 732 380-0995
 New York *(G-9800)*
Dimarzio Inc.................E..... 718 442-6655
 Staten Island *(G-15666)*
Guitar Specialist Inc.................G..... 914 533-5589
 South Salem *(G-15535)*
Hipshot Products Inc.................F..... 607 532-9404
 Interlaken *(G-6747)*
Luthier Musical Corp.................G..... 212 397-6038
 New York *(G-11065)*
Stuart Spector Designs Ltd.................G..... 845 246-6124
 Saugerties *(G-15196)*

MUSICAL INSTRUMENTS: Harmonicas

Jason Ladanye Guitar Piano & H.................E..... 518 527-3973
 Albany *(G-92)*

MUSICAL INSTRUMENTS: Organs

Gluck Orgelbau Inc.................G..... 212 233-2684
 New York *(G-10323)*
Leonard Carlson.................G..... 518 477-4710
 East Greenbush *(G-4403)*

MUSICAL INSTRUMENTS: Reeds

Rico International.................G..... 818 767-7711
 Farmingdale *(G-5099)*

MUSICAL INSTRUMENTS: Strings, Instrument

Albert Augustine Ltd.................D..... 917 661-0220
 New York *(G-9074)*
E & O Mari Inc.................D..... 845 562-4400
 Newburgh *(G-12754)*
Mari Strings Inc.................F..... 212 799-6781
 New York *(G-11148)*

NAME PLATES: Engraved Or Etched

Advanced Graphics Company.................F..... 607 692-7875
 Whitney Point *(G-17219)*
C & M Products Inc.................G..... 315 471-3303
 Syracuse *(G-15880)*
Harold Wood Co Inc.................G..... 716 873-1535
 Buffalo *(G-2990)*
Nameplate Mfrs of Amer.................E..... 631 752-0055
 Farmingdale *(G-5061)*
Precision Design Systems Inc.................E..... 585 426-4500
 Rochester *(G-14592)*
The Gramecy Group.................G..... 518 348-1325
 Clifton Park *(G-3710)*
White Plains Rubber Stamp Name.................G..... 914 949-1900
 White Plains *(G-17187)*

NAMEPLATES

Decal Makers Inc.................E..... 516 221-7200
 Bellmore *(G-817)*
Island Nameplate Inc.................G..... 845 651-4005
 Florida *(G-5213)*

NAMEPLATES

Signature Name Plate Co Inc ....G....... 585 321-9960
Rochester *(G-14686)*

NATIONAL SECURITY FORCES

Metadure Defense & SEC LLC ....F....... 631 249-2141
Farmingdale *(G-5049)*

NATIONAL SECURITY, GOVERNMENT: Army

United States Dept of Army ....C....... 315 772-7538
Watertown *(G-16674)*

NATURAL BUTANE PRODUCTION

Center State Propane LLC ....G....... 315 841-4044
Waterville *(G-16677)*
Green Buffalo Fuel LLC ....F....... 716 768-0600
Tonawanda *(G-16168)*

NATURAL GAS DISTRIBUTION TO CONSUMERS

Noco Incorporated ....G....... 716 833-6626
Tonawanda *(G-16187)*

NATURAL GAS LIQUIDS PRODUCTION

Aggressive Energy LLC ....E....... 718 836-9222
Brooklyn *(G-1570)*
Nfe Management LLC ....F....... 212 798-6100
New York *(G-11423)*
Western Oil and Gas JV Inc ....G....... 914 967-4758
Rye *(G-15069)*

NATURAL GAS PRODUCTION

County Energy Corp ....G....... 718 626-7000
Brooklyn *(G-1808)*
East Resources Inc ....G....... 716 373-0944
Allegany *(G-200)*
Flownet LLC ....G....... 716 685-4036
Lancaster *(G-7316)*
Green Buffalo Fuel LLC ....F....... 716 768-0600
Tonawanda *(G-16168)*
Ipp Energy LLC ....G....... 607 773-3307
Binghamton *(G-928)*
Reserve Gas Company Inc ....G....... 716 937-9484
Alden *(G-182)*
Talisman Energy USA Inc ....G....... 607 562-4000
Horseheads *(G-6595)*

NATURAL GAS TRANSMISSION & DISTRIBUTION

Lenape Energy Inc ....G....... 585 344-1200
Alexander *(G-187)*
Lenape Resources Inc ....F....... 585 344-1200
Alexander *(G-188)*

NATURAL GASOLINE PRODUCTION

20 Bliss St Inc ....G....... 716 326-2790
Westfield *(G-17044)*

NATURAL PROPANE PRODUCTION

Paraco Gas Corporation ....G....... 845 279-8414
Brewster *(G-1225)*
Paraco Gas Corporation ....F....... 800 647-4427
Rye Brook *(G-15073)*

NAUTICAL & NAVIGATIONAL INSTRUMENT REPAIR SVCS

Moor Electronics Inc ....G....... 716 821-5304
Buffalo *(G-3075)*

NAVIGATIONAL SYSTEMS & INSTRUMENTS

Lockheed Martin Corporation ....A....... 315 456-0123
Liverpool *(G-7531)*

NET & NETTING PRDTS

Apex Texicon Inc ....E....... 516 239-4400
New York *(G-9173)*

NETS: Laundry

Sky Laundromat Inc ....F....... 718 639-7070
Jamaica *(G-6949)*

NEW & USED CAR DEALERS

Auto Sport Designs Inc ....F....... 631 425-1555
Huntington Station *(G-6697)*

NEWS DEALERS & NEWSSTANDS

Chronicle Express ....F....... 315 536-4422
Penn Yan *(G-13508)*

NEWS FEATURE SYNDICATES

Hearst Business Media Corp ....F....... 631 650-4441
Great River *(G-5851)*
Hearst Corporation ....A....... 212 649-2000
New York *(G-10438)*
New York Times Company ....B....... 212 556-1234
New York *(G-11410)*

NEWS PICTURES GATHERING & DISTRIBUTING SVCS

Kraus Organization Limited ....G....... 212 686-5411
New York *(G-10888)*

NEWS SYNDICATES

Thomson Reuters Corporation ....A....... 646 223-4000
New York *(G-12329)*

NEWSPAPERS & PERIODICALS NEWS REPORTING SVCS

Dow Jones & Company Inc ....E....... 212 597-5983
New York *(G-9915)*

NEWSPAPERS, WHOLESALE

Best Line Inc ....G....... 917 670-6210
Staten Island *(G-15646)*
Nyt Capital LLC ....F....... 212 556-1234
New York *(G-11488)*

NEWSSTAND

Division Street News Corp ....F....... 518 234-2515
Cobleskill *(G-3736)*

NICKEL ALLOY

Nickel Group LLC ....G....... 212 706-7906
Rockaway Park *(G-14786)*

NONCURRENT CARRYING WIRING DEVICES

Chase Corporation ....F....... 212 644-7281
New York *(G-9586)*
Chase Corporation ....F....... 631 243-6380
Deer Park *(G-4117)*
Chase Corporation ....F....... 631 827-0476
Northport *(G-13009)*
Complete SEC & Contrls Inc ....F....... 631 421-7200
Huntington Station *(G-6700)*
Delta Metal Products Co Inc ....E....... 718 855-4200
Brooklyn *(G-1852)*
Lapp Insulator Company LLC ....F....... 585 768-6221
Le Roy *(G-7411)*
Lapp Insulators LLC ....C....... 585 768-6221
Le Roy *(G-7412)*
Zierick Manufacturing Corp ....D....... 800 882-8020
Mount Kisco *(G-8648)*

NONFERROUS: Rolling & Drawing, NEC

Continental Cordage Corp ....D....... 315 655-9800
Cazenovia *(G-3443)*
Cpp-Syracuse Inc ....E....... 315 687-0014
Chittenango *(G-3632)*
Eco-Bat America LLC ....C....... 845 692-4414
Middletown *(G-8439)*
Medi-Ray Inc ....D....... 877 898-3003
Tuckahoe *(G-16271)*
Nationwide Precision Pdts Corp ....B....... 585 272-7100
Rochester *(G-14529)*
Selectrode Industries Inc ....D....... 631 547-5470
Huntington Station *(G-6723)*
Sigmund Cohn Corp ....D....... 914 664-5300
Mount Vernon *(G-8734)*

NONMETALLIC MINERALS: Support Activities, Exc Fuels

Crystal Ceres Industries Inc ....D....... 716 283-0445
Niagara Falls *(G-12808)*

NOTARIES PUBLIC

Chesu Inc ....F....... 239 564-2803
East Hampton *(G-4407)*

NOTEBOOKS, MADE FROM PURCHASED MATERIALS

Anne Taintor Inc ....G....... 718 483-9312
Brooklyn *(G-1613)*

NOTIONS: Button Blanks & Molds

Connection Mold Inc ....G....... 585 458-6463
Rochester *(G-14286)*

NOTIONS: Pins, Straight, Steel Or Brass

Karp Overseas Corporation ....E....... 718 784-2105
Maspeth *(G-8148)*

NOTIONS: Studs, Shirt, Exc Precious/Semi Metal/Stone

Columbia Button Nailhead Corp ....F....... 718 386-3414
Brooklyn *(G-1792)*

NOVELTIES

Best Priced Products Inc ....G....... 914 345-3800
Elmsford *(G-4735)*
Fish & Crown Ltd ....D....... 212 707-9603
New York *(G-10173)*
Jacobs Juice Corp ....G....... 646 255-2860
Brooklyn *(G-2132)*
Jpm Fine Woodworking LLC ....G....... 516 236-7605
Jericho *(G-7074)*
Orlandi Inc ....D....... 631 756-0110
Farmingdale *(G-5071)*
Orlandi Inc ....E....... 631 756-0110
Farmingdale *(G-5072)*

NOVELTIES & SPECIALTIES: Metal

Buttons & Trimcom Inc ....F....... 212 868-1971
New York *(G-9484)*
Criterion Bell & Specialty ....E....... 718 788-2600
Brooklyn *(G-1819)*
Split Rock Trading Co Inc ....G....... 631 929-3261
Wading River *(G-16526)*
Stylebuilt Accessories Inc ....E....... 917 439-0578
East Rockaway *(G-4472)*

NOVELTIES: Paper, Made From Purchased Materials

National Advertising & Prtg ....G....... 212 629-7650
New York *(G-11346)*
P C I Paper Conversions Inc ....F....... 315 437-1641
Syracuse *(G-16009)*

NOVELTIES: Plastic

Buttons & Trimcom Inc ....F....... 212 868-1971
New York *(G-9484)*
Frisch Plastics Corp ....E....... 973 685-5936
Hartsdale *(G-5998)*
GPM Associates LLC ....E....... 585 335-3940
Dansville *(G-4077)*
Kling Magnetics Inc ....E....... 518 392-4000
Chatham *(G-3558)*
Pelican Products Co Inc ....E....... 718 860-3220
Bronx *(G-1423)*
Ppr Direct Inc ....F....... 718 965-8600
Brooklyn *(G-2432)*
Royal Industries Inc ....E....... 718 369-3046
Brooklyn *(G-2511)*
Skd Distribution Corp ....E....... 718 525-6000
Jericho *(G-7088)*

NOVELTY SHOPS

Mgd Brands Inc ....D....... 516 545-0150
Plainview *(G-13620)*

NOZZLES & SPRINKLERS Lawn Hose

Artys Sprnklr Svc Instllation ....F....... 516 538-4371
East Meadow *(G-4418)*

PRODUCT SECTION

OILS: Orange

NOZZLES: Spray, Aerosol, Paint Or Insecticide
Sono-Tek Corporation .... D 845 795-2020
  Milton *(G-8484)*

NUCLEAR REACTORS: Military Or Indl
Energy Nuclear Operations .... E 315 342-0055
  Oswego *(G-13331)*

NURSERIES & LAWN & GARDEN SPLY STORES, RETAIL: Fertilizer
Scotts Company LLC .... E 631 289-7444
  Yaphank *(G-17400)*

NURSERIES & LAWN & GARDEN SPLY STORES, RETAIL: Sod
E F Lippert Co Inc .... F 716 373-1100
  Allegany *(G-199)*

NURSERIES & LAWN & GARDEN SPLY STORES, RETAIL: Top Soil
East Coast Mines Ltd .... E 631 653-5445
  East Quogue *(G-4450)*
Grosso Materials Inc .... F 845 361-5211
  Montgomery *(G-8594)*
Hampton Sand Corp .... G 631 325-5533
  Westhampton *(G-17057)*

NURSERIES & LAWN/GARDEN SPLY STORE, RET: Lawnmowers/Tractors
Kelley Farm & Garden Inc .... E 518 234-2332
  Cobleskill *(G-3738)*

NURSERY & GARDEN CENTERS
Birkett Mills .... G 315 536-3311
  Penn Yan *(G-13506)*
G & S Farm & Home Inc .... G 716 542-9922
  Akron *(G-23)*

NUTS: Metal
Buckley Qc Fasteners Inc .... E 716 662-1490
  Orchard Park *(G-13255)*
Dependable Acme Threaded Pdts .... G 516 338-4700
  Westbury *(G-16976)*
Zierick Manufacturing Corp .... D 800 882-8020
  Mount Kisco *(G-8648)*

OFFICE EQPT WHOLESALERS
Artistic Products LLC .... E 631 435-0200
  Hauppauge *(G-6026)*
Automecha International Ltd .... E 607 843-2235
  Oxford *(G-13363)*
DAF Office Networks Inc .... F 315 699-7070
  Cicero *(G-3644)*
Finesse Creations Inc .... F 718 692-2100
  Brooklyn *(G-1973)*

OFFICE EQPT, WHOLESALE: Duplicating Machines
Media Technologies Ltd .... F 631 467-7900
  Eastport *(G-4584)*

OFFICE FIXTURES: Exc Wood
Air Crafters Inc .... C 631 471-7788
  Ronkonkoma *(G-14857)*
Evans & Paul LLC .... E 516 576-0800
  Plainview *(G-13600)*

OFFICE FIXTURES: Wood
Bauerschmidt & Sons Inc .... D 718 528-3500
  Jamaica *(G-6898)*

OFFICE FURNITURE REPAIR & MAINTENANCE SVCS
Davies Office Refurbishing Inc .... C 518 426-7188
  Albany *(G-71)*
Jim Quinn .... F 518 356-0398
  Schenectady *(G-15270)*

OFFICE SPLY & STATIONERY STORES
American Office Supply Inc .... F 516 294-9444
  Westbury *(G-16967)*
Flynns Inc .... E 212 339-8700
  New York *(G-10182)*
Tripi Engraving Co Inc .... E 718 383-6500
  Brooklyn *(G-2682)*

OFFICE SPLY & STATIONERY STORES: Office Forms & Splys
A & D Offset Printers Ltd .... G 516 746-2476
  Mineola *(G-8486)*
Action Graphics Services Inc .... F 607 785-1951
  Vestal *(G-16438)*
Datagraphic Business Systems .... G 516 485-9069
  Brentwood *(G-1180)*
Grant Hamilton .... F 716 652-0320
  East Aurora *(G-4371)*
Idc Printing & Sty Co Inc .... G 516 599-0400
  Lynbrook *(G-7951)*
J P Printing Inc .... G 516 293-6110
  Farmingdale *(G-5015)*
Kleer-Fax Inc .... D 631 225-1100
  Amityville *(G-303)*
Richard Ruffner .... F 631 234-4600
  Central Islip *(G-3509)*
Rmd Holding Inc .... G 845 628-0030
  Mahopac *(G-8001)*
Short Run Forms Inc .... D 631 567-7171
  Bohemia *(G-1133)*

OFFICE SPLY & STATIONERY STORES: Writing Splys
Tefft Publishers Inc .... G 518 692-9290
  Greenwich *(G-5894)*

OFFICE SPLYS, NEC, WHOLESALE
DAF Office Networks Inc .... F 315 699-7070
  Cicero *(G-3644)*
Falconer Printing & Design Inc .... F 716 665-2121
  Falconer *(G-4899)*
Rike Enterprises Inc .... F 631 277-8338
  Islip *(G-6812)*
Robert Tabatznik Assoc Inc .... F 845 336-4555
  Kingston *(G-7209)*

OFFICES & CLINICS OF DENTISTS: Prosthodontist
Goldberg Prosthetic & Orthotic .... F 631 689-6606
  East Setauket *(G-4484)*

OFFICES & CLINICS OF DRS, MED: Specialized Practitioners
Erika T Schwartz MD PC .... G 212 873-3420
  New York *(G-10058)*

OFFICES & CLINICS OF HEALTH PRACTITIONERS: Nutritionist
Everlast Worldwide Inc .... E 212 239-0990
  New York *(G-10093)*

OIL & GAS FIELD MACHINERY
Basin Holdings US LLC .... E 212 695-7376
  New York *(G-9332)*
Derrick Corporation .... C 716 683-9010
  Buffalo *(G-2909)*
Schlumberger Technology Corp .... C 607 378-0200
  Horseheads *(G-6592)*
Smith International Inc .... F 585 265-2330
  Ontario *(G-13215)*

OIL FIELD MACHINERY & EQPT
Anchor Commerce Trading Corp .... G 516 881-3485
  Atlantic Beach *(G-468)*
Desmi-Afti Inc .... E 716 662-0632
  Orchard Park *(G-13269)*

OIL FIELD SVCS, NEC
Alba Fuel Corp .... G 718 931-1700
  Bronx *(G-1266)*
Bluebar Oil Co Inc .... F 315 245-4328
  Blossvale *(G-997)*

Direct Oil LLC .... G 914 495-3073
  Thornwood *(G-16119)*
Gas Field Specialists Inc .... D 716 378-6422
  Horseheads *(G-6579)*
Marcellus Energy Services LLC .... E 607 236-0038
  Candor *(G-3378)*
Petro Inc .... G 516 686-1900
  Hicksville *(G-6387)*
Rpc Inc .... E 347 873-3935
  Elmont *(G-4728)*
Schneider Amalco Inc .... F 917 470-9674
  New York *(G-11991)*
U S Energy Development Corp .... D 716 636-0401
  Getzville *(G-5605)*

OIL ROYALTY TRADERS
Schneider Amalco Inc .... F 917 470-9674
  New York *(G-11991)*

OILS & GREASES: Blended & Compounded
Battenfeld-American Inc .... E 716 822-8410
  Buffalo *(G-2835)*

OILS & GREASES: Lubricating
Axel Plastics RES Labs Inc .... E 718 672-8300
  Woodside *(G-17318)*
Battenfeld Grease Oil Corp NY .... E 716 695-2100
  North Tonawanda *(G-12960)*
Baums Castorine Company Inc .... G 315 336-8154
  Rome *(G-14805)*
Bestline International RES Inc .... E 518 631-2177
  Schenectady *(G-15235)*
Black Bear Company Inc .... E 718 784-7330
  Long Island City *(G-7687)*
Blaser Swisslube Holding Corp .... F 845 294-3200
  Goshen *(G-5733)*
Castoleum Corporation .... F 914 664-5877
  Mount Vernon *(G-8670)*
Chemlube International LLC .... F 914 381-5800
  Harrison *(G-5979)*
Chemlube Marketing Inc .... F 914 381-5800
  Harrison *(G-5980)*
Finish Line Technologies Inc .... E 631 666-7300
  Hauppauge *(G-6077)*
Inland Vacuum Industries Inc .... F 585 293-3330
  Churchville *(G-3638)*
Interdynamics .... F 914 241-1423
  Mount Kisco *(G-8631)*
Loobrica International Corp .... G 347 997-0296
  Staten Island *(G-15700)*
Noco Incorporated .... G 716 833-6626
  Tonawanda *(G-16187)*
Oil and Lubricant Depot LLC .... F 718 258-9220
  Amityville *(G-318)*
Ore-Lube Corporation .... F 631 205-0030
  Bellport *(G-836)*
Polycast Industries Inc .... F 631 595-2530
  Bay Shore *(G-726)*
Specialty Silicone Pdts Inc .... E 518 885-8826
  Ballston Spa *(G-609)*
Tribology Inc .... E 631 345-3000
  Yaphank *(G-17405)*

OILS: Essential
Torre Products Co Inc .... G 212 925-8989
  New York *(G-12375)*

OILS: Lubricating
R H Crown Co Inc .... E 518 762-4589
  Johnstown *(G-7123)*

OILS: Lubricating
Blaser Production Inc .... F 845 294-3200
  Goshen *(G-5732)*
Mdi Holdings LLC .... A 212 559-1127
  New York *(G-11203)*
Monroe Fluid Technology Inc .... E 585 392-3434
  Hilton *(G-6418)*
Tallmans Express Lube .... G 315 266-1033
  New Hartford *(G-8812)*

OILS: Orange
Solvents Company Inc .... F 631 595-9300
  Kingston *(G-7210)*

OILS: Still

E and V Energy Corporation ....F 315 786-2067
  Watertown (G-16651)

OINTMENTS

Saratoga Pharmaceuticals Inc ....F 518 894-1875
  Clifton Park (G-3706)

ON-LINE DATABASE INFORMATION RETRIEVAL SVCS

Endava Inc ....G 212 920-7240
  New York (G-10032)
News Corporation ....C 212 416-3400
  New York (G-11416)
Penton Media Inc ....B 212 204-4200
  New York (G-11608)

OPERATOR: Apartment Buildings

Gallagher Printing Inc ....E 716 873-2434
  Buffalo (G-2962)
Hospitality Inc ....E 212 268-1930
  New York (G-10511)

OPERATOR: Nonresidential Buildings

Omega Industries & Development ....E 516 349-8010
  Plainview (G-13625)

OPHTHALMIC GOODS

21st Century Optics Inc ....E 347 527-1079
  Long Island City (G-7643)
Accu Coat Inc ....G 585 288-2330
  Rochester (G-14166)
Bausch & Lomb Holdings Inc ....G 585 338-6000
  New York (G-9335)
Bausch & Lomb Incorporated ....B 585 338-6000
  Rochester (G-14225)
Bausch & Lomb Incorporated ....B 585 338-6000
  Rochester (G-14226)
Designs For Vision Inc ....C 631 585-3300
  Ronkonkoma (G-14894)
Esc Control Electronics LLC ....E 631 467-5328
  Sayville (G-15208)
Eyeworks Inc ....G 585 454-4470
  Rochester (G-14366)
Glasses USA LLC ....F 212 784-6094
  New York (G-10309)
Lens Lab ....G 718 379-2020
  Bronx (G-1381)
Lens Lab Express ....G 718 921-5488
  Brooklyn (G-2211)
Lens Lab Express of Graham Ave ....G 718 486-0117
  Brooklyn (G-2212)
Lens Lab Express Southern Blvd ....G 718 626-5184
  Astoria (G-448)
North Bronx Retinal & Ophthlmi ....G 347 535-4932
  Bronx (G-1413)
Oakley Inc ....D 212 575-0960
  New York (G-11491)
Surgical Design Corp ....F 914 273-2445
  Armonk (G-421)
Wyeth Holdings LLC ....D 845 602-5000
  Pearl River (G-13469)

OPHTHALMIC GOODS WHOLESALERS

21st Century Optics Inc ....E 347 527-1079
  Long Island City (G-7643)
Lens Lab Express Southern Blvd ....G 718 626-5184
  Astoria (G-448)
Winchester Optical Company ....E 607 734-4251
  Elmira (G-4705)

OPHTHALMIC GOODS: Frames & Parts, Eyeglass & Spectacle

Art-Craft Optical Company Inc ....E 585 546-6640
  Rochester (G-14213)
His Vision Inc ....E 585 254-0022
  Rochester (G-14437)
Zyloware Corporation ....D 914 708-1200
  Port Chester (G-13762)

OPHTHALMIC GOODS: Frames, Lenses & Parts, Eyeglasses

Eye Deal Eyewear Inc ....G 716 297-1500
  Niagara Falls (G-12817)

Moscot Wholesale Corp ....G 212 647-1550
  New York (G-11310)
Optika Eyes Ltd ....G 631 567-8852
  Sayville (G-15213)
Winchester Optical Company ....E 607 734-4251
  Elmira (G-4705)

OPHTHALMIC GOODS: Lenses, Ophthalmic

Co-Optics America Lab Inc ....E 607 432-0557
  Oneonta (G-13179)
Tri-Supreme Optical LLC ....D 631 249-2020
  Farmingdale (G-5134)

OPHTHALMIC GOODS: Spectacles

Modo Retail LLC ....E 212 965-4900
  New York (G-11289)

OPHTHALMIC GOODS: Temples & Fronts, Ophthalmic

Kathmando Valley Preservation ....F 212 727-0074
  New York (G-10818)

OPTICAL GOODS STORES

Hart Specialties Inc ....D 631 226-5600
  Amityville (G-292)
Match Eyewear LLC ....E 516 877-0170
  Westbury (G-17009)
Optika Eyes Ltd ....G 631 567-8852
  Sayville (G-15213)
Parker Warby Retail Inc ....E 646 517-5223
  New York (G-11575)

OPTICAL GOODS STORES: Opticians

Eyeglass Service Industries ....G 914 666-3150
  Bedford Hills (G-803)
Lens Lab Express ....G 718 921-5488
  Brooklyn (G-2211)

OPTICAL INSTRUMENTS & APPARATUS

Aeroflex Incorporated ....B 516 694-6700
  Plainview (G-13578)
Applied Image Inc ....E 585 482-0300
  Rochester (G-14209)
Carl Zeiss Inc ....C 914 747-1800
  Thornwood (G-16117)
Halo Optical Products Inc ....D 518 773-4256
  Gloversville (G-5713)
Hart Specialties Inc ....D 631 226-5600
  Amityville (G-292)
Kevin Freeman ....G 631 447-5321
  Patchogue (G-13426)
Leica Microsystems Inc ....G 716 686-3000
  Depew (G-4262)
Lumetrics Inc ....F 585 214-2455
  Rochester (G-14484)
Plx Inc ....E 631 586-4190
  Deer Park (G-4189)
Westchester Technologies Inc ....E 914 736-1034
  Peekskill (G-13486)

OPTICAL INSTRUMENTS & LENSES

21st Century Optics Inc ....E 347 527-1079
  Long Island City (G-7643)
Aeroflex Plainview Inc ....B 516 694-6700
  Plainview (G-13579)
Anorad Corporation ....C 631 380-2100
  East Setauket (G-4476)
Apollo Optical Systems Inc ....E 585 272-6170
  West Henrietta (G-16868)
Binoptics LLC ....D 607 257-3200
  Ithaca (G-6823)
CK Coatings ....G 585 502-0425
  Le Roy (G-7404)
Corning Tropel Corporation ....C 585 377-3200
  Fairport (G-4852)
CVI Laser LLC ....D 585 244-7220
  Rochester (G-14297)
Dorsey Metrology Intl Inc ....E 845 229-2929
  Poughkeepsie (G-13895)
Dynamic Laboratories Inc ....G 631 231-7474
  Ronkonkoma (G-14895)
Eele Laboratories LLC ....F 631 244-0051
  Bohemia (G-1063)
Exfo Burleigh Pdts Group Inc ....D 585 301-1530
  Canandaigua (G-3345)

Genesis Vision Inc ....E 585 254-0193
  Rochester (G-14397)
Gradient Lens Corporation ....E 585 235-2620
  Rochester (G-14412)
Gurley Precision Instrs Inc ....C 518 272-6300
  Troy (G-16237)
Isp Optics Corporation ....D 914 591-3070
  Irvington (G-6773)
Keon Optics Inc ....F 845 429-7103
  Stony Point (G-15775)
Match Eyewear LLC ....E 516 877-0170
  Westbury (G-17009)
Micatu Inc 888 705-8836
  Horseheads (G-6582)
Navitar Inc ....D 585 359-4000
  Rochester (G-14530)
Nikon Instruments Inc ....D 631 547-4200
  Melville (G-8343)
Novanta Inc 818 341-5151
  Syracuse (G-16000)
Optics Plus Inc ....G 716 744-2636
  Tonawanda (G-16190)
Optipro Systems LLC ....D 585 265-0160
  Ontario (G-13208)
Orafol Americas Inc ....E 585 272-0290
  West Henrietta (G-16886)
Planar Optics Inc ....E 585 671-0100
  Webster (G-16729)
Rochester Photonics Corp ....D 585 387-0674
  Rochester (G-14646)
RPC Photonics Inc ....F 585 272-2840
  Rochester (G-14661)
Santa Fe Manufacturing Corp ....E 631 234-0100
  Hauppauge (G-6183)
Schott Corporation ....D 315 255-2791
  Auburn (G-517)
Spectral Systems LLC ....E 845 896-2200
  Hopewell Junction (G-6559)
Stefan Sydor Optics Inc ....E 585 271-7300
  Rochester (G-14702)
Steven John Opticians ....G 718 543-3336
  Bronx (G-1465)
Surgical Design Corp ....F 914 273-2445
  Armonk (G-421)
Synergy Intrntnal Optrnics LLC ....E 631 277-0500
  Ronkonkoma (G-14991)
Tele-Vue Optics Inc ....E 845 469-4551
  Chester (G-3619)
US Optical LLC ....E 315 463-4800
  East Syracuse (G-4578)
Va Inc ....E 585 385-5930
  Rochester (G-14750)
Victory Vision Care Inc ....G 718 622-2020
  Brooklyn (G-2726)
Welch Allyn Inc ....A 315 685-4100
  Skaneateles Falls (G-15472)

OPTICAL SCANNING SVCS

Printech Business Systems Inc ....F 212 290-2542
  New York (G-11720)

OPTOMETRIC EQPT & SPLYS WHOLESALERS

Orafol Americas Inc ....E 585 272-0290
  West Henrietta (G-16886)

ORAL PREPARATIONS

Robell Research Inc ....G 212 755-6577
  New York (G-11888)

ORDNANCE

Dyno Nobel Inc ....D 845 338-2144
  Ulster Park (G-16285)
Island Ordnance Systems LLC ....F 516 746-2100
  Mineola (G-8518)
Magellan Aerospace NY Inc ....C 718 699-4000
  Corona (G-4001)
Mil-Spec Industries Corp ....G 516 625-5787
  Glen Cove (G-5621)

ORGAN TUNING & REPAIR SVCS

Kerner and Merchant ....G 315 463-8023
  East Syracuse (G-4548)

ORGANIZATIONS: Medical Research

Encysive Pharmaceuticals Inc ....E 212 733-2323
  New York (G-10031)

PRODUCT SECTION

ORGANIZATIONS: Noncommercial Biological Research

Nxxi Inc .... F 914 701-4500
  Purchase *(G-13962)*

ORGANIZATIONS: Professional

Physicalmind Institute .... F 212 343-2150
  New York *(G-11655)*
Public Relations Soc Amer Inc .... E 212 460-1400
  New York *(G-11746)*

ORGANIZATIONS: Religious

Albany Catholic Press Assoc .... G 518 453-6688
  Albany *(G-38)*
American Jewish Congress Inc .... E 212 879-4500
  New York *(G-9123)*
Nationwide Custom Services .... G 845 365-0414
  Tappan *(G-16081)*
Seneca Media Inc .... D 607 324-1425
  Hornell *(G-6566)*
United Synggue Cnsrvtive Jdism .... E 212 533-7800
  New York *(G-12467)*

ORGANIZATIONS: Research Institute

Alo Acquisition LLC .... G 518 464-0279
  Albany *(G-45)*
Katikati Inc .... G 585 678-1764
  West Henrietta *(G-16883)*

ORGANIZATIONS: Scientific Research Agency

Loobrica International Corp .... G 347 997-0296
  Staten Island *(G-15700)*

ORGANIZERS, CLOSET & DRAWER Plastic

Cubbies Unlimited Corporation .... F 631 586-8572
  Deer Park *(G-4124)*
Plascoline Inc .... F 917 410-5754
  New York *(G-11673)*

ORNAMENTS: Christmas Tree, Exc Electrical & Glass

Criterion Bell & Specialty .... E 718 788-2600
  Brooklyn *(G-1819)*
Patience Brewster Inc .... F 315 685-8336
  Skaneateles *(G-15464)*

ORTHOPEDIC SUNDRIES: Molded Rubber

Advanced Back Technologies .... G 631 231-0076
  Hauppauge *(G-6009)*
Certified Health Products Inc .... E 718 339-7498
  Brooklyn *(G-1770)*
Newyork Pedorthic Associates .... G 718 236-7500
  Brooklyn *(G-2371)*

OSCILLATORS

Centroid Inc .... E 516 349-0070
  Plainview *(G-13586)*

OUTLETS: Electric, Convenience

Andrew Marc Outlet .... G 631 727-2520
  Riverhead *(G-14138)*
Bronx New Way Corp .... G 347 431-1385
  Bronx *(G-1289)*
Dollar Popular Inc .... G 914 375-0361
  Yonkers *(G-17437)*
RE 99 Cents Inc .... G 718 639-2325
  Woodside *(G-17349)*

PACKAGE DESIGN SVCS

Force Digital Media Inc .... G 631 243-0243
  Deer Park *(G-4143)*
Maxworld Inc .... G 212 242-7588
  New York *(G-11189)*
Sky Dive .... D 845 858-6400
  Port Jervis *(G-13792)*
Titherington Design & Mfg .... F 518 324-2205
  Plattsburgh *(G-13704)*

PACKAGED FROZEN FOODS WHOLESALERS, NEC

Bagelovers Inc .... F 607 844-3683
  Dryden *(G-4320)*

PACKAGING & LABELING SVCS

Atlantic Essential Pdts Inc .... D 631 434-8333
  Hauppauge *(G-6027)*
Bfma Holding Corporation .... G 607 753-6746
  Cortland *(G-4014)*
Ccmi Inc .... G 315 781-3270
  Geneva *(G-5571)*
F M Howell & Company .... D 607 734-6291
  Elmira *(G-4684)*
Klg Usa LLC .... A 845 856-5311
  Port Jervis *(G-13788)*
Marietta Corporation .... B 607 753-0982
  Cortland *(G-4034)*
Nice-Pak Products Inc .... B 845 365-2772
  Orangeburg *(G-13236)*
Nutra Solutions USA Inc .... E 631 392-1900
  Deer Park *(G-4183)*
Orlandi Inc .... D 631 756-0110
  Farmingdale *(G-5071)*
Orlandi Inc .... E 631 756-0110
  Farmingdale *(G-5072)*
Paul Michael Group Inc .... G 631 585-5700
  Ronkonkoma *(G-14966)*
Piezo Electronics Research .... F 845 735-9349
  Pearl River *(G-13463)*
Princeton Label & Packaging .... E 609 490-0800
  Patchogue *(G-13433)*
Products Superb Inc .... G 315 923-7057
  Clyde *(G-3731)*
Professional Disposables Inc .... A 845 365-1700
  Orangeburg *(G-13244)*
Sugar Foods Corporation .... E 212 753-6900
  New York *(G-12227)*
Universal Packg Systems Inc .... A 631 543-2277
  Commack *(G-3845)*
Valentine Packaging Corp .... F 718 418-6000
  Maspeth *(G-8175)*
Weather Products Corporation .... G 315 474-8593
  Syracuse *(G-16069)*

PACKAGING MATERIALS, INDL: Wholesalers

Philpac Corporation .... E 716 875-8005
  Buffalo *(G-3124)*

PACKAGING MATERIALS, WHOLESALE

Patco Tapes Inc .... G 718 497-1527
  Maspeth *(G-8164)*
Technical Library Service Inc .... F 212 219-0770
  Brooklyn *(G-2649)*
Technical Packaging Inc .... F 516 223-2300
  Baldwin *(G-562)*
Terphane Holdings LLC .... G 585 657-5800
  Bloomfield *(G-990)*
W N Vanalstine & Sons Inc .... D 518 237-1436
  Cohoes *(G-3761)*

PACKAGING MATERIALS: Paper

Allen-Bailey Tag & Label Inc .... D 585 538-2324
  Caledonia *(G-3276)*
Anasia Inc .... G 718 588-1407
  Bronx *(G-1275)*
Apexx Omni-Graphics Inc .... D 718 326-3330
  Maspeth *(G-8119)*
Ares Box LLC .... D 718 858-8760
  Brooklyn *(G-1624)*
Bemis Company Inc .... C 631 794-2900
  Edgewood *(G-4594)*
Berry Plastics Corporation .... B 315 986-6270
  Macedon *(G-7984)*
CCL Label Inc .... C 716 852-2155
  Buffalo *(G-2868)*
Classic Labels Inc .... E 631 467-2300
  Patchogue *(G-13417)*
Colad Group LLC .... C 716 961-1776
  Buffalo *(G-2880)*
Craft Packaging Inc .... G 718 633-4045
  Brooklyn *(G-1388)*
De Luxe Packaging Corp .... E 416 754-4633
  Saugerties *(G-15183)*
Depot Label Company Inc .... G 631 467-2952
  Patchogue *(G-13418)*

PACKAGING MATERIALS: Plastic Film, Coated Or Laminated

General Fibre Products Corp .... D 516 358-7500
  New Hyde Park *(G-8835)*
General Trade Mark La .... E 718 979-7261
  Staten Island *(G-15677)*
Idesco Corp .... F 212 889-2530
  New York *(G-10557)*
International Paper Company .... C 585 663-1000
  Rochester *(G-14452)*
K Sidrane Inc .... E 631 393-6974
  Farmingdale *(G-5021)*
Multi Packaging Solutions Inc .... C 516 488-2000
  Hicksville *(G-6375)*
Multi Packaging Solutions Inc .... C 646 885-0157
  New York *(G-11324)*
Nameplate Mfrs of Amer .... E 631 752-0055
  Farmingdale *(G-5061)*
Nova Packaging Ltd Inc .... E 914 232-8406
  Katonah *(G-7133)*
Pactech Packaging LLC .... D 585 458-8008
  Rochester *(G-14566)*
Pactiv LLC .... C 518 562-6101
  Plattsburgh *(G-13684)*
Paperworks Industries Inc .... F 913 621-0922
  Baldwinsville *(G-573)*
Penta-Tech Coated Products LLC .... F 315 986-4098
  Macedon *(G-7989)*
Pliant LLC .... B 315 986-6286
  Macedon *(G-7990)*
Print Pack Inc .... C 404 460-7000
  Farmingdale *(G-5088)*
Printex Packaging Corporation .... E 631 234-4300
  Islandia *(G-6801)*
Quality Circle Products Inc .... D 914 736-6600
  Montrose *(G-8614)*
Rynone Packaging Corp .... G 607 565-8173
  Waverly *(G-16707)*
Saint-Gobain Prfmce Plas Corp .... C 518 642-2200
  Granville *(G-5781)*
Sealed Air Corporation .... E 518 370-1693
  Schenectady *(G-15295)*
Shaant Industries Inc .... E 716 366-3654
  Dunkirk *(G-4350)*
Time Release Sciences Inc .... E 716 823-4580
  Buffalo *(G-3219)*
Transcntinental Ultra Flex Inc .... B 718 272-9100
  Brooklyn *(G-2674)*
Valley Industrial Products Inc .... E 631 385-9300
  Huntington *(G-6689)*
Vitex Packaging Group Inc .... F 212 265-6575
  New York *(G-12557)*
Westrock Mwv LLC .... C 212 688-5000
  New York *(G-12618)*

PACKAGING MATERIALS: Paper, Coated Or Laminated

American Packaging Corporation .... C 585 254-9500
  Rochester *(G-14198)*
Cove Point Holdings LLC .... F 212 599-3388
  New York *(G-9740)*
Patco Tapes Inc .... G 718 497-1527
  Maspeth *(G-8164)*
Tri-Plex Packaging Corporation .... E 212 481-6070
  New York *(G-12401)*

PACKAGING MATERIALS: Paper, Thermoplastic Coated

F M Howell & Company .... D 607 734-6291
  Elmira *(G-4684)*
Smart USA Inc .... E 718 416-4400
  Glendale *(G-5663)*

PACKAGING MATERIALS: Plastic Film, Coated Or Laminated

Allied Converters Inc .... E 914 235-1585
  New Rochelle *(G-8886)*
Ecoplast & Packaging LLC .... G 718 996-0800
  Brooklyn *(G-1901)*
Folene Packaging LLC .... G 917 626-6740
  Brooklyn *(G-1992)*
Kal Pac Corp .... F 845 457-7013
  Montgomery *(G-8597)*
Mason Transparent Package Inc .... E 718 792-6000
  Bronx *(G-1388)*
Packstar Group Inc .... D 716 853-1688
  Buffalo *(G-3111)*
Pregis LLC .... D 518 743-3100
  Glens Falls *(G-5697)*

Employee Codes: A=Over 500 employees, B=251-500, C=101-250, D=51-100, E=20-50, F=10-19, G=5-9

PACKAGING MATERIALS: Plastic Film, Coated Or Laminated

RMS Packaging Inc .... F 914 205-2070
  Peekskill *(G-13481)*
Universal Packg Systems Inc .... A 631 543-2277
  Commack *(G-3845)*
W E W Container Corporation .... E 718 827-8150
  Brooklyn *(G-2740)*

PACKAGING MATERIALS: Polystyrene Foam

24 Seven Enterprises Inc .... G 845 563-9033
  New Windsor *(G-8928)*
Calpac Incorporated .... F 631 789-0502
  Amityville *(G-279)*
Cellect LLC .... C 508 744-6906
  Saint Johnsville *(G-15092)*
Chesu Inc .... F 239 564-2803
  East Hampton *(G-4407)*
Chocolate Delivery Systems Inc .... D 716 854-6050
  Buffalo *(G-2872)*
First Qlty Packg Solutions LLC .... F 516 829-3030
  Great Neck *(G-5811)*
Interntnal Bus Cmmncations Inc .... E 516 352-4505
  New Hyde Park *(G-8842)*
Jamestown Container Corp .... D 716 665-4623
  Falconer *(G-4904)*
Jem Container Corp .... F 516 349-7770
  Plainview *(G-13612)*
Knoll Printing & Packaging Inc .... E 516 621-0100
  Syosset *(G-15826)*
Lamar Plastics Packaging Ltd .... E 516 378-2500
  Freeport *(G-5408)*
Orcon Industries Corp .... D 585 768-7000
  Le Roy *(G-7417)*
Printex Packaging Corporation .... D 631 234-4300
  Islandia *(G-6801)*
R D A Container Corporation .... E 585 247-2323
  Gates *(G-5563)*
Sealed Air Corporation .... C 518 370-1693
  Schenectady *(G-15295)*
Shell Containers Inc (ny) .... E 516 352-4505
  New Hyde Park *(G-8861)*
Snow Craft Co Inc .... E 516 739-1399
  New Hyde Park *(G-8862)*
Stephen Gould Corporation .... G 212 497-8180
  New York *(G-12195)*
Technical Packaging Inc .... E 516 223-2300
  Baldwin *(G-562)*
W Stuart Smith Inc .... E 585 742-3310
  Victor *(G-16512)*
Walnut Packaging Inc .... E 631 293-3836
  Farmingdale *(G-5140)*

PACKAGING MATERIALS: Resinous Impregnated Paper

Cameo Process Corp .... G 914 948-0082
  White Plains *(G-17092)*

PACKAGING: Blister Or Bubble Formed, Plastic

Di Domenico Packaging Co Inc .... G 718 727-5454
  Staten Island *(G-15665)*
Formatix Corp .... E 631 467-3399
  Ronkonkoma *(G-14901)*

PACKING & CRATING SVC

Precision Techniques Inc .... D 718 991-1440
  Bronx *(G-1434)*

PACKING MATERIALS: Mechanical

Bag Arts Ltd .... G 212 684-7020
  New York *(G-9302)*
Gaddis Industrial Equipment .... F 516 759-3100
  Locust Valley *(G-7631)*
Technical Packaging Inc .... F 516 223-2300
  Baldwin *(G-562)*
Thermal Foams/Syracuse Inc .... E 315 699-8734
  Cicero *(G-3652)*
Unique Packaging Corporation .... G 514 341-5872
  Champlain *(G-3548)*

PACKING SVCS: Shipping

Miller Enterprises CNY Inc .... G 315 682-4999
  Manlius *(G-8075)*

PACKING: Metallic

Commercial Gaskets New York .... F 212 244-8130
  New York *(G-9685)*

PADDING: Foamed Plastics

Arm Rochester Inc .... F 585 354-5077
  Rochester *(G-14210)*
Philpac Corporation .... E 716 875-8005
  Buffalo *(G-3124)*

PADS: Desk, Exc Paper

Star Desk Pad Co Inc .... E 914 963-9400
  Yonkers *(G-17486)*

PADS: Desk, Paper, Made From Purchased Materials

General Diaries Corporation .... F 516 371-2244
  Inwood *(G-6758)*

PADS: Mattress

Continental Quilting Co Inc .... E 718 499-9100
  Brooklyn *(G-1800)*
Kravet Fabrics Inc .... D 516 293-2000
  Bethpage *(G-869)*

PAGERS: One-way

Bayside Beepers & Cellular .... G 718 343-3888
  Glen Oaks *(G-5640)*

PAINT STORE

Atlas Coatings Group Corp .... D 718 469-8787
  Brooklyn *(G-1648)*
Mercury Paint Corporation .... D 718 469-8787
  Brooklyn *(G-2298)*
Nautical Marine Paint Corp .... E 718 462-7000
  Brooklyn *(G-2354)*
Starlite Pnt & Varnish Co Inc .... G 718 292-6420
  Bronx *(G-1464)*

PAINTING SVC: Metal Prdts

Aircraft Finishing Corp .... F 631 422-5000
  West Babylon *(G-16767)*
Artistic Innovation Inc .... F 914 968-3021
  Yonkers *(G-17416)*
Buffalo Finishing Works Inc .... G 716 893-5266
  Buffalo *(G-2851)*
Buffalo Metal Finishing Co .... G 716 883-2751
  Buffalo *(G-2856)*
Color Craft Finishing Corp .... F 631 563-3230
  Bohemia *(G-1038)*
D & I Finishing Inc .... G 631 471-3034
  Bohemia *(G-1048)*
Duzmor Painting Inc .... G 585 768-4760
  Le Roy *(G-7407)*
Industrial Paint Services Corp .... F 607 687-0107
  Owego *(G-13352)*
Keymark Corporation .... A 518 853-3421
  Fonda *(G-5316)*
Mac Artspray Finishing Corp .... F 718 649-3800
  Brooklyn *(G-2249)*
McHugh Painting Co Inc .... F 716 741-8077
  Clarence *(G-3665)*
Rims Like New Inc .... F 845 537-0396
  Middletown *(G-8460)*
Tailored Coatings Inc .... E 716 893-4869
  Buffalo *(G-3209)*

PAINTS & ADDITIVES

Atlas Coatings Group Corp .... D 718 469-8787
  Brooklyn *(G-1648)*
Farrow and Ball Inc .... G 212 752-5544
  New York *(G-10139)*
Fougera Pharmaceuticals Inc .... C 631 454-7677
  Melville *(G-8321)*
General Coatings Tech Inc .... E 718 821-1232
  Ridgewood *(G-14108)*
Inglis Co Inc .... G 315 475-1315
  Syracuse *(G-15963)*
Liberty Panel Center Inc .... F 718 647-2763
  Brooklyn *(G-2216)*
Mercury Paint Corporation .... D 718 469-8787
  Brooklyn *(G-2298)*
Reddi Car Corp .... F 631 589-3141
  Sayville *(G-15214)*

PRODUCT SECTION

Sml Brothers Holding Corp .... D 718 402-2000
  Bronx *(G-1457)*
Starlite Pnt & Varnish Co Inc .... G 718 292-6420
  Bronx *(G-1464)*
T J Ronan Paint Corp .... E 718 292-1100
  Bronx *(G-1470)*
Talyarps Corporation .... D 914 699-3030
  Pelham *(G-13496)*
Talyarps Corporation .... E 914 699-3030
  Mount Vernon *(G-8735)*

PAINTS & ALLIED PRODUCTS

A & B Color Corp (del) .... G 718 441-5482
  Kew Gardens *(G-7157)*
Amsterdam Color Works Inc .... F 718 231-8626
  Bronx *(G-1274)*
Angiotech Biocoatings Corp .... E 585 321-1130
  Henrietta *(G-6292)*
Anthony River Inc .... F 315 475-1315
  Syracuse *(G-15855)*
Atc Plastics LLC .... E 212 375-2515
  New York *(G-9245)*
B & F Architectural Support Gr .... E 212 279-6488
  New York *(G-9287)*
Barson Composites Corporation .... E 516 752-7882
  Old Bethpage *(G-13126)*
Benjamin Moore & Co .... E 518 736-1723
  Johnstown *(G-7108)*
Cytec Industries Inc .... F 716 372-9650
  Olean *(G-13142)*
Deluxe Paint .... F 718 768-9494
  Brooklyn *(G-1853)*
Eric S Turner & Company Inc .... F 914 235-7114
  New Rochelle *(G-8898)*
Excel Paint Applicators Inc .... E 347 221-1968
  Inwood *(G-6755)*
Fayette Street Coatings Inc .... G 315 488-5401
  Syracuse *(G-15942)*
Fayette Street Coatings Inc .... F 315 488-5401
  Liverpool *(G-7519)*
Garco Manufacturing Corp Inc .... E 718 287-3330
  Brooklyn *(G-2013)*
Heany Industries Inc .... D 585 889-2700
  Scottsville *(G-15336)*
Inhance Technologies LLC .... E 716 825-9031
  Buffalo *(G-3009)*
Insulating Coatings Corp .... F 607 723-1727
  Binghamton *(G-927)*
Jrlon Inc .... D 315 597-4067
  Palmyra *(G-13409)*
Nautical Marine Paint Corp .... E 718 462-7000
  Brooklyn *(G-2354)*
Nortek Powder Coating LLC .... F 315 337-2339
  Rome *(G-14826)*
Peter Kwasny Inc .... G 727 641-1462
  Hauppauge *(G-6161)*
T C Dunham Paint Company Inc .... G 914 969-4202
  Yonkers *(G-17489)*
Yewtree Millworks Corp .... G 914 320-5851
  Yonkers *(G-17501)*

PAINTS & VARNISHES: Plastics Based

Industrial Finishing Products .... F 718 342-4871
  Brooklyn *(G-2104)*

PAINTS, VARNISHES & SPLYS, WHOLESALE: Paints

A & B Color Corp (del) .... G 718 441-5482
  Kew Gardens *(G-7157)*
Benjamin Moore & Co .... E 518 736-1723
  Johnstown *(G-7108)*

PALLET REPAIR SVCS

Four-Way Pallet Corp .... E 631 351-3401
  Huntington Station *(G-6706)*

PALLETIZERS & DEPALLETIZERS

Arpac LLC .... F 315 471-5103
  Syracuse *(G-15858)*

PALLETS

A D Bowman & Son Lumber Co .... E 607 692-2595
  Castle Creek *(G-3417)*
Dwa Pallet Inc .... G 518 746-1047
  Hudson Falls *(G-6641)*
Just Wood Pallets Inc .... G 718 644-7013
  New Windsor *(G-8940)*

PRODUCT SECTION

PAPER PRDTS: Infant & Baby Prdts

North Shore Pallet Inc .... G 631 673-4700
Huntington Station *(G-6719)*
Pooran Pallet Inc .... G 718 938-7970
Bronx *(G-1431)*
Sanjay Pallets Inc .... G 347 590-2485
Bronx *(G-1447)*
Steven Coffey Pallet S Inc .... G 585 261-6783
Rochester *(G-14704)*

PALLETS & SKIDS: Wood

Berry Industrial Group Inc .... G 845 353-8338
Nyack *(G-13045)*
Best Pallet & Crate LLC .... G 518 438-2945
Albany *(G-55)*
Chemung Cty Assc Retrd Ctzns .... C 607 734-6151
Elmira *(G-4675)*
Curran Renewable Energy LLC .... E 315 769-2000
Massena *(G-8193)*
Dimensional Mills Inc .... G 518 746-1047
Hudson Falls *(G-6640)*
Four-Way Pallet Corp .... E 631 351-3401
Huntington Station *(G-6706)*
McIntosh Box & Pallet Co Inc .... F 315 789-8750
Geneva *(G-5582)*
McIntosh Box & Pallet Co Inc .... E 315 446-9350
Rome *(G-14820)*
Nefab Packaging North East LLC .... E 518 346-9105
Scotia *(G-15328)*
Pallet Services Inc .... E 585 647-4020
Rochester *(G-14569)*
Reuter Pallet Pkg Sys Inc .... G 845 457-9937
Montgomery *(G-8602)*

PALLETS: Wood & Metal Combination

Pallet Division Inc .... G 585 328-3780
Rochester *(G-14568)*

PALLETS: Wooden

Abbot & Abbot Box Corp .... F 888 930-5972
Long Island City *(G-7646)*
B & B Lumber Company Inc .... D 315 492-1786
Jamesville *(G-7045)*
Clements Burrville Sawmill .... G 315 782-4549
Watertown *(G-16645)*
Crawford Furniture Mfg Corp .... C 716 483-2102
Jamestown *(G-6985)*
Custom Shipping Products Inc .... F 716 355-4437
Clymer *(G-3733)*
D & F Pallet Inc .... F 716 672-2984
Fredonia *(G-5372)*
Essex Box & Pallet Co Inc .... E 518 834-7279
Keeseville *(G-7137)*
G & H Wood Products LLC .... F 716 372-5510
Olean *(G-13148)*
Great Lakes Specialties .... E 716 672-4622
Fredonia *(G-5374)*
Lindley Wood Works Inc .... F 607 523-7786
Lindley *(G-7496)*
McIntosh Box & Pallet Co Inc .... D 315 675-8511
Bernhards Bay *(G-858)*
Neville Mfg Svc & Dist Inc .... F 716 834-3038
Cheektowaga *(G-3582)*
Northeast Pallet & Cont Co Inc .... F 518 271-0535
Troy *(G-16244)*
Orleans Pallet Company Inc .... F 585 589-0781
Albion *(G-167)*
Pallets Inc .... E 518 747-4177
Fort Edward *(G-5343)*
Pallets R US Inc .... E 631 758-2360
Bellport *(G-837)*
Paul Bunyan Products Inc .... E 315 696-6164
Cortland *(G-4039)*
Peco Pallet Inc .... E 914 376-5444
Irvington *(G-6776)*
Peter C Herman Inc .... E 315 926-4100
Marion *(G-8098)*
Shepards Sawmill .... G 585 638-5664
Holley *(G-6493)*
Vansantis Development Inc .... E 315 461-0113
Liverpool *(G-7554)*
Wolfe Lumber Mill Inc .... G 716 772-7750
Gasport *(G-5560)*

PANEL & DISTRIBUTION BOARDS: Electric

Allied Circuits LLC .... E 716 551-0285
Buffalo *(G-2803)*
Claddagh Electronics Ltd .... E 718 784-0571
Long Island City *(G-7700)*

PANELS: Building, Wood

Harvest Homes Inc .... E 518 895-2341
Delanson *(G-4233)*

PANELS: Cardboard, Die-Cut, Made From Purchased Materials

Hubray Inc .... F 800 645-2855
North Baldwin *(G-12907)*

PANELS: Wood

Northeast Panel & Truss LLC .... E 845 339-3656
Kingston *(G-7205)*

PAPER & BOARD: Die-cut

All Out Die Cutting Inc .... E 718 346-6666
Brooklyn *(G-1587)*
American Dsplay Die Ctters Inc .... E 212 645-1274
New York *(G-9117)*
Art Industries of New York .... E 212 633-9200
New York *(G-9211)*
Borden & Riley Paper Co Inc .... E 718 454-9494
Hollis *(G-6494)*
Dia .... G 212 675-4097
New York *(G-9867)*
General Die and Die Cutng Inc .... D 516 665-3584
Roosevelt *(G-15004)*
General Fibre Products Corp .... D 516 358-7500
New Hyde Park *(G-8835)*
Glens Falls Business Forms Inc .... F 518 798-6643
Queensbury *(G-13996)*
Kleer-Fax Inc .... D 631 225-1100
Amityville *(G-303)*
Leather Indexes Corp .... D 516 827-1900
Hicksville *(G-6363)*
Manufacturers Indexing Pdts .... G 631 271-0956
Halesite *(G-5905)*
Mid Island Die Cutting Corp .... C 631 293-0180
Farmingdale *(G-5053)*
Miken Companies Inc .... D 716 668-6311
Buffalo *(G-3065)*
New York Cutting & Gumming Co .... E 212 563-4146
Middletown *(G-8454)*
Norampac New York City Inc .... C 718 340-2100
Maspeth *(G-8158)*
Orange Die Cutting Corp .... C 845 562-0900
Newburgh *(G-12772)*
Paperworld Inc .... E 516 221-2702
Bellmore *(G-819)*
Precision Diecutting Inc .... G 315 776-8465
Port Byron *(G-13736)*
Premier Packaging Corporation .... E 585 924-8460
Victor *(G-16496)*
S & S Prtg Die-Cutting Co Inc .... F 718 388-8990
Brooklyn *(G-2522)*
Spectrum Prtg Lithography Inc .... E 212 255-3131
New York *(G-12158)*
Welsh Gold Stampers Inc .... E 718 984-5031
Staten Island *(G-15754)*

PAPER CONVERTING

Aigner Label Holder Corp .... F 845 562-4510
New Windsor *(G-8930)*
Beetins Wholesale Inc .... F 718 524-0899
Staten Island *(G-15645)*
Best Time Processor LLC .... G 917 455-4126
Richmond Hill *(G-14069)*
Eagles Nest Holdings LLC .... E 513 874-5270
New York *(G-9959)*
Felix Schoeller North Amer Inc .... C 315 298-5133
Pulaski *(G-13946)*
Gardei Industries LLC .... F 716 693-7100
North Tonawanda *(G-12973)*
Gavin Mfg Corp .... E 631 467-0040
Farmingdale *(G-4997)*
Global Tissue Group Inc .... E 631 924-3019
Medford *(G-8245)*
Graphic Cntrls Acqisition Corp .... B 716 853-7500
Buffalo *(G-2978)*
Graphic Controls Holdings Inc .... F 716 853-7500
Buffalo *(G-2979)*
Interface Performance Mtls .... F 315 346-3100
Beaver Falls *(G-794)*
Katz Group Americas Inc .... E 716 995-3071
Sanborn *(G-15122)*
Marketing Group International .... G 631 754-8095
Northport *(G-13016)*

Millcraft Paper Company .... E 716 856-5135
Buffalo *(G-3066)*
Northeastern Paper Corp .... G 631 659-3634
Huntington *(G-6670)*
Noteworthy Industries Inc .... C 518 842-2662
Amsterdam *(G-364)*
P C I Paper Conversions Inc .... C 315 437-1641
Syracuse *(G-16006)*
Pack America Corp .... G 212 508-6666
New York *(G-11554)*
Paradigm Mktg Consortium Inc .... E 516 677-6012
Syosset *(G-15835)*
Pkk Inc .... E 716 257-3451
Cattaraugus *(G-3439)*
RB Converting Inc .... G 607 777-1325
Binghamton *(G-945)*
S D Warren Company .... D 914 696-5544
White Plains *(G-17165)*
Trinity Packaging Corporation .... E 914 273-4111
Armonk *(G-422)*
VIP Paper Trading Inc .... E 212 382-4642
New York *(G-12546)*
Waymor1 Inc .... D 518 677-8511
Cambridge *(G-3310)*
Waymor1 Inc .... E 518 677-8511
Cambridge *(G-3311)*

PAPER MANUFACTURERS: Exc Newsprint

Albany International Corp .... C 518 445-2230
Menands *(G-8365)*
Ampac Paper LLC .... A 845 778-5511
Walden *(G-16530)*
Atlas Recycling LLC .... E 212 925-3280
New York *(G-9257)*
Burrows Paper Corporation .... D 315 823-2300
Little Falls *(G-7497)*
Carta Usa LLC .... E 585 436-3012
Rochester *(G-14260)*
Clearwater Paper Corporation .... D 315 287-1200
Gouverneur *(G-5744)*
Dunmore Corporation .... D 845 279-5061
Brewster *(G-1217)*
Euro Fine Paper Inc .... G 516 238-5253
Garden City *(G-5503)*
Freeport Paper Industries Inc .... D 631 851-1555
Central Islip *(G-3497)*
Georgia-Pacific LLC .... A 518 561-3500
Plattsburgh *(G-13664)*
International Paper Company .... A 518 585-6761
Ticonderoga *(G-16126)*
International Paper Company .... C 845 986-6409
Tuxedo Park *(G-16284)*
International Paper Company .... C 607 775-1550
Conklin *(G-3869)*
International Paper Company .... C 315 797-5120
Utica *(G-16345)*
Lenaro Paper Co Inc .... F 631 439-8800
Central Islip *(G-3502)*
Minimill Technologies Inc .... F 315 692-4557
Syracuse *(G-15991)*
Mohawk Fine Papers Inc .... E 518 237-1741
Cohoes *(G-3752)*
Mohawk Fine Papers Inc .... B 518 237-1740
Cohoes *(G-3751)*
Omniafiltra LLC .... E 315 346-7300
Beaver Falls *(G-795)*
Paper Solutions Inc .... F 718 499-4226
Brooklyn *(G-2404)*
Sca Tissue North America LLC .... E 518 692-8434
Greenwich *(G-5892)*
Sca Tissue North America LLC .... C 518 583-2785
Saratoga Springs *(G-15172)*
Verso Corporation .... B 212 599-2700
New York *(G-12526)*
Verso Paper Management LP .... A 781 320-8660
New York *(G-12527)*
Verso Paper Management LP .... C 212 599-2700
New York *(G-12528)*

PAPER PRDTS: Feminine Hygiene Prdts

Maxim Hygiene Products Inc .... F 516 621-3323
Mineola *(G-8523)*
Rochester Midland Corporation .... C 585 336-2200
Rochester *(G-14643)*

PAPER PRDTS: Infant & Baby Prdts

Kas Direct LLC .... E 516 934-0541
Westbury *(G-17001)*

Employee Codes: A=Over 500 employees, B=251-500
C=101-250, D=51-100, E=20-50, F=10-19, G=5-9

PAPER PRDTS: Molded Pulp Prdts

Fibercel Packaging LLC ....E 716 933-8703
Portville *(G-13874)*

PAPER PRDTS: Napkins, Sanitary, Made From Purchased Material

Precare Corp ....G 631 667-1055
Hauppauge *(G-6168)*

PAPER PRDTS: Pattern Tissue

Stephen Singer Pattern Co Inc ....F 212 947-2902
New York *(G-12196)*

PAPER PRDTS: Pressed & Molded Pulp & Fiber Prdts

Pactiv LLC ....G 585 394-1525
Canandaigua *(G-3351)*

PAPER PRDTS: Pressed Pulp Prdts

Huhtamaki Inc ....A 315 593-5311
Fulton *(G-5461)*

PAPER PRDTS: Sanitary

Amscan Inc ....C 914 345-2020
Elmsford *(G-4732)*
Attends Healthcare Inc ....A 212 338-5100
New York *(G-9259)*
Becks Classic Mfg Inc ....D 631 435-3800
Brentwood *(G-1178)*
Cellu Tissue - Long Island LLC ....C 631 232-2626
Central Islip *(G-3489)*
Crosstex International Inc ....D 631 582-6777
Hauppauge *(G-6058)*
First Quality Products Inc ....F 516 829-4949
Great Neck *(G-5812)*
Georgia-Pacific LLC ....A 518 561-3500
Plattsburgh *(G-13664)*
Monthly Gift Inc ....G 888 444-9661
New York *(G-11302)*
Nice-Pak Products Inc ....B 845 365-2772
Orangeburg *(G-13236)*
Precare Corp ....G 631 524-5171
Hauppauge *(G-6167)*
Professional Disposables Inc ....A 845 365-1700
Orangeburg *(G-13244)*
Sqp Inc ....C 518 831-6800
Schenectady *(G-15299)*
Waymor1 Inc ....E 518 677-8511
Cambridge *(G-3311)*

PAPER PRDTS: Toilet Paper, Made From Purchased Materials

Deluxe Packaging Corp ....F 845 246-6090
Saugerties *(G-15184)*

PAPER PRDTS: Toweling Tissue

Crosstex International Inc ....D 631 582-6777
Hauppauge *(G-6058)*

PAPER PRDTS: Towels, Napkins/Tissue Paper, From Purchd Mtrls

Cascades Tssue Group-Sales Inc ....D 518 238-1900
Waterford *(G-16608)*
Florelle Tissue Corporation ....E 647 997-7405
Brownville *(G-2784)*
N3a Corporation ....D 516 284-6799
Inwood *(G-6762)*
Procter & Gamble Company ....C 646 885-4201
New York *(G-11726)*
Select Products Holdings LLC ....E 855 777-3532
Huntington *(G-6681)*
US Alliance Paper Inc ....C 631 254-3030
Edgewood *(G-4619)*

PAPER, WHOLESALE: Fine

Lenaro Paper Co Inc ....F 631 439-8800
Central Islip *(G-3502)*

PAPER, WHOLESALE: Printing

Chesu Inc ....F 239 564-2803
East Hampton *(G-4407)*

Malone Industrial Press Inc ....G 518 483-5880
Malone *(G-8013)*

PAPER: Absorbent

Cascades Tssue Group-Sales Inc ....E 819 363-5100
Waterford *(G-16609)*
National Paper Converting Inc ....G 607 687-6049
Owego *(G-13356)*

PAPER: Adding Machine Rolls, Made From Purchased Materials

Gaylord Bros Inc ....D 315 457-5070
North Syracuse *(G-12944)*
Paperworld Inc ....E 516 221-2702
Bellmore *(G-819)*

PAPER: Adhesive

Avery Dennison Corporation ....C 845 680-3873
Orangeburg *(G-13220)*
Cove Point Holdings LLC ....F 212 599-3388
New York *(G-9740)*
Label Makers Inc ....E 631 319-6329
Bohemia *(G-1090)*
Oaklee International Inc ....G 631 436-7900
Ronkonkoma *(G-14958)*
Rochester 100 Inc ....C 585 475-0200
Rochester *(G-14633)*
Stoney Croft Converters Inc ....F 718 608-9800
Staten Island *(G-15741)*
Triangle Label Tag Inc ....G 718 875-3030
Brooklyn *(G-2679)*

PAPER: Art

Donne Dieu ....G 212 226-0573
New York *(G-9905)*

PAPER: Bristols

Bristol Core Inc ....F 585 919-0302
Canandaigua *(G-3336)*
Bristol/White Plains ....F 914 681-1800
White Plains *(G-17088)*

PAPER: Building, Insulating & Packaging

CCT (us) Inc ....F 716 297-7509
Niagara Falls *(G-12803)*
Howard J Moore Company Inc ....E 631 351-8467
Plainview *(G-13606)*

PAPER: Business Form

Bigrow Paper Mfg Corp ....F 718 624-4439
Brooklyn *(G-1695)*
Chem-Puter Friendly Inc ....E 631 331-2259
Mount Sinai *(G-8654)*
Datagraphic Business Systems ....G 516 485-9069
Brentwood *(G-1180)*
United Data Forms Inc ....F 631 218-0104
Bohemia *(G-1151)*

PAPER: Card

Lion Die-Cutting Co Inc ....E 718 383-8841
Brooklyn *(G-2229)*

PAPER: Chemically Treated, Made From Purchased Materials

Micro Essential Laboratory ....E 718 338-3618
Brooklyn *(G-2310)*

PAPER: Cigarette

Schweitzer-Mauduit Intl Inc ....C 518 329-4222
Ancram *(G-375)*

PAPER: Cloth, Lined, Made From Purchased Materials

Albany International Corp ....D 518 447-6400
Menands *(G-8366)*

PAPER: Coated & Laminated, NEC

3 Star Papers Limited ....F 718 499-5481
Brooklyn *(G-1514)*
A-One Laminating Corp ....G 718 266-6002
Brooklyn *(G-1540)*

Adflex Corporation ....E 585 454-2950
Rochester *(G-14173)*
C & R De Santis Inc ....E 718 447-5076
Staten Island *(G-15653)*
CCL Label Inc ....C 716 852-2155
Buffalo *(G-2868)*
Classic Labels Inc ....E 631 467-2300
Patchogue *(G-13417)*
Dunmore Corporation ....D 845 279-5061
Brewster *(G-1217)*
Fibermark North America Inc ....E 315 376-3571
Lowville *(G-7937)*
Greenbush Tape & Label Inc ....E 518 465-2389
Albany *(G-83)*
K Sidrane Inc ....E 631 393-6974
Farmingdale *(G-5021)*
Liberty Label Mfg Inc ....F 631 737-2365
Holbrook *(G-6457)*
Miken Companies Inc ....E 716 668-6311
Buffalo *(G-3065)*
Mohawk Fine Papers Inc ....B 518 237-1740
Cohoes *(G-3751)*
New York Cutting & Gumming Co ....E 212 563-4146
Middletown *(G-8454)*
Overnight Labels Inc ....E 631 242-4240
Deer Park *(G-4186)*
P C I Paper Conversions Inc ....E 315 437-1641
Syracuse *(G-16006)*
Princeton Label & Packaging ....E 609 490-0800
Patchogue *(G-13433)*
S & S Prtg Die-Cutting Co Inc ....F 718 388-8990
Brooklyn *(G-2522)*

PAPER: Corrugated

General Fibre Products Corp ....D 516 358-7500
New Hyde Park *(G-8835)*

PAPER: Envelope

Tag Envelope Co Inc ....E 718 389-6844
College Point *(G-3809)*

PAPER: Filter

Andex Corp ....E 585 328-3790
Rochester *(G-14204)*
Hollingsworth & Vose Company ....E 518 695-8000
Greenwich *(G-5889)*
Knowlton Technologies LLC ....C 315 782-0600
Watertown *(G-16661)*

PAPER: Insulation Siding

Donald Bruhnke ....F 212 600-1260
New York *(G-9897)*

PAPER: Kraft

APC Paper Company Inc ....D 315 384-4225
Norfolk *(G-12897)*
Kapstone Container Corporation ....D 518 842-2450
Amsterdam *(G-352)*
Scalamandre Wallpaper Inc ....B 631 467-8800
Hauppauge *(G-6185)*

PAPER: Parchment

Palisades Paper Inc ....G 845 354-0333
Spring Valley *(G-15597)*

PAPER: Printer

Batavia Legal Printing Inc ....G 585 768-2100
Le Roy *(G-7403)*
Summit Financial Printing LLC ....E 212 913-0510
New York *(G-12233)*

PAPER: Specialty

Cottrell Paper Company Inc ....E 518 885-1702
Rock City Falls *(G-14777)*
Dunn Paper - Natural Dam Inc ....D 315 287-1200
Gouverneur *(G-5745)*
Fibermark North America Inc ....D 315 782-5800
Brownville *(G-2783)*
Gratitude & Company Inc ....G 607 277-3188
Ithaca *(G-6845)*
Potsdam Specialty Paper Inc ....D 315 265-4000
Potsdam *(G-13881)*

PRODUCT SECTION

PAPER: Tissue

Burrows Paper Corporation .... E 315 348-8491
  Lyons Falls *(G-7977)*
Burrows Paper Corporation .... D 315 823-2300
  Little Falls *(G-7498)*
North End Paper Co Inc .... G 315 593-8100
  Fulton *(G-5471)*
Precare Corp .... G 631 667-1055
  Hauppauge *(G-6168)*

PAPER: Wrapping

Flower Cy Tissue Mills Co Inc .... E 585 458-9200
  Rochester *(G-14376)*

PAPER: Writing

Automation Papers Inc .... E 315 432-0565
  Syracuse *(G-15862)*

PAPERBOARD

Alpine Paper Box Co Inc .... E 718 345-4040
  Brooklyn *(G-1595)*
American Wire Tie Inc .... E 716 337-2412
  North Collins *(G-12926)*
Interface Performance Mtls Inc .... D 518 686-3400
  Hoosick Falls *(G-6540)*
Ms Paper Products Co Inc .... G 718 624-0248
  Brooklyn *(G-2342)*
Multi Packaging Solutions Inc .... D 812 422-4104
  Hicksville *(G-6376)*
Niagara Fiberboard Inc .... E 716 434-8881
  Lockport *(G-7605)*
Pactiv LLC .... E 585 248-1213
  Pittsford *(G-13573)*
Professional Packg Svcs Inc .... E 518 677-5100
  Eagle Bridge *(G-4357)*
Royal Industries Inc .... E 718 369-3046
  Brooklyn *(G-2511)*
Solomon Schwimmer .... G 718 625-5719
  Brooklyn *(G-2583)*

PAPERBOARD CONVERTING

Allied Converters Inc .... E 914 235-1585
  New Rochelle *(G-8886)*
Deltacraft Paper Company LLC .... C 716 856-5135
  Buffalo *(G-2906)*
Mid-York Press Inc .... D 607 674-4491
  Sherburne *(G-15393)*
Winghing 8 Ltd .... G 718 439-0021
  Brooklyn *(G-2760)*

PAPERBOARD PRDTS: Building Insulating & Packaging

Greenfiber Albany Inc .... E 518 842-1470
  Gloversville *(G-5712)*
Shell Containers Inc (ny) .... E 516 352-4505
  New Hyde Park *(G-8861)*

PAPERBOARD PRDTS: Container Board

Cascades Cntnerboard Packg Inc .... C 450 923-3031
  Niagara Falls *(G-12802)*
Kapstone Container Corporation .... D 518 842-2450
  Amsterdam *(G-352)*
Westrock - Solvay Llc .... C 315 484-9050
  Syracuse *(G-16070)*
Westrock CP LLC .... D 315 484-9050
  Syracuse *(G-16071)*

PAPERBOARD PRDTS: Folding Boxboard

Burt Rigid Box Inc .... F 607 433-2510
  Oneonta *(G-13176)*
Di Domenico Packaging Co Inc .... G 718 727-5454
  Staten Island *(G-15665)*
Enterprise Folding Box Co Inc .... E 716 876-6421
  Buffalo *(G-2941)*
Paper Box Corp .... D 212 226-7490
  New York *(G-11563)*
Westrock Rkt Company .... C 770 448-2193
  Syracuse *(G-16072)*

PAPERBOARD PRDTS: Kraft Linerboard

Continental Kraft Corp .... G 516 681-9090
  Jericho *(G-7063)*

PAPERBOARD PRDTS: Packaging Board

Farrington Packaging Corp .... E 315 733-4600
  Utica *(G-16331)*

PAPERBOARD PRDTS: Pressboard

Fibermark North America Inc .... D 315 782-5800
  Brownville *(G-2783)*

PAPERBOARD: Boxboard

Prestige Box Corporation .... E 516 773-3115
  Great Neck *(G-5833)*

PAPERBOARD: Liner Board

Cascades Cntnerboard Packg Inc .... C 716 285-3681
  Niagara Falls *(G-12801)*
Greenpac Mill LLC .... D 716 299-0560
  Niagara Falls *(G-12829)*
Westrock Mwv LLC .... C 212 688-5000
  New York *(G-12618)*

PAPIER-MACHE PRDTS, EXC STATUARY & ART GOODS

Specialty Quality Packg LLC .... D 914 580-3200
  Scotia *(G-15331)*

PARACHUTES

National Military Industries .... G 908 782-1646
  Palenville *(G-13397)*
National Parachute Industries .... E 908 782-1646
  Palenville *(G-13398)*
Yoland Corporation .... E 718 499-4803
  Brooklyn *(G-2776)*

PARKING LOTS

Deans Paving Inc .... G 315 736-7601
  Marcy *(G-8091)*

PARTITIONS & FIXTURES: Except Wood

All American Metal Corporation .... E 516 623-0222
  Freeport *(G-5384)*
American Standard Mfg Inc .... E 518 868-2512
  Central Bridge *(G-3482)*
Avf Inc .... F 951 360-7111
  Buffalo *(G-2827)*
Bobrick Washroom Equipment Inc .... D 518 877-7444
  Clifton Park *(G-3697)*
Bridge Metal Industries LLC .... C 914 663-9200
  Mount Vernon *(G-8667)*
Dakota Systems Mfg Corp .... G 631 249-5811
  Farmingdale *(G-4973)*
E-Systems Group LLC .... E 607 775-1100
  Conklin *(G-3868)*
Hergo Ergonomic Support .... E 718 894-0639
  Maspeth *(G-8143)*
Joldeson One Aerospace Inds .... D 718 848-7396
  Ozone Park *(G-13380)*
La Mar Lighting Co Inc .... D 631 777-7700
  Farmingdale *(G-5032)*
Mass Mdsg Self Selection Eqp .... E 631 234-3300
  Bohemia *(G-1102)*
Maximum Security Products Corp .... E 518 233-1800
  Waterford *(G-16613)*
Milton Merl & Associates Inc .... G 212 634-9292
  New York *(G-11271)*
Mobile Media Inc .... E 845 744-8080
  Pine Bush *(G-13548)*
Modu-Craft Inc .... G 716 694-0709
  Tonawanda *(G-16182)*
Sturdy Store Displays Inc .... E 718 389-9919
  Brooklyn *(G-2616)*
Traco Manufacturing Inc .... G 585 343-2434
  Batavia *(G-651)*

PARTITIONS WHOLESALERS

CNA Specialties Inc .... G 631 567-7929
  Sayville *(G-15206)*

PARTITIONS: Nonwood, Floor Attached

All American Metal Corporation .... G 516 223-1760
  Freeport *(G-5383)*
Global Steel Products Corp .... C 631 586-3455
  Deer Park *(G-4147)*
Inscape (new York) Inc .... D 716 665-6210
  Falconer *(G-4902)*

Knickerbocker Partition Corp .... D 516 546-0550
  Freeport *(G-5406)*

PARTITIONS: Solid Fiber, Made From Purchased Materials

Westrock Rkt Company .... C 770 448-2193
  Camillus *(G-3328)*

PARTITIONS: Wood & Fixtures

Artone LLC .... D 716 664-2232
  Jamestown *(G-6972)*
Champion Millwork Inc .... E 315 463-0711
  Syracuse *(G-15892)*
Custom Countertops Inc .... G 716 685-2871
  Depew *(G-4253)*
Dbs Interiors Corp .... F 631 491-3013
  West Babylon *(G-16788)*
Deakon Homes and Interiors .... F 518 271-0342
  Troy *(G-16233)*
Encore Retail Systems Inc .... F 718 385-3443
  Brooklyn *(G-1923)*
Evans & Paul Unlimited Corp .... E 212 255-7272
  New York *(G-10088)*
Farrington Packaging Corp .... E 315 733-4600
  Utica *(G-16331)*
Fina Cabinet Corp .... G 718 409-2900
  Mount Vernon *(G-8681)*
Gaughan Construction Corp .... G 718 850-9577
  Richmond Hill *(G-14074)*
Gotham City Industries Inc .... E 985 851-5474
  Scarsdale *(G-15217)*
Greenleaf Cabinet Makers LLC .... F 315 432-4600
  Syracuse *(G-15954)*
Hamlet Products Inc .... F 914 665-0307
  Mount Vernon *(G-8689)*
Heartwood Specialties Inc .... G 607 654-0102
  Hammondsport *(G-5955)*
Home Ideal Inc .... G 718 762-8998
  Flushing *(G-5251)*
Industrial Support Inc .... D 716 662-2954
  Buffalo *(G-3006)*
Integrated Wood Components Inc .... E 607 467-1739
  Deposit *(G-4278)*
Inter State Laminates Inc .... E 518 283-8355
  Poestenkill *(G-13724)*
L Builders Supply Inc .... B 518 355-7190
  Schenectady *(G-15275)*
Little Wolf Cabinet Shop Inc .... E 212 734-1116
  New York *(G-11013)*
Michael P Mmarr .... G 315 623-9380
  Constantia *(G-3881)*
New Dimensions Office Group .... D 718 387-0995
  Brooklyn *(G-2361)*
Premier Woodworking Inc .... E 631 236-4100
  Hauppauge *(G-6171)*
Steelcraft Manufacturing Co .... F 718 277-2404
  Brooklyn *(G-2603)*
Stein Industries Inc .... E 631 789-2222
  Amityville *(G-325)*
Unico Inc .... F 845 562-9255
  Newburgh *(G-12782)*
Universal Designs Inc .... G 718 721-1111
  Long Island City *(G-7910)*
Winerackscom Inc .... E 845 658-7181
  Tillson *(G-16130)*

PARTITIONS: Wood, Floor Attached

Steeldeck Ny Inc .... F 718 599-3700
  Brooklyn *(G-2604)*

PARTS: Metal

All-State Diversified Pdts Inc .... E 315 472-4728
  Syracuse *(G-15848)*
Alliance Innovative Mfg Inc .... E 716 822-1626
  Lackawanna *(G-7242)*
Ross Metal Fabricators Inc .... E 631 586-7000
  Deer Park *(G-4202)*
Zone Fabricators Inc .... F 718 272-0200
  Ozone Park *(G-13388)*

PARTY & SPECIAL EVENT PLANNING SVCS

Proof 7 Ltd .... F 212 680-1843
  New York *(G-11735)*

PASTES, FLAVORING

American Almond Pdts Co Inc .... E 718 875-8310
  Brooklyn *(G-1599)*

PATENT OWNERS & LESSORS

PATENT OWNERS & LESSORS
Compositech Ltd.................................C....... 516 835-1458
  Woodbury *(G-17284)*
Eagle Telephonics Inc ....F....... 631 471-3600
  Bohemia *(G-1059)*
General Microwave Corporation...........F....... 516 802-0900
  Syosset *(G-15824)*
Rainforest Inc ....F....... 212 575-7620
  New York *(G-11790)*

PATTERNS: Indl
A & T Tooling LLC ....G....... 716 601-7299
  Lancaster *(G-7297)*
Armstrong Mold Corporation................E....... 315 437-1517
  East Syracuse *(G-4504)*
Armstrong Mold Corporation................D....... 315 437-1517
  East Syracuse *(G-4505)*
Bianca Group Ltd................................G....... 212 768-3011
  New York *(G-9388)*
City Pattern Shop Inc..........................F....... 315 463-5239
  Syracuse *(G-15895)*
IBlt Inc ....E....... 212 768-0292
  New York *(G-10546)*
K & H Precision Products Inc ....E....... 585 624-4894
  Honeoye Falls *(G-6532)*
Studio One Leather Design Inc............F....... 212 760-1701
  New York *(G-12221)*
W N R Pattern & Tool Inc ....G....... 716 681-9334
  Lancaster *(G-7346)*
Wolff & Dungey Inc ....E....... 315 475-2105
  Syracuse *(G-16074)*

PAVERS
Lomin Construction Company ....G....... 516 759-5734
  Glen Head *(G-5636)*
Technopaving New York Inc................G....... 631 351-6472
  Huntington Station *(G-6725)*

PAVING BREAKERS
Mike Wilke..G....... 585 482-5230
  Webster *(G-16727)*

PAVING MATERIALS: Prefabricated, Concrete
Copeland Coating Company Inc..........F....... 518 766-2932
  Nassau *(G-8771)*

PAVING MIXTURES
Dolomite Products Company Inc ....E....... 315 524-1998
  Rochester *(G-14316)*
Dolomite Products Company Inc ....F....... 607 324-3636
  Hornell *(G-6561)*
Dolomite Products Company Inc ....E....... 585 586-2568
  Penfield *(G-13498)*
Dolomite Products Company Inc ....F....... 585 768-7295
  Le Roy *(G-7405)*
Rock Iroquois Products Inc ....E....... 585 381-7010
  Rochester *(G-14655)*

PENCILS & PENS WHOLESALERS
Mark Dri Products Inc.........................C....... 516 484-6200
  Bethpage *(G-873)*
Pda Panache Corp ....G....... 631 776-0523
  Bohemia *(G-1116)*

PENS & PARTS: Ball Point
Effanjay Pens Inc ....E....... 212 316-9565
  Long Island City *(G-7726)*
Gotham Pen Co Inc ....E....... 212 675-7904
  Yonkers *(G-17449)*
Mercury Pen Company Inc..................G....... 518 899-9653
  Ballston Lake *(G-583)*

PENS & PARTS: Cartridges, Refill, Ball Point
STS Refill America LLC ....G....... 516 934-8008
  Hicksville *(G-6395)*

PENS & PENCILS: Mechanical, NEC
A & L Pen Manufacturing Corp............D....... 718 499-8966
  Brooklyn *(G-1527)*
Aakron Rule Corp................................C....... 716 542-5483
  Akron *(G-19)*
Harper Products Ltd ....C....... 516 997-2330
  Westbury *(G-16994)*

Henry Morgan.....................................F....... 718 317-5013
  Staten Island *(G-15683)*
Pelican Products Co Inc ....E....... 718 860-3220
  Bronx *(G-1423)*

PERFUME: Concentrated
Takasago Intl Corp USA ....D....... 845 751-0799
  Harriman *(G-5975)*
Thompson Ferrier LLC ....G....... 212 244-2212
  New York *(G-12326)*

PERFUME: Perfumes, Natural Or Synthetic
Christian Dior Perfumes LLC...............E....... 212 931-2200
  New York *(G-9610)*
Delbia Do Company Inc......................G....... 718 585-2226
  Bronx *(G-1312)*
Elias Fragrances Inc ....F....... 718 693-6400
  Rye Brook *(G-15070)*
Flavormatic Industries Inc ....E....... 845 297-9100
  Wappingers Falls *(G-16567)*

PERFUMES
Alan F Bourguet..................................F....... 516 883-4315
  Port Washington *(G-13797)*
Cassini Parfums Ltd ....G....... 212 753-7540
  New York *(G-9541)*
Coty US LLC ....C....... 212 389-7000
  New York *(G-9731)*
Coty US LLC ....B....... 212 389-7000
  Uniondale *(G-16291)*
Estee Lauder Inc 631 531-1000
  Melville *(G-8316)*
F L Demeter Inc ....E....... 516 487-5187
  Great Neck *(G-5808)*
Fragrance Acquisitions LLC ....D....... 845 534-9172
  Newburgh *(G-12755)*
Fragrance Outlet Inc ....F....... 845 928-1408
  Central Valley *(G-3523)*
Hogan Flavors & Fragrances ....E....... 212 598-4310
  New York *(G-10493)*
JP Filling Inc......................................D....... 845 534-4793
  Mountainville *(G-8748)*
Le Labo Inc..E....... 212 532-7206
  New York *(G-10942)*
Le Labo Inc..E....... 646 719-1740
  Brooklyn *(G-2201)*
Perfume Americana Inc ....E....... 212 683-8029
  New York *(G-11615)*
Perfume Amrcana Whlesalers Inc ......F....... 212 683-8029
  New York *(G-11616)*
Perfumers Workshop Intl Ltd..............G....... 212 644-8950
  New York *(G-11617)*
Selective Beauty Corporation..............F....... 585 336-7600
  New York *(G-12024)*
Value Fragrances Inc..........................G....... 845 294-5726
  Goshen *(G-5741)*

PERLITE: Processed
Skyline LLC ....E....... 631 403-4131
  East Setauket *(G-4492)*

PERSONAL APPEARANCE SVCS
Womens Health Care PC ....G....... 718 850-0009
  Richmond Hill *(G-14088)*

PERSONAL CREDIT INSTITUTIONS: Consumer Finance Companies
Steel Partners Holdings LP ....E....... 212 520-2300
  New York *(G-12189)*

PESTICIDES
Alco Industries Inc.............................E....... 740 254-4311
  Round Lake *(G-15036)*
AP&g Co Inc ....D....... 718 492-3648
  Brooklyn *(G-1615)*

PET ACCESS: Collars, Leashes, Etc, Exc Leather
American Leather Specialties..............D....... 800 556-6488
  Brooklyn *(G-1603)*

PET COLLARS, LEASHES, MUZZLES & HARNESSES: Leather
Dog Good Products LLC ....G....... 212 789-7000
  New York *(G-9895)*
Finger Lakes Lea Crafters LLC ....F....... 315 252-4107
  Auburn *(G-494)*
Max 200 Performance Dog Eqp...........E....... 315 776-9588
  Port Byron *(G-13735)*

PET SPLYS
Clara Papa ....G....... 315 733-2660
  Utica *(G-16311)*
Four Paws Products Ltd.....................D....... 631 436-7421
  Ronkonkoma *(G-14902)*
Grand Island Animal Hospital ....E....... 716 773-7645
  Grand Island *(G-5760)*
Hrg Group Inc ....E....... 212 906-8555
  New York *(G-10524)*
Image Tech ....F....... 716 635-0167
  Buffalo *(G-3002)*
Kittywalk Systems Inc ....G....... 516 627-8418
  Port Washington *(G-13833)*
Petland Discounts Inc ....E....... 516 821-3194
  Hewlett *(G-6311)*
Pets n People Inc ....G....... 631 232-1200
  Hauppauge *(G-6162)*
Spectrum Brands Inc ....B....... 631 232-1200
  Hauppauge *(G-6195)*
Unique Petz LLC ....E....... 212 714-1800
  New York *(G-12462)*

PET SPLYS WHOLESALERS
American Leather Specialties..............D....... 800 556-6488
  Brooklyn *(G-1603)*
Clara Papa ....G....... 315 733-2660
  Utica *(G-16311)*

PETROLEUM & PETROLEUM PRDTS, WHOLESALE Engine Fuels & Oils
Bass Oil Company Inc ....E....... 718 628-4444
  Brooklyn *(G-1672)*

PETROLEUM & PETROLEUM PRDTS, WHOLESALE: Bulk Stations
Hess Corporation................................B....... 212 997-8500
  New York *(G-10464)*

PETROLEUM PRDTS WHOLESALERS
Industrial Raw Materials LLC..............F....... 212 688-8080
  Plainview *(G-13607)*
Noco Incorporated..............................G....... 716 833-6626
  Tonawanda *(G-16187)*

PEWTER WARE
Quest Bead & Cast Inc ....G....... 212 354-1737
  New York *(G-11771)*
Silver City Group Inc ....G....... 315 363-0344
  Sherrill *(G-15408)*

PHARMACEUTICAL PREPARATIONS: Adrenal
Central Islip Pharmacy Inc..................G....... 631 234-6039
  Central Islip *(G-3490)*

PHARMACEUTICAL PREPARATIONS: Barbituric Acid
872 Hunts Point Pharmacy Inc ....G....... 718 991-3519
  Bronx *(G-1251)*

PHARMACEUTICAL PREPARATIONS: Druggists' Preparations
Asence Inc ....E....... 347 335-2606
  New York *(G-9226)*
Bristol-Myers Squibb Company ....E....... 315 432-2000
  East Syracuse *(G-4512)*
Century Grand Inc..............................F....... 212 925-3838
  New York *(G-9569)*
Cognigen Corporation ....D....... 716 633-3463
  Buffalo *(G-2878)*
Drt Laboratories LLC ....G....... 845 547-2034
  Airmont *(G-14)*

PRODUCT SECTION

PHARMACEUTICALS

Flushing Pharmacy Inc.................................C...... 718 260-8999
 Brooklyn *(G-1989)*
Fougera Pharmaceuticals Inc....................C...... 631 454-7677
 Hicksville *(G-6346)*
Global Alliance For Tb................................E...... 212 227-7540
 New York *(G-10310)*
Ima Life North America Inc......................C...... 716 695-6354
 Tonawanda *(G-16173)*
Kingston Pharma LLC...............................G...... 315 705-4019
 Massena *(G-8197)*
Marietta Corporation..................................B...... 607 753-6746
 Cortland *(G-4033)*
Ony Inc Baird Researchpark....................E...... 716 636-9096
 Buffalo *(G-3102)*
Pace Up Pharmaceuticals LLC................G...... 631 450-4495
 Lindenhurst *(G-7478)*
Pharbest Pharmaceuticals Inc.................E...... 631 249-5130
 Farmingdale *(G-5077)*
Pharmavantage LLC..................................G...... 631 321-8171
 Babylon *(G-551)*
Pine Pharmaceuticals LLC.......................G...... 716 248-1025
 Tonawanda *(G-16193)*
Triceutical Inc...F...... 631 249-0003
 Bronx *(G-1477)*
Wavodyne Therapeutics Inc.....................G...... 954 632-6630
 West Henrietta *(G-16900)*

PHARMACEUTICAL PREPARATIONS: Medicines, Capsule Or Ampule

Futurebiotics LLC......................................E...... 631 273-6300
 Hauppauge *(G-6082)*
Nanorx Inc..G...... 914 671-0224
 Chappaqua *(G-3553)*

PHARMACEUTICAL PREPARATIONS: Penicillin

G C Hanford Manufacturing Co...............C...... 315 476-7418
 Syracuse *(G-15946)*

PHARMACEUTICAL PREPARATIONS: Pills

A & Z Pharmaceutical Inc..........................D...... 631 952-3802
 Hauppauge *(G-6006)*

PHARMACEUTICAL PREPARATIONS: Pituitary Gland

Pituitary Society...F...... 212 263-6772
 New York *(G-11669)*

PHARMACEUTICAL PREPARATIONS: Proprietary Drug PRDTS

G S W Worldwide LLC................................D...... 646 437-4800
 New York *(G-10231)*
Ip Med Inc...G...... 516 766-3800
 Oceanside *(G-13082)*
Time-Cap Laboratories Inc.......................C...... 631 753-9090
 Farmingdale *(G-5131)*

PHARMACEUTICAL PREPARATIONS: Solutions

Container Tstg Solutions LLC..................F...... 716 487-3300
 Jamestown *(G-6983)*
Container Tstg Solutions LLC..................F...... 716 487-3300
 Sinclairville *(G-15453)*
Guosa Life Sciences Inc...........................F...... 516 481-1540
 North Baldwin *(G-12906)*
Kent Chemical Corporation......................E...... 212 521-1700
 New York *(G-10838)*
Medek Laboratories Inc............................E...... 845 943-4988
 Monroe *(G-8562)*
Mskcc Rmipc..F...... 212 639-6212
 New York *(G-11319)*
Pall Corporation...A...... 516 484-5400
 Port Washington *(G-13852)*
R J S Direct Marketing Inc........................F...... 631 667-5768
 Deer Park *(G-4197)*
Sterrx LLC...E...... 518 324-7879
 Plattsburgh *(G-13699)*
Zitomer LLC..G...... 212 737-5560
 New York *(G-12715)*

PHARMACEUTICAL PREPARATIONS: Tablets

Aiping Pharmaceutical Inc........................G...... 631 952-3802
 Hauppauge *(G-6012)*

Bli International Inc...................................C...... 631 940-9000
 Deer Park *(G-4109)*
Chartwell Pharma Nda B2 Holdin............G...... 845 268-5000
 Congers *(G-3854)*
Eckerson Drugs Inc...................................F...... 845 352-1800
 Spring Valley *(G-15583)*
Innovative Labs LLC..................................D...... 631 231-5522
 Hauppauge *(G-6097)*
Invagen Pharmaceuticals Inc...................C...... 631 949-6367
 Central Islip *(G-3499)*
Marken LLP..G...... 631 396-7454
 Farmingdale *(G-5041)*
Satnam Distributors LLC..........................G...... 516 802-0600
 Jericho *(G-7084)*

PHARMACEUTICAL PREPARATIONS: Water, Sterile, For Injections

Sterrx LLC...F...... 518 324-7879
 Plattsburgh *(G-13700)*

PHARMACEUTICALS

3v Company Inc..E...... 718 858-7333
 Brooklyn *(G-1517)*
5th Avenue Pharmacy Inc.........................G...... 718 439-8585
 Brooklyn *(G-1520)*
888 Pharmacy Inc......................................F...... 718 871-8833
 Brooklyn *(G-1523)*
A & Z Pharmaceutical Inc..........................C...... 631 952-3800
 Hauppauge *(G-6007)*
Abraxis Bioscience LLC............................G...... 716 773-0800
 Grand Island *(G-5750)*
Actavis Laboratories Ny Inc.....................C...... 631 693-8000
 Copiague *(G-3889)*
Actinium Pharmaceuticals Inc..................F...... 732 243-9495
 New York *(G-9021)*
Advance Pharmaceutical Inc....................E...... 631 981-4600
 Holtsville *(G-6500)*
Affymax Inc...G...... 650 812-8700
 New York *(G-9054)*
Alfred Khalily Inc..F...... 516 504-0059
 Great Neck *(G-5787)*
Allied Pharmacy Products Inc..................F...... 516 374-8862
 Woodmere *(G-17310)*
Altaire Pharmaceuticals Inc......................C...... 631 722-5988
 Aquebogue *(G-383)*
American Bio Medica Corp.......................D...... 518 758-8158
 Kinderhook *(G-7167)*
American Regent Inc.................................B...... 631 924-4000
 Shirley *(G-15411)*
Amneal Pharmaceuticals LLC...................E...... 908 231-1911
 Brookhaven *(G-1505)*
Amneal Pharmaceuticals NY LLC............E...... 631 952-0214
 Brookhaven *(G-1506)*
Anacor Pharmaceuticals Inc.....................C...... 212 733-2323
 New York *(G-9143)*
Angiogenex Inc..G...... 347 468-6799
 New York *(G-9158)*
Anterios Inc..G...... 212 303-1683
 New York *(G-9167)*
Aoi Pharma Inc...F...... 212 531-5970
 New York *(G-9171)*
Apothecus Pharmaceutical Corp.............F...... 516 624-8200
 Oyster Bay *(G-13366)*
Atlantic Essential Pdts Inc.......................D...... 631 434-8333
 Hauppauge *(G-6027)*
Auven Therapeutics MGT LP....................F...... 212 616-4000
 New York *(G-9269)*
Auxilium Pharmaceuticals Inc..................F...... 484 321-2022
 Rye *(G-15054)*
Azurrx Biopharma Inc................................F...... 646 699-7855
 Brooklyn *(G-1654)*
Barc Usa Inc...E...... 516 719-1052
 New Hyde Park *(G-8818)*
Barr Laboratories Inc................................C...... 845 362-1100
 Pomona *(G-13728)*
BASF Corporation......................................B...... 914 785-2000
 Tarrytown *(G-16087)*
Bausch & Lomb Holdings Inc..................G...... 585 338-6000
 New York *(G-9335)*
Bausch & Lomb Incorporated..................B...... 585 338-6000
 Rochester *(G-14225)*
Beyondspring Phrmceuticals Inc............F...... 646 305-6387
 New York *(G-9385)*
Bicon Pharmaceutical Inc.........................F...... 631 593-4199
 Deer Park *(G-4107)*
Biospecifics Technologies Corp..............G...... 516 593-7000
 Lynbrook *(G-7948)*
Bristol-Myers Squibb Company...............A...... 212 546-4000
 New York *(G-9464)*

Bristol-Myers Squibb Company...............C...... 516 832-2191
 Garden City *(G-5497)*
Campbell Alliance Group Inc....................E...... 212 377-2740
 New York *(G-9509)*
Cancer Targeting Systems.......................G...... 212 965-4534
 New York *(G-9511)*
Cellvation Inc...G...... 212 554-4520
 New York *(G-9556)*
Cerovene Inc..F...... 845 359-1101
 Orangeburg *(G-13221)*
Cerovene Inc..F...... 845 267-2055
 Valley Cottage *(G-16377)*
Chartwell Pharmaceuticals LLC...............D...... 845 268-5000
 Congers *(G-3855)*
Cleveland Biolabs Inc................................E...... 716 849-6810
 Buffalo *(G-2876)*
Combe Incorporated.................................C...... 914 694-5454
 White Plains *(G-17095)*
Contract Pharmacal Corp.........................E...... 631 231-4610
 Hauppauge *(G-6052)*
Contract Pharmacal Corp.........................C...... 631 231-4610
 Hauppauge *(G-6053)*
Contract Pharmacal Corp.........................E...... 631 231-4610
 Hauppauge *(G-6054)*
Contract Pharmacal Corp.........................D...... 631 231-4610
 Hauppauge *(G-6055)*
Contract Pharmacal Corp.........................C...... 631 231-4610
 Hauppauge *(G-6056)*
Contract Pharmacal Corp.........................E...... 631 231-4610
 Hauppauge *(G-6057)*
Contract Phrmctcals Ltd Nagara..............C...... 716 887-3400
 Buffalo *(G-2888)*
Cortice Biosciences Inc............................F...... 646 747-9090
 New York *(G-9727)*
CRS Nuclear Services LLC.......................C...... 716 810-0688
 Cheektowaga *(G-3565)*
Delcath Systems Inc.................................E...... 212 489-2100
 New York *(G-9838)*
Dipexium Pharmaceuticals Inc.................C...... 212 269-2834
 New York *(G-9881)*
Dr Reddys Laboratories NY Inc...............F...... 518 827-7702
 Middleburgh *(G-8418)*
DSM Nutritional Products LLC.................B...... 518 372-5155
 Schenectady *(G-15249)*
Edlaw Pharmaceuticals Inc......................E...... 631 454-6888
 Farmingdale *(G-4985)*
Eli Lilly and Company................................F...... 516 622-2244
 New Hyde Park *(G-8832)*
Encysive Pharmaceuticals Inc..................E...... 212 733-2323
 New York *(G-10031)*
Enumeral Biomedical Corp.......................G...... 347 227-4787
 New York *(G-10046)*
Enzo Life Sciences Inc..............................E...... 631 694-7070
 Farmingdale *(G-4988)*
Enzo Life Sciences Intl Inc.......................E...... 610 941-0430
 Farmingdale *(G-4989)*
Eon Labs Inc...F...... 516 478-9700
 New Hyde Park *(G-8833)*
Epic Pharma LLC.......................................C...... 718 276-8600
 Laurelton *(G-7387)*
Forest Laboratories LLC...........................C...... 212 421-7850
 New York *(G-10185)*
Forest Laboratories LLC...........................D...... 212 421-7850
 Hauppauge *(G-6080)*
Forest Laboratories LLC...........................C...... 631 858-6010
 Commack *(G-3831)*
Fortress Biotech Inc..................................F...... 781 652-4500
 New York *(G-10187)*
Fougera Pharmaceuticals Inc...................C...... 631 454-7677
 Melville *(G-8321)*
Fresenius Kabi Usa LLC............................B...... 716 773-0053
 Grand Island *(G-5758)*
Fresenius Kabi USA LLC...........................E...... 716 773-0800
 Grand Island *(G-5759)*
Geritrex LLC...E...... 914 668-4003
 Mount Vernon *(G-8682)*
Geritrex Holdings Inc................................G...... 914 668-4003
 Mount Vernon *(G-8683)*
Glaxosmithkline LLC.................................E...... 845 341-7590
 Montgomery *(G-8593)*
Glaxosmithkline LLC.................................E...... 845 797-3259
 Wappingers Falls *(G-16571)*
Glaxosmithkline LLC.................................E...... 585 738-9025
 Rochester *(G-14406)*
Glaxosmithkline LLC.................................E...... 716 913-5679
 Buffalo *(G-2975)*
Glaxosmithkline LLC.................................D...... 518 239-6901
 East Durham *(G-4387)*
Glaxosmithkline LLC.................................E...... 518 852-9637
 Mechanicville *(G-8228)*

Employee Codes: A=Over 500 employees, B=251-500
C=101-250, D=51-100, E=20-50, F=10-19, G=5-9

2017 Harris
New York Manufacturers Directory

1287

PHARMACEUTICALS — PRODUCT SECTION

Greentree Pharmacy Inc .... F 718 768-2700
  Brooklyn *(G-2054)*
Healthone Pharmacy Inc .... F 718 495-9015
  Brooklyn *(G-2069)*
Hi-Tech Pharmacal Co Inc .... B 631 789-8228
  Amityville *(G-294)*
Hogil Pharmaceutical Corp .... F 914 681-1800
  White Plains *(G-17121)*
Hospira Inc .... C 716 684-9400
  Buffalo *(G-2997)*
Ibio Inc .... G 302 355-0650
  New York *(G-10545)*
Immune Pharmaceuticals Inc .... F 646 440-9310
  New York *(G-10573)*
Intercept Pharmaceuticals Inc .... D 646 747-1000
  New York *(G-10625)*
International Life Science .... G 631 549-0471
  Huntington *(G-6663)*
Intra-Cellular Therapies Inc .... E 212 923-3344
  New York *(G-10645)*
Invagen Pharmaceuticals Inc .... B 631 231-3233
  Hauppauge *(G-6099)*
Izun Pharmaceuticals Corp .... G 212 618-6357
  New York *(G-10672)*
Jerome Stvens Phrmceuticals Inc ... F 631 567-1113
  Bohemia *(G-1082)*
JRS Pharma LP .... E 845 878-8300
  Patterson *(G-13441)*
Kadmon Corporation LLC .... G 212 308-6000
  New York *(G-10799)*
Kadmon Holdings Inc .... C 212 308-6000
  New York *(G-10800)*
Kannalife Sciences Inc .... G 516 669-3219
  Lloyd Harbor *(G-7567)*
Kbl Healthcare LP .... G 212 319-5555
  New York *(G-10824)*
Klg Usa LLC .... A 845 856-5311
  Port Jervis *(G-13788)*
Linden Care LLC .... G 516 221-7600
  Woodbury *(G-17293)*
Lion Biotechnologies Inc .... F 212 946-4856
  New York *(G-11004)*
Liptis Pharmaceuticals USA Inc ..... A 845 627-0260
  Spring Valley *(G-15592)*
LNK International Inc .... D 631 435-3500
  Hauppauge *(G-6114)*
LNK International Inc .... D 631 435-3500
  Hauppauge *(G-6115)*
LNK International Inc .... D 631 435-3500
  Hauppauge *(G-6116)*
LNK International Inc .... D 631 543-3787
  Hauppauge *(G-6117)*
LNK International Inc .... D 631 435-3500
  Hauppauge *(G-6118)*
LNK International Inc .... D 631 231-3415
  Hauppauge *(G-6119)*
LNK International Inc .... D 631 231-4020
  Hauppauge *(G-6120)*
Luitpold Pharmaceuticals Inc .... B 631 924-4000
  Shirley *(G-15423)*
Macrochem Corporation .... G 212 514-8094
  New York *(G-11090)*
Mallinckrodt LLC .... A 607 538-9124
  Hobart *(G-6426)*
Maxus Pharmaceuticals Inc .... F 631 249-0003
  Farmingdale *(G-5045)*
Medtech Products Inc .... F 914 524-6810
  Tarrytown *(G-16096)*
Mentholatum Company .... E 716 677-2500
  Orchard Park *(G-13284)*
Neurotrope Inc .... G 973 242-0005
  Irvington *(G-6774)*
Norwich Pharmaceuticals Inc ...... B 607 335-3000
  Norwich *(G-13033)*
Novartis Corporation .... E 212 307-1122
  New York *(G-11462)*
Novartis Corporation .... C 845 368-6000
  Suffern *(G-15795)*
Novartis Corporation .... D 718 276-8600
  Laurelton *(G-7388)*
Novartis Pharmaceuticals Corp .... G 718 276-8600
  Laurelton *(G-7389)*
Noven Pharmaceuticals Inc .... E 212 682-4420
  New York *(G-11464)*
Nutra-Scientifics LLC .... G 917 238-8510
  Pomona *(G-13731)*
Nutrascience Labs Inc .... E 631 247-0660
  Farmingdale *(G-5068)*
NV Prrcone MD Cosmeceuticals ... G 212 734-2537
  New York *(G-11475)*

NY Phrmacy Compounding Ctr Inc ... G 201 403-5151
  Astoria *(G-451)*
Ohr Pharmaceutical Inc .... F 212 682-8452
  New York *(G-11498)*
Oligomerix Inc .... G 914 997-8877
  New York *(G-11500)*
Ony Inc .... E 716 636-9096
  Amherst *(G-257)*
Opthotech Corp .... F 212 845-8200
  New York *(G-11517)*
P & L Development LLC .... D 516 986-1700
  Westbury *(G-17015)*
P & L Development LLC .... D 516 986-1700
  Westbury *(G-17016)*
P & L Development LLC .... D 516 986-1700
  Westbury *(G-17017)*
Par Pharmaceutical Inc .... B 845 425-7100
  Spring Valley *(G-15598)*
Par Phrmceutical Companies Inc ... E 845 573-5500
  Chestnut Ridge *(G-3624)*
Par Sterile Products LLC .... E 845 573-5500
  Chestnut Ridge *(G-3625)*
Perrigo Company .... E 718 960-9900
  Bronx *(G-1425)*
Perrigo New York Inc .... F 718 901-2800
  Bronx *(G-1426)*
Perrigo New York Inc .... B 718 960-9900
  Bronx *(G-1427)*
Pfizer HCP Corporation .... E 212 733-2323
  New York *(G-11635)*
Pfizer Inc .... A 212 733-2323
  New York *(G-11636)*
Pfizer Inc .... B 518 297-6611
  Rouses Point *(G-15042)*
Pfizer Inc .... C 914 437-5868
  White Plains *(G-17159)*
Pfizer Inc .... C 937 746-3603
  New York *(G-11637)*
Pfizer Inc .... G 212 733-6276
  New York *(G-11638)*
Pfizer Inc .... C 804 257-2000
  New York *(G-11639)*
Pfizer Inc .... E 212 733-2323
  New York *(G-11640)*
Pfizer Overseas LLC .... E 212 733-2323
  New York *(G-11641)*
Pharmaceutic Labs LLC .... F 518 608-1060
  Albany *(G-119)*
Polygen Pharmaceuticals Inc ...... E 631 392-4044
  Edgewood *(G-4608)*
Precision Pharma Services Inc .... C 631 752-7314
  Melville *(G-8349)*
Prestige Brands Holdings Inc ..... D 914 524-6800
  Tarrytown *(G-16101)*
Prime Pack LLC .... F 732 253-7734
  New York *(G-11708)*
Progenics Pharmaceuticals Inc ... D 646 975-2500
  New York *(G-11729)*
Quadpharma LLC .... G 877 463-7823
  Clarence *(G-3670)*
Quogue Capital LLC .... G 212 554-4475
  New York *(G-11775)*
Randob Labs Ltd .... G 845 534-2197
  Cornwall *(G-3991)*
Rapha Pharmaceuticals Inc .... G 956 229-0049
  Valley Cottage *(G-16385)*
Regeneron Pharmaceuticals Inc ... B 914 847-7000
  Tarrytown *(G-16103)*
Regenron Hlthcare Slutions Inc ... A 914 847-7000
  Tarrytown *(G-16104)*
Relmada Therapeutics Inc .... E 646 677-3853
  New York *(G-11825)*
Retrophin LLC .... G 212 983-1310
  New York *(G-11846)*
Rij Pharmaceutical Corporation .... E 845 692-5799
  Middletown *(G-8459)*
Rls Holdings Inc .... G 716 418-7274
  Clarence *(G-3671)*
Rohto USA Inc .... G 716 677-2500
  Orchard Park *(G-13295)*
Ropack USA Inc .... F 631 482-7777
  Commack *(G-3840)*
S1 Biopharma Inc .... G 201 839-0941
  New York *(G-11948)*
Salutem Group LLC .... G 347 620-2640
  New York *(G-11960)*
Saptalis Pharmaceuticals LLC ..... F 631 231-2751
  Hauppauge *(G-6184)*
Scarguard Labs LLC .... F 516 482-8050
  Great Neck *(G-5839)*

Sciarra Laboratories Inc .... G 516 933-7853
  Hicksville *(G-6393)*
Sciegen Pharmaceuticals Inc ...... E 631 434-2723
  Hauppauge *(G-6186)*
Sciegen Pharmaceuticals Inc ...... C 631 434-2723
  Hauppauge *(G-6187)*
Scienta Pharmaceuticals LLC ...... G 845 589-0774
  Valley Cottage *(G-16388)*
Seidlin Consulting .... G 212 496-2043
  New York *(G-12020)*
Shrineeta Pharmacy .... G 212 234-7959
  New York *(G-12055)*
Shrineeta Pharmacy Inc .... G 212 234-7959
  New York *(G-12056)*
Siga Technologies Inc .... E 212 672-9100
  New York *(G-12066)*
Silarx Pharmaceuticals Inc .... E 845 352-4020
  Carmel *(G-3405)*
Silver Oak Pharmacy Inc .... G 718 922-3400
  Brooklyn *(G-2557)*
Sincerus LLC .... G 800 419-2804
  Brooklyn *(G-2563)*
Skills Alliance Inc .... G 646 492-5300
  New York *(G-12091)*
Spri Clinical Trials .... F 718 616-2400
  Brooklyn *(G-2590)*
Stemline Therapeutics Inc .... E 646 502-2311
  New York *(G-12193)*
Steri-Pharma LLC .... F 315 473-7180
  Syracuse *(G-16046)*
Strativa Pharmaceuticals .... F 201 802-4000
  Spring Valley *(G-15602)*
Sunquest Pharmaceuticals Inc .... F 855 478-6779
  Syosset *(G-15840)*
Synergy Pharmaceuticals Inc ..... E 212 297-0020
  New York *(G-12262)*
Syntho Pharmaceuticals Inc ...... E 631 755-9898
  Farmingdale *(G-5122)*
Tg Therapeutics Inc .... E 212 554-4484
  New York *(G-12307)*
Tishcon Corp .... C 516 333-3056
  Westbury *(G-17033)*
Tishcon Corp .... C 516 333-3050
  Westbury *(G-17034)*
Tmp Technologies Inc .... D 716 895-6100
  Buffalo *(G-3220)*
Tocare LLC .... G 718 767-0618
  Whitestone *(G-17215)*
Tongli Pharmaceuticals USA Inc ... F 212 842-8837
  Flushing *(G-5302)*
Tonix Phrmceuticals Holdg Corp .. F 212 980-9155
  New York *(G-12367)*
Topiderm Inc .... C 631 226-7979
  Amityville *(G-329)*
Topix Pharmaceuticals Inc .... E 631 225-5757
  Amityville *(G-330)*
Transparency Life Sciences LLC .. F 862 252-1216
  New York *(G-12393)*
Ucb Pharma Inc .... B 919 767-2555
  Rochester *(G-14739)*
United-Guardian Inc .... E 631 273-0900
  Hauppauge *(G-6220)*
Unither Manufacturing LLC .... C 585 475-9000
  Rochester *(G-14743)*
Venus Pharmaceuticals Intl Inc ... F 631 249-4140
  Hauppauge *(G-6223)*
Viropro Inc .... E 650 300-5190
  New York *(G-12548)*
Vitalis LLC .... G 646 831-7338
  New York *(G-12555)*
Vitane Pharmaceuticals Inc .... E 845 267-6700
  Congers *(G-3862)*
Wyeth Holdings LLC .... D 845 602-5000
  Pearl River *(G-13469)*
X-Gen Pharmaceuticals Inc .... G 607 562-2700
  Big Flats *(G-883)*
X-Gen Pharmaceuticals Inc .... C 631 261-8188
  Elmira *(G-4707)*
X-Gen Pharmaceuticals Inc .... E 607 562-2700
  Horseheads *(G-6596)*
Xstelos Holdings Inc .... G 212 729-4962
  New York *(G-12684)*
Ys Marketing Inc .... F 718 778-6080
  Brooklyn *(G-2778)*

PHARMACEUTICALS: Mail-Order Svc

Alphabet Holding Company Inc .... E 631 200-2000
  Ronkonkoma *(G-14865)*
Greentree Pharmacy Inc .... F 718 768-2700
  Brooklyn *(G-2054)*

PRODUCT SECTION

PHOTOGRAPHIC EQPT & SPLYS

Nbty Inc ....D...... 631 244-2021
  Ronkonkoma (G-14952)
Nbty Inc ....A...... 631 200-2000
  Ronkonkoma (G-14953)

PHARMACEUTICALS: Medicinal & Botanical Prdts

Albany Molecular Research Inc ....F...... 518 433-7700
  Rensselaer (G-14043)
Albany Molecular Research Inc ....F...... 518 512-2000
  Rensselaer (G-14044)
Alo Acquisition LLC ....G...... 518 464-0279
  Albany (G-45)
Amri Rensselaer ....A...... 518 512-2000
  Albany (G-47)
Collaborative Laboratories ....D...... 631 689-0200
  East Setauket (G-4479)
GE Healthcare Inc ....F...... 516 626-2799
  Port Washington (G-13819)
Immudyne Inc ....F...... 914 244-1777
  Mount Kisco (G-8629)
Kannalife Sciences Inc ....G...... 516 669-3219
  Lloyd Harbor (G-7567)
Nbty Inc ....F...... 631 200-2000
  Bayport (G-759)
Regeneron Pharmaceuticals Inc ....E...... 518 488-6000
  Rensselaer (G-14050)
Regeneron Pharmaceuticals Inc ....F...... 518 488-6000
  Rensselaer (G-14051)
Setauket Manufacturing Co ....G...... 631 231-7272
  Ronkonkoma (G-14984)
Stauber Prfmce Ingredients Inc ....G...... 845 651-4443
  Florida (G-5215)

PHARMACIES & DRUG STORES

Far Rockaway Drugs Inc ....F...... 718 471-2500
  Far Rockaway (G-4922)
J P R Pharmacy Inc ....F...... 718 327-0600
  Far Rockaway (G-4923)
Nucare Pharmacy Inc ....F...... 212 426-9300
  New York (G-11470)
Nucare Pharmacy West LLC ....F...... 212 462-2525
  New York (G-11471)

PHONOGRAPH NEEDLES

Grado Laboratories Inc ....F...... 718 435-5340
  Brooklyn (G-2046)

PHONOGRAPH RECORDS WHOLESALERS

Hope International Productions ....F...... 212 247-3188
  New York (G-10504)
Sony Music Holdings Inc ....A...... 212 833-8000
  New York (G-12137)

PHONOGRAPH RECORDS: Prerecorded

Abkco Music & Records Inc ....E...... 212 399-0500
  New York (G-9004)
Eks Manufacturing Inc ....F...... 917 217-0784
  Brooklyn (G-1907)
Hope International Productions ....F...... 212 247-3188
  New York (G-10504)
Ulster-Greene County A R C ....G...... 845 331-8451
  Kingston (G-7220)

PHOSPHATES

International Ord Tech Inc ....D...... 716 664-1100
  Jamestown (G-7003)
Mdi Holdings LLC ....A...... 212 559-1127
  New York (G-11203)

PHOTOCOPY MACHINES

Cannon Industries Inc ....D...... 585 254-8080
  Rochester (G-14258)
Facsimile Cmmncations Inds Inc ....D...... 212 741-6400
  New York (G-10125)
Xerox Corporation ....D...... 212 633-8190
  New York (G-12676)
Xerox Corporation ....D...... 212 330-1386
  New York (G-12677)

PHOTOCOPYING & DUPLICATING SVCS

A & D Offset Printers Ltd ....G...... 516 746-2476
  Mineola (G-8486)
A Q P Inc ....G...... 585 256-1690
  Rochester (G-14161)
Action Graphics Services Inc ....F...... 607 785-1951
  Vestal (G-16438)
All Ready Inc ....G...... 607 722-0826
  Conklin (G-3864)
Apple Press ....G...... 914 723-6660
  White Plains (G-17079)
Avalon Copy Centers Amer Inc ....D...... 315 471-3333
  Syracuse (G-15863)
Avalon Copy Centers Amer Inc ....E...... 716 995-7777
  Buffalo (G-2825)
Capital Dst Print & Imaging ....G...... 518 456-6773
  Schenectady (G-15238)
Carges Entps of Canandaigua ....G...... 585 394-2600
  Canandaigua (G-3338)
Cds Productions Inc ....F...... 518 385-8255
  Schenectady (G-15241)
Chakra Communications Inc ....E...... 607 748-7491
  Endicott (G-4798)
Clarion Publications Inc ....F...... 585 243-3530
  Geneseo (G-5564)
Clarsons Corp ....F...... 585 235-8775
  Rochester (G-14278)
Constas Printing Corporation ....G...... 315 474-2176
  Syracuse (G-15905)
Dealer-Presscom Inc ....G...... 631 589-0434
  Bohemia (G-1053)
Evolution Impressions Inc ....D...... 585 473-6600
  Rochester (G-14361)
Fairmount Press ....G...... 212 255-2300
  New York (G-10130)
Fambus Inc ....G...... 607 785-3700
  Endicott (G-4807)
Fedex Office & Print Svcs Inc ....G...... 718 982-5223
  Staten Island (G-15673)
Graphic Fabrications Inc ....G...... 516 763-3222
  Rockville Centre (G-14791)
Graphicomm Inc ....G...... 716 283-0830
  Niagara Falls (G-12826)
Graphics of Utica ....G...... 315 797-4868
  Remsen (G-14040)
Jon Lyn Ink Inc ....G...... 516 546-2312
  Merrick (G-8386)
Leader Printing Inc ....F...... 516 546-1544
  Merrick (G-8388)
Mercury Print Productions Inc ....C...... 585 458-7900
  Rochester (G-14504)
Miller Enterprises CNY Inc ....G...... 315 682-4999
  Manlius (G-8075)
Multiple Imprssons of Rchester ....G...... 585 546-1160
  Rochester (G-14525)
National Reproductions Inc ....E...... 212 619-3800
  New York (G-11349)
North Delaware Printing Inc ....G...... 716 692-0576
  Tonawanda (G-16188)
Persch Service Print Inc ....G...... 716 366-2677
  Dunkirk (G-4347)
Rapid Print and Marketing Inc ....G...... 585 924-1520
  Victor (G-16499)
Shipmtes/Printmates Holdg Corp ....D...... 518 370-1158
  Scotia (G-15330)
Shiprite Software Inc ....G...... 315 733-6191
  Utica (G-16359)
Silver Griffin Inc ....F...... 518 272-7771
  Troy (G-16255)
Spectrum Graphics & Print ....F...... 845 473-4400
  Poughkeepsie (G-13933)
Twin Counties Pro Printers Inc ....F...... 518 828-3278
  Hudson (G-6636)
William J Ryan ....G...... 585 392-6200
  Hilton (G-6421)
Woodbury Printing Plus + Inc ....G...... 845 928-6610
  Central Valley (G-3529)

PHOTOELECTRIC DEVICES: Magnetic

MMC Magnetics Corp ....F...... 631 435-9888
  Hauppauge (G-6141)
Truebite Inc ....E...... 607 785-7664
  Vestal (G-16455)

PHOTOENGRAVING SVC

Atlas Graphics Inc ....G...... 516 997-5527
  Westbury (G-16970)
Koehlr-Gibson Mkg Graphics Inc ....E...... 716 838-5960
  Buffalo (G-3035)
Rapid Service Engraving Co ....G...... 716 896-4555
  Buffalo (G-3154)

PHOTOFINISHING LABORATORIES

Eastman Kodak Company ....B...... 585 724-4000
  Rochester (G-14328)

PHOTOGRAPH DEVELOPING & RETOUCHING SVCS

Digital Evolution Inc ....E...... 212 732-2722
  New York (G-9876)

PHOTOGRAPHIC EQPT & SPLY: Sound Recordg/Reprod Eqpt, Motion

Kelmar Systems Inc ....F...... 631 421-1230
  Huntington Station (G-6714)

PHOTOGRAPHIC EQPT & SPLYS

Alanelli Psle ....G...... 212 828-6600
  New York (G-9070)
Astrodyne Inc ....G...... 516 536-5755
  Oceanside (G-13073)
AVI-Spl Employee ....B...... 212 840-4801
  New York (G-9277)
Carestream Health Inc ....B...... 585 627-1800
  Rochester (G-14259)
Chemung Cty Assc Retrd Ctzns ....C...... 607 734-6151
  Elmira (G-4675)
Cpac Inc ....E...... 585 382-3223
  Leicester (G-7420)
Creatron Services Inc ....E...... 516 437-5119
  Floral Park (G-5201)
Eastman Kodak Company ....B...... 585 724-4000
  Rochester (G-14338)
Ebsco Industries Inc ....G...... 585 398-2000
  Farmington (G-5149)
Emda Inc ....F...... 631 243-6363
  Edgewood (G-4597)
Garys Loft ....G...... 212 244-0970
  New York (G-10250)
Henrys Deals Inc ....E...... 347 821-4685
  Brooklyn (G-2073)
Kodak Alaris Inc ....B...... 585 290-2891
  Rochester (G-14471)
Kogeto Inc ....G...... 646 490-8169
  New York (G-10868)
Labgrafix Printing Inc ....G...... 516 280-8300
  Lynbrook (G-7953)
Lanel Inc ....F...... 516 437-5119
  Floral Park (G-5205)
Lowel-Light Manufacturing Inc ....E...... 718 921-0600
  Brooklyn (G-2238)
Mirion Technologies Ist Corp ....D...... 607 562-4300
  Horseheads (G-6584)
Norazza Inc ....G...... 716 706-1160
  Buffalo (G-3093)
Rockland Colloid Corp ....G...... 845 359-5559
  Piermont (G-13545)
Stallion Technologies Inc ....G...... 315 622-1176
  Liverpool (G-7548)
Thermo Cidtec Inc ....E...... 315 451-9410
  Liverpool (G-7553)
Tiffen Acquisition LLC ....F...... 631 273-2500
  Hauppauge (G-6215)
Tiffen Acquisition LLC ....D...... 631 273-2500
  Hauppauge (G-6216)
Tiffen Company LLC ....G...... 631 273-2500
  Hauppauge (G-6217)
Vishay Thin Film LLC ....C...... 716 283-4025
  Niagara Falls (G-12889)
Xerox Corporation ....F...... 585 423-4711
  Rochester (G-14768)
Xerox Corporation ....B...... 212 716-4000
  New York (G-12675)
Xerox Corporation ....E...... 914 397-1319
  White Plains (G-17188)
Xerox Corporation ....D...... 585 425-6100
  Fairport (G-4888)
Xerox Corporation ....E...... 845 918-3147
  Suffern (G-15803)
Xerox Corporation ....D...... 585 423-5090
  Webster (G-16744)
Xerox Corporation ....C...... 585 264-5584
  Rochester (G-14770)
Xerox Corporation ....D...... 716 831-3300
  Buffalo (G-3259)

PHOTOGRAPHIC EQPT & SPLYS WHOLESALERS — PRODUCT SECTION

PHOTOGRAPHIC EQPT & SPLYS: WHOLESALERS

Alanelli Psle	G	212 828-6600	
New York (G-9070)			
AVI-Spl Employee	B	212 840-4801	
New York (G-9277)			
Rockland Colloid Corp	G	845 359-5559	
Piermont (G-13545)			

PHOTOGRAPHIC EQPT & SPLYS: Cameras, Aerial

Fluxdata Incorporated .... G 800 425-0176
 Rochester (G-14377)
Geospatial Systems Inc .... F 585 427-8310
 West Henrietta (G-16880)

PHOTOGRAPHIC EQPT & SPLYS: Cameras, Still & Motion Pictures

Critical Imaging LLC .... E 315 732-5020
 Utica (G-16318)

PHOTOGRAPHIC EQPT & SPLYS: Developers, Not Chemical Plants

Eastchester Photo Services .... G 914 961-6596
 Eastchester (G-4582)

PHOTOGRAPHIC EQPT & SPLYS: Editing Eqpt, Motion Picture

Avid Technology Inc .... E 212 983-2424
 New York (G-9278)
Kyle Editing LLC .... G 212 675-3464
 New York (G-10898)

PHOTOGRAPHIC EQPT & SPLYS: Film, Sensitized

Eastman Kodak Company .... D 585 722-2187
 Rochester (G-14327)
Eastman Kodak Company .... B 585 724-4000
 Rochester (G-14328)
Eastman Kodak Company .... D 585 724-5600
 Rochester (G-14329)
Eastman Kodak Company .... D 585 722-9695
 Pittsford (G-13558)
Eastman Kodak Company .... D 585 726-6261
 Rochester (G-14330)
Eastman Kodak Company .... D 585 724-4000
 Rochester (G-14331)
Eastman Kodak Company .... F 800 698-3324
 Rochester (G-14332)
Eastman Kodak Company .... D 585 722-4385
 Rochester (G-14333)
Eastman Kodak Company .... D 585 588-5598
 Rochester (G-14334)
Eastman Kodak Company .... C 585 726-7000
 Rochester (G-14335)
Eastman Kodak Company .... G 585 722-4007
 Rochester (G-14336)
Eastman Kodak Company .... D 585 588-3896
 Rochester (G-14337)
Eastman Park Micrographics Inc .... E 866 934-4376
 Rochester (G-14339)
Truesense Imaging Inc .... C 585 784-5500
 Rochester (G-14733)

PHOTOGRAPHIC EQPT & SPLYS: Graphic Arts Plates, Sensitized

Gpc International Inc .... G 631 752-9600
 Melville (G-8322)

PHOTOGRAPHIC EQPT & SPLYS: Plates, Sensitized

Apexx Omni-Graphics Inc .... D 718 326-3330
 Maspeth (G-8119)

PHOTOGRAPHIC EQPT & SPLYS: Printing Eqpt

Jack L Popkin & Co Inc .... G 718 361-6700
 Kew Gardens (G-7163)
Printer Components Inc .... G 585 924-5190
 Fairport (G-4871)

PHOTOGRAPHIC EQPT & SPLYS: Processing Eqpt

All-Pro Imaging Corp .... E 516 433-7676
 Melville (G-8292)

PHOTOGRAPHIC EQPT & SPLYS: Shutters, Camera

Va Inc .... E 585 385-5930
 Rochester (G-14750)

PHOTOGRAPHIC EQPT & SPLYS: Toners, Prprd, Not Chem Plnts

Efam Enterprises LLC .... E 718 204-1760
 Long Island City (G-7725)
Hilord Chemical Corporation .... E 631 234-7373
 Hauppauge (G-6094)
Konica Mnolta Sups Mfg USA Inc .... D 845 294-8400
 Goshen (G-5736)
Lasertech Crtridge RE-Builders .... G 518 373-1246
 Clifton Park (G-3698)
Toner-N-More Inc .... G 718 232-6200
 Brooklyn (G-2662)

PHOTOGRAPHIC EQPT/SPLYS, WHOL: Cameras/Projectors/Eqpt/Splys

Bescor Video Accessories Ltd .... F 631 420-1717
 Farmingdale (G-4952)

PHOTOGRAPHIC LIBRARY SVCS

Kraus Organization Limited .... G 212 686-5411
 New York (G-10888)

PHOTOGRAPHIC PEOCESSING CHEMICALS

Champion Photochemistry Inc .... D 585 760-6444
 Rochester (G-14271)

PHOTOGRAPHIC PROCESSING EQPT & CHEMICALS

Air Techniques Inc .... B 516 433-7676
 Melville (G-8291)
Seneca TEC Inc .... G 585 381-2645
 Fairport (G-4878)
Sima Technologies LLC .... G 412 828-9130
 Hauppauge (G-6191)

PHOTOGRAPHIC SENSITIZED GOODS, NEC

Turner Bellows Inc .... E 585 235-4456
 Rochester (G-14735)

PHOTOGRAPHIC SVCS

Labgrafix Printing Inc .... G 516 280-8300
 Lynbrook (G-7953)

PHOTOGRAPHY SVCS: Commercial

Folio Graphics Co Inc .... G 718 763-2076
 Brooklyn (G-1993)

PHOTOGRAPHY SVCS: Portrait Studios

Classic Album .... E 718 388-2818
 Brooklyn (G-1786)
Classic Album LLC .... D 718 388-2818
 Brooklyn (G-1787)

PHOTOGRAPHY SVCS: Still Or Video

Dynamic Photography Inc .... G 516 381-2951
 Roslyn (G-15019)

PHOTOTYPESETTING SVC

Digital Color Concepts Inc .... E 212 989-4888
 New York (G-9875)

PHOTOVOLTAIC Solid State

Besicorp Ltd .... F 845 336-7700
 Kingston (G-7179)
Onyx Solar Group LLC .... G 917 951-9732
 New York (G-11513)
Solar Thin Films Inc .... F 516 341-7787
 Uniondale (G-16299)

PHYSICAL FITNESS CENTERS

Womens Health Care PC .... G 718 850-0009
 Richmond Hill (G-14088)

PHYSICIANS' OFFICES & CLINICS: Medical doctors

M H Mandelbaum Orthotic .... F 631 473-8668
 Port Jefferson (G-13777)
Paradigm Spine LLC .... E 212 367-7274
 New York (G-11569)
Smn Medical PC .... F 844 362-2428
 Rye (G-15068)

PICTURE FRAMES: Metal

Access Display Group Inc .... F 516 678-7772
 Freeport (G-5380)
Bristol Gift Co Inc .... F 845 496-2821
 Washingtonville (G-16598)
Custom Frame & Molding Co .... F 631 491-9091
 West Babylon (G-16786)
Dobrin Industries Inc .... G 800 353-2229
 Lockport (G-7581)
Elias Artmetal Inc .... F 516 873-7501
 Mineola (G-8507)
Frame Shoppe & Art Gallery .... G 516 365-6014
 Manhasset (G-8060)
Inter Pacific Consulting Corp .... G 718 460-2787
 Flushing (G-5252)
Picture Perfect Framing .... G 718 851-1884
 Brooklyn (G-2418)
Structural Industries Inc .... C 631 471-5200
 Bohemia (G-1137)

PICTURE FRAMES: Wood

Amci Ltd .... D 718 937-5858
 Long Island City (G-7656)
Apf Manufacturing Company LLC .... E 914 963-6300
 Yonkers (G-17415)
Cdnv Wood Carving Frames Inc .... F 914 375-3447
 Yonkers (G-17426)
Drummond Framing Inc .... F 212 647-1701
 New York (G-9932)
FG Galassi Moulding Co Inc .... G 845 258-2100
 Goshen (G-5734)
Fred M Lawrence Co Inc .... E 718 786-7227
 Bay Shore (G-701)
Galas Framing Services .... F 718 706-0007
 Long Island City (G-7747)
Grant-Noren .... G 845 726-4281
 Westtown (G-17070)
House of Heydenryk Jr Inc .... F 212 206-9611
 New York (G-10518)
Hubray Inc .... F 800 645-2855
 North Baldwin (G-12907)
Interntonal Consmr Connections .... F 516 481-3438
 West Hempstead (G-16856)
Lco Destiny LLC .... B 315 782-3302
 Watertown (G-16662)
North American Enclosures Inc .... E 631 234-9500
 Central Islip (G-3507)
Picture Perfect Framing .... G 718 851-1884
 Brooklyn (G-2418)
Regence Picture Frames Inc .... E 718 779-0888
 Lynbrook (G-7959)
Structural Industries Inc .... C 631 471-5200
 Bohemia (G-1137)

PICTURE FRAMING SVCS, CUSTOM

Frame Shoppe & Art Gallery .... G 516 365-6014
 Manhasset (G-8060)
Galas Framing Services .... F 718 706-0007
 Long Island City (G-7747)
Interntonal Consmr Connections .... F 516 481-3438
 West Hempstead (G-16856)

PICTURE PROJECTION EQPT

Just Lamps of New York Inc .... F 716 626-2240
 Buffalo (G-3022)

PIECE GOODS & NOTIONS WHOLESALERS

Hpk Industries LLC .... F 315 724-0196
 Utica (G-16338)
J & M Textile Co Inc .... F 212 268-8000
 New York (G-10674)
Triangle Label Tag Inc .... G 718 875-3030
 Brooklyn (G-2679)

PRODUCT SECTION

PIECE GOODS, NOTIONS & DRY GOODS, WHOL: Textile Converters

Company	Code	Phone
Bank-Miller Co Inc Pelham *(G-13489)*	E	914 227-9357
Klauber Brothers Inc New York *(G-10859)*	E	212 686-2531
La Lame Inc New York *(G-10909)*	G	212 921-9770

PIECE GOODS, NOTIONS & DRY GOODS, WHOL: Textiles, Woven

Company	Code	Phone
Kowa American Corporation New York *(G-10882)*	E	212 303-7800
Mutual Sales Corp Long Island City *(G-7817)*	E	718 361-8373
Zorlu USA Inc New York *(G-12719)*	F	212 689-4622

PIECE GOODS, NOTIONS & DRY GOODS, WHOLESALE: Fabrics, Knit

Company	Code	Phone
Continental Knitting Mills Deer Park *(G-4120)*	G	631 242-5330

PIECE GOODS, NOTIONS & DRY GOODS, WHOLESALE: Fabrics, Lace

Company	Code	Phone
Empire Bias Binding Co Inc Long Island City *(G-7730)*	F	718 545-0300
Penn & Fletcher Inc Long Island City *(G-7839)*	F	212 239-6868
Super-Trim Inc New York *(G-12241)*	E	212 255-2370

PIECE GOODS, NOTIONS & DRY GOODS, WHOLESALE: Sewing Access

Company	Code	Phone
Bfma Holding Corporation Cortland *(G-4014)*	G	607 753-6746

PIECE GOODS, NOTIONS & OTHER DRY GOODS, WHOLESALE: Bridal

Company	Code	Phone
Alvina Vlenta Couture Collectn New York *(G-9108)*	G	212 921-7058

PIECE GOODS, NOTIONS & OTHER DRY GOODS, WHOLESALE: Buttons

Company	Code	Phone
Emsig Manufacturing Corp Hudson *(G-6613)*	F	518 828-7301
Hemisphere Novelties Inc Yonkers *(G-17453)*	E	914 378-4100

PIECE GOODS, NOTIONS & OTHER DRY GOODS, WHOLESALE: Fabrics

Company	Code	Phone
Creation Baumann USA Inc Rockville Centre *(G-14790)*	E	516 764-7431
Eu Design LLC New York *(G-10081)*	G	212 420-7788
Sifonya Inc New York *(G-12065)*	G	212 620-4512

PIECE GOODS, NOTIONS & OTHER DRY GOODS, WHOLESALE: Woven

Company	Code	Phone
Citisource Industries Inc New York *(G-9625)*	E	212 683-1033

PIECE GOODS, NOTIONS/DRY GOODS, WHOL: Drapery Mtrl, Woven

Company	Code	Phone
Richloom Fabrics Corp New York *(G-11869)*	F	212 685-5400
Scalamandre Silks Inc New York *(G-11982)*	D	212 980-3888

PIECE GOODS, NOTIONS/DRY GOODS, WHOL: Linen Piece, Woven

Company	Code	Phone
Simple Elegance New York Inc Brooklyn *(G-2562)*	F	718 360-1947

PIECE GOODS, NOTIONS/DRY GOODS, WHOL: Sewing Splys/Notions

Company	Code	Phone
Artistic Ribbon Novelty Co Inc New York *(G-9220)*	E	212 255-4224

PILLOWS: Sponge Rubber

Company	Code	Phone
Schlegel Systems Inc Rochester *(G-14674)*	C	585 427-7200

PINS

Company	Code	Phone
Pin Pharma Inc New York *(G-11661)*	G	212 543-2583
Pin Pretty Inc Brooklyn *(G-2421)*	G	718 887-5290
Pins N Needles New York *(G-11666)*	G	212 535-6222
Pni Capital Partners Westbury *(G-17019)*	G	516 466-7120

PIPE & FITTING: Fabrication

Company	Code	Phone
Accord Pipe Fabricators Inc Jamaica *(G-6892)*	E	718 657-3900
Advanced Thermal Systems Inc Lancaster *(G-7298)*	E	716 681-1800
Albany Nipple and Pipe Mfg Troy *(G-16218)*	E	518 270-2162
Arcadia Mfg Group Inc Green Island *(G-5853)*	E	518 434-6213
Arcadia Mfg Group Inc Menands *(G-8367)*	E	518 434-6213
Cobey Inc Buffalo *(G-2877)*	D	716 362-9550
Cwr Manufacturing Corporation East Syracuse *(G-4521)*	D	315 437-1032
Daikin Applied Americas Inc Auburn *(G-491)*	D	315 253-2771
Fixture Hardware Mfg Corp Brooklyn *(G-1980)*	E	718 499-9422
Flatcut LLC Brooklyn *(G-1983)*	E	212 542-5732
Greene Technologies Inc Greene *(G-5866)*	D	607 656-4166
H & H Metal Specialty Inc Jamestown *(G-6997)*	E	716 665-2110
J D Steward Inc Flushing *(G-5256)*	G	718 358-0169
James Woerner Inc Farmingdale *(G-5016)*	G	631 454-9330
Juniper Elbow Co Inc Middle Village *(G-8414)*	C	718 326-2546
Juniper Industries Florida Inc Middle Village *(G-8415)*	G	718 326-2546
Leo International Inc Brooklyn *(G-2213)*	E	718 290-8005
Leroy Plastics Inc Le Roy *(G-7413)*	D	585 768-8158
Long Island Pipe Supply Inc Flushing *(G-5267)*	G	718 456-7877
Long Island Pipe Supply Inc Troy *(G-16222)*	G	518 270-2159
Long Island Pipe Supply Inc Garden City *(G-5516)*	E	516 222-8008
Met Weld International LLC Altamont *(G-210)*	D	518 765-2318
Micromold Products Inc Yonkers *(G-17467)*	E	914 969-2850
Rochester Tube Fabricators Rochester *(G-14653)*	G	585 254-0290
Standex Air Dist Pdts Inc Medina *(G-8283)*	E	585 798-0300
Tag Flange & Machining Inc Oceanside *(G-13100)*	E	516 536-1300
Truly Tubular Fitting Corp Mount Vernon *(G-8742)*	F	914 664-8686
Wedco Fabrications Inc College Point *(G-3810)*	G	718 852-6330

PIPE & FITTINGS: Cast Iron

Company	Code	Phone
Cpp - Guaymas Chittenango *(G-3631)*	C	315 687-0014
Dragon Trading Inc New York *(G-9923)*	G	212 717-1496

PIPE & FITTINGS: Pressure, Cast Iron

Company	Code	Phone
Acme Nipple Mfg Co Inc Buffalo *(G-2796)*	G	716 873-7491
Penner Elbow Company Inc Elmhurst *(G-4665)*	F	718 526-9000

PIPE CLEANERS

Company	Code	Phone
R V Dow Enterprises Inc Rochester *(G-14619)*	F	585 454-5862

PIPE JOINT COMPOUNDS

Company	Code	Phone
Continental Buchanan LLC Buchanan *(G-2785)*	D	703 480-3800

PIPE: Concrete

Company	Code	Phone
Binghamton Precast & Sup Corp Binghamton *(G-893)*	E	607 722-0334
Roman Stone Construction Co Bay Shore *(G-738)*	E	631 667-0566

PIPE: Extruded, Aluminum

Company	Code	Phone
North American Pipe Corp Jericho *(G-7079)*	F	516 338-2863

PIPE: Plastic

Company	Code	Phone
Advanced Distribution System Palisades *(G-13400)*	D	845 848-2357
BMC LLC Buffalo *(G-2844)*	E	716 681-7755
Hancor Inc Waverly *(G-16703)*	D	607 565-3033
Micromold Products Inc Yonkers *(G-17467)*	E	914 969-2850
National Pipe & Plastics Inc Vestal *(G-16451)*	C	607 729-9381
North American Pipe Corp Jericho *(G-7079)*	F	516 338-2863
Prince Rubber & Plas Co Inc Buffalo *(G-3136)*	E	225 272-1653

PIPE: Seamless Steel

Company	Code	Phone
Davidson Corporation Brooklyn *(G-1843)*	G	718 439-6300

PIPE: Sheet Metal

Company	Code	Phone
Lane Enterprises Inc Ballston Spa *(G-601)*	E	518 885-4385
Standex Air Dist Pdts Inc Medina *(G-8283)*	E	585 798-0300

PIPES & TUBES: Steel

Company	Code	Phone
Coventry Manufacturing Co Inc Mount Vernon *(G-8674)*	E	914 668-2212
Handy & Harman White Plains *(G-17118)*	E	914 461-1300
Liberty Pipe Incorporated Mineola *(G-8521)*	G	516 747-2472
Markin Tubing LP Buffalo *(G-3056)*	F	585 495-6211
McHone Industries Inc Salamanca *(G-15101)*	D	716 945-3380
Micromold Products Inc Yonkers *(G-17467)*	E	914 969-2850
Stony Brook Mfg Co Inc Calverton *(G-3298)*	E	631 369-9530
Super Steelworks Corporation Deer Park *(G-4215)*	G	718 386-4770
Tricon Piping Systems Inc Canastota *(G-3375)*	F	315 655-4178
Welded Tube Usa Inc Lackawanna *(G-7250)*	D	716 828-1111

PIPES & TUBES: Welded

Company	Code	Phone
Oriskany Mfg Tech LLC Yorkville *(G-17525)*	E	315 732-4962

PIPES: Steel & Iron

Company	Code	Phone
Cs Manufacturing Limited Alfred *(G-193)*	E	607 587-8154
Lino International Inc Great Neck *(G-5821)*	G	516 482-7100

PIPES: Tobacco

Company	Code	Phone
Ryers Creek Corp Corning *(G-3980)*	E	607 523-6617
S M Frank & Company Inc New Windsor *(G-8951)*	G	914 739-3100

Employee Codes: A=Over 500 employees, B=251-500
C=101-250, D=51-100, E=20-50, F=10-19, G=5-9

2017 Harris
New York Manufacturers Directory

PISTONS & PISTON RINGS

Fcmp Inc .... F 716 692-4623
  Tonawanda (G-16160)

PLACEMATS: Plastic Or Textile

Baby Signature Inc .... G 212 686-1700
  New York (G-9298)
NY Cutting Inc .... G 845 368-1459
  Airmont (G-17)

PLANING MILLS: Independent, Exc Millwork

Embassy Millwork Inc .... F 518 839-0965
  Amsterdam (G-344)

PLANING MILLS: Millwork

Mind Designs Inc .... G 631 563-3644
  Farmingville (G-5160)

PLANT CARE SVCS

Plant-Tech2o Inc .... G 516 483-7845
  Hempstead (G-6285)

PLAQUES: Clay, Plaster/Papier-Mache, Factory Production

B & R Promotional Products .... G 212 563-0040
  New York (G-9288)

PLAQUES: Picture, Laminated

B & R Promotional Products .... G 212 563-0040
  New York (G-9288)
Donorwall Inc .... F 212 766-9670
  New York (G-9907)
Executive Creations Inc .... G 212 422-2640
  New York (G-10105)
International Bronze Manufac .. F 516 248-3080
  Albertson (G-155)
Kelly Foundry & Machine Co 315 732-8313
  Utica (G-16346)

PLASMAS

C T M Industries Ltd .... E 718 479-3300
  Jamaica (G-6899)
Coral Blood Service .... F 800 483-4888
  Elmsford (G-4743)
D C I Plasma Center Inc .... G 914 241-1646
  Mount Kisco (G-8625)
Lake Immunogenics Inc .... F 585 265-1973
  Ontario (G-13205)

PLASTER WORK: Ornamental & Architectural

American Wood Column Corp .. G 718 782-3163
  Brooklyn (G-1610)

PLASTIC COLORING & FINISHING

Color Craft Finishing Corp .... F 631 563-3230
  Bohemia (G-1038)

PLASTIC PRDTS

Dpi of Rochester LLC .... G 585 325-3610
  Rochester (G-14317)
G and G Service .... G 518 785-9247
  Latham (G-7363)
Kc Tag Co .... G 518 842-6666
  Amsterdam (G-353)
Micron Powder Industries LLC . F 718 851-0011
  Brooklyn (G-2311)
Sabic Innovative Plastics .... E 713 448-7474
  East Greenbush (G-4404)

PLASTIC PRDTS REPAIR SVCS

All Spec Finishing Inc .... E 607 770-9174
  Binghamton (G-886)

PLASTICIZERS, ORGANIC: Cyclic & Acyclic

Wecare Organics LLC .... E 315 689-1937
  Jordan (G-7131)

PLASTICS FILM & SHEET

Astra Products Inc .... G 631 464-4747
  Copiague (G-3895)
Curbell Incorporated .... G 315 434-7240
  East Syracuse (G-4520)
Dunmore Corporation .... D 845 279-5061
  Brewster (G-1217)
Farber Plastics Inc .... E 516 378-4860
  Freeport (G-5397)
Farber Trucking Corp .... E 516 378-4860
  Freeport (G-5398)
Favorite Plastic Corp .... G 718 253-7000
  Brooklyn (G-1961)
Kings Film & Sheet Inc .... E 718 624-7510
  Brooklyn (G-2175)
Maco Bag Corporation .... C 315 226-1000
  Newark (G-12735)
Royal Plastics Corp .... F 718 647-7500
  Brooklyn (G-2513)

PLASTICS FILM & SHEET: Polyethylene

Clear View Bag Company Inc .. C 518 458-7153
  Albany (G-64)
Nationwide Tarps Incorporated D 518 843-1545
  Amsterdam (G-361)
Potential Poly Bag Inc .... G 718 258-0800
  Brooklyn (G-2430)
Sentinel Products Corp .... F 518 568-7036
  Saint Johnsville (G-15098)

PLASTICS FILM & SHEET: Polyvinyl

Shaant Industries Inc .... E 716 366-3654
  Dunkirk (G-4350)

PLASTICS FILM & SHEET: Vinyl

Ace Canvas & Tent Corp .... F 631 648-0614
  Ronkonkoma (G-14848)
Latham International Inc .... F 518 346-5292
  Schenectady (G-15276)
Latham International Inc .... G 518 783-7776
  Latham (G-7368)
Nuhart & Co Inc .... D 718 383-8484
  Brooklyn (G-2379)
Orafol Americas Inc .... E 585 272-0309
  Henrietta (G-6297)
Plascal Corp .... G 516 249-2200
  Farmingdale (G-5081)
Pocono Pool Products-North ... E 518 283-1023
  Rensselaer (G-14049)
Robeco/Ascot Products Inc ...... G 516 248-1521
  Garden City (G-5530)
Vinyl Materials Inc .... G 631 586-9444
  Deer Park (G-4224)

PLASTICS FINISHED PRDTS: Laminated

Advanced Assembly Services Inc .. G .. 716 217-8144
  Angola (G-378)
Anthony River Inc .... F 315 475-1315
  Syracuse (G-15855)
Blue Sky Plastic Production ..... F 718 366-3966
  Brooklyn (G-1703)
Inter State Laminates Inc .... E 518 283-8355
  Poestenkill (G-13724)
La Mart Manufacturing Corp .... G 718 384-6917
  Brooklyn (G-2188)
Solid Surface Acrylics Inc .... F 716 743-1870
  North Tonawanda (G-12994)
Synthetic Textiles Inc .... G 716 842-2598
  Buffalo (G-3206)
Unico Special Products Inc ..... E 845 562-9255
  Newburgh (G-12783)

PLASTICS MATERIAL & RESINS

Alco Industries Inc .... E 740 254-4311
  Round Lake (G-15036)
American Acrylic Corporation .. E 631 422-2200
  West Babylon (G-16770)
Ashley Resin Corp .... G 718 851-8111
  Brooklyn (G-1639)
Atc Plastics LLC .... E 212 375-2515
  New York (G-9245)
Axel Plastics RES Labs Inc ..... E 718 672-8300
  Woodside (G-17318)
Bairnco Corporation .... G 914 461-1300
  White Plains (G-17081)
Barrett Bronze Corp .... E 914 699-6060
  Mount Vernon (G-8665)
Ccmi Inc .... G 315 781-3270
  Geneva (G-5571)
Clarence Resins and Chemicals .. G .. 716 406-9804
  Clarence Center (G-3673)
CN Group Incorporated .... A 914 358-5690
  White Plains (G-17094)
Cytec Industries Inc .... D 716 372-9650
  Olean (G-13142)
Cytec Olean Inc .... D 716 372-9650
  Olean (G-13143)
Dice America Inc .... G 585 869-6200
  Victor (G-16473)
Durez Corporation .... F 716 286-0100
  Niagara Falls (G-12812)
E I Du Pont De Nemours & Co E 716 876-4420
  Buffalo (G-2924)
Endurart Inc .... E 212 473-7000
  New York (G-10034)
GE Plastics .... G 518 475-5011
  Selkirk (G-15355)
General Vy-Coat LLC .... E 718 266-6002
  Brooklyn (G-2019)
International Casein Corp Cal .. G 516 466-4363
  Great Neck (G-5816)
Macneil Polymers Inc .... F 716 681-7755
  Buffalo (G-3054)
Maviano Corp .... G 845 494-2598
  Monsey (G-8575)
MB Plastics Inc .... F 718 523-1180
  Greenlawn (G-5874)
Mitsui Chemicals America Inc . E 914 253-0777
  Rye Brook (G-15072)
Momentive Performance Mtls Inc .. D . 914 784-4807
  Tarrytown (G-16098)
Nationwide Tarps Incorporated D 518 843-1545
  Amsterdam (G-361)
Parker-Hannifin Corporation .... E 315 926-4211
  Marion (G-8097)
Polycast Industries Inc .... G 631 595-2530
  Bay Shore (G-726)
Sabic Innovative Plas US LLC . B 518 475-5011
  Selkirk (G-15358)
Saga International Recycl LLC G 718 621-5900
  Brooklyn (G-2529)
Saint-Gobain Prfmce Plas Corp C 518 642-2200
  Granville (G-5781)
SC Medical Overseas Inc .... G 516 935-8500
  Jericho (G-7085)
Solid Surfaces Inc .... E 585 292-5340
  Rochester (G-14692)
Telechemische Inc .... G 845 561-3237
  Newburgh (G-12781)
Terphane Holdings LLC .... E 585 657-5800
  Bloomfield (G-990)
Tmp Technologies Inc .... D 716 895-6100
  Buffalo (G-3052)
Toray Holding (usa) Inc .... E 212 697-8150
  New York (G-12372)
Toray Industries Inc .... E 212 697-8150
  New York (G-12373)
Transpo Industries Inc .... E 914 636-1000
  New Rochelle (G-8926)
Tri-Seal Holdings Inc .... D 845 353-3300
  Blauvelt (G-977)
Unico Inc .... F 845 562-9255
  Newburgh (G-12782)
Wilsonart Intl Holdings LLC ..... E 516 935-6980
  Bethpage (G-879)
WR Smith & Sons Inc .... G 845 620-9400
  Nanuet (G-8763)

PLASTICS MATERIALS, BASIC FORMS & SHAPES WHOLESALERS

Fibre Materials Corp .... E 516 349-1660
  Plainview (G-13602)
Plastic-Craft Products Corp ..... E 845 358-3010
  West Nyack (G-16925)

PLASTICS PROCESSING

A & G Heat Sealing .... G 631 724-7764
  Smithtown (G-15481)
A-1 Products Inc .... G 718 789-1818
  Brooklyn (G-1538)
Adirondack Plas & Recycl Inc . E 518 746-9212
  Argyle (G-408)
All American Precision TI Mold F 585 436-3080
  West Henrietta (G-16865)
American Visuals Inc .... G 631 694-6104
  Farmingdale (G-4941)
Brandys Mold and Tool Ctr Ltd F 585 334-8333
  West Henrietta (G-16871)
Buffalo Polymer Processors Inc E 716 537-3153
  Holland (G-6480)

Cdj Stamping Inc ..... G 585 224-8120
Rochester *(G-14263)*

Centro Inc ..... B 212 791-9450
New York *(G-9567)*

Commodore Plastics LLC ..... E 585 657-7777
Bloomfield *(G-985)*

Continental Latex Corp ..... F 718 783-7883
Brooklyn *(G-1799)*

CSP Technologies Inc ..... E 518 627-0051
Amsterdam *(G-342)*

Custom Lucite Creations Inc ..... F 718 871-2000
Brooklyn *(G-1827)*

Dacobe Enterprises LLC ..... F 315 368-0093
Utica *(G-16320)*

Dawnex Industries Inc ..... F 718 384-0199
Brooklyn *(G-1844)*

Eck Plastic Arts Inc ..... E 607 722-3227
Binghamton *(G-909)*

Fei Products LLC ..... E 716 693-6230
North Tonawanda *(G-12972)*

Formed Plastics Inc ..... D 516 334-2300
Carle Place *(G-3388)*

Gantz-Newman LLC ..... F 631 249-0680
Farmingdale *(G-4996)*

Genpak LLC ..... C 845 343-7971
Middletown *(G-8442)*

Germanow-Simon Corporation ..... E 585 232-1440
Rochester *(G-14399)*

Gifford Group Inc ..... F 212 569-8500
New York *(G-10293)*

Imperial Polymers Inc ..... G 718 387-4741
Brooklyn *(G-2099)*

Inhance Technologies LLC ..... E 716 825-9031
Buffalo *(G-3009)*

Innovative Plastics Corp ..... C 845 359-7500
Orangeburg *(G-13230)*

Jamestown Mvp LLC ..... G 716 846-1418
Falconer *(G-4906)*

Johnson Manufacturing Co ..... G 631 472-1184
Bayport *(G-758)*

L I C Screen Printing Inc ..... E 516 546-7289
Merrick *(G-8387)*

Major-IPC Inc ..... G 845 292-2200
Liberty *(G-7438)*

Md4 Holdings Inc ..... F 315 434-1869
East Syracuse *(G-4549)*

Mettowee Lumber & Plastics Co ..... C 518 642-1100
Granville *(G-5777)*

Mold-A-Matic Corporation ..... E 607 433-2121
Oneonta *(G-13189)*

Nalge Nunc International Corp ..... A 585 586-8800
Rochester *(G-14527)*

Nathan Boning Co LLC ..... G 212 244-4781
New York *(G-11342)*

P V C Molding Technologies ..... F 315 331-1212
Newark *(G-12740)*

Patmian LLC ..... B 212 758-0770
New York *(G-11579)*

Plastic Works ..... G 914 576-2050
New Rochelle *(G-8920)*

Plastic-Craft Products Corp ..... E 845 358-3010
West Nyack *(G-16925)*

Plasticycle Corporation ..... E 914 997-6882
White Plains *(G-17160)*

Prince Rubber & Plas Co Inc ..... E 225 272-1653
Buffalo *(G-3136)*

Richlar Industries Inc ..... F 315 463-5144
East Syracuse *(G-4559)*

Rimco Plastics Corp ..... E 607 739-3864
Horseheads *(G-6590)*

Royce Associates A Ltd Partnr ..... G 516 367-6298
Jericho *(G-7083)*

Russell Plastics Tech Co Inc ..... C 631 963-8602
Lindenhurst *(G-7481)*

Seal Reinforced Fiberglass Inc ..... E 631 842-2230
Copiague *(G-3926)*

Seal Reinforced Fiberglass Inc ..... G 631 842-2230
Copiague *(G-3927)*

Shamrock Plastics & Tool Inc ..... G 585 328-6040
Rochester *(G-14683)*

Silvatrim Corp ..... C 212 675-0933
New York *(G-12075)*

Structural Industries Inc ..... C 631 471-5200
Bohemia *(G-1137)*

Superior Plus Cnstr Pdts Corp ..... F 315 463-5144
East Syracuse *(G-4569)*

Teva Womens Health Inc ..... F 716 693-6230
North Tonawanda *(G-13002)*

Toray Industries Inc ..... G 212 697-8150
New York *(G-12373)*

Tulip Molded Plastics Corp ..... D 716 282-1261
Niagara Falls *(G-12885)*

Unifab Inc ..... G 585 235-1760
Rochester *(G-14742)*

Unifuse LLC ..... F 845 889-4000
Staatsburg *(G-15619)*

United Plastics Inc ..... G 718 389-2255
Brooklyn *(G-2701)*

Usheco Inc ..... F 845 658-9200
Kingston *(G-7223)*

Viele Manufacturing Corp ..... B 718 893-2200
Bronx *(G-1490)*

Vinyl Materials Inc ..... E 631 586-9444
Deer Park *(G-4224)*

W Kintz Plastics Inc ..... C 518 296-8513
Howes Cave *(G-6601)*

Zan Optics Products Inc ..... E 718 435-0533
Brooklyn *(G-2781)*

Zone Fabricators Inc ..... F 718 272-0200
Ozone Park *(G-13388)*

PLASTICS SHEET: Packing Materials

Edco Supply Corporation ..... D 718 788-8108
Brooklyn *(G-1903)*

Knoll Printing & Packaging Inc ..... E 516 621-0100
Syosset *(G-15826)*

Precision Packaging Pdts Inc ..... C 585 638-8200
Holley *(G-6491)*

Tri-Seal Holdings Inc ..... D 845 353-3300
Blauvelt *(G-977)*

PLASTICS: Blow Molded

Confer Plastics Inc ..... C 800 635-3213
North Tonawanda *(G-12967)*

PLASTICS: Cast

Albest Metal Stamping Corp ..... D 718 388-6000
Brooklyn *(G-1576)*

Miller Technology Inc ..... G 631 694-2224
Farmingdale *(G-5056)*

PLASTICS: Extruded

Albany International Corp ..... C 607 749-7226
Homer *(G-6515)*

Burnham Polymeric Inc ..... G 518 792-3040
Fort Edward *(G-5340)*

Certainteed Corporation ..... B 716 827-7560
Buffalo *(G-2870)*

Christi Plastics Inc ..... G 585 436-8510
Rochester *(G-14275)*

E & T Plastic Mfg Co Inc ..... D 718 729-6226
Long Island City *(G-7722)*

East Cast Clor Compounding Inc ..... G 631 491-9000
West Babylon *(G-16790)*

Eastern Industrial Steel Corp ..... G 845 639-9749
New City *(G-8785)*

Finger Lakes Extrusion Corp ..... E 585 905-0632
Canandaigua *(G-3346)*

Kleer-Fax Inc ..... D 631 225-1100
Amityville *(G-303)*

Pawling Engineered Pdts Inc ..... C 845 855-1000
Pawling *(G-13452)*

Phoenix Services Group LLC ..... E 518 828-6611
Hudson *(G-6631)*

Streamline Plastics Co Inc ..... E 718 401-4000
Bronx *(G-1466)*

PLASTICS: Finished Injection Molded

A R V Precision Mfg Inc ..... G 631 293-9643
Farmingdale *(G-4927)*

Alliance Precision Plas Corp ..... C 585 426-5310
Rochester *(G-14189)*

Alliance Precision Plas Corp ..... E 585 426-5310
Rochester *(G-14190)*

Aluminum Injection Mold Co LLC ..... G 585 502-6087
Le Roy *(G-7402)*

Anna Young Assoc Ltd ..... C 516 546-4400
Freeport *(G-5388)*

Aztec Tool Co Inc ..... E 631 243-1144
Edgewood *(G-4593)*

Colonie Plastics Corp ..... C 631 434-6969
Bay Shore *(G-686)*

Epp Team Inc ..... D 585 454-4995
Rochester *(G-14354)*

Everblock Systems LLC ..... G 844 422-5625
New York *(G-10089)*

H & H Hulls Inc ..... G 518 828-1339
Hudson *(G-6616)*

Harbec Inc ..... D 585 265-0010
Ontario *(G-13203)*

J T Systematic ..... G 607 754-0929
Endwell *(G-4836)*

Joe Pietryka Incorporated ..... D 845 855-1201
Pawling *(G-13450)*

K & H Precision Products Inc ..... E 585 624-4894
Honeoye Falls *(G-6532)*

Leidel Corporation ..... E 631 244-0900
Bohemia *(G-1093)*

M & M Molding Corp ..... C 631 582-1900
Central Islip *(G-3503)*

PMI Industries LLC ..... E 585 464-8050
Rochester *(G-14586)*

Primoplast Inc ..... F 631 750-0680
Bohemia *(G-1121)*

Sterling Molded Products Inc ..... E 845 344-4546
Middletown *(G-8463)*

Viapack Inc ..... F 718 729-5500
Long Island City *(G-7915)*

PLASTICS: Injection Molded

American Casting and Mfg Corp ..... D 800 342-0333
Plainview *(G-13581)*

American Casting and Mfg Corp ..... G 516 349-7010
Plainview *(G-13582)*

Anka Tool & Die Inc ..... E 845 268-4116
Congers *(G-3851)*

Armstrong Mold Corporation ..... E 315 437-1517
East Syracuse *(G-4504)*

Armstrong Mold Corporation ..... D 315 437-1517
East Syracuse *(G-4505)*

Autronic Plastics Inc ..... D 516 333-7577
Central Islip *(G-3485)*

Avanti U S A Ltd ..... F 716 695-5800
Tonawanda *(G-16141)*

Barton Tool Inc ..... G 716 665-2801
Falconer *(G-4892)*

Binghamton Precision Tool Inc ..... G 607 772-6021
Binghamton *(G-894)*

Cambridge Security Seals LLC ..... E 845 520-4111
Pomona *(G-13729)*

Carolina Precision Plas LLC ..... D 631 981-0743
Ronkonkoma *(G-14885)*

Cast-All Corporation ..... E 516 741-4025
Mineola *(G-8502)*

Cast-All Corporation ..... E 516 741-4025
Mineola *(G-8503)*

Century Mold Company Inc ..... D 585 352-8600
Rochester *(G-14266)*

Century Mold Mexico LLC ..... G 585 352-8600
Rochester *(G-14267)*

Champlain Plastics Inc ..... D 518 297-3700
Rouses Point *(G-15041)*

Chenango Valley Tech Inc ..... E 607 674-4115
Sherburne *(G-15389)*

Clifford H Jones Inc ..... F 716 693-2444
Tonawanda *(G-16153)*

CPI of Falconer Inc ..... E 716 664-4444
Falconer *(G-4894)*

Craftech Industries Inc ..... D 518 828-5001
Hudson *(G-6611)*

Cs Manufacturing Limited ..... E 607 587-8154
Alfred *(G-193)*

Currier Plastics Inc ..... D 315 255-1779
Auburn *(G-490)*

Cy Plastics Works Inc ..... E 585 229-2555
Honeoye *(G-6523)*

East Pattern & Model Corp ..... E 585 461-3240
Fairport *(G-4856)*

Em-Kay Molds Inc ..... G 716 895-6180
Buffalo *(G-2935)*

Ernie Green Industries Inc ..... D 585 295-8951
Rochester *(G-14356)*

Ernie Green Industries Inc ..... C 585 647-2300
Rochester *(G-14357)*

Ernie Green Industries Inc ..... D 585 647-2300
Rochester *(G-14358)*

Extreme Molding LLC ..... E 518 326-9319
Watervliet *(G-16684)*

Faro Industries Inc ..... F 585 647-6000
Rochester *(G-14368)*

Felchar Manufacturing Corp ..... A 607 723-3106
Binghamton *(G-914)*

G N R Plastics Inc ..... G 631 724-8758
Smithtown *(G-15487)*

Galt Industries Inc ..... G 212 758-0770
New York *(G-10243)*

Gen-West Associates LLC ..... G 315 255-1779
Auburn *(G-497)*

Employee Codes: A=Over 500 employees, B=251-500
C=101-250, D=51-100, E=20-50, F=10-19, G=5-9

2017 Harris
New York Manufacturers Directory

1293

PLASTICS: Injection Molded

Genesee Precision Inc .... E 585 344-0385
  Batavia *(G-634)*
Hansa Plastics Inc .... F 631 269-9050
  Kings Park *(G-7171)*
Ilion Plastics Inc .... F 315 894-4868
  Ilion *(G-6741)*
Illinois Tool Works Inc .... D 860 435-2574
  Millerton *(G-8479)*
Imco Inc .... E 585 352-7810
  Spencerport *(G-15570)*
Inteva Products LLC .... B 248 655-8886
  New York *(G-10643)*
K & H Industries Inc .... F 716 312-0088
  Hamburg *(G-5930)*
K & H Industries Inc .... E 716 312-0088
  Hamburg *(G-5931)*
Kobe Steel USA Holdings Inc .... G 212 751-9400
  New York *(G-10866)*
Master Molding Inc .... F 631 694-1444
  Farmingdale *(G-5044)*
Midbury Industries Inc .... F 516 868-0600
  Freeport *(G-5414)*
Milne Mfg Inc .... F 716 772-2536
  Gasport *(G-5559)*
Minico Industries Inc .... G 631 595-1455
  Bay Shore *(G-719)*
Natech Plastics Inc .... E 631 580-3506
  Ronkonkoma *(G-14949)*
New York Manufactured Products .... F 585 254-9353
  Rochester *(G-14532)*
Nordon Inc .... D 585 546-6200
  Rochester *(G-14538)*
Oneida Molded Plastics LLC .... C 315 363-7990
  Oneida *(G-13161)*
P M Plastics Inc .... F 716 662-1255
  Orchard Park *(G-13286)*
Peninsula Plastics Ltd .... D 716 854-3050
  Buffalo *(G-3118)*
Polymer Engineered Pdts Inc .... D 585 426-1811
  Rochester *(G-14588)*
Precision Techniques Inc .... D 718 991-1440
  Bronx *(G-1434)*
Pylantis New York LLC .... G 310 429-5911
  Groton *(G-5901)*
Rochling Advent Tool & Mold LP .... E 585 254-2000
  Rochester *(G-14654)*
Sonoco-Crellin Inc .... C 518 392-2000
  Chatham *(G-3560)*
Southern Tier Plastics Inc .... D 607 723-2601
  Binghamton *(G-952)*
Staroba Plastics Inc .... F 716 537-3153
  Holland *(G-6484)*
Stuart Mold & Manufacturing .... F 716 488-9765
  Falconer *(G-4914)*
Surprise Plastics Inc .... C 718 492-6355
  Brooklyn *(G-2634)*
Syntec Technologies Inc .... E 585 768-2513
  Rochester *(G-14712)*
Syracuse Plastics LLC .... C 315 637-9881
  Liverpool *(G-7551)*
T A Tool & Molding Inc .... F 631 293-0172
  Farmingdale *(G-5123)*
Tessy Plastics Corp .... B 315 689-3924
  Skaneateles *(G-15466)*
Titherington Design & Mfg .... F 518 324-2205
  Plattsburgh *(G-13704)*
Toolroom Express Inc .... D 607 723-5373
  Conklin *(G-3876)*
Trimac Molding Services .... G 607 967-2900
  Bainbridge *(G-555)*
Turbo Plastics Corp Inc .... F 631 345-9768
  Yaphank *(G-17406)*

PLASTICS: Molded

Abr Molding Andy LLC .... F 212 576-1821
  Ridgewood *(G-14098)*
Ace Molding & Tool Inc .... G 631 567-2355
  Bohemia *(G-1007)*
Baird Mold Making Inc .... G 631 667-0322
  Bay Shore *(G-674)*
Chocolate Delivery Systems Inc .... D 716 854-6050
  Buffalo *(G-2872)*
Craftech .... D 518 828-5011
  Chatham *(G-3557)*
Dutchland Plastics Corp .... C 315 280-0247
  Sherrill *(G-15405)*
Egli Machine Company Inc .... E 607 563-3663
  Sidney *(G-15439)*
Engineered Molding Tech LLC .... F 518 482-2004
  Albany *(G-78)*

Form-Tec Inc .... E 516 867-0200
  Freeport *(G-5399)*
ISO Plastics Corp .... D 914 663-8300
  Mount Vernon *(G-8694)*
K2 Plastics Inc .... G 585 494-2727
  Bergen *(G-847)*
Mechanical Rubber Pdts Co Inc .... F 845 986-2271
  Warwick *(G-16594)*
Mercury Plastics Corp .... F 718 498-5400
  Brooklyn *(G-2299)*
Mirage Moulding Mfg Inc .... F 631 843-6168
  Farmingdale *(G-5057)*
Molding Decor Inc .... F 718 377-2930
  Brooklyn *(G-2329)*
Monarch Plastics Inc .... F 716 569-2175
  Frewsburg *(G-5451)*
Msi-Molding Solutions Inc .... E 315 736-2412
  Rome *(G-14822)*
Niagara Fiberglass Inc .... E 716 822-3921
  Buffalo *(G-3087)*
Pawling Corporation .... C 845 855-1000
  Pawling *(G-13451)*
Peconic Plastics Inc .... F 631 653-3676
  Quogue *(G-14015)*
Pii Holdings Inc .... G 716 876-9951
  Buffalo *(G-3126)*
Piper Plastics Corp .... E 631 842-6889
  Copiague *(G-3918)*
Polymer Conversions Inc .... D 716 662-8550
  Orchard Park *(G-13290)*
Protective Industries Inc .... F 716 876-9951
  Buffalo *(G-3139)*
Protective Industries Inc .... C 716 876-9855
  Buffalo *(G-3140)*
Pulse Plastics Products Inc .... E 718 328-5224
  Bronx *(G-1436)*
Pvc Container Corporation .... C 518 672-7721
  Philmont *(G-13541)*
Sonoco-Crellin Intl Inc .... B 518 392-2000
  Chatham *(G-3561)*
Sweet Tooth Enterprises LLC .... E 631 752-2888
  West Babylon *(G-16835)*
Termatec Molding Inc .... F 315 483-4150
  Sodus *(G-15505)*
Thermold Corporation .... C 315 697-3924
  Canastota *(G-3374)*

PLASTICS: Polystyrene Foam

ABI Packaging Inc .... E 716 677-2900
  West Seneca *(G-16938)*
Advanced Plstic Fbrctions Corp .... G 631 231-4466
  Hauppauge *(G-6010)*
Berry Plastics Corporation .... B 315 986-6270
  Macedon *(G-7984)*
Burnett Process Inc .... G 585 254-8080
  Rochester *(G-14252)*
Cellect Plastics LLC .... D 518 568-7036
  Saint Johnsville *(G-15093)*
Curbell Plastics Inc .... F 585 426-1690
  Rochester *(G-14295)*
Dura Foam Inc .... E 718 894-2488
  Maspeth *(G-8133)*
General Vy-Coat LLC .... E 718 266-6002
  Brooklyn *(G-2019)*
Great American Industries Inc .... G 607 729-9331
  Vestal *(G-16449)*
Hopp Companies Inc .... F 516 358-4170
  New Hyde Park *(G-8841)*
Latham International Inc .... G 518 783-7776
  Latham *(G-7368)*
Latham Pool Products Inc .... E 260 432-8731
  Latham *(G-7370)*
Lewis & Myers Inc .... G 585 494-1410
  Bergen *(G-848)*
Par-Foam Products Inc .... C 716 855-2066
  Buffalo *(G-3112)*
Pliant LLC .... B 315 986-6286
  Macedon *(G-7990)*
Professional Packg Svcs Inc .... E 518 677-5100
  Eagle Bridge *(G-4357)*
Rimco Plastics Corp .... E 607 739-3864
  Horseheads *(G-6590)*
Saint-Gobain Prfmce Plas Corp .... C 518 642-2200
  Granville *(G-5781)*
Sealed Air Corporation .... C 518 370-1693
  Schenectady *(G-15294)*
Skd Distribution Corp .... E 718 525-6000
  Jericho *(G-7088)*
Strux Corp .... E 516 768-3969
  Lindenhurst *(G-7485)*

Tmp Technologies Inc .... D 716 895-6100
  Buffalo *(G-3220)*
TSS Foam Industries Corp .... F 585 538-2321
  Caledonia *(G-3283)*

PLASTICS: Thermoformed

Bo-Mer Plastics LLC .... E 315 252-7216
  Auburn *(G-486)*
Cjk Manufacturing LLC .... F 585 663-6370
  Rochester *(G-14277)*
Marval Industries Inc .... D 914 381-2400
  Mamaroneck *(G-8038)*
Pactiv Corporation .... C 518 743-3100
  Glens Falls *(G-5694)*
Weather Products Corporation .... G 315 474-8593
  Syracuse *(G-16069)*

PLATEMAKING SVC: Color Separations, For The Printing Trade

Absolute Color Corporation .... G 212 868-0404
  New York *(G-9007)*
Eastern Color Stripping Inc .... F 631 563-3700
  Bohemia *(G-1060)*
Lane Park Litho Plate .... E 212 255-9100
  New York *(G-10925)*
Lazer Incorporated .... E 336 744-8047
  Rochester *(G-14476)*
Leo P Callahan Inc .... F 607 797-7314
  Binghamton *(G-933)*
Micro Publishing Inc .... G 212 533-9180
  New York *(G-11253)*
Torch Graphics Inc .... E 212 679-4334
  New York *(G-12374)*

PLATEMAKING SVC: Embossing, For The Printing Trade

Aldine Inc (ny) .... D 212 226-2870
  New York *(G-9079)*

PLATEMAKING SVC: Gravure, Plates Or Cylinders

Charles Henricks Inc .... F 212 243-5800
  New York *(G-9581)*
Miroddi Imaging Inc .... G 516 624-6898
  Oyster Bay *(G-13372)*

PLATES

Adflex Corporation .... E 585 454-2950
  Rochester *(G-14173)*
Circle Press Inc .... D 212 924-4277
  New York *(G-9621)*
Csw Inc .... F 585 247-4010
  Rochester *(G-14293)*
David Fehlman .... G 315 455-8888
  Syracuse *(G-15922)*
Dowd - Witbeck Printing Corp .... F 518 274-2421
  Troy *(G-16234)*
Gallant Graphices Ltd Inc .... E 845 868-1166
  Stanfordville *(G-15627)*
Gazette Press Inc .... E 914 963-8300
  Rye *(G-15056)*
Karr Graphics Corp .... E 718 784-9390
  Long Island City *(G-7779)*
Kristen Graphics Inc .... F 212 929-2183
  New York *(G-10890)*
Mutual Engraving Company Inc .... D 516 489-0534
  West Hempstead *(G-16861)*
P & H Thermotech Inc .... E 585 624-1310
  Lima *(G-7447)*
Rigidized Metals Corporation .... E 716 849-4703
  Buffalo *(G-3158)*
Rotation Dynamics Corporation .... E 585 352-9023
  Spencerport *(G-15573)*
Syracuse Computer Forms Inc .... E 315 478-0108
  Syracuse *(G-16050)*
Tobay Printing Co Inc .... E 631 842-3300
  Copiague *(G-3934)*
Tripi Engraving Co Inc .... E 718 383-6500
  Brooklyn *(G-2682)*
Welsh Gold Stampers Inc .... E 718 984-5031
  Staten Island *(G-15754)*

PRODUCT SECTION

PLATES: Paper, Made From Purchased Materials

Amscan Inc .... D 845 469-9116
  Chester *(G-3599)*
Amscan Inc .... D 845 782-0490
  Harriman *(G-5970)*
Apexx Omni-Graphics Inc .... D 718 326-3330
  Maspeth *(G-8119)*
Pactiv LLC .... C 518 562-6101
  Plattsburgh *(G-13684)*

PLATES: Plastic Exc Polystyrene Foam

Apexx Omni-Graphics Inc .... D 718 326-3330
  Maspeth *(G-8119)*
Pactiv LLC .... C 585 393-3229
  Canandaigua *(G-3353)*

PLATING & FINISHING SVC: Decorative, Formed Prdts

Northeast Paving Concepts LLC .... G 518 477-1338
  East Schodack *(G-4473)*

PLATING & POLISHING SVC

Abetter Processing Corp .... F 718 252-2223
  Brooklyn *(G-1547)*
Epner Technology Incorporated .... E 718 782-8722
  Brooklyn *(G-1930)*
Hartchrom Inc .... F 518 880-0411
  Watervliet *(G-16686)*
McAlpin Industries Inc .... E 585 544-5335
  Rochester *(G-14501)*
North East Finishing Co Inc .... F 631 789-8000
  Copiague *(G-3917)*
Praxair Surface Tech Inc .... C 845 398-8322
  Orangeburg *(G-13242)*
Precious Plate Inc .... D 716 283-0690
  Niagara Falls *(G-12862)*
Tcmf Inc .... D 607 724-1094
  Binghamton *(G-954)*
Wilco Finishing Corp .... E 718 417-6405
  Brooklyn *(G-2751)*

PLATING COMPOUNDS

Coventya Inc .... G 315 768-6635
  Oriskany *(G-13306)*

PLATING SVC: Chromium, Metals Or Formed Prdts

West Falls Machine Co Inc .... F 716 655-0440
  East Aurora *(G-4380)*

PLATING SVC: Electro

Airmarine Electroplating Corp .... G 516 623-4406
  Freeport *(G-5381)*
Astro Electroplating Inc .... E 631 968-0656
  Bay Shore *(G-673)*
Berkman Bros Inc .... E 718 782-1827
  Brooklyn *(G-1686)*
Bfg Manufacturing Services Inc .... E 716 362-0888
  Buffalo *(G-2841)*
Dan Kane Plating Co Inc .... F 212 675-4947
  New York *(G-9797)*
Dura Spec Inc .... F 718 526-3053
  North Baldwin *(G-12904)*
Electro Plating Service Inc .... F 914 948-3777
  White Plains *(G-17104)*
Epner Technology Incorporated .... E 718 782-5948
  Brooklyn *(G-1929)*
Eric S Turner & Company Inc .... F 914 235-7114
  New Rochelle *(G-8898)*
Finest Cc Corp .... G 917 574-4525
  Bronx *(G-1331)*
Frontier Plating .... G 716 896-2811
  Buffalo *(G-2959)*
Genesee Vly Met Finshg Co Inc .... G 585 232-4412
  Rochester *(G-14745)*
Greene Technologies Inc .... D 607 656-4166
  Greene *(G-5866)*
Interplex Industries Inc .... F 718 961-6512
  College Point *(G-3790)*
John Larocca & Son Inc .... G 631 423-5256
  Huntington Station *(G-6712)*
Kent Electro-Plating Corp .... F 718 358-9599
  Dix Hills *(G-4292)*
Key Tech Finishing .... E 716 832-1232
  Buffalo *(G-3029)*
Keystone Corporation .... E 716 832-1232
  Buffalo *(G-3031)*
Mid Hudson Plating Inc .... G 845 849-1277
  Poughkeepsie *(G-13916)*
Rayco of Schenectady Inc .... F 518 212-5113
  Amsterdam *(G-366)*
Sandys Bumper Mart Inc .... G 315 472-8149
  Syracuse *(G-16031)*
T & M Plating Inc .... E 212 967-1110
  New York *(G-12264)*
Tripp Plating Works Inc .... E 716 894-2424
  Buffalo *(G-3225)*
Tronic Plating Co Inc .... F 516 293-7883
  Farmingdale *(G-5135)*
Vernon Plating Works Inc .... F 718 639-1124
  Woodside *(G-17360)*
Victoria Plating Co Inc .... D 718 589-1550
  Bronx *(G-1489)*

PLATING SVC: Gold

Empire Metal Finishing Inc .... E 718 545-6700
  Astoria *(G-440)*
Sherrill Manufacturing Inc .... C 315 280-0727
  Sherrill *(G-15407)*

PLATING SVC: NEC

Aircraft Finishing Corp .... F 631 422-5000
  West Babylon *(G-16767)*
Buffalo Metal Finishing Co .... G 716 883-2751
  Buffalo *(G-2856)*
Coating Technology Inc .... E 585 546-7170
  Rochester *(G-14282)*
Galmer Ltd .... G 718 392-4609
  Long Island City *(G-7748)*
Nas CP Corp .... D 718 961-6757
  College Point *(G-3799)*
Nassau Chromium Plating Co Inc .... E 516 746-6666
  Mineola *(G-8526)*
Programatic Platers Inc .... F 718 721-4330
  East Elmhurst *(G-4396)*
Reynolds Tech Fabricators Inc .... E 315 437-0532
  East Syracuse *(G-4558)*
Rochester Overnight Pltg LLC .... D 585 328-4590
  Rochester *(G-14645)*
Silverman & Gorf Inc .... G 718 625-1309
  Brooklyn *(G-2558)*
US Electroplating Corp .... G 631 293-1998
  West Babylon *(G-16837)*

PLAYGROUND EQPT

Bears Management Group Inc .... G 585 624-5694
  Lima *(G-7443)*
Billy Beez Usa LLC .... F 315 741-5099
  Syracuse *(G-15869)*
Billy Beez Usa LLC .... F 646 606-2249
  New York *(G-9399)*
Billy Beez Usa LLC .... F 845 915-4709
  West Nyack *(G-16913)*
Eastern Jungle Gym Inc .... E 845 878-9800
  Carmel *(G-3399)*
Imagination Playground LLC .... G 212 463-0334
  New York *(G-10567)*

PLEATING & STITCHING FOR THE TRADE: Decorative & Novelty

A Trusted Name Inc .... F 716 326-7400
  Westfield *(G-17045)*

PLEATING & STITCHING FOR TRADE: Permanent Pleating/Pressing

Pleating Plus Ltd .... F 201 863-2991
  Orangeburg *(G-13240)*
Stanley Pleating Stitching Co .... E 718 392-2417
  Long Island City *(G-7886)*
Stylist Pleating Corp .... F 718 384-8181
  Brooklyn *(G-2617)*

PLEATING & STITCHING SVC

Acme Pleating & Fagoting Corp .... F 212 674-3737
  New York *(G-9018)*
Athletic Cap Co Inc .... E 718 398-1300
  Staten Island *(G-15641)*
Custom Patches Inc .... E 845 679-6320
  Woodstock *(G-17362)*
Milaaya Inc .... G 212 764-6386
  New York *(G-11265)*
Pass Em-Entries Inc .... F 718 392-0100
  Long Island City *(G-7835)*
Todd Walbridge .... G 585 254-3018
  Rochester *(G-14727)*

PLEATING & TUCKING FOR THE TRADE

Vogue Too Plting Stitching EMB .... F 212 354-1022
  New York *(G-12565)*

PLUGS: Electric

K & H Industries Inc .... F 716 312-0088
  Hamburg *(G-5930)*

PLUMBING & HEATING EQPT & SPLY, WHOL: Htg Eqpt/Panels, Solar

Vincent Genovese .... G 631 281-8170
  Mastic Beach *(G-8205)*

PLUMBING & HEATING EQPT & SPLY, WHOLESALE: Hydronic Htg Eqpt

Flushing Boiler & Welding Co .... G 718 463-1266
  Brooklyn *(G-1988)*

PLUMBING & HEATING EQPT & SPLYS WHOLESALERS

Bobrick Washroom Equipment Inc ...... D 518 877-7444
  Clifton Park *(G-3697)*

PLUMBING & HEATING EQPT & SPLYS, WHOL: Plumbing Fitting/Sply

Brodco Inc .... E 631 842-4477
  Lido Beach *(G-7440)*
Everflow Supplies Inc .... E 908 436-1100
  Brooklyn *(G-1940)*
Great American Industries Inc .... G 607 729-9331
  Vestal *(G-16449)*
Long Island Pipe Supply Inc .... E 516 222-8008
  Garden City *(G-5516)*
P E Guerin .... D 212 243-5270
  New York *(G-11548)*

PLUMBING & HEATING EQPT & SPLYS, WHOL: Plumbng/Heatng Valves

Flow-Safe Inc .... E 716 662-2585
  Orchard Park *(G-13270)*

PLUMBING & HEATING EQPT & SPLYS, WHOL: Water Purif Eqpt

Empire Division Inc .... D 315 476-6273
  Syracuse *(G-15936)*
Neptune Soft Water Inc .... F 315 446-5151
  Syracuse *(G-15997)*

PLUMBING & HEATING EQPT & SPLYS, WHOLESALE: Brass/Fittings

Coronet Parts Mfg Co Inc .... E 718 649-1750
  Brooklyn *(G-1805)*

PLUMBING & HEATING EQPT & SPLYS, WHOLESALE: Sanitary Ware

Porcelain Refinishing Corp .... F 516 352-4841
  Flushing *(G-5283)*

PLUMBING FIXTURES

ER Butler & Co Inc .... E 212 925-3565
  New York *(G-10055)*
G Sicuranza Ltd .... G 516 759-0259
  Glen Cove *(G-5616)*
L A S Replacement Parts Inc .... F 718 583-4700
  Bronx *(G-1376)*
Liberty Brass Turning Co Inc .... E 718 784-2911
  Westbury *(G-17005)*
Malyn Industrial Ceramics Inc .... G 716 741-1510
  Clarence Center *(G-3679)*
Martin Brass Works Inc .... G 718 523-3146
  Jamaica *(G-6928)*
P E Guerin .... D 212 243-5270
  New York *(G-11548)*

PLUMBING FIXTURES

Roccera LLC .... F 585 426-0887
  Rochester *(G-14632)*
Toto USA Inc .... G 917 237-0665
  New York *(G-12380)*
Toto USA Inc .... G 770 282-8686
  New York *(G-12381)*
Watermark Designs Holdings Ltd .... D 718 257-2800
  Brooklyn *(G-2745)*

PLUMBING FIXTURES: Brass, Incl Drain Cocks, Faucets/Spigots

A B S Brass Products Inc .... F 718 497-2115
  Brooklyn *(G-1532)*
Acme Parts Inc .... E 718 649-1750
  Brooklyn *(G-1556)*
Coronet Parts Mfg Co Inc .... E 718 649-1750
  Brooklyn *(G-1805)*
Coronet Parts Mfg Co Inc .... E 718 649-1750
  Brooklyn *(G-1806)*
Diamond Brass Corp .... G 718 418-3871
  Brooklyn *(G-1859)*
Jacknob International Ltd .... D 631 546-6560
  Hauppauge *(G-6101)*
Royal Line LLC .... F 800 516-7450
  Wantagh *(G-16563)*

PLUMBING FIXTURES: Plastic

An-Cor Industrial Plastics Inc .... D 716 695-3141
  North Tonawanda *(G-12954)*
Bow Industrial Corporation .... D 518 561-0190
  Champlain *(G-3538)*
Darman Manufacturing Coinc .... F 315 724-9632
  Utica *(G-16321)*
Gms Hicks Street Corporation .... E 718 858-1010
  Brooklyn *(G-2032)*
On Point Reps Inc .... G 518 258-2268
  Montgomery *(G-8599)*
Quality Enclosures Inc .... E 631 234-0115
  Central Islip *(G-3508)*

POINT OF SALE DEVICES

Hopp Companies Inc .... F 516 358-4170
  New Hyde Park *(G-8841)*
Kenney Manufacturing Displays .... F 631 231-5563
  Brentwood *(G-1188)*
Powa Technologies Inc .... F 347 344-7848
  New York *(G-11691)*

POLISHING SVC: Metals Or Formed Prdts

Barnes Metal Finishing Inc .... F 585 798-4817
  Medina *(G-8265)*
Control Electropolishing Corp .... F 718 858-6634
  Brooklyn *(G-1801)*

POLYESTERS

Perfect Poly Inc .... E 631 265-0539
  Nesconset *(G-8777)*
Terphane Inc .... D 585 657-5800
  Bloomfield *(G-991)*

POLYPROPYLENE RESINS

Exxonmobil Chemical Company .... C 315 966-1000
  Macedon *(G-7986)*

POLYTETRAFLUOROETHYLENE RESINS

Saint-Gobain Prfmce Plas Corp .... C 518 686-7301
  Hoosick Falls *(G-6545)*

POLYVINYL CHLORIDE RESINS

Adam Scott Designs Inc .... E 212 420-8866
  New York *(G-9024)*
Kent Chemical Corporation .... E 212 521-1700
  New York *(G-10838)*
Newmat Northeast Corp .... F 631 253-9277
  West Babylon *(G-16816)*

POPCORN & SUPPLIES WHOLESALERS

Terrells Potato Chip Co Inc .... D 315 437-2786
  Syracuse *(G-16057)*

PORCELAIN ENAMELED PRDTS & UTENSILS

Chamart Exclusives Inc .... G 914 345-3870
  Elmsford *(G-4740)*

POSTERS

Candid Worldwide LLC .... G 212 799-5300
  Long Island City *(G-7694)*
Clear Channel Outdoor Inc .... F 212 812-0000
  New York *(G-9641)*

POTTERY

Konstantinos Floral Decorators .... G 718 434-3603
  Brooklyn *(G-2180)*

POTTERY: Laboratory & Indl

Saint Gobain Grains & Powders .... A 716 731-8200
  Niagara Falls *(G-12870)*
Saint-Gbain Advnced Crmics LLC .... C 716 278-6066
  Niagara Falls *(G-12871)*

POULTRY & POULTRY PRDTS WHOLESALERS

Vineland Kosher Poultry Inc .... F 718 921-1347
  Brooklyn *(G-2728)*

POULTRY & SMALL GAME SLAUGHTERING & PROCESSING

Advanced Frozen Foods Inc .... E 516 333-6344
  Westbury *(G-16961)*
Campanellis Poultry Farm Inc .... G 845 482-2222
  Bethel *(G-860)*
Goya Foods Inc .... D 716 549-0076
  Angola *(G-380)*
Hoskie Co Inc .... D 718 628-8672
  Brooklyn *(G-2088)*
JW Consulting Inc .... G 845 325-7070
  Monroe *(G-8558)*
MB Food Processing Inc .... B 845 436-5001
  South Fallsburg *(G-15520)*
Murray Bresky Consultants Ltd .... B 845 436-5001
  South Fallsburg *(G-15521)*
Vineland Kosher Poultry Inc .... F 718 921-1347
  Brooklyn *(G-2728)*

POULTRY SLAUGHTERING & PROCESSING

Alle Processing Corp .... C 718 894-2000
  Maspeth *(G-8115)*
Hlw Acres LLC .... G 585 591-0795
  Attica *(G-473)*

POWDER PUFFS & MITTS

American Puff Corp .... D 516 379-1300
  Freeport *(G-5387)*
Penthouse Manufacturing Co Inc .... B 516 379-1300
  Freeport *(G-5418)*

POWDER: Metal

Buffalo Tungsten Inc .... D 716 759-6353
  Depew *(G-4251)*
Cws Powder Coatings Company LP .... G 845 398-2911
  Blauvelt *(G-970)*
Handy & Harman .... E 914 461-1300
  White Plains *(G-17118)*
Hje Company Inc .... G 518 792-8733
  Queensbury *(G-13999)*
Imerys Steelcasting Usa Inc .... D 716 278-1634
  Niagara Falls *(G-12835)*
Oerlikon Metco (us) Inc .... F 716 270-2228
  Amherst *(G-256)*
Reed Systems Ltd .... F 845 647-3660
  Ellenville *(G-4637)*
Tam Ceramics Group of Ny LLC .... D 716 278-9400
  Niagara Falls *(G-12880)*

POWDER: Silver

Ames Advanced Materials Corp .... D 518 792-5808
  South Glens Falls *(G-15522)*
Ames Goldsmith Corp .... E 518 792-7435
  Glens Falls *(G-5669)*

POWER GENERATORS

Ener-G Cogen LLC .... G 718 551-7170
  New York *(G-10035)*
Independent Field Svc LLC .... G 315 559-9243
  Syracuse *(G-15962)*
Intelligen Power Systems LLC .... G 212 750-0373
  Old Bethpage *(G-13129)*

K Road Moapa Solar LLC .... F 212 351-0535
  New York *(G-10795)*
Power Gneration Indus Engs Inc .... F 315 633-9389
  Bridgeport *(G-1235)*

POWER SPLY CONVERTERS: Static, Electronic Applications

Albatros North America Inc .... E 518 381-7100
  Ballston Spa *(G-590)*
Orbit International Corp .... D 631 435-8300
  Hauppauge *(G-6155)*
Recom Power Inc .... G 718 855-9713
  Brooklyn *(G-2483)*

POWER SUPPLIES: All Types, Static

3835 Lebron Rest Eqp & Sup Inc .... E 212 942-8258
  New York *(G-8973)*
Applied Concepts Inc .... E 315 696-6676
  Tully *(G-16273)*
Applied Power Systems Inc .... E 516 935-2230
  Hicksville *(G-6322)*
Arstan Products International .... E 516 433-1313
  Hicksville *(G-6324)*
BC Systems Inc .... E 631 751-9370
  Setauket *(G-15374)*
Behlman Electronics Inc .... G 631 435-0410
  Hauppauge *(G-6033)*
Espey Mfg & Electronics Corp .... E 518 245-4400
  Saratoga Springs *(G-15151)*
Hipotronics Inc .... C 845 279-8091
  Brewster *(G-1220)*
Idt Energy Inc .... E 877 887-6866
  Jamestown *(G-7002)*
Orbit International Corp .... C 631 435-8300
  Hauppauge *(G-6154)*
Ultravolt Inc .... D 631 471-4444
  Ronkonkoma *(G-14996)*
Walter G Legge Company Inc .... E 914 737-5040
  Peekskill *(G-13485)*

POWER SUPPLIES: Transformer, Electronic Type

Applied Power Systems Inc .... E 516 935-2230
  Hicksville *(G-6322)*
Bright Way Supply Inc .... F 718 833-2882
  Brooklyn *(G-1717)*
Hammond Manufacturing Co Inc .... F 716 630-7030
  Cheektowaga *(G-3573)*
Tdk-Lambda Americas Inc .... F 631 967-3000
  Hauppauge *(G-6207)*

POWER SWITCHING EQPT

Switching Power Inc .... D 631 981-7231
  Ronkonkoma *(G-14990)*

POWER TOOLS, HAND: Grinders, Portable, Electric Or Pneumatic

Dean Manufacturing Inc .... F 607 770-1300
  Vestal *(G-16446)*

POWER TOOLS, HAND: Hammers, Portable, Elec/Pneumatic, Chip

Rbhammers Corp .... F 845 353-5042
  Blauvelt *(G-973)*

POWER TRANSMISSION EQPT WHOLESALERS

Peerless-Winsmith Inc .... C 716 592-9311
  Springville *(G-15614)*
United Richter Electrical Mtrs .... F 716 855-1945
  Buffalo *(G-3235)*

POWER TRANSMISSION EQPT: Aircraft

Precision Gear Incorporated .... C 718 321-7200
  College Point *(G-3802)*

POWER TRANSMISSION EQPT: Mechanical

Babbitt Bearings Incorporated .... D 315 479-6603
  Syracuse *(G-15865)*
Borgwarner Morse TEC Inc .... C 607 257-6700
  Ithaca *(G-6828)*
Borgwarner Morse TEC Inc .... B 607 257-6700
  Ithaca *(G-6826)*

PRODUCT SECTION

BW Elliott Mfg Co LLC .... B 607 772-0404
  Binghamton *(G-900)*
Champlain Hudson Power Ex Inc .... G 518 465-0710
  Albany *(G-61)*
Cierra Industries Inc .... F 315 252-6630
  Auburn *(G-488)*
Designatronics Incorporated .... B 516 328-3300
  New Hyde Park *(G-8826)*
Eaw Electronic Systems Inc .... G 845 471-5290
  Poughkeepsie *(G-13897)*
Fait Usa Inc .... G 215 674-5310
  New York *(G-10131)*
Hudson Power Transmission Co .... G 718 622-3869
  Brooklyn *(G-2090)*
Huron TI & Cutter Grinding Co .... E 631 420-7000
  Farmingdale *(G-5008)*
Kaddis Manufacturing Corp .... G 585 624-3070
  Honeoye Falls *(G-6533)*
Ls Power Equity Partners LP .... G 212 615-3456
  New York *(G-11055)*
Maine Power Express LLC .... G 518 465-0710
  Albany *(G-99)*
Metallized Carbon Corporation .... C 914 941-3738
  Ossining *(G-13323)*
On Line Power Technologies .... G 914 968-4440
  Yonkers *(G-17470)*
Package One Inc .... D 518 344-5425
  Schenectady *(G-15285)*
Renold Holdings Inc .... G 716 326-3121
  Westfield *(G-17050)*
Renold Inc .... D 716 326-3121
  Westfield *(G-17051)*
Sepac Inc .... E 607 732-2030
  Elmira *(G-4700)*
Watson Bowman Acme Corp .... D 716 691-8162
  Amherst *(G-271)*

PRECAST TERRAZZO OR CONCRETE PRDTS

Accurate Precast .... F 718 345-2910
  Brooklyn *(G-1552)*
Coastal Pipeline Products Corp .... E 631 369-4000
  Calverton *(G-3288)*
Coral Cast LLC .... E 516 349-1300
  Plainview *(G-13592)*
Key Cast Stone Company Inc .... E 631 789-2145
  Amityville *(G-302)*
Northeast Concrete Pdts Inc .... F 518 563-0700
  Plattsburgh *(G-13681)*
Superior Aggregates Supply LLC .... E 516 333-2923
  Lindenhurst *(G-7488)*
Superior Walls Upstate NY Inc .... D 585 624-9390
  Lima *(G-7449)*
Superior Wlls of Hdson Vly Inc .... E 845 485-4033
  Poughkeepsie *(G-13937)*

PRECIOUS METALS

Handy & Harman .... E 914 461-1300
  White Plains *(G-17118)*

PRECIOUS METALS WHOLESALERS

Wallace Refiners Inc .... G 212 391-2649
  New York *(G-12582)*

PRECIOUS STONES & METALS, WHOLESALE

Jacoby Enterprises LLC .... G 718 435-0289
  Brooklyn *(G-2133)*
S Kashi & Sons Inc .... F 212 869-9393
  Great Neck *(G-5837)*

PRECIOUS STONES WHOLESALERS

Gumuchian Fils Ltd .... F 212 593-3118
  New York *(G-10383)*
Incon Gems Inc .... F 212 221-8560
  New York *(G-10583)*
Jim Wachtler Inc .... G 212 755-4367
  New York *(G-10734)*

PRERECORDED TAPE, CD & RECORD STORES: Video Discs/Tapes

Sony Broadband Entertainment .... F 212 833-6800
  New York *(G-12131)*

PRERECORDED TAPE, CD/RECORD STORES: Video Tapes, Prerecorded

Society For The Study .... G 212 822-8806
  New York *(G-12114)*

PRERECORDED TAPE, COMPACT DISC & RECORD STORES

Taste and See Entrmt Inc .... G 516 285-3010
  Valley Stream *(G-16429)*

PRESSED FIBER & MOLDED PULP PRDTS, EXC FOOD PRDTS

Avco Industries Inc .... F 631 851-1555
  Central Islip *(G-3486)*
Cascades Tissue Group - NY Inc .... C 518 238-1900
  Wynantskill *(G-17379)*
Interntnal Bus Cmmncations Inc .... E 516 352-4505
  New Hyde Park *(G-8842)*

PRESSES

Bars Precision Inc .... F 585 742-6380
  Fairport *(G-4846)*
Win Set Technologies LLC .... F 631 234-7077
  Centereach *(G-3474)*

PRIMARY METAL PRODUCTS

Bridge Components Inc .... G 716 731-1184
  Sanborn *(G-15113)*
Cintube Ltd .... F 518 324-3333
  Plattsburgh *(G-13659)*
New Project LLC .... G 718 788-3444
  Brooklyn *(G-2362)*
Specialty Fabricators .... E 631 256-6982
  Oakdale *(G-13062)*

PRINT CARTRIDGES: Laser & Other Computer Printers

Guttz Corporation of America .... F 914 591-9600
  Irvington *(G-6770)*
Hf Technologies LLC .... E 585 254-5030
  Hamlin *(G-5950)*
New York Cartridge Exchange .... G 212 840-2227
  New York *(G-11396)*
Northeast Toner Inc .... G 518 899-5545
  Ballston Lake *(G-585)*
Printer Components Inc .... G 585 924-5190
  Fairport *(G-4871)*
Qls Solutions Group Inc .... E 716 852-2203
  Buffalo *(G-3144)*
Recharge Net Inc .... G 585 546-1060
  Rochester *(G-14621)*
Smartoners Inc .... G 718 975-0197
  Brooklyn *(G-2572)*
Summit Technologies LLC .... E 631 590-1040
  Holbrook *(G-6475)*

PRINTED CIRCUIT BOARDS

A A Technology Inc .... E 631 913-0400
  Ronkonkoma *(G-14845)*
Ace Electronics Inc .... F 914 773-2000
  Hawthorne *(G-6242)*
Advance Circuit Technology Inc .... E 585 328-2000
  Rochester *(G-14175)*
Advance Micro Power Corp .... F 631 471-6157
  Ronkonkoma *(G-14852)*
Advanced Digital Info Corp .... E 607 266-4000
  Utica *(G-6816)*
Advanced Manufacturing Svc Inc .... E 631 676-5210
  Ronkonkoma *(G-14854)*
American Quality Technology .... F 607 777-9488
  Binghamton *(G-887)*
American Technical Ceramics .... B 631 622-4700
  Huntington Station *(G-6695)*
Ansen Corporation .... G 315 393-3573
  Ogdensburg *(G-13111)*
Ansen Corporation .... C 315 393-3573
  Ogdensburg *(G-13112)*
Bryit Group LLC .... F 631 563-6903
  Holbrook *(G-6433)*
Bsu Inc .... E 607 272-8100
  Ithaca *(G-6829)*
Buffalo Circuits Inc .... G 716 662-2113
  Orchard Park *(G-13256)*

PRINTERS' SVCS: Folding, Collating, Etc

C & D Assembly Inc .... E 607 898-4275
  Groton *(G-5897)*
C A M Graphics Co Inc .... E 631 842-3400
  Farmingdale *(G-4955)*
Chautauqua Circuits Inc .... G 716 366-5771
  Dunkirk *(G-4335)*
Cygnus Automation Inc .... E 631 981-0909
  Bohemia *(G-1047)*
Della Systems Inc .... E 631 580-0010
  Ronkonkoma *(G-14893)*
Falconer Electronics Inc .... D 716 665-4176
  Falconer *(G-4898)*
Geometric Circuits Inc .... D 631 249-0230
  Holbrook *(G-6448)*
Hazlow Electronics Inc .... E 585 325-5323
  Rochester *(G-14431)*
I3 Assemblies Inc .... G 607 238-7077
  Binghamton *(G-923)*
I3 Electronics Inc .... C 866 820-4820
  Endicott *(G-4811)*
IEC Electronics Corp .... B 315 331-7742
  Newark *(G-12732)*
IEC Electronics Wire Cable Inc .... D 585 924-9010
  Newark *(G-12733)*
Irtronics Instruments Inc .... F 914 693-6291
  Ardsley *(G-405)*
Isine Inc .... G 631 913-4400
  Ronkonkoma *(G-14914)*
Jabil Circuit Inc .... B 845 471-9237
  Poughkeepsie *(G-13908)*
Mpl Inc .... E 607 266-0480
  Ithaca *(G-6864)*
NEa Manufacturing Corp .... E 516 371-4200
  Inwood *(G-6763)*
Oakdale Industrial Elec Corp .... F 631 737-4090
  Ronkonkoma *(G-14957)*
Ormec Systems Corp .... E 585 385-3520
  Rochester *(G-14552)*
Park Electrochemical Corp .... C 631 465-3600
  Melville *(G-8347)*
Performance Technologies Inc .... D 585 256-0200
  Rochester *(G-14576)*
Procomponents Inc .... E 516 683-0909
  Westbury *(G-17023)*
Rce Manufacturing LLC .... G 631 856-9005
  Commack *(G-3839)*
Rochester Industrial Ctrl Inc .... D 315 524-4555
  Ontario *(G-13212)*
Rumsey Corp .... G 914 751-3640
  Yonkers *(G-17482)*
S K Circuits Inc .... F 703 376-8718
  Oneida *(G-13166)*
Sag Harbor Industries Inc .... E 631 725-0440
  Sag Harbor *(G-15080)*
Sanmina Corporation .... B 607 689-5000
  Owego *(G-13359)*
Sheltred Wkshp For Dsabled Inc .... C 607 722-2364
  Binghamton *(G-951)*
Sopark Corp .... C 716 822-0434
  Buffalo *(G-3191)*
Stetron International Inc .... F 716 854-3443
  Buffalo *(G-3197)*
Surf-Tech Manufacturing Corp .... F 631 589-1194
  Bohemia *(G-1138)*
Transistor Devices Inc .... E 631 471-7492
  Ronkonkoma *(G-14992)*
Windsor Technology LLC .... F 585 461-2500
  Rochester *(G-14764)*

PRINTERS & PLOTTERS

Blue Skies .... G 631 392-1140
  Deer Park *(G-4110)*
CNy Business Solutions .... G 315 733-5031
  Utica *(G-16312)*
Inner Workings Inc .... E 646 352-4394
  New York *(G-10601)*
Lexmark International Inc .... E 212 949-1090
  New York *(G-10980)*
Mdi Holdings LLC .... A 212 559-1127
  New York *(G-11203)*
Mg Imaging .... G 212 704-4073
  New York *(G-11245)*
Secuprint Inc .... F 585 341-3100
  Rochester *(G-14680)*
X Brand Editions .... G 718 482-7646
  Long Island City *(G-7927)*

PRINTERS' SVCS: Folding, Collating, Etc

JP Signs .... G 518 569-3907
  Chazy *(G-3562)*

Employee Codes: A=Over 500 employees, B=251-500
C=101-250, D=51-100, E=20-50, F=10-19, G=5-9

PRINTERS' SVCS: Folding, Collating, Etc

Shield Press Inc ....G....... 212 431-7489
  New York (G-12050)

PRINTERS: Computer

Control Logic Corporation ....G....... 607 965-6423
  West Burlington (G-16841)
Future Star Digatech..............................F....... 718 666-0350
  Brooklyn (G-2008)
Hf Technologies LLC...........................E....... 585 254-5030
  Hamlin (G-5950)
Tpg Printers Inc..................................B....... 607 273-5310
  Ithaca (G-6879)
Transact Technologies Inc ....D....... 607 257-8901
  Ithaca (G-6880)

PRINTERS: Magnetic Ink, Bar Code

Advanced Barcode Technology ....F....... 516 570-8100
  Great Neck (G-5784)
CPW Direct Mail Group LLC................E....... 631 588-6565
  Farmingdale (G-4964)
Jadak Technologies Inc......................D....... 315 701-0678
  North Syracuse (G-12950)
Paxar Corporation................................E....... 845 398-3229
  Orangeburg (G-13238)

PRINTING & BINDING: Book Music

Bridge Enterprises Inc........................G....... 718 625-6622
  Brooklyn (G-1715)

PRINTING & BINDING: Books

Book1one LLC...................................G....... 585 458-2101
  Rochester (G-14242)
Hamilton Printing Company Inc ....C....... 518 732-2161
  Troy (G-16238)
Logical Operations Inc.........................C....... 585 350-7000
  Rochester (G-14482)
Syracuse Cultural Workers Prj ....F....... 315 474-1132
  Syracuse (G-16051)

PRINTING & BINDING: Pamphlets

Bmg Printing and Promotion LLC ....G....... 631 231-9200
  Bohemia (G-1026)

PRINTING & EMBOSSING: Plastic Fabric Articles

Acorn Products Corp............................F....... 315 894-4868
  Ilion (G-6739)
Mountain T-Shirts Inc ....G....... 518 943-4533
  Catskill (G-3432)
Patrick Rohan...................................G....... 718 781-2573
  Monticello (G-8607)
Starline Usa Inc..................................C....... 716 773-0100
  Grand Island (G-5770)

PRINTING & ENGRAVING: Card, Exc Greeting

Abigal Press Inc ....D....... 718 641-5350
  Ozone Park (G-13375)
New York Sample Card Co Inc............E....... 212 242-1242
  New York (G-11407)
Printery ....G....... 516 922-3250
  Oyster Bay (G-13373)
Proof 7 Ltd ....F....... 212 680-1843
  New York (G-11735)

PRINTING & ENGRAVING: Financial Notes & Certificates

Doremus FP LLC..................................E....... 212 366-3800
  New York (G-9909)
Merrill New York Company Inc ....C....... 212 229-6500
  New York (G-11235)
Superior Print On Demand..................G....... 607 240-5231
  Vestal (G-16454)
Table Tops Paper Corp ....G....... 718 598-7832
  Brooklyn (G-2642)

PRINTING & ENGRAVING: Invitation & Stationery

Batavia Press LLC ....E....... 585 343-4429
  Batavia (G-624)
Jon Lyn Ink Inc ....G....... 516 546-2312
  Merrick (G-8386)

Lion In The Sun Park Slope Ltd...........G....... 718 369-4006
  Brooklyn (G-2230)
Sammba Printing Inc ....G....... 516 944-4449
  Port Washington (G-13862)

PRINTING & ENGRAVING: Plateless

K & B Stamping Co Inc......................G....... 914 664-8555
  Mount Vernon (G-8696)

PRINTING & ENGRAVING: Poster & Decal

BDR Creative Concepts Inc ....F....... 516 942-7768
  Farmingdale (G-4951)

PRINTING & STAMPING: Fabric Articles

Casual Friday Inc................................F....... 585 544-9470
  Rochester (G-14262)
Hollywood Advertising Banners............E....... 631 842-3000
  Copiague (G-3906)

PRINTING & WRITING PAPER WHOLESALERS

Argo Lithographers Inc ....E....... 718 729-2700
  Long Island City (G-7669)
Shipmtes/Printmates Holdg Corp........D....... 518 370-1158
  Scotia (G-15330)
Table Tops Paper Corp ....G....... 718 598-7832
  Brooklyn (G-2642)

PRINTING EQPT & SUPPLIES: Illustration & Poster Woodcuts

Patrick Rohan...................................G....... 718 781-2573
  Monticello (G-8607)

PRINTING INKS WHOLESALERS

I N K T Inc ....F....... 212 957-2700
  New York (G-10540)
Interntnl Publcatns Media Grup ....G....... 917 604-9602
  New York (G-10640)
Won & Lee Inc ....E....... 516 222-0712
  Garden City (G-5538)

PRINTING MACHINERY

A-Mark Machinery Corp......................F....... 631 643-6300
  West Babylon (G-16762)
Anand Printing Machinery Inc ....G....... 631 667-3079
  Deer Park (G-4098)
Awt Supply Corp ....E....... 516 437-9105
  Elmont (G-4717)
Bartizan Data Systems LLC ....E....... 914 965-7977
  Yonkers (G-17419)
Castleragh Printcraft Inc.....................D....... 516 623-1728
  Freeport (G-5392)
Copier & Printer Supply LLC ....G....... 585 329-1077
  Mendon (G-8380)
Daige Products Inc ....F....... 516 621-2100
  Albertson (G-153)
Davis International Inc.........................G....... 585 421-8175
  Fairport (G-4854)
Halm Industries Co Inc.......................D....... 516 676-6700
  Glen Head (G-5632)
Halm Instrument Co Inc......................D....... 516 676-6700
  Glen Head (G-5633)
Hodgins Engraving Co Inc..................D....... 585 343-4444
  Batavia (G-639)
Innotech Graphic Eqp Corp ....G....... 845 268-6900
  Valley Cottage (G-16379)
International Imaging Mtls Inc ....B....... 716 691-6333
  Amherst (G-246)
Mekatronics Incorporated ....E....... 516 883-6805
  Port Washington (G-13844)
Micro Powders Inc ....E....... 914 332-6400
  Tarrytown (G-16097)
Mount Vernon Machine Inc ....E....... 845 268-9400
  Valley Cottage (G-16382)
Newport Business Solutions Inc...........F....... 631 319-6129
  Bohemia (G-1110)
Package Print Technologies ....E....... 716 871-9905
  Buffalo (G-3110)
Paxar Corporation................................E....... 845 398-3229
  Orangeburg (G-13238)
Perretta Graphics Corp ....E....... 845 473-0550
  Poughkeepsie (G-13925)
Prim Hall Enterprises Inc ....F....... 518 561-7408
  Plattsburgh (G-13691)

Southern Graphic Systems LLC..........E....... 315 695-7079
  Phoenix (G-13544)
Specilty Bus Mchs Holdings LLC ....E....... 212 587-9600
  New York (G-12154)
Sterling Toggle Inc ....F....... 631 491-0500
  West Babylon (G-16832)
Super Web Inc ....E....... 631 643-9100
  West Babylon (G-16834)
Universal Metal Fabricators ....F....... 845 331-8248
  Kingston (G-7221)
Vits International Inc...........................E....... 845 353-5000
  Blauvelt (G-979)
Voodoo Manufacturing Inc..................G....... 646 893-8366
  Brooklyn (G-2736)
Woerner Industries Inc ....E....... 585 436-1934
  Rochester (G-14765)

PRINTING MACHINERY, EQPT & SPLYS: Wholesalers

Boxcar Press Incorporated ....E....... 315 473-0930
  Syracuse (G-15873)
Davis International Inc.........................G....... 585 421-8175
  Fairport (G-4854)
Info Label Inc......................................F....... 518 664-0791
  Halfmoon (G-5911)
Super Web Inc ....E....... 631 643-9100
  West Babylon (G-16834)

PRINTING TRADES MACHINERY & EQPT REPAIR SVCS

Interntnal Strpping Diecutting ....G....... 718 383-7720
  Brooklyn (G-2113)
Jack L Popkin & Co Inc......................G....... 718 361-6700
  Kew Gardens (G-7163)

PRINTING, COMMERCIAL Newspapers, NEC

Buffalo Newspress Inc ....C....... 716 852-1600
  Buffalo (G-2858)
Expedi-Printing Inc ....C....... 516 513-0919
  Great Neck (G-5807)
Kim Jae Printing Co Inc......................G....... 212 691-6289
  Roslyn Heights (G-15028)
Kurrier Inc..G....... 718 389-3018
  Brooklyn (G-2181)
Republican Registrar Inc.....................G....... 315 497-1551
  Moravia (G-8617)
Stellar Printing Inc..............................D....... 718 361-1600
  Long Island City (G-7890)
Webster Printing Corporation...............F....... 585 671-1533
  Webster (G-16742)

PRINTING, COMMERCIAL: Announcements, NEC

Kates Paperie Ltd ....G....... 212 966-3904
  New York (G-10817)

PRINTING, COMMERCIAL: Bags, Plastic, NEC

Bags Unlimited Inc..............................E....... 585 436-6282
  Rochester (G-14221)
Dynamic Packaging Inc.......................F....... 718 388-0800
  Brooklyn (G-1887)
Flexo Transparent Inc.........................C....... 716 825-7710
  Buffalo (G-2951)

PRINTING, COMMERCIAL: Business Forms, NEC

Bfc Print Network Inc ....G....... 716 838-4532
  Amherst (G-228)
Endeavor Printing LLC ....G....... 718 570-2720
  Long Island City (G-7731)
General Business Supply Inc ....D....... 518 720-3939
  Watervliet (G-16685)
Kinaneco Inc...E....... 315 468-6201
  Syracuse (G-15974)
Lifeforms Printing.................................G....... 716 685-4500
  Depew (G-4263)
McAuliffe Paper Inc.............................E....... 315 453-2222
  Liverpool (G-7534)
Select-A-Form Inc...............................D....... 631 981-3076
  Holbrook (G-6470)
Short Run Forms Inc ....D....... 631 567-7171
  Bohemia (G-1133)
United Print Group Inc.........................F....... 718 392-4242
  Long Island City (G-7908)

PRODUCT SECTION

PRINTING, COMMERCIAL: Screen

PRINTING, COMMERCIAL: Calendars, NEC

Won & Lee Inc .... E 516 222-0712
   Garden City *(G-5538)*

PRINTING, COMMERCIAL: Cards, Visiting, Incl Business, NEC

Create-A-Card Inc .... G 631 584-2273
   Saint James *(G-15087)*

PRINTING, COMMERCIAL: Certificates, Security, NEC

De La Rue North America Inc .... G 518 463-7621
   Albany *(G-72)*

PRINTING, COMMERCIAL: Circulars, NEC

Linda Campbell .... G 718 994-4026
   Bronx *(G-1382)*

PRINTING, COMMERCIAL: Decals, NEC

Love Unlimited NY Inc .... E 718 359-8500
   Westbury *(G-17008)*
Seri Systems Inc .... E 585 272-5515
   Rochester *(G-14682)*

PRINTING, COMMERCIAL: Envelopes, NEC

Argo Envelope Corp .... D 718 729-2700
   Long Island City *(G-7667)*
Design Distributors Inc .... D 631 242-2000
   Deer Park *(G-4130)*
Diversified Envelope Ltd .... F 585 615-4697
   Rochester *(G-14312)*
Dupli Graphics Corporation .... G 315 422-4732
   Syracuse *(G-15926)*
Ehs Group LLC .... G 914 937-6162
   Port Chester *(G-13744)*
Federal Envelope Inc .... F 212 243-8380
   New York *(G-10148)*
Hudson Envelope Corporation .... E 212 473-6666
   New York *(G-10525)*
Matt Industries Inc .... C 315 472-1316
   Syracuse *(G-15984)*
Poly-Flex Corp .... F 631 586-9500
   Edgewood *(G-4607)*
Precision Envelope Co Inc .... G 631 694-3990
   Farmingdale *(G-5086)*
Sentinel Printing Inc .... G 516 334-7400
   Westbury *(G-17026)*
Shipman Printing Inds Inc .... E 716 504-7700
   Niagara Falls *(G-12876)*

PRINTING, COMMERCIAL: Imprinting

Burr & Son Inc .... G 315 446-1550
   Syracuse *(G-15877)*
Casual Home Worldwide Inc .... G 631 789-2999
   Amityville *(G-280)*
Genesis One Unlimited .... G 516 208-5863
   West Hempstead *(G-16854)*
Issacs Yisroel .... G 718 851-7430
   Brooklyn *(G-2117)*
Total Solution Graphics Inc .... G 718 706-1540
   Long Island City *(G-7903)*

PRINTING, COMMERCIAL: Invitations, NEC

Alpine Business Group Inc .... G 212 989-4198
   New York *(G-9102)*
Color Card LLC .... F 631 232-1300
   Central Islip *(G-3491)*

PRINTING, COMMERCIAL: Labels & Seals, NEC

American Casting and Mfg Corp .... D 800 342-0333
   Plainview *(G-13581)*
Cenveo Inc .... F 716 686-0100
   Depew *(G-4252)*
Classic Labels Inc .... E 631 467-2300
   Patchogue *(G-13417)*
Crisray Printing Corp .... E 631 293-3770
   Farmingdale *(G-4965)*
General Trade Mark La .... E 718 979-7261
   Staten Island *(G-15677)*
Greenbush Tape & Label Inc .... E 518 465-2389
   Albany *(G-83)*
Hammer Packaging Corp .... B 585 424-3880
   West Henrietta *(G-16881)*
Info Label Inc .... F 518 664-0791
   Halfmoon *(G-5911)*
Janco Press Inc .... F 631 563-3003
   Bohemia *(G-1081)*
Kroger Packaging Inc .... E 631 249-6690
   Farmingdale *(G-5029)*
Labels Inter-Global Inc .... F 212 398-0006
   New York *(G-10912)*
Niagara Label Company Inc .... F 716 542-3000
   Akron *(G-25)*
Precision Label Corporation .... F 631 270-4490
   Farmingdale *(G-5087)*
Print Pack Inc .... C 404 460-7000
   Farmingdale *(G-5088)*
Tapemaker Sales Co Inc .... G 516 333-0592
   Westbury *(G-17029)*
Triangle Label Tag Inc .... G 718 875-3030
   Brooklyn *(G-2679)*

PRINTING, COMMERCIAL: Letterpress & Screen

Drns Corp .... F 718 369-4530
   Brooklyn *(G-1881)*
Farthing Press Inc .... G 716 852-4674
   Buffalo *(G-2945)*
L I C Screen Printing Inc .... E 516 546-7289
   Merrick *(G-8387)*
Quist Industries Ltd .... F 718 243-2800
   Brooklyn *(G-2468)*
Regal Screen Printing Intl .... G 845 356-8181
   Spring Valley *(G-15601)*

PRINTING, COMMERCIAL: Literature, Advertising, NEC

A M & J Digital .... G 518 434-2579
   Menands *(G-8363)*
Bizbash Media Inc .... E 646 638-3600
   New York *(G-9406)*
Grado Group Inc .... G 718 556-4200
   Staten Island *(G-15680)*
Landlord Guard Inc .... F 212 695-6505
   New York *(G-10924)*
Nomad Editions LLC .... F 212 918-0992
   Bronxville *(G-1502)*
North American DF Inc .... G 718 698-2500
   Staten Island *(G-15711)*

PRINTING, COMMERCIAL: Magazines, NEC

Aspect Printing Inc .... E 347 789-4284
   Brooklyn *(G-1640)*
Hearst Corporation .... B 212 767-5800
   New York *(G-10441)*
L & M Uniserv Corp .... G 718 854-3700
   Brooklyn *(G-2185)*
R D Manufacturing Corp .... G 914 238-1000
   Pleasantville *(G-13716)*

PRINTING, COMMERCIAL: Periodicals, NEC

Willis Mc Donald Co Inc .... F 212 366-1526
   New York *(G-12638)*

PRINTING, COMMERCIAL: Post Cards, Picture, NEC

4 Over 4com Inc .... G 718 932-2700
   Astoria *(G-431)*

PRINTING, COMMERCIAL: Promotional

A & P Master Images .... F 315 793-1934
   Utica *(G-16304)*
Bobley-Harmann Corporation .... G 516 433-3800
   Ronkonkoma *(G-14880)*
Cooper & Clement Inc .... E 315 454-8135
   Syracuse *(G-15907)*
Excell Print & Promotions Inc .... G 914 437-8668
   White Plains *(G-17107)*
Fulcrum Promotions & Prtg LLC .... G 203 909-6362
   New York *(G-10221)*
Gary Stock Corporation .... G 914 276-2700
   Croton Falls *(G-4061)*
Medallion Associates Inc .... E 212 929-9130
   New York *(G-11207)*
PDQ Shipping Services .... G 845 255-5500
   New Paltz *(G-8877)*
Printech Business Systems Inc .... F 212 290-2542
   New York *(G-11720)*

Scancorp Inc .... F 315 454-5596
   Syracuse *(G-16032)*
Swift Multigraphics LLC .... G 585 442-8000
   Rochester *(G-14709)*
Syracuse Letter Company Inc .... F 315 476-8328
   Bridgeport *(G-1237)*
Xpress Printing Inc .... G 516 605-1000
   Plainview *(G-13647)*

PRINTING, COMMERCIAL: Publications

Advance Finance Group LLC .... D 212 630-5900
   New York *(G-9035)*
Barnett Paul Inc .... E 212 673-3250
   New York *(G-9322)*
Beis Moshiach Inc .... E 718 778-8000
   Brooklyn *(G-1679)*
Check-O-Matic Inc .... G 845 781-7675
   Monroe *(G-8552)*
Dental Tribune America LLC .... F 212 244-7181
   New York *(G-9848)*
Graphic Printing .... G 718 701-4433
   Bronx *(G-1348)*
Graphics 247 Corp .... G 718 729-2470
   Long Island City *(G-7753)*
Merchandiser Inc .... G 315 462-6411
   Clifton Springs *(G-3714)*
New York Christan Times Inc .... G 718 638-6397
   Brooklyn *(G-2363)*
Nys Nyu-Cntr Intl Cooperation .... E 212 998-3680
   New York *(G-11487)*
River & Sound Publication LLC .... G 631 225-7100
   Copiague *(G-3923)*
Sephardic Yellow Pages .... E 718 998-0299
   Brooklyn *(G-2543)*

PRINTING, COMMERCIAL: Screen

A Tradition of Excellence Inc .... G 845 638-4595
   New City *(G-8781)*
Active World Solutions Inc .... G 718 922-9404
   Brooklyn *(G-1559)*
Adco Innvtive Prmtnal Pdts Inc .... G 716 805-1076
   East Aurora *(G-4364)*
Advanced Graphics Company .... F 607 692-7875
   Whitney Point *(G-17219)*
Albert Siy .... G 718 359-0389
   Flushing *(G-5224)*
Arca Ink .... E 518 798-0100
   Queensbury *(G-13991)*
Arena Graphics Inc .... G 516 767-5108
   Port Washington *(G-13801)*
Atlantic Coast Embroidery Inc .... G 631 283-2175
   Southampton *(G-15539)*
Barnaby Prints Inc .... F 845 477-2501
   Greenwood Lake *(G-5896)*
Bidpress LLC .... G 267 973-8876
   New York *(G-9389)*
C & C Athletic Inc .... G 845 713-4670
   Walden *(G-16531)*
Control Research Inc .... G 631 225-1111
   Amityville *(G-282)*
Copy Color Inc .... F 212 889-6202
   New York *(G-9720)*
Custom Sportswear Corp .... G 914 666-9200
   Bedford Hills *(G-800)*
D B F Associates .... G 718 328-0005
   Bronx *(G-1307)*
Dkm Sales LLC .... E 716 893-7777
   Buffalo *(G-2916)*
Efs Designs .... G 718 852-9511
   Brooklyn *(G-1906)*
Freeport Screen & Stamping .... E 516 379-0330
   Freeport *(G-5401)*
Fresh Prints LLC .... E 917 826-2752
   New York *(G-10210)*
Gould J Perfect Screen Prtrs .... F 607 272-0099
   Ithaca *(G-6844)*
Graph-Tex Inc .... F 607 756-7791
   Cortland *(G-4027)*
Graph-Tex Inc .... F 607 756-1875
   Cortland *(G-4028)*
Graphics Plus Printing Inc .... E 607 299-0500
   Cortland *(G-4029)*
Gruber Display Co Inc .... F 718 882-8220
   Bronx *(G-1349)*
Handone Studios Inc .... G 585 421-8175
   Fairport *(G-4857)*
Hanson Sign & Screen Process .... F 716 484-8564
   Falconer *(G-4901)*
Herrmann Group LLC .... G 716 876-9798
   Kenmore *(G-7148)*

Employee Codes: A=Over 500 employees, B=251-500
C=101-250, D=51-100, E=20-50, F=10-19, G=5-9

PRINTING, COMMERCIAL: Screen

Human Technologies Corporation ....F 315 735-3532
  Utica *(G-16340)*
Island Silkscreen Inc ....G 631 757-4567
  East Northport *(G-4437)*
J Kendall LLC ....G 646 739-4956
  Yonkers *(G-17457)*
J M L Productions Inc ....D 718 643-1674
  Brooklyn *(G-2126)*
J N White Associates Inc ....D 585 237-5191
  Perry *(G-13524)*
Kenmar Shirts Inc ....E 718 824-3880
  Bronx *(G-1371)*
Knucklehead Embroidery Inc ....G 607 797-2725
  Johnson City *(G-7098)*
Logomax Inc ....G 631 420-0484
  Farmingdale *(G-5036)*
Loremanss Embroidery Engrav ....G 518 834-9205
  Keeseville *(G-7139)*
Mastercraft Decorators Inc ....E 585 223-5150
  Fairport *(G-4863)*
Mastro Graphic Arts Inc ....E 585 436-7570
  Rochester *(G-14499)*
Matthew-Lee Corporation ....F 631 226-0100
  Lindenhurst *(G-7471)*
Metro Creative Graphics Inc ....E 212 947-5100
  New York *(G-11241)*
Mixture Screen Printing ....G 845 561-2857
  Newburgh *(G-12767)*
Mv Corp Inc ....C 631 273-8020
  Bay Shore *(G-720)*
New Art Signs Co Inc ....G 718 443-0900
  Glen Head *(G-5637)*
Northwind Graphics ....G 518 899-9651
  Ballston Spa *(G-605)*
One In A Million Inc ....G 516 829-1111
  Valley Stream *(G-16417)*
Paratore Signs Inc ....G 315 455-5551
  Syracuse *(G-16010)*
PDM Studios Inc ....G 716 694-8337
  Tonawanda *(G-16192)*
Personal Graphics Corporation ....G 315 853-3421
  Westmoreland *(G-17063)*
Peter Papastrat ....G 607 723-8112
  Binghamton *(G-942)*
Pierrepont Visual Graphics ....G 585 305-9672
  Rochester *(G-14585)*
Print Shoppe ....G 315 792-9585
  Utica *(G-16356)*
Rainbow Lettering ....G 607 732-5751
  Elmira *(G-4699)*
Richs Stiches EMB Screenprint ....G 845 621-2175
  Mahopac *(G-8000)*
Round Top Knit & Screening ....G 518 622-3600
  Round Top *(G-15040)*
Royal Tees Inc ....G 845 357-9448
  Suffern *(G-15800)*
RR Donnelley & Sons Company ....D 518 438-9722
  Albany *(G-129)*
Sand Hill Industries Inc ....G 518 885-7991
  Ballston Spa *(G-608)*
Screen The World Inc ....F 631 475-0023
  Holtsville *(G-6508)*
Shore Line Monogramming Inc ....F 914 698-8000
  Mamaroneck *(G-8047)*
Shykat Promotions ....G 866 574-2757
  Forestville *(G-5336)*
Sign Shop Inc ....G 631 226-4145
  Copiague *(G-3928)*
Silk Screen Art Inc ....F 518 762-8423
  Johnstown *(G-7126)*
Spst Inc ....G 607 798-6952
  Vestal *(G-16453)*
Stromberg Brand Corporation ....F 914 739-7410
  Valley Cottage *(G-16391)*
T L F Graphics Inc ....D 585 272-5500
  Rochester *(G-14716)*
Tara Rific Screen Printing Inc ....G 718 583-6864
  Bronx *(G-1472)*
Ter-El Engraving Co Inc ....G 315 455-5597
  Syracuse *(G-16056)*
Todd Walbridge ....G 585 254-3018
  Rochester *(G-14727)*
U All Inc ....E 518 438-2558
  Albany *(G-144)*
Universal Screening Associates ....F 718 232-2744
  Brooklyn *(G-2708)*
Unlimited Ink Inc ....G 631 582-0696
  Hauppauge *(G-6221)*
Viking Athletics Ltd ....E 631 957-8000
  Lindenhurst *(G-7492)*
Voss Signs LLC ....E 315 682-6418
  Manlius *(G-8076)*
Zacks Enterprises Inc ....E 800 366-4924
  Orangeburg *(G-13248)*

PRINTING, COMMERCIAL: Stamps, Trading, NEC

Ashton-Potter USA Ltd ....C 716 633-2000
  Williamsville *(G-17233)*

PRINTING, COMMERCIAL: Stationery, NEC

Hart Reproduction Services ....G 212 704-0556
  New York *(G-10423)*

PRINTING, COMMERCIAL: Tags, NEC

Actioncraft Products Inc ....G 516 883-6423
  Port Washington *(G-13795)*
Industrial Test Eqp Co Inc ....E 516 883-6423
  Port Washington *(G-13824)*
Itc Mfg Group Inc ....F 212 684-3696
  New York *(G-10669)*

PRINTING, LITHOGRAPHIC: Advertising Posters

First Displays Inc ....F 347 642-5972
  Long Island City *(G-7742)*
V C N Group Ltd Inc ....G 516 223-4812
  North Baldwin *(G-12911)*

PRINTING, LITHOGRAPHIC: Calendars

Redi Records Payroll ....F 718 854-6990
  Brooklyn *(G-2486)*

PRINTING, LITHOGRAPHIC: Color

ABC Check Printing Corp ....F 718 855-4702
  Brooklyn *(G-1546)*
Chakra Communications Inc ....E 716 505-7300
  Lancaster *(G-7309)*
Crawford Print Shop Inc ....G 607 359-4970
  Addison *(G-5)*
Create-A-Card Inc ....G 631 584-2273
  Saint James *(G-15087)*
Digital United Color Prtg Inc ....F 845 986-9846
  Warwick *(G-16588)*
E & J Offset Inc ....G 718 663-8850
  Mount Vernon *(G-8680)*
Industrial Color Inc ....G 212 334-4667
  New York *(G-10591)*
Print Bear LLC ....G 518 703-6098
  New York *(G-11715)*
Raith America Inc ....E 518 874-3000
  Troy *(G-16250)*
Select-A-Form Inc ....D 631 981-3076
  Holbrook *(G-6470)*
Spectrum Prtg Lithography Inc ....F 212 255-3131
  New York *(G-12158)*

PRINTING, LITHOGRAPHIC: Decals

Aro-Graph Corporation ....G 315 463-8693
  Syracuse *(G-15857)*
Decal Makers Inc ....E 516 221-7200
  Bellmore *(G-817)*
Decal Techniques Inc ....G 631 491-1800
  Bay Shore *(G-692)*
Paper House Productions Inc ....E 845 246-7261
  Saugerties *(G-15190)*

PRINTING, LITHOGRAPHIC: Fashion Plates

Chan Luu LLC ....E 212 398-3163
  New York *(G-9577)*

PRINTING, LITHOGRAPHIC: Forms & Cards, Business

Batavia Press LLC ....E 585 343-4429
  Batavia *(G-624)*
Color Card LLC ....F 631 232-1300
  Central Islip *(G-3491)*
Perfect Forms and Systems Inc ....F 631 462-1100
  Smithtown *(G-15494)*
Webb-Mason Inc ....E 716 276-8792
  Buffalo *(G-3250)*

PRINTING, LITHOGRAPHIC: Forms, Business

Precision Envelope Co Inc ....G 631 694-3990
  Farmingdale *(G-5086)*

PRINTING, LITHOGRAPHIC: Letters, Circular Or Form

F & D Services Inc ....F 718 984-1635
  Staten Island *(G-15672)*

PRINTING, LITHOGRAPHIC: Menus

Ready Check Glo Inc ....G 516 547-1849
  East Northport *(G-4444)*

PRINTING, LITHOGRAPHIC: Offset & photolithographic printing

Ace Printing & Publishing Inc ....F 718 939-0040
  Flushing *(G-5221)*
Distinctive Printing Inc ....G 212 727-3000
  New York *(G-9886)*
G & P Printing Inc ....G 212 274-8092
  New York *(G-10229)*
Iron Horse Graphics Ltd ....G 631 537-3400
  Bridgehampton *(G-1234)*
Kaymil Printing Company Inc ....G 212 594-3718
  New York *(G-10822)*
Mdi Holdings LLC ....A 212 559-1127
  New York *(G-11203)*
Printing Sales Group Limited ....E 718 258-8860
  Brooklyn *(G-2449)*
Progressive Color Graphics ....E 212 292-8787
  Great Neck *(G-5834)*
Remsen Graphics Corp ....G 718 643-7500
  Brooklyn *(G-2491)*
Rgm Signs Inc ....G 718 442-0598
  Staten Island *(G-15732)*
Superior Print On Demand ....G 607 240-5231
  Vestal *(G-16454)*

PRINTING, LITHOGRAPHIC: On Metal

A I P Printing & Stationers ....G 631 929-5529
  Wading River *(G-16522)*
Avon Reproductions Inc ....E 631 273-2400
  Hauppauge *(G-6031)*
Challenge Graphics Svcs Inc ....E 631 586-0171
  Deer Park *(G-4115)*
Cherry Lane Lithographing Corp ....E 516 293-9294
  Plainview *(G-13587)*
David Helsing ....G 607 796-2681
  Horseheads *(G-6573)*
Denton Advertising Inc ....F 631 586-4333
  Bohemia *(G-1055)*
Graphic Artisan Ltd ....G 845 368-1700
  Suffern *(G-15790)*
Hks Printing Company Inc ....F 212 675-2529
  New York *(G-10487)*
Mansfield Press Inc ....F 212 265-5411
  New York *(G-11141)*
Messenger Press ....G 518 885-9231
  Ballston Spa *(G-603)*
Seneca West Printing Inc ....G 716 675-8010
  West Seneca *(G-16954)*

PRINTING, LITHOGRAPHIC: Periodicals

Quantum Color Inc ....F 716 283-8700
  Niagara Falls *(G-12865)*

PRINTING, LITHOGRAPHIC: Post Cards, Picture

Anne Taintor Inc ....G 718 483-9312
  Brooklyn *(G-1613)*

PRINTING, LITHOGRAPHIC: Promotional

21st Century Fox America Inc ....D 212 852-7000
  New York *(G-8967)*
China Imprint LLC ....G 585 563-3391
  Rochester *(G-14274)*
Gmp LLC ....D 914 939-0571
  Port Chester *(G-13747)*
In-Step Marketing Inc ....F 212 797-3450
  New York *(G-10579)*
R & L Press Inc ....G 718 447-8557
  Staten Island *(G-15726)*

PRODUCT SECTION

PRINTING: Commercial, NEC

Source One Promotional Product ....G....... 516 208-6996
  Merrick (G-8393)

PRINTING, LITHOGRAPHIC: Publications

Canyon Publishing Inc ....F....... 212 334-0227
  New York (G-9516)
Hudson Park Press Inc ....G....... 212 929-8898
  New York (G-10526)
Post Road ....F....... 203 545-2122
  New York (G-11690)
Print By Premier LLC ....G....... 212 947-1365
  New York (G-11716)

PRINTING, LITHOGRAPHIC: Tags

Kwik Ticket Inc ....F....... 718 421-3800
  Brooklyn (G-2183)
Paxar Corporation ....E....... 845 398-3229
  Orangeburg (G-13238)

PRINTING, LITHOGRAPHIC: Tickets

Worldwide Ticket Craft ....D....... 516 538-6200
  Merrick (G-8394)

PRINTING, LITHOGRAPHIC: Transfers, Decalcomania Or Dry

Royal Tees Inc ....G....... 845 357-9448
  Suffern (G-15800)

PRINTING: Books

Cct Inc ....G....... 212 532-3355
  New York (G-9552)
Kravitz Design Inc ....G....... 212 625-1644
  New York (G-10889)
North Country Books Inc ....G....... 315 735-4877
  Utica (G-16352)
Twp America Inc ....G....... 212 274-8090
  New York (G-12435)
Vicks Lithograph & Prtg Corp ....C....... 315 272-2401
  Yorkville (G-17527)

PRINTING: Books

450 Ridge St Inc ....G....... 716 754-2789
  Lewiston (G-7432)
B-Squared Inc ....E....... 212 777-2044
  New York (G-9296)
Bedford Freeman & Worth ....C....... 212 576-9400
  New York (G-9342)
Centrisource Inc ....G....... 716 871-1105
  Tonawanda (G-16152)
E Graphics Corporation ....G....... 718 486-9767
  Brooklyn (G-1892)
Electronic Printing Inc ....G....... 631 218-2200
  Bohemia (G-1066)
Experiment LLC ....G....... 212 889-1659
  New York (G-10108)
Flare Multicopy Corp ....E....... 718 258-8860
  Brooklyn (G-1982)
Hachette Book Group USA Inc ....E....... 212 364-1200
  New York (G-10392)
Hudson Valley Paper Works Inc ....F....... 845 569-8883
  Newburgh (G-12764)
In-House Inc ....F....... 718 445-9007
  College Point (G-3787)
Literary Classics of US ....F....... 212 308-3560
  New York (G-11008)
Printing Factory LLC ....F....... 718 451-0500
  Brooklyn (G-2447)
Promotional Sales Books LLC ....G....... 212 675-0364
  New York (G-11731)
R D Manufacturing Corp ....G....... 914 238-1000
  Pleasantville (G-13716)
Royal Fireworks Printing Co ....F....... 845 726-3333
  Unionville (G-16302)
Steffen Publishing Inc ....D....... 315 865-4100
  Holland Patent (G-6488)
Sterling Pierce Company Inc ....E....... 516 593-1170
  East Rockaway (G-4471)
Stop Entertainment Inc ....F....... 212 242-7867
  Monroe (G-8564)
The Nugent Organization Inc ....G....... 212 645-6600
  Oceanside (G-13101)
Tobay Printing Co Inc ....E....... 631 842-3500
  Copiague (G-3934)
Vicks Lithograph & Prtg Corp ....C....... 315 736-4544
  Yorkville (G-17528)
Worzalla Publishing Company ....C....... 212 967-7909
  New York (G-12667)

PRINTING: Broadwoven Fabrics. Cotton

Mountain T-Shirts Inc ....G....... 518 943-4533
  Catskill (G-3432)

PRINTING: Checkbooks

Deluxe Corporation ....B....... 845 362-4054
  Spring Valley (G-15580)
Deluxe Corporation ....B....... 212 472-7222
  New York (G-9842)

PRINTING: Commercial, NEC

2 1 2 Postcards Inc ....E....... 212 767-8227
  New York (G-8962)
461 New Lots Avenue LLC ....G....... 347 303-9305
  Brooklyn (G-1519)
5 Stars Printing Corp ....F....... 718 461-4612
  Flushing (G-5220)
A & A Graphics Inc II ....G....... 516 735-0078
  Seaford (G-15343)
A C Envelope Inc ....G....... 516 420-0646
  Farmingdale (G-4926)
A Graphic Printing Inc ....G....... 212 233-9696
  New York (G-8987)
Academy Printing Services Inc ....G....... 631 765-3346
  Southold (G-15557)
Accel Printing & Graphics ....G....... 914 241-3369
  Mount Kisco (G-8621)
Adflex Corporation ....E....... 585 454-2950
  Rochester (G-14173)
Adirondack Pennysaver Inc ....E....... 518 563-0100
  Plattsburgh (G-13650)
Allsafe Technologies Inc ....D....... 716 691-0400
  Amherst (G-222)
Alpina Copyworld Inc ....F....... 212 683-3511
  New York (G-9101)
Alvin J Bart & Sons Inc ....C....... 718 417-1300
  Glendale (G-5645)
Always Printing ....G....... 914 481-5209
  Port Chester (G-13739)
AMA Precision Screening Inc ....F....... 585 293-0820
  Churchville (G-3633)
Amax Printing Inc ....F....... 718 384-8600
  Maspeth (G-8116)
American Office Supply Inc ....F....... 516 294-9444
  Westbury (G-16967)
Amerikom Group Inc ....D....... 212 675-1329
  New York (G-9132)
Ansun Graphics Inc ....F....... 315 437-6869
  Syracuse (G-15854)
Apple Enterprises Inc ....E....... 718 361-2200
  Long Island City (G-7662)
April Printing Co Inc ....F....... 212 685-7455
  New York (G-9185)
Argo Lithographers Inc ....E....... 718 729-2700
  Long Island City (G-7669)
Arista Innovations Inc ....E....... 516 746-2262
  Mineola (G-8408)
Artistic Typography Corp ....G....... 212 463-8880
  New York (G-9221)
Artistics Printing Corp ....G....... 516 561-2121
  Franklin Square (G-5360)
Artscroll Printing Corp ....E....... 212 929-2413
  New York (G-9224)
Asn Inc ....E....... 718 894-0800
  Maspeth (G-8120)
Balajee Enterprises Inc ....G....... 212 629-6150
  New York (G-9308)
Bartolomeo Publishing Inc ....G....... 631 420-4949
  West Babylon (G-16774)
Baseline Graphics Inc ....F....... 585 223-0153
  Fairport (G-4847)
Bedford Freeman & Worth ....C....... 212 576-9400
  New York (G-9342)
Beebie Printing & Art Agcy Inc ....G....... 518 725-4528
  Gloversville (G-5708)
Benchemark Printing Inc ....D....... 518 393-1361
  Schenectady (G-15234)
Berkshire Business Forms Inc ....F....... 518 828-2600
  Hudson (G-6610)
Bestype Digital Imaging LLC ....F....... 212 966-6886
  New York (G-9374)
Big Apple Sign Corp ....E....... 212 629-3650
  New York (G-9392)
Body Builders Inc ....G....... 718 492-7997
  Brooklyn (G-1708)
Bondy Printing Corp ....G....... 631 242-1510
  Bay Shore (G-679)
BP Beyond Printing Inc ....G....... 516 328-2700
  Hempstead (G-6266)

Bradley Marketing Group Inc ....G....... 212 967-6100
  New York (G-9449)
Brooks Litho Digital Group Inc ....G....... 631 789-4500
  Deer Park (G-4112)
C F Print Ltd Inc ....F....... 631 567-2110
  Deer Park (G-4113)
Cama Graphics Inc ....F....... 718 707-9747
  Long Island City (G-7692)
Century Direct LLC ....C....... 212 763-0600
  Islandia (G-6789)
Chakra Communications Inc ....E....... 607 748-7491
  Endicott (G-4798)
Christian Bus Endeavors Inc ....F....... 315 788-8560
  Watertown (G-16644)
Chroma Communications Inc ....G....... 631 289-8871
  Medford (G-8240)
CHv Printed Company ....F....... 516 997-1101
  East Meadow (G-4419)
Citiforms Inc ....G....... 212 334-9671
  New York (G-9623)
Classic Album ....E....... 718 388-2818
  Brooklyn (G-1786)
Colad Group LLC ....D....... 716 961-1776
  Buffalo (G-2880)
Colonial Label Systems Inc ....E....... 631 254-0111
  Bay Shore (G-685)
Colonial Tag & Label Co Inc ....F....... 516 482-0508
  Great Neck (G-5799)
Comgraph Sales Service ....G....... 716 601-7243
  Elma (G-4646)
Commercial Press Inc ....G....... 315 274-0028
  Canton (G-3381)
Copy Room Inc ....F....... 212 371-8600
  New York (G-9721)
Copy X/Press Ltd ....D....... 631 585-2200
  Ronkonkoma (G-14888)
Curtis Prtg Co The Del Press ....G....... 518 477-4820
  East Greenbush (G-4402)
Custom Prtrs Guilderland Inc ....F....... 518 456-2811
  Guilderland (G-5902)
D G M Graphics Inc ....F....... 516 223-2220
  Merrick (G-8383)
DArcy Printing and Lithog ....G....... 212 924-1554
  New York (G-9809)
Dash Printing Inc ....G....... 212 643-8534
  New York (G-9812)
Data Flow Inc ....G....... 631 436-9200
  Medford (G-8242)
Delft Printing Inc ....G....... 716 683-1100
  Lancaster (G-7311)
DEW Graphics Inc ....E....... 212 727-8820
  New York (G-9865)
Digital Evolution Inc ....G....... 212 732-2722
  New York (G-9876)
Digital Print Services ....G....... 877 832-1200
  Buffalo (G-2914)
Direct Print Inc ....F....... 212 987-6003
  New York (G-9882)
Dit Prints Incorporated ....G....... 518 885-4400
  Ballston Spa (G-594)
Division Den-Bar Enterprises ....G....... 914 381-2220
  Mamaroneck (G-8033)
Dupli Graphics Corporation ....C....... 315 234-7286
  Syracuse (G-15925)
Dutchess Plumbing & Heating ....G....... 845 889-8255
  Staatsburg (G-15618)
E&I Printing ....F....... 212 206-0506
  New York (G-9954)
Eagle Envelope Company Inc ....G....... 607 387-3195
  Trumansburg (G-16265)
Elm Graphics Inc ....G....... 315 737-5984
  New Hartford (G-8803)
Enterprise Press Inc ....C....... 212 741-2111
  New York (G-10043)
Evenhouse Printing ....G....... 716 649-2666
  Hamburg (G-5925)
Evergreen Corp Central NY ....F....... 315 454-4175
  Syracuse (G-15939)
Excellent Printing Inc ....G....... 718 384-7272
  Brooklyn (G-1944)
Excelsus Solutions LLC ....E....... 585 533-0003
  Rochester (G-14363)
Exotic Print and Paper Inc ....F....... 212 807-0465
  New York (G-10107)
Eye Graphics & Printing Inc ....F....... 718 488-0606
  Brooklyn (G-1948)
F A Printing ....G....... 212 974-5982
  New York (G-10115)
Falconer Printing & Design Inc ....F....... 716 665-2121
  Falconer (G-4899)

Fedex Office & Print Svcs Inc................G....... 718 982-5223
Staten Island (G-15673)
First2print Inc..G....... 212 868-6886
New York (G-10169)
Flp Group LLC...F....... 315 252-7583
Auburn (G-496)
Force Digital Media Inc...........................G....... 631 243-0243
Deer Park (G-4143)
Franklin Packaging Inc..........................G....... 631 582-8900
Northport (G-13011)
Fred Weidner & Son Printers.................G....... 212 964-8676
New York (G-10205)
Freeville Publishing Co Inc....................F....... 607 844-9119
Freeville (G-5435)
G&J Graphics Inc....................................G....... 718 409-9874
Bronx (G-1340)
Gallant Graphics Ltd Inc........................E....... 845 868-1166
Stanfordville (G-15627)
Garrett J Cronin.......................................G....... 914 761-9299
White Plains (G-17111)
Gatehouse Media LLC............................D....... 585 598-0030
Pittsford (G-13561)
GE Healthcare Fincl Svcs Inc.................G....... 212 713-2000
New York (G-10263)
Gem Reproduction Services Corp.........G....... 845 298-0172
Wappingers Falls (G-16570)
Gem West Inc..G....... 631 567-4228
Patchogue (G-13420)
Genie Instant Printing Co Inc.................F....... 212 575-8258
New York (G-10277)
Grand Meridian Printing Inc..................E....... 718 937-3888
Long Island City (G-7752)
Graphic Lab Inc.......................................E....... 212 682-1815
New York (G-10353)
Haig Press Inc...E....... 631 582-5800
Hauppauge (G-6088)
Hi-Tech Packg World-Wide LLC.............G....... 845 947-1912
New Windsor (G-8939)
Horace J Metz..G....... 716 873-9103
Kenmore (G-7149)
Hospitality Inc...E....... 212 268-1930
New York (G-10511)
I N K T Inc..F....... 212 957-2700
New York (G-10540)
Idc Printing & Sty Co Inc........................G....... 516 599-0400
Lynbrook (G-7951)
Image Typography Inc............................G....... 631 218-6932
Holbrook (G-6450)
Impress Graphic Technologies..............F....... 516 781-0845
Westbury (G-16996)
Impressive Imprints................................F....... 716 692-0905
North Tonawanda (G-12977)
Imtech Graphics Inc................................F....... 212 282-7010
New York (G-10576)
Incodema3d LLC.....................................F....... 607 269-4390
Ithaca (G-6849)
Integrated Graphics Inc..........................G....... 212 592-5600
New York (G-10616)
Iron Horse Graphics Ltd.........................G....... 631 537-3400
Bridgehampton (G-1234)
Jack J Florio Jr...G....... 716 434-9123
Lockport (G-7595)
Japan Printing & Graphics Inc...............G....... 212 406-2905
New York (G-10700)
Joed Press..G....... 212 243-3620
New York (G-10748)
John Auguliaro Printing Co....................G....... 718 382-5283
Brooklyn (G-2145)
Jomar Industries Inc...............................E....... 845 357-5773
Airmont (G-16)
Jomart Associates Inc.............................E....... 212 627-2153
Islandia (G-6798)
Kallen Corp..G....... 212 242-1470
New York (G-10805)
Kenan International Trading..................G....... 718 672-4922
Corona (G-4000)
Key Computer Svcs of Chelsea..............D....... 212 206-8060
New York (G-10840)
L Loy Press Inc..G....... 716 634-5966
Buffalo (G-3040)
L T Sales Corp..F....... 631 886-1390
Wading River (G-16523)
Lake Placid Advertisers Wkshp..............E....... 518 523-3359
Lake Placid (G-7275)
LAM Western New York Inc....................G....... 716 856-0308
Buffalo (G-3045)
Lauricella Press Inc.................................E....... 516 931-5906
Brentwood (G-1189)
Lennons Litho Inc....................................F....... 315 866-3156
Herkimer (G-6304)

Leo Paper Inc...G....... 917 305-0708
New York (G-10970)
Levon Graphics Corp..............................D....... 631 753-2022
Farmingdale (G-5035)
Linden Forms & Systems Inc.................E....... 212 219-1100
Brooklyn (G-2226)
M C Packaging Corporation...................E....... 631 643-3763
Babylon (G-550)
Magazines & Brochures Inc...................G....... 716 875-9699
Tonawanda (G-16178)
Makerbot Industries LLC........................G....... 347 457-5758
New York (G-11118)
Mason Transparent Package Inc...........E....... 718 792-6000
Bronx (G-1388)
Master Image Printing Inc......................G....... 914 347-4400
Elmsford (G-4763)
Measurement Incorporated....................E....... 914 682-1969
White Plains (G-17136)
Media Signs LLC.....................................G....... 718 252-7575
Brooklyn (G-2292)
Mega Graphics Inc..................................G....... 914 962-1402
Yorktown Heights (G-17513)
Menu Solutions Inc.................................D....... 718 575-5160
Bronx (G-1391)
Merlin Printing Inc..................................E....... 631 842-6666
Amityville (G-312)
Merrill Communications LLC.................G....... 212 620-5600
New York (G-11232)
Merrill Corporation.................................D....... 917 934-7300
New York (G-11233)
Middletown Press....................................G....... 845 343-1895
Middletown (G-8451)
Miken Companies Inc..............................D....... 716 668-6311
Buffalo (G-3065)
Mimeocom Inc...B....... 212 847-3000
New York (G-11273)
Mini Graphics Inc....................................D....... 516 223-6464
Hauppauge (G-6139)
Mod-Pac Corp..C....... 716 873-0640
Buffalo (G-3071)
Mpe Graphics Inc....................................F....... 631 582-8900
Bohemia (G-1106)
Multi Packaging Solutions Inc................E....... 646 885-0157
New York (G-11324)
Nathan Printing Express Inc..................G....... 914 472-0914
Scarsdale (G-15221)
New Deal Printing Corp..........................G....... 718 729-5800
New York (G-11382)
New York Legal Publishing.....................G....... 518 459-1100
Menands (G-8377)
Newport Business Solutions Inc...........F....... 631 319-6129
Bohemia (G-1110)
Niagara Sample Book Co Inc.................F....... 716 284-6151
Niagara Falls (G-12850)
Noble Checks Inc....................................G....... 212 537-6241
Brooklyn (G-2373)
North American Graphics Inc................F....... 212 725-2200
New York (G-11455)
North Six Inc..F....... 212 463-7227
New York (G-11458)
Ontario Label Graphics Inc.....................F....... 716 434-8505
Lockport (G-7609)
Origin Press Inc.......................................G....... 516 746-2262
Mineola (G-8530)
Pace Editions Inc....................................G....... 212 675-7431
New York (G-11550)
Paulin Investment Company..................E....... 631 957-8500
Amityville (G-320)
Penny Lane Printing Inc.........................D....... 585 226-8111
Avon (G-542)
Photo Agents Ltd....................................G....... 631 421-0258
Huntington (G-6674)
Pony Farm Press & Graphics................G....... 607 432-9020
Oneonta (G-13192)
Premier Ink Systems Inc........................E....... 845 782-5802
Harriman (G-5973)
Presstek Printing LLC.............................F....... 585 266-2770
Rochester (G-14599)
Print City Corp...F....... 212 487-9778
New York (G-11717)
Print House Inc..D....... 718 443-7500
Brooklyn (G-2445)
Print Mall..G....... 718 437-7700
Brooklyn (G-2446)
Printed Image..G....... 716 821-1880
Buffalo (G-3137)
Printfacility Inc..G....... 212 349-4009
New York (G-11721)
Printing Max New York Inc.....................G....... 718 692-1400
Brooklyn (G-2448)

Printing Prmtnal Solutions LLC.............F....... 315 474-1110
Syracuse (G-16014)
Printing Resources Inc...........................E....... 518 482-2470
Albany (G-124)
Printout Copy Corp.................................E....... 718 855-4040
Brooklyn (G-2450)
Printworks Printing & Design................G....... 315 433-8587
Syracuse (G-16015)
Priority Printing Entps Inc......................F....... 646 285-0684
New York (G-11723)
Publimax Printing Corp..........................G....... 718 366-7133
Ridgewood (G-14121)
Quadra Flex Corp....................................G....... 607 758-7066
Cortland (G-4042)
Quality Graphics West Seneca..............G....... 716 668-4528
Cheektowaga (G-3588)
Quality Impressions Inc..........................G....... 646 613-0002
New York (G-11767)
Quality Offset LLC..................................G....... 347 342-4660
Long Island City (G-7854)
R & M Graphics of New York..................F....... 212 929-0294
New York (G-11779)
Rfn Inc..F....... 516 764-5100
Bay Shore (G-733)
Richard Ruffner.......................................F....... 631 234-4600
Central Islip (G-3509)
Rike Enterprises Inc...............................F....... 631 277-8338
Islip (G-6812)
RIT Printing Corp....................................F....... 631 586-6220
Bay Shore (G-735)
Rose Graphics LLC.................................F....... 516 547-6142
West Babylon (G-16823)
Ross-Ellis Ltd..G....... 212 260-9200
Valley Stream (G-16426)
RR Donnelley & Sons Company............F....... 716 763-2613
Lakewood (G-7294)
RR Donnelley & Sons Company............G....... 646 755-8125
New York (G-11930)
S & S Graphics Inc..................................F....... 914 668-4230
Mount Vernon (G-8728)
S L C Industries Incorporated................F....... 607 775-2299
Binghamton (G-948)
Salamanca Press Penny Saver..............E....... 716 945-1500
Salamanca (G-15105)
Scan-A-Chrome Color Inc.....................G....... 631 532-6146
Copiague (G-3925)
Scotti Graphics Inc.................................E....... 212 367-9602
Long Island City (G-7872)
SDS Business Cards Inc........................F....... 516 747-3131
Syosset (G-15839)
Shapeways Inc..D....... 914 356-5816
New York (G-12043)
Sharp Printing Inc...................................G....... 716 731-3994
Sanborn (G-15127)
Silver Griffin Inc......................................F....... 518 272-7771
Troy (G-16255)
Sino Printing Inc.....................................F....... 212 334-6896
New York (G-12086)
Soho Letterpress Inc..............................F....... 718 788-2518
Brooklyn (G-2578)
Solarz Bros Printing Corp.......................G....... 718 383-1330
Brooklyn (G-2582)
Spaulding Law Printing Inc....................G....... 315 422-4805
Syracuse (G-16042)
Spectrum Prtg Lithography Inc.............F....... 212 255-3131
New York (G-12158)
Speedy Enterprise of USA Corp............G....... 718 463-3000
Flushing (G-5295)
St James Printing Inc.............................G....... 631 981-2095
Ronkonkoma (G-14989)
Standwill Packaging Inc.........................E....... 631 752-1236
Farmingdale (G-5113)
Starcraft Press Inc..................................G....... 718 383-6700
Long Island City (G-7887)
Starfire Printing Inc................................G....... 631 736-1495
Holtsville (G-6509)
Structured 3d Inc....................................G....... 346 704-2614
Amityville (G-326)
Syracuse Label Co Inc...........................D....... 315 422-1037
Liverpool (G-7550)
T S O General Corp.................................E....... 631 952-5320
Brentwood (G-1195)
T&K Printing Inc......................................F....... 718 439-9454
Brooklyn (G-2640)
T-Base Communications USA Inc.........E....... 315 713-0013
Ogdensburg (G-13123)
Tapemaker Supply Company LLC.........G....... 914 693-3407
Hartsdale (G-6001)
Tcmf Inc...D....... 607 724-1094
Binghamton (G-954)

PRODUCT

1302 2017 Harris New York Manufacturers Directory (G-0000) Company's Geographic Section entry number

PRODUCT SECTION

PRINTING: Letterpress

Tele-Pak Inc ....E 845 426-2300
  Monsey *(G-8585)*
The Gramecy Group ....G 518 348-1325
  Clifton Park *(G-3710)*
Thomson Press (india) Limited ....G 646 318-0369
  Long Island City *(G-7901)*
Top Copi Reproductions Inc ....F 212 571-4141
  New York *(G-12368)*
Toppan Vite (new York) Inc ....D 212 596-7747
  New York *(G-12371)*
Toprint Ltd ....G 718 439-0469
  Brooklyn *(G-2667)*
Tri-Lon Clor Lithographers Ltd ....E 212 255-6140
  New York *(G-12400)*
United Graphics Inc ....E 716 871-2600
  Buffalo *(G-3234)*
USA Custom Pad Corp ....E 607 563-9550
  Sidney *(G-15445)*
Varick Street Litho Inc ....G 646 843-0800
  New York *(G-12506)*
Venus Printing Company ....F 212 967-8900
  Hewlett *(G-6316)*
Veterans Offset Printing Inc ....G 585 288-2900
  Rochester *(G-14752)*
Weicro Graphics Inc ....E 631 253-3360
  West Babylon *(G-16840)*
Were Forms Inc ....G 585 482-4400
  Rochester *(G-14761)*
Westprint Inc ....G 212 989-3805
  New York *(G-12617)*
Westypo Printers Inc ....G 914 737-7394
  Peekskill *(G-13487)*
Wheeler/Rinstar Ltd ....F 212 244-1130
  New York *(G-12622)*
Willco Fine Art Ltd ....F 718 935-9567
  New York *(G-12632)*
William J Ryan ....G 585 392-6200
  Hilton *(G-6421)*
Wilson Press LLC ....E 315 568-9693
  Seneca Falls *(G-15372)*
Worldwide Ticket Craft ....D 516 538-6200
  Merrick *(G-8394)*
X Myles Mar Inc ....E 212 683-2015
  New York *(G-12673)*
X Press Screen Printing ....G 716 679-7788
  Dunkirk *(G-4353)*
XI Graphics Inc ....G 212 929-8700
  New York *(G-12680)*

PRINTING: Engraving & Plate

Allstate Sign & Plaque Corp ....F 631 242-2828
  Deer Park *(G-4093)*
Custom House Engravers Inc ....F 631 567-3004
  Bohemia *(G-1046)*
D & A Offset Services Inc ....F 212 924-0612
  New York *(G-9780)*

PRINTING: Flexographic

Astro Label & Tag Ltd ....G 718 435-4474
  Brooklyn *(G-1641)*
Gemson Graphics Inc ....G 516 873-8400
  Albertson *(G-154)*
Marlow Printing Co Inc ....E 718 625-4949
  Brooklyn *(G-2274)*
Transcntinental Ultra Flex Inc ....B 718 272-9100
  Brooklyn *(G-2674)*
Vitex Packaging Group Inc ....F 212 265-6575
  New York *(G-12557)*
W N Vanalstine & Sons Inc ....D 518 237-1436
  Cohoes *(G-3761)*

PRINTING: Gravure, Business Form & Card

Alamar Printing Inc ....F 914 993-9007
  White Plains *(G-17074)*
Alfa Card Inc ....G 718 326-7107
  Glendale *(G-5643)*

PRINTING: Gravure, Color

Clarion Publications Inc ....F 585 243-3530
  Geneseo *(G-5564)*
Kinaneco Inc ....E 315 468-6201
  Syracuse *(G-15974)*

PRINTING: Gravure, Forms, Business

American Print Solutions Inc ....G 718 208-2309
  Brooklyn *(G-1607)*

PRINTING: Gravure, Imprinting

C C Industries Inc ....F 518 581-7633
  Saratoga Springs *(G-15146)*

PRINTING: Gravure, Job

Leonardo Printing Corp ....G 914 664-7890
  Mount Vernon *(G-8700)*
Sommer and Sons Printing Inc ....F 716 822-4311
  Buffalo *(G-3190)*

PRINTING: Gravure, Labels

Adflex Corporation ....E 585 454-2950
  Rochester *(G-14173)*
Janco Press Inc ....F 631 563-3003
  Bohemia *(G-1081)*
Liberty Label Mfg Inc ....F 631 737-2365
  Holbrook *(G-6457)*
Niagara Label Company Inc ....F 716 542-3000
  Akron *(G-25)*
Trust of Colum Unive In The Ci ....F 212 854-2793
  New York *(G-12412)*

PRINTING: Gravure, Promotional

Gemini Manufacturing LLC ....C 914 375-0855
  White Plains *(G-17113)*

PRINTING: Gravure, Rotogravure

Advanced Printing New York Inc ....G 212 840-8108
  New York *(G-9045)*
Benton Announcements Inc ....F 716 836-4100
  Buffalo *(G-2839)*
Color Industries LLC ....G 718 392-8301
  Long Island City *(G-7703)*
Copy Corner Inc ....G 718 388-4545
  Brooklyn *(G-1803)*
Ecoplast & Packaging LLC ....G 718 996-0800
  Brooklyn *(G-1901)*
Gruner + Jahr USA Group Inc ....B 866 323-9336
  New York *(G-10376)*
Image Sales & Marketing Inc ....G 516 238-7023
  Massapequa Park *(G-8186)*
Jack J Florio Jr ....G 716 434-9123
  Lockport *(G-7595)*
Karr Graphics Corp ....E 718 784-9390
  Long Island City *(G-7779)*
Krepe Kraft Inc ....B 716 826-7086
  Buffalo *(G-3037)*
Lane Park Graphics Inc ....G 914 273-5898
  Patterson *(G-13442)*
McG Graphics Inc ....G 631 499-0730
  Dix Hills *(G-4294)*
Mod-Pac Corp ....D 716 447-9013
  Buffalo *(G-3072)*
Paya Printing of NY Inc ....G 516 625-8346
  Albertson *(G-157)*
SRC Liquidation Company ....G 716 631-3900
  Williamsville *(G-17255)*
Tele-Pak Inc ....E 845 426-2300
  Monsey *(G-8585)*
Vitex Packaging Group Inc ....F 212 265-6575
  New York *(G-12557)*

PRINTING: Gravure, Stamps, Trading

Ashton-Potter USA Ltd ....C 716 633-2000
  Williamsville *(G-17233)*

PRINTING: Gravure, Stationery

Mrs John L Strong & Co LLC ....F 212 838-3775
  New York *(G-11317)*
Mutual Engraving Company Inc ....D 516 489-0534
  West Hempstead *(G-16861)*

PRINTING: Gravure, Wrappers

Gooding Co Inc ....E 716 434-5501
  Lockport *(G-7592)*

PRINTING: Laser

Amsterdam Printing & Litho Inc ....F 518 792-6501
  Queensbury *(G-13988)*
CPW Direct Mail Group LLC ....E 631 588-6565
  Farmingdale *(G-4964)*
Data Palette Info Svcs LLC ....D 718 433-1060
  Port Washington *(G-13807)*
Diamond Inscription Tech ....F 646 366-7944
  New York *(G-9873)*
Doctor Print Inc ....E 631 873-4560
  Hauppauge *(G-6066)*
PBR Graphics Inc ....G 518 458-2909
  Albany *(G-115)*

PRINTING: Letterpress

6727 11th Ave Corp ....F 718 837-8787
  Brooklyn *(G-1521)*
Brodock Press Inc ....D 315 735-9577
  Utica *(G-16310)*
Chenango Union Printing Inc ....G 607 334-2112
  Norwich *(G-13022)*
Craig Envelope Corp ....E 718 786-4277
  Long Island City *(G-7706)*
Design Printing Corp ....G 631 753-9801
  Farmingdale *(G-4975)*
Eastwood Litho Inc ....E 315 437-2626
  Syracuse *(G-15929)*
Edgian Press Inc ....G 516 931-2114
  Hicksville *(G-6342)*
Efficiency Printing Co Inc ....F 914 949-8611
  White Plains *(G-17103)*
F & B Photo Offset Co Inc ....G 516 431-5433
  Island Park *(G-6779)*
Fairmount Press ....F 212 255-2300
  New York *(G-10130)*
Forward Enterprises Inc ....F 585 235-7670
  Rochester *(G-14379)*
Frederick Coon Inc ....E 716 683-6812
  Elma *(G-4648)*
Gazette Press Inc ....E 914 963-8300
  Rye *(G-15056)*
Golos Printing Inc ....G 607 732-1896
  Elmira Heights *(G-4710)*
Grover Cleveland Press Inc ....F 716 564-2222
  Amherst *(G-244)*
H T L & S Ltd ....F 718 435-4474
  Brooklyn *(G-2060)*
Harmon and Castella Printing ....F 845 471-9163
  Poughkeepsie *(G-13905)*
HI Speed Envelope Co Inc ....F 718 617-1600
  Mount Vernon *(G-8690)*
Hill Crest Press ....G 518 943-0671
  Catskill *(G-3429)*
Johnnys Ideal Printing Co ....G 518 828-6666
  Hudson *(G-6621)*
Judith Lewis Printer Inc ....G 516 997-7777
  Westbury *(G-17000)*
Kaufman Brothers Printing ....G 212 563-1854
  New York *(G-10820)*
Kaymil Printing Company Inc ....G 212 594-3718
  New York *(G-10822)*
Linco Printing Inc ....E 718 937-5141
  Long Island City *(G-7789)*
Louis Heindl & Son Inc ....G 585 454-5080
  Rochester *(G-14483)*
M T M Printing Co Inc ....F 718 353-3297
  College Point *(G-3796)*
Malone Industrial Press Inc ....G 518 483-5880
  Malone *(G-8013)*
Mark T Westinghouse ....G 518 678-3262
  Catskill *(G-3431)*
Maspeth Press Inc ....G 718 429-2363
  Maspeth *(G-8149)*
Midgley Printing Corp ....G 315 475-1864
  Syracuse *(G-15988)*
Mines Press Inc ....C 914 788-1800
  Cortlandt Manor *(G-4052)*
Moore Printing Company Inc ....G 585 394-1533
  Canandaigua *(G-3349)*
P & W Press Inc ....E 646 486-3417
  New York *(G-11547)*
Patrick Ryans Modern Press ....F 518 434-2921
  Albany *(G-114)*
S & S Prtg Die-Cutting Co Inc ....F 718 388-8990
  Brooklyn *(G-2522)*
Seneca West Printing Inc ....G 716 675-8010
  West Seneca *(G-16954)*
Source Envelope Inc ....G 866 284-0707
  Farmingdale *(G-5111)*
Star Press Pearl River Inc ....G 845 268-2294
  Valley Cottage *(G-16389)*
Stony Point Graphics Ltd ....G 845 786-3322
  Stony Point *(G-15777)*
Tovie Asarese Royal Prtg Co ....G 716 885-7692
  Buffalo *(G-3223)*
Tri Kolor Printing & Sty ....F 315 474-6753
  Syracuse *(G-16061)*
Weeks & Reichel Printing Inc ....G 631 589-1443
  Sayville *(G-15215)*

Employee Codes: A=Over 500 employees, B=251-500
C=101-250, D=51-100, E=20-50, F=10-19, G=5-9

PRINTING: Letterpress

William Charles Prtg Co Inc ....E 516 349-0900
 Plainview *(G-13646)*

PRINTING: Lithographic

2 1 2 Postcards Inc ....E 212 767-8227
 New York *(G-8962)*
2 X 4 Inc ....E 212 647-1170
 New York *(G-8963)*
3g Graphics LLC ....G 716 634-2585
 Amherst *(G-218)*
450 Ridge St Inc ....G 716 754-2789
 Lewiston *(G-7432)*
518 Prints LLC ....G 518 674-5346
 Averill Park *(G-532)*
6727 11th Ave Corp ....F 718 837-8787
 Brooklyn *(G-1521)*
A C Envelope Inc ....G 516 420-0646
 Farmingdale *(G-4926)*
A Esteban & Company Inc ....E 212 989-7000
 New York *(G-8984)*
A Esteban & Company Inc ....E 212 714-2227
 New York *(G-8985)*
Accuprint ....G 518 456-2431
 Albany *(G-34)*
Adirondack Publishing Co Inc ....E 518 891-2600
 Saranac Lake *(G-15134)*
Advanced Business Group Inc ....F 212 398-1010
 New York *(G-9042)*
Advanced Digital Printing LLC ....E 718 649-1500
 New York *(G-9043)*
Advertising Lithographers ....F 212 966-7771
 New York *(G-9050)*
Albert Siy ....G 718 359-0389
 Flushing *(G-5224)*
Aldine Inc (ny) ....D 212 226-2870
 New York *(G-9079)*
Alexander Polakovich ....G 718 229-6200
 Bayside *(G-766)*
All Color Business Spc Ltd ....G 516 420-0649
 Deer Park *(G-4091)*
All Time Products Inc ....G 718 464-1400
 Queens Village *(G-13974)*
Alpina Copyworld Inc ....F 212 683-3511
 New York *(G-9101)*
Alpine Business Group Inc ....G 212 989-4198
 New York *(G-9102)*
Amax Printing Inc ....F 718 384-8600
 Maspeth *(G-8116)*
American Business Forms Inc ....D 716 836-5111
 Amherst *(G-223)*
American Icon Industries Inc ....G 845 561-1299
 Newburgh *(G-12749)*
American Print Solutions Inc ....E 718 246-7800
 Brooklyn *(G-1606)*
Amsterdam Printing & Litho Inc ....F 518 842-6000
 Amsterdam *(G-332)*
Amsterdam Printing & Litho Inc ....E 518 842-6000
 Amsterdam *(G-333)*
Answer Printing Inc ....F 212 922-2922
 New York *(G-9166)*
Arcade Inc ....A 212 541-2600
 New York *(G-9193)*
Argo Envelope Corp ....D 718 729-2700
 Long Island City *(G-7667)*
Argo Lithographers Inc ....E 718 729-2700
 Long Island City *(G-7669)*
Art Digital Technologies LLC ....F 646 649-4820
 Brooklyn *(G-1634)*
Art Scroll Printing Corp ....F 212 929-2413
 New York *(G-9214)*
Artina Group Inc ....E 914 592-1850
 Elmsford *(G-4734)*
Artscroll Printing Corp ....E 212 929-2413
 New York *(G-9224)*
Asn Inc ....F 718 894-0800
 Maspeth *(G-8120)*
Atlas Print Solutions Inc ....E 212 949-8775
 New York *(G-9256)*
Avm Printing Inc ....F 631 351-1331
 Hauppauge *(G-6030)*
B D B Typewriter Supply Works ....E 718 232-4800
 Brooklyn *(G-1659)*
Badoud Communications Inc ....C 315 472-7821
 Syracuse *(G-15866)*
Ballantrae Lithographers Inc ....E 914 592-3275
 White Plains *(G-17083)*
Baum Christine and John Corp ....G 585 621-8910
 Rochester *(G-14224)*
Beastons Budget Printing ....G 585 244-2721
 Rochester *(G-14227)*

Benchemark Printing Inc ....D 518 393-1361
 Schenectady *(G-15234)*
Benjamin Printing Inc ....F 315 788-7922
 Adams *(G-2)*
Bennett Multimedia Inc ....F 718 629-1454
 Brooklyn *(G-1682)*
Bennett Printing Corporation ....F 718 629-1454
 Brooklyn *(G-1683)*
Bernard Hall ....G 585 425-3340
 Fairport *(G-4848)*
Bevilacque Group LLC ....F 212 414-8858
 New York *(G-9382)*
Billing Coding and Prtg Inc ....G 718 827-9409
 Brooklyn *(G-1697)*
Bittner Company LLC ....F 585 214-1790
 Rochester *(G-14233)*
Bk Printing Inc ....G 315 565-5396
 East Syracuse *(G-4511)*
Bluesoho ....G 646 805-2583
 New York *(G-9425)*
Boka Printing Inc ....G 607 725-3235
 Binghamton *(G-898)*
Boncraft Inc ....D 716 662-9720
 Tonawanda *(G-16146)*
Bondy Printing Corp ....G 631 242-1510
 Bay Shore *(G-679)*
Boulevard Printing ....G 716 837-3800
 Tonawanda *(G-16147)*
Boxcar Press Incorporated ....E 315 473-0930
 Syracuse *(G-15873)*
BP Beyond Printing Inc ....G 516 328-2700
 Hempstead *(G-6266)*
Brodock Press Inc ....D 315 735-9577
 Utica *(G-16310)*
Brooks Litho Digital Group Inc ....G 631 789-4500
 Deer Park *(G-4112)*
Brown Printing Company ....E 212 782-7800
 New York *(G-9471)*
Business Card Express Inc ....E 631 669-3400
 West Babylon *(G-16779)*
C & R De Santis Inc ....E 718 447-5076
 Staten Island *(G-15653)*
C K Printing ....G 718 965-0388
 Brooklyn *(G-1744)*
C To C Design & Print Inc ....F 631 885-4020
 Ronkonkoma *(G-14882)*
Caboodle Printing Inc ....G 716 693-6000
 Williamsville *(G-17237)*
Cadmus Journal Services Inc ....E 212 736-2002
 New York *(G-9496)*
Cadmus Journal Services Inc ....D 607 762-5365
 Conklin *(G-3866)*
Canandaigua Msgnr Incorporated ....D 585 394-0770
 Canandaigua *(G-3337)*
Candid Litho Printing Ltd ....D 212 431-3800
 Long Island City *(G-7693)*
Carlara Group Ltd ....G 914 769-2020
 Pleasantville *(G-13712)*
Castlereagh Printcraft Inc ....D 516 623-1728
 Freeport *(G-5392)*
Cathedral Corporation ....C 315 338-0021
 Rome *(G-14808)*
Catskill Delaware Publications ....F 845 887-5200
 Callicoon *(G-3284)*
Cazar Printing & Advertising ....G 718 446-4606
 Corona *(G-3994)*
Cds Productions Inc ....F 518 385-8255
 Schenectady *(G-15241)*
Cenveo Inc ....F 716 686-0100
 Depew *(G-4252)*
Chromagraphics Press Inc ....G 631 367-6160
 Melville *(G-8302)*
Circle Press Inc ....D 212 924-4277
 New York *(G-9621)*
Classic Color Graphics Inc ....G 516 822-9090
 Hicksville *(G-6330)*
Classic Color Graphics Inc ....G 516 822-9090
 Hicksville *(G-6331)*
Cody Printing Corp ....G 718 651-8854
 Woodside *(G-17324)*
Coe Displays Inc ....G 718 937-5658
 Long Island City *(G-7702)*
Colad Group LLC ....D 716 961-1776
 Buffalo *(G-2880)*
Color-Aid Corporation ....G 212 673-5500
 Hudson Falls *(G-6639)*
Commercial Print & Imaging ....E 716 597-0100
 Buffalo *(G-2882)*
Community Media LLC ....E 212 229-1890
 New York *(G-9689)*

Community Newspaper Group LLC ....F 607 432-1000
 Oneonta *(G-13181)*
Compass Printing Plus ....F 518 891-7050
 Saranac Lake *(G-15135)*
Compass Printing Plus ....G 518 523-3308
 Saranac Lake *(G-15136)*
Compucolor Associates Inc ....E 516 358-0000
 New Hyde Park *(G-8823)*
Copy Stop Inc ....G 914 428-5188
 White Plains *(G-17097)*
Coral Color Process Ltd ....E 631 543-5200
 Commack *(G-3829)*
Coral Graphic Services Inc ....C 516 576-2100
 Hicksville *(G-6336)*
Cosmos Communications Inc ....C 718 482-1800
 Long Island City *(G-7705)*
Coughlin Printing Group ....G 315 788-8560
 Watertown *(G-16647)*
Courier Printing Corp ....E 607 467-2191
 Deposit *(G-4277)*
Cronin Enterprises Inc ....G 914 345-9600
 Elmsford *(G-4745)*
Daily Record ....F 585 232-2035
 Rochester *(G-14299)*
Dan Trent Company Inc ....G 716 822-1422
 Buffalo *(G-2901)*
Dark Star Lithograph Corp ....G 845 634-3780
 New City *(G-8782)*
Datorib Inc ....G 631 698-6222
 Selden *(G-15351)*
Dawn Paper Co Inc ....G 516 596-9110
 East Rockaway *(G-4469)*
Deanco Digital Printing LLC ....F 212 371-2025
 Sunnyside *(G-15805)*
Delaware Graphics LLC ....G 716 627-7582
 Lake View *(G-7280)*
Denton Publications Inc ....D 518 873-6368
 Elizabethtown *(G-4626)*
Dependable Lithographers Inc ....F 718 472-4200
 Long Island City *(G-7712)*
Design Distributors Inc ....D 631 242-2000
 Deer Park *(G-4130)*
Designlogocom Inc ....E 212 564-0200
 New York *(G-9856)*
Digital Color Concepts Inc ....E 212 989-4888
 New York *(G-9875)*
Digital Imaging Tech LLC ....G 518 885-4400
 Ballston Spa *(G-593)*
Diversified Envelope Ltd ....F 585 615-4697
 Rochester *(G-14312)*
Division Street News Corp ....F 518 234-2515
 Cobleskill *(G-3736)*
Donmar Printing Co ....F 516 280-2239
 Westbury *(G-16978)*
Donnelley Financial LLC ....B 212 425-0298
 New York *(G-9906)*
Dovelin Printing Company Inc ....F 718 302-3951
 Brooklyn *(G-1876)*
Dual Print & Mail LLC ....G 716 775-8001
 Grand Island *(G-5754)*
Dual Print & Mail LLC ....D 716 684-3825
 Cheektowaga *(G-3568)*
Dupli Graphics Corporation ....C 315 234-7286
 Syracuse *(G-15925)*
E B B Graphics Inc ....F 516 750-5510
 Westbury *(G-16979)*
E L Smith Printing Co Inc ....E 201 373-0111
 New City *(G-8784)*
E W Smith Publishing Co ....F 845 562-1218
 New Windsor *(G-8937)*
Eagle Graphics Inc ....G 585 244-5006
 Rochester *(G-14324)*
East Coast Thermographers Inc ....E 718 321-3211
 College Point *(G-3782)*
Eastwood Litho Inc ....E 315 437-2626
 Syracuse *(G-15929)*
Echo Appellate Press Inc ....G 516 432-3601
 Long Beach *(G-7640)*
Edwards Graphic Co Inc ....G 718 548-6858
 Bronx *(G-1325)*
Efficiency Printing Co Inc ....F 914 949-8611
 White Plains *(G-17103)*
Entermarket ....G 914 437-7268
 Mount Kisco *(G-8627)*
Enterprise Press Inc ....C 212 741-2111
 New York *(G-10043)*
Evolution Impressions Inc ....D 585 473-6600
 Rochester *(G-14361)*
Executive Prtg & Direct Mail ....G 914 592-3200
 Elmsford *(G-4752)*

PRODUCT SECTION — PRINTING: Lithographic

Company	Code	Phone
F5 Networks Inc — New York (G-10122)	G	888 882-7510
Falconer Printing & Design Inc — Falconer (G-4899)	F	716 665-2121
Fao Printing — Brooklyn (G-1959)	F	718 282-3310
Fasprint — Malone (G-8009)	G	518 483-4631
Final Touch Printing Inc — Spring Valley (G-15585)	F	845 352-2677
First Line Printing Inc — Woodside (G-17329)	F	718 606-0860
Fiveboro Printing & Supplies — Brooklyn (G-1979)	G	718 431-9500
Flower City Printing Inc — Rochester (G-14375)	G	585 512-1235
Flynns Inc — New York (G-10182)	E	212 339-8700
Franklin Printing Group Ltd — Cedarhurst (G-3457)	G	516 569-1248
Fx Silk Screen Printing I — Rochester (G-14385)	E	585 266-6773
G W Canfield & Son Inc — Utica (G-16334)	G	315 735-5522
Gannett Stllite Info Ntwrk LLC — West Nyack (G-16917)	E	845 578-2300
Garden City Printers & Mailers — West Hempstead (G-16853)	F	516 485-1600
Gatehouse Media LLC — Canandaigua (G-3347)	D	585 394-0770
Gazette Press Inc — Rye (G-15056)	G	914 963-8300
Global Graphics Inc — Flushing (G-5244)	F	718 939-4967
Gn Printing — Long Island City (G-7750)	E	718 784-1713
Gotham Ink Corp — Syosset (G-15825)	G	516 677-1969
Government Data Publication — Brooklyn (G-2045)	E	347 789-8719
GPM Associates LLC — Dansville (G-4077)	E	585 335-3940
Grand Prix Litho Inc — Holbrook (G-6449)	E	631 242-4182
Graphic Fabrications Inc — Rockville Centre (G-14791)	G	516 763-3222
Graphicomm Inc — Niagara Falls (G-12826)	G	716 283-0830
Great Eastern Color Lith — Poughkeepsie (G-13903)	D	845 454-7420
Great Impressions Inc — New York (G-10356)	F	212 989-8555
Green Girl Prtg & Msgnr Inc — New York (G-10360)	G	212 575-0357
Grover Cleveland Press Inc — Amherst (G-244)	F	716 564-2222
Guaranteed Printing Svc Co Inc — Long Island City (G-7755)	E	212 929-2410
Haig Press Inc — Hauppauge (G-6088)	E	631 582-5800
Hamptons Magazine — Southampton (G-15545)	E	631 283-7125
Hearst Corporation — Albany (G-86)	A	518 454-5694
Hempstead Sentinel Inc — Hempstead (G-6273)	F	516 486-5000
Hooek Produktion Inc — New York (G-10503)	G	212 367-9111
Horne Organization Inc — Yonkers (G-17454)	F	914 572-1330
Huckleberry Inc — Hauppauge (G-6096)	G	631 630-5450
Hugh F McPherson Inc — Cheektowaga (G-3575)	G	716 668-6107
Hunt Graphics Inc — Coram (G-3944)	G	631 751-5349
I 2 Print Inc — Long Island City (G-7762)	F	718 937-8800
Impala Press Ltd — Ronkonkoma (G-14911)	G	631 588-4262
Ink Well — Brooklyn (G-2107)	G	718 253-9736
Instant Again LLC — Rochester (G-14449)	E	585 436-8003
Instant Stream Inc — New York (G-10611)	E	917 438-7182
Interstate Litho Corp — Brentwood (G-1185)	D	631 232-6025
J A T Printing Inc — Huntington (G-6664)	G	631 427-1155
J F B & Sons Lithographers — Lake Ronkonkoma (G-7278)	D	631 467-1444
J P Printing Inc — Farmingdale (G-5015)	G	516 293-6110
J V Haring & Son — Staten Island (G-15691)	F	718 720-1947
Jack J Florio Jr — Lockport (G-7595)	G	716 434-9123
Jam Printing Publishing Inc — Elmsford (G-4758)	G	914 345-8400
Jane Lewis — Binghamton (G-930)	G	607 722-0584
Japan Printing & Graphics Inc — New York (G-10700)	G	212 406-2905
Jfb Print Solutions Inc — Lido Beach (G-7441)	G	631 694-8300
Jon Lyn Ink Inc — Merrick (G-8386)	G	516 546-2312
Joseph Paul — Brooklyn (G-2149)	G	718 693-4269
Jurist Company Inc — Long Island City (G-7774)	G	212 243-8008
Kader Lithograph Company Inc — Long Island City (G-7777)	C	917 664-4380
Kaleidoscope Imaging Inc — New York (G-10802)	E	212 631-9947
Karr Graphics Corp — Long Island City (G-7779)	G	718 784-9390
Keeners East End Litho Inc — East Hampton (G-4412)	G	631 324-8565
Keller Bros & Miller Inc — Buffalo (G-3028)	G	716 854-2374
Key Brand Entertainment Inc — New York (G-10839)	C	212 966-5400
Kim Jae Printing Co Inc — Roslyn Heights (G-15028)	G	212 691-6289
King Lithographers Inc — Mount Vernon (G-8698)	E	914 667-4200
Kling Magnetics Inc — Chatham (G-3558)	E	518 392-4000
Kolcorp Industries Ltd — New York (G-10871)	F	212 354-0400
L & K Graphics Inc — Deer Park (G-4161)	G	631 667-2269
L Loy Press Inc — Buffalo (G-3040)	G	716 634-5966
Label Gallery Inc — Norwich (G-13030)	E	607 334-3244
Lake Placid Advertisers Wkshp — Lake Placid (G-7275)	E	518 523-3359
Laser Printer Checks Corp — Monroe (G-8559)	G	845 782-5837
Laumont Labs Inc — New York (G-10936)	E	212 664-0595
Lehmann Printing Company Inc — New York (G-10963)	G	212 929-2395
Leigh Scott Enterprises Inc — Bellerose (G-810)	G	718 343-5440
Leonard Martin Bus Systems — New City (G-8787)	G	845 638-9350
Li Script LLC — Woodbury (G-17292)	E	631 321-3850
Liberty Label Mfg Inc — Holbrook (G-6457)	E	631 737-2365
Litho Partners Inc — New York (G-11009)	E	212 627-9225
Litmor Publishing Corp — Hicksville (G-6364)	F	516 931-0012
Lmg National Publishing Inc — Fairport (G-4862)	E	585 598-6874
Loudon Ltd — East Northport (G-4441)	G	631 757-4447
Love Unlimited NY Inc — Westbury (G-17008)	E	718 359-8500
Magazines & Brochures Inc — Tonawanda (G-16178)	G	716 875-9699
Magjak Printing Corporation — Port Chester (G-13753)	G	914 939-8800
Marks Corpex Banknote Co — Bay Shore (G-715)	G	631 968-0277
Marlow Printing Co Inc — Brooklyn (G-2274)	E	718 625-4949
Master Image Printing Inc — Elmsford (G-4763)	G	914 347-4400
Mc Squared Nyc Inc — New York (G-11193)	F	212 947-2260
McG Graphics Inc — Dix Hills (G-4294)	G	631 499-0730
Mdr Printing Corp — Manhasset (G-8062)	G	516 627-3221
Merrill New York Company Inc — New York (G-11235)	C	212 229-6500
Michael K Lennon Inc — Westhampton Beach (G-17059)	E	631 288-5200
Mickelberry Communications Inc — New York (G-11252)	G	212 832-0303
Microera Printers Inc — Rochester (G-14509)	E	585 783-1300
Middletown Press — Middletown (G-8451)	G	845 343-1895
Midgley Printing Corp — Syracuse (G-15988)	G	315 475-1864
Miken Companies Inc — Buffalo (G-3065)	D	716 668-6311
Miller Enterprises CNY Inc — Manlius (G-8075)	G	315 682-4999
Minuteman Press Inc — Nanuet (G-8759)	G	845 623-2277
Minuteman Press Intl Inc — Jamaica (G-6932)	G	718 343-5440
Mod-Pac Corp — Buffalo (G-3072)	D	716 447-9013
Monarch Graphics Inc — Central Islip (G-3504)	F	631 232-1300
Moneast Inc — Wappingers Falls (G-16575)	G	845 298-8898
Multimedia Services Inc — Corning (G-3976)	E	607 936-3186
Multiple Imprssons of Rchester — Rochester (G-14525)	G	585 546-1160
Mutual Engraving Company Inc — West Hempstead (G-16861)	D	516 489-0534
Myrtle Leola Inc — Hempstead (G-6281)	G	516 228-2312
Nameplate Mfrs of Amer — Farmingdale (G-5061)	E	631 752-0055
Nash Printing Inc — Plainview (G-13623)	F	516 935-4567
NCR Corporation — Ithaca (G-6866)	C	607 273-5310
New Goldstar 1 Printing Corp — New York (G-11388)	G	212 343-3909
New York Digital Print Center — Whitestone (G-17212)	G	718 767-1953
New York Press & Graphics Inc — Albany (G-106)	F	518 489-7089
North Delaware Printing Inc — Tonawanda (G-16188)	G	716 692-0576
Northern NY Newspapers Corp — Watertown (G-16668)	C	315 782-1000
Observer Daily Sunday Newsppr — Dunkirk (G-4346)	D	716 366-3000
Office Grabs NY Inc — Brooklyn (G-2386)	G	212 444-1331
Old Ue LLC — Long Island City (G-7829)	B	718 707-0700
Orlandi Inc — Farmingdale (G-5071)	D	631 756-0110
Orlandi Inc — Farmingdale (G-5072)	E	631 756-0110
P D R Inc — Plainview (G-13626)	G	516 829-5300
Pace Editions Inc — New York (G-11550)	G	212 675-7431
Paladino Prtg & Graphics Inc — Flushing (G-5277)	G	718 279-6000
Pama Enterprises Inc — Great Neck (G-5828)	G	516 504-6300
Parkside Printing Co Inc — Jericho (G-7081)	F	516 933-5423
Parrinello Printing Inc — Buffalo (G-3115)	F	716 633-7780
Paya Printing of NY Inc — Albertson (G-157)	G	516 625-8346
PDM Litho Inc — Long Island City (G-7836)	E	718 301-1740
Persch Service Print Inc — Dunkirk (G-4347)	G	716 366-2677
Phoenix Graphics Inc — Rochester (G-14582)	E	585 232-4040
Photo Agents Ltd — Huntington (G-6674)	G	631 421-0258
Pic A Poc Enterprises Inc — Ronkonkoma (G-14970)	G	631 981-2094
Pine Bush Printing Co Inc — Albany (G-122)	G	518 456-2431
Platinum Printing & Graphics — Farmingdale (G-5082)	G	631 249-3325
Play-It Productions Inc — Port Washington (G-13856)	F	212 695-6530

Employee Codes: A=Over 500 employees, B=251-500
C=101-250, D=51-100, E=20-50, F=10-19, G=5-9

Pop Printing Incorporated	F	212 808-7800	Brooklyn ***(G-2429)***
Post Community Media LLC	C	518 374-4141	Saratoga Springs ***(G-15167)***
Pre Cycled Inc	G	845 278-7611	Brewster ***(G-1227)***
Preebro Printing	G	718 633-7300	Brooklyn ***(G-2437)***
Presstek Printing LLC	F	585 266-2770	Rochester ***(G-14599)***
Prestige Envelope & Lithograph	F	631 521-7043	Merrick ***(G-8391)***
Prestone Press LLC	C	347 468-7900	Long Island City ***(G-7845)***
Pricet Printing	G	315 655-0369	Cazenovia ***(G-3451)***
Print & Graphics Group	G	518 371-4649	Clifton Park ***(G-3704)***
Print Better Inc	G	347 348-1841	Ridgewood ***(G-14119)***
Print Center Inc	G	718 643-9559	Cold Spring Harbor ***(G-3770)***
Print Cottage LLC	F	516 369-1749	Massapequa Park ***(G-8189)***
Print Management Group Corp	G	212 213-1555	New York ***(G-11718)***
Print Market Inc	G	631 940-8181	Deer Park ***(G-4193)***
Print Media Inc	D	212 563-4040	New York ***(G-11719)***
Print On Demand Initiative Inc	F	585 239-6044	Rochester ***(G-14600)***
Print Shop	G	607 734-4937	Horseheads ***(G-6589)***
Print Solutions Plus Inc	G	315 234-3801	Liverpool ***(G-7545)***
Printcorp Inc	E	631 696-0641	Ronkonkoma ***(G-14971)***
Printech Business Systems Inc	F	212 290-2542	New York ***(G-11720)***
Printers 3 Inc	F	631 351-1331	Hauppauge ***(G-6172)***
Printing Resources Inc	E	518 482-2470	Albany ***(G-124)***
Printing Spectrum Inc	F	631 689-1010	East Setauket ***(G-4490)***
Printing X Press Ions	G	631 242-1992	Dix Hills ***(G-4296)***
Printinghouse Press Ltd	G	212 719-0990	New York ***(G-11722)***
Printutopia	F	718 788-1545	Brooklyn ***(G-2451)***
Printz and Patternz LLC	G	518 944-6020	Schenectady ***(G-15286)***
Professional Solutions Print	G	631 231-9300	Hauppauge ***(G-6174)***
Profile Printing & Graphics	G	631 273-2727	Hauppauge ***(G-6175)***
Psychonomic Society Inc	E	512 381-1494	New York ***(G-11743)***
Quad/Graphics Inc	B	212 672-1300	New York ***(G-11764)***
Quad/Graphics Inc	E	718 706-7600	Long Island City ***(G-7851)***
Quad/Graphics Inc	A	212 206-5535	New York ***(G-11765)***
Quad/Graphics Inc	A	212 741-1001	New York ***(G-11766)***
Quality Graphics Tri State	G	845 735-2523	Pearl River ***(G-13465)***
R Hochman Papers Incorporated	F	516 466-6414	Brooklyn ***(G-2472)***
Rapid Print and Marketing Inc	G	585 924-1520	Victor ***(G-16499)***
Rapid Reproductions LLC	G	607 843-2221	Oxford ***(G-13364)***
Rapid Service Engraving Co	G	716 896-4555	Buffalo ***(G-3154)***
REM Printing Inc	G	518 438-7338	Albany ***(G-128)***
Resonant Legal Media LLC	E	212 687-7100	New York ***(G-11840)***
Rheinwald Printing Co Inc	F	585 637-5100	Brockport ***(G-1246)***
Richard Ruffner	F	631 234-4600	Central Islip ***(G-3509)***
RIT Printing Corp	F	631 586-6220	Bay Shore ***(G-735)***
Rmf Print Management Group	F	716 683-4351	Depew ***(G-4273)***
Robert Portegello Graphics	G	718 241-8118	Brooklyn ***(G-2500)***
Robert Tabatznik Assoc Inc	F	845 336-4555	Kingston ***(G-7209)***
Rosen Mandell & Immerman Inc	E	212 691-2277	New York ***(G-11916)***
Rv Printing	G	631 567-8658	Holbrook ***(G-6469)***
Ry-Gan Printing Inc	G	585 482-7770	Rochester ***(G-14663)***
Ryan Printing Inc	E	845 535-3235	Blauvelt ***(G-974)***
Sammba Printing Inc	G	516 944-4449	Port Washington ***(G-13862)***
Sample News Group LLC	D	315 343-3800	Oswego ***(G-13340)***
SDS Business Cards Inc	F	516 747-3131	Syosset ***(G-15839)***
Seaboard Graphic Services LLC	E	315 652-4200	Liverpool ***(G-7547)***
Seifert Graphics Inc	F	315 736-2744	Oriskany ***(G-13313)***
Sentinel Printing Inc	G	516 334-7400	Westbury ***(G-17026)***
Shipmtes/Printmates Holdg Corp	D	518 370-1158	Scotia ***(G-15330)***
Sign World Inc	E	212 619-9000	Brooklyn ***(G-2554)***
Sizzal LLC	E	212 354-6123	Long Island City ***(G-7878)***
Sloane Design Inc	G	212 539-0184	New York ***(G-12099)***
Source Envelope Inc	G	866 284-0707	Farmingdale ***(G-5111)***
South Bridge Press Inc	G	212 233-4047	New York ***(G-12144)***
Speedcard Inc	G	631 472-1904	Holbrook ***(G-6473)***
Spring Printing Inc	F	718 797-2818	Brooklyn ***(G-2591)***
St James Printing Inc	G	631 981-2095	Ronkonkoma ***(G-14989)***
St Lawrence County Newspapers	D	315 393-1003	Ogdensburg ***(G-13122)***
Star Press Pearl River Inc	G	845 268-2294	Valley Cottage ***(G-16389)***
Steffen Publishing Inc	D	315 865-4100	Holland Patent ***(G-6488)***
Sterling North America Inc	E	631 243-6933	Hauppauge ***(G-6201)***
Sterling Pierce Company Inc	E	516 593-1170	East Rockaway ***(G-4471)***
Sterling United Inc	G	716 835-9290	Amherst ***(G-262)***
Stevens Bandes Graphics Corp	F	212 675-1128	New York ***(G-12202)***
Stony Brook University	E	631 632-6434	Stony Brook ***(G-15772)***
Studley Printing & Publishing	F	518 563-1414	Plattsburgh ***(G-13701)***
Summit Print & Mail LLC	G	716 433-1014	Lockport ***(G-7616)***
Sun Printing Incorporated	E	607 337-3034	Norwich ***(G-13037)***
Syracuse Computer Forms Inc	E	315 478-0108	Syracuse ***(G-16050)***
Sz - Design & Print Inc	F	845 352-0395	Monsey ***(G-8583)***
Taylor	G	518 954-2832	Amsterdam ***(G-369)***
Technipoly Manufacturing Inc	E	718 383-0363	Brooklyn ***(G-2650)***
Teller Printing Corp	G	718 486-3662	Brooklyn ***(G-2653)***
The Kingsbury Printing Co Inc	G	518 747-6606	Hudson Falls ***(G-6650)***
Tobay Printing Co Inc	E	631 842-3300	Copiague ***(G-3934)***
Tom & Jerry Printcraft Forms	E	914 777-7468	Mamaroneck ***(G-8048)***
Torsaf Printers Inc	G	516 569-5577	Hewlett ***(G-6314)***
Transaction Printer Group	G	607 274-2500	Ithaca ***(G-6881)***
Transcntinental Ultra Flex Inc	B	718 272-9100	Brooklyn ***(G-2674)***
Transcontinental Printing GP	G	716 626-3078	Amherst ***(G-267)***
Tri-Lon Clor Lithographers Ltd	E	212 255-6140	New York ***(G-12400)***
Tri-Star Offset Corp	E	718 894-5555	Maspeth ***(G-8173)***
Triad Printing Inc	G	845 343-2722	Middletown ***(G-8466)***
Tripi Engraving Co Inc	E	718 383-6500	Brooklyn ***(G-2682)***
Troy Sign & Printing	G	718 994-4482	Bronx ***(G-1479)***
Unique Printing Company LLC	G	718 386-2519	Flushing ***(G-5305)***
Upstate Printing Inc	F	315 475-6140	Syracuse ***(G-16064)***
Vanguard Graphics LLC	C	607 272-1212	Ithaca ***(G-6882)***
Variable Graphics LLC	G	212 691-2323	New York ***(G-12505)***
Vectra Inc	G	718 361-1000	Long Island City ***(G-7911)***
Vic-Gina Printing Company Inc	G	914 636-0200	New Rochelle ***(G-8927)***
Vicks Lithograph & Prtg Corp	C	315 736-9344	Yorkville ***(G-17528)***
Vicks Lithograph & Prtg Corp	C	315 272-2401	Yorkville ***(G-17527)***
VIP Printing	G	718 641-9361	Howard Beach ***(G-6599)***
Virgil Mountain Inc	G	212 378-0007	New York ***(G-12547)***
Wallkill Valley Publications	E	845 561-0170	Newburgh ***(G-12786)***
Walnut Printing Inc	G	718 707-0100	Long Island City ***(G-7917)***
Wappingers Falls Shopper Inc	E	845 297-3723	Wappingers Falls ***(G-16578)***
Webster Printing Corporation	F	585 671-1533	Webster ***(G-16742)***
Westmore Litho Corp	G	718 361-9403	Long Island City ***(G-7920)***
Westprint Inc	G	212 989-3805	New York ***(G-12617)***
William Boyd Printing Co Inc	C	518 339-5832	Latham ***(G-7385)***
William J Kline & Son Inc	D	518 843-1100	Amsterdam ***(G-374)***
William J Ryan	G	585 392-6200	Hilton ***(G-6421)***
Wilson Press LLC	E	315 568-9693	Seneca Falls ***(G-15372)***
Winner Press Inc	E	718 937-7715	Long Island City ***(G-7924)***
Won & Lee Inc	E	516 222-0712	Garden City ***(G-5538)***
Wynco Press One Inc	G	516 354-6145	Glen Oaks ***(G-5641)***
X Myles Mar Inc	E	212 683-2015	New York ***(G-12673)***
X-L Envelope and Printing Inc	F	716 852-2135	Buffalo ***(G-3258)***
Yorktown Printing Corp	C	914 962-2526	Yorktown Heights ***(G-17522)***
Zacmel Graphics LLC	G	631 944-6031	Huntington ***(G-6692)***
Zenger Group Inc	E	716 871-1058	Tonawanda ***(G-16217)***

PRINTING: Offset

514 Adams Corporation	G	516 352-6948	Franklin Square ***(G-5359)***
A & D Offset Printers Ltd	G	516 746-2476	Mineola ***(G-8486)***
A & M Litho Inc	E	516 342-9727	Bethpage ***(G-861)***
A Q P Inc	G	585 256-1690	Rochester ***(G-14161)***
Act Communications Group Inc	F	631 669-2403	West Islip ***(G-16902)***
Action Graphics Services Inc	F	607 785-1951	Vestal ***(G-16438)***
Ad Vantage Press	G	212 941-8355	New York ***(G-9023)***
Ads-N-Color Inc	E	718 797-0900	Brooklyn ***(G-1564)***
Advantage Press Inc	F	518 584-3405	Saratoga Springs ***(G-15142)***
Advantage Printing Inc	F	718 820-0688	Kew Gardens ***(G-7158)***
Advantage Quick Print Inc	G	212 989-5644	New York ***(G-9047)***
Agrecolor Inc	F	516 741-8700	Mineola ***(G-8491)***

PRODUCT

PRODUCT SECTION

PRINTING: Offset

Company	Code	Phone
Ahw Printing Corp — Oceanside (G-13072)	F	516 536-3600
Alamar Printing Inc — White Plains (G-17074)	F	914 993-9007
Albany Letter Shop Inc — Albany (G-39)	G	518 434-1172
All Color Offset Printers Inc — Farmingdale (G-4936)	G	516 420-0649
All Ready Inc — Conklin (G-3864)	G	607 722-0826
Allen William & Company Inc — Glendale (G-5644)	C	212 675-6461
Allstatebannerscom Corporation — Long Island City (G-7652)	G	718 300-1256
Alpha Printing Corp — Syracuse (G-15851)	F	315 454-5507
Alpina Color Graphics Inc — New York (G-9100)	G	212 285-2700
Amsterdam Printing & Litho Inc — Queensbury (G-13987)	G	518 792-6501
Apple Press — White Plains (G-17079)	G	914 723-6660
Ares Printing and Packg Corp — Brooklyn (G-1625)	C	718 858-8760
Arista Innovations Inc — Mineola (G-8496)	E	516 746-2262
Arnold Printing Corp — Ithaca (G-6819)	F	607 272-7800
Arnold Taylor Printing Inc — Bellmore (G-813)	G	516 781-0564
Atlantic Color Corp — Shirley (G-15413)	E	631 345-3800
Automatic Press Inc — New York (G-9267)	G	212 924-5573
B & P Jays Inc — Buffalo (G-2830)	G	716 668-8408
Bajan Group Inc — Latham (G-7355)	G	518 464-2884
Barone Offset Printing Corp — Mohegan Lake (G-8543)	G	212 989-5500
Bartolomeo Publishing Inc — West Babylon (G-16774)	G	631 420-4949
Bates Jackson Engraving Co Inc — Buffalo (G-2834)	E	716 854-3000
Beacon Press Inc — White Plains (G-17084)	G	212 691-5050
Beehive Press Inc — Bronx (G-1281)	G	718 654-1200
Bel Aire Offset Corp — Flushing (G-5229)	G	718 539-8333
Benchmark Graphics Ltd — New York (G-9358)	F	212 683-1711
Beyer Graphics Inc — Commack (G-3824)	D	631 543-3900
Bishop Print Shop Inc — Edmeston (G-4622)	G	607 965-8155
Bmg Printing and Promotion LLC — Bohemia (G-1026)	G	631 231-9200
Brennans Quick Print Inc — Glens Falls (G-5673)	G	518 793-4999
Bridge Printing Inc — Long Island City (G-7690)	G	212 243-5390
Brown Printers of Troy Inc — Troy (G-16228)	F	518 235-4080
Brownstone Capitl Partners LLC — New York (G-9473)	G	212 889-0069
Canaan Printing Inc — Bayside (G-768)	F	718 729-3100
Canastota Publishing Co Inc — Canastota (G-3365)	G	315 697-9010
Canfield & Tack Inc — Rochester (G-14257)	D	585 235-7710
Capital Dst Print & Imaging — Schenectady (G-15238)	G	518 456-6773
Carges Entps of Canandaigua — Canandaigua (G-3338)	G	585 394-2600
Carnels Printing Inc — Port Washington (G-13803)	G	516 883-3355
Carr Communications Group LLC — Vestal (G-16444)	F	607 748-0481
Cayuga Press Cortland Inc — East Syracuse (G-4516)	E	888 229-8421
Cedar West Inc — Ronkonkoma (G-14886)	G	631 467-1444
Chakra Communications Inc — Endicott (G-4798)	E	607 748-7491
Chenango Union Printing Inc — Norwich (G-13022)	G	607 334-2112
Cilyox Inc — Buffalo (G-2874)	F	716 853-3809
Clarsons Corp — Rochester (G-14278)	F	585 235-8775
Cohber Press Inc — West Henrietta (G-16873)	D	585 475-9100
Color Carton Corp — Bronx (G-1302)	D	718 665-0840
Colorfast — New York (G-9674)	F	212 929-2440
Colorfully Yours Inc — Bay Shore (G-687)	F	631 242-8600
Combine Graphics Corp — Forest Hills (G-5322)	G	212 695-4044
Commerce Offset Ltd — Thornwood (G-16118)	G	914 769-6671
Commercial Press Inc — Canton (G-3381)	G	315 274-0028
Complemar Print LLC — Buffalo (G-2884)	F	716 875-7238
Composite Forms Inc — Port Chester (G-13740)	F	914 937-1808
Concept Printing Inc — Nyack (G-13047)	G	845 353-4040
Conkur Printing Co Inc — New York (G-9701)	E	212 541-5980
Consolidated Color Press Inc — New York (G-9704)	F	212 929-8197
Constas Printing Corporation — Syracuse (G-15905)	F	315 474-2176
Coral Graphic Services Inc — Hicksville (G-6335)	C	516 576-2100
Craig Envelope Corp — Long Island City (G-7706)	E	718 786-4277
Creative Forms Inc — New York (G-9749)	G	212 431-7540
Creative Printing Corp — New York (G-9750)	G	212 226-3870
Dani Lu Inc — Latham (G-7360)	E	518 782-5411
Dealer-Presscom Inc — Bohemia (G-1053)	F	631 589-0434
Dell Communications Inc — New York (G-9840)	F	212 989-3434
Delta Press Inc — High Falls (G-6400)	E	212 989-3445
Design Lithographers Inc — New York (G-9853)	G	212 645-8900
Design Printing Corp — Farmingdale (G-4975)	G	631 753-9801
Dick Bailey Service Inc — Brooklyn (G-1863)	F	718 522-4363
Dispatch Graphics Inc — New York (G-9884)	F	212 307-5943
Doco Quick Print Inc — Watertown (G-16650)	G	315 782-6623
Dowd - Witbeck Printing Corp — Troy (G-16234)	F	518 274-2421
DP Murphy Co Inc — Deer Park (G-4132)	D	631 673-9400
Dupli Graphics Corporation — Syracuse (G-15926)	G	315 422-4732
East Ridge Quick Print — Rochester (G-14325)	F	585 266-4911
Eastern Hills Printing — Clarence (G-3659)	G	716 741-3300
Eastside Printers — East Syracuse (G-4527)	F	315 437-6515
Edgian Press Inc — Hicksville (G-6342)	G	516 931-2114
Eleanor Ettinger Inc — New York (G-9995)	E	212 925-7474
Elmat Quality Printing Ltd — Cedarhurst (G-3456)	F	516 569-5722
Empire Press Co — Brooklyn (G-1921)	G	718 756-9500
Engrav-O-Type Press Inc — Rochester (G-14351)	F	585 262-7590
Excel Graphics Services Inc — New York (G-10101)	F	212 929-2183
Excelsior Graphics Inc — New York (G-10104)	G	212 730-6200
F & B Photo Offset Co Inc — Island Park (G-6779)	G	516 431-5433
F & T Graphics Inc — Hauppauge (G-6075)	F	631 643-1000
F J Remey Co Inc — Mineola (G-8511)	G	516 741-5112
Fambus Inc — Endicott (G-4807)	G	607 785-3700
Farthing Press Inc — Buffalo (G-2945)	F	716 852-4674
Federal Envelope Inc — New York (G-10148)	F	212 243-8380
Finer Touch Printing Corp — Port Washington (G-13815)	F	516 944-8000
Fitch Graphics Ltd — New York (G-10175)	E	212 619-3800
Five Star Prtg & Mailing Svcs — New York (G-10176)	F	212 929-0300
Flare Multicopy Corp — Brooklyn (G-1982)	E	718 258-8860
Flower City Printing Inc — Rochester (G-14374)	C	585 663-9000
Flp Group LLC — Auburn (G-496)	F	315 252-7583
Fort Orange Press Inc — Albany (G-81)	E	518 489-3233
Forward Enterprises Inc — Rochester (G-14379)	F	585 235-7670
Francis Emory Fitch Inc — New York (G-10199)	E	212 619-3800
Frederick Coon Inc — Elma (G-4648)	F	716 683-6812
Freeville Publishing Co Inc — Freeville (G-5435)	F	607 844-9119
Fulton Newspapers Inc — Fulton (G-5457)	E	315 598-6397
Gallagher Printing Inc — Buffalo (G-2962)	F	716 873-2434
Gallant Graphices Ltd Inc — Stanfordville (G-15627)	E	845 868-1166
Gateway Prtg & Graphics Inc — Hamburg (G-5926)	G	716 823-3873
Gbv Promotions Inc — Bay Shore (G-702)	F	631 231-7300
Gem Reproduction Services Corp — Wappingers Falls (G-16570)	G	845 298-0152
Gemson Graphics Inc — Albertson (G-154)	G	516 873-8400
General Business Supply Inc — Watervliet (G-16685)	D	518 720-3939
Geneva Printing Company Inc — Geneva (G-5579)	G	315 789-8191
Glens Falls Printing LLC — Glens Falls (G-5681)	F	518 793-0555
Golos Printing Inc — Elmira Heights (G-4710)	G	607 732-1896
Grand Meridian Printing Inc — Long Island City (G-7752)	E	718 937-3888
Graphic Dimensions Press Inc — Brooklyn (G-2049)	F	718 252-4003
Graphics of Utica — Remsen (G-14040)	G	315 797-4868
Graphics Plus Printing Inc — Cortland (G-4029)	F	607 299-0500
Greenwood Graphics Inc — Hicksville (G-6353)	F	516 822-4856
H T L & S Ltd — Brooklyn (G-2060)	F	718 435-4474
Harmon and Castella Printing — Poughkeepsie (G-13905)	F	845 471-9163
Heritage Printing Center — Plattsburgh (G-13669)	G	518 563-8240
Hi Speed Envelope Co Inc — Mount Vernon (G-8690)	F	718 617-1600
Hill Crest Press — Catskill (G-3429)	G	518 943-0671
Hillside Printing Inc — Jamaica (G-6919)	F	718 658-6719
Hospitality Graphics Inc — New York (G-10510)	G	212 643-6700
Hudson Envelope Corporation — New York (G-10525)	E	212 473-6666
Hudson Printing Co Inc — New York (G-10527)	E	718 937-8600
In-House Inc — College Point (G-3787)	F	718 445-9007
Ink-It Printing Inc — College Point (G-3788)	G	718 229-5590
International Newsppr Prtg Co — Glen Head (G-5635)	E	516 626-6095
Interstate Thermographers Corp — White Plains (G-17124)	G	914 948-1745
Iver Printing Inc — Flushing (G-5255)	G	718 275-2070
J & J Printing Inc — Syracuse (G-15964)	G	315 458-7411
Jacobs Press Inc — Auburn (G-503)	F	315 252-4861
James Conolly Printing Co — Rochester (G-14459)	E	585 426-4150

Employee Codes: A=Over 500 employees, B=251-500
C=101-250, D=51-100, E=20-50, F=10-19, G=5-9

JDS Graphics Inc	F	973 330-3300	New York	(G-10711)
Johnnys Ideal Printing Co	G	518 828-6666	Hudson	(G-6621)
Judith Lewis Printer Inc	G	516 997-7777	Westbury	(G-17000)
Kas-Ray Industries Inc	F	212 620-3144	New York	(G-10812)
Kaufman Brothers Printing	G	212 563-1854	New York	(G-10820)
Kent Associates Inc	G	212 675-0722	New York	(G-10837)
Kenyon Press Inc	E	607 674-9066	Sherburne	(G-15392)
Kimsco Business Systems Inc	G	516 599-5658	Lynbrook	(G-7952)
Kinaneco Inc	E	315 468-6201	Syracuse	(G-15974)
Kingsbury Printing Co Inc	G	518 747-6606	Queensbury	(G-14002)
Knickerbocker Graphics Svcs	F	212 244-7485	New York	(G-10861)
L I F Publishing Corp	E	631 345-5200	Shirley	(G-15422)
L K Printing Corp	G	914 761-1944	White Plains	(G-17132)
L M N Printing Company Inc	E	516 285-8526	Valley Stream	(G-16411)
Lee Printing Inc	G	718 237-1651	Brooklyn	(G-2205)
Lennons Litho Inc	F	315 866-3156	Herkimer	(G-6304)
Levon Graphics Corp	D	631 753-2022	Farmingdale	(G-5035)
Lithomatic Business Forms Inc	G	212 255-6700	New York	(G-11010)
Louis Heindl & Son Inc	G	585 454-5080	Rochester	(G-14483)
Lynmar Printing Corp	G	631 957-8500	Amityville	(G-306)
M L Design Inc	G	212 233-0213	New York	(G-11075)
M T M Printing Co Inc	F	718 353-3297	College Point	(G-3796)
Madison Printing Corp	G	607 273-3535	Ithaca	(G-6857)
Malone Industrial Press Inc	G	518 483-5880	Malone	(G-8013)
Manifestation-Glow Press Inc	G	718 380-5259	Fresh Meadows	(G-5444)
Marcal Printing Inc	G	516 942-9500	Hicksville	(G-6367)
Marcy Printing Inc	G	718 935-9100	Brooklyn	(G-2268)
Mark T Westinghouse	G	518 678-3262	Catskill	(G-3431)
Marsid Group Ltd	G	516 334-1603	Carle Place	(G-3396)
Mason & Gore Inc	E	914 921-1025	Rye	(G-15063)
Medallion Associates Inc	E	212 929-9130	New York	(G-11207)
Mercury Print Productions Inc	C	585 458-7900	Rochester	(G-14504)
Mib Industries Inc	E	718 497-2200	Ridgewood	(G-14114)
Mid Atlantic Graphics Corp	E	631 345-3800	Shirley	(G-15425)
Mid-York Press Inc	D	607 674-4491	Sherburne	(G-15393)
Midstate Printing Corp	E	315 475-4101	Syracuse	(G-15989)
Mikam Graphics LLC	D	212 684-9393	New York	(G-11264)
Miller Printing & Litho Inc	G	518 842-0001	Amsterdam	(G-356)
Mines Press Inc	C	914 788-1800	Cortlandt Manor	(G-4052)
Mitchell Prtg & Mailing Inc	F	315 343-3531	Oswego	(G-13335)
MJB Printing Corp	G	631 581-0177	Islip	(G-6811)
Monte Press Inc	G	718 325-4999	Bronx	(G-1403)
Moore Printing Company Inc	G	585 394-1533	Canandaigua	(G-3349)
Nesher Printing Inc	G	212 760-2521	New York	(G-11371)
New Horizon Graphics Inc	E	631 231-8055	Hauppauge	(G-6147)
New York Typing & Printing Co	G	718 268-7900	Forest Hills	(G-5327)
Newburgh Envelope Corp	G	845 566-4211	Newburgh	(G-12770)
Newport Graphics Inc	E	212 924-2600	New York	(G-11414)
Newsgraphics of Delmar Inc	E	518 439-5363	Delmar	(G-4245)
Northeast Commercial Prtg Inc	G	518 459-5047	Albany	(G-109)
Northeast Prtg & Dist Co Inc	E	518 563-8214	Plattsburgh	(G-13683)
Official Offset Corporation	E	631 957-8500	Amityville	(G-317)
Olympic Press Inc	F	212 242-4934	New York	(G-11502)
Orbis Brynmore Lithographics	G	212 987-2100	New York	(G-11522)
Orffeo Printing & Imaging Inc	G	716 681-5757	Lancaster	(G-7328)
Ozipko Enterprises Inc	G	585 424-6740	Rochester	(G-14560)
P & W Press Inc	E	646 486-3417	New York	(G-11547)
Panther Graphics Inc	E	585 546-7163	Rochester	(G-14571)
Patrick Ryans Modern Press	F	518 434-2921	Albany	(G-114)
Paul Michael Group Inc	G	631 585-5700	Ronkonkoma	(G-14966)
Peachtree Enterprises Inc	E	212 989-3445	Long Island City	(G-7837)
Perception Imaging Inc	F	631 676-5262	Holbrook	(G-6466)
Petcap Press Corporation	F	718 609-0910	Long Island City	(G-7840)
Petit Printing Corp	G	716 871-9490	Getzville	(G-5603)
Pioneer Printers Inc	F	716 693-7100	North Tonawanda	(G-12986)
Pollack Graphics Inc	G	212 727-8400	New York	(G-11681)
Positive Print Litho Offset	G	212 431-4850	New York	(G-11689)
Press of Fremont Payne Inc	G	212 966-6570	New York	(G-11700)
Printroc Inc	F	585 461-2556	Rochester	(G-14601)
Pro Printing	G	516 561-9700	Lynbrook	(G-7957)
Progressive Graphics & Prtg	G	315 331-3635	Newark	(G-12741)
Prompt Printing Inc	G	631 454-6524	Farmingdale	(G-5089)
Quad/Graphics Inc	A	518 581-4000	Saratoga Springs	(G-15168)
Quadrangle Quickprints Ltd	G	631 694-4464	Melville	(G-8351)
Quicker Printer Inc	G	607 734-8622	Elmira	(G-4698)
Quickprint	G	585 394-2600	Canandaigua	(G-3356)
R & J Graphics Inc	F	631 293-6611	Farmingdale	(G-5095)
R D Printing Associates Inc	F	631 390-5964	Farmingdale	(G-5096)
Rasco Graphics Inc	G	212 206-0447	New York	(G-11802)
Reflex Offset Inc	G	516 746-4142	Deer Park	(G-4199)
Register Graphics Inc	E	716 358-2921	Randolph	(G-14018)
Resonant Legal Media LLC	D	800 781-3591	New York	(G-11841)
Rmd Holding Inc	G	845 628-0030	Mahopac	(G-8001)
Rosemont Press Incorporated	E	212 239-4770	New York	(G-11915)
Sand Hill Industries Inc	G	518 885-7991	Ballston Spa	(G-608)
Sanford Printing Inc	G	718 461-1202	Flushing	(G-5290)
Scotti Graphics Inc	E	212 367-9602	Long Island City	(G-7872)
Searles Graphics Inc	F	631 345-2202	Yaphank	(G-17401)
Security Offset Services Inc	G	631 944-6031	Huntington	(G-6680)
Shield Press Inc	G	212 431-7489	New York	(G-12050)
Shipman Printing Inds Inc	E	716 504-7700	Niagara Falls	(G-12876)
Shoreline Publishing Inc	G	914 738-7869	Pelham	(G-13494)
Spectrum Graphics & Print	F	845 473-4400	Poughkeepsie	(G-13933)
Speedway Press Inc	G	315 343-3531	Oswego	(G-13341)
St Gerard Enterprises Inc	F	631 473-2003	Port Jeff STA	(G-13770)
St Vincent Press Inc	F	585 325-5320	Rochester	(G-14699)
Standwill Packaging Inc	E	631 752-1236	Farmingdale	(G-5113)
Star Quality Printing Inc	F	631 273-1900	Hauppauge	(G-6200)
Steval Graphics Concepts Inc	F	516 576-0220	Plainview	(G-13636)
Stevenson Printing Co Inc	G	516 676-1233	Glen Cove	(G-5629)
Stony Point Graphics Ltd	G	845 786-3322	Stony Point	(G-15777)
Stubbs Printing Inc	G	315 769-8641	Massena	(G-8201)
Stylistic Press Inc	F	212 675-0797	New York	(G-12225)
Suffolk Copy Center Inc	G	631 665-0570	Bay Shore	(G-745)
Summit Graphics	G	716 433-1014	Lockport	(G-7615)
T C Peters Printing Co Inc	G	315 724-4149	Utica	(G-16361)
The Nugent Organization Inc	F	212 645-6600	Oceanside	(G-13101)
Thomas Group Inc	F	212 947-6400	New York	(G-12319)
Top Copi Reproductions Inc	F	212 571-4141	New York	(G-12368)
Toppan Printing Co Amer Inc	E	212 975-9060	New York	(G-12370)
Total Concept Graphic Inc	G	212 229-2626	New York	(G-12378)
Tovie Asarese Royal Prtg Co	G	716 885-7692	Buffalo	(G-3223)
Trade Mark Graphics Inc	G	718 306-0001	Brooklyn	(G-2673)
Tremont Offset Inc	G	718 892-7333	Bronx	(G-1474)
Tri Kolor Printing & Sty	F	315 474-6753	Syracuse	(G-16061)
Tri-Town News Inc	E	607 561-3515	Sidney	(G-15442)
Tropp Printing Corp	G	212 233-4519	New York	(G-12409)
Tucker Printers Inc	D	585 359-3030	Henrietta	(G-6298)
Twenty-First Century Press Inc	F	716 837-0800	Buffalo	(G-3227)
Twin Counties Pro Printers Inc	F	518 828-3278	Hudson	(G-6636)
Unicom Graphic Communications	G	212 221-2456	New York	(G-12452)
V & J Graphics Inc	G	315 363-1933	Oneida	(G-13169)
Valentine Printing Corp	G	718 444-4400	Brooklyn	(G-2716)
Veterans Offset Printing Inc	G	585 288-2900	Rochester	(G-14752)
Viatech Pubg Solutions Inc	E	631 968-8500	Bay Shore	(G-754)
Vincys Printing Ltd	F	518 355-4363	Schenectady	(G-15309)
Vivona Business Printers Inc	G	516 496-3453	Syosset	(G-15842)
Wall Street Business Pdts Inc	E	212 563-4014	New York	(G-12580)
Warren Printing Inc	F	212 627-5000	Long Island City	(G-7918)
Wayne Printing Inc	F	914 761-2400	White Plains	(G-17182)
Weeks & Reichel Printing Inc	G	631 589-1443	Sayville	(G-15215)
Weicro Graphics Inc	E	631 253-3360	West Babylon	(G-16840)
Westchester Mailing Service	E	914 948-1116	White Plains	(G-17184)
Westypo Printers Inc	G	914 737-7394	Peekskill	(G-13487)
William Charles Prtg Co Inc	E	516 349-0900	Plainview	(G-13646)

PRODUCT SECTION

Winson Surnamer Inc ....G....... 718 729-8787
  Long Island City *(G-7925)*
Woodbury Printing Plus + Inc ....G....... 845 928-6610
  Central Valley *(G-3529)*
Zenger Partners LLC ....E....... 716 876-2284
  Kenmore *(G-7152)*

PRINTING: Pamphlets

Willis Mc Donald Co Inc ....F....... 212 366-1526
  New York *(G-12638)*

PRINTING: Photo-Offset

Academy Printing Services Inc ....G....... 631 765-3346
  Southold *(G-15557)*
Allied Reproductions Inc ....E....... 212 255-2472
  New York *(G-9090)*
D G M Graphics Inc ....F....... 516 223-2220
  Merrick *(G-8383)*
Genie Instant Printing Co Inc ....F....... 212 575-8258
  New York *(G-10277)*
Leader Printing Inc ....F....... 516 546-1544
  Merrick *(G-8388)*
National Reproductions Inc ....E....... 212 619-3800
  New York *(G-11349)*
Pronto Printer ....G....... 914 737-0800
  Cortlandt Manor *(G-4053)*
Rapid Rays Printing & Copying ....G....... 716 852-0550
  Buffalo *(G-3153)*
Scriven Duplicating Service ....G....... 518 233-8180
  Troy *(G-16253)*
Three Star Offset Printing ....F....... 516 867-8223
  Freeport *(G-5431)*

PRINTING: Photogravure

Dijifi LLC ....F....... 646 519-2447
  Brooklyn *(G-1864)*

PRINTING: Photolithographic

BP Digital Imaging LLC ....G....... 607 753-0022
  Cortland *(G-4016)*

PRINTING: Rotary Photogravure

Mastro Graphic Arts Inc ....E....... 585 436-7570
  Rochester *(G-14499)*

PRINTING: Rotogravure

American Packaging Corporation .....C....... 585 254-9500
  Rochester *(G-14198)*

PRINTING: Screen, Broadwoven Fabrics, Cotton

D & R Silk Screening Ltd ....F....... 631 234-7464
  Central Islip *(G-3494)*
Dynamic Screenprinting ....G....... 518 487-4256
  Albany *(G-74)*
Judscott Handprints Ltd ....F....... 914 347-5515
  Elmsford *(G-4759)*
Loremanss Embroidery Engrav ....F....... 518 834-9205
  Keeseville *(G-7139)*
Printery ....G....... 315 253-7403
  Auburn *(G-514)*
Seo Ryung Inc ....F....... 718 321-0755
  Flushing *(G-5291)*
Steve Poli Sales ....G....... 315 487-0394
  Camillus *(G-3324)*
Tramwell Inc ....G....... 315 789-2762
  Geneva *(G-5587)*
Ward Sales Co Inc ....G....... 315 476-5276
  Syracuse *(G-16068)*
Z Best Printing Inc ....F....... 631 595-1400
  Deer Park *(G-4230)*

PRINTING: Screen, Fabric

Apple Imprints Apparel Inc ....E....... 716 893-1130
  Buffalo *(G-2817)*
Apsco Sports Enterprises Inc ....D....... 718 965-9500
  Brooklyn *(G-1620)*
Aro-Graph Corporation ....G....... 315 463-8693
  Syracuse *(G-15857)*
Art Flag Company Inc ....F....... 212 334-1890
  New York *(G-9210)*
Creative Images & Applique ....D....... 718 821-8700
  Maspeth *(G-8126)*
Dirt T Shirts Inc ....E....... 845 336-4230
  Kingston *(G-7187)*

Galli Shirts and Sports AP ....G....... 845 226-7305
  Stormville *(G-15779)*
Human Technologies Corporation ...F....... 315 735-3532
  Utica *(G-16340)*
Irene Cerone ....G....... 315 668-2899
  Brewerton *(G-1204)*
J M L Productions Inc ....D....... 718 643-1674
  Brooklyn *(G-2126)*
Kevin J Kassman ....G....... 585 529-4245
  Rochester *(G-14469)*
Mart-Tex Athletics Inc ....E....... 631 454-9583
  Farmingdale *(G-5043)*
Park Avenue Imprints LLC ....G....... 716 822-5737
  Buffalo *(G-3113)*
Printz and Patternz LLC ....F....... 518 944-6020
  Schenectady *(G-15286)*
Rainbow Lettering ....G....... 607 732-5751
  Elmira *(G-4699)*
Randy Sixberry ....G....... 315 265-6211
  Potsdam *(G-13883)*
Special Tees ....E....... 718 980-0987
  Staten Island *(G-15735)*
Wicked Smart LLC ....F....... 518 459-2855
  Watervliet *(G-16692)*

PRINTING: Screen, Manmade Fiber & Silk, Broadwoven Fabric

Efs Designs ....G....... 718 852-9511
  Brooklyn *(G-1906)*
Intertex USA Inc ....F....... 212 279-3601
  New York *(G-10641)*
Judscott Handprints Ltd ....F....... 914 347-5515
  Elmsford *(G-4759)*
Mv Corp Inc ....C....... 631 273-8020
  Bay Shore *(G-720)*
Rescuestuff Inc ....G....... 718 318-7570
  Peekskill *(G-13480)*
Screen Gems Inc ....G....... 845 561-0036
  New Windsor *(G-8953)*
Valley Stream Sporting Gds Inc ......E....... 516 593-7800
  Lynbrook *(G-7966)*

PRINTING: Thermography

Bco Industries Western NY Inc ....E....... 716 877-2800
  Tonawanda *(G-16144)*
Business Card Express Inc ....E....... 631 669-3400
  West Babylon *(G-16779)*
Eaglesome Graphics Inc ....F....... 716 665-1116
  Jamestown *(G-6989)*
East Coast Thermographers Inc ......E....... 718 321-3211
  College Point *(G-3782)*
Fineline Thermographers Inc ....F....... 718 643-1100
  Brooklyn *(G-1972)*
Interstate Thermographers Corp ......G....... 914 948-1745
  White Plains *(G-17124)*
Karr Graphics Corp ....F....... 718 784-9390
  Long Island City *(G-7779)*

PROFESSIONAL EQPT & SPLYS, WHOLESALE: Analytical Instruments

Peyser Instrument Corporation ....E....... 631 841-3600
  West Babylon *(G-16818)*

PROFESSIONAL EQPT & SPLYS, WHOLESALE: Engineers', NEC

Advanced Tchncal Solutions Inc ......F....... 914 214-8230
  Yorktown Heights *(G-17506)*

PROFESSIONAL EQPT & SPLYS, WHOLESALE: Optical Goods

Carl Zeiss Inc ....C....... 914 747-1800
  Thornwood *(G-16117)*
Dynamic Laboratories Inc ....E....... 631 231-7474
  Ronkonkoma *(G-14895)*
Lens Lab Express ....G....... 718 921-5488
  Brooklyn *(G-2211)*
Moscot Wholesale Corp ....G....... 212 647-1550
  New York *(G-11310)*
Spectrum Thin Films Inc ....E....... 631 901-1010
  Hauppauge *(G-6196)*
Tri-Supreme Optical LLC ....D....... 631 249-2020
  Farmingdale *(G-5134)*

PROFESSIONAL EQPT & SPLYS, WHOLESALE: Scientific & Engineerg

Avanel Industries Inc ....F....... 516 333-0990
  Westbury *(G-16971)*
VWR Education LLC ....C....... 585 359-2502
  West Henrietta *(G-16899)*

PROFESSIONAL EQPT & SPLYS, WHOLESALE: Theatrical

Steeldeck Ny Inc ....F....... 718 599-3700
  Brooklyn *(G-2604)*

PROFILE SHAPES: Unsupported Plastics

Chelsea Plastics Inc ....F....... 212 924-4530
  New York *(G-9589)*
Franklin Poly Film Inc ....E....... 718 492-3523
  Brooklyn *(G-2002)*
Howard J Moore Company Inc ....E....... 631 351-8467
  Plainview *(G-13606)*
Mitsui Chemicals America Inc ....E....... 914 253-0777
  Rye Brook *(G-15072)*
Ontario Plastics Inc ....E....... 585 663-2644
  Rochester *(G-14550)*

PROGRAM ADMIN, GOVT: Air, Water & Solid Waste Mgmt, Local

City of Kingston ....F....... 845 331-2490
  Kingston *(G-7184)*
Incorporated Village Garden Cy ....C....... 516 465-4020
  Garden City *(G-5510)*

PROMOTION SVCS

Drns Corp ....F....... 718 369-4530
  Brooklyn *(G-1881)*
Shykat Promotions ....G....... 866 574-2757
  Forestville *(G-5336)*

PROTECTION EQPT: Lightning

Heary Bros Lghtning Protection ....E....... 716 941-6141
  Springville *(G-15612)*
Tii Technologies Inc ....E....... 516 364-9300
  Edgewood *(G-4616)*

PUBLIC RELATIONS & PUBLICITY SVCS

Studley Printing & Publishing ....F....... 518 563-1414
  Plattsburgh *(G-13701)*

PUBLISHERS: Art Copy

Classic Collections Fine Art ....G....... 914 591-4500
  White Plains *(G-17093)*

PUBLISHERS: Art Copy & Poster

Hazan Cohen Group LLC ....F....... 646 827-0030
  New York *(G-10432)*
Luminary Publishing Inc ....F....... 845 334-8600
  Kingston *(G-7199)*
Pace Editions Inc ....E....... 212 421-3237
  New York *(G-11549)*
Space 150 ....C....... 612 332-6458
  Brooklyn *(G-2587)*

PUBLISHERS: Atlases

Directory Major Malls Inc ....G....... 845 348-7000
  Nyack *(G-13049)*

PUBLISHERS: Book

Alba House Publishers ....E....... 718 698-2759
  Staten Island *(G-15633)*
Alm Media LLC ....B....... 212 457-9400
  New York *(G-9095)*
Alm Media Holdings Inc ....B....... 212 457-9400
  New York *(G-9096)*
American Inst Chem Engineers ....D....... 646 495-1355
  New York *(G-9121)*
Arbor Books Inc ....E....... 201 236-9990
  New York *(G-9191)*
Aspen Publishers Inc ....A....... 212 771-0600
  New York *(G-9235)*
Assouline Publishing Inc ....G....... 212 989-6769
  New York *(G-9241)*
Ateres Publishing & Bk Bindery ....F....... 718 935-9355
  Brooklyn *(G-1645)*

Employee Codes: A=Over 500 employees, B=251-500
C=101-250, D=51-100, E=20-50, F=10-19, G=5-9

Atlas & Company LLC ....G 212 234-3100
New York *(G-9254)*
Barrons Educational Series Inc ....D 631 434-3311
Hauppauge *(G-6032)*
Bear Port Publishing Company ....F 212 337-8577
New York *(G-9339)*
Beauty Fashion Inc ....E 212 840-8800
New York *(G-9340)*
Bedford Freeman & Worth ....C 212 576-9400
New York *(G-9342)*
Bedrock Communications ....G 212 532-4150
New York *(G-9345)*
Benchmark Education Co LLC ....D 914 637-7200
New Rochelle *(G-8888)*
Birchbrook Press ....G 607 746-7453
Delhi *(G-4236)*
Bloomsbury Publishing Inc ....D 212 419-5300
New York *(G-9418)*
Bmg Rights Management (us) LLC ....E 212 561-3000
New York *(G-9430)*
Bobley-Harmann Corporation ....G 516 433-3800
Ronkonkoma *(G-14880)*
Burns Archive Photographic Dis ....G 212 889-1938
New York *(G-9481)*
Byliner Inc ....E 415 680-3608
New York *(G-9488)*
Canopy Books LLC ....G 516 354-4888
Floral Park *(G-5198)*
CCC Publications Inc ....G 718 306-1008
Brooklyn *(G-1767)*
Conde Nast ....E 212 630-3642
New York *(G-9696)*
Cornell University ....G 607 255-0897
Ithaca *(G-6835)*
Davis Ziff Publishing Inc ....D 212 503-3500
New York *(G-9829)*
Divine Phoenix LLC ....A 585 737-1482
Skaneateles *(G-15459)*
Dorling Kindersley Publishing ....D 212 213-4800
New York *(G-9910)*
Dwj Books LLC ....G 631 899-4500
Sag Harbor *(G-15078)*
Eagle Art Publishing Inc ....G 212 685-7411
New York *(G-9957)*
Editions Schellmann Inc ....G 212 219-1821
New York *(G-9982)*
Edwin Mellen Press Inc ....E 716 754-2796
Lewiston *(G-7434)*
Entertainment Weekly Inc ....C 212 522-5600
New York *(G-10044)*
F P H Communications ....G 212 528-1728
New York *(G-10116)*
Fairchild Publications Inc ....A 212 630-4000
New York *(G-10128)*
Family Publishing Group Inc ....E 914 381-7474
Mamaroneck *(G-8034)*
Feminist Press Inc ....G 212 817-7929
New York *(G-10152)*
Franklin Report LLC ....G 212 639-9100
New York *(G-10204)*
Future Us Inc ....D 844 779-2822
New York *(G-10228)*
Ggp Publishing Inc ....F 914 834-8896
Harrison *(G-5984)*
Gq Magazine ....G 212 286-2860
New York *(G-10344)*
Grey House Publishing Inc ....E 845 483-3535
Poughkeepsie *(G-13904)*
Grey House Publishing Inc ....E 518 789-8700
Amenia *(G-216)*
Grolier International Inc ....G 212 343-6100
New York *(G-10368)*
Haights Cross Cmmnications Inc ....E 212 209-0500
New York *(G-10395)*
Haights Cross Operating Co ....E 914 289-9400
White Plains *(G-17116)*
Harpercollins Publishers LLC ....E 212 553-4200
New York *(G-10415)*
Harvard University Press ....D 212 337-0280
New York *(G-10425)*
Hazan Cohen Group LLC ....F 646 827-0030
New York *(G-10432)*
Hdt Group LLC ....G 914 490-2107
New York *(G-10434)*
Holiday House Inc ....F 212 688-0085
New York *(G-10496)*
Incisive Rwg Inc ....C 212 457-9400
New York *(G-10581)*
Jim Henson Company Inc ....E 212 794-2400
New York *(G-10733)*
Juris Publishing Inc ....E 631 351-5430
Huntington *(G-6665)*
Kensington Publishing Corp ....D 212 407-1500
New York *(G-10836)*
Learningexpress LLC ....E 646 274-6454
New York *(G-10948)*
Legal Strategies Inc ....G 516 377-3940
Merrick *(G-8389)*
Lexis Publishing ....C 518 487-3000
Menands *(G-8373)*
Lippincott Massie McQuilkin L ....F 212 352-2055
New York *(G-11006)*
Literary Classics of US ....F 212 308-3360
New York *(G-11008)*
Living Well Innovations Inc ....G 646 517-3200
Hauppauge *(G-6113)*
M&M Printing Inc ....F 516 796-3020
Carle Place *(G-3394)*
M/B Midtown LLC ....F 212 477-2495
New York *(G-11079)*
Macmillan College Pubg Co Inc ....F 212 702-2000
New York *(G-11086)*
Martha Stewart Living ....B 212 827-8000
New York *(G-11166)*
Mathisen Ventures Inc ....G 212 986-1025
New York *(G-11179)*
McBooks Press Inc ....G 607 272-2114
Ithaca *(G-6859)*
McGraw-Hill School Educatn LLC ....A 646 766-2060
New York *(G-11200)*
Mediaplanet Publishing Hse Inc ....E 646 922-1409
New York *(G-11211)*
Meegenius Inc ....G 212 283-7285
New York *(G-11219)*
Merkos Llnyonei Chinuch Inc ....E 718 778-0226
Brooklyn *(G-2300)*
Micro Publishing Inc ....G 212 533-9180
New York *(G-11253)*
N A R Associates Inc ....G 845 557-8713
Barryville *(G-620)*
New Press ....E 212 629-8802
New York *(G-11392)*
New York Legal Publishing ....G 518 459-1100
Menands *(G-8377)*
New York Qrtrly Foundation Inc ....F 917 843-8825
Brooklyn *(G-2368)*
News Corporation ....C 212 416-3400
New York *(G-11416)*
Nova Science Publishers Inc ....F 631 231-7269
Hauppauge *(G-6149)*
Omniumedia LLC ....G 516 593-2735
Elmont *(G-4725)*
Options Publishing LLC ....F 603 429-2698
New York *(G-11518)*
Other Press LLC ....G 212 414-0054
New York *(G-11534)*
Oxford University Press LLC ....B 212 726-6000
New York *(G-11542)*
Oxford University Press LLC ....G 212 726-6000
New York *(G-11543)*
Ozmodyl Ltd ....G 212 226-0622
New York *(G-11545)*
Pace Walkers of America Inc ....F 631 444-2147
Port Jefferson *(G-13778)*
Palgrave Macmillan Ltd ....G 646 307-5028
New York *(G-11556)*
Papercutz Inc ....G 646 559-4681
New York *(G-11566)*
Pearson Education Inc ....E 845 340-8700
Kingston *(G-7206)*
Pearson Education Inc ....F 212 782-3337
New York *(G-11591)*
Pearson Education Inc ....E 212 366-2000
New York *(G-11592)*
Pearson Education Inc ....F 201 236-7000
West Nyack *(G-16924)*
Penguin Random House LLC ....E 212 782-1000
New York *(G-11603)*
Penguin Random House LLC ....C 212 366-2377
Albany *(G-117)*
Penton Business Media Inc ....F 914 949-8500
White Plains *(G-17150)*
Phaidon Press Inc ....E 212 652-5400
New York *(G-11643)*
Philipp Feldheim Inc ....G 845 356-2282
Nanuet *(G-8760)*
Picador USA ....F 646 307-5629
New York *(G-11658)*
Poetry Mailing List Marsh Hawk ....G 516 766-1891
Oceanside *(G-13090)*
Poets House Inc ....F 212 431-7920
New York *(G-11680)*
Preserving Chrstn Publications ....G 315 942-6617
Boonville *(G-1167)*
Prestel Publishing Inc ....G 212 995-2720
New York *(G-11701)*
Princton Archtctural Press LLC ....E 212 995-9620
New York *(G-11714)*
Pro Publica Inc ....D 212 514-5250
New York *(G-11725)*
Prometheus Books Inc ....E 716 691-2158
Amherst *(G-258)*
PSR Press Ltd ....F 716 754-2266
Lewiston *(G-7435)*
Rapid Intellect Group Inc ....F 518 929-3210
Chatham *(G-3559)*
Readers Dgest Yung Fmilies Inc ....E 914 238-1000
Pleasantville *(G-13719)*
Reading Room Inc ....G 212 463-1029
New York *(G-11812)*
Relx Inc ....C 607 772-2600
Conklin *(G-3873)*
Repertoire International De Ll ....E 212 817-1990
New York *(G-11835)*
Rizzoli Intl Publications Inc ....F 212 387-3572
New York *(G-11882)*
Rosen Publishing Group Inc ....C 212 777-3017
New York *(G-11917)*
S P Books Inc ....G 212 431-5011
New York *(G-11946)*
Scholastic Corporation ....G 212 343-6100
New York *(G-11997)*
Scholastic Inc ....E 212 343-6100
New York *(G-11999)*
Scholium International Inc ....G 516 883-8032
Port Washington *(G-13863)*
Seven Stories Press Inc ....G 212 226-8760
New York *(G-12032)*
Sheridan House Inc ....G 914 725-5431
Scarsdale *(G-15223)*
Simon & Schuster Inc ....D 212 698-7000
New York *(G-12079)*
Simon Schuster Digital Sls Inc ....D 212 698-4391
New York *(G-12081)*
Six Boro Publishing ....G 347 589-6756
New York *(G-12089)*
Skyhorse Publishing Inc ....E 212 643-6816
New York *(G-12096)*
Soul Journ LLC ....F 646 823-9882
New York *(G-12142)*
Springer Customer Svc Ctr LLC ....B 212 460-1500
New York *(G-12172)*
Square One Publishers Inc ....F 516 535-2010
Garden City Park *(G-5542)*
Station Hill of Barrytown ....G 845 758-5293
Barrytown *(G-619)*
Steffen Publishing Inc ....D 315 865-4100
Holland Patent *(G-6488)*
Stonesong Press LLC ....G 212 929-4600
New York *(G-12208)*
Storybooks Forever ....F 716 822-7845
Buffalo *(G-3198)*
Studio Fun International Inc ....E 914 238-1000
White Plains *(G-17172)*
Sweet Mouth Inc ....E 800 433-7758
New York *(G-12253)*
Targum Press USA Inc ....G 248 355-2266
Brooklyn *(G-2646)*
Teachers College Columbia Univ ....E 212 678-3929
New York *(G-12287)*
Thornwillow Press Ltd ....G 212 980-0738
New York *(G-12331)*
Time Home Entertainment Inc ....E 212 522-1212
New York *(G-12342)*
Time Inc ....E 212 522-1212
New York *(G-12343)*
Turtle Pond Publications LLC ....G 212 579-4393
New York *(G-12428)*
Verso Inc ....G 718 246-8160
Brooklyn *(G-2723)*
W W Norton & Company Inc ....G 212 354-5500
New York *(G-12574)*
William H Sadlier Inc ....C 212 233-3646
New York *(G-12634)*
Wolters Kluwer US Inc ....F 212 894-8920
New York *(G-12652)*
Woodward/White Inc ....F 718 509-6082
Brooklyn *(G-2764)*
YS Publishing Co Inc ....G 212 682-9360
New York *(G-12699)*

PRODUCT

Zinepak LLC F 212 706-8621
New York (G-12713)
Zola Books Inc E 917 822-4950
New York (G-12718)

PUBLISHERS: Book Clubs, No Printing

Humana Press Inc E 212 460-1500
New York (G-10530)

PUBLISHERS: Books, No Printing

Abbeville Press Inc E 212 366-5585
New York (G-9001)
Aip Publishing LLC C 516 576-2200
Melville (G-8290)
Amereon Ltd G 631 298-5100
Mattituck (G-8206)
American Institute Physics Inc C 516 576-2410
Melville (G-8293)
Amherst Media Inc G 716 874-4450
Buffalo (G-2809)
Annuals Publishing Co Inc G 212 505-0950
New York (G-9165)
Anthroposophic Press Inc G 518 851-2054
Clifton Park (G-3695)
Baywood Publishing Company G 631 691-1270
Amityville (G-277)
Bertelsmann Pubg Group Inc A 212 782-1000
New York (G-9371)
Binghamton University D 607 777-2316
Binghamton (G-896)
Boardman Simons Publishing E 212 620-7200
New York (G-9432)
British American Publishing D 518 786-6000
Latham (G-7356)
Cambridge University Press D 212 337-5000
New York (G-9507)
Campus Course Paks Inc G 516 877-3967
Garden City (G-5499)
Castle Connolly Medical Ltd E 212 367-8400
New York (G-9543)
CB Publishing LLC G 516 354-4888
Floral Park (G-5199)
Central Cnfrnce of Amrcn Rbbis F 212 972-3636
New York (G-9563)
Chain Store Age Magazine G 212 756-5000
New York (G-9574)
Church Publishing Incorporated G 212 592-1800
New York (G-9615)
Cinderella Press Ltd G 212 431-3130
New York (G-9616)
Clarkson N Potter Inc F 212 782-9000
New York (G-9635)
Columbia University Press Inc E 212 459-0600
New York (G-9678)
Columbia University Press Inc E 212 459-0600
New York (G-9679)
Columbia University Press Inc E 212 459-0600
New York (G-9680)
Confrtrnity of Prescious Blood G 718 436-1120
Brooklyn (G-1797)
Continuum Intl Pubg Group Inc F 646 649-4215
New York (G-9712)
Cross Border Usa Inc G 212 425-9649
New York (G-9756)
Daheshist Publishing Co Ltd F 212 581-8360
New York (G-9787)
Definition Press Inc F 212 777-4490
New York (G-9836)
Delaney Books Inc F 516 921-8888
Syosset (G-15819)
Demos Medical Publishing LLC F 516 889-1791
New York (G-9844)
Eleanor Ettinger Inc E 212 925-7474
New York (G-9995)
Elsevier Engineering Info Inc E 201 356-6800
New York (G-10014)
Facts On File Inc D 212 967-8800
New York (G-10126)
Farrar Straus and Giroux LLC E 212 741-6900
New York (G-10138)
Folio Graphics Co Inc G 718 763-2076
Brooklyn (G-1993)
Foxhill Press Inc E 212 995-9620
New York (G-10196)
Frank Merriwell Inc F 516 921-8888
Syosset (G-15823)
Gildan Media Corp F 718 459-6299
Flushing (G-5243)
Government Data Publication E 347 789-8719
Brooklyn (G-2045)
Grand Central Publishing C 212 364-1200
New York (G-10347)
Graphis Inc F 212 532-9387
New York (G-10354)
Guilford Publications Inc D 212 431-9800
New York (G-10382)
Hachette Book Group Inc B 212 364-1200
New York (G-10391)
Harpercollins Publishers LLC D 212 207-7000
New York (G-10416)
Harry N Abrams Incorporated D 212 206-7715
New York (G-10419)
Hearst Business Media Corp F 631 650-4441
Great River (G-5851)
Hearst Corporation A 212 649-2000
New York (G-10438)
Hearst Corporation E 212 649-2275
New York (G-10447)
Helvetica Press Incorporated G 212 737-1857
New York (G-10456)
Henry Holt and Company LLC D 646 307-5095
New York (G-10459)
Highline Media LLC C 859 692-2100
New York (G-10475)
Hippocrene Books Inc G 212 685-4371
New York (G-10482)
Houghton Mifflin Harcourt Pubg E 212 420-5800
New York (G-10515)
Houghton Mifflin Harcourt Pubg C 914 747-2709
Thornwood (G-16121)
Hudson Park Press Inc G 212 929-8898
New York (G-10526)
Infobase Publishing Company G 212 967-8800
New York (G-10595)
Jonathan David Publishers Inc F 718 456-8611
Middle Village (G-8413)
Judaica Press Inc G 718 972-6202
Brooklyn (G-2156)
K T A V Publishing House Inc F 201 963-9524
Brooklyn (G-2165)
Kodansha USA Inc G 917 322-6200
New York (G-10867)
Le Book Publishing Inc G 212 334-5252
New York (G-10940)
Lee & Low Books Incorporated F 212 779-4400
New York (G-10957)
Little Bee Books Inc G 212 321-0237
New York (G-11011)
Liveright Publishing Corp G 212 354-5500
New York (G-11015)
Looseleaf Law Publications Inc F 718 359-5559
Flushing (G-5268)
Macmillan Publishers Inc A 646 307-5151
New York (G-11088)
Macmillan Publishing Group LLC E 212 674-5151
New York (G-11089)
Malhame Publs & Importers Inc E 631 694-8600
Bohemia (G-1101)
Marshall Cavendish Corp E 914 332-8888
Tarrytown (G-16095)
Mary Ann Liebert Inc D 914 740-2100
New Rochelle (G-8917)
McGraw-Hill School Education H B 646 766-2000
New York (G-11199)
Medikidz Usa Inc G 646 895-9319
New York (G-11216)
Melcher Media Inc F 212 727-2322
New York (G-11222)
Meredith Corporation D 515 284-2157
New York (G-11230)
Mesorah Publications Ltd E 718 921-9000
Brooklyn (G-2302)
Modern Language Assn Amer Inc C 646 576-5000
New York (G-11288)
Monacelli Press LLC G 212 229-9925
New York (G-11298)
Mondo Publishing Inc E 212 268-3560
New York (G-11299)
Monthly Review Foundation Inc G 212 691-2555
New York (G-11303)
Moznaim Publishing Co Inc G 718 853-0525
Brooklyn (G-2337)
Mud Puddle Books Inc G 212 647-9168
New York (G-11322)
NBM Publishing Inc G 212 643-5407
New York (G-11363)
New City Press Inc G 845 229-0335
Hyde Park (G-6735)
New Directions Publishing F 212 255-0230
New York (G-11384)
North Shore Home Improver F 631 474-2824
Port Jeff STA (G-13767)
North-South Books Inc E 212 706-4545
New York (G-11459)
P J D Publications Ltd G 516 626-0650
New Hyde Park (G-8855)
Parachute Publishing LLC E 212 337-6743
New York (G-11567)
Penguin Random House LLC B 212 782-9000
New York (G-11604)
Penguin Random House LLC A 212 572-6162
New York (G-11605)
Penguin Random House LLC A 212 782-9000
New York (G-11606)
Peter Mayer Publishers Inc F 212 673-2210
New York (G-11632)
Peter Pauper Press Inc E 914 681-0144
White Plains (G-17158)
Primedia Special Interest Publ D 212 726-4300
New York (G-11709)
Pwxyz LLC G 212 377-5500
New York (G-11761)
Quarto Group Inc E 212 779-0700
New York (G-11770)
Relx Inc E 212 309-8100
New York (G-11826)
Research Centre of Kabbalah G 718 805-0380
Richmond Hill (G-14079)
Richard C Owen Publishers Inc F 914 232-3903
Somers (G-15512)
Rizzoli Intl Publications Inc E 212 387-3400
New York (G-11881)
Ryland Peters & Small Inc G 646 791-5410
New York (G-11941)
Scholastic Inc A 800 724-6527
New York (G-11998)
Second Chance Press Inc G 631 725-1101
Sag Harbor (G-15081)
Soho Press Inc G 212 260-1900
New York (G-12119)
Springer Adis Us LLC E 212 460-1500
New York (G-12171)
Springer Publishing Co LLC E 212 431-4370
New York (G-12174)
Springer Scnce + Bus Media LLC C 781 871-6600
New York (G-12175)
STf Services Inc E 315 463-8506
East Syracuse (G-4567)
Syracuse University Press Inc E 315 443-5534
Syracuse (G-16055)
Teasurebox Publishing LLC G 718 506-4354
Jamaica (G-6955)
Tom Doherty Associates Inc E 212 388-0100
New York (G-12360)
Trusted Media Brands Inc A 914 238-1000
New York (G-12413)
Trusted Media Brands Inc F 646 293-6025
New York (G-12414)
Unisystems Inc E 212 826-0850
New York (G-12463)
United Synggue Cnsrvtive Jdism E 212 533-7800
New York (G-12467)
Vaad LHafotzas Sichoes F 718 778-5436
Brooklyn (G-2715)
Vandam Inc F 212 929-0416
New York (G-12499)
Vantage Press Inc E 212 736-1767
New York (G-12504)
Vaultcom Inc E 212 366-4212
New York (G-12511)
Waldman Publishing Corporation F 212 730-9590
New York (G-12579)
Westsea Publishing Co Inc G 631 420-1110
Farmingdale (G-5143)
William S Hein & Co Inc D 716 882-2600
Getzville (G-5606)
William S Hein & Co Inc D 716 882-2600
Buffalo (G-3256)
Wolters Kluwer US Inc E 631 517-8060
Babylon (G-553)
Workman Publishing Co Inc C 212 254-5900
New York (G-12660)
Workman Publishing Co Inc C 212 254-5900
New York (G-12661)

PUBLISHERS: Catalogs

AR Media Inc E 212 352-0731
New York (G-9187)
Christopher Anthony Pubg Co F 516 826-9205
Wantagh (G-16555)

Employee Codes: A=Over 500 employees, B=251-500
C=101-250, D=51-100, E=20-50, F=10-19, G=5-9
2017 Harris
New York Manufacturers Directory
1311

PUBLISHERS: Catalogs — PRODUCT SECTION

Company	Code	Phone
Marian Goodman Gallery Inc — New York (G-11149)	E	212 977-7160
Select Information Exchange — New York (G-12023)	F	212 496-6435

PUBLISHERS: Comic Books, No Printing

Company	Code	Phone
Archie Comic Publications Inc — Pelham (G-13488)	D	914 381-5155
Clp Pb LLC — New York (G-9646)	E	212 340-8100
Continuity Publishing Inc — New York (G-9710)	F	212 869-4170
Interntnl Publcatns Media Grup — New York (G-10640)	G	917 604-9602
Marvel Entertainment LLC — New York (G-11170)	C	212 576-4000
NBM Publishing Inc — New York (G-11363)	E	212 643-5407

PUBLISHERS: Directories, NEC

Company	Code	Phone
Black Book Photography Inc — New York (G-9409)	F	212 979-6700
Catholic News Publishing Co — Mamaroneck (G-8027)	F	914 632-7771
Easy Book Publishing Inc — Albany (G-75)	G	518 459-6281
Foundation Center Inc — New York (G-10190)	C	212 620-4230
Hearst Business Media — Uniondale (G-16296)	D	516 227-1300
Highline Media LLC — New York (G-10475)	C	859 692-2100
Supermedia LLC — New York (G-12243)	D	212 513-9700
Thomas Publishing Company LLC — New York (G-12321)	B	212 695-0500

PUBLISHERS: Directories, Telephone

Company	Code	Phone
Hola Publishing Co — Long Island City (G-7761)	G	718 424-3129

PUBLISHERS: Guides

Company	Code	Phone
Family Publications Ltd — New York (G-10133)	F	212 947-2177
Fredonia Pennysaver Inc — Fredonia (G-5373)	G	716 679-1509
Metro Group Inc — Lockport (G-7601)	G	716 434-4055
Mt Morris Shopper Inc — Mount Morris (G-8653)	G	585 658-3520
Network Journal Inc — New York (G-11375)	C	212 962-3791
Worldscale Association NYC — New York (G-12664)	G	212 422-2786

PUBLISHERS: Magazines, No Printing

Company	Code	Phone
21st Century Fox America Inc — New York (G-8967)	D	212 852-7000
2600 Enterprises Inc — Saint James (G-15086)	F	631 474-2677
Adirondack Life Inc — Jay (G-7054)	F	518 946-2191
Advance Magazine Publs Inc — New York (G-9040)	C	212 450-7000
Advanced Research Media Inc — East Setauket (G-4474)	F	631 751-9696
Adventure Publishing Group — New York (G-9049)	E	212 575-4510
Alm Media LLC — New York (G-9095)	B	212 457-9400
Alm Media Holdings Inc — New York (G-9096)	B	212 457-9400
America Press Inc — New York (G-9113)	E	212 581-4640
American Inst Chem Engineers — New York (G-9121)	D	646 495-1355
Analysts In Media (aim) Inc — New York (G-9145)	E	212 488-1777
Animal Fair Media Inc — New York (G-9162)	F	212 629-0392
Art & Understanding Inc — Albany (G-50)	E	518 426-9010
Arthur Frommer Magazines LLC — New York (G-9217)	F	646 695-6739
Associated Bus Publications Co — New York (G-9239)	E	212 490-3999
Atlantic Monthly Group Inc — New York (G-9251)	E	202 266-7000
Beauty Fashion Inc — New York (G-9340)	E	212 840-8800
Bedford Communications Inc — New York (G-9344)	E	212 807-8220
Bellerophon Publications Inc — New York (G-9351)	E	212 627-9977
Bertelsmann Pubg Group Inc — New York (G-9371)	A	212 782-1000
Beverage Media Group Inc — New York (G-9380)	C	212 571-3232
Blue Horizon Media Inc — New York (G-9421)	F	212 661-7878
Brant Art Publications Inc — New York (G-9454)	E	212 941-2800
Brant Publications Inc — New York (G-9455)	E	212 941-2800
Buffalo Spree Publishing Inc — Buffalo (G-2859)	E	716 783-9119
C Q Communications Inc — Hicksville (G-6328)	E	516 681-2922
Carol Group Ltd — New York (G-9532)	C	212 505-2030
Center For Inquiry Inc — Amherst (G-231)	F	716 636-4869
Cfo Publishing LLC — New York (G-9572)	E	212 459-3004
Commonweal Foundation Inc — New York (G-9687)	F	212 662-4200
Consumers Union US Inc — Yonkers (G-17429)	B	914 378-2000
Crain Communications Inc — New York (G-9745)	C	212 210-0100
Daily Beast Company LLC — New York (G-9788)	D	212 445-4600
Data Key Communication LLC — Fayetteville (G-5164)	F	315 445-2347
Dennis Publishing Inc — New York (G-9847)	D	646 717-9500
Discover Media LLC — New York (G-9883)	E	212 624-4800
Dj Publishing Inc — Port Washington (G-13810)	E	516 767-2500
Doctorow Communications Inc — New City (G-8783)	F	845 708-5166
Dotto Wagner — Oswego (G-13330)	G	315 342-8020
Dow Jones & Company Inc — New York (G-9915)	E	212 597-5983
Ducts Webzine Association — Brooklyn (G-1882)	F	718 383-6728
E W Williams Publications — New York (G-9953)	G	212 661-1516
Earl G Graves Pubg Co Inc — New York (G-9960)	D	212 242-8000
EC Publications Inc — New York (G-9973)	F	212 728-1844
Essence Communications Inc — New York (G-10064)	C	212 522-1212
Et Publishing Intl LLC — New York (G-10075)	F	212 838-7220
Executive Business Media Inc — Westbury (G-16983)	E	516 334-3030
Faces Magazine Inc — Poughkeepsie (G-13898)	F	201 843-4004
Family Publishing Group Inc — Mamaroneck (G-8034)	E	914 381-7474
Foundation For Cultural Review — New York (G-10191)	F	212 247-6980
Fridge Magazine Inc — New York (G-10211)	G	212 997-7673
Frozen Food Digest Inc — New York (G-10213)	E	212 557-8600
Fun Media Inc — New York (G-10223)	E	646 472-0135
Getting The Word Out Inc — Saranac Lake (G-15137)	G	518 891-9352
Golfing Magazine — Hicksville (G-6352)	G	516 822-5446
Graphis Inc — New York (G-10354)	F	212 532-9387
Gruner + Jahr Prtg & Pubg Co — New York (G-10375)	C	212 463-1000
Halcyon Business Publications — Westbury (G-16993)	F	516 338-0900
Hamptons Magazine — Southampton (G-15545)	E	631 283-7125
Harpers Magazine Foundation — New York (G-10417)	E	212 420-5720
Hart Energy Publishing Lllp — New York (G-10422)	G	212 621-4621
Haymarket Group Ltd — New York (G-10429)	F	212 239-0855
Haymarket Media Inc — New York (G-10430)	C	646 638-6000
Hearst Bus Communications Inc — New York (G-10435)	G	212 649-2000
Hearst Business Media — Uniondale (G-16296)	D	516 227-1300
Hearst Business Media Corp — Great River (G-5850)	G	631 650-6151
Hearst Business Media Corp — Great River (G-5851)	F	631 650-4441
Hearst Corporation — New York (G-10438)	A	212 649-2000
Hearst Corporation — New York (G-10442)	D	516 382-4580
Hearst Corporation — New York (G-10447)	E	212 649-2275
Hearst Holdings Inc — New York (G-10449)	F	212 649-2000
Herman Hall Communications — Brooklyn (G-2077)	F	718 941-1879
Historic TW Inc — New York (G-10484)	D	212 484-8000
Icd Publications Inc — Islandia (G-6796)	E	631 246-9300
Imek Media LLC — New York (G-10570)	E	212 422-9000
Intellitravel Media Inc — New York (G-10620)	F	646 695-6700
Interhellenic Publishing Inc — New York (G-10628)	G	212 967-5016
Interview Inc — New York (G-10642)	E	212 941-2900
Irish America Inc — New York (G-10659)	E	212 725-2993
Keller International Pubg LLC — Port Washington (G-13832)	E	516 829-9210
Lagardere North America Inc — New York (G-10916)	E	212 477-7373
Lebhar-Friedman Inc — New York (G-10951)	E	212 756-5000
Lebhar-Friedman Inc — New York (G-10952)	C	212 756-5000
Locations Magazine — New York (G-11019)	E	212 288-4745
Los Angeles Mag Holdg Co Inc — New York (G-11044)	E	212 456-7777
Mac Fadden Holdings Inc — New York (G-11081)	E	212 614-3980
Macfadden Cmmnctions Group LLC — New York (G-11083)	C	212 979-4800
Macmillan Holdings LLC — New York (G-11087)	G	212 576-9428
Mag Inc — Ithaca (G-6858)	E	607 257-6970
Manhattan Media LLC — New York (G-11130)	E	212 268-8600
Mann Publications Inc — New York (G-11135)	E	212 840-6266
Mansueto Ventures LLC — New York (G-11142)	C	212 389-5300
Maritime Activity Reports — New York (G-11153)	E	212 477-6700
Mark Levine — New York (G-11155)	F	212 677-4457
Martha Stewart Living — New York (G-11166)	B	212 827-8000
Martha Stewart Living Omni LLC — New York (G-11167)	B	212 827-8000
Martinelli Holdings LLC — Rye (G-15062)	E	302 504-1361
Mass Appeal Magazine — Brooklyn (G-2279)	G	718 858-0979
McCall Pattern Company — New York (G-11195)	C	212 465-6800
Mergent Inc — New York (G-11231)	B	212 413-7700
Miami Media LLC — New York (G-11247)	F	212 268-8600
Music & Sound Retailer Inc — Port Washington (G-13847)	E	516 767-2500
Nation Company LP — New York (G-11344)	E	212 209-5400
National Review Inc — New York (G-11350)	E	212 679-7330
Nature America Inc — New York (G-11357)	B	212 726-9200
New Art Publications Inc — Brooklyn (G-2359)	F	718 636-9100

2017 Harris New York Manufacturers Directory

(G-0000) Company's Geographic Section entry number

Newsgraphics of Delmar Inc E 518 439-5363
Delmar *(G-4245)*
Nickelodeon Magazines Inc G 212 541-1949
New York *(G-11427)*
Nihao Media LLC G 609 903-4264
New York *(G-11430)*
Nsgv Inc E 212 367-3167
New York *(G-11466)*
Nsgv Inc E 212 367-4118
New York *(G-11467)*
Nyemac Inc G 631 668-1303
Montauk *(G-8591)*
Nylon LLc E 212 226-6454
New York *(G-11482)*
Nyrev Inc E 212 757-8070
New York *(G-11486)*
Paper Publishing Company Inc E 212 226-4405
New York *(G-11565)*
Parents Guide Network Corp E 212 213-8840
New York *(G-11571)*
Penhouse Media Group Inc C 212 702-6000
New York *(G-11607)*
Photo Industry Inc F 516 364-0016
Woodbury *(G-17295)*
Preparatory Magazine Group D 718 761-4800
Staten Island *(G-15724)*
Prescribing Reference Inc D 646 638-6000
New York *(G-11699)*
Professnal Spt Pblications Inc D 212 697-1460
New York *(G-11728)*
Q Communications Inc G 212 594-6520
New York *(G-11762)*
Quest Media Llc F 646 840-3404
New York *(G-11772)*
Ramholtz Publishing Inc D 718 761-4800
Staten Island *(G-15727)*
Rd Publications Inc C 914 238-1000
Pleasantville *(G-13717)*
Readers Dgest Latinoamerica SA B 914 238-1000
Pleasantville *(G-13718)*
Readers Digest Assn Incthe F 414 423-0100
New York *(G-11811)*
Readers Digest Assn Incthe F 914 238-1000
Mount Kisco *(G-8644)*
Real Estate Media Inc E 212 929-6976
New York *(G-11813)*
Relx Inc E 212 463-6644
New York *(G-11827)*
Retail Management Pubg Inc F 212 981-0217
New York *(G-11845)*
Rfp LLC E 212 838-7733
New York *(G-11855)*
Risk Society Management Pubg E 212 286-9364
New York *(G-11879)*
Rsl Media LLC G 212 307-6760
New York *(G-11931)*
Ruby Newco LLC G 212 852-7000
New York *(G-11933)*
Sandow Media LLC F 646 805-0200
New York *(G-11966)*
Scholastic Corporation G 212 343-6100
New York *(G-11997)*
Scholastic Inc A 800 724-6527
New York *(G-11998)*
Smart & Strong LLC E 212 938-2051
New York *(G-12100)*
Society For The Study G 212 822-8806
New York *(G-12114)*
Sound Communications Inc E 516 767-2500
Port Washington *(G-13866)*
Sports Illustrated For Kids E 212 522-1212
New York *(G-12166)*
Spotlight Publications LLC G 914 345-9473
Elmsford *(G-4787)*
Suburban Publishing Inc F 845 463-0542
Poughkeepsie *(G-13936)*
Sussex Publishers Inc E 212 260-7210
New York *(G-12247)*
Techweb LLC F 516 562-5000
Manhasset *(G-8066)*
Testa Communications Inc E 516 767-2500
Port Washington *(G-13868)*
Thomas Publishing Company LLC G 212 695-0500
New York *(G-12323)*
Time Inc E 212 522-1633
New York *(G-12344)*
Time Inc A 212 522-1212
New York *(G-12345)*
Time Inc E 212 522-0361
New York *(G-12346)*
Time Inc Affluent Media Group B 212 382-5600
New York *(G-12347)*
Time Warner Companies Inc D 212 484-8000
New York *(G-12350)*
Trusted Media Brands Inc A 914 238-1000
New York *(G-12413)*
Trusted Media Brands Inc F 646 293-6025
New York *(G-12414)*
TV Guide Magazine Group Inc D 212 852-7500
New York *(G-12431)*
U S Japan Publication NY Inc G 212 252-8833
New York *(G-12438)*
Ulster Publishing Co Inc E 845 334-8205
Kingston *(G-7219)*
US Frontline News Inc E 212 922-9090
New York *(G-12486)*
US Weekly LLC D 212 484-1616
New York *(G-12489)*
Vending Times Inc F 516 442-1850
Rockville Centre *(G-14802)*
Veranda Publications Inc G 212 903-5206
New York *(G-12519)*
Virtual Urth F 914 793-1269
Bronxville *(G-1504)*
Visionaire Publishing LLC E 646 434-6091
New York *(G-12553)*
Weider Publications LLC C 212 545-4800
New York *(G-12604)*
Welcome Magazine Inc F 716 839-3121
Amherst *(G-272)*
Western New York Family Mag G 716 836-3486
Buffalo *(G-3253)*
Wine & Spirits Magazine Inc G 212 695-4660
New York *(G-12641)*
Wine On Line International G 212 755-4363
New York *(G-12642)*
Working Mother Media Inc D 212 351-6400
New York *(G-12659)*
Wsn Inc G 212 924-7620
New York *(G-12670)*

PUBLISHERS: Maps

Vandam Inc F 212 929-0416
New York *(G-12499)*

PUBLISHERS: Miscellaneous

212 Media LLC E 212 710-3092
New York *(G-8966)*
ABRA Media Inc G 518 398-1010
Pine Plains *(G-13554)*
Absolute Color Corporation G 212 868-0404
New York *(G-9007)*
Adcomm Graphics Inc E 212 645-1298
West Babylon *(G-16765)*
Add Associates Inc G 315 449-3474
Cicero *(G-3641)*
Affluent Design Inc F 631 655-2556
Mastic Beach *(G-8204)*
Albany Student Press Inc E 518 442-5665
Albany *(G-43)*
Albion-Holley Pennysaver Inc D 585 589-5641
Albion *(G-161)*
Alfred Mainzer Inc E 718 392-4200
Long Island City *(G-7650)*
All Times Publishing LLC E 315 422-7011
Syracuse *(G-15847)*
American Hsptals Patient Guide F 518 346-1099
Schenectady *(G-15230)*
American Media Inc D 212 545-4800
New York *(G-9124)*
Amy Pak Publishing Inc G 585 964-8188
Holley *(G-6489)*
ARC Music Corporation F 212 492-9414
New York *(G-9192)*
Argus Media Inc F 646 376-6130
New York *(G-9201)*
Art Asiapacific Publishing LLC G 212 255-6003
New York *(G-9209)*
Award Publishing Limited G 212 246-0405
New York *(G-9283)*
Blood Moon Productions Ltd G 718 556-9410
Staten Island *(G-15649)*
Brownstone Publishers Inc E 212 473-8200
New York *(G-9474)*
Bucket Links LLC G 212 290-2900
New York *(G-9475)*
Bulkley Dunton E 212 863-1800
New York *(G-9477)*
Burdick Publications Inc G 315 685-9500
Skaneateles *(G-15456)*
Bys Publishing LLC G 315 655-9431
Cazenovia *(G-3442)*
Cambridge Whos Who Pubg Inc E 516 833-8440
Uniondale *(G-16290)*
Castle Connolly Medical Ltd E 212 367-8400
New York *(G-9543)*
Cayuga Press Cortland Inc E 888 229-8421
East Syracuse *(G-4516)*
Cherry Lane Magazine LLC D 212 561-3000
New York *(G-9591)*
City Post Express Inc G 718 995-8690
Jamaica *(G-6904)*
Coastal Publications Inc F 631 725-1700
Sag Harbor *(G-15076)*
Communications & Energy Corp F 315 446-5723
Syracuse *(G-15903)*
Community Cpons Frnchising Inc E 516 277-1968
Glen Cove *(G-5613)*
Community Newsppr Holdings Inc D 716 282-2311
Niagara Falls *(G-12806)*
Complete Publishing Solutions G 212 242-7321
New York *(G-9691)*
Comps Inc F 516 676-0400
Glen Cove *(G-5614)*
Consumers Union US Inc B 914 378-2000
Yonkers *(G-17429)*
Cornell University G 607 255-0897
Ithaca *(G-6835)*
Couture Press F 310 734-4831
New York *(G-9739)*
Custom Publishing Group Ltd G 212 840-8800
New York *(G-9770)*
D C I Technical Inc F 516 355-0464
Franklin Square *(G-5362)*
Dailycandy Inc E 646 230-8719
New York *(G-9794)*
Dapper Dads Inc G 917 903-8045
Brooklyn *(G-1839)*
Desi Talk LLC F 212 675-7515
New York *(G-9850)*
DK Publishing F 212 366-2000
New York *(G-9888)*
Dlc Comprehensive Medical PC F 718 857-1200
Brooklyn *(G-1868)*
Draper Associates Incorporated F 212 255-2727
New York *(G-9924)*
Dwell Life Inc E 212 382-2010
New York *(G-9943)*
Eastern Harbor Media G 212 725-9260
New York *(G-9964)*
Economy 24/7 Inc E 917 403-8876
Brooklyn *(G-1900)*
Educa Publishing Inc G 516 472-0678
Great Neck *(G-5804)*
Elsevier Engineering Info Inc E 201 356-6800
New York *(G-10014)*
Enjoy City North Inc D 607 584-5061
Binghamton *(G-913)*
Ethis Communications Inc G 212 791-1440
White Plains *(G-17106)*
Experiment Publishing LLC G 212 889-1273
New York *(G-10109)*
F+w Media Inc E 212 447-1400
New York *(G-10119)*
Fantasy Sports Media Group Inc E 416 917-6002
New York *(G-10137)*
Federated Media Publishing LLC G 917 677-7976
New York *(G-10149)*
Fidazzel Inc G 917 557-3860
Bronx *(G-1330)*
First Games Publr Netwrk Inc D 212 983-0501
New York *(G-10166)*
Fitzgerald Publishing Co Inc G 914 793-5016
Yonkers *(G-17444)*
Food52 Inc G 718 596-5560
Brooklyn *(G-1994)*
Fordham University F 718 817-4795
Bronx *(G-1335)*
Gannett Co Inc D 607 352-2702
Johnson City *(G-7093)*
Gds Publishing Inc F 212 796-2000
New York *(G-10262)*
Gen Publishing Inc D 914 834-3880
New Rochelle *(G-8905)*
Genius Media Group Inc F 509 670-7502
Brooklyn *(G-2020)*
Global Grind Digital E 212 840-9399
New York *(G-10319)*
Government Data Publication E 347 789-8719
Brooklyn *(G-2045)*

PRODUCT

Grey House Publishing Inc ....E 518 789-8700
Amenia *(G-216)*
Grey House Publishing Inc ....E 845 483-3535
Poughkeepsie *(G-13904)*
Gruner & Jahr USA ....F 212 782-7870
New York *(G-10374)*
Guest Informat LLC ....F 212 557-3010
New York *(G-10380)*
Guilford Publications Inc ....D 212 431-9800
New York *(G-10382)*
Haines Publishing Inc ....E 315 252-2178
Auburn *(G-499)*
Hampton Press Incorporated ....G 646 638-3800
New York *(G-10402)*
Harpercollins ....G 212 207-7000
New York *(G-10414)*
Hearst Communications Inc ....F 212 649-2000
New York *(G-10437)*
Hearst Corporation ....E 212 830-2980
New York *(G-10443)*
Helium Media Inc ....G 917 596-4081
New York *(G-10454)*
Hibert Publishing LLC ....F 914 381-7474
Rye *(G-15059)*
Home Service Publications ....G 914 238-1000
Pleasantville *(G-13714)*
Humor Rainbow Incorporated ....E 646 402-9113
New York *(G-10532)*
Iahcp Inc ....E 631 650-2499
Islip *(G-6809)*
Intuition Publishing Limited ....G 212 838-7115
New York *(G-10648)*
Jackdaw Publications ....F 914 962-6911
Amawalk *(G-214)*
Jewish Heritage For Blind ....G 718 338-4999
Brooklyn *(G-2139)*
Jobson Medical Information LLC ....C 212 274-7000
New York *(G-10745)*
John Szoke Graphics Inc ....G 212 219-8300
New York *(G-10753)*
Kalel Partners LLC ....F 347 561-7804
Flushing *(G-5258)*
Korangy Publishing Inc ....D 212 260-1332
New York *(G-10877)*
Kraus Organization Limited ....G 212 686-5411
New York *(G-10888)*
Kyra Communications Corp ....F 516 783-6244
Seaford *(G-15344)*
L & L Trucking Inc ....E 315 339-2550
Rome *(G-14818)*
Language and Graphics Inc ....G 212 315-5266
New York *(G-10927)*
Leadership Directories Inc ....E 212 627-4140
New York *(G-10946)*
Ledes Group Inc ....F 212 840-8800
New York *(G-10956)*
Lightbulb Press Inc ....E 212 485-8800
New York *(G-10993)*
Lino Press Inc ....E 718 665-2625
Bronx *(G-1383)*
Llcs Publishing Corp ....F 718 569-2703
Brooklyn *(G-2232)*
Lucky Peach LLC ....G 212 228-0031
New York *(G-11059)*
Macmillan Academic Pubg Inc ....F 212 226-1476
New York *(G-11085)*
Mailers-Pblsher Wlfare Tr Fund ....G 212 869-5986
New York *(G-11111)*
Marketresearchcom Inc ....F 212 807-2600
New York *(G-11161)*
Mary Ann Liebert Inc ....D 914 740-2100
New Rochelle *(G-8917)*
Media Transcripts Inc ....E 212 362-1481
New York *(G-11209)*
Medical Information Systems ....G 516 621-7200
Port Washington *(G-13842)*
Mens Journal LLC ....D 212 484-1616
New York *(G-11225)*
Merchant Publishing Inc ....F 212 691-6666
New York *(G-11227)*
Merrill Corporation Inc ....D 212 620-5600
New York *(G-11234)*
Millennium Medical Publishing ....F 212 995-2211
New York *(G-11266)*
Minyanville Media Inc ....E 212 991-6200
New York *(G-11280)*
Monthly Review Foundation Inc ....G 212 691-2555
New York *(G-11303)*
Morey Publishing ....E 516 284-3300
Farmingdale *(G-5060)*
Mortgage Press Ltd ....E 516 409-1400
Wantagh *(G-16560)*
Mtm Publishing Inc ....G 212 242-6930
New York *(G-11320)*
Multi-Health Systems Inc ....D 800 456-3003
Cheektowaga *(G-3580)*
Musical Links Production LLC ....G 516 996-1522
Valley Stream *(G-16414)*
My Publisher Inc ....G 212 935-5215
New York *(G-11332)*
National Health Prom Assoc ....E 914 421-2525
White Plains *(G-17139)*
National Rding Styles Inst Inc ....F 516 921-5500
Syosset *(G-15831)*
New York Legal Publishing ....G 518 459-1100
Menands *(G-8377)*
Newbay Media LLC ....F 516 944-5940
Port Washington *(G-13848)*
Nihao Media LLC ....G 609 903-4264
New York *(G-11430)*
Nybg ....G 718 817-8700
Bronx *(G-1414)*
O Val Nick Music Co Inc ....G 212 873-2179
New York *(G-11489)*
Oakwood Publishing Co ....G 516 482-7720
Great Neck *(G-5824)*
One Story Inc ....G 917 816-3659
Brooklyn *(G-2393)*
Online Publishers Association ....E 646 473-1000
New York *(G-11510)*
Openroad Integrated Media Inc ....E 212 691-0900
New York *(G-11515)*
Options Publishing LLC ....F 603 429-2698
New York *(G-11518)*
Osprey Publishing Inc ....G 212 419-5300
New York *(G-11533)*
Outlook Newspaper ....E 845 356-6261
Suffern *(G-15796)*
Outreach Publishing Corp ....G 718 773-0525
Brooklyn *(G-2399)*
Pace Editions Inc ....G 212 675-7431
New York *(G-11550)*
Paragon Publishing Inc ....G 718 302-2093
Brooklyn *(G-2406)*
Per Annum Inc ....E 212 647-8700
New York *(G-11612)*
Petersons Nelnet LLC ....C 609 896-1800
Albany *(G-118)*
Phillifox Music ....F 646 260-9300
New York *(G-11648)*
Press Express ....G 914 592-3790
Elmsford *(G-4773)*
Primary Wave Publishing LLC ....G 212 661-6990
New York *(G-11705)*
Professnal Spt Pblications Inc ....F 516 327-9500
Elmont *(G-4726)*
Publishers Clearing House LLC ....E 516 249-4063
Melville *(G-8350)*
Quality Pattern Corp ....D 212 704-0355
New York *(G-11768)*
R W Publications Div of Wtrhs ....E 716 714-5620
Elma *(G-4653)*
Record Press Inc ....G 212 619-4949
New York *(G-11814)*
Regan Arts LLC ....F 646 488-6613
New York *(G-11820)*
Reliable Press II Inc ....F 718 840-5812
Brooklyn *(G-2489)*
Repertoire International De Ll ....E 212 817-1990
New York *(G-11835)*
Rockefeller University ....G 212 327-8568
New York *(G-11897)*
Rolling Stone Magazine ....G 212 484-1616
New York *(G-11909)*
Rosemont Press Incorporated ....G 212 239-4770
Deer Park *(G-4201)*
Rough Guides US Ltd ....D 212 414-3635
New York *(G-11921)*
Rsl Media LLC ....G 212 307-6760
New York *(G-11931)*
Sacks and Company New York ....G 212 741-1000
New York *(G-11952)*
Sag Harbor Express ....G 631 725-1700
Sag Harbor *(G-15079)*
Scepter Publishers ....G 212 354-0670
New York *(G-11984)*
Seabay Media Holdings LLC ....G 212 457-7790
New York *(G-12009)*
Selby Marketing Associates Inc ....F 585 377-0750
Fairport *(G-4876)*
Sephardic Yellow Pages ....E 718 998-0299
Brooklyn *(G-2543)*
Sharedbook Inc ....E 646 442-8840
New York *(G-12045)*
Sing Tao Newspapers NY Ltd ....E 212 699-3800
New York *(G-12084)*
Slosson Edctl Publications Inc ....F 716 652-0930
East Aurora *(G-4379)*
Social Science Electronic Pubg ....F 585 442-8170
Rochester *(G-14690)*
Sony Music Holdings Inc ....A 212 833-8000
New York *(G-12137)*
Southampton Town Newspapers ....E 631 283-4100
Southampton *(G-15552)*
Spinmedia Group Inc ....D 646 274-9110
New York *(G-12164)*
Stephen Singer Pattern Co Inc ....F 212 947-2902
New York *(G-12196)*
STf Services Inc ....E 315 463-8506
East Syracuse *(G-4567)*
Straight Arrow Publishing Co ....C 212 484-1616
New York *(G-12210)*
Strathmore Directories Ltd ....E 516 997-2525
Westbury *(G-17028)*
Student Lifeline Inc ....E 516 327-0800
Franklin Square *(G-5367)*
Summit Communications ....G 914 273-5504
Armonk *(G-420)*
Super Express USA Pubg Corp ....F 212 227-5800
Richmond Hill *(G-14086)*
Tablet Publishing Company Inc ....E 718 965-7333
Brooklyn *(G-2643)*
Taylor & Francis Group LLC ....C 212 216-7800
New York *(G-12281)*
Te Neues Publishing Company ....F 212 627-9090
New York *(G-12285)*
Theskimm Inc ....F 212 228-4628
New York *(G-12315)*
Thomson Reuters Corporation ....F 212 393-9461
New York *(G-12328)*
Thomson Reuters Corporation ....A 646 223-4000
New York *(G-12329)*
Trader Interntnal Publications ....G 914 631-6856
Sleepy Hollow *(G-15475)*
Treiman Publications Corp ....G 607 657-8473
Berkshire *(G-854)*
Tribune Entertainment Co Del ....E 203 866-2204
New York *(G-12404)*
Tribune Media Services Inc ....B 518 792-9914
Queensbury *(G-14013)*
Triumph Learning LLC ....E 212 652-0200
New York *(G-12408)*
Trusted Media Brands Inc ....A 914 238-1000
New York *(G-12413)*
Turbo Express Inc ....G 718 723-3686
Jamaica *(G-6960)*
Two Palms Press Inc ....F 212 965-8598
New York *(G-12434)*
Ucc Guide Inc ....F 518 434-0909
Albany *(G-145)*
Underline Communications LLC ....F 212 994-4340
New York *(G-12449)*
Unify360 LLC ....G 718 213-7687
Hollis *(G-6499)*
USA Custom Pad Corp ....E 607 563-9550
Sidney *(G-15445)*
Value Line Inc ....D 212 907-1500
New York *(G-12497)*
Vending Times Inc ....F 516 442-1850
Rockville Centre *(G-14802)*
Vendome Group LLC ....D 646 795-3899
New York *(G-12516)*
Viamedia Corporation ....G 718 485-7792
Brooklyn *(G-2724)*
Viewfinder Inc ....G 212 831-0939
New York *(G-12543)*
Vincys Printing Ltd ....F 518 355-4363
Schenectady *(G-15309)*
VWR Education LLC ....C 585 359-2502
West Henrietta *(G-16899)*
Watchanish LLC ....F 917 558-0404
New York *(G-12594)*
Wayuga Community Newspapers ....E 315 754-6229
Red Creek *(G-14027)*
Welcome Rain Publishers LLC ....G 212 686-1909
New York *(G-12606)*
Won & Lee Inc ....E 516 222-0712
Garden City *(G-5538)*
Yam TV LLC ....G 917 932-5418
New York *(G-12688)*

PUBLISHERS: Music Book

Boydell & Brewer Inc .... F 585 275-0419
Rochester *(G-14243)*
Congress For Jewish Culture .... G 212 505-8040
New York *(G-9700)*
Simmons-Boardman Pubg Corp .... G 212 620-7200
New York *(G-12078)*

PUBLISHERS: Music Book & Sheet Music

Boosey & Hawkes Inc .... E 212 358-5300
New York *(G-9439)*
Bourne Music Publishers .... F 212 391-4300
New York *(G-9444)*
C F Peters Corp .... E 718 416-7800
Glendale *(G-5648)*
Carbert Music Inc .... E 212 725-9277
New York *(G-9523)*
Downtown Music LLC .... G 212 625-2980
New York *(G-9920)*
Franklin-Douglas Inc .... F 516 883-0121
Port Washington *(G-13816)*
Lagunatic Music & Filmworks .... F 212 353-9600
New York *(G-10917)*
Lefrak Entertainment Co Ltd .... G 212 586-3600
New York *(G-10960)*
Reservoir Media Management Inc .... F 212 675-0541
New York *(G-11839)*
Sony/Atv Music Publishing LLC .... E 212 833-7730
New York *(G-12138)*
Verse Music Group LLC .... G 212 564-0977
New York *(G-12525)*

PUBLISHERS: Music, Book

Euphorbia Productions Ltd .... G 212 533-1700
New York *(G-10082)*
G Schirmer Inc .... G 212 254-2100
New York *(G-10232)*
G Schirmer Inc .... E 845 469-4699
Chester *(G-3607)*
Largo Music Inc .... G 212 756-5080
New York *(G-10929)*
Music Sales Corporation .... G 212 254-2100
New York *(G-11327)*
Peer International Corp .... E 212 265-3910
New York *(G-11596)*
Peermusic III Ltd .... G 212 265-3910
New York *(G-11598)*
Peermusic Ltd .... F 212 265-3910
New York *(G-11599)*

PUBLISHERS: Music, Sheet

Abkco Music & Records Inc .... E 212 399-0300
New York *(G-9004)*
Charing Cross Music Inc .... G 212 541-7571
New York *(G-9580)*
Historic TW Inc .... D 212 484-8000
New York *(G-10484)*
Integrated Copyright Group .... E 615 329-3999
New York *(G-10615)*
Ludlow Music Inc .... F 212 594-9795
New York *(G-11060)*
Michael Karp Music Inc .... G 212 840-3285
New York *(G-11249)*
Mom Dad Publishing Inc .... E 646 476-9170
New York *(G-11296)*
Screen Gems-EMI Music Inc .... D 212 786-8000
New York *(G-12007)*
Shapiro Bernstein & Co Inc .... F 212 588-0878
New York *(G-12044)*
Time Warner Companies Inc .... D 212 484-8000
New York *(G-12350)*

PUBLISHERS: Newsletter

Alm Media LLC .... B 212 457-9400
New York *(G-9095)*
Alm Media Holdings Inc .... B 212 457-9400
New York *(G-9096)*
Aspen Publishers Inc .... A 212 771-0600
New York *(G-9235)*
Energy Intelligence Group Inc .... E 212 532-1112
New York *(G-10038)*
Fischler Hockey Service .... F 212 749-4152
New York *(G-10172)*
Grant Hamilton .... F 716 652-0320
East Aurora *(G-4371)*
Hart Energy Publishing Lllp .... G 212 621-4621
New York *(G-10422)*
London Theater News Ltd .... F 212 517-8608
New York *(G-11025)*
Mathisen Ventures Inc .... G 212 986-1025
New York *(G-11179)*
New Direct Product Corp .... G 212 929-0515
New York *(G-11383)*
Redspring Communications Inc .... E 518 587-0547
Saratoga Springs *(G-15170)*

PUBLISHERS: Newspaper

50+ Lifestyle .... G 631 286-0058
Bellport *(G-824)*
A Zimmer Ltd .... D 315 422-7011
Syracuse *(G-15845)*
Advance Magazine Publs Inc .... C 212 450-7000
New York *(G-9040)*
Advertiser Publications Inc .... F 845 783-1111
Chester *(G-3598)*
Afro Times Newspaper .... F 718 636-9500
Brooklyn *(G-1568)*
After 50 Inc .... G 716 832-9300
Lancaster *(G-7299)*
Albany Student Press Inc .... E 518 442-5665
Albany *(G-43)*
Algemeiner Journal Inc .... G 718 771-0400
Brooklyn *(G-1583)*
Almanac .... G 845 334-8206
Kingston *(G-7176)*
American Media Inc .... D 212 545-4800
New York *(G-9124)*
Amnews Corporation .... E 212 932-7400
New York *(G-9137)*
Angel Media and Publishing .... G 845 727-4949
West Nyack *(G-16911)*
Artvoice .... F 716 881-6604
Buffalo *(G-2820)*
Bangla Patrika Inc .... G 718 482-9923
Long Island City *(G-7681)*
Best Line Inc .... G 917 670-6210
Staten Island *(G-15646)*
Bizeventz Inc .... G 315 579-3901
Syracuse *(G-15871)*
Brooklyn Journal Publications .... E 718 422-7400
Brooklyn *(G-1729)*
Brooklyn Rail Inc .... F 718 349-8427
Brooklyn *(G-1730)*
Bureau of National Affairs Inc .... E 212 687-4530
New York *(G-9479)*
Business Journals .... F 212 790-5100
New York *(G-9483)*
Camden News Inc .... G 315 245-1849
Camden *(G-3312)*
Canandaigua Msgnr Incorporated .... D 585 394-0770
Canandaigua *(G-3337)*
Canarsie Courier Inc .... F 718 257-0600
Brooklyn *(G-1752)*
Carib News Inc .... F 212 944-1991
New York *(G-9525)*
Cdc Publishing LLC .... E 215 579-1695
Morrisville *(G-8619)*
China Daily Distribution Corp .... F 212 537-8888
New York *(G-9596)*
China Newsweek Corporation .... F 212 481-2510
New York *(G-9601)*
Chinese Medical Report Inc .... G 718 359-5676
Flushing *(G-5232)*
Chronicle Express .... F 315 536-4422
Penn Yan *(G-13508)*
Citizen Publishing Corp .... F 845 627-1414
Nanuet *(G-8754)*
CNY Business Review Inc .... F 315 472-3104
Syracuse *(G-15898)*
Community Media Group LLC .... F 518 439-4949
Delmar *(G-4244)*
Community Media LLC .... E 212 229-1890
New York *(G-9689)*
Community Newsppr Holdings Inc .... D 716 282-2311
Niagara Falls *(G-12806)*
Cortland Standard Printing Co .... D 607 756-5665
Cortland *(G-4022)*
CT Publications Co .... G 718 592-2196
Corona *(G-3996)*
Daily Freeman .... F 845 331-5000
Kingston *(G-7186)*
Delaware County Times Inc .... G 607 746-2176
Delhi *(G-4237)*
Der Yid Inc .... E 718 797-3900
Brooklyn *(G-1856)*
Digital One USA Inc .... F 718 396-4890
Flushing *(G-5238)*
Division Street News Corp .... F 518 234-2515
Cobleskill *(G-3736)*
Dow Jones & Company Inc .... B 609 627-2999
New York *(G-9913)*
Dray Enterprises Inc .... F 585 768-2201
Le Roy *(G-7406)*
East Hampton Ind News Inc .... E 631 324-2500
East Hampton *(G-4408)*
Economist Newspaper NA Inc .... F 212 554-0676
New York *(G-9980)*
Ecuador News Inc .... F 718 205-7014
Woodside *(G-17327)*
El Diario LLC .... C 212 807-4600
Brooklyn *(G-1908)*
Fairchild Publications Inc .... A 212 630-4000
New York *(G-10128)*
Finger Lakes Media Inc .... F 607 243-7600
Dundee *(G-4327)*
Finger Lakes Printing Co Inc .... E 315 789-3333
Geneva *(G-5576)*
Fire Island Tide Publication .... F 631 567-7470
Sayville *(G-15210)*
Five Islands Publishing Inc .... F 631 583-5345
Bronx *(G-1332)*
Gallagher Printing Inc .... E 716 873-2434
Buffalo *(G-2962)*
Gannett Co Inc .... G 585 924-3406
Farmington *(G-5151)*
Gannett Co Inc .... D 607 798-1234
Vestal *(G-16448)*
Gannett Co Inc .... E 914 278-9315
New Rochelle *(G-8903)*
Gannett Co Inc .... G 585 346-4150
Lakeville *(G-7284)*
Gannett Stllite Info Ntwrk Inc .... F 914 381-3400
Mamaroneck *(G-8035)*
Gatehouse Media LLC .... E 315 792-5000
Utica *(G-16336)*
Gatehouse Media LLC .... D 607 936-4651
Corning *(G-3973)*
Gatehouse Media LLC .... D 585 394-0770
Canandaigua *(G-3347)*
Gatehouse Media LLC .... C 607 324-1425
Hornell *(G-6564)*
General Media Strategies Inc .... G 212 586-4141
New York *(G-10273)*
Gleaner Company Ltd .... F 718 657-0788
Jamaica *(G-6915)*
Great North Road Media Inc .... F 646 619-1355
New York *(G-10358)*
Hagedorn Communications Inc .... D 914 636-7400
New Rochelle *(G-8906)*
Haitian Times Inc .... G 718 230-8700
New Rochelle *(G-8907)*
Hamodia Corp .... F 718 853-9094
Brooklyn *(G-2064)*
Hearst Corporation .... A 518 454-5694
Albany *(G-86)*
Hickville Illustrated News .... D 516 747-8282
Mineola *(G-8513)*
Hispanic Com Pub Inc .... F 718 224-5863
Bayside *(G-772)*
Hyatt Times Square New York .... F 212 398-2158
New York *(G-10536)*
Indian Time .... F 518 358-9531
Hogansburg *(G-6427)*
Informa Uk Ltd .... G 646 957-8966
New York *(G-10597)*
Investmentwires Inc .... G 212 331-8995
New York *(G-10651)*
Irish Tribune Inc .... F 212 684-3366
New York *(G-10661)*
Jewish Journal .... G 718 630-9350
Brooklyn *(G-2140)*
Jobs Weekly Inc .... F 716 648-5627
Hamburg *(G-5929)*
Korea Times New York Inc .... G 718 729-5555
Long Island City *(G-7786)*
L & M Publications Inc .... E 516 378-3133
Garden City *(G-5513)*
Lee Newspapers Inc .... G 518 673-3237
Palatine Bridge *(G-13395)*
Life Time Fitness Inc .... G 914 290-5100
Harrison *(G-5987)*
Lmg National Publishing Inc .... E 585 598-6874
Fairport *(G-4862)*
Long Island Business News .... E 631 737-1700
Ronkonkoma *(G-14933)*
Long Island Catholic Newspaper .... E 516 594-1212
Roosevelt *(G-15007)*

PRODUCT

Employee Codes: A=Over 500 employees, B=251-500
C=101-250, D=51-100, E=20-50, F=10-19, G=5-9
2017 Harris
New York Manufacturers Directory
1315

Long Islander Newspapers LLC .... G 631 427-7000
Huntington *(G-6669)*
Malone Newspapers Corp .... E 518 483-2000
Malone *(G-8014)*
Manhattan Times Inc .... F 212 569-5800
New York *(G-11134)*
Mark I Publications Inc .... E 718 205-8000
Rego Park *(G-14035)*
Market Place Publications .... E 516 997-7909
Carle Place *(G-3395)*
Massapequa Post .... E 516 798-5100
Massapequa Park *(G-8188)*
Mendon Hnoye FLS Lima Sentinel .... G 585 624-5470
Honeoye Falls *(G-6534)*
Merchandiser Inc .... G 315 462-6411
Clifton Springs *(G-3714)*
Mortgage Press Ltd .... E 516 409-1400
Wantagh *(G-16560)*
Nassau County Publications .... G 516 481-5400
Hempstead *(G-6283)*
New York IL Bo Inc .... F 718 961-1538
Flushing *(G-5272)*
New York Times Company .... F 212 556-4300
New York *(G-11411)*
News Corporation .... C 212 416-3400
New York *(G-11416)*
Newspaper Delivery Solutions .... G 718 370-1111
Staten Island *(G-15710)*
Nick Lugo Inc .... F 212 348-2100
New York *(G-11426)*
Nikkei Visual Images Amer Inc .... G 212 261-6200
New York *(G-11433)*
North Country This Week .... G 315 265-1000
Potsdam *(G-13880)*
Northern NY Newspapers Corp .... C 315 782-1000
Watertown *(G-16668)*
Noticia Hispanoamericana Inc .... E 516 223-5678
Baldwin *(G-560)*
Nyp Holdings Inc .... D 718 260-2500
Brooklyn *(G-2385)*
Observer Daily Sunday Newsppr .... D 716 366-3000
Dunkirk *(G-4346)*
Oneida Publications Inc .... E 315 363-5100
Oneida *(G-13163)*
Ottaway Newspapers Inc .... F 845 343-2181
Middletown *(G-8455)*
Panagraphics Inc .... G 716 312-8088
Orchard Park *(G-13287)*
Peace Times Weekly Inc .... G 718 762-6500
Flushing *(G-5280)*
Pearson Inc .... D 212 641-2400
New York *(G-11594)*
Pipe Dream .... E 607 777-2515
Binghamton *(G-943)*
Putnam Cnty News Recorder LLC .... F 845 265-2468
Cold Spring *(G-3764)*
Quality Guides .... G 716 326-3163
Westfield *(G-17049)*
Realtimetraderscom .... E 716 632-6600
Buffalo *(G-3155)*
Record Advertiser .... E 716 693-1000
North Tonawanda *(G-12988)*
Rheinwald Printing Co Inc .... F 585 637-5100
Brockport *(G-1246)*
Rizzoli Intl Publications Inc .... F 212 308-2000
New York *(G-11883)*
Rochester Democrat & Chronicle .... E 585 232-7100
Rochester *(G-14641)*
Rocket Communications Inc .... F 716 873-2594
Buffalo *(G-3162)*
Royal News Corp .... F 212 564-8972
New York *(G-11926)*
Russkaya Reklama Inc .... E 718 769-3000
Brooklyn *(G-2518)*
Sag Harbor Express .... G 631 725-1700
Sag Harbor *(G-15079)*
Salamanca Press Penny Saver .... E 716 945-1500
Salamanca *(G-15105)*
Sample News Group LLC .... D 315 343-3800
Oswego *(G-13340)*
Satellite Network Inc .... F 718 336-2698
Brooklyn *(G-2536)*
Sb New York Inc .... D 212 457-7790
New York *(G-11980)*
Schneps Publications Inc .... E 718 224-5863
Bayside *(G-775)*
Seabay Media Holdings LLC .... G 212 457-7790
New York *(G-12009)*
Seneca Media Inc .... D 607 324-1425
Hornell *(G-6566)*
Sing Tao Newspapers NY Ltd .... F 212 431-9030
Brooklyn *(G-2565)*
Smithtown News Inc .... E 631 265-2100
Smithtown *(G-15498)*
Southampton Town Newspapers .... F 631 288-1100
Westhampton Beach *(G-17061)*
Spectator Publishing Co Inc .... E 212 854-9550
New York *(G-12155)*
Spring Publishing Corporation .... G 718 782-0881
Brooklyn *(G-2592)*
Star Sports Corp .... E 516 773-4075
Great Neck *(G-5842)*
Star-Gazette Fund Inc .... C 607 734-5151
Elmira *(G-4702)*
Stratconglobal Inc .... G 212 989-2355
New York *(G-12211)*
Straus Newspapers Inc .... E 845 782-4000
Chester *(G-3617)*
Sun-Times Media Group Inc .... E 716 945-1644
Salamanca *(G-15110)*
Syracuse Catholic Press Assn .... G 315 422-8153
Syracuse *(G-16049)*
Tegna Inc .... C 716 849-2222
Buffalo *(G-3212)*
Tenney Media Group .... D 315 853-5569
Clinton *(G-3722)*
The Sandhar Corp .... G 718 523-0819
Jamaica *(G-6958)*
Tompkins Weekly Inc .... G 607 539-7100
Ithaca *(G-6878)*
Tri-Village Publishers Inc .... D 518 843-1100
Amsterdam *(G-371)*
Ubm Inc .... A 212 600-3000
New York *(G-12440)*
Ubm LLC .... A 516 562-5085
New York *(G-12441)*
Urdu Times .... G 718 297-8700
Jamaica *(G-6961)*
USA Today International Corp .... G 703 854-3400
New York *(G-12491)*
W H White Publications Inc .... G 914 725-2500
Dobbs Ferry *(G-4304)*
Wallkill Lodge No 627 F&Am .... F 845 778-7148
Walden *(G-16538)*
Webster Ontrio Wlwrth Pnnysver .... F 585 265-3620
Webster *(G-16741)*
Weekly Ajkal .... F 718 565-2100
Jackson Heights *(G-6889)*
Weekly Business News Corp .... G 212 689-5888
New York *(G-12603)*
West Seneca Bee Inc .... D 716 632-4700
Williamsville *(G-17259)*
Westbury Times .... D 516 747-8282
Mineola *(G-8539)*
William J Kline & Son Inc .... D 518 843-1100
Amsterdam *(G-374)*
Workers Vanguard .... E 212 732-7862
New York *(G-12658)*
Yated Neeman Inc .... F 845 369-1600
Monsey *(G-8586)*

PUBLISHERS: Newspapers, No Printing

21st Century Fox America Inc .... D 212 852-7000
New York *(G-8967)*
21st Century Fox America Inc .... G 845 735-1116
Pearl River *(G-13454)*
A C J Communications Inc .... F 631 587-5612
Babylon *(G-544)*
Albany Catholic Press Assoc .... G 518 453-6688
Albany *(G-38)*
Alm Media LLC .... B 212 457-9400
New York *(G-9095)*
Alm Media Holdings Inc .... B 212 457-9400
New York *(G-9096)*
American City Bus Journals Inc .... E 716 541-1654
Buffalo *(G-2806)*
American Sports Media LLC .... G 585 377-9636
Rochester *(G-14200)*
Angola Pennysaver Inc .... F 716 549-1164
Angola *(G-379)*
Architects Newspaper LLC .... F 212 966-0630
New York *(G-9195)*
Auburn Publishing Co .... D 315 253-5311
Auburn *(G-480)*
Bee Publications Inc .... D 716 632-4700
Williamsville *(G-17235)*
Belsito Communications Inc .... F 845 534-9700
New Windsor *(G-8932)*
Blue and White Publishing Inc .... F 215 431-3339
New York *(G-9420)*
Boonville Herald Inc .... G 315 942-4449
Boonville *(G-1164)*
Buffalo Law Journal .... G 716 541-1600
Buffalo *(G-2853)*
Business First of New York .... E 716 854-5822
Buffalo *(G-2862)*
Business First of New York .... E 518 640-6800
Latham *(G-7357)*
Catskill Mountain Publishing .... F 845 586-2601
Arkville *(G-411)*
Chase Media Group .... F 914 962-3871
Yorktown Heights *(G-17509)*
Clarion Publications Inc .... F 585 243-3530
Geneseo *(G-5564)*
Community Newspaper Group LLC .... F 607 432-1000
Oneonta *(G-13181)*
Community Newspaper Group LLC .... E 518 565-4114
Plattsburgh *(G-13660)*
Community Newsppr Holdings Inc .... D 716 693-1000
Niagara Falls *(G-12805)*
Community Newsppr Holdings Inc .... E 716 439-9222
Lockport *(G-7577)*
Courier-Life Inc .... C 718 260-2500
Brooklyn *(G-1810)*
Daily Cornell Sun .... E 607 273-0746
Ithaca *(G-6836)*
Daily Orange Corporation .... E 315 443-2314
Syracuse *(G-15920)*
Dale Press Inc .... E 718 543-6200
Bronx *(G-1310)*
Danet Inc .... F 718 266-4444
Brooklyn *(G-1838)*
Dans Paper Inc .... D 631 537-0500
Southampton *(G-15542)*
Das Yidishe Licht Inc .... G 718 387-3166
Brooklyn *(G-1840)*
Dbg Media .... G 718 599-6828
Brooklyn *(G-1845)*
Ecclesiastical Communications .... F 212 688-2399
New York *(G-9974)*
Empire Publishing Inc .... F 516 829-4000
Far Rockaway *(G-4921)*
Expositor Newspapers Inc .... G 585 427-2468
Rochester *(G-14365)*
Four Directions Inc .... E 315 829-8388
Vernon *(G-16434)*
Freetime Magazine Inc .... G 585 473-2266
Rochester *(G-14382)*
French Morning LLC .... G 646 290-7463
New York *(G-10209)*
FT Publications Inc .... D 212 641-6500
New York *(G-10218)*
FT Publications Inc .... E 212 641-2420
New York *(G-10219)*
Fulton Newspapers Inc .... E 315 598-6397
Fulton *(G-5457)*
Gannett Stllite Info Ntwrk Inc .... E 914 965-5000
Yonkers *(G-17447)*
Gannett Stllite Info Ntwrk LLC .... E 845 578-2300
West Nyack *(G-16917)*
Gatehouse Media LLC .... G 607 776-2121
Bath *(G-656)*
Gateway Newspapers Inc .... G 845 628-8400
Mahopac *(G-7996)*
Good Health Healthcare Newsppr .... F 585 421-8109
Victor *(G-16479)*
Hellenic Corporation .... F 212 986-6881
New York *(G-10455)*
Highline Media LLC .... C 859 692-2100
New York *(G-10475)*
Hudson Valley Black Press .... G 845 562-1313
Newburgh *(G-12762)*
Impremedia LLC .... D 212 807-4785
Brooklyn *(G-2101)*
India Abroad Publications Inc .... D 212 929-1727
New York *(G-10588)*
Irish Echo Newspaper Corp .... F 212 482-4818
New York *(G-10660)*
Jewish Press Inc .... C 718 330-1100
Brooklyn *(G-2141)*
Jewish Week Inc .... E 212 921-7822
New York *(G-10727)*
John Lor Publishing Ltd .... E 631 475-1000
Patchogue *(G-13425)*
Johnson Newspaper Corporation .... E 518 483-4700
Malone *(G-8011)*
Journal Register Company .... D 518 584-4242
Saratoga Springs *(G-15161)*
Korea Times New York Inc .... D 718 784-4526
Long Island City *(G-7785)*

Korea Times New York Inc ....G.... 718 961-7979
Flushing (G-5262)
Lebhar-Friedman Inc ....E.... 212 756-5000
New York (G-10951)
Lebhar-Friedman Inc ....C.... 212 756-5000
New York (G-10952)
Lee Enterprises Incorporated ....C.... 518 792-3131
Glens Falls (G-5686)
Local Media Group Inc ....E.... 845 341-1100
Middletown (G-8446)
Local Media Group Inc ....F.... 845 340-4910
Kingston (G-7197)
Manchester Newspaper Inc ....E.... 518 642-1234
Granville (G-5775)
Manhattan Media LLC ....E.... 212 268-8600
New York (G-11130)
Miami Media LLC ....F.... 212 268-8600
New York (G-11247)
Moneysaver Advertising Inc ....F.... 585 593-1275
Bolivar (G-1160)
National Herald Inc ....E.... 718 784-5255
Long Island City (G-7820)
National Parts Peddler Newsppr ....G.... 315 699-7583
Cicero (G-3649)
Neighbor To Neighbor News Inc ....G.... 585 492-2525
Arcade (G-397)
New Ski Inc ....E.... 607 277-7000
Ithaca (G-6867)
New York Cvl Srvc Emplys Pblsh ....F.... 212 962-2690
New York (G-11398)
New York Daily Challenge Inc ....F.... 718 636-9500
Brooklyn (G-2364)
New York Observer Llc ....D.... 212 887-8460
New York (G-11405)
News Communications Inc ....F.... 212 689-2500
New York (G-11415)
News Report Inc ....E.... 718 851-6607
Brooklyn (G-2370)
Newspaper Publisher LLC ....F.... 607 775-0472
Conklin (G-3871)
Nordic Press Inc ....G.... 212 686-3356
New York (G-11452)
Northern Tier Publishing Corp ....F.... 914 962-4748
Yorktown Heights (G-17514)
Novoye Rsskoye Slovo Pubg Corp ....D.... 646 460-4566
Brooklyn (G-2378)
Nyc Community Media LLC ....F.... 212 229-1890
Brooklyn (G-2384)
Oak Lone Publishing Co Inc ....E.... 518 792-1126
Glens Falls (G-5693)
Page Front Group Inc ....G.... 716 823-8222
Lackawanna (G-7246)
Patchogue Advance Inc ....E.... 631 475-1000
Patchogue (G-13430)
Publishing Group America Inc ....F.... 646 658-0550
New York (G-11747)
Richner Communications Inc ....G.... 516 569-4000
Lawrence (G-7399)
Rochester Business Journal ....E.... 585 546-8303
Rochester (G-14636)
Rochester Catholic Press ....F.... 585 529-9530
Rochester (G-14637)
S I Communications Inc ....F.... 914 725-2500
Scarsdale (G-15222)
Seneca Media Inc ....F.... 585 593-5300
Wellsville (G-16758)
Sing Tao Newspapers NY Ltd ....E.... 212 699-3800
New York (G-12084)
Southampton Town Newspapers ....E.... 631 283-4100
Southampton (G-15552)
Spartacist Publishing Co ....E.... 212 732-7860
New York (G-12148)
Steffen Publishing Inc ....D.... 315 865-4100
Holland Patent (G-6488)
Stuart Communications Inc ....F.... 845 252-7414
Narrowsburg (G-8769)
Tablet Publishing Company Inc ....E.... 718 965-7333
Brooklyn (G-2643)
Tefft Publishers Inc ....G.... 518 692-9290
Greenwich (G-5894)
Thestreet Inc ....D.... 212 321-5000
New York (G-12316)
Times Beacon Record Newspapers ....F.... 631 331-1154
East Setauket (G-4494)
Times Review Newspaper Corp ....E.... 631 354-8031
Mattituck (G-8211)
Tioga County Courier ....G.... 607 687-0108
Owego (G-13360)
Tribco LLC ....E.... 718 357-7400
Whitestone (G-17216)
Tricycle Foundation Inc ....G.... 800 873-9871
New York (G-12405)
Tupper Lake Free Press Inc ....G.... 518 359-2166
Tupper Lake (G-16281)
Ulster Publishing Co Inc ....E.... 845 334-8205
Kingston (G-7219)
Ulster Publishing Co Inc ....F.... 845 255-7005
New Paltz (G-8881)
US Hispanic Media Inc ....G.... 212 885-8000
Brooklyn (G-2713)
Wallkill Valley Publications ....E.... 845 561-0170
Newburgh (G-12786)
Wappingers Falls Shopper Inc ....E.... 845 297-3723
Wappingers Falls (G-16578)
Wave Publishing Co Inc ....F.... 718 634-4000
Rockaway Beach (G-14783)
Westfair Communications Inc ....E.... 914 694-3600
White Plains (G-17186)
Westmore News Inc ....G.... 914 939-6864
Port Chester (G-13761)
Westside News Inc ....F.... 585 352-3411
Spencerport (G-15574)
World Journal LLC ....C.... 718 746-8889
Whitestone (G-17218)
World Journal LLC ....E.... 718 445-2277
Flushing (G-5310)
Yonkers Time Publishing Co ....F.... 914 965-4000
Yonkers (G-17503)

PUBLISHERS: Pamphlets, No Printing

McCall Pattern Company ....C.... 212 465-6800
New York (G-11195)
Spartacist Publishing Co ....E.... 212 732-7860
New York (G-12148)

PUBLISHERS: Patterns, Paper

McCall Pattern Company ....C.... 212 465-6800
New York (G-11195)

PUBLISHERS: Periodical, With Printing

Economist Newspaper Group Inc ....C.... 212 541-0500
New York (G-9979)
Eidosmedia Inc ....F.... 646 795-2100
New York (G-9988)
Frost Publications Inc ....G.... 845 726-3232
Westtown (G-17068)
Gruner + Jahr USA Group Inc ....B.... 866 323-9336
New York (G-10376)
H W Wilson Company Inc ....B.... 718 588-8635
Bronx (G-1350)
Nylon Media Inc ....E.... 212 226-6454
New York (G-11483)
Playbill Incorporated ....E.... 212 557-5757
New York (G-11674)
Sky Art Media Inc ....G.... 917 355-9022
New York (G-12094)
The PRS Group Inc ....F.... 315 431-0511
East Syracuse (G-4571)
Yale Robbins Inc ....D.... 212 683-5700
New York (G-12687)

PUBLISHERS: Periodicals, Magazines

21st Century Fox America Inc ....D.... 212 447-4600
New York (G-8968)
A Guideposts Church Corp ....C.... 212 251-8100
New York (G-8988)
Advance Magazine Publs Inc ....D.... 212 286-2860
New York (G-9039)
American Jewish Committee ....G.... 212 891-1400
New York (G-9122)
American Towman Network Inc ....F.... 845 986-4546
Warwick (G-16586)
AMG Supply Company LLC ....E.... 212 790-6370
New York (G-9135)
Annointed Buty Ministries LLC ....G.... 646 867-3796
Brooklyn (G-1614)
Archaelogy Magazine ....E.... 718 472-3050
Long Island City (G-7666)
Backstage LLC ....E.... 212 493-4243
Brooklyn (G-1662)
Bedford Freeman & Worth ....C.... 212 576-9400
New York (G-9342)
Berger & Wild LLC ....G.... 646 415-8459
New York (G-9363)
Binah Magazines Corp ....G.... 718 305-5200
Brooklyn (G-1698)
BJ Magazines Inc ....G.... 212 367-9705
New York (G-9407)
Bnei Aram Soba Inc ....F.... 718 645-4460
Brooklyn (G-1707)
Business Tech Communications ....F.... 516 354-5205
Garden City (G-5498)
Bust Inc ....G.... 212 675-1707
Brooklyn (G-1741)
Cambridge University Press ....D.... 212 337-5000
New York (G-9507)
Choice Magazine Listening Inc ....G.... 516 883-8280
Port Washington (G-13805)
CNY Business Review Inc ....F.... 315 472-3104
Syracuse (G-15898)
College Calendar Company ....F.... 315 768-8242
Whitesboro (G-17192)
Complex Media Inc ....G.... 917 793-5831
New York (G-9692)
Cornell University ....E.... 607 254-2473
Ithaca (G-6834)
Crains New York Business ....E.... 212 210-0250
New York (G-9747)
Davis Ziff Publishing Inc ....D.... 212 503-3500
New York (G-9829)
Delaware County Times Inc ....G.... 607 746-2176
Delhi (G-4237)
Denton Publications Inc ....E.... 518 561-9680
Plattsburgh (G-13661)
Departures Magazine ....E.... 212 382-5600
New York (G-9849)
Disney Publishing Worldwide ....D.... 212 633-4400
White Plains (G-17101)
Dissent Magazine ....F.... 212 316-3120
New York (G-9885)
Dow Jones Aer Company Inc ....A.... 212 416-2000
New York (G-9916)
Downtown Media Group LLC ....F.... 646 723-4510
New York (G-9919)
Envy Publishing Group Inc ....G.... 212 253-9874
New York (G-10047)
Fairchild Publications Inc ....A.... 212 630-4000
New York (G-10128)
Fairchild Publishing LLC ....G.... 212 286-3897
New York (G-10129)
Fashion Calendar International ....G.... 212 289-0420
New York (G-10143)
Frontiers Unlimited Inc ....G.... 631 283-4663
Southampton (G-15543)
Genomeweb LLC ....F.... 212 651-5636
New York (G-10278)
Glamour Magazine ....G.... 212 286-2860
New York (G-10305)
Global Finance Magazine ....G.... 212 447-7900
New York (G-10314)
Global Finance Media Inc ....F.... 212 447-7900
New York (G-10315)
Golden Owl Publishing Company ....G.... 914 962-6911
New York (G-10333)
Good Times Magazine ....G.... 516 280-2100
Carle Place (G-3390)
Guernica ....F.... 914 414-7318
Brooklyn (G-2055)
Hammer Communications Inc ....F.... 631 261-5806
Northport (G-13012)
Hamptons Media LLC ....G.... 631 283-6900
Southampton (G-15546)
Healthy Way of Life Magazine ....G.... 718 616-1681
Brooklyn (G-2070)
Hearst Business Publishing Inc ....F.... 212 969-7500
New York (G-10436)
Hearst Corporation ....D.... 212 649-4271
New York (G-10444)
Hearst Corporation ....D.... 212 204-4300
New York (G-10445)
Holmes Group The Inc ....G.... 212 333-2300
New York (G-10500)
I On Youth ....G.... 716 832-6509
Buffalo (G-3001)
Industry Forecast ....G.... 914 244-8617
Mount Kisco (G-8630)
Ink Publishing Corporation ....G.... 347 294-1220
Brooklyn (G-2106)
Institutional Invester ....G.... 212 224-3300
New York (G-10613)
Intelligne The Ftr Cmptng Nwsl ....F.... 212 222-1123
New York (G-10619)
L F International Inc ....D.... 212 756-5000
New York (G-10902)
L I F Publishing Corp ....E.... 631 345-5200
Shirley (G-15422)
Latina Media Ventures LLC ....E.... 212 642-0200
New York (G-10933)

PRODUCT

Employee Codes: A=Over 500 employees, B=251-500
C=101-250, D=51-100, E=20-50, F=10-19, G=5-9
2017 Harris
New York Manufacturers Directory
1317

Laurtom Inc .... E 914 273-2233
Mount Kisco (G-8634)
Long Island Catholic Newspaper .... E 516 594-1212
Roosevelt (G-15007)
Lucky Magazine .... F 212 286-6220
New York (G-11058)
Magazine I Spectrum E .... E 212 419-7555
New York (G-11098)
Magnificat Inc .... F 914 502-1820
Yonkers (G-17464)
Media Press Corp .... E 212 791-6347
New York (G-11208)
Meredith Corporation .... F 212 499-2000
New York (G-11229)
Morris Communications Co LLC .... E 212 620-9580
New York (G-11307)
Nation Magazine .... E 212 209-5400
New York (G-11345)
National Marketing Services .... F 516 942-9595
Roslyn Heights (G-15030)
Nervecom Inc .... F 212 625-9914
New York (G-11369)
New York Media LLC .... C 212 508-0700
New York (G-11403)
Newbay Media LLC .... F 516 944-5940
Port Washington (G-13848)
Next Step Publishing Inc .... F 585 742-1260
Victor (G-16494)
Njf Publishing Corp .... G 631 345-5200
Shirley (G-15427)
Northeast Group .... D 518 563-8214
Plattsburgh (G-13682)
Nova Science Publishers Inc .... F 631 231-7269
Hauppauge (G-6149)
Nsgv Inc .... E 212 367-3100
New York (G-11468)
Pearson Education Inc .... F 201 236-7000
West Nyack (G-16924)
Penton Media Inc .... B 212 204-4200
New York (G-11608)
Periodical Services Co Inc .... F 518 822-9300
Hudson (G-6630)
Professnal Spt Pblications Inc .... D 516 327-9500
Elmont (G-4727)
Ralph Martinelli .... E 914 345-3055
Elmsford (G-4775)
Relx Inc .... B 212 633-3900
New York (G-11828)
Res Media Group Inc .... F 212 320-3750
New York (G-11838)
Rolling Stone Magazine .... G 212 484-1616
New York (G-11909)
Rough Draft Publishing LLC .... F 212 741-4773
New York (G-11920)
Rye Record .... G 914 713-3213
Rye (G-15067)
Saveur Magazine .... E 212 219-7400
New York (G-11977)
Shoreline Publishing Inc .... G 914 738-7869
Pelham (G-13494)
Small Business Advisors Inc .... F 516 374-1387
Atlantic Beach (G-470)
Smooth Magazine .... F 212 925-1150
New York (G-12110)
Spin Magazine Media .... G 212 231-7400
New York (G-12163)
Springer Healthcare LLC .... E 212 460-1500
New York (G-12173)
Standard Analytics Io Inc .... G 917 882-5422
New York (G-12181)
Staten Island Parent Magazine .... G 718 761-4800
Staten Island (G-15739)
Steffen Publishing Inc .... D 315 865-4100
Holland Patent (G-6488)
Surface Magazine .... E 646 805-0200
New York (G-12246)
Swaps Monitor Publications Inc .... F 212 742-8550
New York (G-12249)
Teen Fire Magazine .... G 646 415-3703
New York (G-12294)
Time Out New York Partners LP .... D 646 432-3000
New York (G-12348)
TMC Usa LLC .... G 518 587-8920
Saratoga Springs (G-15175)
Trend Pot Inc .... E 212 431-9970
New York (G-12397)
Ubm Inc .... A 212 600-3000
New York (G-12440)
US China Magazine .... E 212 663-4333
New York (G-12484)
Vibe Media Group LLC .... D 212 448-7300
New York (G-12536)
Vickers Stock Research Corp .... E 212 425-7500
New York (G-12537)
Vogue Magazine .... D 212 286-2860
New York (G-12564)
Wallkill Valley Publications .... E 845 561-0170
Newburgh (G-12786)
Westfair Communications Inc .... E 914 694-3600
White Plains (G-17186)
Winsight LLC .... G 646 708-7309
New York (G-12648)
Womens E News Inc .... G 212 244-1720
New York (G-12653)

PUBLISHERS: Periodicals, No Printing

Academy of Political Science .... G 212 870-2500
New York (G-9008)
Alcoholics Anonymous Grapevine .... F 212 870-3400
New York (G-9078)
Association For Cmpt McHy Inc .... D 212 869-7440
New York (G-9240)
Athlon Spt Communications Inc .... E 212 478-1910
New York (G-9250)
Bernhard Arnold & Company Inc .... G 212 907-1500
New York (G-9367)
Boardman Simons Publishing .... E 212 620-7200
New York (G-9432)
Brownstone Publishers Inc .... E 212 473-8200
New York (G-9474)
Buffalo Spree Publishing Inc .... G 585 413-0040
Rochester (G-14249)
Capital Reg Wkly Newsppr Group .... F 518 674-2841
Averill Park (G-533)
Cdc Publishing LLC .... E 215 579-1695
Morrisville (G-8619)
Conde Nast .... E 212 630-3642
New York (G-9696)
Conference Board Inc .... C 212 759-0900
New York (G-9699)
Congress For Jewish Culture .... G 212 505-8040
New York (G-9700)
Crain News Service .... G 212 254-0890
New York (G-9746)
Economist Intelligence Unit NA .... D 212 554-0600
New York (G-9978)
Fahy-Williams Publishing Inc .... F 315 781-6820
Geneva (G-5575)
Francis Emory Fitch Inc .... E 212 619-3800
New York (G-10199)
Global Entity Media Inc .... G 631 580-7772
Ronkonkoma (G-14905)
Government Data Publication .... E 347 789-8719
Brooklyn (G-2045)
Grants Financial Publishing .... F 212 809-7994
New York (G-10352)
Hamptons Media LLC .... E 646 835-5211
New York (G-10403)
Hearst Corporation .... E 212 649-3100
New York (G-10439)
Hearst Corporation .... A 518 454-5694
Albany (G-86)
Highline Media LLC .... C 859 692-2100
New York (G-10475)
Human Life Foundation Inc .... G 212 685-5210
New York (G-10529)
Impressions Inc .... G 212 594-5954
New York (G-10575)
International Center For Postg .... G 607 257-5860
Ithaca (G-6851)
Leadership Directories Inc .... E 212 627-4140
New York (G-10946)
Mathisen Ventures Inc .... G 212 986-1025
New York (G-11179)
McCarthy LLC .... F 646 862-5354
New York (G-11196)
Modern Farmer Media Inc .... F 518 828-7447
Hudson (G-6628)
National Prof Resources .... E 914 937-8879
Port Chester (G-13755)
Parade Publications Inc .... D 212 450-7000
New York (G-11568)
Pati Inc .... F 718 244-6788
Jamaica (G-6938)
Pointwise Information Service .... F 315 457-4111
Liverpool (G-7542)
Psychonomic Society Inc .... E 512 381-1494
New York (G-11743)
Real Est Book of Long Island .... F 516 364-5000
Syosset (G-15837)
Shugar Publishing .... G 631 288-4404
Westhampton Beach (G-17060)
Simmons-Boardman Pubg Corp .... G 212 620-7200
New York (G-12078)
Spc Marketing Company .... G 631 661-2727
West Islip (G-16907)
Suffolk Community Council Inc .... G 631 434-9277
Deer Park (G-4214)
Swift Fulfillment Services .... G 516 593-1198
Lynbrook (G-7964)
Thestreet Inc .... D 212 321-5000
New York (G-12316)
Thomson Rters Tax Accnting Inc .... D 212 367-6300
New York (G-12330)
Trader Interntnal Publications .... G 914 631-6856
Sleepy Hollow (G-15475)
Ubm LLC .... A 516 562-5085
New York (G-12441)
Urban Racercom .... G 718 279-2202
Bayside (G-777)
Value Line Inc .... D 212 907-1500
New York (G-12497)
Value Line Publishing LLC .... C 212 907-1500
New York (G-12498)
World Guide Publishing .... E 800 331-7840
New York (G-12662)

PUBLISHERS: Posters

History Publishing Company LLC .... G 845 398-8161
Palisades (G-13401)

PUBLISHERS: Racing Forms & Programs

Daily Racing Form Inc .... C 212 366-7600
New York (G-9792)

PUBLISHERS: Sheet Music

Carl Fischer LLC .... E 212 777-0900
New York (G-9526)
Kendor Music Inc .... F 716 492-1254
Delevan (G-4235)
Warner Music Inc .... D 212 275-2000
New York (G-12589)

PUBLISHERS: Shopping News

Freeville Publishing Co Inc .... F 607 844-9119
Freeville (G-5435)
Greater Rchster Advertiser Inc .... E 585 385-1974
East Rochester (G-4460)
Service Advertising Group Inc .... F 718 361-6161
Long Island City (G-7875)
Skylark Publications Ltd .... G 607 535-9866
Watkins Glen (G-16696)
Sneaker News Inc .... G 347 687-1588
New York (G-12111)

PUBLISHERS: Technical Manuals

Dayton T Brown Inc .... B 631 589-6300
Bohemia (G-1052)
Elsevier Inc .... B 212 633-3773
New York (G-10015)
Mosby Holdings Corp .... G 212 309-8100
New York (G-11308)

PUBLISHERS: Technical Manuals & Papers

Cambridge Info Group Inc .... F 301 961-6700
New York (G-9506)
Clearstep Technologies LLC .... G 315 952-3628
Camillus (G-3322)

PUBLISHERS: Technical Papers

Humana Press Inc .... E 212 460-1500
New York (G-10530)
Ideas International Inc .... E 914 937-4302
Rye Brook (G-15071)

PUBLISHERS: Telephone & Other Directory

Auto Market Publications Inc .... G 631 667-0500
Deer Park (G-4105)
Business Directory Inc .... F 718 486-8099
Brooklyn (G-1740)
Dex Media Inc .... E 603 263-2811
Buffalo (G-2911)
Dex Media Inc .... E 315 251-3300
Buffalo (G-2912)
Fashiondex Inc .... G 914 271-6121
New York (G-10145)

PRODUCT SECTION

PUBLISHING & PRINTING: Directories, NEC

Golf Directories USA Inc .... G 516 365-5351
  Manhasset *(G-8061)*
Infoservices International .... F 631 549-1805
  Cold Spring Harbor *(G-3769)*
Israeli Yellow Pages .... E 718 520-1000
  Kew Gardens *(G-7162)*
Korean Yellow Pages .... F 718 461-0073
  Flushing *(G-5263)*
Maximillion Communications LLC .... D 212 564-3945
  New York *(G-11188)*
Yellow Pages Inc .... G 845 639-6060
  New City *(G-8795)*

PUBLISHERS: Textbooks, No Printing

Allworth Communications Inc .... F 212 777-8395
  New York *(G-9094)*
Amsco School Publications Inc .... D 212 886-6500
  New York *(G-9141)*
Bedford Freeman & Worth .... D 212 375-7000
  New York *(G-9343)*
Booklinks Publishing Svcs LLC .... G 718 852-2116
  Brooklyn *(G-1709)*
Brown Publishing Network Inc .... G 212 682-3330
  New York *(G-9472)*
Cornell University .... D 607 277-2338
  Ithaca *(G-6833)*
E W Williams Publications .... G 212 661-1516
  New York *(G-9953)*
John Wiley & Sons Inc .... D 845 457-6250
  Montgomery *(G-8596)*
Oxford Book Company Inc .... C 212 227-2120
  New York *(G-11538)*
Peter Lang Publishing Inc .... F 212 647-7700
  New York *(G-11631)*
Project Energy Savers LLC .... F 718 596-4231
  Brooklyn *(G-2454)*
Stanley M Indig .... G 718 692-0648
  Brooklyn *(G-2597)*
W W Norton & Company Inc .... C 212 354-5500
  New York *(G-12573)*
Wordwise Inc .... G 914 232-5366
  Katonah *(G-7135)*
Worth Publishers Inc .... C 212 475-6000
  New York *(G-12666)*

PUBLISHERS: Trade journals, No Printing

Access Intelligence LLC .... A 212 204-4269
  New York *(G-9009)*
American Institute Physics Inc .... C 516 576-2410
  Melville *(G-8293)*
Aspen Publishers Inc .... A 212 771-0600
  New York *(G-9235)*
Baywood Publishing Company .... G 631 691-1270
  Amityville *(G-277)*
Demos Medical Publishing LLC .... F 516 889-1791
  New York *(G-9844)*
Elmont North Little League .... G 516 775-8210
  Elmont *(G-4719)*
Hatherleigh Company Ltd .... G 607 538-1092
  Hobart *(G-6425)*
Humana Press Inc .... E 212 460-1500
  New York *(G-10530)*
International Data Group Inc .... E 212 331-7883
  New York *(G-10632)*
Japan America Learning Ctr Inc .... F 914 723-7600
  Scarsdale *(G-15218)*
Luria Communications Inc .... G 631 329-4922
  East Hampton *(G-4413)*
Marketing Edge .... G 212 790-1512
  New York *(G-11160)*
Mary Ann Liebert Inc .... D 914 740-2100
  New Rochelle *(G-8917)*
McMahon Publishing Company .... D 212 957-5300
  New York *(G-11202)*
NCM Publishers Inc .... G 212 691-9100
  New York *(G-11364)*
Public Relations Soc Amer Inc .... E 212 460-1400
  New York *(G-11746)*
Pwxyz LLC .... G 212 377-5500
  New York *(G-11761)*
Relx Inc .... E 212 309-8100
  New York *(G-11826)*
Schnell Publishing Company Inc .... F 212 791-4200
  New York *(G-11995)*
Security Letter .... G 212 348-1553
  New York *(G-12015)*
Springer Adis Us LLC .... E 212 460-1500
  New York *(G-12171)*
Springer Publishing Co LLC .... E 212 431-4370
  New York *(G-12174)*
Springer Scnce + Bus Media LLC .... C 781 871-6600
  New York *(G-12175)*
Thomas International Pubg Co .... G 212 613-3441
  New York *(G-12320)*
Thomas Publishing Company LLC .... B 212 695-0500
  New York *(G-12321)*
Westchester Law Journal Inc .... G 914 948-0715
  White Plains *(G-17183)*

PUBLISHING & BROADCASTING: Internet Only

Ai Media Group Inc .... F 212 660-2400
  New York *(G-9064)*
Aleteia Usa Inc .... G 914 502-1855
  Yonkers *(G-17410)*
Bdg Media Inc .... B 917 951-9768
  New York *(G-9337)*
Byliner Inc .... E 415 680-3608
  New York *(G-9488)*
Classpass Inc .... E 646 701-2172
  New York *(G-9638)*
East Meet East Inc .... G 650 450-4446
  New York *(G-9963)*
Entrainant Inc .... G 212 946-4724
  New York *(G-10045)*
Epost International Inc .... G 212 352-9390
  New York *(G-10051)*
Equityarcade LLC .... G 678 232-1301
  Brooklyn *(G-1931)*
Golden Eagle Marketing LLC .... G 212 726-1242
  New York *(G-10330)*
Hearst Digital Studios Inc .... E 212 969-7552
  New York *(G-10448)*
Ibt Media Inc .... E 646 867-7100
  New York *(G-10548)*
Learnvest Inc .... G 212 675-6711
  New York *(G-10949)*
Media Trust LLC .... G 212 802-1162
  New York *(G-11210)*
Medical Daily Inc .... E 646 867-7100
  New York *(G-11213)*
Mindbodygreen LLC .... E 347 529-6952
  Brooklyn *(G-2317)*
Narratively Inc .... E 203 536-0332
  Brooklyn *(G-2349)*
Nimbletv Inc .... G 646 502-7010
  New York *(G-11434)*
Playlife LLC .... G 646 207-9082
  New York *(G-11675)*
Qworldstar Inc .... E 212 768-4500
  New York *(G-11778)*
Renegade Nation Online LLC .... G 212 868-9000
  New York *(G-11834)*
Riot New Media Group Inc .... G 604 700-4896
  Brooklyn *(G-2495)*
Sagelife Parenting LLC .... G 315 299-5713
  Syracuse *(G-16030)*
Seymour Science LLC .... G 516 699-8404
  Great Neck *(G-5840)*
Standard Analytics Io Inc .... G 917 882-5422
  New York *(G-12181)*
Statebook LLC .... G 845 383-1991
  Kingston *(G-7212)*
Thehuffingtonpostcom Inc .... E 212 245-7844
  New York *(G-12311)*
Total Webcasting Inc .... G 845 883-0909
  New Paltz *(G-8879)*
Trading Edge Ltd .... G 347 699-7079
  Ridgewood *(G-14128)*
Vidbolt Inc .... G 716 560-8944
  Buffalo *(G-3242)*
Zazoom LLC .... F 212 321-2100
  New York *(G-12706)*

PUBLISHING & PRINTING: Art Copy

Avalon Copy Centers Amer Inc .... D 315 471-3333
  Syracuse *(G-15863)*
Avalon Copy Centers Amer Inc .... E 716 995-7777
  Buffalo *(G-2825)*
Color Unlimited Inc .... G 212 802-7547
  New York *(G-9673)*
Soho Editions Inc .... E 914 591-5100
  Mohegan Lake *(G-8545)*

PUBLISHING & PRINTING: Book Clubs

Christian Book Publishing .... E 646 559-2533
  New York *(G-9607)*
Dreams To Print .... G 718 483-8020
  Brooklyn *(G-1879)*

PUBLISHING & PRINTING: Book Music

Ai Entertainment Holdings LLC .... F 212 247-6400
  New York *(G-9063)*
Alfred Publishing Co Inc .... D 315 736-1572
  Oriskany *(G-13303)*
Faces Magazine Inc .... D 845 454-7420
  Poughkeepsie *(G-13899)*
Kobalt Music Pubg Amer Inc .... D 212 247-6204
  New York *(G-10865)*

PUBLISHING & PRINTING: Books

450 Ridge St Inc .... G 716 754-2789
  Lewiston *(G-7432)*
Adir Publishing Co .... F 718 633-9437
  Brooklyn *(G-1562)*
Apollo Investment Fund VII LP .... G 212 515-3200
  New York *(G-9176)*
Bertelsmann Inc .... E 212 782-1000
  New York *(G-9370)*
Booklyn Artists Alliance .... G 718 383-9621
  Brooklyn *(G-1710)*
Callaway Arts & Entrmt Inc .... F 212 798-3168
  New York *(G-9502)*
Crabtree Publishing Inc .... E 212 496-5040
  New York *(G-9742)*
D C I Technical Inc .... F 516 355-0464
  Franklin Square *(G-5362)*
H W Wilson Company Inc .... B 718 588-8635
  Bronx *(G-1350)*
Interntnl Publcatns Media Grup .... G 917 604-9602
  New York *(G-10640)*
James Morgan Publishing .... G 212 655-5470
  New York *(G-10697)*
Klutz .... E 650 687-2600
  New York *(G-10860)*
Library Tales Publishing Inc .... G 347 394-2629
  New York *(G-10985)*
Metro Creative Graphics Inc .... E 212 947-5100
  New York *(G-11241)*
Multi Packaging Solutions Inc .... E 646 885-0157
  New York *(G-11324)*
Nationwide Custom Services .... G 845 365-0414
  Tappan *(G-16081)*
Natural E Creative LLC .... F 516 488-1143
  New Hyde Park *(G-8849)*
News India USA Inc .... F 212 675-7515
  New York *(G-11418)*
Pearson Inc .... D 212 641-2400
  New York *(G-11594)*
Pearson Longman LLC .... C 917 981-2200
  New York *(G-11595)*
Pearson Longman LLC .... E 212 641-2400
  White Plains *(G-17147)*
Samuel French Inc .... E 212 206-8990
  New York *(G-11962)*
T G S Inc .... G 516 629-6905
  Locust Valley *(G-7634)*
Whittier Publications Inc .... G 516 432-8120
  Oceanside *(G-13106)*
Windows Media Publishing LLC .... E 917 732-7892
  Brooklyn *(G-2759)*

PUBLISHING & PRINTING: Catalogs

Global Video LLC .... D 516 222-2600
  Woodbury *(G-17288)*
Gooding & Associates Inc .... F 631 749-3313
  Shelter Island *(G-15387)*
Mexico Independent Inc .... E 315 963-3763
  Mexico *(G-8396)*
Sentinel Printing Services Inc .... D 845 562-1218
  New Windsor *(G-8954)*
Thomas Publishing Company LLC .... D 212 629-2127
  New York *(G-12322)*

PUBLISHING & PRINTING: Comic Books

Medikidz Usa Inc .... G 646 895-9319
  New York *(G-11216)*

PUBLISHING & PRINTING: Directories, NEC

Hibu Inc .... C 516 730-1900
  East Meadow *(G-4425)*
Want-Ad Digest Inc .... F 518 279-1181
  Troy *(G-16262)*

Employee Codes: A=Over 500 employees, B=251-500
C=101-250, D=51-100, E=20-50, F=10-19, G=5-9

2017 Harris
New York Manufacturers Directory

PUBLISHING & PRINTING: Guides

Gametime Media Inc ....G....... 212 860-2090
New York (G-10246)
Open-Xchange Inc ....F....... 914 332-5720
Tarrytown (G-16099)

PUBLISHING & PRINTING: Magazines: publishing & printing

Advance Magazine Publs Inc ....D....... 212 286-2860
New York (G-9036)
Advance Magazine Publs Inc ....A....... 212 286-2860
New York (G-9037)
Advance Magazine Publs Inc ....D....... 212 790-4422
New York (G-9038)
Advance Magazine Publs Inc ....D....... 212 697-0126
New York (G-9041)
Alpha Media Group Inc ....B....... 212 302-2626
New York (G-9099)
American Graphic Design Awards ....G....... 212 696-4380
New York (G-9118)
American Intl Media LLC ....F....... 845 359-4225
White Plains (G-17077)
American Jewish Congress Inc ....E....... 212 879-4500
New York (G-9123)
Artnews Ltd ....F....... 212 398-1690
New York (G-9223)
Aspire One Communications LLC ....F....... 201 281-2998
Cornwall (G-3986)
Barsky Ventures LLC ....G....... 212 265-8890
New York (G-9327)
Bazaar ....G....... 212 903-5497
New York (G-9336)
Bertelsmann Inc ....E....... 212 782-1000
New York (G-9370)
Blackbook Media Corp ....E....... 212 334-1800
New York (G-9410)
Bondi Digital Publishing LLC ....G....... 212 405-1655
New York (G-9435)
Boy Scouts of America ....G....... 212 532-0985
New York (G-9446)
Bz Media LLC ....F....... 631 421-4158
Melville (G-8299)
Capco Marketing ....F....... 315 699-1687
Baldwinsville (G-567)
City and State Ny LLC ....E....... 212 268-0442
New York (G-9627)
City Real Estate Book Inc ....G....... 516 593-2949
Valley Stream (G-16403)
Civil Svc Rtred Employees Assn ....F....... 718 937-0290
Long Island City (G-7699)
Clarion Publications Inc ....F....... 585 243-3530
Geneseo (G-5564)
CMX Media LLC ....E....... 917 793-5831
New York (G-9649)
Commentary Inc ....F....... 212 891-1400
New York (G-9684)
Conde Nast International Inc ....D....... 212 286-2860
New York (G-9697)
Convenience Store News ....G....... 214 217-7800
New York (G-9713)
Credit Union Journal Inc ....G....... 212 803-8200
New York (G-9753)
Davler Media Group LLC ....E....... 212 315-0800
New York (G-9830)
Distinction Magazine Inc ....E....... 631 843-3522
Melville (G-8311)
Dow Jones & Company Inc ....B....... 609 627-2999
New York (G-9913)
Equal Opprtnity Pblcations Inc ....F....... 631 421-9421
Melville (G-8314)
Excelsior Publications ....G....... 607 746-7600
Delhi (G-4238)
Hearst Corporation ....E....... 212 903-5366
New York (G-10440)
Hearst Corporation ....D....... 212 903-5000
New York (G-10446)
Hello and Hola Media Inc ....E....... 212 807-4795
Brooklyn (G-2072)
Hnw Inc ....F....... 212 258-9215
New York (G-10492)
Homesell Inc ....F....... 718 514-0346
Staten Island (G-15684)
Icarus Enterprises Inc ....G....... 917 969-4461
New York (G-10550)
Index Magazine ....G....... 212 243-1428
New York (G-10587)
Intercultural Alliance Artists ....G....... 917 406-1202
Flushing (G-5253)
Jobson Medical Information LLC ....C....... 212 274-7000
New York (G-10745)
Kbs Communications LLC ....F....... 212 765-7124
New York (G-10825)
L Magazine LLC ....F....... 212 807-1254
Brooklyn (G-2186)
Latino Show Magazine Inc ....G....... 718 709-1151
Woodhaven (G-17307)
Ltb Media (usa) Inc ....D....... 212 447-9555
New York (G-11057)
Luminary Publishing Inc ....F....... 845 334-8600
Kingston (G-7199)
M Shanken Communications Inc ....C....... 212 684-4224
New York (G-11077)
Marie Claire USA ....D....... 212 841-8493
New York (G-11150)
Meredith Corporation ....C....... 212 557-6600
New York (G-11228)
Meredith Corporation ....D....... 515 284-2157
New York (G-11230)
Metrosource Publishing Inc ....F....... 212 691-5127
New York (G-11242)
Mishpacha Magazine Inc ....G....... 718 686-9339
Brooklyn (G-2319)
New Hope Media LLC ....G....... 646 366-0830
New York (G-11390)
Niche Media Holdings LLc ....E....... 702 990-2500
New York (G-11424)
Northside Media Group LLC ....F....... 917 318-6513
Brooklyn (G-2375)
Northside Media Group LLC ....E....... 917 318-6513
Brooklyn (G-2376)
Odyssey Mag Pubg Group Inc ....C....... 212 545-4800
New York (G-11497)
Penton Media Inc ....G....... 212 204-4200
New York (G-11609)
Ragozin Data ....E....... 212 674-3123
Long Island City (G-7856)
Redbook Magazine ....F....... 212 649-3331
New York (G-11815)
Rnd Enterprises Inc ....F....... 212 627-0165
New York (G-11886)
Rodale Inc ....B....... 212 697-2040
New York (G-11900)
Romantic Times Inc ....F....... 718 237-1097
Brooklyn (G-2503)
Ross Communications Associates ....F....... 631 393-5089
Melville (G-8353)
Securities Data Publishing Inc ....G....... 212 631-1411
New York (G-12014)
Source Media Inc ....B....... 212 803-8200
New York (G-12143)
Stuff Magazine ....G....... 212 302-2626
New York (G-12222)
Summit Professional Networks ....D....... 212 557-7480
New York (G-12234)
T V Trade Media Inc ....F....... 212 288-3933
New York (G-12269)
Thomas Publishing Company LLC ....G....... 212 290-7297
New York (G-12324)
Time Inc ....E....... 212 522-1212
New York (G-12343)
Towse Publishing Co ....F....... 914 235-3095
New Rochelle (G-8925)
Trans-High Corporation ....E....... 212 387-0500
New York (G-12391)
TV Guide Magazine LLC ....G....... 212 852-7500
New York (G-12430)
Ubm LLC ....F....... 516 562-5000
New York (G-12442)
Universal Cmmncations of Miami ....C....... 212 986-5100
New York (G-12469)
Uptown Media Group LLC ....E....... 212 360-5073
New York (G-12476)
Urbandaddy Inc ....F....... 212 929-7905
New York (G-12482)
US News & World Report Inc ....C....... 212 716-6800
New York (G-12488)
Vanity Fair ....F....... 212 286-6052
New York (G-12501)
Wall Street Reporter Magazine ....D....... 212 363-2600
New York (G-12581)
Watch Journal LLC ....G....... 212 229-1500
New York (G-12593)
Wenner Media LLC ....C....... 212 484-1616
New York (G-12611)
World Business Media LLC ....F....... 212 344-0759
Massapequa Park (G-8191)

PUBLISHING & PRINTING: Music, Book

Alley Music Corp ....E....... 212 779-7977
New York (G-9088)
Atlas Music Publishing LLC ....G....... 646 502-5170
New York (G-9255)
Finger Lakes Massage Group ....F....... 607 272-9024
Ithaca (G-6841)
Johnny Bienstock Music ....E....... 212 779-7977
New York (G-10755)
Princess Music Publishing Co ....E....... 212 586-0240
New York (G-11712)
Spirit Music Group Inc ....E....... 212 533-7672
New York (G-12165)
Universal Edition Inc ....D....... 917 213-2177
New York (G-12470)
Wmg Acquisition Corp ....F....... 212 275-2000
New York (G-12650)

PUBLISHING & PRINTING: Newsletters, Business Svc

An Group Inc ....G....... 631 549-4090
Melville (G-8295)
Answer Printing Inc ....F....... 212 922-2922
New York (G-9166)
Ceo Cast Inc ....F....... 212 732-4300
New York (G-9570)
Church Bulletin Inc ....F....... 631 249-4994
West Babylon (G-16784)
Froebe Group LLC ....G....... 646 649-2150
New York (G-10212)
Portfolio Media Inc ....C....... 646 783-7100
New York (G-11687)
Retirement Insiders ....G....... 631 751-1329
Setauket (G-15378)
Scholastic Inc ....D....... 212 343-7100
New York (G-12000)
Shop Smart Central Inc ....G....... 914 962-3871
Yorktown Heights (G-17519)
Ubm Inc ....A....... 212 600-3000
New York (G-12440)

PUBLISHING & PRINTING: Newspapers

All Island Media Inc ....C....... 631 698-8400
Edgewood (G-4592)
All Island Media Inc ....E....... 516 942-8400
Hicksville (G-6319)
American Sports Media ....G....... 585 924-4250
Victor (G-16460)
Angie Mangino ....G....... 347 489-4009
Staten Island (G-15638)
AR Publishing Company Inc ....F....... 212 482-0303
New York (G-9188)
Asahi Shimbun America Inc ....F....... 212 398-0257
New York (G-9225)
Beth Kobliner Company LLC ....G....... 212 501-8407
New York (G-9376)
Bornomala USA Inc ....G....... 347 753-2355
Jackson Heights (G-6887)
Bradford Publications Inc ....C....... 716 373-2500
Olean (G-13137)
Brasilans Press Pblcations Inc ....E....... 212 764-6161
New York (G-9456)
Buffalo News Inc ....A....... 716 849-4401
Buffalo (G-2857)
Capital Region Wkly Newspapers ....E....... 518 877-7160
Albany (G-60)
Carefree Daily Money Managemen ....G....... 631 751-1281
Setauket (G-15375)
Chester West County Press ....G....... 914 684-0006
Mount Vernon (G-8671)
Christian Press Inc ....G....... 718 886-4400
Flushing (G-5233)
City Newspaper ....G....... 585 244-3329
Rochester (G-14276)
Classic News ....G....... 718 698-5256
Staten Island (G-15659)
Colors Fashion Inc ....F....... 212 629-0401
New York (G-9675)
Community Newsppr Holdings Inc ....E....... 585 798-1400
Medina (G-8269)
Copia Interactive LLC ....E....... 212 481-0520
New York (G-9719)
Crain News Service ....G....... 212 254-0890
New York (G-9746)
Daily Gazette Company ....B....... 518 374-4141
Schenectady (G-15246)
Daily Gazette Company ....C....... 518 395-3060
Schenectady (G-15247)

PRODUCT

Daily Mail & Greene Cnty News ..... F 518 943-2100
Catskill *(G-3427)*

Daily Muse Inc ..... F 646 861-0284
New York *(G-9789)*

Daily Racing Form ..... F 212 514-2180
New York *(G-9791)*

Daily Record ..... F 585 232-2035
Rochester *(G-14299)*

Daily World Press Inc ..... F 212 922-9201
New York *(G-9793)*

Der Blatt Inc ..... F 845 783-1148
Monroe *(G-8553)*

Document Journal Inc ..... G 917 287-2141
New York *(G-9894)*

DOT Publishing ..... F 315 593-2510
Fulton *(G-5456)*

Dow Jones & Company Inc ..... C 212 597-5600
New York *(G-9914)*

Dow Jones & Company Inc ..... E 212 597-5983
New York *(G-9915)*

East Hampton Star Inc ..... E 631 324-0002
East Hampton *(G-4409)*

El Aguila ..... G 212 410-2450
New York *(G-9991)*

Epoch Times International Inc ..... G 212 239-2808
New York *(G-10050)*

Event Journal Inc ..... G 516 470-1811
Bethpage *(G-866)*

Evercore Partners Svcs E LLC ..... A 212 857-3100
New York *(G-10090)*

Exhibits & More ..... G 585 924-4040
Victor *(G-16476)*

Firefighters Journal ..... E 718 391-0283
Long Island City *(G-7741)*

Francepress LLC ..... G 646 202-9828
New York *(G-10198)*

Fredonia Pennysaver Inc ..... G 716 679-1509
Fredonia *(G-5373)*

Gannett Co Inc ..... E 516 484-7510
Port Washington *(G-13818)*

Gannett Co Inc ..... D 585 232-7100
Rochester *(G-14387)*

Gannett Stllite Info Ntwrk Inc ..... D 585 798-1400
Medina *(G-8272)*

Gannett Stllite Info Ntwrk LLC ..... C 845 454-2000
Poughkeepsie *(G-13900)*

Gatehouse Media LLC ..... D 585 598-0030
Pittsford *(G-13561)*

Gatehouse Media LLC ..... F 315 866-2220
Herkimer *(G-6300)*

Gatehouse Media MO Holdings ..... G 530 846-3661
Pittsford *(G-13562)*

Glens Falls Newspapers Inc ..... G 518 792-3131
Glens Falls *(G-5680)*

Guidance Group Inc ..... F 631 756-4618
Melville *(G-8325)*

Hearst Business Media Corp ..... F 631 650-4441
Great River *(G-5851)*

Hearst Corporation ..... A 212 649-2000
New York *(G-10438)*

Hearst Corporation ..... E 212 649-2275
New York *(G-10447)*

Herald Newspapers Company Inc ..... A 315 470-0011
Syracuse *(G-15959)*

Herald Press Inc ..... G 718 784-5255
Long Island City *(G-7758)*

Herald Publishing Company LLC ..... G 315 470-2022
New York *(G-10460)*

High Ridge News LLC ..... G 718 548-7412
Bronx *(G-1357)*

Home Reporter Inc ..... E 718 238-6600
Brooklyn *(G-2085)*

IMG The Daily ..... G 212 541-5640
New York *(G-10572)*

Investment News ..... E 212 210-0100
New York *(G-10650)*

Investors Business Daily Inc ..... F 212 626-7676
New York *(G-10652)*

Johnson Acquisition Corp ..... F 518 828-1616
Hudson *(G-6622)*

Journal News ..... G 914 694-5000
White Plains *(G-17130)*

Journal News ..... G 845 578-2324
West Nyack *(G-16920)*

Journal Register Company ..... D 212 257-7212
New York *(G-10770)*

Journal Register Company ..... E 212 257-7212
New York *(G-10771)*

Kch Publications Inc ..... E 516 671-2360
Glen Cove *(G-5619)*

Korea Central Daily News Inc ..... D 718 361-7700
Long Island City *(G-7784)*

Latin Business Chronicle ..... G 305 441-0002
New York *(G-10932)*

Lee Publications Inc ..... D 518 673-3237
Palatine Bridge *(G-13396)*

LI Community Newspapers Inc ..... G 516 747-8282
Mineola *(G-8520)*

Litmor Publishing Corp ..... F 516 931-0012
Hicksville *(G-6364)*

Livingston County News ..... G 585 243-1234
Geneseo *(G-5566)*

Local Media Group Inc ..... B 845 341-1100
Middletown *(G-8447)*

Local Media Group Inc ..... F 845 794-3712
Monticello *(G-8605)*

Long Island Cmnty Nwsppers Inc ..... D 516 482-4490
Mineola *(G-8522)*

Long Island Cmnty Nwsppers Inc ..... F 631 427-7000
Huntington *(G-6668)*

Louis Vuitton North Amer Inc ..... G 212 644-2574
New York *(G-11051)*

Lowville Newspaper Corporation ..... G 315 376-3525
Lowville *(G-7940)*

Made Fresh Daily ..... G 212 285-2253
New York *(G-11092)*

Main Street Connect LLC ..... F 203 803-4110
Armonk *(G-417)*

Markets Media LLC ..... G 646 442-4646
New York *(G-11162)*

Melmont Fine Pringng/Graphics ..... G 516 939-2253
Bethpage *(G-874)*

Mid-York Press Inc ..... D 607 674-4491
Sherburne *(G-15393)*

Midway News Inc ..... G 212 628-3009
New York *(G-11260)*

Ming Pao (new York) Inc ..... F 212 334-2220
New York *(G-11277)*

Ming Pao (new York) Inc ..... D 718 786-2888
Long Island City *(G-7813)*

Minority Reporter Inc ..... G 585 225-3628
Rochester *(G-14515)*

Moneypaper Inc ..... F 914 925-0022
Rye *(G-15064)*

Neighbor Newspapers ..... G 631 226-2636
Farmingdale *(G-5063)*

New Living Inc ..... G 631 751-8819
Patchogue *(G-13428)*

New Media Investment Group Inc ..... B 212 479-3160
New York *(G-11391)*

New York Daily News ..... G 212 248-2100
New York *(G-11399)*

New York Press Inc ..... E 212 268-8600
New York *(G-11406)*

New York Times Company ..... B 212 556-1234
New York *(G-11410)*

New York Times Company ..... F 718 281-7000
Flushing *(G-5273)*

New York University ..... E 212 998-4300
New York *(G-11412)*

New York1 News Operations ..... F 212 379-3311
New York *(G-11413)*

News India Usa LLC ..... G 212 675-7515
New York *(G-11417)*

News India USA Inc ..... F 212 675-7515
New York *(G-11418)*

News of The Highlands Inc ..... F 845 534-7771
Cornwall *(G-3990)*

Newsday LLC ..... B 631 843-4050
Melville *(G-8341)*

Newsday LLC ..... C 631 843-3135
Melville *(G-8342)*

Newspaper Association Amer Inc ..... E 212 856-6300
New York *(G-11420)*

Newspaper Times Union ..... F 518 454-5676
Albany *(G-108)*

Nikkei America Inc ..... E 212 261-6200
New York *(G-11432)*

Nyt Capital LLC ..... F 212 556-1234
New York *(G-11488)*

Outlook Newspaper ..... E 845 356-6261
Suffern *(G-15796)*

Owego Pennysaver Press Inc ..... F 607 687-2434
Owego *(G-13358)*

Pearson Longman LLC ..... E 212 641-2400
White Plains *(G-17147)*

Pennysaver Group Inc ..... F 914 966-1400
Yonkers *(G-17476)*

Post Community Media LLC ..... C 518 374-4141
Saratoga Springs *(G-15167)*

Post Journal ..... F 716 487-1111
Jamestown *(G-7023)*

Prospect News ..... F 212 374-2800
New York *(G-11738)*

R W Publications Div of Wtrhs ..... E 716 714-5620
Elma *(G-4653)*

R W Publications Div of Wtrhs ..... E 716 714-5620
Elma *(G-4654)*

Record ..... G 518 270-1200
Saratoga Springs *(G-15169)*

Record Review LLC ..... F 914 244-0533
Bedford Hills *(G-807)*

Ridgewood Times Prtg & Pubg ..... E 718 821-7500
Ridgewood *(G-14122)*

Right World View ..... E 914 406-2994
Purchase *(G-13971)*

Ruby Newco LLC ..... G 212 852-7000
New York *(G-11933)*

S G New York LLC ..... F 631 698-8400
Edgewood *(G-4610)*

S G New York LLC ..... E 631 665-4000
Bohemia *(G-1128)*

Second Amendment Foundation ..... G 716 885-6408
Buffalo *(G-3180)*

Seneca County Area Shopper ..... G 607 532-4333
Ovid *(G-13347)*

Service Advertising Group Inc ..... F 718 361-6161
Long Island City *(G-7875)*

Shelter Island Reporter Inc ..... G 631 749-1000
Shelter Island *(G-15388)*

Sing Tao Newspapers NY Ltd ..... E 718 821-0123
Brooklyn *(G-2566)*

South Shore Tribune Inc ..... G 516 431-5628
Island Park *(G-6784)*

Spartan Publishing Inc ..... F 716 664-7373
Jamestown *(G-7029)*

Sports Pblications Prod NY LLC ..... D 212 366-7700
New York *(G-12167)*

Sports Reporter Inc ..... G 212 737-2750
New York *(G-12169)*

Ssrja LLC ..... F 718 725-7020
Jamaica *(G-6950)*

St Lawrence County Newspapers ..... D 315 393-1003
Ogdensburg *(G-13122)*

Star Community Pubg Group LLC ..... C 631 843-4050
Melville *(G-8357)*

Straus Communications ..... F 845 782-4000
Chester *(G-3616)*

The Earth Times Foundation ..... G 718 297-0488
Brooklyn *(G-2656)*

Tri-Town News Inc ..... E 607 561-3515
Sidney *(G-15442)*

Tribune Entertainment Co Del ..... E 203 866-2204
New York *(G-12404)*

Trilake Three Press Corp ..... G 518 359-2462
Tupper Lake *(G-16280)*

Ulster County Press Office ..... G 845 687-4480
High Falls *(G-6402)*

Unified Media Inc ..... F 917 595-2710
New York *(G-12454)*

Vnovom Svete ..... G 212 302-9480
New York *(G-12562)*

Vpj Publication Inc ..... E 718 845-3221
Howard Beach *(G-6600)*

Vus Is Neias LLC ..... G 347 627-3999
Brooklyn *(G-2738)*

W M T Publications Inc ..... F 585 244-3329
Rochester *(G-14755)*

Wayuga Community Newspapers ..... E 315 754-6229
Red Creek *(G-14027)*

Wayuga Community Newspapers ..... G 315 594-2506
Wolcott *(G-17281)*

Weisbeck Publishing Printing ..... G 716 937-9226
Alden *(G-186)*

West Publishing Corporation ..... E 212 922-1920
New York *(G-12614)*

William B Collins Company ..... D 518 773-8272
Gloversville *(G-5729)*

Williamsburg Bulletin ..... G 718 387-0123
Brooklyn *(G-2755)*

World Journal LLC ..... F 718 871-5000
Brooklyn *(G-2766)*

Yoga In Daily Life - NY Inc ..... G 718 539-8548
College Point *(G-3811)*

PUBLISHING & PRINTING: Pamphlets

Newkirk Products Inc ..... C 518 862-3200
Albany *(G-107)*

Employee Codes: A=Over 500 employees, B=251-500
C=101-250, D=51-100, E=20-50, F=10-19, G=5-9

2017 Harris
New York Manufacturers Directory

1321

PRODUCT

PUBLISHING & PRINTING: Patterns, Paper

Royalty Network Inc .... G 212 967-4300
　New York *(G-11928)*

PUBLISHING & PRINTING: Shopping News

Adirondack Pennysaver Inc .... E 518 563-0100
　Plattsburgh *(G-13650)*
Badoud Communications Inc .... C 315 472-7821
　Syracuse *(G-15866)*
City of New York .... E 718 965-8787
　Brooklyn *(G-1782)*
Rheinwald Printing Co Inc .... F 585 637-5100
　Brockport *(G-1246)*
S G New York LLC .... E 631 665-4000
　Bohemia *(G-1128)*
Salamanca Press Penny Saver .... E 716 945-1500
　Salamanca *(G-15105)*
Tenney Media Group .... D 315 853-5569
　Clinton *(G-3722)*

PUBLISHING & PRINTING: Technical Manuals

Dohnsco Inc .... G 516 773-4800
　Manhasset *(G-8059)*
Service Education Incorporated .... G 585 264-9240
　Victor *(G-16502)*

PUBLISHING & PRINTING: Textbooks

Bright Kids Nyc Inc .... E 917 539-4575
　New York *(G-9460)*
Codesters Inc .... G 646 232-1025
　New York *(G-9664)*
Iat Interactive LLC .... E 914 273-2233
　Mount Kisco *(G-8628)*
McGraw-Hill Glbl Edctn Hldngs .... D 646 766-2000
　New York *(G-11198)*
Pearson Education Holdings Inc .... A 201 236-6716
　New York *(G-11593)*
Peri-Facts Academy .... G 585 275-6037
　Rochester *(G-14577)*
Petersons Nelnet LLC .... C 609 896-1800
　Albany *(G-118)*
Warodean Corporation .... G 718 359-5559
　Flushing *(G-5307)*

PUBLISHING & PRINTING: Trade Journals

Beer Marketers Insights Inc .... G 845 507-0040
　Suffern *(G-15786)*
Forum Publishing Co .... G 631 754-5000
　Centerport *(G-3476)*
Guilford Publications Inc .... D 212 431-9800
　New York *(G-10382)*
H F W Communications Inc .... F 315 703-7979
　East Syracuse *(G-4535)*
Hotelinteractive Inc .... F 631 424-7755
　Smithtown *(G-15488)*
Institute of Electrical and El .... E 212 705-8900
　New York *(G-10612)*
Lockwood Trade Journal Co Inc .... E 212 391-2060
　Long Island City *(G-7793)*
Med Reviews LLC .... E 212 239-5860
　New York *(G-11206)*
Primedia Special Interest Publ .... D 212 726-4300
　New York *(G-11709)*
Strathmore Directories Ltd .... E 516 997-2525
　Westbury *(G-17028)*

PUBLISHING & PRINTING: Yearbooks

Neff Holding Company .... G 914 595-8200
　Armonk *(G-418)*
Visant Secondary Holdings Corp .... G 914 595-8200
　Armonk *(G-423)*

PULP MILLS

APC Paper Company Inc .... D 315 384-4225
　Norfolk *(G-12897)*
Cenibra Inc .... G 212 818-8242
　New York *(G-9561)*
Central Nat Pulp & Ppr Sls Inc .... A 914 696-9000
　Purchase *(G-13955)*
International Paper Company .... C 607 775-1550
　Conklin *(G-3869)*
ITT Engineered Valves LLC .... E 662 257-6982
　Seneca Falls *(G-15363)*
ITT Industries Holdings Inc .... G 914 641-2000
　White Plains *(G-17129)*

Parsons & Whittemore Inc .... E 914 937-9009
　Port Chester *(G-13756)*
Parsons Whittemore Entps Corp .... E 914 937-9009
　Port Chester *(G-13757)*

PULP MILLS: Mech Pulp, Incl Groundwood & Thermomechanical

Norton Pulpstones Incorporated .... G 716 433-9400
　Lockport *(G-7608)*

PULP MILLS: Mechanical & Recycling Processing

Advanced Recovery & Recycl LLC .... F 315 450-3301
　Baldwinsville *(G-565)*
Suffolk Indus Recovery Corp .... D 631 732-6403
　Coram *(G-3951)*

PULP MILLS: Soda Pulp

R D S Mountain View Trucking .... G 315 823-4265
　Little Falls *(G-7503)*

PUMICE

A&B Conservation LLC .... G 845 282-7272
　Monsey *(G-8566)*

PUMP GOVERNORS: Gas Machines

Dormitory Authority - State NY .... G 631 434-1487
　Brentwood *(G-1182)*

PUMPS

Air Flow Pump Corp .... G 718 241-2800
　Brooklyn *(G-1571)*
Air Techniques Inc .... B 516 433-7676
　Melville *(G-8291)*
American Ship Repairs Company .... F 718 435-5570
　Brooklyn *(G-1609)*
Armstrong Pumps Inc .... D 716 693-8813
　North Tonawanda *(G-12955)*
Buffalo Pumps Inc .... C 716 693-1850
　North Tonawanda *(G-12963)*
Curaegis Technologies Inc .... F 585 254-1100
　Rochester *(G-14294)*
Daikin Applied Americas Inc .... C 315 253-2771
　Auburn *(G-491)*
Federal Pump Corporation .... E 718 451-2000
　Brooklyn *(G-1963)*
Fisonic Corp .... F 716 763-0295
　New York *(G-10174)*
Fluid Handling LLC .... G 716 897-2800
　Cheektowaga *(G-3571)*
Gardner Dnver Oberdorfer Pumps .... E 315 437-0361
　Syracuse *(G-15948)*
Goulds Pumps Incorporated .... A 315 568-2811
　Seneca Falls *(G-15360)*
Goulds Pumps Incorporated .... B 315 258-4949
　Auburn *(G-498)*
ITT Corporation .... C 315 568-2811
　Seneca Falls *(G-15362)*
ITT Fluid Technology Corp .... B 914 641-2000
　White Plains *(G-17127)*
ITT Goulds Pumps Inc .... A 914 641-2129
　Seneca Falls *(G-15364)*
ITT Water Technology Inc .... B 315 568-2811
　Seneca Falls *(G-15365)*
John N Fehlinger Co Inc .... F 212 233-5656
　New York *(G-10752)*
Ketcham Pump Co Inc .... F 718 457-0800
　Woodside *(G-17347)*
Linde LLC .... D 716 773-7552
　Grand Island *(G-5763)*
Lufkin Industries LLC .... E 585 593-7930
　Wellsville *(G-16753)*
Mannesmann Corporation .... D 212 258-4000
　New York *(G-11136)*
McWane Inc .... B 607 734-2211
　Elmira *(G-4694)*
Oberdorfer Pumps Inc .... E 315 437-0361
　Syracuse *(G-15601)*
Oyster Bay Pump Works Inc .... F 516 922-3789
　Hicksville *(G-6381)*
Pulsafeeder Inc .... C 585 292-8000
　Rochester *(G-14609)*
Sihi Pumps Inc .... E 716 773-6450
　Grand Island *(G-5769)*
Voss Usa Inc .... C 212 995-2255
　New York *(G-12570)*

Wastecorp Pumps LLC .... F 888 829-2783
　New York *(G-12592)*
Westmoor Ltd .... F 315 363-1500
　Sherrill *(G-15410)*
Xylem Inc .... F 716 862-4123
　Seneca Falls *(G-15373)*
Xylem Inc .... C 315 258-4949
　Auburn *(G-529)*
Xylem Inc .... B 914 323-5700
　Rye Brook *(G-15075)*

PUMPS & PARTS: Indl

Century-Tech Inc .... F 718 326-9400
　Hempstead *(G-6267)*
Fisonic Corp .... F 212 732-3777
　Long Island City *(G-7743)*
Stavo Industries Inc .... F 845 331-4552
　Kingston *(G-7213)*

PUMPS & PUMPING EQPT REPAIR SVCS

A & C/Furia Electric Motors .... F 914 949-0585
　White Plains *(G-17072)*
American Ship Repairs Company .... F 718 435-5570
　Brooklyn *(G-1609)*
Daves Electric Motors & Pumps .... F 212 982-2930
　New York *(G-9817)*
Sunset Ridge Holdings Inc .... F 716 487-1458
　Jamestown *(G-7034)*

PUMPS & PUMPING EQPT WHOLESALERS

Electric Motors and Pumps Inc .... G 718 935-9118
　Brooklyn *(G-1910)*
Gny Equipment LLC .... F 631 667-1010
　Bay Shore *(G-703)*

PUMPS, HEAT: Electric

Economy Pump & Motor Repair .... G 718 433-2600
　Astoria *(G-438)*

PUMPS: Domestic, Water Or Sump

Geopump Inc .... G 585 798-6666
　Medina *(G-8273)*
Liberty Pumps Inc .... C 585 494-1817
　Bergen *(G-849)*
Pentair Water Pool and Spa Inc .... E 845 452-5500
　Lagrangeville *(G-7258)*
Trench & Marine Pump Co Inc .... E 212 423-9098
　Bronx *(G-1475)*
Water Cooling Corp .... G 718 723-6500
　Rosedale *(G-15015)*

PUMPS: Measuring & Dispensing

Aptargroup Inc .... C 845 639-3700
　Congers *(G-3852)*
Charles Ross & Son Company .... D 631 234-0500
　Hauppauge *(G-6044)*
Economy Pump & Motor Repair .... G 718 433-2600
　Astoria *(G-438)*
Pulsafeeder Inc .... C 585 292-8000
　Rochester *(G-14609)*
Schlumberger Technology Corp .... C 607 378-0200
　Horseheads *(G-6592)*
Valois of America Inc .... C 845 639-3700
　Congers *(G-3861)*

PUMPS: Vacuum, Exc Laboratory

Ebara Technologies Inc .... D 845 896-1370
　Hopewell Junction *(G-6548)*
Graham Corporation .... B 585 343-2216
　Batavia *(G-636)*
Kinequip Inc .... F 716 694-5000
　Buffalo *(G-3032)*
Precision Plus Vacuum Parts .... D 716 297-2039
　Sanborn *(G-15125)*

PUNCHES: Forming & Stamping

Pivot Punch Corporation .... D 716 625-8000
　Lockport *(G-7610)*
Precise Punch Corporation .... F 716 625-8000
　Lockport *(G-7611)*

PURIFICATION & DUST COLLECTION EQPT

Buffalo Bioblower Tech LLC .... G 716 625-8618
　Lockport *(G-7573)*

PRODUCT SECTION

RADIO, TV/CONSUMER ELEC STORES: Antennas, Satellite Dish

Hilliard Corporation .... B 607 733-7121
   Elmira *(G-4690)*
Hilliard Corporation .... F 607 733-7121
   Elmira *(G-4691)*
Low-Cost Mfg Co Inc .... G 516 627-3282
   Carle Place *(G-3393)*
Oneida Air Systems Inc .... E 315 476-5151
   Syracuse *(G-16004)*

PURSES: Women's

Formart Corp .... F 212 819-1819
   New York *(G-10186)*

PUSHCARTS & WHEELBARROWS

Truxton Corp .... G 718 842-6000
   Bronx *(G-1480)*

QUICKLIME

Minerals Technologies Inc .... E 212 878-1800
   New York *(G-11276)*

RACE TRACK OPERATION

P S M Group Inc .... E 716 532-6686
   Forestville *(G-5335)*

RACEWAYS

Pole Position Raceway .... G 716 683-7223
   Cheektowaga *(G-3586)*

RACKS & SHELVING: Household, Wood

American Epoxy and Metal Inc .... G 718 828-7828
   Scarsdale *(G-15216)*

RACKS: Display

Eazy Movements .... G 716 837-2083
   Buffalo *(G-2931)*

RACKS: Garment, Exc Wood

All Racks Industries Inc .... G 212 244-1069
   New York *(G-9085)*
ASAP Rack Rental Inc .... G 718 499-4495
   Brooklyn *(G-1638)*
Lifestyle-Trimco .... E 718 257-9101
   Brooklyn *(G-2219)*
Millennium Stl Rack Rntals Inc .... G 212 594-2190
   Brooklyn *(G-2316)*
Ted-Steel Industries Ltd .... G 212 279-3878
   New York *(G-12293)*

RACKS: Garment, Wood

Lifestyle-Trimco .... E 718 257-9101
   Brooklyn *(G-2219)*

RACKS: Pallet, Exc Wood

Frazier Industrial Company .... D 315 539-9256
   Waterloo *(G-16626)*

RADAR SYSTEMS & EQPT

Artemis Inc .... G 631 232-2424
   Hauppauge *(G-6025)*
Itt LLC .... B 914 641-2000
   White Plains *(G-17125)*
ITT Corporation .... D 914 641-2000
   Seneca Falls *(G-15361)*
ITT Corporation .... D 315 568-2811
   Seneca Falls *(G-15362)*
ITT Inc .... G 914 641-2000
   White Plains *(G-17128)*
Laufer Wind Group LLC .... F 212 792-3912
   New York *(G-10935)*
Penetradar Corporation .... F 716 731-2629
   Niagara Falls *(G-12859)*
Systems Drs C3 Inc .... B 716 631-6200
   Buffalo *(G-3207)*
Telephonics Corporation .... A 631 755-7000
   Farmingdale *(G-5127)*
Traffic Logix Corporation .... G 866 915-6449
   Spring Valley *(G-15603)*

RADIATORS, EXC ELECTRIC

Original Convector Specialist .... G 718 342-5820
   Brooklyn *(G-2395)*

RADIO & TELEVISION COMMUNICATIONS EQUIPMENT

Actv Inc (del Corp) .... D 212 995-9500
   New York *(G-9022)*
Airnet Communications Corp .... F 516 338-0008
   Westbury *(G-16963)*
Anaren Holding Corp .... G 212 415-6700
   New York *(G-9148)*
Ashly Audio Inc .... E 585 872-0010
   Webster *(G-16713)*
AVI-Spl Employee .... B 212 840-4801
   New York *(G-9277)*
Benchmark Media Systems Inc .... E 315 437-6300
   Syracuse *(G-15868)*
Chyronhego Corporation .... D 631 845-2000
   Melville *(G-8303)*
CJ Component Products LLC .... G 631 567-3733
   Oakdale *(G-13057)*
Clever Devices Ltd .... E 516 433-6100
   Woodbury *(G-17283)*
Commscope Technologies LLC .... F 315 768-3573
   Marcy *(G-8090)*
Edo LLC .... A 631 630-4200
   Amityville *(G-286)*
Electro-Metrics Corporation .... E 518 762-2600
   Johnstown *(G-7109)*
Eni Technology Inc .... B 585 427-8300
   Rochester *(G-14353)*
Fujitsu Ntwrk Cmmnications Inc .... F 845 731-2000
   Pearl River *(G-13457)*
GE Mds LLC .... C 585 242-9600
   Rochester *(G-14389)*
Griffon Corporation .... E 212 957-5000
   New York *(G-10363)*
Gurley Precision Instrs Inc .... C 518 272-6300
   Troy *(G-16237)*
Hand Held Products Inc .... B 315 554-6000
   Skaneateles Falls *(G-15468)*
Harris Corporation .... A 585 244-5830
   Rochester *(G-14422)*
Harris Corporation .... B 585 244-5830
   Rochester *(G-14428)*
Harris Corporation .... F 718 767-1100
   Whitestone *(G-17208)*
Harris Corporation .... B 585 244-5830
   Rochester *(G-14429)*
Icon Enterprises Intl Inc .... E 718 752-9764
   Long Island City *(G-7763)*
It Commodity Sourcing Inc .... G 718 677-1577
   Brooklyn *(G-2118)*
L-3 Communications Corporation .... A 631 436-7400
   Hauppauge *(G-6108)*
L-3 Communications Corporation .... C 585 742-9100
   Victor *(G-16487)*
Mark Peri International .... F 516 208-6824
   Oceanside *(G-13087)*
Mini-Circuits Fort Wayne LLC .... B 718 934-4500
   Brooklyn *(G-2318)*
Mirion Tech Imaging LLC .... E 607 562-4300
   Horseheads *(G-6583)*
Motorola Solutions Inc .... C 718 330-2163
   Brooklyn *(G-2336)*
Motorola Solutions Inc .... C 518 869-9517
   Albany *(G-103)*
Movin On Sounds and SEC Inc .... E 516 489-2350
   Franklin Square *(G-5365)*
Navitar Inc .... D 585 359-4000
   Rochester *(G-14530)*
NBC Universal LLC .... E 718 482-8310
   Long Island City *(G-7822)*
Panvidea Inc .... F 212 967-9613
   New York *(G-11561)*
Quanta Electronics Inc .... F 631 961-9953
   Centereach *(G-3472)*
Quintel Usa Inc .... E 585 420-8364
   Rochester *(G-14617)*
Rodale Wireless Inc .... E 631 231-0044
   Hauppauge *(G-6179)*
Ruhle Companies Inc .... E 914 287-4000
   Valhalla *(G-16372)*
Sdr Technology Inc .... G 716 583-1249
   Alden *(G-183)*
Sequential Electronics Systems .... E 914 592-1345
   Elmsford *(G-4783)*
Shoretel Inc .... G 877 654-3573
   Rochester *(G-14684)*
Spectralink Corporation .... D 212 372-6997
   New York *(G-12156)*
STI-Co Industries Inc .... E 716 662-2680
   Orchard Park *(G-13297)*
Telephonics Corporation .... A 631 755-7000
   Farmingdale *(G-5127)*
Telxon Corporation .... E 631 738-2400
   Holtsville *(G-6512)*
W & W Manufacturing Co .... F 516 942-0011
   Deer Park *(G-4225)*
Whirlwind Music Distrs Inc .... D 585 663-8820
   Rochester *(G-14762)*
Zetek Corporation .... F 212 668-1485
   New York *(G-12710)*

RADIO & TELEVISION REPAIR

NCR Corporation .... C 516 876-7200
   Jericho *(G-7078)*

RADIO BROADCASTING & COMMUNICATIONS EQPT

Apex Airtronics Inc .... E 718 485-8560
   Brooklyn *(G-1616)*
Appairent Technologies Inc .... G 585 214-2460
   West Henrietta *(G-16869)*
Fleetcom Inc .... F 914 776-5582
   Yonkers *(G-17445)*
Global Tower LLC .... G 561 995-0320
   La Fargeville *(G-7235)*
Hamtronics Inc .... G 585 392-9430
   Rochester *(G-14419)*
Imagine Communications Corp .... F 212 303-4200
   New York *(G-10568)*
L-3 Communications Corporation .... D 631 436-7400
   Hauppauge *(G-6110)*
Motorola Solutions Inc .... C 518 348-0833
   Halfmoon *(G-5912)*
North American MBL Systems Inc .... E 718 898-8700
   Woodside *(G-17341)*
Persistent Systems LLC .... E 212 561-5895
   New York *(G-11626)*
Wireless Communications Inc .... G 845 353-5921
   Nyack *(G-13056)*

RADIO BROADCASTING STATIONS

Hearst Business Media Corp .... F 631 650-4441
   Great River *(G-5851)*
Hearst Corporation .... A 212 649-2000
   New York *(G-10438)*
Iheartcommunications Inc .... C 585 454-4884
   Rochester *(G-14445)*
New York Times Company .... B 212 556-1234
   New York *(G-11410)*

RADIO COMMUNICATIONS: Airborne Eqpt

Eni Mks Products Group .... F 585 427-8300
   Rochester *(G-14352)*

RADIO RECEIVER NETWORKS

Cntry Cross Communications LLC .... F 386 758-9696
   Jamestown *(G-6982)*
Iheartcommunications Inc .... C 585 454-4884
   Rochester *(G-14445)*
Iheartcommunications Inc .... E 212 603-4660
   New York *(G-10564)*

RADIO, TELEVISION & CONSUMER ELECTRONICS STORES: Eqpt, NEC

Electrotech Service Eqp Corp .... E 718 626-7700
   Astoria *(G-439)*
Parrys .... F 315 824-0002
   Hamilton *(G-5949)*
Pass & Seymour Inc .... B 315 468-6211
   Syracuse *(G-16011)*
Sound Source Inc .... G 585 271-5370
   Rochester *(G-14693)*

RADIO, TV & CONSUMER ELECTRONICS: VCR & Access

Elite Cellular Accessories Inc .... E 877 390-2502
   Deer Park *(G-4136)*

RADIO, TV/CONSUMER ELEC STORES: Antennas, Satellite Dish

L-3 Communications Corporation .... D 631 231-1700
   Hauppauge *(G-6109)*

Employee Codes: A=Over 500 employees, B=251-500
C=101-250, D=51-100, E=20-50, F=10-19, G=5-9

RAILINGS: Prefabricated, Metal

Paragon Aquatics .... E 845 452-5500
  Lagrangeville *(G-7257)*

RAILINGS: Wood

Blooming Grove Stair Co .... F 845 783-4245
  Monroe *(G-8550)*
Blooming Grove Stair Co .... G 845 791-4016
  Monticello *(G-8604)*
D K P Wood Railings & Stairs .... F 631 665-8656
  Bay Shore *(G-690)*
Deer Pk Stair Bldg Mllwk Inc .... E 631 363-5000
  Blue Point *(G-998)*
Rockaway Stairs Ltd .... G 718 945-0047
  Far Rockaway *(G-4924)*
Stairworld Inc .... G 718 441-9722
  Richmond Hill *(G-14085)*

RAILROAD CAR RENTING & LEASING SVCS

Acf Industries Holding Corp .... G 212 702-4363
  New York *(G-9016)*
Buffalo Investors Corp .... G 212 702-4363
  New York *(G-9476)*
Highcrest Investors LLC .... D 212 702-4323
  New York *(G-10474)*
Starfire Holding Corporation .... E 914 614-7000
  White Plains *(G-17169)*

RAILROAD CAR REPAIR SVCS

Acf Industries Holding Corp .... G 212 702-4363
  New York *(G-9016)*
Ebenezer Railcar Services Inc .... E 716 674-5650
  West Seneca *(G-16943)*
Highcrest Investors LLC .... D 212 702-4323
  New York *(G-10474)*
Starfire Holding Corporation .... E 914 614-7000
  White Plains *(G-17169)*

RAILROAD CARGO LOADING & UNLOADING SVCS

Packstar Group Inc .... D 716 853-1688
  Buffalo *(G-3111)*

RAILROAD EQPT

Alstom Signaling Inc .... E 585 274-8700
  Schenectady *(G-15229)*
Alstom Transportation Inc .... E 212 692-5353
  New York *(G-9104)*
Bombardier Mass Transit Corp .... B 518 566-0150
  Plattsburgh *(G-13655)*
CAF Usa Inc .... D 607 737-3004
  Elmira Heights *(G-4709)*
Cox & Company Inc .... C 212 366-0200
  Plainview *(G-13593)*
Eagle Bridge Machine & Tl Inc .... E 518 686-4541
  Eagle Bridge *(G-4356)*
Ebenezer Railcar Services Inc .... E 716 674-5650
  West Seneca *(G-16943)*
Era-Contact Usa LLC .... F 631 524-5530
  Hauppauge *(G-6072)*
Gray Manufacturing Inds LLC .... F 607 281-1325
  Hornell *(G-6565)*
Horne Products Inc .... G 631 293-0773
  Farmingdale *(G-5007)*
Hudson Machine Works Inc .... C 845 279-1413
  Brewster *(G-1221)*
Knorr Brake Holding Corp .... G 315 786-5356
  Watertown *(G-16659)*
Peck & Hale LLC .... E 631 589-2510
  West Sayville *(G-16937)*
Semec Corp .... F 518 825-0160
  Plattsburgh *(G-13696)*
Strato Transit Components LLC .... G 518 686-4541
  Eagle Bridge *(G-4359)*
Twinco Mfg Co Inc .... E 631 231-0022
  Hauppauge *(G-6219)*
Westcode Incorporated .... E 607 766-9881
  Binghamton *(G-959)*

RAILROAD EQPT & SPLYS WHOLESALERS

Horne Products Inc .... G 631 293-0773
  Farmingdale *(G-5007)*

RAILROAD EQPT, EXC LOCOMOTIVES

Bombardier Transportation .... D 607 324-0216
  Hornell *(G-6560)*
Kawasaki Rail Car Inc .... C 914 376-4700
  Yonkers *(G-17459)*
Transco Railway Products Inc .... E 716 824-1219
  Blasdell *(G-967)*

RAILROAD EQPT: Brakes, Air & Vacuum

Knorr Brake Company LLC .... G 518 561-1387
  Plattsburgh *(G-13674)*
Knorr Brake Truck Systems Co .... B 315 786-5200
  Watertown *(G-16660)*
New York Air Brake LLC .... C 315 786-5219
  Watertown *(G-16665)*
Westinghouse A Brake Tech Corp .... D 518 561-0044
  Plattsburgh *(G-13708)*

RAILROAD EQPT: Cars & Eqpt, Dining

Acf Industries Holding Corp .... G 212 702-4363
  New York *(G-9016)*
Buffalo Investors Corp .... G 212 702-4363
  New York *(G-9476)*
Highcrest Investors LLC .... D 212 702-4323
  New York *(G-10474)*
Starfire Holding Corporation .... E 914 614-7000
  White Plains *(G-17169)*

RAILROAD EQPT: Cars & Eqpt, Rapid Transit

Westinghouse A Brake Tech Corp .... F 914 347-8650
  Elmsford *(G-4793)*

RAILROAD EQPT: Cars & Eqpt, Train, Freight Or Passenger

General Electric Company .... E 845 567-7410
  Newburgh *(G-12757)*

RAILROAD EQPT: Cars, Maintenance

Koshii Maxelum America Inc .... E 845 471-0500
  Poughkeepsie *(G-13911)*

RAILROAD EQPT: Locomotives & Parts, Indl

Niagara Cooler Inc .... G 716 434-1235
  Lockport *(G-7604)*
Rand Machine Products Inc .... D 716 665-5217
  Falconer *(G-4908)*

RAILROAD EQPT: Lubrication Systems, Locomotive

American Motive Power Inc .... E 585 335-3132
  Dansville *(G-4075)*

RAILROAD RELATED EQPT: Railway Track

Applied Technology Mfg Corp .... E 607 687-2200
  Owego *(G-13350)*
Railworks Transit Systems Inc .... E 212 502-7900
  New York *(G-11788)*

RAILS: Steel Or Iron

Artistic Ironworks Inc .... G 631 665-4285
  Bay Shore *(G-672)*

RAMPS: Prefabricated Metal

Landmark Group Inc .... D 845 358-0350
  Valley Cottage *(G-16380)*

RAZORS: Electric

Harrys Inc .... E 888 212-6855
  New York *(G-10421)*

REAL ESTATE AGENCIES & BROKERS

Yale Robbins Inc .... D 212 683-5700
  New York *(G-12687)*

REAL ESTATE AGENTS & MANAGERS

Directory Major Malls Inc .... G 845 348-7000
  Nyack *(G-13049)*

REAL ESTATE OPERATORS, EXC DEVELOPERS: Apartment Hotel

Atlas Bituminous Co Inc .... F 315 457-2394
  Syracuse *(G-15860)*

REAL ESTATE OPERATORS, EXC DEVELOPERS: Commercial/Indl Bldg

Bertelsmann Inc .... E 212 782-1000
  New York *(G-9370)*
E F Thresh Inc .... G 315 437-7301
  East Syracuse *(G-4526)*
Penhouse Media Group Inc .... C 212 702-6000
  New York *(G-11607)*

RECLAIMED RUBBER: Reworked By Manufacturing Process

Rubberform Recycled Pdts LLC .... F 716 478-0404
  Lockport *(G-7614)*

RECORD BLANKS: Phonographic

Chesky Records Inc .... F 212 586-7799
  New York *(G-9592)*
Europadisk LLC .... E 718 407-7300
  Long Island City *(G-7733)*

RECORDERS: Sound

Interaction Insight Corp .... G 800 285-2950
  New York *(G-10622)*

RECORDING HEADS: Speech & Musical Eqpt

Felluss Recording .... G 212 727-8055
  New York *(G-10151)*
Fine Sounds Group Inc .... F 212 364-0219
  New York *(G-10165)*

RECORDING TAPE: Video, Blank

VDO Lab Inc .... G 914 949-1741
  White Plains *(G-17179)*

RECORDS & TAPES: Prerecorded

Columbia Records Inc .... F 212 833-8000
  New York *(G-9677)*
Cult Records LLC .... G 718 395-2077
  New York *(G-9765)*
Dorling Kindersley Publishing .... F 212 213-4800
  New York *(G-9910)*
Emusiccom Inc .... D 212 201-9240
  New York *(G-10028)*
Extreme Group Holdings LLC .... F 212 833-8000
  New York *(G-10111)*
High Quality Video Inc .... F 212 686-9534
  New York *(G-10473)*
His Productions USA Inc .... G 212 594-3737
  New York *(G-10483)*
Imago Recording Company .... G 212 751-3033
  New York *(G-10569)*
Lefrak Entertainment Co Ltd .... G 212 586-3600
  New York *(G-10960)*
Pete Levin Music Inc .... G 845 247-9211
  Saugerties *(G-15192)*
Pivot Records LLC .... F 718 417-1213
  Brooklyn *(G-2424)*
Recorded Anthology of Amrcn Mus ...... F 212 290-1695
  Brooklyn *(G-2484)*
Roadrunner Records Inc .... E 212 274-7500
  New York *(G-11887)*
Side Hustle Music Group LLC .... F 800 219-4003
  New York *(G-12060)*
Sony Broadband Entertainment .... F 212 833-6800
  New York *(G-12131)*
Sony Music Entertainment Inc .... A 212 833-8000
  New York *(G-12134)*
Sony Music Entertainment Inc .... B 212 833-8500
  New York *(G-12135)*
Sony Music Entertainment Inc .... E 212 833-5057
  New York *(G-12136)*
Sony Music Holdings Inc .... A 212 833-8000
  New York *(G-12137)*
Taste and See Entrmt Inc .... G 516 285-3010
  Valley Stream *(G-16429)*
Warner Music Group Corp .... B 212 275-2000
  New York *(G-12588)*
Warner Music Inc .... D 212 275-2000
  New York *(G-12589)*

PRODUCT SECTION

RECORDS OR TAPES: Masters

Bridge Records Inc ....G....... 914 654-9270
  New Rochelle *(G-8890)*
John Marshall Sound Inc ....G....... 212 265-6066
  New York *(G-10751)*
Masterdisk Corporation.........................F....... 212 541-5022
  Elmsford *(G-4764)*
Peer-Southern Productions Inc ....E....... 212 265-3910
  New York *(G-11597)*
Sterling Sound Inc ....E....... 212 604-9433
  New York *(G-12198)*
Wea International Inc ....D....... 212 275-1300
  New York *(G-12601)*

RECOVERY SVCS: Metal

Island Recycling Corp ....G....... 631 234-6688
  Central Islip *(G-3500)*

RECREATIONAL & SPORTING CAMPS

Steel Excel Inc..D....... 914 461-1300
  White Plains *(G-17171)*

RECTIFIERS: Electrical Apparatus

Ems Development Corporation ....D....... 631 924-4736
  Yaphank *(G-17390)*

RECTIFIERS: Solid State

Electronic Devices Inc...........................E....... 914 965-4400
  Yonkers *(G-17440)*

RECYCLABLE SCRAP & WASTE MATERIALS WHOLESALERS

Metalico Aluminum Recovery Inc..........E....... 315 463-9292
  Syracuse *(G-15986)*

RECYCLING: Paper

Andritz Inc ....E....... 518 745-2988
  Glens Falls *(G-5670)*
Georgia-Pacific Corrugared LLC ....D....... 585 343-3800
  Batavia *(G-635)*
Harvest Technologies Inc......................G....... 518 899-7124
  Ballston Spa *(G-599)*
Owasco Recycling Center ....G....... 315 252-0332
  Auburn *(G-512)*
Recommunity Recycling ....B....... 845 926-1071
  Beacon *(G-789)*
Sierra Processing LLC ....F....... 518 433-0020
  Schenectady *(G-15297)*

REELS: Cable, Metal

Hannay Reels Inc ....C....... 518 797-3791
  Westerlo *(G-17042)*
Reelcology Inc..F....... 845 258-1880
  Pine Island *(G-13553)*

REFINERS & SMELTERS: Aluminum

Metalico Aluminum Recovery Inc..........E....... 315 463-9292
  Syracuse *(G-15986)*

REFINERS & SMELTERS: Antimony, Primary

Zerovalent Nanometals Inc ....G....... 585 298-8592
  Rochester *(G-14774)*

REFINERS & SMELTERS: Cobalt, Primary

Umicore USA Inc....................................E....... 919 874-7171
  Glens Falls *(G-5700)*

REFINERS & SMELTERS: Copper

Sherburne Metal Sales Inc ....F....... 607 674-4441
  Sherburne *(G-15395)*
Tecnofil Chenango SAC ....E....... 607 674-4441
  Sherburne *(G-15398)*

REFINERS & SMELTERS: Copper, Secondary

Ben Weitsman of Albany LLC................E....... 518 462-4444
  Albany *(G-53)*

REFINERS & SMELTERS: Gold

General Refining & Smelting ....G....... 516 538-4747
  Hempstead *(G-6270)*

General Refining Corporation................G....... 516 538-4747
  Hempstead *(G-6271)*

REFINERS & SMELTERS: Lead, Secondary

Eco-Bat America LLC ....C....... 845 692-4414
  Middletown *(G-8439)*

REFINERS & SMELTERS: Nonferrous Metal

Advanced Precision Technology............F....... 845 279-3540
  Brewster *(G-1207)*
Amt Incorporated ....E....... 518 284-2910
  Sharon Springs *(G-15383)*
Cora Materials Corp..............................F....... 516 488-6300
  New Hyde Park *(G-8824)*
General Refining & Smelting ....G....... 516 538-4747
  Hempstead *(G-6270)*
Germanium Corp America Inc ....F....... 315 853-4900
  Clinton *(G-3719)*
Karbra Company ....C....... 212 736-9300
  New York *(G-10809)*
Parfuse Corp ....E....... 516 997-1795
  Westbury *(G-17018)*
Pluribus Products Inc............................E....... 718 852-1614
  Brooklyn *(G-2427)*
S & W Metal Trading Corp ....G....... 212 719-5070
  New York *(G-11944)*
Scepter Inc..E....... 315 568-4225
  Seneca Falls *(G-15367)*
Sims Group USA Holdings Corp ....D....... 718 786-6031
  Long Island City *(G-7877)*
Special Metals Corporation...................D....... 716 366-5663
  Dunkirk *(G-4351)*

REFINERS & SMELTERS: Platinum Group Metal Refining, Primary

AAA Catalytic Recycling Inc ....F....... 631 920-7944
  Farmingdale *(G-4928)*

REFINERS & SMELTERS: Silicon, Primary, Over 99% Pure

Globe Metallurgical Inc..........................D....... 716 804-0862
  Niagara Falls *(G-12825)*

REFINERS & SMELTERS: Silver

Rochester Silver Works LLC..................G....... 585 743-1610
  Rochester *(G-14648)*
Umicore Technical Materials ....C....... 518 792-7700
  Glens Falls *(G-5699)*

REFINERS & SMELTERS: Zinc, Primary, Including Slabs & Dust

Hh Liquidating Corp ....A....... 646 282-2500
  New York *(G-10471)*

REFINING LUBRICATING OILS & GREASES, NEC

Industrial Oil Tank Service ....F....... 315 736-6080
  Oriskany *(G-13311)*
Safety-Kleen Systems Inc ....F....... 716 855-2212
  Buffalo *(G-3174)*

REFINING: Petroleum

California Petro Trnspt Corp..................G....... 212 302-5151
  New York *(G-9500)*
Global Earth Energy ....G....... 716 332-7150
  Buffalo *(G-2976)*
Hess Corporation...................................B....... 212 997-8500
  New York *(G-10464)*
Hess Oil Virgin Island Corp...................A....... 212 997-8500
  New York *(G-10467)*
Hess Pipeline Corporation.....................B....... 212 997-8500
  New York *(G-10468)*
Naval Stores Co ....F....... 914 664-5877
  Mount Vernon *(G-8709)*
Petre Alii Petroleum...............................G....... 315 785-1037
  Watertown *(G-16670)*

REFRACTORIES: Alumina Fused

Global Alumina Corporation..................G....... 212 351-0000
  New York *(G-10311)*
Global Alumina Services Co ....B....... 212 309-8060
  New York *(G-10312)*

REFRIGERATION & HEATING EQUIPMENT

REFRACTORIES: Brick

Capitol Restoration Corp ....G....... 516 783-1425
  North Bellmore *(G-12915)*

REFRACTORIES: Brick

Saint-Gobain Strl Ceramics ....A....... 716 278-6233
  Niagara Falls *(G-12873)*

REFRACTORIES: Clay

Filtros Ltd ....E....... 585 586-8770
  East Rochester *(G-4459)*
Upstate Refractory Svcs Inc ....E....... 315 331-2955
  Newark *(G-12746)*

REFRACTORIES: Graphite, Carbon Or Ceramic Bond

Blasch Precision Ceramics Inc.............D....... 518 436-1263
  Menands *(G-8369)*
Surmet Ceramics Corporation ....F....... 716 875-4091
  Buffalo *(G-3204)*

REFRACTORIES: Nonclay

American Securities LLC ....E....... 716 696-3012
  Tonawanda *(G-16138)*
Ask Chemicals Hi-Tech LLC ....D....... 607 587-9146
  Alfred Station *(G-195)*
Ceramaterials LLC ....G....... 518 701-6722
  Port Jervis *(G-13781)*
Filtros Ltd ....E....... 585 586-8770
  East Rochester *(G-4459)*
Monofrax LLC...C....... 716 483-7200
  Falconer *(G-4907)*
Rembar Company LLC ....E....... 914 693-2620
  Dobbs Ferry *(G-4302)*
Saint-Gobain Dynamics Inc ....F....... 716 278-6007
  Niagara Falls *(G-12872)*
Silicon Carbide Products Inc ....E....... 607 562-8599
  Horseheads *(G-6593)*
Unifrax I LLC..C....... 716 696-3000
  Tonawanda *(G-16210)*
Zircar Refr Composites Inc ....E....... 845 651-4481
  Florida *(G-5218)*
Zircar Zirconia Inc.................................E....... 845 651-3040
  Florida *(G-5219)*

REFRACTORIES: Plastic

Hoffmans Trade Group LLC ....G....... 518 250-5556
  Troy *(G-16239)*

REFRACTORY CASTABLES

Hanyan & Higgins Company Inc...........G....... 315 769-8838
  Massena *(G-8196)*

REFRACTORY MATERIALS WHOLESALERS

Upstate Refractory Svcs Inc ....E....... 315 331-2955
  Newark *(G-12746)*

REFRIGERATION & HEATING EQUIPMENT

A&S Refrigeration Equipment ....G....... 718 993-6030
  Bronx *(G-1255)*
Aeroseal LLC...F....... 315 373-0765
  East Syracuse *(G-4499)*
Besicorp Ltd ....F....... 845 336-7700
  Kingston *(G-7179)*
Bombardier Trnsp Holdings USA ....D....... 607 776-4791
  Bath *(G-654)*
Carrier Corporation................................A....... 315 432-6000
  Syracuse *(G-15889)*
Carrier Corporation................................B....... 315 432-6000
  Syracuse *(G-15888)*
Columbia Pool Accessories Inc ....G....... 718 993-0389
  Bronx *(G-1303)*
Environmental Temp Systems LLC ......G....... 516 640-5818
  Mineola *(G-8508)*
Fts Systems Inc.....................................D....... 845 687-5300
  Stone Ridge *(G-15763)*
GM Components Holdings LLC ....B....... 716 439-2463
  Lockport *(G-7590)*
Healthway Products Company ....E....... 315 207-1410
  Oswego *(G-13332)*
Hydro-Air Components Inc ....C....... 716 827-6510
  Buffalo *(G-3000)*
Kedco Inc..F....... 516 454-7800
  Farmingdale *(G-5025)*

Employee Codes: A=Over 500 employees, B=251-500
C=101-250, D=51-100, E=20-50, F=10-19, G=5-9

REFRIGERATION & HEATING EQUIPMENT

Manning Lewis Div Rubicon Inds .... E 908 687-2400
 Brooklyn *(G-2262)*
Mgr Equipment Corp .... E 516 239-3030
 Inwood *(G-6761)*
Nationwide Coils Inc .... G 914 277-7396
 Mount Kisco *(G-8636)*
Niagara Blower Company .... C 800 426-5169
 Tonawanda *(G-16186)*
Parker-Hannifin Corporation .... D 716 685-4040
 Lancaster *(G-7331)*
Rayco Enterprises Inc .... D 716 685-6860
 Lancaster *(G-7337)*
Solitec Incorporated .... F 315 298-4213
 Pulaski *(G-13952)*
Supermarket Equipment Depo Inc .... G 718 665-6200
 Bronx *(G-1467)*
Trane US Inc .... D 718 721-8844
 Long Island City *(G-7905)*
Trane US Inc .... G 914 593-0303
 Elmsford *(G-4788)*
Trane US Inc .... E 315 234-1500
 East Syracuse *(G-4573)*
Trane US Inc .... E 518 785-1315
 Latham *(G-7380)*
Trane US Inc .... E 585 256-2500
 Rochester *(G-14729)*
Trane US Inc .... E 716 626-1260
 Buffalo *(G-3224)*
Trane US Inc .... E 631 952-9477
 Plainview *(G-13639)*
Universal Parent and Youth .... E 917 754-2426
 Brooklyn *(G-2707)*
York International Corporation .... D 718 389-4152
 Long Island City *(G-7929)*

REFRIGERATION EQPT & SPLYS WHOLESALERS

Maplewood Ice Co Inc .... E 518 499-2345
 Whitehall *(G-17190)*

REFRIGERATION EQPT: Complete

American Refrigeration Inc .... G 212 699-4000
 New York *(G-9127)*
Atmost Refrigeration Co Inc .... E 518 828-2180
 Hudson *(G-6608)*
Foster Refrigerators Entp .... F 518 671-6036
 Hudson *(G-6614)*
Millrock Technology Inc .... E 845 339-5700
 Kingston *(G-7201)*
S & V Restaurant Eqp Mfrs Inc .... E 718 220-1140
 Bronx *(G-1445)*

REFRIGERATION REPAIR SVCS

Colburns AC Rfrgn .... F 716 569-3695
 Frewsburg *(G-5449)*

REFRIGERATION SVC & REPAIR

Foster Refrigerators Entp .... F 518 671-6036
 Hudson *(G-6614)*
Heat-Timer Corporation .... E 212 481-2020
 Bronx *(G-1354)*
Medi-Ray Inc .... D 877 898-3003
 Tuckahoe *(G-16271)*

REFRIGERATORS & FREEZERS WHOLESALERS

Acme Kitchenettes Corp .... E 518 828-4191
 Hudson *(G-6604)*

REFUSE SYSTEMS

APC Paper Company Inc .... D 315 384-4225
 Norfolk *(G-12897)*

REGULATORS: Generator Voltage

Marvel Equipment Corp Inc .... G 718 383-6597
 Brooklyn *(G-2278)*

REGULATORS: Power

Emerson Network Power .... F 607 724-2484
 Binghamton *(G-911)*
Trac Regulators Inc .... E 914 699-9352
 Mount Vernon *(G-8739)*

REGULATORS: Transmission & Distribution Voltage

Telephone Sales & Service Co .... E 212 233-8505
 New York *(G-12295)*

REGULATORS: Transmission & Distribution Voltage

Precision Electronics Inc .... F 631 842-4900
 Copiague *(G-3919)*

RELAYS & SWITCHES: Indl, Electric

C D A Inc .... G 631 473-1595
 Nesconset *(G-8774)*
Select Controls Inc .... E 631 567-9010
 Bohemia *(G-1131)*

RELAYS: Electronic Usage

Dri Relays Inc .... D 631 342-1700
 Hauppauge *(G-6067)*
Hasco Componets .... E 516 328-9292
 New Hyde Park *(G-8840)*
Precision Electronics Inc .... F 631 842-4900
 Copiague *(G-3919)*

RELIGIOUS SPLYS WHOLESALERS

Cathedral Candle Co .... D 315 422-9119
 Syracuse *(G-15890)*
Leiter Sukkahs Inc .... G 718 436-0303
 Brooklyn *(G-2209)*
Malhame Publs & Importers Inc .... E 631 694-8600
 Bohemia *(G-1101)*
Rose Solomon Co .... E 718 855-1788
 Brooklyn *(G-2506)*

REMOVERS & CLEANERS

G & M Dege Inc .... F 631 475-1450
 East Patchogue *(G-4447)*
Rapid Removal LLC .... F 716 665-4663
 Falconer *(G-4909)*

REMOVERS: Paint

Nochem Paint Stripping Inc .... G 631 563-2750
 Blue Point *(G-999)*

RENTAL CENTERS: General

Grayhawk Leasing LLC .... G 914 767-6000
 Somers *(G-15510)*

RENTAL SVCS: Business Machine & Electronic Eqpt

Neopost USA Inc .... E 631 435-9100
 Hauppauge *(G-6146)*
Pitney Bowes Inc .... E 212 564-7548
 New York *(G-11667)*
Pitney Bowes Inc .... E 203 356-5000
 New York *(G-11668)*
Pitney Bowes Inc .... E 516 822-0900
 Hicksville *(G-6389)*

RENTAL SVCS: Costume

Rubies Costume Company Inc .... B 718 846-1008
 Richmond Hill *(G-14081)*
Rubies Costume Company Inc .... D 631 777-3300
 Bay Shore *(G-741)*
Rubies Costume Company Inc .... A 631 951-3688
 Bay Shore *(G-742)*
Rubies Costume Company Inc .... C 718 846-1008
 Richmond Hill *(G-14083)*
Rubies Costume Company Inc .... E 516 326-1500
 Melville *(G-8354)*

RENTAL SVCS: Electronic Eqpt, Exc Computers

Sentry Technology Corporation .... E 631 739-2000
 Ronkonkoma *(G-14982)*

RENTAL SVCS: Eqpt, Theatrical

Martin Chafkin .... G 718 383-1155
 Brooklyn *(G-2276)*
Mutual Sales Corp .... E 718 361-8373
 Long Island City *(G-7817)*

Production Resource Group LLC

Production Resource Group LLC .... D 212 589-5400
 Armonk *(G-419)*
Production Resource Group LLC .... E 845 567-5700
 New Windsor *(G-8948)*

RENTAL SVCS: Invalid Splys

Konrad Prosthetics & Orthotics .... G 516 485-9164
 West Hempstead *(G-16858)*

RENTAL SVCS: Live Plant

Plant-Tech2o Inc .... G 516 483-7845
 Hempstead *(G-6285)*

RENTAL SVCS: Pallet

Peco Pallet Inc .... E 914 376-5444
 Irvington *(G-6776)*

RENTAL SVCS: Tent & Tarpaulin

Ace Canvas & Tent Corp .... F 631 648-0614
 Ronkonkoma *(G-14848)*
Classic Awnings Inc .... F 716 649-0390
 Hamburg *(G-5920)*

RENTAL: Video Tape & Disc

Simulaids Inc .... D 845 679-2475
 Saugerties *(G-15194)*

REPEATERS: Passive

Innovative Power Products Inc .... E 631 563-0088
 Holbrook *(G-6452)*

REPRODUCTION SVCS: Video Tape Or Disk

Bertelsmann Inc .... E 212 782-1000
 New York *(G-9370)*
Play-It Productions Inc .... F 212 695-6530
 Port Washington *(G-13856)*
Professional Tape Corporation .... G 516 656-5519
 Glen Cove *(G-5625)*

RESEARCH, DEV & TESTING SVCS, COMM: Chem Lab, Exc Testing

Advanced Polymer Solutions LLC .... G 516 621-5800
 Port Washington *(G-13796)*

RESEARCH, DEVELOPMENT & TEST SVCS, COMM: Business Analysis

Economist Intelligence Unit NA .... D 212 554-0600
 New York *(G-9978)*

RESEARCH, DEVELOPMENT & TEST SVCS, COMM: Cmptr Hardware Dev

Argon Corp .... F 516 487-5314
 Great Neck *(G-5792)*
Digitronik Dev Labs Inc .... G 585 360-0043
 Rochester *(G-14308)*
Mitsui Chemicals America Inc .... E 914 253-0777
 Rye Brook *(G-15072)*

RESEARCH, DEVELOPMENT & TEST SVCS, COMM: Research, Exc Lab

Dowa International Corp .... F 212 697-3217
 New York *(G-9917)*
Intra-Cellular Therapies Inc .... E 212 923-3344
 New York *(G-10645)*

RESEARCH, DEVELOPMENT & TESTING SVCS, COMM: Research Lab

MTI Instruments Inc .... F 518 218-2550
 Albany *(G-104)*

RESEARCH, DEVELOPMENT & TESTING SVCS, COMMERCIAL: Medical

Health Care Originals Inc .... G 585 967-1398
 West Henrietta *(G-16882)*
Rohto USA Inc .... G 716 677-2500
 Orchard Park *(G-13295)*

PRODUCT SECTION

RETAIL STORES: Awnings

RESEARCH, DEVELOPMENT & TESTING SVCS, COMMERCIAL: Opinion
SOS International LLC ....E...... 212 742-2410
  New York *(G-12140)*

RESEARCH, DVLPMT & TESTING SVCS, COMM: Merger, Acq & Reorg
Toppan Vite (new York) Inc ....D...... 212 596-7747
  New York *(G-12371)*

RESEARCH, DVLPT & TEST SVCS, COMM: Mkt Analysis or Research
International Data Group Inc ....E...... 212 331-7883
  New York *(G-10632)*

RESIDENTIAL REMODELERS
Andike Millwork Inc ....G...... 718 894-1796
  Maspeth *(G-8118)*
Di Fiore and Sons Custom Wdwkg ....G...... 718 278-1663
  Long Island City *(G-7715)*
Majestic Home Imprvs Distr ....G...... 718 853-5079
  Brooklyn *(G-2253)*

RESINS: Custom Compound Purchased
Advance Chemicals Usa Inc ....G...... 718 633-1030
  Brooklyn *(G-1565)*
Ampacet Corporation ....A...... 914 631-6600
  Tarrytown *(G-16086)*
Atc Plastics LLC ....E...... 212 375-2515
  New York *(G-9245)*
Lahr Recycling & Resins Inc ....F...... 585 425-8608
  Fairport *(G-4860)*
Marval Industries Inc ....D...... 914 381-2400
  Mamaroneck *(G-8038)*
Polyset Company Inc ....E...... 518 664-6000
  Mechanicville *(G-8229)*
Si Group Inc ....C...... 518 347-4200
  Schenectady *(G-15296)*
Solepoxy Inc ....D...... 716 372-6300
  Olean *(G-13153)*

RESISTORS
Dahua Electronics Corporation ....E...... 718 886-2188
  Flushing *(G-5236)*
Hvr Advnced Pwr Components Inc ....F...... 716 693-4700
  Cheektowaga *(G-3576)*
Kionix Inc ....C...... 607 257-1080
  Ithaca *(G-6856)*
Microgen Systems Inc ....G...... 585 214-2426
  West Henrietta *(G-16884)*
Micropen Technologies Corp ....D...... 585 624-2610
  Honeoye Falls *(G-6535)*
Passive-Plus Inc ....F...... 631 425-0938
  Huntington *(G-6673)*
Stetron International Inc ....F...... 716 854-3443
  Buffalo *(G-3197)*
Virtue Paintball LLC ....G...... 631 617-5560
  Hauppauge *(G-6226)*
Vishay Americas Inc ....C...... 315 938-7575
  Henderson *(G-6290)*
Vishay Thin Film LLC ....C...... 716 283-4025
  Niagara Falls *(G-12889)*

RESISTORS & RESISTOR UNITS
Micropen Technologies Corp ....D...... 585 624-2610
  Honeoye Falls *(G-6535)*

RESORT HOTELS
Quinn and Co of NY Ltd ....E...... 212 868-1900
  New York *(G-11774)*

RESPIRATORS
Medical Acoustics LLC ....F...... 716 218-7353
  Buffalo *(G-3061)*

RESTAURANT EQPT REPAIR SVCS
Applince Installation Svc Corp ....E...... 716 884-7425
  Buffalo *(G-2818)*
Hobart Corporation ....E...... 631 864-3440
  Commack *(G-3835)*
Ronbar Laboratories Inc ....F...... 718 937-6755
  Long Island City *(G-7864)*

RESTAURANT EQPT: Carts
A-Plus Restaurant Equipment ....F...... 718 522-2656
  Brooklyn *(G-1542)*
All Star Carts & Vehicles Inc ....D...... 631 666-5581
  Bay Shore *(G-668)*

RESTAURANT EQPT: Food Wagons
Carts Mobile Food Eqp Corp ....E...... 718 788-5540
  Brooklyn *(G-1761)*
Kinplex Corp ....E...... 631 242-4800
  Edgewood *(G-4604)*
Restaurant 570 8th Avenue LLC ....F...... 646 722-8191
  New York *(G-11844)*

RESTAURANT EQPT: Sheet Metal
E G M Restaurant Equipment Mfg ....G...... 718 782-9800
  Brooklyn *(G-1891)*
Shanghai Stove Inc ....F...... 718 599-4583
  Brooklyn *(G-2550)*

RESTAURANTS: Full Svc, American
Empire Brewing Company Inc ....D...... 315 925-8308
  Syracuse *(G-15935)*

RESTAURANTS: Full Svc, Seafood
Fire Island Sea Clam Co Inc ....G...... 631 589-2199
  West Sayville *(G-16935)*

RESTAURANTS: Limited Svc, Coffee Shop
Aphrodites ....G...... 718 224-1774
  Whitestone *(G-17200)*

RESTAURANTS: Limited Svc, Ice Cream Stands Or Dairy Bars
Blue Pig Ice Cream Factory ....G...... 914 271-3850
  Croton On Hudson *(G-4062)*
Purity Ice Cream Co Inc ....F...... 607 272-1545
  Ithaca *(G-6872)*

RESTAURANTS: Limited Svc, Lunch Counter
Roslyn Bread Company Inc ....E...... 516 625-1470
  Roslyn Heights *(G-15031)*

RESUME WRITING SVCS
Graphic Dimensions Press Inc ....F...... 718 252-4003
  Brooklyn *(G-2049)*
Key Computer Svcs of Chelsea ....D...... 212 206-8060
  New York *(G-10840)*

RETAIL BAKERY: Bagels
999 Bagels Inc ....G...... 718 915-0742
  Brooklyn *(G-1524)*
A T A Bagel Shoppe Inc ....G...... 718 352-4948
  Bayside *(G-764)*
Bagel Grove Inc ....E...... 315 724-8015
  Utica *(G-16309)*
Bagel Lites LLC ....G...... 855 813-7888
  Long Island City *(G-7680)*
M & M Bagel Corp ....F...... 516 295-1222
  Cedarhurst *(G-3459)*
Mds Hot Bagels Deli Inc ....G...... 718 438-5650
  Brooklyn *(G-2289)*

RETAIL BAKERY: Bread
Addeo Bakers Inc ....F...... 718 367-8316
  Bronx *(G-1263)*
Giovanni Bakery Corp ....F...... 212 695-4296
  New York *(G-10300)*
Harrison Bakery West ....E...... 315 422-1468
  Syracuse *(G-15957)*
Rock Hill Bakehouse Ltd ....E...... 518 743-1627
  Gansevoort *(G-5489)*
Roslyn Bread Company Inc ....E...... 516 625-1470
  Roslyn Heights *(G-15031)*
Tosca Brick Oven Pizza Real ....G...... 718 430-0026
  Bronx *(G-1473)*

RETAIL LUMBER YARDS
Axtell Bradtke Lumber Co ....G...... 607 265-3850
  Masonville *(G-8107)*
Deer Pk Stair Bldg Mllwk Inc ....E...... 631 363-5000
  Blue Point *(G-998)*
Guldenschuh Logging & Lbr LLC ....G...... 585 538-4750
  Caledonia *(G-3280)*
Lowville Farmers Coop Inc ....E...... 315 376-6587
  Lowville *(G-7939)*

RETAIL STORES, NEC
Exhibits & More ....G...... 585 924-4040
  Victor *(G-16476)*
Mark F Rosenhaft N A O ....G...... 516 374-1010
  Cedarhurst *(G-3460)*

RETAIL STORES: Alarm Signal Systems
Lifewatch Inc ....F...... 800 716-1433
  Hewlett *(G-6310)*
Personal Alarm SEC Systems ....F...... 212 448-1944
  New York *(G-11627)*
Table Tops Paper Corp ....F...... 718 598-7832
  Brooklyn *(G-2642)*

RETAIL STORES: Alcoholic Beverage Making Eqpt & Splys
Dutch Spirits LLC ....F...... 518 398-1022
  Pine Plains *(G-13555)*

RETAIL STORES: Aquarium Splys
C B Management Services Inc ....F...... 845 735-2300
  Pearl River *(G-13455)*

RETAIL STORES: Artificial Limbs
Creative Orthotics Prosthetics ....F...... 607 734-7215
  Elmira *(G-4678)*
Goldberg Prosthetic & Orthotic ....F...... 631 689-6606
  East Setauket *(G-4484)*
Green Prosthetics & Orthotics ....G...... 716 484-1088
  Jamestown *(G-6996)*
Hanger Inc ....G...... 718 575-5504
  Forest Hills *(G-5323)*
Konrad Prosthetics & Orthotics ....F...... 516 485-9164
  West Hempstead *(G-16858)*
Lehneis Orthotics Prosthetic ....F...... 631 360-3859
  Hauppauge *(G-6112)*
Lehneis Orthotics Prosthetic ....G...... 631 369-3115
  Riverhead *(G-14146)*
M H Mandelbaum Orthotic ....F...... 631 473-8668
  Port Jefferson *(G-13777)*
North Shore Orthtics Prsthtics ....G...... 631 928-3040
  Port Jeff STA *(G-13768)*
Orthotic & Prosthetic Images ....F...... 516 292-8726
  Hempstead *(G-6284)*
Prosthetic Rehabilitation Ctr ....G...... 845 565-8255
  Newburgh *(G-12777)*
Ultrapedics Ltd ....G...... 718 748-4806
  Brooklyn *(G-2696)*

RETAIL STORES: Audio-Visual Eqpt & Splys
Audio Video Invasion Inc ....F...... 516 345-2636
  Plainview *(G-13583)*
Tony Baird Electronics Inc ....G...... 315 422-4430
  Syracuse *(G-16060)*

RETAIL STORES: Awnings
Acme Awning Co Inc ....F...... 718 409-1881
  Bronx *(G-1262)*
Alley Cat Signs Inc ....F...... 631 924-7446
  Middle Island *(G-8406)*
Atlantic Steinway Awng II LLC ....G...... 718 729-2965
  Long Island City *(G-7677)*
Awning Mart Inc ....G...... 315 699-5928
  Cicero *(G-3642)*
City Signs Inc ....G...... 718 375-5933
  Brooklyn *(G-1784)*
Dart Awning Inc ....F...... 718 945-4224
  Freeport *(G-5393)*
Di Sanos Creative Canvas Inc ....G...... 315 894-3137
  Frankfort *(G-5351)*
Graphic Signs & Awnings Ltd ....G...... 718 227-6000
  Staten Island *(G-15681)*
Kenan International Trading ....G...... 718 672-4922
  Corona *(G-4000)*
Lanza Corp ....G...... 914 937-6360
  Port Chester *(G-13751)*
Lotus Awnings Enterprises Inc ....G...... 718 965-4824
  Brooklyn *(G-2237)*
Mauceri Sign Inc ....F...... 718 656-7700
  Jamaica *(G-6929)*

RETAIL STORES: Awnings

Proof Industries Inc .... G 631 694-7663
  Farmingdale *(G-5090)*
Rgm Signs Inc .... G 718 442-0598
  Staten Island *(G-15732)*
Space Sign .... F 718 961-1112
  College Point *(G-3808)*
Steinway Awning II LLC .... F 718 729-2965
  Astoria *(G-459)*

RETAIL STORES: Cake Decorating Splys

Pfeil & Holing Inc .... D 718 545-4600
  Woodside *(G-17346)*

RETAIL STORES: Canvas Prdts

Brock Awnings Ltd .... F 631 765-5200
  Hampton Bays *(G-5960)*
Geordie Magee Uphl & Canvas .... G 315 676-7679
  Brewerton *(G-1203)*

RETAIL STORES: Cleaning Eqpt & Splys

Collinite Corporation .... G 315 732-2282
  Utica *(G-16313)*
Empire Division Inc .... D 315 476-6273
  Syracuse *(G-15936)*

RETAIL STORES: Concrete Prdts, Precast

Riefler Concrete Products LLC .... C 716 649-3260
  Hamburg *(G-5940)*

RETAIL STORES: Cosmetics

Borghese Inc .... E 212 659-5318
  New York *(G-9441)*
Exquis LLC .... F 845 537-5380
  Harriman *(G-5971)*
Malin + Goetz Inc .... F 212 244-7771
  New York *(G-11121)*
New Avon LLC .... A 212 282-8500
  New York *(G-11380)*
Temptu Inc .... G 212 675-4000
  New York *(G-12299)*

RETAIL STORES: Electronic Parts & Eqpt

G B International Trdg Co Ltd .... C 607 785-0938
  Endicott *(G-4809)*
I Trade Technology Ltd .... G 615 348-7233
  Suffern *(G-15792)*
Industrial Support Inc .... D 716 662-2954
  Buffalo *(G-3006)*
Ross Electronics Ltd .... E 718 569-6643
  Haverstraw *(G-6240)*

RETAIL STORES: Engine & Motor Eqpt & Splys

Electric Motors and Pumps Inc .... G 718 935-9118
  Brooklyn *(G-1910)*

RETAIL STORES: Farm Eqpt & Splys

Birkett Mills .... G 315 536-3311
  Penn Yan *(G-13506)*

RETAIL STORES: Fiberglass Materials, Exc Insulation

Architectural Fiberglass Corp .... E 631 842-4772
  Copiague *(G-3892)*

RETAIL STORES: Fire Extinguishers

C E King & Sons Inc .... G 631 324-4944
  East Hampton *(G-4406)*
Sausbiers Awning Shop Inc .... G 518 828-3748
  Hudson *(G-6633)*

RETAIL STORES: Gravestones, Finished

Woodside Granite Industries .... G 585 589-6500
  Albion *(G-171)*

RETAIL STORES: Hearing Aids

Benway-Haworth-Lwlr-Iacosta He .... F 518 432-4070
  Albany *(G-54)*

RETAIL STORES: Ice

Henry Newman LLC .... F 607 273-8512
  Ithaca *(G-6847)*

South Shore Ice Co Inc .... F 516 379-2056
  Roosevelt *(G-15009)*

RETAIL STORES: Infant Furnishings & Eqpt

Mam USA Corporation .... F 914 269-2500
  Purchase *(G-13961)*

RETAIL STORES: Medical Apparatus & Splys

Medical Action Industries Inc .... C 631 231-4600
  Hauppauge *(G-6129)*
NY Orthopedic Usa Inc .... D 718 852-5330
  Brooklyn *(G-2382)*
Sundance Enterprises Inc .... G 914 946-2942
  White Plains *(G-17173)*

RETAIL STORES: Mobile Telephones & Eqpt

2p Agency Usa Inc .... G 212 203-5586
  Brooklyn *(G-1513)*
Sima Technologies LLC 412 828-9130
  Hauppauge *(G-6191)*

RETAIL STORES: Monuments, Finished To Custom Order

Presbrey-Leland Inc .... G 914 949-2264
  Valhalla *(G-16371)*
St Raymond Monument Co .... G 718 824-3600
  Bronx *(G-1462)*

RETAIL STORES: Motors, Electric

A & C/Furia Electric Motors .... F 914 949-0585
  White Plains *(G-17072)*
Economy Pump & Motor Repair .... G 718 433-2600
  Astoria *(G-438)*
Emes Motor Inc .... G 718 387-2445
  Brooklyn *(G-1919)*

RETAIL STORES: Orthopedic & Prosthesis Applications

Arimed Orthotics Prosthetics P .... F 718 875-8754
  Brooklyn *(G-1626)*
Creative Orthotics Prosthetics .... G 607 771-4672
  Binghamton *(G-903)*
Klemmt Orthotics & Prosthetics .... G 607 770-4400
  Johnson City *(G-7097)*
Ortho Medical Products .... G 212 879-3700
  New York *(G-11528)*
Orthocraft Inc .... G 718 692-0113
  Brooklyn *(G-2396)*
Progressive Orthotics Ltd .... F 631 447-3860
  East Patchogue *(G-4449)*
Progressive Orthotics Ltd .... G 631 732-5556
  Selden *(G-15353)*
Prosthetics By Nelson Inc .... F 716 894-6666
  Cheektowaga *(G-3587)*
Sampsons Prsthtic Orthotic Lab .... E 518 374-6011
  Schenectady *(G-15291)*

RETAIL STORES: Pet Food

J & M Feed Corporation .... G 631 281-2152
  Shirley *(G-15421)*

RETAIL STORES: Photocopy Machines

Printer Components Inc .... G 585 924-5190
  Fairport *(G-4871)*
Recharge Net Inc .... G 585 546-1060
  Rochester *(G-14621)*

RETAIL STORES: Religious Goods

A-1 Skull Cap Corp .... E 718 633-9333
  Brooklyn *(G-1539)*
J Lowy Co .... G 718 338-7324
  Brooklyn *(G-2124)*
Moznaim Publishing Co Inc .... G 718 853-0525
  Brooklyn *(G-2337)*
Y & A Trading Inc .... F 718 436-6333
  Brooklyn *(G-2772)*

RETAIL STORES: Stones, Crystalline, Rough

Amendola MBL & Stone Ctr Inc .... D 914 997-7968
  White Plains *(G-17076)*
Hanson Aggregates PA LLC .... E 585 624-1220
  Honeoye Falls *(G-6530)*

RETAIL STORES: Telephone Eqpt & Systems

ABS Talkx Inc .... G 631 254-9100
  Bay Shore *(G-664)*

RETAIL STORES: Tents

Leiter Sukkahs Inc .... G 718 436-0303
  Brooklyn *(G-2209)*

RETAIL STORES: Water Purification Eqpt

Neptune Soft Water Inc .... F 315 446-5151
  Syracuse *(G-15997)*

RETAIL STORES: Welding Splys

Haun Welding Supply Inc .... F 607 846-2289
  Elmira *(G-4689)*

REUPHOLSTERY & FURNITURE REPAIR

Furniture Doctor Inc .... G 585 657-6941
  Bloomfield *(G-988)*
Henry B Urban Inc .... E 212 489-3308
  New York *(G-10457)*
KPP Ltd .... G 516 338-5201
  Westbury *(G-17004)*
White Plains Drapery Uphl Inc .... E 914 381-0908
  Mamaroneck *(G-8050)*

REUPHOLSTERY SVCS

Anthony Lawrence of New York .... E 212 206-8820
  Long Island City *(G-7661)*

RIBBONS & BOWS

Artistic Ribbon Novelty Co Inc .... E 212 255-4224
  New York *(G-9220)*
Phoenix Ribbon Co Inc .... G 212 239-0155
  New York *(G-11651)*

RIBBONS, NEC

Essential Ribbons Inc .... G 212 967-4173
  New York *(G-10065)*
Fashion Ribbon Co Inc .... E 718 482-0100
  Long Island City *(G-7738)*

RIBBONS: Machine, Inked Or Carbon

International Imaging Mtls Inc .... B 716 691-6333
  Amherst *(G-246)*

RIDING APPAREL STORES

Robert Viggiani .... G 914 423-4046
  Yonkers *(G-17481)*

RIVETS: Metal

John Hassall LLC .... D 516 334-6200
  Westbury *(G-16998)*

ROAD MATERIALS: Bituminous, Not From Refineries

Alliance Paving Materials Inc .... G 315 337-0795
  Rome *(G-14803)*
R Schleider Contracting Corp .... G 631 269-4249
  Kings Park *(G-7174)*
Rochester Asphalt Materials .... G 585 381-7010
  Rochester *(G-14634)*

ROBOTS: Assembly Line

Automated Cells & Eqp Inc .... E 607 936-1341
  Painted Post *(G-13389)*
Honeybee Robotics Ltd .... E 212 966-0661
  Brooklyn *(G-2087)*
J H Robotics Inc .... E 607 729-3758
  Johnson City *(G-7096)*
McHone Industries Inc .... D 716 945-3380
  Salamanca *(G-15101)*

ROCK SALT MINING

American Rock Salt Company LLC .... E 585 991-6878
  Retsof *(G-14054)*

ROCKET LAUNCHERS

CIC International Ltd .... D 212 213-0089
  Brooklyn *(G-1779)*

PRODUCT SECTION — SALT

ROCKETS: Space & Military
Lockheed Martin Corporation ....A 315 456-0123
  Liverpool (G-7531)
Lws Precision Deburring Inc ....F 631 580-0472
  Ronkonkoma (G-14935)

RODS: Extruded, Aluminum
Jem Threading Specialties Inc ....G 718 665-3341
  Bronx (G-1365)

RODS: Plastic
Comco Plastics Inc ....E 718 849-9000
  Woodhaven (G-17305)
Great Lakes Plastics Co Inc ....E 716 896-3100
  Buffalo (G-2981)

RODS: Steel & Iron, Made In Steel Mills
Hitachi Metals America Ltd ....E 914 694-9200
  Purchase (G-13958)
Mardek LLC ....G 585 735-9333
  Pittsford (G-13569)

RODS: Welding
Aufhauser Corporation ....F 516 694-8696
  Plainview (G-13584)
Aufhauser Manufacturing Corp ....E 516 694-8696
  Plainview (G-13585)

ROLL COVERINGS: Rubber
Finzer Holding LLC ....E 315 597-1147
  Palmyra (G-13406)

ROLL FORMED SHAPES: Custom
Inscape (new York) Inc ....D 716 665-6210
  Falconer (G-4902)
Lakeside Capital Corporation ....E 716 664-2555
  Jamestown (G-7015)
Rolite Mfg Inc ....E 716 683-0259
  Lancaster (G-7340)

ROLLED OR DRAWN SHAPES, NEC: Copper & Copper Alloy
Sherburne Metal Sales Inc ....F 607 674-4441
  Sherburne (G-15395)

ROLLERS & FITTINGS: Window Shade
Geigtech East Bay LLC ....F 844 543-4437
  New York (G-10264)
Windowtex Inc ....G 877 294-3580
  Garden City Park (G-5545)

ROLLING MILL EQPT: Galvanizing Lines
Eaton Electric Holdings LLC ....C 607 756-2821
  Cortland (G-4025)

ROLLING MILL MACHINERY
Anthony Manufacturing Inc ....G 631 957-9424
  Lindenhurst (G-7454)
Ivy Classic Industries Inc ....E 914 632-8200
  New Rochelle (G-8913)
Johnston Dandy Company ....G 315 455-5773
  Syracuse (G-15969)
Mannesmann Corporation ....D 212 258-4000
  New York (G-11136)
Polymag Tek Inc ....F 585 235-8390
  Rochester (G-14587)

ROLLS & BLANKETS, PRINTERS': Rubber Or Rubberized Fabric
Enbi Indiana Inc ....E 585 647-1527
  Rochester (G-14349)
Package Print Technologies ....F 716 871-9905
  Buffalo (G-3110)

ROLLS: Rubber, Solid Or Covered
Idg LLC ....E 315 797-1000
  Utica (G-16341)
Rotation Dynamics Corporation ....E 585 352-9023
  Spencerport (G-15573)

ROOFING MATERIALS: Asphalt
Johns Manville Corporation ....E 518 565-3000
  Plattsburgh (G-13673)
Marathon Roofing Products Inc ....F 716 685-3340
  Orchard Park (G-13282)

ROOFING MATERIALS: Sheet Metal
Brothers Roofing Supplies Co ....E 718 779-0280
  East Elmhurst (G-4389)
Pal Aluminum Inc ....G 516 937-1990
  Hicksville (G-6383)
Pal Aluminum Inc ....E 718 262-0091
  Jamaica (G-6937)

ROOFING MEMBRANE: Rubber
Millhouse 1889 LLC ....G 631 259-4777
  Northport (G-13017)

ROPE
Gladding Braided Products LLC ....E 315 653-7211
  South Otselic (G-15531)

ROTORS: Motor
Taro Manufacturing Company Inc ....F 315 252-9430
  Auburn (G-523)

RUBBER
David Fehlman ....G 315 455-8888
  Syracuse (G-15922)
Integrated Liner Tech Inc ....E 518 621-7422
  Rensselaer (G-14048)
Liberty Tire Recycling LLC ....E 716 433-7370
  Lockport (G-7597)
Release Coatings New York Inc ....G 585 593-2335
  Wellsville (G-16756)

RUBBER PRDTS: Automotive, Mechanical
Bridgestone APM Company ....D 419 423-9552
  Sanborn (G-15114)

RUBBER PRDTS: Mechanical
Apple Rubber Products Inc ....C 716 684-7649
  Lancaster (G-7304)
Delford Industries Inc ....D 845 342-3901
  Middletown (G-8436)
Finzer Holding LLC ....E 315 597-1147
  Palmyra (G-13406)
Mechanical Rubber Pdts Co Inc ....F 845 986-2271
  Warwick (G-16594)
Moldtech Inc ....E 716 685-3344
  Lancaster (G-7327)
Ms Spares LLC ....G 607 223-3024
  Clay (G-3683)
Pawling Corporation ....C 845 855-1000
  Pawling (G-13451)
Pawling Corporation ....D 845 373-9300
  Wassaic (G-16600)
Pawling Engineered Pdts Inc ....C 845 855-1000
  Pawling (G-13452)
Pilot Products Inc ....F 718 728-2141
  Long Island City (G-7843)
R & A Industrial Products ....G 716 823-4300
  Buffalo (G-3150)
The Centro Company Inc ....G 914 533-2200
  South Salem (G-15537)
Triangle Rubber Co Inc ....E 631 589-9400
  Bohemia (G-1147)

RUBBER PRDTS: Medical & Surgical Tubing, Extrudd & Lathe-Cut
Pexco LLC ....E 518 792-1199
  Glens Falls (G-5696)

RUBBER PRDTS: Oil & Gas Field Machinery, Mechanical
Camso Manufacturing Usa Ltd ....D 518 561-7528
  Plattsburgh (G-13657)

RUBBER PRDTS: Reclaimed
Cementex Latex Corp ....F 212 741-1770
  New York (G-9558)
Zylon Corporation ....F 845 425-9469
  Monsey (G-8587)

RUBBER PRDTS: Silicone
Canton Bio-Medical Inc ....E 518 283-5963
  Poestenkill (G-13722)
Depco Inc ....F 631 582-1995
  Hauppauge (G-6061)
Silicone Products & Technology ....C 716 684-1155
  Lancaster (G-7343)
Specialty Silicone Pdts Inc ....E 518 885-8826
  Ballston Spa (G-609)
Vasquez Tito ....F 212 944-0441
  New York (G-12510)

RUBBER PRDTS: Sponge
Tmp Technologies Inc ....D 716 895-6100
  Buffalo (G-3220)

RUBBER PRDTS: Wet Suits
Great American Industries Inc ....G 607 729-9331
  Vestal (G-16449)

RUBBER STRUCTURES: Air-Supported
Continental Latex Corp ....F 718 783-7883
  Brooklyn (G-1799)

RUGS: Hand & Machine Made
Mark Nelson Designs LLC ....F 646 422-7020
  New York (G-11156)
Mgk Group Inc ....E 212 989-2732
  New York (G-11246)
Renaissnce Crpt Tapestries Inc ....F 212 696-0080
  New York (G-11831)
Safavieh Inc ....B 516 945-1900
  Port Washington (G-13860)

RULERS: Metal
Gei International Inc ....E 315 463-9261
  East Syracuse (G-4533)

SAFES & VAULTS: Metal
Gardall Safe Corporation ....E 315 432-9115
  Syracuse (G-15947)
Schwab Corp ....E 585 381-4900
  Rochester (G-14675)
Schwab Corp ....C 812 547-2956
  Rochester (G-14676)

SAFETY EQPT & SPLYS WHOLESALERS
Valeo ....G 800 634-2704
  Yonkers (G-17495)

SAILBOAT BUILDING & REPAIR
Allen Boat Co Inc ....G 716 842-0800
  Buffalo (G-2802)
Cellboat Development Corp ....G 800 973-4659
  Melville (G-8301)

SAILS
Allen Boat Co Inc ....G 716 842-0800
  Buffalo (G-2802)
Doyle-Hild Sailmakers ....G 718 885-2255
  Bronx (G-1317)
Haarstick Sailmakers Inc ....F 585 342-5200
  Rochester (G-14418)
Melbourne C Fisher Yacht Sails ....G 631 673-5055
  Huntington Station (G-6716)
Ulmer Sales LLC ....F 718 885-1700
  Bronx (G-1484)

SALES PROMOTION SVCS
Platinum Sales Promotion Inc ....G 718 361-0200
  Long Island City (G-7844)

SALT
Cargill Incorporated ....D 607 535-6300
  Watkins Glen (G-16694)
Real Co Inc ....G 347 433-8549
  Valley Cottage (G-16386)
Roto Salt Company Inc ....E 315 536-3742
  Penn Yan (G-13519)
Topaz Industries Inc ....F 631 207-0700
  Holtsville (G-6513)
US Salt LLC ....D 607 535-2721
  Watkins Glen (G-16698)

Employee Codes: A=Over 500 employees, B=251-500
C=101-250, D=51-100, E=20-50, F=10-19, G=5-9

SALT & SULFUR MINING

Morton Salt Inc F 585 493-2511
Silver Springs *(G-15451)*

SAMPLE BOOKS

Dickard Widder Industries Inc C 718 326-3700
Maspeth *(G-8131)*
Federal Sample Card Corp D 718 458-1344
Elmhurst *(G-4660)*
New York Sample Card Co Inc E 212 242-1242
New York *(G-11407)*
Niagara Sample Book Co Inc F 716 284-6151
Niagara Falls *(G-12850)*

SAND & GRAVEL

110 Sand Company E 631 694-2822
Melville *(G-8286)*
110 Sand Company F 631 694-2822
West Babylon *(G-16761)*
A Colarusso and Son Inc E 518 828-3218
Hudson *(G-6603)*
Barrett Paving Materials Inc G 607 723-5367
Binghamton *(G-890)*
Belangers Gravel & Stone Inc G 585 728-3906
Wayland *(G-16709)*
Bonsal American Inc E 631 208-8073
Calverton *(G-3286)*
Callanan Industries Inc E 845 331-6868
Kingston *(G-7182)*
Chenango Asphalt Products F 607 334-3117
Norwich *(G-13021)*
Dalrymple Grav & Contg Co Inc F 607 739-0391
Pine City *(G-13550)*
Dalrymple Holding Corp E 607 737-6200
Pine City *(G-13551)*
E Tetz & Sons Inc D 845 692-4486
Middletown *(G-8437)*
East Coast Mines Ltd E 631 653-5445
East Quogue *(G-4450)*
Frew Run Gravel Products Inc G 716 569-4712
Frewsburg *(G-5450)*
Genoa Sand & Gravel Lnsg G 607 533-4551
Freeville *(G-5436)*
Greenebuild LLC F 917 562-0556
Brooklyn *(G-2053)*
Hanson Aggregates East LLC E 315 548-2911
Phelps *(G-13533)*
Johnson S Sand Gravel Inc G 315 771-1450
La Fargeville *(G-7237)*
Lafarge North America Inc E 716 651-9235
Lancaster *(G-7322)*
Lafarge North America Inc E 518 756-5000
Ravena *(G-14023)*
McEwan Trucking & Grav Produc G 716 609-1828
East Concord *(G-4385)*
Milestone Construction Corp G 718 459-8500
Rego Park *(G-14037)*
New York Sand & Stone LLC G 718 596-2897
Maspeth *(G-8157)*
Northeast Solite Corporation E 845 246-2177
Mount Marion *(G-8652)*
R G King General Construction G 315 583-3560
Adams Center *(G-4)*
R J Valente Gravel Inc E 518 279-1001
Cropseyville *(G-4060)*
Rd2 Construction & Dem LLC F 718 980-1650
Staten Island *(G-15728)*
Republic Construction Co Inc G 914 235-3654
New Rochelle *(G-8924)*
Robinson Concrete Inc E 315 253-6666
Auburn *(G-516)*
Seneca Stone Corporation G 607 737-6200
Pine City *(G-13552)*
Smith Sand & Gravel Inc G 315 673-4124
Marcellus *(G-8089)*
Speyside Holdings LLC E 845 928-2221
Highland Mills *(G-6414)*
Syracuse Sand & Gravel LLC G 315 548-8207
Fulton *(G-5475)*
Tilcon New York Inc D 845 358-3100
West Nyack *(G-16929)*
Titus Mountain Sand & Grav LLC G 518 483-3740
Malone *(G-8018)*
Tri City Highway Products Inc E 607 722-2967
Binghamton *(G-957)*
Tri-City Highway Products Inc E 518 294-9964
Richmondville *(G-14090)*
Troy Sand & Gravel Co Inc F 518 674-2854
West Sand Lake *(G-16932)*

United Materials LLC G 716 662-0564
Orchard Park *(G-13301)*
US Allegro Inc E 347 408-6601
Maspeth *(G-8174)*

SAND MINING

110 Sand Company G 631 694-2822
West Babylon *(G-16760)*
Country Side Sand & Gravel G 716 988-3271
Collins *(G-3815)*
Dicks Concrete Co Inc E 845 374-5966
New Hampton *(G-8799)*
H L Robinson Sand & Gravel F 607 659-5153
Candor *(G-3377)*
Hampton Sand Corp G 631 325-5533
Westhampton *(G-17057)*
Rush Gravel Corp G 585 533-1740
Honeoye Falls *(G-6536)*
Sparrow Mining Co G 718 519-6600
Bronx *(G-1460)*
Tilcon New York Inc E 845 942-0602
Tomkins Cove *(G-16131)*

SAND: Hygrade

New Jersey Pulverizing Co Inc G 516 921-9595
Syosset *(G-15832)*
Precision Elctro Mnrl Pmco Inc E 716 284-2484
Niagara Falls *(G-12863)*

SANDSTONE: Crushed & Broken

County Line Stone Co Inc E 716 542-5435
Akron *(G-21)*
Shelby Crushed Stone Inc F 585 798-4501
Medina *(G-8281)*

SANITARY SVCS: Waste Materials, Recycling

Crumbrubber Technology Inc F 718 468-3988
Hollis *(G-6496)*
Hampton Sand Corp G 631 325-5533
Westhampton *(G-17057)*
Ivi Services Inc D 607 729-5111
Binghamton *(G-929)*
Kore Infrastructure LLC G 646 532-9060
Glen Cove *(G-5620)*
Twin County Recycling Corp F 516 827-6900
Westbury *(G-17038)*

SANITARY WARE: Metal

Advance Tabco Inc D 631 242-8270
Edgewood *(G-4591)*
Kenbenco Inc F 845 246-3066
Saugerties *(G-15186)*
Metpar Corp D 516 333-2600
Westbury *(G-17011)*
Unico Inc F 845 562-9255
Newburgh *(G-12782)*

SANITATION CHEMICALS & CLEANING AGENTS

Aireactor Inc F 718 326-2433
Maspeth *(G-8113)*
American Wax Company Inc E 718 392-8080
Long Island City *(G-7658)*
Bennett Manufacturing Co Inc C 716 937-9161
Alden *(G-175)*
Car-Freshner Corporation D 315 788-6250
Watertown *(G-16642)*
Cleanse TEC E 718 346-9111
Brooklyn *(G-1788)*
Colgate-Palmolive Company A 212 310-2000
New York *(G-9667)*
Cpac Inc E 585 382-3223
Leicester *(G-7420)*
Crescent Marketing Inc C 716 337-0145
North Collins *(G-12927)*
Crosstex International Inc D 631 582-6777
Hauppauge *(G-6058)*
James Richard Specialty Chem G 914 478-7500
Hastings On Hudson *(G-6004)*
Micro Powders Inc E 914 332-6400
Tarrytown *(G-16097)*
Olin Chlor Alkali Logistics C 716 278-6411
Niagara Falls *(G-12857)*
P S M Group Inc E 716 532-6686
Forestville *(G-5335)*
Rochester Midland Corporation C 585 336-2200
Rochester *(G-14643)*

Safetec of America Inc D 716 895-1822
Buffalo *(G-3173)*
Synco Chemical Corporation E 631 567-5300
Bohemia *(G-1140)*
Tribology Inc E 631 345-3000
Yaphank *(G-17405)*
Us Nonwovens Corp C 631 952-0100
Brentwood *(G-1199)*

SASHES: Door Or Window, Metal

A G M Deco Inc F 718 624-6200
Brooklyn *(G-1533)*
A G M Deco Inc F 718 624-6200
Brooklyn *(G-1534)*
Hopes Windows Inc C 716 665-5124
Jamestown *(G-7000)*
Thermal Tech Doors Inc E 516 745-0100
Garden City *(G-5534)*

SATCHELS

Barclay Brown Corp F 718 376-7166
Brooklyn *(G-1668)*

SATELLITES: Communications

Geosync Microwave Inc G 631 760-5567
Hauppauge *(G-6084)*
Globecomm Systems Inc C 631 231-9800
Hauppauge *(G-6086)*
Loral Space & Commnctns Holdng E 212 697-1105
New York *(G-11032)*
Loral Space Communications Inc E 212 697-1105
New York *(G-11033)*
Loral Spacecom Corporation E 212 697-1105
New York *(G-11034)*
Orbcomm Inc G 703 433-6396
Utica *(G-16355)*
Village Video Productions Inc G 631 752-9311
West Babylon *(G-16839)*

SAW BLADES

Allway Tools Inc D 718 792-3636
Bronx *(G-1269)*
Amana Tool Corp D 631 752-1300
Farmingdale *(G-4939)*
Diamond Saw Works Inc E 716 496-7417
Chaffee *(G-3532)*
Dinosaw Inc E 518 828-9942
Hudson *(G-6612)*
Suffolk McHy & Pwr Tl Corp G 631 289-7153
Patchogue *(G-13435)*

SAWDUST & SHAVINGS

Bono Sawdust Supply Co Inc G 718 446-1374
Corona *(G-3993)*

SAWDUST, WHOLESALE

Attica Package Company Inc F 585 591-0510
Attica *(G-472)*

SAWING & PLANING MILLS

A D Bowman & Son Lumber Co E 607 692-2595
Castle Creek *(G-3417)*
Angelica Forest Products Inc G 585 466-3205
Angelica *(G-376)*
Axtell Bradtke Lumber Co G 607 265-3850
Masonville *(G-8107)*
B & J Lumber Co Inc G 518 677-3845
Cambridge *(G-3304)*
Baillie Lumber Co LP E 315 942-5284
Boonville *(G-1163)*
Bissel-Babcock Millwork Inc F 716 761-6976
Sherman *(G-15401)*
Brookside Lumber Inc F 315 497-0937
Moravia *(G-8616)*
Capital Sawmill Service G 518 479-0729
Nassau *(G-8770)*
Casters Custom Sawing F 315 387-5104
Sandy Creek *(G-15131)*
Clements Burrville Sawmill G 315 782-4549
Watertown *(G-16645)*
Cote Hardwood Products Inc F 607 898-5737
Locke *(G-7568)*
Crawford Furniture Mfg Corp C 716 483-2102
Jamestown *(G-6985)*
Donver Incorporated F 716 945-1910
Kill Buck *(G-7166)*

PRODUCT SECTION SCREW MACHINE PRDTS

Farney Lumber Corporation ....F 315 346-6013
   Lowville *(G-7936)*
Greene Lumber Co LP ....E 607 278-6101
   Davenport *(G-4080)*
Hawkeye Forest Products LP ....F 608 534-6156
   Hamburg *(G-5928)*
J & J Log & Lumber Corp ....D 845 832-6535
   Dover Plains *(G-4315)*
Jdlr Enterprises LLC ....G 315 813-2911
   Sherrill *(G-15406)*
Johnston Forest Products Inc ....G 607 363-2947
   East Branch *(G-4384)*
Lyons & Sullivan Inc ....G 518 584-1523
   Saratoga Springs *(G-15162)*
McDonough Hardwoods Ltd ....E 315 829-3449
   Vernon Center *(G-16437)*
Meltz Lumber Co of Mellenville ....E 518 672-7021
   Hudson *(G-6626)*
Mettowee Lumber & Plastics Co ....C 518 642-1100
   Granville *(G-5777)*
Owletts Saw Mills ....G 607 525-6340
   Woodhull *(G-17309)*
Pallets Inc ....E 518 747-4177
   Fort Edward *(G-5343)*
PDJ Inc ....E 315 655-8824
   Cazenovia *(G-3450)*
Piccini Industries Ltd ....E 845 365-0614
   Orangeburg *(G-13239)*
Potter Lumber Co Inc ....E 716 373-1260
   Allegany *(G-203)*
Rudy Stempel & Family Sawmill ....G 518 872-0431
   East Berne *(G-4381)*
Russell Bass ....F 607 637-5253
   Hancock *(G-5967)*
S Donadic Woodworking Inc ....D 718 361-9888
   Sunnyside *(G-15809)*
Saw Mill Pediatrics Pllc ....G 914 449-6064
   Pleasantville *(G-13720)*
Scotts Company LLC ....E 631 289-7444
   Yaphank *(G-17400)*
Simplicity Bandsaw Inc ....G 716 557-8805
   Hinsdale *(G-6424)*
Spiegel Woodworks Inc ....F 845 336-8090
   Kingston *(G-7211)*
St Lawrence Lumber Inc ....G 315 649-2990
   Three Mile Bay *(G-16123)*
Swanson Lumber ....G 716 499-1726
   Gerry *(G-5593)*
Tupper Lake Hardwoods Inc ....E 518 359-8248
   Tupper Lake *(G-16282)*
Urrey Lumber ....G 518 827-4851
   Middleburgh *(G-8419)*
Wagner Millwork Inc ....D 607 687-5362
   Owego *(G-13361)*

SAWING & PLANING MILLS: Custom

Gutchess Freedom Inc ....D 716 492-2824
   Freedom *(G-5378)*

SAWMILL MACHINES

Cannonsville Lumber Inc ....G 607 467-3380
   Deposit *(G-4276)*

SAWS & SAWING EQPT

Kelley Farm & Garden Inc ....E 518 234-2332
   Cobleskill *(G-3738)*

SCAFFOLDS: Mobile Or Stationary, Metal

Beeche Systems Corp ....D 518 381-6000
   Scotia *(G-15324)*
Safeworks LLC ....F 800 696-5577
   Woodside *(G-17352)*

SCALES & BALANCES, EXC LABORATORY

A & K Equipment Incorporated ....G 705 428-3573
   Watertown *(G-16633)*
Circuits & Systems Inc ....E 516 593-4301
   East Rockaway *(G-4468)*
Itin Scale Co Inc ....E 718 336-5900
   Brooklyn *(G-2120)*

SCALES: Baby

Scale-Tronix Inc ....F 914 948-8117
   Skaneateles *(G-15465)*

SCALP TREATMENT SVCS

British Science Corporation ....G 212 980-8700
   Staten Island *(G-15652)*

SCANNING DEVICES: Optical

Broadnet Technologies Inc ....F 315 443-3694
   Syracuse *(G-15875)*
Cal Blen Electronic Industries ....F 631 242-6243
   Deer Park *(G-4114)*
Jadak LLC ....F 315 701-0678
   North Syracuse *(G-12949)*
T&K Printing Inc ....F 718 439-9454
   Brooklyn *(G-2640)*

SCISSORS: Hand

Klein Cutlery LLC ....D 585 928-2500
   Bolivar *(G-1159)*

SCRAP & WASTE MATERIALS, WHOLESALE: Ferrous Metal

Blue Tee Corp ....G 212 598-0880
   New York *(G-9422)*
Massena Metals Inc ....F 315 769-3846
   Massena *(G-8198)*

SCRAP & WASTE MATERIALS, WHOLESALE: Metal

Umicore USA Inc ....E 919 874-7171
   Glens Falls *(G-5700)*

SCRAP & WASTE MATERIALS, WHOLESALE: Plastics Scrap

Fiber USA Corp ....G 718 888-1512
   Flushing *(G-5241)*

SCRAP & WASTE MATERIALS, WHOLESALE: Rags

Yankee Corp ....F 718 589-1377
   Bronx *(G-1495)*

SCREENS: Projection

Dnp Electronics America LLC ....D 212 503-1060
   New York *(G-9892)*

SCREENS: Window, Metal

Alumil Fabrication Inc ....F 845 469-2874
   Newburgh *(G-12748)*
Bison Steel Incorporated ....G 716 683-0900
   Depew *(G-4248)*
Norandex Inc Vestal ....G 607 786-0778
   Vestal *(G-16452)*
Renewal By Andersen LLC ....E 631 843-1716
   Farmingdale *(G-5098)*
Window Tech Systems Inc ....E 518 899-9000
   Ballston Spa *(G-611)*

SCREENS: Woven Wire

Star Wire Mesh Fabricators ....G 212 831-4933
   New York *(G-12185)*

SCREW MACHINE PRDTS

Acme Precision Screw Pdts Inc ....F 585 328-2028
   Rochester *(G-14170)*
Albert Gates Inc ....D 585 594-9401
   North Chili *(G-12924)*
All Type Screw Machine Pdts ....G 516 334-5100
   Westbury *(G-16965)*
Anderson Precision Inc ....D 716 484-1148
   Jamestown *(G-6971)*
Andros Manufacturing Corp ....F 585 663-5700
   Rochester *(G-14205)*
Brinkman Intl Group Inc ....G 585 429-5000
   Rochester *(G-14245)*
Broda Machine Co Inc ....F 716 297-3221
   Niagara Falls *(G-12799)*
C R C Manufacturing Inc ....F 585 254-8820
   Rochester *(G-14255)*
C&C Automatics Inc ....E 315 331-1436
   Newark *(G-12730)*
Century Metal Parts Corp ....E 631 667-0800
   Bay Shore *(G-682)*
Craftech Industries Inc ....D 518 828-5001
   Hudson *(G-6611)*
Curtis Screw Co Inc ....E 716 898-7800
   Buffalo *(G-2896)*
Elmira Grinding Works Inc ....F 607 734-1579
   Wellsburg *(G-16747)*
Emory Machine & Tool Co Inc ....E 585 436-9610
   Farmington *(G-5150)*
Five Star Tool Co Inc ....E 585 328-9580
   Rochester *(G-14372)*
Globe Electronic Hardware Inc ....F 718 457-0303
   Woodside *(G-17332)*
Gsp Components Inc ....F 585 436-3377
   Rochester *(G-14414)*
Hanco Metal Products Inc ....F 212 787-5992
   Brooklyn *(G-2066)*
I W Industries Inc ....C 631 293-9494
   Melville *(G-8330)*
J & J Swiss Precision Inc ....E 631 243-5584
   Deer Park *(G-4154)*
Jordan Products Inc ....E 585 385-7777
   Penfield *(G-13500)*
Kaddis Manufacturing Corp ....F 585 624-3070
   Honeoye Falls *(G-6533)*
Kathleen B Mead ....G 585 247-0146
   Rochester *(G-14468)*
Ktd Screw Machine Inc ....G 631 243-6861
   Deer Park *(G-4160)*
Lexington Machining LLC ....D 585 235-0880
   Rochester *(G-14478)*
Lexington Machining LLC ....G 585 235-0880
   Rochester *(G-14479)*
Liberty Brass Turning Co Inc ....E 718 784-2911
   Westbury *(G-17005)*
M Manastrip-M Corporation ....G 518 664-2089
   Clifton Park *(G-3699)*
Manacraft Precision Inc ....F 914 654-0967
   Pelham *(G-13493)*
Manth-Brownell Inc ....C 315 687-7263
   Kirkville *(G-7227)*
Marmach Machine Inc ....F 585 768-8800
   Le Roy *(G-7414)*
Micro Threaded Products Inc ....G 585 288-0080
   Rochester *(G-14508)*
Miggins Screw Products Inc ....G 845 279-2307
   Brewster *(G-1224)*
Muller Tool Inc ....E 716 895-3658
   Buffalo *(G-3077)*
Multimatic Products Inc ....D 800 767-7633
   Ronkonkoma *(G-14947)*
Murphy Manufacturing Co Inc ....G 585 223-0100
   Fairport *(G-4865)*
Norwood Screw Machine Parts ....F 516 481-6644
   Mineola *(G-8528)*
Precision Machine Tech LLC ....D 585 467-1840
   Rochester *(G-14595)*
R P M Machine Co ....G 585 671-3744
   Webster *(G-16732)*
Ranney Precision ....F 716 731-6418
   Niagara Falls *(G-12866)*
Selflock Screw Products Co Inc ....E 315 541-4464
   Syracuse *(G-16037)*
Supply Technologies (ny) ....F 212 966-3310
   Albany *(G-139)*
Supreme Screw Products Inc ....F 718 293-6600
   Plainview *(G-13637)*
T & L Automatics Inc ....C 585 647-3717
   Rochester *(G-14715)*
TAC Screw Products Inc ....F 585 663-5840
   Rochester *(G-14717)*
Taylor Metalworks Inc ....C 716 662-3113
   Orchard Park *(G-13298)*
Teale Machine Company Inc ....D 585 244-6700
   Rochester *(G-14719)*
Thuro Metal Products Inc ....E 631 435-0444
   Brentwood *(G-1196)*
Thuro Metal Products Inc ....E 631 435-0444
   Brentwood *(G-1196)*
Townline Machine Co Inc ....F 315 462-3413
   Clifton Springs *(G-3716)*
Tri-Technologies Inc ....E 914 699-2001
   Mount Vernon *(G-8741)*
Trihex Manufacturing Inc ....G 315 589-9331
   Williamson *(G-17227)*
Triple Point Manufacturing ....G 631 218-4988
   Bohemia *(G-1149)*
Umbro Machine & Tool Co Inc ....F 845 876-4669
   Rhinebeck *(G-14059)*
Vanguard Metals Inc ....F 631 234-6500
   Central Islip *(G-3514)*

SCREW MACHINE PRDTS

Verns Machine Co Inc .... E 315 926-4223
   Marion *(G-8103)*

SCREW MACHINES

Johnson Mch & Fibr Pdts Co Inc .... F 716 665-2003
   Jamestown *(G-7014)*
Swiss Specialties Inc .... F 631 567-8800
   Wading River *(G-16527)*

SCREWS: Metal

Anthony Manno & Co Inc .... G 631 445-1834
   Deer Park *(G-4099)*
John F Rafter Inc .... G 716 992-3425
   Eden *(G-4587)*
Kinemotive Corporation .... E 631 249-6440
   Farmingdale *(G-5028)*
Radax Industries Inc .... E 585 265-2055
   Webster *(G-16733)*
Socket Products Mfg Corp .... G 631 232-9870
   Islandia *(G-6803)*
Tamperproof Screw Company Inc .... F 516 931-1616
   Hicksville *(G-6397)*

SEALANTS

Deal International Inc .... E 585 288-4444
   Rochester *(G-14304)*
J M Canty Inc .... E 716 625-4227
   Lockport *(G-7593)*
R-Co Products Corporation .... F 800 854-7657
   Lakewood *(G-7293)*
Saint-Gobain Prfmce Plas Corp .... C 518 642-2200
   Granville *(G-5781)*
Walsh & Hughes Inc .... G 631 427-5904
   Huntington Station *(G-6728)*

SEARCH & DETECTION SYSTEMS, EXC RADAR

Frequency Electronics Inc .... B 516 794-4500
   Uniondale *(G-16295)*
Saab Defense and SEC USA LLC .... F 315 445-5009
   East Syracuse *(G-4560)*
U S Tech Corporation .... F 315 437-7207
   East Syracuse *(G-4575)*
Virtualapt Corp .... G 917 293-3173
   Brooklyn *(G-2730)*
VJ Technologies Inc .... E 631 589-8800
   Bohemia *(G-1154)*

SEARCH & NAVIGATION SYSTEMS

1robotics LLC .... G 845 369-6770
   Airmont *(G-10)*
901 D LLC .... E 845 369-1111
   Airmont *(G-11)*
Ametek Inc .... D 585 263-7700
   Rochester *(G-14202)*
Amherst Systems Inc .... C 716 631-0610
   Buffalo *(G-2810)*
Aventura Technologies Inc .... E 631 300-4000
   Commack *(G-3822)*
C Speed LLC .... E 315 453-1043
   Liverpool *(G-7514)*
C-Flex Bearing Co Inc .... F 315 895-7454
   Frankfort *(G-5350)*
Clayton Dubilier & Rice Fun .... E 212 407-5200
   New York *(G-9640)*
Computer Instruments Corp .... E 516 876-8400
   Westbury *(G-16975)*
Cox & Company Inc .... E 212 366-0200
   Plainview *(G-13593)*
Drs-Electronic Warfare & Netwo .... B 716 631-6200
   Buffalo *(G-2919)*
Dyna-Empire Inc .... C 516 222-2700
   Garden City *(G-5500)*
Edo LLC .... G 631 630-4000
   Amityville *(G-285)*
Edo LLC .... A 631 630-4200
   Amityville *(G-286)*
Emergency Beacon Corp .... F 914 576-2700
   New Rochelle *(G-8896)*
Flightline Electronics Inc .... D 585 742-5340
   Victor *(G-16478)*
Harris Corporation .... C 703 668-6239
   Rome *(G-14812)*
Inficon Inc .... C 315 434-1149
   East Syracuse *(G-4541)*
Joldeson One Aerospace Inds .... D 718 848-7396
   Ozone Park *(G-13380)*

Kerns Manufacturing Corp .... C 718 784-4044
   Long Island City *(G-7780)*
L-3 Cmmnctons Fgn Holdings Inc .... E 212 697-1111
   New York *(G-10903)*
L-3 Cmmunications Holdings Inc .... D 212 697-1111
   New York *(G-10905)*
L-3 Communications Corporation .... B 212 697-1111
   New York *(G-10906)*
Lockheed Martin Corporation .... A 607 751-2000
   Owego *(G-13354)*
Lockheed Martin Corporation .... D 607 751-7434
   Owego *(G-13355)*
Lockheed Martin Corporation .... D 212 697-1105
   New York *(G-11021)*
Lockheed Martin Corporation .... E 716 297-1000
   Niagara Falls *(G-12844)*
Lockheed Martin Global Inc .... D 315 456-2982
   Liverpool *(G-7532)*
Logitek Inc .... D 631 567-1100
   Bohemia *(G-1094)*
Magellan Aerospace NY Inc .... C 718 699-4000
   Corona *(G-4001)*
Metro Dynmc Scntific Instr Lab .... F 631 842-4300
   Copiague *(G-3914)*
Mirion Technologies Ist Corp .... D 607 562-4300
   Horseheads *(G-6584)*
Northrop Grumman Corporation .... A 703 280-2900
   Bethpage *(G-876)*
Norwich Aero Products Inc .... D 607 336-7636
   Norwich *(G-13032)*
Orthstar Enterprises Inc .... D 607 562-2100
   Horseheads *(G-6586)*
Rodale Wireless Inc .... E 631 231-0044
   Hauppauge *(G-6179)*
Transistor Devices Inc .... F 631 471-7492
   Ronkonkoma *(G-14992)*
Tusk Manufacturing Inc .... E 631 567-3349
   Bohemia *(G-1150)*
U E Systems Incorporated .... E 914 592-1220
   Elmsford *(G-4790)*
Vacuum Instrument Corporation .... D 631 737-0900
   Ronkonkoma *(G-14997)*
Worldwide Arntcal Cmpnents Inc .... F 631 842-3780
   Copiague *(G-3939)*
Worldwide Arntcal Cmpnents Inc .... G 631 842-3780
   Copiague *(G-3940)*

SEAT BELTS: Automobile & Aircraft

Davis Restraint Systems Inc .... F 631 563-1500
   Bohemia *(G-1051)*

SEATING: Bleacher, Portable

E & D Specialty Stands Inc .... E 716 337-0161
   North Collins *(G-12928)*

SEATING: Chairs, Table & Arm

Chair Factory .... E 718 363-2383
   Brooklyn *(G-1771)*

SECRETARIAL SVCS

New York Typing & Printing Co .... G 718 268-7900
   Forest Hills *(G-5327)*

SECURITY CONTROL EQPT & SYSTEMS

Aabacs Group Inc .... F 718 961-3577
   College Point *(G-3774)*
Albatros North America Inc .... E 518 381-7100
   Ballston Spa *(G-590)*
Altronix Corp .... D 718 567-8181
   Brooklyn *(G-1596)*
Atlantic Electronic Tech LLC .... G 800 296-2177
   Brooklyn *(G-1646)*
BDB Technologies LLC .... G 800 921-4270
   Brooklyn *(G-1675)*
C & G Video Systems Inc .... G 315 452-1490
   Liverpool *(G-7513)*
Comsec Ventures International .... G 518 523-1600
   Lake Placid *(G-7273)*
Detekion Security Systems Inc .... F 607 729-7179
   Vestal *(G-16447)*
Eyelock Corporation .... E 914 619-5570
   New York *(G-10112)*
Eyelock LLC .... G 855 393-5625
   New York *(G-10113)*
Fire Fox Security Corp .... G 917 981-9280
   Brooklyn *(G-1974)*
Forte Network .... E 631 390-9050
   East Northport *(G-4436)*

Innovative Video Tech Inc .... F 516 840-2587
   Hauppauge *(G-6098)*
Issco Corporation .... E 212 732-8748
   Garden City *(G-5512)*
Mkj Communications Corp .... F 212 206-0072
   New York *(G-11286)*
Napco Security Tech Inc .... B 631 842-9400
   Amityville *(G-314)*
National Security Systems Inc .... E 516 627-2222
   Manhasset *(G-8063)*
Protex International Corp .... D 631 563-4250
   Bohemia *(G-1124)*
Teltech Security Corp .... G 718 871-8800
   Brooklyn *(G-2654)*

SECURITY DEVICES

Avalonics Inc .... G 516 238-7074
   Levittown *(G-7424)*
Century Systems Ltd .... G 718 543-5991
   Bronx *(G-1294)*
Custom Sound and Video .... E 585 424-5000
   Rochester *(G-14296)*
Dyson-Kissner-Moran Corp .... E 212 661-4600
   Poughkeepsie *(G-13896)*
Fairview Bell and Intercom .... G 718 627-8621
   Brooklyn *(G-1953)*
Fiber Instrument Sales Inc .... C 315 736-2206
   Oriskany *(G-13309)*
Hampton Technologies LLC .... E 631 924-1335
   Medford *(G-8248)*
Hawk-I Security Inc .... G 631 656-1056
   Hauppauge *(G-6092)*
Highlander Realty Inc .... E 914 235-8073
   New Rochelle *(G-8911)*
Manhole Brrier SEC Systems Inc .... E 516 741-1032
   Kew Gardens *(G-7165)*
News/Sprts Microwave Rentl Inc .... E 619 670-0572
   New York *(G-11419)*
Parabit Systems Inc .... E 516 378-4800
   Roosevelt *(G-15008)*
Scorpion Security Products Inc .... G 607 724-9999
   Binghamton *(G-949)*
Securevue Inc .... G 631 587-5850
   West Islip *(G-16906)*
Security Defense System .... G 718 357-6200
   Whitestone *(G-17214)*
Security Dynamics Inc .... F 631 392-1701
   Bohemia *(G-1130)*
Triton Infosys Inc .... E 877 308-2388
   New York *(G-12406)*
Verifyme Inc .... G 212 994-7002
   New York *(G-12522)*
Videotec Security Incorporated .... G 518 825-0020
   Plattsburgh *(G-13706)*

SECURITY PROTECTIVE DEVICES MAINTENANCE & MONITORING SVCS

Basil S Kadhim .... G 888 520-5192
   New York *(G-9330)*
Security Defense System .... G 718 357-6200
   Whitestone *(G-17214)*

SECURITY SYSTEMS SERVICES

Indegy Inc .... E 866 801-5394
   New York *(G-10586)*
Intralinks Holdings Inc .... E 212 543-7700
   New York *(G-10646)*
Synergx Systems Inc .... D 516 433-4700
   Woodside *(G-17358)*
World Business Media LLC .... F 212 344-0759
   Massapequa Park *(G-8191)*

SEMICONDUCTOR & RELATED DEVICES: Read-Only Memory Or ROM

Monolithic Coatings Inc .... G 914 621-2765
   Sharon Springs *(G-15384)*

SEMICONDUCTOR CIRCUIT NETWORKS

Interplex Industries Inc .... F 718 961-6212
   College Point *(G-3790)*

SEMICONDUCTOR DEVICES: Wafers

Thermoaura Inc .... F 518 880-2125
   Albany *(G-142)*

(G-0000) Company's Geographic Section entry number

PRODUCT SECTION

SHADES: Lamp & Light, Residential

SEMICONDUCTORS & RELATED DEVICES

Able Electronics Inc ....F 631 924-5386
  Bellport *(G-825)*
Accumetrics Inc ....F 716 684-0002
  Latham *(G-7352)*
Accumetrics Associates Inc ....F 518 393-2200
  Latham *(G-7353)*
Advis Inc ....G 585 568-0100
  Caledonia *(G-3275)*
Aeroflex Holding Corp ....E 516 694-6700
  Plainview *(G-13577)*
Aeroflex Plainview Inc ....C 631 231-9100
  Hauppauge *(G-6011)*
Atlantis Energy Systems Inc ....G 916 438-2930
  Poughkeepsie *(G-13890)*
Beech Grove Technology Inc ....G 845 223-6844
  Hopewell Junction *(G-6547)*
Bga Technology LLC ....F 631 750-4600
  Bohemia *(G-1025)*
CAM Touchview Products Inc ....F 631 842-3400
  Farmingdale *(G-4956)*
Central Semiconductor Corp ....D 631 435-1110
  Hauppauge *(G-6041)*
Ceres Technologies Inc ....D 845 247-4701
  Saugerties *(G-15181)*
Cold Springs R & D Inc ....F 315 413-1237
  Syracuse *(G-15901)*
Compositech Ltd ....C 516 835-1458
  Woodbury *(G-17284)*
Convergent Med MGT Svcs LLC ....G 718 921-6159
  Brooklyn *(G-1802)*
Cooper Power Systems LLC ....B 716 375-7100
  Olean *(G-13140)*
Corning Incorporated ....E 607 248-1200
  Corning *(G-3965)*
Corning Incorporated ....A 607 974-9000
  Corning *(G-3962)*
Corning Incorporated ....G 607 974-6729
  Painted Post *(G-13391)*
Corning Specialty Mtls Inc ....G 607 974-9000
  Corning *(G-3970)*
Crystalonics Inc ....F 631 981-6140
  Ronkonkoma *(G-14891)*
Curtiss-Wright Controls ....G 631 756-4740
  Farmingdale *(G-4967)*
Cypress Semiconductor Corp ....F 631 261-1358
  Northport *(G-13010)*
Dionics-Usa Inc ....G 516 997-7474
  Westbury *(G-16977)*
Elite Semi Conductor Products ....G 631 884-8400
  Lindenhurst *(G-7463)*
Endicott Interconnect Tech Inc ....A 866 820-4820
  Endicott *(G-4802)*
Freescale Semiconductor Inc ....G 585 425-4000
  Pittsford *(G-13560)*
General Semiconductor Inc ....G 631 300-3818
  Hauppauge *(G-6083)*
Globalfoundries US Inc ....F 512 457-3900
  Hopewell Junction *(G-6551)*
Gs Direct LLC ....G 212 902-1000
  New York *(G-10377)*
Gurley Precision Instrs Inc ....C 518 272-6300
  Troy *(G-16237)*
H K Technologies Inc ....G 212 779-0100
  New York *(G-10390)*
Hi-Tron Semiconductor Corp ....E 631 231-1500
  Hauppauge *(G-6093)*
Hipotronics Inc ....C 845 279-8091
  Brewster *(G-1220)*
I3 Electronics Inc ....B 866 820-4820
  Endicott *(G-4812)*
Ilc Holdings Inc ....G 631 567-5600
  Bohemia *(G-1076)*
Ilc Industries LLC ....E 631 567-5600
  Bohemia *(G-1077)*
International Bus Mchs Corp ....A 845 894-2121
  Hopewell Junction *(G-6553)*
International Bus Mchs Corp ....C 800 426-4968
  Hopewell Junction *(G-6554)*
Intex Company Inc ....D 718 336-3491
  Brooklyn *(G-2114)*
Isine Inc ....G 631 913-4400
  Ronkonkoma *(G-14914)*
J H Rhodes Company Inc ....F 315 829-3600
  Vernon *(G-16436)*
Lakestar Semi Inc ....F 212 974-6254
  New York *(G-10919)*
Lasermax Inc ....D 585 272-5420
  Rochester *(G-14474)*
Lightspin Technologies Inc ....G 301 656-7600
  Endwell *(G-4837)*
Logitek Inc ....D 631 567-1100
  Bohemia *(G-1094)*
M C Products ....E 631 471-4070
  Holbrook *(G-6459)*
Marcon Services ....G 516 223-8019
  Freeport *(G-5411)*
Marktech International Corp ....E 518 956-2980
  Latham *(G-7373)*
Materion Brewster LLC ....D 845 279-0900
  Brewster *(G-1223)*
McG Electronics Inc ....E 631 586-5125
  Deer Park *(G-4172)*
Mellanox Technologies Inc ....D 408 970-3400
  New York *(G-11223)*
Micro Contract Manufacturing ....G 631 738-7874
  Ronkonkoma *(G-14941)*
Micro Semicdtr Researches LLC ....G 646 863-6070
  New York *(G-11254)*
Microchip Technology Inc ....C 607 785-5992
  Endicott *(G-4819)*
Micromem Technologies ....F 212 672-1806
  New York *(G-11255)*
Mini-Circuits Fort Wayne LLC ....B 718 934-4500
  Brooklyn *(G-2318)*
Navitar Inc ....D 585 359-4000
  Rochester *(G-14530)*
Procomponents Inc ....E 516 683-0909
  Westbury *(G-17023)*
Riverhawk Company LP ....E 315 624-7171
  New Hartford *(G-8809)*
RSM Electron Power Inc ....D 631 586-7600
  Deer Park *(G-4203)*
RSM Electron Power Inc ....D 631 586-7600
  Hauppauge *(G-6181)*
Ruhle Companies Inc ....E 914 287-4000
  Valhalla *(G-16372)*
Schott Corporation ....D 315 255-2791
  Auburn *(G-517)*
Schott Lithotec USA Corp ....D 845 463-5300
  Elmsford *(G-4781)*
Semitronics Corp ....E 516 223-0200
  Freeport *(G-5425)*
Sencer Inc ....G 315 536-3474
  Penn Yan *(G-13520)*
Sendyne Corp ....G 212 966-0663
  New York *(G-12028)*
Silicon Pulsed Power LLC ....G 610 407-4700
  Clifton Park *(G-3707)*
Sinclair Technologies Inc ....E 716 874-3682
  Hamburg *(G-5942)*
Solartech Renewables LLC ....F 646 675-1853
  Poughkeepsie *(G-13931)*
Spectron Glass & Electronics ....F 631 582-5600
  Hauppauge *(G-6193)*
Stetron International Inc ....F 716 854-3443
  Buffalo *(G-3197)*
Sumitomo Elc USA Holdings Inc ....G 212 490-6610
  New York *(G-12232)*
Super Conductor Materials Inc ....F 845 368-0240
  Suffern *(G-15801)*
Swissbit Na Inc ....G 914 935-1400
  Port Chester *(G-13760)*
Symwave Inc ....G 949 542-4400
  Hauppauge *(G-6205)*
Tel Technology Center Amer LLC ....E 512 424-4200
  Albany *(G-141)*
Telephonics Corporation ....E 631 549-6000
  Huntington *(G-6683)*
Thales Laser SA ....D 585 223-2370
  Fairport *(G-4884)*
Tlsi Incorporated ....D 631 470-8880
  Huntington *(G-6688)*
University At Albany ....E 518 437-8686
  Albany *(G-147)*
Vgg Holding LLC ....G 212 415-6700
  New York *(G-12533)*
Viking Technologies Ltd ....E 631 957-8000
  Lindenhurst *(G-7493)*
Vistec Lithography Inc ....F 518 874-3184
  Troy *(G-16260)*
Widetronix Inc ....G 607 330-4752
  Ithaca *(G-6885)*
Zastech Inc ....E 516 496-4777
  Syosset *(G-15843)*

SENSORS: Temperature For Motor Windings

Irtronics Instruments Inc ....F 914 693-6291
  Ardsley *(G-405)*

SENSORS: Temperature, Exc Indl Process

Titan Controls Inc ....F 516 358-2407
  New York *(G-12354)*

SEPARATORS: Metal Plate

Motivair Corporation ....E 716 691-9222
  Amherst *(G-252)*

SEPTIC TANKS: Concrete

Bistrian Cement Corporation ....F 631 324-1123
  East Hampton *(G-4405)*
H F Cary & Sons ....G 607 598-2563
  Lockwood *(G-7627)*
Suffolk Cement Precast Inc ....F 631 727-4432
  Calverton *(G-3299)*

SEPTIC TANKS: Plastic

Roth Global Plastics Inc ....E 315 475-0100
  Syracuse *(G-16026)*

SERVICES, NEC

G and G Service ....G 518 785-9247
  Latham *(G-7363)*

SERVOMOTORS: Electric

Magna Products Corp ....E 585 647-2280
  Rochester *(G-14489)*

SEWAGE & WATER TREATMENT EQPT

City of Kingston ....F 845 331-2490
  Kingston *(G-7184)*
Clearcove Systems Inc ....F 585 734-3012
  Victor *(G-16467)*
Ewt Holdings III Corp ....G 212 644-5900
  New York *(G-10096)*
Ferguson Enterprises Inc ....E 800 437-1146
  New Hyde Park *(G-8834)*
Incorporated Village Garden Cy ....C 516 465-4020
  Garden City *(G-5510)*
Northeast Water Systems LLC ....G 585 943-9225
  Kendall *(G-7144)*
Yr Blanc & Co LLC ....G 716 800-3999
  Buffalo *(G-3261)*

SEWAGE TREATMENT SYSTEMS & EQPT

Environment-One Corporation ....C 518 346-6161
  Schenectady *(G-15252)*
Orege North America Inc ....G 770 862-9388
  New York *(G-11525)*
Richard R Cain Inc ....F 845 229-7410
  Hyde Park *(G-6736)*

SEWER CLEANING EQPT: Power

Dyna-Vac Equipment Inc ....F 315 865-8084
  Stittville *(G-15762)*
Pathfinder 103 Inc ....G 315 363-4260
  Oneida *(G-13165)*

SEWING CONTRACTORS

TSS Foam Industries Corp ....F 585 538-2321
  Caledonia *(G-3283)*

SEWING MACHINES & PARTS: Indl

Herbert Jaffe Inc ....G 718 392-1956
  Long Island City *(G-7759)*
Tompkins Srm LLC ....G 315 422-8763
  Syracuse *(G-16059)*

SEWING, NEEDLEWORK & PIECE GOODS STORE: Needlework Gds/Sply

Viking Athletics Ltd ....E 631 957-8000
  Lindenhurst *(G-7492)*

SEWING, NEEDLEWORK & PIECE GOODS STORES: Sewing & Needlework

Great Adirondack Yarn Company ....F 518 843-3381
  Amsterdam *(G-349)*

SHADES: Lamp & Light, Residential

Custom Lampshades Inc ....F 718 254-0500
  Brooklyn *(G-1826)*

*Employee Codes: A=Over 500 employees, B=251-500
C=101-250, D=51-100, E=20-50, F=10-19, G=5-9*

SHADES: Lamp Or Candle

SHADES: Lamp Or Candle
- Artemis Studios Inc ....D...... 718 788-6022
  Brooklyn *(G-1635)*
- Blanche P Field LLC ....E...... 212 355-6616
  New York *(G-9412)*
- Diane Studios Inc ....D...... 718 788-6007
  Brooklyn *(G-1861)*
- Jamaica Lamp Corp ....E...... 718 776-5039
  Queens Village *(G-13980)*
- Our Own Candle Company Inc ....F...... 716 769-5000
  Findley Lake *(G-5177)*
- Ray Gold Shade Inc ....F...... 718 377-8892
  Brooklyn *(G-2480)*

SHADES: Window
- Mechoshade Systems Inc ....C...... 718 729-2020
  Long Island City *(G-7808)*
- Solar Screen Co Inc ....G...... 718 592-8222
  Corona *(G-4007)*
- Windowcraft Inc ....F...... 516 294-3580
  Garden City Park *(G-5544)*

SHALE MINING, COMMON
- Callahan & Nannini Quarry Inc ....G...... 845 496-4323
  Salisbury Mills *(G-15112)*
- Grosso Materials Inc ....F...... 845 361-5211
  Montgomery *(G-8594)*

SHALE: Expanded
- Norlite Corporation ....B...... 518 235-0030
  Cohoes *(G-3754)*

SHAPES & PILINGS, STRUCTURAL: Steel
- Markin Tubing Inc ....C...... 585 495-6211
  Wyoming *(G-17381)*
- Pecker Iron Works LLC ....G...... 914 665-0100
  Mount Kisco *(G-8639)*
- Rochester Structural LLC ....E...... 585 436-1250
  Rochester *(G-14651)*

SHEATHING: Paper
- Sabin Robbins Paper Company ....E...... 513 874-5270
  New York *(G-11950)*

SHEET METAL SPECIALTIES, EXC STAMPED
- Aero-Data Metal Crafters Inc ....C...... 631 471-7733
  Ronkonkoma *(G-14856)*
- Asm USA Inc ....G...... 212 925-2906
  New York *(G-9233)*
- Choppy V M & Sons LLC ....E...... 518 266-1444
  Troy *(G-16231)*
- Construction Parts Whse Inc ....G...... 315 445-1310
  East Syracuse *(G-4519)*
- Custom Sheet Metal Corp ....G...... 315 463-9105
  Syracuse *(G-15916)*
- Dayton T Brown Inc ....B...... 631 589-6300
  Bohemia *(G-1052)*
- Franchet Metal Craft Inc ....E...... 718 658-6400
  Jamaica *(G-6913)*
- P R B Metal Products Inc ....F...... 631 467-1800
  Ronkonkoma *(G-14961)*
- Penasack Machine Company Inc ......E...... 585 589-7044
  Albion *(G-168)*
- Service Mfg Group Inc ....F...... 716 893-1482
  Buffalo *(G-3183)*

SHEET MUSIC STORES
- Golfing Magazine ....G...... 516 822-5446
  Hicksville *(G-6352)*

SHEET MUSIC, WHOLESALE
- Carl Fischer LLC ....E...... 212 777-0900
  New York *(G-9526)*

SHEETING: Laminated Plastic
- Advanced Structures Corp ....F...... 631 667-5000
  Deer Park *(G-4088)*

SHEETS & STRIPS: Aluminum
- Alcoa Fastening Systems ....G...... 585 368-5049
  Rochester *(G-14185)*
- Alcoa Inc ....D...... 212 836-2674
  New York *(G-9077)*

SHEETS: Fabric, From Purchased Materials
- Elegant Linen Inc ....E...... 718 871-3535
  Brooklyn *(G-1913)*

SHELVES & SHELVING: Wood
- Forecast Consoles Inc ....E...... 631 253-9000
  Hauppauge *(G-6079)*
- Karp Associates Inc ....D...... 631 768-8300
  Melville *(G-8332)*

SHELVING: Office & Store, Exc Wood
- Abaco Steel Products Inc ....G...... 631 589-1800
  Bohemia *(G-1002)*
- Jack Luckner Steel Shelving Co .....D...... 718 363-0500
  Maspeth *(G-8147)*
- Lucia Group Inc ....G...... 631 392-4900
  Deer Park *(G-4168)*
- Tri-Boro Shlving Prtition Corp ....F...... 434 315-5600
  Ridgewood *(G-14129)*
- Tri-Boro Shlving Prtition Corp ....F...... 718 782-8527
  Ridgewood *(G-14130)*
- Your Furniture Designers Inc ....G...... 845 947-3046
  West Haverstraw *(G-16848)*

SHERARDIZING SVC: Metals Or Metal Prdts
- Superior Metals & Processing ....G...... 718 545-7500
  Long Island City *(G-7896)*

SHIELDS OR ENCLOSURES: Radiator, Sheet Metal
- Interior Metals ....E...... 718 439-7324
  Brooklyn *(G-2110)*
- Radiation Shielding Systems ....F...... 888 631-2278
  Suffern *(G-15799)*
- Rand Products Manufacturing Co ...G...... 518 374-9871
  Schenectady *(G-15288)*
- Steelcraft Manufacturing Co ....F...... 718 277-2404
  Brooklyn *(G-2603)*

SHIMS: Metal
- McD Metals LLC ....F...... 518 456-9694
  Albany *(G-100)*
- Romac Electronics Inc ....E...... 516 349-7900
  Plainview *(G-13632)*

SHIP BLDG & RPRG: Drilling & Production Platforms, Oil/Gas
- Cgsi Group LLC ....F...... 516 986-5503
  Bronx *(G-1296)*

SHIP BUILDING & REPAIRING: Cargo Vessels
- Reynolds Shipyard Corporation ......F...... 718 981-2800
  Staten Island *(G-15731)*

SHIP BUILDING & REPAIRING: Cargo, Commercial
- Steelways Inc ....E...... 845 562-0860
  Newburgh *(G-12780)*

SHIP BUILDING & REPAIRING: Ferryboats
- Robert E Derecktor Inc ....D...... 914 698-0962
  Mamaroneck *(G-8045)*

SHIP BUILDING & REPAIRING: Lighthouse Tenders
- Highland Museum & Lighthouse .....F...... 508 487-1121
  Cairo *(G-3272)*

SHIP BUILDING & REPAIRING: Offshore Sply Boats
- Weldrite Closures Inc ....E...... 585 429-8790
  Rochester *(G-14760)*

SHIP BUILDING & REPAIRING: Radar Towers, Floating
- Standard Ascnsion Towers Group ...D...... 716 681-2222
  Depew *(G-4274)*

SHIP BUILDING & REPAIRING: Rigging, Marine
- Clark Rigging & Rental Corp ....F...... 585 265-2910
  Webster *(G-16717)*
- Dragon Trading Inc ....G...... 212 717-1496
  New York *(G-9923)*

SHIP BUILDING & REPAIRING: Tankers
- McQuilling Partners Inc ....E...... 516 227-5718
  Garden City *(G-5519)*

SHIPBUILDING & REPAIR
- Alpha Marine Repair ....E...... 718 816-7150
  Staten Island *(G-15636)*
- Caddell Dry Dock & Repr Co Inc ....C...... 718 442-2112
  Staten Island *(G-15654)*
- Excelco Developments Inc ....E...... 716 934-2651
  Silver Creek *(G-15448)*
- Excelco/Newbrook Inc ....D...... 716 934-2644
  Silver Creek *(G-15449)*
- George G Sharp Inc ....E...... 212 732-2800
  New York *(G-10281)*
- Godfrey Prpeller Adjusting Svc ......G...... 718 768-3744
  Brooklyn *(G-2035)*
- Huntington Ingalls Inc ....E...... 518 884-3834
  Saratoga Springs *(G-15159)*
- May Ship Repair Contg Corp ....E...... 718 442-9700
  Staten Island *(G-15705)*
- Metalcraft Marine Us Inc ....F...... 315 501-4015
  Cape Vincent *(G-3384)*
- Moran Shipyard Corporation ....C...... 718 981-5600
  Staten Island *(G-15707)*
- Moran Towing Corporation ....G...... 718 981-5600
  Staten Island *(G-15708)*
- Port Everglades Machine Works ....F...... 516 367-2280
  Plainview *(G-13630)*
- Scarano Boat Building Inc ....E...... 518 463-3401
  Albany *(G-131)*
- Stidd Systems Inc ....E...... 631 477-2400
  Greenport *(G-5877)*
- United Ship Repair Inc ....F...... 718 237-2800
  Brooklyn *(G-2702)*
- Viking Mar Wldg Ship Repr LLC ....F...... 718 758-4116
  Brooklyn *(G-2727)*

SHIPPING AGENTS
- Hastings Hide Inc ....G...... 516 295-2400
  Lawrence *(G-7391)*

SHOCK ABSORBERS: Indl
- Kyntec Corporation ....G...... 716 810-6956
  Buffalo *(G-3038)*
- Taylor Devices Inc ....C...... 716 694-0800
  North Tonawanda *(G-13001)*

SHOE & BOOT ACCESS
- Randall Loeffler Inc ....F...... 212 226-8787
  New York *(G-11800)*

SHOE & BOOT MATERIALS: Laces, Leather
- U-Lace LLC ....G...... 716 848-0939
  Rochester *(G-14738)*

SHOE MATERIALS: Body Parts, Outers
- Awap Inc ....G...... 516 481-4070
  Uniondale *(G-16289)*

SHOE MATERIALS: Counters
- Counter Evolution ....G...... 212 647-7505
  New York *(G-9733)*
- Custom Countertops Inc ....G...... 716 646-1579
  Orchard Park *(G-13268)*
- Custom Countertops Inc ....G...... 716 685-2871
  Depew *(G-4253)*
- Custom Design Kitchens Inc ....F...... 518 355-4446
  Duanesburg *(G-4325)*

SHOE MATERIALS: Quarters
- Priscilla Quart Co Firts ....G...... 516 365-2755
  Manhasset *(G-8064)*
- Tread Quarters ....G...... 800 876-6676
  Rochester *(G-14730)*

PRODUCT SECTION

SHOE MATERIALS: Rands
Rand Luxury Inc..................................G...... 212 655-4505
  New York *(G-11798)*

SHOE MATERIALS: Rubber
Kiklord LLC...G...... 917 859-1700
  Long Beach *(G-7641)*
Le Chameau USA Inc......................G...... 646 356-0460
  New York *(G-10941)*

SHOE MATERIALS: Sole Parts
MBA Orthotics Inc..............................G...... 631 392-4755
  Bay Shore *(G-716)*

SHOE MATERIALS: Uppers
Upper 90 Soccer & Sport................G...... 718 643-0167
  Brooklyn *(G-2710)*
Upper East Vererinary Center........G...... 212 369-8387
  New York *(G-12473)*
Upper Manhattan Arts Project........G...... 914 980-9805
  Ardsley *(G-407)*
Upper Ninty LLC..................................G...... 646 863-3105
  New York *(G-12474)*

SHOE REPAIR SHOP
Arimed Orthotics Prosthetics P......F...... 718 875-8754
  Brooklyn *(G-1626)*

SHOE STORES
GH Bass & Co.....................................B...... 212 381-3900
  New York *(G-10290)*
Givi Inc...G...... 212 586-5029
  New York *(G-10303)*
Kcp Holdco Inc...................................A...... 212 265-1500
  New York *(G-10827)*
Kenneth Cole Productions Inc.......B...... 212 265-1500
  New York *(G-10833)*
Nine West Footwear Corporation.....B...... 800 999-1877
  New York *(G-11435)*
Wallico Shoes Corp..........................G...... 212 826-7171
  New York *(G-12583)*

SHOE STORES: Children's
Jakes Sneakers Inc..........................G...... 718 233-1132
  Brooklyn *(G-2134)*

SHOE STORES: Custom
Bandier Corp.......................................F...... 212 242-5400
  New York *(G-9313)*

SHOE STORES: Orthopedic
Arimed Orthotics Prosthetics P......F...... 718 875-8754
  Brooklyn *(G-1626)*

SHOE STORES: Women's
Lsil & Co Inc..G...... 914 761-0998
  White Plains *(G-17134)*

SHOES & BOOTS WHOLESALERS
Ashko Group LLC..............................F...... 212 594-6050
  New York *(G-9229)*
Nine West Footwear Corporation.....B...... 800 999-1877
  New York *(G-11435)*
Wallico Shoes Corp..........................G...... 212 826-7171
  New York *(G-12583)*

SHOES: Athletic, Exc Rubber Or Plastic
Custom Sports Lab Inc...................G...... 212 832-1648
  New York *(G-9771)*
Kicks Closet Sportswear Inc.........G...... 347 577-0857
  Bronx *(G-1372)*
Mango Usa Inc...................................E...... 718 998-6050
  Brooklyn *(G-2258)*
Mayberry Shoe Company Inc.......G...... 315 692-4086
  Manlius *(G-8074)*
McM Products USA Inc...................E...... 646 756-4090
  New York *(G-11201)*
Reebok International Ltd................C...... 718 370-0471
  Staten Island *(G-15729)*
Vsg International LLC.....................G...... 718 300-8171
  Brooklyn *(G-2737)*

SHOES: Ballet Slippers
La Strada Dance Footwear Inc.....G...... 631 242-1401
  Deer Park *(G-4163)*

SHOES: Canvas, Rubber Soled
Inkkas LLC...G...... 646 845-9803
  New York *(G-10600)*
Little Eric Shoes On Madison........G...... 212 717-1513
  New York *(G-11012)*
Mango Usa Inc...................................E...... 718 998-6050
  Brooklyn *(G-2258)*
Vans Inc..F...... 631 724-1011
  Lake Grove *(G-7268)*
Vans Inc..F...... 718 349-2311
  Brooklyn *(G-2720)*

SHOES: Infants' & Children's
Everlast Worldwide Inc....................E...... 212 239-0990
  New York *(G-10093)*
GH Bass & Co.....................................B...... 212 381-3900
  New York *(G-10290)*
Reebok International Ltd................C...... 914 948-3719
  White Plains *(G-17163)*
SM New York..F...... 718 446-1800
  Long Island City *(G-7880)*
Steven Madden Ltd..........................B...... 718 446-1800
  Long Island City *(G-7892)*

SHOES: Men's
Air Skate & Air Jump Corp.............F...... 212 967-1201
  Brooklyn *(G-1572)*
Bm America LLC................................E...... 201 438-7733
  New York *(G-9427)*
Coach Inc..B...... 212 594-1850
  New York *(G-9656)*
Detny Footwear Inc...........................G...... 212 423-1040
  New York *(G-9860)*
GH Bass & Co.....................................B...... 212 381-3900
  New York *(G-10290)*
Kcp Holdco Inc...................................A...... 212 265-1500
  New York *(G-10827)*
Kenneth Cole Productions LP.......E...... 212 265-1500
  New York *(G-10832)*
Kenneth Cole Productions Inc.......B...... 212 265-1500
  New York *(G-10833)*
Lake View Manufacturing LLC.....F...... 315 364-7892
  King Ferry *(G-7168)*
Nicholas Kirkwood LLC..................G...... 646 559-5239
  New York *(G-11425)*
Phillips-Van Heusen Europe..........F...... 212 381-3500
  New York *(G-11649)*
Pvh Corp...D...... 212 381-3500
  New York *(G-11756)*
Rockport Company LLC.................D...... 631 243-0418
  Deer Park *(G-4200)*
Rockport Company LLC.................G...... 718 271-3627
  Elmhurst *(G-4666)*
Steven Madden Ltd..........................D...... 845 348-7026
  West Nyack *(G-16927)*
Steven Madden Ltd..........................E...... 212 736-3283
  New York *(G-12200)*
Steven Madden Ltd..........................B...... 718 446-1800
  Long Island City *(G-7892)*
T O Dey Service Corp......................F...... 212 683-6300
  New York *(G-12267)*
Tic TAC Toes Mfg Corp...................D...... 518 773-8187
  Gloversville *(G-5726)*

SHOES: Men's, Dress
NY Accessory Group Ltd Lblty.....G...... 212 989-6350
  New York *(G-11476)*

SHOES: Men's, Sandals
Neumann Jutta New York Inc........F...... 212 982-7048
  New York *(G-11376)*

SHOES: Orthopedic, Men's
Jerry Miller Molded Shoes Inc......F...... 716 881-3920
  Buffalo *(G-3017)*
Pedifix Inc..E...... 845 277-2850
  Brewster *(G-1226)*
Tru Mold Shoes Inc...........................E...... 716 881-4484
  Buffalo *(G-3226)*

SHOES: Orthopedic, Women's
Jerry Miller Molded Shoes Inc......F...... 716 881-3920
  Buffalo *(G-3017)*
Pedifix Inc..E...... 845 277-2850
  Brewster *(G-1226)*
T O Dey Service Corp......................F...... 212 683-6300
  New York *(G-12267)*
Tru Mold Shoes Inc...........................E...... 716 881-4484
  Buffalo *(G-3226)*

SHOES: Plastic Or Rubber
Anthony L & S LLC...........................G...... 212 386-7245
  New York *(G-9168)*
Deckers Outdoor Corporation.......B...... 212 486-2509
  New York *(G-9835)*
Detny Footwear Inc...........................G...... 212 423-1040
  New York *(G-9860)*
Homegrown For Good LLC............F...... 857 540-6361
  New Rochelle *(G-8912)*
Nike Inc...E...... 212 226-5433
  New York *(G-11431)*
Nike Inc...E...... 631 242-3014
  Deer Park *(G-4181)*
Nike Inc...E...... 631 960-0184
  Islip Terrace *(G-6815)*
Skechers USA Inc.............................F...... 718 585-3024
  Bronx *(G-1456)*
Timing Group LLC............................F...... 646 878-2600
  New York *(G-12353)*
Wallico Shoes Corp..........................G...... 212 826-7171
  New York *(G-12583)*

SHOES: Plastic Soles Molded To Fabric Uppers
Steven Madden Retail Inc..............F...... 718 446-1800
  Long Island City *(G-7893)*

SHOES: Rubber Or Rubber Soled Fabric Uppers
Crocs Inc..F...... 212 362-1655
  New York *(G-9755)*
Crocs Inc..F...... 845 928-3002
  Central Valley *(G-3521)*

SHOES: Women's
Akh Group LLC..................................G...... 646 320-8720
  New York *(G-9066)*
Alpargatas Usa Inc...........................E...... 646 277-7171
  New York *(G-9098)*
Coach Inc..B...... 212 594-1850
  New York *(G-9656)*
Detny Footwear Inc...........................G...... 212 423-1040
  New York *(G-9860)*
Everlast Worldwide Inc....................E...... 212 239-0990
  New York *(G-10093)*
GH Bass & Co.....................................B...... 212 381-3900
  New York *(G-10290)*
Kenneth Cole Productions Inc.......B...... 212 265-1500
  New York *(G-10833)*
Lake View Manufacturing LLC.....F...... 315 364-7892
  King Ferry *(G-7168)*
Nicholas Kirkwood LLC..................G...... 646 559-5239
  New York *(G-11425)*
Nine West Footwear Corporation.....B...... 800 999-1877
  New York *(G-11435)*
Right Fit Shoes LLC.........................G...... 212 575-9445
  New York *(G-11872)*
SM New York..F...... 718 446-1800
  Long Island City *(G-7880)*
Steven Madden Ltd..........................D...... 718 446-1800
  New York *(G-12201)*
Steven Madden Ltd..........................B...... 718 446-1800
  Long Island City *(G-7892)*
Tic TAC Toes Mfg Corp...................D...... 518 773-8187
  Gloversville *(G-5726)*

SHOES: Women's, Dress
Attitudes Footwear Inc....................G...... 212 754-9113
  New York *(G-9260)*
Mango Usa Inc...................................E...... 718 998-6050
  Brooklyn *(G-2258)*

SHOES: Women's, Sandals
Neumann Jutta New York Inc........F...... 212 982-7048
  New York *(G-11376)*

SHOPPING CENTERS & MALLS

Northpoint Trading Inc ....F....... 212 481-8001
  New York *(G-11460)*
Premier Fixtures LLC ....D....... 631 236-4100
  Hauppauge *(G-6170)*

SHOT PEENING SVC

Metal Improvement Company LLC ....D....... 607 533-7000
  Lansing *(G-7349)*

SHOWCASES & DISPLAY FIXTURES: Office & Store

Aarco Products Inc ....F....... 631 924-5461
  Yaphank *(G-17384)*
Abbott Industries Inc ....E....... 718 291-0800
  Jamaica *(G-6891)*
Dejah Associates Inc ....E....... 631 265-2185
  Bay Shore *(G-694)*
Four S Showcase Manufacturing ....G....... 718 649-4900
  Brooklyn *(G-2001)*
Glaro Inc ....D....... 631 234-1717
  Hauppauge *(G-6085)*
Ledan Inc ....E....... 631 239-1226
  Northport *(G-13014)*
Manhattan Display Inc ....G....... 718 392-1365
  Long Island City *(G-7802)*
Mega Vision Inc ....G....... 718 228-1065
  Brooklyn *(G-2295)*
Steven Kraus Associates Inc ....G....... 631 923-2033
  Huntington *(G-6682)*
Visual Millwork & Fixture Mfg ....D....... 718 267-7800
  Woodside *(G-17361)*

SHOWER STALLS: Metal

CNA Specialties Inc ....G....... 631 567-7929
  Sayville *(G-15206)*
ITR Industries Inc ....E....... 914 964-7063
  Yonkers *(G-17456)*

SHOWER STALLS: Plastic & Fiberglass

ITR Industries Inc ....E....... 914 964-7063
  Yonkers *(G-17456)*

SHREDDERS: Indl & Commercial

Chester Shred-It/West ....E....... 914 347-4460
  Valhalla *(G-16365)*

SIDING & STRUCTURAL MATERIALS: Wood

Greater Niagara Bldg Ctr Inc ....F....... 716 299-0543
  Niagara Falls *(G-12827)*
Gutchess Lumber Co Inc ....C....... 607 753-3393
  Cortland *(G-4030)*
L J Valente Inc ....G....... 518 674-3750
  Averill Park *(G-535)*
Mohawk Metal Mfg & Sls ....G....... 315 853-7663
  Westmoreland *(G-17062)*
Tri-State Brick & Stone NY Inc ....D....... 212 366-0300
  New York *(G-12402)*
Upstate Increte Incorporated ....G....... 585 254-2010
  Rochester *(G-14747)*

SIDING MATERIALS

Texture Plus Inc ....E....... 631 218-9200
  Bohemia *(G-1143)*

SIGN LETTERING & PAINTING SVCS

Sign Shop Inc ....G....... 631 226-4145
  Copiague *(G-3928)*

SIGN PAINTING & LETTERING SHOP

Clinton Signs Inc ....G....... 585 482-1620
  Webster *(G-16719)*
Lanza Corp ....G....... 914 937-6360
  Port Chester *(G-13751)*
Paratore Signs Inc ....G....... 315 455-5551
  Syracuse *(G-16010)*
Ray Sign Inc ....F....... 518 377-1371
  Schenectady *(G-15289)*
Santoro Signs Inc ....G....... 716 895-8875
  Buffalo *(G-3176)*
Ter-El Engraving Co Inc ....G....... 315 455-5597
  Syracuse *(G-16056)*

SIGNALING APPARATUS: Electric

Intelligent Traffic Systems ....G....... 631 567-5994
  Bohemia *(G-1078)*
L-3 Cmmnctns Fgn Holdings Inc ....E....... 212 697-1111
  New York *(G-10903)*
L-3 Cmmunications Holdings Inc .....D....... 212 697-1111
  New York *(G-10905)*
L-3 Communications Corporation .....B....... 212 697-1111
  New York *(G-10906)*
North Hills Signal Proc Corp ....F....... 516 682-7740
  Syosset *(G-15834)*
Werma (usa) Inc ....G....... 315 414-0200
  East Syracuse *(G-4580)*

SIGNALING DEVICES: Sound, Electrical

Sensor Films Incorporated ....E....... 585 738-3500
  Victor *(G-16501)*

SIGNALS: Railroad, Electric

Alstom Signaling Inc ....B....... 585 783-2000
  Schenectady *(G-15228)*
Alstom Signaling Inc ....G....... 585 274-8700
  Schenectady *(G-15229)*
Star Headlight Lantern Co Inc ....C....... 585 226-9500
  Avon *(G-543)*
Twinco Mfg Co Inc ....E....... 631 231-0022
  Hauppauge *(G-6219)*

SIGNALS: Traffic Control, Electric

Apex Signal Corporation ....D....... 631 567-1100
  Bohemia *(G-1017)*
Comet Flasher Inc ....G....... 716 821-9595
  Buffalo *(G-2881)*
General Traffic Equipment Corp ....F....... 845 569-9000
  Newburgh *(G-12758)*
Power Line Constructors Inc ....E....... 315 853-6183
  Clinton *(G-3721)*

SIGNALS: Transportation

Alstom Transportation Inc ....G....... 800 717-4477
  West Henrietta *(G-16866)*

SIGNS & ADVERTISING SPECIALTIES

A B C Mc Cleary Sign Co Inc ....F....... 315 493-3550
  Carthage *(G-3407)*
A M S Sign Designs ....G....... 631 467-7722
  Centereach *(G-3469)*
Aakron Rule Corp ....C....... 716 542-5483
  Akron *(G-19)*
ABC Windows and Signs Corp ....F....... 718 353-6210
  College Point *(G-3775)*
Accurate Signs & Awnings Inc ....F....... 718 788-0302
  Brooklyn *(G-1553)*
Acme Signs of Baldwinsville ....G....... 315 638-4865
  Baldwinsville *(G-564)*
Ad Makers Long Island Inc ....F....... 631 595-9100
  Deer Park *(G-4087)*
Adirondack Sign Perfect Inc ....G....... 518 409-7446
  Saratoga Springs *(G-15141)*
All Signs ....G....... 973 736-2113
  Staten Island *(G-15635)*
All Star Awnings & Signs ....F....... 516 742-8469
  Mineola *(G-8492)*
Alley Cat Signs Inc ....F....... 631 924-7446
  Middle Island *(G-8406)*
Allied Decorations Co Inc ....F....... 315 637-0273
  Syracuse *(G-15849)*
American Car Signs Inc ....G....... 518 227-1173
  Duanesburg *(G-4324)*
Architectural Sign Group Inc ....F....... 516 326-1800
  Elmont *(G-4716)*
Artscroll Printing Corp ....E....... 212 929-2413
  New York *(G-9224)*
Asi Sign Systems Inc ....G....... 646 742-1320
  New York *(G-9230)*
Asi Sign Systems Inc ....G....... 716 775-0104
  Grand Island *(G-5751)*
Atlantic Steinway Awng II LLC ....G....... 718 729-2965
  Long Island City *(G-7677)*
Atomic Signworks ....G....... 315 779-7446
  Watertown *(G-16635)*
B Barine Inc ....E....... 718 499-5650
  Brooklyn *(G-1657)*
Bedford Precision Parts Corp ....E....... 914 241-2211
  Bedford Hills *(G-799)*
Bmg Printing and Promotion LLC ....G....... 631 231-9200
  Bohemia *(G-1026)*

Buckeye Corrugated Inc ....D....... 585 924-1600
  Victor *(G-16465)*
Bulow & Associates Inc ....G....... 716 838-0298
  Tonawanda *(G-16150)*
Cab Signs Inc ....E....... 718 479-2424
  Brooklyn *(G-1745)*
Central Rede Sign Co Inc ....G....... 716 213-0797
  Tonawanda *(G-16151)*
Chautauqua Sign Co Inc ....G....... 716 665-2222
  Falconer *(G-4893)*
City Signs Inc ....G....... 718 375-5933
  Brooklyn *(G-1784)*
Climax Packaging Inc ....C....... 315 376-8000
  Lowville *(G-7935)*
Coe Displays Inc ....G....... 718 937-5658
  Long Island City *(G-7702)*
Colad Group LLC ....G....... 716 961-1776
  Buffalo *(G-2880)*
Colonial Redi Record Corp ....E....... 716 972-7433
  Brooklyn *(G-1791)*
Community Products LLC ....E....... 845 658-8351
  Rifton *(G-14133)*
Crown Sign Systems Inc ....F....... 914 375-2118
  Yonkers *(G-17433)*
Custom Display Manufacture ....G....... 516 783-6491
  North Bellmore *(G-12920)*
Decree Signs & Graphics Inc ....F....... 973 278-3603
  Floral Park *(G-5202)*
Design A Sign of Putnam Inc ....G....... 845 279-5328
  Brewster *(G-1216)*
Designplex LLC ....G....... 845 358-6647
  Nyack *(G-13048)*
Display Producers Inc ....C....... 718 904-1200
  New Rochelle *(G-8895)*
Displays & Beyond Inc ....F....... 718 805-7786
  Glendale *(G-5651)*
East End Sign Design Inc ....G....... 631 399-2574
  Mastic *(G-8202)*
Eastern Concepts Ltd ....F....... 718 472-3377
  Sunnyside *(G-15807)*
Eastern Metal of Elmira Inc ....D....... 607 734-2295
  Elmira *(G-4679)*
Elderlee Incorporated ....C....... 315 789-6670
  Oaks Corners *(G-13069)*
Elite Signs Inc ....G....... 718 993-7342
  Pomona *(G-13730)*
Executive Sign Corp ....G....... 212 397-4050
  Cornwall On Hudson *(G-3992)*
Exhibit Corporation America ....E....... 718 937-2600
  Long Island City *(G-7734)*
Fastsigns ....F....... 518 456-7446
  Albany *(G-79)*
Flado Enterprises Inc ....G....... 716 668-6400
  Depew *(G-4258)*
Flair Display Inc ....D....... 718 324-9330
  Bronx *(G-1333)*
Fletcher Enterprises Inc ....G....... 716 837-7446
  Tonawanda *(G-16163)*
Forrest Engraving Co Inc ....F....... 845 228-0200
  New Rochelle *(G-8901)*
Fortune Sign ....G....... 646 383-8682
  Brooklyn *(G-1997)*
Fossil Industries Inc ....E....... 631 254-9200
  Deer Park *(G-4145)*
G I Certified Inc ....G....... 212 397-1945
  New York *(G-10230)*
Graphic Signs & Awnings Ltd ....G....... 718 227-6000
  Staten Island *(G-15681)*
Graphitek Inc ....F....... 518 686-5966
  Hoosick Falls *(G-6539)*
Greyline Signs Inc ....G....... 716 947-4526
  Derby *(G-4283)*
Hl Tech Signs of NY Inc ....G....... 516 794-7880
  East Meadow *(G-4424)*
Hollywood Signs Inc ....G....... 917 577-7333
  Brooklyn *(G-2083)*
ID Signsystems Inc ....E....... 585 266-5750
  Rochester *(G-14442)*
Ideal Signs Inc ....G....... 718 292-9196
  Bronx *(G-1359)*
Image360 ....G....... 585 272-1234
  Rochester *(G-14446)*
Impressive Imprints Inc ....G....... 631 293-6161
  Farmingdale *(G-5010)*
International Bronze Manufac ....F....... 516 248-3080
  Albertson *(G-155)*
International Patterns Inc ....D....... 631 952-2000
  Plainview *(G-13609)*
Jaf Converters Inc ....E....... 631 842-3131
  Copiague *(G-3908)*

(G-0000) Company's Geographic Section entry number

Jal Signs Inc .... F 516 536-7280
Baldwin *(G-559)*
Jax Signs and Neon Inc .... G 607 727-3420
Endicott *(G-4815)*
Jay Turoff .... F 718 856-7300
Brooklyn *(G-2136)*
Jem Sign Corp .... G 516 867-4466
Hempstead *(G-6275)*
JP Signs .... G 518 569-3907
Chazy *(G-3562)*
Kenan International Trading .... G 718 672-4922
Corona *(G-4000)*
Knr Fragrances & Cosmetics Inc .... F 631 586-8500
Edgewood *(G-4605)*
KP Industries Inc .... F 516 679-3161
North Bellmore *(G-12922)*
Kraus & Sons Inc .... F 212 620-0408
New York *(G-10887)*
L I C Screen Printing Inc .... E 516 546-7289
Merrick *(G-8387)*
L Miller Design Inc .... G 631 242-1163
Deer Park *(G-4162)*
L Y Z Creations Ltd Inc .... E 718 768-2977
Brooklyn *(G-2187)*
Lanco Corporation .... C 631 231-2300
Ronkonkoma *(G-14929)*
Lanza Corp .... G 914 937-6360
Port Chester *(G-13751)*
Letterama Inc .... G 516 349-0800
West Babylon *(G-16807)*
Lifestyle-Trimco .... E 718 257-9101
Brooklyn *(G-2219)*
Linear Signs Inc .... F 631 532-5330
Lindenhurst *(G-7468)*
M Santoliquido Corp .... F 914 375-6674
Yonkers *(G-17463)*
Marigold Signs Inc .... F 516 433-7446
Hicksville *(G-6369)*
Maxworld Inc .... G 212 242-7588
New York *(G-11189)*
Mekanism Inc .... E 212 226-2772
New York *(G-11221)*
Metropolitan Sign & Riggin .... G 718 231-0010
Bronx *(G-1395)*
Metropolitan Signs Inc .... G 315 638-1448
Baldwinsville *(G-572)*
Midwood Signs & Design Inc .... G 718 499-9041
Brooklyn *(G-2312)*
Millennium Signs & Display Inc .... E 516 292-8000
Hempstead *(G-6280)*
Miller Mohr Display Inc .... G 631 941-2769
East Setauket *(G-4487)*
Mixture Screen Printing .... G 845 561-2857
Newburgh *(G-12767)*
Modulex New York Inc .... G 646 742-1320
New York *(G-11290)*
Monasani Signs Inc .... G 631 266-2635
East Northport *(G-4442)*
Morris Brothers Sign Svc Inc .... G 212 675-9130
New York *(G-11306)*
Movinads & Signs LLC .... G 518 378-3000
Halfmoon *(G-5913)*
Mr Sign Usa Inc .... F 718 218-3321
Brooklyn *(G-2340)*
Nameplate Mfrs of Amer .... E 631 752-0055
Farmingdale *(G-5061)*
New Art Signs Co Inc .... G 718 443-0900
Glen Head *(G-5637)*
New Dimensions Research Corp .... C 631 694-1356
Melville *(G-8340)*
New Kit On The Block .... G 631 757-5655
Bohemia *(G-1109)*
Noel Assoc .... G 516 371-5420
Inwood *(G-6764)*
Norampac New York City Inc .... C 718 340-2100
Maspeth *(G-8158)*
North Shore Neon Sign Co Inc .... E 718 937-4848
Flushing *(G-5275)*
Northeastern Sign Corp .... G 315 265-6657
South Colton *(G-15516)*
Northern Awning & Sign Company .... G 315 782-8515
Watertown *(G-16667)*
Nysco Products LLC .... D 718 792-9000
Bronx *(G-1415)*
On The Mark Digital Printing & .... G 716 823-3373
Hamburg *(G-5935)*
Orlandi Inc .... D 631 756-0110
Farmingdale *(G-5071)*
Orlandi Inc .... E 631 756-0110
Farmingdale *(G-5072)*
Penn Signs Inc .... E 718 797-1112
Brooklyn *(G-2414)*
Precision Signscom Inc .... D 631 842-5060
Amityville *(G-323)*
Premier Sign Systems LLC .... E 585 235-0390
Rochester *(G-14598)*
Promotional Development Inc .... D 718 485-8550
Brooklyn *(G-2455)*
Qcr Express Corp .... G 888 924-5888
Astoria *(G-453)*
Quick Sign F X .... F 516 249-6531
Farmingdale *(G-5094)*
Resonant Legal Media LLC .... D 800 781-3591
New York *(G-11841)*
Rgm Signs Inc .... G 718 442-0598
Staten Island *(G-15732)*
Riverwood Sgns By Dndev Dsigns .... G 845 229-0282
Hyde Park *(G-6737)*
Rosenwach Tank Co Inc .... F 718 274-3250
Long Island City *(G-7867)*
Royal Promotion Group Inc .... D 212 246-3780
New York *(G-11927)*
Rpf Associates Inc .... G 631 462-7446
Commack *(G-3841)*
Rsquared Ny Inc .... D 631 521-8700
Edgewood *(G-4609)*
Santoro Signs Inc .... G 716 895-8875
Buffalo *(G-3176)*
Saxton Corporation .... E 518 732-7705
Castleton On Hudson *(G-3420)*
Sellco Industries Inc .... E 607 756-7594
Cortland *(G-4045)*
Seneca Signs LLC .... G 315 446-9420
Syracuse *(G-16038)*
Sign & Signs .... G 718 941-6200
Brooklyn *(G-2552)*
Sign A Rama Inc .... G 631 952-3324
Hauppauge *(G-6190)*
Sign A Rama of Syracuse .... G 315 446-9420
Syracuse *(G-16041)*
Sign Company .... G 212 967-2113
New York *(G-12069)*
Sign Design Group New York Inc .... F 718 392-0779
Long Island City *(G-7876)*
Sign Expo Enterprises .... F 212 925-8585
New York *(G-12070)*
Sign Group Inc .... E 718 438-7103
Brooklyn *(G-2553)*
Sign Guys LLC .... G 315 253-4276
Auburn *(G-518)*
Sign Here Enterprises LLC .... G 914 328-3111
Hartsdale *(G-6000)*
Sign Studio Inc .... F 518 266-0877
Troy *(G-16254)*
Sign Up Now Inc .... G 516 221-3394
Bellmore *(G-822)*
Sign Works Incorporated .... E 914 592-0700
Elmsford *(G-4784)*
Sign World Inc .... E 212 619-9000
Brooklyn *(G-2554)*
Signature Industries Inc .... F 516 679-5177
Freeport *(G-5427)*
Signs Inc .... G 518 483-4759
Malone *(G-8017)*
Signs Ink Ltd .... F 914 739-9059
Yorktown Heights *(G-17520)*
Signs of Success Ltd .... E 516 295-6000
Lynbrook *(G-7961)*
Smith Graphics Inc .... G 631 420-4180
Farmingdale *(G-5110)*
Snyders Neon Displays Inc .... G 518 857-4100
Colonie *(G-3821)*
Space Sign .... F 718 961-1112
College Point *(G-3808)*
Spanjer Corp .... G 347 448-8033
Long Island City *(G-7881)*
Specialty Signs Co Inc .... F 212 243-8521
New York *(G-12153)*
Spectrum On Broadway .... F 718 932-5388
Woodside *(G-17354)*
Speedy Sign A Rama USA Inc .... G 516 783-1075
Bellmore *(G-823)*
Starlite Media LLC .... G 212 909-7700
New York *(G-12186)*
Stepping Stones One Day Signs .... G 518 237-5774
Waterford *(G-16622)*
Strategic Signage Sourcing LLC .... F 518 450-1093
Saratoga Springs *(G-15174)*
Tech Products Inc .... E 718 442-4900
Staten Island *(G-15748)*
Three Gems Inc .... G 516 248-0388
New Hyde Park *(G-8866)*
Timely Signs of Kingston Inc .... F 845 331-8710
Kingston *(G-7215)*
Todd Walbridge .... G 585 254-3018
Rochester *(G-14727)*
Tru-Art Sign Co Inc .... F 718 658-5068
Jamaica *(G-6959)*
Ultimate Signs & Designs Inc .... E 516 481-0800
Hempstead *(G-6288)*
United Sttes Brnze Sign of Fla .... E 516 352-5155
New Hyde Park *(G-8870)*
Universal Signs and Svc Inc .... E 631 446-1121
Deer Park *(G-4220)*
USA Signs of America Inc .... D 631 254-6900
Deer Park *(G-4221)*
Valle Signs and Awnings .... F 516 408-3440
Uniondale *(G-16301)*
Valley Creek Side Inc .... G 315 839-5526
Clayville *(G-3690)*
Vez Inc .... G 718 273-7002
Staten Island *(G-15752)*
Viana Signs Corp .... F 516 887-2000
Oceanside *(G-13104)*
Victory Signs Inc .... G 315 762-0220
Canastota *(G-3376)*
Visual ID Source Inc .... F 516 307-9759
Mineola *(G-8538)*
Visual Impact Graphics Inc .... G 585 548-7118
Batavia *(G-652)*
Vital Signs & Graphics Co Inc .... G 518 237-8372
Cohoes *(G-3760)*
Voss Signs LLC .... E 315 682-6418
Manlius *(G-8076)*
Wedel Sign Company Inc .... G 631 727-4577
Riverhead *(G-14159)*
Westchester Signs Inc .... G 914 666-7446
Mount Kisco *(G-8646)*
Wizard Equipment Inc .... G 315 414-9999
Syracuse *(G-16073)*
Wl Concepts & Production Inc .... G 516 538-5300
Freeport *(G-5434)*
Woodbury Printing Plus + Inc .... G 845 928-6610
Central Valley *(G-3529)*
X-Press Signs Inc .... G 716 677-0880
West Seneca *(G-16955)*
Yellowpagecitycom .... F 585 410-6688
Rochester *(G-14773)*
Yong Xin Kitchen Supplies Inc .... F 212 995-8908
New York *(G-12696)*
Z-Car-D Corp .... E 631 424-2077
Huntington Station *(G-6730)*

SIGNS & ADVERTISING SPECIALTIES: Artwork, Advertising

Adstream America LLC .... F 845 496-8283
New York *(G-9032)*
Liberty Awnings & Signs Inc .... G 347 203-1470
East Elmhurst *(G-4394)*
National Prfmce Solutions Inc .... D 718 833-4767
Brooklyn *(G-2351)*
Pyx Inc .... G 718 469-4253
Brooklyn *(G-2460)*
Rocket Fuel Inc .... B 212 594-8888
New York *(G-11898)*
United Print Group Inc .... F 718 392-4242
Long Island City *(G-7908)*
Whispr Group Inc .... F 212 924-3979
Brooklyn *(G-2747)*

SIGNS & ADVERTISING SPECIALTIES: Displays, Paint Process

Chameleon Color Cards Ltd .... D 716 625-9452
Lockport *(G-7576)*
Faster-Form Corp .... D 800 327-3676
New Hartford *(G-8804)*
Mechtronics Corporation .... E 845 231-1400
Beacon *(G-786)*
Mechtronics Corporation .... E 845 831-9300
Beacon *(G-787)*
Props Displays & Interiors .... F 212 620-3840
New York *(G-11737)*

SIGNS & ADVERTISING SPECIALTIES: Novelties

Amsterdam Printing & Litho Inc .... F 518 842-6000
Amsterdam *(G-332)*

Employee Codes: A=Over 500 employees, B=251-500
C=101-250, D=51-100, E=20-50, F=10-19, G=5-9
2017 Harris
New York Manufacturers Directory
1337

SIGNS & ADVERTISING SPECIALTIES: Novelties

Amsterdam Printing & Litho Inc .... E 518 842-6000
  Amsterdam *(G-333)*
Dkm Sales LLC .... E 716 893-7777
  Buffalo *(G-2916)*
Jomar Industries Inc .... E 845 357-5773
  Airmont *(G-16)*
Keep America Beautiful Inc .... G 518 842-4388
  Amsterdam *(G-354)*
Kling Magnetics Inc .... E 518 392-4000
  Chatham *(G-3558)*
Mastercraft Manufacturing Co .... G 718 729-5620
  Long Island City *(G-7805)*
National Advertising & Prtg .... G 212 629-7650
  New York *(G-11346)*
Northeast Promotional Group In .... G 518 793-1024
  South Glens Falls *(G-15527)*
Pama Enterprises Inc .... G 516 504-6300
  Great Neck *(G-5828)*
Tempo Industries Inc .... G 516 334-6900
  Westbury *(G-17031)*
Von Pok & Chang New York Inc .... G 212 599-0556
  New York *(G-12568)*

SIGNS & ADVERTISING SPECIALTIES: Scoreboards, Electric

Eversan Inc .... F 315 736-3967
  Whitesboro *(G-17193)*

SIGNS & ADVERTISING SPECIALTIES: Signs

Allstate Sign & Plaque Corp .... F 631 242-2828
  Deer Park *(G-4093)*
Art Parts Signs Inc .... G 585 381-2134
  East Rochester *(G-4453)*
Big Apple Sign Corp .... E 631 342-0303
  Islandia *(G-6788)*
Big Apple Sign Corp .... E 212 629-3650
  New York *(G-9392)*
Checklist Boards Corporation .... G 585 586-0152
  Rochester *(G-14273)*
Dura Engraving Corporation .... E 718 706-6400
  Long Island City *(G-7719)*
Executive Sign Corporation .... G 212 397-4050
  New York *(G-10106)*
Hanson Sign & Screen Process .... E 716 484-8564
  Falconer *(G-4901)*
Hermosa Corp .... E 315 768-4320
  New York Mills *(G-12725)*
Mauceri Sign Inc .... F 718 656-7700
  Jamaica *(G-6929)*
Mohawk Sign Systems Inc .... E 518 842-5303
  Amsterdam *(G-360)*
Nas Quick Sign Inc .... G 716 876-7599
  Buffalo *(G-3081)*
Poncio Signs .... G 718 543-4851
  Bronx *(G-1430)*
Quorum Group LLC .... D 585 798-8888
  Medina *(G-8279)*
Rapp Signs Inc .... F 607 656-8167
  Greene *(G-5867)*
Rome Sign & Display Co .... G 315 336-0550
  Rome *(G-14833)*
Sign Center Inc .... F 212 967-2113
  New York *(G-12068)*
Sign Impressions Inc .... G 585 723-0420
  Rochester *(G-14685)*
Sign Language Inc .... G 585 237-2620
  Perry *(G-13526)*
Suma Industries Inc .... G 646 436-5202
  New York *(G-12230)*
Universal 3d Innovation Inc .... F 516 837-9423
  Valley Stream *(G-16431)*

SIGNS & ADVERTSG SPECIALTIES: Displays/Cutouts Window/Lobby

American Visuals Inc .... G 631 694-6104
  Farmingdale *(G-4941)*
Azar International Inc .... E 845 624-8808
  Nanuet *(G-8751)*
Bridgewater Mdsg Concepts .... F 718 383-5500
  Brooklyn *(G-1716)*
Creative Solutions Group Inc .... B 914 771-4200
  Yonkers *(G-17432)*
Crown Industries Inc .... E 973 672-2277
  New York *(G-9759)*
Display Marketing Group Inc .... E 631 348-4450
  Islandia *(G-6791)*
Display Presentations Ltd .... D 631 951-4050
  Hauppauge *(G-6065)*

DSI Group Inc .... C 800 553-2202
  Maspeth *(G-8132)*
Edge Display Group Entp Inc .... F 631 498-1373
  Bellport *(G-830)*
Hadley Exhibits Inc .... D 716 874-3666
  Buffalo *(G-2985)*
Joseph Struhl Co Inc .... F 516 741-3660
  New Hyde Park *(G-8843)*
King Displays Inc .... F 212 629-8455
  New York *(G-10853)*
Lamar Plastics Packaging Ltd .... D 516 378-2500
  Freeport *(G-5408)*
Mystic Display Co Inc .... F 718 485-2651
  Brooklyn *(G-2345)*
Nationwide Exhibitor Svcs Inc .... F 631 467-2034
  Central Islip *(G-3505)*
New Style Signs Limited Inc .... F 212 242-7848
  New York *(G-11393)*
Newline Products Inc .... E 972 881-3318
  New Windsor *(G-8946)*
Plasti-Vue Corp .... F 718 463-2300
  Flushing *(G-5282)*
Platinum Sales Promotion Inc .... G 718 361-0200
  Long Island City *(G-7844)*
Polyplastic Forms Inc .... F 631 249-5011
  Farmingdale *(G-5083)*
R & J Displays Inc .... F 631 491-3500
  West Babylon *(G-16820)*
Signs & Decal Corp .... E 718 486-6400
  Brooklyn *(G-2555)*
Steel-Brite Ltd .... F 631 589-4044
  Oakdale *(G-13063)*
Timely Signs Inc .... F 516 285-5339
  Elmont *(G-4730)*
Unique Display Mfg Corp .... F 516 546-3800
  Freeport *(G-5433)*
Visual Citi Inc .... C 631 482-3030
  Lindenhurst *(G-7495)*

SIGNS, EXC ELECTRIC, WHOLESALE

Fedex Office & Print Svcs Inc .... G 718 982-5223
  Staten Island *(G-15673)*
Mixture Screen Printing .... G 845 561-2857
  Newburgh *(G-12767)*

SIGNS: Electrical

Artkraft Strauss LLC .... E 212 265-5155
  New York *(G-9222)*
Clinton Signs Inc .... G 585 482-1620
  Webster *(G-16719)*
Flexlume Sign Corporation .... G 716 884-2020
  Buffalo *(G-2950)*
Gloede Neon Signs Ltd Inc .... F 845 471-4366
  Poughkeepsie *(G-13902)*
Motion Message Inc .... F 631 924-9500
  Manorville *(G-8079)*
Olson Sign Company Inc .... G 518 370-2118
  Schenectady *(G-15284)*
Ray Sign Inc .... F 518 377-1371
  Schenectady *(G-15289)*
Spectrum Signs Inc .... E 631 756-1010
  Woodside *(G-17355)*
T J Signs Unlimited LLC .... E 631 273-4800
  Islip *(G-6813)*
Trans-Lux Corporation .... D 800 243-5544
  New York *(G-12392)*
Visual Effects Inc .... F 718 324-0011
  Jamaica *(G-6962)*

SIGNS: Neon

Broadway Neon Sign Corp .... F 908 241-4177
  Ronkonkoma *(G-14881)*
Frank Torrone & Sons Inc .... F 718 273-7600
  Staten Island *(G-15674)*
K & B Stamping Co Inc .... G 914 664-8555
  Mount Vernon *(G-8696)*
Manhattan Neon Sign Corp .... F 212 714-0430
  New York *(G-11131)*
Mds USA Inc .... F 718 358-5588
  Flushing *(G-5269)*
Super Neon Light Co Inc .... F 718 236-5667
  Brooklyn *(G-2624)*
Turoff Tower Graphics Inc .... F 718 856-7300
  Brooklyn *(G-2688)*
Ulrich Sign Co Inc .... E 716 434-0167
  Lockport *(G-7623)*
Yost Neon Displays Inc .... F 716 674-6780
  West Seneca *(G-16956)*

SILICA MINING

American Minerals Inc .... F 646 747-4222
  New York *(G-9125)*
St Silicones Inc .... G 518 664-0745
  Mechanicville *(G-8231)*

SILICON & CHROMIUM

Medima LLC .... C 716 741-0400
  Clarence *(G-3666)*

SILICON WAFERS: Chemically Doped

Isonics Corporation .... G 212 356-7400
  New York *(G-10668)*

SILICONE RESINS

George M Dujack .... G 518 279-1303
  Troy *(G-16236)*
Meliorum Technologies Inc .... G 585 313-0616
  Rochester *(G-14503)*
Pawling Corporation .... C 845 855-1000
  Pawling *(G-13451)*

SILICONES

Crown Delta Corporation .... E 914 245-8910
  Yorktown Heights *(G-17510)*
Momentive Performance Mtls Inc .... A 614 986-2495
  Waterford *(G-16615)*
Momentive Performance Mtls Inc .... E 518 237-3330
  Waterford *(G-16616)*
Momentive Prfmce Mtls Holdings .... A 518 533-4600
  Albany *(G-102)*
Mpm Holdings Inc .... E 518 237-3330
  Waterford *(G-16617)*
Mpm Intermediate Holdings Inc .... E 518 237-3330
  Waterford *(G-16618)*
Mpm Silicones LLC .... A 518 233-3330
  Waterford *(G-16619)*
Specialty Silicone Pdts Inc .... E 518 885-8826
  Ballston Spa *(G-609)*

SILK SCREEN DESIGN SVCS

Buffalo Circuits Inc .... G 716 662-2113
  Orchard Park *(G-13256)*
Gildan Apparel USA Inc .... G 716 759-6273
  Clarence *(G-3662)*
Mainly Monograms Inc .... E 845 624-4923
  West Nyack *(G-16921)*

SILVER ORES

Global Gold Corporation .... F 914 925-0020
  Rye *(G-15058)*

SILVER ORES PROCESSING

Rochester Silver Works LLC .... E 585 477-9501
  Rochester *(G-14647)*

SILVERSMITHS

D W Haber & Son Inc .... E 718 993-6405
  Bronx *(G-1308)*
Denvin Inc .... E 718 232-3389
  Brooklyn *(G-1855)*
R Goldsmith .... F 718 239-1396
  Bronx *(G-1439)*
Swed Masters Workshop LLC .... F 212 644-8822
  New York *(G-12252)*

SILVERWARE

Studio Silversmiths Inc .... E 718 418-6785
  Ridgewood *(G-14125)*

SILVERWARE & PLATED WARE

Oneida International Inc .... G 315 361-3000
  Oneida *(G-13160)*
Oneida Silversmiths Inc .... G 315 361-3000
  Oneida *(G-13164)*

SILVERWARE, SILVER PLATED

Sherrill Manufacturing Inc .... C 315 280-0727
  Sherrill *(G-15407)*

PRODUCT SECTION

SIMULATORS: Flight
BSC Associates LLC ....F....... 607 321-2980
  Binghamton (G-899)
Northrop Grumman Intl Trdg Inc ....G....... 716 626-7233
  Buffalo (G-3096)

SKIN CARE PRDTS: Suntan Lotions & Oils
Doctor Bronze Solar Potions ....E....... 516 775-4974
  Elmont (G-4718)
St Tropez Inc...G....... 800 366-6383
  New York (G-12180)

SKYLIGHTS
Citros Building Materials Co ....E....... 718 779-0727
  East Elmhurst (G-4390)
Gottlieb Schwartz Family ....E....... 718 761-2010
  Staten Island (G-15679)

SLAB & TILE: Precast Concrete, Floor
Duranm Inc ....G....... 914 774-3367
  Cortlandt Manor (G-4049)
Rain Catchers Seamless Gutters ....G....... 516 520-1956
  Bethpage (G-878)

SLABS: Steel
Safespan Platform Systems Inc ....E....... 716 694-1100
  Tonawanda (G-16198)

SLATE PRDTS
Evergreen Slate Company Inc ....D....... 518 642-2530
  Middle Granville (G-8398)
North American Slate Inc ....G....... 518 642-1702
  Granville (G-5778)
Northeast Solite Corporation..................E....... 845 246-2177
  Mount Marion (G-8652)
Sheldon Slate Products Co Inc ....E....... 518 642-1280
  Middle Granville (G-8401)
Vermont Natural Stoneworks ....E....... 518 642-2460
  Middle Granville (G-8403)

SLATE: Dimension
Hadeka Stone Corp.................................G....... 518 282-9605
  Hampton (G-5959)
Hilltop Slate Inc ....E....... 518 642-1453
  Middle Granville (G-8399)
Vermont Multicolor Slate ....G....... 518 642-2400
  Middle Granville (G-8402)

SLINGS: Rope
All-Lifts Incorporated..............................E....... 518 465-3461
  Albany (G-44)

SLIPPERS: House
RG Barry Corporation.............................F....... 212 244-3145
  New York (G-11856)

SMOKE DETECTORS
Fuel Watchman Sales & Service............F....... 718 665-6100
  Bronx (G-1338)
Nrd LLC ....E....... 716 773-7634
  Grand Island (G-5764)

SOAPS & DETERGENTS
Aura Detergent LLC ....F....... 718 824-2162
  Bronx (G-1278)
Baums Castorine Company Inc ....G....... 315 336-8154
  Rome (G-14805)
Chemite Inc..G....... 607 529-3218
  Waverly (G-16700)
Colgate-Palmolive Company ....A....... 212 310-2000
  New York (G-9667)
Colgate-Palmolive Nj Inc ....E....... 212 310-2000
  New York (G-9669)
Combe Incorporated ....C....... 914 694-5454
  White Plains (G-17095)
Cosco Enterprises Inc ....G....... 718 383-4488
  Ridgewood (G-14104)
Cpac Inc ....E....... 585 382-3223
  Leicester (G-7420)
Crosstex International Inc......................D....... 631 582-6777
  Hauppauge (G-6058)
Ecolab Inc ....F....... 716 683-6298
  Cheektowaga (G-3569)
Enviro Service & Supply Corp ....F....... 347 838-6500
  Staten Island (G-15671)
Gfl USA Inc ....G....... 917 297-8701
  Brooklyn (G-2022)
Greenmaker Industries LLC..................F....... 866 684-7800
  Farmingdale (G-5002)
H & H Laboratories Inc ....F....... 718 624-8041
  Brooklyn (G-2057)
H & H Laboratories Inc ....G....... 718 624-8041
  Brooklyn (G-2058)
Jayen Chemical Supplies Inc ....G....... 516 933-3311
  Plainview (G-13611)
Medtech Products Inc ....F....... 914 524-6810
  Tarrytown (G-16096)
Monroe Fluid Technology Inc ....E....... 585 392-3434
  Hilton (G-6418)
Prestige Brands Holdings Inc................D....... 914 524-6800
  Tarrytown (G-16101)
Pro-Line Solutions Inc ....G....... 914 664-0002
  Mount Vernon (G-8719)
Robert Racine..E....... 518 677-0224
  Cambridge (G-3309)
Sabon Management LLC ....F....... 212 982-0968
  New York (G-11951)
Sunfeather Natural Soap Co Inc ....G....... 315 265-1776
  Potsdam (G-13885)

SOAPS & DETERGENTS: Textile
T S Pink Corp ....F....... 607 432-1100
  Oneonta (G-13194)

SOCIAL SERVICES INFORMATION EXCHANGE
Human Life Foundation Inc....................G....... 212 685-5210
  New York (G-10529)

SOCIAL SVCS, HANDICAPPED
Choice Magazine Listening Inc..............G....... 516 883-8280
  Port Washington (G-13805)

SOCIAL SVCS: Individual & Family
Maramont Corporation ....B....... 718 439-8900
  Brooklyn (G-2265)
Suffolk Community Council Inc.............G....... 631 434-9277
  Deer Park (G-4214)

SOFT DRINKS WHOLESALERS
Load/N/Go Beverage Corp ....F....... 585 218-4019
  Rochester (G-14481)
Save More Beverage Corp ....G....... 518 371-2520
  Halfmoon (G-5916)

SOFTWARE PUBLISHERS: Application
Advanced Comfort Systems Inc ....F....... 518 884-8444
  Ballston Spa (G-589)
Amcom Software Inc ....G....... 212 951-7600
  New York (G-9110)
Anbeck Inc..G....... 518 907-0308
  White Plains (G-17078)
Appboy Inc...F....... 504 327-7269
  New York (G-9180)
Astria Solutions Group LLC ....E....... 518 346-7799
  Schenectady (G-15231)
Autodesk Inc..F....... 646 613-8680
  New York (G-9266)
Automated & MGT Solutions LLC ....G....... 518 283-5352
  East Greenbush (G-4401)
Big White Wall Holding Inc ....F....... 917 281-2649
  New York (G-9395)
Bull Street LLC.......................................G....... 212 495-9855
  New York (G-9478)
C S I G Inc ....G....... 845 383-3800
  Kingston (G-7181)
Callaway Digital Arts Inc ....E....... 212 675-3050
  New York (G-9503)
Capital Programs Inc.............................G....... 212 842-4640
  New York (G-9520)
Catalyst Group Inc ....G....... 212 243-7777
  New York (G-9545)
Catch Ventures Inc................................F....... 347 620-4351
  New York (G-9547)
Cbord Group Inc ....C....... 607 257-2410
  Ithaca (G-6831)
Cellufun Inc ....E....... 212 385-2255
  New York (G-9555)
Cloud Rock Group LLC ....G....... 516 967-6023
  Roslyn (G-15017)

SOFTWARE PUBLISHERS: Application

Contactive Inc ....E....... 646 476-9059
  New York (G-9709)
Customshow Inc ....G....... 800 255-5303
  New York (G-9773)
Dbase LLC ....G....... 607 729-0234
  Binghamton (G-907)
Do It Different Inc..................................G....... 917 842-0230
  New York (G-9893)
Document Strategies LLC ....F....... 585 506-9000
  Rochester (G-14315)
Dwnld Inc ....E....... 484 483-6572
  New York (G-9944)
Eft Energy Inc..G....... 212 290-2300
  New York (G-9987)
Elepath Inc...G....... 347 417-4975
  Brooklyn (G-1914)
Empire Innovation Group LLC...............F....... 716 852-5000
  Buffalo (G-2937)
Exchange My Mail Inc ....F....... 516 605-1835
  Jericho (G-7068)
Express Checkout LLC ....G....... 646 512-2068
  New York (G-10110)
Freshop Inc..F....... 585 738-6035
  Rochester (G-14383)
Galaxy Software LLC ....G....... 631 244-8405
  Oakdale (G-13058)
Ghostery Inc ....G....... 917 262-2530
  New York (G-10291)
Grantoo LLC ....G....... 646 356-0460
  New York (G-10351)
Identifycom Inc......................................G....... 212 235-0000
  New York (G-10556)
Incentivate Health LLC ....G....... 518 469-8491
  Saratoga Springs (G-15160)
INTEL Corporation.................................D....... 408 765-8080
  Getzville (G-5599)
Jpm and Associates ....F....... 516 483-4699
  Uniondale (G-16297)
Kontrolscan Inc ....G....... 917 743-0481
  Scarsdale (G-15219)
Liiiike Shopping Inc ....F....... 914 271-2001
  New York (G-10996)
Lookbooks Media Inc ....F....... 646 737-3360
  New York (G-11029)
Luluvise Inc ....E....... 914 309-7812
  New York (G-11064)
Madhat Inc ....G....... 518 947-0732
  New York (G-11093)
Meethappy Inc ....F....... 917 903-0591
  Seaford (G-15346)
Microstrategy Incorporated ....F....... 888 537-8135
  New York (G-11257)
Molabs Inc ....G....... 310 721-6828
  New York (G-11293)
Mpr Magazine App Inc ....E....... 718 403-0303
  Brooklyn (G-2338)
Nervve Technologies Inc ....E....... 716 800-2250
  Buffalo (G-3083)
Nitel Inc ....G....... 347 731-1558
  Brooklyn (G-2372)
Omx (us) Inc ....A....... 646 428-2800
  New York (G-11504)
One-Blue LLC ....G....... 212 223-4380
  New York (G-11509)
Pefin Technologies LLC ....F....... 917 715-3720
  New York (G-11600)
Pexip Inc ....E....... 703 338-3544
  New York (G-11634)
Pingmd Inc...G....... 212 632-2665
  New York (G-11662)
Piwik Pro LLC ....E....... 888 444-0049
  New York (G-11670)
Pocket Solutions Inc.............................G....... 631 355-1073
  Brookhaven (G-1509)
Proginet Corporation.............................F....... 516 535-3600
  Garden City (G-5527)
Prospector Network ....E....... 212 601-2781
  New York (G-11739)
Pts Financial Technology LLC..............E....... 844 825-7634
  New York (G-11745)
Quovo Inc ....E....... 646 216-9437
  New York (G-11777)
Raleigh and Drake Pbc ....F....... 212 625-8212
  New York (G-11791)
Responcer Inc..G....... 917 572-0895
  New York (G-11843)
Robert Ehrlich ....G....... 516 353-4617
  New York (G-11890)
Robot Fruit Inc ....F....... 631 423-7250
  Huntington (G-6677)

Seed Media Group LLC E 646 502-7050
New York *(G-12016)*

Serendipity Consulting Corp F 914 763-8251
South Salem *(G-15536)*

Signpost Inc F 646 503-4231
New York *(G-12074)*

Sitecompli LLC F 800 564-1152
New York *(G-12088)*

Smn Medical PC F 844 362-2428
Rye *(G-15068)*

Spring Inc G 646 732-0323
New York *(G-12170)*

Striata Inc D 212 918-4677
New York *(G-12214)*

Superchat LLC G 212 352-8581
New York *(G-12242)*

Synced Inc G 917 565-5591
New York *(G-12259)*

Tep Events International Inc F 646 393-4723
New York *(G-12301)*

Theirapp LLC E 212 896-1255
New York *(G-12312)*

Thing Daemon Inc E 917 696-5794
New York *(G-12317)*

Tootter Inc E 212 300-7489
Brooklyn *(G-2664)*

Tpa Computer Corp F 877 866-6044
Carmel *(G-3406)*

Trac Medical Solutions Inc G 518 346-7799
Schenectady *(G-15306)*

Treauu Inc G 703 731-0196
New York *(G-12395)*

Trendlytics Innvation Labs Inc G 415 971-4123
New York *(G-12398)*

Ufn LLC G 800 533-1787
Fishkill *(G-5188)*

Usq Group LLC G 212 777-7751
New York *(G-12493)*

Virtual Frameworks Inc F 646 690-8207
New York *(G-12549)*

West Internet Trading Company G 415 484-5848
New York *(G-12612)*

White Label Partners LLC G 917 445-6650
New York *(G-12626)*

Whiteboard Ventures Inc F 855 972-6346
New York *(G-12628)*

Winesoft International Corp G 914 400-6247
Yonkers *(G-17500)*

Wink Inc E 212 389-1382
New York *(G-12646)*

Wink Labs Inc E 916 717-0437
New York *(G-12647)*

Xborder Entertainment LLC G 518 726-7036
Plattsburgh *(G-13710)*

Yooconnect1 LLC G 212 726-2062
New York *(G-12697)*

SOFTWARE PUBLISHERS: Business & Professional

Aarfid LLC G 716 992-3999
Eden *(G-4585)*

Abel Noser Solutions Ltd E 646 884-6440
New York *(G-9003)*

Appfigures Inc F 212 343-7900
New York *(G-9181)*

Arcserve (usa) LLC E 866 576-9742
Islandia *(G-6786)*

Aspen Research Group Ltd G 212 425-9588
New York *(G-9236)*

Auric Technology LLC F 212 573-0911
New York *(G-9265)*

Automated Office Systems Inc F 516 396-5555
Valley Stream *(G-16401)*

Aycan Medical Systems LLC F 585 271-3078
Rochester *(G-14219)*

B601 V2 Inc G 646 391-6431
New York *(G-9297)*

Beyondly Inc F 646 658-3665
New York *(G-9384)*

Big Data Bizviz LLC G 716 803-2367
West Seneca *(G-16939)*

Boundless Spatial Inc E 646 831-5531
New York *(G-9443)*

Boxbee Inc G 646 612-7839
New York *(G-9445)*

Broadway Technology LLC E 646 912-6450
New York *(G-9466)*

Business Integrity Inc G 718 238-2008
New York *(G-9482)*

Ca Inc A 800 225-5224
New York *(G-9491)*

Caminus Corporation D 212 515-3600
New York *(G-9508)*

Careconnector G 919 360-2987
Brooklyn *(G-1758)*

Checkm8 Inc F 212 268-0048
New York *(G-9588)*

Chequedcom Inc E 888 412-0699
Saratoga Springs *(G-15149)*

Clarityad Inc G 646 397-4198
New York *(G-9634)*

Clearview Social Inc G 801 414-7675
Buffalo *(G-2875)*

Connecticut Bus Systems LLC G 914 696-1900
White Plains *(G-17096)*

Conversant LLC G 212 471-9570
New York *(G-9714)*

Cross Border Transactions LLC G 914 631-0878
Tarrytown *(G-16089)*

Curaegis Technologies Inc F 585 254-1100
Rochester *(G-14294)*

Cureatr Inc F 212 203-3927
New York *(G-9768)*

Dartcom Incorporated G 315 790-5456
New Hartford *(G-8802)*

Debt Resolve Inc G 914 949-5500
White Plains *(G-17100)*

Dow Jones & Company Inc E 212 597-5983
New York *(G-9915)*

Dropcar Inc G 212 464-8860
New York *(G-9931)*

EBM Care Inc G 212 500-5000
New York *(G-9972)*

Efront Financial Solutions Inc E 212 220-0660
New York *(G-9986)*

Elodina Inc G 646 402-5202
New York *(G-10013)*

EMC Corporation E 212 899-5500
New York *(G-10021)*

Endava Inc G 212 920-7240
New York *(G-10032)*

Enterprise Management Tech LLC G 212 835-1557
New York *(G-10042)*

Equilend Holdings LLC E 212 901-2200
New York *(G-10052)*

EZ Systems US Inc C 212 634-6899
Brooklyn *(G-1950)*

Floored Inc F 908 347-5845
New York *(G-10180)*

Forwardlane Inc F 310 779-8590
New York *(G-10188)*

Fusion Telecom Intl Inc C 212 201-2400
New York *(G-10227)*

Gifts Software Inc E 904 438-6000
New York *(G-10294)*

Globalquest Solutions Inc F 716 601-3524
Williamsville *(G-17245)*

Heartland Commerce Inc E 845 920-0800
Pearl River *(G-13458)*

Hovee Inc F 646 249-6200
New York *(G-10522)*

Inprotopia Corporation F 917 338-7501
New York *(G-10610)*

Intelligize Incorporated G 571 612-8580
New York *(G-10618)*

Kindling Inc F 212 400-6296
New York *(G-10851)*

Klara Technologies Inc F 844 215-5272
New York *(G-10858)*

Latchable Inc E 646 833-0604
New York *(G-10931)*

Laurus Development Inc F 716 823-1202
Buffalo *(G-3047)*

Liftforward Inc F 917 693-4993
New York *(G-10989)*

Livetiles Corp F 917 472-7887
New York *(G-11016)*

Market Factory Inc F 212 625-9988
New York *(G-11158)*

Micro Systems Specialists Inc G 845 677-6150
Millbrook *(G-8476)*

NBC Internet Inc B 212 315-9016
New York *(G-11362)*

Oracle Corporation B 516 247-4500
Mineola *(G-8529)*

Oracle Corporation B 585 383-1998
Rochester *(G-14551)*

Oracle Corporation B 212 508-7700
New York *(G-11519)*

Oracle Corporation C 212 508-7700
New York *(G-11520)*

Orangenius Inc F 631 742-0648
New York *(G-11521)*

Orthstar Enterprises Inc D 607 562-2100
Horseheads *(G-6586)*

Pb Mapinfo Corporation A 518 285-6000
Troy *(G-16246)*

Pegasystems Inc E 212 626-6550
New York *(G-11601)*

Pitney Bowes Software Inc F 518 272-0014
Troy *(G-16248)*

Powa Technologies Inc E 347 344-7848
New York *(G-11691)*

Pricing Engine Inc F 917 549-3289
New York *(G-11703)*

Principia Partners LLC D 212 480-2270
New York *(G-11713)*

Purebase Networks Inc G 646 670-8964
New York *(G-11752)*

Quality and Asrn Tech Corp G 646 450-6762
Ridge *(G-14093)*

Relavis Corporation E 212 995-2900
New York *(G-11823)*

Ringlead Inc F 310 906-0545
Huntington *(G-6676)*

Rision Inc G 212 987-2628
New York *(G-11878)*

Ritnoa Inc E 212 660-2148
Bellerose *(G-811)*

RPS Holdings Inc E 607 257-7778
Ithaca *(G-6874)*

Sapphire Systems Inc F 212 905-0100
New York *(G-11970)*

Sefaira Inc E 855 733-2472
New York *(G-12018)*

Shake Inc F 650 544-5479
New York *(G-12040)*

Siemens Product Life Mgmt Sftw E 585 389-8699
Fairport *(G-4879)*

Solve Advisors Inc G 646 699-5041
Rockville Centre *(G-14799)*

Squond Inc E 718 778-6630
Brooklyn *(G-2593)*

Stop N Shop LLC G 518 512-9657
Albany *(G-138)*

Structuredweb Inc E 201 325-3110
New York *(G-12217)*

Styleclick Inc D 212 329-0300
New York *(G-12224)*

Successware Remote LLC G 716 842-1439
Buffalo *(G-3199)*

Symphony Talent LLC D 212 999-9000
New York *(G-12257)*

Team Builders Inc F 718 979-1005
Staten Island *(G-15747)*

Technology Crossover MGT VII C 212 808-0200
New York *(G-12289)*

Telmar Information Services E 212 725-3000
New York *(G-12297)*

Thinktrek Inc F 212 884-8399
New York *(G-12318)*

Tika Mobile Inc F 516 635-1696
New York *(G-12340)*

Transportgistics Inc F 631 567-4100
Mount Sinai *(G-8657)*

Trueex LLC E 646 786-8526
New York *(G-12410)*

Tyme Global Technologies LLC E 212 796-1950
New York *(G-12437)*

Varsity Monitor LLC G 212 691-6292
New York *(G-12509)*

Velocity Outsourcing LLC E 212 891-4043
New York *(G-12515)*

Virtuvent Inc G 646 845-0387
New York *(G-12551)*

Vita Rara Inc G 518 369-7356
Troy *(G-16261)*

Wercs Ltd E 518 640-9200
Latham *(G-7384)*

Whentech LLC F 212 571-0042
New York *(G-12623)*

Ypis of Staten Island Inc G 718 815-4557
Staten Island *(G-15755)*

SOFTWARE PUBLISHERS: Computer Utilities

BMC Software Inc E 212 730-1389
New York *(G-9429)*

PRODUCT

Simply Logic Labs LLC ....G....... 516 626-6228
Roslyn Heights (G-15032)
Wagner Technical Services Inc..........F....... 845 566-4018
Newburgh (G-12785)

SOFTWARE PUBLISHERS: Education

Accelify Solutions LLC..........E....... 888 922-2354
Brooklyn (G-1550)
Brainpop LLC..........E....... 212 574-6017
New York (G-9451)
Childrens Progress Inc..........E....... 212 730-0905
New York (G-9595)
Classroom Inc..........E....... 212 545-8400
New York (G-9639)
Coalition On Positive Health..........F....... 212 633-2500
New York (G-9660)
Cognotion Inc..........G....... 347 692-0640
New York (G-9665)
Comet Informatics LLC..........G....... 585 385-2310
Pittsford (G-13557)
Health Care Compliance..........E....... 516 478-4100
Jericho (G-7070)
Isabella Products Inc..........F....... 516 699-8404
Great Neck (G-5818)
Isimulate LLC..........G....... 877 947-2831
Albany (G-91)
Jumprope Inc..........G....... 347 927-5867
New York (G-10787)
Learningateway LLC..........G....... 212 920-7969
Brooklyn (G-2203)
Maven Marketing LLC..........G....... 615 510-3248
New York (G-11183)
Multimedia Plus Inc..........F....... 212 982-3229
New York (G-11326)
Nemaris Inc..........E....... 646 794-8648
New York (G-11366)
Parlor Labs Inc..........G....... 646 217-0918
New York (G-11576)
Playfitness Corp..........G....... 917 497-5443
Staten Island (G-15722)
San Jae Educational Resou..........G....... 845 364-5458
Pomona (G-13733)
Scholastic Corporation..........G....... 212 343-6100
New York (G-11997)
Scholastic Inc..........A....... 800 724-6527
New York (G-11998)
Schoolnet Inc..........C....... 646 496-9000
New York (G-12001)
Standardware Inc..........G....... 914 738-6382
Pelham (G-13495)
Teachergaming LLC..........F....... 866 644-9323
New York (G-12286)
Teachley LLC..........G....... 347 552-1272
Staten Island (G-15746)
Tequipment Inc..........D....... 516 922-3508
Huntington Station (G-6726)
Time To Know Inc..........F....... 212 230-1210
New York (G-12349)
Trovvit Inc..........G....... 718 908-5376
Brooklyn (G-2685)
Virtusphere Inc..........F....... 607 760-2207
Binghamton (G-958)
Wireless Generation Inc..........G....... 212 213-8177
Brooklyn (G-2762)

SOFTWARE PUBLISHERS: Home Entertainment

Avalanche Studios New York Inc..........D....... 212 993-6447
New York (G-9272)
Clever Goats Media LLC..........G....... 917 512-0340
New York (G-9642)
E H Hurwitz & Associates..........G....... 718 884-3766
Bronx (G-1321)
Magic Numbers Inc..........G....... 646 839-8578
New York (G-11105)
Mdcare911 LLC..........G....... 917 640-4869
Brooklyn (G-2287)
Reentry Games Inc..........G....... 646 421-0080
New York (G-11817)
Udisense Inc..........G....... 858 442-9875
New York (G-12443)
Urthworx Inc..........G....... 646 373-7535
New York (G-12483)
Vizbee Inc..........G....... 650 787-1424
New York (G-12560)

SOFTWARE PUBLISHERS: NEC

2k Inc..........G....... 646 536-3007
New York (G-8969)
30dc Inc..........G....... 212 962-4400
New York (G-8970)
30dc Inc..........F....... 212 962-4400
New York (G-8971)
6n Systems Inc..........G....... 518 583-6400
Halfmoon (G-5907)
A K A Computer Consulting Inc..........G....... 718 351-5200
Staten Island (G-15630)
A2ia Corp..........G....... 917 237-0390
New York (G-8996)
Accela Inc..........F....... 631 563-5005
Ronkonkoma (G-14846)
Adl Data Systems Inc..........E....... 914 591-1800
Hawthorne (G-6243)
Adobe Systems Inc..........E....... 212 471-0904
New York (G-9029)
Adobe Systems Incorporated..........E....... 212 471-0904
New York (G-9030)
Adtech Us Inc..........C....... 212 402-4840
New York (G-9033)
Advanced Cmpt Sftwr Consulting..........G....... 718 300-3577
Bronx (G-1264)
Andigo New Media Inc..........G....... 212 727-8445
New York (G-9153)
Ansa Systems of USA Inc..........G....... 516 887-6855
Valley Stream (G-16400)
Application Security Inc..........D....... 212 912-4100
New York (G-9183)
Apprenda Inc..........D....... 518 383-2130
Troy (G-16225)
Appsbidder Inc..........G....... 917 880-4269
Brooklyn (G-1619)
APS Enterprise Software Inc..........E....... 631 784-7720
Huntington (G-6654)
Archive360 Inc..........E....... 212 731-2438
New York (G-9197)
Articulate Global Inc..........C....... 800 861-4880
New York (G-9218)
Arumai Technologies Inc..........F....... 914 217-0038
Armonk (G-412)
Asite LLC..........D....... 203 545-3089
New York (G-9232)
AT&T Corp..........F....... 212 317-7048
New York (G-9244)
Autodesk Inc..........E....... 607 257-4280
Ithaca (G-6820)
Base Systems Inc..........G....... 845 278-1991
Brewster (G-1211)
BEC Acquisition Co LLC..........G....... 516 986-3050
Melville (G-8296)
Bigwood Systems Inc..........G....... 607 257-0915
Ithaca (G-6822)
Billing Blocks Inc..........F....... 718 442-5006
Staten Island (G-15647)
Blue Wolf Group LLC..........D....... 866 455-9653
New York (G-9423)
BMC Software Inc..........E....... 646 452-4100
New York (G-9428)
Bootstrap Software..........G....... 212 871-2020
New York (G-9440)
Brigadoon Software Inc..........G....... 845 624-0909
Nanuet (G-8752)
Buncee LLC..........F....... 631 591-1390
Calverton (G-3287)
Business Management Systems..........F....... 914 245-8558
Yorktown Heights (G-17508)
Byte Consulting Inc..........G....... 646 500-8606
New York (G-9489)
Ca Inc..........C....... 800 225-5224
New York (G-9492)
California US Holdings Inc..........A....... 212 726-6500
New York (G-9501)
Callidus Software Inc..........F....... 212 554-7300
New York (G-9504)
Candex Solutions Inc..........G....... 215 650-3214
New York (G-9512)
Cavalry Solutions..........G....... 315 422-1699
Syracuse (G-15891)
Cdml Computer Services Ltd..........G....... 718 428-9063
Fresh Meadows (G-5439)
Ceipal LLC..........G....... 585 351-2934
Rochester (G-14264)
Ceipal LLC..........G....... 585 351-2934
Rochester (G-14265)
Celonis Inc..........G....... 941 615-9670
Brooklyn (G-1769)
Cgi Technologies Solutions Inc..........F....... 212 682-7411
New York (G-9573)
Cinedigm Software..........G....... 212 206-9001
New York (G-9618)
Citixsys Technologies Inc..........G....... 212 745-1365
New York (G-9626)
Clayton Dubilier & Rice Fun..........E....... 212 407-5200
New York (G-9640)
Cloudsense Inc..........G....... 917 880-6195
New York (G-9645)
Commercehub Inc..........G....... 518 810-0700
Albany (G-70)
Commify Technology..........F....... 917 603-1822
New York (G-9686)
Comprehensive Dental Tech..........G....... 607 467-4456
Hancock (G-5963)
Condeco Software Inc..........E....... 917 677-7600
New York (G-9698)
Construction Technology Inc..........G....... 914 747-8900
Valhalla (G-16366)
Coocoo SMS Inc..........F....... 646 459-4260
Huntington (G-6659)
CTI Software Inc..........F....... 631 253-3550
Deer Park (G-4123)
Cuffs Planning & Models Ltd..........G....... 914 632-1883
New Rochelle (G-8893)
Cultureiq Inc..........G....... 212 755-8633
New York (G-9766)
Curemdcom Inc..........B....... 646 224-2201
New York (G-9769)
Cyandia Inc..........F....... 315 679-4268
Syracuse (G-15917)
Cybersports Inc..........G....... 315 737-7150
Utica (G-16319)
Data Implementation Inc..........G....... 212 979-2015
New York (G-9813)
Davel Systems Inc..........G....... 718 382-6024
Brooklyn (G-1841)
Defran Systems Inc..........E....... 212 727-8342
New York (G-9837)
Delivery Systems Inc..........F....... 212 221-7007
New York (G-9839)
Deniz Information Systems..........G....... 212 750-5199
New York (G-9845)
Diligent Board Member Svcs LLC..........E....... 212 741-8181
New York (G-9878)
Diligent Corporation..........C....... 212 741-8181
New York (G-9879)
Dynamo Development Inc..........G....... 212 385-1552
New York (G-9949)
Eastnets Americas Corp..........F....... 212 631-0666
New York (G-9968)
Ebeling Associates Inc..........F....... 518 688-8700
Halfmoon (G-5910)
Electronic Arts Inc..........G....... 212 672-0722
New York (G-9997)
Electronic Business Tech..........F....... 845 353-8549
West Nyack (G-16916)
Elephant Talk Cmmncations Corp..........B....... 866 901-3309
New York (G-10000)
Emblaze Systems Inc..........C....... 212 371-1100
New York (G-10020)
EMC Corporation..........E....... 585 387-9505
East Rochester (G-4457)
Empowrx LLC..........G....... 212 755-3577
New York (G-10024)
Enterprise Tech Group Inc..........F....... 914 588-0327
New Rochelle (G-8897)
Ert Software Inc..........G....... 845 358-5721
Blauvelt (G-971)
Ex El Enterprises Ltd..........F....... 212 489-4500
New York (G-10097)
Exact Solutions Inc..........F....... 212 707-8627
New York (G-10099)
Exacttarget Inc..........G....... 646 560-2275
New York (G-10100)
EZ Newsletter LLC..........F....... 412 943-7777
Brooklyn (G-1949)
F R A M Technologies Inc..........G....... 718 338-6230
Brooklyn (G-1951)
F-O-R Software LLC..........F....... 212 231-9506
New York (G-10120)
F-O-R Software LLC..........E....... 914 220-8800
White Plains (G-17108)
F-O-R Software LLC..........G....... 212 724-3920
New York (G-10121)
Facts On File Inc..........D....... 212 967-8800
New York (G-10126)
Falconstor Software Inc..........F....... 631 777-5188
Melville (G-8318)
Femtech Women Powered Software..........D....... 516 328-2631
Franklin Square (G-5363)
Fidelus Technologies LLC..........D....... 212 616-7800
New York (G-10159)

PRODUCT

Employee Codes: A=Over 500 employees, B=251-500
C=101-250, D=51-100, E=20-50, F=10-19, G=5-9
2017 Harris
New York Manufacturers Directory
1341

Fidesa US Corporation B 212 269-9000
New York *(G-10160)*
Filestream Inc F 516 759-4100
Locust Valley *(G-7629)*
Flexsin F 212 470-9279
New York *(G-10179)*
Flextrade Systems Inc C 516 627-8993
Great Neck *(G-5813)*
Flogic Inc F 914 478-1352
Hastings On Hudson *(G-6003)*
Fog Creek Software Inc G 866 364-2733
New York *(G-10183)*
Formats Unlimited Inc F 631 249-9200
Deer Park *(G-4144)*
Frazer Computing Inc E 315 379-3500
Canton *(G-3383)*
Fuel Data Systems Inc G 800 447-7870
Middletown *(G-8441)*
Games For Change Inc G 212 242-4922
New York *(G-10245)*
Geoweb3d Inc G 607 323-1212
Binghamton *(G-918)*
Glassbox US Inc E 917 378-2933
New York *(G-10308)*
Glitnir Ticketing Inc G 516 390-5168
Levittown *(G-7428)*
Global Applctions Solution LLC G 212 741-9595
New York *(G-10313)*
Globeop Financial Services LLC C 914 670-3600
Harrison *(G-5985)*
Group Commerce Inc F 646 346-0598
New York *(G-10370)*
Hailo Network Usa Inc G 646 561-8552
New York *(G-10396)*
Happy Software Inc G 518 584-4668
Saratoga Springs *(G-15158)*
Heineck Associates Inc G 631 207-2347
Bellport *(G-832)*
High Performance Sftwr USA Inc E 866 616-4958
Valley Stream *(G-16409)*
Hinge Inc F 502 445-3111
New York *(G-10481)*
Hudson Software Corporation E 914 773-0400
Elmsford *(G-4755)*
Huntington Services Inc G 516 795-8500
Massapequa *(G-8179)*
IAC Search LLC E 212 314-7300
New York *(G-10543)*
Iac/Interactivecorp C 212 314-7300
New York *(G-10544)*
Inboxmind LLC G 646 773-7726
New York *(G-10580)*
Incycle Software Corp G 212 626-2608
New York *(G-10584)*
Indegy Inc E 866 801-5394
New York *(G-10586)*
Infinity Augmented Reality Inc G 917 677-2084
New York *(G-10593)*
Info Quick Solutions E 315 463-1400
Liverpool *(G-7525)*
Infobase Publishing Company G 212 967-8800
New York *(G-10595)*
Infor Global Solutions Inc D 646 336-1700
New York *(G-10596)*
Informa Solutions Inc E 516 543-3733
Garden City *(G-5511)*
Informatica LLC F 212 845-7650
New York *(G-10598)*
Informerly Inc G 646 238-7137
New York *(G-10599)*
Innovation MGT Group Inc F 800 889-0987
Shirley *(G-15420)*
Insight Unlimited Inc G 914 861-2090
Chappaqua *(G-3552)*
Intellicheck Mobilisa Inc E 360 344-3233
Jericho *(G-7072)*
International Bus Mchs Corp F 914 345-5219
Armonk *(G-414)*
International Bus Mchs Corp E 914 499-2000
Armonk *(G-415)*
International MGT Netwrk F 646 401-0032
New York *(G-10637)*
Internodal International Inc E 631 765-0037
Southold *(G-15559)*
Intralinks Holdings Inc E 212 543-7700
New York *(G-10646)*
Invision Inc G 212 557-5554
New York *(G-10653)*
Irv Inc E 212 334-4507
New York *(G-10663)*

Joseph A Filippazzo Software G 718 987-1626
Staten Island *(G-15693)*
Kaseya US Sales LLC D 415 694-5700
New York *(G-10813)*
Kastor Consulting Inc G 718 224-9109
Bayside *(G-773)*
Key Computer Svcs of Chelsea D 212 206-8060
New York *(G-10840)*
Keynote Systems Corporation G 716 564-1332
Buffalo *(G-3030)*
Latham Software Sciences Inc F 518 785-1100
Latham *(G-7371)*
Lincdoc LLC G 585 563-1669
East Rochester *(G-4465)*
Magsoft Corporation G 518 877-8390
Clifton Park *(G-3701)*
Maler Technologies Inc G 212 391-2070
New York *(G-11120)*
Marcus Goldman Inc F 212 431-0707
New York *(G-11147)*
McAfee Inc G 646 728-1440
New York *(G-11194)*
Mealplan Corp G 909 706-8398
New York *(G-11205)*
Medical Transcription Billing A 631 863-1198
New York *(G-11214)*
Medidata Solutions Inc B 212 918-1800
New York *(G-11215)*
Medius Software Inc F 877 295-0058
New York *(G-11217)*
Meta Pharmacy Systems Inc E 516 488-6189
Garden City *(G-5522)*
Microcad Trning Consulting Inc G 617 923-0500
Lagrangeville *(G-7256)*
Microcad Trning Consulting Inc G 631 291-9484
Hauppauge *(G-6135)*
Microsoft Corporation D 585 240-6037
Rochester *(G-14513)*
Microsoft Corporation A 914 323-2150
White Plains *(G-17138)*
Microsoft Corporation F 212 245-2100
New York *(G-11256)*
Microsoft Corporation D 516 380-1531
Hauppauge *(G-6137)*
Midas Mdici Group Holdings Inc G 212 792-0920
New York *(G-11258)*
Mml Software Ltd E 631 941-1313
East Setauket *(G-4488)*
Mobile Data Systems Inc G 631 360-3400
Nesconset *(G-8776)*
Mobile Hatch Inc G 212 314-7300
New York *(G-11287)*
Mobileapp Systems LLC G 716 667-2780
Buffalo *(G-3070)*
Nastel Technologies Inc D 631 761-9100
Melville *(G-8338)*
Navatar Consulting Group Inc E 212 863-9655
New York *(G-11360)*
Navatar Consulting Group Inc E 212 863-9655
New York *(G-11361)*
Netegrity Inc C 631 342-6000
Central Islip *(G-3506)*
Netologic Inc E 212 269-3796
New York *(G-11372)*
Netsuite Inc G 646 652-5700
New York *(G-11373)*
Network Components LLC F 212 799-5890
New York *(G-11374)*
Neverware Inc F 516 302-3223
New York *(G-11378)*
New Triad For Collaborative E 212 873-9610
New York *(G-11394)*
Nikish Software Corp G 631 754-1618
Hauppauge *(G-6148)*
Olympic Software & Consulting G 631 351-0655
Melville *(G-8344)*
Ontra Presentations LLC G 212 213-1315
New York *(G-11512)*
Openfin Inc G 917 450-8822
New York *(G-11514)*
Operative Media Inc C 212 994-8930
New York *(G-11516)*
Os33 Inc G 708 336-3466
New York *(G-11529)*
Overture Media Inc G 917 446-7455
New York *(G-11537)*
Pap Chat Inc G 516 350-1888
Brooklyn *(G-2403)*
Par Technology Corporation D 315 738-0600
New Hartford *(G-8808)*

Patient Portal Tech Inc F 315 638-2030
Baldwinsville *(G-574)*
Patron Technology Inc G 212 271-4328
New York *(G-11583)*
Peer Software Incorporated G 631 979-1770
Hauppauge *(G-6160)*
Perry Street Software Inc G 415 935-1429
New York *(G-11625)*
Platform Experts Inc G 646 843-7100
Brooklyn *(G-2426)*
Poly Software International G 845 735-9301
Pearl River *(G-13464)*
Portable Tech Solutions LLC F 631 727-8084
Calverton *(G-3295)*
Portfolio Decisionware Inc E 212 947-1326
New York *(G-11686)*
Portware LLC D 212 425-5233
New York *(G-11688)*
Practicepro Software Systems G 516 222-0010
Garden City *(G-5526)*
Pretlist G 646 368-1849
New York *(G-11702)*
Professional Access LLC G 212 432-2844
Chappaqua *(G-3554)*
Pupa Tek Inc G 631 664-7817
Huntington *(G-6675)*
Quartet Financial Systems Inc F 845 358-6071
New York *(G-11769)*
Radnor-Wallace G 516 767-2131
Port Washington *(G-13858)*
Rational Retention LLC E 518 489-3000
Albany *(G-127)*
Razorfish LLC G 212 798-6600
New York *(G-11808)*
Red Oak Software Inc G 585 454-3170
Rochester *(G-14622)*
Reliant Security E 917 338-2200
New York *(G-11824)*
Revana Inc E 212 244-6137
New York *(G-11849)*
Robly Digital Marketing LLC E 917 238-0730
New York *(G-11895)*
Robocom Us LLC F 631 861-2045
Farmingdale *(G-5101)*
Rockport Pa LLC F 212 482-8580
New York *(G-11899)*
Roomactually LLC G 646 388-1922
New York *(G-11914)*
Rovi Corporation C 212 524-7000
New York *(G-11922)*
Rovi Corporation C 212 824-0355
New York *(G-11923)*
S C T F 585 467-7740
Rochester *(G-14664)*
Safe Passage International Inc F 585 292-4910
Rochester *(G-14665)*
Sakonnet Technology LLC E 212 849-9267
New York *(G-11955)*
Salentica Systems Inc E 212 672-1777
New York *(G-11957)*
Sas Institute Inc F 212 757-3826
New York *(G-11975)*
Sculptgraphicz Inc G 646 837-7302
Brooklyn *(G-2540)*
Secured Services Inc G 866 419-3900
New York *(G-12013)*
Segovia Technology Co F 212 868-4412
New York *(G-12019)*
Servicenow Inc F 914 318-1168
New York *(G-12031)*
Shiprite Software Inc G 315 733-6191
Utica *(G-16359)*
Shoretel Inc G 877 654-3573
Rochester *(G-14684)*
Shritec Consultants Inc G 516 621-7072
Albertson *(G-160)*
Similarweb Inc F 347 685-5422
West Nyack *(G-16926)*
Skystem LLC G 877 778-3320
New York *(G-12098)*
Slyde Inc F 917 331-2114
Long Island City *(G-7879)*
Sneakers Software Inc F 800 877-9221
New York *(G-12112)*
Social Bicycles Inc E 917 746-7624
Brooklyn *(G-2576)*
Softlink International E 914 574-8197
White Plains *(G-17168)*
Software & General Services Co G 315 986-4184
Walworth *(G-16552)*

PRODUCT

1342 2017 Harris New York Manufacturers Directory (G-0000) Company's Geographic Section entry number

PRODUCT SECTION

SPACE VEHICLE EQPT

Somml Health LLC ....G..... 518 880-2170 Albany *(G-135)*	X Function Inc ....E..... 212 231-0092 New York *(G-12672)*	Prism Solar Technologies Inc ....E..... 845 883-4200 Highland *(G-6407)*
Soroc Technology Corp ....G..... 716 849-5913 Buffalo *(G-3192)*	Ymobiz Inc ....F..... 917 470-9280 New York *(G-12694)*	Solar Energy Systems LLC ....F..... 718 389-1545 Brooklyn *(G-2580)*
SS&c Technologies Inc ....E..... 212 503-6400 New York *(G-12177)*	Zedge Inc ....D..... 330 577-3424 New York *(G-12708)*	**SOLDERS**
Sticky ADS TV Inc ....G..... 646 668-1346 New York *(G-12204)*	**SOFTWARE PUBLISHERS: Operating**	Braze Alloy Inc ....G..... 718 815-5757 Staten Island *(G-15651)*
Strada Soft Inc ....G..... 718 556-6940 Staten Island *(G-15742)*	**Systems**	Indium Corporation of America ......E..... 800 446-3486 Clinton *(G-3720)*
Structured Retail Products ....G..... 212 224-3692 New York *(G-12216)*	Enterprise Network of New York ......F..... 516 263-0641 Brooklyn *(G-1925)*	Indium Corporation of America ......E..... 315 793-8200 Utica *(G-16342)*
Successware Inc ....F..... 716 565-2338 Williamsville *(G-17256)*	J9 Technologies Inc ....E..... 412 586-5038 New York *(G-10684)*	Indium Corporation of America ......E..... 315 381-2330 Utica *(G-16343)*
Suite Solutions Inc ....E..... 716 929-3050 Amherst *(G-263)*	Northrop Grumman Systems Corp ..E..... 315 336-0500 Rome *(G-14827)*	Jewelers Solder Supply Inc ....F..... 718 637-1256 Brooklyn *(G-2138)*
Super Software ....G..... 845 735-0000 New City *(G-8794)*	**SOFTWARE PUBLISHERS: Publisher's**	**SOLID CONTAINING UNITS: Concrete**
Sutton Place Software Inc ....G..... 631 421-1737 Melville *(G-8358)*	Avocode Inc ....F..... 646 934-8410 New York *(G-9280)*	Heidenhain International Inc............C..... 716 661-1700 Jamestown *(G-6999)*
Sybase Inc ....D..... 212 596-1100 New York *(G-12255)*	Brainworks Software Dev Corp ....G..... 631 563-5000 Sayville *(G-15204)*	**SOLVENTS**
Symantec Corporation ....D..... 631 656-0185 Smithtown *(G-15499)*	Catholic News Publishing Co ....F..... 914 632-7771 Mamaroneck *(G-8027)*	Solvents Company Inc ....F..... 631 595-9300 Kingston *(G-7210)*
Symantec Corporation ....D..... 646 487-6000 New York *(G-12256)*	Ceros Inc ....E..... 347 744-9250 New York *(G-9571)*	**SONAR SYSTEMS & EQPT**
Synco Technologies Inc ....G..... 212 255-2031 New York *(G-12260)*	Datadog Inc ....E..... 866 329-4466 New York *(G-9814)*	Lockheed Martin Corporation ....E..... 315 456-6604 Syracuse *(G-15980)*
Syntel Inc ....F..... 212 785-9810 New York *(G-12263)*	Digital Associates LLC ....G..... 631 983-6075 Smithtown *(G-15485)*	Lockheed Martin Overseas ....E..... 315 456-0123 Liverpool *(G-7533)*
Syrasoft LLC ....F..... 315 708-0341 Baldwinsville *(G-578)*	Hyperlaw Inc ....F..... 212 873-6982 New York *(G-10537)*	**SOUND EQPT: Electric**
Systems Trading Inc ....G..... 718 261-8900 Melville *(G-8359)*	Irene Goodman Literary Agency .....G..... 212 604-0330 New York *(G-10657)*	Audible Difference Inc ....F..... 212 662-4848 Brooklyn *(G-1651)*
Targetprocess Inc ....F..... 607 346-0621 Amherst *(G-265)*	Maz Digital Inc ....E..... 646 692-9799 New York *(G-11191)*	Audible Difference Inc ....G..... 212 662-4848 Brooklyn *(G-1652)*
Teacup Software Inc ....G..... 212 563-9288 Brooklyn *(G-2648)*	Mediapost Communications LLC ....E..... 212 204-2000 New York *(G-11212)*	Isolation Technology Inc ....G..... 631 253-3314 West Babylon *(G-16796)*
Tel Tech International ....E..... 516 393-5174 Melville *(G-8360)*	Mnn Holding Company LLC ....F..... 404 558-5251 Brooklyn *(G-2326)*	Magic Tech Co Ltd ....G..... 516 539-7944 West Hempstead *(G-16859)*
Tensa Software ....F..... 914 686-5376 White Plains *(G-17177)*	On Demand Books LLC ....G..... 212 966-2222 New York *(G-11505)*	**SOUND EQPT: Underwater**
Terranua US Corp ....F..... 212 852-9028 New York *(G-12303)*	Spektrix Inc ....G..... 646 741-5110 New York *(G-12159)*	L-3 Cmmnctons Ntronix Holdings...D..... 212 697-1111 New York *(G-10904)*
Thomson Reuters Corporation.........A..... 646 223-4000 New York *(G-12329)*	Tradewins Publishing Corp..............G..... 631 361-6916 Smithtown *(G-15501)*	**SOUND REPRODUCING EQPT**
Tradepaq Corporation ....F..... 914 332-9174 Tarrytown *(G-16109)*	Vortex Ventures Inc ....G..... 516 946-8345 North Baldwin *(G-12912)*	Citation Manufacturing Co Inc.........G..... 845 425-6868 Spring Valley *(G-15579)*
Tss-Transport Snltn Sstms ....G..... 917 267-8534 New York *(G-12417)*	**SOFTWARE PUBLISHERS: Word Processing**	Samson Technologies Corp.............D..... 631 784-2200 Hauppauge *(G-6182)*
Ttg LLC ....G..... 917 777-0959 New York *(G-12418)*	Cegid Corporation ....F..... 212 757-9038 New York *(G-9553)*	Vtb Holdings Inc...............................G..... 914 345-2255 Valhalla *(G-16373)*
Tunaverse Media Inc ....G..... 631 778-8350 Hauppauge *(G-6218)*	**SOFTWARE TRAINING, COMPUTER**	**SOYBEAN PRDTS**
Two Rivers Computing Inc ....G..... 914 968-9239 Yonkers *(G-17493)*	Microcad Trning Consulting Inc ......G..... 617 923-0500 Lagrangeville *(G-7256)*	Cayuga Enterprise 21 ....G..... 607 441-9166 Manlius *(G-8069)*
U X World Inc....................................G..... 914 375-6167 Hawthorne *(G-6255)*	**SOLAR CELLS**	**SPACE VEHICLE EQPT**
Upstate Records Management LLC ......E..... 518 834-1144 Keeseville *(G-7142)*	Atlantis Energy Systems Inc...........F..... 845 486-4052 Poughkeepsie *(G-13889)*	Gb Aero Engine LLC ....B..... 914 925-9600 Rye *(G-15057)*
Value Spring Technology Inc ....F..... 917 705-4658 Harrison *(G-5994)*	Ely Beach Solar LLC ....G..... 718 796-9400 New York *(G-10017)*	GKN Aerospace Monitor Inc ....B..... 562 619-8558 Amityville *(G-289)*
Varnish Software Inc ....G..... 201 857-2832 New York *(G-12507)*	Idalia Solar Technologies LLC.........G..... 212 792-3913 New York *(G-10553)*	L-3 Cmmnctons Fgn Holdings Inc........E..... 212 697-1111 New York *(G-10903)*
Varonis Systems Inc ....C..... 877 292-8767 New York *(G-12508)*	Nationwide Tarps Incorporated ....D..... 518 843-1545 Amsterdam *(G-361)*	L-3 Cmmunications Holdings Inc ...D..... 212 697-1111 New York *(G-10905)*
Vehicle Tracking Solutions LLC ......E..... 631 586-7400 Commack *(G-3846)*	Renewable Energy Inc ....G..... 718 690-2691 Little Neck *(G-7510)*	L-3 Communications Corporation........A..... 631 436-7400 Hauppauge *(G-6108)*
Vertana Group LLC ....F..... 646 706-7210 New York *(G-12529)*	Schott Solar Pv Inc ....G..... 888 457-6527 Elmsford *(G-4782)*	L-3 Communications Corporation........B..... 212 697-1111 New York *(G-10906)*
Vhx Corporation ....F..... 347 689-1446 New York *(G-12534)*	Yingli Green Enrgy Amricas Inc ......E..... 888 686-8820 New York *(G-12692)*	Lockheed Martin Corporation ....E..... 716 297-1000 Niagara Falls *(G-12844)*
Vicarious Visions Inc ....D..... 518 283-4090 Troy *(G-16259)*	**SOLAR HEATING EQPT**	Magellan Aerospace NY Inc ....C..... 718 699-4000 Corona *(G-4001)*
Visible Systems Corporation ....E..... 508 628-1510 Oneida *(G-13170)*	Atlantis Energy Systems Inc...........G..... 916 438-2930 Poughkeepsie *(G-13890)*	Moog Inc ....A..... 716 652-2000 Elma *(G-4651)*
Visual Listing Systems Inc ....G..... 631 689-7222 East Setauket *(G-4496)*	Atlantis Solar Inc..............................F..... 916 226-9183 Potsdam *(G-13877)*	Saturn Industries Inc ....E..... 518 828-9956 Hudson *(G-6632)*
Vormittag Associates Inc ....C..... 800 824-7776 Ronkonkoma *(G-14999)*	I-Evolve Techonology Services ......F..... 801 566-5268 Amherst *(G-245)*	Servotronics Inc ....C..... 716 655-5990 Elma *(G-4655)*
Watchitoo Inc ....G..... 212 354-5888 New York *(G-12595)*	Integrated Solar Tech LLC ....G..... 914 249-9364 Port Chester *(G-13749)*	SKF USA Inc ....D..... 716 661-2869 Falconer *(G-4912)*
Wetpaintcom Inc ....E..... 206 859-6300 New York *(G-12620)*	Mx Solar USA LLC ....C..... 732 356-7300 New York *(G-11330)*	Turbine Engine Comp Utica ....A..... 315 768-8070 Whitesboro *(G-17197)*
Wing Tel Inc ....G..... 347 508-5802 New York *(G-12645)*	Nanopv Corporation ....C..... 609 851-3666 Liverpool *(G-7536)*	
Wizq Inc ....F..... 586 381-9048 New York *(G-12649)*	New Energy Systems Group............C..... 917 573-0302 New York *(G-11385)*	
Woodbury Systems Group Inc ....G..... 516 364-2653 Woodbury *(G-17304)*		

Employee Codes: A=Over 500 employees, B=251-500
C=101-250, D=51-100, E=20-50, F=10-19, G=5-9

SPARK PLUGS: Internal Combustion Engines

Unison Industries LLC..................B........607 335-5000
  Norwich (G-13039)

SPARK PLUGS: Internal Combustion Engines

Karlyn Industries Inc..................F........845 351-2249
  Southfields (G-15556)

SPAS

461 New Lots Avenue LLC..................G........347 303-9305
  Brooklyn (G-1519)
Epic Beauty Co LLC..................G........212 327-3059
  New York (G-10049)
Skincare Products Inc..................G........917 837-5255
  New York (G-12093)

SPEAKER SYSTEMS

Covington Sound..................G........646 256-7486
  Bronx (G-1305)
L A R Electronics Corp..................G........716 285-0555
  Niagara Falls (G-12840)
Professional Technology Inc..................G........315 337-4156
  Rome (G-14830)
Pure Acoustics Inc..................G........718 788-4411
  Brooklyn (G-2457)

SPECIAL EVENTS DECORATION SVCS

Allied Decorations Co Inc..................F........315 637-0273
  Syracuse (G-15849)
Hotelinteractive Inc..................F........631 424-7755
  Smithtown (G-15488)
Ubm LLC..................A........516 562-5085
  New York (G-12441)

SPECIALTY FOOD STORES: Coffee

Coffee Holding Co Inc..................D........718 832-0800
  Staten Island (G-15661)
Death Wish Coffee Company LLC..................F........518 400-1050
  Round Lake (G-15037)
Orens Daily Roast Inc..................G........212 348-5400
  New York (G-11526)

SPECIALTY FOOD STORES: Health & Dietetic Food

Ajes Pharmaceuticals LLC..................E........631 608-1728
  Copiague (G-3891)
Alphabet Holding Company Inc..................E........631 200-2000
  Ronkonkoma (G-14865)
Cosmic Enterprise..................G........718 342-6257
  Brooklyn (G-1807)
Nbty Inc..................D........631 244-2021
  Ronkonkoma (G-14952)
Nbty Inc..................A........631 200-2000
  Ronkonkoma (G-14953)
Only Natural Inc..................F........516 897-7001
  Island Park (G-6783)
Setauket Manufacturing Co..................G........631 231-7272
  Ronkonkoma (G-14984)

SPECIALTY FOOD STORES: Juices, Fruit Or Vegetable

Mayer Bros Apple Products Inc..................D........716 668-1787
  West Seneca (G-16952)
Nantucket Allserve Inc..................B........914 612-4000
  Elmsford (G-4770)
Schutt Cider Mill..................F........585 872-2924
  Webster (G-16734)

SPERM BANK

Daxor Corporation..................E........212 244-0555
  New York (G-9831)

SPONGES: Plastic

3M Company..................B........716 876-1596
  Tonawanda (G-16132)

SPOOLS: Fiber, Made From Purchased Materials

Syraco Products Inc..................E........800 581-5555
  Syracuse (G-16047)

SPOOLS: Indl

McIntosh Box & Pallet Co Inc..................E........315 446-9350
  Rome (G-14820)

SPORTING & ATHLETIC GOODS: Bags, Golf

Athalon Sportgear Inc..................G........212 268-8070
  New York (G-9249)
Premiumbag LLC..................G........718 657-6219
  Jamaica (G-6941)

SPORTING & ATHLETIC GOODS: Balls, Baseball, Football, Etc

Sky Bounce Ball Company Inc..................G........516 305-4883
  Hewlett (G-6313)

SPORTING & ATHLETIC GOODS: Bowling Alleys & Access

Hootz Family Bowling Inc..................F........518 756-4668
  Ravena (G-14021)

SPORTING & ATHLETIC GOODS: Bowling Pins

Qubicaamf Worldwide LLC..................C........315 376-6541
  Lowville (G-7941)

SPORTING & ATHLETIC GOODS: Bows, Archery

Perfect Form Manufacturing LLC..................G........585 500-5923
  West Henrietta (G-16890)

SPORTING & ATHLETIC GOODS: Boxing Eqpt & Splys, NEC

Everlast Worldwide Inc..................E........212 239-0990
  New York (G-10093)

SPORTING & ATHLETIC GOODS: Camping Eqpt & Splys

Adirondack Outdoor Center..................G........315 369-2300
  Old Forge (G-13132)
J R Products Inc..................G........716 633-7565
  Clarence Center (G-3677)

SPORTING & ATHLETIC GOODS: Cartridge Belts

Car Doctor Motor Sports LLC..................G........631 537-1548
  Water Mill (G-16603)

SPORTING & ATHLETIC GOODS: Driving Ranges, Golf, Electronic

Paddock Chevrolet Golf Dome..................E........716 504-4059
  Tonawanda (G-16191)

SPORTING & ATHLETIC GOODS: Dumbbells & Other Weight Eqpt

TDS Fitness Equipment..................E........607 733-6789
  Elmira (G-4704)

SPORTING & ATHLETIC GOODS: Fishing Bait, Artificial

Fishing Valley LLC..................G........716 523-6158
  Lockport (G-7586)
Makiplastic..................G........716 772-2222
  Gasport (G-5558)

SPORTING & ATHLETIC GOODS: Fishing Eqpt

Cortland Line Mfg LLC..................E........607 756-2851
  Cortland (G-4018)
Fly-Tyers Carry-All LLC..................E........607 821-1460
  Charlotteville (G-3555)
Rome Specialty Company Inc..................E........315 337-8200
  Rome (G-14834)
Sampo Inc..................E........315 896-2606
  Barneveld (G-617)

SPORTING & ATHLETIC GOODS: Fishing Tackle, General

Sea Isle Custom Rod Builders..................G........516 868-8855
  Freeport (G-5424)

SPORTING & ATHLETIC GOODS: Game Calls

Quaker Boy Inc..................E........716 662-3979
  Orchard Park (G-13292)

SPORTING & ATHLETIC GOODS: Gymnasium Eqpt

Peloton Interactive Inc..................E........818 571-7236
  New York (G-11602)

SPORTING & ATHLETIC GOODS: Hockey Eqpt & Splys, NEC

Hart Sports Inc..................G........631 385-1805
  Huntington Station (G-6707)
Kohlberg Sports Group Inc..................G........914 241-7430
  Mount Kisco (G-8633)

SPORTING & ATHLETIC GOODS: Lacrosse Eqpt & Splys, NEC

Maverik Lacrosse LLC..................A........516 213-3050
  New York (G-11184)
Tosch Products Ltd..................G........315 672-3040
  Camillus (G-3325)

SPORTING & ATHLETIC GOODS: Pools, Swimming, Exc Plastic

Asia Connection LLC..................F........212 369-4644
  New York (G-9231)
Charm Mfg Co Inc..................E........607 565-8161
  Waverly (G-16699)
Imperial Pools Inc..................C........518 786-1200
  Latham (G-7365)
Latham Pool Products Inc..................C........518 951-1000
  Latham (G-7369)
Polytech Pool Mfg Inc..................F........718 492-8991
  Brooklyn (G-2428)

SPORTING & ATHLETIC GOODS: Pools, Swimming, Plastic

Florida North Inc..................F........518 868-2888
  Sloansville (G-15479)
Hinspergers Poly Industries..................E........585 798-6625
  Medina (G-8275)
Swimline Corp..................E........631 254-2155
  Edgewood (G-4613)
Wilbar International Inc..................D........631 951-9800
  Hauppauge (G-6235)

SPORTING & ATHLETIC GOODS: Protective Sporting Eqpt

Fist Inc..................G........718 643-3478
  Brooklyn (G-1976)

SPORTING & ATHLETIC GOODS: Shafts, Golf Club

Elmira Country Club Inc..................G........607 734-6251
  Elmira (G-4681)

SPORTING & ATHLETIC GOODS: Shooting Eqpt & Splys, General

Otis Products Inc..................C........315 348-4300
  Lyons Falls (G-7978)

SPORTING & ATHLETIC GOODS: Skateboards

Blades..................F........212 477-1059
  New York (G-9411)

SPORTING & ATHLETIC GOODS: Skates & Parts, Roller

Chapman Skateboard Co Inc..................G........631 321-4773
  Deer Park (G-4116)

PRODUCT SECTION

SPORTING & ATHLETIC GOODS: Target Shooting Eqpt

Devin Mfg Inc .... F 585 496-5770
  Arcade *(G-391)*

SPORTING & ATHLETIC GOODS: Team Sports Eqpt

Adpro Sports Inc .... D 716 854-5116
  Buffalo *(G-2798)*
Warrior Sports Inc .... G 315 536-0937
  Penn Yan *(G-13523)*

SPORTING & ATHLETIC GOODS: Tennis Eqpt & Splys

Rottkamp Tennis Inc .... E 631 421-0040
  Huntington Station *(G-6720)*

SPORTING & REC GOODS, WHOLESALE: Camping Eqpt & Splys

Adirondack Outdoor Center .... G 315 369-2300
  Old Forge *(G-13132)*
Johnson Outdoors Inc .... C 607 779-2200
  Binghamton *(G-931)*

SPORTING & RECREATIONAL GOODS & SPLYS WHOLESALERS

Everlast Sports Mfg Corp .... E 212 239-0990
  New York *(G-10092)*
Graph-Tex Inc .... G 607 756-1875
  Cortland *(G-4028)*
Refuel Inc .... G 917 645-2974
  New York *(G-11818)*
Walsh & Hughes Inc .... G 631 427-5904
  Huntington Station *(G-6728)*

SPORTING & RECREATIONAL GOODS, WHOL: Sharpeners, Sporting

Dead Ringer LLC .... G 585 355-4685
  Rochester *(G-14303)*

SPORTING & RECREATIONAL GOODS, WHOLESALE: Boat Access & Part

Brock Awnings Ltd .... F 631 765-5200
  Hampton Bays *(G-5960)*
Di Sanos Creative Canvas Inc .... G 315 894-3137
  Frankfort *(G-5351)*
Katherine Blizniak .... G 716 674-8545
  West Seneca *(G-16950)*

SPORTING & RECREATIONAL GOODS, WHOLESALE: Fishing

Fly-Tyers Carry-All LLC .... G 607 821-1460
  Charlotteville *(G-3555)*

SPORTING & RECREATIONAL GOODS, WHOLESALE: Fishing Tackle

Hemisphere Novelties Inc .... E 914 378-4100
  Yonkers *(G-17453)*

SPORTING & RECREATIONAL GOODS, WHOLESALE: Fitness

Valeo .... G 800 634-2704
  Yonkers *(G-17495)*

SPORTING & RECREATIONAL GOODS, WHOLESALE: Hot Tubs

Charm Mfg Co Inc .... E 607 565-8161
  Waverly *(G-16699)*

SPORTING & RECREATIONAL GOODS, WHOLESALE: Skiing

Sundown Ski & Sport Shop Inc .... E 631 737-8600
  Lake Grove *(G-7267)*

SPORTING & RECREATIONAL GOODS, WHOLESALE: Watersports

Great American Industries Inc .... G 607 729-9331
  Vestal *(G-16449)*

SPORTING GOODS

Absolute Fitness US Corp .... D 732 979-8582
  Bayside *(G-765)*
Apparel Production Inc .... G 212 278-8362
  New York *(G-9179)*
Azizi Ltd .... F 212 869-6550
  New York *(G-9286)*
Bob Perani Sport Shops Inc .... G 585 427-2930
  Rochester *(G-14239)*
Buffalo Sports Inc .... G 716 826-7700
  Blasdell *(G-961)*
Burnt Mill Smithing .... G 585 293-2380
  Churchville *(G-3634)*
Burton Corporation .... D 802 862-4500
  Champlain *(G-3539)*
City Sports Inc .... G 212 730-2009
  New York *(G-9630)*
Cooperstown Bat Co Inc .... F 607 547-2415
  Fly Creek *(G-5314)*
Cooperstown Bat Co Inc .... G 607 547-2415
  Cooperstown *(G-3884)*
Cy Plastics Works Inc .... E 585 229-2555
  Honeoye *(G-6523)*
Everlast Sports Mfg Corp .... E 212 239-0990
  New York *(G-10092)*
Excellent Art Mfg Corp .... F 718 388-7075
  Inwood *(G-6756)*
Genetclly Enhnced Athc RES Inc .... G 631 750-3195
  Hicksville *(G-6348)*
Good Show Sportwear Inc .... F 212 334-8751
  New York *(G-10338)*
Grand Slam Safety LLC .... G 315 766-7008
  Croghan *(G-4059)*
Hana Sportswear Inc .... E 315 639-6332
  Dexter *(G-4285)*
Herrmann Group LLC .... G 716 876-9798
  Kenmore *(G-7148)*
Jag Manufacturing Inc .... E 518 762-9558
  Johnstown *(G-7116)*
Johnson Outdoors Inc .... C 607 779-2200
  Binghamton *(G-931)*
Macgregor Golf North Amer Inc .... D 646 840-5200
  New York *(G-11084)*
Mattel Inc .... F 716 714-8514
  East Aurora *(G-4374)*
Michael Britt Inc .... G 516 248-2010
  Mineola *(G-8525)*
Muscle Sports Products .... G 631 755-1388
  Bohemia *(G-1107)*
Nalge Nunc International Corp .... A 585 586-8800
  Rochester *(G-14527)*
North Coast Outfitters Ltd .... E 631 727-5580
  Riverhead *(G-14150)*
PNC Sports .... G 516 665-2244
  Deer Park *(G-4190)*
Pocono Pool Products-North .... E 518 283-1023
  Rensselaer *(G-14049)*
PRC Liquidating Company .... E 212 823-9626
  New York *(G-11694)*
Promats Athletics LLC .... E 607 746-8911
  Delhi *(G-4241)*
Radar Sports LLC .... G 516 678-1919
  Oceanside *(G-13091)*
Rawlings Sporting Goods Co Inc ..... D 315 429-8511
  Dolgeville *(G-4307)*
Rising Stars Soccer Club CNY .... F 315 381-3096
  Westmoreland *(G-17064)*
Roscoe Little Store Inc .... G 607 498-5553
  Roscoe *(G-15012)*
Sportsfield Specialties Inc .... E 607 746-8911
  Delhi *(G-4243)*
Stephenson Custom Case Company .... E 905 542-8762
  Niagara Falls *(G-12878)*
Vertical Lax Inc .... G 518 669-3699
  Albany *(G-148)*
Viking Athletics Ltd .... E 631 957-8000
  Lindenhurst *(G-7492)*
Watson Adventures LLC .... G 212 564-8293
  New York *(G-12598)*
Xpogo LLC .... G 717 650-5232
  New York *(G-12682)*
Zumiez Inc .... F 585 425-8720
  Victor *(G-16515)*

SPORTING GOODS STORES, NEC

A Trusted Name Inc .... F 716 326-7400
  Westfield *(G-17045)*
Arena Graphics Inc .... G 516 767-5108
  Port Washington *(G-13801)*
Burnt Mill Smithing .... G 585 293-2380
  Churchville *(G-3634)*
Cooperstown Bat Co Inc .... F 607 547-2415
  Fly Creek *(G-5314)*
Cooperstown Bat Co Inc .... G 607 547-2415
  Cooperstown *(G-3884)*
Glenda Inc .... G 718 442-8981
  Staten Island *(G-15678)*
Graph-Tex Inc .... G 607 756-1875
  Cortland *(G-4028)*
Great American Bicycle LLC .... E 518 584-8100
  Saratoga Springs *(G-15155)*
Pda Panache Corp .... G 631 776-0523
  Bohemia *(G-1116)*
Shore Line Monogramming Inc .... F 914 698-8000
  Mamaroneck *(G-8047)*
Vic Demayos Inc .... G 845 626-4343
  Accord *(G-1)*

SPORTING GOODS STORES: Camping Eqpt

Johnson Outdoors Inc .... C 607 779-2200
  Binghamton *(G-931)*

SPORTING GOODS STORES: Fishing Eqpt

Sea Isle Custom Rod Builders .... G 516 868-8855
  Freeport *(G-5424)*

SPORTING GOODS STORES: Playground Eqpt

Eastern Jungle Gym Inc .... E 845 878-9800
  Carmel *(G-3399)*

SPORTING GOODS STORES: Skateboarding Eqpt

Chapman Skateboard Co Inc .... G 631 321-4773
  Deer Park *(G-4116)*

SPORTING GOODS STORES: Specialty Sport Splys, NEC

Genetclly Enhnced Athc RES Inc .... G 631 750-3195
  Hicksville *(G-6348)*

SPORTING GOODS STORES: Tennis Goods & Eqpt

Walsh & Hughes Inc .... G 631 427-5904
  Huntington Station *(G-6728)*

SPORTING GOODS: Archery

Copper John Corporation .... F 315 258-9269
  Auburn *(G-489)*
Fenway Holdings LLC .... E 212 757-0606
  New York *(G-10153)*
Outdoor Group LLC .... C 585 201-5358
  West Henrietta *(G-16888)*
Shehawken Archery Co Inc .... F 607 967-8333
  Bainbridge *(G-554)*

SPORTING GOODS: Fishing Nets

Koring Bros Inc .... G 888 233-1292
  New Rochelle *(G-8916)*
Osprey Boat .... G 631 331-4153
  Mount Sinai *(G-8656)*

SPORTING GOODS: Sailboards

Alternatives For Children .... E 631 271-0777
  Dix Hills *(G-4290)*

SPORTING GOODS: Surfboards

Bungers Surf Shop .... G 631 244-3646
  Sayville *(G-15205)*
Pilgrim Surf & Supply .... G 718 218-7456
  Brooklyn *(G-2419)*

Employee Codes: A=Over 500 employees, B=251-500
C=101-250, D=51-100, E=20-50, F=10-19, G=5-9

SPORTING/ATHLETIC GOODS: Gloves, Boxing, Handball, Etc

Fownes Brothers & Co Inc .... E 212 683-0150
New York *(G-10194)*
Fownes Brothers & Co Inc .... E 518 752-4411
Gloversville *(G-5711)*
Olympia Sports Company Inc .... F 914 347-4737
Elmsford *(G-4772)*

SPORTS APPAREL STORES

Gametime Sportswear Plus LLC .... G 315 724-5893
Utica *(G-16335)*
Hanesbrands Inc .... G 212 576-9300
New York *(G-10406)*
JM Studio Inc .... F 646 546-5514
New York *(G-10743)*
Refuel Inc .... G 917 645-2974
New York *(G-11818)*
Unlimited Ink Inc .... E 631 582-0696
Hauppauge *(G-6221)*

SPORTS PROMOTION SVCS

Professnal Spt Pblications Inc .... D 212 697-1460
New York *(G-11728)*

SPOUTING: Plastic & Fiberglass Reinforced

Saint-Gobain Prfmce Plas Corp .... E 518 283-5963
Poestenkill *(G-13725)*

SPRAYING & DUSTING EQPT

Spfm Corp .... G 718 788-6800
Brooklyn *(G-2588)*

SPRAYING EQPT: Agricultural

Fountainhead Group Inc .... C 315 736-0037
New York Mills *(G-12722)*

SPRAYS: Artificial & Preserved

Jenray Products Inc .... E 914 375-5596
Yonkers *(G-17458)*

SPRINGS: Coiled Flat

Angelica Spring Company Inc .... F 585 466-7892
Angelica *(G-377)*
Newport Magnetics Inc .... G 315 845-8878
Newport *(G-12791)*
Whiting Door Mfg Corp .... D 716 542-3070
Akron *(G-31)*

SPRINGS: Leaf, Automobile, Locomotive, Etc

Whitesboro Spring & Alignment .... F 315 736-4441
Whitesboro *(G-17198)*

SPRINGS: Mechanical, Precision

Lee Spring Company LLC .... C 718 362-5183
Brooklyn *(G-2206)*
Unimex Corporation .... C 718 236-2222
Brooklyn *(G-2699)*

SPRINGS: Precision

Fennell Spring Company LLC .... D 607 739-3541
Horseheads *(G-6577)*
Kinemotive Corporation .... E 631 249-6440
Farmingdale *(G-5028)*

SPRINGS: Sash Balances

Pullman Mfg Corporation .... G 585 334-1350
Rochester *(G-14608)*

SPRINGS: Steel

Chet Kruszkas Service Inc .... F 716 662-7450
Orchard Park *(G-13261)*
Isolation Dynamics Corp .... E 631 491-5670
West Babylon *(G-16795)*
Lee Spring Company LLC .... C 718 362-5183
Brooklyn *(G-2206)*
Midstate Spring Inc .... E 315 437-2623
Syracuse *(G-15990)*
Temper Corporation .... E 518 853-3467
Fonda *(G-5317)*

SPRINGS: Wire

Ajax Wire Specialty Co Inc .... F 516 935-2333
Hicksville *(G-6318)*
Barnes Group Inc .... G 315 457-9200
Syracuse *(G-15867)*
Commerce Spring Corp .... F 631 293-4844
Farmingdale *(G-4961)*
Commercial Communications LLC .... G 845 343-9078
Middletown *(G-8432)*
Lee Spring LLC .... E 718 236-2222
Brooklyn *(G-2207)*
Midstate Spring Inc .... E 315 437-2623
Syracuse *(G-15990)*
Teka Precision Inc .... G 845 753-1900
Nyack *(G-13055)*
The Caldwell Manufacturing Co .... D 585 352-3790
Rochester *(G-14721)*
The Caldwell Manufacturing Co .... E 585 352-2803
Victor *(G-16508)*
Unimex Corporation .... D 212 755-8800
New York *(G-12458)*

SPRINKLING SYSTEMS: Fire Control

Allied Inspection Services LLC .... F 716 489-3199
Falconer *(G-4891)*
Gem Fabrication of NC .... G 704 278-6713
Garden City *(G-5508)*
Long Island Pipe Supply Inc .... E 516 222-8008
Garden City *(G-5515)*
Reliable Autmtc Sprnklr Co Inc .... B 914 829-2042
Elmsford *(G-4776)*
Sentry Automatic Sprinkler .... F 631 723-3095
Riverhead *(G-14156)*
Tyco Simplexgrinnell .... E 315 437-9664
East Syracuse *(G-4574)*
Tyco Simplexgrinnell .... E 716 483-0079
Jamestown *(G-7040)*
Tyco Simplexgrinnell .... D 315 337-6333
Taberg *(G-16076)*

STAGE LIGHTING SYSTEMS

Altman Stage Lighting Co Inc .... C 914 476-7987
Yonkers *(G-17412)*
Methods Tooling & Mfg Inc .... E 845 246-7100
Mount Marion *(G-8651)*
Ric-Lo Productions Ltd .... E 845 469-2285
Chester *(G-3613)*
Sir Industries Inc .... G 631 234-2444
Hauppauge *(G-6192)*

STAINLESS STEEL

American Chimney Supplies Inc .... G 631 434-2020
Hauppauge *(G-6020)*
Bryant Manufacturing Wny Inc .... F 716 894-8282
Buffalo *(G-2847)*
Dakota Systems Mfg Corp .... G 631 249-5811
Farmingdale *(G-4973)*
Hallock Fabricating Corp .... G 631 727-2441
Riverhead *(G-14144)*
Qsf Inc .... G 585 247-6200
Gates *(G-5562)*
Recon Construction Corp .... E 718 939-1305
Little Neck *(G-7509)*
Sims Group USA Holdings Corp .... D 718 786-6031
Long Island City *(G-7877)*
Tdy Industries LLC .... E 716 433-4411
Lockport *(G-7617)*
Viraj - USA Inc .... G 516 280-8380
Garden City *(G-5535)*

STAIRCASES & STAIRS, WOOD

A W Hamel Stair Mfg Inc .... F 518 346-3031
Schenectady *(G-15226)*
Adirondack Stairs Inc .... F 845 246-2525
Saugerties *(G-15178)*
Capital District Stairs Inc .... G 518 383-2449
Halfmoon *(G-5909)*
Island Stairs Corp .... G 347 645-0560
Staten Island *(G-15689)*
Mestel Brothers Stairs & Rails .... C 516 496-4127
Syosset *(G-15828)*
Monroe Stair Products Inc .... E 845 783-4245
Monroe *(G-8563)*
Monroe Stair Products Inc .... G 845 791-4016
Monticello *(G-8606)*
Quality Stair Builders Inc .... F 631 694-0711
Farmingdale *(G-5093)*

S R Sloan Inc .... D 315 736-7730
Whitesboro *(G-17195)*
Stated Island Stair Inc .... G 718 317-9276
Staten Island *(G-15738)*
Staten Island Stair Inc .... G 718 317-9276
Staten Island *(G-15740)*
United Rockland Holding Co Inc .... E 845 357-1900
Suffern *(G-15802)*

STAMPED ART GOODS FOR EMBROIDERING

Dirt T Shirts Inc .... E 845 336-4230
Kingston *(G-7187)*

STAMPING SVC: Book, Gold

Mines Press Inc .... C 914 788-1800
Cortlandt Manor *(G-4052)*

STAMPINGS: Automotive

P R B Metal Products Inc .... F 631 467-1800
Ronkonkoma *(G-14961)*
Utica Metal Products Inc .... D 315 732-6163
Utica *(G-16364)*

STAMPINGS: Metal

4m Precision Industries Inc .... D 315 252-8415
Auburn *(G-476)*
Able National Corp .... E 718 386-8801
Brooklyn *(G-1549)*
Acro Industries Inc .... C 585 254-3661
Rochester *(G-14171)*
Advanced Structures Corp .... F 631 667-5000
Deer Park *(G-4088)*
Afco Systems Inc .... C 631 424-3935
Farmingdale *(G-4931)*
All Out Die Cutting Inc .... E 718 346-6666
Brooklyn *(G-1587)*
Arnell Inc .... G 516 486-7098
Hempstead *(G-6265)*
Arro Tool & Die Inc .... E 716 763-6203
Lakewood *(G-7287)*
B & R Tool Inc .... G 718 948-2729
Staten Island *(G-15642)*
B H M Metal Products Co .... G 845 292-5297
Kauneonga Lake *(G-7136)*
Bailey Manufacturing Co LLC .... E 716 965-2731
Forestville *(G-5333)*
Barnes Group Inc .... G 315 457-9200
Syracuse *(G-15867)*
Bel-Bee Products Incorporated .... F 845 353-0300
West Nyack *(G-16912)*
Bowen Products Corporation .... G 315 498-4481
Nedrow *(G-8772)*
C & H Precision Tools Inc .... E 631 758-3806
Holtsville *(G-6502)*
Cameo Metal Products Inc .... E 718 788-1106
Brooklyn *(G-1751)*
Cannon Industries Inc .... D 585 254-8080
Rochester *(G-14258)*
Cep Technologies Corporation .... E 914 968-4100
Yonkers *(G-17427)*
Check-Mate Industries Inc .... E 631 491-1777
West Babylon *(G-16782)*
Chivvis Enterprises Inc .... F 631 842-9055
Copiague *(G-3897)*
Cobbe Industries Inc .... E 716 287-2661
Gerry *(G-5592)*
Coda Resources Ltd .... D 718 649-1666
Brooklyn *(G-1790)*
Compar Manufacturing Corp .... E 212 304-2777
New York *(G-9690)*
Crosby Company .... E 716 852-3522
Buffalo *(G-2893)*
Dayton Rogers New York LLC .... D 585 349-4040
Rochester *(G-14302)*
Dunkirk Metal Products Wny LLC .... E 716 366-2555
Dunkirk *(G-4339)*
Eaton Electric Holdings LLC .... C 607 756-2821
Cortland *(G-4025)*
Endicott Precision Inc .... C 607 754-7076
Endicott *(G-4803)*
Engineering Mfg Tech LLC .... D 607 754-7111
Endicott *(G-4805)*
Falso Industries Inc .... E 315 463-0266
Syracuse *(G-15941)*
Forsyth Industries Inc .... E 716 652-1070
Buffalo *(G-2953)*

PRODUCT SECTION

STEEL FABRICATORS

Freeport Screen & Stamping ....E...... 516 379-0330
  Freeport *(G-5401)*
Gasser & Sons Inc ....C...... 631 543-6600
  Commack *(G-3832)*
Gleason Works ....A...... 585 473-1000
  Rochester *(G-14408)*
Great Lakes Pressed Steel Corp ....E...... 716 885-4037
  Buffalo *(G-2982)*
Greene Technologies Inc ....D...... 607 656-4166
  Greene *(G-5866)*
International Ord Tech Inc ....D...... 716 664-1100
  Jamestown *(G-7003)*
Johnson & Hoffman LLC ....D...... 516 742-3333
  Carle Place *(G-3392)*
Lamparts Co Inc ....F...... 914 723-8986
  Mount Vernon *(G-8699)*
Magic Novelty Co Inc ....E...... 212 304-2777
  New York *(G-11104)*
Mantel & Mantel Stamping Corp ....G...... 631 467-1916
  Ronkonkoma *(G-14937)*
Marex Aquisition Corp ....C...... 585 458-3940
  Rochester *(G-14497)*
Matov Industries Inc ....E...... 718 392-5060
  Long Island City *(G-7806)*
McHone Industries Inc.........................D...... 716 945-3380
  Salamanca *(G-15101)*
National Die & Button Mould Co ....E...... 201 939-7800
  Brooklyn *(G-2350)*
OEM Solutions Inc ....G...... 716 864-9324
  Clarence *(G-3667)*
P R B Metal Products Inc ....F...... 631 467-1800
  Ronkonkoma *(G-14961)*
P&G Metal Components Corp ....D...... 716 896-7900
  Buffalo *(G-3108)*
Precision Photo-Fab Inc ....D...... 716 821-9393
  Buffalo *(G-3133)*
Precision Tl Die & Stamping Co ....F...... 516 561-0041
  Valley Stream *(G-16420)*
Premier Metals Group ....E...... 585 436-4020
  Rochester *(G-14597)*
Pronto Tool & Die Co Inc ....E...... 631 981-8920
  Ronkonkoma *(G-14972)*
Quality Metal Stamping LLC ....G...... 516 255-9000
  Rockville Centre *(G-14797)*
R G Flair Co Inc ....E...... 631 586-7311
  Bay Shore *(G-730)*
Richter Metalcraft Corporation ....E...... 845 895-2025
  Wallkill *(G-16545)*
Rochester Stampings Inc ....F...... 585 467-5241
  Rochester *(G-14649)*
Sharon Metal Stamping Corp ....G...... 718 828-4510
  Bronx *(G-1451)*
Simplex Manufacturing Co Inc ....F...... 315 252-7524
  Auburn *(G-519)*
Stampcrete International Ltd ....E...... 315 451-2837
  Liverpool *(G-7549)*
Stamped Fittings Inc............................E...... 607 733-9988
  Elmira Heights *(G-4713)*
Stever-Locke Industries Inc ....G...... 585 624-3450
  Honeoye Falls *(G-6538)*
Stewart Efi LLC ....D...... 914 965-0816
  Yonkers *(G-17487)*
Superior Washer & Gasket Corp ....D...... 631 273-8282
  Hauppauge *(G-6203)*
Tooling Enterprises Inc ....F...... 716 842-0445
  Buffalo *(G-3222)*
Tri-Technologies Inc ....E...... 914 699-2001
  Mount Vernon *(G-8741)*
TRW Automotive Inc ....B...... 315 255-3311
  Auburn *(G-525)*
TRW Automotive US LLC ....C...... 315 255-3311
  Auburn *(G-526)*
Universal Shielding Corp ....E...... 631 667-7900
  Deer Park *(G-4219)*
V Lake Industries Inc ....G...... 716 885-9141
  Buffalo *(G-3239)*
Village Metals Inc ....G...... 585 271-1250
  Rochester *(G-14754)*
W & H Stampings Inc ....E...... 631 234-6161
  Hauppauge *(G-6229)*
Web Associates Inc ....G...... 716 883-3477
  Buffalo *(G-3249)*
WR Smith & Sons Inc ....G...... 845 620-9400
  Nanuet *(G-8763)*

STANDS & RACKS: Engine, Metal

Devin Mfg Inc ....F...... 585 496-5770
  Arcade *(G-391)*

STARTERS: Motor

Con Rel Auto Electric Inc ....E...... 518 356-1646
  Schenectady *(G-15245)*

STATIC ELIMINATORS: Ind

Nrd LLC ....E...... 716 773-7634
  Grand Island *(G-5764)*

STATIONARY & OFFICE SPLYS, WHOLESALE: Laser Printer Splys

Interntnl Publcatns Media Grup ....G...... 917 604-9602
  New York *(G-10640)*
Printer Components Inc ....G...... 585 924-5190
  Fairport *(G-4871)*

STATIONARY & OFFICE SPLYS, WHOLESALE: Stationery

F J Remey Co Inc ....E...... 516 741-5112
  Mineola *(G-8511)*
One In A Million Inc ....G...... 516 829-1111
  Valley Stream *(G-16417)*
Tripi Engraving Co Inc ....E...... 718 383-6500
  Brooklyn *(G-2682)*

STATIONER'S SUNDRIES: Rubber

Hampton Art LLC ....E...... 631 924-1335
  Medford *(G-8247)*
Rubber Stamps Inc ....E...... 212 675-1180
  Mineola *(G-8535)*

STATIONERY & OFFICE SPLYS WHOLESALERS

Argo Lithographers Inc ....E...... 718 729-2700
  Long Island City *(G-7669)*
Atlaz International Ltd ....F...... 516 239-1854
  Lawrence *(G-7390)*
Kas-Ray Industries Inc ....F...... 212 620-3144
  New York *(G-10812)*
Kleer - View Index Co Inc ....G...... 718 896-3800
  Woodside *(G-17335)*
Labels Inter-Global Inc ....F...... 212 398-0006
  New York *(G-10912)*

STATIONERY PRDTS

Bak USA Technologies Corp ....E...... 716 248-2704
  Buffalo *(G-2831)*
Cos TEC Manufacturing Corp ....G...... 631 589-7170
  Bohemia *(G-1039)*
Dynamic Intl Mfrs & Distrs Inc ....F...... 347 993-1914
  Suffern *(G-15788)*
Innovative Designs LLC ....E...... 212 695-0892
  New York *(G-10605)*
International Design Assoc Ltd ....G...... 212 687-0333
  New York *(G-10633)*
Kleer-Fax Inc ....D...... 631 225-1100
  Amityville *(G-303)*
Leather Indexes Corp ....E...... 516 827-1900
  Hicksville *(G-6363)*
Moleskine America Inc ....E...... 646 461-3018
  New York *(G-11294)*
P C I Paper Conversions Inc ....F...... 315 437-1641
  Syracuse *(G-16006)*
Paper Magic Group Inc ....B...... 631 521-3682
  New York *(G-11564)*
Westrock Mwv LLC ....C...... 212 688-5000
  New York *(G-12618)*

STATIONERY: Made From Purchased Materials

Allen William & Company Inc ....C...... 212 675-6461
  Glendale *(G-5644)*

STATUARY & OTHER DECORATIVE PRDTS: Nonmetallic

Design Research Ltd ....C...... 212 228-7675
  New York *(G-9854)*
Gallery 91 ....G...... 212 966-3722
  New York *(G-10242)*

STATUES: Nonmetal

Barrett Bronze Inc ....E...... 914 699-6060
  Mount Vernon *(G-8665)*

Dream Statuary Inc ....G...... 718 647-2024
  Brooklyn *(G-1878)*
Jonas Louis Paul Studios Inc ....G...... 518 851-2211
  Hudson *(G-6623)*

STEAM SPLY SYSTEMS SVCS INCLUDING GEOTHERMAL

Caithness Equities Corporation ....E...... 212 599-2112
  New York *(G-9498)*

STEEL & ALLOYS: Tool & Die

B H M Metal Products Co ....G...... 845 292-5297
  Kauneonga Lake *(G-7136)*
Fuller Tool Incorporated ....F...... 315 891-3183
  Newport *(G-12790)*
Spin-Rite Corporation ....F...... 585 266-5200
  Rochester *(G-14695)*

STEEL FABRICATORS

760 NI Holdings ....E...... 716 821-1391
  Buffalo *(G-2791)*
A & T Iron Works Inc ....F...... 914 632-8992
  New Rochelle *(G-8883)*
A-Fab Initiatives Inc ....G...... 716 877-5257
  Buffalo *(G-2793)*
A/C Design & Fabrication Corp ....E...... 718 227-8100
  Staten Island *(G-15632)*
AAA Welding and Fabrication of ....G...... 585 254-2830
  Rochester *(G-14163)*
Abalon Precision Mfg Corp ....F...... 718 589-5682
  Mount Vernon *(G-8659)*
Abalon Precision Mfg Corp ....F...... 718 589-5682
  Mount Vernon *(G-8660)*
Acadia Stairs ....G...... 845 765-8600
  Fishkill *(G-5180)*
Accucut Inc ....G...... 631 567-2868
  West Sayville *(G-16933)*
Achilles Construction Co Inc ....G...... 718 389-4717
  Mount Vernon *(G-8662)*
Ackroyd Metal Fabricators Inc ....F...... 518 434-1281
  Menands *(G-8364)*
Advanced Thermal Systems Inc ....E...... 716 681-1800
  Lancaster *(G-7298)*
Advantage Machining Inc ....F...... 716 731-6418
  Niagara Falls *(G-12795)*
Aero-Data Metal Crafters Inc ....C...... 631 471-7733
  Ronkonkoma *(G-14856)*
Airflex Corp ....D...... 631 752-1219
  Farmingdale *(G-4932)*
Aldo Frustacci Iron Works Inc ....F...... 718 768-0707
  Brooklyn *(G-1578)*
All-City Metal Inc ....E...... 718 937-3975
  Maspeth *(G-8114)*
Alp Steel Corp ....E...... 716 854-3030
  Buffalo *(G-2804)*
American Aerogel Corporation ....E...... 585 328-2140
  Rochester *(G-14196)*
Asp Industries Inc ....E...... 585 254-9130
  Rochester *(G-14217)*
Atlantis Equipment Corporation ....F...... 518 733-5910
  Stephentown *(G-15756)*
B H M Metal Products Co ....G...... 845 292-5297
  Kauneonga Lake *(G-7136)*
B P Nash Co Inc ....F...... 315 445-1310
  East Syracuse *(G-4509)*
Barber Welding Inc ....E...... 315 834-6645
  Weedsport *(G-16746)*
Barker Steel LLC ....E...... 518 465-6221
  Albany *(G-52)*
Barry Steel Fabrication Inc ....F...... 716 433-2144
  Lockport *(G-7571)*
Bear Metal Works Inc ....F...... 716 824-4350
  Buffalo *(G-2836)*
Bennett Manufacturing Co Inc ....C...... 716 937-9161
  Alden *(G-175)*
Bereza Iron Works Inc ....F...... 585 254-6311
  Rochester *(G-14229)*
Blackstone Advanced Tech LLC ....C...... 716 665-5410
  Jamestown *(G-6975)*
Bms Manufacturing Co Inc ....E...... 607 535-2426
  Watkins Glen *(G-16693)*
Bob Murphy Inc ....F...... 607 729-3553
  Vestal *(G-16442)*
Bombardier Transportation ....D...... 607 324-0216
  Hornell *(G-6560)*
Bombardier Trnsp Holdings USA ....D...... 607 776-4791
  Bath *(G-654)*
Bristol Metals Inc ....F...... 585 657-7665
  Bloomfield *(G-982)*

Employee Codes: A=Over 500 employees, B=251-500
C=101-250, D=51-100, E=20-50, F=10-19, G=5-9

2017 Harris
New York Manufacturers Directory

1347

Buffalo Metal Forming Inc......................G....... 716 856-4575
West Seneca *(G-16941)*
Burnt Hills Fabricators Inc....................F........ 518 885-1115
Ballston Spa *(G-592)*
C & C Custom Metal Fabricators...........G....... 631 235-9646
Hauppauge *(G-6039)*
C & C Metal Fabrications Inc................F....... 315 598-7607
Fulton *(G-5453)*
C & T Tool & Instrument Co...................E....... 718 429-1253
Woodside *(G-17321)*
Cameron Mfg & Design Inc....................C....... 607 739-3606
Horseheads *(G-6571)*
Carpenter Industries Inc.........................F....... 315 463-4284
Syracuse *(G-15886)*
Castle Harvester Co Inc..........................G....... 585 526-5884
Seneca Castle *(G-15359)*
CBM Fabrications Inc............................E....... 518 399-8023
Ballston Lake *(G-581)*
Chautauqua Machine Spc LLC..............F....... 716 782-3276
Ashville *(G-427)*
Christian Fabrication LLC.....................G....... 315 822-0135
West Winfield *(G-16957)*
Cives Corporation...................................C....... 315 287-2200
Gouverneur *(G-5743)*
Cobbe Industries Inc.............................E....... 716 287-2661
Gerry *(G-5592)*
Cobra Operating Industries LLC...........G....... 607 639-1700
Afton *(G-9)*
Columbia Metal Fabricators...................G....... 631 476-7527
Port Jeff STA *(G-13765)*
Computerized Metal Bending Ser..........F....... 631 249-1177
West Babylon *(G-16785)*
Cottonwood Metals Inc..........................E....... 646 807-8674
Bohemia *(G-1040)*
County Fabricators.................................F....... 914 741-0219
Pleasantville *(G-13713)*
Cyncal Steel Fabricators Inc..................F....... 631 254-5600
Bay Shore *(G-689)*
D N Gannon Fabricating Inc...................G....... 315 463-7466
Syracuse *(G-15919)*
Dennies Manufacturing Inc....................E....... 585 393-4646
Canandaigua *(G-3342)*
Diversified Manufacturing Inc................F....... 716 681-7670
Lancaster *(G-7312)*
Donald Stefan..G....... 716 492-1110
Chaffee *(G-3533)*
Dynasty Metal Works Inc........................G....... 631 284-3719
Riverhead *(G-14141)*
E & Y General Cnstr Co Inc....................F....... 718 567-7011
Staten Island *(G-15667)*
E B Atlas Steel Corp...............................F....... 716 876-0900
Buffalo *(G-2922)*
Eastern Manufacturing Inc......................F....... 716 741-4572
Clarence Center *(G-3674)*
Eastern Welding Inc................................G....... 631 727-0306
Riverhead *(G-14142)*
Elevator Accessories Mfg.......................F....... 914 739-7004
Peekskill *(G-13477)*
Elmira Metal Works Inc...........................G....... 607 734-9813
Elmira *(G-4683)*
Empire Industrial Systems Corp...........F....... 631 242-4619
Bay Shore *(G-699)*
Empire Metal Fabricators Inc.................G....... 585 288-2140
Rochester *(G-14347)*
Eps Iron Works Inc..................................G....... 516 294-5840
Mineola *(G-8509)*
Erie Engineered Products Inc...............E....... 716 206-0204
Lancaster *(G-7314)*
Everfab Inc...D....... 716 655-1550
East Aurora *(G-4370)*
Excel Industries Inc.................................E....... 716 542-5468
Clarence *(G-3661)*
Farmingdale Iron Works Inc...................G....... 631 249-5995
Farmingdale *(G-4991)*
Feinstein Iron Works Inc.........................E....... 516 997-8300
Westbury *(G-16985)*
Fence Plaza Corp....................................G....... 718 469-2200
Brooklyn *(G-1966)*
Five Corners Repair Inc..........................F....... 585 322-7369
Bliss *(G-980)*
Flagpoles Incorporated..........................D....... 631 751-5500
East Setauket *(G-4483)*
Fort Miller Group Inc...............................B....... 518 695-5000
Greenwich *(G-5887)*
Frazier Industrial Company....................D....... 315 539-9256
Waterloo *(G-16626)*
Gasport Welding & Fabg Inc...................F....... 716 772-7205
Gasport *(G-5557)*
George Industries LLC............................C....... 607 748-3371
Endicott *(G-4810)*

Gibraltar Industries Inc..........................D....... 716 826-6500
Buffalo *(G-2974)*
Glenridge Fabricators Inc.......................F....... 718 456-2297
Glendale *(G-5655)*
Hallock Fabricating Corp.......................G....... 631 727-2441
Riverhead *(G-14144)*
Hansen Steel..E....... 585 398-2020
Farmington *(G-5152)*
Homer Iron Works LLC............................G....... 607 749-3963
Homer *(G-6519)*
Hudson Steel Fabricators......................E....... 585 454-3923
Rochester *(G-14440)*
Industrial Fabricating Corp....................E....... 315 437-3353
East Syracuse *(G-4539)*
Industrial Support Inc.............................D....... 716 662-2954
Buffalo *(G-3006)*
Inscape (new York) Inc...........................D....... 716 665-6210
Falconer *(G-4902)*
Irony Limited Inc......................................G....... 631 329-4065
East Hampton *(G-4411)*
Irv Schroder & Sons Inc..........................E....... 518 828-0194
Stottville *(G-15781)*
Irving Woodlands LLC.............................E....... 607 723-4862
Conklin *(G-3870)*
J F M Sheet Metal Inc..............................G....... 631 737-8494
Ronkonkoma *(G-14916)*
J M Haley Corp..D....... 631 845-5200
Farmingdale *(G-5013)*
Jaab Precision Inc...................................G....... 631 218-3725
Ronkonkoma *(G-14918)*
James Woerner Inc..................................G....... 631 454-9330
Farmingdale *(G-5016)*
Jbs LLC...E....... 518 346-0001
Scotia *(G-15327)*
Jentsch & Co Inc......................................G....... 716 852-4111
Buffalo *(G-3016)*
Joy Edward Company..............................E....... 315 474-3360
East Syracuse *(G-4547)*
Jpw Structural Contracting Inc..............E....... 315 432-1111
Syracuse *(G-15971)*
K & E Fabricating Co Inc.........................F....... 716 829-1829
Buffalo *(G-3023)*
Kal Manufacturing Corporation.............E....... 585 265-4310
Webster *(G-16726)*
KDO Industries Inc..................................G....... 631 608-4612
Amityville *(G-301)*
King Steel Iron Work Corp.....................F....... 718 384-7500
Brooklyn *(G-2174)*
Kleinfelder John.......................................G....... 716 753-3163
Mayville *(G-8216)*
Knj Fabricators LLC................................F....... 347 234-6985
Bronx *(G-1374)*
Koenig Iron Works Inc.............................E....... 718 433-0900
Long Island City *(G-7782)*
Kryten Iron Works Inc..............................G....... 914 345-0990
Hawthorne *(G-6249)*
Leading Edge Fabrication.......................G....... 631 274-9797
Deer Park *(G-4164)*
Lindenhurst Fabricators Inc..................G....... 631 226-3737
Lindenhurst *(G-7467)*
M & L Steel & Ornamental Iron..............F....... 718 816-8660
Staten Island *(G-15701)*
Major-IPC Inc..G....... 845 292-2200
Liberty *(G-7438)*
Marex Aquisition Corp.............................C....... 585 458-3940
Rochester *(G-14497)*
Mason Industries Inc...............................C....... 631 348-0282
Hauppauge *(G-6126)*
Maspeth Steel Fabricators Inc...............G....... 718 361-9192
Long Island City *(G-7804)*
Maspeth Welding Inc...............................E....... 718 497-5430
Maspeth *(G-8150)*
Metal Concepts..G....... 845 592-1863
Beacon *(G-788)*
Metal Crafts Inc..G....... 718 443-3333
Brooklyn *(G-2303)*
Metal Fab LLC..G....... 607 775-3200
Binghamton *(G-936)*
Metal Works of NY Inc.............................G....... 718 525-9440
Jamaica *(G-6930)*
Miscellnous Ir Fabricators Inc..............E....... 518 355-1822
Schenectady *(G-15280)*
Mobile Mini Inc...F....... 315 732-4555
Utica *(G-16349)*
Monarch Metal Fabrication Inc..............G....... 631 563-8967
Bohemia *(G-1105)*
Nathan Steel Corp....................................F....... 315 797-1335
Utica *(G-16351)*
Nci Group Inc..D....... 315 339-1245
Rome *(G-14824)*

New Vision Industries Inc.......................F....... 607 687-7700
Endicott *(G-4820)*
New York Manufactured Products.........F....... 585 254-9353
Rochester *(G-14532)*
North E Rggers Erectors NY Inc............E....... 518 842-6377
Amsterdam *(G-362)*
North Eastern Fabricators Inc...............E....... 718 542-0450
New York *(G-11457)*
Northeast Fabricators LLC.....................D....... 607 865-4031
Walton *(G-16549)*
Oehlers Wldg & Fabrication Inc.............F....... 716 821-1800
Buffalo *(G-3098)*
Orange County Ironworks LLC...............E....... 845 769-3000
Montgomery *(G-8600)*
Oriskany Mfg Tech LLC...........................E....... 315 732-4962
Yorkville *(G-17525)*
P & H Inc...E....... 631 231-7660
Hauppauge *(G-6157)*
P K G Equipment Incorporated..............E....... 585 436-4650
Rochester *(G-14564)*
Patsy Strocchia & Sons Iron Wo............F....... 516 625-8800
Albertson *(G-156)*
Pcx Aerostructures LLC.........................E....... 631 249-7901
Ronkonkoma *(G-14967)*
Pcx Aerostructures LLC.........................E....... 631 467-2632
Farmingdale *(G-5075)*
Peralta Metal Works Inc..........................G....... 718 649-8661
Brooklyn *(G-2416)*
Perma Tech Inc...E....... 716 854-0707
Buffalo *(G-3122)*
Pierce Industries LLC.............................E....... 585 458-0888
Rochester *(G-14584)*
Portfab LLC..E....... 718 542-3600
Amityville *(G-322)*
Precision Metals Corp.............................E....... 631 586-5032
Bay Shore *(G-727)*
Precision Polish LLC...............................E....... 315 894-3792
Frankfort *(G-5356)*
Prime Materials Recovery Inc................G....... 315 697-5251
Canastota *(G-3371)*
Productand Design Inc............................F....... 718 858-2440
Brooklyn *(G-2452)*
R & J Sheet Metal Distrs Inc..................G....... 518 433-1525
Albany *(G-125)*
R&S Steel LLC..E....... 315 281-0123
Rome *(G-14831)*
Ramsey Charles Company......................F....... 845 338-1464
Kingston *(G-7208)*
Raulli and Sons Inc..................................D....... 315 479-6693
Syracuse *(G-16018)*
REO Welding Inc.......................................F....... 518 238-1022
Cohoes *(G-3756)*
Risa Management Corp...........................E....... 718 361-2606
Maspeth *(G-8167)*
RJ Precision LLC.....................................G....... 585 768-8030
Stafford *(G-15622)*
Robert E Derecktor Inc............................D....... 914 698-0962
Mamaroneck *(G-8045)*
Romar Contracting Inc............................G....... 845 778-2737
Walden *(G-16535)*
Roth Design & Consulting Inc................E....... 718 209-0193
Brooklyn *(G-2509)*
Rothe Welding Inc....................................G....... 845 246-3051
Saugerties *(G-15193)*
Rs Automation..F....... 585 589-0199
Albion *(G-169)*
Rus Industries Inc....................................E....... 716 284-7828
Niagara Falls *(G-12869)*
Schenectady Steel Co Inc.......................D....... 518 355-3220
Schenectady *(G-15293)*
Schenectady Steel Co Inc.......................E....... 607 275-0086
Ithaca *(G-6875)*
Schneider Brothers Corporation...........E....... 315 458-8369
Syracuse *(G-16034)*
Schuler-Subra Inc....................................G....... 716 893-3100
Buffalo *(G-3177)*
Seibel Modern Mfg & Wldg Corp...........D....... 716 683-1536
Lancaster *(G-7342)*
Sentry Metal Blast Inc..............................E....... 716 285-5241
Niagara Falls *(G-12875)*
Sherco Services LLC................................F....... 516 676-3028
Glen Cove *(G-5627)*
Silverstone Shtmtl Fbrications..............G....... 718 422-0380
Brooklyn *(G-2559)*
Specialty Steel Fabg Corp.......................F....... 718 893-6326
Bronx *(G-1461)*
Specialty Wldg & Fabg NY Inc................D....... 315 426-1807
Syracuse *(G-16043)*
Standard Steel Fabricators....................F....... 518 765-4820
Voorheesville *(G-16519)*

PRODUCT

1348 2017 Harris New York Manufacturers Directory (G-0000) Company's Geographic Section entry number

PRODUCT SECTION

STRUCTURAL SUPPORT & BUILDING MATERIAL: Concrete

Steel Tech SA LLC .... G 845 786-3691
  Thiells *(G-16114)*
Stone Well Bodies & Mch Inc .... F 315 497-3512
  Genoa *(G-5590)*
STS Steel Inc .... D 518 370-2693
  Schenectady *(G-15301)*
Sunlight US Co Inc .... G 716 826-6500
  Buffalo *(G-3201)*
Supreme Steel Inc .... F 631 884-1320
  Lindenhurst *(G-7489)*
Team Fabrication Inc .... G 716 655-4038
  West Falls *(G-16845)*
Titan Steel Corp .... F 315 656-7046
  Kirkville *(G-7229)*
Triboro Iron Works Inc .... G 718 361-9600
  Long Island City *(G-7906)*
Triton Builders Inc .... E 631 841-2534
  Amityville *(G-331)*
Tropical Driftwood Originals .... G 516 623-0980
  Roosevelt *(G-15010)*
Tymetal Corp .... E 518 692-9930
  Greenwich *(G-5895)*
Ulster Precision Inc .... E 845 338-0995
  Kingston *(G-7218)*
United Iron Inc .... E 914 667-5700
  Mount Vernon *(G-8745)*
United Structure Solution Inc .... F 347 227-7526
  New York *(G-12466)*
Universal Metal Works LLC .... F 315 598-7607
  Fulton *(G-5476)*
Vance Metal Fabricators Inc .... D 315 789-5626
  Geneva *(G-5588)*
Vulcan Iron Works Inc .... G 631 395-6846
  Manorville *(G-8082)*
Ward Steel Company Inc .... E 315 451-4566
  Liverpool *(G-7555)*
Welding Metallurgy Inc .... E 631 253-0500
  Hauppauge *(G-6231)*
Whitacre Engineering Company .... G 315 622-1075
  Liverpool *(G-7556)*
Winters Railroad Service Inc .... G 716 337-2668
  North Collins *(G-12932)*

STEEL MILLS

Albaluz Films LLC .... G 347 613-2321
  New York *(G-9072)*
Allvac .... F 716 433-4411
  Lockport *(G-7569)*
Baker Tool & Die .... G 716 694-2025
  North Tonawanda *(G-12958)*
Belmet Products Inc .... E 718 542-8220
  Bronx *(G-1283)*
China Industrial Steel Inc .... G 646 328-1502
  New York *(G-9598)*
Coventry Manufacturing Co Inc .... E 914 668-2212
  Mount Vernon *(G-8674)*
DAgostino Iron Works Inc .... G 585 235-8850
  Rochester *(G-14298)*
David Fehlman .... G 315 455-8888
  Syracuse *(G-15922)*
Dunkirk Specialty Steel LLC .... C 716 366-1000
  Dunkirk *(G-4340)*
Hmi Metal Powders .... C 315 839-5421
  Clayville *(G-3688)*
Jaquith Industries Inc .... E 315 478-5700
  Syracuse *(G-15966)*
Juniper Elbow Co Inc .... C 718 326-2546
  Middle Village *(G-8414)*
Kenbenco Inc .... F 845 246-3066
  Saugerties *(G-15186)*
Nucor Steel Auburn Inc .... B 315 253-4561
  Auburn *(G-511)*
Republic Steel Inc .... B 716 827-2800
  Blasdell *(G-965)*
Standex Air Dist Pdts Inc .... E 585 798-0300
  Medina *(G-8283)*
Universal Stainless & Alloy .... C 716 366-1000
  Dunkirk *(G-4352)*

STEEL, COLD-ROLLED: Sheet Or Strip, From Own Hot-Rolled

Renco Group Inc .... G 212 541-6000
  New York *(G-11832)*

STEEL, COLD-ROLLED: Strip NEC, From Purchased Hot-Rolled

Worthington Industries Inc .... D 315 336-5500
  Rome *(G-14840)*

STEEL, HOT-ROLLED: Sheet Or Strip

Jfe Engineering Corporation .... F 212 310-9320
  New York *(G-10728)*
Jfe Steel America Inc .... G 212 310-9320
  New York *(G-10729)*

STEEL: Cold-Rolled

Aero-Data Metal Crafters Inc .... C 631 471-7733
  Ronkonkoma *(G-14856)*
Clover Wire Forming Co Inc .... E 914 375-0400
  Yonkers *(G-17428)*
Gibraltar Industries Inc .... D 716 826-6500
  Buffalo *(G-2974)*
Hitachi Metals America Ltd .... E 914 694-9200
  Purchase *(G-13958)*
Northeast Cnstr Inds Inc .... F 845 565-1000
  Montgomery *(G-8598)*
Sunlight US Co Inc .... G 716 826-6500
  Buffalo *(G-3201)*

STEEL: Galvanized

Elderlee Incorporated .... C 315 789-6670
  Oaks Corners *(G-13069)*

STEEL: Laminated

Advantech Industries Inc .... C 585 247-0701
  Rochester *(G-14181)*

STENCILS

Crafters Workshop Inc .... G 914 345-2838
  Elmsford *(G-4744)*

STONE: Cast Concrete

Alp Stone Inc .... F 718 706-6166
  Long Island City *(G-7653)*
Corinthian Cast Stone Inc .... E 631 920-2340
  Wyandanch *(G-17374)*

STONE: Dimension, NEC

Dominic De Nigris Inc .... E 718 597-4460
  Bronx *(G-1316)*
Finger Lakes Stone Co Inc .... F 607 273-4646
  Ithaca *(G-6842)*
Hillburn Granite Company Inc .... G 845 357-8900
  Hillburn *(G-6415)*
Suffolk Granite Manufacturing .... E 631 226-4774
  Lindenhurst *(G-7486)*

STONE: Quarrying & Processing, Own Stone Prdts

Callanan Industries Inc .... E 845 331-6868
  Kingston *(G-7182)*
Dalrymple Holding Corp .... E 607 737-6200
  Pine City *(G-13551)*
Graymont Materials Inc .... E 518 561-5200
  Plattsburgh *(G-13667)*
Hanson Aggregates PA LLC .... E 315 789-6202
  Oaks Corners *(G-13070)*
New York Marble and Stone Corp .... F 718 729-7272
  Maspeth *(G-8156)*
Rock Iroquois Products Inc .... F 585 381-7010
  Rochester *(G-14655)*
Thalle Industries Inc .... E 914 762-3415
  Briarcliff Manor *(G-1231)*

STONEWARE CLAY MINING

Devonian Stone New York Inc .... E 607 655-2600
  Windsor *(G-17272)*

STORE FIXTURES, EXC REFRIGERATED: Wholesalers

Action Rack Display Mfg .... F 718 257-7111
  Brooklyn *(G-1558)*
Alrod Associates Inc .... F 631 981-2193
  Ronkonkoma *(G-14866)*
Artistry In Wood of Syracuse .... F 315 431-4022
  East Syracuse *(G-4506)*
Leo D Bernstein & Sons Inc .... E 212 337-9578
  New York *(G-10968)*

STORE FIXTURES: Exc Wood

Alrod Associates Inc .... F 631 981-2193
  Ronkonkoma *(G-14866)*

Fixture Hardware Mfg Corp .... E 718 499-9422
  Brooklyn
Hamlet Products Inc .... F 914 665-0307
  Mount Vernon *(G-8689)*
Yaloz Mould & Die Co Inc .... E 718 389-1131
  Brooklyn *(G-2773)*

STORE FIXTURES: Wood

Abbott Industries Inc .... E 718 291-0800
  Jamaica *(G-6891)*
Alrod Associates Inc .... F 631 981-2193
  Ronkonkoma *(G-14866)*
Custom Wood Inc .... G 718 927-4700
  Brooklyn *(G-1828)*
Falvo Manufacturing Co Inc .... F 315 738-7682
  Utica *(G-16330)*
L & J Interiors Inc .... E 631 218-0838
  Bohemia *(G-1089)*
Longo Commercial Cabinets Inc .... E 631 225-4290
  Lindenhurst *(G-7469)*
Madjek Inc .... D 631 842-4475
  Amityville *(G-308)*
Premier Fixtures LLC .... D 631 236-4100
  Hauppauge *(G-6170)*
Three R Enterprises Inc .... E 585 254-5050
  Rochester *(G-14725)*
Wares of Wood .... E 315 964-2983
  Williamstown *(G-17229)*

STORE FRONTS: Prefabricated, Metal

Eastern Storefronts & Mtls Inc .... F 631 471-7065
  Ronkonkoma *(G-14897)*
Empire Archtctural Systems Inc .... E 518 773-5109
  Johnstown *(G-7110)*
Gamma North Corporation .... E 716 902-5100
  Alden *(G-178)*
Pk30 System LLC .... F 212 473-8050
  Stone Ridge *(G-15764)*

STORE FRONTS: Prefabricated, Wood

Empire Archtctural Systems Inc .... E 518 773-5109
  Johnstown *(G-7110)*

STRAPPING

Gibraltar Industries Inc .... D 716 826-6500
  Buffalo *(G-2974)*
Precision Spclty Fbrctions LLC .... E 716 824-2108
  Buffalo *(G-3134)*
Sunlight US Co Inc .... G 716 826-6500
  Buffalo *(G-3201)*

STRAPS: Apparel Webbing

H Group .... F 212 719-5500
  New York *(G-10389)*

STRAPS: Bindings, Textile

Ambind Corp .... G 716 836-4365
  Buffalo *(G-2805)*
New York Binding Co Inc .... E 718 729-2454
  Long Island City *(G-7825)*

STRAPS: Braids, Textile

La Lame Inc .... G 212 921-9770
  New York *(G-10909)*

STRAPS: Cotton Webbing

Sturges Manufacturing Co Inc .... D 315 732-6159
  Utica *(G-16360)*

STRAWS: Drinking, Made From Purchased Materials

Last Straw Inc .... E 516 371-2727
  Lawrence *(G-7393)*
Plastirun Corporation .... E 631 273-2626
  Brentwood *(G-1193)*
Sqp Inc .... C 518 831-6800
  Schenectady *(G-15299)*

STRUCTURAL SUPPORT & BUILDING MATERIAL: Concrete

Cossitt Concrete Products Inc .... F 315 824-2700
  Hamilton *(G-5947)*
Geotech Associates Ltd .... G 631 286-0251
  Brookhaven *(G-1507)*

Employee Codes: A=Over 500 employees, B=251-500
C=101-250, D=51-100, E=20-50, F=10-19, G=5-9

STUDIOS: Artist's

Donne Dieu.....................................G...... 212 226-0573
New York *(G-9905)*

STUDIOS: Sculptor's

Surving Studios...............................F...... 845 355-1430
Middletown *(G-8464)*

STUDS & JOISTS: Sheet Metal

Studco Building Systems US LLC......E...... 585 545-3000
Webster *(G-16736)*

SUBMARINE BUILDING & REPAIR

Electric Boat Corporation..................D...... 518 884-1270
Ballston Spa *(G-596)*
Electric Boat Corporation..................C...... 518 884-1596
Rock City Falls *(G-14778)*

SUBSCRIPTION FULFILLMENT SVCS: Magazine, Newspaper, Etc

Viatech Pubg Solutions Inc.................E...... 631 968-8500
Bay Shore *(G-754)*

SUGAR SUBSTITUTES: Organic

Cumberland Packing Corp..................B...... 718 858-4200
Brooklyn *(G-1824)*
Flavors Holdings Inc..........................G...... 212 572-8677
New York *(G-10178)*
Sugar Foods Corporation...................E...... 212 753-6900
New York *(G-12227)*

SUNDRIES & RELATED PRDTS: Medical & Laboratory, Rubber

Geri-Gentle Corporation....................G...... 917 804-7807
Brooklyn *(G-2021)*
Impladent Ltd....................................G...... 718 465-1810
Jamaica *(G-6921)*
Jamestown Scientific Inds LLC...........F...... 716 665-3224
Jamestown *(G-7012)*
Life Medical Technologies LLC..........F...... 845 894-2121
Hopewell Junction *(G-6556)*
Remedies Surgical Supplies...............G...... 718 599-5301
Brooklyn *(G-2490)*
Tmp Technologies Inc........................D...... 585 495-6231
Wyoming *(G-17383)*

SUNROOMS: Prefabricated Metal

Latium USA Trading LLC....................D...... 631 563-4000
Holbrook *(G-6455)*
Pei Liquidation Company...................F...... 315 431-4697
East Syracuse *(G-4554)*
Sunbilt Solar Pdts By Sussman..........D...... 718 297-0228
Jamaica *(G-6954)*

SUPERMARKETS & OTHER GROCERY STORES

Ives Farm Market...............................G...... 315 592-4880
Fulton *(G-5463)*
Melita Corp..C...... 718 392-7280
Bronx *(G-1390)*
Ravioli Store Inc.................................G...... 718 729-9300
Long Island City *(G-7858)*
TLC-Lc Inc..E...... 212 756-8900
New York *(G-12355)*

SURFACE ACTIVE AGENTS

BASF Corporation..............................B...... 914 785-2000
Tarrytown *(G-16087)*
Bigsky Technologies LLC....................G...... 585 218-9499
Rochester *(G-14231)*
Halmark Architectural Finshg............E...... 718 272-1831
Brooklyn *(G-2063)*
Momentum Performance Mtls Inc.....D...... 914 784-4807
Tarrytown *(G-16098)*
Suit-Kote Corporation........................F...... 716 683-8850
Buffalo *(G-3200)*

SURFACE ACTIVE AGENTS: Oils & Greases

Comander Terminals LLC...................F...... 516 922-7600
Oyster Bay *(G-13368)*

SURGICAL & MEDICAL INSTRUMENTS WHOLESALERS

Derm/Buro Inc...................................G...... 516 694-8300
Plainview *(G-13596)*

SURGICAL APPLIANCES & SPLYS

Proficient Surgical Eqp Inc.................G...... 516 487-1175
Port Washington *(G-13857)*

SURGICAL APPLIANCES & SPLYS

Argon Medical Devices Inc................G...... 585 321-1130
Henrietta *(G-6293)*
Arimed Orthotics Prosthetics P..........F...... 718 875-8754
Brooklyn *(G-1626)*
Avanti U S A Ltd.................................F...... 716 695-5800
Tonawanda *(G-16141)*
Backtech Inc......................................G...... 973 279-0838
New York *(G-9300)*
Byer California...................................E...... 212 944-8989
New York *(G-9487)*
Community Products LLC..................E...... 845 658-7720
Chester *(G-3603)*
Community Products LLC..................E...... 518 589-5103
Elka Park *(G-4631)*
Creative Orthotics Prosthetics...........G...... 607 431-2526
Oneonta *(G-13183)*
Cy Plastics Works Inc........................E...... 585 229-2555
Honeoye *(G-6523)*
Depuy Synthes Inc.............................C...... 607 271-2500
Horseheads *(G-6574)*
Derm/Buro Inc...................................G...... 516 694-8300
Plainview *(G-13596)*
Far Rockaway Drugs Inc....................E...... 718 471-2500
Far Rockaway *(G-4922)*
Fenway Holdings LLC.........................E...... 212 757-0606
New York *(G-10153)*
Grand Slam Holdings LLC..................E...... 212 583-5000
New York *(G-10348)*
Greatbatch Inc...................................D...... 716 759-5200
Clarence *(G-3663)*
Hanger Inc...G...... 718 575-5504
Forest Hills *(G-5323)*
Hanger Prsthetcs & Ortho Inc............F...... 607 277-6620
Ithaca *(G-6846)*
Hanger Prsthetcs & Ortho Inc............D...... 518 446-1774
Albany *(G-85)*
Hanger Prsthetcs & Ortho Inc............E...... 585 292-9510
Rochester *(G-14420)*
Harvy Surgical Supply Corp...............E...... 718 939-1122
Flushing *(G-5249)*
Hersco-Orthotic Labs Corp................E...... 718 391-0416
Long Island City *(G-7760)*
Howmedica Osteonics Corp...............G...... 518 783-1880
Latham *(G-7364)*
Huron TI & Cutter Grinding Co..........E...... 631 420-7000
Farmingdale *(G-5008)*
Instrumentation Laboratory Co.........C...... 845 680-0028
Orangeburg *(G-13231)*
J P R Pharmacy Inc............................F...... 718 327-0600
Far Rockaway *(G-4923)*
Konrad Prosthetics & Orthotics..........G...... 516 485-9164
West Hempstead *(G-16858)*
Ldc..G...... 516 822-2499
Bethpage *(G-871)*
Mayflower Splint Co...........................E...... 631 549-5131
Dix Hills *(G-4293)*
Medline Industries Inc.......................B...... 845 344-3301
Middletown *(G-8450)*
New England Orthotic & Prost..........F...... 845 471-7777
Poughkeepsie *(G-13921)*
Nortech Laboratories Inc...................F...... 631 501-1452
Farmingdale *(G-5067)*
Nova Health Systems Inc..................G...... 315 798-9018
Utica *(G-16353)*
Nucare Pharmacy Inc........................F...... 212 426-9300
New York *(G-11470)*
Nucare Pharmacy West LLC..............F...... 212 462-2525
New York *(G-11471)*
Overhead Door Corporation..............D...... 518 828-7652
Hudson *(G-6629)*
Pall Biomedical Inc............................C...... 516 484-3600
Port Washington *(G-13851)*
Pall Corporation.................................A...... 607 753-6041
Cortland *(G-4035)*
Pall Corporation.................................A...... 607 753-6041
Cortland *(G-4036)*
Pall Corporation.................................A...... 516 484-2818
Port Washington *(G-13853)*

Pall Corporation.................................A...... 607 753-6041
Cortland *(G-4037)*
Premier Brands of America Inc..........C...... 914 667-6200
Mount Vernon *(G-8717)*
Scientific Plastics Inc..........................F...... 212 967-1199
New York *(G-12004)*
Silipos Holding LLC............................E...... 716 283-0700
Niagara Falls *(G-12877)*
SPS Medical Supply Corp...................D...... 585 359-0130
Rush *(G-15052)*
Syracuse Prosthetic Center Inc..........G...... 315 476-9697
Syracuse *(G-16054)*
TDS Fitness Equipment......................E...... 607 733-6789
Elmira *(G-4704)*
Tumble Forms Inc..............................G...... 315 429-3101
Dolgeville *(G-4309)*
Turbine Engine Comp Utica...............A...... 315 768-8070
Whitesboro *(G-17197)*
Ultrapedics Ltd...................................E...... 718 748-4806
Brooklyn *(G-2696)*
Upstate Medical Solutions Inc............G...... 716 799-3782
Buffalo *(G-3236)*
Wyeth Holdings LLC..........................D...... 845 602-5000
Pearl River *(G-13469)*

SURGICAL EQPT: See Also Instruments

Abyrx Inc...F...... 914 357-2600
Irvington *(G-6766)*
Avery Biomedical Devices Inc............F...... 631 864-1600
Commack *(G-3823)*
Conmed Corporation.........................B...... 315 797-8375
Utica *(G-16316)*
Hub Surgical & Orthopedic Sups........G...... 718 585-5415
Bronx *(G-1358)*
Lake Region Medical Inc....................C...... 716 662-5025
Orchard Park *(G-13279)*
Schilling Forge Inc.............................G...... 315 454-4421
Syracuse *(G-16033)*
Surgical Design Corp.........................F...... 914 273-2445
Armonk *(G-421)*
T G M Products Inc............................G...... 631 491-0515
Wyandanch *(G-17377)*

SURGICAL IMPLANTS

Agnovos Healthcare LLC....................G...... 646 502-5860
New York *(G-9058)*
Bionic Eye Technologies Inc..............G...... 845 505-5254
Fishkill *(G-5181)*
Paradigm Spine LLC..........................E...... 212 367-7274
New York *(G-11569)*
Prosthodontic & Implant Den.............G...... 212 319-6363
New York *(G-11740)*

SURVEYING SVCS: Aerial Digital Imaging

Systems Drs C3 Inc............................B...... 716 631-6200
Buffalo *(G-3207)*

SVC ESTABLISHMENT EQPT & SPLYS WHOLESALERS

Architectural Textiles USA Inc............E...... 212 213-6972
New York *(G-9196)*
Compumatic Time Recorders Inc.......G...... 718 531-5749
North Bellmore *(G-12917)*
Licenders...G...... 212 759-5200
New York *(G-10986)*
Mirandy Products Ltd........................E...... 516 489-6800
South Hempstead *(G-15530)*

SVC ESTABLISHMENT EQPT, WHOL: Cleaning & Maint Eqpt & Splys

Jad Corp of America...........................E...... 718 762-8900
College Point *(G-3792)*
Paradigm Mktg Consortium Inc..........E...... 516 677-6012
Syosset *(G-15835)*

SVC ESTABLISHMENT EQPT, WHOLESALE: Beauty Parlor Eqpt & Sply

Ivy Enterprises Inc.............................C...... 516 621-9779
Port Washington *(G-13826)*
Ralph Payne.......................................G...... 718 222-4200
Brooklyn *(G-2477)*

PRODUCT SECTION

TABLEWARE: Household & Commercial, Semivitreous

SVC ESTABLISHMENT EQPT, WHOLESALE: Firefighting Eqpt

Simplexgrinnell LP .... G 845 774-4120
  Harriman *(G-5974)*

SVC ESTABLISHMENT EQPT, WHOLESALE: Laundry Eqpt & Splys

Coinmach Service Corp .... A 516 349-8555
  Plainview *(G-13588)*
CSC Serviceworks Inc .... E 516 349-8555
  Plainview *(G-13594)*
CSC Serviceworks Holdings .... E 516 349-8555
  Plainview *(G-13595)*
G A Braun Inc .... D 315 475-3123
  North Syracuse *(G-12943)*
Low-Cost Mfg Co Inc .... G 516 627-3282
  Carle Place *(G-3393)*
Spin Holdco Inc .... G 516 349-8555
  Plainview *(G-13635)*

SWEEPING COMPOUNDS

Bono Sawdust Supply Co Inc .... G 718 446-1374
  Corona *(G-3993)*

SWIMMING POOL ACCESS: Leaf Skimmers Or Pool Rakes

Swimline International Corp .... C 631 254-2155
  Edgewood *(G-4614)*

SWIMMING POOL EQPT: Filters & Water Conditioning Systems

Abe Pool Service .... G 845 473-7730
  Hyde Park *(G-6733)*
Pentair Water Pool and Spa Inc .... E 845 452-5500
  Lagrangeville *(G-7258)*
Pleatco LLC .... D 516 609-0200
  Glen Cove *(G-5624)*

SWIMMING POOL SPLY STORES

Clean All of Syracuse LLC .... G 315 472-9189
  Syracuse *(G-15897)*

SWIMMING POOLS, EQPT & SPLYS: Wholesalers

Asia Connection LLC .... F 212 369-4644
  New York *(G-9231)*
Imperial Pools Inc .... C 518 786-1200
  Latham *(G-7365)*

SWITCHBOARDS & PARTS: Power

Electric Swtchbard Sltions LLC .... G 718 643-1105
  New Hyde Park *(G-8831)*

SWITCHES

Bassin Technical Sales Co .... E 914 698-9358
  Mamaroneck *(G-8024)*
Delta Metal Products Co Inc .... E 718 855-4200
  Brooklyn *(G-1852)*
Sector Microwave Inds Inc .... D 631 242-2245
  Deer Park *(G-4208)*

SWITCHES: Electric Power

Adeptronics Incorporated .... G 631 667-0659
  Bay Shore *(G-665)*
Marquardt Switches Inc .... C 315 655-8050
  Cazenovia *(G-3449)*
Transistor Devices Inc .... E 631 471-7492
  Ronkonkoma *(G-14992)*

SWITCHES: Electric Power, Exc Snap, Push Button, Etc

Atlas Switch Co Inc .... E 516 222-6280
  Garden City *(G-5495)*

SWITCHES: Electronic

C A M Graphics Co Inc .... E 631 842-3400
  Farmingdale *(G-4955)*
Dortronics Systems Inc .... E 631 725-0505
  Sag Harbor *(G-15077)*

Kearney-National Inc .... F 212 661-4600
  New York *(G-10828)*
NEa Manufacturing Corp .... E 516 371-4200
  Inwood *(G-6763)*
Scientific Components Corp .... B 718 934-4500
  Brooklyn *(G-2538)*
Secs Inc .... E 914 667-5600
  Mount Vernon *(G-8732)*
Spectron Glass & Electronics .... F 631 582-5600
  Hauppauge *(G-6193)*
Spectron Systems Technology .... F 631 582-5600
  Hauppauge *(G-6194)*

SWITCHES: Electronic Applications

Dortronics Systems Inc .... E 631 725-0505
  Sag Harbor *(G-15077)*
Machine Components Corp .... E 516 694-7222
  Plainview *(G-13617)*
Switches and Sensors Inc .... F 631 924-2167
  Yaphank *(G-17404)*

SWITCHES: Silicon Control

Senera Co Inc .... F 516 639-3774
  Valley Stream *(G-16427)*

SWITCHES: Starting, Fluorescent

Monarch Electric Products Inc .... G 718 583-7996
  Bronx *(G-1402)*

SWITCHES: Time, Electrical Switchgear Apparatus

Ems Development Corporation .... D 631 924-4736
  Yaphank *(G-17390)*

SWITCHGEAR & SWITCHBOARD APPARATUS

Alarm Controls Corporation .... E 631 586-4220
  Deer Park *(G-4090)*
All City Switchboard Corp .... E 718 956-7244
  Long Island City *(G-7651)*
C A M Graphics Co Inc .... E 631 842-3400
  Farmingdale *(G-4955)*
Cooper Power Systems LLC .... B 716 375-7100
  Olean *(G-13140)*
Inertia Switch Inc .... E 845 359-8300
  Orangeburg *(G-13229)*
Marquardt Switches Inc .... C 315 655-8050
  Cazenovia *(G-3449)*
Schneider Electric Usa Inc .... C 646 335-0220
  New York *(G-11993)*
Select Controls Inc .... E 631 567-9010
  Bohemia *(G-1131)*
Sinclair Technologies Inc .... E 716 874-3682
  Hamburg *(G-5942)*

SWITCHGEAR & SWITCHGEAR ACCESS, NEC

Cooper Industries LLC .... E 315 477-7000
  Syracuse *(G-15909)*
Electrotech Service Eqp Corp .... E 718 626-7700
  Astoria *(G-439)*

SWORDS

Starfire Swords Ltd Inc .... E 607 589-7244
  Spencer *(G-15564)*

SYNTHETIC RESIN FINISHED PRDTS, NEC

General Composites Inc .... E 518 963-7333
  Willsboro *(G-17265)*

SYRUPS, DRINK

Pepsi-Cola Metro Btlg Co Inc .... G 914 767-6000
  White Plains *(G-17152)*

SYRUPS, FLAVORING, EXC DRINK

3v Company Inc .... E 718 858-7333
  Brooklyn *(G-1517)*
H Fox & Co Inc .... E 718 385-4600
  Brooklyn *(G-2059)*

SYSTEMS INTEGRATION SVCS

Binghamton Simulator Co Inc .... E 607 321-2980
  Binghamton *(G-895)*
Medsim-Eagle Simulation Inc .... F 607 658-9354
  Endicott *(G-4818)*
New Media Investment Group Inc .... B 212 479-3160
  New York *(G-11391)*
Telxon Corporation .... E 631 738-2400
  Holtsville *(G-6512)*

SYSTEMS INTEGRATION SVCS: Local Area Network

Cables and Chips Inc .... E 212 619-3132
  New York *(G-9493)*

SYSTEMS SOFTWARE DEVELOPMENT SVCS

Ex El Enterprises Ltd .... F 212 489-4500
  New York *(G-10097)*
Inprotopia Corporation .... F 917 338-7501
  New York *(G-10610)*
Intellicheck Mobilisa Inc .... E 360 344-3233
  Jericho *(G-7072)*
Napco Security Tech Inc .... B 631 842-9400
  Amityville *(G-314)*
Roomactually LLC .... G 646 388-1922
  New York *(G-11914)*
Sale 121 Corp .... D 240 855-8988
  New York *(G-11956)*
Schoolnet Inc .... C 646 496-9000
  New York *(G-12001)*

TABLE OR COUNTERTOPS, PLASTIC LAMINATED

Allegany Laminating and Supply .... G 716 372-2424
  Allegany *(G-198)*
Contempra Design Inc .... G 718 984-8586
  Staten Island *(G-15662)*
Kitchen Specialty Craftsmen .... G 607 739-0833
  Elmira *(G-4693)*
Lif Distributing Inc .... F 631 630-6900
  Islandia *(G-6799)*
Red White & Blue Entps Corp .... G 718 565-8080
  Woodside *(G-17350)*
Wilsonart Intl Holdings LLC .... E 516 935-6980
  Bethpage *(G-879)*

TABLECLOTHS & SETTINGS

Broder Mfg Inc .... G 718 366-1667
  Brooklyn *(G-1718)*
Royal Copenhagen Inc .... F 845 454-4442
  Poughkeepsie *(G-13929)*

TABLES: Lift, Hydraulic

Columbus McKinnon Corporation .... C 716 689-5400
  Getzville *(G-5595)*
Columbus McKinnon Corporation .... C 716 689-5400
  Getzville *(G-5597)*
Columbus McKinnon Corporation .... C 716 689-5400
  Getzville *(G-5598)*

TABLETS & PADS: Book & Writing, Made From Purchased Material

Duck Flats Pharma .... G 315 689-3407
  Elbridge *(G-4625)*
USA Custom Pad Corp .... E 607 563-9550
  Sidney *(G-15445)*

TABLEWARE OR KITCHEN ARTICLES: Commercial, Fine Earthenware

Green Wave International Inc .... G 718 499-3371
  Brooklyn *(G-2051)*
Korin Japanese Trading Corp .... E 212 587-7021
  New York *(G-10878)*

TABLEWARE: Household & Commercial, Semivitreous

Jill Fenichell Inc .... G 718 237-2490
  Brooklyn *(G-2142)*

Employee Codes: A=Over 500 employees, B=251-500
C=101-250, D=51-100, E=20-50, F=10-19, G=5-9

TABLEWARE: Plastic

Pactiv LLC .... A 585 393-3149
  Canandaigua *(G-3354)*
Q Squared Design LLC .... E 212 686-8860
  New York *(G-11763)*
Supreme Poultry Inc .... G 718 472-0300
  Long Island City *(G-7897)*

TABLEWARE: Vitreous China

Carmona Nyc LLC .... G 718 227-6662
  Rego Park *(G-14031)*

TAGS & LABELS: Paper

Auto Data Systems Inc .... F 631 831-7427
  Deer Park *(G-4104)*
Depot Label Company Inc .... G 631 467-2952
  Patchogue *(G-13418)*
K Sidrane Inc .... E 631 393-6974
  Farmingdale *(G-5021)*
Sml USA Inc .... E 212 736-8800
  New York *(G-12107)*
Stickershopcom Inc .... G 631 563-4323
  Holbrook *(G-6474)*
Web-Tech Packaging Inc .... F 716 684-4520
  Lancaster *(G-7347)*

TAGS: Paper, Blank, Made From Purchased Paper

Allen-Bailey Tag & Label Inc .... D 585 538-2324
  Caledonia *(G-3276)*
Jerry Tomaselli .... F 718 965-1400
  Brooklyn *(G-2137)*
Tag Envelope Co Inc .... E 718 389-6844
  College Point *(G-3809)*

TAILORS: Custom

Adrian Jules Ltd .... D 585 342-5886
  Rochester *(G-14174)*

TALLOW: Animal

Baker Commodities Inc .... E 585 482-1880
  Rochester *(G-14222)*

TANK REPAIR SVCS

David Isseks & Sons Inc .... E 212 966-8694
  New York *(G-9820)*

TANKS & OTHER TRACKED VEHICLE CMPNTS

Lourdes Industries Inc .... D 631 234-6600
  Hauppauge *(G-6121)*
Tecmotiv (usa) Inc .... E 905 669-5911
  Niagara Falls *(G-12882)*

TANKS: Concrete

Preload Concrete Structures .... E 631 231-8100
  Hauppauge *(G-6169)*

TANKS: Cryogenic, Metal

North American Svcs Group LLC .... F 518 885-1820
  Ballston Spa *(G-604)*

TANKS: Fuel, Including Oil & Gas, Metal Plate

Cardinal Tank Corp .... E 718 625-4350
  Brooklyn *(G-1757)*
Crown Tank Company LLC .... G 855 276-9682
  Horseheads *(G-6572)*
Stutzman Management Corp .... F 800 735-2013
  Lancaster *(G-7344)*

TANKS: Lined, Metal

Amherst Stnless Fbrication LLC .... E 716 691-7012
  Amherst *(G-225)*
General Oil Equipment Co Inc .... E 716 691-7012
  Amherst *(G-243)*
Modutank Inc .... F 718 392-1112
  Long Island City *(G-7815)*

TANKS: Military, Including Factory Rebuilding

Federal Prison Industries .... C 845 386-6819
  Otisville *(G-13344)*

TANKS: Plastic & Fiberglass

An-Cor Industrial Plastics Inc .... D 716 695-3141
  North Tonawanda *(G-12954)*
Chem-Tek Systems Inc .... F 631 253-3010
  Bay Shore *(G-683)*
Norwesco Inc .... F 607 687-8081
  Owego *(G-13357)*

TANKS: Standard Or Custom Fabricated, Metal Plate

Gasport Welding & Fabg Inc .... F 716 772-7205
  Gasport *(G-5557)*
Stainless Metals Inc .... F 718 784-1454
  Woodside *(G-17356)*
Stavo Industries Inc .... F 845 331-4552
  Kingston *(G-7213)*
Steelways Inc .... E 845 562-0860
  Newburgh *(G-12780)*
Taylor Tank Company Inc .... F 718 434-1300
  Brooklyn *(G-2647)*

TANKS: Storage, Farm, Metal Plate

Bigbee Steel and Tank Company .... E 518 273-0801
  Watervliet *(G-16679)*

TANKS: Water, Metal Plate

David Isseks & Sons Inc .... E 212 966-8694
  New York *(G-9820)*
Water Cooling Corp .... G 718 723-6500
  Rosedale *(G-15015)*

TANKS: Wood

Rosenwach Tank Co Inc .... E 212 972-4411
  Astoria *(G-455)*

TANNERIES: Leather

Colonial Tanning Corporation .... G 518 725-7171
  Gloversville *(G-5709)*
Simco Leather Corporation .... E 518 762-7100
  Johnstown *(G-7127)*
Wood & Hyde Leather Co Inc .... E 518 725-7105
  Gloversville *(G-5730)*

TAPE DRIVES

Matrox Graphics Inc .... G 518 561-4417
  Plattsburgh *(G-13677)*

TAPES, ADHESIVE: Medical

Eis Inc .... D 585 426-5330
  Rochester *(G-14341)*
Tape Systems Inc .... F 914 668-3700
  Mount Vernon *(G-8736)*

TAPES: Audio Range, Blank

Orpheo USA Corp .... G 212 464-8255
  New York *(G-11527)*
West African Movies .... G 718 731-2190
  Bronx *(G-1494)*

TAPES: Coated Fiberglass, Pipe Sealing Or Insulating

GM Insulation Corp .... F 516 354-6000
  Elmont *(G-4721)*

TAPES: Gummed, Cloth Or Paper Based, From Purchased Matls

Patco Tapes Inc .... G 718 497-1527
  Maspeth *(G-8164)*

TAPES: Magnetic

Professional Tape Corporation .... E 516 656-5519
  Glen Cove *(G-5625)*

TAPES: Pressure Sensitive

Adchem Corp .... C 631 727-6000
  Riverhead *(G-14137)*
Kleen Stik Industries Inc .... F 718 984-5031
  Staten Island *(G-15696)*
Merco Hackensack Inc .... G 845 357-3699
  Hillburn *(G-6416)*
T L F Graphics Inc .... E 585 272-5500
  Rochester *(G-14716)*
Tape-It Inc .... E 631 243-4100
  Bay Shore *(G-750)*
Tri Star Label Inc .... G 914 237-4800
  Mount Vernon *(G-8740)*
Valley Industrial Products Inc .... E 631 385-9300
  Huntington *(G-6689)*

TARGET DRONES

Enlighten Air Inc .... G 917 656-1248
  New York *(G-10041)*

TELECOMMUNICATION SYSTEMS & EQPT

Aines Manufacturing Corp .... E 631 471-3900
  Islip *(G-6806)*
Alcatel-Lucent USA Inc .... D 516 349-4900
  Plainview *(G-13580)*
Clayton Dubilier & Rice Fun .... E 212 407-5200
  New York *(G-9640)*
Corning Incorporated .... E 607 248-1200
  Corning *(G-3965)*
Corning Incorporated .... G 607 974-6729
  Painted Post *(G-13391)*
Corning Incorporated .... A 607 974-9000
  Corning *(G-3962)*
Data Transmission Essentials .... F 516 378-8820
  Harrison *(G-5983)*
ESi Cases & Accessories Inc .... E 212 883-8838
  New York *(G-10061)*
Forerunner Technologies Inc .... E 631 337-2100
  Bohemia *(G-1067)*
Harris Corporation .... E 585 244-5830
  Rochester *(G-14427)*
Interdgital Communications LLC .... C 631 622-4000
  Melville *(G-8331)*
Kelta Inc .... E 631 789-5000
  Edgewood *(G-4602)*
L-3 Communications Corporation .... A 631 436-7400
  Hauppauge *(G-6108)*
Parabit Systems Inc .... E 516 378-4800
  Roosevelt *(G-15008)*
Performance Technologies Inc .... D 585 256-0200
  Rochester *(G-14576)*
Shoretel Inc .... G 877 654-3573
  Rochester *(G-14684)*
Telephonics Corporation .... E 631 755-7659
  Farmingdale *(G-5126)*
Telephonics Corporation .... A 631 755-7000
  Farmingdale *(G-5127)*
Tii Technologies Inc .... E 516 364-9300
  Edgewood *(G-4616)*

TELECOMMUNICATIONS CARRIERS & SVCS: Wired

Forerunner Technologies Inc .... E 631 337-2100
  Bohemia *(G-1067)*
Fusion Telecom Intl Inc .... C 212 201-2400
  New York *(G-10227)*
Globecomm Systems Inc .... C 631 231-9800
  Hauppauge *(G-6086)*
Hnw Inc .... F 212 258-9215
  New York *(G-10492)*
Human Electronics Inc .... G 315 724-9850
  Utica *(G-16339)*
Key Computer Svcs of Chelsea .... D 212 206-8060
  New York *(G-10840)*

TELEMARKETING BUREAUS

S & H Uniform Corp .... D 914 937-6800
  White Plains *(G-17164)*

TELEMETERING EQPT

L-3 Cmmnctons Fgn Holdings Inc .... E 212 697-1111
  New York *(G-10903)*
L-3 Cmmunications Holdings Inc .... D 212 697-1111
  New York *(G-10905)*
L-3 Communications Corporation .... B 631 231-1700
  Hauppauge *(G-6107)*

PRODUCT SECTION

TEXTILE FINISHING: Chemical Coating Or Treating

L-3 Communications Corporation ....D...... 607 721-5465
  Kirkwood *(G-7234)*
L-3 Communications Corporation ....D...... 631 231-1700
  Hauppauge *(G-6109)*
L-3 Communications Corporation ....B...... 212 697-1111
  New York *(G-10906)*

TELEPHONE ANSWERING SVCS

Milne Mfg Inc ....F....... 716 772-2536
  Gasport *(G-5559)*

TELEPHONE BOOTHS, EXC WOOD

Clark Specialty Co Inc ....E....... 607 776-3193
  Bath *(G-655)*
Parabit Systems Inc ....G...... 516 378-4800
  Roosevelt *(G-15008)*

TELEPHONE EQPT INSTALLATION

Telecommunication Concepts ....G...... 315 736-8523
  Whitesboro *(G-17196)*
Teltech Security Corp ....G...... 718 871-8800
  Brooklyn *(G-2654)*

TELEPHONE EQPT: NEC

ABS Talkx Inc ....G...... 631 254-9100
  Bay Shore *(G-664)*
Access 24 ....G...... 845 358-5397
  Valley Cottage *(G-16374)*
Audio-Sears Corp ....D...... 607 652-7305
  Stamford *(G-15623)*
Brook Telephone Mfg & Sup Co ....F....... 718 449-4222
  Brooklyn *(G-1719)*
Call Forwarding Technologies ....G...... 516 621-3600
  Greenvale *(G-5879)*
Eagle Telephonics Inc ....F....... 631 471-3600
  Bohemia *(G-1059)*
I D Tel Corp ....F....... 718 876-6000
  Staten Island *(G-15685)*
R I R Communications Systems ....G...... 718 706-9957
  Mount Vernon *(G-8722)*
R I R Communications Systems ....E....... 718 706-9957
  Mount Vernon *(G-8723)*
Siemens Corporation ....E....... 905 528-8811
  Buffalo *(G-3186)*
Siemens Corporation ....F....... 202 434-7800
  New York *(G-12062)*
Siemens Industries Inc ....F....... 607 936-9512
  Corning *(G-3981)*
Siemens USA Holdings Inc ....B....... 212 258-4000
  New York *(G-12064)*
Telecommunication Concepts ....G...... 315 736-8523
  Whitesboro *(G-17196)*
Toshiba Amer Info Systems Inc ....B....... 949 583-3000
  New York *(G-12376)*

TELEPHONE SVCS

Tempo Industries Inc ....G...... 516 334-6900
  Westbury *(G-17031)*

TELEPHONE SWITCHING EQPT

Redcom Laboratories Inc ....C....... 585 924-6567
  Victor *(G-16500)*

TELEPHONE: Fiber Optic Systems

Fiber Instrument Sales Inc ....C....... 315 736-2206
  Oriskany *(G-13309)*
Fiberwave Corporation ....C....... 718 802-9011
  Brooklyn *(G-1968)*
Fujitsu Ntwrk Cmmnications Inc ....F....... 845 731-2000
  Pearl River *(G-13457)*
Kent Optronics Inc ....F....... 845 897-0138
  Hopewell Junction *(G-6555)*
Sandstone Technologies Corp ....G...... 585 785-5537
  Rochester *(G-14667)*
Sandstone Technologies Corp ....G...... 585 785-5537
  Rochester *(G-14668)*
Splice Technologies Inc ....G...... 631 924-8108
  Manorville *(G-8081)*
Terahertz Technologies Inc ....G...... 315 736-3642
  Oriskany *(G-13316)*

TELEPHONE: Headsets

Quality One Wireless LLC ....C....... 631 233-3371
  Ronkonkoma *(G-14974)*

TELEPHONE: Sets, Exc Cellular Radio

Maia Systems LLC ....G...... 718 206-0100
  Jamaica *(G-6927)*
Powermate Cellular ....G...... 718 833-9400
  Brooklyn *(G-2431)*

TELEVISION BROADCASTING & COMMUNICATIONS EQPT

Basil S Kadhim ....G...... 888 520-5192
  New York *(G-9330)*

TELEVISION BROADCASTING STATIONS

21st Century Fox America Inc ....D...... 212 852-7000
  New York *(G-8967)*
General Electric Company ....A....... 518 385-4022
  Schenectady *(G-15257)*
Hearst Business Media Corp ....F....... 631 650-4441
  Great River *(G-5851)*
Hearst Corporation ....A....... 212 649-2000
  New York *(G-10438)*
New York Times Company ....B....... 212 556-1234
  New York *(G-11410)*
Tegna Inc ....C....... 716 849-2222
  Buffalo *(G-3212)*
Tribune Entertainment Co Del ....E....... 203 866-2204
  New York *(G-12404)*

TELEVISION SETS

Jwin Electronics Corp ....D...... 516 626-7188
  Port Washington *(G-13831)*
Toshiba America Inc ....E....... 212 596-0600
  New York *(G-12377)*

TELEVISION: Cameras

Silicon Imaging Inc ....G...... 518 374-3367
  Niskayuna *(G-12896)*

TELEVISION: Closed Circuit Eqpt

AG Adriano Goldschmied Inc ....G...... 845 928-8616
  Central Valley *(G-3520)*
Click It Inc ....D...... 631 686-2900
  Hauppauge *(G-6047)*
Sartek Industries Inc ....G...... 631 473-3555
  Port Jefferson *(G-13779)*
Sentry Technology Corporation ....F....... 800 645-4224
  Ronkonkoma *(G-14983)*
Vicon Industries Inc ....C....... 631 952-2288
  Hauppauge *(G-6225)*

TEMPERING: Metal

Elmira Heat Treating Inc ....E....... 607 734-1577
  Elmira *(G-4682)*

TENT REPAIR SHOP

Custom Canvas Manufacturing Co ....E....... 716 852-6372
  Buffalo *(G-2897)*

TENTS: All Materials

Air Structures Amercn Tech Inc ....E....... 914 937-4500
  Port Chester *(G-13737)*
Dhs Systems LLC ....F....... 845 359-6066
  Orangeburg *(G-13224)*
Johnson Outdoors Inc ....C....... 607 779-2200
  Binghamton *(G-931)*
Kraus & Sons Inc ....F....... 212 620-0408
  New York *(G-10887)*
Leiter Sukkahs Inc ....G...... 718 436-0303
  Brooklyn *(G-2209)*
Select Fabricators Inc ....F....... 585 393-0650
  Canandaigua *(G-3357)*
Toptec Products LLC ....F....... 631 421-9800
  Melville *(G-8361)*

TERMINAL BOARDS

Veja Electronics Inc ....D...... 631 321-6086
  Deer Park *(G-4222)*

TERRA COTTA: Architectural

Boston Valley Pottery Inc ....D...... 716 649-7490
  Orchard Park *(G-13254)*

TEST KITS: Pregnancy

Northeast Doulas ....G...... 845 621-0654
  Mahopac *(G-7999)*
Working Family Solutions Inc ....G...... 845 802-6182
  Saugerties *(G-15198)*

TESTERS: Battery

Sorfin Yoshimura Ic Disc Ltd ....G...... 516 802-4600
  Woodbury *(G-17300)*
Walter R Tucker Entps Ltd ....E....... 607 467-2866
  Deposit *(G-4282)*

TESTERS: Environmental

Caltex International Ltd ....E....... 315 425-1040
  Syracuse *(G-15883)*
Nexgen Enviro Systems Inc ....E....... 631 226-2930
  Lindenhurst *(G-7475)*
Niagara Scientific Inc ....D...... 315 437-0821
  East Syracuse *(G-4552)*

TESTERS: Integrated Circuit

Epoch Microelectronics Inc ....E....... 914 332-8570
  Valhalla *(G-16367)*
Xelic Incorporated ....F....... 585 415-2764
  Pittsford *(G-13575)*

TESTERS: Physical Property

G E Inspection Technologies LP ....C....... 315 554-2000
  Skaneateles *(G-15460)*
Gleason Corporation ....A....... 585 473-1000
  Rochester *(G-14407)*
Gleason Works ....A....... 585 473-1000
  Rochester *(G-14408)*
Gurley Precision Instrs Inc ....C....... 518 272-6300
  Troy *(G-16237)*

TESTERS: Water, Exc Indl Process

Ewt Holdings III Corp ....G...... 212 644-5900
  New York *(G-10096)*

TEXTILE & APPAREL SVCS

Gould J Perfect Screen Prtrs ....F....... 607 272-0099
  Ithaca *(G-6844)*
New York Knitting Processor ....G...... 718 366-3469
  Ridgewood *(G-14115)*
Newcastle Fabrics Corp ....G...... 718 388-6600
  Brooklyn *(G-2369)*
RAK Finishing Corp ....E....... 718 416-4242
  Howard Beach *(G-6598)*

TEXTILE BAGS WHOLESALERS

Adam Scott Designs Inc ....E....... 212 420-8866
  New York *(G-9024)*
Nochairs Inc ....G...... 917 748-8731
  New York *(G-11449)*

TEXTILE CONVERTERS: Knit Goods

Bank-Miller Co Inc ....E....... 914 227-9357
  Pelham *(G-13489)*
Hofset Fabrics Ltd ....G...... 718 522-6228
  Brooklyn *(G-2082)*
Sextet Fabrics Inc ....F....... 516 593-0608
  East Rockaway *(G-4470)*

TEXTILE FABRICATORS

Dream Green Productions ....G...... 917 267-8920
  Warwick *(G-16589)*

TEXTILE FINISH: Chem Coat/Treat, Fire Resist, Manmade

American Spray-On Corp ....E....... 212 929-2100
  New York *(G-9128)*
Beckmann Converting Inc ....E....... 518 842-0073
  Amsterdam *(G-334)*

TEXTILE FINISHING: Chemical Coating Or Treating

Reynolds Drapery Service Inc ....F....... 315 845-8632
  Newport *(G-12792)*

Employee Codes: A=Over 500 employees, B=251-500
C=101-250, D=51-100, E=20-50, F=10-19, G=5-9

2017 Harris
New York Manufacturers Directory

1353

TEXTILE FINISHING: Dyeing, Broadwoven, Cotton

TEXTILE FINISHING: Dyeing, Broadwoven, Cotton
- B & K Dye Cutting Inc .... G 718 497-5216
  Brooklyn *(G-1656)*
- Dyenamix Inc .... G 212 941-6642
  New York *(G-9945)*

TEXTILE FINISHING: Dyeing, Finishing & Printng, Linen Fabric
- American Country Quilts & Lin .... G 631 283-5466
  Southampton *(G-15538)*
- China Ting Fashion Group (usa) ..... G 212 716-1600
  New York *(G-9602)*
- Duck River Textiles Inc .... G 212 679-2980
  New York *(G-9936)*

TEXTILE FINISHING: Dyeing, Manmade Fiber & Silk, Broadwoven
- Dyenamix Inc .... G 212 941-6642
  New York *(G-9945)*
- Eastern Silk Mills Inc .... G 212 730-1300
  New York *(G-9966)*

TEXTILE FINISHING: Embossing, Cotton, Broadwoven
- Lee Dyeing Company NC Inc .... F 518 736-5232
  Johnstown *(G-7118)*

TEXTILE FINISHING: Embossing, Man Fiber & Silk, Broadwoven
- Knucklehead Embroidery Inc .... G 607 797-2725
  Johnson City *(G-7098)*

TEXTILE FINISHING: Silk, Broadwoven
- Raxon Fabrics Corp .... F 212 532-6816
  New York *(G-11804)*

TEXTILE FINISHING: Sponging, Cotton, Broadwoven, Trade
- Basiloff LLC .... G 646 671-0353
  New York *(G-9331)*

TEXTILE PRDTS: Hand Woven & Crocheted
- HMS Productions Inc .... D 212 719-9190
  New York *(G-10489)*

TEXTILE: Finishing, Cotton Broadwoven
- All About Art Inc .... F 718 321-0755
  Flushing *(G-5225)*
- Carolyn Ray Inc .... G 914 476-0619
  Yonkers *(G-17424)*
- Central Textiles Inc .... F 212 213-8740
  New York *(G-9566)*
- Marcel Finishing Corp .... E 718 381-2889
  Plainview *(G-13618)*
- Prismatic Dyeing & Finshg Inc ...... D 845 561-1800
  Newburgh *(G-12775)*
- Santee Print Works .... F 212 997-1570
  New York *(G-11969)*

TEXTILE: Finishing, Raw Stock NEC
- Ben-Sak Textile Inc .... G 212 279-5122
  New York *(G-9356)*
- Flexene Corp .... E 631 491-0580
  West Babylon *(G-16792)*
- Hosel & Ackerson Inc .... G 212 575-1490
  New York *(G-10509)*
- Majestic Rayon Corporation .... E 212 929-6443
  New York *(G-11115)*
- Marcel Finishing Corp .... E 718 381-2889
  Plainview *(G-13618)*
- National Spinning Co Inc .... E 212 382-6400
  New York *(G-11351)*
- Newcastle Fabrics Corp .... G 718 388-6600
  Brooklyn *(G-2369)*
- Prismatic Dyeing & Finshg Inc ...... D 845 561-1800
  Newburgh *(G-12775)*
- Skin Prints Inc .... G 845 920-8756
  Pearl River *(G-13466)*

TEXTILE: Goods, NEC
- Alok Inc .... G 212 643-4360
  New York *(G-9097)*
- Priva USA Inc .... G 518 963-4074
  Willsboro *(G-17266)*
- Southern Adrndck Fbr Prdcrs CP .. G 518 692-2700
  Greenwich *(G-5893)*

TEXTILES
- Schneider Mills Inc .... F 212 768-7500
  New York *(G-11994)*
- Stern & Stern Industries Inc .... D 607 324-4485
  Hornell *(G-6567)*

TEXTILES: Bagging, Jute
- Ivi Services Inc .... D 607 729-5111
  Binghamton *(G-929)*

TEXTILES: Fibers, Textile, Rcvrd From Mill Waste/Rags
- Ace Drop Cloth Canvas Pdts Inc ... E 718 731-1550
  Bronx *(G-1260)*

TEXTILES: Flock
- Solivaira Specialties Inc .... D 716 693-4009
  North Tonawanda *(G-12996)*
- Solvaira Specialties Inc .... C 716 693-4040
  North Tonawanda *(G-12997)*

TEXTILES: Linen Fabrics
- David King Linen Inc .... F 718 241-7298
  Brooklyn *(G-1842)*
- Novita Fabrics Furnishing Corp ..... F 516 299-4500
  Glen Cove *(G-5623)*
- Sabbsons International Inc .... F 718 360-1947
  Brooklyn *(G-2528)*
- Simple Elegance New York Inc .... F 718 360-1947
  Brooklyn *(G-2562)*
- TRM Linen Inc .... G 718 686-6075
  Brooklyn *(G-2683)*

TEXTILES: Linings, Carpet, Exc Felt
- G Fried Carpert Service .... E 516 333-3900
  Westbury *(G-16989)*

TEXTILES: Mill Waste & Remnant
- Dean Trading Corp .... F 718 485-0600
  Brooklyn *(G-1847)*
- Federal Prison Industries .... D 518 897-4000
  Ray Brook *(G-14024)*
- S Hellerman Inc .... F 718 622-2995
  Brooklyn *(G-2526)*

TEXTILES: Tops & Top Processing, Manmade Or Other Fiber
- Jo-Vin Decorators Inc .... E 718 441-9350
  Woodhaven *(G-17306)*

THEATRICAL LIGHTING SVCS
- Creative Stage Lighting Co Inc ...... E 518 251-3302
  North Creek *(G-12933)*

THEATRICAL PRODUCERS & SVCS
- Congress For Jewish Culture .... G 212 505-8040
  New York *(G-9700)*
- Peermusic Ltd .... F 212 265-3910
  New York *(G-11599)*

THEATRICAL SCENERY
- Center Line Studios Inc .... F 845 534-7143
  New Windsor *(G-8934)*
- Costume Armour Inc .... F 845 534-9120
  Cornwall *(G-3987)*
- Hudson Scenic Studio Inc .... C 914 375-0900
  Yonkers *(G-17455)*
- King Displays Inc .... F 212 629-8455
  New York *(G-10853)*
- Production Resource Group LLC .. D 212 589-5400
  Armonk *(G-419)*
- Production Resource Group LLC .. D 845 567-5700
  New Windsor *(G-8948)*

Stiegelbauer Associates Inc .... E 718 624-0835
  Brooklyn *(G-2608)*

THERMOMETERS: Indl
- Kessler Thermometer Corp .... G 631 841-5500
  West Babylon *(G-16804)*
- Oden Machinery Inc .... E 716 874-3000
  Tonawanda *(G-16189)*

THERMOMETERS: Liquid-In-Glass & Bimetal
- Germanow-Simon Corporation ...... E 585 232-1440
  Rochester *(G-14399)*

THERMOMETERS: Medical, Digital
- Accuvein Inc .... G 816 997-9400
  Cold Spring Harbor *(G-3767)*

THERMOPLASTIC MATERIALS
- Belsul America Corp .... F 212 520-1827
  New York *(G-9352)*
- Plexi Craft Quality Products .... F 212 924-3244
  New York *(G-11677)*

THERMOPLASTICS
- ADC Acquisition Company .... E 518 377-6471
  Niskayuna *(G-12893)*

THERMOSETTING MATERIALS
- Empire Plastics Inc .... E 607 754-9132
  Endwell *(G-4835)*

THREAD: All Fibers
- Albany International Corp .... C 607 749-7226
  Homer *(G-6515)*
- United Thread Mills Corp .... G 516 536-3900
  Oceanside *(G-13102)*

THREAD: Embroidery
- American Quality Embroidery .... G 631 467-3200
  Ronkonkoma *(G-14869)*
- One In A Million Inc .... G 516 829-1111
  Valley Stream *(G-16417)*

TICKET OFFICES & AGENCIES: Theatrical
- London Theater News Ltd .... F 212 517-8608
  New York *(G-11025)*

TIES, FORM: Metal
- American Wire Tie Inc .... E 716 337-2412
  North Collins *(G-12926)*

TILE: Asphalt, Floor
- Shenfield Studio LLC .... F 315 436-8869
  Syracuse *(G-16040)*

TILE: Brick & Structural, Clay
- Stone and Bath Gallery .... G 718 438-4500
  Brooklyn *(G-2609)*

TILE: Drain, Clay
- Bistrian Cement Corporation .... F 631 324-1123
  East Hampton *(G-4405)*

TILE: Fireproofing, Clay
- Certified Flameproofing Corp .... G 631 265-4824
  Smithtown *(G-15484)*
- Noroc Enterprises Inc .... E 718 585-3230
  Bronx *(G-1412)*

TILE: Mosaic, Ceramic
- Artsaics Studios Inc .... G 631 254-2558
  Deer Park *(G-4103)*

TILE: Stamped Metal, Floor Or Wall
- Surving Studios .... F 845 355-1430
  Middletown *(G-8464)*

TILE: Terrazzo Or Concrete, Precast
- Foro Marble Co Inc .... E 718 852-2322
  Brooklyn *(G-1996)*

PRODUCT SECTION

TOOLS: Hand, Engravers'

Walter G Legge Company Inc ....G....... 914 737-5040
  Peekskill *(G-13485)*

TILE: Vinyl, Asbestos

Allied Tile Mfg Corp ....G....... 718 647-2200
  Brooklyn *(G-1592)*

TILE: Wall & Floor, Ceramic

Aremco Products Inc ....F....... 845 268-0039
  Valley Cottage *(G-16376)*
Dal-Tile Corporation ....G....... 914 835-1801
  Harrison *(G-5982)*
Lazer Marble & Granite Corp ....G....... 718 859-9644
  Brooklyn *(G-2197)*

TILE: Wall & Floor, clay

Quality Components Framing Sys ....F....... 315 768-1167
  Whitesboro *(G-17194)*

TILE: Wall, Enameled Masonite, Made From Purchased Materials

Soavedra Masonry Inc ....G....... 347 695-5254
  Harrison *(G-5990)*

TIMBER PRDTS WHOLESALERS

Guldenschuh Logging & Lbr LLC ....G....... 585 538-4750
  Caledonia *(G-3280)*

TIMING DEVICES: Electronic

Eversan Inc ....F....... 315 736-3967
  Whitesboro *(G-17193)*
Infitec Inc ....D....... 315 433-1150
  East Syracuse *(G-4543)*

TIRE & INNER TUBE MATERIALS & RELATED PRDTS

Handy & Harman Ltd ....A....... 914 461-1300
  White Plains *(G-17120)*
Roli Retreads Inc ....E....... 631 694-7670
  Farmingdale *(G-5102)*
Sph Group Holdings LLC ....G....... 212 520-2300
  New York *(G-12162)*

TIRE CORD & FABRIC

Albany International Corp ....C....... 518 445-2230
  Menands *(G-8365)*
Designatronics Incorporated ....B....... 516 328-3300
  New Hyde Park *(G-8826)*
Haines Equipment Inc ....E....... 607 566-8531
  Avoca *(G-537)*
York Industries Inc ....E....... 516 746-3736
  Garden City Park *(G-5546)*

TIRE INFLATORS: Hand Or Compressor Operated

Vac Air Service Inc ....F....... 716 665-2206
  Jamestown *(G-7042)*

TIRES & INNER TUBES

East Coast Intl Tire Inc ....F....... 718 386-9088
  Maspeth *(G-8136)*
New York CT Loc246 Seiu Wel BF ......G....... 212 233-0616
  New York *(G-11397)*

TIRES: Auto

McCarthy Tire Svc Co NY Inc ....F....... 518 449-5185
  Menands *(G-8375)*

TITANIUM MILL PRDTS

Titanium Dem Remediation Group ....F....... 716 433-4100
  Lockport *(G-7619)*

TOBACCO LEAF PROCESSING

Schweitzer-Mauduit Intl Inc ....C....... 518 329-4222
  Ancram *(G-375)*

TOBACCO: Chewing

National Tobacco Company LP ....F....... 212 253-8185
  New York *(G-11353)*

TOBACCO: Chewing & Snuff

Elab Smokers Boutique ....G....... 585 865-4513
  Rochester *(G-14343)*

TOBACCO: Cigarettes

East End ....F....... 716 532-2622
  Collins *(G-3816)*
Jacobs Tobacco Company ....E....... 518 358-4948
  Hogansburg *(G-6428)*
Juicy Vapor LLC ....F....... 855 525-8429
  Amherst *(G-248)*
Philip Morris Intl Inc ....C....... 917 663-2000
  New York *(G-11645)*
PMI Global Services Inc ....E....... 917 663-2000
  New York *(G-11679)*
R J Reynolds Tobacco Company ....C....... 716 871-1553
  Tonawanda *(G-16196)*
Revolution Vapor LLC ....G....... 518 627-4133
  Amsterdam *(G-367)*
Schweitzer-Mauduit Intl Inc ....C....... 518 329-4222
  Ancram *(G-375)*
Seneca Manufacturing Company ....G....... 716 945-4400
  Salamanca *(G-15106)*
Seneca Nation Enterprise ....F....... 716 934-7430
  Irving *(G-6765)*
Vector Group Ltd ....B....... 212 409-2800
  New York *(G-12512)*

TOBACCO: Cigars

American Cigar ....G....... 718 969-0008
  Fresh Meadows *(G-5438)*
Davidoff Gneva Madison Ave Inc ....G....... 212 751-9060
  New York *(G-9828)*
Mafco Consolidated Group Inc ....F....... 212 572-8600
  New York *(G-11096)*
Martinez Hand Made Cigars ....G....... 212 239-4049
  New York *(G-11169)*

TOBACCO: Smoking

Mafco Consolidated Group Inc ....F....... 212 572-8600
  New York *(G-11096)*

TOILET FIXTURES: Plastic

Metpar Corp ....D....... 516 333-2600
  Westbury *(G-17011)*

TOILET PREPARATIONS

H & H Laboratories Inc ....F....... 718 624-8041
  Brooklyn *(G-2057)*
H & H Laboratories Inc ....G....... 718 624-8041
  Brooklyn *(G-2058)*
King Research Inc ....E....... 718 788-0122
  Brooklyn *(G-2172)*
MZB Accessories LLC ....D....... 718 472-7500
  Long Island City *(G-7818)*

TOILETRIES, COSMETICS & PERFUME STORES

Estee Lauder Companies Inc ....A....... 212 572-4200
  New York *(G-10069)*
Estee Lauder Inc ....A....... 212 572-4200
  New York *(G-10072)*
Estee Lauder Inc ....D....... 631 531-1000
  Melville *(G-8316)*
International Design Assoc Ltd ....G....... 212 687-0333
  New York *(G-10633)*
Rev Holdings Inc ....A....... 212 527-4000
  New York *(G-11848)*
Revlon Holdings Inc ....D....... 212 527-4000
  New York *(G-11853)*
RGI Group Incorporated ....E....... 212 527-4000
  New York *(G-11858)*

TOILETRIES, WHOLESALE: Hair Preparations

EL Erman International Ltd ....G....... 212 444-9440
  Brooklyn *(G-1909)*

TOILETRIES, WHOLESALE: Perfumes

Elias Fragrances Inc ....F....... 718 693-6400
  Rye Brook *(G-15070)*
Elite Parfums Ltd ....D....... 212 983-2640
  New York *(G-10007)*
Eternal Love Parfums Corp ....G....... 516 921-6100
  Syosset *(G-15821)*
Scent-A-Vision Inc ....E....... 631 424-4905
  Huntington Station *(G-6722)*
Sundial Fragrances & Flavors ....E....... 631 842-8800
  Amityville *(G-328)*
Symrise Inc ....E....... 845 469-7675
  Chester *(G-3618)*
Value Fragrances Inc ....E....... 845 294-5726
  Goshen *(G-5741)*

TOILETRIES, WHOLESALE: Toilet Preparations

Bare Escentuals Inc ....G....... 646 537-0070
  New York *(G-9319)*
Quality King Distributors Inc ....C....... 631 439-2027
  Ronkonkoma *(G-14973)*

TOILETRIES, WHOLESALE: Toiletries

Bfma Holding Corporation ....G....... 607 753-6746
  Cortland *(G-4014)*
Gassho Body & Mind Inc ....G....... 518 695-9991
  Schuylerville *(G-15320)*
Robell Research Inc ....G....... 212 755-6577
  New York *(G-11888)*

TOMBSTONES: Terrazzo Or Concrete, Precast

Eaton Brothers Corp ....G....... 716 649-8250
  Hamburg *(G-5922)*

TOOL & DIE STEEL

Baker Tool & Die & Die ....G....... 716 694-2025
  North Tonawanda *(G-12959)*

TOOLS: Carpenters', Including Levels & Chisels, Exc Saws

Nyc District Council Ubcja ....G....... 212 366-7500
  New York *(G-11478)*

TOOLS: Hand

Allway Tools Inc ....D....... 718 792-3636
  Bronx *(G-1269)*
Ames Companies Inc ....E....... 607 739-4544
  Pine Valley *(G-13556)*
Best Way Tools By Anderson Inc ....G....... 631 586-4702
  Deer Park *(G-4106)*
Circo File Corp ....G....... 516 922-1848
  Oyster Bay *(G-13367)*
Coastel Cable Tools Inc ....E....... 315 471-5361
  Syracuse *(G-15899)*
Dead Ringer LLC ....G....... 585 355-4685
  Rochester *(G-14303)*
Dresser-Argus Inc ....G....... 718 643-1540
  Brooklyn *(G-1880)*
Huron TI & Cutter Grinding Co ....E....... 631 420-7000
  Farmingdale *(G-5008)*
Hydramec Inc ....G....... 585 593-5190
  Scio *(G-15321)*
Ivy Classic Industries Inc ....E....... 914 632-8200
  New Rochelle *(G-8913)*
North Pk Innovations Group Inc ....G....... 716 699-2031
  Ellicottville *(G-4643)*
Robinson Tools LLC ....G....... 585 586-5432
  Penfield *(G-13503)*
Schilling Forge Inc ....E....... 315 454-4421
  Syracuse *(G-16033)*
Snyder Manufacturing Inc ....E....... 716 945-0354
  Salamanca *(G-15107)*
U S Air Tool Co Inc ....F....... 631 471-3300
  Ronkonkoma *(G-14994)*
Winters Railroad Service Inc ....G....... 716 337-2668
  North Collins *(G-12932)*
York Industries Inc ....E....... 516 746-3736
  Garden City Park *(G-5546)*

TOOLS: Hand, Engravers'

Edward C Lyons Company Inc ....G....... 718 515-5361
  Bronx *(G-1323)*
Edward C Muller Corp ....F....... 718 881-7270
  Bronx *(G-1324)*

Employee Codes: A=Over 500 employees, B=251-500
C=101-250, D=51-100, E=20-50, F=10-19, G=5-9

2017 Harris
New York Manufacturers Directory

TOOLS: Hand, Jewelers'

Boucheron Joaillerie USA Inc .... G 212 715-7330
 New York *(G-9442)*
Empire Devleopment .... G 716 789-2097
 Mayville *(G-8215)*
The Swatch Group U S Inc .... G 212 297-9192
 New York *(G-12310)*

TOOLS: Hand, Mechanics

Classic Tool Design Inc .... E 845 562-8700
 New Windsor *(G-8935)*

TOOLS: Hand, Plumbers'

Design Source By Lg Inc .... E 212 274-0022
 New York *(G-9855)*
Metro City Group Inc .... G 516 781-2500
 Bellmore *(G-818)*

TOOLS: Hand, Power

Allied Motion Technologies Inc .... C 315 782-5910
 Watertown *(G-16634)*
Awt Supply Corp .... G 516 437-9105
 Elmont *(G-4717)*
Black & Decker (us) Inc .... B 914 235-6300
 Brewster *(G-1212)*
Black & Decker (us) Inc .... G 716 884-6220
 Buffalo *(G-2843)*
Black & Decker (us) Inc .... G 631 952-2008
 Hauppauge *(G-6035)*
Dynabrade Inc .... C 716 631-0100
 Clarence *(G-3658)*
Great American Tool Co Inc .... G 716 646-5700
 Hamburg *(G-5927)*
Huck International Inc .... C 845 331-7300
 Kingston *(G-7191)*
Ivy Classic Industries Inc .... E 914 632-8200
 New Rochelle *(G-8913)*
Meritool LLC .... F 716 699-6005
 Ellicottville *(G-4642)*
New York Industrial Works Inc .... G 718 292-0615
 Bronx *(G-1409)*
P & F Industries Inc .... C 631 694-9800
 Melville *(G-8346)*
Reimann & Georger Corporation .... E 716 895-1156
 Buffalo *(G-3156)*
Stature Electric Inc .... B 315 782-5910
 Watertown *(G-16672)*
Stephen Hanley .... D 718 729-3360
 Long Island City *(G-7891)*

TOOTHBRUSHES: Electric

Quip Nyc Inc .... G 703 615-1076
 Brooklyn *(G-2467)*

TOOTHBRUSHES: Exc Electric

Colgate-Palmolive Company .... A 212 310-2000
 New York *(G-9667)*
Marketshare LLC .... G 631 273-0598
 Brentwood *(G-1191)*
Violife LLC .... G 914 207-1820
 Yonkers *(G-17497)*

TOOTHPASTES, GELS & TOOTHPOWDERS

Colgat-Plmolive Centl Amer Inc .... G 212 310-2000
 New York *(G-9666)*
Colgate-Palmolive Company .... A 212 310-2000
 New York *(G-9667)*
Colgate-Palmolive Company .... B 718 506-3961
 Queens Village *(G-13975)*
Colgate-Palmolive Globl Trdg .... G 212 310-2000
 New York *(G-9668)*
Quip Nyc Inc .... G 703 615-1076
 Brooklyn *(G-2467)*

TOWELS: Indl

Blu Sand LLC .... G 212 564-1147
 New York *(G-9419)*

TOWELS: Linen & Linen & Cotton Mixtures

Blc Textiles Inc .... E 516 791-4500
 Mineola *(G-8499)*

TOWERS, SECTIONS: Transmission, Radio & Television

Fred A Nudd Corporation .... E 315 524-2531
 Ontario *(G-13201)*

TOYS

Church Communities NY Inc .... E 518 589-5103
 Elka Park *(G-4629)*
Church Communities NY Inc .... E 518 589-5103
 Elka Park *(G-4630)*
Creative Kids Far East Inc .... C 845 368-0246
 Airmont *(G-13)*
Dana Michele LLC .... G 917 757-7777
 New York *(G-9798)*
Drescher Paper Box Inc .... F 716 854-0288
 Buffalo *(G-2918)*
Habermaass Corporation .... F 315 685-8919
 Skaneateles *(G-15462)*
Jim Henson Company Inc .... E 212 794-2400
 New York *(G-10733)*
Joel Zelcer .... F 917 525-6790
 Brooklyn *(G-2144)*
Jupiter Creations Inc .... G 917 493-9393
 New York *(G-10790)*
Kidtellect Inc 017 803-1456
 New York *(G-10841)*
Kling Magnetics Inc .... E 518 392-4000
 Chatham *(G-3558)*
Master Juvenile Products Inc .... F 845 647-8400
 Ellenville *(G-4635)*
Mattel Inc .... F 716 714-8514
 East Aurora *(G-4374)*
Ogosport LLC .... G 718 554-0777
 Brooklyn *(G-2387)*
Readent Inc .... F 212 710-3004
 White Plains *(G-17162)*
Sandbox Brands Inc .... G 212 647-8877
 New York *(G-11965)*
Toymax Inc .... G 212 633-6611
 New York *(G-12384)*
Vogel Applied Technologies .... G 212 677-3136
 New York *(G-12563)*
Way Out Toys Inc .... G 212 689-9094
 New York *(G-12599)*
Whats Next Manufacturing Inc .... E 585 492-1014
 Arcade *(G-402)*

TOYS & HOBBY GOODS & SPLYS, WHOLESALE: Arts/Crafts Eqpt/Sply

Multi Packaging Solutions Inc .... E 646 885-0157
 New York *(G-11324)*

TOYS & HOBBY GOODS & SPLYS, WHOLESALE: Balloons, Novelty

OH How Cute Inc .... G 347 838-6031
 Staten Island *(G-15719)*

TOYS & HOBBY GOODS & SPLYS, WHOLESALE: Educational Toys

Global Video LLC .... D 516 222-2600
 Woodbury *(G-17288)*

TOYS & HOBBY GOODS & SPLYS, WHOLESALE: Toys & Games

Last Straw Inc .... E 516 371-2727
 Lawrence *(G-7393)*
Way Out Toys Inc .... G 212 689-9094
 New York *(G-12599)*

TOYS & HOBBY GOODS & SPLYS, WHOLESALE: Toys, NEC

Toymax Inc .... G 212 633-6611
 New York *(G-12384)*

TOYS & HOBBY GOODS & SPLYS, WHOLESALE: Video Games

Barron Games Intl Co LLC .... F 716 630-0054
 Buffalo *(G-2832)*

TOYS, HOBBY GOODS & SPLYS WHOLESALERS

Creative Kids Far East Inc .... C 845 368-0246
 Airmont *(G-13)*
Fierce Fun Toys LLC .... G 646 322-7172
 New York *(G-10162)*
Habermaass Corporation .... F 315 685-8919
 Skaneateles *(G-15462)*

TOYS: Dolls, Stuffed Animals & Parts

Community Products LLC .... E 518 589-5103
 Elka Park *(G-4631)*
Cosmetics Plus Ltd .... G 516 768-7250
 Amagansett *(G-213)*
Dana Michele LLC .... G 917 757-7777
 New York *(G-9798)*
Jim Henson Company Inc .... E 212 794-2400
 New York *(G-10733)*
Jupiter Creations Inc .... G 917 493-9393
 New York *(G-10790)*
Madame Alexander Doll Co LLC .... D 212 244-4500
 New York *(G-11091)*

TOYS: Electronic

Littlebits Electronics Inc .... D 917 464-4577
 New York *(G-11014)*
Wobbleworks Inc .... G 415 987-1534
 New York *(G-12651)*

TOYS: Video Game Machines

C T A Digital Inc .... E 845 513-0433
 Monroe *(G-8551)*

TRADE SHOW ARRANGEMENT SVCS

Alm Media LLC .... B 212 457-9400
 New York *(G-9095)*
Alm Media Holdings Inc .... B 212 457-9400
 New York *(G-9096)*
International Data Group Inc .... E 212 331-7883
 New York *(G-10632)*
Relx Inc .... F 212 309-8100
 New York *(G-11826)*

TRADERS: Commodity, Contracts

Demeo Brothers Inc .... F 212 268-1400
 New York *(G-9843)*

TRAILERS & PARTS: Boat

Performance Custom Trailer .... G 518 504-4021
 Lake George *(G-7263)*

TRAILERS & PARTS: Truck & Semi's

Cross Country Mfg Inc .... F 607 656-4103
 Greene *(G-5863)*
Cross Country Mfg Inc .... F 607 656-4103
 Greene *(G-5864)*
Davis Trailer World LLC .... F 585 538-6640
 York *(G-17505)*
G L 7 Sales Plus Ltd .... G 631 696-8290
 Coram *(G-3942)*
General Welding & Fabg Inc .... G 716 652-0033
 Elma *(G-4649)*
Seneca Truck & Trailer Inc .... G 315 781-1100
 Geneva *(G-5586)*
Stone Well Bodies & Mch Inc .... F 315 497-3512
 Genoa *(G-5590)*

TRAILERS & TRAILER EQPT

Rolling Star Manufacturing Inc .... E 315 896-4767
 Barneveld *(G-616)*

TRAILERS: Bus, Tractor Type

Full Service Auto Body Inc .... F 718 831-9300
 Floral Park *(G-5204)*

TRAILERS: Semitrailers, Truck Tractors

Blue Tee Corp .... G 212 598-0880
 New York *(G-9422)*

TRANSDUCERS: Electrical Properties

American Aerospace Contrls Inc .... E 631 694-5100
 Farmingdale *(G-4940)*

PRODUCT SECTION

TRUCK & BUS BODIES: Truck, Motor Vehicle

Pcb Group Inc .... E 716 684-0001
   Depew *(G-4268)*
Ruhle Companies Inc .... E 914 287-4000
   Valhalla *(G-16372)*

TRANSDUCERS: Pressure

Dylix Corporation .... E 719 773-2985
   Grand Island *(G-5755)*
Kinemotive Corporation .... E 631 249-6440
   Farmingdale *(G-5028)*

TRANSFORMERS: Control

Current Controls Inc .... C 585 593-1544
   Wellsville *(G-16750)*

TRANSFORMERS: Distribution

Electron Coil Inc .... D 607 336-7414
   Norwich *(G-13027)*
Ems Development Corporation .... D 631 345-6200
   Yaphank *(G-17391)*
Kepco Inc .... E 718 461-7000
   Flushing *(G-5259)*
Kepco Inc .... D 718 461-7000
   Flushing *(G-5260)*
Kepco Inc .... E 718 461-7000
   Flushing *(G-5261)*
Schneider Electric It Corp .... F 646 335-0216
   New York *(G-11992)*

TRANSFORMERS: Distribution, Electric

Hale Electrical Dist Svcs Inc .... G 716 818-7595
   Wales Center *(G-16540)*
Siemens Corporation .... F 202 434-7800
   New York *(G-12062)*
Siemens USA Holdings Inc .... B 212 258-4000
   New York *(G-12064)*

TRANSFORMERS: Electric

Niagara Transformer Corp .... D 716 896-6500
   Buffalo *(G-3091)*
Transistor Devices Inc .... E 631 471-7492
   Ronkonkoma *(G-14992)*

TRANSFORMERS: Electronic

Atlantic Transformer Inc .... F 716 795-3258
   Barker *(G-612)*
Beta Transformer Tech Corp .... E 631 244-7393
   Bohemia *(G-1024)*
Data Device Corporation .... B 631 567-5600
   Bohemia *(G-1049)*
Esc Control Electronics LLC .... E 631 467-5328
   Sayville *(G-15208)*
Exxelia-Raf Tabtronics LLC .... E 585 243-4331
   Piffard *(G-13547)*
NEa Manufacturing Corp .... E 516 371-4200
   Inwood *(G-6763)*
Todd Systems Inc .... D 914 963-3400
   Yonkers *(G-17490)*
Urban Technologies Inc .... G 716 672-2709
   Fredonia *(G-5376)*

TRANSFORMERS: Ignition, Domestic Fuel Burners

Frederick Cowan & Company Inc .... F 631 369-0360
   Riverhead *(G-14143)*

TRANSFORMERS: Power Related

Arstan Products International .... F 516 433-1313
   Hicksville *(G-6324)*
Berkshire Transformer .... G 631 467-5328
   Central Islip *(G-3487)*
Buffalo Power Elec Ctr De .... E 716 651-1600
   Depew *(G-4250)*
Cooper Power Systems LLC .... B 716 375-7100
   Olean *(G-13140)*
Exxelia-Raf Tabtronics LLC .... E 585 243-4331
   Piffard *(G-13547)*
K Road Power Management LLC .... F 212 351-0535
   New York *(G-10796)*
Piller Usa Inc .... E 845 695-6600
   Middletown *(G-8456)*
Ram Transformer Technologies .... F 914 632-3988
   New Rochelle *(G-8922)*
Sag Harbor Industries Inc .... E 631 725-0440
   Sag Harbor *(G-15080)*

Schneider Electric Usa Inc .... F 585 377-1313
   Penfield *(G-13504)*
Spellman High Vltage Elec Corp .... B 631 630-3000
   Hauppauge *(G-6197)*
Spence Engineering Company Inc .... C 845 778-5566
   Walden *(G-16536)*
Sunward Electronics Inc .... F 518 687-0030
   Troy *(G-16257)*
Switching Power Inc .... D 631 981-7231
   Ronkonkoma *(G-14990)*
Veeco Instruments Inc .... C 516 349-8300
   Plainview *(G-13643)*

TRANSFORMERS: Specialty

Dyco Electronics Inc .... D 607 324-2030
   Hornell *(G-6562)*
Mitchell Electronics Corp .... E 914 699-3800
   Mount Vernon *(G-8707)*

TRANSLATION & INTERPRETATION SVCS

Language and Graphics Inc .... G 212 315-5266
   New York *(G-10927)*
SOS International LLC .... E 212 742-2410
   New York *(G-12140)*

TRANSMISSIONS: Motor Vehicle

A-Line Technologies Inc .... F 607 772-2439
   Binghamton *(G-884)*
Auburn Bearing & Mfg Inc .... G 315 986-7600
   Macedon *(G-7982)*
Pro Torque .... E 631 218-8700
   Bohemia *(G-1122)*
Terrys Transmission .... G 315 458-4333
   North Syracuse *(G-12952)*

TRANSPORTATION EPQT & SPLYS, WHOLESALE: Acft/Space Vehicle

Nell-Joy Industries Inc .... E 631 842-8989
   Copiague *(G-3915)*

TRANSPORTATION EPQT/SPLYS, WHOL: Marine Propulsn Mach/Eqpt

William J Blume Worldwide Svcs .... G 914 723-6185
   Saratoga Springs *(G-15177)*

TRANSPORTATION EQPT & SPLYS WHOLESALERS, NEC

Stidd Systems Inc .... E 631 477-2400
   Greenport *(G-5877)*
Worldwide Arntcal Cmpnents Inc .... G 631 842-3780
   Copiague *(G-3940)*

TRANSPORTATION: Local Passenger, NEC

Hampton Transport Inc .... F 631 716-4445
   Coram *(G-3943)*

TRAP ROCK: Crushed & Broken

Dolomite Products Company Inc .... E 585 586-2568
   Penfield *(G-13498)*
Tilcon New York Inc .... B 845 358-4500
   West Nyack *(G-16928)*
Tilcon New York Inc .... E 845 778-5591
   Walden *(G-16537)*
Tilcon New York Inc .... D 845 358-3100
   West Nyack *(G-16929)*

TRAPS: Animal & Fish, Wire

Cuba Specialty Mfg Co Inc .... F 585 567-4176
   Fillmore *(G-5175)*

TRAPS: Stem

John N Fehlinger Co Inc .... F 212 233-5656
   New York *(G-10752)*

TRAVEL AGENCIES

Mapeasy Inc .... F 631 537-6213
   Wainscott *(G-16529)*
Quinn and Co of NY Ltd .... E 212 868-1900
   New York *(G-11774)*
Rfp LLC .... E 212 838-7733
   New York *(G-11855)*

TRAVEL TRAILERS & CAMPERS

All Star Carts & Vehicles Inc .... D 631 666-5581
   Bay Shore *(G-668)*

TRAYS: Cable, Metal Plate

Mono-Systems Inc .... E 716 821-1344
   Buffalo *(G-3074)*

TRAYS: Plastic

Commodore Machine Co Inc .... F 585 657-6916
   Bloomfield *(G-984)*
SAV Thermo Inc .... F 631 249-9444
   West Babylon *(G-16826)*
Tully Products Inc .... G 716 773-3166
   Grand Island *(G-5771)*

TROPHIES, NEC

All American Awards Inc .... F 631 567-2025
   Bohemia *(G-1011)*
Dwm International Inc .... F 646 290-7448
   Long Island City *(G-7721)*
Endurart Inc .... E 212 473-7000
   New York *(G-10034)*

TROPHIES, PEWTER

Valerie Bohigian .... G 914 631-8866
   Sleepy Hollow *(G-15476)*

TROPHIES, PLATED, ALL METALS

Csi International Inc .... E 716 282-5408
   Niagara Falls *(G-12809)*

TROPHIES, SILVER

Atlantic Trophy Co Inc .... G 212 684-6020
   New York *(G-9253)*

TROPHIES, WHOLESALE

Ter-El Engraving Co Inc .... G 315 455-5597
   Syracuse *(G-16056)*

TROPHIES: Metal, Exc Silver

A D Mfg Corp .... F 516 352-6161
   Floral Park *(G-5189)*
C & M Products Inc .... G 315 471-3303
   Syracuse *(G-15880)*
Classic Medallics Inc .... E 718 392-5410
   Mount Vernon *(G-8672)*
New Dimension Awards Inc .... G 718 236-8200
   Brooklyn *(G-2360)*

TROPHY & PLAQUE STORES

Displays & Beyond Inc .... F 718 805-7786
   Glendale *(G-5651)*
International Bronze Manufac .... F 516 248-3080
   Albertson *(G-155)*
Jem Sign Corp .... G 516 867-4466
   Hempstead *(G-6275)*
Ter-El Engraving Co Inc .... G 315 455-5597
   Syracuse *(G-16056)*

TRUCK & BUS BODIES: Ambulance

Jeffersonville Volunteer .... E 845 482-3110
   Jeffersonville *(G-7059)*

TRUCK & BUS BODIES: Motor Vehicle, Specialty

Abasco Inc .... E 716 649-4790
   Hamburg *(G-5918)*
Kurtz Truck Equipment Inc .... F 607 849-3468
   Marathon *(G-8084)*
Rexford Services Inc .... G 716 366-6671
   Dunkirk *(G-4349)*

TRUCK & BUS BODIES: Truck, Motor Vehicle

Demartini Oil Equipment Svc .... G 518 463-5752
   Glenmont *(G-5667)*
Eastern Welding Inc .... G 631 727-0306
   Riverhead *(G-14142)*
Marros Equipment & Trucks .... F 315 539-8702
   Waterloo *(G-16630)*
Renaldos Sales and Service Ctr .... G 716 337-3760
   North Collins *(G-12931)*

Employee Codes: A=Over 500 employees, B=251-500, C=101-250, D=51-100, E=20-50, F=10-19, G=5-9

TRUCK & BUS BODIES: Truck, Motor Vehicle

Unicell Body Company Inc .... E 716 853-8628
  Buffalo (G-3231)
USA Body Inc .... G 315 852-6123
  De Ruyter (G-4082)
Weld-Built Body Co Inc .... E 631 643-9700
  Wyandanch (G-17378)

TRUCK BODIES: Body Parts

Brunner International Inc .... C 585 798-6000
  Medina (G-8268)
Concrete Mixer Supplycom Inc .... G 716 375-5565
  Olean (G-13139)
Ekostinger Inc .... F 585 739-0450
  Rochester (G-14342)
Fiberglass Replacement Parts .... G 716 893-6471
  Buffalo (G-2946)
General Welding & Fabg Inc .... G 585 697-7660
  Rochester (G-14392)
Tectran Mfg Inc .... D 800 776-5549
  Buffalo (G-3211)
Unicell Body Company Inc .... F 716 853-8628
  Schenectady (G-15307)

TRUCK GENERAL REPAIR SVC

Chet Kruszkas Service Inc .... F 716 662-7450
  Orchard Park (G-13261)
Riverview Industries Inc .... G 845 265-5284
  Cold Spring (G-3765)

TRUCK PAINTING & LETTERING SVCS

Jem Sign Corp .... G 516 867-4466
  Hempstead (G-6275)
Monasani Signs Inc .... G 631 266-2635
  East Northport (G-4442)

TRUCK PARTS & ACCESSORIES: Wholesalers

Chet Kruszkas Service Inc .... F 716 662-7450
  Orchard Park (G-13261)
Unicell Body Company Inc .... E 716 853-8628
  Buffalo (G-3231)

TRUCKING & HAULING SVCS: Garbage, Collect/Transport Only

Suffolk Indus Recovery Corp .... D 631 732-6403
  Coram (G-3951)

TRUCKING, DUMP

Alice Perkins .... F 716 378-5100
  Salamanca (G-15099)
Ribble Lumber Inc .... G 315 536-6221
  Penn Yan (G-13518)

TRUCKING: Except Local

Platinum Sales Promotion Inc .... G 718 361-0200
  Long Island City (G-7844)

TRUCKING: Local, Without Storage

Clark Concrete Co Inc .... G 315 478-4101
  Syracuse (G-15896)
Haley Concrete Inc .... F 716 492-0849
  Delevan (G-4234)
J & S Logging Inc .... E 315 262-2112
  South Colton (G-15515)
Little Valley Sand & Gravel .... G 716 938-6676
  Little Valley (G-7511)

TRUCKS & TRACTORS: Industrial

Arlington Equipment Corp .... G 518 798-5867
  Queensbury (G-13992)
ASAP Rack Rental Inc .... G 718 499-4495
  Brooklyn (G-1638)
B & J Delivers Inc .... G 631 524-5550
  Brentwood (G-1177)
Channel Manufacturing Inc .... E 516 944-6271
  Port Washington (G-13804)
Ducon Technologies Inc .... F 631 694-1700
  New York (G-9937)
Ducon Technologies Inc .... G 631 420-4900
  Farmingdale (G-4979)
E-One Inc .... D 716 646-6790
  Hamburg (G-5921)
Mettler-Toledo Inc .... C 607 257-6000
  Ithaca (G-6860)

Raymond Consolidated Corp .... C 800 235-7200
  Greene (G-5868)
Raymond Corporation .... A 607 656-2311
  Greene (G-5869)
Raymond Corporation .... E 315 643-5000
  East Syracuse (G-4557)
Speedways Conveyors Inc .... E 716 893-2222
  Buffalo (G-3195)
Win-Holt Equipment Corp .... G 516 222-0433
  Garden City (G-5537)

TRUCKS: Forklift

Continental Lift Truck Inc .... F 718 738-4738
  South Ozone Park (G-15532)
Jamestown Industrial Trcks Inc .... F 716 893-6105
  Buffalo (G-3014)
Raymond Corporation .... C 607 656-2311
  East Syracuse (G-4555)
Raymond Corporation .... B 315 463-5000
  East Syracuse (G-4556)
Raymond Sales Corporation .... G 607 656-2311
  Greene (G-5870)
Stanley Industrial Eqp LLC .... G 315 656-8733
  Kirkville (G-7228)

TRUCKS: Indl

Meteor Express Inc .... F 718 551-9177
  Jamaica (G-6931)
Pb08 Inc .... G 347 866-7353
  Hicksville (G-6385)
Ward Lafrance Truck Corp .... E 518 893-1865
  Saratoga Springs (G-15176)

TRUNKS

Junk In My Trunk Inc .... G 631 420-5865
  Farmingdale (G-5019)

TRUSSES: Wood, Floor

Niagara Truss & Pallet LLC .... F 716 433-5400
  Lockport (G-7607)

TRUSSES: Wood, Roof

L Builders Supply Inc .... B 518 355-7190
  Schenectady (G-15275)
Northeast Panel & Truss LLC .... E 845 339-3656
  Kingston (G-7205)
P & R Truss Co .... E 716 496-5484
  Chaffee (G-3535)
Pdj Components Inc .... E 845 469-9191
  Chester (G-3611)
Proof Industries Inc .... G 631 694-7663
  Farmingdale (G-5090)
Rochester Lumber Company .... E 585 924-7171
  Farmington (G-5155)
S R Sloan Inc .... D 315 736-7730
  Whitesboro (G-17195)
Steele Truss Company Inc .... E 518 562-4663
  Plattsburgh (G-13698)
Ufp New York LLC .... G 315 381-5093
  Clinton (G-3723)
Ufp New York LLC .... E 716 496-5484
  Chaffee (G-3536)
Ufp New York LLC .... E 518 828-2888
  Hudson (G-6637)
Ufp New York LLC .... E 607 563-1556
  Sidney (G-15443)

TUBE & TUBING FABRICATORS

Coventry Manufacturing Co Inc .... E 914 668-2212
  Mount Vernon (G-8674)
Ram Fabricating LLC .... E 315 437-6654
  Syracuse (G-16017)
Spinco Metal Products Inc .... D 315 331-6285
  Newark (G-12743)
Star Tubing Corp .... G 716 483-1703
  Jamestown (G-7031)
Tube Fabrication Company Inc .... F 716 673-1871
  Fredonia (G-5375)

TUBES: Finned, For Heat Transfer

CMS Heat Transfer Division Inc .... E 631 968-0084
  Bohemia (G-1037)

TUBES: Generator, Electron Beam, Beta Ray

E-Beam Services Inc .... G 516 622-1422
  Hicksville (G-6341)

TUBES: Paper

Caraustar Industries Inc .... G 716 874-0393
  Buffalo (G-2867)

TUBES: Paper Or Fiber, Chemical Or Electrical Uses

Industrial Paper Tube Inc .... F 718 893-5000
  Bronx (G-1361)

TUBES: Steel & Iron

Markin Tubing LP .... F 585 495-6211
  Buffalo (G-3056)
TI Group Auto Systems LLC .... G 315 568-7042
  Seneca Falls (G-15371)

TUBES: Vacuum

New Sensor Corporation .... D 718 937-8300
  Long Island City (G-7824)

TUBES: Wrought, Welded Or Lock Joint

Markin Tubing LP .... D 585 495-6211
  Wyoming (G-17380)
Markin Tubing Inc .... C 585 495-6211
  Wyoming (G-17381)

TUBING: Flexible, Metallic

Conrad Blasius Equipment Co .... G 516 753-1200
  Plainview (G-13590)

TUBING: Glass

Gray Glass Inc .... E 718 217-2943
  Queens Village (G-13978)

TUBING: Plastic

Finger Lakes Extrusion Corp .... E 585 905-0632
  Canandaigua (G-3346)
Hancor Inc .... D 607 565-3033
  Waverly (G-16703)

TUBING: Seamless

TI Group Auto Systems LLC .... G 315 568-7042
  Seneca Falls (G-15371)

TUNGSTEN CARBIDE

Buffalo Tungsten Inc .... D 716 759-6353
  Depew (G-4251)
Niagara Refining LLC .... E 716 706-1400
  Depew (G-4266)

TUNGSTEN CARBIDE POWDER

Golden Egret LLC .... G 516 922-2839
  East Norwich (G-4446)

TURBINE GENERATOR SET UNITS: Hydraulic, Complete

Hdm Hydraulics LLC .... D 716 694-8004
  Tonawanda (G-16170)
Signa Chemistry Inc .... F 212 933-4101
  New York (G-12071)

TURBINES & TURBINE GENERATOR SET UNITS, COMPLETE

Ingersoll-Rand Company .... E 716 896-6600
  Buffalo (G-3008)

TURBINES & TURBINE GENERATOR SET UNITS: Gas, Complete

General Electric Company .... B 518 385-3716
  Schenectady (G-15259)
General Electric Company .... B 518 385-2211
  Schenectady (G-15261)

TURBINES & TURBINE GENERATOR SETS

Awr Energy Inc .... F 585 469-7750
  Plattsburgh (G-13652)
Beowawe Binary LLC .... E 646 829-3900
  New York (G-9362)
Cooper Turbocompressor Inc .... B 716 896-6600
  Buffalo (G-2890)

PRODUCT SECTION

VITAMINS: Natural Or Synthetic, Uncompounded, Bulk

M Manastrip-M Corporation ....G...... 518 664-2089
  Clifton Park *(G-3699)*
Make-Waves Instrument Corp ....E....... 716 681-7524
  Depew *(G-4264)*
Micromold Products Inc ....E....... 914 969-2850
  Yonkers *(G-17467)*
Rand Machine Products Inc ....D....... 716 665-5217
  Falconer *(G-4908)*
Ross Valve Mfg ....G...... 518 274-0961
  Troy *(G-16251)*
Sigmamotor Inc ....E....... 716 735-3115
  Middleport *(G-8423)*
Spence Engineering Company Inc ....C...... 845 778-5566
  Walden *(G-16536)*
Steel & Obrien Mfg Inc ....D....... 585 492-5800
  Arcade *(G-400)*
Sure Flow Equipment Inc ....E....... 800 263-8251
  Tonawanda *(G-16204)*
William E Williams Valve Corp ....E....... 718 392-1660
  Long Island City *(G-7922)*

VALVES & REGULATORS: Pressure, Indl

Doyle & Roth Mfg Co Inc ....F....... 212 269-7840
  New York *(G-9921)*
Spence Engineering Company Inc ....C...... 845 778-5566
  Walden *(G-16536)*
Total Energy Fabrication Corp ....G...... 580 363-1500
  North Salem *(G-12940)*

VALVES: Aerosol, Metal

901 D LLC ....E....... 845 369-1111
  Airmont *(G-11)*
Chapin International Inc ....C...... 585 343-3140
  Batavia *(G-627)*
Chapin Manufacturing Inc ....C...... 585 343-3140
  Batavia *(G-628)*
Fabritex Inc ....G...... 706 376-6584
  New York *(G-10124)*
Jordan Panel Systems Corp ....E....... 631 754-4900
  East Northport *(G-4439)*
Peak Motion Inc ....G...... 716 534-4925
  Clarence *(G-3668)*
Peelle Company ....G...... 631 231-6000
  Hauppauge *(G-6159)*

VALVES: Aircraft

Valvetech Inc ....E....... 315 548-4551
  Phelps *(G-13538)*

VALVES: Aircraft, Control, Hydraulic & Pneumatic

Young & Franklin Inc ....D....... 315 457-3110
  Liverpool *(G-7559)*

VALVES: Aircraft, Fluid Power

Dmic Inc ....F....... 716 743-4360
  North Tonawanda *(G-12969)*
Moog Inc ....A....... 716 652-2000
  Elma *(G-4651)*
Tactair Fluid Controls Inc ....C...... 315 451-3928
  Liverpool *(G-7552)*

VALVES: Control, Automatic

ADC Industries Inc ....E....... 516 596-1304
  Valley Stream *(G-16398)*

VALVES: Fluid Power, Control, Hydraulic & pneumatic

Aerco International Inc ....C...... 845 580-8000
  Blauvelt *(G-969)*
BW Elliott Mfg Co LLC ....B....... 607 772-0404
  Binghamton *(G-900)*
Direkt Force LLC ....E....... 716 652-3022
  East Aurora *(G-4369)*
Dsti Inc ....G...... 716 557-2362
  Olean *(G-13145)*
Dynamic Sealing Tech Inc ....G...... 716 376-0708
  Olean *(G-13146)*

VALVES: Gas Cylinder, Compressed

Caithness Equities Corporation ....E....... 212 599-2112
  New York *(G-9498)*

VALVES: Hard Rubber

Inflation Systems Inc ....E....... 914 381-8070
  Mamaroneck *(G-8036)*

VALVES: Indl

Air System Products Inc ....F....... 716 683-0435
  Lancaster *(G-7300)*
Byelocorp Scientific Inc ....E....... 212 785-2580
  New York *(G-9486)*
Curtiss-Wright Flow Ctrl Corp ....C...... 631 293-3800
  Farmingdale *(G-4968)*
Curtiss-Wright Flow Ctrl Corp ....C...... 631 293-3800
  Farmingdale *(G-4969)*
Dresser-Rand LLC ....A....... 585 596-3100
  Wellsville *(G-16751)*
Flow-Safe Inc ....E....... 716 662-2585
  Orchard Park *(G-13270)*
J H Buscher Inc ....G...... 716 667-2003
  Orchard Park *(G-13276)*
McWane Inc ....B....... 607 734-2211
  Elmira *(G-4694)*
Murphy Manufacturing Co Inc ....E....... 585 223-0100
  Fairport *(G-4865)*
Plattco Corporation ....E....... 518 563-4640
  Plattsburgh *(G-13687)*
Precision Valve & Automtn Inc ....C...... 518 371-2684
  Cohoes *(G-3755)*
Syraco Products Inc ....E....... 800 581-5555
  Syracuse *(G-16047)*
Town Food Service Eqp Co Inc ....F....... 718 388-5650
  Brooklyn *(G-2672)*
Trac Regulators Inc ....E....... 914 699-9352
  Mount Vernon *(G-8739)*
William E Williams Valve Corp ....E....... 718 392-1660
  Long Island City *(G-7922)*

VALVES: Plumbing & Heating

Everflow Supplies Inc ....E....... 908 436-1100
  Brooklyn *(G-1940)*
Lemode Plumbing & Heating ....E....... 718 545-3336
  Astoria *(G-447)*
Smiths Gas Service Inc ....G...... 518 438-0400
  Albany *(G-134)*
Venco Sales Inc ....E....... 631 754-0782
  Huntington *(G-6691)*

VALVES: Regulating & Control, Automatic

Digital Home Creations Inc ....G...... 585 576-7070
  Webster *(G-16721)*
Tyco Simplexgrinnell ....E....... 315 437-9664
  East Syracuse *(G-4574)*

VALVES: Water Works

Flomatic Corporation ....E....... 518 761-9797
  Glens Falls *(G-5678)*

VARNISHES, NEC

John C Dolph Company Inc ....E....... 732 329-2333
  Schenectady *(G-15271)*
Royce Associates A Ltd Partnr ....G...... 516 367-6298
  Jericho *(G-7083)*
Si Group Inc ....C...... 518 347-4200
  Rotterdam Junction *(G-15035)*

VEGETABLE STANDS OR MARKETS

Lakeside Cider Mill Farm Inc ....G...... 518 399-8359
  Ballston Lake *(G-582)*

VEHICLES: All Terrain

Kens Service & Sales Inc ....F....... 716 683-1155
  Elma *(G-4650)*

VEHICLES: Recreational

Adirondack Power Sports ....G...... 518 481-6269
  Malone *(G-8006)*
Bullet Industries Inc ....G...... 585 352-0836
  Spencerport *(G-15568)*

VENDING MACHINES & PARTS

Cubic Trnsp Systems Inc ....F....... 212 255-1810
  New York *(G-9764)*
Vengo Inc ....G...... 866 526-7054
  Long Island City *(G-7912)*

VENTILATING EQPT: Metal

Air Louver & Damper Inc ....E....... 718 392-3232
  Maspeth *(G-8112)*
Air Louver & Damper Inc ....F....... 718 392-3232
  Long Island City *(G-7649)*
GM Sheet Metal Inc ....F....... 718 349-2830
  Brooklyn *(G-2031)*
Imperial Damper & Louver Co ....E....... 718 731-3800
  Bronx *(G-1360)*
M&G Duravent Inc ....F....... 518 463-7284
  Albany *(G-98)*
Spence Engineering Company Inc ....C...... 845 778-5566
  Walden *(G-16536)*

VENTILATING EQPT: Sheet Metal

Empire Ventilation Eqp Co Inc ....F....... 718 728-2143
  Florida *(G-5212)*
Lambro Industries Inc ....D....... 631 842-8088
  Amityville *(G-304)*

VENTURE CAPITAL COMPANIES

Circle Peak Capital MGT LLC ....E....... 646 230-8812
  New York *(G-9620)*
Victoire Latam Asset MGT LLC ....F....... 212 319-6550
  New York *(G-12538)*

VETERINARY PHARMACEUTICAL PREPARATIONS

Ark Sciences Inc ....G...... 646 943-1520
  Islandia *(G-6787)*
H W Naylor Co Inc ....F....... 607 263-5145
  Morris *(G-8618)*

VIBRATORS: Concrete Construction

Ozteck Industries Inc ....E....... 516 883-8857
  Port Washington *(G-13850)*

VIDEO & AUDIO EQPT, WHOLESALE

Lanel Inc ....G...... 516 437-5119
  Floral Park *(G-5205)*
National Prof Resources ....E....... 914 937-8879
  Port Chester *(G-13755)*
Professional Tape Corporation ....G...... 516 656-5519
  Glen Cove *(G-5625)*
Video Technology Services Inc ....F....... 516 937-9700
  Syosset *(G-15841)*

VIDEO EQPT

Video Technology Services Inc ....F....... 516 937-9700
  Syosset *(G-15841)*

VIDEO PRODUCTION SVCS

Amherst Media Inc ....G...... 716 874-4450
  Buffalo *(G-2809)*
Scholastic Inc ....A....... 800 724-6527
  New York *(G-11998)*

VIDEO REPAIR SVCS

Video Technology Services Inc ....F....... 516 937-9700
  Syosset *(G-15841)*

VIDEO TAPE PRODUCTION SVCS

NCM Publishers Inc ....G...... 212 691-9100
  New York *(G-11364)*
Physicalmind Institute ....F....... 212 343-2150
  New York *(G-11655)*

VINYL RESINS, NEC

Manufacturers Indexing Pdts ....G...... 631 271-0956
  Halesite *(G-5905)*

VISUAL COMMUNICATIONS SYSTEMS

L & M Welding LLC ....G...... 516 220-1722
  Freeport *(G-5407)*
Vicon Industries Inc ....C...... 631 952-2288
  Hauppauge *(G-6225)*

VITAMINS: Natural Or Synthetic, Uncompounded, Bulk

Abh Natures Products Inc ....E....... 631 249-5783
  Edgewood *(G-4589)*

VITAMINS: Natural Or Synthetic, Uncompounded, Bulk

Ajes Pharmaceuticals LLC ....E...... 631 608-1728
  Copiague *(G-3891)*
Alphabet Holding Company Inc ....E...... 631 200-2000
  Ronkonkoma *(G-14865)*
Gemini Pharmaceuticals Inc ....C...... 631 543-3334
  Commack *(G-3833)*
Healthee Endeavors Inc ....G...... 718 653-5499
  Bronx *(G-1353)*
Healthy N Fit Intl Inc ....F...... 914 271-6040
  Croton On Hudson *(G-4064)*
Natural Organics Inc ....C...... 631 293-0030
  Melville *(G-8339)*
Nbty Inc..F...... 631 244-2065
  Ronkonkoma *(G-14951)*
Nbty Inc..F...... 518 452-5813
  Albany *(G-105)*
Nbty Inc..D...... 631 244-2021
  Ronkonkoma *(G-14952)*
Nbty Inc..A...... 631 200-2000
  Ronkonkoma *(G-14953)*
Nbty Inc..D...... 631 200-7338
  Ronkonkoma *(G-14954)*
Nbty Inc..F...... 631 588-3492
  Holbrook *(G-6464)*
Nbty Manufacturing LLC ....E...... 631 567-9500
  Ronkonkoma *(G-14955)*
Nutraqueen LLC............................F...... 347 368-6568
  New York *(G-11473)*
Only Natural Inc ....F...... 516 897-7001
  Island Park *(G-6783)*
Princeton Sciences.......................G...... 845 368-1214
  Airmont *(G-18)*
Vitalize Labs LLC ....G...... 212 966-6130
  New York *(G-12556)*
Vitamix Laboratories Inc ....E...... 631 465-9245
  Commack *(G-3847)*
Wellquest International Inc ....G...... 212 689-9094
  New York *(G-12608)*

VITAMINS: Pharmaceutical Preparations

Bi Nutraceuticals Inc ....D...... 631 232-1105
  Central Islip *(G-3488)*
Bronson Nutritionals LLC ....E...... 631 750-0000
  Hauppauge *(G-6038)*
Danbury Pharma LLC ....E...... 631 393-6333
  Farmingdale *(G-4974)*
FB Laboratories Inc ....E...... 631 750-0000
  Hauppauge *(G-6076)*
Kabco Pharmaceuticals Inc ....G...... 631 842-3600
  Amityville *(G-300)*
Natural Organics Laboratories ......B...... 631 957-5600
  Amityville *(G-315)*
Natures Bounty Inc ....F...... 631 567-9500
  Bohemia *(G-1108)*
Natures Bounty Inc ....A...... 631 580-6137
  Ronkonkoma *(G-14950)*
Natures Value Inc ....C...... 631 846-2500
  Coram *(G-3946)*
Nutraceutical Wellness LLC ....G...... 888 454-3320
  New York *(G-11472)*
Tishcon Corp................................C...... 516 333-3056
  Westbury *(G-17032)*
Tishcon Corp................................C...... 516 333-3050
  Westbury *(G-17035)*
Unipharm Inc ....E...... 212 564-3634
  New York *(G-12459)*
Very Best Irtj................................F...... 914 271-6585
  Croton On Hudson *(G-4066)*
Wellmill LLC ....F...... 631 465-9245
  Farmingdale *(G-5142)*

WALL COVERINGS WHOLESALERS

Scalamandre Wallpaper Inc ....B...... 631 467-8800
  Hauppauge *(G-6185)*

WALLPAPER & WALL COVERINGS

Adelphi Paper Hangings ....G...... 518 284-9066
  Sharon Springs *(G-15382)*
Flavor Paper Ltd...........................F...... 718 422-0230
  Brooklyn *(G-1985)*
Gerald McGlone ....G...... 518 482-2613
  Colonie *(G-3820)*
Larkin Anya Ltd ....G...... 718 361-1827
  Long Island City *(G-7788)*
Sunnyside Decorative Prints Co ...G...... 516 671-1935
  Glen Cove *(G-5630)*

WALLPAPER: Made From Purchased Paper

Lulu DK LLC ....G...... 212 223-4234
  New York *(G-11063)*

WALLS: Curtain, Metal

A&B McKeon Glass Inc ....G...... 718 525-2152
  Staten Island *(G-15631)*
Pierce Steel Fabricators ....F...... 716 372-7652
  Olean *(G-13152)*

WAREHOUSE CLUBS STORES

Brucci Ltd ....E...... 914 965-0707
  Yonkers *(G-17422)*

WAREHOUSING & STORAGE FACILITIES, NEC

Acme Signs of Baldwinsville ....G...... 315 638-4865
  Baldwinsville *(G-564)*
Cambridge University Press ....D...... 212 337-5000
  New York *(G-9507)*
Eastern Welding Inc......................G...... 631 727-0306
  Riverhead *(G-14142)*
Medical Action Industries Inc ....C...... 631 231-4600
  Hauppauge *(G-6129)*

WAREHOUSING & STORAGE, REFRIGERATED: Frozen Or Refrig Goods

Adirondack Ice & Air Inc ....F...... 518 483-4340
  Malone *(G-8005)*

WAREHOUSING & STORAGE: General

George G Sharp Inc ....E...... 212 732-2800
  New York *(G-10281)*
Ivi Services Inc ....D...... 607 729-5111
  Binghamton *(G-929)*
Lighting Holdings Intl LLC ....F...... 845 306-1850
  Purchase *(G-13960)*
Platinum Sales Promotion Inc ......G...... 718 361-0200
  Long Island City *(G-7844)*
Wayuga Community Newspapers ..G...... 315 594-2506
  Wolcott *(G-17281)*

WAREHOUSING & STORAGE: General

Baby Uv/Kids Uv Inc ....F...... 917 301-9020
  Brooklyn *(G-1661)*
Canfield & Tack Inc ....D...... 585 235-7710
  Rochester *(G-14257)*
Dayleen Intimates Inc ....E...... 914 969-5900
  Yonkers *(G-17435)*

WAREHOUSING & STORAGE: Refrigerated

Crescent Duck Farm Inc ....E...... 631 722-8700
  Aquebogue *(G-384)*

WARM AIR HEATING & AC EQPT & SPLYS, WHOLESALE Air Filters

R P Fedder Corp............................E...... 585 288-1600
  Rochester *(G-14618)*

WARM AIR HEATING/AC EQPT/SPLYS, WHOL Dehumidifiers, Exc Port

MSP Technologycom LLC ....G...... 631 424-7542
  Centerport *(G-3480)*

WASHCLOTHS

1510 Associates LLC ....G...... 212 828-8720
  New York *(G-8960)*

WASHERS: Metal

Superior Washer & Gasket Corp ...D...... 631 273-8282
  Hauppauge *(G-6203)*

WASHERS: Plastic

Fibre Materials Corp ....E...... 516 349-1660
  Plainview *(G-13602)*

WASHERS: Spring, Metal

J T D Stamping Co Inc ....E...... 631 643-4144
  West Babylon *(G-16799)*

WATCH STRAPS, EXC METAL

International Time Products ....G...... 516 931-0005
  Jericho *(G-7073)*
Roma Industries LLC ....G...... 212 268-0723
  New York *(G-11910)*

WATCHCASES

American Time Mfg Ltd ....F...... 585 266-5120
  Rochester *(G-14201)*

WATCHES

Croton Watch Co Inc ....E...... 800 443-7639
  West Nyack *(G-16915)*
E Gluck Corporation......................C...... 718 784-0700
  Little Neck *(G-7508)*
First Sbf Holding Inc ....G...... 845 425-9882
  Valley Cottage *(G-16378)*
Geneva Watch Company Inc ....E...... 212 221-1177
  New York *(G-10276)*
Life Watch Technology Inc ....D...... 917 669-2428
  Flushing *(G-5266)*
Visage Swiss Watch LLC ....E...... 212 594-7991
  New York *(G-12552)*

WATCHES & PARTS, WHOLESALE

E Gluck Corporation......................C...... 718 784-0700
  Little Neck *(G-7508)*

WATER PURIFICATION EQPT: Household

Atlantic Ultraviolet Corp................E...... 631 234-3275
  Hauppauge *(G-6028)*
Vivreau Advanced Water Systems ..F...... 212 502-3749
  New York *(G-12559)*
Water Energy Systems LLC ....G...... 844 822-7665
  New York *(G-12596)*

WATER SUPPLY

Ewt Holdings III Corp ....G...... 212 644-5900
  New York *(G-10096)*

WATER TREATMENT EQPT: Indl

Business Advisory Services ....G...... 718 337-3740
  Far Rockaway *(G-4919)*
City of Olean ....G...... 716 376-5694
  Olean *(G-13138)*
City of Oneonta ....G...... 607 433-3470
  Oneonta *(G-13178)*
Integrated Water Management .....G...... 607 844-4276
  Dryden *(G-4321)*
Metro Group Inc ....D...... 718 392-3616
  Long Island City *(G-7811)*
Neptune Soft Water Inc ....F...... 315 446-5151
  Syracuse *(G-15997)*
New Windsor Waste Water Plant ...F...... 845 561-2550
  New Windsor *(G-8944)*
Ossining Village of Inc ....G...... 914 202-9668
  Ossining *(G-13325)*
R C Kolstad Water Corp ....E...... 585 216-2230
  Ontario *(G-13210)*
Water Treatment Services Inc ......G...... 914 241-2261
  Bedford Hills *(G-808)*

WATER: Mineral, Carbonated, Canned & Bottled, Etc

Global Brands Inc ....G...... 845 358-1212
  Nyack *(G-13052)*
Just Beverages LLC ....G...... 480 388-1133
  Glens Falls *(G-5683)*
New York Spring Water Inc ....E...... 212 777-4649
  New York *(G-11408)*
Nirvana Inc...................................C...... 315 942-4900
  Forestport *(G-5331)*
Saratoga Spring Water Company ..E...... 518 584-6363
  Saratoga Springs *(G-15171)*

WATER: Pasteurized & Mineral, Bottled & Canned

Ariesun Inc ....E...... 866 274-3049
  Mount Vernon *(G-8663)*
Mayer Bros Apple Products Inc .....D...... 716 668-1787
  West Seneca *(G-16952)*
Water Resources Group LLC ....G...... 631 824-9088
  Cold Spring Harbor *(G-3771)*

PRODUCT SECTION

WATER: Pasteurized, Canned & Bottled, Etc
Crystal Rock LLC .... E 716 626-7460
  Buffalo (G-2894)
Let Water Be Water LLC .... G 212 627-2630
  New York (G-10976)
Superleaf LLC .... G 607 280-9198
  Brooklyn (G-2629)

WATERPROOFING COMPOUNDS
Ics Penetron International Ltd .... F 631 928-8282
  East Setauket (G-4485)

WAVEGUIDES & FITTINGS
M W Microwave Corp .... F 516 295-1814
  Lawrence (G-7394)

WAX REMOVERS
Comfort Wax Incorporated .... F 718 204-7028
  Astoria (G-434)

WAXES: Mineral, Natural
Koster Keunen Waxes Ltd .... F 631 589-0400
  Sayville (G-15212)

WAXES: Paraffin
Industrial Raw Materials LLC .... F 212 688-8080
  Plainview (G-13607)
Kent Chemical Corporation .... E 212 521-1700
  New York (G-10838)

WAXES: Petroleum, Not Produced In Petroleum Refineries
Premier Ingridients Inc .... G 516 641-6763
  Great Neck (G-5832)

WEATHER STRIPS: Metal
Accurate Metal Weather Strip .... G 914 668-6042
  Mount Vernon (G-8661)

WEAVING MILL, BROADWOVEN FABRICS: Wool Or Similar Fabric
Loomstate LLC .... E 212 219-2300
  New York (G-11031)

WEDDING CHAPEL: Privately Operated
Silver Griffin Inc .... F 518 272-7771
  Troy (G-16255)

WEIGHING MACHINERY & APPARATUS
Measupro Inc .... F 845 425-8777
  Spring Valley (G-15596)
Mettler-Toledo Inc .... C 607 257-6000
  Ithaca (G-6860)
S R Instruments Inc .... E 716 693-5977
  Tonawanda (G-16297)
Weighing & Systems Tech Inc .... F 518 274-2797
  Troy (G-16263)

WELDING & CUTTING APPARATUS & ACCESS, NEC
McAllisters Precision Wldg Inc .... F 518 221-3455
  Menands (G-8374)

WELDING EQPT
Apogee Translite Inc .... E 631 254-6975
  Deer Park (G-4100)
Lubow Machine Corp .... F 631 226-1700
  Copiague (G-3911)
Riverview Industries Inc .... G 845 265-5284
  Cold Spring (G-3765)
Vante Inc .... F 716 778-7691
  Newfane (G-12789)

WELDING EQPT & SPLYS WHOLESALERS
Haun Welding Supply Inc .... G 315 592-5012
  Fulton (G-5460)
Matheson Tri-Gas Inc .... F 518 439-0362
  Feura Bush (G-5173)

WELDING EQPT: Electrical
3krf LLC .... G 516 208-6824
  Oceanside (G-13071)
FWC Networks Inc .... F 718 408-1558
  Brooklyn (G-2009)

WELDING MACHINES & EQPT: Ultrasonic
Branson Ultrasonics Corp .... E 585 624-8000
  Honeoye Falls (G-6525)
Sonicor Inc .... G 631 920-6555
  West Babylon (G-16830)

WELDING REPAIR SVC
303 Contracting Inc .... E 716 896-2122
  Orchard Park (G-13249)
A & J Machine & Welding Inc .... F 631 845-7586
  Farmingdale (G-4925)
AAA Welding and Fabrication of .... G 585 254-2830
  Rochester (G-14163)
Accurate Welding Service Inc .... G 516 333-1730
  Westbury (G-16960)
Acro-Fab Ltd .... E 315 564-6688
  Hannibal (G-5969)
Airweld Inc .... G 631 924-6366
  Ridge (G-14091)
Aj Genco Mch Sp McHy Rdout Svc .... F 716 664-4925
  Falconer (G-4889)
Allen Tool Phoenix Inc .... E 315 463-7533
  East Syracuse (G-4501)
Alliance Services Corp .... F 516 775-7600
  Floral Park (G-5190)
Alliance Welding & Steel Fabg .... F 516 775-7600
  Floral Park (G-5191)
Alloy Metal Works Inc .... G 631 694-8163
  Farmingdale (G-4937)
Alpine Machine Inc .... F 607 272-1344
  Ithaca (G-6818)
ARC TEC Wldg & Fabrication Inc .... G 718 982-9274
  Staten Island (G-15639)
Athens Iron Fabrication Inc .... F 718 424-7799
  Woodside (G-17317)
Atlantis Equipment Corporation .... E 518 733-5910
  Stephentown (G-15756)
Barber Welding Inc .... E 315 834-6645
  Weedsport (G-16746)
Benemy Welding & Fabrication .... G 315 548-8500
  Phelps (G-13530)
Bms Manufacturing Co Inc .... E 607 535-2426
  Watkins Glen (G-16693)
Bracci Ironworks Inc .... F 718 629-2374
  Brooklyn (G-1711)
Brenseke George Wldg Ir Works .... G 631 271-4870
  Deer Park (G-4111)
Broadalbin Manufacturing Corp .... E 518 883-5313
  Broadalbin (G-1240)
Bruce Pierce .... E 716 731-9310
  Sanborn (G-15115)
C G & Son Machining Inc .... E 315 964-2430
  Williamstown (G-17228)
CBM Fabrications Inc .... E 518 399-8023
  Ballston Lake (G-581)
Certified Fabrications Inc .... E 716 731-8123
  Sanborn (G-15117)
Competicion Mower Repair .... E 516 280-6584
  Mineola (G-8254)
Cs Automation Inc .... F 315 524-5123
  Ontario (G-13198)
Custom Laser Inc .... E 716 434-8600
  Lockport (G-7578)
D & G Welding Inc .... G 716 873-3088
  Buffalo (G-2899)
Deck Bros Inc .... E 716 852-0262
  Buffalo (G-2904)
Dennies Manufacturing Inc .... E 585 393-4646
  Canandaigua (G-3342)
Donald Stefan .... G 716 492-1110
  Chaffee (G-3533)
Dorgan Welding Service .... G 315 462-9030
  Phelps (G-13531)
E B Industries LLC .... E 631 293-8565
  Farmingdale (G-4982)
Eagle Welding Machine .... G 315 594-1845
  Wolcott (G-17279)
Etna Tool & Die Corporation .... F 212 475-4350
  New York (G-10079)
Excelco/Newbrook Inc .... D 716 934-2644
  Silver Creek (G-15449)
F M L Industries Inc .... G 607 749-7273
  Homer (G-6517)

WELDING REPAIR SVC
Flushing Boiler & Welding Co .... G 718 463-1266
  Brooklyn (G-1988)
Formac Welding Inc .... G 631 421-5525
  Huntington Station (G-6705)
G & C Welding Co Inc .... G 516 883-3228
  Port Washington (G-13817)
Gasport Welding & Fabg Inc .... F 716 772-7205
  Gasport (G-5557)
Gc Mobile Services Inc .... G 914 736-9730
  Cortlandt Manor (G-4051)
Genco John .... G 716 483-5446
  Jamestown (G-6994)
General Welding & Fabg Inc .... G 716 652-0033
  Elma (G-4649)
General Welding & Fabg Inc .... G 716 568-7958
  Williamsville (G-17244)
General Welding & Fabg Inc .... G 716 824-1572
  Blasdell (G-963)
General Welding & Fabg Inc .... G 716 681-8200
  Buffalo (G-2972)
General Welding & Fabg Inc .... G 716 304-3622
  Niagara Falls (G-12824)
Guthrie Heli-ARC Inc .... G 585 548-5053
  Bergen (G-846)
Hadfield Inc .... F 631 981-4314
  Ronkonkoma (G-14909)
Hadleys Fab-Weld Inc .... G 315 926-5101
  Marion (G-8095)
Hansen Steel .... E 585 398-2020
  Farmington (G-5152)
Hartman Enterprises Inc .... D 315 363-7300
  Oneida (G-13156)
Haskell Machine & Tool Inc .... F 607 749-2421
  Homer (G-6518)
Haun Welding Supply Inc .... F 607 846-2289
  Elmira (G-4689)
Haun Welding Supply Inc .... G 315 592-5012
  Fulton (G-5460)
Homer Iron Works LLC .... G 607 749-3963
  Homer (G-6519)
Huntington Welding & Iron .... G 631 423-3331
  Huntington Station (G-6709)
Ingleside Machine Co Inc .... D 585 924-4363
  Farmington (G-5153)
Kon Tat Group Corporation .... G 718 207-5022
  Brooklyn (G-2179)
L & S Metals Inc .... E 716 692-6865
  North Tonawanda (G-12980)
Lagasse Works Inc .... G 315 946-9202
  Lyons (G-7973)
Lagoe-Oswego Corp .... E 315 343-3160
  Rochester (G-14473)
Linita Design & Mfg Corp .... E 716 566-7753
  Lackawanna (G-7244)
M and M Industrial Welding .... G 631 451-6044
  Medford (G-8254)
M M Welding .... E 315 363-3980
  Oneida (G-13158)
Maple Grove Corp .... E 585 492-5286
  Arcade (G-396)
Maspeth Welding Inc .... E 718 497-5430
  Maspeth (G-8150)
Meades Welding and Fabricating .... G 631 581-1555
  Islip (G-6810)
Mega Tool & Mfg Corp .... E 607 734-8398
  Elmira (G-4695)
Miller Metal Fabricating Inc .... E 585 359-3400
  Rochester (G-14514)
Modern Mechanical Fab Inc .... G 518 298-5177
  Champlain (G-3544)
Mooradian Hydraulics & Eqp Co .... G 518 766-3866
  Castleton On Hudson (G-3419)
Ms Spares LLC .... G 607 223-3024
  Clay (G-3683)
New Age Ironworks Inc .... F 718 277-1895
  Brooklyn (G-2358)
New York Manufacturing Corp .... G 585 254-9353
  Rochester (G-14533)
North Country Welding Inc .... G 315 788-9718
  Watertown (G-16666)
NY Iron Inc .... F 718 302-9000
  Long Island City (G-7827)
Phillip J Ortiz Manufacturing .... G 845 226-7030
  Hopewell Junction (G-6557)
Phoenix Welding & Fabg Inc .... G 315 695-2223
  Phoenix (G-13543)
Pro-Tech Wldg Fabrication Inc .... E 585 436-9855
  Rochester (G-14603)
Qsf Inc .... G 585 247-6200
  Gates (G-5562)

Employee Codes: A=Over 500 employees, B=251-500
C=101-250, D=51-100, E=20-50, F=10-19, G=5-9

2017 Harris
New York Manufacturers Directory

WELDING REPAIR SVC

Quality Industrial Services .... F 716 667-7703
  Orchard Park *(G-13294)*
Reliable Welding & Fabrication .... G 631 758-2637
  Patchogue *(G-13434)*
REO Welding Inc .... F 518 238-1022
  Cohoes *(G-3756)*
Rini Tank & Truck Service .... F 718 384-6606
  Brooklyn *(G-2494)*
Rj Welding & Fabricating Inc .... G 315 523-1288
  Clifton Springs *(G-3715)*
Robert M Brown .... F 607 426-6250
  Montour Falls *(G-8611)*
Rothe Welding Inc .... G 845 246-3051
  Saugerties *(G-15193)*
S & D Welding Corp .... G 631 454-0383
  West Babylon *(G-16824)*
S J B Fabrication .... F 716 895-0281
  Buffalo *(G-3171)*
Smithers Tools & Mch Pdts Inc .... D 845 876-3063
  Rhinebeck *(G-14058)*
Strecks Inc .... E 518 273-4410
  Watervliet *(G-16689)*
Tangent Machine & Tool Corp .... E 631 249-3088
  Farmingdale *(G-5124)*
Technapulse LLC .... G 631 234-8700
  Hauppauge *(G-6209)*
Tek Weld .... F 631 694-5503
  Hauppauge *(G-6211)*
Tracey Welding Co Inc .... G 518 756-6309
  Coeymans *(G-3746)*
Watkins Welding and Mch Sp Inc .... G 914 949-6168
  White Plains *(G-17181)*
Waynes Welding Inc .... E 315 768-6146
  Yorkville *(G-17530)*
Welding and Brazing Svcs Inc .... G 607 397-1009
  Richfield Springs *(G-14062)*
Welding Chapter of New York .... G 212 481-1496
  New York *(G-12607)*
West Metal Works Inc .... E 716 895-4900
  Buffalo *(G-3252)*

WELDING SPLYS, EXC GASES: Wholesalers

Austin Industries Inc .... G 585 589-1353
  Albion *(G-162)*

WELDING TIPS: Heat Resistant, Metal

JE Monahan Fabrications LLC .... F 518 761-0414
  Queensbury *(G-14001)*
National Maint Contg Corp .... D 716 285-1583
  Niagara Falls *(G-12849)*

WELDMENTS

Glenridge Fabricators Inc .... F 718 456-2297
  Glendale *(G-5655)*
Industrial Fabricating Corp .... E 315 437-8234
  East Syracuse *(G-4540)*
Miller Metal Fabricating Inc .... G 585 359-3400
  Rochester *(G-14514)*

WHEELBARROWS

Clopay Ames True Tmper Hldng .... F 516 938-5544
  Jericho *(G-7062)*

WHEELCHAIR LIFTS

S & H Enterprises Inc .... G 888 323-8755
  Queensbury *(G-14010)*

WHEELCHAIRS

Crosley Medical Products Inc .... F 631 595-2547
  Deer Park *(G-4122)*
Future Mobility Products Inc .... E 716 783-9130
  Buffalo *(G-2961)*
Gadabout USA Wheelchairs Inc .... F 585 338-2110
  Rochester *(G-14386)*
Palmer Industries Inc .... G 607 754-8741
  Endicott *(G-4822)*
Palmer Industries Inc .... E 607 754-2957
  Endicott *(G-4823)*
Palmer Industries Inc .... G 607 754-1954
  Endicott *(G-4824)*
Skil-Care Corporation .... C 914 963-2040
  Yonkers *(G-17484)*
Vcp Mobility Inc .... B 718 356-7827
  Staten Island *(G-15751)*
VSM Investors LLC .... F 212 351-1600
  New York *(G-12571)*

WHEELS

Wheel & Tire Depot Ex Corp .... G 914 375-2100
  Yonkers *(G-17498)*

WHEELS & PARTS

Bam Enterprises Inc .... G 716 773-7634
  Grand Island *(G-5753)*
Factory Wheel Warehouse Inc .... G 516 605-2131
  Plainview *(G-13601)*
Motor Components LLC .... D 607 737-8011
  Elmira Heights *(G-4711)*

WHEELS: Abrasive

Eraser Company Inc .... C 315 454-3237
  Mattydale *(G-8212)*
Jta USA Inc .... G 718 722-0902
  Brooklyn *(G-2155)*

WHEELS: Buffing & Polishing

Barker Brothers Incorporated .... D 718 456-6400
  Ridgewood *(G-14101)*
Dimanco Inc .... G 315 797-0470
  Utica *(G-16324)*
Divine Brothers Company .... C 315 797-0470
  Utica *(G-16327)*

WHEELS: Iron & Steel, Locomotive & Car

Nitro Wheels Inc .... F 716 337-0709
  North Collins *(G-12930)*

WIGS & HAIRPIECES

M and J Hair Center Inc .... F 516 872-1010
  Garden City *(G-5518)*
Moti Inc .... F 718 436-4280
  Brooklyn *(G-2335)*

WIGS, WHOLESALE

Rev Holdings Inc .... A 212 527-4000
  New York *(G-11848)*
Revlon Holdings Inc .... D 212 527-4000
  New York *(G-11853)*
RGI Group Incorporated .... E 212 527-4000
  New York *(G-11858)*

WIND TUNNELS

United Wind Inc .... F 800 268-9896
  Brooklyn *(G-2704)*

WINDINGS: Coil, Electronic

American Precision Inds Inc .... C 716 691-9100
  Amherst *(G-224)*
American Precision Inds Inc .... D 716 652-3600
  East Aurora *(G-4365)*
American Precision Inds Inc .... D 585 496-5755
  Arcade *(G-386)*
Mohawk Electro Techniques Inc .... D 315 896-2661
  Barneveld *(G-615)*
Precision Electronics Inc .... F 631 842-4900
  Copiague *(G-3919)*

WINDMILLS: Electric Power Generation

EDP Renewables North Amer LLC .... G 518 426-1650
  Albany *(G-76)*
Wind Solutions LLC .... G 518 813-8029
  Esperance *(G-4840)*

WINDOW & DOOR FRAMES

Action Bullet Resistant .... F 631 422-0888
  West Islip *(G-16903)*
D D & L Inc .... F 607 729-9131
  Binghamton *(G-906)*
Deronde Doors and Frames Inc .... F 716 895-8888
  Buffalo *(G-2908)*
J Sussman Inc .... E 718 297-0228
  Jamaica *(G-6922)*
Jaidan Industries Inc .... F 516 944-3650
  Port Washington *(G-13827)*
Kasson & Keller Inc .... A 518 853-3421
  Fonda *(G-5315)*
Master Window & Door Corp .... F 718 782-5407
  Brooklyn *(G-2281)*
New Bgnnngs Win Door Dstrs LLC .... G 845 214-0698
  Poughkeepsie *(G-13920)*

PRODUCT SECTION

Sunrise Door Solutions .... G 631 464-4139
  Copiague *(G-3930)*
Window Rama Enterprises Inc .... G 631 462-9054
  Commack *(G-3849)*

WINDOW BLIND REPAIR SVCS

Window-Fix Inc .... E 718 854-3475
  Brooklyn *(G-2757)*

WINDOW FRAMES & SASHES: Plastic

Hart To Hart Industries Inc .... G 716 492-2709
  Chaffee *(G-3534)*
JSM Vinyl Products Inc .... F 516 775-4520
  New Hyde Park *(G-8844)*
Northeast Windows Usa Inc .... E 516 378-6577
  Merrick *(G-8390)*

WINDOW FRAMES, MOLDING & TRIM: Vinyl

Eastern Enterprise Corp .... F 718 727-8600
  Staten Island *(G-15670)*
Kasson & Keller Inc .... A 518 853-3421
  Fonda *(G-5315)*
Tri-State Window Factory Corp .... D 631 667-8600
  Deer Park *(G-4218)*
Vinyline Window and Door Inc .... F 914 476-3500
  Yonkers *(G-17496)*
Window Tech Systems Inc .... E 518 899-9000
  Ballston Spa *(G-611)*

WINDOW TRIMMING SVCS

New Business Solutions Inc .... E 631 789-1500
  Amityville *(G-316)*

WINDOWS, LOUVER: Metal

Grover Aluminum Products Inc .... E 631 475-3500
  Patchogue *(G-13421)*

WINDOWS: Frames, Wood

SSP Window Cleaning Corp .... F 917 750-2619
  Brooklyn *(G-2594)*

WINDOWS: Storm, Wood

Lasser Products Incorporated .... G 585 249-5180
  Rochester *(G-14475)*

WINDOWS: Wood

J Zeluck Inc .... E 718 251-8060
  Brooklyn *(G-2128)*
Kelly Window Systems Inc .... E 631 420-8500
  Farmingdale *(G-5026)*
Pella Corporation .... B 516 385-3622
  Albertson *(G-158)*
Pella Corporation .... B 516 385-3622
  Albertson *(G-159)*
Pella Corporation .... B 607 223-2023
  Johnson City *(G-7100)*
Pella Corporation .... B 607 231-8550
  Johnson City *(G-7101)*
Pella Corporation .... B 607 231-8550
  Johnson City *(G-7102)*
Pella Corporation .... B 607 238-2812
  Johnson City *(G-7103)*
Pella Corporation .... B 607 238-2812
  Johnson City *(G-7104)*
Royal Windows Mfg Corp .... E 631 435-8888
  Bay Shore *(G-740)*
Stealth Archtctral Windows Inc .... F 718 821-6666
  Brooklyn *(G-2601)*
Window Technologies LLC .... F 402 464-0202
  New York *(G-12640)*

WINE & DISTILLED ALCOHOLIC BEVERAGES WHOLESALERS

Constellation Brands Inc .... D 585 678-7100
  Victor *(G-16469)*
Levindi .... F 212 572-7000
  New York *(G-10978)*
Liquid Management Partners LLC .... F 516 775-5050
  New Hyde Park *(G-8846)*

WINE CELLARS, BONDED: Wine, Blended

Hickory Road Land Co LLC .... G 607 243-9114
  Dundee *(G-4330)*

PRODUCT SECTION

WOMEN'S & CHILDREN'S CLOTHING WHOLESALERS, NEC

Solstars Inc .... G 212 605-0430
   New York *(G-12126)*
Tickle Hill Winery .... G 607 546-7740
   Hector *(G-6262)*
Wine Services Inc .... G 631 722-3800
   Riverhead *(G-14160)*

WIRE

Bekaert Corporation .... E 716 830-1321
   Amherst *(G-227)*
CFS Enterprises Inc .... E 718 585-0500
   Bronx *(G-1295)*
EB Acquisitions LLC .... D 212 355-3310
   New York *(G-9971)*
Hanes Supply Inc .... E 518 438-0139
   Albany *(G-84)*
Island Industries Corp .... G 631 451-8825
   Coram *(G-3945)*
Lee Spring Company LLC .... C 718 362-5183
   Brooklyn *(G-2206)*
Liberty Fabrication Inc .... G 718 495-5735
   Brooklyn *(G-2215)*
Nupro Technologies LLC .... F 412 422-5922
   Canandaigua *(G-3350)*
Owl Wire & Cable LLC .... C 315 697-2011
   Canastota *(G-3370)*
Spectrum Cable Corporation .... G 585 235-7714
   Rochester *(G-14694)*
Tappan Wire & Cable Inc .... C 845 353-9000
   Blauvelt *(G-976)*
Web Associates Inc .... G 716 883-3377
   Buffalo *(G-3249)*

WIRE & CABLE: Aluminum

Irtronics Instruments Inc .... F 914 693-6291
   Ardsley *(G-405)*
SI Partners Inc .... G 516 433-1415
   Hicksville *(G-6394)*

WIRE & CABLE: Nonferrous, Aircraft

United States Dept of Army .... C 315 772-7538
   Watertown *(G-16674)*

WIRE & WIRE PRDTS

369 River Road Inc .... E 716 694-5001
   North Tonawanda *(G-12953)*
Abbott Industries Inc .... E 718 291-0800
   Jamaica *(G-6891)*
Albest Metal Stamping Corp .... D 718 388-6000
   Brooklyn *(G-1576)*
All-Lifts Incorporated .... E 518 465-3461
   Albany *(G-44)*
American Wire Tie Inc .... E 716 337-2412
   North Collins *(G-12926)*
Angelica Spring Company Inc .... F 585 466-7892
   Angelica *(G-377)*
Bayshore Wire Products Corp .... F 631 451-8825
   Coram *(G-3941)*
Better Wire Products Inc .... E 716 883-3377
   Buffalo *(G-2840)*
Cable Management Solutions Inc .... E 631 674-0004
   Bay Shore *(G-680)*
Clover Wire Forming Co Inc .... E 914 375-0400
   Yonkers *(G-17428)*
Compar Manufacturing Corp .... E 212 304-2777
   New York *(G-9690)*
Continental Cordage Corp .... D 315 655-9800
   Cazenovia *(G-3443)*
Cuddeback Machining Inc .... G 585 392-5889
   Hilton *(G-6417)*
Engineering Mfg Tech LLC .... D 607 754-7111
   Endicott *(G-4805)*
Eraser Company Inc .... C 315 454-3237
   Mattydale *(G-8212)*
Flanagans Creative Disp Inc .... F 845 858-2542
   Port Jervis *(G-13784)*
Flatcut LLC .... G 212 542-5732
   Brooklyn *(G-1983)*
Greene Technologies Inc .... D 607 656-4166
   Greene *(G-5866)*
Hitachi Metals America Ltd .... E 914 694-9200
   Purchase *(G-13958)*
Interstate Wood Products Inc .... E 631 842-4488
   Amityville *(G-296)*
Kehr-Buffalo Wire Frame Co Inc .... E 716 897-2288
   Buffalo *(G-3027)*
Lubow Machine Corp .... F 631 226-1700
   Copiague *(G-3911)*

Magic Novelty Co Inc .... E 212 304-2777
   New York *(G-11104)*
Oneida Sales & Service Inc .... E 716 822-8205
   Buffalo *(G-3101)*
Peck & Hale LLC .... E 631 589-2510
   West Sayville *(G-16937)*
Quality Industrial Services .... F 716 667-7703
   Orchard Park *(G-13294)*
Rose Fence Inc .... F 516 223-0777
   Baldwin *(G-561)*
SCI Bore Inc .... G 212 674-7128
   New York *(G-12003)*
Selectrode Industries Inc .... D 631 547-5470
   Huntington Station *(G-6723)*
Sigmund Cohn Corp .... D 914 664-5300
   Mount Vernon *(G-8734)*
Teka Precision Inc .... G 845 753-1900
   Nyack *(G-13055)*
Trylon Wire & Metal Works Inc .... E 718 542-4472
   Bronx *(G-1481)*
Utility Engineering Co .... F 845 735-8900
   Pearl River *(G-13468)*

WIRE CLOTH & WOVEN WIRE PRDTS, MADE FROM PURCHASED WIRE

G Bopp USA Inc .... G 845 296-1065
   Wappingers Falls *(G-16569)*
Sinclair International Company .... E 518 798-2361
   Queensbury *(G-14012)*

WIRE FABRIC: Welded Steel

Sheltred Wkshp For Dsabled Inc .... C 607 722-2364
   Binghamton *(G-951)*
Technical Wldg Fabricators LLC .... F 518 463-2229
   Albany *(G-140)*

WIRE FENCING & ACCESS WHOLESALERS

Master-Halco Inc .... F 631 585-8150
   Ronkonkoma *(G-14939)*

WIRE MATERIALS: Copper

Camden Wire Co Inc .... A 315 245-3800
   Camden *(G-3313)*
International Wire Group .... G 315 245-3800
   Camden *(G-3315)*
Omega Wire Inc .... D 315 689-7115
   Jordan *(G-7130)*
Omega Wire Inc .... B 315 245-3800
   Camden *(G-3318)*
Owi Corporation .... G 315 245-4305
   Camden *(G-3319)*
Performance Wire & Cable Inc .... F 315 245-2594
   Camden *(G-3320)*

WIRE MATERIALS: Steel

American Wire Tie Inc .... E 716 337-2412
   North Collins *(G-12926)*
Continental Cordage Corp .... D 315 655-9800
   Cazenovia *(G-3443)*
E B Iron Art LLC .... F 716 876-7510
   Buffalo *(G-2923)*
Hitachi Metals America Ltd .... E 914 694-9200
   Purchase *(G-13958)*
Hohmann & Barnard Inc .... E 631 234-0600
   Hauppauge *(G-6095)*
Omega Wire Inc .... D 315 689-7115
   Jordan *(G-7130)*
Rolling Gate Supply Corp .... G 718 366-5258
   Glendale *(G-5661)*
Rose Fence Inc .... F 516 223-0777
   Baldwin *(G-561)*
Sigmund Cohn Corp .... D 914 664-5300
   Mount Vernon *(G-8734)*

WIRE PRDTS: Ferrous Or Iron, Made In Wiredrawing Plants

Forsyth Industries Inc .... E 716 652-1070
   Buffalo *(G-2953)*
Handy & Harman .... E 914 461-1300
   White Plains *(G-17118)*

WIRE PRDTS: Steel & Iron

Handy & Harman Ltd .... A 914 461-1300
   White Plains *(G-17120)*

Sph Group Holdings LLC .... G 212 520-2300
   New York *(G-12162)*

WIRE WHOLESALERS

Awt Supply Corp .... G 516 437-9105
   Elmont *(G-4717)*

WIRE: Barbed

Cobra Systems Inc .... F 845 338-6675
   Bloomington *(G-993)*

WIRE: Barbed & Twisted

Cobra Manufacturing Corp .... G 845 514-2505
   Lake Katrine *(G-7269)*

WIRE: Communication

Caldwell Bennett Inc .... E 315 337-8540
   Oriskany *(G-13305)*
Corning Optcal Cmmncations LLC .... F 607 974-7543
   Corning *(G-3969)*

WIRE: Mesh

Aeroflex Incorporated .... B 516 694-6700
   Plainview *(G-13578)*

WIRE: Nonferrous

Camden Wire Co Inc .... A 315 245-3800
   Camden *(G-3313)*
Colonial Wire & Cable Co Inc .... D 631 234-8500
   Hauppauge *(G-6049)*
Continental Cordage Corp .... D 315 655-9800
   Cazenovia *(G-3443)*
Convergent Cnnctivity Tech Inc .... G 845 651-5250
   Florida *(G-5211)*
Corning Cable Systems Cr Un .... G 607 974-9000
   Corning *(G-3960)*
Corning Incorporated .... G 646 521-9600
   New York *(G-9726)*
International Wire Group Inc .... B 315 245-2000
   Camden *(G-3316)*
Jaguar Industries Inc .... F 845 947-1800
   Haverstraw *(G-6237)*
Kris-Tech Wire Company Inc .... E 315 339-5268
   Rome *(G-14817)*
Leviton Manufacturing Co Inc .... B 631 812-6000
   Melville *(G-8334)*
Rdi Inc .... F 914 773-1000
   Mount Kisco *(G-8643)*
Rockland Insulated Wire Cable .... G 845 429-3103
   Haverstraw *(G-6239)*
Siemens Corporation .... F 202 434-7800
   New York *(G-12062)*
Siemens USA Holdings Inc .... B 212 258-4000
   New York *(G-12064)*
Sinclair Technologies Inc .... E 716 874-3682
   Hamburg *(G-5942)*
Steelflex Electro Corp .... D 516 226-4466
   Lindenhurst *(G-7483)*
Tappan Wire & Cable Inc .... C 845 353-9000
   Blauvelt *(G-976)*
United Wire Technologies Inc .... E 315 675-3558
   Cleveland *(G-3692)*
Universal Builders Supply Inc .... F 845 758-8801
   Red Hook *(G-14030)*
Whirlwind Music Distrs Inc .... G 585 663-8820
   Rochester *(G-14762)*

WIRE: Nonferrous, Appliance Fixture

County WD Applnc & TV Srvc of .... F 585 328-7417
   Rochester *(G-14290)*

WIRE: Steel, Insulated Or Armored

Able Industries Inc .... F 914 739-5685
   Cortlandt Manor *(G-4048)*
Aerospace Wire & Cable Inc .... E 718 358-2345
   College Point *(G-3776)*

WOMEN'S & CHILDREN'S CLOTHING WHOLESALERS, NEC

Alpha 6 Distributions LLC .... F 516 801-8290
   Locust Valley *(G-7628)*
Arteast LLC .... G 212 965-8787
   New York *(G-9216)*
Avon Products Inc .... C 212 282-5000
   New York *(G-9281)*

Employee Codes: A=Over 500 employees, B=251-500
C=101-250, D=51-100, E=20-50, F=10-19, G=5-9

WOMEN'S & CHILDREN'S CLOTHING WHOLESALERS, NEC

Cejon Inc .... E 201 437-8788
 New York *(G-9554)*
Cotton Express Inc .... E 212 921-4588
 New York *(G-9729)*
D-C Theatricks .... G 716 847-0180
 Buffalo *(G-2900)*
Design Archives Inc .... G 212 768-0617
 New York *(G-9851)*
Grand Knitting Mills Inc .... E 631 226-5000
 Amityville *(G-290)*
Halmode Apparel Inc .... A 212 819-9114
 New York *(G-10398)*
Item-Eyes Inc .... D 631 321-0923
 New York *(G-10670)*
JM Originals Inc .... C 845 647-3003
 Ellenville *(G-4634)*
Kate Spade & Company .... B 212 354-4900
 New York *(G-10816)*
Kenmar Shirts Inc .... E 718 824-3880
 Bronx *(G-1371)*
Lloyds Fashions Inc .... D 631 435-3353
 Brentwood *(G-1190)*
M Hidary & Co Inc .... D 212 736-6540
 New York *(G-11073)*
Maggy Boutique Ltd .... E 212 997-5222
 New York *(G-11101)*
Mango Usa Inc .... E 718 998-6050
 Brooklyn *(G-2258)*
Moresca Clothing and Costume .... F 845 331-6012
 Ulster Park *(G-16286)*
New York Popular Inc .... D 718 499-2020
 Brooklyn *(G-2367)*
Only Hearts Ltd .... E 718 783-3218
 New York *(G-11511)*
Penfli Industries Inc .... F 212 947-6080
 Great Neck *(G-5830)*
Soho Apparel Ltd .... G 212 840-1109
 New York *(G-12118)*
Therese The Childrens Collectn .... G 518 346-2315
 Schenectady *(G-15305)*
United Knitwear International .... G 212 354-2920
 New York *(G-12465)*

WOMEN'S & GIRLS' SPORTSWEAR WHOLESALERS

Argee America Inc .... G 212 768-9840
 New York *(G-9199)*
Casuals Etc Inc .... D 212 838-1319
 New York *(G-9544)*
Danice Stores Inc .... F 212 665-0389
 New York *(G-9803)*
F & J Designs Inc .... G 212 302-8755
 New York *(G-10114)*
Jacques Moret Inc .... C 212 354-2400
 New York *(G-10692)*
Jaxis Inc .... G 212 302-7611
 Brooklyn *(G-2135)*
Lollytogs Ltd .... D 212 502-6000
 New York *(G-11024)*
Main Street Fashions Inc .... F 212 764-2613
 New York *(G-11112)*
Morelle Products Ltd .... F 212 391-8070
 New York *(G-11304)*
Noah Enterprises Ltd .... G 212 736-2888
 New York *(G-11448)*
S2 Sportswear Inc .... F 347 335-0713
 Brooklyn *(G-2527)*
Sterling Possessions Ltd .... G 212 594-0418
 New York *(G-12197)*

WOMEN'S CLOTHING STORES

Elie Tahari Ltd .... F 212 398-2622
 New York *(G-10001)*
Jlnw Inc .... D 212 719-4666
 Long Island City *(G-7771)*
Joseph (uk) Inc .... G 212 570-0077
 New York *(G-10763)*
Mee Accessories LLC .... C 917 262-1000
 New York *(G-11218)*
Saint Laurie Ltd .... E 212 643-1916
 New York *(G-11954)*
Uniqlo USA LLC .... F 877 486-4756
 New York *(G-12460)*

WOMEN'S CLOTHING STORES: Ready-To-Wear

Hillary Merchant Inc .... G 646 575-9242
 New York *(G-10476)*

Phillips-Van Heusen Europe .... F 212 381-3500
 New York *(G-11649)*
Pvh Corp .... D 212 381-3500
 New York *(G-11756)*
Stallion Inc .... E 718 706-0111
 Long Island City *(G-7882)*

WOMEN'S SPECIALTY CLOTHING STORES

Dvf Studio LLC .... D 212 741-6607
 New York *(G-9942)*

WOMEN'S SPORTSWEAR STORES

A H Schreiber Co Inc .... D 212 594-7234
 New York *(G-8989)*
Central Apparel Group Ltd .... F 212 868-6505
 New York *(G-9562)*
Mainly Monograms Inc .... E 845 624-4923
 West Nyack *(G-16921)*
Royal Tees Inc .... G 845 357-9448
 Suffern *(G-15800)*

WOOD FENCING WHOLESALERS

Interstate Wood Products Inc .... E 631 842-4488
 Amityville *(G-296)*
Master-Halco Inc .... F 631 585-8150
 Ronkonkoma *(G-14939)*

WOOD PRDTS

Aid Wood Working .... F 631 244-7768
 Bohemia *(G-1010)*
Polanco Mills Woodwork .... G 845 271-3639
 West Haverstraw *(G-16846)*

WOOD PRDTS: Clothespins

Green Renewable Inc .... E 518 658-2233
 Berlin *(G-856)*

WOOD PRDTS: Display Forms, Boot & Shoe

Encore Retail Systems Inc .... F 718 385-3443
 Brooklyn *(G-1923)*

WOOD PRDTS: Engraved

Lanwood Industries Inc .... E 718 786-3000
 Bay Shore *(G-711)*

WOOD PRDTS: Furniture Inlays, Veneers

American Woods & Veneers Works ... E 718 937-2195
 Long Island City *(G-7659)*

WOOD PRDTS: Jalousies, Glass, Wood Framed

Paul David Enterprises Inc .... G 646 667-5530
 New York *(G-11584)*

WOOD PRDTS: Ladders & Stepladders

York Ladder Inc .... G 718 784-6666
 Long Island City *(G-7930)*

WOOD PRDTS: Mantels

Funda-Mantels LLC .... G 631 399-3223
 Mastic *(G-8203)*

WOOD PRDTS: Moldings, Unfinished & Prefinished

Adriatic Wood Products Inc .... E 718 922-4621
 Brooklyn *(G-1563)*
Attica Millwork Inc .... F 585 591-2333
 Attica *(G-471)*
Fire Island Sea Clam Co Inc .... G 631 589-2199
 West Sayville *(G-16935)*
Old World Mouldings Inc .... G 631 563-8660
 Bohemia *(G-1113)*
Scanga Woodworking Corp .... G 845 265-9115
 Cold Spring *(G-3766)*
Spiegel Woodworks Inc .... G 845 336-8090
 Kingston *(G-7211)*

WOOD PRDTS: Mulch Or Sawdust

Premium Mulch & Materials Inc .... F 631 320-3666
 Coram *(G-3949)*
Wholesale Mulch & Sawdust Inc .... G 607 687-2637
 Owego *(G-13362)*

WOOD PRDTS: Novelties, Fiber

Cowee Forest Products Inc .... E 518 658-2233
 Berlin *(G-855)*
Graphics Slution Providers Inc .... G 845 677-5088
 Lagrangeville *(G-7253)*
Ryers Creek Corp .... E 607 523-6617
 Corning *(G-3980)*

WOOD PRDTS: Outdoor, Structural

Wolski Wood Works Inc .... G 718 577-9816
 Flushing *(G-5308)*

WOOD PRDTS: Panel Work

Danbury Creek Inc .... G 315 822-5640
 West Winfield *(G-16958)*
Empire Building Products Inc .... G 518 695-6094
 Schuylerville *(G-15319)*

WOOD PRDTS: Rulers & Rules

Aakron Rule Corp .... C 716 542-5483
 Akron *(G-19)*
Aakron Rule Corp .... D 716 542-5483
 Akron *(G-20)*

WOOD PRDTS: Shavings & Packaging, Excelsior

RWS Manufacturing Inc .... G 518 361-1657
 Queensbury *(G-14009)*

WOOD PRDTS: Shoe Trees

R P M Industries Inc .... E 315 255-1105
 Auburn *(G-515)*

WOOD PRDTS: Silo Staves

Unadilla Silo Company Inc .... D 607 369-9341
 Sidney *(G-15444)*

WOOD PRDTS: Survey Stakes

T Eason Land Surveyor .... G 631 474-2200
 Port Jeff STA *(G-13772)*

WOOD PRDTS: Trellises

Finger Lakes Trellis Supply .... G 315 904-4007
 Williamson *(G-17223)*

WOOD PRDTS: Trophy Bases

Cherry Creek Woodcraft Inc .... E 716 988-3211
 South Dayton *(G-15518)*
M A Moslow & Bros Inc .... E 716 896-2950
 Buffalo *(G-3052)*

WOOD PRDTS: Window Backs, Store Or Lunchroom, Prefabricated

Vitarose Corp of America .... G 718 951-9700
 Brooklyn *(G-2733)*

WOOD PRDTS: Yard Sticks

Cfp Purchasing Inc .... G 705 806-0383
 Flushing *(G-5231)*

WOOD PRODUCTS: Reconstituted

Bedford Wdwrk Instllations Inc .... G 914 764-9434
 Bedford *(G-796)*
Northeastern Products Corp .... E 518 623-3161
 Warrensburg *(G-16580)*
Zircar Refr Composites Inc .... F 845 651-2200
 Florida *(G-5217)*

WOOD TREATING: Creosoting

Colorspec Coatings Intl Inc .... F 631 472-8251
 Holbrook *(G-6440)*
Osmose Holdings Inc .... A 716 882-5905
 Depew *(G-4267)*

WOOD TREATING: Flooring, Block

Wego International Floors LLC .... F 516 487-3510
 Great Neck *(G-5849)*

WOOD TREATING: Structural Lumber & Timber

Bestway Enterprises Inc ....E 607 753-8261
  Cortland (G-4012)
Bestway of New York Inc......................G....... 607 753-8261
  Cortland (G-4013)
Genesee Reserve Buffalo LLC...............E 716 824-3116
  Buffalo (G-2973)

WOODWORK & TRIM: Interior & Ornamental

Beaver Creek Industries Inc...................G....... 607 545-6382
  Canaseraga (G-3362)
Inform Studio Inc ....F 718 401-6149
  Bronx (G-1362)
Miller Blaker Inc ....D....... 718 665-3930
  Bronx (G-1398)
Props Displays & Interiors ....F 212 620-3840
  New York (G-11737)
Upstate Door Inc ....D....... 585 786-3880
  Warsaw (G-16585)
Vander Heyden Woodworking ....G....... 212 242-0525
  New York (G-12500)
Wood Innovations of Suffolk ....G....... 631 698-2345
  Medford (G-8263)

WOODWORK: Carved & Turned

Architectural Dctg Co LLC ....E 845 483-1340
  Poughkeepsie (G-13888)
Lanza Corp ....G....... 914 937-6360
  Port Chester (G-13751)
Superior Wood Turnings ....F 716 483-1254
  Jamestown (G-7037)

WOODWORK: Interior & Ornamental, NEC

A Losee & Sons.....................................G....... 516 676-3060
  Glen Cove (G-5608)
American Wood Column Corp................G....... 718 782-3163
  Brooklyn (G-1610)
Bauerschmidt & Sons Inc ....D....... 718 528-3500
  Jamaica (G-6898)
Brauen Construction ....G....... 585 492-0042
  Arcade (G-390)
Custom Wood Inc ....G....... 718 927-4700
  Brooklyn (G-1828)
DAngelo Home Collections Inc..............G....... 917 267-8920
  Warwick (G-16587)
DC Contracting & Building Corp ....F 631 385-1117
  Huntington Station (G-6701)
Ignelzi Interiors Inc ....E 718 464-0279
  Queens Village (G-13979)
Kng Construction Co Inc ....F 212 595-1451
  Warwick (G-16593)
Michael Bernstein Design Assoc ....E 718 456-9277
  Brooklyn (G-2308)
Nordic Interior Inc ....C....... 718 456-7000
  Maspeth (G-8159)
Siegfrieds Basement Inc ....F 212 629-3523
  New York (G-12061)

WOOL: Grease

Sivko Furs Inc ....G....... 607 698-4827
  Canisteo (G-3379)

WOVEN WIRE PRDTS, NEC

Joldeson One Aerospace Inds ....D....... 718 848-7396
  Ozone Park (G-13380)

WRITING FOR PUBLICATION SVCS

Mosby Holdings Corp ....G....... 212 309-8100
  New York (G-11308)

X-RAY EQPT & TUBES

AFP Imaging Corporation ....F 914 592-6665
  Mount Kisco (G-8622)
Air Techniques Inc ....B....... 516 433-7676
  Melville (G-8291)
American Access Care LLC ....F 631 582-9729
  Hauppauge (G-6019)
Biodex Medical Systems Inc ....C....... 631 924-9000
  Shirley (G-15416)
Dra Imaging PC ....E 845 296-1057
  Wappingers Falls (G-16566)
Flow X Ray Corporation ....D....... 631 242-9729
  Deer Park (G-4142)
Mitegen LLC ....G....... 607 266-8877
  Ithaca (G-6862)
Multiwire Laboratories Ltd ....G....... 607 257-3378
  Ithaca (G-6865)
New York Imaging Service Inc ....F 716 834-8022
  Tonawanda (G-16184)
Phantom Laboratory Inc.........................F 518 692-1190
  Greenwich (G-5891)
Photo Medic Equipment Inc...................D....... 631 242-6600
  Bay Shore (G-723)
R M F Health Management L L C ....E 718 854-5400
  Wantagh (G-16562)
RC Imaging Inc ....G....... 585 392-4336
  Hilton (G-6420)
Star X-Ray Co Inc ....E 631 842-3010
  Woodbury (G-17301)
Surescan Corporation ....E 607 321-0042
  Binghamton (G-953)
VJ Technologies Inc ....E 631 589-8800
  Bohemia (G-1154)
Wolf X-Ray Corporation ....D....... 631 242-9729
  Deer Park (G-4227)

X-RAY EQPT REPAIR SVCS

RC Imaging Inc ....G....... 585 392-4336
  Hilton (G-6420)

YARN & YARN SPINNING

Advanced Yarn Technologies Inc ....E 518 239-6600
  Durham (G-4354)
Colortex Inc ....G....... 212 564-2000
  New York (G-9676)
Missiontex Inc ....G....... 718 532-9053
  Brooklyn (G-2322)
National Spinning Co Inc ....E 212 382-6400
  New York (G-11351)
St Regis Sportswear Ltd ....G....... 518 725-6767
  Gloversville (G-5722)
United Thread Mills Corp ....G....... 516 536-3900
  Oceanside (G-13102)

YARN MILLS: Twisting

Majestic Rayon Corporation ....E 212 929-6443
  New York (G-11115)

YARN WHOLESALERS

Colortex Inc ....G....... 212 564-2000
  New York (G-9676)
Great Adirondack Yarn Company...........F 518 843-3381
  Amsterdam (G-349)
National Spinning Co Inc ....E 212 382-6400
  New York (G-11351)

YARN: Embroidery, Spun

Printz and Patternz LLC ....G....... 518 944-6020
  Schenectady (G-15286)

YARN: Manmade & Synthetic Fiber, Spun

Ultrafab Inc ....C....... 585 924-2186
  Farmington (G-5158)

YARN: Natural & Animal Fiber, Spun

Great Adirondack Yarn Company...........F 518 843-3381
  Amsterdam (G-349)

YARN: Specialty & Novelty

A Thousand Cranes Inc ....F 212 724-9596
  New York (G-8993)
K F I Inc ....F 516 546-2904
  Roosevelt (G-15006)
La Lame Inc ....G....... 212 921-9770
  New York (G-10909)

YARN: Weaving, Twisting, Winding Or Spooling

Marsha Fleisher.....................................F 845 679-6500
  Woodstock (G-17364)

YOGURT WHOLESALERS

Fage USA Holdings...............................G....... 518 762-5912
  Johnstown (G-7113)
Kesso Foods Inc ....G....... 718 777-5303
  East Elmhurst (G-4393)

ZIRCONIUM

Prince Minerals LLC ....D....... 646 747-4222
  New York (G-11711)

Employee Codes: A=Over 500 employees, B=251-500
C=101-250, D=51-100, E=20-50, F=10-19, G=5-9